Bielefelder Katalog

Jazz

Compact Discs, MusiCassetten, Schallplatten, DVD's, SACD's

2004

42. Jahrgang
Frühjahr 2004

Etwa 500 Neueintragungen
Über 6.100 Datenträger
Über 63.100 Titel
Über 13.200 Interpreten
178 Label

Mit CD-ROM (für Windows©)

€ 24,50

NEW MEDIA VERLAG • Nürnberg

Inhalt

4	Impressum
5	Vorwort
6	Preface
7	Wie findet man was
8	How to find what
9	Die Instrumente
10	Firmenverzeichnis
13	Das Oldie-Markt-Magazin
19	Farbiger Coverteil
35	Titelverzeichnis
355	Interpretenverzeichnis
687	Labelverzeichnis

Update-CD-ROM mit zeitnahem Datenbestand laufend

Der nächste Katalog plus CD-ROM erscheint am 16. April 2005

Impressum

Erscheinungsweise: einmal jährlich im April
(CD-ROM-Updates laufend)

Herausgeber und Verlag:
Martin Reichold
New Media Verlag, Nürnberg
© 2004 by New Media-Verlag

Bestellungen vom Fachhandel:
Tel.: (0711) 182-15 06
Fax: (0711) 182- 27 15 06
email: iwalz@scw-media.de

Bestellungen von Privat:
Tel.: (0711) 182- 26 26
Fax: (0711) 182- 17 56
email: bestellservice@scw-media.de

Bestellungen von Update-CD-ROM´s:
Tel.: (08631) 162-785
Fax: (08631) 162-786
email: info@plattensammeln.de
(10,- € zzgl. Versandkosten)

Vertrieb:
SCW-Media Vertriebs GmbH & Co.KG
70138 Stuttgart

Vertrieb Schweiz:
TUDOR AG, Zürich, Tel. 01/4 91 72 50

Foreign mail orders: by land 34,50 €;
By airmail 50,00 € per copy.
Please send a cheque with the exact indication of the requested catalogues issues or transfer the amount with the corresponding indication to SCW-Media Vertriebs GmbH & Co.KG, Stuttgart with account no. 10 03 53 35 00 at the Baden-Württembergische Bank AG Stuttgart, bank no. 600 200 30.

Objektleitung: Fabian Leibfried
Tel.: (07042) 76 46

Anzeigenverkauf: Julia Bamboschek
Tel.: (07473) 953 188
Fax: (07473) 953 177

Vertriebsleitung: Ralf Günther
Tel.: (0711) 182 16 87

Titelfoto: Pat Metheny / Willi Kuper

Datenverarbeitung, Layout: Trieb, Mühldorf

Druck: OZ, Rheinfelden

Redaktion:
Manfred Scheffner
Postfach 60 07 32, 81207 München
Fax: (089) 834 68 91
email: mscheffner@motorpresse.de

Systemvoraussetzungen CD-ROM:
Hardware: PC ab Pentium II 300 MHz mit 50 MB freiem Arbeitsspeicher und ca. 2 MB Festplattenspeicher; Betriebssystem: Windows 98, ME, NT, 2000 oder XP; Browser: Internet Explorer ab Version 5.0 oder Netscape Navigator ab Version 6

Nachdruck, fotomechanische oder elektronische Wiedergabe, auch einzelner Teile, nur mit Genehmigung des Verlages

Printed in Germany

Verlag
New Media Verlag GmbH
Parkstr. 13, 90409 Nürnberg

ISSN 0721-7153
ISBN 3-926886-41-2
(früher 3-89113-137-2 bei Vereinigte Motor-Verlage, Stuttgart)

Vorwort

Von Frank Zappa ist der böse Ausspruch:

"Jazz ist nicht tot – er riecht nur komisch"

überliefert. Tatsächlich neigte er gegen Ende seiner Karriere selbst zu dem von ihm karikierten Stil und dieses Beispiel zeigt nicht nur die Langlebigkeit dieses Stils – sie demonstriert auch seine Wandlungsfähigkeit.

Das ist eine Eigenschaft, die den Jazz von einer Musik der Freudenhäuser in New Orleans zu einem der Bestandteile der offiziellen Kultur werden ließ. Deswegen sind für ihn Schicksalsschläge, die den Popmarkt hart treffen, weniger schlimm als für die Vertreter der leichten Muse.

Auf dem Level, den der Jazz erreicht hat, ist ein Schrumpfungsprozeß wesentlich leichter zu verkraften als auf den Höhen, die in den 80er Jahren die Pop- und Rockmusik erreichte. Dies demonstriert auch der erneut angewachsene Umfang dieses Katalogs, den der neue Verlag zudem mit einigen Zusätzen versehen hat, die den ansonsten rein statistischen Katalogteil aufwerten sollen:

Dazu zählt zum einen der Fototeil mit den Hüllen etlichen der neuen Platten, aber zum anderen auch die CD-ROM, die im Vergleich zu der Vergangenheit diesmal wirklich sehr gut zu gebrauchen ist.

Insgesamt ist das wie wir hoffen, ein Katalog, der den Vergleich mit der Vergangenheit nicht nur aushält, sondern ihn auch übertrifft. Natürlich mussten aufgrund von Versäumnissen der Vorbesitzer kleine Abstriche gemacht werden, was die Neu-Eintragungen betrifft, die diesmal nicht den sonst üblichen Umfang erreichen.

Doch der Rest – von der Druckaufbereitung bis zur Gestaltung und zum Inhalt – wurde genauso sorgfältig gestaltet wie zuvor.

Dies gilt auch für den Katalog insgesamt, der den Jazz-Fans das nächste Jahr ein ebenso zuverlässiger Begleiter sein soll, wie es seine Vorgänger waren.

Dazu wünsche ich Ihnen, dem Leser, viele erfüllte Stunden voller Informationen.

Ihr
Martin Reichold
Herausgeber
27.4.2004

Preface

Frank Zappa once said in his typical sardonic way

„Jazz isn't dead – it just smells funny".

He himself tended to play this music, that he carricated so bitterly, at the end of his career.

This example shows not only the long life of this musical style, it demonstrates also its ability to change. That is a capacity, that carried Jazz from the red light district in New Orleans into the halls and temples of the official culture.

Because of this it endures heavy blows, that hit the popmarket much harder than the colleagues in the Jazz-corner.

On the level, to which the Jazz has climbed, a process of shrinking results can absorbed much easier than on the heights, which the Pop- and Rockmusic has reached in the eighties.

That shows the even more grown volume of this catalogue, that is enriched with some features by the new publishing house, that should make more out of the once pure statistical part.

That means in the first place the part with pictures of the covers of the new records, but on the other hand also the finally very good to use CD-ROM, that is not the enemy of the user, but its friend.

All in all this book is one, as we hope, that is as good to use as its predecessors.

Unfortunately we had to make some concessions to the very stressful process of putting together the new catalogue, thanks to the actions of the old publishing house, to lock out the editor from the catalogue-program for months before the sale of the book. Still:

This catalogue is again thicker than the one before and should be a friend for all lovers of jazz-records – as in the past.

I hope, you share this impression.

Sincerely
Martin Reichold
Publisher
27.4.2004

Wie findet man was?

Der Katalog besteht aus vier Teilen:

1. **Farbiger Cover-Teil**
2. **Titelverzeichnis**
3. **Interpretenverzeichnis**
4. **Label-/Vertriebsverzeichnis**

Farbteil

Der **1. Teil** enthält einen Auszug aus LP-, CD-, MC-, DVD und SACD-Cover

Datenteil

NEU: Zur besseren Übersicht sind die ersten Zeilen der einzelnen Einträge grau hinterlegt. Die Trennung der einzelnen Datenteile erfolgt durch das Zeichen | ‚da diese Trennung besser erkennbar ist als ein Komma.

Der **2. Teil** enthält in alphabetischer Reihenfolge alle im Katalog aufgeführten Titel mit dem Hinweis, auf welcher Platte dieses Stück ist und von welcher Formation (in alphabetischer Reihenfolge des ersten Buchstabens - z.B. **W**oody Herman and his Orchestra) es gespielt wird. Steht hier ein : hinter dem Titel, so ist das ein Oberbegriff für ein mehrteiliges Stück (z.B. Medley oder Suite). Ein - hinter dem Titel bedeutet, dass dieser nur ein Teil eines Medleys ist und nicht ausgespielt wird.

Wenn Sie einen Musiker suchen und wissen möchten, auf welchen Platten dieser mitwirkt, so können Sie im **3. Teil** nachsehen und finden in alphabetischer Reihenfolge alle Interpreten mit dem dazugehörigen Hinweis, auf welchen Platten diese zu hören sind, in welcher Formation (in alphabetischer Reihenfolge des ersten Buchstaben **W**oody Herman and his Orchestra) und welches Instrument sie dort spielen.

Der **4. Teil** enthält die Haupteinträge (Labelverzeichnis). Hier finden Sie, alphabetisch nach Labeln geordnet und in aufsteigender Reihenfolge der Bestellnummern, alle Platten des Kataloges. Die Angaben gliedern sich wie folgt:

- <u>Bestellnummer (es sind jeweils eigene Nummern für die verschiedenen Datenträger möglich)</u>
- <u>Obertitel der Platte</u>
- <u>EAN-Nummer</u> (soweit vorhanden)
  Zur besseren Übersicht sind diese Daten unterstrichen
- Formation (soweit ein Name vorhanden ist)
- Angabe der einzelnen Titel
- Aufnahmeort und Aufnahmedatum (soweit vorhanden)
- Leiter der Formation
- Interpreten mit Angabe der Instrumente
- Zusatzinformationen (soweit vorhanden) **fett gedruckt**

Zur besseren Übersicht wurden die einzelnen Bereiche in Graustufen gedruckt.

Alle neu aufgenommenen Titel sind im **4. Teil *fett und kursiv*** dargestellt.

How To Find What?

This catalogue consist of four sections:

1. **Coloured Photographs of Record Covers**
2. **Title Index**
3. **Artists Index**
4. **Label-/Distribution Index**

Coloured Photographs of Record Covers

The first section contains an excerpt from new LP-, MC-, DVD- and SACD-Covers.

Data section

New: The first lines of each insert are black on grey, for a better overview. The separation of the parts ensues by the sign , because this separation is much better recognizable than a comma.

Section 2 contains all titles listed in the catalogue in alphabetic order with reference to the records on which they appear and to the artists (in alphabetical order - e.g. **W**oody Herman and his Orchestra). If the code : follows a title then the piece is a medley or a suite composed of several individual pieces. The code - indicates that the preceding title is only part of a medley and is not played in its entirety.

Section 3 lists all artists in alphabetical order as well as the records on which they appear, the group or band in which they appear (in alphabetical order - e.g. **W**oody Herman and his Orchestra) and the instruments featured.

Section 4 is the main index (label index). All records in this catalogue are listed here. The system follows here:

- List number (each different kind of record may have a list number of its own)
- Title of record
- EAN-Number (if available) (These datas are underlined for a better overviewed)
- Listing of the tracks
- Location and date of each recording (if available)
- Head of formation
- Musicians with listing of their instruments
- Additional informations (if available) **bold letters**

For a better overview the different listings were printed in different shades of grey.

All newly listed titles are market in the **4th section** in *bold and italics*.

Die Instrumente

International gebräuchliche Abkürzungen:

alto-fl	alto flute		**mel**	mellophone
alto-h	alto horn		**org**	organ
as	alto-saxophone		**perc**	percussion
b	bass		**p**	piano
b-cl	bass-clarinet		**reeds**	saxophones / clarinets
b-g	bass-guitar		**sax**	saxophones, reeds
b-sax	bass-saxophone		**ss**	soprano-saxophones
b-tb	bass-trombone		**strings**	string section
b-tp	bass-trumpet		**tb**	trombone
bj	banjo		**tp**	trumpet
bo	bongos		**ts**	tenor-saxophone
bs	bariton-saxophone		**tu**	tuba
cello	violoncello		**v**	violine
cga	conga		**vib**	vibraphone
cl	clarinet		**voc**	vocal
co	cornet		**v-tb**	valve trombone
dr	drums		**wdb**	washboard
el-b	electric-bass		**xyl**	xylophone
el-g	electric-guitar			
engl-h	english-horn		**Sonstige Abkürzungen:**	
fl	flute			
fl-h	flugelhorn		**acc**	accompeniment
fr-h	french-horn		**arr**	arranger
g	guitar		**cond**	conducted
harm	harmonica		**ld**	bandleader
mand	mandoline		**Vol**	Volume (Folge)
mel	mellophone			

Firmenadressen

Album Records
Martin Buntrock Music
Braunfelder Allee 18
46286 Dorsten
Tel. 02369 248129
Fax 02369 22171
eMail
Internet

Aliso Records
Benhauser Straße 5
33100 Paderborn
Tel. 05251 54 14 37
Fax
eMail
Internet

ART BY HEART
Christian Willisohn & Rainer Schmidt GbR
Ehrenbürgstraße 9
81249 München
Tel. 089 870941
Fax 089 8714331
eMail artbyheart@t-online.de
Internet www.artbyheart.de

ATM Records
Postfach 54
28877 Grasberg
Tel. 04208 3228
Fax 04208 1082
eMail atmrecord@aol.com
Internet

Baer family records GmbH
Postfach 1154
27727 Hambergen
Tel. 04794 1399
Fax 04794 1574
eMail
Internet www.baer-family.de

Birth Records
Günter Hampel
Phil.-Reis-Straße 10
37075 Göttingen
Tel. 0551 31871
Fax 0551 31742
eMail www.jazzpages.com
Internet www.bekkoame.or.jp

BMG - Ariola - Classics
Neumarkter Str. 28
81673 München
Tel. 089 4136 98 88
Fax 089 4136 91 67
eMail cus01@bertelsmann.de
Internet

Connexion Agency
Ali Haurand
Konrad-Adenauer-Ring 10
41747 Viersen
Tel. 02162 18408
Fax 02162 15373
eMail connexion@jazzbox.com
Internet www.jazzbox.com

Creative Works Records
Mike Wider
Ronmatt 2
6037 Root
Tel. 0041-41 4504482
Fax 0041-41 4504482
eMail
Internet

DELTA Music GmbH
Europa-Allee 59
50226 Frechen
Tel. 02234 95012-0
Fax 02234 95012-40
eMail
Internet

ECM Export
Pasingerstr. 94
82166 Gräfelfing
Tel. 089 85 10 48
Fax 089 854 56 52
eMail order@ecmrecords.com
Internet www.ecmrecords.com

EDEL Distribution GmbH
a division of 'edel records GmbH'
Wichmannstraße 4
22607 Hamburg
Tel. 040 89085500
Fax 040 891610
eMail
Internet www.edel.com

Edition Soundmaster Musikproduktion
Römerstraße 23
80801 München
Tel.
Fax
eMail
Internet

Efa Medien GmbH
Billwerder Neuer Deich 334 a
20539 Hamburg
Tel. 040 7891700
Fax 040 782783
eMail
Internet

Ego Records
And Books Publisher GmbH
Hellabrunner Straße 30
81543 München
Tel. 089 664911
Fax 089 664035
eMail
Internet

EMI Electrola GmbH
Im Mediapark 8 a
50670 Köln
Tel. 0221 4905-2400
Fax 0221 4902-111
eMail
Internet www.emimusic.de

ENJA RECORDS
P.O.Box 190333
80603 München
Tel. 089 180 063 11
Fax 089 180 063 13
eMail info@enjarecords.com
Internet www.enjarecords.com

FENN MUSIC Service GmbH
Bundesstr. 4
21521 Dassendorf
Tel. 04104 9600-11 oder 9600-1
Fax 04104 9600-13
eMail fenn-music@t-online.de
Internet

Free Flow Music Produktion
c/o Schildberg
Sternstraße 11
60318 Frankfurt
Tel. 069 540177
Fax 069 54801606
eMail
Internet

GGG
Verlag und Mailorder
St.-Michel-Straße 3-4
39112 Magdeburg
Tel.
Fax
eMail
Internet

GLM Georg Löffler Musikverlag
Schillerstraße 7 (1. OG)
80336 München
Tel. 089 54884 79-5
Fax 089 54884 79-9
eMail glm@glm.de
Internet www.glm.de

Firmenadressen

HR Media Lizenz- und Verlagsges. mbH

Bertramstraße 8
60320   Frankfurt
Tel.   069   15543-30
Fax   069   15543-22
eMail   cscheffler@hr-online.de
Internet

Jazz-Network

Martinstraße 42 - 44
73728   Esslingen
Tel.   0711   3966294
Fax   0711   3966295
eMail   vertrieb@jazz-network.com
Internet www.jazz-network.com

Naxos Deutschland
Musik und Video Vertriebs GmbH
Wienburgstraße 171 a
48147   Münster
Tel.   0251   924060-0
Fax   0251   9240610
eMail   info@naxos.de
Internet

IN+OUT Records GmbH

Klarastr. 45
79106   Freiburg
Tel.   0761   2023647
Fax   0761   2023648
eMail   inandout@t-online.de
Internet www.inandout-records.com

Jazzpoint Records
G&J Records International
Entengasse 12
74189   Weinsberg
Tel.   07134   21019
Fax   07134   21118
eMail   jazzpointrecords@t-online.de
Internet www.jazzpages.com/Jerry Felix

Peta Music
Norbert Stein
Eiserweg 14 a
51503   Rösrath
Tel.   02205   82605
Fax   02205   86865
eMail   patamusic@compuserve.com
Internet www.patamusic.de

Indigo Records
Matthias Petzold
Freiheitsstraße 8
50321   Brühl
Tel.   02232   25971
Fax   02232   211898
eMail
Internet www.petzold-jazz-de/indigo-records.

M.A. Music
Stefan Haake
Multatulilaan 64
1215 BK Hilversum
Tel.
Fax
eMail
Internet www.mamusic.de

Phono Spezialverkauf

Postfach
70162   Stuttgart
Tel.   0711   182-1494
Fax   0711   182-1867
eMail
Internet

JA-RO Medien GmbH

Bismarckstraße 83
28203   Bremen
Tel.   0421   78811
Fax   0421   794196
eMail
Internet

MicNic Records

Saarlandstraße 6c
22303   Hamburg
Tel.   040   390 3693
Fax   040   390 3693
eMail
Internet www.stringthing.de

Salko Production

P.O.Box 323
8803   Rüschlikon
Tel.   0041-1 724 1766
Fax   0041-1 724 3112
eMail   mmm@salko-promotion.com
Internet www.salko-promotion.com

Jazz Connaisseur
Jörg + Doris Koran
Maiacherstraße 2
8916   Jonen
Tel.   0041-56 3643131
Fax   0441-56 6344065
eMail   www.jazzconnaisseur@bluewin.ch
Internet www.jazzconnaisseur.ch

Minor Music Records Gmbh

Osterladekop 68
21635   Jork
Tel.   04162   912000
Fax   04162   912001
eMail   minormusic@aol.com
Internet www.minormusic.de

Sony Music Entertainment GmbH
(Soulfood)
Bellevuestraße 3
10785   Berlin
Tel.   030   138 88-0
Fax   030   138 88-7440
eMail
Internet

Jazz Haus Musik

Venloer Straße 40
50672   Köln
Tel.   0221   952994-50
Fax   0221   952994-90
eMail   jhm@jazzhausmusik.de
Internet www.jazzhausmusik.de

Nabel Records

Rochusstraße 61
52062   Aachen
Tel.
Fax
eMail
Internet

sunny moon Musikvertrieb
Volker Dueck GdbR
Gustav-cords-Straße 19
50733   Köln
Tel.   0221   130 56 10
Fax   0221   130 56 119
eMail   mail@sunny-moon.com
Internet www.sunny-moon.com

Jazz4ever
Alfred Mangold
Schwander Straße 17
90459   Nürnberg
Tel.
Fax
eMail
Internet

Nagel-Heyer Records GmbH

Rugenbarg 85
22549   Hamburg
Tel.   040   801884 oder 830846
Fax   040   8002232
eMail   nhrjazz@aol.com
Internet www.nagelheyer.de

Trick Music Records Distribution

Spitalstraße 1
97499   Traunstadt
Tel.   09528   1324
Fax   09528   629
eMail
Internet

Firmenadressen

Triptychon Musikproduktion
Agentur für Design und Kulturkomm. GmbH
Lerchenfeldstraße 16
80528   München
Tel.
Fax
eMail
Internet

True Muze Records

Hohenesch 61 A
22765   Hamburg
Tel.   040   397568
Fax   040   397568
eMail   truemuze@voices.de
Internet   www.voices.de/truemuze.html

Tutu Records

Max-Zimmermann-Straße 2
82319   Starnberg
Tel.   08151   16539
Fax   08151   12549
eMail   tutu@jazzrecords.com
Internet   www.jazzrecords.com/tutu

Universal Music Germany

Stralauer Allee 1
10245   Berlin
Tel.   030   52007-01
Fax   030   52007-09
eMail
Internet   www.universalmusic.de

Warner Classics & Jass Germany

Oberbaumbrücke 1
20457   Hamburg
Tel.   040   30339-0
Fax   040   30339-333
eMail
Internet   www.warnermusic.de

Zomba Records

Benzstrasse, Industriegebiet
35797   Merenberg
Tel.   02325   6972-00
Fax   02325   6972-22
eMail
Internet

Zyx Music GmbH

Benzstraße, Industriegebiet
35797   Merenberg
Tel.   06471   505-0
Fax   06471   505-199
eMail   zyxinfo@zyx.de
Internet   www.zyx.de / www.zyxmusic.co

Das Oldie-Markt-Magazin

Das Gold im Plattenschrank – Abteilung Jazz

Es gilt, eine der hartnäckigsten Legenden im Sammlerbereich aufzuklären: Jazz ist nicht viel wert.

Schon lange ist diese Aussage ebenso obsolet wie die früher vielleicht bestehende Trennung zwischen Rock, Pop und Jazz bei den Plattensammlern. Spätestens seit den 90er Jahren hat sich ein stilübergreifendes Gebiet entwickelt, das im Grenzbereich zwischen Jazz und Rock angesiedelt ist und jenseits von solchen Stil-Hybriden wie Jazzrock oder Souljazz Künstler und Veröffentlichungen in die teuersten Segmente befördert hat, die lange nur Spezialisten und Fachleuten ein Begriff waren.

Das fand in den 90er Jahren des letzten Jahrhunderts seinen Ausdruck auch auf solchen gut verkauften Samplern wie den CDs des Hamburger *Mojo*-Clubs, auf denen ohne eine enge Eingrenzung auf einen Stil die Grenzbereiche zwischen Jazz, Soul und Rock abgegrast wurden. Dies war bereits ein Resultat von den stetig wachsenden Preisen auf dem Sammlermarkt für Veröffentlichungen solcher Firmen wie **Blue Note, Saba und MPS**, um nur drei der wichtigsten zu nennen.

Dabei werden die meisten der begehrten Platten durch drei Kriterien definiert: Zum einen der stilistischen Einordnung in ein Feld, das man ganz grob als Modern Jazz bezeichnen kann. Dazu gehören die schon lange populären Jazzrock-Produktionen ebenso wie die Avantgarde (auch inklusive des Free Jazz), der Verbindungen mit der schwarzen Musik (besonders dem Soul) und der Weiterentwicklung des Be-Bop.

Dies führt direkt zum zweiten Kriterium: Das Zeitfenster. Dies öffnete sich in den 50er Jahren und dauerte bis in die 70er Jahre, wobei die Höhepunkte allgemein in den 60er Jahren liegen.

Sieht man sich beispielsweise die Preisentwicklung von **Saba/MPS** an, tauchen die mit Abstand höchsten Preise in der Zeit von 1966-68 auf. Platten von Art van Damme, Wolfgang Lauth, Wolfgang Dauner, Dieter Reith und anderen Künstlern erreichen regelmäßig Preise im dreistelligen Euro-Bereich. Das dritte Kriterium schließlich betrifft wie beim Rock auch die großen Namen: Das reicht von deutschen Größen wie Volker Kriegel, Wolfgang Dauner oder Albert Mangelsdorff (die Liste ließe sich beliebig verlängern) bis zu den Stars der Moderne aus den USA und Europa. Ihre Originale auf solchen Labeln wie **Impulse, Prestige** oder **Blue Note** haben immer gute Preise erzielt und das hat sich nicht geändert – im Gegenteil: Sie halten nicht nur ihren Wert, sondern steigern ihn noch.

Eine Einschränkung ist für das Verständnis dieser Ausführungen freilich unerlässlich: Alles, was hier über den Wert von Jazzplatten gesagt wurde, gilt ausschließlich für das Vinyl. CDs sind – und da unterscheidet sich der Markt im Jazz in keinster Weise vom Rock – Gebrauchsware, deren Wert bestenfalls dem Ladenpreis entspricht. Deswegen sollte man seine Sammlung einmal daraufhin untersuchen, ob man Platten besitzt, auf die die angesprochenen Kriterien zutreffen.

Eine Zeitschrift wie der Oldie-Markt kann nicht nur Sammlungen auffüllen, sie kann auch zur Vergoldung des eigenen Plattenbestands genützt werden.

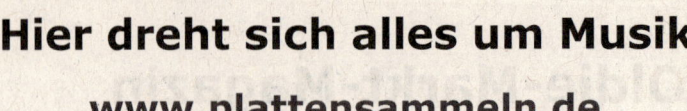

Hier dreht sich alles um Musik

www.plattensammeln.de

Der leichte Einstieg in die Internetseiten von Oldie-Markt und FunWithMusic.

Vinyl bleibt Vinyl

FunWithMusic	Plattenbewertung
Oldie-Markt-Auktionen	Vinyl-Abkürzungen
Oldie-Markt Magazin	Auktionstermine
OM-Services/Events	Oldie-Markt Depots
Oldie-Markt Archiv	Fanclubs, Partnerlinks
OM-Probeheft / Abo	Bieten / Anbieten
Highlight des Monats	Auktionsergebnisse
Kostenlose Downloads	
WEBSHOP Musik - ROCK&POP-Kataloge	
WEBSHOP HiFi	Vinyl bleibt Vinyl
	Stereoscopie
	WEBSHOP Foto

(c) Peter Trieb
D 84453 Mühldorf

Surfen Sie doch einfach einmal

Internet: www.plattensammeln.de

Bei Fragen im Bereich eMail-Gebote und Software für die
Oldie-Markt-Auktionen helfen wir gerne:
**Datenerfassung und Computerworks für das
OLDIE-MARKT-MAGAZIN:**

Peter Trieb - Datentechnik
Postfach 1165 - D 84442 Mühldorf
Tel (+49) 08631 - 162785
Fax (+49) 08631 - 162786
Email: info@plattensammeln.de

Software für Kleinanzeigen im Oldie-Markt
Software für Auktionsgebote
ROCK&POP-Preiskataloge
Software zur Pflege der eigenen Sammlung

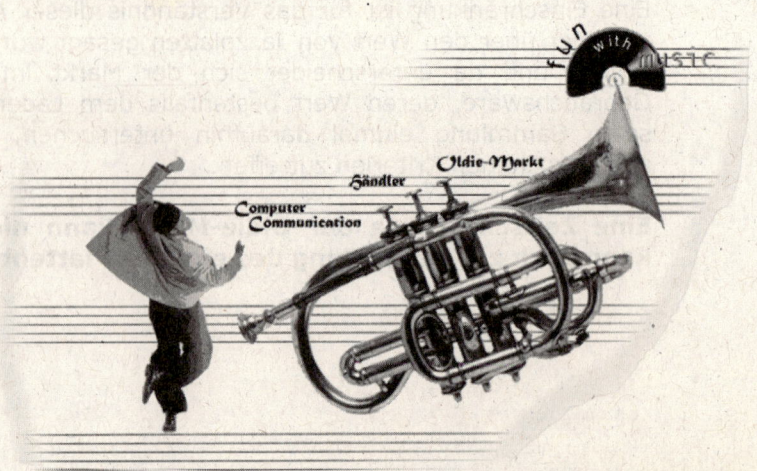

Notizen

Notizen

Europas größte Fachzeitschrift für Platten- und CD-Sammler

The Best of OLDIE-MARKT

Ein Angebot unter Freunden

Her damit.
Sofort.

Und zwar jeden Monat.

Im Abo.

| Bitte ausschneiden und einsenden |

New Media Verlag GmbH
Abo-Service
Postfach 21 04 40

90122 Nürnberg

Die Rockgeschichte frei Haus

| Bitte ausschneiden und einsenden |

New Media Verlag GmbH
Abo-Service
Postfach 21 04 40

90122 Nürnberg

Unser Dankeschön für Ihre Vermittlung

○ Eine Folge »The Story Of Rock« Ihrer Wahl (Band_____)

○ 20 kostenlose Anzeigenzeilen im OLDIE-MARKT

○ Die Repertoire/Edel Contraire-CD

_____

○ Ich bin Abonnent des OLDIE-MARKT

| Bitte ausschneiden und einsenden |

New Media Verlag GmbH
Abo-Service
Postfach 21 04 40

90122 Nürnberg

Her damit. Und zwar jeden Monat.

Bitte liefern Sie mir jeden Monat mein ganz persönliches Heft. Das Abonnement beginnt ab der nächsterreichbaren Ausgabe.

Ich wünsche die angekreuzte, jährliche Zahlungsweise (Inland € 85,20 inkl. Mwst. und Porto, Ausland € 94,60 inkl. Porto):

☐ gegen Rechnung (Bitte kein Geld einsenden. Rechnung abwarten!)

☐ durch Bankeinzug. Die Einzugsermächtigung erlischt mit Kündigung des Abonnements.

Kontonummer _____ BLZ _____

Name und Ort der Bank: _____

Vor- und Zuname _____

Straße _____

PLZ, Ort _____

Unterschrift _____

Mir ist bekannt, daß ich diesen Vertrag innerhalb einer Woche widerrufen kann. Es genügt eine schriftliche Mitteilung innerhalb der Widerrufsfrist an den Verlag. Von dieser Garantie habe ich Kenntnis genommen und bestätige dies durch meine zweite Unterschrift.

Datum _____ Unterschrift _____

Oldie-Markt — Europas größte Fachzeitschrift für Platten- und CD-Sammler

Ihre »Story Of Rock«-Bestellung

Ich möchte meine Bestellung wie folgt bezahlen:

☐ ein Band für € 10,-
☐ Bände für _____

oder zum Spartarif im voraus:

☐ 8 Bände für € 75,- (Ich spare € 5,-!)
☐ 16 Bände für € 150,- (ich erhalte 16 Bände zum Preis von 15 und spare € 10,-!)

Name _____ Vorname _____

Straße/Nr. _____

PLZ _____ Ort _____

Datum _____ Unterschrift _____

Bitte senden Sie kein Geld, Sie erhalten eine Rechnung. Danke.

Widerrufsrecht: Sie garantieren mir, daß ich diese Vereinbarung innerhalb einer Woche ab heute ohne Angaben von Gründen beim New Media Verlag, Abo-Service, Parkstraße 13, 90409 Nürnberg, schriftlich widerrufen kann. Zur Wahrung dieser Frist genügt die rechtzeitige Absendung des Widerrufs.

Datum _____ Unterschrift _____

Das »Oldie-Markt«-Freundschaftsabo

Als Vermittler eines neuen »Oldie-Markt«-Abonnenten liefern Sie mir bitte die umseitig angekreuzte Prämie an folgende Adresse:

Name, Vorname _____

Straße/Nr. _____

PLZ/Wohnort _____

Die Zusendung der Prämie erfolgt, sobald der neue Abonnent bezahlt hat.

Ja, ich bin der neue Abonnent von »Oldie-Markt«:

Senden Sie mir »Oldie-Markt« ab dem nächst erreichbaren Heft für mindestens 1 Jahr frei Haus. Der Preis für ein »Oldie-Markt«-Jahresabonnement beträgt € 85,20. »Oldie-Markt« wurde während der letzten drei Monate nicht an diese Adresse geliefert.

Name, Vorname des neuen Abonnenten _____

Straße/Nr. _____

PLZ/Wohnort _____

Prämienempfänger und Abonnent dürfen nicht demselben Haushalt angehören.

Bitte Rechnung abwarten, keine Vorauszahlung leisten (€ 85,20 in 12 Monaten).

Datum/Unterschrift _____

Widerrufsrecht: Ich kann diese Vereinbarung innerhalb einer Frist von sieben Tagen widerrufen. Die Frist beginnt mit Absendung dieser Bestellung. Zur Wahrung der Frist genügt die rechtzeitige Absendung des Widerrufs an den New Media Verlag, Abo-Service, Parkstraße 13, 90409 Nürnberg.
Ich bestätige dies mit meiner zweiten Unterschrift

Unterschrift _____

Oldie-Markt — Europas größte Fachzeitschrift für Platten- und CD-Sammler

Cover - Auswahl

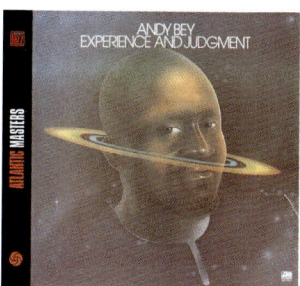 Andy Bay-Experience .. (Warner)
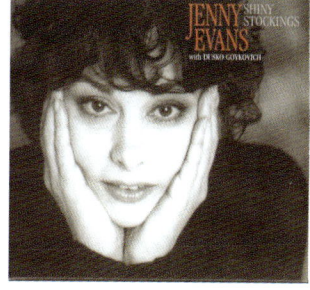 Jenny Evans - Shiny Stockings
 The Cactus of Knowledge (enja)
 A night at birdland (Warner)

 Cotton Club Stomp (Warner)
 Chicago Speak Easy (Warner)
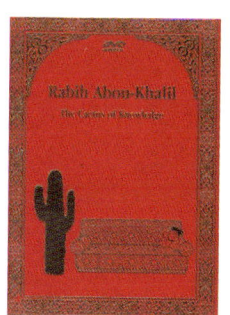 The Cactus of Kowledge - DVD
 52'nd Street (warner)

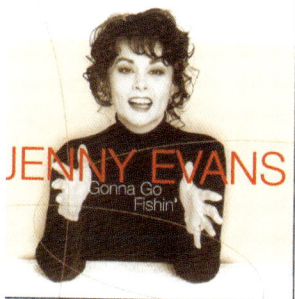 Jenny Evans - Gonna Go Fishin'
 Dhafer Youssef (enja)
 Renaud Garcia-Fons (enja)
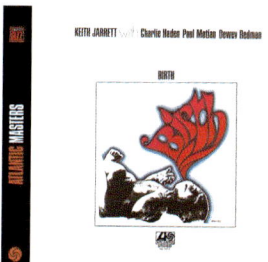 Keith Jarrett - (Warner)

 Ferenc Snétberger-Balance (enja)
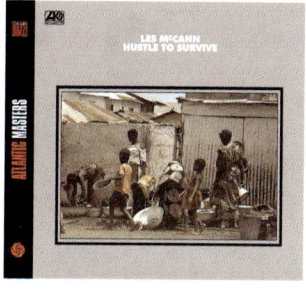 Les McCann (Warner)
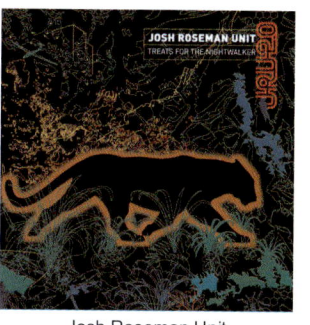 Josh Roseman Unit
 Joana MacGregor - Play

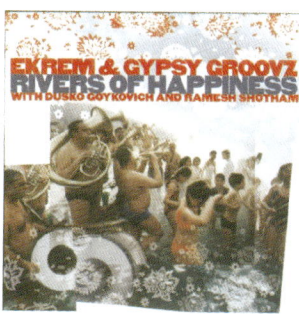 Rivers of Happiness
 Myriam Alter - IF
 Jackson (Warner)
 Jean-Louis Matinier-Confluences

 Harlem House Rent Party (Warner)
 carlos bica & azul
 Sandra Weckert - Bar Jazz
 Colossus of Sound

Cover - Auswahl

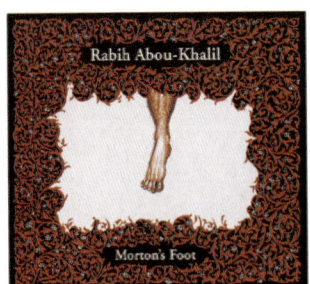
Morton's Foot

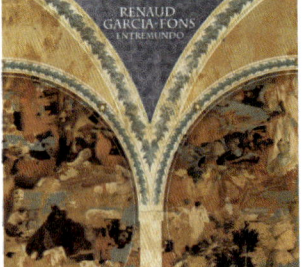
Renaud Garcia-Fons-Entremundo

The Owner Of the River Bank

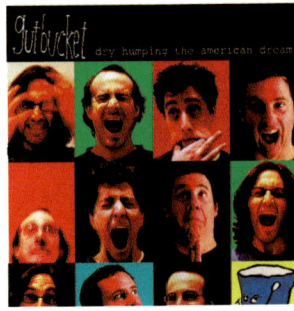
dry humping the american dream

Alexi Toumarila Quartet (Warner)

jenny evans - nuages

Joyosa

Crawford - more soul (Warner)

McCann - Second Movement (Warner)

Ray Charles presents - Fathead (Warner)

Bennie Wallace - The Nearness of you

uwai

Samba Do Mar

Mahmoud Turkmani - zâkira

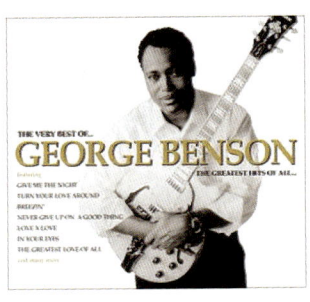
Benson - very best of

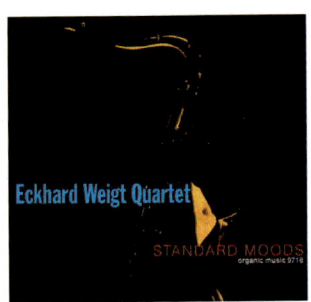
Standard Moods (Organic Music)

Márcio Tubino (Organic Music)

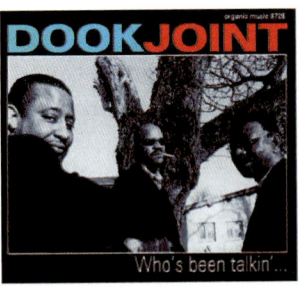
DOOK JOINT (Organic Music)

Scenario - jazz the Beatles (Organic)

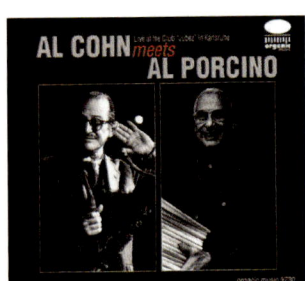
Al Cohn meets Al Porcino (Organic)

Marc Schmolling Trio (Organic Music)

Wanja Slavin meets Marc Schmolling

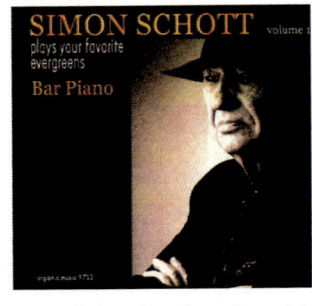
Simon Schott - Bar Piano (Organic)

Bembeya Jazz (Fenn)

Cover - Auswahl

Kora Jazz Trio (Fenn)

Jim Pepper - Flying Eagle (Fenn)

Mingus (Fenn)

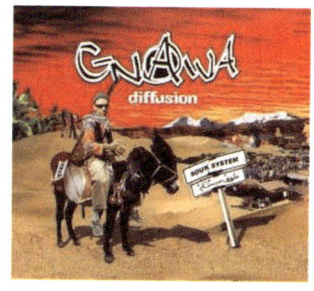
Gnoawa - diffusion (Warner)

Passport - Back to Brazil (Warner)

cafe brasil 2 (Warner)

Nascimento - Pietá (Warner)

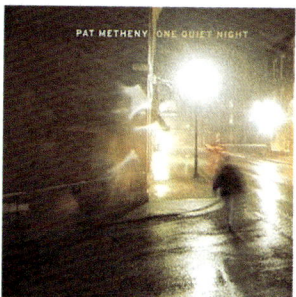
Theny - One quiet night (Warner)

Soulongue (Warner)

Norton - Original Score (Warner)

space night vol. IX (Warner)

Pastorius - Punk Jazz (Warner)

Music from the Nonesuch (Warner)

Donald Harrison jr. (Fenn)

Bill Frisell (Warner)

Thomas Lersen (Warner)

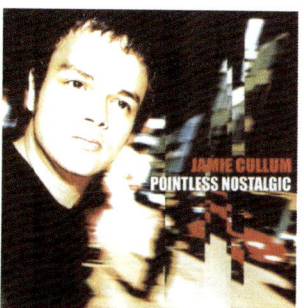
Jamie Collum (Fenn)

stacey kent - The boy next door (Fenn)

Alan Holdsworth Group - Live (Fenn)

Frank Kroll - Landscape (Fenn)

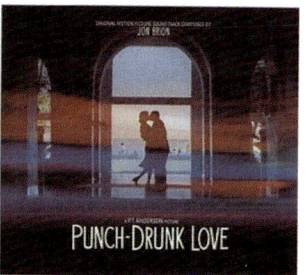
Punch Drunk (Warner)

Java-Court Gamalan V.II (Warner)

Dave Holland (ECM)

Egberto Gismonti (ECM)

Cover - Auswahl

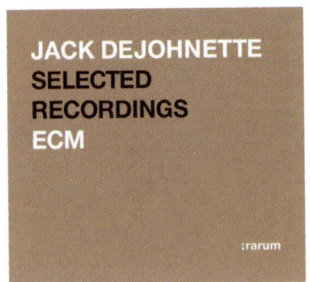
Jack Dejohnette (ECM)

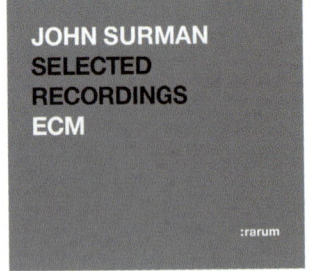
John Surman (ECM)

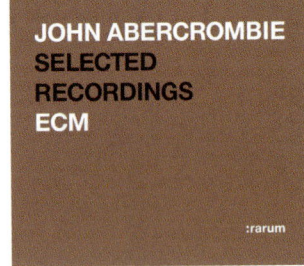
John Abercrombie (ECM)

Carla Bely (ECM)

Paul Motian (ECM)

Tomasz Stanko (ECM)

Eberhard Weber (ECM)

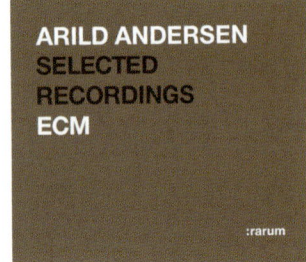
Erild Andersen (ECM)

Jon Christensen (ECM)

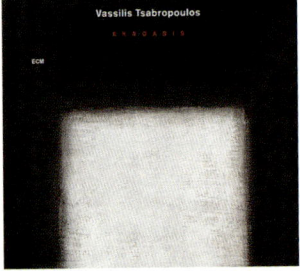
Vassilis Tsabropoulos (ECM)

Rosslyn (ECM)

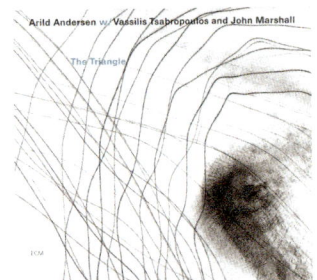
The Triangle (EMC)

Enrico Rava (EMC)

FREE AND EQUAL (EMC)

Tribute to Lester (EMC)

Sofienberg Variations (EMC)

Promises Kept (EMC)

Responsorium (ECM)

Rugace (ECM)

Tord Gustavsen Trio (ECM)

VINDONISSA (ECM)

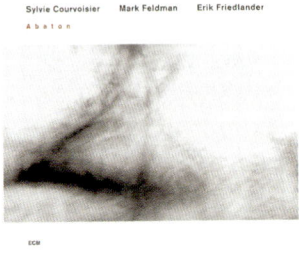
Abaton (ECM)

The Rain (ECM)

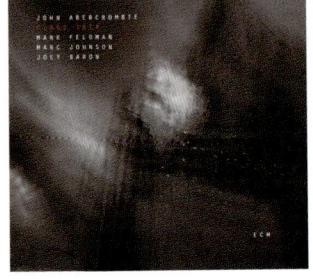
CLASS TRIP (ECM)

Cover - Auswahl

Memory-Vision (ECM)

Terra Nostra (ECM)

Napoli's Walls (ECM)

Angles of Repose

Universal Syncopations (EMC)

Live At Birdland (ECM)

Suspended Night (ECM)

Evening Falls (ECM)

Which Way is East

Looking for America

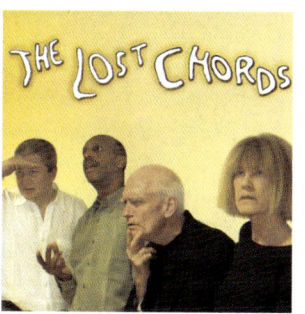
The Lost Chords

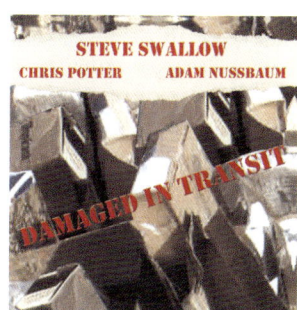
Damaged in Transit

jo ambros - wanderlust (Fenn)

Archie Shepp - Swing Low (Fenn)

Stephane Grappelli (Fenn)

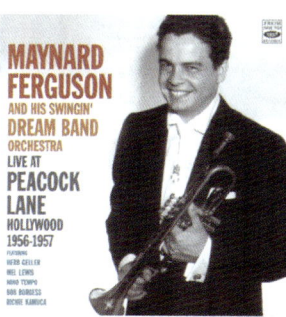
Maynard Ferguson (Fenn)

Yusef Lateef-Lost in sound (Fresh Sound)

bud shank - alone together (Fresh Sound)

Kurt Rosenwinkel Trio (Fenn)

New York-Barcelona Crossing (Fenn)

Chris Cheek - Vine (Fenn)

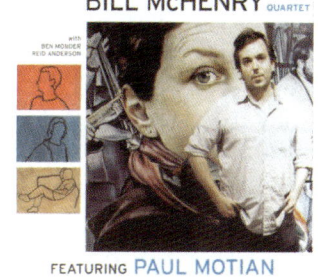
Bill McHenry Quartet (Fenn)

Saxophonic Soul and Blues (Fenn)

Venice - Christian Elsässer Trio (Organic)

Cover - Auswahl

Doubel bass (SteepleChase)

Chet Baker - Paul Bley (SteepleChase)

Duke Jordan Trio (SteepleChase)

Larry Schneider Quartet (SteepleChase)

Louis Smith Quintet (SteepleChase)

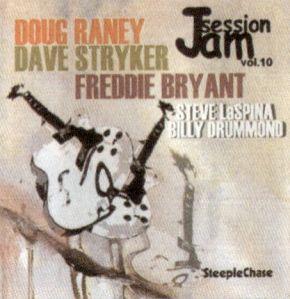
Jam Session Vol 10 (SteepleChase)

Dave Ballou (SteepleChase)

Duke Robillard & Herb Ellis (Storyville)

Thelonious Monk Quartet (Storyville)

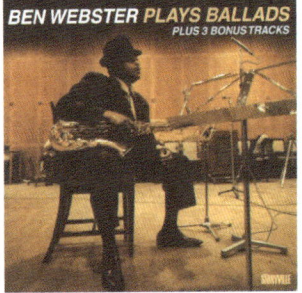
Ben Webster Plays Ballads (Storyville)

The Duke In Munich (Storyville)

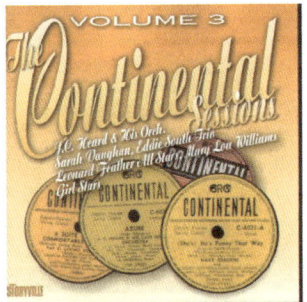
Continental Sessions Vol. 3 (Storyville)

Illinois Jaque Quartet (Storyville)

Dexter Gordon (Storyville)

Zoot Sims (Storyville)

Clark Terry - OW (Storyville)

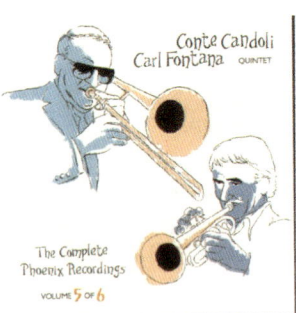
Candoli-Fontana Quintet (Fenn)

The Carl Fontana Quartet (Fenn)

Stefania Tallini Trio (yvp)

Ralph Sutton - Live (nagel heyer)

Butch Miles (nagel heyer)

Pete York Jazz All Stars (nagel heyer)

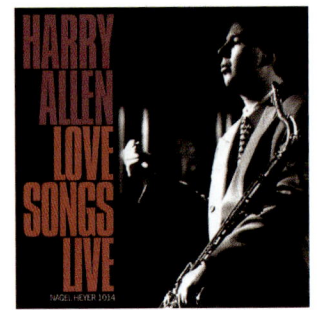
Harry Allen - Love songs (nagel heyer)

Terell Stafford (nagel heyer)

Cover - Auswahl

 Martin Sasse Trio (nagel heyer)
 Eric Reed - Happiness (nagel heyer)
 2GETHER (nagel heyer)
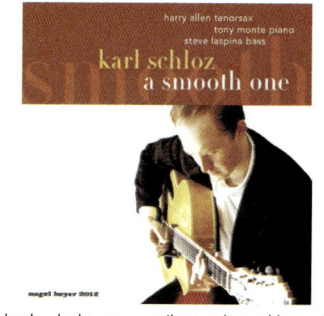 karl scholz - a smooth one (nagel heyer)

 Ken Peplowski Quartet (nagel heyer)
 Lyambiko-Out of this mood (nagel heyer)
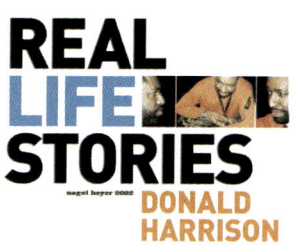 Donald Harrison (nagel - heyer)
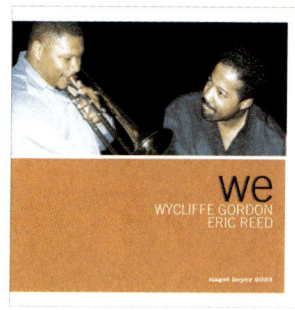 Gordon / Reed - WE (nagel heyer)

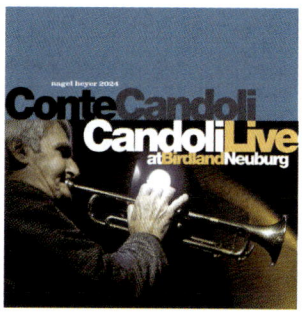 Candoli Live (nagel heyer)
 Claudio Roditi - Three for one (nh)
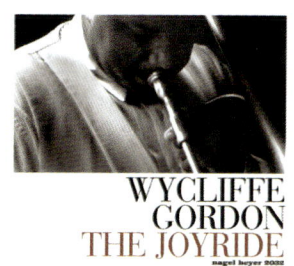 Wycliffe Gordon - The Joyride (nh)
 Lyambiko - Shades of Delight (nh)

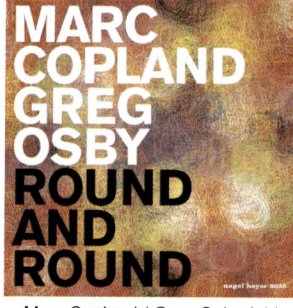 Marc Copland / Greg Osby (nh)
 Roy Powell - Solace (nagel heyer)
 Wayne Escoffery-Intuition (nagel heyer)
 Zona Sul - Pure Love (nagel heyer)

 Frode Berg - Pig it! (nagel heyer)
 Donald Harrison - Heroes (nagel heyer)
 Martin Sasse Trio - close encounter (nh)
 Robert Stewart (nagel heyer)

 Darren Barrett (nagel heyer)
 Masso / Peplowski - Just Friends (nh)
 soulmates (nagel heyer)
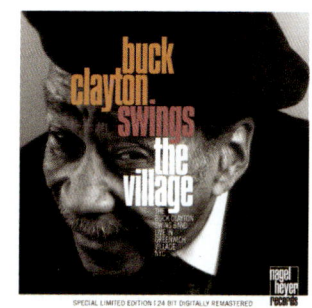 buck clayton - swings the village (nh)

Cover - Auswahl

Warren Vaché - My shining hour (nh)

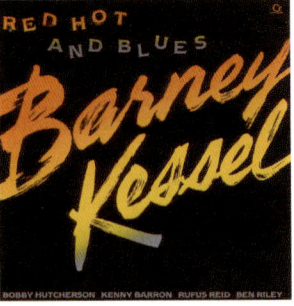
Barney Kessel (Contemporairy)

Harrell (Contemporairy)

Tom Harrell - Visions (Contemporairy)

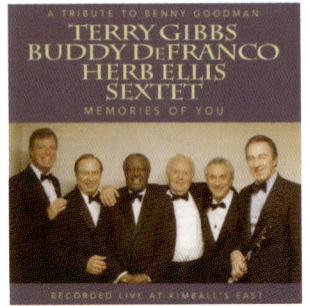
A Tribute to Benny Goodman (Contemp.)

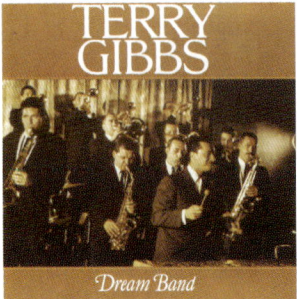
Terry Gibbs - Dream Band (Contemp.)

Fitzgerald - Ellington (Pablo)

Duke Ellington (Pablo)

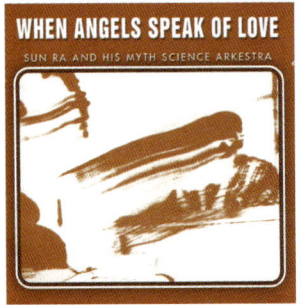
When Anels Speak Of Love (Evidance)

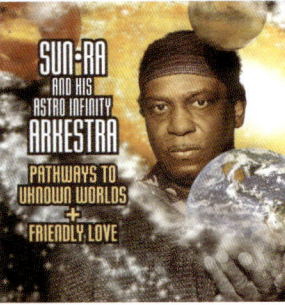
Pathways To Uknown Worlds

It took so long (Einstein Music)

Sonny Rollins (Milestone)

Chico O'Farrill (Milestone)

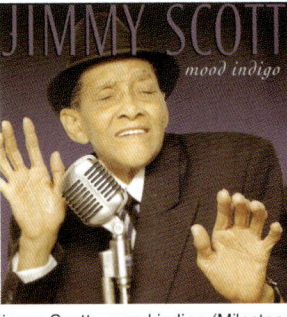
Jimmy Scott - mood indigo (Milestone)

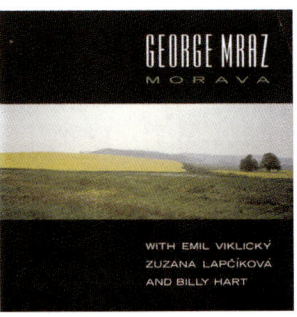
George Mraz - Morava (Milestone)

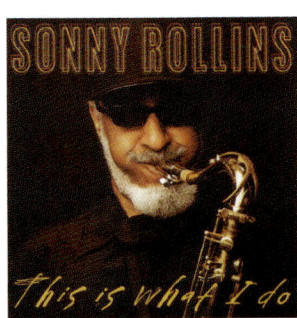
Sonny Rollins - This is what I do

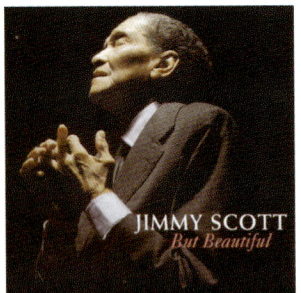
Jimmy Scott - But Beautiful (Milestone)

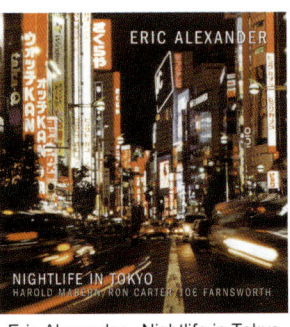
Eric Alexander - Nightlife in Tokyo

jimmy scott - MOON GLOW (Milestone)

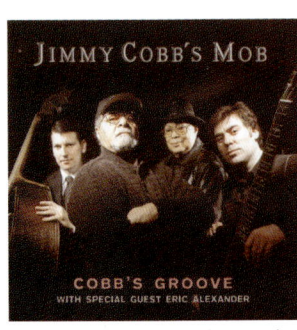
Jimmy Cobb's Mob (Milestone)

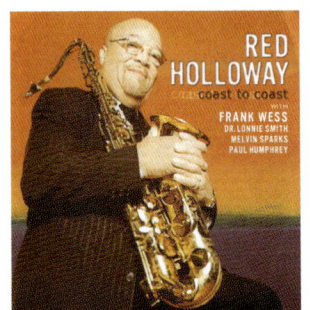
Red Holloway - coast to coast

The Modern Jazz Quartett (prestige)

Clifford Brown Memorial (prestige)

John Coltrane - Soultrane (prestige)

Cover - Auswahl

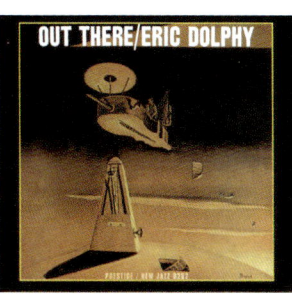
Eric Dolphy - Out There (prestige)

Thelonious Monk (Riverside)

the hawk flies high (Riverside)

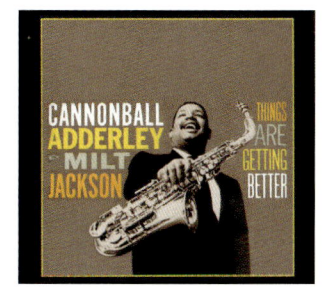
Cannonball Adderley With Milt Jackson

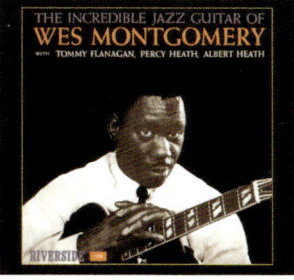
Wes Montgomery (Riverside)

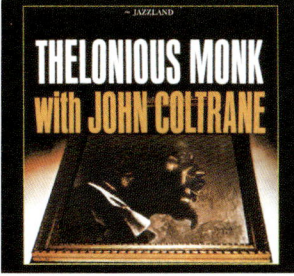
Thelonious Monk (Jazzland)

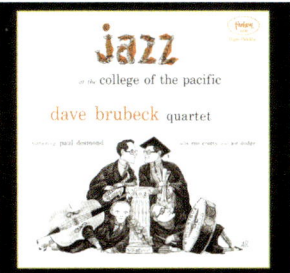
dave brubeck quartet (Fantasy)

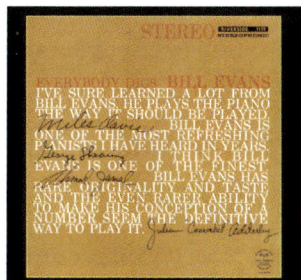
Bill Evans-Everybody Digs (Riverside)

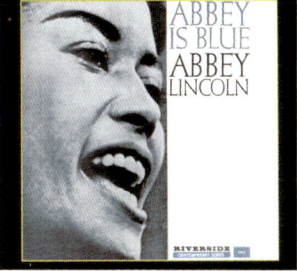
Abbey Lincoln - Abbey is Blue

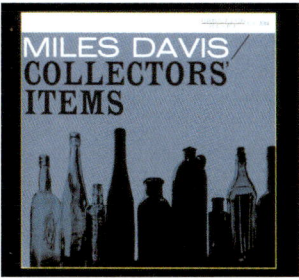
Miles Davis - Collector's Items

Chet (Riverside)

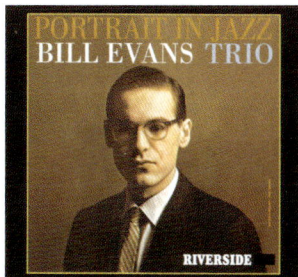
Bill Evans Trio (Riverside)

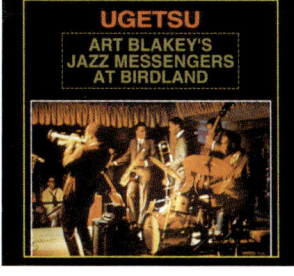
Art Blakey's Jazz Messengers

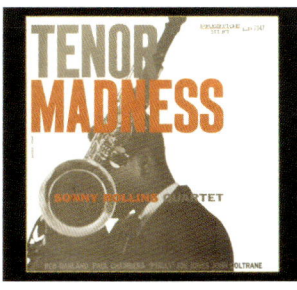
Sonny Rollins Quartet (prestige)

Cookin' with the Miles Davos Quintet

John Coltrane - Lush Life (prestige)

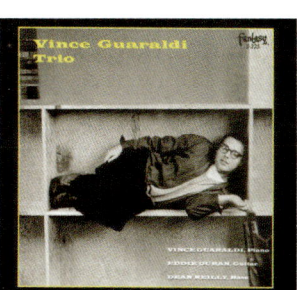
Vince Guaraldi Trio (Fantasy)

Ornette Coleman (Jazz Classics)

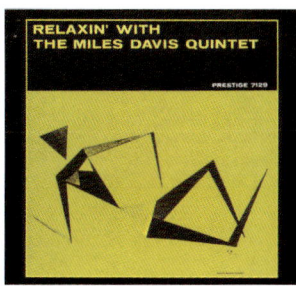
The Miles Davis Quintet (prestige)

sonny rollins - plus 4 (prestige)

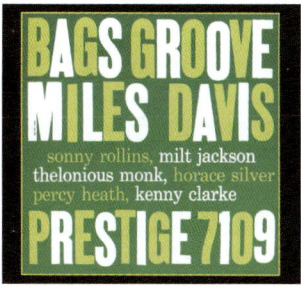
Miles Davis - Bags Groove (prestige)

Sonny Rollins - Saxophone Colossus

gene ammons - boss tenor

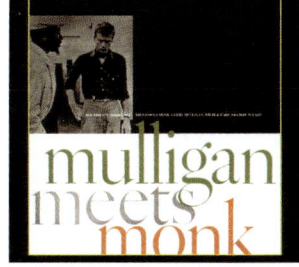
mulligan meets monk

Cover - Auswahl

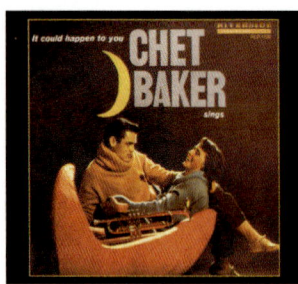 Chet Baker Sings (Riverside)
 McCoy Tyner - Sahara (Milestone)
 Hampton Hawes Trio
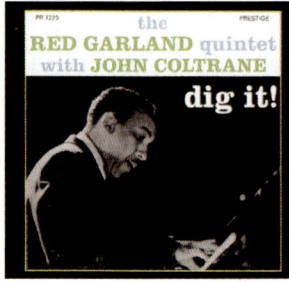 Red Garland Quintet (prestige)

 nippon soul (Riverside)
 Yusef Lateef - Eastern Sounds
 The Eddie "Lockjaw" Davis Cookbook
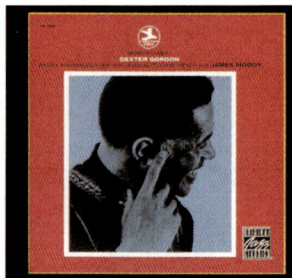 Dexter Gordon (Prestige)

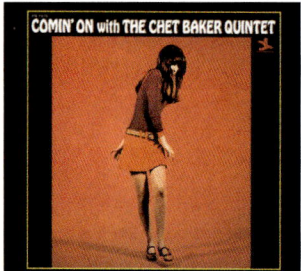 The Chet Baker Quintet
 Blues Sonata-Charlie Byrd (Riverside)
 Mingus By Five
 Olaf Kübler - Midnight Soul

 Dee Dee Bridgewater
 Vintage Dolphy (enja)
 diana krall - stepping out
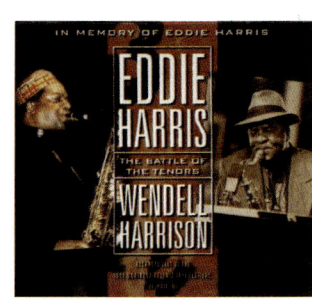 The Battle Of The Tenors

 David Murray - Creole Project
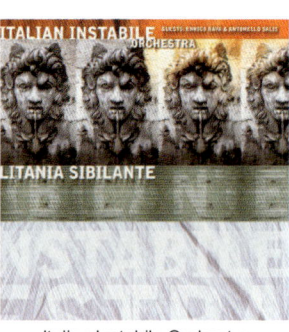 Italian Instabile Orchestra
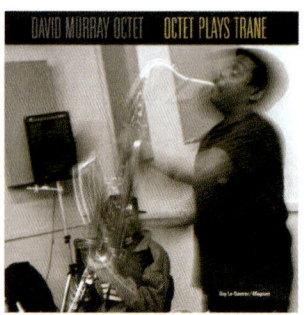 David Murray Octet - ..Plays Trane
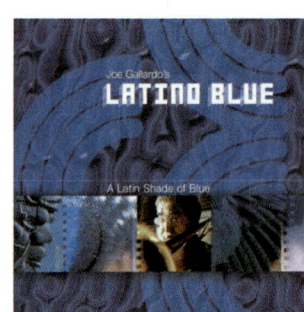 Joe Gallardo's Latino Blue

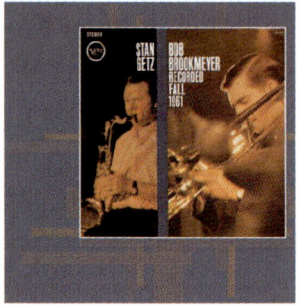 Stan Getz - Bob Brookmeyer (Verve)
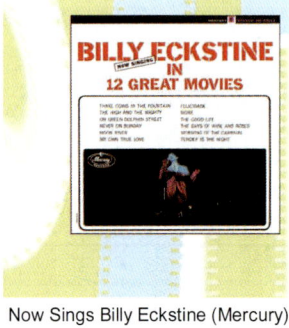 Now Sings Billy Eckstine (Mercury)
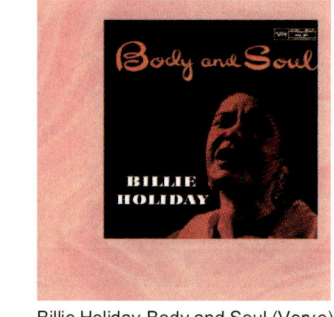 Billie Holiday-Body and Soul (Verve)
 Al Cohn-Zoot Sims Quintet (Mercury)

Cover - Auswahl

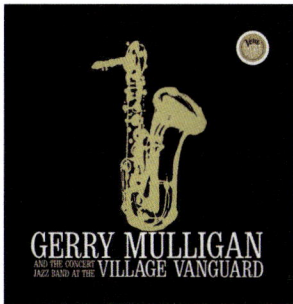 Gerry Mulligan - Village Vanguard

 Lionel Hampton-Jazz in Paris (Gitanes)

 Saxophones à Saint-Germain de Prés

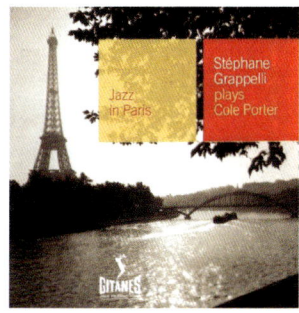 Stephané Grapelli plays Cole Porter

 Henri Crolla & co - Notre ami Django

 Gérard Badini - The Swing Machine

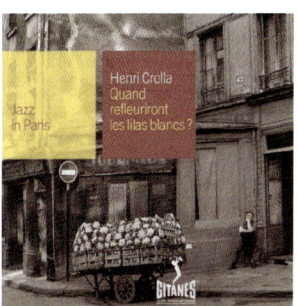 Henri Crolla (Gitanes)

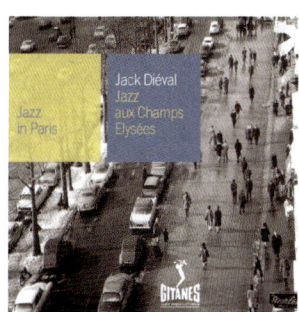 Jack Diéval - Jazz aux Champs Elysées

 Dizzy Gillespie & his Operatic Strings

 Stéphane Grapelli - Django (Gitanes)

 Bobby Jaspar - Jeux de quartes

 Blosom Dearie - The Pianist (Gitanes)

 Esbjörn Svensson Trio (Act)

 Tim Hagans with Norrbotten Big Band

 Geir Lysne - Suite for Jazz Orchestra

 Der Rote Bereich (Act)

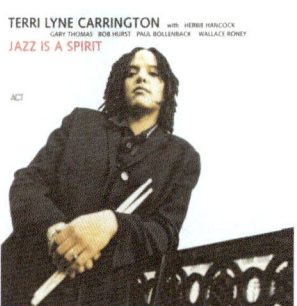 Terri Lyne Carrington-Jazz is a Spirit

 Nils Landgren - Senitmental Journey

 Nguyên Lê Purple (Act)

 David Binney - Balance (Act)

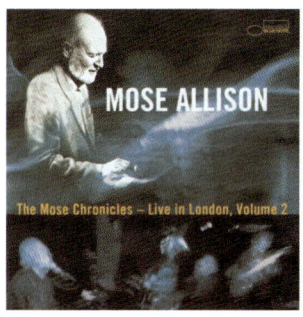 Mose Allison Live in London (BlueNote)

 Cannonball - Takes Charge (Capitol)

 Medeski Martin And Wood - Uninvisible

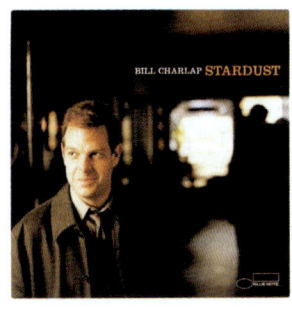 Bill Charlap - Stardust (BlueNote)

Cover - Auswahl

 grant green - ballads (BlueNote)
 Benny Waters - Birdland Birthday
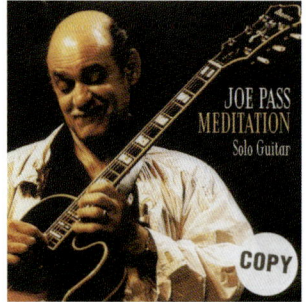 Joe Pass - Meditation
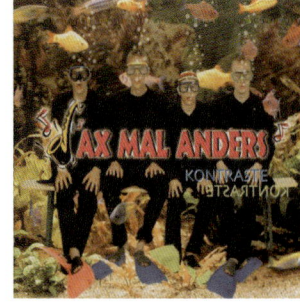 Sax Mal Anders - Kontraste

 Django Reinhardt - Souvenirs
 Schlaier Hirt Duo
 attila zoller + helmut kagerer
 byron stripling (nagel heyer)

 A Jazz Salute To the Big Apple
 Terell Stafford (nagel heyer)
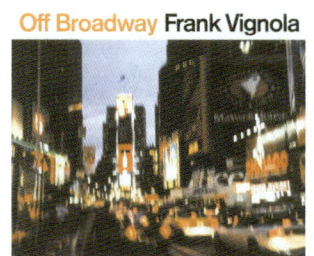 Frank Vignola-Off Broadway (nagel heyer)
 Martin Sasse Trio - Here We Come

 Joachim Schoenecker - in the moment
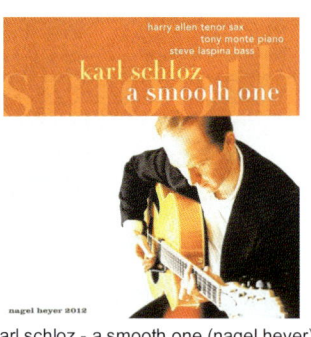 karl schloz - a smooth one (nagel heyer)
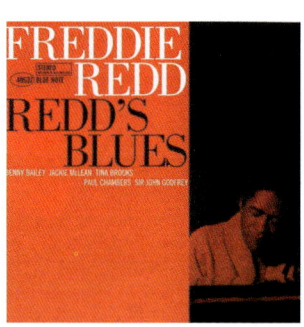 Freddie Redd - Redd's Blues
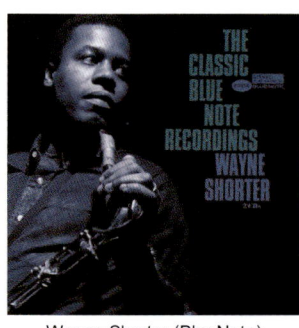 Wayne Shorter (BlueNote)

 cannonball adderley - ballads
 Duke Ellington - Money Jungle (BlueNote)
 (Blue Note)
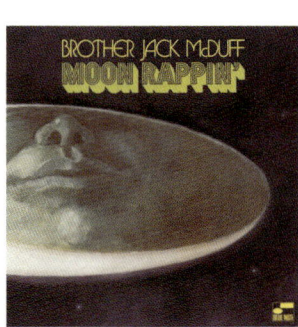 Brother Jack McDuff (BlueNote)

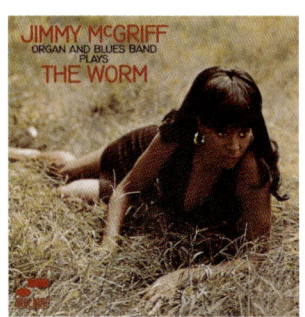 Jimmy McGriff - The Worm (BlueNote)
 Richard Groove Holmes (BlueNote)
 Jason Moran - Modernistic
 Sarah Vaughan - Vaughan and violins

Cover - Auswahl

 stefanie schlesinger - what love is

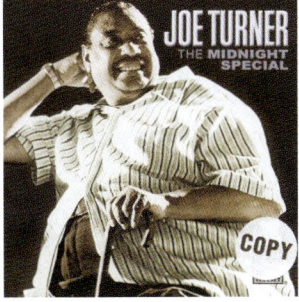 Joe Turner - The Midnight Special

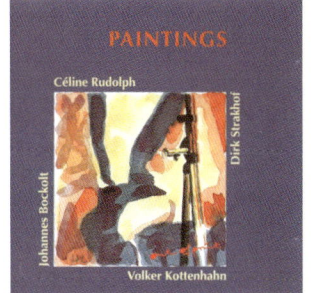 Paintings

 Book Of Travels - By Céline Rudolph

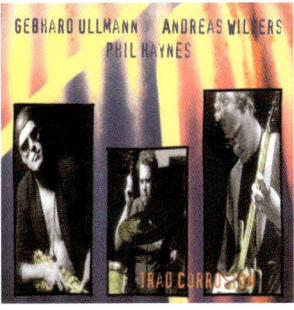 Trad Corrosion

 Tim Sund

 Fishland Canyon

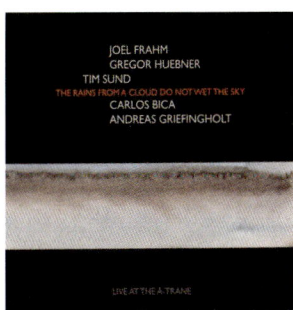 Live At The A-Trane

 Tim Sund Trio - Trialogue

 Ansgar Striepens Quintet

 Windstärke 4 - Lunar oder Solar?

 Tempel Bigband - Album 03

 Arnulf Ochs - in the meantime

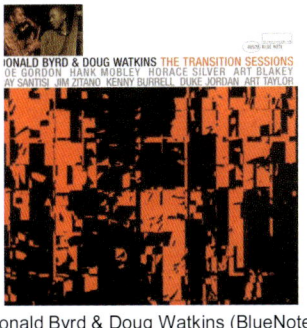 Donald Byrd & Doug Watkins (BlueNote)

 hank mobley thinking of home (BlueNote)

 chick corea - the complete "IS" session

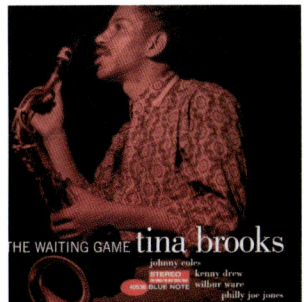 tina brooks - The Waiting Game (BlueNote)

 Dizzy Gillespie - AFRO

 The Source and Different Cikadas (ECM)

 Steve Tibbetts (ECM)

 Paolo Damiani (ECM)

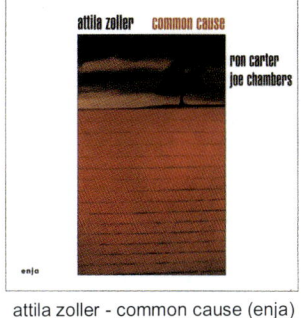 attila zoller - common cause (enja)

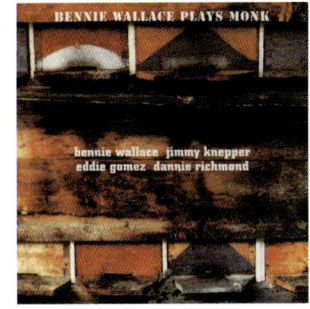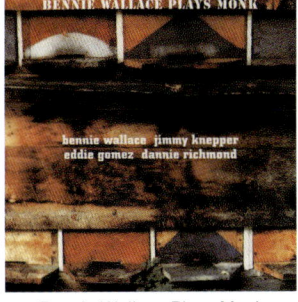 Bennie Wallace Plays Monk

 SLICKAPHONICS (enja)

Cover - Auswahl

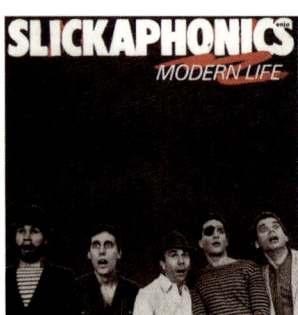 Slickaphonics - Modern Life (enja)
 nils wogram - speed life
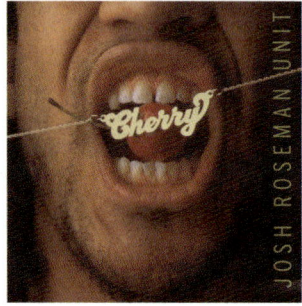 Josh Roseman Unit - Cherry
 Trio Ivoire

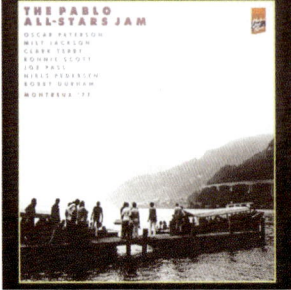 The Pablo All-Stars Jam
 Sal Nistico - Heavyweights
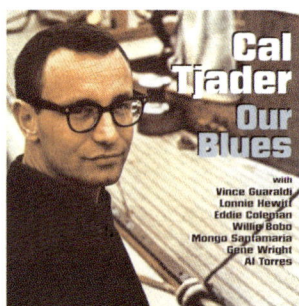 Cal Tjader - Our Blues
 Cleanhead & Cannonball

 Frank Strozier - Long Night
 Joe Pass - Montreux '77
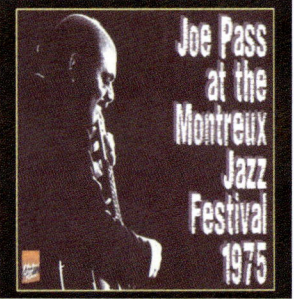 Joe Pass - Montreux Festival 1975
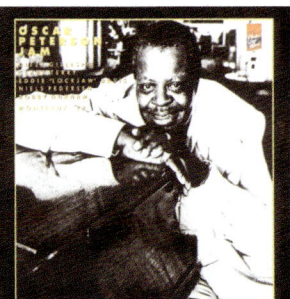 Oscar Peterson Jam

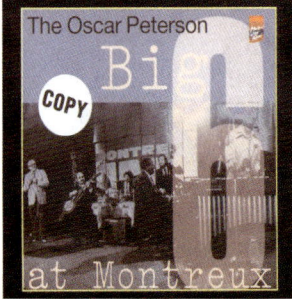 The Oscar Peterson Big 6
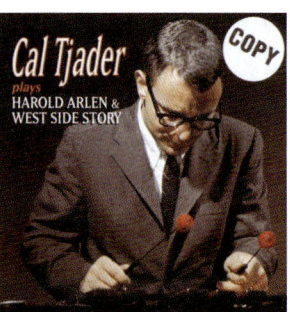 Cal Tjader plays Harold Arlen ...
 This is Oscar Peterson (bluebird)
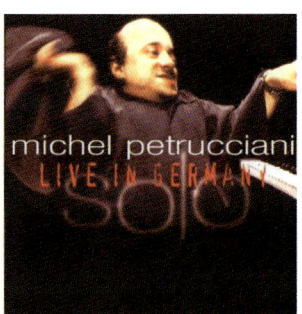 michel petrucciani - Live In Germany

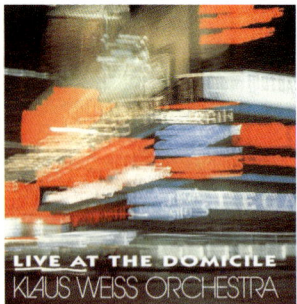 Klaus Wiess Orchestra - Live
 Norbert Stein / Pata Masters Live ..
 Volker Schlott - The 12 Seasons
 Trio Larose 'Debut' (JAZZ 'n' ARTS)

 Eric Reed - Happiness (nagel heyer)
 warren vache and bill charlap
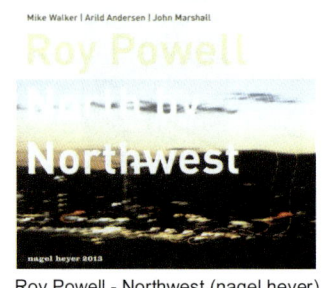 Roy Powell - Northwest (nagel heyer)
 wayne escoffery - times change

Cover - Auswahl

Marcus Printup - The New Boogaloo

Michel Petrucciani-100 Hearts (BlueNote)

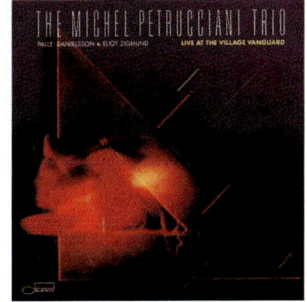
The Michel Petrucciani Trio (BlueNote)

Sing A Song Of Basie

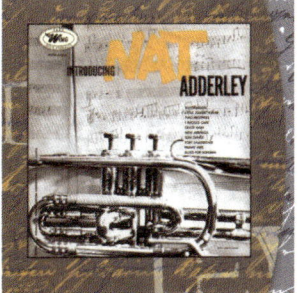
Adderley - Introducing NAT (Wing)

stan getz and the col sounds (Verve)

Eddie Costa Quartet (Coral)

Bing Sings Whilst Bregmn Swings

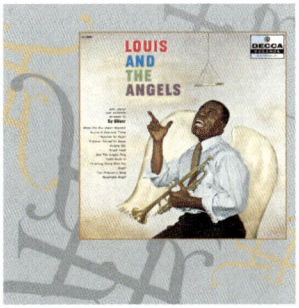
Louis And the Angels (DECCA)

Louis and The Good Book (DECCA)

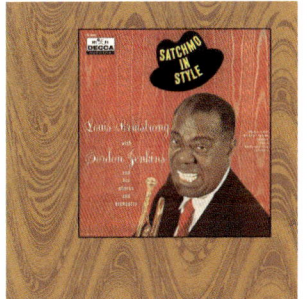
Satchmo In Style (DECCA)

Michael Brecker-Nearness Of You (Verve

Kenny Barron & Regina Carter (Verve)

Gillespie - Have Trumpet Will Excite!

DIZ and GETZ

Margaret Whiting sings the ... (Verve)

swingle singers (Philips)

swingle singers - Getting Romantic

Stan Gets - Café Montmartre

Lionel Hampton Quintet (Clef)

Kenny Burrell - Blues (Verve)

Blossom Dearie Sings (Verve)

Jesse van Ruller - Trio

Archie Shepp - Steam (enja)

Cover - Auswahl

John Scofield - Shinola (enja)

Archie Shepp - Soul Song (enja)

Michael Riessler - Honig Und Asche

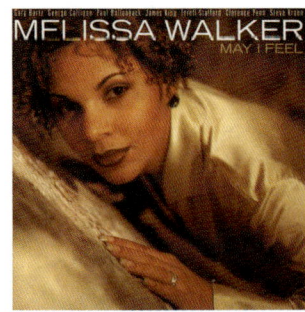
Melissa Walker - May I Feel

Melissa Walker - Moment of Truth

Gianluigi Trovesi Nonet

Paquito D'Rivera - Habanera

Dhafer Youssef - electric sufi

Nils Wogram - Odd And Awkward

new art saxophone quartet

Mahmoud Turkmani - Fyaka

Ramon Valle - Danza Negra (ACT)

Ella Fitzgerald - Whisper Not (Verve)

Wes Montgomery - Willow Weep For Me

!Ole Tormé! - Goes South (Verve)

???

John Coltrane - A Love Supreme

Hancock-Brecker-Hargrove (Verve)

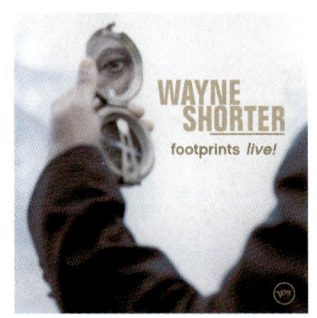
Wayne Shorter - footprints live!(Verve)

At Newport (Verve)

Brown / Roach at Basin Street (Mercury)

Gianluigi Trovesi - Dedalo

Lutz Wichert Trio - Ambiguous

Anita O'Day - Incomparable! (Verve)

Teil 1
Titelverzeichnis

Legende: Zeile 1: Liedtitel • Zeile 2: Interpret (Gruppe) | Plattentitel | Label | Bestellnummer

007
Five Up High | Five Up High | Timeless | CD SJP 417

008
Albert Mangelsdorff Quartet | Shake,Shuttle And Blow | Enja | ENJ-9374 2

01/799
Allan Holdsworth Group | The Sixteen Man Of Tain | Cream Records | CR 610-2

0274
Wendi Slaton Group | Back Here Again | Justice Records | JR 0602-2

1 Nite Stand
Ralph Towner-Gary Burton | Matchbook | ECM | 1056(835014-2)

1 x 6
Andy Kirk And His Twelve Clouds Of Joy | Live Sessions 1937 | Jazz Anthology | JA 5133

1,2,3,
Will Osborne And His Orchestra | The Uncollected:Will Osborne | Hindsight | HSR 197

1,4,4,
Elefanten | Faust | KlangRäume | 30150

1.2.79
Wolfgang Haffner International Jazz Quintet | Whatever It Is | Jazz 4 Ever Records:Jazz Network | J4E 4714
European Jazz Youth Orchestra | Swinging Europe 3 | dacapo | DCCD 9461

1.4.E:M
Jerome Cooper-Oliver Lake Duo | For The People | Hat Art | 7 (1Ro7)

10 Anos
Don Grusin Group | No Borders | GRP | GRP 96762

10 Estrella
Hans Reichel | Shamghaied On Tor Road | FMP | CD 46

10 YR Dance
John Wolf Brennan-Daniele Patumi | Ten Zentences | L+R Records | CDLR 45066

100 Dollar Bill
Roberto Gatto Group feat. John Scofield | Ask | Inak | 8802

100 Hearts
Steve Tibbetts Group | Big Map Idea | ECM | 1380

100 Moons
Swim Two Birds | Apsion | VeraBra Records | CDVBR 2101-2

100+8
Zollsounds 4 feat. Lee Konitz | Open Hearts | Enja | 9123-2

101 Eastbound
Dave Holland Qartet | Extensions | ECM | 1410(841778-2)

101 Fahrenheit(Slow Meltdown)
Malta And His Orchestra | Obsession | JVC | ???

10th Of February(dedicated to Efim Alperin)
Yosuke Yamashita New York Trio With Ravi Coltrane | Wind Of The Age | Verve | 557008-2

10th Variation:Forward Motion
Chico Hamilton Trio | Trio! | Soul Note | 121246-2

111-44
Oliver Nelson Quintet | Images | Prestige | P 24060
Phil Woods Quintet | Gratitude | Denon Compact Disc | CY-1316

117th Street
Ted Rosenthal | Maybeck Recital Hall Series Volume Thirty-Eight | Concord | CCD 4648

117th Street(alt.take)
Bernhard Arndt | Insight Insight | FMP | OWN-90005

11th Variation:Nuage
Ron Carter With Strings | Pastels | Original Jazz Classics | OJCCD 665-2(M 9073)

12 + 12
Tom Varner Quartet | Tom Varner Quartet | Soul Note | 121017-2

12 De Fevereio
Maya Homburger | G.Ph.Thelemann | MAYA Recordings | MCD 9302

1-2 Spoon
Berliner Saxophon Quartet | 12 Notes 4 Musicians And The Blues | BIT | 11150

12 Tones Old
Les Brown And His Orchestra | The Uncollected: Les Brown | Hindsight | HSR 103

1-2-3-4-Jump
Woody Herman And His Orchestra | Chubby Jackson-The Happy Monster:Small Groups 1944-1947 | Cool & Blue | C&B-CD 109
The Radio Years: Woody Herman And His First Herd 1944 | Hindsight | HSR 134

1239A
Air Mail | Light Blues | Amadeo | 835305-2

125th Street Congress
Woody Herman And His Orchestra | Old Gold Rehearsals 1944 | Jazz Unlimited | JUCD 2079

125th Street Prophet
The Radio Years: Woody Herman And His First Herd 1944 | Hindsight | HSR 134

125th Street, New York
Clark Terry Quintet | Top And Bottom Brass | Original Jazz Classics | OJCCD 764-2(RLP 1137)

12-99
New England Ragtime Ensemble | The Art Of The Rag | GM Recordings | GM 3018 CD(882950)

12th Street Rag
Benny Moten's Kansas City Orchestra | The Complete Bennie Moten Vol.1/2 | RCA | NL 89881(2) DP
Cy Laurie Jazz Band | Chattanooga Stomp | Lake | LACD 61
Elmer Snowden Quartet | Harlem Banjo | Original Jazz Classics | OJCCD 1756-2
Lionel Hampton And His All Stars | Masters Of Jazz Vol.8 | RCA | NL 89540 DP
Louis Armstrong And His All Stars | Louis Armstrong:Complete 1950-1951 All Stars Decca Recordings | Definitive Records | DRCD 11188
Essential Jazz | CBS | 473686-2
Sidney Bechet And His New Orleans Feetwarmers | Sidney Bechet 1932-1943: The Bluebird Sessions | Bluebird | ND 90317
Masters Of Jazz Vol.3 | RCA | NL 89719 DP

12th Variation:Two For One(Finale)
Rimak | Back In Town | Jazzline | ???

12x12=143
Jimmy Smith And Wes Montgomery With Orchestra | Jimmy & Wes-The Dynamic Duo | Verve | 521445-2

13 (Death March)
Jimmy Smith And Wes Montgomery With The Oliver Nelson Orchestra | Talkin' Jazz:Roots Of Acid Jazz | Verve | 529580-2
Jazz For A Sunday Afternoon All Stars | Village Vanguard Live Sessions No.2 | LRC Records | CDC 9012

13 For Piano And Two Orchestras
Leroy Simpson | Blues From The Deep South | Anthology of the Blues | AB 5604

13 Steps
Pat Martino Quintet | Stone Blue | Blue Note | 830822-2

1-3-234
Duck Baker | Duck Baker Plays The Music Of Herbie Nichols | Avant | AVAN 040

1374
Michel Petrucciani Trio | Michel Plays Petrucciani | Blue Note | 748679-2

13th
Albert Mangelsdorff Quartet | Three Originals:Never Let It End-A Jazz Tune I Hope-Triple Entente | MPS | 529090-2

13th Floor
Return To The Wide Open Spaces | Live At The Caravan Of Dreams | Amazing Records | AMCD 1021

13th House
The Heath Brothers Orchestra | Jazz Family | Concord | CCD 4846

15 W 40
Louie Bellson's Magic 7 | Louie Bellson's Magic 7 | Concord | CCD 4742

16 Bars
Count Basie And His Orchestra | Count Basie 1954 | Jazz Society | AA 526/527

16:55
Shep Fields And His New Music | The Uncollected:Shep Fields | Hindsight | HSR 160

16-Bar-Blues
Geoffrey McCabe Quartet | Teseract Complicity | Timeless | SJP 212

16th St. Baptist Church
Karl Ratzer | Dancing On A String | CMP Records | CMP 13

17 West
Eric Dolphy Quartet | Out There | New Jazz | NJSA 8252-6
Eric Dolphy:The Complete Prestige Recordings | Prestige | 9 PRCD-4418-2
Harold Danko Quintet | Prestigious-A Tribute To Eric Dolphy | Steeplechase | SCCD 31508

18 Carrots For Rabbit
Gerry Mulligan-Johnny Hodges Quintet | The Silver Collection: Gerry Mulligan Meets The Saxophonists | Verve | 827436-2 PMS

18 Grad Minus
Koch-Schütz-Studer & El Nil Troop | Heavy Cairo Trafic | Intuition Records | INT 3175-2

18,Maamal El Sokar
Tarheel Slim | No Time At All | Trix Records | TRIX 3310

18th Century Ballroom
Toots Thielemans Quintet | Man Bites Harmonica! | Original Jazz Classics | OJCCD 1738-2(RLP 1125)

18th Hole
Fats Waller And His Rhythm And His Orchestra | The Jazz Collector Edition: Fats Waller | Laserlight | 15711

1919 March
Papa Bue's Viking Jazzband | Greatest Hits | Storyville | 6.23336 AF

1934
Heiner Goebbels/Alfred Harth | Berold Brecht:Zeit wird knapp | Riskant | 568-72414

1944 Stomp
Deep Creek Jazzuits | Again | Jazz Pure Collection | AU 31615 CD

1951
Robert Previt Quintet | Bump The Renaissance | Sound Aspects | sas CD 008

1972 Bronze Medalist
The Bad Plus | The Bad Plus | Fresh Sound Records | FSNT 107 CD
Eddie Harris Group | The Best Of Eddie Harris | Atlantic | 7567-81370-2

1974 Blues
Art Blakey And The Jazz Messengers | In This Korner | Concord | CJ 68

1983 A Merman I Should Turn To Be
Nguyen Le Trio With Guests | Purple:Celebrating Jimi Hendrix | ACT | 9410-2
Yusef Lateef Quartet | 1984 | MCA | AS 84

1987-1988
Fun Horns | Surprise | Jazzpoint | JP 1029 CD

1989 Song
Bob Holman | Live At Knitting Factory Vol.4 | Enemy | EMCD 118(03518)

1991
Ronnie Burrage Septet | Shuttle | Sound Hills | SSCD 8052

1st Movement:Villa Radieuse
Jan Garbarek | All Those Born With Wings | ECM | 1324(831394-2)

1st Piece
John LaPorta Septet | Theme And Variations | Fantasy | FCD 24776-2

1st Variation:Basso Profundo
Alfred 23 Harth QuasarQuartet | POPending EYE | free flow music | ffm 0493

1st2nd3rd&4th
Terje Rypdal Quartet With The Bergen Chamber Ensemble | Lux Aeterna | ECM | 1818(017070-2)

1th Movement:Luminous Galaxy
Ralph Towner | Trios/Solos | ECM | 1025(833328-2)

1x12
Denny Christianson Big Band | Suite Mingus | Justin Time | Just 15

2
Carla Bley Band | Amarcord Nino Rota | Hannibal | HNBL 9301

2 Bulgarische Zigeunerlieder
Hans Kumpf + Anatolij Vapirow Trio | Jam Session Leningrad | Fusion | 8004

2 Dans Un Café
Hyde Park After Dark | Hyde Park After Dark | Bee Hive | BH 7014

2 Degrees East 3 Degrees West
Modern Jazz Quartet | Live 1956 | Jazz Anthology | JA 5207

2 J
Joachim Raffel Quintet | Circlesongs | Acoustic Music Records | 312.1093.2

2 Scenes From '...Liebt Mich Nicht'(for two pianos)
Bill Frisell-Vernon Reid Duo | Smash & Scatteration | Minor Music | 005

2 Stromland
The Rosenberg Trio With Orchestra | Noches Calientes | Verve | 557022-2

2 The Night
Harmonica Slim Blues Group | Black Bottom Blues | Trix Records | TRIX 3323

2 Violones(Vermelho)
Martin Classen Quartet | Stop & Go | Acoustic Music Records | 319.1033.2

2,4,4,
Sachi Hayasaka & Stir Up! | 2.26 | Enja | 8014-2

2.Arrival-
Jerome Cooper-Oliver Lake Duo | For The People | Hat Art | 7 (1Ro7)

2:19 Blues
Chilton/Fawkes Feetwarmers | Melody Maker Tribute To Louis Armstrong Vol.2 | Jazz Colours | 874768-2
Estella Mama Yancey With Axel Zwingenberger | Axel Zwingenberger And The Friends Of Boogie Woogie Vol.4: The Blues Of Mama Yancey | Vagabond | VRCD 8.88009
George Lewis And His Band | George Lewis At Manny's Tavern 1949 | American Music | AMCD-85
Ian Wheeler Jazz Band | Ian Wheeler At Farnham Maltings | Lake | LACD 32
Louis Armstrong And His Orchestra | Jazz:The Essential Collection Vol.2 | IN+OUT Records | 78012-2
Louis Armstrong Vol.3-Louis With Guest Stars | MCA | 1306

2:25
Bruce Forman Quintet | 20/20 | Muse | MR 5273

20 Years After
Gerry Mulligan/Astor Piazolla Group | Gerry Mulligan/Astor Piazolla 1974 | Accord | 556642

20 Years Ago
Gerry Mulligan/Astor Piazolla 1974 | Accord | 556642

20.000 Dominosteine
Jeff Berlin Group | Crossroads | Denon Compact Disc | CY-18077

200 Horses
Tubby Hayes Orchestra | 200% Proof | Master Mix | CHECD 00105

20-20
Nehemiah 'Skip' James | Skip James-King Of The Delta Blues Singers | Biograph | BLP 12029

211 E 11 Street
Joe Magnarelli Quintet | Mr.Mags | Criss Cross | Criss 1200

21th Street Stomp
The Duke Ellington Orchestra | Digital Duke | GRP | GRP 95482

23 Degrees North-82 Degrees West
Sonny Boy Williamson & The Yardbirds | 1963 Live In London | L+R Records | CDLR 42020

23 Xiprers
Duck Baker | Duck Baker Plays The Music Of Herbie Nichols | Avant | AVAN 040

2300 Skiddoo
Oscar Klein-Philadelphia Jerry Ricks | Blues Panorama Vol.2 | Koch Records | 322 423
Roswell Rudd Quintet | Regeneration | Soul Note | 121054-2

2300 Skiddoo(alt.take)
Brodmann-Pausch Percussion Duo | Percussion Duo | Fiala Music | JFJ 92002

23rd Psalm
Duke Ellington And His Orchestra | Black Brown And Beige | CBS | CK 65566

23rd Psalm(alt.take)
Hugh Lawson Trio | Colours | Soul Note | 121052-2

24 Nanno
Aki Takase-Rudi Mahall | Duet For Eric Dolphy | Enja | 9109-2

245
Eric Dolphy Sextet | Saxophones | West Wind | WW 2013

245(alt.take)
Jerome Harris Sextet | Hidden In Plain View | New World Records | 80472-2

24h Street Blues
Julian Priester Quintet | Keep Swingin' | Original Jazz Classics | SMJ 6081

24th Street Blues
Johnny Griffin Quartet | The Kerry Dancers | Original Jazz Classics | OJCCD 1952-2(RLP 9420)

25 1-2 Daze
Jane Ira Bloom Quartet | Mighty Lights | Enja | 4044 (807519)

2513
John Tchicai-Pierre Dorge | Ball At Louisiana | Steeplechase | SCCD 31174

26 Bars
Dave Ballou Trio | Volition | Steeplechase | SCCD 31460

26-2
John Coltrane Quartet | John Coltrane-The Heavyweight Champion:The Complete Atlantic Recordings | Atlantic | 8122-71984-2
The Coltrane Legacy | Atlantic | SD 1553
OAM Trio | Trilingual | Fresh Sound Records | FSNT 070 CD
Steve Davis Quintet | The Jaunt | Criss Cross | Criss 1113
Anthony Braxton Quartet | Seven Compositions 1978 | Moers Music | 01066

29 Ways
Johnny Littlejohn Group | When Your Best Friend Turns Your Back On You | JSP Records | JSPCD 246

2nd Movement:Fjelldapen
Costa & Cataldo Music Project | Picture Number One | SPLASC(H) Records | H 141

2nd Movement:Tween Dusk And Down In Via Urbana
Konstantin Wienstroer-Veit Lange-Felix Elsner | Unfinished Business | Green House Music | CD 1005

2nd Order Kinetic
Jan Garbarek | All Those Born With Wings | ECM | 1324(831394-2)

2nd Piece
Jimmy Giuffre 4 | Quasar | Soul Note | 121108-2

2nd Variation:Jazz Canon
Globe Unity Orchestra | 20th Anniversary | FMP | CD 45

2x2-
Eddie Clearwater And His Orchestra | Two Times Nine | Charly | CRB 1025

3
John Thomas & Lifeforce | 3000 Worlds | Nabel Records:Jazz Network | CD 4604
Kenny Wheeler Sextet | Deer Wan | ECM | 1102

3 And 3
Eddie Daniels Quartet | Eddie Daniels...This Is Now | GRP | GRP 96352

3 East
Chris Jarrett | Fire | Edition Collage | EC 443-2

3 Folk Songs
Masqualero | Bande A Part | ECM | 1319

3 For 5
Jon Burr Trio | 3 For All | Cymekob | CYK 806-2

3 For Civility
Klaus Treuheit Trio | 3 In 1 | Klaus Treuheit Production | KTMP 2001

3 Letters(part 1-3)
Mario Pavone Septet | Song For (Septet) | New World Records | 80452-2

3 Minutes Of Pure Entertainment
Bruce Barth Quartet | Where Eagles Fly | Fresh Sound Records | FSNT 090 CD

3 More Minors
Bernhard Arndt | Insight Insight | FMP | OWN-90005

3 Steps Up Clark
Vinny Golia Quintet | Regards From Norma Desmond | Fresh Sound Records | FSNT 008 CD

3 Things For The Practitioner-
Crystal | Clear | Black-Hawk | BKH 51501

3 Views Of Secret
Sören Fischer Quartet | Don't Change Your Hair For Me | Edition Collage | EC 513-2
John McLaughlin Trio | Que Alegria | Verve | 837280-2

3 Willows
Roscoe Mitchell And The Sound Ensemble | 3 x 4 Eye | Black Saint | 120050-2

3,4,4,
Steve Adams/Ken Filiano Quartet | Anacrusis | Nine Winds Records | NW 0128

3/4 & 1/4 8
Suzanne Dean Group | I Wonder | Nova | NOVA 9028-2

3000 Miles Ago
Milt Jackson With The Monty Alexander Trio | The Best Of Milt Jackson | Pablo | 2405405-2

3000 Worlds
Luigi Archetti | Das Ohr | ATM Records | ATM 3804-AH

317 East 32nd Street
Lee Konitz-Ted Brown Quartet | Dig-It | Steeplechase | SCCD 31466

32 Lunch-
Wolfgang Muthspiel Trio | Perspective | Amadeo | 533466-2

32-20 Blues
Martin Schmitt | Handful Of Blues | ESM Records | ESM 9303

324 Blues
Handful Of Blues | AH Records | ESM 9303

34 Skidoo
Bill Evans Trio | The Complete Fantasy Recordings | Fantasy | 9FCD 1012-2
The Complete Fantasy Recordings | Fantasy | 9FCD 1012-2
The Paris Concert-Edition Two | Blue Note | 60311-1
How My Heart Sings! | Original Jazz Classics | OJCCD 369-2
Bill Evans-Montreux II | CBS | 481264-2

34° South

Keith Jarrett Trio | Inside Out | ECM | 1780(014005-2)

341 Free Fade
Bajazzo | Harlequin Galaxy | Edition Collage | EC 519-2

3438
Anthony Braxton | Saxophone Improvisations Series F | America | AM 011/012

35 Basic-
Michel Petrucciani Sextet | Both Worlds | Dreyfus Jazz Line | FDM 36590-2

35 Seconds Of Music And More
Sonic Fiction | Changing With The Times | Naxos Jazz | 86034-2

39-25-39
Fuchs-van Hove-Hollinger Trio | Berliner Begegnung | FMP | SAJ 47

3-D Montevideo
Bill Laswell/Jones Hellborg Group | Niels & The New York Street Percussionists | ITM Records | ITM 1453

3-In-1 Without The Oil
Roland Kirk Quartet | Domino | Verve | 543833-2
Alte Leidenschaften | Sketches Of Pain | L+R Records | CDLR 45042

3rd Movement:Escalator
Costa & Cataldo Music Project | Picture Number One | SPLASC(H) Records | H 141

3rd Movement:Rosati At Popolo Square
Rodney Jones Group | The Undiscoverd Few | Blue Note | 496902-2

3rd Piece
Peter Ponzol Trio | Prism | View | VS 114 IMS

3rd Type Blues
John LaPorta Septet | Theme And Variations | Fantasy | FCD 24776-2

3rd Variation:Tribute To Bird
Rainer Tempel Big Band | Melodies Of '98 | Jazz 4 Ever Records:Jazz Network | J4E 4744

3X3
Rova Saxophone Quartet | This This This This | Moers Music | 01080

4 Ballade
Tòme XX | Third Degree | Jazz Haus Musik | JHM 0063 CD

4 Berth Out Front
Clyde Hart All Stars | Charlie Parker:The Complete 1944-1948 Small Group Sessions(Studio Recordings-Master Takes),Vol.1 | Blue Moon | BMCD 1007

4 For Piano And Orchestra
Kenny Wheeler Sextet | Deer Wan | ECM | 1102

4 KH
Christian Willisohn | Boogie Woogie And Some Blues | Blues Beacon | BLU-1007 2

4 Meade
| Love Every Moment | Concord | CCD 4534

4 On 6
Joe Lovano Trio | Trio Fascination | Blue Note | 833114-2

4 On The Floor
Cedar Walton Quartet | Eastern Rebellion | Timeless | CD SJP 101

4,4,4,
Chico Hamilton Trio | Trio! | Soul Note | 121246-2

400 Years Ago Tomorrow
Oliver Kent Trio | 400 Years Ago Tomorrow | Mons Records | MR 874814

416 East 10th Street
The International Blues Duo | To The World | Crosscut | CCR 1007

42639
Strange Meeting | Stadtgarten Series Vol.3 | Jazz Haus Musik | JHM 1003 SER

42nd Street
Family Of Percussion | Message To The Enemies Of Time | Nagara | MIX 1016-N

42nd Street Theme
Pekka Pöyry With Band/Orchestra | Happy Peter | Leo Records | 016

44 Blues
Hound Dog Taylor & The House Rockers | Hound Dog Taylor And The House Rockers | Sonet | 198045(SNTF 676)
Roosevelt Sykes | Roosevelt Sykes(1929-1941) | Story Of Blues | CD 3542-2

440
Orchestra Jazz Siciliana | Orchestra Jazz Siciliana Plays The Music Of Carla Bley | Watt | XtraWatt/4
McCoy Tyner Quartet | 44th Street Suite | Red Baron | 469284-2

45-8
Herbie Nichols Trio | The Bethlehem Session | Affinity | AFF 759

45Grad Angle
Roscoe Mitchell-Anthony Braxton | Roscoe Mitchell Duets With Anthony Braxton | Sackville | 3016

4th Movement:Toccata
Jan Garbarek | All Those Born With Wings | ECM | 1324(831394-2)

4th Piece
Yosuke Yamashita New York Trio With Joe Lovano | Kurdish Dance | Verve | 517708-2

4th Variation:Images
Javier Feierstein Quartet | Wysiwyg | Fresh Sound Records | FSNT 040 CD

4x3
Cedar Walton Quartet | Eastern Rebellion | Timeless | CD SJP 101

5 AM:Locked In Amazement
Joe Pass/Niels-Henning Orsted-Pedersen Duo | Chops | Original Jazz Classics | OJCCD 786-2(2310830)

5 Blues
Georg Hofmann-Lucas Niggli Duo | Mute Songs & Drumscapes | Creative Works Records | CW CD 1022-2

5 For Elvin
Dave Holland Quintet | The Razor's Edge | ECM | 1353

5 Four Six
Remember Shakti | The Believer | Verve | 549044-2

5 Miles To Wrentham
Paul Motian Quintet | The Story Of Maryam | Soul Note | 121074-2

5,4,4,
Jerome Cooper-Oliver Lake Duo | For The People | Hat Art | 7 (1Ro7)

50 Ways To Leave Your Lover
John C. Marshall Group | Same Old Story | Traditional Line | TL 1317
National Youth Jazz Orchestra | In Control | Ronnie Scott's Jazz House | JHCD 037

50.000 KLeine Wichtigtuer
Azimuth | Outubro | Milestone | M 9097

500 Miles High
Chick Corea And Return To Forever | Compact Jazz: Chick Corea | Polydor | 831365-2
Stan Getz Quartet | Round Midnight | Jazz Door | JD 1266

500 Miles High(alt.take)
John Zorn Group | Downtown Lullaby | Depth Of Field | DOF-2

500.000 Caricias Del Cielo
Nils Landgren Funk Unit With Guests | 5000 Miles | ACT | 9271-2

5000 Miles
Bill Mays/Ray Drummond | One To One 2 | dmp Digital Music Productions | CD 482

502 Blues
Harold Danko Trio | 3/4 Three Of Four | Steeplechase | SCCD 31444
Jimmy & Stacy Rowles Quartet | Sometimes I'm Happy Sometimes I'm Blue | Orange Blue | ???

50-21
Tommy Flanagan Trio With Kenny Burrell | Beyond The Bluebird | Timeless | CD SJP 350

518
Christof Griese Quartet | 52nd Return | Jazz 4 Ever Records:Jazz Network | J4E 4728

52nd Street
Hans Koller Groups And Orchestra | Hans Koller Masterpieces | MPS | 529078-2
Wheelz With Ingrid Jensen | Around The World I | ACT | 9247-2

52nd Street Theme
Bud Powell Quartet | Parisian Thoroughfare | Pablo | CD 2310976-2
The Legacy | Jazz Door | JD 1204
Bud Powell Quintet | The Amazing Bud Powell Vol.1 | Blue Note | 300366
Fats Navarro/Tadd Dameron:Complete Blue Note & Capitol Sessions | Definitive Records | DRCD 11191
Dizzy Gillespie And His Orchestra | Dizzy Gillespie:Night In Tunisia | Dreyfus Jazz Line | FDM 36734-2
Dizzier And Dizzier | RCA | 26685172
Dizzy Gillespie Septet | Dizzy Gillespie-Diz Delights | RCA | CL 89804 SF
Hank Mobley Quintet | Mobley's Message | Prestige | VIJ 5040
Kenny Clarke And His 52nd Street Boys | Fats Navarro:The 1946-1949 Small Group Sessions(Studio Recordings-Master Takes),Vol.1 | Blue Moon | BMCD 1016
Oscar Peterson Trio | Compact Jazz: Oscar Peterson Plays Jazz Standards | Verve | 833283-2
Quintet Of The Year | The Quintet-Jazz At Massey Hall | Debut | DSA 124-6
Charles Mingus-The Complete Debut Recordings | Debut | 12 DCD 4402-2
Red Rodney Quintet | Bird Lives! | Muse | MCD 5371
Sonny Rollins & Co. | Now's The Time! | RCA | 2132335-2
The Nagel-Heyer Allstars | Uptown Lowdown:A Jazz Salute To The Big Apple | Nagel-Heyer | CD 2004
Walter Davis Trio | Live Au Dreher | Harmonia Mundi | PJC 222005

52nd Street Theme-
Charlie Parker All Stars | More Unissued Vol.1 | Royal Jazz | RJD 505
Charlie Parker Quintet | Bird At St. Nick's | Original Jazz Classics | OJC20 041-2(JWS 500)
Charlie Parker At Birdland And Cafe Society | Cool & Blue | C&B-CD 108

53rd And Greenwood
Danny Gatton Septet | New York Stories Volume One | Blue Note | 798959-2

5-5-7
Bobby Hackett-Jack Teagarden All Stars | Coast Concert/Jazz Ultimate | Dormouse | DMI CDX 02(882984)

56-
Andy McKee And NEXT with Hamiet Bluiett | Sound Root | Mapleshade | 04432

57 Varieries
| In Pursuite Of The 13th Note | Talkin' Loud | 848493-2

59
Nat Adderley Orchestra | Double Expusure | Prestige | P 10090

597-59
Vienna Art Orchestra | Nightride Of A Lonely Saxophoneplayer | Moers Music | 02054/5 CD

5th Movement:Lux Aeterna
Archie Shepp-Jasper Van't Hof | The Fifth Of May | L+R Records | LR 45004

5th Piece
L.A. Underground | Black/Note | Red Records | 123259-2

5th Symphony
John LaPorta Septet | Theme And Variations | Fantasy | FCD 24776-2

5th Variation:Jazz Fugue
Charlie Parker With Machito And His Orchestra | Bird On Verve-Vol.4:Machito Jazz With Flip And Bird | Verve | 817445-1 IMS

6 D'Octubre
Donald Byrd Quintet | Royal Flush | Blue Note | 869476-7

601 1-2 North Polar St.
Corey Harris | Betwen Midnight And Day | Alligator Records | ALCD 4837

61 Highway
Honeyboy Edwards | White Windows | Evidence | ECD 26039-2

'62
Meade Lux Lewis Trio | Cat House Piano | Verve | 557098-2

632nd Street Theme
Johnny Griffin Sextet | The Little Giant | Original Jazz Classics | OJCCD 136-2(R 1149)

63rd Street Theme
Little Giant | Milestone | M 47054

64 Bars On Wilshire Boulevard
Alvin Queen Quintet | Alvin Queen In Europe | Nilva | NQ 3401 IMS

6-4 Mambo
Herbie Harper Quartet | Jazz In Hollywood:Herbie Harper | Original Jazz Classics | OJCCD 1887-2(Nocturne NLP-1/NLP-7)

6-Nix-Pix-Flix
The New Stan Getz Quartet | Getz Au Go Go | CTI Records | PDCTI 1124-2

6th Piece
John LaPorta Septet | Theme And Variations | Fantasy | FCD 24776-2

6th Variation:From The Cool School
Larry Coryell | Bolero | String | BLE 233850

7 Anéis
U.P. Wilson Band | On My Way | Red Lightnin' | RL 0078

7 Notes,7 Days,7 Planets
Berlin Jazz Composers Orchestra(JayJayBeCe) | How Rook | BIT | 11185

70's Child
Erroll Garner Quartet | Plays Misty | Fresh Sound Records | FSR-CD 0158

7-11 Jump
Erroll Garner Trio | Contrasts | Verve | 558077-2
Ella Fitzgerald With Marty Paich's Dektette | Ella Swings Lightly | Verve | 517535-2

720 In The Book
Jan Savitt And His Top Hatters | The Uncollected:Jan Svitt | Hindsight | HSR 213

720 In The Books-
Martin Taylor Quartet | Change Of Heart | Linn Records | AKD 016

73 Degrees Kalvin(Variation-3)
Anthony Braxton-George Lewis Duo | Donaueschingen (Duo) 1976 | Hat Art | CD 6150

7-4
Ted Curson Quartet | Tears For Dolphy | Black Lion | BLCD 760190

74 Miles Away
Cannonball Adderley Quintet | The Best Of Cannonball Adderley:The Capitol Years | Capitol | 795482-2
Russel Gunn Group | Ethnomusicology Vol.1 | Atlantic | 7567-83165-2

74 Miles Away(intro)
Blind Idiot God | Cyclotron | Avant | AVAN 010

77 Throughshine Slip
John Zorn Group | Downtown Lullaby | Depth Of Field | DOF-2

7th Ave. South
Bobby Watson & Horizon | Post-Mowtown Bop | Blue Note | 795148-2

7th D
Jasper Van't Hof | Solo Piano | Timeless | CD SJP 286

7th Floor
Jack Wilkins Quintet | Mexico | CTI Records | CTI 1004-2

7th Variation:Changing Times
Joel Palsson Group | Prim | Naxos Jazz | 86049-2

7x2 New Orleans
Charlie Parker With Machito And His Orchestra | Bird On Verve-Vol.4:Machito Jazz With Flip And Bird | Verve | 817445-1 IMS

8 Counts For Rita
Jimmy Smith-Eddie Harris Trio | All The Way | Milestone | MCD 9251-2
Terry Gibbs Quartet | Take It From Me | Impulse(MCA) | JAS 60 (AS 58)

8,5
Billy Drummond Quintet | Native Colours | Criss Cross | Criss 1057

8/4 Beat
Pat Metheny Quartet | 80/81 | ECM | 1180/81 (843169-2)

80
Gary McFarland And His Orchestra | America The Beautiful | Gryphon | 6.24452 AT

81
Rein de Graaff Quintet | New York Jazz | Timeless | CD SJP 130

88 Basie Street
The Frank Capp Juggernaut | Play It Again Sam | Concord | CCD 4747

8th Variation:Two Brothers
Gunter Hampel And His Galaxie Dream Band | Unity Dance-European Concert | Birth | 0013

9:20 Special
Count Basie And His Orchestra | Swingin' The Blues | Arco | 3 ARC 111
Dompsey Wright Quintet | The Wright Approach | Fresh Sound Records | FSR 501(Andex S 3006)
Jonah Jones Quartet | Jumpin' With A Shuffle | Pathe | 1547711(Capitol ST 1404)
Ray Bryant Trio | Ray Bryant Plays Basie & Ellington | EmArCy | 832235-2 PMS
Stan Kenton And His Orchestra | Journey Into Capricorn | Creative World | STD 1077

900 Miles
Terry Callier Duo | The New Folk Sound Of Terry Callier | Prestige | PRCD 11026-2
Gregor Hübner Quintet | Januschke's Time | Satin Doll Productions | SDP 1034-1 CD

910,Columbus Ave
Charlie Hunter Quartet | Ready...Set...Shango! | Blue Note | 837101-2

911
Peter Leitch Sextet | From Another Perspective | Concord | CCD 4535

9-12
Antonio Hart Quintet With Guests And Strings | It's All Good | Novus | 4163183-2

928
Michel Petrucciani With The Graffiti String Quartet | Marvellous | Dreyfus Jazz Line | FDM 36564-2

92's Last
Haruko Nara Group | My Favorite Things | Jazz City | 660.53.021

99 Flavors
Ray Barretto & New World Spirit | Taboo | Concord | CCD 4601

996
Deborah Henson-Conant | Alterd Ego | Laika Records | 35100962
Deborah Henson-Conant Group | Deborah Henson-Conant:Best Of Instrumental Music | Laika Records | 35101322
Gordon Beck | With A Heart In My Song | JMS | 044-1

9th Variation:Lucidity
James P.Johnson | Rare Piano Rags | Jazz Anthology | JA 5120

A Baby's Smile
Vic Lewis West Coast All Stars | Vic Lewis Presenting A Celebration Of Contemporary West Coast Jazz | Candid | CCD 79711/12

A Backward Glance
Dinah Washington With The Belford Hendricks Orchestra | Compact Jazz:Dinah Washington Sings The Blues | Mercury | 832573-2 PMS

A Ballad
Gerry Mulligan Tentette | The Birth Of The Cool Vol.2 | Capitol | 798935-2
Spyro Gyra | City Kids | MCA | 2292-50456-1
Michael Smith Quartet | Austin Stream | FMP | SAJ 09

A Ballad For A Doll
Klaus Ignatzek Quintet | Live | Acoustic Music Records | 319.1097.2

A Ballad For Jai
Lee Konitz-Martial Solal Duo | Live At The Berlin Jazz Days 1980 | MPS | 68289

A Baptist Beat
Hank Mobley Quintet | Roll Call | Blue Note | 540030-2)
Red Rodney Sextet | Serge Chaloff Memorial | Cool & Blue | C&B-CD 102

A Basin Street Ballad
John Rapson Octet | bing | Sound Aspects | sas CD 036

A Bear Playing Double Bass And The Black Woman-
Omer Simeon Trio | That's My Stuff | Frog | DGF 7

A Beautiful Friendship -> (This Is The End Of...) A Beautiful Friendship

A Belt Of Asteroids
Staple Singers | Great Day | Milestone | MCD 47027-2

A Better Place
Billy Taylor And His Orchestra | Solo | Taylor Made Records | T 1002

A Bientot
Thilo Wolf Big Band | Swing It! | MDL-Jazz | CD 1915(CD 052)

A Bird In The Hand
James Moody Quartet With Roy Ayers And Chris Potter | Moody's Party | Telarc Digital | CD 83382

A Bit Of Basie
Howard Rumsey's Lighthouse All-Stars | Oboe/Flute | Original Jazz Classics | OJCCD 154-2(C 3520)
Billy Taylor And His Orchestra | Solo | Taylor Made Records | T 1002

A Blossom Fell
Sue Raney With The Billy May Orchestra | Songs For A Raney Day | Capitol | 300015(TOCJ 6129)

A Blue Collection:
Loft Line | Visitors | Acoustic Music Records | 319.1085.2

A Blue Robe In The Distance
Don Braden Quartet | Landing Zone | Landmark | LCD 1539-2

A Blues
Wild Bill Davison All Stars | The Idividualism Of Wild Bill Davison | Savoy | SJL 2229 (801205)

A Blues For Mickey-O
Peter Leitch Quintet | Portraits And Dedications | Criss Cross | Criss 1039

A Blues Mood
Django Reinhardt With Duke Ellington And His Orchestra | Django Reinhardt:Souveniers | Dreyfus Jazz Line | FDM 36744-2

A Blues Riff
Duke Ellington And His Famous Orchestra | The Complete Duke Ellington-Vol.11 | CBS | CBS 88242

A Blues Serenade
Johnny Hodges Orchestra | The Complete Duke Ellington-Vol.11 | CBS | CBS 88242

A Bow To The Classics
Dave Liebman/Gil Goldstein | West Side Story(Today) | Owl Records | 061 CD

A Boy On A Dolphin(Tina Tue)
Art Ensemble Of Chicago | A Jackson In Your House/Message To Our Folks | Affinity | AFF 752

A Brand New Song
Guy Cabay Quartet | The Ghost Of McCoy's Castle | B.Sharp Records | CDS 101

A Breath Away
Eddie Baccus Quartet | Rahsaan/The Complete Mercury Recordings Of Roland Kirk | Mercury | 846630-2

A Breath In The Wind
Wallace Roney Quintet | Seth Air | Muse | MCD 5441

A Bright Pearl
Mahalia Jackson With Orchestra | In Memoriam Mahalia Jackson | CBS | 66501

A Brilliant Madness
Mark Whitfield Quartet | 7th Avenue Stroll | Verve | 529223-2

A Case Of Plus 4's
Steve Lacy-Mal Waldron | Vol.1:Round Midnight | Hat Art | CD 6172(2)

A Case Of You
Barbara Dennerlein Group | Junkanoo | Verve | 537122-2

A Cat Strikes Back
Mal Waldron/Marion Brown | Songs Of Love And Regret | Freelance | FRL-CD 006

A Certain Sadness
Astrud Gilberto With The Walter Wanderley Quiutet | Verve Jazz Masters 9:Astrud Gilberto | Verve | 519824-2
Astrud Gilberto With The Walter Wanderley Quartet | A Certain Smile A Certain Sadness | Verve | 557449-2

A Certain Smile
Mingus Dynasty | Chair In The Sky | Warner | 99081

A Change Is Gonna Come
Willie Mabon | Willie Mabon | Blues Classics(L+R) | CDLR 82003

A Chaos With Some Kind Of Order
George Winston | Linus & Lucy-The Music Of Vince Guaraldi | Windham Hill | 34 11187-2

A Charlie Brown Thanksgiving
Cat Anderson & The Ellington All-Stars | Cat Anderson | Swing | SW 8412 IMS

A 'Chat' With Cat
Cat Anderson And His All Stars | Ellingtonians In Paris | Jazztime(EMI) | 251275-2
A Chicken Ain't Nothin' But A Bird
Louis Jordan And His Tympany Five | Louis Jordan Vol.2-Knock Me Out | Swingtime(Contact) | ST 1012
A Chicken Named Fido
Abbey Lincoln And Her Orchestra | Devil's Got Your Tongue | Verve | 513574-2
A Child Is Born
Bill Evans Quintet | The Complete Fantasy Recordings | Fantasy | 9FCD 1012-2
Bobby Lyle Trio | Night Breeze | Electric Bird | K 28P 6457
Dick Johnson Orchestra | Swing Shift | Concord | CJ 167
Enrico Pieranunzi Trio | New Lands | Timeless | CD SJP 211
Jimmy Smith Trio | The Master II | Blue Note | 855466-2
Joe Bonner | New Beginnings | Evidence | TR 125
Mel Lewis Quartet | Mel Lewis And Friends | Horizon | MLJ 716
Oscar Peterson | Tracks | MPS | 68084
Paul Kuhn Trio | Play It Again Paul | IN+OUT Records | 77040-2
Pepper Adams Quartet | Pepper | Enja | ENJ-9079 2
Singers Unlimited + The Oscar Peterson Trio | In Tune | MPS | 68085
Tete Montoliu | The Music I Like To Play Vol.2 | Soul Note | 121200-2
Thad Jones-Mel Lewis Orchestra | Body And Soul | West Wind Orchestra Series | 2407 CD
Tommy Flanagan And Hank Jones | Our Delights | Original Jazz Classics | GXY 5113
Warren Vaché Sextet | Blues Walk | Dreamstreet | DR 101
A Child Is Born-
Louis Mazetier | Good Vibrations | Jazz Connaisseur | JCCD 9521-2
Michel Petrucciani | 100 Hearts | Blue Note | 538329-2
Oscar Peterson And His Trio | Live At The Blue Note | Telarc Digital | CD 83304
A Child's Prayer
Jane Ira Bloom-Fred Hersch Duo | As One | JMT Edition | 919003-2
A Child's Song(For Charlie Haden)
Dick Robertson And His Orchestra | The New York Session Man | Timeless | CBC 1-008
A Christmas Song
Duke Ellington And His Orchestra | Yale Concert | Fantasy | F 9433
A Chromatic Love Affair
Abbey Lincoln And Her Orchestra | Devil's Got Your Tongue | Verve | 513574-2
A Circle Of Love
The Pilgrim Jubilee Singers | Walk On/The Old Ship Of Zion | Mobile Fidelity | MFCD 756
A City Called Heaven
Dutch Swing College Band | Digital Dutch | Philips | 814068-2 PMS
A Clear Day And No Memories
Danny Gatton Septet | New York Stories Volume One | Blue Note | 798959-2
A Closer Look
Warren Bernhardt Quintet | Family Album | dmp Digital Music Productions | CD 499
A Closer View
Andre Persiani Trio | Out Of This World | Black & Blue | 33185
A Cockeyed Optimist
Modern Jazz Quartet | Odds Against Tomorrow | Blue Note | 793415-2
A Colloquial Dream(Scenes In The City)
Charles Mingus Septet | RCA Victoe 80th Anniversary(Bonus-CD) | RCA | RCMJ 68969-2
A Colloquial Dream(Scenes In The City-alt.take)
Charles Mingus Orchestra | Tijuana Moods(The Complete Edition) | RCA | 2663840-2
Tijuana Moods(The Complete Edition) | RCA | 2663840-2
Tijuana Moods(The Complete Edition) | RCA | 2663840-2
A Colloquial Dream(Scenes In The City-short-take-1)
The Baltimore Syndicate | The Baltimore Syndicate | Paddle Wheel | KICJ 72
A Column Of Birds
Vienna Art Orchestra | Standing...What? | Amadeo | 519816-2
A Cool Talk
Ronaldo Folegatti Groups | Sound Of Watercolors | AH Records | AH 403001-11
A Cradle Song
Judy Niemack With The Kenny Werner Quartet | ...Night And The Music | Freelance | FRL-CD 026
A Creature Of Many Faces
Joelle Leandre-Carlos Zingaro | Ecritures | Adda | 590038
A Cry From The Heart
Hot Stuff | Hot Stuff! Celebrating Early Jazz | Lake | LACD 40
A Dance To Summer
Steve Kuhn Quartet | Non-Fiction | ECM | 1124
A Dandy Line
Chet Baker Septet | Chet Baker-Grey December | Pacific Jazz | 797160-2
A Dark Spell
Eberhard Weber Quartet | Works | ECM | 825429-2
A Day At The Races
First House | Erendira | ECM | 1307
A Day Away
Taku Sugimoto | Oposite | HatNOIR | 802
A Day In Ocho Rios
George Wallington Trio | The Piano Collection Vol.2 | Vogue | 21610222
A Day In The Life
Conte Candoli-Carl Fontana Quintet | The Complete Phoenix Recordings Vol.5 | Woofy Productions | WPCD 125
A Day In The Life Of A Fool(Carnival)
Derek Smith Trio | Love For Sale | Progressive | PRO 7002 IMS
A Day To Mourn
Art Porter Group | Straight To The Point | Verve | 517997-2
A Daydream
Putte Wickman And The Hal Galper trio | Time To Remember | Dragon | DRCD 378
A Dear One
Time To Remember | Dragon | DRCD 378
A Dear One(alt.take)
Georgie Fame & The Danish Radio Big Band | Endangered Species | Music Mecca | CD 1040-2
A Deeper Season
Michael Schiefel | I Don't Belong | Traumton Records | 4433-2
A Delicate Atmosphere
Marian McPartland Trio With Strings | Marian McPartland With Strings | Concord | CCD 4745
A Delta So Old
Furio Di Castri-Paolo Fresu | Urlo | yvp music | CD 3035
A Deserting Love Affair
Jeff Beal | Contemplations | Triloka Records | 320204-2
A Different Kind Of Freedom
Jerry Bergonzi And Joachim Kühn | Signed By | Adda | ZZ 84104
A Dime Away From A Hotdog
Oscar Brown Jr. And His Group | Movin' On | Rhino | 8122-73678-2
Bob Moses Quartet | Wheels Of Colored Light | Open Minds | OM 2412-2
A Distant Spring
Sonny Simmons Quintet | Staying On The Watch | ESP Disk | ESP 1030-2
A Dog's Life
XIAME | Pensa! | VeraBra Records | CDVBR 2106-2
A Dream Of You
Roy Hargrove Quartet | Family | Verve | 527630-2
Ranee Lee And Her Quartet | Seasons Of Love | Justin Time | JUST 103-2
A Face Without A Name
Bill Evans-Eddie Gomez Duo | The Complete Fantasy Recordings | Fantasy | 9FCD 1012-2
Egberto Gismonti Group | Infancia | ECM | 1428
A Fala Da Paixao
Al Grey Quintet | Al Grey featuring Arnett Cobb and Jimmy Forrest | Black & Blue | BLE 233143
A Family Song
Tony Williams Lifetime | Spectrum:The Anthology | Verve | 537075-2
A Fantasic Story
Paul Horn/David Friesen | Heart To Heart | Golden Flute Records | GFR 2002
A Farewell To Maria
Kölner Saxophon Mafia With V.Nick Nikitakis | Kölner Saxophon Mafia Proudly Presents | Jazz Haus Musik | JHM 0046 CD
A Fat Morgana
Benny Carter And His Orchestra | The Various Facets Of A Genius 1929-1940 | Black & Blue | BLE 59.230 2
A Felicidade(Happiness)
Bob Brookmeyer And His Orchestra | Jazz-Club: Vibraphone | Verve | 840034-2
Gal Costa-Herbie Hancock | Antonio Carlos Jobim And Friends | Verve | 531556-2
George Cables Trio | Skylark | Steeplechase | SCCD 31381
Kenny Drew Trio | Dark Beauty | Steeplechase | SCS 1016
Niels-Henning Orsted-Pedersen Quartet | Jaywalkin' | Steeplechase | SCCD 31041
A Few Words By Cannonball...
Cannonball Adderley Quintet | Live In San Francisco | Riverside | RISA 1157-6
Patrick Tompert Trio | Moche! | Satin Doll Productions | SDP 1035-1 CD
A Few Words For Galileo
Johnny Griffin Quartet | NYC Underground | Galaxy | GXY 5132
A Fickle Sonance
Curtis Counce Group | Landslide | Original Jazz Classics | OJCCD 606-2
A Final Bars
Gary Dial-Dick Oatts Quartet With Brass Ensemble | Brassworks | dmp Digital Music Productions | CD 477
A Fine Romance
Billie Holiday And Her All Stars | Billie Holiday:The Great American Songbook | Verve | 523003-2
Billie Holiday And Her Orchestra | Billie Holiday:The Quintessential Vol.2(1936) | CBS | 460060-2
Derek Smith Trio | Derek Smith Trio Plays Jerome Kern | Progressive | PRO 7055 IMS
Ella Fitzgerald And Louis Armstrong With The Oscar Peterson Quartet | The Jazz Collector Edition: Ella & Louis | Laserlight | 15706
A Fine Romance | Verve | 523827-2
Compact Jazz: Ella Fitzgerald/Louis Armstrong | Verve | 835313-2
Ella Fitzgerald With Orchestra | Essential Ella | Verve | 523990-2
Ella Fitzgerald With The Nelson Riddle Orchestra | The Complete Ella Fitzgerald Song Books of Harold Arlen, Irving Berlin, Duke Ellington, George & Ira Gershwin, Jerome Kern, Johnny Mercer, Cole Porter And Rogers & Hart | Verve | 519832-2
Erroll Garner Trio | Erroll Garner Plays Gershwin & Kern | EmArCy | 826224-2 PMS
J.R. Monterose Sextet | Jaywalkin' | Fresh Sound Records | FSR-CD 320
Margaret Whiting With Russel Garcia And His Orchestra | Margaret Whiting Sings The Jerome Kern Song Book | Verve | 559553-2
Marian McPartland | Maybeck Recital Hall Series Volume Nine | Concord | CCD 4460
Stephane Grappelli Group | Plays Jerome Kern | GRP | GRP 95422
A Fitting Epitaph
Stan Getz With The Eddie Sauter Orchestra | Stan Getz Plays The Music Of Mickey One | Verve | 531232-2
A Five Day Live-
Chuck Marohnic | Permutations | Steeplechase | SCS 1155
A Flower
Eddie Daniels/Bucky Pizzarelli Duo | Blue Bossa | Choice | CHCD 71002
A Flower Is A Lovesome Thing
Dave Burrell | Plays Ellington & Monk | Denon Compact Disc | DC-8550
Duke Ellington And His Orchestra | Unknown Session | CBS | 467180-2
Elvin Jones Sextet | It Don't Mean A Thing... | Enja | ENJ-8066 2
John Hicks Trio | Something To Life For | HighNote Records | HCD 7019
Kristian Jorgensen Quartet With Monty Alexander | Meeting Monty | Stunt Records | STUCD 01212
Mal Waldron/Marion Brown | Songs Of Love And Regret | Freelance | FRL-CD 006
Seldon Powell Sextet | Seldon Powell Sextet | Fresh Sound Records | FSR 588(Roost 2220)
The Duke Ellington Orchestra | Music Is My Mistress | Limelight | 820801-2 IMS
Vince Guaraldi Trio | A Flower Is A Lovesome Thing | Original Jazz Classics | OJC 235(F 3257)
A Foggy Day(In London Town)
Art Tatum-Buddy DeFranco Quartet | The Tatum Group Masterpieces | Pablo | 2625706
Benny Carter Quintet | Cosmopolite | Verve | 521673-2
Billie Holiday And Her Orchestra | Embraceable You | Verve | 817359-1 IMS
Bireli Lagrene Quartet | Blue Eyes | Dreyfus Jazz Line | FDM 36591-2
Bob Florence Trio | Bob Florence Trio | Fresh Sound Records | FSR-CD 0303
Cannonball Adderley Quintet | Cannonball Adderley Birthday Celebration | Fantasy | FANCD 6087-2
Cannonball Adderley:Sophisticated Swing-The EmArCy Small Group Sessions | Verve | 528408-2
Cannonball Adderley With Richard Hayman's Orchestra | Julian Cannonball Adderley And Strings/Jump For Joy | Verve | 528699-2
Charles Mingus Jazz Workshop | Pithecanthropus Erectus | Atlantic | 7567-81456-2
Charles Mingus Quintet | Charles Mingus-The Complete Debut Recordings | Debut | 12 DCD 4402-2
Charles Mingus Quintet Plus Max Roach | The Charlie Mingus Quintet Plus Max Roach | Debut | VIJ 5011 IMS
Chuck Brown And The Second Chapter Band | Timeless | Minor Music | 801068
Claude Williamson Trio | The Fabulous Claude Williamson Trio | Fresh Sound Records | FSR-CD 0051
Dinah Washington With Her All Stars | Verve Jazz Masters 19:Dinah Washington | Verve | 518200-2
Ella Fitzgerald And Louis Armstrong With The Oscar Peterson Quartet | The Jazz Collector Edition: Ella & Louis | Laserlight | 15706
Welcome To Jazz: Ella Fitzgerald | Koch Records | 322 078 D1
Compact Jazz: Ella Fitzgerald/Louis Armstrong | Verve | 835313-2
Ella Fitzgerald With The Nelson Riddle Orchestra | Ella Sings Gershwin-Vol. 2 | Metro | 2682023 IMS
Ella Fitzgerald-Joe Pass Duo | Joe Pass:A Man And His Guitar | Original Jazz Classics | OJCCD 8806-2
Elliot Lawrence Band | Plays Tiny Kahn And Johnny Mandel Arrangements | Fantasy | 0902109(F 3219)
George Benson Group/Orchestra | George Benson Anthology | Warner | 8122-79934-2
George Benson Quartet | It's Uptown | CBS | 502469-2
Essential Jazz | CBS | 473686-2
George Van Eps | Legends | Concord | CCD 4616
Herb Ellis Trio With Hendrik Meurkens | Burnin' | Acoustic Music Records | 319.1164.2
Jimmy Raney Quintet | Jimmy Raney/A | Original Jazz Classics | OJC-1706(P 7089)
Lajos Dudas Quintet | Talk Of The Town | double moon | CHRDM 71012
Lee Konitz-Franco D'Andrea | 12 Gershwin In 12 Keys | Philology | W 312.2
Marcus Roberts Trio | Gershwin For Lovers | CBS | 477752-2
Nicole Metzger With The Christoph Mudrich Trio | Nicole Metzger Sings Gershwin | Blue Concept | BCCD 97/01
Oscar Peterson Trio | Oscar Peterson:The Gershwin Songbooks | Verve | 529698-2
Oscar Peterson:Exclusively For My Friends | MPS | 513830-2
Patti Page With Pete Rugolo And HisOrchestra | Patti Page In The Land Of Hi-Fi | Verve | 538320-2
Pierre Spiers Sextet feat. Stephane Grappelli | Special Stephane Grappelli | Jazztime(EMI) | 251286-2
Ronny Lang Quartet | Basie Street | Fresh Sound Records | FSR-CD 0501
Roy Eldridge With The Oscar Peterson Quartet | Compact Jazz: Oscar Peterson & Friends | Verve | 835315-2
Sarah Vaughan And Her Trio | The Complete Sarah Vaughan Live In Japan | Mobile Fidelity | MFCD 844-2
Sauter-Finegan Orchestra | The Return Of The Doodletown Fifers | EMI Records | ED 2607691
Tatum-Carter-Bellson Trio | The Tatum Group Masterpieces | Pablo | 2310732
Thilo Wolf Trio | I Got Rhythm | MDL-Jazz | CD 1911(CD 050)
A Foggy Day(In London Town-78rpm master take)
Charles Mingus Quintet | Charles Mingus-The Complete Debut Recordings | Debut | 12 DCD 4402-2
A Foggy Day(In London Town-alt.take)
Hank Jones Trio | Compassion | Black & Blue | BB 879.2
A Foggy Day(In London Town-LP master take)
Steve Lacy Nine | Futurities Part II | Hat Art | CD 6032
A Fool For You
Little Joe Blue Group | The Blues Vol.4 | Big Bear | 156401
A Foxy Chick And A Cool Cat
Perico Sambeat Group | Ademuz | Fresh Sound Records | FSNT 041 CD
A Free K
Donald Brown Sextet | Cause And Effect | Muse | MCD 5447
A French Touch
Pete Magadini Quintet | Night Dreamers | Timeless | CD SJP 317
A Friend's DAT Machine Makes
Keshavan Maslak Trio | Maslak One Thousand | Waterland | WM 004
A Fuego Lento
Modern Jazz Quartet feat.Jimmy Giuffre | MJQ 40 | Atlantic | 7567-82330-2
A Fugue For Music Inn
The MJQ At Music Inn | Atlantic | 90049-1 TIS
A Full Moon Ritual
Kölner Saxophon Mafia | Go Commercial... | Jazz Haus Musik | JHM 0065 CD
A Funkful Of House
Jimmy Smith Trio | Paris Jazz Concert:Jimmy Smith And The Trio | Laserlight | 36159
A Funky Blues Called I Don't Know
Billy Cobham Group | A Funky Thide Of Sings | Atlantic | ATL 50189
A Gainsbourg
Lou Levy Trio | My Old Flame | Fresh Sound Records | FSR-CD 312
A Gal In C
Barbara Carroll | Barbara Carroll At The Piano | Discovery | DS 847 IMS
A Gal In Calico
Dave McKenna | Dancing In The Dark And Other Music Of Arthur Schwartz | Concord | CCD 4292
Miles Davis Quartet | Green Haze | Prestige | P 24064
A Gathering In A Clearing
Cat Anderson And His All Stars | Ellingtonians In Paris | Jazztime(EMI) | 251275-2
A Gem From Tiffany
Shelly Manne And His Men | At The Black Hawk Vol.4 | Original Jazz Classics | OJCCD 659-2(S 7580)
At The Blackhawk Vol.4 | Contemporary | C 7580
A Gem From Tiffany(Theme)
At The Black Hawk Vol.2 | Original Jazz Classics | OJCCD 657-2(S 7578)
At The Black Hawk Vol.5 | Original Jazz Classics | OJCCD 660-2
At The Blackhawk Vol.2 | Contemporary | C 7578
A Ghost Called M
Anita Boyer & Her Tomboyers | Nat King Cole Trio:The MacGregor Years 1941/45 | Music & Arts | CD 911
A Ghost Of A Chance
Lenny Hambro Quintet | The Nature Of Things | Fresh Sound Records | LSP 15821(Epic LN 3361)
Sonny Stitt Quartet | Constellation | Muse | MCD 5323
The Yamaha International Allstar Band | Hapy Birthday Jazzwelle Plus | Nagel-Heyer | CD 005
Wild Bill Davis-Eddie Lockjaw Davis Quartet | Live! | Black & Blue | 33308
A Girl Like You
Stan Getz With The Eddie Sauter Orchestra | Stan Getz Plays The Music Of Mickey One | Verve | 531232-2
A Girl Named Jenny
Stan Getz Plays The Music Of Mickey One | Verve | 531232-2
A Girl Named Jenny-
Chris Cheek Sextet | A Girl Named Joe | Fresh Sound Records | FSNT 032 CD
A Girl Named Joe
Andrew Cyrille Quartet | Special People | Soul Note | SN 1012
A Girl Named Rigmor
Mark Soskin Quartet | Calypso & Jazz-Around The Corner | Paddle Wheel | KICJ 175
A Glimmer Of Sepal
Peppino D'Agostino | A Glimpse Of Times Past | Acoustic Music Records | 319.1157.2
A Go Go
Inez Andrews And The Andrewettes | The Famous Spiritual + Gospel Festival Of 1965 | L+R Records | LR 44005
A Good Man Is Hard To Find
Big Maybelle With Orchestra | Roots Of Rock 'N' Roll, Vol. 5: Ladies Sing The Blues | Savoy | SJL 2233
Kid Ory's Creole Jazz Band | Kid Ory's Creole Jazz Band | Good Time Jazz | GTCD 12008-2
Ralph Sutton | More At Cafe Des Copains | Sackville | SKCD2-2036
A Good Top Tongue
Ben Sidran Group | A Good Travel Agent | VeraBra Records | CDVBR 2095-2
A Good 'Un
Guy Klucevsek-Phillip Johnston | Tales From The Cryptic | Winter&Winter | 910088-2
A Goyish Kind Of Blues
Rabih Abou-Khalil Group | Yara | Enja | ENJ-9360 2
A Gracious Man
Joe Newman Quartet | In A Mellow Mood | Stash Records | ST 219 IMS
A Grand Night For Swinging
Leslie Drayton Orchestra | Love Is A Four-Letter Word | Optimism | ER 1003
A Gush Of Periwinkles
Ella Fitzgerald With Sy Oliver And His Orchestra | Ella Fitzgerald:The Decca Years 1949-1954 | Decca | 050668-2
A Guy Is A Guy
Jason Miles Group | Jason Miles World Tour | Lipstick Records | LIP 890212
A Handful Of Fives
Roland Kirk Quartet | The Inflated Tear | Atlantic | 7567-90045-2
Annie Ross With The Johnny Spence Orchestra | Annie Ross Sings A Handful Of Songs | Fresh Sound Records | FSR-CD 0061
A Handful Of Stars
Jack Nimitz Quartet | Confirmation | Fresh Sound Records | FSR CD 5006
Serge Chaloff Quartet | California Cool | Blue Note | 780707-2
Stan Getz Quartet | Stan Getz And The 'Cool' Sounds | Verve | 547317-2
Best Of The West Coast Sessions | Verve | 537084-2
Stan Getz Highlights | Verve | 847430-2
Stan Getz:East Of The Sun-The West Coast Sessions | Verve | 531935-2
A Handful O'Soul
James Weiman Trio | People Music | TCB Records | TCB 96302
A Happy Afternoon
Makoto Ozone Trio | The Trio | Verve | 537503-2
A Hard Day's Night

TITELVERZEICHNIS

Gary McFarland Orchestra | Soft Samba | Verve | MV 2102 IMS
Peggy Lee With Lou Levy's Orchestra | Pass Me By/Big Spender | Capitol | 535210-2
Ute Kannenberg Quartet | Kannenberg On Purpose | Jazz Haus Musik | JHM 0109 CD
Christoph Thewes-Rudi Mahall Quartet | Quartetto Pazzo | Jazz Haus Musik | JHM 0122 CD

A Hard Night's Day
Tom Mega + Band | Songs & Prayers | ITM Records | ITM 1491

A Hatful Of Dandruff
Joe McPhee Trio | Sweet Freedom-Now What? | Hat Art | CD 6162

A Heart Is Not A Toy
Skinnay Ennis And His Orchestra | The Uncollected:Skinnay Ennis | Hindsight | HSR 164 (835575)

A Helluva Town
Putney Dandridge Band | Putney Dandridge 1935-1936 | Timeless | CBC 1-023

A Hot Time In The Old Town
Miff Mole And His Molers | Jazz Classics In Digital Stereo: Red Nichols And Miff Mole | CDS Records Ltd. | RPCD 627(CD 664)

A House Is Not A Home
Bill Evans Trio | I Will Say Goodbye | Original Jazz Classics | OJCCD 761-2(F 9593)
Dakota Staton With The Groove Holmes Sextet | Dakota Staton | LRC Records | CDC 9017
Eric Alexander Quintet | Summit Meeting | Milestone | MCD 9322-2
Joe Sample Group | Invitation | Warner | 9362-45209.2
John Tank Quartet | Canadian Sunset | TCB Records | TCB 20902
Stan Getz With The Richard Evans Orchestra | What The World Needs Now-Stan Getz Plays Bacharach And David | Verve | 557450-2
Steve Kuhn Trio | Porgy | Jazz City | 660.53.012

A House Is Not A Home(alt.take)
Sun Ra And His Solar Arkestra | Heliocentric Worlds Vol.2 | ESP Disk | ESP 1017-2

A Hundred Years From Today
Doris Day With Orchestra | The Uncollected:Doris Day | Hindsight | HSR 200
June Christy With Orchestra | This Is June Christy/June Christy Recalls Those Kenton Days | Capitol | 535209-2
June Christy With The Pete Rugolo Orchestra | June Christy Recalls Those Kenton Days | EMI Records | 1599311
Maxine Sullivan With The Scott Hamilton Quintet | Swingin' Sweet | Concord | CCD 4351

A Hymn Of Sorrow-
Hendrik Meurkens Octet | Sambahia | Concord | CCD 4474

A Japanese Waltze
Rhythm Aces | Jabbo Smith 1929-1938 | Retrieval | RTR 79013

A John Coltrane Blues
Gato Barbieri Septet | Gato Barbieri:The Complete Flying Dutchman Recordings 1969-1973 | RCA | 2154555-2

A Johnny Hodges Medley:
Duke Ellington And His Orchestra | Yale Concert | Original Jazz Classics | OJCCD 664-2
Paul Tardif Septet | Points Of Departure | Koch Jazz | KOC 3-7800-2

A Jump Ahead
Earl Hines And His Orchestra | Fatha Vol.1 | Zeta | ZET 710

A Keen Bat
Jack McDuff Quartet With Orchestra | Prelude:Jack McDuff Big Band | Prestige | PRCD 24283-2

A Kettle Of Fish
Jacques Schwarz-Bart/James Hurt Quartet | Immersion | Fresh Sound Records | FSNT 057 CD

A Kick In The Bone
Joe Maneri Quartet | In Full Cry | ECM | 1617(537048-2)

A Kind Of Birth
Bill Carrothers Quartet | The Electric Bill | Dreyfus Jazz Line | FDM 36631-2

A Kindred Spirit
Cindy Blackman Quartet | In The Now | HighNote Records | HCD 7024

A Kiss To Build A Dream On
Benny Bailey Septet | Big Brass | Candid | CCD 79011
Buddy Tate Quartet | The Ballad Artistry Of Buddy Tate | Sackville | SKCD2-3034
Louis Armstrong And His All Stars | En Concert Avec Europe 1 | Laserlight | 710415
Louis Armstrong And His All Stars/Orchestra | Do You Know What It Means To Miss New Orleans? | Verve | 837919-2
Louis Armstrong With Sy Oliver And His Orchestra | Louis Armstrong-All Time Greatest Hits | MCA | MCD 11032
Maryland Jazzband Of Cologne | Jazz In Schloss Gracht | USW Records | G 6710
Weslia Whitefield With The Mike Greensill Duo | Nice Work... | Landmark | LCD 1544-2

A La Cabeza
Kenny Burrell With Rufus Reid | A La Carte | Muse | MR 5317(952092)

A La French
Bebo Valdés Trio | El Arte Del Sabor | Blue Note | 535193-2

A La Loma De Belen-
Mehldau & Rossy Trio | When I Fall In Love | Fresh Sound Records | FSNT 007 CD

A La Loss
Mongo Santamaria And His Band | Sabroso | Original Jazz Classics | OJCCD 281-2

A La Luna
Bebo Valdés Group | Bebo Rides Again | Messidor | 15834 CD

A La Mode
Arturo Sandoval And The Latin Train Band | Arturo Sandoval & The Latin Train | GRP | GRP 98202

A La P.P.
Patrick Bebelaar Quartet | Never Thought It Could Happen | dml-records | CD 007

A La Prima Vera Corta Que Tuvimos
Jean-Pierre Catoul Quintet | Modern Gardens | B.Sharp Records | CDS 076

A La Table
Michael Mantler Group With The Danish Concert Radio Orchestra | Many Have No Speech | Watt | 19(835580-2)

A L'Abattoir
Mundell Lowe Quintet | Mundell's Moods | Nagel-Heyer | CD 065

A Lad Named Charlie
Oscar Brown Jr. And His Group | Movin' On | Rhino | 8122-73678-2

A Ladiesman
Helen Merrill With The Dick Katz Group | A Shade Of Difference | EmArCy | 558851-2

A Lady Must Live
Pearl Bailey With Orchestra | Come On Let's Play With Pearlie Mae | Roulette | CDP 793274-2

A Laugh For Rory
Roland Kirk Quartet | The Inflated Tear | Atlantic | 7567-90045-2
Ray Anthony And His Orchestra | Ray Anthony Plays Steve Allen | Fresh Sound Records | 054 2602341(Capitol T 1086)

A L'Encre Rouge
Tito Burns And His Sextet | Bebop In Britain | Esquire | CD ESQ 100-4

A Letter To Mr. B
Guitar Slim And His Band | The Things That I Used To Do | Ace Records | CDCHD 318

A Life
Mike Westbrook Concert Band | Release | Deram | 844851-2

A Life Unfolds
John Pizzarelli Trio | Kisses In The Rain | Telarc Digital | CD 83491

A Line For Two
Les McCann Group | Listen Up! | Musicmasters | 65139-2

A Little Barefoot Soul
Big Maybelle With The Ernie Wilkins Orchestra | Roots Of Rock 'N' Roll, Vol. 5: Ladies Sing The Blues | Savoy | SJL 2233

A Little Bit Of Basie
Eddie Clearwater And His Orchestra | Two Times Nine | Charly | CRB 1025

A Little Bit Of This And A Little Bit Of That
Chuck Foster And His Orchestra | The Uncollected: Chuck Foster | Hindsight | HSR 115

A Little Booker
Lee Ritenour Sextet | Alive In L.A. | GRP | GRP 98822

A Little Bumpin'
Art Blakey And The Jazz Messengers | The Witch Doctor | Blue Note | 521957-2

A Little Busy
Best Of Blakey 60 | Blue Note | 493072-2
Bobby Timmons Trio | Moanin' | Milestone | M 47031

A Little Doctor
Herbert Joos | Still Life | Extraplatte | 316139

A Little Fourplay
Fourplay | Fourplay...Yes,Please! | Warner | 9362-47694-2
John Surman-Tony Levin Duo | Live At Moers Festival | Ring | 01006

A Little Gypsy
Oscar Peterson | Tracks | MPS | 68084

A Little Jazz Exercise
Thilo Wolf Big Band | Swing It! | MDL-Jazz | CD 1915(CD 052)

A Little Les Of Lou's Blues
Eb Davis Bluesband | Good Time Blues | Acoustic Music Records | AMC 1016

A Little Max(Parfait)
Ellington/Mingus/Roach Trio | Money Jungle | Blue Note | 538227-2

A Little Max(Parfait)(alt.take)
Stan Kenton And His Orchestra | Hits In Concert | Creative World | ST 1074

A Little New York Midtown Music
Sammy Kaye And His Orchestra | The Uncollected:Sammy Kaye, Vol.2 | Hindsight | HSR 163

A Little Piece Of Heaven
Lennart Ginman-Kirk Lightsey Quartet | 1991 | Stunt Records | STUCD 19003

A Little Push
Jesse Davis Quartet | First Insight | Concord | CCD 4796

A Little Taste
Cannonball Adderley Quintet | Spontaneous Combustion-The Savoy Sessions | Savoy | ???
Johnny Hodges Orchestra | Jazz Legacy 62: Johnny Hodges-Jumpin' | Vogue | 500112
Cannonball Adderley Quintet | Discoveries | Savoy | SV 0251

A Little Tear
Count Basie And His Orchestra | En Concert Avec Europe 1 | Laserlight | 710411/12

A Little Twist
Harold Harris Trio | Here's Harold | Vee Jay Recordings | VJR 501

A Long Drink Of The Blues(take 1)
Jackie McLean Sextet | A Long Drink Of The Blues | Original Jazz Classics | OJCCD 253-2(NJ 8253)

A Long Drink Of The Blues(take 2)
Henry Kaiser-Jim O'Rourke | Tomorrow Knows Where You Live | Victo | CD 014

A Long Way
Michael Mantler Group | Michael Mantler: No Answer/Silence | Watt | 2/5(543374-2)
Bobby Jaspar-Don Rendell Septet | Bobby Jaspar Featuring Dave Amram | Vogue | 21606392

A Long Way From Home
Mark Whitfield Quartet | The Marksman | Warner | 7599-26321-2
Kazda | New Strategies Of Riding | ITM Records | ITM 1492

A Los Tilingos
Junior Parker With Orchestra feat.Jimmy McGriff | Little Junior Parker | LRC Records | CDC 9002

A Lot Of Livin' To Do
Pat Metheny Trio | Trio 99-00 | Warner | 9362-47632-2
Stan Kenton And His Orchestra | Stan Kenton-Jean Turner | Creative World | ST 1046

A Lot Of Things
Mahavishnu Orchestra | The Inner Mounting Flame | CBS | CK 65523

A Lotus On Irish Streams
Eric Reed Trio | Musicale | Impulse(MCA) | 951196-2

A Love Divine
David Torkanowsky Group | Steppin' Out | Line Records | COCD 9.00900 O

A Love Supreme(part 1:Acknowledgement)
John Coltrane Quartet | Jazz Gallery:John Coltrane Vol.2 | RCA | 2127276-2

A Love Supreme(Suite):
A Love Supreme | Ingo | 11

A Love Supreme:
John Coltrane:The Classic Quartet-Complete Impulse Studio Recordings | Impulse(MCA) | 951280-2
Peter Herborn Group With The WDR Big Band | Traces Of Trane | JMT Edition | 514002-2

A Lovely Way To Spend An Evening
Curtis Fuller Quintet | The Opener | Blue Note | 300173(1567)
Oscar Peterson Trio With Herb Ellis | Three Originals:Motion&Emotions/Tristeza On Piano/Hello Herbie | MPS | 521059-2
Raymond Scott And His Orchestra | The Uncollected:Raymond Scott Vol.2 | Hindsight | HSR 211

A Lover Is Blue
Gene Ammons Quartet | The Gene Ammons Story: The 78 Era | Prestige | P 24058

A Lull At Dawn
Barney Bigard And His Orchestra | The Great Ellington Units | RCA | ND 86751
Elvin Jones Sextet | It Don't Mean A Thing... | Enja | ENJ-8066 2

A Lunar Tune
John Stevens Orchestra | A Luta Continua | Konnex Records | KCD 5056

A Luz Da Sombra-
Peter Brötzmann | Nothing To Say-A Suite Of Breathless Motion Dedicated To Oscar Wild | FMP | CD 73

A Madia Luz
Joe Haider Trio | A Magyar-The Hungarian-Die Ungarische | JHM Records | JHM 3626

A Magyar-The Hungarian-Die Ungarische
Avery Sharpe Sextet | Unspoken Words | Sunnyside | SSC 1029 D

A Man And A Woman
Herbie Mann-Tamiko Jones | The Best Of Herbie Mann | Atlantic | 7567-81369-2
Robert Conti | Solo Guitar | Trend | TR 519 Direct-to-Disc

A Mandala To Liberation
Werner Lüdi Sunnymoon | Sunnymoon | Creative Works Records | CW LP 1009

A Man's Best Friend Is A Bed
Cadavre Exquis | Cadavre Exquis | Creative Works Records | CW CD 1014-1

A March Is An Introduction
Pino Minafra Sud Ensemble | Sudori | Victo | CD 034

A Married Man's A Fool
Milt Jackson Septet | Night Mist | Pablo | 2312124

A Matter Of Intensity
Klaus König Orchestra | Reviews | Enja | ENJ-9061 2

A Matter Of Taste
John Abercrombie Trio | While We're Young | ECM | 1489

A Matter Of Time
Banda Città Ruvo Di Puglia | La Banda/Banda And Jazz | Enja | ENJ-9326 2

A Me,Fanciulla(La Traviata)
Andy Kirk And His Orchestra | A Mellow Bit Of Rhythm | RCA | 2113028-2

A Melody
Gene Ammons-Sonny Stitt Quintet | We'll Be Together Again | Original Jazz Classics | OJCCD 708-2(P 7606)

A Metropolitan Affair
Dino Saluzzi Trio | Responsorium | ECM | 1816(017069-2)

A Mi Hermano Celso
Paquito D'Rivera Orchestra | Tropicana Nights | Chesky | JD 186

A Minor Blues In F
Lee Konitz Trio | Three Guys | Enja | ENJ-9351 2
Lee Konitz-Albert Mangelsdorff Duo | Art Of The Duo | Enja | 5059-2

A Minor Delight
Lucky Thompson-Emmett Berry Quintet | Lucky Thompson | Swing | SW 8404 IMS

A Minor Goof
Jukka Tolonen & Coste Apetrea | Touch Wood | Sonet | 147128

A Moment Alone
Keith Jarrett Trio | Somewhere Before | Atlantic | 7567-81455-2

A Moment For Tears
Joe Haider Trio | A Magyar-The Hungarian-Die Ungarische | JHM Records | JHM 3626

A Moment In Montreux
Bob James Trio | Bold Conceptions | Verve | 557454-2

A Moment's Notice
Bud Powell Trio | Ups 'N Downs | Mainstream | MD CDO 724

A Monastic Calling
Benny Carter Quartet | Swingin' The Twenties | Original Jazz Classics | OJCCD 339-2

A Monday Date
Earl Hines | The Earl | Naxos Jazz | 8.120581 CD
George Zack-George Wettling Duo | Commodore Classics-George Zack/George Wettling:Barrelhouse Piano | Commodore | 6.25895 AG
Louis Armstrong And His Hot Five | Heebie Jeebies | Naxos Jazz | 8.120351 CD
Wild Bill Davison And His Commodores | Wild Bill Davison:The Commodore Master Takes | Commodore | CMD 14052

A Monk In A Simple Room
Irene Schweizer/Andrew Cyrille | Irene Schweizer-Andrew Cyrille | Intakt Records | CD 008

A Monk's Dream
Johnny Griffin Quartet | Return Of The Griffin | Galaxy | GXY 5117

A Mural From Two Perspectives
Duke Ellington | Duke Ellington Live At The Whitney | Impulse(MCA) | 951173-2
Frank Carlberg Group | Variations On A Summer Day | Fresh Sound Records | FSNT 083 CD

A Music
Matthias Daneck's N.O.W. | Seven Portraits Of Obviously Unpredictable Mood Swings And Subsequent Behaviour | Satin Doll Productions | SDP 1012-1 CD

A New Day
Stan Kenton And His Orchestra | Stan Kenton Conducts The Jazz Compositions Of Dee Barton | Creative World | ST 1022

A New Hymn
Tacuma-Puschnig Duo | Gemini-Gemini | ITM-Pacific | ITMP 970063

A New Job
Craig Bailey Band | A New Journey | Candid | CCD 79725

A New Journey
Roy Hargrove Quintet | Diamond In The Rough | Novus | PD 90471

A New Orleans Overture
Brian Trainor Quintet | Brian Trainor:Portraits | Candid | CCD 79731

A New Place:Arrival-Scenery-Imps Walk-Rest
Peter Erskine Group | Motion Poet | Denon Compact Disc | CY-72582

A New Shade Of Blues
Pee Wee Ellis Quintet With Guests | A New Shift | Minor Music | 801060

A New Shift
Aydin Esen Group | Pictures | Jazz City | 660.53.007

A New Spirit(für Michael)
Klaus Ignatzek Quintet | All Systems Go | Candid | CCD 79738

A Newton
Mickey Tucker Quartet | Blues In Five Dimensions | Steeplechase | SCCD 31258

A Nice Idea
Jay Clayton-Jim Knapp Collective | Tito's Acid Trip | ITM-Pacific | ITMP 970072

A Night In Bongolia
Simon Cato Spang-Hansen Quartet | Identified | dacapo | DCCD 9448

A Night In Copenhagen
Sun Ra And His Arkestra | Sun Ra And His Cosmo Dicipline Arkestra | LEO | LR 149

A Night In Lisbon
Poncho Sanchez Band With Tito Puente | Chile Con Soul | Concord | CCD 4406

A Night In The Mountains
Jon Hiseman Group | Night In The Sun | Kuckuck | 055

A Night In Tunisia
Art Blakey And The Jazz Messengers | A Night At Birdland Vol. 1 | Blue Note | 532146-2
Live In Stockholm 1959 | DIW | DIW 313 CD
Jazz In Paris:Paris Jam Session | EmArCy | 832692-2 PMS
Paris Jazz Concert:Art Blakey & The Jazz Messengers | Laserlight | 36158
Theory Of Art | RCA | ND 86286(886235)
At The Club St.Germain | RCA | ND 74897(2)
Live In Holland 1958 | Bandstand | BDCD 1532
Art Blakey & The Jazz Messengers: Olympia, May 13th, 1961 | Laserlight | 36128
Live In Stockholm 1959 | Dragon | DRCD 182
Art Blakey And The Jazz Messengers(Art Blakey Quintet) | Clifford Brown:The Complete Blue Note And Pacific Recordings | Blue Note | 834195-2
Art Pepper Quartet | A Night At The Surf Club Vol.2 | EPM Musique | FDC 5154
Art Pepper:The Complete Village Vanguard Sessions | Contemporary | 9CCD-4417-2
New York Album | Galaxy | GXY 5154
Arturo Sandoval And His Cuban Jazz Masters | Tumbaito | Inak | 2003
Boyd Raeburn And His Orchestra | Experiments In Big Band Jazz-1945 | Musicraft | MVS 505 IMS
Bud Powell Trio | The Amazing Bud Powell Vol.1 | Blue Note | 300366
Blue Note Cafe Paris 1961 | ESP Disk | ESP 1066-2
Cal Tjader Sextet | A Night At The Blackhawk | Original Jazz Classics | OJC 278(F 8026)
Charlie Parker Septet | Jazz Gallery:Charlie Parker Vol.1 | RCA | 2114174-2
Count Basie Big Band | The Montreux '77 Collection | Pablo | 2620107
Dexter Gordon Quartet | Our Man In Paris | Blue Note | 591722-2
Billie's Bounce | Steeplechase | SCCD 36028
Dizzy Gillespie And His Orchestra | Dizzy Gillespie:Night In Tunisia | Dreyfus Jazz Line | FDM 36734-2
Compact Jazz:Dizzy Gillespie | Mercury | 832574-2 PMS
Dizzier And Dizzier | RCA | 26685172
Dizzy Gillespie And The United Nation Orchestra | 7.Zelt-Musik-Festival:Jazz Events | Zounds | CD 2730001
Live At The Royal Festival Hall | Enja | ENJ-6044 2
Dizzy Gillespie Group | Triple Play:Dizzy Gillespie-The Final Recordings | Telarc Digital | CD 83451
Dizzy Gillespie Quintet | Copenhagen Concert | Steeplechase | SCCD 36024
Don Bennett Trio | Solar | Candid | CCD 79723
Duke Jordan Trio | Flight To Jordan | Savoy | 650118(881918)
Ella Fitzgerald With The Lou Levy Quartet | Compact Jazz: Ella Fitzgerald | Verve | 831367-2
Ella Fitzgerald-First Lady Of Song | Verve | 517898-2
Elmo Hope Ensemble | Hope From Rikers Island | Chiaroscuro | CR 2009
Elmo Hope Trio | Last Sessions Vol.2 | Inner City | IC 1037 IMS
Frank Morgan With The Rodney Kendrick Trio | Bop! | Telarc Digital | CD 83413

A Night In Tunisia · Bielefelder Katalog · 39 · Jazz • Ausgabe 2004 · A Taste Of Honey

George Cables Trio | BluesOlogy | Steeplechase | SCCD 31434
Heinz Von Hermann Jazz Ahead | A Standard Treatment | Mons Records | MR 874320
Itchy Fingers | Full English Breakfast | Enja | ENJ-7085 2
Jack McDuff Orchestra | Write On, Capt'n | Concord | CCD 4568
Jeff Hamilton Trio | Jeff Hamilton Trio Live | Mons Records | MR 874777
Jimmy Forrest Sextet | Live At The Barrel | Prestige | P 7858
Jimmy Smith Trio | Jimmy Smith: Grazy Baby | Blue Note | 784030-2
Joe Albany Trio | Birdtown Birds | Steeplechase | SCCD 31003
John Clayton Big Band | Tribute To... | Timeless | JC 11005
Jon Faddis Quintet | Legacy | Concord | CCD 4291
Junior Mance | Here 'Tis | Sackville | SKCD2-3050
Kenny Dorham Sextet | Round Midnight At The Cafe Bohemia | Blue Note | 300105(1524)
Les Double Six | Les Double Six | RCA | 2164314-2
Les McCann Trio | Plays The Shout | Pacific Jazz | LN 10083
Max Roach Quintet | Drum Conversation | Enja | 4074-2
Miles Davis Quartet | The Musings Of Miles | Original Jazz Classics | OJCCD 004-2
Green Haze | Prestige | P 24064
Mundell Lowe-Tete Montoliu | Mundell Lowe & Tete Montoliu Vol.2:Sweet'n Lovely | Fresh Sound Records | FSR-CD 0162
Poncho Sanchez And His Orchestra | Sonando | Concord | CCD 4201
Quintet Of The Year | The Quintet-Jazz At Massey Hall | Debut | DSA 124-6
Charlie Parker The Immortal Sessions Vol.2:1949-1953 | SAGA Jazz Classics | EC 3319-2
Ran Blake | Something To Live For | HatOLOGY | 527
Return To The Wide Open Spaces | Live At The Caravan Of Dreams | Amazing Records | AMCD 1021
Sebastiaan De Krom Sextet | 13th Jazz Hoeilaart International Europ' Jazz Contest 91 | B.Sharp Records | CDS 086
Sonny Rollins Trio | A Night At The Village Vanguard | Blue Note | 499795-2
A Night At The Village Vanguard Vol.2 | Blue Note | 300203(BNJ 61014)
Sonny Rollins:The Blue Note Recordings | Blue Note | 821371-2
Stan Getz Quintet | West Coast Jazz | Verve | 557549-2
Stan Getz Highlights | Verve | 847430-2
Stan Getz:East Of The Sun-The West Coast Sessions | Verve | 531935-2
Sylvain Luc-André Ceccarelli-Jean Marc Jafet | SUD | Dreyfus Jazz Line | FDM 36612-2
Teddy Charles Quartet | Ezz-Thetic | Prestige | P 7827
Charlie Parker All Stars | Charlie Parker 1950-1951:The Complete Bird At Birdland Vol.1 | Fat Boy Jazz | FBB 901

A Night In Tunisia Suite:
Art Blakey And The Jazz Messengers | A Night In Tunisia | RCA | 2663896-2

A Night In Tunisia(alt.take)
Art Pepper Quartet | Art Pepper:The Complete Galaxy Recordings | Galaxy | 16GCD 1016-2
Bud Powell Trio | The Amazing Bud Powell Vol.1 | Blue Note | 532136-2
Bud Powell:The Complete Blue Note And Roost Recordings | Blue Note | 830083-2

A Night In Tunisia(Interlude)
Dizzy Gillespie And His Orchestra | Jazz Gallery:Dizzy Gillespie | RCA | 2114165-2
Charlie Parker Septet | Charlie Parker On Dial, Vol.1 | Spotlite | SPJ 101

A Night Of Love
Kai Winding Septet | Early Bones | Prestige | P 24067

A Night To Remember
Catch Up | Catch Up Vol. 1 | Calig | 30613

A Nightingale Sang In Berkeley Square
Bill Carrothers-Bill Stewart | Bill Carrothers Duets With Bill Stewart | Dreyfus Jazz Line | FDM 37002-2
Christian Josi With The Harry Allen Quartet | I Walk With My Feet Off The Ground | Master Mix | CHECD 00111
Debbie Poryes Trio | Trio | Timeless | SJP 203
Ed Neumeister Quintet | Ed Neumeister Quartet/Quintet | Timescrapper | TSCR 9614
Ellis Marsalis | Jazz Piano Vol.2 | CBS | 486639-2
Glenn Miller And His Orchestra | Original Recordings From 1938 to 1942,Vol.2 | RCA | 2118549-2
Herb Ellis-Ross Tompkins Duo | A Pair To Draw To | Concord | CJ 17
Marian McPartland Trio | Marion McPartland At The Hickory House | Savoy | SJL 2248 (801856)
Mel Tormé And His Band | Fujitsu-Concord Jazz Festival In Japan '90 | Concord | CCD 4481
Rosemary Clooney And Her Sextet | Rosemary Clooney Sings Ballads | Concord | CCD 4282
Scott Hamilton Quartet | Live At Brecon Jazz Festival | Concord | CCD 4649
Stan Getz-Bob Brookmeyer Quintet | Stan Getz-Bob Brookmeyer Recorded Fall 1961 | Verve | 813359-1 IMS
Stephane Grappelli Quartet | Verve Jazz Masters 11:Stéphane Grappelli | Verve | 516758-2
Stephane Grappelli With The Diz Disley Trio | Violinspiration | MPS | 68058
The Mel Lewis Jazz Orchestra | To You-A Tribute To Mel Lewis | Limelight | 820832-2 IMS
Thilo Wolf Big Band | Mr. Grooverix | MDL-Jazz | CD 1925(CD 053)

A Nite In Tunisia
Babs Gonzales Group | Properly Presenting Babs Gonzales | Fresh Sound Records | FSR 702(835422)

A Nite In Tunisia -> A Night In Tunisia

A Northern Tale
Niels-Henning Orsted-Pedersen/Sam Jones Quintet | Double Bass | Steeplechase | SCS 1055(Audiophile Pressing)

A Notation
Dirk Schreurs-Walter Baeken Group | Beyond Ballads | B.Sharp Records | CDS 100

A Pad On Edge Of Town
Keith Jarrett With String Quartet | In The Light | ECM | 1033/4

A Pagan Hymn
Eddie Taylor Blues Band | Stormy Monday | Blues Beacon | BLU-1004 2

A Pale Smile
Clarence Williams | The Music Of New Orleans | RCA | NL 89724 DP

A Pear For Satie
Louie Bellson Quintet | Skin Deep | Verve | 559825-2

A Pedrinha Cai
J.C. Higginbotham's Big Eight | Giants Of Small-Band Swing Vol.2 | Original Jazz Classics | OJCCD 1724-2

A Pepper Poem
Mal Waldron & Jim Pepper | Art Of The Duo | Tutu Records | 888106-2*
Mahalia Jackson With Choir/Orchestra/Falls-Jones Ensemble | This Is Mahalia Jackson | CBS | 66241

A Poison Tree
Mike Westbrook Trio | Love For Sale | Hat Art | CD 6061

A Porter's Love Song To A Chambermaid
Red Norvo And His Orchestra | Jivin The Jeep | Hep | CD 1019
Duke Ellington And His Famous Orchestra | Duke Ellington:Ko-Ko | Dreyfus Jazz Line | FDM 36717-2

A Portrait Of Bert Williams
In A Mellow Tone | RCA | 2113029-2

A Portrait Of Bud Powell
Pat Martino Quartet | Desperado | Original Jazz Classics | OJCCD 397-2(P 7795)

A Portrait Of Diana
Wayne Horvitz Group | Pigpen-V As In Victim | Avant | AVAN 027

A Portrait Of Robert Thompson(As A Young Man)
Loren MazzaCane Connors | A Possible Dawn | HatNOIR | 801

A Powdered Wig
Chico Freeman-Clyde Criner Duo | Tradition In Transition | Elektra | MUS K 52412

A Prayer 4 The Blind
Donny McCaslin Quartet | Exile And Discovery | Naxos Jazz | 86014-2

A Prayer For My Family
Warren Bernhardt Quintet | Reflections | dmp Digital Music Productions | CD 489

A Prescription For The Blues
Acoustic Affaire | Mira | Jazz 'n' Arts Records | JNA 1303

A Present With A View
Pili-Pili | Boogaloo | JA & RO | JARO 4174-2

A Presi Dee
Svend Asmussen-Kenny Drew Quartet | Prize/Winners | Matrix | MTX 1001 IMS

A Pretty Girl Is Like A Melody
Earl Hines | Americans Swinging In Paris:Earl Hines | EMI Records | 539661-2
Le Jazz En France Vol.15:Earl Hunes Paris Session 1965 | Pathe | 1552611

A Pretty Girl(A Cadillac And Some Money)
David S.Ware Trio | Birth Of A Being | Hat Art | W

A Question Of Doing It
The Four Brothers | Together Again! | RCA | 2179623-2

A Quick One
Herbie Hancock Quartet | Herbie Hancock Quartet | CBS | SRCS 9343

A Quick Sketch
Sherrie Maricle/John Mastroianni Quintet | Cookin' On All Burners | Stash Records | ST-CD 24(881828)

A Quiet Place
M'Boom | Collage | Soul Note | SN 1059
Take 6 | Goldmine | Reprise | 7599-25670-2
Wes Montgomery With The Don Sebesky Orchestra | Bumpin' | Verve | 539062-2

A Quiet Thing
Richie Beirach | Self Portrait | CMP Records | CMP CD 51

A Quivering Sound Of The Mountain Stream
Claude Luter Quartet | Blue Clarinet | Vogue | 502612

A Quote From Clifford Brown
Roland Kirk Quintet | Rahsaan/The Complete Mercury Recordings Of Roland Kirk | Mercury | 846630-2
Karl Denson Group | The Red Snapper | Minor Music | 801024

A Red Hat
Rex Stewart And His Orchestra | Porgy And Bess Revisited | Swing | SW 8414 IMS

A Remark You Made
Eddie Louiss Quartet | Flomela | Dreyfus Jazz Line | FDM 36578-2

A Rhyme For Angela
Moacir Santos Group | Opus 3, No. 1 | Discovery | DS 795 IMS

A Ritual
Juanjo Dominguez | Che Guitarra | ALISO Records | AL 1025

A Roberto Grela
Arthur Prysock With The Red Prysock Band | A Rockin' Good Way | Milestone | M 9139

A Rockin' Good Way
Dinah Washington And Brook Benton With The Belford Hendricks Orchestra | Brook Benton-Dinah Washington:The Two Of Us | Verve | 526467-2

A Rosa Negra-
Stan Kenton And His Orchestra | The Kenton Touch | Creative World | ST 1033

A Royal Wedding Suite:
Mavis Staples-Lucky Peterson | Spirituals&Gospel:Dedicated To Mahalia Jackson | Verve | 533562-2

A Sack Full Of Soul
Roland Kirk Quartet | Talkin' Verve-Roots Of Acid Jazz:Roland Kirk | Verve | 533101-2
The Gospelaire Of Dayton,Ohio | Can I Get A Witness/Bones In The Valley | Mobile Fidelity | MFCD 763

A Sailboat In The Moonlight
Dick Jurgens And His Orchestra | The Radio Years: Dick Jurgens And His Orchestra 1937-39 | London | HMP 5046 AN

A Searching Spirit
Jeremy Davenport Quartet | Maybe In A Dream | Telarc Digital | CD 83409

A Shade Of Jade
Joe Henderson Septet | Mode For Joe | Blue Note | 591894-2
Joe Henderson Sextet | In Pursuit Of Blackness | Milestone | M 9034
Yoron Israel Connection | A Gift For You | Freelance | FRL-CD 024

A Shanty In Old Shanty Town
Salvatore Bonafede Trio | Plays | Ken Music | 660.56.017

A Sheep Out Of A Foam
Red Allen And His Orchestra | Take It Edmond Hall With Your Clarinet That Ballet | Queen-Disc | 020

A Shifting Design
Dave McKenna | Dancing In The Dark And Other Music Of Arthur Schwartz | Concord | CCD 4292

A Shine On Your Shoes
Dave Frishberg Quintet | Let's Eat Home | Concord | CCD 4402

A Ship Without A Sail
Ella Fitzgerald With The Buddy Bregman Orchestra | The Best Of The Song Books:The Ballads | Verve | 521867-2
The Complete Ella Fitzgerald Song Books of Harold Arlen, Irving Berlin, Duke Ellington, George & Ira Gershwin, Jerome Kern, Johnny Mercer, Cole Porter And Rogers & Hart | Verve | 519832-2
Sarah Vaughan With Hal Mooney's Orchestra | Sarah Vaughan Sings Broadway:Grat Songs From Hit Shows | Verve | 526464-2

A Short One
Matthias Bätzel Trio | Green Dumplings | JHM Records | JHM 3618

A Short Story
Susan Weinert Band | Mysterious Stories | VeraBra Records | CDVBR 2111-2

A Short Story About Tofu
Tom Scott Group | Steamline | GRP | GRP 95552

A Shot In The Dark
Tony Scott With The Bill Evans Trio | A Day In New York | Fresh Sound Records | FSR-CD 0160(2)

A Sight A Song
Gil Scott-Heron Sextet | The Revolution Will Not Be Televised | RCA | ND 86994(874175)

A Significant Look Of Birch Grove
Enrico Pieranunzi Quartet | From Always To Now | EdiPan | NPG 803

A Silent Tear
Roy Powell Quartet | North By Northwest | Nagel-Heyer | CD 2013

A Simple Answer
Jimmy Rowles-Red Mitchell Quartet | I'm Glad There Is You | Contemporary | CCD 14032-2

A Simple Matter Of Conviction
Bill Evans Trio | A Simple Matter Of Conviction | Verve | 23MJ 3040 IMS

A Simple Need
Dave Weckl Band | Synergy | Stretch Records | SCD 9022-2

A Single Petal Of A Rose
Dollar(Abdullah Ibrahim) Brand | Ode To Duke Ellington | West Wind | WW 0020

A Sinner Kissed An Angel
Herbie Mann Quartet With Strings | Love And The Weather | Bethlehem | BET 6009-2(BCP 63)
Louis Armstrong With Sy Oliver's Choir And Orchestra | Louis Armstrong-Heavenly Music | Ambassador | CLA 1916

A Sleepin' Bee
Ada Montellanico With The Jimmy Cobb Trio | The Encounter | Philology | W 66.2

A Sleeping Bee
Bill Evans | Conversations With Myself | Verve | 521409-2
Bill Evans Trio | The Complete Bill Evans On Verve | Verve | 527953-2
The Complete Bill Evans On Verve | Verve | 527953-2
Trio (Motian Peacock)-Duo(Hall) | Verve | 2-2509 IMS
Bill Evans Trio:The Last Waltz | Milestone | 8MCD 4430-2
The Jazz Giants Play Harold Arlen:Blues In The Night | Prestige | PCD 24201-2
Bill Evans:The Secret Sessions | Milestone | 8MCD 4421-2
Emily | Moon Records | MCD 060-2
Bill Evans:The Secret Sessions | Milestone | 8MCD 4421-2
Trio 64 | Verve | 539058-2
Christian Josi With The Harry Allen Quartet | I Walk With My Feet Off The Ground | Master Mix | CHECD 00111
Kenny Burrell Quintet | Soul Call | Original Jazz Classics | OJCCD 846-2(P 7315)
Kim Parker With The Kenny Drew Trio | Havin' Myself A Time | Soul Note | 121033-2
Phil Woods Sextet | Live | Novus | ND 83104

A Sleepy Lagoon
Hank Mobley And His Orchestra | A Slic Of The Top | Blue Note | 833588-2

A Slight Smile
Duke Ellington And His Famous Orchestra | Duke Ellington:The Blanton-Webster Band | Bluebird | 21 13181-2

A Slip Of The Lip(Can Sink A Ship)
Duke Ellington And His Orchestra | The Indispensable Duke Ellington,Vol.7/8 | RCA | ND 89274

A Small Ballad
Kip Hanrahan Group | Vertical's Currency | American Clave | AMCL 1010-2

A Smile In The Subway
David Friedman Quintet | Futures Passed | Enja | 2068

A Smooth One
Ellis Larkins Trio | A Smooth One | Black & Blue | BLE 59.123 2
Les Blue Stars | Jazz In Paris:Les Blue Stars-Pardon My English/Henri Salvador-Plays The Blues | EmArCy | 013035-2
Mani Neumeir-Peter Hollinger | Monsters Of Drums-Live | ATM Records | ATM 3821-AH

A So
Modern Jazz Quartet | Odds Against Tomorrow | Blue Note | 793415-2

A Song
Stan Getz Quintet With The Boston Pops Orchestra | Stan Getz And Arthur Fiedler At Tanglewood | RCA | 2136406-2

A Song For Anna Sophia
Anthony Wonsey Quintet | Open The Gates | Criss Cross | Criss 1162

A Song For Jack
Ramsey Lewis Group | Sky Islands | GRP | GRP 97452

A Song For Richard
Wolfhound-Anne Haigis | The Never Ending Story | BELL Records | BLR 84025

A Song For You
Carmen McRae And Her Trio | Live | Jazz Door | JD 1280

A Song Of Joy-
Hal Schaefer And His Orchestra | The RCA Victor Jazz Workshop | Fresh Sound Records | NL 45975(RCA LPM 1199)

A Song Was Born
Louis Armstrong And His All Stars | Louis Armstrong & His All Stars | Laserlight | 15773
From The Big Band To The All Stars (1946-1956) | RCA | ND 89279

A Sound For Sore Ears
The Heath Brothers | Brotherly Love | Antilles | ???

A Spire
George Adams Sextet | Soung Suggestions | ECM | 1141
Charley Patton | Founder Of The Delta Blues | Yazoo | YAZ 1020

A Star Stood Still
Thierry Lang Quintet | Nan | Blue Note | 498492-2

A Statement
Herbie Mann's Californians | Great Ideas Of Western Man | Original Jazz Classics | OJCCD 1065-2(RLP 245)

A Stella Performance
Stan Kenton And His Orchestra | Live At Brigham Young University | Creative World | STD 1039

A Story Tale
Peter Wölpl Group | Mr. Wölps & Dr. Fudge | Blue Flame | 40422(3984042-2)

A Story Within The Story
Coleman Hawkins With The Ramblers | The Hawk In Holland | Ace Of Club | ACL 1247

A Stranger Called The Blues
June Christy With The Pete Rugolo Orchestra | Something Cool(The Complete Mono & Stereo Versions) | Capitol | 534069-2
Kenny Drew Trio | If You Could See Me Now | Steeplechase | SCS 1034

A Stranger In Town
Mel Tormé With The Tony Osborne Orchestra | Compact Jazz: Mel Torme | Verve | 833282-2 PMS
Dinah Washington With Orchestra | Ballads | Roulette | 537559-2

A Stranger On Earth
Cindy Blackman Quartet | In The Now | HighNote Records | HCD 7024

A Streetcar Named Desire
Allotria Jazz Band | 69-89 Good Times | Elite Special | 30224

A Strich In Time
Roland Kirk Quartet | Domino | Verve | 543833-2
Roland Kirk With The Stan Tracy Trio | Gifts And Messages | Ronnie Scott's Jazz House | JHAS 606

A String Of Pearls
Benny Goodman And His Orchestra | Recorded Live In Stockholm-1970 | Verve | 820471-2
Glenn Miller And His Orchestra | The Unforgettable Glenn Miller | RCA | PD 89260
Glenn Miller-The Great Instrumentals 1938-1942 | Retrieval | RTR 79001
A Legendary Performer-Previously Unreleased Live Recordings | RCA | NL 89212 DP
The Very Best Of Glenn Miller | RCA | PL 89009 AO

A String Of Pearls-
Benny Goodman And His Orchestra | Big City Swing | Decca | TAB 5

A Suite In 8 Pictures
Jacques Stotzem | Fingerprint | Acoustic Music Records | 319.1129.2

A Summer Child
Charlie Elgart Group | Signs Of Life | RCA | PD 83045

A Sunbonnet Blue
Billy Eckstine With Bobby Tucker And His Orchestra | Billy Eckstine:Billy's Best! | Verve | 526440-2

A Sunday Kind Of Love
Earl Hines | The Indispensable Earl Hines Vol.5/6:The Bob Thiele Sessions | RCA | ND 89618

A Sure Thing
Blue Mitchell And His Orchestra | The Jazz Giants Play Jerome Kern:Yesterdays | Prestige | PCD 24202-2
Jonathan Schwartz & Quintet | Anyone Would Love You | Muse | MCD 5325

A Sweet Defeat
Buck Clayton-Buddy Tate Quintet | Kansas City Nights | Prestige | P 24040

A Swinging Doll
Ernie Wilkins And His Orchestra | The Big New Band Of The '60s | Fresh Sound Records | FSCD 2006

A Tail Of A B-Tune
Thomas Hass Group | A Honeymoon Too Soon | Stunt Records | STUCD 19601

A Taste For Passion
Klaus Ignatzek Group Feat.Dave Liebman | The Spell | Nabel Records:Jazz Network | CD 4614

A Taste Of Caramel
Andy And The Bey Sisters | Andy Bey And The Bey Sisters | Prestige | PCD 24245-2

A Taste Of Honey
Chet Baker With Bobby Scott | Baby Breeze | Verve | 538328-2
David Matthews Trio With Gary Burton | American Pie | Sweet Basil | 660.55.005
Lionel Hampton And His All Star Jazz Inner Circle | En Concert Avec Europe 1 | Laserlight | 710375/76
Lionel Hampton Quintet | You Better Know It | Impulse(MCA) | IMP 12972
Paul Desmond Quartet | Planet Jazz:Paul Desmond | Planet Jazz | 2152061-2

TITELVERZEICHNIS

Paul Desmond-Greatest Hits | RCA | CL 89809 SF
Quincy Jones And His Orchestra | Rahsaan/The Complete Mercury Recordings Of Roland Kirk | Mercury | 846630-2
Big Band Bossa Nova | Verve | 557913-2
Sarah Vaughan And Her Band | Misty Blue:Sweet Sisters Swing Songs Of Sorrow And Sadness | Blue Note | 521151-2
Sarah Vaughan With Her Sextet | Sarah Sings Soulfully | Roulette | CDP 798445-2
Shorty Rogers Big Band | Jazz Waltz | Discovery | DS 843 IMS

A Taste Of Living-
Gene McDaniels And His Band | Another Tear Falls | Charly | CRB 1136

A Tender Farewell To A Spanish Woman
Helen Merrill With The Roger Kellaway Trio | Clear Oot Of This World | EmArCy | 510691-2 PMS

A Theme In 3-4
Ron Carter Trio | The Golden Striker | Blue Note | 590831-2
Stan Kenton And His Orchestra | Festival Of Modern Amarican Jazz | Status | CD 101(882197)

A Thousand Autumns
Makoto Kuriya Quintet | X-Based Music | Paddle Wheel | KICJ 171

A Thousand Dreams
Fats Waller And His Rhythm | Fifty Thousand Killer Watts Of Jive | Ember | CJS 842

A Thousand Evenings
Snooks Eaglin | Blues From New Orleans Vol.1 | Storyville | SLP 119

A Thousand Years
Peter Kowald Group | When The Is Out You Don't See Stars | FMP | CD 38

A Thursday In October
Joe Bonner Quartet | Suite For Chocolate | Steeplechase | SCCD 31215

A Time For Love
Agneta Baumann And Her Quintet | A Time For Love | Touché Music | TMcCD 006
Art Farmer With Orchestra | Gentle Eyes | Mainstream | MD CDO 716
Bill Evans | The Complete Bill Evans On Verve | Verve | 527953-2
Alone | Verve | 598319-2
Alone | Verve | 598319-2
Ultimate Bill Evans selected by Herbie Hancock | Verve | 557536-2
Bill Perkins Quintet | Quietly There | Original Jazz Classics | OJCCD 1776-2
Earl Klugh-Gloria Agostine | Late Night Guitar | Blue Note | 498573-2
Eric Alexander Quartet | Man With A Horn | Milestone | MCD 9293-2
Ernestine Anderson With The Hank Jones Trio | Hello Like Before | Concord | CCD 4031
Joe Locke Quartet | Wire Walker | Steeplechase | SCCD 31332
Joe Williams With The Robert Farnon Orchestra | Joe Williams:Triple Play | Telarc Digital | CD 83461
Lex Jasper Trio With Orchestra | Lexpression | Limetree | MCD 0016
Milt Jackson-Oscar Peterson | Milt Jackson Birthday Celebration | Fantasy | FANCD 6079-2
Monty Alexander Trio | Overseas Special | Concord | CCD 4253
Oscar Peterson-Milt Jackson Quartet | Reunion Blues | MPS | 817490-1
Shirley Horn With Strings | Here's To Life | Verve | 511879-2
Singers Unlimited With The Pat Williams Orchestra | The Singers Unlimited:Magic Voices | MPS | 539130-2
Feeling Free | MPS | 68103
Irene Kral With Alan Broadbent | Where Is Love? | Choice | CHCD 71012

A Time For Love-
George Adams-Don Pullen Quartet | Breakthrough | Blue Note | BT 85122

A To Z Blues
Phillip Johnston's Big Trouble | The Unknown | Avant | AVAN 037

A Tonal Group:
Duke Ellington And His Orchestra | Duke Ellington:Complete Prestige Carnegie Hall 1946-1947 Concerts | Definitive Records | DRCD 11211

A Tooth Lost
Elliot Lawrence And His Orchestra | Big Band Sound | Fresh Sound Records | FSCD 2003

A Touch Of Berlin
Hank Mobley And His Orchestra | A Slic Of The Top | Blue Note | 833588-2

A Touch Of Boogie Woogie
Clifford Jordan-Ran Blake Groups | Masters From Different Worlds | Mapleshade | 01732

A Touch Of Kin
Mark Egan Group | A Touch Of Light | GRP | GRP 95722

A Touch Of Silver
Hal McKusick Quintet | Triple Exposure | Original Jazz Classics | OJCCD 1811-2(P 7135)

A Touch Of The Blues
The Visitors | Motherland | Muse | MR 5094

A Town In Your Heart
Carlos Bica Group | Azul | Traumton Records | 4425-2

A Tragédia De Um Homem Condenado A Ser Um Poeta
Massimo Urbani Quartet | Easy To Love | Red Records | NS 208

A Tree Frog Tonality
Harry James And His Orchestra | The Uncollected:Harry James, Vol.5 | Hindsight | HSR 142

A Triangle(Dance,Jealousy,Blues)-
Jimmy Ponder Quintet | Come On Down | Muse | MCD 5375

A Tribute To John Coltrane:
Ed Schuller & Mack Goldbury | Art Of The Duo: Savignyplatz | Tutu Records | 888206-2*

A Tribute To Munir
Ernie K-Doe Group | New Orleans:A Musical Gumbo Of Jazz,Blues & Gospel | Mardi Gras Records | MG 5005

A Tribute To Someone
Herbie Hancock Septet | My Point Of View | Blue Note | 521226-2
Larry Willis Sextet | A Tribute To Someone | audioquest Music | AQCD 1022

A Tribute Two
Nat King Cole Trio | Any Old Time | Giants Of Jazz | GOJ 1031

A Trip
Jimmy Ponder With Orchestra | Jimmy Ponder | LRC Records | CDC 9031

A Trout No Doubt
Ralph Sharon Sextet feat. Sue Sharon | Mr.& Mrs. Jazz | Fresh Sound Records | FSR 2028(Bethlehem BCP 13)

A Tune For Humming
Mel Tormé With The George Shearing Trio | A Vintage Year | Concord | CJ 341

A Tune For Mac
Horace Parlan Sextet | Happy Frame Of Mind | Blue Note | 869784-7

A Turtle's Dream
Willis Jackson Quintet | At Large | Prestige | PCD 24243-2

A Twist Of Blues
Don Redman And His Orchestra | Shakin' The Africann | Hep | 1001

A Uma Escrava Que lhe Ocultou O Sol
Ernst Reijseger & Tenore E Cuncordu De Orosei | Colla Voche | Winter&Winter | 910037-2

A Una Rosa(Voche É Notte Antica)
David Friedman Quartet | Of The Wind's Eye | Enja | ENJ-3089 2

A Vampire Dances(Symmetry)
Max Roach Quartet | Conversations | Milestone | M 47061

A Variation
Clusone 3 | An Hour With... | HatOLOGY | 554

A Velvet Affair
Hank Jones Quartet | Just For Fun | Original Jazz Classics | OJCCD 471-2

A View From My Mind's Eye
National Youth Jazz Orchestra | A View From The Hill | Ronnie Scott's Jazz House | JHCD 044

A Walk In The Centerpoint
Eberhard Weber Group | Endless Days | ECM | 1748(013420-2)

A Walk In The Garrigue
Brad Mehldau Trio | Places | Warner | 9362-47693-2

A Walk In The Park
Kenny Werner Group | Beauty Secrets | RCA | 2169904-2

A Walkin' Thing
Benny Carter Sextet | Jazz Giant | Original Jazz Classics | OJC20 167-2(C 7555)

A Walking Thing
Kenny Dorham Quintet | Kenny Dorham | Bainbridge | BT 1048

A Waltz For Fran
Steve Williamson Quintet | A Waltz For Grace | Verve | 843088-2 PMS

A Waste Land
Paul Desmond Quartet | Desmond | Original Jazz Classics | OJCCD 712-2(F 3235/8082)

A Watchman's Carroll
Paul Desmond Quartet Featuring Don Elliott | Original Jazz Classics | OJC 119(F 3235)

A Wave Groove
Phil Minton/Veryan Weston | Ways | ITM Records | ITM 1420

A Weaver Of Dreams
Monty Alexander Trio | Threesome | Soul Note | 121152-2
Steve Klink Trio | Feels Like Home | Minor Music | 801092

A Wedding In Cherokee County
Grant Green Trio | Grant's First Stand | Blue Note | 521959-2

A Wee Bit O'Green
Canadian Brass | Take The A Train | RCA | 2663455-2

A Week In Paris
Peter Giger | Family Of Percussion | Nagara | MIX 1010-N

A Wheel Within A Wheel
N.Y. Hardbop Quintet | A Whisper Away | TCB Records | TCB 98702

A Window To The Soul
Mel Lewis Septet | Got' Cha | Fresh Sound Records | FSR-CD 0073

A Wishing Doll
Eddie Higgins Trio | Those Quiet Days | Sunnyside | SSC 1052 D

A Woman Alone With The Blues
Dorothy Wilson Gospel Express | O How Beautiful | L+R Records | CDLR 44019

A Woman Is A Sometime Thing
Louis Armstrong And Ella Fitzgerald With Russell Garcia's Orchestra | The Complete Ella Fitzgerald And Louis Armstrong On Verve | Verve | 537284-2
Ray Charles-Cleo Laine With The Frank DeVol Orchestra & Chorus | Porgy And Bess | London | 6.30110 EM

A Woman, A Lover, A Friend
Jimmy Jones' Big Eight | Rex Stewart And The Ellingtonians | Original Jazz Classics | OJCCD 1710-2(RLP 144)

A Wonderful Guy
Oscar Peterson Trio With Milt Jackson | Very Tall | Verve | 827821-2
Ruby Braff-Dick Hyman | Younger Than Swingtime-Music From South Pacific | Concord | CCD 4445

A Word-
Stephen Scott Quartet | Vision Quest | Enja | ENJ-9347 2

A Work In Process
Walt Weiskopf Quartet | A World Away | Criss Cross | Criss 1100

A World I Never Made
Marilyn Mazur's Future Song | Small Labyrinths | ECM | 1559(533679-2)

A World Of Gates
Acoustic Art | Interlude | Acoustic Music Records | AMC 1024

A Y
Cal Tjader Quintet | Cal Tjader's Latin Concert | Original Jazz Classics | OJCCD 643-2(F 8014)

A Young Love
Paul Smith Sextet | Cool And Sparkling | Capitol | 300011(TOCJ 6125)

A.B.
David Murray Sextet | Jug-A-Lug | DIW | DIW 894 CD

A.B.Blues
Joe Albany Trio | Live In Paris | Fresh Sound Records | FSCD 1010

A.B.'s Blues
Benny Goodman Sextet | Jazz Live & Rare: Benny Goodman & His Group/Orchestra | Jazzline | ???

A.D. 2016:The Comet
A Tipico Trio | Where The Reeds Are | SPLASC(H) Records | CD H 312-2

A.I.R
Susanne Abbuehl Group | April | ECM | 1766(013999-2)

A.I.R.(All India Radio)
Tim Berne Group | Tim Berne EmpireThe Five Years Plan/Spectres/Songs And Rituals In Real Time | Screwgun | SC 70009

A.L.P.Traum(a deconstruction)
Kalifactors | An Introduction To Kalifactors | Fresh Sound Records | FSNT 143 CD

A.M.
Michael Bisio Quartet | Michael Bisio Quartet In Seattle | Silkheart | SHCD 107

A.M. Romp
Joe Newman Septet | The Count's Men | Fresh Sound Records | FSR-CD 0135

A.R.C.
Phalanx | In Touch | DIW | DIW 8026

A.T.
The Prestige All Stars | All Day Long | Prestige | SMJ 6604

A+B+C+D
Peter Kowald-Maarten Altena Duo | Bass Duets | FMP | CD 102

A>C
A Band Of Friends | Bill Frisell:Songs We Know | Nonesuch | 7559-79468-2
Ornette Coleman-Beauty Is A Rare Thing | Rhino | 8122-71410-2
Peter Kowald-Maarten Altena Duo | Two Making A Triangle | FMP | 0990

A-12
Baden Powell Quartet | En Concert Avec Europe 1 | Laserlight | 710703/04

Aarti
Raphe Malik 5tet | 21st Century Texts | FMP | CD 43

Ababa
Paul Motian Quintet | Misterioso | Soul Note | 121174-2

Abacus
Paul Motian Trio | You Took The Words Right Out Of My Heart | JMT Edition | 514028-2

Abakus
George Colligan | Return To Copenhagen | Steeplechase | SCCD 31519

Abandon All Hope Ye Who Enter Here
Diana Krall Group | The Girl In The Other Room | Verve | 9862246

Abandoned Masquerade
Hugh Masekela Group | Hope | Triloka Records | 320203-2

Abate Fetel
Sylvie Courvoisier Group | Abaton | ECM | 1838/39(157628-2)

Abaton
Jo Ambros Group | Wanderlust | dml-records | CD 016

Abba
Per Gudmundson-Ale Möller-Lene Willemark | Frifot | ECM | 1690(557653-2)

Abba Fader
Frank Ricotti Quartet | Our Point Of View | CBS | 494440-2

Abbamele
Heiner Goebbels/Alfred Harth | Berold Brecht:Zeit wird knapp | Riskant | 568-72414

ABC
Kenny Blake Group | A Lifetime After | Inak | 30372

A-B-C
Thad Jones-Mel Lewis Big Band | The Orchestra | West Wind | WW 2044

Abdullah's Demeanor
Pierre Dorge's New Jungle Orchestra | Giraf | dacapo | DCCD 9440

Abe Teyata
Ronald Shannon Jackson And The Decoding Society | What Spirit Say | DIW | DIW 895 CD

Abend Wird Es Wieder
The Contemporary Alphorn Orchestra | Mytha | Hat Art | CD 6110

Abendlandabend:
Radu Malfatti-Stephan Wittwer Duo | Thrumblin' Malfatti-Wittwer | FMP | 0350

Abendlich Erfolgt Die...
Rainer Tempel Big Band | Melodies Of '98 | Jazz 4 Ever Records:Jazz Network | J4E 4744

Abendlich...
Hans Reichel | Wichlinghauser Blues | FMP | 0150

Abenteuer Unter Wasser
Munich Saxophon Family | Survival Song | JHM Records | JHM 3613
Fats Waller And His Rhythm | The Last Years 1940-1943 | Bluebird | ND 90411(3)

Abercrombie Had A Zombie
American Folk Blues Festival | American Folk Blues Festival 1967 | L+R Records | CDLR 42070

Abf
John Zorn Group | Massada Tree | DIW | DIW 890 CD

Abide With Me
Grand Dominion Jazz Band | The Spiritual Album | Stomp Off Records | CD 1291
Rüdiger Carl | Vorn:Lieder Und Improvisationen Für Akkordeon, Bandoneon Und Ziehharmonika | FMP | 1110

Abide With Me-
Johnny Copeland Group | Jungle Swing | Verve | 527466-2

Abi-gaah!
Lightnin' Hopkins | Lightnin' Hopkins Sings The Blues | Pathe | 2C 068-83075(Imperial)

Ability To Swing
Guillermo Klein & Big Van | El Minotauro | Candid | CCD 79706

Ablution
Lars Gullin Quartet | The Saxophone Collection | Vogue | 21610232
Lee Konitz And Lars Gullin With Hans Koller's New Jazz Stars | Lee Konitz:Move | Moon Records | MCD 057-2
Rein de Graaff Quintet | Nostalgia | Timeless | CD SJP 429

Abolish Bad Architecture
Elvin Jones-Jimmy Garrison Sextet | Illumination! | Impulse(MCA) | IMP 12502

About Birds And Bees
The Three Deuces | Pee Wee Russell:Jazz Original | Commodore | CMD 14042

About Three The Blues
Bishop Norman Williams Group | One For Bird | Evidence | TR 105

About TimeTo Begin
Stephan Diez-Mirrors | Lost In A Dream | BELL Records | BLR 84048

Above & Below
Paul Bley | Blues For Red | Red Records | 123238 2

Above The Rainbow
Paul Bley/Evan Parker/Barre Phillips | Time Will Tell | ECM | 1537

Above The Three Line
Paul Bley Trio | Reality Check | Steeplechase | SCCD 31379

Abow And Below
Allan Holdsworth Group | The Sixteen Man Of Tain | Cream Records | CR 610-2

Abow And Below(reprise)
Darol Anger-Barbara Higbie Duo | Tideline | Windham Hill | WD 1021

Abow The Treetops
Sylvie Courvoisier Group | Y2K | Enja | ENJ-9383 2

Abra
Clifford Jordan Orchestra | Inward Fire | Muse | MR 5128

Abracadabra
The Caribbean Jazz Project | The Caribbean Jazz Project | Inak | 9038

Abraham Arise!
Eartha Kitt And A 100 Voices Gospel Choir | My Way:A Musical Tribute To Rev.Martin Luther King Jr. | Basic | 50015

Abreise Des O.D.D.J.P.-
Frank Kuruc Band | Limits No Limits | Edition Musikat | EDM 023

Abricotine
Karoline Höfler Quartet | Charly Haigl's Festival Band | Satin Doll Productions | SDP 1007-1 CD

Abril
Lindemann Quintet | En Public Aux Faux-nez | Plainisphare | PL 1267-13

Abrupto
Vinko Globokar | 5, Die Sich Nicht Ertragen Können! | FMP | 1180

Abschied Im Dezember
Naßler & Schneider feat. Jörg Ritter | Triologe | Acoustic Music Records | 319.1137.2

Abschiedsgeschenk Eines Obdachlosen-
Christian Doepke | Ten Piano Players,Vol.1 | Green House Music | CD 1002

Abschiedslied
Volker Schlott Quartet | Why Not | Acoustic Music Records | 319.1083.2

Absente
Pata Music Meets Arfi | News Of Roi Ubu | Pata Musik | PATA 10 CD

Absinth
Norbert Stein Pata Masters | Pata Maroc | Pata Musik | PATA 12(AMF 1063)

Absinth In Oudayas
Duke Ellington And His Orchestra | Afro-Bossa | Reprise | 9362-47876-2

Absinthe
Gerry Brown-John Lee Group | Infinite Jones | Keytone | KYT 710

Absolutely
Jabbo Smith And His Orchestra | Jazz Archives Vol.77:Jabbo Smith-The Complete 1929-1938 Sessions | EPM Musique | 158112

Absolutely Maybe
Michael Mantler Orchestra | Hide And Seek | ECM | 1738(549612-2)

Absolutely Nothing
Absolute Ensemble | Absolution | Enja | ENJ-9394 2

Absolution
Lee Morgan Quintet | Live At The Lighthouse | Blue Note | 835228-2

Absolutions
Friedeman Graef-Achim Goettert | Saxoridoo | FMP | OWN-90010

Abstinence Sows Sand
Brigitte Dietrich-Joe Haider Jazz Orchestra | Consequences | JHM Records | JHM 3624

Abstract
Jim Hall-Charlie Haden | Jim Hall & Basses | Telarc Digital | CD 83506

Abstract Blues
Low Flying Aircraft | Low Flying Aircraft | Line Records | COCD 9.00426 O

Abstract Improvisation
Shelly Manne Three | The Three & The Two | Original Jazz Classics | OJCCD 172-2(C 3584)

Abstract Realities
Kxutrio | Riff-ifi | Sound Aspects | sas CD 032

Abstraction
Jackie McLean Quintet | 4, 5 And 6 | Original Jazz Classics | OJC 056(P 7048)
Lennie Tristano Trio | The Rarest Trio/Quartet Sessions 1946/47 | Raretone | 5008 FC

Abstrato
Südpool Jazz Project IV | Südpol Jazz Project IV-Quartet | L+R Records | CDLR 45091

Abundance
Music Revelation Ensemble | In The Name Of... | DIW | DIW 885 CD

Academicians
Baden Powell Trio | Melancholie | Festival | ???

Accarezzame
Stephan Oliva | Jazz 'n (e)motion:Stephan Oliva | RCA | 2155936-2

Accelerated Service
Jazzensemble Des Hessischen Rundfunks | Atmosphering Conditions Permitting | ECM | 1549/50
Hans Koch/Martin Schütz/Marco Käppeli | Accélération | ECM | 1357

Acceleration Controlee
J.F. Jenny Clark | Unison | CMP Records | CMP CD 32

Accent
Ben Webster With Strings | The Warm Mood | Discovery | DS 818 IMS

Accent On Youth
Billy May And His Orchestra | Bacchanalia | Capitol | ED 2604201

Ac-Cent-Tchu-Ate The Positive

Ella Fitzgerald With The Billy May Orchestra | The Harold Arlen Songbook | Verve | 817526-1 IMS
Oscar Peterson Trio | Oscar Peterson Plays The Harold Arlen Song Book | Verve | 589103-2
Susannah McCorkle With The Allen Farnham Orchestra | From Bessie To Brazil | Concord | CCD 4547

Accepting The Chalice
Nils Petter Molvaer Group | Khmer | ECM | 1560(537798-2)

Access-
Andy Sheppard Group | Rhythm Method | Blue Note | 827798-2

Accidental Meeting
Art Blakey And The Jazz Messengers | One For All | A&M Records | 395329-2

Ace In The Hole
Connie Francis With Orchestra | The Swinging Connie Francis | Audiophile | ACD-286
Ella Fitzgerald With The Buddy Bregman Orchestra | The Complete Ella Fitzgerald Song Books of Harold Arlen, Irving Berlin, Duke Ellington, George & Ira Gershwin, Jerome Kern, Johnny Mercer, Cole Porter And Rogers & Hart | Verve | 519832-2
Lizzie Miles And Her Trio | Lizzie Miles | American Music | AMCD-73

Ace In The Hole(alt.take)
Jabbo Smith And His Rhythm Aces | Big Band Bounce & Boogie-Jabbo Smith:Sweet 'N' Low Down | Affinity | AFS 1029

Ach Bitt'rer Winter
Daniel Schnyder Group | Words Within Music | Enja | ENJ-9369 2

Ach Golgatha,Unsel'ges Golgatha-
Cassiber | The Beauty And The Beast | Riskant | 528-72410

Ach Kina
E.A.O. | E.A.O. | amf records | amf 1020

Ach Lieber Herre Jesu Christ
Fun Horns | Choral Concert(Weihnachtsoratorium/Choräle) | KlangRäume | 30090

Ach, Frl. Annie Wohnt Schon Lang Nicht Hier
Bob Mintzer Big Band | Latin From Manhattan | dmp Digital Music Productions | CD 523

Achirana
Dizzy Reece Quintet | Comin' On | Blue Note | 522019-2

Acht O'Clock Rock
No Nett | Wenn Der Weiße Flieder Wieder Blüht | Jazz Haus Musik | JHM 14

Achtundvierzig
Illinois Jacquet Sextet | Swing's The Thing | Verve | MV 2660 IMS

Acid Jazz
John McLaughlin Group | The Heart Of Things | Verve | 539153-2
Adelhard Roidinger Trio | Computer & Jazz Project I | Thein | TH 100384

Ack Värmeland Du Sköna
Hans van der Sys | Piano Giants Vol.1 | Swingtime | 8201
Michael Naura Quintet | Jazz In Deutschland 1957-1958/Kühl Und Modern | Vagabond | 6.22563 AG
Stan Getz And The Swedish All Stars | Stan Getz:The Complete 1946-1951 Quartet Sessions(Master Takes),Vol.2 | Blue Moon | BMCD 1014

Acknowledgement
John Coltrane Quartet | A Love Supreme | Ingo | 11
Peter Herborn Group With The WDR Big Band | Traces Of Trane | JMT Edition | 514002-2

Acknowledgement-
John Coltrane Quartet | A Love Supreme | Impulse(MCA) | 589945-2
John Coltrane:The Classic Quartet-Complete Impulse Studio Recordings | Impulse(MCA) | 951280-2
John Coltrane Sextet | A Love Supreme | Impulse(MCA) | 589945-2

Acknowledgement(alt,take)
Christian Chevallier And His Orchestra | 6+6 | Fresh Sound Records | 054 2610781(FPX 144)

Aconteceu
Ahmad Jamal Quartet | Life At The Montreal Jazz Festival 1985 | Atlantic | 781699-2

Acorn
Ahmad Jamal Trio | Live In Paris 92 | Birdology | 849408-2

Acqua,Aria,Fioco,Terra
Riccardo Fassi Tankio Band | Il Principe | SPLASC(H) Records | H 180

Acquiescence
Ike Quebec Quartet | The Art Of Ike Quebec | Blue Note | 799178-2

Across Bridges
June Christy With Orchestra | This Is June Christy/June Christy Recalls Those Kenton Days | Capitol | 535209-2

Across The Alley From The Alamo
June Christy With The Pete Rugolo Orchestra | June Christy Recalls Those Kenton Days | EMI Records | 1599311

Across The Bridge
Harold Danko | Ink And Water | Sunnyside | SSC 1008(952101)

Across The Golden Gate
Doctor Clayton's Buddy | Doctor Clayton And His Buddy(1935-1947) | Story Of Blues | CD 3539-2

Across The Midnight Sky
Roy Hargrove Quintet With Joshua Redman | Roy Hargrove Quintet With The Tenors Of Our Time | Verve | 523019-2

Across The Pond
Cyril Haynes Sextet | Don Byas Complete American Small Group Recordings | Definitive Records | DRCD 11213

Across The Sky
Duke Ellington And His Famous Orchestra | Duke Ellington:The Blanton-Webster Band | Bluebird | 21 13181-2

Across The Track Blues
Duke Ellington:Ko-Ko | Dreyfus Jazz Line | FDM 36717-2
Duke Ellington And His Orchestra | Jazz Giants:Duke Ellington | RCA | NL 45179 SI
The Indispensable Duke Ellington Vol.5/6 | RCA | ND 89750

Across The Water
Sebastian Weiss Trio | Polaroid Memory | Fresh Sound Records | FSNT 085 CD
Steve Cárdenas Trio | Shebang | Fresh Sound Records | FSNT 079 CD

Across The Way
Frederica von Stade With The Chris Brubeck-Bill Crofut Ensemble | Across Your Dreams: Frederica von Stade Sings Brubeck | Telarc Digital | CD 80467

Act Natural
Mary Lou Williams Group | Mary Lou's Mass | Mary Records | M 102

Action
Bireli Lagrene Group | Inferno | Blue Note | 748016-2
Wynton Kelly Quartet | Keep It Moving | Milestone | M 47026
Matthew Shipp-Joe Morris | Thesis | HatOLOGY | 506

Action Painting
Jimmy Gordon With Band | 'The Mississippi Mudder' Jimmie Gordon Vol.2(1934-1941) | Story Of Blues | CD 3518-2

Actors
Herbie Hancock Group | Thrust | CBS | CK 64984

Actual Prof
Centrifugal Funk | Centrifugal Funk | Legato | 652508

Actus Tragicus
Bern Nix Trio | Alarms And Excursions | New World Records | 80437-2

Acumulando Puntos
Yosuke Yamashita Quintet | Ways Of Time | Verve | 523841-2

Acute Motelitis
Aera | Hand Und Fu | Erlkönig | 148401

Ad Infinitum
Carla Bley Band | Dinner Music | Watt | 6(825815-2)
Carla Bley-Steve Swallow | Go Together | Watt | 24(517673-2)
Phil Woods And His European Rhythm Machine | At The Montreux Jazz Festival | Verve | 065512-2
Roland Kirk Quartet | Rahsaan/The Complete Mercury Recordings Of Roland Kirk | Mercury | 846630-2

Ad Lib
Benny Goodman Septet | Charlie Christian:Swing To Bop | Dreyfus Jazz Line | FDM 36715-2

Ad Lib Blues
Jazz:The Essential Collection Vol.3 | IN+OUT Records | 78013-2
Lester Young Quintet | Pres And Teddy And Oscar | Verve | 2-2502 IMS
Ruby Braff Sextet | Hustlin' And Bustlin' | Black Lion | BLCD 760908

Ad Lib On Nippon
Duke Ellington And His Orchestra | Duke Ellington: The Champs-Elysees Theater January 29-30th,1965 | Laserlight | 36131
Duke Ellington's Far East Suite | RCA | 2174797-2
Roland Kirk Quartet | Rahsaan/The Complete Mercury Recordings Of Roland Kirk | Mercury | 846630-2

Ad Lib(Hip Chops)
Warne Marsh Quartet | Warne Marsh/4 | Criss Cross | Criss 1004(Mode 125)

Ad Libido
Mick Goodrick-David Liebman-Wolfgang Muthspiel | In The Same Breath | CMP Records | CMP CD 71

Adage A-
Ensemble Modern | Ensemble Modern-Fred Frith:Traffic Continues | Winter&Winter | 910044-2

Adage B-
Ensemble Modern-Fred Frith:Traffic Continues | Winter&Winter | 910044-2

Adage Coda-
Ensemble Modern-Fred Frith:Traffic Continues | Winter&Winter | 910044-2

Adage D-
Terje Rypdal-David Darling Duo | Eos | ECM | 1263

Adagietto
Gianluigi Trovesi Nonet | Round About A Midsummer's Dream | Enja | ENJ-9384 2

Adagietto Bergomasco
Charlie Mariano Trio | Adagio | Lipstick Records | LIP 890242

Adagio
Misha Alperin Trio | Night After Night | ECM | 1769(014431-2)
Paolo Fresu Angel Quartet | Metamorfosi | RCA | 2165202-2
Saxophon And Organ | Above The Clouds | Naxos Jazz | 86041-2
Steve Kuhn With Strings | Promises Kept | ECM | 1815(0675222)
Terje Rypdal Group | Odyssey | ECM | 1067/8
Uschi Brüning And Ernst-Ludwig Petrowsky With The Günter Bartel Trio | Enfant | Aho-Recording | CD 1017

Adagio-
Jacques Loussier Trio | The Best Of Play Bach | Philips | 824664-2
Bach To The Future | Teldec | 2292-44430-2
Play Bach No.5 | Decca | 159194-2
Larry Coryell Quintet | The Coryells | Chesky | JD 192
Swingle Singers | Swingling Telemann | Philips | 586735-2
Swingling Telemann | Philips | 586735-2
Saxophon And Organ | Above The Clouds | Naxos Jazz | 86041-2

Adagio Assai für Streichquartet
Massimo Colombo Trio | Alexander | SPLASC(H) Records | H 177

Adagio From Concierto De Aranjuez
Swingle Singers | Jazz Sebastian Bach Vol.2 | Philips | 542553-2

Adagio From Sonate No.3 In E Major(BWV 1016)
John Zorn Group | Cobra | Hat Art | CD 6040(2)

Adagio Molto-
Vittorino Curci/Pino Minafra/Carlos Actis Dato Group | L'Invenzione Del Verso Sfuso | SPLASC(H) Records | HP 21

Adagio Sostenuto-
Jacques Loussier Trio | Baroque Favorites | Telarc Digital | CD 83516

Adagio(Haydn:Klaviersonate C-Dur)
Enrico Pieranunzi-Bert Van Den Brink | Daedalus' Wings | Challenge | CHR 70069

Adam's Apple
Wayne Shorter Quartet | Wayne Shorter:The Classic Blue Note Recordings | Blue Note | 540856-2
Woody Herman And His Orchestra | Brand New | Original Jazz Classics | OJCCD 1044-2(F 8414)
Olga Konkova Trio | Her Point Of View | Candid | CCD 79757

Adam's Checking In
Dennis Warren's Full Metal Revolutionary Jazz Ensemble | Watch Out! | Accurate | AC 5017

Addé Oya
Chick Corea Trio | Works | ECM | 825426-2

Addie's At It Again
Frank Kuruc Band | Limits No Limits | Edition Musikat | EDM 023

Addis
James Newton | Axum | ECM | 1214

Addis Ababa
Teodross Avery Quartet | My Generation | Impulse(MCA) | 951181-2
John Wolf Brennan | Irisations | Creative Works Records | CW CD 1021-2

ADDR
Lisle Ellis Group | What We Live Fo(u)r | Black Saint | 120156-2

Ade Zur Guten Nacht
Hans Koller Quintet | Kunstkopfindianer | MPS | 9813439

Adea
Stephan Micus | Desert Poems | ECM | 1757(159739-2)

Adela
Eddie Costa Quartet | Guys And Dolls Like Vives | Verve | 549366-2

Adeleide
Perico Sambeat Group | Ademuz | Fresh Sound Records | FSNT 041 CD

Ademuz
Markus Stockhausen Orchestra | Sol Mestizo:Markus Stockhausen Plays The Music Of Enrique Diaz | ACT | 9222-2

Adentro
Dewey Redman Quartet | Soundsigns | Galaxy | GXY 5130

Adeus
Luiz Bonfa/Cafe | Non Stop To Brazil | Chesky | JD 29

Adieu
De 8 Baan | Europ' Jazz Contest Belgium '93 | B.Sharp Records | CDS 097

Adios
Glenn Miller And His Orchestra | The Very Best Of Glenn Miller | RCA | PL 89009 AO
Stan Kenton And His Orchestra | Stan Kenton-The Formative Years | Decca | 589489-2
The Formative Years(1941-1942) | Creative World | ST 1061
Zim Zemarel And His Orchestra | Live At The Hyatt Regency | Hindsight | HSR 230

Adios Iony
Mr.Acker Bilk And His Paramount Jazz Band | Mr. Acker Bilk Starportrait | Aves | 156503

Adios Nonino
Phil Woods Quintet | Astor& Elis | Chesky | JD 146
Joe Roccisano Orchestra | Leave Your Mind Behind | Landmark | LCD 1541-2

Adios Panama-
Jon Hassell Group | Earthquake | Tomato | 2696122

Adjacent
Mara! | Ruino Vino | Laika Records | 35100792

Adje
Horace Silver Quintet With Brass | Horace Silver Retrospective | Blue Note | 495576-2

Adjustment
Manfred Schoof Quintet | The First Jazz Sampler: 25 Years Of Jazz | L+R Records | LS 40012

Adlerflug
Jo Jones Orchestra | The Main Man | Pablo | 2310799

Administratosphäre
Peter Beets New York Trio | Peter Beets New York Trio | Criss Cross | Criss 1214

Adorée
Bruce Williams Quartet | Brotherhood | Savant Records | SCD 2004

Adrian
Moacir Santos Group | Opus 3, No. 1 | Discovery | DS 795 IMS

Adriatica
Dusko Goykovich Quintet | Soul Connection | Enja | ENJ-8044 2
Walt Weiskopf Quintet | Anytown | Criss Cross | Criss 1169

Adrift
Diederik Wissels Quintet | Kamook | B.Sharp Records | CDS 083
Curtis Fuller And Hampton Hawes With French Horns | Curtis Fuller And Hampton Hawes With French Horns | Original Jazz Classics | OJCCD 1942-2(NJ 8305)

A-Drift
Saxophon And Organ | Above The Clouds | Naxos Jazz | 86041-2

Adventures
Harry Betts And His Orchestra | The Jazz Soul Of Doctor Kildare | Fresh Sound Records | FSR 634(Choreo/Ava AS 6)

Advise And Consent
Paul Desmond With Strings | Desmond Blue | RCA | 2663898-2
Desmond Blue | RCA | 2663898-2

Advise And Consent(alt.take)
Guido Guidoboni Quintet | Xoanon | SPLASC(H) Records | H 145

Aeolio
Rainer Glas/Chris Beier/Leszek Zadlo | Space | clearaudio | WOR 181 CD

Aerial Boundaries
Carmen Leggio Quintet | Aerial View | Dreamstreet | DR 103

Aerial View
Masqualero | Aero | ECM | 1367

Aero
Tom Scott Orchestra | Target | Atlantic | 7567-80106-2

Aeroflotz
Lotz Of Music | Puasong Daffriek | Laika Records | LK 94-054

Aerofloz
String Thing | String Thing:Alles Wird Gut | MicNic Records | MN 2

Aerofunk
Palatino | Palationo Chap.3 | EmArCy | 013610-2

Aeroidea
Charly Antolini Trio | Knock Out 2000 | Inak | 9053

AFAP
Abbey Lincoln With Orchestra | Abbey Lincoln's Affair-A Story Of A Girl In Love | Blue Note | 781199-2

Affirmation
MOKAVE | MOKAVE Vol.2 | audioquest Music | AQCD 1007

AFKaP
Bob Neloms | Pretty Music | India Navigation | IN 1050

Afraid Of What Might Be
Benny Goodman And His Orchestra | This Is Benny Goodman | RCA | NL 89224 DP

Afreeka
Jan Garbarek Quartet | Afric Pepperbird | ECM | 1007 (2301007)

Africa
John Coltrane Quartet With Brass | Africa/Brass | Impulse(MCA) | GRJ 80042
Mandingo Griot Society | Mandingo Griot Society | Flying Fish | FF 70076
Pat Martino Quintet | Think Tank | Blue Note | 592009-2
Pharoah Sanders Quartet | Africa | Timeless | CD SJP 253
The Vivino Brothers Band | Chitlins Parmigiana | dmp Digital Music Productions | CD 492

Africa And Aviation
Ged Hone's New Orleans Boys | Throwing Stones At The Sun | Lake | LACD 28

Africa Blues
Seis Del Solar | Seis Del Solar:Alternate Roots | Messidor | 15831 CD

Africa(1.version)
John Coltrane Quartet With Brass | The Complete Africa/Brass Sessions | Impulse(MCA) | 952168-2

Africa(alt.take)
Irene Schweizer/Louis Moholo | Irene Schweizer-Louis Moholo | Intakt Records | CD 006

Africain
Cheik Tidiana Fall Trio | African Magic | Circle Records | RK 17-5679/17 IMS

African Bossa Nova
Dave Brubeck Quartet | 25th Anniversary Reunion | A&M Records | 396998-2

African Child
Randy Weston Orchestra | The Spirits Of Our Ancestors | Verve | 511857-2

African Dance
Dave Brubeck Quartet | 25th Anniversary Reunion | A&M Records | 396998-2

African Dawn
Mount Everest | Jazz I Sverige '79 | Caprice | CAP 1177

African Drum Suite(part 1)
Archie Shepp Orchestra | The Cry Of My People | Impulse(MCA) | 9861488

African Drum Suite(part 2)
Beaver Harris & Davis S.Ware | African Drums | Owl Records | 018356-2

African Drums
African Drums | Owl Records | 09

African Fairytale
NDR Radio Philharmonic Orchestra | Colossus Of Sound | Enja | ENJ-9460 2

African Fanfare
Cécile Verny Quartet | Got A Ticket | double moon | DMCD 1002-2

African Flower
Conrad Herwig-Andy LaVerne | Shades Of Light | Steeplechase | SCCD 31520
Ellery Eskelin Trio | Forms | Open Minds | OM 2403-2
Klaus Ignatzek International Quintet | African Flower | Acoustic Music Records | 319.1125.2
Michel Petrucciani | Promenade With Duke | Blue Note | 780590-2
Pago Libre | Pago Libre | L+R Records | CDLR 45105

African Lady
Al Grey And His Allstars | Snap Your Fingers | Verve | 9860307
Max Roach All Stars | Candid Dolphy | Candid | CCD 79033

African Lady(take 4)
Loft Line | Source | Laika Records | 35101122

African Line
Dave Holland Trio | Triplicate | ECM | 1373

African Lullaby
Triocolor | Colours Of Ghana | ACT | 9285-2

African Magic
Nina Simone Trio | My Baby Just Cares For Me | Charly | CR 30217

African Market
Abdullah Ibrahim With The NDR Big Band | Ekapa Lodumo | TipToe | TIP-888840 2
Abdullah Ibrahim | South African Sunshine | Pläne | CD 88778

African Marketplace
Abdullah Ibrahim Trio | Cape Town Flowers | TipToe | TIP-888826 2
Abdullah Ibrahim Trio With The Munich Radio Symphony Orchestra | African Symphony | Enja | ENJ-9410 2
Dollar Brand Orchestra | Abdullah Ibrahim-African Marketplace | Elektra | ELK K 52217
Dave Doran Group | Rhythm Voice | Plainisphare | PL 1267-109 CD

African Piano
Abdullah Ibrahim | Fats Duke And Monk | Sackville | SKCD2-3048

African Queen
Sandy Brown's Jazz Band | Best Of British Jazz From The BBC Jazz Club Vol.2 | Upbeat Jazz | URCD 119

African Ripples
Fats Waller | Fats Waller-The Joint Is Jumpin' | RCA | ND 86288(874182)

African River
Akili | Akili | M.A Music | NU 730-2
Dollar(Abdullah Ibrahim) Brand Group | African River | Enja | ENJ-6018 2
Errol Parker And The Contemporary Jazz Ensemble | African Samba | Sahara | 1006

African Skies
The Brecker Brothers | Out Of The Loop | GRP | GRP 97842
Mongo Santamaria Orchestra | Skins | Milestone | MCD 47038-2

African Street Parade
Dado Moroni Trio | What's New? | SPLASC(H) Records | CD H 378-2
African Suite:
Dollar Brand | Ancient Africa | Japo | 60005(2360005)
African Sunrise
Randy Weston Orchestra | The Spirits Of Our Ancestors | Verve | 511857-2
African Sunrise-
Paul Wertico Trio | Don't Be Scared Anymore | Premonition | 790748-2
African Symphony:
Dave Brubeck Quartet | 25th Anniversary Reunion | A&M Records | 396998-2
African Waltz
Cannonball Adderley And His Orchestra | African Waltz | Original Jazz Classics | OJC 258(RLP 9377)
Africana
Dizzy Gillespie And His Orchestra | Gillespiana And Carnegie Hall Concert | Verve | 519809-2
Africana-
Ana Caram Group | Maracana | Chesky | JD 104
Africans Unite
Ayibobo | Ayibobo:Freestyle | DIW | DIW 877 CD
Afrilude
Affinity | Affinity Plays Nine Modern Jazz Classics | Music & Arts | CD 834
Afrique
Art Blakey And The Jazz Messengers | Best Of Blakey 60 | Blue Note | 493072-2
Count Basie And His Orchestra | Jazz Special-Afrique | RCA | CL 42784 DP
Dave Weckl Group | Hard-Wired | GRP | GRP 97602
Duke Ellington And His Orchestra | The Afro-Eurasian Eclipse-A Suite In Eight Parts | Original Jazz Classics | OJCCD 645-2(F 9498)
Eric Marienthal Group | Round Trip | GRP | GRP 95862
Afro
Rimak | Back In Town | Jazzline | ???
Afro Blake
Abbey Lincoln With The Max Roach Sextet | Abbey Is Blue | Original Jazz Classics | OJC20 069-2(RLP 1153)
Afro Blue
Andy Summers Trio | The Last Dance Of Mr.X | RCA | 2668937-2
Cal Tjader Quintet | Concerts In The Sun | Fantasy | FCD 9688-2
Concerts In The Sun | Fantasy | FCD 9688-2
Cal Tjader Sextet | Monterey Concerts | Prestige | PCD 24026-2
Carme Canela With The Joan Monné Trio | Introducing Carme Canela | Fresh Sound Records | FSNT 014 CD
Colin Dunwoodie Quartet | Glad To See You | Edition Collage | EC 460-2
Wind Moments | Take Twelve On CD | TT 009-2
Dave Valentine Group | Legends | GRP | GRP 95192
Dizzy Gillespie Orchestra | Summertime | Pablo | 2308229-2
John Coltrane Quartet | Afro Blue Impressions | Pablo | 2PACD 2620101
The Best Of John Coltrane | Pablo | 2405417-2
Coltrane Live At Birdland | MCA | 2292-54654-2
John Patitucci Group | Imprint | Concord | CCD 4881
McCoy Tyner And The Latin All-Stars | McCoy Tyner And The Latin All-Stars | Telarc Digital | CD 83462
Michel Petrucciani | Date With Time | Owl Records | 064 CD
Poncho Sanchez And His Orchestra | Para Todos | Concord | CCD 4600
Afro Blues-
Jean-Paul Bourelly Group | Saints & Sinners | DIW | DIW 872 CD
Afro Dio
Ayibobo | Ayibobo:Freestyle | DIW | DIW 877 CD
Afro Party
Grant Green With Orchestra | The Final Comedown(Soundtrack) | Blue Note | 581678-2
Ugetsu | There's Something On The Way | Mons Records | MR 874806
Afro Tang
Jasper Van't Hof | Pili-Pili | Warner | 2292-40458-2
Afro Timento
Pili-Pili | Pili-Pili | JA & RO | JARO 4141-2
Franco D'Andrea Trio | Franco D'Andrea Trio | yvp music | 3021
Afro.Cuban Drum Suite
Dennis Charles Quartet | Spirit Of New Jazz | Silkheart | SHCD 130
Afro-Bossa
Duke Ellington And His Orchestra | En Concert Avec Europe 1 | Laserlight | 710433/34
James Williams Sextet | Up To The Minute Blues | DIW | DIW 882 CD
Afro-Centric
Steve Erquiaga Group | Erkiology | Windham Hill | 34 10127-2
Poncho Sanchez And His Orchestra | Afro-Cuban Fantasy | Concord | CCD 4847
Afro-Cuban Jazz Suite
Charlie Parker With Machito And His Orchestra | The Latin Bird | Memo Music | HDJ 4076
Afrodisia
Kenny Dorham Octet | Afro-Cuban | Blue Note | 746815-2
Nueva Manteca | Afrodisia | Timeless | CD SJP 355
Shelly Manne And His Men | Jimmy Giuffre:The Complete 1947-1953 Small Group Sessions,Vol.2 | Blue Moon | BMCD 1047
Afro-Eurasian Eclipse:,The
Eddie Lockjaw Davis Orchestra | Afro-Jaws | Original Jazz Classics | OJCCD 403-2(RLP 9373)
Afro-Jaws
Bill Coleman And His Orchestra | From Boogie To Funk | Polydor | 2445035 IMS
Afromotive In Blue
Luis Agudo | Afrorera | Red Records | VPA 185
Afro-Transdabubian Groove
JoAnne Brackeen Trio | AFT | Timeless | CD SJP 115
Aften(Evening)
Flemming Agerskov Quintet | Face To Face | dacapo | DCCD 9445
Aftenland
Jan Garbarek-Kjell Johnsen Duo | Aftenland | ECM | 1169(839304-2)
Affinity | Affinity Plays Nine Modern Jazz Classics | Music & Arts | CD 834
After
Ellis Marsalis Quartet | Whistle Stop | CBS | 474555-2
Wynton Marsalis Quartet | J Mood | CBS | 468712-2
After All
Bob Berg-Mike Stern Group | Games | Jazz Door | JD 1275
Duke Ellington And His Famous Orchestra | Duke Ellington & His Famous Orchestra | Forlane | UCD 19003
René Pretschner | Floating Pictures | Green House Music | CD 1001
Ronnie Earl & The Broadcasters | Soul Searchin' | Black Top | BT 1042 CD
Vienna Art Orchestra | Duke Ellington's Sound Of Love | TCB Records | TCB 99802
After All This Years
McKinney's Cotton Pickers | The Complete McKinney's Cotton Pickers Vol.3/4 | RCA | NL 89738(2) DP
After Celan
Charlie Mariano Sextet | The Jazz Scene:San Francisco | Fantasy | FCD 24760-2
After Coffee
Nat Pierce-Dick Collins Nonet/Charlie Mariano Sextet | Original Jazz Classics | OJC 118(F 3224)
After Dark
Von Freeman Quartet | Serenade & Blues | Chief Records | CD 3
After Dinner
Ull Möck Trio | Drilling | Satin Doll Productions | SDP 1023-1 CD
After Eight
Roscoe Mitchell With The Brus Trio | After Fallen Leaves | Silkheart | SHCD 126
After Glow
Christopher Hollyday Quartet | The Natural Moment | Novus | PD 83118
Nat Pierce And His Orchestra | Big Band At The Savoy Ballroom | RCA | 2130073-2
Wollie Kaiser Timeghost | New Traces For Old Aces | Jazz Haus Musik | JHM 0102 CD
Andreas Hansl | Dualism | UAK | UAK 1
After Hours
Bob Hall Trio | Alone With The Blues | Lake | LACD 44
Christian Willisohn-Boris Vanderlek | Blues News | Blues Beacon | BLU-1019 2
Dizzy Gillespie-Sonny Rollins-Sonny Stitt Sextet | Sonny Side Up | Verve | 521426-2
Eddie Playboy Taylor & The Blueshounds | Ready For Eddie | Big Bear | 146407
Jay McShann Quartet | Roll' Em | Black & Blue | BLE 233022
Jimmy Smith Trio | Groovin' At Smalls' Paradise | Blue Note | 499777-2
John Campbell Trio | After Hours | Contemporary | CCD 14053-2
Lafayette Leake | American Folk Blues Festival '70 | L+R Records | LS 42021
Ray Bryant | Inimitable | Jazz Connaisseur | JCCD 9430-2
Alone At Montreux | 32 Jazz | 32128
Sarah Vaughan With The Paul Weston Orchestra | Ella,Billie,Sarah,Aretha,Mahalia | CBS | 473733-2
Bob Hall | No.29 | BELL Records | BLR 84038
After Hours Rock
JATP All Stars | JATP In Tokyo | Pablo | 2620104-2
After Hours Session: Sweethearts On Parade And Dixie
Sammy Price Quintet | Roots Of Rock 'N' Roll, Vol. 7: Rib Joint | Savoy | SJL 2240 (801886)
After My Work Each Day
Michael Mantler Group | Michael Mantler: No Answer/Silence | Watt | 2/5(543374-2)
Chick Corea | Piano Improvisations-Vol.2 | ECM | 1020(829190-2)
After Noon Song
Tony Purrone Trio | Rascality | Steeplechase | SCCD 31514
After PM
Jimmy Rowles-Eric Von Essen | Lilac Time | Kokopelli Records | KOKO 1297
After School Swing Session(Swinging With Symphony Sid)
Johnny King Septet | The Meltdown | Enja | ENJ-9329 2
After Six
Michael Sagmeister Quintet | Here And Now | Acoustic Music Records | 319.1146.2
After Supper
Count Basie And His Orchestra | Basie On Roulette, Vol. 1: E : MC 2 : Count Basie Orchestra+Neal HeftArrangeme | Roulette | CDP 793273-2
After The Ball
The Bourbon Street Stompers | I Like Dixieland | Bainbridge | BT 1019
After The Cosmic Rain
Return To Forever | Return To The 7th Galaxy-Return To Forever:The Anthology | Verve | 533108-2
John Coltrane Quartet | Dear Old Stockholm | Impulse(MCA) | GRP 11202
After The Crescent
Courtney Pine Group | Modern Day Jazz Stories | Verve | 529028-2
After The Damaja
Fourplay | Fourplay | Warner | 7599-26656-2
After The Dance
Jimmy McGriff Quintet | Blue To The Bone | Milestone | MCD 9163-2
After The Day Is Done
Matthew Brubeck & David Widelock | Giraffes In A Hurry | B&W Present | BW 042
After The Fact
John Scofield Groups | Quiet | Verve | 533185-2
Peter Ehwald Trio | Away With Words:The Music Of John Scofield | Jazz Haus Musik | JHM 0128 CD
Mercy Dee Walton Trio | Pity And A Shame | Original Blues Classics | OBCCD 552-2(BV 1039)
After The Gold Rush
Matthias Frey Trio | Y | Jazzline | ???
After The Morning
John Hicks Trio | Power Trio | Novus | PD 90547(847028)
Peter Leitch Quartet | Trio/Quartet '91 | Concord | CCD 4480
Nils Landgren Funk Unit | Paint It Blue:A Tribute To Cannonball Adderley | ACT | 9243-2
After The Party
Maynard Ferguson And His Orchestra | Straightaway Jazz Themes | Fresh Sound Records | FSR 656(Roulette R 52076)
After The Rain
Dave Liebman With Gunnar Mossblad And The James Madison University Jazz Esemble | The Music Of John Coltrane | Candid | CCD 79531
Duke Pearson Sextet | Midnight Blue(The [Be]witching Hour) | Blue Note | 854365-2
Enrico Pieranunzi Trio | Moon Pie | yvp music | CD 3011
Harold Danko | After The Rain | Steeplechase | SCCD 31356
Jimmy Ponder Quartet | Mean Street-No Bridges | Muse | MCD 5324
Joe McPhee | As Serious As Your Life | HatOLOGY | 514
John Coltrane Quartet | The Mastery Of John Coltrane/Vol. 2: To The Beat Of A Different Drum | MCA | IZ 9346/2
John Coltrane Quintet | Impressions | Impulse(MCA) | 543416-2
John Hicks | Maybeck Recital Hall Series Volume Seven | Concord | CCD 4442
LeeAnn Ledgerwood | Compassion | Steeplechase | SCCD 31477
Michel Legrand Orchestra | After The Rain | Original Jazz Classics | 2312139
After The Snow The Fragrance
Chris Cody Coalition | Oasis | Naxos Jazz | 86018-2
After The Storm
Maggie Nichols-Peter Nu | Don't Assume | LEO | LR 145
After Theatre Jump
Woody Herman And His Orchestra | Woody Herman 1954 And 1959 | Status | DSTS 1021
After While
Paul Nash Ensemble | Second Impression | Soul Note | SN 1107
After Words
Herbie Mann Quartet | Herbie Mann Plays | Bethlehem | BET 6010-2(BCP 58)
After You
Bob Berg-Mike Stern Group | Games | Jazz Door | JD 1275
George Shearing & Barry Tuckwell With Orchestra | Plays The Music Of Cole Porter | Concord | CCD 42010
Marc Johnson Trio | Right Brain Patrol | JMT Edition | 849153-2
After You've Gone
Al Casey Quartet | A Tribute To Fats | Jazzpoint | JP 1044 CD
Al Porcino Big Band | Al Porcino Big Band Live! | Organic Music | ORGM 9717
Allotria Jazz Band | All That Jazz | Elite Special | 730217
Art Tatum | Masters Of Jazz Vol.8:Art Tatum | Storyville | SLP 4108
Benny Goodman And His All Star Sextet | Verve Jazz Masters 33:Benny Goodman | Verve | 844410-2
On Stage | Decca | 6.28101 DP
Benny Goodman And His Orchestra | The Yale University Muisc Library Vol.5 | Limelight | 820827-2 IMS
Benny Goodman Quartet | Teddy Wilson | LRC Records | CDC 9003
Benny Goodman Trio | Planet Jazz:Benny Goodman | Planet Jazz | 2152054-2
Jazz Collection:Benny Goodman | Laserlight | 24396
Jazz Drumming Vol.1(1927-1937) | Fenn Music | FJD 2701
Bill Coleman Quintet | Bill Coleman | Swing | SW 8402 IMS
Bobby Hackett Quintet | At The Roosevelt Grill | Chiaroscuro | CR 161
Concord Festival All Stars | After You've Gone | Concord | CCD 6006
Count Basie And His Orchestra | 100 Ans De Jazz:Count Basie | RCA | 2177831-2
Masters Of Jazz Vol.5 | RCA | NL 89530 DP
Dan Barrett Sextet | Reunion With Al | Arbors Records | ARCD 19124
Dinah Washington With The Eddie Chamblee Orchestra | Dinah Sings Bessie Smith | Verve | 538635-2
Django Reinhardt And The Quintet Du Hot Club De France | The Indispensable Django Reinhardt | RCA | ND 70929
Eddie Lockjaw Davis Quartet | Jaws Strikes Again | Black & Blue | BLE 233101
Ella Fitzgerald With The Bill Doggett Orchestra | Ella Fitzgerald-First Lady Of Song | Verve | 517898-2
Erroll Garner Trio | The Erroll Garner Collection Vol.2: Dancing On The Ceiling | EmArCy | 834935-2 PMS
Fats Waller And His Rhythm | Live At The Yacht Club | Giants Of Jazz | GOJ 1029
Isidore 'Tuts' Washington | The Larry Borenstein Collection Vol.3:Isidore 'Tuts' Washington-New Orleans Piano | 504 Records | 504CD 32
JATP All Stars | JATP-1940's | Verve | MV 9070/72 IMS
The Complete Jazz At The Philharmonic On Verve 1944-1949 | Verve | 523893-2
Jay McShann Quartet | The Man From Muskogee | Sackville | SKCD2-3005
Joe Venuti Quartet | Jazz-Club: Violin | Verve | 840039-2
Joscho Stephan Group | Swinging Strings | Acoustic Music Records | 319.1195.2
Kansas City Six | From Spiritual To Swing | Vanguard | VCD 169/71
Keith Smith Hefty Jazz All Stars | Swing Is Here Again | Lake | LACD 80
Lester Young And His Band | Lester Young:The Complete 1936-1951 Small Group Sessions(Studio Recordings-Master Takes),Vol.3 | Blue Moon | BMCD 1003
Magnificant Seventh's with Milton Batiste And Alton Carson | Best Of New Orleans:Bourbon Street Jazz After Dark | Mardi Gras Records | MG 1022
Mick Mulligan's Magnolia Jazz Band With George Melly | Great British Traditional Bands Vol.7:Mick Mulligan & George Melly | Lake | LACD 66
Neil Richardson Singers With The Metropole Orchestra | A Beautiful Friendship | Koch Jazz | 3-6909-2
Nick Brignola Quartet | New York Bound | Interplay | IP 7719
Quintet Du Hot Club De France | Djangology | Bluebird | 2663957-2
Django Reinhardt:Nuages | Arkadia Jazz | 71431
Sidney Bechet And His Feetwarmers | Sidney Bechet:Summertime | Dreyfus Jazz Line | FDM 36712-2
Jazz In Paris:Sidney Bechet Et Claude Luther | EmArCy | 159821-2 PMS
Sidney Bechet And His New Orleans Feetwarmers | Sidney Bechet 1932-1943: The Bluebird Sessions | Bluebird | ND 90317
Stephane Grappelli Group | Stephane Grappelli:Live In San Francisco | Storyville | 4960723
Stephane Grappelli Quartet | Stephane Grappelli | LRC Records | CDC 9014
Sue Raney With The Alan Broadbent Sextet | In Good Company | Discovery | DSCD 974(889498)
The New York Allstars | Broadway | Nagel-Heyer | CD 003
The Tremble Kids All Stars | The Tremble Kids All Stars Play Chicago Jazz! | Nagel-Heyer | CD 043
Theresa Brewer With The Stephane Grappelli Quartet | On The Road Again | Doctor Jazz | FW 38448
Woody Allen Trio | Wild Man Blues | RCA | 2663353-2
Zoot Sims-Al Cohn-Phil Woods Sextet | Jazz Alive:A Night At The Half Note | Blue Note | 494105-2
Art Tatum | Art Tatum:20th Century Piano Genius | Verve | 531763-2
After You've Gone-
Jaki Byard Quartet | The Last From Lennie's | Prestige | PRCD 11029-2
Simon Schott | Bar Piano: Simon Schott Plays Your Favorite Evergreens Vol.2 | Organic Music | ORGM 9735
Ray Brown With The Marty Paich Orchestra | Bass Hit! | Verve | 559829-2
After You've Gone(alt.take)
Seger Ellis With Louis Armstrong And His Orchestra | Louis Armstrong-Louis In New York Vol.5 | CBS | 466965-2
Afterglow
Eddie Daniels/Bucky Pizzarelli Duo | Blue Bossa | Choice | CHCD 71002
Afterlife Calypso
Ahmad Jamal Quartet | Ahmad Jamal Á L'Olympia | Dreyfus Jazz Line | FDM 36629-2
Aftermath
Andrew Cyrille Trio | Good To Go,With A Tribute To Bu | Soul Note | 121292-2
Bill Evans Group | Escape | Escape | ESC 03650-2
Aftermath The Fourth Movement-
Kevin Eubanks Group | Turning Point | Blue Note | 798170-2
Afternoon
Misha Alperin Quintet | North Story | ECM | 1596
Mundell Lowe-Hendrik Meurkens Quartet | When Lights Are Lowe | Acoustic Music Records | 319.1190.2
Afternoon Blues
Richard Grossman Trio | Where The Sky Ended | HatOLOGY | 541
Afternoon In August
Lester Bowie's New York Organ Ensemble | Funky T. Cool T. | DIW | DIW 853 CD
Afternoon In Paris
Cedar Walton Trio | Manhattan Afternoon | Criss Cross | Criss 1082
Horace Parlan Quintet | Glad I Found You | Steeplechase | SCCD 31194
John Lewis | Afternoon In Paris | Dreyfus Jazz Line | FDM 36507-2
Stephane Grappelli Quartet | Compact Jazz:Stephane Grappelli | MPS | 831370-2 PMS
Xanadu All Stars | Xanadu At Montreux Vol.1 | Vogue | 506614
Afternoon Of A Dawn(part 1-4)
Jack Teagarden And His Orchestra | A Standard Library Of Jazz Vol. 1 | Storyville | SLP 700
Afternoon Of A Georgia Faun
Charlie Barnet And His Orchestra | Clap Hands,Here Comes Charlie! | Bluebird | ND 86273
Aftershock
Bill McHenry Quartet | Rest Stop | Fresh Sound Records | FSNT 033 CD
Afterthought
George Colligan | Small Room | Steeplechase | SCCD 31470
Les Spann Quintet | Gemini | Original Jazz Classics | OJCCD 1948-2(JLP 9355)
Michel Camilo Trio | Triangulo | Telarc Digital | CD 83549
Billy Taylor Trio | Custom Taylored | Fresh Sound Records | FSR-CD 0205
Afterthoughts
Mike Wofford | Afterthoughts | Discovery | DS 784 IMS
Trinity | Trinity | L+R Records | LR 40002
Afterthoughts Of A Dream
American Jazz Philharmonic(The New American Orchestra) | American Jazz Philharmonic | GRP | GRP 97302
Again
Bill Frisell Trio | Bill Frisell With Dave Hollnad And Elvin Jones | Nonesuch | 7559-79624-2
Live | Gramavision | GCD 79504
The Three Sounds | Standards | Blue Note | 821281-2
Again And Again
Karlheinz Miklin Trio | Echoes Of Illyria | Amadeo | 829448-1
Again And Again,Again
World Music Meeting | World Music Meeting | Eigelstein | 568-72224
Again Anew
Jo Swan And Her Quartet | Primal Schmaltz | Timbre | TRCD 004
Again Never
Anderson-Harris-Lewis-Valente | Slideride | Hat Art | CD 6165
Against The Grain
Edgar Winter Group | I'm Not A Kid Anymore | L+R Records | CDLR 42076
Against The Wall
Eric Person Trio | Prophecy | Soul Note | 121287-2
Agathon
Bobby Watson Group | Urban Renewal | Kokopelli Records | KOKO 1309
Aged In Wood
Ronald Shannon Jackson And The Decoding Society | What Spirit Say | DIW | DIW 895 CD

Ageless
Elvin Jones Sextet | Poly-Currents | Blue Note | 784331-2

Aggayu
Sabu L. Martinez Group | Palo Congo | Blue Note | 522665-2

Aggo Elegua
Bessie Smith With Her Down Home Trio | Bessie Smith-The Complete Recordings Vol.1 | CBS | 467895-2

Aggression
Eric Dolphy-Booker Little Quintet | The Great Concert Of Eric Dolphy | Prestige | P 34002
Eric Dophy Quintet | Eric Dolphy:The Complete Prestige Recordings | Prestige | 9 PRCD-4418-2
Tom Williams Quintet | Introducing Tom Williams | Criss Cross | Criss 1064

Agir Dalbughi
Curlew | North America | Moers Music | 02042

Agitation
Miles Davis Quintet | No (More) Blues | Jazz Door | JD 1224
Victor Feldman Quartet | The Artful Dodger | Concord | CCD 4038

Agitato
John Wolf Brennan | The Well-Prepared Clavier/Das Wohlpräparierte Klavier | Creative Works Records | CW CD 1032-2

Agitato(medium)-
Ketil Bjornstad Group | The Sea II | ECM | 1633(537341-2)

Agnes
Cecil McBee Sextet | Music For The Source | Enja | 3019-2

Agnus Dei
Joe Masters Orchestra & Choir | The Jazz Mass By John Masters | Discovery | DS 785 IMS

Agnus Dei Plus
Natascha Majevskaja | Orgel Ist Mehr...In Bamberg Vol.2 | Orgel ist mehr! | OIM/BA/1999-2 CD

Agnus Dei(Mozart:Litaniae Lauretanae KV 195)
Karl Ratzer Group | Gumbo Dive | RST-Records | 91540-2

Agra
Geoff Keezer Quartet | Here And Now | Blue Note | 796691-2

Agram
Evan Parker/Barry Guy/Paul Lytton | Imaginary Values | MAYA Recordings | MCD 9401

Agua De Beber(Water To Drink)
Antonio Carlos Jobim With The Claus Ogerman Orchestra | Compact Jazz: Best Of Bossa Nova | Verve | 833269-2
Astrud Gilberto With Antonio Carlos Jobim And The Marty Paich Orchestra | The Antonio Carlos Jobim Songbook | Verve | 525472-2
The Astrud Gilberto Album | Verve | 823009-1
Astrud Gilberto With The Marty Paich Orchestra | Verve Jazz Masters 9:Astrud Gilberto | Verve | 519824-2
Tempo Jazz Edition Vol.3-Stayin' Cool | Verve | 847902-2
Gonzalo Rubalcaba-Herbie Hancock Quintet | Antonio Carlos Jobim And Friends | Verve | 531556-2
Götz Tangerding Group | A La Ala - A Voice In Jazz | Bhakti Jazz | BK 22
Sadao Watanabe Sextet | Bossa Nova Concert | Denon Compact Disc | DC-8556

Agua De Beber(Water To Drink-reprise)
Ruben Blades Y Seis Del Solar | Agua De Luna | Messidor | 15964 CD

Agua De Paz
Jazz Crusaders | Chile Con Soul | Pacific Jazz | 590957-2

Agua Dulce
Poncho Sanchez Band | El Conguero | Concord | CJ 286

Agua Mae Agua
Darrell Grant Quintet | The New Bop | Criss Cross | Criss 1106

Aguamarinha
Irakere | Catalina | Messidor | 15955

Aguas De Marco(Waters Of March)
Antonio Carlos Jobim-Elis Regina Group | The Antonio Carlos Jobim Songbook | Verve | 525472-2
Elis Regina Group | Compact Jazz: Antonio Carlos Jobim | Verve | 843273-2
Tom Jobim Group | Montreux Jazz Festival | ACT | 9001-2

Aguas De Oxala
Egberto Gismonti | Danca Das Cabecas | ECM | 1089

Aguas Luminosas
Luis Agudo | Afrosamba | Red Records | VPA 172

Aguilar
Gary Lucas | Skeleton On The Feast | Enemy | EMCD 126(03526)

Agung
dAs prOjekT | dAs prOjekT | Foolish Music | FM 211288

Ägypten
Christoph Mudrich Trio feat. Sir Henry | Christmas In Blue | Blue Concept | BCCD 93/03

Ah' That's Freedom
Aaron Sachs Sextet | Jazzville Vol.3 | Fresh Sound Records | FSR 565(Dawn DLP 1114)

Ah! So
Rod Levitt Orchestra | The Dynamic Sound Patterns Of The Rod Levitt Orchestra | Original Jazz Classics | OJCCD 1955-2(RS 9471)

Ah! Spain
Bert Ambrose And His Orchestra | The Bands That Matter | Eclipse | ECM 2044

Ah! Vita Bella
Jean-Michel Defaye Trio | Morat Jazz Trio | Forlane | UCD 16650

Ah! Vous Dirais-Je,Maman
John Stevens Dance Orchestra | Ah! | View | VS 111 IMS

Ah, George, We Hardly Knew Ya'
Christian Von Der Golz Trio | Sophie Said | Mons Records | MR 874828

Ahaha
Nathan Davis Quartet | Rules Of Freedom | Hot House Records | HH 1002 IMS

Ahayu-Da
Les Brown And His Orchestra | The Uncollected: Les Brown And His Orchestra 1949-Vol.2 | Hindsight | HSR 132

Ahi Lingua, Ai Baci
Jones Hellborg | The Silent Life | Demon Records | DEM 026

Ah-Ite
The Catholics | Simple | Laika Records | 35100802

Ah-Kah-Kah
Art Farmer Quintet | Foolish Memories | L+R Records | CDLR 45008

Ah-Leu-Cha
Bud Shank-Shorty Rogers Quintet | California Concert | Contemporary | CCD 14012-2
Charlie Parker All Stars | The Savoy Recordings 2 | Savoy | 650108(881908)
Miles Davis Quintet | Miles Davis With John Coltrane | CBS | CBS 88029
Miles Davis Sextet | Miles & Monk At Newport | CBS | SRCS 5698
Sphere | Bird Songs | Verve | 837032-2

Ahmad The Terrible
Ahmad Jamal Trio | Ahmad's Blues | Jazz Society(Vogue) | 670507

Ahmad's Blues
Horace Silver Quintet | Jazz Has... A Sense Of Humor | Verve | 050293-2

Ah-Ma-Tell
Bob Berg Group | Riddles | Stretch Records | SCD 9008-2

Ahoom Mbram-
Poncho Sanchez Orchestra | Bien Sabroso! | Concord | CCD 4239

Aichuri, The Song Man
Hilton Ruiz Trio | Hilton Ruiz Trio | Jazz Publications | JPV 8004

Aida
Miles Davis Group | This Is Jazz:Miles Davis Electric | CBS | CK 65449

AIDS
Martial Solal | The Solosolal | MPS | 68221

Aila
Georg Ruby-Wollie Kaiser | Ruby Domesticus Vugaris | Jazz Haus Musik | JHM 26
Ruby & Puntin | Stadtgarten Series Vol.6 | Jazz Haus Musik | JHM 1006 SER

Aila-
Christine Tobin Band | Aililiu | Babel | BDV 9501

Aim
Jimmy Woods Sextet | Conflict | Original Jazz Classics | OJCCD 1954-2(S 7612)

Aim(alt.take)
James Moody Quintet With Strings | James Moody/Frank Foster:Sax Talk | Vogue | 2113410-2

Ain Ghazel
Clarence Gatemouth Brown Quartet | Cold Storage | Black & Blue | BLE 59.096 2

Aina's Travels
Rolf Schimmermann Group | Suru | B&W Present | BW 009

Ainbusk
Laurindo Almeida/Carlos Barbosa-Lima/Charlie Byrd Quintet | Music Of The Brazilian Masters | Concord | CCD 4389

Ain't Got Time
Bing Crosby And Rosemarie Clooney With The Billy May Orchestra | Fancy Meeting You Here | RCA | 2663859-2

Ain't A-Hankerin'
Milt Jackson Quartet | Ain't But A Few Of Us Left | Pablo | 2310873-2

Ain't But A Few Of Us Left
Buddy Johnson And His Orchestra | Buddy And Ella Johnson 1953-1964 | Bear Family Records | BCD 15479 DH

Ain't But One
Peg Leg Sam | Medicine Show Man | Trix Records | TRIX 3302

Ain't Cha Glad
Teddy Wilson | Solo:Teddy Wilson Plays Cole Porter And Fat Waller | Jazz Colours | 874715-2

Ain't Cha Got Me(Where You Want Me)
Bob Wilber-Dick Wellstood | The Duet | Progressive | PCD 7080

Ain't Goin' No Place
Bob Crosby And His Orchestra | So Far So Good | Halcyon | DHDL 132

Ain't Got No Home
Nina Simone Quartet | Nina Simone | The Rising Sun Collection | RSC 0004

Ain't Got Nothing But The Blues
Schmid-Hübner-Krill | Time Makes The Tune | Mons Records | MR 874825

Ain't I Got You
Don Redman And His Orchestra | Doin' The New Low Down | Hep | 1004

Ain't It Funky Now
Grant Green Orchestra | Green Is Beautiful | Blue Note | 300275(4342)
Blue Breaks Beats Vol.2 | Blue Note | 789907-2
Jimmy McGriff Band | Jimmy McGriff featuring Hank Crawford | LRC Records | CDC 9001(874373)

Ain't Misbehavin'
Al Casey Quintet | Buck Jumpin' | Original Jazz Classics | OJCCD 675-2(SV 2007)
Art Tatum | Esquire's All-American Hot Jazz Sessions | RCA | ND 86757
Benny Goodman Quintet | B.G. In Hi-Fi | Capitol | 792864-2
Billie Holiday And Her All Stars | Billie Holiday Story Vol.4:Lady Sings The Blues | Verve | 521429-2
Stay With Me | Verve | 511523-2
Buddy Tate-Nat Simkins-Houston Person Sextet | Just Friends:The Tenors Of Buddy Tate, Nat Simkins, Houston Person | Muse | MCD 5418
Cat Anderson And His Orchestra | Ellingtonians In Paris | Jazztime(EMI) | 251275-2
Charleston Chasers | The Charleston Chasers 1929-1931 | VJM | VLP 44 IMS
Count Basie And His Orchestra | Sixteen Men Swinging | Verve | 2-2517 IMS
Don Ewell | Free 'N' Easy | Good Time Jazz | GTCD 10046-2
Dorothy Donegan-Jay McShann Duo | Piano Giants Vol.1 | Swingtime | 8201
Echoes Of New Orleans | Live At Sweet Basil | Big Easy Records | BIG CD-005
Ella Fitzgerald With The Count Basie Orchestra | A Classy Pair | Pablo | 2312132-2
Fats Waller | Fats Waller-The Joint Is Jumpin' | RCA | ND 86288(874182)
Fats Waller And His Rhythm | Fats Waller:The Complete Associated Transcription Sessions 1935-1939 | Jazz Unlimited | JUCD 2076
Private Acetates And Film Soundtracks | Jazz Anthology | JA 5148
Fess Williams And His Orchestra | Fess Williams-The Complete Sessions 1929 Vol.1 | Harlequin | HQ 2039 IMS
George Van Eps | The Concord Jazz Guitar Collection Volume 3 | Concord | CCD 4507
Harry Edison Quintet | Edison's Light | Original Jazz Classics | OJCCD 804-2(2310780)
The Best Of Harry Edison | Pablo | 2310847
Houston Person Sextet | Wild Flower | Muse | MR 5161
Jimmy Rushing With The Dave Brubeck Quartet | Brubeck & Rushing | CBS | CK 65727
Jimmy Smith Quartet | Off The Top | Elektra | MUS K 52418
Joe Williams With The Count Basie All Stars | Basie-Bennett | Roulette | 7938992
Judy Carmichael Quintet | Two-Handed Stride | Progressive | PRO 7065 IMS
Louis Armstrong And His All Stars | Greatest Hits | CBS | 21058
Best Of The Complete RCA Victor Recordings | RCA | 2663636-2
The Louis Armstrong Selection | CBS | 467278-2
Louis Armstrong And His Orchestra | Jazz Gallery:Louis Armstrong Vol.1 | RCA | 2114166-2
Louis Armstrong Vol.4: Hot Fives & Sevens | JSP Records | JSPCD 315
Marcus Pintrup Quartet | Nocturnal Traces | Blue Note | 493676-2
Maxine Sullivan And Her Band | Maxine Sullivan Sings | Fresh Sound Records | FSR-CD 0178
Milt Jackson All Stars | The Best Of Milt Jackson | Pablo | 2405405-2
Papa Bue's Viking Jazzband | Live At Slukefter,Tivoli | Music Mecca | CD 1028-2
Peggy Serra-Oscar Pettiford | Jazzville | Dawn | DCD 114
Ralph Sutton-Jay McShann Quartet | The Last Of The Whorehouse Piano Players Vol. 2 | Chaz Jazz | CJ 104
Sarah Vaughan With The Jimmy Jones Orchestra | Sarah Vaughan In Hi-Fi | CBS | CK 65117
Sonny Stitt Quartet | Prestige First Sessions, Vol.2 | Prestige | PCD 24115-2
Stephane Grappelli With The Diz Disley Trio | Violinspiration | MPS | 68058
Willie 'The Lion' Smith | Pork And Beans | Black Lion | BLCD 760144

Ain't Misbehavin'-
Earl Hines | Live At The New School | Chiaroscuro | CR 157
Fats Waller | Fifty Thousand Killer Watts Of Jive | Ember | CJS 842
Teddy Wilson Trio | Ben & Teddy | Sackville | SKCD2-2056

Ain't No Love In Town
Stan Kenton And His Orchestra | Artistry In Rhythm | Creative World | ST 1043

Ain't No Sunshine
Jim Kahr Group | Burnin' The Blues | Acoustic Music Records | 319.1044.2
Rodney Jones Group | Soul Manifesto | Blue Note | 530499-2
Bobby Bland And His Band | Bobby Bland The Voice: Duke Recordings 1959-1969 | Ace Records | CDCHD 323

Ain't No Use
Count Basie And His Orchestra | Count Basie Orchestra featuring Arthur Prysock | CTI Records | PDCTI 1123-2
Sarah Vaughan And Her Band | The Devine One | Fresh Sound Records | FSR 659(Roulette R 52060)
Memphis Minnie(Mamie Smith) | Memphis Jamboree 1927-1936 | Yazoo | YAZ 1021

Ain't Nobody
Nils Landgren Funk Unit | Live In Montreux | ACT | 9265-2
Duke Ellington And His Orchestra | Highlights From The Duke Ellington Centennial Edition | RCA | 2663672-2

Ain't Nobody Nowhere Nothin' Without God
Grand Dominion Jazz Band | Half And Half | Stomp Off Records | CD 3989

Ain't Nobody Here But Us Chickens
Louis Jordan Quintet | Great Rhyhtm & Blues-Vol.1 | Bulldog | BDL 1000

Ain't Nobody's Bizness If I Do
B.B.King And His Band | Live At San Quentin | MCA | MCD 06103
B.B.King With The Philip Morris Super Band | Live At The Apollo | MCA | MCA 09637
Helen Humes And Her All Stars | On The Sunny Side Of The Street | Black Lion | BLCD 760185
Stan Getz Quintet | Stan Getz-The Complete Roost Sessions | The Jazz Factory | JFCD 22839

Ain't Nobody's Business
Jim Kahr Group | Back To Chicago | Acoustic Music Records | AMC 1027
Billie Holiday With The Mal Waldron Trio | At Monterey 1958 | Black-Hawk | BKH 50701

Ain't Nobody's Business But My Own
Ella Fitzgerald With Louis Jordan And His Tympany Five | Ella:The Legendary American Decca Recordings | GRP | GRP 46482

Ain't Nobody's Business If I Do
Billie Holiday With The Count Basie Orchestra | Birdland All Stars At Carnegie Hall | Roulette | CDP 798660-2

Ain't She Sweet
Benny Green Trio | That's Right! | Blue Note | 784467-2
Erroll Garner Trio | The Erroll Garner Selection | CBS | 471624-2
Jazz Family | New Orleans Stomp | Jazz Family Production | CD 63591
Jimmy Smith Trio | Jimmy Smith Plays Fats Waller | Blue Note | 869943-4
Michael Moore-Bill Charlap | Concord Duo Series Volume Nine | Concord | CCD 4678
Carsten Dahl Trio | Will You Make My Soup Hot & Silver | Storyville | STCD 4203

Ain't Sorry Blues
The Goofus Five | The Goofus Five feat. Adrian Rollini | Timeless | CBC 1-017

Ain't That A Rockin'
Ella Mae Morse With Orchestra | Sensational Ella Mae Morse | Pathe | 1566211

Ain't That Good News
Naylor's Seven Aces | Oliver Naylor 1924-25 | Retrieval | RTR 79008

Ain't That Just Like A Woman
Diane Schuur And Her Band | Talkin' 'Bout You | GRP | GRP 95672

Ain't That Nothin'
Milt Jackson-Ray Brown Quartet | It Don't Mean A Thing If You Can't Tap Your Foot To It | Original Jazz Classics | OJCCD 601-2
Big John Patton Quartet | Blue'n Soul-Do The Jerk | Blue Note | 799105-2

Ain't That Peculiar
George Benson Group/Orchestra | George Benson Anthology | Warner | 8122-79934-2
George Benson Quartet | It's Uptown | CBS | 502469-2
Ramsey Lewis Trio With Orchestra | Ramsey Lewis | Chess | 6.24473 AL

Ain't That Something
Cab Calloway And His Orchestra | Soundtracks And Broadcastings | Jazz Anthology | 550232

Ain't Thinkin' 'Bout It
Lew Del Gatto Septet | Katewalk | Naxos Jazz | 86058-2

Ain't Too Proud To Beg
Mitchell's Jazz Kings | Le Jazz En France Vol.1:Premiers Jazz Bands | Pathe | 1727251

Ain't You A Mess
Champion Jack Dupree Group | Chamion Jack Dupree | EPM Musique | FDC 5504

Air
Alice Coltrane Quintet | Joe Henderson:The Milestone Years | Milestone | 8MCD 4413-2
Bobby Hutcherson Sextet | Components | Blue Note | 829027-2
Dollar Brand | Ancient Africa | Japo | 60005(2360005)
Gabriele Hasler-Roger Hanschel Duo | Pigeon | Jazz Haus Musik | JHM 0120 CD
Guido Mazzon-Umberto Petrin-Tiziano Tononi | Other Line | SPLASC(H) Records | CD H 317-2
Matthias Spillmann Septet | Something About Water | JHM Records | JHM 3620
Mike Richmono-Andy LaVerne | For Us | Steeplechase | SCCD 31101
Papa Bue's Viking Jazzband | Church Concert | Timeless | CD TTD 571

Air Afrique(Wind)
Gary Bartz Quintet | Libra | Milestone | M 9006

Air And Fire
Salvatore Bonafede Trio | Plays | Ken Music | 660.56.017

Air Dancing
Herbie Hancock Quartet | The Herbie Hancock Quartet Live | Jazz Door | JD 1270
Stanley Cowell Trio | We Three | DIW | DIW 8017

Air From Other Planets
Shelly Manne Jazz Quartet | Interpretations | Trend | TR 525 Direct-to-Disc

Air From The Suite In D (Bach)
Rudy Linka Trio | Always Double Czech! | Enja | ENJ-9301 2

Air Mail Special
Allotria Jazz Band | 69-89 Good Times | Elite Special | 30224
Ella Fitzgerald With The Don Abney Trio | Ella Fitzgerald, Billie Holiday And Carmen McRae At Newport | Verve | 559809-2
Jam Session | Coleman Hawkins-Rare Broadcasts Area 1950 | Jazz Anthology | JA 5217
Lionel Hampton And His Orchestra | Lionel Hampton:Flying Home | Dreyfus Jazz Line | FDM 36735-2
Made In Japan | Timeless | CD SJP 175
Lionel Hampton Quartet | Air Mail Special | Verve | MV 2547 IMS
Lionel Hampton Quintet | Hamp's Blues | LRC Records | CDC 7973
Oscar Peterson Quartet | Norman Granz' Jazz At The Philharmonic HARTFORD, 1953 | Pablo | 2308240-2
Thilo Wolf Quartet | I Got Rhythm | MDL-Jazz | CD 1911(CD 050)
Wolfgang Schlüter's Swing Revival | Swing der 30er-40er Jahre | Koala Records | Panda 11(941331)

Air Mail Special(alt.take)
Lionel Hampton And His Orchestra | Jazz Gallery:Lionel Hampton Vol.1 | RCA | 2114170-2

Air On The G String
Jacques Loussier Trio | The Best Of Play Bach | Philips | 824664-2
Jacques Loussier Plays Bach | Telarc Digital | CD 83411
John Scofield Quartet | Rough House | Enja | 3033-2

Air Sculpture
Ornette Coleman & Prime Time Band | Of Human Feelings | Antilles | AN 2001(802385)

Air(cut)
Cecil Taylor Quartet | Cecil Taylor: Air | Candid | CCD 79046

Air(take 21)
Cecil Taylor: Air | Candid | CCD 79046

Air(take 24)
Cecil Taylor: Air | Candid | CCD 79046

Air(take 9)
Klaus Ignatzek Trio | Airballoon | Nabel Records:Jazz Network | CD 4651

Airballoon
Klaus Ignatzek-Martin Wind Duo | Obrigado | Acoustic Music Records | 319.1113.2

Air-Conditioned Jungle
Duke Ellington And His Orchestra | Duke Ellington:Complete Prestige Carnegie Hall 1946-1947 Concerts | Definitive Records | DRCD 11211

Aire De Buenos Aires
Gerry Mulligan/Astor Piazolla Group | Gerry Mulligan/Astor Piazolla 1974 | Accord | 556642

Aire Puro
Andy Fusco Quintet | Big Man's Blues | Double Time Records | DTRCD-116

Airegin
Art Pepper Plus Eleven | Modern Jazz Classics | Original Jazz Classics | OJC20 341-2

TITELVERZEICHNIS

A Treasury Of Modern Jazz Classics | Mobile Fidelity | MFCD 805
Bill Evans-Don Elliott | Tenderly | Milestone | MCD 9317-2
Bill Holman And His Orchestra | The Fabulous Bill Holman | Sackville | 2013
Chet Baker-Stan Getz Quintet | The Stockholm Concerts | Verve | 537555-2
Chris Potter Quartet | Sundiata | Criss Cross | Criss 1107
Eddie Harris Group | Live In Berlin | Timeless | CD SJP 289
Hubert Laws And His Orchestra | In The Beginning | CTI | ZK 65127
Jan Erik Kongshaug Group | The Other World | ACT | 9267-2
John Hicks Trio | I'll Give You Something To Remember Me By... | Limetree | MCD 0023
Lambert, Hendricks And Ross | The Swingers | Blue Note | AFF 131
Miles Davis Quintet | Bags' Groove | Original Jazz Classics | OJC20 245-2
Cookin' With The Miles Davis Quintet | Original Jazz Classics | OJC20 128-2
Peter Leitch Trio | On A Misty Night | Criss Cross | Criss 1026
Stan Getz Quartet | Stan Getz:The Golden Years Vol.2(1958-1961) | Moon Records | MCD 040-2
Tete Montoliu | Words Of Love | Steeplechase | SCCD 31084
Wes Montgomery Quartet | The Incredible Guitar Of Wes Montgomery | Original Jazz Classics | OJC20 036-2
Wes Montgomery-The Complete Riverside Recordings | Riverside | 12 RCD 4408-2
Phil Woods Quartet | At The Vanguard | Antilles | AN 1013(802736)

Air-Lines
Günter Christmann | Off | Moers Music | 01070

Airport Sadness
Bob Brookmeyer New Quartet | Paris Suite | Challenge | CHR 70026

Airwaves
Ray Anderson Alligatory Band | Don't Mow Your Lawn | Enja | ENJ-8070 2
Fra-Fra Sound | Panja-Gazz +4 | Jazz Pure Collection | AU 31619 CD

Aisha
John Coltrane Group | Olé Coltrane | Atlantic | 7567-81349-2
John Coltrane: The Legend 'Ole' | Atlantic | ATL 40286
John Coltrane Sextet | The Art Of John Coltrane - The Atlantic Years | Atlantic | SD 2-313

Aisokey
Karim Ziad Groups | Ifrikya | ACT | 9282-2

Ait Oumrar
Bheki Mseleku Group | Beauty Of Sunrise | Verve | 531868-2

Aka Lotan
Yutaka Yokokura Group | Yutaka | GRP | GRP 95572

Aketé Oba Oba
Klaus Treuheit Trio | Full House | Klaus Treuheit Production | R&M 2-8003

Akicita
Axel Fischbacher Group | Moods | Blue Flame | 40082(2132484-2)

Akira
Horace Tapscott Trio | Horace Tapscott In New York | Interplay | IP 7724

Akkaya
Tome XX | The Red Snapper | Jazz Haus Musik | JHM 0047 CD
Pierre Michelot Orchestra | Jazz In Paris:Pierre Michelot-Round About The Bass | EmArCy | 832309-2 PMS

Akomado(for Babaluaye)
Ronnie Earl & The Broadcasters | Blues And Forgiveness | Crosscut | CCD 11042

Akzente
Renaud Garcia-Fons Quartet | Alboreá | Enja | ENJ-9057 2

Al Camarón
Tanzorchester Der Original Teddies | Teddy Stauffer:Rare And Historical Jazz Recordings | Elite Special | 9522009

Al Hadba(The Hunchback Lady)
Charlie Mariano Trio | Mariano | VeraBra Records | CDVBR 2124-2

Al Hadji
Billy Brooks' El Babaku | Jazz Meets Africa:Noon In Tunisia-El Babaku | MPS | 531720-2

Al Hizam Al Dhahbi
Hanschel-Hübsch-Schipper | Planet Blow Chill | Jazz Haus Musik | JHM 0087 CD

Al Kaphra
Jam Session | Bird's Eyes-Last Unissued Vol.12 | Philology | W 842.2

Al Mal Tiempo Buena Cara
| Box:Billy Tipton Memorial Saxophone Quartet | New World Records | 80495-2

Al Ur
Pedro Iturralde Quintet With Paco De Lucia | Jazz Meets Europe:Flamenco Jazz/From Sticksland With Love | MPS | 531847-2

Alabama
John Coltrane Quartet | The Gentle Side Of John Coltrane | Impulse(MCA) | 951107-2
Coltrane Live At Birdland | MCA | 2292-54654-2
Gregor Hilden-Hans D. Riesop Group | Compared To What...? | Wonderland Records | 319.9014.2

Alabama Concerto(Benson Brooks, 1st movement):
Beryl Bryden And The Louisiana Dandies | Beryl Bryden:Queen Of Blues And Washboard | Elite Special | 72430

Alabama Jubilee
Percy Humphrey's Jazz Band | New Orleans Traditional Jazz Legends:Kid Thomas/Thomas Jefferson/Percy Humphrey | Mardi Gras Records | MG 9003

Alabama Song
Brass Attack | Brecht Songs | Tutu Records | 888190-2*
Dee Dee Bridgewater With Band | This Is New | Verve | 016884-2
Dee Dee Bridgewater Sings Kurt Weil | EmArCy | 9809601
Jugend Jazzorchester Sachsen-Anhalt | Jugend Jazzorchester Sachsen-Anhalt Spielt Kurt Weill | Born&Bellmann | 972806 CD
Rias Big Band Berlin + Strings | Weill | Mons Records | MR 874347

Alabamy Bound
Ken Colyer's Skiffle Group | The Famous Manchester Free Trade Hall Concert | 504 Records | 504CD 50
Quintet Du Hot Club De France | Django/Django In Rome 1949-1050 | BGO Records | BGOCD 366
Santa Pecora & The Tailgaters | Recorded In New Orleans Vol. 2 | Good Time Jazz | GTCD 12020-2
Stephane Grappelli Quintet | Feeling + Finesse = Jazz | Atlantic | 7567-90140-2
Stephane Grappelli-Bucky Pizzarelli Duo | Duet | Ahead | 33755

Aladdin's Lamp
Michal Urbaniak Quartet | Songbird | Steeplechase | SCCD 31278

Alamode
Budd Johnson Quintet | Blues A La Mode | Affinity | AFF 169

Alar
SamulNori | Record Of Changes | CMP Records | CMP CD 3002

Alarm
Polyphonix | Alarm | Jazz 'n' Arts Records | 0300
Marty Grosz & The Collectors Items Cats | Thanks | J&M Records | J&MCD 502

Alas Alert
Koch-Schütz-Studer & El Nil Troop | Heavy Cairo Trafic | Intuition Records | INT 3175-2

Alaschaan Aref Albi Ma'ak
Danny Gottlieb Group | Aquamarine | Atlantic | 781806-1

Alaude
Claudio Lodati Dac'Corda | Voci | SPLASC(H) Records | H 154

Alba-
Mads Vinding Trio | The Kingdom | Stunt Records | STUCD 19703

Albacin-
BBFC | Cherchez L'Erreur | Plainisphare | PL 1267-1

Albatros
Jan Akkerman Group | Puccini's Cafe | Inak | 9027

Albatros Song
Bobby Hackett And His Jazz Band | Gotham Jazz Scene/Big T's Dixieland Band | Dormouse | DMI CDX 03(882985)

Albert Ayler-
Leroy Jenkins Trio | The Legend Of Ai Glatson | Black Saint | BSR 0022

Albert Ayler In A Spiritual Light
Alte Leidenschaften | Alte Leidenschaften | Carsten Hormes Musikverlag | 807446

Alberta
Champion Jack Dupree Group | The Death Of Louis | Vogue | 655502
Leadbelly[Huddie Ledbetter] | Alabama Bound | RCA | ND 90321(847151)

Alberti Y Chile
Brötzmann, van Hove, Bennink + Albert Mangelsdorff | Live In Berlin '71 | FMP | CD 34/35

Albert's Love Theme
Paul Bley Trio | Paul Bley With Gary Peacock | ECM | 1003
Ramblin' | Affinity | AFF 37

Albert's Waltz
Snooks Eaglin / Robert Pete Williams | Rural Blues | Fantasy | F 24716

Albi
Albinia Jones With Don Byas' Swing Seven | Don Byas Complete American Small Group Recordings | Definitive Records | DRCD 11213

Alborada Y Son
Renaud Garcia-Fons Quartet | Alboreá | Enja | ENJ-9057 2

Alboreá
Ragtime Specht Groove Trio | Mr. Woodpeckers Special | Intercord | 130001

Albuquerque Bar Band
Juan Serrano Group | Sabor Flamenco | Concord | CCD 4490

Alcantara
George Duke Orchestra | Save The Country | Pacific Jazz | LN 10127

Alchemy-
Larry Vuckovich Trio | Blues For Red | Hot House Records | HH 1001 IMS

Aldebaran
UMO Jazz Orchestra | UMO Jazz Orchestra | Naxos Jazz | 86010-2

Aldgate East(mend the gap under ground)
Didier Lockwood Quartet + Bob Malach | Fasten Seat Belts | MPS | 68283

Alec Le Temps
Horace Tapscott Quintet | Alee! The Phantom | Arabesque Recordings | AJ 0119

Alegria
Klaus Doldinger & Passport | Lifelike | Warner | 2292-46478-2
Passport | Ataraxia | Atlantic | 2292-42148-2
Carbonell Austin 'Bola' Group | Carmen | Messidor | 15814 CD

Alegrinho(Amarelo)
Egberto Gismonti Group | Musica De Sobrevivencia | ECM | 1509(519706-2)

Alegrinho(No.2)
Astor Piazzolla Y Su Orquesta | Pulsacion | West Wind Latina | 2220 CD

Aleppo
Black Note | Nothin' But Swing | Impulse(MCA) | IMP 11772

Alesia
European Music Orchestra | Guest | Soul Note | 121299-2

Alexander The Great
Parham-Pickett Apollo Syncopators | Alexander Where's That Band?-Paramount Recordings 1926-1928 | Frog | DGF 13

Alexander's Fugue
Swingle Singers With The Modern Jazz Quartet | Place Vendome | Philips | 824545-2 PMS

Alexander's Ragtime Band
Alix Combelle Et Son Orchestre | Le Jazz En France Vol.11:Bill Coleman 1935-1937(Tome 1) | Pathe | 1552571
Benny Goodman And His Orchestra | The Birth Of Swing | Bluebird | ND 90601(3)
Chubby Jackson And His All Star Big Band | Chubby Takes Over | Fresh Sound Records | FSR-CD 324
Cy Coleman Trio | Cy Coleman | Fresh Sound Records | FSR 635(Seeco CELP 402)
Ella Fitzgerald With Paul Weston And His Orchestra | Cheek To Cheek-The Irving Berlin Song Book | Verve | 533829-2
Erroll Garner Trio | The Best Of Erroll Garner | CBS | CBS 52706
Golden Gate Quartet | Spirituals To Swing 1955-69 | EMI Records | 791569-2
Hatchett's Swingtette | Stephane's Tune | Naxos Jazz | 8.120570 CD
Longstreet Jazzband | New York,New York | Elite Special | 73436
Louis Armstrong With Luis Russell And His Orchestra | Louis Armstrong Vol.7-Satchmo's Discoveries | MCA | 1326
Teddy Buckner And The All Stars | Teddy Buckner And The All Stars | Dixieland Jubilee | DJ 507

Alfie
Bill Evans Trio | The Complete Bill Evans On Verve | Verve | 527953-2
Bill Evans:The Secret Sessions | Milestone | 8MCD 4421-2
Live In Paris 1972 Vol.3 | France's Concert | FCD 125
Re: Person I Knew | Original Jazz Classics | OJCCD 749-2(F 9608)
Verve Jazz Masters 5:Bill Evans | Verve | 519821-2
Bill Evans:The Secret Sessions | Milestone | 8MCD 4421-2
Bill Evans-Montreux II | CBS | 481264-2
Jaco Pastorius Group | Live In New York City Volume Three | Big World | BW 1003
Maynard Ferguson Orchestra | Maynard Ferguson Orchestra 1967 | Just A Memory | JAS 9504-2
Sarah Vaughan With The Hal Mooney Orchestra | It's A Man's World | Mercury | 589487-2
Stan Getz With The Richard Evans Orchestra | What The World Needs Now-Stan Getz Plays Bacharach And David | Verve | 557450-2
Stella Levitt With The Jacques Pelzer Quartet | Stella Levitt | Adda | 590066

Alfie(2)
Bill Evans Trio | The Complete Bill Evans On Verve | Verve | 527953-2
Albert Mangelsdorff-John Scofield | Internationales Jazzfestival Münster | Tutu Records | 888110-2*

Alfie's Theme
D-Code | D-Code And Introducing Ben Herman | Timeless | CD SJP 359
Sonny Rollins Quintet | First Moves | Jazz Door | JD 1271

Alfie's Theme Differently
Ignaz Netzer-Dirk Sommer Quartet | Schnappschuss | Jazz Classics | AU 11082

Alfonsina Y El Mar
Gabriel Pérez Group | Alfonsina | Jazz 4 Ever Records:Jazz Network | J4E 4751

Alfonsina Y El Mar-
Alfonsina | Jazz 4 Ever Records:Jazz Network | J4E 4751

Alfonsina Y El Mar(Tema)
Andrew Hill Quartet | Judgment! | Blue Note | 870079-6

Alfred In Wonderland
Jimmy Smith Trio | Jimmy Smith: Grazy Baby | Blue Note | 784030-2

Algebra
Joan Abril Quintet | Eric | Fresh Sound Records | FSNT 092 CD
Keith Jarrett - Jack DeJohnette | Ruta + Daitya | ECM | 1021(513776-2)

Algeria
Henry Red Allen's All Stars | World On A String | RCA | ND 82497847084)

Algo Bueno
Roy Eldridge-Dizzy Gillespie With The Oscar Peterson Quartet | The Complete Verve Roy Eldridge Studio Sessions | Verve | 9861278
Róy And Diz | Verve | 521647-2

Algo Bueno(Woody'n You)
Dizzy Gillespie And His Orchestra | RCA Victor 80th Anniversary Vol.3:1940-1949 | RCA | 2668779-2
Curtis Fuller Quintet | Bone & Bari | Blue Note | 300180(1572)

Al-Hallaj
Kenny Drew Jr. Trio | Third Phase | Jazz City | 660.53.002

Ali And Frazier
Henry Busse And His Shuffle Rhythm Orchestra | The Uncollected:Henry Busse,Vol.2 | Hindsight | HSR 193 (835574)

Ali Shuffle
Paul Desmond Quartet | Bossa Antigua | RCA | 2174795-2

Alianca
Ellery Eskelin + Han Bennink | Dissonant Characters | HatOLOGY | 534

Alice Blue Gown
Muggsy Spanier And His Ragtimers | Commodore Classics-Muggsy Spanier:Nick's New York | Commodore | 6.25494 AG

Alice Blues
Christoph Spendel Trio | Back To Basics | Blue Flame | 40072(2132485-2)

Alice In Wonderland
Bill Evans Trio | Bill Evans:The Secret Sessions | Milestone | 8MCD 4421-2
More From The Vanguard | Milestone | M 9125
Dave Brubeck Quartet | Dave Digs Disney | CBS | 21060
Eddie Gomez-Michael Okun Duo | Live In Moscow | B&W Present | BW 038
John Abercrombie-Marc Johnson-Peter Erskine | John Abercrombie/Marc Johnson/Peter Erskine | ECM | 1390(837756-2)
Mary Fettig Quintet | In Good Company | Concord | CJ 273
Oscar Peterson | Oscar Peterson:Exclusively For My Friends | MPS | 513830-2

Alice In Wonderland(alt.take)
Bill Evans Trio | Sunday At The Village Vanguard | Original Jazz Classics | OJC20 140-2
Al Rapone & The Zydeco Express | Troubled Woman | Traditional Line | TL 1306

Alice My Dear-
Dan Gottshall Group | The Golem Shuffle | Timbre | TRCD 002

Alien Cult
Hans Reichel | Coco Bolo Nights | FMP | CD 10

Alien Prints(For D.Sharpe)
Michael Mantler-Don Preston | Alien | Watt | 15

Alien(part 1-4)
Nils Wogram Quartet | Speed Life | Enja | ENJ-9346 2

Alien's Earworm
Loved By Millions | Loved By Millions | ITM Records | 0011

Alignment
Kahil El'Zabar's The Ritual Trio | Alika Rising | Sound Aspects | sas CD 040

Ali's Nest
Babik Reinhardt Group | Babik Reinhardt-Live | Melodie | 400032

Alison
Joe Pass | Jazz At The Philharmonic:The Montreux Collection | Pablo | PACD 5306-2
Highlights Of The Montreux Jazz Festival 1975 | Pablo | 2625707

Alive
Phil Woods And His European Rhythm Machine | Americans Swinging In Paris:Phil Woods | EMI Records | 539654-2

Alive And Well
Le Jazz En France-Vol.8 | Pathe | 1727321

Alkony
Jazz Orchester Rheinland-Pfalz | Kazzou | Jazz Haus Musik | LJBB 9104

Alkuin
Kölner Saxophon Mafia | Live | Jazz Haus Musik | JHM 12

All
Horace Silver Sextet With Vocals | Horace Silver Retrospective | Blue Note | 495576-2
Ornette Coleman Quartet | Beauty Is A Rare Thing:Ornette Coleman-The Complete Atlantic Recordings | Atlantic | 8122-71410-2
Peter O'Mara Quintet | Back Seat Driver | Enja | 9126-2

All Aboard
Muddy Waters Band | Good News-Muddy Waters, Vol.3 | Red Lightnin' | SC 002

All About Love
Lonnie Plaxico Group | Iridescence | Muse | MCD 5427

All About My Girl
Jimmy McGriff Trio | So Blue So Funky-Heroes Of The Hammond | Blue Note | 796563-2
Pullin' Out The Stops! The Best Of Jimmy McGriff | Blue Note | 830724-2

All About Rosie
George Russell And His Orchestra | Bill Evans:Piano Player | CBS | CK 65361

All About Rosie(3rd Section-alt.take)
Gerry Mulligan Concert Jazz Band | The Complete Verve Gerry Mulligan Concert Band | Verve | 9860613

All About Rosie(part 1&2)
The Complete Verve Gerry Mulligan Concert Band | Verve | 9860613

All About Rosie(part 3)
Michel Bisceglia Quintet | About Stories | RCA | 2153080-2

All Across The City
Bill Evans-Jim Hall | Trio (Motian Peacock)-Duo(Hall) | Verve | 2-2509 IMS
Tony Purrone Quartet | Six-String Delight | Steeplechase | SCCD 31438

All Africa
Max Roach Group | Live In Europe 1964-Freedom Now Suite | Magnetic Records | MRCD 110

All Alone
Richie Kamuca Quartet | Drop Me Off In Harlem | Concord | CJ 39
Tal Farlow Trio | Chromatic Palette | Concord | CCD 4154
Thelonious Monk | Thelonious Monk-The Complete Riverside Recordings | Riverside | 15 RCD 022-2
Howard Alden Trio | Silver Anniversary Set | Concord | CCD 7002

All Along The Sunstream
Peter Herborn Group With The Auryn String Quartet | Something Personal | JMT Edition | 849156-2

All Apologies
Little Milton And His Band | Little Milton | Chess | 427013

All Bird's Children
Phil Woods Quintet | All Bird's Children | Concord | CCD 4441

All Blues
Anthony Braxton-Lee Konitz-Chick Corea Sextet | Woodstock Jazz Festival Vol.2 | Douglas Music | DM 10009
Bob Brookmeyer Quartet | Old Friends | Storyville | STCD 8292
Candid Jazz Masters | The Candid Jazz Masters:For Miles | Candid | CCD 79710
Carsten Dahl Trio | Will You Make My Soup Hot & Silver | Storyville | STCD 4203
Chet Baker Quintet | All Blues | Arco | 3 ARC 102
Chet Baker With The NDR-Bigband | Chet Baker-The Legacy Vol.1 | Enja | ENJ-9021 2
The Last Concert Vol.I+II | Enja | ENJ-6074 22
Christoph Spendel Trio | Back To Basics | Blue Flame | 40072(2132485-2)
Dennis Rowland Group | A Vocal Celebration Of Miles Davis | Concord | CCD 4751
Eric Kloss Quartet | About Time | Prestige | PRCD 24268-2
Ernestine Anderson With Orchestra | Three Ladies Of Jazz:Live In New York | Jazz Door | JD 12102
George Benson Quartet | The Electrifying George Benson | Affinity | AFF 140
Harry Allen And Randy Sandke Meets The RIAS Big Band Berlin | The Music Of The Trumpet Kings | Nagel-Heyer | CD 037
Howard Roberts Quartet | The Real Howard Roberts | Concord | CCD 4053
Jimmy McGriff-Hank Crawford Quartet | Blues Groove | Telarc Digital | CD 83381
Kenny Burrell And The Jazz Heritage All-Stars | Live At The Blue Note | Concord | CCD 4731
Miles Davis Quintet | Greatest Hits | CBS | CK 65418
No (More) Blues | Jazz Door | JD 1224
Miles Davis Sextet | Miles Davis Classics | CBS | CBS 88138
Milt Jackson Quintet | Milt Jackson At The Kosei Nenkin | Pablo | 2620103-2
Monty Alexander Trio | Threesome | Soul Note | 121152-2
Peter Mac Guire Quartet | Midnight | Jazz Pure Collection | AU 31617 CD

Ray Bryant Trio | All Blues | Pablo | 2310820
Ron McClure Quartet | McJolt | Steeplechase | SCCD 31262
Steve Turre Group | Rhythm Within | Verve | 527159-2
Take 6 | Tonight Take 6 | Warner | 9362-47611-2
Terry Smith With The Tony Lee Trio | British Jazz Artists Vol. 2 | Lee Lambert | LAM 002
Warren Vaché Sextet | Horn Of Plenty | Muse | MCD 5524
Willy Vande Walle Quartet | Midnight | Jazz Pure Collection | AU 31617 CD

All Blues(Intro)
The Kenny Clarke-Francy Boland Big Band | Two Originals:Sax No End/All Blues | MPS | 523525-2

All By Myself
Ella Fitzgerald With Paul Weston And His Orchestra | The Complete Ella Fitzgerald Song Books of Harold Arlen, Irving Berlin, Duke Ellington, George & Ira Gershwin, Jerome Kern, Johnny Mercer, Cole Porter And Rogers & Hart | Verve | 519832-2
Memphis Slim And His Band | The Blues Is Everywhere | Vogue | 655503
Memphis Slim With Willie Dixon | Jazz In Paris:Memphis Slim/Willie Dixon Aux Trois Mailletz | EmArCy | 658148 IMS

All By Myself-
Sammy Rimington's New Orleans Quartet | Clarinet King In Norway | Herman Records | HJCD 1001

All Cat's Whiskers And Bee's Knees
Diane Schuur And Her Band | Pure Schuur | GRP | GRP 96282

All Choked Up
Jackie McLean-Dexter Gordon Quintet | The Meeting | Steeplechase | SCCD 31006

All Day Long
Remy Filipovitch Trio | All Day Long | Album | AS 22927
Rusty Bryant Quintet | Rusty Bryant Returns | Original Jazz Classics | OJCCD 331-2(P 7626)
The Prestige All Stars | All Day Long | Prestige | SMJ 6604

All Fall Down
The Meeting | Update | Hip Bop | HIBD 8008

All Feets Can Dance
John Surman-John Warren Group | The Brass Project | ECM | 1478

All For A Shadow
Jimmy Dawkins With Big Voice Odom | All For Business | Delmark | 900207 AO

All For Nothing
Adrian Mears Quintet | All For One | Enja | 9124-2

All For The Love Of Lil
Louis Jordan And His Tympany Five | Five Guys Named Moe | Bandstand | BDCD 1531

All For You
Shankar Trio | Vision | ECM | 1261(811969-2)
Joe Sample Group | Spellbound | Rhino | 81273726-2

All God's Children
Lars Gullin Octet | Lars Gullin 1951/52 Vol.5:First Walk | Dragon | DRCD 380
Stan Getz Quintet | The Great English Concert 1958 | Jazz Groove | JG 007 IMS

All God's Children Got A Home In The Universe
Al Haig Trio | Jazz Will O'-The -Wisp | Fresh Sound Records | FSR-CD 0038

All God's Chillun Got Rhythm
Bud Powell Trio | The Genius Of Bud Powell | Verve | 821690-1
Bud Powell:Complete 1947-1951 Blue Note,Verve & Roost Recordings | The Jazz Factory | JFCD 22837
Bunny Berigan And His Orchestra | The Indispensable Bunny Berigan 1937-1939 | RCA | NL 89744(2) DP
Henri Chaix Trio | Jumpin' Punkins | Sackville | SKCD2-2020
John Colianni Trio With Lew Tabackin | Blues-O-Matic | Concord | CCD 4367
Martial Solal Trio | At Newport '63 | RCA | 2125768-2
Mel Tormé With The George Shearing Duo | An Evening With George Shearing & Mel Torme | Concord | CCD 4190
Sonny Stitt Trio | The Boss Men | Prestige | PCD 24253-2
Sonny Stitt With The Bud Powell Trio | Genesis | Prestige | P 24044
Stan Getz Quartet | Stan Getz In Europe | Laserlight | 24657
The Best Of The Jazz Saxophone | LRC Records | CDC 8520

All God's Chillun Got Rhythm-
Joe Williams And Friends | At Newport '63 | RCA | 2663919-2
Joe Williams And His Band | Planet Jazz:Joe Williams | Planet Jazz | 2165370-2
Uli Wewelsiep And His Quartet | ...My Favourite Stories | Aho-Recording | CD 1002

All God's Chillun Got Rhythm(false start)
Duke Ellington And His Famous Orchestra | The Complete Duke Ellington-Vol. 9 | CBS | CBS 88210

All Heart
Ella Fitzgerald With The Duke Ellington Orchestra | Ella Fitzgerald Sings The Duke Ellington Song Book Vol.2 | Verve | 2615033 IMS

All Heart(Second Movement)
The Complete Ella Fitzgerald Song Books of Harold Arlen, Irving Berlin, Duke Ellington, George & Ira Gershwin, Jerome Kern, Johnny Mercer, Cole Porter And Rogers & Hart | Verve | 519832-2

All I Care
Etta James With Orchestra | Peaches | Chess | 427014

All I Do Is Dream Of You
Bennie Green Quintet | Walkin' And Talkin' | Blue Note | 868296-2
Great British Jazz Band | The Great British Jazz Band:Jubilee | Candid | CCD 79720
Jaye P. Morgan With Marion Evens And His Orchestra | Just You Just Me | Fresh Sound Records | ND 38627
Mick Mulligan's Magnolia Jazz Band | Great British Traditional Bands Vol.7:Mick Mulligan & George Melly | Lake | LACD 66
Ella Fitzgerald With Benny Carter's Magnificent Seven | 30 By Ella | Capitol | 520090-2

All I Do Is Dream Of You-
Benny Goodman Trio | Benny Goodman-The Complete Capitol Trios | Capitol | 521225-2

All I Do Is Dream Of You(II)
Art Kassel And His 'Kassels-In-The-Air' Orchestra | The Uncollected:Art Kassel, Vol.2 | Hindsight | HSR 170

All I Need
Susanne Abbuehl Group | April | ECM | 1766(013999-2)
Errol Dixon with Mickey Baker & The Alex Sanders Funk Time Band | Fighting The Boogie | Bellaphon | BCH 33021

All I Need Is You
John Pizzarelli Group | Let There Be Love | Telarc Digital | CD 83518

All I Touch
Eric Lugosch | Kind Heroes | Acoustic Music Records | 319.1188.2

All I Wanna Ever Do
Martin Schmitt | Handful Of Blues | AH Records | ESM 9303

All I Want
Emborg-Larsen Quintet | Heart Of The Matter | Stunt Records | STUCD 19102
Peter Bolte Trio | Trio | Jazz Haus Musik | JHM 0095 CD
Swim Two Birds | Sweet Reliet | Laika Records | 35101182
HR Big Band With Marjorie Barnes And Frits Landesbergen And Strings | Swinging Christmas | hr music.de | hrmj 012-02 CD

All I Want For Christmas
Osie Johnson And His Orchestra | A Bit Of The Blues | Fresh Sound Records | NL 45989(RCA LPM 1369)

All In Fun
Margaret Whiting With Russel Garcia And His Orchestra | Margaret Whiting Sings The Jerome Kern Song Book | Verve | 559553-2
Mike Wofford Trio | Plays Jerome Kern, Vol. 3 | Discovery | DS 827 IMS

All In Love Is Fair
Carmen McRae with the Cal Tjader Orchestra | Heat Wave | Concord | CCD 4189

All In Time
Cécile Verny Quartet | Métisse | double moon | CHRDM 71010

All Is Gone
Conrad Herwig Sextet | Unseen Universe | Criss Cross | Criss 1194

All Is Real
Gunter Hampel And His Galaxie Dream Band | All Is Real | Birth | 0028
Don Pullen Quintet | The Sixth Sense | Black Saint | 120088-2

All Love
Mel Tormé And His All-Star Quintet | Sing, Sing, Sing | Concord | CCD 4542

All Members
Lee Morgan Quintet | We Remember You | Fresh Sound Records | FSCD 1024

All Morning Long
Red Garland Quintet | John Coltrane-The Prestige Recordings | Prestige | 16 PCD 4405-2
Red Garland Quintet feat.John Coltrane | Jazz Junction | Prestige | P 24023

All My Life
Carroll Gibbons And The Savoy Hotel Orpheans | Brighter Than The Sun | Saville Records | SVL 174 IMS
Frank Wess Sextet | Commodore Classics-Frank Wess:Wess Of The Moon | Commodore | 6.25897 AG
Jay McShann | A Tribute To Fats Waller | Sackville | 3019

All My Love,Always
Erroll Garner | Erroll Garner | Verve | 846191-2 PMS

All My Loving
Wolfgang Muthspiel Group | Loaded, Like New | Amadeo | 527727-2

All My Relations
Dee Bell-Eddie Duran Sextet | One By One | Concord | CJ 271

All My Tomorrows
Carol Kidd With The Sandy Taylor Trio | All My Tomorrows | Linn Records | AKD 005
Mark Murphy And His Orchestra | What A Way To Go | Muse | MCD 5419
Weslia Whitefield With The Mike Greensill Quartet | Teach Me Tonight | HighNote Records | HCD 7009

All Neon Like
Christopher Hollyday Quartet | The Natural Moment | Novus | PD 83118

All Night Long
Kenny Burrell Septet | All Day Long And All Night Long | Prestige | P 24025
Otis Grand Blues Band With Guests | Nothing Else Matters | Sequel Records | NEG CD 272
Sandy Graham And Her Quintet | Sandy Graham | Muse | MCD 5425
Louise Johnson Group | Paramounth Piano Blues Vol.1(1928-1932) | Black Swan Records | HCD-12011

All Night Through
Klaus Weiss Trio | L.A.Calling | L+R Records | CDLR 45033

All Of A Sudden My Heart Sings
Duke Ellington And His Orchestra | Duke Ellington:The Complete RCA-Victor Mid-Forties Recordings(1944-1946) | RCA | 2663394-2
Erroll Garner Trio | Contrasts | Verve | 558077-2
Frances Faye With The Russ Garcia Orchestra | I'm Wild Again | Fresh Sound Records | FSR 2031(Bethlehem BCP 23)
Rebecca Coupe Franks Group | All Of A Sudden | Justice Records | JR 0902-2

All Of Me
Adam Makowicz Quintet | Moonray | RCA | PL 83003
Billie Holiday With Eddie Heywood And His Orchestra | Billie Holiday 'Control Booth' Series,Vol.1(1940-41) | Jazz Unlimited | JUCD 2014
Billie Holiday With The Carl Drinkard Trio | Misty Blue:Sweet Sisters Swing Songs Of Sorrow And Sadness | Blue Note | 521151-2
Billie Holiday With The Count Basie Orchestra | Birdland All Stars At Carnegie Hall | Roulette | CDP 798660-2
Billie Holiday With The JATP All Stars | The Complete Jazz At The Philharmonic On Verve 1944-1949 | Verve | 523893-2
Billie Holiday Story Vol.1:Jazz At The Philharmonic | Verve | 521642-2
Billie Holiday With The Ray Ellis Orchestra | Billie Holiday-Her Last Recordings | Jazz Magazine | 40197
Bireli Lagrene Ensemble | Routes To Django & Bireli Swing '81 | Jazzpoint | JP 1055 CD
Bob Wallis Storyville Jazzmen | Best Of British Jazz From The BBC Jazz Club Vol.1 | Upbeat Jazz | URCD 118
Dee Dee Pierce And His New Orleans Stompers | In Binghampton,N.Y. Vol.Three | American Music | AMCD-81
Dinah Washington With The Terry Gibbs Band | Verve Jazz Masters 40:Dinah Washington | Verve | 522055-2
Dinah Washington With The Urbie Green Sextet | Newport Jazz Festival 1958,July 3rd-6th Vol.2:Mulligan The Main Man | Phontastic | NCD 8814
Django Reinhardt And The Quintet Du Hot Club De France | Django Reinhardt:Djangology | EMI Records | 780659-2
Duke Ellington And His Orchestra | Live | Affinity | AFF 28
Live At Click Restaurant Philadelphia 1949-Vol.4 | Raretone | 5005 FC
Florian Bührich Quintet | endlich Jazz...? | Jazz 4 Ever Records:Jazz Network | J4E 4764
Frank Sinatra With The Count Basie Orchestra | You Make Me Fee So Young:Sinatra At The Sands | Traditional Line | TL 1348
Frankie Laine With Carl Fischer And His Orchestra | The Uncollected:Frankie Laine | Hindsight | HSR 198 (835569)
George Benson Quartet + Guests | The George Benson Cookbook | CBS | 502470-2
George Paxton And His Orchestra | The Uncollected:George Paxton | Hindsight | HSR 183
Hal Schaefer | Solo, Duo, Trio | Discovery | DSCD 975(889499)
Helen Merrill And Her Band | You And The Night And The Music | Verve | 537087-2
JATP All Stars | Jazz Gallery:Billie Holiday Vol.1(1933-49) | RCA | 2119542-2
Jenny Evans And Her Quintet | Shiny Stockings | Enja | ENJ-9317 2
Jimmy Dorsey And His Orchestra | The Uncollected:Jimmy Dorsey, Vol.3 | Hindsight | HSR 165
John Crocker Quartet | All Of Me | Timeless | CD TTD 585
Johnny Hodges With The Al Waslon Trio | A Man And His Music | Storyville | SLP 4073
King Pleasure And His Band | King Pleasure Golden Days | Fresh Sound Records | FSR-CD 0108
Lajos Dudas Quintet | Nightlight | double moon | DMCHR 71030
Lars Gullin Quartet | Lars Gullin 1955/56 Vol.1 | Dragon | DRCD 224
Lee Konitz Quartet | Inside Hi-Fi | Rhino | 790669-1
Lee Konitz Trio | Motion | Verve | 557107-2
Lester Young Quartet | Verve Jazz Masters 30:Lester Young | Verve | 521859-2
Pres And Teddy And Oscar | Verve | 2-2502 IMS
Louis Armstrong And His All Stars | Greatest Hits | CBS | 21058
Ambassador Satch | CBS | CK 64926
Louis Armstrong And His Orchestra | This Is Jazz:Louis Armstrong Sings | CBS | CK 65039
Magnificant Seventh's with Milton Batiste And Alton Carson | Best Of Bourbon Street Jazz | Mardi Gras Records | MG 1009
Nat Gonella's Georgia Jazz Band | Runnin' Wild | Harlequin | HQ 3003 IMS
Oscar Klein's Anniversary Band | Moonglow | Nagel-Heyer | CD 021
Oscar Peterson Trio | A Jazz Portrait Of Frank Sinatra | Verve | 825769-2
Peanuts Hucko Sextet | Tribute To Louis Armstrong And Benny Goodman | Timeless | TTD 541/42
Roy Eldridge And The Jimmy Ryan All Stars | Little Jazz And The Jimmy Ryan All-Stars | Original Jazz Classics | OJCCD 1058-2(DRE 1001)
Roy Eldridge Quartet | The Best Of Roy Eldridge | Pablo | 2310857
Sarah Vaughan And Her Trio | The Complete Sarah Vaughan Live In Japan | Mobile Fidelity | MFCD 844-2
Sarah Vaughan With The Jimmy Jones Trio | Linger Awhile | Pablo | 2312144-2
Scott Hamilton Quartet | The Great Appearance | Progressive | PCD 7026
Stephane Grappelli Quartet With Phil Woods | Stephane Grappelli | Jazz Classics | AU 36017 CD
Thilo Wolf Big Band | Mr. Grooverix | MDL-Jazz | CD 1925(CD 053)
Willie Lewis And His Entertainers | Le Jazz En France Vol.3 | Pathe | 1727271

All Of My Love
Lee Konitz Trio | Another Shade Of Blue | Blue Note | 498222-2

All Of Us
Meredith d'Ambrosio | Another Time | Sunnyside | SSC 1017 D

All Of You
Bill Evans | The Complete Fantasy Recordings | Fantasy | 9FCD 1012-2
Eloquence | Fantasy | F 9618
Bill Evans Quintet | Summertime | Jazz City | 660.53.018
Bill Evans Trio | Bill Evans:The Complete Live At The Village Vanguard 1961 | Riverside | 3RCD 1961-2
Live In Stockholm 1965 | Royal Jazz | RJD 519
The Legendary Bill Evans Trio-The Legendary 1960 Birdland Sessions | Cool & Blue | C&B-CD 106
More From The Vanguard | Milestone | M 9125
Conte Candoli-Carl Fontana Quintet | The Complete Phoenix Recordings Vol.4 | Woofy Productions | WPCD 124
Denny Zeitlin-David Friesen Duo | Concord Duo Series Volume Eight | Concord | CCD 4639
Ella Fitzgerald With The Buddy Bregman Orchestra | The Complete Ella Fitzgerald Song Books of Harold Arlen, Irving Berlin, Duke Ellington, George & Ira Gershwin, Jerome Kern, Johnny Mercer, Cole Porter And Rogers & Hart | Verve | 519832-2
Ernie Wilkins And His Orchestra | Here Comes The Swingin' Mr.Wilkins | Fresh Sound Records | FSR 511(Everest LPBR 5077)
Hendrik Meurkens Quintet | Slidin' | Concord | CCD 4628
Joe Locke Quintet | Present Tense | Steeplechase | SCCD 31257
Keith Jarrett Trio | Standards In Norway | ECM | 1542(521717-2)
Kenny Burrell Quintet | Kenny Burrell | Original Jazz Classics | OJCCD 019-2(P 7088)
Larry Willis Trio | How Do You Keep The Music Playing? | Steeplechase | SCCD 31312
Mary Fettig Quintet | In Good Company | Concord | CJ 273
Michael Cochrane Trio | Gesture Of Faith | Steeplechase | SCCD 31459
Miles Davis Quintet | Round About Midnight | CBS | 460605-2
Live In Stockholm | Dragon | DRCD 228
The Miles Davis Selection | CBS | 465699-2
Miles Davis In Stockholm Complete | Dragon | DRCD 228
Modern Jazz Quartet | The Complete Modern Jazz Quartet Prestige & Pablo Recordings | Prestige | 4PRCD 4438-2
The Jazz Giants Play Cole Porter:Night And Day | Prestige | PCD 24203-2
Modern Jazz Quartet | Prestige | P 24005
Phineas Newborn Jr. Quartet | Stockholm Jam Session Vol.1 | Steeplechase | SCCD 36025
Stan Kenton And His Orchestra | Stan Kenton At Ukiah 1959 | Status | CD 109(882969)
Thilo Wagner Trio | Wagner,Mörike.Beck,Finally. | Nagel-Heyer | CD 078
Tiziana Ghiglioni With The Kenny Drew Trio | Sounds Of Love | Soul Note | SN 1056

All Of You(alt.take)
Bill Evans Trio | Bill Evans:The Complete Live At The Village Vanguard 1961 | Riverside | 3RCD 1961-2
Sunday At The Village Vanguard | Original Jazz Classics | OJC20 140-2
Guido Mazzon-Umberto Petrin-Tiziano Tononi | Other Line | SPLASC(H) Records | CD H 317-2

All One Can Get
Dinah Washington With Lucky Thompson And His All Stars | The Complete Dinah Washington Vol.1 | Official | 3004

All Or Nothing
Leni Stern Group | Closer To The Light | Enja | ENJ-6034 2
Al Jarreau With Band | Heart's Horizon | i.e. Music | 557851-2

All Or Nothing At All
André Holst With Chris Dean's European Swing Orchestra | That's Swing | Nagel-Heyer | CD 079
Anthony Ortega Trio | Scattered Clouds | HatOLOGY | 555
Bob Cooper And His Orchestra | Shifting Winds | Affinity | AFF 59
Diana Krall Trio | Love Scenes | Impulse(MCA) | 951234-2
Don Braden Quartet | The Fire Within | RCA | 2663297-2
Frances Wayne With Neal Hefti And His Orchestra | Songs For My Man | Fresh Sound Records | LSP 15822(Epic LN 3222)
George Cables Trio | I Mean You | Steeplechase | SCCD 31334
Harry James And His Orchestra | Welcome To Jazz: Harry James | Koch Records | 321 983 D1
Jack Teagarden And His Orchestra | Jack Teagarden 1943 | Queen-Disc | 040
John Coltrane Quartet | Ballads | Impulse(MCA) | MCD 05885
John Coltrane:The Classic Quartet-Complete Impulse Studio Recordings | Impulse(MCA) | 951280-2
John Coltrane:Standards | Impulse(MCA) | 549914-2
Johnny Pace With The Chet Baker Quintet | Chet Baker Introduces Johnny Pace | Original Jazz Classics | OJCCD 433-2(RLP 12-292)
Kurt Rosenwinkel Trio | East Coast Love Affair | Fresh Sound Records | FSNT 016 CD
Mark Turner Quartet | Ballad Session | Warner | 9362-47631-2
Meredith d'Ambrosia With The Eddie Higgins Trio | Love Is Not A Game | Sunnyside | SSC 1051 D
Niels Lan Doky Quartet | Daybreak | Storyville | STCD 4160
Sarah Vaughan Plus Two | Sarah + 2 | Fresh Sound Records | FSR 605(Roulette R 52118)
Stan Kenton And His Orchestra | Two Much | Creative World | ST 1067
Wayne Shorter Quintet | Wayning Moments | Vee Jay Recordings | VJ 014

All Or Nothing At All(alt.take)
Wayning Moments | Vee Jay Recordings | VJ 014

All Right Be That Way
Jacques Stotzem | Clear Night | Acoustic Music Records | AMC 1013

All Soul
Mark Nauseef/Miroslav Tadic Group | The Snake Music | CMP Records | CMP CD 60

All Star
Barney Kessel With The Monty Alexander Trio | Spontaneous Combustion | Contemporary | C 14033

All Sweets
Klaus Ignatzek Quintet | All Systems Go | Candid | CCD 79738

All That Dust
Mildred Bailey With The Eddie Sauter Orchestra | Me And The Blues | Savoy | SV 0200(MG 6032)

All That Jazz
Mel Tormé With The Mort Garson Orchestra | Grandes Voix Du Jazz | CBS | 467147-2

All That Matters
Fats Waller And His Rhythm | The Last Years 1940-1943 | Bluebird | ND 90411(3)

All That Meat And No Potatoes
Lennie Baldwin's Dauphin Street Six | The Golden Years Of Revival Jazz.Vol.3 | Storyville | STCD 5508
Louis Armstrong And His All Stars | Satch Plays Fats(Complete) | CBS | CK 64927
The Louis Armstrong Selection | CBS | 467278-2

All The Cats Join In
The Buck Clayton Legacy | Encore Live | Nagel-Heyer | CD 018
Stanley Jordan | Magic Touch | Blue Note | 746092-2

All The Children
Helmut Kagerer-Peter Bernstein Quartet | April In New York | Jardis Records | JRCD 9818

All The Chords I Know
Jazz Guitar Highlights 1 | Jardis Records | JRCD 20141
Stephen Scott Sextet | Something To Consider | Verve | 849557-2

All The Girls Go Crazy
Chris Barber's Jazz And Blues Band | 40 Years Jubilee | Timeless | CD TTD 589
Mr.Acker Bilk And His Paramount Jazz Band | New Orleans Days | Lake | LACD 36

TITELVERZEICHNIS

The Stable Roof Jazzband | From New Orleans To Amsterdam | Timeless | CD TTD 578

All The Girls Go Crazy About The Way I Walk

Monty Sunshine's Jazz Band | Best Of British Jazz From The BBC Jazz Club Vol.5 | Upbeat Jazz | URCD 125

All The Love

Lester Bowie Group | All The Magic! | ECM | 1246/47

All The Rest Is The Same

Steve Rochinski-Jim Stinnett | Otherwise | Jardis Records | JRCD 20133

All The Shirts I Own

Tom Mega + Band | Backyards Of Pleasure | ITM Records | ITM 1432

All The Strings You Are

Bobby Bradford With The Frank Sullivan Trio | Bobby Bradford Live:One Night Stand | Soul Note | 121168-2

All The Things You Ain't

Jimmy Dorsey And His Orchestra | The Uncollected:Jimmy Dorsey, Vol.2 | Hindsight | HSR 153

All The Things You Are

Al Porcino Big Band | In Oblivion | Jazz Mark | 106 Digital
Art Pepper-Shorty Rogers Quintet | Art Pepper & Shorty Rogers:Complete Lighthouse Sessions | The Jazz Factory | JFCD 22836
Art Tatum | Art Tatum-The Complete Pablo Solo Masterpieces | Pablo | 7 PACD 4404-2
The Tatum Solo Masterpieces Vol. 3 | Pablo | 2310730
Art Tatum-Ben Webster Quartet | The Tatum Group Masterpieces Vol.8 | Pablo | PACD20 431-2
Art Tatum-The Complete Pablo Group Masterpieces | Pablo | 6 PACD 4401-2
The Tatum Group Masterpieces | Pablo | 2310737-2
Art Van Damme Group | State Of Art | MPS | 841413-2
Artie Shaw And His Orchestra | This Is Artie Shaw | RCA | NL 89411 DP
Baden Powell Trio | Poema On Guitar | MPS | 68089
Benny Carter Quartet | Cookin' At Carlos I | Musicmasters | 5033-2
Bill Evans Trio | The Complete Fantasy Recordings | Fantasy | 9FCD 1012-2
Bill Evans/Hank Jones/Red Mitchell | Moods Unlimited | Paddle Wheel | KICJ 65
Billy Butterfield And His Orchestra | The Uncollected:Billy Butterfield | Hindsight | HSR 173
Bireli Lagrene Quartet | Acoustic Moments | Blue Note | 795263-2
Brad Mehldau Trio | Art Of The Trio Vol.4: Back At The Vanguard | Warner | 9362-47463-2
Bruce Forman Quartet With Bobby Hutcherson | There Are Times | Concord | CCD 4332
Carmen McRae And Her Quintet | Velvet Soul | LRC Records | CDC 7970
Charlie Parker And The Swedish All Stars | Complete Bird In Sweden | Definitive Records | DRCD 11216
Chet Baker Quartet | The Best Of Chet Baker Plays | Pacific Jazz | 797161-2
Chet Baker Quintet | Out Of Nowhere | Milestone | MCD 9191-2
Connie Crothers Trio | Perception | Steeplechase | SCCD 31022
Dave Brubeck Quartet | Jazz At The College Of The Pacific | Original Jazz Classics | OJC20 047-2(F 3223)
The Dave Brubeck Quartet feat. Paul Desmond In Concert | Fantasy | FCD 60-013
Stardust | Fantasy | FCD 24728-2
Dave Liebman Quintet | Return Of The Tenor:Standards | Double Time Records | DTRCD-109
Dieter Fischer Trio | Trio Music | Jardis Records | JRCD 9925
Dizzy Gillespie Big Band | Bird's Eyes-Last Unissued Vol.13 | Philology | W 843.2
Dizzy Gillespie Sextet | In The Beginning | Prestige | P 24030
Don Friedman | Avenue Of The Americas | Owl Records | 019
Duke Ellington And His Orchestra | Happy Birthday Duke Vol.3 | Laserlight | 15785
Ella Fitzgerald With The Nelson Riddle Orchestra | Love Songs:The Best Of The Song Books | Verve | 531762-2
The Complete Ella Fitzgerald Song Books of Harold Arlen, Irving Berlin, Duke Ellington, George & Ira Gershwin, Jerome Kern, Johnny Mercer, Cole Porter And Rogers & Hart | Verve | 519832-2
Gerry Mulligan Quartet | Reunion With Chet Baker | Blue Note | 746857-2
Gonzalo Rubalcaba Trio | Discovery-Live At Montreux | Blue Note | 795478-2
Greetje Kauffeld With The Metropole Orchestra | My Favorite Ballads | Koch Jazz | 3-6902-2
Hampton Hawes Trio | Hampton Hawes Trio Vol.1 | Original Jazz Classics | OJC20 316-2(C 3505)
Hank Garland Group | Jazz Winds From New Directions | CBS | 492532-2
Jerry Wiggins Trio | The Piano Collection Vol.1 | Vogue | 21610242
Jimmy Heath Quintet | On The Trail | Original Jazz Classics | OJCCD 1854-2
Jimmy Smith | The Sounds Of Jimmy Smith | Blue Note | 300158(1556)
Joe Albany-Warne Marsh Trio | The Right Combination | Original Jazz Classics | OJCCD 1749-2
Joe Henderson With The Keith Greko Trio | Last Train Outta Flagstaff | Concept | VL 4 IMS
Joe Pass | Solo Guitar | Pablo | 2310974-2
Joe Pass:A Man And His Guitar | Original Jazz Classics | OJCCD 8806-2
Joe Pass:A Man And His Guitar | Original Jazz Classics | OJCCD 8806-2
Live At Long Beach City College | Pablo | 2308239-2
Junior Mance | Jubilation | Sackville | SKCD2-2046
Keith Jarrett Trio | Tribute | ECM | 1420/21
Kenny Werner Trio | Live At Visiones | Concord | CCD 4675
Lanfranco Malaguti/Enzo Pietropaoli/Fabrizio Sferra | Sound Investigations | SPLASC(H) Records | H 143
Lars Gullin Quartet | Made In Sweden Vol.2: 24.3.1951-12.12.1952 | Magnetic Records | MRCD 113
Lee Konitz & The Gerry Mulligan Quartet | Konitz Meets Mulligan | Pacific Jazz | 746847-2
Lee Konitz Quintet | The Saxophon Collection | Vogue | 21610232
Lennie Tristano Quartet | That's Jazz Vol.15: Lennie Tristano | Atlantic | ATL 50245
Liz Story/Joel DiBartolo | My Foolish Heart | Windham Hill | 34 11115-2
Louis Armstrong And His All Stars | Historic Barcelona Concerts At Windsor Palace 1955 | Fresh Sound Records | FSR-CD 3004
Margaret Whiting With Russel Garcia And His Orchestra | Margaret Whiting Sings The Jerome Kern Song Book | Verve | 559553-2
Marion McPartland Trio | Great Britain's | Savoy | SV 0160(MG 12016)
Massimo Urbani-Mike Melillo | Duet Improvisations For Yardbird | Philology | 214 W 4
Michel Petrucciani Trio | Michel Petrucciani:Concert Inédits | Dreyfus Jazz Line | FDM 36607-2
Modern Jazz Quartet | The Complete Modern Jazz Quartet Prestige & Pablo Recordings | Prestige | 4PRCD 4438-2
Modern Jazz Quartet | Prestige | P 24005
The MJQ Box | Prestige | 7711-2
Oscar Peterson-Ray Brown Duo | Oscar Peterson:Get Happy | Dreyfus Jazz Line | FDM 36738-2
Tenderly | Verve | MV 2662 IMS
Oscar Pettiford Quartet | Vienna Blues:The Complete Session | Black Lion | BLCD 760104
Paul Bley Quartet | Rejoicing | Steeplechase | SCCD 31274
Paul Desmond-Gerry Mulligan Quartet | RCA Victor 80th Anniversary Vol.5:1960-1969 | RCA | 2668781-2
Paul Desmond-Greatest Hits | RCA | CL 89809 SF
The Ballad Of Paul Desmond | RCA | 21429372
Victor Jazz History Vol.13:Modern Jazz-Cool & West Coast | RCA | 2135732-2
Peter Fessler Quartet | Foot Prints | Minor Music | 801058
Phil Woods Quartet | Ornithology:Phil Salutes Bird | Philology | W 69.2
Quintet Of The Year | The Quintet-Jazz At Massey Hall | Original Jazz Classics | OJC20 044-2
The Quintet-Jazz At Massey Hall | Debut | DSA 124-6
Charlie Parker The Immortal Sessions Vol.2:1949-1953 | SAGA Jazz Classics | EC 3319-2
Red Rodney Sextet | Home Free | Muse | MR 5135
Rene Thomas Trio | Guitar Genius | RTBF Records | 16001
Ron Carter-Jim Hall Duo | Live At Village West | Concord | CJ 245
Sarah Vaughan And The Count Basie Orchestra | Sarah Vaughan Birthday Celebration | Fantasy | FANCD 6090-2
Send In The Clowns | Pablo | 2312130-2
Schnuckenack Reinhardt Quintet | 15.3.1973 | Intercord | 160031
Shirley Scott Trio | Skylark | Candid | CCD 79705
Sidney Bechet With The Martial Solal Trio | Sidney Bechet | Vogue | 000001 GK
Singers Unlimited | The Singers Unlimited:Magic Voices | MPS | 539130-2
A Capella III | MPS | 68245
Sonny Rollins Trio | Jazz Profile:Sonny Rollins | Blue Note | 823516-2
Sonny Rollins-Coleman Hawkins Quintet | The Complete Sonny Rollins RCA Victor Recordings | RCA | 2668675-2
Sonny Stitt Quintet | The Champ | 32 Jazz | 32084
The Page Cavanaugh Trio | The Digital Page | Star Line Productions | SLCD 9001(875581)
Thelonious Monk Quartet | Monk's Mood | Naxos Jazz | 8.120588 CD
Thelonious Monk:Complete 1947-1952 Blue Note Recordings | The Jazz Factory | JFCD 22838
Thomas Clausen-Pyysalo Severi | Turn Out The Stars | Storyville | STCD 4215
Traubeli Weiß Ensemble | Dreaming Of You | Edition Collage | EC 468-2
Tyrone Brown String Sextet | Song Of The Sun | Naxos Jazz | 86038-2
Wes Montgomery Quartet | Fingerpickin' | Pacific Jazz | 837987-2

All The Things You Are-

Bill Evans | Alone | Verve | 598319-2
Cecil Payne Quintet | Bird Gets The Worm | Muse | MR 5061
Norman Granz Jam Session | Bird: The Complete Charlie Parker On Verve | Verve | 837141-2
Charlie Parker Jam Session | Verve | 833564-2 PMS
Toto Blanke-Rudolf Dasek | Two Much Guitar! | ALISO Records | AL 1022
Charles Mingus Quintet | Mingus At The Bohemia | Debut | VIJ 5010 IMS

All The Things You Are In C Sharp Minor

Mingus At The Bohemia | Original Jazz Classics | OJC20 045-2

All The Things You Are In C Sharp Minor(alt.take)

Art Pepper-Warne Marsh Quintet | The Way It Is | Original Jazz Classics | OJCCD 389-2

All The Things You Are(alt.take)

Bobby Jaspar Quartet | Bobby Jaspar & His Modern Jazz | Vogue | 21559512

All The Things You Are(take 1)

Lee Konitz Quintet | Lee Konitz/Bob Brookmeyer:Quintets | Vogue | 2111503-2

All The Things You Are(take 2)

Lee Konitz/Bob Brookmeyer:Quintets | Vogue | 2111503-2

All The Things You Are(take 5)

Charles Mingus Quintet | Charles Mingus-The Complete Debut Recordings | Debut | 12 DCD 4402-2

All The Things You C

Charles Mingus-The Complete Debut Recordings | Debut | 12 DCD 4402-2

All The Things You C(alt.take)

Charles Mingus Quartet | Charles Mingus Presents Charles Mingus | Candid | CCD 79005

All The Things You Could Be By Now If Sigmund Freud's Wife Was Your Mother

Gunter Hampel And His Galaxie Dream Band | All The Things You Could Be If Charles Mingus Was Your Daddy | Birth | CD 031

All The Things You Could Be If Charles Mingus Was Your Daddy

Gunter Hampel Quintet | Legendary: The 27th Of May 1997 | Birth | CD 045
Andy Lumpp | Dreamin' Man | Nabel Records:Jazz Network | CD 4662

All The Things You Where

Coleman Hawkins With The Frank Hunter Orchestra | Hawk Talk | Fresh Sound Records | FSR-CD 0130

All The Way

Billie Holiday With The Ray Ellis Orchestra | Last Recordings | Verve | 835370-2 PMS
Eddie Boyd Blues Band | Five Long Years | L+R Records | CDLR 72009
Herbie Nichols Trio | The Bethlehem Session | Affinity | AFF 759
Oliver Nelson Quintet | The Jazz Giants Play Sammy Cahn:It's Magic | Prestige | PCD 24226-2
Taking Care Of Business | Original Jazz Classics | OJCCD 1784-2(NJ 8233)
Uri Caine | Solitaire | Winter&Winter | 910075-2
Vince Jones Group | Tell Me A Secret | Intuition Records | INT 3072-2
Wes Montgomery With Orchestra | Pretty Blue | Milestone | M 47030
Toots Thielemans-Kenny Werner Duo | Toots Thielemans & Kenny Werner | EmArCy | 014722-2

All The Way-

Albert King Blues Band | The Lost Session | Stax | SCD 8534-2

All The Way Down

Etta James & The Roots Band | Burnin' Down he House | RCA | 3411633-2
Louie Bellson Septet | Louie Bellson Jam | Original Jazz Classics | OJCCD 802-2(2310838)

All The Way Home-

| All The Way To Sendai | Enja | ENJ-6030 2

All The Wrongs You've Done To Me

Eva Taylor With Clarence Williams' Blue Five | Louis Armstrong And The Blues Singers 1924-1930 | Affinity | AFS 1018(6)

All Them Chicken

Joe Henderson And His Orchestra | Canyon Lady | Milestone | M 9057

All Things Considered

Los Angeles Jazz Quartet | Conversation Piece | Naxos Jazz | 86045-2

All This And Heaven Too

Frank Sinatra With The Tommy Dorsey Orchestra | The Popular Sinatra Vol.1 | RCA | 2668711-2

All This Could Lead To Love

Charles Lloyd-Billy Higgins | Which Way Is East | ECM | 1878/79(9811796)

All This Is That

Henry Johnson Group | Missing You | Inak | 30292

All Through The Day

Barbara Lea And The Legendary Lawson-Haggart Jazz Band | You're The Cats! | Audiophile | ACD-252

All Through The Night

Deborah Henson-Conant | Naked Music | Laika Records | LK 94-051
Dick Hyman | Cole Porter:All Through The Night | Musicmasters | 5060-2
Ella Fitzgerald With The Buddy Bregman Orchestra | The Complete Ella Fitzgerald Song Books of Harold Arlen, Irving Berlin, Duke Ellington, George & Ira Gershwin, Jerome Kern, Johnny Mercer, Cole Porter And Rogers & Hart | Verve | 519832-2
Kenny Clarke-Francy Boland Big Band | En Concert Avec Europe 1 | Laserlight | 710413/14
Phil Woods Quartet | The Macerata Concert | Philology | 214 W 1/2/3

All Through The Night-

S.E.M. Ensemble | Virtuosity With Purpose | Ear-Rational | ECD 1034

All Too Soon

Bennie Wallace Quintet | The Art Of The Saxophone | Denon Compact Disc | CY-1648
Buddy Tate Quintet feat.Clark Terry | Tate-A-Tate | Original Jazz Classics | OJC 184(SV 2014)
Duke Ellington And His Famous Orchestra | Three Great Swing Saxophones | RCA | NL 90405
Duke Ellington:Ko-Ko | Dreyfus Jazz Line | FDM 36717-2
Ben Webster-Cotton Tail | RCA | 63667902
Jazz:The Essential Collection Vol.3 | IN+OUT Records | 78013-2
In A Mellow Tone | RCA | 2113029-2
Duke Ellington And His Orchestra | Welcome To Jazz: Duke Ellington | Koch Records | 321 943 D1
Duke Ellington-Count Basie | CBS | 473753-2
Duke Ellington Small Band | The Intimacy Of The Blues | Original Jazz Classics | OJCCD 624-2
Duke Ellington Trio | Piano Reflections | Capitol | 792863-2
Ella Fitzgerald With The Duke Ellington Orchestra | Ella Fitzgerald Sings The Duke Ellington Song Book Vol.2 | Verve | 2615033 IMS
Love Songs:The Best Of The Song Books | Verve | 531762-2
The Complete Ella Fitzgerald Song Books of Harold Arlen, Irving Berlin, Duke Ellington, George & Ira Gershwin, Jerome Kern, Johnny Mercer, Cole Porter And Rogers & Hart | Verve | 519832-2
Freddy Cole With Band | A Circle Of Love | Fantasy | FCD 9674-2
George Shearing And His Quintet With Peggy Lee | Beauty And The Beat | Pathe | EMS 1158(Capitol ST 1219)
Pee Wee Russell-Coleman Hawkins Septet | Jazz Reunion | Candid | CS 9020
Peter Leitch Trio | Trio/Quartet '91 | Concord | CCD 4480
Scott Hamilton Quintet | The Second Set | Concord | CCD 4254
Charles Mingus And His Orchestra | Mingus At Monterey | Prestige | P 24100

All Walks Of Life

Keith Jarrett - Jack DeJohnette | Ruta + Daitya | ECM | 1021(513776-2)

All We Got

Gigi Gryce-Clifford Brown Octet | Clifford Brown:The Complete Paris Sessions Vol.3 | Vogue | 21457302

All Your Love

Al Jones Blues Band | Watch This! | Blues Beacon | BLU-1024 2

All Yours

Lars Gullin Quartet | Made In Sweden Vol.1: 1949 to March 1951 | Magnetic Records | MRCD 106

Alla

Dave Brubeck Sextet | Bravo! Brubeck! | CBS | CK 65723

Alla En El Rancho Grande

Tommy Dorsey And His Clambake Seven | Having Wonderful Time | RCA | 2121824-2

Alle Jahre Wieder

Mark Shane's X-Mas Allstars | What Would Santa Say? | Nagel-Heyer | CD 055

Alle Jahre Wieder-

Joe Kienemann Trio | Liedgut:Amsel,Drossel,Swing & Funk | yvp music | CD 3095

Alle Vögel Sind Schon Da

Albert Mangelsdorff-Lee Konitz | Albert Mangelsdorff And His Friends | MPS | 067375-2

Al-Lee

Ron Carter-Richard Galliano Duo | Panamanhattan | fnac Muisc | 662015

Allée Des Brouillards

Gary Peacock Quartet | Voice From The Past-Paradigm | ECM | 1210(517768-2)

Allegory

Klaus Doldinger's Passport | Oceanliner | Warner | 2292-46479-2
Bishop Norman Williams Group | One For Bird | Evidence | TR 105

Allegretto-

Maarten Van Regteren | Live Performances | FMP | SAJ 10

Allegretto Grazioso(Mozart:Klaviersonate B-Dur)

Astor Piazzolla With Orchestra Of St. Luke's | Concierto Para Bandoneon-Tres Tangos | Nonesuch | 7559-79174-2

Allegretto Molto Marcato-

Tamia/Pierre Favre | Solitudes | ECM | 1446

Allegria

Positive Knowledge | Invocation No.9 | Music & Arts | CD 909

Allegro

John Zorn Group | Cobra | Hat Art | CD 6040(2)
Paolo Damiani Quintet | Poor Memory | SPLASC(H) Records | HP 07

Allegro-

Jacques Loussier Trio | Reflections Of Bach | Teldec | 2292-44431-2
Play Bach Aux Champs-Élyssées | Decca | 159203-2
Play Bach Aux Champs-Élyssées | Decca | 159203-2
Ravel's Bolero | Telarc Digital | CD 83466
Raymond Fol Big Band | Jazz In Paris:Raymond Fol-Les 4 Saisons | EmArCy | 548791-2
Jazz In Paris:Raymond Fol-Les 4 Saisons | EmArCy | 548791-2
Jazz In Paris:Raymond Fol-Les 4 Saisons | EmArCy | 548791-2
Jazz In Paris:Raymond Fol-Les 4 Saisons | EmArCy | 548791-2
Jazz In Paris:Raymond Fol-Les 4 Saisons | EmArCy | 548791-2
Swingle Singers | Swingling Telemann | Philips | 586735-2
Swingling Telemann | Philips | 586735-2
Swingling Telemann | Philips | 586735-2
Swingle Singers Singing Mozart | Philips | 548538-2
Viktoria Tabatchnikowa-Eugenij Belov | Troika | ALISO Records | AL 1036
Troika | ALISO Records | AL 1036
Ensemble Indigo | Reflection | Enja | ENJ-9417 2

Allegro Apassionato-

Reflection | Enja | ENJ-9417 2

Allegro Assai-

Paquito D'Rivera Group With The Absolute Ensemble | Habanera | Enja | ENJ-9395 2

Allegro Ben Ritmato E Decisco

Habanera | Enja | ENJ-9395 2

Allegro Ben Ritmato E Decisco(2)

Friedemann Graef-Albrecht Riermeier Duo | Exit | FMP | 0820

Allegro from Concerto Grosso Op.6 No.4 in A Minor(Haendel)

Swingle Singers | Swingle Singers Singing Mozart | Philips | 548538-2

Allegro from Piano Sonata No.5 in G Major(KV 283)

Swingle Singers Getting Romantic | Philips | 586736-2

Allegro from Piano Sonata Op.26 In A Flat Major(L.v.Beethoven)

Hans Reichel | Wichlinghauser Blues | FMP | 0150

Allegro Furioso

Nikolai Kapustin | Kapustin Plays Kapustin-A Jazz Portrait | VIST | MK 417051

Allegro Marcato-

Jacques Loussier Trio | The Best Of Play Bach | Philips | 824664-2

Allegro Moderato-

George Gruntz Concert Jazz Band | Live At The Jazz Fest Berlin | TCB Records | TCB 99452

Allegro Non Molto-

Raymond Fol Big Band | Jazz In Paris:Raymond Fol-Les 4 Saisons | EmArCy | 548791-2
Percussion Project Rostock | First Catalogue | KlangRäume | 30170

Allegro Risoluto-

John Zorn Group | Cobra | Hat Art | CD 6040(2)

Allegro Spiritual

Gary Burton Group | Tango | Concord | CCD 4793

Allegro Tranquillo-

George Gruntz Concert Jazz Band | Live At The Jazz Fest Berlin | TCB Records | TCB 99452

Allegro-Andante-Finale

Jürgen Knieper Quintet | State Of Things | Jazz Haus Musik | JHM 0104 CD

Alleh Hopp!

John Schröder-Henrik Walsdorff-Uli Jenneßen | Freedom Of Speech | FMP | OWN-90011

Allemande

Klaus Doldinger's Passport | Earthborn | Atlantic | 2292-46477-2
Peter Fulda Trio With Céline Rudolph | Silent Dances | Jazz 4 Ever Records:Jazz Network | J4E 4731
Jacques Loussier Trio | Play Bach Aux Champs-Élyssées | Decca | 159203-2

Allemande-

L.A.4 | The L.A.Four Scores! | Concord | CCD 6008

Allemande Deux

Joachim Kühn | The Diminished Augmented System | EmArCy | 542320-2

Allemande(from Partita 2)
Allan Vaché-Harry Allen Quintet | Allan And Allan | Nagel-Heyer | CD 074
Allen And Allen
52nd Street All Stars | Esquire's All-American Hot Jazz Sessions | RCA | ND 86757
Allen's Alley
Art Pepper Quartet | Art Lives | Galaxy | GXY 5145
Laurie's Choice | Laserlight | 17012
Dizzy Gillespie/Max Roach | Max+Dizzy | A&M Records | 396404-2
Alles In Ordnung
Hans Lüdemann | The Natural Piano | Jazz Haus Musik | JHM 0075 CD
Alles Ist Hin(Song of the Mbuti Pygmies-German Folk Song)
Klaus Spencker Trio | Invisible | Jardis Records | JRCD 9409
Alles Quart
Kölner Saxophon Mafia | Space Player | Jazz Haus Musik | JHM 0132 CD
Alles Roger,Buck?
Michael Mantler Group With The Danish Concert Radio Orchestra | Many Have No Speech | Watt | 19(835580-2)
Alles Scheint Rand
Dieter Ilg Trio With Wolfgang Muthspiel | Folk Songs | Jazzline | JL 11146-2
Alles Wird Gut
Amani A.W.-Murray Quintet | Amani A.W.-Murray | GRP | GRP 96332
Allez Oop
Members Of The Basie Band | Lester Young:The Complete 1936-1951 Small Group Sessions(Studio Recordings-Master Takes),Vol.6 Rare Items | Blue Moon | BMCD 1006
Alliance
Wayne Krantz Trio | 2 Drinks Minimum | Enja | ENJ-9043 2
Alliance-
John Hyman's Bayou Stompers | The Owls' Hoot | Frog | DGF 2
Alligator Crawl
Dave Frishberg Quintet | Getting Some Fun Out Of Life | Concord | CJ 37
Dill Jones | Jazz Piano Masters | Chiaroscuro | CR 170
Fats Waller | Fats Waller-The Joint Is Jumpin' | RCA | ND 86288(874182)
Louis Armstrong And His Hot Seven | The Louis Armstrong Selection Vol.1 | CBS | 474764-2
Alligator Hop
King Oliver's Creole Jazz Band | Louis Armstrong With King Oliver Vol.1 | Village(Jazz Archive) | VILCD 003-2
Alligator Pecadillo
Louis Armstrong And His All Stars | Louis Armstrong Plays W.C.Handy | CBS | CK 64925
Alligator Story
Screamin' Jay Hawkins & The Chicken Hawks | Live And Crazy | Black & Blue | BLE 59.731 2
Allnächtlich Im Traum
Pete York Group | String Time In New York | BELL Records | BLR 84015
Allons A Lafayette
Stephan Noel Lang Trio | Echoes | Nagel-Heyer | CD 2033
Allright !
Count Basie And His Orchestra | Count On The Coast Vol.1 | Phontastic | NCD 7555
Allright Okay You Win
En Concert Avec Europe 1 | Laserlight | 710411/12
Diane Schuur With Orchestra | Blues For Schuur | GRP | GRP 98632
The Best Of Diane Schuur | GRP | GRP 98882
Joe Williams With The Count Basie Orchestra | Having the Blues Under European Sky | LRC Records | CDC 7684
All's Well That Ends
Peter Erskine Orchestra | Peter Erskine | Contemporary | CCD 14010-2
All-Star Strut
Brew Moore Quintet | Svinget 14 | Black Lion | BLCD 760164
Allusion I
Lee Konitz-Frank Wunsch | Into It(Solos & Duos) | West Wind | WW 2090
Alma Alegre(Happy Soul)
Tito Puente's Latin Ensemble And Orchestra | Un Poco Loco | Concord | CCD 4329
Alma Latina
Paquito D'Rivera Orchestra | A Night In Englewood | Messidor | 15829 CD
Alma Via
Pedro Javier Gonzales | Internationales Guitarren Festival '94 | ALISO Records | AL 1030
Almandina
Vince Guaraldi Trio | Cast Your Fate To The Wind | Original Jazz Classics | OJCCD 437-2(F 8089)
Alma-Ville
Heiner Goebbels-Alfred Harth Duo | Vom Sprengen Des Gartens | FMP | SAJ 20
Almenrausch
Duke Ellington And His Orchestra & Choir | Second Sacred Concert | America | AM 006/007
Almost A Simple Blues
Louis Stewart-Heiner Franz Quartet | Winter Song | Jardis Records | JRCD 9005
Axel Zwingenberger | Powerhouse Boogie | Vagabond | 6.24210 AS-Digital
Almost Always
Vincent Herring Quintet | Dawnbird | Landmark | LCD 1533-2
Almost Blue
Kendra Shank With The Larry Willis Quartet | Afterglow | Mapleshade | 02132
Almost Blues
The Barone Brothers Band | Blues & Other Happy Moments | Palo Alto | PA 8004
Almost Cried
Robert Pete Williams | Free Again | Original Blues Classics | OBCCD 553-2(BV 1026)
Almost Epilog
Don Friedman Quartet | My Foolish Heart | Steeplechase | SCCD 31545
Almost Everything
My Foolish Heart | Steeplechase | SCCD 31534
Don Friedman Trio | Almost Everything | Steeplechase | SCCD 31368
Almost Fast
New On The Corner | Left Handed | Jazz 4 Ever Records:Jazz Network | J4E 4758
Almost Gentle
Pete Yellin Quartet | Pete Yellin's European Connection:Live! | Jazz 4 Ever Records:Jazz Network | J4E 4722
Almost Gently
John Bergamo | On The Edge | CMP Records | CMP CD 27
Almost Inside
Bill Saxton Quartet | Atymony | Jazzline | JL 11136-2
Almost Like Being In Love
Benny Carter Quartet | Summer Serenade | Storyville | STCD 4047
Bernard Peiffer Trio | Jazz In Paris:Bernard Peiffer-La Vie En Rose | EmArCy | 013980-2
Bud Powell Trio | Swingin' With Bud | RCA | 2113041-2
Charlie Parker Big Band | Bird On Verve-Vol.7:Charlie Parker Big Band | Verve | 817448-1 IMS
Charlie Parker With The Joe Lipman Orchestra | Charlie Parker Big Band | Verve | 559835-2
Chet Baker Quintet | Time After Time | I.R.D. Records | TDMCD 004
Chris Connor With The John Lewis Quartet | Chris Connor | Atlantic | 7567-80769-2
Don Elliott Octet | Don Elliott:Mellophone | Fresh Sound Records | FSR 2009(Bethlehem BCP 12)
Ella Fitzgerald With The Marty Paich Orchestra | Ella Sings Broadway | Verve | 549373-2
Etta Jones With Her Trio | Something Nice | Original Jazz Classics | OJCCD 221-2(P 7194)
Gerry Mulligan Quartet With Lee Konitz | Complete 1953 The Haig Performances | The Jazz Factory | JFCD 22861
Jack McDuff Quintet | Color Me Blue | Concord | CCD 4516
Jon Hendricks And The All Stars | Boppin' At The Blue Note | Telarc Digital | CD 83320
Lee Konitz & The Gerry Mulligan Quartet | Konitz Meets Mulligan | Pacific Jazz | 746847-2
Lester Young Quartet | Live At The Royal Roost | Jazz Anthology | JA 5214
Lozenzo Petrocca Quartet | Stop It | Edition Musikat | EDM 018
Martial Solal Trio | Balade Du 10 Mars | Soul Note | 121340-2
Pat Thomas With Band | Jazz Patterns | Fresh Sound Records | Strand SLS CD 1015
Ross Tompkins-Joe Venuti Quintet | Live At Concord '77 | Concord | CJ 51
Sonny Rollins With The Modern Jazz Quartet | Welcome To Jazz: Sonny Rollins | Koch Records | 322 079 D1
Sonny Rollins With The Modern Jazz Quintet | Vintage Sessions | Prestige | P 24096
Teddy Edwards Quartet | Midnight Creeper | HighNote Records | HCD 7011
Weslia Whitefield With The Mike Greensill Quartet | Teach Me Tonight | HighNote Records | HCD 7009
Almost One Hour
Louis Armstrong With Orchestra | Ramblin' Rose | H&L Records | 6.24131 AO
Almost Pretty
Nils Gessinger Orchestra | Ducks 'N' Cookies | GRP | GRP 98302
Almost There
Gebhard Ullmann Quartet | Kreuzberg Park East | Soul Note | 121371-2
Almost Unisons
Eddie Allen Quintet | R 'N' B | Enja | ENJ-9033 2
Almost You
Misha Mengelberg Trio | Who's Bride | Avant | AVAN 038
Alna's Connexus
Armando Bertozzi Trio | Armando Bertozzi Trioz | Penta Flowers | CDPIA 014
Aloe Evra
Aera | Humanum Est | Erlkönig | 148400
Alois,Wir Entkommen Ihm Nicht
Christian Minh Doky Quintet | The Sequel | Storyville | STCD 4175
Alone
Eric Dolphy Quintet | Stockholm Sessions | Enja | 3055 (807503)
Lars Gullin Quartet | Lars Gullin 1951/52 Vol.5:First Walk | Dragon | DRCD 380
Lars Gullin 1951/52 Vol.5:First Walk | Dragon | DRCD 380
Lionel Hampton And His Orchestra | The Great Hamptologia, Vol. 1 | MGM | 2304527 IMS
Misha Alperin Quintet | North Story | ECM | 1596
Paul Smoker Trio | Alone | Sound Aspects | sas CD 018(32018)
Alone Again Suite
Berry Lipman Orchestra | Easy Listening Vol.1 | Sonia | CD 77280
Alone Again(Naturally)
Gene Ammons Septet | Goodbye | Original Jazz Classics | OJCCD 1081-2(P 100939)
Johnny Griffin Quartet | NYC Underground | Galaxy | GXY 5132
Tok Tok Tok | 50 Ways To Leave Your Lover | Einstein Music | EM 91051
Woody Herman And His Orchestra | The Raven Speaks | Original Jazz Classics | OJCCD 663-2(F 9416)
Herbie Hancock Quintet | Takin' Off | Blue Note | 837643-2
Alone And I
Herbie Hancock:The Complete Blue Note Sixties Sessions | Blue Note | 495569-2
Mark Turner Quintet | Ballad Session | Warner | 9362-47631-2
The Original Five Blind Boys Of Mississippi | Oh Lord-Stand By Me/Marching Up To Zion | Ace Records | CDCHD 341
Alone At Last
Ken Peplowski Quintet | Sunny Side | Concord | CCD 4376
Alone In The Morning
Joe Newman Septet | The Count's Men | Fresh Sound Records | FSR-CD 0135
Alone Together
Allen Farnham Trio | Play-Cation | Concord | CCD 4521
Anthony Ortega Trio | Scattered Clouds | HatOLOGY | 555
Art Farmer Quartet | Early Art | Original Jazz Classics | OJCCD 880-2(NJ 8258)
Farmer 's Market | Prestige | P 24032
Bill Mays/Ray Drummond | One To One | dmp Digital Music Productions | CD 473
Bruce Gertz Quintet | Third Eye | RAM Records | RMCD 4509
Chet Baker Quartet | Sings Again | Timeless | CD SJP 238
Chico Hamilton And Euphoria | Arroyo | Soul Note | 121241-2
Elliot Lawrence And His Orchestra | The Elliot Lawrence Big Band Swings Cohn & Kahn | Fantasy | FCD 24761-2
Eric Dolphy-Richard Davis Duo | Music Matador | Fresh Sound Records | FSR-CD 0304
Great Jazz Trio | Standard Collection Vol.2 | Limetree | MCD 0032
Herb Ellis-Stuff Smith Sextet | Herb Ellis & Stuff Smith:Together | Koch Jazz | KOC 3-7805-2
Jessica Williams/Dick Berk | A Song That I Heard | Hep | CD 2061
Jimmie Lunceford And His Orchestra | The King Of Big Band Jazz | Festival | Album 146
Joe Pass-John Pisano | Joe Pass-John Pisano:Duets | Pablo | 2310959-2
Joe Williams With The Harry 'Sweets' Edison Quintet | Together | Fresh Sound Records | FSR-CD 23(882188)
Joey DeFrancesco Quartet | All About My Girl | Muse | MCD 5528
Keith Copeland Trio | Live At Limerick | Steeplechase | SCCD 31469
Ken Peplowski Quintet | Illumination | Concord | CCD 4449
Masha Bijlsma Band | Lebo | Jazzline | JL 11145-2
Meredith d'Ambrosia Group | Shadowland | Sunnyside | SSC 1060 D
Michael 'Patches' Stewart Group | Blue Patches | Hip Bop | HIBD 8016
Mikesch Van Grümmer | Bar-Piano | Timeless | CD SJP 362
Miles Davis Quintet | Charles Mingus-The Complete Debut Recordings | Debut | 12 DCD 4402-2
Milestone Jazz Stars | Milestone Jazz Stars in Concert | Milestone | MCD 55006-2
Oscar Peterson-Dizzy Gillespie Duo | Oscar Peterson & Dizzy Gillespie | Pablo | 2310740-2
Paul Desmond Quartet | Paul Desmond-Greatest Hits | RCA | CL 89809 SF
Take Ten | RCA | 63661462
Paul Robertson Quintet | Old Friends, New Friends | Palo Alto | PA 8013
Pepper Adams Quintet | Conjuration | Reservoir | RSR CD 113(882637)
Rahn Burton Trio | The Poem | DIW | DIW 610 CD
Reykjavik Jazz Quartet with Guy Barker | Hot House | Ronnie Scott's Jazz House | JHCD 032
Soesja Citroen Group | Songs For Lovers And Losers | Challenge | CHR 70034
Sonny Rollins And The Contemporary Leaders | Sonny Rollins-The Freelance Years:The Complete Riverside & Contemporary Recordings | Riverside | 5 RCD 4427-2
Sonny Stitt Quartet | New York Jazz | Verve | 517050-2
Steve Kuhn Trio | Looking Back | Concord | CCD 4446
Tete Montoliu | The Music I Like To Play Vol.1 | Soul Note | 121180-2
The Atlantic String Trio | First Meeting | Factory Outlet Records | 2001-1 CD
The Mastersounds | A Date With The Mastersounds | Original Jazz Classics | OJC 282(F 8062)
Tough Young Tenors | Alone Together | Antilles | 848767-2(887317)
Yoshiko Kishino Trio | Photograph | GRP | GRP 98842
Alone Together-
Ahmad Jamal Trio | Live In Paris 92 | Birdology | 849408-2
Joe Beck-Ali Ryerson | Django | dmp Digital Music Productions | CD 530
Bill Evans Trio | The Complete Bill Evans On Verve | Verve | 527953-2
Alone Together(2)
The Complete Bill Evans On Verve | Verve | 527953-2
Alone Together(3)
Axel Beineke Jazz Trio | Let's Be True | Edition Collage | EC 469-2
Alone Together(alt.take)
Herb Ellis-Stuff Smith Sextet | Herb Ellis & Stuff Smith:Together | Koch Jazz | KOC 3-7805-2
Alone Too Long
Tommy Flanagan | Alone Too Long | Denon Compact Disc | DC-8572
Alone With A Lovely Girl
(Little)Jimmy Scott With The Billy Taylor Orchestra | Everybody's Somebody's Fool | Decca | 050669-2
Alone With A Memory
Rodney Whitaker Quintet | Ballads And Blues-The Brooklyn Session | Criss Cross | Criss 1167
Alone With My Thoughts Of You
Bob Hall Trio | Alone With The Blues | Lake | LACD 44
Alone, Alone and Alone
Terumasa Hino Quintet | Taro 's Mood | Enja | 2028
Along Came Betty
Art Blakey & The All Star Jazz Messengers | Aurex Jazz Festival '83 | Eastworld | EWJ 80270
Art Blakey And The Jazz Messengers | Anthenagin | Prestige | P 10076
Live In Stockholm 1959 | DIW | DIW 313 CD
Art Farmer/Benny Golson Jazztet | The Jazztet-Real Time | Contemporary | CCD 14034-2
John Swana Quintet | Introducing John Swana | Criss Cross | Criss 1045
Pat Martino Quartet | Consciousness | Muse | MCD 5039
Along Came John
John Patton Quintet | Along Came John | Blue Note | 0675614
Art Blakey And The Jazz Messengers | At The Club St.Germain | RCA | ND 74897(2)
Along Came Manon
George Benson And His Orchestra | Giblet Gravy | Verve | 543754-2
Along Came Mary
The Modern Jazz Disciples | Disciples Blues | Prestige | PCD 24263-2
Along Come Cheryl
David Benoit Group With.Symphony Orchestra | Inner Motion | GRP | GRP 96212
Alore Domore
Karim Ziad Groups | Ifrikya | ACT | 9282-2
Alouhid
Stefon Harris Group | Black Action Figure | Blue Note | 499546-2
Alovi
Flavio Ambrosetti Septet | Flavio Ambrosetti Anniversary | Enja | ENJ-9027 2
Alpenbride
Boury | Für Herrn Keupert | Jazz Haus Musik | JHM 16
Alpha
Christian Chevallier And His Orchestra | Formidable! | Fresh Sound Records | 054 2611130l(Columbia FP 1067)
Ornette Coleman Quintet | Something Else | Contemporary | C 7551
Andy Laverne Quartet | Liquid Silver | dmp Digital Music Productions | CD 449
Alpha Centauri
Swingrass | SwinGrass '83 | Antilles | AN 1014(802737)
Alphabet Call
Adrian Mears & Johannes Enders Quintet | Discoveries | Enja | 8022-2
Alpine Dialogue:
The Contemporary Alphorn Orchestra | Mytha | Hat Art | CD 6110
Alpsegen
Rabih Abou-Khalil/Michael Armann Duo | Compositions & Improvisations | MMP-Records | 170857
Already Alright
David Benoit Group With Symphony Orchestra | Shadows | GRP | GRP 96542
Alright
Steve Gibbons Band | Birmingham To Memphis | Linn Records | AKD 019
Alright,Okay,You Win
Chris Barber's Jazz Band | The Traditional Jazz Scene Vol.2 | Teldec | 2292-43997-2
Count Basie And His Orchestra | Live In Basel 1956 | Jazz Helvet | JH 05
Ella Fitzgerald With The Tommy Flanagan Trio | Jazz Collection:Ella Fitzgerald | Laserlight | 24397
Ella Johnson With Orchestra | Swing Me | Official | 6009
Jenny Evans And Her Quintet | Shiny Stockings | Enja | ENJ-9317 2
Joe Williams With Red Holloway & His Blues All-Stars | Nothin' But The Blues | Delos | DE 4001
Peggy Lee With Orchestra | Pass Me By/Big Spender | Capitol | 535210-2
Frederic Rabold Inspiration Orchestra | Relaxing Walk | Fusion | 8019
Al's Hallucinations
Alix Combelle Trio | Le Jazz En France Vol.13:Alix Combelle 1937-1940(Tome 1) | Pathe | 1552591
Al's In
Jason Seizer Quintet | Patience | Acoustic Music Records | 319.1087.2
Alskar Barnet Modernfamnen
John Scofield Quartet | Sampler | Enja | 2000
Alster Promenade
Alguimia | Alguimia 'U' | Fresh Sound Records | FSNT 023 CD
Alta Fidelitat
Gabriel Pérez Group | Alfonsina | Jazz 4 Ever Records:Jazz Network | J4E 4751
Alta Paz
Alex Cline Group | The Lamp And The Star | ECM | 1372
Altar Stone
Mario Fragiacomo Orchestra | Trieste Ieri Un Secolo Fa | SPLASC(H) Records | HP 08
Alter Be Tyar
Donald Byrd Sextet | Harlem Blues | Landmark | LCD 1516-2
Alter Ego
Franz Koglmann Tentet | Ich | Hat Art | CD 6033
Altered Ego
Greg Osby Quintet | Mindgames | JMT Edition | 919021-2
Kenny Barron Trio | Live at Bradley's | EmArCy | 549099-2
Kevin Eubanks Trio | Live At Bradley's | Blue Note | 830133-2
Roy Hargrove Quintet With Guests | The Vibe | Novus | PD 90668
Alternate Blues Four
All Stars | The Alternate Blues | Pablo | 2312136
Alternate Blues One
The Alternate Blues | Pablo | 2312136
Alternate Blues Three
The Alternate Blues | Pablo | 2312136
Alternate Blues Two
Mike Melillo Trio | Alternate Changes For Bud | Red Records | NS 211
Alternate Root
Ron Carter Sextet | New York Slick | Original Jazz Classics | OJCCD 916-2(M 9096)
Alternate Route
David Moss Duos | Time Stories | Intakt Records | CD 054
Although
Wayne Krantz Trio | Long To Be Loose | Enja | ENJ-7099 2
Although One Began
Alex de Grassi Quartet | Altiplano | RCA | PL 83016
Alto Music
Renaud Garcia-Fons | Navigatore | Enja | ENJ-9418 2
Alto Pais
Renaud Garcia-Fons Group | Navigatore | Enja | ENJ-9418 2
Hal McKusick Octet | In A Twentieth-Century Drawing Room | Fresh Sound Records | ND 12584
Alto-Itis
Oliver Nelson Sextet | The Prestige Legacy Vol.2:Battles Of Saxes | Prestige | PCD 24252-2
Eric Dolphy:The Complete Prestige Recordings | Prestige | 9 PRCD-4418-2
Phil & Quill | Phil & Quill | Original Jazz Classics | OJCCD 215-2(P 7115)
Altonality

TITELVERZEICHNIS

Kid Thomas' Dixieland Band | New Orleans Traditional Jazz Legends:Kid Thomas | Mardi Gras Records | MG 9004

Altos E Baixos
Jimmy Dorsey And His Orchestra | Jimmy Dorsey And His Orchestra | Jazz Anthology | JA 5221

Altruvista
Paul Horn Group feat. Egberto Gismonti | The Altitude Of The Sun | Black Sun Music | 15002-2

Aluminum Baby
Herb Pomeroy Orchestra | Life Is A Many Splendored Gig | Fresh Sound Records | FSR-CD 84(882191)
Rahsaan Roland Kirk Quartet | Here Comes The Whistleman | Atlantic | ATL 40389(SD 3007)

Aluminum(7,57%)
David Moss Duos | Time Stories | Intakt Records | CD 054

Alvin
Tony Lakatos Quintet | Generation X | Jazzline | JL 11149-2

Alvorada
Giger-Lenz-Maron | Where The Hammer Hangs | Nagara | MIX 1015-N

Always
Benny Goodman And His Orchestra | The Birth Of Swing | Bluebird | ND 90601(3)
Bill Evans Trio | The Complete Bill Evans On Verve | Verve | 527953-2
Trio 64 | Verve | 539058-2
Bill Frisell Trio | Bill Frisell With Dave Hollnad And Elvin Jones | Nonesuch | 7559-79624-2
Billie Holiday And Her All Stars | Billie Holiday:The Great American Songbook | Verve | 523003-2
Stay With Me | Verve | 511523-2
Ella Fitzgerald With Paul Weston And His Orchestra | Love Songs:The Best Of The Song Books | Verve | 531762-2
Frank Wess Meets The Paris-Barcelona Swing Connection | Paris-Barcelona Connection | Fresh Sound Records | FSNT 002 CD
Hank Garland Group | Jazz Winds From New Directions | CBS | 492532-2
Kai Winding's New Jazz Group | Loaded:Vido Musso/Stan Getz | Savoy | SV 0227(MG 12074)
Lionel Hampton Trio | Lionel Hampton's Paris All Stars | Vogue | 21511502
Lionel Hampton:Real Crazy | Vogue | 2113409-2
Michael Brecker Quintet | Nearness Of You-The Ballad Book | Verve | 549705-2
Michele Hendricks And Her Trio | Me And My Shadow | Muse | MCD 5404

Always And Forever
Perry Robinson-Badal Roy-Nana Vasconcelos | Kundalini | Improvising Artists Inc. | 123856-2

Always Broke
Henry Hall And The BBC Dance Orchestra | Help Yourself To Happiness | Saville Records | SVL 156 IMS

Always Say Goodbye
Joe Magnarelli Septet | Always There | Criss Cross | Criss 1141

Always There
George Shearing And His Quintet With Peggy Lee | Beauty And The Beat | Pathe | EMS 1158(Capitol ST 1219)

Always True To You In My Fashion
Ella Fitzgerald With The Buddy Bregman Orchestra | The Complete Ella Fitzgerald Song Books of Harold Arlen, Irving Berlin, Duke Ellington, George & Ira Gershwin, Jerome Kern, Johnny Mercer, Cole Porter And Rogers & Hart | Verve | 519832-2
John Balke Group | Saturation | EmArCy | 538160-2

Always With A Purpose
Nat King Cole And His Trio | Combo USA | Affinity | CD AFS 1002

Always You
Kühn/Nauseef/Newton/Tadic | Let's Be Generous | CMP Records | CMP CD 53

Always!
Ella Fitzgerald With Paul Weston And His Orchestra | The Complete Ella Fitzgerald Song Books of Harold Arlen, Irving Berlin, Duke Ellington, George & Ira Gershwin, Jerome Kern, Johnny Mercer, Cole Porter And Rogers & Hart | Verve | 519832-2

Always(alt.take 1)
Bill Evans Trio | The Complete Bill Evans On Verve | Verve | 527953-2

Always(alt.take 2)
Trio 64 | Verve | 539058-2

Always(alt.take)
Trio 64 | Verve | 539058-2

Always(incompl.take)
Michael Bocian | Premonition:Solo Debut For Nylon String Guitar | Enja | 9118-2

Always,Never And Forever
Hank Jones Meets Cheik-Tidiana Seck | Sarala | Verve | 528783-2

Aly Kawélé
Jeff 'Tain' Watts Trio | MegaWatts | Sunnyside | SSC 1055 D

Am Berg
Dagobert Böhm Sextet | Acoustic Moods | Jazzline | ???

Am Fluss
The Alpine Experience | Rosa Loui | TCB Records | TCB 03042

Am I Blue
Connie Francis With Orchestra | The Swinging Connie Francis | Audiophile | ACD-286
Dorothy Donegan | Makin' Whoopee | Black & Blue | BLE 59.146 2
Herb Ellis-Joe Pass | Two For The Road | Original Jazz Classics | 2310714
Jay McShann Trio | Swingmatism | Sackville | SKCD2-3046
Kenny Davern And His Jazz Band | East Side, West Side | Arbors Records | ARCD 19137
The Travelers | The Dorsey Brothers' Orchestra Vol.2 | Jazz Oracle | BDW 8005

Am I Too Late?
Budd Johnson Quartet | Mr.Bechet | Black & Blue | BB 882.2

Am I Waisting My Time
Giorgio Gaslini Trio | Schumann Reflections | Soul Note | SN 1120

Am Leuchtenden Sommermorgen
String Thing | String Thing:Alles Wird Gut | MicNic Records | MN 2

Am Meer
Dave Burrell | Windward Passages | Hat Art | CD 6138

Am Rande:
Ekkehard Jost & Chromatic Alarm | Von Zeit Zu Zeit | Fish Music | FM 005 CD

Am Sausenden Webstuhl Der Zeit
Uli Beckerhoff Quintet | Original Motion Picture Soundtrack:Das Geheimnis(Secret Of Love) | Nabel Records:Jazz Network | CD 4666

Am See
Old Merrytale Jazz Band | 25 Jahre Old Merrytale Jazzband Hamburg | Intercord | 155043

Am Sonntag Will Mein Süsser Mit Mir Segeln Gehn
Alberto Marsico Quintet | Them That's Got | Organic Music | ORGM 9705

Am Südlichen Ende Der Bar
Ulli Bögershausen | Christmas Carols | Laika Records | 35101622

Am Weihnachtsbaum Die Lichter Brennen
Brad Mehldau | Places | Warner | 9362-47693-2

Am Zauberberg
Joe Diorio/Robben Ford Quartet | Minor Elegance | MGI Records | MGR CD 1012

Ama Tu Sonrisa
Darius Brubeck And The Nu Jazz Connection | African Tributes | B&W Present | BW 023

Amad
Duke Ellington And His Orchestra | Duke Ellington's Far East Suite | RCA | 2174797-2

Amad(alt.take)
Renaud Garcia-Fons Quartet | Alboreá | Enja | ENJ-9057 2

Amadu
The African Jazz Pioneers | Live At The Montreux Jazz Festival | Intuition Records | INT 3099-2

Amager-Dans-
Victor De Diego Group | Amaia | Fresh Sound Records | FSNT 012 CD

Amaia
Rabih Abou-Khalil Group | Nafas | ECM | 1359(835781-2)

Amal Hayati
Rabih Abou-Khalil Quartet | Bitter Harvest | MMP-Records | 170884

Amalgame
Michel Petrucciani | Oracle's Destiny | Owl Records | 032 CD

Amaliya
Noma Kosazana & Uli Lenz | Art Of The Duo: Trouble In Paradise | Tutu Records | 888144-2*

Amamponda
Louis Moholo's Viva-La-Black | Exile | Ogun | OGCD 003

Amanda
Big John Patton Quartet | The Organization! The Best Of Big John Patton | Blue Note | 830728-2
Duke Pearson Sextet | Joe Henderson-The Blue Note Years | Blue Note | 789287-2
Stephane Grappelli-Alan Clare Duo | Stardust | Black Lion | CD 877630-2

Amandamena
Horace Tapscott | The Tapscott Sessions Vol.7 | Nimbus | NS 2147

Amandla
Miles Davis Group | Miles In Montreux | Jazz Door | JD 1287/88

Amanecer
Rene Toledo Group | The Dreamer | GRP | GRP 96772

Amanha(Tomorrow)
Nat Adderley Group | Soul Of The Bible | Capitol | 358257-2

Amani
Maria Joao-Aki Takase | Looking For Love:Live At The Leverkusen Jazz Festival | Enja | 5075-2

Amarchaj
Jaki Byard | Amarcord Nino Rota | Hannibal | HNBL 9301

Amarma
George Shearing Trio & The Robert Farnon Orchestra | On Target | MPS | 68280

Amaryllis
Oregon | Crossing | ECM | 1291(825323-2)
Tony Oxley Sextet | 4 Compositions For Sextet | CBS | 494437-2

Amass
Inge Brandenburg mit Kurt Edelhaben und seinem Orchester | Why Don't You Take All Of Me | Bear Family Records | BCD 15614 AH

Amateur D'Amour
Furio Di Castri-Paolo Fresu | Urlo | yvp music | CD 3035

Amazing Grace
Cassandra Wilson | Dance To The Drums Again | CBS | CK 53451(DIW 863)
Christopher Murrell-Robert Irving III | Full Circle:Gospels And Spirituals | Nagel-Heyer | NHR SP 3
Cleo Brown | Living In The Afterglow | Audiophile | ACD-216
David Murray Quartet | Spirituals | DIW | DIW 841 CD
First Revolution Singers | A Cappella Gospel Anthology | Tight Harmony Records | TH 199404
Fumio Yasuda | Schumann's Bar Music | Winter&Winter | 910081-2
Gene Harris Group | In His Hands | Concord | CCD 4758
Herb Ellis Quintet | Roll Call | Justice Records | JR 1001-2
Papa Bue's Viking Jazzband | Church Concert | Timeless | CD TTD 571
Charlie Haden-Hank Jones | Steal Away | Verve | 527249-2

Amazing Grace-
Richard Stoltzman & Woody Herman's Thundering Herd | Ebony | RCA | ???

Amazing Love
Count Basie And His Orchestra | Compact Jazz: Count Basie & Joe Williams | Verve | 835329-2 PMS

Amazon
Jeremy Steig-Eddie Gomez Group | Rain Forest | CMP Records | CMP 12

Amazonas
Glen Velez Group | Assyrian Rose | CMP Records | CMP CD 42

Ambacharm
Pili-Pili | Jakko | JA & RO | JARO 4131-2

Ambandru
Bud Shank Quartet | Live At The Haig | Choice | CHCD 71030

Ambassador Blues
Live At The Haig | Concept | VL 2 IMS

Amber Captive
Spyro Gyra | Freetime | MCA | 2292-50417-1

Amber Sounds
Peter Erskine Trio | You Never Know | ECM | 1497(517353-2)

Amber Waves
Kenneth Knudsen-Christian Skeel | Music For Eyes | dacapo | DCCD 9433

Amberish-
Marian McPartland Trio With Strings | Marian McPartland With Strings | Concord | CCD 4745

Ambiance Pourpre
Eddie Harris Group | Live In Berlin | Timeless | CD SJP 289

Ambiguity
Lutz Wichert Trio | Ambiguous | Edition Musikat | EDM 068

Ambiguous
Klaus Ignatzek | Magic Secret | Nabel Records:Jazz Network | LP 4617

Ambleside
Chet Baker Quartet | Quartet | Pacific Jazz | 855453-2

Ambra
Sylvain Luc | Solo Ambre | Dreyfus Jazz Line | FDM 36650-2

Ambre
Dave King Group | Wildcat | Off The Wall Records | OTW 9501-CD

Ambrosia Mama
Gianluigi Trovesi Octet | Les Hommes Armés | Soul Note | 121311-2

Amely
Herbert Joos Trio | Ballade Noire | free flow music | ffm 0392
Bernard Purdie's Soul To Jazz | Bernard Purdie's Soul To Jazz II | ACT | 9253-2

Amen
Christopher Murrell-Robert Irving III | Full Circle:Gospels And Spirituals | Nagel-Heyer | NHR SP 3
David Bond Group | L'Essence | ITM-Pacific | ITMP 970056
Fritz Münzer Quintet | Jazz für junge Leute:Live im HR 1962 | Jazz 'n' Arts Records | C 01
Golden Gate Quartet | Best Of Golden Gate Quartet | Sonia | CD 77285
John Coltrane Quartet | John Coltrane:The Classic Quartet-Complete Impulse Studio Recordings | Impulse(MCA) | 951280-2
Johnny Thompson & The Pennsylvania District Choir | Live At Lausanne | Bellaphon | BCH 33007
Willie Humphrey Jazz Band | New Orleans Traditional Jazz Legends:Willie Humphrey | Mardi Gras Records | MG 9002

America
Dave Grusin Orchestra | David Grusin Presents West Side Story | N2K | 43062
Rhein Brass And Friends | Kant Park | Mons Records | MR 874318

America Drinks And Goes Home
Art Hodes-Jim Galloway | Art Hodes-The Final Sessions | Music & Arts | CD 782

America The Beautiful
Christian Jacob Trio | Time Lines | Concord | CCD 4801
Eartha Kitt And A 100 Voices Gospel Choir | My Way:A Musical Tribute To Rev.Martin Luther King Jr. | Basic | 50015
Richie Cole Quintet | Signature | Milestone | MCD 9162-2

American Bandstand(aka American Bandstand Thing)
Dieter Köhnlein | Three Faces(At Least) | Aho-Recording | CD 1022

American Boy
Michael Gregory | The Way We Used To Do | TipToe | TIP-888806 2

American Dream
Charlie Haden Quartet With Orchestra | American Dreams | Verve | 064096-2

American Dreams
Vincent Herring Sextet | American Experience | Limelight | 820826-2

American Garage
Pat Metheny Group | Unity Village | Jazz Door | JD 1246

American Indian:Song Of Sitting Bull
Richard Stoltzman & Woody Herman's Thundering Herd | Ebony | RCA | ???

American Patrol
Glenn Miller And His Orchestra | In The Mood | Intercord | 125403
Glenn Miller-The Great Instrumentals 1938-1942 | Retrieval | RTR 79001
The Ultimate Glenn Miller-22 Original Hits From The King Of Swing | RCA | 2113137-2
Play Selections From The Glenn Miller Story And Other Hits | RCA | NL 89073
Max Greger Und Sein Orchester | Swing Tanzen Gestattet | Vagabond | 6.28415 DP

American Rhythm
Sidney Bechet And His All Stars | Bechet/Nicholas/Mezzrow:Spirits Of New Orleans | Vogue | 2113408-2

American Woman
Dizzy Gillespie Quintet | Dizzie Gillespie: Salle Pleyel/Olympia | Laserlight | 36132

Americana
Keith Jarrett | Dark Intervals | ECM | 1379(837342-2)
Scott Colley Sextet | Portable Universe | Freelance | FRL-CD 027
Ricky Ford Quartet | American-African Blues | Candid | CCD 79528

Amerino
Eddie Louiss-Michel Petrucciani | Conférence De Presse | Dreyfus Jazz Line | FDM 36568-2

Ameskeri
Alex Riel Sextet | Unriel | Stunt Records | STUCD 19707

Amethyst
Pocket Change | Random Axis | Passport Jazz | ???

Ameva
Cecil Taylor | Live At Sweet Basil | Sound Hills | SSCD 8066

Amici
Fabio Morgera Quintet | The Pursuit | Ken Music | 660.56.014

Amidst A Yesterday's Presence
Marc Copland Quartet | Second Look | Savoy | CY 18001

Amigos De Longe
Jamie Findlay | Amigos Del Corazon | Acoustic Music Records | 319.1100.2

Amischa
Xu Feng Xia | Difference And Similarity | FMP | CD 96

Amman Amman
Bengt Berger & Bitter Funeral Beer Band | Praise Drumming | Dragon | DRLP 142

Ammazare Il Tempo
Phil Minton/Roger Turner Duo | Ammo | LEO | LR 116

Ammons' Joy
Gene Ammons And His All Stars | The Big Sound | Prestige | P 24098
Albert Ammons Rhythm Kings | The King Of Boogie Woogie | Blues Classics | BC 27

Amnesia
Duck Baker | The Clear Blue Sky | Acoustic Music Records | 319.1065.2

Amoeba
Frank Kimbrough Quintet | The Herbie Nichols Project | Soul Note | 121313-2

Amoeba's Dance
Asita Hamidi & Arcobaleno | Mosaic | Laika Records | 8695067

Amoebe
Art Pepper Quartet | Among Friends | Discovery | DSCD 837

Among The Hops
Art Ensemble Of Chicago | Among The People | Praxis | CM 103

Amonkst
Ana Caram Group | Amazonia | Chesky | JD 45

Amor
Eddie Brunner Und Die Original Teddies | Teddy Stauffer:Rare And Historical Jazz Recordings | Elite Special | 9522009

Amor En Paz(Once I Loved)
Carlos Barbosa-Lima | Plays The Music Of Luiz Bonfa And Cole Porter | Concord | CCD 42008

Amor Flamenco
Laurindo Almeida Quartet | Brazilliance Vol.1 | Pacific Jazz | 796339-2

Amores Que Matan
Michael Riessler & Singer Pur with Vincent Courtois | Ahi Vita | ACT | 9417-2

Amor-Lamento Della Ninfa
Count Basie And His Orchestra | Basie On Roulette, Vol. 21: The Legend | Vogue | 500021

Amorosa(Bossa Nova)
Count Down | Jazz Society(Vogue) | 670503

Amoroso
Louie Bellson Big Band | Big Band Jazz From The Summit | Fresh Sound Records | R 52087(Roulette)

Amorous Cat
Amos Milburn Trio | Chicken Shack Boogie | Pathe | 1561411(Aladdin)

Amour Et Beauté
Milt Bernhart Brass Ensemble | Modern Brass | Fresh Sound Records | NL 45662(RCA LPM 1123)

Amour, Amour
Hot Club De Norvege With Guests | Swinging With Jimmy | Hot Club Records | HCRCD 082

Amourette
Titi Winterstein Sextet | Djinee Tu Kowa Ziro | Boulevard | BLD 501 CD

Amoureux
Great Guitars | Great Guitars | Concord | CCD 4023

Amparo
Manfredo Fest Quartet | Just Jobim | dmp Digital Music Productions | CD 524

Ampurdan
Toto Blanke-Rudolf Dasek | Meditation | ALISO Records | AL 1026
Guy Klucevsek-Phillip Johnston | Tales From The Cryptic | Winter&Winter | 910088-2

Am-Scray
Brad Mehldau | Places | Warner | 9362-47693-2

Amsterdam
Harry Beckett Trio | Les Jardins Du Casino | West Wind | WW 2080

Amsterdam Blues
Chris Potter Quartet | Unspoken | Concord | CCD 4775

Amtrak
Art Blakey Ensemble | Orgy In Rhythm Vol.2 | Blue Note | 300157(1555)

Amurado
Heinz Sauer 4tet | Exchange 2 | free flow music | ffm 0998

Amuse Gueule
Ken McIntyre Quartet | Home | Steeplechase | SCCD 31039

Amy And Joseph
Greetje Bijma Kwintet | Tales Of A Voice | TipToe | TIP-888808 2

Amy Camus
Tana Reid Quintet | Blue Motion | Paddle Wheel | KICJ 172

An Addition To The Family
Billy Bang Quintet | Invitation | Soul Note | 121036-2

An Affair Ro Remember
Lynne Arriale Trio | Live At Montreux | TCB Records | TCB 20252
Russell Malone Quartet | Look Who's Here | Verve | 543543-2

An Affair To Remember
Warren Vaché Quintet | Warren Plays Warrey | Nagel-Heyer | CD 033
Chet Baker Quartet | Quartet | Pacific Jazz | 855453-2

An Atypical Affair
Big Joe Williams | Nine String Guitar Blues | Delmark | 900203 AO

An Die Musik
Paul Giger Trio | Vindonissa | ECM | 1836(066069-2)

An Ear On Buddha's Belly
Nat Gonella And His Georgians | Mister Rhythm Man | EMI Records | EG 2601881

An Evening In Sao Paulo
Lajos Dudas Quintet | Contrasts | Rillophon | 801031-320

An Evening In Thessaloniki-At The Oriental Gates
Tim Berne Quartet | Mutant Variations | Soul Note | 121091-2

An Evening With Jerry
Herbert Joos | The Philosophy Of The Fluegelhorn | Japo | 60004 IMS
An Evening With Vincent Van Ritz
Atlanta Jazzband | Welcome To Dr. Jazz | Dr.Jazz Records | 8600-2
An Exercise
Human Feel | Welcome To Malpesta | New World Records | 80450-2
An How I Hoped For Your Love
John Surman With String Quartet | Coruscating | ECM | 1702(543033-2)
An Illusive Shadow
John Surman | A Biography Of The Rev. Absolom Dawe | ECM | 1528(523749-2)
An Image
Lee Konitz With Strings | Lee Konitz Meets Jimmy Giuffre | Verve | 527780-2
An Intrigant Melody
Shorty Rogers And His Orchestra Feat. The Giants | An Invisible Orchard | Fresh Sound Records | 49560 CD(RCA)
An Occasional Man
Ann Richards With The Jack Sheldon Quartet | Ann,Man! | Atlantic | AMCY 1071
Med Flory and his Orchestra | Jazz Wave | Fresh Sound Records | JLP 1066(Jubilee)
An Ocean Goes To Sea(or voce e maluco)
Dave Bartholomew And His Orchestra | Shrimp And Gumbo | Pathe | 1566311
An Oscar For Treadwell
Charlie Parker Quintet | Verve Jazz Masters 15:Charlie Parker | Verve | 519827-2
An Oscar For Treadwell(alt.take)
Charlie Parker And His Orchestra | Bird: The Complete Charlie Parker On Verve | Verve | 837141-2
An Oscar For Treadwell(take 3)
Bird: The Complete Charlie Parker On Verve | Verve | 837141-2
An Oscar For Treadwell(take 4)
Urs Blöchlinger Trio | (Aesth)eti(c)k Als Widerstand | Plainisphare | PL 1267-3/4
An Oyster In Paris
Berlin Contemporary Jazz Orchestra | Berlin Contemporary Jazz Orchestra | ECM | 1409
Ana
Kenny Wheeler Quintet | The Widow In The Window | ECM | 1417(843198-2)
Thomas Hufschmidt & Tyron Park | Pepila | Acoustic Music Records | 319.1034.2
Anaconda
Oliver Nelson Sextet | Soul Battle | Original Jazz Classics | OJC 325(P 7223)
Anacrusis
Don Cherry Group | Don Cherry-The Sonet Recordings:Eternal Now/Live Ankara | Verve | 533049-2
Anadolu Havasi(turkish folk material)
Mehmet Ergin Group | Beyond The Seven Hills | MCA | MCD 70020
Analog Guy
Alexander von Schlippenbach Trio | Elf Bagatellen | FMP | CD 27
Ananda Nadamadum Tillai Sankara
Big Bill Broonzy | Trouble In Mind | Spotlite | SPJ 900
Ananta(Song Of Creation)
Family Of Percussion | Message To The Enemies Of Time | Nagara | MIX 1016-N
Anasazi
Yusef Lateef Quintet | Other Sounds | Original Jazz Classics | OJCCD 399-2(NJ 8218)
Anastasia
Don Pullen's African-Brazilian Connection | Ode To Live-A Tribute To George Adams | Blue Note | 789233-2
Anatelio
Don Byas Quintet | Lover Man | Vogue | 2115470-2
Anatolia
Nexus | Urban Shout | SPLASC(H) Records | H 170
Anatomy
John Coltrane-Paul Quinichette Quintet | John Coltrane-The Prestige Recordings | Prestige | 16 PCD 4405-2
Prestige All Stars | Interplay For Two Trumpets And Two Tenors | Prestige | VIJ 5028
Interplay | Original Jazz Classics | OJCCD 292-2(P 7112)
Anatomy Of A Murder
Duke Ellington And His Orchestra | Duke 56/62 Vol.1 | CBS | 88653
Anatomy Of A Murder(Sountrack):
M-Base Collective | Anatomy Of A Groove | DIW | DIW 864 CD
Anazing Grace
Giorgio Gaslini | Four Pieces | Dischi Della Quercia | Q 28015
ANC
Richie Beirach/John Abercrombie | Emerald City | Line Records | COCD 9.00522 O
Ancestors
George Colligan Quartet | Desire | Fresh Sound Records | FSNT 071 CD
Ancestra Wisdom
Horace Tapscott | The Tapscott Sessions Vol.6 | Nimbus | NS 2036
Ancestral Meditation
Urs Blöchlinger Trio | (Aesth)eti(c)k Als Widerstand | Plainisphare | PL 1267-3/4
Ancestral Spring(part 1-3)
Michael Formanek Quintet | Wide Open Space | Enja | ENJ-6032 2
Ancha Es Castilla
Firehouse Five Plus Two | Goes To Sea | Good Time Jazz | 10028
Anchors Aweigh
Louis Gallaud | Punch Miller/Louis Gallaud | American Music | AMCD-68
Ancient Cape
Özay With Band | Antiquared Love | Basic | 50004
Ancient Footprints
Jugendjazzorchester NW | Back To The Roots | Jugendjazzorchester NW | JJO 002
Ancient Saga
Eric Person Trio | Prophecy | Soul Note | 121287-2
Ancona Danza
Ganelin Trio | Da Capo | Enja | 4036
And
The Danish Radio Jazz Orchestra | Nice Work | dacapo | DCCD 9446
And Rhythm - ...And Rhythm
John Stevens Trio | Application Interaction And ... | Spotlite | SPJ 513
And Baby Makes Three
Gus Mancuso Quintet | Introducing Gus Mancuso | Fresh Sound Records | 3233(Fantasy)
Peter Sonntag Sextet | Words Written In Stone | amf records | maj 1011
And Don't You Forget It
Roger Kellaway Quartet | A Portrait Of Roger Kellaway | Fresh Sound Records | FSR-CD 0147
And Finally...The Oasis
Abdullah Ibrahim-Carlos Ward Duo | Live At Sweet Basil Vol.1 | Black-Hawk | BKH 50204
And Flowers Pick Themselves(Song Of Hope)
O'Mara-Darling-Elgart | O'Mara-Darling-Elgart | Line Records | COCD 9.00670 O
And He Loved His Brother Till The End - ...And He Loved His Brother Till The End
Dino Saluzzi-Anthony Cox-David Friedman | Rios | VeraBra Records | CDVBR 2156-2
Stan Kenton And His Orchestra | The Early Years | Capitol | 166219-2
And Hopefully,So Will You
Rudy Linka Trio | Always Double Czech! | Enja | ENJ-9301 2
And I Love Her
Gary McFarland Orchestra | Soft Samba | Verve | MV 2102 IMS
Sarah Vaughan And Her Band | Songs Of The Beatles | Atlantic | 16037-2
Sarah Vaughan With Orchestra | Song Of The Beatles | Atlantic | SD 16037
And I Love You So
Thad Jones-Mel Lewis Orchestra | A Touch Of Class | West Wind Orchestra Series | 2402 CD
And It's Supposed To Be Love
Franck Amsallem-Tim Ries-Leon Parker | Is That So? | Sunnyside | SSC 1071 D
And Maybe You'll Be There
Clare Fischer Group | Lembrancas | Concord | CCD 4404
And More...
Noctett | Contraste | Cain | CL 4794
And Now
Myra Melford-Han Bennink | Eleven Ghosts | HatOLOGY | 507
And Now-
Nat King Cole Trio | Straighten Up And Fly Right | Pro-Arte | CDD 558
And Now The Queen
Paul Bley | Alone,Again | Improvising Artists Inc. | 123840-2
Paul Bley Quintet | Barrage | ESP Disk | ESP 1008-2
And Now The Queer
Art Farmer Quartet | Warm Valley | Concord | CCD 4212
And Other
Muneer B.Fennell & The Rhythm String Band | An Encounter With Higher Forces | double moon | CHRDM 71019
And Peace Is A Lonely Quest Together
Astrud Gilberto With Antonio Carlos Jobim And The Marty Paich Orchestra | The Astrud Gilberto Album | Verve | 823009-1
And Satisfy
AM 4 | ...And She Answered | ECM | 1394
And She Answered: When You Return To Me, I Will Open Quick The Cage Door, I Will Let The Red Bird Flee
Mitch Seidman Quartet | How 'Bout It? | Jardis Records | JRCD 20135
And She Remembers Me
Tal Farlow Quartet | Autumn In New York | Verve | 2304321 IMS
And So It Goes
Daniel Flors Group | When Least Expected | Fresh Sound Records | FSNT 080 CD
Jill Seifers And Her Quartet | The Waiting | Fresh Sound Records | FSNT 072 CD
Frank Wess And His Orchestra | Tryin' To Make My Blues Turn Green | Concord | CCD 4592
And So To Sleep Again
Coleman Hawkins And His Orchestra | The Hawk Talks | Affinity | AFF 139
And The Angels Sing
Benny Goodman And His Orchestra | Camel Caravan Broadcast 1939 Vol.1 | Phontastic | NCD 8817
The Benny Goodman Story | Capitol | 833569-2
Della Reese With The Neal Hefti Orchestra | Della | RCA | 2663912-2
Don Lanphoro/Camillc Pcterson Duo | Don Loves Midge | Hep | 2027
Etta Jones And Her Quartet | Hollar! | Original Jazz Classics | OJCCD 1061(PR 7284)
Glenn Miller And His Orchestra | Original Recordings From 1938 to 1942,Vol.2 | RCA | 2118549-2
Louis Armstrong With Sy Oliver's Choir And Orchestra | Louis Armstrong-Heavenly Music | Ambassador | CLA 1916
Tommy Dorsey And His Orchestra | Tommy Dorsey In Concert | RCA | NL 89780 DP
And The Angels Sing-
Benny Goodman And His Orchestra | Big City Swing | Decca | TAB 5
And The Father Said...(Intermediate)
Mark Kramer Trio | Evita En Jazz | Telarc Digital | CD 83422
And The Rest Are What They Are - ...And The Rest Are What They Are
Billy Jenkins And Fun Horns | East/West Now Wear The Same Vest | Babel | BDV 9601
And Their White Tigers
Counterculture | Art Gecko | B&W Present | BW 025
And Then
Billy Cobham Trio | The Art Of Three | IN+OUT Records | 77045-2
And Then Again
Bobby Watson Sextet | No Question About It | Blue Note | 790262-2
Kenny Barron Quartet | Invitation | Criss Cross | Criss 1044
And Then I Knew
Holly Slater Quartet | The Mood Was There | Ronnie Scott's Jazz House | JHCD 053
And Then I Wrote
George Shearing With The Montgomery Brothers | Wes Montgomery-The Complete Riverside Recordings | Riverside | 12 RCD 4408-2
Wes Montgomery Quintet | Wes And Friends | Milestone | M 47013
And Then It Had To Be You - ...And Then It Had To Be You
Sammy Kaye And His Orchestra | The Uncollected:Sammy Kaye,Vol.3 | Hindsight | HSR 207
And Then My Love I Found You
Dizzy Gillespie And Arturo Sandoval Quintet | To A Finland Station | Original Jazz Classics | OJCCD 733-2(2310889)
And Then She Stopped
Louie Bellson Septet | Prime Time | Concord | CCD 4064
And Then She Wept
Hank Jones Quintet | Hank Jones Quartet-Quintet | Savoy | SV 0147(MG 12037)
And Then You'll Know
Jessica Williams Trio | ...And Then,There's This! | Timeless | CD SJP 345
And These Few Words - ...And These Few Words
Geri Allen Group | Maroons | Blue Note | 799493-2
And Time Goes On
Freddie Redd Sextet | Everybody Loves A Winner | Milestone | MCD 9187-2
And We Were Lovers
Ahmad Jamal Quartet | Nature(The Essence Part III) | Atlantic | 3984-23105-2
Patrick Williams Orchestra | Come On And Shine | MPS | 68199
And What
Herbie Hancock Septet | My Point Of View | Blue Note | 521226-2
And What If I Don't
Herbie Hancock:The Complete Blue Note Sixties Sessions | Blue Note | 495569-2
Cantaloupe Island | Blue Note | 829331-2
Bianca Ciccu With The Randy Brecker Quintet | The Gusch | ITM Records | ITM 1440
And When I Die
Liane Carroll Quartet | Dolly Bird | Ronnie Scott's Jazz House | JHCD 051
And When You Are Young(dedicated to Bob Kennedy)
Phil Woods And His European Rhythm Machine | Phil Woods/Slide Hampton 1968 Jazz | Jazztime(EMI) | 781253-2
And Zero
Bebo Valdés Group | Bebo Rides Again | Messidor | 15834 CD
Andalucia
The Caribbean Jazz Project | Island Stories | Inak | 30392
Andante
Chico Hamilton Quintet | With Strings Attached/The Three Faces Of Chico | Warner | 9362-47874-2
Jacques Loussier Trio | Play Bach No.3 | Decca | 157892-2
La Gaia Scienza | Love Fugue-Robert Schumann | Winter&Winter | 910049-2
Rene Bottlang | Infront | Owl Records | 022
Saxophon And Organ | Above The Clouds | Naxos Jazz | 86041-2
Andante-
Jacques Loussier Trio | Ravel's Bolero | Telarc Digital | CD 83466
Swingle Singers | Swingle Singers Singing Mozart | Philips | 548538-2
Massimo Colombo Trio | Alexander | SPLASC(H) Records | H 177
Andante Cantabile In Modo De Blues-
Paquito D'Rivera Group With The Absolute Ensemble | Habanera | Enja | ENJ-9395 2
Andante Con Moto A Poco Rubato
Jean-Michel Defaye Trio | Morat Jazz Trio | Forlane | UCD 16650
Andante from String Quartet Op.29 No.13 in A Minor(Schubert,D 804)
Swingle Singers | Swingle Singers Getting Romantic | Philips | 586736-2
Andante from String Quartet Op.44 No.1 In D Major(Mendelssohn-Bartholdy)
Swingling Telemann | Philips | 586735-2
Andante Moderato-
Eugen Cicero Trio | Swings Tschaikowsky & Liszt | MPS | 88039-2
Andantino From Tchaikovsky Symphony No.4(2nd movement)
Joelle Leandre-Carlos Zingaro | Ecritures | Adda | 590038
Andantino(Sonata In C-Mino)-
Ramon Valle Trio | No Escape | ACT | 9424-2
Andar Por Dentro
Louis Smith Quintet | Louisville | Steeplechase | SCCD 31552
Ande
Here Comes Louis Smith | Blue Note | 852438-2
Andere
Der Rote Bereich | Risky Business | ACT | 9407-2
Anderes Obst
Birka | Jazz I Sverige '78 | Caprice | CAP 1145
Andina
Al Di Meola Group | Tiramisu | Manhattan | CDP 7469952
Andre Heyward Interlude
Andy McKee And NEXT with Hamiet Bluiett | Sound Root | Mapleshade | 04432
Andreas Fleischmann
Willie Williams Quartet | Spirit Willie | Enja | ENJ-7045 2
Andre's Mood
Elmar Kräling | Pianomusic | FMP | 0560
Andre's Turn
Don Pullen Trio | Random Thoughts | Blue Note | 794347-2
Andy & Andy
Ernie Watts-Chick Corea Quartet | 4Tune | West Wind | WW 2105
Anecdote 1
Sylvie Courvoisier Group | Ocre | Enja | ENJ-9323 2
Anecdote 2
Ocre | Enja | ENJ-9323 2
Anecdote 3
Ocre | Enja | ENJ-9323 2
Anecdote 4
John Coltrane-Wilbur Harden Sextet | Africa-The Savoy Sessions | Savoy | ???
Anekdoten
Lozenzo Petrocca Quartet | Stop It | Edition Musikat | EDM 018
Anema E Core
Steve LaSpina Quintet | When I'm Alone | Steeplechase | SCCD 31376
Angel
Billy Usselton Sextet | Modern Jazz Gallery | Fresh Sound Records | KXL 5001(252282-1 Kapp)
Gunter Hampel And His Galaxie Dream Band | Ruomi | Birth | 0023
Louis Armstrong With Sy Oliver's Choir And Orchestra | Louis Armstrong-Heavenly Music | Ambassador | CLA 1916
Peter Möltgen Quartet | Mellow Acid | Edition Collage | EC 495-2
Pinguin Moschner-Joe Sachse | If 69 Was 96/The Music Of Jimi Hendrix | Aho-Recording | CD 1016
Angel Blue
Stan Levey's Sextet | Grand Stan | Fresh Sound Records | FSR 2000(Bethlehem BCP 71)
Angel Child
Louis Armstrong With Sy Oliver's Choir And Orchestra | Louis Armstrong-Heavenly Music | Ambassador | CLA 1916
Angel Eyes
Ahmad Jamal Trio | Live At The Alhambra | Vogue | 655002
Alvin Queen Quartet | Introducing:RTB Big Band | Plainisphare | PL 1267-23
Anita O'Day With The Russ Garcia Orchestra | Verve Jazz Masters 49:Anita O'Day | Verve | 527653-2
Archie Shepp Quartet | Black Ballad | Timeless | CD SJP 386
Benny Carter Sextet | Cosmopolite | Verve | 521673-2
Bob Cooper Quartet | Milano Blues | Fresh Sound Records | FSR-CD 0179
Carol Kidd With The Sandy Taylor Trio | All My Tomorrows | Linn Records | AKD 005
Chris Connor And Her Quartet | Chris In Person | Atlantic | AMCY 1063
Dave Brubeck Quartet | Angel Eyes | CBS | SRCS 9368
Denise Jannah And Her Band | A Heart Full Of Music | Timeless | CD SJP 414
Ella Fitzgerald And Paul Smith | The Intimate Ella | Verve | 839838-2
Ella Fitzgerald With Orchestra | Welcome To Jazz: Ella Fitzgerald | Koch Records | 322 078 D1
Ella Fitzgerald With Sy Oliver And His Orchestra | Ella Fitzgerald 75th Birthday Celebration:The Original Decca Recordings | GRP | GRP 26192
Eric Alexander Quartet | Two Of A Kind | Criss Cross | Criss 1133
Freddy Cole With Band | A Circle Of Love | Fantasy | FCD 9674-2
Gary Thomas Group | Till We Have Faces | JMT Edition | 514000-2
Gene Ammons Quintet | Gene Ammons-Greatest Hits Vol.1:The Sixties | Original Jazz Classics | OJCCD 6005-2
Heiner Franz Trio | A Window To The Soul | Jardis Records | JRCD 8801
Helen Merrill With The Gary Peacock Trio | Sposin' | Storyville | SLP 1014
Herb Ellis-Joe Pass | Two For The Road | Original Jazz Classics | 2310714
Jenny Evans And Her Quintet | Gonna Go Fishin' | Enja | ENJ-9403 2
Joachim Kühn-Rolf Kühn | Love Stories | IN+OUT Records | 77061-2
Joe Albany-Warne Marsh Trio | The Right Combination | Original Jazz Classics | OJCCD 1749-2
Kenny Burrell With The Don Sebesky Orchestra | Blues-The Common Ground | Verve | 589101-2
Kenny Colman With The London Philharmonic Orchestra | Dreamscape | Justin Time | JTR 8466-2
Larry Schneider Trio | Freedom Jazz Dance | Steeplechase | SCCD 31390
Marion Brown | Recollections-Ballads And Blues For Saxophone | Creative Works Records | CW LP 1001
McCoy Tyner Big Band | The Turning Point | Birdology | 513163-2
Modern Jazz Quartet | Live 1956 | Jazz Anthology | JA 5207
Paul Desmond Quartet | Victor Jazz History Vol.13:Modern Jazz-Cool & West Coast | RCA | 2135732-2
Phil Upchurch Group | Whatever Happened To The Blues | VeraBra Records | CDVBR 2066-2
Ray Draper Quintet | A Tuba Jazz | Fresh Sound Records | FSR-CD 20(882173)
Scott Hamilton With Strings | Scott Hamilton With Strings | Concord | CCD 4538
Singers Unlimited With The Robert Farnon Orchestra | Sentimental Journey | MPS | 68102
Tom Mega + Band | A Moon Of Roses | ITM Records | ITM 1487
Viktoria Tolstoy With The Jacob Karlzon Trio & Strings | Blame It On My Youth | Kaza(EMI) | 536620-2
Willis Jackson Sextet | Gravy | Prestige | PCD 24254-2
Wynton Marsalis With Art Blakey And His Jazz Messengers | Wynton Marsalis:Jodi | Memo Music | Gate 7013
Angel Eyes(alt.take)
Ute Kannenberg Quartet | Kannenberg On Purpose | Jazz Haus Musik | JHM 0109 CD
Angel Eyes(Intro)-
Donald Byrd Quintet | Groovin' For Nat | Black Lion | BLP 60134
Angel Face
Bill Evans-Jim Hall | Trio (Motian Peacock)-Duo(Hall) | Verve | 2-2509 IMS
Ultimate Bill Evans selected by Herbie Hancock | Verve | 557536-2
Coleman Hakins And His Orchestra | Body And Soul | RCA | 26685152
Coleman Hawkins And His All Stars | Fats Navarro:The 1946-1949 Small Group Sessions(Studio Recordings-Master Takes),Vol.2 | Blue Moon | BMCD 1017
Hank Jones Trio | Bluesette | Black & Blue | BLE 233168
Angel Food
Bob Crosby And His Orchestra | So Far So Good | Halcyon | DHDL 132

TITELVERZEICHNIS

Angel In The Night
Clifford Jordan Quartet | Firm Roots | Steeplechase | SCCD 31033
Original Phalanx | Original Phalanx | DIW | DIW 801 CD

Angel Oak
Nels Cline Quintet | Angelica | Enja | ENJ-5063 2

Angel Song
Tony Williams Quintet | Angel Street | Blue Note | 748494-2

Angel Voice
Art Pepper Quintet | The Return Of Art Pepper -The Complete Art Pepper Aladdin Recordings Vol.1 | Blue Note | 870601-9

Angel Wings
Klaus Doldinger Jubilee | Doldinger Jubilee '75 | Atlantic | ATL 50186

Angel(alt take)
Gunter Hampel And His Galaxie Dream Band | Angel | Birth | 009

Angela
Eliane Elias Quartet | Eliane Elias Plays Jobim | Blue Note | 793089-2
Lee Morgan Quintet | We Remember You | Fresh Sound Records | FSCD 1024
The Rippingtons | Moonlighting | GRP | GRP 96052

Angela Mia
Louis Armstrong With Sy Oliver's Choir And Orchestra | Louis Armstrong-Heavenly Music | Ambassador | CLA 1916

Angelica
Bob Mover Trio Feat. Paul Bley And John Abercrombie | The Night Bathers | Justin Time | Just 14
Harold Danko Quartet | The Feeling Of Jazz | Steeplechase | SCCD 31392
Richard Wyands Trio | Get Out Of Town | Steeplechase | SCCD 31401

Angelique
Clark Terry & Chico O Farril Orchestra | Spanish Rice | Verve | 9861050

Angelitos Negros
Perry Robinson Quartet | Perry Robinson Quartet | Timescrapper | TSCR 9613

Angelology
Angelo Debarre Group | Angelo Debarre | Hot Club Records | HCRCD 116

Angels
Albert Ayler Group | Spirits Rejoice | ESP Disk | ESP 1020-2
Geri Allen Sextet | The Gathering | Verve | 557614-2
Keith Jarrett Group | Treasure Island | MCA | 2292-54623-2

Angels And Artiface
Sunny Murray Orchestra | Big Chief | Pathe | 1727561

Angel's Idea
Doctor Clayton Band | Gotta Find My Baby | Swingtime(Contact) | BT 2005

Angels' Share
Charlie Byrd | The Charlie Byrd Christmas Album | Concord | CCD 42004

Angels We Have Heard On High
Jan Harrington Sextet | Jan Harrington's Christmas In New Orleans | Nagel-Heyer | NHR SP 4
Keith Foley | Music For Christmas | dmp Digital Music Productions | CD 452

Angels(part 1-5)
Los Angeles Neophonic Orchestra | Stan Kenton Conducts The Los Angeles Neophonic Orchestra | Capitol | 494502-2

Angie
Ulli Bögershausen | Ageless Guitar Solos | Laika Records | 8695071
Bud Revels Group | Survivors | Enja | ENJ-6066 2

Anglar(Angels)
David Torn/Geoffrey Gordon | Best Laid Plans | ECM | 1284

Angle Of Incidents
Michael Brecker Quindectet | Wide Angles | Verve | 076142-2

Angle Of Repose
Ahmad Mansour Quartet | Episode | Timeless | CD SJP 341

Angola
Johnny Dyani Quartet | Angolian Cry | Steeplechase | SCCD 31209

Angry
Richard Fairhurst Quartet | The Hungry Ants | Babel | BDV 9504

Angry Blackbird
Nancy Harrow Group | Lost Lady | Soul Note | 121263-2

Angry Dragon
Cheik Tidiana Fall Trio | African Magic | Circle Records | RK 17-5679/17 IMS

Angst
Daniel Schnyder Group | Tanatula | Enja | ENJ-9302 2
New Winds | Digging It Harder From Afar | Victo | CD 028

Angu
David S. Ware Quartet | Great Bliss Vol.1 | Silkheart | SHCD 127

Aniexty
Aldo Romano Quartet | Canzoni | Enja | 9102-2

Anika
Anima Trio | Blue In Green | Anima Records | DV-CD 003

Animal Dance
Modern Jazz Quartet | Longing For The Continent | LRC Records | CDC 7678(874386)
Modern Jazz Quartet And The All-Star Jazz Band | Jazz Dialogue | Philips | PHCE 3018 PMS

Animali In Marcia
Enrico Rava 4uartet | Animals | Inak | 8801

Anisa
Fats Waller And His Rhythm | The Indispensable Fats Waller Vol.7/8(1938-1940) | RCA | 2126417-2

Anita's Dance
Gil Evans Orchestra | Live At The Public Theater Vol.1(New York 1980) | Black-Hawk | BKH 525 CD

Anja
Ana Caram Group | Blue Bossa | Chesky | JD 219

Ankunft
Fun Horns | Surprise | Jazzpoint | JP 1029 CD

Ankunft Des Orchesters Der Deutschen Jazzpolizei-
Marcus Sukiennik Big Band | A Night In Tunisia Suite(7 Variationen über Dizzy Gillespie's 'A Night In Tunisia') | Jazz Haus Musik | ohne Nummer

Anlauf
Hannes Clauss Quartett | Dances | Acoustic Music Records | 319.1161.2

Anlipark
Earl Hines | Another Monday Date | Prestige | P 24043

Ann
Earl Hines And His Orchestra | The Indispensable Earl Hines Vol.1/2 | RCA | 2126407-2

Ann Arbor Boogie
Karl Ratzer Group | Gumbo Dive | RST-Records | 91540-2

Ann,Wonderful One
Chet Baker Quintet | Chet Baker Plays & Sings | West Wind | WW 2108

Anna
Chick Corea | Expressions | GRP | GRP 97732
Cindy Blackman Quartet | Trio + Two | Freelance | FRL-CD 015
Gene Ammons Septet | Gene Ammons Bossa Nova | Original Jazz Classics | OJCCD 351-2(PR 7257)
Remember Shakti | The Believer | Verve | 549044-2

Anna Sophia
Juan Garcia Esquivel Orchestra | Juan's Again | RCA | 2168206-2

Anna(El Negro Zumbo)
Gray Gordon And His Tic-Toc Rhythm Orchestra | The Uncollected Gray Gordon | Hindsight | HSR 206

Annäherung
George Gruntz Trio With Franco Ambrosetti | Mock-Lo-Motion | TCB Records | TCB 95552

Anna's Cat
George Shearing | Favorite Things | Telarc Digital | CD 83398

Annie
John Goldsby Sextet | Viewpoint | Nagel-Heyer | CD 2014
Billy May And His Orchestra With Members Of The Jimmy Lunceford Orchestra | Great Swing Classics In Hi-Fi | Capitol | 521223-2

Annie Laurie
Don Byas And The All Star Rhythm Section | Don Byas Complete American Small Group Recordings | Definitive Records | DRCD 11213

Tiny Grimes Quintet | Tiny Grimes:The Complete 1944-1950 Vol.2(1947-1950) | Blue Moon | BMCD 6006

Annie's Dance
Annie Ross And Her Quartet | Annie Ross & King Pleasure Sings | Original Jazz Classics | OJC 217(P 7128)

Anniversary Song
Django Reinhardt And The Quintet Du Hot Club De France | Django Reinhardt Portrait | Barclay | DALP 2/1939
Quintet Du Hot Club De France | Verve Jazz Masters 38:Django Reinhardt | Verve | 516931-2
Michael Riessler Group | Orange | ACT | 9274-2

Annonce-
Art Blakey And The Jazz Messengers | Swiss Radio Days Jazz Series Vol.6:Art Blakey's Jazz Messengers | TCB Records | TCB 02062

Announcement
Bopland Boys | Jazz West Coast Live-Hollywood Jazz Vol.2: Bopland Boys | Savoy | SV 0165
Chet Baker-Stan Getz Quintet | The Stockholm Concerts | Verve | 537555-2
Dave Liebman Trio | Spirit Renewed | Owl Time Line | 3819112
Oscar Peterson With Orchestra | A Royal Wedding Suite | Original Jazz Classics | OJCCD 973-2(2312129)
Stan Getz Quartet With Chet Baker | Stan Getz-Chet Baker:Quintessence Vol.1 | Concord | CCD 4807
Charlie Parker And His Orchestra | Bird's Eyes Last Unissued Vol.18 | Philology | W 848.2

Announcement by Al Anderson
John Fischer-Hans Kumpf Quartet | Jam Session Moscow | Fusion | 8005

Announcement by Art Blakey
Art Blakey And The Jazz Messengers | At The Cafe Bohemia Vol.2 | Blue Note | 532149-2
Swiss Radio Days Jazz Series Vol.2:Art Blakey's Jazz Messengers | TCB Records | TCB 02022
Jimmy Smith Quintet | Cool Blues | Blue Note | 535587-2

Announcement by Babs Gonzales
Junior Mance Quartet | At Town Hall Vol.1 | Enja | 9085-2

Announcement by Dannie Richmond
Digby Fairweather And His Friends | North Sea Festival Vol.1 | Jazz Colours | 874758-2

Announcement by Johnny Mercer
Art Blakey And The Jazz Messengers | Jazzbühne Berlin '80 | Repertoire Records | REPCD 4909-CC

Announcement by Leonard Feather
Billie Holiday With The Carl Drinkard Trio | Billie's Blues | Blue Note | 748786-2
Billie Holiday With Bobby Tucker | The Complete Jazz At The Philharmonic On Verve 1944-1949 | Verve | 523893-2

Announcement by Norman Granz
Billie Holiday Story Vol.1:Jazz At The Philharmonic | Verve | 521642-2
Billie Holiday With The Mal Waldron Trio | Billie Holiday Story Vol.1:Jazz At The Philharmonic | Verve | 521642-2
JATP All Stars | Jazz At The Philharmonic 1957 | Tax | CD 3703-2
The Complete Jazz At The Philharmonic On Verve 1944-1949 | Verve | 523893-2
The Complete Jazz At The Philharmonic On Verve 1944-1949 | Verve | 523893-2
Meade Lux Lewis | The Complete Jazz At The Philharmonic On Verve 1944-1949 | Verve | 523893-2
Art Blakey And The Jazz Messengers | A Night At Birdland Vol. 1 | Blue Note | 532146-2

Announcement by Pee Wee Marquette
Meet You At The Jazz Corner Of The World | Blue Note | 535565-2
Birdland Stars | Birdland Stars 1956 | Bluebird | 63 66159-2

Announcement by Pee Wee Marquette and Art Blakey
Pete Allen's Jazz Band | North Sea Festival Vol.2 | Jazz Colours | 874759-2

Announcement by 'Symphony Sid Torin'
Barry Harris Septet | Interpertations Of Monk | DIW | DIW 395/8 CD

Announcement by Willis Connover
Art Ensemble Of Chicago | Urban Bushmen | ECM | 1211/12

Announcement Of Victory-
Joe McPhee & Survival Unit II | At WBAI's Free Music Store | Hat Art | CD 6197

Annoying Neighbour
Macrino-Rovagna Ensemble | New Age Jazz | Penta Flowers | CDPIA 003

Anos Despues(Years Later)
Ana Caram Group | Rio After Dark | Chesky | JD 28

Another
Klaus Koch | Basse Partout | Creative Works Records | CW CD 1011-1

Another Ambience
Victor Lewis Trio | Three Way Conversations | Red Records | 123276-2

Another Aspect
Vince Weber | The Boogie Man | Rüssl Räckords | 062-29597

Another Chance
Ingolf Burkhardt-Ludwig Nuß Quintet | Jazzed Friends | Mons Records | MR 874780

Another Dozen
Bud Powell Trio | Time Was | Bluebird | ND 86367

Another Dream
Dieter Köhnlein-Uwe Kropinski | In Und Um C | Aho-Recording | AHO CD 1015(CD 661)

Another Earth
John Lewis With The Gary McFarland Orchestra | Essence | Atlantic | AMCY 1097

Another Fine Mess
Interjazz IV | Good Old Circus | FMP | SAJ 33

Another Goodun'
Charlie Parker All Stars | The Complete Savoy Studio Sessions | Savoy | 886421

Another Hair-Do
Charlie Parker Quintet | Bird/The Savoy Recordings (Master Takes) | Savoy | SJL 2201 (801177)

Another Kind Of Soul
Bop City | Bop City:Hip Strut | Hip Bop | HIBD 8013

Another Language
Roy Hargrove Quintet | Family | Verve | 527630-2

Another Level
Steve Coleman Group | Motherland Pulse | JMT Edition | 919001-2
Steve Coleman Quintet | Jump On It | Enja | 4094

Another Meaning Of The Blues
Myra Melford-Han Bennink | Eleven Ghosts | HatOLOGY | 507

Another Nat
Furio Romano Quartet | What Colour For A Tale | SPLASC(H) Records | CD H 351-2

Another Night In Tunisia
Jasper Van't Hof Group | Blau | ACT | 9203-2

Another Night In Tunisia(for Georg Baselitz)
Lonnie Johnson | Another Night To Cry | Original Blues Classics | OBCCD 550-2(BV 1062)

Another One
Oscar Pettiford All Stars | Oscar Pettiford | Polydor | MP 2346 IMS

Another Shade Of Blue
Louie Bellson's Magic 7 | Louie Bellson's Magic 7 | Concord | CCD 4742

Another Time Another Place
Benny Carter Quartet With Dizzy Gillespie | In The Mood For Swing | Limelight | 820806-2 IMS

Another Valley
The Dolphins | Malayan Breeze | dmp Digital Music Productions | CD 474

Another Way Around
Phil Minton/Veryan Weston | Ways | ITM Records | ITM 1420

Another World
Andy LaVerne Trio | Another World | Steeplechase | SCCD 31086

Another World Is Possible
Another World | Steeplechase | SCCD 31086

Another Year
Dave Liebman Quintet | Return Of The Tenor:Standards | Double Time Records | DTRCD-109

Anouman
Henri Crolla Orchestra | Jazz In Paris:Henri Crolla-Notre Ami Django | EmArCy | 014062-2
Joe Pass Quartet | Summer Night | Pablo | 2310939-2
The Rosenberg Trio | The Rosenberg Trio:The Collection | Verve | 537152-2
Poncho Sanchez And His Orchestra | Para Todos | Concord | CCD 4600

Anstatt-Dass Song(I)
Brass Attack | Brecht Songs | Tutu Records | 888190-2*

Anstatt-Dass Song(II)
African Force | Palanquin's Pole | ITM Records | ITM 1433

Answer My Love
Götz Tangerding Group | First Step | Bhakti Jazz | BR 20

Answering Service
John Abercrombie Quartet | The Toronto Concert | Maracatu | MAC 940003

Ant Steps On An Elephant's Toe
Jim Black Alasnoaxis | Splay | Winter&Winter | 910076-2

Ant Work Song
Dexter Gordon Quartet | The Apartment | Steeplechase | SCCD 31025

Antarktisch
Al Haig Sextet | Early Getz | Prestige | P 24088

Ante Room
Stan Getz:The Complete 1948-1952 Quintet Sessions(Master Takes) | Blue Moon | BMCD 1015

Antes Que Seja Tarde
8 Bold Souls | Ant Farm | Arabesque Recordings | AJ 0114

Anthem
Gary Burton Septet | Gary Burton & Friends-Six Pack | GRP | GRP 96852
Mitchel Forman | Childhood Dreams | Soul Note | SN 1050
Rick Margitza Septet | Color | Blue Note | 792279-2

Anthropology
All Stars | Bird's Eyes Last Unissued Vol.21:Bird On TV/Bird On Bandbox | Philology | W 851.2
Art Pepper Plus Eleven | Modern Jazz Classics | Original Jazz Classics | OJC20 341-2
A Treasury Of Modern Jazz Classics | Mobile Fidelity | MFCD 805
Art Pepper Trio | Art Pepper:The Complete Galaxy Recordings | Galaxy | 16GCD 1016-2
Artworks | Galaxy | GXY 5148
Bud Powell Trio | The Legacy | Jazz Door | JD 1204
Dizzy Gillespie And His Orchestra | Dizzy Gillespie:Night In Tunisia | Dreyfus Jazz Line | FDM 36734-2
Jazz Gallery:Dizzy Gillespie | RCA | 2114165-2
Dizzy Gillespie Septet | Dizzy Gillespie-Diz Delights | RCA | CL 89804 SF
Lewis Keel Quintet | Coming Out Swinging | Muse | MCD 5438
Paul Kuhn Trio | Play It Again Paul | IN+OUT Records | 77040-2
Peter Herbolzheimer Rhythm Combination & Brass | More Bebop | Koala Records | CD P 6

Anthropology(incomplete)
Eye Of The Hurricane | Eye Of The Hurricane | Aho-Recording | AHO CD 1007(CD 662)

Anti Climax
Muneer B.Fennell & The Rhythm String Band | An Encounter With Higher Forces | double moon | CHRDM 71019

Anti Ego Groove
Don Rendell And Pete Martin With The Joe Palin Trio | Live At The Avgarde Gallery Manchaster | Spotlite | SPJ 501

Antiphon
Harold Danko Quintet | The Harold Danko Quartet feat.Gregory Herbert | Inner City | IC 1029 IMS

Antonia
The Tango Kings | The Tango Kings | Big World | BW 2016

Antonico
Gato Barbieri Group | Gato Barbieri:The Complete Flying Dutchman Recordings 1969-1973 | RCA | 2154555-2

Antonio Das Mortes
Gato Barbieri Sextet | Gato Barbieri:The Complete Flying Dutchman Recordings 1969-1973 | RCA | 2154555-2

Antonio's Song
Aki Takase Trio | Clapping Music | Enja | 8090-2

Ants
Double Drums Project | Double Drums Project | BIT | 11264

Anu Anu
Glenn Miller And His Orchestra | The Genius Of Glenn Miller Vol.1 | RCA | ND 90090

Anxienty-The Colonal Of Mortal Life
Cindy Blackman Quintet | Code Red | Muse | MCD 5365

Any Moment Now
Buddy Johnson And His Orchestra | Buddy And Ella Johnson 1953-1964 | Bear Family Records | BCD 15479 DH

Any Day Now
Gerd Baumann-Alessandro Ricciarelli Quartet | Say No More | Edition Collage | EC 489-2
Hank Crawford-Jimmy McGriff Quartet | On The Blue Side | Milestone | M 9177

Any Minute
Chris Barber-Barry Martin Band | Collaboration | GHB Records | BCD 40

Any Old Time
Artie Shaw And His Orchestra | Jazz Gallery:Billie Holiday Vol.1(1933-49) | RCA | 2119542-2
Planet Jazz:Swing | Planet Jazz | 2169651-2
This Is Artie Shaw | RCA | NL 89411 DP
Nat King Cole Trio | Any Old Time | Giants Of Jazz | GOJ 1031

Any Old Time Of the Day
David Benoit Group | Shaken Not Stirred | GRP | GRP 97872

Any Other World
Berlin Contemporary Jazz Orchestra | The Morlocks And Other Pieces | FMP | CD 61

Any Place I Hang My Hat Is Home
Rosemary Clooney And Her Band | Sings The Lyrics Of Johnny Mercer | Concord | CCD 4333

Any Time
Duke Ellington And His Famous Orchestra | The Complete Duke Ellington-vol. 4 | CBS | CBS 88035

Any Time Any Day Any Where
Lionel Hampton And His Orchestra | The Complete Lionel Hampton Vol.1/2(1937-1938) | RCA | 2115525-2

Any Way You Can
Bessie Smith With Fletcher Henderson | Bessie Smith-The Complete Recordings Vol.1 | CBS | 467895-2

Anya Goes East
Asgard | Songs Of G. | Acoustic Music Records | 319.1042.2

Anyday
Five Blind Boys Of Alabama | The Five Blind Boys Of Alabama | Heritage Records | HT 315 IMS

Anyone
George Shearing | Favorite Things | Telarc Digital | CD 83398

Anything Can Happen
Michael Feinstein With Burton Lane | Michael Feinstein Sings The Burton Lane Songbook Vol.1 | Nonesuch | 7559-79243-2

Anything Can Swing-
Benny Goodman And His Orchestra | Camel Caravan Broadcast 1939 Vol.2 | Phontastic | NCD 8818
The Birth Of Swing | Bluebird | ND 90601(3)

Anything Goes
Chris Connor With Band | Chris Connor | Atlantic | 7567-80769-2
Claude Williamson Trio | The Fabulous Claude Williamson Trio | Fresh Sound Records | FSR-CD 0051
Ella Fitzgerald With The Buddy Bregman Orchestra | The Complete Ella Fitzgerald Song Books of Harold Arlen, Irving Berlin, Duke Ellington, George & Ira Gershwin, Jerome Kern, Johnny Mercer, Cole Porter And Rogers & Hart | Verve | 519832-2

John T. Williams Quartet | Modern Jazz Gallery | Fresh Sound Records | KXL 5001(252282-1 Kapp)
Singers Unlimited | A Capella III | MPS | 68245

Anything Goes-
Clark Terry Octet | Clark Terry | Verve | 537754-2

Anything You Wanna Do(I Wanna Do With You)
Fletcher Henderson And His Sextet | New-York December 1950 | Jazz Anthology | JA 5185

Anytime Anyplace
| Little Jimmy Scott | Specialty | SPCD 2170-2

Anytime Anyplace Anywhere
Slim Gaillard Group | Anytime Anyplace Anywhere | Hep | CD 2020

Anytime Tomorrow
Nils Landgren Funk Unit | Fonk Da World | ACT | 9299-2

Anytime,Anywhere
Urbanator | Urbanator II | Hip Bop | HIBD 8012
Walt Weiskopf Quintet | Anytown | Criss Cross | Criss 1169

Anyway...Was There Ever Nothing?
Kölner Saxophon Mafia With Guests | Kölner Saxophon Mafia: 20 Jahre Saxuelle Befreiung | Jazz Haus Musik | JHM 0115 CD

Anywhere I Lay My Head
Bob Helm's Jazz Band | Hotter Than That | Stomp Off Records | CD 1310

Aon
Didier Lockwood Quartet + Bob Malach | Fasten Seat Belts | MPS | 68283

Aos Pes Da Cruz
Baden Powell Quartet | En Concert Avec Europe 1 | Laserlight | 710703/04

Apaches-
Trio Neue Deutsche Blasmusik | Vier Stücke Für Das Trio Neue Deutsche Blasmusik | Misp Records | CD 512

Aparajita,The Lady From The East
Furio Romano Quartet | What Colour For A Tale | SPLASC(H) Records | CD H 351-2

Aparis
Paul Smith Quartet | I Just Love Jazz Piano | Savoy | SV 0117(MG 12100)

Apart Together
Kostas Konstantinou-Vassilis Tsabropoulos | Concentric Cycles | Nabel Records:Jazz Network | CD 4698

Apartement 103
Loverly | Play World Wild Music | ITM Records | ITM 1419

Apartment 512
Tete Montoliu | Boston Concert | Steeplechase | SCS 1152/3

Apasionado
Jean-Luc Ponty Quintet | Sonata Erotica | Affinity | AFF 133

Apathy
Larry Coryell-Kenny Barron | Shining Hour | 32 Jazz | 32112

Ape Woman
Unit X | Rated X | Timescrapper | TSCR 9618

Apeiron
Lennie Tristano Trio | The Rarest Trio/Quartet Sessions 1946/47 | Raretone | 5008 FC

Apes And Peacocks-
Ralph Schweizer Big Band | DAY Dream | Chaos | CACD 8177
Billy Drummond Quartet | The Gift | Criss Cross | Criss 1083

Apex Blues
Dutch Swing College Band | DSC Live 1974 | DSC Production | PA 1013 (801068)
Great British Jazz Band | The Great British Jazz Band:Jubilee | Candid | CCD 79720
Jazz Jokers | Jazz-Jokers | Jazzpoint | JP 1024 LP
The Tremble Kids | The Tremble Kids:The Of 40 Years | BELL Records | BLR 84060

Aphrodesia
Barry Deister Quintet | East/West Dialogue | L+R Records | CDLR 45037

Apne Havner(Open Harbours)
Ralph Peterson Quintet | The Art Of War | Criss Cross | Criss 1206

Apollo Tropical
Dave Brubeck Quartet | Near-Myth | Original Jazz Classics | OJC 236(F 3319)

Apologies
Mezz Mezzrow And His Orchestra | Jazz Drumming Vol.1(1927-1937) | Fenn Music | FJD 2701

Apologize
Michael Urbaniak Trio | My One And Only Love | Steeplechase | SCCD 31159

Apology Nicaragua
Gregor Hilden Group | Westcoast Blues | Acoustic Music Records | 319.1162.2

Apostle Man
Jimmy Smith Quartet | On The Sunny Side | Blue Note | LT 1092

Apostrophe
Lars Gullin Group | Made In Sweden Vol.2: 24.3.1951-12.12.1952 | Magnetic Records | MRCD 113

Apothegm
Kenny Clarke Meets The Detroit Jazzmen | Kenny Clarke Meets The Detroit Jazz Men | Savoy | SV 0243(SJL 1111)

Appalachian Dance
Richard Carr Trio | Along The Edge | Nabel Records:Jazz Network | CD 4683

Appalachian Gamelan
LeeAnn Ledgerwood Trio | Transition | Steeplechase | SCCD 31468

Appalachian Green
Aldo Romano Quintet | Night Diary | Owl Records | 018

Appear
Roscoe Mitchell | Sound Songs | Delmark | DE 493(2)

Appel Direct
Quintet Du Hot Club De France | Swing '35 -'39 | Eclipse | ECM 2051

Applause
Engelbert Wrobel's Swing Society | Live At Sägewerk | Timeless | CD TTD 588

Apple Avenue
Ralph Flanagan And His Orchestra | Dance Again Part 2 | Magic | DAWE 75

Apple Core
Gerry Mulligan Concert Jazz Band | En Concert Avec Europe 1 | Laserlight | 710382/83

Apple Honey
Woody Herman And His Orchestra | Jazz Live & Rare: Woody Herman 1945-1947 | Jazzline | ???
The Radio Years: Woody Herman And His First Herd 1944 | Hindsight | HSR 134

Applejackin'
Herbie Nichols Trio | Herbie Nichols:The Complete Blue Note Recordings | Blue Note | 859352-2
Herbie Nichols:The Complete Blue Note Recordings | Blue Note | 859352-2

Applejackin'(alt.take)
Tamia | Senza Tempo | T-Records | T 1002 CD

Apples(aka Gino)
Buddy Rich And His Orchestra | Big Swing Face | Pacific Jazz | 837989-2
John Stevens Trio | Application Interaction And ... | Spotlite | SPJ 513

Appreciation
Ahmad Jamal Trio | Live In Paris 1992 | Dreyfus Jazz Line | FDM 37019-2
Live In Paris 92 | Birdology | 849408-2

Approaching The Sea
Joe McPhee Trio | Sweet Freedom-Now What? | Hat Art | CD 6162

Après Un Reve(Fauré)
Michael Weiss Quintet | Presenting Michael Weiss | Criss Cross | Criss 1022

April
Lee Konitz Nonet | The Lee Konitz Nonet | Chiaroscuro | CR 186
Uwe Kropinski/David Friesen | Dancing With The Bass | ITM Records | 0031

April 8th
Charlie Mariano Quintet | Boston Days | Fresh Sound Records | FSR-CD 0207

April Day-
Dannie Richmond Quintet | The Last Mingus Band A.D. | Landmark | LCD 1537-2

April Fool
Eric Dolphy Quintet | Eric Dolphy:The Complete Prestige Recordings | Prestige | 9 PRCD-4418-2
Maynard Ferguson Sextet | Magnitude | Mainstream | MD CDO 712

April In My Heart
Billie Holiday With Teddy Wilson And His Orchestra | Billie Holiday:The Quintessential Vol.6(1938) | CBS | 466313-2

April In Paris
Bireli Lagrene Quartet | Blue Eyes | Dreyfus Jazz Line | FDM 36591-2
Blossom Dearie Trio | April In Paris | Fresh Sound Records | FSR 555(Barclay 74017)
Bob Mintzer Big Band | Homage To Count Basie | dmp Digital Music Productions | CD 529
Bud Powell Trio | The Best Of Bud Powell On Verve | Verve | 523392-2
Bud Powell:Complete 1947-1951 Blue Note,Verve & Roost Recordings | The Jazz Factory | JFCD 22837
Charlie Lewis Trio | JazzIn Paris:Harlem Piano In Montmartre | EmArCy | 018447-2
Charlie Parker Groups | Welcome To Jazz: Charlie Parker | Koch Records | 322 075 D1
Charlie Parker With Strings | The Verve Years (1950-51) | Verve | 2-2512 IMS
Bird: The Complete Charlie Parker On Verve | Verve | 837141-2
Charlie Parker With Strings:The Master Takes | Verve | 523984-2
Charlie Parker The Immortal Sessions Vol.2:1949-1953 | SAGA Jazz Classics | EC 3319-2
Charlie Parker The Immortal Sessions Vol.2:1949-1953 | SAGA Jazz Classics | EC 3319-2
Cindy Blackman Quartet | Works On Canvas | HighNote Records | HCD 7038
Coleman Hawkins And His All Stars | Fats Navarro:The 1946-1949 Small Group Sessions(Studio Recordings-Master Takes),Vol.2 | Blue Moon | BMCD 1017
Coleman Hawkins With Many Albam And His Orchestra | The Hawk In Paris | Bluebird | 63 51059-2
Count Basie And His Orchestra | Verve Jazz Masters 2:Count Basie | Verve | 519819-2
The Great 1959 Band In Concert | Jazz Groove | 003 IMS
Swing | Stereoplay-CD | CD 697042
Compact Jazz: The Sampler | Verve | 831376-2
Ella Fitzgerald And Louis Armstrong With The Oscar Peterson Quartet | Ella And Louis | Verve | 543304-2
The Complete Ella Fitzgerald And Louis Armstrong On Verve | Verve | 537284-2
Welcome To Jazz: Ella Fitzgerald | Koch Records | 322 078 D1
Ella Fitzgerald With The Count Basie Orchestra | Ella Fitzgerald-First Lady Of Song | Verve | 517898-2
Ella Fitzgerald With The Don Abney Trio | Ella Fitzgerald, Billie Holiday And Carmen McRae At Newport | Verve | 559809-2
Elliot Lawrence And His Orchestra | The Uncollected:Elliot Lawrence | Hindsight | HSR 182
JATP All Stars | Jazz At The Philharmonic 1957 | Tax | CD 3703-2
Jenny Evans And Her Quintet | Shiny Stockings | Enja | ENJ-9317 2
Jimmy McGriff Trio | Georgia On My Mind | LRC Records | CDC 8513
Joe Pass | I Remember Charlie Parker | Original Jazz Classics | OJC 602(2312109)
Joe Williams And Friends | Joe Williams At Newport '63 | RCA | NL 70119
Joe Williams And His Band | Planet Jazz:Joe Williams | Planet Jazz | 2165370-2
Karl Ratzer Group | Gumbo Dive | RST-Records | 91540-2
Lionel Hampton Quartet | The Lional Hampton Quintet | Verve | 589100-2
Mel Tormé | Mel Torme | Glendale | GLS 6007 IMS
Nat King Cole With The Nelson Riddle Orchestra | The Piano Style Of Nat King Cole | Capitol | 781203-2
Peter Leitch-Heiner Franz | At First Sight | Jardis Records | JRCD 9611
Ran Blake | Epistrophy | Soul Note | 121177-2
Sarah Vaughan With The Clifford Brown All Stars | Sarah Vaughan | EmArCy | 9860779
Sarah Vaughan | Verve | 543305-2
Brownie-The Complete EmArCy Recordings Of Clifford Brown | EmArCy | 838306-2
Sauter-Finegan Orchestra | The Return Of The Doodletown Fifers | EMI Records | ED 2607691
Singers Unlimited | A Capella 2 | MPS | 821860-2
Stephen Scott | Parker's Mood | Verve | 527907-2
Super Sax & L.A.Voices | Supersax & L.A.Voices Vol.3:Straighten Up And Fly Right | CBS | CBS 40547
Thelonious Monk | Pure Monk | Milestone | M 47004
Thelonious Monk-The Complete Riverside Recordings | Riverside | 15 RCD 022-2
Thelonious Monk Quartet | Paris Jazz Concert:Theloniuos Monk And His Quartet | Laserlight | 17250
San Francisco Holiday | Milestone | MCD 9199-2
Thelonious Monk Trio | The Complete Genius | Blue Note | LA 579
Thelonious Monk:The Complete Blue Note Recordings | Blue Note | 830363-2
Thelonious Monk:Complete 1947-1952 Blue Note Recordings | The Jazz Factory | JFCD 22838
Wild Bill Davis | Greatest Organ Solos Ever! | Jazz Connaisseur | JCCD 8702-2
Wild Bill Davis Quartet | Live At Swiss Radio Studio Zürich | Jazz Connaisseur | JCCD 8701-2
Wynton Marsalis Quartet | Marsalis Standard Time Vol.1 | CBS | 451039-2

April In Paris(alt.take)
Thelonious Monk Quartet | MONK. | CBS | CK 86564
Thelonious Monk Trio | Genius Of Modern Music,Vol.1 | Blue Note | 532138-2
More Genius Of Thelonious Monk | Blue Note | 300194(BNJ 61011)

April In Portugal
Franz Koglmann Tentet | A White Line | Hat Art | CD 6048

April Joy
Eddie Lang | Pioneers Of Jazz Guitar 1927-1939 | Retrieval | RTR 79015

April Mist
Tom Harrell Quintet | Sail Away | Original Jazz Classics | OJCCD 1095-2(C- 14054-2)
Axel Zwingenberger | Boogie Woogie Live | Vagabond | VRCD 8.85007

April Mood
Roland Kirk Quartet | Rahsaan/The Complete Mercury Recordings Of Roland Kirk | Mercury | 846630-2

April Morning
ETC & Jerry Bergonzi | ETC Plus One | Red Records | 123249-2

April Skies
Chick Corea | Originals | Stretch Records | SCD 9029-2

April Wind
Lee Konitz-Gil Evans | Hereos | Verve | 511621-2 PMS

April's Fool
Klaus Ignatzek Quintet | Silent Horns | Candid | CCD 79729

Apsis
Joaquin Chacón-Uffe Markussen European Quintet | Time | Fresh Sound Records | FSNT 051 CD

Apunte
Renaud Garcia-Fons | Entremundo | Enja | ENJ-9464 2

Aqa Jan
Brubeck/LaVerne Trio | See How It Feels | Black-Hawk | BKH 51401

Aqua De Beber-
Greetje Kauffeld With Jerry Van Rooyen And Jiggs Whigham And The Rias Big Band | Greetje Kauffeld Meets Jerry Van Rooyen And Jiggs Whigham With The Rias Big Band | Mons Records | MR 874786

Aqua Rapida
Georg Ruby Group | Stange Loops | Jazz Haus Musik | JHM 0057 CD

Aquamarin
Dick Heckstall-Smith & John Etheridge Group | Obsession Fees | R&M Digital Music | 2-8002

Aquarela Do Brazil
Joey Baron Trio | RAIsedpleasuredot | New World Records | 80449-2

Aquarian Rain
David S. Ware Quartet | Flight If I | DIW | DIW 856 CD

Aquarium
Tabla & Strings | Islands Everywhere | Tutu Records | 888208-2*

Aquarium Suite
Barney Kessel Quintet | Aquarius-The Music From Hair | Black Lion | BLCD 760222

Aquarius
Inga Lühning With Trio | Lühning | Jazz Haus Musik | JHM 0111 CD
J.J.Johnson Sextet | J.J.Inc. | CBS | CK 65296

Aquatintes-Coloured Water
Tony Aless Orchestra | Tony Aless And His Long Island Suite | Fresh Sound Records | RLP 2202(Roost)

Aquellas Cartas
Marc Ribot Y Los Cubanos Postizos | The Proshetic Cubans | Atlantic | 7567-83116-2

Aqui Como Alla
Charles Davis Trio | Nomadic Instincts | L+R Records | CDLR 45048

Arabesco
Tobias Langguth Band | One Note Bossa | Jardis Records | JRCD 9510

Arabeske
Ahmad Jamal Quartet | Crystal | Atlantic | 781793-2

Arabesque
Steve Halpern-Daniel Kobialka | Recollections | Gramavision | 18-7823-1

Arabian Hip
Duke Ellington And His Cotton Club Orchestra | Duke Ellington's Jungle Style | Black & Blue | BLE 59.234 2

Arabian Night-
Don Cherry/Ed Blackwell | El Corazon | ECM | 1230

Arabian Nightingale(Dedicated to Om Kaltsom)
John Kirby And His Band | 1940 | Jazz Anthology | 550252

Arabian Waltz
Rabih Abou-Khalil Group | Tarab | Enja | ENJ-7083 2
Sandole Brothers | The Sandole Brothers | Fantasy | FCD 24763-2

Arabu
Michael Riessler Group | Orange | ACT | 9274-2

Arabuno-
Louis Stewart Quintet | Milesian Source | Ronnie Scott's Jazz House | NSPL 18555

Aranjuez
The Super Guitar Fusion | Aranjuez | RCA | PL 40866 AS

Arbeit
Ben Waltzer Quintet | In Metropolitan Motion | Fresh Sound Records | FSNT 082 CD

Arbella
Arnold Ross Trio | The Piano Collection Vol.1 | Vogue | 21610242

Arbolé
Piirpauke | Piirpauke-Global Servisi | JA & RO | JARO 4150-2
Alex Riel Trio | Emergence | Red Records | 123263-2

Arbor Place Blues
Doneda-Rogers-Le Quan | Open Paper Tree | FMP | CD 68

ARC
Lisle Ellis Group | Elevations | Victo | CD 027

Arc And Point
Michael Brecker Group | Time Is Of The Essence | Verve | 547844-2

Arc Of The Pendulum
James Emery Quartet | Standing On A Whale... | Enja | ENJ-9312 2

ARC,Into Distant Night
Janice Borla With Band | Lunar Octave | dmp Digital Music Productions | CD 3004

Architektur
Joey Baron Trio | Tongue In Groove | JMT Edition | 849158-2

Arco
Volker Schlott & Reinmar Henschke | Influence | Acoustic Music Records | 319.1043.2

Arco I
Horn Knox | The Song Is You | JHM Records | JHM 3625

Arco II
Christoph Haberer Group | Pulsation | Jazz Haus Musik | JHM 0066 CD

Arco Iris
Clyde Criner Group | Behind The Sun | RCA | PD 83029

Arco Saltando
Hartmut Kracht | Kontrabass Pur | Jazz Haus Musik | JHM 0103 CD

Arco(reprise)
Günter Christmann | Solomusiken FÄr Posaune Und Kontraba | Ring | 01032

Arcosanti
Howard Riley | Duality | View | VS 0020 IMS

Arctic Barbecue
Eero Koivistoinen Sextet | Picture In Three Colours | Line Records | COCD 9.00515 O

Ardor
Chuck Foster And His Orchestra | The Uncollected:Chuck Foster, Vol.2 | Hindsight | HSR 171(835576)

Are We There Yet
Pat Metheny Group | Letter From Home | Geffen Records | GED 24245
Count Basie And His Orchestra With Tony Bennett | Basie On Roulette, Vol. 5: Strike Up The Band | Vogue | 500005

Are You All The Things
Bill Evans Trio | Re: Person I Knew | Original Jazz Classics | OJCCD 749-2(F 9608)
Bill Evans-Eddie Gomez Duo | The Complete Fantasy Recordings | Fantasy | 9FCD 1012-2
Bill Evans Trio | Bill Evans:From The 70's | Original Jazz Classics | OJCCD 1069-2(F 9630)

Are You All The Things(take 3)
Jean-Paul Bourelly Group | Tribute To Jimi | DIW | DIW 893 CD

Are You Experienced?
Gary Lucas | Skeleton On The Feast | Enemy | EMCD 126(03526)

Are You Going With Me
Pat Metheny Group | Travels | ECM | 1252/53
Count Basie And His Orchestra With Tony Bennett | Basie-Bennett | Roulette | 7938992

Are You In The Mood
Quintet Du Hot Club De France | Django Reinhardt:Djangology | EMI Records | 780659-2
Stephane Grappelli Quintet | Hommage A Django Reinhardt | Festival | Album 120

Are You Living Humble
Lisa Bassenge Trio With Guests | A Sight, A Song | Minor Music | 801100

Are You Lonesome Tonight
Wollie Kaiser Timeghost | Tust Du Fühlen Gut | Jazz Haus Musik | JHM 0060 CD
Buddy Guy Blues Band | The Blues Giant | Black & Blue | BLE 59.900 2

Are You Phoenix?
Kid Thoams Valentine Jazz Band | The Dance Hall Years | American Music | AMCD-48

Are You Real
Art Blakey And The Jazz Messengers | Jazz In Paris:Art Blakey-1958-Paris Olympia | EmArCy | 832659-2 PMS
Hot Tracks For Cool Cats Vol.2 | Polydor | 816380-2

Are You Stickin'
Duke Ellington And His Orchestra | Duke Elliongton:Complete Prestige Carnegie Hall 1943-1944 Concerts | Definitive Records | DRCD 11210

Are You Sticking
The Indispensable Duke Ellington,Vol.7/8 | RCA | ND 89274

Are You Surprised?
John McLaughlin Trio | Electric Guitarist | CBS | 467093-2

TITELVERZEICHNIS

***Aren't You Glad You're Yo*u**
Mel Tormé With The George Shearing Trio | Mel & George 'Do' World War II | Concord | CCD 4471
Aren't You Kind Of Glad We Did
Lola Albright With The Dean Elliott Orchestra | Lola Wants You | Fresh Sound Records | FSR-CD 0007
Areous Vlor Ta
Asgard | Songs Of G. | Acoustic Music Records | 319.1042.2
Aretha
29th Street Saxophone Quartet | The Real Deal | New Note Records | ???
Argen's Bag
Steve Houben Quartet | Blue Circumstances | Igloo | IGL 102
Argentia
Thelonious Monk Quartet | Thelonious Monk-The Complete Riverside Recordings | Riverside | 15 RCD 022-2
Argentiera
Orchestre National De Jazz | Charmediterranéen | ECM | 1828(018493-2)
Argentiera(2)
Michael Naura-Wolfgang Schlüter Duo | Country Children | ECM | 803 SP
Argentyna
Mara Et Nana Vasconcelos | Ntsano | Red Records | VPA 171
Argo
Paolino Dalla Porta Quartet | Canguri Urbani | SPLASC(H) Records | H 174
Aria And Variations from Suite for Harpsichord in E Major(Haendel)
Franco D'Andrea Quartet | Live | Red Records | VPA 195
Aria From Orchester Suite No.3 In D Major(BWV 1068)
Jacques Loussier Trio | Play Bach No.2 | Decca | 157562-2
Aria In D Major(BWV 1068)
Play Bach Live In Concert | Decca | 6.22597 AO
Aria(from Orchestra Suite No.3 In D Major BWV 1068)
Tiziana Ghiglioni And The Strings Ensemble | Tiziana Ghiglioni Sings Gaslini | Soul Note | 121297-2
Ariadne's Thread
Spyro Gyra & Guests | Love & Other Obsessions | GRP | GRP 98112
Ariana
La Vienta | Night Dance | Telarc Digital | CD 83359
Ariang-
Oregon | Oregon | ECM | 1258(811711-2)
Arianne
Nathalie Lorriers Quartet | Nympheas | Igloo | IGL 088
Aries
Don Patterson Quintet | Why Not... | Muse | MR 5148
Sandor Szabo | Gaia And Aries | Acoustic Music Records | 319.1146.2
Ariescene
Freddie Hubbard Sextet | Ready For Freddie | Blue Note | 84085 (GXK 8203)
Arietta
Hank Jones Trio | Arigato | Progressive | PRO 7004
Ario
Bud Shank Quartet | At Jazz Alley | Contemporary | C 14027
Arise
Norbert Stein Pata Orchester | Ritual Life | Pata Musik | PATA 5(JHM 50) CD
Gary Burton | Alone At Last | Atlantic | 7567-80762-2
Arise Her Eyes-
Gary Burton Quartet With Chamber Orchestra | Seven Songs For Quartet And Chamber Orchestra | ECM | 1040
Arise!
Jimmy Greene Group | Brand New World | RCA | 2663564-2
Arise,Her Eyes
Vanessa Rubin With Orchestra | Pastiche | Novus | 4163152-2
Aris's Mode
Duke Ellington And His Orchestra | New Orleans Suite | Rhino | 812273670-2
Aristocracy A La Jean Lafitte
That's Jazz Vol.31: New Orleans Suite | Atlantic | ATL 50403
Arizona Stars(dedicated to Judith)
Gabriele Hasler Group | Listening To Löbering | Foolish Music | FM 211389
Ark
Alan Braufman Quintet | Valley Of Search | India Navigation | IN 1024
Arkansas Blues
Fred Elizalde And His Orchestra | Fred Elizalde And His Anglo American Band | Retrieval | RTR 79011
Marcus Roberts | If I Could Be With You | Novus | 4163149-2
Arlequin
Denny Christianson Big Band | More Pepper | Justin Time | JUST 19
Arlmyn Trangent
David Binney Group | Balance | ACT | 9411-2
Arlmyn Trangent Reliv
Oliver Augst-Rüdiger Carl-Christoph Korn | Blank | FMP | OWN-90013
Arm In Arm-
Arcado String Trio | Live In Europe | Avant | AVAN 058
Armageddon
Willie Williams Trio | WW3 | Enja | ENJ-8060 2
Armageddon-
Steve Coleman And Five Elements | Rhythm People | Novus | PL 83092
Armando's Rhumba
Chick Corea | Originals | Stretch Records | SCD 9029-2
Chick Corea-Gary Burton | Native Sense-The New Duets | Stretch Records | SCD 9014-2
Chick Corea & Origin | Change | Stretch Records | SCD 9023-2
Armenonville
Fats Waller And His Rhythm | Breakin' The Ice-The Early Years Part 1(1934-1935) | Bluebird | 63 66618-2
Armonica
Michael Leonhart Quartet | Aardvark Poses | Sunnyside | SSC 1070 D
Arneckestr.29
Arnett Cobb & His Orchestra | The Complete Apollo Sessions | Vogue | 500116
Arnold's Dead
Hot Rod Rumble Orchestra | Hot Rod Rumble | Fresh Sound Records | 054 2607941(Liberty LRP 3048)
Aromas
Ron Carter Sextet | New York Slick | Original Jazz Classics | OJCCD 916-2(M 9096)
Aromatic
Chico Hamilton Quintet | Passin ' Thru | Impulse(MCA) | JAS 17 (AS 29)
Around Again
Paul Bley Group | The Paul Bley Group | Soul Note | SN 1140
Around Bartók Bagatelle No.4
Beirach-Hübner-Mraz | Round About Bartok | ACT | 9276-2
Around Bartók's World
Round About Bartok | ACT | 9276-2
Around Dubrawuschka
Round About Bartok | ACT | 9276-2
Around Kodaly's World
Michael Mantler Group | Silence | Watt | 5 (2313105)
Around Me Sits The Night
Michael Mantler: No Answer/Silence | Watt | 2/5(543374-2)
$$hide$$ | $$Titelverweise | |
Around Midnight -> Round About Midnight
Around Musica Callada No.19
Richard Beirach Trio | Round About Federico Mompou | ACT | 9296-2
Around Musica Callada No.27
Beirach-Hübner-Mraz | Round About Bartok | ACT | 9276-2
Around Porumbescu Balada
Round About Bartok | ACT | 9276-2
Around Salcam De Vara
Round About Bartok | ACT | 9276-2
Around Scrijabin Prelude op.16
Round About Bartok | ACT | 9276-2
Around Stenkarasin
Marc Johnson Trio | Magic Labyrith | JMT Edition | 514018-2
Around The Bend
Jimmy Witherspoon And His Quartet | Blues Around The Clock | Original Blues Classics | OBCCD 576-2(P 7314)
Around The Corner
Makoto Ozone Trio | Pandora | Verve | 549629-2
Mark Soskin Quartet | Calypso & Jazz-Around The Corner | Paddle Wheel | KICJ 175
Around The World
Bill Barron-Ted Curson Quintet | The Leopard | Fresh Sound Records | CR 2010
Arouss Labneh-
Bill Smith Quartet | Folk Jazz U.S.A. | Original Jazz Classics | OJCCD 1956-2(S 7591)
A-Roving
Bob Brookmeyer New Quartet | Paris Suite | Challenge | CHR 70026
Arpege
Christy Doran-John Wolf Brennan | Henceforward | Line Records | COCD 9.00871 O
Arrak
Eddie Tower Orchester | Swing tanzen verboten | Vagabond | 6.28360 DP
Arrival
Never Been There | Ambience | VeraBra Records | CDVBR 2030-2
Wolfgang Puschnig-Jamaladeen Tacuma Group With Guests | Journey Into The Gemini Territory | ITM-Pacific | ITMP 970091
Arrival At The Castle
Joe Zawinul Group | Zawinul | Atlantic | 7567-81375-2
Arrival In New York
Billy Jenkins And Fun Horns | Mayfest '94 | Babel | BDV 9502
Arrivee
Sidney Bechet With Orchestra | La Nuit Es Une Sorciere | Vogue | 21134142
Arriving-
Buddy Childers Big Band | Just Buddy's | Candid | CCD 79761
Arriving Soon
Cannonball Adderley Quintet | What I Mean | Milestone | M 47053
Cannonball Adderley Quintet Plus | Original Jazz Classics | OJC20 306-2
Eddie Cleanhead Vinson With The Cannonball Adderley Quintet | Cleanhead & Cannonball | Landmark | LCD 1309-2(882857)
Nat Adderley Quintet | Talkin' About You | 32 Jazz | 32082
Arrivivederci Roma
Ramón Diaz Group | O Si No Que? | Fresh Sound Records | FSNT 044 CD
Arroro-
Marion Brown-Gunter Hampel Duo | Reeds 'N Vibes | Improvising Artists Inc. | 123855-2
Arrows
Billy Cobham Group | Inner Conflicts | Atlantic | ATL 50475
Arroyo
Jerome Harris Quintet | In Passing | Muse | MCD 5386
Arroz Con Pollo
Sonny Rollins Quintet | Easy Living | Milestone | M 9080
Ars Vivendi
Elliott Sharp Carbon | Datacide | Enemy | EMCD 116(03516)
Art-
Jane Ira Bloom Quartet | Art And Aviation | Arabesque Recordings | AJ 0107
Art Deco
Dave Ballou Quartet | Rothko | Steeplechase | SCCD 31525
Don Cherry Quartet | Art Deco | A&M Records | 395258-2 PMS
Art Meets Mr. Beautiful
Robert Previt Quintet | Bump The Renaissance | Sound Aspects | sas CD 008
Arte Povera
Orchestre National De Jazz | Charmediterranéen | ECM | 1828(018493-2)
Artefact(part 1-2)
Stan Kenton And His Orchestra | Adventures In Time | Capitol | 855454-2
Artemis And Apollo
John Zorn Naked City | Absinthe | Avant | AVAN 004
Arthur Rainbow
Angelo Di Pippo Quintet | Arthur Street | Stash Records | ST-CD 557(875135)
Arthur's Blues
Art Pepper Quartet | Arthur's Blues | Original Jazz Classics | OJCCD 680-2
Mark Feldman Quartet | The Chromatic Persuaders | Konnex Records | KCD 5063
Arthur's Seat
Paul Horn Group | Paul Horn In India | Blue Note | 84551
Article Four
Andreas Willers Octet | The Ground Music | Enja | ENJ-9368 2
Articulate Tumbling(Slight Return)
Rodney Jones Orchestra | Articulation | Timeless | CD SJP 125
Artillerie Lourde
Quintet Du Hot Club De France | Jazz Legacy 58: Django Reinhardt-Rythme Futur-Radio Sessions 1947 Vol | Vogue | 500108
Django Reinhardt Quintet | Djangology 49 | Bluebird | NL 90448
Artillerie Lourde(Heavy Artillery)
1239A | Artistry | Verve | 847956-2
Artistry In Rhythm
Stan Kenton And His Orchestra | Mellophonium Magic | Status | CD 103(882199)
Stan Kenton With The Danish Radio Big Band | Stan Kenton With The Danish Radio Big Band | Storyville | STCD 8340
The Four Freshman With Stan Kenton And His Orchestra | Live At Butler University | Creative World | STD 1059
Artistry In Rhythm(Closing Theme)
Stan Kenton And His Orchestra | Festival Of Modern American Jazz | Status | CD 101(882197)
Artistry In Rhythm(Opening Theme)
The Complete MacGregor Transcriptions Vol.1 | Naxos Jazz | 8.120517 CD
Aruanda
$$hide$$ | $$Titelverweise | |
Aruanda -> Take Me To Aruanda
Aruba
Larry Coryell-Emily Remler Duo | Together | Concord | CJ 289
Arun
Christina Nielsen Quintet | From This Time Forward | Stunt Records | STUCD 19503
As
Pat Metheny Group With Orchestra | Secret Story | Geffen Records | GED 24468
As A Flower Blossom(I Am Running To You)
Gregor Hotz | Solo/+Nicholas Bussmann | FMP | OWN-90012
As Catch Can
Gerry Mulligan Quartet | Americans In Sweden | Tax | CD 3711-2
Art Ensemble Of Chicago | Tribute To Lester | ECM | 1808(017066-2)
As Clear As The Sun
Gerry Mulligan-Bill Mays | Triple Play:Gerry Mulligan | Telarc Digital | CD 83453
As Everybody Sees I'm Oldfashioned
Mind Games With Claudio Roditi | Live | Edition Collage | EC 501-2
Vocal Moments | Take Twelve On CD | TT 008-2
Pat Metheny & Lyle Mays | As Falls Wichita, So Falls Wichita Falls | ECM | 1190(821416-2)
As Falls Wichita So Fall Wichita Falls
Pat Metheny Group | Travels | ECM | 1252/53
Charles Blenzig Group | Say What You Mean | Big World | BW 2009
As Flores
David Fathead Newman Octet | Back To Basics | Milestone | MCD 9188-2
As Historias De Domingos
Michael Brecker Group | Time Is Of The Essence | Verve | 547844-2
As I Am
Pat Metheny Group | Quartet | Geffen Records | GED 24978
Uri Caine | Solitaire | Winter&Winter | 910075-2
Stephan Micus | Implosions | Japo | 60017(2360017)
As I Crossed A Bridge Of Dreams
Greetje Bijma Trio | Barefoot | Enja | ENJ-8038 2
As I Drive By
Lonnie Plaxico Orchestra | With All Your Heart | Muse | MCD 5525
As I Love You
Lucky Four | Lucky Four | Tutu Records | 888108-2
As If It Were A Bridge
Gunter Hampel Next Generation | Next Generation | Birth | CD 043
Art Ensemble Of Chicago | Live In Berlin | West Wind | WW 2051
As If We Knew
Franz De Byl | Verdammt Allein | Moers Music | 02022
As Is
Kathy Stobart Quintet | Arbeia | Spotlite | SPJ 509
Gunter Hampel And His Galaxie Dream Band | A Place To Be With Us | Birth | 0032
As Long As I Live
Allan Vaché-Antti Sarpila Quintet | The Second Sampler | Nagel-Heyer | NHR SP 6
Allotria Jazz Band | Cleared For Take Off | Elite Special | 73331
Count Basie Trio | For The First Time | Pablo | 2310712-2
Ella Fitzgerald With The Billy May Orchestra | The Complete Ella Fitzgerald Song Books of Harold Arlen, Irving Berlin, Duke Ellington, George & Ira Gershwin, Jerome Kern, Johnny Mercer, Cole Porter And Rogers & Hart | Verve | 519832-2
The Harold Arlen Songbook | Verve | 817526-1 IMS
Joe Pass-Jimmy Rowles Duo | Checkmate | Original Jazz Classics | OJCCD 975-2(2310865)
Joe Pass:A Man And His Guitar | Original Jazz Classics | OJCCD 8806-2
Johannes Rediske Sextet | Re-Disc Bounce | Bear Family Records | BCD 16119 AH
June Christy With The Pete Rugolo Orchestra | The Song Is June | Capitol | 855455-2
Lena Horne With The Horace Henderson Orchestra | Planet Jazz:Lena Horne | Planet Jazz | 2165373-2
Lennie Niehaus Sextet | Lennie Niehaus Vol.5:The Sextet | Original Jazz Classics | OJCCD 1944-2(C 3524)
Lew Stone And His Orchestra | The Bands The Matter | Eclipse | ECM 2047
Lurlean Hunter And Her All Stars | Blue & Sentimantel | Atlantic | AMCY 1081
Maxine Sullivan With The Bob Wilber Quartet | Clse As Pages In A Book | Audiophile | ACD-203
Oscar Peterson Trio | Oscar Peterson Plays The Harold Arlen Song Book | Verve | 589103-2
Red McKenzie With The Spirits Of Rhythm | Spirit Of Rhythm 1932-34 | Retrieval | RTR 79004
Ruby Braff-Dick Hyman | A Pipe Organ Recital Plus One | Concord | CCD 43003
Tal Farlow Quintet | Tal Farlow Plays The Music Of Harold Arlen | Verve | MV 2589 IMS
As Long As Now
Hampton Hawes Trio With The Blue Strings | Hampton Hawes Plays Movie Musicals | Fresh Sound Records | FSR-CD 0065
As Long As She Needs Me
Fats Waller And His Rhythm | I'm Gonna Sit Right Down...The Early Years-Part 2(1935-1936) | Bluebird | 63 66640-2
As Long As There's Music
Fred Hersch Trio | Point In Time | Enja | ENJ-9035 2
Freddy Christman Quartet | Deutsches Jazz Fesival 1954/1955 | Bear Family Records | BCD 15430
Hampton Hawes-Charlie Haden Duo | As Long As There's Music | Artists House | AH 4 IMS
Johnny Smith Quartet | The Sound Of Johnny Smith Guitar | Fresh Sound Records | FSR 583(Roost 2246)
The Waltzer-McHenry Quartet | Jazz Is Where You Find It | Fresh Sound Records | FSNT 021 CD
Coleman Hawkins All Stars | Coleman Hawkins | West Wind | WW 2034
As Of Yet
Arthur Blythe Quartet | Illusions | CBS | SRCS 7188
As Quiet As It Kept
Jay Hoggard Quartet | Love Is The Answer | Muse | MCD 5527
As The Crow Flies
David Friesen | Paths Beyond Tracing | Steeplechase | SCCD 31138
As Time Goes By
Allotria Jazz Band | All That Jazz | Elite Special | 730217
Bill Evans-Bob Brookmeyer Quartet | As Time Goes By | Blue Note | LT 1100
Billie Holiday With Eddie Heywood And His Orchestra | The Commodore Series | Decca | 180008 AG
Bud Shank Quartet | That Old Feeling | Contemporary | C 14019
Dave McKenna | Dave Fingers McKenna | Chiaroscuro | CR 175
Dexter Gordon Quintet | The Other Side Of Round Midnight | Blue Note | 746397-2
Ernestine Anderson And Her Trio | Late At Night | Paddle Wheel | KICJ 113
Germaine Bazzle & Friends | New New Orleans Music: Vocal Jazz | Line Records | COCD 9.00918 O
Jaye P. Morgan With Marion Evens And His Orchestra | Just You Just Me | Fresh Sound Records | ND 38627
Kenny Colman With The London Philharmonic Orchestra | Dreamscape | Justin Time | JTR 8466-2
Lee Gibson With The Metropole Orchestra | Night Songs | Koch Jazz | 3-6911-2
Maynard Ferguson Orchestra | Storm | ARG Jazz | 21374872
Richie Cole Quintet | Keeper Of The Flame | Muse | MR 5192
Sam 'The Man' Taylor Orchestra | Back Beat-The Rhythm Of The Blues Vol.5 | Mercury | 511270-2 PMS
Singers Unlimited With The Robert Farnon Orchestra | Sentimental Journey | MPS | 68102
Vince Jones Group | Watch What Happens | Intuition Records | INT 3070-2
Boots Randolph-Richie Cole Sextet | Yakety Madness! | Palo Alto | PA 8041
As Time Goes By-
Duke Jordan Trio | When You're Smiling | Steeplechase | SCCD 37023/24
As We Are
George Howard Group | Asphalt Gardens | Palo Alto | PA 8035
As You Once Were
Sun Ra And His Arkestra | Sound Of Joy | Delmark | DE 414
As You Wish-
Baden Powell | Le Coeur De Baden Powell | Festival | FLD 633
Asabache
Christian Chevallier And His Orchestra | 6+6 | Fresh Sound Records | 054 2610781(FPX 144)
Asante
Glenn Spearman Double Trio | Smokehouse | Black Saint | 120157-2
Ascenseur
Barry Harris | Listen To Barry Harris | Original Jazz Classics | OJCCD 999-2(R 9392)
Ascension(edition I)
John Coltrane And His Orchestra | The Major Works Of John Coltrane | Impulse(MCA) | GRP 21132
Ascension(edition II)
The Major Works Of John Coltrane | Impulse(MCA) | GRP 21132
Ascent
John Coltrane Quartet | John Coltrane:The Classic Quartet-Complete Impulse Studio Recordings | Impulse(MCA) | 951280-2
Tom Beckham Quartet | Suspicions | Fresh Sound Records | FSNT 075 CD
Daniel Carter Quartet | Other Dimensions In Music | Silkheart | SHCD 120
Ascot Gavotte
Shelly Manne And His Friends | My Fair Lady | Mobile Fidelity | MFCD 809

Asfalto
Pablo Ziegler And His Quintet For New Tango | Asfalto-Street Tango | RCA | 2663266-2
Ash
Seger Ellis | Prairie Blues-The Music Of Seger Ellis | AZURE Compact Disc | AZ-CD-22
Ash Wednesday
Bola Sete Quintet | Bossa Nova | Original Jazz Classics | OJC 286(F 8349)
Ashby Man
Ted Pilzecker Group | Destinations | Mons Records | CD 1885
Ashes To Ashes
Doug Wieselman-Bill Frisell Duo | Todos Santos | Sound Aspects | sas CD 019
Ashkabad
John Zorn Group | Masada One | DIW | DIW 888 CD
Asi
Conexion Latina | Calorcito | Enja | ENJ-4072 2
Asi Es La Vida
Orquesta Conexion Latina | Un Poco Loco | Enja | ENJ-5023 2
Asi Sin Pensar
Christina Nielsen Quintet | From This Time Forward | Stunt Records | STUCD 19503
Asia Minor
Emil Mangelsdorff Quartet | Meditation | L+R Records | CDLR 45088
Asian Lullaby
JoAnne Brackeen Trio | Where Legends Dwell | Ken Music | 660.56.021
Asia's Theme
Soul Rebels | Let Your Mind Be Free | Mardi Gras Records | MG 1020
Asiatic Race
David Murray Quartet | For Aunt Louise | DIW | DIW 901 CD
Asiatic Raes
Jack DeSalvo-Arthur Lipner | Liquide Stones | Tutu Records | 888132-2
Asiento
Marc Ducret | Detail | Winter&Winter | 910003-2
Asile
Barbara Dennerlein Quartet | Orgelspiele | Böhm Records | 65145 IMS
Ask A Woman Who Knows
Lowell Fulsom Band | Tramp/Soul | Ace Records | CDCHD 339
Ask Me Now
Bennie Wallace Trio | Live At The Public Theater | Enja | 9127-2
Elvin Jones Sextet | It Don't Mean A Thing... | Enja | ENJ-8066 2
George Shearing/Hank Jones | The Spirit Of 176 | Concord | CCD 4371
Henri Chaix Trio | Jive At Five | Sackville | SKCD2-2035
Joe Henderson Trio | The State Of The Tenor Vol.1&2 | Blue Note | 828879-2
Joe Temperley Quartet With Strings | Easy To Remember | Hep | CD 2083
Joe Viera Sextet | Kontraste | Calig | 30619
Marion Brown-Gunter Hampel Duo | Gemini | Birth | CD 037
Mark Levin Quintet | Concepts | Concord | CJ 234
Muhal Richard Abrams Septet | Interpertations Of Monk | DIW | DIW 395/8 CD
Paul Motian Electric Bebop Band | Reincarnation Of A Love Bird | JMT Edition | 514016-2
Perico Sambeat Quartet | Dual Force | Ronnie Scott's Jazz House | JHCD 031
Steve Lacy Quartet | Reflections-Steve Lacy Plays Thelonious Monk | Original Jazz Classics | OJCCD 063-2
Steve Lacy-Charlie Rouse | That's The Way I Feel Now-A Tribute To Thelonious Monk | A&M Records | AMLM 66600
Thelonious Monk | Solo Monk | CBS | 471248-2
Thelonious Monk Quintet | The Blue Note Years-The Best Of Thelonious Monk | Blue Note | 796636-2
Thelonious Monk-The Complete Riverside Recordings | Riverside | 15 RCD 022-2
Jazz Profile:Thelonious Monk | Blue Note | 823518-2
The Best Of Thelonious Monk:The Blue Note Years | Blue Note | 795636-2
Thelonious Monk Trio | Thelonious Monk:Misterioso | Dreyfus Jazz Line | FDM 36743-2
Genius Of Modern Music,Vol.2 | Blue Note | 300404
Ask Me Now(alt.take)
Thelonious Monk Quartet | More Genius Of Thelonious Monk | Blue Note | 300194(BNJ 61011)
Thelonious Monk Trio | Thelonious Monk:The Complete Blue Note Recordings | Blue Note | 830363-2
Ask Yourself Why
Kent Sangster Quartet | Adventures | Jazz Focus | JFCD 006
Asking For Trouble
June Christy With The Bob Cooper Orchestra | Do Re Mi | Fresh Sound Records | 054 2607961(Capitol T 1586)
Aspects Of Duke:
Carola Grey & Noisy Mama | Girls Can't Hit! | Lipstick Records | LIP 8945-2
Aspects Of Mother Earth
| Sonic Fiction | Hat Art | CD 6043
Aspen
The Rippingtons | Live In L.A. | GRP | GRP 97182
Aspen Leaf
Miniature | I Can't Put My Finger On It | JMT Edition | 849147-2
Aspettando Caterina
Kenny Burrell-Grover Washington Jr. Quintet | Togethering | Blue Note | BT 85106
Asphaltwirbel, Fleisch Vom Rind, Smogalarm
Gary Burton Sextet | Gary Burton & Friends-Six Pack | GRP | GRP 96852
Asphodéle
Jack Millman Quartet | Four More | Fresh Sound Records | FSR-CD 0217
Aspirations
Kenny Wheeler Quintet | The Widow In The Window | ECM | 1417(843198-2)
Aspire
Anthony Braxton Duo/Quintet | Dances & Orations | Music & Arts | CD 923
Asr
Miles Davis Quintet | Ascenseur Pour LÉchafaud | Fontana | 836305-2
Assassinat(3 takes)
Gunter Hampel Group | Music From Europe | ESP Disk | ESP 1042-2
Assembly Field
Javon Jackson Group | A Look Within | Blue Note | 836490-2
Assim Nao Da
Jasper Van't Hof Groups | The Selfkicker | MPS | 68164
Assonance
Acoustic Affaire | Mira | Jazz 'n' Arts Records | JNA 1303
Assszonyság
Badi Assad | Solo | Chesky | JD 99
Astara
Gary Lucas/Walter Horn | Skeleton On The Feast | Enemy | EMCD 126(03526)
Asthma
Big Band De Lausanne & Charles Papasoff | Astor | TCB Records | TCB 95502
Astor Place
Kristian Jorgensen Quartet With Monty Alexander | Meeting Monty | Stunt Records | STUCD 01212
Astor Samba
The Tango Kings | The Tango Kings | Big World | BW 2016
Astoria Blues
Jones And Collins Astoria Hot Eight | Victor Jazz History Vol.1:New Orleans & Dixieland | RCA | 2128555-2
Astorlogie
Fernando Tarrés And The Arida Conta Group With Guests | The Outsider | Savant Records | SCD 2002
Astrakan Café(1)
Anouar Brahem Trio | Astrakan Café | ECM | 1718(159494-2)
Astrakan Café(2)
Armen Donelian Sextet | Secrets | Sunnyside | SSC 1031 D
Astral Projection
Joe McPhee Po Music | Oleo & A Future Retrospective | Hat Art | 3514
Astral Traveling
Pharoah Sanders Orchestra | Thembi | Impulse(MCA) | JAS 53 (AS 9206)
Pharoah Sanders Quintet | Red Hot On Impulse | Impulse(MCA) | GRP 11512
Astral Traveling(alt.take)
World Saxophone Quartet | Moving Right Along | Black Saint | 120127-2
As-Tu Le Cafard
Sidney Bechet With Claude Luter And His Orchestra | In Concert | Vogue | 655625
Asturiana
Bola Sete Trio | Tour Do Force:The Bola Sete Trios | Fantasy | FCD 24766-2
Asturias
Om | Cerberus | Japo | 60032
Asymptote
Charlie Mariano Sextet | October | CMP Records | CMP 2
At A Dixie Roadside Diner
Duke Ellington And His Orchestra | The Indispensable Duke Ellington Vol.5/6 | RCA | ND 89750
At A Fergana Bazar
Alvin Alcorn' 'Gay Paree' Stompers | Alvin Alcorn/Harrison Verret | American Music | AMCD-65
At A Georgia Camp Meeting
Sidney Bechet And His New Orleans Feetwarmers | The Commodore Story | Commodore | CMD 24002
Chico Freeman Quartet | Tradition In Transition | Elektra | MUS K 52412
At A Glance
Bob Crosby And His Orchestra | Bob Crosby And His Orchestra Vol.9(1939):Them There Eyes | Halcyon | DHDL 128
At A Loss
Dave Brubeck Quartet | Stardust | Fantasy | FCD 24728-2
At Dawning
J.P.Torres Band | Trombone Man | RMM Records | 660.58.085
At Dusk
John Surman With String Quartet | Coruscating | ECM | 1702(543033-2)
Frank Speer Acoustic Quartet | Dread Nay | Jazz 4 Ever Records:Jazz Network | J4E 4734
At Ghanaba's Place
John Blake Sextet | Quest | Sunnyside | SSC 1058 D
At Home
Niko Schäuble Quintet | On The Other Hand | Naxos Jazz | 86011-2
At Home-
John Lindberg | Comin' & Goin' | LEO | LR 104
At Home In The Universe(for Stuart Kauffman)
Benny Goodman And His Orchestra | The Benny Goodman Caravans Vol.5:Jumpin' At The Woodside | Giants Of Jazz | GOJ 1042
At Large
(Little)Jimmy Scott And His Quintet | All The Way | Warner | 7599-26955-2
At Last
Arthur Prysock With The Red Prysock Band | This Guy's In Love With You | Milestone | MCD 9146-2
Chet Baker Quartet | At Last! | Original Jazz Classics | OJCCD 480-2
Dan Moretti Quintet | Some Time Inside | Black-Hawk | BKH 51901
Dirk Strakhof & Batoru | Arabesque | Nabel Records:Jazz Network | CD 4696
DMP Big Band | Glenn Miller Project | dmp Digital Music Productions | CD 519
Etta James & The Roots Band | Burnin' Down he House | RCA | 3411633-2
Etta James With Orchestra | Peaches | Chess | 427014
Glenn Miller And His Orchestra | A Legendary Performer-Previously Unreleased Live Recordings | RCA | NL 89212 DP
The Ultimate Glenn Miller-22 Original Hits From The King Of Swing | RCA | 2113137-2
Glenn Miller Orchestra | Glenn Miller Serenade | CBS | 487445-2
Glenn Miller Revival Orchestra | Forever-From The Forties To The... | Timeless | CD JC 11013
Lou Rawls And His Orchestra | At Last | Blue Note | 791937-2
The Three Sounds | The Best Of The Three Sounds | Blue Note | 827323-2
At Last-
Warren Vaché Quintet | Warren Plays Warrey | Nagel-Heyer | CD 033
Gogi Grant With The Dennis Farnon Orchestra | Welcome To My Heart | Fresh Sound Records | ND 42126
At Long Last First
Bill Henderson With The Oscar Peterson Trio | Vocal Classics | Verve | 837937-2
At Long Last Love
Count Basie And His Orchestra | This Time By Basie | Reprise | 9362-45162-2
Frank Sinatra With The Red Norvo Quintet(Sextet!) | Live In Australia,1959 | Blue Note | 837513-2
Grant Green Quartet | I Want To Hold Your Hand | Blue Note | 300261(4202)
At Lulu White's
Bennie Wallace Trio | The Old Songs | audioquest Music | AQCD 1017
At McKies'
Om | Cerberus | Japo | 60032
At Night-
Ernst Bier-Mack Goldsbury Quartet | At Night When You Go To Sleep | Timescrapper | TSCR 9611
At Night When You Go To Sleep
The Danish Radio Jazz Orchestra | This Train:The Danish Radio Jazz Orchestra Plays The Music Of Ray Pitts | dacapo | DCCD 9428
At Our House
MOKAVE | MOKAVE Vol.1 | audioquest Music | AQCD 1006
At Ronnie's
The Kenny Clarke-Francy Boland Big Band | Two Originals:Sax No End/All Blues | MPS | 523525-2
At Saturday
Fumio Yasuda | Schumann's Bar Music | Winter&Winter | 910081-2
At Schumann's
| Max And Pee Wee At The Copley Terrace 1945 | Jazzology | JCD-15
At Sundown
Benny Goodman Trio | Benny Goodman:The Complete 1947-1949 Small Group Sessions Vol.2(1947-1949) | Blue Moon | BMCD 1043
Bobby Hackett And His Orchestra | Commodore Classics-Bobby Hackett/Miff Mole | Commodore | 6.26171 AG
Bud Freeman And His Summa Cum Laude Orchestra | Chicago/Austin High School Jazz In Hi-Fi | RCA | 2113031-2
Earl Hines Trio | Fatha | CBS | CBS 21104
Humphrey Lyttelton-Acker Bilk Band | Humph & Acker-Together For The Very First Time! | Calligraph | CLGCD 027
Oscar Peterson Trio | Masters Of Jazz Vol.7 | RCA | NL 89721 DP
Ray Anthony And His Orchestra | Swingin' On Campus! | Pathe | 1566131(Capitol T 645)
The King Sisters With Frank DeVol's Orchestra | The Uncollected:The King Sisters | Hindsight | HSR 168
Ella Fitzgerald With Benny Carter's Magnificent Seven | 30 By Ella | Capitol | 520090-2
At Sundown-
Jimmie Lunceford And His Orchestra | The Original Jimmy Lunceford Orchestra | Jazz Anthology | JA 5224
At Sunrise
Stefania Tallini Trio | New Life | yvp music | CD 3114
At Sunset
Claus Stötter's Nevertheless | Die Entdeckung Der Banane | Jazz 'n' Arts Records | JNA 1403
At Swim Two Birds
Die Entdeckung Der Banane | Jazz 'n' Arts Records | JNA 1403
At Swin Two Birds(final theme)
Kamikaze Ground Crew | The Scenic Route | New World Records | 80400-2
At The Ball
James P.Johnson's Blue Note Jazzmen | Hot Jazz On Blue Note | Blue Note | 835811-2
At The Ball(alt.take)
Juez | There's A Room | Stunt Records | 18806
At The Codfish Ball
Tommy Dorsey And His Clambake Seven | The Music Goes Round And Round | RCA | ND 83140(847123)
The Best Of Tommy Dorsey And His Clambake Seven | Retrieval | RTR 79012
At The Cross
First Revolution Singers | A Cappella Gospel Anthology | Tight Harmony Records | TH 199404
At The Crossroad
| Jazz Classics In Digital Stereo: Coleman Hawkins 1927-1939 | CDS Records Ltd. | RPCD 600(CD 698)
At The End Of The Day
Mark Dresser Trio | The Cabinet Of Dr. Caligari(Music For The Silent Film) | Knitting Factory Works | KFWCD 155
At The Fireman's Ball
Frisco Syncopators | Firehouse Stomp | Stomp Off Records | CD 1245
At The Gate
Flim & The BB's | Big Notes | dmp Digital Music Productions | CD 454
At The Horse Show
Allotria Jazz Band | Swing That Music | Elite Special | 73232
At The Jazz Band Ball
Bix Beiderbecke Orchestra/Gang | The Golden Age Of Bix Beiderbecke | EMI Records | CD MFP 6046
Bobby Hackett And His Jazz Band | Gotham Jazz Scene/Big T's Dixieland Band | Dormouse | DMI CDX 03(882985)
Chris Barber's Jazz And Blues Band | Oldtime Festival | BELL Records | BLR 84005
Dutch Swing College Band | DSC Live 1974 | DSC Production | PA 1013 (801068)
Franz Koglmann Tentet | A White Line | Hat Art | CD 6048
Joe Venuti-Dave McKenna Duo | Alone At The Palace | Chiaroscuro | CR 160
Muggsy Spanier And His Ragtime Band | Victor Jazz History Vol.19:Dixieland Revival | RCA | 2135738-2
Stars Of Jazz | Stars Of Jazz Vol.1 | Jazzology | JCD-62
The Chicago All Stars | Planet Jazz:Bud Freeman | Planet Jazz | 2161240-2
Victor Jazz History Vol.18:Chicago Jazz(1924-64) | RCA | 2135737-2
This Is Jazz All Stars | World's Greatest Jazz Concert Vol.1 | Jazzology | JCD-301
At The Last Moment
Ok Nok...Kongo | Moonstone Journey | dacapo | DCCD 9444
At The Lotus Lake
Brian Lynch Quintet | At The Main Event | Criss Cross | Criss 1070
At The Movies
Andreas Maile Quartet | Mailensteine | Satin Doll Productions | SDP 1022-1 CD
At The Regency
We Three | The Drivin' Beat | Organic Music | ORGM 9707
At The Rio Bar
Lezlie Anders And Her Band | With Love,Lezlie | Celebrity | CYCD 74801
At The Swing Cat's Ball
Werner Bühler Quartet | At The Swinging Organ | MWM Records | MWM 005
At The Top Of The Hill(A Double Left)
Victor Mendoza Group | If Only You Knew | L+R Records | CDLR 45019
At The Vanguard
Bob Hall Quartet | At The Window | Lake | LACD 23
At Your Earliest Hesitation-
Mind Games With Claudio Roditi | Live | Edition Collage | EC 501-2
Ata
Benny Carter Group | Wonderland | Pablo | 2310922-2
Atacando
Karlheinz Miklin Quartet | Last Waltz | Acoustic Music Records | 319.1126.2
Ataraxi
Klaus Doldinger & Passport | Lifelike | Warner | 2292-46478-2
Ataraxia
Passport | Ataraxia | Atlantic | 2292-42148-2
Ataraxia(part 1&2)
Jorge Pardo Band | Cicadas | ACT | 9209-2
Atavachron
Andy LaVerne/Dave Samuels | Fountainhead | Steeplechase | SCCD 31261
Atemlinie für Horn und Tamtam
Steve Nelson Quartet | Communications | Criss Cross | Criss 1034
Aterragio Africano:Do Not Remain Seated!
Thad Jones-Mel Lewis Orchestra | Swiss Radio Days Jazz Series Vol.4:Thad Jones-Mel Lewis Orchestra | TCB Records | TCB 02042
A-Tisket A-Tasket
Chick Webb And His Orchestra | Ella:The Legendary American Decca Recordings | GRP | GRP 46482
Dick Jurgens And His Orchestra | The Uncollected: Dick Jurgens, Vol.2 | Hindsight | HSR 138
Ella Fitzgerald With Frank De Vol And His Orchestra | Verve Jazz Masters 6:Ella Fitzgerald | Verve | 519822-2
Ella Fitzgerald With Orchestra | Basin Street Blues | Intercord | 125404
Ella Fitzgerald With The Frank DeVol Orchestra | Get Happy! | Verve | 523321-2
Ella Fitzgerald With The Hank Jones Trio | The Complete Jazz At The Philharmonic On Verve 1944-1949 | Verve | 523893-2
Ella Fitzgerald With The Lou Levy Quartet | For The Love Of Ella Fitzgerald | Verve | 841765-2
Compact Jazz: Ella Fitzgerald | Verve | 831367-2
Ella Fitzgerald With The Tommy Flanagan Quartet | Ella Fitzgerald:Newport Jazz Festival-Live at Carnegie Hall | CBS | C2K 66809
Glenn Miller And His Orchestra | Jazz Collection:Glenn Miller | Laserlight | 24367
Oscar Peterson Quartet | A Tribute To My Friends | Pablo | 2310902-2
The Sunshine Terrace Swing Band | Swinging In A New Mood | Vagabond | 6.22997 AS
A-Tisket A-Tasket(Theme)
Ella Fitzgerald And Her Famous Orchestra | The Radio Years 1940 | Jazz Unlimited | JUCD 2065
Ella Fitzgerald Vol.2-Forever Young | Swingtime(Contact) | ST 1007
Atitled Valse
The Clarke/Duke Project | The Clarke/Duke Project 2 | Epic | EK 38934
Atlanta Blues
Louis Armstrong And His All Stars | Louis Armstrong Plays W.C.Handy | CBS | CK 64925
The Louis Armstrong Selection | CBS | 467278-2
Atlanta Rag
Blind Willie McTell | Blind Willie McTell-Death Cell Blues | Biograph | BLP C 14
Atlanta,GA
The Danish Radio Jazz Orchestra | This Train:The Danish Radio Jazz Orchestra Plays The Music Of Ray Pitts | dacapo | DCCD 9428
Atlantic Avenue
Wild Bill Davis Quartet | Live At Swiss Radio Studio Zürich | Jazz Connaisseur | JCCD 8701-2
Atlantic City
Georg Wadenius Group | Cleo | Four Leaf Clover | FLC 5097 CD
Atlantis
Miroslav Vitous | Emergence | ECM | 1312
Atlantis Suite:
Michael Riessler Group | Orange | ACT | 9274-2

Atlas
Sonny Stitt And His West Coast Friends | Atlas Blues Blow And Ballade | Eastworld | CP 32-5428

Atlas Blues
Eddie Bert Sextet | The Human Factor | Fresh Sound Records | FSR-CD 5005

Atmos
Phil Haynes' 4 Horns & What | 4 Horns & What? | Open Minds | OM 2402-2

Atomic Cafe
Ray McKinley & His Orchestra | Borderline | Savoy | SV 0203(MG 12024)

Atomic Peace
Perry Robinson Quartet | The Traveler | Chiaroscuro | CR 190

Atom-Sex-Kino
Alfred 23 Harth-John Zorn | Plan Eden | Creative Works Records | CW LP 1008

Atonal Citizen
Nornert Stein Pata Masters | Live In Australia | Pata Musik | PATA 15 CD

Atonal Citizen II
Gerardo Iacoucci Modern Big Band | Great News From Italy | yvp music | CD 3030

Atsui Sugoku
Bosho | Live At The Knitting Factory New York City,Vol.1 | Enemy | EMCD 111(03511)

Attack Of Sharon The Herbovore
Kevin Bruce Harris Quartet | Folk Songs-Folk Tales | TipToe | TIP-888807 2

Attaining
John Coltrane Quartet | John Coltrane:The Classic Quartet-Complete Impulse Studio Recordings | Impulse(MCA) | 951280-2
Jeff 'Tain' Watts Quartet | Citizen Tain | CBS | CK 69551

Attention
Charly Antolini Orchestra | Charly Antolini | Jazz Magazine | 48017
Jazz Orchester Rheinland-Pfalz | Kazzou | Jazz Haus Musik | LJBB 9104

Attention-
Enrico Rava Quartet | Il Giro Del Giorno In 80 Mondi | Black Saint | BSR 0011

Au Bar Du Petit Bac
Joelle Leandre-Carlos Zingaro | Ecritures | Adda | 590038

Au Clair De La Femme
Five + Jazz Comfort | Brazz | Memo Music | MM 6061

Au Contraire
Pino Minafra Sud Ensemble | Sudori | Victo | CD 034

Au Grand Large
BBFC | Live | Plainisphare | PL 1267-14

Au Lait
Pat Metheny Group | Offramp | ECM | 1216(817138-2)
Hannes Clauss Quartett | Walk | Acoustic Music Records | 319.1074.2

Au Privave
Anima Trio | Blue In Green | Anima Records | DV-CD 003
Cannonball Adderley Quintet | Wes Montgomery-The Complete Riverside Recordings | Riverside | 12 RCD 4408-2
Charlie Parker And His Orchestra | Bird On Verve-Vol.5:The Magnificent Charlie Parker | Verve | 817446-1 IMS
Charlie Parker Quintet | Charlie Parker:The Best Of The Verve Years | Verve | 527815-2
Swedish Schnapps + | Verve | 849393-2
Chet Baker Quintet | Out Of Nowhere | Milestone | MCD 9191-2
Coliseum Jazz Trio | Coliseum Jazz Trio | EdiPan | NGP 810
Gianni Basso European Quartet | Lunet | SPLASC(H) Records | H 101
Jimmy Bruno Trio With Bobby Watson | Live At Birdland | Concord | CCD 4768
Joe Albany Trio | Portrait Of A Legend | Fresh Sound Records | FSR-CD 317
Joe Bonner Trio | Parade | Steeplechase | SCCD 31116
Oscar Peterson Big 6 | Oscar Peterson At The Montreux Jazz Festival 1975 | Original Jazz Classics | 2310747
Patrick Tompert Trio | Patrick Tompert Trio Live | Satin Doll Productions | SDP 1029-1 CD
Peter Herbolzheimer Rhythm Combination & Brass | Bigband Bebop | Koala Records | CD P 5
Sergio Salvatore Trio | Tune Up | GRP | GRP 97632
Warne Marsh-Lee Konitz Quintet | Warne Marsh-Lee Konitz,Vol.3 | Storyville | SLP 4096

Au Privave-
Cannonball Adderley And The Poll Winners | The Cannonball Adderley Collection Vol.4:C.Adderley And The Poll Winners | Landmark | CAC 1304-2(882340)

Au Privave(alt.take)
Cannonball Adderley Quintet | Wes Montgomery-The Complete Riverside Recordings | Riverside | 12 RCD 4408-2
Charlie Parker And His Orchestra | Bird On Verve-Vol.5:The Magnificent Charlie Parker | Verve | 817446-1 IMS

Au Privave(take 2)
Bird: The Complete Charlie Parker On Verve | Verve | 837141-2

Au Privave(take 3)
Charlie Parker Quintet | Jazz-Club: Trumpet | Verve | 840038-2

Aubade
Takashi Yoshimatsu | Tender Toys:Shin-Ichi Fukuda | Denon Compact Disc | CO-18053

Aube
Transition Jazz Group | Richard's Rumba | SPLASC(H) Records | H 182

Aube Rouge Á Grozny
Barney Wilen Quintet | Wild Dogs Of The Ruwenzori | IDA Record | 020 CD

Audience's Excitement
Max Roach Quintet | The Hardbop Academy | Affinity | AFF 773

Audrey
Bud Powell Trio | Bud Powell:The Complete Blue Note And Roost Recordings | Blue Note | 830083-2
David Friesen Trio | The Name Of A Woman | Intuition Records | INT 3334-2
Eddie Cleanhead Vinson With The Cannonball Adderley Quintet | Eddie 'Cleanhead' Vinson With The Cannonball Adderley Quintet | Milestone | MCD 9324-2
Mel Lewis Quintet | Mellifous | Landmark | LCD 1543-2

Audrey Hepburn
Roni Ben-Hur With The Barry Harris Trio | Backyard | TCB Records | TCB 95902

Auf Alle Felle
Papa Bue's Viking Jazzband | Schlafe Mein Prinzchen | Storyville | 6.23327 AF

Auf Dem Jahrmarkt
Ernst Jandl Mit Band | Bist Eulen? | Extraplatte | EX 316141

Auf Dem Meere
Stefan Pelzl's Juju feat. Idris Muhammad | Juju | L+R Records | CDLR 45026

Auf Den Straßen Zu Singen
The Contemporary Alphorn Orchestra | Mytha | Hat Art | CD 6110

Auf Einer Burg-
Don Byron-Joe Berkovitz | Tuskegee Experiments | Nonesuch | 7559-79280-2

Auf Einer Burg(Robert Schumann)
Das Böse Ding | Cleanhappydirty | Acoustic Music Records | 319.1090.2

Auf Erden
Erika Rojo & Tim Sund | Das Lied | Nabel Records:Jazz Network | CD 4684

Auf Erden Und Im Paradies-
Jazzensemble Des Hessischen Rundfunks | Atmosphering Conditions Permitting | ECM | 1549/50

Auf In Den Wald
Der Rote Bereich | Der Rote Bereich 3 | Jazz 4 Ever Records:Jazz Network | J4E 4740

Auf In Den Wald-
Grubenklangorchester | Bergmannsleben | CMP Records | CMP 18

Auf Spurensuche
Jack Hylton And His Orchestra | The Bands That Matter | Eclipse | ECM 2046

August Blues
Franck Avitabile Trio With Louis Petrucciani | In Tradition | Dreyfus Jazz Line | FDM 36594-2

August In Paris
Rick Margitza Quartet | Game Of Chance | Challenge | CHR 70044

August Moon
Benny Carter With The Rutgers University Orchestra | Harlem Renaissance | Limelight | 844299-2 IMS

August Moon(alt.take)
Donald Johnston Quartet | There's No Forgetting You | Bhakti Jazz | BR 30

August Morning
Vorläufiges Amtliches Endergebnis | Stadtgarten Series Vol.7 | Jazz Haus Musik | JHM 1007 SER

Augusta
Richard Zimmerman | The Complete Works Of Scott Joplin | Laserlight | 15945

Augustine
Helmut Nieberle-Helmut Kagerer | Skyliner | ART BY HEART | ABH 2001 2
Der Rote Bereich | Der Rote Bereich | Jazz 4 Ever Records:Jazz Network | J4E 4715

Auk And Dromedary
Dieter Ilg Trio | Fieldwork | Jazzline | JL 11155-2

Auld Lang Syne
Marcus Roberts | Prayer For Peace | Novus | ND 90585(847064)

Auld Lang Syne:
Rüdiger Carl | Vorn:Lieder Und Improvisationen Für Akkordeon, Bandoneon Und Ziehharmonika | FMP | 1110

Auma
Wayne Shorter Quartet | Footprints Live! | Verve | 589679-2

Aung San Suu Kyi
Wayne Shorter-Herbie Hancock | 1+1:Herbie Hancock-Wayne Shorter | Verve | 537564-2
André Previn Trio | Gigi | Original Jazz Classics | OJCCD 407-2(C 7548)

Aunt Hagar's Blues
Art Tatum | Art Tatum-The Complete Pablo Solo Masterpieces | Pablo | 7 PACD 4404-2
Art Tatum:Complete Capitol Recordings | Definitive Records | DRCD 11192
Don Ewell | Don Ewell-Live At The 100 Club | Solo Art | SACD-89
Humphrey Lyttelton And His Band | Movin' And Groovin' | Black Lion | BLCD 760504
Jeanie Lambe And The Danny Moss Septet | Three Great Concerts:Live In Hamburg 1993-1995 | Nagel-Heyer | CD 019
Ken Colyer's Jazzmen | Ken Colyer's Jazzmen In Concert 1959 | Dine-A-Mite Jazz | DJCD-001
King Oliver And His Dixie Syncopators | Papa Joe | MCA | 1309
Louis Armstrong And His All Stars | The Louis Armstrong Selection | CBS | 467278-2
Ted Lewis And His Band | The Jazzworthy Ted Lewis | Retrieval | RTR 79014

Aura-
King & Moore | Cliff Dance | Justice Records | JR 0803-2

Auratune
Bud Shank-Shorty Rogers Quintet | California Concert | Contemporary | CCD 14012-2

Aurora
Beaver Harris | African Drums | Owl Records | 09
Ralph Towner-Gary Burton | Matchbook | ECM | 1056(835014-2)
Scott Colley Trio | This Place | Steeplechase | SCCD 31443

Aurora-
Jukka Tolonen Group | Impressions | Sonet | 147126

Aurora Borealis Suite:
Marc Ribot Y Los Cubanos Postizos | The Prosthetic Cubans | Atlantic | 7567-83116-2

Aurora En Pekin
Anne Morre | Anne Morre | Bellaphon | BCH 33008

Aurora(part 1)
Jean-Luc Ponty Quintet | Aurora | Atlantic | 7567-81543-2

Aurora(part 2)
The Very Best Of Jean-Luc Ponty | Rhino | 8122-79862-2
Francois Jeanneau | Ephemere | Owl Records | 07

Auroville
Klaus Doldinger's Passport | Running In Real Time | Warner | 2292-40633-2

Auryn
Stefano Battaglia Trio | Auryn | SPLASC(H) Records | CD H 162-2

Aus
Pinguin Moschner-Joe Sachse | If 69 Was 96/The Music Of Jimi Hendrix | Aho-Recording | CD 1016

Aus Alten Märchen Winkt Es
Ulrich Gumpert Workshop Band/DDR | Unter Anderem: 'N Tango Für Gitti | FMP | 0600

Aus Meinen Tränen Spriessen
Rade Soric Quartet | Mixturiosities | Edition Collage | EC 502-2

Aus:Morgenstern-Lieder
A Band Of Friends | Teatime Vol.1 | Poise | Poise 01

Aus:Philipp Keller 'Ärmliche Verhältnisse'
Steve Coleman And Five Elements | The Sonic Language Of Myth | RCA | 2164123-2

Ausar(Reincarnation)
Ingo Bartz/Karl Schumweber | First Catalogue | KlangRäume | 30170

Ausgetragen-
KLaus Treuheit-Stefan Poetzsch | 2 Duos | Klaus Treuheit Production | GR 9412(CD 160)

Ausklang-
Buddy DeFranco-Terry Gibbs Quintet | Jazz Party-First Time Together | Palo Alto | PA 8011

Ausrichtung
Das Böse Ding | Cleanhappydirty | Acoustic Music Records | 319.1090.2

Ausstellung-
Lily White Group | Somewhere Between Truth & Fiction | Knitting Factory Works | KFWCD 153

Autism Cap
Sonny Terry & Brownie McGhee | The 1958 London Sessions | Sequel Records | NEX CD 120

Autobio
Frank Minion With The Tommy Flanagan Quartet | The Soft Land Of Make Believe | Fresh Sound Records | FSR 2013(Bethlehem BCP 6052)

Autodienst Mitte
Herbie Hancock Group | Future Shock | CBS | SRCS 9508

Autogen
Billy Mitchell Sextet | This Is Billy Mitchell | Smash | 065507-2

Automation
Dodo Marmarosa Quartet | The Chicago Sessions | Argo | ARC 502 D

Automne(Vivaldi)
Bryan Lee Group With Guests | Live at The Old Absinthe House Bar...Friday Night | Blues Beacon | BLU-1029 2

Automobile Blues
Clifford Hayes' Louisville Stompers | Frog Hop | Frog | DGF 10

Autumn
Bob Florence Big Band | Westlake | Discovery | DS 832 IMS

Autumn Day In Balkans(O Zi De Toamna In Balcani)
Don Friedman | Avenue Of The Americas | Owl Records | 019

Autumn In New York
Al Porcino Big Band | In Oblivion | Jazz Mark | 106 Digital
Barney Wilen With The Bud Powell Trio | More Unissued Vol.1 | Royal Jazz | RJD 507
Billie Holiday And Her Orchestra | Welcome To Jazz: Billie Holiday | Koch Records | 322 082 D1
Bireli Lagrene Quartet | Blue Eyes | Dreyfus Jazz Line | FDM 36591-2
Blossom Dearie Quartet | April In Paris | Fresh Sound Records | FSR 555(Barclay 74017)
Bud Powell Trio | Bud Powell:The Complete Blue Note And Roost Recordings | Blue Note | 830083-2
Buddy Tate Trio | Midnight Slows Vol.4 | Black & Blue | BLE 194682
Charlie Parker With The Joe Lipman Orchestra | Charlie Parker With Strings:The Master Takes | Verve | 523984-2
Charlie Parker Big Band | Verve | 559835-2
Chet Baker Quartet | Jazz In Paris:Chet Baker Quartet Plays Standards | EmArCy | 014378-2 PMS
Chet Baker Trio | The Touch Of Your Lips | Steeplechase | SCCD 31122
Chet Baker With String-Orchestra And Voices | Chet Baker With Fifty Italian Strings | Original Jazz Classics | OJC20 492-2(JLP 921)
Chet Baker With The Radio Orchestra Baden-Baden | Live In Paris 1960-63 & Nice 1975 | France's Concert | FCD 123
Curtis Fuller Quintet | Blues-ette Part II | Savoy | CY 75624
Ella Fitzgerald And Louis Armstrong With The Oscar Peterson Quartet | The Best Of Ella Fitzgerald And Louis Armstrong On Verve | Verve | 537909-2
Ella And Louis Again,Vol.1 | Verve | 2304501 IMS
The Complete Ella Fitzgerald And Louis Armstrong On Verve | Verve | 537284-2
Ella And Louis Again | Verve | 825374-2
Ella Fitzgerald With Orchestra | The Best Is Yet To Come | Original Jazz Classics | OJCCD 889-2(2312138)
Errol Parker | A Tribute To Monk | Sahara | 1012
George Coleman Quartet | Amsterdam After Dark | Timeless | CD SJP 129
Great Jazz Trio | The Club New Yorker | Denon Compact Disc | DC-8567
Harald Banter Ensemble | Deutsches Jazz Fesival 1954/1955 | Bear Family Records | BCD 15430
Harry James And His Orchestra | The Uncollected:Harry James, Vol.5 | Hindsight | HSR 142
Jay McShann | Jay McShann At Cafe Des Copains | Sackville | SKCD2-2024
John Colianni | Prime Cuts | Jazz Connaisseur | JCCD 9935-2
Kenny Burrell Quartet | Blue Lights-Vol. 1 | Blue Note | 300235(1596)
Kenny Dorham Sextet | The Complete Round About Midnight At The Cafe Bohemia | Blue Note | 533775-2
Round Midnight At The Cafe Bohemia | Blue Note | 300105(1524)
Louis Hayes Sextet | The Crawl | Candid | CCD 79045
Maria Baptist Trio | Crazy Dreams | BIT | 11194
Mel Torme With The Great American Song Book Orchestra | The Great American Song Book | Telarc Digital | CD 83328
Modern Jazz Quartet | The Complete Modern Jazz Quartet Prestige & Pablo Recordings | Prestige | 4PRCD 4438-2
Modern Jazz Quartet | Prestige | P 24005
Singers Unlimited | A Capella 2 | MPS | 821860-2
Stan Kenton And His Orchestra | Portraits On Standards | Creative World | ST 1042
Stan Seltzer Trio | Stan Seltzer Trio | Fresh Sound Records | HIFI R 202 CD
Tete Montoliu | Songs For Love | Enja | ENJ-2040 2
Tete Montoliu Trio | Catalonian Nights | Steeplechase | SCCD 31148

Autumn In New York-
Dorothy Donegan Trio | Live At The Widder Bar 1986 | Timeless | CD SJP 247
Jack Sheldon-Ross Tompkins | On My Own | Concord | CCD 4529
Stan Getz-Lionel Hampton Quintet | Hamp And Getz | Verve | 831672-2
Tete Montoliu Trio | Live At Keystone Corner | Timeless | CD SJP 138

Autumn In New York(78 rpm-take)
Bud Powell Trio | The Amazing Bud Powell Vol.2 | Blue Note | 532137-2

Autumn In New York(alt.take 1)
The Amazing Bud Powell Vol.2 | Blue Note | 532137-2

Autumn In New York(alt.take 2)
Charles Mingus Workshop | Charles Mingus-The Complete Debut Recordings | Debut | 12 DCD 4402-2

Autumn In New York(take 1)
Charles Mingus-The Complete Debut Recordings | Debut | 12 DCD 4402-2

Autumn In New York(take 2)
Jean-Michel Pilc Trio | Welcome Home | Dreyfus Jazz Line | FDM 36630-2

Autumn In Newfane
Frederica von Stade With The Chris Brubeck-Bill Crofut Ensemble | Across Your Dreams: Frederica von Stade Sings Brubeck | Telarc Digital | CD 80467

Autumn Into Fall
John Swana Quintet | The Feeling's Mutual | Criss Cross | Criss 1090

Autumn Leaves
Ahmad Jamal Quintet | The Essence Part 1 | Dreyfus Jazz Line | FDM 37007-2
Ahmad Jamal Septet | Live In Paris 1996 | Dreyfus Jazz Line | FDM 37020-2
Ahmad Jamal Trio | Live At The Alhambra | Vogue | 655002
Arthur Prysock And His Orchestra | Morning,Noon And Night:The Collection | Verve | 557484-2
Benny Carter Quintet | Take The 'A' Train | Fresh Sound Records | FSR-CD 0306
Benny Waters Quartet | Swinging Again | Jazzpoint | JP 1037 CD
Bill Doggett And His Orchestra | Dance Awhile | Sing | 585
Bill Evans Trio | Live In Paris 1972 Vol.2 | France's Concert | FCD 114
Bill Evans:The Secret Sessions | Milestone | 8MCD 4421-2
Emily | Moon Records | MCD 060-2
Yesterday I Heard The Rain | Bandstand | BDCD 1535
Portrait In Jazz | Original Jazz Classics | OJC20 088-2
Bill Evans/Jazzhouse | Milestone | MCD 9151-2
Bill Evans Trio With Jeremy Steig | What's New | Enoch's Music | 57271053
Billy May And His Orchestra | Billy May's Big Fat Brass | Capitol | EMS 1155
Bireli Lagrene Ensemble | Bireli Lagrene 15 | Antilles | 802503
Bireli Lagrene Trio | Live In Marciac | Dreyfus Jazz Line | FDM 36567-2
Bob Berg Quintet | The Best Of Bob Berg On Denon | Denon Compact Disc | DC-8593
Bobby Timmons Trio | Moanin' | Milestone | M 47031
Booker Ervin Quintet | Down In The Dumps | Savoy | SV 0245(SJL 1119)
Bruce Forman Quartet | Pardon Me | Concord | CCD 4368
Cannonball Adderley Quintet | Somethin' Else | Blue Note | 746338-2
Somethin' Else | Blue Note | 495329-2
Miles Davis:The Blue Note And Capitol Recordings | Blue Note | 827475-2
Miles Davis:The Best Of The Capitol/Blue Note Years | Blue Note | 798287-2
Cannonball Adderley Sextet | The Japanese Concerts | Milestone | M 47029
Carl Allen And Manhattan Projects | Piccadilly Square | Timeless | CD SJP 406
Chet Baker With The Don Sebesky Orchestra | She Was Too Good To Me | Epic | 450954-2
Chuck Brown And The Second Chapter Band | Timeless | Minor Music | 801068
Chuck Marohnic Trio | Pages Of Stone | ITM-Pacific | ITMP 970064
David S. Ware Quartet | Third Ear Recitation | DIW | DIW 870 CD
Denny Christianson Big Band | More Pepper | Justin Time | JUST 19
Dizzy Gillespie And His Orchestra | Dizzy's Diamonds-Best Of The Verve Years | Verve | 513875-2
Dizzy Gillespie Quintet | The Great Modern Jazz Trumpet | Festival | 402151
European Jazz Trio | Nowegian Wood | Timeless | CD SJP 322
Frances Wayne With Neal Hefti And His Orchestra | Songs For My Man | Fresh Sound Records | LSP 15822(Epic LN 3222)
Frank Morgan Sextet | Frank Morgan | Vogue | 655018
Gene Ammons-Sonny Stitt Quintet | Left Bank Encores | Prestige | PRCD 11022-2
Jazz-Club: Tenor Sax | Verve | 840031-2
Helen Merrill + Ron Carter | Duets | Mercury | 838097-2 PMS

Jacky Terrasson Trio | Smile | Blue Note | 542413-2
James Moody Quartet | Feelin' It Together | Muse | MCD 5020
Jenny Evans And Band | Girl Talk | ESM Records | ESM 9306
Girl Talk | Enja | ENJ-9363 2
Live At The Allotria | BELL Records | BLR 90003
Jimmy Forrest Quintet | Most Much! | Original Jazz Classics | OJCCD 350-2(P 7218)
Jimmy Smith Trio | Incredible Jimmy Smith Vol.3 | Blue Note | 300106(1525)
Joachim Kühn Quartet | Standards/Live | ITM Records | ITM 1484
Joe Pass | Virtuoso No.4 | Pablo | 2640102
Junior Mance | Jubilation | Sackville | SKCD2-2046
Keith Jarrett Trio | Still Live | ECM | 1360/61(835008-2
Tokyo '96 | ECM | 1666(539955-2)
Kenny Burrell Quintet | Sunup To Sundown | Contemporary | CCD 14065-2
Lanfranco Malaguti/Enzo Pietropaoli/Fabrizio Sferra | Sound Investigations | SPLASC(H) Records | H 143
Larry Schneider Quartet | Blind Date | Steeplechase | SCCD 31317
Lee Konitz Quartet | Jazz a 1 Juan | Steeplechase | SCCD 31072
Matthew Shipp Trio | The Multiplication Table | HatOLOGY | 516
Miles Davis Quintet | Stockholm 1960 | Royal Jazz | RJD 509
Nat Adderley Quintet | We Remember Cannon | IN+OUT Records | 7012-2
Nat Adderley Sextet | Autumn Leaves-Live At Sweet Basil | Sweet Basil | 660.55.013
Oscar Peterson Trio | Compact Jazz:Oscar Peterson | Mercury | 830698-2
Oscar Peterson-Dizzy Gillespie Duo | Oscar Peterson & Dizzy Gillespie | Pablo | 2310740-2
Oscar Peterson-Stephane Grappelli Quartet | Jazz In Paris:Oscar Peterson-Stephane Grappelli Quartet Vol.2 | EmArCy | 013029-2
Patrick Tompert Trio | Patrick Tompert Trio Live | Satin Doll Productions | SDP 1029-1 CD
Paul Desmond Orchestra | Late Lament | Bluebird | ND 90207
Paul Desmond With Strings | The Ballad Of Paul Desmond | RCA | 21429372
Desmond Blue | RCA | 2663898-2
Pedro Iturralde Quartet | Pedro Iturralde Quartet feat. Hampton Hawes | Fresh Sound Records | FSR 546(Hispavox 550-4020411)
Ray Barretto + New World Spirit | My Summertime | Owl Records | 835830-2
Rogall & Van Buggenum | Two Piano Jazz: Live | Jazzline | ???
Ron Holloway Group | Slanted | Milestone | MCD 9219-2
Sarah Vaughan With The Roland Hanna Quartet | Sarah Vaughan Birthday Celebration | Fantasy | FANCD 6090-2
Scott Hamilton Quartet | East Of The Sun | Concord | CCD 4583
Stan Getz All Stars | Stan Getz Live(The Great Jazz Gala '80) | Jazz Classics | CD CA 36005
Stan Getz Quintet | Live At Palm Beach Casino, Cannes 1980 | Rare Bid | BID 155504
Stan Kenton And His Orchestra | Innovations-Live 1951 | Bandstand | BDCD 1519
Stanley Jordan Trio | Festival International De Jazz De Montreal | Spectra | 9811660
Stolen Moments | Blue Note | 797159-2
Tal Farlow Quartet | Poppin' And Burnin' | Verve | 815236-1 IMS
Thomas Clausen Trio With Gary Burton | Flowers And Trees | M.A Music | A 805-2
Thomas Stabenow-Lothar Schmitz | Basspartout For Guitar | Bassic-Sound | 003
Tierney Sutton And Her Trio | Blue In Green | Telarc Digital | CD 83522
Tommy Flanagan And Hank Jones | Our Delights | Original Jazz Classics | GXY 5113
Toots Thielemans/Jonny Teupen/Paul Kuhn And Friends | Just Friends | Jazzline | ???
Trio Karel Boehlee | Switch | Timeless | CD SJP 206
Wynton Marsalis Quartet | Live At Blues Alley | CBS | 487323-2

Autumn Leaves-
Mel Tormé And Cleo Laine With The John Dankworth Orchestra | Nothing Without You | Concord | CCD 4515
Paul Desmond With Strings | Desmond Blue | RCA | 2663898-2

Autumn Leaves(alt.take 1)
Wynton Kelly Trio | Wynton Kelly! | Vee Jay Recordings | VJ 011

Autumn Leaves(alt.take 2)
Wynton Kelly! | Vee Jay Recordings | VJ 011

Autumn Leaves(alt.take)
Stan Getz Quintet | Stan Getz-The Complete Roost Sessions | The Jazz Factory | JFCD 22839

Autumn Leaves(mono version)
Bill Evans Trio | Spring Leaves | Milestone | M 47034

Autumn Mood
McCoy Tyner Quintet | Double Exposure | LRC Records | CDC 9040

Autumn Nocturne
Benny Goodman And His Orchestra | Swing Swing Swing-Rare Recordings From The Yale University Music Library | Limelight | 844312-2
Claude Thornhill And His Orchestra | Snowfall | Fresh Sound Records | NL 46030(RCA)
Esmeralda Ferrara Group | Day By Day | Philology | W 129.2
Lew Del Gatto Septet | Katewalk | Naxos Jazz | 86058-2
Sonny Rollins Quintet | Just Once | Jazz Door | JD 12121
Billy Butler Quintet | Guitar Soul | Original Jazz Classics | OJC 334(P 7734)

Autumn Nocturne-
Spyro Gyra | Catching The Sun | MCA | ???

Autumn Picture
Wolfgang Muthspiel Group | In & Out | Amadeo | 521385-2

Autumn Rose
Toshiko Akiyoshi-Lew Tabackin Big Band | Farewell | JAM | 003 IMS

Autumn Serenade
Johnny Hartman With The John Coltrane Quartet | John Coltrane And Johnny Hartman | Impulse(MCA) | 951157-2
Mel Tormé With Rob McConnell And The Boss Brass | Velvet & Brass | Concord | CCD 4667

Autumn's Reverie
Steve Khan Quartet | Eyewitness | Antilles | AN 1018(802758)

Avalon
Arne Domnerus Quintet | Sugar Fingers | Phontastic | NCD 8831
Art Farmer/Benny Golson Jazztet | Met The Jazztet | Chess | CHD 91550(872338)
Art Pepper Quartet | Art Pepper:The Complete Galaxy Recordings | Galaxy | 16GCD 1016-2
Landscape | Original Jazz Classics | OJCCD 676-2(GXY 5128)
Benny Goodman And His Orchestra | Jazz Collection:Benny Goodman | Laserlight | 24396
Live At The International World Exhibition Brussels, 1958 | Jazz Anthology | 550172
Benny Goodman Quintet | Berlin 1980 | TCB Records | TCB 43022
Coleman Hawkins With Michel Warlop And His Orchestra | Django Reinhardt And His American Friends:Paris 1935-1937 | Memo Music | HDJ 4124
Dutch Swing College Band | Still Blowing Strong - 34 Years | DSC Production | PA 1022 (801071)
Erroll Garner Trio | This Is Erroll Garner 2 | CBS | 68219
Jack Sheldon-Ross Tompkins | On My Own | Concord | CCD 4529
Jazz At Carnegie Hall All Stars | Ella Fitzgerald:Newport Jazz Festival-Live at Carnegie Hall | CBS | C2K 66809
John Crocker Quartet | Easy Living | Timeless | CD TTD 561
Lionel Hampton With Milt Buckner And The All Stars | Alive & Jumping | MPS | 821283-1
Louis Armstrong With The Dukes Of Dixieland | Great Alternatives | Chiaroscuro | CR 2003
Roberto Cipelli Quartet | Moona Moore | SPLASC(H) Records | H 173
Sarah Vaughan With Orchestra | !Viva! Vaughan | Mercury | 549374-2
Schnuckenack Reinhardt Quintet | 15.3.1973 | Intercord | 160031
Terry Gibbs-Buddy DeFranco-Herb Ellis Sextet | Memories Of You-A Tribute To Benny Goodman | Contemporary | CCD 14066-2
The Tremble Kids | 25 Jahre The Tremble Kids | Intercord | 180036
Warne Marsh Quintet With Art Pepper | Jazz Of Two Cities | Fresh Sound Records | FSR-CD 342
Wedeli Köhler Group | Swing & Folk | Jazzpoint | JP 1067 CD
West Coast Jam Session | Live At The Trade Winds 1952 | Fresh Sound Records | FSCD 1001
Wolfgang Schlüter Quintet | Good Vibrations | Extra Records & Tapes | 11522

Avalon(alt.take)
Charles Moffett Quintet | The Gift | Savoy | SV 0217(MG 12194)

Avantgarde Noise Pollution
Larry Goldings Quartet | Caminhos Cruzados | Novus | 4163184-2

Avatar
Chris Jarrett | Short Stories For Piano | Edition Musikat | EDM 056

Ave Crux
Al Di Meola Group | Winter Nights | Telarc Digital | CD 83458

Avenue
String Band Featuring Isao Suzuki | String Band Featuring Isao Suzuki | Flying Disk | VIDC 601 Direct Disc

Avenue A
Count Basie And His Orchestra | The Uncollected:Count Basie | Hindsight | HSR 224 (835571)

Avenue C
Prez's Hat Vol.3 | Philology | 214 W 8
Lambert, Hendricks And Ross | Sing A Song Of Basie | Verve | 543827-2
Lambert,Hendricks & Ross:Sing A Song Of Basie | CTI Records | PDCTI 1115-2

Avenue Of Stars
Don Friedman | Avenue Of The Americas | Owl Records | 019

Avenue(Footprints)
Rocky Boyd Quintet | Ease It | Blue Moon | BMCD 1606

Avila And Tequila
Ingrid Jensen Quintet | Here On Earth | Enja | ENJ-9313 2
Toon Van Vliet Quartet | Toon Van Vliet | BVHAAST | 059

Avisale A La Vecina
The Conga Kings | The Conga Kings | Chesky | JD 193

Avotcja One
Chico Freeman-Arthur Blythe Sextet | Luminous | Ronnie Scott's Jazz House | JHCD 010

Avskjed
Ketil Bjornstad Group | Early Years | EmArCy | 013271-2

Avskjet Pa Forskudd(Farewell In Advance)
Natraj | Meet Me Anywhere | Dorian Discovery | DIS-80119

Awakening
Ian Carr's Nucleos | Awakening/Live At The Theaterhaus | BELL Records | BLR 83752
Mahavishnu Orchestra | The Inner Mounting Flame | CBS | CK 65523
Mark Soskin Quartet | Overjoyed | Jazz City | 660.53.020
Rabih Abou-Khalil Group | Tarab | Enja | ENJ-7083 2
Spyro Gyra | Carnaval | MCA | 2292-50418-1
Steve Williamson Sextet | A Waltz For Grace | Verve | 843088-2 PMS

Awakening Ancestores
Craig Harris Sextet | Aboriginal Affairs | India Navigation | IN 1060

Awakening-Midweek
Henry Threadgill Sextet | Easily Slip Into Another World | RCA | PD 83025(874076)

Aware
Steve Coleman And The Council Of Balance | Genesis & The Opening Of The Way | RCA | 2152934-2

Awareness
Sangoma Everett Trio | Fresh Air | IDA Record | 018 CD

Away
John Scofield Groups | Quiet | Verve | 533185-2
Joint Venture | Mirrors | Enja | ENJ-7049 2

Away From The Crowd
Roger Sturgis With Lovie Jordan's Elks Rendez-Vous Band | Louis Jordan-Let The Good Times Roll: The Complete Decca Recordings 1938-1954 | Bear Family Records | BCD 15557 IH

Away From You
Shelly Manne Quartet | Rex-From The Broadway Musical oRex o | Discovery | DS 783 IMS

Away In The Manger
The Four Freshmen | Freshmas! | Ranwood | RCD 8239(875344)

Away We Go
Buddy Rich Big Band | The New One! | Pacific Jazz | 494507-2

Away We Go(alt.take)
John Scofield Groups | Quiet | Verve | 533185-2

Away With Words
Carmen McRae With The Norman Simmons Trio | Live At Century Plaza | Atlantic | AMCY 1075

Awful Lonely
Paul Chambers Quartet | Ease It | Affinity | AFF 115

Awful Sad
Bill Holman Octet | Group Activity | Affinity | AFF 65

Awkwarder
Karim Ziad Groups | Ifrikya | ACT | 9282-2

Awra
Frank Kuruc Band | Limits No Limits | Edition Musikat | EDM 023

Äwwi Metall
Glenn Spearman Double Trio | Smokehouse | Black Saint | 120157-2

Axes 'N X-Legs
Erhard Hirt | Guitar Solo | FMP | OWN-90003

Axioma
Paul Bley | Axis | Improvising Artists Inc. | 123853-2

Axum
Bebo Valdés Trio | El Arte Del Sabor | Blue Note | 535193-2

Ay Que Me Vango Cayendo-
Carlos Bica & Azul | Twist | Enja | ENJ-9386 2

Ay,Ay,Ay
Hamiet Bluiett Quintet | Endangered Species | India Navigation | IN 1025

Ayiko Ayiko
Okay Temiz Group | Magnet Dance | TipToe | TIP-888819 2

Ayler Songs-
Hipsters In The Zone | Into The Afro-Latin Bag | Nabel Records:Jazz Network | CD 4663

Ayola
Luis Agudo & Friends | Dona Fia | Red Records | 123244-2

Ay-Tete-Fee
Friedeman Graef-Achim Goettert | Saxoridoo | FMP | OWN-90010

Azalea
Chris Potter Group | Traveling Mercies | Verve | 018243-2
Dado Moroni Trio | Insights | Jazz Focus | JFCD 007
Louis Armstrong And His All Stars With Duke Ellington | The Beautiful American | Jazz Society(Vogue) | 670501
Sonny Rollins Group | Nucleus | Original Jazz Classics | OJCCD 620-2(M 9064)

Azalea(alt.take)
Jamie Findlay | Wings Of Light | Acoustic Music Records | 319.1076.2

Azerbaizan Albatross
Oriental Wind | Life Road | JA & RO | JARO 4113-2

Azeri
Walter Benton Quintet | Out Of This World | Milestone | MCD 47087-2

Azil
Andy Lumpp | Piano Solo | Nabel Records:Jazz Network | CD 4646

Azimuth
Azimuth | Azimuth | ECM | 1099
Andy Lumpp | Piano Solo | Nabel Records:Jazz Network | CD 4646

Azimuth(for Renate Otta)
Jens Schliecker & Nils Rohwer | Duo Fantasie:Piano Meets Vibes | Acoustic Music Records | 319.1094.2

Azul Azul Cielo
Carlos Bica Group | Azul | Traumton Records | 4425-2

Azul É O Mar
Eddie Louiss-Richard Galliano Duo | Face To Face | Dreyfus Jazz Line | FDM 36627-2

Azul Tiple
The Three Sounds | Black Orchid | Blue Note | 821289-2

Azule Scrape
Cannonball Adderley And The Poll Winners | The Cannonball Adderley Collection Vol.4:C.Adderley And The Poll Winners | Landmark | CAC 1304-2(882340)

Azule Serape
Cannonball Adderley Quintet | Cannonball Adderley Birthday Celebration | Fantasy | FANCD 6087-2
At The Lighthouse | Capitol | 531572-2
The Cannonball Adderley Collection Vol.5:At The Lighthouse | Landmark | CAC 1305-2(882344)
Cannonball Adderley-Nat Adderley Quintet | What Is This Thing Called Soul:In Europe-Live! | Original Jazz Classics | OJCCD 801-2(2308238)
Nat Adderley Quintet | Talkin' About You | 32 Jazz | 32082

Azure
Bunny Berigan And His Orchestra | The Indispensable Bunny Berigan 1937-1939 | RCA | NL 89744(2) DP
David Fathead Newman Sextet | Mr.Gentle, Mr.Cool:A Tribute To Duke Ellington | Kokopelli Records | KOKO 1300
Ella Fitzgerald And Barney Kessel | Ella Fitzgerald Day Dream:The Best Of The Duke Ellington Song Book | Verve | 527223-2
Ella Fitzgerald-Barney Kessel | Ella Fitzgerald Sings The Duke Ellington Songbook | Verve | 559248-2
The Complete Ella Fitzgerald Song Books of Harold Arlen, Irving Berlin, Duke Ellington, George & Ira Gershwin, Jerome Kern, Johnny Mercer, Cole Porter And Rogers & Hart | Verve | 519832-2

Azure-Te
Junior Mance Trio | Happy Time | Original Jazz Classics | VIJ 5049
Mary Lou Williams Quartet | Mary Lou Williams:The London Sessions | Vogue | 21409312
Wild Bill Davis Quartet | Live At Swiss Radio Studio Zürich | Jazz Connaisseur | JCCD 8701-2
John Colianni | Prime Cuts | Jazz Connaisseur | JCCD 9935-2

Azure-Te(Paris Blues)
Kenny Burrell Quartet | Stormy Monday Blues | Fantasy | FCD 24767-2
Ray Anderson Trio | Azurety | Hat Art | CD 6155

Azzura
Milford Graves Trio | B bi | IPS Records | 004

B 4 U Said
Rob Mullins Group | Tokyo Nights | Nova | NOVA 9026-2

B And A
Billy Butler Quintet | Guitar Soul | Original Jazz Classics | OJC 334(P 7734)

B B 5
Milford Graves Trio | B bi | IPS Records | 004

B Blues
Trio Concepts | Trio Concepts More | yvp music | CD 3019

B Flat Swing
Teddy Wilson And His Orchestra | The Rarest 1937-42 | Everybody's | 1003
Teddy Wilson Sextet | Take It Edmond Hall With Your Clarinet That Ballet | Queen-Disc | 020

B For BB
Hank Mobley Quintet | Jazz Message No.2 | Savoy | SV 0158(MG 12092)

B Funk
Rene Thomas Quintet | Guitar Genius | RTBF Records | 16001

B Minor Waltz (For Ellaine)
Quiet Now | Inside The Waltz | Blue Concept | BCCD 94/01

B&G (Midwestern Nights Dream)
Greg Cohen Sextet | Way Low | DIW | DIW 918 CD

B.B.
Grover Mitchell & His All-Star Orchestra | Hip Shakin' | Ken Music | 660.56.005

B.B.B. Bag's Barney Blues
Serge Forté Trio | Vaina | Laika Records | LK 90-021

B.B.Bemol
Mark Dresser Quintet | Force Green | Soul Note | 121273-2

B.B.King Intro
B.B.King And His Band | B. B. King, 1949-1950 | Anthology of the Blues | AB 5611

B.C.Special
Warren Vaché And The New York City All-Star Big Band | Swingtime! | Nagel-Heyer | CD 059

B.D. Blues
Duke Ellington And Count Basie With Their Orchestras | First Time! | CBS | CK 65571

B.D.B.
First Time! | CBS | CK 65571

B.D.B.(alt.take)
Andy LaVerne Trio | Between Mars & Earth | Steeplechase | SCCD 31478

B.E.
Robert Balzar Trio | Travelling | Jazzpoint | JP 1050 CD
Bennie Green Sextet | Soul Stirrin' | Blue Note | 300233(1599)

B.I.B. & Little Waltz
Wilbur Harden Sextet | Tanganyika Strut | Jazz Anthology | JA 5163

B.L.
Bireli Lagrene Ensemble | Routes To Django & Bireli Swing '81 | Jazzpoint | JP 1055 CD
John Carter Quintet | Variations On Selected Themes For Jazz Quintet | Moers Music | 01056

B.Quick
Sonny Rollins Quartet | Taking Care Of Business | Prestige | P 24082
Thilo Wolf Big Band | Swing It! | MDL-Jazz | CD 1915(CD 052)

B.Swift
Sonny Rollins Quartet | Taking Care Of Business | Prestige | P 24082
Frank Morgan Sextet | Frank Morgan | Vogue | 655018

B.T.
Buddy Tate Quartet | The Ballad Artistry Of Buddy Tate | Sackville | SKCD2-3034

B+B Calypso
Peter Kowald-Maarten Altena Duo | Bass Duets | FMP | CD 102

B-40 M23-6K RS-4-W
Charly Antolini Trio | Knock Out 2000 | Inak | 9053

B-4-U Leave
Jane Ira Bloom Quintet | The Nearness | Arabesque Recordings | AJ 0120

Ba Binga
MOKAVE | MOKAVE Vol.2 | audioquest Music | AQCD 1007

BA(e)SF,Oder Die Kunst Der Fugendichting
Dirk Raulf Group | Theater I (Bühnenmusik) | Poise | Poise 07

Baal(Theater Oberhausen)
Laurindo Almeida Quartet | Brazilliance Vol.1 | Pacific Jazz | 796339-2

Baba
Trilok Gurtu Group | Living Magic | CMP Records | CMP CD 50

Baba(for Ramana Maharashi)
Albrecht Riermeier Quartet | Four Drummers Drumming | Riff Records | CD RIFF 902-2

Babalu Ayé
Slim Gaillard And His Internationally Famous Orchestra | Slim Gailard Laughing In Rhythm-The Best Of The Verve Years | Verve | 521651-2

Babble On
Ulla Oster Group | Beyond Janis | Jazz Haus Musik | JHM 0052 CD

Babe(1)
Beyond Janis | Jazz Haus Musik | JHM 0052 CD

Babe(2)
Baden Powell Ensemble | Samba Triste | Accord | 102772

Babik
Django Reinhardt And The Quintet Du Hot Club De France | The Very Best Of Django Reinhardt | Decca | 6.28441 DP

Babo-Ling
Michael Naura Quintet | Vanessa | ECM | 1053

Babs Mood For Love
Michael Bisio Quartet | Michael Bisio Quartet In Seattle | Silkheart | SHCD 107

TITELVERZEICHNIS

Baby Baby
John Lee Hooker Trio | I Feel Good | Memo Music | HDJ 4038
Rose Murphy Trio | Rose Murphy(The Chee-Chee Girl) | RCA | 2153222-2

Baby Baby All The Time
Frankie Laine With Buck Clayton And His Orchestra | Jazz Spectacular | CBS | CK 65507
Frankie Laine With Carl Fischer's Orchesrtra | The Uncollected:Frankie Lane Vol.2 | Hindsight | HSR 216 (835570)
Nat King Cole Trio | The Best Of The Nat King Cole Trio:The Vocal Classics(1942-1946) | Blue Note | 833571-2
Oscar Peterson Trio | On The Town | Verve | 543834-2
Stan Kenton-June Christy | Duet | Capitol | 789285-2

Baby Baby Baby
Memphis Slim With Willie Dixon | Jazz In Paris:Memphis Slim/Willie Dixon Aux Trois Mailletz | EmArCy | 658148 IMS

Baby Breeze
Chet Baker Sextet | Compact Jazz: Chet Baker | Verve | 840632-2 PMS

Baby Brown
New Orleans Rhythm Kings | Big Band Bounce & Boogie-Muggsy Spanier:Hesitatin' Blues | Affinity | AFS 1030

Baby Don't Worry 'Bout Me
Buddy Johnson And His Orchestra | Buddy And Ella Johnson 1953-1964 | Bear Family Records | BCD 15479 DH

Baby Don't You Cry
Freddie Roach Quartet | Mo' Greens Please | Blue Note | 869698-3

Baby Don't You Go Way Mad
Lowell Fulsom Band | San Francisco Blues | Black Lion | BLCD 760176

Baby Don't You Quit Now
Ella Fitzgerald And Her All Stars | All That Jazz | Pablo | 2310938-2
Harlem Mamfats | I'm So Glad | Queen-Disc | 062

Baby Don't You Tell On Me
John Lee Hooker | I Wanna Dance All Night | America | AM 6101

Baby Dreams
Night Ark | Moments | RCA | PD 83028(874049)

Baby Elephant Walk
Don Ewell's Hot Four | A Portrait Of George Lewis | Lake | LACD 50

Baby Gorilla Walk
George Wallington And His Band | George Wallington Showcase | Blue Note | BNJ 71003

Baby Hear My Humble Plea
Dan Pickett | 1949 Country Blues | Krazy Kat | KK 811 IMS

Baby I Got My Eyes On You
John Lee Hooker Group | Lonesome Mood | Chess | MCD 01365

Baby I'm A Legend
Kenny Hagood With John Lewis' Orchestra | The Bebop Boys | Savoy | WL 70547 (809278)

Baby It's Cold Outside
Jimmy Smith-Wes Montgomery Quartet | Christmas Cookin' | Verve | 513711-2
Ray Charles With Orchestra | Portrait In Music | London | 6.28338 DP

Baby Let Me Hold Your Hand
Mose Allison Trio | Mose Allison Sings The 7th Son | Prestige | PR20 7279-2
Nils Landgren First Unit And Guests | Nils Landgren-The First Unit | ACT | 9292-2

Baby Let Me Kiss You
Rahsaan Roland Kirk & The Vibration Society | Rahsaan Rahsaan | Atlantic | ATL 40127(SD 1575)

Baby M's Bayou Blues
Carl Anderson Group | Pieces Of A Heart | GRP | GRP 96122

Baby Please Don't Go
Charles Musselwhite | Mellow-Dee | Crosscut | CCD 11013
Lightnin' Hopkins | The Blues Vol.2 | Intercord | 158601
Mose Allison Trio | Mose Alife!/Wild Man On The Loose | Warner | 8122-75439-2
High Jinks! The Mose Allison Trilogy | CBS | J3K 64275
Muddy Waters Blues Band | Feathers And Sons | Chess | CHD 92522(872344)

Baby Plum
Jacky Terrasson Group | What It Is | Blue Note | 498756-2
Larry Johnson & Nat Riddles | Johnson! Where Did You Get That Sound? New York Really Has The Blues | L+R Records | LR 42046

Baby Sis
Max Roach Quintet | Dizzy Gillespie:Pleyel Jazz Concert 1948 + Max Roach Quintet 1949 | Vogue | 21409412
Michael Cochrane Trio | Gesture Of Faith | Steeplechase | SCCD 31459

Baby What You Want Me To Do
Christian Willisohn Group | Blues On The World | Blues Beacon | BLU-1025 2
Etta James With Band | The Late Show-Recorded Live At Marla's Memory Lane Supper Club Vol.2 | Fantasy | FCD 9655-2
Etta James With Orchestra | Peaches | Chess | 427014

Baby What's The Matter With You
Roy Eldridge Quintet | Rockin' Chair | Verve | MV 2686 IMS

Baby Won't You Please Come Home
Al Hibbler With Gerald Wilson's Orchestra | Monday Every Day | Discovery | DS 842 IMS
Bessie Smith With Clarence Williams | Bessie Smith-The Complete Recordings Vol.1 | CBS | 467895-2
Bill Coleman Orchestra | Bill Coleman | Swing | SW 8402 IMS
Della Reese With The Neal Hefti Orchestra | Della | RCA | 2663912-2
Della | RCA | 2663912-2
Dinah Washington With Orchestra | Ballads | Roulette | 537559-2
Dinah Washington With The Don Costa Orchestra | Drinking Again | M&M Records | R 25183(Roulette)
Heiner Franz' Swing Connection | Heiner Franz' Swing Connection | Jardis Records | JRCD 9817
Helen Humes And Her All Stars | Swingin' With Helen | Original Jazz Classics | OJCCD 608-2
Jack Teagarden And His Band | The Club Hangover Broadcast | Arbors Records | ARCD 19150/51
Kid Ory's Creole Jazz Band | Song Of The Wanderer | Verve | 2304542 IMS
Louis Armstrong And His Orchestra | Mostly Blues | Ember | CJS 850
Mama Estella Yancey With Erwin Helfer | Maybe I'll Cry | Steeplechase | SCB 9001
McKinney's Cotton Pickers | The Complete McKinney's Cotton Pickers Vol.3/4 | RCA | NL 89738(2) DP
Miles Davis Quintet | Ballads | CBS | 461099-2
Muggsy Spanier And His Band | This Is Jazz Vol.1 | Jazzology | JCD 1025/26
Sarah Vaughan Plus Two | Sarah + 2 | Fresh Sound Records | FSR 605(Roulette R 52118)
Shirley Horn Trio with Buck Hill | I Remember Miles | Verve | 557109-2
Sidney Bechet And His New Orleans Feetwarmers | Sidney Bechet 1932-1943: The Bluebird Sessions | Bluebird | ND 90317
This Is Jazz All Stars | World's Greatest Jazz Concert Vol.1 | Jazzology | JCD-301

Baby Won't You Please Come Home(alt.take)
John Lee Hooker | Half A Stranger | Mainstream | MD CDO 903

Baby You Can Count On Me
Cousin Joe With Earl Bostic And His Orchestra | Cousin Joe From New Orleans In His Prime | Oldie Blues | OL 8008

Baby You Got What It Takes
Joe Williams And Marlena Shaw With The Norman Simmons Quintet | In Good Company | Verve | 837932-2

Baby You Know
Eddie 'Blues Man' Kirkland Band | It's The Blues Man! | Original Blues Classics | OBCCD 513-2(Tru 15010)

Baby(Baby, Baby, Baby)
Dinah Washington And Brook Benton With The Belford Hendricks Orchestra | Brook Benton-Dinah Washington:The Two Of Us | Verve | 526467-2

Baby, I Don't Cry Over You
Sonny Terry & Brownie McGhee | Sonny Terry And Brownie McGhee At Suger Hill | Original Blues Classics | OBCCD 536-2(F 8091)

Baby, I Knocked On Your Door
John Lee Hooker | Half A Stranger | Mainstream | MD CDO 903

Baby, It Must be Love
Ella Fitzgerald With Ellis Larkins | Ella:The Legendary American Decca Recordings | GRP | GRP 46482

Baby, What Else Can I Do?
Taj Mahal And The International Rhythm Band | Taj Mahal | The Rising Sun Collection | RSC 0003

Baby,Let's Be Friends
Jesse Price And His Orchestra | Swingin' Small Combos Kansas City Style Vol.1 | Blue Moon | BMCD 6019

Baby,Rub My Achin' Head
Norman Connors Orchestra | Beyond A Dream | Arista Novus | AN 3021 (802062)

Babylon Falls-
Kenny Blake Group | Interior Design | Heads Up Records | 889010

Baby's Birthday Party
Keith Nichols Cotton Club Orchestra With Claus Jacobi & Bent Persson | Syncopated Jamboree | Stomp Off Records | CD 1234

Baby's Gonna Go, Bye Bye
Grant Green Trio | Grant's First Stand | Blue Note | 521959-2

Baby's Minor Lope
Sidney Bechet Trio | Sidney Bechet | Vogue | 000001 GK

Baccara
Kenny Barron Quintet | Sambao | EmArCy | 512736-2

Bach
Jeff Berlin Group | Crossroads | Denon Compact Disc | CY-18077

Bach And Me
Peter Herbert Group | B-A-C-H A Chromatic Universe | Between The Lines | btl 013(Efa 10183)

B-A-C-H Bass
B-A-C-H A Chromatic Universe | Between The Lines | btl 013(Efa 10183)

B-A-C-H Bass-Clarinet
Eugen Cicero Quartet | Jazz Bach | Timeless | CD SJP 216

Bach Goes To Town
Benny Goodman And His Orchestra | Benny Goodman Forever | RCA | NL 89955(2) DP

Bach In Mind
Peter Herbert Group | B-A-C-H A Chromatic Universe | Between The Lines | btl 013(Efa 10183)

B-A-C-H Piano
Ornette Coleman & Prime Time | Tone Dialing | Verve | 527483-2

Bach To The Blues
Peter Herbert Group | B-A-C-H A Chromatic Universe | Between The Lines | btl 013(Efa 10183)

B-A-C-H Trumpet
Warne Marsh Quartet | Ne Plus Ultra | Hat Art | CD 6063

Bachafillen
Jazz Crusaders | The Best Of The Jazz Crusaders | Pacific Jazz | 789283-2
John Zorn Group | Masada Seven | DIW | DIW 915 CD

Bachianas Brasileiras
Gato Barbieri Sextet | The Third World | RCA | 2179617-2

Bachianas Brasileiras-
Gato Barbieri:The Complete Flying Dutchman Recordings 1969-1973 | RCA | 2154555-2

Bachianas Brazileiras(No.5)
Jackie Cain With The Don Sebesky Orchestra | Jazzin' The Classics | CBS | 474751-2

Bachiao
Frederic Hand Ensemble | Jazz Antiqua | Musicmasters | 65150-2

Bach's Blues-
The New York Saxophone Quartet | The New York Saxophone Quartet | Stash Records | ST 210 IMS

Back Again
Shorty Rogers/Bud Shank Quintet | Back Again | Concept | VL 1 IMS

Back And Forth
Lee Konitz | Lee Konitz 'Self Portrait'(In Celebration Of Lee Konitz' 70th Birthday) | Philology | W 121.2

Back At The Chicken Shack
Jimmy Smith Quartet | The Best Of Jimmy Smith | Blue Note | 791140-2
Fourmost Return | Milestone | MCD 9311-2
Jimmy Smith Trio | En Concert Avec Europe 1 | Laserlight | 710379/80
Rodney Jones Quintet | Right Now | Minor Music | 801054

Back Bay Shuffle
Swingle Singers | Back To Swing | Aves | 161530
Gerry Mulligan-Johnny Hodges Quintet | Gerry Mulligan Meets Johnny Hodges | Verve | 2304476 IMS

Back Beat
Verve Jazz Masters 35:Johnny Hodges | Verve | 521857-2
Louis Moholo-Evan Parker-Pule Pheto-Gibo Pheto-Barry Guy Quintet | Bush Fire | Ogun | OGCD 009

Back Beat Boogie
Harry James And His Orchestra | Harry James | Jazz Magazine | 40199

Back Country Suite For Piano, Bass And Drums:
Big Joe Williams | Big Joe Williams-The Final Years | Verve | 519943-2

Back Door
Washboard Sam & His Washboard Band | Harmonica And Washboard Blues | Black & Blue | BLE 59.252 2

Back Door Blues
Joe Stone | St. Louis Blues 1929-1935 | Yazoo | YAZ 1030

Back Door Getaway
Big Joe Turner With Axel Zwingenberger | Boogie Woogie Jubilee | Vagabond | VRCD 8.81010

Back Door Getaway (2nd version)
Lowell Fulsom Band | Tramp/Soul | Ace Records | CDCHD 339

Back Down To The Tropics'
Kokomo Arnold | King Of The Bottelneck Guitar | Black & Blue | BLE 59.250 2

Back From Where We Came
Opposite Corner | Back From Where We Came | Dragon | DRLP 70

Back Home
Bob Berg Quintet | Cycles | Denon Compact Disc | CY 72745
Gil Scott-Heron/Brian Jackson Group | Winter In America | Strata East Records | 660.51.015
Myriam Alter Quintet | Silent Walk | Challenge | CHR 70035
Phineas Newborn Jr. Quartet | Fabulous Phineas | RCA | 2179622-2
Phineas Newborn Jr. Trio | Back Home | Original Jazz Classics | OJCCD 971-2(C 7648)
Warne Marsh Quintet | Back Home | Criss Cross | Criss 1023
Wolfgang Schmid Group | Another Moonsong | BELL Records | BLR 84046
Wolfgang Bernreither-Golly-Rudy Bayer Group | I Wonder Why | L+R Records | CDLR 42079

Back Home Again In Indiana
Ann Richards With The Bill Marx Trio | Live At The Losers/We Remember Mildred Bailey | Vee Jay Recordings | VJ 018
Art Tatum | The Story Of Jazz Piano | Laserlight | 24653
The V-Discs | Black Lion | BLP 60114
Solos 1937 & Classic Piano Solos | Forlane | UCD 19010
Art Tatum Trio | Art Tatum:Complete Capitol Recordings | Definitive Records | DRCD 11192
Ben Webster Quartet | Live At The Jazzhus Montmartre,Vol.1 | Jazz Colours | 874710-2
Bill Coleman Quintet | Dicky Wells & Bill Coleman In Paris | Affinity | CD AFS 1004
Bobby Hackett-Jack Teagarden All Stars | Coast Concert/Jazz Ultimate | Dormouse | DMI CDX 02(882984)
Bud Powell Trio | Bud Powell:Bouncing With Bud | Dreyfus Jazz Line | FDM 36725-2
Bud Powell:Complete 1947-1951 Blue Note,Verve & Roost Recordings | The Jazz Factory | JFCD 22837
Charlie Parker at 'Bob Reisner presents Bird' | Bird's Eyes Last Unissued Vol.25 | Philology | W 855.2
Dave Brubeck Quartet | Interchanges '54 | CBS | 467917-2
Dave Brubeck Trio | The Dave Brubeck Trio | Fantasy | FCD 24726-2
Erroll Garner Trio | Gems | CBS | 21062
The Complete Savoy Sessions Vol.1 | Savoy | WL 70521 (809292)
Harry Edison Quartet | The Inventive Mr. Edison | Fresh Sound Records | 054 2402661(Pacific Jazz PJ 11)
JATP All Stars | Norman Granz' JATP: Carnegie Hall 1949 | Pablo | PACD 5311-2
Jay Jay Johnson-Milt Jackson Quartet | Jazz Legacy 30: J.J.Johnson/Milt Jackson-A Date In New York Vol.1 | Vogue | 500080
Joe Bushkin Trio | The Jazz Keyboards of Joe Bushkin/Marian McPartland/Bobby Scott/Lennie Tristano | Savoy | SV 0224(MG 12043)
Johnny Griffin Quartet | Live at The Jazzhus Montmartre,Copenhagen Vol.1 | Jazz Colours | 874723-2
Lester Young With The Oscar Peterson Quartet | Jazz Gallery:Lester Young Vol.2(1946-59) | RCA | 2119541-2
The Pres-ident Plays | Verve | 831670-2 PMS
Lester Young-Nat Cole Trio | Lester Young 'Rarities' | Moon Records | MCD 048-2
Lester Young:The Complete Aladdin Sessions | Blue Note | 832787-2
Lester Young:The Complete1936-1951 Group Sessions(Studio Recordings-Master Takes),Vol.1 | Blue Moon | BMCD 1001
Lionel Hampton Quintet | The Complete Lionel Hampton Quartets And Quintets With Oscar Peterson On Verve | Verve | 559797-2
Lou Levy Trio | Jazz In Four Colors | Fresh Sound Records | ND 74401
Louis Armstrong And His All Stars | Historic Barcelona Concerts At Windsor Palace 1955 | Fresh Sound Records | FSR-CD 3004
Masters Of Jazz Vol.1:Louis Armstrong | Storyville | STCD 4101
Louis Armstrong:Complete 1950-1951 All Stars Decca Recordings | Definitive Records | DRCD 11188
The Great Performer | Traditional Line | TL 1304
Minton's Playhouse All Stars | Thelonious Monk:After Hours At Minton's | Definitive Records | DRCD 11197
Oscar Klein's Jazz Show | Oscar Klein's Jazz Show Vol.2 | Jazzpoint | JP 1048 CD
Oscar Peterson Duo | Digital At Montreux | Pablo | 2308224-2
Oscar Peterson Trio | Masters Of Jazz Vol.7 | RCA | NL 89721 DP
Planet Music:Oscar Peterson | RCA | 2165365-2
Oscar Peterson-Joe Pass Duo | Oscar Pterson Et Joe Pass A La Salle Pleyel | Pablo | 2CD 2625705
Live At Salle Pleyel, Paris | Pablo | 2625705
Pete Fountain With Orchestra | The Best Of Pete Fountain | MCA | MCD 4032
Re-Birth Jazz Band | Do Whatcha Wanna | Mardi Gras Records | MG 1003
Richie Kamuca Octet | Jazz Erotica | Fresh Sound Records | FSR-CD 500(881696)
Sam Newsome Quintet | Sam I Am | Criss Cross | Criss 1056
Sonny Criss Quintet | At The Crossroad | Fresh Sound Records | 252962-1(Peacock PLP 91)
Sweet Emma Barrett And Herr Bell Boys | Mardi Grax Day 1960-Live | 504 Records | 504CD 67
The Birdlanders | The Birdlanders | Fresh Sound Records | FSR-CD 0170
Wild Bill Davison With The Dutch Swing College Band | Dixieland Jubilee Vol.4 | Intercord | 155024

Back Home Again In Indiana-
Tierney Sutton Group | Unsung Heroes | Telarc Digital | CD 83477

Back Home Again In Indiana(alt.take)
Lionel Hampton Quartet | The Complete Lionel Hampton Quartets And Quintets With Oscar Peterson On Verve | Verve | 559797-2

Back Home Again In Indiana(false start)
Lester Young Quintet | Pres/The Complete Savoy Recordings | Savoy | WL 70505 (809309)

Back Home Blues
Charlie Parker Quintet | Bird On Verve-Vol.6:South Of The Border | Verve | 817447-1 IMS

Back Home Blues(take 1)
Charlie Parker And His Orchestra | Bird: The Complete Charlie Parker On Verve | Verve | 837141-2

Back Home Blues(take 2)
Lightnin' Hopkins | Sittin' In With Lightnin' Hopkins | Mainstream | MD CDO 905

Back In The Day
Message | The Art Of Blakey | Paddle Wheel | KICJ 162

Back Of J.
Gabriele Hasler-Georg Ruby | Spider's Lovesong | Foolish Music | FM 211893

Back On Earth
Furry Lewis | Shake 'Em On Down | Fantasy | F 24703

Back O'Town Blues
Louis Armstrong And His All Stars | Rare Performances Of The 50's And The 60's | CBS | CBS 88669
Louis Armstrong And His Orchestra | Best Of The Complete RCA Victor Recordings | RCA | 2663636-2
Louis Armstrong-Satchmo's Greatest Hits | RCA | CL 89799

Back Road
Bob Berg Sextet | Back Roads | Denon Compact Disc | CY-79042

Back Row Hi Jinx
Les McCann Group | On The Soul Side | Musicmasters | 65112-2

Back Seat Betty
Miles Davis Group | The Man With The Horn | CBS | 468701-2
Peter O'Mara Quintet | Back Seat Driver | Enja | 9126-2

Back Stabbers
Dexter Gordon Quintet | Homecoming-Live At The Village Vanguard | CBS | CBS 88232

Back To A Place
Klaus Weiss Quintet | On Tour | Calig | 30623

Back To Back
Montgomery Brothers | Groove Yard | Original Jazz Classics | OJCCD 139-2(R 9362)
The Riverside Reunion Band | Hi-Fly | Milestone | MCD 9228-2

Back To Brooklyn
Marilyn Mazur's Future Song | Small Labyrinths | ECM | 1559(533679-2)

Back To Dreamfog Mountain
Bazillus | The Regulator | ACT | 9206-2

Back To Eternity
Om | OM with Dom Um Romao | Japo | 60022 IMS

Back To L.A.
Lajos Dudas Trio | Chamber Music Live | Pannon Jazz/Classic | PCL 8004

Back To New Orleans
Sonny Terry & Brownie McGhee | Back To New Orleans | Fantasy | FCD 24708-2

Back To Normal
Vienna Art Orchestra | Two Little Animals | Moers Music | 02066 CD

Back To The Apple
Count Basie And His Orchestra | Atomic Swing | Roulette | 497871-2
Count Basie & His Orchestra:Fresno,California April 24,1959 | Jazz Unlimited | JUCD 2039
Nighthawks | CitizenWayne | Call It Anything | CIA 4004-2

Back To The Blues-
Luther Johnson Blues Band | Luther´s Blues | Black & Blue | BLE 59.519 2

Back To The Church
Art Farmer/Benny Golson Jazztet | Back To The City | Original Jazz Classics | C 14020

Back To The Land
Lester Young Trio | Lester Young:Blue Lester | Dreyfus Jazz Line | FDM 36729-2
Lester Young Trio | Verve | 521650-2

Back To The Source
Enrico Rava Quartet | Il Giro Del Giorno In 80 Mondi | Black Saint | BSR 0011

Back To The Tropics
Kokomo Arnold | Bottleneck Guitar Trendsetters Of The 1930's | Yazoo | YAZ 1049

Back To You
John Lee Hooker | Get Back Home | Black & Blue | BLE 59.023 2

Back Up
Joe Locke Quartet | Longing | Steeplechase | SCCD 31281

Back Water Blues
Archie Shepp-Horace Parlan Duo | 1rst Set | 52e Rue Est | RECD 015
Dinah Washington With Her All Stars | Compact Jazz: Dinah Washington | Mercury | 830700-2 PMS
Dinah Washington With The Eddie Chamblee Orchestra | Jazz-Club: Vocal | Verve | 840029-2
Firma Kischke | Nix Als The Blues-Live Im Allgäu | Jazz Classics | AU 11126 Digital
Ottilie Patterson With The Pat Halcox Quartet | Trad Tavern | Philips | 838397-2 PMS

Bäckahästen
Sweetman With His South Side Groove Kings | Austin Backalley Blue | Mapleshade | 02752

Backbiting(Ton Soni)
Walter Norris-George Mraz Duo | Hues Of Blues | Concord | CCD 4671

Backé
Jim Black Quartet | Alasnoaxis | Winter&Winter | 910061-2

Backfloatpedal
Birka | Jazz I Sverige '78 | Caprice | CAP 1145

Background Music
Lee Konitz-Sal Mosca Duo | Spirits | Milestone | M 9038
Lee Konitz-Warne Marsh Sextet | That's Jazz Vol.21: Lee Konitz & Warne Marsh | Atlantic | ATL 50298
Warne Marsh Quintet | Jazz Exchange Volume One | Storyville | SLP 4001

Backlash
Nina Simone And Orchestra | Planet Jazz:Nina Simone | Planet Jazz | 2165372-2

Backlash Blues
Johnny Griffin-Sal Nistico-Roman Schwaller Sextet | Three Generations Of Tenorsaxophone | JHM Records | JHM 3611

Backlog
Sal Nistico/Stan Tracey Quintet | Live In London | Steam | SJ 112

Backspace
Gerry Mulligan Quartet With Brassensemble and Guests | Dragonfly | Telarc Digital | CD 83377

Backstage At Stuff's
Count Basie And His Orchestra | The Indispensable Count Basie | RCA | ND 89758

Backstairs
Christian Bleiming & His Boogie Boys | Jivin' Time | Acoustic Music Records | AMC 1010

Backtalk
Willis Jackson Quintet | Together Again: Willis Jackson With Jack McDuff | Prestige | PRCD 24284-2

Backtrack(Twistin' Train)
Steve Khan Trio | Let's Call This | Polydor | 849563-2

Backward Country Boy Blues
Ahmad Mansour Quintet | Is Really This It ? | Plainisphare | PAV 805

Backward Glance
Vienna Art Orchestra | Vienna Art Orchestra Plays For Jean Cocteau | Amadeo | 529290-2

Backwood Mating
John Patitucci | Sketchbook | GRP | GRP 96172

Backwoods
Buddy Rich Big Band | Backwoods Siseman/Pieces Of Dream | Laserlight | 24655

Backwoods Sideman
Eje Thelin Group | Hypothesis | MRC | 066-45421

Back-Woods Song
Nick Brignola Quartet | On A Different Level | Reservoir | RSR CD 112(882636)

Backyard Blues
Big Joe Turner With Axel Zwingenberger | Boogie Woogie Jubilee | Vagabond | VRCD 8.81010

Backyard Boogie
Miles Davis Group | Tutu | Warner | 7599-25490-2

Backyard Ritual
Andreas Schnerman Sextet | Welcome To My Backyard | Edition Collage | EC 535-2

Backyard Suite
Gebhard Ullmann-Andreas Willers | Playful '93 | Nabel Records:Jazz Network | CD 4659

Backyard Thang
Mani Neumeir | Privat | ATM Records | ATM 3803-AH

Bacon
Walt Dickerson Quartet | Impressions Of A Patch Of Blue | Verve | 559929-2

Bad Actin' Woman
Jack Teagarden And His Orchestra | Jazz Original | Charly | CD 80

Bad Ass
Cousin Joe With The Mezzrow-Bechet Septet | Cousin Joe:The Complete 1945-1947 Vol.1 (1945-1946) | Blue Moon | BMCD 6001

Bad Bad Whiskey
King Curtis Band | Trouble In Mind | Original Blues Classics | OBCCD 512-2(Tru 15001)

Bad Blues
Dave Spencer & The Bluebirds | Live In Europe | Crosscut | CCD 11047

Bad Condition
Otis Spann/Robert Lockwood Jr. With James Oden | Otis Spann And His Piano | Crosscut | CCR 1004(Candid)

Bad Feelin'
Katie Kern | Still Young | Jazzpoint | JP 1070 CD

Bad Feeling
Blind Blake | Blind Blake-Bootleg Rum Dum Blues | Biograph | BLP 12003

Bad Girl
Chris Potter Quartet | Pure | Concord | CCD 4637

Bad Habit
Trilok Gurtu Group | Bad Habits Die Hard | CMP Records | CMP CD 80

Bad Hat Blues
Lou Donaldson Quartet | Good Gracious | Blue Note | 854325-2

Bad John
Kostas Konstantinou-Vassilis Tsabropoulos | Concentric Cycles | Nabel Records:Jazz Network | CD 4698

Bad Ladder
Smokey Hogg | Texas Blues | Anthology of the Blues | AB 5605

Bad Loser
B.B.King And His Band | Singin' The Blues/The Blues | Ace Records | CDCHD 320

Bad Luck And Troubles
Albert King Blues Band | Door To Door | Chess | 515021

Bad Party
Lightnin' Hopkins | Houston's King Of The Blues | Blues Classics | BC 30

Bad Time
Dook Joint | Who's Been Talkin'... | Organic Music | ORGM 9728

Bad Times
Blaufrontal With Hank Roberts & Mark Feldman | Bad Times Roll | Jazz Haus Musik | JHM 0061 CD

Bad Times Roll
Ahmad Jamal Orchestra | Night Song | MoJazz | 530303-2

Bada Blues
Ornette Coleman & Prime Time | Tone Dialing | Verve | 527483-2

Badhra
Weather Report | Tale Spinnin' | CBS | CBS PC 33417

Badinerie
Mikesch Van Grümmer | Bar-Piano | Timeless | CD SJP 362

Badinerie from Suite No.2 in B Minor(BWV 1067)
The Steamboat Rats | ...Got That Swing | Elite Special | 73435

Badland
Blauer Hirsch | Cyberpunk | FMP | 1240

Badobe Ya
Jean-Paul Bourelly & The BluWave Bandits | Rock The Cathartic Spirits:Vibe Music And The Blues! | DIW | DIW 911 CD

Bafiology-
Louis Sclavis Quartet | Acoustic Quartet | ECM | 1526

Bafouée
John Scofield Trio | En Route | Verve | 9861357

Bag
Lou Stein Duo | Stompin' 'Em Down | Chiaroscuro | CR 173

Bag Of Dreams
Count Basie Big Band | The Montreux '77 Collection | Pablo | 2620107

Bag Of Jewels
Count Basie And His Orchestra | The Atomic Band Live In Europe | Bandstand | BDLP 1506

Bagatelle
Dutch Jazz Orchestra | Portrait Of A Silk Thread | Kokopelli Records | KOKO 1310
Lanny Morgan Quintet | It's About Time | Palo Alto | PA 8007

Bagdad By Bus
Ben Wolfe Sextet | Bagdad Theater | Mons Records | MR 874827

Baghdad By The Bay
Urs Blöchlinger Trio | (Aesth)eti(c)k Als Widerstand | Plainisphare | PL 1267-3/4

Bagpipe Song
Lajos Dudas Quartet | Nightlight | double moon | DMCHR 71030

Bagpiper
Stan Kenton And His Orchestra | Kenton Showcase | Creative World | ST 1026

Bag's & Trane
John Coltrane-Milt Jackson Quintet | Bags & Trane | Rhino | 8122-73685-2
Stan Kenton And His Orchestra | By Request Vol.1 | Creative World | ST 1036

Bags And Rags
Al Haig Trio | Al Haig Today! | Fresh Sound Records | FSR-CD 0006

Bag's Groove
Bud Powell Trio | My Devotion | Jazz Society(Vogue) | 670512
Hampten Hawes | The Challenge | Storyville | SLP 1013
Harry Sweets Edison Quintet | Swingin' 'Sweets' | L+R Records | CDLR 45076
Howard Rumsey's Lighthouse All-Stars | Oboe/Flute | Original Jazz Classics | OJCCD 154-2(C 3520)
Humair-Louiss-Ponty | Volume 2 | Dreyfus Jazz Line | FDM 36510-2
Jack Millman Quartet | Four More | Fresh Sound Records | FSR-CD 0217
Joey & 'Papa' John DeFrancesco Group | All In The Family | HighNote Records | HCD 7021
Mal Waldron Trio | You And The Night And The Muisc | Paddle Wheel | K 28P 6272
Miles Davis Quintet | To Bags...With Love:Memorial Album | Pablo | 2310967-2
Milt Jackson Orchestra | Big Mouth | Original Jazz Classics | OJCCD 865-2(2310867)
Milt Jackson Sextet | Jackson, Johnson, Brown And Company | Pablo | 2310897-2
Modern Jazz Quartet | The Modern Jazz Quartet | Atlantic | 7567-81331-2
Modern Jazz Quartet With Sonny Rollins | The Modern Jazz Quartet At Music Inn With Sonny Rollins,Vol.2 | Atlantic | 7567-80794-2
Monday Night At Birdland | Monday Night At Birdland | Fresh Sound Records | FSR-CD 31(882175)
Oscar Peterson Trio | Compact Jazz: Oscar Peterson Plays Jazz Standards | Verve | 833283-2
Ray Brown Trio | Some Of My Best Friends Are The Piano Players | Telarc Digital | CD 83373
Steve Hobbs Sextet | Cultural Diversity | Timeless | CD SJP 375
Toots Thielemans Quartet | Jazz In Paris:Toots Thielemans-Blues Pour Flirter | EmArCy | 549403-2 PMS
Vibes Summit | Vibes Summit | MPS | 68208

Bag's Groove(alt.take)
Duke Pearson Trio | Bag's Groove | Black Lion | BLCD 760149

Bag's Groove(take 1)
Miles Davis And The Modern Jazz Giants | Miles Davis And The Modern Jazz Giants | Prestige | P 7650

Bag's Groove(take 2)
Miles Davis All Stars | Milt Jackson Birthday Celebration | Fantasy | FANCD 6079-2
Miles Davis And The Modern Jazz Giants | Miles Davis And The Modern Jazz Giants | Prestige | P 7650

Bags New Groove
Modern Jazz Quartet | Together Again | Pablo | PACD20 244-2(2308244)
Paul Desmond And The Modern Jazz Quartet | Paul Desmond With The Modern Jazz Quartet | CBS | JK 57337

Bags Of Blues
Ray Charles-Milt Jackson Quintet | Soul Meeting | Atlantic | SD 1360
Ray Charles-Milt Jackson Sextet | That's Jazz Vol.4: Soul Meeting | Atlantic | ATL 50234

Bah U Bah
Bobbi Humphrey Group | Montreux Summit Vol.1 | CBS | 478607-2

Bahia
Archie Shepp Quartet feat. Jeanna Lee | African Moods | Circle Records | RK 29-61084/29 IMS
Gato Barbieri Group | Masters Of Jazz Vol.9 | RCA | NL 89722
Gato Barbieri:The Best Of The Early Years | RCA | 2663523-2
Gato Chapter Four: Alive In New York | MCA | AS 9303
Jan Garbarek Trio | Madar | ECM | 1515(519075-2)
Joe Gallardo's Latino Blue | A Latin Shade Of Blue | Enja | ENJ-9421 2
John Coltrane Quartet | Bahia | Original Jazz Classics | OJCCD 415-2
Jazz Gallery:John Coltrane Vol.1 | RCA | 2119540-2
Spies & Guests | By The Way Of The World | Telarc Digital | CD 83305

Bahia Blanca
Herbie Mann Group | Opalescence | Kokopelli Records | KOKO 1298

Bahia Do Sol
Passport | Iguacu | Atlantic | 2292-46031-2
Volker Kriegel Group | Topical Harvest | MPS | 821279

Bahia Praia
Keith Copeland Trio | Postcard From Vancouver | Jazz Focus | JFCD 023

Baia
Laurindo Almeida/Carlos Barbosa-Lima/Charlie Byrd Quintet | Music Of The Brazilian Masters | Concord | CCD 4389
Stan Getz-Charlie Byrd Sextet | Compact Jazz: Best Of Bossa Nova | Verve | 833269-2
Stan Getz/Charlie Byrd:Jazz Samba | CTI Records | PDCTI 1104-2
Mel Tormé And Cleo Laine With The John Dankworth Orchestra | Nothing Without You | Concord | CCD 4515

Baiao Blues
Duo Fenix | Karai-Eté | IN+OUT Records | 7009-2

Baiao De Dois
Ronaldo Folegatti Groups | Sound Of Watercolors | AH Records | AH 403001-11

Baiao Kathrin
Stefanie Schlesinger And Her Group | What Love Is | Enja | ENJ-9434 2
Egberto Gismonti Group | Sol Do Meio Dia | ECM | 1116(829117-2)

Baiao Malandro
Glen Moore -Rabih Abou-Khalil | Nude Bass Ascending... | Intuition Records | INT 3192-2

Baida
Dick Heckstall-Smith & John Etheridge Group | Live 1990 | L+R Records | CDLR 45028

Bailando
Juan Serrano Group | Sabor Flamenco | Concord | CCD 4490

Bailarina
Marc Ribot Y Los Cubanos Postizos | Nuy Divertido(Very Entertaining) | Atlantic | 7567-83293-2

Baile Baile Baile
Joe Pass-John Pisano | Joe Pass:Guitar Virtuoso | Pablo | 4 PACD 4423-2

Bailewick
Joe Pass-John Pisano:Duets | Pablo | 2310959-2
Astor Piazzolla Group | The Rough Dancer And The Cyclical Night(Tango Apasionado) | American Clave | AMCL 1019-2

Bailophone Dance
Raymond Boni | L'Homme Etoile | Hat Art | 3510

Bajo Andaluz
Jack Costanzo Group | Latin Fever:The Wild Rhythms Of Jack Costanza | Capitol | 590955-2

Bajo Numero Uno
The World Saxophone Quartet | Point Of No Return | Moers Music | 01034 CD

Bakai
Cal Massey Sextet | Blues To Coltrane | Candid | CCD 79029
John Coltrane Sextet | Coltrane | Original Jazz Classics | OJC20 020-2
John Coltrane-The Prestige Recordings | Prestige | 16 PCD 4405-2
Eddy Louiss Trio | Tabataba(Soundtrack) | Nocturne Productions | NTCD 106

Bakean(Paisiblement)
Blind Lemon Jefferson | Blind Lemon Jefferson | Milestone | MCD 47022-2

Baker's Daughter
Shorty Baker-Doc Cheatham Quintet | Shorty & Doc | Original Jazz Classics | OJCCD 839-2(SV 2021)

Baker's Dozen
Nguyen Le Trio | Bakida | ACT | 9275-2

Bakida
Duke Ellington And His Famous Orchestra | Duke Ellington:The Blanton-Webster Band | Bluebird | 21 13181-2

Bakiff
Duke Ellington & His Famous Orchestra | Forlane | UCD 19003
Duke Ellington And His Orchestra | Carnegie Hall Concert January 1943 | Prestige | 2PCD 34004-2
The Best Of Duke Ellington | Capitol | 831501-2

Bakija
Shorty Rogers And His Giants | Way Up There | Fresh Sound Records | 1270(Atlantic)

Bal Masque
Charlie Haden-Carlos Paredes | Dialogues | Polydor | 843445-2 PMS

Balada Para Un Loco
Kudsi Erguner/Süleyman Erguner | Sufi Music Of Turkey | CMP Records | CMP CD 3005

Balahto
Henri Guédon Et L'Orchestre D'Harmonie Du Havre | L'Opera Triangulaire | Messidor | 15997 CD

Balance
David Binney Group | Balance | ACT | 9411-2
Eje Thelin Group | Eje Thelin Group Live '76 | Caprice | CAP 2007:1-2
Martin Theurer | Moon Mood | FMP | 0700

Balance Of Happiness
Ull Möck Trio | Drilling | Satin Doll Productions | SDP 1023-1 CD

Balanced Time
Munich Saxophon Family | Balanced | Edition Collage | EC 487-2

Balanced-Im Gleichgewicht
Peter Kowald/Julius Hemphill | Duos: America | FMP | 1270

Balancing Act
Chicago Underground Trio | Possible Cube | Delmark | DE 511

Balanco No Samba
Baden Powell Ensemble | Apaixonado | MPS | 68090

Balantofe
Chet Baker & The Boto Brasilian Quartet | Chet Baker & The Boto Brasilian Quartet | Dreyfus Jazz Line | FDM 36511-9

Balao
Stan Kenton And His Orchestra | By Request Vol.1 | Creative World | ST 1036

Balcony Rock
Hal Galper Trio | Invitation To A Concert | Concord | CCD 4455

Balet
David Doucet Group | Quand Jai Parti | Rounder Records | CDRR 6040

Bali
Elements | Illumination | RCA | PD 83031(874013)
Charlie Barnet And His Orchestra | Charlie Barnet Big Band 1967 | Creative World | ST 1056

Bali Ha'i
Ruby Braff-Dick Hyman | Younger Than Swingtime-Music From South Pacific | Concord | CCD 4445
Stan Kenton And His Orchestra | The Stage Door Swings | Capitol | EMS 1159

Bali Run
Pierre Dorge & New Jungle Orchestra | Different Places Different Bananas | Olufsen Records | DOCD 5079

Balkan Blue
Dusko Goykovich Sextet | Dusko Goykovich Portrait | Enja | ENJ-9427 2

Balkan Blues
Dusko Goykovich Quintet With The NDR Radio-Philharmonie,Hannover | Balkan Blues | Enja | ENJ-9320 2

Balkan Blues(A Jazz Suite by Dusko Goykovich)
Orage Then Blue Orchestra | Orange Then Blue | GM Recordings | GM 3006(807787)

Balkan Dance
Chris Barber's Jazz And Blues Band | Sideways | Black Lion | 147009

Balkanale
Florin Niculescu Quartet | Four Friends | Jardis Records | JRCD 9923

Balkanals
Wheelz With Ingrid Jensen | Around The World I | ACT | 9247-2

Ball Bearings
Lluis Vidal Trio | Milikituli | Fresh Sound Records | FSNT 009 CD

Ball De Capvespre
Orquestra De Cambra Teatre Lliure | Orquestra De Cambra Teatre Lliure and Lluis Vidal Trio feat.Dave Liebman | Fresh Sound Records | FSNT 027 CD
Klaus Ignatzek Group | Live At Leverkusener Jazztage | Nabel Records:Jazz Network | CD 4630

Ball Games
Martin Kolbe-Ralf Illenberger Quartet | Waves/Colouring The Leaves | BELL Records | BLR 83751

Ball The Jack
Professor Longhair And His Band | New Orleans Piano | Sequel Records | RSA CD 808

Ballad
Gerry Mulligan Concert Jazz Band | Verve Jazz Masters 36:Gerry Mulligan | Verve | 523342-2
Verve Jazz Masters Vol.60:The Collection | Verve | 529866-2
Hot Channels-John Tchicai Orchestra | Merlin Vibrations | Plainisphare | PL 1267-10
Kevin Harris & Militia | Kevin Harris & Militia | TipToe | TIP-888802 2
Oliver Lake Quartet | Holding Together | Black Saint | BSR 0009
Paul Bley-Paul-Motian Duo | Notes | Soul Note | 121190-2
Phil Minton | A Doughnut In One Hand | FMP | CD 91
Roscoe Mitchell | Nonaah | Nessa | N 9/10
Super Jazz Trio | The Super Jazz Trio | RCA | PL 45367
Chris Potter & Jazzpar Septet | This Will Be | Storyville | STCD 4245

Ballad-
Jürgen Sturm's Sidestream | Blue News | Nabel Records:Jazz Network | LP 4606
Willem Breuker Kollektief | Sensemayá | BVHAAST | CD 9509

Ballad For A Dead Child
David Murray Quartet | Flowers For Albert | India Navigation | IN 1026

Ballad For A.(Little Rose)
McCoy Tyner Octet | Together | Milestone | M 9087

Ballad For Anna
Frank Marocco Quintet | Road To Marocco | Discovery | DS 854 IMS

Ballad For Attila
Jack McDuff Quartet | The Last Goodun' | Prestige | PRCD 24274-2

Ballad For Baby
Soul Summit | Prestige | PCD 24118-2(P 7234/7275)

Ballad For Bernt

TITELVERZEICHNIS

Leni Stern Sextet | Clairvoyant | Passport Jazz | ???

Ballad For Friends
Klaus Ignatzek Quintet | Son Of Gaudi | Nabel Records:Jazz Network | CD 4660

Ballad For G.B.
Curtis Fuller Quintet | Four On The Outside | Timeless | CD SJP 124

Ballad For Line
Gust Williams Tsilis Quintet | Sequestered Days | Enja | ENJ-6094 2

Ballad For Miles
Stefan Karlsson Quintet | The Road Not Taken | Justice Records | JR 0702-2

Ballad For Monsieur
Stan Getz With The Eddie Louiss Trio | Dynasty | Verve | 839117-2

Ballad For My People-
Simon Nabatov | Loco Motion | ASP Records | 11988

Ballad For Nori
West End Avenue 4 | City Jazz | L+R Records | CDLR 45098

Ballad For Sting
Randy Weston | Marrakech In The Cool Of The Evening | Verve | 521588-2

Ballad For The Children
Tony Coe-Roger Kellaway | British-American Blue | Between The Lines | btl 007(Efa 10177-2)

Ballad For The Russian Princess
Soren Lee Trio | Soren Lee Trio | L+R Records | CDLR 45072

Ballad For The Unborn
West End Avenue 4 | City Jazz | L+R Records | CDLR 45098

Ballad For Tillie
Nils Petter Molvaer Group | Elegy For Africa | Nabel Records:Jazz Network | CD 4678

Ballad For Tinga Tinga
Joe Lovano Quartet | Tones Shapes & Colors | Soul Note | 121132-2

Ballad For Two Girls
Trilok Gurtu Group | Crazy Saints | CMP Records | CMP CD 66

Ballad For Ulli
Herb Geller Quartet | To Benny & Johnny | Hep | CD 2084

Ballad For Very Tired And Very Sad Lotus Eaters
John Marshall Quintet | Theme Of No Repeat | Organic Music | ORGM 9719
Johnny Hodges And The Ellington All-Stars Without Duke | Duke's In Bed | Verve | 2304383 IMS
Paul Eßer-Gerd Dudek-Ali Haurand-Jiri Strivin | Jazz Und Lyrik:Schinderkarren Mit Buffet | Konnex Records | KCD 5108

Ballad For W.L.
Stivin-Van Den Broeck-Haurand | Bordertalk | Konnex Records | KCD 5068
Kent Sangster Quartet | Adventures | Jazz Focus | JFCD 006

Ballad In B Minor-
Benny Goodman And His Orchestra | The Birth Of Swing | Bluebird | ND 90601(3)

Ballad In C Minor
Don Friedman Trio | Flashback | Original Jazz Classics | SMJ 6094

Ballad In G-Major
Bernard Peiffer Trio | Jazz In Paris:Bernard Peiffer-La Vie En Rose | EmArCy | 013980-2

Ballad Medley:
Art Blakey And The Jazz Messengers | Reflections in Blue | Timeless | SJP 128
Cecil Payne Quintet | Bright Moments | Spotlite | SPJ LP 21
Dizzy Gillespie-Roy Eldridge Sextet | The Complete Verve Roy Eldridge Studio Sessions | Verve | 9861278
Eddie Condon All Stars | Ringside At Condons | Savoy | SV 0231(MG 12055)
Howard Riley Trio | Flight | FMR | FMR CD 26
JATP All Stars | Welcome To Jazz At The Philharmonic | Fantasy | FANCD 6081-2
Jazz At The Philharmonic-Frankfurt 1952 | Pablo | PACD 5305-2
Joe Viera Sextet | Kontraste | Calig | 30619
Louie Bellson Septet | Louie Bellson Jam | Original Jazz Classics | OJCCD 802-2(2310838)
Mel Lewis And His Sextet | The Lost Art | Limelight | 820815-2 IMS
Norman Granz Jam Session | Jazz-Club: Tenor Sax | Verve | 840031-2
Roy Eldridge-Benny Carter Quintet | The Complete Verve Roy Eldridge Studio Sessions | Verve | 9861278
The Urban Sessions/New Jazz Sound | Verve | 531637-2
Roy Eldridge-Dizzy Gillespie With The Oscar Peterson Quartet | Roy And Diz | Verve | 521647-2
Stan Getz-Lionel Hampton Quintet | Hamp And Getz | Verve | 831672-2
Tenor Tribute | Tenor Tribute | Soul Note | SN 1184
The Tenor Triangle & The Melvin Rhyne Trio | Tell It Like It Is | Criss Cross | Criss 1089

Ballad Of Hix Blewitt
George Russell Smalltet | The RCA Victor Jazz Workshop | RCA | 2159144-2

Ballad Of Hix Blewitt(alt.take)
Vince Guaraldi-Bola Sete Quartet | From All Sides | Original Jazz Classics | OJCCD 989-2(F 3-362)

Ballad Of The Runaway Horse
Chris Connor With The Ralph Sharon Orchestra | Sings Ballad Of The Sad Cafe | Atlantic | AMCY 1067

Ballad Of The Sad Young Men
Ack Van Rooyen And The Metropole Orchestra | Colores | Koala Records | CD P 21
Art Pepper Quartet | No Limit | Contemporary | COP 019
Mark Murphy And His Sextet | Bop For Kerouac | Muse | MCD 5253
Stefan Scaggiari Trio | That's Ska-jär-é | Concord | CCD 4510

Ballad Of Thelonious Monk
Adam Makowicz | From My Window | Candid | CRS 1028 IMS

Ballad To J.S.B.
Jaki Byard Quartet | Family Man | 32 Jazz | 32171

Ballada
Zbigniew Namyslowski Quintet | Winobranie | Power Bros | 00121

Ballade
Charlie Parker All Stars | Charlie Parker:The Best Of The Verve Years | Verve | 527815-2
Charlie Parker Groups | Welcome To Jazz: Charlie Parker | Koch Records | 322 075 D1
Chris Jarrett | Live In Tübingen | Edition Collage | EC 490-2
Dave Brubeck Quartet feat. Bill Smith | Brubeck A La Mode | Original Jazz Classics | OJCCD 200-2
Hans Joachim Roedelius/Alexander Czjzek | Weites Land | Amadeo | 831627-2
J.J.Johnson With The Brass Orchestra | The Brass Orchestra | Verve | 537321-2
Paul Bley | Alone Again | DIW | DIW 319 CD

BallAde
Philippe Caillat Group | French Connection,Dirty Rats | JA & RO | 003(08-4103)

Ballade
Tamia/Pierre Favre | De La Nuit... Le Jour | ECM | 1364(835249-2)
Zbigniew Namyslowski Quartet | Namyslovski | Inner City | IC 1048 IMS

Ballade And Allegro
Art Farmer Sextet | PH.D. | Contemporary | CCD 14055-2

Ballade Für Juliane
Brodmann-Pausch Percussion Duo | Percussion Duo | Fiala Music | JFJ 92002

Ballade Noire
Urs Blöchlinger | (Aesth)eti(c)k Als Widerstand | Plainisphare | PL 1267-3/4

Ballade Pour Adrenalin
Catherine-Escoude-Lockwood Trio | Catherine-Escoude-Lockwood | BS Records | BS 84002

Ballade Pour Marion
Richard Galliano-Gabriele Mirabassi Duo | Coloriage | Quadrivium | SCA 031

Finküberthurm | Fink Über Thurm | Jazz Haus Musik | JHM 44 CD

Ballade Über Die Frage:Wovon Lebt Der Mensch
Uwe Kropinski/Volker Schlott | Dinner For Two | Acoustic Music Records | 319.1057.2

Ballade Vom Weib Und Dem Soldaten
Brass Attack | Brecht Songs | Tutu Records | 888190-2*

Ballade Von Der Sexuellen Hörigkeit
Del Ferro/Overwater/Paeffgen | Evening Train | Acoustic Music Records | 319.1063.2

Balladi
Muhal Richard Abrams Group | 1-OQA+19 | Black Saint | 120017-2

Balladin
Mal Waldron Trio | Free At Last | ECM | 1001

Balladina
Christy Doran-John Wolf Brennan | Henceforward | Line Records | COCD 9.00871 O

Ballads For Trane:
Loren Stilllman Quartet | Cosmos | Soul Note | 121310-2

Balladyna
Bobby Watson & Open Form Trio | Appointment In Milano | Red Records | VPA 184

Ballantine For Valentine
Chet Baker Sextet | Chet Baker-The Italian Sessions | Bluebird | ND 82001

Ballata In Forma Di Blues
Chet Is Back | RCA | NL 70578 AG

Balld For Djole
Freddy Martin And His Orchestra | The Uncollected:Freddy Martin,Vol.4 | Hindsight | HSR 205

Ballet On The Moon
Gil Melle Quartet | Primitive Modern | Original Jazz Classics | OJCCD 1712-2(PR 7040)

Ballimaran
Hank Mobley Quintet | Dippin' | Blue Note | 746511-2

Ballin' The Jack
Bunk Johnson's Jazz Band | Bunk Johnson 1944/45 | American Music | AMCD-12
Freddy Martin And His Orchestra | The Uncollected: Freddy Martin, Vol.3 | Hindsight | HSR 190
Golden Gate Quartet | Spirituals To Swing 1955-69 | EMI Records | 791569-2
Hal Smith-Keith Ingham-Bobby Gordon | Music From The Mauve Decades | Sackville | SKCD2-2033
Kid Ory's Creole Jazz Band | Kid Ory:Creole Classics 1944-1947 | Naxos Jazz | 8.120587 CD
Singleton Palmer And His Dixieland Band | New Orleans Legends | Vogue | 655603
The European Jazz Ginats | Jazz Party | Nagel-Heyer | CD 009
The Tremble Kids All Stars | Dixieland At Its Best | BELL Records | BLR 89091

Balloonman
Chinese Compass | Chinese Compass | dacapo | DCCD 9443

Ballroom
Steve Swallow Group | Swallow | Watt | XtraWatt/6
Lloyd Glenn Quartet | Old Time Shuffle | Black & Blue | BLE 59.077 2

Balm In The Gilead
First Revolution Singers | A Cappella Gospel Anthology | Tight Harmony Records | TH 199404
Nina Simone Trio | Let It Be Me | Verve | 831437-1

Balsa
Matrix | Harvest | Pablo | 2312121

Baltimore
Julia Hülsmann Trio With Anna Lauvergnac | Come Closer | ACT | 9702-2
Nina Simone And Orchestra | Baltimore | Epic | 476906-2
Nina Simone Trio | Let It Be Me | Verve | 831437-1

Baltimore Oriole
Chris Connor With The Richard Wess Orchestra | Witchcraft | Atlantic | AMCY 1068
Keith Ingham Sextet | A Star Dust Melody | Sackville | SKCD2-2051

Ba-Lue Bolivar Ba-Lues-Are
Thelonious Monk Quartet | Live At The Jazz Workshop-Complete | CBS | C2K 65189
Live At The It Club:Complete | CBS | C2K 65288
Thelonious Monk Quintet | Brillance | Milestone | M 47023
Sonny Rollins-The Freelance Years:The Complete Riverside & Contemporary Recordings | Riverside | 5 RCD 4427-2
Thelonious Monk-The Complete Riverside Recordings | Riverside | 15 RCD 022-2
GRP All-Star Big Band | All Blues | GRP | GRP 98002

Ba-Lue Bolivar Ba-Lues-Are-
Ted Rosenthal Sextet | Images Of Monk | The Jazz Alliance | TJA 10023

Balzwaltz
Wolfgang Lackerschmid Group | Mallet Connection | Bhakti Jazz | BR 33
Ray Brown Trio | Bam Bam Bam | Concord | CCD 4375

Bamako
Ulli Bögershausen | Best Of Ulli Bögershausen | Laika Records | LK 93-045

Baman Bia
Jim Pepper Sextet | The Path | Enja | 5087-2

Bamboo
Mike Mainieri Group | Jazz Life Vol.2:From Seventh At Avenue South | Storyville | 4960763
Mike Mainieri Orchestra | Wanderlust | NYC-Records | NYC 6002 2

Bamboo Forest
Norbert Stein Pata Masters | Pata Maroc | Pata Musik | PATA 12(AMF 1063)

Bamboo Interior
Gerry Brown-John Lee Group | Infinite Jones | Keytone | KYT 710

Bambra
Sal Nistico Sextet | Neo/Nistico | Bee Hive | BH 7006

Bambuzal
Scales Brothers Group | Our House | Enja | 9106-2

Banana Plantation
Christoph Spendel Group | Spendel | L+R Records | CDLR 45014

Bananas
Draft | Traveling Birds | Jazz Haus Musik | JHM 68 CD

Bananera
Herbie Harper Quartet | Jazz In Hollywood:Herbie Harper | Original Jazz Classics | OJCCD 1887-2(Nocturne NLP-1/NLP-7)

Band Call
Duke Ellington And His Orchestra | Happy Birthday Duke Vol.4 | Laserlight | 15786
Oscar Peterson Trio | The Sound Of The Trio | Verve | 543321-2
En Concert Avec Europe 1 | Laserlight | 710443/48
Louis Armstrong And His All Stars With Duke Ellington | Louis Armstrong-Duke Ellington:The Great Summit-Complete Session | Roulette | 524546-2

Band discussion on Cotton Tail
First Avenue | First Avenue | ECM | 1194

Band Eight
First Avenue | ECM | 1194

Band Five
First Avenue | ECM | 1194

Band Four
Florian Ross Quartet With The Event String Ensemble | Suite For Soprano Sax And String Orchestra | Naxos Jazz | 86037-2

Band Intro
Art Taylor's Wailers | Wailin' At The Vanguard | Verve | 519677-2

Band Introductions
Simon Phillips Group | Out Of The Blue | Lipstick Records | LIP 8964-2

Band One
Jeannie And Jimmy Cheatham & The Sweet Baby Blues Band | Basket Full Of Blues | Concord | CCD 4501

Band Seven
First Avenue | First Avenue | ECM | 1194

Band Six
Buddy Guy Band | Buddy Guy | Chess | 427006

Band Three
First Avenue | First Avenue | ECM | 1194

Band Two
Evan Parker | Process And Reality | FMP | CD 37

Bang Bang
John Lee Hooker Group | Lonesome Mood | Chess | MCD 01365

Bang Goes The Drum
Blossom Dearie Quartet | Give Him The Ooh-La-La | Verve | 517067-2
Randy Brecker Quintet | Score | Blue Note | 781202-2

Bangu Jabour
Rena Rama | Inside-Outside | Caprice | CAP 1182

Bang-Up Blues
Soriba Kouyaté Quartet | Live In Montreux | ACT | 9414-2

Bani
Phil Woods Quintet & The Festival Orchestra | Celebration! | Concord | CCD 4770

Bank Float
Joachim Kühn | Dynamics | CMP Records | CMP CD 49

Banty Rooster Blues
Dollar Brand Trio | The Children Of Africa | Enja | ENJ-2070 2

Banyana-The Children Of Africa
Tome XX | The Red Snapper | Jazz Haus Musik | JHM 0047 CD

Bao Ding
Errol Parker Tentet | Live At The Wollman Auditorium | Sahara | 1014

Baptismal
Dave Liebman Quartet | The Elements:Water | Arkadia Jazz | 71043

Bar Blues
Nighthawks | CitizenWayne | Call It Anything | CIA 4004-2

Bar Talk
Paul Glasse Group | Paul Glasse | Amazing Records | AMCD 1022

Bar Utopia
Willis Jackson Quintet | Bar Wars | Muse | MCD 6011

Barakaat
Abdullah Ibrahim Trio And A String Orchestra | African Suite | TipToe | TIP-888832 2
Abdullah Ibrahim Trio With The Munich Radio Symphony Orchestra | African Symphony | Enja | ENJ-9410 2
Abdullah Ibrahim Trio | Cape Town Revisited | TipToe | TIP-888836 2

Barakaat(The Blessing)
Galden-Sonnenschein | Boiling Point | Aho-Recording | CD 1004

Barasco
Lazaro Ros Con Mezcla | Cantos | Intuition Records | INT 3080-2

Barasuayo
The Halfway House Orchestra | The Halfway House Orchestra-The Complete Recordings In Chronological Order | Jazz Oracle | BDW 8001

Barbados
Axel Beineke Jazz Trio | Let's Be True | Edition Collage | EC 469-2
Charlie Parker All Stars | The Savoy Recordings 2 | Savoy | 650108(881908)
Chet Baker Sextet | Chet Is Back | RCA | NL 70578 AG
David Hazeltine Sextet | Good-Hearted People | Criss Cross | Criss 1210
Joe Albany Trio | Live In Paris | Fresh Sound Records | FSCD 1010
Montgomery Brothers | Wes'Best | America | AM 6092
Phineas Newborn Jr. Quartet | That's Jazz Vol.39: Here Is Phineas | Atlantic | ATL 50522
Sheila Jordan/Harvie Swartz | Old Time Feeling | Muse | MCD 5366
Tommy Flanagan 3 | The Montreux '77 Collection | Pablo | 2620107

Barbados Carnival
Lew Del Gatto Septet | Katewalk | Naxos Jazz | 86058-2

Barbara
Fred Elizalde And His Orchestra | An Evening At The Savoy | Decca | DDV 5011/12
Jimmy Ponder Quintet | Come On Down | Muse | MCD 5375

Barbara Song
Joachim Kühn Trio | Musik Aus Der Dreigroschenoper | Verve | 532498-2

Barbara's Theme
Gerry Mulligan Concert Jazz Band | The Complete Verve Gerry Mulligan Concert Band | Verve | 9860613
Verve Jazz Masters 36:Gerry Mulligan | Verve | 523342-2
Compact Jazz: Gerry Mulligan Concert Jazz Band | Verve | 838933-2

Barbary Coast
Freddie Redd Trio | San Francisco Suite | Original Jazz Classics | OJCCD 1748-2

Barbizon Blues
Sammy Price Quintet | Roots Of Rock 'N' Roll, Vol. 7: Rib Joint | Savoy | SJL 2240 (801886)

Barb's Song To The Wizard
Bob Crosby And His Orchestra | The Uncollected:Bob Crosby Vol.2 | Hindsight | HSR 209

Barcarole
Jack Teagarden And His Orchestra | A Standard Library Of Jazz Vol. 1 | Storyville | SLP 700
Rhoda Scott | Rhoda Scott:Alone | Verve | 537635-2
Jan Fryderyk Trio | tri-o (tri-ou) Trio n. | Jazzline | ???

Bärchen
Brad Mehldau | Elegiac Cycle | Warner | 9362-47357-2

Bard
Brian Trainor Quintet | Brian Trainor:Portraits | Candid | CCD 79731

Bare Necessities
Tom Christensen Quartet | Gualala | Naxos Jazz | 86050-2

Barefoot
Vincent Chancey Quartet | Welcome Mr. Chancey | IN+OUT Records | 7020-1

Barefoot Bahian Girl
Jelly Jaw Short | St. Louis Town 1927-1932 | Yazoo | YAZ 1003

Barefoot Stomper
Cannonball Adderley Quartet | Takes Charge | Blue Note | 534071-2

Barefoot Sunday Blues
Mel Rhyne Sextet | Organ-izing | Original Jazz Classics | OJCCD 1055-2(JLP 916)
Cannonball Adderley Quartet | Takes Charge | Blue Note | 534071-2

Barefoot Sunday Blues(alt.take)
Mose Allison Trio | High Jinks! The Mose Allison Trilogy | CBS | J3K 64275

Barengo
Fischbacher Group & Modern String Quartet | Fischbacher Group & Modern String Quartet | Dr.Jazz Records | 8608-2

Bargain Day
Renaud Garcia-Fons & Jean-Louis Matinier | Fuera | Enja | ENJ-9364 2

Bari
Schnuckenack Reinhardt Sextet | Starportrait Schnuckenack Reinhardt | Intercord | 155012

Barium
Bud Shank Quartet | After You,Jeru | Fresh Sound Records | FSR-CD 5026

Bark For Barksdale
Gerry Mulligan Quartet | Chet Baker:Complete 1952 Fantasy & Pacific Jazz Sessions | Definitive Records | DRCD 11233
Gerry Mulligan:Pleyel Concert Vol.1 | Vogue | 21409422
Gerry Mulligan:Pleyel Concert Vol.2 | Vogue | 21409432

Bark For Barksdale-
Sonny Terry & Brownie McGhee | Brownie McGhee & Sonny Terry At The 2nd Fret:Recorded Live | Original Blues Classics | OBCCD 561-2

Barn 12
Dick Oatts Trio | All Of Three | Steeplechase | SCCD 31422

Barnacle Bill The Sailor
Louis Jordan's Elks Rendez-Vous Band | Louis Jordan Vol.1-Hoodoo Man | Swingtime(Contact) | ST 1011

Barney Goin' Easy(I'm Checkin' Out Goin' Bye)
Charlie Ventura And His Orchestra | It's All Bop To Me | Fresh Sound Records | LPM 1135(RCA)

Barney Rose
Tony Lakatos Quintet | Generation X | Jazzline | JL 11149-2

Barney's Blues
Bud Powell Quartet | Pianology | Moon Records | MCD 055-2

Butch Miles-Howard Alden Sextet | Cookin' | Nagel-Heyer | CD 5003
Buddy Rich Quintet | Buddy And Sweets | Verve | 841433-2

Barney's Bugle(Blues)
Barney Wilen Quartet | Newport '59 | Fresh Sound Records | FSR-CD 0165

Barnyard Boogie
Meyer-Fleck-Marshall | Unconnon Ritual | CBS | SK 62891

Baronesse
NAD | Ghosts | ITM Records | ITM 1454

Baroque Flamenco
Deborah Henson-Conant Group | Deborah Henson-Conant:Best Of Instrumental Music | Laika Records | 35101322
Deborah Henson-Conant Trio | Just For You | Laika Records | LK 95-063
New York Voices | New York Voices | GRP | GRP 95892

Baroque Steps
Paul Desmond Quintet | Desmond | Original Jazz Classics | OJCCD 712-2(F 3235/8082)

Baroque(Chorale Prelude)
Hot Club De Norvege With Guests | Swinging With Jimmy | Hot Club Records | HCRCD 082

Barra Da Tijuca
Canoneo | Canodeo | Passport Jazz | ???

Barrel House Bessie From Basin Street
Bob Crosby And His Orchestra | The Uncollected:Bob Crosby | Hindsight | HSR 192

Barrel Of Keys
Albert Mangelsdorff Quartet | Shake,Shuttle And Blow | Enja | ENJ-9374 2

Barrel Without Bottom
Ramona And Her Gang | The Indispensable Jack Teagerden(1928-1957) | RCA | ND 89613

Barrelhouse Woman
Will Ezell | Boogie Woogie | Laserlight | 24321
Tom Shaka | Hit From The Heart | Crosscut | CCD 11025

Barri De La Coma
Paul Hock Quartet | Fresh Fruit | Timeless | CD SJP 343

Barroom Room Serenade
Fabio Morgera Quintet | The Pursuit | Ken Music | 660.56.014

Barry McGuigan
Richie Vitale Quintet | The Richie Vitaleo Quintet feat.Ralph Lalama | TCB Records | TCB 96402

Barry's Bop
Fats Navarro Quintet | Fats Navarro:The 1946-1949 Small Group Sessions(Studio Recordings-Master Takes),Vol.2 | Blue Moon | BMCD 1017

Bartók Goes New Orleans
Antonio Hart Quintet With Guests And Strings | It's All Good | Novus | 4163183-2

Barzakh
Daniel Humair Trio | Humair/Jeanneau/Texier | Owl Records | 014734-2

Bas De Lou
David Friedman Trio | Ternaire | Deux Z | ZZ 84107

Basculement Du Désir
Hank Mobley Quintet | Hank Mobley | Blue Note | 0675622

Base On Balls
Carla Bley Band | 4X4 | Watt | 30(159547-2)

Baseball
Modern Jazz Quartet | Live At The Lighthouse | Mobile Fidelity | MFCD 827
Live At The Lighthouse | Atlantic | AMCY 1102

Basel
Ella Fitzgerald With The Count Basie Orchestra | Bluella:Ella Fitzgerald Sings The Blues | Pablo | 2310960-2

Basella
A Perfect Match-Basie And Ella | Pablo | 2312110-2

Basheer
Kenny Dorham Octet | Afro-Cuban | Blue Note | 0675619

Basheer's Dream
Afro-Cuban | Blue Note | 746815-2

Bashin'
Jimmy Smith Trio | Bashin' | Verve | 2304481 IMS

Basia
N.Y. Hardbop Quintet | A Whisper Away | TCB Records | TCB 98702

Basic Basic
Jimmy Heath Quartet | You've Changed | Steeplechase | SCCD 31292

Basic Blue
Mary Lou Williams-Cecil Taylor Quartet | Embraced | Pablo | 2620108

Basic Instinct
Norbert Stein Pata Masters | Graffiti | Pata Musik | PATA 9 CD
We Three With Roman Schwaller | East Coasting | Organic Music | ORGM 9702
Cool Blue | House In The Country | Foolish Music | FM 211591

Basic Structures
Don Bagley Trio | Basically Bagley | Blue Moon | BMCD 1601

Basically Blue
Buddy Rich And His Orchestra | Swingin' New Big Band | Pacific Jazz | 835232-2

Basically Blues
The Ritz | Movin' Up | Denon Compact Disc | CY-72526

Basie And Bean
Count Basie And His Orchestra | 100 Ans De Jazz:Count Basie | RCA | 2177831-2

Basie Basement
The Indispensable Count Basie | RCA | ND 89758

Basie Boogie
The Uncollected:Count Basie | Hindsight | HSR 224 (835571)
The Legendary Count Basie | CBS | 26033

Basie Like
En Concert Avec Europe 1 | Laserlight | 710706/07

Basie Power
Ronny Lang And His All-Stars | Basie Street | Fresh Sound Records | FSR-CD 0501

Basie Thought
Count Basie And His Orchestra | The Best Of The Big Bands Vol.2 | LRC Records | CDC 8528

Basie!
Oscar Peterson-Harry Edison Duo | Oscar Peterson & Harry Edison | Original Jazz Classics | OJCCD 738-2(2310741)
The Count Basie Orchestra | Live At El Morocco | Telarc Digital | CD 83312

Basiec Jump
Count Basie And His Orchestra | Live In Antibes 1968 | France's Concert | FCD 112

Basie's Basement
Woody Herman And His Orchestra | Old Gold Rehearsals 1944 | Jazz Unlimited | JUCD 2079
Big Band Bounce & Boogie-Woody Herman:Pre-Herds | Affinity | AFS 1027

Basin Street
Rey DeMichel Orchestra | For Bloozers Only! | Fresh Sound Records | CHS 2503(Challenge)

Basin Street Blues
Albert Nicholas With Alan Elsdon's Band | Albert Nicholas With Alan Elsdon's Band Vol.2 | Jazzology | JCD-269
Benny Bailey Quintet | The Satchmo Legacy | Enja | ENJ-9407 2
Benny Goodman And His Orchestra | Camel Caravan Broadcast 1939 Vol.1 | Phontastic | NCD 8817
Benny Goodman's 1934 Dodge All-Star Recordings(Complete) | Circle | CCD-111
Dixie Kings Meets Sharp & Flats | The World Is Waiting For The Sunrise | Express | CA 38-1027
Duke Ellington And His Orchestra | The Rare Broadcast Recordings 1952 | Jazz Anthology | JA 5213
Dutch Swing College Band | Albert Nicholas & The Dutch Swing College Band | Storyville | STCD 5522
Dutch Swing College Band & Teddy Wilson | The Dutch Swing College Band & Teddy Wilson | DSC Production | PA 008 (801065)
Ella Fitzgerald And Her Orchestra | Jazz Collection:Ella Fitzgerald | Laserlight | 24397
Ella Fitzgerald With Orchestra | Basin Street Blues | Intercord | 125404
Ella Fitzgerald With Sy Oliver And His Orchestra | Ella Fitzgerald 75th Birthday Celebration:The Original Decca Recordings | GRP | GRP 26192
Esquire Metropolitan Opera House Jam Session | Jazz Live & Rare: The First And Second Esquire Concert | Jazzline | ???
Frank 'Big Boy' Goudie With Burt Bales | Frank 'Big Boy' Goudie With Amos White | American Music | AMCD-50
Golden Gate Quartet | Spirituals To Swing 1955-69 | EMI Records | 791569-2
Gottfried Böttger-Joe Penzlin Duo | Take Two | L+R Records | CDLR 40030
Henry Red Allen Band With Jack Teagarden | At Newport | Verve | 817792-1 IMS
Jack Teagarden And His Sextet | Compact Jazz: Best Of Dixieland | Verve | 831375-2
Jack Teagarden-Earl Hines All Stars | In England 1957 | Jazz Groove | JG 001 IMS
Joe Newman And His Orchestra | The Complete Joe Newman RCA-Victor Recordings(1955-1956):The Basie Days | RCA | 2122613-2
Katie Webster | The Many Faces Of Katie Webster | Schubert Records | SCH- 103
Kid Ory's Creole Jazz Band | Kid Ory At The Green Room Vol.2 | American Music | AMCD-43
Louis Armstrong And His All Stars | Rare Performances Of The 50's And The 60's | CBS | CBS 88669
Satchmo-A Musical Autobiography Vol.2 | MCA | 2-4174
In Concert At The Pasadena Civic Auditorium | Vogue | 655601
Louis Armstrong:Wintergarden 1947/Blue Note 1948 | Storyville | STCD 8242
Satchmo In Stockholm | Queen-Disc | 053
Louis Armstrong And His Orchestra | Louis Armstrong:Fireworks | Dreyfus Jazz Line | FDM 36710-2
Laughin' Louie | RCA | ND 90404
Louis Armstrong-Satchmo's Greatest Hits | RCA | CL 89799
Jazz:The Essential Collection Vol.2 | IN+OUT Records | 78012-2
Louis Armstrong-The Complete RCA Victor Recordings | RCA | 2668682-2
Louis Armstrong Sings The Blues | Bluebird | 63 66244-2
Magnificant Seventh's with Milton Batiste And Alton Carson | Best Of Bourbon Street Jazz | Mardi Gras Records | MG 1009
Miles Davis Quintet | Ballads | CBS | 461099-2
Mr.Acker Bilk And His Paramount Jazz Band | Mr. Acker Bilk Starportrait | Aves | 156503
Muggsy Spanier And His Dixieland All Stars | At Club Hangover-Vol. 2 | Storyville | SLP 249
Papa Bue's Viking Jazzband | On Stage | Timeless | CD TTD 511
Pete Fountain Quartet | Do You Know What It Means To Miss New Orleans | GHB Records | BCD 300
Red Allen Band | Red Allen With Jack Teagarden And Kid Ory At Newport | Verve | MV 2624 IMS
Roy Eldridge With The George Williams Orchestra | Rockin' Chair | Verve | MV 2686 IMS
Ruby Braff-Roger Kellaway | Inside & Out | Concord | CCD 4691
Silver Leaf Jazz Band | Streets And Scenes Of New Orleans | Good Time Jazz | GTCD 15001-2
The New York Allstars | Broadway | Nagel-Heyer | CD 003
The Sidney Bechet Society | Jam Session Concert | Nagel-Heyer | CD 076
This Is Jazz All Stars | Jazz Live & Rare: This Is Jazz Radio Series-Live 1947 | Jazzline | ???

Baskenmütze
Jeannie And Jimmy Cheatham & The Sweet Baby Blues Band | Basket Full Of Blues | Concord | CCD 4501

Basket Of Fruit
Glenn Miller And His Orchestra | Glenn Miller:The Complete Studio Recordings Vol.2:In The Mood | Memo Music | HDJ 4115

Basking Tiger
Michel Legrand Big Band | Le Jazz Grand | Gryphon | 6.23951 AT

Basquiat
Pete LaRoca Quartet | Basra | Blue Note | 300262

Bass-
Jaco Pastorius Group | Live In New York City Volume Three | Big World | BW 1003

Bass Blues
Hans Laib Sextet | German Authentics-Mannheim Area 1956/1957/1962 | Hohner Records | ohne Nummer(1)
John Coltrane Quartet | John Coltrane | Prestige | P 24003
John Coltrane With The Red Garland Trio | John Coltrane-The Prestige Recordings | Prestige | 16 PCD 4405-2
Lee Konitz-Hein Van De Geyn | Hein Van De Geyn Meets Lee Konitz | September | CD 5110

Bass Desires
Peter Erskine Trio | ELB | ACT | 9289-2
The Hudson Project | The Hudson Project | Stretch Records | SCD 9024-2

Bass Duet
Ron Carter Quintet | Eric Dolphy:The Complete Prestige Recordings | Prestige | 9 PRCD-4418-2
Wayne Darling Group | The Art Of The Bass Vol.1 | Laika Records | 35101652

Bass Encounters
Bill Evans Quintet | Quintessence | Original Jazz Classics | OJCCD 698-2(F 9529)

Bass Face
The Complete Fantasy Recordings | Fantasy | 9FCD 1012-2
Chubby Jackson Sextet | Chubby Jackson-The Happy Monster:Small Groups 1944-1947 | Cool & Blue | C&B-CD 109

Bass Fantasie On Musica Callada No.1
Don Cherry Group | Don Cherry-The Sonet Recordings:Eternal Now/Live Ankara | Verve | 533049-2

Bass Figure For Ballatune(two pianos and three piano players)
Jamaaladeen Tacuma Group | Dreamscape | DIW | DIW 904 CD

Bass Folk Song
Return To Forever | Jazz-Club: Bass | Verve | 840037-2
Woody Herman And The New Thundering Herd | Woody Herman:Thundering Herd | Original Jazz Classics | OJCCD 841-2
Albert Ammons | Boogie Woogie | Laserlight | 24321

Bass Goin' Crazy
Boogie Woggie Classics | Blue Note | BLP 1209
Werner Lener Trio | My Own | Satin Doll Productions | SDP 1013-1 CD

Bass Hit
Jamaaladeen Tacuma Group | Dreamscape | DIW | DIW 904 CD

Bass Line
Christy Doran Group | Cor Por Ate Art | JMT Edition | 849155-2

Bass On Balls
Meade Lux Lewis | Boogie Woogie, Stride & The Piano Blues | Blue Note | 799099-2

Bass Vibes
Marilyn Crispell-Tim Berne | Inference | Music & Arts | CD 851

Bassclarinet
Theo Jörgensmann Quartet | Song Of BoWaGe | CMP Records | CMP 8

Basses Three-O
Louie Bellson's Magic 7 | Louie Bellson's Magic 7 | Concord | CCD 4742

Bassic
Wild And Peaceful | Tempo Jazz Edition Vol.1-Talkin' Loud | Talkin' Loud | 848362-2

Bass-Ically Speaking
Bud Powell Trio | Jazz At Massey Hall,Vol.2 | Original Jazz Classics | OJCCD 111-2(DLP 9)
Billy Taylor Trio | Charles Mingus-The Complete Debut Recordings | Debut | 12 DCD 4402-2

Bass-Ically Speaking(alt.take 1)
Jazz At Massey Hall,Vol.2 | Original Jazz Classics | OJCCD 111-2(DLP 9)

Bass-Ically Speaking(alt.take 2)
Jazz At Massey Hall,Vol.2 | Original Jazz Classics | OJCCD 111-2(DLP 9)

Bass-Ically Speaking(alt.take 3)
Jazz At Massey Hall,Vol.2 | Original Jazz Classics | OJCCD 111-2(DLP 9)

Bassically Taps
Matalex | Proud | Lipstick Records | LIP 8957-2

Basslines
Duke Ellington And His Orchestra | Duke Ellington All Star Road Band | Doctor Jazz | ZL 70968(2) (809318)

Basso Profundo
Duke Ellington:Complete Prestige Carnegie Hall 1946-1947 Concerts | Definitive Records | DRCD 11211

Bassride
Markus Stockhausen Quartet | Joyosa | Enja | ENJ-9468 2

Basswave
Wolfgang Puschnig-Jamaladeen Tacuma Group With Guests | Journey Into The Gemini Territory | ITM-Pacific | ITMP 970091

Bastard
Reichel-Knipsel Duo | Erdmännchen | FMP | 0400

Bat Dance
Anthony Ortega With The Nat Pierce Orchestra | Earth Dance | Fresh Sound Records | FSR-CD 325

Bat Man's Blues
Tony Ortega Octet | Jazz For Young Moderns | Fresh Sound Records | FSR 2006(Bethlehem BCP 79)

Bata Balaio
David Earle Johnson Group | Skin Deep Yeah! | CMP Records | CMP 20

Bath Thing
Ed Schuller Group feat. Dewey Redman | The Force | Tutu Records | 888166-2*

Bathing Beauties
Flim & The BB's | The Further Adventures | dmp Digital Music Productions | CD 462
Alberto Marsico Quintet | Them That's Got | Organic Music | ORGM 9705

Bathman Blues
Frank Gambale-Allan Holdsworth Group | Truth In Shredding | Legato | HW 652507

Batida Diferente
Joe Kienemann Trio | Integration | yvp music | CD 3023

Batik
Geri Allen Sextet | The Nurturer | Blue Note | 795139-2

Batland
Taylor's Wailers | Taylor's Wailers | Original Jazz Classics | OJCCD 094-2(P 7117)

Batman-
Pierre Dorge's New Jungle Orchestra | Giraf | dacapo | DCCD 9440

Baton-
Nils Petter Molvaer Group | Elegy For Africa | Nabel Records:Jazz Network | CD 4678

Batoru
Ken Schaphorst Big Band | Purple | Naxos Jazz | 86030-2

Bats In The Belfry
Dennis Gonzales New Dallasangels | The Desert Wind | Silkheart | SHCD 124

Battangó
André Previn-Russ Freeman | Double Play! | Original Jazz Classics | OJC 157(C 7537)

Battle Cry
Ryan Kisor Quartet | Battle Cry | Criss Cross | Criss 1145

Battle Hymn Of The Republic
Herbie Mann Group | That's Jazz Vol.37: Memphis Underground | Atlantic | ATL 50520
Joe Newman/Joe Wilder Quintet | Hangin' Out | Concord | CCD 4262
Monty Alexander Trio | Perception! | MPS | 68042
Shorty Rogers-Bud Shank And The Lighthouse All Stars | Eight Brothers | Candid | CCD 79521

Battle Hymn Of The Republican
Laurent De Wilde Sextet | Time Change | Warner | 8573-84315-2

Battle In A Box
Coleman Hawkins And His Sax Ensemble | Rare Dates Without The Duke 1944/49 | Raretone | 5011 FC

Battle Of Swing(Le Jazz Hot)
Duke Ellington And His Famous Orchestra | Duke Ellington Playing The Blues 1927-1939 | Black & Blue | BLE 59.232 2

Battle Of The Saxes
Stan Getz And His Four Brothers | The Prestige Legacy Vol.2:Battles Of Saxes | Prestige | PCD 24252-2
Stan Getz Five Brothers Bop Tenor Sax Stars | Stan Getz:Imagination | Dreyfus Jazz Line | FDM 36733-2
Helmut Kagerer/Helmut Nieberle | Wes Trane | Edition Collage | EC 453-2

Battle Of Twins
Guitar Moments | Take Twelve On CD | TT 006-2

Battle Royal
Frank Wess-Harry Edison Orchestra | Dear Mr. Basie | Concord | CCD 4420

Battle Royal(rehersal take)
Grant Green With Orchestra | The Final Comedown(Soundtrack) | Blue Note | 581678-2

Battle Scene
The Final Comedown(Soundtrack) | Blue Note | 581678-2
Freddie Hubbard Sextet | Life Flight | Blue Note | BT 85139

Battlefield
Ron Ringwood's Gospel Messengers | You Can Lean On Me | Inak | 9040

Battleground
Stan Getz Five Brothers Bop Tenor Sax Stars | Zoot Sims:The Featured Sessions With Great Leaders 1949-1954 | Blue Moon | BMCD 1037

Battleship
Badi Assad Group | Echoes Of Brazil | Chesky | JD 154

Batucada(Nos E O Rio)
Tamba Trio | Tamba Trio Classics | EmArCy | 536958-2

Baubles
Benny Carter With The Oscar Peterson Trio | Benny Carter Meets Oscar Peterson | Original Jazz Classics | 2310926

Baubles Bangles And Beads
Bill Evans Trio | The Complete Bill Evans On Verve | Verve | 527953-2
Bud Shank-Lou Levy | Lost In The Stars-Bud Shank And Lou Levy Play The Sinatra Songbook | Fresh Sound Records | FSR-CD 0183
Chuck Wayne/Joe Puma Duo | Interactions | Candid | CRS 1004 IMS
Gerry Mulligan Quartet | Gerry Mulligan Quartet At Storyville | Pacific Jazz | 794472-2
Live In Stockholm-Vol.1 | Ingo | 3
Oscar Peterson Trio | The Jazz Soul Of Oscar Peterson/Affinity | Verve | 533100-2
Zoot Sims Quartet | Soprano Sax | Pablo | 2310770-2

Baubles Bangles And Beads(alt.take)
Franck Band | Liebeslieder | Jazz Haus Musik | JHM 35 CD

Bauerntanz(7)
Dufte | Jazz Haus Musik | JHM 0054 CD

Bauerntanz(8)
Uwe Walter | Tauta | Ear-Rational | ECD 1037

Bavarian Square Dance
Volker Schlott Quartet | Akribik | Acoustic Music Records | 319.1165.2

Bay Area Blues
Hendrik Meurkens Octet | Sambahia | Concord | CCD 4474

Bay City
Charlie Haden Trio | The Montreal Tapes | Verve | 537670-2
Turk Murphy And His Jazz Band | Turk Murphy's San Francisco Jazz-Vol.2 | Good Time Jazz | 12027

Bayou
Jimmy Smith Trio | The Champ-Jimmy Smith At The Organ Vol.2 | Blue Note | 300093(1514)

Bayou Fever
Jack DeJohnette Quartet | New Directions | ECM | 1128

McCoy Tyner Octet | Together | Milestone | M 9087

Bayou Red
Andrew Hill Sextet | Grass Roots | Blue Note | 522672-2
Mongo Santamaria Orchestra | The Watermelon Man | Milestone | M 47012

Bayrischer Wald
Tal Farlow Trio | A Sign Of The Times | Concord | CCD 4026

Bazalicka
Peter A. Schmid Trio With Guests | Profound Sounds In An Empty Reservoir | Creative Works Records | CW CD 1033

Bazar
Daniel Küffer Quartet | Daniel Küffer Quartet | Satin Doll Productions | SDP 1010-1 CD

BB 14
A Band Of Friends | Teatime Vol.2 | Poise | Poise 06/2

BB 35
Teatime Vol.2 | Poise | Poise 06/2

BB 45
Teatime Vol.2 | Poise | Poise 06/2

BB 9
Big Eye Louis Nelson Band | Big Eye Louis Nelson:1949 Sessions & Live At Luthjens | American Music | AMCD-7

Bb Blues
Kid Thoams Valentine Jazz Band | The Dance Hall Years | American Music | AMCD-48

Be
Franco Ambrosetti And Friends | Movies | Enja | ENJ-5035 2

Be Ass Em Dorp
Estelle Edson With Oscar Pettiford And His All Stars | Lucky Thompson Vol.1-Test Pilot | Swingtime(Contact) | ST 1005

Be Bop Romp
Fats Navarro Quintet | Fats Navarro:The 1946-1949 Small Group Sessions(Studio Recordings-Master Takes),Vol.2 | Blue Moon | BMCD 1017

Be Bop Salat I
Olaf Kübler Quartet | When I'm 64 | Village | VILCD 1016-2

Be Bop Salat II
Sebastian Gramss Underkarl | Jazzscene | TCB Records | TCB 99102

Be Careful It's My Heart
Tommy Dorsey And His Orchestra | Forever | RCA | NL 89859 DP

Be Fair With Me Baby
John Wolf Brennan | The Beauty Of Fractals | Creative Works Records | CW CD 1017-1

Be Flat
Willisau And More Live | Creative Works Records | CW CD 1020-2
The Well-Prepared Clavier/Das Wohlpräparierte Klavier | Creative Works Records | CW CD 1032-2

Be Flat(QEH Live Version)
Tyrone Washington Quintet | Do Right | Blue Labor | BL 102

Be Gone
Nguyen Le Trio | Million Waves | ACT | 9221-2

Be Good
Kenny Clarke And His Orchestra | Americans Swinging In Paris:James Moody | EMI Records | 539653-2

Be Good Girl
Lee Ritenour Group | Banded Together | Elektra | 960358-1

Be Happy
Knut Kiesewetter With Orchestra | Jazz Again | Polydor | 2372016

Be Here Now
The Ravens | Old Man River | Savoy | SV 0260

Be In Two Minds
Pili-Pili | Be In Two Minds | JA & RO | JARO 4134-2
Bobby Jaspar Quartet | At Ronnie Scott's 1962 | Mole Jazz | Mole 11

Be Me-Little Me
Jeri Brown With Band feat. Leon Thomas | Zaius | Justin Time | JUST 117-2

Be My Husband
Freddy Martin And His Orchestra | The Uncollected: Freddy Martin, Vol.3 | Hindsight | HSR 190

Be My Love
Earl Bostic Sextet | Alto Magic In Hi Fi | Sing | 597
Kenny Dorham Quintet | Kenny Dorham Quintet | Debut | VIJ 5006 IMS
Ray Charles With Orchestra | True To Life | London | 6.23291 AO

Be My Love(take 2)
Kenny Dorham Quintet | Kenny Dorham Quintet | Original Jazz Classics | OJCCD 113-2(DLP 9)

Be My Woman
Jeri Brown With Band feat. Leon Thomas | Zaius | Justin Time | JUST 117-2

Be Nice
Howard Johnson & Gravity | Gravity!!! | Verve | 531021-2

Be Ooo Ba
Barry Altschul Trio | Brahma | Sackville | 3023

Be Sure I'll Let You Know
Airto Moreira And The Gods Of Jazz | Killer Bees | B&W Present | BW 041

Be There For You
Stan Getz Sextet | Billy Highstreet Samba | EmArCy | 838771-2

Be There Then
Koko Taylor With The Mighty Joe Young Group | I Got What It Takes | Sonet | 198212(SNTF 687)

Beach Samba
Astrud Gilberto With The Don Sebesky Orchestra | Compact Jazz: Astrud Gilberto | Verve | 831369-2

Beachparty
Tony Kinsey Orchestra | Thames Suite | Spotlite | SPJ 504

Beacon
Polyphonix | Alarm | Jazz 'n' Arts Records | 0300

Beacon Park
Jochen Feucht Quartet | Signs On Lines | Satin Doll Productions | SDP 1019-1 CD

Beacons
| All At Once At Any Time | Victo | CD 029

Beads
International Jazz Consensus | Beak To Beak | Nabel Records:Jazz Network | LP 4602

Beale Street
Donald Byrd Sextet | Blackjack | Blue Note | 784466-2
Jesse Fuller One Man Band | Brother Lowdown | Fantasy | F 24707

Beale Street After Dark
A Salute To Eddie Condon | A Salute To Eddie Condon | Nagel-Heyer | CD 004

Beale Street Blues
Alberta Hunter | Planet Jazz:Female Jazz Vocalists | Planet Jazz | 2169656-2
Victor Jazz History Vol.20:Jazz & The Blues | RCA | 2135739-2
Earl Hines | Four Jazz Giants:Earl Hines Plays Tributes To W.C.Handy,Hoagy Carmichael And Louis Armstrong | Solo Art | SACD-111/112
Fats Waller With Alberta Hunter | The Indispensable Fats Waller Vol.1/2 | RCA | 2122616-2
Jelly Roll Morton's Red Hot Peppers | Doctor Jazz | Black & Blue | BLE 59.227 2
Louis Armstrong And His All Stars | Louis Armstrong Plays W.C.Handy | CBS | CK 64925
The Louis Armstrong Selection | CBS | 467278-2
Red Nichols And His Five Pennies | Red Nichols And His Five Pennies | Laserlight | 15743
Summit Reunion | Jazz Im Amerikahaus,Vol.5 | Nagel-Heyer | CD 015
The Tremble Kids | Dixieland Jubilee | Intercord | 155057
Tommy Dorsey And His Orchestra | This Is Tommy Dorsey Vol. 2 | RCA | 26.28041 DP

Beams
Sister Rosetta Tharpe And Her Group | Gospel Train | Mercury | 841134-2

Beams On Heaven
Elliott Sharp Carbon | Sili/Contemp/Tation | Ear-Rational | ECD 1018

Bean And The Boys
Bud Powell Trio | The Genius Of Bud Powell-Vol.2 | Verve | 2-2526 IMS
Coleman Hawkins All Star Octet | Milt Jackson Birthday Celebration | Fantasy | FANCD 6079-2
Bean And The Boys | Prestige | PCD 24124-2
Coleman Hawkins Quintet | The Rare Live Performance 1958/59 | Jazz Anthology | JA 5231
Coleman Hawkins With The Göran Lindberg Trio | Coleman Hawkins At The Golden Circle | Dragon | DRCD 265
Hot Mallets | Hot Mallets...Live! | JHM Records | JHM 3610
Jackie McLean Quartet | Makin' The Changes | Original Jazz Classics | OJCCD 197-2(NJ 8231)
Tommy Flanagan | Alone Too Long | Denon Compact Disc | DC-8572

Bean At The Met
Coleman Hawkins Quintet | Ultimate Coleman Hawkins selected by Sonny Rollins | Verve | 557538-2
Johnny Hodges Orchestra | Jazz Legacy 9: Johnny Hodges-The Rabbit In Paris | Vogue | 500059

Bean Bag Boogie
Coleman Hawkins Quintet | The Hawk Swings Vol.2 | Fresh Sound Records | FSR CD 0015

Bean Stalkin'
Eddie Lockjaw Davis Trio | Eddie 'Lockjaw' Davis His Tenor Saxophone And Trio | Sing | 506

Beans And Cornbread
Louis Jordan And His Tympany Five | Louis Jordan-Let The Good Times Roll: The Complete Decca Recordings 1938-1954 | Bear Family Records | BCD 15557 IH
Louis Jordan Quintet | Great Rhyhtm & Blues-Vol.1 | Bulldog | BDL 1000

Bean's Blues
Ray Gaskins | Can't Stp | Lipstick Records | LIP 8946-2

Bean's Talking Again
Joe McPhee | Variations On A Blue Line: 'Round Midnight | Hat Art | O

Bear Bones
T.S. Monk Sextet | Take One | Blue Note | 799614--2

Bear Right At Burma
Tom Harrell Orchestra | Labyrinth | RCA | 2668512-2

Beartoes
Chet Baker Quartet | The Best Of Chet Baker Plays | Pacific Jazz | 797161-2

Bea's Flat
Shelly Manne And His Men | Swinging Sounds | Original Jazz Classics | OJCCD 267-2(C 3516)

Beast
Jazz Pistols | 3 On The Moon | Lipstick Records | LIP 8965-2

Beast Of Burdon
Jan Garbarek Quartet | Afric Pepperbird | ECM | 1007 (2301007)

Beat 70
Pat Metheny Group | The Road To You | Geffen Records | GED 24601
Rochester/Veasley Band | One Minute Of Love | Gramavision | GR 8505-2

Beat Me Daddy Eight To The Bar
Freddie Slack With Orchestra | Boogie Woogie On The 88 | Official | 12000

Beat Stone
Xu Feng Xia | Difference And Similarity | FMP | CD 96

Beata
Slim Gaillard And His Flat Foot Floogie Boys | Slim And Slam Vol.2 | Tax | m- 8043

Beatrice
Doug Raney Quintet | Lazy Bird | Steeplechase | SCCD 31200
Jim Snidero Quartet | Storm Rising | Ken Music | 660.56.006
Joe Henderson Trio | The State Of The Tenor Vol.1&2 | Blue Note | 828879-2
Kevin Hays Quintet | Sweetear | Steeplechase | SCCD 31282
Sam Rivers Quartet | Lazuli | Timeless | CD SJP 291
Stan Getz Quartet | Bossas And Ballads:The Lost Sessions | Verve | 9901098
Steve Slagle Quartet | Spread The Words | Steeplechase | SCCD 31354
Joe Locke Quintet | Present Tense | Steeplechase | SCCD 31257

Beats Up
Frederic Rabold Crew | Open House | Calig | 30612

Beat-Up Team
Howard Rumsey's Lighthouse All-Stars | Sunday Jazz A La Lighthouse Vol.2 | Original Jazz Classics | OJCCD 972-2(S 2501)

Beau Boy
Jackie McLean Quintet | Jackie McLean & Co. | Original Jazz Classics | OJCCD 074-2(P 7087)

Beau Koo Jack
Ed Blackwell Project | Vol.1:What It Is? | Enja | ENJ-7089 2

Beau Regard
Mark Helias Quintet | Attack The Future | Enja | ENJ-7019 2

Beau Rivage
Howard Alden-Dan Barrett Quintet | The A.B.Q Salutes Buck Clayton | Concord | CCD 4395

Beaute Bleue
J.R. Monterose Quintet | J.R.Monterose | Blue Note | BLP 1536

Beautiful Black Eyes
Chet Baker Quartet | Live In Chateauvallon 1978 | France's Concert | FCD 128

Beautiful Brown Eyes
Michel Petrucciani/Ron McClure | Cold Blues | Owl Records | 042 CD

Beautiful Colours
Klaus Ignatzek Quintet | Is That So? | Koala Records | CD P 24

Beautiful Dreamer
Phil Haynes Quartet | Phil Haynes & Free Country | Premonition | 790744-2

Beautiful E.
Pepper Adams-Donald Byrd Sextet | Out Of This World Vol.1 | Fresh Sound Records | FSR 638(Warwick W 2041)

Beautiful Fractals
Elvira Plenar-Vitold Rek | Elvira Plenar-Vitold Rek | L+R Records | CDLR 45089

Beautiful Friendship
Peter Guidi Quartet | Beautiful Friendship | Timeless | CD SJP 352

Beautiful Land
Nina Simone With Orchestra | Nina Simone-The 60s Vol.1: Ne Me Quitte Pas | Mercury | 838543-2 PMS

Beautiful Life
Abdullah Ibrahim Group | Mantra Mode | TipToe | TIP-888810 2

Beautiful Love
Bill Evans Trio | Spring Leaves | Milestone | M 47034
Masters Of The Modern Piano | Verve | 2-2514 IMS
Bill Evans At Town Hall | Verve | 831271-2
The Paris Concert-Edition One | Blue Note | MUS 96.0164-1
Don Friedman Quintet | Hot Knepper And Pepper | Progressive | PRO 7036 IMS
John Abercrombie Trio | Straight Flight | JAM | 5001 IMS
John Blake Sextet | Maiden Dance | Gramavision | GR 8309-2
Maximilian Geller Quartet feat. Melanie Bong | Vocal Moments | Take Twelve On CD | TT 008-2
McCoy Tyner | Monk's Dream | Memo Music | HDJ 4019
Michel Petrucciani/Niels-Henning Orsted-Pedersen | Michel Petrucciani:Concert Inédits | Dreyfus Jazz Line | FDM 36607-2
Pete Malinverni Trio | This Time | Reservoir | RSR CD 147
Steve Nelson Trio | Full Nelson | Sunnyside | SSC 1044 D
Sun Ra Arkestra | Hours After | Black Saint | 120111-2

Beautiful Love(alt.take)
Jackie McLean & The Macband | Fire & Love | Blue Note | 493254-2

Beautiful People
Miroslav Vitous Quartet | First Meeting | ECM | 1145

Beautiful Place To
Cootie Williams And His Orchestra | Duke Ellington's Trumpets | Black & Blue | BLE 59.231 2

Beautiful Swan Lady
Eric Alexander Quartet | Two Of A Kind | Criss Cross | Criss 1133

Beauty
Thomas Brendgens-Mönkemeyer | Beauty | Jardis Records | JRCD 20138
Leroy Jenkins Quartet | Space Minds,New Worlds,Survival America | Tomato | 2696512

Beauty Is A Rare Thing
New Winds | The Cliff | Sound Aspects | sas CD 025
Ornette Coleman Quartet | Beauty Is A Rare Thing:Ornette Coleman-The Complete Atlantic Recordings | Atlantic | 8122-71410-2
Paul Plimley-Lisle Ellis | Kaleidoscopes(Ornette Coleman Songbook) | Hat Art | CD 6117

Beauty Is Rarity-
Peter Herborn's Acute Insights | Peter Herborn's Acute Insights | JMT Edition | 919017-2

Beauty Is...
Bheki Mseleku Group | Beauty Of Sunrise | Verve | 531868-2

Beauty's In The Eye
Montgomery Brothers | Groove Brothers | Milestone | M 47051

Beaux J.Poo Boo
Les McCann Orchestra | Invitation To Openess | Atlantic | SD 1603
Count Basie And His Orchestra | Basie Boogie | CBS | 21063

Beaver Junction
BBFC | Cherchez L'Erreur | Plainisphare | PL 1267-1

Bebé
Tok Tok Tok | Love Again | Einstein Music | EM 01081

Bebeep
Charles 'Bobo' Shaw & The Human Arts Ensemble | P'nk J'zz | Muse | MR 5232

Bebop
Bud Powell Trio | Bud Powell Paris Sessions | Pablo | PACD 2310972-2
More Unissued Vol.1 | Royal Jazz | RJD 507
Dizzy Gillespie Quintet | Something Old Something New | Verve | 558079-2
Dizzy Gillespie Septet | Verve Jazz Masters 25:Stan Getz & Dizzy Gillespie | Verve | 521852-2
Dizzy Gillespie Sextet | Triple Play:Dizzy Gillespie-The Final Recordings | Telarc Digital | CD 83451
For Musicians Only | For Musicians Only | Verve | 837435-2
George Wallington - Phil Woods Quintet | Leonard Feather Presents Bop | Polydor | MP 2333 IMS
John Coltrane-Milt Jackson Quintet | John Coltrane-The Heavyweight Champion:The Complete Atlantic Recordings | Atlantic | 8122-71984-2
Atlantic Jazz: Bebop | Atlantic | 7567-81702-2
Kenny Barron Trio | Wanton Spirit | Verve | 522364-2
Slide Hampton & The Jazz Masters | Dedicated To Diz | Telarc Digital | CD 83323
Sonny Clark Trio | Sonny Clark Trio | Blue Note | 533774-2
Sonny Criss Sextet | California Boppin' 1947 | Fresh Sound Records | FSR-CD 0156
Super Sax | Supersax Plays Bird | Blue Note | 796264-2
Tito Puente Orchestra | Special Delivery | Concord | CCD 4732

Bebop Baby
Yvonne Walter With Band | Thrills | Mons Records | MR 874805

Bebop Blues
Sonny Stitt Sextet | In The Beginning | Original Jazz Classics | OJCCD 1771-2(G 204)

Bebop In Pastel
Kenny Dorham Quintet | The Bebop Boys | Savoy | WL 70547 (809278)

Bebop Love Song
Vic Lewis West Coast All Stars | Vic Lewis Presenting A Celebration Of Contemporary West Coast Jazz | Candid | CCD 79711/12
Alberto Barattini Quartet | Panta Rei | SPLASC(H) Records | H 175

Bebopper
The Gordons With The Hank Jones Trio | Autobiography In Jazz | Original Jazz Classics | OJC 115(DEB 198)

Because
Stanley Jordan | Standards Vol.1 | Blue Note | 746333-2

Because I Love You
George Robert-Tom Harrell Quintet | Sun Dance | Contemporary | CCD 14037-2

Because My Baby Don't Mean May Be Now
George Olsen And His Music | The Clasic Years In Digital Stereo: Dance Bands USA | CDS Records Ltd. | RPCD 302(CD 650)
The New York Allstars | The First Sampler | Nagel-Heyer | NHR SP 5
Randy Sandke Meets Bix Beiderbecke | Nagel-Heyer | CD 3002
Brook Benton With Fred Norman's Orchestra | Brook Benton-Dinah Washington:The Two Of Us | Verve | 526467-2

Because Of Once Upon A Time
Fats Waller And His Rhythm | Breakin' The Ice-The Early Years Part 1(1934-1935) | Bluebird | 63 66618-2

Because Of Rain
Nat King Cole And His Trio | Combo USA | Affinity | CD AFS 1002
Peter Lehel Quartet | Heavy Rotation | Satin Doll Productions | SDP 1024-1 CD

Because Of The Bass
A Band Of Friends | Because Of You | Chesky | JD 63

Because Of You
Peter Herbolzheimer Rhythm Combination & Brass | Colors Of A Band | Mons Records | MR 874799

Bechet Medley:
David Murray Big Band | Live At Sweet Basil Vol.1 | Black Saint | 120085-2

Bechet's Creole Blues
Sidney Bechet With Claude Luter And His Orchestra | Sidney Bechet | Vogue | 000001 GK

Beck's Blues
Deborah Henson-Conant | Alterd Ego | Laika Records | 35100962
Charlie Mariano Quartet | Crystal Balls | CMP Records | CMP 10

Becoming
Sonny Sharrock/Nicky Skopelitis | Faith Moves | CMP Records | CMP CD 52

Bed And Breakfast
Hip Linkchain Group | Airbusters | Evidence | ECD 26038-2

Bedalia
Gambit Jazzmen With Tim Laughlin | King Of The Mardi Gras | Lake | LACD 54

BedouinTrail
Dave Holland Quintet | Point Of View | ECM | 1663(557020-2)
Pharoah Sanders Group | Journey To The One | Evidence | ECD 22016-2

Bedroom Blues
Sippie Wallace With Roosevelt Sykes | Blues Roots Vol.6 | Storyville | 6.23705 AG

Bedruthan Steps
Peter Ehwald Trio | Away With Words:The Music Of John Scofield | Jazz Haus Musik | JHM 0128 CD

Bedside Manner
Geri Allen Group | Maroons | Blue Note | 799493-2

Bedtime Story
Paolo Fresu Angel Quartet | Metamorfosi | RCA | 2165202-2

Bee
Peter Erskine Trio | ELB | ACT | 9289-2
Henry Threadgill Very Very Circus | Spirit Of Nuff...Nuff | Black Saint | 120134-2

Bee Gee
J.J.Johnson Quintet | J.J. Johnson's Jazz Quintets | Savoy | SV 0151(MG 12106)

Bee Tango-Waltz
Booker Little Quartet | Booker Little | Bainbridge | BT 1041

Bee Tee's Minor Plea
Eric Dolphy-Booker Little Quintet | The Great Concert Of Eric Dolphy | Prestige | P 34002

Bee Vamp
Eric Dophy Quintet | Eric Dolphy:The Complete Prestige Recordings | Prestige | 9 PRCD-4418-2

Thierry Bruneau 4tet feat. Mal Waldron | Live At De Kave | Serene Records | SER 01

Bee Vamp(alt.take)
Medeski Martin & Wood With Guests | It's A Jungle In Here | Gramavision | R2 79495

Beebe
Jimmy Dorsey And His Orchestra | The Radio Years | London | HMG 5022 AN

Beedees
Claudio Fasoli/Kenny Wheeler/J.F. Jenny-Clark | Land | Nueva Records | IN 802

Beedle Um Bum
Blind Willie McTell | Last Session | Original Blues Classics | OBCCD 517-2
Bourbon St.Jazzband Luzern | I Must Have It | Elite Special | 76347
McKinney's Cotton Pickers | McKinney's Cotton Pickers 1928/1930 | Zeta | ZET 743

Been A Son
Billy Boy Arnold Group | Eldorado Cadillac | Alligator Records | ALCD 4836

Been Gone Too Long
Woody Mann-Jo Ann Kelly | Been Here And Gone | Acoustic Music Records | 319.1174.2

Beepdurple
Daniel Schnyder Group | Words Within Music | Enja | ENJ-9369 2

Beep-Hop(Duo For Soprano Saxophone And Bass Trombone)
Jack Walrath Group | Revenge Of The Fat People | Stash Records | ST 221 IMS

Beer Barrel Polka
Bob Crosby And His Orchestra | The Summer Of '39-Bob Crosby's Camel Caravan | Giants Of Jazz | GOJ 1037
Jimmie Gordon Band | Jimmie Gordon 1934-1941 | Story Of Blues | CD 3510-2

Bees
Mark Whitfield Group | Patrice | Warner | 7599-26659-2

Bee's Blues
Roy Eldridge Sextet | Decidedly | Pablo | PACD 5314-2
Eric Reed Trio | Soldier's Hymn-Dedicated To Art Blakey | Candid | CCD 79511

Beethoven
Laurindo Almeida Trio | Outra Vez | Concord | CCD 4497

Beethoven's Moonlight Sonata
Leith Stevens All Stars | Jazz Themes From The Wild One(Soundtrack) | Fresh Sound Records | 252280-1(Decca DL 8349)

Befiehl Du Deine Wege
Pat Martino Quintet | Think Tank | Blue Note | 592009-2

Befor You Ask
Dave Liebman | Time Immemorial | Enja | ENJ-9389 2

Before
Joshua Redman Quartet | Passage Of Time | Warner | 9362-47997-2
Paolo Fresu Sextet | Ensalada Mistica | SPLASC(H) Records | CD H 415-2

Before Birth(for Joseph Beuys)
Christian Wallumrod Trio | No Birch | ECM | 1628(537344-2)

Before Church
Ann Malcom With The Kenny Barron Quartet | Incident'ly | Sound Hills | SSCD 8053

Before Dawn
George Wallington Quintet | Jazz Editions Presents: Jazz At Hotchkiss | Savoy | SV 0119(MG 12122)

Before Sunrise
David Torn/Geoffrey Gordon | Best Laid Plans | ECM | 1284

Before The Bitter Wind
Emborg-Larsen Quintet | Heart Of The Matter | Stunt Records | STUCD 19102

Before Us
Mark Murphy With Azymuth And Guests | Night Mood | Milestone | MCD 9145-2

Before We Were Born
Hamiet Bluiett Resolution | Resolution | Black Saint | 120014-2

Begegnungen(Meetings)
Jimmy Smith Trio | Bashin' | Verve | 2304481 IMS

Beggin'
Blind Lemon Jefferson | Blind Lemon Jefferson | Biograph | BLP 12000

Begin The Beguine
Art Tatum | Art Tatum:Over The Rainbow | Dreyfus Jazz Line | FDM 36727-2
Art Tatum:Over The Rainbow | Dreyfus Jazz Line | FDM 36727-2
Art Tatum-The Complete Pablo Solo Masterpieces | Pablo | 7 PACD 4404-2
Standards | Black Lion | CD 877646-2
Jazz:The Essential Collection Vol.2 | IN+OUT Records | 78012-2
Art Tatum:20th Century Piano Genius | Verve | 531763-2
Solos 1937 & Classic Piano Solos | Forlane | UCD 19010
Artie Shaw And His Orchestra | Planet JazzArtie Shaw | Planet Jazz | 2152057-2
Artie Shaw, Vol.1 | Musicraft | MVS 503 IMS
Planet Jazz:Swing | Planet Jazz | 2169651-2
In The Blue Room/In The Café Rouge | RCA | 2118527-2
Carlos Barbosa-Lima | Plays The Music Of Luiz Bonfa And Cole Porter | Concord | CCD 42008
Charlie Parker Sextet | Charlie Parker-South Of The Border | Verve | 527779-2
The Cole Porter Song Book | Verve | 823250-1
Dave Liebman Trio | Plays The Music Of Cole Porter | Red Records | 123236-2
Eddie Heywood And His Orchestra | The Commodore Story | Commodore | CMD 24002
Ella Fitzgerald With The Buddy Bregman Orchestra | The Complete Ella Fitzgerald Song Books of Harold Arlen, Irving Berlin, Duke Ellington, George & Ira Gershwin, Jerome Kern, Johnny Mercer, Cole Porter And Rogers & Hart | Verve | 519832-2
Gene Krupa And His Orchestra | Gene Krupa Plays Gerry Mulligan Arrangements | Verve | 2304430 IMS
Juan Garcia Esquivel Orchestra | Juan's Again | RCA | 2168206-2
Louie Bellson And His Jazz Orchestra | Air Mail Special-A Salute To The Big Band Masters | Limelight | 820824-2 IMS
Peter Herbolzheimer Orchestra | Music For Swinging Dancers Vol.4: Close To You | Koala Records | CD P 12
The Houdini's | The Houdini's Play The Big Five | Challenge | CHR 70027
Tiny Grimes And His Rockin' Highlanders | Tiny Grimes:The Complete 1950-1954,Vol.4 | Blue Moon | BMCD 6008

Begin The Beguine-
Simon Schott | Bar Piano: Simon Schott Plays Your Favorite Evergreens Vol.1 | Organic Music | ORGM 9733
Chubby Jackson And His Fifth Dimensional Jazz Group | Bebop Enters Sweden | Dragon | DRCD 318

Begin The Blues
Jay Clayton And Her Quintet | Circle Dancing | Sunnyside | SSC 1076 D

Beginning
Paul Bley | Lyrics | SPLASC(H) Records | CD H 348-2

Beginning-
Gregorio-Gustafsson-Nordeson | Background Music | HatOLOGY | 526

Beginning Of The End
Inner Visuals | Songs Of Berlin | KlangRäume | 30040

Begona-Blues
International Hashva Orchestra | All's Well | TCB Records | TCB 99602

Behind Bars
Stephan Micus | Behind Eleven Deserts | Intuition Records | INT 2042-2

Behind Eleven Deserts
Ronald Shannon Jackson And The Decoding Society | Decode Yourself | Island | ILPS 9827(804685)

Behind The Clouds-Your Face
Scarlet Rivera Trio | Behind The Crimson Veil | Erdenklang | 40702

Behind The Fridge
Dizzy Gillespie Orchestra | Bahiana | Pablo | 2625708

Behind The Plow
Anthony Davis | Middle Passage | Gramavision | GR 8401-2

Behind The Scenes
Stephen Scott Trio | Aminah's Dream | Verve | 517996-2

Behind The Yashmak
Steve LaSpina Quartet | New Horizon | Steeplechase | SCCD 31313

Behold
Jimmy Knepper Sextet | I Dream Too Much | Soul Note | 121092-2

Bei Dir War Es Immer So Schön
Ekkehard Jost Ensemble | Weimarer Balladen | Fish Music | FM 004 CD
Frank Castenier Group | For You,For Me For Evermore | EmArCy | 9814976
Georg Ruby Village Zone | Mackeben Revisited:The Ufa Years | Jazz Haus Musik | JHM 0121 CD
Joe Kienemann Trio | Integration | yvp music | CD 3023
Wolfgang Lauth Quartet | Lauther | Bear Family Records | BCD 15717 AH
Cowws Quintet | Grooves 'N' Loops | FMP | CD 59

Bei Mir Bist Du Schön
Benny Goodman Quartet | Benny Goodman Forever | RCA | NL 89955(2) DP
Cal Tjader Quintet | Tjader Plays Mambo | Original Jazz Classics | OJCCD 274-2(F 3221)
Cal Tjader's Modern Mambo Sextet | Tjader Plays Mambo | Original Jazz Classics | OJC 274(F 3221)
Garland Wilson | Jazz Piano Vol.1 | Jazztime(EMI) | 251282-2
Jimmy Rushing And His Band | The You And Me That Used To Be | RCA | ND 86460
June Christy With Orchestra | This Is June Christy/June Christy Recalls Those Kenton Days | Capitol | 535209-2
Lionel Hampton And His Orchestra | A True Collectors Item | Jazz Archive | 90.506-2
Mick Mulligan's Magnolia Jazz Band With George Melly | Great British Traditional Bands Vol.7:Mick Mulligan & George Melly | Lake | LACD 66
Mr.Acker Bilk And His Paramount Jazz Band | New Orleans Days | Lake | LACD 36
The Andrew Sisters | The Andrew Sisters | ASV | AJA 5096
The Tremble Kids | The Tremble Kids:The Of 40 Years | BELL Records | BLR 84060

Beia Flor
Louie Bellson And His All-Star Orchestra | Duke Ellington:Black, Brown & Beige | Musicmasters | 65096-2

Beija-Flor
Petra Straue & The Moonmen | Voices Around My House | Satin Doll Productions | SDP 1016-1 CD

Bein' Green
Homesick James | Got To Move | Trix Records | TRIX 3320

Being Here With You
Peter Kuhn Quartet | The Kill | Soul Note | SN 1043

Being In The Frontline
Abbey Lincoln With The Rodney Kendrick Trio And Guests | A Turtle's Dream | Verve | 527382-2

Being Me
Yvonne Walter With Band | Thrills | Mons Records | MR 874805

Being With You
Andy Rinehart Group | Jason's Chord | CMP Records | CMP CD 1003

Beirach
Gebhard Ullmann-Andreas Willers | Playful '93 | Nabel Records:Jazz Network | CD 4659

Beirut
Rabih Abou-Khalil Group | Blue Camel | Enja | ENJ-7053 2
Dewey Redman-Cecil Taylor-Elvin Jones | Momentum Space | Verve | 559944-2

Bekei
The Voodoo Gang | Return Of The Turtle-Old And New Songs From Africa | Enja | 9112-2

Bela
Pata Horns | New Archaic Music | Pata Musik | PATA 4(JHM 42) CD

Béla
Tania Maria Ensemble | Love Explosion | Concord | CCD 4230

Belare
Rabih Abou-Khalil Quartet | Bitter Harvest | MMP-Records | 170884

Beleba
Papa Bue's Viking Jazzband | The Golden Years Of Revival Jazz,Vol.14 | Storyville | STCD 5519

Belelia
Kenny Barron Quintet | Sambao | EmArCy | 512736-2

Belfast Area
Steve Houben Trio | 3 | B.Sharp Records | CDS 071

Belief
M.T.B. | Consenting Adults | Criss Cross | Criss 1177

Believe Beleft Below
Odetta With The Buck Clayton Sextet | Odetta And The Blues | Original Blues Classics | OBCCD 509-2(RLP 9417)

Believe I'll Go
Little Milton And His Band | Little Milton | Chess | 427013

Believe It Beloved
Fats Waller And His Rhythm | Breakin' The Ice-The Early Years Part 1(1934-1935) | Bluebird | 63 66618-2
Mark Murphy With Azymuth And Guests | Night Mood | Milestone | MCD 9145-2

Believe You Me
Terje Rypdal-Miroslav Vitous-Jack DeJohnette Trio | Terje Rypdal Miroslav Vitous Jack DeJohnette | ECM | 1125(825470-2)

Believer
Deborah Henson-Conant | Alter Ego | Laika Records | 35100852

Belinda
Alterd Ego | Laika Records | 35100962
Eddie Brunner Und Die Original Teddies | Teddy Stauffer:Rare And Historical Jazz Recordings | Elite Special | 9522009

Belisco
Rickey Kelly Group | My Kind Of Music | New Note Records | NNR 001

Belkis
Remember Shakti | Saturday Night In Bombay | Verve | 014184-2

Bell' Alla
Jon Eardley Quintet | Namely Me' -Jon Eardley | Spotlite | SPJ LP 17

Bell Boy Blues
Todd Rhodes And His Septet | Dance Music That Hits The Spot! | Swingtime(Contact) | ST 1020

Bella
Gerard Pansanel Quintet | Voices | Owl Time Line | 3819102

Bella And Herr T.
Dizzy Gillespie & The Mitchell-Ruff Duo | Dizzy Gillespie And Mitchell-Ruff | Mainstream | MD CDO 721

Bella Ciao
Ran Blake | The Blue Potato And Other Outrages | Milestone | M 9021
Thomas Stabenow Trio | Clips | UJQ Production | 1

Bella Donna
Philip Harper Sextet | The Thirteenth Moon | Muse | MCD 5520

Bella Ragazza
Curtis Counce Group | Sonority | Contemporary | CCD 7655-2

Bella Vista
Franco & Lorenzo Petrocca | Italy | Edition Musikat | EDM 062

Bellamonte
Benny Green Trio | These Are Soulful Days | Blue Note | 499527-2

Bellarosa
Clifford Brown Quintet | More Memorable Tracks | Blue Note | 300195(BNJ 61001)
Pinguin Moschner | The Flight Of The Humble Beast | Born&Bellmann | 980205 CD

Belle Of The Ball
Walter Norris Trio | Lush Life | Concord | CCD 4457

Belles
Bireli Lagrene Group | Gipsy Project | Dreyfus Jazz Line | FDM 36626-2

Belleville
Django Reinhardt And The Quintet Du Hot Club De France | Django Reinhardt:Djangology | EMI Records | 780659-2
Joe Pass Quartet | Summer Night | Pablo | 2310939-2
Quintet Du Hot Club De France | Verve Jazz Masters 38:Django Reinhardt | Verve | 516931-2
Django Reinhardt-Stephane Grappelli | Ace Of Club | ACL 1158
Enrico Rava 4uartet | Animals | Inak | 8801

Bellflower
Junie C. Cobb And His New Hometown Band | Chicago-The Living Legends:Junie C. Cobb | Original Jazz Classics | OJCCD 1825-2(RLP 9415)

Bellows
Ahmad Jamal Trio | Chicago Revisited | Telarc Digital | CD 83327
Albert Ayler Group | Bells-Prophecy | ESP Disk | ESP 1010-2

Bells
Fred Wesley And The Horny Horns | The Final Blow | Sequel Records | NED CD 270
Wolfgang Lackerschmid Group | Gently But Deep | Lady Hamilton Productions | BR 39

Belluard
Pete Brown Quintet | The Changing Face Of Harlem-The Savoy Sessions | Savoy | SJL 2208 (801184)

Belly Button Rave
Count Basie And His Orchestra | Li'l Ol' Groovemaker...Basie | Verve | 821799-2 PMS

Belly Roll
Lonnie Brooks Blues Band | Wound Up Tight | Sonet | SNTF 974(941974)

Belly Up
Billy May And His Orchestra Plus Guests | The Capitol Years | EMI Records | EMS 1275

Bellydance On A Chessboard
Henk De Jonge Trio With Willem Breuker And Alex Coke | Jumping Shark | BVHAAST | CD 9103

Belo Horizonte
Sigi Schwab & Percussion Academia | Rondo A Tre | Melos Music | CDGS 703

Belonging
Joshua Redman Quartet | Beyond | Warner | 9362-47465-2

Belonging(Lopsided Lullaby)
Furio Di Castri-Paolo Fresu | Urlo | yvp music | CD 3035

Bemoanable Lady
Andy Summers Group | Green Chimneys:The Music Of Thelonious Monk | RCA | 2663472-2

Bemsha Swing
Bill Evans | Verve Jazz Masters 5:Bill Evans | Verve | 519821-2
Conversations With Myself | Verve | 521409-2
Bobby Hutcherson Quintet | Color Schemes | Landmark | LCD 1508-2
Don Cherry Quartet | Art Deco | A&M Records | 395258-2 PMS
Esbjörn Svensson Trio(E.S.T.) | EST Plays Monk | ACT | 9010-2
EST Plays Monk | RCA | 2137680-2
J.J.Johnson And His Orchestra | J.J.! | RCA | 2125727-2
John Coltrane-Don Cherry Quartet | John Coltrane-The Heavyweight Champion:The Complete Atlantic Recordings | Atlantic | 8122-71984-2
The Avantgarde | Rhino | 8122-79892-2
That's Jazz Vol.40: The Avant-Garde | Atlantic | ATL 50523
Karl Berger-Ray Anderson Duo | Conversations | IN+OUT Records | 77027-2
Keith Copeland Trio | Postcard From Vancouver | Jazz Focus | JFCD 023
Kenny Burrell Quartet | Midnight At The Village Vanguard | Paddle Wheel | KICJ 178
Klaus Suonsaari Quintet | True Colours | L+R Records | CDLR 45080
Miles Davis And The Modern Jazz Giants | Thelonious Monk:85th Birthday Celebration | zyx records | FANCD 6076-2
Miles Davis And The Modern Jazz Giants | Prestige | P 7650
Monk By Five | Monk By Five | Touché Music | TMcCD 012
Peter Weniger Trio | I Mean You | Mons Records | MR 874300
Soren Lee Trio | Soren Lee Trio | L+R Records | CDLR 45072
Thelonious Monk Quartet | Live In Stockholm 1961 | Dragon | DRLP 151/152
Pianology | Moon Records | MCD 055-2
Live At The It Club:Complete | CBS | C2K 65288
Thelonious Monk In Stockholm | Duke Records | D 1020
Thelonious Monk Quintet | Sonny Rollins-The Freelance Years:The Complete Riverside & Contemporary Recordings | Riverside | 5 RCD 4427-2
Thelonious Monk-The Complete Riverside Recordings | Riverside | 15 RCD 022-2
Thelonious Monk Trio | Thelonious Monk:The Complete Prestige Recordings | Prestige | 3 PRCD 4428-2
The Prestige Legacy Vol.1:The High Priests | Prestige | PCD 24251-2
Wallace Roney Quintet | Munchin' | Muse | MCD 5533
Medeski Martin & Wood With Guests | It's A Jungle In Here | Gramavision | R2 79495

Ben
Monty Alexander Trio | Reunion In Europe | Concord | CCD 4231
Krystall Klear And The Buells | Our Night Together | K2B2 Records | 2169

Ben Blew
Warne Marsh Quintet | Modern Jazz Gallery | Fresh Sound Records | KXL 5001(252282-1 Kapp)

Ben J Man
John Stein Quintet | Jazz Guitar Highlights 1 | Jardis Records | JRCD 20141
Pete Johnson's Housewarmin' | Jazz:The Essential Collection Vol.3 | IN+OUT Records | 78013-2

Ben Rides Out
Pete Johnson All Stars | All Star Swing Groups-The Savoy Sessions | Savoy | WL 70533 (809316)

Bend It
Johnny Hodges Orchestra | Duke Ellington And Johnny Hodges Plus Others | Verve | 2304417 IMS

Bend One
Paul Motian Trio With Chris Potter And Larry Grenadier | Paul Motian Trio 2000 + One | Winter&Winter | 910032-2

Bend Over Backwards
Steve Swallow Quintet | Always Pack Your Uniform On Top | Watt | XtraWatt/10(543506-2)
Albert Collins Blues Band | Cold Snap | Sonet | SNTF 969(941969)

Bending New Corners
Glen Velez-Layne Redmond | Internal Combustion | CMP Records | CMP CD 23

Beneath An Evening Sky
Ralph Towner Quintet | Old Friends New Friends | ECM | 1153
Ralph Towner-David Darling | Works | ECM | 823268-1
Mino Cinelu-Kenny Barron | Swamp Sally | Verve | 532268-2

Beneath The Earth
Larry Coryell-Alphonse Mouzon Quartet | Back Together Again | Atlantic | ATL 50382

Beneath The Little Green Trees
Chick Corea Electric Band | Beneath The Mask | GRP | GRP 96492

Beneath The Mask
Alvin Queen-Bill Saxton Sextet | Ashanti | Divox | CDX 48703

Benedictus-
Clemens Maria Peters/Reinhold Bauer | Quadru Mana/Quadru Mania | Edition Collage | EC 464-2

Benedikt
Mario Schiano Sextet | Benefit Concert To Repurchae The Pendulum For Mr.Fourcault | SPLASC(H) Records | HP 20

Bengal Blues
Bobo Stenson Trio | War Orphans | ECM | 1604(539723-2)

Bengali Blue
Schnuckenack Reinhardt Sextet | Starportrait Schnuckenack Reinhardt | Intercord | 155012

Bennie's Diggin'

Gunther Klatt And Elephantrombones | Live At Leverkusen | Enja | 5069-2

Benny
Benny Goodman And His Orchestra | 40th Anniversary Concert-Live At Carnegie Hall | London | 820349-2

Benny Goodman Medley:
Live At Carnegie Hall-40th Anniversary Concert | Decca | 6.28451 DP

Benny Sent Me
George Benson Quartet + Guests | The George Benson Cookbook | CBS | 502470-2

Benny's Back
The Sextet | Jazz Workshop Presents The Sextet | somethin'else | 300252(TOCJ 5586)

Benny's Bounced Blues
Benny Waters Quartet | Swinging Again | Jazzpoint | JP 1037 CD
Benny Goodman Septet feat.Count Basie | Charlie Christian:Swing To Bop | Dreyfus Jazz Line | FDM 36715-2

Benny's Bugle
Live 1939/1941 | Jazz Anthology | JA 5181
Oscar Peterson Trio | The Paris Concert | Pablo | 2PACD 2620112
Johnny 'Hammond' Smith Quartet | Good 'Nuff | Prestige | PRCD 24282-2

Benny's Diggin'
Eddie Jefferson With Orchestra | The Main Man | Inner City | IC 1033 IMS

Ben's Blues
Ben Webster Quartet | Jazz At Ronnie Scott's | Ronnie Scott's Jazz House | JHAS 612

Benson's Rider
Jim Hall-Christian McBride | Jim Hall & Basses | Telarc Digital | CD 83506

Benusan
New Orleans Klezmer Allstars | Manichalfwitz | Gert Town Records | GT-1117

Beppo
Ralph Towner-Gary Peacock | A Closer View | ECM | 1602(531623-2)
Badi Assad | Rhythms | Chesky | JD 137

Berberlied
Aldo Romano Trio | Il Piacere | Owl Records | 013575-2

Berceuse
Christoph Stiefel Trio | Sweet Paradox | Jazzline | JL 11148-2
Jan Fryderyk | Piano Works: Live Recordings | Jazzline | ???

Berceuse Basque
Jan Fryderyk Trio | tri-o (tri-ou) Trio n. | Jazzline | ???

Berceuse(Michael Baumgartner)
Thierry Péala Group | Inner Traces:A Kenny Wheeler Songbook | Naive | 226102

Berga
Bireli Lagrene Group | Bireli Lagrene 'Highlights' | Jazzpoint | JP 1027 CD
Down In Town | Island | 205863-320
Jan Jankeje Quintet | Zum Trotz | Jazzpoint | JP 1016 CD
Vienna Art Orchestra And Voices | Swiss Swing | Moers Music | 02060 CD

Berget Det Bla(Blue Mountain)
Flim & The BB's | Big Notes | dmp Digital Music Productions | CD 454

Berimbau
Astrud Gilberto With The Gil Evans Orchestra | Silver Collection: The Astrud Gilberto Album | Verve | 823451-2 PMS
Maximilian Geller Quartet feat. Sabina Sciubba | Maimilian Geller Goes Bossa Encore | Edition Collage | EC 505-2
Shigeharu Mukai Group | Mukai Meets Gilberto | Denon Compact Disc | DC-8569

Berimbau Do Sul
Paulinho Da Costa Orchestra | Agora | Original Jazz Classics | OJCCD 630-2(2310785)

Berimbau Variations
Quiet Now | Inside The Waltz | Blue Concept | BCCD 94/01

Berkeley Campus Blues
Dave Doran Group | Rhythm Voice | Plainisphare | PL 1267-109 CD

Berlin Babes
John Tchicai-Vitold Rek Duo | Art Of The Duo:Satisfaction | Enja | 7033-2

Berlin, Dein Gesicht Hat Sommersprossen
Heiner Goebbels/Alfred Harth | Indianer Für Morgen | Riskant | 568-72401

Berliner Zimmer
Der Rote Bereich | Love Me Tender | ACT | 9286-2

Berlin-Mitte
The Splendid Master Gnawa Musicians Of Morocco | The Splendid Master Gnawa Musicians Of Morocco | Verve | 521587-2

Bernardo
Louie Bellson Sextet | Louie Bellson Jazz Giants | Limelight | 820822-2 IMS

Bernfest '96
Don Byron Quartet | Romance With The Unseen | Blue Note | 499545-2

Bernhard Goetz,James Ramseur And Me
Eddie Cleanhead Vinson With The Cannonball Adderley Quintet | Cleanhead & Cannonball | Landmark | LCD 1309-2(882857)

Bernice's Bounce
A Band Of Friends | The Best Of The Gerry Mulligan Quartet With Chet Baker | Pacific Jazz | 795481-2

Bernie's Tune
All Stars | Bird's Eyes Last Unissued Vol.21:Bird On TV/Bird On Bandbox | Philology | W 851.2
Art Pepper Plus Eleven | Modern Jazz Classics | Original Jazz Classics | OJC20 341-2
A Treasury Of Modern Jazz Classics | Mobile Fidelity | MFCD 805
Buddy Rich-Gene Krupa Orchestra | Krupa And Rich | Verve | 521643-2
Buddy Tate Quintet | The Great Buddy Tate | Concord | CJ 163
Charlie Ventura Quintet | The New Charlie Ventura In Hi-Fi | Harlequin | HQ 2009(Baton BL 1202) IMS
Chubby Jacksons Big Three Plus | Jazz From Then Till Now | Fresh Sound Records | FSR 504(Everest LPBR 5041)
Gene Krupa And Buddy Rich Band | Krupa And Rich | Verve | 817109-1 IMS
Gerry Mulligan Quartet | Chet Baker:Complete 1952 Fantasy & Pacific Jazz Sessions | Definitive Records | DRCD 11233
Live In Stockholm-Vol.2 | Ingo | 6
Gerry Mulligan Quartet With Lee Konitz | Complete 1953 The Haig Performances | The Jazz Factory | JFCD 22861
Les Blue Stars | Jazz In Paris:Les Blue Stars-Pardon My English/Henri Salvador-Plays The Blues | EmArCy | 013035-2
Michael Rabinowitz Quartet | Gabrielle's Balloon | Jazz Focus | JFCD 011
Stan Kenton And His Orchestra | At The Las Legas Tropicana | Capitol | 835245-2

Bernie's Tune(Ad Lib)
Charlie Ventura Quintet | The New Charlie Ventura In Hi-Fi | Harlequin | HQ 2009(Baton BL 1202) IMS

Bert
Jerome Cooper | The Unpredictability Of Predictability | About Time | AT 1002

Besame Mucho
Art Pepper Quartet | Among Friends | Discovery | DSCD 837
Art Pepper:The Complete Galaxy Recordings | Galaxy | 16GCD 1016-2
Among Friends | Interplay | IP 7718
Artie Shaw Sextet | Artie Shaw:The Last Recordings | Limelight | 820847-2 IMS
Christof Sänger & Cuban Fantasy | Moliendo Café | Mons Records | MR 874302
Dave Liebman Quintet | Besame Mucho And Other Latin Jazz Standards | Red Records | 123260-2
Dave Pike Quartet | Pike's Peak | Epic | 489772-2
Dexter Gordon Quartet | American Classic | Discovery | 71009-2
Grant Green Sextet | The Latin Bit | Blue Note | 300051(4111)
Juan Garcia Esquivel Orchestra | Juan's Again | RCA | 2168206-2
Julia Hülsmann Trio | Julia Hülsmann-Marc Muellbauer-Rainer Winch Trio | BIT | 11218
Kermit Ruffins Septet | The Big Butter & Egg Man | Justice Records | JR 1102-2
Michel Petrucciani | Michel Petrucciani:Concert Inédits | Dreyfus Jazz Line | FDM 36607-2
Live In Germany | Dreyfus Jazz Line | FDM 36597-2
Michel Petrucciani With The Graffiti String Quartet | Marvellous | Dreyfus Jazz Line | FDM 36564-2
Nat King Cole Trio | Any Old Time | Giants Of Jazz | GOJ 1031
Ronald Muldrow Trio | Yesterdays | Enja | 8020-2
Thilo Kreitmeier & Group | Soul Call | Organic Music | ORGM 9711
Torsten Zwingenberger & Band With Guests | Open Sunroof | Blackbird Records | BD 41012
Wes Montgomery Trio | Boss Guitar | Original Jazz Classics | OJCCD 261-2
Wes Montgomery-The Complete Riverside Recordings | Riverside | 12 RCD 4408-2
Doug Raney Quartet | Rainey '96 | Steeplechase | SCCD 31397

Besame Mucho(alt.take)
Barney Wilen Quintet | La Note Bleue | IDA Record | 010 CD

Beside A Brook
Dick Jurgens And His Orchestra | The Uncollected: Dick Jurgens, Vol.2 | Hindsight | HSR 138

Beside Manner
Art Farmer Sextet | The Company I Keep-Art Farmer Meets Tom Harrell | Arabesque Recordings | AJ 0112

Bess Oh Where's My Bess
John Towner Quartet | The John Towner Touch | Fresh Sound Records | KL 1055(Kapp)
Louis Armstrong And Ella Fitzgerald With Russell Garcia's Orchestra | The Complete Ella Fitzgerald And Louis Armstrong On Verve | Verve | 537284-2
Miles Davis With Gil Evans & His Orchestra | Porgy And Bess | CBS | CK 65141
The Miles Davis Selection | CBS | 465699-2

Bess You Is My Woman Now
Ella Fitzgerald And Louis Armstrong With The Russell Garcia Orchestra | Porgy And Bess | Verve | ???
Ivan Julien Orchestra | Jazz In Paris:Porgy & Bess | EmArCy | 013039-2
Joel Weiskopf Trio | The Search | Criss Cross | Criss 1174
Louis Armstrong And Ella Fitzgerald With Russell Garcia's Orchestra | The Complete Ella Fitzgerald And Louis Armstrong On Verve | Verve | 537284-2
Lynne Arriale Trio | When You Listen | dmp Digital Music Productions | CD 511
Miles Davis With Gil Evans & His Orchestra | The Miles Davis Selection | CBS | 465699-2
Mundell Lowe's Jazzmen | Porgy And Bess | RCA | PL 43552
Oscar Peterson Trio | Porgy And Bess | Verve | 519807-2
Oscar Peterson-Joe Pass Duo | Porgy And Bess | Original Jazz Classics | OJCCD 829-2(2310779)
Paolo Fresu Quartet | Kind Of Porgy & Bess | RCA | 21951952
Pete Christlieb Quartet | Coversations With Warne Vol.2 | Criss Cross | Criss 1103

Bess You Is My Woman Now-
Cal Tjader Quartet | Our Blues | Fantasy | FCD 24771-2
Dave Grusin Band With Orchestra | The Orchestral Album | GRP | GRP 97972

Bessarabia
Ma Rainey And Her Band | Ma Rainey | Milestone | MCD 47021-2

Bessie Couldn't Help It
Humphrey Lyttelton-Acker Bilk Band | More Humph & Acker | Calligraph | CLGCD 030

Bessie Harris
Sunnyland Slim Band | The Ralph Bass Sessions Vol.4 | Red Lightnin' | RL 0056

Bessie's Blues
Conrad Herwig-Andy LaVerne | Shades Of Light | Steeplechase | SCCD 31520
Elvin Jones Jazz Machine | Live In Japan-Tokyo April 1978 | Konnex Records | KCD 5041
John Abercrombie Trio | Straight Flight | JAM | 5001 IMS
John Coltrane Quartet | The Best Of John Coltrane-His Greatest Years | MCA | AS 9200-2
McCoy Tyner Quintet | 44th Street Suite | Red Baron | 469284-2

Bessie's Blues-
John Coltrane Quartet | John Coltrane:The Classic Quartet-Complete Impulse Studio Recordings | Impulse(MCA) | 951280-2

Bessie's Blues(first version-incomplete)
Barrett Deems Big Band | Groovin' Hard | Delmark | DE 505

Best Laid Plans
John Pizzarelli Sextet | My Blue Heaven | Chesky | JD 38

Best Of Friends
John Scofield Quintet | Electric Outlet | Gramavision | GR 8405-2

Betcha By Golly Wow
Members Only...Too! | The Way You Make Me Feel | Muse | MCD 5348

Betcha' I Getcha'
Ella Fitzgerald And Her Famous Orchestra | Ella Fitzgerald Vol.2-Forever Young | Swingtime(Contact) | ST 1007

Bethena-A Concert Waltz
New England Conservatory Ragtime Ensemble | More Scott Joplin Rags | London | HMG 5009 AN

Betrum Narfoli
John Benson Brooks' Orchestra | Folk Jazz U.S.A. | RCA | PM 43767

Bette Davis
Anouar Brahem Quartet | Conte De L'Incroyable Amour | ECM | 1457(511959-2)

Bettements
Keshavan Maslak Group | Better And Better | LEO | LR 150

Better Call Me Now
Sonny Boy Williamson Group | Sonny Boy Williamson(1937-1947) | RCA | 2126418-2

Better Days Ahead
Jazz Orchester Rheinland-Pfalz | Like Life | Jazz Haus Musik | LJBB 9405
Pat Metheny Group | Letter From Home | Geffen Records | GED 24245
In Concert | Jazz Door | JD 1231
Peter Herbolzheimer Rhythm Combination & Brass | Colors Of A Band | Mons Records | MR 874799

Better Git It In Your Soul
Charles Mingus Jazz Workshop | Thirteen Pictures:The Charles Mingus Anthology | Rhino | R2 71402
Charles Mingus Orchestra | Mingus Mingus Mingus | Impulse(MCA) | 951170-2
Charles Mingus -Passions Of A Man | Atlantic | ATL 60143
Charles Mingus Quintet | Charles Minus-Live | Affinity | CD AFS 778
Charles Mingus Live | Affinity | AFF 19
Dean Magraw | Broken Silence | Acoustic Music Records | 319.1054.2
Maceo Parker Group | Roots Revisited | Minor Music | 801015
Mingus Dynasty | Live At Montreux | Atlantic | 99145
Pepper Adams Octet | Pepper Adams Plays Charlie Mingus | Fresh Sound Records | FSR-CD 0177
Woody Herman And The Young Thundering Herd With Friends | Woody And Friends At Monterey Jazz Festival 1979 | Concord | CCD 4170

Better Git It In Your Soul-
Ramón Diaz Group | O Si No Que? | Fresh Sound Records | FSNT 044 CD
Charles Mingus Group | Charles Mingus:Alternate Takes | CBS | CK 65514

Better Git It In Your Soul(alt.take)
Ben Webster-Harry Sweets Edison Quintet | Ben And Sweets | CBS | CK 40853

Better Not Now
Terje Rypdal Group | Odyssey | ECM | 1067/8

Better Off With You
Terje Rypdal Quartet | Works | ECM | 825428-1

Better Than Anything
Bob Dorough/Bill Takas Duo | Sing And Swing | Red Records | NS 204
Keshavan Maslak Group | Better And Better | LEO | LR 150

Better Than The Average Man
Anthony Braxton Duo/Quintet | Dances & Orations | Music & Arts | CD 923

Better Than Words
Rob Bargad Sextet | Better Times | Criss Cross | Criss 1086

Better Times
John Marshall Quintet | Dreamin' On The Hudson | Organic Music | ORGM 9713

Better To Know
Luther Johnson Blues Band | Luther´s Blues | Black & Blue | BLE 59.519 2

Better World
Ted Rosenthal | Maybeck Recital Hall Series Volume Thirty-Eight | Concord | CCD 4648

Betty
Erik Truffaz Quartet Quintet | Out Of A Dream | Blue Note | 855855-2
Chris Barber's Jazz Band With Sonny Terry And Brownie McGhee | Echoes Of Harlem | Lake | LACD 87

Betty Grable
Max [Blues] Bailey Group | Obscure Blues Shouters Vol.1 | Blue Moon | BMCD 6010

Between
Gregorio-Gustafsson-Nordeson | Background Music | HatOLOGY | 526

Between 8th And 9th Mission Street
Vince Guaraldi Quartet | Modern Jazz From San Francisco | Original Jazz Classics | OJC 272(F 3213)

Between I And E
Ravi Coltrane Quintet | From The Round Box | RCA | 2173923-2

Between Memory And Presentiment
Art Tatum | Art Tatum:Memories Of You | Black Lion | BLCD 7608-2

Between Midnight And Day
John Taylor Trio | Rosslyn | ECM | 1751(159924-2)

Between Moons
Jochen Feucht Quartet | Signs On Lines | Satin Doll Productions | SDP 1019-1 CD

Between Now And Then
Myra Melford Trio | Now & Now | Enemy | EMCD 131(03531)

Between Our Eeys
Jeff Gardner-Gary Peacock | Alchemy | fnac Muisc | 662016

Between The Clouds
Loren Stilllman Quartet | How Swee It Is | Nagel-Heyer | CD 2031

Between The Devil And God
Alvino Rey And His Orchestra | The Uncollected: Alvino Rey And His Orchestra 1946 | Hindsight | HSR 121

Between The Devil And The Deep Blue Sea
Bob Stewart With The Mat Mathes Quintet | The 4 Most + Bob Stewart | Dawn | DCD 112
Cal Tjader Quartet | Plays Harold Arlen | Original Jazz Classics | OJC 285(F 8072)
Dicky Wells And His Orchestra | Django Reinhardt And His American Friends:Paris 1935-1937 | Memo Music | HDJ 4124
Ella Fitzgerald And Her Trio | The Greatest Jazz Concert In The World | Pablo | 2625704-2
Ella Fitzgerald With The Billy May Orchestra | The Complete Ella Fitzgerald Song Books of Harold Arlen, Irving Berlin, Duke Ellington, George & Ira Gershwin, Jerome Kern, Johnny Mercer, Cole Porter And Rogers & Hart | Verve | 519832-2
The Harold Arlen Songbook | Verve | 817526-1 IMS
Elliot Lawrence And His Orchestra | Mullenium | CBS | CK 65678
Ellis Larkins Trio | A Smooth One | Black & Blue | BLE 59.123 2
Hal Kemp And His Orchestra | The Radio Years: Hal Kemp And His Orchestra 1934 | Hindsight | HSR 143
John Williams Band | Plays The Music Of Harold Arlen | Discovery | DSCD 891(881472)
Jonathan Schwartz & Quintet | Anyone Would Love You | Muse | MCD 5325
Oscar Peterson Trio | Oscar Peterson Plays The Harold Arlen Song Book | Verve | 589103-2
En Concert Avec Europe 1 | Laserlight | 710443/48
Oscar Peterson-Roy Eldridge Duo | Oscar Peterson & Roy Eldridge | Original Jazz Classics | OJCCD 727-2(2310739)
Paris Washboard | 10'eme Anniversaire:Love For Sale | Stomp Off Records | CD 1326
Roy Eldridge 4 | Montreux '77 | Original Jazz Classics | OJCCD 373-2
The Montreux '77 Collection | Pablo | 2620107
Ruby Braff And His Big City Six | Little Big Horn | Fresh Sound Records | FSR-CD 321
Ruby Braff Quartet | Live At The Regattabar | Arbors Records | ARCD 19131
Tommy Flanagan Trio | Plays The Music Of Harold Arlen | EmArCy | DIW 25030

Between The Devil And The Deep Blue Sea-
Roy Eldridge And The Jimmy Ryan All Stars | Little Jazz And The Jimmy Ryan All-Stars | Original Jazz Classics | OJCCD 1058-2(DRE 1001)

Between The Devil And The Deep Blue Sea(alt.take)
Teddy Wilson | Piano Solos | Affinity | CD AFS 1016

Between The Fourth And Fifth Step
Dave Samuels Group | Natural Selections | GRP | GRP 96562

Between The Lines
Zaza Miminoshvili-Zurab J. Gadnidze Duo | The Shin | Acoustic Music Records | 319.1172.2

Between The Sheets
Fourplay | Between The Sheets | Warner | 9362-45340-2
Johnny 'Hammond' Smith Quintet | Discovery:Grover Washington Jr.-The First Recordings | Prestige | PCD 11020-2
Frank Haunschild & Tom Van Der Geld | Getting Closer | Acoustic Music Records | 319.1170.2

Between Two Islands
Bertha Hope Trio | Between Two Kings | Minor Music | 801025

Between You And Me
Jean-Luc Ponty Quintet | Aurora | Atlantic | SD 19158

Between You And Me And The Gatepost
Curtis Mosby And His Dixieland Blue-Blowers | Curtis Mosby And Henry Star | Jazz Oracle | BDW 8003

Beulah's Boogie
Lionel Hampton And His Orchestra | Jay Bird | Black Lion | 127032
Wes Montgomery:Complete Recordings With Lionel Hampton | Definitive Records | DRCD 11242

Bevan Beeps
Tadd Dameron And His Orchestra | The Lost Sessions | Blue Note | 521484-2

Beverly Hills Blues
Rolf Kühn And His Orchestra | Rolf Kühn-Picture CD | Blue Flame | 40162(2132489-2)

Beware
Louis Jordan And His Tympany Five | Louis Jordan-Let The Good Times Roll: The Complete Decca Recordings 1938-1954 | Bear Family Records | BCD 15557 IH
Wilbur Ware Quintet | The Chicago Sound | Original Jazz Classics | OJCCD 1737-2(RLP 12-252)

Bewitched Bothered And Bewildered
André Previn And His Pals | Pal Joey | Original Jazz Classics | OJCCD 637-2(S 7543)
Bucky Pizzarelli | Solo Flight | Stash Records | ST-CD 573(875903)
Chick Corea And Origin | A Week At The Blue Note | Stretch Records | SCD 9020-2
Earl Klugh Trio | The Earl Klugh Trio Volume One | Warner | 7599-26750-2
Ella Fitzgerald And The Paul Smith Quartet | The Best Of The Song Books | Verve | 519804-2
Ella Fitzgerald With Orchestra | Essential Ella | Verve | 523990-2
Ella Fitzgerald With The Buddy Bregman Orchestra | The Rodgers And Hart Songbook | Verve | 821693-1
Ella Fitzgerald With The Paul Smith Quartet | Ella Fitzgerald-First Lady Of Song | Verve | 517898-2

Fran Warren With The Marty Paich Orchestra | Hey There! Here's Fran Warren | Fresh Sound Records | Tops T 1585 CD
George Coleman Quartet | I Could Write A Book:The Music Of Richard Rodgers | Telarc Digital | CD 83439
June Christy With The Johnny Guarnieri Quintet | June Christy And The Johnny Guarnieri Quintet (1949) | Jazz Unlimited | JUCD 2084
Kenny Drew Trio | Jazz Impressions Of Pal Joey | Original Jazz Classics | SMJ 6106
Laura Fygi With Band | Bewitched | Verve | 514724-2
Leith Stevens All Stars | Jazz Themes From The Wild One(Soundtrack) | Fresh Sound Records | 252280-1(Decca DL 8349)
Paul Desmond Quartet | Easy Living | RCA | 2174796-2
Masters Of Jazz Vol.13 | RCA | CL 42790 AG
Rosemary Clooney And Her Sextet | Rosemary Clooney Sings Ballads | Concord | CCD 4282
Sonny Red (Kyner) Sextet | Images:Sonny Red | Original Jazz Classics | OJC 148(J 974)
Stan Getz And The Oscar Peterson Trio | The Silver Collection: Stan Getz And The Oscar Peterson Trio | Verve | 827826-2
Stan Kenton And His Orchestra | Adventures In Standards | Creative World | ST 1025

Bewitched Bothered And Bewildered-
Charlie Parker Quintet | Charlie Parker At Birdland And Cafe Society | Cool & Blue | C&B-CD 108

Beyond A Shadow Of Doubt
Larry Young Quartet | Unity | Blue Note | GXK 8205 (84221)

Beyond All Limits
Tony Reedus Quartet | Minor Thang | Criss Cross | Criss 1117

Beyond Category(Third Movement)
Ella Fitzgerald With The Duke Ellington Orchestra | The Complete Ella Fitzgerald Song Books of Harold Arlen, Irving Berlin, Duke Ellington, George & Ira Gershwin, Jerome Kern, Johnny Mercer, Cole Porter And Rogers & Hart | Verve | 519832-2

Beyond Darkness
George Cables Quartet | Circles | Contemporary | C 14015

Beyond The Blue
Artie Shaw And His Orchestra | This Is Artie Shaw Vol. 2 | RCA | NL 89411 DP

Beyond The Blue Horizon
Engelbert Wrobel-Chris Hopkins-Dan Barrett Sextet | Harlem 2000 | Nagel-Heyer | CD 082
Stan Kenton And His Orchestra | Back To Balbao | Creative World | ST 1031

Beyond The Horizon
Bob Mintzer Big Band | Urban Contours | dmp Digital Music Productions | CD 467

Beyond The Mirage
Lotte Anker/Mette Petersen Quartet | Beyond The Mist | Stunt Records | STUCD 18908

Beyond The Sea(La Mer)
Django Reinhardt And The Quintet Du Hot Club De France | The Indispensable Django Reinhardt | RCA | ND 70929
Mehmet Ergin Group | Beyond The Seven Hills | MCA | MCD 70020

Beyond The Seventh Galaxy
John Surman | Upon Reflection | ECM | 1148(825472-2)

Beyond The Shadow
Toshinori Kondo & Ima | Red City Smoke | JA & RO | JARO 4173-2

Beyond The Sorrow
Nicholas Payton Quintet | Nick@Night | Verve | 547598-2

Beyond The Stars
McCoy Tyner Trio With Woodwinds And Strings | Fly With The Wind | Original Jazz Classics | OJCCD 699-2(M 9067)

Beyond These Walls
Batida | Batida | Timeless | CD SJP 200

Beyond Words
Les McCann Group | Music Lets Me Be | MCA | 28916 XOT

Bhagavad
Charlie Mariano & The Karnataka College Of Percussion | Jyothi | ECM | 1256

Bhajan
Live | VeraBra Records | CDVBR 2034-2
Khan Jamal Trio | Three | Steeplechase | SCCD 31201

Bharati
Charles Lloyd Quintet | Hyperion With Higgins | ECM | 1784(014000-2)
Matthias Müller Quartet | Bhavam | Jazz Haus Musik | JHM 0126 CD

Bhavan Ballade
Bhavam | Jazz Haus Musik | JHM 0126 CD

Bhavan Rock
Trygve Seim Group | Different Rivers | ECM | 1744(159521-2)

Bhavana
Trygve Seim-Oyvind Braekke-Per Oddvar Johansen Orchestra | The Source And Different Cikadas | ECM | 1764(014432-2)
Roy Hargrove Sextet | Diamond In The Rough | Novus | PD 90471

Bianca
Egberto Gismonti/Nana Vasconcelos | Duas Vozes | ECM | 1279
Fritz Hauser | Pensieri Bianchi | Hat Art | CD 6067

Bible Travels
Geoff Keezer Group | Turn Up The Quiet | CBS | 488830-2

Bica
José Luis Gutiérrez Trio | Núcleo | Fresh Sound Records | FSNT 039 CD

Bicéfalo
Thomas Horstmann-Markus Zaja | Somewhere | Factory Outlet Records | 400004-2

Bicinium 1
Somewhere | Factory Outlet Records | 400004-2

Bicinium 2
Andre Hodeir And His Jazz Group De Paris | Jazz In Paris:Le Jazz Groupe De Paris Joue André Hodeir | EmArCy | 548792-2

Bicinum
Bill Mays/Ed Bickert | Concord Duo Series Volume Seven:Bill Mays-Ed Bickert | Concord | CCD 4626

Bicycle Built For Two
Billy Taylor And His Orchestra | Taylor Made Jazz | Fresh Sound Records | LP 650(Argo)

Bidin' My Time
Johnny Hartman And His Orchestra | Unforgettable | Impulse(MCA) | IMP 11522
Nat King Cole With The Billy May Orchestra | Let's Face The Music | Capitol | EMS 1112
Teddi King With Al Cohn And His Orchestra | Bidin' My Time | Fresh Sound Records | 14465 CD(RCA)
Ruby Braff-George Barnes Quartet | Plays Gershwin | Concord | CCD 6005

Bienvenidos Al Mundo
Lu Watters' Yerba Buena Jazz Band | San Francisco Style | Good Time Jazz | 12003

Biff Baff Buff
Schmilz | Schmilz | Creative Works Records | CW CD 1041

Biffhei-No!
Henry Allen Jr. And His New York Orchestra | Victor Jazz History Vol.6:Harlem Jazz(1928-33) | RCA | 2128560-2

Bifurcation
John Coltrane-Duke Ellington Quartet | Duke Ellington & John Coltrane | Impulse(MCA) | 951166-2

Big
Jack Teagarden And His Swingin' Gates | Commodore Classics In Swing | Commodore | 9031-72723-2

Big Alice
Dannie Richmond Quintet | Three Or Four Shades Of Dannie Richmond Quintet | Tutu Records | 888120-2*

Big Alice & John Henry
Big Nick Nicholas Quintet | Big And Warm | India Navigation | IN 1061

Big Bad Bob
Paul Barbarin's New Orleans Band | Streets Of The City | 504 Records | 504CD 9

Big Bad Jug
Idris Muhammad-Gary Bartz | Right Now | Cannonball Records | CBD 27105

Big Bang
Billy Bang Quartet | Big Bang Theory | Justin Time | JUST 135-2

Big Banng-
Yusef Lateef Ensemble | Rahsaan Roland Kirk-Yusef Lateef:Seperate But Equal | 32 Jazz | 32111

Big Bear
Lu Watters' Yerba Buena Jazz Band | The San Francisco Style Vol.2:Watters' Original & Ragtime | Good Time Jazz | GTCD 12002-2

Big Ben Blues
Wild Bill Davison With The Eddie Condon All Stars | Wild Bill Davison | Storyville | SLP 4005

Big Bertha
Memphis Slim And His Band | Soul Blues | Ember | EMB 3422

Big Bill's Guitar
Lightnin' Hopkins | I've Been Buked And Scorned | Ember | EMB 3423

Big Bob
Klaus Kreuzeder & Henry Sincigno | Saxappeal | Trick Music | TM 9013 MC

Big Bop
Richie Cole Septet | Alto Madness | Muse | MCD 5155

Big Bossa
Toots Thielemans With Orchestra | Old Friend | Polydor | 2925029 IMS
Bud Freeman And His Summa Cum Laude Orchestra | It's Got To Be The Eel, A Tribute To Bud Freeman | Affinity | CD AFS 1008

Big Boy
Wolverine Orchestra | Bix Beiderbecke & The Wolverines | Village(Jazz Archive) | VILCD 008-2

Big Boy Blues
Bill Coleman Orchestra | Bill Coleman | Swing | SW 8402 IMS
Johnny Hodges Orchestra | Triple Play | RCA | ND 90208(847147)

Big Butter And Egg Man From The West
Charlie Byrd Quartet | Charlie Byrd In Greenwich Village | Milestone | M 47049
Jimmy Dorsey And His Orchestra | The Uncollected:Jimmy Dorsey And His Orchestra, Vol.4 | Hindsight | HSR 178
Muggsy Spanier And His Ragtime Band | The Great 16 | RCA | 2113039-2
Wild Bill Davison And His Commodores | Wild Bill Davison:The Commodore Master Takes | Commodore | CMD 14052

Big Byrd
Lightnin' Hopkins | Lightnin' Strikes Back | Charly | CRB 1031

Big Chief Battle Axe
Furry Lewis | Shake 'Em On Down | Fantasy | F 24703

Big City
Ernestine Anderson With The Hank Jones Trio | Big City | Concord | CCD 4214
Wolfgang Puschnig Group With Ernst Jandl | Mixed Metaphors | Amadeo | 527266-2

Big City Blues
George Russell's New York Big Band | New York Big Band | Soul Note | 121039-2
Gerry Mulligan Concert Jazz Band | Verve Jazz Masters 36:Gerry Mulligan | Verve | 523342-2
Blossom Dearie Trio | Sweet Blossom Dearie | Philips | PHCE 1019 PMS

Big City Life
Edgar Winter Group | I'm Not A Kid Anymore | L+R Records | CDLR 42076

Big Crwod
Sonny Stitt Trio | The Boss Men | Prestige | PCD 24253-2

Big C's Rock
Elliott Lawrence Orchestra | Jazz Goes Broadway | Fresh Sound Records | NL 45905(RCA Vik LX 1113)

Big Ears,Wet Nose
The Bad Plus | These Are The Vistas | CBS | 510666-2

Big Eater
Jack Teagarden's Big Eight | Jazz Gallery:Jack Teagerden | RCA | 2114175-2

Big Eight Blues
Jack Teagarden/Pee Wee Russell | Original Jazz Classics | OJCCD 1708-2(RLP 141)

Big Fat Alice's Blues
Dexter Gordon Quartet | Love For Sale | Steeplechase | SCCD 36018

Big Fat Lady
Louis Armstrong And His Hot Five | Louis Armstrong-The Hot Fives Vol.1 | CBS | 460821-2

Big Fat Mama
Cousin Joe With Band | Cousin Joe:The Complete 1945-1947 Vol.2(1946-1947) | Blue Moon | BMCD 6002
James 'Son' Thomas | James 'Son' Thomas | Blues Classics(L+R) | CDLR 82006
Oscar Peterson Trio | At Zardis' | Pablo | 2CD 2620118
Tampa Red Band | Tampa Red 1928-1942:It's Tight Like That | Story Of Blues | CD 3505-2

Big Fat Orange
Leadbelly[Huddie Ledbetter] | Huddie Ledbetter | Fantasy | F 24715

Big Foot
Greg Osby Quartet | Banned In New York | Blue Note | 496860-2
Hampton Hawes Trio | Bird Song | Original Jazz Classics | OJCCD 1035-2
Hilton Ruiz Trio | Piano Man | Steeplechase | SCCD 31036
Joe Thomas And His Orchestra | Joe Thomas:The Complete Recordings 1945-1950 | Blue Moon | BMCD 1051
Max Roach Orchestra | Standard Time | EmArCy | 814190-1 IMS
Red Rodney Quintet | Bird Lives! | Muse | MCD 5371

Big Foot Jump
Greg Osby Quartet | Banned In New York | Blue Note | 496860-2

Big Foot(excerpt)
Charlie Jordan | St. Louis Blues 1929-1935 | Yazoo | YAZ 1030

Big Fun
Steve Argüelles Quintet | Busy Listening | Babel | BDV 9406

Big Gig In Pajala
Howard Rumsey's Lighthouse All-Stars | Howard Rumsey's Lighthouse All Stars Vol.3 | Original Jazz Classics | OJCCD 266-2(C 3508)

Big Girls
David Torkanowsky Group | Steppin' Out | Line Records | COCD 9.00900 O

Big Heart
Rimak | Back In Town | Jazzline | ???

Big Idea
The Brecker Brothers | Return Of The Brecker Brothers | GRP | GRP 96842
Erskine Hawkins And His Orchestra | The Original Tuxedo Junction | RCA | ND 90363(874142)

Big Inside
John Scofield Quintet | Works For Me | Verve | 549281-2

Big J
Big Jay McNeely Band | Big Jay In 3-D | Sing | 650

Big Joe
Sammy Price And His Bluesicians | 1944 World Jam Session | Progressive | PCD 7074

Big John
Grant Green Trio | Blues For Lou | Blue Note | 521438-2

Big John Grady
Benny Goodman And His Orchestra | The Indispensable Benny Goodman(Big Band) Vol.5/6(1938-1939) | RCA | 2122621-2

Big John's Special
More Camel Caravans | Phontastic | NCD 8843/4
More Camel Caravans | Phontastic | NCD 8843/4
1938 Carnegie Hall Concert | CBS | 450983-2
Wrappin' It Up-The Harry James Years Part 2 | Bluebird | 63 66549-2
Sun Ra Arkestra | Sunrise In Different Dimensions | HatOLOGY | 568

Big Joy
Greetje Bijma Kwintet | Dark Moves | BVHAAST | 076(835643)

Big Kids
Bob Stewart Groups | Then & Now | Postcards | POST 1014

Big Legged Woman
Memphis Slim | Steady Rolling Blues | Original Blues Classics | OBCCD 523-2(BV 1075)

Big Lip Blues
| Meeting In Brooklyn | Babel | BDV 9405

Big Love
Willie Humphrey Jazz Band | New Orleans Traditional Jazz Legends:Willie Humphrey | Mardi Gras Records | MG 9002

Big Mac
Reichlich Weiblich | Live At Moers Festival '87 | Moers Music | 02064 CD

Big Mama's Back In Town
Herb Pomeroy Orchestra | Life Is A Many Splendored Gig | Fresh Sound Records | FSR-CD 84(882191)

Big Music
Michael Chertock | Cinematic Piano-Solo Piano Music From The Movies | Telarc Digital | CD 80357

Big Nick
John Coltrane Quartet | John Coltrane:The Classic Quartet-Complete Impulse Studio Recordings | Impulse(MCA) | 951280-2
John Coltrane-Duke Ellington Quartet | Duke Ellington & John Coltrane | Impulse(MCA) | 951166-2
Kevin Hays Trio | Ugly Beauty | Steeplechase | SCCD 31297
Special EFX | Confidential | GRP | GRP 95812

Big Noise From Winnetka
Bob Haggart/Ray Bauduc | Jazz Drumming Vol.3(1938-1939) | Fenn Music | FJD 2703
Chris Barber's Jazz And Blues Band | Chris Barber:40 Years Jubilee Concert | Storyville | 4990013
Henry Mancini And His Orchestra | The Blues And The Beat | Fresh Sound Records | ND 74409
Terry Lightfoot And His Band | Stardust | Upbeat Jazz | URCD 104
The Royal Air Force HQ Bomber Command Sextet | RAF HQ Bomber Command Sextet | Celebrity | CYCD 74508

Big Oak Basin
Humphrey Lyttelton And His Band | Take It From The Top-A Dedication To Duke Ellington | Black Lion | BLCD 760516

Big 'P'
Cannonball Adderley Quintet | The Cannonball Adderley Collection Vol.5:At The Lighthouse | Landmark | CAC 1305-2(882344)
Jimmy Heath And His Orchestra | Fast Company | Milestone | M 47025

Big Paul
Kenny Burrell-John Coltrane Quintet | Kenny Burrell & John Coltrane | New Jazz | NJSA 8276-2
Kenny Burrell & John Coltrane | Original Jazz Classics | OJC20 300-2
Cannonball Adderley Quintet | Julian Cannonball Adderlry: Salle Pleyel/Olympia | Laserlight | 36126

Big Pea
Bonobo Club | Bonobo Club | PAO Records | PAO 10690

Big Pow Wow-
Eric Alexander Quartet | Nightlife In Tokyo | Milestone | MCD 9330-2

Big R.C.
Cannon's Jug Stompers | Memphis Blues 1928-1930 | RCA | 2126409-2

Big Red
Count Basie And His Orchestra | Hall Of Fame | Verve | MV 2645 IMS

Big Red Peaches
Herb Ellis Quintet | Nothing But The Blues | Verve | 521674-2

Big Red's Boogie Woogie
Arnett Cobb Quartet | Arnett Cobb Is Back | Progressive | PRO 7037 IMS

Big Schlepp
Johnny Hodges Orchestra | Duke Ellington And Johnny Hodges Plus Others | Verve | 2304417 IMS

Big Shoe
Jimmy Bruno Trio | Sleight Of Hand | Concord | CCD 4532

Big Six
Jay Anderson Sextet | Local Color | dmp Digital Music Productions | CD 507

Big Sky
Michael Davis Group | Midnight Crossing | Lipstick Records | LIP 890035

Big Spender
Michael Formanek Septet | Low Profile | Enja | ENJ-8050 2

Big Stockings
Billie Holiday | My Greatest Songs | MCA | MCD 18767

Big Stuff
Count Basie And His Orchestra | En Concert Avec Europe 1 | Laserlight | 710706/07
Gil Evans And Ten | Gil Evans And Ten | Original Jazz Classics | OJC 346(P 7120)
Gil Evans And Ten | Prestige | PRSA 7120-6
Milt Jackson With The Count Basie Orchestra | Milt Jackson + Count Basie + The Big Band Vol.1 | Pablo | 2310822-2
Miriam Klein And Her Allstars | Ladylike-Miriam Klein Sings Billie Holiday | MPS | 523379-2

Big Swing Face
Kenny Wheeler Sextet | Uncovered Heart | Sunnyside | SSC 1048 D

Big Time
Harold Mabern Trio | Lookin' On The Bright Side | DIW | DIW 614 CD

Big Top
Music Revelation Ensemble | Elec.Jazz | DIW | DIW 839 CD

Big Top-
Lester Young And His Orchestra | It Don't Mean A Thing (If It Ain't Got That Swing) | Verve | MV 2685 IMS

Big Yellow Taxi
The New Orleans Spiritualettes | I Believe | Sound Of New Orleans | SONO 6012

Biggie's Ride
Dabiré Gabin | Kontômé | Nueva Records | IN 816

Big'n And The Bear
Clark Terry-Red Mitchell Duo | Jive At Five | Enja | 6042-2

Bigos
Rich Perry Quartet | Hearsay | Steeplechase | SCCD 31515

Biji
Ulf Meyer & Martin Wind Group | Kinnings | Storyville | STCD 8374
Ralph Burns And His Ensemble | Bijou | Fresh Sound Records | FSR 2014(Bethlehem BCP 68)

Bijou
Woody Herman And His Orchestra | Compact Jazz: Woody Herman | Verve | 835319-2 PMS
Woody Herman And The New Thundering Herd | The 40th Anniversary Carnegie Hall Concert | RCA | 2159151-2

Bijou(Rhumba A La Jazz)
Woody Herman's First Herd | This Is Jazz:Woody Herman | CBS | CK 65040

Bijoy The Poodle
Hilaria Kramer 6 | Trigon | SPLASC(H) Records | H 191

Biko In Bonn
Louis Hayes-Woody Shaw Quintet | Swiss Radio Days Jazz Series Vol.5:Louis Hayes-Woody Shaw Quintet | TCB Records | TCB 02052

Bilbao
Gil Evans Orchestra | The Great Arrangers | MCA | IA 9340/2
Dave Douglas Quintet | Convergence | Soul Note | 121316-2

Bilbao Song
Gil Evans Orchestra | Out Of The Cool | Impulse(MCA) | 951186-2
Out Of The Cool | CTI Records | PDCTI 1114-2
Rias Big Band Berlin + Strings | Weill | Mons Records | MR 874347

Bild An Der Wand
Henning Berg Quartet | Minnola | Jazz Haus Musik | JHM 0127 CD

Bilder Einer Umstellung
Blaufrontal | Blaufrontal | Jazz Haus Musik | JHM 0037 CD

Bilder,Köpfe,Gesichte
Paul Eßer-Gerd Dudek-Ali Haurand-Jiri Strivin | Jazz Und Lyrik:Schinderkarren Mit Buffet | Konnex Records | KCD 5108

Bilderfluß:
Brigitte Dietrich-Joe Haider Jazz Orchestra | Consequences | JHM Records | JHM 3624

TITELVERZEICHNIS

Bilein
Don Menza And The Joe Haider Trio | Bilein | JHM Records | JHM 3608
Joe Haider Trio | Grandfather's Garden | JHM Records | JHM 3619
Ivan Lins Group | Montreux Jazz Festival | ACT | 9001-2

Bill
Greetje Kauffeld Trio | The Song Is You | Munich Records | BM 150258
Morgana King And Her Band | A Fine Romance | Verve | 523827-2
Shorty Rogers And His Giants | Martians Stay Home | Atlantic | 50714

Bill B.
Cal Tjader Sextet | Black Hawk Nights | Fantasy | FCD 24755-2
Adrian Bentzon's Jazzband | The Golden Years Of Revival Jazz,Vol.4 | Storyville | STCD 5509

Bill Bailey Won't You Please Come Home
Alvin Alcorn Band With George Lewis | George Lewis With Red Allen-The Circle Records | American Music | AMCD-71
Charlie Love Jazz Band | Kid Sheik With Charlie Love And His Cado Jazz Band | 504 Records | 504CD 21
Chris Barber Original Jazzband Of 1954 | Chris Barber:40 Years Jubilee Concert | Storyville | 4990013
Chris Barber-Barry Martin Band | Collaboration | GHB Records | BCD 40
Chubby Jacksons Big Three Plus | Jazz From Then Till Now | Fresh Sound Records | FSR 504(Everest LPBR 5041)
Duke Ellington And His Orchestra | The Duke Live In Santa Monica Vol.2 | Queen-Disc | 070
Firehouse Five Plus Two | Dixieland Favorites | Good Time Jazz | FCD 60-008
George Lewis And His New Orleans Jazzband | Sounds Of New Orleans Vol.7 | Storyville | STCD 6014
Kid Ory's Creole Jazz Band | Kid Ory:Creole Classics 1944-1947 | Naxos Jazz | 8.120587 CD
Lizzie Miles With The George Lewis Band | Lizzie Miles | American Music | AMCD-73
Louis Armstrong And His All Stars | The Best Live Concert | Festival | ???
Monty Sunshine's Jazz Band | South | Timeless | CD TTD 583

Bill Coleman Blues
Bill Coleman-Django Reinhardt Duo | Django Reinhardt 1910-1953 | Jazztime(EMI) | 790560-2

Bill Evans
Lyle Mays Trio | Fictionary | Geffen Records | GED 24521

Bill Evans-Eddie Gomez
David Fathead Newman Sextet | Fathead:Ray Charles Presents David Newman | Atlantic | 8122-73708-2

Bill For Bennie
John Scofield Septet | Gracy Under Pressure | Blue Note | 798167-2

Bill Street Blues
Bill Coleman Quintet | Dicky Wells & Bill Coleman In Paris | Affinity | CD AFS 1004

Bill,Budd And Butter
Don Sebesky Orchestra | I Remember Bill-A Tribute To Bill Evans | RCA | 2668929-2

Billboard March
Klaus Treuheit Trio | Steinway Afternoon | clearaudio | 42016 CD

Billets Doux
Quintet Du Hot Club De France | Swing '35 -'39 | Eclipse | ECM 2051

Billi
Richard Galliano | Concert Inédits | Dreyfus Jazz Line | FDM 36606-2

Billie-Doo
Thad Jones Quintet | Magnificent Thad Jones | Blue Note | 300109(1527)

Billie's Blues
Billie Holiday And Her All Stars | The Billie Holiday Song Book | Verve | 823246-2
Billie Holiday And Her Band | Billie Holiday Broadcast Performances Vol.1 | ESP Disk | ESP 3002-2
Billie Holiday With Eddie Heywood And His Orchestra | Billie Holiday:The Complete Commodore Recordings | GRP | AFS 1019-8
Billie Holiday With The Mal Waldron Trio | Billie Holiday 1948-1959 | Royal Jazz | RJD 508

Billie's Blues(aka I Love My Man)
Billie Holiday With The JATP All Stars | Jazz At The Philharmonic:Best Of The 1940's Concerts | Verve | 557534-2
Billie Holiday With Eddie Heywood And His Orchestra | Billie Holiday:The Complete Commodore Recordings | GRP | AFS 1019-8

Billie's Bossa
Albert Ayler Quartet | My Name Is Albert Ayler | Black Lion | BLCD 760211

Billie's Bounce
Art Pepper-George Cables Duo | Art Pepper:The Complete Galaxy Recordings | Galaxy | 16GCD 1016-2
Goin' Home | Original Jazz Classics | GXY 5143
Buddy Rich Septet | Tuff Dude | Denon Compact Disc | 33C38-7972
Charlie Parker's Beboppers | The Savoy Recordings 1 | Savoy | 650107(881907)
Count Basie Jam Session | Count Basie Jam Session At The Montreux Jazz Festival 1975 | Original Jazz Classics | OJC20 933-2(2310750)
Count Basie Sextet | The Best Of Count Basie | Pablo | 2405408-2
Eddie Bert With The Hank Jones Trio | Musician Of The Year | Savoy | SV 0183(MG 12015)
Ella Fitzgerald With The Tommy Flanagan Trio | Bluella:Ella Fitzgerald Sings The Blues | Pablo | 2310960-2
The Montreux '77 Collection | Pablo | 2620107
Frank Morgan Quartet | Yardbird Suite | Original Jazz Classics | OJCCD 1060-2(C 14045)
Gary Bartz-Sonny Fortune Quintet | Alto Memories | Verve | 523268-2
George Benson Quintet | Blue Benson | Polydor | 2391242 IMS
George Wallington - Phil Woods Quintet | Leonard Feather Presents Bop | Polydor | MP 2333 IMS
J.J.Johnson & Stan Getz With The Oscar Peterson Quartet | A Life In Jazz:A Musical Biography | Verve | 535119-2
Jam Session | Jam Session Vol.2 | Steeplechase | SCCD 31523
James Moody And His Band | Moody's Blues | Vogue | 655016
John Lewis-Hank Jones Duo | An Evening With Two Grand Pianos | Little David | LD 59657
Kirk Lightsey Quartet | Everything Is Changed | Sunnyside | SSC 1020 D
Louis Stewart-Martin Taylor | Acoustic Guitar Duets | Jardis Records | JRCD 9613
Mal Waldron Trio | You And The Night And The Muisc | Paddle Wheel | K 28P 6272
Martin Taylor Trio | Skye Boat | Concord | CJ 184
Michel Petrucciani/Niels-Henning Orsted-Pedersen | Michel Petrucciani:Concert Inédits | Dreyfus Jazz Line | FDM 36607-2
Oscar Peterson And His Trio | Encore At The Blue Note | Telarc Digital | CD 83356
Oscar Peterson Trio | En Concert Avec Europe 1 | Laserlight | 710443/48
Red Garland Quintet | Saying Something | Prestige | P 24090
Shelly Manne Two | The Three & The Two | Original Jazz Classics | OJCCD 172-2(C 3584)
Stan Getz Orchestra | Heart Place | Memo Music | HDJ 4025
The Metronome All Stars | Metronome All-Stars 1956 | Verve | MV 2510 IMS

Billie's Bounce-
Phineas Newborn Jr. Trio | Tivoli Encounter | Storyville | STCD 8221
Charlie Parker's Reboppers | The Complete Savoy Studio Sessions | Savoy | 886421

Billie's Heart
Billie & Dee Dee Pierce | De De Pierce With Billie Pierce In Binghampton,NY,Vol.2 | American Music | AMCD-80

Billows Of Rhythm
Jessica Williams | Intuition | Jazz Focus | JFCD 010

Bill's Blues
Bill Smith With The Enrico Pieranunzi Trio | Sonorities | EdiPan | NPG 801

Bill's Mill
Count Basie And His Orchestra | 100 Ans De Jazz:Count Basie | RCA | 2177831-2
Count Basie-Basie's Basement | RCA | ???
The Indispensable Count Basie | RCA | ND 89758

Billumba-Palo Congo
Ella Fitzgerald And Her Famous Orchestra | Ella Fitzgerald:The Early Years-Part 2 | GRP | GRP 26232

Billy Bauer's Tune
Billy Byers' Jazz Workshop | The Jazz Workshop | Fresh Sound Records | NL 46046(RCA LPM 1269)

Billy Boy
Oscar Peterson Trio | The Sound Of The Trio | Verve | 543321-2
The Trio-Live From Chicago | Verve | 823008-2
Red Garland Trio | Jazz Piano Vol.2 | CBS | 486639-2
Sahib Shihab Quintet | Conversations | Black Lion | BLCD 760169

Billy Boy's Blues
Marilyn Crispell-Gerry Hemingway Duo | Marilyn Crispell And Gerry Hemingway Duo | Knitting Factory Works | KFWCD 117

Billy Goat Stomp
Jelly Roll Morton's Red Hot Peppers | The Complete Jelly Roll Morton-Vol.1/2 | RCA | ND 89768

Billy Highstreet Samba
Bill Jennings-Leo Parker Quintet | Billy In The Lion's Den | Swingtime(Contact) | ST 1025

Billy The Bowl
Horstmann-Wiedmann-Danek | Billy The Kid | Factory Outlet Records | FOR 2001-3 CD

Billy The Kid
Manfred Christl Farnbach-Oliver Spieß Group | Groovin' | clearaudio | 42021 CD

Billy's Bounce
Ron McClure Quintet | Closer To Your Tears | Steeplechase | SCCD 31413

Bim Bom
Joao Gilberto Trio | Getz/Gilberto-Recorded Live At Carnegie Hall | CTI Records | PDCTI 1129-2
Mind Games | Mind Games Plays The Music Of Stan Getz & Astrud Gilberto | Edition Collage | EC 515-2
Sadao Watanabe And His Brazilian Friends | Sadao Meets Brazilian Friends | Denon Compact Disc | DC-8557
Tania Maria/Nils-Henning Orsted-Pederson Duo | Tania Maria & Nils-Henning Orsted-Pedersen | Accord | ACV 130010

Bimbo
Ragtime Specht Groove Trio | Mr. Woodpeckers Special | Intercord | 130001

Bimbo Blue
Cannonball Adderley Quintet | Cannonball Adderley:Sophisticated Swing-The EmArCy Small Group Sessions | Verve | 528408-2

Bimini
Jim Hall Trio Feat. Tom Harrell | These Roots | Denon Compact Disc | CY-30002
Michel Petrucciani feat. Jim Hall and Wayne Shorter | Michel Petrucciani:The Blue Note Years | Blue Note | 789916-2
Sun Ra And His Astro-Infinity Arkestra | Atlantis | Evidence | ECD 22067-2

Bimwa Swing
The Sea Ensemble | Manzara | Red Records | VPA 122

Bingo
Airto Moreira/Flora Purim Group | Jazz Unlimited | IN+OUT Records | 7017-2
Eddie Lockjaw Davis Quintet | Jaws In Orbit | Original Jazz Classics | OJCCD 322-2(P 7171)

Bingo Domingo
Eddie Lockjaw Davis-Johnny Griffin Quintet | Live At Minton's | Prestige | P 24099

BingoIngo
Per Gudmundson-Ale Möller-Lene Willemark | Frifot | ECM | 1690(557653-2)

Bingsjö Stora Langdans-
Darrell Grant Quartet | Black Art | Criss Cross | Criss 1087

Binky's Beam
Rabih Abou-Khalil Group | Yara | Enja | ENJ-9360 2

Bint El Bahr
Kühn/Nauseef/Newton/Tadic | Let's Be Generous | CMP Records | CMP CD 53

Biography
Mick Goodrick Trio | Biorhythms | CMP Records | CMP CD 46

Bioy
Stanley Cowell Sextet | Setup | Steeplechase | SCCD 31349

Bird
Philly Joe Jones Septet | Drum Song | Milestone | GXY 5153

Bird Alone
James Weiman Trio | People Music | TCB Records | TCB 96302

Bird Brain
Charles Mingus Group | Mingus Ah Um | CBS | CK 65512

Bird Calls
Charles Mingus Septet | Charles Mingus:The Complete 1959 Columbia Recordings | CBS | C3K 65145
Charles Mingus Sextet | Nostalgia In Times Square/The Immortal 1959 Sessions | CBS | 88337

Bird Calls(alt.take)
Liane Carroll Quartet | Dolly Bird | Ronnie Scott's Jazz House | JHCD 051

Bird Day
Bob Rockwell Trio | The Bob Rockwell Trio | Steeplechase | SCS 1242

Bird Feathers
Paul Motian Electric Bebop Band | Europe | Winter&Winter | 910063-2
Eddie Daniels Group | To Bird With Love | GRP | GRP 95442

Bird Flight
Charlie Haden Quartet With Orchestra | American Dreams | Verve | 064096-2

Bird Food
Denny Zeitlin-Charlie Haden Duo | Time Remembers One Time Once | ECM | 1239
Joe Lovano-Gonzalo Rubalcaba | Flying Colors | Blue Note | 856092-2
Ornette Coleman Quartet | Change Of The Century | Atlantic | 7567-81341-2
Beauty Is A Rare Thing:Ornette Coleman-The Complete Atlantic Recordings | Atlantic | 8122-71410-2
Ryan Kisor Quartet | Power Source | Criss Cross | Criss 1196

Bird In The High Room
Roger Hanschel/Gabriele Hasler | Go In Green | Jazz Haus Musik | JHM 0073 CD

Bird Jet
Teddy Edwards Quintet | Teddy Edwards:Steady With Teddy 1946-1948 | Cool & Blue | C&B-CD 115

Bird Medley:
Charley Patton | Founder Of The Delta Blues | Yazoo | YAZ 1020

Bird Of Paradise
Charlie Parker Quintet | Live At Carnegie Hall | Bandstand | BDCD 1518
Sadao Watanabe With The Great Jazz Trio | Bird Of Paradise | Flying Disk | VJJ 6017

Bird Out Of Cage
Chris Barber's Jazz Band | Trad Tavern | Philips | 838397-2 PMS

Bird Song
Ingrid Sertso/Karl Berger Group | Jazz Dance | ITM Records | ITM 1427
Tommy Flanagan Trio | Let's Play The Music Of Thad Jones | Enja | ENJ-8040 2

Bird Talk
Ellen Christi With Menage | Live At Irving Plaza | Soul Note | SN 1097

Bird World War
Leroy Jenkins Quintet | Leroy Jenkins Live! | Black Saint | 120122-2

Birdboy
New England Ragtime Ensemble | The Art Of The Rag | GM Recordings | GM 3018 CD(882950)

Birdland
Weather Report With The Manhattan Transfer | In Performance At The Playboy Jazz Festival | Elektra | MUS 96.0298-1

Birdland After Dark
Buck Clayton-Buddy Tate Quintet | Kansas City Nights | Prestige | P 24040

Birdland Betty
Bud Powell Trio | Planet Jazz:Bud Powell | Planet Jazz | 2152064-2

Birdland Blues
Time Was | Bluebird | ND 86367

Birdlike
Ryan Kisor Quartet | Battle Cry | Criss Cross | Criss 1145

Birds
Tomato Kiss | Tomato Kiss | Nabel Records:Jazz Network | CD 4624
Zbigniew Seifert | Solo Violin | MRC | 066-45088

Birds And Flies
Marilyn Lerner Group | Birds Are Returning | Jazz Focus | JFCD 022

Birds At Dawn
Wolfgang Schlüter-Christoph Spendel Duo | Dualism | MPS | 68285

Bird's Eye
Sonny Stitt Quartet | Sonny Stitt With The New Yorkers | Fresh Sound Records | FSR 570(Roost 2226)

Birds In Springtime Gone By
Joe Maneri-Joe Morris-Mat Maneri | Three Men Walking | ECM | 1597

Bird's In The Belfry
Friedeman Graef-Achim Goettert | Saxoridoo | FMP | OWN-90010

Bird's Nest Bound
Charlie Parker Quartet | Charlie Parker On Dial, Vol.2 | Spotlite | SPJ 102

Birds Of A Feather
Gene Krupa And His Orchestra | Gene Krupa Plays Gerry Mulligan Arrangements | Verve | 2304430 IMS

Birds Of A Feather-
Taku Sugimoto | Oposite | HatNOIR | 802

Birds Of Paradise
Marco Cerletti Group | Random And Providence | VeraBra Records | CDVBR 2039-2
Nils Petter Molvaer Group | Elegy For Africa | Nabel Records:Jazz Network | CD 4678

Birds Of Passage
Evan Parker-Hans Koch | Duets,Dithyrambisch | FMP | CD 19/20

Bird's Perspective
Max Roach Double Quartet | Easy Winners | Soul Note | 121109-2

Bireli
Bireli Lagrene Group | A Tribute To Django Reinhardt | Jazzpoint | JP 1061 CD
Bireli Lagrene Ensemble | Routs To Django-Live At The 'Krokodil' | Jazzpoint | JP 1056 CD

Bireli Blues 1979
Routes To Django & Bireli Swing '81 | Jazzpoint | JP 1055 CD
Bireli Lagrene | Bireli Lagrene 'Highlights' | Jazzpoint | JP 1027 CD

Bireli Hi Gogoro
Bireli Lagrene Ensemble | Bireli Swing '81 | Jazzpoint | JP 1009 CD
Routes To Django & Bireli Swing '81 | Jazzpoint | JP 1055 CD
Routs To Django-Live At The 'Krokodil' | Jazzpoint | JP 1056 CD

Bireli Swing 1979
Routes To Django & Bireli Swing '81 | Jazzpoint | JP 1055 CD
Bireli Lagrene Group | Bireli Lagrene 'Highlights' | Jazzpoint | JP 1027 CD
Piirpauke | Birgi Bühtüi | JA & RO | 004(08-4104)

Birkelunden
JATP All Stars | The Exciting Battle-JATP Stockholm '55 | Pablo | 2310713-2

Birk's Works
Bob James Trio | Bold Conceptions | Verve | 557454-2
Dave Pike With The Cedar Walton Trio | Pike's Groove | Criss Cross | Criss 1021
Dizzy Gillespie And His Orchestra | Dizzy's Diamonds-Best Of The Verve Years | Verve | 513875-2
Dizzy Gillespie Group | New Faces | GRP | GRP 95122
Dizzy Gillespie Quintet | Pleyel Concert 1953 | Vogue | 655608
Dizzy Gillespie Sextet | Live At The Village Vanguard | Blue Note | 780507-2
GRP All-Star Big Band | All Blues | GRP | GRP 98002
Jay Clayton And Her Quartet | Live At Jazz Alley | ITM-Pacific | ITMP 970065
Milt Jackson Septet | Bebop | East-West | ???
Red Garland Quintet | Soul Junction | Original Jazz Classics | OJCCD 481-2
John Coltrane-The Prestige Recordings | Prestige | 16 PCD 4405-2
Red Garland Quintet feat.John Coltrane | Jazz Junction | Prestige | P 24023

Birkshire Blues
Roland Kirk Quartet | Rahsaan/The Complete Mercury Recordings Of Roland Kirk | Mercury | 846630-2
Ethel Waters And Her Band | Ethel Waters 1929-1939 | Timeless | CBC 1-007

Birmingham Bounce
Dick Wellstood | Live at The Sticky Wicket | Arbors Records | ARCD 19188

Birmingham Papa
Frisco Syncopators | Firehouse Stomp | Stomp Off Records | CD 1245

Birth Death Regeneration
Quincy Jones And His Orchestra | The Birth Of A Band | Fontana | 6430130

Birth Of A Butterfly
Jaco Pastorius Groups | Holiday For Pans | Sound Hills | SSCD 8001

Birth Of Janet
Sandor Szabo | Gaia And Aries | Acoustic Music Records | 319.1146.2

Birth Of The Blues
Earl Hines | Live In Milano 1966 | Nueva Records | JU 315

Birth Of The Cool(Theme)
Catch Up | Catch Up II | Calig | 30615

Birthday Blues
Scapes | Changes In Time | Timeless | CD SJP 361

Birthday With Oliver
Klaus Ignatzek Group | Live In Switzerland | Nabel Records:Jazz Network | LP 4627

Birthdays
Arcado String Trio | Live In Europe | Avant | AVAN 058

Bismillah
Don Cherry Quartet | Complete Communion | Blue Note | 522673-2

Bismillah-
Maurice McIntyre Ensemble | Humility In The Light Of The Creator | Delmark | 900252 AO

Bit Bytes Bugs
Billy Taylor Trio With Candido | The Billy Taylor Trio With Candido | Original Jazz Classics | OJCCD 015-2(P 7051)

Bit Of Blue
Joey Baron Quartet | We'll Soon Find Out | Intuition Records | INT 3515-2

Bit O'Water
Babamadu | Babamadu | Enja | 9093-2

Bitches Brew
Miles Davis Group | Live At The Fillmore East | CBS | C2K 65139
Live At The Fillmore East | CBS | C2K 65139
Miles Davis Quintet | Paraphernalia | JMY(Jazz Music Yesterdays) | JMY 1013-2

Bitches Brew-
Miles Davis Group | Live At The Fillmore East | CBS | C2K 65139
Miles Davis Sextet | Black Beauty-Miles Davis At Filmore West | CBS | C2K 65138
Charlie Rouse Band | Two Is One | Strata East Records | 660.51.012

Bite
Michel Petrucciani Quintet | Michel Petrucciani Live | Blue Note | 780589-2
Steve Swallow Group | Real Book | Watt | XtraWatt/7(521637-2)

Bite Your Grandmother
John Zorn Group | Masada One | DIW | DIW 888 CD

Bitin'
Gijs Hendriks Quartet | Print Collection | yvp music | 3012

Bits And Pieces

Wolfgang Fuchs | Solos & Duets | FMP | OWN-90004
Bits For Bitz
Peter Lehel Quartet | Heavy Rotation | Satin Doll Productions | SDP 1024-1 CD
Bits Of Blues
Ernst Jandl Mit Band | Bist Eulen? | Extraplatte | EX 316141
Bitte-meeh!
Giorgio Gaslini Trio | Schumann Reflections | Soul Note | SN 1120
Bitter Funeral Beer
Rabih Abou-Khalil Quartet | Bitter Harvest | MMP-Records | 170884
Bitter Street
David Hazeltine Quartet | A World For Her | Criss Cross | Criss 1170
Bitter Sweet Waltz
Extempore | Bitternis | Jazz Haus Musik | JHM 01
Bittersweet
Buddy Johnson And His Orchestra | Walkin' | Official | 6008
Glenn Wilson/Rory Stuart | Bittersweet | Sunnyside | SSC 1057 D
Shpere | Four For All | Verve | 831674-2
Bittersweet Passages
Dave Burrell Trio | High Won-High Two | Black Lion | BLCD 760206
Bitty Ditty
Miles Davis-Milt Jackson Quintet | Milt Jackson Birthday Celebration | Fantasy | FANCD 6079-2
Pepper Adams-Donald Byrd Sextet | Pepper Adams&Donald Byrd:Stardust | Bethlehem | BET 6000-2(BCP 6029)
Philippe Caillat Group | Stream Of Time | Laika Records | LK 92-030
Bivalence
Nico Morelli Trio | Behind The Window | yvp music | CD 3042
Bizarre
Dave King Group | Wildcat | Off The Wall Records | OTW 9501-CD
Bizarre Roundabout
The Hungarian Bop-Art Orchestra | Elephants Of The Milky Way | B&W Present | BW 014
Björnen
John C. Marshall Group | Same Old Story | Traditional Line | TL 1317
Bla
Hans Koch | Uluru | Intakt Records | CD 014
Black
Jon Eardley Quartet | From Hollywood To New York | Original Jazz Classics | OJCCD 1746-2
Black Action Figure
David Murray Quartet | Black & Black | Red Baron | 471577-2
Black And Blind
Al Casey Quintet | Serenade In Blue | Savoy | SV 0232(MG 12057)
Black And Blue
Albert Nicholas With The Henri Chaix Trio | Kornhaus Theater Baden 1969 | Sackville | SKCD2-2045
Carmen McRae With The Red Holloway Quintet | Fine And Mellow | Concord | CCD 4342
Edmond Hall With The Ralph Sutton Group | Edmond Hall With The Ralph Sutton Group | Storyville | STCD 6052
Ethel Waters And Her Band | Ethel Waters 1929-1939 | Timeless | CBC 1-007
Jonah Jones With Dave Pochonet & His All Stars | Jonah Jones | Swing | SW 8408 IMS
Louis Armstrong And His All Stars | Louis Armstrong & The All Stars 1965 | EPM Musique | FDC 5100
The Louis Armstrong Selection | CBS | 467278-2
Louis Armstrong:The Great Chicago Concert 1956 | CBS | C2K 65119
At Symphony Hall,Boston | Laserlight | 15728
Louis Armstrong And His All Stars/Orchestra | St.Louis Blues | Black Lion | 127035
Louis Armstrong And His Orchestra | Jazz Gallery:Louis Armstrong Vol.1 | RCA | 2114166-2
Muggsy Spanier And His Ragtime Band | Jazz Classics In Digital Stereo: Muggsy Spanier 1931 & 1939 | CDS Records Ltd. | REB 687
Planet Jazz:Jazz Trumpet | Planet Jazz | 2169654-2
The Ragtime Band Sessions 1939 | Bluebird | 63 66550-2
Ralph Sutton-Kenny Davern Trio | Ralph Sutton & Kenny Davern | Chaz Jazz | CJ 105
Rod Mason And His Hot Five | Tribute To Fats Waller | Jazz Colours | 874730-2
Roy Eldridge And His Orchestra | Frenchie Roy | Vogue | 655009
Roy Eldridge Septet | Roy Eldridge And His Little Jazz Vol.2 | Vogue | 21559522
Teddy Buckner And His Dixieland Band | A Salute To Louis Armstrong | Dixieland Jubilee | GNPD 505
The World's Greatest Jazzband | Live | Atlantic | 790982-2
Black And Blue(alt.take)
Roy Eldridge And The Jimmy Ryan All Stars | Little Jazz And The Jimmy Ryan All-Stars | Original Jazz Classics | OJCCD 1058-2(DRE 1001)
DeParis Brothers Orchestra | Commodore Classics-De Paris Brothers/Edmond Hall: Jimmy Ryans/Uptown Soc. | Commodore | 6.24296 AG
Black And Blues
Al Jarreau With Band | Jarreau | i.e. Music | 557847-2
Abdullah Ibrahim Quartet | Duke's Memories | String | BLE 233853
Black And Brown Cherries
Dollar Brand Quintet | South Africa | Enja | 5007 Digital (807535)
Black And Tan Fantasy
Cat Anderson & The Ellington All-Stars | Cat Anderson | Swing | SW 8412 IMS
Cat Anderson And His Orchestra | Ellingtonians In Paris | Jazztime(EMI) | 251275-2
Duke Ellington And His Orchestra | The Best Of Duke Ellington | Capitol | 831501-2
Highlights From The Duke Ellington Centennial Edition | RCA | 2663672-2
Duke Ellington:The Complete RCA-Victor Mid-Forties Recordings(1944-1946) | RCA | 2663394-2
Cotton Club Stomp | Naxos Jazz | 8.120509 CD
Carnegie Hall 1943 | Jazz Anthology | JA 5117
Ellington At Newport 1956(Complete) | CBS | CK 64932
Louis Armstrong & Duke Ellington | Avenue | AVINT 1006
Duke Ellington Playing The Blues 1927-1939 | Black & Blue | BLE 59.232 2
Duke Ellington At Tanglewood Vol.1 | Queen-Disc | 049
Duke Ellington Trio | Legends Of The 20th Century | EMI Records | 522048-2
Joe Temperley Quintet | Double Duke | Naxos Jazz | 86032-2
Louis Armstrong-Duke Ellington Group | The Complete Louis Armstrong & Duke Ellington Sessions | Roulette | 793844-2
Ran Blake | Duke Dreams/The Legacy Of Strayhorn-Ellington | Soul Note | SN 1027
Thelonious Monk Trio | The Thelonious Monk Memorial Album | Milestone | MCD 47064-2
Black And Tan Fantasy-
Duke Ellington And His Orchestra | Carnegie Hall Concert December 1947 | Prestige | 2PCD 24075-2
Live In Paris 1959 | Affinity | CD AFS 777
Ella Fitzgerald And Duke Ellington:Cote D'Azure Concerts on Verve | Verve | 539033-2
Duke Ellington At The Alhambra | Pablo | PACD 5313-2
Hot Summer Dance | Red Baron | 469285-2
Black And Tan Fantasy(alt.take)
Louis Armstrong And His All Stars With Duke Ellington | Louis Armstrong-Duke Ellington:The Great Summit-Complete Session | Roulette | 524546-2
Duke Ellington And His Orchestra | Jazz Archives Vol.77:Jabbo Smith-The Complete 1929-1938 Sessions | EPM Musique | 158112
Black And White
Hans Koller Big Band | New York City | MPS | 9813437
New York City | MPS | 68235
Black And White Rag
Lu Watters' Yerba Buena Jazz Band | The San Francisco Style Vol.1:Dawn Club Favorites | Good Time Jazz | GTCD 12001-2
Black Baroness
Charles Mingus Quintet | Changes One & Two | Atlantic | 60108
Black Bats And Poles
Bourbon Street | Jazzpuzzle | GIC | GD 4.1411
Black Beauty
Duke Ellington | The Complete Duke Ellington-Vol. 1 | CBS | CBS 67264
Duke Ellington And His Orchestra | Highlights From The Duke Ellington Centennial Edition | RCA | 2663672-2
Duke Ellington | Bluebird | ND 86641(3)
Black Beauty-
Ruby Braff Trio | Ruby Braff Trio:In Concert | Storyville | 4960543
The Washingtonians | Duke Ellington:Complete Original American Decca Recordings | Definitive Records | DRCD 11196
Black Beauty(part 1-4):
Lillian Boutté And Her Group | You've Gotta Love Pops:Lillian Boutté Sings Louis Armstrong | ART BY HEART | ABH 2005 2
Black Benny
Leadbelly[Huddie Ledbetter] | Huddie Ledbetter | Fantasy | F 24715
Black Bottom Blues
Harmonica Slim Blues Group | Black Bottom Blues | Trix Records | TRIX 3323
Black Bottom Stomp
Jelly Roll Morton's Red Hot Peppers | Planet Jazz Sampler | Planet Jazz | 2152326-2
Planet Jazz:Jelly Roll Morton | Planet Jazz | 2152060-2
The Jelly Roll Morton Centennial-His Complete Victor Recordings | Bluebird | ND 82361
Doctor Jazz | Black & Blue | BLE 59.227 2
Thomas Heberer-Dieter Manderscheid | Chicago Breakdown:The Music Of Jelly Roll Morton | Jazz Haus Musik | JHM 0038 CD
Veterinary Street Jazz Band | Everybody Stomp | Elite Special | 730220
Christy Doran's New Bag With Muthuswamy Balasubramoniam | Black Box | double moon | CHRDM 71022
Black Box
Johnny Hodges And Leon Thomas With The Oliver Nelson Orchestra | 3 Shades Of Blues | RCA | 2147787-2
Black Brown And Beige (Excerpts)
Duke Ellington And His Orchestra | Duke Ellington:Complete Prestige Carnegie Hall 1946-1947 Concerts | Definitive Records | DRCD 11211
Black Brown And Beige:
Carnegie Hall Concert December 1944 | Prestige | 2PCD 24073-2
Duke Ellington | Bluebird | ND 86641(3)
Black Brown And Beige | CBS | CK 65566
Black Brown And Beige | CBS | CK 65566
Black Brown And Beige | CBS | CK 65566
Duke Ellington -Carnegie Hall Concert | Ember | 800851-370(EMBD 2001)
The Indispensable Duke Ellington Vol.11/12 | RCA | 2115524-2
Black Butterfly
Dick Sudhalter Band | Melodies Heard,Melodies Sweet... | Challenge | CHR 70055
Sarah Vaughan And Her Band | Duke Ellington Song Book Two | Pablo | CD 2312116
Sarah Vaughan With Orchestra | Sarah Vaughan Birthday Celebration | Fantasy | FANCD 6090-2
Stan Tracey With Roy Babbington | Plays Duke Ellington | Mole Jazz | Mole 10
Bobby Short Sextet | Songs Of New York | Telarc Digital | CD 83346
Black Byrd
Lightnin' Hopkins | Bluesville: Lightnin' Hopkins | Prestige | 61141
Black Cat
Lightnin Hopkins-A Legend In His Own Time | Anthology of the Blues | AB 5608
Black Cat On The Fence
Rod Mason Band | Dixieland Forever Vol.2 | BELL Records | BLR 89046
Black Coffee
Duke Pearson Trio | Profile | Blue Note | GXK 8212 (84022)
Ella Fitzgerald And Paul Smith | Verve Jazz Masters 46:Ella Fitzgerald-The Jazz Sides | Verve | 527655-2
The Intimate Ella | Verve | 839838-2
Ella Fitzgerald-First Lady Of Song | Verve | 517898-2
Ella Fitzgerald With Gordon Jenkins And His Orchestra | Ella:The Legendary American Decca Recordings | GRP | GRP 46482
Ella Fitzgerald With The Hank Jones Trio | Jazz At The Philharmonic:The Ella Fitzgerald Set | Verve | 815147-1 IMS
International Chicago-Jazz Orchestra | That's A Plenty | JHM Records | JHM 3621
Jacintha With Band And Strings | Lush Life | Groove Note | GRV 1011-2(Gold CD 2011)
Jeanie Lambe And The Danny Moss Quartet | The Blue Noise Session | Nagel-Heyer | CD 052
Jenny Evans And Her Quintet | Gonna Go Fishin' | ESM Records | ESM 9307
Gonna Go Fishin' | Enja | ENJ-9403 2
Phineas Newborn Jr. Trio | Please Send Me Someone To Love | Contemporary | C 7622
Ruth Brown With The Thad Jones-Mel Lewis Orchestra | Fine Brown Frame | Capitol | 781200-2
Sarah Vaughan With The Jimmy Jones Trio | Linger Awhile | Pablo | 2312144-2
Sarah Vaughan With The Joe Lippman Orchestra | Sarah Vaughan:Lover Man | Dreyfus Jazz Line | FDM 36739-2
Sonny Criss Quartet | This Is Criss | Original Jazz Classics | OJCCD 430-2(P 7511)
Jazz In Paris:Saxophones Á Saint-Germain Des Prés | EmArCy | 014060-2
Sonny Criss Quintet | Blues Pour Flirter | Polydor | 2445034 IMS
Black Comedy
Miles Davis Quintet | Miles Davis Quintet 1965-1968 | CBS | C6K 67398
Miles In The Sky | CBS | CK 65684
Black Comedy(alt.take)
Miles Davis Quintet 1965-1968 | CBS | C6K 67398
Cassandra Wilson Group | Blue Light 'Til Dawn | Blue Note | 781357-2
Black Crow
Diana Krall Group | The Girl In The Other Room | Verve | 9862246
Inga Lühning With Trio | Lühning | Jazz Haus Musik | JHM 0111 CD
Mikio Masuda Trio | Black Daffodils | JVC | JVC 9030-2
Black Danube(James Brown In 3-4 Time)
Sax Appeal Saxophone Quartet plus Claudio Fasoli | Giotto | Soul Note | 121309-2
Black Desciples
Jessica Williams | Ain't Misbehavin' | Candid | CCD 79763
Black Diamond
Peter O'Mara Quintet | Back Seat Driver | Enja | 9126-2
Roland Kirk Quartet | Talkin' Verve-Roots Of Acid Jazz:Roland Kirk | Verve | 533101-2
Wayne Shorter Quintet | Introducing Wayne Shorter | Vee Jay Recordings | VJ 007
Black Diamond And Pink Whispers
Eddie Daniels Group | Blackwood | GRP | GRP 95842
Black Elk(Buddy Red Bow)
Alice Moore | St.Louis Girls(1929-1937) | Story Of Blues | CD 3536-2
Black Eyed Peas And Rice
Ernst Höllerhagen And His Band | Ernst Höllerhagen 1942-1948 | Elite Special | 9522001
Black Eyes
Chet Baker Quartet | In Paris Vol.2 | West Wind | WW 2059
Black Eyes(alt.take)
Christian Willisohn Group | Live At Marians | ART BY HEART | ABH 2006 2
Black Fantasy
Lloyd Glenn Quartet | Old Time Shuffle | Black & Blue | BLE 59.077 2
Black Flower
Claude Williamson Trio | La Fiesta | Discovery | DS 862 IMS
Black Forest Myth
Hampton Hawes Trio | Blues For Bud | Black Lion | BLCD 760126
Black Gal
Walter Horton Band | Mumbles Walter Horton:Mouth Harp Maestro | Ace Records | CDCH 252
Black Gammon
Steve Coleman And Metrics | The Way Of The Cipher | Novus | 2131690-2
Black Genghis
Steve Coleman's Music Live In Paris | Novus | 2131691-2
Black Groove
Charles Earland Septet | Charles Earland In Concert | Prestige | PRCD 24267-2
Black Gun
Archie Shepp And His Band | Black Gypsy | America | AM 6099
Black Halo
Henry Threadgill Sextet | Easily Slip Into Another World | RCA | PD 83025(874076)
Black Hills
Amiri Baraka And His Blue Ark | Amiri Baraka:Real Song | Enja | 8098-2
Black Hole
Malachi Thompson's Freebop Band | Freebop Now!(20th Anniversary Of The Freebop Band) | Delmark | DE 506
Black Ice
Lyle Mays | Improvisations For Expanded Piano | Warner | 9362-47284-2
The Jeff Lorber Fusion | Soft Space | Inner City | IC 1056 IMS
Black Inside
Jason Seizer Quartet | Serenity | Acoustic Music Records | 319.1152.2
Black Is The Color Of My True Love's Hair
Geoff Keezer Quartet | World Music | CBS | 472811-2
Joachim Kühn And The Radio Philharmonie Hannover NDR With Jazz Soloists | Europeana | ACT | 9220-2
Joe Sample Group | Invitation | Warner | 9362-45209.2
John Benson Brooks' Orchestra | Folk Jazz U.S.A. | RCA | PM 43767
Johnny Smith Quartet | Johnny Smith And His New Quartet | Fresh Sound Records | FSR-CD 80(882190)
Mike Nock | Talisman | Enja | 3071
Nina Simone | Nina Simone After Hours | Verve | 526702-2
Nina Simone Quartet | Nina Simone-The 60s Vol.3:Work Song | Mercury | 838545-2 PMS
Joe Henderson Sextet | Joe Henderson:The Milestone Years | Milestone | 8MCD 4413-2
Black Is The Color(Of My True Love's Mind)
Paul Bley/Jimmy Giuffre | The Life Of A Trio:Saturday | Owl Records | 014731-2
Black Ivory
Glen Gray And The Casa Loma Orchestra | The Radio Years | London | HMG 5028 AN
Black Knight
Kenny Clarke And His Orchestra | Kenny Clarke | Swing | SW 8411 IMS
Black Lightning
Abdullah Ibrahim-Carlos Ward Duo | Live At Sweet Basil Vol.1 | Black-Hawk | BKH 50204
Black Magic
Rössler/Kühn/Heidepriem/Stefanski Quartet | Coloured | Fusion | 8015
Black Market
Jaco Pastorius Trio | Live In Italy & Honestly | Jazzpoint | JP 1059 CD
James Spaulding Sextet | Songs Of Courage | Muse | MCD 5382
Ake Stan Hasselgard Septet | Young Clarinet | Dragon | DRLP 163
Black Maybe
Mary Johnson | St.Louis Girls(1929-1937) | Story Of Blues | CD 3536-2
Black Minuet-
Joe Henderson And His Orchestra | Black Miracle | Milestone | M 9066
Black Miracle
Guy Cabay Quartet | The Ghost Of McCoy's Castle | B.Sharp Records | CDS 101
Black Moon
David Pritchard Quintet | Light-Year | Inner City | IC 1047 IMS
Black Moonlight-
Jack Hylton And His Orchestra | The Talk Of The Town | Saville Records | SVL 164 IMS
Black Mountain Side
Rahsaan Roland Kirk And His Orchestra | Left & Right | Atlantic | ATL 40235(SD 1518)
Black Myth-
Brian Melvin Trio | Old Voices | Timeless | CD SJP 396
Black Narcissus
Donald Brown | Piano Short Stories | Space Time Records | BG 9601
Frank Morgan All Stars | Reflections | Original Jazz Classics | OJCCD 1046-2(C 14052)
Reflections | Contemporary | CCD 14052-2
Joe Henderson Quintet | Joe Henderson:The Milestone Years | Milestone | 8MCD 4413-2
Tony Purrone Trio | Rascality | Steeplechase | SCCD 31514
Charles Brown | Great Rhythm & Blues-Vol.1 | Bulldog | BDL 1001
Black Night
James Booker | Boogie Woogie And Ragtime Piano Contest | Gold Records | 11035 AS
Black Nightgown
Gerry Mulligan Concert Jazz Band | The Complete Verve Gerry Mulligan Concert Band | Verve | 9860613
En Concert Avec Europe 1 | Laserlight | 710382/83
Black Nile
Cyrille Bugnon Quartet | Southern Perspective | TCB Records | TCB 98302
Jeff 'Tain' Watts Trio | MegaWatts | Sunnyside | SSC 1055 D
Malachi Thompson's Freebop Band | Freebop Now!(20th Anniversary Of The Freebop Band) | Delmark | DE 506
Wayne Shorter Quintet | Night Dreamer | Blue Note | 784173-2
Charles Brown Band | Drifting Blues | Pathe | 1546611(Score SLP 4011)
Black Or White
Cal Tjader's Orchestra | Several Shades Of Jade/Breeze From The East | Verve | 537083-2
Black Orchid
Woody Herman's 2nd Herd | The Herd Rides Again...In Stereo | Evidence | ECD 22010-2
Black Orpheus
Conte Candoli Quartet | Candoli Live | Nagel-Heyer | CD 2024
Dan Faulk Trio | Spirit In The Night | Fresh Sound Records | FSNT 024 CD
Dylan Cramer Quartet | All Night Long | Nagel-Heyer | CD 073
Freddie Hubbard Quartet | Topsy | Enja | ENJ-7025 2
Great Jazz Trio | Standard Collection Vol.2 | Limetree | MCD 0032
Thomas Karl Fuchs Trio | Colours And Standards | Edition Collage | EC 509-2
Wayne Shorter Quintet | Wayning Moments | Vee Jay Recordings | VJ 014
Black Orpheus Suite
Vince Guaraldi-Bola Sete Quartet | Live At El Matador | Original Jazz Classics | OJC 289(F 8371)
Black Out
Joseph Jarman-Don Moye Trio | Black Paladins | Black Saint | BSR 0042
Black Pastels
Jamaaladeen Tacuma Group | Dreamscape | DIW | DIW 904 CD
Black Pearls
John Coltrane Quintet | Black Pearls | Prestige | P 24037
Wallace Roney Quintet | Seth Air | Muse | MCD 5441
Black Polo-Necks
Duke Ellington And His Orchestra | Paris Jazz Party | Affinity | AFF 57
Black Rock Park
Rahsaan Roland Kirk Group | Natural Black Inventions:Roots Strata | Atlantic | ATL 40185(SD 1578)
Black Satin
Miles Davis Group | In Concert | CBS | C2K 65140
Black Satin-
James Williams Sextet | Alter Ego | Sunnyside | SSC 1007(952096)
Black Sea

James Blood Ulmer With The Quartet Indigo | Harmolodic Guitar With Strings | DIW | DIW 878 CD

Black Sheep Blues
Buck Clayton Swing Band | Blues Of Summer | Nagel-Heyer | NH 1011
Howard Alden-Dan Barrett Quintet | Swing Street | Concord | CCD 4349

Black Six Blues
Barbecue Bob | Chocolate To The Bone | Yazoo | YAZ 2005

Black Snake
Barrelhouse Jazzband | 25 Jahre Barrelhouse Jazzband Frankfurt | Intercord | 155030

Black Snake Blues
Victoria Spivey With Buster Bailey's Blues Blasters | Songs We Taught Your Mother | Original Blues Classics | OBCCD 520-2
Blind Lemon Jefferson | Blind Lemon Jefferson-Master Of The Blues | Biograph | BLP 12015

Black Talk
Jimmy Smith Trio | I'm Movin' On | Blue Note | 832750-2
Joachim Kühn & The String Orchestra | Cinemascope/Piano | MPS | 88037-2

Black Temple
Clint Houston Quartet | Inside The Plain Of The Elliptic | Timeless | SJP 132

Black Trees
Steve Gut & The RTB Big Band | Mr.C.T. | Timeless | CD SJP 428

Black Unity
Arnett Cobb With The Red Garland Trio | Blue An Sentimental | Prestige | PCD 24122-2(PR 7227/MV 14)

Black Velvet
Hamiet Bluiett Quartet | Sankofa/Rear Garde | Soul Note | 121238-2

Black Yard Sonata-
Steve Tibbetts Group | Big Map Idea | ECM | 1380

Black Year
Johnny Smith | Legends | Concord | CCD 4616

Black,As In Buhaina
Louie Bellson And His All-Star Orchestra | Duke Ellington:Black, Brown & Beige | Musicmasters | 65096-2

Blackberry Blossoms
Erskine Butterfield | Part-Time Boogie | Harlequin | HQ 2050

Blackbird
Brad Mehldau Trio | The Art Of The Trio Vol.1 | Warner | 9362-46260-2
Dave Valentine Group | The Hawk | GRP | GRP 95152
Horst Faigle's Jazzkrement | Gans Normal | Jazz 4 Ever Records:Jazz Network | J4E 4748
Jaco Pastorius With Orchestra | Word Of Mouth | Warner | 7599-23525-2
Lynne Arriale Trio | Inspiration | TCB Records | TCB 22102
Sabina Sciubba-Paulo Cardoso | VoceBasso | Organic Music | ORGM 9703
Sarah Vaughan And Her Band | Songs Of The Beatles | Atlantic | 16037-2
Sarah Vaughan With Orchestra | Song Of The Beatles | Atlantic | SD 16037
Terri Lyne Carrington Group | Real Life Story | Verve | 837697-2
Vertrauensbildende Maßnahmen | Stadtgarten Series Vol.7 | Jazz Haus Musik | JHM 1007 SER

Blackbird,Bye Bye
Tommy Smith Quartet | Standards | Blue Note | 796452-2

Blacker Black's Revenge
Esther Phillips With Orchestra | The Best Of Esther Phillips | CTI | 63036

Blackhawk Blues
Shelly Manne And His Men | At The Blackhawk Vol.3 | Contemporary | C 7579

Blackjack
Donald Byrd Sextet | Blackjack | Blue Note | 821286-2
Blackjack | Blue Note | 784466-2
Ray Charles And His Orchestra | Yes Indeed! Ray Charles | Atlantic | 50917(SD 8025)
Warne Marsh Quintet | Modern Jazz Gallery | Fresh Sound Records | KXL 5001(252282-1 Kapp)

Blackmail
Sun Ra And His Intergalactic Solar Arkestra | Space Is The Place(Soundtrack) | Evidence | ECD 22070-2

Blacknuss
Craig Harris And Tailgater's Tales | Blackout In The Square Root Of Soul | JMT Edition | 919015-2

Blackout In The Square Root Of Soul
Bobbi Humphrey Group | Bobbi Humphrey:Blue Breakbeats | Blue Note | 494706-2

Blacksmith Blues-
Kazumi Watanabe Quartet | Lonesome Cat | Denon Compact Disc | 38C38-7017

Blackwell's Message
Anliker-Parker-Schmid-Senn-Solothurnmann | September Winds | Creative Works Records | CW CD 1038/39

Blackwood
Eddie Daniels Group | Blackwood | GRP | GRP 95842

Blakey's Blues
Art Blakey And The Jazz Messengers | Blakey's Theme | West Wind | WW 2045

Blamann(Blue Moon)
Lena Willemark-Ale Möller Group | Agram | ECM | 1610

Blamari
Agneta Baumann And Her Quartet | Comes Love... | Touché Music | TMcCD 011

Blame It On My Youth
Anders Lindskog Trio | Fine Together | Touché Music | TMcCD 010
Art Farmer Quintet | Blame It On My Youth | Contemporary | CCD 14042-2
Bucky Pizzarelli-John Pizzarelli Duo | The Complete Guitar Duos(The Stash Sessions) | Stash Records | ST-CD 536(889114)
Juan Tizol With The Nat King Cole Quartet | The Complete After Midnight Sessions | Capitol | 748328-2
Keith Jarrett Trio | The Cure | ECM | 1440(849650-2)
Ken Peplowski Quintet | Double Exposure | Concord | CJ 344
Max Kaminsky Quintet | When Summer Is Gone | Chiaroscuro | CR 176
Paul Kuhn Trio | Blame It On My Youth | Timbre | TRCD 003
Trine-Lise Vaering With The Bobo Stenson Trio And Guests | When I Close My Eyes | Stunt Records | STUCD 19602

Blame It On My Youth-
Ralph Sutton And His Allstars | Echoes Of Spring:The Complete Hamburg Concert | Nagel-Heyer | CD 038
Black Eagle Jazz Band | Black Eagle Jazz Band | Stomp Off Records | CD 1224

Blame It On The Boers
Lennie Tristano | Live At Birdland 1949 | Jazz Records | JR-1 CD

Blanc Sur Blanc
Enrico Rava Quartet | The Pilgrim And The Stars | ECM | 1063(847322-2)

Blancasnow
Enrico Rava Quintet | Easy Living | ECM | 1760(9812050)
Furio Di Castri | Solo | SPLASC(H) Records | HP 04

Blanche Touquatuox
Crane River Jazz Band | The Crane River Jazz Band | Cadillac | SGC/MEL CD 202

Blanket On The Beach
Stanley Turrentine And His Quartet | Pieces Of Dream | Original Jazz Classics | OJCCD 831-2(F 9465)

Blanket On The Beach(alt.take)
Abdullah Ibrahim Trio With The Munich Radio Symphony Orchestra | African Symphony | Enja | ENJ-9410 2

Blanton
String Orchestra | African Suite | TipToe | TIP-888832 2
Peter A. Schmid Trio With Guests | Profound Sounds In An Empty Reservoir | Creative Works Records | CW CD 1033

Blasblues
Archie Shepp Group | Blase | Charly | CD 77

Blau De Nit

Julia Hülsmann Trio | Julia Hülsmann-Marc Muellbauer-Rainer Winch Trio | BIT | 11218

Blau Klang(for Ernst W. Nay)
European Trumpet Summit | European Trumpet Summit | Konnex Records | KCD 5064

Blaublusen
Habarigani | Habarigani | Hat Art | CD 6007

Blaues Lied
Klaus Müller-Ekkehard Rössle | Auf Und Davon | Jazz Haus Musik | JHM 0091 CD

Blaues Wunder
Matthias Schubert Quartet | Blue And Grey Suite | Enja | ENJ-9045 2

Blauwe Sliert
| The Nixa 'Jazz Today' Collection | Lake | LACD 48

Blazing
Ron Affif Quartet | Vierd Blues | Pablo | 2310954-2

Ble
Jon Burr Quartet | In My Own Words | Cymekob | CYK 804-2

Blee Blop Blues
Count Basie And His Orchestra | Basie Rides Again | Verve | MV 2643 IMS

Bleibender Ruhm
M.L.A.Blek | M.L.A. oBlek o | FMP | SAJ 32

Blekete
Duke Ellington And His Orchestra | Up In Duke's Workshop | Original Jazz Classics | OJCCD 633-2(2310815)

Blem
Cuban All Stars | Passaporte | Enja | ENJ-9019 2

Blessed
Paul Chambers Sextet | Paul Chambers-1st Bassman | Vee Jay Recordings | VJ 004
Dave Brubeck Trio & Gerry Mulligan | Live At The Berlin Philharmonie | CBS | 67261

Blessed Assurance
Gene Ammons Quartet | Preachin' | Original Jazz Classics | OJCCD 792-2(P 7270)
Sammy Rimington Band With Thais Clark | Blessed Assurance | SAM Records | SAM CD 001

Blessed Wind
Joice Walton & Blackout With Guests | Downsville Girl | Line Records | LICD 9.01303

Blessing In Disguise
Trilok Gurtu Group | Crazy Saints | CMP Records | CMP CD 66

Blessing The World
Amina Claudine Myers Sextet | Country Girl | Minor Music | 1012

Bleu Et Blue
Irene Schweizer | Many And One Direction | Intakt Records | CD 044

Bleue
Duke Ellington And His Orchestra | A True Collectors Item | Jazz Archive | 90.105-2

Bli-Blip
Duke Ellington And His Famous Orchestra | Harlem Roots-Jazz On Film:The Big Bands | Storyville | SLP 6000
Ella Fitzgerald With The Duke Ellington Orchestra | The Complete Ella Fitzgerald Song Books of Harold Arlen, Irving Berlin, Duke Ellington, George & Ira Gershwin, Jerome Kern, Johnny Mercer, Cole Porter And Rogers & Hart | Verve | 519832-2

Blic
Julia Hülsmann Trio | Julia Hülsmann-Marc Muellbauer-Rainer Winch Trio | BIT | 11218

Blick In Die Welt
Paul Desmond-Gerry Mulligan Quartet | Two Of A Mind | RCA | 2179620-2

Blight Of The Fumble Bee
Mike Westbrook Orchestra | The Orchestra Of Smith's Academy | Enja | ENJ-9358 2

Dlighters
Ted Brown Quintet | In Good Company | Criss Cross | Criss 1020 (835608)

Blind Blake's Rag
Henry Brown-Ike Rogers | Paramount Piano Blues Vol.2(1927-1932) | Black Swan Records | HCD-12012

Blind Date
Larry Schneider Quartet | Blind Date | Steeplechase | SCCD 31317
Ull Möck Trio | How High The Moon | Satin Doll Productions | SDP 1006-1 CD

Blind Faith
Blind Joe Hill One-Man-Blues Band | First Chance | L+R Records | LR 42059

Blind Man, Blind Man
Herbie Hancock Septet | Herbie Hancock:The Complete Blue Note Sixties Sessions | Blue Note | 495569-2
Cantaloupe Island | Blue Note | 829331-2
My Point Of View | Blue Note | 521226-2

Blind Man, Blind Man(alt.take)
Herbie Hancock:The Complete Blue Note Sixties Sessions | Blue Note | 495569-2
Franco Morone | The South Wind | Acoustic Music Records | 319.1115.2

Blind Willie
Last Exit | Best Of Last Exit-Live | Enemy | EMCD 110(03510)

Blinde Kuh
Jimmy Witherspoon And His Band | Midnight Lady Called The Blues | Muse | MCD 5327

Blissed(Selfchatter Mix)
David Fathead Newman Septet | Still Hard Times | Muse | MCD 5283

Blitzkrieg Baby(You Can't Bomb Me)
Una Mae Carlisle Septet | Lester Young:The Complete 1936-1951 Small Group Sessions(Studio Recordings-Master Takes),Vol.6 Rare Items | Blue Moon | BMCD 1006

Blizzard Of Lies
Dave Frishberg Trio | Classics | Concord | CCD 4462

Blocks And Dots
Larry Coryell Group | Larry Coryell+Live From Bahia | CTI Records | CTI 1005-2

Blok
Drei Vom Rhein | Starke Gesten | Mons Records | MR 874782

Bloo Denim
John Wolf Brennan | Text, Context, Co-Text & Co-Co-Text | Creative Works Records | CW CD 1025-2

Bloo(m)himwhom
Future Shock | It's Great | BVHAAST | 067(807058)

Blood
Pastorius-Metheny-Bley-Ditmas | Jaco | Jazz Door | JD 1286
Mal Waldron Trio | Mal, Dance And Soul | Tutu Records | 888102-2*

Blood And Guts
James Blood Ulmer With The Quartet Indigo | Harmolodic Guitar With Strings | DIW | DIW 878 CD

Blood Count
Charles Lloyd Quintet | Lift Every Voice | ECM | 1832/33(018783-2)
Chet Baker-Stan Getz Quintet | The Stockholm Concerts | Verve | 537555-2
Duke Ellington And His Orchestra | Highlights From The Duke Ellington Centennial Edition | RCA | 2663672-2
And His Mother Called Him Bill | RCA | 2125762-2
Hank Jones Trio | The Oracle | EmArCy | 846376-2 PMS
Jim Snidero Quintet | Mixed Bag | Criss Cross | Criss 1032
John Gross-Putter Smith-Larry Koonse | Three Play | Nine Winds Records | NWCD 0133
Norris Turney Quartet | Big Sweet N' Blue | Mapleshade | 02632
Stan Getz Quartet | Soul Eyes | Concord | CCD 4783
Vic Juris Quartet | Moonscape | Steeplechase | SCCD 31402

Blood Duster
Herlin Riley Quintet | Watch What You're Doing | Criss Cross | Criss 1179

Bloody Mary
Buddy Rich Orchestra | Compact Jazz: Buddy Rich | Verve | 823295-2 PMS

Bloody Nose
Hot Lips Page Orchestra | The Black Swing Tradition | Savoy | SJL 2246 (801854)

Blook's Dues
Khan Jamal Trio | The Traveller | Steeplechase | SCCD 31217

Bloomdido
Charlie Parker Quintet | Charlie Parker: The Verve Years (1948-50) | Verve | 2-2501 IMS
Compact Jazz: Charlie Parker | Verve | 833288-2
Ultimate Dizzy Gillespie | Verve | 557535-2
Charlie Parker:The Best Of The Verve Years | Verve | 527815-2
Charlie Parker:Bird's Best Bop On Verve | Verve | 527452-2
Charlie Parker-Dizzy Gillespie Quintet | Thelonious Monk:Misterioso | Dreyfus Jazz Line | FDM 36743-2
Christopher Hollyday Quintet | Christopher Hollyday | Novus | PD 83055
Hank Jones Trio | A Jazz Par 91 Project | Storyville | STCD 4180
Super Sax & L.A.Voices | Supersax & L.A.Voices Vol.2 | CBS | FC 39925

Bloomination
Luther Allison Blues Band | Love Me Mama | Delmark | 900202 AO

Bloos For Baby B
Zoot Sims Quartet | The Best Of Zoot Sims | Pablo | 2405406-2

Blooz...First Thaingh 'Dis Moanin'
Billy Usselton Sextet | Modern Jazz Gallery | Fresh Sound Records | KXL 5001(252282-1 Kapp)

Blossom
The Crossover Ensemble | The River:Image Of Time And Life | dacapo | DCCD 9434
George Winston | Winter Into Spring | Windham Hill | 34 11019-2

Blow
Jan Garbarek Quartet | Afric Pepperbird | ECM | 1007 (2301007)

Blow By Blow
Duke Ellington And His Orchestra | Harlem | Pablo | 2308245-2

Blow By Blow-
Verve Jazz Masters 20:Introducing | Verve | 519853-2
Johnny Frigo Sextet | I Love John Frigo...He Swings | Mercury | 9861061

Blow Fiddle Blow
Vital Information | Where We Come From | Intuition Records | INT 3218-2

Blow Fish Blues
Billy Butler Quintet | Guitar Soul | Original Jazz Classics | OJC 334(P 7734)

Blow For The Crossing
Reverend Blind Gary Davis | Gospel, Blues And Street Songs | Original Blues Classics | OBCCD 524-2(RLP 148)

Blow My Friend
Klaus Lenz Band | Aufbruch | View | VS 002 IMS

Blow That Man Down
Jack Teagarden And His Orchestra | A Standard Library Of Jazz Vol. 2 | Storyville | SLP 704
Count Basie And His Orchestra | Lester Leaps In-Vol.2 1939/1940 | CBS | CBS 88668

Blow Top Blues
Lionel Hampton And His Septet | Jazz Gallery:Lionel Hampton Vol.1 | RCA | 2114170-2

Blow Wind Blow
Muddy Waters Blues Band | Unreleased In The West-2 | Moon Records | MCD 017-2

Blow Your Mind
Ray Anderson Alligatory Band | Don't Mow Your Lawn | Enja | ENJ-8070 2

Blow Your Own Horn
Illinois Jacquet And His Orchestra | Illinois Jacquet:All Stars Studio Recordings 1945-1947(Master Takes) | Blue Moon | BMCD 1011

Blowin' In The Wind
Stan Getz With Strings And Voices | Reflections | Verve | 523322-2
Ed Barron And His Orchestra | Clyde Bernhardt:The Complete Recordings Vol.2 (1949-1953) | Blue Moon | BMCD 6017

Blowin' Omni
Chuck Darling | Harmonica Blues | Yazoo | YAZ 1053

Blowin' The Blues Away
Horace Silver Quintet | Blowin' The Blues Away | Blue Note | 495342-2
Horace Silver Retrospective | Blue Note | 495576-2
Paul Williams Orchestra | Paul Williams:The Complete Recordings Vol.2 (1949-1952) | Blue Moon | BMCD 6021

Blowing Up A Storm
Woody Herman's 2nd Herd | The Herd Rides Again...In Stereo | Evidence | ECD 22010-2

Blown Chairs
John Zorn Group | Spillane | Nonesuch | 7559-79172-2

Blowout-
Ax Genrich Group | Psychedelic Guitar | ATM Records | ATM 3809-AH

Blow-Up
Galliano-Portal | Blow Up | Dreyfus Jazz Line | FDM 36589-2
Guido Manusardi Trio | Introduction | Penta Flowers | CDPIA 009
Richard Galliano-Michel Portal | Concert Inédits | Dreyfus Jazz Line | FDM 36606-2

Blu Gnu
Orchestra Vielharmonie | More Like Brahms | Blackbird Records | BD 40308

Blue
Earl Hines And His Orchestra | Earl Hines Vol.1-South Side Swing | MCA | 1311
John Abercrombie Trio | Gateway 2 | ECM | 1105(847323-2)
Klaus Kreuzeder & Franz Benton | Big little Gigs: First Takes Live | Trick Music | TM 0112 CD
Lisa Bassenge Trio | A Sight, A Song | Minor Music | 801100
Lisa Bassenge Trio With Guests | A Sight, A Song | Minor Music | 801100
Loose Tubes | Jazzbühne Berlin '87 | Repertoire Records | REPCD 4916-WZ
Parallel Realities | Parallel Realities:Live... | Jazz Door | JD 1251/52
Terje Rypdal And The Chasers | Blue | ECM | 1346(831516-2)
Uli Wewelsiep And His Septet | ...My Favourite Stories | Aho-Recording | CD 1002
Hans Koller & The International Brass Company | The Horses | L+R Records | LR 40008

Blue Afternoon
Gloria Lynne And Her Band/Orchestra | Starry Eyes | Verve | 539777-2

Blue Ammons
Lonnie Johnson With Elmer Snowden | Lonnie Johnson With Elmer Snowden Vol.2:Blues Ballads And Jumpin' Jazz | Original Blues Classics | OBCCD 570-2

Blue And Broken Hearted
Eddie Condon All Stars | Jazz Festival Vol. 1 | Storyville | 4960733
Harry Gold And His Famous Pieces Of Eight | Dixie! | Harlequin | HQ 3001 IMS
Wild Bill Davison With The Alex Welsh Band | Memories | Jazzology | JCD-201

Blue And Brown
Clifford Brown Quartet | Clifford Brown:The Complete Paris Sessions Vol.3 | Vogue | 21457302

Blue And Disgusted
Memphis Slim | Bluesville: Memphis Slim | Prestige | 61143

Blue And Green
Christof Lauer Trio | Evidence | CMP Records | CMP CD 70

Blue And Orange
Arnett Cobb And The Muse All Stars | Live At Sandy's | Muse | MR 5191

Blue And Sentimental
Cal Tjader Sextet | A Night At The Blackhawk | Original Jazz Classics | OJC 278(F 8026)
Count Basie Sextet | The Swinging Count | Verve | MV 2646 IMS
Don Byas Quartet | Don Byas Complete 1946-1951 European Small Group Master Takes | Definitive Records | DRCD 11214
Eddie Lockjaw Davis Quartet | Jaws Strikes Again | Black & Blue | BLE 233101
Erroll Garner Trio | The Greatest Garner | Rhino | SD 1227
Hank Jones Trio | Bluesette | Black & Blue | BLE 233168

Illinois Jacquet And His Orchestra | How High The Moon | Prestige | P 24057
Newport Jazz Festival All-Stars | Bern Concert '89 | Concord | CCD 4401
The Buck Clayton Legacy | All The Cats Join In(Buck Clayton Rememberd) | Nagel-Heyer | CD 006
Encore Live | Nagel-Heyer | CD 018
The New York Allstars | Count Basie Remembered Vol.2 | Nagel-Heyer | CD 041
The Tremble Kids | Dixieland Jubilee | Intercord | 155032

Blue And Sentimental-
Lester Young Septet | Laughin' To Keep From Cryin' | Verve | 543301-2
The Ritz feat.Clark Terry | Almost Blue | Denon Compact Disc | CY-77999

Blue Angel
Franz Koglmann Monoblue Quartet | L'Heure Bleue | Hat Art | CD 6093
Tal Farlow Trio | Chromatic Palette | Concord | CCD 4154

Blue Aura
Dave Bargeron Quartet | Barge Burns...Slide Flies | Mapleshade | 02832

Blue Avenue
Steve Lacy Sextet | Songs | Hat Art | CD 6045

Blue Ballad
Wolfgang Engstfeld-Peter Weiss Quartet | Upside Down | Drops Special | CD 1

Blue Bash
Jimmy Smith Quartet | Compact Jazz: Jimmy Smith | Verve | 831374-2
Kenny Burrell-Jimmy Smith Trio | Blue Bash | Verve | 557453-2
Orchestra Vielharmonie | From BeBand To BigBop | AH Records | CD 1-90

Blue Because Of You
Earl Hines | Le Jazz En France Vol.15:Earl Hunes Paris Session 1965 | Pathe | 1552611
Lionel Hampton And His Orchestra | Lionel Hampton:Flying Home | Dreyfus Jazz Line | FDM 36735-2
Lionel Hampton With The Nat King Cole Trio | Lionel Hampton-Historical Recording Sessions 1939-1941 | RCA | PM 42417

Blue Belles Of Harlem
Duke Ellington And His Orchestra | Duke Ellington:Complete Prestige Carnegie Hall 1943-1944 Concerts | Definitive Records | DRCD 11210

Blue Bells
Stan Getz Quintet | Stan Getz And The 'Cool' Sounds | Verve | 547317-2
The Three Sounds | Introducing The Three Sounds | Blue Note | 300234(1600)

Blue Bells Goodbye
The Storyville Jassband | Trad Tavern | Timeless | CD TTD 577

Blue Bells Of Harlem
Jasper Van't Hof Group | Blue Corner | ACT | 9228-2

Blue Bells(for Sam Francis)
Sammy Price And His Bluesicians | Sammy Price:Blues & Boogie | Vogue | 2111509-2

Blue Birdland
Maynard Ferguson With The Birdland Dreamband | The Birdland Dream Band Vol.1 | Fresh Sound Records | 58110 CD(RCA)

Blue Birdland(alt.take)
Matrix | Harvest | Pablo | 2312121

Blue Blood Blues
James Dapogny's Chicago Jazz Band | Laughing At Life | Discovery | 74006-2
Jelly Roll Morton And His Orchestra | The Complete Jelly Roll Morton-Vol.7/8 | RCA | 2126411-2

Blue Blues
Helmut Zacharias mit seinen Verzauberten Geigen | Ich Habe Rhythmus | Bear Family Records | BCD 15642 AH
Jo Mikowich Group | Strom Thunder Lightning | yvp music | CDX 48805

Blue Bolero
Eddie Daniels Quartet | Real Time | Chesky | JD 118

Blue Bolero(fragment 1)
Abdullah Ibrahim Trio | African Magic | TipToe | TIP-888845 2

Blue Bolero(fragment 2)
African Magic | TipToe | TIP-888845 2

Blue Bolero(fragment 3)
African Magic | TipToe | TIP-888845 2

Blue Bolero(fragment 4)
Thelonious Monk Quartet | Monk's Dream | CBS | CK 63536

Blue Bolivar Blues
Monk's Dream | CBS | CK 63536

Blue Bolivar Blues(alt.take)
Bill Allred-Roy Williams Quintet | Absolutely | Nagel-Heyer | CD 024

Blue Bones
Hugh Lawson Trio | Prime Time | Storyville | 3 IMA

Blue Bossa
Bobby McFerrin-Chick Corea | Play | Blue Note | 795477-2
Chet Baker-Wolfgang Lackerschmid Duo | Ballads For Two | Inak | 856
Dianne Mower And Her Group | A Song For You | Jazz City | 660.53.023
Joe Henderson Quartet | Joe Henderson:The Milestone Years | Milestone | 8MCD 4413-2
Joe Henderson Quintet | Page One | Blue Note | 498795-2
The Blue Note Years-The Best Of Joe Henderson | Blue Note | 795627-2
Joe Henderson-The Blue Note Years | Blue Note | 789287-2
Joe Henderson Trio | The Standard Joe | Red Records | 123248-2
Lou Donaldson Quintet | Birdseed | Milestone | MCD 9198-2
Louis Stewart | Jazz Guitar Highlights 1 | Jardis Records | JRCD 20141
McCoy Tyner And The Latin All-Stars | McCoy Tyner And The Latin All-Stars | Telarc Digital | CD 83462
Tommy Flanagan 3 | The Montreux '77 Collection | Pablo | 2620107
Tommy Flanagan Trio | The Best Of Tommy Flanagan | Pablo | 2405410-2

Blue Boy
Jutta Gruber & The Martin Schrack Trio | Keep Hanging On | yvp music | CD 3043

Blue Boye's Blues
Abdullah Ibrahim | South African Sunshine | Pläne | CD 88778

Blue Breeze
Brew Moore & His Playboys | In The Beginning...Bebop | Savoy | SV 0169(MG 12119)

Blue Brew
Memphis Slim | Bluesville: Memphis Slim | Prestige | 61143

Blue Bud Blues-
Bud Powell Quartet | The Legacy | Jazz Door | JD 1204

Blue Calypso
Mal Waldron-John Coltrane Sextet | Wheelin' | Prestige | P 24069

Blue Camel
Scott Hamilton Quartet | My Romance | Concord | CCD 4710

Blue Cee
Charles Mingus Quintet | Charles Mingus-Passion Of A Man:The Complete Atlantic Recordings 1956-1961 | Atlantic | 8122-72871-2
Sebastian Gramss Underkarl | 20th Century Jazz Cover-Live | TCB Records | TCB 96202

Blue Cellophane
Duke Ellington And His Orchestra | Duke Ellington:The Complete RCA-Victor Mid-Forties Recordings(1944-1946) | RCA | 2663394-2

Blue Champagne
Charlie Spivak And His Orchestra | The Uncollected: Charlie Spivak | Hindsight | HSR 105

Blue Chaser
Clark Terry-Bob Brookmeyer Quintet | Clark Terry-Bobby Brookmeyer Quintet | Mainstream | MD CDO 728

Blue Ching
Art Blakey And The Jazz Messengers | Pisces | Blue Note | GXK 8151

Blue Chip
Pata Blue Chip | Pata Blue Chip | Pata Musik | PATA 13(amf 1064)
Herbie Nichols Trio | The Third World | Blue Note | 84552

Blue Chopsticks
Roswell Rudd Quintet | Regeneration | Soul Note | 121054-2

Blue Circle
Steve Houben Quartet | Blue Circumstances | Igloo | IGL 102

Blue Clouds
Eddie Boyd And His Blues Band | Eddie Boyd And His Blues Band Featuring Peter Green | Crosscut | CCR 1002

Blue Comedy
Art Farmer Quintet | Farmer 's Market | Prestige | P 24032

Blue Concept
Nat Adderley Sextet | Much Brass | Original Jazz Classics | OJCCD 848-2(R 1143)
Gene Ammons Quartet | A Stranger In Town | Prestige | PRCD 24266-2

Blue Coolade
Jasper Van't Hof Group | Blau | ACT | 9203-2

Blue Corner(for Bettina Blohm)
Jim Tomlinson Quintet | Only Trust Your Heart | Candid | CCD 79758

Blue Corners
Buck Clayton-Buddy Tate Quintet | Kansas City Nights | Prestige | P 24040

Blue Creek
Buddy Tate-Al Grey Quintet | Just Jazz | Reservoir | RSR CD 110(882634)
James Carter Group | Conversin' With The Elders | Atlantic | 7567-82988-2
Maneri/Morris/Maneri | Out Right Now | HatOLOGY | 561

Blue Dado
Ada Montellanico With The Jimmy Cobb Trio | The Encounter | Philology | W 66.2

Blue Daniel
Cannonball Adderley Quintet | At The Lighthouse | Capitol | 531572-2
The Cannonball Adderley Collection Vol.5:At The Lighthouse | Landmark | CAC 1305-2(882344)
Conte Candoli With The Joe Haider Trio | Conte Candoli Meets The Joe Haider Trio | JHM Records | JHM 3602
Frank Rosolino Quartet | Frank Talks! | Storyville | STCD 8284
Frank Strazzeri And His Woodwinds West | Somebody Loves Me | Fresh Sound Records | FSR-CD 5003
P.J. Perry Quartet | Worth Waiting For | The Jazz Alliance | TJA 10007
Shelly Manne And His Men | At The Blackhawk Vol.1 | Contemporary | C 7577
At The Black Hawk Vol.1 | Original Jazz Classics | OJCCD 656-2(S 7577)

Blue Daniel(alt.take)
Tommy Dorsey And His Orchestra | The Indispensable Tommy Dorsey Vol.1/2 | RCA | 2126405-2

Blue Day
Scrapper Blackwell | The Virtuoso Guitar Of Scrapper Blackwell | Yazoo | YAZ 1019

Blue Deco
Dave Stryker Quartet | Blue Degrees | Steeplechase | SCCD 31315

Blue Desert
New Art Saxophone Quartet | Songs And Dances | Enja | ENJ-9420 2

Blue Devil Jump
Sun Ra | Monorails And Satellites | Evidence | ECD 22013-2

Blue Dip
UMO Jazz Orchestra | UMO Jazz Orchestra | Naxos Jazz | 86010-2

Blue Dreams
Sonny Thompson Quintet/Sharps And Flats | Sonny Thompson:The Complete Recordings Vol.1 (1946-1948) | Blue Moon | BMCD 6024

Blue Ebony
Herbie Mann Sextet | Just Wailin' | Original Jazz Classics | OJCCD 900-2(NJ 8211)

Blue Echo
Rex Stewart Septet | Rendezvous With Rex | Affinity | AFF 165

Blue Energy
Klaus Ignatzek Group | Live At Leverkusener Jazztage | Nabel Records:Jazz Network | CD 4630
Klaus Ignatzek Jazztet | Return Voyage(To The Golden Age Of Hard Bop) | Candid | CCD 79716

Blue Eyes
Werner Bühler Quartet | At The Swinging Organ | MWM Records | MWM 005

Blue Fable
Guido Manusardi Trio | Introduction | Penta Flowers | CDPIA 009

Blue Farouq
Mel Rhyne Sextet | Organ-izing | Original Jazz Classics | OJCCD 1055-2(JLP 916)
Duke Ellington And His Famous Orchestra | Duke Ellington Playing The Blues 1927-1939 | Black & Blue | BLE 59.232 2

Blue Flame
Woody Herman And His Orchestra | La Fiesta | West Wind Orchestra Series | 2400 CD

Blue Flame(Theme)
Old Gold Rehearsals 1944 | Jazz Unlimited | JUCD 2079
La Fiesta | West Wind Orchestra Series | 2400 CD

Blue Flower
Al Ryerson Quintet | Blue Flute | Red Baron | 471576-2

Blue For Lou-
Humphrey Lyttelton And His Band | Delving Back With Humph:Humphrey Lyttelton 1948-1949 | Lake | LACD 72

Blue Funk
Jack Teagarden And His Band | Meet Me Where They Play The Blues | Good Time Jazz | GTCD 12063-2
Jack Teagarden And His Orchestra | Jazz Original | Charly | CD 80
Tal Farlow Quintet | The Guitar Artistry Of Tal Farlow | Verve | MV 2588 IMS

Blue Fuse No.1(rehersal)
Duke Ellington And His Orchestra | Ella Fitzgerald And Duke Ellington:Cote D'Azure Concerts on Verve | Verve | 539033-2

Blue Fuse No.2(rehersal)
Cootie Williams And His Orchestra | Rhythm And Jazz In The Mid Forties | Official | 3014

Blue Gardenia
Dinah Washington And Her Orchestra | For Those In Love | EmArCy | 514073-2
Compact Jazz:Dinah Washington Sings The Blues | Mercury | 832573-2 PMS
Mark Murphy-Joe Lo Duca | Mark Murphy Sings Nat Cing Cole,Volumes 1&2 | Muse | MCD 6001

Blue Gardenia(alt.take)
Willis Jackson Quintet | Soul Night Live! | Prestige | PRCD 24273-2

Blue Gator
Gene Ammons And His All Stars | Blue Gene | Original Jazz Classics | OJC20 192-2(P 7146)

Blue Gene
Russell Gunn Quartet | Young Gunn | Muse | MCD 5539

Blue Genius
Ray Charles-Milt Jackson Quintet | That's Jazz Vol.4: Soul Meeting | Atlantic | ATL 50234

Blue Ghost
Chet Baker Quartet | Broken Wings | Adda | 581020

Blue Gilles
In Paris Vol.2 | West Wind | WW 2059

Blue Goose
Duke Ellington And His Famous Orchestra | Passion Flower 1940-46 | Bluebird | 63 66616-2

Blue Gown
Barney Kessel Quartet | Feeling Free | Original Jazz Classics | OJC 179(C 7618)

Blue Grass Groove
Wardell Gray Quartet | Wardell Gray:Light Gray 1948-1950 | Cool & Blue | C&B-CD 116

Blue Greens
David Fathead Newman-Marchel Ivery With The Rein De Graaff Trio | Blue Greens & Beans | Timeless | CD SJP 351

Blue Greens 'N Beans
Gene Ammons Quintet | Blue Groove | Prestige | MPP 2514

Blue Harlem
Scott Hamilton And Friends | Blues,Bop & Ballads | Concord | CCD 4866

Blue Haze
John Graas Quintet | French Horn Jazz | Fresh Sound Records | KL 1046(Kapp)
Miles Davis Quartet | Welcome To Jazz: Miles Davis Vol.2 | Koch Records | 321 975 D1

Blue Head
Cedar Walton Trio | Cedar Walton-Ron Carter-Jack DeJohnette | Limetree | MCD 0021

Blue Heaven
Hal Mooney Orchestra & The Gene Lowell Singers | Big Band And Voices | Bainbridge | BT 1008

Blue Horizon
Sidney Bechet's Blue Note Jazzmen | Jazz Classics Vol.1 | Blue Note | 789384-2

Blue Hour
Barney Wilen Quintet | Barney Wilen Quintet | Fresh Sound Records | FSR-CD 0048

Blue Hymn
Leipziger Saxophon Quartet + Rolf Von Nordenskjöld | Passages: Leipziger Saxophon Quartet Plays Rolf Von Nordenskjöld | BIT | 11158

Blue Ideas
Fritz Münzer Tentet | Blue Ideas | Jazz 'n' Arts Records | 0200
The Be-Bop Boys | The Modern Jazz Piano Album | Savoy | WL 70510(2)(SJL 2247) DP

Blue In Green
Bill Evans Trio | Live In Paris 1972 Vol.3 | France's Concert | FCD 125
Bill Evans:The Secret Sessions | Milestone | 8MCD 4421-2
Bill Evans:The Secret Sessions | Milestone | 8MCD 4421-2
The Legendary Bill Evans Trio-The Legendary 1960 Birdland Sessions | Cool & Blue | C&B-CD 106
Bill Perkins-Bud Shank Quintet | Serious Swingers | Contemporary | CCD 14031-2
Charlie Haden Quartet West | In Angel City | Verve | 837031-2
Chet Baker Meets Space Jazz Trio | Little Girl Blue | Philology | W 21.2
Don Sebesky Orchestra | I Remember Bill-A Tribute To Bill Evans | RCA | 2668929-2
Eric Le Lann Group | New York | OMD | VB 053 CD
Gebhard Ullmann Quartet | Per-Dee-Doo | Nabel Records:Jazz Network | CD 4640
Gonzalo Rubalcaba Trio | The Blessing | Blue Note | 797197-2
Grant Green Quartet | The Best Of The Jazz Guitars | LRC Records | CDC 8531(874372)
Harold Danko Trio | 3/4 Three Of Four | Steeplechase | SCCD 31444
Joe Diorio | Italy | MGI Records | MGR CD 1010
Marc Copland Quintet | Stompin' At The Savoy | Denon Compact Disc | CY-75853
Miles Davis Quintet | Kind Of Blue | CBS | CK 64935
Miles Davis Sextet | The Miles Davis Selection | CBS | 465699-2
Ralph Simon Magic Club | Music For The Millenium | Postcards | POST 1015
Rich Perry Trio | Doxy | Steeplechase | SCCD 31473
The Atlantic String Trio | First Meeting | Factory Outlet Records | 2001-1 CD
Thomas Stabenow-Lothar Schmitz | Swet Peanuts | Bassic-Sound | CD 007
Tony Purrone Trio | Rascality | Steeplechase | SCCD 31514
Wallace Roney Quintet | Verses | Muse | MCD 5335

Blue In Green(alt.take)
Al Jarreau With Band | Heaven And Earth | i.e. Music | 557852-2

Blue In Green(Tapestry):
Tom Harrell Orchestra | Labyrinth | RCA | 2668512-2

Blue Interlude
Michel Warlop Et Son Orchestre | Le Jazz En France Vol.4 | Pathe | 1727281

Blue Interlude(C-Minor Prelude[Chopin])
Edmond Hall's All Star Quintet | Edmond Hall Profoundly Blue | Blue Note | 821260-2

Blue Invasion
Cootie Williams And His Rug Cutters | The Complete Duke Ellington-Vol.11 | CBS | CBS 88242

Blue Jay
Jessica Williams Quartet | Jassica's Blues | Jazz Focus | JFCD 018

Blue Jay Way
Lew Stone And His Band | Lew Stone And His Band | Decca | DDV 5005/6 DT

Blue Jean
Duke Ellington And His Orchestra | Duke Ellington In Hamilton | Radiex Music | RDX-1000

Blue Jean Beguine
Sophisticated Lady | Jazz Society(Vogue) | 670502

Blue Jewels
Jim Hall Trio | It's Nice To Be With You -Jim Hall In Berlin | MPS | 843035-2 PMS

Blue Juice
Jimmy McGriff Organ Blues Band | The Worm | Blue Note | 538699-2
Pullin' Out The Stops! The Best Of Jimmy McGriff | Blue Note | 830724-2

Blue Kind Of Mind
Claude Bolling And The Show Biz Band | Swing Party | Decca | 6.22983 AO

Blue Lace
Art Blakey And The Jazz Messengers | The Freedom Rider | Blue Note | 870076-5

Blue Lester
Lester Young Quintet | Jazz Gallery:Lester Young Vol.1(1936-46) | RCA | 2114171-2
Nat Pierce/Dick Collins Nonet | Nat Pierce-Dick Collins Nonet/Charlie Mariano Sextet | Original Jazz Classics | OJC 118(F 3224)

Blue Life
Ben Webster Sextet | The Jeep Is Jumping | Black Lion | BLCD 760147

Blue Light
Benny Carter And His Orchestra | Americans Swinging In Paris:Benny Carter | EMI Records | 539647-2

Blue Light Blues
Django Reinhardt All Star Sessions | Capitol | 531577-2
Django Reinhardt:Djangology | EMI Records | 780659-2

Blue Light Boogie(part 1)
Louis Jordan And His Tympany Five | Louis Jordan-Let The Good Times Roll: The Complete Decca Recordings 1938-1954 | Bear Family Records | BCD 15557 IH

Blue Light Boogie(part 2)
Cassandra Wilson Group | Blue Light 'Til Dawn | Blue Note | 781357-2

Blue Light 'Till Dawn
Rössler/Kühn/Heidepriem/Stefanski Quartet | Coloured | Fusion | 8015

Blue Lights
Coleman Hawkins All Stars | The Hawk Flies High | Original Jazz Classics | OJC 027(R 12-223)

Blue Lilacs
John Stevens Sextet | Freebop | Affinity | AFF 101

Blue Lips
David Moss-Michael Rodach | Fragmentary Blues | Traumton Records | 4432-2

Blue Loop Garow
Harry Allen With The John Pizzarelli Trio | Harry Allen Meets The John Pizzarelli Trio | Novus | 2137397-2

Blue Lou
All Star Band | Jazz Drumming Vol.3(1938-1939) | Fenn Music | FJD 2703
Alvino Rey And His Orchestra | The Uncollected: Alvino Rey And His Orchestra 1946 | Hindsight | HSR 121
Art Tatum | Art Tatum-The Complete Pablo Solo Masterpieces | Pablo | 7 PACD 4404-2
The Tatum Solo Masterpieces Vol.9 | Pablo | 2310835
Art Tatum Trio | The Tatum Group Masterpieces | Pablo | 2310735-2
Benny Carter And His Band | The Best Of The Jazz Saxophones Vol.2 | LRC Records | CDC 8529
Benny Carter Sextet | Jazz Giant | Original Jazz Classics | OJC20 167-2(C 7555)

Benny Goodman And His Orchestra | The Hits Of Benny Goodman | Capitol | 791212-2
Django Reinhardt And The Quintet Du Hot Club De France | Django Reinhardt:Djangology | EMI Records | 780659-2
Ella Fitzgerald With Sy Oliver And His Orchestra | Ella:The Legendary American Decca Recordings | GRP | GRP 46482
Ella Fitzgerald 75th Birthday Celebration:The Original Decca Recordings | GRP | GRP 26192
Harry Arnold Big Band | Big Band Classics 1957-58 | Dragon | DRLP 139/140
JATP All Stars | J.A.T.P. In London 1969 | Pablo | 2CD 2620119
Jay McShann Trio | Airmail Special | Sackville | SKCD2-3040
Lionel Hampton All Stars | Jazz In Paris:Lionel Hampton-Ring Dem Bells | EmArCy | 159825-2 PMS
Lionel Hampton And His Orchestra | Hamp's Big Band | RCA | 2121821-2
Mundell Lowe Trio | Souvenirs-A Tribute To Nick Ceroli | The Jazz Alliance | TJA 10011
Paolo Tomelleri-Fritz Hartschuh Quintet | Milan Swing | L+R Records | CDLR 45070
The All Star Band | The Indispensable Bunny Berigan 1937-1939 | RCA | NL 89744(2) DP

Blue Mambo
Ketil Bjornstad | New Life | EmArCy | 017265-2

Blue Man
Big Boy Knox | Texas Piano Blues 1929-1948 | Story Of Blues | CD 3509-2

Blue Me
Guido Manusardi Quartet | Bra Session | SPLASC(H) Records | H 125

Blue Midnight
Stephan Oliva Trio | Fantasm | RCA | 2173925-2
Chick Corea Electric Band II | Paint The World | GRP | GRP 97412

Blue Miles
Art Blakey And The Jazz Messengers | Blue Night | Timeless | CD SJP 217

Blue Minor
Sonny Clark Quintet | Cool Struttin' | Blue Note | 746513-2

Blue Mizz
James P.Johnson's Blue Note Jazzmen | Jazz:The Essential Collection Vol.3 | IN+OUT Records | 78013-2
The Blue Note Jazzmen | Blue Note | 821262-2

Blue Mizz(alt.take)
Charlie Byrd | Solo Flight | Original Jazz Classics | OJCCD 1093-2(RS 9498)

Blue Mobile
J.J.Johnson Quintet | First Sessions 1949/50 | Prestige | P 24081

Blue Mode
Jay Jay Johnson's Bebopers | Genesis | Prestige | P 24044

Blue Mode(2 takes)
Les Jazz Modes | Les Jazz Modes | Dawn | DCD 104

Blue Monday
Jay McShann Quintet | What A Wonderful World | Groove Note | GRV 1005-2
Carey Bell And His Blues Band | Blues Harp | Delmark | 900201 AO

Blue Monk
Aki Takase-David Murray | Blue Monk | Enja | 7039-2
Barney Wilen Quartet | Tilt | Vogue | 21559492
Bill Evans | Conversations With Myself | Verve | 521409-2
Brew Moore Quartet | If I Had You | Steeplechase | SCCD 36016
Cedar Walton Quartet | Third Set | Steeplechase | SCCD 31179
The Maestro | Muse | MCD 6008
Clark Terry-Don Friedman | Clark Terry:One On One | Chesky | JD 198
Dexter Gordon With The Junior Mance Trio | At Montreux | Prestige | P 7861
Donald Byrd Quintet | Harlem Blues | Landmark | LCD 1516-2
Gary Burton-Makoto Ozone | Face To Face | GRP | GRP 98052
George Shearing Septet | George Shearing In Dixieland | Concord | CCD 4388
John Gordon's Trombones Unlimited | Live In Concert | Mons Records | CD 1890
Kai Winding-J.J.Johnson Quintet | The Great Kai & J.J. | Impulse(MCA) | 951225-2
Karin Krog With The Dexter Gordon Quartet | Some Other Spring | Storyville | STCD 4045
Larry Coryell | Twelve Frets To One Octave | Koch Records | 322 657
McCoy Tyner-Bobby Hutcherson Duo | Manhattan Moods | Blue Note | 828423-2
Pee Wee Russell-Henry Red Allen Quintet | The College Concerts | MCA | JAS 78(AS 9137)
Ron Carter Quartet | Piccolo | Milestone | M 55004
Sam Newsome Quartet | This Masquerade | Steeplechase | SCCD 31503
Thelonious Monk | Alone In San Francisco | Original Jazz Classics | OJC 231(RLP 1158)
Thelonious Monk-The Complete Riverside Recordings | Riverside | 15 RCD 022-2
Thelonious Monk Quartet | Evidence | Milestone | M 9115
Live In Paris, Alhambra 1964 Vol.1 | France's Concert | FCD 135
En Concert Avec Europe 1 | Laserlight | 710377/78
Thelonious Monk In Copenhagen | Storyville | STCD 8283
Thelonious Monk In Stockholm | Duke Records | D 1020
Thelonious Monk Quintet | European Tour | LRC Records | CDC 7683(874371)
Thelonious Monk Trio | Thelonious Monk:The Complete Prestige Recordings | Prestige | 3 PRCD 4428-2
Thelonious Monk With Art Blakey's Jazz Messengers | Art Blakey's Jazz Messengers With Thelonious Monk | Atlantic | SD 1278

Blue Monk(alt.take)
Nguyen Le Trio | Nguyen Le:3 Trios | ACT | 9245-2

Blue Monkey
Peter Herborn Group With The Auryn String Quartet | Something Personal | JMT Edition | 849156-2

Blue Mood
Erwin Lehn Orchester | Jazz Made In Germany | MPS | 88053-2

Blue Moon
Art Tatum | The Art Tatum Solo Masterpieces | Pablo | 2625703
Bengt Hallberg Quartet | Hallberg's Hot Accordion In The Foreground | Phontastic | NCD 7532
Benny Waters Quartet | Hurry On Down | Storyville | STCD 8264
Betty Roche And Her All Stars | Sigin'& Swingin' | Original Jazz Classics | OJCCD 1718-2(P 7187)
Billie Holiday And Her Orchestra | Billie Holiday: The First Verve Sessions | Verve | 2610027
Billie Holiday And Her Trio | Billie Holiday 1948-1959 | Royal Jazz | RJD 508
Billy Butterfield And His Orchestra | The Uncollected:Billy Butterfield | Hindsight | HSR 173
Bob Crosby And His Orchestra | 1946 | Jazz Anthology | JA 5142
Buck Clayton Jam Session | Buck Clayton Jam Session Vol.2 | Blue Moon | BMCD 3045
Charles Mingus-Spaulding Givens Duo | Strings And Keys | Fantasy | 0902110(Debut DLP 1)
Clifford Brown With Strings | Brownie-The Complete EmArCy Recordings Of Clifford Brown | EmArCy | 838306-2
Coleman Hawkins With Michel Warlop And His Orchestra | Django Reinhardt All Star Sessions | Capitol | 531577-2
Coleman Hawkins In Europe | Timeless | CBC 1-006
Dicky Wells And His Orchestra | Trombone Four-In-Hand | Affinity | AFF 168
Ella Fitzgerald With The Buddy Bregman Orchestra | The Rodgers And Hart Songbook | Verve | 821693-1
Herb Ellis-Red Mitchell | Doggin' Around | Concord | CCD 4372
Joe Pass | The Jazz Giants Play Rodgers & Hart:Blue Moon | Prestige | PCD 24205-2
Joe Pass With Red Mitchell | Finally | EmArCy | 512603-2 PMS
Johnny Hodges Orchestra | Johnny Hodges At The Sportpalast, Berlin | Pablo | 2CD 2620102
Julie London With Howard Roberts And Red Mitchell | Julie Is Her Name Vol.2 | Pathe | 1566201(Liberty LRP 3100)
Kenny Barron Trio | Live at Bradley's | EmArCy | 549099-2
Louis Armstrong And His All Stars | Mack The Knife | Pablo | 2310941-2
Message | The Art Of Blakey | Paddle Wheel | KICJ 162
Oscar Peterson Trio | Masters Of Jazz Vol.7 | RCA | NL 89721 DP
The Song Is You-The Best Of The Verve Songbooks | Verve | 531558-2
Pierre Spiers Sextet feat. Stephane Grappelli | Special Stephane Grappelli | Jazztime(EMI) | 251286-2
Roy Eldridge And His Orchestra | The Complete Verve Roy Eldridge Studio Sessions | Verve | 9861278
Roy Eldridge Quintet | Roy Eldridge 'Littel Jazz'-The Best Of The Verve Years | Verve | 523338-2
Roy Eldridge-Dizzy Gillespie With The Oscar Peterson Quartet | The Complete Verve Roy Eldridge Studio Sessions | Verve | 9861278
Roy And Diz | Verve | 521647-2
Spaulding Givens/Charles Mingus | Debut Rarities Vol.2 | Original Jazz Classics | OJCCD 1808-2
Stan Seltzer Trio | Stan Seltzer Trio | Fresh Sound Records | HIFI R 202 CD
The Basie-Ites | How High The Moon | Fresh Sound Records | FSR 637(Jubilee JGM 5004)

Blue Moon-
Oscar Peterson Trio | This Is Oscar Peterson | RCA | 2663990-2

Blue Moon(alt.take)
Allen Lowe/Stacy Philips | Dark Was The Night-Cold Was The Ground | Music & Arts | CD 811

Blue Motel Room
Joachim Raffel Sextet | ...In Motion | Jazz 4 Ever Records:Jazz Network | J4E 4746

Blue Motion
Tana Reid Quintet | Blue Motion | Paddle Wheel | KICJ 172

Blue 'N' Boogie
Claude Williamson Trio | Live! The Sermon | Fresh Sound Records | FSR 105
Dexter Gordon-Benny Bailey Quintet | Round Midnight | Steeplechase | SCCD 31290
Dizzy Gillespie Sextet | In The Beginning | Prestige | P 24030
Giants Of Jazz | Live | Jazz Door | JD 1277
J.J.Johnson Sextet | J.J.Inc. | CBS | CK 65296
JATP All Stars | Dizzy's Diamonds-Best Of The Verve Years | Verve | 513875-2
Miles Davis All Stars | The J.J.Johnson Memorial Album | Prestige | PRCD 11025-2
Miles Davis Sextet | Tune Up | Prestige | P 24077
Sonny Criss Sextet | The Sonny Criss Memorial Album | DIW | DIW 302 CD
Wes Montgomery Quintet | Full House | Original Jazz Classics | OJC20 106-2
Wycliffe Gordon Quintet | What You Dealin' With | Criss Cross | Criss 1212

Blue 'N' Boogie(alt.take)
Claudio Roditi With The Metropole Orchestra | Metropole Orchestra | Mons Records | MR 874767

Blue Nights-
Chris Jarrett | Piano Moments | Take Twelve On CD | TT 007-2
Alice Coltrane Quintet | Red Hot On Impulse | Impulse(MCA) | GRP 11512

Blue Nile
Steven Halpern-Dalles Smith | Threshold | Gramavision | 18-7301-1

Blue Note Boogie
James P.Johnson | Boogie Woogie, Stride & The Piano Blues | Blue Note | 799099-2

Blue Note Singes Again
Mel Lewis Quintet | Mellifous | Landmark | LCD 1543-2

Blue Odyssey
Count Basie And His Orchestra | Count On The Coast Vol.1 | Phontastic | NCD 7555

Blue On Blue
Basie On Roulette, Vol. 16: Not Now I'll Tell You When | Vogue | 500016

Blue Orchid
Per Carsten Quintet | Via | dacapo | DCCD 9462
Bob Crosby And His Orchestra | The Bob Crosby Orchestra Vol.10:High Society(1939) | Halcyon | DHDL 130

Blue Orchids
Glenn Miller And His Orchestra | The Original Sounds Of The Swing Era Vol. 5 | RCA | CL 05514 DP

Blue Paintings
Lionel Hampton And His Orchestra | Lionel Hampton's Paris All Stars | Vogue | 21511502

Blue Panassie
Lionel Hampton:Real Crazy | Vogue | 2113409-2

Blue Pearl
Bud Powell Trio | Alternate Takes | Blue Note | BST 84430
Claude Williamson Trio | Live! At The Jazz Bakery | Fresh Sound Records | FSR-CD 5014
Bud Powell Trio | Blue Trails-The Rare Tracks | Blue Note | 300191

Blue Pearl(alt.take)
Duke Ellington And His Orchestra | Highlights From The Duke Ellington Centennial Edition | RCA | 2663672-2

Blue Pepper(Far East Of The Blues)
Duke Ellington's Far East Suite | RCA | 2174797-2
Bob Cooper Sextet | COOP! The Music Of Bob Cooper | Original Jazz Classics | OJCCD 161-2

Blue Planet
Glenn Wilson Quartet | Blue Porpoise Avenue | Sunnyside | SSC 1074 D

Blue Prelude
Jim Beebe's Chicago Jazz | A Sultry Serenade | Delmark | DE 230
The 4 Most | The 4 Most + Bob Stewart | Dawn | DCD 112
Woody Herman And His Orchestra | The Band That Plays The Blues | Naxos Jazz | 8.120527 CD

Blue Prince
Eubie Blake | The Eighty-Six Years Of Eubie Blake | CBS | 22223

Blue Red
Oscar Klein's Jazz Show | Oscar Klein's Jazz Show Vol.2 | Jazzpoint | JP 1048 CD

Blue Reed
Shorty Rogers And The Big Band | The Swingin' Nutcracker | Fresh Sound Records | ND 42121

Blue Reverie
Cootie Williams And His Orchestra | Duke Ellington's Trumpets | Black & Blue | BLE 59.231 2

Blue Ribbon Rag
Hatchett's Swingtette | Stephane's Tune | Naxos Jazz | 8.120570 CD

Blue Riff
Al Jolson With Orchestra | Al Jolson-Great Original Performances(1926-1932) | CDS Records Ltd. | RPCD 300

Blue Rol
Gene Ammons Septet | The Gene Ammons Story: The 78 Era | Prestige | P 24058

Blue Rondo A La Turk
Dave Brubeck Quartet | The Dave Brubeck Quartet At Carnegie Hall | CBS | 66234
Time Out | CBS | CK 65122
The Dave Brubeck Selection | CBS | 467279-2

Blue Room
Billy Mitchell Quintet | Swing...Nor Spring! | Savoy | SV 0188(MG 12062)
Chick Webb And His Orchestra | The King Of Big Band Jazz | Festival | Album 146
Ella Fitzgerald With The Buddy Bregman Orchestra | The Complete Ella Fitzgerald Song Books of Harold Arlen, Irving Berlin, Duke Ellington, George & Ira Gershwin, Jerome Kern, Johnny Mercer, Cole Porter And Rogers & Hart | Verve | 519832-2
Miles Davis Sextet | Miles Davis And Horns | Original Jazz Classics | OJC20 053-2(P 7025)
Welcome To Jazz: Miles Davis | Koch Records | 321 944 D1
Red Garland Trio | Prestige Moodsville Vol.1 | Original Jazz Classics | OJCCD 360-2(MV 1)
Red Norvo Quintet | Red's 'X' Sessions | Fresh Sound Records | NL 46034(RCA)
Sonny Rollins Quartet | Sonny Rollins On Impulse | MCA | 2292-54613-2

Blue Room-
Count Basie And His Orchestra | Prez's Hat Vol.2 | Philology | 214 W 7

Blue Room(alt.take)
G.Q.Williams & Dave Collett | Back To The Boogie | Jazz Colours | 874735-2

Blue Rose
Paul Eßer-Gerd Dudek-Ali Haurand-Jiri Strivin | Jazz Und Lyrik:Schinderkarren Mit Buffet | Konnex Records | KCD 5108
Ran Blake | Duke Dreams/The Legacy Of Strayhorn-Ellington | Soul Note | SN 1027
Rosemary Clooney With The Duke Ellington Orchestra | Blue Rose | CBS | CK 65506
System Tandem | Reunion | Supraphon | 11 1224-2
Richard Wyands Trio | Then Here And Now | Storyville | STCD 8269

Blue Rose(alt.take)
Milt Jackson-Wes Montgomery Quintet | Bags Meets Wes! | Original Jazz Classics | OJC20 234-2(RLP 9407)

Blue Roz
Wes Montgomery-The Complete Riverside Recordings | Riverside | 12 RCD 4408-2
Wes Montgomery-The Complete Riverside Recordings | Riverside | 12 RCD 4408-2

Blue Roz(alt.take)
Wes Montgomery Quintet | Wes And Friends | Milestone | M 47013

Blue Sands
Paul Gonsalves-Earld Hines Quartet | It Don't Mean A Thing If It Ain't Got That Swing | Jazz Colours | 874766-2

Blue Serge
Bill Evans-Eddie Gomez Duo | The Complete Fantasy Recordings | Fantasy | 9FCD 1012-2
Duke Ellington And His Famous Orchestra | Duke Ellington:The Blanton-Webster Band | Bluebird | 21 13181-2
Jazz:The Essential Collection Vol.2 | IN+OUT Records | 78012-2
Ben Webster-Cotton Tail | RCA | 63667902
Duke Ellington And His Orchestra | Jazz Live & Rare: The Immortal Duke Ellington | Jazzline | ???
Kenny Clarke Quintet | Jazz In Paris:Kenny Clarke Sextet Plays André Hodair | EmArCy | 834542-2 PMS
Serge Chaloff Quintet | Serge Chaloff Memorial | Cool & Blue | C&B-CD 102
Woody Herman And The New Thundering Herd | The 40th Anniversary Carnegie Hall Concert | RCA | 2159151-2

Blue Seven
Shirley Scott Quintet | Blue Seven | Original Jazz Classics | OJCCD 1050-2(P 7376)
Sonny Rollins Quartet | Saxophone Colossus And More | Prestige | P 24050
Chicago Blues All Stars '78 | Live In Montreux | Black & Blue | BLE 59.530 2

Blue Shift
Ted Des Plantes' Washboard Wizards | Midnight Stomp | Stomp Off Records | CD 1231

Blue Skies
André Previn Sextet | Music At Sunset | Jazz Colours | 874738-2
Art Tatum | Art Tatum:Complete Capitol Recordings | Capitol | 821325-2
Art Tatum-The Complete Pablo Solo Masterpieces | Pablo | 7 PACD 4404-2
Art Tatum:Complete Capitol Recordings | Definitive Records | DRCD 11192
Cassandra Wilson Trio | Cheek To Cheek-The Irving Berlin Song Book | Verve | 533829-2
Count Basie And His Orchestra | Count Basie And His Great Vocalists | CBS | CK 66374
Della Reese With The Neal Hefti Orchestra | Della | RCA | 2663912-2
Dick Hyman | There Will Never Be Another You | Jazz Connaisseur | JCCD 9831-2
14 Jazz Piano Favorites | Music & Arts | CD 622
Dinah Washington And Her Band | Verve Jazz Masters 40:Dinah Washington | Verve | 522055-2
Dr.John With The John Clayton Big Band | Dr.John-Afterglow | Blue Thumb | GRB 70002
Duke Ellington And His Orchestra | Sophisticated Lady | Jazz Society(Vogue) | 670502
Ella Fitzgerald With The Paul Weston Orchestra | Ella Fitzgerald-First Lady Of Song | Verve | 517898-2
Get Happy! | Verve | 523321-2
Ellis Larkins | Maybeck Recital Hall Series Volume Twenty-Two | Concord | CCD 4533
Glenn Miller And His Orchestra | Meadowbrook Ballroom Vol.2 | Magic | DAWE 81
John Mehegan | Johnny Mehegan's Reflections | Savoy | SV 0204(MG 12028)
Louis Armstrong And His Orchestra | Louis Armstrong Radio Days | Moon Records | MCD 056-2
Ralph Sutton Trio | Pocketful Of Dreams | Sackville | SKCD2-3062
Tommy Dorsey And His Orchestra | Planet Jazz:Frank Sinatra & Tommy Dorsey | Planet Jazz | 2152067-2
Tommy Dorsey And His Orchestra With Frank Sinatra | RCA | 2115518-2

Blue Skies-
Giacomo Gates With The Harold Danko Quartet | Blue Skies | dmp Digital Music Productions | CD 3001
Lars Moller Group | Colours | Stunt Records | STUCD 19711

Blue Skies(and Fletcher Henderson)
Duke Ellington And His Orchestra | Duke Ellington And His Orchestra 1943,Vol.1 | Circle | CCD-101

Blue Skies(Trumpets No End)
Chick Webb And His Orchestra | The King Of Big Band Jazz | Festival | Album 146
Duke Ellington And His Orchestra | Duke Ellington:Complete Musicraft Recordings | Definitive Records | DRCD 11215
Ella Fitzgerald With Paul Weston And His Orchestra | Get Happy | Verve | 813391-1 IMS

Blue Skies(unedited version)
Jan Garbarek Group | Photo With Blue Skie, White Clouds, Wires, Windows And A Red Roof | ECM | 1135 (843168-2)

Blue Sky
Stephan Kurmann Strings | Alive | TCB Records | TCB 96152

Blue Sky-
Toshinori Kondo & Ima | Red City Smoke | JA & RO | JARO 4173-2

Blue Sky Battlezone
Memphis Slim | Boogie Woogie Piano | CBS | CBS 21106

Blue Slit
Sonny Stitt Quartet | Saxophone Supremacy | Verve | MV 2687 IMS

Blue Sonny
Sonny Red (Kyner) Sextet | Images:Sonny Red | Original Jazz Classics | OJC 148(J 974)

Blue Soul
Lowell Fulsom Band | Lowell Fulson | Chess | 427007

Blue Spanish Eyes
Robert Jeanne Quartet | Quartets | B.Sharp Records | CDS 084

Blue Spring
Kenny Dorham Quartet | Quiet Kenny | Original Jazz Classics | OJC 250(NJ 8225)

Blue Star
Benny Carter Quartet | Summer Serenade | Storyville | STCD 4047

Blue Stomp
Nornert Stein Pata Masters | Live In Australia | Pata Musik | PATA 15 CD
Hal Singer-Charlie Shavers Quintet | Blue Stompin' | Original Jazz Classics | OJCCD 834-2(P 7153)

Blue Stompin'
Charlie Mariano-Chris Hinze Quintet | Blue Stone | Black Lion | BLCD 760203

Blue Stride
Hot Club De Norvege With Guests | Swinging With Jimmy | Hot Club Records | HCRCD 082

Blue Suede Shoes
Sam 'The Man' Taylor Orchestra | Back Beat-The Rhythm Of The Blues Vol.5 | Mercury | 511270-2 PMS

Blue Sun
Ralph Towner | Works | ECM | 823268-1

Blue Tattoo
Sue Raney With The Billy May Orchestra | Songs For A Raney Day | Capitol | 300015(TOCJ 6129)

Blue Thoughts
Franz Jackson's Original Jass All-Stars feat. Bob Shoffner | Chicago-The Living Legends:Franz Jackson | Original Jazz Classics | OJCCD 1824-2(RLP 9406)

Blue Tide
Charles Mingus-Spaulding Givens Duo | Strings And Keys | Fantasy | 0902110(Debut DLP 1)
David Kikoski Trio | Presage | Freelance | FRL-CD 011

Blue Tone
Bob Rockwell Quartet | Shades Of Blue | Steeplechase | SCCD 31378

Blue Top
Ernie Watts-Christof Sänger | Blue Topaz | Laika Records | 35101352

Blue Topaz
Uwe Kropinski/Volker Schlott | Dinner For Two | Acoustic Music Records | 319.1057.2

Blue Train
GRP All-Star Big Band | GRP All-Star Big Band:Live! | GRP | GRP 97402
GRP 10th Anniversary | GRP | GRP 96722
John Coltrane Sextet | Blue Train(The Ultimate Blue Train) | Blue Note | 853428-0
1949-1959, Blue Note's Three Decades Of Jazz, Vol. 1 | Blue Note | 89903
Jazz Gallery:John Coltrane Vol.1 | RCA | 2119540-2
The Ultimate Blue Train | Blue Note | 853428-2
Kenny Werner Trio | Live At Visiones | Concord | CCD 4675

Blue Train(alt.take)
John Coltrane Sextet | Blue Trails-The Rare Tracks | Blue Note | 300191
Gebhard Ullmann Quartet | Kreuzberg Park East | Soul Note | 121371-2

Blue Trees(Song Of Fantasy)
Clifford Hayes' Louisville Stompers | Frog Hop | Frog | DGF 10

Blue Turning Grey Over Me
Charlie Byrd-Ginny Byrd | Byrd's Word! | Original Jazz Classics | OJCCD 1054-2(R 9448)
Dick Sudhalter Band | Melodies Heard,Melodies Sweet... | Challenge | CHR 70055
Earl Hines Quartet | Another Monday Date | Prestige | PRCD 24043-2
Fawkes-Turner Quintet | The Controversial Bruce Turner:That's The Blues, Dad | Lake | LACD 49
Louis Armstrong And His All Stars | The Louis Armstrong Selection | CBS | 467278-2
Louis Armstrong And His Orchestra | Louis Armstrong-St.Louis Blues Vol.6 | CBS | 467919-2
Loverfield Jazzband | Swissmade In Holland | Timeless | CD TTD 601

Blue Turning Grey Over You
Deep Creek Jazzuits | At Night | Jazz Pure Collection | AU 31620 CD
Fats Waller And His Rhythm | The Indispensable Fats Waller Vol.5/6 | RCA | 2126416-2
Teddy Wilson | Blues For Thomas Waller | Black Lion | BLCD 760131

Blue Turning Grey Over You(alt.take)
Das Pferd | Blue Turns To Grey | VeraBra Records | CDVBR 2065-2

Blue Variations
Arthur Prysock And His Orchestra | Morning,Noon And Night:The Collection | Verve | 557484-2

Blue Velvet
Gene Ammons Quartet | Brother Jug! | Prestige | PR20 7792-2
Glenn Miller Orchestra | Glenn Miller Serenade | CBS | 487445-2
Houston Person Quintet | The Party | Muse | MCD 5451

Blue Violin
Art Farmer Quintet | Manhattan | Soul Note | SN 1026

Blue Wail
Scott Hamilton Quartet | Live At Brecon Jazz Festival | Concord | CCD 4649

Blue Waltz
Eddie Daniels Group | Blackwood | GRP | GRP 95842

Blue Waters
Bill Lowe/Philippe Crettien Quintet | Sunday Train | Konnex Records | KCD 5051

Blue Whale
Jeff Beck-Jan Hammer Duo | Wired | Epic | ???

Blue Window
Art Farmer-Fritz Pauer Duo | Azure | Soul Note | 121126-2

Blue Yodel No.9 (Standin' On The Corner)
| Bright's Spot | Savoy | SV 0220(MG 6041)

Blue(2000)
Thilo Berg Big Band | Carnival Of Life | Mons Records | CD 1887

Blue(Prayer)
Sarah Vaughan With The Michel Legrand Orchestra | Sarah Vaughan With Michel Legrand | Mainstream | MD CDO 703

Blueberry Hill
Jan Jankeje's Party And Swingband | Mobil | Jazzpoint | JP 1068 CD
Jimmy Dorsey And His Orchestra | The Uncollected: Jimmy Dorsey | Hindsight | HSR 101
Louis Armstrong And His All Stars | The Jazz Collector Edition: Louis Armstrong | Laserlight | 15700
Rare Performances Of The 50's And The 60's | CBS | CBS 88669
In Concert At The Pasadena Civic Auditorium | Vogue | 655601
Louis Armstrong And His All Stars/Orchestra | The Wonderful World Of Louis Armstrong | MCA | 2292-57202-2
Louis Armstrong With Gordon Jenkins And His Orchestra And Choir | Louis Armstrong-My Greatest Songs | MCA | MCD 18347
Louis Armstrong-All Time Greatest Hits | MCA | MCD 11032
Louis Armstrong With Orchestra | High Society | Intercord | 125400
Mose Allison Trio | Mose Allison:Greatest Hits | Original Jazz Classics | OJCCD 6004-2
Mr.Acker Bilk And His Paramount Jazz Band | White Cliffs Of Dover | Intercord | 125408
Warren Ceasar And The Creole Zydeco Snap Band | The Crowd Pleaser | Sound Of New Orleans | SONO 1035

Blueberry Rhyme
Albert Bover-Horacio Fumero | Duo | Fresh Sound Records | FSNT 025 CD

Bluebird
Art Pepper With The Sonny Clark Trio | Art Pepper:Complete Straight Ahead Sessions | The Jazz Factory | JFCD 22847
Charlie Parker Quintet | Encores-The Savoy Sessions | Savoy | SJL 1107 (801156)
Joe Albany Trio | Portrair Of A Legend | Fresh Sound Records | FSR-CD 317
Bird Lives! | Interplay | IP 7723
Pippo Cataldo-Giuseppe Costa Septet | Picture Number Two | SPLASC(H) Records | CD H 325-2

Bluebird Of Delhi(alt.take)
Duke Ellington And His Orchestra | Victor Jazz History Vol.12:Ellingtonia | RCA | 2135731-2

Bluebird Of Delhi(Mynah)
Charlie Parker All Stars | Charlie Parker Memorial Vol.1 | Savoy | SV 0101(MG 12000)

Blueduette
Bob Sawyer's Jazz Band | Blue Yodelers | Retrieval | RTR 79020

Bluego
Thelonious Monk | Pure Monk | Milestone | M 47004

Bluehawk
Thelonious Monk-The Complete Riverside Recordings | Riverside | 15 RCD 022-2

Bluejays
Aurora | Aurora | Denon Compact Disc | CY-73148

Blueport
Gerry Mulligan Concert Jazz Band | The Complete Verve Gerry Mulligan Concert Band | Verve | 9860613
The Complete Verve Gerry Mulligan Concert Band | Verve | 9860613
Verve Jazz Masters 36:Gerry Mulligan | Verve | 523342-2
En Concert Avec Europe 1 | Laserlight | 710382/83
Gerry Mulligan Quartet | Americans In Sweden | Tax | CD 3711-2
Red Rodney Sextet | The 3 R's | Muse | MR 5290

Blues
Art Blakey And The Jazz Messengers | A Night At Birdland Vol. 3 | Blue Note | 300192(BNJ 61002)
Billy Eckstine And His Orchestra | Billy Eckstine Sings | Savoy | SJL 1127 (801176)
Count Basie And His Orchestra | Live! | Laserlight | 15797
Dee Dee Pierce And His New Orleans Stompers | In Binghampton,N.Y. Vol.Three | American Music | AMCD-81
Django Reinhardt And The Quintet Du Hot Club De France | Swing De Paris | Arco | 3 ARC 110
Eddie Condon And His Jazz Band | Eddie Condon Days | CBS | CBS 88032
JATP All Stars | Jazz At The Philharmonic-The First Concert | Verve | 521646-2
The Complete Jazz At The Philharmonic On Verve 1944-1949 | Verve | 523893-2
The Complete Jazz At The Philharmonic On Verve 1944-1949 | Verve | 523893-2
Jay McShann And His Orchestra | Early Bird | Spotlite | SPJ 120
Kid Ory's Creole Jazz Band | Kid Ory '44-'46 | American Music | AMCD-19
Laszlo Süle Band | Silence Fiction | AH Records | CD 90025
Lionel Hampton And His Orchestra | European Tour 1953 | Royal Jazz | RJD 517
Mark Turner Quintet | Yam Yam | Criss Cross | Criss 1094
Oscar Peterson Four | Return To Happiness-JATP At Yoyogi National Stadium,Tokyo | Pablo | 2620117-2
Paul Bley Trio | Paul Bley With Gary Peacock | ECM | 1003
Indian Summer | Steeplechase | SCCD 31286
World Saxophone Quartet | Requiem For Julius | Justin Time | JUST 137-2

Blues-
Dizzy Gillespie Orchestra | Monterey Jazz Festival 1975 | Storyville | 4960213
Dizzy Gillespie Quintet | En Concert Avec Europe 1 | Laserlight | 710705
Wild Bill Davison All Stars | The Eddie Condon Floor Show Vol.1 | Queen-Disc | 030

Blues 2
Blues Comany And Guests | Damn! Let's Jam | Inak | 9009

Blues After All
Benny Golson Quintet | Gone With Golson | Original Jazz Classics | OJCCD 1850-2

Blues After Midnight
Heinz Sauer & Bob Degen With Carey Bell | Blues After Sunrise | L+R Records | LR 40017

Blues All Day
Richard 'Groove' Holmes Sextet | Blues All Day Long | Muse | MCD 5358

Blues Alley
Jim Galloway Trio | Music Is My Life | Sackville | SK2CD-5006

Blues And The Abstract Truth
Jimmy Smith With The Oliver Nelson Orchestra | Jimmy Smith:Best Of The Verve Years | Verve | 527950-2
Oliver Nelson And His Orchestra | More Blues And The Abstract Truth | Impulse(MCA) | 951212-2
More Blues And The Abstract Truth | MCA | 2292-54643-2

Blues And Tonic
Jack McDuff Quartet | Honeydripper | Original Jazz Classics | OJC 222(P 7199)

Blues And Trouble
Wolfgang Bernreither-Golly-Rudy Bayer Group | I Wonder Why | L+R Records | CDLR 42079

Blues Ar Easy To Write
Arnett Cobb Quintet | Smooth Sailing | Original Jazz Classics | OJCCD 323-2

Blues Around Dusk
Lowell Fulsom Band | Tramp/Soul | Ace Records | CDCHD 339

Blues At Blue Note
Edmond Hall's Blue Note Jazzmen | Hot Jazz On Blue Note | Blue Note | 835811-2

Blues At Blue Note(alt.take)
Oliver Strauch Group | City Lights | Blue Concept | BCCD 94/03

Blues Back
McCoy Tyner Trio | Reaching Fourth | Impulse(MCA) | 951255-2

Blues Backstage
Lambert, Hendricks And Ross | Lambert,Hendricks & Ross:Sing A Song Of Basie | CTI Records | PDCTI 1115-2

Blues Before Freud
Tete Montoliu | Lunch In L.A. | Original Jazz Classics | C 14004

Blues Before Midnight
Champion Jack Dupree | American Folk Blues Festival '70 | L+R Records | LS 42021

Blues Before Sunrise
John Lee Hooker | Blues Before Sunrise | Bulldog | BDL 1011

Blues Blue
Sonny Clark Trio | Blues Mambo | West Wind | WW 2103

Blues Bred In The Bone
Budd Johnson Quintet | Let's Swing | Original Jazz Classics | OJCCD 1720-2(SV 2015)

Blues By Five
Miles Davis Quintet | Cookin' With The Miles Davis Quintet | Original Jazz Classics | OJC20 128-2
Warne Marsh Quintet | Jazz Exchange Volume One | Storyville | SLP 4001

Blues Changes
Coleman Hawkins Quintet | The Big 3 | CBS | AK 40950
Ray Bryant Trio | Through The Years-The 60th Birthday Special Recordings Vol.1 | EmArCy | 512764-2 PMS

Blues Chat
David Murray Octet | Home | Black Saint | BSR 0055

Blues Chorale
Johnny Smith Quartet | The Sound Of Johnny Smith Guitar | Fresh Sound Records | FSR 583(Roost 2246)

Blues Clair
Django Reinhardt Quartet | Django Reinhardt:Djangology | EMI Records | 780659-2

Blues Connotation
Buddy DeFranco Group | Blues Bag | Affinity | AFF 55
Cody Moffett Septet | Evidence | Telarc Digital | CD 83343
Lew Tabackin Quartet | Lou Tabackin Quartet | Eastworld | EWJ 90025
Ornette Coleman Quartet | This Is Our Music | Atlantic | 7567-80767-2
Beauty Is A Rare Thing:Ornette Coleman-The Complete Atlantic Recordings | Atlantic | 8122-71410-2
Renee Rosnes Trio | Art & Soul | Blue Note | 499997-2
Tom Harrell Sextet | Upswing | Chesky | JD 103

Blues De Lux
Alain Goraguer Orchestra | Jazz In Paris:Jazz & Cinéma Vol.1 | EmArCy | 548318-2 PMS

Blues De Memphis(1)
Jazz In Paris:Jazz & Cinéma Vol.1 | EmArCy | 548318-2 PMS

Blues De Memphis(2)
Sidney Bechet With Claude Luter And His Orchestra | Sidney Bechet | Vogue | 000001 GK

Blues Dove
Woody Herman And His Orchestra | The Band That Plays The Blues | Naxos Jazz | 8.120527 CD

Blues Dream
Bill Frisell Trio | Bill Frisell With Dave Hollnad And Elvin Jones | Nonesuch | 7559-79624-2
Bill Frisell Band | Blues Dream | Nonesuch | 7559-79615-2

Blues Dream(reprise)
Albert Mangelsdorff Quintet | Tension | L+R Records | CDLR 71002

Blues Dues
Joe Pass | Joe Pass:A Man And His Guitar | Original Jazz Classics | OJCCD 8806-2
Live At Long Beach City College | Pablo | 2308239-2
Peter O'Mara Quartet | Wind Moments | Take Twelve On CD | TT 009-2
Eddie Gomez Trio | Down Stretch | Black-Hawk | BKH 531 CD

Blues En Mineur
Hot Club De Norvege | Moreno | Hot Club Records | HCRCD 120

Blues En Si Bémol
Hampton Hawes Trio | Blues For Bud | Black Lion | BLCD 760126

Blues Etude
Oscar Peterson And His Trio | At The Blue Note: Last Call | Telarc Digital | CD 83314
Oscar Peterson Trio | Verve Jazz Masters 16:Oscar Peterson | Verve | 516320-2
Paris Jazz Concert:Oscar Peterson | Laserlight | 36155

Blues Etude(Concert closing)
Coleman Hawkins Trio | Thanks For The Memory | EPM Musique | FDC 5159

Blues Five Spot
Thelonious Monk Quartet | Misterioso | Original Jazz Classics | OJC20 206-2
Thelonious Monk-The Complete Riverside Recordings | Riverside | 15 RCD 022-2
Blues Five Spot | Milestone | M 9124

Blues Foll
Jon Lloyd Quartet | Four And Five | HatOLOGY | 537

Blues For 2
Zoot Sims-Joe Pass Duo | Blues For Two | Original Jazz Classics | 2310879 Digital

Blues For 3+1
Sebastian Weiss Trio | Polaroid Memory | Fresh Sound Records | FSNT 085 CD

Blues For A Bave Drummer
Dave Shepherd Sextet | Jazz Me Blues | Jazz Colours | 874700-2

Blues For A Hip King
Dollar Brand | African Dawn | Enja | ENJ-4030 2
Abdullah Ibrahim | Fats Duke And Monk | Sackville | SKCD2-3048

Blues For Alf
Joe Haider Trio | Grandfather's Garden | JHM Records | JHM 3619
Count Basie And His Orchestra | The Best Of Count Basie | Pablo | 2405408-2

Blues For Alfy
Al Haig-Jimmy Raney Quartet | Special Brew | Spotlite | SPJ LP 8

Blues For Alice
Charlie Parker And His Orchestra | Bird: The Complete Charlie Parker On Verve | Verve | 837141-2
Charlie Parker Quintet | Bird On Verve-Vol.6:South Of The Border | Verve | 817447-1 IMS
Swedish Schnapps + | Verve | 849393-2
Lanny Morgan Quartet | A Suite For Yardbird | Fresh Sound Records | FSR-CD 5023
Rahsaan Roland Kirk With The George Gruntz Trio | Rahsaan Rolnd Kirk:Dog Years In The Fourth Ring | 32 Jazz | 32032
Red Rodney Quintet | One For Bird | Steeplechase | SCCD 31238
Super Sax | Supersax Dynamite | MPS | 68210

Blues For Alice(alt.take)
Joe Pass | The Best Of Joe Pass | Pablo | 2405419-2

Blues For Alician
Joe Pass:A Man And His Guitar | Original Jazz Classics | OJCCD 8806-2
Salvatore Bonafede Quartet | Nobody's Perfect | Penta Flowers | CDPIA 022

Blues For All The Monsters
Emil Mangelsdorff Quartet & Sebastian Norden | Allen Ginsberg: Das Geheul | Trion | 5101/2

Blues For Alvina
Freddie Hubbard Sextet | Minor Mishap | Black Lion | BLP 60122

Blues For Andrew Hill
George Robert-Dado Moroni | Youngbloods | Mons Records | CD 1897

Blues For Angel
Joe Pass | Joe Pass:Guitar Virtuoso | Pablo | 4 PACD 4423-2
Red Garland Trio | Red Garland Trio | Original Jazz Classics | OJC 224(MV 6)

Blues For Art
Eddie Higgins Trio | Those Quiet Days | Sunnyside | SSC 1052 D

Blues For Barclay
Django Reinhardt And The Quintet Du Hot Club De France | Django Reinhardt Portrait | Barclay | DALP 2/1939

Blues For Basie
Joe Pass | Virtuoso No.2 | Pablo | 2310788-2

Blues For Bessie
Bud Powell Trio | Strictly Powell | RCA | 6351423-2

Blues For Betsy
Jimmy Ponder Sextet | Jump | Muse | MCD 5347

Blues For Big Scotia-
Jessica Williams Quartet | Jassica's Blues | Jazz Focus | JFCD 018

Blues For Bill Basie
Barney Kessel Quintet | Red Hot And Blues | Contemporary | CCD 14044-2

Blues For Bird
Nicolas Simion Group | Black Sea | Tutu Records | 888134-2*
Oscar Peterson-Dizzy Gillespie Duo | Oscar Peterson & Dizzy Gillespie | Pablo | 2310740-2

Blues For Birks
Oscar Peterson-Joe Pass Duo | Oscar Pterson Et Joe Pass A La Salle Pleyel | Pablo | 2CD 2625705

Blues For Bise
Live At Salle Pleyel, Paris | Pablo | 2625705

Blues For Blanche
Art Pepper Quartet | Art Pepper:The Complete Galaxy Recordings | Galaxy | 16GCD 1016-2

Blues For Blanche(alt.take)
Artworks | Galaxy | GXY 5148

Blues For Blanche(alt.take-2)
Duke Ellington Quartet | The Golden Duke | Prestige | P 24029

Blues For Blanton
Steve Nelson Quartet | Communications | Criss Cross | Criss 1034

Blues For Bohenia
Ronnie Earl & The Broadcasters | Soul Searchin' | Black Top | BT 1042 CD

Blues For Buddy
Peter Bernstein Quartet | Signs Of Life | Criss Cross | Criss 1095

Blues For Butterball
Jimmy Smith With The Claus Ogerman Orchestra | Any Number Can Win | Verve | 557447-2

Blues For C.A.
Red Holloway Quartet | Red Holloway & Company | Concord | CJ 322

Blues For C.M.
Dave Holland Quintet | The Razor's Edge | ECM | 1353
Hank Jones Trio | The Oracle | EmArCy | 846376-2 PMS

Blues For C.T.
Charles McPherson Quartet | Come Play With Me | Arabesque Recordings | AJ 0117

Blues For Charles
Patrick Tompert Trio | Patrick Tompert Trio Live | Satin Doll Productions | SDP 1029-1 CD
Larry Coryell | Twelve Frets To One Octave | Koch Records | 322 657

Blues For Charlie
Thilo Kreitmeier & Group | Changes | Organic Music | ORGM 9725
Count Basie Kansas City Septem | Mostly Blues...And Some Others | Pablo | 2310919-2
Blues For Charlie Parker
Tony Scott With The Horst Jankowski Trio | Dedications | Line Records | COCD 9.00803
Blues For Chris
Oscar Peterson Septet | The Silent Partner | Pablo | 2312103
Blues For Chu
Charles McPherson Quintet | First Flight Out | Arabesque Recordings | AJ 0113
Blues For Cindy
Harry Verbeke Quartet | Short Speech | Timeless | SJP 136
Blues For Clarinet
Jimmy Hamilton And The New York Jazz Quintet | Jimmy Hamilton And The New York Jazz Quintet | Fresh Sound Records | FSCD 2002
Blues For D.P.
Ron Carter Quartet | The Bass And I | somethin'else | 300258(TOCJ 5585)
Blues For David
David Murray Group | Interboogieology | Black Saint | 120018-2
Blues For Deac'n Cone
Johnny 'Hammond' Smith Sextet | Open House | Milestone | MCD 47089-2
Blues For De-De
Kenny Burrell-Jimmy Smith Quartet | Blue Bash | Verve | 557453-2
Blues For Del
Stanley Turrentine Orchestra | New Time Shuffle | Blue Note | LT 993 (GXK 8189)
Blues For Dexter
Milt Jackson Sextet | Bag's Opus | Blue Note | 784458-2
Blues For Django And Mezz
Larry Coryell-Philip Catherine Quartet | Jazz-Club: Guitar | Verve | 840035-2
Blues For Django And Stephane
Paul Smoker Trio | Mississippi River Rat | Sound Aspects | sas 006
Blues For Donna
Sonny Red (Kyner) Quintet | Images:Sonny Red | Original Jazz Classics | OJC 148(J 974)
Blues For Dorte
Ben Webster-Don Byas Quintet | Ben Webster/Don Byas | Jazz Magazine | 48018
Blues For Douglaston
Sammy Price Sextet | Fire | Black & Blue | BLE 233079
Blues For Duke
Sonny Stitt Quartet | Blues For Duke | Muse | MR 5129
Blues For Edith
Milt Jackson With Strings | The Best Of Milt Jackson | Pablo | 2405405-2
Blues For Ellis
Randy Weston | Marrakech In The Cool Of The Evening | Verve | 521588-2
Blues For Eric
Curtis Peagler Quartet | I'll Be Around | Pablo | 2310930
Blues For Eric(Dolphy)
Wilton Gaynair Quintet | Alpharian | Konnex Records | KCD 5032
Blues For Erica
Clark Terry Quintet | Top And Bottom Brass | Original Jazz Classics | OJCCD 764-2(RLP 1137)
Blues For Felix
Giorgio Azzolini Trio | Giorgia Mood | SPLASC(H) Records | H 144
Blues For Fred-
Joe Pass | Blues For Fred | Pablo | 2310931-2
Blues For Fun
Paul Desmond Quartet | Masters Of Jazz Vol.13 | RCA | CL 42790 AG
Blues For Gemini
Gene Harris-Scott Hamilton Quintet | At Last | Concord | CCD 4434
Blues For Gene
Milt Jackson Sextet | The Harem | Musicmasters | 5061-2
Blues For George
Klaus Doldinger Quartet | Bluesy Toosy | ACT | 9200-2
Blues For Gonzi-
Jazz Pistols | 3 On The Moon | Lipstick Records | LIP 8965-2
Blues For Gwen
Oscar Peterson Trio With Herb Ellis | Hello Herbie | MPS | 821846-2
Blues For H.G.
Three Originals:Motion&Emotions/Tristeza On Piano/Hello Herbie | MPS | 521059-2
Tony Lee Trio | British Jazz Artists Vol. 1 | Lee Lambert | LYN 3416
Blues For Heard
Art Pepper Quartet | Art Pepper:The Complete Village Vanguard Sessions | Contemporary | 9CCD-4417-2
Art Pepper:The Complete Village Vanguard Sessions | Contemporary | 9CCD-4417-2
Art Pepper:The Complete Village Vanguard Sessions | Contemporary | 9CCD-4417-2
Blues For Heard(alt.take)
Art Pepper:The Complete Village Vanguard Sessions | Contemporary | 9CCD-4417-2
Art Pepper:The Complete Village Vanguard Sessions | Contemporary | 9CCD-4417-2
Art Pepper:The Complete Village Vanguard Sessions | Contemporary | 9CCD-4417-2
Blues For Heard(alt.take-2)
Art Pepper:The Complete Village Vanguard Sessions | Contemporary | 9CCD-4417-2
Art Pepper:The Complete Village Vanguard Sessions | Contemporary | 9CCD-4417-2
Blues For Heard(alt.take-3)
Jazz Passengers | Plain Old Joe | Knitting Factory Works | KFWCD 139
Blues For Henry
Stan Getz With The Oscar Peterson Trio | Stan Getz Highlights | Verve | 847430-2
Emily Remler Quartet | Retrospective Volume Two: Compositions | Concord | CCD 4463
Blues For Howard
Hugh Masekela Quintet | The African Connection | MCA | IA 9343/2
Blues For Ian
Bireli Lagrene Quartet | My Favorite Django | Dreyfus Jazz Line | FDM 36574-2
Blues For Ike
Django Reinhardt And His Rhythm | Peche Á La Mode-The Great Blue Star Sessions 1947/1953 | Verve | 835418-2
Django Reinhardt And The Quintet Du Hot Club De France | Django Reinhardt Portrait | Barclay | DALP 2/1939
Count Basie And His Orchestra | Basie Bounce | Affinity | CD AFS 1001
Blues For Ilene
Doctor Ross | The Blues Vol. 5 | Big Bear | 156042
Blues For J
Jimmy Smith Trio | Organ Grinder Swing | Verve | 543831-2
Ed Blackwell Trio | Walls-Bridges | Black Saint | 120153-2
Blues For J.P.
Stefan Karlsson Quintet | Room 292 | Justice Records | JR 0701-2
Blues For Jackie
Pete Yellin Quartet | Pete Yellin's European Connection:Live! | Jazz 4 Ever Records:Jazz Network | J4E 4722
Giorgio Rosciglione Quartet | Giorgio Rosciglione Quartet | Penta Flowers | CDPIA 013
Blues For Jacque
Hampton Hawes Trio | The Trio Vol.2 | Original Jazz Classics | OJCCD 318-2
Blues For Jacques
Cinzia Gizzi Trio | Trio & Sextet | Penta Flowers | CDPIA 017
Blues For Janet
Herb Ellis-Stuff Smith Sextet | Herb Ellis & Stuff Smith:Together | Koch Jazz | KOC 3-7805-2

Blues For Jimmy Yancey
Don Thompson Quartet | Beautiful Friendship | Concord | CJ 243
Blues For Joe
Wild Bill Davis Quartet | Organ 1959 | Jazz Anthology | JA 5132
Blues For Joe Turner
Count Basie And His Orchestra With Joe Turner & Eddie Cleanhead Vinson | Kansas City Shout | Pablo | 2310859-2
Blues For Junior
Herb Ellis Quintet | Nothing But The Blues | Verve | 521674-2
Roll Call | Justice Records | JR 1001-2
Blues For Khan
Albert Nicholas Sextet | Bechet/Nicholas/Mezzrow:Spirits Of New Orleans | Vogue | 2113408-2
Blues For Klaus
Eddy Louiss | Sang Mele | Nocturne Productions | NTCD 101
Blues For Lady J.
Benny Bailey With The Bernhard Pichl Trio | On The Corner | Jazz 4 Ever Records:Jazz Network | J4E 4726
Cat Anderson & The Ellington All-Stars | Cat Anderson | Swing | SW 8412 IMS
Blues For Laurence
Cat Anderson And His Orchestra | Ellingtonians In Paris | Jazztime(EMI) | 251275-2
Blues For Lennie
Art Pepper Quartet | Thursday Night At The Village Vanguard | Original Jazz Classics | OJCCD 694-2(7642)
Blues For Les
Art Pepper:The Complete Village Vanguard Sessions | Contemporary | 9CCD-4417-2
Budd Johnson And The Four Brass Giants | Budd Johnson And The Four Brass Giants | Original Jazz Classics | OJC 209(RLP 9343)
Blues For Little Jazz
Lionel Hampton Sextet | Big Band Bounce And Boogie:In The Bag-Lionel Hampton | Affinity | AFS 1017
Blues For Lorraine
Paris Session 1956 | Jazztime(EMI) | 251274-2
Blues For Lucky Lakatos
Benny Carter All Stars | Benny Carter All Stars | Sonet | SNTF 947(941484)
Blues For Mama
Robin Kenyatta Quartet | Live At Cully-Blues For Mama Doll | Jazz Dance Records | 1989
Blues For Mannie
Steve Wilson Quintet | Blues For Marcus | Criss Cross | Criss 1073
Blues For Marina
Werner Bühler Quartet | At The Swinging Organ | MWM Records | MWM 005
Blues For Martha
Joe Pass | The Montreux '77 Collection | Pablo | 2620107
Blues For Martin
Lester Young And His Orchestra | Jammin The Blues | Jazz Anthology | JA 5110
Blues For Mary Jane
Stan Getz Quartet | Best Of The West Coast Sessions | Verve | 537084-2
Stan Getz:East Of The Sun-The West Coast Sessions | Verve | 531935-2
Blues For Me
The International Jazz Group | The International Jazz Group Vol.2 | Swing | SW 8416
Blues For Mike
Melvin Rhyne Trio | Kojo | Criss Cross | Criss 1164
Blues For Miles
Four French Horns Plus Rhythm | Four French Horns | Savoy | SV 0214(MG 12173)
Blues For Monty
Joe Pass Quartet | Live At Yoshi's | Pablo | 2310951-2
Blues For Mr.Broadway
Oliver Nelson And His Orchestra | More Blues And The Abstract Truth | MCA | 2292-54643-2
Blues For Musidisc
John Lee Hooker | Burning Hell | Original Blues Classics | OBCCD 555-2(RLP 008)
Blues For My Baby
Memphis Slim Group | The Real Folk Blues | Chess | CHD 9270(872290)
Blues For Nat
Count Basie-Zoot Sims Quartet | Basie & Zoot | Original Jazz Classics | OJCCD 822-2(2310745)
Blues For Nat Cole
Jürgen Seefelder Meets Azymuth | Rio De Janeiro | ITM Records | ITM 1444
Blues For New Orleans
Duke Ellington And His Orchestra | That's Jazz Vol.31: New Orleans Suite | Atlantic | ATL 50403
Blues For Newport
Dave Brubeck Sextet | Nightshift | Telarc Digital | CD 83351
Blues For Nica
Joe Bonner-Johnny Dyani | Suburban Fantasies | Steeplechase | SCCD 31176
Blues For Nils
Kenny Drew-Bo Stief Duo | Kenny Drew/Solo-Duo | Storyville | STCD 8274
Joe Pass | Joe Pass At The Montreux Jazz Festival 1975 | Original Jazz Classics | OJC20 934-2(2310752)
Blues For Nina
Count Basie Kansas City 7 | Count Basie Kansas City 7 | Pablo | 2310908-2
Blues For Norman
JATP All Stars | Early Modern | Milestone | M 9035
The Complete Jazz At The Philharmonic On Verve 1944-1949 | Verve | 523893-2
Lionel Hampton Quartet | The Complete Lionel Hampton Quartets And Quintets With Oscar Peterson On Verve | Verve | 559797-2
The Trumpet Kings | The Trumpet Kings At The Montreux Jazz Festival 1975 | Original Jazz Classics | OJCCD 445-2
Blues For Nothing
Richard Davis Sextet | Dealin' | Muse | MR 5027
Blues For Pablo
Miles Davis + 19 | The Miles Davis Selection | CBS | 465699-2
The RCA Victor Jazz Workshop | The Arrangers-The RCA Victor Jazz Workshop | Bluebird | ND 86471
Blues For Pam
Count Basie-Oscar Peterson Quartet | Night Rider | Original Jazz Classics | OJC 688(2310843)
Blues For Pat
Pat Metheny Trio | Rejoicing | ECM | 1271(817795-2)
Joe Haider Jazz Orchestra featuring Mel Lewis | Mel Lewis Meets The Joe Haider Jazz Orchestra | JHM Records | JHM 3604
Blues For Peter Schilperoort
Bob Rockwell Trio | The Bob Rockwell Trio | Steeplechase | SCS 1242
Blues For Philly Joe
Sonny Rollins Quartet | Jazz Profile:Sonny Rollins | Blue Note | 823516-2
Newk's Time | Blue Note | 576752-2
Soren Lee Quartet | Soren Lee Quartet | L+R Records | CDLR 45073
Blues For Piney Brown
Michal Urbaniak With The Horace Parlan Trio | Take Good Care Of My Heart | Steeplechase | SCCD 31195
Blues For Pluto
Woody Herman And The New Thundering Herd | Woody Herman:Thundering Herd | Original Jazz Classics | OJCCD 841-2
Blues For Poland
Jack Dieval And The J.A.C.E. All-Stars | Jazz In Paris:Jack Diéval-Jazz Aux Champs Elysées | EmArCy | 018419-2
Blues For Polydor
Don Grolnick Septet | Nighttown | Blue Note | 798689-2
Blues For Rebecca
Larry Vuckovich Trio | Blues For Red | Hot House Records | HH 1001 IMS

Blues For René
Coleman Hawkins With The Oscar Peterson Quartet | The Genius Of Coleman Hawkins | Verve | 539065-2
Blues For René(alt.take)
Gene Harris | Maybeck Recital Hall Series Volume Twenty-Three | Concord | CCD 4536
Blues For Roberta
Philip DeGruy | Innuendo Out The Other | NYC-Records | NYC 6013-2
Blues For Ron
Frank Morgan-George Cables Duo | Double Image | Contemporary | CCD 14035-2
Blues For Ruby
Charles Earland Septet | Infant Eyes | Muse | MR 5181
Blues For Ruurd
Chuck Mangione Quintet | Jazz Brother | Milestone | M 47042
Blues For Sammy
Pharoah Sanders Quartet | Live | Evidence | TR 116
Blues For Sarge
New York Jazz Quartet | Blues For Sarka | Enja | 3025-2
Blues For Shorty Bill
Axel Zwingenberger | Boogie Woogie Live | Vagabond | VRCD 8.85007
Blues For Sippie Wallace
Joe Pass | Montreux '77 | Original Jazz Classics | OJC20 382-2(2308212)
Blues For Sitges
The Montreux '77 Collection | Pablo | 2620107
Blues For Smedley
Lady Bass & The Real Gone Guys | Lady Be Good | L+R Records | CDLR 40029
Blues For Smoke
Christian Minh Doky Quartet | Appreciation | Storyville | STCD 4169
Blues For Stanley
Gene Harris Quartet | A Little Piece Of Heaven | Concord | CCD 4578
Blues For Steph & Stuff
Oscar Peterson Quintet | Oscar Peterson Meets Roy Hargrove And Ralph Moore | Telarc Digital | CD 83399
Blues For Stitt
Adam Makowicz | The Solo Album | Verve | 517888-2
Blues For Tango
Dakota Staton With The Groove Holmes Sextet | Dakota Staton | LRC Records | CDC 9017
Blues For Tatum
Thomas Heidepriem Quartet | Brooklyn Shuffle | L+R Records | CDLR 45084
Blues For Tenorsaxophon
Steve Martland Band | The Orchestra Of Smith's Academy | Enja | ENJ-9358 2
Blues For Terenzi
Jiggs Whigham With The WDR Big Band | The Third Stone | Koala Records | CD P 4
Blues For Terry
Olivier Peters Sextet | The Open Door | NCC Jazz | NCC 8501
Blues For The Barbecue
Peter Schärli Special Sextet feat.Glenn Ferris and Tom Varner | Blues For The Beast | Enja | 9103-2
Blues For The Blues
Harry Sweets Edison Sextet | The Soul Of Ben Webster | Verve | 527475-2
Blues For The Blues(alt.take)
Sammy Price Septet | Barrelhouse And Blues | Black Lion | BLCD 760159
Blues For The Champ Of The Champs
Albert Nicholas And His New Orleans Friends | Jazz In Paris:Classic Jazz At Saint-Germain-Des-Prés | EmArCy | 013045-2
Blues For The Flitsch
Sonny Morris And The Delta Jazz Band | For The Good Old Boys | Lake | LACD 63
Blues For The Groundskeeper
Alex Norris Quintet | A New Beginning | Fresh Sound Records | FSNT 081 CD
Blues For The Guardian Angels
Joe Pass Duo | Northsea Nights | Pablo | 2308221
Blues For The Hague
Richie Hart Quartet | Remembering Wes | Blue Flame | 40222
Blues For The Moment
Rodney Jones Quintet | Rodney Jones-The 'X' Field | Musicmasters | 65147-2
Blues For The New Millenium
Randy Johnston Quartet | In A-Chord | Muse | MCD 5512
Blues For The Night People
Charlie Byrd Trio | Midnight Guitar | Savoy | SV 0247(SJL 1121)
Blues For The Old Men
Yusef Lateef Quartet | Blues For The Orient | Prestige | P 24035
Blues For The Orient
Scott Hamilton Quintet | Scott Hamilton, 2 | Concord | CCD 4061
Blues For The Saints
Quadrant | Quadrant | Original Jazz Classics | OJCCD 498-2
Blues For The Weasel
Joe Pass-John Pisano | Joe Pass-John Pisano:Duets | Pablo | 2310959-2
Blues For The Wee Folk
Ronnie Earl & The Broadcasters | Blues And Forgiveness | Crosscut | CCD 11042
Blues For Tomi-Oka
Port Of Harlem Seven | Jazz Classics Vol.2 | Blue Note | 789385-2
Blues For Tomorrow
Thelonious Monk Septet | Thelonious Monk-The Complete Riverside Recordings | Riverside | 15 RCD 022-2
Blues For Val
Joe Pass | The Montreux '77 Collection | Pablo | 2620107
Blues For Valerie
Ingolf Burkhardt-Ludwig Nuß Quintet | Jazzed Friends | Mons Records | MR 874780
Blues For Welshie
Michael Naura Quintet | Jazz In Deutschland 1957-1958/Kühl Und Modern | Vagabond | 6.22563 AG
Blues For Wes
Ran Blake | Wende | Owl Records | 05
Blues For Willarene
Tete Montoliu Trio | I Wanna Talk About You | Steeplechase | SCS 1137
Blues For Yano San
Nat Su Quartet | The J.Way | Fresh Sound Records | FSNT 038 CD
Blues For Yard
Sonny Stitt Quartet | Symphony Hall Swing | Savoy | WL 70830 (809327)
Blues For Yesterday
Louis Armstrong And His Hot Seven | Louis Armstrong:A 100th Birthday Celebration | RCA | 2663694-2
Louis Armstrong-The Complete RCA Victor Recordings | RCA | 2668682-2
Gerald Wilson's Orchestra Of The 90's | Jenna | Discovery | DSCD 964(881985)
Blues For Yolanda(incompl.take)
Coleman Hawkins And Ben Webster With The Oscar Peterson Quartet | Coleman Hawkins Encounters Ben Webster | Verve | 521427-2
Blues For Yolanda(Mono take)
Coleman Hawkins Encounters Ben Webster | Verve | 521427-2
Blues For Yolanda(Stereo take)
Booker Ervin Quartet | Lament For Booker Ervin | Enja | 2054-2
Blues For Zain
Art Ensemble Of Chicago | Vol.1:Ancient To The Future | DIW | DIW 8014
Blues Force
Emil Mangelsdorff Quartet | This Side Up | L+R Records | CDLR 45065
Blues Forever Variations
Clark Terry Sextet | Free And Oozy | Blue Moon | BMCD 3076
Blues From Havana

John Lewis Quartet | Mirjana | Ahead | 33750

Blues From The East
Thomas Morris And His Seven Hot Babies | Victor Jazz History Vol.5:Harlem Jazz(1921-28) | RCA | 2128559-2

Blues F-T
Jackie McLean Quintet | Bluesnik | Blue Note | 784067-2

Blues Für Hendricks Mama
Johnny Dodds And His Chicago Boys | King Of The New Orleans Clarinet | Black & Blue | BLE 59.235 2

Blues Go Away
George Barnes Quartet | Blues Going Up | Concord | CJ 43

Blues Impromptus
Lee Konitz-Gil Evans | Hereos | Verve | 511621-2 PMS

Blues In 12 Bars-
Carla Bley Band | 4X4 | Watt | 30(159547-2)

Blues In 12 Other Bars-
Big Bill Broonzy | Blues Legacy 10: Big Bill Broonzy-Feelin' Low Down | Vogue | 512510

Blues In 6-8
George Shearing Trio | Jazz Moments | Capitol | 832085-2

Blues In A Minor
Modern Jazz Quartet | A Night At The Opera | Jazz Door | JD 1244

Blues In A Riff
Raymond Burke's Big Three | Raymond Burke And Cie Frazier With Butch Thompson In New Orleans | 504 Records | 504CD 27

Blues In B Flat
Bill Henderson And His Friends | Live At The Times | Discovery | DS 779 IMS
Modern Jazz Quartet | Blues On Bach | Atlantic | 7567-81393-2
Richie Kamuca Quintet | Richie Kamuca's Charlie | Concord | CJ 96
Tatum-Carter-Bellson Trio | The Tatum Group Masterpieces | Pablo | 2625706

Blues In B Flat(alt.take)
Gerry Mulligan-Ben Webster Quintet | The Complete Gerry Mulligan Meets Ben Webster Sessions | Verve | 539055-2

Blues In B Flat(incompl.take)
Gene Harris Quartet | A Little Piece Of Heaven | Concord | CCD 4578

Blues In C
Tatum-Carter-Bellson Trio | The Tatum Group Masterpieces | Pablo | 2310732

Blues In C Minor
Modern Jazz Quartet | A Night At The Opera | Jazz Door | JD 1244

Blues In E Flat
Red Norvo And His Swing Octet | Knock On Wood | Affinity | CD AFS 1017

Blues In Englewood Cliffs
Ben Webster With The Kenny Drew Trio | Swiss Radio Days Jazz Series:Ben Webster-Dexter Gordon | TCB Records | TCB 02102

Blues In F
Buddy Bolden's Blues | Buddy Bolden's Blues | ITM Records | ITM 14101

Blues In Five Dimensions
Mickey Tucker Quartet | Blues In Five Dimensions | Steeplechase | SCCD 31258

Blues In G
Joe Pass | Live At Long Beach City College | Pablo | 2308239-2
Ray Bryant | Blue Moods | EmArCy | 842438-2 PMS

Blues In H(B)
Count Basie And His Orchestra | Chairman Of The Board | Roulette | 581664-2

Blues In Hoss' Flat
Live In Antibes 1968 | France's Concert | FCD 112

Blues In Hoss' Flat(Blues In Frankie's Flat)
| Cecil's Boogie | Jazz Colours | 874749-2

Blues In Maude's Flat
Thilo Kreitmeier Quintet | Mo' Better Blues | Organic Music | ORGM 9706
Charlie Haden Trio | The Montreal Tapes | Verve | 537483-2

Blues In Motion
Charlie Haden-Paul Motian Trio Feat.Geri Allen | Etudes | Soul Note | 121162-2

Blues In My Heart
Art Tatum | The Art Tatum Solo Masterpieces | Pablo | 2625703
Dick Katz Trio | 3wayPlay | Reservoir | RSR CD 127(875790)
Milt Jackson Septet | Night Mist | Pablo | 2312124
Scott Hamilton Quartet | After Hours | Concord | CCD 4755

Blues In My Music Room
Gary Smulyan Quartet And Brass | Blue Suite | Criss Cross | Criss 1189

Blues In My Sleep
Earl Hines Sextet | The Dukeless Gang | Queen-Disc | 041

Blues In Orbit
Gil Evans Orchestra | Svengali | ACT | 9207-2
Müller Braig Jazz Unit | Secret Information | SemaDenga Music | R 001B

Blues In Orbit(aka Tender)
Phil Woods Sextet | Young Woods | Fresh Sound Records | FSR-CD 0182

Blues In Quandary
Stan Kenton And His Orchestra | One Night Stand | Choice | CHCD 71051

Blues In Riff
By Request Vol.1 | Creative World | ST 1036

Blues In Suburbia
Stan Getz With The Kurt Edelhagen Orchestra | Stan Getz | Laserlight | 15761

Blues In The Air
Sidney Bechet And His New Orleans Feetwarmers | Sidney Bechet:Summertime | Dreyfus Jazz Line | FDM 36712-2
Sidney Bechet 1932-1943: The Bluebird Sessions | Bluebird | ND 90317
The Tremble Kids All Stars | The Tremble Kids All Stars Play Chicago Jazz! | Nagel-Heyer | CD 043
Sidney Bechet And His New Orleans Feetwarmers | Sidney Bechet 1932-1943: The Bluebird Sessions | Bluebird | ND 90317

Blues In The Background
Lalo Schifrin Trio With The London Philharmonic | Jazz Meets The Symphony | East-West | 4509-92004-2

Blues In The Basement
Shelly Manne All Stars | A Night On The Coast | Moon Records | MLP 008-1

Blues In The Bergerie
Lightnin' Hopkins | Blues In My Bottle | Original Blues Classics | OBCCD 506-2(BV 1045)

Blues In The Burying Ground
Frank Wess And His Orchestra | Tryin' To Make My Blues Turn Green | Concord | CCD 4592

Blues In The Closet
Bud Powell Trio | The Legacy | Jazz Door | JD 1204
Chet Baker Sextet | Chet Is Back | RCA | NL 70578 AG
Harry Sweets Edison Sextet | Mr.Swing Harry Edison | Verve | 559868-2
Horace Parlan Trio | Like Someone In Love | Steeplechase | SCCD 31178
Kenny Drew Trio | In Concert | Steeplechase | SCCD 31106
Red Garland Trio | Rediscovered Masters | Prestige | P 24078
Sarane Ferret Group | Tribute To Django | France's Concert | FCD 124
Tal Farlow Quartet | The Tal Farlow Album | Verve | MV 2584 IMS
Toots Thielemans With The Shirley Horn Trio | For My Lady | EmArCy | 510133-2
Walter Bishop Jr. Trio | Speak Low | Muse | MR 5066

Blues In The Dark
Jimmy Rushing With The Count Basie Orchestra | Big Band Bounce And Boogie Woogie:Good Mornin' Blues-Jimmy Rushing | Affinity | AFS 1002
Original Motion Picture Soundtrack | Kansas City | Verve | 529554-2

Blues In The Night
Art Pepper Quintet With Strings | Art Pepper:The Complete Galaxy Recordings | Galaxy | 16GCD 1016-2
Artie Shaw And His Orchestra | This Is Artie Shaw Vol. 2 | RCA | NL 89411 DP
Billy Eckstine With The Billy May Orchestra | Once More With Feeling | Roulette | 581862-2
Boots Mussuli Quartet | Little Man | Affinity | AFF 67
Cal Tjader Quartet | Jazz At The Blackhawk | Original Jazz Classics | OJCCD 436-2(F 8096)
Cal Tjader Quartet With Strings | Plays Harold Arlen | Original Jazz Classics | OJC 285(F 8072)
Dee Daniels With The Trio Johan Clement | Close Encounter Of The Swingin' Kind | Timeless | CD SJP 312
Ella Fitzgerald With The Billy May Orchestra | For The Love Of Ella Fitzgerald | Verve | 841765-2
The Complete Ella Fitzgerald Song Books of Harold Arlen, Irving Berlin, Duke Ellington, George & Ira Gershwin, Jerome Kern, Johnny Mercer, Cole Porter And Rogers & Hart | Verve | 519832-2
The Harold Arlen Songbook | Verve | 817526-1 IMS
Jimmy Smith With The Lalo Schifrin Orchestra | The Cat | CTI Records | PDCTI 1110-2
Jimmy Witherspoon And His All Stars | Blues For Easy Livers | Original Blues Classics | OBCCD 585-2(PR 7475)
Julie London With Russ Garcia And His Orchestra | About The Blues/London By Night | Capitol | 535208-2
Larry Vuckovich Quintet | Tres Palabras | Concord | CCD 4416
Louis Armstrong With The Oscar Peterson Quartet | Louis Armstrong Meets Oscar Peterson | Verve | 825713-2
Louis Armstrong With The Russell Garcia Orchestra | Compact Jazz: Louis Armstrong | Verve | 833293-2
Nat King Cole Trio With Anita Boyer | The Legendary 1941-44 Broadcast Transcriptions | Music & Arts | CD 808
Peggy Lee With Benny Goodman And His Sextet | Peggy Lee & Benny Goodman:The Complete Recordings 1941-1947 | CBS | C2K 65686
Pete Candoli Septet | Blues When Your Lover Has Gone | Fresh Sound Records | FSR 518(Somerset SF 17200)
Rey DeMichel Orchestra | For Bloozers Only! | Fresh Sound Records | CHS 2503(Challenge)
Shorty Rogers And His Orchestra | Swings | Bluebird | ND 83012
Stan Kenton And His Orchestra | Stan Kenton In New Jersey | Status | CD 104(882200)

Blues In The Night(alt.take)
Jimmie Lunceford And His Orchestra | Big Band Bounce & Boogie:Strictly Lunceford | Affinity | AFS 1003

Blues In The Pulpit
Leonard Feather's Blue Six | Clyde Bernhardt:The Complete Recordings Vol.1 (1945-1948) | Blue Moon | BMCD 6016

Blues In Thirds
Sidney Bechet Trio | Sidney Bechet 1932-1943: The Bluebird Sessions | Bluebird | ND 90317
Earl Hines-Piano Man | Bluebird | NK 86750
Earl Hines | Live In Milano 1966 | Nueva Records | JU 315

Blues In Thirds-
Gerry Mulligan-Paul Desmond Quartet | Blues In Time | Verve | POCJ 1919 PMS

Blues In Time
Buddy Collette Quintet | Flute Talk | Soul Note | SN 1165

Blues In Twos
Tom Harrell Quintet | Live At The Village Vanguard | RCA | 2663910-2

Blues In Una Sea
Krystall Klear And The Buells | Our Night Together | K2B2 Records | 2169

Blues Intermezzo
Andy McKee And NEXT with Hamiet Bluiett | Sound Root | Mapleshade | 04432

Blues Is A Woman
T-Bone Walker And His Band | Classics Of Modern Blues | Blue Note | 84550

Blues Legacy
John Coltrane-Milt Jackson Quintet | The Coltrane Legacy | Atlantic | SD 1553
Cousin Joe With The Blueshounds | The Blues Vol.3 | Big Bear | 156400

Blues Lundvall
Roy Haynes Quintet | Te-Vou! | Dreyfus Jazz Line | FDM 36569-2

Blues March
Art Blakey And The Jazz Messengers | The Art Of Jazz | IN+OUT Records | 77028-2
Live In Stockholm 1959 | DIW | DIW 313 CD
Night In Tunisia | Philips | 800064-2
The Best Of Blue Note Vol.2 | Blue Note | 797960-2
Paris Jazz Concert:Art Blakey & The Jazz Messengers | Laserlight | 36158
Jazz-Club: Drums | Verve | 840033-2
Benny Golson Sextet | Domingo | Dreyfus Jazz Line | FDM 36557-2
Gene Harris Group | Alley Cats | Concord | CCD 4859

Blues March For Europe No.1
Art Blakey And The Jazz Messengers | Planet Jazz:Lee Morgan | Planet Jazz | 2161238-2
Martial Solal And The Kentonians | Martial Solal:The Complete Vogue Recordings Vol.3 | Vogue | 21606372

Blues Mess Around
Modern Jazz Quartet | Blues At Carnegie Hall | Philips | PHCE 3019 PMS

Blues Milanese
John Coltrane Quartet With Brass | Africa/Brass | Impulse(MCA) | JAS 8 (AS 6)

Blues Minor
Africa/Brass | Impulse(MCA) | GRJ 80042

Blues Montmartre
Frank Morgan Sextet | Bird Calls 2 | Savoy | 650111(881911)

Blues My Naughty Sweetie Gives To Me
Blue Barron And His Orchestra | The Uncollected: Blue Barron | Hindsight | HSR 110
Dutch Swing College Band Meets Billy Butterfield | Swing That Music | DSC Production | PA 1009 (801066)
Firehouse Five Plus Two | The Firehouse Five Story Vol. 1 | Good Time Jazz | 12010
Henrik Johansen's Jazzband | The Golden Years Of Revival Jazz,Vol.13 | Storyville | STCD 5518
Humphrey Lyttelton And His Band | Jazz From The Island Vol.2 | Jazz Colours | 874703-2
Ralph Sutton Trio | Easy Street | Sackville | SKCD2-2040

Blues 'N' Bells
Lester Young And His Band | Lester Young:The Complete 1936-1951 Small Group Sessions(Studio Recordings-Master Takes),Vol.4 | Blue Moon | BMCD 1004

Blues 'N' Dues Et Cetera
George Gruntz Concert Jazz Band | Blues 'N Dues Et Cetera | Enja | ENJ-6072 2
Hampton Hawes Trio | The Sermon | Original Jazz Classics | OJCCD 1067-2(C 7653)

Blues N/C
Bernt Rosengren Big Band | Jazz In Sweden | Caprice | CAP 1214

Blues No.1
Bill Evans-Don Elliott | Tenderly | Milestone | MCD 9317-2
Count Basie Quartet | The Soloist | Jazz Anthology | 550002
Ken Colyer And His Jazz Band | Ken Colyer-The Unknown New Orleans Sessions With Raymond Burke 1952-1953 | 504 Records | 504CD 23

Blues No.2
Bill Evans-Don Elliott | Tenderly | Milestone | MCD 9317-2
Count Basie Quartet | The Soloist | Jazz Anthology | 550002
Jochen Feucht Trio | Signs On Lines | Satin Doll Productions | SDP 1019-1 CD
Ken Colyer And His Jazz Band | Ken Colyer-The Unknown New Orleans Sessions With Raymond Burke 1952-1953 | 504 Records | 504CD 23
Miles Davis Quintet | Circle In The Round | CBS | 467898-2
Miles Davis Sextet | Someday My Prince Will Come | CBS | CK 65919
Ray Bryant | Alone At Montreux | 32 Jazz | 32128
Allan Vaché-Antti Sarpila & 1 Sextet | Summit Meeting | Nagel-Heyer | CD 027

Blues No.3
Count Basie Quartet | The Soloist | Jazz Anthology | 550002
Ray Bryant | Alone With The Blues | Original Jazz Classics | OJC 249(NJ 8213)

Blues No.4
Florian Poser Group | Pacific Tales | Acoustic Music Records | 319.1124.2

Blues No.5(Blues For Kurtchen)
Ray Bryant | The Montreux '77 Collection | Pablo | 2620107

Blues Not To Lose
Steve Slagle Quartet | Alto Blue | Steeplechase | SCCD 31416

Blues Of Summer
Oscar Peterson | Solo | Pablo | 2310975-2

Blues Of The Prairies
Oscar Peterson Trio | Gitanes Jazz 'Round Midnight: Oscar Peterson | Verve | 511036-2 PMS
Mezzrow-Bechet Quintet | Masters Of Jazz Vol.4:Sidney Bechet | Storyville | STCD 4104

Blues O'Mighty
Oliver Nelson And His Orchestra | More Blues And The Abstract Truth | MCA | 2292-54643-2

Blues On Account
Hubert Sumlin & Carey Bell | Gamblin' Woman | L+R Records | LR 42008

Blues On Down
Albert Ammons | Commodore Classics-Albert Ammons: Boogie Woogie And The Blues | Commodore | 6.24297 AG

Blues On My Mind
Blue Mitchell Quintet | The Riverside Collection: Blues On My Mind | Original Jazz Classics | OJCCD 6009-2
Cal Collins Quartet | Blues On My Mind | Concord | CJ 95
Joshua Redman Quartet | Ludwigsburger Jazztage | Chaos | CACD 8055-3

Blues On Parade
Woody Herman And His Orchestra | The Band That Plays The Blues | Naxos Jazz | 8.120527 CD

Blues On Parade-
Leroy Vinnegar Quartet | Walkin' The Basses | Contemporary | CCD 14068-2

Blues On Purpose
Nina Simone With Orchestra | Nina Simone-The 60s Vol.1: Ne Me Quitte Pas | Mercury | 838543-2 PMS

Blues On Sunday
Walter 'Foots' Thomas And His All Stars | Unissued Bean & Ben Takes 1944 | Harlequin | HQ 2032 IMS

Blues On The Champ-Elysées
Avery Sharpe Sextet with McCoy Tyner | Unspoken Words | Sunnyside | SSC 1029 D

Blues On The Corner
McCoy Tyner Big Band | Journey | Birdology | 519941-2
McCoy Tyner Quartet | Joe Henderson-The Blue Note Years | Blue Note | 789287-2

Blues On The World
Axel Zwingenberger | Boogie Woogie Live | Vagabond | VRCD 8.85007

Blues On Top
Ike Quebec With The Three Sounds | The Lost Sessions | Blue Note | 521484-2

Blues Open
Cannonball Adderley Quintet | Cannonball And Eight Giants | Milestone | M 47001

Blues Oriental
Cannonball Adderley-Milt Jackson Quintet | Milt Jackson Birthday Celebration | Fantasy | FANCD 6079-2
Lu Watters' Jazz Band | Blues Over Bodega | Good Time Jazz | GTCD 12066-2

Blues Over Bodega
Larry Garner Group | Baton Rouge | Verve | 529467-2

Blues Pour Flirter No.2
Claude Luter Quartet | Blue Clarinet | Vogue | 502612

Blues Primitif
Django Reinhardt And The Quintet Du Hot Club De France | Django Reinhardt Portrait | Barclay | DALP 2/1939
David Hazeltine Quartet | Blues Quarters Vol.1 | Criss Cross | Criss 1188

Blues Quodlibet
Jessica Williams Trio | Inventions | Jazz Focus | JFCD 008

Blues Reconstruction
Glen Gray And The Casa Loma Orchestra | Swingin' Decade! Sounds Of The Great Bands Of The 40's | Pathe | 1566171(Capitol ST 1289)

Blues Riff
Wes Montgomery Trio | Wes Montgomery-The Complete Riverside Recordings | Riverside | 12 RCD 4408-2

Blues Riff(alt.take)
Art Pepper Quintet | Art Pepper Quintet Live At Donte's 1968 | Fresh Sound Records | FSCD 1039/2

Blues Roots
Lonnie Johnson Quintet | Blues By Lonnie Johnson | Original Blues Classics | OBCCD 502-2(BV 1007)

Blues Sonata:
Sandy Brown's Jazz Band | The Golden Years Of Revival Jazz,Vol.8 | Storyville | STCD 5513

Blues Stampede
Rodney Jones Quintet | Rodney Jones-The 'X' Field | Musicmasters | 65147-2

Blues Suite
Trombone Summit | Trombone Summit | MPS | 68272

Blues The Most
Hampton Hawes Trio | Hampton Hawes Trio Vol.1 | Original Jazz Classics | OJC20 316-2(C 3505)
Count Basie And His Orchestra With Billy Eckstine | Basie On Roulette, Vol. 8: Basie/Eckstine Inc. | Vogue | 500008

Blues Time
Dusko Goykovich Quintet | Soul Connection | Enja | ENJ-8044 2
Warren Vaché Quintet | Warren Plays Warrey | Nagel-Heyer | CD 033

Blues Times(2)
Blues Of Summer | Nagel-Heyer | NH 1011
Gil Fuller And His Orchestra | The Bebop Boys | Savoy | WL 70547 (809278)

Blues To Be There
Danny Moss-Roy Williams Quintet | Ellington For Lovers | Nagel-Heyer | NH 1009
Duke Ellington And His Orchestra | Essential Jazz | CBS | 473686-2

Blues To Be There-
Ellington At Newport 1956(Complete) | CBS | CK 64932
John Coltrane Quartet | John Coltrane-The Heavyweight Champion:The Complete Atlantic Recordings | Atlantic | 8122-71984-2

Blues To Bechet
Jazz Gallery:John Coltrane Vol.2 | RCA | 2127276-2
John Coltrane Trio | Coltrane Plays The Blues | Atlantic | 7567-81351-2
Steve Gut-Michael Blam | Mr.C.T. | Timeless | CD SJP 428

Blues To Coltrane
Eric Reed Quintet | Musicale | Impulse(MCA) | 951196-2

Blues To Come)
John Coltrane Quartet | John Coltrane-The Heavyweight Champion:The Complete Atlantic Recordings | Atlantic | 8122-71984-2

Blues To Elvin
Coltrane Plays The Blues | Rhino | 8122-79966-2
Coltrane Plays The Blues | Atlantic | 7567-81351-2
John Coltrane-The Heavyweight Champion:The Complete Atlantic Recordings | Atlantic | 8122-71984-2

Blues To Elvin(alt.take 1)
Coltrane Plays The Blues | Rhino | 8122-79966-2
John Coltrane-The Heavyweight Champion:The Complete Atlantic Recordings | Atlantic | 8122-71984-2

Blues To Elvin(alt.take 2)
Coltrane Plays The Blues | Rhino | 8122-79966-2
John Coltrane-The Heavyweight Champion:The Complete Atlantic Recordings | Atlantic | 8122-71984-2

Blues To Elvin(false start)

TITELVERZEICHNIS

Greg Tardy Band | Serendipity | Impulse(MCA) | 951258-2
Blues To Professor Pickens
Art Hodes' International Trio | Blues To Save The Trees | L+R Records | CDLR 40015
Blues To The Lonely(Lonely Blues)
John Coltrane Quartet | John Coltrane-The Heavyweight Champion:The Complete Atlantic Recordings | Atlantic | 8122-71984-2
Blues To You
John Coltrane Trio | Coltrane Plays The Blues | Rhino | 8122-79966-2
Coltrane Plays The Blues | Atlantic | 7567-81351-2
John Coltrane Quartet | John Coltrane-The Heavyweight Champion:The Complete Atlantic Recordings | Atlantic | 8122-71984-2
Blues To You(alt.take 1)
John Coltrane Trio | Coltrane Plays The Blues | Rhino | 8122-79966-2
John Coltrane Quartet | John Coltrane-The Heavyweight Champion:The Complete Atlantic Recordings | Atlantic | 8122-71984-2
Blues To You(alt.take 2)
John Coltrane Trio | Coltrane Plays The Blues | Rhino | 8122-79966-2
Don Rendell Nine | Earth Music | Spotlite | SPJ 515
Blues Triste
Tummy Young's Big Seven | The Classic Swing Of Buck Clayton | Original Jazz Classics | OJCCD 1709-2(RLP 142)
Blues Up And Down
Dexter Gordon-Johnny Griffin Quintet | Live At Carnegie Hall | CBS | CK 65312
Eddie Lockjaw Davis-Johnny Griffin Quintet | Tough Tenors Back Again! | Storyville | STCD 8298
Gene Ammons-Sonny Stitt Quintet | Left Bank Encores | Prestige | PRCD 11022-2
Scott Hamilton-Ken Peplowski-Spike Robinson Septet | Groovin' High | Concord | CCD 4509
Blues Valse
Daniel Schnyder & The Modern Art Septet | Secret Cosmos | Enja | ENJ-5055 2
Blues Velvet
Barney Wilen Quartet | New York Romance | Sunnyside | SSC 1067 D
Blues Walk
Clifford Brown-Max Roach Quintet | Verve Jazz Masters 44:Clifford Brown and Max Roach | Verve | 528109-2
Dexter Gordon Quartet | Body And Soul | Black Lion | CD 877628-2
Lou Donaldson Quintet | The Best Of Lou Donaldson Vol.1(1957-1967) | Blue Note | 827298-2
Blues Waltz
The Latin Jazz Quintet | Hot Sauce | Prestige | PCD 24128-2
Blues With Helen
Members Of The Basie Band | Lester Young:The Complete 1936-1951 Small Group Sessions(Studio Recordings-Master Takes),Vol.6 Rare Items | Blue Moon | BMCD 1006
Blues With Lips
Clifford Gibson | Beat You Doing It | Yazoo | YAZ 1027
Blues Without Woe
Bennie Wallace With Yosuke Yamashita | Brilliant Corners | Denon Compact Disc | CY-30003
Blues!
Charlie Parker Quartet | Bird On Verve-Vol.2:Bird & Diz | Verve | 817443-1 IMS
Blues(fast)
Charlie Parker | Verve | 539757-2
Stuff Smith With The Jean Claude Pelletier Orchestra | Live In Paris 1965 | France's Concert | FCD 120
Blues(Largo)-
JATP All Stars | The Complete Jazz At The Philharmonic On Verve 1944-1949 | Verve | 523893-2
Blues(Pres)
Count Basie And His Orchestra | Lester Leaps In-Vol.2 1939/1940 | CBS | CBS 88668
Blues(Young Man)-
Jazzensemble Des Hessischen Rundfunks | Atmosphering Conditions Permitting | ECM | 1549/50
Blues, Eternal Turn On
Leo Smith Group | Procession Of The Great Ancestry | Chief Records | CD 6
Bluesanova
Tom Browne Quintet | Hot Jazz Bisquits | Hip Bop | HIBD 8801
Johnny Hodges Orchestra | The Soul Of Ben Webster | Verve | 527475-2
Blues-A-Plenty
Günter Lenz Springtime | Majorleague | L+R Records | CDLR 45063
Bluesdoctor
Merseysippi Jazz Band 1954-1957 | Mersey Tunnel Jazz | Lake | LACD 85
Bluesette
Hank Jones | Maybeck Recital Hall Series Volume Sixteen | Concord | CCD 4502
Joe Pass | Live At Long Beach City College | Pablo | 2308239-2
Morgana King With Orchestra | A Taste Of Honey | Mainstream | MD CDO 707
Rhoda Scott Trio | Jazz In Paris:Rhoda Scott-Live At The Olympia | EmArCy | 549879-2 PMS
Stochelo Rosenberg Group | Gypsy Swing | Verve | 527806-2
Tito Puente And His Ensemble | On Broadway | Concord | CCD 4207
Toots Thielemans Sextet | Toots Thielemans Live | Polydor | 2491003 IMS
Bluesiando
Kenny Burrell Quintet | Kenny Burrell-Bluesin' Around | CBS | FC 38507
Bluesin' In Cadaques
McCoy Tyner | Monk's Dream | Memo Music | HDJ 4019
Bluesnote
Sonny Rollins Quintet | Sonny Rollins:The Blue Note Recordings | Blue Note | 821371-2
Jim Hall | Dedications & Inspirations | Telarc Digital | CD 83365
Bluesology
Cal Tjader Quintet | At Grace Cathedral | Fantasy | F 9521
Joe Pass Quintet | One For My Baby | Pablo | 2310936-2
Kenny Drew/Niels-Henning Orsted-Pedersen Duo | Duo 2 | Steeplechase | SCS 1010
Milt Jackson Quartet | First Recording | Jazz Anthology | JA 5130
Modern Jazz Quartet | Fontessa | Rhino | 8122-73687-2
European Concert | Atlantic | SD 2-603
Ray Brown Trio | Summerwind-Live At The Loa | Concord | CCD 4426
Bluesongo
Sonny Rollins Quintet | Masters Of Jazz Vol.14 | RCA | CL 42874 AG
Bluesville
Harold Harris Trio | Here's Harold | Vee Jay Recordings | VJR 501
Blueswil
Barney Kessel With The Monty Alexander Trio | Spontaneous Combustion | Contemporary | C 14033
Bluesy
Massimo Moriconi Trio & Guests | Massimo Moriconi Trio & Guests | Penta Flowers | CDPIA 016
Bluesy Sue
Klaus Doldinger Quartet | Bluesy Toosy | ACT | 9200-2
Blueth?
Dave Brubeck Quartet | Adventures In Time | CBS | CBS 66291
Bluing
Miles Davis Sextet | Dig | Prestige | P 24054
Bluma
Bireli Lagrene Ensemble | Routes To Django & Bireli Swing '81 | Jazzpoint | JP 1055 CD
Jaco Pastorius Trio | Jaco Pastorius Broadway Blues & Theresa | Jazzpoint | JP 1053 CD
Heavy'n Jazz | Jazzpoint | JP 1036 CD
Jaco Pastorius Heavy'n Jazz & Stuttgart Aria | Jazzpoint | JP 1058 CD
Bluma-
Gabriele Hasler-Elvira Plenar-Andreas Willers | Sonetburger-Nach Texten Von Oskar Pastior | Foolish Music | FM 211793
Blunduffel Hendelechs
John Zorn Naked City | Naked City-Grand Guignol | Avant | AVAN 002
Blunt Object
Orchestra Jazz Siciliana | Orchestra Jazz Siciliana Plays The Music Of Carla Bley | Watt | XtraWatt/4
Jan Garbarek Quartet | Afric Pepperbird | ECM | 1007 (2301007)
Blut(Lullaby)
Jeff 'Tain' Watts Quartet | Citizen Tain | CBS | CK 69551
Blutopia
Duke Ellington And His Orchestra | Duke Elliongton:Complete Prestige Carnegie Hall 1943-1944 Concerts | Definitive Records | DRCD 11210
Bl-You-Uuz
Michel Portal-Martial Solal | Fast Mood | RCA | 2169310-2
BMG No.5
String Thing | String Thing:Turtifix | MicNic Records | MN 4
B-Movie Bang Bang Bang
Donald Byrd Quintet | Byrd In Flight | Blue Note | 852435-2
Bo Diddley
John Abercrombie Trio | Tactics | ECM | 1623(533680-2)
Bo Diddy
Tiziana Simona With The Mal Waldron Quartet | Flakes | ITM Records | ITM 1437
Boar Jibu
Shorty Rogers And His Orchestra Feat. The Giants | Short Stops | RCA | NL 85917(2)
Bob
The Mel Lewis Jazz Orchestra | To You-A Tribute To Mel Lewis | Limelight | 820832-2 IMS
Bob Marley
Sacbe | Sacbe-Street Corner | Discovery | DS 864 IMS
Bob Nouveau
The Lounge Lizards | Voice Of Chunk | VeraBra Records | CDVBR 2025-2
Bob White(Whatcha Gonna Swing Tonight)
Carmen McRae With Orchestra | Birds Of A Feather | Decca | 589515-2
Dick Hyman | Maybeck Recital Hall Series Volume Three | Concord | CCD 4415
Bobblehead
Jimmy Cobb's Mob | Cobb's Groove | Milestone | MCD 9334-2
Chas Burchell Quintet | Unsong Hero:The Undiscovered Genius Of Chas Burchell | IN+OUT Records | 7026-2
Bobblin'
The Three Sounds | The Best Of The Three Sounds | Blue Note | 827323-2
Bobby In Bassoonville
Tim Berne-Marc Ducret-Tom Rainey | Big Satan | Winter&Winter | 910005-2
Bobby Raconte Une Histoire
Chris Barber's Jazz Band | The Great Re-Union Concert | Intercord | 157011
Bobby's New Mood
Joe Carter Band | The Ralph Bass Sessions Vol.5 | Red Lightnin' | RL 0057
Bobok
Charlie Parker Quintet | Bird At The Roost-The Savoy Sessions | Savoy | SJL 1108 (801157)
Bob's Boys
Prestige All Stars | Tenor Conclave | Original Jazz Classics | OJCCD 127-2
Helmut Nieberle & Cordes Sauvages | Salut To Django | Jardis Records | JRCD 9926
Bob's Chops
Essence All Stars | Hub Art | Hip Bop | HIBD 8005
Bock To Bock(Back To Back)
Wes Montgomery Orchestra | Fingerpickin' | Pacific Jazz | 837987-2
Bodas De Prata
Paul Horn Group feat. Egberto Gismonti | The Altitude Of The Sun | Black Sun Music | 15002 2
Bodi
Eric Kloss Quintet | Bodies' Warmth | Muse | MR 5077
Bodmin Moor
Herbie Mann Sextet | Let Me Tell You | Milestone | M 47010
Bo-Do
Julius Hemphill Quartet | Flat Out Jump Suite | Black Saint | BSR 0040
Body & Mention
Gregor Hilden-Hans D. Riesop Group | Compared To What...? | Wonderland Records | 319.9014.2
Body And Soul
Adam Makowicz | The Solo Album | Verve | 517888-2
Albert Dailey Trio | That Old Feeling | Steeplechase | SCCD 31107
Art Pepper | Artworks | Galaxy | GXY 5148
Art Pepper-George Cables Duo | Art Pepper:The Complete Galaxy Recordings | Galaxy | 16GCD 1016-2
Art Pepper-Shorty Rogers Quintet | Art Pepper & Shorty Rogers:Complete Lighthouse Sessions | The Jazz Factory | JFCD 22836
Art Tatum | The Standard Sessions: Art Tatum 1935-1943 Transcriptions | Music & Arts | CD 673
Standards | Black Lion | CD 877646-2
Art Tatum:20th Century Piano Genius | Verve | 531763-2
Solos 1937 & Classic Piano Solos | Forlane | UCD 19010
Benny Carter And His Orchestra | Further Definitions | Impulse(MCA) | JAS 14 (AS 12)
Benny Golson Group | Tenor Legacy | Arkadia Jazz | 70742
Benny Goodman Trio | 1938 Carnegie Hall Concert | CBS | 450983-2
Jazz Collection:Benny Goodman | Laserlight | 24396
Benny Goodman:The Complete Small Combinations Vol.1/2(1935-1937) | RCA | ND 89753
The Benny Goodman Trio And Quartet Sessions Vol.1-After You've Gone | Bluebird | ND 85631
Bill Mays Group | Kaleidoscope | The Jazz Alliance | TJA 10013
Billie Holiday And Her Orchestra | Billie Holiday:The Quintessential Vol.8/9(1939-1942) | CBS | 477837-2
Billie Holiday With The JATP All Stars | The Complete Jazz At The Philharmonic On Verve 1944-1949 | Verve | 523893-2
Billie Holiday Story Vol.1:Jazz At The Philharmonic | Verve | 521642-2
Billy Ross Quartet | The Sound:A Tribute To Stan Getz | Milestone | MCD 9227-2
Bluiett's Barbeque Band | Bluiett's Barbeque Band | Mapleshade | 04032
Brocksi-Quartett | Drums Boogie | Bear Family Records | BCD 15988 AH
Bruce Turner Quartet | The Dirty Bopper | Calligraph | CLG LP 003 IMS
Bud Powell Trio | Bud Powell In Paris | Discovery | DS 830 IMS
Bud Powell:Complete 1947-1951 Blue Note,Verve & Roost Recordings | The Jazz Factory | JFCD 22837
Buddy DeFranco-Terry Gibbs Quintet | Jazz Party-First Time Together | Palo Alto | PA 8011
Charles Mingus Group | Mysterious Blues | Candid | CCD 79042
Charles Mingus Quartet | Live In Chateauvallon 1972 | France's Concert | FCD 134
Charlie Haden-Kenny Barron | Night And The City | Verve | 539961-2
Charlie Parker | The Complete 'Bird Of The Bebop' | Stash Records | ST-CD 535(889113)
Christian Münchinger Quartet | Live At Moods! | Mons Records | MR 874321
Christoph Sänger | Live At The Montreal Jazz Festival | Laika Records | 35100822
Chu Berry And His Jazz Orchestra | Chu Berry: Berry Story | Zeta | ZET 738
Coleman Hawkins And His Orchestra | Planet Jazz:Coleman Hawkins | Planet Jazz | 2152055-2
Planet Jazz:Jazz Greatest Hits | Planet Jazz | 2169648-2
Body And Soul | Naxos Jazz | 8.120532 CD
The Indispensable Coleman Hawkins 1927-1956:Body And Soul | RCA | ND 89277
Coleman Hawkins Quartet | Verve Jazz Masters 43:Coleman Hawkins | Verve | 521856-2
Supreme | Enja | ENJ-9009 2
Coleman Hawkins Quintet | The Great Tenors | Jazz Anthology | JA 5205
Coleman Hawkins With Billy Byers And His Orchestra | The Indispensable Coleman Hawkins 1927-1956:Body And Soul | RCA | ND 89277
Coleman Hawkins With Different Bands | 100 Ans De Jazz:Coleman Hawkins | RCA | 2177832-2
Coleman Hawkins With The Adrian Acea Trio | Coleman Hawkins At The Golden Circle | Dragon | DRCD 265
Coleman Hawkins With The Thore Ehrlings Orchestra | Coleman Hawkins At The Golden Circle | Dragon | DRCD 265
Coleman Hawkins With The Tommy Flanagan Trio | Saxophones | West Wind | WW 2013
Cozy Cole All Stars | Concerto For Cozy | Jazz Anthology | JA 5161
Dakota Staton With The Dave Berkman Trio | Dakota Staton | Muse | MCD 5401
Dexter Gordon Quartet | King Neptune | Steeplechase | SCCD 36012
Ballads For Tenor | Jazz Colours | 874709-2
Dexter Gordon Quintet | Round Midnight(Soundtrack) | CBS | 70300
Dick Wellstood | Dick Wellstood-Alone | Solo Art | SACD-73
Don Byas Quartet | Americans Swinging In Paris:Don Byas | EMI Records | 539655-2
Don Byas Complete 1946-1951 European Small Group Master Takes | Definitive Records | DRCD 11214
Duke Ellington And His Orchestra feat.Dizzy Gillespie | Concert At Carnegie Hall | Atlantis | ATS 2 D
Eddie Condon All Stars | Eddie Condon Town Hall Concerts Vol.1 | Jazzology | JCECD-1001
Eddie Lockjaw Davis Quartet | Jaws | Original Jazz Classics | OJCCD 218-2(P 7154)
Eddie 'Lockjaw' Davis/Sonny Stitt | LRC Records | CDC 9028
Elisabeth Kontomanou & Jean-Michel Pilc | Hands & Incantation | Steeplechase | SCCD 31484
Engelbert Wrobel-Chris Hopkins-Dan Barrett Sextet | Harlem 2000 | Nagel-Heyer | CD 082
Ernestine Anderson With George Shearing | Great Moments With Ernestine Anderson | Concord | CCD 4582
Erroll Garner Trio | 1945 | Zeta | ZET 713
The Complete Savoy Sessions Vol.1 | Savoy | WL 70521 (809292)
Eugen Apostolidis Quartet | Imaginary Directions | Edition Collage | EC 503-2
Fatty George Combo | Jazz In Deutschland 1957-1958/Kühl Und Modern | Vagabond | 6.22563 AG
Fred Hersch | Maybeck Recital Hall Series Volume Thirty-One | Concord | CCD 4596
Freddie Hubbard Sextet | Keystone Bop | Fantasy | F 9615
Gene Krupa-Charlie Ventura Trio | Commodore Classics-Town Hall Concert 1945 | Commodore | 6.26169 AG
George Wettling Jazz Band | George Wettling Jazz Band | JSP Records | 1103
Gerry Mulligan Concert Jazz Band | The Complete Verve Gerry Mulligan Concert Band | Verve | 9860613
En Concert Avec Europe 1 | Laserlight | 710382/83
Glenn Miller And His Orchestra | Glenn Miller Live-15 Rare Broadcast Performances From 1940-1942 | RCA | NL 89485 AG
Helen Humes And The Muse All Stars | Helen Humes And The Muse All Stars | Muse | MCD 5473
Jam Session | Jam Session Vol.9 | Steeplechase | SCCD 31554
Miles Davis | Royal Jazz | RJD 514
Jason Moran Trio | The Bandwagon | Blue Note | 591893-2
Jason Seizer With The Larry Goldings Trio | Sketches | Organic Music | ORGM 9710
JATP All Stars | JATP-1940's | Verve | MV 9070/72 IMS
Jazz At The Philharmonic-The First Concert | Verve | 521646-2
The Complete Jazz At The Philharmonic On Verve 1944-1949 | Verve | 523893-2
The Complete Jazz At The Philharmonic On Verve 1944-1949 | Verve | 523893-2
Jay McShann | Jay McShann At Cafe Des Copains | Sackville | SKCD2-2024
Jeanie Bryson With The Ronnie Mathews Trio | Live at Warsaw Jazz Festival 1991 | Jazzmen Records | 660.50.002
Jimmy Smith Trio | Groovin' At Smalls' Paradise Vol.2 | Blue Note | 300222(1586)
Joe Albany-Warne Marsh Trio | The Right Combination | Original Jazz Classics | OJCCD 1749-2
Joe Maneri-Mat Maneri | Blessed | ECM | 1661(557365-2)
Joe Pass | University Of Akron Concert | Pablo | 2308249-2
Joe Turner | Stride By Stride | Solo Art | SACD-106
John Coltrane Quartet | Jazz Gallery:John Coltrane Vol.2 | RCA | 2127276-2
Live At Birdland | Charly | CD 68
The Art Of John Coltrane - The Atlantic Years | Atlantic | SD 2-313
Johnny Smith Quartet | The Johnny Smith Foursome | Fresh Sound Records | FSR 581(Roost 2223)
Junior Mance Trio | Milestones | Sackville | SKCD2-3065
Ken McIntyre Quartet | Hindsight | Steeplechase | SCCD 31014
Knut Kiesewetter Train | Knut Kiesewetter | Jazz Magazine | 48020
Lee Konitz-Frank Wunsch | Frank-Lee Speaking | West Wind | WW 2081
Lester Young Quintet | Pres Lives-The Savoy Sessions | Savoy | WL 70528 (SJL 1109) SF
Lester Young-Nat Cole Trio | Lester Young:The Complete Aladdin Sessions | Blue Note | 832787-2
Lester Young:The Complete 1936-1951 Small Group Sessions(Studio Recordings-Master Takes),Vol.2 | Blue Moon | BMCD 1002
Lionel Hampton Sextet | Americans Swinging In Paris:Lionel Hampton | EMI Records | 539649-2
Le Jazz En France-Vol.6 | Pathe | 1727301
Louis Armstrong With The Russell Garcia Orchestra | Verve Jazz Masters 1:Louis Armstrong | Verve | 519818-2
Louis Smith Quintet | Silvering | Steeplechase | SCCD 31336
Martin Taylor Trio | Skye Boat | Concord | CJ 184
Minton's Playhouse All Stars | Thelonious Monk:After Hours At Minton's | Definitive Records | DRCD 11197
Mundell Lowe-Mike Wofford | Souvenirs-A Tribute To Nick Ceroli | The Jazz Alliance | TJA 10011
Nat King Cole Trio | The Legendary 1941-44 Broadcast Transcriptions | Music & Arts | CD 808
Old Merrytale Jazz Band | Hot Time | Intercord | 160002
Oscar Peterson Quartet | Verve Jazz Masters 37:Oscar Peterson Plays Broadway | Verve | 516893-2
Oscar Peterson | Jazz Magazine | 40198
Paul Desmond With Strings | Masters Of Jazz Vol.13 | RCA | CL 42790 AG
Paul Gonsalves Quartet | Tell The Way It Is | Impulse(MCA) | JAS 27 (AS 55)
Pee Wee Russell-Henry Red Allen Quintet | The College Concerts | MCA | JAS 78(AS 9137)
Peter Weniger-Hubert Nuss | Private Concert | Mons Records | CD 1878
Quintet Du Hot Club De France | Django Reinhardt:Djangology | EMI Records | 780659-2
Rene Thomas Trio | Guitar Genius | RTBF Records | 16001
Roots | Salutes The Saxophone | IN+OUT Records | 7016-2
Roy Eldridge & His Orchestra | Big Band Bounce And Boogie:Tippin' Out | Affinity | AFS 1016
Sarah Vaughan And Her Trio | Swingin' Easy | EmArCy | 514072-2
Sarah Vaughan With Her Quartet | One Night Stand-The Town Hall Concert 1947 | Blue Note | 832139-2
Sarah Vaughan-Ray Brown | Sarah Vaughan Birthday Celebration | Fantasy | FANCD 6090-2
Scott Hamilton Quartet | The Great Appearance | Progressive | PCD 7026
Sonny Stitt Quartet | New York Jazz | Verve | 517050-2
Stan Getz Quintet | Stan Getz Plays | Verve | 2304387 IMS

Verve Jazz Masters 8:Stan Getz | Verve | 519823-2
Stan The Man | Verve | 815239-1 IMS
Stan Kenton And His Orchestra | The Kenton Era | Creative World | ST 1030
Stefano D'Anna Trio | Leapin' In | SPLASC(H) Records | CD H 374-2
Stephane Grappelli Quartet | Jazz In Paris:Stephane Grappelli-Improvisations | EmArCy | 549242-2 PMS
Grapelli Story | Verve | 515807-2
Stephane Grappelli Trio | I Hear Music | RCA | 2179624-2
Stephane Grappelli-Django Reinhard | A Swinging Affair | Decca | 6.24725 AO
Steve Allen Sextet | Steve Allen Plays Jazz Tonight | Concord | CCD 4548
Steve Grossman Trio | Way Out East Vol.2 | Red Records | 123183-2
Sun Ra And His Astro-Infinity Arkestra | Holiday For Soul Dance | Evidence | ECD 22011-2
Szakcsi Trio | Straight Ahead | GRP | GRP 97582
Ted Brown Trio | Free Spirit | Criss Cross | Criss 1031
Tete Montoliu Trio | Catalonian Fire | Steeplechase | SCCD 31017
The New York Allstars | Hey Ba-Ba-Re-Bop!! The New York Allstars Play Lionel Hampton Vol.1 | Nagel-Heyer | CD 047
The Newport Jazz Festival All-Stars | The Newport Jazz Festival All-Stars | Concord | CJ 260
Thelonious Monk | Live In Stockholm 1961 | Dragon | DRLP 151/152
Thelonious Monk-The Complete Riverside Recordings | Riverside | 15 RCD 022-2
Monk Alone:The Complete Columbia Solo Studio Recordings | CBS | C2K 65495
Thelonious Monk In Copenhagen | Storyville | STCD 8283
Blues Five Spot | Milestone | M 9124
Thelonious Monk Quartet | Thelonious Monk In Italy | Original Jazz Classics | OJCCD 488-2(RLP 9443)
Thelonious Monk In Stockholm | Duke Records | D 1020
Tiny Grimes Quintet | Some Groovy Fours | Black & Blue | BB 874.2
Tony Scott And The All Stars | Body And Soul Revisited | GRP | GRP 16272
Tony Scott-Bill Evans Quintet | A Day In New York | Fresh Sound Records | FSR-CD 0160(2)
Torsten Zwingenberger's Swingburger | Groovy At The Movie | Moustache Music | 02 03 37 72 86
Tuck Andress | Reckless Precision | Windham Hill | 34 10124-2
Walter Norris | Maybeck Recital Hall Series Volume Four | Concord | CCD 4425
Wes Montgomery Quintet | Wes Montgomery-The Complete Riverside Recordings | Riverside | 12 RCD 4408-2
Wilbur Ware Quintet | The Chicago Sound | Original Jazz Classics | OJCCD 1737-2(RLP 12-252)
Woody Herman And His Orchestra | Verve Jazz Masters 54:Woody Herman | Verve | 529903-2
Live At Peacock Lane, Hollywood | Bandstand | BDCD 1508

Body And Soul-
Klaus Ignatzek Quintet | All Systems Go | Candid | CCD 79738
Sir Charles Thompson | Playing My Way | Jazz Connaisseur | JCCD 9313-2
Sonny Clark | Sonny Clark 1954 Memorial Album | The Jazz Factory | JFCD 22834
Tenor Tribute | Tenor Tribute | Soul Note | SN 1184

Body And Soul(alt.take)
Art Tatum And His Swingsters | Art Tatum:Complete Original American Decca Recordings | Definitive Records | DRCD 11200
Joe Henderson Trio | The Standard Joe | Red Records | 123248-2
John Coltrane Quartet | Coltrane's Sound | Atlantic | 7567-81358-2
Stan Kenton And His Orchestra | Adventures In Jazz | Capitol | 521222-2
Thelonious Monk | Monk's Dream | CBS | CK 63536
Monk Alone:The Complete Columbia Solo Studio Recordings | CBS | C2K 65495
Wes Montgomery Quintet | Movin' Along | Original Jazz Classics | OJC20 089-2
Wes Montgomery-The Complete Riverside Recordings | Riverside | 12 RCD 4408-2
Louis Armstrong With The Russell Garcia Orchestra | I've Got The World On A String/Louis Under The Stars | Verve | 2304428 IMS

Body And Soul(take 2)
Stephane Grappelli Group | Satin Doll | Accord | 440162

Bodyguard From Scotland Yard
Louis Armstrong And His All Stars | Satchmo At Symphony Hall | GRP | GRP 16612

Boff Boff(Mop Mop)
Coleman Hawkins And Leonard Feather's All Stars | Commodore Classics In Swing | Commodore | 9031-72723-2

Bofinger
Soul Saxophone Quartet | New Orleans:A Musical Gumbo Of Jazz,Blues & Gospel | Mardi Gras Records | MG 5005

Bogalusa
Jude Taylor And His Burning Flames | Autentic Bayou Blues-Best Of Zydeco | Mardi Gras Records | MG 5011

Bogenlampe
Nana | Schwarze Nana | Jazz Haus Musik | JHM 23

Bogey's Blues
Maurice Magnoni Orchestra | New York Suite | L+R Records | CDLR 45077

Bogie
Lionel Hampton And His Sextet | Lionel Hampton-Historical Recording Sessions 1939-1941 | RCA | PM 42417

Bohemia After Dark
Cannonball Adderley Quintet | Live In San Francisco | Riverside | RISA 1157-6
En Concert Avec Europe 1 | Laserlight | 710466
Julian Cannonball Adderlry: Salle Pleyel/Olympia | Laserlight | 36126
Cannonball Adderley Septet | Spontaneous Combustion | Savoy | 650104(881904)
Dorothy Ashby-Frank Wess Quartet | In A Minor Groove | Prestige | PCD 24120-2(P 7140/NJ 8209)
Kenny Clarke All Stars | Bohemia After Dark | Savoy | SV 0107(MG 12017)
Oscar Pettiford All Stars | Oscar Pettiford | Polydor | MP 2346 IMS
Roy Hargrove-Antonio Hart Quintet | The Tokyo Sessions | Novus | 4163164-2

Boina
Jeff Jarvis Group | When It Rains | Jazz Pure Collection | AU 31612 CD

Boira Al Montensy
Gus Viseur Sextet | Gus Viseur A Bruxelles | Harmonia Mundi | PJC 222006

Bojangles
Duke Ellington And His Famous Orchestra | Duke Ellington:Ko-Ko | Dreyfus Jazz Line | FDM 36717-2
Ben Webster-Cotton Tail | RCA | 63667902
Duke Ellington And His Orchestra | The Indispensable Duke Ellington Vol.5/6 | RCA | ND 89750
Lincoln Center Jazz Orchestra | Portraits By Ellington | CBS | 472814-2
The Danish Radio Big Band | A Little Bit Of Duke | dacapo | DCCD 9420
Jimmy Knepper Sextet | I Dream Too Much | Soul Note | 121092-2

Bolbol
Kollektiv | Kollektiv feat. Jonas Hellborg | ITM Records | ITM 1434

Bolerepi
Caterina Valente-Catherine Michel | Girltalk | Nagel-Heyer | NH 1015

Bolero
Charlie Haden/Christian Escoudé | Duo | Dreyfus Jazz Line | FDM 36505-2
Freddie Slack With Orchestra | Boogie Woogie On The 88 | Official | 12000
Jacques Loussier Trio | Ravel's Bolero | Telarc Digital | CD 83466
Mike Richmono-Andy LaVerne | For Us | Steeplechase | SCCD 31101
Quintet Du Hot Club De France | Django Reinhardt-Un Géant Sur Son Image | Melodie | 400052
Yosuke Yamashita New York Trio With Ravi Coltrane | Canvas In Vigor | Verve | 537008-2

Bolero (No.139-part 1)
Gunter Hampel And His Galaxie Dream Band | Journey To The Song Within | Birth | 0017

Bolero (No.139-part 2)
Anita O'Day With Gene Krupa And His Orchestra | Let Me Off Uptown:Anita O'Day With Gene Krupa | CBS | CK 65625

Bolero At The Savoy
Count Basie And His Orchestra | The Count And The President-Vol.1 1936 & 1939 | CBS | CBS 88667

Bolero De Habana
Jack Millman And His All-Stars | Jack Millman And His All-Stars | Fresh Sound Records | FSR-CD 0502

Bolero In D
Hendrik Meurkens Quintet | Slidin' | Concord | CCD 4628

Bolero Potpourri:
Ronaldo Folegatti Groups | Sound Of Watercolors | AH Records | AH 403001-11

Bolero Triste
Jacky Terrasson-Emmanuel Pahud Quartet | Into The Blue | Blue Note | 557257-2

Boléro(Ravel)
Carlos Garnett Group | The New Love | Muse | MR 5133

Bolgar Ritmus
Albert Mangelsdorff Quartet | Shake,Shuttle And Blow | Enja | ENJ-9374 2

Bolghatty Dreams
Bola Sete Quintet | The Incomparable Bola Sete | Original Jazz Classics | OJC 288(F 8364)

Bolinha De Papel
Willis Jackson Sextet | Single Action | Muse | MCD 5179

Bolivar Blues
Paul Bley Quartet | Rejoicing | Steeplechase | SCCD 31274

Bolivia
Cody Moffett Septet | Evidence | Telarc Digital | CD 83343
Gato Barbieri Group | Gato Barbieri:The Complete Flying Dutchman Recordings 1969-1973 | RCA | 2154555-2
Monty Alexander Quartet | Saturday Night | Limetree | MCD 0024
Louis Stewart Quintet | Milesian Source | Ronnie Scott's Jazz House | NSPL 18555

Bom Dia
Tania Maria's Nouvelle Vague | Alive & Cooking | West Wind Latina | 2221 CD

Bomba Puertoriquene
Daniel Schnyder Orchestra | Decoding The Message | Enja | ENJ-6036 2

Bombay Vice
Mark Egan Group | A Touch Of Light | GRP | GRP 95722

Bomsu
Bill Charlap Trio | Distant Star | Criss Cross | Criss 1131

Bon Sueno
Zachary Richard Group | Best Of Jazz Fest-Live From New Orleans | Mardi Gras Records | MG 1011

Bon Voyage
McCoy Tyner Trio | Bon Voyage | Timeless | CD SJP 260

Bona Fide
Vladimir Tolkachev-Yuri Yukechev | Homo Liber | LEO | LR 114

Bone
Tiziana Ghiglioni And Her Band | SONB-Something Old Something New Something Borrowed Something Blue | SPLASC(H) Records | CD H 370-2

Bone Blue
Kenny Garrett Group | Black Hope | Warner | 9362-45017-2

Bone Dry
R.Angus-J.Greinke | Crossing Ngoli | Ear-Rational | ECD 1033

Bone Up Blues
Scales Brothers Group | Our House | Enja | 9106-2

Bonehenge Suite:
J.J.Johnson Quintet | J.J. Johnson's Jazz Quintets | Savoy | SV 0151(MG 12106)

Bones Don't Cry
Dogs Don't Sing In The Rain | Bones For Breakfast | Edition Collage | EC 472-2

Bones For Breakfast
Clifford Brown All Stars | Zoot Sims:The Featured Sessions With Great Leaders 1949-1954 | Blue Moon | BMCD 1037

Bones Jive
Mick Karn Group | Bestial Cluster | CMP Records | CMP CD 1002

Bonewith
Alexi Tuomarila Quartet | 02 | Finladia Jazz | 0927-49148-2

Bone-Yard Jive
The Arkansas Travelers | Red Nichols And Miff Mole 1927 | Village(Jazz Archive) | VILCD 015-2

Bonga
Irene Schweizer/Pierre Favre | Irene Schweizer & Pierre Favre | Intakt Records | CD 009

Bongo Beep
Charlie Parker Sextet | Charlie Parker On Dial, Vol.6 | Spotlite | SPJ 106

Bongo Interlude
Astral Project | Astral Project | Astral Project | no No.

Bonita
Horace Silver Sextet | The Cape Verdean Blues | Blue Note | 576753-2
Illinois Jacquet Septet | Illinois Flies Again | Argo | ARC 503 D
Mongo Santamaria And His Orchestra | Live At Jazz Alley | Concord | CCD 4427
Sarah Vaughan With Band | Copacabana | Pablo | 2312125
Bluiett's Barbeque Band | Bluiett's Barbeque Band | Mapleshade | 04032

Bonito Tema
Hubert Rostaing Et Son Orchestre | Jazz In Paris:Clarinettes À Saint-Germain Des Prés | EmArCy | 013543-2

Bonjour Tristesse, Ca Va?
Septer Bourbon | Septer Bourbon-The Smile Of The Honeycakehorse | Jazzline | JL 11151-2

Bonzo Blues
Booker Ervin Quartet | That's It | Candid | CCD 79014

Boo
Mal Waldron Trio | Free At Last | ECM | 1001
Jackie McLean Quintet | Demon's Dance | Blue Note | 784345-2

Boo Boo's Back In Town
Andy Summers Group | Green Chimneys:The Music Of Thelonious Monk | RCA | 2663472-2

Boo Boo's Birthday
Joe Henderson Trio | The State Of The Tenor-Live At The Village Vanguard Vol.2 | Blue Note | 746426-2
Kenny Drew Jr. Quartet | The Rainbow Connection | Jazz City | 660.53.010
T.S. Monk Group | Monk On Monk | N2K | 43052

Boo Wah
The Birdlanders | The Birdlanders | Fresh Sound Records | FSR-CD 0170

Boo-Dah
City Ramblers | The Fantastic Skiffle Festival | Decca | 6.28422 DP

Boogaloo
Pili-Pili | Boogaloo | JA & RO | JARO 4174-2
Tim Hagans With Norrbotten Big Band | Future Miles | ACT | 9235-2
Charles Kynard Quintet | Reelin' With The Feelin' | Original Jazz Classics | OJC 333(P 7688)

Boogalooin'
Couch Ensemble | Winnetou | Jazz 'n' Arts Records | JNA 1503

Boogalule
Blind Lemon Jefferson | Blind Lemon Jefferson-Master Of The Blues | Biograph | BLP 12015

Boogie
Rimak | Back In Town | Jazzline | ???

Boogie And Drums
Gary McFarland Orchestra | The Great Arrangers | MCA | IA 9340/2

Boogie Blues
Anita O'Day With The Gary McFarland Orchestra | Verve Jazz Masters 49:Anita O'Day | Verve | 527653-2
All The Sad Youn Men | Verve | 517065-2
Cecil Gant | Cecil Gant:The Complete Recordings Vol.1 (1944) | Blue Moon | BMCD 6022
Oscar Klein | Oscar Klein Pickin' The Blues-Vol. 1 | Intercord | 150005

Boogie Bop
Matthew Brubeck & David Widelock | Really! | Jazzpoint | JP 1030 CD

Boogie Bored
Jeanne Carroll Trio | My Style Is Different | L+R Records | CDLR 42075

Boogie Call Blues
Sammy Price Quintet | Roots Of Rock 'N' Roll, Vol. 7: Rib Joint | Savoy | SJL 2240 (801886)

Boogie De Lux
Axel Zwingenberger | Powerhouse Boogie | Vagabond | 6.24210 AS-Digital

Boogie Down
Ernestine Anderson With The Clayton-Hamilton Jazz Orchestra | Boogie Down | Concord | CCD 4407

Boogie Down-
Gottfried Böttger-Joe Penzlin Duo | Take Two | L+R Records | CDLR 40030

Boogie Du Printemps
The Birmingham Boogie Boys | Blues Women | Krazy Kat | KK 793 IMS

Boogie For Chuck Berry
Memphis Slim Trio | Boogie For All My Friends | Black & Blue | BLE 59.741 2

Boogie For Real
Memphis Slim | Boogie For All My Friends | Black & Blue | BLE 59.741 2

Boogie Für Geige
The Mojo Bluesband | Shake That Boogie | Gold Records | 11048

Boogie Out In The Field
Flim & The BB's | Big Notes | dmp Digital Music Productions | CD 454

Boogie Stomp Shuffle
Charles Mingus Orchestra | Nostalgia In Times Square/The Immortal 1959 Sessions | CBS | 88337
Joe Viera Sextet | Kontraste | Calig | 30619

Boogie Stop Shuffle
Randy Sandke Sextet | Get Happy | Concord | CCD 4598
Kevin Mahogany With The WDR Big Band And Guests | Pussy Cat Dues:The Music Of Charles Mingus | Enja | ENJ-9316 2

Boogie Stop Shuffle-
Melvin Sparks Group | I'm A 'Gittar' Player | Cannonball Records | CBD 27101

Boogie Woogie
Albert Ammons | From Spiritual To Swing | Vanguard | VCD 169/71
Albert Ammons-Pete Johnson | The Boogie Woogie Boys | Storyville | 6.28469 DP
Ben Webster Quartet | Ultimate Ben Webster selected by James Carter | Verve | 557537-2
Big Bill Broonzy | Last Session-Vol.1/The Big Bill Broonzy Story | Verve | 2304559 IMS
Buddy Tate Quintet | Buddy Tate-The Texas Twister | New World Records | 80352-2
Jack Teagarden And His Orchestra | Masters Of Jazz Vol.10:Jack Teagarden | Storyville | STCD 4110

Boogie Woogie A La Parisienne
Sammy Price Quintet | Le Jazz En France Vol.14:Boogie Woogie A La Parisienne | Pathe | 1552601

Boogie Woogie Be With Me
Erwin Helfer | Chicago Piano | Steeplechase | SCB 9010

Boogie Woogie Blues
Albert Ammons | Boogie Woggie Classics | Blue Note | BLP 1209

Boogie Woogie Bossa Nova
Tok Tok Tok | 50 Ways To Leave Your Lover | Einstein Music | EM 91051
Axel Zwingenberger | Boogie Woogie Breakdown | Vagabond | VRCD 8.78013

Boogie Woogie Breakdown
Teddy Stauffer Und Seine Original Teddies | Hot Jazz & Swing Mit Teddy Stauffer's Original Teddies | Elite Special | 9522002

Boogie Woogie Came To Town
Andy Kirk And His Orchestra | A Mellow Bit Of Rhythm | RCA | 2113028-2

Boogie Woogie Cocktail
Kenny Kersey Trio | The Complete Jazz At The Philharmonic On Verve 1944-1949 | Verve | 523893-2
Axel Zwingenberger-Vince Weber | The Boogiemeisters | Vagabond | VRCD 8.99026

Boogie Woogie Country Girl
Big Joe Turner And His Band | Big Joe Turner Greatest Hits | Sequel Records | RSA CD 809

Boogie Woogie Dream
Taps Miller And His Orchestra | Buck Clayton Rarities Vol.1 | Swingtime(Contact) | ST 1024

Boogie Woogie Jubilee
Axel Zwingenberger | Boogie Woogie Classics | Vagabond | VRCD 8.92023

Boogie Woogie Jump
Pete Johnson | The Boogie Woogie Boys | Storyville | SLP 229

Boogie Woogie Mess Around
Sammy Price Septet | Barrelhouse And Blues | Black Lion | BLCD 760159

Boogie Woogie On St. Louis Blues
Earl Hines And His Orchestra | Boogie Woogie Hits-Various Artists | RCA | CL 89803 SF
The Earl | Naxos Jazz | 8.120581 CD
Earl Hines With Paul Barron's Orchestra | Jazz In V.Discs Vol.1 | Collection Hugues Panassié | CTPL 001

Boogie Woogie Plate
Albert Ammons-Pete Johnson | The Boogie Woogie Boys | Storyville | 6.28469 DP

Boogie Woogie Round The Clock
Vince Weber | The Boogie Man | Rüssl Räckords | 062-29597

Boogie Woogie Stomp
Albert Ammons | 1939-1949, Blue Note's Three Decades Of Jazz, Vol. 1 | Blue Note | 89902
Joachim Palden | Boogie Woogie And Ragtime Piano Contest | Gold Records | 11034 AS

Boogie Woogie Waltz
Weather Report | Sweetnighter | CBS | 485102-2
B.B.King And His Band | Singin' The Blues/The Blues | Ace Records | CDCHD 320

Boogie Woogie(I May Be Wrong)
Count Basie And His Orchestra | Count Basie At Newport | Verve | 2304414 IMS

Boo-Go-Loo
Monty Alexander's Ivory & Steel | To The Ends Of The Earth | Concord | CCD 4721

Book Of Slim
Mark Feldman Quartet | Book Of Tells | Enja | ENJ-9385 2

Book Of Tells
Keith Jarrett | Book Of Ways | ECM | 1344/45(831396-2)

Book Of Ways(part One: 1-10)
Book Of Ways | ECM | 1344/45(831396-2)

Book Of Ways(part Two: 1-9)
Stacy Kent With The Jim Tomlinson Quintet | The Boy Next Door | Candid | CCD 79797

Bookends
Lars Duppler Sextet | Palindrome 6tet | Jazz Haus Musik | JHM 0131 CD

Booker
Randy Sandke Quintet | The Chase | Concord | CCD 4642

Booker's Blues
Booker Little Sextet | Victory And Sorrow | Affinity | AFF 124

Booker's Bossa
Cedar Walton | Blues For Myself | Red Records | NS 205

Booker's Waltz

Eric Dolphy-Booker Little Quintet | Eric Dolphy Birthday Celebration | Fantasy | FANCD 6085-2
Eric Dophy Quintet | Eric Dolphy:The Complete Prestige Recordings | Prestige | 9 PRCD-4418-2
Amos Hoffman Quartet | The Dreamer | Fresh Sound Records | FSNT 060 CD

Bookie & Ofi
John Hicks Trio | Inc.1 | DIW | DIW 817 CD

Bookie's Blues
Steve Lacy Trio | Bye-Ya | Freelance | FRL-CD 025

Book's Bossa
John Hicks Trio | Inc.1 | DIW | DIW 817 CD

Boola Boola
Teddy Stauffer Und Seine Original Teddies | Hot Jazz & Swing Mit Teddy Stauffer's Original Teddies | Elite Special | 9522002

Boombye
Joe Liggins Quintet | Great Rhythm & Blues-Vol.6 | Bulldog | BDL 1005

Boomerang
Charlie Barnet And His Orchestra | Charlie Barnet Big Band 1967 | Creative World | ST 1056
Lonnie Brooks Blues Band | Wound Up Tight | Sonet | SNTF 974(941974)
Soviet Jazz Ensemble | Boomerang | Mobile Fidelity | MFCD 908

Boop Bop Bing Bash
George Braith Quartet | Soul Stream | Blue Note | 870167-0

Boo's Bloos
Mike LeDonne Quintet | 'Bout Time | Criss Cross | Criss 1033

Boo's Tune
James Moody And His Band | Moody's Blues | Vogue | 655016

Bootin' It
Christine Chatman And Her Band | Sammy Price Vol.1-Singing With Sam | Swingtime(Contact) | BT 2002

Booty Rock
Oliver Nelson Quintet | Oliver Nelson Feat. Kenny Dorham | Original Jazz Classics | OJCCD 227-2(NJ 8224)

Booze Baby Blues
| Time To Move On | Acoustic Music Records | 319.1088.2

Boozer
Red Norvo Septet | Jazz Profile:Dexter Gordon | Blue Note | 823514-2

Bop
Jimmy Giuffre:Complete 1947-1952 Master Takes | Definitive Records | DRCD 11212

Bop Boogie
Charles Blenzig Group | Say What You Mean | Big World | BW 2009

Bop City Flamenco
Lionel Hampton And His Orchestra | Jazz Flamenco | RCA | 2136400-2

Bop Goes The Leesel
Lee Konitz Quartet | Konitz | Black Lion | BLCD 760922

Bop Kick
Nat King Cole Trio | Vocal Classics & Instrumental Classics | Capitol | 300014(TOCJ 6128)

Bop Or Not To Be
Colin Dunwoodie Quartet | Wind Moments | Take Twelve On CD | TT 009-2
Bill Heid Trio | Bop Rascal | Savant Records | SCD 2009

Bop To The Boogie
Dusko Goykovich Quintet | Bebop City | Enja | ENJ-9015 2

Bop-Be
Ben Sidran Sextet | Bop City | Antilles | 848816-2(889649)

Bo-Peep
Barbara Dennerlein Quintet | Bebab | Bebab Records | 250964(880159)

Boperation
Howard McGhee-Fats Navarro Sextet | Fats Navarro/Tadd Dameron:Complete Blue Note & Capitol Sessions | Definitive Records | DRCD 11191

Bophal
Chris Hunter And His Orchestra | Scarborough Fair | Paddle Wheel | KICJ 5

Boplicity
Gerry Mulligan Orchestra | Re-Birth Of The Cool | GRP | GRP 96792
Martial Solal Trio | Martial Solal At Newport '63 | RCA | 2174803-2
At Newport '63 | RCA | 2125768-2
Miles Davis And His Orchestra | The Complete Birth Of The Cool | Capitol | 494550-2
Birth Of The Cool | Capitol | 530117-2
Miles Davis:The Blue Note And Capitol Recordings | Blue Note | 827475-2
Miles Davis With Gil Evans Orchestra, The George Gruntz Concert Jazz Band And Guests | Miles & Quincy Live At Montreux | Warner | 9362-45221-2
Ron McCroby Quintet | Ron McCroby Plays Puccolo | Concord | CJ 208

Boplics
Dodo Marmarosa Quartet | Dodo's Bounce | Fresh Sound Records | FSCD 1019

Boppin' The Blues
Ray Brown All Stars(The Be Bop Boys) | The Dizzy Gillespie Story | Savoy | SV 0177(MG 12110)

Boptical Illusion
Les Brown And His Orchestra | The Uncollected: Les Brown And His Orchestra 1949-Vol.2 | Hindsight | HSR 132

Boram Xam Xam
Axel Beineke Jazz Trio | Let's Be True | Edition Collage | EC 469-2

Bordell 1900
Jim Hall Quartet | Grand Slam | Telarc Digital | CD 83485

Bordercross
Bill Cunliffe Quintet | Bill Plays Bud | Naxos Jazz | 86024-2

Borderline
Horace Parlan Quintet | Speakin' My Piece | Blue Note | 868848-3
Ray McKinley & His Orchestra | Borderline | Savoy | SV 0203(MG 12024)
Universal-International Orchestra | Touch Of Evil | Fresh Sound Records | FSR 610(Challenge CHL 602)

Borderline(for Paco Leva)
Marty Cook Group feat. Monty Waters | Borderlines | Tutu Records | 888122-2*

Borderlines No. One
Borderlines | Tutu Records | 888122-2*

Borderlines No. Two
Stivin-Van Den Broeck-Haurand | Bordertalk | Konnex Records | KCD 5068

Bordertalk
Julius Hemphill Trio | Live From The New Music Cafe | Music & Arts | CD 731

Borgia's Stick
Stephan Micus | Implosions | Japo | 60017(2360017)

Borkenkind
Evan Parker | Process And Reality | FMP | CD 37

Born Cross-Eyed(Remembering Fuller)
J.B.Lenoir | J.B.Lenoir | Blues Classics(L+R) | CDLR 82001

Born Happy
Bent Axen Quintet(Jazz Quintet '60) | Axen | Steeplechase | SCCD 36003

Born In The USA
K.C. Douglas | K.C.'s Blues | Original Blues Classics | OBCCD 533-2(BV 1023)

Born In Trouble
Linda Hopkins And Her All Stars | How Blue Can You Get | Palo Alto | PA 8034

Born On The Bayou
Joe Sample Group | Ashes To Ashes | Warner | 7599-26318-2

Born To Be Bad
Agneta Baumann Group | Sentimental Lady | Touché Music | TMcCD 017

Born To Be Blue
Bob Rockwell Trio | Born To Be Blue | Steeplechase | SCCD 31333
Charles Thomas All Stars Trio | The Finishing Touch! | Space Time Records | BG 9602
Chet Baker With Bobby Scott And Kenny Burrell | Baby Breeze | Verve | 538328-2
Dexter Gordon Trio | Lullaby For A Monster | Steeplechase | SCCD 31156
Ella Fitzgerald With The Lou Levy Quartet | Clap Hands,Here Comes Charlie! | Verve | 835646-2
Freddie Hubbard And His Orchestra | Born To Be Blue | Original Jazz Classics | OJCCD 734-2(2312134)
Freddie Hubbard Sextet | The Best Of Freddie Hubbard | Pablo | 2405415-2
George Shearing-Marion McPartland Duo | Alone Together | Concord | CCD 4171
Grant Green Quintet | Born To Be Blue | Blue Note | 784432-2
Helen Merrill And Her Band | Brownie:Homage To Clifford Brown | Verve | 522363-2
Helen Merrill With The Quincy Jones Orchestra | Brownie-The Complete EmArCy Recordings Of Clifford Brown | EmArCy | 838306-2
James Carter Quartet | The Real Quietstorm | Atlantic | 7567-82742-2
Jan Lundgren Trio With Herb Geller | Stockholm Get-Together | Fresh Sound Records | FSR CD 5007
Maynard Ferguson And His Orchestra | Si Si M.F. | Fresh Sound Records | R 52084(Roulette)
Melvin Rhyne Quartet | Boss Organ | Criss Cross | Criss 1080
Ray Charles With Orchestra | Portrait In Music | London | 6.28338 DP
Soesja Citroen And Her Trio | Here And Now | Challenge | CHR 70003
Wes Montgomery Quartet | The Alternative Wes Montgomery | Milestone | MCD 47065-2
Wes Montgomery Quintet | Wes Montgomery-The Complete Riverside Recordings | Riverside | 12 RCD 4408-2
Full House | Original Jazz Classics | OJC20 106-2
Wes Montgomery With Orchestra | Compact Jazz: Wes Montgomery Plays The Blues | Verve | 835318-2 PMS
Wynton Kelly Trio | New Faces-New Sounds:Piano Interpretations | Blue Note | 784456-2

Born To Be Wild
Cassandra | Enten Eller | SPLASC(H) Records | H 176

Born To Blow The Blues
Marilyn Moore With Don Abney And His Orchestra | Moody | Affinity | AFF 157

Born To Live The Blues
Blind John Davis | You Better Cut That Out | Steeplechase | SCB 9008

Born To Play
Larry Garner Group | Too Blues | JSP Records | JSPCD 249

Born Under A Bad Sign
Albert King Blues Band | Wednesday Night In San Francisco | Stax | SCD 8556-2
Blues Power No.4: Albert King-King Of The Blues Guitar | Atlantic | 40494
Peter Green | Black & White Blues-The Little Red Rooster | Chess | 2292-44598-1
Firma Kischke | Nix Als The Blues-Live Im Allgäu | Jazz Classics | AU 11126 Digital

Born With The Blues
Memphis Slim And His Band | Memphis Slim:Born To Boogie | Memo Music | HDJ 4007

Borneo
Temperance Seven | 33 Not Out | Upbeat Jazz | URCD 103

Boroquinho
Peter Leitch Trio | Trio/Quartet '91 | Concord | CCD 4480

Borrowed Time
Silje Nergard Group with Strings | Nightwatch | EmArCy | 9865648

Borrowing Moons
Bob Barnard Quintet | New York Notes | Sackville | SKCD2-3061

Borzeguim
Bo Diddley And Chuck Berry | Two Great Guitars | Chess | CH 9170

Boscaglia
Cecil Payne Quartet | Casbah | Empathy Records | E 1005

Bosna Calling
Double Trio(Trio De Clarinettes&Arcado) | Green Dolphy Suite | Enja | ENJ-9011 2

Bosnia
Greetje Bijma Trio | Barefoot | Enja | ENJ-8038 2
Mark Dresser Quintet | Force Green | Soul Note | 121273-2

Boss Blues
Hank Mobley Septet | Third Season | Blue Note | LT 1081

Boss City
Wes Montgomery With The Oliver Nelson Orchestra | Talkin' Jazz:Roots Of Acid Jazz | Verve | 529580-2
Goin' Out Of My Head | CTI Records | PDCTI 1107-2

Boss Lady
Joe Lovano-Gonzalo Rubalcaba | Flying Colors | Blue Note | 856092-2

Boss Town
Chick Corea Trio | Circling In | Blue Note | 84555

Bossa Antigua
Milt Jackson And Big Brass | For Someone I Love | Original Jazz Classics | OJCCD404-2(RLP 9478)

Bossa Beguine
Joe Diorio-Hal Crook 4et | Narayani | RAM Records | RMCD 4522

Bossa For Egberto
Greg Abate Quintet | Straight Ahead | Candid | CCD 79530

Bossa G-
Richie Cole-Hank Crawford Quintet | Bossa International | Milestone | MCD 9180-2

Bossa Nova
Friedrich Gulda-Klaus Weiss Duo | It 's All One | MPS | 68059

Bossa Nova Do Marilla
Monty Alexander Trio | The Way It Is | MPS | 68223

Bossa Nova In Blue
Rob McConnell Jive 5 | Jive 5 | Concord | CCD 4437

Bossa Rocka
George Benson Quartet + Guests | The George Benson Cookbook | CBS | 502470-2
Lee Konitz-Peggy Stern Sextet | Lunasea | Soul Note | 121249-2

Bossalero
Joe Venuti Quartet | Happy Joe | Vagabond | 6.23757 AO

Bossango
Michel Philip Mossman Sextet | Mama Soho | TCB Records | TCB 98102

Boston Beans
Dexter Gordon Quartet | Power! | Prestige | P 24087

Boston Bernie
More Power | Original Jazz Classics | OJC20 815-2(P 7680)
L.T.D. | Prestige | PCD 11018-2
Conrad Herwig Quintet | The Amulet | Ken Music | 660.56.016

Boston In 3-4
Phil Moerke Group feat. Victor Mendoza | Multi Colors | Jazz Pure Collection | AU 31625 CD

Boston Summer
Charlie Mariano Group | Boston All Stars/New Sound From Boston | Original Jazz Classics | OJCCD 1745-2

Boswil Boogie
Paul Quinichette And His Orchestra | Paul Quinichete:All Stars Sessions 1951-1953 | Blue Moon | BMCD 1012

Both
Paul Bley Trio | Ramblin' | Affinity | AFF 37

Both Sides Now
Singers Unlimited | A Capella | MPS | 815671-1
Paul Glasse Group | Paul Glasse | Amazing Records | AMCD 1022

Both Sides Of The Coin
Steps Ahead | Steps Ahead | Elektra | 7559-60168-2
Bobby Hutcherson Group | Ambos Mundos(Both Worlds) | Landmark | LCD 1522-2

Bo-Till
Joe Henderson Group | Double Rainbow | Verve | 527222-2

Boto
Lorenzo Petrocca Quartet Feat. Bruno De Filippi | Insieme | Edition Musikat | EDM 002

Botta E Risposta
Marc Moulin Group | Top Secret | Blue Note | 536034-2

Bottle Blues
Buddy Tate Octet | Swinging Like Tate | Affinity | AFF 171

Bottom
Brownie McGhee & Sonny Terry Quartet | Climbin' Up | Savoy | SV 0256(MG 12118)

Bottom Groove
Head Heart & Hands | The Best Of Head Heart & Hands | Blue Flame | 40061

Bottom Of The Mirror
Anne LeBaron Quintet | Phantom Orchestra | Ear-Rational | ECD 1035

Bottoms Up
Lennie Niehaus Quintet | Vol.1:The Quintets | Original Jazz Classics | OJC 319(C 3518)

Bötz
Conrad Bauer | Flüchtiges Glück | Riskant | 568-722417

Bou Naouara
Juxoli | Juxoli | Pannon Jazz/Classic | PJ 1009

Bouboule
Philippe Caillat Special Project | Melodic Travel | Laika Records | LK 689-012
Batoru | Tree Of Sounds | Nabel Records:Jazz Network | CD 4685

Bouché
Frank Paul Schubert Quartet | Der Verkauf Geht Weiter | Jazz Haus Musik | JHM 0114 CD
Chet Baker Quintet | Cool Burnin' With The Chet Baker Quintet | Prestige | PR20 7496-2

Boudoir
Cootie Williams And His Orchestra | Duke Ellington's Trumpets | Black & Blue | BLE 59.231 2

Boulder Buff
Glenn Miller And His Orchestra | The Glenn Miller Story Vol.4 | RCA | NL 89223 AG

Boulevard
Maarten Altena Ensemble | Quotl | Hat Art | CD 6029

Boulevard Of Broken Dreams
Art Tatum | The Jazz Giants Play Harry Warren:Lullaby Of Broadway | Prestige | PCD 24204-2
The Tatum Solo Masterpieces Vol.12 | Pablo | 2310870
Hal Kemp And His Orchestra | The Radio Years: Hal Kemp And His Orchestra 1934 | Hindsight | HSR 143
Juan Garcia Esquivel Orchestra | Juan's Again | RCA | 2168206-2
Marjorie Lee With The John T.Williams Quintet | Remembering With Marjorie Lee | Fresh Sound Records | Beaumonde BR 100 CD

Boum
Grosses Tanzorchester Vom Palace-Hotel St.Moritz | Hot Jazz & Swing Mit Teddy Stauffer's Original Teddies | Elite Special | 9522002

Bounce
Virgil Gonsalves Sextet | Jazz In Hollywood:Virgil Gonsalves/Steve White | Original Jazz Classics | OJCCD 1889-2(Nocturne NLP-8/NLP-9)

Bounce Blues
Ben Webster With The Oscar Peterson Quartet | King Of The Tenors | Verve | 519806-2

Bounce Blues(alt.take)
John Kirby And His Band | 1940 | Jazz Anthology | 550252

Bounce The Ball(Do Da Dittle Um Day)
Louis Jordan And His Tympany Five | Louis Jordan Vol.1-Hoodoo Man | Swingtime(Contact) | ST 1011

Bouncin' Around
Django Reinhardt Trio | Django Reinhardt:Djangology | EMI Records | 780659-2

Bouncing Around
Peter Bocage With His Creole Serenaders | New Orleans-The Living Legends:Peter Bocage | Original Jazz Classics | OJCCD 1835-2

Bouncing Baby
Sugar Chile Robinson Trio | Go Boy Go | Oldie Blues | OL 2828

Bouncing The Celeste
Coleman Hakins And His Orchestra | Body And Soul | RCA | 26685152

Bouncing With Bean
Johnny Hodges Sextet | Masters Of Jazz Vol.9:Johnny Hodges | Storyville | STCD 4109

Bouncing With Bud
Billy Cobham Trio | The Art Of Three | IN+OUT Records | 77045-2
Bud Powell Quintet | Bud Powell:Bouncing With Bud | Dreyfus Jazz Line | FDM 36725-2
The Amazing Bud Powell Vol.1 | Blue Note | 300366
Fats Navarro And Tadd Dameron:The Complete Blues Note And Capitol Recordings | Blue Note | 833373-2
Larry Vuckovich Sextet | City Sounds,Village Voices | Palo Alto | PA 8012

Bouncing With Bud(alt.master)
Bud Powell's Modernists | The Fabulous Fats Navarro Vol.1 | Blue Note | 0677207
Bud Powell Quintet | The Amazing Bud Powell Vol.1 | Blue Note | 532136-2

Bouncing With Bud(alt.take 1)
Fats Navarro/Tadd Dameron:Complete Blue Note & Capitol Sessions | Definitive Records | DRCD 11191

Bouncing With Bud(alt.take 2)
Fats Navarro And Tadd Dameron:The Complete Blues Note And Capitol Recordings | Blue Note | 833373-2

Bound For The Beauty Of The South
Corey Harris | Betwen Midnight And Day | Alligator Records | ALCD 4837

Bound To Miss Me
Bern Nix Trio | Alarms And Excursions | New World Records | 80437-2

Bounding
Blue Note All Stars | Town Hall Concert | Blue Note | 497811-2

Bouquet
Bobby Hutcherson Quartet | Happenings | Blue Note | 300285
Phil Woods Quintet | Bouquet/Fujitsu-Concord Jazz Festival In Japan '87 | Concord | CCD 4377

Bouquet Of Blues
Johnny Hodges And The Ellington Men | The Big Sound | Verve | MV 2525 IMS

Bourbon Street Jingling Jollies
Duke Ellington And His Orchestra | That's Jazz Vol.31: New Orleans Suite | Atlantic | ATL 50403

Bourbon Street Parade
Chris Barber's Jazz And Blues Band | The Streets Of New Orleans | Jazz Colours | 874705-2
Cy Laurie Jazz Band | Chattanooga Stomp | Lake | LACD 61
Dutch Swing College Band | Ain't Nobody's Business | DSC Production | PA 002 (801059)
Jazzkränzchen Immergrün | Jazzkränzchen Immergrün | Swingtime | 8209
Paul Barbarin And His Band | Atlantic Jazz: New Orleans | Atlantic | 7567-81700-2
George Lewis/Paul Barbarin | Storyville | SLP 4049
Sharkey Bonano And His Band | Sounds Of New Orleans Vol.4 | Storyville | STCD 6011

Bourée
Lajos Dudas Quartet | Nightlight | double moon | DMCHR 71030

Bouree(BWW 966)
Muneer B.Fennell & The Rhythm String Band | An Encounter With Higher Forces | double moon | CHRDM 71019

Bourelly Broad Stroke
An Encounter With Higher Forces | double moon | CHRDM 71019

Bourelly's Brush Stroke
Hans Theessink Group | Journey On | Minor Music | 801062

Bourgeois Blues
Huddie Ledbetter | Blues Roots Vol.1 | Storyville | 6.23700 AG

Bourree(BWV 807)
Joe Gordon Quintet | Blakey | Verve | 538634-2

Bow Jest
Illinois Jacquet Sextet | Swing's The Thing | JSP Records | 1078

Bow Road

Original Dixieland Jazz Band | ODJB-The First Recordings | Timeless | CBC 1-009

Bowery 1
Franz Koglmann Quintet | Opium | Between The Lines | btl 011(Efa 10181-2)

Bowery 2
Enrico Rava Quintet | Andanada | Soul Note | SN 1064

Bowing Bowing
Jean-Luc Ponty Quintet | Upon The Wings Of Music | Atlantic | 7567-81495-2

Box 702
Cousin Joe With The Sammy Price Quartet | Cousin Joe:The Complete 1945-1947 Vol.2(1946-1947) | Blue Moon | BMCD 6002

Box The Music
Rahsaan Roland Kirk With The George Gruntz Trio | Rahsaan Rolnd Kirk:Dog Years In The Fourth Ring | 32 Jazz | 32032

Boxer Boogie
Jan Jankeje's Party And Swingband | Mobil | Jazzpoint | JP 1068 CD
Jazz Jokers | Jazz-Jokers | Jazzpoint | JP 1024 LP
Bireli Lagrene Ensemble | Routs To Django-Live At The 'Krokodil' | Jazzpoint | JP 1056 CD

Boxer's Boogie
Routes To Django & Bireli Swing '81 | Jazzpoint | JP 1055 CD
Bireli Lagrene Group | Bireli Lagrene 'Highlights' | Jazzpoint | JP 1027 CD
Gigi Gryce Quintet | The Rat Race Blues | Original Jazz Classics | OJCCD 081-2(NJ 8262)

Boy From New Orleans
Your Neighborhood Saxophone Quartet | Boogie Stop Shuffle | Coppens | CCD 3004(882623)

Boy Meets Horn
Bill Berry's L.A.Big Band | Hello Rev. | Concord | CCD 4027
Duke Ellington And His Orchestra | Duke Ellington And His Orchestra 1943,Vol.1 | Circle | CCD-101
Duke Ellington's Masterpieces Vol.1: 1938-1940 | Black & Blue | BLE 59.233 2
J.J. Johnson-Al Grey Sextet | Things Are Getting Better All The Time | Pablo | 2312141

Boy What A Night
Ella Fitzgerald With The Nelson Riddle Orchestra | Ella Sings Gershwin-Vol. 2 | Metro | 2682023 IMS

Boys
Loope | Prinz Henry | ITM Records | ITM 1447

Boys From Harlem
Harry Beckett-Marilyn Mazur-Chris McGregor Group | Grandmother's Teaching | ITM Records | 0028

Boys On The Corner
Rob Mullins Group | Tokyo Nights | Nova | NOVA 9026-2

Bra Joe From Kilimanjaro
Dollar Brand | Ancient Africa | Japo | 60005(2360005)

Brace
Rick Margitza Septet | Color | Blue Note | 792279-2

Braceful
Rinus Groeneveld Trio | Dare To Be Different | Timeless | CD SJP 321

Bracondale
Urs Leimgruber Quartet | Reflexionen | Timeless | SJP 199

Bradley's Beans
Phil Woods Quintet + One | Flash | Concord | CCD 4408

Brad's Bag
International Hashva Orchestra | All's Well | TCB Records | TCB 99602

Brahm's...I Think
Bryan Lee Group With Guests | Live at The Old Absinthe House Bar...Friday Night | Blues Beacon | BLU-1029 2

Brain Change
Volker Schlott Quartet | Akribik | Acoustic Music Records | 319.1165.2

Brain Dead
Simon Spang-Hanssen & Maneklar | Wondering | dacapo | DCCD 9436

Brain Forest
George Gruntz Concert Jazz Band | Global Exellence | TCB Records | TCB 21172

Brainwasher
Buck Hill Quartet | Easy To Love | Steeplechase | SCCD 31160

Brake's Sake
Daniel Humair Trio | Triple Hip Trip | Owl Records | 014 CD

Bram Van Velde
Tomasz Stanko-Manfred Bründl-Michael Riessler | Suite Talk | ITM-Pacific | ITMP 970081

Branching Out
Ketil Bjornstad Group | The Sea II | ECM | 1633(537341-2)

Brand
Jeannie Cheatham And Jimmy Cheatham Band | Sweet Baby Blues | Concord | CCD 4258

Brand New Razor
Count Basie And His Orchestra | Planet Jazz:Count Basie | Planet Jazz | 2152068-2

Brand New Wagon
100 Ans De Jazz:Count Basie | RCA | 2177831-2
Victor Jazz History Vol.20:Jazz & The Blues | RCA | 2135739-2

Brandenburg Gate
Dave Brubeck Quintet | The Quartet | LRC Records | CDC 7681(974377)

Brandy And Beer
Super Session | Welcome & Alive | Vagabond | 6.28604 DP

Brandyn
Christoph Sänger Trio | Imagination | Laika Records | 35100752
Scolohofo | Oh! | Blue Note | 542081-2
Lionel Hampton And His Orchestra | Jay Bird | Black Lion | 127032

Brash
Gato Barbieri Sextet | El Pampero | RCA | FD 10151

Brasil Postal
Willie Rodriguez Jazz Quartet | Flatjacks | Milestone | MCD 9331-2

Brasileira
JoAnne Brackeen Quartet | Breath Of Brazil | Concord | CCD 4479

Brasilero
Chick Corea | Originals | Stretch Records | SCD 9029-2

Brasilian Suite
Gijs Hendriks-Beaver Harris Quartet | Sound Compound | yvp music | CD 3009

Brasilliance
Norbert Emminger Quintet | In The Park | Edition Collage | EC 521-2

Brasov In The Clouds
Chris Barber's Brass Band | Take Me Back To New Orleans | Black Lion | 157007

Brass Rings
Herbie Nichols Trio | Herbie Nichols:The Complete Blue Note Recordings | Blue Note | 859352-2

Brass Rings(alt.take)
European Tuba Quartet | Heavy Metal-Light Industry | FMP | 1200

Brassmen's Holiday
Dave Douglas Tiny Bell Trio | Wandering Souls | Winter&Winter | 910042-2

Brath-A-Thon
Oscar Klein's Jazz Show | Oscar Klein's Jazz Show | Jazzpoint | JP 1043 CD

Bratislava Fantasy
A' Portrait Of Jan Jankeje | Jazzpoint | JP 1054 CD
Dom Um Romao Group | Dom Um Romao | Muse | MCD 6012

Bravo
Tethered Moon | Chansons D'Edith Piaf | Winter&Winter | 910048-2

Bravo Pour Le Clown
Hal Di Meola Group | Casino | CBS | 468215-2

Bravoto Fantasia-
Victor Feldman Septet | Suite Sixteen | Original Jazz Classics | OJCCD 1768-2C 3541)

Brazil
Art Pepper Quartet | One September Afternoon | Original Jazz Classics | OJCCD 678-2(GXY 5141)
Chick Corea | Standards | Stretch Records | SCD 9028-2
Django Reinhardt And The Quintet Du Hot Club De France | Peche Á La Mode-The Great Blue Star Sessions 1947/1953 | Verve | 835418-2
Django Reinhardt Portrait | Barclay | DALP 2/1939
Django Reinhardt Quartet | Jazz In Paris:Django Reinhardt-Nuages | EmArCy | 018428-2
Ferenc Snétberger | The Budapest Concert | TipToe | TIP-888823 2
Gato Barbieri Group | The Third World Revisited | Bluebird | ND 86995
Grant Green Sextet | The Latin Bit | Blue Note | 300051(4111)
Nils Wogram Quintet | New York Conversations | Mons Records | MR 874658
Mel Tormé And Cleo Laine With The John Dankworth Orchestra | Nothing Without You | Concord | CCD 4515

Brazil At Union Sqare
Miroslav Vitous Group | Universal Syncopations | ECM | 1863(038506-2)

Brazil Waves
Antonio Carlos Jobim With Orchestra | This Is Jazz:Bossa Nova | CBS | CK 65045

Brazilia
John Coltrane Quartet | John Coltrane:The Classic Quartet-Complete Impulse Studio Recordings | Impulse(MCA) | 951280-2
John Coltrane-Eric Dolphy Quartet | John Coltrane:The Complete 1961 Village Vanguard Recordings | Impulse(MCA) | 954322-2
Larry Coryell-Brian Keane-Diego Cortez | Bolero | String | BLE 233850

Brazilian Bossa Galore
Bola Sete Quintet | Bossa Nova | Original Jazz Classics | OJC 286(F 8349)

Brazilian Fondue
John Goldsby Sextet | Viewpoint | Nagel-Heyer | CD 2014

Brazilian Hat Trick
Lalo Schifrin Trio With The London Philharmonic | Jazz Meets The Symphony | East-West | 4509-92004-2

Brazilian Impressions
Michel Petrucciani | Live In Germany | Dreyfus Jazz Line | FDM 36597-2

Brazilian Like
Michel Petrucciani Sextet | Both Worlds | Dreyfus Jazz Line | FDM 36590-2
Al Cohn-Zoot Sims Quintet | Body & Soul | Muse | MCD 5356

Brazilian Rhyme
Sergio Salvatore Sextet | Sergio Salvatore | GRP | GRP 97202

Brazilian Rosewood
Oscar Castro-Neves Orchestra | Brazilian Scandals | JVC | ???

Brazilian Sketch
Tom Harrell Quintet | Form | Contemporary | CCD 14059-2

Brazilian Song
Laurindo Almeida-Charlie Byrd Quartet | Brazilian Soul | Concord | CCD 4150

Brazilian Suite
Michel Petrucciani Group | Playground | Blue Note | 795480-2

Brazilian Suite No.1
Music | Blue Note | 792563-2

Brazilian Suite No.2
Sun Ra And His Myth Science Arkestra | Fate In A Pleasant Mood/When Sun Comes Out | Evidence | ECD 22068-2

Brazilian Sunset
Astrud Gilberto With Orchestra | Astrud Gilberto | Jazz Magazine | 43003

Brazilian Waves
Manfredo Fest Quintet | Braziliana | dmp Digital Music Productions | CD 459

Brazilienza
Charlie Byrd Trio With Bud Shank | Brazilville | Concord | CCD 4173

Bread And Tears
Joe Lovano Sextet | Tenor Legacy | Blue Note | 827014-2

Bread And Wine
Leroy Carr | Leroy Carr-Singin' The Blues | Biograph | BLP C 9

Bread Winner
Kenny Clarke Quintet | Verve Jazz Masters 45:Kenny Burrell | Verve | 527652-2
Kenny Burrell Quintet | Guitar Forms | Verve | 521403-2

Bread Winner(alt.take 1)
Guitar Forms | Verve | 521403-2

Bread Winner(alt.take 2)
Guitar Forms | Verve | 521403-2

Bread Winner(alt.take 3)
Guitar Forms | Verve | 521403-2

Bread Winner(alt.take 4)
Esbjörn Svensson Trio(E.S.T.) | E.S.T. Live | ACT | 9295-2

Breadbasket
Liz Story | Solid Colors | Windham Hill | TA-C- 1023

Break City
Nina Simone Quartet | Nina Simone-The 60s Vol.3:Work Song | Mercury | 838545-2 PMS

Break 'Em Down
Big Joe Williams | Baby Please Don't Go | Swingtime(Contact) | BT 2007

Break It Down
Fourplay | Heartfelt | RCA | 2663916-2

Break It Out
Toots Thielemans With Orchestra | Your Precious Love | B.Sharp Records | CDS 099

Break Tune
Arthur Blythe Quartet | Calling Card | Enja | ENJ-9051 2
Bert Ambrose And His Orchestra | Happy Days | Saville Records | SVL 147 IMS

Breakdown Blues
Kieler Saxophon Quartett | JazzNord | KlangRäume | 30100

Breake The Ice
Klaus Koch | Basse Partout | Creative Works Records | CW CD 1011-1

Breakfast Am Vierwaldstädter See Oder Vollmundiger Gesang Nach Einer Vollmondnacht
Willisau And More Live | Creative Works Records | CW CD 1020-2
Buddy Morrow And His Orchestra | The Uncollected:Buddy Morrow | Hindsight | HSR 154

Breakfast With A.
Marjorie Barnes With Band | The Sentimantal Touch Of Albert Van Dam | RCA | PL 70465 TIS

Breakin' Down
Benny Goodman And His Orchestra | The Birth Of Swing | Bluebird | ND 90601(3)

Breaking
Archie Shepp Quartet feat. Annette Lowman | Lover Man | Timeless | CD SJP 287

Breaking It In
Myra Melford Trio | Alive In The House Of Saints | HatOLOGY | 570(2)

Breaking Up
Lois Lane With The Metropole Orchestra | Sensual Songs | Koch Jazz | 3-6901-2

Breath
Jaki Byard Trio | Foolin' Myself | Soul Note | 121125-2
Welcome To The Maze | Welcome To The Maze:Puzzle | Nabel Records:Jazz Network | CD 4671
Leszek Zadlo Quartet | Breath | Enja | ENJ-6026 2

Breathe
Roberto Perera Group | Harp And Soul | Inak | 30362

Breathing
Karl Berger-Dave Holland-Ed Blackwell | Crystal Fire | Enja | 7029-2

Breathing Space
Barbara Thompson's Paraphernalia | Breathless | VeraBra Records | CDVBR 2057-2

Breathless
Ozzie Nelson And His Orchestra | The Uncollected: Ozzie Nelson | Hindsight | HSR 107

Breathless(short cut)
Azimuth | Azimuth '85 | ECM | 1298

Breathtaking
David Friesen-Michael Brecker | Two For The Show | ITM-Pacific | ITMP 970079

Breeze
Mr.Acker Bilk And His Paramount Jazz Band | The Golden Years Of Revibal Jazz,Vol.15 | Storyville | STCD 5520
Steve Lacy-Maarten Altena | High,Low And Order | Hat Art | CD 6069

Breeze Valley
Dumoustiers Stompers | Back Water Blues | Black & Blue | BLE 59.219 2

Breezin'
George Benson Group/Orchestra | George Benson Anthology | Warner | 8122-79934-2
Joe Sullivan Trio | The Piano Artistry Of Joe Sullivan | Jazz Unlimited | JUCD 2051

Breezin' Along With The Breeze
Charlie Shavers With The Al Waslon Trio | A Man And His Music | Storyville | SLP 4073

Breezy And The Bass
Henry Threadgill-Craig Harris Group | Hip Hop Be Bop | ITM Records | ITM 1480

Bregenz(part 1)
Keith Jarrett | Concerts(Bregenz/München) | ECM | 1227/9

Bregenz(part 2)
Concerts(Bregenz) | ECM | 1227(827286-2)

Bregenz,May 28, 1981(part 1 + 2)
Ahmed El-Salamouny/Gilson De Assis | Tango Brasileiro | FSM | FCD 97725

Brejeiro-
Trevor Watts Moiré Music Drum Orchestra | A Wider Embrace | ECM | 1449

Brekete Takai
Flim & The BB's | Neon | dmp Digital Music Productions | CD 458

Bremen(part 1)
Keith Jarrett | Solo-Concerts(Bremen-Lausanne) | ECM | 1035/7(827747-2)

Bremen(part 2a)
Solo-Concerts(Bremen-Lausanne) | ECM | 1035/7(827747-2)

Bremen(part 2b)
Cedar Walton | Maybeck Recital Hall Series Volume Twenty-Five | Concord | CCD 4546

Bresilien
Tiziana Ghiglioni And Her Quartet | Yet Time | SPLASC(H) Records | CD H 150-2

Bretagne
Plas Johnson-Red Holloway Quintet | Keep That Groove Going! | Milestone | MCD 9319-2

Brethreren!
Del Ferro/Overwater/Paeffgen | Evening Train | Acoustic Music Records | 319.1063.2

Brew's Blues
Barre Phillips | Call Me When You Get There | ECM | 1257

Brexterity
Roy Hargrove Quintet | Family | Verve | 527630-2

Brian's Bounce
Rita Reys With The Nederlands Metropole Orchestra | Once Upon A Summertime | Koch Jazz | 3-6919-2

Briar Patch
Mongo Santamaria And His Rhythm Afro-Cubanos | Afro Roots | Prestige | PCD 24018-2(F 8012/8032)

Brick Top
Billie & Dee Dee Pierce Trio | New Orleans-The Living Legends:Billie And Dede Pierce | Original Blues Classics | OBCCD 534-2(RLP 370)

Bricks
Jimmy McGriff Orchestra | City Lights | JAM | 002 IMS

Bride's March
Flora Purim And Her Sextet | 500 Miles High-Flora Purim At Montreux | Milestone | M 9070

Bridge Call
Mighty Sam McClain Group | Sledgehammer Soul & Down Home Blues | audioquest Music | AQCD 1042

Bridgehampton South
Gerry Mulligan Concert Jazz Band | The Complete Verve Gerry Mulligan Concert Band | Verve | 9860613

Bridgehampton South(alt.take)
The Complete Verve Gerry Mulligan Concert Band | Verve | 9860613

Bridgehampton Strut
The Complete Verve Gerry Mulligan Concert Band | Verve | 9860613

Bridgehampton Strut(alt.take)
Andy Bey Group | Tuesdays In Chinatown | Minor Music | 801099

Bridges
Billy Oskay/Michael O'Domhnaill | Nightnoise | Windham Hill | WD 1031
Janice Borla With Band | Lunar Octave | dmp Digital Music Productions | CD 3004

Bridges(Travessia)
Duke Jordan | Duke Jordan-Solo Masterpieces Vol.2 | Steeplechase | SCCD 31300

Bridging
Barney Kessel Quintet | Yesterday | Black Lion | BLCD 760183

Brief And Die Pharisäer
Eddie Daniels Quartet | Brief Encounter | Muse | MCD 5154

Brief Hesitation
Jimmy Giuffre Trio | Live In Europe Vol.1 | Raretone | 5018 FC

Brigas, Nunca Mais(No More Quarrels)
Klaus Ignatzek International Quintet | African Flower | Acoustic Music Records | 319.1125.2
Warren Bernhardt Trio | So Real | dmp Digital Music Productions | CD 532

Bright Angel Falls
Earl Hines Sextet | Swingin' Away | Black Lion | BLCD 760210

Bright Boy
Cecil Scott And His Bright Boys | Harlem Big Bands | Timeless | CBC 1-010

Bright Eyes
Bill Holman And His Orchestra | The Fabulous Bill Holman | Sackville | 2013
Chris Hirson-Geoff Goodman | Human Lives | Acoustic Music Records | 319.1112.2

Bright Lights
Dook Joint | Who's Been Talkin'... | Organic Music | ORGM 9728

Bright Lights Big City
Eddie Cleanhead Vinson With The Cannonball Adderley Quintet | Cleanhead & Cannonball | Landmark | LCD 1309-2(882857)
Jimmy Reed | The Blues Vol.2 | Intercord | 158601

Bright Mississippi
Danilo Perez Quartet | Panamonk | Impulse(MCA) | 951190-2
David Murray Quartet | David Murray-Saxmen | Red Baron | JK 57758
Roy Haynes Trio | The Roy Haynes Trio | Verve | 543534-2
Russell Malone Quartet | Sweet Georgia Peach | Impulse(MCA) | 951282-2
T.S. Monk Group | Monk On Monk | N2K | 43052
Thelonious Monk Quartet | Paris Jazz Concert:Thelonious Monk And His Quartet | Laserlight | 17250
Live In Paris 1964 | France's Concert | FCD 132x2
En Concert Avec Europe 1 | Laserlight | 710377/78
Live At Monterey Jazz Festival,1963 | Jazz Unlimited | JUCD 2045/2046

Bright Mississippi(alt.take)
Live At The Jazz Workshop-Complete | CBS | C2K 65189
Cecil Payne Quintet | Bright Moments | Spotlite | SPJ LP 21

Bright Nights
Stanley Cowell Sextet | Setup | Steeplechase | SCCD 31349

Bright Reign
John Tchicai & Strange Brothers | Darktown Highlights | Storyville | SLP 1015

Bright Size Life
Pat Metheny Trio | Part Metheny Trio Live | Warner | 9362-47907-2
Grand Dominion Jazz Band | Half And Half | Stomp Off Records | CD 3989

Brighter Days
The Dave McMurdo Jazz Orchestra | Fire & Song | Sackville | SK2CD-5004

TITELVERZEICHNIS

Brighter Days For You
The Danish Radio Jazz Orchestra | This Train:The Danish Radio Jazz Orchestra Plays The Music Of Ray Pitts | dacapo | DCCD 9428
Brighter Daze
Al Bowlly With The Ray Noble Orchestra | The Classic Years In Digital Stereo: Al Bowlly With Ray Noble | CDS Records Ltd. | REB 649
Brilliant Corners
Gary Bartz Quintet | Reflections Of Monk | Steeplechase | SCCD 31248
Johannes Mössinger New York Trio with Joe Lovano | Monk's Corner | double moon | DMCHR 71032
Junko Onishi Trio | Live At The Village Vanguard | Blue Note | 833418-2
Steve Lacy-Roswell Rudd Quartet | School Days | Hat Art | CD 6140
Thelonious Monk Quintet | Thelonious Monk:85th Birthday Celebration | zyx records | FANCD 6076-2
Sonny Rollins-The Freelance Years:The Complete Riverside & Contemporary Recordings | Riverside | 5 RCD 4427-2
The Thelonious Monk Memorial Album | Milestone | MCD 47064-2
Ellery Eskelin + Han Bennink | Dissonant Characters | HatOLOGY | 534
Brindemos
Ran Blake | Realization Of A Dream | Owl Records | 012
Bring Back The Time When (If)
Cootie Williams And His Orchestra | Rhythm And Jazz In The Mid Forties | Official | 3014
Bring It All Down
Deborah Henson-Conant | Alterd Ego | Laika Records | 35100962
Freddie Hubbard Orchestra | Mistral | Liberty | LT 1110
Bring It On Home
Christian Willisohn Group | Live At Marians | ART BY HEART | ABH 2006 2
Christian Willisohn-Boris Vanderlek-Ludwig Seuss | Blues News | Blues Beacon | BLU-1019 2
Doug MacLeod Group | Blues Masters | audioquest Music | AQCD 1034
Rubberlegs Williams With Herbie Fields' Band | Obscure Blues Shouters Vol.2 | Blue Moon | BMCD 6011
Sonny Boy Williamson Band | The Real Folk Blues | Chess | CHD 9272(872292)
Bring It Up, Van Dyke
Cannon's Jug Stompers | Memphis Blues 1928-1930 | RCA | 2126409-2
Bring Me Flowers While I'm Living
Champion Jack Dupree | Blues Roots Vol.8 | Storyville | 6.23707 AG
Brings Goodness
Count Basie Kansas City Septem | Mostly Blues...And Some Others | Pablo | 2310919-2
Bris
Poncho Sanchez Orchestra | Bien Sabroso! | Concord | CCD 4239
Brisa Do Mar
Moments Quartet | Original Moments | Fresh Sound Records | FSNT 052 CD
Brisas
Ahmed El-Salamouny/Gilson De Assis | Calunga | FSM | FCD 97753
Brite 'N' Sunny Babe
Tony Coe-Roger Kellaway | British-American Blue | Between The Lines | btl 007(Efa 10177-2)
British-American Blue
Red Norvo And His Orchestra | Red Play The Blues | RCA | 2113034-2
Broad Jump
Ozzie Nelson And His Orchestra | The Uncollected: Ozzie Nelson | Hindsight | HSR 107
Broadbottom
Lew Stone And His Band | Lew Stone And His Band | Decca | DDV 5005/6 DT
Broadland
Bennie Wallace Trio | One Night With Blue Note Vol.2 | Blue Note | BT 85114 Digital
Broadway
Concord All Stars | Tour De Force | Concord | CCD 4172
Count Basie And His Orchestra | Count Basie-The Best Of The Roulette Years | Roulette | CDP 797969-2
Prez's Hat Vol.4 | Philology | 214 W 9
David Chesky-Romero Lubambo Duo | The New York Chorinhos | Chesky | JD 39
Dexter Gordon Quartet | Dexter Gordon Birthday Celebration | Fantasy | FANCD 6082-2
L.T.D. | Prestige | PCD 11018-2
Dexter Gordon:The Complete Blue Note Sixties Sessions | Blue Note | 834200-2
True Blue | Blue Note | 534032-2
Earl Hines Trio | Fatha | CBS | CBS 21104
Ernie Wilkins And His Orchestra | Here Comes The Swingin' Mr.Wilkins | Fresh Sound Records | FSR 511(Everest LPBR 5077)
Gerry Mulligan Quartet With Lee Konitz | Complete 1953 The Haig Performances | The Jazz Factory | JFCD 22861
Howard Rumsey's Lighthouse All-Stars | Jazz Invention | Contemporary | C 14051
Jaki Byard Quartet | Live! At Lennie's On The Turnpike | Prestige | PCD 24121-2(P 7419/7477)
Mel Tormé With Orchestra | Comin' Home Baby!/Sings Sunday In New York | Warner | 8122-75438-2
Monty Alexander Trio | Monty Alexander In Tokyo | Pablo | 2310836
Rodney Whitaker Groups | ChildrenOf The Light | DIW | DIW 907 CD
Stan Getz Quartet | 'Round Midnight In Paris | Bandstand | BDCD 1503
Tal Farlow Trio | Tal | Verve | MV 2565 IMS
The Clayton Brothers | It's All In The Family | Concord | CJ 138
The New York Allstars | Broadway | Nagel-Heyer | CD 003
The Three Sounds | Here We Come | Blue Note | BNJ 71009(BST 84088)
Zim Zemarel And His Orchestra | Live At The Hyatt Regency | Hindsight | HSR 230
Charlie Parker Quintet | Summit Meeting At Birdland | CBS | CBS 82291
Broadway Blues
Jaco Pastorius Trio | Jaco Pastorius Broadway Blues & Theresa | Jazzpoint | JP 1053 CD
Heavy'n Jazz | Jazzpoint | JP 1036 CD
Joe Lovano-Greg Osby Quintet | Friendly Fire | Blue Note | 499125-2
John Zorn Group | Spy Vs. Spy-The Music Of Ornette Coleman | Nonesuch | 7559-60844-2
Junko Onishi Trio | Wow | somethin'else | 300032(TOCJ 5547)
Broadway Blues-
Dave Brubeck Quartet | Jazz Impressions Of New York | CBS | CK 46189
Broadway Lady
Ben Selvin And His Orchestra | Cheerful Little Earful | Saville Records | SVL 165 IMS
Broadway Rose-
RMS | Centennial Park | MMC | CDP 7900102
Broadway(alt.take)
Kai Winding Sextet | Trombone By Three | Original Jazz Classics | OJCCD 091-2(P 7023)
Brocksi Foxtrot
Juxoli | Juxoli | Pannon Jazz/Classic | PJ 1009
Broke Down Engine Blues
Blind Willie McTell(as 'Blind Sammy') | The Early Years | Yazoo | YAZ 1005
Broken Arrow In A Bathub
Ian Shaw With The Adrian York Quartet | Ghostsongs | Ronnie Scott's Jazz House | JHCD 025
Broken Heart
The Original Five Blind Boys Of Mississippi | Oh Lord-Stand By Me/Marching Up To Zion | Ace Records | CDCHD 341
Broken Hearted Blues
Lightnin' Hopkins | Really The Blues | America | AM 6080
Broken House
Uli Gutscher Quintet | Inspiration | Edition Collage | EC 462-2
Broken Shadows
Old And New Dreams | Playing | ECM | 1205
Ornette Coleman Septet | Broken Shadows | CBS | SRCS 7098
Broken Silence
Salamander | Spirit Of Fire | amf records | amf 1017
Broken Stone
Billy Bang Quintet | Rainbow Gladiator | Soul Note | 121016-2
Broken Wing
Chet Baker Quartet | Broken Wings | Adda | 581020
In Paris Vol.2 | West Wind | WW 2059
Evan Parker | Process And Reality | FMP | CD 37
Norbert Gottschalk With The Matthias Bröde Quartet | Norbert Gottschalk:Two Sessions | Dr.Jazz Records | 8605-2
Bronx Blues
Eddie Bert-JR. Montrose Quintet | Live At Birdland | Fresh Sound Records | FSR-CD 0198
Bronze Dance
Joshua Redman Quartet | Passage Of Time | Warner | 9362-47997-2
Ben Wolfe Trio | 13 Sketches | Mons Records | MR 874791
Brooklyn
Hans Koller Big Band | New York City | MPS | 68235
Brooklyn Blue
Sieverts-Enders-Salfellner Trio | Brooklyn Blue | Jazz 4 Ever Records:Jazz Network | J4E 4732
Brooklyn Bridge
David Chesky-Romero Lubambo Duo | The New York Chorinhos | Chesky | JD 39
Lance Bryant With The Christoph Spendel Trio | West End Avenue II | Nabel Records:Jazz Network | CD 4644
Yosuke Yamashita New York Trio | Kurdish Dance | Verve | 517708-2
Brother Aintz
Stanley Blume Quartet | Movin' Up | Organic Music | ORGM 9709
Brother Al
Ralph Abelein Group | Mr. B's Time Machine | Satin Doll Productions | SDP 1042-1 CD
Brother B
Blue Mitchell Sextet | The Riverside Collection: Blues On My Mind | Original Jazz Classics | OJCCD 6009-2
Brother 'Ball
Niko Schäuble Quintet | On The Other Hand | Naxos Jazz | 86011-2
Brother Can You Spare A Dime
Barbara Sutton Curtis | Old Fashioned Love | Sackville | SKCD2-2042
Dave Stryker Trio | All The Way | Steeplechase | SCCD 31455
Lew Stone And His Band | Lew Stone And His Band | Decca | DDV 5005/6 DT
Brother Elijah
Kjell Jansson Quartet | Back From Where We Came | Touché Music | TMcCD 009
Brother G.
Albert King Blues Band | I'm In A Phone Booth,Baby | Fantasy | F 9633
Brother Grimm
Houston Person Sextet | Goodness! | Original Jazz Classics | OJC20 332-2(P 7678)
Brother H.
Donald Byrd Orchestra With Brass & Voices | I'm Tryin'To Get Home | Blue Note | 84188
Brother Jack
Jack McDuff Quartet | Brother Jack | Prestige | PR20 7174-2
Mark Whitfield Group | Patrice | Warner | 7599-26659-2
Big Joe Williams | Baby Please Don't Go | Swingtime(Contact) | BT 2007
Brother Joe
European Jazz Ensemble | European Jazz Ensemble 25th Anniversary | Konnex Records | KCD 5100
European Trumpet Summit | European Trumpet Summit | Konnex Records | KCD 5064
Jiri Stivin-Ali Haurand | Just The Two Of Us | Konnex Records | KCD 5095
Bill Saxton Quartet | Atymony | Jazzline | JL 11136-2
Brother John
Elvin Jones Quartet | Familiar Ground | West Wind | WW 2104
Yusef Lateef Quintet | Live at Pep's Vol.2 | Impulse(MCA) | 547961-2
Horace Silver Quintet | A Prescription For The Blues | Impulse(MCA) | 951238-2
Brother John And Brother Gene
Ben Webster Sextet | Lions Abroad Volume One:Tenor Titans | Black Lion | BLCD 7620-2
Brother Kenny
Dizzy Gillespie Sextet | Musician: Composer Raconteur | Pablo | 2620116
Brother Leo
Jesse Fuller One Man Band | Brother Lowdown | Fantasy | F 24707
Brother Nasheet
Charles Lloyd Quartet | The Call | ECM | 1522(517719-2)
Brother On The Rooftop
Ray Barretto + New World Spirit | My Summertime | Owl Records | 835830-2
Brother Soul
Lou Donaldson Quintet | Blue Breakbeats:Lou Donaldson | Blue Note | 494709-2
Brother Terry
Ray Barretto & New World Spirit | Taboo | Concord | CCD 4601
Brother Ty
Eddie Harris Group | The Versatile Eddie Harris | Atlantic | SD 8807
Brother Where Are You
Annette Lowman With Three Of A Kind, Fred Wesley And Rodney Jones | Brown Baby:A Tribute To Oscar Brown Jr. | Minor Music | 801061
Bernard Purdie's Soul To Jazz | Bernard Purdie's Soul To Jazz | ACT | 9242-2
Freddy Cole With The Eric Alexander Band | Love Makes The Changes | Fantasy | FCD 9681-2
Karl Ratzer Group | Moon Dancer | Enja | ENJ-9357 2
Brother Wind
Jan Garbarek Group | Twelve Moons | ECM | 1500(519500-2)
Brother Wind March
Bob Mintzer Big Band | Only In New York | dmp Digital Music Productions | CD 501
Brotherhood
Archie Shepp Group | Live At The Pan African Festival | Affinity | AFF 41
Brotherhood Of Man
Clark Terry With The Oscar Peterson Trio | Oscar Peterson Trio + One | Verve | 558075-2
Claude Williamson Quartet | Theatre Party | Fresh Sound Records | FSR 551(Contract 15003)
Brotherly Love
Louis Jordan And His Tympany Five | Louis Jordan Vol.2-Knock Me Out | Swingtime(Contact) | ST 1012
Brothers
Rolf Kühn-Joachim Kühn | Brothers | VeraBra Records | CDVBR 2184-2
Sonny Stitt Quartet | Brothers 4 | Prestige | PCD 24261-2
Brothers 4
Joe Beck-David Sanborn Orchestra With Strings | Beck&Sanborn | CTI | ZK 40805
Brothers And Sisters
Axel Zwingenberger-Torsten Zwingenberger | Boogie Woogie Bros. | Vagabond | VRCD 8.88015
Brothers Boogie
Little Brother Montgomery Trio | Tasty Blues | Original Blues Classics | OBCCD 554-2(BV 1012)
Brown Baby
Eddie Edinborough And His New Orleans Wild Cats | The New Orleans Wild Cats | VJM | VLP 38 IMS
Brown Ballad
Duke Ellington And His Orchestra | Carnegie Hall Concert-Vol. 1 | Jazz Anthology | JA 5140
Brown Boy
Chet Baker With The Enrico Pieranunzi Quartet | Soft Journey | EdiPan | NGP 805
Brown Eyes
Klaus Kreuzeder & Henry Sincigno | Sax As Sax Can-Alive | Trick Music | TM 9312 CD
Temperance Seven | The Writing On The Wall | Upbeat Jazz | URCD 108
Brown Funk(for Ray)
The Ink Spots | If I Didn't Care | Pro-Arte | CDD 555
Brown Prance
Don Lanphere Quintet Feat. Jon Pugh Plus Two | Into Somewhere | Hep | 2022
Brown Silk
Big Bill Broonzy (as Big Bill Johnson) | The Young Big Bill Broonzy | Yazoo | YAZ 1011
Brown Sugar
Jack DeJohnette Quartet | The DeJohnette Complex | Original Jazz Classics | OJCCD 617-2
Brown Warm and Wintery
Jack Wilkins Quartet | The Jack Wilkins Quartet | Chiaroscuro | CR 156
Brownie Eyes
Clifford Brown-Gigi Gryce Sextet | Alternate Takes | Blue Note | BST 84428
Brownie Meets Bee Tee
Bobby Shew-Chuck Findley Quintet | Trumpets No End | Delos | DE 4003(882204)
Brownie Speaks
Roland Hanna Trio | Persia My Dear | DIW | DIW 805 CD
Brownout
Cold Sweat | Cold Sweat Plays J.B. | JMT Edition | 919025-2
Brown's Dance
Ray Brown Trio | Don't Get Sassy | Telarc Digital | CD 83368
Brownskin Gal (I Got My Eyes On You)
Jesse Fuller | San Francisco Bay Blues | Original Blues Classics | OBCCD 537-2(S 10051)
Sonny Rollins Quartet | The Complete Sonny Rollins RCA Victor Recordings | RCA | 2668675-2
Sonny Rollins Septet | Sonny Rollins & Co.Vol.3:What's New/Vol.4:Our Man In Jazz | RCA | 741091/92
Brown-Skinned Gal In The Calico Gown
Duke Ellington And His Orchestra | The Indispensable Duke Ellington,Vol.7/8 | RCA | ND 89274
Snooks Eaglin | That's All Right | Original Blues Classics | OBCCD 568-2(BV 1046)
Browser
Vinnie Colaiuta Group | Vinnie Colaiuta | Stretch Records | SCD 9007-2
Brückenpfeiler
Rimaak | Rimaak | Moers Music | 02016
Brujo
Ralph Towner | Trios/Solos | ECM | 1025(833328-2)
Susanne Lundeng Quartet | Waltz For The Red Fiddle | Laika Records | 35101402
Brun Halling(Brown Halling)
Peter Brötzmann | Brötzmann/Solo | FMP | 0360
Bruremarsj
Dave Brubeck Quartet | Time Out/Time Further Out | CBS | CBS 22013
Bruschetta
Junko Onishi Trio | Wow | somethin'else | 300032(TOCJ 5547)
Brush Lightly
Louie Bellson Big Band | London Scene | Concord | CJ 157
Brush Strokes
Louie Bellson Quintet | Peaceful Thunder | Musicmasters | 65074-2
Brush Thing
Dick Hyman | Cole Porter:All Through The Night | Musicmasters | 5060-2
Brushes And Brass
Count Basie And His Orchestra | The Great 1959 Band In Concert | Jazz Groove | 003 IMS
Brush-Wind
Joos-Czelusta-Konrad Trio | Blow!!! | FMP | 0370
Brütsch Over Troubled Water
The New Roman Schwaller Jazzquartet | Welcome Back From Outer Space | JHM Records | JHM 3605
Carlo Actis Dato Quartet | Ankara Twist | SPLASC(H) Records | CD H 302-2
Brutto Tempo
Vienna Art Orchestra | Artistry In Rhythm-A European Suite | TCB Records | TCB 01102
B's Dilemma
Duke Ellington And His Orchestra | Welcome To Jazz: Duke Ellington | Koch Records | 321 943 D1
BT-U
George Gruntz Jazz Group feat. Jean-Luc Ponty & The Bedouins | Jazz Meets Africa:Noon In Tunisia-El Babaku | MPS | 531720-2
Bubba And The Whale
Jimmy Smith Trio | A New Sound A New Star:Jimmy Smith At The Organ | Blue Note | 857191-2
Bubbis
The Champ-Jimmy Smith At The Organ Vol.2 | Blue Note | 300093(1514)
Bubbles
Count Basie And His Orchestra | Americans In Sweden: Roy Eldridge 1957-Count Basie 1954 | Jazz Society | AA 514
Sam Rivers' Rivbea All-Star Orchestra | Culmination | RCA | 2168311-2
Lawrence Welk And His Orchestra | Here's That Band Again | Naxos Jazz | 8.120619 CD
Bubbles,Bangles And Beans
Klaus Lenz Band | Wiegenlied | View | VS 001 IMS
Buche Y Pluma 'Na Ma'
Brötzman-Laswell-Evans-Helborg | Ode To A Tractor | Demon Records | DEM 030
Buck
Jesse Fuller | The Lone Cat | Original Blues Classics | OBCCD 526-2
Buck Jumpin'
Buck Clayton And His Orchestra | Buck Clayton:Buck Special | Vogue | 2111513-2
Bucket
Plas Johnson Sextet | The Blues | Concord | CCD 4015
Bucket(2001)
Ray Anderson-Han Bennink-Christy Doran | Cheer Up | Hat Art | CD 6175
Bucket's Got A Hole In It
Kid Ory's Creole Jazz Band | New Orleans | CBS | 21061
Louis Armstrong And His All Stars | Louis Armstrong:Complete 1950-1951 All Stars Decca Recordings | Definitive Records | DRCD 11188
Louis Armstrong And His All Stars/Orchestra | Do You Know What It Means To Miss New Orleans? | Verve | 837919-2
Percy Humphrey-Louis Nelson Jazz Band | New Orleans To Scandinavia | Storyville | SLP 232
Buckie Wuckie
John Carter Quintet | Night Fire | Black Saint | BSR 0047
Buckin' The Blues
Esquire All-American Award Winners | RCA Victor 80th Anniversary Vol.3:1940-1949 | RCA | 2668779-2
The Buck Clayton Legacy | Encore Live | Nagel-Heyer | CD 018
Fats Waller And His Rhythm | The Last Years 1940-1943 | Bluebird | ND 90411(3)
Buck's Business
Thelonious Monk Quartet | Thelonious Monk-The Complete Riverside Recordings | Riverside | 15 RCD 022-2
Buck's County Blues
Charlie Byrd Sextet | Byrd's Word! | Original Jazz Classics | OJCCD 1054-2(R 9448)
Buck's Hill
Blind Blake | Blind Blake-Bootleg Rum Dum Blues | Biograph | BLP 12003
Bucky Bucky Pizzarelli
Anca Parghel | Carpathian Colors | Nabel Records:Jazz Network | CD 4656
Buco
Carpathian Colors | Nabel Records:Jazz Network | CD 4656
Bucovina
Miles Davis And His Orchestra | Miles Davis:Early Milestones 1945-1949 | Naxos Jazz | 8.120607 CD

Bud-
Ellery Eskelin + Han Bennink | Dissonant Characters | HatOLOGY | 534

Bud On Bach
Bud Powell Trio | More Unissued Vol.1 | Royal Jazz | RJD 507
Andy LaVerne | In The Mood For A Classic-Andy LaVerne Plays Bud Powell | Steeplechase | SCCD 31342

Bud Powell
Ernie Watts-Chick Corea Quartet | 4Tune | West Wind | WW 2105

Budapest
Deborah Henson-Conant Group | Budapest | Laika Records | LK 93-039
Deborah Henson-Conant Trio | Just For You | Laika Records | LK 95-063
Hartmut Kracht | Kontrabass Pur | Jazz Haus Musik | JHM 0103 CD
James Newton Septet | James Newton | Gramavision | GR 8205-2

Budapest Encore
Ferenc Snétberger | The Budapest Concert | TipToe | TIP-888823 2

Budapest Mood
Ben Webster And His Associates | Tenor Giants | Verve | 2610046

Budd Johnson
JATP All Stars | Compact Jazz: Coleman Hawkins/Ben Webster | Verve | 833296-2

Buddhi
Kokomo Arnold | King Of The Bottelneck Guitar | Black & Blue | BLE 59.250 2

Budding Dancers
Gene DiNovi Trio | Renaissance Of A Jazz Master | Candid | CCD 79708

Budding Memories
Leo Smith Creative Orchestra | Budding Of A Rose | Moers Music | 02026

Buddy
Marilyn Middleton Pollock & Steve Mellor's Chicago Hoods | Red Hot And Blue | Lake | LACD 42

Buddy Bolden
Bunk Johnson With Bertha Gonsoulin | Bunk Johnson In San Francisco | American Music | AMCD-16

Buddy Bolden's Blues
Chris Barber's Brass Band | Take Me Back To New Orleans | Black Lion | 157007
Rod Mason-Ray Foxley | Six For Two | BELL Records | BLR 84035
Warren Vaché With Michael Moore | Horn Of Plenty | Muse | MCD 5524

Buddy Boy
Lightnin' Hopkins | Blues In My Bottle | Original Blues Classics | OBCCD 506-2(BV 1045)

Buddy's Blues
Buddy Rich Band | Krupa And Rich | Verve | 817109-1 IMS
Buddy Rich Orchestra | Compact Jazz: Gene Krupa & Buddy Rich | Verve | 835314-2 PMS

Buddy's Boogie
Buddy Johnson And His Orchestra | Buddy And Ella Johnson 1953-1964 | Bear Family Records | BCD 15479 DH
Walkin' | Official | 6008

Buddy's Groove
Alex Welsh And His Jazz Band | Dixieland To Duke-The Melrose Folio | Dormouse | DM 7 IMS

Buddy's Habits
King Oliver's Jazz Band | Louis Armstrong With King Oliver Vol.2 | Village(Jazz Archive) | VILCD 012-2

Buddy's Rock
Buddy Rich And His Orchestra | Buddy Rich Presented by Lionel Hampton | Jazz Classics | CD CA 36014

Budgie
Buddy Montgomery Quintet | So Why Not? | Landmark | LCD 1518-2

Budnike
Bud Powell Trio | Birdland '53 | Fresh Sound Records | FSCD 1017

Budo
Miles Davis And His Orchestra | The Complete Birth Of The Cool | Capitol | 494550-2
The Complete Birth Of The Cool | Capitol | 494550-2
Birth Of The Cool | Capitol | 530117-2
Miles Davis:The Blue Note And Capitol Recordings | Blue Note | 8274752
Miles Davis Nonet | The Real Birth Of The Cool | Bandstand | BDCD 1512
Peter Herbolzheimer Rhythm Combination & Brass | Bigband Bebop | Koala Records | CD P 5
Stan Getz Quintet | Jazz At Storyville Vol.2 | Fresh Sound Records | FSR 630(Roost RLP 411)

Budo(alt.take)
Stan Getz-The Complete Roost Sessions | The Jazz Factory | JFCD 22839

Bud's Blues
Claude Williamson Trio | Tribute To Bud | Eastworld | EWJ 90009
Sonny Stitt With The Bud Powell Trio | Genesis | Prestige | P 24044

Bud's Bubble
Bud Powell Trio | More Unissued Vol.1 | Royal Jazz | RJD 507

Bue
Glen Gray And The Casa Loma Orchestra | The Radio Years: Glen Gray And The Casa Loma Orchestra 1943-46 | London | HM-A 5050 AN

Buenavista
Jan Garbarek Group | I Took Up The Runes | ECM | 1419(843850-2)

Bueno Hora, Buenos Vientos
Mark Kramer Trio | Evita En Jazz | Telarc Digital | CD 83422

Buffalo
Michael Weiss Trio | Milestones | Steeplechase | SCCD 31449

Buffalo Rhythm
Ted Wallace And His Orchestra | Adrian Rollini Groups 1924-27 | Village(Jazz Archive) | VILCD 023-2

Buffalo Wings
Lonnie Mack Band | Second Sight | Sonet | SNTF 968(941968)

Bug In A Rug
Jimmy McGriff Orchestra | Swingin' The Blues-Jumpin' The Blues | Laserlight | 24654

Bug Out
Jimmy McGriff-Funkiest Little Band In The Kand | LRC Records | CDC 9046(874379)

Bugle Boy March
Chris Barber's Jazz Band | Ice Cream | Storyville | 6.23326 AF
George Lewis And The Barry Martyn Band | For Dancers Only | GHB Records | BCD 37

Bugle Call Rag
Benny Goodman And His Orchestra | Planet Jazz:Benny Goodman | Planet Jazz | 2152054-2
The Benny Goodman Story | Capitol | 833569-2
Carlo Krahmer's Chicagoans | Delving Back With Humph:Humphrey Lyttelton 1948-1949 | Lake | LACD 72
Dicky Wells And His Orchestra | Americans Swinging In Paris:Dicky Wells | EMI Records | 539664-2
Django Reinhardt And His American Friends:Paris 1935-1937 | Memo Music | HDJ 4124
Jack Linx And His Birmingham Society Serenaders | Jack Linx And Maurice Sigler | Jazz Oracle | BDW 8018
JATP All Stars | The Complete Jazz At The Philharmonic On Verve 1944-1949 | Verve | 523893-2
Jazz At The Philharmonic:Best Of The 1940's Concerts | Verve | 557534-2
Kenny Baker And His Orchestra | Date With The Dozen | Dormouse | DM 9 IMS
New Orleans All Stars | At The Dixieland Jubilee | Dixieland Jubilee | DJ 502
Phil Mason's New Orleans All-Stars | You Do Something To Me! | Lake | LACD 33
Roy Eldridge And His Central Plaza Dixielanders | Roy Eldridge 'Littel Jazz'-The Best Of The Verve Years | Verve | 523338-2
The Metronome All Stars | The Indispensable Coleman Hawkins 1927-1956:Body And Soul | RCA | ND 89277

Bugle Call Rag-
Louis Armstrong And His All Stars | Louis Armstrong:Complete 1950-1951 All Stars Decca Recordings | Definitive Records | DRCD 11188

Bugs
Jazz Pistols | Special Treatment | Lipstick Records | LIP 8971-2
Charles Mingus Group | Reincarnation Of A Love Bird | Candid | CS 9026

Buhaina
Milt Jackson Quintet | Opus De Funk | Prestige | P 24048
The MJQ Box | Prestige | 7711-2

Buhaina's Valediction
Bob Wilber Octet | Bean:Bob Wilber's Tribute To Coleman Hawkins | Arbors Records | ARCD 19144

Buh-De-Daht
Harry Roy And His Orchestra | May Fair Nights | Saville Records | SVL 171 IMS

Building
Horace Heidt And His Musical Knights | The Uncollected:Horace Heidt | Hindsight | HSR 194

Building No.1
Art Ensemble Of Chicago | Complete Live In Japan-April 22, 1984 Tokyo | DIW | DIW 815/16 CD

Built For Comfort
Larry O'Neill With The Houston Person Quintet | You Got Me Runnin' | Muse | MCD 5426

Bukka's Jitterbug Swing
Keshavan Maslak Trio | Loved By Millions | LEO | LR 105

Bukowsky-Chapter 1
Rabih Abou-Khalil Group | Bukra | Enja | ENJ-9372 2

Bukra
Alfred 23 Harth QuasarQuartet | POPending EYE | free flow music | ffm 0493

BukzokWestWostokSude
Duke Ellington And His Orchestra | In The Uncommon Market | Pablo | 2308247-2

Bula
Jimmy Dorsey And His Orchestra | Perfidia | Laserlight | 15768

Bula-Beige
Cecil Taylor Orchestra | Into The Hot | Impulse(MCA) | IMP 12922

Bulbs
Michael Riessler Group | Tentations D'Abélard | Wergo | WER 8009-2

Bulegria
Los Jovenes Flamencos With The WDR Big Band And Guests | Jazzpana | ACT | 9212-2

Buleria
Pedro Javier Gonzales | Internationales Guitarren Festival '94 | ALISO Records | AL 1030
Raphael Fays Group | Voyages | Acoustic Music Records | AMC 1015

Bulerias
Mel Lewis And His Sextet | The Lost Art | Limelight | 820815-2 IMS

Bulgaria
Kenny Werner Trio | Introducing The Trio | Sunnyside | SSC 1038 D

Bulgarian Folk Tune
For Free Hands | Eastern Moods | Laika Records | 35101502

Bulgarian Suite
Eastern Moods | Laika Records | 35101502

Bulgarskie Devoitsche
Big Bill Broonzy (as Big Bill Johnson) | Do That Guitar Rag | Yazoo | YAZ 1035

Bullet Bag
Lincoln Center Jazz Orchestra | Big Train | CBS | CK 69860

Bullet Train
Mike Mainieri Group | Jazz Life Vol.2:From Seventh At Avenue South | Storyville | 4960763
Mike Mainieri Orchestra | Wanderlust | NYC-Records | NYC 6002 2
Billy Sheehan-John Novello-Dennis Chambers | Niacin | Stretch Records | SCD 9011-2

Bullfight
Roy Haynes Septet | Thank You Thank You | Galaxy | GXY 5103

Bullroarer
Barry Harris Sextet | Bull's Eye! | Original Jazz Classics | OJCCD 1082-2(P 7600)

Bull's Eye
NRG Ensemble | This Is My House | Delmark | DE 485

Bullues Bullose
Branford Marsalis Quartet | Reqiem | CBS | 69655-2

Bullworth
Cecil Taylor Unit | Cecil Tayler Unit In Japan, Vol.1 | Konnex Records | KCD 5039

Bumble Bee Blues
Tampa Red | Tampa Red 1928-1942:It's Tight Like That | Story Of Blues | CD 3505-2

Bumble Bee Stomp
Benny Goodman And His Orchestra | Wrappin' It Up-The Harry James Years Part 2 | Bluebird | 63 66549-2

Bumpin'
Les McCann Group | Listen Up! | Musicmasters | 65139-2
Wes Montgomery With The Don Sebesky Orchestra | Bumpin' | Verve | 539062-2
Verve Jazz Masters 14:Wes Montgomery | Verve | 519826-2
Jimmy Ponder Quintet | To Reach A Dream | Muse | MCD 5394

Bumpin' On Sunset
Wes Montgomery Quintet With The Claus Ogerman Orchestra | Talkin' Jazz:Roots Of Acid Jazz | Verve | 529580-2
Tequila | CTI Records | PDCTI 1118-2
Wes Montgomery Trio | Tequila | Verve | 547769-2

Bumpin' On Sunset(alt.take)
George Wallington And His Band | George Wallington Showcase | Blue Note | BNJ 71003

Bums
Enrico Rava Quintet | Andanada | Soul Note | SN 1064

Bunch Of Banners
Duke Ellington And His Famous Orchestra | Duke Ellington Playing The Blues 1927-1939 | Black & Blue | BLE 59.232 2

Bundle O'Funk
John Lee Hooker | John Lee Hooker | Original Jazz Classics | 61140

Bundle Up And Go
Foday Musa Suso | The Dreamtime | CMP Records | CMP CD 3001

Bunk Johnson Talking Records(9:29)
Lennie Niehaus Octet | Lennie Niehaus Vol.3:The Octet No.2 | Contemporary | COP 017

Bunk's Blues
Art Pepper Orchestra | The Artistry Of Pepper | Pacific Jazz | 797194-2

Bunny
Gerry Mulligan-Johnny Hodges Quintet | The Silver Collection: Gerry Mulligan Meets The Saxophonists | Verve | 827436-2 PMS
Shorty Rogers And His Giants | Short Stops | RCA | NL 85917(2)

Bunny Hop Mambo
Duke Ellington And His Orchestra | Happy Birthday Duke Vol.5 | Laserlight | 15787

Bunt Sind Schon Die Wälder
Art Blakey And The Jazz Messengers | One For All | A&M Records | 395329-2

Burglar King
Barry Harris Quintet | Stay Right With It | Milestone | M 47050

Burgundy
George Young Quartet | Burgundy | Paddle Wheel | K 28P 6449

Burgundy Street Blues
George Lewis And His Jazzband | George Lewis In Japan Vol.1 | GHB Records | BCD 14
George Lewis And His New Orleans Stompers | Hot Jazz On Blue Note | Blue Note | 835811-2
George Lewis And His Ragtime Band | The Second Bakersfield Concert,1954 | Storyville | SLP 4022

Burkina Faso
Paul Bley/Evan Parker/Barre Phillips | Time Will Tell | ECM | 1537

Burlesque
Gabriele Mirabassi Trio | Latakia Blend | Enja | ENJ-9441 2

Burley E Perique
Gary Peacock-Ralph Towner | Oracle | ECM | 1490(521350-2)

Burly Hello
Paul Howard's Quality Serenaders | Early Hamp | Affinity | CD AFS 1011

Burn My Body
Ann Phillips And The Kermit Leslie Orchestra | Born To Be Blue | M&M Records | R 25090(Roulette)

Burnin' Hell
Bob Crosby And His Orchestra | Swing Legens:Bob Crosby | Nimbus Records | NI 2011

Burnin' The Candle At Both Ends
James Dapogny's Chicago Jazz Band | Original Jelly Roll Blues | Discovery | 74008-2

Burnin' The Iceberg
Jelly Roll Morton And His Orchestra | The Complete Jelly Roll Morton-Vol.3/4 | RCA | NL 89769(2) DP

Burning
Chris McGregor | Piano Song Vol.1 | Musica | MUS 3019

Burning Fingers
James Blood Ulmer Quartet | Black And Blues | DIW | DIW 845 CD

Burning Of The Midnight Lamp
Nguyen Le Trio With Guests | Purple:Celebrating Jimi Hendrix | ACT | 9410-2
Pinguin Moschner-Joe Sachse | If 69 Was 96/The Music Of Jimi Hendrix | Aho-Recording | CD 1016

Burning Spear
Kenny Burrell With The Don Sebesky Orchestra | Blues-The Common Ground | Verve | 589101-2
Peter Kowald Group | When The Is Out You Don't See Stars | FMP | CD 38

Burning Temple
James Blood Ulmer Blues Experience | Live at The Bayerischer Hof | IN+OUT Records | 7018-2

Burning Up
Steve Tibbetts Group | Bye Bye Safe Journey | ECM | 1270
The Crusaders With The Royal Philharmonic Orchestra | Royal Jam | MCA | ???

Burnleigh
Steve Tibbetts Group | The Fall Of Us All | ECM | 1527(521144-2)

Burnt Offering
Milt Buckner Quintet | Organ | Jazz Anthology | JA 5178

Burried In Blue
Johnny Richards And His Orchestra | Something Else By Johnny Richards | Affinity | AFF 155

Burst
Peter Kowald Group | When The Is Out You Don't See Stars | FMP | CD 38

Bursts
Borah Bergman | Bursts Of Joy | Chiaroscuro | CR 158

Burt's Pad
Oscar Pettiford Sextet | Oscar Pettiford Sextet | Vogue | 21409452

Bu's Beat
Ronnie Cuber Quartet | In A New York Minute | Steeplechase | SCCD 31372

Buschka
Peter A. Schmid Duos | Duets,Dialogues & Duels | Creative Works Records | CW CD 1034

Buschwerk:
Osman Ismen Project | Jazz Eastern | CBS | 489840-2

Bush Baby
Arthur Blythe Quintet | Illusions | CBS | SRCS 7188
Johnny Griffin Sextet | Bush Dance | Galaxy | GXY 5126

Bush Magic
Meade Lux Lewis Duo | Cat House Piano | Verve | 557098-2

Bushman In The Desert
Louis Hayes Sextet | The Crawl | Candid | CCD 79045

Bushman Song
John Stubblefield Quintet | Bushman Song | Enja | 5015 (807538)

Bushman Triumphant-
Jeanne Lee Group | Natural Affinities | Owl Records | 018352-2

Bushwhacked-
New Winds | The Cliff | Sound Aspects | sas CD 025

Business As Usual
The Blue Bird Society Orchestra | The Blue Bird Society Orchestra | Stash Records | ST 268 IMS

Business You're Doin'
Mark Whitfield Quartet | 7th Avenue Stroll | Verve | 529223-2

Buss(Right On Togo)
Henry Busse And His Shuffle Rhythm Orchestra | The Uncollected:Henry Busse,Vol.2 | Hindsight | HSR 193 (835574)

Buster Rides Again
Hound Dog Taylor & The House Rockers | Natural Boogie | Sonet | 198044(SNTF 678)

Buster's Tune
Return To The Wide Open Spaces | Live At The Caravan Of Dreams | Amazing Records | AMCD 1021

But Anyway
Ada Montellanico With The Jimmy Cobb Trio | The Encounter | Philology | W 66.2

But Beautiful
Art Pepper Quartet | Friday Night At The Village Vanguard | Original Jazz Classics | OJCCD 695-2(C 7643)
Arthur's Blues | Original Jazz Classics | OJCCD 680-2
Art Pepper:The Complete Galaxy Recordings | Galaxy | 16GCD 1016-2
Art Pepper:The Complete Village Vanguard Sessions | Contemporary | 9CCD-4417-2
Art Pepper-George Cables Duo | Art Lives | Galaxy | GXY 5145
Art Van Damme & The Singers Unlimited | Invitation | MPS | 68107
Benny Carter Quintet | New York Nights | Musicmasters | 65154-2
Bill Evans Trio | Getting Sentimental | Milestone | MCD 9346-2
His Last Concert In Germany | West Wind | WW 2022
Bill Evans Trio:The Last Waltz | Milestone | 8MCD 4430-2
Bill Evans Trio:The Last Waltz | Milestone | 8MCD 4430-2
Turn Out The Stars | Dreyfus Jazz Line | FDM 36553-2
Homecoming | Milestone | MCD 9291-2
Bill Evans-Eddie Gomez Duo | The Complete Fantasy Recordings | Fantasy | 9FCD 1012-2
Eloquence | Fantasy | F 9618
Bill Holman Band | A View From The Side | JVC | JVC 2050-2
Blue Mitchell And His Orchestra | A Blue Time | Milestone | M 47055
Curtis Fuller Sextet | Boss Of The Soul-Stream Trombone | Fresh Sound Records | FSR-CD 0209
Dave Pell Octet feat. Lucy Ann Polk | Plays Burke And Van Heusen | Fresh Sound Records | KL 1034(Kapp)
Eddie Lockjaw Davis Quartet | The Cookbook | Prestige | P 24039
Eddie Lockjaw Davis Quintet | The Eddie Lockjaw Davis Cookbook Vol.1 | Original Jazz Classics | OJCCD 652-2(P 7141)
Gene Ammons Quartet | The Gene Ammons Story: Gentle Jug | Prestige | P 24079
Harry Allen Quartet | Love Songs Live! | Nagel-Heyer | NH 1014
Herb Ellis-Ray Brown Sextet | Hot Tracks | Concord | CCD 6012
Jimmy Smith Trio | Standards | Blue Note | 821282-2
Joe Pass Quartet | The Complete 'Catch Me' Sessions | Blue Note | LT 1053
Kenny 'Pancho' Hagood With The Joe Sample Trio | Cool Whalin' - Bebop Vocals | Spotlite | SPJ 135
Kenny Dorham Sextet | But Beautiful | Milestone | M 47036
Lew Soloff Quartet | But Beautiful | Paddle Wheel | K32Y 6205
Lois Lane With The Metropole Orchestra | Sensual Songs | Koch Jazz | 3-6901-2
Patty Peterson Group | The More I See You | Jazz Pure Collection | AU 31614 CD
Sir Charles Thompson | Playing My Way | Jazz Connaisseur | JCCD 9313-2
Soesja Citroen And Her Trio | Here And Now | Challenge | CHR 70003

TITELVERZEICHNIS

Stan Getz Quartet | Best Of The West Coast Sessions | Verve | 537084-2
Stan Getz:East Of The Sun-The West Coast Sessions | Verve | 531935-2
Stan Getz With The Bill Evans Trio | The Chick Corea-Bill Evans Sessions | Verve | 2610036
But Beautiful | Jazz Door | JD 1208
Stan Kenton And His Orchestra | Sophisticated Approach | Creative World | ST 1018
Tony Bennett-Bill Evans | The Tony Bennett-Bill Evans Album | Original Jazz Classics | OJC20 439-2(F 9489)
Tony Perkins With The Marty Paich Orchestra | Tony Perkins | Fresh Sound Records | LN 3394(Epic)
Waymon Reed Quintet | 46th And 8th | Artists House | AH 10 IMS

But Beautiful-
Hank Jones Trio | Arigato | Progressive | PRO 7004

But For Love
Peter Ehwald Trio | Away With Words:The Music Of John Scofield | Jazz Haus Musik | JHM 0128 CD
Marlena Shaw With Orchestra | From The Depths Of My Soul | Blue Note | 84443

But Happy(Fugue IV)
George Cables Trio | Phantom Of The City | Contemporary | C 14014

But I Know It When I See It
Eddie Marshall Quintet | Dance Of The Sun | Timeless | CD SJP 109

But I'll Be Back
George Shearing & Barry Tuckwell With Orchestra | Plays The Music Of Cole Porter | Concord | CCD 42010

But It's O.K.
Michel Grailler | In A Spring Way | Red Records | VPA 133

But Not For Me
Ahmad Jamal Trio | At The Pershing | Affinity | CD AFS 780
Ben Webster-Bill Coleman Sextet | A Tribute To Gershwin | Jazz Colours | 874707-2
Bernard Berkhout's Swingmates | Air Mail Special | Timeless | CD SJP 360
Billie Holiday And Her Orchestra | Embraceable You | Verve | 817359-1 IMS
Bud Freeman All Stars | The Bud Freeman All-Star Sessions | Prestige | PRCD 24286-2
The Bud Freeman All Stars | Original Jazz Classics | OJC 183(SV 2012)
Buddy Greco Quartet | Route 66-A Personal Tribute To Nat King Cole | Celebrity | CYCD 71901
Chet Baker Quartet | Chet Baker-The Legacy Vol.2:I Remember You | Enja | ENJ-9077 2
Let's Get Lost: The Best Of Chet Baker Sings | Pacific Jazz | 792932-2
Chet Baker | Carlyne | 695015
Chet Baker Trio | Strollin' | Enja | ENJ-5005 2
Chet Baker In Bologna | Dreyfus Jazz Line | FDM 36558-9
Christian Elsässer Trio | Venice | Organic Music | ORGM 9727
Claudio Roditi Quintet | Milestones | Candid | CCD 79515
Dusko Goykovich-Oscar Pettiford | Dusko Goykovich Portrait | Enja | ENJ-9427 2
Eddie Lockjaw Davis Quartet | Eddie Lockjaw Davis With Shirley Scott | Original Jazz Classics | OJC 218(P 7154)
Ella Fitzgerald With Ellis Larkins | Ella:The Legendary American Decca Recordings | GRP | GRP 46482
Ella Fitzgerald With Orchestra | Essential Ella | Verve | 523990-2
Ella Fitzgerald With The Nelson Riddle Orchestra | Oh Lady Be Good:The Best Of The Gershwin Songbook | Verve | 529581-2
Ella Sings Gershwin-Vol. 1 | Metro | 2682004 IMS
Georgie Fame With The Ellen Helmus Sextet | A Portrait Of Chet | Four Leaf Clover | FLC 108 CD
J.J.Johnson Quintet | Vivian | Concord | CCD 4523
Jimmy Smith Trio | Jimmy Smith At The Organ | Blue Note | 300154(1512)
Joe Puma Quartet | Wild Kitten | Dawn | DCD 109
John Coltrane Quartet | My Favorite Things | Atlantic | 8122-75204-2
John Pizzarolli Trio And Friends | After Hours | Novus | 4163191-2
Klaus Ignatzek | Gershwin Songs | Nabel Records:Jazz Network | CD 4631
Lee Konitz-Franco D'Andrea | 12 Gershwin In 12 Keys | Philology | W 312.2
Luca Flores | For Those I Never Knews | SPLASC(H) Records | CD H 439-2
Modern Jazz Quartet | The Complete Modern Jazz Quartet Prestige & Pablo Recordings | Prestige | 4PRCD 4438-2
Modern Jazz Quartet | Prestige | P 24005
Nicole Metzger With The Christoph Mudrich Trio | Nicole Metzger Sings Gershwin | Blue Concept | BCCD 97/01
Oliver Jones | Just 88 | Enja | ENJ-8062 2
Oscar Pettiford/Dusko Goykovic | Jazz Legacy Baden Baden Unreleased Radio Tapes | Jazzline | ???
Ran Blake | That Certain Feeling(George Gershwin Songbook) | Hat Art | CD 6077
Red Garland Trio | Crossings | Original Jazz Classics | OJCCD 472-2
Rosemary Clooney With Les Brown & His Band Of Renown | Aurex Jazz Festival '83 | Eastworld | EWJ 80268
Ruby Braff-George Barnes Quartet | Plays Gershwin | Concord | CCD 6005
Urbie Green And His Orchestra | The Message | Fresh Sound Records | NL 46033(RCA)

But Not For Me-
Bill Evans | Eloquence | Fantasy | F 9618
Johnny Hodges Orchestra | The Rabbit's Work On Verve In Chronological Order, Vol. 6 | Verve | 2304446 IMS

But Not For Me(take 1)
Miles Davis Quintet | Tune Up | Prestige | P 24077

But Not For Me(take 2)
Ben Webster-Bill Coleman Sextet | Ben Webster Meets Bill Coleman | Black Lion | BLCD 760141

But On The Other Hand
Roseanna Vitro With The Ken Werner Group | Catchin' Some Rays-The Music Of Ray Charles | Telarc Digital | CD 83419

But She's My Buddy's Chick
King Curtis Band | Trouble In Mind | Original Blues Classics | OBCCD 512-2(Tru 15001)

But Where's te Moon?
Phillip Johnston's Big Trouble | The Unknown | Avant | AVAN 037

Butch And Butch
Oliver Nelson & His Sextet | Three Dimensions | MCA | IA 9335/2
Oliver Nelson And His Orchestra | Blues And The Abstract Truth | CTI Records | PDCTI 1122-2
Astor Piazzolla Group | The Rough Dancer And The Cyclical Night(Tango Apasionado) | American Clave | AMCL 1019-2

Butter(For Yo' Popcorn)
French Toast | French Toast | Electric Bird | KICD 1000

Buttercups
Chas. Creath's Jazz-O-Maniacs | The Classic Years In Digital Stereo: Hot Town | CDS Records Ltd. | RPCD 616(CD 647)

Butterflies & Zebras
Sandra King With Band | Songbirds Special | Blue Flame | 40562(2132444-2)

Butterflies That I Feel Inside Me
Bianca Ciccu With The Randy Brecker Quintet | The Gusch | ITM Records | ITM 1440

Butterfly
Herbie Hancock Group | Directstep | CBS | SRCS 9503
Karl Denson Group | The Red Snapper | Minor Music | 801024

Butterfly Dreams
Flora Purim And Her Sextet | Butterfly Dreams | Original Jazz Classics | OJCCD 315-2
Jon Jang & The Pan-Asian Arkestra | Tiananmen! | Soul Note | 121223-2

Butterfly's Debut
Jay McShann And His Orchestra | Jimmy Witherspoon & Jay McShann | Black Lion | BLCD 760173

Button Nose
Maynard Ferguson With The Birdland Dreamband | The Birdland Dream Band Vol.1 | Fresh Sound Records | 58110 CD(RCA)

Button Up Your Overcoat
Johnny Mercer With Paul Weston's Orchestra | The Uncollected:Johnny Mercer | Hindsight | HSR 152

Buttons & Bows
Sonny Criss Quintet | Sonny Criss Quartet Feat. Wynton Kelly | Fresh Sound Records | FSR-CD 318

Butt's Delight
At The Crossroad | Fresh Sound Records | 252962-1(Peacock PLP 91)

Buy One, Get None Free
Andy LaVerne | Buy One, Get One Free | Steeplechase | SCCD 31319

Buy This Record
Kenny Clarke-Martial Solal Sextet | Roy Haynes/Kenny Clarke:Transatlantic Meetings | Vogue | 2111512-2

Buzz Me
Louis Jordan And His Tympany Five | Louis Jordan Greatest Hits-Vol.2 | MCA | 1337

Buzzard Breath
Ray Run No Star Band | I Got Gershwin | Jazzline | ???

Buzzard Song
Louis Armstrong And Ella Fitzgerald With Russell Garcia's Orchestra | The Complete Ella Fitzgerald And Louis Armstrong On Verve | Verve | 537284-2
Miles Davis With Gil Evans & His Orchestra | Porgy And Bess | CBS | CK 65141
The Miles Davis Selection | CBS | 465699-2
Ray Charles-Cleo Laine With The Frank DeVol Orchestra & Chorus | Porgy And Bess | London | 6.30110 EM

Buzzard Variation
Ray Pizzi Quintet | The Love Letter | Discovery | DS 801 IMS

Buzzin' Around
Lionel Hampton And His All Stars | Masters Of Jazz Vol.8 | RCA | NL 89540 DP

Buzzy
Charlie Parker All Stars | Charlie Parker:The Complete 1944-1948 Small Group Sessions(Studio Recordings-Master Takes),Vol.3 | Blue Moon | BMCD 1009
Major Holley With The Joe Van Enkhuizen Trio | Major Step | Timeless | CD SJP 364
Red Rodney Quintet | One For Bird | Steeplechase | SCCD 31238

Bwaata
Joe Henderson Quintet | Multiple | Original Jazz Classics | OJCCD 763-2(M 9050)
Anka Darghel-Klaus Ignatzek Quartet | Soul My Secret Place | Blue Flame | 40152(2132487-2)

Bweebida Bwobbida
Gerry Mulligan Quartet | Gerry Mulligan Quartet At Storyville | Pacific Jazz | 794472-2

Bweebida Bwobbida(remake)
Ed Schuller Quartet feat. Dewey Redman | Mu-Point | Tutu Records | 888154-2*

B-Well(for Ed Blackwell)
Anthony Braxton Quartet | Anthony Braxton | Affinity | AFF 15

By All Means
Florian Ross Quintet | Seasons And Places | Naxos Jazz | 86029-2

By Any Means Necessary
Plas Johnson Band | The Warm Sound Of Plas Johnson Tenor Sax Vol.1:Midnight Blue | Blue Moon | BMCD 3060

By Heart
Chick Webb And His Orchestra | The King Of Big Band Jazz | Festival | Album 146

By My Side
John Rae Quintet | Opus De Jazz Vol.2-John Rae | Savoy | SV 0179(MG 12156)

By Myself
Buddy Montgomery | Maybeck Recital Hall Series Volume Fifteen | Concord | CCD 4494
Hod O'Brien Trio | Have Piano...Will Swing! | Fresh Sound Records | FSR-CD 5030
Joe Pass | Blues For Fred | Pablo | 2310931-2
Lena Horne With The Lennie Hayton Orchestra | Lena Goes Latin | DRG | MRS 510 IMS
Miriam Klein | By Myself | L+R Records | LR 40001
Ruby Braff-Dick Hyman | Ruby Braff And Dick Hyman Play Nice Tunes | Arbors Records | ARCD 19141
Sheila Jordan And Her Quartet | Confirmation | East Wind | EW 8024 IMS
Trudy Desmond With The Roger Kellaway Trio | Tailor Made | The Jazz Alliance | TJA 10015

By Now
Madrid Jazz Group | Unreleased Madrid Jazz Sessions 1964-1981 | Fresh Sound Records | FSR-CD 3003

By Strauss
Morton Halle Quartet | The Eagle | Curling Legs Prod. | C.L.P. CD 017

By The Beautiful Sea
Betty Carter And Her Orchestra | Out There With Betty Carter | Fresh Sound Records | 252964-1(Peacock PLP 90)

By The Bend Of The River-
Jiri Stivin & Co. | Reduta Live | clearaudio | LT 0010-2 531

By The Fireside
Ray Noble And His Orchestra | The Radio Years | London | HMG 5019 AN

By The Fjord
Barney Wilen Quintet | Wild Dogs Of The Ruwenzori | IDA Record | 020 CD

By The Light Of The Silver Moon
The Sidewalks Of New York | Tin Pan Alley:The Sidewalks Of New York | Winter&Winter | 910038-2
Frankie Laine With Carl Fischer's Orchesrtra | The Uncollected:Frankie Lane Vol.2 | Hindsight | HSR 216 (835570)

By The Numbers
John Coltrane With The Red Garland Trio | The Last Trane | Original Jazz Classics | OJC 394(P 7378)
Borah Bergman | A New Frontier | Soul Note | 121030-2

By The River Saint Marie
Johnny Mercer With Paul Weston's Orchestra | The Uncollected:Johnny Mercer | Hindsight | HSR 152
Stan Kenton And His Orchestra | The Kenton Era | Creative World | ST 1030

By The Sea
Moscow Art Trio | Music | JA & RO | JARO 4214-2
Zsolt Kutas Trio | Europ' Jazz Contest '95 | B.Sharp Records | CDS 107

By The Sleepy Lagoon
Gabriele Hasler-Roger Hanschel Duo | Pigeon | Jazz Haus Musik | JHM 0120 CD

By The Time
Alex Welsh And His Band | If I Had A Talking Picture | Black Lion | BLCD 760521

By The Time I Get To Phoenix
Oscar Peterson Trio | En Concert Avec Europe 1 | Laserlight | 710443/48
Oscar Peterson With Orchestra | Motions & Emotions | MPS | 821289-2 PMS
Oscar Peterson Trio | Paris Jazz Concert:Oscar Peterson | Laserlight | 36155

By The Time I Get To Phoenix-
Carmen Cavallaro And His Orchestra | The Uncollected: Carmen Cavallaro | Hindsight | HSR 112

By The Way
Kim Pensyl Group | Eyes Of Wonder | GRP | GRP 97102

By The Way(part 1&2)
Rebecka Gordon Quartet | Yiddish'n Jazz | Touché Music | TMcCD 014

By The Wayside Stand A Tree
Steve Wilson Quartet | Four For Time | Criss Cross | Criss 1115

By Weary Well
Keith Jarrett | Byablue | Impulse(MCA) | MCD 10648

Byablue
Keith Jarrett Quartet | Byablue | Impulse(MCA) | MCD 10648
Paul Motian Quintet | Misterioso | Soul Note | 121174-2

Bye
Ed Neumeister Trio | The Mohican And The Great Spirit | TCB Records | TCB 01072

Bye And Bye
Louis Armstrong With Gordon Jenkins And His Orchestra And Choir | Satchmo In Style | Verve | 549594-2
Louis Armstrong With The Dukes Of Dixieland | Sweetheart-Definite Alternatives | Chiaroscuro | CR 2006
Mr.Acker Bilk And His Paramount Jazz Band | New Orleans Days | Lake | LACD 36

Bye Bye Baby
Count Basie And His Orchestra | Count Basie-Basie's Basement | RCA | ???

Bye Bye Benjamino
Pete Fountain With Orchestra | The Best Of Pete Fountain | MCA | MCD 4032

Bye Bye Blackbird
Ben Webster With The Oscar Peterson Trio | Ben Webster Meets Oscar Peterson | Verve | 521448-2
Verve Jazz Masters 43:Ben Webster | Verve | 525431-2
Ben Webster Meets Oscar Peterson | Verve | 829167-2
Buck Clayton And His Band | Jammin' At Condon's Vol.2 | Nueva Records | JU 312
Charlie Shavers With The Al Waslon Trio | A Man And His Music | Storyville | SLP 4073
Dave Liebman Quintet | Return Of The Tenor:Standards | Double Time Records | DTRCD-109
Don Friedman Quartet | My Foolish Heart | Steeplechase | SCCD 31534
Donald 'Duck' Harrison Quintet | Full Circle | Sweet Basil | 660.55.003
Gene Ammons-Sonny Stitt Quintet | God Bless Jug And Sonny | Prestige | PCD 11019-2
Gianni Basso & Guido Manusardi | Maestro+Maestro=Exciting Duo | SPLASC(H) Records | H 103
Henning Berg-Andreas Genschel Duo | Beim 5.Kölner Jazz Haus Festival 1982 | Jazz Haus Musik | JHM 13
Jeanette MacLeod With The Frieder Berlin Swing Project | The Voice Of Swing | Satin Doll Productions | SDP 1001-1 CD
Jimmy Scott With Band | But Beautiful | Milestone | MCD 9321-2
Jimmy Smith Trio | On The Sunny Side | Blue Note | LT 1092
Joe Lovano With The Junko Onishi Trio | Tenor Time | somethin'else | 300230(TOCJ 5584)
John Coltrane Quartet | John Coltrane-Live Trane:The European Tours | Pablo | 7PACD 4433-2
The Complete Graz Concert Vol.1 | Magnetic Records | MRCD 104
The Best Of John Coltrane | Pablo | 2405417-2
Keith Jarrett Trio | Bye Bye Blackbird | ECM | 1467(513074-2)
Kenny 'Pancho' Hagood With The Joe Sample Trio | Cool Whalin' - Bebop Vocals | Spotlite | SPJ 135
Marion Montgomery And Her Quintet | Nice And Easy | Ronnie Scott's Jazz House | JHCD 011
Miles Davis Quintet | Miles Davis In Person-Friday Night At The Blackhawk,San Francisco,Vol.1 | CBS | C4K 87106
The Miles Davis Selection | CBS | 465699-2
Newport Jazz Festival 1958,July 3rd-6th,Vol.1:Mostly Miles | Phontastic | NCD 8813
Miles Davis Sextet | Miles Davis All Stars Live in 1958-59 | Jazz Band Records | EBCD 2101-2(882858)
Monty Alexander Trio | Live In Holland | Verve | 835627-2 PMS
Niels Tausk Quartet | Pall Mall Export Swing Award: Swing Night | EMI Records | CDP 748910-2
Oscar Peterson | My Favorite Instrument | MPS | 821843-2 PMS
Papa John De Francesco Quintet | Comin' Home | Muse | MCD 5531
Pierre Michelot Orchestra | Jazz In Paris:Pierre Michelot-Round About The Bass | EmArCy | 832309-2 PMS
Rahsaan Roland Kirk Group | The Man Who Cried Fire | Night Records | VNCD 1(887047)
Roy Eldridge Quartet | The Best Of Roy Eldridge | Pablo | 2310857
Terumasa Hino Quartet | Unforgettable | Blue Note | 781191-2
The Mills Brothers | The Mills Brothers Story | Storyville | 4960233
The New York Allstars | Broadway | Nagel-Heyer | CD 003
The Steve Davis Project | Quality Of Silence | dmp Digital Music Productions | CD 522
Tim Warfield Sextet | A Whisper In The Midnight | Criss Cross | Criss 1122

Bye Bye Blackbird-
The Minstrel Stars | The Minstrel Stars | Upbeat Jazz | URCD 105

Bye Bye Blues
Arzo Youngblood | Living Country Blues USA,Vol.9:Mississippi Moan | L+R Records | LR 42039
Benny Carter Big Band | On The Air | Nueva Records | JU 327
Charlie Mariano Boston All Stars | Boston All Stars/New Sound From Boston | Original Jazz Classics | OJCCD 1745-2
Dixieland Jug Blowers | The Dixieland Jug Blowers | Yazoo | YAZ 1054
Jazzkränzchen Immergrün | Bavarian Jazz Live | Calig | 30620/21
Lew Tabackin Trio | Tabackin | Inner City | IC 1038 IMS
Mose Allison Trio | Creek Bank | Prestige | PCD 24055-2
Oscar Peterson Jam | Montreux '77-The Art Of The Jam Session | Pablo | 2620106
Singers Unlimited With The Clare Fischer Orchestra | Compact Disc:The Singers Unlimited | MPS | 831373-2 PMS
Stan Levey With Howard Rumsey's Lighthouse All Stars | Drummin' The Blues | Liberty | LPR 3064

Bye Bye Blues-
Simon Schott | Bar Piano: Simon Schott Plays Your Favorite Evergreens Vol.1 | Organic Music | ORGM 9733
Amos Milburn Quintet | Chicken Shack Boogie | Pathe | 1561411(Aladdin)

Bye Bye Booze
Shirley Horn Quintet | Light Out Of Darkness(A Tribute To Ray Charles) | Verve | 519703-2

Bye Bye Love
Vince Jones Group | Here's To The Miracles | Intuition Records | INT 3198-2
Benny Goodman And His Orchestra | More Camel Caravans | Phontastic | NCD 8841/2

Bye Bye Pretty Baby
Benny Goodman Trio | Benny Goodman:The Complete 1947-1949 Small Group Sessions Vol.2(1947-1949) | Blue Moon | BMCD 1043
Louie Bellson Septet | Louie Bellson Jam | Original Jazz Classics | OJCCD 802-2(2310838)

Bye Bye To All Birds-
Miles Davis Quintet | Miles Davis In Person-Friday Night At The Blackhawk,San Francisco,Vol.1 | CBS | C4K 87106

Bye Bye(Theme)
Memphis Slim And His Band | Memphis Slim:Born To Boogie | Memo Music | HDJ 4007

Bye George
Freddy Martin And His Orchestra | The Hits Of Freddy Martin | Capitol | 791222-2

Bye-Ya
Donny McCaslin Quartet | Exile And Discovery | Naxos Jazz | 86014-2
Neal Kirkwood Octet | Neal Kirkwood Octet | Timescrapper | TSCR 9612
Paul Motian Trio | Monk In Motian | JMT Edition | 919020-2
Ricky Ford Quartet | Flying Colors | Muse | MR 5227
Steve Lacy Quartet | The Mal Waldron Memorial Album:Soul Eyes | Prestige | PRCD 11024-2
Steve Lacy Trio | Bye-Ya | Freelance | FRL-CD 025
Thelonious Monk Trio | Thelonious Monk | Original Jazz Classics | OJC20 010-2(P 7027)
Thelonious Monk:The Complete Prestige Recordings | Prestige | 3 PRCD 4428-2

Zoot Sims Quartet | The Big Stampede | Biograph | BLP 12064

Bye-Ya-
Sebastian Gramss-Lömsch Lehmann | knoM.T | Jazz Haus Musik | JHM 0107 CD
Steve Khan | Evidence | Novus | ND 83074

Bye-Yard
Ahmad Mansour Quintet | Penumbra | Timeless | CD SJP 404

Bypass
James Blood Ulmer With The Quartet Indigo | Harmolodic Guitar With Strings | DIW | DIW 878 CD

Byrdlike
V.S.O.P. | The Quintet | CBS | 88273

Byrd's Word
Teddy Charles New Directions Quartet With Booker Little And Booker Ervin | Jazz In The Garden At The Museum Of Modern Art | Fresh Sound Records | FSR-CD 0212

Byron Get One Free
Christoph Spendel Group | Spendel | L+R Records | CDLR 45014

C & H Sugar
Chico Freeman Sextet | Destiny's Dance | Original Jazz Classics | OJCCD 799-2(C 14008)

C & M
Mike LeDonne Sextet | Soulmates | Criss Cross | Criss 1074

C Jam Blues
Brocksi-Quintett | Drums Boogie | Bear Family Records | BCD 15988 AH
Buck Clayton All Stars feat.Ben Webster | Ben And Buck | Sackville | SKCD2-2037
Cat Anderson And His All Stars | Ellingtonians In Paris | Jazztime(EMI) | 251275-2
Dave Brubeck Quartet | Newport '58:Brubeck Plays Ellington | CBS | 450317-1
DMP Big Band | DMP Big Band Salutes Duke Ellington | dmp Digital Music Productions | CD 520
Duke Ellington And His Famous Orchestra | Duke Ellington:The Blanton-Webster Band | Bluebird | 21 13181-2
Sophisticated Lady | RCA | 26685162
Duke Ellington And His Orchestra | Duke Ellington And His Orchestra 1943,Vol.1 | Circle | CCD-101
All Star Road Band Vol.2 | Doctor Jazz | ZL 70969(2) (809319)
Happy Birthday Duke Vol.3 | Laserlight | 15785
Live At Empire Hotel Hollywood L.A. February 1949-Vol.3 | Raretone | 5004 FC
Duke Ellington Trio | Legends Of The 20th Century | EMI Records | 522048-2
Duke Ellington's Jazz Group | Duke Ellington's Jazz Group | Jazz Anthology | JA 5145
Ella Fitzgerald With The Jazz At Carnegie All-Stars | Newport Jazz Festival - Live At Carnegie Hall | CBS | CBS 68279
Gerald Albright Group | Live At Birdland West | Atlantic | 7567-82334-2
Gottfried Böttger-Joe Penzlin Duo | Take Two | L+R Records | CDLR 40030
Grover Mitchell & His All-Star Orchestra | Hip Shakin' | Ken Music | 660.56.005
Helmut Zacharias & His Sax-Team | Ich Habe Rhythmus | Bear Family Records | BCD 15642 AH
Horace Parlan Trio | Movin' And Groovin' | Blue Note | 0677187
Blue Note Plays Ellington And Strayhorn | Blue Note | 520809-2
JATP All Stars | The Complete Jazz At The Philharmonic On Verve 1944-1949 | Verve | 523893-2
Jazz At Carnegie Hall All Stars | Ella Fitzgerald:Newport Jazz Festival-Live at Carnegie Hall | CBS | C2K 66809
Johnny Hodges Orchestra | Jazz Special-The 40's & 60's | RCA | CL 43236 AF
Lonnie Johnson With Elmer Snowden | Lonnie Johnson With Elmer Snowden Vol.2:Blues Ballads And Jumpin' Jazz | Original Blues Classics | OBCCD 570-2
Monty Alexander/John Clayton | The Duke Ellington Song Book | MPS | 821151-1
New Emily Jazz Orchestra | Neanthropus Retractus | SPLASC(H) Records | HP 10
Oscar Peterson All Stars | The Greatest Jazz Concert In The World | Pablo | 2625704-2
Oscar Peterson Quartet | Victor Jazz History Vol.20:Jazz & The Blues | RCA | 2135739-2
Oscar Peterson Trio | The London Concert | Pablo | 2CD 2620111
Night Train | Verve | 821724-2
Red Norvo Trio | Rare 1950-51 Transcriptions | Queen-Disc | 061
Stuff Smith-Svend Asmussen Quintet | Hot Violins | Storyville | STCD 4170
Toots Thielemans Group | Live | Polydor | 831694-2 PMS

C Jam Funk
Bill McHenry Quartet | Graphic | Fresh Sound Records | FSNT 056 CD

C Major Tune
Lennie Tristano | The New Tristano | Atlantic | 7567-80475-2

C Minor Complex
Howard Alden-Dan Barrett Quintet | The A.B.Q Salutes Buck Clayton | Concord | CCD 4395

C To G Jam Blues
Toots Thielemans Sextet | Toots Thielemans Live | Polydor | 2491003 IMS

C&D
Marc Van Roon Trio With David Liebman | Falling Stones | Mons Records | MR 874730

C. & D.
Badiane | Flavours | Acoustic Music Records | 319.1071.2

C.B. No.1
Count Basie And His Orchestra | Warm Breeze | Pablo | 2312131-2

C.C.A.
Alec Seward & Friends | Late One Saturday Evening | Blue Labor | BL 103

C.C.Rider
Jimmy Witherspoon And His All Stars | Jimmy Witherspoon | Laserlight | 17069

C.J.
John McNeil Quintet | Faun | Steeplechase | SCCD 31117

C.M.A.
Julius Hemphill | Bluy Boyé | Screwgun | SC 70008

C.M.J.
Milt Jackson-Ray Brown Jam | Montreux '77-The Art Of The Jam Session | Pablo | 2620106

C.P.W.
Mr.Acker Bilk And His Paramount Jazz Band | Golden Hour Of Acker Bilk And His Paramount Jazz Band | Golden Hour | 88 368 XAT

C.T.A.
Chet Baker-Art Pepper Sextet | Playboys | Pacific Jazz | 794474-2
Chick Corea Electric Band II | Paint The World | GRP | GRP 97412
Lee Morgan Quartet | Candy | Blue Note | 300057(1590)
Miles Davis Sextet | Miles Davis:The Blue Note And Capitol Recordings | Blue Note | 827475-2
Miles Davis Vol.1 | Blue Note | 300081(1501)
Miles Davis Vol.1 | Blue Note | 300081(1501)

C.T.A.(alt.take)
Miles Davis:The Blue Note And Capitol Recordings | Blue Note | 827475-2

C.T.Kangaroo
Enrico Rava Quartet | Il Giro Del Giorno In 80 Mondi | Black Saint | BSR 0011

C3PO(Variations On Sergej Kuryokhin's 'The Situation Of The Asian Proletariat In America')
Five + Jazz Comfort | Brazz | Memo Music | MM 6061

Ca' Purange(Jungle Soul)
Gene Ammons Septet | Gene Ammons Bossa Nova | Original Jazz Classics | OJCCD 351-2(PR 7257)

Ca Va Mieux
Helmut Zacharias Quintet | Ich Habe Rhythmus | Bear Family Records | BCD 15642 AH

ca. mid March 1949
David Schnitter Sextet | Thundering | Muse | MR 5197

Cabala
Geri Allen Trio | Segments | DIW | DIW 833 CD

Cabaret
Ella Fitzgerald With The Tommy Flanagan Trio | Ella Fitzgerald In Budapest | Pablo | PACD 5308-2
Louis Armstrong And His All Stars | The Jazz Collector Edition: Louis Armstrong | Laserlight | 15700
Live At The Cote D'Azur | Bandstand | BDCD 1521
Louis Armstrong And His All Stars With The Robert Mersey Orchestra | Greatest Hits | CBS | 21058

Cabin Fever
Mills Blue Rhythm Band | Rhythm Spasm | Hep | CD 1015

Cabin In The Sky
Jack Walrath And The Masters Of Supense | Out Of The Tradition | Muse | MCD 5403
Ruby Braff And His New England Songhounds | Ruby Braff And His New England Songhounds Vol.2 | Concord | CCD 4504
Stan Getz And The Swedish All Stars | Stockholm Sessions '58 | Dragon | DRLP 157/158

Cabin In The Sky-
Ahmad Jamal Quartet | Nature(The Essence Part III) | Atlantic | 3984-23105-2
Mike Wofford | Afterthoughts | Discovery | DS 784 IMS

Cabin In The Sky(medley):
Ahmad Jamal Quartet | Nature(The Essence Part III) | Atlantic | 3984-23105-2
Stan Getz And The Swedish All Stars | Stockholm Sessions '58 | Dragon | DRLP 157/158

Cabo De La Guardia-
Charly Antolini Quintet | Crash | BELL Records | BLR 84002

Cabu
Shelly Manne And His Men | At The Black Hawk Vol.4 | Original Jazz Classics | OJCCD 659-2(S 7580)
At The Blackhawk Vol.4 | Contemporary | C 7580

Cabu(alt.take)
Mehmet Ergin Group | Beyond The Seven Hills | MCA | MCD 70020

Caccaroo Boohoo
Al Di Meola Group | Scenario | CBS | 25718-2

Cachita
Cuarteto Las D'Aida Y Su Grupo | Soy La Mulata | L+R Records | CDLR 45059

Cactus Tree
Jean-Pierre Pasquier Group | Firegold | Plainisphare | PAV 810

Cada 2x3
Thierry Lang-Daniel Perrin | Tusitala | Plainisphare | PL 1267-105 CD

Cadenoc Du Milicu
Fairy Tale Trio | Jazz Across The Border | Wergo | SM 1531-2

Cadence In Green
Willem Breuker Kollektief | Sensemayá | BVHAAST | CD 9509

Cadencia-
Aldo Romano Group | AlmaLatina | Owl Records | 018364-2

Cadenza
David S. Ware Quartet | Great Bliss Vol.1 | Silkheart | SHCD 127
Alvin Batiste Ensemble | Musique D'Afrique Nouvelle Orleans | India Navigation | IN 1064

Cadenze
Melvin Taylor Quartet | Plays The Blues For You | Isabel | BLE 59.920 2

Cadillac Slim
Benny Carter And His Chocolate Dandies | Coleman Hawkins & Benny Carter | Swing | SW 8403 IMS

Cadillac Taxi
Scott Hamilton-Warren Vaché Orchestra | Skyscrapers | Concord | CJ 111

Caé Caé
Gene Ammons Septet | Gene Ammons Bossa Nova | Original Jazz Classics | OJCCD 351-2(PR 7257)

Cafe
Egberto Gismonti Group | Sol Do Meio Dia | ECM | 1116(829117-2)
Janice Borla With Band | Lunar Octave | dmp Digital Music Productions | CD 3004
Rich Perry & Harold Danko | Cancoes Do Brasil | Steeplechase | SCCD 31463

Café 1930
Villa-Lobos Duo | Orage Moon | Acoustic Music Records | 319.1155.2

Cafe Aristoxenos
Duke Ellington And His Orchestra | Such Sweet Thunder | CBS | CK 65568

Cafe Au Lait(Lucky)
Duke 56/62 Vol.1 | CBS | 88653

Cafe Au Lait(Lucky-outtakes)
Joe Beck-David Sanborn Orchestra With Strings | Beck&Sanborn | CTI | ZK 40805

Café Com Leite
Terra Brazil | Café Com Leite | art-mode-records | AMR 2101

Café Com Leite(part 2)
Oscar Castro-Neves Orchestra | Brazilian Scandals | JVC | ???

Cafe Fatal-
Giovanni Mirabassi Trio | Architectures | Sketch | SKE 333010

Cafe L'amour
Michal Urbaniak Quartet | Live In New York | L+R Records | CDLR 45041

Cafe Montmartre-
Stan Getz Quartet | Stan Getz At Large Plus!,Vol.1 | Jazz Unlimited | JUCD 2001

Cafe Noir
Juraj Galan-Norbert Dömling | Playing For Love | BELL Records | BLR 84026

Cafe Subway Blues
Gebhard Ullmann Quartet | Basement Research | Soul Note | 121271-2

Cafe Vue
Johnny King Quintet | Notes From The Underground | Enja | ENJ-9067 2

Cafeine
Jacinte/Juan-José Mosalini Trio | Tango, Mi Corazón | Messidor | 15911 CD

Caged Bird
Abbey Lincoln With The Archie Shepp Quintet | Painted Lady | ITM Records | ITM 1422

Cagey
Eddy Louiss Trio & Fanfare | Sentimental Feeling | Dreyfus Jazz Line | FDM 36600-2

Cahuenga
Baden Powell | Live In Hamburg | Acoustic Music Records | 319.1037.2

Cain And Abel
Louis Armstrong And His Orchestra | Ambassador Louis Armstrong Vol.7(1940-1941) | Ambassador | CLA 1907

Cain Of Chance
Ruben Blades Y Seis Del Solar | Escenas | Messidor | 15939 CD

Cain's Brand
Jugendjazzorchester NW | Turning Around | Jugendjazzorchester NW | JJ 005

Cairns For Courtney
Amina Claudine Myers Group | In Touch | RCA | PL 83064

Cairo
John G. Smith Quartet | Roadside Picnic | RCA | PD 74002

Cairo Cadenza
John Zorn Naked City | Naked City-Grand Guignol | Avant | AVAN 002

Caithness To Kerry
Christian Wegscheider Trio | Live | Village | VILCD 1015-2

Cajin
Eric Lugosch | Black Key Blues | Acoustic Music Records | 319.1148.2

Cakewalk
Alberta Hunter With The Red Onion Jazz Babies | Louis Armstrong And The Blues Singers 1924-1930 | Affinity | AFS 1018(6)

Cakewalkin' Babies From Home
Barrelhouse Jazzband | 25 Jahre Barrelhouse Jazzband Frankfurt | Intercord | 155030
Dick Hyman-Louis Mazetier Duo | Barrel Of Keys | Jazz Connaisseur | JCCD 0140-2
Eva Taylor With Clarence Williams' Blue Five | Louis Armstrong And The Blues Singers 1924-1930 | Affinity | AFS 1018(6)
Henrik Johansen's Jazzband | The Golden Years Of Revival Jazz,Vol.2 | Storyville | STCD 5507
Humphrey Lyttelton And His Band | Delving Back With Humph:Humphrey Lyttelton 1948-1949 | Lake | LACD 72
Turk Murphy And His Jazz Band | Turk Murphy's San Francisco Jazz-Vol.2 | Good Time Jazz | 12027

Calaba
The Caribbean Jazz Project | Island Stories | Inak | 30392

Calcutta
Champion Jack Dupree Group | Back Home In New Orleans | Rounder Records | BB 9502

Calcutta Cutie
Wayne Horvitz Group | 4+1 Ensemble | Intuition Records | INT 3224-2

Calder-
Albert Collins & The Ice Breakers | Frozen Alive | Sonet | 147129

Caldonia
Bill Ramsey & His Trio | Caldonia And More... | Bear Family Records | BCD 16151 AH
Christian Bleiming & His Boogie Boys | Jivin' Time | Acoustic Music Records | AMC 1010
Woody Herman And His Orchestra | The Legends Of Swing | Laserlight | 24659
La Fiesta | West Wind Orchestra Series | 2400 CD

Caldonia Boogie
Woody Herman And The New Thundering Herd | The 40th Anniversary Carnegie Hall Concert | RCA | 2159151-2

Calgary
James Williams Sextet | James Williams Meets The Saxophone Masters | DIW | DIW 868 CD

Cali Mist
Edward Vesala Trio With Orchestra | Bad Luck Good Luck | Leo Records | 015

Calidad
Machito And His Orchestra | Afro-Cuban Jazz Moods | Original Jazz Classics | OJC20 447-2

Calidocopico-
Astor Piazzolla Y Su Quinteto Tango Nuevo | Live In Wien, Vol.1 | Messidor | 15916

California
Jean-Luc Ponty Quartet | Live At Donte's | Blue Note | 835635-2
Steve Klink Funk Unit | Places To Come From,Places To Go | Minor Music | 801098
The Minstrel Stars | The Minstrel Stars | Upbeat Jazz | URCD 105

California Crawl
Lane Hardin | The Greatest In Country Blues Vol.3(1929-1956) | Story Of Blues | CD 3523-2

California Dreaming
CTI All Stars | CTI Summer Jazz At The Hollywood Bowl-Live One | CTI | 63026
A Salute To Eddie Condon | A Salute To Eddie Condon | Nagel-Heyer | CD 004

California Here I Come
Bill Evans Trio | The Complete Bill Evans On Verve | Verve | 527953-2
The Complete Bill Evans On Verve | Verve | 527953-2
The Complete Bill Evans On Verve | Verve | 527953-2
Bill Evans:The Secret Sessions | Milestone | 8MCD 4421-2
Bill Evans/Jazzhouse | Milestone | MCD 9151-2
Firehouse Five Plus Two | Around The World | Good Time Jazz | GTCD 10044-2
Ray Noble And His Orchestra | The Radio Years | London | HMG 5019 AN
Bill Evans Trio | The Complete Bill Evans On Verve | Verve | 527953-2

California Here I Come(2)
The Complete Bill Evans On Verve | Verve | 527953-2
The Complete Bill Evans On Verve | Verve | 527953-2
Eddie Condon And His Band | Early Hamp | Affinity | CD AFS 1011

Calisto
Cecil Taylor Trio | Trance | Black Lion | BLCD 760220

Call 911
Karen Mantler Group | Karen Mantler And Her Cat Arnold Get The Flu | Watt | XtraWatt/5

Call A Doctor
Andrew Cyrille-Milford Graves Duo | Dialogue Of The Drums | IPS Records | 001

Call From The Sea
John Lee Hooker Trio | I Feel Good | Memo Music | HDJ 4038

Call It What You Wanna
Ahmad Jamal Trio | At The Top-Poinciana Revisited | Impulse(MCA) | JAS 15 (AS 9176)

Call Me
Brook Benton With The Belford Hendricks Orchestra | Brook Benton-Dinah Washington:The Two Of Us | Verve | 526467-2
Jimmy Smith-Wes Montgomery Quartet | Further Adventures Of Jimmy And Wes | Verve | 519802-2
Oscar Peterson Sextet | Soul Espanol | Limelight | 510439-2
Salvatore Bonafede Trio | Plays | Ken Music | 660.56.017

Call Me Bop
Archie Shepp Quartet | New Thing At Newport | Impulse(MCA) | JAS 22 (AS 94)

Call Me Happy
Earl Hines And His Orchestra | The Indispensable Earl Hines Vol.1/2 | RCA | 2126407-2

Call Money
| Time To Move On | Acoustic Music Records | 319.1088.2

Call Of The Canyon
Frank Sinatra With The Tommy Dorsey Orchestra | The Popular Sinatra Vol.1 | RCA | 2668711-2

Call Of The West
Dave Brubeck Orchestra | Two Generations Of Brubeck | Atlantic | SD 1645

Call Stone
Klaus König Orchestra | Time Fragments:Seven Studies In Time And Motion | Enja | ENJ-8076 2

Call That Going,Call That On
Jimmy Johnson Band | Heap See | Blue Phoenix | BLP 233720

Calling
Hugo Rignold Quintet | The Classic Years In Digital Stereo: Hot Violins | CDS Records Ltd. | RPCD 312(CD 680)

Calling Dr.Funk
The Be-Bop Boys | Fats Navarro:The 1946-1949 Small Group Sessions(Studio Recordings-Master Takes),Vol.1 | Blue Moon | BMCD 1016

Calling Home
Cecil Taylor Quartet | The Eight | Hat Art | CD 6036

Calling The Cows
Nils Landgren-Esbjörn Svensson | Layers Of Light | ACT | 9281-2

Calling The Goats
Joachim Raffel Quintet | Circlesongs | Acoustic Music Records | 312.1093.2

Calling You
Herbie Mann Group | Opalescence | Kokopelli Records | KOKO 1298
Holly Cole Trio | Misty Blue:Sweet Sisters Swing Songs Of Sorrow And Sadness | Blue Note | 521151-2
Ian Shaw With The Adrian York Quartet | Ghostsongs | Ronnie Scott's Jazz House | JHCD 025

Calling(2001)
Paul Horn-Steven Halpern | Connections | Gramavision | 18-7838-1

Calm
Miriam Alter Quintet | Alter Ego | Intuition Records | INT 3258-2

Calm Down
The Bang | Omonimo | Nueva Records | NC 3011

Calmer Of Tempest-
Peter Kowald/Vincent Chancey | Duos: America | FMP | 1270
Calorcito
Jacques Demierre/Maurice Magnoni | Disque | Plainisphare | PAV 802
Cal's Bluedo
Cal Tjader's Orchestra | Talkin Verve/Roots Of Acid Jazz:Cal Tjader | Verve | 531562-2
Poncho Sanchez And His Orchestra | Sonando | Concord | CCD 4201
Calvados
Billy Harper Quintet | Billy Harper Quintet In Europe | Soul Note | 121001-2
Calvin
Ulli Jünemann-Morton Ginnerup European Jazz Project | The Exhibition | Edition Collage | EC 518-2
Calvin's Song(One For Mum)
Duke Ellington Orchestra | Only God Can Make A Tree | Musicmasters | 65117-2
Calypso
Kenny Barron Trio | Landscape | Limetree | MCD 0020
Mike Westbrook Brass Band | The Paris Album | Polydor | 2655008 IMS
Calypso Blues
Errol Dixon Trio | In The Groove | Bellaphon | BCH 33001
Nat King Cole Duo | Nat King Cole:The Snader Telescriptions | Storyville | 4960103
Oscar Peterson With Orchestra | With Respect To Nat | Verve | 557486-2
Mark Murphy-Bob Magnusson | Mark Murphy Sings Nat Cing Cole,Volumes 1&2 | Muse | MCD 6001
Calypso Bulbosa
The Rippingtons | Moonlighting | GRP | GRP 96052
Calypso Falto
Charlie Hunter-Leon Parker | Duo | Blue Note | 499187-2
Calypso For Grampa
Freddie Hubbard & The Festival All Stars | Sweet Return | Atlantic | 780108-1
Calypso Major
Abdullah Ibrahim Septet | No Fear, No Die(S'en Fout La Mort):Original Soundtrack | TipToe | TIP-888815 2
Calypso Minor
Joe Locke-Phil Markowitz Quartet | Restless Dreams | Chief Records | CD 1
Calypso Walk
Uli Binetsch's Own Bone | Boone Up Blues | Rockwerk Records | CD 011001
Calypsodelic
Leonard Feather All Stars | Night Blooming | Mainstream | MD CDO 719
Camden Maret
Chicago Blues All Stars | American Folk Blues Festival '70 | L+R Records | LS 42021
Camel
Chris McGregor's Brotherhood Of Breath | Liv At Willisau | Ogun | OGCD 001
Camel Hop
Benny Goodman And His Orchestra | Jazz Giants:Benny Goodman | RCA | NL 89731 SI
Camel Walk
Woody Herman And His Orchestra | Verve Jazz Masters 54:Woody Herman | Verve | 529903-2
Woody Herman-1963 | Philips | 589490-2
Compact Jazz: Woody Herman | Verve | 835319-2 PMS
Camille
Bill Crosby All Stars | Bill Crosby-My Appreciation | Verve | 847892-2 PMS
Caminando Al Mar(für Bobolina)
Ralph Towner-John Abercrombie | Five Years Later | ECM | 1207
Caminhos Cruzados
Jim Tomlinson Quintet | Brazilian Sketches | Candid | CCD 79769
Larry Goldings Quartet | Caminhos Cruzados | Novus | 4163184-2
Cedar Walton | Maybeck Recital Hall Series Volume Twenty-Five | Concord | CCD 4546
Caminito
Toto Blanke-Rudolf Dasek | Mona Lisa | ALISO Records | AL 1037
Carlos Mascardini | Internationales Guitarren Festival '99 | ALISO Records | AL 1038
Camino De Las Tropas
Clemens Maria Peters/Reinhold Bauer | Quadru Mana/Quadru Mania | Edition Collage | EC 464-2
Camino Inka
Bajazzo | Caminos | Edition Collage | EC 485-2
Caminos
Ruben Blades Y Seis Del Solar With Band | Buscando America | Messidor | 15924
Camouflage
Don Wilkerson Quintet | Preach Brother! | Blue Note | 0677212
Camp Meeting
Eddie Lockjaw Davis-Johnny Griffin Quintet | The Toughest Tenors | Milestone | M 47035
Lionel Hampton All Stars | The Changing Face Of Harlem, Vol. 2 | Savoy | SJL 2224 (801200)
Camp Meeting Blues
Jacques Gauthé's Creole Rice Yerba Buena Jazz Band | Cassoulet Stomp | Stomp Off Records | CD 1170
Camp Out
Lonnie Mack Band | Second Sight | Sonet | SNTF 968(941968)
Campanile
Eliana Elias Trio | Crosscurrents | Denon Compact Disc | CY-2180
Camporondo
Dave Brubeck Quartet | Dave Brubeck's Greatest Hits | CBS | 465703-2
Camptown Races
Gone With The Wind | CBS | SRCS 9362
The Bourbon Street Stompers | I Like Dixieland | Bainbridge | BT 1019
Can Anyone Explain
Ella Fitzgerald With Sy Oliver And His Orchestra | Ella:The Legendary American Decca Recordings | GRP | GRP 46482
Louis Armstrong And Ella Fitzgerald With Sy Oliver's Orchestra | Ambassador Louis Armstrong Vol.18:Because Of You(1950-1953) | Ambassador | CLA 1918
Can Call Us
Heinz | Stadtgarten Series Vol.6 | Jazz Haus Musik | JHM 1006 SER
Can He Excuse My Wrongs
Jimmy Smith Quartet | So Blue So Funky:Heroes Of The Hammond Vol.2 | Blue Note | 829092-2
Can Heat
Marc Ducret Group | News From The Front | JMT Edition | 849148-2
Can I Go Like This
Ray Russell Quartet | Dragon Hill | CBS | 494435-2
Can Y Gwynt
Charles Mingus Trio And Voices | Debut Rarities Vol.4:The Charles Mingus Groups | Original Jazz Classics | OJCCD 1829-2
Can You Blame Me
Honey Gordon With The Hank Jones Trio | Autobiography In Jazz | Original Jazz Classics | OJC 115(DEB 198)
Can You Fee The Subway
John Kaizan Neptune Quintet | Jazzen | Denon Compact Disc | CY-1570
Can You Keep It?
Nat King Cole Trio | Love Songs | Nimbus Records | NI 2010
Can You Look Me In The Eyes
Roberto Gatto with Michael Brecker | Notes | Inak | 8805
Can You See The Dancing Gnomes?
Sun Ra Arkestra | Cosmo Omnibus Imagiable Illusion/Live At Pit-Inn,Tokyo | DIW | DIW 824 CD
Canada
Wolfgang Engstfeld-Peter Weiss Quartet | Upside Down | Drops Special | CD 1
Canadian 4
Paul Williams Group | Roots Of Rock 'N' Roll, Vol. 6: Honkers & Screamers | Savoy | SJL 2234 (801210)
Canadian Domino
Attilio Zanchi Group | Early Spring | SPLASC(H) Records | H 129
Canadian Sunset
Claude Williams Quintet | Claude Williams-King Of Kansas City | Progressive | PCD 7100
Gene Ammons Quintet | Greatest Hits | Prestige | P 10084
Giovanni Hidalgo Ensemble | Worldwide | RMM Records | 660.58.026
Hank Crawford Orchestra | Groove Master | Milestone | MCD 9182-2
Little Brother Montgomery | Little Brother Montgomery | Aves | 146502
Sonny Stitt Quartet | Sonny's Back | Muse | MR 5204
Wes Montgomery Trio | Wes Montgomery-The Complete Riverside Recordings | Riverside | 12 RCD 4408-2
Blind John Davis | You Better Cut That Out | Steeplechase | SCB 9008
Canadian Sunset-
Sunnyland Slim Blues Band | Decoration Day | L+R Records | CDLR 72007
Canal Street Blues
Frl. Mayer's Hinterhaus Jazzer | Frl. Mayer's Hinterhaus Jazzer | Jazz Classics | AU 11097
Henry Red Allen And His Orchestra | Compact Jazz: Best Of Dixieland | Verve | 831375-2
King Oliver's Creole Jazz Band | King Oliver's Creole Jazzband-The Complete Set | Retrieval | RTR 79007
Cancao De Embalar
Tamba Trio | Tamba Trio Classics | EmArCy | 536958-2
Cancao Do Sol
Stan Getz Quartet | Live At Montmartre(CD=Stan's Party) | Steeplechase | SCCD 37021/22
Grooveyard featuring Red Holloway | Grooveyard Featuring Red Holloway | JHM Records | JHM 3607
Cancion-
Machito And His Orchestra | Afro Cuban Jazz | Verve | 833561-1
Cancion Del Fuego Fatuo
Gato Barbieri Sextet | The Third World | RCA | 2179617-2
Cancion Del Llamero-
Gato Barbieri:The Complete Flying Dutchman Recordings 1969-1973 | RCA | 2154555-2
Cancion Di Argentna
Todd Coolman Trio With Joe Henderson | Lexicon | Double Time Records | DTRCD-104
Cancion Sefardi
Ramón Diaz Group | O Si No Que? | Fresh Sound Records | FSNT 044 CD
Cancion Turca
Baden Powell And His Orchestra | Canta Vinicius De Moraes E Paolo Cesar Pinheiro | Festival | 114911
Canco De No Fer Res
Elisabet Raspall Grup | Lila | Fresh Sound Records | FSNT 058 CD
Canco Neta
Ahmed El-Salamouny/Gilson De Assis | Tango Brasileiro | FSM | FCD 97725
Candela(Yo Si Como Candela)-
Bucky Pizzarelli | Solo Flight | Stash Records | ST-CD 573(875903)
Candelight
Inga Lühning With Trio | Lühning | Jazz Haus Musik | JHM 0111 CD
Jess Stacy | Commodore Classics-Jess Stacy And Friends | Commodore | 6.24298 AG
Candelight-
Vaughn Monroe And His Orchestra | Vaughn Monroe And His Orchestra 1943 | Circle | CCD-45
Candelights
The Washington Guitar Quintet | Aquarelle | Concord | CCD 42016
Howard Alden-Dan Barrett Quintet | The A.B.Q Salutes Buck Clayton | Concord | CCD 4395
Candle
Jack McDuff Quartet With Orchestra | Prelude:Jack McDuff Big Band | Prestige | PRCD 24283-2
Candlelight
Dave Holland Quintet | Prime Directive | ECM | 1698(547950-2)
Candlelight Vigil
Jerome Harris Group | Algorithms | Minor Music | 1011
Candombre
Peter Fulda Trio With Céline Rudolph | Silent Dances | Jazz 4 Ever Records:Jazz Network | J4E 4731
Candratala
Pete LaRoca Quartet | Basra | Blue Note | 300262
Candy
Harold Ashby Quartet | Presenting Harold Ashby | Progressive | PRO 7040 IMS
John Pizzarelli Collection | One Night With You | Chesky | JD 153
Kenny Davern-Flip Phillips Quintet | John & Joe | Chiaroscuro | CR 199
Nat King Cole Quartet | After Midnight | Capitol | 520087-2
Nat King Cole Trio | Any Old Time | Giants Of Jazz | GOJ 1031
Candy-
The Frank Capp/Nat Pierce Juggernaut Feat. Ernestine Anderson | Live At Alley Cat | Concord | CCD 4336
Cannis-
The Clayton Brothers | It's All In The Family | Concord | CJ 138
Cannon Ball Blues
Jelly Roll Morton's Red Hot Peppers | Doctor Jazz | Black & Blue | BLE 59.227 2
Cannonball
Emily Remler Quartet | Take Two | Concord | CCD 4195
Orexis | Orexis | Intercord | 160075
J.J.Johnson Septet | Pinnacles | Original Jazz Classics | M 9093
Cannonball's Theme
George Robert Quartet | Inspiration | TCB Records | TCB 20852
Cannonizing
Machito And His Afro Cuban Jazz Ensemble | Machito And His Afro Cuban Jazz Ensemble | Caliente | Hot 120
Cannon's Theme
Gregorio-Gustafsson-Nordeson | Background Music | HatOLOGY | 526
Canon
Kamikaze Ground Crew | The Scenic Route | New World Records | 80400-2
Canon Canon
Jacques Loussier Trio | Baroque Favorites | Telarc Digital | CD 83516
Can't Afford To Live,Can't Afford To Die
Rosa Henderson With James P. Johnson | Rosa Henderson 1923-1931 | Retrieval | RTR 79016
Can't Buy Me Love
Ella Fitzgerald With The Johnny Spence Orchestra | Ella Fitzgerald-First Lady Of Song | Verve | 517898-2
Grooveyard Meets Houston Person | Basic Instinct | Organic Music | ORGM 9701
Klaus Ignatzek | Plays Beatles Songs | Nabel Records:Jazz Network | CD 4643
Michel Leeb And Gérard Badini 'Super Swing Machine' | Certains Leeb Jazz | Dreyfus Jazz Line | FDM 36586-2
Can't Dance
Ann Burton And Her Quartet | Am I Blue | Keytone | KYT 711
Can't Find A Word To Say
Queen Sylvia With The Jimmy Dawkins Band | Midnight Baby | L+R Records | CDLR 72003
Can't Get Enough
Keith Ingham Trio | A Star Dust Melody | Sackville | SKCD2-2051
Can't Get Out Of This Mood
Harry Edison Quartet | Can't Get Out Of This Mood... | Orange Blue | OB 006 CD
Maynard Ferguson Orchestra With Chris Connor | Two's Company | Roulette | 837201-2
Sarah Vaughan With George Treadwell And His Allstars | Sarah Vaughan:Lover Man | Dreyfus Jazz Line | FDM 36739-2
Nina Simone With The Bob Mercey Orchestra | The Amazing Nina Simone | Official | 6002
Can't Get You Out Of My Head
Claire Martin With The Jim Mullen Quartet And Special Guests | Devil May Care | Linn Records | AKD 021
Can't Help Falling In Love
Hamiet Bluiett Group | Same Space | Justin Time | JUST 109-2
Can't Help Lovin' Dat Man
Clifford Brown With Strings | Brownie-The Complete EmArCy Recordings Of Clifford Brown | EmArCy | 838306-2
Earl Hines Trio | Boogie Woogie On St.Louis Blues | Prestige | MPP 2515
Ella Fitzgerald With The Nelson Riddle Orchestra | The Complete Ella Fitzgerald Song Books of Harold Arlen, Irving Berlin, Duke Ellington, George & Ira Gershwin, Jerome Kern, Johnny Mercer, Cole Porter And Rogers & Hart | Verve | 519832-2
June Christy And Her Orchestra | Early June | Fresh Sound Records | FSCD 1011
Louis Armstrong And His All Stars | The Legendary Berlin Concert Part 2 | Jazzpoint | JP 1063 CD
The Best Live Concert | Festival | ???
Marilyn Middleton Pollock With The Lake Records All-Star Jazzband |
Marilyn Middleton Pollock With The Lake Records All-Star Jazzband | Lake | LACD 35
Sammy Price-J.C.Heard | Boogie And Jazz Classics | Black & Blue | BLE 59.111 2
Wrobel-Roberscheuten-Hopkins Jam Session | Jammin' At The IAJRC Convention Hamburg 1999 | Nagel-Heyer | CD 066
Ella Fitzgerald With The Lou Levy Quartet | Ella Returns To Berlin | Verve | 837758-2
Can't Help Lovin' Dat Man-
Gene Ammons Quintet | Fine And Mellow | Prestige | PRCD 24281-2
Can't Help Myself
Abbey Lincoln With Hank Jones | When There Is Love | Verve | 519697-2
Can't Judge A Book By Its Cover
Champion Jack Dupree Quintet | Blues Power No.8:Champion Jack Dupree - Blues From The Gutter | Atlantic | 40526
Can't Let It Go
Muddy Waters Blues Band | Feathers And Sons | Chess | CHD 92522(872344)
Can't Make You Stay
Sister Rosetta Tharpe And Her Group | Gospel Train | Mercury | 841134-2
Can't No Grave Hold My Body Down
Red Garland Trio | Can't See For Lookin' | Original Jazz Classics | OJCCD 918-2(PR 7276)
Can't See For Lookin'
The Hawks | Dave Bartholomew Presents The Hawks | Pathe | 1561371(Imperial)
Can't Sit Down
Stanley Jordan Group | Flying Home | Blue Note | 748682-2
Can't Stand Your Funk
Howlin' Wolf Band | The Back Door Wolf | Chess | 515013
Can't We Be Friends
Anita O'Day With The Bill Holman Orchestra | Incomparable! Anita O'Day | Verve | 589516-2
Art Tatum | Art Tatum-The Standard Transcriptions | Music & Arts | CD 919
Standards | Black Lion | CD 877646-2
Bob Keene Septet | Solo For Seven | Fresh Sound Records | FSR 641(Andex A 4001)
Buddy Rich And His Sextet | Buddy Rich Just Sings | Verve | MV 2689 IMS
Concord Jazz All Stars | Concord Jazz All Stars At The Northsea Jazz Festival | Concord | CJ 205
Ella Fitzgerald And Louis Armstrong With The Oscar Peterson Quartet | The Jazz Collector Edition: Ella & Louis | Laserlight | 15706
Satchmo/What A Wonderful World | Verve | 837786-2
Ella Fitzgerald-First Lady Of Song | Verve | 517898-2
Ella Fitzgerald With The Frank DeVol Orchestra | Ella Fitzgerald Sings Sweet Songs For Swingers | Verve | 9860417
Frankfurt Swing All Stars | Can't We Be Friends | Joke Records | JLP 219
George Shearing-Neil Swainson Duo | Dexterity | Concord | CCD 4346
Jeanie Lambe And The Danny Moss Quartet | Three Great Concerts:Live In Hamburg 1993-1995 | Nagel-Heyer | CD 019
Joe Albany | Joe Albany At Home | Spotlite | SPJ LP 1 (JA 1)
Joe Pass-Jimmy Rowles Duo | Joe Pass:A Man And His Guitar | Original Jazz Classics | OJCCD 8806-2
Karrin Allyson And Her Sextet | Sweet Home Cookin' | Concord | CCD 4593
Ralph Sutton Quartet | The Ralph Sutton Quartet With Ruby Braff,Vol.2 | Storyville | STCD 8246
Ray Linn And The Chicago Stompers | Chicago Jazz | Trend | TR 515 Direct-to-Disc
Sarah Vaughan With Hal Mooney's Orchestra | Sarah Vaughan Sings Broadway:Grat Songs From Hit Shows | Verve | 526464-2
Sonny Stitt Quartet | Kaleidoscope | Original Jazz Classics | OJCCD 060-2(P 7077)
Toni Harper With The Oscar Peterson Quartet | Toni | Verve | MV 2684 IMS
Woody Herman And His Orchestra | The Uncollected: Woody Herman And His Orchestra 1937 | Hindsight | HSR 116
Can't We Be Friends-
Roy Eldridge-Dizzy Gillespie With The Oscar Peterson Quartet | Roy And Diz | Verve | 521647-2
Can't We Talk It Over
Tex Beneke And His Orchestra | Dancer's Delight | Magic | DAWE 79
Betty Carter And Her Trio | The Audience With Betty Carter | Bet-Car | MK 1003
Can't We Try Love Again
Lightnin' Hopkins | Lightnin' Hopkins Sings The Blues | Pathe | 2C 068-83075(Imperial)
Can't You Line 'Em
Leadbelly With The Golden Gate Jubilee Quartet | Alabama Bound | RCA | ND 90321(847151)
Cantabile
Jacques Loussier Trio | Ravel's Bolero | Telarc Digital | CD 83466
Cantado La Melodia
Tuck And Patti | Love Warriors | Windham Hill | 34 10116-2
Cantador(Like A Lover)
Blue Note All Stars | Town Hall Concert | Blue Note | 497811-2
Cantaloupe Island
Donald Byrd Orchestra With Brass & Voices | His Majesty King Funk/Up With Donald Byrd | Verve | 527474-2
Herbie Hancock Quartet | Herbie Hancock:The Complete Blue Note Sixties Sessions | Blue Note | 495569-2
Cantaloupe Island | Blue Note | 829331-2
Blue N' Groovy | Blue Note | 780679-2
Herbie Hancock Quintet | One Night With Blue Note Vol.1 | Blue Note | BT 85113 Digital
Tony Purrone Trio | The Tonester | Steeplechase | SCCD 31495
Cantaloupe Woman
Zoot Sims And His Orchestra | Recado Bossa Nova | Fresh Sound Records | FSR-CD 0189
Cantar A Vida
Ronny Lang Quartet | Basie Street | Fresh Sound Records | FSR-CD 0501
Canticle
Kenny Wheeler-Sonny Greenwich Quintet | Kenny And Sonny Live At The Montreal Bistro | Justin Time | JUST 114-2
Cantiga De Santa Maria
Frederic Hand Ensemble | Jazz Antiqua | Musicmasters | 65150-2
Cantile With Response
First House | Cantilena | ECM | 1393
Cantilena
Baden Powell + Janine | Jazz Meets Brasil | MPS | 533133-2
Canto

Clare Fischer Orchestra And 2+2 | And Sometime Voices | Discovery | DS 852 IMS

Canto A La Lluvia-
Rumbata | Canto Al Caribe | Timeless | CD JC 11019

Canto Das Tres Racas
Baden Powell Ensemble | Samba Triste | Accord | 102772

Canto De Ossanha
Caterina Valente With The Count Basie Orchestra | Caterina Valente '86 | Mobile Fidelity | MFCD 889
Charlie Haden-Carlos Paredes | Dialogues | Polydor | 843445-2 PMS

Canto De Xango
Charlie Haden And The Liberation Music Orchestra | Dream Keeper | Polydor | 847876-2

Canto Del Viento
Michel Godard Ensemble | Castel Del Monte | Enja | ENJ-9362 2

Canto Della Sibilla
Gary Smulyan Quintet | The Lure Of Beauty | Criss Cross | Criss 1049

Canto Indio
Ekkehard Jost & Chromatic Alarm | Wintertango | Fish Music | FM 008 CD

Canto Intervale
Franz Koglmann Pipetet | Cantos I-IV | Hat Art | CD 6123

Canto Latino(Latin Chant)
Paul Desmond Quartet With The Don Sebesby Orchestra | From The Hot Afternoon | Verve | 543487-2

Canto Latino(Latin Chant-alt.take)
Mario Bauzá And The Afro-Cuban Jazz Orchestra | 944 Columbus | Messidor | 15828 CD

Cantor
Leny Andrade And The Fred Hersch Trio | Mayden Voyage | Chesky | JD 113

Cantos Canarios-
Francesca Simone Trio | Guardia Li | Minor Music | 801093

Cantu Un Pucnu
Cornelius Claudio Kreusch | Talking To A Goblin | Edition Collage | EC 441-2

Cantus
Michael Riessler Group | Tentations D'Abélard | Wergo | WER 8009-2
Ralph Abelein Group | Mr. B's Time Machine | Satin Doll Productions | SDP 1042-1 CD

Cantus Interruptus
Gianluigi Trovesi Octet | Les Hommes Armés | Soul Note | 121311-2

Canvas 1:Y-Rism
Hans Lüdemann Rism | Unitarism | Jazz Haus Musik | JHM 0067 CD

Canvas 2:Die Musik Des Erich Zann
Unitarism | Jazz Haus Musik | JHM 0067 CD

Canvas 3:Ungeist Und Geist
JoAnne Brackeen Trio | Invitation | Black Lion | BLCD 760218

Canyon Lady
Oregon | Distant Hills | Vanguard | VSD 79341

Canzone Di Peppe
Paolo Damiani Quintet | Poor Memory | SPLASC(H) Records | HP 07

Canzone Dolce:Unresistable!
Nino De Rose Solo/Duo/Trio/Quartet | Compagno Eros | EdiPan | NPG 809

Canzonetta
Joe Daniels And His Hot Shots | Steppin' Out To Swing | Saville Records | SVL 167 IMS

Caos
Antonello Salis | Salis! | SPLASC(H) Records | H 136

Cape To Cairo Suite(Hommage to Mandela)
Abdullah Ibrahim | Knysna Blue | TipToe | TIP-888816 2

Cape Verdean Song-
Hubert Laws Quartet | The Laws Of Jazz | Atlantic | 8122-71636-2

Capers
Steve Lacy Three | N.Y.Capers & Quirks | HatOLOGY | 532
Dave Stryker Quintet | Changing Times | Steeplechase | SCCD 31510

Capra Black
Art Farmer-Gigi Gryce Quintet | When Farmer Met Gryce | Original Jazz Classics | OJC 072(P 7085)

Capri
Jay Jay Johnson Sextet | Clifford Brown:The Complete Blue Note And Pacific Recordings | Blue Note | 834195-2

Capri(alt.take)
Clifford Brown:The Complete Blue Note And Pacific Recordings | Blue Note | 834195-2

Capricci Cavalleschi
Gijs Hendriks Quartet | Gentlemania | yvp music | CD 3028

Capriccio
John Zorn Group | Cobra | Hat Art | CD 6040(2)

Caprice
Christoph Sänger Trio | Caprice | Laika Records | LK 94-057

Caprice Francis(por F.Poulenc)
Slim And Slam | Slim & Slam:Original 1938-39 Recordings Vol.2 | Tax | S 2-2

Capricho DeAbuela
Arturo Sandoval Group | Flight To Freedom | GRP | GRP 96342

Capricio Arabe
Billy Taylor Quartet | Where've You Been? | Concord | CJ 145

Capricorn
Joe Haider Trio | Katzenvilla | JHM Records | JHM 3622
Miles Davis Quintet | Water Babies | CBS | CBS PC 34396
Pat Metheny Trio | Trio 99-00 | Warner | 9362-47632-2
Stephane Grappelli Quartet | Stephane Grappelli '80 | Blue Silver | BS 3002

Caprifischer
J.J.Johnson Sextet | The Eminent J.J.Johnson Vol.1 | Blue Note | BLP 1505 (CDP 7815052)

Captain Bligh
Alexander von Schlippenbach And Sven-Ake Johansson | Live 1976/77 | FMP | CD 111

Captain Caribe
Earl Klugh With Orchestra | Living Inside Your Love | Blue Note | 748385-2

Captain Crunch(Meets The Cereal Killer)
Doc Severinsen And Xebron | Doc Severinsen And Xebron | Passport Jazz | ???

Captain Jetter
Zoot Sims Quintet | Zoot Sims | Swing | SW 8417

Captain Marvel
Chick Corea Quartet | Verve Jazz Masters 20:Introducing | Verve | 519853-2
Chick Corea's Return To Forever | Verve Jazz Masters 3:Chick Corea | Verve | 519820-2
Jack Wilkins Quintet | Mexico | CTI Records | CTI 1004-2
Stan Getz Quartet | The Lyrical Stan Getz | CBS | 460819-2
Stan Getz Quintet | Captain Marvel | CBS | 468412-2

Captain Nasty
Denny Christianson Big Band | More Pepper | Justin Time | JUST 19

Captain Senor Mouse
Return To Forever | Return To The 7th Galaxy-Return To Forever:The Anthology | Verve | 533108-2
Jack McDuff Orchestra | Write On, Capt'n | Concord | CCD 4568

Capture Of The Wolf
Blue Box | Captured Dance Floor | TipToe | TIP-888801 2

Capuchin Swing
Joey Baron Trio | RAIsedpleasuredot | New World Records | 80449-2

Car 1
Miles Davis Sextet | Circle In The Round | CBS | 467898-2

Car 2
Big Jay McNeely & Christian Rannenberg | Blues At Daybreak | Acoustic Music Records | AMC 1018

Car Machine Blues
Billy Drummond Quartet | The Gift | Criss Cross | Criss 1083

Cara Bruja-
Dave Samuels Group | Natural Selections | GRP | GRP 96562

Cara Lucia
Tome XX | Stadtgarten Series Vol.4 | Jazz Haus Musik | JHM 1004 SER

Cara Mia
Gene Ammons Septet | A Stranger In Town | Prestige | PRCD 24266-2
Lou Donaldson Quartet | Good Gracious | Blue Note | 854325-2

Caracas
Blue Breakbeats:Lou Donaldson | Blue Note | 494709-2

Caraculiambro
Eddy Louiss-Michel Petrucciani | Conference De Presse Vol.2 | Dreyfus Jazz Line | FDM 36573-2

Caramba
Lee Morgan Quintet | Lee Morgan:Blue Breakbeats | Blue Note | 494704-2

Caran
Ahmad Jamal Trio | Live In Paris 1992 | Dreyfus Jazz Line | FDM 37019-2

Caravan
Live In Paris 92 | Birdology | 849408-2
Archie Shepp Quartet | Day Dream | Denon Compact Disc | DC-8547
Art Blakey And The Jazz Messengers | Standards | Paddle Wheel | 292 E 6026
Art Pepper Quartet | Art Pepper:The Complete Village Vanguard Sessions | Contemporary | 9CCD-4417-2
Art Pepper:The Complete Village Vanguard Sessions | Contemporary | 9CCD-4417-2
Art Pepper With The Duke Jordan Trio | Art Pepper With Duke Jordan In Copenhagen 1981 | Galaxy | 2GCD 8201-2
Art Tatum | Art Tatum-The Complete Pablo Solo Masterpieces | Pablo | 7 PACD 4404-2
The Jazz Giants Play Duke Ellington:Caravan | Prestige | PCD 24227-2
The Art Tatum Solo Masterpieces | Pablo | 2625703
Ben Webster Quintet | At The Renaissance | Contemporary | COP 026
Ben Webster-Don Byas Quintet | Ben Webster/Don Byas | Jazz Magazine | 48018
Bernard Berkhout's Swingmates | Air Mail Special | Timeless | CD SJP 360
Brocksi-Quintett | Drums Boogie | Bear Family Records | BCD 15988 AH
Buell Neidlinger Sextet | Buellgrass-Big Day At Ojai | K2B2 Records | 2369
Charles Blenzig Group | Say What You Mean | Big World | BW 2009
Clifford Brown All Stars | Jazz Gallery:Clifford Brown | RCA | 2114176-2
Coleman Hawkins Quintet | Body And Soul | West Wind | WW 2018
Dave Brubeck Quartet | Back Home | Concord | CCD 4103
Dieter Fischer Trio | Jazz Guitar Highlights 1 | Jardis Records | JRCD 20141
Dinah Washington With The Quincy Jones Orchestra | The Swingin' Miss 'D' | Verve | 558074-2
Dirty Dozen Brass Band | My Feet Can't Fail Me Now | Concord | CCD 43005
Dizzy Gillespie With THE Orchestra | One Night In Washington | Elektra | 96-0300-1 TIS
DMP Big Band | DMP Big Band Salutes Duke Ellington | dmp Digital Music Productions | CD 520
Duke Ellington And His Famous Orchestra | The Complete Duke Ellington-Vol. 8 | CBS | CBS 88185
Duke Ellington And His Orchestra | Planet Jazz:Duke Ellington | Planet Jazz | 2152053-2
Carnegie Hall Concert January 1946 | Prestige | 2PCD 24074-2
Duke Ellington And His Orchestra feat. Paul Gonsalves | Original Jazz Classics | OJCCD 623-2
The Best Of Duke Ellington | Capitol | 831501-2
Jazz Group 1964 | Jazz Anthology | 550192
100 Years Duke | Laserlight | 24906
Duke Ellington:The Complete RCA-Victor Mid-Forties Recordings(1944-1946) | RCA | 2663394-2
Ellington On The Air | Ember | CJS 840
Soul Call | Verve | 539785-2
The Duke At Fargo 1940 | Storyville | STCD 8316/17
Happy Birthday Duke Vol.2 | Laserlight | 15784
Live At Click Restaurant Philadelphia 1949-Vol.4 | Raretone | 5005 FC
Eddy Howard And His Orchestra | The Uncollected:Eddy Howard, Vol.2 | Hindsight | HSR 156
Ella Fitzgerald With The Duke Ellington Orchestra | Ella Fitzgerald Sings The Duke Ellington Songbook | Verve | 559248-2
The Complete Ella Fitzgerald Song Books of Harold Arlen, Irving Berlin, Duke Ellington, George & Ira Gershwin, Jerome Kern, Johnny Mercer, Cole Porter And Rogers & Hart | Verve | 519832-2
Ella Fitzgerald With The Lou Levy Trio | Ella In Rome-The Birthday Concert | Verve | 835454-2
Ellington/Mingus/Roach Trio | Money Jungle | Blue Note | 538227-2
Ellis Marsalis | Duke In Blue | CBS | CK 63631
Frank Morgan All Stars | Reflections | Original Jazz Classics | OJCCD 1046-2(C 14052)
Reflections | Contemporary | CCD 14052-2
Freddie Hubbard Quintet | Topsy | Enja | ENJ-7025 2
Freddie Hubbard Sextet | The Artistry Of Freddy Hubbard | Impulse(MCA) | 951179-2
George Colligan | Small Room | Steeplechase | SCCD 31470
Gonzalo Rubalcaba Trio | The Trio | somethin'else | 494442-2
Inner Voyage | Blue Note | 499241-2
Great Jazz Trio With String Quartet | N.Y. Sophisticate-A Tribute To Duke Ellington | Denon Compact Disc | DC-8575
Hank Jones Trio With The Meridian String Quartet | Hank Jones With The Meridian String Quartet | LRC Records | CDC 9026
Horst Gmeinwieser 'One Cue Big Band' | Bigband-Fieber | Media Arte | CD 06569209(BRW)
Hot Mallets | Hot Mallets...Live | Jazzcharge | JC 8302
Jenny Evans And Her Quintet | Shiny Stockings | ESM Records | ESM 9305
Shiny Stockings | Enja | ENJ-9317 2
Jerome Richardson Sextet | Midnight Oil | Original Jazz Classics | OJCCD 1815-2(NJ 8205)
Johannes Rediske Quintet | Re-Disc Bounce | Bear Family Records | BCD 16119 AH
John Fedchock New York Big Band | John Fedchock New York Big Band | Reservoir | RSR CD 138
Kenny Drew Trio | The Kenny Drew Trio | Original Jazz Classics | OJC20 065-2(RLP 224)
Kevin Mahogany With Orchestra | Songs And Moments | Enja | ENJ-8072 2
Kosh | Groovy Strings | Elite Special | 73325
Lawrence Brown Quintet | Compact Jazz: Duke Ellington And Friends | Verve | 833291-2
Leon Lee Dorsey Quintet | The Watcher | Landmark | LCD 1540-2
Lou Donaldson Quintet | Wailing With Lou | Blue Note | 300145(1545)
Max Greger Quintet | Night Train | Polydor | 543393-2
Maynard Ferguson And His Big Bop Nouveau Band | These Cats Can Swing! | Concord | CCD 4669
Michel Petrucciani | Promenade With Duke | Blue Note | 780590-2
Michel Petrucciani:Concert Inédits | Dreyfus Jazz Line | FDM 36607-2
Milt Jackson Quartet | Mostly Duke | Pablo | 2310944-2
Mind Games With Philip Catherine | Pretty Fonky | Edition Collage | EC 482-2
Monty Alexander/John Clayton | The Duke Ellington Song Book | MPS | 821151-1
Nat King Cole Sextet | After Midnight | Capitol | 520087-2
Nat King Cole Trio | Nat King Cole Trio Transcriptions Vol.1 | Naxos Jazz | 8.120512 CD
Paul Smoker Trio | Alone | Sound Aspects | sas CD 018(32018)
Quadrant | All Too Soon-Quadrant Toasts Duke Ellington | Original Jazz Classics | OJCCD 450-2
Randy Weston Quartet | Randy Weston Portraits Of Duke Ellington | Verve | 841312-2
Rolf Kühn Quintet | Rolf Kühn And His Sound Of Jazz | Fresh Sound Records | FSR-CD 326
Ron Holloway Group | Slanted | Milestone | MCD 9219-2
Sir Roland Hanna | Duke Ellington Piano Solos | Musicmasters | 5045-2
Thelonious Monk Trio | Thelonious Monk-The Complete Riverside Recordings | Riverside | 15 RCD 022-2
Todd Coolman Trio With Joe Henderson | Lexicon | Double Time Records | DTRCD-104
Unknown Trio | The King Jazz Story Vol. 7+8 | Storyville | SLP 820/21
Wes Montgomery With Orchestra | Tempo Jazz Edition Vol.3-Stayin' Cool | Verve | 847902-2
Wes Montgomery With The Johnny Pate Orchestra | Verve Jazz Masters 14:Wes Montgomery | Verve | 519826-2
West Coast Jazz Summit | West Coast Jazz Summit | Mons Records | MR 874773
Wild Bill Moore Quintet | Bottom Groove | Milestone | MCD 47098-2
Woody Herman And The Young Thundering Herd With Friends | Woody And Friends At Monterey Jazz Festival 1979 | Concord | CCD 4170
Zoot Sims Quartet | Zoot Sims | Storyville | STCD 8367
| Barrelhouse Jazzband Plays Duke Ellington | L+R Records | LR 40026

Caravan-
Charlie Parker Quartet | Bird's Eyes Last Unissued Vol.21:Bird On TV/Bird On Bandbox | Philology | W 851.2
Dick Wellstood | Dick Wellstood-Alone | Solo Art | SACD-73
Duke Ellington | Masters Of Jazz Vol.6:Duke Ellington | Storyville | STCD 4106
On The Corner With The Philharmonic Orchestra,Würzburg | On The Corner feat. Benny Bailye | Mons Records | MR 874807
Oscar Peterson Quartet | Oscar Peterson Live! | Pablo | 2310940-2
Oscar Peterson Trio | The London Concert | Pablo | 2CD 2620111
Rebop | To Duke | Blue Concept | BCCD 93/01
John Blake Sextet | Maiden Dance | Gramavision | GR 8309-2

Caravan(A Tribute to Charlie Antolini)
Oscar Klein Band | Pick-A-Blues Live | Jazzpoint | JP 1071
Bernard Peiffer | Jazz In Paris:Bernard Peiffer-La Vie En Rose | EmArCy | 013980-2

Caravan(Intro)-
Edmond Hall Quartet With Teddy Wilson | Commodore Classics In Swing | Commodore | 9031-72723-2

Caravan(The Boss Man)
Roy Eldridge Quartet | Rare Broadcasts | Duke Records | D 1010

Caravanserai
Chet Baker Plays/Chet Baker Sings | Cool Cat | Timeless | CD SJP 262

Carcrash
Charlie Parker And His Orchestra | Bird On Verve-Vol.1:Charlie Parker With Strings | Verve | 817442-1 IMS

Cardboard
Charlie Parker:The Best Of The Verve Years | Verve | 527815-2
Charlie Parker Septet | Charlie Parker: The Verve Years (1948-50) | Verve | 2-2501 IMS
David Kikoski Trio | Surf's Up | Criss Cross | Criss 1208
Bob Hall Trio | Alone With The Blues | Lake | LACD 44

Cardeosa
Thom Rotella Group | Without Words | dmp Digital Music Productions | CD 476

Cardinal Points
Jean-Michel Pilc Quintet | Cardinal Points | Dreyfus Jazz Line | FDM 36649-2
Mosalini/Beytelmann/Caratini | Inspiration Del Tango | Eigelstein | 568-72223

Cards
Roscoe Mitchell Quartet | Roscoe Mitchell Quartet | Sackville | 2009

Care Free
Carmen Cavallaro And His Orchestra | The Uncollected: Carmen Cavallaro | Hindsight | HSR 112

Carefree
Sun Ra & His Omniverse Arkestra | Destination Unknown | Enja | 7071-2

Careful
George Shearing-Jim Hall Duo | First Edition | Concord | CCD 4177
Mitch Seidman-Fred Fried-Harvie Swartz | This Over That | Jardis Records | JRCD 9816
Schwarz-Hübner Duo | Elegie | dml-records | CD 012
The Jimmy Giuffre 3 | The Easy Way | Verve | 2304491 IMS
Dreamtime | Bunny Up | Affinity | AFF 109

Careless
Glenn Miller And His Orchestra | Candelight Miller | RCA | 2668716-2
Glenn Miller:The Complete Studio Recordings Vol.2:In The Mood | Memo Music | HDJ 4115

Careless Love Blues
Allotria Jazz Band | Cleared For Take Off | Elite Special | 73331
Art Hodes' International Trio | Blues To Save The Trees | L+R Records | CDLR 40015
Billie & Dee Dee Pierce Trio | New Orleans-The Living Legends:Billie And Dede Pierce | Original Blues Classics | OBCCD 534-2(RLP 370)
Bunk Johnson's Jazz Band | The King Of The Blues | American Music | AMCD-1
Dutch Swing College Band | Souvenirs From Holland, Vol. 1 | DSC Production | PA 003 (801060)
Joe Newman Septet | The Count's Men | Fresh Sound Records | FSR-CD 0135
Mr.Acker Bilk And His Paramount Jazz Band | New Orleans Days | Lake | LACD 36

Careless Love Blues(alt.take)
George Lewis And His New Orleans Stompers | George Lewis & His New Orleans Stompers Vol.1 | American Music | AMCD-100

Careless Whisper
Eddy Howard And His Orchestra | The Uncollected: Eddy Howard | Hindsight | HSR 119

Carey Line
Max Kaminsky And His Dixieland Bashers | Jazz On The Campus Ltd. | RCA | 2136408-2

Cargo Area
Infinity & Alphonse Mouzon | Now | Inak | 9004

Cargo Treu Banya-
Ralph Towner | Ana | ECM | 1611(537023-2)

Carib Crib(1)
Ana | ECM | 1611(537023-2)

Carib Crib(2)
Wes Montgomery Quintet | Movin' | Milestone | M 47040

Cariba
Full House | Original Jazz Classics | OJC20 106-2
Wes Montgomery-The Complete Riverside Recordings | Riverside | 12 RCD 4408-2

Cariba(alt.take)
Humphrey Lyttelton-Jim Galloway Quintet | Music Is My Life | Sackville | SK2CD-5006

Caribbean Clipper
Glenn Miller And His Orchestra | Jazz Collection:Glenn Miller | Laserlight | 24367
Glenn Miller And The Army Air Force Band | I Sustain The Wings Vol.3(September 1943) | Magic | DAWE 78

Caribbean Connection
Cannonball Adderley Quintet | Spontaneous Combustion | Savoy | 650104(881904)

Caribbean Firedance
Joe Henderson Septet | Joe Henderson-The Blue Note Years | Blue Note | 789287-2
Judy Niemack With The Fred Hersch Trio | Long As You're Living | Freelance | FRL-CD 014

Caribbean Parade
Jakob Magnusson Group | Time Zone | Optimism | GBJ 2002

Caribbean Sky
Georg Wadenius Group | Cleo | Four Leaf Clover | FLC 5097 CD

Caribé
Monty Alexander Sextet | Cobilimbo | MPS | 68188

Caribea
Conexion Latina | Mambo 2000 | Enja | ENJ-7055 2

Caribe-Cha
Ray Barretto And His Orchestra | Handprints | Concord | CCD 4473
Cariffity
Paolo Fresu Sextet | Mamut: Music For A Mime | SPLASC(H) Records | CD H 127-2
Carinoso
Gato Barbieri Septet | Gato Barbieri:The Complete Flying Dutchman Recordings 1969-1973 | RCA | 2154555-2
Carioca
Dick Johnson-Dave McKenna Duo | Spider's Blues | Concord | CJ 135
Hampton Hawes Trio | The Trio-Vol.1 | Original Jazz Classics | OJC 316(C 3515)
Hampton Hawes Trio Vol.1 | Original Jazz Classics | OJC20 316-2(C 3505)
Helmut Zacharias mit seinem Orchester | Ich Habe Rhythmus | Bear Family Records | BCD 15642 AH
Juan Garcia Esquivel Orchestra | Juan's Again | RCA | 2168206-2
Kai Winding All Stars | Jay And Kai | Savoy | SV 0163(MG 12010)
Oscar Peterson Trio | Night Train Vol. 3 | Verve | 711071 IMS
Carissima
Bob Mintzer Big Band | Latin From Manhattan | dmp Digital Music Productions | CD 523
Carla
Jimmy Giuffre 3 | Emphasis,Stuttgart 1961 | Hat Art | CD 6072
Paul Bley/Niels-Henning Orsted-Pedersen Duo | Paul Bley-NHOP | Steeplechase | SCCD 31005
Carlito's Reise
Rinde Eckert Group | Story In,Story Out | Intuition Records | INT 3507-2
Carlo Dreams
Alfred 23 Harth With Mani Neumeier | Red Art | Creative Works Records | CW LP 1004
Carlos
Bireli Lagrene Ensemble | Routes To Django & Bireli Swing '81 | Jazzpoint | JP 1055 CD
Carlos Bica-Ana Brandao Group | DIZ | Enja | ENJ-9414 2
Benny Green Trio | Testifyin'!-Live at The Village Vanguard | Blue Note | 798171-2
Carlypso
Michael Kersting Quintet | Michael Kersting 'Five' | Bassic-Sound | CD 004
Carma
Chuck Wayne And His Orchestra | String Fever | Fresh Sound Records | NL 46067(RCA LX 1098)
Carmel Rise
JoAnne Brackeen Trio | Keyed Up | CBS | 83868
Carmela Dame La Llave
Nathan Davis Quintet | Two Originals:Happy Girl/The Hip Walk | MPS | 539082-2
Carmen
Peter Lemer Quintet | Local Colour | ESP Disk | ESP 1057-2
Giorgio Gaslini Globo Quartet | Ballets | Soul Note | 121320-2
Carmen's Cool
Christian Escoude Octet | Gipsy Waltz | EmArCy | 838772-2
Carmilla
Ray Mantilla Space Station | Synergy | Red Records | VPA 198
Carmouflage
Bob Mintzer Big Band | Carmouflage | dmp Digital Music Productions | CD 456
Carnation
Carla Bley-Steve Swallow | Go Together | Watt | 24(517673-2)
Carnation-
Aparis | Aparis | ECM | 1404
Carnaval
Barry Finnerty Quintet | Straight Ahead | Arabesque Recordings | AJ 0116
Carnaval De La Gente
Pierre Favre Ensemble | Singing Drums | ECM | 1274
Carnaval Of The Four
Thom Rotella Group | Without Words | dmp Digital Music Productions | CD 476
Carnegie Blues
Oscar Peterson-Ray Brown Duo | The Complete Jazz At The Philharmonic On Verve 1944-1949 | Verve | 523893-2
Kenny Burrell All Stars | Ellington Is Forever | Fantasy | F 79005
Carney
Achim Kaufmann Trio | Weave | Jazz 4 Ever Records:Jazz Network | J4E 4737
Carnies
Andy Lumpp Trio With Andy Przybielski | Music From Planet Earth | Nabel Records:Jazz Network | CD 4687
Carnival
Artie Shaw And His Orchestra | Artie Shaw And His Orchestra 1949 | Limelight | 820817-2 IMS
Dave McKenna Trio | Plays The Music Of Harry Warren | Concord | CJ 174
Harry James And His Orchestra | More Harry James In Hi-Fi | Capitol | EMS 1148
Randy Weston Quintet | Carnival | Freedom | FCD 741004
Stan Kenton And His Orchestra | By Request Vol.2 | Creative World | ST 1040
Carnival Of Colors
Thilo Berg Big Band | Carnival Of Life | Mons Records | CD 1887
Carnival Samba(aka Carnaval)
Jeremy Steig-Eddie Gomez Group | Rain Forest | CMP Records | CMP 12
Carol-
Lennie Tristano | The New Tristano | Atlantic | 7567-80475-2
Deborah Henson-Conant | The Gift:15 Weihnachtslieder der Erde | Laika Records | 35100992
Carol Of The Bells
George Winston | December | Windham Hill | 34 11025-2
Carol Of The Bells-
Singers Unlimited | Christmas | MPS | 821859-2
Carole Lombard
Humair-Louiss-Ponty | Volume 2 | Dreyfus Jazz Line | FDM 36510-2
Carolina In The Morning
Benny Goodman And His Orchestra | Camel Caravan Broadcast 1939 Vol.3 | Phontastic | NCD 8819
Brad Gowans And His New York Nine | Jazz On The Campus Ltd. | RCA | 2136408-2
Carolina Moon
Ken Colyer's Jazzmen | Ken Colyer's Jazzmen Serenading Auntie-BBC Recordings 1955-1960 | Upbeat Jazz | URCD 111
Thelonious Monk Sextet | Thelonious Monk:The Complete Blue Note Recordings | Blue Note | 830363-2
Genius Of Modern Music,Vol.1 | Blue Note | 781510-2
Carolina Shout
Fats Waller | Fats Waller-The Joint Is Jumpin' | RCA | ND 86288(874182)
James P.Johnson | From Spiritual To Swing | Vanguard | VCD 169/71
Rare Piano Rags | Jazz Anthology | JA 5120
Joe Turner | I Understand | Black & Blue | BLE 59.153 2
Marcus Roberts | If I Could Be With You | Novus | 4163149-2
Oscar Peterson Trio | Two Originals:Walking The Line/Another Day | MPS | 533549-2
This Is Jazz All Stars | Jazz Live & Rare: This Is Jazz Radio Series-Live 1947 | Jazzline | ???
Carolina Shout-
Cliff Jackson | Carolina Shout | Black Lion | BLCD 760194
Caroline's Dance
Singers Unlimited | Christmas | MPS | 821859-2
Carol's Bridge
John Abercrombie Trio | While We're Young | ECM | 1489
Carol's Carol
Jean-Luc Ponty Quartet | Giants | MPS | 68265
Carol's Interlude
Art Blakey And The Jazz Messengers | Art Blakey/The Jazz Messengers | CBS | CK 62265
Carol's Interlude(alt.take)
Art Blakey/The Jazz Messengers | CBS | CK 62265
Carolyn
Pepper Adams Quintet | Pepper Adams Plays Charlie Mingus | Fresh Sound Records | FSR-CD 0177
Carolyn V.
J.J.Johnson Sextet | Heroes | Verve | 528864-2
Carona Glass And Lady Maggie
Manfredo Fest Quintet With Scott Hamilton | Oferenda | Concord | CCD 4539
Carousel
Mulgrew Miller Trio | With Our Own Eyes | Novus | 4163171-2
Carpe Noctem-
Dixieland Jug Blowers | Louisville Stomp-The Complete Sessions Of The Dixieland Jug Blowers | Frog | DGF 6
Carpet Ride
Stan Getz-Bill Evans Quartet | Stan Getz & Bill Evans | Verve | 833802-2
Carpetbagger's Theme
Chet Baker Quintet | Comin' On With The Chet Baker Quintet | Prestige | PR20 7478-2
Carpsie's Groove
Yannick Rieu Trio | Sweet Geom | Victo | CD 030
Carrer 8,5
Fritz Krisse Quartet | Soulcolours | Laika Records | 35100782
Carrer De Campos
Max Greger And His Orchestra | European Jazz Sounds | Polydor | 829257-1 IMS
Carretera Austral
McCoy Tyner Trio | McCoy Tyner With Stanley Clarke And Al Foster | Telarc Digital | CD 83488
Carribean Clipper
Cannonball Adderley Quintet | Spontaneous Combustion-The Savoy Sessions | Savoy | ???
Carrosso
Jacques Pirotton Trio | Soty | B.Sharp Records | CDS 087
Carry Me Back To Old Virginia
Eddie Heywood Sextet | Commodore Classics-Eddie Heywood:The Biggest Little Band In The Forties | Commodore | 6.25493 AG
Carry Me Home
Eric Person Trio | Prophecy | Soul Note | 121287-2
Carry On No.1
Carmen McRae With The Dixie Flyers | Just A Little Lovin' | Atlantic | AMCY 1079
Carry That Weight
Walter Coleman | Cincinnati Blues(1928-1936) | Story Of Blues | CD 3519-2
Carson City Stage
Chet Baker Quartet | Chet Baker Quartet Live Vol.3: May Old Flame | Pacific Jazz | 531573-2
The Best Of Chet Baker Plays | Pacific Jazz | 797161-2
The Contemporary Alphorn Orchestra | Mythahorns 2 | Hat Art | CD 6151
Carta De Amor
Egberto Gismonti Trio | ZigZag | ECM | 1582
Azimuth | Outubro | Milestone | M 9097
Cartoon
Paul Bley Trio | Closer | ESP Disk | ESP 1021-2
Caruso
Dylan Cramer Quartet | All Night Long | Nagel-Heyer | CD 073
Franco & Lorenzo Petrocca | Italy | Edition Musikat | EDM 062
Franco Ambrosetti Sextet | Grazie Italia | Enja | ENJ-9379 2
Richard Galliano Group | French Touch | Dreyfus Jazz Line | FDM 36596-2
Richard Galliano Trio | Gallianissimo! The Best Of Richard Galliano | Dreyfus Jazz Line | FDM 36616-2
Graef-Schippa-Moritz | Orlando Frames | Nabel Records:Jazz Network | CD 4690
Carved From The Monkey's Cage
Earl Hines And His Orchestra | Deep Forest | Hep | 1003
Carvin' The Bird(alt.take 2)
Charlie Parker All Stars | Charlie Parker Story On Dial Vol.1:West Coast Days | Capitol | 300009(TOCJ 6123)
Carvin The Rock
Clifford Brown Quintet | More Memorable Tracks | Blue Note | 300195(BNJ 61001)
Carvin' The Rock(alt.take 1)
More Memorable Tracks | Blue Note | 300195(BNJ 61001)
Casa De Luz
Bud Shank Quintet | Jazz In Hollywood:Bud Shank/Lou Levy | Original Jazz Classics | OJCCD 1890-2(Nocturne NLP-2/NLP-10)
Casa Forte
Peter Herbolzheimer Rhythm Combination & Brass | Latin Groove | Koala Records | CD P 13
Casa Oscura
Baden Powell Ensemble | Samba Triste | Accord | 102772
Casa Velha
Baden Powell Trio | Samba Triste | Festival | 114861
Casaba
Essence All Stars | Afro Cubano Chant | Hip Bop | HIBD 8009
Casablanca
G.Q.Williams & Dave Collett | Back To The Boogie | Jazz Colours | 874735-2
Archie Shepp And His Band | Black Gypsy | America | AM 6099
Casanova's Lament
Mulo Francel-Evelyn Huber | Tango Lyrico | Fine Music | FM 102-2
Cascade
Charlie Mariano Group | Cascade | Keytone | KYT 707
Cascade Infinity
Chick Corea Electric Band | Eye Of The Beholder | GRP | GRP 95642
Cascade(part 1+2)
Christy Doran-John Wolf Brennan | Henceforward | Line Records | COCD 9.00871 O
Cascades
Oliver Nelson And His Orchestra | Blues And The Abstract Truth | CTI Records | PDCTI 1122-2
Scott Joplin | Welcome To Jazz: Scott Joplin | Koch Records | 321 945 D1
Cascatas
Art Farmer Quintet | From Vienna With Art | MPS | 9811443
Cascavelo
Carlo Actis Dato/Laura Culver | Zig Zag | SPLASC(H) Records | H 186
Casey Jones
Joe Newman Septet | The Count's Men | Fresh Sound Records | FSR-CD 0135
Cash For Your Trash
Louis Armstrong And His Orchestra | Louis Armstrong Vol.8:1941-1942 | Ambassador | CLA 1908
Cashmere
Herbie Mann-Bill Evans Quartet | That's Jazz Vol.8: Nirvana | Atlantic | ATL 50238
Casi Te Amo
Emilio Solla Y Afines | Folcolores | Fresh Sound Records | FSWJ 001
Casino
Norman Connors Orchestra | Beyond A Dream | Arista Novus | AN 3021 (802062)
Cassandra
Dave Brubeck Quartet | Time In | CBS | 474635-2
Cast Away
Eva Taylor With Clarence Williams' Blue Five | Louis Armstrong 1924-25 | Village(Jazz Archive) | VILCD 009-2
Cast Your Fate To The Wind
David Benoit Group | Waiting For Spring | GRP | GRP 95952
Larry Vuckovich Quartet With Jon Hendricks | Cast Your Fate | Palo Alto | PA 8042
Franz Koglmann Group | Venus In Transit | Between The Lines | btl 017(Efa 10186)
Casta Diva
Glenda Powrie Group | Asha | Muse | MCD 5392
Caster Starb Für Eure Sünden(Floyd Westermann)
Dave Brubeck Quartet | The Dave Brubeck Quartet At Carnegie Hall | CBS | 66234
Castle Of Air
Henry Mancini And His Orchestra | Combo! | RCA | 2147794-2
Castle Rock
Jake Hanna's Kansas City Express | Kansas City Express | Concord | CJ 22
Johnny Hodges Orchestra | The Rabbit's Work On Verve In Chronological Order Vol. 1: 1951 | Verve | 2304447 IMS
Scott Hamilton Quartet | Organic Duke | Concord | CCD 4623
Castle Walk
Cedar Walton Quartet With Abbey Lincoln | The Maestro | Muse | MCD 6008
Castles In Heaven
Barbara Thompson's Paraphernalia | Mother Earth | VeraBra Records | CDVBR 2005-2
Castles In The Air
Marian McPartland Trio With Strings | Marian McPartland With Strings | Concord | CCD 4745
Castles Made Of Sand
Gil Evans Orchestra | PLay The Music Of Jimi Hendrix | RCA | 2663872-2
NDR Big Band feat. Inga Rumpf | The Spirit Of Jimi Hendrix | Extra Records & Tapes | 11542
Castles Made Of Sand-
Tuck And Patti | Love Warriors | Windham Hill | 34 10116-2
John Carter Octet | Castles Of Ghana | Gramavision | GR 8603-2
Castles Of Spain
Mitch Watkins Quartet | Curves | Enja | ENJ-6054 2
Castling
Eje Thelin Group | Hypothesis | MRC | 066-45421
Cat And Mouse
Joshua Redman Quintet | Freedom In The Groove | Warner | 9362-46330-2
Cat Battles
Luther Allison Blues Band | South Side Safari | Red Lightnin' | RL 0036
Cat Dance
Schlaier-Hirt Duo | Don't Walk Outside Thos Area | Chaos | CACD 8186
Cat I See
Jimmy Smith With The Oliver Nelson Orchestra | Peter & The Wolf | Verve | 547264-2
Cat In A Tree
Blind Lemon Jefferson | Blind Lemon Jefferson-Master Of The Blues | Biograph | BLP 12015
Cat Meal
Clark Terry Septet | Clark Terry | Verve | 537754-2
Cat 'N Mouse
John Abercrombie-Andy LaVerne Quartet | Now It Can Be Played | Steeplechase | SCCD 31314
Cat On The Stairs
Oleg Plotnikov Trio | My Little Rolly | Timeless | CD SJP 435
Cat Walks
Mal Waldron Trio | Left Alone | Bethlehem | BET 6024-2(BCP 6045)
Catability
John Zorn Naked City | Heretic-Jeux Des Dames Cruelles | Avant | AVAN 001
Catalina
Irakere | Catalina | Messidor | 15955
Catalogue
Frank Strazzeri And His Woodwinds West | Somebody Loves Me | Fresh Sound Records | FSR-CD 5003
Catalyst
Peter O'Mara Quartet | Wind Moments | Take Twelve On CD | TT 009-2
Scott Colley Sextet | Portable Universe | Freelance | FRL-CD 027
Catania
Reuben Brown Trio | Ice Shape | Steeplechase | SCCD 31423
Catastrophe
Günter Christmann Group | Vario II | Moers Music | 01084
Catavento
Paul Desmond Quartet With The Don Sebesby Orchestra | From The Hot Afternoon | Verve | 543487-2
Catavento(alt.take)
Pat Martino Quartet | Interchange | Muse | MCD 5529
Catch
The Houdini's | Kickin' In The Frontwindows | Timeless | CD SJP 405
Catch A Satch
Snooky Young-Marshal Royal Sextet | Snooky & Marshal's Album | Concord | CCD 4055
Catch The Blues
Don Grusin Group | Native Land | GRP | GRP 97192
Catch Up With The Count
Fabio Jegher Trio | Time Zone-Fabio Jegher Boston & L.A.Trios | Red Records | VPA 175
Catémbe
Ray Gelato Giants | The Full Flavour | Linn Records | AKD 034
Catering
New Winds | Traction | Sound Aspects | sas CD 044
Catfish
Buddy Guy-Junior Wells Band | Alone & Acoustic | Isabel | BLE 59.910 2
Catfish Blues
James 'Son' Thomas | Living Country Blues USA Vol.5: Mississippi Delta Blues | L+R Records | LR 42035
Cathedral In A Suitcase
Hal Crook Trio | Hero Workship | RAM Records | RMCD 4531
Cathedrale Sans Nom
Stephane Metraux/Bernard Ogay | Oxymore | Plainisphare | PAV 803
Catherine
Singers Unlimited + The Oscar Peterson Trio | In Tune | MPS | 68085
Cats
Gary Meek Groups | Gary Meek | Lipstick Records | LIP 890032
Cat's Cradle
Vic Juris Quintet | Bleeker Street | Muse | MR 5265
Cat's Cradle Conference Rag
Yosuke Yamashita New York Trio | Spider | Verve | 531271-2
Cats On The Roof
Fred Hersch Trio | Point In Time | Enja | ENJ-9035 2
Cat's Paws
Jean-Luc Ponty Quartet | Fables | Atlantic | 781276-2
Catta
Joe Chambers Sextet | The Almoravid | 32 Jazz | 32099
Cattin'
John Coltrane-Paul Quinichette Quintet | John Coltrane-The Prestige Recordings | Prestige | 16 PCD 4405-2
Coleman Hawkins Quartet | Body And Soul | Naxos Jazz | 8.120532 CD
Cattin' At Keynote
Dave Pike Quintet | Carnavals | Prestige | PCD 24248-2
Cattin' Latin
Bob Crosby And His Orchestra | The Uncollected:Bob Crosby Vol.2 | Hindsight | HSR 209
Catu
Don Grusin Group | Raven | GRP | GRP 96022
Catwalk
Prestige All Stars | John Coltrane-The Prestige Recordings | Prestige | 16 PCD 4405-2
Tony Lakatos Quintet | Different Moods | Lipstick Records | LIP 890112
Caucasian Bird Riffles
Chuck Israels International Trio | Meeting On Hvar | Anima Records | DV-CD 001
Caught In Love
Mel Tormé With The George Shearing Trio | An Evening At Charlie's | Concord | CCD 4248
Caution Blues
Earl Hines | The Earl | Naxos Jazz | 8.120581 CD
Cautious Heart

Hot Lips Page With Simon Brehms Kvintett | Americans In Sweden: Hot Lips Page 1951-Rex Stewart 1947 | Jazz Society | AA 513

Cavalcade Of Boogie
Boogie Woogie Trio | Boogie Woogie | Laserlight | 24321
Django Reinhardt And The Quintet Du Hot Club De France | Django Reinhardt:Djangology | EMI Records | 780659-2

Cavallette
Baden Powell And His Orchestra | Canta Vinicius De Moraes E Paolo Cesar Pinheiro | Festival | 114911

Cavaquinho
Folklore E Bossa Nova Do Brasil | Jazz Meets Brasil | MPS | 533133-2

Cavatina(Theme From The Deerhunter)
Submedia | Submedia | Nine Winds Records | NWCD 0137

Cave Souvenir
Spanish Fly | Rags To Britches | Knitting Factory Works | KFWCD 114

Caverns Beneath The Zoth
Christy Doran's New Bag With Muthuswamy Balasubramoniam | Black Box | double moon | CHRDM 71022

Caviar
Johnny Smith Quintet | Moonlight In Vermont | Roulette | 596593-2

Cavu
Zoot Sims:The Complete 1944-1954 Small Group Sessions(Master Takes),Vol.3 | Blue Moon | BMCD 1040

CCS
Christian Christl | Tribute To Willie Dixon | Acoustic Music Records | AMC 1014

CD-ROM Track
John Coltrane Sextet | The Ultimate Blue Train | Blue Note | 853428-2

Ce Qu'a De Pis
Diederik Wissels Trio | Tender Is The Night | Jazz Pure Collection | AU 31616 CD

Ce Qu'elle Dit
Ricky Ford Quintet | Manhattan Plaza | Muse | MR 5188

Cedar Lane
Cyril Haynes Sextet | Don Byas Complete American Small Group Recordings | Definitive Records | DRCD 11213

Cedar Tree
Eddie Harris Trio | Eddie Who? | Timeless | CD SJP 244

Cedar's Blues
John Critchinson-Art Themen Quartet | First Moves | Ronnie Scott's Jazz House | JHCD 052

Cedo D'Amanhã
Dave McMurdo Jazz Orchestra | Different Paths | Sackville | SKCD2-2034

Cego Aderaldo
Nana Vasconcelos-Egberto Gismonti Duo And Strings | Saudades | ECM | 1147
Baden Powell Quartet | Canto On Guitar | MPS | 68157

Celebracao De Nupcias
Billy Taylor Trio | You Tempt Me | Taylor Made Records | T 1004

Celebrate Life
Herb Geller Quartet | Playing Jazz:The Musical Autobiography Of Herb Geller | Fresh Sound Records | FSR-CD 5011

Celebration
Dave Holland Quintet | Seeds Of Time | ECM | 1292
Dusko Goykovich Quartet | Celebration | DIW | DIW 806 CD
Joe Bonner Sextet | Angel Eyes | Muse | MR 5114

Celebration(7)
Gary Peacock | December Poems | ECM | 1119

Celebrations
Gianluigi Trovesi-Gianni Coscia | In Cerca Di Cibo | ECM | 1703(543034-2)

Celebre Mazurka Alterata
Charlie Parker Quartet | The Verve Years (1950-51) | Verve | 2-2512 IMS

Celebrity
JATP All Stars | Bird: The Complete Charlie Parker On Verve | Verve | 837141-2
Conte Candoli Sextet | Howard Rumsey Presents Conte Candoli & Lee Morgan:Double Or Nothin' | Fresh Sound Records | FSR-CD 0197

Celeste
Pilz-Niebergall-Schmitt Trio | Celeste | Trion | 3901
Meade Lux Lewis | Kings & Queens Of Ivory Vol.1 | MCA | 1329

Celeste Rocks
Memphis Slim | Steady Rolling Blues | Original Blues Classics | OBCCD 523-2(BV 1075)

Celestial Boogie
McCoy Tyner Trio | Trident | Original Jazz Classics | OJC20 720-2(M 9063)

Celestial Chant
Edmond Hall's Celeste Quartet | Edmond Hall Profoundly Blue | Blue Note | 821260-2

Celestial Guests
Stanley Cowell Trio | Close To You Alone | DIW | DIW 6003 CD

Celia
Bud Powell Trio | The Genius Of Bud Powell | Verve | 821690-1
Bud Powell:Complete 1947-1951 Blue Note,Verve & Roost Recordings | The Jazz Factory | JFCD 22837
Charles Mingus And His Orchestra | Great Moments With Charles Mingus | MCA | MCA 2-4128 (802130)
Charles Mingus Sextet | New York Sketchbook | Charly | CD 19
Chick Corea | Remembering Bud Powell | Stretch Records | SCD 9012-2
Phineas Newborn Jr. Quartet | Stockholm Jam Session, Vol.2 | Steeplechase | SCCD 36026

Celians Song
Gary Peacock Quartet | Guamba | ECM | 1352

Celina
Thomasz Stanko Quartet | Matka Joanna | ECM | 1544(523986-2)
Vincent Courtois Trio | The Fitting Room | Enja | ENJ-9411 2

Celine(part 1-3)
Havana Flute Summit | Havana Flute Summit | Naxos Jazz | 86005-2

Cell Walk For Celeste
Cecil Taylor Quartet | Cell Walk For Celeste | Candid | CS 9034

Cella/No Quiere Postre)
Ernst Höllerhagen Quintet | Ernst Höllerhagen 1942-1948 | Elite Special | 9522001

Cello Di Buddha
Oscar Pettiford Trio | Jazz Legacy Baden Baden Unreleased Radio Tapes | Jazzline | ???

Cellular Expansions
The Oom Maw Maw | Roger's Living Room | Timeless | CD SJP 353

Celtic Song
Alain Everts | Terra Nueva | Acoustic Music Records | 319.1103.2

Celtig Princess
Boulou Ferre Quartet | Relax And Enjoy | Steeplechase | SCS 1210

Cement Mixer Putti Putti
Arne Birger's Jazzsjak | The Golden Years Of Revival Jazz,Vol.10 | Storyville | STCD 5515

Cementary Blues
| In Pursuite Of The 13th Note | Talkin' Loud | 848493-2

Centerpiece
Conte Candoli-Carl Fontana Quintet | The Complete Phoenix Recordings Vol.6 | Woofy Productions | WPCD 126
Dee Daniels With The Trio Johan Clement | Close Encounter Of The Swingin' Kind | Timeless | CD SJP 312
Harry Sweets Edison And The Golden Horns | Live At The Iridium | Telarc Digital | CD 83425
James Williams Sextet | James Williams Meets The Saxophone Masters | DIW | DIW 868 CD
John Coltrane-Milt Jackson Quintet | The Coltrane Legacy | Atlantic | SD 1553
Nat Adderley Quintet | Remembering Dinah-A Salute To Dinah Washington | Hot Shot Records | HSR 8313-2
Ray Brown Group | Super Bass | Telarc Digital | CD 83393

Centers
Brubeck/LaVerne Trio | See How It Feels | Black-Hawk | BKH 51401

Central Avenue Breakdown
Lionel Hampton And His Orchestra | Planet Jazz:Lionel Hampton | Planet Jazz | 2152059-2
Lionel Hampton:Flying Home | Dreyfus Jazz Line | FDM 36735-2
Lionel Hampton And The Just Jazz All Stars | Lionel Hampton And The Just Jazz All Stars | GNP Crescendo | GNPD 15

Central Avenue Breakdown(2nd version)
Leon Lee Dorsey Quintet | The Watcher | Landmark | LCD 1540-2

Central Guitar
Hans Koller Big Band | New York City | MPS | 9813437

Central Park
New York City | MPS | 68235

Central Park North
Buddy Morrow And His Orchestra | The Uncollected:Buddy Morrow | Hindsight | HSR 154

Central Park West
Jean Toussaint Quartet | Impressions Of Coltrane | September | CD 5104
John Coltrane Quartet | John Coltrane-The Heavyweight Champion:The Complete Atlantic Recordings | Atlantic | 8122-71984-2
The Very Best Of John Coltrane | Rhino | 8122-79778-2
Coltrane's Sound | Atlantic | 7567-81358-2
The Art Of John Coltrane - The Atlantic Years | Atlantic | SD 2-313
Larry Nocella/Dannie Richmond Quartet | Everything Happens To Me | Red Records | VPA 167

Central Station
William McCoy | Going Away Blues 1926-1935 | Yazoo | YAZ 1018

Ceora
Eddie Henderson Quintet | Think On Me | Steeplechase | SCCD 31264

C'era Una Strega,C'era Una Fata
Gianluigi Trovesi With The Orchestra Da Camera Di Nembro Enea Salmeggia | Around Small Fairy Tales | Soul Note | 121341-2
Aldo Romano Group | AlmaLatina | Owl Records | 018364-2

C'era Una Volta
United Women's Orchestra | Virgo Supercluster | Jazz Haus Musik | JHM 0123 CD

Cerasarda
Om | Cerberus | Japo | 60032

Cerco Un Paese Innocente(part 1-4):
Martin Classen Quartet | Cereal | Acoustic Music Records | 319.1122.2

Cereal Killer
Bobby Scott Septet | The Compositions Of Bobby Scott | Fresh Sound Records | FSR 2020(Bethlehem BCP 8)

Ceremony In Starlight
Karlheinz Miklin Quintet & KUG Big Band | KH Miklin Quinteto Argentina & KUG Big Band | TCB Records | TCB 21232

Cergah Sirto
Don Byas Quintet | Lover Man | Vogue | 2115470-2

Certi Angoli
Enrico Rava With The Michael Flügel Quartet | Live At Birdland Neuburg | double moon | CHRDM 71011

Certi Angoli Secreti
Christian Minh Doky Quintet | The Sequel | Storyville | STCD 4175

Cesse
Anouar Brahem Trio | Le Pas Du Chat Noir | ECM | 1792(016373-2)

C'est Ailleurs
Rocky Cole With Al Cohn And His Orchestra | Smooth & Rocky | M&M Records | R 25113(Roulette)

C'Est La Vie
Blossom Dearie Trio | Blossom Dearie Sings & Plays Songs Of Chelsea | Master Mix | CHECD 2

C'est Le Son Qui La (Remini) Scene
Ella Fitzgerald With The Nelson Riddle Orchestra | Dream Dancing | Original Jazz Classics | OJCCD 1072-2(2310814)

C'Est Magnifique
George Masso Sextet | C'Est Magnifique! | Nagel-Heyer | CD 060
Mitchell's Jazz Kings | Le Jazz En France Vol.1:Premiers Jazz Bands | Pathe | 1727251

C'Est Si Bon
Bireli Lagrene Trio | Live In Marciac | Dreyfus Jazz Line | FDM 36567-2
Louis Armstrong And His All Stars | Jazz Festival Vol.1 | Storyville | 4960733
Historic Barcelona Concerts At Windsor Palace 1955 | Fresh Sound Records | FSR-CD 3004
Masters Of Jazz Vol.1:Louis Armstrong | Storyville | STCD 4101
Louis Armstrong With Sy Oliver And His Orchestra | Ambassador Louis Armstrong Vol.18:Because Of You(1950-1953) | Ambassador | CLA 1918
Louis Armstrong-My Greatest Songs | MCA | MCD 18347
Satchmo Serenaders | Verve | 543792-2
Mr.Acker Bilk And His Paramount Jazz Band | White Cliffs Of Dover | Intercord | 125408

C'Est Si Bon-
TSF+Daniel Huck | Drolement Vocal! | IDA Record | 013 CD

CFK
Christof Griese Quartet With Davis Milne | New Friends | Jazz 4 Ever Records:Jazz Network | J4E 4736

CH & HC
Cal Tjader's Orchestra | Several Shades Of Jade/Breeze From The East | Verve | 537083-2

Cha Cha Cha
Tito Puente Orchestra | Goza Mi Timbal | Concord | CCD 4399

Cha Cha Cha Du Luop
Junior Wells Blues Band | Mesing With The Kid | Charly | CRB 1133

Chabootie
Gene Ammons Septet | The Gene Ammons Story: The 78 Era | Prestige | P 24058

Chaboud
Santos Chillemi Group | Trinidad | Maracatu | MAC 940001

Chaconne
Noel Akchoté-Marc Ribot-Eugene Chadbourne | Lust Corner | Winter&Winter | 910019-2

Chadology
Buddy DeFranco-Terry Gibbs Quintet | Holiday For Swing | Contemporary | C 14047

Chagall-
The Jazz Passengers | Implement Yourself | New World Records | 80398-2

Chain 'Em Down
James Wiggins With Blind Leroy Garnett | Paramounth Piano Blues Vol.1(1928-1932) | Black Swan Records | HCD-12011

Chain Gang
Kokomo Arnold | King Of The Bottelneck Guitar | Black & Blue | BLE 59.250 2

Chain Of Fools
Herbie Mann Group | Memphis Underground | Atlantic | 7567-81364-2
That's Jazz Vol.37: Memphis Underground | Atlantic | ATL 50520
Thursday Diva | Folow Me | dmp Digital Music Productions | CD 509

Chain Reaction
Hank Mobley Quintet | Straight No Filter | Blue Note | BST 84435
Peter Bolte-Marcio Doctor | Zeitraum | Jazz Haus Musik | JHM 0113 CD
The Crusaders | The Best Of The Crusaders | MCA | 2292-50536-1

Chains Of Love
Bobby Bland And His Band | Bobby Bland The Voice: Duke Recordings 1959-1969 | Ace Records | CDCHD 323

Chairman Mao
Don Cherry Group | Old And New Dreams | Black Saint | 120013-2

Chalabati
Randy Weston With The Splendid Master Gnawa Musicians Of Morocco | The Splendid Master Gnawa Musicians Of Morocco | Verve | 521587-2

Chalmeau
Bob Degen Trio With Zbigniew Namyslowski | Joy | Dr.Jazz Records | 8611-2

Chameleon
Louie Bellson And His Orchestra | The Louis Bellson Explosion | Original Jazz Classics | OJCCD 728-2(2310755)
Maynard Ferguson And His Orchestra | Chameleon | CBS | 467091-2

Chameleon,Madrepore And A Wind Rose
Chico Hamilton Quintet | Chico Hamilton Quintet feat. Eric Dolphy | Fresh Sound Records | FSCD 1004

Champagne-
Astrud Gilberto With The Shigeharu Mukai Group | Mukai Meets Gilberto | Denon Compact Disc | DC-8569

Champak Odours
Alfred 23 Harth Group | Sweet Paris | free flow music | ffm 0291

Champ-De-Mars
Eric Schultz Quintet | Space And Time Ensemble | Naxos Jazz | 86066-2

Champion Jack's Boogie
Mal Waldron Trio | Impressions | Original Jazz Classics | OJCCD 132-2(NJ 8242)

Champ's Housewarming
Enrico Rava Quintet And String Quartet | Rava String Band | Soul Note | 121114-2

Chance
John Abercrombie Quartet | Getting There | ECM | 1321(833494-2)
Kenny Kirkland Trio | Kenny Kirkland | Verve | 543037-2

Chance It
Miles Davis All Stars | Miles Davis Vol.1 | Blue Note | 532610-2
Miles Davis Sextet | Miles Davis:The Blue Note And Capitol Recordings | Blue Note | 827475-2
Miles Davis Vol.1 | Blue Note | 300081(1501)

Chance Meeting
Meyer-Fleck-Marshall | Unconnon Ritual | CBS | SK 62891

Chances
Ben Sidran/Clementine Quintet | Spread Your Wings And Fly Now | Orange Blue | ???

Chandoha
Charlie Mariano Quintet | Boston Days | Fresh Sound Records | FSR-CD 0207

Chandra
Keith Jarrett Trio | At The Deer Head Inn | ECM | 1531(517720-2)
John McLaughlin Group | Remember Shakti | Verve | 559945-2

Chandrakauns
Peter Materna Quartet | Aquarius | Jazzline | JL 11142-2

Change
Duke Jordan Trio | Change A Pace | Steeplechase | SCCD 31135

Change In Rhythm
Hannibal Marvin Peterson Sextet | One With The Wind | Muse | MCD 5523

Change My Ways
Duke Ellington And His Orchestra | The Rare Broadcast Recordings 1953 | Jazz Anthology | JA 5220

Change Of Colours
Emborg-Larsen Quintet | Heart Of The Matter | Stunt Records | STUCD 19102

Change Of Mind
Peter Erskine Orchestra | Peter Erskine | Contemporary | CCD 14010-2

Change Of Pace
Tom Harrell Quintet | Moon Alley | Criss Cross | Criss 1018

Change Of The Century
Ornette Coleman Quartet | Beauty Is A Rare Thing:Ornette Coleman-The Complete Atlantic Recordings | Atlantic | 8122-71410-2
Lajos Dudas Quintet | Jubilee Edition | double moon | CHRDM 71020

Change Of Time
Peter O'Mara Sextet | Stairway | Enja | 7077-2

Change Parners
Art Farmer Quartet | A Work Of Art | Concord | CJ 179

Change Partners
Ella Fitzgerald With Paul Weston And His Orchestra | The Complete Ella Fitzgerald Song Books of Harold Arlen, Irving Berlin, Duke Ellington, George & Ira Gershwin, Jerome Kern, Johnny Mercer, Cole Porter And Rogers & Hart | Verve | 519832-2
The Blue Bird Society Orchestra | The Blue Bird Society Orchestra | Stash Records | ST 268 IMS

Change The Guard
Giorgio Rosciglione Quartet | Giorgio Rosciglione Quartet | Penta Flowers | CDPIA 013

Change The World
Vincent Herring Quintet | Change The World | Musicmasters | 65163-2

Change Up
Jane Ira Bloom Quartet | Mighty Lights | Enja | 4044 (807519)

Change(Makes You Want To Hustle)
Margaret Johnson With Clarence Williams' Blue Five | Louis Armstrong And The Blues Singers 1924-1930 | Affinity | AFS 1018(6)

Changes
Connie Jones & Dick Sudhalter Group | Live at The Vineyard | Challenge | CHR 70054
Frank Morgan And The McCoy Tyner Trio | Major Changes | Contemporary | C 14039
McCoy Tyner Trio With Michael Brecker | Infinity | Impulse(MCA) | IMP 11712
Paul Whiteman And His Orchestra | The Indispensable Bix Beiderbecke(1924-1930) | RCA | ND 89572
Thilo Kreitmeier & Group | Changes | Organic Music | ORGM 9725
Threeo | Racing Time | L+R Records | CDLR 45103

Changes Has Come
Albert Ammons | The First Day | Blue Note | 798450-2

Changes Of Season
New Association | Four Wheel Drive | Inak | 8702

Changes(reprise)
Krakatau | Volition | ECM | 1466

Changgo
Earl Hines Quartet | Jazz Legacy 26: Earl Hines/Jimmy Rushing-Blues And Things | Vogue | 500076

Changing Colors
Cees Slinger Octet | Live At The Northsea Jazz Festival | Limetree | MLP 198244

Changing Places
Greg Tardy Band | Crazy Love | DuBat Music | CD 26293

Changing Song
Dave Stryker Quintet | Changing Times | Steeplechase | SCCD 31510

Chango
Milton Cardona With The Eya Arania Ensemble | Bembe | American Clave | AMCL 1004

Chango Chango
New Generation Cuban All Stars | The New Generation Cuban All Stars Vol.1:Antes De Nuestro Tiempo | Messidor | 15941

Chank
Poncho Sanchez Band | Cambios | Concord | CCD 4439

Channel Surfer
Chuck Loeb Group | Simple Things | dmp Digital Music Productions | CD 504

Chan's House Of Jazz
Bobby Hutcherson Group | Skyline | Verve | 559616-2

Chan's Song
Eliana Elias Quartet | Illusions | Blue Note | BLJ 46994
Jens Bunge Group | Meet You In Chicago | Jazz 4 Ever Records:Jazz Network | J4E 4749
Lafayette Harris Jr. Quartet | Lafayette Is Here | Muse | MCD 5507
Christian McBride/Nicholas Payton/Mark Whitfield | Fingerpainting-The Music Of Herbie Hancock | Verve | 537856-2

Chanson Anonyme
Louis Smith Quintet | Prancin' | Steeplechase | SCCD 31121

Chanson Pour La Nuit
Michel Godard-Miroslav Tadic-Mark Nauseef | Loose Wires | Enja | ENJ-9071 2

Chanson Pour Lise
Louis Sclavis Group | Chine | IDA Record | 012 CD

Chant
Coleman Hawkins All Stars | The Hawk Flies High | Original Jazz Classics | OJC 027(R 12-223)
Fourplay | Between The Sheets | Warner | 9362-45340-2
George Young Orchestra | Chant | Electric Bird | K32Y 6033
Jiggs Whigham Quintet | Hope | Mons Records | CD 1888
Peter Bernstein Quintet | Brain Dance | Criss Cross | Criss 1130

Chant D'Exil

Vocal Summit | Sorrow Is Not Forever-Love Is | Moers Music | 02004 CD

Chant For Ibeji
Ivo Perlman Group | Children Of Ibeji | Enja | ENJ-7005 2

Chant For Logum
Children Of Ibeji | Enja | ENJ-7005 2

Chant For Oshala
Children Of Ibeji | Enja | ENJ-7005 2

Chant For Oshum
T.K.Blue Group | Another Blue | Arkadia Jazz | 70351

Chant Of The Groove
Coleman Hawkins Big Band | Big Band 1940 | Jazz Anthology | 550132

Chant Of The Soil
Keith Jarrett Quartet | Nude Ants | ECM | 1171/72(829119-2)
Andy Anderson's Pelican State Jazz Band | Prelude To The Revival Vol.1 | American Music | AMCD-40

Chant Of The Weed
Don Redman And His Orchestra | The Complete McKinney's Cotton Pickers Vol.5 Plus Don Redman & His Orchestra | RCA | NL 89161 (809233)

Chantez Les Bas
Louis Armstrong And His All Stars | The Louis Armstrong Selection | CBS | 467278-2

Chao
Baden Powell | Le Coeur De Baden Powell | Festival | FLD 633

Chaos' Order
Steve Coleman And Metrics | The Way Of The Cipher | Novus | 2131690-2

Chaos(Tech Jump)
Steve Coleman's Music Live In Paris | Novus | 2131691-2

Chaotic Romance
Stuff Smith And Stephane Grappelli With The Oscar Peterson Quartet | Violins No End | Pablo | 2310907-2

Chaperon
Ahmad Jamal Quartet | Nature(The Essence Part III) | Atlantic | 3984-23105-2
Gina Sbu/Etienne Brunet Group | Aller Simple | ITM Records | ITM 1458

Chapter XI
Mario Pavone Septet | Song For (Septet) | New World Records | 80452-2

Chaque Jour
Clark Terry Orchestra | Clark Terry | Swing | SW 8406 IMS

Character Study
Alfred 23 Harth-Bob Degen Duo | Melchior | Biber Records | BI 6240

Characteristically B.H.
Ran Blake | Realization Of A Dream | Owl Records | 012

Charade
Johnny Hartman And His Quintet | I Just Dropped By To Say Hello | MCA | 951176-2
Mel Tormé With Band And Symphony Orchestra | A New Album | Paddle Wheel | KICJ 128
Sahib Shihab Sextet | Conversations | Black Lion | BLCD 760169
Secret Agent Men | Secret Agent Men | Paddle Wheel | KICJ 135
The Capp/Pierce Orchestra | Juggernaut Strikes Again | Concord | CCD 4183

Charanga
Rabih Abou-Khalil | Il Sospiro | Enja | ENJ-9440 2

Charao Et Tout-
Juan Carlos Quintero Group | Juan Carlos Quintero | Nova | NOVA 9024-2

Charbon
Walter Blanding Quintet | The Olive Tree | Criss Cross | Criss 1186

Charcoal Blues
Azimuth With Ralph Towner | Depart | ECM | 1163

Charcoal Traces-
Cecil Taylor Quartet | Jazz Advance | Blue Note | 784462-2

Charged Particles
George Duke Group | I Love The Blues | MPS | 817488-1

Charise
Joachim Kühn | Charisma | Atlantic | ATL 50352

Charisma
Bud Shank Quartet | Misty Eyes | West Wind | WW 2031

Charles M.
Dave Brubeck Quartet | Adventures In Time | CBS | CBS 66291

Charleston
Quintet Du Hot Club De France | L'Essentiel Django Reinhardt | EMI Records | 780671-2

Charleston Alley
Joe Reisman And His Orchestra | Party Night At Joe's | Fresh Sound Records | NL 46027(RCA LPM 1476)

Charleston Rag
Thomas Morris And His Seven Hot Babies | Victor Jazz History Vol.5:Harlem Jazz(1921-28) | RCA | 2128559-2

Charlie
Oscar Peterson Quartet | Night Child | Original Jazz Classics | OJCCD 1030-2(2312108)
Tarika Blue | Tarika Blue | Chiaroscuro | CR 164

Charlie Brown
George Winston | Linus & Lucy-The Music Of Vince Guaraldi | Windham Hill | 34 11187-2

Charlie Brown And His All Stars
Vince Guaraldi Group | Charlie Brown's Holiday Hits | Fantasy | FCD 9682-2

Charlie Brown Theme
Charlie Ventura Quartet | Euphoria | Savoy | SJL 2243 (801889)

Charlie M
Lester Bowie | All The Magic! | ECM | 1246/47

Charlie Parker Place
Clifford Jordan Big Band | Play What You Feel | Mapleshade | 03232

Charlie's Ant
Charlie Byrd Trio | Great Guitars | Concord | CCD 6004

Charlie's Blues
Charley Booker Band | Mississippi Blues | Anthology of the Blues | AB 5609

Charlies Fingers
Paul Howard's Quality Serenaders | Early Hamp | Affinity | CD AFS 1011

Charlie's Song
Edith Steyer... Posterity Quintet | ...On The Right Track | Jazz 4 Ever Records:Jazz Network | J4E 4745

Charlie's Tone
Anthony Braxton | Wesleyan(12 Altosolos) 1992 | Hat Art | CD 6128

Charlotte's Piccolo
Ralph Towner-Gary Burton | Slide Show | ECM | 1306

Charlotte's Tangle
Paul Millns | Finally Falls The Rain | BELL Records | BLR 84707

Charmaine
Bill Henderson With The Oscar Peterson Trio | Vocal Classics | Verve | 837937-2

Charmaine-
Squeeze Me Jazzband | Salute To Uncle Bijou | Jazz Pure Collection | AU 31623 CD

Charmediterranéen
Louis Sclavis Sextet | Les Violences De Rameau | ECM | 1588(533128-2)

Charmes
Les Violences De Rameau | ECM | 1588(533128-2)

Charmes(II)
Jacques Pirotton Quartet | Artline | B.Sharp Records | CDS 070

Charms Of The Night Sky
George Lewis-Douglas Ewart | George Lewis-Douglas Ewart | Black Saint | BSR 0026

Chaser
Eddie Daniels Quintet | Nepenthe | GRP | GRP 96072
Claude Hopkins And His Orchestra | Big Bands Uptown 1931-40 | MCA | 1323

Chasin' The Bird
Charlie Parker Quintet | The Best Of Bird On Savoy | Savoy | 650109(881909)
Red Rodney Quintet | Bird Lives! | Muse | MCD 5371
Super Sax | Chasin' The Bird | MPS | 821867-1
Charlie Parker Quintet | The Complete Savoy Sessions Vol.3 | Savoy | WL 70548 (809291)

Chasin' The Blues
Bruce Forman Quartet | Coast To Coast | Candid | CRS 1026 IMS

Chasin' The Gyssy
Michael Hornstein Quartet | Innocent Green | Enja | 9099-2

Chasin' The Trane
John Coltrane Quartet | The Best Of John Coltrane | Pablo | 2405417-2
Live At The Village Vanguard | MCA | 2292-54627-2
John Coltrane Trio | Live At The Village Vanguard:The Master Takes | Impulse(MCA) | 951251-2
John Coltrane-His Greatest Years, Vol. 3 | MCA | AS 9278
John Coltrane-Eric Dolphy Quartet | John Coltrane:The Complete 1961 Village Vanguard Recordings | Impulse(MCA) | 954322-2
The Other Village Vanguard Tapes | Impulse(MCA) | MCD 04137
Borah Bergman-Andrew Cyrille | The Human Factor | Soul Note | 121212-2

Chasin' The Voodoo
Lionel Hampton And His Orchestra | Lionel Hampton-Historical Recording Sessions 1939-1941 | RCA | PM 42417

Chasing Chicken
Klaus Ignatzek Quintet | Silent Horns | Candid | CCD 79729

Chasing Reality:
Ronnell Bright Trio | Jazz In Paris:Piano Aux Champs Elysées | EmArCy | 014059-2

Chasing The Bird
Charlie Parker All Stars | Miles Davis:Early Milestones 1945-1949 | Naxos Jazz | 8.120607 CD
The Moscow Sax Quintet | The Jazznost Tour | Arkadia Jazz | 71161

Chasing The White Rabbit
Cannonball Adderley Septet | Spontaneous Combustion | Savoy | 650104(881904)

Chat Imaginaire
Pata Music Meets Arfi | News Of Roi Ubu | Pata Musik | PATA 10 CD
Clark Terry Orchestra | Color Changes | Candid | CCD 79009

Chat Qui Peche(A Cat That Fishes)
Thomas Horstmann-Markus Zaja | Somewhere | Factory Outlet Records | 400004-2

Chateau Bellevue
Franz Koglmann Pipetet | The Use Of Memory | Hat Art | CD 6078

Chattanooga Choo Choo
Glenn Miller And His Orchestra | Planet Jazz:Glenn Miller | Planet Jazz | 2152056-2
The Unforgettable Glenn Miller | RCA | PD 89260
Planet Jazz:Jazz Greatest Hits | Planet Jazz | 2169648-2
Planet Jazz:Big Bands | Planet Jazz | 2169649-2
Glenn Miller | Koch Records | 321 941 D1
The Very Best Of Glenn Miller | RCA | PL 89009 AO
Glenn Miller Revival Orchestra | Forever-From The Forties To The... | Timeless | CD JC 11013
Sultans Of Swing | This Joint Is Jumping | Mons Records | MR 874319

Chattanooga Stomp
King Oliver's Jazz Band | Louis Armstrong With King Oliver Vol.1 | Village(Jazz Archive) | VILCD 003-2

Chatterbox
Nat Adderley Sextet | In The Bag | Original Jazz Classics | OJCCD 648-2(JLP 975)
Bill Evans Quintet | Summertime | Jazz City | 660.53.018

Chattin' With Chet
Nina Simone Quartet | Nina Simone-The 60s Vol.2:Mood Indigo | Mercury | 838544-2 PMS

Chava Meets The Tango Man
Buddy Rich Big Band | Mercy Mery | Pacific Jazz | 854331-2

Chazz
Mal Waldron Quartet | One Entrance, Many Exits | Palo Alto | PA 8014

Chazzanova
Four Trombones | Charles Mingus-The Complete Debut Recordings | Debut | 12 DCD 4402-2
Thad Jones Quintet | Thad Jones | Original Jazz Classics | OJCCD 625-2(DEB 127)
North Sea Jazz Tentet | North Sea Jazz Tentet(Part One) | September | CD 5105

Cheaper To Keep Her
Memphis Slim And His Solid Band | The Ambassador Of The Blues | Official | 6016

Check And Double Check
Bernhard Pichl Trio | On The Corner | Jazz 4 Ever Records:Jazz Network | J4E 4726

Check It Out
Martin Taylor Trio | Skye Boat | Concord | CJ 184

Check Up
Lee Konitz Duo | The Lee Konitz Duets | Original Jazz Classics | OJCCD 466-2

Checkered Hat
Norris Turney Quartet | Big Sweet N' Blue | Mapleshade | 02632

Checkered Past
Sonny Boy Williamson Band | The Real Folk Blues | Chess | CHD 9272(872292)

Checkin' With Chuck(theme)
Mike Westbrook Orchestra | On Duke's Birthday | Hat Art | CD 6021

Checking In At Hotel Le Prieure
Buddy Guy-Junior Wells Band | Drinkin' TNT 'N' Smokin' Dynamite | Sequel Records | NEM CD 687

Checkmate
Ernie Henry Quintet | Presenting Ernie Henry | Original Jazz Classics | OJC 102(RLP 222)

Cheek To Cheek
Allan Vaché Sextette plus Warren Vaché Jr. | Swing And Other Things | Arbors Records | ARCD 19171
Bernard Peiffer Trio | Jazz In Paris:The Bernard Peiffer Trio Plays Standards | EmArCy | 018425-2
Beryl Booker Trio | Don Byas Featuring Mary Lou Williams Trio & Beryl Booker Trio | Vogue | 21610212
Billie Holiday And Her All Stars | Billie Holiday:The Great American Songbook | Verve | 523003-2
Ella Fitzgerald And Louis Armstrong With The Oscar Peterson Quartet | The Jazz Collector Edition: Ella & Louis | Laserlight | 15706
Satchmo/What A Wonderful World | Verve | 837786-2
Ella Fitzgerald With Paul Weston And His Orchestra | Ella Fitzgerald Sings The Irving Berlin Song Book | Verve | 543830-2
The Complete Ella Fitzgerald Song Books of Harold Arlen, Irving Berlin, Duke Ellington, George & Ira Gershwin, Jerome Kern, Johnny Mercer, Cole Porter And Rogers & Hart | Verve | 519832-2
Elliot Lawrence And His Orchestra | The Uncollected:Elliot Lawrence | Hindsight | HSR 182
George Van Eps | Legends | Concord | CCD 4616
Joe Pass | Blues For Fred | Pablo | 2310931-2
Kai Winding All Stars | Kai Winding All Stars | Fresh Sound Records | FSR 627(Roost RLP 408)
Oliver Jones Trio | Requestfully Yours | Justin Time | Just 11
Peter Herbolzheimer Orchestra | Music For Swinging Dancers,Vol.3.Cheek To Cheek | Koala Records | CD P 10
Ray Anderson Quintet | Wishbone | Gramavision | GV 79454-2(882568)
Roy Williams With The Eddie Thompson Trio | Something Wonderful | Hep | 2015
Stephen Scott Trio | Vision Quest | Enja | ENJ-9347 2
Tana Reid Quintet | Passing Thoughts | Concord | CCD 4505

Cheek To Cheek-
Allen Farnham Quartet | Play-Cation | Concord | CCD 4521

Cheeky
Michael Heise Trio | Touchdown | Storyville | STCD 4213
Barbara Thompson's Paraphernalia | Breathless | VeraBra Records | CDVBR 2057-2

Cheeky(short cut)
Jim Black Alasnoaxis | Splay | Winter&Winter | 910076-2

Cheepa Vs, Cheep
Jerry Van Rooyen With The WDR Big Band | Swing & Balladen | WDR | 2141013-2

Cheerful Little Earful
George Barnes Quartet | Blues Going Up | Concord | CJ 43

Cheerin' Rag
James Blood Ulmer Quartet | Blues Preacher | DIW | DIW 869 CD

Cheerlessness
Art Van Damme Group | State Of Art | MPS | 841413-2

Cheers
Blue Box | Captured Dance Floor | TipToe | TIP-888801 2
Charly Antolini Orchestra | Charly Antolini | Jazz Magazine | 48017
Charles Brackeen Quartet | Bannar | Silkheart | SH 105

Cheese Cake
Dexter Gordon Quartet | Dexter Gordon:The Complete Blue Note Sixties Sessions | Blue Note | 834200-2

Chega De Saudade(No More Blues)
Betty Bennett And Her Quintet | The Song Is You | Fresh Sound Records | FSR-CD 186(889843)
Dizzy Gillespie And His Orchestra | Compact Jazz:Dizzy Gillespie | Mercury | 832574-2 PMS
Dizzy Gillespie Septet | The Antonio Carlos Jobim Songbook | Verve | 525472-2
Eliane Elias Group | Fantasia | Blue Note | 796146-2
Gary Burton | Atlantic Jazz: Introspection | Atlantic | 7567-81710-2
James Morrison Quartet | Snappy Doo | Warner | 9031-71211-2
L.A.4 | Executive Suite | Concord | CCD 4215
Manfredo Fest Quintet | Jungle Cat | dmp Digital Music Productions | CD 470
Roman Schwaller Jazz Quartet | Clubdate | Jazz 4 Ever Records:Jazz Network | J4E 4713
Stan Getz With The Gary McFarland Orchestra | Verve Jazz Masters 53:Stan Getz-Bossa Nova | Verve | 529904-2
Compact Jazz: Best Of Bossa Nova | Verve | 833269-2
Stochelo Rosenberg Trio | Seresta | Hot Club Records | HCRCD 059
Hendrik Meurkens With The Rio Samba-Jazz Group | Clear Of Clouds | Concord | CCD 4531

Chega De Saudade(No More Blues-part 2)
Dusko Goykovich Quartet | Samba Do Mar | Enja | ENJ-9473 2

Chega De Saudare
Samba Trio | Tristeza | Timeless | CD SJP 169

Chejudo
Chet Baker Quintet | Chet Baker In Paris | Fresh Sound Records | FSR Box 1(Barclay)

Che-Low
Fats Waller | London Sessions 1938-39 | Jazztime(EMI) | 251271-2

Chelsea Bells (For Hern)
Gary Burton-Steve Swallow | Works | ECM | 823267-2

Chelsea Bridge
Ben Webster Sextet | Perdido | Moon Records | MCD 070-2
Ben Webster With Orchestra And Strings | Ultimate Ben Webster selected by James Carter | Verve | 557537-2
Bennie Wallace Quartet | Bennie Wallace | audioquest Music | AQCD 1051
Bob Haggart's Swing Three | Hag Leaps In | Arbors Records | ARCD 19156
Duke Ellington And His Famous Orchestra | Jazz:The Essential Collection Vol.2 | IN+OUT Records | 78012-2
Sophisticated Lady | RCA | 26685162
Duke Ellington And His Orchestra | Highlights From The Duke Ellington Centennial Edition | RCA | 2663672-2
En Concert Avec Europe 1 | Laserlight | 710433/34
Passion Flower | Moon Records | MCD 074-2
Duke Ellington: The Champs-Elysees Theater January 29-30th,1965 | Laserlight | 36131
The Indispensable Duke Ellington,Vol.7/8 | RCA | ND 89274
Ella Fitzgerald With The Duke Ellington Orchestra | The Complete Ella Fitzgerald Song Books of Harold Arlen, Irving Berlin, Duke Ellington, George & Ira Gershwin, Jerome Kern, Johnny Mercer, Cole Porter And Rogers & Hart | Verve | 519832-2
Gerry Mulligan-Ben Webster Quintet | Gerry Mulligan Meets Ben Webster | Verve | 841661-2 PMS
The Silver Collection: Gerry Mulligan Meets The Saxophonists | Verve | 827436-2 PMS
Gijs Hendriks Quartet & Guests | Gentlemania | yvp music | CD 3028
Günter Wehinger Quartet | As Promised | Minor Music | 801031
Günther Klatt Quartet | Internationales Jazzfestival Münster | Tutu Records | 888110-2*
Harry Verbeke/Carlo de Wijs Quartet | Plays Romantic Ballads | Timeless | CD SJP 230
Jesper Thilo Quintet feat. Hank Jones | A Jazz Par 91 Project | Storyville | STCD 4178
Jimmy Raney-Doug Raney Quartet | Stolen Moments | Steeplechase | SCCD 31118
Joe Henderson Sextet | Joe Henderson:The Milestone Years | Milestone | 8MCD 4413-2
Joe Lovano | Blue Note Plays Ellington And Strayhorn | Blue Note | 520809-2
Kenny Burrell All Stars | Ellington Is Forever | Fantasy | F 79005
Louis Stewart-Heiner Franz Quartet | Jazz Guitar Highlights 1 | Jardis Records | JRCD 20141
Martin Krusche Quintet | Friendship Pagoda | Naxos Jazz | 86057-2
Sarah Vaughan And Her Band | Duke Ellington Song Book Two | Pablo | CD 2312116
Sarah Vaughan With The Mike Wofford Trio | Sarah Vaughan Birthday Celebration | Fantasy | FANCD 6090-2
Scott Hamilton Quintet | Race Point | Concord | CCD 4492
Tommy Flanagan Trio | The Tommy Flanagan Tokyo Recital | Original Jazz Classics | 2310724
Wild Bill Davis | Greatest Organ Solos Ever! | Jazz Connaisseur | JCCD 8702-2
Art Blakey And The Jazz Messengers | Reflections in Blue | Timeless | SJP 128

Chelsea Bridge-
Rex Allen's Swing Express | Ellington For Lovers | Nagel-Heyer | NH 1009
Roy Eldridge-Benny Carter Quintet | The Complete Verve Roy Eldridge Studio Sessions | Verve | 9861278
The Urban Sessions/New Jazz Sound | Verve | 531637-2

Chelsea Bridge(alt.take)
The Complete Verve Roy Eldridge Studio Sessions | Verve | 9861278

Chelsea Bridge(alt.take)-
Chris Hunter Quartet | This Is Chris | Paddle Wheel | K32Y 6261

Chelsea Courtyard
Frank Strozier Quintet | What's Goin' On | Steeplechase | SCD 17001 Direct Disc

Chelsea Morning
Singers Unlimited With Rob McConnell And The Boss Brass | The Singers Unlimited With Rob McConnell And The Boss Brass | MPS | 817486-1

Chemischer Urlaub
Doran/Studer/Burri/Magnenat | Musik Für Zwei Kontrabässe, Elektrische Gitarre & Schlagzeug | ECM | 1436

Chemistries(I)
Musik Für Zwei Kontrabässe, Elektrische Gitarre & Schlagzeug | ECM | 1436

Chemistries(II)
Mark Nauseef Group | Personal Note | CMP Records | CMP 16

Cheremies Folk Song
Conte Candoli Quintet | West Coast Wailers | Fresh Sound Records | 1268(Atlantic)

Cheri(Dudu)
Micheline Day Et Son Quatuor Swing | Jazz In Paris:Django Reinhardt-Django Et Compagnie | EmArCy | 549241-2 PMS

Cheri,Est-Ce Que Tu M'Aimes?
Art Lande-Jan Garbark | Red Lanta | ECM | 1038(829383-2)
Cherifen Dream Of Renate
Adam Makowicz-George Mraz Duo | Classic Jazz Duets | Stash Records | ST 216 IMS
Cherokee
Art Pepper Quartet | Art Pepper:The Complete Village Vanguard Sessions | Contemporary | 9CCD-4417-2
Art Pepper:The Complete Village Vanguard Sessions | Contemporary | 9CCD-4417-2
Art Pepper:The Complete Village Vanguard Sessions | Contemporary | 9CCD-4417-2
Art Pepper Quintet | Art Pepper:Tokyo Debut | Galaxy | GCD 4201-2
Art Pepper-Shorty Rogers Quintet | Art Pepper & Shorty Rogers:Complete Lighthouse Sessions | The Jazz Factory | JFCD 22836
Art Tatum | Esquire's All-American Hot Jazz Sessions | RCA | ND 86757
Ashley Alexander Big Band | Power Slide | Pausa | PR 7178(952087)
Bud Powell Trio | The Bud Powell Trio | Debut | VIJ 5002 IMS
Bud Powell:Complete 1947-1951 Blue Note,Verve & Roost Recordings | The Jazz Factory | JFCD 22837
Jazz At Massey Hall,Vol.2 | Original Jazz Classics | OJCCD 111-2(DLP 9)
Charlie Barnet And His Orchestra | Planet Jazz:Big Bands | Planet Jazz | 2169649-2
RCA Victor 80th Anniversary Vol.2:1930-1939 | RCA | 2668778-2
Chet Baker Trio | Chet Baker-Philip Catherine-Jean Louis Rassinfosse | Igloo | IGL 034
Clifford Brown-Max Roach Quintet | Clifford Brown-Max Roach:Alone Together-The Best Of The Mercury Years | Verve | 526373-2
Verve Jazz Masters Vol.60:The Collection | Verve | 529866-2
Verve Jazz Masters 44:Clifford Brown and Max Roach | Verve | 528109-2
Study In Brown | EmArCy | 814646-2
Brownie-The Complete EmArCy Recordings Of Clifford Brown | EmArCy | 838306-2
Concord All Stars | Concord All Stars On Cape Cod | Concord | CCD 4530
Dado Moroni Trio | Insights | Jazz Focus | JFCD 007
Dee Dee Bridgewater With Her Trio | Live In Paris | Verve | 014317-2
Dexter Gordon Quartet | Love For Sale | Steeplechase | SCCD 36018
Don Byas Quartet | Don Byas Complete American Small Group Recordings | Definitive Records | DRCD 11213
Savoy Jam Party-The Savoy Sessions | Savoy | WL 70512 (809315)
Donald Harrison With The Guardians Of The Flame And The Mardi Gras Indians | Indian Blues | Candid | CCD 79514
Freddie Hubbard Quintet | Topsy | Enja | ENJ-7025 2
George Braith Quartet | Double Your Pleasure | Paddle Wheel | KICJ 114
Gustav Brom Big Band | Legenda | Musica | 700003-2
Jackie And Roy | Full Circle | Contemporary | CCD 14046-2
Jam Session | Bird's Eyes-Last Unissued Vol.12 | Philology | W 842.2
Jeff Hamilton Trio With Frits Landesbergen | Dynavibes | Mons Records | MR 874794
Jimmy Raney Sextet | Jimmy Raney Visits Paris | Fresh Sound Records | FSR 561(Dawn DLP 1120)
Joe Pass | Virtuoso | Pablo | 2310708-2
Joe Pass:A Man And His Guitar | Original Jazz Classics | OJCCD 8806-2
Joe Pass Quartet | Nuages | Pablo | 2310961-2
Joe Wilder Quartet | Wilder' N' Wilder | Savoy | SV 0131(MG 12063)
John Lewis | Evolution | Atlantic | 7567-83211-2
John Mehegan Trio | I Just Love Jazz Piano | Savoy | SV 0117(MG 12100)
Johnny Smith Quintet | Moonlight In Vermont | Roulette | 300016
Kurt Henkels Und Sein Orchester | Swing Tanzen Gestattet | Vagabond | 6.28415 DP
Lee Konitz Quartet | Lullaby Of Birdland | Candid | CCD 79709
Lee Konitz Terzet | Dovetail | Sunnyside | SSC 1003(952100)
Lee Konitz With The Bert Van Den Brink Trio | Dialogues | Challenge | CHR 70053
Lucky Thompson Quartet | Live In Switzerland 1968/69 | Jazz Helvet | JH 03
Nancy King-Glen Moore Group | Impending Bloom | Justice Records | JR 0801-2
Pierre Michelot Orchestra | Jazz In Paris:Pierre Michelot-Round About The Bass | EmArCy | 832309-2 PMS
Sonny Stitt Quartet | Autumn In New York | Black Lion | CD 877642-2
Stan Getz Quartet | Born To Be Blue | Bandstand | BDCD 1533
Stan Getz With Ib Glindemann And His Orchestra | Stan Getz | Laserlight | 15761
Stan Getz-Lionel Hampton Quintet | Hamp And Getz | Verve | 831672-2
Stan Kenton And His Orchestra | Contemporary Concepts | Creative World | ST 1003
Ted Heath And His Orchestra | Swing Is King | Decca | 6.28129 DP
The Tough Tenors With The Antonio Farao European Trio | Tough Tenors | Jazz 4 Ever Records:Jazz Network | J4E 4761
Three Of A Kind | Drip Some Grease | Minor Music | 801056
Tommy Flanagan Trio | Lady Be Good...For Ella | Groovin' High | 521617-2
Two-Bone Big Band | Two-Bone Big Band | MKW-Records | ???
Warren Vaché Trio | Live at The Vineyard | Challenge | CHR 70028
Wynton Kelly Trio | New Faces-New Sounds:Piano Interpretations | Blue Note | 784456-2
Cherokee-
Simon Schott | Bar Piano: Simon Schott Plays Your Favorite Evergreens Vol.2 | Organic Music | ORGM 9735
The Tenor Triangle & The Melvin Rhyne Trio | Tell It Like It Is | Criss Cross | Criss 1089
Cherokee(alt.take)
Clifford Brown-Gigi Gryce Sextet | Alternate Takes | Blue Note | BST 84428
John Dennis Trio | Charles Mingus-The Complete Debut Recordings | Debut | 12 DCD 4402-2
Herb Ellis-Joe Pass | Two For The Road | Original Jazz Classics | 2310714
Cherry
Alex Riel Quartet | D.S.B. Kino | Stunt Records | STUCD 19811
Allan Vaché-Antti Sarpila & 1 Sextet | Summit Meeting | Nagel-Heyer | CD 027
Arnett Cobb Quartet | Arnett Cobb Is Back | Progressive | PRO 7037 IMS
Benny Goodman And His Orchestra | Benny Goodman Vol.2: Clarinet A La King | CBS | 460829-2
Billy Strayhorn's Septet | Cue For Saxophone | Affinity | AFF 166
Harry James And His Orchestra | Trumpet Blues:The Best Of Harry James | Capitol | 521224-2
Welcome To Jazz: Harry James | Koch Records | 321 983 D1
Kenny Davern And The Rhythm Men | Kenny Davern And The Rhythm Men | Arbors Records | ARCD 19147
Lou Donaldson Quintet | Birdseed | Milestone | MCD 9198-2
Oscar Peterson-Count Basie Quartet | Satch And Josh...Again | Pablo | 2310802-2
Snooky Young-Marshal Royal Sextet | Snooky & Marshal's Album | Concord | CCD 4055
Woody Herman And His Orchestra | Big Band Bounce & Boogie-Woody Herman:Pre-Herds | Affinity | AFS 1027
Cherry Blossom
Howard Alden-Dan Barrett Quintet | Swing Street | Concord | CCD 4349
Cherry Float
Big Bill Broonzy | Big Bill Broonzy-1930's Blues | Biograph | BLP C 15
Cherry Point
Count Basie And His Orchestra | Breakfast Dance And Barbecue | Roulette | 531791-2
En Concert Avec Europe 1 | Laserlight | 710706/07
Count Basie & His Orchestra:Fresno,California April 24,1959 | Jazz Unlimited | JUCD 2039
Stanley Turrentine Quintet | Stanley Turrentine | Blue Note | 84506
Cherry Red
Big Joe Turner With Axel Zwingenberger | Boogie Woogie Jubilee | Vagabond | VRCD 8.81010
Big Joe Turner With Pete Johnson And His Boogie Woogie Boys | Boogie Woogie And More | Official | 6028
Big Joe Turner With The Milt Buckner Trio | Texas Style | Black & Blue | BLE 59.547 2
Count Basie And His Orchestra | En Concert Avec Europe 1 | Laserlight | 710706/07
Count Basie And His Orchestra With Joe Turner & Eddie Cleanhead Vinson | Kansas City Shout | Pablo | 2310859-2
Jay McShann Quintet | Live! | Black & Blue | 33309
Jay McShann-Milt Buckner Quartet | Kansas City Memories | Black & Blue | BLE 59.057 2
Vince Weber | Blues 'N Boogie | Rüssl Räckords | 064-32295
Cherryco
John Coltrane-Don Cherry Quartet | The Avantgarde | Rhino | 8122-79892-2
Atlantic Jazz: The Avant-Garde | Atlantic | 7567-81709-2
That's Jazz Vol.40: The Avant-Garde | Atlantic | ATL 50523
Cheryl
David Hazeltine Quartet | Blues Quarters Vol.1 | Criss Cross | Criss 1188
George Shearing Trio | Compact Jazz:George Shearing | MPS | 833284-2 PMS
Herb Geller Quartet | Birdland Stomp | Fresh Sound Records | FSR-CD 0174
Joe Van Enkhuizen Trio | Blues Ahead | Timeless | CD SJP 356
Phineas Newborn Jr. Trio | A World Of Piano | Contemporary | C 7600
Eddie Daniels Group | To Bird With Love | GRP | GRP 95442
Cheryl Blues
Charlie Parker Quintet | Bird's Eyes-Last Unissued Vol.2+3 | Philology | W 12/15.2
Chesire Hotel
Joe Lovano Quartet | Tones Shapes & Colors | Soul Note | 121132-2
Chess With Mal
Cecil Payne Quartet | Patterns Of Jazz | Savoy | SV 0135(MG 12147)
Chestnut Street Ramble(Vine Street Ramble)
Andy Lumpp Trio With Andy Przybielski | Music From Planet Earth | Nabel Records:Jazz Network | CD 4687
Chet
Chet Baker And His Orchestra | Chet Baker In Paris-The Complete Barclay Recordings Vol.1 | EmArCy | 837474-2 PMS
Chet's Ballad
Lee Konitz-Wolfgang Lackerschmid Quintet | Chet Baker:The Legacy Vol.3:Why Shouldn't You Cry | Enja | ENJ-9337 2
Chet's Ballad(Why Shouldn't You Cry)
Chet Baker Quartet | Deep In A Dream Of You | Moon Records | MCD 026-2
Chetu
Gijs Hendriks Quartet | Feedles | Timeless | SJP 146
Chevere
Kamafra | Kamafra Live | Edition Musikat | EDM 072
Louis Conte Group | La Cocina Caliente | Denon Compact Disc | CY-30001
Chevrolet
Eubie Blake | The Eighty-Six Years Of Eubie Blake | CBS | 22223
Chew Chew Chew
Ella Fitzgerald And Her Orchestra | Live From The Roseland Ballroom New York 1940 | Jazz Anthology | 550032
Cheyenne
Nils Landgren First Unit And Guests | Nils Landgren-The First Unit | ACT | 9292-2
Martin Taylor Quintet | Spirit Of Django | Linn Records | AKD 030
Chez Laurette
Miles Davis Quintet | Compact Jazz: Miles Davis | Philips | 838254-2
Chez Le Photographie Du Motel
Kosh | Groovy Strings | Elite Special | 73325
Chez Moi
Bobby Short With The Alden-Barrett Quintet | Swing That Music | Telarc Digital | CD 83317
Gigi Gryce-Clifford Brown Octet | Planet Jazz:Clifford Brown | Planet Jazz | 2161239-2
The Rosenberg Trio | Caravan | Verve | 523030-2
Chhota Mitha
John Wolf Brennan | Irisations | Creative Works Records | CW CD 1021-2
Chi
Charlie Parker Quartet | The Verve Years(1952-54) | Verve | 2-2523 IMS
Chi Chi
Charlie Parker | Verve | 539757-2
Charlie Parker:Bird's Best Bop On Verve | Verve | 527452-2
Hank Mobley Quartet | Complete 'The Jazz Message Sessions With Kenny Clarke' | The Jazz Factory | JFCD 22858
Junior Cook Quartet | Somethin's Cookin' | Muse | MR 5218
Chi Chi(2 false starts)
Charlie Parker Quartet | Charlie Parker | Verve | 539757-2
Chi Chi(alt,take 1)
Bird On Verve-Vol.7:Charlie Parker Big Band | Verve | 817448-1 IMS
Chi Chi(alt.take 2)
Charlie Parker | Verve | 539757-2
Chi Chi(alt.take 3)
Bird On Verve-Vol.7:Charlie Parker Big Band | Verve | 817448-1 IMS
Chi Chi(take 1-6)
David Benoit Group | Shaken Not Stirred | GRP | GRP 97872
Chi Gong
Francesca Simone Trio | Guardia Li | Minor Music | 801093
Chi Ventu
Nicolas Simion Quartet feat. Tomasz Stanko | Dinner For Don Carlos | Tutu Records | 888146-2*
Chiacona For Chet
Voices | Für Wilhelm E. | Trion | 3105
Chiaroscuro
Yosuke Yamashita | Banslikana | Enja | 2080
Chic Chic Chico
Lew Tabackin Quartet | I'll Be Seeing You | Concord | CCD 4528
Chicago
Benny Goodman Quartet | The Benny Goodman Caravans Vol.5:Jumpin' At The Woodside | Giants Of Jazz | GOJ 1042
Buddy Rich And His Orchestra | Swingin' New Big Band | Pacific Jazz | 835232-2
Buddy Rich Big Band | The New One! | Pacific Jazz | 494507-2
Buddy Tate Quintet | Buddy Tate-The Texas Twister | New World Records | 80352-2
Eddie Condon And The Chicagoans | Chicago And All That Jazz! | Verve | MV 2535 IMS
Muggsy Spanier And His Huge Dixieland Band | Columbia-The Gem Of The Ocean | Mobile Fidelity | MFCD 857
Oscar Peterson Trio | The Trio-Live From Chicago | Verve | 823008-2
Quintet Du Hot Club De France | Django Reinhardt:Djangology | EMI Records | 780659-2
Stephane Grappelli Quartet | At The Winery | Concord | CCD 4139
The Yamaha International Allstar Band | Hapy Birthday Jazzwelle Plus | Nagel-Heyer | CD 005
Tommy Dorsey And His Orchestra | This Is Tommy Dorsey Vol. 2 | RCA | 26.28041 DP
Chicago Blues
The Bucktown Five | Bix Beiderbecke | Milestone | MCD 47019-2
Chicago Breakdown
Giorgio Gaslini Quintet | Multipli | Soul Note | 121220-2
Vince Weber | The Boogie Man | Rüssl Räckords | 062-29597
Chicago Buzz
Johnny Griffin Quartet | Introducing Johnny Griffin | Blue Note | 746536-2
Chicago Flyer
Mezzrow-Bechet Septet | The Prodigious Bechet-Mezzrow Quintet & Septet | Festival | Album 117
Chicago High Life
Albert Ammons | Boogie Woogie | Laserlight | 24321
Chicago In Mind
Boogie Woggie Classics | Blue Note | BLP 1209
Chicago Melodie
Lovie Austin And Her Serenaders | Johnny Dodds Vol.2 | Village(Jazz Archive) | VILCD 017-2
Chicago Serenade
Natty Dominique's Creole Dance Band | Natty Dominique's Creole Dance Band | American Music | AMCD-18
Chicharera
Crash | Every Day A Trial | JA & RO | 005(08-4105)
Chick On The Water
Sieverts-Enders-Salfellner Trio | Brooklyn Blue | Jazz 4 Ever Records:Jazz Network | J4E 4732
Chicken
Carla Bley/Andy Sheppard/Steve Swallow | Song With Legs | Watt | 26(527069)
Fat Boogie Horns | Fat Boogie Horns(Rhythm And Soul Big Band) | Paul Records | PP 4002
Jaco Pastorius Trio | Jaco Pastorius Broadway Blues & Theresa | Jazzpoint | JP 1053 CD
Loren Stillman Quartet | How Swee It Is | Nagel-Heyer | CD 2031
Maceo Parker Group | Mo' Roots | Minor Music | 801018
Mississippi John Hurt | The Best Of Mississippi John Hurt | Vanguard | VCD 19/20
Chicken Dog
Mel Brown Quintet | Chicken Fat | Impulse(MCA) | 9861047
Chicken Fat
Steve Kuhn Quartet | Raindrops/Steve Kuhn Live In New York | Muse | MR 5106
Chicken Feet
Wolfgang Lauth Quartet | Lauther | Bear Family Records | BCD 15717 AH
Jimmy Johnson Band | Heap See | Blue Phoenix | BLP 233720
Chicken Rhythm
Slim Gaillard Group | Slim & Slam:Original 1938-39 Recordings Vol.2 | Tax | S 2-2
Chicken Soup
| Modern Walkin':Greatest Hits Volume 1 | Satin Doll Productions | SDP 1008-1 CD
Chicken Today,Feathers Tomorrow
Jugendjazzorchester NW | Back From The States | Jugendjazzorchester NW | JJO 004
Chicken Wings
Frank Stokes | Creator Of The Memphis Blues | Yazoo | YAZ 1056
Chicky-Mo, Craney-Crow
Tania Maria Quintet | Piquant | Concord | CCD 4151
Chico Cuadradino
Baden Powell Trio | Samba Triste | Festival | 114861
Chico's Love Song
Donald Byrd Sextet | The Creeper | Blue Note | LT 1096
Chief
Kenny Garrett Quartet | KG Standard Of Language | Warner | 9362-48404-2
Chief Blackwater
Jam Session | Jam Session Vol.4 | Steeplechase | SCCD 31527
Chief Crazy Horse
Scott Kreitzer Group | New York State Of Mind | Jazz City | 660.53.022
Bob Porter Orchestra | Meeting You | B.Sharp Records | 1002
Chihuahua Dreams
Phil Urso Quartet | Brothers And Other Mothers, Vol. 2 | Savoy | SJL 2236 (801212)
Child At Heart
Bill Frisell Trio | Live | Gramavision | GCD 79504
Child Of A Disordered Brain
Earl Hines | The Earl | Naxos Jazz | 8.120581 CD
Child Of All Nations
Avantgarden Party | Into The Blue | Stunt Records | 18906
Child Of Nature
SWR Big Band | Jazz In Concert | Hänssler Classics | CD 93.004
Enrico Pieranunzi Quintet | Don't Forget The Poet | Challenge | CHR 70065
Child Of The Sea
Thierry Péala Group | Inner Traces:A Kenny Wheeler Songbook | Naive | 226102
Child On The Porch
Jack Bruce Group | Somethinelse | CMP Records | CMP CD 1001
Childhood
Mitchel Forman | Childhood Dreams | Soul Note | SN 1050
Children At Play
Lajos Dudas Trio | Talk Of The Town | double moon | CHRDM 71012
Sachi Hayasaka & Stir Up! | 2.26 | Enja | 8014-2
Children Games
Chris Potter Group | Traveling Mercies | Verve | 018243-2
Children Go
David & Roselyn Group | Gospel From The Streets Of New Orleans | Sound Of New Orleans | SONO 1033
Children Go Where I Send Thee
Stars Of Faith | Black Nativity | Black & Blue | BLE 59.065 2
Children Go Where I Send You
Betty Carter And Her Trio | Betty Carter Album | Bet-Car | MK 1002
Children Of Sanchez
Gil Evans Orchestra | There Comes A Time | RCA | 2131392-2
Children Of The Fire-
Mose Allison And His Orchestra | The Earth Wants You | Blue Note | 827640-2
Children Of The Night
Billy May And His Orchestra | Billy May's Big Fat Brass/Bill's Bag | Capitol | 535206-2
Bob Berg Group | Riddles | Stretch Records | SCD 9008-2
Gary Bartz Quintet | Shadows | Timeless | CD SJP 379
Children Play
Tommy Smith Sextet | Paris | Blue Note | 780612-2
Children Song No.8
Villa-Lobos Duo | Orage Moon | Acoustic Music Records | 319.1155.2
Children's Dance
Dieter Köhnlein-Volker Schlott | Sweet Ballad Sweet | Aho-Recording | AHO CD 1032(CD 660)
Children's Games
Singers Unlimited + The Oscar Peterson Trio | In Tune | MPS | 68085
Children's Garden
Mingus Big Band | Live In Time | Dreyfus Jazz Line | FDM 36583-2
Children's Hunt
Thilo von Westernhagen Group | Forgotten Gardens | Acoustic Music Records | AMC 1011
Children's Play Song
Bill Evans Quartet With Orchestra | From Left To Right | Verve | 557451-2
Paul Motian Quartet | Bil Evans | JMT Edition | 834445-2
Children's Song
Bob Mintzer Big Band | Departure | dmp Digital Music Productions | CD 493
Chick Corea/Gary Burton | Crystal Silence | ECM | 1024(831331-2)
Chick Corea-Gary Burton | Works | ECM | 825426-2
Ulli Bögershausen | Sologuitar | Laika Records | 35101132
Chick Corea And Return To Forever | Light As A Feather | Polydor | 557115-2
Children's Song(alt.take)
Eberhard Weber | Pendulum | ECM | 1518(519707-2)
Children's Song(No.1)
Chick Corea | Originals | Stretch Records | SCD 9029-2
Children's Song(No.15)
Gary Burton-Chick Corea | Duet | ECM | 1140(829941-2)
Giulio Granata/Christian Gilardi | Cornici & Children's Song | Nueva Records | NC 2002
Children's Song(No.2)
Renee Rosnes Trio | Art & Soul | Blue Note | 499997-2
Children's Song(No.3)
Gary Burton-Chick Corea | Duet | ECM | 1140(829941-2)

Children's Song(No.5)
Chick Corea | Originals | Stretch Records | SCD 9029-2
Children's Song(No.6)
Peter Sprague Quartet | Na Pali Coast | Concord | CJ 277
Children's Song(That Old Man)
Andy LaVerne | Jazz Piano Lineage | dmp Digital Music Productions | CD 463
Children's Songs(No.1-20)
Johannes Cernota | Sparta | JA & RO | JARO 4136-2
Children's Songs(No.3,6,17,18,19)
Michel Bisceglia Quintet | About Stories | RCA | 2153080-2
Children's World
The J.B. Horns | Funky Good Time/Live | Gramavision | R2 79485
Child's Eyes
Charles Gayle | Unto I Am | Victo | CD 032
Child's Play
Chick Corea Electric Band | Inside Out | GRP | GRP 96012
Ralph Towner-John Abercrombie | Five Years Later | ECM | 1207
Chile And Beans O'Voutee
Poncho Sanchez Band With Tito Puente | Chile Con Soul | Concord | CCD 4406
Chill
Joshua Redman Quartet | MoodSwing | Warner | 9362-45643-2
Teo Macero And His Orchestra | Impressions Of Charles Mingus | Palo Alto | PA 8046
Chil-Lee
Jimmy Lunceford And His Orchestra | Rhythm Business | Hep | 1013
Chilli Peppers
David Fathead Newman Quintet | Chillin' | HighNote Records | HCD 7036
Chillin'
Art Lande Trio | Skylight | ECM | 1208
Chillum
Andrew Hill Quartet | Shades | Soul Note | 121113-2
Chim Chim Cheree
John Coltrane Quartet | The Best Of John Coltrane-His Greatest Years, Vol. 2 | MCA | AS 9223
Wes Montgomery With The Oliver Nelson Orchestra | Goin' Out Of My Head | CTI Records | PDCTI 1107-2
Chime This
Michael Brecker Group | The Cost Of Living | Jazz Door | JD 1260
Chimes
Sam Morrison Group | Natural Layers | Chiaroscuro | CR 184
Chimes Blues
Chris Barber's Jazz Band | The Great Re-Union Concert | Intercord | 157011
Dutch Swing College Band | Digital Date | Philips | 834087-2
Chimes In Blues
Sonny Simmons Group | Backwoods Suite | West Wind | WW 2074
Chin Lang
Lonnie Plaxico Group | Plaxico | Muse | MCD 5389
China Boy
Bechet-Spanier Big Four | Spreadin Joy (Original Recordings 1940-50) | Naxos Jazz | 8.120531 CD
Benny Goodman Quartet | Welcome To Jazz: Benny Goodman | Koch Records | 321 973 D1
Benny Goodman Trio | Jazz Drumming Vol.1(1927-1937) | Fenn Music | FJD 2701
The Benny Goodman Trio And Quartet Sessions Vol.1-After You've Gone | Bluebird | ND 85631
Bud Freeman And His Summa Cum Laude Orchestra | A String Of Swingin' Pearls | RCA | 2113035-2
Frankfurt Swing All Stars | Jive At Five | L+R Records | CDLR 40025
Glenn Hardman And His Hammond Five | Lester Young:The Complete1936-1951 Group Sessions(Studio Recordings-Master Takes),Vol.1 | Blue Moon | BMCD 1001
Henry Red Allen Band With Jack Teagarden | At Newport | Verve | 817792-1 IMS
Lionel Hampton With The Oscar Peterson Quartet | Compact Jazz: Lionel Hampton | Verve | 833287-2
Oscar Peterson Trio | The Complete Young Oscar Peterson(1945-1949) | RCA | 2122612-2
Masters Of Jazz Vol.7 | RCA | NL 89721 DP
Sidney Bechet Quartet | Sidney Bechet Sessions | Storyville | SLP 4028
Stephane Grappelli And His Hot Four | Jazz In Paris:Django Reinhardt-Swing From Paris | EmArCy | 159853-2 PMS
Django Reinhardt Vol. 1 | Decca | 180020 AG
The New York Allstars | Randy Sandke Meets Bix Beiderbecke | Nagel-Heyer | CD 3002
The Rosenberg Trio | Tribute To Django Reinhardt | EmArCy | 9811568
The Tremble Kids All Stars | Dixieland At Its Best | BELL Records | BLR 89091
China Boy(alt.take)
Muggsy Spanier And His V-Disc All Stars | Muggsy Spanier And Bud Freeman:V-Discs 1944-45 | Jazz Unlimited | JUCD 2049
China Boy(false start 1)
Muggsy Spanier And Bud Freeman:V-Discs 1944-45 | Jazz Unlimited | JUCD 2049
China Boy(false start 2)
Muggsy Spanier And Bud Freeman:V-Discs 1944-45 | Jazz Unlimited | JUCD 2049
China Boy(false start 3)
David Murray Octet | Dark Star(The Music Of The Grateful Dead) | Astor Place | TCD 4002
China Nights
Cal Tjader With The Lalo Schifrin Orchestra | Several Shades Of Jade/Breeze From The East | Verve | 537083-2
China Party
Lionel Hampton And His All Stars | Masters Of Jazz Vol.8 | RCA | NL 89540 DP
Chinatown
George Lewis Ragtime Jazz Band Of New Orleans | The Oxford Series Vol.14 | American Music | AMCD-34
Rahn Burton Trio | The Poem | DIW | DIW 610 CD
Südpool Jazz Project IV | Südpool Jazz Project IV-Quartet | L+R Records | CDLR 45091
Alex Welsh And His Band | Wonderful Dixieland Vol.2 | Sonia | CD 77269
Chinatown My Chinatown
George Girard & His New Orleans Five | Sounds Of New Orleans Vol.6 | Storyville | STCD 6013
Louis Armstrong And His All Stars | Louis Armstrong | Forlane | UCD 19002
The Alex Welsh Legacy Band | The Sound Of Alex Vol.1 | Nagel-Heyer | CD 070
The Mills Brothers | Four Boys And A Guitar | CBS | CK 57713
Chinese Lamp
Alvino Rey And His Orchestra | The Uncollected:Alvino Rey,Vol.2 | Hindsight | HSR 167
Chinesisches Gedicht No.3
Yusef Lateef Quartet | Blues For The Orient | Prestige | P 24035
Chinoir
Duke Ellington And His Orchestra | The Afro-Eurasian Eclipse-A Suite In Eight Parts | Original Jazz Classics | OJCCD 645-2(F 9498)
Chinoiserie
Jazz Collection:Duke Ellington | Laserlight | 24369
Lincoln Center Jazz Orchestra | Live In Swing City-Swingin' With Duke | CBS | CK 69898
Chinq Miau
Amalgam | Another Time | View | VS 100 IMS
Chippie
Ornette Coleman Quintet | Something Else | Contemporary | C 7551
This Is Jazz All Stars | World's Greatest Jazz Concert Vol.1 | Jazzology | JCD-301
Chippyn'
Elmo Hope Quintet | Trio And Quartet | Blue Note | 784438-2
Chips
Woody Herman's Four Chips | Boogie Woogie-Great Original Performances 1928-1941 | CDS Records Ltd. | RPCD 601
Chiquilin De Bachin
Charlie Byrd Trio | Byrd By The Sea | Fantasy | F 9466
Chiquito Loco
Shorty Rogers And His Giants | The Big Shorty Rogers Express | RCA | 2118519-2
Shorty Rogers And His Orchestra Feat. The Giants | Short Stops | RCA | NL 85917(2)
Chiri-Biri-Bin
Alberta Hunter With Buster Bailey's Blues Blasters | Songs We Taught Your Mother | Original Blues Classics | OBCCD 520-2
Chirpin' The Blues
Alberta Hunter With The Charlie Shavers Quartet | Charlie Shavers And The Blues Singers 1938-1939 | Timeless | CBC 1-025
Chisa
Dollar(Abdullah Ibrahim) Brand Group | African River | Enja | ENJ-6018 2
The Brazz Brothers | Ngoma | Laika Records | 35101562
Abdullah Ibrahim | Fats Duke And Monk | Sackville | SKCD2-3048
Chit Chattin'
Herbie Nichols Trio | Herbie Nichols Trio | Blue Note | 300098(1519)
Chitlin's
Ken McIntyre Trio With Strings | Ken McIntyre:The Complete United Artists Sessions | Blue Note | 857200-2
Chittham Irangaayo
Neal Hefti Sextet | The Changing Face Of Harlem, Vol. 2 | Savoy | SJL 2224 (801200)
Chittlins Con Carne
Kenny Burrell Quintet | Midnight Blue | Blue Note | 495335-2
Cordon Blue | Blue Note | 789915-2
Ch'l Energy
Paul Giger Trio | Alpstein | ECM | 1426(847940-2)
Chlauseschuppel
Vienna Art Choir | From No Art To Mo-(z)-Art | Moers Music | 02002 CD
Chloe
Art Tatum | Art Tatum:Complete Original American Decca Recordings | Definitive Records | DRCD 11200
Cal Tjader's Modern Mambo Quintet(Sextet) | Mambo With Tjader | Original Jazz Classics | OJCCD 271-2(F 3202)
Charlie Mariano Sextet | Charlie Mariano Plays | Fresh Sound Records | FSR-CD 115(882423)
Duke Ellington And His Orchestra | The Indispensable Duke Ellington Vol.5/6 | RCA | ND 89750
Jimmy Slyde With The Milt Buckner Trio | Special Tap Dance-Four Dancing Masters | Black & Blue | BLE 191652
Ken Colyer's All Stars | The Sunny Side Of Ken Colyer | Upbeat Jazz | URCD 113
Louis Armstrong With Gordon Jenkins And His Orchestra And Choir | Louis Armstrong-All Time Greatest Hits | MCA | MCD 11032
Nat Adderley Quartet | Naturally! | Original Jazz Classics | OJCCD 1088-2(JLP 947)
Old Merrytale Jazz Band | 25 Jahre Old Merrytale Jazzband Hamburg | Intercord | 155043
Chloe (Song Of The Swamp)
Duke Ellington And His Famous Orchestra | Duke Ellington:Ko-Ko | Dreyfus Jazz Line | FDM 36717-2
Duke Ellington:The Blanton-Webster Band | Bluebird | 21 13181-2
Ben Webster-Cotton Tail | RCA | 63667902
Chloé Meets Gershwin
Michel Petrucciani Sextet | Both Worlds | Dreyfus Jazz Line | FDM 36590-2
Art Tatum | Art Tatum:Complete Original American Decca Recordings | Definitive Records | DRCD 11200
Chloe(Song Of The Swamp)
Jutta Hipp Quintet | Cool Dogs & Two Oranges | L+R Records | LR 41006
Chocolate Chip
Trio Concepts | Trio Concepts More | yvp music | CD 3019
Chocolate Rock
Cannonball Adderley With The Bill Russo Orchestra | Julian Cannonball Adderley And Strings/Jump For Joy | Verve | 528699-2
Chocolate Shake
Duke Ellington And His Orchestra | The Indispensable Duke Ellington,Vol.7/8 | RCA | ND 89274
Jean-Paul Bourelly & The BluWave Bandits | Rock The Cathartic Spirits:Vibe Music And The Blues! | DIW | DIW 911 CD
Chocomotive
Alix Combelle Et Son Orchestre | Buck Clayton:Buck Special | Vogue | 2111513-2
Chodhanai Thanthu
Sabu L. Martinez Group | Palo Congo | Blue Note | 522665-2
Choferito-Plena
Gust Williams Tsilis Quintet | Sequestered Days | Enja | ENJ-6094 2
Choices
Michael Brecker Group | The Cost Of Living | Jazz Door | JD 1260
Choir
James Newton | Flutes! | Circle Records | RK 7-7677/7 IMS
Choisya
Irene Schweizer | Hexensabbat | FMP | 0500
Chokr
Mongo Santamaria Orchestra | Skins | Milestone | MCD 47038-2
Choo Choo Ch' Boogie
Louis Jordan Quintet | Great Rhythm & Blues-Vol.1 | Bulldog | BDL 1000
Choose Now
Tadd Dameron And His Orchestra | Clifford Brown Memorial | Original Jazz Classics | OJC20 017-2(P 7055)
Clifford Brown Memorial | Original Jazz Classics | OJC20 017-2(P 7055)
Choose Now(alt.take)
Art Ensemble Of Chicago | Among The People | Praxis | CM 103
Chop Suey
Slide Hampton Quartet | Phil Woods/Slide Hampton 1968 Jazz | Jazztime(EMI) | 781253-2
Chopiniana
Neal Kirkwood Octet | Neal Kirkwood Octet | Timescrapper | TSCR 9612
Chopin's Waterloo
Oscar Peterson-Clark Terry Duo | Oscar Peterson & Clark Terry | Original Jazz Classics | OJCCD 806-2(2310742)
Chops
First Brass | First Brass | M.A Music | NU 158-3
Chops A La Salsa
Nils Wogram Quartet | Round Trip | Enja | ENJ-9307 2
Chopska
Art Kassel And His 'Kassels-In-The-Air' Orchestra | The Uncollected:Art Kassel, Vol.2 | Hindsight | HSR 170
Choqueno(For Chuck Smart)
Cassiber | Man Or Monkey | Riskant | 6.28624
Choral
Charlie Mariano Quartet | Warum Bist Du Traurig(Why Are You So Sad) | B&W Present | BW 019
Dino Saluzzi | Andina | ECM | 1375(837186-2)
Gary Burton Quartet | The New Quartet | ECM | 1030
Jacques Loussier Trio | Portrait | Decca | 6.28511 DO
Olaf Tarenskeen | Decisions | Acoustic Music Records | 319.1144.2
Thomas Horstmann-Markus Zaja | Somewhere | Factory Outlet Records | 400004-2
Wolf Mayer Dialects | Roots And Wings | Triptychon | 300201
Holger Mantey | Piano Total | NCC Jazz | NCC 8506
Choral 'Erbarm Dich Mein O Herre Gott'(BWV 721)
Wolf Mayer Dialects | Roots And Wings | Triptychon | 300201
Choral Fantasie I
Manfred Schulze Bläserquintett | Viertens | FMP | 1230
Choral Jesus Bleibet Meine Freude(BWV 147)
Jacques Loussier Trio | Play Bach No.2 | Decca | 157562-2
Swingle Singers | Jazz Sebastian Bach Vol.2 | Philips | 542553-2
Jacques Loussier Trio | Play Bach | Accord | 500372
Choral No.1 'Wachet Auf Ruft Uns Die Stimme'(BWV 645)
Swingle Singers | Jazz Sebastian Bach | Philips | 542552-2
Jacques Loussier Trio | Play Bach No.4 | Decca | 157893-2
Choral No.16 'Christ Unser Herr Zum Jordan Kam'(BWV 684)
Play Bach | Accord | 500372
Choral Nr.1 Wachet Auf Ruft Uns Die Stimme(BWV 645)
Play Bach No.5 | Decca | 159194-2
Choral Nr.1(BWV 645)
Anders Jormin With Brass Quartet | Xieyi | ECM | 1762(013998-2)
Choral(1)
Jacques Loussier Trio | Play Bach No.1 | Festival | FLD 725
Choral(2)
Chris Potter Quartet | Moving On | Concord | CCD 4723
Chorale
Dave Brubeck Quintet | Reunion | Original Jazz Classics | OJCCD 150-2
Jacques Loussier Trio | Focus On Jacques Loussier | Decca | FOS-R 5/6
Paul Giger Trio | Vindonissa | ECM | 1836(066069-2)
Slide Hampton Orchestra | World Of Trombones | Black Lion | CD 877641-2
Chris Potter & Jazzpar Septet | This Will Be | Storyville | STCD 4245
Chorale-
Kamikaze Ground Crew | The Scenic Route | New World Records | 80400-2
Chorale No.1
Jacques Loussier Trio | Play Bach No.2 | Accord | 500182
Chorale(BWV 859)
The Best Of Play Bach | Philips | 824664-2
Chorale:Jesu You Of Man's Desiring
Willem Breuker Kollektief And Djazzex | Dance Plezier-Joy Of Dance | BVHAAST | CD 9513
Chorar
Christy Doran | What A Band | Hat Art | CD 6105
Chordless
Nat Adderley And His Orchestra | Work Songs | Milestone | M 47047
Chords
Heinz Sauer Quartet | Metal Blossoms | L+R Records | LR 40019
Chorinho Para Ele
Galliano-Portal | Blow Up | Dreyfus Jazz Line | FDM 36589-2
Chorinho Pra Ele
David Chesky-Romero Lubambo Duo | The New York Chorinhos | Chesky | JD 39
Chorinho(Speedy Gonzales)
Live Recordings From The Streets | Fun Horns Live In South America-Natural Music | KlangRäume | 30060
Choro
Vince Guaraldi-Bola Sete Quartet | From All Sides | Original Jazz Classics | OJCCD 989-2(F 3-362)
Choro Porteno
Gilberto Gil With Band | Montreux Jazz Festival | ACT | 9001-2
Chorovod
Irakere | Yemayá | Blue Note | 498239-2
Chorrino
Cecil Taylor Unit | Dark To Themselves | Enja | ENJ-2084 2
Chorus Of Seed
Blue Box | Blue Box Live:Time We Sign | TipToe | TIP-888813 2
Chorus(part 1 & 2)
Marc Ribot Y Los Cubanos Postizos | The Proshetic Cubans | Atlantic | 7567-83116-2
Choserito Plena
| All At Once At Any Time | Victo | CD 029
Chovendo Na Roseira(Double Rainbow)
Carlos Barbosa-Lima/Sharon Isbin Duo | Brazil With Love | Concord | CCD 4320
Sarah Vaughan With Band | Copacabana | Pablo | 2312125
Benny Carter With The Rutgers University Orchestra | Harlem Renaissance | Limelight | 844299-2 IMS
Chris 'N' Diz
JATP Jam Session | Lester Young 'Rarities' | Moon Records | MCD 048-2
Chris's Blues
Chico Hamilton Quintet | Newport Jazz Festival 1958,July 3rd-6th Vol.2:Mulligan The Main Man | Phontastic | NCD 8814
Chrissie
Stars Of Faith | Black Nativity | Black & Blue | BLE 59.065 2
Christal Walls
Gianluigi Trovesi Trio | Les Boites A Musique | SPLASC(H) Records | CD H 152-2
Christel's Theme
Flip Phillips Sextet | A Real Swinger | Concord | CJ 358
Christiane
Bishop Norman Williams Group | The One Mind Experience-The Bishop | Evidence | TR 101
Christina
Christoph Spendel Group | Raspail Hotel | Trion | 3104
George Wallington And His Band | George Wallington Showcase | Blue Note | BNJ 71003
Christina's Sang
Eugen Cicero-Decebal Badila | Swinging Piano Classics | IN+OUT Records | 77047-2
Christina's Song
Amina Claudine Myers Trio | The Circle Of Time | Black Saint | 120078-2
Christmas Comes To Us All Once Year
Joe Turner With Pete Johnson And His Orchestra | Tell Me Pretty Baby | Arhoolie | CD 333
Christmas Dreams
Trombone Summit | Jazz-Club: Trombone | Verve | 840040-2
Christmas In New Orleans
Jan Harrington Sextet | Jan Harrington's Christmas In New Orleans | Nagel-Heyer | NHR SP 4
Jim Galloway-Jay McShann Quartet | Jim & Jay's Christmas | Sackville | SKCD2-3054
Maryland Jazzband Of Cologne feat. Papa Don Vappie And Erny Elly | Christmas In New Orleans | Maryland Records | MJCD 0895
Christmas Is Coming
Ulli Bögershausen | Christmas Carols | Laika Records | 35101622
Christmas Lullaby
Mel Tormé And His Trio With The Cincinnati Sinfonietta | Christmas Songs- | Telarc Digital | CD 83315
Christmas Night In Harlem
The Orchestra | New Skies | dacapo | DCCD 9463
Christmas Quarrels
Dave Liebman Group | New Vista | Arkadia Jazz | 71041
Christmas Song
Niels Lan Doky Quartet | Friendship | Milestone | MCD 9183-2
Christmas Time In New Orleans
Kenny Drew Jr. Trio | Jazz City Christmas,Vol.1 | Jazz City | 660.53.006
Christmas Time Is Here
Vince Guaraldi Trio | A Charlie Brown Christmas | Fantasy | FSA 8431-6
Vince Guaraldi Group | Charlie Brown's Holiday Hits | Fantasy | FCD 9682-2
Christmas Time Is Here(vocal)
Vince Guaraldi Trio | A Charlie Brown Christmas | Fantasy | FSA 8431-6
Things | Blues For The Last Punk | Jazzpoint | JP 1026 MC
Christo Redentor
Duke Pearson Quintet | The Blue Testament | Blue Note | 780703-2
Christopher Columbus
Humphrey Lyttelton And His Band | Compact Jazz: Best Of Dixieland | Verve | 831375-2
Jimmy Archey With Michel Attenoux And His Orchestra | Jazz In Paris:Classic Jazz At Saint-Germain-Des-Prés | EmArCy | 013045-2
The Royal Air Force HQ Bomber Command Sextet | RAF HQ Bomber Command Sextet | Celebrity | CYCD 74508
Wild Bill Davison & Papa Bue | Wild Bill Davison & Papa Bue | Storyville | SLP 250
Christopher Columbus-
Benny Goodman And His Orchestra | Live At Carnegie Hall-40th Anniversary Concert | Decca | 6.28451 DP
Christopher Jr.

Christopher Murrell-Robert Irving III | Full Circle:Gospels And Spirituals | Nagel-Heyer | NHR SP 3

Christopher Murrell Speaking
Sonny Stitt-Sadik Hakim Quartet | Sonny Stitt Meets Sadik Hakim | Progressive | PRO 7034 IMS

Christopher's Bossa
Kenny Barron Group | Things Unsee | Verve | 537315-2

Chromatic Fantasy
Jacques Loussier Trio | The Best Of Play Bach | Philips | 824664-2
New Orleans Klezmer Allstars | Manichalfwitz | Gert Town Records | GT-1117

Chromatic Mousetrap
Franco D'Andrea Trio | Franco D'Andrea Trio | yvp music | 3021

Chromosphere
John Coltrane Sextet | Coltrane | Original Jazz Classics | OJC20 020-2

Chronic Blues
John Coltrane-The Prestige Recordings | Prestige | 16 PCD 4405-2
David Moss Duos | Time Stories | Intakt Records | CD 054

Chronology
Larry Schneider Quartet | Ornettology | Steeplechase | SCCD 31461
Ornette Coleman Quartet | The Shape Of Jazz To Come | Atlantic | 7567-81339-2

Chrysanthemen Blues
Johannes Rediske Quintet | Re-Disc Bounce | Bear Family Records | BCD 16119 AH
Ken Colyer's Jazzmen | Ken Colyer's Jazzmen On Tour | GHB Records | BCD 16

Chuckin'
Clark Terry Septet | Clark Terry | Verve | 537754-2

Chuereihe
The Contemporary Alphorn Orchestra | Mytha | Hat Art | CD 6110

Chug Chug Boogie
Gerry Mulligan Concert Jazz Band | The Complete Verve Gerry Mulligan Concert Band | Verve | 9860613

Chuggin'
Verve Jazz Masters 36:Gerry Mulligan | Verve | 523342-2
Gerry Mulligan Orchestra | New-York December 1960 | Jazz Anthology | JA 5236

Chumbida
Blind Blake | Blind Blake-That Lovin' I Crave | Biograph | BLP 12050

Chun-King
Landes Jugend Jazz Orchester Hessen | Touch Of Lips | hr music.de | hrmj 004-01 CD

Chunky
Marcos Valle With Orchestra | Samba '68 | Verve | 559516-2

Chup Chup Away
D.D.Jackson Group | Anthem | RCA | 2663606-2

Church
James Blood Ulmer Trio | Odyssey | CBS | 25602

Church Bell Tone
Sauter-Finegan Orchestra | The Return Of The Doodletown Fifers | EMI Records | ED 2607691

Churchhouse Blues
God Is My Co-Pilot | Mir Shlufn Nisht | Avant | AVAN 032

Churnin' Man Blues
Frank Lowe And The Memphis Four | Fresh | Black Lion | BLCD 760214

Ciacona
George Gruntz Quartet | Doldinger Jubilee | Atlantic | ATL 60073

Ciacona(from Partita 2)
Frank Kuruc Band | Limits No Limits | Edition Musikat | EDM 023

Ciano Marco
Mal Waldron Trio | Impressions | Original Jazz Classics | OJCCD 132-2(NJ 8242)

Ciao Ciao
Stanley Turrentine Quartet | The Roots Of Acid Jazz | Impulse(MCA) | IMP 12042
Let It Go | Impulse(MCA) | IMP 11042

Cicconi
Peter Rühmkorf Mit Dem Michael Naura Trio | Kein Apolloprogramm Für Lyrik | ECM | 801 SP

Cielito Lindo
Ed Thigpen Quintet | Out Of The Storm | Verve | 557100-2
Wilbur DeParis And His New New Orleans Band | Wilbur DeParis At Symphony Hall | Atlantic | 7567-82268-2

Cielito Lindo-
L.A.4 | The L.A.Four Scores! | Concord | CCD 6008

Ciftik
Tete Montoliu | Yellow Dolphin Street/Catalonian Folk Songs | Timeless | CD SJP 107/116

Ci-lc für Flöte uns Viola
Slow Poke | Redemption | Intuition Records | INT 3260-2

Cilantro
Passport | Garden Of Eden | Atlantic | 2292-44147-2

Cildren's Dance
Big Joe Turner With Axel Zwingenberger | Boogie Woogie Jubilee | Vagabond | VRCD 8.81010

Cimarrob St.Breakdown
Toto Blanke-Rudolf Dasek | Mona Lisa | ALISO Records | AL 1037

Cimicurri
Don Pullen' s African-Brazilian Connection | Kele Mou Bana | Blue Note | 798166-2

Cincinnati Baby
Jesse Fuller | Jesse Fuller's Favorites | Original Blues Classics | OBCCD 528-2(P 7368)

Cincinnati Blues
Jesse Fuller One Man Band | Brother Lowdown | Fantasy | F 24707

Cinco Minutos Sin Ti
Tom Harrell Group | The Art Of Rhythm | RCA | 2668924-2

Cinderella
Poncho Sanchez And His Orchestra | A Night At Kimball's East | Concord | CCD 4472

Cinderella Song
Glenn Miller And His Orchestra | The Glenn Miller Collection | RCA | ???

Cinderella's Curfew
Tony Ortega Octet | Jazz For Young Moderns | Fresh Sound Records | FSR 2006(Bethlehem BCP 79)

Cinderella's Waltz
Louie Bellson Big Band | Dynamite! | Concord | CCD 4105

Cindy
Traubeli Weiß Ensemble | Guitar Moments | Take Twelve On CD | TT 006-2

Cindy Cindy
Deborah Henson-Conant | Alter Ego | Laika Records | 35100962
Cecil Taylor/Buell Neidlinger Trio | New York City R&B | Candid | CCD 79017

Cindy's Main Mood
Chris Potter Quintet | Presenting Chriss Potter | Criss Cross | Criss 1067

Cinema Paradiso(Love Theme)
Charlie Haden-Pat Metheny | Beyond The Missouri Sky | Verve | 537130-2

Cinema Paradiso(Main Theme)
Sammy Price | Jazz In Paris:Sammy Price And Doc Cheatham Play Gershwin | EmArCy | 018426-2

Cinema's Boogie
Gato Barbieri Quartet | In Search Of The Mystery | ESP Disk | ESP 1049-2

Cinnamon And Clove
Dom Um Romao Group | Dom Um Romao | Muse | MCD 6012

Cintec De Legan
Gateway | In The Moment | ECM | 1574(529346-2)

Cinucen
Richard Todd Quintet | Rickter Scale | GM Recordings | GM 3015 CD(882952)

Ciranda Nordestina
Egberto Gismonti | Works | ECM | 823269-2

Ciranda(1)
Marcio Tubino Group | Festa Do Olho | Organic Music | ORGM 9723

Ciranda(2)
Ahmad Mansour Quintet | Penumbra | Timeless | CD SJP 404

Circa
Tony Williams Lifetime | Spectrum:The Anthology | Verve | 537075-2

Circa 1990
Ego | Verve | 559512-2

Circa 45
Dave Brubeck Orchestra | Two Generations Of Brubeck | Atlantic | SD 1645

Circeo
Chico Freeman Quartet | No Time Left | Black Saint | 120036-2

Circle
George Cables Trio | Circles | Contemporary | C 14015
Miles Davis Quintet | Miles Smiles | CBS | CK 65682
Miles Davis Quintet 1965-1968 | CBS | C6K 67398
Nils Wogram Quartet | Speed Life | Enja | ENJ-9346 2
Ron Jackson Quartet | Thinking Of You | Muse | MCD 5515

Circle Dance-
Marilyn Crispell-Gary Peacock-Paul Motian | Amaryllis | ECM | 1742(013400-2)
Jay Clayton And Her Quintet | Circle Dancing | Sunnyside | SSC 1076 D

Circle In The Round
Miles Davis Sextet | Circle In The Round | CBS | 467898-2
Circle In The Round | CBS | 467898-2
Vince Jones Group | It All Ends Up In Tears | Intuition Records | INT 3069-2

Circle In The Square
Matthias Frey Group | Liquid Crystal | Inak | 9026

Circle K
Daniel Schnyder Septet | The City | Enja | ENJ-6002 2

Circle Nightmare
Christy Doran-John Wolf Brennan | Henceforward | Line Records | COCD 9.00871 O

Circle Of Coherence
Duke Ellington And His Orchestra | Such Sweet Thunder | CBS | CK 65568

Circle Of Fourth
Such Sweet Thunder | CBS | CK 65568

Circle Of Fourth(stereo-LP-master)
Hamiet Bluiett Group | ...You Don't Need To Know...If You Have To Ask | Tutu Records | 888128-2*

Circle Of Prayer
Ken Peplowski Quintet | The Natural Touch | Concord | CCD 4517

Circle Waltz
Daniel Humair Trio | Triple Hip Trip | Owl Records | 014 CD

Circle(Solo)
Bryan Lee And The Jump Street Five | The Blues Is... | Blues Beacon | BLU-1012 2

Circles
Cindy Blackman Quintet | Code Red | Muse | MCD 5365
Maarten Van Regteren | Live Performances | FMP | SAJ 10
Paul Quinichette Septet | On The Sunny Side | Original Jazz Classics | OJCCD 076-2(P 7103)
Dennis Moorman | Circles Of Destiny | India Navigation | IN 1055

Circlesong No.5(Where To Go...)
Lennie Niehaus Octet | Lennie Niehaus Vol.3:The Octet No.2 | Contemporary | COP 017

Circling The Square
Sergio Vesely With Band | Personas | Messidor | 15914

Circuito
Gonzalo Rubalcaba | Imagine | Blue Note | 830491-2

Circuito(II)
Gonzalo Rubalcaba Quartet | Rapsodia | Blue Note | 828264-2

Circuito(III)
Gonzalo Rubalcaba & Cuban Quartet | Antiguo | Blue Note | 837717-2

Circuito(IV)
Dean Magraw Group | Kitchen Man | Acoustic Music Records | 319.1133.2

Circus
Ed Bickert Trio | Third Floor Richard | Concord | CCD 4380
Howard Riley Trio | Flight | FMR | FMR CD 26

Circus '68 '69
Jim Hall Sextet | Textures | Telarc Digital | CD 83402

Ciribiribin
Benny Goodman And His Orchestra | Benny Goodman Forever | RCA | NL 89955(2) DP
Harry James And His Orchestra | The Golden Trumpet Of Harry James | London | 820178-2 IMS
Trumpet Blues:The Best Of Harry James | Capitol | 521224-2
Harry James:Concerto For Orchestra 1939-1941 | Naxos Jazz | 8.120618

Ciruja(to Paul Montero)
The Saxophone Choir | The Saxophone Choir | Soul Note | 121129-2

Cisco
Dom Um Romao With Orchestra | Hotmosphere | Original Jazz Classics | OJCCD 977-2(2310777)

Cissy Strut
J.C. Dook Quartet | Travelin' Man | Organic Music | ORGM 9734
Jaco Pastorius Trio | Live In New York City Volume Two | Big World | BW 1002

Cité De La Musique
Branford Marsalis Trio | The Beautiful Ones Are Not Yet Born | CBS | 468896-2

Citrus To Ceder-
Peter Lemer Quintet | Local Colour | ESP Disk | ESP 1057-2

City Boy
Mahalia Jackson | Amazing Grace | Intercord | 125402

City Dance
Chick Corea Electric Band | The Chick Corea Electric Band | GRP | GRP 95352

City Gate
George Adams-Don Pullen Quartet | City Gates | Timeless | SJP 181

City Home
Mose Allison Trio | High Jinks! The Mose Allison Trilogy | CBS | J3K 64275

City Lights
Breeze | Groovin' Jazz Regensburg | I-Records | IR 319101
Jimmy McGriff Orchestra | City Lights | JAM | 002 IMS
Lee Morgan Sextet | City Lights | Blue Note | 300183(1575)
Oscar Peterson Quartet | Oscar Peterson Live! | Pablo | 2310940-2
Live At The Northsea Jazz Festival | Pablo | 2620115-2

City Monsters
Billy Oskay/Michael O'Domhnaill | Nightnoise | Windham Hill | WD 1031

City Of Eyes
Diederik Wissels Quintet | Kamook | B.Sharp Records | CDS 083

City Of Lights
Geoffrey McCabe Quartet | Teseract Complicity | Timeless | SJP 212

City Scape
Tana Reid Sextet | Passing Thoughts | Concord | CCD 4505

City Speak
Lance Bryant With The Christoph Spendel Trio | West End Avenue II | Nabel Records:Jazz Network | CD 4644

City Speed
Airto Moreira And The Gods Of Jazz | Killer Bees | B&W Present | BW 041

Cityscapes
Alain Everts | Terra Nueva | Acoustic Music Records | 319.1103.2

Ckara's Smile
Singers Unlimited | The Singers Unlimited:Magic Voices | MPS | 539130-2

Clair
A Capella 2 | MPS | 821860-2

Claire
Bireli Lagrene Quartet | My Favorite Django | Dreyfus Jazz Line | FDM 36574-2

Claire De Lune
Jacques Loussier Trio | Jacques Loussier Trio Plays Debussy | Telarc Digital | CD 83511

Claire's Song
Phil Woods Quintet | Mile High Jazz:Live In Denver | Concord | CCD 4739

Clair-Obscur
Duane Eubanks Sextet | My Shining Hour | TCB Records | TCB 99202

Clairvoyance II
Eddie Allen Quintet | R 'N' B | Enja | ENJ-9033 2

Clairvoyant
The Capitol Jazzmen | Jazz:The Essential Collection Vol.3 | IN+OUT Records | 78013-2

Clambake In B-Flat
The Hollywood Session:The Capitol Jazzmen | Jazz Unlimited | JUCD 2044
Sonny Thompson And His Orchestra | Cat On The Keys | Swingtime(Contact) | ST 1027

Clap City
Benny Goodman And His Orchestra | All Of Me | Black Lion | 127034

Clap Hands Here Comes Charlie
Lambert, Hendricks And Ross | The Swingers | Blue Note | AFF 131
Claude Bolling And The Show Biz Band | Swing Party | Decca | 6.22983 AO

Clap Yo' Hands
Dick Hyman | The Gershwin Songbook:Jazz Variations | Musicmasters | 65094-2

Clapperclowe
Dizzy Gillespie Quintet | Dizzy Gillespie Plays In Paris | Vogue | 21409402

Claquent Les Voiles
Bill Potts And His Orchestra | The Jazz Soul Of Porgy And Bess | Capitol | 795132-2

Clara Linda
Winanda Del Sur | Luny Y Mar | Challenge | CHR 70037

Clara,Don't You Be Downhearted
Bik Bent Braam | Howdy | Timeless | CD SJP 388

Clarabell
Eddie Daniels Group | Blackwood | GRP | GRP 95842

Clarence's Place
Louis Hayes Quintet | Quintessential Lou | TCB Records | TCB 99652

Claressence
Dave Holland Quintet | Extended Play | ECM | 1864/65(038505-2)
Maria Joao With Band | Fábula | Verve | 533216-2

Claridade
Clarinet Summit | Clarinet Summit In Concert At The Public Theater | India Navigation | IN 1062 CD

Clarinet Games
Duke Ellington And His Famous Orchestra | Duke Ellington's Jungle Style | Black & Blue | BLE 59.234 2

Clarinet Lament
Duke Ellington And His Orchestra | Jazz:The Essential Collection Vol.2 | IN+OUT Records | 78012-2

Clarinet Lament(Barney's Concerto)
Buddy Tate With The Humphrey Lyttelton Band | Buddy Tate With Humphrey Lyttelton And Ruby Braff | Jazz Colours | 874713-2

Clarinet Marmalade
Fred Elizalde And His Orchestra | An Evening At The Savoy | Decca | DDV 5011/12
Louis Armstrong And His All Stars | Ambassador Satch | CBS | CK 64926
Louis Delisle's Band | Echoes From New Orleans | Storyville | SLP 212
Pete Daily's Rhythm Kings | Jazz Band Ball | Good Time Jazz | GTCD 12005-2
The Royal Air Force HQ Bomber Command Sextet | RAF HQ Bomber Command Sextet | Celebrity | CYCD 74508

Clarinet Zone
Benny Goodman Trio | Big Band Bounce And Boogie:Clarinetitis/The Young BG-Benny Goodman | Affinity | AFS 1018

Clarion Call
Frank Gordon Sextet | Clarion Echoes | Soul Note | 121096-2

Clark Bars
George Wein And The Newport All Stars | Swing That Music | CBS | CK 53317

Clark:
Clark Terry Orchestra | Clark Terry | Swing | SW 8406 IMS

Clasanova
Jacques Pirotton Trio | Soty | B.Sharp Records | CDS 087

Class In Swing:
Amiri Baraka with David and Steve McCall | New Music-New Poetry | India Navigation | IN 1048

Class Trip
Don Redman And His Orchestra | The Complete McKinney's Cotton Pickers Vol.5 Plus Don Redman & His Orchestra | RCA | NL 89161 (809233)

Classic Emotion
Ulli Bögershausen | Ageless Guitar Solos | Laika Records | 8695071

Classical Gas
Mike Garson | Avant Garson | Contemporary | C 14003

Classifica Avulsa
James Booker | The Piano Prince From New Orleans | Aves | 146509

Claude
Gary Burton Quartet With Eberhard Weber | Passengers | ECM | 1092(835016-2)

Claude And Betty
Claude Williamson Trio | Salute To Bud | Affinity | AFF 72

Claudette Colbert
Gary Smulyan Quartet | Homage | Criss Cross | Criss 1068

Claudia
Steve Turre With String Quartet | In The Spur Of The Moment | Telarc Digital | CD 83484

Claudia Luna
Danilo Perez Quintet | Danilo Perez | Novus | 4163148-2

Clave For Collin
Simon Nabatov, String Gang & Percussion | Inside Lookin' Out | Tutu Records | 888104-2*
Poncho Sanchez And His Orchestra | A Night With Poncho Sanchez Live:Bailar | Concord | CCD 4558

Clawback
Screamin' Jay Hawkins & The Chicken Hawks | Live And Crazy | Black & Blue | BLE 59.731 2

Claw-Til-Da
Yosuke Yamashita Trio | Clay | Enja | 2052 (807597)

Clay's Blues
Howard Alden-Dan Barrett Quintet | The A.B.Q Salutes Buck Clayton | Concord | CCD 4395

Clean
Jack Wilkins Alien Army | Alien Army | Musicmasters | 65049-2

Cleanhead Blues
Eddie Cleanhead Vinson And The Muse All Stars | Lave At Sandy's | Muse | MR 5208
Eddie Cleanhead Vinson Orchestra | Back In Town | Charly | CRB 1046

Cleaning Up For Jenny-
Pee Wee Ellis Quartet | Sepia Tonality | Minor Music | 801040

Cleaning Windows
Tim Berne Quartet | Mutant Variations | Soul Note | 121091-2

Clear The Bridge
Dexter Gordon Quartet | Dexter Gordon | Blue Note | 84502

Clear-Cut Boogie
Fats Waller | Fats At The Organ | ASV | AJA 5007

Clementine
Duke Ellington And His Famous Orchestra | Passion Flower 1940-46 | Bluebird | 63 66616-2
Ella Fitzgerald With The Duke Ellington Orchestra | The Complete Ella Fitzgerald Song Books of Harold Arlen, Irving Berlin, Duke Ellington, George & Ira Gershwin, Jerome Kern, Johnny Mercer, Cole Porter And Rogers & Hart | Verve | 519832-2
Lonnie Johnson | Blues Masters Vol.4 | Storyville | STCD 8004

Cleopatra And The African Knight
Johnny 'Hammond' Smith Quartet | Open House | Milestone | MCD 47089-2

Machito And His Afro-Cuban Salseros | Mucho Macho | Pablo | 2625712-2
Clic
Harold Danko Quartet | The First Love Song | Jazz City | 660.53.011
Clicky Clacky
Bobby Jaspar All Stars | Bobby Jaspar | Fresh Sound Records | 84063(Barclay)
Cliff Cliff
Clifford Jordan Quintet | Cliff Craft | Blue Note | BLP 1582
Cliff Walk
Billy Barber | Shades Of Gray | dmp Digital Music Productions | CD 445
Cliffhanger
David Moss Duos | Time Stories | Intakt Records | CD 054
Clifford's Kappa
N.Y. Hardbop Quintet | A Mere Bag Of Shells | TCB Records | TCB 20702
Climax
Duncan Swift | Ragtime | Jazz Colours | 874731-2
Climax Rag
Mr.Acker Bilk And His Paramount Jazz Band | New Orleans Days | Lake | LACD 36
Climb Every Mountain
Brad Dutz | Brad Dutz | Nine Winds Records | NWCD 0141
Climbing
Diane Schuur With The Count Basie Orchestra | Diane Shuur & The Count Basie Orchestra | GRP | GRP 95502
Climbing The Mountain
Paul Bley | Lyrics | SPLASC(H) Records | CD H 348-2
Clint
Jeff Berlin | Taking Notes | Denon Compact Disc | CY-18043
Clockwise
Billy Higgins Quartet | Soweto | Red Records | VPA 141
George Benson Quartet | It's Uptown | CBS | 502469-2
Timeless All Stars | It's Timeless | Timeless | CD SJP 178
Clockwork Lemon
Henri Renaud Sextet | Henri Reanaud Trio,Sextet & All Stars | Vogue | 21606382
Cloe
Nico Morelli Trio | Behind The Window | yvp music | CD 3042
Clopin Clopant
Stephane Grappelli Quintet | Hommage A Django Reinhardt | Festival | Album 120
Clo's Blues
Oscar Peterson Quartet With Coleman Hawkins | Des Femmes Disparaissent/Les Tricheurs(Original Soundtracks) | Fontana | 834752-2 PMS
Close
Paul Bley | Lyrics | SPLASC(H) Records | CD H 348-2
Close As Pages In A Book
Jimmy Knepper Quintet | Idol Of The Flies | Affinity | AFF 89
Close Enough For Jazz
Agneta Baumann Group | Sentimental Lady | Touché Music | TMcCD 017
Close Enough For Love
Bruce Dunlap Trio | The Rhythm Of Wings | Chesky | JD 92
Claire Martin With The Jim Mullen Quartet And Special Guests | Devil May Care | Linn Records | AKD 021
Jack Bruce Group | Somethinelse | CMP Records | CMP CD 1001
Monty Alexander | Maybeck Recital Hall Series Volume Forty | Concord | CCD 4658
Stan Getz Quartet | The Dolphin | Concord | CCD 4158
Close Enough For Love-
Arne Birger's Jazzsjak | The Golden Years Of Revival Jazz,Vol.8 | Storyville | STCD 5513
Close Fit Blues
Chris Barber's Jazz Band | The Golden Years Of Revival Jazz,Vol.2 | Storyville | STCD 5507
Clarence Williams' Blue Seven | Clarence Williams Vol.2(1927) | Village(Jazz Archive) | VILCD 022-2
Close Hearing
Sonny Boy Williamson Band | More Real Folk Blues | Chess | CHD 9277(872297)
Close Near
Jimmie Lunceford And His Orchestra | The Golden Swing Years | Storyville | SLP 828
Close Quarters
John Kirby And His Orchestra | TheComplete Una Mae Carlisle(1940-1942) And John Kirby(1941-1942) | RCA | ND 89484
Close To Home
Dirk Strakhof & Batoru | Arabesque | Nabel Records:Jazz Network | CD 4696
Close To The Black Sea
Liam Noble | Close Your Eyes | FMR | FMR CD 25
Close To The Edge
Frank Lewe Quintet | Live From Soundscape | DIW | DIW 399 CD
Close To You
Erroll Garner Sextet | Magician & Gershwin And Kern | Telarc Digital | CD 83337
Peter Herbolzheimer Orchestra | Music For Swinging Dancers Vol.4: Close To You | Koala Records | CD P 12
Earl Hines | Live | Black & Blue | BLE 59.305 2
Close To You Alone
Art Pepper Quartet | One September Afternoon | Original Jazz Classics | OJCCD 678-2(GXY 5141)
Stanley Cowell Trio | Close To You Alone | DIW | DIW 6003 CD
Close Your Eyes
Art Blakey And The Jazz Messengers | Art Blakey & The Jazz Messengers: Olympia, May 13th, 1961 | Laserlight | 36128
Live In Stockholm 1959 | Dragon | DRCD 182
Bob Howard With The Hank Jones Trio | In A Sentimental Mood | Stash Records | ST 266 IMS
Chris Flory Quartet | For All We Know | Concord | CCD 4403
Eric Kloss Quartet | About Time | Prestige | PRCD 24268-2
Frank Wess Meets The Paris-Barcelona Swing Connection | Paris-Barcelona Connection | Fresh Sound Records | FSNT 002 CD
Freddie Brocksieper And His Boys | Freddie's Boogie Blues | Bear Family Records | BCD 16388 AH
Gene Ammons Quintet | Boss Tenor | Original Jazz Classics | OJC20 297-2(P-7180)
Guy Barker With The London Metropolitan Orchestra | What Love Is | EmArCy | 558331-2
Harry Edison-Eddie Lockjaw Davis Quintet | Jawbreakers | Original Jazz Classics | OJCCD 487-2(RLP 9430)
Jason Rebello Group | Keeping Time | Novus | 2112904-2
Lew Stone And His Band | Lew Stone And His Band | Decca | DDV 5005/6 DT
Roy Eldridge-Benny Carter Quintet | The Urban Sessions/New Jazz Sound | Verve | 531637-2
Steve Laury Quartet | Keepin' The Faith | Denon Compact Disc | CY-75283
Close Your Eyes And Listen
Gerry Mulligan/Astor Piazolla Group | Gerry Mulligan/Astor Piazolla 1974 | Accord | 556642
Close Your Eyes(78rpm-take)
Roy Eldridge-Benny Carter Quintet | The Urban Sessions/New Jazz Sound | Verve | 531637-2
Closed Mouth Blues
Yusef Lateef Ensemble | Nocturnes | Atlantic | 7567-81977-2
Closed Space
Maria Joao Quintet | Conversa | Nabel Records:Jazz Network | CD 4628
Closed System
Axel Zwingenberger With The Mojo Blues Band And Red Holloway | Axel Zwingenberger And The Friends Of Boogie Woogie,Vol.8 | Vagabond | VRCD 8.93019
Closedown
Arturo Sandoval Group | Hot House | N2K | 43072
Closer
Paul Bley | Open, To Love | ECM | 1023
Homage To Carla | Owl Records | 013427-2
Paul Bley Quartet | Fragments | ECM | 1320
Paul Bley Trio | Closer | ESP Disk | ESP 1021-2
Joey Baron Quartet | We'll Soon Find Out | Intuition Records | INT 3515-2
Closer Than You Think
Don Byron Quartet | Romance With The Unseen | Blue Note | 499545-2
Closer To Home
Billy Bang | Bangception | HatOLOGY | 517
Closer To The Light
Dizzy Gillespie And His Orchestra | Closer To The Source | Atlantic | 7567-80776-2
Closer To The Source
Deborah Henson-Conant | Just For You | Laika Records | LK 95-063
Closer To You
Naked Music | Laika Records | LK 94-051
Ron McClure Quintet | Closer To Your Tears | Steeplechase | SCCD 31413
Closest To The Sun
Rod Williams Quartet | Destiny Express | Muse | MCD 5412
Closing
Jackie McLean Quartet | Dr. Jackle | Steeplechase | SCCD 36005
Johnny Griffin Quartet | Jazz Life Vol.1:From Village Vanguard | Storyville | 4960753
Closing-
Glenn Miller And The Army Air Force Band | I Sustain The Wings Vol.3(September 1943) | Magic | DAWE 78
Closing Announcement
Duke Ellington And His Orchestra | Duke Ellington In Hamilton | Radiex Music | RDX-1000
Closing Scene
Dee Dee Pierce And His New Orleans Stompers | In Binghampton,N.Y. Vol.Four | American Music | AMCD-82
Closing Theme
Joe Henderson Quintet | At The Lighthouse | Milestone | M 9028
Roland Kirk Quintet | Petite Fleur | Moon Records | MCD 027-2
Closing Time Blues
The Sauter-Finegan Orchestra | That's All | Magic | DAWE 80
Clothes Line Ballet
Fats Waller | Piano Solos | RCA | ND 89741
Ralph Sutton | Maybeck Recital Hall Series Volume Thirty | Concord | CCD 4586
Ralph Sutton Trio | Ralph Sutton Trio-Sunday Session | Sackville | SKCD2-2044
Cloud Castles
Collin Walcott Quartet | Cloud Dance | ECM | 1062(825469-2)
Cloud Dance
Christopher Dell Quartet | Other Voices, Other Rooms | L+R Records | CDLR 45093
Cloudburst
Jon Hendricks With The Larry Vuckovich Trio | Jon Hendricks | Enja | 4032-2
Clouds
Cannonball Adderley With Sergio Mendes And The Bossa Rio Quartet | Cannonball's Bossa Nova | Blue Note | 522667-2
David Darling | Journal October | ECM | 1161
Great Guitars | Great Guitars/Straight Tracks | Concord | CCD 4421
Niels-Henning Orsted-Pedersen Quartet | Dancing On The Tables | Steeplechase | SCS 1125(Audiophile Pressing)
Quintet Du Hot Club De France | Djangology Vol.1 | Naxos Jazz | 8.120515 CD
Tomas Franck With The Mulgrew Miller Trio | Tomas Franck In New York | Criss Cross | Criss 1052
Franco D'Andrea Trio | Volte | Owl Records | 052 CD
Clouds In Green
Arild Andersen Quartet | Clouds In My Mind | ECM | 1059
Clouds In My Heart
Muddy Waters Group | Back In His Early Days, Vol.1+2 | Red Lightnin' | SC 001/2
Clouds In The Mountain
Michael Bolivar Group | Hangin' Out | Clarity Recordings | CCD-1009
Clouds Over Bew York
Anton Fier Group | Dreamspeed | Avant | AVAN 009
Clouds(Nuages)
Cannonball Adderley With Sergio Mendes And The Bossa Rio Quartet | Cannonball's Bossa Nova | Blue Note | 522667-2
Clouds(single-version)
Geoff Keezer Group | Other Spheres | DIW | DIW 871 CD
Cloudy
Manhattan Jazz Quintet | Caravan | Paddle Wheel | 292 E 6002
Steve Lacy | Stabs | FMP | SAJ 05
Cloudy Morning
Mary Lou Williams Trio | Mary Lou Williams Trio-Roll 'Em(1944) | Solo Art | SACD-43
Clouseau
Catch Up | Catch Up II | Calig | 30615
Club Madness
Billy Jenkins And Fun Horns | East/West Now Wear The Same Vest | Babel | BDV 9601
Club Vinyl
Cindy Blackman Quartet | Cindy Blackman Telepathy | Muse | MCD 5437
Clusters(part 1&2)
Count Basie And His Orchestra | The Soloist | Jazz Anthology | 550002
C'Mon Baby
Lisle Atkinson Quartet | Bass Contra Bass | Storyville | STCD 8270
C'Mon Baby(alt.take)
Coleman Hawkins Sextet | Hawk Eyes | Original Jazz Classics | OJCCD 294-2
C'Mon In
Unit X | Rated X | Timescrapper | TSCR 9618
CMW
Ray Mantilla Quintet | Mantilla | Inner City | IC 1052 IMS
Coal Black Shine
Longstreet Jazzband | New York,New York | Elite Special | 73436
Sidney Bechet And His New Orleans Feetwarmers | Sidney Bechet 1932-1943: The Bluebird Sessions | Bluebird | ND 90317
Coal Cart Blues
Louis Armstrong Quartet | Louis Armstrong Vol.3-Louis With Guest Stars | MCA | 1306
Coal Train
Jeff Williams Quintet | Coalescence | Steeplechase | SCCD 31308
Coarser And Finer
The Fantasy Band | The Fantasy Band | dmp Digital Music Productions | CD 496
Coastline
Oliver Pospiech's Small Big Band | Cool Blue | Mons Records | MR 874809
Coba
David Becker Tribune | In Motion | Bluemoon | R 27-7916-2
Cobalt Blue
Charlie Shavers Quintet | Live! | Black & Blue | 33307
Cobb's Idea
Arnett Cobb Quintet | Smooth Sailing | Original Jazz Classics | OJCCD 323-2
Cobb's Mob
Cannonball Adderley Quintet | Cannonball Adderley:Sophisticated Swing-The EmArCy Small Group Sessions | Verve | 528408-2
Cobbweb
Monty Alexander Sextet | Cobilimbo | MPS | 68188
Cobilimbo
Acoustic Affaire | Mira | Jazz 'n' Arts Records | JNA 1303
Cobra
European Trumpet Summit | European Trumpet Summit | Konnex Records | KCD 5064
Jimmy Giuffre-Paul Bley-Steve Swallow | Conversations With A Goose | Soul Note | 121258-2
Ron Holloway Group | Struttin' | Milestone | MCD 9238-2
Cob's Groove
Duke Ellington And His Orchestra | Goin' Up | Duke Records | D 1011
Cochbamba
Carlos Barbosa-Lima | Music Of The Americas | Concord | CCD 4461
Cocktails For Two
Art Tatum | Art Tatum:Complete Original American Decca Recordings | Definitive Records | DRCD 11200
Coleman Hawkins And Ben Webster With The Oscar Peterson Quartet | Verve Jazz Masters Vol.60:The Collection | Verve | 529866-2
Coleman Hawkins And Confreres | Coleman Hawkins And Confreres | Verve | 835255-2 PMS
Coleman Hawkins-Roy Eldridge Quintet | Coleman Hawkins And Roy Eldridge At The Opera House | Verve | 2304432 IMS
Javon Jackson-Billy Pierce Quintet | Burnin' | Criss Cross | Criss 1139
Louis Armstrong And His All Stars | The Best Live Concert | Festival | ???
Coco Quebrado
Svend Asmussen Sextet | Svend Asmussen At Slukafter | Phontastic | NCD 8804
Cocoanut Calypso
David S. Ware Quartet | Earthquation | DIW | DIW 892 CD
Cocodrilo
Africa Djole | Kaloum | FMP | SAJ 26
Coconut & Banana
Ken McIntyre Trio | Chasing The Sun | Steeplechase | SCCD 31114
Coconut Bread
Maynard Ferguson Band | Live From San Francisco | ARG Jazz | 21374892
Coda
Dizzy Gillespie Sextet | Dizzie Gillespie: Salle Pleyel/Olympia | Laserlight | 36132
Jazz Indeed | Who The Moon Is | Traumton Records | 4427-2
Joe Harriott Quintet | Free Form | EmArCy | 538184-2
Quintet For A Day | What We Live | New World Records | 80553-2
Code
Maarten Altena Ensemble | Code | Hat Art | CD 6094
Code Carnival
Jeff Hittman-Yoshitaka Uematsu Quintet | Mosaic | Soul Note | 121137-2
Code M.D.
Cindy Blackman Quintet | Code Red | Muse | MCD 5365
Codetta
New Emily Jazz Orchestra | Neanthropus Retractus | SPLASC(H) Records | HP 10
Codona
Al Fairweather Band | Fairweather Friends Made To Measure | Lake | LACD 75
Coffaro's Theme
Skip Martin Orchestra | The Music From Mickey Spillane's Mike Hammer | Fresh Sound Records | ND 42124
Coffee & Kisses
Una Mae Carlisle With John Kirby And His Orchestra | TheComplete Una Mae Carlisle(1940-1942) And John Kirby(1941-1942) | RCA | ND 89484
Coffee And Kisses
Lightnin' Hopkins | Bluesville: Lightnin' Hopkins | Prestige | 61141
Coffee Groove
Lightnin' Strikes Back | Charly | CRB 1031
Coffee Pot
Gene DiNovi Trio | Live At The Montreal Bistro | Candid | CCD 79726
Coffee Time
Gerald Wiggins Trio | Mary Lou Williams/Gerry Wiggins:On Vogue | Vogue | 2111505-2
Cohen Owes Me Ninety Seven Dollars
Al Cohn And His Orchestra | The Jazz Workshop:Four Brass One Tenor | RCA | PM 45164
Col Legno
Bruno Tommaso Orchestra | Su Un Tema Di Jerome Kern | SPLASC(H) Records | HP 18
Colchiques Dans Les Prés
Jude Swift Group | Music For Your Neighborhood | Nova | NOVA 8917-2
Cold Afternoon Blues
Eddie C. Campbell & Tip On In | Let's Pick It | Black Saint | 9007
Cold Cold Heart
Nat King Cole With The Billy May Orchestra | Let's Face The Music | Capitol | EMS 1112
Cold Day Of February
Jack McDuff Group | Bringin' It Home | Concord | CCD 4855
Cold Duck Time
Les McCann-Eddie Harris Quintet | Swiss Movements | Atlantic | 7567-81365-2
Cold In Hand
Bessie Smith With Louis Armstrong And Fred Longshaw | Louis Armstrong And The Blues Singers 1924-1930 | Affinity | AFS 1018(6)
Cold In Hand Blues
Joe Louis Walker & The Boss Talkers | Cold Is The Night | Ace Records | CDCHM 208
Cold Miner
Peter Brötzmann | No Nothing: Brötzmann Solo | FMP | CD 32
Cold Nose
Johnny Copeland Band | Make My Home Where Hang My Hat | Edsel | Fiend 4
Cold Smoke
Blind Idiot God | Cyclotron | Avant | AVAN 010
Cold Sweat
Cold Sweat | Cold Sweat Plays J.B. | JMT Edition | 919025-2
Eric St-Laurent-Thomy Jordi-Thomas Alkier feat. Helge Schneider | Rock,Jazz & Music:Laut! | BIT | 11212
Poncho Sanchez And His Orchestra | A Night At Kimball's East | Concord | CCD 4472
Cold Turkey-
Double Trio(Trio De Clarinettes&Arcado) | Green Dolphy Suite | Enja | ENJ-9011 2
Cold Water Music
Muddy Waters Quartet | Folk Singer | Chess | CH 9261
Cole Capers
Allotria Jazz Band | Cleared For Take Off | Elite Special | 73331
Cole Slave
Chris Barber's Jazz Band | Elite Syncopations-Great British Traditional Jazzbands Vol.2 | Lake | LACD 43
Colemanology
Don Cherry/Nana Vasconcelos/Collin Walcott | Codona | ECM | 1132(829371-2)
Colemanwonder:
Peter Giger | Illigitimate Music | Nagara | MIX 1014-N
Colla Parta
Chris Barber's Jazz Band | Chris Barber Special | Black Lion | 157004
Colla Voche
Stan Kenton And His Orchestra | One Night Stand | Choice | CHCD 71051
Collaboration
Stan Kenton In Hi-Fi | Capitol | EMS 1149
Collage
Rudy Linka Quartet | News From Home | ARTA Records | F 1 0026-2511
Gene Harris And The Philip Morris All-Stars | Live | Concord | CCD 4808
Collard Greens And Black Eyed Peas
Bud Powell Trio | The Amazing Bud Powell Vol.2 | Blue Note | 532137-2
Bud Powell:The Complete Blue Note And Roost Recordings | Blue Note | 830083-2
Collard Greens And Black Eyed Peas(alt.take)
Bud Powell:The Complete Blue Note And Roost Recordings | Blue Note | 830083-2
Collect Calls
Blue Box | Stambul Boogie | Enja | 5025 Digital (807542)
Collection Blues
Count Basie Sextet | Highlights Of The Montreux Jazz Festival 1975 | Pablo | 2625707

Collector's Choice
Bob Degen Trio | Catability | Enja | ENJ-9332 2
Colleen
Fritz Krisse Quartet | Soulcolours | Laika Records | 35100782
James Emery | Exo Eso | FMP | SAJ 59
Colleur De Nuit
The Golden Gate Orchestra | The California Ramblers With Adrian Rollini | Village(Jazz Archive) | VILCD 011-2
Collision Cruise
Salvatore Bonafede Trio | Plays | Ken Music | 660.56.017
Colonel Rykken's Southern Fried Chicken
Don Grusin Group | No Borders | GRP | GRP 96762
Color Of Mind
Billy Pierce Quartet | The Complete William The Conqueror Sessions | Sunnyside | SSC 9013 D
Coloratura-
Duke Ellington And His Orchestra | The Jazz Collector Edition: Duke Ellington | Laserlight | 15710
Colores
Richard Galliano Quartet | Viaggio | Dreyfus Jazz Line | FDM 36562-9
Coloriage
Richard Galliano-Gabriele Mirabassi Duo | Coloriage | Quadrivium | SCA 031
Colors
Lonnie Plaxico Group | Iridescence | Muse | MCD 5427
Michel Petrucciani Trio | Trio In Tokyo | Dreyfus Jazz Line | FDM 36605-2
Pharoah Sanders Septet | The Best Of Pharoah Sanders | MCA | AS 9229
World Saxophone Quartet With The African Drums | Four Now | Justin Time | JUST 83-2
Colors Of Love
Yutaka Yokokura Group | Yutaka | GRP | GRP 95572
Colours
Sam Rivers Winds Of Manhattan | Colours | Black Saint | 120064-2
Uli Gutscher Quintet | Inspiration | Edition Collage | EC 462-2
Colours Of Sky
Uli Beckerhoff Group | Stay | Nabel Records:Jazz Network | CD 4636
Colours Of The Late Afternoon
Walton Ornato | Magic Mountain | Black Sun Music | 15016-2
Coltrane
Miles Davis Quintet | Live In Stockholm | Dragon | DRLP 90/91
Columbine Polka Mazurka
Dave Valentine Quintet | Live At The Blue Note | GRP | GRP 95682
Columbus Stockade Blues
Pete Fountain With Orchestra | The Best Of Pete Fountain | MCA | MCD 4032
Columbus,Ohio
Jin Hi Kim Group | Sargeng | Ear-Rational | ECD 1014
Combination
Ku-umba Frank Lacy & The Poker Bigband | Songs From The Musical 'Poker' | Tutu Records | 888150-2*
J.B.& His Hawks | Combination Blues | Charly | CRB 1042
Combinations
Urs Blüchlinger Tettet | Neurotica | Hat Art | 2008 Digital
Combo Suite:
Michael Feinstein With Jule Styne | Michael Feinstein Sings The Jule Styne Songbook | Nonesuch | 7559-79274-2
Come A Little Closer-
The Buck Clayton Legacy | All The Cats Join In(Buck Clayton Remembered) | Nagel-Heyer | CD 006
Come Again
The First Sampler | Nagel-Heyer | NHR SP 5
Gabriele Hasler-Roger Hanschel Duo | Love Songs | Foolish Music | FM 211003
Come Again,Sweet Love Doth Now Invite
Stars Of Faith | Black Nativity | Black & Blue | BLE 59.065 2
Come And Dance With Me
Son House-Woody Mann | Been Here And Gone | Acoustic Music Records | 319.1174.2
Come And Get It
Glen Gray And His Orchestra | Great Swing Classics In Hi-Fi | Capitol | 521223-2
Louis Jordan And His Tympany Five | Louis Jordan-Let The Good Times Roll: The Complete Decca Recordings 1938-1954 | Bear Family Records | BCD 15557 IH
Joe Lee Wilson Quintet | Secrets From The Sun | Inner City | IC 1042 IMS
Come A'Runnin'
Joachim Kühn | The Diminished Augmented System | EmArCy | 542320-2
Come As It Goes
Joice Walton & Blackout With Guests | Downsville Girl | Line Records | LICD 9.01303
Come Back
Champion Jack Dupree Group | Champ's Housewarming | Vagabond | VRCD 8.88014
Come Back Baby
The Blues Of Champion Jack Dupree,Vol.1 | Storyville | STCD 8019
Joe Williams And His Band | Planet Jazz:Joe Williams | Planet Jazz | 2165370-2
Joe Williams With The Harry 'Sweets' Edison Quintet | Live! A Swingin' Night At Birdland | Fresh Sound Records | FSR-CD 22(882187)
Little Walter Blues Band | Blues Roots Vol. 15: Little Walter | Chess | 6.24805 AG
Come Back Jack
Ernie Andrews With The Frank Wess Quartet | The Great City | Muse | MCD 5543
Come Back Lucky
Tony Scott Group | African Bird-Come Back Mother Africa | Soul Note | 121083-2
Come Back Sweet Papa
George Lewis Session | George Lewis/Paul Barbarin | Storyville | SLP 4049
The World's Greatest Jazzband | Live | Atlantic | 790982-2
Come Back To Me
Klaus Ignatzek Trio | Airballoon | Nabel Records:Jazz Network | CD 4651
Lonnie Plaxico Group | Iridescence | Muse | MCD 5427
Ramsey Lewis Group | Sky Islands | GRP | GRP 97452
Steve Laury Trio | Passion | Denon Compact Disc | CY-79043
Come Back To Sorento
Ramsey Lewis Trio | Down To Earth | Verve | 538329-2
Stan Kenton And His Orchestra | Artistry In Rhythm | Creative World | ST 1043
Come Back To Sorento(alt.take)
Jerry Bergonzi And Joachim Kühn | Signed By | Adda | ZZ 84104
Come Be With Me
Elise Einarsdotter-Olle Steinholz | Sketches Of Roses | Touché Music | TMcCD 008
Come Bright Sunshine
Sally Blair And The Bethlehem Orchestra | Squeeze Me | Fresh Sound Records | FSR 2023(Bethlehem BCP 6009)
Come Candela
Mongo Santamaria And His Orchestra | Live At Jazz Alley | Concord | CCD 4427
Come Closer
Sammy Kaye And His Orchestra | The Uncollected:Sammy Kaye, Vol.2 | Hindsight | HSR 163
Come Dance With Me
Ronnie Cuber Orchestra | Passion Fruit | Electric Bird | K 28P 6347
Shirley Horn With The Quincy Jones Orchestra | Loads Of Love + Shirley Horn With Horns | Mercury | 843454-2
Jeff Beck Sextet | Wired | Epic | ???
Come Day Go Day
Otis Spann/Robert Lockwood Jr. With James Oden | Otis Spann And His Piano | Crosscut | CCR 1004(Candid)
Come Fly With Me
Count Basie And His Orchestra | Compact Jazz: Count Basie-The Standards | Verve | 841197-2
Jermaine Landsberger Trio & Gina | Samba In June | Edition Collage | EC 524-2
LaVerne Butler With Band | No Looking Back | Chesky | JD 91
Come Gone
Sonny Rollins Trio | Contemporary Sonny Rollins-Alternate Takes | Contemporary | C 7651
Way Out West | Original Jazz Classics | OJC20 337-2(S 7530)
Come Gone(alt.take)
Sonny Rollins-The Freelance Years:The Complete Riverside & Contemporary Recordings | Riverside | 5 RCD 4427-2
Hatchett's Swingtette | In The Mood | Decca | RFL 11
Come Here Lovely Dovey
Count Basie And His Orchestra | Count Basie Orchestra featuring Arthur Prysock | CTI Records | PDCTI 1123-2
Come Home Again
Buddy Childers With The Russ Garcia Strings | Artistry In Jazz | Candid | CCD 79735
Helen Merrill + Ron Carter | Duets | Mercury | 838097-2 PMS
Come In From The Rain
James Booker | Boogie Woogie And Ragtime Piano Contest | Gold Records | 11035 AS
Come In Out Of The Rain
Oscar Moore Trio | Oscar Moore And Friends | Fresh Sound Records | FSR-CD 0202
Come Oekotopia
David Digs Orchestra | Realworld | Palo Alto | PA 8037
Come On
Otis Spann Band | The Blues Never Die! | Original Blues Classics | OBCCD 530-2(P 7391)
Rosemary Clooney With Les Brown & His Band Of Renown | Aurex Jazz Festival '83 | Eastworld | EWJ 80268
Come On And See About Me
Doctor Ross With The Blueshounds | Jivin' The Blues | Big Bear | 146409
Come On And Stomp Stomp Stomp
Allister Wylie And His Coronoado Hotel Orchestra | Jazz Museum-Hot Dance Bands Of The Twenties,Vol.2 | MCA | 52057 (801842)
Come On Baby
Shakti | Natural Elements | CBS | 82329
Come On Back
Stan Kenton And His Orchestra | By Request Vol.6 | Creative World | ST 1069
Come On Children Let's Sing
Mahalia Jackson | In Memoriam Mahalia Jackson | CBS | 66501
Come On Home
Big Maceo Merriweather | Big Maceo Vol.2 | Blues Classics | BC 29
Duke Ellington And His Orchestra | The Rare Broadcast Recordings 1953 | Jazz Anthology | JA 5220
Junior Mance-Martin Rivera Duo | For Dancer's Only | Sackville | SKCD2-3031
Come On Home(Comin' Home)
Lloyd Smith's Gut-Bucketeers | That's My Stuff | Frog | DGF 7
Come On In My Kitchen
Guitar Slim | The Introduction To Living Country Blues USA | L+R Records | LS 42030
Robert Johnson | Robert Johnson-King Of The Delta Blues | CBS | 493006-2
Come On In My Kitchen(alt.take)
Pee Wee Ellis Quintet With Guests | A New Shift | Minor Music | 801060
Come On In The House
Buddy Guy & Junior Wells With The Chicago Blues All Stars '78 | Live In Montreux | Black & Blue | BLE 59.530 2
Come On Mule
The Pete Haycock Band | Livin' It | L+R Records | CDLR 42073
Come Out Wherever You Are
Gerry Mulligan Quartet | Live In Stockholm 1957 | Nueva Records | JU 324
Michael Feinstein With Jule Styne | Michael Feinstein Sings The Jule Styne Songbook | Nonesuch | 7559-79274-2
Come Out With Me
Aldo Romano Quartet | Canzoni | Enja | 9102-2
Come Rain Or Come Shine
Ada Montellanico With The Jimmy Cobb Trio | The Encounter | Philology | W 66.2
Art Blakey And The Jazz Messengers | Hard Champion | Paddle Wheel | K32Y 6209
Art Pepper Quartet | Intensity | Original Jazz Classics | OJCCD 387-2
Art Tatum | Art Tatum-The Complete Pablo Solo Masterpieces | Pablo | 7 PACD 4404-2
Solos 1937 & Classic Piano Solos | Forlane | UCD 19010
Ben Webster With Orchestra And Strings | Music For Loving:Ben Webster With Strings | Verve | 527774-2
Benny Goodman Septet | Benny Goodman:The King Of Swing | Musicmasters | 65130-2
Bill Evans Trio | The Complete Bill Evans On Verve | Verve | 527953-2
Spring Leaves | Milestone | M 47034
How Deep Is The Ocean | West Wind | WW 2055
The Legendary Bill Evans Trio-The Legendary 1960 Birdland Sessions | Cool & Blue | C&B-CD 106
Bill Holman And His Orchestra | The Fabulous Bill Holman | Sackville | 2013
Bobby Troup Quartet | Bobby Troup Plays Johnny Mercer | Affinity | AFF 174
Cal Tjader Quartet | Plays Harold Arlen | Original Jazz Classics | OJC 285(F 8072)
Charlie Mariano Quartet | Nat Pierce-Dick Collins Nonet/Charlie Mariano Sextet | Original Jazz Classics | OJC 118(F 3224)
Chick Corea-Gayle Moran | Chic Corea And Friends | Memo Music | HDJ 4017
Count Basie And His Orchestra | The Greatest | Verve | MV 2650 IMS
Diane Schuur With Orchestra | Timeless | GRP | GRP 91030-1(808727)
Eddie Higgins Quartet | Zoot's Hyms | Sunnyside | SSC 1064 D
Ella Fitzgerald With The Billy May Orchestra | The Silver Collection: Ella Fitzgerald-The Songbooks | Verve | 823445-2 PMS
The Complete Ella Fitzgerald Song Books of Harold Arlen, Irving Berlin, Duke Ellington, George & Ira Gershwin, Jerome Kern, Johnny Mercer, Cole Porter And Rogers & Hart | Verve | 519832-2
The Harold Arlen Songbook | Verve | 817526-1 IMS
Ella Fitzgerald With The Tommy Flanagan Trio | The Montreux '77 Collection | Pablo | 2620107
Gerry Mulligan And His Orchestra | The Silver Collection: Gerry Mulligan Meets The Saxophonists | Verve | 827436-2 PMS
Gerry Mulligan Concert Jazz Band | The Complete Verve Gerry Mulligan Concert Band | Verve | 9860613
The Complete Verve Gerry Mulligan Concert Band | Verve | 9860613
En Concert Avec Europe 1 | Laserlight | 710382/83
Jenny Evans And Her Quintet | Whisper Not | ESM Records | Panda 16(941336)
Joe Henderson With The Keith Greko Trio | Last Train Outta Flagstaff | Concept | VL 4 IMS
Joe Pass | Virtuoso No.4 | Pablo | 2640102
Joe Pass/Niels-Henning Orsted-Pedersen Duo | Chops | Original Jazz Classics | OJCCD 786-2(2310830)
Joe Sample Group | Invitation | Warner | 9362-45209.2
John Abercrombie Quartet | November | ECM | 1502(519073-2)
John Collins Trio | The Incredible John Collins | Nilva | NQ 3412 IMS
John Coltrane Quintet | The Jazz Giants Play Harold Arlen:Blues In The Night | Prestige | PCD 24201-2
John Coltrane-The Prestige Recordings | Prestige | 16 PCD 4405-2
John Hicks-Ray Drummond | Two Of A Kind | Evidence | ECD 22017-2
John Williams Band | Plays The Music Of Harold Arlen | Discovery | DSCD 891(881472)
Johnny Smith Quartet | The Sound Of Johnny Smith Guitar | Fresh Sound Records | FSR 583(Roost 2246)
June Christy With Orchestra | June Christy Recalls Those Kenton Days | EMI Records | 1599311
Kenny Burrell Trio | Kenny Burrell In New York | Muse | MR 5241
Kenny Drew Trio | The Riverside Collection: Kenny Drew | Original Jazz Classics | OJCCD 6007-2
Les Brown And His Band Of Renown | Digital Swing | Fantasy | FCD 9650-2
Lew Tabackin Trio | Tabackin | Inner City | IC 1038 IMS
Martin Schmitt | Handful Of Blues | AH Records | ESM 9303
Monica Zetterlund With The Bill Evans Trio | Bill Evans-Monica Zetterlund | West Wind | WW 2073
Nancy Wright With Caesar Giovannini +6 | You Make Me Feel So Young! | Fresh Sound Records | Concert-Disc CD 43 CD
Oscar Peterson Trio | Verve Jazz Masters 37:Oscar Peterson Plays Broadway | Verve | 516893-2
Oscar Peterson Plays The Harold Arlen Song Book | Verve | 589103-2
The Song Is You-The Best Of The Verve Songbooks | Verve | 531558-2
Oscar Peterson Plays The Harold Arlen Song Book | Verve | 589103-2
Paul Kuhn Orchestra feat. Gustl Mayer | Street Of Dreams | Mons Records | MR 874800
Peter Fessler Quartet | Foot Prints | Minor Music | 801058
Plas Johnson Band | Rockin' With The Plas | Pathe | 2C 068-86529(Capitol)
Ray Charles And His Orchestra | The Best Of The Blues Singers Vol.2 | LRC Records | CDC 9007
Sarah Vaughan With The Jimmy Jones Orchestra | Sarah Vaughan In Hi-Fi | CBS | CK 65117
Wes Montgomery Quintet | Full House | Original Jazz Classics | OJC20 106-2
Woody Herman And His Orchestra | King Cobra | Original Jazz Classics | OJCCD 1068-2(F 9499)
Wynton Kelly Trio | Wynton Kelly! | Vee Jay Recordings | VJ 011
Zoot Sims-Bucky Pizzarelli Duo | A Summer Thing | Laserlight | 15754
Come Rain Or Come Shine-
André Previn Trio | Jazz At The Musikverein | Verve | 537704-2
Come Rain Or Come Shine(alt.take 1)
Monica Zetterlund With The Bill Evans Trio | The Complete Bill Evans On Verve | Verve | 527953-2
Come Rain Or Come Shine(alt.take 2)
James Clay Quintet | A Double Dose Of Soul | Original Jazz Classics | OJCCD 1790-2(RLP 9349)
Come Rain Or Come Shine(alt.take)
Sarah Vaughan With The Jimmy Jones Orchestra | Sarah Vaughan In Hi-Fi | CBS | CK 65117
| The Clifford Brown Quartet In Paris | Original Jazz Classics | OJCCD 357-2(P 7761)
Come Running To Me
The Dave McMurdo Jazz Orchestra | Fire & Song | Sackville | SK2CD-5004
Come Saturday Morning
Sarah Vaughan With Orchestra | Sweet 'N' Sassy | Roulette | 531793-2
Come Spring
Werner Lener Quartet | Personal Moments | Satin Doll Productions | SDP 1026-1 CD
U.P. Wilson Band | On My Way | Red Lightnin' | RL 0078
Come Sunday
Abbey Lincoln With The Kenny Dorham Quintet | Abbey Is Blue | Original Jazz Classics | OJC20 069-2(RLP 1153)
Abdullah Ibrahim | Desert Flowers | Enja | ENJ-7011 2
André Previn Trio | Uptown | Telarc Digital | CD 83303
Ben Webster And His Orchestra | Masters Of Jazz Vol.5:Ben Webster | Storyville | SLP 4105
Big Band De Lausanne | Duke Ellington's Sacred Music | TCB Records | TCB 20502
Bobby Timmons Orchestra | Quartet And Orchestra | Milestone | MCD 47091-2
Booker Ervin Quartet | The Song Book | Original Jazz Classics | OJCCD 779-2(P 7318)
Canadian Brass | Take The A Train | RCA | 2663455-2
Cannonball Adderley Sextet | The Japanese Concerts | Milestone | M 47029
Cedar Walton Quintet | Cedar! | Original Jazz Classics | OJCCD 462-2
Dizzy Gillespie And His Orchestra | A Portrait Of Duke Ellington | Verve | 817107-1 IMS
A Portrait Of Duke Ellington | Verve | 817107-1 IMS
Duke Ellington And His Famous Orchestra | Passion Flower 1940-46 | Bluebird | 63 66616-2
Duke Ellington And His Orchestra | Duke Ellington:The Complete RCA-Victor Mid-Forties Recordings(1944-1946) | RCA | 2663394-2
Concert Of Sacred Music | RCA | PL 43663
Georges Arvanitas Trio | Rencontre | CBS | 491232-2
Heinz Sauer Quintet | Lost Ends:Live at Alte Oper Frankfurt | free flow music | ffm 0594
Heinz Sauer-Bob Degen Duo | Plaza Lost And Found | L+R Records | CDLR 45044
Michael Moore-Bill Charlap | Concord Duo Series Volume Nine | Concord | CCD 4678
Norris Turney Quartet | Big Sweet N' Blue | Mapleshade | 02632
Oscar Peterson Trio With The Nelson Riddle Orchestra | The Silver Collection: Oscar Peterson | Verve | 823447-2 PMS
Pat Martino Quartet | Exit | Muse | MCD 5075
The Big Three | The Big Three | Original Jazz Classics | OJCCD 805-2(2310757)
The Danish Radio Big Band | A Little Bit Of Duke | dacapo | DCCD 9420
World Saxophone Quartet | Plays Duke Ellington | Nonesuch | 7559-79137-2
Duke Ellington And His Orchestra | Carnegie Hall Concert December 1944 | Prestige | 2PCD 24073-2
Come Sunday-
Duke Ellington | Bluebird | ND 86641(3)
The Indispensable Duke Ellington Vol.11/12 | RCA | 2115524-2
Come Sunday (alt.take)
Black Brown And Beige | CBS | CK 65566
Black Brown And Beige | CBS | CK 65566
Come Sunday(a capella)
Carnegie Hall Concert January 1946 | Prestige | 2PCD 24074-2
Come Sunday(Spiritual)-
Duke Ellington:Complete Prestige Carnegie Hall 1946-1947 Concerts | Definitive Records | DRCD 11211
Come Take My Hand
Marc Puricelli Group | The Shade | Musicmasters | 65146-2
Come To Baby Do
Nat King Cole Trio | The Best Of The Nat King Cole Trio:The Vocal Classics(1942-1946) | Blue Note | 833571-2
Phineas Newborn Jr. Trio | Phineas' Rainbow | RCA | 2131870-2
Come To Mama
Andy LaVerne/Dave Samuels | Fountainhead | Steeplechase | SCCD 31261
Come To Me
Francesca Simone Trio | Guardia Li | Minor Music | 801093
Hank Jones Trio | I Remember You | Black & Blue | BLE 233122
Come Together
Christian Willisohn-Lillian Boutté | Come Together | ART BY HEART | ABH 2002 2
Defunkt | Live At The Knitting Factory | Enemy | EMCD 122(03522)
Mike Westbrook Band | Off Abbey Road | TipToe | TIP-888805 2
Sarah Vaughan And Her Band | Songs Of The Beatles | Atlantic | 16037-2
Sarah Vaughan With Orchestra | Song Of The Beatles | Atlantic | SD 16037
The Real Group | Get Real! | ACT | 9252-2
Come Unto Me
The Pilgrim Jubilee Singers | Walk On/The Old Ship Of Zion | Mobile Fidelity | MFCD 756
Come What May

Canadian Brass | Take The A Train | RCA | 2663455-2

Come What May Places
George Howard Group | Love Will Follow | GRP | GRP 96592

Come Ye
Nina Simone With Orchestra | Nina Simone-The 60s Vol.3:Work Song | Mercury | 838545-2 PMS

Come, Come Crazy
Noma Kosazana & Uli Lenz | Art Of The Duo: Trouble In Paradise | Tutu Records | 888144-2*
Chas Burchell Quartet | Unsong Hero:The Undiscovered Genius Of Chas Burchell | IN+OUT Records | 7026-2

Comeback
Shelly Manne Quintet | Perk Up | Concord | CCD 4021

Comecar De Novo
Ivan Lins Group | Montreux Jazz Festival | ACT | 9001-2

Comencar De Novo
Peter Herbolzheimer Rhythm Combination & Brass | Latin Groove | Koala Records | CD P 13

Comes Love
Alfred Lauer Bigband | Just Music | Mons Records | MR 874819
Artie Shaw And His Orchestra | The Uncollected:Artie Shaw And His Orchestra, Vol.3 | Hindsight | HSR 148
Ella Fitzgerald With Joe Pass | Speak Love | Pablo | 2310888
Flip Phillips-Scott Hamilton Sextet | A Sound Investment | Concord | CCD 4334
Keith Ingham Manhattan Swingtet | We're In The Money | Sackville | SKCD2-2055
Summit Reunion | Jazz Im Amerikahaus,Vol.5 | Nagel-Heyer | CD 015
Sylvia Syms With The Johnny Richards Orchestra | Sylvia Syms Sings | Atlantic | AMCY 1076
Vanessa Rubin With Band | Girl Talk | Telarc Digital | CD 83480
Warren Vaché Quartet | What Is There To Say? | Nagel-Heyer | CD 056
Woody Herman And His Orchestra | Songs For Hip Lovers | Verve | 559872-2
Woody Herman Live 1957 Featuring Bill Harris Vol.1 | Status | CD 107(882500)

Comiat
Gary Lucas | Knitting Factory Tours Europe Way 23-June 15,1991 | Enemy | EMCD 121(03521)

Comin' Down
Chet Baker Sextet | Compact Jazz: Chet Baker | Verve | 840632-2 PMS

Comin' & Goin'
Gunther Schuller With The WDR Radio Orchestra & Rememberance Band | Witchi Tia To, The Music Of Jim Pepper | Tutu Records | 888204-2*

Comin' And Goin'
Jim Pepper Group | Comin' And Goin' | Bellaphon | 290.31.029

Comin' Back
John Kirby And His Orchestra | TheComplete Una Mae Carlisle(1940-1942) And John Kirby(1941-1942) | RCA | ND 89484

Comin' Home Baby
Herbie Mann Group | The Best Of Herbie Mann | Atlantic | 7567-81369-2
The Best Of Herbie Mann | Atlantic | 7567-81369-2
Herbie Mania | Atlantic | ATL 20106
Manhattan Jazz Orchestra | Moritat | Sweet Basil | 660.55.008
Moe Koffman Quartet | Moe Koffman 1967 | Just A Memory | JAS 9505-2
Paul Nero's Blue Sounds | Bluesy Toosy | ACT | 9200-2
Tamami Koyake Quartet | Tamami Koyake First New York Session | Paddle Wheel | KICJ 85
Zachary Breaux Group | Groovin' | Ronnie Scott's Jazz House | JHCD 023

Comin' On
Dizzy Reece Sextet | Comin' On | Blue Note | 522019-2

Comin' On Up
Mezz Mezzrow And His Orchestra | The Complete Sidney Bechet-Vol.5 | RCA | 2115519-2

Comin' Through The Apple
Deborah Henson-Conant | The Celtic Album | Laika Records | 35101022

Comin' Through The Rye
Tommy Dorsey And His Orchestra | The Post-War Era | Bluebird | 63 66156-2

Comin' Thru The Rye Bread
Marty Cook Group feat. Jim Pepper | Internationales Jazzfestival Münster | Tutu Records | 888110-2*

Comin' To Git You
Bill Cunliffe Quintet | Bill Plays Bud | Naxos Jazz | 86024-2

Coming Back, Jamaica
Joe Maneri Quartet | Coming Down The Mountain | HatOLOGY | 501

Coming Home
Roosevelt Sykes Quintet | The Return Of Roosevelt Sykes | Original Blues Classics | OBCCD 546-2

Coming On The Hudson
Thelonious Monk Quartet | Thelonious Monk-The Complete Riverside Recordings | Riverside | 15 RCD 022-2

Coming Through The Rye
Charles Gayle Quartet | Always Born | Silkheart | SHCD 115

Coming Up
Martial Solal Trio | Suite For Trio | MPS | 68201

Comino Island
Speakers And Singers On Radio Spot | Radio Suite | Red Records | 123280-2

Comme Dans Un Train Pour Une Etoile
Vanasse/Vitous | Nouvelle Cuisine | Justin Time | JTR 8406

Comme Il Faut
Anouar Brahem Group | Khomsa | ECM | 1561(527093-2)

Comme Un Départ
Eddie Louiss Quartet | Flomela | Dreyfus Jazz Line | FDM 36578-2

Comme Une Absence
Clementine And Her Trio | Continent Bleu | Orange Blue | OB 004 CD

Common Ground
The Brecker Brothers | The Brecker Brothers Live | Jazz Door | JD 1248

Common Mama
Otis Grand Blues Band With Guests | Nothing Else Matters | Sequel Records | NEG CD 272

Communication
Dewey Redman/Ed Blackwell Duo | Redman And Blackwell In Willisau | Black Saint | 120093-2

Communications '72
Stan Getz With The Michel Legrand Orchestra | Compact Jazz: Michel Legrand | Philips | 840944-2

Communications No.10
The Jazz Composer's Orchestra | Comminications | JCOA | 1001/2

Communications No.11-part 1
Comminications | JCOA | 1001/2

Communications No.11-part 2
Comminications | JCOA | 1001/2

Communications No.8
Comminications | JCOA | 1001/2

Communications No.9
Airto Moreira And The Gods Of Jazz | Killer Bees | B&W Present | BW 041

Community
Glenn Miller And His Orchestra | The Glenn Miller Orchestra:The Early Years | Halcyon | DHDL 129

Como El Viento
David Matthews Trio With Gary Burton | American Pie | Sweet Basil | 660.55.005

Como En Vietnam
Gary Burton-Keith Jarrett Quintet | Gary Burton&Keith Jarrett | Atlantic | SD 1577
Jane Bunnett-Frank Emilio Flynn | Jane Bunnett And The Cuban Piano Masters | Pacific Jazz | 832695-2

Como Fué
Paquito D'Rivera Group | Why Not | CBS | 467137-2

Como O Chines E A Bicicleta
Orquestra Mahatma | A Young Person's Guide | Babel | BDV 9612

Como Se Goza En El Barrio
Terra Brazil | Café Com Leite | art-mode-records | AMR 2101

Como Um Samba De Adeus
The Caribbean Jazz Project | The Caribbean Jazz Project | Inak | 9038

Como Voa As Coisas?
Conexion Latina | Calorcito | Enja | ENJ-4072 2

Como Volver A Tenerte
Jimmy Gourley Trio | Jimmy Gourley And The Paris Heavyweights | 52e Rue Est | RECD 002

Comotion
Toshiyuki Honda With The Chick Corea Trio | Dream | Eastworld | EWJ 90027

Companero
Gunter Hampel Trio | Companion | Birth | 0036

Company
Bob Berg Quintet | Cycles | Denon Compact Disc | CY 72745

Compared To What
Les McCann Quartet | Les Is More | Night Records | VNCD 4(887048)
Les McCann-Eddie Harris Quintet | Swiss Movement | Atlantic | 8122-72452-2
Swiss Movements | Atlantic | 7567-81365-2
Passport And Guests | Doldinger's Best | ACT | 9224-2
Bluesy Toosy | ACT | 9200-2

Compassion
John Coltrane Quartet | First Meditation | Impulse(MCA) | GRP 11182
Milt Jackson With The Monty Alexander Trio | Soul Fusion | Original Jazz Classics | OJCCD 731-2(2310804)
Monty Alexander Trio | Threesome | Soul Note | 121152-2
Paul Bley Trio | Notes On Ornette | Steeplechase | SCCD 31437

Compassion-
Yusef Lateef Ensemble | Nocturnes | Atlantic | 7567-81977-2

Compassion Duration
Chick Corea & Origin | Change | Stretch Records | SCD 9023-2

Compet Gar
Dave Liebman | The Loneliness Of A Long Distance Runner | CMP Records | CMP CD 24

Complainte De La Seine
Barney Wilen Quintet | Jazz In Paris:Jazz & Cinéma Vol.1 | EmArCy | 548318-2 PMS

Complainte Du Chauffeur
Curtis Counce Group | You Get More Bounce With Curtis Counce | Original Jazz Classics | OJCCD 159-2

Complete Communion-
Don Cherry Quartet | Complete Communion | Blue Note | 522673-2

Complete Communion:
Dave Burrell-Beaver Harris Orchestra | In: Sanity | Black Saint | BSR 0006/7

Completely Crazy
Brecker-Engstfeld-Plümer-Weiss | ToGether | Nabel Records:Jazz Network | CD 4648

Completely Different
Tender Variations | Tender Variations(Original Sountrack aus dem Film oDer Windhund o) | Decca | 6.23969 AO

Complicity
Bobby Hutcherson Sextet | Components | Blue Note | 829027-2

Composition 400
Anthony Braxton With The Northwest Creative Orchestra | Eugene(1989) | Black Saint | 120137-2

Compositional Theme Story:Anthems And Folklore
Charles Mingus | Mingus Plays Piano | Mobile Fidelity | MFCD 783

Composizione '92
Adrian Mears & Johannes Enders Quintet | Discoveries | Enja | 8022-2

Compulsion
Miles Davis And His Orchestra | Collector's Items | Original Jazz Classics | OJC20 071-2(P 7044)
Welcome To Jazz: Miles Davis Vol.2 | Koch Records | 321 975 D1
Miles Davis Sextet | The Jazz Giants Play Miles Davis:Milestones | Prestige | PCD 24225-2
Rolf Kühn Sextet | Don't Split | L+R Records | LR 40016

Comrade
Bill Evans Quartet | The Complete Bill Evans On Verve | Verve | 527953-2

Comrade Conrad
Bill Evans Quintet | We Will Meet Again | Warner | 7599-27504-2
Carlos Denia-Uli Glaszmann | Ten Strings For Bill Evans | Edition Musikat | EDM 069
Bill Evans Quartet | The Complete Bill Evans On Verve | Verve | 527953-2

Comrade Conrad(alt.take 1)
The Complete Bill Evans On Verve | Verve | 527953-2

Comrade Conrad(alt.take 2)
Cassandra | Enten Eller | SPLASC(H) Records | H 176

Con Affetto
Wes Montgomery With The Don Sebesky Orchestra | Bumpin' | Verve | 539062-2
Al Gafa Quintet | Leblon Beach | Pablo | 2310782

Con Alma
Claudio Roditi Quartet | Two Of Swords | Candid | CCD 79504
Dizzy Gillespie Group | Bird Songs | Telarc Digital | CD 83421
Dizzy Gillespie Quintet With The Rochester Philharmonic Orchestra | The Symphony Sessions | Sion | Sion 18110
Dizzy Gillspie And His Latin American Rhythm | Afro | Verve | 517052-2
Ellen H. Band | A Gentle Approach | Timeless | SJP 229
Hilton Ruiz Orchestra | Hebros | Telarc Digital | CD 83338
Jimmy Greene Sextet | Introducing Jimmy Greene | Criss Cross | Criss 1181
Lilian Terry With The Dizzy Gillespie Quartet | Oo-Shoo-Be-Doo-Be...Oo,Oo ...Oo,Oo | Soul Note | SN 1147
Oscar Peterson Trio | The Jazz Soul Of Oscar Peterson/Affinity | Verve | 533100-2
Ron McClure Sextet | Double Triangle | Naxos Jazz | 86044-2
Stan Getz Quartet | Compact Jazz: Stan Getz & Friends | Verve | 835317-2
Stan Getz With The Chick Corea Trio | The Chick Corea-Bill Evans Sessions | Verve | 2610036
Takashi Ohi With The Junior Mance Trio | Time Stream | Denon Compact Disc | CY-78898
Wallace Roney Quintet | The Standard Bearer | Muse | MCD 5372
Randy Weston | Marrakech In The Cool Of The Evening | Verve | 521588-2

Con Edison
John Wolf Brennan | The Well-Prepared Clavier/Das Wohlpräparierte Klavier | Creative Works Records | CW CD 1032-2

Con Fuoco(fast)-
Dizzy Reece Sextet | Manhattan Project | Bee Hive | BH 7001

Con Plastillina Verde
Jean-Luc Ponty Quintet | Sonata Erotica-Live At Montreux | Inner City | IC 1003 IMS

Conan
Gonzalo Rubalcaba Group | Live In Havanna | Messidor | 15960 CD

Concentrating
Willie 'The Lion' Smith | Luckey & The Lion:Harlem Piano | Good Time Jazz | GTCD 10035-2

Concentration
The Boswell Sisters | It's The Girls | ASV | AJA 5014

Concentric Circle
Kostas Konstantinou-Vassilis Tsabropoulos | Concentric Cycles | Nabel Records:Jazz Network | CD 4698

Concentric Cycles
Jan Garbarek Quartet | Afric Pepperbird | ECM | 1007 (2301007)

Conception
Bud Powell | Lions Abroad Vol.3:Le Lion Á Paris | Black Lion | BLCD 7622-2
Chet Baker Quintet/NDR Big Band/Radio Orchestra Hannover | The Last Concert Vol.I+II | Enja | ENJ-6074 22
Chet Baker Trio | Chet's Choice | Criss Cross | Criss 1016
Dave McMurdo Jazz Orchestra | Different Paths | Sackville | SKCD2-2034
Frank Strazzeri Trio | Little Giant | Fresh Sound Records | FSR-CD 0184
Gigi Gryce-Clifford Brown Sextet | Planet Jazz:Clifford Brown | Planet Jazz | 2161239-2
Jan Lundgren Trio With Herb Geller | Stockholm Get-Together | Fresh Sound Records | FSR CD 5007
Miles Davis Quintet | Ezz-Thetic | Original Jazz Classics | OJCCD 1726-2(P 7827)

Conception Vessel
Paul Motian-Keith Jarrett | Conception Vessel | ECM | 1028(519279-2)
Marilyn Crispell-Gary Peacock-Paul Motian | Amaryllis | ECM | 1742(013400-2)

Conception Vessel-
Gigi Gryce-Clifford Brown Sextet | Jazz Legacy 3: Clifford Brown-The Complete Paris Collection Vol.1 | Vogue | 500053

Concepts In Blue
The Human Arts Ensemble | The Human Arts Ensemble Live, Vol.2 | Circle Records | RK 12-23578/12 IMS

Concert For Marimba, Harp And Strings
Shep Fields And His Rippling Rhythm Orchestra | The Uncollected:Shep Fields, Vol.2 | Hindsight | HSR 179

Concertina For Clarinet
Schwarz-Hübner Duo | Elegie | dml-records | CD 012

Concertino Cappricioso
Willem Breuker Kollektief | In Holland | BVHAAST | 041/42 (807118)

Concerto A Six:
Mary Lou Williams | Solo Recital-Montreux Jazz Festival 1978 | Pablo | 2308218

Concerto For Bass
George Russell Smalltet | Victor Jazz History Vol.15:Progressive Jazz | RCA | 2135734-2

Concerto For Billy The Kid
The RCA Victor Jazz Workshop | RCA | 2159144-2

Concerto For Billy The Kid(alt.take)
Artie Shaw And His Orchestra | This Is Artie Shaw Vol. 2 | RCA | NL 89411 DP

Concerto For Clarinet(edited)
Cat Anderson & The Ellington All-Stars | Cat Anderson | Swing | SW 8412 IMS

Concerto For Cootie
Cat Anderson And His Orchestra | Ellingtonians In Paris | Jazztime(EMI) | 251275-2
Duke Ellington And His Famous Orchestra | Planet Jazz:Jazz Trumpet | Planet Jazz | 2169654-2
Jazz:The Essential Collection Vol.2 | IN+OUT Records | 78012-2
Duke Ellington:Ko-Ko | Dreyfus Jazz Line | FDM 36717-2
Victor Jazz History Vol.12:Ellingtonia | RCA | 2135731-2
Duke Ellington And His Orchestra | Duke Ellington's Masterpieces Vol.1: 1938-1940 | Black & Blue | BLE 59.233 2

Concerto For Doghouse
Stan Kenton And His Orchestra | The Formative Years(1941-1942) | Creative World | ST 1061

Concerto For Jazz Trombone And Orchestra:
Willem Breuker Kollektief | Sensemayá | BVHAAST | CD 9509

Concerto For Piano
Shelly Manne Jazz Quartet | Interpretations | Trend | TR 525 Direct-to-Disc

Concerto For Solo Trumpet, Percussion And Orchestra
German Jazz Orchestra | German Jazz Orchestra-First Take | Mons Records | MR 874669

Concerto In Jazz(part 1-3)
Richard Galliano With Orchestra | Passatori | Dreyfus Jazz Line | FDM 36601-2

Concerto In Three Movements(for Bandoneon,Harp,Piano And Orchestra)
Miroslav Vitous Quartet | First Meeting | ECM | 1145

Concerto In Three Parts
Jacques Loussier Trio | Play Bach | Decca | 6.28150 DP

Concerto No.1:Le Printemps
Raymond Fol Big Band | Jazz In Paris:Raymond Fol-Les 4 Saisons | EmArCy | 548791-2

Concerto No.2:`L'Été
Jazz In Paris:Raymond Fol-Les 4 Saisons | EmArCy | 548791-2

Concerto No.3:L'Automne
Jazz In Paris:Raymond Fol-Les 4 Saisons | EmArCy | 548791-2

Concerto No.4
Stan Kenton And His Orchestra | Artistry In Voices And Brass | Creative World | ST 1038

Concerto Pour Bandoneon Et Orchestre Aconcagua:Final
Joe Zawinul Group | Concerto Retitled | Atlantic | SD 1694

Concerto To End All Concertos
Stan Kenton And His Orchestra | The Early Years | Capitol | 166219-2

Conchita
Luca Flores | For Those I Never Knews | SPLASC(H) Records | CD H 439-2

Concierto D'Aranjuez
Miles Davis With Gil Evans & His Orchestra | Sketches Of Spain | CBS | CK 65142
Miles Davis Classics | CBS | CBS 88138

Concierto D'Aranjuez(Adagio)
The Rosenberg Trio With Orchestra | Noches Calientes | Verve | 557022-2
Miles Davis With Gil Evans & His Orchestra | Sketches Of Spain | CBS | CK 65142

Concierto D'Aranjuez(part 1)
Live Miles-More From The Legendary Carnegie Hall Concert | CBS | 460064-2

Concierto D'Aranjuez(part 2)
Live Miles-More From The Legendary Carnegie Hall Concert | CBS | 460064-2

Concierto De Charagojazz
Astor Piazzolla With Orchestra Of St. Luke's | Concierto Para Bandoneon-Tres Tangos | Nonesuch | 7559-79174-2

Concierto Para Bandoneon:
Irakere | Misa Negra | Messidor | 15972 CD

Conclusions Of A Dream
Alex Riel Trio | Emergence | Red Records | 123263-2

Concordanza
Gil Evans Orchestra | Verve Jazz Masters 23:Gil Evans | Verve | 521860-2

Concorde
The Individualism Of Gil Evans | Verve | 833804-2 PMS
Joachim Kühn Group | Universal Time | EmArCy | 016671-2
Modern Jazz Quartet | Concorde | Original Jazz Classics | OJC20 002-2
The Complete Modern Jazz Quartet Prestige & Pablo Recordings | Prestige | 4PRCD 4438-2
MJQ 40 | Atlantic | 7567-82330-2
Modern Jazz Quartet | Prestige | P 24005

Concrete Hat
Babamadu | Babamadu | Enja | 9093-2

Condition Blue
Willem Breuker Kollektief | Deadly Sin/Twice A Woman(Sountracks) | BVHAAST | CD 9708

Condorito
Javier Paxarino Group With Glen Velez | Temurá | ACT | 9227-2

Conductus Mundi
NAD | Ghosts | ITM Records | ITM 1454

Con-Fab
Art Farmer Quintet | Farmer 's Market | Prestige | P 24032

Confab In Tempo
Johnny Hodges And The Ellington All-Stars Without Duke | Duke's In Bed | Verve | 2304383 IMS

Conference Mit Mosch
Positive Knowledge | Another Day's Journey | Music & Arts | CD 842

Conference Of The Birds
Vocal Summit | Conference Of The Birds | ITM-Pacific | ITMP 970070

Confessin'
Django Reinhardt Quartet | Jazz In Paris:Django Reinhardt-Nuages | EmArCy | 018428-2
Ella Fitzgerald And Her Famous Orchestra | The Radio Years 1940 | Jazz Unlimited | JUCD 2065
Erroll Garner Trio | Serenade To 'Laura' | Savoy | SV 0221(MG 12003)

Confessin'-
B.B.King And His Band | Completely Live And Well | Charly | CDX 14

Confessin' The Blues
Jay McShann Kansas City Band | Jay McShann Paris All Star Band-A Tribute To Charlie Parker | Musicmasters | 5052-2
Jay McShann Quartet | Goin' To Kansas City | Stony Plain | SPCD 1286
The Man From Muskogee | Affinity | AFF 147

Confessin'(That I Love You)
Earl Hines | Four Jazz Giants:Earl Hines Plays Tributes To W.C.Handy,Hoagy Carmichael And Louis Armstrong | Solo Art | SACD-111/112
Louis Armstrong And His Orchestra | Louis Armstrong And His Big Band Vol.1-The Maturity | Black & Blue | BLE 59.225 2
Teddy Wilson Sextet | I Want To Be Happy | Naxos Jazz | 8.120538 CD

Confessions
Zbigniew Seifert | Solo Violin | MRC | 066-45088

Confidence
Special EFX | Confidential | GRP | GRP 95812

Configuration
29th Street Saxophone Quartet | The Real Deal | New Note Records | ???

Confirmation
Archie Shepp-Chet Baker Quintet | In Memory Of: First And Last Meeting In Frankfurt And Paris 1988 | L+R Records | CDLR 45006
Art Blakey And The Jazz Messengers(Art Blakey Quintet) | Clifford Brown:The Complete Blue Note And Pacific Recordings | Blue Note | 834195-2
Bud Powell Trio | Budism | Steeplechase | SCCD 30007/9
Charlie Parker Quartet | Charlie Parker:The Best Of The Verve Years | Verve | 527815-2
Charlie Parker | Verve | 539757-2
Charlie Parker:Bird's Best Bop On Verve | Verve | 527452-2
Charlie Parker Quintet | Bird At St. Nick's | Original Jazz Classics | OJC20 041-2(JWS 500)
Bird At The Roost Vol.2 | Savoy | WL 70825 (886428)
Datevik With The Larry Willis Quartet | Ballads From The Black Sea | Mapleshade | 04332
Dizzy Gillespie Sextet | To Diz With Love | Telarc Digital | CD 83307
Eddie Jefferson Sextet | The Live-Liest | Muse | MR 5127
George Shearing/Hank Jones | The Spirit Of 176 | Concord | CCD 4371
James Moody Quartet | Sweet And Lovely | Novus | PD 83063
John Lewis-Hank Jones Duo | An Evening With Two Grand Pianos | Little David | LD 59657
Red Rodney Quintet | Then And Now | Chesky | JD 79
Sam Most Sextet | Sam Most Plays Bird, Bud, Monk And Miles | Fresh Sound Records | FSR 2039(Bethlehem BCP 75)
Sonny Stitt Quintet | That's Jazz Vol.24: Stitt Plays Bird | Atlantic | ATL 50301
Tete Montoliu | Boston Concert | Steeplechase | SCS 1152/3
Tommy Flanagan Trio | Eclypso | Enja | 2088-2
Maria Joao-Aki Takase | Looking For Love:Live At The Leverkusen Jazz Festival | Enja | 5075-2

Confirmation(2 false starts)
Charlie Parker Quintet | Bird's Eyes-Last Unissued Vol.2+3 | Philology | W 12/15.2

Confirmation(take 1-3)
George Freeman Quintet | All In The Game | LRC Records | CDC 9037

Conflict
Mike Westbrook Concert Band | Marching Songs Vol.1&2 | Deram | 844853-2

Conflict(alt.take)
Mike Richmond Quartet | Dance For Andy | Steeplechase | SCCD 31267

Confluence
Saxophon And Organ | Above The Clouds | Naxos Jazz | 86041-2

Confluences
Fuchs & Katzer | FinkFarker | FMP | CD 26

Confrontation
Kenny Drew Jr. Quartet | The Rainbow Connection | Jazz City | 660.53.010

Confronting Our Fears
Hal Kemp And His Orchestra | Got A Date With An Angel | Pro-Arte | CDD 553

Conga Brava
Duke Ellington And His Famous Orchestra | Duke Ellington:Ko-Ko | Dreyfus Jazz Line | FDM 36717-2
Ben Webster-Cotton Tail | RCA | 63667902
Duke Ellington And His Orchestra | Crystal Ballroom, Fargo Concert | Jazz Anthology | JA 5229/30
Duke Ellington's Masterpieces Vol.1: 1938-1940 | Black & Blue | BLE 59.233 2
The Conga Kings | Jazz Descargas | Chesky | JD 217

Conga Potpourri:
Lloyd Glenn Quartet | Old Time Shuffle | Black & Blue | BLE 59.077 2

Congalegre
Horace Parlan Quartet | Headin' South | Blue Note | 869065-3

Congeniality
Ornette Coleman Quartet | Beauty Is A Rare Thing:Ornette Coleman-The Complete Atlantic Recordings | Atlantic | 8122-71410-2
The Shape Of Jazz To Come | Atlantic | 7567-81339-2

Congo
Remy Filipovitch-Gediminas Laurinavicius | Open Your Eyes | Album | AS 331108 CD

Congo-
Noodband | Shiver | Moers Music | 01094

Congo Call
Big John Patton Septet | Blue Planet Man | Paddle Wheel | KICJ 168

Congo Square
Festa Group | Montreux Jazz Festival-Live | SPLASC(H) Records | HP 19

Congratulations-
Dakota Staton With The Groove Holmes Sextet | Dakota Staton | LRC Records | CDC 9017

Congratulations To Someone
Mario Bauzá And The Afro-Cuban Jazz Orchestra | 944 Columbus | Messidor | 15828 CD

Congratulations,You Made It This Far
Deborah Henson-Conant | Alter Ego | Laika Records | 35100852

Congratulations,You Made It This Far(The Birthday Song)
Attila Zoller-Jimmy Raney Duo | Jim & I | L+R Records | LR 40006

Connection
Lily White Group | No Pork Long Line | Jazz Focus | JFCD 017

Connie's Blues
Modern Jazz Quartet | The Best Of The Modern Jazz Quartet | Pablo | 2405423-2

Conquistador
Cecil Taylor Sextet | A Blue Conception | Blue Note | 534254-2
Dave Samuels Group | Del Sol | GRP | GRP 96962

Consecutive Seconds
Thelonious Monk And His Orchestra | Who's Afraid Of The Big Band Monk? | CBS | CBS 88034

Consequence
John Coltrane Quartet | First Meditation | Impulse(MCA) | GRP 11182

Consequences
Dave Liebman Ensemble | John Coltrane's Medetation | Arkadia Jazz | 71042
When Granny Sleeps | Welcome | dacapo | DCCD 9447
John Coltrane Quartet | John Coltrane:The Classic Quartet-Complete Impulse Studio Recordings | Impulse(MCA) | 951280-2

Consequences-
29th Street Saxophone Quartet | Underground | Antilles | 848415-2(889151)

Considerung The Snail
Joe Kienemann Trio | Integration | yvp music | CD 3023

Consin
Clarence Penn Quintet | Play-Penn | Criss Cross | Criss 1201

Consolacao
Bola Sete And His New Brazilian Trio | Autentico | Original Jazz Classics | OJC 290(F 8375)

Consolation
Jazz Orchester Rheinland-Pfalz | Last Season | Jazz Haus Musik | LJBB 9706
Kenny Wheeler Ensemble | Muisc For Large & Small Ensembles | ECM | 1415/16
Gunter Hampel Group | Music From Europe | ESP Disk | ESP 1042-2

Constant Travel
Nguyen Le Group | Maghreb And Friends | ACT | 9261-2

Constantine
Benny Carter-Dizzy Gillespie Inc. | Carter Gillespie.Inc. | Original Jazz Classics | OJCCD 682-2(2310781)

Constantinople
Patricia Barber Group | Modern Cool | Blue Note | 521811-2
Franz Koglmann Pipetet | The Use Of Memory | Hat Art | CD 6078

Constantly
Bill Allred-Roy Williams Quintet | The Second Sampler | Nagel-Heyer | NHR SP 6
Fraser MacPherson Quintet | In The Tradition | Concord | CCD 4506

Constellation
Mark Isaacs Quintet | Closer | Naxos Jazz | 86065-2
Sonny Stitt Quartet | Constellation | Muse | MCD 5323

Constellation(part 1-5)
Charlie Parker All Stars | Charlie Parker Memorial Vol.1 | Savoy | SV 0101(MG 12000)

Construct ß 32
Butterbeams And Susie | King Oliver's Creole Jazzband-The Complete Set | Retrieval | RTR 79007

Contact
Ernst Höllerhagen Quartet | Ernst Höllerhagen 1942-1948 | Elite Special | 9522001

Contact Blues
Gonzalo Rubalcaba Quartet | Imagine | Blue Note | 830491-2

Contagio
Rapsodia | Blue Note | 828264-2

Conte De L'Incroyable Amour
Art Blakey And The Jazz Messengers | Buhaina's Delight | Blue Note | 784104-2

Contemplation
Bernhard Reinke Transfusion | Driftin' | Timeless | CD SJP 323
McCoy Tyner Quintet | Prelude And Sonata | Milestone | MCD 9244-2
Passport | Infinity Machine | Atlantic | 2292-44146-2
Peter Herborn Orchestra | Large One | Jazzline | JL 11174-2

Contempo Latinsky
Billy Kyle's Big Eight | Giants Of Small-Band Swing Vol.1 | Original Jazz Classics | OJC- 1723(RLP 143)

Contempt
Peter Bolte-Marcio Doctor | Zeitraum | Jazz Haus Musik | JHM 0113 CD

Contenance
Evan Parker/Barry Guy/Paul Lytton | Imaginary Values | MAYA Recordings | MCD 9401

Contessa Entellina
James Weiman Trio | People Music | TCB Records | TCB 96302

Contigo En La Distancia
Guillermo Marchena Y El Grupo Irazu | Boleros | L+R Records | CDLR 45068

Contimuum
Clementine And The Johnny Griffin Quartet | Continent Bleu | Orange Blue | OB 004 CD

Continental Breakfast
Ralph Towner-Gary Burton | Slide Show | ECM | 1306
Peter Fulda Trio With Céline Rudolph | Silent Dances | Jazz 4 Ever Records:Jazz Network | J4E 4731

Continental Songlines
Lars Danielsson Trio | Continuation | L+R Records | CDLR 45085

Continuation
Passport | 2 Originals Of Passport(Passport-Second Passport) | Atlantic | ATL 60117
Steve Rochinski | Otherwise | Jardis Records | JRCD 20133

Continuation On An Afterthought
Paul Grabowsky Sextet | Tee Vee | VeraBra Records | CDVBR 2050-2

Continuum
Jaco Pastorius Trio | Live In Italy & Honestly | Jazzpoint | JP 1059 CD
Jaco Pastorius' Word Of Mouth Big Band | Invitation | Warner | 92-3876-1
Richie Beirach | Continuum | Eastwind | EWIND 704

Contour
Jackie McLean Quintet | Contour | Prestige | P 24076

Contours
Shorty Rogers And His Orchestra Feat. The Giants | Short Stops | RCA | NL 85917(2)

Contra Post
Astor Piazzolla Group | Tango: Zero Hour | American Clave | AMCL 1013-2

Contractor's Blues
Chuck Israels International Quartet | On Common Ground | Anima Records | DV-CD 002

Contradance
Irakere | Felicidad | Ronnie Scott's Jazz House | JHCD 014

Contradictions
Michel Petrucciani Quintet | Michel Petrucciani Live | Blue Note | 780589-2
Glen Moore Group | Introducing Glen Moore | Elektra | ELK K 52151

Contrary Motion
Ted Heath And His Orchestra | Swing Is King | Decca | 6.28129 DP

Contraste
Dizzy Gillespie And His Orchestra | Afro Cuban Jazz | Verve | 833561-1

Contrasts
Bucky And John Pizzarelli Duo | The Pizzarellis,Bucky And John:Contrasts | Arbors Records | ARCD 19209

Contrasts(Opening Theme)
Jimmy Dorsey And His Orchestra | The Uncollected:Jimmy Dorsey, Vol. 2 | Hindsight | HSR 153

Contre Contre
Mosalini/Beytelmann/Caratini | Inspiration Del Tango | Eigelstein | 568-72223

Contructing Stop
Butterbeams And Susie | Louis Armstrong With King Oliver Vol.2 | Village(Jazz Archive) | VILCD 012-2

Convalescent
Mehldau & Rossy Trio | When I Fall In Love | Fresh Sound Records | FSNT 007 CD
Great Jazz Trio | Threesome | Eastworld | EWJ 90015

Converge
Chick Corea Septet | The Complete 'Is' Sessions | Blue Note | 540532-2

Converge(alt.take)
AMM III | It Had Been An Ordinary Enough Day In Pueblo, Colorado | Japo | 60031

Convergence
Jay Hoggard Quartet | Overview | Muse | MCD 5383

Conversa
Baden Powell + Janine | Jazz Meets Brasil | MPS | 533133-2

Conversaciones En La Plate
Arne Domnerus Favourite Group | Made In Sweden Vol.1: 1949 to March 1951 | Magnetic Records | MRCD 106

Conversation
L.Subramaniam/Stephane Grappelli Group | Conversations | Milestone | M 9130
Mino Cinelu-Kenny Barron | Swamp Sally | Verve | 532268-2
Shankar/Garbarek/Hussain/Gurtu | Song For Everyone | ECM | 1286(823795-2)
Superblue | Superblue | Blue Note | 791731-2
Bill Dixon Sextet | Bill Dixon In Italy-Volume One | Soul Note | 121008-2

Conversation Blues
Rahsaan Roland Kirk Orchestra | Rahsaan Roland Kirk-Yusef Lateef:Seperate But Equal | 32 Jazz | 32111

Conversation In A Flat
Lee Konitz-Hein Van De Geyn | Hein Van De Geyn Meets Lee Konitz | September | CD 5110

Conversation Piece
Dick Meldonian And The Jersey Swingers | Some Of These Days | Progressive | PRO 7033 IMS

Conversation With A Baby
Albert Collins & The Ice Breakers | Ice Pickin' | Sonet | 147107

Conversations At The Mess
Vocal Summit | Sorrow Is Not Forever-Love Is | Moers Music | 02004 CD

Conversations With Sparze
Sahib Shihab Quintet | Conversations | Black Lion | BLCD 760169

Conversing In Blue
Benny Morton's All Stars | The Blue Note Swingtets | Blue Note | 495697-2
Jackie McLean Sextet | 'Bout Soul | Blue Note | 859383-2

Convict 13
Dave Belany And Her Trio | Motivations | Sahara | 1005

Convolution
Frank Gordon Sextet | Clarion Echoes | Soul Note | 121096-2

Coogan's Bluff
Red Rodney Quintet | Prestige First Sessions, Vol.3 | Prestige | PCD 24116-2

Cook-A-Doodle-Doo
Deanna Witkowski Group | Having To Ask | Jazzline | JL 11158-2

Cookey's Song
Tony Kinsey Orchestra | Thames Suite | Spotlite | SPJ 504

Cookie Man
Julian Argüelles-Steve Argüelles | Scapes | Babel | BDV 9614

Cookin'
Christian Rannenberg & The Pink Piano All Stars | Long Way From Home | Acoustic Music Records | AMC 1006

Cookin' At The Continental
GRP All-Star Big Band | All Blues | GRP | GRP 98002
Helmut Kagerer-Peter Bernstein Quartet | April In New York | Jardis Records | JRCD 9818
Horace Silver Quintet | Horace Silver | Blue Note | 84510
Horace Silver Retrospective | Blue Note | 495576-2
Michal Urbaniak Quintet | Music For Violin & Jazz Quartet | JAM | 001 IMS

Cookin'(alt.take)
Ben Webster With The Junior Mance Trio | Tenor Giants | Enja | 2038-2

Cook's Bay
011 Jazz Sextet | Bustring | SPLASC(H) Records | H 114

Cool
CMMC Bigband | Modern Times | Blue Concept | BCCD 93/02

Cool-
Rhein Brass And Friends | Kant Park | Mons Records | MR 874318

Cool Blue
All Stars | Bird's Eyes Last Unissued Vol.21:Bird On TV/Bird On Bandbox | Philology | W 851.2

Cool Blues
Charlie Parker With The Chet Baker Quartet | Chet Baker & Charlie Parker:Complete Jam Sessions | Definitive Records | DRCD 11232
Hampton Hawes Trio | Everybody Likes Hampton Hawes | Original Jazz Classics | OJCCD 421-2
Lars Gullin And The Chet Baker Quartet | Lars Gullin 1955/56 Vol.1 | Dragon | DRCD 224
Charlie Parker Quintet | One Night At Birdland | CBS | CBS 88250

Cool Breeze
Dizzy Gillespie And His Orchestra | Dizzy Gillespie (1946-1949) | RCA | ND 89763
Eric Essix Sextet | First Impressions | Nova | NOVA 8920-2

Cool Cave
Babs Gonzales And His Band | Voilà | Fresh Sound Records | FSR CD 340

Cool Cookin'
Louie Bellson Trio/Quartet/Quintet | Cool Cool Blue | Pablo | 2310899

Cool Day In Hell
Sonny Boy Williamson Band | One Way Out | Chess | CHD 9116(872271)

Cool Eyes
Horace Silver Quintet | Horace Silver Retrospective | Blue Note | 495576-2
Sal Salvador Quartet | A Tribute To The Greats | Fresh Sound Records | FSR 2019(Bethlehem BCP 74)

Cool Fool
Jackie McLean Quintet | Bluesnik | Blue Note | 784067-2

Cool Hopper
Marty Fogel Quartet | Many Bobbing Heads, At Last... | CMP Records | CMP CD 37

Cool Mambo
Harry Allen With The John Pizzarelli Trio | Tenors Anyone? | Novus | 2150684-2

Cool March
André Previn And His Pals | West Side Story | Original Jazz Classics | OJC 422(C 7572)

Cool Mix
Gary Burton Group | Cool Nights | GRP | GRP 96432

Cool Papa N'Diaye
World Saxophone Quartet | Dances And Ballads | Nonesuch | 7559-79164-2

Cool Red
Duke Ellington And His Orchestra | Jazz Collection:Duke Ellington | Laserlight | 24369

Cool Rock
Eddie Bert Sextet | Let's Dig Bert(Eddie That Is) | Fresh Sound Records | FSR 540(Trans-World TWLP 208)

Cool Street
Art Farmer Quintet | Central Avenue Reunion | Contemporary | CCD 14057-2

Cool Struttin'
Sonny Clark Quintet | Cool Struttin' | Blue Note | 746513-2

Cool Sweets
Lester Bowie's New York Organ Ensemble | Funky T. Cool T. | DIW | DIW 853 CD

Cool Train
Lionel Hampton And His Orchestra | The Great Hamptologia, Vol. 1 | MGM | 2304527 IMS

Cool Walk
Oscar Peterson Quintet | Oscar Peterson Meets Roy Hargrove And Ralph Moore | Telarc Digital | CD 83399

Cool Water
Christoph Spendel Group | Milky Way | L+R Records | CDLR 45012

Cool Weasel Boogie
Babs Gonzales And His Orchestra | Cool Whalin' - Bebop Vocals | Spotlite | SPJ 135

Cool Your Motor
Louis Armstrong With The Commanders | Ambassador Louis Armstrong Vol.17:Moments To Remember(1952-1956) | Ambassador | CLA 1917

Cool Yule
Howard McGhee Quintet | Sharp Edge | Black Lion | BLCD 760110

Coolangata
Cyrus Chestnut Sextet | Earth Stories | Atlantic | 7567-82876-2

Cooldaddy's Perspective
Howard McGhee Sextet | Trumpet At Tempo | Spotlite | SPJ 131

Co-Op Blues
Shorty Rogers And His Giants | The Big Shorty Rogers Express | RCA | 2118519-2

TITELVERZEICHNIS

Coop De Graas
Shorty Rogers And His Orchestra Feat. The Giants | Short Stops | RCA | NL 85917(2)

Coordination
Craig Harris And Tailgater's Tales | Shelter | JMT Edition | 919008-2

Cootie
Jam Session | Coleman Hawkins-Rare Broadcasts Area 1950 | Jazz Anthology | JA 5217

Cop Out
Duke Ellington And His Orchestra | Duke Ellington All Star Road Band | Doctor Jazz | ZL 70968(2) (809318)

Copacabana
Fun Horns | First Catalogue | KlangRäume | 30170

Copenhagen
Harry Gold And His Famous Pieces Of Eight | Dixie! | Harlequin | HQ 3001 IMS
Ragtime Specht Groove Trio | Mr. Woodpeckers Special | Intercord | 130001

Copious
Muddy Waters Blues Band | I'm Ready | Blue Sky | 82235

Copyright Royalties
The Carla Bley Band | Social Studies | Watt | 11(831831-2)
Luis Agudo | Afrosamba | Red Records | VPA 172

Coqueta
Hector Martignon Group | Portrait In White And Black | Candid | CCD 79727

Coquette
Bucky And John Pizzarelli Duo | The Pizzarellis,Bucky And John:Contrasts | Arbors Records | ARCD 19209
Charlie Lewis Trio | JazzIn Paris:Harlem Piano In Montmartre | EmArCy | 018447-2
Chris Barber & His New Orleans Friends | Chris Barber Plays With Members Of The Preservation Hall Band | Timeless | CD TTD 573
Jay McShann And His Orchestra | Early Bird | Spotlite | SPJ 120
Ron Eschete | A Closer Look | Concord | CCD 4607

Cora
George Duke Group | George Duke & Feel | MPS | 68023

Coracao
Dave Brubeck Quartet | Dave Brubeck's All-Time Greatest Hits | CBS | 68288

Coral
Gary Burton Quartet | Works | ECM | 823267-2

Coral Negro
Dino Saluzzi Trio | Cité De La Musique | ECM | 1616(533316-2)

Coral Para Mi Pequeno Y Lejano Pueblo
Archie Shepp Quartet | Doodlin' | Inner City | IC 1001 IMS

Corazon
Freddie Hubbard Group | Times Are Changing | Blue Note | B 1-90905

Corbu-
Allan Vaché-Harry Allen Quintet | Allan And Allan | Nagel-Heyer | CD 074

Corcovado(Quiet Nights)
Ana Caram Group | Blue Bossa | Chesky | JD 219
Anna Lauvergnac-Wolfgang Puschnig-Alegre Correa | Anna Lauvergnac | TCB Records | TCB 21132
Astrud Gilberto With The New Stan Getz Quartet | Verve Jazz Masters 9:Astrud Gilberto | Verve | 519824-2
Baden Powell Quartet | Le Genie De Baden Powell | Accord | 114852
Cannonball Adderley With Sergio Mendes And The Bossa Rio Quartet | Cannonball's Bossa Nova | Blue Note | 522667-2
Charlie Byrd Trio With Ken Peplowski | The Bossa Nova Years | Concord | CCD 4468
Franco D'Andrea New Quartet | Jobim | Philology | W 125.2
Getz-Gilberto Quintet | Stan Getz Highlights:The Best Of The Verve Years Vol.2 | Verve | 517330-2
A Life In Jazz:A Musical Biography | Verve | 535119-2
Getz/Gilberto | Polydor | 521414-2
Getz/Gilberto No.2 | Verve | 519800-2
Getz/Gilberto:The Girl From Ipanema | CTI Records | PDCTI 1105-2
Jerry Gonzalez & Fort Apache Band | Moliendo Cafe-To Wisdom The Price | Sunnyside | SSC 1061 D
Larry Coryell-Miroslav Vitous | Dedicated To Bill Evans And Scott LaFaro | Jazzpoint | JP 1021 CD
Laura Fygi With Band | Laura Fygi Live At The North Sea Jazz | Spectra | 9811207
Miles Davis With Gil Evans & His Orchestra | This Is Jazz:Bossa Nova | CBS | CK 65045
Miles Davis With Orchestra | Ballads | CBS | 461099-2
Mind Games | Mind Games Plays The Music Of Stan Getz & Astrud Gilberto | Edition Collage | EC 515-2
Mind Games With Claudio Roditi | Live | Edition Collage | EC 501-2
Monty Alexander Quartet | Triple Treat III | Concord | CCD 4394
Ran Blake-Jeanne Lee | You Stepped Out Of A Cloud | Owl Records | 055 CD
Sonny Stitt With The Zimbo Trio | Sonny Stitt In Brazil | Fresh Sound Records | FSR-CD 0118
Stan Getz Orchestra | Compact Jazz | Verve | 831368-2
Stan Getz Quintet Feat. Astrud Gilberto | Getz/Gilberto | Verve | 589595-2 SACD
Stan Getz Sextet | Compact Jazz: Best Of Bossa Nova | Verve | 833269-2
Tamba Trio | Tamba Trio Classics | EmArCy | 536958-2
The New Stan Getz Quintet Feat. Astrud Gilberto | Getz Au Go Go | CTI Records | PDCTI 1124-2

Corcovado(Quiet Nights,45rpm issue)
Cannonball Adderley With Sergio Mendes And The Bossa Rio Quartet | Cannonball's Bossa Nova | Blue Note | 522667-2

Corcovado(Quiet Nights-alt.take)
Joelle Leandre/Irene Schweizer | Cordial Gratin | FMP | 1160

Cordoba
Warren Bernhardt Quintet | Reflections | dmp Digital Music Productions | CD 489

Corine
Jens Bunge Group | With All My Heart | yvp music | CD 3060

Corinne Corinna
Art Tatum And His Band | Pure Genius | Affinity | AFF 118
Big Joe Turner With The Count Basie Orchestra | Flip Flop And Fly | Original Jazz Classics | OJCCD 1053-2(2310937)
Big Nick Nicholas Quintet | Big And Warm | India Navigation | IN 1061

Corinne Corinna Boogie
Acker Bilk With Ken Colyer's Jazzmen | Together Again | Lake | LACD 53

Corinthian Melodies
Ulrich Gumpert | The Secret Concert | ITM Records | ITM 1461

Corner Pocket
Count Basie And His Orchestra | Basie Bounce | Affinity | CD AFS 1001
A True Collectors Item | Jazz Archive | 90.106-2
Basie In Sweden | Roulette | CDP 759974-2
Milt Jackson With The Count Basie Orchestra | Milt Jackson + Count Basie + The Big Band Vol.1 | Pablo | 2310822-2
Sir Charles Thompson Trio | Robbin's Nest | Paddle Wheel | KICJ 181

Corner Pocket(aka Until I Met You)
Count Basie And His Orchestra | April In Paris | Verve | 521402-2

Corner Pocket(alt.take)
Phil Haynes' 4 Horns & What | 4 Horns & What? | Open Minds | OM 2402-2

Cornet Chop Suey
Funny House Jazzband | That's My Home | Timeless | CD TTD 575
Louis Armstrong And His Hot Five | Heebie Jeebies | Naxos Jazz | 8.120351 CD
Thomas Heberer-Dieter Manderscheid | What A Wonderful World | Jazz Haus Musik | JHM 0118 CD
Oscar Klein-Philadelphia Jerry Ricks | Blues Panorama | Koch Records | 121 705

Cornette
José Luis Gámez Quartet | Colores | Fresh Sound Records | FSNT 028 CD

Anca Parghel With The Klaus Ignatzek Trio | Indian Princess | Blue Flame | 40262(2132488-2)

Corona
Tony Aless Orchestra | Tony Aless And His Long Island Suite | Fresh Sound Records | RLP 2202(Roost)

Corona(alt.take 1)
Clifford Brown All Stars | Brownie-The Complete EmArCy Recordings Of Clifford Brown | EmArCy | 838306-2

Corona(alt.take 2)
Gene Krupa Sextet | The Exciting Gene Krupa | Enoch's Music | 57271033

Corrida
Abraham Burton Quartet | Closest To The Sun | Enja | ENJ-8074 2

Corrida De Toros
Curtis Fuller Quintet | Four On The Outside | Timeless | CD SJP 124

Corrine Corrina Blues
Two Bad Boys | The Voice Of The Blues-Bottleneck Guitar Masterpieces | Yazoo | YAZ 1046

Cortesanos
Chris Barber's Jazz Band | The Outstanding Album | BELL Records | BLR 89300

Cosa Linda
Eric Reed Quintet | Musicale | Impulse(MCA) | 951196-2

Cosa Nostra(Our Thing)
Chico Hamilton And Euphoria | Arroyo | Soul Note | 121241-2

Coscrane
Bud Powell Trio | Time Was | Bluebird | ND 86367

Cosi-
Clare Fischer Group | Machaca | MPS | 68254

Cosmic Biotope-
Sun Ra And His Solar Arkestra | Heliocentric Worlds Vol.2 | ESP Disk | ESP 1017-2

Cosmic Chicken
Herb Robertson Group | Certified | JMT Edition | 849150-2

Cosmic Messenger
Jean-Luc Ponty Sextet | Cosmic Messenger | Atlantic | 7567-81550-2
Curtis Clark | Deep Sea Diver | Nimbus | NS 3580

Cosmic Rays
Ray Charles-Milt Jackson Sextet | Soul Brothers/Soul Meeting | Atlantic | 7567-81951-2
Charlie Parker Quartet | Bird On Verve-Vol.7:Charlie Parker Big Band | Verve | 817448-1 IMS

Cosmic Rays(alt.take)
Bird: The Complete Charlie Parker On Verve | Verve | 837141-2

Cosmic Rays(take 2)
Bird: The Complete Charlie Parker On Verve | Verve | 837141-2

Cosmic Rays(take 5)
The Crusaders | Images | MCA | 250777-1

Cosmic Song
JoAnne Brackeen Trio | Where Legends Dwell | Ken Music | 660.56.021

Cosmic Turtle
Ed Thigpen Rhythm Features | It's Entertainment | Stunt Records | STUCD 19816

Cosmology
Marilyn Crispell Trio | Story Teller | ECM | 1847(0381192)
JoAnne Brackeen Quintet | Fi-Fi Goes To Heaven | Concord | CCD 4316

Cosmosis
Bent Axen Quintet(Jazz Quintet '60) | Axen | Steeplechase | SCCD 36003

Cossak's Farewell
Mongo Santamaria And His Band | Brazilian Sunset | Candid | CCD 79703

Costa Del Oro
Peter O'Mara Quintet | Avenue 'U' | Enja | 6046-2

Cote D'Azur
Bob Wilber-Dick Hyman Sextet | A Perfect Match:A Tribute To Johnny Hodges & Wild Bill Davis | Arbors Records | ARCD 19193

Cottage For Sale
Charles Brown With Orchestra | Boss Of The Blues | Mainstream | MD CDO 908
Etta Jones With The Houston Person Sextet | At Last | Muse | MCD 5511

Cotton Avenue
Sonny Thompson And His Orchestra | Cat On The Keys | Swingtime(Contact) | ST 1027

Cotton Boy Blues
Jimmy McGriff Quintet | Jimmy McGriff-Funkiest Little Band In The Kand | LRC Records | CDC 9046(874379)

Cotton Club
Duke Ellington And His Cotton Club Orchestra | Early Ellington (1927-1934) | Bluebird | ND 86852

Cotton Club Stomp
Duke Ellington And His Orchestra | Highlights From The Duke Ellington Centennial Edition | RCA | 2663672-2
Duke Ellington's Masterpieces Vol.1: 1938-1940 | Black & Blue | BLE 59.233 2

Cotton Eyed Joe
The Real Group | One For All | ACT | 9003-2

Cotton Eyed Joe-
Garfield Akers | The Greatest In Country Blues Vol.1(1927-1930) | Story Of Blues | CD 3521-2

Cotton Field Boogie
Bill Marx And His Trio | My Son The Folk Swinger/Jazz Kaleidoscope | Vee Jay Recordings | VJ 021

Cotton Tail
Ben Webster With The Oscar Peterson Quartet | King Of The Tenors | Verve | 519806-2
Benny Carter And His Orchestra | Further Definitions | Impulse(MCA) | JAS 14 (AS 12)
Bill Berry's L.A.Big Band | Hello Rev. | Concord | CCD 4027
Charlie Byrd Quintet | Du Hot Club De Concord | Concord | CCD 4674
Dave McKenna Quartet | Piano Mover | Concord | CJ 146
Dee Dee Bridgewater With Big Band | Dear Ella | Verve | 539102-2
Dee Dee Bridgewater With Her Trio | Live At Yoshi's | Verve | 543354-2
DMP Big Band | DMP Big Band Salutes Duke Ellington | dmp Digital Music Productions | CD 520
Duke Ellington And His Famous Orchestra | Duke Ellington:Ko-Ko | Dreyfus Jazz Line | FDM 36717-2
Ben Webster-Cotton Tail | RCA | 63667902
Jazz:The Essential Collection Vol.3 | IN+OUT Records | 78013-2
In A Mellow Tone | RCA | 2113029-2
Duke Ellington And His Orchestra | Carnegie Hall Concert January 1943 | Prestige | 2PCD 34004-2
Highlights From The Duke Ellington Centennial Edition | RCA | 2663672-2
Duke Ellington:Complete Prestige Carnegie Hall 1943-1944 Concerts | Definitive Records | DRCD 11210
Big Band Bounce & Boogie:Duke Ellington Presents | Affinity | AFS 1013
Duke Ellington Quartet | Duke's Big 4 | Pablo | 2310703-2
Earl Hines And His Orchestra | Once Upon A Time | MCA | 2292-50608-1
Ella Fitzgerald And Her All Stars | Ella Fitzgerald Sings The Duke Ellington Songbook | Verve | 559248-2
The Complete Ella Fitzgerald Song Books of Harold Arlen, Irving Berlin, Duke Ellington, George & Ira Gershwin, Jerome Kern, Johnny Mercer, Cole Porter And Rogers & Hart | Verve | 519832-2
Ella Fitzgerald And Her Trio With The Duke Ellington Orchestra | The Greatest Jazz Concert In The World | Pablo | 2625704-2
Ella Fitzgerald With The Duke Ellington Orchestra | The Stockholm Concert 1966 | Pablo | 2308242-2
Ella Fitzgerald With The Duke Ellington Orchestra And Jimmy Jones Trio | Ella Fitzgerald And Duke Ellington:Cote D'Azure Concerts on Verve | Verve | 539033-2
Ella Fitzgerald And Duke Ellington:Cote D'Azure Concerts on Verve | Verve | 539033-2
Flip Phillips Sextet | A Real Swinger | Concord | CJ 358
JATP Jam Session | Norman Granz' Jazz At The Philharmonic HARTFORD, 1953 | Pablo | 2308240-2
Joe Temperley Quintet | They All Play The Duke | Jazz Colours | 874740-2
Louis Armstrong-Duke Ellington Group | The Complete Louis Armstrong & Duke Ellington Sessions | Roulette | 793844-2
Oscar Peterson Quartet | A Tribute To My Friends | Pablo | 2310902-2
Oscar Peterson Trio | Oscar Peterson Plays The Duke Ellington Song Book | Verve | 559785-2
Panama Francis And The Savoy Sultans | Grooving | Stash Records | ST 218 IMS
Ray Barretto Orchestra | Portraits In Jazz And Clave | RCA | 2168452-2
Ray Brown Trio With Ulf Wakenius | Duke Ellington...Swings! | Telarc Digital | CD 83429
Roots | Salutes The Saxophone: Tributes To John Coltrane, Dexter Gordon, Sonny Rollins, Ben Webster And Lester Young | IN+OUT Records | 7016-1
Wes Montgomery Quartet | Wes Montgomery-The Complete Riverside Recordings | Riverside | 12 RCD 4408-2
Wes Montgomery Quintet | So Much Guitar! | Original Jazz Classics | OJC20 233-2
The Jazz Giants Play Duke Ellington:Caravan | Prestige | PCD 24227-2
Wycliffe Gordon Quintet | What You Dealin' With | Criss Cross | Criss 1212

Cotton Tail-
Joe Temperley Quintet | Double Duke | Naxos Jazz | 86032-2

Couch Potato
Eddy Louiss Trio | Tabataba(Soundtrack) | Nocturne Productions | NTCD 106

Could It Be You
Duke Ellington And His Orchestra | At The Hurricane:Original 1943 Broadcasts | Storyville | STCD 8359
Uschi Brüning And Ernst-Ludwig Petrowsky With The Günter Bartel Trio | Enfant | Aho-Recording | CD 1017

Could Ja
Chris Barber's Jazz Band With Alex Bradford | Chris Barber Jubille Album-Vol. 4 | Black Lion | 182000

Couldn't It Be You
Art Blakey And The Jazz Messengers | Second Edition | Bluebird | 63 66661-2

Count 'Em
Grant Green Quintet | Born To Be Blue | Blue Note | 784432-2

Count Every Star
Lester Young Quintet | Lester Swings | Verve | 833554-1

Count It
Florian Poser Group | Say Yes! | Edition Collage | EC 452-2

Count It(short cut)
Count Basie Kansas City 7 | Count Basie Kansas City 7 | Original Jazz Classics | OJCCD 690-2(2310908)

Count Me In
The Original Five Blind Boys Of Mississippi | Oh Lord-Stand By Me/Marching Up To Zion | Ace Records | CDCHD 341

Count Me Out
Claude Bolling Trio | A Tribute To My Favorites | Memo Music | HDJ 4068

Count On Me
Lucky Peterson Group | Beyond Cool | Verve | 521147-2

Coun't Place
Jeff Palmer Quartet | Island Universe | Soul Note | 121301-2

Count The Ways
Barry Finnerty Quintet | Straight Ahead | Arabesque Recordings | AJ 0116

Count Your Blessings
James 'Sing' Miller Quartet | New Orleans Traditional Jazz Legends:Sing Miller | Mardi Gras Records | MG 9006
Toshiko Akiyoshi Trio | Finesse | Concord | CCD 4069

Countdown
Brad Mehldau Trio | Introducing Brad Mehldau | Warner | 9362-45997-2
The Art Of The Trio Vol.2 | Warner | 9362-46848-2
Bruce Forman Quartet | The Concord Jazz Guitar Collection Volume 3 | Concord | CCD 4507
John Coltrane Quartet | Giant Steps | Atlantic | 8122-75203-2
The Art Of John Coltrane - The Atlantic Years | Atlantic | SD 2-313
Lou Levy Trio | Tempus Fugue-It | Interplay | IP 7711
Sebastian Gramss Underkarl | Jazzscene | TCB Records | TCB 99102

Countdown(alt.take)
John Coltrane Quartet | Giant Steps | Atlantic | 8122-75203-2
Wilbur Harden Quintet | Countdown | Savoy | 650102(881902)

Counter Block
Count Basie And His Orchestra | Basie On Roulette, Vol. 9: Breakfast Dance And Barbecue | Vogue | 500009

Counterpoise No.2 For Electric Guitar And Trumpet
Count On The Coast Vol.2 | Phontastic | NCD 7575

Countin' The Blues
John Stubblefield Quintet | Countin' The Blues | Enja | ENJ-5051 2

Counting Texas
Art Kassel And His 'Kassels-In-The-Air' Orchestra | The Uncollected:Art Kassel, Vol.2 | Hindsight | HSR 170

Countless Journeys
A Band Of Friends | Art Of The Improviser | Naxos Jazz | 86026-2

Country
Keith Jarrett Quartet | Works | ECM | 825425-1

Country Bama
Hein Känzig Quartet | Grace Of Gravity | Plainisphare | PL 1267-102 CD

Country Boy
John Lee Hooker | It Steve You Right To Suffer | MCA | JAS 74(AS 9103)
Peter Erskine Trio | ELB | ACT | 9289-2
Jack Teagarden And His Orchestra | Think Well Of Me | Verve | 557101-2

Country Club
Richard Zimmerman | The Complete Works Of Scott Joplin | Laserlight | 15945

Country Dance
Barbara Thompson's Paraphernalia | Mother Earth | VeraBra Records | CDVBR 2005-2
Tommy Smith Sextet | Misty Morning And No Time | Linn Records | AKD 040

Country Fair
Woody Mann | Stairwell Serenade | Acoustic Music Records | 319.1072.2

Country Life
Carrie Smith And Her All Stars | Nobody Wants You... | Black & Blue | BLE 59.119 2

Country Mile
Pat Metheny | New Chautauqua | ECM | 1131(825471-2)

Country Poem
Cannonball Adderley Group | Phenix | Fantasy | FCD 79004-2

Country Preacher
Cannonball Adderley Monologues | Radio Nights | Night Records | VNCD 2(887045)
Peppino D'Agostino | Close To The Heart | Acoustic Music Records | 319.1039.2

Country Son
Miles Davis Quintet | Miles Davis Quintet 1965-1968 | CBS | C6K 67398
Miles In The Sky | CBS | CK 65684

Country Son(alt.take)
Miles Davis Quintet 1965-1968 | CBS | C6K 67398
Karl Ratzer Group | Moon Dancer | Enja | ENJ-9357 2

Count's Blues
Count Basie Sextet | The Swinging Count | Verve | MV 2646 IMS

County Jail
Muddy Waters Blues Band | Blues Roots Vol. 11: Muddy Waters | Chess | 6.24801 AG

Coupe
Peter Bolte Quartet | Evocation | Jazz Haus Musik | JHM 0079 CD

Couples
Bob Degen Trio | Catability | Enja | ENJ-9332 2

Courage
Double You | Menschbilder | Jazz Haus Musik | JHM 0062 CD
Monika Linges Quartet | Songing | Nabel Records:Jazz Network | LP 4615

Joshua Redman Quartet | Beyond | Warner | 9362-47465-2
Courage(Assymetric Aria)
Jacques Loussier Trio | Play Bach No.2 | Decca | 157562-2
Courante
Play Bach Aux Champs-Élyssées | Decca | 159203-2
Courante-
Play Bach | Decca | 6.24015 AL
Course Of A Stream
Thomas Heberer | Stella | Poise | Poise 08
Courses
Archie Shepp-Horace Parlan Duo | Trouble In Mind | Steeplechase | SCCD 31139
Courthouse Blues
Clara Smith With The Louis Armstrong Trio | Louis Armstrong And The Blues Singers 1924-1930 | Affinity | AFS 1018(6)
Courthouse Bump
Jelly Roll Morton And His Orchestra | The Complete Jelly Roll Morton-Vol.3/4 | RCA | NL 89769(2) DP
Courtship
Gilbert Paeffgen Trio | Pedestrian Tales | Edition Musikat | EDM 061
Cous Cous
Harold Ashby Quartet | Presenting Harold Ashby | Progressive | PRO 7040 IMS
Cousin Mary
Brad Mehldau With The Rossy Trio | New York-Barcelona Crossing Vol.2 | Fresh Sound Records | FSNT 037 CD
Buddy DeFranco Group | Blues Bag | Affinity | AFF 55
John Coltrane Quartet | John Coltrane-The Heavyweight Champion:The Complete Atlantic Recordings | Atlantic | 8122-71984-2
The Very Best Of John Coltrane | Rhino | 8122-79778-2
John Coltrane-Live Trane:The European Tours | Pablo | 7PACD 4433-2
Afro Blue Impressions | Pablo | 2PACD 2620101
Giant Steps | Atlantic | 8122-75203-2
The Best Of John Coltrane | Atlantic | 7567-81366-2
Countdown | Atlantic | 90462-1 TIS
Stanley Jordan Trio | Festival International De Jazz De Montreal | Spectra | 9811660
Steve Davis Sextet | Crossfire | Criss Cross | Criss 1152
Cousin Mary(alt.take)
John Coltrane Quartet | Giant Steps | Atlantic | 8122-75203-2
Arthur Blythe Group | Hipmotism | Enja | ENJ-6088 2
Cousin Sidney
The Jeff Lorber Fusion | Fusion | Inner City | IC 1026 IMS
Cousins
Paul Bley Trio | Footoose | Savoy | SV 0140(MG 12182)
Woody Herman And His Orchestra | La Fiesta | West Wind Orchestra Series | 2400 CD
Coventry Carol-
Henry Threadgill Sextet | Just The Facts And Pass The Bucket | About Time | AT 1005
Cover The Earth With Your Loveliness
Barre Phillips | Carmouflage | Victo | CD 008
Cow Cow Blues
Bob Zurke And His Delta Rhythm Band | Masters Of Jazz Vol. 11-29 Original Boogie Woogie Hits | RCA | NL 89773 DP
Cowboy
George Shearing Trio | Windows | MPS | 68200
Cowboys Cartoons & Assorted Candy
Joel Weiskopf Quintet | New Beginning | Criss Cross | Criss 1204
Coyote
Dave Grusin Band With Orchestra | The Orchestral Album | GRP | GRP 97972
Coyote Angel-
Peter Erskine Orchestra | Peter Erskine | Original Jazz Classics | OJC 610(C 14010)
Coyote Blues
Peter Erskine | Contemporary | CCD 14010-2
Crab Alley
Ray Charles-Cleo Laine With The Frank DeVol Orchestra & Chorus | Porgy And Bess | London | 6.30110 EM
Crab Man-
Louis Armstrong And Ella Fitzgerald With Russell Garcia's Orchestra | The Complete Ella Fitzgerald And Louis Armstrong On Verve | Verve | 537284-2
Paolo Fresu Quintet | Kind Of Porgy & Bess | RCA | 21951952
Noel Akchoté Trio | Rien | Winter&Winter | 910057-2
Crache
Mulo Francel-Evelyn Huber | Tango Lyrico | Fine Music | FM 102-2
Crack House Blues
Das Böse Ding | Cleanhappydirty | Acoustic Music Records | 319.1090.2
Crackington Haven And Ginger Crackers
Max Roach Quintet | The Hardbop Academy | Affinity | AFF 773
Cracklin'
Clyde Bernhardt And His Kansas City Buddies | Clyde Bernhardt:The Complete Recordings Vol.2 (1949-1953) | Blue Moon | BMCD 6017
Cradle Song
Hal McIntyre And His Orchestra | The Uncollected:Hal McIntyre | Hindsight | HSR 172
Craigie Hill
Peter Bolte Quartet | ...All The April Snow | ITM-Pacific | ITMP 970092
Craniac Trilogy-Part 1:Transport
Vital Information | Where We Come From | Intuition Records | INT 3218-2
Craniac Trilogy-Part 2:The Extraction
Where We Come From | Intuition Records | INT 3218-2
Craniac Trilogy-Part 3:The Implant
Live Around The World Where We Come From Tour '98-'99 | Intuition Records | INT 3296-2
Cranial Jam
Where We Come From | Intuition Records | INT 3218-2
Cranial Joy:Completion
Where We Come From | Intuition Records | INT 3218-2
Cranial Meltdown:Dementia
Show 'Em Where You Live | Intuition Records | INT 3306-2
Cranial No. 6 Mata Hari
Show 'Em Where You Live | Intuition Records | INT 3306-2
Cranial No.1 Right Now
Show 'Em Where You Live | Intuition Records | INT 3306-2
Cranial No.2 The Jinx
Show 'Em Where You Live | Intuition Records | INT 3306-2
Cranial No.3 Azul
Show 'Em Where You Live | Intuition Records | INT 3306-2
Cranial No.4 Where We Live
Show 'Em Where You Live | Intuition Records | INT 3306-2
Cranial No.5 Awaken The Hoodoo
Show 'Em Where You Live | Intuition Records | INT 3306-2
Cranial No.7 Brake Failure
Roland Batik Trio | Streams | Warner | 4509-91745-2
Crape Myrtle
Charly Antolini Quintet | Crash | BELL Records | BLR 84002
Crash Test No.1
Palo Alto | Crash Test | Jazz 'n' Arts Records | JNA 1803
Crash Test No.2
Sylvie Courvoisier Group | Y2K | Enja | ENJ-9383 2
Crasse-Tignasse
Eddie Barclay Et Son Grand Orchestre | Et Voila! | Fresh Sound Records | FSR 515(Barclay 82138)
Crawdad Hole
Brownie McGhee & Sonny Terry | You Hear Me Talkin' | Muse | MR 5131
Crawdad Suite
Larry Johnson & Nat Riddles | Johnson! Where Did You Get That Sound? New York Really Has The Blues | L+R Records | LR 42046
Crawler
Homesick James Quartet | Blues On The Southside | Original Blues Classics | OBCCD 529-2(P 7388)
Crawlin'
John Lee Hooker Group | Everybody Rockin' | Charly | CRB 1014
Crazy
Edgar Winter Group | I'm Not A Kid Anymore | L+R Records | CDLR 42076
Pee Wee Ellis-Horace Parlan | Gentle Men Blue | Minor Music | 801073
Smiley Lewis And His Orchestra | No No | Pathe | 1566321
Crazy Baby
Nat Adderley Quintet | Introducing Nat Adderley | Verve | 543828-2
Compact Jazz: Cannonball Adderley | EmArCy | 842930-2 PMS
Crazy 'Bout A Saxophone
Irving Mills And His Hotsy Totsy Gang | Big Band Bounce And Boogie:Clarinetitis/The Young BG-Benny Goodman | Affinity | AFS 1018
Crazy Chords
Jelly Roll Morton And His Orchestra | The Complete Jelly Roll Morton-Vol.7/8 | RCA | 2126411-2
Crazy Day
Maria Baptist Quartet | Crazy Dreams | BIT | 11194
Crazy Games
Lionel Hampton-Milton 'Mezz' Mezzrow Quartet | Des Femmes Disparaissent/Les Tricheurs(Original Soundtracks) | Fontana | 834752-2 PMS
Crazy He Calls Me
Anita O'Day With The Johnny Mandel Orchestra | Trav'lin Light | Verve | 2304584 IMS
Billie Holiday And Her Trio | Lady Day-The Storyville Concerts | Jazz Door | JD 1215
Billie Holiday With Gordon Jenkins And His Orchestra | Lover Man | MCA | 2292-52317-1
Etta Jones With The Houston Person Sextet | I'll Be Seeing You | Muse | MCD 5351
Crazy Horse
Gust Williams Tsilis Quintet | Sequestered Days | Enja | ENJ-6094 2
Crazy House
Sweetman With His South Side Groove Kings | Austin Backalley Blue | Mapleshade | 02752
Crazy Legs And Friday Strut
Jay McShann Quintet | What A Wonderful World | Groove Note | GRV 1005-2
Jay McShann-Buddy Tate Duo | Crazy Legs & Friday Strut | Sackville | 3011
Crazy Love(Crazy Music)
Dinah Washington And Her Sextet | Newport Jazz Festival 1958,July 3rd-6th Vol.4:Blues In The Night No.2 | Phontastic | NCD 8816
Brownie McGhee & Sonny Terry | Blues Is My Companion | Aves | 146508
Crazy Moon
Jesper Thilo Quintet Plus One | Don't Count' Him Out | Music Mecca | CD 1035-2
Crazy Red-
| Jazz Classics In Digital Stereo: Coleman Hawkins 1927-1939 | CDS Records Ltd. | RPCD 600(CD 698)
Crazy Rhythm
Art Tatum | Art Tatum At The Piano Vol.2 | GNP Crescendo | GNP 9026
Bill Coleman Quintet | Really I Do | Black & Blue | BLE 59.162 2
Buck Clayton And His Band | The Doctor Jazz Series Vol.3:Buck Clayton | Storyville | STCD 6043
Coleman Hawkins And His All Star Jam Band | Django Reinhardt All Star Sessions | Capitol | 531577-2
The Various Facets Of A Genius 1929-1940 | Black & Blue | BLE 59.230 2
Dave Brubeck Quartet | Jazz At The College Of The Pacific Vol.2 | Original Jazz Classics | OJCCD 1076-2
Django Reinhardt And His Quintet | Bruxelles/Paris | Accord | 403222
Donald Brown Quintet | Donald Byrd & Doug Watkins:The Tradition Sessions | Blue Note | 540528-2
Ella Fitzgerald With The Tommy Flanagan Trio | Ella Fitzgerald In Budapest | Pablo | PACD 5308-2
Emil Mangelsdorff Swingin' Oil Drops | Emil Mangelsdorff Swinging Oildrops 1966 | L+R Records | LR 41002
Harry James And His Orchestra | Harry James | Jazz Magazine | 40199
Henri Chaix Trio | Jive At Five | Sackville | SKCD2-2035
Johnny Mercer With Paul Weston's Orchestra | The Uncollected:Johnny Mercer | Hindsight | HSR 152
Mark Murphy With The Ralph Burns Orchestra | Crazy Rhythm:His Debut Recordings | Decca | 050670-2
Martial Solal/Daniel Humair | Daniel Humair Surrounded 1964-1987 | Blue Flame | 40322(2132163-2)
Oscar Peterson-Roy Eldridge Duo | Jousts | Pablo | 2310817
Red Garland Trio | It's A Blue World | Original Jazz Classics | OJCCD 1028-2(P 7838)
Red Norvo Trio | Red Norvo Trio | Original Jazz Classics | OJCCD 641-2(F 3-19)
Stephane Grappelli Group | Golden Hour Of Stephane Grappelli | Golden Hour | GH 650
Steve White Quintet | Jazz In Hollywood:Virgil Gonsalves/Steve White | Original Jazz Classics | OJCCD 1889-2(Nocturne NLP-8/NLP-9)
Crazy Rhythm(Schräger Rhythmus)
Big Sid Catlett And His Orchestra | The Small Black Groups | Storyville | 4960523
Crazy Riffin
Trilok Gurtu Group | Crazy Saints | CMP Records | CMP CD 66
Crazy Sakari
Bill Mays/Ed Bickert | Concord Duo Series Volume Seven:Bill Mays-Ed Bickert | Concord | CCD 4626
Crazy She Calls Me
John Gordon's Trombones Unlimited | Live In Concert | Mons Records | CD 1890
Lee Konitz Quintet | Very Cool | Verve | 2304344 IMS
Rob McConnell Septet With Harry 'Sweets' Edison | Live At The 1990 Concord Jazz Festival-First Set | Concord | CCD 4451
Vince Jones Group | Spell | Intuition Records | INT 3067-2
Von Freeman Quartet | Live At The Dakota | Premonition | 790750-2
Dutch Swing College Band | Digital Date | Philips | 834087-2
Crazy Strings
David Murray Quartet | Shakill's II | DIW | DIW 884 CD
Crazy With You
Carla Bley/Andy Sheppard/Steve Swallow | Song With Legs | Watt | 26(527069)
Crazy Without You
Percfect Trouble | Perfect Trouble | Moers Music | 02070 CD
Cream
Glen Moore Group | Introducing Glen Moore | Elektra | ELK K 52151
Creation
Randy Weston African Rhythm | Khepera | Verve | 557821-2
Pamela Fries Group | Alarming States | Nueva Records | NC 1011
Creative Stopper
Jean-Paul Bourelly & The BluWave Bandits | Rock The Cathartic Spirits:Vibe Music And The Blues! | DIW | DIW 911 CD
Creatoxygenology
Jerry Bergonzi Quartet | Inside Out | Red Records | 123230-2
Creature Talk
Brad Dutz | Brad Dutz | Nine Winds Records | NWCD 0141
Crebe De Chet
Jazzensemble Des Hessischen Rundfunks | Jazz Messe-Messe Für Unsere Zeit | hr music.de | hrmj 003-01 CD
Credo
Joe Masters Orchestra & Choir | The Jazz Mass By John Masters | Discovery | DS 785 IMS
Creek Bank
Bill Frisell | Ghost Town | Nonesuch | 7559-79583-2
Creep
Céline Rudolph And Her Trio | Paintings | Nabel Records:Jazz Network | CD 4661
Creep Into Your Dream
Dick Oatts-Dave Santoro Quartet | Meru | Red Records | 123274-2
Creeper
Elliott Sharp-Zeena Parkins | Psycho-Acoustic | Victo | CD 026
Creepin' Home
Horace Silver Quintet | Horace Silver | Blue Note | 300097(1518)
Creeps,Bloodhounds And Badies
Hugh Lawson Trio | Colours | Soul Note | 121052-2
Creole
Mongo Santamaria And His Band | Mongo At The Village Gate | Original Jazz Classics | OJCCD 490-2(RLP 9529)
Mongo Santamaria Orchestra | The Watermelon Man | Milestone | M 47012
Creole Jazz
Mr.Acker Bilk And His Paramount Jazz Band | Dixieland Collection | Aves | 146534
Creole Love Call
Albert Mangelsdorff | Tromboneliness | MPS | 68129
Chris Barber With Zenith Hot Stompers | The Chris Barber Collection | Timeless | CD TTD 582
Duke Ellington And His Orchestra | The Jazz Collector Edition: Cotton Club Days | Laserlight | 15707
Early Ellington (1927-1934) | Bluebird | ND 86852
Cotton Club Stomp | Naxos Jazz | 8.120509 CD
This Is Duke Ellington | RCA | NL 89234 DP
Carnegie Hall Concert-Vol. 2 | Jazz Anthology | JA 5141
In The Sixties | RCA | PD 89565
Funny House Jazzband | That's My Home | Timeless | CD TTD 575
Kid Ory's Creole Jazz Band | This Kid's The Greatest! | Good Time Jazz | GTCD 12045-2
Lee Konitz-Albert Mangelsdorff Duo | Art Of The Duo | Enja | 5059-2
Oscar Klein's Anniversary Band | Moonglow | Nagel-Heyer | CD 021
Papa Bue's Viking Jazzband | Barber-Bue Concerts | Storyville | 671196
Rias Big Band | The Music Of Duke Ellington | Mons Records | MR 874306
Roland Kirk Quartet | The Inflated Tear | Atlantic | 7567-90045-2
Sy Oliver Orchestra | Yes Indeed | Black & Blue | BLE 59.049 2
Creole Love Call-
Duke Ellington And His Orchestra | Ella Fitzgerald And Duke Ellington:Cote D'Azure Concerts on Verve | Verve | 539033-2
Duke Ellington At The Alhambra | Pablo | PACD 5313-2
Hot Summer Dance | Red Baron | 469285-2
Creole Rhapsody(part 1)
Victor Jazz History Vol.12:Ellingtonia | RCA | 2135731-2
Creole Rhapsody(part 2)
The Jungle Band | Duke Ellington:Complete Original American Decca Recordings | Definitive Records | DRCD 11196
Creole Song
Kid Ory's Creole Jazz Band | Kid Ory And Jimmy Noone | Avenue | AVINT 1015
Archie Shepp & The New York Contemporary Five | Archie Shepp & The New York Contemporary Five | Storyville | SLP 1010
Crepescule With Nellie
Thelonious Monk Quartet | Blues Five Spot | Milestone | M 9124
Barry Altschul Sextet | Another Time Another Place | Muse | MR 5176
Crepuscular Air
Django Reinhardt And The Quintet Du Hot Club De France | Planet Jazz:Django Reinhardt | Planet Jazz | 2152071-2
Crepuscule
Francois Jeanneau | Ephemere | Owl Records | 07
Quintet Du Hot Club De France | Django Reinhardt:Djangology | EMI Records | 780659-2
Crepuscule With Nellie
Esbjörn Svensson Trio(E.S.T.) | EST Plays Monk | RCA | 2137680-2
Jim Pepper With The Claudine Francois Trio | Camargue | Pan Music | PMC 1106
Muhal Richard Abrams | Interpertations Of Monk | DIW | DIW 395/8 CD
T.S. Monk Group | Monk On Monk | N2K | 43052
Thelonious Monk Quartet | Thelonious Monk:85th Birthday Celebration | zyx records | FANCD 6076-2
Live In Stockholm 1961 | Dragon | DRLP 151/152
The Paris Concert | Charly | CD 74
Thelonious Monk:The Complete Blue Note Recordings | Blue Note | 830363-2
Thelonious Monk In Copenhagen | Storyville | STCD 8283
Live at The Five Spot,NYC | Blue Note | 799786-2
Crepuscule With Nellie(alt.take)
Thelonious Monk Septet | Thelonious Monk-The Complete Riverside Recordings | Riverside | 15 RCD 022-2
Crepusculo Y Aurora-
Frank Morgan Sextet | Frank Morgan | Vogue | 655018
Crescendo In Blue
Duke Ellington And His Orchestra | Duke Ellington:Complete Prestige Carnegie Hall 1946-1947 Concerts | Definitive Records | DRCD 11211
Crescent
Harold Mabern Trio | Straight Street | DIW | DIW 608 CD
John Coltrane Quartet | John Coltrane-His Greatest Years, Vol. 3 | MCA | AS 9278
John Coltrane Quintet | John Coltrane Live In Japan | Impulse(MCA) | GRP 41022
Marc Copland Trio | Haunted Heart & Other Ballads | HatOLOGY | 581
Peter O'Mara Sextet | Stairway | Enja | 7077-2
Crescent Moon-
Billy Cobham Group | Total Eclipse | Atlantic | ATL 50098
Crescent(first version)
John Coltrane Quartet | Coltrane in Japan Vol. 2 | MCA | 2292-54620-2
Cricket Sing For Anamaria
Klaus König Orchestra | Times Of Devastation/Poco A Poco | Enja | ENJ-6014 22
Cries For South Africa
Tok Tok Tok | 50 Ways To Leave Your Lover | Einstein Music | EM 91051
Crime Of Crimes
Tony Williams Quintet | The Story Of Neptune | Blue Note | 798169-2
Crimée Rome
Ken Peplowski & Friends | It's A Lonesome Old Town' | Concord | CCD 4673
Crimian Dance
Jack Bruce Group | Somethinelse | CMP Records | CMP CD 1001
Crimp Cut
Joe Henderson Quartet | Relaxin' At Camarillo | Original Jazz Classics | OJCCD 776-2(C 14006)
Crimson Lake
Guillermo Gregorio Trio | Red Cube(d) | HatOLOGY | 531
Cris De Balaines
Gianluigi Trovesi Nonet | Round About A Midsummer's Dream | Enja | ENJ-9384 2
Crisbell
Michel Godard Ensemble | Castel Del Monte | Enja | ENJ-9362 2
Everette DeVan Quartet | East Of The Sun | Organic Music | ED 2
Crisis
The Poll Winners | Poll Winners Three | Original Jazz Classics | OJCCD 692-2(C 7576)
Tim Hagans-Marcus Printup Septet | Hub Songs | Blue Note | 859509-2
Willie Bobo Group | Bobo's Beat | Roulette | 590954-2
Woody Herman And The New Thundering Herd | The 40th Anniversary Carnegie Hall Concert | RCA | 2159151-2
Crisis Stuff
Main Stream Power Band | Holiday For Swing | MWM Records | MWM 006
Crisp Day
Frank Kimbrough Quintet | The Herbie Nichols Project | Soul Note | 121313-2
Criss Cross
Billy Pierce Quartet | Rolling Monk | Paddle Wheel | KICJ 154
Esbjörn Svensson Trio(E.S.T.) | EST Plays Monk | RCA | 2137680-2
Kenny Drew Jr. Quartet | The Flame Within | Jazz City | 660.53.017
Thelonious Monk Quartet | Live At Monterey Jazz Festival,1963 | Jazz Unlimited | JUCD 2045/2046
Thelonious Monk Quintet | The Complete Genius | Blue Note | LA 579
Jazz Profile:Thelonious Monk | Blue Note | 823518-2

Thelonious Monk:Complete 1947-1952 Blue Note Recordings | The Jazz Factory | JFCD 22838
Thelonious Monk Trio | The London Collection Vol.2 | Black Lion | BLCD 760116

Criss Cross-
Milt Jackson Quintet | Thelonious Monk:The Complete Blue Note Recordings | Blue Note | 830363-2

Criss Cross(alt.take)
Thelonious Monk Quintet | Thelonious Monk:Complete 1947-1952 Blue Note Recordings | The Jazz Factory | JFCD 22838

Cristo Redentor
Donald Byrd Septet + Voices | A New Perspective | Blue Note | 499006-2
Renaud Garcia-Fons Group | Entremundo | Enja | ENJ-9464 2

Cristobal
Manfred Schoof Quintet | Light Lines | Japo | 60019(2360019)

Critic's Choice
Harry Edison-Buck Clayton Orchestra | Swing Trumpet Kings:Harry Edison Swings Buck Clayton And Vice Versa/Red Allen Plays King Oliver/Swing Goes Dixie | Verve | 533263-2

Critics,Promotors And Producers
Ran Blake | Realization Of A Dream | Owl Records | 012

Cro-Magnon Nights
Herbie Nichols Trio | Herbie Nichols:The Complete Blue Note Recordings | Blue Note | 859352-2

Cro-Magnon Nights(alt.take)
Roberto Perera Group | Seduction | Inak | 30302

Cromosoni
Massimo Ciolli Quartet | Cronopios | SPLASC(H) Records | H 171

Crooked Blues
King & Moore | Potato Radio | Justice Records | JR 0802-2

Crooked Timber
Willie Baker | The Georgia Blues 1927-1933 | Yazoo | YAZ 1012

Crooner Song
Jabbo Smith And His Rhythm Aces | Jabbo Smith 1929-1938 | Retrieval | RTR 79013

Croquet Ballet
Kühn/Humair/Jenny-Clark | Tripple Entente | EmArCy | 558690-2

Croquis
Bud Powell Trio | Strictly Powell | RCA | 6351423-2

Cross Breeding
Ornette Coleman Quartet | Ornette On Tenor | Atlantic | 8122-71455-2
Chubby Jackson And His Orchestra | Chubby Jackson-The Happy Monster:Small Groups 1944-1947 | Cool & Blue | C&B-CD 109

Cross Currents
Albert King Blues Band | Thursday Night In San Francisco | Stax | MPS 8557

Cross My Heart
Nick Woodland Quartet | Live Fireworks | Blues Beacon | BLU-1027 2
Sonny Boy Williamson Blues Band | Sonny Boy Williamson | Chess | 427004

Cross Purpose
Lauren Newton Quartet | Timbre | Hat Art | 3511

Cross Road Blues
Robert Johnson | Robert Johnson-King Of The Delta Blues | CBS | 493006-2

Cross Road Blues(alt.take)
Jimmy Giuffre Trio | Paris Jazz Concert:Jimmy Giuffre | Laserlight | 17249

Cross Roads
Pat Metheny Group | American Garage | ECM | 1155(827134-2)

Cross The Heartland
Works | ECM | 823270-2

Cross Your Heart
Elliot Lawrence And His Orchestra | The Uncollected:Elliot Lawrence | Hindsight | HSR 182
Martial Solal Quartet | Martial Solal-The Vogue Recordings Vol.1:Trios & Quartet | Vogue | 21115142(875744)

Cross-Collateral
Tacuma-Puschnig Duo | Gemini-Gemini | ITM-Pacific | ITMP 970063

Crossing
T.K.Blue Group | Another Blue | Arkadia Jazz | 70351

Crossing-
Robin Williamson Group | Skirting The River Road | ECM | 1785(016372-2

Crossing Brooklyn Ferry
Stephan Micus | Towards The Wind | ECM | 1804(159453-2)

Crossing Dark Rivers
Ernst Bier-Mack Goldsbury Quartet | At Night When You Go To Sleep | Timescrapper | TSCR 9611

Crossing Over
Anthony Cox Quartet | Factor Of Faces | Minor Music | 801035

Crossing The Border
The Yamaha International Allstar Band | Hapy Birthday Jazzwelle Plus | Nagel-Heyer | CD 005
Werner Lüdi-William Parker-Shoji Hano | Ki West/East | Intakt Records | CD 051

Crossing The Channel
Bud Powell Trio | Duke Jordan New York/Bud Powell Paris | Vogue | 21457272

Crossing The Corpus Callosum
Chico Freeman Quintet | Destiny's Dance | Original Jazz Classics | OJCCD 799-2(C 14008)

Crossing The Sudan
Cecil Taylor | Silent Tongues | Black Lion | CD 877633-2

Crosspoints
Kevin Hays Quintet | Crossroad | Steeplechase | SCCD 31324

Crossroads
Charlie Haden Trio | The Montreal Tapes | Verve | 523295-2

Crossroads Blues
Winston Mankunku Band | Crossroads | ITM Records | ITM 1441

Crosstalk
Lou Donaldson Sextet | The Time Is Right | Blue Note | 868498-0

Crosstown Trafic
NDR Big Band feat. Inga Rumpf | The Spirit Of Jimi Hendrix | Extra Records & Tapes | 11542

Crosswind
Uli Trepte Group | Real Time Music | ATM Records | ATM 3820-AH

Crosswise Blues
Dick Crouch Septet | Kandeen Love Song | Spotlite | SPJ 507

Crow's Nest
Bruce Dunlap Trio | The Rhythm Of Wings | Chesky | JD 92

Cruise Control
Jean-Pierre Pasquier Group | Cap Sud | Plainisphare | PAV 804

Cruisin' For A Bluesin'
Bobby Hutcherson Quintet | Cruisin' The Bird | Landmark | LCD 1517-2

Crumbles
Ned Rothenberg | Dix Improvisations, Victoriaville 1989 | Victo | CD 009

Crush Dance
Art Ensemble Of Chicago | Live In Berlin | West Wind | WW 2051

Cry
Ray Charles With Orchestra | Portrait In Music | London | 6.28338 DP

Cry A Blue Tear-
Art Blakey And The Jazz Messengers | Moanin' | Blue Note | 300321

Cry Me A River
Barney Wilen Quartet | New York Romance | Sunnyside | SSC 1067 D
Brian Lynch Quintet | At The Main Event | Criss Cross | Criss 1070
Charlie Ventura Quintet | The New Charlie Ventura In Hi-Fi | Harlequin | HQ 2009(Baton BL 1202) IMS
David Hazeltine Quartet | Blues Quarters Vol.1 | Criss Cross | Criss 1188
Dinah Washington With The Belford Hendricks Orchestra | What A Diff'rence A Day Makes! | Verve | 543300-2
Ella Fitzgerald With The Lou Levy Quartet | Clap Hands,Here Comes Charlie! | Verve | 835646-2
Francesca Simone Trio | Guardia Li | Minor Music | 801093
J.J.Johnson Quartet | Jazz Legends | CBS | 471684-2
Jack McDuff Quintet | Color Me Blue | Concord | CCD 4516
Louis Smith Quartet | Ballads For Lulu | Steeplechase | SCCD 31268
Ray Brown Trio | Soular Energy | Concord | CJ 268
Stefanie Schlesinger And Her Group | What Love Is | Enja | ENJ-9434 2
Tania Maria Sextet | Taurus | Concord | CCD 4175

Cry Me Not
Freddie Hubbard Sextet | Ballads In Blue-Big Sounds For The Small Hours | Blue Note | 796098-2
Billy Harper Orchestra | Capra Black | Strata East Records | 660.51.022

Cry Of Hunger
Gil Evans Orchestra | Svengali | ACT | 9207-2

Cry To The Stars
Jimmy Giuffre 3 | Jimmy Giuffre 3, 1961 | ECM | 1438/39(849644-2)

Cry Want
Flight, Bremen 1961 | Hat Art | CD 6071
Jimmy Giuffre Trio | Live In Europe Vol.1 | Raretone | 5018 FC

Cry(If You Want To)
Bobby Bland And His Band | Bobby Bland The Voice: Duke Recordings 1959-1969 | Ace Records | CDCHD 323

Cryin' All Day
Charles Mingus And His Orchestra | Charles Mingus-Passion Of A Man:The Complete Atlantic Recordings 1956-1961 | Atlantic | 8122-72871-2

Cryin' Blues
Charles Mingus Jazz Workshop | Blues & Roots | Atlantic | 8122-75205-2
Blues & Roots | Atlantic | 7567-81336-2
Charles Mingus Orchestra | Charles Mingus -Passions Of A Man | Atlantic | ATL 60143

Crying
James Blood Ulmer Quartet | Black And Blues | DIW | DIW 845 CD

Crying Blues
The Blues Woman With The Buddy Banks Sextet | Buddy Banks:The Complete Recordings 1945-1949 | Blue Moon | BMCD 6015

Crying In Hiroshima
Estella Mama Yancey With Axel Zwingenberger | Axel Zwingenberger And The Friends Of Boogie Woogie Vol.4: The Blues Of Mama Yancey | Vagabond | VRCD 8.88009

Crying In My Sleep
Mahalia Jackson | Welcome To Europe | CBS | SPR 32

Crying My Heart Out For You
Ella Fitzgerald With The Chick Webb Orchestra | Let's Get Together | Laserlight | 17003

Crying Song
Okschila Tatanka | Wounded Knee-Lyrik Und Jazz | Wergo | SM 1088-2

Crying Song(II)
Brownie McGhee And His Jook Block Busters | Home Town Blues | BGO Records | BGOCD 75

Crying Won't Make Me Stay
Bruce Gertz Quintet | Blueprint | Freelance | FRL-CD 017

Crystal Beat
Charlie Mariano Quartet | Crystal Balls | CMP Records | CMP 10

Crystal Illusions
Tom Schuman Group | Extremities | GRP | GRP 96252

Crystal Moment
Dave Grusin Sextet | Out Of The Shadow | GRP | GRP 95112

Crystal Morning
Katrina Krimsky-Trevor Watts | Stella Malu | ECM | 1199
Lee Ritenour Septet | Friendship | JVC | JVC 2009-2

Crystal Palace
Mulgrew Miller Quartet | The Countdown | Landmark | LCD 1519-2

Crystal Silence
Chick Corea/Gary Burton | Crystal Silence | ECM | 1024(831331-2)
Chick Corea-Gary Burton | In Concert, Zürich, October 28, 1979 | ECM | 1182/83
Conrad Herwig-Andy LaVerne | Shades Of Light | Steeplechase | SCCD 31520
Dave Valentine Group | Legends | GRP | GRP 95192

Crystall Bells
Larry Coryell-Alphonse Mouzon Quartet | Back Together Again | Atlantic | ATL 50382

Crystals
Larry Schneider Quintet | So Easy | Label Bleu | LBLC 6516(881241)

Csardas
Schnuckenack Reinhardt Sextet | Starportrait Schnuckenack Reinhardt | Intercord | 155012

Csardas Macabre
Lajos Dudas Quintet | Contrasts | Rillophon | 801031-320

C-Smooth
Tony Lakatos Quintet | Generation X | Jazzline | JL 11149-2

CT
Bheki Mseleku Group | Timelessness | Verve | 521306-2

Cuando Tu No Estas(When You Are Not There)
Victor Mendoza Group | This Is Why | RAM Records | RMCD 4515

Cuando,Cuando,Que Sera?
Carlo Actis Dato Quartet | Ankara Twist | SPLASC(H) Records | CD H 302-2

Cuban Fantasy
Cal Tjader Quintet | Concert On The Campus | Original Jazz Classics | OJC 279(F 8044)
Kenny Clarke-Francy Boland Big Band | Three Latin Adventures | MPS | 529095-2

Cuban Fever:
Stan Kenton With The Danish Radio Big Band | Stan Kenton With The Danish Radio Big Band | Storyville | STCD 8340

Cuban Fire Suite
Charlie Parker With The Woody Herman Orchestra | Bird's Eyees Last Unissued Vol.23 | Philology | W 853.2

Cuban Love Song
Victor Feldman Orchestra | Latinsville | Contemporary | CCD 9005-2
Mario Bauzá And His Afro-Cuban Jazz Orchestra | Tanga | Messidor | 15819 CD

Cuban Patato Chip
Louis Armstrong With Luis Russell And His Orchestra | Louis Armstrong Vol.7-Satchmo's Discoveries | MCA | 1326

Cuban Pete
Slim Gaillard Quartet | Cement Mixer Put-Ti Put-Ti | Folklyric | 9038

Cubana Be
Dizzy Gillespie And His Orchestra | The Greatest Of Dizzy Gillespie | RCA | 2113164-2

Cubana Bop
The Greatest Of Dizzy Gillespie | RCA | 2113164-2

Cubano Be
| Latin Jazz | CBS | 472683-2

Cubano Chant
Cal Tjader Quintet | Concerts In The Sun | Fantasy | FCD 9688-2
Concerts In The Sun | Fantasy | FCD 9688-2
Cal Tjader's Latin Concert | Original Jazz Classics | OJCCD 643-2(F 8014)
Essence All Stars | Afro Cubano Chant | Hip Bop | HIBD 8009
Hot Jazz Bisquits | Hip Bop | HIBD 8801
Junior Mance Quartet | That Lovin' Feelin' | Milestone | MCD 47097-2
Oscar Peterson | Jazz At The Philharmonic:The Montreux Collection | Pablo | PACD 5306-2
Highlights Of The Montreux Jazz Festival 1975 | Pablo | 2625707
Werner Lener Trio | My Own | Satin Doll Productions | SDP 1013-1 CD
Mario Bauzá And The Afro-Cuban Jazz Orchestra | 944 Columbus | Messidor | 15828 CD

Cubism
Mark Turner Quintet | Yam Yam | Criss Cross | Criss 1094

Cublak Cublak Suweng
Mongo Santamaria Orchestra | Soca Me Nice | Concord | CCD 4362

Cuchara
Hilton Ruiz Group | A Moment's Notice | Novus | PD 83123

Cuchy Frito Man
Cal Tjader's Orchestra | Soul Burst | Verve | 557446-2
Hans Theessink Group | Call Me | Minor Music | 801022

Cuckoo
Toto Blanke-Rudolf Dasek | Meditation | ALISO Records | AL 1026
George Wallington Trio | Our Delight | Prestige | P 24093

Cuckoo's Egg
UMO Jazz Orchestra | UMO Jazz Orchestra | Naxos Jazz | 86010-2

Cüd Ba-Rith
Steve Coleman Quintet | Jump On It | Enja | 4094

Cuddles
Terry Gibbs Septet | Early Getz | Prestige | P 24088

Cueca Del Árbol
Santa Maria/Auberson Duo | Piano Duo Plus | Plainisphare | PL 1267-8

Cuenta,Cuenta
Ruben Blades Y Seis Del Solar | Escenas | Messidor | 15939 CD

Cuesta Abajo
Paul Nero Sound | Doldinger Jubilee | Atlantic | ATL 60073

Cuius Animam
Hank Jones With Oliver Nelson's Orchestra | Happenings | Impulse(MCA) | JAS 61(AS 9132)

Cultural Value
Rodney Whitaker Groups | ChildrenOf The Light | DIW | DIW 907 CD

Culture And Sensivity
Soul Rebels | Let Your Mind Be Free | Mardi Gras Records | MG 1020

Culture Of One
Tom Browne Groups | Mo' Jamaica Funk | Hip Bop | HIBD 8002

Culture Shock(Let's Dance)
West Coast All Stars | Best From The West:Modern Sounds From California-A Musical Blindfold Test | Fresh Sound Records | BLP 5059/5060(Blue Note)

Culver City Park
Eddie Condon All Stars | Town Hall Concerts Vol.11 | Jazzology | JCD 1021/23

Cumbanchero
Jack Costanzo Group | Latin Fever:The Wild Rhythms Of Jack Costanza | Capitol | 590955-2
Jackie Terrasson Trio | Jacky Terrasson | Blue Note | 829351-2

Cumba's Dance
Jacky Terrasson Trio | Alive | Blue Note | 859651-2
Clifford Jordan Quintet | Mosaic | Milestone | MCD 47092-2

Cumberland Court
Charles Mingus Orchestra | Cumbia & Jazz Fusion | Atlantic | 8122-71785-2

Cumbia & Jazz Fusion
Thirteen Pictures:The Charles Mingus Anthology | Rhino | R2 71402
Dannie Richmond Quintet | The Last Mingus Band A.D. | Landmark | LCD 1537-2

Cumi Cumi
Jean-Paul Céléa-Francois Couturier Quintet | Passagio | Nocturne Productions | NPCD 509

Cunning Lee
Jimmy Knepper Quintet | Cunningbird | Steeplechase | SCCD 31061

Cunningbird
Cecil Taylor Orchestra Of Two Continents | Segments II | Soul Note | 121089-2

Cup Bearers
James Moody Quintet | Moving Forward | Novus | PD 83026
Junior Cook Quartet | The Place To Be | Steeplechase | SCCD 31240
Tommy Flanagan Trio | Eclypso | Enja | 2088-2

Cupcake
Charles Mingus Trio And Voices | Debut Rarities Vol.4:The Charles Mingus Groups | Original Jazz Classics | OJCCD 1829-2

Cupid
Honi Gordon With The Jaki Byard Quintet | Honi Gordon Sings | Original Jazz Classics | OJCCD 1783-2(P 7230)
Ralph Burns And His Orchestra | Ralph Burns Conducts Ralph Burns | Raretone | 5017 FC

Curacao
Cal Tjader's Orchestra | Soul Burst | Verve | 557446-2
Paul Desmond Quartet | Bossa Antigua | RCA | 2174795-2

Curacao Dolorosa
Paul Desmond-Gerry Mulligan Quartet | The Ballad Of Paul Desmond | RCA | 21429372
Jorge Strunz-Ardeshir Farah Group | Guitars | Milestone | MCD 9136-2

Curio In Trivia(in memory of Hugo Pratt)
Stan Kenton And His Orchestra | The Christy Years | Creative World | ST 1035

Current Event
Butch Morris Orchestra | Current Trends In Racism In Modern America(A Work In Progress) | Sound Aspects | sas CD 4010

Cursum
Toots Thielemans Sextet | Toots Thielemans Live | Polydor | 2491003 IMS

Curtains Dream
Ran Blake-Houston Person Duo | Suffield Gothic | Soul Note | 121077-2

Curtsy
Sacbe | Sacbe-Street Corner | Discovery | DS 864 IMS

Curveball
Flim & The BB's | The Further Adventures | dmp Digital Music Productions | CD 462

Cushion Foot Stomp
Mike Durham's West Jesmond Rhythm Kings | Shake 'Em Loose | Lake | LACD 45

Custard Puff
Jim Pepper Group | Comin' And Goin' | Bellaphon | 290.31.029

Cut
Karoline Höfler Quartet | Charly Haigl's Festival Band | Satin Doll Productions | SDP 1007-1 CD

Cut Me Loose,Charlie
Sonny Terry Trio | Robbin' The Grave | Blue Labor | BL 101

Cut Plug
Mongo Santamaria Orchestra | The Watermelon Man | Milestone | M 47012

Cute
Art Van Damme Group | State Of Art | MPS | 841413-2
Barrett Deems Big Band | Groovin' Hard | Delmark | DE 505
Count Basie And His Orchestra | Breakfast Dance And Barbecue | Roulette | 531791-2
En Concert Avec Europe 1 | Laserlight | 710411/12
Basie On Roulette, Vol. 2: Basie Plays Hefti | Vogue | 500002
DMP Big Band | Carved In Stone | dmp Digital Music Productions | CD 512
Gerry Hayes-Charlie Antolini Quintet | Swing Explosion | BELL Records | BLR 84061
Horst Gmeinwieser 'One Cue Big Band' | Bigband-Fieber | Media Arte | CD 06569209(BRW)
Les McCann Trio | Plays The Shout | Pacific Jazz | LN 10083
Oscar Peterson Trio | The London Concert | Pablo | 2CD 2620111
Patrick Tompert Trio | Moche! | Satin Doll Productions | SDP 1035-1 CD
Paul Moer Trio | Live At The Pour House | Fresh Sound Records | FSCD 1025
Shirley Scott Quartet | Queen Of The Organ | Impulse(MCA) | GRP 11232
Freddie Redd Sextet | Redd's Blues | Blue Note | 540537-2

Cute Doot
Hank Mobley And His Orchestra | A Slic Of The Top | Blue Note | 833588-2

Cutie
Sonny Rollins Quartet | Sonny Rollins-The Freelance Years:The Complete Riverside & Contemporary Recordings | Riverside | 5 RCD 4427-2
Sonny Rollins:Brown Skin Girl | Memo Music | HDJ 4041

Cyberola
Mike Nock Trio | Not We But One | Naxos Jazz | 86006-2

Cycle One: Namaste
David Darling Group | Cycles | ECM | 1219

Cycle Song
Cycles | ECM | 1219

Cycle Three: Quintet And Coda

Cycles | ECM | 1219

Cycle Two: Trio
Ahmad Jamal Trio with Orchestra | Pittsburgh | Atlantic | 7567-8209-2

Cycles
Andreas Willers Octet | The Ground Music | Enja | ENJ-9368 2
Teddy Charles New Directions Quartet With Booker Little And Booker Ervin | Jazz In The Garden At The Museum Of Modern Art | Fresh Sound Records | FSR-CD 0212

Cyclic Episode
Lotte Anker-Marilyn Crispell-Marilyn Mazur | Poetic Justice | dacapo | DCCD 9460

Cyclic Sight Song
Uli Trepte Group | Real Time Music | ATM Records | ATM 3820-AH

Cyclologie
Bingi Miki And The Inner Galaxy Orchestra Of Japan With Gu | Montreux Jazz | Gryphon | 6.24396 AT

Cyclops
J.J.Johnson-Nat Adderley Quintet | The Yokohama Concert | Pablo | 2620109

Cymbalism
Roy Haynes Quartet | Cymbalism | Original Jazz Classics | OJCCD 1079-2(NJ 8287)

Cymbalismn-
Manny Albam-Ernie Wilkins And Their Orchestra | Drum Suite/Son Of Drum Suite | RCA | 2136409-2

Cymbal-Promenade
Chico Hamilton | Dancing To A Different Drummer | Soul Note | 121291-2

Cymbeline(Schaupielhaus Bonn)
Eric Kloss Quartet | Eric Kloss & The Rhythm Section | Prestige | PCD 24125-2(P 7689/7793)

Cynthia's In Love
Cannonball Adderley And His Orchestra | Verve Jazz Masters 31:Cannonball Adderley | Verve | 522651-2
Cannonball Adderley Group | Julian 'Cannonball' Adderley | EmArCy | 830381-2
Don Byas Quartet | Don Byas Complete American Small Group Recordings | Definitive Records | DRCD 11213
George Shearing Group | Two Originals:Light,Airy And Swinging/Continental Experience/On Target | MPS | 523522-2

Cyp
Hans Theessink | Hans Theessink:Solo | Minor Music | 801047

Cypress Grove Blues
Nehemiah 'Skip' James | Skip James-King Of The Delta Blues Singers | Biograph | BLP 12029

Cyra
Hank Jones Trio | The Jazz Trio Of Hank Jones | Savoy | SV 0184(MG 12023)

Czar
Martin Taylor Quintet With Guests | Spirit Of Django:Years Apart | Linn Records | AKD 058

D & E
Oscar Peterson Trio | Verve Jazz Masters 16:Oscar Peterson | Verve | 516320-2
Tete Montoliu Trio | Catalonian Nights | Steeplechase | SCCD 31148

D And E
Modern Jazz Quartet | MJQ 40 | Atlantic | 7567-82330-2
The Complete Modern Jazz Quartet Prestige & Pablo Recordings | Prestige | 4PRCD 4438-2

D And E Blues
Jazz-Club: Piano | Verve | 840032-2

D And E Blues(alt.take)
Topsy-This One's For Basie | Original Jazz Classics | OJCCD 1073-2(2310917)
Karl Denson Group | Herbal Turkey Breast | Minor Music | 801032

D Minor Concerto:
Freddie Hubbard All Stars | MMTC(Monk,Miles,Trane And Cannon) | Musicmasters | 65132-2

D Minor Mint
Glen Gray And The Casa Loma Orchestra | Shall We Swing? | Creative World | ST 1055

D Natural Blues
Art Pepper Quartet | In San Francisco | Fresh Sound Records | FSCD 1005

D Trane
Jimmy Heath And His Orchestra | Fast Company | Milestone | M 47025

D.B.B.
Blind Lemon Jefferson | Blind Lemon Jefferson-Master Of The Blues | Biograph | BLP 12015

D.B.Blues
Lester Young And His Band | Jazz Gallery:Lester Young Vol.1(1936-46) | RCA | 2114171-2
Lester Young Quintet | Norman Granz' Jazz At The Philharmonic HARTFORD, 1953 | Pablo | 2308240-2
Lester Young With The Bill Potts Trio | Lester Young In Washington,DC 1956:Vol.4 | Pablo | 2308230
Milt Jackson Septet | Night Mist | Pablo | 2312124

D.B.Exchange
Albert Ayler Group | Spirits Rejoice | ESP Disk | ESP 1020-2

D.C.
Tome XX | Natura Morte | Jazz Haus Musik | JHM 32

D.C.Divertimento
George Russell's New York Band | Live In An American Time Spiral | Soul Note | 121049-2

D.Day For Eric
Franck Band | Liebeslieder | Jazz Haus Musik | JHM 35 CD

D.Jazz
Danny Moss Meets Buddha's Gamblers | A Swingin' Affair | Nagel-Heyer | CD 034

D.M. Blues
Blues Of Summer | Nagel-Heyer | NH 1011
Dick Morrissey Quartet | Jazz At Ronnie Scott's | Ronnie Scott's Jazz House | JHAS 612

D.Nee No
Cesc Miralta Quartet | Carretera Austal | Fresh Sound Records | FSNT 149 CD

D.O. Priorat
Django Reinhardt Quartet | Jazz In Paris:Django Reinhardt-Nuits De Saint-Germain-Des-Prés | EmArCy | 018427-2

D.R. Blu
Django Reinhardt And His Quintet | Django Reinhardt Vol. 7 | Decca | 180026 AG

D.T.Blues
Christy Doran-Fredy Studer-Stephan Wittwer | Red Twist & Tuned Arrow | ECM | 1342

D.T.E.T.
Brian Lynch Sextet | In Process | Ken Music | 660.56.011

Da Da Dapp
Mr.Acker Bilk And His Paramount Jazz Band | I Think The Best Thing About This Record Is The Music | BELL Records | BLR 84014

Da Fonk
Your Neighborhood Saxophone Quartet | Boogie Stop Shuffle | Coppens | CCD 3004(882623)

Daahoud
Clifford Brown All Stars | Zoot Sims:The Featured Sessions With Great Leaders 1949-1954 | Blue Moon | BMCD 1037
Clifford Brown-Max Roach Quintet | Clifford Brown-Max Roach:Alone Together-The Best Of The Mercury Years | Verve | 526373-2
Jazz Gallery:Clifford Brown | RCA | 2114176-2
Compact Jazz: Clifford Brown | EmArCy | 842933-2 PMS
Pure Genius | Elektra | MUS K 52388
Oscar Peterson Trio | En Concert Avec Europe 1 | Laserlight | 710443/48
Oscar Peterson-The London House Sessions | Verve | 531766-2
Oscar Peterson Trio With The All Star Big Band | Bursting Out/Swinging Brass | Verve | 529699-2
Phineas Newborn Jr. Trio | A World Of Piano | Original Jazz Classics | OJC 175(C 7600)
Red Garland Trio | Jazz-Club: Piano | Verve | 840032-2
Rob Schneiderman Trio | Keepin' In The Groove | Reservoir | RSR CD 144
Wallace Roney Quintet | Munchin' | Muse | MCD 5533

Daahoud(alt.take)
Clifford Brown-Max Roach Quintet | Brownie-The Complete EmArCy Recordings Of Clifford Brown | EmArCy | 838306-2
Stephen Scott Quartet | Vision Quest | Enja | ENJ-9347 2

Da'At
Curtis Fuller-Slide Hampton Quintet | Two Bones | Blue Note | GXK 8166

D'Accord Mon Pote Boogie
Sammy Price | Le Jazz En France Vol.14:Boogie Woogie A La Parisienne | Pathe | 1552601

Dackelwackel
Art Taylor Quintet | Taylor's Tenors | Prestige | VIJ 5034

Dad Can Dig
Louis Jordan And His Tympany Five | Go Blow Your Horn-Part 2 | Pathe | 1546680(Aladdin)

Daddy Banks-
Hamiet Bluiett Quartet | Sankofa/Rear Garde | Soul Note | 121238-2

Daddy Dig
Bob Helm's Jazz Band | Hotter Than That | Stomp Off Records | CD 1310

Daddy Gonna Tell You No Lie
Ma Rainey With Georgia Tom | Ma Rainey | Milestone | MCD 47021-2

Daddy Longlegs
Chuck Loeb Group | Memory Lane | dmp Digital Music Productions | CD 517
Dexter Gordon Quartet | Dexter Gordon Plays-The Bethlehem Years | Fresh Sound Records | FSR-CD 154(882891)

Daddy Redux
J.B.Lenoir Blues Band | J. B. Lenoir | Chess | 427003

Daddy Wong Legs
WDR Big Band | Harlem Story | Koala Records | CD P 7

Daddy-O
$$hide$$ | $$Titelverweise | |

Daddy-O -> Swingin' With Dady-O

Daddy's Home
Patricia Covair With Satin Blues And The Larks Of New Orleans | New Orleans After Dark | Challenger Productions | AE 1000-2

Daddy's Rap
Dade | In The Shade | Big World | BW 2001

Dado
In The Shade | Big World | BW 2001

Da-Duh-Dah
Dimitrios Vassilakis Daedalus Project | Labyrinth | Candid | CCD 79776

Daedalus
Enrico Pieranunzi-Bert Van Den Brink | Daedalus' Wings | Challenge | CHR 70069

Dager Pa Skajaeret(Days By The Shore)
Sippie Wallace With Axel Zwingenberger | Sippie Wallace/Axel Zwingenberger And The Friends Of Boogie Woogie Vol.1 | Vagabond | VRCD 8.84002

Dago Hill
Carlos Bica Group | Azul | Traumton Records | 4425-2

Dagobert
Der Rote Bereich | Zwei | Jazz 4 Ever Records:Jazz Network | J4E 4727

Dah Blessing
Joe Maneri Quartet | Dahabenzapple | Hat Art | CD 6188

Dahomey Dance
Harold Danko | After The Rain | Steeplechase | SCCD 31356
John Coltrane Group | Olé Coltrane | Atlantic | 7567-81349-2
John Coltrane: The Legend 'Ole' | Atlantic | ATL 40286
Pili-Pili | Hotel Babo | JA & RO | JARO 4147-2
Tom Scott Group | Them Changes | GRP | GRP 96132

Daily Affirmation
Georgie Auld And His Orchestra | The Most Versatile Saxophonist Of Our Time-Georgie Auld,Vol.1 | Musicraft | MVS 501 IMS

Daily Rose
Jazzerie Feat. Roberto Ottaviano | Another Day | SPLASC(H) Records | H 156

Daisy Bell-
Joe McPhee | Graphics | Hat Art | I/J

Daisy 's Dream
Elliott Sharp-Zeena Parkins | Psycho-Acoustic | Victo | CD 026

Dakar
John Coltrane Sextet | The Mal Waldron Memorial Album:Soul Eyes | Prestige | PRCD 11024-2
Prestige All Stars | After Hours | Prestige | P 24107
The Prestige All Stars | Olio | Original Jazz Classics | OJCCD 1004-2(P 7084)
David Murray Quartet | Deep River | DIW | DIW 830 CD

Dakhut
Itchy Fingers | Live | Enja | ENJ-6076 2
1239A | Artistry | Verve | 847956-2

Dakota Kid
David Matthews Trio With Strings | Jazz Ballads With Strings | Sweet Basil | 660.55.012

Dakota Song
Jim Pepper Quartet | Dakota Song | Enja | 5043-2

Dalens Ande
Roy Eldridge Quintet | The Complete Verve Roy Eldridge Studio Sessions | Verve | 9861278

Dale's Wail
Roy Eldridge 'Littel Jazz'-The Best Of The Verve Years | Verve | 523338-2

Dale's Wail(alt.take 1)
The Complete Verve Roy Eldridge Studio Sessions | Verve | 9861278

Dale's Wail(alt.take 2)
The Complete Verve Roy Eldridge Studio Sessions | Verve | 9861278

Dale's Wail(alt.take.3)
Willem Breuker Kollektief | To Remain | BVHAAST | CD 8904

Dali's Himmelfahrt
Vinny Valentino & Here No Evil | Now And Again | dmp Digital Music Productions | CD 3003

Dallas Blues
George Lewis Trio | The Oxford Series Vol.9 | American Music | AMCD-29

Dallas Delight
Duke Ellington And His Orchestra | The Indispensable Duke Ellington Vol.3/4(1930-1934) | RCA | 2122620-2

Dalliance Of Eagles
Boyd Raeburn And His Orchestra | Man With The Horns | Savoy | WL 70534 (809300)

Damaged But Good
Ray Anderson Lapis Lazuli Band | Funkorific | Enja | ENJ-9340 2
Passport | Cross-Collateral | Atlantic | 2292-44145-2

Damals
Heinz Sauer 4tet | Exchange 2 | free flow music | ffm 0998

Damals Vor Jahren
Abdullah Ibrahim Trio | Cape Town Revisited | TipToe | TIP-888836 2

Damara Blue
Abdullah Ibrahim Trio And A String Orchestra | African Suite | TipToe | TIP-888832 2
Abdullah Ibrahim Trio With The Munich Radio Symphony Orchestra | African Symphony | Enja | ENJ-9410 2
Peter Fulda | Fin De Siècle | Jazz 4 Ever Records:Jazz Network | J4E 4724

Dame Un Cachito Pa'huele
Hans Reichel-Rüdiger Carl Duo | Buben...Plus | FMP | CD 78

Dameronia
Tadd Dameron-Fats Navarro Sextet | Fats Navarro:Nostalgia | Dreyfus Jazz Line | FDM 36736-2
Fats Navarro/Tadd Dameron:Complete Blue Note & Capitol Sessions | Definitive Records | DRCD 11191

Dameronia(alt.master)
Fats Navarro/Tadd Dameron:Complete Blue Note & Capitol Sessions | Definitive Records | DRCD 11191

Dammed Black Blues
Wolfgang Dauner Trio | Dream Talk | L+R Records | LR 41004

Damn If I Know (The Stroller)
Leon Thomas With Band | Spirits Known And Unknown | RCA | 2663876-2

Damn Nam
Super Black Blues Vol.II | RCA | 2663874-2
Leon Thomas In Berlin | RCA | 2663877-2

Damn Nam(Ain't Goin' To Vietnam)
Blues Comany And Guests | Damn! Let's Jam | Inak | 9009

Damned I Love You Not
Harold Danko Trio | Trilix | Steeplechase | SCCD 31551

Damned If I Know
Steve Wilson Quintet | New York Summit | Criss Cross | Criss 1062

Danca Comigo
Duo Gismonti-Vasconcelos | Jazzbühne Berlin '84 | Repertoire Records | REPCD 4906-CC

Danca Das Cabecas
Paul Horn Group feat. Egberto Gismonti | The Altitude Of The Sun | Black Sun Music | 15002-2

Danca Do Brasil
Bob Enevoldsen Sextet | Jazz In Hollywood:Harry Babasin/Bob Enevoldsen | Original Jazz Classics | OJCCD 1888-2(Nocturne NLP3/NLP-6)

Danca Dos Escravos(Preto)
Egberto Gismonti & Academia De Dancas | Sanfona | ECM | 1203/04(829391-2)

Danca Dos Pes-
Luiz Bonfa/Cafe | Non Stop To Brazil | Chesky | JD 29

Danca Solitaria
Duo Gismonti-Vasconcelos | Jazzbühne Berlin '84 | Repertoire Records | REPCD 4906-CC

Danca Solitaria(No.2)
Egberto Gismonti Group | Infancia | ECM | 1428

Danca(No.1)
Infancia | ECM | 1428

Danca(No.2)
Egberto Gismonti/Nana Vasconcelos | Duas Vozes | ECM | 1279

Dancando
Jeff Gardner-Gary Peacock | Alchemy | fnac Muisc | 662016

Dance
Eric Watson Trio | Conspiracy | Owl Records | 027
John Surman Orchestra | John Surman | Deram | 844883-2
Paul Motian Quintet | Misterioso | Soul Note | 121174-2
Stephan Oliva Trio | Fantasm | RCA | 2173925-2
Takashi Yoshimatsu | Tender Toys:Shin-Ichi Fukuda | Denon Compact Disc | CO-18053
Urs Leimgruber Quartet | Reflexionen | Enja | 5057 (807653)

Dance-
Roscoe Mitchell-Muhal Richard Abrams | Duets And Solos | Black Saint | 120133-2

Dance Benita Dance
Joe Diorio/Ira Sullivan | The Breeze And I | RAM Records | RMCD 4508

Dance Cadaverous
Wayne Shorter Quintet | Speak No Evil | Blue Note | 499001-2

Dance Cadaverous(alt.take)
Bud Shank/Bill Mays | Explorations:1980 | Concord | CCD 42002

Dance Dreams
Billy Harper Quintet | Black Saint | Black Saint | 120001-2

Dance For A King(fragment 1)
Glenn Horiuchi Quartet | Oxnard Beet | Soul Note | 121228-2

Dance For M
Gunter Hampel | Dances | Birth | 002

Dance For The Comet
Gianlugi Trovesi Quartet With The WDR Big Band | Dedalo | Enja | ENJ-9419 2

Dance For The East No.2
Gianluigi Trovesi Octet | Les Hommes Armés | Soul Note | 121311-2

Dance For The King(fragment 2)
Gianlugi Trovesi Quartet With The WDR Big Band | Dedalo | Enja | ENJ-9419 2

Dance For The King(fragment 3)
Gunter Hampel | Dances | Birth | 002

Dance Hall
Clifford Hayes' Louisville Stompers | Frog Hop | Frog | DGF 10

Dance In The Cart(Sabra In Caruta)
James Blood Ulmer Group | Music Speaks Louder Than Words:James Blood Ulmer Plays The Music Of Ornette Coleman | DIW | DIW 910 CD

Dance In Thy Soul
Frank Kimbrough Quintet | The Herbie Nichols Project | Soul Note | 121313-2

Dance Line
Fred Elizalde And His Orchestra | Fred Elizalde And His Anglo American Band | Retrieval | RTR 79011

Dance Me Love
Bright Moments | Return Of The Lost Tribe | Delmark | DE 507

Dance No.1
Duke Ellington And His Orchestra | Duke Ellington:Complete Prestige Carnegie Hall 1946-1947 Concerts | Definitive Records | DRCD 11211
Lincoln Center Jazz Orchestra | Portraits By Ellington | CBS | 472814-2

Dance No.2
Duke Ellington And His Orchestra | Duke Ellington:Complete Prestige Carnegie Hall 1946-1947 Concerts | Definitive Records | DRCD 11211

Dance No.3
Duke Ellington:Complete Prestige Carnegie Hall 1946-1947 Concerts | Definitive Records | DRCD 11211

Dance No.4
Duke Ellington:Complete Prestige Carnegie Hall 1946-1947 Concerts | Definitive Records | DRCD 11211

Dance No.5
Duke Ellington:Complete Prestige Carnegie Hall 1946-1947 Concerts | Definitive Records | DRCD 11211

Dance Of Dospat
Ed Sarath Quintet | Last Day In May | Konnex Records | KCD 5042

Dance Of Gaia
Christoph Spendel Group | Radio Exotic | L+R Records | CDLR 70001

Dance Of The 3-Legged Elves
Michael Marcus Quintet | Under The Wire | Enja | ENJ-6064 2

Dance Of The Demented Pigeon
Paul Horn Group | The Magic Of Findhorn | Golden Flute Records | GFR 2003

Dance Of The Global Village
Johnny Hodges Orchestra | Johnny Hodges:The Complete 1937-1940 Small Group Sessions(Master Takes),Vol.2 | Blue Moon | BMCD 1020

Dance Of The Gremlins
Count Basie And His Orchestra | Prez's Hat Vol.2 | Philology | 214 W 7

Dance Of The Infidels
Bud Powell Quintet | Bud Powell:Bouncing With Bud | Dreyfus Jazz Line | FDM 36725-2
The Amazing Bud Powell Vol.1 | Blue Note | 300366
Fats Navarro And Tadd Dameron:The Complete Blues Note And Capitol Recordings | Blue Note | 833373-2
Bud Powell Trio | Pianology | Moon Records | MCD 055-2
Charlie Parker Quartet | New York All Star Sessions | Bandstand | BDCD 1507

Dance Of The Infidels(alt.master)
Bud Powell Quintet | Fats Navarro/Tadd Dameron:Complete Blue Note & Capitol Sessions | Definitive Records | DRCD 11191

Dance Of The Infidels(alt.take)
Fats Navarro And Tadd Dameron:The Complete Blues Note And Capitol Recordings | Blue Note | 833373-2

Dance Of The Night Child
Red Norvo Quintet | Knock On Wood | Affinity | CD AFS 1017

Dance Of The One's Beyond-
Sputnik 27 | But Where's The Moon? | dml-records | CD 011

Dance Of The One's Beyond(2)-

Rob Van Den Broeck Quintet | Free Fair | Timeless | SJP 122

Dance Of The Pisachas
Babamadu | Babamadu | Enja | 9093-2

Dance Of The Robot People
Tippett-Kellers-Tippett | Twilight Etchings | FMP | CD 65

Dance Of The Silver Skeezix
Richard Sussman Quintet | Free Fall | Inner City | IC 1045 IMS

Dance Of The Spider People
Hot Lips Page And His Hot Seven | The Changing Face Of Harlem-The Savoy Sessions | Savoy | SJL 2208 (801184)

Dance Of The Tumblers
Chico Hamilton | Dancing To A Different Drummer | Soul Note | 121291-2

Dance On The Water
John Serry Quintet | Enchantress | Telarc Digital | CD 83392

Dance Only With Me
Eddie Higgins Trio | Portrait In Black And White | Sunnyside | SSC 1072 D

Dance Romance
James Newton Orchestra | Water Mystery | Gramavision | GR 8407-2

Dance Stone
Kent Carter String Trio | The Willisau Suites | ITM-Pacific | ITMP 970077

Dance The Way You Dance
Cassandra Wilson Group | Dance To The Drums Again | CBS | CK 53451(DIW 863)

Dance Until Dawn
Les Brown And His Orchestra | Les Brown And His Orchestra 1944 & 1946 | Circle | CCD-90

Dance With Me
Deborah Henson-Conant | Naked Music | Laika Records | LK 94-051
Deborah Henson-Conant Trio | Just For You | Laika Records | LK 95-063
Ingrid Sertso And Her Sextet | Dance With Me | Enja | 8024-2
The Charles Ford Band | A Reunion Live | Crosscut | CCD 11043

Dance(2)
Hayden Chisholm | Circe | Jazz Haus Musik | JHM 0081 CD

Dance(3)
Wolfgang Muthspiel Sextet | Black & Blue | Amadeo | 517653-2

Dance(4)
Hayden Chisholm | Circe | Jazz Haus Musik | JHM 0081 CD

Dance(5)
Circe | Jazz Haus Musik | JHM 0081 CD

Dance(6)
Circe | Jazz Haus Musik | JHM 0081 CD

Dance(7)
Chris Jarrett | Fire | Edition Collage | EC 443-2

Dance(from 2 dances)
Marion Brown Sextet | Marion Brown In Sommerhausen | Calig | 30605

Dance,You Monster,To My Soft Song!
Jazz Orchester Rheinland-Pfalz | Last Season | Jazz Haus Musik | LJBB 9706
Landes Jugend Jazz Orchester Hessen | Touch Of Lips | hr music.de | hrmj 004-01 CD
Maria Schneider Jazz Orchestra | Evanescence | Enja | ENJ-8048 2

Dancer's Call
Tex Beneke And His Orchestra | Dancer's Delight | Magic | DAWE 79

Dancers In Love
Duke Ellington And His Famous Orchestra | Duke Ellington:The Complete RCA-Victor Mid-Forties Recordings(1944-1946) | RCA | 2663394-2
Duke Ellington Trio | Piano Reflections | Capitol | 792863-2
Howard Alden Trio With Monty Alexander | Snowy Morning Blues | Concord | CCD 4424

Dancers In Love-
Duke Ellington And His Orchestra | The Jazz Collector Edition: Duke Ellington | Laserlight | 15710

Dancesaball
Dave Brubeck Quartet | Once When I Was Very Young | Limelight | 844298-2 IMS

Dancin' Feet
Lonnie Smith Quintet | The Lost Grooves | Blue Note | 831883-2

Dancin' In An Easy Groove
Quincy Jones All Stars | Go West Man | Fresh Sound Records | ABC 186 (Paramount)

Dancin' To The Coffee Machine
Mighty Sam McClain Group | Sledgehammer Soul & Down Home Blues | audioquest Music | AQCD 1042

Dancing
Marilyn Crispell | Contrasts: Live At Yoshi's | Music & Arts | CD 930

Dancing Alone
Heads Up Super Band | Live at The Berks Jazz Fest | Inak | 30462

Dancing Cats
Franco D'Andrea New Quartet | Ballads And Rituals | Philology | W 127.2

Dancing Derwish
Things | Mother Nature | Jazzpoint | JP 1028 CD

Dancing Dolls
Ron Marvin & Remy Filipovitch | Mysterious Traveler | Album | AS 44677 CD

Dancing Dolphins
Ronaldo Folegatti Groups | Sound Of Watercolors | AH Records | AH 403001-11

Dancing Foot
Lutz Häfner Quintet | Things & Thoughts | Mons Records | MR 874309

Dancing In The Dark
Art Tatum | Art Tatum:Over The Rainbow | Dreyfus Jazz Line | FDM 36727-2
Art Tatum:Over The Rainbow | Dreyfus Jazz Line | FDM 36727-2
Art Tatum-The Complete Pablo Solo Masterpieces | Pablo | 7 PACD 4404-2
Art Tatum:Complete Capitol Recordings | Definitive Records | DRCD 11192
Bill Evans Trio | The Complete Bill Evans On Verve | Verve | 527953-2
Trio (Motian Peacock)-Duo(Hall) | Verve | 2-2509 IMS
Buddy DeFranco Quintet | Chip Off The Old Bop | Concord | CCD 4527
Cannonball Adderley Quintet | Somethin' Else | Blue Note | 746338-2
Miles Davis:The Blue Note And Capitol Recordings | Blue Note | 827475-2
Charlie Parker With Strings | Bird With Strings-Live At The Apollo, Carnegie Hall & Birdland | CBS | CBS 82292
Charlie Parker With The Joe Lipman Orchestra | Charlie Parker With Strings:The Master Takes | Verve | 523984-2
Charlie Parker Big Band | Verve | 559835-2
Chet Baker And The Mike Melillo Trio With Orchestra | Symphonically | Soul Note | 121134-2
Don Elliott Quartet | Jazz-Club: Vibraphone | Verve | 840034-2
Erroll Garner Trio | The Concert Garner | Jazz Groove | 008 IMS
Frank Wess And His Orchestra | The Long Road | Prestige | PCD 24247-2
Fred Astaire With The Oscar Peterson Sextet | Fred Astaire Steppin' Out:Astaire Sings | Verve | 523006-2
Lars Gullin Quartet | Lars Gullin 1951/52 Vol.5:First Walk | Dragon | DRCD 380
Lars Gullin 1951/52 Vol.5:First Walk | Dragon | DRCD 380
Les Jazz Modes | Jazzville '56 Vol.1 | Fresh Sound Records | FSR 619(Dawn DLP 1101)
Paul Kuhn Quintet | Deutsches Jazz Fesival 1954/1955 | Bear Family Records | BCD 15430
Peter Leitch-John Hicks | Duality | Reservoir | RSR CD 134
Sarah Vaughan And Her Trio | Sarah Vaughan At Mister Kelly's | EmArCy | 832791-2 PMS
Sonny Clark Trio | Blue Eyes-Sinatra Songs The Blue Note Way | Blue Note | 789914-2
Tony Bennett With The Ralph Burns Orchestra | My Heart Sings | Fresh Sound Records | LSP 15825(CBS CS 8458)
Zoot Sims Quartet | Zoot Sims:The Complete 1944-1954 Small Group Sessions(Master Takes),Vol.2 | Blue Moon | BMCD 1039

Dancing In The Sky
Ramsey Lewis Trio/And Orchestra | The Best Of Ramsey Lewis | Chess | 515022

Dancing In The Township
Melissa Walker And Her Band | May I Feel | Enja | ENJ-9335 2

Dancing Meadow(suite in 5 parts)
Buddy Rich And His Orchestra | RCA Victor 80th Anniversary Vol.6:1970-1979 | RCA | 2668782-2

Dancing Nitely
Maynard Ferguson With The Rolf Hans Müller Orchestra | Trumpet Rhapsody | MPS | 68224

Dancing On The Ceiling
Charlie Parker Quintet | Charlie Parker At Storyville | Blue Note | 785108-2
Chet Baker Quartet | Sings/It Could Happen To You | Original Jazz Classics | OJC20 303-2
Dorothy Ashby Quartet | The Jazz Harpist | Savoy | SV 0194(MG 6039)
Ella Fitzgerald With The Buddy Bregman Orchestra | The Rodgers And Hart Song Book, Vol.1 | Verve | 821579-2 PMS
Georgie Fame With The Ellen Helmus Sextet | A Portrait Of Chet | Four Leaf Clover | FLC 108 CD
Jones-Brown-Smith | Rockin' In Rhythm | Concord | CCD 4032
Les Jazz Modes | Jazzville '56 Vol.1 | Fresh Sound Records | FSR 619(Dawn DLP 1101)
Ralph Flanagan And His Orchestra | Dance Again Part 2 | Magic | DAWE 75
Willis Jackson Sextet | Together Again: Willis Jackson With Jack McDuff | Prestige | PRCD 24284-2
Mal Waldron Quartet feat. Jim Pepper | The Git-Go At Utopia,Volume Two | Tutu Records | 888148-2*

Dancing On The Flames
Mal Waldron Trio | Mal, Dance And Soul | Tutu Records | 888102-2*
Clark Terry-Bob Brookmeyer Quintet | The Power Of Positive Swinging | Mainstream | JK 57117

Dancing On The Tables
The Real Group | Get Real! | ACT | 9252-2

Dancing Queen-
Sun Ra And His Myth Science Arkestra | Fate In A Pleasant Mood/When Sun Comes Out | Evidence | ECD 22068-2

Dancing Shoes
Clare Fischer With The Metropole Orchestra | The Latin Side | Koch Jazz | 3-6907-2

Dancing Trees
Charles Lloyd Quintet | Hyperion With Higgins | ECM | 1784(014000-2)

Dancing Waters,Big Sur To Bahia
Ray Barretto And His Orchestra | Handprints | Concord | CCD 4473

Dancing With A Beautiful Lady
Andy Lumpp | Piano Solo | Nabel Records:Jazz Network | CD 4646

Dancing With A Beautiful Lady(for Galel)
Jack Jackson And His Orchestra | Things Are Looking Up | Saville Records | SVL 173 IMS

Dancing With Daniela
Flim & The BB's | Neon | dmp Digital Music Productions | CD 458

Dancing With Nature Spirits
Joe Venuti And His New Yorkers | The Big Bands Of Joe Venuti Vol.1 (1928-30) | JSP Records | 1111

Dancing With The Morning
Christoph Spendel | Dreams & Melodies | Software Music | SOWA 107

Dancing Without Reindeers
Cristina Zavalloni Quartet | Danse A Rebours | yvp music | CD 3053

Dando Vueltas
Bob Cunningham Quartet | Walking Bass | Nilva | NQ 3411 IMS

Danger Street
Deborah Henson-Conant | Naked Music | Laika Records | LK 94-051

Danger Zone
Deborah Henson-Conant Trio | Just For You | Laika Records | LK 95-063
Diamond, Angel & Crooks | More Where That Came From | Intuition Records | INT 3061-2
Peter Bernstein Quintet | Brain Dance | Criss Cross | Criss 1130

Dangerous
Wes Montgomery Trio | Wes Montgomery-The Complete Riverside Recordings | Riverside | 12 RCD 4408-2
Original Dixieland Jazz Band | Original Dixieland Jazz Band | RCA | ND 90026

Dangerous Ground
Buster Benton Blues Band | Blues At The Top | Black & Blue | BLE 59.001 2

Danielle
Zoot Sims Quintet | The Swinger | Pablo | 2310861

Daniel's Blues
Gary Dial-Dick Oatts Quartet With Brass Ensemble | Brassworks | dmp Digital Music Productions | CD 477

Danke Bestens
Vienna Art Orchestra | Blues For Brahms | Amadeo | 839105-2

Danke,Frau Hofrat
Joelle Leandre-Rüdiger Carl | Blue Goo Park | FMP | CD 52

Dankeschoen
Duke Ellington And His Orchestra | Jazz Legacy 11: Duke Ellington-Ellington Moods | Vogue | 500061

Danny Boy (Londonderry Air)
Art Tatum | Art Tatum:20th Century Piano Genius | Verve | 531763-2
The Art Tatum Solo Masterpieces | Pablo | 2625703
Ben Webster With The Stan Tracy Trio | Ben Webster Plays Ballads | Storyville | SLP 4118
Bill Evans Trio | Empathy+A Simple Matter Of Conviction | Verve | 837757-2 PMS
Danny Walch Quintet | D's Mood | Steeplechase | SCCD 31428
Glenn Miller And His Orchestra | The Glenn Miller Carnegie Hall Concert | RCA | NL 81506
Herb Ellis-Remo Palmier Quartet | Windflower | Concord | CJ 56
Joe Beck-Ali Ryerson | Django | dmp Digital Music Productions | CD 530
Scott Hamilton Sextet | In New York City | Concord | CCD 4070
Stephane Grappelli Quartet | I Hear Music | RCA | 2179624-2
Planet Jazz:Stephane Grappelli | RCA | 2165366-2
Steve Kuhn | Mostly Ballads | New World Records | 80351-2
Werner Lener Trio | My Own | Satin Doll Productions | SDP 1013-1 CD
Charles Earland Sextet | Smokin' | Muse | MR 5126

Danny-O
Conrad Janis And His Tailgate Band | Conrad Janis And His Tailgate Band Vol.2 | GHB Records | BCD-81

Danny's Dream
Lars Sjösten Octet Feat. Lee Konitz | Dedicated To Lee-Lars Sjösten Plays The Music Of Lars Gullin | Dragon | DRLP 66

Dans Des Grenouilles
Mal Waldron Trio | Breaking New Ground | Eastwind | EWIND 712

Dans La Nuit(1)
Louis Sclavis Group | Dans La Nuit | ECM | 1805(589524-2)

Dans La Nuit(2)
Dans La Nuit | ECM | 1805(589524-2)

Dans La Nuit(3)
Stephane Grappelli Quartet | Jazz In Paris:Stephane Grappelli-Improvisations | EmArCy | 549242-2 PMS

Dans La Vie
Grapelli Story | Verve | 515807-2
Stefano Maltese Open Music Orchestra | Hanging In The Sky | SPLASC(H) Records | H 139

Dans Les Rues D'Antibes
Max Collie And His Rhythm Aces | World Champions Of Jazz | Black Lion | BLCD 760512
Sidney Bechet With Claude Luter And His Orchestra | Salle Pleyel 31 January 52 | Vogue | 655001

Dans Ma Roulotte
Teddy Stauffer Und Seine Original Teddies | Teddy Stauffer:Rare And Historical Jazz Recordings | Elite Special | 9522009

Dans Mon Ile
André Ricros-Louis Sclavis Group | Le Partage Des Eaux | Silex | Y 225003 IMS

Danse
Cristina Zavalloni Quartet | Danse A Rebours | yvp music | CD 3053

Danse Brisée
Ray Drummond Sextet | Excursion | Arabesque Recordings | AJ 0106

Danse Norvegienne
Django Reinhardt And The Quintet Du Hot Club De France | Django Reinhardt Portrait | Barclay | DALP 2/1939
Quintet Du Hot Club De France | Django Reinhardt:Souveniers | Dreyfus Jazz Line | FDM 36744-2
Duke Ellington And His Orchestra | Hot Summer Dance | Red Baron | 469285-2

Dansere
Eddie Lockjaw Davis-Shirley Scott Sextet | Bacalao | Original Jazz Classics | OJCCD 1090-2(P 7178)

Dansero
Ulrich Gumpert | Satie: Trois Gymnopédies | ITM Records | ITM 1451

Dansir
ULG | Spring | Laika Records | 35101382

Dansk Morgenzarrar-
The Duke Ellington Orchestra | Music Is My Mistress | Limelight | 820801-2 IMS

Dante Extra Vergine
Scarlet Rivera Trio | Behind The Crimson Veil | Erdenklang | 40702

Dany
Guido Manusardi | Love And Peace: Solo Piano Performance | SPLASC(H) Records | HP 02

Danza Le Los Nanigos
Ramon Valle Quintet | Ramon Valle Plays Ernesto Lecuona | ACT | 9404-2

Danza Negra
Trio Terracota | Savia | Acoustic Music Records | 319.1193.2

Danza Sul Posta
Franco Morone | Guitarea | Acoustic Music Records | 319.1046.2

Danzarin
Carl Kress-Dick McDonough | Pioneers Of Jazz Guitar 1927-1939 | Retrieval | RTR 79015

Daphne
Bireli Lagrene Quartet | My Favorite Django | Dreyfus Jazz Line | FDM 36574-2
Bireli Lagrene Trio | Live At The Carnegie Hall: A Tribute To Django Reinhardt | Jazzpoint | JP 1040 CD
Django Reinhardt And The Quintet Du Hot Club De France | Planet Jazz:Django Reinhardt | Planet Jazz | 2152071-2
The Indispensable Django Reinhardt | RCA | ND 70929
Eddie South/Stephane Grappelli Quintet | Django Reinhardt:Djangology | EMI Records | 780659-2
Quintet Du Hot Club De France | Djangology | Bluebird | 2663957-2
Verve Jazz Masters 38:Django Reinhardt | Verve | 516931-2
Django Reinhardt-Stephane Grappelli | Ace Of Club | ACL 1158
Stephane Grappelli Quintet | Grapelli Story | Verve | 515807-2
Atlantic Jazz: Mainstream | Atlantic | 7567-81704-2
Stephane Grappelli Trio | Live | Justin Time | JTR 8469-2
Häns'che Weiss-Vali Mayer Duo | Just Play II | MMM Records | CD 1303

Daphne-
Stephane Grappelli Quartet | Jazz-Club: Violin | Verve | 840039-2
Stephane Grappelli Trio | How High The Moon | Memo Music | HDJ 4020

Daphne's Madness
Sigi Schwab & Percussion Academia | Rondo A Tre | Melos Music | CDGS 703

Dapper Dan
Joe Pass | Virtuoso Live! | Pablo | 2310948-2

Dar Es Salam
Lluis Vidal Trio | Milikituli | Fresh Sound Records | FSNT 009 CD

D'Ara Endavant
Jazzensemble Des Hessischen Rundfunks | Atmosphering Conditions Permitting | ECM | 1549/50

Darauf Der Schnee Danach
Inno | Insonnie | SPLASC(H) Records | CD H 321-2

Dardanella
Art Tatum | Art Tatum:Complete Capitol Recordings | Definitive Records | DRCD 11192
Ernst Höllerhagen Quintet | Ernst Höllerhagen 1942-1948 | Elite Special | 9522001
Louis Armstrong And His All Stars | At The Pasadena Civic Auditorium | GNP Crescendo | GNP 11001
Louis Katzman And The Brunswick Orchestra | Jazz Museum-Hot Dance Bands Of The Twenties,Vol.2 | MCA | 52057 (801842)

Dare I Ask?
New York Voices | New York Voices | GRP | GRP 95892

Daria
Hamiet Bluiett Quartet | Ballads & Blues:Live At The Village Vanguard | Soul Note | 121288-2

Darien Mode
Ron McClure Quartet | Dream Team | Steeplechase | SCCD 31435

Darizm
Darji With The Hank Jones Quartet | Darji Meets Hank Jones | Timeless | SJP 171

Dark
Paris Jazz Quintet | The Paris Jazz Quintet | TCB Records | TCB 21112

Dark And Curious
Tampa Red | Don't Jive Me | Original Blues Classics | OBCCD 549-2

Dark Before Dawn
T.S. Monk Sextet | Changing Of The Guard | Blue Note | 789050-2

Dark Blue
Rez Abbasi Group | Out Of Body | String Jazz | SJRCD 1021

Dark Bones
Jackie McLean Septet | Rhythm Of The Earth | Dreyfus Jazz Line | FDM 37009-2

Dark Corner
Ben Webster Septet | The Big 3 | CBS | AK 40950

Dark Corners
Duke Ellington And His Orchestra | Duke Ellington | Laserlight | 15753

Dark Drops
Al Di Meola Groups | Guitar Heroes Vol.1:Al Di Meola | Zounds | CD 2700044001

Dark Eye Tango
Hal Di Meola Group | Casino | CBS | 468215-2
Art Tatum Trio | Art Tatum:Over The Rainbow | Dreyfus Jazz Line | FDM 36727-2

Dark Eyes
Art Tatum:Over The Rainbow | Dreyfus Jazz Line | FDM 36727-2
Chuck Foster And His Orchestra | The Uncollected: Chuck Foster | Hindsight | HSR 115
Dizzy Gillespie Septet | Verve Jazz Masters 25:Stan Getz & Dizzy Gillespie | Verve | 521852-2
Don Byas Quartet | Don Byas Complete American Small Group Recordings | Definitive Records | DRCD 11213
Gene Krupa Trio | The Complete Jazz At The Philharmonic On Verve 1944-1949 | Verve | 523893-2
Gillespie-Stitt-Getz Septet | Diz And Getz | Verve | 2-2521 IMS
Itzak Perlman With The Oscar Peterson Quartet | Side By Side | Telarc Digital | CD 83341
Jo Jones Orchestra | The Main Man | Pablo | 2310799
Papa Bue's Viking Jazzband With Wingy Manone | A Tribute To Wingy Manone | Storyville | SLP 210
Ray Gelato Giants | The Full Flavour | Linn Records | AKD 034
Stan Kenton And His Orchestra | Sketches On Standards | Creative World |
For Musicians Only | For Musicians Only | Verve | 837435-2

Dark Eyes(alt.take)
Wynton Kelly Quartet | Wynton Kelly-Piano | Original Jazz Classics | OJCCD 401-2(RLP 12-254)
Slam Stewart Quartet | The Complete Savoy Sessions Vol.1 | Savoy | WL 70521 (809292)

Dark Glasses-
Friedrich Gulda Septet | Friedrich Gulda At Birdland | Fresh Sound Records | ND 12587

Dark Glow
J.A. Deane | Nomad | Victo | CD 035
Dark Matter
Anthony Cox Quartet | Dark Metals | Minor Music | 801019
Dark Nebula
Ben Sidran Group | Old Songs For New The Depression | Antilles | 846132-2(889648)
Dark Nines
JMOG | JMOG | Sackville | SKCD2-2031
Dark Rapture
Nat King Cole Trio | Nat King Cole Trio Transcriptions Vol.1 | Naxos Jazz | 8.120512 CD
Dark Rapture-
Joachim Kühn-Walter Quintus | Dark | Ambiance(Blue Flame) | AMB 1
Dark Rooms
Berlin Skyscaper | Butch Morris Conducts Berlin Skyscraper '95 | FMP | CD 92/93
Dark Space
Philippe Caillat Special Project | Melodic Travel | Laika Records | LK 689-012
Oregon | Distant Hills | Vanguard | VSD 79341
Dark Spirit
David Murray Octet | Dark Star(The Music Of The Grateful Dead) | Astor Place | TCD 4002
Dark Tales
Chuck Israels International Quartet | On Common Ground | Anima Records | DV-CD 002
Dark,But Lovely
Matthias Daneck's N.O.W. | Seven Portraits Of Obviously Unpredictable Mood Swings And Subsequent Behaviour | Satin Doll Productions | SDP 1012-1 CD
Darker Than Light-
Paul Bley Duo | Sonor | Soul Note | SN 1085
Darkness
Stephan Micus | Darkness And Light | ECM | 1427(847272-2)
Darkness And Light(part 1-3)
Stan Getz With The Eddie Sauter Orchestra | Stan Getz Plays The Music Of Mickey One | Verve | 531232-2
Darkness Before The Day-
Terje Rypdal Group | Odyssey | ECM | 1067/8
Darkness Falls
Richie Beirach | Self Portrait | CMP Records | CMP CD 51
Darkness On The Delta
Mr.Acker Bilk And His Paramount Jazz Band | New Orleans Days | Lake | LACD 36
Darkness On The Delta Suite
The Golden Years Of Revival Jazz,Vol.10 | Storyville | STCD 5515
Darkness On The Delta(alt.take)
Peter Madsen Group | Snuggling Snakes | Minor Music | 801030
Darkness Rising
Bengt Berger & Bitter Funeral Beer Band | Praise Drumming | Dragon | DRLP 142
Darktown Strutters Ball
Bunk Johnson With Bertha Gonsoulin | Bunk Johnson In San Francisco | American Music | AMCD-16
Darkwood(1)
David Darling | Cello | ECM | 1464(511982-2)
Darkwood(2)
Cello | ECM | 1464(511982-2)
Darkwood(3)
Dark Wood | ECM | 1519(523750-2)
Darkwood(4)
Dark Wood | ECM | 1519(523750-2)
Darkwood(5)
Dark Wood | ECM | 1519(523750-2)
Darkwood(6)
Dark Wood | ECM | 1519(523750-2)
Darkwood(7)
Dwight Dickerson Trio | Sooner Or Later | Discovery | DS 792 IMS
Darling
Loren Stillman Quartet | How Swee It Is | Nagel-Heyer | CD 2031
Darling Clementine
John Benson Brooks' Orchestra | Folk Jazz U.S.A. | RCA | PM 43767
Darling Je Vous Aime Beaucoup
Buddy Collette Sextet | Jazz For Lovers | Original Jazz Classics | OJCCD 1764-2(SP 5002)
Darling Nelly Gray
Loverfield Jazzband | Swissmade In Holland | Timeless | CD TTD 601
Darn That Dream
Akio Sasajima-Ron Carter | Akioustically Sound | Muse | MCD 5448
Alex Smith Quintet | Jazzville Vol.2 | Fresh Sound Records | FSR 601(Dawn DLP 1107)
Andrew Hill | Verona Rag | Soul Note | 121110-2
Art Farmer/Slide Hampton Quintet | In Concert | Enja | ENJ-4088 2
Art Pepper-George Cables Duo | Tete-A-Tete | Original Jazz Classics | OJCCD 843-2(GXY 5147)
Art Pepper:The Complete Galaxy Recordings | Galaxy | 16GCD 1016-2
Art Pepper:The Complete Galaxy Recordings | Galaxy | 16GCD 1016-2
Bill Evans-Jim Hall | Undercurrent | Blue Note | 538228-2
Billie Holiday And Her Band | Verve Jazz Masters 47:Billie Holiday Sings Standards | Verve | 527650-2
Billie Holiday And Her Orchestra | Body And Soul | Verve | 2304340 IMS
Chet Baker Big Band | Chet Baker Big Band | Fresh Sound Records | 054 2607921(Pacific 1229)
Clifford Brown-Max Roach Quintet | Brownie-The Complete EmArCy Recordings Of Clifford Brown | EmArCy | 838306-2
Conte Candoli With The Joe Haider Trio | Conte Candoli Meets The Joe Haider Trio | JHM Records | JHM 3602
Conte Candoli-Carl Fontana Quintet | The Complete Phoenix Recordings Vol.4 | Woofy Productions | WPCD 124
Count Basie And His Orchestra | From Southland Cafe Boston 1940 | Jazz Anthology | 550022
Dexter Gordon Quartet | Dexter Gordon Plays-The Bethlehem Years | Fresh Sound Records | FSR-CD 154(882891)
Dinah Washington With The Clifford Brown All Stars | Verve Jazz Masters 19:Dinah Washington | Verve | 518200-2
Eric Alexander Sextet | Full Range | Criss Cross | Criss 1098
George Shearing With The Montgomery Brothers | Wes Montgomery-The Complete Riverside Recordings | Riverside | 12 RCD 4408-2
Georgie Auld And His Orchestra | Cool California | Savoy | WL 70511(2)(SJL 2254) DP
Gerry Mulligan Quartet | California Concerts Vol.1 | Pacific Jazz | 746860-2
Jack Millman Quintet | Four More | Fresh Sound Records | FSR-CD 0217
Jimmy Smith Trio With Lou Donaldson | Jimmy Smith Trio With L.D. | Blue Note | 300200(BNJ 61013)
Joe Wilder Quartet | Wilder' N' Wilder | Savoy | SV 0131(MG 12063)
John Basile Quartet | The Desmond Project | Chesky | JD 156
John Swana Sextet | John Swana And Friends | Criss Cross | Criss 1055
Leo Parker Quartet | First Sessions 1949/50 | Prestige | P 24081
Louis Stewart-Martin Taylor | Acoustic Guitar Duets | Jardis Records | JRCD 9613
Luca Flores Trio | Sounds And Shades Of Sound | SPLASC(H) Records | CD H 320-2
Miles Davis And His Orchestra | The Complete Birth Of The Cool | Capitol | 494550-2
Birth Of The Cool | Capitol | 530117-2
Miles Davis:The Blue Note And Capitol Recordings | Blue Note | 827475-2
Nick Brignola Quartet | Raincheck | Reservoir | RSR CD 108(882632)
Oscar Peterson-Joe Pass Duo | Live At Salle Pleyel, Paris | Pablo | 2625705
Rein De Graaff | Be-Bop, Ballads & Blues | Timeless | CD SJP 354
Sauter-Finegan Orchestra | The Return Of The Doodletown Fifers | EMI Records | EP 2607691
Soren Lee Quartet | Soren Lee Quartet | L+R Records | CDLR 45073
Stan Getz Quartet | Born To Be Blue | Bandstand | BDCD 1533
Ted Brown Trio | Free Spirit | Criss Cross | Criss 1031
Thelonious Monk | Thelonious Monk Collection | Black Lion | BLCD 7601-2
Thelonious Monk Trio | Thelonious Monk-The Complete Riverside Recordings | Riverside | 15 RCD 022-2
Tom Harrell | Labyrinth | RCA | 2668512-2
All Star Trumpet Spectacular | The Second Progressive Records All Star Trumpet Spectacular | Progressive | PRO 7017 IMS
Darn That Dream(alt.take)
Horace Parlan Trio | Hi-Fly | Steeplechase | SCCD 31417
Kenny Dorham Quintet | Kenny Dorham Quintet | Original Jazz Classics | OJCCD 113-2(DLP 9)
Darth Songs
David Murray Quintet | Remembrances | DIW | DIW 849 CD
Darvanan
Dodo Marmarosa Quartet | Dodo's Bounce | Fresh Sound Records | FSCD 1019
Das Biest
Drei Vom Rhein | Drei Vom Rhein | Mons Records | CD 1896
Das Gaslied-
Uli Beckerhoff Quintet | Original Motion Picture Soundtrack:Das Geheimnis(Secret Of Love) | Nabel Records:Jazz Network | CD 4666
Das Geheimnis
Der Rote Bereich | Der Rote Bereich 3 | Jazz 4 Ever Records:Jazz Network | J4E 4740
Das Geht Doch Nicht
Pata Music Meets Arfi | La Belle Et La Bête | Pata Musik | PATA 14(amf 1066)
Das Gespräch Im Schloss
Chris Barber's Jazzband & das Große Rundfunkorchester Berlin,DDR | Jazz Zounds: Chris Barber | Zounds | CD 2720007
Das Gibt's Nur Einmal
Inge Brandenburg mit Werner Müller und seinem Orchester | Why Don't You Take All Of Me | Bear Family Records | BCD 15614 AH
Ekkehard Jost Trio | Some Other Tapes | Fish Music | FM 009/10 CD
Das Grüne Pferd
A Band Of Friends | Teatime Vol.2 | Poise | Poise 06/2
Das Haus:
Kölner Saxophon Mafia With Dieter Wellershoff | Kölner Saxophon Mafia Proudly Presents | Jazz Haus Musik | JHM 0046 CD
Das Ich Und Seine Augenblicke
European Jazz Quintet | European Jazz Quintet | EGO | 4012
Das Ist Ein Flöten Und Geigen
Slawterhaus | Slawterhaus Live | Victo | CD 013
Das Ist Mein Leben(John Trudell)
Blaufrontal | Blaufrontal | Jazz Haus Musik | JHM 0037 CD
Das Jagen Ist Des Saxophonisten Lust
Horst Grabosch Quartet | Alltage | Jazz Haus Musik | JHM 80 CD
Das Leben Ist Wie Ein Pfeifen
Vladimir Estragon | Three Quarks For Muster Mark | TipToe | TIP-888803 2
Das Lied Vom Surabaya-Johnny
Anirahtak und die Jürgen Sturm Band | Das Kurt Weill Programm | Nabel Records:Jazz Network | CD 4638
Das Lied Von Den Braunen Inseln
Jugend Jazzorchester Sachsen-Anhalt | Jugend Jazzorchester Sachsen-Anhalt Spielt Kurt Weill | Born&Bellmann | 972806 CD
Das Loch In Der Banane
Manfred Dierkes | It's About Time | Acoustic Music Records | 319.1176.2
Das Morsealphabet
Sven Ake Johansson-Alexander von Schlippenbach Duo | Kalfaktor A.Falke Und Andere Lieder | FMP | 0970
Das Raumschiff
Baden Powell Solo/Group | Tristeza On Guitar | MPS | 68087
Das Rosas
Franz Bauer Quintet | Plüschtier | Jazz Haus Musik | JHM 0097 CD
Das Schweigen Des R.
Peter Kowald/Barry Guy | Paintings | FMP | 0960
Das Step
Boury | Moderne Zeiten-Musik Und Tanz | Jazz Haus Musik | JHM 11
Das Virus
Mani Neumeir Group | Privat | ATM Records | ATM 3803-AH
Das War 1999
Alfred 23 Harth Group | Gestalt Et Jive | Moers Music | 02038
Dat Dere
Art Blakey And The Jazz Messengers | Live At Birdland | Fresh Sound Records | FSCD 1020
Art Blakey & The Jazz Messengers: Olympia, May 13th, 1961 | Laserlight | 36128
Billy May And His Orchestra | Billy May's Big Fat Brass/Bill's Bag | Capitol | 535206-2
Bobby Timmons Trio | Moanin' | Milestone | M 47031
In Person | Original Jazz Classics | OJC20 364-2(RLP 9391)
Brad Mehldau With The Rossy Trio | New York-Barcelona Crossing Vol.2 | Fresh Sound Records | FSNT 037 CD
Cannonball Adderley Quintet | Them Dirty Blues | Blue Note | 495447-2
Them Dirty Blues | Capitol | 495447-2
The Cannonball Adderley Collection Vol.1:Them Dirty Blues | Landmark | CAC 1301-2(882341)
Hank Crawford Septet | More Soul | Atlantic | 8122-73709-2
Hank Jones Trio | I Remember You | Black & Blue | BLE 233122
Jenny Evans And Band | Girl Talk | ESM Records | ESM 9306
Girl Talk | Enja | ENJ-9363 2
Live At The Allotria | BELL Records | BLR 90003
Michael Logan Quartet | Night Out | Muse | MCD 5458
Monty Budwig Septet | Dig | Concord | CJ 79
Randy Johnston Quartet | Somewhere In The Night | HighNote Records | HCD 7007
Wayne Bartlett With The Thomas Hufschmidt Group | Tokyo Blues | Laika Records | 35101212
Woody Shaw Quintet | Imagination | 32 Jazz | 32090
Dat Dere(alt.take)
Cannonball Adderley Quintet | Them Dirty Blues | Capitol | 495447-2
The Cannonball Adderley Collection Vol.1:Them Dirty Blues | Landmark | CAC 1301-2(882341)
Dat Dere(Theme)
Bobby Timmons Trio | In Person | Original Jazz Classics | OJC20 364-2(RLP 9391)
The Enriquillo Winds | Melodia Para Congas | Mapleshade | 04632
Date In The Morning
Wolfgang Lauth Quartet | Lauther | Bear Family Records | BCD 15717 AH
Date On Wax
Lionel Hampton Quintet | The Complete Lionel Hampton Quartets And Quintets With Oscar Peterson On Verve | Verve | 559797-2
Date With Oscar
Lionel Hampton With The Oscar Peterson Quartet | Verve Jazz Masters 26:Lionel Hampton with Oscar Peterson | Verve | 521853-2
Buddy Rich And His Orchestra | Live Sessions At The Palladium, Hollywood | Jazz Anthology | JA 5206
Dating
Kölner Saxophon Mafia-Drümmele Maa-Elima | Baboma | Jazz Haus Musik | JHM 33
Datune
Ray Anderson Quintet | Blues Bred In The Bone | Enja | ENJ-5081 2
Niels-Henning Orsted-Pedersen/Kenneth Knudsen Duo | Pictures | Steeplechase | SCCD 31068
Daughter's Waltz
Alfred 23 Harth Group | Sweet Paris | free flow music | ffm 0291
Dauphine
Crane River Jazz Band | The Crane River Jazz Band | Cadillac | SGC/MEL CD 202
Davenport Blues
Bix And His Rhythm Jugglers | Riverboat Shuffle | Naxos Jazz | 8.120584 CD
Gil Evans Orchestra | Pacific Standart Time | Blue Note | 84494
Jack Teagarden And His Orchestra | Jazz Original | Charly | CD 80
Red And Miff's Stompers | Red & Miff | Saville Records | SVL 146 IMS
Miff Mole And His Molers | Red Nichols And Miff Mole 1927 | Village(Jazz Archive) | VILCD 015-2
Dave's Tune
David Fathead Newman Sextet | Resurgence! | Muse | MR 5234
David And Goliath
Big Band De Lausanne | Duke Ellington's Sacred Music | TCB Records | TCB 20502
David The King
David Murray Quintet | Children | Black Saint | 120089-2
David's Theme
Richard Carr Trio | Along The Edge | Nabel Records:Jazz Network | CD 4683
David's Tumbao-
David Murray Big Band | Live At Sweet Basil Vol.2 | Black Saint | 120095-2
Dawn
Joachim Schoenecker Quartet | In The Moment | Nagel-Heyer | CD 2009
Karlheinz Miklin Quintet & KUG Big Band | KH Miklin Quinteto Argentina & KUG Big Band | TCB Records | TCB 21232
Kenny Barron Quintet | Sunset To Dawn | Muse | MCD 6014
Niels-Henning Orsted-Pedersen Trio | The Eternal Traveller | Pablo | 2310910
Ornette Coleman Trio | The Best Of Ornette Coleman:The Blue Note Years | Blue Note | 823372-2
Sun Ra Arkestra | The Sun Ra Arkestra Meets Salah Ragab In Egypt | Praxis | CM 106
David Darling | Dark Wood | ECM | 1519(523750-2)
Dawn-
Jack Walrath-Ralph Reichert Sextet | Solidarity | ACT | 9241-2
Bill Evans Quartet | Living In The Crest Of A Wave | Elektra | MUS 96.0349-1
Dawn Bird
Buck Clayton's Big Four | The Classic Swing Of Buck Clayton | Original Jazz Classics | OJCCD 1709-2(RLP 142)
Dawn Dance
Freddie Redd Trio | San Francisco Suite | Original Jazz Classics | OJCCD 1748-2
Dawn Song
Dean Magraw Group | Kitchen Man | Acoustic Music Records | 319.1133.2
Dawn Vision
Johannes Enders Quartet | Kyoto | Organic Music | ORGM 9726
Dawning Dance
Mongo Santamaria And His Band | Brazilian Sunset | Candid | CCD 79703
Dawn's Light
Susan Weinert Band | Point Of View | Intuition Records | INT 3272-2
Day
Gordon Beck | Dreams | JMS | 049-2
Day After Day(Leaving)
Cosmo Intini & The Jazz Set | Seeing The Cosmic | SPLASC(H) Records | H 121
Day And Night
Tana Reid Quintet | Blue Motion | Paddle Wheel | KICJ 172
Day By Day
(Little)Jimmy Scott And His Quintet With Horns And Strings | Lost And Found | Sequel Records | RSA CD 804
Astrud Gilberto With The Claus Ogerman Orchestra | Silver Collection: The Astrud Gilberto Album | Verve | 823451-2 PMS
Ernestine Anderson With The Clayton-Hamilton Jazz Orchestra | Boogie Down | Concord | CCD 4407
Lennie Niehaus Quintet | Vol.1:The Quintets | Original Jazz Classics | OJC 319(C 3518)
Oscar Peterson Trio With Herb Ellis | Three Originals:Motion&Emotions/Tristeza On Piano/Hello Herbie | MPS | 521059-2
Peter Fessler Quartet | Foot Prints | Minor Music | 801058
Rickey Woodard Quartet | California Cooking | Candid | CCD 79509
Ron McClure Quartet | Pink Cloud | Naxos Jazz | 86002-2
Sonny Phillips Septet | I Concentrate On You | Muse | MR 5157
Chick Corea And His Orchestra | My Spanish Heart | Polydor | 543303-3
Day Danse
Al Haig Trio | Invitation | Spotlite | SPJ LP 4 (AH 4)
Day Dream
Bob Cooper Sextet | COOP! The Music Of Bob Cooper | Original Jazz Classics | OJCCD 161-2
Chris Connor With The Al Cohn Orchestra | Free Spirits | Atlantic | AMCY 1077
Danny Walch Quintet | D's Mood | Steeplechase | SCCD 31428
Duke Ellington And His Orchestra | The Jazz Collector Edition: Duke Ellington | Laserlight | 15710
Eddie Duran Trio | Ginza | Concord | CJ 94
Ella Fitzgerald With The Duke Ellington Orchestra | The Best Of The Song Books:The Ballads | Verve | 521867-2
The Complete Ella Fitzgerald Song Books of Harold Arlen, Irving Berlin, Duke Ellington, George & Ira Gershwin, Jerome Kern, Johnny Mercer, Cole Porter And Rogers & Hart | Verve | 519832-2
Forward Motion | Reminiscence | Linn Records | AKD 024
Harry Allen-Tommy Flanagan | Day Dream | RCA | 2167152-2
Jack Sheldon Quartet | Stand By For The Jack Sheldon Quartet | Concord | CJ 229
Johnny Hodges Orchestra | The Rabbit's Work On Verve In Chronological Order Vol. 2: 1951-52 | Verve | 2304448 IMS
Passion Flower 1940-46 | Bluebird | 63 66616-2
Marian McPartland Quartet | Plays The Music Of Billy Strayhorn | Concord | CCD 4326
Red Richards | Dreamy | Sackville | SKCD2-3053
Sarah Vaughan With Small Group & Orchestra | Duke Ellington Song Book One | Pablo | CD 2312111
Smiley Winters-Mark Levine Duo | Smiley & Me | Concord | CCD 4352
Stan Kenton And His Orchestra | Stan Kenton-Jean Turner | Creative World | ST 1046
Steve Slagle Quartet | Spread The Words | Steeplechase | SCCD 31354
Toshiko Akiyoshi Trio | A Tribute To Billy Strayhorn | JAM | 5003 IMS
André Previn Trio | Uptown | Telarc Digital | CD 83303
Day Dream-
David Shea Group | Shock Corridor | Avant | AVAN 013
Day Dream(take 1)
Spaulding Givens Trio | Debut Rarities Vol.2 | Original Jazz Classics | OJCCD 1808-2
Day Dream(take 2)
LaVerne Butler With The Rob Bargad Band | Day Dreamin' | Chesky | JD 117
Day Dreaming
Mike Wofford Trio | Plays Jerome Kern, Vol. 1 | Discovery | DS 808 IMS
Day Five
Klaus Ignatzek Group | Day For Night | Nabel Records:Jazz Network | CD 4639
Day For Night
Jacaranda | Timeless | CD SJP 292
Day Four
Al Porcino Big Band | Al Porcino Big Band Live! | Organic Music | ORGM 9717
Day In Day Out
Allen Harris With The Metropole Orchestra | Here Comes Allen Harris... | Mons Records | MR 874771
Billie Holiday And Her All Stars | Billie Holiday:The Great American Songbook | Verve | 523003-2
Billie Holiday And Her Orchestra | Embraceable You | Verve | 817359-1 IMS
Cal Tjader Quintet | Concerts In The Sun | Fantasy | FCD 9688-2
Concerts In The Sun | Fantasy | FCD 9688-2

TITELVERZEICHNIS

Chris Connor With The Ronnie Ball Orchestra | A Portrait Of Chris | Atlantic | AMCY 1073
Duke Ellington And His Orchestra | Ellington On The Air | Ember | CJS 840
Ella Fitzgerald With The Nelson Riddle Orchestra | Ella Fitzgerald Sings The Johnny Mercer Songbook | Verve | 539057-2
The Johnny Mercer Songbook | Verve | 823247-2 PMS
Jeanie Lambe And The Danny Moss Quartet | The Blue Noise Session | Nagel-Heyer | CD 052
Jimmy Smith Trio | I'm Movin' On | Blue Note | 832750-2
Marty Elkins And Her Sextet | Fuse Blues | Nagel-Heyer | CD 062
Mel Tormé And His Trio | Night At The Concord Pavillion | Concord | CCD 4433
Stan Kenton And His Orchestra | Road Show Vol.1 | Creative World | ST 1019
The Couriers Of Jazz | The Couries Of Jazz-England's Greatest Combo | Fresh Sound Records | Carlton STCD 116

Day Number One
Kahil El'Zabar Quartet | Sacred Love | Sound Aspects | sas CD 021

Day Of The Dark Bright Light
Michiel Borstlap Sextet | Michiel Borstlap:The Sextet Live! | Challenge | CHR 70030

Day One
John Coltrane Quartet | Transition | Impulse(MCA) | GRP 11242

Day Seven
Steve Coleman And The Council Of Balance | Genesis & The Opening Of The Way | RCA | 2152934-2

Day Six
Genesis & The Opening Of The Way | RCA | 2152934-2

Day Three
Mongo Santamaria Orchestra | Soca Me Nice | Concord | CCD 4362

Day Tripper
Martin Taylor | Martin Taylor Artistry | Linn Records | AKD 020

Day Two
Joe Carter Quartet Feat. Art Farmer | My Foolish Heart | Empathy Records | E 1004

Daybreak
Chet Baker Trio | Daybreak | Steeplechase | SCS 1142(Audiophile Pressing)
Ethel Azama With The Marty Paich Orchestra | Cool Heat | Fresh Sound Records | 054 2600411(Liberty LRP 3142)
Keith Ingham Trio | A Star Dust Melody | Sackville | SKCD2-2051
Meredith d'Ambrosia With The Eddie Higgins Trio | Love Is Not A Game | Sunnyside | SSC 1051 D
Scheer Music | Rappin' It Up | Palo Alto | PA 8025
Tommy Dorsey And His Orchestra | Frank Sinatra And The Tommy Dorsey Orchestra | RCA | 2668701-2
Tommy Dorsey In Concert | RCA | NL 89780 DP

Daybreak Delight
Duke Ellington And His Cotton Club Orchestra | Early Ellington (1927-1934) | Bluebird | ND 86852

Daybreak Express
Duke Ellington And His Orchestra | The Classic Years In Digital Stereo: Hot Town | CDS Records Ltd. | RPCD 616(CD 647)
The Cotton Club Legend | RCA | NL 89506 AG

Daybreak Serenade
Stu Goldberg Group | Eye Of The Beholder | MPS | 68282

Daydream
Florian Poser-Klaus Ignatzek Duo | Springdale | Acoustic Music Records | 319.1166.2
Errol Parker | Live At St.Peter's Church | Sahara | 1009

Daydreaming
Paul Gonsalves Septet | Ellingtonia Moods & Blues | RCA | 2147793-2

Daylie Double
J.J.Johnson Quintet | The Eminent J.J.Johnson Vol.2 | Blue Note | 532144-2

Daylie Double(alt.take)
Ahmad Mansour Quintet | Penumbra | Timeless | CD SJP 404

Days Beyond Recall
Bunk Johnson-Sidney Bechet Sextet | Jazz Classics Vol.1 | Blue Note | 789384-2

Days In Paris
Thilo Wolf Trio With Randy Brecker,Chuck Loeb & New York Strings | A Swinging Hour In New York | Mons Records | MR 874801

Days Like Open Wounds
Mose Allison Quartet | The Mose Chronicles-Live In London,Vol.2 | Blue Note | 529748-2

Days Like This
Mose Allison Trio | The Word From Mose | Atlantic | 8122-72394-2
That's Jazz Vol.19: Mose Allison | Atlantic | ATL 50249

Days Of The Fifth Period
| Florian Poser Plays His Favourite Standards | Acoustic Music Records | 319.1067.2

Days Of Wine And Roses
Bill Evans Trio | His Last Concert In Germany | West Wind | WW 2022
Consecration 2 | Timeless | CD SJP 332
Bill Frisell Band | Is That You? | Nonesuch | 7559-60956-2
Billy Eckstine With Bobby Tucker And His Orchestra | Billy Eckstine Now Singing In 12 Great Movies | Verve | 589307-2
Bireli Lagrene & Jaco Pastorius | Stuttgart Aria | Jazzpoint | JP 1019 LP
Bireli Lagrene Trio | Live In Marciac | Dreyfus Jazz Line | FDM 36567-2
Dexter Gordon Quartet | Swiss Nights-Vol. 1 | Steeplechase | SCCD 31050
Tangerine | Original Jazz Classics | OJCCD 1041-2(P 10091)
Dexter Gordon Birthday Celebration | Fantasy | FANCD 6082-2
Dexter Gordon-Benny Bailey Quintet | Revelation | Steeplechase | SCCD 31373
Dieter Reith Trio | Reith On! | MPS | 557423-2
Dizzy Gillespie Quintet | The Cool World/Dizzy Goes Hollywood | Verve | 531230-2
Eddie Lockjaw Davis Quartet | Jaw's Blues | Enja | 3097-2
Ernestine Anderson With The Hank Jones Trio | Live From Concord To London | Concord | CCD 4054
Francois Magnin Trio | M.J. | Plainisphare | PAV 806
George Barnes Quartet | Plays So Good | Concord | CCD 4067
Herb Ellis Quartet | An Evening With Herb Ellis | Jazz Focus | JFCD 019
Jaco Pastorius Trio | Jaco Pastorius Heavy'n Jazz & Stuttgart Aria | Jazzpoint | JP 1058 CD
Jaco Pastorius Broadway Blues & Theresa | Jazzpoint | JP 1053 CD
Jimmy Raney-Doug Raney Duo | Duets | Steeplechase | SCCD 31134
Jimmy Smith Trio | Paris Jazz Concert:Jimmy Smith And The Trio | Laserlight | 36159
Joe Bawelino Quartet & Martin Stegner | Happy Birthday Stéphane | Edition Collage | EC 458-2
Joe Henderson With The Wynton Kelly Trio | Straight No Chaser | Verve | 531561-2
Kenny Colman With The London Philharmonic Orchestra | Dreamscape | Justin Time | JTR 8466-2
Lajos Dudas Quintet | Some Great Songs | double moon | DMCD 1005-2
Lambert, Hendricks And Bavan | Havin' A Ball-Live At The Village Gate | RCA | 2122111-2
McCoy Tyner Trio | Nights Of Ballads And Blues | Impulse(MCA) | JAS 35 (AS 39)
Michel Petrucciani Trio | Michel Petrucciani-The Owl Years:Days Of Wine And Roses | Owl Records | 548301-2
Milt Jackson And Big Brass | For Someone I Love | Original Jazz Classics | OJCCD404-2(RLP 9478)
Norbert Gottschalk-Frank Haunschild | The Art Of The Duo:Favorite Songs | Mons Records | MR 874813
Oscar Peterson Trio | We Get Request | Verve | 521442-2
Oscar Peterson-Harry Edison Duo | Oscar Peterson & Harry Edison | Original Jazz Classics | OJCCD 738-2(2310741)
Pat Martino Quartet | Exit | Muse | MCD 5075
Ray Brown Trio | Bam Bam Bam | Concord | CCD 4375
Ron McClure Quartet | Tonite Only | Steeplechase | SCCD 31288
Sonny Criss Quartet | This Is Criss | Original Jazz Classics | OJCCD 430-2(P 7511)
Stuttgarter Gitarren Trio | Stuttgarter Gitarren Trio Vol.2 | Edition Musikat | EDM 034
Sunday Night Orchestra | Voyage Out | Mons Records | MR874305
The Widespread Depression Orchestra | Time To Jump And Shout | Stash Records | ST 212 IMS
Tony Bennett-Bill Evans | The Tony Bennett-Bill Evans Album | Original Jazz Classics | OJC20 439-2(F 9489)
Toots Thielemans Group | Live | Polydor | 831694-2 PMS
Toots Thielemans Quartet With Orchestra | Bluesette | CBS | CDCOL 26604
Warren Bernhardt Trio | Ain't Life Grand | dmp Digital Music Productions | CD 478
Wes Montgomery Trio | Wes Montgomery-The Complete Riverside Recordings | Riverside | 12 RCD 4408-2
Willis Jackson Sextet | Gravy | Prestige | PCD 24254-2
Willy Vande Walle Quartet | Midnight | Jazz Pure Collection | AU 31617 CD

Days Of Yore
Sebastian Gramss Underkarl | Jazzscene | TCB Records | TCB 99102

Dayton,Ohio 1903
Oscar Peterson Trio | The Greatest Jazz Concert In The World | Pablo | 2625704-2

D-Cup And Up
Weather Report | Domino Theory | CBS | 25839-2

Dding Dek
The Ganelin Trio | Vide | LEO | LR 117

De Berlin-
Alex Alves | Verde | Acoustic Music Records | 319.1169.2

De Ce Trait Enchante
Brötzmann, van Hove, Bennink | Balls | FMP | 0020

De De
The Poll Winners | The Poll Winners Ride Again | Original Jazz Classics | OJC 607(C 7556)

De Deele Dee Do
Lisa Bassenge Trio | Going Home | Minor Music | 801091

De Doo Doo Doo De Da Da
Keith Jarrett Quintet | Fort Yawuh | Impulse(MCA) | 547966-2

De Drums
Ana Caram Group | Maracana | Chesky | JD 104

De Grine Kusine
Joachim Schoenecker Quartet | In The Moment | Nagel-Heyer | CD 2009

De Haan
Jackie McLean-Michael Carvin Duo | Antiquity | Steeplechase | SCCD 31028

De La Raiz A La Copa
Louis Jordan And His Tympany Five | Louis Jordan-Let The Good Times Roll: The Complete Decca Recordings 1938-1954 | Bear Family Records | BCD 15557 IH

De Laff's On You
Louis Jordan-Let The Good Times Roll: The Complete Decca Recordings 1938-1954 | Bear Family Records | BCD 15557 IH
Loose Tubes | Jazzbühne Berlin '87 | Repertoire Records | REPCD 4916-WZ

De Luzern-
Joan Monné Trio | Mireia | Fresh Sound Records | FSNT 100 CD

De Mica En Mica
Alguimia | Alguimia 'U' | Fresh Sound Records | FSNT 023 CD

De Moment Una Samba
Trinity | Trinity | Steeplechase | SCCD 31171

De Repente
Barbara Thompson | Songs From The Center Of The Earth | Black Sun Music | 15014-2

De Romeria
Art Farmer Quartet Feat Jim Hall | To Sweden With Love | Atlantic | AMCY 1016

De Som Blaeser Ud...(He Who Blows Out...)
Amsterdam String Trio | Winter Theme | Winter&Winter | 910060-2

De Spul
Alfred 23 Harth Group | Sweet Paris | free flow music | ffm 0291

De St.Cloud-
Deep Creek Jazzuits | Again | Jazz Pure Collection | AU 31615 CD

De Tout Ton Coeur
René Marino Rivero | Che Bandoneon | ALISO Records | AL 1020

De Tübingen-
Red Records All Stars | Together Again For The First Time | Red Records | 123275-2

De Vuelta A Casa
Maarten Altena Octet | Rif | Hat Art | CD 6056

Deacon Jones
Big Jay McNeely And His Orchestra | Deacon Rides Again | Pathe | 1546691(Imperial)

Dead Indeed
James Dapogny's Chicago Jazz Band | Original Jelly Roll Blues | Discovery | 74008-2

Dead Man Blues
Jelly Roll Morton | Blues And Rag From Piano Rolls | Jazz Anthology | 550122
Jelly Roll Morton's Red Hot Peppers | Jelly Roll Morton-Doctor Jazz | RCA | CL 89808 SF
Doctor Jazz | Black & Blue | BLE 59.227 2
Birth Of The Hot | Bluebird | 63 66641-2

Dead Shrimp Blues
John Zorn Naked City | Naked City-Grand Guignol | Avant | AVAN 002

Deadweight
John Scofield Quartet | A Go Go | Verve | 539979-2

Deadzy
Choo Choo Light:Stammberger-Rädler-Schöne | Choo Choo Light | G.N.U. Records | CD A 92.007

Dealin'(take 1)
Prestige All Stars | John Coltrane-The Prestige Recordings | Prestige | 16 PCD 4405-2
Mal Waldron-John Coltrane Sextet | Wheelin' | Prestige | P 24069

Dealin'(take 2)
Prestige All Stars | John Coltrane-The Prestige Recordings | Prestige | 16 PCD 4405-2
Eddie Burns Group | Treat Me Like I Treat You | Moonshine | BLP 106

Dealing With The Devil
Ralph Abelein Group | Mr. B's Time Machine | Satin Doll Productions | SDP 1042-1 CD

Deancing
The Intergalactic Maiden Ballet feat. John Zorn | Square Dance | TipToe | TIP-888804 2

Dear Arnold
Stephane Grappelli Trio | I Hear Music | RCA | 2179624-2

Dear Ben
Bill Watrous And His Orchestra | Reflections | Soundwings | SW 2104(807408)

Dear Dessa
Monty Alexander Trio | Steamin' | Concord | CCD 4636

Dear Ear
Prestige Jazz Quartet | The Mal Waldron Memorial Album:Soul Eyes | Prestige | PRCD 11024-2

Dear Elaine
The Prestige Jazz Quartet | The Prestige Jazz Quartet | Original Jazz Classics | OJCCD 1937-2(P 7108)
Dee Dee Bridgewater-Kenny Burrell | Dear Ella | Verve | 539102-2

Dear Ella
Kenny Burrell And The Jazz Heritage All-Stars | Live At The Blue Note | Concord | CCD 4731

Dear Father
Stan Kenton And His Orchestra | National Anthems Of The World | Creative World | ST 1060

Dear Heart
Sarah Vaughan With Orchestra | Sarah Vaughan Sings The Mancini Songbook | Verve | 558401-2
Al Jones Blues Band | Paying Our Dues | Dues | AJBB 01

Dear John
Loverly | Play World Wild Music | ITM Records | ITM 1419
N.Y. Hardbop Quintet | A Mere Bag Of Shells | TCB Records | TCB 20702

Dear Little Pipistrelle
Avishai Cohen Trio | The Trumpet Player | Fresh Sound Records | FSNT 161 CD

Dear Lord
Dave Liebman Quintet | Homage To John Coltrane | Owl Records | 018357-2
Harold Mabern-Kieran Overs | Philadelphia Bound | Sackville | SKCD2-3051
John Coltrane Quartet | John Coltrane-His Greatest Years, Vol. 3 | MCA | AS 9278
Coltrane Spiritual | Impulse(MCA) | 589099-2
Marilyn Crispell | Live In San Francisco | Music & Arts | CD 633

Dear Lord(breakdowns and alt.take)
Matt Renzi-Jimmy Weinstein-Masa Kamaguchi Trio | Lines And Ballads | Fresh Sound Records | FSNT 065 CD

Dear Max
Martin Sasse Trio | Here We Come | Nagel-Heyer | CD 2008

Dear McCoy
Fred Van Hove | Verloren Maandag | FMP | SAJ 11

Dear Mr. Florence
Sabine&Markus Setzer | Between The Words | Lipstick Records | LIP 8970

Dear Mr. P.
Albert Mangelsdorff Trio | Live In Montreux | MPS | 68261

Dear Mr.Palmer
Jackie McLean Quintet | 'Bout Soul | Blue Note | 859383-2

Dear Old Southland
Louis Armstrong And His All Stars | The Complete Town Hall Concert 17.May 1947 | RCA | ND 89746

Dear Old Southland-
Art Taylor's Wailers | Wailin' At The Vanguard | Verve | 519677-2

Dear Old Stockholm
Don Lanphere Quintet Feat. Jon Pugh Plus Two | Into Somewhere | Hep | 2022
Duane Eubanks Sextet | My Shining Hour | TCB Records | TCB 99202
John Coltrane Quintet | Impressions | Impulse(MCA) | 543416-2
Jutta Hipp Trio | Jutta Hipp At The Hickory House Vol.1 | Blue Note | 300094(1515)
Miles Davis Quintet | This Is Jazz:Miles Davis Plays Ballads | CBS | CK 65038
Round About Midnight | CBS | 460605-2
Miles Davis Sextet | Miles Davis:The Best Of The Capitol/Blue Note Years | Blue Note | 798287-2
Miles Davis Vol.1 | Blue Note | 300081(1501)
Saxophone Connection | Saxophone Connection | L+R Records | CDLR 45046
Stan Getz Quintet | The Best Of The Jazz Saxophone | LRC Records | CDC 8520

Dear Rain
John Abercrombie Trio | While We're Young | ECM | 1489
Carmen McRae And Her Quartet | Carmen Sings Monk | RCA | 2663841-2

Dear Ruby(Ruby My Dear)
Carmen McRae with the Clifford Jordan Quartet | The Collected Carmen McRae | RCA | 2668713-2
T.S. Monk Group | Monk On Monk | N2K | 43052

Dear Rudy
Primal Blue | Primal Blue | Hip Bop | HIBD 8006

Dear,If You Change
Mike Mainieri Group | An American Diary:The Dreaming | NYC-Records | NYC 6026-2

Dearborn St. Breakdown
Pat Martino Quartet | Desperado | Original Jazz Classics | OJCCD 397-2(P 7795)

Dearborn Walk
Benny Goodman Original Quartet | Benny Goodman:The King Of Swing | Musicmasters | 65130-2

Dearest
The Original Benny Goodman Quartet | The Yale University Music Library:Benny Goodman Vol.10 | Musicmasters | 65129-2

Dearie's Blues
Miles Davis Quintet | Miles Davis With John Coltrane | CBS | CBS 88029

Dearly Beloved
Cal Tjader's Modern Mambo Quintet(Sextet) | Mambo With Tjader | Original Jazz Classics | OJCCD 271-2(F 3202)
Dave Stryker Trio | All The Way | Steeplechase | SCCD 31455
Jack Sheldon And The Swedish All Stars | Blues In The Night | Phontastic | PHONT 7569
John Coltrane Quartet | John Coltrane:The Classic Quartet-Complete Impulse Studio Recordings | Impulse(MCA) | 951280-2
June Christy And Her Orchestra | The Misty Miss Christy | Pathe | 1566141(Capitol T 725)
McCoy Tyner-Bobby Hutcherson Duo | Manhattan Moods | Blue Note | 828423-2
Ruth Price With Shelly Manne & His Men | Ruth Prica With Shelly Manne & His Men At The Manne Hole | Original Jazz Classics | OJCCD 1770-2(S 7590)
Sonny Rollins Quartet | Sonny Rollins & Co | Bluebird | ND 82496
The Jazz Giants Play Jerome Kern:Yesterdays | Prestige | PCD 24202-2
Sonny Rollins & Co.Vol.3:What's New/Vol.4:Our Man In Jazz | RCA | 741091/92
Wes Montgomery Trio | Wes Montgomery-The Complete Riverside Recordings | Riverside | 12 RCD 4408-2
Norman Granz Jam Session | Bird: The Complete Charlie Parker On Verve | Verve | 837141-2

Dearly Beloved-
Charlie Parker Jam Session | Verve | 833564-2 PMS

Death Blues
Robert Pete Williams | Free Again | Original Blues Classics | OBCCD 553-2(BV 1026)

Death Chant
Reverend Blind Gary Davis | When I Die I 'll Live Again | Fantasy | F 24704

Death In The Carwash
Stephan Wittwer | World Of Strings | Intakt Records | CD 017

Death Letter
Son House | Death Letter | Edsel | CD 167

Death Rolls
Sara Martin With Clarence Williams And His Orchestra | Jazz Classics In Digital Stereo: King Oliver Volume Two 1927 To 1930 | CDS Records Ltd. | ZCF 788

Deauville
Dan Moretti Quintet | Some Time Inside | Black-Hawk | BKH 51901

Debased Line
Defunkt | Defunkt/Heroes | DIW | DIW 838 CD

Deborah
Jean-Paul Céléa-Francois Couturier Quintet | Passagio | Nocturne Productions | NPCD 509

Deborah's Theme
Jeff Williams Quintet | Coalescence | Steeplechase | SCCD 31308

Debut
Oscar Peterson-Ray Brown Duo | Tenderly | Verve | MV 2662 IMS

Decafinata
Dave Douglas Quartet | Charms Of The Night Sky | Winter&Winter | 910015-2

Decafinata-
Things | Blues For The Last Punk | Jazzpoint | JP 1026 MC

Deccaphonie
Blind Lemon Jefferson | Blind Lemon Jefferson-Master Of The Blues | Biograph | BLP 12015

December
Niels Lan Doky Trio | Close Encounter | Storyville | STCD 4173
Walt Weiskopf Quartet | A World Away | Criss Cross | Criss 1100

December Greenwings
Marilyn Crispell-Gary Peacock-Paul Motian | Amaryllis | ECM | 1742(013400-2)
Jacques Pirotton Quintet | Artline | B.Sharp Records | CDS 070

December Remember
Claudio Fasoli Jazz Group | Hinterland | EdiPan | NPG 804

Decending Grace
Cindy Blackman Quintet | Arcane | Muse | MCD 5341

Decepticon
Beboppin' | Beboppin' | Limetree | MLP 198403

Deception
Miles Davis And His Orchestra | Birth Of The Cool | Capitol | 530117-2
Miles Davis:The Blue Note And Capitol Recordings | Blue Note | 827475-2
Randy Sandke Sextet | Get Happy | Concord | CCD 4598

Deceptively Yours
Art Blakey And The Jazz Messengers | The Jazz Messengers At The Cafe Bohemia Vol. 1 | Blue Note | 300087(1507)

Decicifering The Message
John LaPorta Quartet | The Most Minor | Fresh Sound Records | FSR-CD 0208

Decidedly
Thelonious Monk-Gerry Mulligan Quartet | 'Round Midnight | Milestone | M 47067

Decidedly(alt.take)
Thelonious Monk-The Complete Riverside Recordings | Riverside | 15 RCD 022-2

Decimas
Art Blakey And The Jazz Messengers | At The Cafe Bohemia Vol.1 | Blue Note | 532148-2

Deciphering The Message
At The Cafe Bohemia Vol.3 | Blue Note | 300193(BNJ 61007)

Decision
Sonny Rollins Quintet | Sonny Rollins | Blue Note | 84508
The Blue Note Years-The Best Of Sonny Rollins | Blue Note | 793203-2
Sonny Rollins:The Blue Note Recordings | Blue Note | 821371-2
Jazz Gallerie:Sonny Rollins Vol.1 | RCA | 2127283-2
Tony Lakatos With The Martin Sasse Trio | Feel Alright | Edition Collage | EC 494-2
Byron Allen Trio | The Byron Allen Trio | ESP Disk | ESP 1005-2

Decisione
Ruben Blades Y Seis Del Solar With Band | Buscando America | Messidor | 15924

Decisions
Russell Gunn Group | Love Requiem | HighNote Records | HCD 7020

Deck The Halls
Kevin Gibbs Trio | Christmas Presence | Concord | CCD 4432

Deconstructed
Eric Felten-Jimmy Knepper Group | T-Bop | Soul Note | 121196-2

Decoy
Steve Adams/Ken Filiano Quartet | Anacrusis | Nine Winds Records | NW 0128

Decrescendo-
Joachim Ullrich Orchestra | Faces Of The Duke | Jazz Haus Musik | JHM 0045 CD

Decrescendo Suite:
Billy Taylor Trio With Candido | The Billy Taylor Trio With Candido | Original Jazz Classics | OJCCD 015-2(P 7051)

De-Dah
Gianlugi Trovesi Quartet With The WDR Big Band | Dedalo | Enja | ENJ-9419 2

Dedalo
Paolo Fresu Sextet | Mamut: Music For A Mime | SPLASC(H) Records | CD H 127-2

De-Dar
Ben Webster And His Associates | Ben Webster And Associates | Verve | 835254-2
JATP All Stars | Compact Jazz: Coleman Hawkins/Ben Webster | Verve | 833296-2

Dedicated
Johnny Dyani Septet | Afrika | Steeplechase | SCS 1186(Audiophile Pressing)

Dedicated Abdullah Ibrahim
Anthony Braxton | For Alto | Delmark | 900253/4 DX

Dedicated To Lee
Lars Sjösten Octet Feat. Lee Konitz | Dedicated To Lee-Lars Sjösten Plays The Music Of Lars Gullin | Dragon | DRLP 66

Dedicated To Lee(alt.take)
Keith Tippett-Louis Moholo Duo | No Gossip | FMP | SAJ 28

Dedicated To Mingus
Anthony Braxton | For Alto | Delmark | 900253/4 DX

Dedicated To Thomas Mapfumo
(Little)Jimmy Scott And His Quartet With Horns And Strings | Lost And Found | Sequel Records | RSA CD 804

Dedicated To You
Carmen McRae With The Shirley Horn Trio | Sarah-Dedicated To You | Novus | PD 90546
James Williams Quartet | Everything I Love | Concord | CJ 104
Keith Jarrett Trio | Somewhere Before | Atlantic | 7567-81455-2
Standards In Norway | ECM | 1542(521717-2)
Klaus Treuheit Trio | Steinway Afternoon | clearaudio | 42016 CD

Dedication
Arild Andersen Quartet | Shimri | ECM | 1082
Coleman Hawkins And The Chocolate Dandies | The Commodore Story | Commodore | CMD 24002
Mal Waldron-David Friesen Duo | Dedication | Soul Note | SN 1178
Stu Goldberg | Piru | MPS | 68262
Thilo von Westernhagen Group | Theatre | SHP Records | SHP 203

Dedication To Tom Harrell
Andrew Hill Sextet | Point Of Departure | Blue Note | 499007-2

Dedication(alt.take)
Leonid Chizhik | Leonid Chizhik In Concert | Mobile Fidelity | MFCD 887

Dedications
Jukkis Uotila Group | Avenida | Stunt Records | 18807
Paul Schwarz/Bernd Konrad | Sali | Creative Works Records | CW LP 1003
Lanfranco Malaguti Quintet | Top Jazz From Italy-The Winners Of Musica Jazz Critics Poll '88 | yvp music | CD 3018

Dee Blues
Booker Ervin Quintet | Cookin' | Savoy | SV 0150(MG 12154)

Dee Dee
Ornette Coleman Trio | The Best Of Ornette Coleman:The Blue Note Years | Blue Note | 823372-2

Dee Dee's Dance
Joe Roland Quartet With String Quartet | Joltin' Joe | Savoy | SV 0215(MG 12039)

Dee Gee
Lee Morgan Sextet | Taru | Blue Note | 522670-2

Dee Lawd
Enrico Pieranunzi Trio | Deep Down | Soul Note | 121121-2

'Deed I Do
Bill Evans Trio | The Complete Bill Evans On Verve | Verve | 527953-2
Billie Holiday With The Ray Ellis Orchestra | Last Recordings | Verve | 835370-2 PMS
Buck Clayton All Stars feat.Jimmy Rushing | Copenhagen Concert | Steeplechase | SCC 6006/7
Diane Schuur And Her Band | Pure Schuur | GRP | GRP 96282
Dixie-O-Naires | Strike Up The Band | Timeless | CD TTD 576
Ella Fitzgerald With The Count Basie Orchestra | Ella & Basie-On The Sunny Side Of The Street | Verve | 821576-2
Frank Strazzeri | Nobody Else But Me | Fresh Sound Records | FSR-CD 5020
Houston Person Quartet | In A Sentimental Mood | HighNote Records | HCD 7060
Jackie And Roy With The Charlie Ventura Band | Jackie And Roy:Jazz Classics By Charlie Ventura's Band | Savoy | SV 0218(MG 6057)
Jimmy Rushing And His All Stars | Jimmy Rushing And The Big Brass/Rushing Lullabies | CBS | CK 65118
Joe Pass-Jimmy Rowles Duo | Joe Pass:A Man And His Guitar | Original Jazz Classics | OJCCD 8806-2
John Bunch Trio | The Best Thing For You | Concord | CJ 328
Keith Nichols Cotton Club Orchestra With Claus Jacobi & Bent Persson | Syncopated Jamboree | Stomp Off Records | CD 1234
Meade Lux Lewis | Meade Lux Lewis 1939-1054 | Story Of Blues | CD 3506-2
Paolo Tomelleri-Fritz Hartschuh Quintet | Milan Swing | L+R Records | CDLR 45070
Peanuts Hucko All Stars | Tribute To Benny Goodman | Timeless | CD TTD 513
Red Norvo Trio | The Red Norvo Trios | Prestige | P 24108
Rob McConnell Trio | Trio Sketches | Concord | CCD 4591
Ruby Braff And His Big City Six | Little Big Horn | Fresh Sound Records | FSR-CD 321
Ruby Braff-Scott Hamilton Sextet | A Sailboat In The Moonlight | Concord | CCD 4296
Stephane Grappelli Quartet | Stephane Grappelli | LRC Records | CDC 9014
The Sidney Bechet Society | Jam Session Concert | Nagel-Heyer | CD 076
Marion Montgomery And Her Quartet | I Gotta Right To Sing... | Ronnie Scott's Jazz House | JHCD 003

Deed-Lee-Yah
Lambert, Hendricks And Bavan | At Newport '63 | RCA | 2125757-2

Deedles' Blues
Johannes Cernota | Sparta | JA & RO | JARO 4136-2

D'Eedriophtalma-
Max Roach Quintet | Conversations | Milestone | M 47061

Deeds Not Words
Thomas Heberer | Mouth | Poise | Poise 09

Deeds(2002)
The Danish Radio Jazz Orchestra | This Train:The Danish Radio Jazz Orchestra Plays The Music Of Ray Pitts | dacapo | DCCD 9428

Deelirium
Ekkehard Jost Quartet | Deep | Fish Music | FM 007 CD

Deep
Herb Ellis Trio | Herb Mix | Concord | CJ 181

Deep As Love
Jimi Sumen Group | Paintbrush,Rock Penstemon | CMP Records | CMP CD 61

Deep Blue
Avishai Cohen Group | Devotion | Stretch Records | SCD 9021-2

Deep Creek
Jelly Roll Morton And His Orchestra | The Jelly Roll Morton Centennial-His Complete Victor Recordings | Bluebird | ND 82361
Wynton Marsalis Group | Standard Time Vol.6:Mr.Jelly Lord | CBS | CK 69872
Jelly Roll Morton And His Orchestra | Didn't He Ramble | Black & Blue | BLE 59.228 2

Deep Dish Chicago(Blues for Sooze)
Rudy Rotta Quartet | Live In Kansas City | Acoustic Music Records | 319.1138.2

Deep Forest
Earl Hines | Live In Milano 1966 | Nueva Records | JU 315
Earl Hines And His Orchestra | The Earl | Naxos Jazz | 8.120581 CD

Deep Henderson
Bert Ambrose And His Orchestra | Saturday Night | Decca | DDV 5003/4 DT

Deep In A Dream
Bob Cooper And His Orchestra | Shifting Winds | Affinity | AFF 59
Charlie Mariano With The Don Sebesky Orchestra | A Jazz Portrait Of Charlie Mariano | Fresh Sound Records | FSR-CD 0176
Chet Baker-Steve Houben Sextet | Chet Baker-Steve Houben | 52e Rue Est | RECD 019
Hank Mobley Quintet | Curtain Call | Blue Note | 300202
Helen O'Connel With Irv Orton's Orchestra | The Uncollected:Helen O'Connell | Hindsight | HSR 217
Dave Brubeck Trio | All The Things We Are | Atlantic | 7567-81399-2

Deep In A Dream-
Mel Tormé And His Trio | Night At The Concord Pavillion | Concord | CCD 4433

Deep In Green
Stanley Turrentine And His Orchestra | Pieces Of Dream | Original Jazz Classics | OJCCD 831-2(F 9465)

Deep In Love
Joe Haider Quartet | The Essential Point | Jazz Publications | JPV 8403

Deep In The Water
René Pretschner Trio | Floating Pictures | Green House Music | CD 1001
Charles Owens New York Art Ensemble | Charles Owens Plays The Music Of Harry Warren | Discovery | DS 811 IMS

Deep Low
Ma Rainey With The Tub Jug Washboard Band | Ma Rainey | Milestone | MCD 47021-2

Deep Morgan Blues
Michal Urbaniak Group | Fusion | CBS | CK 65525

Deep Night
Art Tatum-Buddy DeFranco Quartet | The Tatum Group Masterpieces | Pablo | 2625706
Sonny Clark Quintet | Cool Struttin' | Blue Note | 746513-2

Deep Night(alt.take)
Ron Marvin & Remy Filipovitch | Mysterious Traveler | Album | AS 44677 CD

Deep Ocean
Lucky Thompson Trio | Tricotism | Impulse(MCA) | GRP 11352

Deep Paths
Shelly Manne Orchestra | Cool California | Savoy | WL 70511(2)(SJL 2254) DP

Deep Purple
Art Tatum | Jazz:The Essential Collection Vol.2 | IN+OUT Records | 78012-2
The Art Tatum Solo Masterpieces | Pablo | 2625703
Art Tatum Sextet | The Tatum Group Masterpieces | Pablo | 2310731
Artie Shaw And His Orchestra | This Is Artie Shaw | RCA | NL 89411 DP
Benny Goodman Quartet | Camel Caravan Broadcast 1939 Vol.2 | Phontastic | NCD 8818
The Benny Goodman Caravans-The Small Groups Vol.1 | Giants Of Jazz | GOJ 1034
Buddy DeFranco Quartet | Jazz Tones | Verve | MV 2610 IMS
Don Elliott Octet | Don Elliott:Mellophone | Fresh Sound Records | FSR 2009(Bethlehem BCP 12)
Erroll Garner Trio | Relaxin' | Vogue | 500117
Jimmy Smith Trio | The Champ-Jimmy Smith At The Organ Vol.2 | Blue Note | 300093(1514)
Kai Winding Quintet | Kai Winding-Bop City:Small Groups 1949-1951 | Cool & Blue | C&B-CD 110
Lars Gullin Quartet | Lars Gullin 1951/52 Vol.5:First Walk | Dragon | DRCD 380
Made In Sweden Vol.1: 1949 to March 1951 | Magnetic Records | MRCD 106
Soprano Summit | Chalumeau Blue | Chiaroscuro | CR 148
Buddy Bertinat-Jack Trommer | Hot Jazz & Swing Mit Teddy Stauffer's Original Teddies | Elite Special | 9522002

Deep Purple-
Glenn Miller And His Orchestra | 15 Rare Broadcast-Performances From 1943-1944 | RCA | NL 89499 AG
Simon Schott | Bar Piano: Simon Schott Plays Your Favorite Evergreens Vol.2 | Organic Music | ORGM 9735
Willis Jackson Quintet | Together Again: Willis Jackson With Jack McDuff | Prestige | PRCD 24284-2
Art Tatum | Art Tatum:Complete Original American Decca Recordings | Definitive Records | DRCD 11200

Deep River
Archie Shepp-Horace Parlan Duo | 2nd Set | 52e Rue Est | RECD 016
Charlie Shavers Quartet | Swing Along With Charlie Shavers | Fresh Sound Records | FSR-CD 327
First Revolution Singers | A Cappella Gospel Anthology | Tight Harmony Records | TH 199404
Golden Gate Quartet | Americans Swinging In Paris:Golden Gate Quartet | EMI Records | 539659-2
Spirituals To Swing 1955-69 | EMI Records | 791569-2
Grant Green Quintet | Feelin' The Spirit | Blue Note | 746822-2
Hank Crawford Orchestra | Midnight Ramble | Milestone | MCD 9112-2
Jack Teagarden And His Orchestra | Jack Teagarden | Queen-Disc | 027
Stan Kenton And His Orchestra | The Complete MacGregor Transcriptions Vol.1 | Naxos Jazz | 8.120517 CD
Toshiko Mariano Quartet | Live At Birdland | Fresh Sound Records | FSCD 1021

Deep River-
John Campbell | A Man And His Blues | Crosscut | CCD 11019

Deep Sea
Klaus Kreuzeder & Henry Sincigno | Sax As Sax Can-Alive | Trick Music | TM 9312 CD
Ida Cox And Her All Star Band | I Can't Quit My Man | Affinity | CD AFS 1015

Deep Song
Masha Bijlsma Band | Lebo | Jazzline | JL 11145-2
Benny Bailey Quintet | Live At Grabenhalle, St.Gallen | TCB Records | TCB 8940

Deep Steelze Kick
Kip Hanrahan Groups | Tenderness | American Clave | AMCL 1016-2

Deep Thought
James Carter Quartet | The Real Quietstorm | Atlantic | 7567-82742-2

Deep Throat Blues
Pinguin Moschner | Tuba Love Story | Sound Aspects | sas 005

Deep Trouble
Michael Shrieve Group | Two Doors | CMP Records | CMP CD 74

Deeper
Glen Moore Group | Introducing Glen Moore | Elektra | ELK K 52151

Defiance
Eddie Palmieri Group | Arbete | RMM Records | 660.58.087

Definition Of A Dog
Joachim Raffel Trio | ...In Motion | Jazz 4 Ever Records:Jazz Network | J4E 4746

Definitions
Clark Terry Sextet | Clark Terry-Remember The Time | Mons Records | MR 874762

Deformation
Klaus Ignatzek Quartet | Blue Energy | Red Records | RR 217

Degnello
Banda Cittá Ruvo Di Puglia | La Banda/Banda And Jazz | Enja | ENJ-9326 2

Deh,Non Volerli Vittime E Finale(Norma)
Conrad Gozzo And His Sextet | GOZ The Great | Fresh Sound Records | LPM 1124(RCA)

Deiling Er Jorden
Laurent Coq Quartet | Jaywalker | Enja | 9111-2

Dein Herz(1)
Kodexx Sentimental | Das Digitale Herz | Poise | Poise 02

Dein Herz(2)
Joe Kienemann Trio | Integration | yvp music | CD 3023

Dein Ist Mein Ganzes Herz
Willem Breuker Kollektief | In Holland | BVHAAST | 041/42 (807118)

Deja
Soledad Bravo With Band | Volando Voy | Messidor | 15966 CD
Anouar Brahem Trio | Le Pas Du Chat Noir | ECM | 1792(016373-2)

Déjà La Nuit
Ahmad Jamal Orchestra | Night Song | MoJazz | 530303-2

Deja Vu
Roswell Rudd-Archie Shepp Group | Live In New York | EmArCy | 013482-2
Donald & Peggy Knaack | Inside The Plactic Lotus | Hat Art | 3517

Dejala En La Puntica
Michel Portal | !Dejarme Solo! | Dreyfus Jazz Line | FDM 36506-2

Dejection Blues
Ray Brown Trio With Ulf Wakenius | Seven Steps To Heaven | Telarc Digital | CD 83384
Maarten Altena Octet | Rif | Hat Art | CD 6056

Del Cenote
Django Reinhardt And The Quintet Du Hot Club De France | The Very Best Of Django Reinhardt | Decca | 6.28441 DP

Del Sasser
Cannonball Adderley Quintet | Them Dirty Blues | Capitol | 495447-2
The Cannonball Adderley Collection Vol.1:Them Dirty Blues | Landmark | CAC 1301-2(882341)
Tommy Chase Quartet | Hard! | Contemporary | BOP 5

Delarna
Tommy Flanagan Trio | Overseas | Original Jazz Classics | OJCCD 1033-2(P 7134)

Delarna(alt.take)
John Lewis Trio | Improvised Meditations & Excursions | Atlantic | AMCY 1104

Delauney's Dilemma
Modern Jazz Quartet | Live 1956 | Jazz Anthology | 550062
The Complete Modern Jazz Quartet Prestige & Pablo Recordings | Prestige | 4PRCD 4438-2
MJQ 40 | Atlantic | 7567-82330-2
Modern Jazz Quartet | Prestige | P 24005
Ray Brown Quartet | Summerwind | BELL Records | BLR 84017

Dele...,Don!!
Jerome Richardson Sextet | Midnight Oil | Original Jazz Classics | OJCCD 1815-2(NJ 8205)

Deli Guelema
Junior Mance Trio | Softly As In A Morning Sunrise | Enja | 8080-2

Delia
| The Nixa 'Jazz Today' Collection | Lake | LACD 48

Deliberation
Ugetsu | There's Something On The Way | Mons Records | MR 874806

Delicatessen
Stephane Grappelli Quartet | Stephane Grappelli & Friends In Paris | Accord | 500762

Delicious
Carlos Bica-Ana Brandao Group | DIZ | Enja | ENJ-9414 2

Delilah
Cecil Payne Sextet | Payne's Window | Delmark | DE 509
Clifford Brown-Max Roach Quintet | Brownie-The Complete EmArCy Recordings Of Clifford Brown | EmArCy | 838306-2
David Moss | My Favorite Things | Intakt Records | CD 022
Milt Jackson-Wes Montgomery Quintet | Wes Montgomery-The Complete Riverside Recordings | Riverside | 12 RCD 4408-2
Yusef Lateef Quintet | Live at Pep's Vol.2 | Impulse(MCA) | 547961-2
Gong! | Savoy | SJL 2226 (801202)

Delilah(alt.take)
Wes Montgomery Quintet | Wes And Friends | Milestone | M 47013

Delirium
Harold Land Quintet | Groove Yard | Original Jazz Classics | OJCCD 162-2
Red And Miff's Stompers | Victor Jazz History Vol.4:New York Jazz | RCA | 2128558-2
The Montgomery Brothers | Wes Montgomery-The Complete Riverside Recordings | Riverside | 12 RCD 4408-2
Miff Mole And His Molers | Red Nichols And Miff Mole 1927 | Village(Jazz Archive) | VILCD 015-2

Delmar Rag
Jimmy Smith Trio | En Concert Avec Europe 1 | Laserlight | 710379/80

Delon's Blues
Jimmy Smith With The Lalo Schifrin Orchestra | Jimmy Smith:Best Of The Verve Years | Verve | 527950-2

TITELVERZEICHNIS

The Cat | CTI Records | PDCTI 1110-2
James Moody Boptet | Americans Swinging In Paris:James Moody | EMI Records | 539653-2

Delooney
David Friesen Trio | The Name Of A Woman | Intuition Records | INT 3334-2

Delores
Eric Person Trio | Prophecy | Soul Note | 121287-2

Delphine
Ahmad Mansour Quartet | Episode | Timeless | CD SJP 341

Delta
John Wolf Brennan | Irisations | Creative Works Records | CW CD 1021-2
Big Joe Williams | Big Joe Williams | Blues Classics(L+R) | CDLR 82004

Delta City Blues
Cootie Williams And His Orchestra | Duke Ellington's Trumpets | Black & Blue | BLE 59.231 2

Deluge
Dave Stryker Quartet | Full Moon | Steeplechase | SCCD 31345
Wayne Shorter Quartet | Juju | Blue Note | 837644-2

Deluxe
Archie Shepp Orchestra | Mama Too Tight | Impulse(MCA) | 951248-2

Dem Basses-
John Patton Quintet | Blue John | Blue Note | 870009-3

Dem Tambourines
Don Wilkerson Quintet | Blue Bop! | Blue Note | BNSLP 2
Jean-Luc Ponty Quintet | Civilized Evil | Atlantic | SD 16020

Democrat Man
Dado Moroni Trio | Insights | Jazz Focus | JFCD 007

Demon Sanctuary
Michael Carvin Quintet | Between Me And You | Muse | MCD 5370

Den Atem Ausgetauscht
Jens Winther Group | Looking Through | Storyville | STCD 4127

Den Blomstertid Nu Kommer
Moscow Art Trio | Music | JA & RO | JARO 4214-2

Den Endelause(The Eternal One)
Terje Rypdal Trio | Works | ECM | 825428-1

Den Forste Sne
ULG | Spring | Laika Records | 35101382

Den Gamle Gjonne
Jens Winther And The WDR Big Band | The Escape | dacapo | DCCD 9437

Den Gra Dame(The Grey Lady)
Arild Andersen Quintet | Masqualero | Odin | LP 08

Den Lille Sang-
Christoph Haberer Group | Pulsation | Jazz Haus Musik | JHM 0066 CD

Den Lille Sang(Til Gerd):
Mats Eden-Jonas Simonson With The Cikada String Quartet | Milvus | ECM | 1660

Den Lyckliga(Beate Virgine)
The Real Group | Jazz:Live | ACT | 9258-2

Den Of Sins
Svend Asmussen Sextet | Svend Asmussen Collection Vol.14 | Swan Music | CD 2514-2

Denial
Miles Davis Sextet | Dig | Prestige | P 24054

Denn Wovon Lebt Der Mensch
Tom Coster Groups | From The Street | JVC | JVC 2053-2

Dentology
Tampa Red | Bottleneck Guitar | Yazoo | YAZ 1039

Depart
Depart | Depart | Moers Music | 02058 CD

Departure
Gebhard Ullmann Trio | Suite Noire | Nabel Records:Jazz Network | CD 4649
Jon Balke w/Magnetic North Orchestra | Further | ECM | 1517
Klaus Doldinger's Passport | Oceanliner | Warner | 2292-46479-2
McCoy Tyner Sextet | Focal Point | Original Jazz Classics | OJCCD 1009-2(M 9072)
New Orchestra Workshop | The Future Is N.O.W. | Nine Winds Records | NWCD 0131

Departure-
Diana Krall Group | The Girl In The Other Room | Verve | 9862246

Departure Bay
Jimmy Jones' Big Eight | Rex Stewart And The Ellingtonians | Original Jazz Classics | OJCCD 1710-2(RLP 144)

Departure From Planet Earth
Ellery Eskelin Trio | Kulak, 29 & 30 | HatOLOGY | 521

Departures
André Ricros-Louis Sclavis Group | Le Partage Des Eaux | Silex | Y 225003 IMS

Depiction
Duke Ellington And His Orchestra | Live At Carnegie Hall 1964 Vol.1 | Nueva Records | JU 322

Depk
Gary Burton And Friends | Departure | Concord | CCD 4749

Der 13.Wunsch(Dornröschens Taufe)
The Fraterman | Spielerlaubnis | Aho-Recording | CD 1014

Der 3.Weltkrieg Von Der Tribüne Aus Gesehen-
Adam Noidlt-Intermission | Eine Permanent Helle Fläche | Jazz Haus Musik | JHM 53 CD

Der 7.Sinn-Jay Jay
Rias Big Band Berlin + Strings | Weill | Mons Records | MR 874347

Der Ägypter
Voices | Für Wilhelm E. | Trion | 3105

Der Alb
Blaufrontal | Blaufrontal | Jazz Haus Musik | JHM 0037 CD

Der Almanach
Double You | Menschbilder | Jazz Haus Musik | JHM 0062 CD

Der Alptraum
Albert Mangelsdorff | Albert Mangelsdorff-Solo | MPS | 68287

Der Alte Und Der Kranke
Rias Big Band Berlin + Strings | Weill | Mons Records | MR 874347

Der Arumatische Klangbefeuchter(to Paul Bley)
Modern Walkin' | Modern Walkin'-Live In Japan | Satin Doll Productions | SDP 1009-1 CD

Der Atlas
Buddy Bolden's Blues | Buddy Bolden's Blues | ITM Records | ITM 14101

Der Betrunkene Pinguin
Blaufrontal | Blaufrontal | Jazz Haus Musik | JHM 0037 CD

Der Blaue Reiter
Sven Ake Johansson-Alexander von Schlippenbach Duo | Kalfaktor A.Falke Und Andere Lieder | FMP | 0970

Der Bug Hat Zwei Fübe
Ernst-Ludwig Petrowsky Trio | SelbDritt | FMP | 0890

Der Buschmeister
Giorgio Gaslini Trio | Schumann Reflections | Soul Note | SN 1120

Der Die Das Blueneon
Eugen Rödel Trio | As Time Goes By | Jazzpoint | JP 1014 LP

Der Du Die Zeit In Händen Hast
Heiner Goebbels/Alfred Harth | Indianer Für Morgen | Riskant | 568-72401

Der Eine Zupft Den Anderen
Septer Bourbon | Septer Bourbon-The Smile Of The Honeycakehorse | Jazzline | JL 11151-2

Der Fahle Zwerg Auf Dem Kahlen Berg
Mathias Götz-Windstärke 4 | Lunar Oder Solar? | Jazz 'n' Arts Records | JNA 1002

Der Fels
Thilo Wolf Quartet With Strings | I Got Rhythm | MDL-Jazz | CD 1911(CD 050)

Der Frühling(W.F.Bach)
Franz Koglmann Pipetet & Ran Blake | Orte Der Geometrie | Hat Art | CD 6018

Der Glöckner
Peter Brötzmann | Brötzmann/Solo | FMP | 0360

Der Grüne Treibt
Morgenland/Yarinistan | Vielleicht | Riskant | 568-72229

Der Hat Vergeben Das Ewig' Leben Der Nicht Die Musik Liebt
Daniel Schnyder Group | Words Within Music | Enja | ENJ-9369 2

Der Heiland Fällt Vor Seinem Vater Nieder-
Michael Sell Ensemble | Der Heilig'n Landmusik | Misp Records | MISP 509

Der Herr Ist Mein Getreuer Hirt
Sven Ake Johansson-Alexander von Schlippenbach Duo | Kalfaktor A.Falke Und Andere Lieder | FMP | 0970

Der Himmel Über Pingsdorf
Überfall | Next To Silence | GIC | DL 4.1871

Der Hut-Trick-
Matzeit-Daerr | September | Jazz Haus Musik | JHM 0125 CD

Der Indianer
Alfred 23 Harth | Plan Eden | Creative Works Records | CW LP 1008

Der Kanonsong
Fritz Hauser & Stephan Grieder | The Mirror | Hat Art | CD 6037

Der Kleine Prinz
Heiner Goebbels/Alfred Harth | Indianer Für Morgen | Riskant | 568-72401

Der Landwal
Tome XX | Stadtgarten Series Vol.4 | Jazz Haus Musik | JHM 1004 SER

Der Laufende Hase
Henrichs-Kuchenbuch-Rilling | Ohpsst | FMP | SAJ 22

Der Leiermann
Guru Guru | Guru Guru/Uli Trepte | ATM Records | ATM 3815-AH

Der LSD-Marsch
Boury | Moderne Zeiten-Musik Und Tanz | Jazz Haus Musik | JHM 11

Der Mann Im Fahrstuhl(Text Heiner Müller)
Uli Beckerhoff Quintet | Original Motion Picture Soundtrack:Das Geheimnis(Secret Of Love) | Nabel Records:Jazz Network | CD 4666

Der Mann Mit Dem Kreuz
Heinz | Der Spion | Jazz Haus Musik | JHM 30

Der Mond Ist Aufgegangen
Joachim Kühn Trio | Musik Aus Der Dreigroschenoper | Verve | 532498-2

Der Musikant
Pata Trio | Lucy Und Der Ball | Jazz Haus Musik | JHM 34

Der Pflaumenbaum
Heiner Goebbels/Alfred Harth | Berold Brecht:Zeit wird knapp | Riskant | 568-72414

Der Polizwar
Rainer Tempel Big Band | Album 03 | Jazz 'n' Arts Records | JNA 1102

Der Professor
Heiner Goebbels/Alfred Harth | Indianer Für Morgen | Riskant | 568-72401

Der Regenmann
Matzeit-Daerr | September | Jazz Haus Musik | JHM 0125 CD
Heiner Goebbels/Alfred Harth | Indianer Für Morgen | Riskant | 568-72401

Der Richter Briet
Uri Caine Ensemble | Wagner E Venezia | Winter&Winter | 910013-2

Der Ritt Der Walküren
Theo Jörgensmann | Laterna Magica | CMP Records | CMP 19

Der Sonnengesang Des Franziskus
Brötzmann, van Hove, Bennink + Albert Mangelsdorff | Outspan Nr. 1 | FMP | 0180

Der Streichholzhändler
Heiner Goebbels/Alfred Harth | Indianer Für Morgen | Riskant | 568-72401

Der Tag Ist Seiner Höhe Nah(Partita)
Rüdiger Carl | Vorn:Lieder Und Improvisationen Für Akkordeon, Bandoneon Und Ziehharmonika | FMP | 1110

Der Taucher
Paul Eßer-Gerd Dudek-Ali Haurand-Jiri Strivin | Jazz Und Lyrik:Schinderkarren Mit Buffet | Konnex Records | KCD 5108

Der Taugenichts
Charles Davis & Captured Moments | Strange Goodbyes | L+R Records | CDLR 45101

Der Tisch Ist Gedeckt
Ton-Art | Zu | Hat Art | CD 6034

Der Verkauf Geht Weiter
Mani Neumeir-Peter Hollinger | Monsters Of Drums-Live | ATM Records | ATM 3821-AH

Der Verrückt Gewordene Schrotthaufen
Pata Music Meets Arfi | La Belle Et La Bête | Pata Musik | PATA 14(amf 1066)

Der Verzauberte Garten
Boury | Moderne Zeiten-Musik Und Tanz | Jazz Haus Musik | JHM 11

Der Vogel
KoKo & Co | Orte Der Geometrie | Hat Art | CD 6018

Der Vogel-
Trio KoKoKo | Good Night | Creative Works Records | CW LP 1002

Der Wahn Im Grund
Ernst Jandl Mit Band | Bist Eulen? | Extraplatte | EX 316141

Der Zufallsgenerator III
Henk De Jonge Trio With Willem Breuker | Henk De Jonge Trio | BVHAAST | 058

Derek's Blues
Phil Grenadier Quintet | Sweet Transients | Fresh Sound Records | FSNT 093 CD

Derelict
Niels-Henning Orsted-Pedersen/Ulf Wakenius Duo | Those Who Were | Verve | 533232-2

Derfor Kan Vort Oje Glaedes
Catalogue | Pénétration | Hat Art | CD 6187

Derniere Regard
Renaud Garcia-Fons & Jean-Louis Matinier | Fuera | Enja | ENJ-9364 2

Derniere Route
Charlie Byrd And Carlos Barbosa-Lima With The Washington Guitar Quartet | Charlie Byrd/The Washington Guitar Quartet | Concord | CCD 42014

Derrick's Delight
Andy Jaffe Sextet | Manhattan Projections | Stash Records | ST-CD 549(875045)

Dersu
8 Bold Souls | 8 Bold Souls | Open Minds | OM 2409-2

Dervish
Matthias Frey Group | Frequency Of Vision | Lipstick Records | LIP 890052

Dervish On The Glory B
Peter A. Schmid Trio With Guests | Profound Sounds In An Empty Reservoir | Creative Works Records | CW CD 1033

Derwisch
Art Blakey And The Jazz Messengers | Des Femmes Disparaissent/Les Tricheurs(Original Soundtracks) | Fontana | 834752-2 PMS

Des Fetes
Hans Reichel | Bonobo | FMP | 0280

Des Rayons Et Des Ombres
Alexander von Schlippenbach And Martin Theurer | Rondo Brilliante | FMP | 1040

Des Voiliers
Ana Caram Group | Blue Bossa | Chesky | JD 219

Desafinado
Antonio Carlos Jobim With The Claus Ogerman Orchestra | Compact Jazz: Antonio Carlos Jobim | Verve | 843273-2
Art Pepper Quartet | Artworks | Galaxy | GXY 5148
Coleman Hawkins Septet | Latin On Impulse! Various Artists | Impulse(MCA) | IMP 12762
Don Friedman Quartet | My Foolish Heart | Steeplechase | SCCD 31545
My Foolish Heart | Steeplechase | SCCD 31534
Eliane Elias Quartet | Eliane Elias Plays Jobim | Blue Note | 793089-2
Ella Fitzgerald With The Marty Paich Orchestra | Compact Jazz: Ella Fitzgerald | Verve | 831367-2
Franco D'Andrea New Quartet | Jobim | Philology | W 125.2
Getz-Gilberto Quintet | Getz/Gilberto:The Girl From Ipanema | CTI Records | PDCTI 1105-2
Manfredo Fest Quartet | Just Jobim | dmp Digital Music Productions | CD 524
Stan Getz Quartet | The Art Of Saxophone | Laserlight | 24652
Stan Getz Quintet | Verve Jazz Masters 53:Stan Getz-Bossa Nova | Verve | 529904-2
Compact Jazz: Best Of Bossa Nova | Verve | 833269-2
Stan Getz Sextet | Compact Jazz | Verve | 831368-2
Stan Getz With The Joao Gilberto Trio & Orchestra | The Carnegie Hall Concert | Jazz Door | JD 1221
Stan Getz-Charlie Byrd Sextet | Stan Getz Highlights | Verve | 847430-2
Ultimate Stan Getz selected by Joe Henderson | Verve | 557532-2
Stan Getz/Charlie Byrd:Jazz Samba | CTI Records | PDCTI 1104-2

Desafinado(45rpm issue)
Henri Texier Quintet | Colonel Skopje | Label Bleu | LBLC 6523(881998)

Desassossec
Charles Fambrough Group | Keeper Of The Spirit | audioquest Music | AQCD 1033

Descarga Cachao
Cal Tjader's Orchestra | Soul Burst | Verve | 557446-2

Descarga Cubana
The Conga Kings | The Conga Kings | Chesky | JD 193

Descending Motion
Terje Rypdal Trio | Descendre | ECM | 1144

Descendre
Works | ECM | 825428-1

Descension
Christof Lauer Quartet | Christof Lauer | CMP Records | CMP CD 39

Descent
Ricky Ford Quartet | American-African Blues | Candid | CCD 79528

Descisions,Descisions
Stan Kenton And His Orchestra | Kenton '76 | Creative World | STD 1076

Description Du Tunnel
José Luis Gámez Quintet | Rumbo Dorte | Fresh Sound Records | FSNT 089 CD

Desde Dentro
University Six | University Six Vol.One 1925-26 | Harlequin | HQ 2036 IMS

Desert
Steve Tibbetts/Tim Weinhold Duo | Steve Tibbetts | ECM | bzz- 77

Desert Air
Mark Helias Group | Desert Blue | Enja | ENJ-6016 2

Desert Cry
Horace Tapscott With The Pan-African Peoples Arkestra | Live At The I.U.C.C. | Nimbus | NS 357

Desert Moonlight
Blue Room Ensemble | Solitude | Foolish Music | FM 211993

Desert Places
Ornette Coleman & Prime Time | Virgin Beauty | CBS | 489433-2

Desert Poem
Bruce Forman Quartet | Full Circle | Concord | CJ 251

Desert Rose
Stuff Smith Quartet | Stuff Smith+Dizzy Gillespie+Oscar Peterson | Verve | 521676-2

Desert Song
Stanley Clarke Groups | Stanley Clarke Best | Zounds | CD 2700020089
Jimmy Rowles Trio | Grandpaws | Candid | CRS 1014 IMS

Desert Sun
Michel Portal | !Dejarme Solo! | Dreyfus Jazz Line | FDM 36506-2

Desert View
Mark Turner Quartet | Dharma Days | Warner | 9362-47998-2

Deserted Floor
Spark Plug Smith | Country Blues Collector Items Vol.2(1931-1937) | Story Of Blues | CD 3540-2

Desesperacion
Hendrik Meurkens Band | Poema Brasileiro | Concord | CCD 4728

Desierto
Tom Harrell Quintet | Live At The Village Vanguard | RCA | 2663910-2

Design
Stan Kenton And His Orchestra | At The Las Legas Tropicana | Capitol | 835245-2

Desinterresse En Deviatie,Opnieuw En Opnieuw
Charles Lloyd-Billy Higgins | Which Way Is East | ECM | 1878/79(9811796)

Desire
George Colligan Quartet | Desire | Fresh Sound Records | FSNT 071 CD
George Mraz Quartet | Morava | Milestone | MCD 9309-2
Sam Rivers Quartet | Lazuli | Timeless | CD SJP 291

Desirée
Jan Garbarek-Bobo Stenson Quartet | Witchi-Tai-To | ECM | 1041(833330-2)

Desireless
Phil Haynes Quartet | Continuum:The Passing | Owl Time Line | 3819072

Desmond Blue
Paul Desmond With Strings | Planet Jazz:Paul Desmond | Planet Jazz | 2152061-2
Masters Of Jazz Vol.13 | RCA | CL 42790 AG
Silvia Droste And Her Quartet | Audiophile Voicings | BELL Records | BLR 84004

Desolacion
Jan Garbarek Group | Visible World | ECM | 1585(529086-2)

Desolate Mountains(I)
Visible World | ECM | 1585(529086-2)

Desolate Mountains(II)
Visible World | ECM | 1585(529086-2)

Desolate Mountains(III)
Ted Curson Quartet | Tears For Dolphy | Black Lion | BLCD 760190

Desolation Sound
Conexion Latina | Calorcito | Enja | ENJ-4072 2

Despacito
Allen Farnham Quintet | 5th House | Concord | CCD 4413

Despairing Little Trumpet
Lutz Wichert Trio | Ambiguous | Edition Musikat | EDM 068

Despedida Sincopada
Ikue Mori Trio | Painted Desert | Avant | AVAN 030

Desperado
Cousin Joe With Band | Cousin Joe:The Complete 1945-1947 Vol.1 (1945-1946) | Blue Moon | BMCD 6001

Desperate Move
Cassandra Wilson And Her Trio | Live | JMT Edition | 849149-2

Dessacy
Ayibobo | Ayibobo:Freestyle | DIW | DIW 877 CD

Dessert
Chick Corea/Gary Burton | Crystal Silence | ECM | 1024(831331-2)

Dessert Air
Gary Burton-Chick Corea | Works | ECM | 823267-2

Destination
Loft Line | Visitors | Acoustic Music Records | 319.1085.2

Destino-
Alan Braufman Quintet | Valley Of Search | India Navigation | IN 1024

Destiny
Eje Thelin Group | Hypothesis | MRC | 066-45421
Viktoria Tolstoy With The Jacob Karlzon Trio | Blame It On My Youth | Kaza(EMI) | 536620-2

Destruction Into Energy-
Ahmed El-Salamouny/Claudio Menandro | Aquarela | FSM | FCD 97770

Det Kimer Na Til Julefest
Alex Möller-Lena Willemark Group | Hästen Och Tranan | ACT | 9244-2

Det Virkelige Ord(The True Word)
Marc Ducret | Detail | Winter&Winter | 910003-2

Detail - (Detail)
Mario Neunkirchen Quintet | Long Distance | Laika Records | LK 94-060

Detailed Instructions
Detlef Schönenberg | Detlef Sch nenberg spielt Schlagzeug | FMP | SAJ 04

Detour Ahead
Bill Evans Trio | Waltz For Debby | Original Jazz Classics | OJC20 210-2
Live In Paris 1972 Vol.3 | France's Concert | FCD 125

More From The Vanguard | Milestone | M 9125
Bob Brookmeyer Quartet | Oslo | Concord | CCD 4312
Concord Festival All Stars | After You've Gone | Concord | CCD 6006
Gloria Lynne And Her Band | No Detour Ahead | Muse | MCD 5414
Larry Schneider-Andy LaVerne Duo | Bill Evans...Person We Know | Steeplechase | SCCD 31307
Milt Jackson Quintet | Goodbye | CTI | 6038
Steve Davis Sextet | Dig Deep | Criss Cross | Criss 1136
Vince Jones With The Benny Green Quartet | One Day Spent | Intuition Records | INT 3087-8(CD-Single)

Detour Ahead(alt.take)
Bill Evans Trio | Waltz For Debby | Original Jazz Classics | OJC20 210-2
Junior Cook Quartet | Something's Cookin' | Muse | MCD 5470

Deus Xango
Gerry Mulligan/Astor Piazolla Group | Gerry Mulligan/Astor Piazolla 1974 | Accord | 556642

Devastating Cherub
Johnny O'Neal Trio | Coming Out | Concord | CJ 228

Devi(Song Of The Childhood)
Piludu Quattro | Room 626 | Jazz 4 Ever Records:Jazz Network | J4E 4721

Deviation Lozari
Archie Shepp All Stars | Devil Blues-The Essential Archie Shepp | Circle Records | RK 33-7884/33 IMS

Devil Blues
George Adams-Don Pullen Quartet | More Funk | Palcoscenico | PAL 15003

Devil Dance
John Thomas Group | Dreams Illusions Nightmares And Other Realities | Nabel Records:Jazz Network | LP 4611

Devil Head
Eric Reed Orchestra | Happiness | Nagel-Heyer | CD 2010

Devil In A Dress
Mose Allison Trio | Autumn Song | Original Jazz Classics | OJCCD 894-2(P 7189)

Devil In The Moon
Chicago Blues Session | Chicago Blues Session | Southland | SCD 10

Devil May Care
Claire Martin With The Jim Mullen Quartet And Special Guests | Devil May Care | Linn Records | AKD 021
Glenn Miller And His Orchestra | Glenn Miller | Memo Music | HDJ 4116
Kendra Shank With The Larry Willis Trio | Afterglow | Mapleshade | 02132

Devil Whip
Rodach | Himmel Und Hölle-Heaven And Hell | Traumton Records | 4434-2

Devil With The Blue Herrt
Charles Mingus Orchestra | Me Myself An Eye | Atlantic | 50571

Devil Woman
Charles Mingus Quintet With Roland Kirk | Oh Yeah | Atlantic | 90667-1 TIS
Buddy Childers Quintet | Sam Songs | Fresh Sound Records | LJH 6009(Liberty)

Devil's Disciples
Olaf Kübler Quartet | Midnight Soul | Village | VILCD 1024-2
Sonny Sharrock | Sonny Sharrock Guitar | Enemy | EMCD 102(03502)

Devil's Highway-
Bunny Berigan And His Orchestra | Bunny Berigan | Atlantis | ATS 7

Devil's In My Den
Ahmad Jamal Quartet With Stanley Turrentine | Nature(The Essence Part III) | Atlantic | 3984-23105-2
Ahmad Jamal Septet | Live In Paris 1996 | Dreyfus Jazz Line | FDM 37020-2
Jimmy Rowles | Jimmy Rowles/Subtle Legend Vol.1 | Storyville | STCD 8287

Devil's Island
Stacy Rowles With The Jimmy Rowles Quartet | Tell It Like It Is | Concord | CJ 249

Devil's Pulpit
Four Or More Flutes | Influtenza | L+R Records | CDLR 45079

Devine Love
Terence Blanchard Quintet | Romantic Defiance | CBS | 480489-2

Devlus
Fun Horns & Baticun | Live And Latin | KlangRäume | 30110

Devotion
Coleman Hawkins-Freddy Johnson | Thanks For The Memory | EPM Musique | FDC 5159

Dew And Mud
Jimmy Heath Sextet | The Riverside Collection: Jimmy Heath-Nice People | Original Jazz Classics | OJCCD 6006-2

Dew Drops
Eye Of The Hurricane | Eye Of The Hurricane | Aho-Recording | AHO CD 1007(CD 662)

Dewey Square
Don Sickler Orchestra | Tribute To Charlie Parker Vol.2 | Dreyfus Jazz Line | FDM 37015-2
Donald Byrd Quintet | House Of Byrd | Prestige | P 24066
Sphere | Bird Songs | Verve | 837032-2

Dexter Digs In
Eddie Jefferson And His Band | Come Along With Me | Original Jazz Classics | OJCCD 613-2(P 7698)

Dexterity
Charlie Parker Quintet | Jazz Gallery:Charlie Parker Vol.1 | RCA | 2114174-2
Paul Chambers Quartet | High Step | Blue Note | 84482
Sadao Watanabe With The Great Jazz Trio | Bird Of Paradise | Flying Disk | VJJ 6017

Dexter's Deck
David Murray Quartet | Davis Murray Special Quartet | CBS | CK 52955(DIW 843)

Dexter's Minor Mad
Dexter Gordon And His Boys | Nostalgia | Savoy | SV 0123(MG 12133)

Dextiny's Dance
Fats Navarro:The 1946-1949 Small Group Sessions(Studio Recordings-Master Takes),Vol.2 | Blue Moon | BMCD 1017

Dextrose
Dexter Gordon Quintet | Long Tall Dexter | Savoy | 650117(881917)

Dharma Days
Jasper Van't Hof-Charlie Mariano-Steve Swallow | Brutto Tempo | Intuition Records | INT 3309-2

Dhatuvardhani
Johannes Cernota | Sparta | JA & RO | JARO 4136-2

D'Holothuries-
Tina Brooks Quintet | The Waiting Game | Blue Note | 540536-2

Dhyana
Toast Man Quartet Plus Friends | One For Leonardo | SPLASC(H) Records | CD H 379-2

Di Wing
Louis Sclavis Group | Dans La Nuit | ECM | 1805(589524-2)

Dia Dia(1)
Dans La Nuit | ECM | 1805(589524-2)

Dia Dia(2)
Tete Montoliu | Lush Life | Steeplechase | SCS 1216

Diabelli Variatios(Ludwig van Beethoven, Opus 120)
The Kenny Clarke-Francy Boland Big Band | Two Originals:Sax No End/All Blues | MPS | 523525-2

Diablo's Dance
Shorty Rogers And His Giants | Short Stops | RCA | NL 85917(2)

Diabolo
Buddy Rich Big Band | The New One! | Pacific Jazz | 494507-2

Diabolus
The Atlantic Jazz Trio | Some Other Time | Factory Outlet Records | FOR 2002-1 CD
The Atlantic String Trio | First Meeting | Factory Outlet Records | FOR 2501-1 CD

Diabolus(A Fragment)
First Meeting | Factory Outlet Records | 2001-1 CD

Diabolus(alt.take)
Steve Schroyder-Hans Cousto | Klänge Bilder Welten | Musik Vision | CD 051

Dial 'B' For Beauty
Sonny Clark All Stars | Dial S For Sonny | Blue Note | 0675621

Dial S For Sonny
Red Rodney-Ira Sullivan Quintet | Night And Day | Muse | MR 5274

Dialectes
Greg Osby Group | Art Forum | Blue Note | 837319-2

Dialing In
Eero Koivistoinen Quintet | Dialog | L+R Records | CDLR 45094

Dialog
Gabriele Hasler Group | Gabriele Hasler's Rosensrücke | Foolish Music | FM 211096

Dialog On Lamm
Conrad Bauer-Johannes Bauer | Bauer Bauer | Intakt Records | CD 040

Dialogue
Double Drums Project | Double Drums Project | BIT | 11264
Joshua Redman Quartet | MoodSwing | Warner | 9362-45643-2
Lee Konitz With The Bert Van Den Brink Trio | Dialogues | Challenge | CHR 70053
Mike Westbrook Orchestra | Bar Utopia-A Big Band Cabaret | Enja | ENJ-9333 2
Patti Austin And Her Band | Patti Austin Live | GRP | GRP 96822

Dialogue Amour
Peter Finger | Between The Lines | Acoustic Music Records | 319.1079.2

Dialogue No.1
Dieter Köhnlein-Volker Schlott | Sweet Ballad Sweet | Aho-Recording | AHO CD 1032(CD 660)

Dialogue(I)
Gabriele Hasler-Georg Ruby | Spider's Lovesong | Foolish Music | FM 211893

Dialogue(II)
Natty Dominique's Creole Dance Band | Natty Dominique's Creole Dance Band | American Music | AMCD-18

Diamond Cut Diamond
Dudu Pukwana Group | Ubagile | Jazz Colours | 874744-2

Diamonds Are A Girl's Best Friend
Laura Fygi With Band | Laura Fygi Live At The North Sea Jazz | Spectra | 9811207
Pearl Bailey With Orchestra | Pearl Bailey-The Best Of The Roulette Years | Roulette | CDP 796483-2

Diamonds In The Light
Tom Mega + Band | Songs & Prayers | ITM Records | ITM 1491

Diamonds On The Move
Andy Lumpp | Dreamin' Man | Nabel Records:Jazz Network | CD 4662

Diana
Art Pepper Quartet | So In Love | Artists House | AH 9412 IMS
Jimmy Jewell Sextet | From The First Time I Met You | Affinity | AFF 5
Klaus Suonsaari Quartet | True Colours | L+R Records | CDLR 45080
Tomasz Gaworek-Schodrok | Found In The Flurry Of The World | Acoustic Music Records | 319.1073.2

Diana(alt.take)
Dick Wellstood | Live at The Sticky Wicket | Arbors Records | ARCD 19188

Diane
Art Pepper Quartet | Gettin' Together | Original Jazz Classics | OJCCD 169-2
Art Pepper Quintet | Gettin' Together | Contemporary | COP 023
Bill Watrous Quartet | Bill Watrous In London | Mole Jazz | MOLE 7
Miles Davis Quintet | Steamin' | Original Jazz Classics | OJC20 391-2
Mingus Dynasty | Mingus' Sounds Of Love | Soul Note | 121142-2
World's Greatest Jazzband | Bob Haggart & Yank Lawson | Timeless | TTD 533

Diane-
Eddie Condon And His Band | Comodore Condon Vol. 1 | London | DHMC 1/2 DT

Diane's Melody
Jaki Byard Trio | Sunshine Of My Soul | Original Jazz Classics | OJCCD 1946-2(PR 7550)
Ricky Ford Quintet | Manhattan Plaza | Muse | MR 5188

Diarabi
Steve Masakowski Quartet | Just Friends-A Gathering In Tribute To Emily Remler(Vol.2) | Justice Records | JR 0503-2

Diary If The Same Dream
Evan Parker | Process And Reality | FMP | CD 37

Diary Suite(part 1-3)
A Band Of Friends | Teatime Vol.1 | Poise | Poise 01

Diary:25.2.1996
Teatime Vol.1 | Poise | Poise 01

Diary:26.11.1995
Teatime Vol.1 | Poise | Poise 01

Diary:26.12.1995
Teatime Vol.1 | Poise | Poise 01

Diary:28.1.1996
Teatime Vol.1 | Poise | Poise 01

Diary:28.4.1996
Teatime Vol.1 | Poise | Poise 01

Diary:31.3.1996
Adonis Rose Quintet | Song For Donise | Criss Cross | Criss 1146

Dias(Solea)
Ronald Muldrow Quartet | Diaspora | Enja | 8086-2

Diäthylaminoäthyl
Keith Jarrett Quintet | Shades | MCA | 62742 (801433)

Dichotomy
Uri Caine Ensemble | Love Fugue-Robert Schumann | Winter&Winter | 910049-2

Dichterliebe(Robert Schumann op.48):
John Stowell-Bebo Ferra | Elle | Jardis Records | JRCD 20028

Diciembre
Dirk Berger Quartet | Garagenjazz | Jazz Haus Musik | JHM 0090 CD

Dick
Duke Ellington And His Orchestra | Up In Duke's Workshop | Original Jazz Classics | OJCCD 633-2(2310815)

Dick Is Slick
Lost Tribe | Lost Tribe | Windham Hill | 34 10143-2

Dickie's Dream
Jay McShann Orchestra | The Big Apple Bash | Atlantic | 90047-1 TIS

Dicky Wells Blues
Dicky Wells Quartet | Dicky Wells & Bill Coleman In Paris | Affinity | CD AFS 1004

Did I Get You Right
Joe Williams With The Thad Jones-Mel Lewis Orchestra | Joe Williams | LRC Records | CDC 9005874375)

Did I Remember
International Allstars | The Second Sampler | Nagel-Heyer | NHR SP 6
Ken Peplowski Quintet | Illumination | Concord | CCD 4449

Did I Say Anything
Brainstorm feat. Chico Freeman | The Mystical Dreamer | IN+OUT Records | 7006-2

Did I Say Anything,Prelude
Guy Barker Quintet | Into The Blue | Verve | 527656-2

Did They Ever Tell Cousteau?
Ben Webster Quartet | Did You Call | Nessa | N 8

Did You Call Her Today
Harry Allen Quartet | Jazz Im Amerika Haus,Vol.1 | Nagel-Heyer | CD 011
Les Blue Stars | Jazz In Paris:Les Blue Stars-Pardon My English/Henri Salvador-Plays The Blues | EmArCy | 013035-2

Did You Ever
Jimmy Witherspoon With The Ben Webster Quintet | That's Jazz Vol.30: Jimmy Witherspoon & Ben Webster | Warner | WB 56295

Did You Expect That...?
Dogs Don't Sing In The Rain | Wind Moments | Take Twelve On CD | TT 009-2
Abdullah Ibrahim | South African Sunshine | Pläne | CD 88778

Did You Hear That Sound
Gil Scott-Heron Sextet | The Revolution Will Not Be Televised | RCA | ND 86994(874175)

Did You Mean It
Pinguin Moschner | The Flight Of The Humble Beast | Born&Bellmann | 980205 CD

Did You See Harold Vick?
Leonardo Pedersen's Jazzkapel | Harry Sweets Edison-Eddie Lockjaw Davis-Richard Boone | Storyville | SLP 271

Diddleybop
Christian Willisohn Group | Blues On The World | Blues Beacon | BLU-1025 2

Diddlin'
Clark Terry Sextet | Yes The Blues | Pablo | 2312127

Didg.
Hayden Chisholm | Circe | Jazz Haus Musik | JHM 0081 CD

Didg.(2)
Art Pepper Orchestra | The Artistry Of Pepper | Pacific Jazz | 797194-2

Didjeridoo
Christofer Varner | Christofer Varner-Solo | G.N.U. Records | CD A 96.010

Didn't It Rain
Jan Harrington And Friends | I Feel The Spirit | Nagel-Heyer | NHR SP 7
Mahalia Jackson | In Memoriam Mahalia Jackson | CBS | 66501

Didn't Know About You-
Eugene Holmes | Spirituals | Schubert Records | SCH- 102

Didn't Rain
Louis Armstrong With Sy Oliver's Choir And Orchestra | Louis And The Good Book | Verve | 940130-0
Louis And The Good Book | Verve | 549593-2
Mahalia Jackson And Her Trio | Live In Antibes 1968 | France's Concert | FCD 122

Didn't We
Dexter Gordon With The Kenny Drew Trio | Swiss Radio Days Jazz Series:Ben Webster-Dexter Gordon | TCB Records | TCB 02102
Gene Ammons Quartet | Brother Jug! | Prestige | PR20 7792-2
Greetje Kauffeld With The Metropole Orchestra | My Favorite Ballads | Koch Jazz | 3-6902-2

Didn't You
Count Basie And His Orchestra | April In Paris | Verve | 521402-2

Didn't You(alt.take)
Andreas Lonardoni Group | Snooze | Lipstick Records | LIP 8956-2

Die Alte Mär Und Das Mann
Uri Caine Ensemble | Love Fugue-Robert Schumann | Winter&Winter | 910049-2

Die Alten Bösen Lieder
No Nett | Zur Lage Der Nation | Jazz Haus Musik | JHM 10

Die Augenbraue
Kölner Saxophon Mafia With Guests | Kölner Saxophon Mafia: 20 Jahre Saxuelle Befreiung | Jazz Haus Musik | JHM 0115 CD

Die Aura Des Wahns
Landes Jugend Jazz Orchester Hessen | Magic Morning | Mons Records | CD 1905

Die Axt Geschwungen-
Bermuda Viereck | Noblesse Galvanisee | Plainisphare | PL 1267-20/21

Die Diebe Von Bagdad
A Band Of Friends | Teatime Vol.1 | Poise | Poise 01

Die Drei Faulen
Orexis | Orexis | Intercord | 160075

Die Einladung
Kölner Saxophon Mafia | Die Eiserne Nachtigall | Jazz Haus Musik | JHM 28

Die Entdeckung Der Banane
Emil Mangelsdorff Quartet & Sebastian Norden | Allen Ginsberg: Das Geheul | Trion | 5101/2

Die Familie
Peter Koch | Die Farbe Blau | Born&Bellmann | 972306 CD

Die Fee
Das Böse Ding | Cleanhappydirty | Acoustic Music Records | 319.1090.2

Die Flüsse Hinauf
Allotria Jazz Band | All That Jazz | Elite Special | 730217

Die Frage Nach Dem Warum
Freddie Brocksieper And His Boys | Freddie's Boogie Blues | Bear Family Records | BCD 16388 AH

Die Ganze Welt Ist Himmelblau
Pata Horns | New Archaic Music | Pata Musik | PATA 4(JHM 42) CD

Die Himmel Brennen-
Michael Riessler Group | Tentations D'Abélard | Wergo | WER 8009-2

Die Horen Des Astrolabius
Peter Finger Und Gäste | InnenLeben | Acoustic Music Records | AMC 1019

Die Jodlerin Von Teheran
Barre Phillips-Peter Kowald Duo | Die Jungen: Random Generators | FMP | 0680

Die Lerche
Horst Faigle's Jazzkrement | Gans Normal | Jazz 4 Ever Records:Jazz Network | J4E 4748

Die Letzten Helden
Pata Music Meets Arfi | La Belle Et La Bête | Pata Musik | PATA 14(amf 1066)

Die Liebe
Uli Beckerhoff Quintet | Original Motion Picture Soundtrack:Das Geheimnis(Secret Of Love) | Nabel Records:Jazz Network | CD 4666
Norbert Stein Pata Orchester | Die Wilden Pferde Der Armen Leute | Pata Musik | JHM 39

Die Lieder Der Deutschen-
Extempore | Bitternis | Jazz Haus Musik | JHM 01

Die Matriarchin
Kölner Saxophon Mafia With Guests | Kölner Saxophon Mafia: 20 Jahre Saxuelle Befreiung | Jazz Haus Musik | JHM 0115 CD
Wittek/Kaiser/Manderscheid | Jazz...Oder Was? | Jazz Haus Musik | JHM 27

Die Maus Und Die Auster
Kölner Saxophon Mafia | Live | Jazz Haus Musik | JHM 12

Die Moritat Von Mackie Messer
Joachim Kühn Trio | Musik Aus Der Dreigroschenoper | Verve | 532498-2

Die Moritat Von Mackie Messer(I)
Brass Attack | Brecht Songs | Tutu Records | 888190-2*

Die Moritat Von Mackie Messer(II)
Matthias Rosenbauer-Gerhard Gschlößl | Duo 1 | Jazz 4 Ever Records:Jazz Network | J4E 4763

Die Mücke
Norbert Stein Pata Orchester | Ritual Life | Pata Musik | PATA 5(JHM 50) CD

Die Mühle
Roland Gyarmati Trio | Querelle Soundtrack | Jazzpoint | 1012 Maxi Single

Die Nacht Ist Gekommen,Drin Wir Ruhen Sollen
Karl Scharnweber Trio | Choral Concert | Nabel Records:Jazz Network | CD 4642

Die Nacht Ist Kommen
Alfred Lauer Bigband | Just Music | Mons Records | MR 874819

Die Nacht Ist Vorgedrungen
Bobo Stenson Trio | Serenity | ECM | 1740/41(543611-2)

Die Nachtigall
Vladimir Estragon | Three Quarks For Muster Mark | TipToe | TIP-888803 2

Die Namen
Helmut 'Joe' Sachse | Solo | FMP | 1070

Die Phasen Der Nacht
Vienna Art Orchestra | Serapionsmuisc | Moers Music | 02050

Die Rose,Die Lilie,Die Taube
Elefanten | Faust | KlangRäume | 30150

Die Schöne
Franz Koglmann Pipetet | Orte Der Geometrie | Hat Art | CD 6018

Die Seeräuber Jenny

Joachim Kühn Trio | Musik Aus Der Dreigroschenoper | Verve | 532498-2

Die Stadt:
Urs Blöchlinger | (Aesth)eti(c)k Als Widerstand | Plainisphare | PL 1267-3/4

Die Sweet Dé Snove(-18,-19)
Ralph R.Hübner-Christoph Lauer | Moabiter Blues | L+R Records | CDLR 45040

Die Trommel Und Ihr Rhythmus
Viktoria Tabatchnikowa-Eugenij Belov | Troika | ALISO Records | AL 1036

Die Uhr-
Pata Music Meets Arfi | News Of Roi Ubu | Pata Musik | PATA 10 CD

Die Ultravioletten Dinge,Die Uns Verboten Waren
Amman Boutz | Some Other Tapes | Fish Music | FM 009/10 CD

Die Ungelösten Fragen Der Sippe Valdez
Peter Bolte-Marcio Doctor | Zeitraum | Jazz Haus Musik | JHM 0113 CD

Die Unzertrennlichen
Hans Lüdemann Rism | Unitarism | Jazz Haus Musik | JHM 0067 CD

Die Vereinigung-The Unification
Cassiber | Man Or Monkey | Riskant | 6.28624

Die Viool Komt Wel Terug
Heiner Goebbels/Alfred Harth | Berold Brecht:Zeit wird knapp | Riskant | 568-72414

Die Weisheit Von Le Comte Lautréamont
Norbert Stein Pata Orchester | Die Wilden Pferde Der Armen Leute | Pata Musik | JHM 39

Die Welt Ist Immer Wieder Schön(Hörspiel-Collage)
Brodmann-Pausch Percussion Duo | Are You Serious? | Jazz 4 Ever Records:Jazz Network | J4E 4718

Die Wende
Modern String Quartet | Elephants & Strings | Upsolute Music Records | UMR 102 ST

Die Zuhälter Ballade
Brass Attack | Brecht Songs | Tutu Records | 888190-2*
Rias Big Band Berlin + Strings | Weill | Mons Records | MR 874347

Diebstahl Im Basar
Don Byron Quartet | Tuskegee Experiments | Nonesuch | 7559-79280-2

Diego Rivera
Branford Marsalis Quartet | Royal Garden Blues | CBS | 468704-2

Dienstag
Willem Breuker Kollektief | Sensemayá | BVHAAST | CD 9509

Dies De Nens I Nenes
Eduardo M.Kohan Trio | Dies Irae | Hat Art | 3507

Different Rivers
John Stevens Orchestra | A Luta Continua | Konnex Records | KCD 5056

Differentes Planetes
Sheila Jordan-Mark Murphy Group | One For Junior | Muse | MCD 5489

Diffusion 8
Prestige All Stars | Three Trumpets | Original Jazz Classics | OJCCD 1801-2(P 7092)

Dig
Lew Tabackin Quartet | What A Little Moonlight Can Do | Concord | CCD 4617
Miles Davis Sextet | Dig | Prestige | P 24054

Dig A Pony-
Jack McDuff Quartet With Orchestra | Prelude:Jack McDuff Big Band | Prestige | PRCD 24283-2

Dig Cousin Will
Steve Davis Sextet | Dig Deep | Criss Cross | Criss 1136

Dig Dis
Tommy Dorsey And His Orchestra | Tommy Dorsey And His Orchestra With Frank Sinatra | RCA | 2115518-2

Dig It
Jimmy McGriff Orchestra | Swingin' The Blues-Jumpin' The Blues | Laserlight | 24654

Dig On It
Jimmy McGriff-Funkiest Little Band In The Kand | LRC Records | CDC 9046(874379)

Dig This
Manfredo Fest Quintet | Jungle Cat | dmp Digital Music Productions | CD 470

Diga Diga Do
Dick Charlesworth And His City Gents | The Golden Years Of Revival Jazz,Vol.4 | Storyville | STCD 5509
Duke Ellington And His Orchestra | Hot From The Cotton Club | EMI Records | EG 2605671
Elmer Snowden Quartet | Harlem Banjo | Original Jazz Classics | OJCCD 1756-2

Digature Of The Line
Tambastics | Tambastics | Music & Arts | CD 704

Diggin' Bones
Charlie Parker All Stars | Charlie Parker Anthology | Accord | 500122

Diggin' My Potatoes
Big Bill Broonzy | An Evening With Big Bill Broonzy,Vol.2 | Storyville | STCD 8017
Lonnie Donegan Skiffle Group | Barber 's Best | Decca | 6.28128 DP

Digital Wildlife
Kodexx Sentimental | Das Digitale Herz | Poise | Poise 02

Digitales Herz(1)
Das Digitale Herz | Poise | Poise 02

Digitales Herz(2)
Ray Pizzi Group | Conception | Pablo | 2310795

Dilemma
Bola Sete Quintet | Bossa Nova | Original Jazz Classics | OJC 286(F 8349)

Dillu
The Latin Jazz Quintet | Hot Sauce | Prestige | PCD 24128-2

Dim Light Raga
J.B.& His Hawks | Combination Blues | Charly | CRB 1042

Dim The Light
Mongo Santamaria And His Band | Sabroso | Original Jazz Classics | OJCCD 281-2

Dimelo
Jasper Van't Hof | Un Mondo Illusorio | Challenge | CHR 70059

Diminishing
Bireli Lagrene Group | Down In Town | Island | 205863-320

Diminuendo And Crescendo In Blue
Duke Ellington And His Orchestra | All Star Road Band Vol.2 | Doctor Jazz | ZL 70969(2) (809319)
The Legendary Duke Ellington | Ember | CJS 852
Duke Ellington At The Alhambra | Pablo | PACD 5313-2
Duke Ellington | Laserlight | 15753

Diminuendo And Crescendo In Blue-
Duke Ellington:Complete Prestige Carnegie Hall 1946-1947 Concerts | Definitive Records | DRCD 11211

Diminuendo In Blue
Verve Jazz Masters 20:Introducing | Verve | 519853-2

Diminuendo In Blue-
Verve Jazz Masters 4:Duke Ellington | Verve | 516338-2
Duke Ellington And His Famous Orchestra | The Complete Duke Ellington-Vol. 9 | CBS | CBS 88210

Dimma
First House | Cantilena | ECM | 1393

Dimple
George Gruntz Concert Jazz Band | 25 Years George Gruntz Concert Jazz Band:The World's Greatest Unknown Hits | TCB Records | TCB 96602

Din Di(Jin Je)
Okay Temiz Group | Magnet Dance | TipToe | TIP-888819 2

Dina
Stefano Di Battista Quintet | A Prima Vista | Blue Note | 497945-2

DinA3
Benny Goodman And His Orchestra | Benny Goodman's 1934 Dodge All-Star Recordings(Complete) | Circle | CCD-111

Dinah
Benny Goodman Quartet | Benny Goodman:The Complete Small Combinations Vol.1/2(1935-1937) | RCA | ND 89753
Count Basie And His Orchestra | The Uncollected:Count Basie | Hindsight | HSR 224 (835571)
Prez's Hat Vol.3 | Philology | 214 W 8
Dicky Wells Septet | Dicky Wells & Bill Coleman In Paris | Affinity | CD AFS 1004
Doc Cheatham-Nicholas Payton Group | Doc Cheatham & Nicholas Payton | Verve | 537062-2
Fats Waller And His Rhythm | I'm Gonna Sit Right Down...The Early Years-Part 2(1935-1936) | Bluebird | 63 66640-2
George Lewis And His New Orleans Jazzband | Sounds Of New Orleans Vol.7 | Storyville | STCD 6014
Herbie Harper Quintet | The Complete Nocturne Recordings:Jazz In Hollywood Series Vol.1 | Fresh Sound Records | NR 3CD-101
The Complete Nocturne Recordings:Jazz In Hollywood Series Vol.1 | Fresh Sound Records | NR 3CD-101
Jazz In Hollywood:Herbie Harper | Original Jazz Classics | OJCCD 1887-2(Nocturne NLP-1/NLP-7)
Jimmy Raney Sextet | Jimmy Raney Visits Paris | Fresh Sound Records | FSR 561(Dawn DLP 1120)
Lionel Hampton And His Orchestra | Planet Jazz:Lionel Hampton | Planet Jazz | 2152059-2
Three Great Swing Saxophones | RCA | NL 90405
Lionel Hampton Quintet | The Complete Lionel Hampton Quartets And Quintets With Oscar Peterson On Verve | Verve | 559797-2
Louis Armstrong And His Orchestra | Armstrong Forever-Vol. 1 | CBS | CBS 52027
Paris Washboard | Waiting For The Sunrise | Stomp Off Records | CD 1261
The Mills Brothers | The Mills Brothers Story | Storyville | 4960233
The Mills Brothers With Orchestra | Four Boys And A Guitar | CBS | CK 57713
Thelonious Monk | Solo Monk | CBS | 471248-2

Dinah-
Louis Armstrong And His Orchestra | Laughin' Louie | RCA | ND 90404
Louis Armstrong-Satchmo's Greatest Hits | RCA | CL 89799

Dinah(alt.take)
Louis Armstrong-The Complete RCA Victor Recordings | RCA | 2668682-2

Dindi
Astrud Gilberto With Antonio Carlos Jobim And The Marty Paich Orchestra | The Astrud Gilberto Album | Verve | 823009-1
Astrud Gilberto With The Marty Paich Orchestra | Silver Collection: The Astrud Gilberto Album | Verve | 823451-2 PMS
Boel-Emborg-Vinding-Riel | Shadow Of Love | Stunt Records | 18803
Flora Purim And Her Sextet | Butterfly Dreams | Original Jazz Classics | OJCCD 315-2
Folklore E Bossa Nova Do Brasil | Jazz Meets Brasil | MPS | 533133-2
Jackie And Roy | Star Sounds | Concord | CJ 115
Peter Fessler Group | Eastside Moments | Minor Music | 801078
Sarah Vaughan And Her Band | Sarah Vaughan Birthday Celebration | Fantasy | FANCD 6090-2
Sarah Vaughan With Band | Copacabana | Pablo | 2312125
Singers Unlimited With Rob McConnell And The Boss Brass | The Singers Unlimited With Rob McConnell And The Boss Brass | MPS | 817486-1
Terrie Richard With The Harry Allen Quartet | I Cried For You | Master Mix | CHECD 00107
Zoot Sims-Joe Pass Duo | Blues For Two | Original Jazz Classics | 2310879 Digital

Diner Au Motel
Bob Smith Band | Radio Face | dmp Digital Music Productions | CD 483

Dinette
Django Reinhardt And The Quintet Du Hot Club De France | Planet Jazz:Django Reinhardt | Planet Jazz | 2152071-2
Django Reinhardt Quintet | Django/Django In Rome 1949-1050 | BGO Records | BGOCD 366
Quintet Du Hot Club De France | Django Reinhardt:Djangology | EMI Records | 780659-2

Ding Dong Baby
Benny Moten's Kansas City Orchestra | The Complete Bennie Moten Vol.1/2 | RCA | NL 89881(2) DP

Ding Dong Daddy-
Mick Mulligan's Magnolia Jazz Band With George Melly | Best Of British Jazz From The BBC Jazz Club Vol.4 | Upbeat Jazz | URCD 122

Ding Dong! The Witch Is Dead
Ella Fitzgerald With The Billy May Orchestra | The Harold Arlen Songbook | Verve | 817526-1 IMS

Ding-A-Ling-A-Ling
Vienna Art Orchestra | Serapionsmuisc | Moers Music | 02050

Dingo
Craig Harris Sextet | Aboriginal Affairs | India Navigation | IN 1060

Dingy-Dong Day
Carla Bley Band | Dinner Music | Watt | 6(825815-2)

Dining Alone
Lincoln Center Jazz Orchestra | Big Train | CBS | CK 69860

Dining Car
Barney Wilen Quintet | Barney Wilen Quintet | Fresh Sound Records | FSR-CD 0048

Dink's Blues
Jack McDuff Quartet | Honeydripper | Original Jazz Classics | OJC 222(P 7199)

Dink's Dream
Walter Bishop Jr. Group | Summertime | Fresh Sound Records | FSR-CD 0011

Dinner
Lew Stone And His Orchestra | The Bands The Matter | Eclipse | ECM 2047

Dinner For One Please James
Eddy Howard And His Orchestra | The Uncollected: Eddy Howard | Hindsight | HSR 119

Dinner For One Please James(alt.take)
Jasper Van't Hof | Solo Piano | Timeless | CD SJP 286

Dinner With Friends
Jazz Don't Panic | Jazz Don't Panic | G.N.U. Records | CD A 95.013(Maxi-Single)

Dinosaur
Karl Denson Group | Herbal Turkey Breast | Minor Music | 801032

Dinosaurs' Dispute
Tchangodei Trio | Jeux D'Ombres | Volcanic Records | 30030

Diogenes-
Danny Richmond Quintet | Dionysius | Red Records | VPA 161

Dippermouth Blues
Dutch Swing College Band | Albert Nicholas & The Dutch Swing College Band | Storyville | STCD 5522
Ed Hall And The All Star Stompers | This Is Jazz Vol.3 | Storyville | SLP 4069
Glenn Miller And His Orchestra | Meadowbrook Ballroom Vol.2 | Magic | DAWE 81
King Oliver's Creole Jazz Band | Jazz:The Essential Collection Vol.1 | IN+OUT Records | 78011-2
Louis Armstrong With King Oliver Vol.1 | Village(Jazz Archive) | VILCD 003-2
Louis Armstrong With Jimmy Dorsey And His Orchestra | Big Band Bounce & Boogie-Louis Armstrong:Struttin' With Some Barbecue | Affinity | AFS 1024
Louis Armstrong With The Dukes Of Dixieland | Sweetheart-Definite Alternatives | Chiaroscuro | CR 2006
Muggsy Spanier And His Dixieland All Stars | At Club Hangover-Vol. 2 | Storyville | SLP 249
Wild Bill Davison All Stars | The Idividualism Of Wild Bill Davison | Savoy | SJL 2229 (801205)
Kid Thomas And His Algiers Stompers | Sonnets From Algiers' | American Music | AMCD-53

Direct Input
Wolf Mayer Dialects | Roots And Wings | Triptychon | 300201

Directed-Undirected
Horace Silver Ensemble | Silver 'N Strings Play The Music Of The Spheres | Blue Note | LWB 1033

Direction Discovered-
Copenhagen Art Ensemble | Shape To Twelve | dacapo | DCCD 9430

Direction Switch
Bob Belden Ensemble | Treasure Island | Sunnyside | SSC 1041 D

Directions
Miles Davis Group | Live At The Fillmore East | CBS | C2K 65139
Miles Davis Quintet | Paraphernalia | JMY(Jazz Music Yesterdays) | JMY 1013-2

Directions-
Weather Report | Weathe Report Live In Tokyo | CBS | 489208-2
Fenton Robinson Blues Group | Somebody Loan Me A Dime | Sonet | 4705

Direvision
Diego Carraresi Trio | Attrezzo | SPLASC(H) Records | H 140

Dirge
Duke Ellington And His Orchestra | Duke Elliongton:Complete Prestige Carnegie Hall 1943-1944 Concerts | Definitive Records | DRCD 11210

Dirge For Dorsey
James Newton Quintet | The Mystery School | India Navigation | IN 1046

Dirt
The Mills Brothers | Four Boys And A Guitar | CBS | CK 57713

Dirt Road Blues
Urs Leimgruber/John Wolf Brennan | Mountain Hymn | L+R Records | CDLR 45002

Dirty Dog Blues
Billy Hart Band | Amethyst | Arabesque Recordings | AJ 0105

Dirty Money Blues
Roland Kirk Quartet | Rahsaan/The Complete Mercury Recordings Of Roland Kirk | Mercury | 846630-2

Dirty Money Blues(alt.take)
Roosevelt Sykes | Roosevelt Sykes(1929-1941) | Story Of Blues | CD 3542-2

Dirty Old Man
Toots Thielemans Sextet | Toots Thielemans Live | Polydor | 2491003 IMS

Dirty Sanchez
Dick Heckstall-Smith & John Etheridge Group | Obsession Fees | R&M Digital Music | 2-8002

Dirty Showtunes
Louis Jordan And His Tympany Five | Louis Jordan-Let The Good Times Roll: The Complete Decca Recordings 1938-1954 | Bear Family Records | BCD 15557 IH

Dirty Snake
Victoria Spivey | Better Boot That Thing-Great Women Blues Singers Of The 1920's | Bluebird | 63 66065 2

Dis
Gebbia/Kowald/Sommer | Cappuccini Klang | SPLASC(H) Records | CD H 383-2

Dis' Place This
Willie Bobo Group | Juicy | Verve | 519857-2

Dis-Advantages
Juicy | Verve | 519857-2

Dis-Advantages(alt.take)
David Bowne Trio | One Way Elevator | DIW | DIW 920 CD

Disappear Here
Chico O'Farrill's Orchestra | Afro Cuban Jazz | Verve | 833561-1

Disappearing Act
Eddie Jefferson With The James Moody Septet | There I Go Again | Prestige | P 24095

Disc Jockey Jump
Gerry Mulligan And The Sax Section | The Gerry Mulligan Songbook | Pacific Jazz | 833575-2
The All Star Sextet | Bebop In Britain | Esquire | CD ESQ 100-4

Disc Jockey Jump(alt.take)
Chicago Blues Session | Chicago Blues Session | Southland | SCD 10

Disciples Blues
Chuck Loeb Groups | Mediterranean | dmp Digital Music Productions | CD 494

Discipline
Sun Ra And His Intergalactic Solar Arkestra | Space Is The Place(Soundtrack) | Evidence | ECD 22070-2

Discipline Seres
Memphis Slim Duo | Memphis Slim Story | Arco | 3 ARC 108

Disco Monk
John Handy Group | Handy Dandy Man | Inak | 8618

Discovering Metal
Chick Corea Quartet | Time Warp | Stretch Records | GRS 00152

Discovery-
Leroy Jenkins Quartet | Space Minds,New Worlds,Survival America | Tomato | 2696512

Discussing Repertoire
Max Greger And His Orchestra | European Jazz Sounds | Polydor | 829257-1 IMS

Disguise The Limit
Sun Ra Arkestra | Sunrise In Different Dimensions | HatOLOGY | 568

Dishes
Jimmy McGriff Sextet | McGriff's House Party | Milestone | MCD 9300-2

Dishin' The Dirt
Dizzy Atmosphere | Dizzy Atmosphere | Original Jazz Classics | OJCCD 1762-2

Disillusion Blues
Oliver Nelson And His Orchestra | Black Brown And Beautiful | RCA | ND 86993

Dislocated In Natran
Sabina Sciubba-Paulo Cardoso | VoceBasso | Organic Music | ORGM 9703

Dismal
Pat Metheny Group | Quartet | Geffen Records | GED 24978

Dismantling Utopia
Le Petit Chien | Woof | Enja | 9122-2

Displacement
Eddie Palmieri Group | Vortex | RMM Records | 660.58.116

Dissertation On The Blues
Herb Robertson Quintet | 'X'-cerpts:Live At Willisau | JMT Edition | 919013-2

Dissipation
Gunter Hampel Group | Music From Europe | ESP Disk | ESP 1042-2

Dissonance No.1
Joe Pass | Virtuoso No.3 | Original Jazz Classics | OJC20 684-2(2310805)

Dissonance No.2
Ellery Eskelin + Han Bennink | Dissonant Characters | HatOLOGY | 534

Distances
Elisabet Raspall Quintet | Triangles | Fresh Sound Records | FSNT 018 CD

Distàncies
Chico Hamilton Quartet | Euphoria | Master Mix | CHECD 7

Distant Cousins
Reiner Witzel Group | Passage To The Ear | Nabel Records:Jazz Network | CD 4668

Distant Desire
Steve LaSpina Quintet | Distant Dream | Steeplechase | SCCD 31448

District Six
Abdullah Ibrahim Trio | Cape Town Revisited | TipToe | TIP-888836 2
African Magic | TipToe | TIP-888845 2
Johannes Cernota | Sparta | JA & RO | JARO 4136-2

Di-Ta-Tedo
Luke Jones & His Five Joes | Luke Jones:The Complete Recordings 1946-1949 | Blue Moon | BMCD 6012

Dites-Moi
Les Brown And His Orchestra | South Pacific | Capitol | ED 2604131

Ditscheriduddel

Seamus Blake Quintet/Sextet | Four Track Mind | Criss Cross | Criss 1126

Diuturnal
Enrico Rava Quartet | Opening Night | ECM | 1224

Diva
Tiziana Simona With The Kenny Wheeler Quartet | Gigolo | ITM Records | 0014

Divans
Conrad Herwig Quintet | With Every Breath | Ken Music | 660.56.008

Diverse Tune X(alternate)
Charlie Parker Quintet | Bird On Verve-Vol.1:Charlie Parker With Strings | Verve | 817442-1 IMS

Diverse(Segment)
Anouar Brahem Quartet | Conte De L'Incroyable Amour | ECM | 1457(511959-2)

Diversion
Brad Dutz | Brad Dutz | Nine Winds Records | NWCD.0141

Diversions
Lluis Vidal | Lluis Vidal Piano Solo | Fresh Sound Records | FSNT 001 CD

Divertiment
Ahmad Jamal Trio with Orchestra | Pittsburgh | Atlantic | 7567-8209-2

Divertimento
Astor Piazzolla Group | Onda Nueve | West Wind Latina | 2213 CD
Eddie Daniels Quartet With The London Philharmonia Orchestra | Breakthrough | GRP | GRP 95332
Shelly Manne And His Men | Shelly Manne Vol.2 | Original Jazz Classics | OJCCD 1910-2(C 2511)

Divertimento Per Cinque
Ekkehard Jost & Chromatic Alarm | Von Zeit Zu Zeit | Fish Music | FM 005 CD
Red Norvo Sextet | Music To Listen To Red Norvo By | Original Jazz Classics | OJCCD 1015-2(C 7534)

Divertimento(in 4 movements)
Peter Herbert Group | B-A-C-H A Chromatic Universe | Between The Lines | btl 013(Efa 10183)

Divi Blasli
Jimmy Giuffre Three | Free Fall | CBS | CK 65446

Divided Man
Louis Sclavis Group | Napoli's Walls | ECM | 1857(038504-2)

Divinazione Moderna I
Napoli's Walls | ECM | 1857(038504-2)

Divinazione Moderna II
Walt Dickerson/Richard Davis | Divine Gemini | Steeplechase | SCS 1089

Divinidad
Don Cherry Group | Multi Kulti | A&M Records | 395323-2

Divinity-Tree
Woody Shaw Trio | The Iron Man | Muse | MR 5160

Diwen
Bud Freeman Trio | The Joy Of Sax | Chiaroscuro | CR 135

Dixieland
Art Tatum | Art Tatum-The Standard Transcriptions | Music & Arts | CD 919

Dixieland Band
Masters Of Jazz Vol.8:Art Tatum | Storyville | SLP 4108

Dixieland Jass Band One Step
Original Dixieland 'Jass' Band | Victor Jazz History Vol.1:New Orleans & Dixieland | RCA | 2128555-2

Dixieland Shuffle
Boulou Ferre-Elios Ferre Duo | Gypsy Dreams | Steeplechase | SCCD 31140

Dixie's Dilemma
Warne Marsh Quintet | Intuition | Capitol | 852771-2

Dixital
Miki N'Doye Orchestra | Joko | ACT | 9403-2

Dizzier and Dizzier
Dizzy Gillespie And His Orchestra | The Greatest Of Dizzy Gillespie | RCA | 2113164-2

Dizzy Atmosphere
Dizzy Gillespie Quintet | Something Old Something New | Verve | 558079-2
Dizzy Gillespie Sextet | In The Beginning | Prestige | P 24030

Dizzy Gillespie Fireworks
Anthony Parenti And His Famous Melody Boys | Victor Jazz History Vol.1:New Orleans & Dixieland | RCA | 2128555-2

Dizzy Meets Sonny
Charles Mingus Group | Victor Jazz History Vol.14:Hard Bop | RCA | 2135733-2

Dizzy Moods
Charles Mingus Orchestra | New Tijuana Moods | Bluebird | ND 85644
Mingus Big Band | Que Viva Mingus! | Dreyfus Jazz Line | FDM 36593-2
Charles Mingus Orchestra | New Tijuana Moods | Bluebird | ND 85644

Dizzy Moods(short-take-1)
Tijuana Moods(The Complete Edition) | RCA | 2663840-2

Dizzy Moods(short-take-2)
Dizzy Gillespie And The United Nation Orchestra | Live At The Royal Festival Hall | Enja | ENJ-6044 2

Dizzy Spells
Benny Goodman Quartet | Benny Goodman:The Complete Small Combinations Vol.3/4 | RCA | ND 89754
Teddy Wilson Sextet | Teddy Wilson presented by Lionel Hampton | Jazz Classics | AU 36007 CD

Dizzy's Blues
Dizzy Gillespie Band | Dizzy Gillespie At Newport | Verve | 513754-2 PMS

Dizzy's Business
Cannonball Adderley Sextet | Cannonball Adderley In New York | Original Jazz Classics | OJC20 142-2(RLP 9404)
Court-Candiotto Quintet | Live In Montreux | Plainisphare | PAV 811
Dave Brubeck Quartet | Blue Rondo | Concord | CCD 4317

DJ Apollo Interlude
| All At Once At Any Time | Victo | CD 029

Djambo
Pili-Pili | Jakko | JA & RO | JARO 4131-2

Djamo Djamo
Tony Scott & The Indonesian All Stars | Jazz Meets Asia:Sakura Sakura-Jazz Meets India-Djanger Bali | MPS | 533132-2

Django
Bill Evans-Eddie Gomez Duo | The Complete Fantasy Recordings | Fantasy | 9FCD 1012-2
Bill Evans:Piano Player | CBS | CK 65361
Bob Wilber Quintet | A Man And His Music | J&M Records | J&MCD 503
Chet Baker With The NDR-Bigband | My Favourite Songs: The Last Great Concert Vol.1 | Enja | ENJ-5097 2
Chet Baker-The Legacy Vol.1 | Enja | ENJ-9021 2
The Last Concert Vol.I+II | Enja | ENJ-6074 22
NDR Big Band-Bravissimo | ACT | 9232-2
Christian Escoude Octet | Gipsy Waltz | EmArCy | 838772-2
Fraser MacPherson Trio | Live At The Planetarium | Concord | CJ 92
Gil Evans Orchestra | Pacific Standart Time | Blue Note | 84494
Herbie Mann And His Orchestra | Super Mann | Atlantic | ATL 50569
Joe Pass Quartet | For Django | Pacific Jazz | 300007(PJ 85)
John Eaton | It Seems Like Old Times | Chiaroscuro | CR 174
John Lewis | Afternoon In Paris | Dreyfus Jazz Line | FDM 36507-2
John Lewis Sextet | John Lewis:Kansas City Breaks | Red Baron | JK 57759
Jukka Tolonen Group | Impressions | Sonet | 147126
Modern Jazz Quartet | The Complete Modern Jazz Quartet Prestige & Pablo Recordings | Prestige | 4PRCD 4438-2
The Complete Modern Jazz Quartet Prestige & Pablo Recordings | Prestige | 4PRCD 4438-2
Milt Jackson Birthday Celebration | Fantasy | FANCD 6079-2
The Complete Modern Jazz Quartet Prestige & Pablo Recordings | Prestige | 4PRCD 4438-2
MJQ 40 | Atlantic | 7567-82330-2
Atlantic Jazz: Mainstream | Atlantic | 7567-81704-2
European Concert | Atlantic | SD 2-603
Modern Jazz Quartet And The All-Star Jazz Band | Jazz Dialogue | Philips | PHCE 3018 PMS
Oscar Peterson Trio | Compact Jazz:Oscar Peterson | Mercury | 830698-2
Ray Bryant | Through The Years-The 60th Birthday Special Recordings Vol.1 | EmArCy | 512764-2 PMS
Montreux '77 | Original Jazz Classics | OJC 371(2308201)
Robert Norman In Different Groups | The Best Of Robert Norman(1941-1989) | Hot Club Records | HCRCD 085
Roland Kirk Quintet | Rahsaan/The Complete Mercury Recordings Of Roland Kirk | Mercury | 846630-2
Ron Carter-Cedar Walton Duo | Heart & Soul | Timeless | CD SJP 158
Stephane Grappelli Quintet | Grapelli Story | Verve | 515807-2
Feeling + Finesse = Jazz | Atlantic | 7567-90140-2
Stochelo Rosenberg Group | Gypsy Swing | Verve | 527806-2
Svend Asmussen-Kenny Drew Quartet | Prize/Winners | Matrix | MTX 1001 IMS
Tete Montoliu Trio | The Man From Barcelona | Timeless | CD SJP 368
The Rosenberg Trio With Frits Landesbergen | The Rosenberg Trio:The Collection | Verve | 537152-2
The Super Guitar Fusion | Aranjuez | RCA | PL 40866 AS
Vince Guaraldi Trio | Vince Guaraldi Trio | Original Jazz Classics | OJC20 149-2(F 3225)
Vladimir Shafranov Trio | White Nights | The Jazz Alliance | TJA 10018
Larry Coryell | Privat Concert | Acoustic Music Records | 319.1159.2

Django(alt.take)
Bireli Lagrene Ensemble | Bireli Swing '81 | Jazzpoint | JP 1009 CD

Djangology
Routes To Django & Bireli Swing '81 | Jazzpoint | JP 1055 CD
Bireli Lagrene Group | A Tribute To Django Reinhardt | Jazzpoint | JP 1061 CD
Bireli Lagrene Trio | Live At The Carnegie Hall: A Tribute To Django Reinhardt | Jazzpoint | JP 1040 CD
Christian Escoude Quartet | Plays Django Reinhardt | EmArCy | 510132-2
Henri Crolla Orchestra | Jazz In Paris:Henri Crolla-Notre Ami Django | EmArCy | 014062-2
Quintet Du Hot Club De France | Djangology | Bluebird | 2663957-2
Django Reinhardt-Un Géant Sur Son Image | Melodie | 400052
Stephane Grappelli Quintet | Hommage A Django Reinhardt | Festival | Album 120

Django's Blues
Django Reinhardt And The Quintet Du Hot Club De France | Django Reinhardt Portrait | Barclay | DALP 2/1939
The Indispensable Django Reinhardt | RCA | ND 70929

Django's Castle(Manoir De Mes Reves)
Joe Pass Quartet | For Django | Pacific Jazz | 300007(PJ 85)

Django's Tiger
Renaud Garcia-Fons Group | Oriental Bass | Enja | ENJ-9334 2

Djani
Norbert Stein Pata Masters | Pata Maroc | Pata Musik | PATA 12(AMF 1063)

Djema Voices
George Gruntz Jazz Group feat. Jean-Luc Ponty & The Bedouins | Jazz Meets Africa:Noon In Tunisia-El Babaku | MPS | 531720-2

Djinji's Corner
Joe Pisano And Friends | Joe Pisano:Among Friends | Pablo | 2310956-2

D-Joe
Joe Pass Quartet | Summer Night | Pablo | 2310939-2

Dlidi Clidi
Jackie And Roy | East Of Suez | Concord | CJ 149

DNA
Wes Montgomery Quartet | The Incredible Guitar Of Wes Montgomery | Original Jazz Classics | OJC20 036-2

D-Natural Blues
Montgomery Brothers | Groove Brothers | Milestone | M 47051

Do
Noodband | Shiver | Moers Music | 01094

Do I Crazy?
Alphonse Mouzon Group | By All Means | MPS | 817485-1

Do I Love You
Ella Fitzgerald With The Buddy Bregman Orchestra | The Complete Ella Fitzgerald Song Books of Harold Arlen, Irving Berlin, Duke Ellington, George & Ira Gershwin, Jerome Kern, Johnny Mercer, Cole Porter And Rogers & Hart | Verve | 519832-2
Peggy Lee With George Shearing | Beauty And The Beat | Capitol | 542308-2
Peggy Lee With The David Barbour And Billy May Bands | The Uncollected:Peggy Lee | Hindsight | HSR 220
Scott Hamilton Quartet | Apples And Oranges | Concord | CJ 165

Do I Love You Because You're Beautiful
John Coltrane Quintet | Black Pearls | Prestige | P 24037
John Coltrane-The Prestige Recordings | Prestige | 16 PCD 4405-2
Mel Tormé With Orchestra | That's All Mel Tormé | CBS | CK 65165

Do I Move You?
Ernie Andrews With Orchestra | From The Heart | Discovery | DS 825 IMS

Do It Again
Dick Hyman | The Gershwin Songbook:Jazz Variations | Musicmasters | 65094-2
Ruby Braff Trio | Cornet Chop Suey | Concord | CCD 4606
Shirley Horn Trio | I Loe You, Paris | Verve | 523486-2
Dirty Dozen Brass Band | Live:Mardi Gras In Montreux | Rounder Records | CDRR 2052

Do It The Hard Way
Georgie Fame With The Ellen Helmus Sextet | A Portrait Of Chet | Four Leaf Clover | FLC 108 CD

Do Like Eddie
Christian Griese Group | Affinities:My Berlin Phone Book | BIT | 11216

Do Me A Favour
Fats Waller And His Rhythm | Breakin' The Ice-The Early Years Part 1(1934-1935) | Bluebird | 63 66618-2

Do Not Disturb
Jack Dieval And The J.A.C.E. All-Stars | Jazz In Paris:Jack Diéval-Jazz Aux Champs Elysées | EmArCy | 018419-2
Sal Nistico With Joe Haider Trio | Just For Fun | EGO | 4002

Do Nothin' Till You Hear From Me
Anders Lindskog Trio | Fine Together | Touché Music | TMcCD 010
Anita O'Day With The Gary McFarland Orchestra | All The Sad Youn Men | Verve | 517065-2
Art Tatum | Art Tatum-The Complete Pablo Solo Masterpieces | Pablo | 7 PACD 4404-2
The Tatum Solo Masterpieces Vol.6 | Pablo | 2310791
Ben Webster With Orchestra And Strings | Music For Loving:Ben Webster With Strings | Verve | 527774-2
Bill Mays/Ed Bickert | Concord Duo Series Volume Seven:Bill Mays-Ed Bickert | Concord | CCD 4626
Billie Holiday And Her All Stars | Stay With Me | Verve | 511523-2
Diana Krall Trio | Stepping Out | Enja | ENJ-8042 2
Duke Ellington And His Orchestra | Jazz Special-The Popular Duke Ellington | RCA | NL 89095 AG
Carnegie Hall 1943 | Jazz Anthology | JA 5117
Duke Ellington -Carnegie Hall Concert | Ember | 800851-370(EMBD 2001)
Ella Fitzgerald And Her All Stars | The Best Of The Song Books:The Ballads | Verve | 521867-2
The Complete Ella Fitzgerald Song Books of Harold Arlen, Irving Berlin, Duke Ellington, George & Ira Gershwin, Jerome Kern, Johnny Mercer, Cole Porter And Rogers & Hart | Verve | 519832-2
Joe Pass Trio | Portraits Of Duke Ellington | Pablo | 2310716-2
June Christy With Orchestra | The Best Of June Christy | Capitol | 792588-2
Louis Armstrong With The Russell Garcia Orchestra | I've Got The World On A String/Louis Under The Stars | Verve | 2304428 IMS
Louis Armstrong-Duke Ellington Group | The Complete Louis Armstrong & Duke Ellington Sessions | Roulette | 793844-2
Mose Allison Quartet | The Mose Chronicles-Live In London,Vol.2 | Blue Note | 529748-2
Mose Allison Trio | Autumn Song | Original Jazz Classics | OJCCD 894-2(P 7189)
Mose Allison Sings The 7th Son | Prestige | PR20 7279-2
Nat King Cole Trio | The Legendary 1941-44 Broadcast Transcriptions | Music & Arts | CD 808
Oscar Peterson Trio | Oscar Peterson Plays The Duke Ellington Song Book | Verve | 559785-2
Patti Page With Lou Stein's Music | The Uncollected:Patti Page | Hindsight | HSR 223
Rex Stewart-Cootie Williams Orchestra | Together 1957 | Jazz Anthology | JA 5201
Ross Tompkins-Joe Venuti Quintet | Live At Concord '77 | Concord | CJ 51
Stan Kenton And His Orchestra | By Request Vol.3 | Creative World | ST 1062
Tom Williams Quintet | Straight Street | Criss Cross | Criss 1091
Von Freeman Quartet | Live At The Dakota | Premonition | 790750-2
Wycliffe Gordon Group | Slidin' Home | Nagel-Heyer | CD 2001
Wynton Kelly Trio | Kelly Blue | Original Jazz Classics | OJC20 033-2(RLP 1142)
Kelly Blue | Riverside | RISA 1142-6
New Faces-New Sounds:Piano Interpretations | Blue Note | 784456-2
Billy Eckstine With Bobby Tucker And His Orchestra | No Cover No Minimum | Blue Note | 798583-2

Do Nothin' Till You Hear From Me-
Duke Ellington | Duke Ellington Live At The Whitney | Impulse(MCA) | 951173-2
Duke Ellington And His Orchestra | Duke Ellington's 70th Birthday Concert | Blue Note | 837746-2
Ellis Marsalis | Duke In Blue | CBS | CK 63631
Rex Allen's Swing Express | Keep Swingin' | Nagel-Heyer | CD 016
Steve White Quartet | In The Spur Of The Moment | Telarc Digital | CD 83484

Do Nothin' Till You Hear From Me(alt.take)
Duke Ellington And His Orchestra | Duke Ellington And His Orchestra 1943,Vol.1 | Circle | CCD-101

Do Nothing Till You're True
Incognito | Positivity | Talkin' Loud | 518260-2

Do Right Woman, Do Right Man
Milan Swoboda Prague Big Band | Poste Restante | Jazz Pure Collection | AU 31626 CD

Do That Then
Jimmie Gordon Band | Jimmie Gordon 1934-1941 | Story Of Blues | CD 3510-2

Do The Do
Rebecca Coupe Franks Group | All Of A Sudden | Justice Records | JR 0902-2

Do The Jangle
King Curtis Band | King Curtis-Blow Man Blow | Bear Family Records | BCD 15670 CI

Do The Monkey
Jack Hylton And His Orchestra | Swing | Saville Records | SVL 158 IMS

Do U See The Way?
High Steppers Brass Band | New Orleans Jazz Greatest Hits | Sound Of New Orleans | SONO 1032

Do What Cha Wanna
Billy Cobham-George Duke Band | Live On Tour In Europe | Atlantic | ATL 50316

Do What Ory Say
Rod Mason's Hot Five | Tribute To Louis Armstrong | Jazz Colours | 874736-2

Do What You Do Do
Barbara Lea And The Legendary Lawson-Haggart Jazz Band | You're The Cats! | Audiophile | ACD-252

Do You Call That A Buddy
Louis Jordan And His Tympany Five | Louis Jordan Vol.2-Knock Me Out | Swingtime(Contact) | ST 1012

Do You Call That A Buddy(Dirty Cat)
Blue Barron And His Orchestra | The Uncollected: Blue Barron | Hindsight | HSR 110

Do You Have A Name
Pat Martino Trio | The Return | Muse | MCD 5328

Do You Hear The Voices That You Left Behind
Shirley Scott Quintet | Oasis | Muse | MCD 5388

Do You Know The Way To San Jose?
Horst Jankowski Orchestra With Voices | Jankowskeynotes | MPS | 9814806
Gerry Mulligan-Scott Hamilton Quintet | Soft Light & Sweet Music | Concord | CCD 4300

Do You Know What It Means To Miss New Orleans
Archie Shepp Quartet | Black Ballald | Timeless | CD SJP 386
Beryl Bryden And The Piccdilly Six | Beryl Bryden:Queen Of Bues And Washboard | Elite Special | 72430
Billie Holiday | New Orleans-Original Motion Picture Soundtrack | Giants Of Jazz | GOJCD 1025
Kenny Drew Trio | Duo | Steeplechase | SCS 1002
Louis Armstrong And His All Stars | Jazz Giants:Louis Armstrong | RCA | NL 89823 SI
Louis Armstrong At The Eddie Condon Floor Show Vol.1 | Queen-Disc | 010
Louis Armstrong And His Dixieland Seven | Louis Armstrong:C'est Si Bon | Dreyfus Jazz Line | FDM 36730-2
Louis Armstrong:A 100th Birthday Celebration | RCA | 2663694-2
Swing Legends:Louis Armstrong | Nimbus Records | NI 2012
Best Of The Complete RCA Victor Recordings | RCA | 2663636-2
Louis Armstrong-Satchmo's Greatest Hits | RCA | CL 89799
Planet Jazz:Male Jazz Vocalists | Planet Jazz | 2169657-2
Victor Jazz History Vol.19:Dixieland Revival | RCA | 2135738-2
Martin Taylor-Chet Atkins | Portraits | Linn Records | AKD 048
Papa Bue's Viking Jazzband With Wingy Manone | A Tribute To Wingy Manone | Storyville | SLP 210
Walter Davis Jr. Quartet | Illumination | Jazz City | 660.53.004

Do You Know What It Means To Miss New Orleans-
Clarinet Jazz Trio | Live At Birdland Neuburg | Birdland | BN 003
Art Blakey And The Jazz Messengers | Art Blakey And The Jazz Messengers | MCA | AS 7 (254624-2)

Do You Know Why
Max Bennett Quintet | Max Bennett Plays | Fresh Sound Records | FSR 2015(Bethlehem BCP 50)

Do You Know Why Stars Come Out At Night
New On The Corner | Left Handed | Jazz 4 Ever Records:Jazz Network | J4E 4758
Zipflo Reinhardt Group | Light Of The Future | MPS | 68274

Do You Like Pastrami?
Taylor's Weatherbirds | John Byrd & Walter Taylor(1929-1931) | Story Of Blues | CD 3517-2

Do You Mind(If I Hang Around)?
Dave Frishberg Trio | Classics | Concord | CCD 4462

Do You Read Me?
Jim McNeely Quartet And The WDR Big Band | East Coast Blow Out | Lipstick Records | LIP 890072

Do You Remember Me?
The Crusaders | The Best Of The Crusaders | MCA | 2292-50536-1

Do You Remember?(Jimi)
Phil Moerke Group feat. Victor Mendoza | Multi Colors | Jazz Pure Collection | AU 31625 CD

Do You Thing Of Me?
Grafitti | Good Groove | Lipstick Records | LIP 890202

Do You Think We'll Ever Find It?
Amina Claudine Myers Trio | The Circle Of Time | Black Saint | 120078-2

Do You Wanna Jump Children

TITELVERZEICHNIS

Joe Williams And Friends | Joe Williams At Newport '63 | RCA | NL 70119

Do You Wanna Jump Children-

At Newport '63 | RCA | 2663919-2
Joe Williams And His Band | Planet Jazz:Joe Williams | Planet Jazz | 2165370-2
New York Voices | What's Inside | GRP | GRP 97002

Do You Want To Know A Secret?

Wolfgang Muthspiel Trio | Perspective | Amadeo | 533466-2

Do Your Duty

Billie Holiday With Sy Oliver And His Orchestra | Jazz Gallery:Billie Holiday Vol.1(1933-49) | RCA | 2119542-2

Dobbin' With Redd Foxx

Mikel Andueza Quintet | BCN | Fresh Sound Records | FSNT 036 CD

Doble Nacionalidad

Dusko Goykovich Big Band | Balkan Connection | Enja | ENJ-9047 2

Doboy

Dusko Goykovich Quartet | Celebration | DIW | DIW 806 CD

Doc Phil

Kenny Garrett Quartet | KG Standard Of Language | Warner | 9362-48404-2

Doc Tone's Short Speech

J.J.Johnson Quintet | Live At The Village Vanguard | EmArCy | 848327-2

Dock 'C'

Paul Bollenback Group | Soul Groove | Challenge | CHR 70064

Doctone

Don Braden Quartet | The Fire Within | RCA | 2663297-2

Doctor

Gary Burton Quintet | Dreams So Real | ECM | 1072
Bluesiana | Bluesiana II | Windham Hill | 34 10133-2

Doctor Honoris Causa

Weather Report | Weathe Report Live In Tokyo | CBS | 489208-2

Doctor Honoris Causa-

Marco Tamburini Quartet | Thinking Of You | Penta Flowers | CDPIA 021

Doctor Jazz

Horace Silver Quintet | A Prescription For The Blues | Impulse(MCA) | 951238-2
Jack Teagarden And His Jazz Band | Gotham Jazz Scene/Big T's Dixieland Band | Dormouse | DMI CDX 03(882985)
Jelly Roll Morton's Red Hot Peppers | Doctor Jazz | Black & Blue | BLE 59.227 2

Doctor's Blues

Ron Carter Quartet | Etudes | Discovery | 71012-2

Documentation

Trigon | Oglinda | JA & RO | JARO 4215-2

Doda

Tok | Paradox | Japo | 60029

Dodge City

Sonny Red (Kyner) Quintet | Images:Sonny Red | Original Jazz Classics | OJC 148(J 974)

Dodge The Dodo

Dave Frishberg Trio | Classics | Concord | CCD 4462

Dodgin' The Dean

Ambrose & His Orchestra | Champagne Cocktail | Ace Of Club | ACL 1246

Dodo

Dick Hyman | The Gershwin Songbook:Jazz Variations | Musicmasters | 65094-2

Does Mama Know You're Out?

Klaus König Orchestra | The Heart Project | Enja | ENJ-9338 2

Does Money Matter

Teddy Stauffer Und Seine Original Teddies | Teddy Stauffer:Rare And Historical Jazz Recordings | Elite Special | 9522009

Does Time Go By?

Lonnie Donegan Skiffle Group | Dixieland Jubilee Vol.4 | Intercord | 155024

Dog House Blues

The Jumping Notes Dixieland-Band | C'Est Si Bon | Elite Special | 73444

Dog River

Rozie Trio | Afro Algonquin | Moers Music | 01078

Dog With A Bone

Alex Welsh And His Band | Wonderful Dixieland Vol.2 | Sonia | CD 77269

Doggin' Around

Buddy Tate-Dollar Brand Quartet | Buddy Tate Meets Dollar Brand | Chiaroscuro | CR 165
Harry Sweets Edison And The Golden Horns | Live At The Iridium | Telarc Digital | CD 83425

Doggy Boy

Johannes Enders Quartet | Home Ground | Enja | 9105-2

Dogs From Afar

Michael Brecker Group | Now You See It...(Now You Don't) | GRP | GRP 96222

Dogs In The Wine Shopnyc

Fritz Hauser Duo | Zwei | Hat Art | CD 6010

Dogs Of Somerville

Bob Crosby And His Orchestra | Swing Legens:Bob Crosby | Nimbus Records | NI 2011

Dogtown Blues

Aki Takase Trio | ABC | Eastwind | EWIND 703

Doin' The Bone

Chris Barber's Jazz And Blues Band | Sideways | Black Lion | 147009

Doin' The New Low Down

WDR Big Band | Harlem Story | Koala Records | CD P 7

Doin' The Shout

Roland Kirk With The Jack McDuff Trio | Kirk's Work | Original Jazz Classics | OJC20 459-2(P 7210)

Doin' The Sixty-Eight

Roland Kirk-Jack McDuff Quartet | Pre-Rahsan | Prestige | P 24080

Doin' The Thing

Horace Silver Quintet | Doin' The Thing - The Horace Silver Quintet At The Village Gate | Blue Note | 300414

Doin' Time

T-Bone Walker prob.With Jim Wynn And His Orchestra | Hot Leftovers | Pathe | 1561451(Imperial)

Doina Olt

Dixie Hummingbirds | Live | Mobile Fidelity | MFCD 771

Doj-Doj

Eje Thelin Quartet | Ejs Thelin 1966 With Barney Wilen | Dragon | DRCD 366
George Cables Trio | Skylark | Steeplechase | SCCD 31381

Dolemite

Erskine Hawkins And His Orchestra | The Original Tuxedo Junction | RCA | ND 90363(874142)

Doll

Hamiet Bluiett Quintet | Dangerously Suite | Soul Note | 121018-2

Doll Baby-

Hamiet Bluiett | Birthright-A Solo Blues Concert | India Navigation | IN 1030

Doll Of The Bride

Don Cherry/Ed Blackwell | Mu(The Complete Session) | Affinity | AFF 774

Dollar Shot

Peter Hertmans Quartet | Waiting | Timeless | CD SJP 418

Dolores

Miles Davis Quintet | Miles Davis Quintet 1965-1968 | CBS | C6K 67398
Tommy Dorsey And His Orchestra | Frank Sinatra And The Tommy Dorsey Orchestra | RCA | 2668701-2
V.S.O.P. | The Quintet | CBS | 88273

Dolorosa

Bert Saeger Jazz Quintet | Live At The Yardbird Suite | L+R Records | CDLR 45023

Dolphin Dance

Ahmad Jamal Trio | Freeflight | Impulse(MCA) | GRP 11332
Bill Evans Trio | I Will Say Goodbye | Original Jazz Classics | OJCCD 761-2(F 9593)
Bill Evans:The Secret Sessions | Milestone | 8MCD 4421-2
Bunny Brunel Group | Dedication | Accord | 500362
Christian McBride/Nicholas Payton/Mark Whitfield | Fingerpainting-The Music Of Herbie Hancock | Verve | 537856-2
Herbie Hancock Quintet | The Best Of Herbie Hancock | Blue Note | 791142-2
Howard Roberts Quartet | The Real Howard Roberts | Concord | CCD 4053
Toots Thielemans-Kenny Werner Duo | Toots Thielemans & Kenny Werner | EmArCy | 014722-2
Bill Evans Trio | The Complete Fantasy Recordings | Fantasy | 9FCD 1012-2

Dolphin Dance-(Excerpts)

Re: Person I Knew | Original Jazz Classics | OJCCD 749-2(F 9608)
Count Basie And His Orchestra | Hall Of Fame | Verve | MV 2645 IMS

Dolphy No.1

Jaki Byard Quartet | The Last From Lennie's | Prestige | PRCD 11029-2

Dolphy No.2

Eric Dolphy-Ron Carter | Other Aspects | Blue Note | BT 85131

Dolphy's Dance

Charlie Haden-Paul Motian Trio Feat.Geri Allen | Etudes | Soul Note | 121162-2
Geri Allen Group | Maroons | Blue Note | 799493-2

Dolu

Gerwin Eisenhauer's The Gäff Gang feat. Lisa Wahland | Favorite Tunes | Edition Collage | EC 527-2

Dom De Illudir

Claudio Roditi Quintet | Two Of Swords | Candid | CCD 79504

Domani

Steve Lacy Double Sextet | Clangs | Hat Art | CD 6116

Domimonk

Sam Rivers Quartet | Lazuli | Timeless | CD SJP 291

Domination

Washington Phillips | I Am Born To Preach The Gospel | Yazoo | YAZ 2003

Domino

Roland Kirk Quartet | Rahsaan/The Complete Mercury Recordings Of Roland Kirk | Mercury | 846630-2
Domino | Verve | 543833-2
Domino | Verve | 543833-2
Thilo von Westernhagen Group | Theatre | SHP Records | SHP 203
Gary Burton-Steve Swallow | Hotel Hello | ECM | 1055(835586-2)

Domino Biscuit

Weather Report | Domino Theory | CBS | 25839-2

Dominoes

Mark Helias' Open Loose | New School | Enja | ENJ-9413 2
Michael Formanek Quintet | Extented Animation | Enja | ENJ-7041 2

Domino's Intro

Toto Blanke-Rudolf Dasek | Meditation | ALISO Records | AL 1026

Dominus, Vobistu?

Poncho Sanchez And His Orchestra | A Night At Kimball's East | Concord | CCD 4472

Don Camelone

Christof Sänger & Cuban Fantasy | Moliendo Café | Mons Records | MR 874302

Don Carlos

Dudek-Van Den Broek-Haurand | Crossing Level | Konnex Records | KCD 5077

Don Cherry

Jiri Stivin-Ali Haurand | Just The Two Of Us | Konnex Records | KCD 5095
Don Byas All Stars | Don Byas Complete American Small Group Recordings | Definitive Records | DRCD 11213

Don Quijote Und Die Warteschlangen

Charles Fambrough Group | The Proper Angle | CTI Records | CTI 1002-2

Don Quixote

Egberto Gismonti/Nana Vasconcelos | Duas Vozes | ECM | 1279
Harris Simen Group | New York Connection | Eastwind | EWIND 701

Dona Luchi

Kenny Barron Group With Trio De Paz | Canta Brazil | EmArCy | 017993-2

Dona Maria

Trio Da Paz With Special Guests | Black Orpheus | Kokopelli Records | KOKO 1299

Dona Nobis Pacem

Deborah Henson-Conant | The Gift:15 Weihnachtslieder der Erde | Laika Records | 35100992

Dona Nobis Pacem-

Azimuth | Light As A Feather | Milestone | M 9089

Donald

Wolfgang Schlüter-Christoph Spendel Duo | Dualism | MPS | 68285

Donald Mu-

Phineas Newborn Jr. Trio | Look Out-Phineas Is Back | Pablo | 2310801

Donau

Brötzmann, van Hove, Bennink | Brötzmann, van Hove, Bennink | FMP | 0130

Doncha Hear Me Callin' To Ya

J.J. Johnson-Al Grey Sextet | Things Are Getting Better All The Time | Pablo | 2312141

Done Got Wise

Charles Musselwhite Band | Charles Musselwhite Memphis,Tennessee | Crosscut | CCR 1008

Donegal Cradle Song

Dorothy Donegan Trio | The Many Faces Of Dorothy Donegan | Storyville | STCD 8362

Donegan's Blues

The Explosive Dorothy Donegan | Progressive | PRO 7056 IMS

Donkey

Paul Bley Trio | Paul Plays Carla | Steeplechase | SCCD 31303

Donna

Miles Davis Sextet | Miles Davis:The Blue Note And Capitol Recordings | Blue Note | 827475-2
Miles Davis Vol.2 | Blue Note | 300082(1502)

Donna Carmen

Matthias Stich & Whisper Not | Bach Lives!! | Satin Doll Productions | SDP 1018-1 CD

Donna Inventia

All Stars | Bird's Eyes Last Unissued Vol.21:Bird On TV/Bird On Bandbox | Philology | W 851.2

Donna Lee

Art Pepper Plus Eleven | Modern Jazz Classics | Original Jazz Classics | OJC20 341-2
A Treasury Of Modern Jazz Classics | Mobile Fidelity | MFCD 805
Art Pepper Quartet | Art Pepper:The Complete Galaxy Recordings | Galaxy | 16GCD 1016-2
Arthur's Blues | Original Jazz Classics | OJCCD 680-2
Artworks | Galaxy | GXY 5148
Bireli Lagrene Trio | Live In Marciac | Dreyfus Jazz Line | FDM 36567-2
Charlie Parker Quintet | The Savoy Recordings 1 | Savoy | 650107(881907)
Eric Dolphy Orchestra | Vintage Dolphy | Enja | ENJ-5045 2
Jam Session | Bird's Eyes-Last Unissued Vol.12 | Philology | W 842.2
Joey DeFrancesco Trio | All About My Girl | Muse | MCD 5528
Lee Konitz-Warne Marsh Sextet | That's Jazz Vol.21: Lee Konitz & Warne Marsh | Atlantic | ATL 50298
Pablo All Star Jam | Montreux '77 | Original Jazz Classics | OJC 385(2620105)
Montreux '77-The Art Of The Jam Session | Pablo | 2620106

Donna Lee-

Jaco Pastorius Trio | Jaco Pastorius Broadway Blues & Theresa | Jazzpoint | JP 1053 CD
Maria Joao-Aki Takase | Looking For Love:Live At The Leverkusen Jazz Festival | Enja | 5075-2

Donna Lee(alt.take)

Art Pepper Plus Eleven | Modern Jazz Classics | Original Jazz Classics | OJC20 341-2
Art Pepper Quartet | Art Pepper:The Complete Galaxy Recordings | Galaxy | 16GCD 1016-2
Charlie Parker All Stars | The Immortal Charlie Parker | Savoy | SV 0102(MG 12001)

Donna(alt.take)

Miles Davis Sextet | Miles Davis:The Blue Note And Capitol Recordings | Blue Note | 827475-2

Donna's Waltz

Jack Dieval Trio | Jazz In Paris:Jack Diéval-Jazz Aux Champs Elysées | EmArCy | 018419-2

Donne Ta Main Et Viens

Ralph Burns And His Orchestra | Ralph Burns Conducts Ralph Burns | Raretone | 5017 FC

Donner-Träume

Irene Schweizer/Han Bennink | Irene Schweizer & Han Bennink | Intakt Records | CD 010

Donnybrook

Klaus Treuheit Trio | Full House | Klaus Treuheit Production | R&M 2-8003

Don's Delight

Billy Bang Quartet | Bang On! | Justin Time | JUST 105-2

Don't

Dave McMurdo Jazz Orchestra | Different Paths | Sackville | SKCD2-2034

Don't Ask

Sonny Rollins Sextet | Don't Ask | Original Jazz Classics | OJCCD 915-2(M 9090)
Steve LaSpina Quartet | New Horizon | Steeplechase | SCCD 31313

Don't Ask Me

Henry Johnson Group | Missing You | Inak | 30292

Don't Axe Me

Benny Goodman Quintet | Slipped Disc, 1945-1946 | CBS | 463337-2

Don't Be Afraid,The Clown's Afraid,Too

Vienna Art Orchestra | The Original Charts Of Duke Ellington & Charles Mingus | Verve | 521998-2

Don't Be Cruel

Jimmy Ponder Quartet | To Reach A Dream | Muse | MCD 5394

Don't Be Mad At Me Pretty Mama

Buddy Johnson And His Orchestra | Buddy And Ella Johnson 1953-1964 | Bear Family Records | BCD 15479 DH

Don't Be Messin'

John Lee Hooker Band | John Lee Hooker-The 1965 London Sessions | Sequel Records | NEB CD 657

Don't Be That Way

Anita O'Day And Her Combo | Pick Yourself Up | Official | 3015
Benny Goodman And His Orchestra | Benny Goodman Bangkok 1956 | TCB Records | TCB 43042
Ella Fitzgerald And Louis Armstrong With The Oscar Peterson Quartet | Ella And Louis Again | Verve | 825374-2
Compact Jazz: Ella Fitzgerald/Louis Armstrong | Verve | 835313-2
Ella Fitzgerald With The Duke Ellington Orchestra | The Greatest Jazz Concert In The World | Pablo | 2625704-2
Ella Fitzgerald-Joe Pass Duo | Take Love Easy | Pablo | 2310702
Joe Pass:A Man And His Guitar | Original Jazz Classics | OJCCD 8806-2
Erroll Garner | Verve Jazz Masters 7:Erroll Garner | Verve | 518197-2
Erroll Garner Quartet | The Fascinating Erroll Garner | Fontana | 6430135
Joe Daniels And His Hot Shots | Steppin' Out To Swing | Saville Records | SVL 167 IMS
Les Blue Stars | Jazz In Paris:Les Blue Stars-Pardon My English/Henri Salvador-Plays The Blues | EmArCy | 013035-2
Lionel Hampton Quintet | The Lional Hampton Quintet | Verve | 589100-2
Little Jazz And His Trumpet Ensemble | Little Jazz Special | Queen-Disc | 066
Stan Kenton And His Orchestra | Two Much | Creative World | ST 1067
Teddy Wilson Trio | Three Little Words | Black & Blue | BLE 233094

Don't Be That Way-

Benny Goodman And His Orchestra | Big City Swing | Decca | TAB 5

Don't Blame Me

Al Casey Quintet | Buck Jumpin' | Original Jazz Classics | OJCCD 675-2(SV 2007)
Art Tatum | Art Tatum:Complete Capitol Recordings | Definitive Records | DRCD 11192
Barney Kessel And His Quintet | To Swing Or Not To Swing | Original Jazz Classics | OJCCD 317-2
Barry Harris | Solo | September | CD 5111
Budd Johnson And The Four Brass Giants | Budd Johnson And The Four Brass Giants | Original Jazz Classics | OJC 209(RLP 9343)
Charlie Parker Quintet | Charlie Parker:The Complete 1944-1948 Small Group Sessions(Studio Recordings-Master Takes),Vol.4 | Blue Moon | BMCD 1010
Charlie Parker With The Cootie Williams Orchestra | Bird's Eyes Last Unissued Vol.22:Don't Blame Me | Philology | W 852.2
Concord Super Band | Concord Super Band | Concord | CJ 80
Dizzy Gillespie Big Band | Bird's Eyes-Last Unissued Vol.13 | Philology | W 843.2
Duke Ellington And His Orchestra | Carnegie Hall Concert-Vol. 1 | Jazz Anthology | JA 5140
Eric Dolphy With Erik Moseholm's Trio | Eric Dolphy:The Complete Prestige Recordings | Prestige | 9 PRCD-4418-2
Erroll Garner Trio | Erroll Garner:Trio | Dreyfus Jazz Line | FDM 36719-2
The Erroll Garner Collection Vol.2: Dancing On The Ceiling | EmArCy | 834935-2 PMS
JATP Jam Session | Return To Happiness-JATP At Yoyogi National Stadium,Tokyo | Pablo | 2620117-2
Joe Thomas And His Orchestra | Joe Thomas:The Complete Recordings 1945-1950 | Blue Moon | BMCD 1051
John Crocker Quartet | All Of Me | Timeless | CD TTD 585
John Lewis | Private Concert | EmArCy | 848267-2
Lennie Tristano Quartet | Anthropology | Spotlite | SPJ 108
Lucky Thompson With The Gerard Pochonet All-Stars | Lucky Thompson:Lucky Sessions | Vogue | 2111510-2
Miles Davis/Tadd Dameron Quintet | Paris Festival International De Jazz, May 1949 | CBS | 485527-2
Nat King Cole Trio | Nat King Cole:For Sentimental Reasons | Dreyfus Jazz Line | FDM 36740-2
The Legendary 1941-44 Broadcast Transcriptions | Music & Arts | CD 808
Ralph Sutton Quartet | The Ralph Sutton Quartet With Ruby Braff,Vol.2 | Storyville | STCD 8246
Randy Weston Trio | How High The Moon | Biograph | BLP 12065
Ruby Braff-Buddy Tate With The Newport All Stars | Ruby Braff-Buddy Tate With The Newport All Stars | Black Lion | BLCD 760138
Sonny Criss Quartet | Jazz In Paris:Saxophones À Saint-Germain Des Prés | EmArCy | 014060-2
Sonny Criss Quintet | Blues Pour Flirter | Polydor | 2445034 IMS
Super Sax & L.A.Voices | Supersax & L.A.Voices | CBS | FC 39140
Thelonious Monk | Monk Alone:The Complete Columbia Solo Studio Recordings | CBS | C2K 65495
Thelonious Monk Quartet | Live At The Jazz Workshop-Complete | CBS | C2K 65189
Tiziana Ghiglioni With Paul Bley | Lyrics | SPLASC(H) Records | CD H 348-2
Ella Fitzgerald With Benny Carter's Magnificent Seven | 30 By Ella | Capitol | 520090-2

Don't Blame Me-

Simon Schott | Bar Piano: Simon Schott Plays Your Favorite Evergreens Vol.2 | Organic Music | ORGM 9735
The Mastersounds | The Mastersounds | Prestige | PRCD 24770-2
Coleman Hawkins Quartet | Ultimate Coleman Hawkins selected by Sonny Rollins | Verve | 557538-2

Don't Blame Me(alt.take)

Eric Dolphy With Erik Moseholm's Trio | Eric Dolphy:The Complete Prestige Recordings | Prestige | 9 PRCD-4418-2
Teddy Wilson | Piano Solos | Affinity | CD AFS 1016

Don't Burn The Candle At Both Ends
Louis Jordan And His Tympany Five | Look Out Sisters-Unissued Film Soundtracks 1944-1948 | Krazy Kat | KK 7415 IMS
Don't Call It Love
Johnny Hodges And The Ellington Men | The Big Sound | Verve | MV 2525 IMS
Don't Call Me I'll Call You
Pierre Boussaguet Trio | Charme | EmArCy | 538468-2
Don't Call On Me
Marilyn Middleton Pollock With The Lake Records All-Star Jazzband |
Marilyn Middleton Pollock With The Lake Records All-Star Jazzband | Lake | LACD 35
Don't Cha Go 'Way Mad
Mel Tormé And His Band | Fujitsu-Concord Jazz Festival In Japan '90 | Concord | CCD 4481
Don't Cha Hear Me Callin' To Ya
John Handy's Louisiana Shakers | John Handy-The Very First Recordings | American Music | AMCD-51
Don't Change Your Mind
Al Jones Blues Band | Watch This! | Blues Beacon | BLU-1024 2
Don't Come Cryin' On My Shoulder
Louis Jordan And His Tympany Five | Louis Jordan Vol.1-Hoodoo Man | Swingtime(Contact) | ST 1011
Don't Cry Baby
Lonnie Johnson | Blues Masters Vol.4 | Storyville | STCD 8004
Don't Cry Cry Baby
Nat King Cole Trio | Rare Live Performences | Jazz Anthology | JA 5175
Don't Cry For Me Argentina
Laurindo Almeida-Charlie Byrd Quartet | Brazilian Soul | Concord | CCD 4150
Mark Kramer Trio | Evita En Jazz | Telarc Digital | CD 83422
Don't Cuddle That Crazy Cat
Hannes Clauss Quartett | Dances | Acoustic Music Records | 319.1161.2
Don't Dream Of Anybody But Me
Mel Tormé With The Mel-Tones | Back In Town | Verve | MV 2675 IMS
Don't Embarrass Me, Baby
Phil Woods Quintet | Phil Woods Plays The Music Of Jim McNeely | TCB Records | TCB 95402
Don't Even Go There
Herbie Hancock Septet | The Lost Sessions | Blue Note | 521484-2
Don't Ever Leave Me
Keith Jarrett Trio | Keith Jarrett At The Blue Note-The Complete Recordings | ECM | 1575/80(527638-2)
Margaret Whiting With Russel Garcia And His Orchestra | Margaret Whiting Sings The Jerome Kern Song Book | Verve | 559553-2
Peggy Lee With The George Shearing Trio | Beauty And The Beat | Capitol | 542308-2
Thad Jones-Mel Lewis Orchestra | Swiss Radio Days Jazz Series Vol.4:Thad Jones-Mel Lewis Orchestra | TCB Records | TCB 02042
Don't Ever Say Goodbye
MJT+3 | MJT+3 | Vee Jay Recordings | VJ 002
Don't Explain
Abbey Lincoln With Her Quintet | Sonny Rollins-The Freelance Years:The Complete Riverside & Contemporary Recordings | Riverside | 5 RCD 4427-2
Abbey Lincoln With The Harold Vick Quartet | Abbey Sings Billie | Enja | 9134-2
Billie Holiday And Her All Stars | The Essential Billie Holiday Carnegie Hall Concert | Verve | 833767-2
Billie Holiday With Bob Haggart And His Orchestra | Jazz Gallery:Billie Holiday Vol.1(1933-49) | RCA | 2119542-2
Carmen McRae And Her Trio With Zoot Sims | For Lady Day Vol.1 | Novus | 4163163-2
Chet Baker And His Orchestra | Compact Jazz: Chet Baker | Verve | 840632-2 PMS
Dexter Gordon Quartet | A Swingin' Affair | Blue Note | 784133-2
George Shearing | The Shearing Piano | Capitol | 531574-2
George Shearing-Brian Torff Duo | On A Clear Day | Concord | CCD 4132
Hartschuh-Reiter-Sauer | Eternal Verities | L+R Records | CDLR 45096
Heinz Sauer Quintet | Lost Ends:Live at Alte Oper Frankfurt | free flow music | ffm 0594
Heinz Sauer-Bob Degen Duo | Plaza Lost And Found | L+R Records | CDLR 45044
Helen Merrill With The Quincy Jones Orchestra | Brownie-The Complete EmArCy Recordings Of Clifford Brown | EmArCy | 838306-2
Herbert Joos Quartet | Herbert Joos Plays Billie Holiday Songs | EmArCy | 522634-2
Melvin Rhyne Quartet | Classmasters | Criss Cross | Criss 1183
Nancy Wilson With The Great Jazz Trio | What's New | Eastworld | EWJ 90014
Nina Simone Quartet | Nina Simone-The 60s Vol.2:Mood Indigo | Mercury | 838544-2 PMS
Patty Waters-Jessica Williams | Love Songs | Jazz Focus | JFCD 012
Dick Katz Quintet | The Line Forms Here | Reservoir | RSR CD 141
Don't Fail Me Baby
Buddy Johnson And His Orchestra | Go Ahead & Rock Rock Rock | Official | 6011
Don't Fall Around Much Anymore
Gunter Hampel And His Galaxie Dream Band | Enfant Terrible | Birth | 0025
Don't Fall Around Much Anymore(take 1)
Enfant Terrible | Birth | 0025
Don't Fall Around Much Anymore(take 2)
Orrin Evans Ortet | Captain Black | Criss Cross | Criss 1154
Don't Fence Me In
Ella Fitzgerald With The Buddy Bregman Orchestra | The Complete Ella Fitzgerald Song Books of Harold Arlen, Irving Berlin, Duke Ellington, George & Ira Gershwin, Jerome Kern, Johnny Mercer, Cole Porter And Rogers & Hart | Verve | 519832-2
Don't Follow The Crowd
Gary Smulyan Quartet With Strings | Gary Smulyan With Strings | Criss Cross | Criss 1129
Don't Forget It
Hans Koller Quartet | Multiple Koller | L+R Records | LR 41003
Don't Forget To Mess Around
Louis Armstrong And His Hot Five | Louis Armstrong-The Hot Fives Vol.1 | CBS | 460821-2
Don't Forget To Smile
Mose Allison Trio | The Word From Mose | Atlantic | 8122-72394-2
Mose In Your Ear | Atlantic | SD 1627
Don't Forgett Fatty
Martin Taylor Trio | Don't Fret | Linn Records | AKD 014
Don't Get Around Much Anymore
Ben Webster All Stars | Compact Jazz: Coleman Hawkins/Ben Webster | Verve | 833296-2
Benny Bailey Quartet With Wayne Bartlett | I Thought About You | Laika Records | 35100762
Benny Carter And His Orchestra | Tickle Toe | Vee Jay Recordings | VJ 024
Billy Jenkins | In The Nude | West Wind | ???
Bob Crosby And His Orchestra | The Uncollected:Bob Crosby | Hindsight | HSR 192
Cat Anderson And His All Stars | Ellingtonians In Paris | Jazztime(EMI) | 251275-2
Concord All Stars | Festival Time | Concord | CJ 117
Dave Brubeck-Lee Konitz Duo | All The Things We Are | Atlantic | 7567-81399-2
David Fathead Newman Sextet | Mr.Gentle, Mr.Cool:A Tribute To Duke Ellington | Kokopelli Records | KOKO 1300
Duke Ellington And His Orchestra | At The Hurricane:Original 1943 Broadcasts | Storyville | STCD 8359
At The Hurricane:Original 1943 Broadcasts | Storyville | STCD 8359
Carnegie Hall Concert January 1943 | Prestige | 2PCD 34004-2
Duke Ellington And His Orchestra 1929-1943 | Storyville | 4960333
Duke Elliongton:Complete Prestige Carnegie Hall 1943-1944 Concerts | Definitive Records | DRCD 11210
Goin' Up | Duke Records | D 1011
Ella Fitzgerald And Her All Stars | Ella Fitzgerald Sings The Duke Ellington Songbook | Verve | 559248-2
The Complete Ella Fitzgerald Song Books of Harold Arlen, Irving Berlin, Duke Ellington, George & Ira Gershwin, Jerome Kern, Johnny Mercer, Cole Porter And Rogers & Hart | Verve | 519832-2
George Shearing Trio | Breakin' Out | Concord | CJ 335
Grace Knight With Orchestra | Come In Spinner | Intuition Records | INT 3052-2
Hampton Hawes Trio | Black California | Savoy | SJL 2215 (801191)
Jenny Evans And The Rudi Martini Quartet | At Loyd's | BELL Records | BLR 90004
Jimmy Hamilton Quartet | Jimmy Hamilton:As Time Goes By | Memo Music | HDJ 4013
Jodie Christian Sextet | Front Line | Delmark | DE 490
Johnny Hodges Orchestra | The Rabbit's Work On Verve In Chronological Order Vol. 3: 1952-54 | Verve | 2304449 IMS
Louis Armstrong With The Russell Garcia Orchestra | I've Got The World On A String/Louis Under The Stars | Verve | 2304428 IMS
Madeline Bell With The Metropole Orchestra | Beat Out That Rhythm On A Drum | Koch Jazz | 3-6910-2
MJT+3 | Walter Perkins' MJT+3/Make Everybody Happy | Vee Jay Recordings | VJ 009
Mose Allison Trio | Mose Allison Sings The 7th Son | Prestige | PR20 7279-2
Nat Adderley With The Three Sounds | Branching Out | Original Jazz Classics | OJCCD 255-2(R 285)
Nat King Cole With Orchestra | Welcome To Jazz: Nat King Cole | Koch Records | 321 981 D1
Oscar Peterson Trio | Oscar Peterson Plays Duke Ellington | Pablo | 2310966-2
The History Of An Artist | Pablo | 2625702-2
Oscar Peterson Plays The Duke Ellington Song Book | Verve | 559785-2
Papa John De Francesco Quintet | Doodlin' | Muse | MCD 5501
Peter Herbolzheimer Rhythm Combination & Brass | Fat Man Boogie | Koala Records | CD P 2
Regal Jazz Band/Smitty Dee's Brass Band | New Orleans Favorites | Sound Of New Orleans | SONO 1040
Sal Salvador Sextet | Starfingers | Bee Hive | BH 7002
Sonny Criss Quintet | Jazz In Paris:Sonny Criss-Mr.Blues Pour Flirter | EmArCy | 549231-2 PMS
Sonny Stitt Quartet | Blues For Duke | Muse | MR 5129
Stan Getz With Ib Glindemann And His Orchestra | Stan Getz | Laserlight | 15761
Woody Herman And His Orchestra | Verve Jazz Masters 54:Woody Herman | Verve | 529903-2
Live At Peacock Lane, Hollywood | Bandstand | BDCD 1508
Compact Jazz: Woody Herman | Verve | 835319-2 PMS
Don't Get Around Much Anymore-
Dollar Brand | Pre Abdullah Ibrahim | Jazz Colours | 874711-2
Jonah Jones Quartet | Harry 'Sweets' Edison/Jonah Jones | LRC Records | CDC 9030
Don't Get Around Much Anymore(alt.take)
Milt Jackson Quintet | Wizard Of The Vibes | Blue Note | 532140-2
Duke Ellington And His Orchestra | Way Low | Duke Records | D 1015
Don't Get Sassy
Ray Brown Trio | Don't Get Sassy | Telarc Digital | CD 83368
Don't Get Scared
Alix Combelle Trio | Le Jazz En France Vol.13:Alix Combelle 1937-1940(Tome 1) | Pathe | 1552591
Don't Give Me That Jive
Oldsmobile Dixieland Jazz Band | Dixieland Jazz(Hungarian) | Jazz Pure Collection | AU 31613 CD
Don't Go
Carmen McRae With The Shorty Rogers Orchestra | The Sound Of Silence | Atlantic | AMCY 1069
Don't Go Don't Go
Muddy Waters Band | Good News-Muddy Waters, Vol.3 | Red Lightnin' | SC 002
Don't Go To Strangers
Henry Johnson Group | Missing You | Inak | 30292
Bishop Norman Williams Group | The One Mind Experience-The Bishop | Evidence | TR 101
Don't Go 'Way Nobody
George Lewis And His New Orleans Stompers | George Lewis And His New Orleans Stompers-Vol. 2 | Blue Note | 81206
Don't Hold It In
Corina Curschellas-John Wolf Brennan | Entupadas | Creative Works Records | CW CD 1013-1
Don't Hurt A Woman-It's A Boomerang
Neil Swainson Quintet | 49th Parallel | Concord | CCD 4396
Don't I Know You
Laura Fygi With Band | Laura Fygi Live At The North Sea Jazz | Spectra | 9811207
Don't It Make My Brown Eyes Blue
Tampa Red Band | Tampa Red 1928-1942:It's Tight Like That | Story Of Blues | CD 3505-2
Don't Jive Me
Louis Armstrong And His Savoy Ballroom Five | Louis Armstrong-The Hot Fives & Hot Sevens Vol.3 | CBS | 465189-2
Don't Knock On My Door
Coronarias Dans | Visitor | Steeplechase | SCCD 31032
Don't Know
Jutta Glaser & Bernhard Sperrfechter | Little Girl Blue | Jazz 'n' Arts Records | JNA 0502
Don't Know Blues
Billie Holiday And Her Orchestra | Rare And Unissued Recordings From The Golden Years,Vol.2 | Queen-Disc | 065
Don't Know Much Abou Love
Stefano Maltese Quintet | Amor Fati | SPLASC(H) Records | H 184
Don't Know What I Would Do
Jim Kahr Group | Incredibly Live! | Acoustic Music Records | 319.1101.2
Don't Know What To Say
Joice Walton & Blackout With Guests | Downsville Girl | Line Records | LICD 9.01303
Don't Know Why
Buddy Guy-Junior Wells Band | Alone & Acoustic | Isabel | BLE 59.910 2
Don't Let It Bother You
Fats Waller And His Rhythm | Breakin' The Ice-The Early Years Part 1(1934-1935) | Bluebird | 63 66618-2
Don't Let It Go To Your Head
Nat King Cole Quintet | After Midnight | Capitol | 520087-2
Ray Gelato Giants | The Full Flavour | Linn Records | AKD 034
Don't Let Me Be Lonely Tonight
Michael Brecker Quintet | Nearness Of You-The Ballad Book | Verve | 549705-2
Rosemary Clooney With The Woody Herman Big Band | My Buddy | Concord | CCD 4226
Don't Let Me Be Misunderstood
Nina Simone Trio/Quartet/Orchestra | Moon Of Alabama | Jazz Door | JD 1214
Nina Simone With Horace Ott's Orchestra | Broadway-Blues-Ballads | Verve | 518190-2
Willem Breuker Kollektief | Deadly Sin/Twice A Woman(Soundtracks) | BVHAAST | CD 9708
Don't Let Me Down-
Christian Scheuber Quintet | Clara's Smile | double moon | DMCHR 71025
Don't Let Me Go
Eddie Harris | A Tale Of Two Cities | Night Records | VNCD 3(887046)
Don't Let Me Lose This Dream
John Patton Quartet | Accent On The Blues | Blue Note | 853924-2
First Class Blues Band | The First Class Blues Band Proudly Presents Mr. Frank Biner | Acoustic Music Records | 319.1062.2
Don't Let That Moon Get Away
Dick Jurgens And His Orchestra | The Uncollected: Dick Jurgens | Hindsight | HSR 111
Don't Let The Moon Get Away
Ku-umba Frank Lacy & The Poker Bigband | Songs From The Musical 'Poker' | Tutu Records | 888150-2*
Don't Let The Sun
Tok Tok Tok | Love Again | Einstein Music | EM 01081
Art Pepper-George Cables Duo | Art Pepper:The Complete Galaxy Recordings | Galaxy | 16GCD 1016-2
Don't Let The Sun Catch You Cryin'
Goin' Home | Original Jazz Classics | GXY 5143
Louis Jordan And His Tympany Five | Five Guys Named Moe | Bandstand | BDCD 1531
Susannah McCorkle With The Ken Peplowski Quintet | No More Blues | Concord | CCD 4370
Don't Let The Sun Catch You Cryin'(alt.take)
Art Pepper-George Cables Duo | Goin' Home | Original Jazz Classics | GXY 5143
Don't Let The Sun Catch You Cryin'(alt.take-2)
Holly Cole And Her Quartet | It Happened One Night | Metro Blue | 852699-0
Don't Let The Teardrops Rust Your Shining Heart
Jean-Luc Ponty Sextet | Cosmic Messenger | Atlantic | 7567-81550-2
Don't Let The World Pass You By
Slim And Slam | Slim & Slam: Original 1940-42 Recordings,Vol.3 | Tax | S 7-2
Don't Look Back
Nat Adderley Septet | Don't Look Back | Steeplechase | SCCD 31059
Super Session | Welcome & Alive | Vagabond | 6.28604 DP
Don't Lose You Mind
Sonny Boy Williamson Band | One Way Out | Chess | CHD 9116(872271)
Don't Love Me
Coleman Hawkins Quartet | Today And Now | MCA | AS 34
Don't Make A Fool Of Me
Humphrey Lyttelton And His Band | ...It Seems Like Yesterday | Calligraph | CLG LP 001 IMS
Don't Mention My Name
Mark Nightingale Quartet | What I Wanted To Say | Mons Records | MR 874763
Don't Mess With Me Baby
Jim Kahr Group | Back To Chicago | Acoustic Music Records | AMC 1027
Don't Mind If I Do
Blueprint Stage | Puzzle | Mons Records | MR 874817
Don't Misunderstand
Sonny Boy Williamson Band | Blues Giants In Concert-More American Folk Blues Festival 1963 | ACT | 9205-2
Don't Mow Your Lawn
Ray Anderson With The George Gruntz Concert Jazz Band | Ray Anderson Big Band Record | Gramavision | R2 79497
Don't Open Here
Etta James With Orchestra | Peaches | Chess | 427014
Don't Say Goodbye
Roberto Perera Group | Harp And Soul | Inak | 30362
Don't Say Goodbye(Just Leave)
Honeyboy Edwards | White Windows | Evidence | ECD 26039-2
Don't Shoot The Banjo Player('Cause We've Done It Already)
John Scofield Sextet | Hand Jive | Blue Note | 827327-2
Don't Shoot The Messenger
Maria Joao-Aki Takase | Looking For Love:Live At The Leverkusen Jazz Festival | Enja | 5075-2
Don't Shout At Me, Daddy
Miles Davis All Stars | Bopping The Blues | Black Lion | CD 877631-2
Don't Sit Under The Apple Tree
Coleman Hawkins Quartet | Today And Now | MCA | AS 34
Glenn Miller And His Orchestra | The Unforgettable Glenn Miller | RCA | PD 89260
Glenn Miller In Concert | RCA | NL 89216 DP
Glenn Miller And His Orchestra/Army Air Force Band | The Best Of Glenn Miller | RCA | NL 83871 AG
Don't Sleep In The Subway
Susan Weinert Band | The Bottom Line | VeraBra Records | CDVBR 2177-2
Don't Smile Too Soon
Tete Montoliu | The Music I Like To Play Vol.1 | Soul Note | 121180-2
Don't Smoke In Bed
Nina Simone Quartet | Nina Simone-The 60s Vol.1: Ne Me Quitte Pas | Mercury | 838543-2 PMS
Nina Simone Trio | My Baby Just Cares For Me | Charly | CR 30217
Don't Speak
ORF-Bigband | Maurische Anekdoten | EGO | 4017
Don't Squawk
Lee Konitz-Warne Marsh Sextet | That's Jazz Vol.21: Lee Konitz & Warne Marsh | Atlantic | ATL 50298
Don't Stand Up
Good Rockin' Charles With The Aces | The Devil's Music:Mississippi And Memphis/Chicago Blues | Red Lightnin' | RL 0033
Don't Stay Out All Night
Wolfhound-Anne Haigis | The Never Ending Story | BELL Records | BLR 84025
Don't Stop
Johnny Copeland Group | Texas Twister | Edsel | 66.23401 AS
Don't Stop The Carnival
Sonny Rollins Quartet | Planet Jazz:Sonny Rollins | Planet Jazz | 2152062-2
The Complete Sonny Rollins RCA Victor Recordings | RCA | 2668675-2
Sonny Rollins Quintet | Sonny Rollins Play G-Man | Milestone | MCD 9150-2
Don't Stop This Train
Modern Jazz Quartet | A Night At The Opera | Jazz Door | JD 1244
Don't Take Your Love From Me
Coleman Hawkins-Milt Jackson Sextet | Bean Bags | Atlantic | AMCY 1105
Inge Brandenburg mit Werner Müller und seinem Orchester | Why Don't You Take All Of Me | Bear Family Records | BCD 15614 AH
Jessica Williams Trio | Higher Standards | Candid | CCD 79736
Jimmy Scott With Band | Over The Rainbow | Milestone | MCD 9314-2
Joe Venuti-Zoot Sims Sextet | Joe Venuti And Zoot Sims | Chiaroscuro | CR 142
John Coltrane Quintet | John Coltrane-The Prestige Recordings | Prestige | 16 PCD 4405-2
Johnny Hodges Orchestra | The Soul Of Ben Webster | Verve | 527475-2
Jordan Sandke & Jaki Byard And Co. | Rhythm Is Our Business | Stash Records | ST 259
Stan Kenton And His Orchestra | Return To Biloxi | Magic | DAWE 35(881848)
Weslia Whitefield With The Mike Greensill Quartet | High Standards | HighNote Records | HCD 7025
Don't Take Your Love From Me(alt.take)
Carmen McRae With The Johnny Keating Orchestra | For Once In My Life | Atlantic | AMCY 1064
Don't Talk(Put Your Head On My Shoulder)
Roy Dunn | Know'd Them All | Trix Records | TRIX 3312
Don't Tell A Man About His Woman
Lew Stone And His Band | Lew Stone And His Band | Decca | DDV 5005/6 DT
Don't Tell Me
Lizzie Miles With Jelly Roll Morton | The Complete Jelly Roll Morton-Vol.5/6 | RCA | 2126410-2
Don't Throw Your Heart Away
Albert King Blues Band | Wednesday Night In San Francisco | Stax | SCD 8556-2
Don't Throw Your Love On Me So Strong
American Blues Legends 79 | American Blues Legends 79 | Big Bear | 146410

TITELVERZEICHNIS

Don't Trust The Mirror
National Youth Jazz Orchestra | A View From The Hill | Ronnie Scott's Jazz House | JHCD 044
Don't Try This At Home
Dizzy Gillespie Sextet | Jambo Caribe | Verve | 557492-2
Don't Try To Keep Up With The Jones
Rod Mason Band | Dixieland Forever | BELL Records | BLR 89025
Don't Turn Your Back On Me
Roy Ayers Group | Roy Ayers-The Essential Groove:Live | Ronnie Scott's Jazz House | JHCD 035
Don't Walk Outside This Area
Eb Davis Bluesband | Good Time Blues | Acoustic Music Records | AMC 1016
Don't Waste Your Time
William Galison-Mulo Franzl Group | Midnight Sun | Edition Collage | EC 508-2
Don't Watch The Girls
Five Blind Boys Of Alabama | The Five Blind Boys Of Alabama | Heritage Records | HT 315 IMS
Don't Worry Be Happy
Lester Bowie's Brass Fantasy | My Way | DIW | DIW 835 CD
Don't Worry 'Bout A Thing
Woody Herman And His Orchestra | Jazzin' Vol.2: The Music Of Stevie Wonder | Fantasy | FANCD 6088-2
Shirley Scott Quintet | Blue Seven | Original Jazz Classics | OJCCD 1050-2(P 7376)
Don't Worry 'Bout It Baby,Here I Am
Al Casey Quintet | Serenade In Blue | Savoy | SV 0232(MG 12057)
Don't Worry 'Bout Me
Art Tatum | The Tatum Solo Masterpieces Vol.5 | Pablo | 2310790
Benny Goodman And His Orchestra | The Benny Goodman Caravans Vol.4 | Giants Of Jazz | GOJ 1039
Bireli Lagrene Ensemble | Routes To Django & Bireli Swing '81 | Jazzpoint | JP 1055 CD
Bobby Wellins Quartet | Don't Worry 'Bout Me | Cadillac | SGCCD 05
Count Basie And His Orchestra | Basie's Timing | MPS | 88016-2
Erroll Garner Trio | Erroll Garner | Verve | 846191-2 PMS
Etta Jones With The Houston Person Sextet | Fine And Mellow/Save Your Love For Me | Muse | MCD 6002
Jimmy Witherspoon And His All Stars | Blues For Easy Livers | Original Blues Classics | OBCCD 585-2(PR 7475)
Joe Newman Quintet | Jive At Five | Prestige | 61159
June Christy And Her Orchestra | Early June | Fresh Sound Records | FSCD 1011
Lynn Hope Band | Lynn Hope And His Tenor Sax | Pathe | 1546661(Aladdin)
Ruby Braff-Dick Hyman | Manhattan Jazz | Musicmasters | 5031-2
Don't Worry 'Bout Me-
Ella Fitzgerald With The Tommy Flanagan Quartet | Newport Jazz Festival - Live At Carnegie Hall | CBS | CBS 68279
Don't Worry 'Bout The Mule
Louis Jordan And His Tympany Five | Louis Jordan-Let The Good Times Roll: The Complete Decca Recordings 1938-1954 | Bear Family Records | BCD 15557 IH
Louis Jordan With The Chris Barber Band | Louis Jordan&Chris Barber | Black Lion | BLCD 760156
Don't You Go Away My Friend
Jeanie Lambe And The Danny Moss Quartet | The Blue Noise Session | Nagel-Heyer | CD 052
Don't You Go Way Mad
Willie 'The Lion' Smith Duo | Willie 'The Lion ' Smith:The Lion's In Town | Vogue | 2111506-2
Don't You Know
Ornette Coleman Quartet | Sound Museum | Verve | 531657-2
Don't You Know I Care (Or Don't You Care I Know)
Clifford Jordan Quintet | Starting Time | Original Jazz Classics | OJC 147(J 952)
Duke Ellington And His Orchestra | Duke Ellington | Bluebird | ND 86641(3)
Ken Peplowski Quintet | Double Exposure | Concord | CJ 344
Eddie Bert Sextet | The Human Factor | Fresh Sound Records | FSR-CD 5005
Don't You Remember?
Bob Cort Skiffle Group | Kings Of Skiffle | Decca | 6.28132 DP
Don't You Think-
Roy Eldridge-Dizzy Gillespie With The Oscar Peterson Quartet | Roy And Diz | Verve | 521647-2
Don't You Want A Man Like Me
Count Basie And His Orchestra | The Indispensable Count Basie | RCA | ND 89758
Don't You Worry 'Bout A Thing
Carmen Lundy With Band | Moment To Moment | Arabesque Recordings | AJ 0102
Donte's Inferno
Leonard Feather All Stars | Night Blooming | Mainstream | MD CDO 719
Doo In Peru
Georgia Melodians | Georgia Melodians 1924-1926 | Timeless | CBC 1-031
Doo Wah Doo
Jay McShann Quartet | Goin' To Kansas City | Stony Plain | SPCD 1286
The Man From Muskogee | Affinity | AFF 147
Doobie Doobie Blues
Amos Hoffman Quartet | The Dreamer | Fresh Sound Records | FSNT 060 CD
Doobie Time
Kenny Baker And His Band | Kenny Baker Presents:The Half Dozen...After Hours | Lake | LACD 88
Doodlin'
Art Blakey And The Jazz Messengers | The History Of Art Blakey And The Jazz Messengers | Blue Note | 797190-2
Dee Dee Bridgewater With Her Quintet | Love And Peace-A Tribute To Horace Silver | Verve | 527470-2
Dizzy Gillespie And His Orchestra | Dizzy Gillespie:Birks Works-The Verve Big Band Sessions | Verve | 527900-2
Dizzy Gillespie Band | Dizzy Gillespie At Newport | Verve | 513754-2 PMS
Mar Murphy With The Ernie Wilkins Orchestra | RAH | Original Jazz Classics | OJCCD 141-2(R 9395)
Martin Schmitt | Handful Of Blues | ESM Records | ESM 9303
Handful Of Blues | AH Records | ESM 9303
The Poll Winners | Exploring The Scene | Original Jazz Classics | OJCCD 969-2(C 7581)
Toni Jannotta Group | Just Jazz | TCB Records | TCB 99052
Doogie
James Dapogny's Chicago Jazz Band | Laughing At Life | Discovery | 74006-2
Doom
Massimo De Mattia Group | The Silent Drama | SPLASC(H) Records | CD H 442-2
Toshinori Kondo | Touchstone | JA & RO | JARO 4172-2
Doom Stone
Noodband | Shiver | Moers Music | 01094
Door
Frank Tannehill | Frank Tannehill(1932-1941) | Story Of Blues | CD 3526-2
Door No.3
Baikida Carroll Quintet | Door Of The Cage | Soul Note | 121123-2
Door To Freedom
Brownie McGhee Trio | Brownie's Blues | Original Blues Classics | OBCCD 505-2(BV 1042)
Doors
Tom Mega + Band | Backyards Of Pleasure | ITM Records | ITM 1432
Doors(Very Short Tales)
Gunter Hampel Group | Cosmic Dancer | Birth | 0024
Doot Dat
Buddy Johnson And His Orchestra | Buddy And Ella Johnson 1953-1964 | Bear Family Records | BCD 15479 DH
Doot Doot Dow
Walter Bishop Jr. Group | Summertime | Fresh Sound Records | FSR-CD 0011
Doozy
Benny Carter And His Orchestra | Further Definitions/Additions To Further Definotions | Impulse(MCA) | 951229-2
Benny Carter Quintet With Jon Hendricks | Benny Carter Songbook Vol.2 | Musicmasters | 65155-2
Dope Music-
Bryan Lee Group | Live at The Old Absinthe House Bar...Saturday Night | Blues Beacon | BLU-1032 2
Doppel
Peter Bolte-Marcio Doctor | Zeitraum | Jazz Haus Musik | JHM 0113 CD
Doppelbelastung
Titi Winterstein Quintet | Saitenstra en | Intercord | 160117
Dorafo
A Band Of Friends | Because Of You | Chesky | JD 63
Doralice
Getz-Gilberto Quintet | Getz/Gilberto:The Girl From Ipanema | CTI Records | PDCTI 1105-2
Stan Getz Quintet Feat. Astrud Gilberto | Getz/Gilberto | Verve | 589595-2 SACD
Terence Blanchard/Donald Harrison Quintet | Discemment | Concord | CCD 43008
DoReMi
Paris Washboard | California Here We Come | Stomp Off Records | CD 1280
Dorham's Epitaph
Kenny Clarke-Francy Boland And Co. | The Golden 8 | Blue Note | 869935-9
Dorica
JoAnne Brackeen Trio | Where Legends Dwell | Ken Music | 660.56.021
Dorkay House
The Blue Notes Legacy | Live In South Afrika 1964 | Ogun | OGCD 007
Dorman Road
Bruce Ditmas & D 3 | Spontaneous Combustion | Tutu Records | 888126-2
Dorme Profundo
Padouk | Padouk | SPLASC(H) Records | H 192
Dorotea's Studie
Peter Herbolzheimer Rhythm Combination & Brass | Friends And Sihouettes | Koala Records | CD P 25
Dorothy
Joe Hill Louis | Joe Hill Louis: The Be-Bop Boy | Bear Family Records | BCD 15524 AH
Dorothy Mae
Dorothy Donegan Trio | The Many Faces Of Dorothy Donegan | Storyville | STCD 8362
Dorothy Runs Away
Sun Ra And His Astro-Infinity Arkestra | Holiday For Soul Dance | Evidence | ECD 22011-2
Dörrmattan
Jimmy Dorsey And His Orchestra | The Radio Years | London | HMG 5022 AN
Dos
Ekkehard Jost-Vinko Globokar | Some Other Tapes | Fish Music | FM 009/10 CD
Dos Á Dos
Pablo Ziegler And His Quintet For New Tango | Asfalto-Street Tango | RCA | 2663266-2
Dos De Tus Mascaras
Hernan Merlo Quintet | Consin | Fresh Sound Records | FSNT 150 CD
Dos Marias
Daniel Messina Band | Imagenes | art-mode-records | 990014
Dos Palabras Necesarias
Quique Sinesi & Daniel Messina | Prioridad A la Emoción | art-mode-records | AMR 21061
Dos Soles
Jonas Hellborg Group | Jonas Hellborg Group | Day Eight Music | DEMCD 025
Dose Hassiu
Dave Spencer & The Bluebirds | Live In Europe | Crosscut | CCD 11047
Dot Com Blues
Mongo Santamaria Orchestra | Skins | Milestone | MCD 47038-2
Dottie
Jacques Demierre/Maurice Magnoni | Disque | Plainisphare | PAV 802
D'Ou La Voix
Anthony Braxton/Mario Pavone | Duets (1993) | Music & Arts | CD 786
Double Bass Hit
Pat Metheny Group | Quartet | Geffen Records | GED 24978
Double Blind
Thomas Stabenow Duo | Clips | UJQ Production | 1
Double Check Stomp-
Chris Barber's Jazz And Blues Band | 40 Years Jubilee | Timeless | CD TTD 589
Double Concerto For Two Electric Guitars And Symphony Orchestra
Rosetta Howard And Her Hep Cats | The 30's Girls | Timeless | CBC 1-026
Double Deal
George Shearing With The Montgomery Brothers | Wes Montgomery-The Complete Riverside Recordings | Riverside | 12 RCD 4408-2
Wes Montgomery Quintet | Wes And Friends | Milestone | M 47013
Double Density-
Miles Donahue Quartet | Double Dribble | Timeless | CD SJP 392
Double Exposure
Herbie Nichols Trio | Herbie Nichols:The Complete Blue Note Recordings | Blue Note | 859352-2
Double Exposure(alt.take)
Harald Rüschenbaum Orchestra | Double Faces | Swingtime | 8206
Double Image
Miles Davis Group | Live In Paris 1969 | Jazz Door | JD 1201
Double Image-
Miles Davis Quintet | Double Image | Moon Records | MCD 010/11-2
Double Mail
Brötzmann-Miller-Moholo Trio | Opened But Hardly Touched | FMP | 0840/50
Double Rainbow -> Chovendo Na Roseira
Double Scotch
Stephane Grappelli Trio With Marcel Azzola | Stephane Grappelli In Toky | Denon Compact Disc | CY-77130
Double Talk
The McGhee-Navarro Boptet | The Fabulous Fats Navarro Vol.2 | Blue Note | 0677208
Double Talk(alt.master)
Howard McGhee-Fats Navarro Sextet | Fats Navarro/Tadd Dameron:Complete Blue Note & Capitol Sessions | Definitive Records | DRCD 11191
Double Tripper
Donald Harrison Trio | Heroes | Nagel-Heyer | CD 2041
Double Trouble
Fourplay | Fourplay...Yes,Please! | Warner | 9362-47694-2
Hampton Hawes Trio | Northern Windows Plus | Prestige | PRCD 24278-2
Muddy Waters Band | Muddy Waters Sings Big Bill Broonzy | Chess | CH 9197
Putney Dandridge Band | Putney Dandridge 1935-1936 | Timeless | CBC 1-023
Double Trouble:
Vanasse/Vitous | Nouvelle Cuisine | Justin Time | JTR 8406
Double Vision
Kölner Saxophon Mafia With Guests | Kölner Saxophon Mafia: 20 Jahre Saxuelle Befreiung | Jazz Haus Musik | JHM 0115 CD
Double Weasel
Hank Mobley Sextet | Hank Mobley With Donald Byrd And Lee Morgan | Blue Note | 300138(1540)
Double Whiskey
George Braith Quartet | Double Your Pleasure | Paddle Wheel | KICJ 114
Double-O
Count Basie And His Orchestra | Basie On Roulette, Vol. 1: E : MC 2 : Count Basie Orchestra+Neal HeftArrangeme | Roulette | CDP 793273-2
Doubt
Leroy Jenkins Quartet | Space Minds,New Worlds,Survival America | Tomato | 2696512
Doubts
Michal Urbaniak Quartet | Songbird | Steeplechase | SCCD 31278
Douce Ambiance
Boulou Ferre-Elios Ferre Duo | Pour Django | Steeplechase | SCCD 31120
Doug The Jitterbug
John King Trio | Electric World | Ear-Rational | ECD 1016
Doughnuts
Lionel Hampton And His All Stars | Masters Of Jazz Vol.8 | RCA | NL 89540 DP
Douglas 64(part 1-3)
Chuck Loeb Group | Jazz City Christmas,Vol.1 | Jazz City | 660.53.006
Doug's Blues
Hank Mobley Quintet | Jazz Message No.2 | Savoy | SV 0158(MG 12092)
Doujie
The Montgomery Brothers | Wes Montgomery-The Complete Riverside Recordings | Riverside | 12 RCD 4408-2
Doujie(alt.take)
The Alternative Wes Montgomery | Milestone | MCD 47065-2
Doujie(take 8)
John Zorn Naked City | Naked City-Grand Guignol | Avant | AVAN 002
Doundounba
Spies & Guests | By The Way Of The World | Telarc Digital | CD 83305
Doust
Ahmed El-Salamouny/Claudio Menandro/Gilson De Assis | Aquarela | FSM | FCD 97770
Douz
Wayne Krantz Trio | 2 Drinks Minimum | Enja | ENJ-9043 2
Dove Gloria
Paolo Fresu Quartet | Angel | RCA | 2155864-2
Dove Niente Accade
Nino De Rose & Friends | Jazz Voices: It's Always Jazz | SPLASC(H) Records | H 124
Down
Chet Baker Trio | Chet Baker In Bologna | Dreyfus Jazz Line | FDM 36558-9
Donald Byrd Quartet | Au Chat Qui Peche 1958 | Fresh Sound Records | FSCD 1028
Miles Davis Sextet | Dig | Prestige | P 24054
Miles Davis-Birdland Days | Fresh Sound Records | FSR-CD 0124
Norbert Gottschalk-Frank Haunschild | The Art Of The Duo:Favorite Songs | Mons Records | MR 874813
Carlos Garnett Quartet | Under Nubian Skies | HighNote Records | HCD 7023
Down Among The Sheltering Palms
Eddie Condon And His Orchestra | Big Band Bounce And Boogie:At The Jazz Band Ball-Eddie Condon | Affinity | AFS 1021
Down At The Landing
John Lee Hooker Band | House Of The Blues | Chess | CHD 9258(872282)
Down At You Buryin'
Lightnin' Hopkins | Lightnin' Hopkins Sings The Blues | Pathe | 2C 068-83075(Imperial)
Down By The Old Mill Stream
Sidney Bechet With Andre Reweliotty And His Orchestra | En Concert Avec Europe 1 | Laserlight | 710440
Down By The Old Well
Albert Ayler Quartet | Lions Abroad Volume One:Tenor Titans | Black Lion | BLCD 7620-2
Down By The Riverside
Benny Green Trio | Testifyin'!-Live at The Village Vanguard | Blue Note | 798171-2
Bob Scobey's Frisco Band | Victor Jazz History Vol.19:Dixieland Revival | RCA | 2135738-2
Bunk Johnson With The Yerba Buena Jazz Band | Bunk & Lu | Good Time Jazz | GTCD 12024-2
Chris Barber & The Ramblers | The Golden Years Of Revival Jazz,Vol.12 | Storyville | STCD 5517
Chris Barber's Jazz And Blues Band | He's Got The Whole World In His Hand | Timeless | CD TTD 599
Chris Barber's Jazz Band | Copulatin' Jazz | Great Southern Records | GS 11025
City Ramblers | Kings Of Skiffle | Decca | 6.28132 DP
Dodo Greene With The Ike Quebec Quintet | The Blue Testament | Blue Note | 780703-2
First Revolution Singers | A Cappella Gospel Anthology | Tight Harmony Records | TH 199404
George Lewis And His Ragtime Band | Jazz At Vesper | Original Jazz Classics | OJCCD 1721-2(RLP 230)
Golden Gate Quartet | Spirituals To Swing 1955-69 | EMI Records | 791569-2
Hampton Hawes Trio | The Sermon | Original Jazz Classics | OJCCD 1067-2(C 7653)
Henry Butler | Blues & More Vol.1 | Windham Hill | 34 10138-2
Jimmy Smith And Wes Montgomery With Orchestra | Jimmy & Wes-The Dynamic Duo | Verve | 521445-2
Jimmy Smith And Wes Montgomery With The Oliver Nelson Orchestra | Jimmy Smith:Best Of The Verve Years | Verve | 527950-2
Jonah Jones Sextet | Harlem Jump And Swing | Affinity | AFF 96
Louis Armstrong With Sy Oliver's Choir And Orchestra | Louis And The Good Book | Verve | 549593-2
Jazz Collection:Louis Armstrong | Laserlight | 24366
Louis Cottrell Trio | New Orleans-The Living Legends:Bourbon Street-The Louis Cottrell Trio | Original Jazz Classics | OJCCD 1836-2
Magnificant Seventh's Brass Band | Authentic New Orleans Jazz Funeral | Mardi Gras Records | MG 1012
Down By The Sycamore Tree
Stan Getz Quartet | Stan Getz:The Complete 1952-1954 Small Group Sessions(Master Takes),Vol.3 | Blue Moon | BMCD 1036
Stan The Man | Verve | 815239-1 IMS
Down Deep
Philippe Pares Et Son Orchestre-Jazz | Le Jazz En France Vol.9:Pionniers Du Jazz Francais 1906-1931 | Pathe | 1552551
Down Down Down
Louis Jordan And His Tympany Five | Look Out Sisters-Unissued Film Soundtracks 1944-1948 | Krazy Kat | KK 7415 IMS
Down For Double
Lambert, Hendricks And Ross | Lambert,Hendricks & Ross:Sing A Song Of Basie | CTI Records | PDCTI 1115-2
Count Basie And His Orchestra | Sixteen Men Swinging | Verve | 2-2517 IMS
Down For The Count
Lambert, Hendricks And Ross | Lambert,Hendricks & Ross:Sing A Song Of Basie | CTI Records | PDCTI 1115-2
Down Here Below
Rodney Kendrick Group | The Secrets Of Rodney Kendrick | Verve | 517558-2
Down Here In The Ground
Anthony Ortega Quintet | Rain Dance | Discovery | DS 788 IMS
Down Here On The Ground
Jimmy Ponder Sextet | Down Here On The Ground | Milestone | M 9121
Oscar Peterson Trio | En Concert Avec Europe 1 | Laserlight | 710443/48
Three Originals:Motion&Emotions/Tristeza On Piano/Hello Herbie | MPS | 521059-2
Richard Elliot Sextet | City Speak | Blue Note | 832620-2

Down Hill Run
Howard McGhee Sextet | Maggie | Savoy | SV 0269
Down Home Blues
Fats Waller | Piano Solos | RCA | ND 89741
Down Home Funk
Memphis Minnie(Mamie Smith) | Blind Willie McTell/Memphis Minnie-Love Changin' Blues | Biograph | BLP 12035
Down Home Rag
Chris Barber's Jazz Band | Best Of British Jazz From The BBC Jazz Club Vol.3 | Upbeat Jazz | URCD 120
Lu Watters' Yerba Buena Jazz Band | The San Francisco Style Vol.2:Watters' Original & Ragtime | Good Time Jazz | GTCD 12002-2
Down Home Where The Blowfish Roam
Wynton Marsalis Quintet | Soul Gestures In Southern Blue Vol.2: Uptown Ruler | CBS | 468660-2
Down In Chihuahua
Stan Kenton And His Orchestra | The Lighter Side | Creative World | ST 1050
Down In Copenhagen
John Williams' Synco Jazzers | Alexander Where's That Band?-Paramount Recordings 1926-1928 | Frog | DGF 13
Down In Honky Tonk Town
Bob Wilber's Bechet Legacy | The Hamburg Concert-Tribute To A Legend | Nagel-Heyer | CD 028
Charlie Love Jazz Band | Kid Sheik With Charlie Love And His Cado Jazz Band | 504 Records | 504CD 21
Paris Washboard | California Here We Come | Stomp Off Records | CD 1280
The Bell Gal & Her Dixieland Boys feat. Jim Robinson | New Orleans-The Living Legends:Sweet Emma | Original Jazz Classics | OJCCD 1832-2
Down In The Depths
Ella Fitzgerald With The Tommy Flanagan Quartet | Ella Fitzgerald:Newport Jazz Festival-Live at Carnegie Hall | CBS | C2K 66809
Wayne Shorter Quintet | Introducing Wayne Shorter | Vee Jay Recordings | VJ 007
Down In The Line
Jay Leonhart-Joe Beck | There's Gonna Be Trouble | Sunnyside | SSC 1006(952110)
Down In Town
Al Bowlly With The Ray Noble Orchestra | The Classic Years In Digital Stereo: Al Bowlly With Ray Noble | CDS Records Ltd. | REB 649
Down On Teddy's Hill
Minton's Playhouse All Stars | Jazz Legacy 64: Charlie Christian-1941 Live Sessions | Vogue | 500114
Down South
Chris Jarrett | Piano Moments | Take Twelve On CD | TT 007-2
Muddy Waters Group | More Real Folk Blues | Chess | CH 9278
Down South Camp Meeting
Benny Goodman And His Orchestra | The Benny Goodman Selection | CBS | 467280-2
Fletcher Henderson And His Orchestra | Wild Party | Hep | 1009
Mark Murphy And His Sextet | Bop For Kerouac | Muse | MCD 5253
Down The Depths Of The 90th Floor
Charley Patton | Founder Of The Delta Blues | Yazoo | YAZ 1020
Down The Line
Sonny Rollins Quintet | Easy Living | Milestone | M 9080
Down The Old Mill Stream
Bert Ambrose And His Orchestra | Saturday Night | Decca | DDV 5003/4 DT
Down The River
International Commission For The Prevention Of Musical Border Control,The | The International Commission For The Prevention Of Musical Border Control | VeraBra Records | CDVBR 2093-2
Andy Narell Group | Down The Road | Windham Hill | 34 10139-2
Down The Road I Go
Urs Leimgruber/John Wolf Brennan | Mountain Hymn | L+R Records | CDLR 45002
Down The Street, 'Round The Corner Blues
Barney Kessel And Friends | Barney Plays Kessel | Concord | CCD 6009
Down The Walkway-
Lightnin' Hopkins Trio | The Blues Of Lightnin' Hopkins | Original Blues Classics | OBCCD 532-2(BV 1019)
Down There Baby
Clifford Jordan Big Band | Play What You Feel | Mapleshade | 03232
Down Through The Years
Clifford Jordan Quintet | Starting Time | Original Jazz Classics | OJC 147(J 952)
Down Time
Axel Zinowsky Quartet | Mindwalk | Acoustic Music Records | 319.1064.2
Down With It
Blossom Dearie Quartet | Verve Jazz Masters 51:Blossom Dearie | Verve | 529906-2
Down With Love
Eddie Condon All Stars | Town Hall Concerts Vol.11 | Jazzology | JCD 1021/23
Marie Bergman With Band | Fruit | Stunt Records | STUCD 19603
Down Yonder
Buddy Johnson And His Orchestra | Go Ahead & Rock Rock Rock | Official | 6011
Downbeats
Vincent Herring Quintet | Dawnbird | Landmark | LCD 1533-2
Downhearted Blues
Lillian Boutté And Her Group | Lipstick Traces(A New Orleans R&B Session) | Blues Beacon | BLU-1011 2
Downside Up
Duke Jordan | Duke Jordan-Solo Masterpieces Vol.2 | Steeplechase | SCCD 31300
Downstairs
Plas Johnson Band | Rockin' With The Plas | Pathe | 2C 068-86529(Capitol)
Downstairs Blues Upstairs
Kenny Burrell Quintet | Guitar Forms | Verve | 521403-2
Downstairs(alt.take 1)
Guitar Forms | Verve | 521403-2
Downstairs(alt.take 2)
Guitar Forms | Verve | 521403-2
Downstairs(alt.take 3)
Guitar Forms | Verve | 521403-2
Downstairs(alt.take 4)
Jay Anderson Sextet | Local Color | dmp Digital Music Productions | CD 507
Downtown
Guido Manusardi Quartet | Bra Session | SPLASC(H) Records | H 125
Paul Bley | Blues For Red | Red Records | 123238 2
Frank Kirchner Group | Frank Kirchner | Laika Records | LK 93-036
Downtown Blues
Edmond Hall Sextet | Commodore Classics In Swing | Commodore | 9031-72723-2
Downtown N.Y.
Alvin Queen-Dusko Goykovich Quintet | A Day In Holland | Sound Hills | NQ 3407 IMS
Downtown Waltz
Art Farmer Quintet | On The Road | Original Jazz Classics | OJCCD 478-2
Doxology
Ronnell Bright Trio | The Ronnell Bright Trio | Fresh Sound Records | FSR 559(Polydor 46106)
Doxology(Memory Of Dick)
Branford Marsalis Trio | Trio Jeepy | CBS | 465134-2
Doxy
Bruce Forman-George Cables Duo | Dynamics | Concord | CJ 279
Dexter Gordon Quartet | Lions Abroad Volume One:Tenor Titans | Black Lion | BLCD 7620-2
Oliver Nelson Quintet | Taking Care Of Business | Original Jazz Classics | OJCCD 1784-2(NJ 8233)
Phil Woods And His European Rhythm Machine | Americans Swinging In Paris:Phil Woods | EMI Records | 539654-2
Le Jazz En France-Vol.8 | Pathe | 1727321
Rich Perry Trio | Doxy | Steeplechase | SCCD 31473
Sonny Rollins Quartet | Sonny Rollins & Co | Bluebird | ND 82496
Dozen Down
Chris Hinze Combination | Summer Dance | Keytone | KYT 701
DPM
Johannes Cernota | Sparta | JA & RO | JARO 4136-2
D'Podophtalma-
Maria Joao/Aki Takase/Niels-Henning Orsted-Pedersen | Alice | Enja | 6096-2
Dr. Dee Dee
Tim Sund Quartet | About Time | Laika Records | LK 93-043
Henry Butler | Blues & More Vol.1 | Windham Hill | 34 10138-2
Dr. Free-Zee
Max Roach Plus Four | Max Roach + 4 | EmArCy | 822673-2 PMS
Dr. Gieler's Presccription
Georg Ruby-Wollie Kaiser | Ruby Domesticus Vugaris | Jazz Haus Musik | JHM 26
Dr. No's Fantasy
Count Basie And His Orchestra | Basie Meets Bond | Capitol | 538225-2
Dr. No's Fantasy(alt.take)
Suzanne Dean Group | I Wonder | Nova | NOVA 9028-2
Dr. R
Pata Trio | Lucy Und Der Ball | Jazz Haus Musik | JHM 34
Dr. Slate
Steve Khan Quartet | Eyewitness | Antilles | AN 1018(802758)
Dr. Wong's Bag
David Torn | Tripping Over God | CMP Records | CMP CD 1007
Dr.Bär(für Onkel Manfred)
Aki Takase | Shima Shoka | Enja | 6062-2
Dr.Demento
Vital Information | Live Around The World Where We Come From Tour '98-'99 | Intuition Records | INT 3296-2
World Trio | World Trio | VeraBra Records | CDVBR 2052-2
Dr.Do-Right
Kölner Saxophon Mafia | Live | Jazz Haus Musik | JHM 12
Dr.Feelgood
Dee Dee Bridgewater With Her Trio | Live In Paris | Verve | 014317-2
Doctor Feelgood-The Original Piano Red | Music Is Medicine | L+R Records | LR 42019
Dr.Jackle
Jackie McLean Quartet | Dr. Jackle | Steeplechase | SCCD 36005
Rene Thomas Quintet | Jazz In Paris:René Thomas-Meeting Mister Thomas | EmArCy | 549812-2
Stanley Cowell Trio | Equipoise | Galaxy | GXY 5125
Lenny White Group | Renderers Of Spirit | Hip Bop | HIBD 8014
Dr.Jackle-Africa Talks To You
Good Fellas | Good Fellas 2 | Paddle Wheel | KICJ 115
Dr.Jazz
Jelly Roll Morton's Red Hot Peppers | Victor Jazz History Vol.2:Black Chicago | RCA | 2128556-2
Dr.Jeckyll & Mr.Hyde
Gil Evans Orchestra | Little Wing | Circle Records | RK 13-101978/13 IMS
Dr.Jive(part 1)
Flora Purim And Her Sextet | Butterfly Dreams | Original Jazz Classics | OJCCD 315-2
Dr.Jive(part 2)
Lotz Of Music | Puasong Daffriek | Laika Records | LK 94-054
Dr.Kimble
Lionel Hampton And His Big Band | Outrageous | Timeless | CD SJP 163
Dr.Moriarty,Suposo
Jukkis Uotila Group | Avenida | Stunt Records | 18807
Dr.Pretty
Enrico Rava Quartet | The Plot | ECM | 1078
Dr.Ra And Mr.Va
Martin Jäger | Boogie Woogie And Ragtime Piano Contest | Gold Records | 11034 AS
Dra Kumba
Adam Noidlt-Intermission | Eine Permanent Helle Fläche | Jazz Haus Musik | JHM 53 CD
Drachentanz
Grant Green Orchestra | Green Is Beautiful | Blue Note | 300275(4342)
Dracula's Breakfast
Flip Phillips Quartet | Flipenstein | Progressive | PRO 7063 IMS
Drafadelic In Db
Chris Flory Quartet | City Life | Concord | CCD 4589
Drag
Duke Ellington And His Orchestra | Yale Concert | Fantasy | F 9433
Drag-
Lou Stein | Stompin' 'Em Down | Chiaroscuro | CR 173
Drag-Dog
Miles Davis Quintet | The Miles Davis Selection | CBS | 471623-2
Draggin' In The Line
Al Cooper And His Savoy Sultans | Big Band Bounce & Boogie:Jump Steady | Affinity | AFS 1009
Dragon City
Arild Andersen Quintet With The Cikada String Quartet | Hyperborean | ECM | 1631(537342-2)
Dragon Dance
Randy Sandke Sextet | The Sandke Brothers | Stash Records | ST-CD 575(875901)
Dragonetti's Dream
Eric Watson Quartet | Full Metal Quartet | Owl Records | 159572-2
Dragonfly
Gerry Mulligan Quartet With Brassensemble and Guests | Dragonfly | Telarc Digital | CD 83377
Dragons Are
Stan Kenton And His Orchestra | Adventures In Blues | Capitol | 520089-2
Dragonwyck
Stan Kenton With The Danish Radio Big Band | Stan Kenton With The Danish Radio Big Band | Storyville | STCD 8340
Louis Cottrell Trio | New Orleans-The Living Legends:Bourbon Street-The Louis Cottrell Trio | Original Jazz Classics | OJCCD 1836-2
Drahtseilakt
Ulrich P. Lask Group | Lask | ECM | 1217
Drain Brain
Phil Minton | A Doughnut In One Hand | FMP | CD 91
Dramatic Interplay
Glenn Miller And The Army Air Force Band | I Sustain The Wings Vol.3(September 1943) | Magic | DAWE 78
Drame
David Moss Duets | Full House | Moers Music | 02010
Draum
Victory Of The Better Man | L'Utopiste | CMP Records | CMP CD 44
Draw
Duke Jordan | When You're Smiling | Steeplechase | SCCD 37023/24
Drawing Down The Moon
Bob Cooper And His Orchestra | Shifting Winds | Affinity | AFF 59
Drawing Room Blues
Duke Ellington-Billy Strayhorn Duo | Solos, Duets And Trios | RCA | ND 82178(847130)
Evan Parker Electro-Acoustic Ensemble | Drawn Inward | ECM | 1693
DrawnInward
George Guesnon | George Guesnon | American Music | AMCD-87
Dream
Billy Cobham Group | By Design | fnac Muisc | 662144
Dinah Washington With The Hal Mooney Orchestra | A Slick Chick(On The Mellow Side)-The Rhythm&Blues Years | EmArCy | 814184-1 IMS
Ella Fitzgerald With The Nelson Riddle Orchestra | The Johnny Mercer Songbook | Verve | 823247-2 PMS
Rob McConnell Jive 5 | Jive 5 | Concord | CCD 4437
Thomas Clausen Trio With Gary Burton | Flowers And Trees | M.A Music | A 805-2
Tom Harrell Orchestra | Time's Mirror | RCA | 2663524-2
Tuck And Patti | Dream | Windham Hill | 34 10130-2
Vince Jones Group | Watch What Happens | Intuition Records | INT 3070-2
Zoot Sims Quintet | Zoot Sims:The Complete 1944-1954 Small Group Sessions(Master Takes),Vol.3 | Blue Moon | BMCD 1040
Dream-
Chick Corea And Gary Burton With A String Quartet | Lyric Suite For Sextet | ECM | 1260
Rosemary Clooney And Her Band | Sings The Lyrics Of Johnny Mercer | Concord | CCD 4333
Allotria Jazz Band | Cleared For Take Off | Elite Special | 73331
Dream A Little Dream Of Me
Dave McKenna | Shadows 'N' Dreams | Concord | CCD 4467
Ella Fitzgerald And Her All Stars | All That Jazz | Pablo | 2310938-2
Ella Fitzgerald And Louis Armstrong With Sy Oliver And His Orchestra | Ella Fitzgerald 75th Birthday Celebration:The Original Decca Recordings | GRP | GRP 26192
Ella Fitzgerald With The Count Basie Orchestra | Ella & Basie-On The Sunny Side Of The Street | Verve | 821576-2
Flip Phillips And His Orchestra | Flip Phillips Complete 1947-1951 Verve Master Takes | Definitive Records | DRCD 11201
Laura Fygi With Band | Bewitched | Verve | 514724-2
Lillian Boutté And Her American Band | Live In Tivoli | Music Mecca | CD 1030-2
Louis Armstrong And His All Stars | What A Wonderful World | MCA | MCD 01876
Nat King Cole Trio | Nat King Cole:Route 66 | Dreyfus Jazz Line | FDM 36716-2
Great Capitol Masters | Pathe | 1566251(Capitol)
Rob McConnell-Ed Bickert-Don Thompson | Three For The Road | Concord | CCD 4765
Dream A Little Dream Of Me-
Roscoe Mitchell And The Note Factory | Nine To Get Ready | ECM | 1651(539725-2)
Dream And Response
Attila Zoller | Attila Zoller:The Last Recordings | Enja | ENJ-9349 2
Dream Boat
Robin Kenyatta Quartet | Beggars And Stealers | Muse | MR 5095
Dream Called Love
Isato Nakagawa | Dream Catcher | Acoustic Music Records | 319.1123.2
Dream Clock
Swim Two Birds | No Regrets | Laika Records | 35101342
Dream Come True
La Vienta | Forgotten Romance | Telarc Digital | CD 83380
Dream Dancing
Jimmy Knepper Quintet | Dream Dancing | Criss Cross | Criss 1024
Mel Tormé With The George Shearing Trio | An Evening At Charlie's | Concord | CCD 4248
Zoot Sims Quartet | Getting Sentimental | Choice | CHCD 71006
On The Korner | Pablo | 2310953-2
Warm Tenor | Pablo | 2310831-2
Dream Drops
Tarika Blue | Tarika Blue | Chiaroscuro | CR 164
Dream For Claudine
Michele Rosewoman And Quintessence | Contrast High | Enja | ENJ-5091 2
Dream Gypsy
Elvin Jones-Takehisa Tanaka Quartet | Elvin Jones Introduces Takehisa Tanaka | Enja | ENJ-7081 2
Dream In June
Bill Laswell/Jones Hellborg Group | Niels & The New York Street Percussionists | ITM Records | ITM 1453
Dream Of A Dying City
Sainkho Namtchylak | Lost Rivers | FMP | CD 42
Dream Of Muskogee
Ralph Flanagan And His Orchestra | Dance Again Part 2 | Magic | DAWE 75
Dream Of Plancton
Pat Metheny Group | Letter From Home | Geffen Records | GED 24245
Dream Of Return
Ensemble FisFüz | SimSim | Peregrina Music | PM 50211
Dream Of The Day
Dave Holland Qartet | Dream Of The Elders | ECM | 1572(529084-2)
Dream Of The Elders
Steve Coleman-Dave Holland | Phase Space | DIW | DIW 865 CD
Dream Of The Old
George Adams-Dannie Richmond Quintet | Gentlemen's Agreement | Soul Note | 121057-2
Dream Of You
Earl Hines Trio | The Indispensable Earl Hines Vol.5/6:The Bob Thiele Sessions | RCA | ND 89618
Jimmie Lunceford And His Orchestra | Jimmy Lunceford - Rythm Is Our Business | MCA | 1302
Oscar Peterson-Milt Jackson Quartet | Reunion Blues | MPS | 817490-1
Dream On
Eddie Gomez Trio | Down Stretch | Black-Hawk | BKH 531 CD
Dream Sequence
Andre Ekyan And His Orchestra | Django Reinhardt:Djangology | EMI Records | 780659-2
Dream Stalker
Paul Horn Group | The Magic Of Findhorn | Golden Flute Records | GFR 2003
Dream Stone
Crusaders | Ghetto Blaster | MCA | ???
Dream Time
Kenny Clarke And His Orchestra | Kenny Clarke | Swing | SW 8411 IMS
Dream Train
Roy Hargrove's Crisol | Habana | Verve | 537563-2
Dream Traveler
Lee Konitz Quartet | The New York Album | Soul Note | SN 1169
Dream Walk(1)
Loft Line | Source | Laika Records | 35101122
Dream Walk(2)
Steve Halpern-Daniel Kobialka | Recollections | Gramavision | 18-7823-1
Dream With You
Rahsaan Roland Kirk Orchestra | Rahsaan Roland Kirk-Yusef Lateef:Seperate But Equal | 32 Jazz | 32111
Dreamed I Hand The Blues
Astrud Gilberto With Antonio Carlos Jobim And The Marty Paich Orchestra | The Astrud Gilberto Album | Verve | 823009-1
Dreamer
Erica Lindsay Quintet | Dreamers | Candid | CCD 79040
Frank Haunschild & Tom Van Der Geld | Getting Closer | Acoustic Music Records | 319.1170.2
McCoy Tyner Quartet | Double Trios | Denon Compact Disc | CY-1128
Sarah Vaughan With Band | Copacabana | Pablo | 2312125
Dreamer(Vivo Sohando)
JoAnne Brackeen Trio | AFT | Timeless | CD SJP 115
Dreamer's Tale
Paulinho Da Costa Orchestra | Happy People | Original Jazz Classics | OJCCD 783-2(2312102)
Dreamflow
Joe Beck Group | Back To Beck | dmp Digital Music Productions | CD 464
Dreamin' Blues
John Marshall Quintet | Dreamin' On The Hudson | Organic Music | ORGM 9713
Dreamin' On The Hudson
Eddie Daniels Quartet With String Quartet | Memos From Paradise | GRP | GRP 95612
Dreaming At...-
Willie Reed | The Blues Of Texas, Arkansas & Louisiana 1927-1932 | Yazoo | YAZ 1004
Dreaming Of Abroad
Art Ensemble Of Chicago | Nice Guys | ECM | 1126

Dreaming Of The Master
Live In Berlin | West Wind | WW 2051
Dreaming Of The North
Adam Rudolph's Moving Pictures | Skyway | Soul Note | 121269-2
Dreaming Of You
Traubeli Weiß Ensemble | Guitar Moments | Take Twelve On CD | TT 006-2
Dreamland
Sidsel Endresen Quartet | So I Write | ECM | 1408(841776-2)
Tony Williams Quintet | Angel Street | Blue Note | 748494-2
Dreams
Niels Lan Doky Quartet | Dreams | Milestone | MCD 9178-2
James Newton Quintet | The Mystery School | India Navigation | IN 1046
Dreams And Realities
Eddie Harris Group | The Versatile Eddie Harris | Atlantic | SD 8807
Dreams Are Made For Children
Danny Toan Trio | Big Foot | Inak | 8613
Dream's Monk
Rabih Abou-Khalil Group | Roots & Sprouts | Enja | ENJ-9373 2
Dreams Of A Dying City
Bob Degen Trio With Zbigniew Namyslowski | Joy | Dr.Jazz Records | 8611-2
Dreams So Real
Cindy Blackman Quartet | Trio + Two | Freelance | FRL-CD 015
Orchestra Jazz Siciliana | Orchestra Jazz Siciliana Plays The Music Of Carla Bley | Watt | XtraWatt/4
Sweet Miss Coffy With The Mississippi Burnin' Blues Revue | Sweet Miss Coffy | Mardi Gras Records | MG 1021
Dreams(If Time Weren't)
Furio Di Castri-Paolo Fresu | Urlo | yvp music | CD 3035
Dreamstepper
Ku-umba Frank Lacy & The Poker Bigband | Songs From The Musical 'Poker' | Tutu Records | 888150-2*
Dreamstuff
Brad Mehldau Trio | Anything Goes | Warner | 9362-48608-2
Dreamsville
Dave Grusin Orchestra | Two For The Road:The Music Of Henry Mancini | GRP | GRP 98652
George Shearing Trio | I Hear A Rhapsody | Telarc Digital | CD 83310
John Stowell-Bebo Ferra | Jazz Guitar Highlights 1 | Jardis Records | JRCD 20141
Oscar Peterson Trio With The Claus Ogermann Orchestra | Three Originals:Motion&Emotions/Tristeza On Piano/Hello Herbie | MPS | 521059-2
Oscar Peterson With Orchestra | Motions & Emotions | MPS | 821289-2 PMS
Sarah Vaughan With Orchestra | Sarah Vaughan Sings The Mancini Songbook | Verve | 558401-2
Stacey Kent With The Jim Tomlison Quintet | Dreamsville | Candid | CCD 79775
Steven King | Acoustic Swing | Acoustic Music Records | 319.1107.2
Wes Montgomery Trio | Wes Montgomery-The Complete Riverside Recordings | Riverside | 12 RCD 4408-2
West Coast All Stars | TV Jazz Themes | Fresh Sound Records | FSR 517(Somerset SF 8800)
Dreamware
Passport | Garden Of Eden | Atlantic | 2292-44147-2
Simon Spang-Hanssen & Maneklar | Wondering | dacapo | DCCD 9436
Dreamworld
Jon Hassell & Farafina | Flash Of The Spirit | Intuition Records | INT 3009-2
Dreamworld(Dance)
Ahmad Jamal Trio | Live In Paris 1992 | Dreyfus Jazz Line | FDM 37019-2
Dreamy
Live In Paris 92 | Birdology | 849408-2
Sarah Vaughan With The Jimmy Jones Orchestra | Jazz Profile | Blue Note | 823517-2
Ballads | Roulette | 537561-2
Dreamy | Fresh Sound Records | SR 52046(Roulette)
Kid Thomas And His Algiers Stompers | Sonnets From Algiers' | American Music | AMCD-53
Dreamy Mood
Harry Roy And His Orchestra | May Fair Nights | Saville Records | SVL 171 IMS
Drebirks
George Gruntz Jazz Ensemble With The Basel Tambours & Pipers | Jazz Meets Europe:Flamenco Jazz/From Sticksland With Love | MPS | 531847-2
Drehung Inform
Naked Ear | Acoustik Guitar Duolog | Acoustic Music Records | AMC 1022
Drei Fragmente Aus der Markus-Pasion
Südpool Jazz Project IV | Südpol Jazz Project IV-Quartet | L+R Records | CDLR 45091
Drei Seelen-Three Souls
Slim Gaillard Quartet | Cement Mixer Put-Ti Put-Ti | Folklyric | 9038
Drei Stücke für Klavier
Eric St-Laurent-Thomy Jordi-Thomas Alkier feat. Helge Schneider | Rock,Jazz & Music:Laut! | BIT | 11212
Dreiunddreissig
Christopher Dell D.R.A. | Future Of The Smallest Form | Jazz 4 Ever Records:Jazz Network | J4E 4754
Dreiundvierzig
Future Of The Smallest Form | Jazz 4 Ever Records:Jazz Network | J4E 4754
Dreiundvierzig A
Del Ferro/Overwater/Paeffgen | Dices | Acoustic Music Records | 319.1139.2
Dre's Blues
John Lindberg Orchestra | Trilogy Of Works For Eleven Instrumentalists | Black Saint | BSR 0082
Drew
Fred Hersch Quintet | Point In Time | Enja | ENJ-9035 2
Drew's Blues
Jackie McLean Quintet | Bluesnik | Blue Note | 784067-2
Kenny Drew Trio | New Faces New Sounds:Introducing The Kenny Drew Trio | Blue Note | 871245-4
Drift
Ray Charles With Orchestra | Ain't It So | London | 6.23864 AP
Drifter
John Lindberg Ensemble | A Tree Frog Tonality | Between The Lines | btl 008(Efa 10178-2)
Bernhard Reinke Transfusion | Driftin' | Timeless | CD SJP 323
Driftin'
Bill Evans-Eddie Gomez Duo | The Complete Fantasy Recordings | Fantasy | 9FCD 1012-2
Charles Brown Band | Boss Of The Blues | Mainstream | MD CDO 908
Herbie Hancock Quintet | Herbie Hancock:The Complete Blue Note Sixties Sessions | Blue Note | 495569-2
Cantaloupe Island | Blue Note | 829331-2
Howard McGhee Sextet | Jazzbrothers | Storyville | SLP 4077
Driftin' Boogie
Little Milton And His Band | Little Milton | Chess | 427013
Drifting
Joel Frahm Quintet | The Rains From A Cloud Do Not Wet The Sky | Nabel Records:Jazz Network | CD 4686
Johnny Littlejohn Group | When Your Best Friend Turns Your Back On You | JSP Records | JSPCD 246
| Meeting In Brooklyn | Babel | BDV 9405
Drifting On A Reed
Coleman Hawkins Quartet | Bean And The Boys | Prestige | PCD 24124-2
Drifting Petals
Ralph Towner-Gary Burton | Matchbook | ECM | 1056(835014-2)

Matchbox Bluesband | Live Recordings Extravaganza! | L+R Records | CDLR 42074
Drilling
Dezona | Hands | Lipstick Records | LIP 8930-2
Drink And Blather
Henry Red Allen And His Orchestra | Harlem Roots-Jazz On Film:Jivin' Time | Storyville | SLP 6003
Drinking Again
Jimmy Witherspoon And His Band | Evenin' Blues | Original Blues Classics | OBCCD 511-2
Drinking Lesson
Peetie Wheatstraw | Peetie Wheatstraw(1930-1941) | Story Of Blues | CD 3541-2
Drinking Music
Gary Bartz Ntu Troop | Harlem Bush Music | Milestone | M 9031
Drip Some Grease
Andy Laster Quintet | Twirler | Sound Aspects | sas CD 035
Drip-Dry
Joe McPhee Trio | Sweet Freedom-Now What? | Hat Art | CD 6162
Driva Man
Max Roach Group | Live In Europe 1964-Freedom Now Suite | Magnetic Records | MRCD 110
Drive
Don Friedman Quartet | Metamorphosis | Original Jazz Classics | OJCCD 1914-2(P 7488)
Morgana King And Her Band | I Just Can't Stop Loving You | Muse | MCD 5408
Drive My Car
Bobby McFerrin Group | Blue Velvet: Crooners, Swooners And Velvet Vocals | Blue Note | 521153-2
[Little Maxie] Bailey Band | Obscure Blues Shouters Vol.1 | Blue Moon | BMCD 6010
Drive Time
Richard Smith Group | Flow | Inak | 30512
Drivin'
Tiny Grimes Quintet | Tiny Grimes:The Complete 1944-1950 Vol.2(1947-1950) | Blue Moon | BMCD 6006
Driving While Black
Petra Straue & The Moonmen | Voices Around My House | Satin Doll Productions | SDP 1016-1 CD
Dromedar
Michael Hornstein-Robert Di Gioia | Dry Red | Edition Collage | EC 486-2
Drommen
Ketil Bjornstad Group | Early Years | EmArCy | 013271-2
Drommen Om Havet(Ocean Dream)
Jens Skou Olsen Group | September Veje | dacapo | DCCD 9451
Drommevise(Dream Song)
Per Gudmundson-Ale Möller-Lene Willemark | Frifot | ECM | 1690(557653-2)
Drömsken
Lena Willemark-Ale Möller Group | Nordan | ECM | 1536(523161-2)
Drömspar-Efterspel
Erhard Hirt | Guitar Solo | FMP | OWN-90003
Drop
Dick Robertson And His Orchestra | The New York Session Man | Timeless | CBC 1-008
Drop Kick Live
Steve Coleman And Five Elements | Victor Jazz History Vol.16:Jazz-Rock & Fusion | RCA | 2135735-2
Drop Me Off In Harlem
Blue Room Ensemble | Solitude | Foolish Music | FM 211993
Bobby Short Trio | Late Night At The Cafe Carlyle | Telarc Digital | CD 83311
Dutch Swing College Band | The Joint Is Jumpin'! | Timeless | CD TTD 594
Ella Fitzgerald With The Duke Ellington Orchestra | The Complete Ella Fitzgerald Song Books of Harold Arlen, Irving Berlin, Duke Ellington, George & Ira Gershwin, Jerome Kern, Johnny Mercer, Cole Porter And Rogers & Hart | Verve | 519832-2
George Cables Trio | One For My Baby | Steeplechase | SCCD 31487
Louis Armstrong And His All Stars With Duke Ellington | The Beautiful American | Jazz Society(Vogue) | 670501
Richie Kamuca Quartet | Drop Me Off In Harlem | Concord | CJ 39
Drop Me Off In Harlem-
Louis Armstrong And His All Stars With Duke Ellington | Louis Armstrong-Duke Ellington:The Great Summit-Complete Session | Roulette | 524546-2
Drop Me Off In Harlem(alt.take)
Duke Ellington And His Famous Orchestra | The Complete Duke Ellington-Vol. 5 | CBS | CBS 88082
Drop That Sack
Lil's Hot Shots | Louis Armstrong Vol.1-Young Louis 'The Side Man' | MCA | 1301
Rod Mason And His Hot Five | Rod Mason's Hot Five feat. Angela Brown | Timeless | CD TTD 563
Drop The Other Shoe
Nat Pierce/Dick Collins Nonet | Nat Pierce-Dick Collins Nonet/Charlie Mariano Sextet | Original Jazz Classics | OJC 118(F 3224)
Drops
Thomas Schmidt Trio | For Good Reasons | Jazz 4 Ever Records:Jazz Network | J4E 4742
Dröttbom Hus
Charles Tolliver Quartet | Live In Berlin-At The Quasimodo Vol.2 | Strata East Records | 660.51.011
Drown In My
Christian Willisohn New Band | Heart Broken Man | Blues Beacon | BLU-1026 2
Drown In My Own Tears
Johnny 'Big Mouse' Walker | Blue Love | Steeplechase | SCB 9005
Shirley Horn Quartet | Light Out Of Darkness(A Tribute To Ray Charles) | Verve | 519703-2
John Balke Group | Saturation | EmArCy | 538160-2
Drowning-
Flip Phillips Quartet | Flip Phillips Complete 1947-1951 Verve Master Takes | Definitive Records | DRCD 11201
Drowsy
Roy Fox And His Orchestra | The Bands That Matter | Eclipse | ECM 2045
Drug Waltz
Jerry Moore Quintet | Ballad Of Birmingham | ESP Disk | ESP 1061-2
Drugstore B.
Richard Carr Trio | Along The Edge | Nabel Records:Jazz Network | CD 4683
Druids
John Surman | A Biography Of The Rev. Absolom Dawe | ECM | 1528(523749-2)
Druid's Circle
Georg Ruby Group | Stange Loops | Jazz Haus Musik | JHM 0057 CD
Drull 4
Ruby & Puntin | Stadtgarten Series Vol.6 | Jazz Haus Musik | JHM 1006 SER
Drum Boogie
Concord Super Band | Concord Super Band II | Concord | CJ 120
Gene Krupa Trio | This Is Jazz | Verve | 2615040 IMS
Terry Lightfoot And His Band | Stardust | Upbeat Jazz | URCD 104
Drum Conversation
Max Roach | At Last! | Original Jazz Classics | OJCCD 480-2
Max Roach | Original Jazz Classics | OJCCD 202-2(DLP 13)
Drum Duo(Art Blakey & Roy Haynes)
Trevor Richards New Orleans Trio | The Trevor Richards New Orleans Trio | Stomp Off Records | CD 1222
Drum Ffarment
Chuck Flores Quintet | Drum Flower | Concord | CJ 49
Drum Interlude
Chick Corea Quartet | Live In Montreux | Stretch Records | SCD 9009-2

Andreas Maile Quartet | Mailensteine | Satin Doll Productions | SDP 1022-1 CD
Drum Intro-
Crusaders | Live In Japan | GRP | GRP 97462
Drum Meets Bum
David Moss Duets | Full House | Moers Music | 02010
Drum Mucis
Paul Motian Quintet | Jack Of Clubs | Soul Note | 121124-2
Drum Organ
Charly Antolini Orchestra | Charly Antolini | Jazz Magazine | 48017
Bill Carrothers-Bill Stewart | Bill Carrothers Duets With Bill Stewart | Dreyfus Jazz Line | FDM 37002-2
Drum Solo
Oregon | Oregon In Performance | Elektra | ELK K 62028
Drum Storm
Charly Antolini Group | Countdown | BELL Records | BLR 84067
Drum Talking
Art Blakey And The Jazz Messengers | Moanin' | Blue Note | 495324-2
Drum Thunder-
Moanin' | Blue Note | 300321
Drum Tunnel
Jack Costanzo Group | Latin Fever:The Wild Rhythms Of Jack Costanza | Capitol | 590955-2
Drum-A-Mania
Torsten Zwingenberger | Drumkid | AH Records | RR 40213
Drumbeats And Heartbeats
Andre Jaume-Joe McPhee Duo | Tales And Prophecies | Hat Art | 12 (2R12)
Drume Negrita
Badi Assad | Solo | Chesky | JD 99
Drum-Pet
Charly Antolini Orchestra | Charly Antolini | Jazz Magazine | 48017
Drums
Charles Mingus Quintet | Charles Mingus-The Complete Debut Recordings | Debut | 12 DCD 4402-2
Charles Mingus Quintet Plus Max Roach | The Charlie Mingus Quintet Plus Max Roach | Debut | VIJ 5011 IMS
Modern Jazz Quartet | Django | Original Jazz Classics | OJC20 057-2
Drums-
Charly Antolini Orchestra | Special Delivery | MPS | 68256
Drums Boogie Woogie
Cécile Verny Quartet | Kekeli | double moon | CHRDM 71028
Drums Call For The Dance
Max Roach Quartet | Max Roach | Original Jazz Classics | OJCCD 202-2(DLP 13)
Drums In The Rain
The Tuba Trio | The Tuba Trio-Vol. 3 | Circle Records | RK 3-2976/3 IMS
Drums Of Heaven
Jaco Pastorius/Brian Melvin Group | Jazz Street | Timeless | CD SJP 258
Drums Unlimited
Archie Shepp-Max Roach Duo | The Long March Part 2 | Hat Art | CD 6042
Drums(alt.take 1)
Charles Mingus Quintet | Charles Mingus-The Complete Debut Recordings | Debut | 12 DCD 4402-2
Drums(alt.take 2)
Brocksi-Quintett | Drums Boogie | Bear Family Records | BCD 15988 AH
Drums-Boogie(aka Drum Boogie)
Milo Fine Free Jazz Ensemble | The Constant Extension Of Inescapable Tradition | Hat Art | H
Drunk
Winck-Büning-Schoenefeld | Truth And The Abstract Blues | Acoustic Music Records | 319.1061.2
Drunk With Majic
Harmonica Slim Blues Group | Black Bottom Blues | Trix Records | TRIX 3323
Drunken Hearted Man
Robert Johnson | Robert Johnson-King Of The Delta Blues | CBS | 493006-2
Drunken Hearted Man(alt.take)
Horace Tapscott Quintet | Alee! The Phantom | Arabesque Recordings | AJ 0119
Drunken Penguin
Volker Schlott Quartet | Why Not | Acoustic Music Records | 319.1083.2
Dry Bones In The Valley
Phil Woods-Gene Quill Sextet | Phil And Quill | RCA | 2159153-2
Dry Four
Misery Loves Company | Magia Ke Miseria | Enja | 9117-2
Dry Humping The American Dream
David Pritchard Quintet | Light-Year | Inner City | IC 1047 IMS
Dry Martino
Michael Blake Group | Drift | Intuition Records | INT 3212-2
Dry Socket
Bud Powell Trio | The Amazing Bud Powell Vol.4 | Blue Note | BLP 1598
Dry Soul
Blind Lemon Jefferson | Blind Lemon Jefferson | Biograph | BLP 12000
Dschungelschweiß
Louis Sclavis-Ernst Reijseger | Et On Ne Parle Pas Du Temps | FMP | CD 66
Du Du Du
Italian Instabile Orchestra | Skies Of Europe | ECM | 1543
Du Du Duchamp-
Clare Fischer And The Brunner-Schwer Steinway | Alone Together | MPS | 68178
Du Gronne,Glitrende Tre
Karl Scharnweber Trio With Timbre | Choral Concert(Passion) | KlangRäume | 30160
Du Hast Glück Bei Den Frau'n Bel Ami
Muhal Richard Abrams Orchestra | Blues Forever | Black Saint | 120061-2
Du Läßt Mich Nicht Los(I'll Never Be Free)
Hans Kennel Group feat. Mark Soskin | Stella | TCB Records | TCB 97102
Du Red'st Allweil Vom Scheiden
Dark | Dark | CMP Records | CMP CD 28
Dual Force
Larry Coryell Quartet | Air Dancing | Jazzpoint | JP 1025 CD
Perico Sambeat Quartet | Dual Force | Ronnie Scott's Jazz House | JHCD 031
Duality
Peter Leitch-John Hicks | Duality | Reservoir | RSR CD 134
Duas Rosas-
Billy Drummond Quartet | Dubai | Criss Cross | Criss 1120
Dubidap
Lionel Hampton And His Septet | Ridin' On The L&N | Affinity | AFS 1037
Duch Feelings-
Billy Hart Group | Oshumare | Gramavision | GR 8502-2
Duck Hunt
Art Lande Trio | Skylight | ECM | 1208
Duck In A Colorful Blanket(For Here)
Greetje Bijma Trio | Barefoot | Enja | ENJ-8038 2
Duck Pond
Art Blakey And The Jazz Messengers | Oh-By The Way | Timeless | CD SJP 165
Duck Theme-
Boyd Raeburn And His Orchestra | Man With The Horns | Savoy | WL 70534 (809300)
Duckaddiction
Buddy Tate Quintet | The Great Buddy Tate | Concord | CJ 163
Duck's Groove
Nils Gessinger Orchestra | Ducks 'N' Cookies | GRP | GRP 98302
Duck's Room
Donald Harrison Quartet | Free To Be | Impulse(MCA) | 951283-2
Duck's Step
Count Basie And His Orchestra | On My Way And Shoutin' Again | Verve | 2304385 IMS

DuduWawa
Jo Mikowich Group | Just A Dream-A Collection For Easy Listening | yvp music | CD 3025

Duel Of Jester And The Tyrant
Return To Forever | Romantic Warrior | CBS | SRCS 9348

Dueling Dovidls
| Little Jimmy Scott | Specialty | SPCD 2170-2

Dueling Tenors
Chick Corea Group | Touchstone | Stretch Records | SCD 9003-2

Duesoprani
Buddy Rich-Gene Krupa Duo | Compact Jazz: Gene Krupa & Buddy Rich | Verve | 835314-2 PMS

Duet
Circle | Paris Concert | ECM | 1018/19(843163-2)
Count Basie And His Orchestra | Count On The Coast Vol.2 | Phontastic | NCD 7575
The Complete Atomic Basie | Roulette | 828635-2
Basie On Roulette, Vol. 1: E : MC 2 : Count Basie Orchestra+Neal HeftArrangeme | Roulette | CDP 793273-2
Tom Mega + Band | Songs & Prayers | ITM Records | ITM 1491
Wild Bill Davison With The Alex Welsh Band | Memories | Jazzology | JCD-201

Duet 1
The Conga Kings | The Conga Kings | Chesky | JD 193

Duet 2
The Conga Kings | Chesky | JD 193

Duet 3
The Conga Kings | Chesky | JD 193

Duet For One
Muhal Richard Abrams Orchestra | Blues Forever | Black Saint | 120061-2

Duet Improvisations(1&2)
Roy Brooks-Geri Allen | Duet In Detroit | Enja | ENJ-7067 2

Duet Solo Dancers
Jones And Collins Astoria Hot Eight | Sizzling The Blues | Frog | DGF 5

Duet Suite
Joaquin Chacón Group | San | Fresh Sound Records | FSNT 015 CD

Dueto
Bob Brookmeyer New Art Orchestra | New Work | Challenge | CHR 70066

Duett Duell
Red Mitchell Quintet | Red Mitchell | Bethlehem | BTM 6825

Dugub
Louis Sclavis Group | Chine | IDA Record | 012 CD

Duke
Abdullah Ibrahim Trio | Yarona | TipToe | TIP-888820 2

Duke 88
African Magic | TipToe | TIP-888845 2
Dollar(Abdullah Ibrahim) Brand Group | African River | Enja | ENJ-6018 2
Stanley Clarke-George Duke Band | Live In Montreux | Jazz Door | JD 1234

Duke Booty
Marcus Roberts Trio | In Honor Of Duke | CBS | CK 63630

Duke Ellington Introduces Ella Fitzgerald
Abdullah Ibrahim(Dollar Brand) | Autobiography | Plainisphare | PL 1267-68 CD

Duke Ellington Medley:
Rex Allen's Swing Express | Ellington For Lovers | Nagel-Heyer | NH 1009
Keep Swingin' | Nagel-Heyer | CD 016
WDR Big Band | Harlem Story | Koala Records | CD P 7

Duke Ellington's Sophisticated Lady Melange
Joe Pass | Live At Long Beach City College | Pablo | 2308239-2

Duke Ellington's Sound Of Love
Charles Mingus Sextet | Changes Two | Rhino | 8122-71404-2
Danny Richmond Quintet | Danny Richmond Plays Charles Mingus | Timeless | CD SJP 148
Joe Lovano Quartet | Live At The Village Vanguard | Blue Note | 829125-2
Joe Lovano Quintet | Village Rhythm | Soul Note | 121182-2
Kevin Mahogany With The Kenny Barron Trio And Ralph Moore | Double Rainbow | Enja | ENJ-7097 2
Mingus Dynasty | Reincarnation | Soul Note | 121042-2
Paolo Fresu Quintet | Ballads | SPLASC(H) Records | CD H 366-2
Peter Leitch Quartet | Colors & Dimensions | Reservoir | RSR CD 140

Duke Vinaccia
Tom Lellis Group | Taken To Heart | Concord | CCD 4574

Duke's Choice(aka Don't Come Back)
Sleepy Matsumoto With New York First Calls | Papillon | Sweet Basil | 660.55.017

Duke's In Bed
Johnny Hodges Orchestra | Ellingtonia '56 | Verve | 2304431 IMS

Duke's Joke
Dizzy Gillespie Quintet | The Cool World/Dizzy Goes Hollywood | Verve | 531230-2

Duke's Place(C Jam Blues)
Ella Fitzgerald With The Duke Ellington Orchestra | The Stockholm Concert 1966 | Pablo | 2308242-2
George Mraz Quartet | Duke's Place | Milestone | MCD 9292-2
John Hicks Trio | Power Trio | Novus | PD 90547(847028)
Louis Armstrong And His All Stars With Duke Ellington | The Beautiful American | Jazz Society(Vogue) | 670501
Oliver Nelson And His Orchestra | Black Brown And Beautiful | RCA | ND 86993

Duke's Place(C Jam Blues-alt.take)
Ernst Bier-Mack Goldsbury Quartet | At Night When You Go To Sleep | Timescrapper | TSCR 9611

Duke's Voice
Mongo Santamaria Orchestra | Skins | Milestone | MCD 47038-2

Dulzura
Peter Compo Quintet | Hot Jazz Violin-Nostalgia In Times Square | Take Twelve On CD | TT 001-2

Dumas
Michel Petrucciani Trio | Michel Petrucciani:Concert Inédits | Dreyfus Jazz Line | FDM 36607-2

Dumb Breaks
Antonio Farao Trio | Black Inside | Enja | ENJ-9345 2

Dumb Show
Jazz Africa All Nations Big Band | Jadu(Jazz Africa Down Under) | Enja | ENJ-9339 2

Dumela Azania
Om | OM with Dom Um Romao | Japo | 60022 IMS

Dümpeln
Matzeit-Daerr | September | Jazz Haus Musik | JHM 0125 CD
Gene Ammons-Sonny Stitt Quartet | Soul Summit | Prestige | PCD 24118-2(P 7234/7275)

Dungo
Foday Musa Suso | The Dreamtime | CMP Records | CMP CD 3001

Dunkin' Bagel
Heiner Goebbels/Alfred Harth | Indianer Für Morgen | Riskant | 568-72401

Dunkle Wolken
Cowws Quintet | Grooves 'N' Loops | FMP | CD 59

Duo Á 3 Voix
Art Pepper-Ron Carter Duo | Art Pepper:The Complete Galaxy Recordings | Galaxy | 16GCD 1016-2

Duo Blues
New York Album | Galaxy | GXY 5154

Duo Derdoo
Jens Schliecker & Nils Rohwer | Duo Fantasie:Piano Meets Vibes | Acoustic Music Records | 319.1094.2

Duo I(Pull Over)
Bill McHenry Quartet | Rest Stop | Fresh Sound Records | FSNT 033 CD

Duo II(Rest Stop)
Kenny Drew/Niels-Henning Orsted-Pedersen Duo | Duo | Steeplechase | SCS 1002

Duo(In Two Parts)
Sadao Watanabe Orchestra & Strings | California Shower | Flying Disk | VIJ 6012

Duogeny
Katrina Krimsky-Trevor Watts | Stella Malu | ECM | 1199
A Band Of Friends | Renè Wohlhauser Werkauswahl 1978-1993 | Creative Works Records | CW CD 1026-2

Duometric für Flöte und Bassklarinette
Donald Byrd Quintet | House Of Byrd | Prestige | P 24066

Dupree Blues
Meade Lux Lewis | Boogie Woogie Trio Vol. 3 | Storyville | SLP 4006

Dupree Special
Champion Jack Dupree | The Death Of Louis | Vogue | 655502

Duquility
Mal Waldron Sextet | Fire Waltz | Prestige | P 24085
Eric Dolphy:The Complete Prestige Recordings | Prestige | 9 PRCD-4418-2
Tiziana Ghiglioni And Her Band | SONB-Something Old Something New Something Borrowed Something Blue | SPLASC(H) Records | CD H 370-2

Durch Dich Wird Die Welt Erst Schön
Rüdiger Carl | Vorn:Lieder Und Improvisationen Für Akkordeon, Bandoneon Und Ziehharmonika | FMP | 1110

Durem
Eddie Chamblee And His Orchestra | Eddie Chamblee:The Complete Recordings 1947-1952 | Blue Moon | BMCD 1049

Durga Durga
Carlos Bica & Azul | Look What They've Done To My Song | Enja | ENJ-9458 2

Durme
Duke Robillard Group | Swing | Demon Records | Fiend CD 191

Dusk
Duke Ellington And His Famous Orchestra | Jazz:The Essential Collection Vol.2 | IN+OUT Records | 78012-2
Duke Ellington:Ko-Ko | Dreyfus Jazz Line | FDM 36717-2
Duke Ellington And His Orchestra | Jazz Giants:Duke Ellington | RCA | NL 45179 SI
Stan Kenton And His Orchestra | Kenton Showcase | Creative World | ST 1026

Dusk: Nightwatch
Geoffrey McCabe Quartet | Teseract Complicity | Timeless | SJP 212

Dusk-Dawn
John Coltrane Quartet | The Mastery Of John Coltrane/Vol. 1: Feelin' Good | MCA | 2292-54641-2
John Coltrane:The Classic Quartet-Complete Impulse Studio Recordings | Impulse(MCA) | 951280-2
Kulu Se Mama | Impulse(MCA) | 543412-2

Dusk-Dawn(alt.take)
Don Neely's Royal Society Jazz Orchestra | Don't Bring Lulu | Stomp Off Records | CD 1250

Dust
Cassiber | Perfect Worlds | Riskant | 568-72418

Dust My Broom
Otis Spann Band | The Blues Never Die! | Original Blues Classics | OBCCD 530-2(P 7391)
Robert Lockwood Jr. | Contrasts | Trix Records | TRIX 3307

Dusty Foot
Bunk Johnson's Jazz Band | Commodore Classica-Old New Orleans Jazz 1942 | Commodore | 6.24547 AG

Dusty Rag
Sonny Morris And The Delta Jazz Band | The Spirit Lives On | Lake | LACD 46

Dutch Rain
Nicolas Thijs Trio | Europ' Jazz Contest Belgium '93 | B.Sharp Records | CDS 097

Duty Free
Sonny Stitt Quartet | Eddie 'Lockjaw' Davis/Sonny Stitt | LRC Records | CDC 9028

Duty Free Suite
Charly Antolini Trio | Knock Out 2000 | Inak | 9053

Dwell On
Charles Lloyd Quartet | The Call | ECM | 1522(517719-2)

Dwija
Kenny Dorham Quintet | The Bopmasters | MCA | IA 9337/2 (801647)

D'ya Love Me?
Blue Box | Blue Box Live:Time We Sign | TipToe | TIP-888813 2

Dyani
Kol Simcha | Contemporary Klezmer | Laika Records | LK 93-048

Dybbuk
Leonard Feather And Ye Olde English Swynge Band | Swingin' Britain-The Thirties | Decca | DDV 5013/14

Dyin' By The Hour
Albert Collins Blues Band | The Master Of The Telecaster | Crosscut | CCR 1011

Dying Gambler's Blues
Memphis Willie B. | Hard Working Man Blues | Original Blues Classics | OBCCD 578-2(BV 1048)

Dying To Get To Europe
Irene Schweizer | Hexensabbat | FMP | 0500

Dynaelo
Stan Kenton And His Orchestra | Stan Kenton On The Air | Status | DSTS 1022

Dynamite's O'Rooney
Don Byas Ree-Boppers | Don Byas Complete 1946-1951 European Small Group Master Takes | Definitive Records | DRCD 11214

Dynamo A
Das Pferd | Das Pferd | ITM Records | ITM 1416

Dyna-Soar
Quincy Jones And His Orchestra | Talkin' Verve-Roots Of Acid Jazz:Roland Kirk | Verve | 533101-2
Heartbop | Wednesday Night | yvp music | CD 3033

Dynasty
Stan Getz With The Eddie Louiss Trio | Dynasty | Verve | 839117-2

Dzogchen Punks
Harry Edison Quintet | The Best Of Harry Edison | Pablo | 2310847

E
Edison's Light | Original Jazz Classics | OJCCD 804-2(2310780)

'E'
Marcus Schinkel Trio | The First Of A Million Tones | Acoustic Music Records | 319.1132.2

E De Lei
John Tchicai-Vitold Rek Duo | Art Of The Duo:Satisfaction | Enja | 7033-2

E La Nave Va
Véronique Gillet And Fernando Freitez With Carlos Franco | Terracota | Acoustic Music Records | 319.1056.2

E Lucevan Le Stelle(Tosca)
Mind Games | Mind Games Plays The Music Of Stan Getz & Astrud Gilberto | Edition Collage | EC 515-2

E Luxo So
Stan Getz-Charlie Byrd Sextet | Jazz Samba | Verve | 521413-2
Stan Getz/Charlie Byrd:Jazz Samba | CTI Records | PDCTI 1104-2

E' Quasi L'Alba-
Tiziana Ghiglioni And The Strings Ensemble | Tiziana Ghiglioni Sings Gaslini | Soul Note | 121297-2

E Senza Fiato-
Piano Seven | Best Of Piano Seven | TCB Records | TCB 01042

E.B.
George Gruntz Concert Jazz Band | First Prize | Enja | ENJ-6004 2

E.D.
Roland Kirk Quartet | Domino | Verve | 543833-2
Marcus Roberts Sextet | The Collected Robert Marcus | RCA | 2668720-2

E.P.W.
Adonis Rose Quintet | Song For Donise | Criss Cross | Criss 1146

E.S.P.
Joey DeFrancesco Group | Reboppin' | CBS | CK 48624
Miles Davis Quintet | Greatest Hits | CBS | CK 65418
Nat Adderley And His Orchestra | Work Songs | Milestone | M 47047
Peter Erskine Orchestra | Peter Erskine | Original Jazz Classics | OJC 610(C 14010)
Peter Erskine | Contemporary | CCD 14010-2

E.T.A.
Robert Watson/Curtis Lundy Quartet | Beatitudes | New Note Records | KM 11867

E.V.G.
Frank Foster And The Loud Minority | The Loud Minority | Mainstream | MD CDO 718

E=MC
Huey Simmons Sextet | Burning Spirits | Contemporary | C 7625/6

Each One (Must) Teach One
Chico Freeman Quintet | Tradition In Transition | Elektra | MUS K 52412

Eager Beaver
Stan Kenton And His Orchestra | At The Rendezvous Vol.1 | Status | CD 102(882198)

Ear Conditioning
Warne Marsh Quintet | Intuition | Capitol | 852771-2

Earful
Modern Jazz Gallery | Fresh Sound Records | KXL 5001(252282-1 Kapp)

Early And Later(part 1)
Sonny Criss Quintet | Jazz In Paris:Saxophones Á Saint-Germain Des Prés | EmArCy | 014060-2
Jazz In Paris:Sonny Criss-Mr.Blues Pour Flirter | EmArCy | 549231-2 PMS

Early And Later(part 2)
Jazz In Paris:Saxophones Á Saint-Germain Des Prés | EmArCy | 014060-2
Al Casey Quintet | Serenade In Blue | Savoy | SV 0232(MG 12057)

Early Autumn
Ben Webster With Orchestra And Strings | Ultimate Ben Webster selected by James Carter | Verve | 557537-2
Billy Ross Quartet | The Sound:A Tribute To Stan Getz | Milestone | MCD 9227-2
Ella Fitzgerald With The Nelson Riddle Orchestra | Ella Fitzgerald Sings The Johnny Mercer Songbook | Verve | 539057-2
The Johnny Mercer Songbook | Verve | 823247-2 PMS
Lorez Alexandria With The Mike Wofford Quartet | Lorez Alexandria Sings The Songs Of Johnny Mercer | Discovery | DS 826 IMS
Stan Kenton And His Orchestra | The Ballad Style Of Stan Kenton | Blue Note | 856688-2
Woody Herman And His Orchestra | Victor Jazz History Vol.15:Progressive Jazz | RCA | 2135734-2
Don Lamond And His Big Swing Band | Extraordinary | Progressive | PRO 7067 IMS

Early Bird
Toto Blanke Group | Fools Paradise | ALISO Records | AL 1019

Early Birds
Cripple Clarence Lofton | Pioneers Of Boogie Woogie | Jazz Anthology | JA 5212

Early In The Morning
Dinah Washington With The Rudy Martin Trio | The Complete Dinah Washington On Mercury Vol.1 | Mercury | 832444-2
Joe Williams With The Jimmy Jones Orchestra | Me And The Blues | RCA | 2121823-2
Louis Jordan And His Tympany Five | Louis Jordan-Let The Good Times Roll: The Complete Decca Recordings 1938-1954 | Bear Family Records | BCD 15557 IH
Look Out Sisters-Unissued Film Soundtracks 1944-1948 | Krazy Kat | KK 7415 IMS

Early Life
Marilyn Crispell | A Concert In Berlin-Summer '83 | FMP | SAJ 46

Early Messenger
Ari Ambrose Quartet | Cylic Episode | Steeplechase | SCCD 31472

Early Minor-
Albert Ammons Rhythm Kings | Big Band Bounce & Boogie-Piano Portraits Vol.1 | Affinity | AFS 1022

Early Morning Blues
John Henry Barbee | Blues Masters Vol.3 | Storyville | STCD 8003
Nat King Cole Trio | Nat King Cole Vol.5 | Laserlight | 15750

Early Morning Rock
Stephen Horenstein Ensemble | Collages Jerusalem '85 | Soul Note | SN 1099

Early Morning Stroll
Chet Baker Sextet | Chet | Original Jazz Classics | OJC20 087-2

Early Morning(Before Daybreak)
Muddy Waters Group | More Real Folk Blues | Chess | CH 9278

Early Session Hop
Lionel Hampton And His Orchestra | The Complete Lionel Hampton Vol.3/4(1939) | RCA | 2122614-2
Ben Webster-Cotton Tail | RCA | 63667902
Lionel Hampton Orchestra | Lionel Hampton Story Vol.2 | Black & Blue | BLE 59.238 2

Early Summer
Chapaka Shaweez | New Orleans Classics | Pathe | 1561351(Imperial)

Early Sunrise Over Cambodia
Sonny Scott | Sonny Scott(1933) | Story Of Blues | CD 3525-2

Early Tide
John Abercrombie Trio | Speak To The Devil | ECM | 1511

Early To Bed
Dusan Bogdanovic Quartet | Early To Rise | Palo Alto | PA 8049

Ear-Mike Song
Freddie Hubbard Sextet | Hub Cap | Blue Note | 542302-2

Earmon Jr.
John Carter | A Suite Of Early American Folk Pieces For Solo-Clarinet | Moers Music | 02014

Ears4Evol
Henning Berg & John Taylor With 'Tango' | Tango & Company | Jazz Haus Musik | JHM 0085 CD

Earspace
Alice Coltrane Sextet | Joe Henderson:The Milestone Years | Milestone | 8MCD 4413-2

Earth
Art Farmer Quartet | Portrait Of Art Farmer | Contemporary | C 7554
David Darling | Dark Wood | ECM | 1519(523750-2)

Earth-
Alex Merck Group | Dog Days | Lipstick Records | LIP 8968-2

Earth Bird
Randy Weston Trio With The Orchestre Du Festival De Monreal | Earth Birth | Verve | 537088-2

Earth Blues
Céline Rudolph And Her Trio | Book Of Travels | Nabel Records:Jazz Network | CD 4672

Earth Chant
Peter Guidi Quartet | Beautiful Friendship | Timeless | CD SJP 352

Earth End
Elvin Jones Quintet | Earth Jones | Palo Alto | PA 8016

Earth Juice
Dave Grusin Quintet | GRP Super Live In Concert | GRP | GRP 16502

Earth Ship
Paul Horn Group | The Magic Of Findhorn | Golden Flute Records | GFR 2003

Earth Sky-
Kahil El'Zabar Quartet | Sacred Love | Sound Aspects | sas CD 021

Earth Song
Sadao Watanabe Group | Earth Step | Verve | 521287-2

Earthborn
The Rippingtons | Tourist In Paradise | GRP | GRP 95882

Earthbound
Pat Martino Quintet | Think Tank | Blue Note | 592009-2

Earthings
Billy Cobham Group | Life & Times | Atlantic | ATL 50253

Earthmusic
Forman/Loeb/Jackson/Haffner | Metro | Lipstick Records | LIP 890232

Ease Back

TITELVERZEICHNIS

Kenny Dorham Quintet | Ease It! | Muse | MR 5053

Ease On Down The Road
Peter Fessler Quartet | Colours Of My Mind | Minor Music | 801063

Easier Said Than Done
Bill Evans Group | Escape | Escape | ESC 03650-2

Easin' In
Count Basie And His Orchestra | En Concert Avec Europe 1 | Laserlight | 710411/12

East
Pat Martino Quintet | East! | Original Jazz Classics | OJCCD 248-2

East 117th Street
Saheb Sarbib Quintet | It Couldn't Happen Without You | Soul Note | 121098-2

East 7th St.Blues
Andrew Hill Quartet | Divine Revelation | Steeplechase | SCCD 31044

East Broadway Run Down
Mat Maneri Quintet | Acceptance | HatOLOGY | 512
Olga Konkova-Per Mathisen Quartet | Northern Crossing | Candid | CCD 79766

East By Northwest
Paul Motian Electric Bebop Band | Flight Of The Blue Jay | Winter&Winter | 910009-2

East Coast
Kurt Rosenwinkel Trio | East Coast Love Affair | Fresh Sound Records | FSNT 016 CD

East Coast Love Affair
Red Mitchell Quintet | Red Mitchell | Bethlehem | BTM 6825

East Coast Trot
Mr.Acker Bilk And His Paramount Jazz Band | New Orleans Days | Lake | LACD 36

East Coasting
Mingus Big Band | Live In Time | Dreyfus Jazz Line | FDM 36583-2

East End Blues
Bill Russo And His Orchestra | Something New, Something Blue | Fresh Sound Records | LSP 15623(CBS CL 1388)

East L.A.
Oscar Pettiford Sextet | The Birdlanders Vol.2 | Original Jazz Classics | OJCCD 1931-2

East Lag
Jukka Tolonen | Mountain Stream | Sonet | 147122

East Of Montenegro
The Dave McMurdo Jazz Orchestra | Fire & Song | Sackville | SK2CD-5004

East Of Suez
Charlie Ventura Quintet | The New Charlie Ventura In Hi-Fi | Harlequin | HQ 2009(Baton BL 1202) IMS

East Of The Night
Al Cohn-Zoot Sims Quintet | From A To Z | RCA | 2147790-2

East Of The Sun West Of The Moon
Billie Holiday And Her Orchestra | Billie Holiday: The First Verve Sessions | Verve | 2610027
Bud Powell Trio | Masters Of The Modern Piano | Verve | 2-2514 IMS
Cal Collins Quartet | Ohio Style | Concord | CCD 4447
Cal Tjader's Orchestra | Several Shades Of Jade/Breeze From The East | Verve | 537083-2
Charlie Parker All Stars | Jazz Gallery:Charlie Parker Vol.1 | RCA | 2114174-2
Charlie Parker With Strings | Bird With Strings-Live At The Apollo, Carnegie Hall & Birdland | CBS | CBS 82292
Charlie Parker The Immortal Sessions Vol.2:1949-1953 | SAGA Jazz Classics | EC 3319-2
Charlie Parker/Dizzy Gillepie Groups | Dizzy Gillespie, Sarah Vaughan & Charlie 'Bird' Parker | Laserlight | 15731
Dakota Staton With Her Quartet | Darling Please Save Your Love For Me | Muse | MCD 5462
Earl Hines | Dinah | RCA | NL 70577
Elvin Jones Jazz Machine | Going Home | Enja | ENJ-7095 2
Engelbert Wrobel's Swing Society | A Heartful(l) Of Swing | NCC Jazz | NCC 8502
George Shearing Quintet/With Strings/Latin Mood | The Best Of George Shearing-All Time Shearing Favorites | Capitol | SM 2104
Jack Teagarden And His Orchestra | Jack Teagarden Plays The Blues And Dixie | Ember | CJS 803
Jesse Davis Quintet | Young At Art | Concord | CCD 4565
Jimmy And Stacy Rowles Quartet | Looking Back | Delos | DE 4009
John Basile Quartet | The Desmond Project | Chesky | JD 156
Lee Konitz With The Bert Van Den Brink Trio | Dialogues | Challenge | CHR 70053
Lester Young Quintet | Lester Young:The Complete 1936-1951 Small Group Sessions(Studio Recordings-Master Takes),Vol.4 | Blue Moon | BMCD 1004
Louis Armstrong With The Russell Garcia Orchestra | I've Got The World On A String/Louis Under The Stars | Verve | 2304428 IMS
Lucky Thompson With Gerard Pochonet And His Orchestra | Lullaby In Rhythm | Biograph | BLP 12061
Maximilian Geller Quartet feat. Melanie Bong | Smile | Edition Collage | EC 461-2
Nick Brignola With The Metropole Orchestra | Spring Is Here | Koch Jazz | 3-6905-2
Oscar Peterson Trio | Masters Of Jazz Vol.7 | RCA | NL 89721 DP
Sarah Vaughan With Orchestra | Tenderly | Bulldog | BDL 1009
Sarah Vaughan With The Jimmy Jones Orchestra | Sarah Vaughan In Hi-Fi | CBS | CK 65117
Stan Getz Quartet | Stan Getz In Europe | Laserlight | 24657
'Round Midnight In Paris | Bandstand | BDCD 1503
Stan Getz Quintet | West Coast Jazz | Verve | 557549-2
Best Of The West Coast Sessions | Verve | 537084-2
Stan Getz:East Of The Sun-The West Coast Sessions | Verve | 531935-2
Stan Kenton And His Orchestra | Mellophonium Magic | Status | CD 103(882199)
Tommy Dorsey And His Orchestra | Frank Sinatra Sings The Standards | RCA | NL 89102 AP
Wild Bill Davison Quartet | Midnight Slows No.1 | Black & Blue | BLE 233026
Zoot Sims Quartet | Zoot Sims:The Complete 1944-1954 Small Group Sessions(Master Takes),Vol.2 | Blue Moon | BMCD 1039
Simon Schott | Bar Piano: Simon Schott Plays Your Favorite Evergreens Vol.1 | Organic Music | ORGM 9733

East Of The Sun West Of The Moon-
Stan Getz-Lionel Hampton Quintet | Hamp And Getz | Verve | 831672-2
Oscar Peterson Trio | This Is Oscar Peterson | RCA | 2663990-2

East Of The Sun West Of The Moon(alt.take)
Sarah Vaughan With The Jimmy Jones Orchestra | Sarah Vaughan In Hi-Fi | CBS | CK 65117

East Print
Furio Di Castri-Paolo Fresu | Urlo | yvp music | CD 3035

East River
Werner Baumgart's Big Band Baden Baden | Jazz Rock & Sweet | MPS | 68252

East River Drive
Attila Zoller Trio | The K & K In New York | L+R Records | LR 40009

East Seventh
John Hicks Trio | East Side Blues | DIW | DIW 828 CD

East Side Medley:
Billy Higgins Quartet | Mr.Billy Higgins | Evidence | ECD 22061-2

East Side Story
Louie Bellson And His Jazz Orchestra | East Side Suite | Musicmasters | 5009-2

East St.Louis
Russell Gunn Quartet | Young Gunn | Muse | MCD 5539

East St.Louis Toodle-Oo
Duke Ellington And His Kentucky Club Orchestra | Duke Ellington:Complete Original American Decca Recordings | Definitive Records | DRCD 11196
Duke Ellington And His Orchestra | Duke Ellington's Jungle Style | Black & Blue | BLE 59.234 2
Humphrey Lyttelton And His Band | A Tribute To Duke Ellington Vol.2 | Jazz Colours | 874719-2
Mills' Ten Black Berries | Jazz Classics In Digital Stereo: Duke Ellington | CDS Records Ltd. | REB 643
| Barrelhouse Jazzband Plays Duke Ellington | L+R Records | LR 40026

East St.Louis Toodle-Oo-
Duke Ellington And His Orchestra | Duke Ellington:Complete Prestige Carnegie Hall 1946-1947 Concerts | Definitive Records | DRCD 11211

East Texas Freezeout-
Lennie Tristano Trio | Requiem | Atlantic | 7567-80804-2

East Thirty-Second
That's Jazz Vol.15: Lennie Tristano | Atlantic | ATL 50245

East Virginia,West Memphis
Billy Harper Quintet | Destiny Is Yours | Steeplechase | SCCD 31260

Easter Blue
Guitar Shorty | Alone In His Field | Trix Records | TRIX 3306

Easter Parade
Oscar Peterson Trio | The Song Is You-The Best Of The Verve Songbooks | Verve | 531558-2
Roy Eldridge And His Orchestra | The Complete Verve Roy Eldridge Studio Sessions | Verve | 9861278
Roy Eldridge Quartet | Frenchie Roy | Vogue | 655009

Easter Song
Henning Schmiedt-Volker Schlott Group | PAmagieRA | Peregrina Music | PM 50081

Eastern Blues
Henry Brown | Paramount Piano Blues Vol.2(1927-1932) | Black Swan Records | HCD-12012

Eastern Chimes Blues
Jon Balke w/Magnetic North Orchestra | Further | ECM | 1517

Eastern Forest
Furio Romano Quartet | What Colour For A Tale | SPLASC(H) Records | CD H 351-2

Eastern Incident
Harry Pepl Trio | Schoenberg Improvations | Amadeo | 843086-2

Eastern Lady
Out Of The Blue | O.T.B. | Blue Note | BT 85118 Digital

Eastern Parkway
David Phillips & Fredance | David Phillips & Freedance | Naxos Jazz | 86061-2

Eastern Princess
Charles Loos Quintet | No Wall, No War(Jazz Ballet) | B.Sharp Records | CDS 090

Eastern Song
Paul Horn And Nexus | The Altitude Of The Sun | Black Sun Music | 15002-2

Eastern Western Promise(part 1&2)
Mark Egan Group | A Touch Of Light | GRP | GRP 95722

Easy Come Easy Go
Klaus Doldinger's Passport | Heavy Nights | Warner | 2292-42006-2
Lucy Reed With The Eddie Higgins Trio | This Is Lucy Reed | Original Jazz Classics | OJCCD 1943-2(F 3243)
Michael Bocian Quartet | Reverence | Enja | 8096-2

Easy Does It
Clark Terry With Bob Lark And The DePaul University Big Band | Clark Terry Express | Reference Recordings | RR-73 CD
Count Basie Trio | For The First Time | Pablo | 2310712-2
Lester Young And His Band | Tenor Triumvirate:Bean & Prez & Chu | Queen-Disc | 051
Oscar Peterson Trio | Night Train | Verve | 521440-2
Night Train | Verve | 821724-2
Ray Brown Trio | Soular Energy | Concord | CJ 268
Steve Slagle Quartet | Spread The Words | Steeplechase | SCCD 31354

Easy Does It(alt.take)
Steve White Quintet | Jazz In Hollywood:Steve White | Original Jazz Classics | OJCCD 1891-2(Nocturne unreleased)

Easy Ernie
Marlena Shaw With Orchestra | From The Depths Of My Soul | Blue Note | 84443

Easy For You
Plas Johnson Sextet | Positively | Concord | CCD 4024

Easy Going
Guido Manusardi Trio | Introduction | Penta Flowers | CDPIA 009

Easy Listening Blues
Nat King Cole Trio | Vocal Classics & Instrumental Classics | Capitol | 300014(TOCJ 6128)
Oscar Peterson Trio | Compact Jazz:Oscar Peterson | Mercury | 830698-2
With Respect To Nat | Verve | 557486-2
Ronnell Bright Trio | The Ronnell Bright Trio | Fresh Sound Records | FSR 559(Polydor 46106)

Easy Living
Ahmad Jamal Trio | Live In Paris 1992 | Dreyfus Jazz Line | FDM 37019-2
Live In Paris 92 | Birdology | 849408-2
Anita O'Day With The Bill Holman Orchestra | Incomparable! Anita O'Day | Verve | 589516-2
Archie Shepp-Mal Waldron | Left Alone Revisited | Enja | 9141-2
Bill Evans Trio | Bill Evans:The Secret Sessions | Milestone | 8MCD 4421-2
Bill Perkins With The Jan Lundgren Trio | Bill Perkins Recreates The Historic Solos Of Lester Young | Fresh Sound Records | FSR-CD 5010
Cannonball Adderley Quintet | Them Dirty Blues | Blue Note | 495447-2
Them Dirty Blues | Capitol | 495447-2
The Cannonball Adderley Collection Vol.1:Them Dirty Blues | Landmark | CAC 1301-2(882341)
Clementine With The Johnny Griffin Quartet | Continent Bleu | Orange Blue | OB 004 CD
Count Basie And His Orchestra | Me And You | Pablo | 2310891-2
Dinah Washington And Her Orchestra | For Those In Love | EmArCy | 514073-2
Dinah Washington With The Quincy Jones Orchestra | Compact Jazz: Dinah Washington | Mercury | 830700-2 PMS
Enrico Rava Quintet | Easy Living | ECM | 1760(9812050)
Etta Jones And Her Quartet | Something Nice | Original Jazz Classics | OJCCD 221-2(P 7194)
Flip Phillips With The Woody Herman Orchestra | Together Flip & Woody | CDS Records Ltd. | CJCD 828
Frank Newton And His Uptown Serenaders | Frankie's Jump | Affinity | CD AFS 1014
George Cables Trio | BluesOlogy | Steeplechase | SCCD 31434
Hal Singer Orchestra | Rent Party | Savoy | SV 0258(SJL 1147)
Hampton Hawes Trio | Hampton Hawes Trio Vol.1 | Original Jazz Classics | OJC20 316-2(C 3505)
Harry Verbeke/Carlo de Wijs Quartet | Plays Romantic Ballads | Timeless | CD SJP 230
Heiner Franz & Friends | Jazz Guitar Highlights 1 | Jardis Records | JRCD 20141
Herb Ellis-Joe Pass Quartet | Seven, Comes Eleven | Concord | CCD 6002
Jackie McLean-John Jenkins Quintet | Alto Madness | Original Jazz Classics | OJCCD 1733-2(P 7114)
Joachim Kühn-Rolf Kühn | Love Stories | IN+OUT Records | 77061-2
Joe Bonner Quartet | The Lost Melody | Steeplechase | SCCD 31227
Joe Zawinul Trio | His Majesty Swinging Nephews 1954-1957 | RST-Records | 91549-2
John Crocker Quartet | Easy Living | Timeless | CD TTD 561
Kenny Burrell-Jimmy Smith Trio | Blue Bash | Verve | 557453-2
Kurt Elling Group | Flirting With Twilight | Blue Note | 531113-2
Lanny Morgan Quintet | It's About Time | Palo Alto | PA 8007
Lee Konitz With Strings | Strings For Holiday:A Tribute To Billie Holiday | Enja | ENJ-9304 2
Lee Konitz-Rich Perry With The Harold Danko Trio | RichLee | Steeplechase | SCCD 31440
Lou Colombo Quintet | I Remember Bobby | Concord | CCD 4435
Marian McPartland | Maybeck Recital Hall Series Volume Nine | Concord | CCD 4460
Miles Davis Quintet | Charles Mingus-The Complete Debut Recordings | Debut | 12 DCD 4402-2
Morgana King With Orchestra | A Taste Of Honey | Mainstream | MD CDO 707
Nat Pierce/Dick Collins Nonet | Nat Pierce-Dick Collins Nonet/Charlie Mariano Sextet | Original Jazz Classics | OJC 118(F 3224)
Paul Desmond Quartet | Easy Living | RCA | 2174796-2
Paul Desmond With Strings | Masters Of Jazz Vol.13 | RCA | CL 42790 AG
Phil Woods Sextet | Young Woods | Fresh Sound Records | FSR-CD 0182
Ray Brown Trio With Joe Lovano | Some Of My Best Friends Are...The Sax Players | Telarc Digital | CD 83388
Ronnie Cuber With The Metropole Orchestra | Passion Fruit | Koch Jazz | 3-6914-2
Ruby Braff And His Orchestra | The Mighty Braff | Affinity | AFF 757
Sarah Vaughan With The Oscar Peterson Quartet | Sarah Vaughan Birthday Celebration | Fantasy | FANCD 6090-2
How Long Has This Been Going On? | Pablo | 2310821-2
Silvia Droste And Her Quartet | Audiophile Voicings | BELL Records | BLR 84004
Sonny Rollins Quartet | Easy Living | Milestone | M 9080
Stan Getz Quartet | Blue Skies | Concord | CCD 4676
Tony Scott Quartet | The Clarinet Album | Philology | W 113.2
Wardell Gray Quartet | Wardell Gray:Light Gray 1948-1950 | Cool & Blue | C&B-CD 116
Zoot Sims Quartet | For Lady Day | Pablo | 2310942-2

Easy Living-
Willis Jackson Quintet | Together Again: Willis Jackson With Jack McDuff | Prestige | PRCD 24284-2
Wardell Gray Quartet | Wardell Gray Memorial Vol.1 | Original Jazz Classics | OJCCD 050-2(P 7008)

Easy Living(alt.take)
Bud Shank/Bob Cooper Sextet | Hello Baden-Baden | Jazzline | ???

Easy Money
Benny Carter Sextet | To Bags...With Love:Memorial Album | Pablo | 2310967-2
The King | Original Jazz Classics | 2310768

Easy On The Heart
Earl Hines And His Orchestra | The Indispensable Earl Hines Vol.1/2 | RCA | 2126407-2

Easy Rhythm
Dixie Rhythm Kings | That's My Stuff | Frog | DGF 7

Easy Rider
Leadbelly[Huddie Ledbetter] | Alabama Bound | RCA | ND 90321(847151)

Easy Street
Duke Ellington And His Famous Orchestra | Duke Ellington & His Famous Orchestra | Forlane | UCD 19003
June Christy With The Pete Rugolo Orchestra | June Christy Recalls Those Kenton Days | EMI Records | 1599311

Easy Swing
Wardell Gray Quartet | Lions Abroad Volume One:Tenor Titans | Black Lion | BLCD 7620-2

Easy To Get
Bud Freeman And His Summa Cum Laude Orchestra | A String Of Swingin' Pearls | RCA | 2113035-2

Easy To Love
Ben Webster Quartet | Three Tenors | Jazz Colours | 874706-2
Billie Holiday With Teddy Wilson And His Orchestra | Billie Holiday:The Quintessential Vol.2(1936) | CBS | 460060-2
Cannonball Adderley Sextet | Nippon Soul | Original Jazz Classics | OJC20 435-2(RLP 9477)
Carmen McRae With The Mat Mathews Quintet | Easy To Love | Bethlehem | BTM 6817
Charlie Parker Quartet With Strings | Concert At Carnegie Hall | Atlantis | ATS 2 D
Charlie Parker With Strings | Charlie Parker:April In Paris | Dreyfus Jazz Line | FDM 36737-2
Bird With Strings-Live At The Apollo, Carnegie Hall & Birdland | CBS | CBS 82292
Bird: The Complete Charlie Parker On Verve | Verve | 837141-2
Bird's Eyes Last Unissued Vol.17 | Philology | W 847.2
Charlie Parker With The Joe Lipman Orchestra | Charlie Parker With Strings:The Master Takes | Verve | 523984-2
Chris Potter Quartet | Pure | Concord | CCD 4637
Don Wilkerson Quartet | The Texas Twister | Original Jazz Classics | OJCCD 1950-2(RLP 1186)
Ella Fitzgerald With The Buddy Bregman Orchestra | The Cole Porter Song Book | Verve | 2683044 IMS
Ella Fitzgerald Sings The Cole Porter Songbook Vol.2 | Verve | 821990-2
Erroll Garner Trio | Gems | CBS | 21062
Gene Ammons Quintet | 'Jug' | Original Jazz Classics | OJCCD 701-2(P 7192)
Jack Millman Quartet | Four More | Fresh Sound Records | FSR-CD 0217
John Campbell | Maybeck Recital Hall Series Volume Twenty-Nine | Concord | CCD 4581
Morgana King With Orchestra | A Taste Of Honey | Mainstream | MD CDO 707
Oscar Peterson Trio | Oscar Peterson Plays The Cole Porter Song Book | Verve | 821987-2
Oscar Peterson-Ray Brown Duo | Keyboard Music By Oscar Peterson | Verve | MV 2666 IMS
Roland Kirk Quintet | Live In Paris 1970 Vol.1 | France's Concert | FCD 109
Sarah Vaughan With Mundell Lowe And George Duvivier | The Man I Love | Jazz Society(Vogue) | 670504
Skinnay Ennis And His Orchestra | The Uncollected:Skinnay Ennis | Hindsight | HSR 164 (835575)
Sonny Stitt-Sadik Hakim Quartet | Sonny Stitt Meets Sadik Hakim | Progressive | PRO 7034 IMS
Sun Ra Quintet | Standards | Black Lion | CD 877643-2

Easy To Love-
Marion Montgomery And Her Quintet | Nice And Easy | Ronnie Scott's Jazz House | JHCD 011
Trudy Desmond With The Ed Bickert Trio | Make Me Rainbows | Koch Jazz | KOC 3-7803-2

Easy To Read
Sarah Vaughan With The Jimmy Jones Trio And The Basie Reed And Brass Sextion | Birdland All Stars At Carnegie Hall | Roulette | CDP 798660-2

Easy To Remember
Harry Babasin Quintet | The Complete Nocturne Recordings:Jazz In Hollywood Series Vol.1 | Fresh Sound Records | NR 3CD-101
Jazz In Hollywood:Harry Babasin/Bob Enevoldsen | Original Jazz Classics | OJCCD 1888-2(Nocturne NLP3/NLP-6)
Liam Noble | Close Your Eyes | FMR | FMR CD 25
John Coltrane Quartet | Ballads | Impulse(MCA) | 589548-2

Easy To Remember(alt.take 1)
Ballads | Impulse(MCA) | 589548-2

Easy To Remember(alt.take 2)
Ballads | Impulse(MCA) | 589548-2

Easy To remember(alt.take 2)
Ballads | Impulse(MCA) | 589548-2

Easy To Remember(alt.take 3)
Ballads | Impulse(MCA) | 589548-2

Easy To Remember(alt.take 4)
Ballads | Impulse(MCA) | 589548-2

Easy To Remember(alt.take 5)
Ballads | Impulse(MCA) | 589548-2

Easy To Remember(alt.take 6)
Buck Clayton Quintet | Jazz In Paris:Peanuts Holland-Buck Clayton-Charlie Singleton | EmArCy | 013032-2

Easy Walker
Coleman Hawkins With The Frank Hunter Orchestra | Hawk Talk | Fresh Sound Records | FSR-CD 0130
Eat That Chicken
Charles Mingus Quintet With Roland Kirk | Oh Yeah | Atlantic | 90667-1 TIS
Eat Time
White Orange | White Orange | Caprice | CAP 1215
Eb Pob
Helen Humes With Roy Milton's Band | E-Baba-Le-Ba The Rhythm And Blues Years | Savoy | WL 70824 (809326)
Ebb
Dave Holland Qartet | Dream Of The Elders | ECM | 1572(529084-2)
Ebb & Flo
Dave Liebman Quartet | The Elements:Water | Arkadia Jazz | 71043
Ebb Tide
Ozzie Nelson And His Orchestra | The Uncollected:Ozzie Nelson, Vol.2 | Hindsight | HSR 189
The Houdini's | Kickin' In The Frontwindows | Timeless | CD SJP 405
Ella Fitzgerald With Benny Carter's Magnificent Seven | 30 By Ella | Capitol | 520090-2
Ebb Tide-
Thad Jones With The Danish Radio Big Band | By Jones I Think We Got It | Atlantic | ATL 50548
Ebony
Jay Clayton And Her Quintet | Circle Dancing | Sunnyside | SSC 1076 D
Ebony Concerto(third movement)
Bob Berg Group | Riddles | Stretch Records | SCD 9008-2
Ebony Queen
McCoy Tyner Quartet | Reflections | Milestone | M 47062
Ebony Rhapsody
Stan Getz-Luiz Bonfa Quartet | Jazz Samba Encore! | Verve | 823613-2
Ebony Samba(first version)
Stan Getz-Luiz Bonfa Quintet | Jazz Samba Encore! | Verve | 823613-2
Ebony Samba(second version)
Duane Eubanks Quintet/Sextet | Second Take | TCB Records | TCB 20602
E-Bossa
Roland Kirk And His Orchestra | Rahsaan/The Complete Mercury Recordings Of Roland Kirk | Mercury | 846630-2
Ebrauqs
Hamiet Bluiett Quartet | EBU | Soul Note | 121088-2
Ecaroh
Art Blakey And The Jazz Messengers | Art Blakey/The Jazz Messengers | CBS | CK 62265
Horace Silver Trio | Horace Silver Trio And Spotlight On Drums:Art Blakey-Sabu | Blue Note | 591725-2
Trio Hein Van Der Gaag | To The Point | Limetree | MLP 0018
Wes Montgomery Trio | Wes Montgomery-The Complete Riverside Recordings | Riverside | 12 RCD 4408-2
Ran Blake Trio | Horace Is Blue:A Silver Noir | HatOLOGY | 550
Ecars
Ornette Coleman Quartet | Ornette On Tenor | Atlantic | 8122-71455-2
Andy LaVerne/Dave Samuels | Fountainhead | Steeplechase | SCCD 31261
Eccentric
Friars Society Orchestra | New Orleans Rhythm Kings | Village(Jazz Archive) | VILCD 004-2
Jack Teagarden And His Orchestra | Jazz Original | Charly | CD 80
Ecclusiastics
Charles Mingus Quintet With Roland Kirk | The Very Best Of Charles Mingus | Rhino | 8122-79988-2
Oh Yeah | Atlantic | 90667-1 TIS
Mingus Dynasty | Reincarnation | Soul Note | 121042-2
Paquito D'Rivera Orchestra | Portraits Of Cuba | Chesky | JD 145
Echo
Steve Swallow Group | Home | ECM | 1160(513424-2)
Toni Jannotta Group | Jazz At The Ranch | TCB Records | TCB 21182
Echoes
Leon Thomas With Band | Spirits Known And Unknown | RCA | 2663876-2
Lou Bennett Trio With The Paris Jazz All Stars | Jazz In Paris | EmArCy | 548790-2
Milt Jackson Big Band | Big Band Bags | Milestone | M 47006
Modern Jazz Quartet | Milt Jackson Birthday Celebration | Fantasy | FANCD 6079-2
The Complete Modern Jazz Quartet Prestige & Pablo Recordings | Prestige | 4PRCD 4438-2
The Best Of The Modem Jazz Quartet | Pablo | 2405423-2
Todd Rhodes And His Orchestra | Dance Music That Hits The Spot! | Swingtime(Contact) | ST 1020
Echoes-
The Crossover Ensemble | The River:Image Of Time And Life | dacapo | DCCD 9434
Mike Westbrook Concert Band | Celebration | Deram | 844852-2
Echoes Of A Memory
Freddie Hubbard Quintet | Backlash | Atlantic | SD 1477
Echoes Of Blue
Lalo Schifrin Trio With The London Philharmonic | Jazz Meets The Symphony | East-West | 4509-92004-2
Echoes Of Duke Ellington
Django Reinhardt And The Quintet Du Hot Club De France | Django Reinhardt:Djangology | EMI Records | 780659-2
Echoes Of France(La Marseillaise)
Bud Shank-Shorty Rogers Quintet | California Concert | Contemporary | CCD 14012-2
Echoes Of Harlem
Charlie Bamet And His Orchestra | Charlie Barnet Vol.1 | Zeta | ZET 749
Duke Ellington And His Orchestra | Live Recording At The Cotton Club-Vol. 2 | Jazz Anthology | JA 5169
Harry Allen And Randy Sandke Meets The RIAS Big Band Berlin | The Music Of The Trumpet Kings | Nagel-Heyer | CD 037
John Kirby And His Band | 1940 | Jazz Anthology | 550252
Shorty Rogers Big Band | Jazz Waltz | Discovery | DS 843 IMS
Echoes Of Harlem-
Duke Ellington And His Orchestra | Duke Ellington:Complete Prestige Carnegie Hall 1946-1947 Concerts | Definitive Records | DRCD 11211
Roy Eldridge Quintet | The Complete Verve Roy Eldridge Studio Sessions | Verve | 9861278
Echoes Of Harlem(10" LP-Master)
Cootie Williams And His Rug Cutters | The Complete Duke Ellington-Vol. 10 | CBS | CBS 88220
Echoes Of Spring
Howard Alden Trio | A Good Likeness | Concord | CCD 4544
Ralph Sutton | Maybeck Recital Hall Series Volume Thirty | Concord | CCD 4586
Willie 'The Lion' Smith | Commodore Classics-Willie 'The Lion' Smith:Composer-Entertainer | Commodore | 6.25491 AG
Echoes Of The Deep
Helen Shapiro & Humphrey Lyttelton And His Band | Echoes Of The Duke | Calligraph | CLG LP 002 IMS
Echoes Of The Jungle
Duke Ellington And His Orchestra | The Indispensable Duke Ellington Vol.3/4(1930-1934) | RCA | 2122620-2
Victor Jazz History Vol.12:Ellingtonia | RCA | 2135731-2
Echo-Side Blue
String Trio Of New York | Area Cone 212 | Black Saint | BSR 0048
Echubelekéo
Christof Lauer-Jens Thomas | Shadows In The Rain | ACT | 9297-2
Ecilop
Rüdiger Carl | Rüdiger Carl Solo | FMP | CD 86
Eclipse
Charles Mingus Orchestra | Tonight At Noon...Three Or Four Shades Of Love | Dreyfus Jazz Line | FDM 36633-2
Charles Mingus:Pre-Bird(Mingus Revisited) | Verve | 538636-2
David Valentine Group | Kalahari | GRP | GRP 95082
Eric Dolphy Quartet | Eric Dolphy Birthday Celebration | Fantasy | FANCD 6085-2
Out There | New Jazz | NJSA 8252-6
Eric Dolphy:The Complete Prestige Recordings | Prestige | 9 PRCD-4418-2
Freddie Hubbard Orchestra | Mistral | Liberty | LT 1110
Jack Walrath And The Masters Of Suspense | Hip Gnosis | TCB Records | TCB 01062
Joe Diorio Trio | More Than Friends | RAM Records | RMCD 4514
Marcus Pintrup Quintet | Unveiled | Blue Note | 837302-2
Eclipse(alt.take)
Lee Morgan Quintet | The Rumproller | Blue Note | 521229-2
Eclipso
Tommy Flanagan Trio | Eclypso | Enja | 2088-2
Eclypse
Gato Barbieri Group | Gato Barbieri:The Complete Flying Dutchman Recordings 1969-1973 | RCA | 2154555-2
Eclypso
Prestige All Stars | John Coltrane-The Prestige Recordings | Prestige | 16 PCD 4405-2
Tommy Flanagan Trio | The Complete 'Overseas' | DIW | DIW 305 CD
John McNeil Sextet | Fortuity | Steeplechase | SCCD 31499
Eco
Marty Hall Band | Tried & True | Blues Beacon | BLU-1030 2
Ecoman
Kamafra | Kamafra Live | Edition Musikat | EDM 072
Ecotopia
Oregon | Ecotopia | ECM | 1354
Beyond Words | Chesky | JD 130
Ecstasy
Buddy Johnson And His Orchestra | Buddy And Ella Johnson 1953-1964 | Bear Family Records | BCD 15479 DH
Elmo Hope Ensemble | Hope From Rikers Island | Chiaroscuro | CR 2009
Frank Kirchner Group | Frank Kirchner | Laika Records | LK 93-036
Oscar Peterson Quintet | Oscar Peterson Meets Roy Hargrove And Ralph Moore | Telarc Digital | CD 83399
Dave Douglas Quartet | A Thousand Evenings | RCA | 2663698-2
Ecstatic
The Human Arts Ensemble | The Human Arts Ensemble Live, Vol.2 | Circle Records | RK 12-23578/12 IMS
Edda
Teodross Avery Quintet | In Other Words | GRP | GRP 97982
Eddie's Blues
Eddie Boyd Blues Band | Five Long Years | L+R Records | CDLR 72009
Eddie's Razzmatazz Rap
Eddie Palmieri Group | Vortex | RMM Records | 660.58.116
Ede Pustefix
Peter Brötzmann-Willi Kellers Duo | Maar Helaas! | FMP | 0800
Edelweiss
Gene Bertoncici Trio | Acoustic Romance | Paddle Wheel | KICJ 155
Eden
Danielsson-Liebman-Christensen-Stenson | Far North | Curling Legs Prod. | C.L.P. CD 013
Edge Of The Wing
Michael Shrieve Group | The Leaving Time | RCA | PD 83032
Edges Of Illusion
Room | Room | Sound Aspects | sas CD 028
Edie
Cannonball Adderley Quintet | Cannonball Adderley:Sophisticated Swing-The EmArCy Small Group Sessions | Verve | 528408-2
Edie McLin
Arcado | Behind The Myth | JMT Edition | 834441-2
Edison's Lights
Harry Edison Quintet | The Best Of Harry Edison | Pablo | 2310847
Edith
Bennie Wallace Quintet | The Art Of The Saxophone | Denon Compact Disc | CY-1648
Edith Variation
Günter Sommer | Hörmusik III:Sächsische Schatulle | Intakt Records | CD 027
Educating People-
Harold Mabern-Kieran Overs | Philadelphia Bound | Sackville | SKCD2-3051
Ee-Ah
Sonny Rollins Quartet | Taking Care Of Business | Prestige | P 24082
Buddy Rich And His Orchestra | Live Sessions At The Palladium, Hollywood | Jazz Anthology | JA 5206
Eeeyyess!
Elmo Hope Trio | HiFiJazz | Fresh Sound Records | FSR-CD 0074
Een Kennis Vind Ik Niks
Serge Chaloff All Stars | The Fable Of Mabel | Black Lion | CD 877627-2
Eerie Dearie
Duke Ellington And His Famous Orchestra | The Complete Duke Ellington-Vol. 5 | CBS | CBS 88082
Efeler(turkish folk material)
Marcello Rosa Quartet | Jass & Jazz | Penta Flowers | CDPIA 008
Effendi
Ray Barretto & New World Spirit | Taboo | Concord | CCD 4601
E-Flat Blues
Fats Waller | The Music Of New Orleans | RCA | NL 89724 DP
Francis Coletta Trio + One | Cris De Balaines | IN+OUT Records | 77030-2
Margaret Johnson With Clarence Williams' Blue Five | The Complete 1923-1926 Clarence Williams Sessions Vol.1 | EPM Musique | FDC 5107
E-Flat Blues(alt.take)
Buster Smith Orchestra | Atlantic Jazz: Kansas City | Atlantic | 7567-81701-2
E-Flat Boogie
Guitar Madness | Guitar Madness | Nueva Records | HM 705
Eftermiddag(Afternoon)
Quartette Indigo | Quartette Indigo | Landmark | LCD 1536-2
Eg Veit I Himmerik Ei Borg(Ich Weiß Im Himmelreich)
Christian McBride Group | Number Two Express | Verve | 529585-2
Egad,Martha
Olga Konkova Trio | Her Point Of View | Candid | CCD 79757
Egberto
Stan Kenton And His Orchestra | Kenton Showcase | Creative World | ST 1026
Egg
Benny Goodman And His Orchestra | Undercurrent Blues | Capitol | 832086-2
Egg Learns To Walk...Suyafhu Seal
Jacques Pirotton Trio | Soty | B.Sharp Records | CDS 087
Egil
Betty Carter And Her Trio | Betty Carter | Bet-Car | MK 1001
Egocentric Molecules
Jean-Luc Ponty Group | Jean-Luc Ponty: Live | Atlantic | ATL 50594
Jean-Luc Ponty Sextet | The Very Best Of Jean-Luc Ponty | Rhino | 8122-79862-2
Johannes Enders Quintet | Bright Nights | Enja | ENJ-9352 2
Egon
Michel Benita Quartet | Preferences | Label Bleu | LBLC 6532(882935)
Egugu
Joseph Jarman-Don Moye | Egwu-Anwu | India Navigation | IN 1033
Egyptain Fantasy
New Orleans Feetwarmers | Jazz:The Essential Collection Vol.1 | IN+OUT Records | 78011-2
Sidney Bechet And His New Orleans Feetwarmers | Spreadin Joy (Original Recordings 1940-50) | Naxos Jazz | 8.120531 CD
Egyptian
Lee Konitz Quartet | Haiku | Nabel Records:Jazz Network | CD 4664
Egyptian Caravan
Al Di Meola Group | Casino | CBS | 468215-2
Egyptian Dance
Al Di Meola Groups | Guitar Heroes Vol.1:Al Di Meola | Zounds | CD 2700044001
Al Di Meola Group | Tour De Force-Live | CBS | 25121-2
Egyptian Fantasy
Sidney Bechet And His New Orleans Feetwarmers | Sidney Bechet 1932-1943: The Bluebird Sessions | Bluebird | ND 90317
Eh-Las-Bas
Terry Lightfoot's Jazzmen | Down On Bourbon Street | Timeless | CD TTD 581
Eiderdown
Bill Evans Trio With Lee Konitz & Warne Marsh | Crosscurrents | Original Jazz Classics | OJCCD 718-2(F 9568)
Lee Konitz Trio | Three Guys | Enja | ENJ-9351 2
Pat LaBarbera Quartet | Virgo Dance | Justin Time | Just 24
Bill Evans Trio With Lee Konitz & Warne Marsh | Crosscurrents | Original Jazz Classics | OJCCD 718-2(F 9568)
Eidolon
Jimmy Giuffre André Jaume | Momentum,Willisay 1988 | HatOLOGY | 508
Eigentlich Bin Ich Hautarzt
Om | Cerberus | Japo | 60032
Eight
Sandy Brown With The Brian Lemon Trio | In The Evening | Hep | CD 2017
Eight Five Five
Xu Feng Xia | Difference And Similarity | FMP | CD 96
Eight Plus Three-
Muthspiel-Peacock-Muthspiel-Motian | Muthspiel-Peacock-Muthspiel-Motian | Amadeo | 519676-2
Eighteen
Pat Metheny Group | Offramp | ECM | 1216(817138-2)
Peter Bolte Quartet | Evocation | Jazz Haus Musik | JHM 0079 CD
Rüdiger Carl | Rüdiger Carl Solo | FMP | CD 86
Eighth Veil
Dick Griffin Septet | The Eighth Wonder & More | Konnex Records | KCD 5059
Eighth Wonder
Eric Lugosch | Black Key Blues | Acoustic Music Records | 319.1148.2
Eighty-One
Glenn Wilson/Rory Stuart | Bittersweet | Sunnyside | SSC 1057 D
Kirk Lightsey Quartet | First Affairs | Limetree | MCD 0015
Miles Davis Quintet | Miles Davis Quintet 1965-1968 | CBS | C6K 67398
Tom Browne Quintet | Another Shade Of Browne | Hip Bop | HIBD 8011
Eiji Kitamura Group | Swing Eiji | Eastworld | ICJ 90001
Ein Anflug Von Sehnsucht
Ulli Bögershausen | Best Of Ulli Bögershausen | Laika Records | LK 93-045
Brötzmann, van Hove, Bennink | Tschüs | FMP | 0230
Ein Blindenhund Und Ein Spazierhund
Gebhard Ullmann Trio | Suite Noire | Nabel Records:Jazz Network | CD 4649
Ein Denkmal Für Rosa Und Karl-
Matthias Rosenbauer-Gerhard Gschlößl | Duo 1 | Jazz 4 Ever Records:Jazz Network | J4E 4763
Ein Dunkles Helles
Cowws Quintet plus Guests | Book/Virtual Cowws | FMP | OWN-90007/9
Ein Feste Burg
Wolf Mayer Trio | I Do Believe In Spring | Triptychon | 400403
Brodmann-Pausch Percussion Duo | Are You Serious? | Jazz 4 Ever Records:Jazz Network | J4E 4718
Ein Flug Über's Kuckucksnest
Bermuda Viereck | Noblesse Galvanisee | Plainisphare | PL 1267-20/21
Ein Ittlige Sprak Hat Ir Eigen Art
Fun Horns | Surprise | Jazzpoint | JP 1029 CD
Ein Jahr Später
Uri Caine Ensemble | Love Fugue-Robert Schumann | Winter&Winter | 910049-2
Ein Jüngling Liebt Ein Mädchen
Gabriele Hasler Group | Gabriele Hasler's Rosensrücke | Foolish Music | FM 211096
Ein Knabe Ist Ein...
Theo Jörgensmann | Laterna Magica | CMP Records | CMP 19
Ein Liebes Paar-
Inge Brandenburg | Why Don't You Take All Of Me | Bear Family Records | BCD 15614 AH
Ein Mann Ist Ein Mann
Vienna Art Orchestra | All That Strauss | TCB Records | TCB 20052
Ein Tag Im Leben Des Jungen L.
Erdmann 2000 | Recovering From y2k | Jazz 4 Ever Records:Jazz Network | J4E 4750
Irene Schweizer/Pierre Favre | Irene Schweizer & Pierre Favre | Intakt Records | CD 009
Ein Unsel In Ali's Bus
Heinz | Bavarian Back Beat | Jazz Haus Musik | JHM 41 CD
Einbahnstrasse
Houston Person-Ron Carter | Now's The Time | Muse | MCD 5421
Einbúinn
Irene Schweizer/Han Bennink | Irene Schweizer & Han Bennink | Intakt Records | CD 010
Eine Kleine März Muzik
Brötzmann-Miller-Moholo Trio | Opened But Hardly Touched | FMP | 0840/50
Eine Kleine Sekunde Vor 4
Petra Straue & The Moonmen | Voices Around My House | Satin Doll Productions | SDP 1016-1 CD
Eine Nacht In Monte Carlo
Adam Noidlt-Intermission | Eine Permanent Helle Fläche | Jazz Haus Musik | JHM 53 CD
Eine Reprise Ist Eine...
Matthias Schubert Quartet | Momentum | Jazzline | JL 11160-2
Eines Tages...-
Marius Ungureanu-Sergiu Nastase-Räto Harder | Musikversuche | Experimente 93 | MU/EX 93
Einmal Ist Keinmal
Nicolas Thijs Trio | Europ' Jazz Contest Belgium '93 | B.Sharp Records | CDS 097
Einsturz
Christopher Dell D.R.A. | Future Of The Smallest Form | Jazz 4 Ever Records:Jazz Network | J4E 4754
Einunddreissig
Future Of The Smallest Form | Jazz 4 Ever Records:Jazz Network | J4E 4754
Einundvierzig
Thilo von Westernhagen Duo | Ardent Desire | SHP Records | SHP 202
Eisemo
H.P.Salentin Group | It's Up To You | Mons Records | MR 874787
Either Or
Dave Grusin Group | Mountain Dance | GRP | GRP 95072
Either Way
Nina Simone Quartet | Nina Simone-The 60s Vol.3:Work Song | Mercury | 838545-2 PMS
Eix
Victor Alcántara Trio | Stabat Mater Inspirations | Organic Music | ORGM 9716
Eja Mater
The Brazz Brothers | Ngoma | Laika Records | 35101562
Ejala
Friedeman Graef-Achim Goettert | Saxoridoo | FMP | OWN-90010
EJP
Abdullah Ibrahim Group | Ekaya(Home) | Black-Hawk | BKH 50205
EKE Blues
Ippe Kätkä Band | Ippe Kätkä Band | Leo Records | 018
Ekpyrosis
Reinhard Flatischler | Transformation | VeraBra Records | CDVBR 2033-2
El Abadonado
Les Misérables Brass Band | Manic Tradition | Popular Arts | NR 5004 CD

TITELVERZEICHNIS

El Agarejo
Lluis Vidal Trio | Tren Nocturn | Fresh Sound Records | FSNT 003 CD
Orquestra De Cambra Teatre Lliure | Orquestra De Cambra Teatre Lliure and Lluis Vidal Trio feat.Dave Liebman | Fresh Sound Records | FSNT 027 CD
Francois Theberge Group | Europ' Jazz Contest '92 Belgium | B.Sharp Records | CDS 092

El Amanecer
Rova Saxophone Quartet | Beat Kennel | Black Saint | 120126-2

El Barrio
Joe Henderson Quartet | Joe Henderson-The Blue Note Years | Blue Note | 789287-2
Mark Helias Group | Loopin' The Cool | Enja | ENJ-9049 2

El Baz
Toto Blanke-Diego Jasca | Sur | ALISO Records | AL 1035

El Bobo
Irazu | Charanga De La Luna | L+R Records | CDLR 45053

El Bosc De Les Fades
Mongo Santamaria And His Band | Sabroso | Original Jazz Classics | OJCCD 281-2

El Bote
Chick Corea And His Orchestra | My Spanish Heart | Polydor | 543303-3

El Bozo(part 1-3)
Bobby McFerrin | The Voice | Elektra | 7559-60366-2

El Brujo
Joe Gallardo Group | Latino Blue | Inak | 853

El Cadete Constitucional
Stan Getz Quartet | Anniversary ! | EmArCy | 838769-2

El Cahon
Al Cohn Quartet | Nonpareil | Concord | CCD 4155

El Cajon
Herb Geller Quartet | Herb Geller Plays The Al Cohn Songbook | Hep | CD 2066
Jim Tomlinson Quintet | Only Trust Your Heart | Candid | CCD 79758
David Benoit Group With Symphony Orchestra | Inner Motion | GRP | GRP 96212

El Camino Real
J.J.Johnson And His Orchestra | J.J.! | RCA | 2125727-2

El Camino(Introduccion-Imitacion)
Mongo Santamaria Orchestra | Olé Ola | Concord | CCD 4387

El Capitan
Avishai Cohen Group | Devotion | Stretch Records | SCD 9021-2

El Cel Puja
Mel Lewis Septet | Got' Cha | Fresh Sound Records | FSR-CD 0073

El Chancho
Nat Adderley Quintet | Natural Soul | Milestone | M 9009

El Chico
Bettina Born-Wolfram Born | Schattenspiel | Born&Bellmann | 993004 CD

El Choclo
Gianluigi Trovesi-Gianni Coscia | In Cerca Di Cibo | ECM | 1703(543034-2)
Mosalini/Beytelmann/Caratini | Inspiration Del Tango | Eigelstein | 568-72223
Stan Kenton And His Orchestra | The Formative Years(1941-1942) | Creative World | ST 1061

El Ciego
Daniel Schnyder Group | Tanatula | Enja | ENJ-9302 2

El Cigaro
Charlie Mariano Trio | Mariano | VeraBra Records | CDVBR 2124-2

El Colibri
Inti-Immimani | De Canto Y Baile | Messidor | 15936 CD

El Corazon
Horacio Molina With Band | Tango Cancion | Messidor | 15910

El Corazon De La Tierra
Daniel Messina Band | Imagenes | art-mode-records | 990014

El Corazon De Mi Pueblo
Paul Bley-Franz Koglmann-Gary Peacock | Anette | HatOLOGY | 564

El Cumbanchero
Mikesch Van Grümmer | Bar-Piano | Timeless | CD SJP 362
Eckart Runge-Jacques Ammon | Cello Tango | Edition Musikat | EDM 053

El Dia Que Me Quieras
Gabriel Pérez Group | Alfonsina | Jazz 4 Ever Records:Jazz Network | J4E 4751
Gato Barbieri Group | Masters Of Jazz Vol.9 | RCA | NL 89722
Gato Barbieri Sextet | Fenix | RCA | FD 10144

El Dimoni Escuat-
Les Misérables Brass Band | Manic Tradition | Popular Arts | NR 5004 CD

El Divorcio
Irakere | Misa Negra | Messidor | 15972 CD

El Escatime
Orquestra De Cambra Teatre Lliure feat. Dave Liebman | Orquestra De Cambra Teatre Lliure and Lluis Vidal Trio feat.Dave Liebman | Fresh Sound Records | FSNT 027 CD
Flor De Tango | Armenonville | Minor Music | 801097

El Esquinazo
Art De Fakt | Art De Fakt-Ray Federman:Surfiction Jazz No.2 | double moon | CHRDM 71007

El Eventones
Harold Ousley Group | The People's Groove | Muse | MR 5107

El Fatha Morgana
Terry Gibbs Quartet | Take It From Me | MCA | AS 58

El Firulete
Arnett Cobb-Tiny Grimes Quintet | Live In Paris 1974 | France's Concert | FCD 133

El Gato
Gato Barbieri Group | Planet Jazz:Gato Barbieri | RCA | 2165364-2
Gato Barbieri:The Complete Flying Dutchman Recordings 1969-1973 | RCA | 2154555-2

El Gaucho
Joe Chambers Quintet | Phantom Of The City | Candid | CCD 79517
Marc Ribot Y Los Cubanos Postizos | Nuy Divertido(Very Entertaining) | Atlantic | 7567-83293-2

El Gaucho Rojo
Laurindo Almeida-Charlie Byrd Quartet | Latin Odyssey | Concord | MC CJ 211C

El Gavilan-
Orquestra De Cambra Teatre Lliure feat. Dave Liebman | Orquestra De Cambra Teatre Lliure and Lluis Vidal Trio feat.Dave Liebman | Fresh Sound Records | FSNT 027 CD

El Gegant Del Pi-
Orquestra De Cambra Teatre Lliure and Lluis Vidal Trio feat.Dave Liebman | Fresh Sound Records | FSNT 027 CD

El Gegant I El Cargol:
Rod Levitt Orchestra | The Dynamic Sound Patterns Of The Rod Levitt Orchestra | Original Jazz Classics | OJCCD 1955-2(RS 9471)

El General
Joe Pass Trio | Intercontinental | MPS | 68121

El Ghalla Ghalletna-
Irakere | A Night At Ronnie Scott's Vol.4 | Ronnie Scott's Jazz House | NARCD 4

El Haris(Anxious)
Frank Lowe & The Saxemple | Inappropriate Choices | ITM-Pacific | ITMP 970062

El Hombre
Pat Martino Trio | Live At Yoshi's | Blue Note | 499749-2
Sun Ra And His Arkestra | Sound Of Joy | Delmark | DE 414

El Juicio(And Extensions Fabulosas)
Karlheinz Miklin All Stars | Carlitos-Karlheinz Miklin In Buenos Aires | Amadeo | 829447-1

El Lugar Y El Momento
Billy Brooks' El Babaku | Jazz Meets Africa:Noon In Tunisia-El Babaku | MPS | 531720-2

El Manicero
Mario Bauzá And His Afro-Cuban Jazz Orchestra | My Time Is Now | Messidor | 15842 CD

El Maranon
Paquito D'Rivera Group | Tico! Tico! | Chesky | JD 34

El Marne
Don Pullen Quartet | The Best Of Don Pullen:The Blue Note Years | Blue Note | 823513-2

El Matador
Vince Guaraldi-Bola Sete Quartet | Live At El Matador | Original Jazz Classics | OJC 289(F 8371)

El Mayor
JoAnne Brackeen Trio | Keyed Up | CBS | 83868

El Monito
Andres Boiarsky Quintet | Into The Light | Reservoir | RSR CD 149

El Nino
Michael Formanek Quintet | Nature Of The Beast | Enja | ENJ-9308 2

El Nino Jesus-
The Oom Maw Maw | Roger's Living Room | Timeless | CD SJP 353

El Noi De La Mare
Cesc Miralta Quartet | Sol De Nit | Fresh Sound Records | FSNT 098 CD

El Nou Mil-Lenni
Charlie Byrd And The Washington Guitar Quartet | Charlie Byrd/The Washington Guitar Quartet | Concord | CCD 42014

El Ojo De Dios
Tangata Rea | Tango Alla Baila | Winter&Winter | 910025-2

El Once
Stefan Karlsson Quartet | Below Zero | Justice Records | JR 0703-2

El Otro
Kölner Saxophon Mafia-Drümmele Maa-Elima | Baboma | Jazz Haus Musik | JHM 33

El Owora Befame-Ko(So, I'll Come Back)
Ruben Blades Y Seis Del Solar With Band | Buscando America | Messidor | 15924

El Pelado
Toto Blanke-Diego Jasca | Sur | ALISO Records | AL 1035

El Pelado(reprise)
Hernan Merlo Quintet | Consin | Fresh Sound Records | FSNT 150 CD

El Pendulo
Dave Samuels Group | Del Sol | GRP | GRP 96962

El Petit Bailet-
Free Flight | Jazzrock-Anthology Vol.3:Fusion | Zounds | CD 27100555

El Pinero(The Pioneer)
Madmo(Two Guitars & Percussion) | Cicles | Acoustic Music Records | 319.1053.2

El Pla De La Calma
Gabriel Pérez Group | Alfonsina | Jazz 4 Ever Records:Jazz Network | J4E 4751

El Portenito
Tangata Rea | Tango Alla Baila | Winter&Winter | 910025-2

El Portenito(Milonga)
Paul Desmond Quartet | Planet Jazz:Paul Desmond | Planet Jazz | 2152061-2

El Prince
Paul Desmond-Greatest Hits | RCA | CL 89809 SF
Take Ten | RCA | 2179621-2
Take Ten | RCA | 63661462
Paul Desmond With Different Groups | 100 Ans De Jazz:Paul Desmond | RCA | 2177830-2

El Prince(alt.take)
Antonio Hart Group | Ama Tu Sonrisa | Enja | ENJ-9404 2

El Professor
Art Lande And Rubisa Patrol | Desert Maraunders | ECM | 1106

El Quinto Regimiento(The First Regiment)
Lluis Vidal Trio | Tren Nocturn | Fresh Sound Records | FSNT 003 CD

El Rabada-
Artie Shaw And His Orchestra | In The Blue Room/In The Café Rouge | RCA | 2118527-2

El Regalo
Ray Noble And His Orchestra | The Radio Years | London | HMG 5019 AN

El Rio Y El Abuelo
Dino Saluzzi Group | Argentina | West Wind Latina | 2201 CD
Little Brother Montgomery's Quintet | New Orleans To Chicago:The Forties | Gannet | CJR 1002

El Rloj De Pastora
Tim Sund Trio | Trialogue | Nabel Records:Jazz Network | CD 4692

El Rojo
Shorty Rogers And His Orchestra Feat. The Giants | An Invisible Orchard | Fresh Sound Records | 49560 CD(RCA)

El Salon De Gutbucket
Göbels-Harth Group | Es Herrscht Uhu Im Land | Japo | 60037 (2360037)

El Salvador
Jimmy Ponder Sextet | Down Here On The Ground | Milestone | M 9121

El Saola
Paolo Fresu Quartet | Angel | RCA | 2155864-2
Gato Barbieri Group | Masters Of Jazz Vol.9 | RCA | NL 89722

El Sino
Gene Ammons Sextet | Red Top-The Savoy Sessions | Savoy | SJL 1103 (801179)

El Sueno
Stan Getz Quartet | The Lost Sessions | Verve | 9801098
Willie Rodriguez Jazz Quartet | Flatjacks | Milestone | MCD 9331-2

El Sueno DeFrances
Irakere | Catalina | Messidor | 15955

El Tata
Mike Nock-Marty Ehrlich | The Waiting Game | Naxos Jazz | 86048-2

El Testament D'Amelia
Tete Montoliu | Tete Montoliu Interpreta A Serrat | Fresh Sound Records | FSR 4004(835319)

El Toreador
Riccardo Fassi-Antonello Salis Duo | Joining | SPLASC(H) Records | H 113

El Toro
Art Blakey And The Jazz Messengers | The Freedom Rider | Blue Note | 870076-5
Chico Hamilton Quintet | Passin ' Thru | MCA | AS 29
Mongo Santamaria Orchestra | The Watermelon Man | Milestone | M 47012

El Ultimo Café
Mind Games | Pretty Fonky | Edition Collage | EC 482-2

El Uncoolito
Inti-Immimani | De Canto Y Baile | Messidor | 15936 CD

El Vigia
Sun Ra And His Arkestra | Sound Of Joy | Delmark | DE 414

El Viti(aka The Matador)
Duke Ellington And His Orchestra | Ella Fitzgerald And Duke Ellington:Cote D'Azure Concerts on Verve | Verve | 539033-2
Ella Fitzgerald And Duke Ellington:Cote D'Azure Concerts on Verve | Verve | 539033-2
Los Jovenes Flamencos | Jazzpana | ACT | 9212-2

El Vito Cante
Los Jovenes Flamencos With The WDR Big Band And Guests | Jazzpana | ACT | 9212-2

El Vito En Gran Tamano
Maynard Ferguson And His Orchestra | New Vintage | CBS | CBS 82282

El Wali Sidi Mimoun
Pete Jolly Trio | Jolly Jumps In | Fresh Sound Records | 12582 CD(RCA)

Ela E Carioca
Charlie Byrd Quartet | Charlie Byrd In Greenwich Village | Milestone | M 47049

Ela Me Deixou
Arthur Blythe Quintet & Guests | Elaborations | CBS | FC 38163

Elaborations
Debriano-Hart-Blythe | 3-Ology | Konnex Records | KCD 5047
The Leaders | Mudfoot | Black-Hawk | BKH 52001 CD

Elan Vital
Dave Brubeck Quartet | Blue Rondo | Concord | CCD 4317

Elastische Dinge(to Anthony Braxton)
John Hicks Quartet | In The Mix | Landmark | LCD 1542-2

Elbow Room
Lennie Niehaus Sextet | Lennie Niehaus Vol.5:The Sextet | Original Jazz Classics | OJCCD 1944-2(C 3524)
Victor Feldman's Generation Band | Smooth | TBA Records | TB 215

Elder Eatmore's Sermon On Generosity
Louis Armstrong With Harry And Choir | Ambassador Louis Armstrong Vol.5(1938-1939) | Ambassador | CLA 1905

Elder Eatmore's Sermon On Throwing Stones
Charley Patton | Founder Of The Delta Blues | Yazoo | YAZ 1020

Eldorado
Donald Byrd Sextet | Blackjack | Blue Note | 784466-2

Eldorado Stomp
Art Blakey And The Jazz Messengers | Blakey | Verve | 538634-2

Eleanor Rigby
Klaus Ignatzek | Plays Beatles Songs | Nabel Records:Jazz Network | CD 4643
Klaus Weiss Orchestra | Live At The Domicile | ATM Records | ATM 3805-AH
Lanfranco Malaguti/Enzo Pietropaoli/Fabrizio Sferra | Something | Nueva Records | NC 1010
Modern Walkin' | Modern Walkin'-Live In Japan | Satin Doll Productions | SDP 1009-1 CD
Oscar Peterson With Orchestra | Motions & Emotions | MPS | 821289-2 PMS
Sarah Vaughan With Orchestra | Song Of The Beatles | Atlantic | SD 16037
Singers Unlimited With The Patrick Williams Orchestra | Compact Disc:The Singers Unlimited | MPS | 831373-2 PMS
Tok Tok Tok | Love Again | Einstein Music | EM 01081
Urszula Dudziak With Orchestra | Ulla | Pop-Eye | PE 101

Eleanor Vance
The Henri Renaud Quintet | Bobby Jaspar/Henri Renaud | Vogue | 21409372

Electric Light
Sippie Wallace With Axel Zwingenberger | An Evening With Sippie Wallace | Vagabond | VRCD 8.86006
Alphonse Mouzon Group | In Search Of A Dream | MPS | 68192

Electric Red
Dhafer Youssef Group | Electric Sufi | Enja | ENJ-9412 2

Electric Sufi
Jack McDuff Sextet | The Reentry | Muse | MCD 5361

Ele-Fun(t)-Horn(s)-
Fun Horns & Baticun | Live And Latin | KlangRäume | 30110

Elegant Flower(for Jazz'min')
Al Di Meola Group | Elegant Gypsy | CBS | 468213-2

Elegant Gypsy Suite
Tour De Force-Live | CBS | 25121-2

Elegant People
Jonas Hellborg | Elegant Punk | Day Eight Music | DEMCD 004

Elegba
Bill Evans Trio With The Claus Ogerman Orchestra | The Complete Bill Evans On Verve | Verve | 527953-2

Elegia
Franco Ambrosetti Quintet | Light Breeze | Enja | ENJ-9331 2
Guido Mazzon-Umberto Petrin-Tiziano Tononi | Other Line | SPLASC(H) Records | CD H 317-2

Elegia Cascais
Pablo Ziegler And His Quintet For New Tango | Asfalto-Street Tango | RCA | 2663266-2

Elegia(Elegy)
Art Tatum | Art Tatum-The Standard Transcriptions | Music & Arts | CD 919

Elegie
Tatum Is Art | Jazz Anthology | JA 5177
Matthias Stich Sevensenses | ...mehrschichtig | Satin Doll Productions | SDP 1038-1 CD
Schwarz-Hübner Duo | Elegie | dml-records | CD 012
Stan Kenton And His Orchestra | The Complete MacGregor Transcriptions Vol.1 | Naxos Jazz | 8.120517 CD

Elegie I:
Schwarz-Hübner Duo | Elegie | dml-records | CD 012

Elegie II:
Elegie | dml-records | CD 012

Elegie III:
Elegie | dml-records | CD 012

Elegie IV:
Paolo Fresu Angel Quartet | Metamorfosi | RCA | 2165202-2

Elegio Del Discount
Enrico Pieranunzi/Enrico Rava | Nausicaa | Quadrivium | SCA 037

Elegua
Jerry Gonzalez & Fort Apache Band | Crossroads | Milestone | MCD 9225-2

Elegy
Art Tatum | Standards | Black Lion | CD 877646-2
Bud Powell Trio | Strictly Powell | RCA | 6351423-2
Harold Danko/Rufus Reid | Mirth Song | Sunnyside | SSC 1001 D

Elegy For A Duck
Oliver Nelson Quartet | Three Dimensions | MCA | IA 9335/2

Elegy For Joe Scott
Ken Peplowski Quartet With The Loren Schoenberg Big Band | A Good Reed | Concord | CCD 4767

Elegy For William Burroughs And Allen Ginsberg
Benny Carter Sextet | Elegy In Blue | Musicmasters | 65115-2

Elektric City
Kollektiv | Kollektiv feat. Jonas Hellborg | ITM Records | ITM 1434

Elektrische Libellen
Cecil Taylor | Garden | Hat Art | CD 6050

Elementary Substance
Balance | Elements | double moon | DMCHR 71033

Elements
Brötzmann, van Hove, Bennink + Albert Mangelsdorff | Live In Berlin '71 | FMP | CD 34/35

Elements & Context
Josep Maria Balanyà | Elements Of Development | Laika Records | 8695070

Elements Of Development Number Four
Elements Of Development | Laika Records | 8695070

Elements Of Development Number Three
Khan Jamal Group | Thinking Of You | Storyville | STCD 4138

Elements Of Poetry 1
Oskar Aichinger Trio | Elelents Of Poetry | Between The Lines | btl 005(Efa 10175-2)

Elements Of Poetry 2
Jukka Tolonen Group | Tolonen! | Sonet | 147117

Elend(Zemlinsky,from Op.27 No.7)
Jimmy Giuffre Trio | The Train And The River | Choice | CHCD 71011

Elephant
Phil Minton And Veryan Weston | Ways Past | ITM Records | ITM 1468

Elephant Business
BBFC | Live | Plainisphare | PL 1267-14

Elephant Hips
Jeremy Steig Quartet Feat. Jan Hammer | Something Else | LRC Records | CDC 8512

Elephant Song
Keith Ingham-Harry Allen Septet | The Back Room Romp | Sackville | SKCD2-3059

Elephant Walk
Art Farmer Septet | Farmer 's Market | Prestige | P 24032

Elephantasy-
Don Cherry Quartet | Complete Communion | Blue Note | 522673-2

Elephantasy:
Steve Beresford Orchestra | Signals For Tea | Avant | AVAN 039

Elephant's Camp
Jean-Luc Ponty Quartet | Fables | Atlantic | 781276-2

Elephant's Walk
Kölner Saxophon Mafia | Go Commercial... | Jazz Haus Musik | JHM 0065 CD

Stefano Maltese Open Music Orchestra | Hanging In The Sky | SPLASC(H) Records | H 139

Elevation

OTB Out Of The Blue | Live At Mt. Fuji | Blue Note | 746784-2

Elevation Of Love

Jon Rose Group | Violin Music In The Age Of Shopping | Intakt Records | CD 038

Eleven

Gil Evans Orchestra | Svengali | ACT | 9207-2

Eleven Dreams

Bill McHenry Quartet | Graphic | Fresh Sound Records | FSNT 056 CD

Eleven Eleven

Wanderlust + Guests | Full Bronte | Laika Records | 35101412

Eleven Elvises

Dave Brubeck Quartet | Adventures In Time | CBS | CBS 66291

Eleven Years Old

The Dave Brubeck Quartet At Carnegie Hall | CBS | 66234

Eleven-One

Urs Leimgruber/John Wolf Brennan | M.A.P. | L+R Records | CDLR 45021

Eleventh Hour

Abdullah Ibrahim Trio | Cape Town Flowers | TipToe | TIP-888826 2
African Magic | TipToe | TIP-888845 2
Greg Gisbert Quintet | Harcology | Criss Cross | Criss 1084

Eleventh Of January

Schmid-Hübner-Krill | Time Makes The Tune | Mons Records | MR 874825

Elfe

Kontrasax | Zanshin/Kontrasax | Jazz Haus Musik | JHM 0130 CD

Elfzehn

Ram-lösa | Ram-lösa In Mesopotamia | Aho-Recording | AHO CD 1008(CD 665)

Elijah

Golden Gate Quartet | Spirituals To Swing 1955-69 | EMI Records | 791569-2
Zion Harmonizers | Thank You Lord | Sound Of New Orleans | SONO 6007

Elinor Powell

Mark Helias Group | The Current Set | Enja | ENJ-5041 2

Elipso

Kelm 3 | Per Anno | dml-records | CD 013

Elis

Phil Woods Quintet | Astor& Elis | Chesky | JD 146

Elite Syncopations

New England Conservatory Ragtime Ensemble | More Scott Joplin Rags | London | HMG 5009 AN

Elizabeth

Ornette Coleman Septet | Broken Shadows | CBS | SRCS 7098

Elke

Ted Heath And His Orchestra | Swing Is King | Decca | 6.28129 DP

Ella Speed

Gil Evans And Ten | Gil Evans And Ten | Prestige | PRSA 7120-6
Huddie Ledbetter | Classics In Jazz-Leadbelly | Pathe | 2C 068-80701(Capitol)

El-Lail(Night)

John Stowell-Bebo Ferra | Elle | Jardis Records | JRCD 20028

Elle

Renaud Garcia-Fons | Légendes | Enja | ENJ-9314 2
Lindemann/Santa Maria Quintet | Piano Duo Plus | Plainisphare | PL 1267-8

Ellen David

Chet Baker With The Ake Johansson Trio | Chet Baker Live In Sweden | Dragon | DRLP 56
Jerry Granelli UFB | News From The Street | VeraBra Records | CDVBR 2146-2

Ellen Waltzing

Bob Brookmeyer New Quartet | Paris Suite | Challenge | CHR 70026

Ellington Ballad Medley:

Satchmo Legacy Band | Salute To Pops-Vol.1 | Soul Note | 121116-2

Ellington Medley:

Buddy Tate-Nat Simkins-Houston Person Sextet | Just Friends:The Tenors Of Buddy Tate, Nat Simkins, Houston Person | Muse | MCD 5418
Dick Wellstood | Piano Giants Vol.2 | Swingtime | 8202

Ellingtonia:

Chris Barber's Jazz And Blues Band | 40 Years Jubilee | Timeless | CD TTD 589
Jimmy Heath Quintet | Peer Pleasure | Landmark | LCD 1514-2

Ellioko(Yoruba Word Foe 'Two'

Oscar Peterson Septet | The Silent Partner | Pablo | 2312103

Ellipsis

Dezsö Lakatos With The Super Trio | Elliptic Dance | Timeless | CD SJP 298

Elm

Richard Beirach Trio | ELM | ECM | 1142

Elma My Dear

Super Trio | Brotherhood Of Man | L+R Records | CDLR 45095

Elmer's Blues

Elmer Snowden | Berlin Festival-Guitar Workshop | MPS | 68159

Elmer's Tune

Glenn Miller And His Orchestra | His Original Recordings | RCA | NL 89026 DP
Mark Murphy With The Ralph Burns Orchestra | Crazy Rhythm:His Debut Recordings | Decca | 050670-2
Peggy Lee With The Benny Goodman Orchestra | Peggy Lee & Benny Goodman:The Complete Recordings 1941-1947 | CBS | C2K 65686
Ray Anthony Orchestra | I Remember Glenn Miller | Aero Space | RA 1011(835474)

Elmer's Tune-

Elmore James And His Broomdusters | Street Talkin' | Muse | MCD 5087

Elogio Del Discanto

Marty Ehrlich-Peter Erskine-Michael Formanek | Relativity | Enja | ENJ-9341 2

Eloi Lament

Dave Frishberg | Live At Vine Street | Original Jazz Classics | OJCCD 832-2(F 9638)

Eloise

Johnny 'Hammond' Smith Quartet | Open House | Milestone | MCD 47089-2
John Lindberg Quartet | Quartet Afterstorm | Black Saint | 120162-2

Elongate

Barbara Jungfer Trio | Vitamin B 3 | yvp music | CD 3097

Eloquence

Passport | Looking Thru | Atlantic | 2292-44144-2
J.J.Johnson Quintet | First Sessions 1949/50 | Prestige | P 24081

Elora

Q4 Orchester Project | Lyon's Brood | Creative Works Records | CW CD 1018-3

El-Qahira

Ellis Marsalis Trio | Heart Of Gold | CBS | CK 47509

Els Angles Triangles

Elliot Lawrence And His Orchestra | The Elliot Lawrence Big Band Swings Cohn & Kahn | Fantasy | FCD 24761-2

El's Bells

Lluis Vidal Trio | Milikituli | Fresh Sound Records | FSNT 009 CD

Els Miquelets D'Espanya

Tete Montoliu | Yellow Dolphin Street/Catalonian Folk Songs | Timeless | CD SJP 107/116

Els Segadors(The Reapers)

Elisabet Raspall Grup | Lila | Fresh Sound Records | FSNT 058 CD

Els Teus Ulls Són Transparents

Pep O'Callaghan Grup | Tot Just | Fresh Sound Records | FSNT 017 CD

Els Vells Temps

Arnold Klos Trio | Crinkle's Garden | Limetree | MLP 198537

Elsa

Bill Evans Trio | Bill Evans:From The 70's | Fantasy | F 9630
Trio '65 | Verve | 2304517 IMS
How Deep Is The Ocean | West Wind | WW 2055
Compact Jazz: Bill Evans | Verve | 831366-2 PMS
Bill Evans:From The 70's | Original Jazz Classics | OJCCD 1069-2(F 9630)
Half Moon Bay | Milestone | MCD 9282-2
Bill Evans-Eddie Gomez Duo | Montreux III | Original Jazz Classics | OJC20 644-2(F 9510)
The Complete Fantasy Recordings | Fantasy | 9FCD 1012-2
Bud Shank Quartet | Heritage | Concord | CJ 58
David Friesen Trio | The Name Of A Woman | Intuition Records | INT 3334-2
Ed Bickert-Lorne Lofsky Quartet | This Is New | Concord | CCD 4414
Joe Temperley Quintet | Double Duke | Naxos Jazz | 86032-2

Elsa-Maria

Kenny Davern-Flip Phillips Quintet | John & Joe | Chiaroscuro | CR 199

Else-Britt's Blues

Mike Nock | Piano Solos | Timeless | SJP 134

Elusive

Tommy Flanagan Trio | Let's Play The Muisc Of Thad Jones | Enja | ENJ-8040 2

Elvedansen

Wynton Marsalis Quintet | Soul Gestures In Southern Blue Vol.1: Thick In The South | CBS | 468659-2

Elvin (Sir) Jones

Barry Finnerty Quintet | Straight Ahead | Arabesque Recordings | AJ 0116

Elvin's Exit

New York Jazz Collective | Everybody Wants To Go To Heaven | Naxos Jazz | 86073-2

Elvin's Guitar Blues

Bob Mintzer Big Band | Art Of The Big Band | dmp Digital Music Productions | CD 479

Elysee

Jay Jay Johnson's Bebopers | Sonny Rollins:Complete 1949-1951 Prestige Studio Recordings | Definitive Records | DRCD 11240

Elysian Fields

Mark Soskin Sextet | 17(Seventeen) | TCB Records | TCB 20652

Elysium

Jay Jay Johnson Sextet | Trombone By Three | Original Jazz Classics | OJCCD 091-2(P 7023)

Em Familia

Duo Gismonti-Vasconcelos | Jazzbühne Berlin '84 | Repertoire Records | REPCD 4906-CC

Em Familia-

Schorn-Puntin Duo | Elephant's Love Affair | NCC Jazz | NCC 8002

Emanacion

Jerome Harris Sextet | Hidden In Plain View | New World Records | 80472-2

Emanation

Michael Sell Doppelquartet | Emanationen | Misp Records | CD 508

Emanations

Mike Cain Trio | Strange Omen | Candid | CCD 79505

Emavungwani(Green Home)

Paul Desmond Quartet | Planet Jazz:Paul Desmond | Planet Jazz | 2152061-2

Embarcadero

Paul Desmond-Greatest Hits | RCA | CL 89809 SF
Take Ten | RCA | 2179621-2
Take Ten | RCA | 63661462

Embarkation

The Herdsmen | The Herdsmen Play Paris | Original Jazz Classics | OJC 116(F 3201)

Embracadero

Paul Desmond With Different Groups | 100 Ans De Jazz:Paul Desmond | RCA | 2177830-2

Embracadero(alt.take)

Elisabeth Kontomanou Group | Embrace | Steeplechase | SCCD 31467

Embraceable You

Adam Makowicz Quartet | Naughty Baby | RCA | 3022-1-N(809279)
Archie Shepp-Horace Parlan Duo | Swing Low | Plainisphare | PL 1267-73 CD
Art Tatum | The Tatum Solo Masterpieces Vol.9 | Pablo | 2310835
Barry Harris-Kenny Barron Quartet | Confirmation | Candid | CCD 79519
Bill Evans Trio | At The Montreux Jazz Festival | Verve | 539758-2
Billie Holiday And Her All Stars | Billie Holiday:The Great American Songbook | Verve | 523003-2
Billie Holiday With Eddie Heywood And His Orchestra | The Commodore Series | Decca | 180008 AG
Bud Powell Trio | Live At Birdland | Queen-Disc | 024
Charlie Parker Quintet | One Night At Birdland | CBS | CBS 88250
More Unissued Vol.2 | Royal Jazz | RJD 506
Christopher Hollyday Quintet | Christopher Hollyday | Novus | PD 83055
Clifford Brown With Strings | The Gershwin Songbook(The Instrumentals) | Verve | 525361-2
Dave Pike & Charles McPherson With The Rein De Graaff Trio | Bluebird | Timeless | CD SJP 302
Django Reinhardt And The Quintet Du Hot Club De France | Django Reinhardt:Djangology | EMI Records | 780659-2
Don Byas Quartet | Don Byas Complete American Small Group Recordings | Definitive Records | DRCD 11213
Duke Jordan Trio | Osaka Concert Vol.1 | Steeplechase | SCCD 31271
Ella Fitzgerald With The Nelson Riddle Orchestra | Ella Sings Gershwin-Vol. 1 | Metro | 2682004 IMS
Erroll Garner | The Fascinating Erroll Garner | Fontana | 6430135
Frank Rosolino Sextet | Kenton Presents: Frank Rosolino | Affinity | AFF 61
Gigi Gryce Quartet | Bird Calls 2 | Savoy | 650111(881911)
Helen Merrill With The Pepper Adams Quintet | Chasin' The Bird(Gershwin) | EmArCy | 558850-2
Helmut Zacharias Sextet | Ich Habe Rhythmus | Bear Family Records | BCD 15642 AH
Herb Geller Quartet | Hot House | Circle Records | RK 30-241184/30
Jackie McLean Quartet | Tribute To Charlie Parker | RCA | PL 43560
James Williams Sextet feat. Clark Terry | Talkin' Trash | DIW | DIW 887 CD
JATP All Stars | JATP-1940's | Verve | MV 9070/72 IMS
Charlie Parker:The Best Of The Verve Years | Verve | 527815-2
The Complete Jazz At The Philharmonic On Verve 1944-1949 | Verve | 523893-2
Jazz At The Philharmonic:Best Of The 1940's Concerts | Verve | 557534-2
Charlie Parker Jazz At The Philharmonic 1949 | Verve | 519803-2
Jimmy Smith Sextet | Open House/Plain Talk | Blue Note | 784269-2
Jo Jones Trio | Jo Jones Trio | EmArCy | 512534-2
Joe Williams With The Norman Simmons Quartet And Supersax | In Good Company | Verve | 837932-2
Johnny Smith Quartet | The Sound Of The Johnny Smith Guitar | Roulette | 531792-2
The Sound Of Johnny Smith Guitar | Fresh Sound Records | FSR 583(Roost 2246)
Oleg Lundstrem Orchestra | In Swing Time | Mobile Fidelity | MFCD 881
Ornette Coleman Quartet | Beauty Is A Rare Thing:Ornette Coleman-The Complete Atlantic Recordings | Atlantic | 8122-71410-2
Peter Leitch Sextet | From Another Perspective | Concord | CCD 4535
Ralph Flanagan And His Orchestra | Dance Again Part 2 | Magic | DAWE 75
Sarah Vaughan With The Clifford Brown All Stars | Sarah Vaughan | EmArCy | 9860779
Brownie-The Complete EmArCy Recordings Of Clifford Brown | EmArCy | 838306-2
Sarah Vaughan With The Dizzy Gillespie Quintet | The Best Of The Jazz Singers | LRC Records | CDC 8517(874388)
Scott Hamilton Quintet | Plays Ballads | Concord | CCD 4386
The Dixieland All Stars | The Dixieland All Stars | Jazz Unlimited | JUCD 2037
The Prestige All Stars | Olio | Original Jazz Classics | OJCCD 1004-2(P 7084)
The Rosenberg Trio With Stephane Grappelli | Caravan | Verve | 523030-2
Zoot Sims Quintet | Zoot Sims And The Gershwin Brothers | Pablo | PASA 2310-744-6
Zoot Sims And The Gershwin Brothers | Original Jazz Classics | OJC20 444-2(2310744)
Benny Goodman Trio | Benny Goodman:The King Of Swing | Musicmasters | 65130-2

Embraceable You-

Dave Burrell | Windward Passages | Hat Art | CD 6138
Jesper Thilo Quintet feat. Harry Edison | Jesper Thilo Quintet feat. Harry Edison | Storyville | STCD 4120
Stephane Grappelli Trio With Marcel Azzola | Stephane Grappelli In Toky | Denon Compact Disc | CY-77130

Embracing Oneness

Mike Nock Quartet | Dark & Curious | VeraBra Records | CDVBR 2074-2

Embracing You

Raymond Boni | L'Homme Etoile | Hat Art | 3510

Embrasse-Moi Bien

René Bottlang Quintet | Round About Bobby-Hommage Á Bobby Lapointe | Plainisphare | PL 1267-91 CD

Embryons Desseches(Erik Satie):

Jack Sheldon And The Swedish All Stars | Blues In The Night | Phontastic | PHONT 7569

Emerald Light

Rebecca Parris With The Gary Burton Group | It's Another Day | GRP | GRP 97382

Emerald Tears

Joint Venture | Mirrors | Enja | ENJ-7049 2

Emergence Of The Spirit-

Tony Williams Lifetime | Emergency! | Verve | 539117-2

Emil Kahl

Stefano Battaglia Trio | Auryn | SPLASC(H) Records | CD H 162-2

Emilio

Ack Van Rooyen And The Metropole Orchestra | Colores | Koala Records | CD P 21

Emily

Bill Evans | Further Conversations With Myself | Verve | 559832-2
Bill Evans Trio | The Complete Bill Evans On Verve | Verve | 527953-2
The Complete Bill Evans On Verve | Verve | 527953-2
Getting Sentimental | Milestone | MCD 9346-2
Bill Evans Trio:The Last Waltz | Milestone | 8MCD 4430-2
Bill Evans Trio:The Last Waltz | Milestone | 8MCD 4430-2
The Best Of Bill Evans Live | Verve | 533825-2
Bill Evans:The Secret Sessions | Milestone | 8MCD 4421-2
Live In Paris 1972 Vol.3 | France's Concert | FCD 125
You're Gonna Hear From Me | Milestone | M 9164
Bill Evans:The Secret Sessions | Milestone | 8MCD 4421-2
Bill Evans:The Secret Sessions | Milestone | 8MCD 4421-2
Yesterday I Heard The Rain | Bandstand | BDCD 1535
David Friesen Trio | The Name Of A Woman | Intuition Records | INT 3334-2
Don Friedman Trio | Almost Everything | Steeplechase | SCCD 31368
Gary McFarland Orchestra | Soft Samba | Verve | MV 2102 IMS
Jiggs Whigham With The WDR Big Band | The Third Stone | Koala Records | CD P 4
Ray Brown Quartet | Brown's Bag | Concord | CCD 6019
Singers Unlimited | The Singers Unlimited:Magic Voices | MPS | 539130-2
A Capella | MPS | 815671-1
Stan Getz With The Bill Evans Trio | But Beautiful | Jazz Door | JD 1208
Zoot Sims With The Nederlands Metropole Orchestra | Only A Rose | Koch Jazz | 3-6916-2

Emily(2)

Bill Evans Trio | The Complete Bill Evans On Verve | Verve | 527953-2
Oscar Peterson Trio | The London Concert | Pablo | 2CD 2620111

Emily(The Americanization Of Emily)

Les Arbuckle Quartet | No More No Les | audioquest Music | AQCD 1019

Eminence

Joe Diorio/Robben Ford Quartet | Minor Elegance | MGI Records | MGR CD 1012

Emlékek

Mynta | Nandu's Dance | Blue Flame | 40782(2132162-2)

Emma

Steve Kuhn Trio | Remembering Tomorrow | ECM | 1573(529035-2)

Emmanuel

Looking Back | Concord | CCD 4446

Empathy

Herbie Mann-Sam Most Quintet | The Epitome Of Jazz | Bethlehem | BET 6011-2(BCP 6067)

Emperor Norton's Hunch

Lu Watters' Yerba Buena Jazz Band | The San Francisco Style Vol.2:Watters' Original & Ragtime | Good Time Jazz | GTCD 12002-2

Emphasis

Jimmy Giuffre 3 | Emphasis,Stuttgart 1961 | Hat Art | CD 6072

Empreintes(Jean-Luc Darbellay)

Aera | Too Much | Spiegelei | 145625

Emptiness(dedicated to Olivier Messian)

Carolyn Breuer-Fee Claassen Quintet With Hermann Breuer | Simply Me | Challenge | CHR 70017

Empty Carrousel

Tiziana Ghiglioni And Her Quartet | Yet Time | SPLASC(H) Records | CD H 150-2

Empty Faces(Vera Cruz)

Jutta Gruber & The Martin Schrack Trio | Keep Hanging On | yvp music | CD 3043

Empty Hearts

Alexander von Schlippenbach And Sven-Ake Johansson | Live 1976/77 | FMP | CD 111

Empty Pockets

Herbie Hancock Quintet | Herbie Hancock:The Complete Blue Note Sixties Sessions | Blue Note | 495569-2
Takin' Off | Blue Note | 837643-2

Empty Pockets(alt.take)

Herbie Hancock:The Complete Blue Note Sixties Sessions | Blue Note | 495569-2
Zipflo Reinhardt Quintet | Oceana | Intercord | 160114

En Cadence

Victor De Diego Group | Amaia | Fresh Sound Records | FSNT 012 CD

En Condicions

Susanne Lundeng Quartet | Waltz For The Red Fiddle | Laika Records | 35101402

En Dance Tel Han Harald(Dance For Harald)

Amsterdam String Trio | Winter Theme | Winter&Winter | 910060-2

En Deuil

Michel Portal | !Dejarme Solo! | Dreyfus Jazz Line | FDM 36506-2

En El Final De La Noche

Hernan Merlo Quintet | Consin | Fresh Sound Records | FSNT 150 CD

En El Mismo Lada

Chuck Loeb Group | Memory Lane | dmp Digital Music Productions | CD 517

En Face

Vigleik Storaas Trio | Bilder | Curling Legs Prod. | C.L.P. CD 018

En Joan Petit

La Vienta | Night Dance | Telarc Digital | CD 83359

En La Felicidad

Afrocuba | Electicism | Ronnie Scott's Jazz House | JHCD 039

En Manzanillo Se Baila El Son-

Francois Jeanneau Quartet | Techniques Douces | Owl Records | 04

En Passant

Shelly Manne And His Men | Checkmate | Contemporary | C 7599
Stefan Bauer-Claudio Puntin-Marcio Doctor | Lingo | Jazz Haus Musik | JHM 0116 CD
Gorka Benitez Trio | Gorka Benitez Trio | Fresh Sound Records | FSNT 073 CD

En Que Toni Chabeli?

Didier Lockwood Quintet | Storyboard | Dreyfus Jazz Line | FDM 36582-2

En Rapport

John LaPorta Octet | Theme And Variations | Fantasy | FCD 24776-2

Anouar Brahem Group | Khomsa | ECM | 1561(527093-2)

En Robe D'Olivier

Lee Konitz And Lars Gullin With Hans Koller's New Jazz Stars | Lee Konitz:Move | Moon Records | MCD 057-2

En Schuiftrompet Voor Julius

Baden Powell | Le Genie De Baden Powell | Festival | 114851

En Souvenir D'Iram

Christoph Oeding Trio | Pictures | Mons Records | MR 874829

En Tres Por Cuatro

David Xirgu Quartet | Idolents | Fresh Sound Records | FSNT 077 CD

En Vista Del Éxito

Bluiett's Barbeque Band | Bluiett's Barbeque Band | Mapleshade | 04032

Encanto

David Valentine Group | Kalahari | GRP | GRP 95082

Enchanted

George Shearing With The Montgomery Brothers | Wes Montgomery-The Complete Riverside Recordings | Riverside | 12 RCD 4408-2

Wes Montgomery Quintet | Wes And Friends | Milestone | M 47013

Enchanted Place

Essence All Stars | Bongobop | Hip Bop | HIBD 8017

Enchantment

Louis Hayes Quintet | Light And Lively | Steeplechase | SCCD 31245

Enchantress

John Serry Quintet | Enchantress | Telarc Digital | CD 83392

Encontros

Batida | Terra Do Sul | Timeless | CD SJP 245

Encore

Claudio Puntin Quartet | Mondo | Jazz Haus Musik | JHM 0134 CD

Friedrich Gulda Trio | Fata Morgana:Live At The Domicile | MPS | 68060

Jimmy Giuffre-André Jaume | Momentum,Willisay 1988 | HatOLOGY | 508

Kropinski-Köhnlein Duo | By The Way | Aho-Recording | AHO CD 1001(CD 664)

Sun Ra & His Arkestra | Live At Montreux | Inner City | IC 1039 IMS

Encore Toi

Keith Jarrett | Eyes Of The Heart | ECM | 1150(825476-2)

Encore(a-b-c)

Bennie Green Quintet | The 45 Session | Blue Note | 300209(BNJ 61020)

Encore:Amen-

Dirty Dozen Brass Band | Live:Mardi Gras In Montreux | Rounder Records | CDRR 2052

Encores:

Baden Powell | Estudos | MPS | 68092

Encounter

Reggie Workman Quintet | Summit Conference | Postcards | POST 1003

Encuentros

John McLaughlin Trio | After The Rain | Verve | 527467-2

Bendik Hofseth Quintet | Colours | Verve | 537627-2

End Of Party

Spyro Gyra | Morning Dance | MCA | ???

End Of Session Jump

Catch Up | Catch Up II | Calig | 30615

End Of The Game

Chet Baker Quintet | Albert's House | Repertoire Records | REPCD 4167-WZ

End Of The Line

Nina Simone Quintet | Nina Simone-The 60s Vol.2:Mood Indigo | Mercury | 838544-2 PMS

End Of Vienna

Ahmad Mansour Quintet | Penumbra | Timeless | CD SJP 404

End Title

Hot Rod Rumble Orchestra | Hot Rod Rumble | Fresh Sound Records | 054 2607941(Liberty LRP 3048)

Endangered Species

Don Pullen Trio | Random Thoughts | Blue Note | 794347-2

Endgame

JATP All Stars | The Complete Jazz At The Philharmonic On Verve 1944-1949 | Verve | 523893-2

Endido

Louis Armstrong And His Orchestra | Louis Armstrong-The Complete RCA Victor Recordings | RCA | 2668682-2

Ending

Das Saxophonorchester Frankfurt | Das Saxophonorchester Frankfurt-Live | FMP | SAJ 40

Hans Koller Big Band | New York City | MPS | 68235

Paul Bley Trio | Ballads | ECM | 1010

Ending It

The New Mel Lewis Quintet | Live | Inak | 8611

Ending With The Theme

Charly Antolini Quartet | Menue/Finale | BELL Records | BLR 84068

Endless

Marty Cook Conspiracy | Phases Of The Moon | Tutu Records | 888160-2*

Ornette Coleman Quartet | Tomorrow Is The Question | Original Jazz Classics | OJC20 342-2(S 7569)

Don Cherry's Eternal Rhythm Group | Eternal Rhythm | MPS | 68225

Endless Boogie(part 27&28)

Eberhard Weber Group | Endless Days | ECM | 1748(013420-2)

Endless Days

George Adams & Blue Brass Connection | Cool Affairs | PAO Records | PAO 10010

Endless Journey

Rolf Schimmermann Group | Suru | B&W Present | BW 009

Endless Melody

A.D.D.Trio | Sic Bisquitus Disintegrat | Enja | ENJ-9361 2

Endless Radiance

Makoto Ozone | Makoto Ozone | CBS | 26198

Endless Sleep

Chick Corea-Gary Burton | In Concert, Zürich, October 28, 1979 | ECM | 1182/83

Endless Trouble Endless Pleasure

Niels Lan Doky Septet | Friendship | Milestone | MCD 9183-2

Endlos

Gerry Hemingway Quintet | Outerbridge Crossing | Sound Aspects | sas CD 017

Endstation Sehnsucht(Theater Oberhausen)

Yusef Lateef Quintet | Gong! | Savoy | SJL 2226 (801202)

Enduring Freedom

Andy Lumpp | Piano Solo | Nabel Records:Jazz Network | CD 4646

Endzeit

Horst Grabosch Quartet | Alltage | Jazz Haus Musik | JHM 80 CD

Enemies Within

Anthony Davis Sextet | Variations In Dream-Time | India Navigation | IN 1056

Energy

Four Keys | Four Keys | MPS | 68241

Energy: Blood

New Art Saxophone Quartet | Songs And Dances | Enja | ENJ-9420 2

Enfant

Ornette Coleman Quartet | Beauty Is A Rare Thing:Ornette Coleman-The Complete Atlantic Recordings | Atlantic | 8122-71410-2

Ornette On Tenor | Atlantic | 8122-71455-2

Uschi Brüning And Ernst-Ludwig Petrowsky With The Günter Bartel Trio | Enfant | Aho-Recording | CD 1017

Enfant Terrible

Jim Snidero Quintet | Blue Afternoon | Criss Cross | Criss 1072

Eng Leise Nische

Indiscreet | Difficult To Contribute Silence | Nabel Records:Jazz Network | LP 4620

Engführung-

Claudio Puntin/Gerdur Gunnarsdóttir | Ýlir | ECM | 1749(158570-2)

Engin Lát Ödrum Frekt

Lincoln Center Jazz Orchestra | Big Train | CBS | CK 69860

Engine

Lonely Universe | Lonely Universe | CMP Records | CMP CD 41

England's Carol(God Rest Ye Merry Gentlemen)

ULG | Spring | Laika Records | 35101382

Englis-

Jack McDuff Quartet With Orchestra | Prelude:Jack McDuff Big Band | Prestige | PRCD 24283-2

English Country Gardens

Fritz Pauer Trio | Blues Inside Out | MPS | 68218

English Jam

Raphael Fays Group | Voyages | Acoustic Music Records | AMC 1015

English Waltz

Eric Reed Trio | Manhattan Melodies | Verve | 050294-2

Enige Nurksen

Al Haig Trio | Invitation | Spotlite | SPJ LP 4 (AH 4)

Enigma

Michael Weiss Quintet | Presenting Michael Weiss | Criss Cross | Criss 1022

Miles Davis Sextet | Miles Davis:The Blue Note And Capitol Recordings | Blue Note | 827475-2

Miles Davis:The Best Of The Capitol/Blue Note Years | Blue Note | 798287-2

Miles Davis Vol.1 | Blue Note | 300081(1501)

Ralph Moore Quartet | Images | Landmark | LCD 1520-2

Georg Ruby | Stadtgarten Series Vol.4 | Jazz Haus Musik | JHM 1004 SER

Enigma(alt.take)

Miles Davis Sextet | Miles Davis:The Blue Note And Capitol Recordings | Blue Note | 827475-2

Enigmatic Ocean(part 1-4)

Jean-Luc Ponty Sextet | The Very Best Of Jean-Luc Ponty | Rhino | 8122-79862-2

Enigmatic Ocean(part 3)

Herb Robertson Quintet | Transparency | JMT Edition | 834402-1

Enitnerrut

Ben Sidran Group | Enivre D'Amour | VeraBra Records | CDVBR 2097-2

Enlightenment

Sun Ra And His Arkestra | Calling Planet Earth | Freedom | FCD 741071

En-Mocion

Kühn/Humair/Jenny-Clark | Tripple Entente | EmArCy | 558690-2

Enna

Bill Russo And His Orchestra | Deep People | Savoy | SV 0186(MG 12045)

Enormous Tots

Archie Shepp Quartet | On Green Dolphin Street | Denon Compact Disc | DC-8587

Ensaio De Escola De Samba(Danca Dos Escravos)

Cecil Taylor | Fly! Fly! Fly! | MPS | 68263

Ensenada

Sylvie Courvoisier Group | Ocre | Enja | ENJ-9323 2

Ensorcelirradiant

Music By...-Barre Phillips Group | Music By... | ECM | 1178

Ente(To Go)

Paul Bley Trio | Not Two, Not One | ECM | 1670(559447-2)

Entelechy

Sammy Price | Midnight Boogie | Black & Blue | BLE 59.025 2

Enter The King

Andy Lumpp | Piano Solo | Nabel Records:Jazz Network | CD 4646

Enter The Malesh

Piano Solo | Nabel Records:Jazz Network | CD 4646

Enter The Malesh(for Handy Van Baren)

Jimmy Giuffre-Paul Bley | Giuffre/Konitz/Connors/Bley | Improvising Artists Inc. | 123859-2

Entering

Art Ensemble Of Chicago | Urban Bushmen | ECM | 1211/12

Entering The City-

Pago Libre | Cinémagique | TCB Records | TCB 01112

Entrance

Keith Jarrett | Dark Intervals | ECM | 1379(837342-2)

Louie Bellson Drum Explosion | Matterhorn | Original Jazz Classics | 2310834

Entranced

Peter Delano Group | Peter Delano | Verve | 519602-2

Entre Amigos

Renaud Garcia-Fons Group | Entremundo | Enja | ENJ-9464 2

Entre Continentes(Buleria)

The Rosenberg Trio | The Rosenberg Trio:The Collection | Verve | 537152-2

Entre Dos Aguas

The Rosenberg Trio With Orchestra | Noches Calientes | Verve | 557022-2

Entre Dos Aguas-

Ulli Bögershausen | Christmas Carols | Laika Records | 35101622

Entre Le Boeuf Et L'Ane Gris

Jacques Stotzem | Straight On | Acoustic Music Records | 319.1030.2

Entre Les Trous De La Memoire

Barbara Thompson Group | Heavenly Bodies | VeraBra Records | CDVBR 2015-2

Barbara Thompson's Paraphernalia | A Cry From The Heart | VeraBra Records | CDVBR 2021-2

Marcio Tubino Group | Festa Do Olho | Organic Music | ORGM 9723

Entre Nos

Raphael Fays Group | Voyages | Acoustic Music Records | AMC 1015

Entre Tinieblas

Quique Sinesi & Daniel Messina | Prioridad A la Emoción | art-mode-records | AMR 21061

Entre Tus Rios

Duke Ellington And His Orchestra | Three Suites | CBS | 467913-2

Entremundo

Oregon | Our First Record | Vanguard | 62162

Entrez Vous

Greg Osby Quintet | Inner Circle | Blue Note | 499871-2

Entruption

Gijs Hendriks Quartet & Clifford Adams | Print Collection | vyp music | 3012

Entry In A Diary

Alfred 23 Harth-Bob Degen Duo | Melchior | Biber Records | BI 6240

Entupadas-Berliner Version(Encounters)

Woody Schabata Quintet | May-Rimba | Amadeo | 829324-2

Entwicklungshelfer-

Joseph Berardi-Kira Vollman | Happy Wretched Family | Victo | CD 033

Enver Left Town

Enver Ismailov & Geoff Warren | Art Of The Duo:Dancing Over The Moon | Tutu Records | 888168-2*

Enver's Mood No.2

Irazu | Charanga De La Luna | L+R Records | CDLR 45053

Envottats De Boira

Junior Cook Quintet | You Leave Me Breathless | Steeplechase | SCCD 31304

Eons

Ornette Coleman Quartet | Beauty Is A Rare Thing:Ornette Coleman-The Complete Atlantic Recordings | Atlantic | 8122-71410-2

Eos

Ornette On Tenor | Atlantic | 8122-71455-2

Terje Rypdal-David Darling Duo | Eos | ECM | 1263

Woody Schabata Quintet | May-Rimba | Amadeo | 829324-2

Eosine

Leo Smith | Creative Music-I | Kabell | 1

Epanados

String Trio Of New York | Rebirth Of A Feeling | Black Saint | BSR 0068

Epicenter

Dave Binney Quintet | Point Game | Owl Time Line | 3819032

Epigraph No.1

Ketil Bjornstad-David Darling | Epigraphs | ECM | 1684(543159-2)

Epigraph No.1(Var.1)

Epigraphs | ECM | 1684(543159-2)

Epigraph No.1(Var.2)

Epigraphs | ECM | 1684(543159-2)

Epigraph No.1(Var.3)

A Band Of Friends | Teatime Vol.1 | Poise | Poise 01

Epilog

Teatime Vol.2 | Poise | Poise 06/2

Andreas Heuser | Continuum | Acoustic Music Records | 319.1086.2

Peter Bolte Quartet | ...All The April Snow | ITM-Pacific | ITMP 970092

Sotto In Su | Vanitas | Poise | Poise 04

Subwave | Subwave | G.N.U. Records | CD A 96.X22

Dave Grusin Band With Orchestra | The Orchestral Album | GRP | GRP 97972

Epilog Mit Umgedrehter Sichel

Der Rote Bereich | Der Rote Bereich 3 | Jazz 4 Ever Records:Jazz Network | J4E 4740

Epilog:Da Ist Holz Vor Der Hütte-

Motus Quartett | Grimson Flames | Creative Works Records | CW CD 1023-2

Epilog:Der Freudenspender Kommt-

Orchestre National De Jazz | Charmediterranéen | ECM | 1828(018493-2)

Epilogo

| Modern Walkin':Greatest Hits Volume 1 | Satin Doll Productions | SDP 1008-1 CD

Epilogue

Bajazzo | Caminos | Edition Collage | EC 485-2

Bill Evans | Everybody Digs Bill Evans | Original Jazz Classics | OJC20 068-2

Bill Evans At Town Hall | Verve | 831271-2

Claudio Puntin/Gerdur Gunnarsdóttir | Ýlir | ECM | 1749(158570-2)

Diederik Wissels Quintet | Kamook | B.Sharp Records | CDS 083

Gary Dial-Dick Oatts Quartet With Strings | Dial And Oatts | dmp Digital Music Productions | CD 465

George Lewis Ensemble | Changing With The Times | New World Records | 80434-2

John Abercrombie Quartet | Class Trip | ECM | 1846(0381182)

John McLaughlin With The Aighette Quartet And Yan Marez | Time Remembered:John McLaughlin Plays Bill Evans | Verve | 519861-2

John Surman-Jack DeJohnette With The London Brass | Printed In Germany | ECM | 1802(017065-2)

John Zorn Group | Cobra | Hat Art | CD 6040(2)

Matthias Müller Quartet | Bhavam | Jazz Haus Musik | JHM 0126 CD

Mikhail Alperin/Arkady Shilkloper | Wave Over Sorrow | ECM | 1396

Miroslav Vitous | Emergence | ECM | 1312

Miroslav Vitous Quintet | Mountain In The Clouds | Atlantic | SD 1622

Roland Hanna | Piano Soliloquy | L+R Records | LR 40003

Epilogue-

Dave Grusin Orchestra | Havana(Original Motion Picture Soundtrack) | GRP | GRP 20032

Epiphany

Kurt Rosenwinkel Quartet | Intuit | Criss Cross | Criss 1160

Gunter Hampel Group | Music From Europe | ESP Disk | ESP 1042-2

Episode

John Surman Orchestra | John Surman | Deram | 844883-2

Sadao Watanabe Group | Go Straight Ahead 'N Make A Left | Verve | 537944-2

Episode D'Azur

Dave Douglas Group | Witness | RCA | 2663763-2

Episode For Taslima Nasrin

James Williams Septet | Progress Report | Sunnyside | SSC 1012(952102)

Episodio:A Flor Da Pele

Clifford Jordan,Sonny Simmons And Prince Lasha With The Bossa Très | Music Matador | Fresh Sound Records | FSR-CD 0304

Epistrophy

Barry Harris Septet | Interpertations Of Monk | DIW | DIW 395/8 CD

Eddie Lockjaw Davis-Johnny Griffin Quintet | The Toughest Tenors | Milestone | M 47035

Geoff Keezer Trio | Trio | Sackville | SKCD2-2039

Kenny Drew Jr. Trio With Stefon Harris | Remembrance | TCB Records | TCB 20202

Peter Leitch-John Hicks | Duality | Reservoir | RSR CD 134

Roswell Rudd Quintet | Regeneration | Soul Note | 121054-2

Simon Nabatov Trio | Three Stories,One End | ACT | 9401-2

Steve Lacy | Remains | Hat Art | CD 6102

Thelonious Monk And His Orchestra | Who's Afraid Of The Big Band Monk? | CBS | CBS 88034

Thelonious Monk Quartet | The Complete Genius | Blue Note | LA 579

Paris Jazz Concert:Theloniuos Monk And His Quartet | Laserlight | 17250

Monk At Newport 1963 & 1965 | CBS | C2K 63905

Thelonious Monk:85th Birthday Celebration | zyx records | FANCD 6076-2

Live In Paris 1964 | France's Concert | FCD 132x2

The Blue Note Years-The Best Of Thelonious Monk | Blue Note | 796636-2

Monk's Mood | Naxos Jazz | 8.120588 CD

Thelonious Monk:The Complete Blue Note Recordings | Blue Note | 830363-2

Thelonious Monk In Copenhagen | Storyville | STCD 8283

Thelonious Monk:Complete 1947-1952 Blue Note Recordings | The Jazz Factory | JFCD 22838

Live at The Five Spot,NYC | Blue Note | 799786-2

Thelonious Monk Quintet | On Tour In Europe | Charly | CD 122

Thelonious Monk Septet | Thelonious Monk-The Complete Riverside Recordings | Riverside | 15 RCD 022-2

Epistrophy(alt.take)

Thelonious Monk With John Coltrane | Jazzland | JZSA 946-6

Thelonious Monk With John Coltrane | Original Jazz Classics | OJC20 039-2

Thelonious Monk Quartet | Live In Switzerland 1966 | Jazz Helvet | JH 06

Epistrophy(theme)

Live In Paris, Alhambra 1964 Vol.1 | France's Concert | FCD 135

Live At The Jazz Workshop-Complete | CBS | C2K 65189

San Francisco Holiday | Milestone | MCD 9199-2

Live At The It Club:Complete | CBS | C2K 65288

Blues Five Spot | Milestone | M 9124

Epitaph

Rabih Abou-Khalil/Michael Armann Duo | Compositions & Improvisations | MMP-Records | 170857

Epitaph For Klook

Jack Walrath-Larry Willis | Portraits In Ivory & Brass | Mapleshade | 02032

Epitaph For Tom

Archie Shepp And His Band | Black Gypsy | America | AM 6099

Epitaph(part 1)

Charles Mingus And His Orchestra | The Complete Town Hall Concert | Blue Note | 828353-2

Epitaph(part 1alt.take)

The Complete Town Hall Concert | Blue Note | 828353-2

Epitaph(part 2)

Diederik Wissels Trio | Tender Is The Night | Jazz Pure Collection | AU 31616 CD

Epizykel(part 1-4)

Antonio Farao Quartet | Thorn | Enja | ENJ-9399 2

Epochè

Air Mail | Light Blues | Amadeo | 835305-2

Epoque

Fats Navarro With The Tadd Dameron Band | Fats Navarro Featured With The Tadd Dameron Band | Milestone | M 47041

Eps Vom Schorsch

John Wolf Brennan | Irisations | Creative Works Records | CW CD 1021-2

Epsilon

Taylor Hawkins Group | Wake Up Call | Fresh Sound Records | FSCD 145 CD

Equal Being

S.E.M. Ensemble | Virtuosity With Purpose | Ear-Rational | ECD 1034

Equalatogram

Joey Baron Quartet | We'll Soon Find Out | Intuition Records | INT 3515-2

Equaled
Thomas Chapin Trio Plus Brass | Insomnia | Knitting Factory Works | KFWCD 132

Eque
Charlie Haden Trio | Folk Songs | ECM | 1170(827705-2)

Equilibrista
Guillermo Gregorio Group | Approximately | Hat Art | CD 6184

Equilibrium
Cecil Payne Quintet | Bright Moments | Spotlite | SPJ LP 21

Equinox
Eddie Daniels Quartet | Nepenthe | GRP | GRP 96072
John Coltrane Quartet | The Very Best Of John Coltrane | Rhino | 8122-79778-2
Coltrane's Sound | Atlantic | 7567-81358-2
The Best Of John Coltrane | Atlantic | 7567-81366-2
Khan Jamal Trio | The Traveller | Steeplechase | SCCD 31217
Stephan Micus | To The Evening Child | ECM | 1486(513780-2)
Tito Puente And His Latin Ensemble | El Rey | Concord | CJ 250

Equipoise
Larry Coryell Quartet | Equipoise | Muse | MCD 5319

Erba Luce
Eugen Cicero Trio | Classics In Rhythm(Bach-Mozart-Chopin-Liszt-Tchaikovsky-Scarlatti) | MPS | 817924-2

Erg
Dylan Fowler Group | Portrait | Acoustic Music Records | 319.1185.2

Erhalt Uns, Herr Bei Deinam Wort
Irene Schweizer-Rüdiger Carl Duo | Die V-Mann Suite | FMP | 0860

Eric
Marcus Miller Group | Tales | Dreyfus Jazz Line | FDM 36571-2
Peter Weniger Quartet | Weirdoes | Mons Records | MR 874826
Maynard Ferguson And His Big Bop Nouveau Band | Brass Attitude | Concord | CCD 4848

Eric Song
Steve Turre Group | TNT | Telarc Digital | CD 83529

Erich, Der Dicke Grüne Delphin Tanzt
Kölner Saxophon Mafia | Mafia Years 1982-86 | Jazz Haus Musik | JHM 0058 CD

Erich, Der Grüne Delphin
Mafia Years 1982-86 | Jazz Haus Musik | JHM 0058 CD

Erich, Der Grüne Delphin Tanzt
Art Ensemble Of Chicago | A Jackson In Your House/Message To Our Folks | Affinity | AFF 752

Eric's Smoozie Blues
Chico Hamilton And Euphoria | My Panamanian Friend-The Music Of Eric Dolphy | Soul Note | 121265-2

Erilinda(Song Of Love)
Klaus Doldinger Group | Back In New York:Blind Date | Atlantic | 3984-26922-2

Erinnerung
Matthias Petzold Esperanto-Music | Lifelines | Indigo-Records | 1001 CD

Erinnerung An Die Opfer Des Golfkrieges(1)
Lifelines | Indigo-Records | 1001 CD

Erinnerung An Die Opfer Des Golfkrieges(2)
Häns'che Weiss Ensemble | Erinnerungen | Elite Special | 733503

Ernestine
Laurindo Almeida/Carlos Barbosa-Lima/Charlie Byrd Quintet | Music Of The Brazilian Masters | Concord | CCD 4389

Ernie's Tune
Dexter Gordon And Orchestra | More Than You Know | Steeplechase | SCS 1030
Dexter Gordon Quartet | Dexter Gordon:Ballads | Blue Note | 796579-2
Dexter Gordon With Orchestra | Strings & Things | Steeplechase | SCCD 31145

Ernst Und Heiter
Art Blakey And The Afro Drum Ensemble | The African Beat | Blue Note | 522666-2

Ero Ti Nr'ojeje
Joe McPhee Group | Old Eyes | Hat Art | CD 6047

Eronel
Christian Münchinger Quartet | Live At Moods! | Mons Records | MR 874321
Esbjörn Svensson Trio(E.S.T.) | EST Plays Monk | RCA | 2137680-2
Matt Renzi-Jimmy Weinstein-Masa Kamaguchi Trio | Lines And Ballads | Fresh Sound Records | FSNT 065 CD
Michael Rabinowitz Quartet | Gabrielle's Balloon | Jazz Focus | JFCD 011
Thelonious Monk Quintet | Thelonious Monk:Misterioso | Dreyfus Jazz Line | FDM 36743-2
The Complete Genius | Blue Note | LA 579
Thelonious Monk:Complete 1947-1952 Blue Note Recordings | The Jazz Factory | JFCD 22838

Erotic Lines
Pekka Pöyry With Band/Orchestra | Happy Peter | Leo Records | 016

Erroling
Claude Bolling Trio | A Tribute To My Favorites | Memo Music | HDJ 4068

Erroll's Bounce
Erroll Garner | Historical First Recording 1944 | Jazz Anthology | 550042
Erroll Garner Solo/Trio/Quartet | Inedits 1946-1947 | Festival | 402791
Erroll Garner Trio | Concert By The Sea | CBS | 451042-2

Erster Tango (Sountrack Querelle)
Bireli Lagrene Ensemble | Routes To Django & Bireli Swing '81 | Jazzpoint | JP 1055 CD
Bireli Lagrene Group | Bireli Lagrene 'Highlights' | Jazzpoint | JP 1027 CD
Bireli Lagrene Quartet | A' Portrait Of Jan Jankeje | Jazzpoint | JP 1054 CD
Eugen Rödel Trio | As Time Goes By | Jazzpoint | JP 1014 LP

Erwartung
Bob Hall | Left Hand Roller | BELL Records | BLR 84034

Erzählung
Cecil Taylor | Erzulie Maketh Scent | FMP | CD 18

E's Flat Ah's Flat Too
Charles Mingus And His Orchestra | Charles Mingus And Friends In Concert | CBS | C2K 64975
Charles Mingus Jazz Workshop | Blues & Roots | Atlantic | 7567-81336-2

E's Flat Ah's Flat Too(alt.take)
Blues & Roots | Atlantic | 8122-75205-2
Ekkehard Jost Quartet | Deep | Fish Music | FM 007 CD

Es Geht Eine Dunkle Wolke Herein
John Wolf Brennan | Flügel | Creative Works Records | CW CD 1037-2
A Band Of Friends | Teatime Vol.2 | Poise | Poise 06/2

Es Gescheh'n Noch Wunder
Elefanten | Faust | KlangRäume | 30150

Es Ist Doch Immer Wieder Schön
Bugge Wesseltoft | It's Snowing On My Piano | ACT | 9260-2

Es Ist Ein Ros Entsprungen
Christoph Lauer & Norwegian Brass | Heaven | ACT | 9420-2
David Gazarov Trio | Let's Have A Merry Christmas With The David Gazarov Trio! | Organic Music | ORGM 9712
HR Big Band With Marjorie Barnes And Frits Landesbergen | Swinging Christmas | hr music.de | hrmj 012-02 CD
Wolfgang Lauth Quartet | Lauther | Bear Family Records | BCD 15717 AH

Es Ist Nur Die Liebe
A Band Of Friends | Teatime Vol.1 | Poise | Poise 01

Es Ist Schön,Viel Zu Schön
Human Music Association | Short Stories | Software Music | SOWA 108

Es Läuft
Heiner Goebbels/Alfred Harth | Berold Brecht:Zeit wird knapp | Riskant | 568-72414

Es Mold Tard
Motus Quartett | Grimson Flames | Creative Works Records | CW CD 1023-2

Es Muß Doch Irgend Einen Ausweg Geben-
Anirahtak und die Jürgen Sturm Band | Das Kurt Weill Programm | Nabel Records:Jazz Network | CD 4638

Es Regnet
Ann Malcom With The Robi Szakcsi Jr. Trio | R.S.V.P. | Mons Records | MR 874301

Es Sungen Drei Engel 2000
Dieter Ilg Trio | Folk Songs | Jazzline | JL 11146-2

Es War Ein Zauberer-
Norbert Stein Pata Masters | Blue Slit | Pata Musik | PATA 8 CD

Es War Einmal
Volker Schlott & Reinmar Henschke | Influence | Acoustic Music Records | 319.1043.2

Es War In Schöneberg
Papa Bue's Viking Jazzband | Schlafe Mein Prinzchen | Storyville | 6.23327 AF

Es Wäre Schön Gewesen
Ton-Art | Zu | Hat Art | CD 6034

Es Wird Einmal Gewesen Sein
The Harlem Ramblers Dixieland-Jazzband | Harlem Ramblers 2000 | Elite Special | 73438

Escapade
Lafayette Harris Jr. Quartet | Lafayette Is Here | Muse | MCD 5507

Escapades For Voice
Airto Moreira/Flora Purim | The Colours Of Life | IN+OUT Records | 001-2

Escape
Bill Evans Group | Escape | Escape | ESC 03650-2
Michel Warlop Et Son Orchestre | Le Jazz En France Vol.4 | Pathe | 1727281

Escape Velocity
Rob Brown Trio | Breath Rhyme | Silkheart | SHCD 122

Escher Sketch
Rüdiger Carl | Rüdiger Carl Solo | FMP | CD 86

Esclavo Triste
Fleurine With Band And Horn Section | Meant To Be! | EmArCy | 159085-2

Escolher
Laurindo Almeida/Carlos Barbosa-Lima/Charlie Byrd Quintet | Music Of The Brazilian Masters | Concord | CCD 4389

Escualo
Orquesta Conexion Latina | Un Poco Loco | Enja | ENJ-5023 2

Eshun Agwe(Yoruba Word For 'Party')
Tiziana Ghiglioni Quartet | Spellbound | yvp music | CD 3058

Esitazione
Rodach | Himmel Und Hölle-Heaven And Hell | Traumton Records | 4434-2

Eskimo Märchen
Philip Catherine/Niels-Henning Orsted-Pedersen With The Royal Copenhagen Chamber Orchestra | Spanish Nights | Enja | ENJ-7023 2

Esmeralda
Ralph Moore Quartet | Who It Is You Are | Denon Compact Disc | CY-75778

Espai
Jessica Williams Trio | Inventions | Jazz Focus | JFCD 008

Espanola
Charlie Byrd And The Washington Guitar Quartet | Charlie Byrd/The Washington Guitar Quartet | Concord | CCD 42014

Esperanca
Charlie Byrd Group | My Inspiration:Music Of Brazil | Concord | CCD 4850

Esperanca Perdida-
Gabriele Hasler Group | Gabriele Hasler's Personal Notebook | Foolish Music | FM 211490

Esperango
Alexi Tuomarila Quartet | 02 | Finladia Jazz | 0927-49148-2

Esperanto
Klaus Doldinger & Passport | Down To Earth | Warner | 4509-93207-2
Kurt Elling Group With Guests | Live In Chicago | Blue Note | 522211-2
Live In Chicago | Blue Note | 522211-2

Esperanto(Intro)
Fourth World | Fourth World | B&W Present | BW 030

Esperanza
Makoto Ozone Trio | The Trio | Verve | 537503-2

Espiritu
Airto Moreira/Flora Purim | The Colours Of Life | IN+OUT Records | 001-2

Espiritual Rain Forest
Ann Malcom With The Kenny Barron Quintet | Incident'ly | Sound Hills | SSCD 8053

Esprit De L'Escalier
Dave Holland Qartet | Dream Of The Elders | ECM | 1572(529084-2)

Esquality
Dream Of The Elders | ECM | 1572(529084-2)

Esquality(II)
Andrew Cyrille Trio | X Man | Soul Note | 121262-2

Esque
Paris Quartet | Paris Quartet | Intakt Records | 012

Esquire Blues
Leonard Feather's Esquire All Stars | Metropolitan Opera House Jam Session | Jazz Anthology | 550212

Esquire Bounce
Esquire Metropolitan Opera House Jam Session | Jazz Live & Rare: The First And Second Esquire Concert | Jazzline | ???
Coleman Hawkins And Leonard Feather's All Stars | Commodore Classics In Swing | Commodore | 9031-72723-2

Essence
Richard Beirach-Masahiko Togashi | Richie Beirach-Masahiko Togashi-Terumasa Hino | Konnex Records | KCD 5043

Essence Of Jazz
Sam Rivers Tuba Trio | Jazz Of The Seventies | Circle Records | RK 6-7376/6 IMS

Essencia Grave
Gebhard Ullmann Trio | Essencia | Between The Lines | btl 017(Efa 10187-2)

Essencia Largo
Yusef Lateef Ensemble | Nocturnes | Atlantic | 7567-81977-2

Essential Element
David Murray-Milford Graves | Real Deal | DIW | DIW 867 CD

Estate(Summer)
Dave Liebman Group | New Vista | Arkadia Jazz | 71041
Ed Bickert-Lorne Lofsky Quartet | This Is New | Concord | CCD 4414
Eric Alexander Quartet | The Second Milestone | Milestone | MCD 9315-2
Franco & Lorenzo Petrocca | Italy | Edition Musikat | EDM 062
George Colligan Trio | Activism | Steeplechase | SCCD 31382
Lorenzo Petrocca Quartet Feat. Bruno De Filippi | Insieme | Edition Musikat | EDM 002
Lynne Arriale Trio | Live At Montreux | TCB Records | TCB 20252
Meredith d'Ambrosio Quartet | Beware Of Spring! | Sunnyside | SSC 1069 D
Michel Petrucciani Trio | Estate | Riviera | RVR 1
Stefanie Schlesinger And Her Group | What Love Is | Enja | ENJ-9434 2
Susannah McCorkle And Her Sextet | Sabia | Concord | CCD 4418
Tex Allen Quintet | Late Night | Muse | MCD 5492
Trio Idea With Jerry Bergonzi | Napoli Connection | Red Records | 123261-2
Woody Shaw Quartet | In My Own Sweet Way | IN+OUT Records | 7003-2
Zona Sul | Pure Love | Nagel-Heyer | CD 3039
Donald Byrd & His Orchestra | Electric Byrd | Blue Note | 836195-2

Estella By Starlight
Reggie Workman Quintet | Summit Conference | Postcards | POST 1003

Estels Foscos En Un Cel Tan Clar
Jan Klare/Tom Lorenz Quartett | Das Böse Ding | Acoustic Music Records | 319.1060.2

Estorias De Alcantara
Vanessa Rubin With Orchestra | Pastiche | Novus | 4163152-2

Estrada Do Sol
Zona Sul | Pure Love | Nagel-Heyer | CD 3039
Maria Joao-Aki Takase Duo | Art Of The Duo Vol.1 | Enja | 8008-2

Estramadura(part 1-3)
Das Pferd | Blue Turns To Grey | VeraBra Records | CDVBR 2065-2

Estrellas
Marco Tamburini Quartet | Thinking Of You | Penta Flowers | CDPIA 021

Estrellita
Dave McKenna | A Handful Of Stars | Concord | CCD 4580

Estrellita(Little Star)
Laurindo Almeida-Charlie Byrd Quartet | Latin Odyssey | Concord | MC CJ 211C

Estrellita(take 2,4-6)
Akili | Akili | M.A Music | NU 730-2

Estuary
Tommy Smith Sextet | Misty Morning And No Time | Linn Records | AKD 040
Josep Maria Balanyà | Elements Of Development | Laika Records | 8695070

Estudi Per A Piano, Pinxitos I Tub De Plastic
Luis Agudo & Friends | Dona Fia | Red Records | 123244-2

Estupenda Graca
Anthony Davis Orchestra | Hemispheres | Gramavision | GR 8303-2

Et La Roue De La Vie
Häns'che Weiss Ensemble | Erinnerungen | Elite Special | 733503

Et Pourquois Pas
Martial Solal Big Band | Martial Solal Big Band | Dreyfus Jazz Line | FDM 36512-2

Et Si Demain
Stephane Grappelli-Martial Solal Duo | Happy Reunion | Owl Records | 013430-2

Et Si L'on Improvisait
Simon Cato Spang-Hansen Quartet | Identified | dacapo | DCCD 9448

Et Si?
Clark Terry Sextet | Clark Terry | Swing | SW 8406 IMS

Etcetera
Joe Locke Quartet | Longing | Steeplechase | SCCD 31281

Été(Vivaldi)
Herbie Mann & The Family Of Mann With Minoru Muraoka,Shomyo & Gagaku | Gagaku & Beyond | Finnadar | SR 9014

Eterna
Perico Sambeat Quartet | Friendship | ACT | 9421-2
Egberto Gismonti & Academia De Dancas | Sanfona | ECM | 1203/04(829391-2)

Eterna-
Ahmed El-Salamouny/Gilson De Assis | Tango Brasileiro | FSM | FCD 97725

Eternal Ascension To A Topless Mountain
Charles Owens Quartet | Eternal Balance | Fresh Sound Records | FSNT 067 CD

Eternal Balance
Jimmy Yancey | The Yancey-Lofton Sessions Vol. 2 | Storyville | SLP 239

Eternal Chant
The Jimmy Giuffre 3 | Music For People,Birds,Butterflies & Mosquitoes | Candid | CRS 1001 IMS

Eternal Child
Thomas Chapin Trio | Third Force | Knitting Factory Works | KFWCD 103

Eternal Heavy Metal
Joe Lovano Trio | Trio Fascination | Blue Note | 833114-2

Eternal Joy
Carlos Garnett Quartet | Fuego En Mi Alma | HighNote Records | HCD 7001

Eternal Spiral
Ahmed Abdullah Sextet | Life's Force | About Time | AT 1001

Eternal Youth
Freddy Martin And His Orchestra | The Uncollected: Freddy Martin, Vol.3 | Hindsight | HSR 190

Eternally
Victor Goines Quintet | Genesis | AFO Records | AFO 92-0428-2

Eternally(short version)
Bob Wilber-Dick Hyman Sextet | A Perfect Match:A Tribute To Johnny Hodges & Wild Bill Davis | Arbors Records | ARCD 19193

Eternity
Steve Eliovson-Collin Walcott | Dawn Dance | ECM | 1198
Mahavishnu Orchestra | Visions Of The Emerald Beyond | CBS | 467904-2

Eternity's Breath(part 1)
Visions Of The Emerald Beyond | CBS | 467904-2

Eternity's Breath(part 2)
Jorge Pardo Band | Cicadas | ACT | 9209-2

Eterno-
Mario Fragiacomo Orchestra | Trieste Ieri Un Secolo Fa | SPLASC(H) Records | HP 08

Ethel
Scott Colley Sextet | Portable Universe | Freelance | FRL-CD 027

Ethereal Mood
Andy LaVerne Quintet | Severe Clear | Steeplechase | SCCD 31273

Ethereggae
Larry Willis Quartet | My Funny Valentine | Jazz City | 660.53.005

Ethiopia
Roy Hargrove-Walter Booker | Family | Verve | 527630-2
Terri Lyne Carrington Quartet | Structure | ACT | 9427-2
Baron-Berne-Roberts Trio | Miniature | JMT Edition | 834423-2

Ethnolog
I Virtuosi Di Cave | I Virtuosi Di Cave | Red Records | VPA 131

Etincelles
Big Three Trio | Willie Dixon-The Big Three Trio | CBS | 467248-2

Etosha
Charlie Mariano Quartet | Deep In A Dream | Enja | ENJ-9423 2
Philippe Macé Group | Aventures | AH Records | PAM 969

Etu Heii
Harry Tavitian/Corneliu Stroe | Transilvanian Suite | LEO | LR 132

Etude
Misha Alperin Quintet | North Story | ECM | 1596
Paul Motian Band | Psalm | ECM | 1222
Stephan Oliva Trio | Fantasm | RCA | 2173925-2
Friedrich Gulda | The Long Road To Freedom | MPS | 88021-2

Etude 22
Jan Fryderyk Trio | tri-o (tri-ou) Trio n. | Jazzline | ???

Etude In Three
Rade Soric Trio | Nahend | Edition Collage | EC 455-2

Etude No.2
Donny McCaslin Quartet | Exile And Discovery | Naxos Jazz | 86014-2

Etude Op.10 No.6 In E Flat Major(Chopin)
The Swingle Singers | Compact Jazz:The Swingle Singers | Mercury | 830701-2 PMS

Etude Op.25 No.2 In F Minor(Chopin)
Ullmann-Wille-Haynes | Trad Corrosion | Nabel Records:Jazz Network | CD 4673

Etude Part 1
Trad Corrosion | Nabel Records:Jazz Network | CD 4673

Etude Part 2
Trad Corrosion | Nabel Records:Jazz Network | CD 4673

Etude Part 3
Trad Corrosion | Nabel Records:Jazz Network | CD 4673

Etude Part 4
Jan Fryderyk | Piano Works: Live Recordings | Jazzline | ???

Etwas
Sven-Ake Johansson | Schlingerland | FMP | SAJ 01

Eu E Voce
The New Stan Getz Quintet Feat. Astrud Gilberto | Getz Au Go Go | Verve | 821725-2
Getz Au Go Go | CTI Records | PDCTI 1124-2

Eu Ja Sei
Caterina Valente-Catherine Michel | Girltalk | Nagel-Heyer | NH 1015

Eu Nao Exixte
Carlos Bica-Ana Brandao Group | DIZ | Enja | ENJ-9414 2

Eu Vim Da Bahia
Eubie Blake | The Eighty-Six Years Of Eubie Blake | CBS | 22223

Eugenia The Bride
Benny Bailey Quartet | I Thought About You | Laika Records | 35100762

Eukalypso
Duke Ellington And His Orchestra | The Intimate Ellington | Original Jazz Classics | OJCCD 730-2(2310787)

Eulogy
World Trio | World Trio | VeraBra Records | CDVBR 2052-2
Air | Live Air | Black Saint | 120034-2

Euphonic Sounds-A Syncopeted Novelty
Morton Gunnar Larsen | Maple Leaf Rag | Herman Records | HJCD 1009

Euphoria
Charlie Ventura Quintet | The New Charlie Ventura In Hi-Fi | Harlequin | HQ 2009(Baton BL 1202) IMS

Euphrates
Baden Powell | Poema On Guitar | MPS | 68089

Euridice
J.J.Johnson And His Orchestra | The Total J.J. Johnson | RCA | 2147791-2

Euro Salsa
Franck Band | Looser | Jazz Haus Musik | JHM 43 CD

Europa
Vital Information | Live Around The World Where We Come From Tour '98-'99 | Intuition Records | INT 3296-2
Charles Earland Septet | Unforgettable | Muse | MCD 5455

Europa(Earth Cry-Heaven's Smile)
Ronnie Foster Group | The Racer | Electric Bird | K 28P 6441

European Echoes
Ornette Coleman Trio | Blue Note's Three Decade Of Jazz 1959-1969, Vol. 1 | Blue Note | 89904

European Echoes(alt.take)
Jaki Byard | Maybeck Recital Hall Series Volume Seventeen | Concord | CCD 4511

European Faces
Charles Lloyd Quartet | Charles Lloyd In Europe | Atlantic | 7567-80788-2

European Fantasy
Cash McCall And The Young Blues Thrillers | Cash McCall | Blues Classics(L+R) | CDLR 82010

European Triangle
Kenny Blake Group | A Lifetime After | Inak | 30372

Eurydice
Weather Report | Weather Report | CBS | 468212-2

Eurydice-
Steve Erquiaga Group | Erkiology | Windham Hill | 34 10127-2

Eva
Christof Lauer Quartet | Christof Lauer | CMP Records | CMP CD 39

Evan
Muddy Waters Group | Back In His Early Days, Vol.1+2 | Red Lightnin' | SC 001/2

Evanescence
Bud Shank Quartet | Bud Shank Plays The Music Of Bill Evans | Fresh Sound Records | FSR-CD 5012

Evanesque
ETC & Jerry Bergonzi | ETC Plus One | Red Records | 123249-2

Evans
Kelm 3 | Per Anno | dml-records | CD 013
Peter Erskine Trio | You Never Know | ECM | 1497(517353-2)

Evans Above
Lounge Lizards | Live In Berlin 1991-Vol.2 | Intuition Records | INT 2055-2

Evan's Drive To Mombasa
Enrico Pieranunzi Trio | Deep Down | Soul Note | 121121-2

Evansong
Charles Lloyd Quartet | All My Relations | ECM | 1557

Evanstide, Where Lotus Bloom
Nancy Wilson With George Shearing And His Quintet | The Swingin's Mutual | Capitol | 799190-2

Evansville
Bruce Dunlap Quintet | About Home | Chesky | JD 59

Evas Pflug
Axel Zwingenberger-Torsten Zwingenberger | Boogie Woogie Bros. | Vagabond | VRCD 8.88015

Eva's Pleasure
Alex Merck & Painted Birds | Minds And Bodies | yvp music | 3003(Demon)

Evasion De Julien
Sun Ra And His Solar Arkestra | Sun Ra Visit Planet Earth/Interstellar Low Ways | Evidence | ECD 22039-2

Evelation
Red Rodney Sextet | Serge Chaloff Memorial | Cool & Blue | C&B-CD 102

Even From Me
Louis Conte Group | La Cocina Caliente | Denon Compact Disc | CY-30001

Even If It Breaks My Heart
Michel Petrucciani With The Graffiti String Quartet | Marvellous | Dreyfus Jazz Line | FDM 36564-2

Even Mice Dance
Michel Petrucciani | Au Theatre Des Champ-Elysees(Paris Concert) | Dreyfus Jazz Line | FDM 36570-2

Even Mice Dance-
Neil Richardson Singers With The Metropole Orchestra | A Beautiful Friendship | Koch Jazz | 3-6909-2

Even Plains
Adam Holzman Group | Overdrive | Lipstick Records | LIP 890252

Even Song
John Scofield-John Abercrombie Quartet | Solar | West Wind | WW 2100

Even Steven
Pierre Dorge & New Jungle Orchestra | Very Hot Even The Moon Is Dancing | Steeplechase | SCCD 31208

Evenin'
Count Basie And His Orchestra | Count Basie At Newport | Verve | 2304414 IMS
Jimmy Witherspoon And His Band | Evenin' Blues | Original Blues Classics | OBCCD 511-2
Ken Peplowski Quintet | The Natural Touch | Concord | CCD 4517
Bill Dixon Sextet | Bill Dixon In Italy - Volume Two | Soul Note | SN 1011

Evening Air
Chris Kase Sextet | Starting Now | Mons Records | MR 874659

Evening Dreams
Michael Brecker Quindectet | Wide Angles | Verve | 076142-2

Evening Faces
Derek Bailey/John Zorn/William Parker | Harras | Avant | AVAN 056

Evening In Atlantis
Art Farmer Quintet | Farmer 's Market | Prestige | P 24032

Evening In Paris
Gigi Gryce Quartet | Lucky Thompson/Gigi Gryce:Street Scenes | Vogue | 2115467-2
Quincy Jones And His Orchestra | That's How I Feel About Jazz | CTI Records | PDCTI 1108-2
Zoot Sims Quintet | Zoot Sims | Swing | SW 8417

Evening Land
Joe Gordon Quintet | Blakey | Verve | 538634-2

Evening Sky
Charles Sullivan Orchestra | Genesis | Inner City | IC 1012 IMS

Evening Song
Oscar Peterson Quartet | A Summer Night In Munich | Telarc Digital | CD 83450
Dizzy Gillespie And His Orchestra | Dizzy's Diamonds-Best Of The Verve Years | Verve | 513875-2

Evenly They Danced
Dave Bargeron Quartet | Barge Burns...Slide Flies | Mapleshade | 02832

Evensong
John Surman Quartet | How Many Clouds Can You See? | Deram | 844882-2

Event
Geoff Keezer Group | Other Spheres | DIW | DIW 871 CD

Eventide
Scott Hamilton Quintet | The Right Time | Concord | CCD 4311
Steven Halpern | Timeless | Gramavision | 18-7833-1

Eventually
Ornette Coleman Quartet | Atlantic Jazz: The Avant-Garde | Atlantic | 7567-81709-2

Eventyr
Annette Peacock With The Cikada String Quartet | An Acrobat's Heart | ECM | 1733(159496-2)

Ever 2 B Gotten
Christoph Spendel Group | Out Of Town | TCB Records | TCB 01032

Ever Since The World Ended
Billy Taylor Trio | Billy Taylor Trio | Prestige | PRCD 24285-2

Ever So Easy
Lucky Thompson Sextet | Accent On Tenor Sax | Fresh Sound Records | FSCD 2001

Ever So Greatful
Harry Sheppard Quintet | This-A-Way That-A-Way | Justice Records | JR 0302-2

Everblue
James Cotton Group | Deep In The Blues | Verve | 529849-2

Everbody's Fishin'
Kol Simcha | Contemporary Klezmer | Laika Records | LK 93-048

Everbody's Freilach
Thad Jones And His Orchestra | Eclipse | Storyville | SLP 4089

Evergreenish
Eef Albers Group | Pyramids | Cris Crazz | CCR 017 IMS

Every Breath You Take
Herbie Nichols Trio | The Bethlehem Session | Affinity | AFF 759

Every Day
Jimmy Witherspoon And His All Stars | Jimmy Witherspoon | Laserlight | 17069
Joe Williams And His Band | Planet Jazz:Joe Williams | Planet Jazz | 2165370-2
Victor Jazz History Vol.10:Kansas City(1935-71) | RCA | 2128564-2

Every Day Is Beautiful
Hal McIntyre And His Orchestra | The Uncollected:Hal McIntyre | Hindsight | HSR 172

Every Girl I See
Tom Talbert Septet | Things As They Are | Seabreeze | CDSB 2038(881572)

Every Little Thing
Claus Boesser-Ferrari | Welcome | Acoustic Music Records | 319.1117.2

Every Man To His Own Profession
Dee Dee Bridgewater With Band | Dee Dee Bridgewater | Atlantic | 7567-80760-2

Every Man Wants Another Man's Woman
Edwin Hawkins Singers | The Best Of The Edwin Hawkins Singers | Warner | 252213-1

Every Moment
Jeff Beal | Contemplations | Triloka Records | 320204-2

Every Night
Joe Williams With The Jimmy Jones Orchestra | Me And The Blues | RCA | 2121823-2

Every Now And Then
Ramona And Her Gang | The Indispensable Jack Teagerden(1928-1957) | RCA | ND 89613

Every Saturday Night
Peter Hertmans Quartet | Waiting | Timeless | CD SJP 418

Every Step Of The Way
David Benoit Group | Every Step Of The Way | GRP | GRP 95582

Every Summer Night
Pat Metheny Group | In Concert | Jazz Door | JD 1231

Every Sunday
John McLaughlin Quintet | Electric Guitarist | CBS | 467093-2

Every Time
Don Elliott Orchestra | Don Elliott Sings | Fresh Sound Records | FSR 2049(Bethlehem BCP 15)

Every Time I Get To Drinking(take 3)
Sarah Vaughan And Her Band | The Devine One | Fresh Sound Records | FSR 659(Roulette R 52060)

Every Time We Say Goodbye
Agneta Baumann And Her Quartet | Comes Love... | Touché Music | TMcCD 011
Andy And The Bey Sisters | Andy Bey And The Bey Sisters | Prestige | PCD 24245-2
Betty Carter And Her Trio | Jazzbühne Berlin '85 | Repertoire Records | REPCD 4901-CC
Bill Evans Trio With Lee Konitz & Warne Marsh | Crosscurrents | Original Jazz Classics | OJCCD 718-2(F 9568)
Chet Baker Quartet | Let's Get Lost | RCA | PL 83054
Dick Whittington Trio | In New York | Concord | CCD 4498
Dinah Washington With The Quincy Jones Orchestra | The Swingin' Miss 'D' | Verve | 558074-2
Dorothy Carless With The Barney Kessel Trio | The Carless Torch | Fresh Sound Records | HIFI R 403 CD
Ella Fitzgerald With The Buddy Bregman Orchestra | The Cole Porter Song Book | Verve | 2683044 IMS
Ella Fitzgerald Sings The Cole Porter Songbook | Verve | 537257-2
The Complete Ella Fitzgerald Song Books of Harold Arlen, Irving Berlin, Duke Ellington, George & Ira Gershwin, Jerome Kern, Johnny Mercer, Cole Porter And Rogers & Hart | Verve | 519832-2
Gail Wynters With The Gordon Brisker Quintet | My Shining Hour | Naxos Jazz | 86027-2
Harry Allen Quartet | Love Songs Live! | Nagel-Heyer | NH 1014
HUM | HUM(Humair-Urtreger-Michelot) | Sketch | SKE 333006
Ingrid Sertso And Her Sextet | Dance With Me | Enja | 8024-2
Jeanne Lee-Mal Waldron | After Hours | Owl Records | 013426-2
Jerri Southern And The Dave Barbour Trio | The Very Thought Of You:The Decca Years 1951-1957 | Decca | 050671-2
John Coltrane Quartet | John Coltrane-The Heavyweight Champion:The Complete Atlantic Recordings | Atlantic | 8122-71984-2
European Impressions | Bandstand | BDLP 1514
The Complete Graz Concert Vol.1 | Magnetic Records | MRCD 104
The Best Of John Coltrane | Pablo | 2405417-2
Live 1962 | Festival | ???
John Mehegan-Kenny Clarke | Johnny Mehegan's Reflections | Savoy | SV 0204(MG 12028)
Kurt Elling Group | This Time Its Love | Blue Note | 493543-2
Larry Schneider Quartet | Just Cole Porter | Steeplechase | SCCD 31291
Lee Konitz-Red Mitchell Duo | I Concentrate On You | Steeplechase | SCCD 31018
Milt Jackson Sextet | The Harem | Musicmasters | 5061-2
P.J. Perry Quartet | Worth Waiting For | The Jazz Alliance | TJA 10007
Rosemary Clooney And Her Band With Strings | For The Duration | Concord | CCD 4444
Sarah Vaughan With Mundell Lowe And George Duvivier | The Roulette Years Vol. One/Two | Roulette | CDP 794983-2
Sonny Rollins Quartet | The Freedom Suite Plus | Milestone | M 47007
Sonny Rollins-The Freelance Years:The Complete Riverside & Contemporary Recordings | Riverside | 5 RCD 4427-2
The Jazz Giants Play Cole Porter:Night And Day | Prestige | PCD 24203-2
Sonny Rollins:Brown Skin Girl | Memo Music | HDJ 4041
The Timeless Art Orchestra | Without Words | Satin Doll Productions | SDP 1005-1 CD
Till Brönner Group | Chattin' With Chet | Verve | 157534-2
Vanessa Rubin With Band | Language Of Love | Telarc Digital | CD 83465
Warren Bernhardt Quintet | Reflections | dmp Digital Music Productions | CD 489

Every Time We Say Goodbye-
Sheila Jordan With The Steve Kuhn Trio | Jazz Child | HighNote Records | HCD 7029

Every Time You're Near
Count Basie And His Orchestra | Verve Jazz Masters 2:Count Basie | Verve | 519819-2

Every Tub
Basie Rides Again | Verve | MV 2643 IMS
Swingin' The Blues | Arco | 3 ARC 111
Oldsmobile Dixieland Jazz Band | Dixieland Jazz(Hungarian) | Jazz Pure Collection | AU 31613 CD

Everybody Blow!
Champion Jack Dupree Group | Jack Dupree-Jimmy Rushing-Muddy Waters | Laserlight | 17062

Everybody Cryin' Mercy
Mose Allison Trio | That's Jazz Vol.19: Mose Allison | Atlantic | ATL 50249

Everybody Loves My Baby
Arne Birger's Jazzsjak | The Golden Years Of Revival Jazz,Vol.8 | Storyville | STCD 5513
Benny Goodman Quartet | Jazz Drumming Vol.2(1937-1938) | Fenn Music | FJD 2702
Firehouse Five Plus Two | The Firehouse Five Story Vol. 1 | Good Time Jazz | 12010
Grady Tate And His Quartet | Body & Soul | Milestone | MCD 9208-2
Lionel Hampton And His All Stars | Masters Of Jazz Vol.8 | RCA | NL 89540 DP
Marilyn Middleton Pollock With The Lake Records All-Star Jazzband |
Marilyn Middleton Pollock With The Lake Records All-Star Jazzband | Lake | LACD 35
Mezzrow-Ladnier Quintet | The Complete Sidney Bechet-Vol.5 | RCA | 2115519-2
Sidney DeParis' Blue Note Jazzmen | The Blue Note Jazzmen | Blue Note | 821262-2
Sippie Wallace With Jim Dapogny's Chicago Jazz Band | Sippie | Atlantic | SD 19350
Vic Dickenson Septet With Ruby Braff | Nice Work | Vanguard | VCD 79610-2
Mezzrow-Ladnier Quintet | The Complete Sidney Bechet-Vol.5 | RCA | 2115519-2

Everybody Loves My Baby(alt.take)
Papa Bue's Viking Jazzband | Greatest Hits | Storyville | 6.23336 AF

Everybody Loves Saturday Night
Sandy Brown's Jazz Band | The Golden Years Of Revival Jazz,Vol.6 | Storyville | STCD 5511
Dinah Washington With Orchestra | Mad About The Boy-The Best Of Dinah Washington | Mercury | 512214-2

Everybody Loves Somebody
Les Brown And His Band Of Renown | Today | MPS | 68118

Everybody Loves Somebody-
New Orleans Rhythm Kings | Victor Jazz History Vol.1:New Orleans & Dixieland | RCA | 2128555-2

Everybody Loves Somebody Sometime
Roy Ayers Group | Roy Ayers-The Essential Groove:Live | Ronnie Scott's Jazz House | JHCD 035

Everybody Loves The Sunshine
Maynard Ferguson With The Birdland Dreamband | The Birdland Dream Band Vol.2 | Fresh Sound Records | 58057 CD(RCA)

Everybody Plays The Game
John Lee Hooker Group | Everybody Rockin' | Charly | CRB 1014

Everybody Wants To Go To Heaven
New York Jazz Collective | Everybody Wants To Go To Heaven | Naxos Jazz | 86073-2

Everybody's Broke
The Real Ambassadors | The Real Ambassadors | CBS | 467140-2

Everybody's Doing It
Tommy Dorsey And His Clambake Seven | The Music Goes Round And Round | RCA | ND 83140(847123)

Everybody's Jumpin'
Dave Brubeck Quartet | The Dave Brubeck Selection | CBS | 467279-2

Everybody's Party
Alonzo Yancey | The Yancey-Lofton Sessions Vol. 1 | Storyville | SLP 238

Everybody's Somebody's Fool
(Little)Jimmy Scott With Orchestra | Little Jimmy Scott-All Over Again | Savoy | SV 0263
Betty Carter With Orchestra | 'Round Midnight | Atlantic | AMCY 1060
Karin Krog With The Dexter Gordon Quartet | Some Other Spring | Storyville | STCD 4045
| Meeting In Brooklyn | Babel | BDV 9405

Everybody's Talkin'-
Louis Armstrong And His Friends | Planet Jazz:Louis Armstrong | Planet Jazz | 2152052-2

Everybody's Talkin'(Echoes)
Jazz Special-His Last Recordings | RCA | ND 89527
Lena Horne And Gabor Szabo | Lena & Gabor | Gryphon | 6.24451 AT

Everyday
Klaus Suonsaari Sextet | Inside Out | Soul Note | 121274-2

Everyday I Have The Blues
B.B.King And His Band | Live At San Quentin | MCA | MCD 06103
Singin' The Blues/The Blues | Ace Records | CDCHD 320
Big Joe Turner With The Pee Wee Crayton-Sonny Stitt Quintet | The Best Of Joe Turner | Pablo | 2405404-2
Count Basie And His Orchestra | The Great 1959 Band In Concert | Jazz Groove | 003 IMS
Live In Basel 1956 | Jazz Helvet | JH 05
Count Basie And His Orchestra With Ella Fitzgerald & Joe Williams | Metronome All-Stars 1956 | Verve | MV 2510 IMS
Harry Allen Quartet | Jazz Im Amerika Haus,Vol.1 | Nagel-Heyer | CD 011
Blues Of Summer | Nagel-Heyer | NH 1011
Helen Humes And Her All Stars | Sneakin' Around | Black & Blue | BLE 233083
Jeanne Carroll Trio | My Style Is Different | L+R Records | CDLR 42075
Jimmy Witherspoon And His All Stars | At The Renaissance | Fresh Sound Records | FSR 579(HiFiJazz J426)
Joe Williams And Friends | Joe Williams At Newport '63 | RCA | NL 70119
Kenny Burrell With The Don Sebesky Orchestra | Blues-The Common Ground | Verve | 589101-2
Lambert, Hendricks And Ross | Sing A Song Of Basie | Verve | 543827-2
Lightnin' Hopkins | Lightnin Hopkins-A Legend In His Own Time | Anthology of the Blues | AB 5608
Piano Red | The Blues Vol. 5 | Big Bear | 156042

Everyday(I Fall In Love)
Joe Williams With The Norman Simmons Quartet | Ballad And Blues Master | Verve | 511354-2 PMS
Kenny Burrell With The Don Sebesky Orchestra | Blues-The Common Ground | Verve | 589101-2

Everydays
Ozzie Nelson And His Orchestra | The Uncollected: Ozzie Nelson | Hindsight | HSR 107

Everyone Is Saying Hello Again
Festa Group | Strings | Nueva Records | NC 3009

Everyone Needs It
Ella Fitzgerald And Her Savoy Eight | Ella Fitzgerald-The Early Years-Part 1 | GRP | GRP 26182

Everything But You
Clark Terry Five | Memories Of Duke | Original Jazz Classics | OJCCD 604-2
Duke Ellington Quartet | Duke's Big 4 | Pablo | 2310703-2
Ella Fitzgerald With The Duke Ellington Orchestra | The Complete Ella Fitzgerald Song Books of Harold Arlen, Irving Berlin, Duke Ellington, George & Ira Gershwin, Jerome Kern, Johnny Mercer, Cole Porter And Rogers & Hart | Verve | 519832-2
Sarah Vaughan | A Celebration Of Duke | Original Jazz Classics | OJC 605(2312119)
Sarah Vaughan With Joe Pass And Mike Wofford | Sarah Vaughan Birthday Celebration | Fantasy | FANCD 6090-2
Eddy Howard And His Orchestra | The Uncollected:Eddy Howard, Vol.2 | Hindsight | HSR 156

Everything Depends On Me
Earl Hines | Another Monday Date | Prestige | P 24043
Earl Hines Quartet | Up To Date With Earl Hines | RCA | 2125726-2

Everything Happens To Me
Al Caiola Quintet | Deep In A Dream | Savoy | SV 0205(MG 12033)
Art Pepper Quartet | Two Altos | Savoy | SV 0161(MG 6069)
Art Pepper Quintet | Live At Donte's Vol.2 | Fresh Sound Records | FSR 5002(835552)
Bill Evans Trio | Trio (Motian Peacock)-Duo(Hall) | Verve | 2-2509 IMS
Bill Evans-Don Elliott | Tenderly | Milestone | MCD 9317-2
Billie Holiday And Her All Stars | Billie Holiday Story Vol.4:Lady Sings The Blues | Verve | 521429-2
Stay With Me | Verve | 511523-2
Branford Marsalis Trio | Bloomington | CBS | 473771-2
Bud Powell Trio | Bud Powell:Complete 1947-1951 Blue Note,Verve & Roost Recordings | The Jazz Factory | JFCD 22837
Charlie Mariano With The Tete Montoliu Trio | It's Standard Time Vol.2 | Fresh Sound Records | FSR-CD 5022
Charlie Parker With Strings | Bird With Strings-Live At The Apollo, Carnegie Hall & Birdland | CBS | CBS 82292
Charlie Parker With Strings:The Master Takes | Verve | 523984-2
Charlie Spivak And His Orchestra | The Uncollected:Charlie Spivak And His Orchestra,Vol.2 | Hindsight | HSR 188(835796)
Chet Baker Trio | Let's Get Lost | RCA | PL 83054
Claire Martin With The Jim Mullen Quartet | The Waiting Game | Linn Records | AKD 018
Dave Brubeck Quartet | Angel Eyes | CBS | SRCS 9368
Duke Jordan Trio | Flight To Denmark | Steeplechase | SCCD 31011
Erroll Garner | Historical First Recording 1944 | Jazz Anthology | 550042
Gene Harris Quartet | Funky Gene's | Concord | CCD 4609
George Shearing Trio | 500 Miles High | MPS | 68219
Houston Person Sextet | The Talk Of The Town | Muse | MCD 5331
Jimmy Raney Quintet | Jimmy Raney Visits Paris Vol.2 | Vogue | 21434802
Too Marvelous For Words | Biograph | BLP 12060
Joe Pass | Solo Guitar | Pablo | 2310974-2
Jon Hendricks Group | A Tribute To Charlie Parker Vol.2 | Storyville | 4960493
Julie London And Her Band | Julie At Home | EMI Records | EMS 1186
Kenny Drew Trio | New Faces New Sounds:Introducing The Kenny Drew Trio | Blue Note | 871245-4
Larry Nocella/Dannie Richmond Quartet | Everything Happens To Me | Red Records | VPA 167
Lewis Keel Quintet | Coming Out Swinging | Muse | MCD 5438
Marshall Royal Quintet | Royal Blue | Concord | CJ 125
Mocambo Jam Session | The Historic Mocambo Sessions '54-Vol.2 | Polydor | MP 2491 IMS
Paolo Fresu Quartet | Angel | RCA | 2155864-2
Paul Desmond Quartet | Desmond | Original Jazz Classics | OJCCD 712-2(F 3235/8082)
Paul Desmond Quartet Featuring Don Elliott | Original Jazz Classics | OJC 119(F 3235)
Ralph Sutton Quartet | Live At Sunnie's Rendezvous Vol.1 | Storyville | STCD 8280
Ray Brown Trio Plus | Bye Bye Blackbird | Paddle Wheel | K 28P 6303
Sonny Rollins Quartet | Sonny Rollins On Impulse | MCA | 2292-54613-2
Stan Getz Quintet | Jazz At Storyville Vol.2 | Fresh Sound Records | FSR 630(Roost RLP 411)
Tal Farlow Quintet | The Legendary Tal Farlow | Concord | CJ 266
Thelonious Monk | Thelonious Monk-The Complete Riverside Recordings | Riverside | 15 RCD 022-2
Monk Alone:The Complete Columbia Solo Studio Recordings | CBS | C2K 65495
Solo Monk | CBS | 471248-2
Till Brönner Group | Chattin' With Chet | Verve | 157534-2
Tina Brooks Quintet | Minor Move | Blue Note | 522671-2
Tommy Dorsey And His Orchestra | Frank Sinatra And The Tommy Dorsey Orchestra | RCA | 2668701-2
Forever | RCA | NL 89859 DP
Warne Marsh Quartet | Warne Marsh/4 | Criss Cross | Criss 1004(Mode 125)

Everything Happens To Me-
Norman Granz Jam Session | Charlie Parker Jam Session | Verve | 833564-2 PMS

Everything Happens To Me(alt.take 1)
Thelonious Monk | Monk Alone:The Complete Columbia Solo Studio Recordings | CBS | C2K 65495

Everything Happens To Me(alt.take 2)
Kenny Drew Trio | New Faces New Sounds:Introducing The Kenny Drew Trio | Blue Note | 871245-4

Everything Happens When You're Gone
Lil' Ed Williams And The Blues Imperials | Roughhousin' | Sonet | SNTF 966(941966)

Everything I Do Is Gonna Be Funky(From Now On)
Lou Donaldson Sextet | Lou Donaldson:The Righteous Reed! The Best Of Poppa Lou | Blue Note | 830721-2

Everything I Have Is Yours
Art Tatum | The Tatum Solo Masterpieces Vol.9 | Pablo | 2310835
Betty Carter And Her Trio | The Audience With Betty Carter | Bet-Car | MK 1003
Billy Eckstine With The Sonny Burke Orchestra | Verve Jazz Masters 22:Billy Eckstine | Verve | 516693-2
Don Lanphere Quintet | Don Loves Midge | Hep | 2027
Greg Marvin Quintet | Workout! | Criss Cross | Criss 1037 (835629)
Maxine Sullivan With The Keith Ingham Quintet | Maxine Sullivan Sings The Music Of Burton Lane | Mobile Fidelity | MFCD 773
N.Y. Hardbop Quintet | A Whisper Away | TCB Records | TCB 98702
Ella Fitzgerald With Benny Carter's Magnificent Seven | 30 By Ella | Capitol | 520090-2

Everything I Have Is Yours-
Phineas Newborn Jr. | Solo Piano | Atlantic | 7567-82272-2

Everything I Love
Bill Evans Trio | Bill Evans:The Secret Sessions | Milestone | 8MCD 4421-2
Bill Evans-Andy LaVerne | Modern Days & Night:Music Of Cole Porter | Double Time Records | DTRCD-120
Dick Hyman | Cole Porter:All Through The Night | Musicmasters | 5060-2
George Shearing & Barry Tuckwell With Orchestra | Plays The Music Of Cole Porter | Concord | CCD 42010
Kim Parker With The Kenny Drew Trio | Havin' Myself A Time | Soul Note | 121033-2
Oliver Pospiech's Small Big Band | Cool Blue | Mons Records | MR 874809
Oscar Peterson-Joe Pass Duo | Live At Salle Pleyel, Paris | Pablo | 2625705
Peter Erskine Trio | You Never Know | ECM | 1497(517353-2)
Ray Brown Trio | Don't Get Sassy | Telarc Digital | CD 83368
Thomas Clausen-Pyysalo Severi | Turn Out The Stars | Storyville | STCD 4215
Zoot Sims Quintet | Zoot Sims | Swing | SW 8417

Everything In Its Right Place
Kirk Lightsey Quartet | Everything Is Changed | Sunnyside | SSC 1020 D

Everything I've Got
Blossom Dearie Quartet | My Funny Valentine-The Rogers & Hart Songbook | Verve | 526448-2
Chris Connor With The Hank Jones Trio | As Time Goes By | Enja | ENJ-7061 2
Chris Connor With The Ralph Sharon Sextet | A Jazz Date With Chris Connor | Atlantic | AMCY 1072
Ella Fitzgerald And The Paul Smith Quartet | Verve Jazz Masters 6:Ella Fitzgerald | Verve | 519822-2
Ella Fitzgerald With The Buddy Bregman Orchestra | The Rodgers And Hart Songbook | Verve | 821693-1
Ella Fitzgerald With The Paul Smith Quartet | Ella Fitzgerald Sings The Rodgers And Hart Song Book | Verve | 537258-2
Hal Serra Trio | Jazzville Vol.4 | Fresh Sound Records | FSR 633(Dawn DLP 1122)
Teddy Wilson | Teddy Wilson Revamps Rodgers & Hart | Chiaroscuro | CR 168

Everything I've Got Belongs To You
Blossom Dearie Trio | At Ronnie Scott's:Blossom Time | EmArCy | 558683-2
Bob Florence Trio | Bob Florence Trio | Fresh Sound Records | FSR-CD 0303
Johnny Pace With The Chet Baker Quintet | Chet Baker Introduces Johnny Pace | Original Jazz Classics | OJCCD 433-2(RLP 12-292)
Lee Konitz And His Orchestra | You And Lee | Verve | 2304444 IMS
The International Jazz Group | The International Jazz Group Vol.2 | Swing | SW 8416

Everything Machine
Wayne Bartlett With The Thomas Hufschmidt Group | Tokyo Blues | Laika Records | 35101212

Everything Matters
Arthur Prysock With The Red Prysock Band | This Guy's In Love With You | Milestone | MCD 9146-2

Everything Must Change
Monty Alexander Trio | Live In Holland | Verve | 835627-2 PMS
Nina Simone And Orchestra | Baltimore | Epic | 476906-2
Ranee Lee And Her Quartet With David Murray | Seasons Of Love | Justin Time | JUST 103-2
Steve Wilson Quartet | Four For Time | Criss Cross | Criss 1115

Everything Reminds Me On You
Lenny Popkin Trio | Falling Free | Candid | CRS 1027 IMS

Everything Seems-
JoAnne Brackeen Trio | Havin' Fun | Concord | CJ 280

Everything That Lives Laments
Louis Jordan With The Nelson Riddle Orchestra | Louis Jordan-Let The Good Times Roll: The Complete Decca Recordings 1938-1954 | Bear Family Records | BCD 15557 IH

Everything That's Made Of Wood
Artie Shaw And His Orchestra | Original Recordings 1937/1938 | Festival | Album 248

Everything's Gonna Be Alright
The Uncollected:Artie Shaw, Vol.5 | Hindsight | HSR 176

Everywhere
Frank Carlberg Group | Variations On A Summer Day | Fresh Sound Records | FSNT 083 CD
Roswell Rudd Sextet | Mixed | Impulse(MCA) | IMP 12702
Woody Herman And The Herd | Woody Herman (And The Herd) At Carnegie Hall | Verve | 559833-2
Woody Herman And The New Thundering Herd | The 40th Anniversary Carnegie Hall Concert | RCA | 2159151-2

Everywhere You Turn
Affinity | Affinity Plays Nine Modern Jazz Classics | Music & Arts | CD 834

Evidence
Bebop And Beyond | Bebop And Beyond | Concord | CJ 244
Big Band Bellaterra | Don't Git Sassy | Fresh Sound Records | FSNT 048 CD
Billy Higgins Quartet | Bridgework | Contemporary | C 14024
Esbjörn Svensson Trio(E.S.T.) | EST Plays Monk | RCA | 2137680-2
Gäel Horellou-David Sauzay Quintet | Gäel Horellou Versus David Sauzay | Fresh Sound Records | FSNT 068 CD
George Cables Quartet | Beyond Forever | Steeplechase | SCCD 31305
Jaki Byard Experience | Pre-Rahsan | Prestige | P 24080
Joey DeFrancesco Group | Reboppin' | CBS | CK 48624
Peter Herborn Group With The Auryn String Quartet | Something Personal | JMT Edition | 849156-2
Thelonious Monk And His Orchestra | Who's Afraid Of The Big Band Monk? | CBS | CBS 88034
Thelonious Monk Quartet | The Complete Genius | Blue Note | LA 579
Thelonious Monk:85th Birthday Celebration | zyx records | FANCD 6076-2
Wizard Of The Vibes | Blue Note | 532140-2
The Blue Note Years-The Best Of Thelonious Monk | Blue Note | 796636-2
Live At The Jazz Workshop-Complete | CBS | C2K 65189
Monk's Mood | Naxos Jazz | 8.120588 CD
Thelonious Monk:Complete 1947-1952 Blue Note Recordings | The Jazz Factory | JFCD 22838
Thelonious Monk Quintet | European Tour | LRC Records | CDC 7683(874371)
Barry Altschul Sextet | Another Time Another Place | Muse | MR 5176

Evidence-
Jeff Jerolamon Quartet | Jeff Jerolamon's Swing Thing! | Candid | CCD 79538
Donald 'Duck' Harrison Quintet | Full Circle | Sweet Basil | 660.55.003

Evidence(We Named It Justice)
Robin Eubanks Group | Karma | JMT Edition | 834446-2

Evigheden(Eternety)
Big Allanbik | Batuque Y Blues | Blues Beacon | BLU-1031 2

Evil
Billy Branch Group | The Blues Keep Following Me Around | Verve | 527268-2
Howlin' Wolf Band | Howlin' Wolf | Chess | 427016

Evil Ambition
Count Basie And His Orchestra | Count Basie Vol.2(1938-1940) | CDS Records Ltd. | RPCD 603

Evil Blues
Washboard Sam | Masters Of Jazz Vol. 15-Blues Giants | RCA | NL 89728 DP

Evil Eye
Bill Holman And His Orchestra | The Fabulous Bill Holman | Sackville | 2013

Evil Eyes
Albinia Jones With Don Byas' Swing Seven | Don Byas Complete American Small Group Recordings | Definitive Records | DRCD 11213

Evil Gal Blues
Leonard Feather All Stars | Night Blooming | Mainstream | MD CDO 719

Evil Ways
Otis Spann/Robert Lockwood Jr. | Otis Spann And His Piano | Crosscut | CCR 1003(Candid)

Evocacao De Jacob
Klaus Doldinger's Passport | Man In The Mirror | Warner | 2292-40253-2

Evocation
Sam Rivers' Rivbea Orchestra | Jazzbühne Berlin '82 | Repertoire Records | REPCD 4910-CC

Evocations
Moacir Santos Group | Opus 3, No. 1 | Discovery | DS 795 IMS

Evolution
Buddy Rich-Gene Krupa Orchestra | Compact Jazz: Gene Krupa & Buddy Rich | Verve | 835314-2 PMS
John Coltrane Sextet | Live In Seatle | Impulse(MCA) | GRP 21462

Evolution Of Mann
William Hooker Trio | The Firmament Fury | Silkheart | SHCD 123

Evonce
Thelonious Monk Sextet | Monk's Mood | Naxos Jazz | 8.120588 CD

Evonce(alt.take)
More Genius Of Thelonious Monk | Blue Note | 300194(BNJ 61011)

Evrev
Oscar Peterson Trio | Verve Jazz Masters 16:Oscar Peterson | Verve | 516320-2
Mel Tormé With Orchestra | That's All Mel Tormé | CBS | CK 65165

Ev'ry Time
Melissa Walker And Her Band | Moment Of Truth | Enja | ENJ-9365 2

Ev's Mad
Louis Moholo's Viva-La-Black | Freedom Tour-Live In South Afrika 1993 | Ogun | OGCD 006

Ewig Denke Ich An Dich(Jet Tenker Alltid Pa Deg)
Martin Auer Quintet | Martin Auer Quintett | Jazz 4 Ever Records:Jazz Network | J4E 4762

Ex 7,2
Lee Konitz With Alan Broadbent | Live-Lee | Milestone | MCD 9329-2

Ex Temp
Gebbia/Kowald/Sommer | Cappuccini Klang | SPLASC(H) Records | CD H 383-2

Exactly Like A Blues
Tom Kubis Big Band | Slightly Off The Ground | Seabreeze | CDSB 109(881861)

Exactly Like You
Al Fairweather Band | Fairweather Friends Made To Measure | Lake | LACD 75
Alix Combelle Et Son Orchestre | Le Jazz En France Vol.11:Bill Coleman 1935-1937(Tome 1) | Pathe | 1552571
Art Hodes | Someone To Watch Over Me-Live At Hanratty's | Muse | MR 5252
Benny Goodman Quartet | Benny Goodman:The Complete Small Combinations Vol.1/2(1935-1937) | RCA | ND 89753
Buck Clayton All Stars feat.Jimmy Rushing | Copenhagen Concert | Steeplechase | SCC 6006/7
Claude Williams Quintet | Claude Williams-King Of Kansas City | Progressive | PCD 7100
Concord All Stars | Festival Time | Concord | CJ 117
Count Basie-Oscar Peterson Quintet | Satch And Josh | Pablo | 2310722-2
Dave Brubeck Quartet | Double Live From The USA & UK | Telarc Digital | CD 83400(2)
Dizzy Gillespie-Stan Getz Sextet | Welcome To Jazz: Dizzy Gillespie | Koch Records | 321 972 D1
Don Byas Group | Don Byas:Midnight At Mintons | HighNote Records | HCD 7044
Etta Jones And Her Band | Ms. Jones To You | Muse | MR 5099
Fran Warren With The Marty Paich Orchestra | Hey There! Here's Fran Warren | Fresh Sound Records | Tops T 1585 CD
Gene Ammons Quartet | Gene Ammons-Greatest Hits Vol.1:The Sixties | Original Jazz Classics | OJCCD 6005-2
Glenn Hardman And His Hammond Five | This Is Jazz:Lester Young | CBS | CK 65042
John Crocker Quartet | All Of Me | Timeless | CD TTD 585
Lionel Hampton All Stars | Jazz In Paris:Lionel Hampton Mai 1956 | EmArCy | 013880-2
Maxine Sullivan With The Art Hodes Sextet | We Just Couldn't Say Goodbye | Audiophile | ACD-128
Oscar Peterson Trio With Herb Ellis | Three Originals:Motion&Emotions/Tristeza On Piano/Hello Herbie | MPS | 521059-2
Oscar Peterson-Major Holley Duo | Oscar Peterson:Get Happy | Dreyfus Jazz Line | FDM 36738-2
Keyboard Music By Oscar Peterson | Verve | MV 2666 IMS
Red Norvo Trio | Rare 1950-51 Trascriptions Vol.2 Plus One Mingus Rarity | Queen-Disc | 063
Ted Heath And His Orchestra | Ted Heath And His Music-It's Swing Time | Magic | DAWE 82
Tommy Dorsey And His Orchestra | Tommy Dorsey In Concert | RCA | NL 89780 DP
Charles Mingus And His Orchestra | Jazz-Club: Tenor Sax | Verve | 840031-2

Exactly Like You-
Frances Faye With The Russ Garcia Orchestra | I'm Wild Again | Fresh Sound Records | FSR 2031(Bethlehem BCP 23)

Exaltation
Pili-Pili | Be In Two Minds | JA & RO | JARO 4134-2
Carla Bley Big Band | The Carla Bley Big Band Goes To Church | Watt | 27(533682-2)

Exaltation-
Oliver Nelson Quartet | Three Dimensions | MCA | IA 9335/2

Excerent!
Paul Bley-Paul Motian Duo | Notes | Soul Note | 121190-2

Excerpts From European Episode:
Jaki Byard Quartet | Family Man | 32 Jazz | 32171

Excerpts From I'll Take The 20
Kenny Burrell Quintet | Guitar Forms | Verve | 521403-2

Excerpts From Prelude No.2
Jaki Byard | Empirical | Muse | MCD 6010

Exclamation
King Pleasure And His Band | Annie Ross & King Pleasure Sings | Original Jazz Classics | OJC 217(P 7128)

Excursion
Bennie Maupin Ensemble | The Jewel In The Lotus | ECM | 1043
Mose Allison Trio | The Mose Chronicles-Live In London,Vol.1 | Blue Note | 529747-2

Excursion And Interlude
Cecil Taylor Quartet | Looking Ahead | Original Jazz Classics | OJC 452(C 7562)

Excuse Me
Muddy Waters Blues Band | Mud In Your Ear | Muse | MCD 6004

Excuse Me For Livin'
Major Holley Trio | Two Big Mice | Black & Blue | BLE 59.124 2

Excuse My Shoes
Greg Osby Quintet | Mindgames | JMT Edition | 919021-2

Excuse Not
Ron McClure Quintet | Closer To Your Tears | Steeplechase | SCCD 31413

Exercise 13
Larry Young Quartet | Testifying | Original Jazz Classics | OJCCD 1793-2(NJ 8249)

Exil-
Mike Nock Quintet | Ozboppin' | Naxos Jazz | 86019-2

Exile:
Nels Cline Trio | Silencer | Enja | ENJ-6098 2

Exile's Gate
Gary Thomas Quartet | Exile's Gate | JMT Edition | 514009-2

Exit
Pat Martino Quartet | Exit | Muse | MCD 5075

Exit Laughing
Brad Mehldau Trio | Art Of The Trio Vol.3: Songs | Warner | 9362-47051-2

Exit Music(for a Film)
Art Of The Trio Vol.4: Back At The Vanguard | Warner | 9362-47463-2
Michael Zilber Quartet | Stranger In Brooklyn | Owl Records | 067 CD

Exit Stage Left
Free Fair + 8 | Free Fair + 8 | Limetree | MLP 198127

Exit To Nowhere
Peter Erskine Group | Motion Poet | Denon Compact Disc | CY-72582

Exodo
(Little)Jimmy Scott And His Quintet With Horns And Strings | Lost And Found | Sequel Records | RSA CD 804

Exodus
Cannonball Adderley Quintet | The Cannonball Adderley Collection Vol.5:At The Lighthouse | Landmark | CAC 1305-2(882344)
Lionel Hampton Orchestra | The Many Sides Of Lionel Hampton | Ember | CJS 805

Exotic Places
Anthony Braxton Quartet | Antony Braxton Piano Quartet,Yoshi 1994 | Music & Arts | CD 849

Expanding
Horace Silver Ensemble | Silver 'N Strings Play The Music Of The Spheres | Blue Note | LWB 1033

Expectations
Sfogliare Albi | Tempo Per | ywp music | CD 3029

Expedicion
Gail Thompson Orchestra | Gail Thompson's Jazz Africa | Enja | ENJ-9053 2

Expedition
Al Cohn Quartet | Nonpareil | Concord | CCD 4155

Experience

TITELVERZEICHNIS

Martin Schmitt | Handful Of Blues | AH Records | ESM 9303

Experience In E
Al Bowlly With Lew Stone And His Band | On The Sentimental Side | Decca | DDV 5009/10

Experiment
Joe Williams With The Ellis Larkin Quintet | Having the Blues Under European Sky | LRC Records | CDC 7684

Experiment In Terror
Henry Mancini And His Orchestra | Experiment In Terror(Sountrack) | Fresh Sound Records | NL 45964(RCA LSP 2442)

Explanation For The Not So Successful Life Of Sheep
Paul Bley | Alone Again | DIW | DIW 319 CD

Explorations
Steve LaSpina Quintet | When I'm Alone | Steeplechase | SCCD 31376
Dennis Moorman | Circles Of Destiny | India Navigation | IN 1055

Explorer
Curtis Counce Quintet | Exploring The Future | Contemporary | BOP 7(Dootone 247)

Exponiert-
Lee Morgan Quintet | Indestructible Lee | Affinity | AFF 762

Exposure
Modern Jazz Quartet & Guests | Third Stream Music | Atlantic | AMCY 1094

Express
The Youngbloods | Switzerjazz | TCB Records | TCB 96452

Expressions
José Luis Gámez Quintet | Rumbo Dorte | Fresh Sound Records | FSNT 089 CD
Lennie Tristano | Lennie Tristano:The Copenhagen Concert | Storyville | 4960603
Lonnie Smith Septet | Live At Club Mozambique | Blue Note | 831880-2
The Quartet | Crossing Level | Konnex Records | KCD 5077
Buddy Montgomery Septet | Ties Of Love | Landmark | LCD 1512-2

Exquisite Tenderness
Jerry Bergonzi 4et | On Again | RAM Records | RMCD 4527

Exstacy
Alonzo Yancey | The Yancey-Lofton Sessions Vol. 2 | Storyville | SLP 239

Extemporaneous
Steve Grossman Quintet | Time To Smile | Dreyfus Jazz Line | FDM 36566-2

Extempore
Count Basie-Oscar Peterson Quintet | The Swinging Count | Verve | MV 2646 IMS

Extension
Keith Jarrett Trio | Still Live | ECM | 1360/61(835008-2
Trombone Summit | Trombone Summit | MPS | 68272

Extensions
P.U.L.S.E. | Amsterdam Groove | ACT | 9262-2
Raphe Malik 5tet | 21st Century Texts | FMP | CD 43

Extra Low
Chet Baker Quintet | Cools Out | Ace Records | CDBOP 013

Extra Virgin
National Jazz Ensemble | National Jazz Ensemble Vol. 2 | Chiaroscuro | CR 151

Extradition
Seamus Blake Quartet | Stranger Things Have Happened | Fresh Sound Records | FSNT 063 CD

Extranjero
Kenny Clarke-Francy Boland Big Band | Three Latin Adventures | MPS | 529095-2

Extrano Sueno-
Milt Jackson And Big Brass | For Someone I Love | Original Jazz Classics | OJCCD404-2(RLP 9478)

Extraordinary Blues
Snowball | Cold Heat | Atlantic | ATL 58036

Extrapolation
John McLaughlin Quartet | Jazz-Club: Guitar | Verve | 840035-2

Extras:
Oscar Klein Band | Pick-A-Blues Live | Jazzpoint | JP 1071
Dee Dee Bridgewater With Band | Dee Dee Bridgewater Sings Kurt Weil | EmArCy | 9809601

Extras:Photo Gallery & Biography
Charles Mingus Quintet | Debut Rarities Vol.4:The Charles Mingus Groups | Original Jazz Classics | OJCCD 1829-2

Extrasensory Perceptions
Lee Konitz With The Charles Mingus Quartet | Autobiography In Jazz | Original Jazz Classics | OJC 115(DEB 198)

Extrasensory Perceptions(alt.take)
Padouk | Padouk | SPLASC(H) Records | H 192

Extreme Jonction
Wayne Peet's Doppler Funk | Plasto! | Nine Winds Records | NW 0126

Exuberante-
Sam Rivers Orchestra | Crystals | Impulse(MCA) | 589760-2

Exultation
Albert Sarko Quintet | Blues And Views(Bagdad Christmas) | Enja | 8018-2

Eye Of The Beholder
Stu Goldberg Group | Eye Of The Beholder | MPS | 68282

Eye Of The Fly
Bernie Senensky Quartet | Wheel Within A Wheel | Timeless | CD SJP 410

Eye Of The Hurricane
Eye Of The Hurricane | Eye Of The Hurricane | Aho-Recording | AHO CD 1007(CD 662)
Mel Lewis And The Jazz Orchestra | Live In Montreux | MPS | 68273

Eye Witness Blues
David Fathead Newman Quintet Plus Clifford Jordan | Blue Head | Candid | CCD 79041
Klaus Weiss Quintet feat. Clifford Jordan | Live At Opus 1 | Jazzline | ???

Eye,Ear,Nose
Jasper Van't Hof | Eye-Ball | Keytone | KYT 706

Eyes Of Love
Eddie Johnson Quartet | Love You Madly | Delmark | DE 515
Oscar Peterson Trio | The Giants | Pablo | 2310796

Eyes Of The Heart(part 1&2)
Kim Pensyl Group | Eyes Of Wonder | GRP | GRP 97102

Eyes So Beautiful As Yours
Eberhard Weber Quartet | Works | ECM | 825429-2

Eyes That Can See In The Dark
Jutta Gruber & The Martin Schrack Trio | Keep Hanging On | yvp music | CD 3043

Eyesight To The Blind
Mose Allison Trio | Mose Allison Sings The 7th Son | Prestige | PR20 7279-2
Sons Of Blues | Live '82 | L+R Records | CDLR 72005

Eyesight To The Blind-
Johnny Dyani Sextet feat.John Tchicai & Dudu Pukwana | Witchdoctor's Son | Steeplechase | SCCD 31098

Ezekiel Saw 'De Wheel
Gary Bartz Quartet | Episode One Children Of Harlem | Challenge | CHR 70001
Jerry Gonzalez & Fort Apache Band | Crossroads | Milestone | MCD 9225-2
Louis Armstrong With Sy Oliver's Choir And Orchestra | Louis And The Good Book | Verve | 549593-2
Montreal Jubilation Gospel Choir | A Capella | Blues Beacon | BLU-1014 2

Ezz-thetic
George Russell Smalltet | The RCA Victor Jazz Workshop | RCA | 2159144-2
George Russell's New York Band | Live In An American Time Spiral | Soul Note | 121049-2
Lee Konitz-Harold Danko Duo | Wild As Springtime | G.F.M. Records | 8002

Ezz-thetic(alt.take)
Barrelhouse Jazzband | 25 Jahre Barrelhouse Jazzband Frankfurt | Intercord | 155030

F
Phillip Wilson Quartet | Live At Moers Festival | Moers Music | 01062

F Minor Stride
Marty Cook Trio | Marty Cook Trio/Quintet | Tutu Records | 888210-2*

F No.6
Lester Bowie Quartet | Fast Last | Muse | MR 5055

F.D.H.
Enrico Rava Quartet | Opening Night | ECM | 1224

F.M.G.(Franz Mark gewidmet)
Franck Band | Looser | Jazz Haus Musik | JHM 43 CD

Fa Fa Fa(The Sad Song)
Tania Maria Ensemble | Outragous | Concord | CCD 4563

Fa Mozzo
Günther Klatt & New York Razzmatazz | Fa Mozzo | Tutu Records | 888138-2

Fable
Matthew Shipp-Joe Morris | Thesis | HatOLOGY | 506
Vassilis Tsabropoulos Trio | Achirana | ECM | 1728(157462-2)
Blasnost | Blasnost | Acoustic Music Records | AMC 1023

Fables
Francois Jeanneau | Ephemere | Owl Records | 07

Fables Aren't Nothing But Doggone Lies
Jesse Fuller One Man Band | Brother Lowdown | Fantasy | F 24707

Fables Of Faubus
Charles Mingus Group | Live In Stockholm 1964 | Royal Jazz | RJD 518
Charles Mingus Sextet | Meditations On Integration | Bandstand | BDCD 1524

Fabrik
Marty Cook Group | Theory Of Strange | Enja | 9107-2

Fac Ut Ardeat
Victor Alcántara Trio | Stabat Mater Inspirations | Organic Music | ORGM 9716

Fac Ut Portem
Cindy Blackman Quintet | Code Red | Muse | MCD 5365

Face In The Water
Salvatore Tranchini Quintet feat. Jerry Bergonzi And Franco Ambrosetti | Radio Suite | Red Records | 123280-2

Face Nord
Wayne Shorter Septet | The All Seeing Eye | Blue Note | 84219 (GXK 8004)

Face The Nation
Marty Cook Group feat. Jim Pepper | Internationales Jazzfestival Münster | Tutu Records | 888110-2*
Seamus Blake Quintet/Sextet | Four Track Mind | Criss Cross | Criss 1126

Face To Face
Baby Face Willette Quartet | Face To Face | Blue Note | 859382-2
Eddie Louiss-Richard Galliano Duo | Face To Face | Dreyfus Jazz Line | FDM 36627-2
Frank Lowe Quartet | Live From Soundscape | DIW | DIW 399 CD
Shakti | Natural Elements | CBS | 82329
Bruce Ditmas Trio | Aeray Dust | Chiaroscuro | CR 195

Faceless Woman
John Zorn Naked City | Naked City-Grand Guignol | Avant | AVAN 002

Faces
Woody Schabata Quintet | May-Rimba | Amadeo | 829324-2

Faces And Places
Ornette Coleman Trio | At The Golden Circle Vol.One | Blue Note | 535518-2

Faces And Places(alt.take)
Gunter Hampel-Christian Weider Duo | Solid Fun | Birth | CD 044

Faces Around
Michel Petrucciani Trio | Pianism | Blue Note | 746295-2

Face's Face
George Duke Trio | Faces In Reflection | MPS | 68022

Facets Squared
Bob Smith Band | Radio Face | dmp Digital Music Productions | CD 483

Facing East
Manfredo Fest Quintet | Braziliana | dmp Digital Music Productions | CD 459

Facing Interviews
Mike Cain Trio | Strange Omen | Candid | CCD 79505

Facing West
Pat Metheny Group With Orchestra | Secret Story | Geffen Records | GED 24468
Charly D'Inverno Trio | Following The Band | Jazz Pure Collection | AU 31622 CD

Factus Est Repente
Steve Tibbetts Group | The Fall Of Us All | ECM | 1527(521144-2)

Fade Away
Joe Bushkin Sextet | Zoot Sims:The Complete 1944-1954 Small Group Sessions(Master Takes),Vol.1 | Blue Moon | BMCD 1038

Fade Up
Stefon Harris Group | Black Action Figure | Blue Note | 499546-2

Faded Beauty
Bobo Stenson Trio | Serenity | ECM | 1740/41(543611-2)

Fader V(Father World)
Boogaloo Joe Jones Sextet | Discovery:Grover Washington Jr.-The First Recordings | Prestige | PCD 11020-2

Fadin'
Lenni-Kalle Taipale Trio | Nothing To Hide | Naxos Jazz | 86035-2

Fading Day
Joelle Leandre-Rüdiger Carl | Blue Goo Park | FMP | CD 52

Fado
Maria Joao With Band | Fábula | Verve | 533216-2

Fafänglighet
Muhal Richard Abrams Orchestra | Mama And Daddy | Black Saint | 120041-2

Fährmann Charon
Jack Jackson And His Orchestra | Things Are Looking Up | Saville Records | SVL 173 IMS

Fair And Warmer
Count Basie And His Orchestra | Atomic Swing | Roulette | 497871-2
Harry Edison Sextet | The Swinger | Verve | 2304538 IMS

Fair Ground
Friedrich-Herbert-Moreno Trio | Voyage Out | Jazz 4 Ever Records:Jazz Network | J4E 4747

Fair Grounds
Mara! | Ruino Vino | Laika Records | 35100792

Fair Kop
Neil Ardley And His Harmony Of The Spheres | Harmony Of The Spheres | Decca | 6.23985 AS

Fair Share
John Surman-Jack DeJohnette | Invisible Nature | ECM | 1796(016376-2)

Fair Trade
Art Farmer Quintet | Modern Art | Blue Note | 784459-2

Fair Weather
Chico Hamilton Quintet | With Strings Attached/The Three Faces Of Chico | Warner | 9362-47874-2
Dado Moroni Trio | Insights | Jazz Focus | JFCD 007
Peter Brötzmann | Nothing To Say-A Suite Of Breathless Motion Dedicated To Oscar Wild | FMP | CD 73

Fairy Tale
Passport | Second Passport | Atlantic | 2292-44143-2
2 Originals Of Passport(Passport-Second Passport) | Atlantic | ATL 60117

Fais Attention P'tit Garcon
Carol Welsman With Band | Inclined | Justin Time | JTR 8478-2

Fais Comme Si
Dizzy Gillespie Quintet | Dizzy Gillespie Plays In Paris | Vogue | 21409402

Faith
Dave Ballou Quintet | On This Day | Steeplechase | SCCD 31504
Jodie Christian Sextet | Front Line | Delmark | DE 490
Kevin Eubanks Group | Spiritalk 2 | Blue Note | 830132-2
Pat Metheny Trio | Part Metheny Trio Live | Warner | 9362-47907-2

Faith Healer
Kip Hanrahan Groups | Tenderness | American Clave | AMCL 1016-2

Faith In The Process
Marc Johnson Group | The Sound Of Summer Running | Verve | 539299-2

Faith On You
Miroslav Vitous Group | Universal Syncopations | ECM | 1863(038506-2)

Faith Run
Nicholas Payton Quintet | Nick@Night | Verve | 547598-2

Faith(for Faith Evans)
Bob Degen | Sandcastle | free flow music | ffm 0897

Faithful
Paul Desmond Quartet With The Don Sebesby Orchestra | From The Hot Afternoon | Verve | 543487-2

Faithful Brother
From The Hot Afternoon | Verve | 543487-2

Faithful Brother(alt.take)
Shlomo Bat-Ain Group | Distant Echoes | VeraBra Records | CDVBR 2018-2

Fajista
Gerry Mulligan-Ben Webster Quintet | Gerry Mulligan Meets Ben Webster | Verve | 841661-2 PMS
The Complete Gerry Mulligan Meets Ben Webster Sessions | Verve | 539055-2

Fajista(alt.take)
The Complete Gerry Mulligan Meets Ben Webster Sessions | Verve | 539055-2

Fajista(incompl.take 1)
The Complete Gerry Mulligan Meets Ben Webster Sessions | Verve | 539055-2

Fajista(incompl.take 2)
Betty Carter And The John Hicks Trio | The Audience With Betty Carter | Verve | 835684-2 PMS

Fake Fuge
Albert Collins Blues Band | Cold Snap | Sonet | SNTF 969(941969)

Fake Paradise
Scalesenders | This And More | Edition Collage | EC 498-2

Falando De Amor
Warren Vaché-Allen Vaché Sextet | Mrs.Vaché's Boys | Nagel-Heyer | CD 050

Falando De Orlando
Thomas Kessler Group | Untitled | Laika Records | LK 92-027

Falcon Hunting, Fishing Methods
Baden Powell And His Orchestra | Canta Vinicius De Moraes E Paolo Cesar Pinheiro | Festival | 114911

Fall
Jerry Bergonzi Quartet | Vertical Reality | Accord | 500642
Miles Davis Quintet | Miles Davis Quintet 1965-1968 | CBS | C6K 67398
Paolo Fresu Quintet | Ballads | SPLASC(H) Records | CD H 366-2

Fall Fog
Elton Dean's Unlimited Saxophone Company | Elton Dean's Unlimited Saxophone Company | Ogun | OGCD 002

Fall Of Leaves
Ben Webster Quartet | See You At The Fair | Impulse(MCA) | JAS 33 (AS 65)

Fall Out
Nat Adderley Sextet | Work Songs | Milestone | M 47047
Wes Montgomery-The Complete Riverside Recordings | Riverside | 12 RCD 4408-2
Roland Kirk Quartet | Now Please Don't You Cry, Beautiful Edith | Verve | 2304519

Fallen Angels
John McLaughlin Group | The Heart Of Things | Verve | 539153-2
Jack Linx And His Birmingham Society Serenaders | Jack Linx And Maurice Sigler | Jazz Oracle | BDW 8018

Fallen Feathers
Larry Willis Trio | Steal Away | audioquest Music | AQCD 1009

Fallen Heroe
Louisiana Repertory Jazz Ensemble Of New Orleans | Marching, Ragging And Mourning:Brass Band Music Of New Orleans 1900-1920 | Stomp Off Records | CD 1197

Fallen Star
Paul Bley/Jimmy Giuffre | The Life Of A Trio:Sunday | Owl Records | 014735-2

Fallen Statue
| Modern Walkin':Greatest Hits Volume 1 | Satin Doll Productions | SDP 1008-1 CD

Fallin'
Ingrid Jensen Quintet | Here On Earth | Enja | ENJ-9313 2
Lars Danielsson Trio | Continuation | L+R Records | CDLR 45085

Falling
Joel Weiskopf Quintet | New Beginning | Criss Cross | Criss 1204

Falling Back
Humphrey Lyttelton And His Band | A Tribute To Humph-Vol.4 | Dormouse | DM 4 IMS

Falling Grace
Bill Evans-Eddie Gomez Duo | The Complete Fantasy Recordings | Fantasy | 9FCD 1012-2
Bunny Brunel Group | Dedication | Accord | 500362
Chick Corea-Gary Burton | In Concert, Zürich, October 28, 1979 | ECM | 1182/83
Elise Einarsdotter-Olle Steinholz | Sketches Of Roses | Touché Music | TMcCD 008
Florian Poser-Klaus Ignatzek Duo | Reunion | Acoustic Music Records | 319.1084.2
George Mraz Quartet | Bottom Line | Milestone | MCD 9272-2
Hal Crook Trio | Hero Workship | RAM Records | RMCD 4531
Lyle Mays Trio | Fictionary | Geffen Records | GED 24521

Falling In Love
Stan Getz Quartet | Stan Getz Cafe Montmartre | EmArCy | 586755-2
Thilo Wolf Big Band | Swing It! | MDL-Jazz | CD 1915(CD 052)

Falling In Love-
Ann Hampton Callaway And Her Band | After Hours | Denon Compact Disc | CY-18042

Falling In Love All Over Again
John McNeil Quintet | Things We Did Last Summer | Steeplechase | SCCD 31231

Falling In Love Is Wonderful
Ahmad Jamal Trio | Ahmad's Blues | Jazz Society(Vogue) | 670507

Falling In Love With Love
Art Blakey And The Jazz Messengers | Straight Ahead | Concord | CCD 4168
Cannonball Adderley With Richard Hayman's Orchestra | Julian Cannonball Adderley And Strings/Jump For Joy | Verve | 528699-2
Christian Minh Doky Quintet | The Sequel | Storyville | STCD 4175
Don Braden Sextet | Wish List | Criss Cross | Criss 1069
Horst Jankowski Quartet | Jankowskinetik | MPS | 9808189
Jack Wilkins Quartet | The Jack Wilkins Quartet | Chiaroscuro | CR 156
Joshua Breakstone Quartet | Remembering Grant Green | Paddle Wheel | KICJ 169
Kenny Dorham Quintet | But Beautiful | Milestone | M 47036
Sonny Rollins-The Freelance Years:The Complete Riverside & Contemporary Recordings | Riverside | 5 RCD 4427-2
Kenny Drew Jr. Trio | Third Phase | Jazz City | 660.53.002
Mal Waldron-John Coltrane Sextet | Wheelin' | Prestige | P 24069
Oliver Jones Trio | Just In Time | Justin Time | JUST 120/1-2
Oscar Peterson Trio | The Jazz Giants Play Rodgers & Hart:Blue Moon | Prestige | PCD 24205-2
The London Concert | Pablo | 2CD 2620111
At Zardis' | Pablo | 2CD 2620118
Paul Kuhn Trio With Greetje Kauffeld | Play It Again Paul | IN+OUT Records | 77040-2
Pete Minger Quartet | Look To The Sky | Concord | CCD 4555
Ron McClure Quartet | Tonite Only | Steeplechase | SCCD 31288

Sonny Phillips Septet | I Concentrate On You | Muse | MR 5157
Walter Norris-George Mraz Duo | Echoes of Enja | Enja | 4000

Falling In Love With You
George Shearing Duo | The Many Faces Of George Shearing | MPS | 68177

Falling Loves
Marty Ehrlich/Anthony Cox | Falling Man | Muse | MCD 5398

Falling Rains Of Life
String Trio Of New York | Intermobility | Arabesque Recordings | AJ 0108

Falling Stars
Willie 'The Lion' Smith Trio | Willie 'The Lion' Smith | Collection Hugues Panassié | CTPL 004/005

Falsa Bahiàna
Gato Barbieri Sextet | Fenix | RCA | FD 10144

False Knot
Doctor Clayton | Doctor Clayton And His Buddy(1935-1947) | Story Of Blues | CD 3539-2

Fäm Fäm
Gabriele Hasler-Elvira Plenar-Andreas Willers | Sonetburger-Nach Texten Von Oskar Pastior | Foolish Music | FM 211793

Familia Faluta Forte
Robert Stewart Quartet | Judgement | Red Records | 123268-2

Familie(part 1)
Gunter Hampel Group | Familie | Birth | 008

Familie(part 2)
Joe Barnikel-Norbert Nagel Group | Zero Gravity | Mons Records | MR 874808

Familles
Hubert Laws All Stars | Aurex Jazz Festival '81:Fusion Super Jam | Eastworld | EWJ 80210

Family
Christian McBride Group | A Family Affair | Verve | 557554-2

Family Affair
James Blood Ulmer Group | Black Rock | CBS | 25064

Family Circle
Ram-lösa | Ram-lösa In Mesopotamia | Aho-Recording | AHO CD 1008(CD 665)

Family Portrait
Ornette Coleman & Prime Time | Tone Dialing | Verve | 527483-2

Family Values
Naima | Family Walk | Nabel Records:Jazz Network | LP 4605

Famone Mumone
Laurindo Almeida-Charlie Byrd Quartet | Brazilian Soul | Concord | CCD 4150

Famoudou's Bone
Charlie Parker Septet | Charlie Parker -The Very Best Of Bird | Warner | WB 66081

Fan It & Cool It
Sippie Wallace With Axel Zwingenberger | An Evening With Sippie Wallace | Vagabond | VRCD 8.86006
Maynard Ferguson And His Orchestra | A Message From Newport | Roulette | CDP 793272-2

Fancifree
Lance Bryant With The Christoph Spendel Trio | West End Avenue II | Nabel Records:Jazz Network | CD 4644

Fancy Colours
Duke Ellington And His Orchestra | Two Great Concerts | Festival | ???

Fancy Dance Song
Chris Connor With The Ralph Sharon Sextet | A Jazz Date With Chris Connor | Atlantic | AMCY 1072

Fancy Free
Richard Davis Quintet | Fancy Free | Galaxy | GXY 5102

Fancy Meeting Karen
Blue Barron And His Orchestra | The Uncollected: Blue Barron | Hindsight | HSR 110

Fancy Meeting You
Count Basie And His Orchestra | Count Basie All Stars | Moon Records | MCD 062-2

Fancy Meeting You Here
Bing Crosby And Rosemarie Clooney With The Billy May Orchestra | Fancy Meeting You Here | RCA | 2663859-2

Fancy Meeting You Here-
Christoph Spendel | Park Street No 92 | EGO | 4009

Fancy Pants
Hal Singer-Charlie Shavers Quintet | Blue Stompin' | Original Jazz Classics | OJCCD 834-2(P 7153)
Max Bennett & Freeway | Images | TBA Records | TBCD 243(881845)

Fancy Place
Marcos Silva And Intersection | Here We Go | Crossover | CR 5004

Fandango
Peter Finger Und Gäste | InnenLeben | Acoustic Music Records | AMC 1019

Fanfare
Franck Band | Liebeslieder | Jazz Haus Musik | JHM 35 CD
Nickendes Perlgras | Die Hintere Vase | Jazz Haus Musik | JHM 0105 CD
Paul Bley Trio | Questions | Steeplechase | SCCD 31205
Steve LaSpina Quartet | Story Time | Steeplechase | SCCD 31396

Fanfare-
Gary Burton Quartet With Orchestra | A Genuine Tong Funeral(Dark Opera Without Words) | RCA | 2119255-2
D.D.Jackson-Hugh Ragin | Paired Down,Vol.1 | Justin Time | JUST 99-2

Fanfare For A Timeshare-
Ella Fitzgerald With The Lou Levy Quartet | Ella Returns To Berlin | Verve | 837758-2

Fanfare For Miles
Billy Taylor And The Jazzmobile Allstars | The Jazzmobile Allstars | Taylor Made Records | T 1003

Fanfare For The Common Man
Woody Herman And The New Thundering Herd | The 40th Anniversary Carnegie Hall Concert | RCA | 2159151-2

Fang
Aldo Romano Quintet | Dreams & Waters | Owl Records | 063 CD

Fannie Mae
Jaco Pastorius Trio | Live In New York City Volume Four | Big World | BW 1004
Live In Italy & Honestly | Jazzpoint | JP 1059 CD
L.C.Williams With Lightnin' Hopkins | Sittin' In With Lightnin' Hopkins | Mainstream | MD CDO 905

Fanny
Wesley Wallace | Paramounth Piano Blues Vol.1(1928-1932) | Black Swan Records | HCD-12011

Fanny Lee Blues
Blind Joe Hill | American Folk Blues Festival Live '85 | L+R Records | CDLR 42065

Fantaguè
Count Basie And His Orchestra | The Complete Atomic Basie | Roulette | 828635-2

Fantail
Basie On Roulette, Vol. 1: E : MC 2 : Count Basie Orchestra+Neal HeftArrangeme | Roulette | CDP 793273-2

Fantasia
John Zorn Group | Cobra | Hat Art | CD 6040(2)
Melanie Bong With Band | Fantasia | Jazz 4 Ever Records:Jazz Network | J4E 4755
Walt Barr Quartet | First Visit | Muse | MR 5172

Fantasia Alla Tango
Jacques Loussier Trio | Focus On Jacques Loussier | Decca | FOS-R 5/6

Fantasia And Fugue In G Minor(BWV 542)
Play Bach No.3 | Decca | 157892-2

Fantasia In C Minor(BWV 906)
Eugen Cicero Trio | Classics In Rhythm(Bach-Mozart-Chopin-Liszt-Tchaikovsky-Scarlatti) | MPS | 817924-2

Fantasia On Which Side Are You On
Vittorino Curci/Pino Minafra/Carlos Actis Dato Group | L'Invenzione Del Verso Sfuso | SPLASC(H) Records | HP 21

Fantasia Suite For Two Guitars:
Eliane Elias Group | Fantasia | Blue Note | 796146-2

Fantasie On Musica Callada No.10
Richard Beirach Trio | Round About Federico Mompou | ACT | 9296-2

Fantasie On Musica Callada No.18
Round About Federico Mompou | ACT | 9296-2

Fantasie On Musica Callada No.19
Jacques Loussier Trio | Play Bach | Decca | 6.30006 DX

Fantasm
Paul Motian Band | Psalm | ECM | 1222
Stephan Oliva Trio | Fantasm | RCA | 2173925-2
Fernand Englebert Group | Fantasmatic | B.Sharp Records | CDS 078

Fantastic
Vanessa Rubin With Band | Language Of Love | Telarc Digital | CD 83465

Fantastic That's You
Ahmad Jamal Quartet | Nature | Dreyfus Jazz Line | FDM 37018-2

Fantastic Vehicle
Nature(The Essence Part III) | Atlantic | 3984-23105-2
Eddie Harris Sextet | A Study In Jazz/Breakfast At Tiffany's | Vee Jay Recordings | VJ 020

Fantastic,That's You
Lanfrenco Malaguti Sextet | Tip Of The Hat! | SPLASC(H) Records | H 116

Fantasy
Tip Of The Hat! | SPLASC(H) Records | H 116
Peter Herbolzheimer Rhythm Combination & Brass | Bandfire | Koala Records | CD P 1
The Fantasy Band | The Fantasy Band | dmp Digital Music Productions | CD 496

Fantasy & Prelude
Bobby Previte's Empty Suits | Slay The Suitors | Avant | AVAN 036

Fantasy Exit
Paul Horn-Steven Halpern | Connections | Gramavision | 18-7838-1

Fantasy For Bass
Kenny Clarke And His Orchestra | Kenny Clarke | Swing | SW 8411 IMS

Fantasy Für Eine Alte Zugsäge
Charlie Byrd Trio | Byrd By The Sea | Fantasy | F 9466

Fantasy In Blues
Art Blakey And The Jazz Messengers | Anthenagin | Prestige | P 10076

Fantasy In D
Eugen Cicero-Decebal Badila | Swinging Piano Classics | IN+OUT Records | 77047-2

Fantasy In D-Minor
Tobias Langguth Band | One Note Bossa | Jardis Records | JRCD 9510

Fantasy In G
Dave Brubeck Quartet | Aurex Jazz Festival '82:Live Special | Eastworld | EWJ 80255

Fantasy Suite For Two Guitars
Django Reinhardt And The Quintet Du Hot Club De France | Django Reinhardt:Djangology | EMI Records | 780659-2

Fantazia
Duke Ellington And His Orchestra | Carnegie Hall Concert-Vol. 2 | Jazz Anthology | JA 5141

Far Away
Benny Golson-Freddie Hubbard Quintet | Stardust | Denon Compact Disc | CY-1838
Red Sun/SamulNori | Then Comes The White Tiger | ECM | 1499

Far Away-
Ari Ambrose Trio | Introducing Ari Ambrose | Steeplechase | SCCD 31450

Far Away Clouds
Hank Mobley Quintet | Far Away Lands | Blue Note | BST 84425

Far Away The South
Aera | Akataki | Spiegelei | 145633

Far Cry
Eric Dolphy Quintet | Far Cry | Original Jazz Classics | OJC20 400-2
Magic | Prestige | P 24053
Jerome Harris Septet | Hidden In Plain View | New World Records | 80472-2
Harold Danko Quintet | Prestigious-A Tribute To Eric Dolphy | Steeplechase | SCCD 31508

Far East
Chico Hamilton Quintet | Gongs East | Discovery | DS 831 IMS

Far East-
Henry Mancini And His Orchestra | Combo! | RCA | 2147794-2

Far East Blues
Arild Andersen Quartet | If You Look Far Enough | ECM | 1493(513902-2)

Far Enough
Misha Alperin Trio | Night After Night | ECM | 1769(014431-2)

Far Far...
Kip Hanrahan Groups | Desire Develops An Edge | American Clave | AMCL 1008-2

Far From Home
Mundell Lowe Quartet | Exciting Modern Guitar | Original Jazz Classics | SMJ 6089

Far Horizon
Linda Sharrock Trio | Live In Vitoria-Gasteiz | Amadeo | 537693-2

Far Mi Deggio
Dave Brubeck Quartet | Time Out/Time Further Out | CBS | CBS 22013

Far Out East
Albert Mangelsdorff | Tromboneliness | MPS | 68129

Far Wells Mill Valley
Charles Mingus Orchestra | Charles Mingus:The Complete 1959 Columbia Recordings | CBS | C3K 65145
James Emery Septet | Spectral Domains | Enja | ENJ-9344 2
Mingus Big Band | Que Viva Mingus! | Dreyfus Jazz Line | FDM 36593-2

Farah' Alaiyna(Joy Upon Us)
Johnny Otis Show(Johnny Otis Band/Dee Williams Band/James Von Streeter Band) | The Original Johnny Otis Show Vol.2 | Savoy | WL 70810(2) (809332)

Fare
Count Basie Quartet | Big Band Bounce And Boogie:Rockin' In Rhythm-Piano Portraits Vol.2 | Affinity | AFS 1028

Fare Thee Well To Harlem
Dave Brubeck Quartet | Jazz:Ted Hot And Cool | CBS | CK 61468

Fare Thee Well, Annabelle
Live | Bandstand | BDCD 1538

Farewell
Karen Mantler Group | Farewell | Watt | XtraWatt/8
Klaus Spencker Trio | Invisible | Jardis Records | JRCD 9409
Laszlo Süle Band | Silence Fiction | AH Records | CD 90025
Mitchel Forman | Childhood Dreams | Soul Note | SN 1050
Ron Affif Quartet | Vierd Blues | Pablo | 2310954-2

Farewell Blues
Benny Carter And His Orchestra | Americans Swinging In Paris:Benny Carter | EMI Records | 539647-2
Django Reinhardt All Star Sessions | Capitol | 531577-2
Django Reinhardt:Djangology | EMI Records | 780659-2
Benny Goodman And His Orchestra | Wrappin' It Up-The Harry James Years Part 2 | Bluebird | 63 66549-2
California Ramblers | The California Ramblers With Adrian Rollini | Village(Jazz Archive) | VILCD 011-2
Glenn Miller And His Orchestra | Glenn Miller And His Orchestra-Swinging Instrumentals | Bluebird | 63 66529-2
Live At Meadowbrook Ballroom 1939 | Magic | DAWE 34(881864)
Muggsy Spanier And His Dixieland All Stars | At Club Hangover-Vol. 2 | Storyville | SLP 249

Farewell Roker Park
Chet Baker Quintet | Albert's House | Repertoire Records | REPCD 4167-WZ

Farewell To B.J.
Mulgrew Miller Trio | From Day To Day | Landmark | LCD 1525-2

Farewell To Erin
Ronnie Taheny Group | Briefcase | Laika Records | 35101152

Farewell To Fools
The Fringe | It's Time For The Fringe | Soul Note | 121205-2

Farewell To Old Friends
Axel Zwingenberger-Torsten Zwingenberger | Boogie Woogie Bros. | Vagabond | VRCD 8.88015

Farewell To Peter
Christie Brothers Stompers | Christie Brothers Stompers | Cadillac | SGC/MEL CD 20/1

Farewell To Storyville
Louis Armstrong And His Band | New Orleans-Original Motion Picture Soundtrack | Giants Of Jazz | GOJCD 1025

Farewell, New York
Jugendjazzorchester NW | Back From The States | Jugendjazzorchester NW | JJO 004

Farha
Salut! | Green & Orange | Edition Collage | EC 488-2

Farina
Little Brother Montgomery | Bajez Copper Station | Blues Beacon | BLU-1002 2

Farmer's Dance
Eddie Cleanhead Vinson & Roomful Of Blues | Eddie Cleanhead Vinson & Roomful Of Blues | Muse | MCD 5282

Farmer's Market
Mark Murphy With Richie Cole And His Orchestra | Stolen Moments | Muse | MCD 5102
Gary Burton Group | Cool Nights | GRP | GRP 96432

Farmer's Trust
René Pretschner | Story Of A Jazz Piano Vol.1 | Green House Music | CD 1013
Louisiana Red With Sunnyland Slim's Blues Band | Reality Blues | L+R Records | LR 42011

Far-Off Sand
Dusko Goykovich Quartet | Celebration | DIW | DIW 806 CD

Farrah´s Eye
Eddie Daniels Quartet | Real Time | Chesky | JD 118

Farruca
Jimmy Smith All Stars | Prime Time | Milestone | MCD 9176-2

Fascinating Rhythm
Art Pepper Quartet | Omega Alpha | Blue Note | LT 1064
Cal Tjader's Orchestra | Tjader Plays Mambo | Original Jazz Classics | OJC 274(F 3221)
Dianne Mower And Her Group | A Song For You | Jazz City | 660.53.023
Ella Fitzgerald With The Nelson Riddle Orchestra | Ella Sings Gershwin-Vol. 2 | Metro | 2682023 IMS
Sings The Ira And George Gershwin Songbook | Verve | 825024-2
George Shearing Septet | George Shearing In Dixieland | Concord | CCD 4388
Jimmy Raney Quintet | Too Marvelous For Words | Biograph | BLP 12060
Klaus Ignatzek | Gershwin Songs | Nabel Records:Jazz Network | CD 4631
Lee Konitz-Franco D'Andrea | 12 Gershwin In 12 Keys | Philology | W 312.2
Louie Bellson Quintet | The Gershwin Songbook(The Instrumentals) | Verve | 525361-2
Martial Solal | Martial Solal:The Complete Vogue Recordings Vol.2 | Vogue | 21409332
Oscar Peterson Trio | The Song Is You-The Best Of The Verve Songbooks | Verve | 531558-2
Pete Candoli Quartet | Fascinating Rhythm | Fresh Sound Records | FSR-CD 0311
Sarah Vaughan With Orchestra | !Viva! Vaughan | Mercury | 549374-2
Scott Hamilton Quartet | Live At Brecon Jazz Festival | Concord | CCD 4649
Stephane Grappelli Quartet | Jazz In Paris:Stephane Grappelli-Improvisations | EmArCy | 549242-2 PMS
Grapelli Story | Verve | 515807-2
Live In San Francisco | Black-Hawk | BKH 51601
The Hi-Lo's With The Marty Paich Dek-tette | Grandes Voix Du Jazz | CBS | 467147-2
The World's Greatest Jazzband | Plays George Gershwin And Rodgers & Hart | Jazzology | JCD-300
Werner Pöhlert Quintet | German Authentics-Mannheim Area 1956/1957/1962 | Hohner Records | ohne Nummer(1)

Fascinating Rhythm-
Sir Roland Hanna | Maybeck Recital Hall Series Volume Thirty-Two | Concord | CCD 4604

Fascination
Marcus Roberts | If I Could Be With You | Novus | 4163149-2

Fase I
Erroll Garner With The Leith Stevens Orchestra | Closeup In Swing/A New Kind Of Love(Music from The Motion Picture) | Telarc Digital | CD 83383

Fast
Joachim Kühn | Cinemascope/Piano | MPS | 88037-2

Fast Bb Blues
Bechet-Mezzrow Feetwarmers | The Best Original Sessions Of Sidney Bechet | Festival | Album 139

Fast Boat To China
Meade Lux Lewis | The Complete Jazz At The Philharmonic On Verve 1944-1949 | Verve | 523893-2

Fast Boogie
Piano Connection | Boogie Woogie & Blues | Elite Special | 73434

Fast Buck
Bob Enevoldsen Quintet | Jazz In Hollywood:Harry Babasin/Bob Enevoldsen | Original Jazz Classics | OJCCD 1888-2(Nocturne NLP3/NLP-6)

Fast City
Stan Levey Sextet | West Coasting | Fresh Sound Records | FSR 2005(Bethlehem BCP 9)

Fast Company
Victor De Diego Group | Amaia | Fresh Sound Records | FSNT 012 CD

Fast Dance
Fred Astaire With The Oscar Peterson Sextet | The Astaire Story | Verve | 835649-2 PMS

Fast Desaster
The Dave McMurdo Jazz Orchestra | Fire & Song | Sackville | SK2CD-5004

Fast Food
Michel Legrand Big Band | Michel Legrand Big Band | Verve | 538937-2
Steve Baker-Chris Jones | Slow Roll | Acoustic Music Records | 319.1070.2

Fast Foot
Reggie Workman Ensemble | Cerebral Caverns | Postcards | POST 1010

Fast Lane
George Robert-Tom Harrell Quintet | Cape Verde | Mons Records | CD 1898
Steve Coleman And Metrics | Steve Coleman's Music Live In Paris | Novus | 2131691-2

Fast Lane Rhythm
Lester Bowie Quintet | Fast Last | Muse | MR 5055

Fast Life
Lightnin' Hopkins | Really The Blues | America | AM 6080

Fast Mood
Dinah Washington With The Teddy Stewart Orchestra | John Coltrane:Complete Recordings With Dizzy Gillespie | Definitive Records | DRCD 11249

Fast Ride
Alix Combelle And His Swing Band | Django Reinhardt:Djangology | EMI Records | 780659-2

Fast Spiral
James Newton Quintet | The Mystery School | India Navigation | IN 1046

Fast Track
Joice Walton & Blackout With Guests | Downsville Girl | Line Records | LICD 9.01303

Fastän
Didier Lockwood Quartet + Bob Malach | Fasten Seat Belts | MPS | 68283

TITELVERZEICHNIS

Fasten Your Seatbelt
James Moody And His Orchestra | James Moody's Moods | Original Jazz Classics | OJC 188(P 7056)

Fat Back
Mongo Santamaria Orchestra | Skins | Milestone | MCD 47038-2

Fat Cakes
Jimmy McGriff Orchestra | Jimmy McGriff-Funkiest Little Band In The Kand | LRC Records | CDC 9046(874379)

Fat Girl
The Houdini's | Kickin' In The Frontwindows | Timeless | CD SJP 405

Fat Horse
Woody Herman And His Orchestra | Sonny Berman:Woodshopper's Holiday 1946 | Cool & Blue | C&B-CD 111

Fat Judy
Big John Patton Quintet | The Organization! The Best Of Big John Patton | Blue Note | 830728-2

Fat Layback
David Bowne Trio | One Way Elevator | DIW | DIW 920 CD

Fat Mama
Beulah Bryant With The Blues Chasers | Blues Women | Krazy Kat | KK 793 IMS

Fat Sam From Birmingham
Frank Foster Quartet | The 1954 Paris Sessions | Vogue | 21622912

Fat Time
Grant-Lyttelton Paseo Jazz Band | A Tribute To Humph-Vol.4 | Dormouse | DM 4 IMS

Fata Morgana
Barbara Dennerlein Group | Take Off | Verve | 527664-2
Evelyn Huber-Mulo Franzl | Rendezvous | Edition Collage | EC 512-2
Hot Club De Norvege With The Vertavo String Quartet | Vertavo | Hot Club Records | HCRCD 095

Fata Morgana Kaputt
Friedrich Gulda Trio | Fata Morgana:Live At The Domicile | MPS | 68060

Fata Turchina
Stan Kenton And His Orchestra | The Uncollected:Stan Kenton, Vol.5 | Hindsight | HSR 157

Fatal Passions
Buddy Tate Band | Rock 'N Roll | Krazy Kat | KK 784 IMS

Fate
Paolo Fresu Sextet feat. David Liebman | Inner Voices | SPLASC(H) Records | CD H 110-2

Fate Of A Child
Jasper Van't Hof Group | Blue Corner | ACT | 9228-2

Fate[Subo](for Konrad Klapheck)
Ray Anderson Sextet | It Just So Happens | Enja | ENJ-5037 2

Fatelet
Earl Hines Quartet | Vintage Hampton | Telarc Digital | CD 83321

Fathead
Lee Morgan Quintet | Sonic Boom | Blue Note | 590414-2
Bobby Broom Quartet | No Hype Blues | Criss Cross | Criss 1109

Father And Son
Cal Massey Sextet | Blues To Coltrane | Candid | CCD 79029
Freddie Hubbard Quintet | Here To Stay | Blue Note | 869788-1

Father Steps In
Earl Hines And His Orchestra | The Earl | Naxos Jazz | 8.120581 CD

Father Time
Chet Baker Quartet | Mr.B | Timeless | CD SJP 192

Father's Got His Glasses On
Grant Green With Orchestra | The Final Comedown(Soundtrack) | Blue Note | 581678-2

Father's Lament
The Final Comedown(Soundtrack) | Blue Note | 581678-2
George Adams-Don Pullen Quartet | Life Line | Timeless | CD SJP 154

Fatima
Lars Danielsson Trio | Continuation | L+R Records | CDLR 45085

Fats Blows
Fats Navarro Quintet | Fats Navarro:The 1946-1949 Small Group Sessions(Studio Recordings-Master Takes),Vol.2 | Blue Moon | BMCD 1017

Fats Waller Medley:
Fats Waller With Morris's Hot Babies | Victor Jazz History Vol.5:Harlem Jazz(1921-28) | RCA | 2128559-2

Fats Waller's Original E-Flat Blues
Bill Doggett And His Orchestra | Wow! | Verve | 549372-2

Fatt Blatt
Lady Bass & The Real Gone Guys | Lady Be Good | L+R Records | CDLR 40029

Fauntain Scene
Grant Green With Orchestra | The Final Comedown(Soundtrack) | Blue Note | 581678-2
Gus Viseur Quintet | Gus Viseur A Bruxelles | Harmonia Mundi | PJC 222006

Faustino No.7
Alguimia | Alguimia 'U' | Fresh Sound Records | FSNT 023 CD

Faustus
Marty Ehrlich Quartet | Song | Enja | ENJ-9396 2

Fauve
Antonio Carlos Jobim With The Claus Ogerman Orchestra | Verve Jazz Masters 13:Antonio Carlos Jobim | Verve | 516409-2

Favela
Charlie Byrd Trio | Sugarloaf Suite | Concord | CCD 4114

Favela(O Morro Nao Tem Vez)
Speakers And Singers On Radio Spot | Radio Suite | Red Records | 123280-2

Favorite Love Affair
8 Bold Souls | 8 Bold Souls | Open Minds | OM 2409-2

Fax I-III
Roger Girod-Peter A.Schmid | Windschief | Creative Works Records | CW CD 1027-2

Fax IV-VI
John Abercrombie Quartet | The Toronto Concert | Maracatu | MAC 940003

Fayka
Les McCann Ltd. | In New York | Pacific Jazz | 792929-2

Fe Cega Faca Amolada
Jerry Gonzalez & Fort Apache Band | Earth Dance | Sunnyside | SSC 1050 D

Fear
Tom Mega + Band | Songs & Prayers | ITM Records | ITM 1491

Fear Of Pain
Barbara Thompson's Paraphernalia | Barbara Thompson's Special Edition | VeraBra Records | CDVBR 2017-2

Fear Of Spiders
Mother Earth | VeraBra Records | CDVBR 2005-2
Eero Koivistoinen Quintet | Dialog | L+R Records | CDLR 45094

Fearful Dark Streets
Chad Wackerman Quartet | Forty Reasons | CMP Records | CMP CD 48

Feast
Matrix | Harvest | Pablo | 2312121

Feast Dance
The Jimmy Giuffre 3 | Music For People,Birds,Butterflies & Mosquitoes | Candid | CRS 1001 IMS

Feather
Eric Dolphy Quartet | Eric Dolphy:The Complete Prestige Recordings | Prestige | 9 PRCD-4418-2
Oliver Lake Quintet | Dedicated To Dolphy | Black Saint | 120144-2

Feather Brain Blues
Chinese Compass | Chinese Compass | dacapo | DCCD 9443

Feather Dance
Count Basie And His Orchestra | Jazz:The Essential Collection Vol.3 | IN+OUT Records | 78013-2

Feather Merchant
Herb Pomeroy Orchestra | Life Is A Many Splendored Gig | Fresh Sound Records | FSR-CD 84(882191)

Feather One's Nest
Clarion Fracture Zone | Blue Shift | VeraBra Records | CDVBR 2075-2

Feather Star
Bob Crosby's Bobcats | The Bob Crosby Orchestra Vol.10:High Society(1939) | Halcyon | DHDL 130

Feathers
Eric Dolphy Quartet | Out There | New Jazz | NJSA 8252-6
Mimmo Cafiero Sextet | I Go | SPLASC(H) Records | H 157

Feathers Dance
Charlie Ventura And His Orchestra | It's All Bop To Me | Fresh Sound Records | LPM 1135(RCA)

February Daze
T.A.O. | Amaremandorle | yvp music | CD 3041

February Fiesta
Benny Carter And His Orchestra | Aspects | Capitol | 852677-2

February Fiesta(alt.take)
Herbie Hancock & Chick Corea | An Evening With Herbie Hancock & Chick Corea In Concert | CBS | SRCS 9346-2

February Waltz
Rüdiger Carl | Rüdiger Carl Solo | FMP | CD 86

Federleicht-Kinderleicht
European Jazz Quintet | Life At Moers Festival | Ring | 01018

Fedja
Louis Prima Group | Jack Pot! | Pathe | 1566231

Feebles Fables And Ferns
Freddie Green And His All Stars | Mr. Rhythm | RCA | 2130072-2

Feed The Fire
Geri Allen Group | Maroons | Blue Note | 799493-2

Fee-Fi-Fo-Fum
Cornelius Claudio Kreusch Group | Scoop | ACT | 9255-2

Feel
George Duke Group | George Duke & Feel | MPS | 68023

Feel All Right
Tony Lakatos With The Martin Sasse Trio | Feel Alright | Edition Collage | EC 494-2

Feel Allright
Nguyen Le Trio | Bakida | ACT | 9275-2

Feel Feliz
Jim Hall Quartet | Grand Slam | Telarc Digital | CD 83485

Feel Free To Come By Any Time You Want
Claudio Roditi Group | Slow Fire | Milestone | MCD 9175-2

Feel It Comin'
Elsie Jones With Smilin' Joe's Sextet | Cousin Joe:The Complete Recordings Vol.3(1947-1955) | Blue Moon | BMCD 6013

Feel Like Going Home
Hans Theessink Group | Journey On | Minor Music | 801062
Muddy Waters Quartet | Folk Singer | Chess | CH 9261

Feel Like Making Love
Monty Sunshine Quartet | Love And Sunshine-Monty Alexander In Concert | MPS | 68043

Feel The Earth Move
Oscar Brown Jr. And His Group | Movin' On | Rhino | 8122-73678-2

Feel The Fire
Ray Gaskins | Can't Stp | Lipstick Records | LIP 8946-2

Feel The Pain
Dave King Group | Wildcat | Off The Wall Records | OTW 9501-CD

Feelgood
Baby Dodds' Jazz Four | Hot Jazz On Blue Note | Blue Note | 835811-2

Feelin' Fine
Hampton Hawes Trio | Hampton Hawes Trio Vol.1 | Original Jazz Classics | OJC20 316-2(C 3505)
Hank Mobley Sextet | The Flip | Blue Note | 593872-2

Feelin' Folsky
John Klemmer Group | Hush | Elektra | 5E-527

Feelin' Good
John Coltrane Quartet | John Coltrane:The Classic Quartet-Complete Impulse Studio Recordings | Impulse(MCA) | 951280-2
John Coltrane Quintet | John Coltrane:Standards | Impulse(MCA) | 549914-2
Otis Spann Band | The Blues Never Die! | Original Blues Classics | OBCCD 530-2(P 7391)
Paul Horn Group | Jupiter 8 | Golden Flute Records | GFR 2004

Feelin' Good(alt.take)
Mel Tormé And Cleo Laine With The John Dankworth Orchestra | Nothing Without You | Concord | CCD 4515

Feelin' It
Donald Harrison Quartet | Free To Be | Impulse(MCA) | 951283-2

Feelin' Jazzy,Baby
Andy Bey | Tuesdays In Chinatown | Minor Music | 801099

Feelin' Low Down
Big Bill Broonzy | Blues Legacy 10: Big Bill Broonzy-Feelin' Low Down | Vogue | 512510

Feeling A Draft
Freddy King Blues Band | Live In Nancy 1975 Vol.2 | France's Concert | FCD 129

Feeling Drowsy
Phil Mason's New Orleans All-Stars | Here's To You | Lake | LACD 41

Feeling Free With Patrick B.
Singers Unlimited With The Pat Williams Orchestra | Feeling Free | MPS | 68103

Feeling Good
Art Blakey And The Jazz Messengers | Feeling Good | Delos | DE 4007
Nina Simone With Hal Mooney's Orchestra | In Concert/I Put A Spell On You | Mercury | 846543-2
Nina Simone With Orchestra | Nina Simone-The 60s Vol.1: Ne Me Quitte Pas | Mercury | 838543-2 PMS
Big Joe Turner And His Band | Big Joe Turner Greatest Hits | Sequel Records | RSA CD 809

Feeling Happy
Oleo | Hope You Get It | Nabel Records:Jazz Network | LP 4603

Feeling Lonely
Louis Mazetier | The Piano Starts Talking | Jazz Connaisseur | JCCD 0243-2

Feeling Lonesome
James Moody Orchestra | The Blues And Other Colors | Original Jazz Classics | OJCCD 954-2(M 9023)

Feeling Low
Memphis Slim Group | The Real Folk Blues | Chess | CHD 9270(872290)

Feelings
Joe Pass | Virtuoso No.2 | Pablo | 2310788-2
Robert Conti | Solo Guitar | Trend | TR 519 Direct-to-Disc
Susuma Arima | Super Touch | JVC | SGS- 4 Direct Disc

Feelings And Things
Ullmann-Willers-Schäuble-Lorenz | Out To Lunch | Nabel Records:Jazz Network | CD 4623

Feels
Steve Klink-Mia Znidaric | Feels Like Home | Minor Music | 801092

Feels Like Home
Django's Music | Django Reinhardt:Djangology | EMI Records | 780659-2

Feet Draggin' Blues
Harry James And His Orchestra | Harry James:Concerto For Orchestra 1939-1941 | Naxos Jazz | 8.120618

Feet First
Steve Swallow Quintet | Always Pack Your Uniform On Top | Watt | XtraWatt/10(543506-2)
Tom Scott Group | Steamline | GRP | GRP 95552

Feet Music
Ornette Coleman & Prime Time | In All Languages | Harmolodic | 531915-2

Feet On The Ground
Shadow Vignettes | Birth Of A Notion | Open Minds | OM 2410-2

Fegefeuer
Fun Horns | Fun Horns Live In South America-Natural Music | KlangRäume | 30060

Feijada
Stan Getz Quartet | Soul Eyes | Concord | CCD 4783

Feijoada De Chocos
Der Rote Bereich | Risky Business | ACT | 9407-2

Stan Getz Quartet | The Lost Sessions | Verve | 9801098
Joe Kienemann Trio | Liedgut:Amsel,Drossel,Swing & Funk | yvp music | CD 3095

Feins Liebchen,Du Sollst Nicht Barfuß Geh'n
Miles Davis Group | Bitches Brew | CBS | C2K 65774

Feio
Claudio Roditi Group | Slow Fire | Milestone | MCD 9175-2

Felicia
Louis Prima And His Orchestra | Remember | Magic | DAWE 12(882656)

Felicidad
Acoustic Jazz Quartet | Acoustic Jazz Quartet | Naxos Jazz | 86033-2

Felicidade
Astrud Gilberto With The Gil Evans Orchestra | Compact Jazz: Astrud Gilberto | Verve | 831369-2
Bruce Forman-George Cables Duo | Dynamics | Concord | CJ 279
Eddie Daniels Quartet | First Prize! | Original Jazz Classics | OJCCD 771-2(P 7506)
Willie Bobo Group | Bobo's Beat | Roulette | 590954-2
Juicy | Verve | 519857-2
Sadao Watanabe Sextet | Bossa Nova Concert | Denon Compact Disc | DC-8556

Feline
Stefon Harris Group | Black Action Figure | Blue Note | 499546-2

Feline Blues
Johnny Parker Trio | The Golden Years Of Revival Jazz,Vol.5 | Storyville | STCD 5510

Feline Stomp
Kenny Ball And His Jazzmen | Saturday Night At The Mill | Decca | 6.23040 AO

Feliz
Herbert Joos Quartet | Fellicat | Sesam Jazz | 1004

Fellini
European Jazz Ensemble | European Jazz Ensemble 25th Anniversary | Konnex Records | KCD 5100
Paolo Fresu Quartet | Angel | RCA | 2155864-2
Kenny Clarke-Francy Boland Big Band | Francy Boland-Fellini 712 | MPS | 9814805

Fellini 712:
Three Latin Adventures | MPS | 529095-2
David Xirgu Quartet | Idolents | Fresh Sound Records | FSNT 077 CD

Fellini Buscando A Benet
Tiziana Ghiglioni And The Strings Ensemble | Tiziana Ghiglioni Sings Gaslini | Soul Note | 121297-2

Fellini Song-
George Russell Smalltet | The RCA Victor Jazz Workshop | RCA | 2159144-2

Fellow Delegates
Baden Powell Trio | Poema On Guitar | MPS | 68089

Feltinha Pro Poeta
Alfred Harth Quintet | This Earth! | ECM | 1264

Female Is The Sun
Patrick Karlhuber Group | So What | Edition Collage | EC 480-2

Femskaft-
ULG | Spring | Laika Records | 35101382

Femspring
The Ferals | Ruff | LEO | LR 138

Fenwyck's Farfel
Doug Raney Quintet | Lazy Bird | Steeplechase | SCCD 31200

Fer Now
Phil Minton/Roger Turner Duo | Ammo | LEO | LR 116

Ferdinando
Roman Schwaller Jazz Quartet | The Bizarre Is Open | Jazz Publications | JPV 8505

Ferma L'Ali
Taps Miller And His Orchestra | Buck Clayton Rarities Vol.1 | Swingtime(Contact) | ST 1024

Fermé La Porta
Svend Asmussen Sextet | Svend Asmussen Collection Vol.14 | Swan Music | CD 2514-2

Ferris Wheel
Rick Margitza Septet | Color | Blue Note | 792279-2

Ferrous
7th Ave.Stompers | Fidgety Feet | Savoy | WL 70509(SJL 1139) SF

Ferry Cross The Mersey
Duke Ellington And His Orchestra | The Duke At Fargo 1940 | Storyville | STCD 8316/17

Ferryboat Serenade
John Lindberg-Albert Mangelsdorff-Eric Watson | Dodging Bullets | Black Saint | 120108-2

Fester Kurs-
Dancing Hands | Jaguar At Halfmoon Lake | Acoustic Music Records | 319.1151.2

Festival
Special EFX | Peace Of The World | GRP | GRP 96402
Steve Nelson Quartet | Communications | Criss Cross | Criss 1034

Festival 48
The Rosenberg Trio | Tribute To Django Reinhardt | EmArCy | 9811568
Wolfgang Lauth Quartet | Noch Lauther | Bear Family Records | BCD 15942 AH

Festival 57
Count Basie Jam Session | Count Basie Jam Session At The Montreux Jazz Festival 1975 | Original Jazz Classics | OJC20 933-2(2310750)

Festival Blues
Count Basie Sextet | The Best Of Count Basie | Pablo | 2405408-2

Festival De Ritmo
Richie Cole Quintet | Profile | Inak | 30222

Festival In Bahia
Max Roach With The New Orchestra Of Boston | Max Roach | Blue Note | 834813-2

Festival Jump
Duke Ellington And His Orchestra | Ellington At Newport 1956(Complete) | CBS | CK 64932

Festival Junction-
Ellington At Newport 1956(Complete) | CBS | CK 64932
Ellington At Newport 1956(Complete) | CBS | CK 64932

Festival Junction(rehersal)-
Die Deutsche All Star Band 1953 | 1.Deutsches Jazz Festival 1953 Frankfurt/Main | Bear Family Records | BCD 15611 AH

Festival Riff
Modern Jazz Quartet | MJQ 40 | Atlantic | 7567 82330-2

Festival Sketch
The Modern Jazz Quartet At Music Inn With Sonny Rollins,Vol.2 | Atlantic | 7567-80794-2
European Concert | Atlantic | SD 2-603

Festive Minor
Franz Koglmann Tentet | A White Line | Hat Art | CD 6048

Fete Foraine
Bensusan & Malherbe | Live Au New Morning | Acoustic Music Records | 319.1142.2

Fetter Mond
Peter Brötzmann/Alfred 23 Harth | Go-No-Go | FMP | 1150

Feuer Und Flamme
Schnuckenack Reinhardt Sextet | Starportrait Schnuckenack Reinhardt | Intercord | 155012

Feuertanz
Freddie Brocksieper Orchester | Shot Gun Boogie | Bear Family Records | BCD 16277 AH

Feuertanz(Ritual Fire Dance)
Manfred Christl Farnbach-Oliver Spieß Group | Bilder | clearaudio | 180492 CD

Fever
Kristin Korb With The Ray Brown Trio And Guests | Introducing Kristin Korb | Telarc Digital | CD 83386
Rigmor Gustafsson With The Nils Landgren Quartet And The Fleshquartet | I Will Wait For You | ACT | 9418-2
Ronnie Laws With Strings And Voices | Fever | Blue Note | 84557

Shirley Horn Trio | The Main Ingredient | Verve | 529555-2
System Tandem | Reunion | Supraphon | 11 1224-2

Fever(alt.take)
Joe Maneri-Joe Morris-Mat Maneri | Three Men Walking | ECM | 1597

Fevered
Antonio Farao Quartet | Next Stories | Enja | ENJ-9430 2

Few Days
Bob Porter Orchestra | Meeting You | B.Sharp Records | 1002

Fiasco
Charlie Haden-Paul Motian Trio Feat.Geri Allen | Etudes | Soul Note | 121162-2
Paul Motian Trio | It Should've Happened A Long Time Ago | ECM | 1283
Stephan Oliva Trio | Fantasm | RCA | 2173925-2
Dan Rose Trio | Conversations | Enja | 8006-2

Fictionary
Lyle Mays Trio | Fictionary | Geffen Records | GED 24521
Jackie McLean Quintet | Jackie's Bag | Blue Note | BST 84051

Fidding The Path
Eddie South Trio | Django Reinhardt:Djangology | EMI Records | 780659-2

Fiddler On The Diddle
Duke Ellington And His Orchestra | Concert In The Virgin Islands | Discovery | DS 841 (807431)

Fiddler On The Roof
Helmut Zacharias mit seinen Verzauberten Geigen | Ich Habe Rhythmus | Bear Family Records | BCD 15642 AH

Fiddler's Boogie
Eric Watson-John Lindberg | Soundpost: Works For Piano And Double Bass | Music & Arts | CD 920

Fiddlin'
The Mills Brothers | Four Boys And A Guitar | CBS | CK 57713

Fiddlin t
Jimmy Smith Trio | Incredible Jimmy Smith Vol.3 | Blue Note | 300106(1525)

Fide Et Amore (By Faith And Love)
Art Taylor Quintet | Taylor's Tenors | Prestige | VIJ 5034

Fidene
The Dorsey Brothers Orchestra | Mood Hollywood | Hep | 1005

Fidgety Feet
Albert Burbank With Kid Ory And His Creole Jazzband | Sounds Of New Orleans Vol.3 | Storyville | STCD 6010
Avery-Tillman Band | Original Zenith Brass Band/Eclipse Alley Five/Avery-Tillman Band | American Music | AMCD-75
Bob Schulz And His Frisco Jazz Band | Travelin' Shoes | Stomp Off Records | CD 1315
Dutch Swing College Band | Souvenirs From Holland, Vol. 2 | DSC Production | PA 004 (801061)
Eddie Condon And His Jazz Band | Eddie Condon Days | CBS | CBS 88032
Fletcher Henderson And His Orchestra | Fletcher Henderson Vol.1-First Impressions | MCA | 1310
Pee Wee Russell And His Orchestra | Muggsy Spanier | Storyville | SLP 4020
Stars Of Jazz | Stars Of Jazz Vol.1 | Jazzology | JCD-62
The Wolverines | Bix Beiderbecke | Milestone | MCD 47019-2

Fiebre Cubana-
Guillermo Marchena Y El Grupo Irazu | Boleros | L+R Records | CDLR 45068

Field And Figure
Glenn Spearman Double Trio | The Fields | Black Saint | 120197-2

Field Day
Charles Sullivan Orchestra | Genesis | Inner City | IC 1012 IMS

Fields Of Flowers
Barbara Thompson's Paraphernalia | Pure Fantasy | VeraBra Records | No. 8

Fields Of Gold
David Friesen Quartet/Trio/Duo/Solo | Star Dance | Inner City | IC 1019 IMS

Fiesta
Buddy Rich Band | Class Of '78 | CDS Records Ltd. | CJCD 832
Chick Corea | Chic Corea And Friends | Memo Music | HDJ 4017
Paquito D'Rivera Group | The Clarinetist Vol.1 | Peregrina Music | PM 50221
Dave Grusin Band With Orchestra | The Orchestral Album | GRP | GRP 97972

Fiesta-
Christof Sänger & Cuban Fantasy | Moliendo Café | Mons Records | MR 874302

Fiesta De Despedida
The Enriquillo Winds | Melodia Para Congas | Mapleshade | 04632

Fiesta De Soneros
Marc Ribot Y Los Cubanos Postizos | The Prosthetic Cubans | Atlantic | 7567-83116-2

Fiesta En El Solar
Juan Martin Group | Through The Moving Window | RCA | PD 83036(874035)

Fiesta Espanola
J.P.Torres Band | Trombone Man | RMM Records | 660.58.085

Fiesta In Blue
Lambert, Hendricks And Ross | Lambert,Hendricks & Ross:Sing A Song Of Basie | CTI Records | PDCTI 1115-2
The Buck Clayton Legacy | The Second Sampler | Nagel-Heyer | NHR SP 6
Encore Live | Nagel-Heyer | CD 018
Cab Calloway And His Orchestra | Soundtracks And Broadcastings | Jazz Anthology | 550232

Fiesta Mojo
Dizzy Gillespie Quintet With The Rochester Philharmonic Orchestra | The Symphony Sessions | Sion | Sion 18110
Dizzy Gillespie Sextet | Dizzy's Diamonds-Best Of The Verve Years | Verve | 513875-2
Luis 'Perico' Ortiz And His Orchestra | In Tradition | Messidor | 15947

Fife 'N' Tambourine Corps
Duke Ellington And His Orchestra | Duke Ellington's 70th Birthday Concert | Blue Note | 837746-2

Fifth (Recognition)-
Jeanfracois Prins Trio With Lee Konitz | All Around Town | TCB Records | TCB 99402

Fifth Corner
Peter O'Mara Quartet | Symmetry | Edition Collage | EC 484-2

Fifth Dimesion
Allen Farnham Quintet | 5th House | Concord | CCD 4413

Fifth House
John Coltrane Quartet | Coltrane Jazz | Atlantic | 7567-81344-2
Marcello Melis Quartet With Gruppo Rubano | The New Village On The Left | Black Saint | BSR 0012

Fifth Impression
Jon Jang & The Pan-Asian Arkestra | Tiananmen! | Soul Note | 121223-2

Fifty Is A Hundred,A Hundred la A Thousand...
Miff Mole's Molers | That's A Plenty | Memo Music | HDJ 4112

Fifty Years
Klaus Doldinger's Passport | Klaus Doldinger Passport Live | Warner | 8573-84132-2

Fifty Years Later
Bob Crosby And His Orchestra | 1946 | Jazz Anthology | JA 5142

Fifty-Fifty Blues
Charles Mingus Sextet | New York Sketchbook | Charly | CD 19

Fig Foot
Dick Wellstood | Dick Wellstood-Alone | Solo Art | SACD-73

Fig Leaf Rag
Ken Colyer's Jazzmen | Ragtime Revisited | Joy | 194

Figger-ration
Luther Allison Blues Band | Let's Try It Again-Live 89 | TIS | LACD 1989-2

Fighting Song
Errol Dixon with Mickey Baker & The Alex Sanders Funk Time Band | Fighting The Boogie | Bellaphon | BCH 33021

Figit Time
Doug Hammond Group | Spaces | DIW | DIW 359 CD

Figs(a de-deconstruction:piano duet)
John Wolf Brennan | Text, Context, Co-Text & Co-Co-Text | Creative Works Records | CW CD 1025-2

Figs(the poem:recited by Macdara Woods))
Draft | Traveling Birds | Jazz Haus Musik | JHM 68 CD

Figure In Blue
Charles Lloyd Quartet | The Call | ECM | 1522(517719-2)

Figure In Blue, Memories Of Duke
Mike Cain Trio | What Means This? | Candid | CCD 79529

Filene's
Brötzmann, van Hove, Bennink | Balls | FMP | 0020

Filet Of Soul
Baden Powell Quartet | Canto On Guitar | MPS | 68157

Filide
Ray Draper Quintet | The Ray Draper Quintet feat. John Coltrane | Prestige | MPP 2507
John Surman | Upon Reflection | ECM | 1148(825472-2)

Filigree
Lauren Newton Quartet | Timbre | Hat Art | 3511

Filigree Snippety
Michael Moore Group | Tunes For Horn Guys | Ramboy Recordings | No.08

Fill The Woods With Laughter
Herbie Hancock Group | Death Wish | CBS | 491981-2

Fille Des Sables
Ensemble Pago Libre | Ensemble Pago Libre | SPLASC(H) Records | CD H 314-2

Filles De Kilimanjaro
Miles Davis Quintet | Miles Davis Quintet 1965-1968 | CBS | C6K 67398
Lucky Thompson Quartet | Lucky Thompson | LRC Records | CDC 9029

Filmballad
Hajo Weber-Ulrich Ingenbold Duo | Winterreise | ECM | 1235

Filters
Claude Williamson Trio | New Departure | Interplay | IP 7717

Filthy McNasty
Eddie Jefferson With The James Moody Quintet | There I Go Again | Prestige | P 24095
Horace Silver Quintet | Paris Blues | Pablo | PACD 5316-2
Doin' The Thing - The Horace Silver Quintet At The Village Gate | Blue Note | 300414
Lajos Dudas Quintet | Nightlight | double moon | DMCHR 71030
Wayne Bartlett With The Thomas Hufschmidt Group | Tokyo Blues | Laika Records | 35101212
The Clayton Brothers Quintet | Siblingity | Warner | 9362-47813-2

Filthy McNasty-
Jazzensemble Des Hessischen Rundfunks | Atmosphering Conditions Permitting | ECM | 1549/50

Fin 89...Oder Was Der Mensch So Braucht
Christoph Haberer Group | Pulsation | Jazz Haus Musik | JHM 0066 CD

Fin De Chantier
Hank Mobley Quintet | Hank Mobley | Blue Note | 0675622

Fin De L'Affaire
Peter Fulda | Fin De Siècle | Jazz 4 Ever Records:Jazz Network | J4E 4724

Final Au Jardin D'Acclimation
Free Fair | Free Fair 2 | Timeless | SJP 141

Final Call(interlude)
Rhein Brass And Friends | Kant Park | Mons Records | MR 874318

Final Inspiration
Henry Mancini And His Orchestra | Experiment In Terror(Sountrack) | Fresh Sound Records | NL 45964(RCA LSP 2442)

Final Truth(part 1)
Jean-Luc Ponty Group | Mystical Adventures | Atlantic | 19333-2

Final Truth(part 1-2)
Marcel Azzola-Itaru Oki Group | Transat Rue Des Orchidées | Zoo Records | J 9001

Final(3 takes)
Bunk Johnson's Jazz Band | Bunk & Leadbelly At New York Town Hall 1947 | American Music | AMCD-46

Finale
Fred Van Hove | Fred Van Hove-Church Organ | FMP | SAJ 25
George Lewis Rag Time Jass Band | Jass At Ohio Union | Storyville | SLP 830/31
Lester Bowie-Phillip Wilson | Duet | Improvising Artists Inc. | 123854-2
Paul Bley | Solo Piano | Steeplechase | SCCD 31236
Paul Bley-Paul Motian Duo | Notes | Soul Note | 121190-2
This Is Jazz All Stars | World's Greatest Jazz Concert Vol.1 | Jazzology | JCD-301

Finale-
Louis Armstrong And His All Stars | The Best Live Concert | Festival | ???

Finale(Friday 12:15 a.m.)
Eric Reed Trio | Pure Imagination | Impulse(MCA) | 951259-2

Finale(Last Trip)
Jacques Loussier Trio | Play Bach | Decca | 6.24015 AL

Finale:
Willem Breuker Kollektief With Strings And Choir | Psalm 122 | BVHAAST | CD 9803

Finale-Presto-
Machito And His Afro-Cuban Salseros | Mucho Macho | Pablo | 2625712-2

Finally
Marco Piludu International Quartet | New York Travels | Jazz 4 Ever Records:Jazz Network | J4E 4733
Red Mitchell-Kenny Barron Duo | The Red Barron Duo | Storyville | STCD 4137
Wolfhound | Halleluja | BELL Records | BLR 84024

Find Aother Animal
Grant And Wilson With The Fletcher Henderson Orchestra | Louis Armstrong And The Blues Singers 1924-1930 | Affinity | AFS 1018(6)

Finding And Believing
The Clarke/Duke Project | The Clarke/Duke Project | Epic | 468223-2

Fine & Brown-
Anson Weeks And His Orchestra | The Radio Years: Anson Weeks And His Hotel Mark Hopkins Orchestra 193 | Hindsight | HSR 146

Fine And Dandy
Art Tatum | Art Tatum At The Piano Vol.2 | GNP Crescendo | GNP 9026
Chet Baker Quintet | Out Of Nowhere | Milestone | MCD 9191-2
Dick Hyman Orchestra | Swing Is Here | Reference Recordings | RR-72 CD
Django Reinhardt And His Quintet | Bruxelles/Paris | Accord | 403222
Earl Hines Trio | Earl Hines:Fine & Dandy | Vogue | 2111508-2
Erroll Garner Trio | The Erroll Garner Selection | CBS | 471624-2
Jam Session | Bird's Eyes-Last Unissued Vol.12 | Philology | W 842.2
Massimo Urbani-Mike Melillo | Duet Improvisations For Yardbird | Philology | 214 W 4
Oscar Peterson Trio | Masters Of Jazz Vol.7 | RCA | NL 89721 DP
Oscar Peterson-Ray Brown Duo | The Complete Jazz At The Philharmonic On Verve 1944-1949 | Verve | 523893-2
Phil Bodner & Company | Fine & Dandy | Stash Records | ST 214 IMS
Red Rodney Sextet | Serge Chaloff Memorial | Cool & Blue | C&B-CD 102

Fine And Dandy(2 takes)
Sonny Stitt Quartet | First Sessions 1949/50 | Prestige | P 24081

Fine And Mellow
Billie Holiday With Frankie Newton And His Orchestra | Billie Holiday:The Complete Commodore Recordings | GRP | 543272-2
Jazz Gallery:Billie Holiday Vol.1(1933-49) | RCA | 2119542-2
The Commodore Series | Decca | 180008 AG
Billie Holiday With The JATP All Stars | Billie Holiday Story Vol.1:Jazz At The Philharmonic | Verve | 521642-2
Carmen McRae And Her Trio With Zoot Sims | For Lady Day Vol.1 | Novus | 4163163-2
Claude Williams Quintet | Claude Williams-King Of Kansas City | Progressive | PCD 7100

Ella Fitzgerald Jam | Fine And Mellow | Pablo | 2310829-2
Erskine Hawkins And His Orchestra | The Complete Erskine Hawkins Vol.1/2 | RCA | 2135552-2
Jimmy Rushing And His Band | The You And Me That Used To Be | RCA | ND 86460
Planet Jazz:Jimmy Rushing | RCA | 2165371-2
Lezlie Anders And Her Band | With Love,Lezlie | Celebrity | CYCD 74801
Ruby Braff Quintet | Ruby Got Rhythm | Jazz Colours | 874716-2
Terence Blanchard Quartet | The Billie Holiday Songbook | CBS | 475926-2

Fine Dinner
Dinah Washington With The Eddie Chamblee Orchestra | Dinah Sings Bessie Smith | Verve | 538635-2

Fine Fat Daddy
Dinah Washington With Walter Buchanan's Orchestra | The Complete Dinah Washington Vol.6 | Official | 3013

Fine Nelly In Fin Alley
Chris Barber's Jazz And Blues Band | He's Got The Whole World In His Hand | Timeless | CD TTD 599

Fine Time To Explain
Anders Lindskog Trio | Fine Together | Touché Music | TMcCD 010

Fine Together
Lars Sjösten Octet Feat. Lee Konitz | Dedicated To Lee-Lars Sjösten Plays The Music Of Lars Gullin | Dragon | DRLP 66

Finesse
Johnny Hodges Orchestra | Johnny Hodges:The Complete 1937-1940 Small Group Sessions(Master Takes),Vol.2 | Blue Moon | BMCD 1020

Finger Of Fear
Pete Rugolo And His Orchestra | Thriller/Richard Diamon(Original Jazz Scores From 2 Classics TV Series) | Fresh Sound Records | FSCD 2015
Steve Coleman And The Mystic Rhythm Society | Myths, Modes And Means | Novus | 2131692-2

Finger Poppin'
Tony Scott And His Orchestra | The Complete Tony Scott | Fresh Sound Records | ND 42132

Finger Rap
Jimmy Giuffre Quartet | Tangents In Jazz | Affinity | AFF 60

Finger Therapy(For Sherman)
Aydin Esen Group | Pictures | Jazz City | 660.53.007

Fingerlips
Pili-Pili | Stolen Moments | JA & RO | JARO 4159-2
Joe Newman-Bill Byers Sextet | Byers' Guide | Fresh Sound Records | FSCD 2004

Fingerprint(I)
Gert Sorensen | Gert Sorensen Plays Poul Ruders | dacapo | 8.224085 CD

Fingerprint(II)
Gert Sorensen Plays Poul Ruders | dacapo | 8.224085 CD

Fingerprint(III)
Chick Corea New Trio | Past,Present & Futures | Stretch Records | SCD 9035-2

Fingers In The Wind
Roland Kirk Quartet | The Inflated Tear | Atlantic | 7567-90045-2
Bill Frisell | Ghost Town | Nonesuch | 7559-79583-2

Fingers Snappin' And Toes Tappin'
We Three With Roman Schwaller | East Coasting | Organic Music | ORGM 9702

Fingersnappin',Foottappin'
Edward Vesala Group | Lumi | ECM | 1339

Fingo
Balthasar Thomass-Tony Pagano Quartet | Double Mind | ACT | 9213-2

Fink-Fank-Funk
The Mastersounds | A Date With The Mastersounds | Original Jazz Classics | OJC 282(F 8062)

Finn Air
Ketil Bjornstad Group | Early Years | EmArCy | 013271-2

Finnes Du Noensteds Ikveld(Are You There,Somewhere,Tonight)
Tiziana Ghiglioni And The Strings Ensemble | Tiziana Ghiglioni Sings Gaslini | Soul Note | 121297-2

Fire
Aparis | Despite The Fire Fighters' Efforts... | ECM | 1496(517717-2)
Chris Jarrett | Fire | Edition Collage | EC 443-2
Piano Moments | Take Twelve On CD | TT 007-2
Conrad Herwig Quintet | Osteology | Criss Cross | Criss 1176
Jens Winther And The IASJ Big Band | The Four Elements | Stunt Records | STUCD 19802
Kayhan Kalhor Trio | The Rain | ECM | 1840(066627-2)
Lee Morgan Quintet | Indestructible Lee | Affinity | AFF 762
Terri Lyne Carrington Quartet | Structure | ACT | 9427-2
The Dave McMurdo Jazz Orchestra | Fire & Song | Sackville | SK2CD-5004

Fire And Rain
Wolfgang Bernreither-Golly-Rudy Bayer Group | I Wonder Why | L+R Records | CDLR 42079

Fire Dance
Keith Jarrett | Dark Intervals | ECM | 1379(837342-2)
Woody Herman And His Orchestra | Road Father | CDS Records Ltd. | ZCJC 829

Fire Revisited
Manfred Schoof/Rainer Brünninghaus | Shadows & Smiles | Wergo | WER 80007-50

Fire Side
Donald Harrison-Terence Blanchard Quintet | Eric Dolphy & Booker Little Remembered Live At Sweet Basil Vol.2 | Paddle Wheel | K32Y 6214

Fire Waltz
Eric Dolphy-Booker Little Quintet | The Great Concert Of Eric Dolphy | Prestige | P 34002
Eric Dophy Quintet | Eric Dolphy:The Complete Prestige Recordings | Prestige | 9 PRCD-4418-2
Jeanne Lee-Mal Waldron | After Hours | Owl Records | 013426-2
Mal Waldron Sextet | The Quest | Original Jazz Classics | OJCCD 082-2(NJ 8269)
Fire Waltz | Prestige | P 24085
Eric Dolphy:The Complete Prestige Recordings | Prestige | 9 PRCD-4418-2
Mal Waldron Trio With Jeanne Lee | Soul Eyes | RCA | 2153887-2
Oliver Lake Quintet | Dedicated To Dolphy | Black Saint | 120144-2

Fire! Fire? FIRE!!!
Lee Morgan Quintet | Expoobident | Vee Jay Recordings | VJ 008

Fireball
Prince Lasha-Sonny Simmons Quintet | Firebirds | Original Jazz Classics | OJCCD 1822-2(C 7617)

Firedance
Chris Beier | Roots | Media Arte | CD 587

Firehouse Stomp
Firehouse Five Plus Two | Goes To A Fire | Good Time Jazz | GTCD 10052-2
Frisco Syncopators | Firehouse Stomp | Stomp Off Records | CD 1245

Fireman Save My Child
Firehouse Five Plus Two | The Firehouse Five Story Vol. 1 | Good Time Jazz | 12010

Fires Of Spring
Mose Allison Sextet | Your Mind Is In Vacation | Atlantic | SD 1691

Fire-Sticks,Chrysanthemums And Moonlight(for Harumi)
Rob Brown Trio | Breath Rhyme | Silkheart | SHCD 122

Firewater
Herbie Hancock Orchestra | Herbie Hancock:The Complete Blue Note Sixties Sessions | Blue Note | 495569-2
Jazz Crusaders | The Best Of The Jazz Crusaders | Pacific Jazz | 789283-2

Firewater(alt.take)
John Lindberg Ensemble | Bounce | Black Saint | 120192-2

Fireworks
Louis Armstrong And His Hot Five | Jazz Gallery:Louis Armstrong Vol.1 | RCA | 2114166-2

TITELVERZEICHNIS

Firm Roots
Count Basie And His Orchestra | Basie's Bag | Telarc Digital | CD 83358
David Fiuczynski-John Medeski Group | Lunar Crush | Gramavision | R2 79498

First (Solo Voice)-
Jackie Terrasson Trio | Reach | Blue Note | 837570-2

First Affair
Hans Reichel-Rüdiger Carl Duo | Buben...Plus | FMP | CD 78

First Bass Line
Marcus Klossek Imagination | Jazz Guitar Highlights 1 | Jardis Records | JRCD 20141

First Bird
As We Are | Jardis Records | JRCD 20134
Curlew | North America | Moers Music | 02042

First Breath
Horace Tapscott | The Tapscott Sessions-Vol.4 | Nimbus | NS 1814

First Cause
Blind Joe Hill One-Man-Blues Band | First Chance | L+R Records | LR 42059

First Circle
Joachim Raffel Quintet | Circlesongs | Acoustic Music Records | 312.1093.2

First Day Of Spring
Louisiana Red | The Blues Purity Of Louisiana Red | Blue Labor | BL 104

First Dream
David Shea Group | Shock Corridor | Avant | AVAN 013

First Encounter
Roland Dahinden/Christian Muthspiel | Trombone Performance | Amadeo | 841330-1

First Impression
Eric Essix Sextet | First Impressions | Nova | NOVA 8920-2

First Lady
Michael Mantler Group With The Danish Radio Concert Orchestra Strings | The School Of Understanding(Sort-Of-An-Opera) | ECM | 1648/49(537963-2)

First Lesson
Freddie Hubbard Orchestra | First Light | CTI | EPC 450562-2

First Light
Freddie Hubbard Sextet | Keystone Bop Vol.2:Friday/Saturday | Prestige | PCD 24163-2
Classics | Fantasy | F 9635
John Abercrombie Trio | Animato | ECM | 1411
John Surman | A Biography Of The Rev. Absolom Dawe | ECM | 1528(523749-2)
Northern Jazz Orchestra | Good News | Lake | LACD 38
Bob Stewart First Line Band | First Line | JMT Edition | 919014-2

First Line
Tolvan Big Band | Tolvan Big Band | Naxos Jazz | 86025-2

First Love
Freddy Christman Quartet | Deutsches Jazz Fesival 1954/1955 | Bear Family Records | BCD 15430
RMS | Centennial Park | MMC | CDP 7900102

First Love(for Thelonious Monk)
Irene Schweizer/George Lewis | Live At Taktlos | Intakt Records | 001

First Meeting
Miroslav Vitous Quartet | First Meeting | ECM | 1145
Wolfgang Puschnig Group With The Amstettner Musikanten | Alpine Aspects | Amadeo | 511204-1

First Movement
Keith Jarrett With The Syracuse Symphony | The Celestial Hawk | ECM | 1175
Steve Cohn Trio | Ittekemasu | ITM-Pacific | ITMP 970059

First Movement-Black-
Duke Ellington And His Orchestra | Duke Elliongton:Complete Prestige Carnegie Hall 1943-1944 Concerts | Definitive Records | DRCD 11210

First Moves
Sonny Sharrock/Nicky Skopelitis | Faith Moves | CMP Records | CMP CD 52

First Rain
Shlomo Bat-Ain Group | Distant Echoes | VeraBra Records | CDVBR 2018-2

First Riddle
Ali Ryerson Quintet | Brasil:Quiet Devotion | Concord | CCD 4762

First Romance
Bob Degen Trio With Zbigniew Namyslowski | Joy | Dr.Jazz Records | 8611-2

First Snow
Dave Holland Quintet | Jumpin' In | ECM | 1269
Stephan Micus | Desert Poems | ECM | 1757(159739-2)
Abbey Lincoln And Her All Stars | The World Is Falling Down | Verve | 843476-2

First Song
Anna Lauvergnac-John Di Martino-Boris Kozlov | Anna Lauvergnac | TCB Records | TCB 21132
Charlie Haden-Egberto Gismonti | In Montreal | ECM | 1746(543813-2)
Geri Allen/Charlie Haden/Paul Motian | In The Year Of The Dragon | JMT Edition | 919027-2
Gonzalo Rubalcaba Trio | Discovery-Live At Montreux | Blue Note | 795478-2
Peter Beets New York Trio | Peter Beets New York Trio | Criss Cross | Criss 1214
Cecil McBee Sextet | Music For The Source | Enja | 3019-2

First Song(For Ruth)
Charlie Haden-Pat Metheny | Beyond The Missouri Sky | Verve | 537130-2
Stan Getz-Kenny Barron | People Time | EmArCy | 510134-2
Stan Getz Cafe Montmartre | EmArCy | 586755-2
Dizzy Gillespie With Orchestra | Stonhenge/Carousel Suite | GM Recordings | GM 3014 CD(882949)

First Step
The New Jazz Composers Octet | First Step Into Reality | Fresh Sound Records | FSNT 059 CD

First Step Into Reality
South Frisco Jazz Band | Got Everything | Stomp Off Records | CD 1240

First Strike
Dave Stryker And The Bill Warfield Big Band | Nomad | Steeplechase | SCCD 31371

First Take
Ornette Coleman Double Quartet | Twins | Atlantic | SD 8810

First Thing This Morning
Vital Information | Live Around The World Where We Come From Tour '98-'99 | Intuition Records | INT 3296-2
Larry Coryell Quartet | Equipoise | Muse | MCD 5319

First Time I Met The Blues
Buddy Guy Group | American Folk Blues Festival '65-Studio Session | L+R Records | LR 42025

First Time Long Time
Michael Shrieve Group | Two Doors | CMP Records | CMP CD 74

First Trip
Herbie Hancock Trio | Herbie Hancock:The Complete Blue Note Sixties Sessions | Blue Note | 495569-2
Joe Henderson Quartet | Tetragon | Original Jazz Classics | OJCCD 844-2(M 9017)
Joe Henderson:The Milestone Years | Milestone | 8MCD 4413-2
Michele Rosewoman Trio | Occasion To Rise | Evidence | ECD 22042-2

First Walk
Chuck And Gap Mangione Quintet | Spring Fever | Original Jazz Classics | OJCCD 767-2(RLP 9405)

First-Time Love
Christian Griese Group | Affinities:My Berlin Phone Book | BIT | 11216

Fisco Place
Bireli Lagrene Ensemble | Routes To Django & Bireli Swing '81 | Jazzpoint | JP 1055 CD
Bireli Lagrene-Philip Catherine | Bireli Lagrene 'Highlights' | Jazzpoint | JP 1027 CD
Fischbacher Group & Modern String Quartet | Fischbacher Group & Modern String Quartet | Dr.Jazz Records | 8608-2

Fish Farm
Eddie Locke Group | Jivin' With The Refuges From Hastings Street | Chiaroscuro | CR 2007

Fish Out Of Water
Eric St.Laurent & Osmose | Eric St-Laurent & Osmose | BIT | 11190

Fish Seller
Terry Lightfoot And His Band | Stardust | Upbeat Jazz | URCD 104

Fisherman Strawberry And Devil Crab
Miles Davis With Gil Evans & His Orchestra | The Miles Davis Selection | CBS | 465699-2

Fisherman's Dance
Peggy Lee With The Quincy Jones Orchestra | Blues Cross Country | Capitol | 520088-2

Fisherman's Wharff
Paolo Fresu Quintet | Kind Of Porgy & Bess | RCA | 21951952

Fishermen,Strawberry And Devil Crab:
David Murray Quartet | For Aunt Louise | DIW | DIW 901 CD

Fishin' Around
Bob Stewart Groups | Then & Now | Postcards | POST 1014

Fishin' With Gramps
James Emery Quartet | Standing On A Whale... | Enja | ENJ-9312 2

Fishing For Minnows
Warne Marsh-Sal Mosca | How Deep How High | Discovery | DS 863 IMS

Fishland Canyon
Horst Faigle's Jazzkrement | Gans Normal | Jazz 4 Ever Records:Jazz Network | J4E 4748

Fishland Curse
Dan Burley With Brownie & Sticks McGhee | Circle Blues Session | Southland | SCD 9

Fit To Be Tired
Jimmy Giuffre-Paul Bley-Steve Swallow | Fly Away Little Bird | Owl Records | 018351-2

Fits
Pheeroan akLaff Group | Fits Like A Glove | Gramavision | GR 8207-2

Fitting
Stan Kenton And His Orchestra | Adventures In Blues | Capitol | 520089-2

Fitz
Slim And Slam | Slim And Slam Vol.2 | Tax | m- 8043

Five
Bill Evans Trio | Live At Balboa Jazz Club Vol.1 | Jazz Lab | JLCD 4(889363)
Bill Evans Trio:The Last Waltz | Milestone | 8MCD 4430-2
The Brilliant | West Wind | WW 2058
Thomas Schiedel | All Alone | AH Records | AH 404001-13

Five Bits
Jo Mikowich Quartet | Jazzin' | yvp music | CD 3039

Five Brothers
Gerry Mulligan Quartet | Complete 1953 The Haig Performances | The Jazz Factory | JFCD 22861
Gerry Mulligan:Pleyel Concert Vol.1 | Vogue | 21409422
Herbie Harper Quintet | Jazz In Hollywood:Herbie Harper | Original Jazz Classics | OJCCD 1887-2(Nocturne NLP-1/NLP-7)
The Complete Nocturne Recordings:Jazz In Hollywood Series Vol.1 | Fresh Sound Records | NR 3CD-101
Herbie Harper Feat.Bud Shank And Bob Gordon | Fresh Sound Records | 054 2600581(Liberty LJH 6003)
Stan Getz Five Brothers Bop Tenor Sax Stars | Stan Getz:Imagination | Dreyfus Jazz Line | FDM 36733-2
Zoot Sims:The Featured Sessions With Great Leaders 1949-1954 | Blue Moon | BMCD 1037

Five Cat Cuts
Julian Argüelles-Steve Argüelles | Scapes | Babel | BDV 9614

Five Fantasies
Old Merrytale Jazz Band | Hot Time | Intercord | 160002

Five Guys Named Moe
Louis Jordan And His Tympany Five | Look Out Sisters-Unissued Film Soundtracks 1944-1948 | Krazy Kat | KK 7415 IMS

Five Long Years
Al Smith With The King Curtis Quintet | Midnight Special | Original Blues Classics | OBCCD 583-2(BV 1013)
Big Moose Walker Group | The Rising Sun Collection | The Rising Sun Collection | RSC 0008

Five Miles To Wrentham
Ernst Höllerhagen Quartet | Ernst Höllerhagen 1942-1948 | Elite Special | 9522001

Five O'Clock Drag
Duke Ellington And His Famous Orchestra | Ben Webster-Cotton Tail | RCA | 63667902

Five O'Clock In The Morning
Count Basie And His Orchestra | Jazz Collection:Count Basie | Laserlight | 24368
Joe Williams With The Harry 'Sweets' Edison Quintet | Live! A Swingin' Night At Birdland | Fresh Sound Records | FSR-CD 22(882187)

Five O'Clock Whistle
Duke Ellington And His Orchestra | Crystal Ballroom, Fargo Concert | Jazz Anthology | JA 5229/30
The Indispensable Duke Ellington Vol.5/6 | RCA | ND 89750

Five Of A Kind
Wolfgang Engstfeld-Peter Weiss Quartet | Upside Down | Drops Special | CD 1

Five Planets In Leo
Bob Crosby's Bobcats | Swing Legens:Bob Crosby | Nimbus Records | NI 2011

Five Point Blues
The World's Greatest Jazzband | Live | Atlantic | 790982-2

Five Spot
Benny Golson Quintet | One More Mem'ry | Timeless | SJP 180

Five Spot After Dark
Shirley Scott Quartet | Blue Flames | Original Jazz Classics | OJCCD 328-2(P 7338)
Twobones | Spiral Stairway | TCB Records | TCB 99752

Five Star
Wardell Gray Quintet | Wardell Gray:Light Gray 1948-1950 | Cool & Blue | C&B-CD 116

Five Will Get You Ten
Emily Remler Quartet | Catwalk | Concord | CCD 4265

Five Years Ago
Bill Evans Trio | Bill Evans:The Secret Sessions | Milestone | 8MCD 4421-2

Five(Closing Theme)
Bill Evans:The Secret Sessions | Milestone | 8MCD 4421-2
The Legendary Bill Evans Trio-The Legendary 1960 Birdland Sessions | Cool & Blue | C&B-CD 106

Fjord March
Peter Guidi Quartet | Beautiful Friendship | Timeless | CD SJP 352

Fjorton Ar Tror Jag Visst Att Jag Var
Wolfgang Fuchs-Hans Schneider-Klaus Huber | Momente | FMP | 0610

Flagrant Fragrant
Glenn Miller And His Orchestra | Glenn Miller In Concert | RCA | NL 89216 DP

Flair
Tomasz Stanko Quintet | Purple Sun | Calig | 30610

Flakey
Ruby Braff Sextet | Ruby Got Rhythm | Jazz Colours | 874716-2

Flambee Montalbanaise
Trio Terracota | Savia | Acoustic Music Records | 319.1193.2

Flame
Keith Jarrett Quintet | Mysteries | MCA | 2292-54642-2

Flamenco Sketches
Frank Minion With The Bill Evans Trio | The Soft Land Of Make Believe | Fresh Sound Records | FSR 2013(Bethlehem BCP 6052)
Miles Davis Sextet | Kind Of Blue | CBS | 480410-2
The Miles Davis Selection | CBS | 465699-2
Ron McClure Trio | Inspiration | Ken Music | 660.56.015

Flamenco Sketches(alt.take)
Lionel Hampton And His Orchestra | Planet Jazz:Lionel Hampton | Planet Jazz | 2152059-2

Flamenco Soul
Jazz Flamenco | RCA | 2136400-2

Flaming Mamie
Duke Ellington And His Cotton Club Orchestra | Early Ellington (1927-1934) | Bluebird | ND 86852

Flaming Youth
Duke Ellington And His Orchestra | The Indispensable Duke Ellington Vol.1/2 | RCA | NL 89749 (809154)

Flamingo
Archie Shepp Quartet | Lady Bird | Denon Compact Disc | DC-8546
Bennie Wallace Trio | The Fourteen Bar Blues | Enja | 3029-2
Cecil Taylor Jazz Unit | The Early Unit 1962 | Ingo | 16
Charlie Mariano With The Tete Montoliu Trio | It's Standard Time Vol.1 | Fresh Sound Records | FSR-CD 5021
Conte Candoli Quintet | West Coast Wailers | Fresh Sound Records | 1268(Atlantic)
Dizzy Gillespie And His Orchestra | Dizzy's Diamonds-Best Of The Verve Years | Verve | 513875-2
Duke Ellington | Duke Ellington Live At The Whitney | Impulse(MCA) | 951173-2
Duke Ellington And His Famous Orchestra | Duke Ellington:The Blanton-Webster Band | Bluebird | 21 13181-2
Harlem Roots-Jazz On Film:The Big Bands | Storyville | SLP 6000
Erroll Garner | The Erroll Garner Collection Vol.4&5 | EmArCy | 511821-2 PMS
Jack McDuff Septet | That's The Way I Feel About It | Concord | CCD 4760
Milt Buckner Trio | Midnight Slows No.1 | Black & Blue | BLE 233026
Oscar Peterson-Stephane Grappelli Quartet | Jazz In Paris:Oscar Peterson-Stephane Grappelli Quartet Vol.1 | EmArCy | 013028-2
Plas Johnson Band | The Warm Sound Of Plas Johnson Tenor Sax Vol.1:Midnight Blue | Blue Moon | BMCD 3060
Ronnie Cuber Group | The Scene Is Clean | Milestone | MCD 9218-2
Spike Robinson With The Eddie Thompson Trio | At Chesters | Hep | CD 2028
Stan Getz Quintet | Stan Getz At The Shrine | Verve | POCJ 1904 PMS
Stephane Grappelli With The George Shearing Trio | Compact Jazz:Jean-Luc Ponty & Stephane Grappelli | MPS | 835320-2 PMS
Tal Farlow Trio | Trilogy | Inner City | IC 1099 IMS
Victor Feldman Trio | The Arrival Of Victor Feldman | Original Jazz Classics | OJC 268(C 7549)

Flamingo-
Phineas Newborn Jr. | Solo Piano | Atlantic | 7567-82272-2
Thad Jones Sextet | The Bop Rebells | Jazz Door | JD 1218

Flamingo Struttin'
Charles Mingus Orchestra | New Tijuana Moods | Bluebird | ND 85644

Flamingo(alt.take)
Thad Jones Sextet | Leonard Feather Presents | Fresh Sound Records | FSR 575(Period PLP 1204)

Flaps
McCoy Tyner Trio | The Early Trios | MCA | IA 9338/2

Flash
Gerry Mulligan Tentette | The Birth Of The Cool Vol.2 | Capitol | 798935-2

Flash On The Spirit(Laughter)
Art Ensemble Of Chicago | Naked | DIW | DIW 818 CD

Flashdance
Bucky Pizzarelli | Love Songs | Stash Records | ST 213 IMS

Flashes
Jess Stacy | Handful Of Keys | ASV | AJA 5073

Flat Backin'
Louis Jordan And His Tympany Five | Louis Jordan-Let The Good Times Roll: The Complete Decca Recordings 1938-1954 | Bear Family Records | BCD 15557 IH

Flat Face
Louis Jordan Vol.1-Hoodoo Man | Swingtime(Contact) | ST 1011

Flat Rate
Cozy Cole All Stars | Concerto For Cozy | Jazz Anthology | JA 5161

Flatbush Minyan Bulgar(Star Trek Edit)
Phil Woods Quartet With Orchestra Strings | Phil Woods/I Remember... | Gryphon | 6.23953 AT

Flatjacks(Just A Minor Bass-A Nova)
Joe Bonner | Devotion | Steeplechase | SCCD 31182

Flaull Clon Sleare
Flautissimo | Flautissimo | Edition Collage | EC 445-2

Flavoids
Edward Vesala Nordic Gallery | Sound & Fury | ECM | 1541

Flavor Lust
George Benson Group | The Best Of The Jazz Guitars | LRC Records | CDC 8531(874372)

Fleche D'Or
Frank Vignola Trio With Ken Peplowski | Let It Happen | Concord | CCD 4625

Flecki's Walk
George Lewis Rag Time Jass Band | Jass At Ohio Union | Storyville | SLP 830/31

Flee As A Bird-
Louis Armstrong And His All Stars | Louis Armstrong-My Greatest Songs | MCA | MCD 18347
Satchmo-A Musical Autobiography Vol.1 | MCA | 2-4173
Louis Armstrong:The New And Revisited Musical Autobiography Vol.1 | Jazz Unlimited | JUCD 2003

Flee Jazz
Mark Nightingale Quartet | What I Wanted To Say | Mons Records | MR 874763

Fleur Carnivore
Carla Bley-Steve Swallow | Go Together | Watt | 24(517673-2)
Carlo Actis Dato Quartet | Bagdad Boogie | SPLASC(H) Records | CD H 380-2

Fleure De L'Eau
Eddie Henderson With The Laurent De Wilde Trio | Colors Of Manhattan | IDA Record | 027 CD

Fleurette Africaine(African Flower)
Gary Burton Quartet | Jazz Special-The Vibe Man | RCA | CL 43237 AF
James Newton Ensemble | The African Flower | Blue Note | 746292-2
John Zorn Naked City | Absinthe | Avant | AVAN 004

Flick Flag
Dexter Gordon Quintet | Dexter Gordon:The Complete Blue Note Sixties Sessions | Blue Note | 834200-2

Flieg Mein Herz
Quartett & Brass | Culloo | Line Records | COCD 9.00919 O

Flies & Mosquitos
NuNu! | Ocean | TipToe | TIP-888837 2

Fliesse Wasser-
Ahmad Jamal Quartet | The Essence Part 1 | Dreyfus Jazz Line | FDM 37007-2

Flight
Claudio Fasoli Quintet | For Once | SPLASC(H) Records | H 126
Jimmy Giuffre 3 | Flight, Bremen 1961 | Hat Art | CD 6071
Prince Lasha Quartet | Inside Story | Enja | 3073
The Jimmy Giuffre 3 | Thesis | Verve | 2304499 IMS

Flight 19
Andrew Hill Sextet | Point Of Departure | Blue Note | 499007-2

Flight 19(alt.take)
Reykjavik Jazz Quartet with Guy Barker | Hot House | Ronnie Scott's Jazz House | JHCD 032

Flight For The Exit-
John Capec And The Family Of Man | Indaba | Intuition Records | INT 3094-2

Flight Of The Blue Jay
Paul Motian Electric Bebop Band | Flight Of The Blue Jay | Winter&Winter | 910009-2
Gerry Mulligan Septet | Gerry Mulligan:Gerry Meets Hamp | Memo Music | HDJ 4009

Flight Of The Fly
Count Basie And His Orchestra | Count Basie-The Best Of The Roulette Years | Roulette | CDP 797969-2

Flight Of The Foo Birds
Count Down | Jazz Society(Vogue) | 670503
Live at The Sands | Reprise | 9362-45946-2
Ain't Misbehavin' | Laserlight | 15778
Basie On Roulette, Vol. 1: E : MC 2 : Count Basie Orchestra+Neal HeftArrangeme | Roulette | CDP 793273-2

Flight Over Rio
Al Di Meola Groups | Guitar Heroes Vol.1:Al Di Meola | Zounds | CD 2700044001
Gary Bartz Candid All Stars | There Goes The Neighborhood! | Candid | CCD 79506

Flight Time
Duke Jordan Trio | Flight To Denmark | Steeplechase | SCCD 31011

Flight To Jordan
Chet Baker Quintet | Chet Baker Plays & Sings | West Wind | WW 2108
Count Basie And His Orchestra | Warm Breeze | Pablo | 2312131-2

Flights Of Fancy
The Bad Plus | These Are The Vistas | CBS | 510666-2

Flim
Flim & The BB's | Vintage BB's | dmp Digital Music Productions | CD 486

Flintstones -> (Meet The) Flintstones

Flip
Shelly Manne Three | The Three & The Two | Original Jazz Classics | OJCCD 172-2(C 3584)

Flip Flop
American Folk Blues Festival | American Folk Blues Festival '80 | L+R Records | CDLS 42013

Flip Flop And Fly
Big Joe Turner With The Benny Waters Quartet | The Best Of The Blues Singers | LRC Records | CDC 8530
Big Joe Turner With The Jesse Stone Band | Big Joe Turner Greatest Hits | Sequel Records | RSA CD 809

Flip Side
Graham Haynes Group | The Griots Footsteps | Verve | 523262-2

Flip The Whip
Woody Herman And His Orchestra | Sonny Berman:Woodshopper's Holiday 1946 | Cool & Blue | C&B-CD 111

Flipo
Duke Ellington And His Orchestra | Duke Ellington:Complete Musicraft Recordings | Definitive Records | DRCD 11215

Flippant Flurry
Duke Ellington And His Orchestra 1947 Vol.4 | Decca | 6.23578 AG

Flipper
Trygve Seim-Oyvind Braekke-Per Oddvar Johansen Orchestra | The Source And Different Cikadas | ECM | 1764(014432-2)
Joe Koinzer Group | Percussive Music | Sesam Jazz | 1002

Flirt
Toots Thielemans Quartet | Jazz In Paris:Toots Thielemans-Blues Pour Flirter | EmArCy | 549403-2 PMS
Mario Schiano-Co Streiff Duo | Unlike | SPLASC(H) Records | CD H 309-2

Flirtbird
Duke Ellington And His Orchestra | Duke Ellington Live ! | EmArCy | 842071-2
Anatomy Of A Murder | CBS | CK 65569

Flirtbird(II)
Duke Ellington-Count Basie | CBS | 473753-2

Floater
Les Brown And His Orchestra | From The Cafe Rouge | Giants Of Jazz | GOJ 1027

Floating
Monika Linges Quartet | Floating | Nabel Records:Jazz Network | CD 4607
Nils Wogram Octet | Odd And Awkward | Enja | ENJ-9416-2
Vlatko Kucan Group | Vlatko Kucan Group | true muze | TUMU CD 9803
New Art Saxophone Quartet | Songs And Dances | Enja | ENJ-9420 2

Floating Away
Depart | Depart | Moers Music | 02058 CD

Floating Circles
Harry Beckett/Keith Tippett | Passion And Possession | ITM Records | ITM 1456

Floating Pictures Sonata No.1[part 1-3](dedicated to Regina Donner)
Wolfgang Puschnig-Jamaladeen Tacuma Group With Guests | Journey Into The Gemini Territory | ITM-Pacific | ITMP 970091

Flocculus
Herb Robertson Quintet | Transparency | JMT Edition | 834402-1

Flood In Franklyn Park
Albert King Blues Band | Crosscut Saw:Albert King In San Francisco | Stax | SCD 8571-2(F 9627)

Floor Dance
Duke Ellington And His Orchestra | Duke Ellington -Carnegie Hall Concert | Ember | 800851-370(EMBD 2001)

Floppy
Franz Koglmann Quintet | Opium | Between The Lines | btl 011(Efa 10181-2)

Flops
Olaf Rupp | Life Science | FMP | CD 109

Flor De Luna
Hermeto Pascoal Orchestra With Strings | Brazilian Adventure | Muse | MCD 6006

Flora
Curtis Clark Quintet | Amsterdam Sunshine | Nimbus | NS 3691

Florence Of Arabia
Miles Davis Quintet | Compact Jazz: Miles Davis | Philips | 838254-2

Florence Sur Les Champs-Elysees
Gitanes Jazz 'Round Midnight: Trumpet | Verve | 511037-2 PMS

Florestal
John McLaughlin And Mahavishnu | Adventures In Radioland | Verve | 519397-2

Floriday Greeting Song-
St.Louis Jimmy Oden With Muddy Waters & His Blues Combo | St.Louis Jimmy Oden 1932-1948 | Story Of Blues | CD 3508-2

Flossie Lou
Clifford Brown-Max Roach Quintet | Verve Jazz Masters 44:Clifford Brown and Max Roach | Verve | 528109-2
More Study In Brown | EmArCy | 814637-2
Helen Merrill With The Quincy Jones Orchestra | Compact Jazz: Clifford Brown | EmArCy | 842933-2 PMS
Clifford Brown-Max Roach Quintet | Brownie-The Complete EmArCy Recordings Of Clifford Brown | EmArCy | 838306-2

Flossie Lou(alt.take 1)
Brownie-The Complete EmArCy Recordings Of Clifford Brown | EmArCy | 838306-2

Flossie Lou(alt.take 2)
Brownie-The Complete EmArCy Recordings Of Clifford Brown | EmArCy | 838306-2

Flossie Lou(alt.take 3)
Clifford Brown And Max Roach At Basin Street | Verve | 589826-2

Flossie Lou(alt.take)
Lotte Anker/Mette Petersen Quartet | Beyond The Mist | Stunt Records | STUCD 18908

Flotando En El Aire
Ketil Bjornstad Group | Water Stories | ECM | 1503(519076-2)

Flotation And Surroundings
Peter A. Schmid Trio With Guests | Profound Sounds In An Empty Reservoir | Creative Works Records | CW CD 1033

Flöten - (F)löten
Hanschel-Hübsch-Schipper | Planet Blow Chill | Jazz Haus Musik | JHM 0087 CD

Flow
Karl Berger Company | With Silence | Enja | 2022

Flow Motian
Jenny Evans And Her Quintet | Nuages | Enja | ENJ-9467 2

Flow My Tears
Nuages | ESM Records | ESM 9308
Greenfish | Perfume Light... | TipToe | TIP-888831 2

Flower Clouds
Gary Peacock | December Poems | ECM | 1119

Flower Crystals
Niels-Henning Orsted-Pedersen Trio | Live At Montmartre Vol.2 | Steeplechase | SCCD 31093

Flower For Kenny
Arnett Cobb & His Orchestra | The Complete Apollo Sessions | Vogue | 500116

Flower Of Now
John Scofield Quartet | Time On My Hands | Blue Note | 792894-2

Flower Song
Häns'che Weiss-Vali Mayer Duo | The Duo Live In Concert | MMM Records | CD 1296

Flowers
Jasper Van't Hof | Flowers Allover If675 | MPS | 68207
Loft Line | Source | Laika Records | 35101122
Phil Woods Quartet With Orchestra & Strings | Round Trip | Verve | 559804-2
Phil Woods/Jim McNeely | Flowers For Hodges | Concord | CCD 4485

Flowers And Trees
Klaus Ignatzek Jazztet | Return Voyage(To The Golden Age Of Hard Bop) | Candid | CCD 79716

Flowers Around Midnight
Charles Mingus Group | Mingus Moves | 32 Jazz | 32131

Flowers In Bloom
Stephan Micus | The Garden Of Mirrors | ECM | 1632(537162-2)

Flowers In Chaos
Mario Rusca Trio | Mario Rusca Trio | Penta Flowers | CDPIA 006

Flowersville
Elliott Sharp + Guitarists | 'Dyners Club | Intakt Records | CD 036

Fluctuations
Clark Terry Quartet | New Blue Horns | Original Jazz Classics | OJC 256(RLP 294)

Flügelflug
Cruising | Milestone | M 47032

Fluid Rustle
Jazz Orchester Rheinland-Pfalz | Kazzou | Jazz Haus Musik | LJBB 9104

Fluorescent Stones In The River
Kölner Jazz Haus Big Band | Open Lines | Jazz Haus Musik | JHM 04

Flurries
John Rapson Octet | bing | Sound Aspects | sas CD 036

Flute
Erhard Hirt | Guitar Solo | FMP | OWN-90003

Flute Bass Blues
Donald Byrd Quintet | Byrd In Paris Vol.1 | Polydor | 833394-2

Flute Blues
Häns'che Weiss-Vali Mayer Duo | Just Play | MMM Records | CD 1298
Bobby Jaspar Quintet | Flute Flight | Original Jazz Classics | OJCCD 1084-2(P 2124)

Flute Bob
Lew Tabackin Trio | Black & Tan Fantasy | JAM | 5005 IMS

Flute Sanjo
James Newton Quintet | The Mystery School | India Navigation | IN 1046

Flute Song
Jimmy Giuffre Trio | Night Dance | Choice | CHCD 71001
Joe Farrell And His Orchestra | The Best Of Joe Farrell | CTI | 63046

Flutin' And Fluglin'
Gebhard Ullmann Quartet | Kreuzberg Park East | Soul Note | 121371-2

Flutter Step
Mulo Francel-Evelyn Huber | Tango Lyrico | Fine Music | FM 102-2

Fluxus
Al Jarreau With Band | All Fly Home | Warner | 7599-27362-2

Fly
David Darling Group | Cycles | ECM | 1219
Farlanders | The Farlander | JA & RO | JARO 4222-2
Kölner Jazz Haus Big Band | Open Lines | Jazz Haus Musik | JHM 04

Fly Away
Barbara Dennerlein Group | Take Off | Verve | 527664-2
Jack McDuff Group | The Heatin' System | Concord | CCD 4644
Sammy Rimington Band With Thais Clark | Blessed Assurance | SAM Records | SAM CD 001
Wolfgang Lackerschmid-Donald Johnston Group | New Singers-New Songs | Bhakti Jazz | BR 31
Cleo Brown | Living In The Afterglow | Audiophile | ACD-216

Fly Away Littel Bird
Bobby Lyle Group | The Journey | Atlantic | 7567-82138-2

Fly Away Spirit
Benny Goodman And His Orchestra | The Benny Goodman Selection | CBS | 467280-2

Fly By Night
Roland Kirk Quintet | The Inflated Tear | Atlantic | 7567-90045-2
Christie Brothers Stompers | Christie Brothers Stompers | Cadillac | SGC/MEL CD 20/1

Fly Down Low
The Intergalactic Maiden Ballet feat. John Zorn | Square Dance | TipToe | TIP-888804 2

Fly Me
Ana Caram Group | Blue Bossa | Chesky | JD 219

Fly Me To The Moon
Anita O'Day And Her Trio | Anita And The Rhythm Section | Glendale | GLS 6001 IMS
Art Farmer Orchestra | Listen To Art Farmer And The Orchestra | Verve | 537747-2
Astrud Gilberto With Orchestra | The Shadow Of Your Smile | Verve | 2304540
Chris Connor With The Herbie Mann Septet | Out Of This World | Affinity | AFF 122
Frank Sinatra With The Count Basie Orchestra | You Make Me Fee So Young:Sinatra At The Sands | Traditional Line | TL 1348
Kenny Drew Jr. Quartet | The Flame Within | Jazz City | 660.53.017
Michael 'Patches' Stewart Group | Blue Patches | Hip Bop | HIBD 8016
Michel Leeb And Gérard Badini 'Super Swing Machine' | Certains Leeb Jazz | Dreyfus Jazz Line | FDM 36586-2
Nat King Cole Trio With George Shearing And Strings | Blue Moon-Blue Note The Night And The Music | Blue Note | 789910-2
Oscar Peterson Quartet | En Concert Avec Europe 1 | Laserlight | 710443/48
Oscar Peterson Trio | Three Originals:Motion&Emotions/Tristeza On Piano/Hello Herbie | MPS | 521059-2
Peggy Lee With Billy May And His Orchestra | Pretty Eyes | Capitol | EMS 1153
Ray Brown Trio With Benny Carter | Some Of My Best Friends Are...The Sax Players | Telarc Digital | CD 83388
Roy Haynes Quartet | Standards On Impulse! | Impulse(MCA) | IMP 12032
Victor Feldman Trio | Jazz At Ronnie Scott's | Ronnie Scott's Jazz House | JHAS 612
Ella Fitzgerald With The Tommy Flanagan Trio | Ella A Nice | Original Jazz Classics | OJC20 442-2

Fly Me To The Moon-
Mel Tormé And Cleo Laine With The John Dankworth Orchestra | Nothing Without You | Concord | CCD 4515
Heinz Sauer Quartet | Metal Blossoms | L+R Records | LR 40019

Fly Off
Lumpp-Read-Küttner Trio | Midnight Sun | Nabel Records:Jazz Network | CD 4612

Fly On
Roscoe Mitchell Quartet | In Walked Buckner | Delmark | DE 510

Fly With The Wind
McCoy Tyner Big Band | The Turning Point | Birdology | 513163-2

Flyfisher
Ellen H. Band | A Gentle Approach | Timeless | SJP 229

Flyin' Hawk
Coleman Hawkins Quartet | Thelonious Monk:The Complete Prestige Recordings | Prestige | 3 PRCD 4428-2
Monk's Mood | Naxos Jazz | 8.120588 CD

Flying
Carmen McRae With The Johnny Keating Orchestra | For Once In My Life | Atlantic | AMCY 1064
Voices | Voices:Live In Rome | Nueva Records | IN 806

Flying At New Morning
Bob Mintzer Big Band | Incredible Journey | dmp Digital Music Productions | CD 451

Flying Back Home
John Tchicai Quartet | Timo's Message | Black Saint | 120094-2

Flying Carpets
Andreas Willers Octet | The Ground Music | Enja | ENJ-9368 2

Flying Circus
Joe Lovano-Gonzalo Rubalcaba | Flying Colors | Blue Note | 856092-2

Flying Colors
Danny Richmond Quintet | Dionysius | Red Records | VPA 161

Flying Cows
German Jazz Orchestra | German Jazz Orchestra-First Take | Mons Records | MR 874669

Flying Down To Rio
Peter Gullin Trio | Untold Story | Dragon | DRCD 315

Flying East
Henry Johnson Group | Missing You | Inak | 30292

Flying High
Tiny Grimes Quintet | Rock The House | Swingtime(Contact) | ST 1016

Flying Home
Arnett Cobb Quartet | Arnett Cobb Is Back | Progressive | PRO 7037 IMS
Benny Goodman Sextet | Charlie Christian:Swing To Bop | Dreyfus Jazz Line | FDM 36715-2
From Spiritual To Swing | Vanguard | VCD 169/71
Compact Jazz: Benny Goodman | Verve | 820543-2
Duke Robillard-Herb Ellis Quintet | Conversation In Swing Guitar | Stony Plain | SPCD 1260
Ella Fitzgerald And Barney Kessel | Jazz Collection:Ella Fitzgerald | Laserlight | 24397
Ella Fitzgerald And Her All Stars | Ella Fitzgerald:Mr.Paganini | Dreyfus Jazz Line | FDM 36741-2
Ella Fitzgerald With Count Basie And His Orchestra | Digital III At Montreux | Original Jazz Classics | OJCCD 996-2(2308223)
Ella Fitzgerald With Orchestra | Basin Street Blues | Intercord | 125404
Frankfurt Swing All Stars | Jive At Five | L+R Records | CDLR 40025
Gerald Wilson's Orchestra Of The 90's | Jenna | Discovery | DSCD 964(881985)
Glenn Miller And The Army Air Force Band | This Is Glenn Miller And The Army Air Force Band | RCA | NL 89217 DP
JATP All Stars | Bird: The Complete Charlie Parker On Verve | Verve | 837141-2
The Complete Jazz At The Philharmonic On Verve 1944-1949 | Verve | 523893-2
The Complete Jazz At The Philharmonic On Verve 1944-1949 | Verve | 523893-2
Jazz At The Philharmonic:Best Of The 1940's Concerts | Verve | 557534-2
Charlie Parker Jazz At The Philharmonic 1949 | Verve | 519803-2
Lionel Hampton And His All Stars | Masters Of Jazz Vol.8 | RCA | NL 89540 DP
Lionel Hampton And His Orchestra | The Black Velvet Band | Bluebird | ND 86571
Victor Jazz History Vol.7:Swing Groups | RCA | 2128561-2
Lionel Hampton Quintet | The Complete Lionel Hampton Quartets And Quintets With Oscar Peterson On Verve | Verve | 559797-2
The Lional Hampton Quintet | Verve | 589100-2
Lionel Hampton With Milt Buckner And The All Stars | Alive & Jumping | MPS | 821283-1
Oscar Peterson Quartet | Masters Of Jazz Vol.7 | RCA | NL 89721 DP
Rob McConnell And The Boss Brass | Our 25th Year | Concord | CCD 4559
Stanley Jordan Group | Flying Home | Blue Note | 748682-2
Ted Heath And His Orchestra | Swing Is King | Decca | 6.28129 DP
Teddy Wilson Trio | Three Little Words | Black & Blue | BLE 233094
Terry Gibbs Dream Band | Terry Gibbs Dream Band Vol.3:Flying Home | Contemporary | CCD 7654-2
Terry Gibbs-Buddy DeFranco-Herb Ellis Sextet | Memories Of You-A Tribute To Benny Goodman | Contemporary | CCD 14066-2
Tito Puente Orchestra | Special Delivery | Concord | CCD 4732

Flying Home(Homeward Bound)
Lionel Hampton And His Orchestra | Big Band Bounce & Boogie-Lionel Hampton:Leapin' With Lionel | Affinity | AFS 1000

Flying Horses
Ullmann-Wille-Haynes | Trad Corrosion | Nabel Records:Jazz Network | CD 4673

Flying In A Nutshell
Stanley Turrentine Orchestra | Stanley Turrentine | Blue Note | 84506

Flying Part(1&2)
Michael Shrieve Group | Two Doors | CMP Records | CMP CD 74

Flying The Coop
Jon Balke w/Magnetic North Orchestra | Further | ECM | 1517

Flying Thing
Giger-Lenz-Maron | Beyond | Nagara | MIX 1011-N

Flyjam
Lars Danielsson Trio | Continuation | L+R Records | CDLR 45085

FM 9X.2
Harry Pepl Trio | Schoenberg Improvations | Amadeo | 843086-2

FNH
Dewey Redman Trio | Tarik | Affinity | AFF 42

Focus
Michael Moore Trio | Monitor | Between The Lines | btl 003(Efa 10173-2)
Tadd Dameron And His Orchestra | Crosscurrents | Affinity | AFF 149

Focus On Sanity
John Coltrane-Don Cherry Quartet | The Avantgarde | Rhino | 8122-79892-2
That's Jazz Vol.40: The Avant-Garde | Atlantic | ATL 50523
Ornette Coleman Quartet | Beauty Is A Rare Thing:Ornette Coleman-The Complete Atlantic Recordings | Atlantic | 8122-71410-2
The Shape Of Jazz To Come | Atlantic | 7567-81339-2

Fodder On My Wings
Ned Rothenberg Trio | Port Of Entry | Intuition Records | INT 3249-2

FoFela-
Calvin Jackson Trio | Cal-Essence:Calvin Jackson At The Piano | Fresh Sound Records | Raynote RR 4001 CD

Fog In The Highlands
Jacky Terrasson Trio | Alive | Blue Note | 859651-2

Fog Taking Over Noe Valley
Joe Pass Quartet | Ira George And Joe-Joe Pass Loves Gershwin | Original Jazz Classics | OJCCD 828-2(2312133)

Foggy Day
Oscar Peterson Trio | Action | MPS | 68073

Fogueira
Ida Cox With The Coleman Hawkins Quintet | Blues For Rampart Street | Original Jazz Classics | OJCCD 1758-2

Folie A Amphion
Django Reinhardt And The Quintet Du Hot Club De France | Django Reinhardt Portrait | Barclay | DALP 2/1939

Folk Forms(No.1)
Charles Mingus Quintet | Charles Mingus-Passion Of A Man:The Complete Atlantic Recordings 1956-1961 | Atlantic | 8122-72871-2
Charles Minus-Live | Affinity | CD AFS 778
Charles Mingus Live | Affinity | AFF 19

Folk Song
Charlie Haden Trio | Folk Songs | ECM | 1170(827705-2)
Works | ECM | 823266-2
Forward Motion | Reminiscence | Linn Records | AKD 024
Lajos Dudas Quintet | Nightlight | double moon | DMCHR 71030
Leszek Zadlo Ensemble | Time Emit | MRC | 066-32858

Rudy Linka Trio | Czech It Out! | Enja | ENJ-9001 2
Woody Shaw With The Tone Jansa Quartet | Woody Shaw With Tone Jansa Quartet | Timeless | CD SJP 221

Folk Song For Rosie
Paul Motian Quintet | Misterioso | Soul Note | 121174-2
Paul Motian Trio | You Took The Words Right Out Of My Heart | JMT Edition | 514028-2
Mike Westbrook Concert Band | Release | Deram | 844851-2

Folk Tale
Ornette Coleman Quartet | Beauty Is A Rare Thing:Ornette Coleman-The Complete Atlantic Recordings | Atlantic | 8122-71410-2
Paul Plimley-Lisle Ellis | Kaleidoscopes(Ornette Coleman Songbook) | Hat Art | CD 6117

Folk Tune-
Christoph Lauer & Norwegian Brass | Heaven | ACT | 9420-2

Folkefreisar Til Oss Kom(Nun Komm,Der Heiden Heiland)
Brian Blade Group | Fellowship | Blue Note | 859417-2

Folklore
Good Fellas | Good Fellas 3 | Paddle Wheel | KICJ 166

Folklore Imaginaire(Miss Moustique)
Elvira Plenar-Vitold Rek | Elvira Plenar-Vitold Rek | L+R Records | CDLR 45089

Folks
Ahmad Jamal Trio | Ahmad Jamal:Waltz For Debby | Memo Music | HDJ 4018

Folksong
Jack Bruce-Bernie Worrell | Monkjack | CMP Records | CMP CD 1010
Steve LaSpina Quartet | New Horizon | Steeplechase | SCCD 31313

Folkus
Michael Urbaniak Trio | My One And Only Love | Steeplechase | SCCD 31159

Folkz
Steve Lacy Quintet | Follies | FMP | SAJ 18

Follow Down
Norbert Gottschalk With The Matthias Bröde Quintet | Norbert Gottschalk:Two Sessions | Dr.Jazz Records | 8605-2

Follow Her Heart
Jan Harrington And Friends | I Feel The Spirit | Nagel-Heyer | NHR SP 7

Follow Him
Chris Connor With The Jimmy Jones Quintet | A Portrait Of Chris | Atlantic | AMCY 1073

Follow Me
Jon Strong Trio | Follow Me | Linn Records | AKD 023
Thursday Diva | Folow Me | dmp Digital Music Productions | CD 509

Follow The Crooked Path(Through It Be Longer)
Kamikaze Ground Crew | The Scenic Route | New World Records | 80400-2

Follow The Leader
Harry Betts And His Orchestra | The Jazz Soul Of Doctor Kildare | Fresh Sound Records | FSR 634(Choreo/Ava AS 6)

Follow Your Heart
Joe Farrell Quintet | The Best Of Joe Farrell | CTI | 63046

Following Behind
Kollektiv | Kollektiv feat. Jonas Hellborg | ITM Records | ITM 1434

Folly Seeing All This
Africa Djole | Kaloum | FMP | SAJ 26

Fond Memories
Steve Lacy-Mal Waldron | Communiqué | Soul Note | 121298-2

Fonk Da World
Future Shock | Handclaps | Timeless | CD SJP 374

Fontainebleau
Tadd Dameron Orchestra | The Magic Touch | Original Jazz Classics | OJCCD 143-2(RLP 9419)

Fontessa
Stan Getz Quintet | Stan Getz:The Golden Years Vol.1(1952-1958) | Moon Records | MCD 039-2

Foo Foo
Bob Hall-George Green Band | Shufflin' The Boogie | Jazz Colours | 874748-2

Foodstamps On The Moon
Blues Comany | Damn! Let's Jam | Inak | 9009

Fool Killer
Mose Allison Trio | The Word From Mose | Atlantic | 8122-72394-2
That's Jazz Vol.19: Mose Allison | Atlantic | ATL 50249

Fool Moon
Deborah Henson-Conant Group | Budapest | Laika Records | LK 93-039

Fool Of The World
Antonello Salis | Salis! | SPLASC(H) Records | H 136

Fool On The Hill
Mulgrew Miller Quintet | Getting To Know You | Novus | 4163188-2
Sarah Vaughan With Orchestra | Song Of The Beatles | Atlantic | SD 16037

Foolin' Around
Jo Jones Trio | Explosive Drums | Black & Blue | BLE 59.080 2

Foolin' Myself
Lee Konitz Trio | Motion | Verve | 557107-2
Teddy Wilson And His Orchestra | The Lester Young Story Vol.1 | CBS | CBS 88223
Warne Marsh-Lee Konitz Quintet | Live At The Club Montmartre,Vol.2 | Storyville | STCD 8202

Fooling Around
Werner Lener Trio | Colours | Satin Doll Productions | SDP 1033-1 CD

Fooling Around Blues
Daniel Guggenheim Group | Daniel Guggenheim Group feat. Jasper van't Hof | Laika Records | LK 990-018

Foolish Dancer
John Abercrombie Quartet | Abercrombie Quartet | ECM | 1164

Foolish Man Blues
Art Farmer Quintet | Foolish Memories | L+R Records | CDLR 45008

Foolish Ways
Taj Mahal Group | Conjure | American Clave | AMCL 1006-2

Fools
Lucy Reed With The Bill Evans Quartet | The Singing Reed | Original Jazz Classics | OJCCD 1777-2(F 3212)

Fool's Paradise
Mose Allison Trio | Singin' Till The Girls Come Home | CBS | FC 38508
High Jinks! The Mose Allison Trilogy | CBS | J3K 64275
Billy Eckstine With Bobby Tucker And His Orchestra | No Cover No Minimum | Blue Note | 798583-2

Fools Rush In
Count Basie And His Orchestra | Basie On Roulette, Vol. 11: Dance Along With Basie | Vogue | 500011
Frank Sinatra With The Tommy Dorsey Orchestra | The Popular Sinatra Vol.1 | RCA | 2668711-2
Glenn Miller And His Orchestra | Original Recordings From 1938 to 1942,Vol.2 | RCA | 2118549-2
Jimmy Dorsey And His Orchestra | The Uncollected: Jimmy Dorsey | Hindsight | HSR 101
Lionel Hampton Quartet | Mostly Ballads | Limelight | 820834-2 IMS
Louis Armstrong With Sy Oliver's Choir And Orchestra | Louis Armstrong-Heavenly Music | Ambassador | CLA 1916
Stan Getz Quintet | Stan Getz-The Complete Roost Sessions | EMI Records | 859622-2
Unearthed Masters-Vol.2: Stan Getz | JAM | 5007 IMS
Tommy Dorsey And His Orchestra | Frank Sinatra Sings The Standards | RCA | NL 89102 AP

Fools Rush In(alt.take)
Stan Getz Quintet | Stan Getz-The Complete Roost Sessions | The Jazz Factory | JFCD 22839

Foot Foolers-In Concert Part 1&2:
Anita Carmichael Quintet | Anita Carmichael | Lipstick Records | LIP 8944-2

Foot Pattin'
Lou Donaldson Quintet | Play The Right Thing | Milestone | MCD 9190-2

Foot Pedal Boogie
Allen Farnham Quartet | Play-Cation | Concord | CCD 4521

Foot Stompin' Blues-
The Fringe | The Return Of The Neanderthal Man | Popular Arts | NR 5006 CD

Footpath Café
Ahmad Jamal Quartet | Life At The Montreal Jazz Festival 1985 | Atlantic | 781699-2

Footprints
Chico Freeman-Arthur Blythe Sextet | Luminous | Ronnie Scott's Jazz House | JHCD 010
GRP All-Star Big Band | GRP 10th Anniversary | GRP | GRP 96722
Jerry Gonzalez & Fort Apache Band | Obatala | Enja | ENJ-5095 2
Lars Moller Quartet | Kaleidoscope | Naxos Jazz | 86022-2
Miles Davis Quintet | Voodoo Down | Moon Records | MCD 063-2
Pat LaBarbera Quartet | Virgo Dance | Justin Time | Just 24
The Atlantic String Trio | First Meeting | Factory Outlet Records | 2001-1 CD
Toninho Horta Trio | Once I Loved | Verve | 513561-2
Wayne Shorter Quartet | The Best Of Wayne Shorter | Blue Note | 791141-2
Kind Of Blue:Blue Note Celebrate The Music Of Miles Davis | Blue Note | 534255-2
Wayne Shorter:The Classic Blue Note Recordings | Blue Note | 540856-2
Ray Noble And His Orchestra | The Radio Years | London | HMG 5027 AN

Footsie Wootsie
Kenny Werner Trio | A Delicate Ballace | RCA | 2151694-2

Footsteps
Metro | Tree People | Lipstick Records | LIP 890312

Foow
AMM III | It Had Been An Ordinary Enough Day In Pueblo, Colorado | Japo | 60031

For A
Stephan Diez-Mirrors | Lost In A Dream | BELL Records | BLR 84048

For A Free Portugal
Mitch Watkins Quartet | Curves | Enja | ENJ-6054 2

For A Thousand Years
Steve Houben Trio | 3 | B.Sharp Records | CDS 071

For A.M.B.
Stephan Micus | Listen To The Rain | Japo | 60040

For Abai And Togshan
Peter Brötzmann Trio | For Adolphe Sax | FMP | 0080

For Adults Only
Michele Rosewoman Trio | Spirit | Blue Note | 836777-2

For Albert
Lucas Heidepriem Quartet | Voicings | IN+OUT Records | 7011-2
Ken Hyder's Talisker | Land Of Stone | Japo | 60018 IMS

For Alene(Arvo Pärt)
Manhattan Jazz Quintet | Manhattan Jazz Quintet Plays Blue Note | Paddle Wheel | K 28P 6480

For All Colours
Frank Foster's Living Color | Twelve Shades Of Black-For All Intents And Purposes | Leo Records | 007

For All We Know
Ben Webster Quartet | Live At The Haarlemse Jazzclub | Limetree | MCD 0040
Billie Holiday With The Ray Ellis Orchestra | Ella,Billie,Sarah,Aretha,Mahalia | CBS | 473733-2
Buddy Tate Quartet | Midnight Slows Vol.2 | Black & Blue | 190552
Cedar Walton Trio | Among Friends | Evidence | ECD 22023-2
Dave Brubeck Quartet | The Dave Brubeck Quartet feat. Paul Desmond In Concert | Fantasy | FCD 60-013
The Great Concerts | CBS | 462403-2
The Dave Brubeck Selection | CBS | 467279-2
Dinah Washington With Orchestra | Ballads | Roulette | 537559-2
Dinah Washington With The Don Costa Orchestra | Drinking Again | M&M Records | R 25183(Roulette)
Ed Kröger Quartet | What's New | Laika Records | 35101172
Eddie Henderson With The Laurent De Wilde Trio | Colors Of Manhattan | IDA Record | 027 CD
Fred Hersch Trio | Dancing In The Dark | Chesky | JD 90
Gary Burton And Friends | Departure | Concord | CCD 4749
Ingrid Sertso And Her Sextet | Dance With Me | Enja | 8024-2
Lee Konitz With Strings | Strings For Holiday:A Tribute To Billie Holiday | Enja | ENJ-9304 2
Les Brown And His Band Of Renown | Digital Swing | Fantasy | FCD 9650-2
Lorez Alexandria And Her Quintet | I'll Never Stop Loving You | Muse | MCD 5457
Mark Murphy-Gary Schunk | Mark Murphy Sings Nat Cing Cole,Volumes 1&2 | Muse | MCD 6001
Monty Alexander | So What | Black & Blue | BLE 59.148 2
Rosemary Clooney And Her Band With Strings | For The Duration | Concord | CCD 4444
Stefan Scaggiari Trio | Stefan Out | Concord | CCD 4659
Till Brönner Quintet With Annette Lowman | My Secret Love | Minor Music | 801051
Tiziana Ghiglioni With The Steve Lacy Quartet | Somebody Special | Soul Note | SN 1156
Wes Montgomery Trio | Wes Montgomery-The Complete Riverside Recordings | Riverside | 12 RCD 4408-2
Weslia Whitefield Trio | Lucky To Be Me | Landmark | LCD 1524-2
Wynton Marsalis Sextet | Hot House Flowers | CBS | 468710-2
Sheila Jordan With The Steve Kuhn Trio | Jazz Child | HighNote Records | HCD 7029

For All You Are
Marilyn Crispell-Tim Berne | Inference | Music & Arts | CD 851

For Amadou
Tenor Saxes | Frankfurt Workshop '78:Tenor Saxes | Circle Records | RK 31-24978/31 IMS

For Art's Sake
Bluesiana | Bluesiana II | Windham Hill | 34 10133-2

For Bernard Moore
Gerry Mulligan-Ben Webster Quintet | Gerry Mulligan Meets Ben Webster | Verve | 841661-2 PMS

For Bessie
Stan Kenton And His Orchestra | Birthday In Britain | Creative World | STD 1065

For Bobby
Gil Evans Orchestra | Little Wing | West Wind | WW 2042

For Brad
Brass Octet And Percussion | Rhys Chatham Factor X | Moers Music | 02008 CD

For Coltrane
Bracha | Bracha | CMP Records | CMP CD 34
Abdullah Ibrahim-Carlos Ward Duo | Live At Sweet Basil Vol.1 | Black-Hawk | BKH 50204

For Count
Billy Sheehan-John Novello-Dennis Chambers | Niacin | Stretch Records | SCD 9011-2

For Dad
A.Spencer Barefield Group | Live At Leverkusener Jazztage | Sound Aspects | sas CD 039

For Dancers Only
Duke Ellington And His Orchestra | Recollections Of The Big Band Era | Atlantic | 90043-2
Don Thompson's Banff Jazz All Stars | Celebration | Jazz Focus | JFCD 024

For Django
Tony Purrone Quartet | Six-String Delight | Steeplechase | SCCD 31438

For Dodo
Matthias Nadolny-Gunnar Plümer | You'll Never Walk Alone | Nabel Records:Jazz Network | CD 4667

For Dolphy
D.D.Jackson-Hamiet Bluiett | Paired Down,Vol.1 | Justin Time | JUST 99-2

For Don C.
Brötzmann, van Hove, Bennink | Brötzmann, van Hove, Bennink | FMP | 0130

For Earth And Stars
Trygve Seim Group | Different Rivers | ECM | 1744(159521-2)

For Edward
Urs Leimgruber/John Wolf Brennan | An Chara-A Cara | L+R Records | CDLR 45007

For Ellington
Modern Jazz Quartet | For Ellington | East-West | 7567-90926-2
Peter Leitch Sextet | From Another Perspective | Concord | CCD 4535

For Emily
Ron McClure Quintet | Inner Account | Steeplechase | SCCD 31329
Don Redman And His Orchestra | For Europeans Only | Steeplechase | SCC 6020/21

For Ever-
Mike Westbrook Concert Band | Release | Deram | 844851-2

For Evermore
Dianne Reeves With Orchestra | For Every Heart | Palo Alto | TB 203

For Every Man There's A Woman
George Shearing-Brian Torff Duo | Blues Alley Jazz | Concord | CCD 4110
Sarah Vaughan With The Hal Mooney Orchestra | It's A Man's World | Mercury | 589487-2
Tal Farlow Septet | Tal Farlow Plays The Music Of Harold Arlen | Verve | MV 2589 IMS

For Example
Lars Sjösten Septet Feat. Lee Konitz | Dedicated To Lee-Lars Sjösten Plays The Music Of Lars Gullin | Dragon | DRLP 66

For Franz
Art Pepper Quartet | Saturday Night At The Village Vanguard | Original Jazz Classics | OJCCD 696-2(C 7644)

For Freddie
Art Lives | Galaxy | GXY 5145
Arthur's Blues | Original Jazz Classics | OJCCD 680-2
Art Pepper:The Complete Galaxy Recordings | Galaxy | 16GCD 1016-2
Art Pepper:The Complete Village Vanguard Sessions | Contemporary | 9CCD-4417-2
Art Pepper:The Complete Village Vanguard Sessions | Contemporary | 9CCD-4417-2
Art Pepper:The Complete Village Vanguard Sessions | Contemporary | 9CCD-4417-2
Bob Cooper/Snooky Young Sextet | In A Mellotone | Contemporary | C 14017

For Freddie(alt.take)
Free Flight | Free Flight-The Jazz/Classic Union | Palo Alto | PA 8024

For Free
Modern Walkin' | Modern Walkin'-Live In Japan | Satin Doll Productions | SDP 1009-1 CD

For Good
Thomas Schmidt Trio | For Good Reasons | Jazz 4 Ever Records:Jazz Network | J4E 4742

For H.-
J.R. Monterose Quintet | Body And Soul | Blue Moon | BMCD 1605

For Harry Carney
Michael Bisio Quartet | Michael Bisio Quartet In Seattle | Silkheart | SHCD 107

For Heaven's Sake
Bill Evans Trio | Trio (Motian Peacock)-Duo(Hall) | Verve | 2-2509 IMS
Trio 64 | Verve | 539058-2
Billie Holiday With The Ray Ellis Orchestra | Lady In Satin | CBS | CK 65144
Blue Mitchell With Strings And Brass | Smooth As The Wind | Original Jazz Classics | OJCCD 871-2(R 9367)
Cal Tjader's Modern Mambo Sextet | Tjader Plays Mambo | Original Jazz Classics | OJC 274(F 3221)
Chet Baker Quartet | Let's Get Lost | RCA | PL 83054
Jesse Davis Quartet | Horn Of Passion | Concord | CCD 4465
Landes Jugend Jazz Orchester Hessen | Magic Morning | Mons Records | CD 1905
Louis Smith Quintet | The Bopsmith | Steeplechase | SCCD 31489
McCoy Tyner-Bobby Hutcherson Duo | Manhattan Moods | Blue Note | 828423-2
Tony Reedus Quartet | Incognito | Enja | ENJ-6058 2
Wes Montgomery Trio | Wes Montgomery-The Complete Riverside Recordings | Riverside | 12 RCD 4408-2
Geoff Keezer Trio | World Music | CBS | 472811-2

For Heaven's Sake-
Ray Brown All Stars(The Be Bop Boys) | The Dizzy Gillespie Story | Savoy | SV 0177(MG 12110)

For Herbie
Simon Nabatov-Nils Wogram | Starting A Story | ACT | 9402-2
Del Ferro/Overwater/Paeffgen | Evening Train | Acoustic Music Records | 319.1063.2

For Hope Of Hope
Tiziana Ghiglioni Sextet | Streams | SPLASC(H) Records | CD H 104-2

For Instance
Michael Mantler Group | Michael Mantler: No Answer/Silence | Watt | 2/5(543374-2)
Michael Mantler Quintet | Live | Watt | 18
Dave Brubeck Quartet | For Iola | Concord | CCD 4259

For Jack And T
Eric Vloeiman Quartet | Bestiarium | Challenge | CHR 70038

For Jammers Only
Cat Anderson And His All Stars | Ellingtonians In Paris | Jazztime(EMI) | 251275-2

For Jan
Peter Erskine Trio | Juni | ECM | 1657(539726-2)
Stan Getz Quartet | Stan Getz/Zoot Sims | LRC Records | CDC 9041

For Jim H.
Bill Perkins Quintet | Swing Spring | Candid | CCD 79752

For Jo Ann
Herb Geller Quintet | A Jazz Song Book | Enja | ENJ-6006 2

For John Coltrane
Albert Ayler Group | Albert Ayler Live In Greenwich Village:The Complete Impulse Recordings | Impulse(MCA) | IMP 22732
Albert Ayler Quartet | Albert Ayler In Greenwich Village | MCA | 2292-54635-2
Ken Hyder's Talisker | Land Of Stone | Japo | 60018 IMS

For John Malachi
Geri Allen Group | Maroons | Blue Note | 799493-2
Fun Horns | Surprise | Jazzpoint | JP 1029 CD

For John T
Joe Maneri-Joe Morris-Mat Maneri | Three Men Walking | ECM | 1597

For Josef Schmid
Sal Mosca | For You | Candid | CRS 1022 IMS

For Kenny Kirkland
Matzeit-Daerr | September | Jazz Haus Musik | JHM 0125 CD
Don Thompson's Banff Jazz All Stars | Celebration | Jazz Focus | JFCD 024

For La Rives
Klaus König Orchestra | Times Of Devastation/Poco A Poco | Enja | ENJ-6014 22

For Lacy
Five For Jazz | Live In Sanremo | SPLASC(H) Records | HP 01

For Lena And Lennie
Quincy Jones And His Orchestra | The Quintessence | Impulse(MCA) | 951222-2
The Quintessential Charts | MCA | IA 9342/2
Draft | Traveling Birds | Jazz Haus Musik | JHM 68 CD

For Lester
Roscoe Mitchell And The Note Factory | Nine To Get Ready | ECM | 1651(539725-2)

For Lester B
Roscoe Mitchell | Sound Songs | Delmark | DE 493(2)

For Lolo

George Adams & Blue Brass Connection | Cool Affairs | PAO Records | PAO 10010

For Louis
George Duke Ensemble | The Aura Will Prevail | MPS | 68025

For 'M' Dance
Hamiet Bluiett Clarinet Family | The Clarinet Family | Black Saint | 120097-2

For Maestro Morricone
Christy Doran | What A Band | Hat Art | CD 6105

For Mary F
Ricky Ford Sextet | Saxotic Stomp | Muse | MCD 5349

For MC
James 'Sugarboy' Crawford Band | Sugarboy Crawford | Chess | 427017

For Me Formidable
The Timeless Art Orchestra | Without Words | Satin Doll Productions | SDP 1005-1 CD

For Mercedes
Jane Bunnett-Don Pullen | New York Duets | Music & Arts | CD 629

For Miles
Mark Dresser Quintet | Force Green | Soul Note | 121273-2

For Miles And Miles
Ian Carr's Nucleos | Awakening/Live At The Theaterhaus | BELL Records | BLR 83752

For Minors Only
Chet Baker-Art Pepper Sextet | Playboys | Pacific Jazz | 794474-2
Fritz Münzer Quintet | Jazz für junge Leute:Live im HR 1962 | Jazz 'n' Arts Records | C 01
Jacques Pelzer Open Sky Unit | Never Let Me Go | Igloo | IGL 084

For Mods Only
Chico Hamilton Quintet | The Dealer | Impulse(MCA) | 547958-2
Morton Gunnar Larsen | Maple Leaf Rag | Herman Records | HJCD 1009

For Monk
Michele Rosewoman Quartet | The Source | Soul Note | SN 1072

For Mr.Thomas
Stephan Micus | Implosions | Japo | 60017(2360017)

For M'schr And Djingis Khan
Bud Freeman And The V-Disc Jumpers | Muggsy Spanier And Bud Freeman:V-Discs 1944-45 | Jazz Unlimited | JUCD 2049

For Musicians Only
Memphis Slim Group | Live In Paris 1963 | France's Concert | FCD 127

For My Father
Bud Powell Trio | Bud Powell Paris Sessions | Pablo | PACD 2310972-2

For My Friends
Count Basie And His Orchestra | Basie's Bag | Telarc Digital | CD 83358

For My Lady
Toots Thielemans With The Shirley Horn Trio | Verve Jazz Masters Vol.59:Toots Thielemans | Verve | 535271-2
For My Lady | EmArCy | 510133-2

For Myself
Sal Mosca | For You | Candid | CRS 1022 IMS

For Nancy
Bill Dixon Orchestra | Thoughts | Soul Note | 121111-2

For Nina
Steve Lacy Nine | Futurities Part II | Hat Art | CD 6032

For No Reason At All In C
Stephan Micus | East Of The Night | Japo | 60041(825655-2)

For Nobuko
Arcado String Trio With The Kölner Rundfunkorchester | For Three Strings And Orchestra | JMT Edition | 849152-2

For Now
David Friedman Quartet | Of The Wind's Eye | Enja | ENJ-3089 2
Larry Schneider Quintet | So Easy | Label Bleu | LBLC 6516(881241)
Ruby Braff And His Men | Easy Now | RCA | 2118522-2
The Mastersounds | A Date With The Mastersounds | Original Jazz Classics | OJC 282(F 8062)

For Once In My Life
Jackie Terrasson Trio | Jacky Terrasson | Blue Note | 829351-2
Kenny Burrell | Lotus Blossom | Concord | CCD 4668

For P.A.
Michael Bisio Quintet | Michael Bisio Quartet In Seattle | Silkheart | SHCD 107

For Pauline
Albert Mangelsdorff Trio | The Wild Point | MPS | 68071

For Peter (Dedicated To Peter Trunk)
Peter Sonntag Quintet | Portraits In The Sign Of... | amf records | maj 1010

For Regulars Only
Dexter Gordon Quintet | Dexter Gordon:The Complete Blue Note Sixties Sessions | Blue Note | 834200-2

For Ruth
Bill Perkins & Frank Strazzeri | Warm Moods | Fresh Sound Records | FSR-CD 0191

For Samuel B.
Don Thompson Quartet | Beautiful Friendship | Concord | CJ 243

For Sentimental Reasons
The Rosenberg Trio | The Rosenberg Trio:The Collection | Verve | 537152-2

For Sephora
The Heath Brothers | As We Were Saying... | Concord | CCD 4777

For Someone I Love
Milt Jackson And His Orchestra | The Best Of Milt Jackson | CTI | 63045
Modern Jazz Quartet | Live At The Lighthouse | Atlantic | AMCY 1102

For Spee's Sakes
Freddie Hubbard Quintet | Hub-Tones | Blue Note | 499008-2

For Spee's Sakes(alt.take)
Julian Dash And His Orchestra | Julian Dash:The Complete Recordings 1950-1953 | Blue Moon | BMCD 1050

For Stompers Only
Stan Getz Quartet | Stan Getz-The Complete Roost Sessions | The Jazz Factory | JFCD 22839

For Susan
Carol Sloane And Her Trio | Heart's Desire | Concord | CCD 4503

For The Beautiful Changing Child
Louis Moholo's Viva-La-Black | Exile | Ogun | OGCD 003

For The Elders
Fred Wesley Group | Swing & Be Funky | Minor Music | 801027
Jack Montrose Quintet | Blues And Vanilla | Fresh Sound Records | ND 74400

For The Good Times
Bert Ambrose And His Orchestra | Happy Days | Saville Records | SVL 147 IMS

For The Love Of Sarah
Louis Hayes Quintet | Light And Lively | Steeplechase | SCCD 31245

For The Moment
Marc Copland Quartet | All Blues At Night | Jazz City | 660.53.026

For The Music
The Real Group | Get Real! | ACT | 9252-2

For The Rest Of My Life
Cyrus Chestnut Trio | You Are My Sunshine | Warner | 9362-48445-2

For The Sainnts
Ugetsu | Cape Town Blues | Naxos Jazz | 86052-2

For The Time Being
The Amsterdam Jazz Quintet With Fee Claassen | Playground | Challenge | CHR 70071
Johnny Hartman And His Orchestra | Unforgettable | Impulse(MCA) | IMP 11522

For The Want Of A Kiss
Cecil Taylor | For Olim | Soul Note | 121150-2

For The Wind Was Green
Fernando Tarrés And The Arida Conta Group With Guests | On The Edges Of White | Muse | MCD 5463

For Those Who Choose
John Stubblefield Quintet | Countin' The Blues | Enja | ENJ-5051 2

For Those Who Still Hear The...
Russell Malone Quartet | Sweet Georgia Peach | Impulse(MCA) | 951282-2

For Toddlers Only
Elvin Jones Quintet | Very Rare & Love And Peace | Konnex Records | KCD 5036

For Tomorrow
McCoy Tyner Group With Voices | Inner Voices | Original Jazz Classics | OJCCD 1039-2(M 9079)
Greg Abate Quintet | Dr. Jeckyll & Mr. Hyde | Candid | CCD 79715

For Tony
Primal Blue | Primal Blue | Hip Bop | HIBD 8006

For Turiya
Charlie Haden-Alice Coltrane | Closeness Duets | Verve | 397000-2
Geri Allen Trio | Live At The Village Vanguard | DIW | DIW 847 CD

For Us
Daniel Guggenheim Group | Daniel Guggenheim Group feat. Jasper van't Hof | Laika Records | LK 990-018

For Ute
David Murray Quartet | Live Vol.2 | India Navigation | IN 1044

For Wayne And Joe
Branford Marsalis Quartet | Black Codes | CBS | 468711-2

For Wise And Ramin
Mike Wofford | Maybeck Recital Hall Series Volume Eighteen | Concord | CCD 4514

For You
Cody Moffett Septet | Evidence | Telarc Digital | CD 83343
Franz Weyerer Quintet | For You | Bassic-Sound | CD 012
The King Sisters With Frank DeVol's Orchestra | The Uncollected:The King Sisters | Hindsight | HSR 168
Wolfgang Engstfeld Quartet | Songs And Ballads | Nabel Records:Jazz Network | CD 4658
Jessica Williams | Arrival | Jazz Focus | JFCD 001

For You For Me For Evermore
Dave McKenna | Teddi King Sings Ira Gershwin | Inner City | IC 1044 IMS
Trudy Desmond Band | My One And Only Love | Justin Time | JTR 8468-2

For You For Me For Evermore-
Modern Jazz Quartet | The Complete Modern Jazz Quartet Prestige & Pablo Recordings | Prestige | 4PRCD 4438-2
The MJQ Box | Prestige | 7711-2

For You My Love
Tom Mega + Band | Backyards Of Pleasure | ITM Records | ITM 1432

For Your Ears Only
Frank Strozier Sextet | Remember Me | Steeplechase | SCCD 31066

For Your Love
Little Johnny Taylor With Band | The Galaxy Years | Ace Records | CDCHD 967

For Your Sound
Stephan Micus | Desert Poems | ECM | 1757(159739-2)

For Yuko
Terra Brazil | Café Com Leite | art-mode-records | AMR 2101

Fora Da Lei
Terje Rypdal Group | If Mountains Could Sing | ECM | 1554(523987-2)

Foran Peisen
Lionel Hampton And His Orchestra | The Great Hamptologia, Vol. 2 | MGM | 2304528 IMS

Forbidden City
Pili-Pili | Hotel Babo | JA & RO | JARO 4147-2

Forbidden Drums
Abraham Burton-Eric McPherson Quartet | Cause And Effect | Enja | ENJ-9377 2

Forbidden Fruit
John Zorn Group With The Kronos Quartet | Spillane | Nonesuch | 7559-79172-2
Nina Simone Groups | You Can Have Him | Memo Music | HDJ 4087

Forbidden Games
Paul Millns Groups | Unsong Heroes | Acoustic Music Records | 319.1143.2

Forbidden Land
Marion Meadows Group | For Lovers Only | Novus | PD 83097

Forbidden Romance
Tambastics | Tambastics | Music & Arts | CD 704

Ford Fiasco
Ricky Ford Septet | Hot Brass | Candid | CCD 79518

'Fore Day Blues
Ida Cox And Her All Star Band | I Can't Quit My Man | Affinity | CD AFS 1015

'Fore Day Creep
Ida Cox With The James P. Johnson Septet | From Spiritual To Swing | Vanguard | VCD 169/71
Tarheel Slim | No Time At All | Trix Records | TRIX 3310

'Fore Day Rider
Jay McShann Quartet | Goin' To Kansas City | Stony Plain | SPCD 1286
The Man From Muskogee | Sackville | SKCD2-3005

Foregone Conclusion
Bireli Lagrene Group | Foreign Affairs | Blue Note | 790967-2

Foreign Fun
The Poll Winners | The Poll Winners Ride Again | Original Jazz Classics | OJC 607(C 7556)

Foreign Intrigue
Tony Williams Sextet | Foreign Intrigue | Blue Note | 746289-2

Foreplay
Cold Sweat | 4 Play | JMT Edition | 834444-2

Forerunner
Ornette Coleman Quartet | Beauty Is A Rare Thing:Ornette Coleman-The Complete Atlantic Recordings | Atlantic | 8122-71410-2
Darrell Grant Quartet | Black Art | Criss Cross | Criss 1087

Foresight And Afterthought
Gary Thomas Quintet | Seventh Quadrant | Enja | 5047 (807550)

Forest Cathedral
Moe Koffman Quartet | Moe Koffman 1967 | Just A Memory | JAS 9505-2

Forest Flower(Sunrise)
Charles Lloyd Quartet | Atlantic Jazz: Introspection | Atlantic | 7567-81710-2
Atlantic Saxophones | Rhino | 8122-71256-2
Chico Hamilton Quartet | Man From Two Worlds | Impulse(MCA) | JAS 48 (AS 59)

Forest Flower(Sunset)
Charles Lloyd Quartet | Forest Flower:Charles Lloyd At Monterey | Atlantic | 8122-71746-2
Atlantic Saxophones | Rhino | 8122-71256-2
Chico Hamilton Quartet | Man From Two Worlds | Impulse(MCA) | JAS 48 (AS 59)

Forever
Klaus Doldinger's Passport | Heavy Nights | Warner | 2292-42006-2
Sandro Cerino Action Quartet | Che Fine Fanno I Personaggi Dei Sogni | SPLASC(H) Records | H 190
James Newton Septet | Romance And Revolution | Blue Note | BT 85134

Forever Gone
Les McCann Group | Listen Up! | Musicmasters | 65139-2

Forever Young
Kitty White With The Benny Carter All Stars | Sweet Talk | Fresh Sound Records | FSR 557(Roulette R 52020)

Forever, For Now
Viktoria Tolstoy Group & Strings | Shining On You | ACT | 9701-2

Foreverly
Jimmy Smith Quintet | Root Down | Verve | 559805-2

Foreveryone Under The Sun
Booker Little Sextet | Victory And Sorrow | Affinity | AFF 124

Foreward Motion
Gunter Hampel Jazz Sextet | Gunter Hampel: The 8th Of Sept.1999 | Birth | CD 049

Foreward To The Past
Lars Duppler Sextet | Palindrome 6tet | Jazz Haus Musik | JHM 0131 CD

Forfait
Per Gudmundson-Ale Möller-Lene Willemark | Frifot | ECM | 1690(557653-2)

Förgäves
Ugetsu | Cape Town Blues | Naxos Jazz | 86052-2

Forget
Steve Tibbetts Group | Exploded View | ECM | 1335
Ray Gelato Giants | The Full Flavour | Linn Records | AKD 034

Forget Full
Paul Millns Groups | Unsong Heroes | Acoustic Music Records | 319.1143.2

Forget Me
Dave McMurdo Jazz Orchestra | Live at Montreal Bistro | Sackville | SKCD2-2029

Forgetful
Chet Baker With String-Orchestra And Voices | Chet Baker With Fifty Italian Strings | Original Jazz Classics | OJC20 492-2(JLP 921)
Christian Josi With The Harry Allen Quartet | I Walk With My Feet Off The Ground | Master Mix | CHECD 00111

Forgive Me
Sonny Terry & Brownie McGhee | Hometown Blues | Mainstream | MD CDO 902

Forgiveness
Liz Story Group | Speechless | RCA | PL 83037

Forgotten Joys,Forsaken Songs
Piirpauke | Piirpauke-Global Servisi | JA & RO | JARO 4150-2
John Tchicai Group | Put Up The Flight | Storyville | SLP 4141

Forgotten Love
Allan Botschinsky Quartet | Last Summer | M.A Music | A 804-2

Forgotten Melody
The Moscow Chambers Jazz Ensemble | Kadans | Mobile Fidelity | MFCD 916

Forgotten Past
Das Pferd | The World Of 'Das Pferd' | ITM Records | ITM 1488

Forgotten Song
Ornette Coleman Quartet | Friends And Neighbors:Ornette Live At Prince Street | RCA | PL 43548

Forlon
Tomasz Stanko Quartet | Leosia | ECM | 1603(531693-2)

Forlorn Walk
Alex Möller-Lena Willemark Group | Hästen Och Tranan | ACT | 9244-2

Form
The Enja Band | The Enja Band-Live At Sweet Basil | Enja | ENJ-8034 2

Formal Schematics
BLU | Rhythm & Blu. | Gramavision | 18-8606-1

Formation
Joe Harriott Quintet | Free Form | EmArCy | 538184-2
Jacob Young Quintet | Evening Falls | ECM | 1876(9811780)

Formerly
| All The Way To Sendai | Enja | ENJ-6030 2

Formiddag(Morning)
Steve Tibbetts Group | The Fall Of Us All | ECM | 1527(521144-2)

Formless
Paul Horn Group | A Special Edition | Black Sun Music | 15003-2

Forms
The Philadelphia Woodwind Quintet | The Music Of Ornette Coleman: Forms + Sounds | RCA | ND 86561(847114)

Forms Of Life
Jean-Luc Ponty | Civilized Evil | Atlantic | SD 16020

Formula
Africa Djole | Percussion Music From Africa | FMP | SAJ 50

Foroya
Ahmed El-Salamouny/Claudio Menandro | Aquarela | FSM | FCD 97770

Forro
Egberto Gismonti Trio | ZigZag | ECM | 1582

Forrobodó
Sven-Ake Johansson Quintet | Six Little Pieces For Quintet | HatOLOGY | 538

Fort Apache
Susan Weinert Band | Point Of View | Intuition Records | INT 3272-2

Fort Carré
Don Cherry Group | Dona Nostra | ECM | 1448(521727-2)

Fort Cherry
Jack Teagarden And His Orchestra | Masters Of Jazz Vol.10:Jack Teagarden | Storyville | STCD 4110

Fort Lauderdale
Nat Adderley Quintet | Compact Jazz: Cannonball Adderley | EmArCy | 842930-2 PMS

Fort Worth
Joe Lovano Quartet | From The Soul | Blue Note | 798636-2
Bessie Tucker | Better Boot That Thing-Great Women Blues Singers Of The 1920's | Bluebird | 63 66065 2

Fortaleza
Arild Andersen Quintet | Masqualero | Odin | LP 08

Forth (Shock, Scatter)-
Keith Jarrett Quintet | Fort Yawuh | Impulse(MCA) | 547966-2

Forth Yawuh
Miroslav Vitous/Jan Garbarek | Atmos | ECM | 1475(513373-2)

Forthcoming
Andrew Cyrille Quartet | Special People | Soul Note | SN 1012

Fortitude And Chaos
Trygve Seim-Oyvind Braekke-Per Oddvar Johansen Orchestra | The Source And Different Cikadas | ECM | 1764(014432-2)

Fort-Jazz
Fourplay | Fourplay...Yes,Please! | Warner | 9362-47694-2

Fortress
The Crossover Ensemble With The Zapolski Quartet | Helios Suite | dacapo | DCCD 9459

Fortryllede Dage(Bewitched Days)
Munich Saxophon Family | Balanced | Edition Collage | EC 487-2

Fortsetzung Folgt Now
Dennis Gonzales New Dallas Quartet | Stefan | Silkheart | SHCD 101

Fortune Cookie
Vocal Summit | Conference Of The Birds | ITM-Pacific | ITMP 970070

Fortune Dance
John Lindberg Ensemble | Bounce | Black Saint | 120192-2

Fortune Seeker
Gary Burton-Keith Jarrett Quintet | Atlantic Jazz: Introspection | Atlantic | 7567-81710-2

Fortune Smiles
Helen Humes With Leonard Feather's Hip-Tet | E-Baba-Le-Ba The Rhythm And Blues Years | Savoy | WL 70824 (809326)

Fortune's Child
Charlie Haden Quartet West | In Angel City | Verve | 837031-2

Fortune's Fame
Vince Jones Group | Future Girl | Intuition Records | INT 3109-2

Fortunes Pet
Beale Street Washboard Band | South Side Chicago Jazz | MCA | MCAD 42326(872083)

Forty And Tight
Get Easy Blues | Frog | DGF 9

Forty Days
Dave Brubeck Trio With Gerry Mulligan And The Cincinnati Symphony Orchestra | Brubeck/Mulligan/Cincinnati | MCA | 252313-1

Forty Days And Forty Nights
Muddy Waters Blues Band | Jack Dupree-Jimmy Rushing-Muddy Waters | Laserlight | 17062

Forty Four Blues
James Wiggins With Blind Leroy Garnett | Paramounth Piano Blues Vol.1(1928-1932) | Black Swan Records | HCD-12011

Forty-Second Street
The Boswell Sisters With The Dorsey Brothers' Orchestra | Everybody Loves My Baby | Pro-Arte | CDD 550
Bud Freeman And His Summa Cum Laude Orchestra | Jazz Gallery:Jack Teagarden | RCA | 2114175-2

Forward
Markus Stockhausen Quartet | Cosi Lontano...Quasi Dentro | ECM | 1371
Booker Little Sextet | Booker Little And Friends | Bethlehem | BTM 6821

Forward March
Antonio Hart Group | Ama Tu Sonrisa | Enja | ENJ-9404 2

Forward Motion
David S. Ware Quartet | Great Bliss Vol.1 | Silkheart | SHCD 127

TITELVERZEICHNIS

Foto Di Famiglia
Riccardo Fassi-Antonello Salis Duo | Joining | SPLASC(H) Records | H 113

Fotografia
Franco & Lorenzo Petrocca | Italy | Edition Musikat | EDM 062
Jermaine Landsberger Trio & Gina | Samba In June | Edition Collage | EC 524-2
Lorenzo Petrocca Organ Trio | Milan In Minor | Jardis Records | JRCD 20136
Maximilian Geller Group | Maximilian Geller Goes Bossa | Edition Collage | EC 496-2
Ornette Coleman Quintet | Body Meta | Verve | 531916-2

Fou Rire
Richard Galliano Quartet | New York Tango | Dreyfus Jazz Line | FDM 36581-2
Richard Galliano Trio | Concert Inédits | Dreyfus Jazz Line | FDM 36606-2

Found Footage
Tomasz Gaworek-Schodrok | Found In The Flurry Of The World | Acoustic Music Records | 319.1073.2

Found On Sordid Streets
Stanley Blume Quartet | Movin' Up | Organic Music | ORGM 9709

Foundation
Lajos Dudas Trio | Chamber Music Live | Pannon Jazz/Classic | PCL 8004

Fountaine Of Tears(part 1&2)
Andy LaVerne/Dave Samuels | Fountainhead | Steeplechase | SCCD 31261

Four
Gene Ammons And His All Stars | Juganthology | Prestige | P 24036
Joe Henderson With The Wynton Kelly Trio | Four! | Verve | 523657-2
King & Moore | Potato Radio | Justice Records | JR 0802-2
Miles Davis New Quintet | Workin' With The Miles Davis Qoartet | Original Jazz Classics | OJC 296(P 7166)
Miles Davis Quartet | Tune Up | Prestige | P 24077
Miles Davis Quintet | En Concert Avec Europe 1 | Laserlight | 710455/58
Ran Blake-Anthony Braxton | A Memory Of Vienna | HatOLOGY | 505
Rob Schneiderman Trio | Keepin' In The Groove | Reservoir | RSR CD 144
Sonny Rollins & Co. | Now's The Time! | RCA | 2132335-2
Sonny Rollins Trio | A Night At The Village Gate Vol.3 | Blue Note | 300204(BNJ 61015)
Jazz Profile:Sonny Rollins | Blue Note | 823516-2
The Alternative Rollins | RCA | PL 43268
Stan Getz Quintet | Best Of The West Coast Sessions | Verve | 537084-2
Stan Getz:East Of The Sun-The West Coast Sessions | Verve | 531935-2

Four-
J.P.Torres Band | Trombone Man | RMM Records | 660.58.085

Four And One
Barney Bigard And His Jazzopators | The Complete Duke Ellington-Vol. 8 | CBS | CBS 88185

Four And One More
Stan Getz And His Five Brothers | Early Getz | Prestige | P 24088
Stan Getz Five Brothers Bop Tenor Sax Stars | Zoot Sims:The Featured Sessions With Great Leaders 1949-1954 | Blue Moon | BMCD 1037
Elvin Jones Trio | Elvin! | Original Jazz Classics | OJCCD 259-2(RLP 9409)

Four Bars Short
George Shearing Quintet | So Rare | Savoy | 650141(882497)

Four Bowls Of Soup
Anita O'Day With The Marty Paich Orchestra | Sings The Winners | Verve | 2304255 IMS

Four Brothers
Art Pepper Plus Eleven | Modern Jazz Classics | Original Jazz Classics | OJC20 341-2
A Treasury Of Modern Jazz Classics | Mobile Fidelity | MFCD 805
Harry Allen With The John Pizzarelli Trio | Tenors Anyone? | Novus | 2150684-2
Jazz Band Ball Orchestra | Plays Fantastic,Fantastic | Timeless | CD TTD 559
Marian McPartland Trio | At Storyville/At The Hickory House | Savoy | SV 0202(MG 12004)
The Four Brothers | Victor Jazz History Vol.13:Modern Jazz-Cool & West Coast | RCA | 2135732-2
The Moscow Sax Quintet | The Jazznost Tour | Arkadia Jazz | 71161
Woody Herman And His Orchestra | Woody Herman:Four Brother | Dreyfus Jazz Line | FDM 36722-2
Woody Herman 1954 And 1959 | Status | DSTS 1021
Woody Herman Big Band | Aurex Jazz Festival '82 | Eastworld | EWJ 80237

Four By Five
McCoy Tyner Trio | Super Trios | Milestone | M 55003

Four Comets
Uli Lenz | Midnight Candy | Enja | 5009

Four Fathers
John Lindberg-Albert Mangelsdorff-Eric Watson | Dodging Bullets | Black Saint | 120108-2

Four Five Six
The Count Basie Orchestra | Long Live The Chief | Denon Compact Disc | CY-1018

Four For Three
Jack Walrath + Sprit Level | Killer Bunnies | Spotlite | SPJ LP 25

Four In Hand
Anthony Braxton Quartet | Six Monk's Compositions(1987) | Black Saint | 120116-2

Four In One
John Abercrombie-Marc Johnson-Peter Erskine | John Abercrombie/Marc Johnson/Peter Erskine | ECM | 1390(837756-2)
John Campbell Trio | Workin' Out | Criss Cross | Criss 1198
Roni Ben-Hur Trio | Sofia's Butterfly | TCB Records | TCB 98802
Steve Slagle Quartet | The Steve Slagle Quartet | Steeplechase | SCCD 31323
Thelonious Monk Quartet Plus Two | At The Blackhawk | Original Jazz Classics | OJCCD 305-2
Thelonious Monk Quintet | Thelonious Monk:Misterioso | Dreyfus Jazz Line | FDM 36743-2
Genius Of Modern Music,Vol.2 | Blue Note | 300404
Genius Of Modern Music,Vol.1 | Blue Note | 781510-2
Thelonious Monk Sextet | In Person | Milestone | M 47033
Danilo Perez Quartet | Panamonk | Impulse(MCA) | 951190-2

Four In One-
Milt Jackson Quintet | Thelonious Monk:The Complete Blue Note Recordings | Blue Note | 830363-2

Four Legends:
Jack DeJohnette Group | Sorcery | Prestige | P 10081

Four Men And A Horse
Wanderlust + Guests | Full Bronte | Laika Records | 35101412

Four Miles
European Tuba Quartet | Low And Behold | Jazz Haus Musik | JHM 0110 CD

Four Miniatures
Dave Douglas Sextet | In Our Lifetime | New World Records | 80471-2

Four O'Clock Blues
Lionel Hampton All Stars | The Changing Face Of Harlem, Vol. 2 | Savoy | SJL 2224 (801200)

Four On Six
Wes Montgomery Quartet | The Small Group Recordings | Verve | 2-2513 IMS
Wes Montgomery Quartet With The Claus Ogerman Orchestra | Willow Weep For Me | Verve | 589486-2
Wynton Kelly Trio With Wes Montgomery | Smokin' At The Half Note | Verve | 2304480 IMS
Wes Montgomery:The Verve Jazz Sides | Verve | 521690-2
Smokin' At The Half Note | CTI Records | PDCTI 1117-2

Four On The Floor
Curtis Fuller Quintet | Four On The Outside | Timeless | CD SJP 124

Four Once More
The Original Benny Goodman Quartet | The Yale University Music Library:Benny Goodman Vol.10 | Musicmasters | 65129-2

Four Openers
Bob Florence Trio | Bob Florence Trio | Fresh Sound Records | FSR-CD 0303

Four Or Five Times
Adrian Bentzon's Jazzband | The Golden Years Of Revival Jazz,Vol.13 | Storyville | STCD 5518
Alan Elsdon Band | Jazz Journeymen | Black Lion | BLCD 760519
Alvin Alcorn' 'Gay Paree' Stompers | Alvin Alcorn/Harrison Verret | American Music | AMCD-65
Bechet-Spanier Big Four | Spreadin Joy (Original Recordings 1940-50) | Naxos Jazz | 8.120531 CD
George Lewis And His New Orleans Ragtime Band | The Beverly Caverns Session | Good Time Jazz | GTCD 12058-2
Jimmie Lunceford And His Orchestra | Big Band Bounce & Boogie:Strictly Lunceford | Affinity | AFS 1003
Jimmy Lunceford And His Orchestra | Rhythm Business | Hep | 1013
Lionel Hampton And His Orchestra | The Complete Lionel Hampton Vol.3/4(1939) | RCA | 2122614-2
Woody Herman And His Orchestra | The Radio Years: Woody Herman And His First Herd 1944 | Hindsight | HSR 134

Four Or Five Times-
Jimmy Noone's Apex Club Orchestra | Jimmy Noone 1928 | Village(Jazz Archive) | VILCD 021-2

Four Or Less
Howard Rumsey's Lighthouse All-Stars | Sunday Jazz A La Lighthouse Vol.2 | Original Jazz Classics | OJCCD 972-2(S 2501)

Four Others
Sunday Jazz A La Lighthouse,Vol.1 | Original Jazz Classics | OJC 151(C 3501)

Four Queasy Pieces
Eric Lugosch | Black Key Blues | Acoustic Music Records | 319.1148.2

Four Steps
Mike Clark-Paul Jackson Quartet | The Funk Stops Here | TipToe | TIP-888811 2

Four String Drive
Joe Venuti's Blue Four | Jazz Classics In Digital Stereo: Joe Venuti/Eddie Lang | CDS Records Ltd. | RPCD 626(CD 644)

Four To Four
Tony Ortega Octet | Jazz For Young Moderns | Fresh Sound Records | FSR 2006(Bethlehem BCP 79)

Four Tom-Toms
Seamus Blake Quintet/Sextet | Four Track Mind | Criss Cross | Criss 1126

Four Winds
David Holland Quartet | Conference Of The Birds | ECM | 1027(829373-2)
Helmut Forsthoff Trio | Four Together | Aho-Recording | CD 1011

Four Winds-
Nina Simone Quartet | Nina Simone-The 60s Vol.3:Work Song | Mercury | 838545-2 PMS

Four Women
Nina Simone Trio | Verve Jazz Masters Vol.58:Nina Simone Sings Nina | Verve | 529867-2
Nnenna Freelon And Her Band | Maiden Voyage | Concord | CCD 4794

Fourmost
Very Saxy | Very Saxy | Original Jazz Classics | OJCCD 458-2
Brad Goode Quartet | By Myself | Steeplechase | SCCD 31506

Fours Bars Shorter
Reedstorm Saxophone Quartet | Reedstorm Saxophone Quartet | Acoustic Music Records | 319.1075.2

Fourth Floor
L.A. Underground | Black/Note | Red Records | 123259-2

Fourth Impression
Ed Blackwell & AJQ-2 | Boogie Live...1958 | AFO Records | AFO 92-1228-2

Fourth Sun
Karlheinz Miklin Quintet & KUG Big Band | KH Miklin Quinteto Argentina & KUG Big Band | TCB Records | TCB 21232

Fourth Waltz
Fourth World | Fourth World | Ronnie Scott's Jazz House | JHCD 026

Fourth World
Mark Helias Group | Desert Blue | Enja | ENJ-6016 2

Fourty Dregrees
Max Roach Quintet | The Hardbop Academy | Affinity | AFF 773

Fous Qui Disiez
Brad Dutz | Brad Dutz | Nine Winds Records | NWCD 0141

Fox Chase
Sonny Terry & Brownie McGhee | The 1958 London Sessions | Sequel Records | NEX CD 120

Foxtrot
Spyro Gyra | Carnaval | MCA | 2292-50418-1

Foxy
Eddie Lockjaw Davis Quintet | 6 Classic Tenors | EPM Musique | FDC 5170

Foxy Lady
Defunkt | Defunkt/Heroes | DIW | DIW 838 CD

Foxy Lady-
Manhattan Jazz Quintet | Funky Strut | Sweet Basil | 660.55.006

Foxy Trot
Norma Winstone With Group | Live At Roccella Jonica | SPLASC(H) Records | CD H 508-2

Fo-Yah
Big Al Sears Band | Sear-iously | Bear Family Records | BCD 15668 AH

Fo-Yah(alt.take)
Bill Frisell | Smash & Scatteration | Minor Music | 005

Fractal Joy
Jeff Beal With The Metropole Orchestra | Concerto For Orchestra | Koch Jazz | 3-6904-2

Fractions
Rolf Kühn And Friends | Affairs:Rolf Kühn & Friends | Intuition Records | INT 3211-2
Dick Wellstood And The Friends Of Fats | Ain't Misbehavin' | Chiaroscuro | CR 183

Fractual Gumbo
Eddie Davis And His Beboppers | Nostalgia | Savoy | SV 0123(MG 12133)

Frag Mich Nicht...
Anders Jormin | Xieyi | ECM | 1762(013998-2)

Fragancia
Andy Bey Group | Tuesdays In Chinatown | Minor Music | 801099

Fragile
Eddie Bert With The Hank Jones Trio | Musician Of The Year | Savoy | SV 0183(MG 12015)
Marco Piludu International Quartet | New York Travels | Jazz 4 Ever Records:Jazz Network | J4E 4733
Nils Landgren Group | Sentimental Journey | ACT | 9409-2
Sarah Jane Morris Group | Blue Valentine | Ronnie Scott's Jazz House | JHCD 038
Ulli Bögershausen | Best Of Ulli Bögershausen | Laika Records | LK 93-045
Klaus Kreuzeder & Franz Benton | Big little Gigs: First Takes Live | Trick Music | TM 0112 CD

Fragile Feeling
Ensemble Modern | Ensemble Modern-Fred Frith:Traffic Continues | Winter&Winter | 910044-2

Fragile Finale
Joe Haider Quintet | Magic Box | JHM Records | JHM 3601

Fragile Youth
Greg Osby Quintet | Inner Circle | Blue Note | 499871-2

Fragmatic Decoding
Rainer Tempel Quintet | Blick In Die Welt | Edition Musikat | EDM 038

Fragment
Thomas Heberer | The Heroic Millepede | ITM Records | ITM 1443

Fragment From Concerto In G Minor For Violin And Strings Op.8 N.2(Summer)
Stan Kenton And His Orchestra | Live At Butler University | Creative World | ST 1058

Fragmentary Blues
Bright Moments | Return Of The Lost Tribe | Delmark | DE 507

Fragments Of A Hologram Rose
Werner Lüdi-Burhan Öcal | Willisau And More Live | Creative Works Records | CW CD 1020-2
Martin Joseph-Eugenio Colombo | Duets And Solos | Red Records | VPA 139

Fragments Of Blues
Peter Brötzmann Group | Die Like A Dog(fragments of music, life and death of Albert Ayler) | FMP | CD 64

Fraises Et Creme Fraiche
Manfredo Fest Quintet | Oferenda | Concord | CCD 4539

Fraligh In Swing(And The Angels Sing)
Ziggy Elman And His Orchestra | Zaggin' With Ziggy | Affinity | CD AFS 1006

Frame-Up
Bruno Tommaso Orchestra | Su Un Tema Di Jerome Kern | SPLASC(H) Records | HP 18

Francavilla
Oliver Lake Quartet | Gallery | Gramavision | GR 8609-2

France Medley:
Jelly Roll Morton | The Jelly Roll Morton Centennial-His Complete Victor Recordings | Bluebird | ND 82361

Francine
Louie Bellson And His Big Band | Live From New York | Telarc Digital | CD 83334

Francis' Delight
Jackie McLean Quintet | Capuchin Swing | Blue Note | 540033-2

Francisco
Soma | Southern Cross | West Wind Latina | 2208 CD

Francois Villon
George Gruntz Trio | Serious Fun | Enja | ENJ-6038 2

Fran-Dance
Miles Davis Quintet | Live In Stockholm | Dragon | DRLP 90/91
Miles Davis Quintet Live In Zürich 1960 | Jazz Unlimited | JUCD 2031

Frank Mills Jr.
Frank Rosolino Sextet | Kenton Presents: Frank Rosolino | Affinity | AFF 61

Frank Talk
Phil Woods-Gene Quill Sextet | Phil And Quill | RCA | 2159153-2

Franken Global
Archie Shepp Sextet | The Way Ahead | Impulse(MCA) | 951272-2

Frankenstein
Edgar Winter Group | I'm Not A Kid Anymore | L+R Records | CDLR 42076

Frankfurt Blues(Now's The Time)
Jutta Hipp Quintet | Cool Dogs & Two Oranges | L+R Records | LR 41006

Frankie And Johnny
Bob Cooper Sextet | COOP! The Music Of Bob Cooper | Original Jazz Classics | OJCCD 161-2
Duke Ellington And His Famous Orchestra | Duke Ellington & His Famous Orchestra | Forlane | UCD 19003
Duke Ellington And His Orchestra | Big Band Bounce And Boogie:Classic Transcriptions-Duke Ellington | Affinity | AFS 1032

Frankie And Johnny-
Memphis Slim | All Kinds Of Blues | Original Blues Classics | OBC-507(BV 1053)

Frankincense & Rosewood
Phil Franklin Jazz Band | Phil Franklin Jazz Band | Timeless | TTD 501

Franklin Street Blues
Bunk Johnson And His New Orleans Band | Victor Jazz History Vol.19:Dixieland Revival | RCA | 2135738-2
Mr.Acker Bilk And His Paramount Jazz Band | 1+2=3:The Best Of Barber And Bilk | Lake | LACD 73

Frankly Speaking
Horace Parlan Quintet | Frank-ly Speaking | Steeplechase | SCS 1076

Frank's Magic
Freddie Brocksieper Und Seine Solisten | Freddie's Boogie Blues | Bear Family Records | BCD 16388 AH

Frank's Melody
Ahmad Jamal Trio | At The Top-Poinciana Revisited | Impulse(MCA) | JAS 15 (AS 9176)

Frantic Desire
Bud Powell Trio | Bud Powell:The Complete Blue Note And Roost Recordings | Blue Note | 830083-2

Frantic Fancies
Illinois Jacquet And His Orchestra | Illinois Jacquet | CBS | EK 64654

Frantic Flight
Cab Calloway And His Orchestra | Duke Ellington/Cab Calloway | Forlane | UCD 19004

Franz-Branntwein(dedicated to F.K.,a dear friend in Vienna)
Matthias Petzold Group With Choir | Psalmen und Lobgesänge für Chor und Jazz-Enseble | Indigo-Records | 1002 CD

Franziskuspsalm 7(All Ihr Völker Klatscht In Die Hände)
Tony Scott With The Bill Evans Trio | A Day In New York | Fresh Sound Records | FSR-CD 0160(2)

Fratzen,I Love The Smell Of Garbage
Wolfgang Schmiedt | 4 Guitars | KlangRäume | 30010

Frauen Sind Keine Engel
Tome XX | Natura Morte | Jazz Haus Musik | JHM 32

Freak In
Alexander Sipiagin Group | Images | TCB Records | TCB 98602

Freakish
Luis Russell And His Orchestra | Harlem Big Bands | Timeless | CBC 1-010

Freaky Deaky
Yakou Tribe | Red & Blue Days | Traumton Records | 4474-2
Rolf Kühn Group | Internal Eyes | Intuition Records | INT 3328-2

Freaky Eyes
Claudio Lodati Dac'Corda | Voci | SPLASC(H) Records | H 154

Freckle Face
The Frank Capp Juggernaut | Play It Again Sam | Concord | CCD 4747

Fred
George Masso Quintet | Just For A Thrill | Sackville | SKCD2-2022
Zoot Sims-Bucky Pizzarelli Duo | Elegiac | Storyville | STCD 8238
Steve Swallow Group | Carla | Watt | XtraWatt/2

Fred And Ethel
Kamikaze Ground Crew | The Scenic Route | New World Records | 80400-2

Freddie Freeloader
Dexter Gordon Quartet | Something Different | Steeplechase | SCS 1136
Gerald Wilson Orchestra | Feelin' Kinda Blues | Pacific Jazz | CDP 79-2
Jon Hendricks And Friends | Freddie Freeloader | Denon Compact Disc | CY-76302
Miles Davis Sextet | The Miles Davis Selection | CBS | 465699-2
Monty Alexander Trio | Full Steam Ahead | Concord | CCD 4287
Wes Montgomery Trio | Portrait Of Wes | Original Jazz Classics | OJCCD 144-2
Wes Montgomery-The Complete Riverside Recordings | Riverside | 12 RCD 4408-2
World Saxophone Quartet With Jack DeJohnette And African Drums | Selim Sivad:A Tribute To Miles Davis | Justin Time | JUST 119-2

Freddie Tooks Jr.
Dejan's Young Olympia Brass Band | Alive And Kicken | Traditional Line | TL 1310

Freddie's Boogie Blues
Marcus Pintrup Quartet | Nocturnal Traces | Blue Note | 493676-2

Freddie's Melody
Freddie King Group | Freddie King Gives You A Bonanza Of Instrumentals | Crosscut | CCR 1010

Freddy C | Bielefelder Katalog 127 Jazz • Ausgabe 2004 | From Four Till Late

Freddie's Yen For Jen
Thomas Francke Group | Rabiator | G.N.U. Records | CD A 96.086
Freddy C
Tom Varner Quartet | Motion/Stillness | Soul Note | SN 1067
Freddy's Step-
Thilo Berg Big Band | Carnival Of Life | Mons Records | CD 1887
Frederiks Contra-
Artie Shaw And His Orchestra | Artie Shaw And His Orchestra 1949 | Limelight | 820817-2 IMS
Fred's Walk
Gloria Lynne And Her Band | No Detour Ahead | Muse | MCD 5414
Free
Ornette Coleman Quartet | Beauty Is A Rare Thing:Ornette Coleman-The Complete Atlantic Recordings | Atlantic | 8122-71410-2
Paul Bley Quintet | The Faboulus Paul Bley Quintet | America | AM 6120
Free Above Sea
Benny Golson Sextet With Curtis Fuller | California Message | Timeless | CD SJP 177
Free And Equal
World Saxophone Quartet | Requiem For Julius | Justin Time | JUST 137-2
Free As A Bird
Mike Westbrook Brass Band | The Paris Album | Polydor | 2655008 IMS
Free At Last
Peter Erskine Trio | ELB | ACT | 9289-2
Rusty Bryant Quartet | Fire Eater | Prestige | PCD 10014-2
29th Street Saxophone Quartet | Underground | Antilles | 848415-2(889151)
Free Bop
Götz Tangerding Group | A La Ala - A Voice In Jazz | Bhakti Jazz | BK 22
Free Cell Block F 'Tis Nazi U.S.A.
Steve Lacy-Eric Watson | Spirit Of Mingus | Freelance | FRL-CD 016
Free Energy
Nils Landgren-Esbjörn Svensson | Swedish Folk Modern | ACT | 9428-2
Free Esbjörn
Gerd Dudek-Rob Van Den Broeck-Ali Haurand | After All | Konnex Records | KCD 5022
Free Fall
Harry Sheppard Quintet | This-A-Way That-A-Way | Justice Records | JR 0302-2
Free Flow
Trevor Watts Moiré Music Drum Orchestra | A Wider Embrace | ECM | 1449
Free Flow-
David S. Ware Quartet | Third Ear Recitation | DIW | DIW 870 CD
Free For All
Frank Rosolino Quintet | Free For All | Original Jazz Classics | OJCCD 1763-2
Free For Mandela
Tenor Saxes | Frankfurt Workshop '78:Tenor Saxes | Circle Records | RK 31-24978/31 IMS
Free Form
Ralph Burns And His Orchestra | Ralph Burns Conducts Ralph Burns | Raretone | 5017 FC
Free Forward And Ahead
Joe Sachse | Ballade Für Jimi Metag | Born&Bellmann | 991503 CD
Free Interlude
Tenor Saxes | Frankfurt Workshop '78:Tenor Saxes | Circle Records | RK 31-24978/31 IMS
Free Jazz
Ornette Coleman Double Quartet | Beauty Is A Rare Thing:Ornette Coleman-The Complete Atlantic Recordings | Atlantic | 8122-71410-2
Free Jazz | Atlantic | 7567-81347-2
Free Jazz(alt.take)
Beauty Is A Rare Thing:Ornette Coleman-The Complete Atlantic Recordings | Atlantic | 8122-71410-2
Free Jazz | Atlantic | 7567-81347-2
Free Love
Kevin Harris & Militia | Kevin Harris & Militia | TipToe | TIP-888802 2
Free My Mind
Oscar Klein Band | Pick-A-Blues Live | Jazzpoint | JP 1071
Nils Landgren-Esbjörn Svensson | Swedish Folk Modern | ACT | 9428-2
Free Nils
Noel Akchoté-Marc Ribot-Eugene Chadbourne | Lust Corner | Winter&Winter | 910019-2
Free No.1
Volker Schlott Quartet | The Day Before | Acoustic Music Records | AMC 1026
Free Notes
Kenny Werner Trio | Introducing The Trio | Sunnyside | SSC 1038 D
Free Piece Suit(e)
Lionel Hampton And His Orchestra | The Paris Session 1953 | Vogue | 655609
Free Press Qui
Lionel Hampton:Real Crazy | Vogue | 2113409-2
Free Range
Dizzy Gillespie With The Lalo Schifrin Orchestra | Free Ride | Pablo | 2310794
Free Ride
Jimmy Smith With Orchestra | The Big Brawl | Milan | CD CH 128(883460)
Free Space
Joshua Redman Quartet | Passage Of Time | Warner | 9362-47997-2
Free Speech,Phase 1
Passage Of Time | Warner | 9362-47997-2
Free Speech,Phase 2
Art Porter Group | Straight To The Point | Verve | 517997-2
Free Step
Masabumi Kikuchi Trio | Feel You | Paddle Wheel | KICJ 141
Free Stylin'
Annette Peacock With The Cikada String Quartet | An Acrobat's Heart | ECM | 1733(159496-2)
Free The Memory
Tim Ries Quintet | Universal Spirits | Criss Cross | Criss 1144
Free To Be
Michele Rosewoman And Quintessence | Guardians Of The Light | Enja | ENJ-9378 2
The Steve Davis Project | Quality Of Silence | dmp Digital Music Productions | CD 522
Free Wheelin'
Matalex | Proud | Lipstick Records | LIP 8957-2
Freedom
Hans Koller Big Band | New York City | MPS | 68235
Freedom-
Jerome Richardson Group | Jazz Station Runaway | TCB Records | TCB 97402
Freedom At Midnight
Jessica Williams Quintet | Joy | Jazz Focus | JFCD 014
Freedom Day
Max Roach Group | Live In Europe 1964-Freedom Now Suite | Magnetic Records | MRCD 110
Freedom Delta
Tommy Vig Orchestra | Encounter With Time | Discovery | DS 780 IMS
Freedom Jazz Dance
Big John Patton Quartet | The Organization! The Best Of Big John Patton | Blue Note | 830728-2
Christoph Stiefel Trio | Dream Of The Camel | Enja | 9135-2
Eddie Harris Quartet | Steps Up | Steeplechase | SCCD 31151
Eddie Harris Quintet | Atlantic Saxophones | Rhino | 8122-71256-2
Eddie Jefferson And His Band | Eddie Jefferson:Vocalease | 32 Jazz | 32123
Essence Of Funk | Essence Of Funk | Hip Bop | HIBD 8007
Larry Schneider Trio | Freedom Jazz Dance | Steeplechase | SCCD 31390
Miles Davis Quintet | Miles Davis Quintet 1965-1968 | CBS | C6K 67398
Miroslav Vitous Group | Atlantic Jazz: Fusion | Atlantic | 7567-81711-2
Miroslav Vitous Quintet | Mountain In The Clouds | Atlantic | SD 1622
Passport And Guests | Doldinger Jubilee Concert | Atlantic | 2292-44175-2
Paul Horn Group | A Special Edition | Black Sun Music | 15003-2
Phil Woods And His European Rhythm Machine | Americans Swinging In Paris:Phil Woods | EMI Records | 539654-2
Le Jazz En France-Vol.8 | Pathe | 1727321
Freedom One Day
Mario Pavone Group | Toulon Days | New World Records | 80420-2
Freedom(part 1)
Charles Mingus And His Orchestra | The Complete Town Hall Concert | Blue Note | 828353-2
Freedom(part 2:aka Clark In The Dark)
Karl Berger-Ingrid Sertso Duo | Conversations | IN+OUT Records | 77027-2
Freedom, Getting There
Bob Mintzer Big Band | Departure | dmp Digital Music Productions | CD 493
Freedomland
Rob Van Den Broeck | Ten Piano Players,Vol.1 | Green House Music | CD 1002
Freefair
Rob Van Den Broeck-Wiro Mahieu | Departures | Green House Music | CD 1004
Kenny Barron-Regina Carter | Freefall | Verve | 549706-2
Freefall
Martin Schütz-Hans Koch Group | Approximations | Intakt Records | CD 018
Freepie
Count Basie Group | Basie Jam | Pablo | 2310718-2
Freeport Jump
Count Basie Jam | Montreux '77-The Art Of The Jam Session | Pablo | 2620106
FreeReggaeHiBop
Joe Sachse | Ballade Für Jimi Metag | Born&Bellmann | 991503 CD
Freestyle
Steve Coleman And Metrics | The Way Of The Cipher | Novus | 2131690-2
Steve Coleman's Music Live In Paris | Novus | 2131691-2
Freeway
Bill Smith Quintet | Americans In Europe | Impulse(MCA) | GRP 11502
Freeway-
Freddie King Group | Freddie King Gives You A Bonanza Of Instrumentals | Crosscut | CCR 1010
Freeway Driver
Christoph Spendel Group | Radio Exotic | L+R Records | CDLR 70001
Freewheelin' At Utopia-
Dutch Swing College Band | Dutch Swing College Band Live In 1960 | Philips | 838765-2
Freeze And Melt
The Joint Is Jumpin'! | Timeless | CD TTD 594
Freezoo
Elmo Hope Trio | Trio And Quartet | Blue Note | 784438-2
Freibier Für Alle
Andy Lumpp | Andy Lump Piano Solo | Nabel Records:Jazz Network | LP 4608(Audiophile)
Freigeweht
Bob Cort Skiffle Group | Kings Of Skiffle | Decca | 6.28132 DP
Freight Train
Kenny Burrell-John Coltrane Quintet | Kenny Burrell & John Coltrane | New Jazz | NJSA 8276-2
Kenny Burrell & John Coltrane | Original Jazz Classics | OJC20 300-2
Kevin Bruce Harris Quartet | Folk Songs-Folk Tales | TipToe | TIP-888807 2
Ralph Peterson Quintet | The Art Of War | Criss Cross | Criss 1206
Frelon Brun (Brown Hornet)
Norbert Stein Pata Masters | Blue Slit | Pata Musik | PATA 8 CD
Fremde
Das Pferd | Das Pferd | ITM Records | ITM 1416
French Diary
David Friesen Group | Waterfall Rainbow | Inner City | IC 1027 IMS
French Fries
Christoph Spendel Group | City Kids | TCB Records | TCB 01052
Frenche Spice
Anita O'Day With The Russ Garcia Orchestra | Sings The Winners | Verve | 2304255 IMS
Frenesi
Artie Shaw And His Orchestra | Planet Jazz:Jazz Greatest Hits | Planet Jazz | 2169648-2
This Is Artie Shaw | RCA | NL 89411 DP
Dave Brubeck Quartet | Stardust | Fantasy | FCD 24728-2
Duke Ellington And His Orchestra | Big Band Bounce And Boogie:Classic Transcriptions-Duke Ellington | Affinity | AFS 1032
Les Brown And His Orchestra | The Uncollected:Les Brown, Vol.4 | Hindsight | HSR 199
Stan Kenton And His Orchestra | Stan Kenton In New Jersey | Status | CD 104(882200)
Fresh Impression
Tommy Dorsey And His Orchestra | The Post-War Era | Bluebird | 63 66156-2
Fressn(1)
Kodexx Sentimental | Das Digitale Herz | Poise | Poise 02
Fressn(2)
Marcio Tubino Group | Festa Do Olho | Organic Music | ORGM 9723
Festa Do Olho
Roy Smeck | Roy Smeck Plays Hawaiian Guitar, Banjo, Ukelele And Guitar | Yazoo | YAZ 1052
Freude Am Fahren
Stephan Meinberg VITAMINE | Horizontal | Jazz Haus Musik | JHM 0106 CD
Freuden Der Verweigerung
Markus Stockhausen Quartet | Joyosa | Enja | ENJ-9468 2
Freund
Alfred 23 Harth Group | Gestalt Et Jive | Moers Music | 02038
Frevo
Charlie Haden-Egberto Gismonti | In Montreal | ECM | 1746(543813-2)
Duo Brazil | Carioca | M.A Music | A 808-2
Egberto Gismonti & Academia De Dancas | Sanfona | ECM | 1203/04(829391-2)
Egberto Gismonti With The Lithuanian State Symphony Orchestra | Meeting Point | ECM | 1586(533681-2)
Fred Hersch Group | Forward Motion | Chesky | JD 55
Trio Da Paz With Special Guests | Black Orpheus | Kokopelli Records | KOKO 1299
Frick & Frack
Steve Lacy | Clinkers | Hat Art | F
Frictitious Paragon
James Newton Ensemble | Suite For Frida Kahlo | audioquest Music | AQCD 1023
Friday Nite
Nat Adderley Quintet | Compact Jazz: Cannonball Adderley | EmArCy | 842930-2 PMS
Friday The 13th
Jon Gordon Quartet/Quintet | Along The Way | Criss Cross | Criss 1138
Thelonious Monk And His Orchestra | In Person | Milestone | M 47033
Thelonious Monk-The Complete Riverside Recordings | Riverside | 15 RCD 022-2
Thelonious Monk Quintet | Thelonious Monk/Sonny Rollins | Original Jazz Classics | OJCCD 059-2
Thelonious Monk:The Complete Prestige Recordings | Prestige | 3 PRCD 4428-2
Tommy Flanagan Trio | Something Borrowed Something Blue | Original Jazz Classics | OJCCD 473-2
Friday The 16th
Johnny Coles Quartet | Ballads For Trumpet | Jazz Colours | 874708-2
Fried Bananas
Dexter Gordon Quartet | More Power | Original Jazz Classics | OJC20 815-2(P 7680)
Live At The Amsterdam Paradiso | Affinity | AFF 751
Karl Denson Trio | Karl Denson Trio | Minor Music | 801041
Fried Buzzard
Woody Herman And His Orchestra | 50th Anniversary Tour | Concord | CCD 4302
Fried Pies
Wes Montgomery Trio | Guitar On The Go | Original Jazz Classics | OJCCD 489-2(RLP 9494)
Wes Montgomery-The Complete Riverside Recordings | Riverside | 12 RCD 4408-2
Wes Montgomery-The Complete Riverside Recordings | Riverside | 12 RCD 4408-2
Fried Pies(alt.take)
The Alternative Wes Montgomery | Milestone | MCD 47065-2
Friedhof In Jerusalem-
Rabih Abou-Khalil/Michael Armann Duo | Compositions & Improvisations | MMP-Records | 170857
Friend In The Mirror
Barondown | Crackshot | Avant | AVAN 059
Friend Lee
Lee Konitz With The Oliver Strauch Group & Peter Decker | Lee Konitz With Oliver Strauch Group & Peter Decker | Edition Collage | EC 497-2
Eddie Cleanhead Vinson & Roomful Of Blues | Eddie Cleanhead Vinson & Roomful Of Blues | Muse | MCD 5282
Friendly Fire
Herb Robertson Group | Certified | JMT Edition | 849150-2
Friendly Galaxy No.2
Russell Garcia Orchestra | I Lead A Charmed Life | Discovery | DS 814 IMS
Friendly Persuation
Lem Winchester Sextet | Lem's Beat | Original Jazz Classics | OJCCD 1785-2(NJ 8239)
Friends
Horace Silver Ensemble | Silver 'N Strings Play The Music Of The Spheres | Blue Note | LWB 1033
Joe Venuti Quartet | Happy Joe | Vagabond | 6.23757 AO
Nils Gessinger Orchestra | Ducks 'N' Cookies | GRP | GRP 98302
Friends And Strangers
Phil Nimmons 'N' Nine Plus Six | The Atlantic Suite/Suite P.E.I./Tributes | Sackville | SK2CD-5003
Friends Forever
Peter Finger | Between The Lines | Acoustic Music Records | 319.1079.2
Friends Forever-
Tuck And Patti | Dream | Windham Hill | 34 10130-2
Friends In High Places
Herb Robertson Group | The Little Trumpet | JMT Edition | 919007-2
Friendship
John McLaughlin-Carlos Santana Group | Electric Guitarist | CBS | 467093-2
Louis Jordan And His Tympany Five | Louis Jordan-Let The Good Times Roll: The Complete Decca Recordings 1938-1954 | Bear Family Records | BCD 15557 IH
Marcello Rosa Sextet | The Blue Rose | Penta Flowers | CDPIA 015
Friesel
Mathias Demoulin-Claude Buri Group | Minging | Jazz Pure Collection | AU 31607 CD
Frim Fram Sauce
Eddie Locke Group | Jivin' With The Refuges From Hastings Street | Chiaroscuro | CR 2007
Les Brown And His Orchestra | Les Brown And His Orchestra 1944 & 1946 | Circle | CCD-90
Nat King Cole Trio | The Small Black Groups | Storyville | 4960523
The Forgotten Years | Giants Of Jazz | GOJ 1013
Frisky
Onix | Stress | Fresh Sound Records | FSR 104 (835273)
Frizz
John Tchicai | Live In Athens | Praxis | CM 101
Frockles
Ben Webster Quintet | The Big 3 | CBS | AK 40950
Frog Dance
Johnny Rondo Duo Plus Mike Cooper | Johnny Rondo Duo Plus Mike Cooper | FMP | SAJ 29
Frog Legs
Sonny Thompson And His Orchestra | Cat On The Keys | Swingtime(Contact) | ST 1027
Frog Me
Liz Story Group | Speechless | RCA | PL 83037
Frog Songs
Bill Connors | Swimming With A Hole In My Body | ECM | 1158
Frog Stroke
Lovie Austin And Her Serenaders | Johnny Dodds Vol.2 | Village(Jazz Archive) | VILCD 017-2
Froggie Moore
Jelly Roll Morton | Jelly Roll Morton-24 Rare Recordings Of Piano Solos 1923-1926 | Retrieval | RTR 79002
King Oliver's Creole Jazz Band | Louis Armstrong With King Oliver Vol.1 | Village(Jazz Archive) | VILCD 003-2
Frog-I-More
Bob Schulz And His Frisco Jazz Band | Thanks Turk! | Stomp Off Records | CD 1288
Frog's Legs
Keith Foley | Music For Christmas | dmp Digital Music Productions | CD 452
Fröhliche Weihnacht Überall
Eric St-Laurent-Thomy Jordi-Thomas Alkier feat. Helge Schneider | Rock,Jazz & Music:Laut! | BIT | 11212
From A Little Acorns
Wayne Krantz Trio | Long To Be Loose | Enja | ENJ-7099 2
From A Little Croaking Sound
John Patitucci Group | Sketchbook | GRP | GRP 96172
From A Rainy Night
Al Cohn-Zoot Sims Quintet | From A To Z | RCA | 2147790-2
From A To Z
Dave Frishberg Quintet | Let's Eat Home | Concord | CCD 4402
From Anywhere To Somewhere
Vera Guimaraes Group | Stirring The Forest | West Wind Latina | 2202 CD
From Bechet,Fats And Byas
Roland Kirk Quartet | Rip Rig And Panic/Now Please Don't You Cry Beautiful Edith | EmArCy | 832164-2 PMS
From Boogie To Funk(part 1)
Bill Coleman Septet | Jazz In Paris:Bill Coleman-From Boogie To Funk | EmArCy | 549401-2 PMS
From Boogie To Funk(part 2)
Bill Coleman And His Orchestra | From Boogie To Funk | Polydor | 2445035 IMS
From Branch To Branch
Andrew Hill | From California With Love | Artists House | AH 9 IMS
From Coast To Coast
Malcolm Goldstein-Peter Niklas Wilson | Goldstein-Wilson | true muze | TUMU CD 9801
From 'Configurations In Darkness'
Mal Waldron-Nicolas Simion | Art Of The Duo:The Big Rochade | Tutu Records | 888186-2*
From Dark Into The Light
Mal Waldron Trio | Soul Eyes | RCA | 2153887-2
From Dipper To Satchmo
Lucky Thompson And His Lucky Seven | Esquire's All-American Hot Jazz Sessions | RCA | ND 86757
From Four Till Late
Gianlugi Trovesi Quartet With The WDR Big Band | Dedalo | Enja | ENJ-9419 2
From G To G

TITELVERZEICHNIS

Esbjörn Svensson Trio(E.S.T.) | Est-From Gagarin's Point Of View | ACT | 9005-2

From Gagarin's Point Of View
Tomasz Stanko Quartet | Almost Green | Leo Records | 008

From Loosened Soil
Thomas Sliomis/Daunik Lazro Duo | Phonorama | Praxis | GM 1002

From Me To You
Chris Barber's Jazz Band | Chris Barber Special | Black Lion | 157004

From Mexico To Bali
Buster Benton Blues Band | Blues At The Top | Black & Blue | BLE 59.001 2

From Monday On
Temperance Seven | The Writing On The Wall | Upbeat Jazz | URCD 108

From Now On
Jim Hall Trio Feat. Tom Harrell | These Roots | Denon Compact Disc | CY-30002

From Now On(We're One)
Barbara Thompson's Paraphernalia | Live In Concert | MCA | 2292-50425-1

From Ocean To The Clouds-
Nelson Rangell Group | Playing For Keeps | GRP | GRP 95932

From Russia With Love
Gary McFarland Orchestra | Soft Samba | Verve | MV 2102 IMS

From Stockholm To Bejing
Michele Rosewoman Quintet | Harvest | Enja | ENJ-7069 2

From Tear To Here
Die Elefanten | Wasserwüste | Nabel Records:Jazz Network | CD 4634

From The Beginning
Jo Swan And Her Quartet | Primal Schmaltz | Timbre | TRCD 004

From The Body
Trine-Lise Vaering With The Bobo Stenson Trio And Guests | When I Close My Eyes | Stunt Records | STUCD 19602

From The Bottom
Zbigniew Namyslowski-Remy Filipovitch Quintet | Go! | Album | AS 66919 CD

From The Bottom Drawer
Harry James And His Orchestra | Harry James & His Orchestra Feat.Frank Sinatra | CBS | CK 66377

From The Chalk Cliffs
Diamond, Angel & Crooks | More Where That Came From | Intuition Records | INT 3061-2

From The Distance
Taj Mahal Group | Conjure | American Clave | AMCL 1006-2

From The Green Hill - ...From The Green Hill
Greg Abate Quintet | Dr. Jeckyll & Mr. Hyde | Candid | CCD 79715

From The Heart
Jack DeJohnette Quartet | Oneness | ECM | 1637(537343-2)
Jim McNeely Trio | From The Heart | Owl Records | 045 CD

From The Hot Afternoon
Paul Desmond Quartet With The Don Sebesby Orchestra | From The Hot Afternoon | Verve | 543487-2

From The Hot Afternoon(alt.take 1)
From The Hot Afternoon | Verve | 543487-2

From The Hot Afternoon(alt.take 2)
Steve Davis Sextet | Crossfire | Criss Cross | Criss 1152

From The Love Of A Woman
Zbigniew Namyslowski-Remy Filipovitch Quintet | Go! | Album | AS 66919 CD

From The Other Side
Jack McDuff Orchestra | Write On, Capt'n | Concord | CCD 4568

From The Second Shelf
Buddy Rich And His Orchestra | Compact Jazz: Buddy Rich | Verve | 823295-2 PMS

From The Window-
Triocolor | Colours Of Ghana | ACT | 9285-2

From The Wizard
Jimmy Giuffre-Lee Konitz | Giuffre/Konitz/Connors/Bley | Improvising Artists Inc. | 123859-2

From This Moment On
Chris Connor With The Herbie Mann Septet | This Is Chris | CTI Records | PDCTI 1127-2
Cy Coleman Trio | Cy Coleman | Fresh Sound Records | FSR 635(Seeco CELP 402)
Ella Fitzgerald With The Buddy Bregman Orchestra | The Cole Porter Song Book | Verve | 2683044 IMS
Love Songs:The Best Of The Song Books | Verve | 531762-2
The Complete Ella Fitzgerald Song Books of Harold Arlen, Irving Berlin, Duke Ellington, George & Ira Gershwin, Jerome Kern, Johnny Mercer, Cole Porter And Rogers & Hart | Verve | 519832-2
John Jenkins Quintet | John Jenkins | Blue Note | 300181(1573)
Jonah Jones Quartet | Jonah Jones At The Embers | RCA | 2118523-2
Manfred Junker Quartet | Cole Porter-Live! | Edition Collage | EC 531-2
Marion McPartland Trio | From This Moment On | Concord | CJ 86
Sarah Vaughan And The Count Basie Orchestra | Send In The Clowns | Pablo | 2312130-2
Weslia Whitefield With The Mike Greensill Quartet | High Standards | HighNote Records | HCD 7025

From Time To Time
Paul Motian Trio | Motian In Tokyo | JMT Edition | 849154-2
Daniel Humair Sextet | 9.11 pm Town Hall | Label Bleu | LBLC 6517(881628)

From Uganda
Joe Zawinul Group | Concerto Retitled | Atlantic | SD 1694

Frosty
Clarence Gatemouth Brown Band | Alright Again! | Edsel | Fiend 2

Frozen Footsteps
Edward Vesala Group | Lumi | ECM | 1339

Frozen Melody
Andy Laverne Quartet | Frozen Music | Steeplechase | SCCD 31244

Frozen Sun
Gene Ammons And His Orchestra | Free Again | Prestige | P 10040

Frühling,Sommer,Herbst
Ulli Bögershausen | Best Of Ulli Bögershausen | Laika Records | LK 93-045
String Thing | String Thing:Turtifix | MicNic Records | MN 4

Frühlingsvorhersage
Don Weller Spring Quartet | Commit No Nuisance | Affinity | AFF 44

Fruit Of The Bottom
Ed Frank Quintet | New New Orleans Music: Jump Jazz | Line Records | COCD 9.00916 O

Fruitcase
Tummy Young's Big Seven | The Classic Swing Of Buck Clayton | Original Jazz Classics | OJCCD 1709-2(RLP 142)

Frustration
Duke Ellington And His Orchestra | Duke Ellington:Complete Studio Transcriptions | Definitive Records | DRCD 11199

FS Five
Craig Harris Group | F-Stops | Soul Note | 121255-2

Fuchsia Swing Song
Sam Rivers Quartet | A Blue Conception | Blue Note | 534254-2
Batman | Naked City | Nonesuch | 7559-79238-2

Fuck The Facts
Wollie Kaiser Timeghost | Tust Du Fühlen Gut | Jazz Haus Musik | JHM 0060 CD

Fuckin' You Know Man
Om | Jazz In Switzerland 1930-1975 | Elite Special | 9544002/1-4

Fue
Buster Williams Trio | Tokudo | Denon Compact Disc | DC-8549

Fuga
Viktoria Tabatchnikowa-Eugenij Belov | Troika | ALISO Records | AL 1036
Yosuke Yamashita New York Trio | Wind Of The Age | Verve | 557008-2

Fuga in e-Moll(Bach BWV 548)
Pierre Favre | Solo Now | MPS | 68067

Fugato
Heiner Goebbels-Alfred Harth Duo | Hommage/Vier F uste FÄr Hans Eisler | FMP | SAJ 08

Fughata For Harpsichord
Bob Florence And His Orchestra | Here And Now | Fresh Sound Records | 054 2607951(Liberty)

Fugitive Fandangos
Anthony Davis Sextet | Variations In Dream-Time | India Navigation | IN 1056

Fuglsang
Jacques Loussier Trio | Play Bach No.2 | Accord | 500182

Fugue-
Stan Kenton And His Orchestra | A Concert In Progressive Jazz | Creative World | ST 1037

Fugue from Concert Op.3 No.11 in D Minor(Vivaldi)
Swingle Singers | Swingle Singers Singing Mozart | Philips | 548538-2

Fugue from Sonata for Violin and Piano in A Major (KV 402)
Modern Jazz Quartet And Laurindo Almeida | Collaboration | Philips | 30JD-10093 PMS

Fugue In A Minor
Dave Brubeck Octet | The Dave Brubeck Octet | Original Jazz Classics | OJCCD 101-2(F 3239)

Fugue In Bop Themes
Ketil Bjornstad | The Bach Variations | EmArCy | 017267-2

Fugue In C Sharp Minor(BWV 849)
Swingle Singers | Jazz Sebastian Bach | Philips | 542552-2

Fugue In D Minor(BWV 1080)
Swingling Telemann | Philips | 586735-2

Fugue In D Minor(Georg Muffat)
Jazz Sebastian Bach Vol.2 | Philips | 542553-2

Fugue In G Major(BWV 541)
Kenny Burrell Quintet | Introducing Kenny Burrell | Blue Note | 300104(1523)

Fugue No.1 In C Major(BWV 846)
Jacques Loussier Trio | Play Bach No.2 | Decca | 157562-2

Fugue No.1 In G Minor(BWV 861)
David Matthews & The Manhattan Jazz Orchestra | Back To Bach | Milestone | MCD 9312-2

Fugue No.2
Jacques Loussier Trio | Play Bach No.1 | Decca | 157561-2

Fugue No.2 In C Minor(BWV 847)
Swingle Singers | Jazz Sebastian Bach | Philips | 542552-2

Fugue No.2 In C Minor(BWV 871)
Jazz Sebastian Bach Vol.2 | Philips | 542553-2

Fugue No.21 In B Flat Major(BWV 866)
Jacques Loussier Trio | Jacques Loussier Plays Bach | Telarc Digital | CD 83411

Fugue No.5 In D Major(BWV 850)
Swingle Singers | Jazz Sebastian Bach | Philips | 542552-2
Jazz Sebastian Bach | Philips | 542552-2

Fugue No.5 In D Major(BWV 874)
Hank Jones With Oliver Nelson's Orchestra | Happenings | Impulse(MCA) | JAS 61(AS 9132)

Fugue-A-Ditty-
Duke Ellington And His Orchestra | Duke Ellington:Complete Prestige Carnegie Hall 1946-1947 Concerts | Definitive Records | DRCD 11211

Fugue'n And Alludin'
Roland Kirk Quintet | Rahsaan/The Complete Mercury Recordings Of Roland Kirk | Mercury | 846630-2
Wollie Kaiser Timeghost | Tust Du Fühlen Gut | Jazz Haus Musik | JHM 0060 CD

Fühlgut
Jiri Stivin-Ali Haurand | Just The Two Of Us | Konnex Records | KCD 5095

Fuhrmann
Renaud Garcia-Fons Group | Navigatore | Enja | ENJ-9418 2

Fui Piedra
Alain Goraguer Orchestra | Jazz In Paris | EmArCy | 548793-2

Fuite Du Rouquin
Jan Jankeje Mlada Muzika | Sokol | Jazzpoint | 1002

Fuji
Céline Rudolph And Her Trio | Paintings | Nabel Records:Jazz Network | CD 4661

Fuji Colors
Milt Jackson-Ray Brown Quintet | Fuji Mama | West Wind | WW 2054

Fulano De Tal...
McCoy Tyner Quintet | Asante | Blue Note | 493384-2

Fulfilment
Edward Vesala Nordic Gallery | Sound & Fury | ECM | 1541

Fulflandia
Oliver Jones Quintet | Lights Of Burgundy | Justin Time | Just 6

Full Circle
Jackie And Roy | Full Circle | Contemporary | CCD 14046-2
Oregon | Our First Record | Vanguard | 62162

Full Deep And Mellow
Hamiet Bluiett | Walkin' & Talkin' | Tutu Records | 888172-2*

Full Deep And Mellow-
Choo Choo Light:Stammberger-Rädler-Schöne | Choo Choo Light | G.N.U. Records | CD A 92.007

Full English Breakfast
Ian Carr Sextet | Old Heartland | MMC | 7910712

Full Force
Roscoe Mitchell | Sound Songs | Delmark | DE 493(2)

Full House
Wes Montgomery Quintet | Full House | Original Jazz Classics | OJC20 106-2
Red Sun/SamulNori | Then Comes The White Tiger | ECM | 1499

Full House(part 1)
Then Comes The White Tiger | ECM | 1499

Full House(part 2)
Eric Watson Quartet | Full Metal Quartet | Owl Records | 159572-2

Full Metal Quartet
Ahmad Khatab Salim And His Orchestra | Blues Suite | Savoy | SV 0142(MG 12132)

Full Moon
Magnus' Trio | Dangerous Game | Mikado Records | MK 94-209
Olivier Peters Quartet Feat.Joan Johnson | Wings Of Spring | Village Music | VM 1002
Steve Slagle Quartet | Alto Blue | Steeplechase | SCCD 31416

Full Moon Dogs
Peter Materna Quartet | Full Moon Party | Village | VILCD 1021-2

Full Moon Party
Peggy Lee With The Benny Goodman Orchestra | Peggy Lee & Benny Goodman:The Complete Recordings 1941-1947 | CBS | C2K 65686

Full Moon(Noche De Luna)
Sidsel Endresen-Bugge Wesseltoft | Nightsong | ACT | 9004-2

Full Moon-High Noon
Miles Davis Group | Miles Davis Live From His Last Concert In Avignon | Laserlight | 24327

Full Nelson
Tutu | Warner | 7599-25490-2
Time After Time | Jazz Door | JD 1256/57

Fuller & Fuller
Cannonball Adderley Quintet | Cannonball's Sharpshooters | Mercury | 826986-2 PMS

Fuller Bop Man
Cannonball's Sharpshooters | Mercury | 826986-2 PMS

Fuller Bop Man(alt.take)
Art Blakey And The Jazz Messengers | Keystone 3 | Concord | CJ 196

Fuller Love
Art Collection-The Best Of Art Blakey And The Jazz Messengers | Concord | CCD 4495

Fullmoon(in Fuhlsbüttel)
Keith Jarrett Group | Treasure Island | MCA | 2292-54623-2

Fully Mechanized Peaks
Irene Schweizer/Pierre Favre | Irene Schweizer & Pierre Favre | Intakt Records | CD 009

Fum Fum Fum
Cannonball Adderley Quintet | Mercy Mercy Mercy | Capitol | 829915-2

Fun
Clifford Jordan Quartet | Repetition | Soul Note | 121084-2
Modern Jazz Quartet feat.Jimmy Giuffre | MJQ 40 | Atlantic | 7567-82330-2
The MJQ At Music Inn | Atlantic | 90049-1 TIS

Fun For
Kenny Clarke And His Orchestra | Kenny Clarke | Swing | SW 8411 IMS

Fun In The Church
Gary Meek Groups | Gary Meek | Lipstick Records | LIP 890032

Fun In The Sun
Lee Konitz Quartet | Haiku | Nabel Records:Jazz Network | CD 4664

Fun Keys
Delle-Bätzel-Bätzel-Seidel-Schlüter | Wherever You've Gone | Wonderland Records | WR 005

Fun Ride
Warren Bernhardt Trio | Warren Bernhardt Trio | dmp Digital Music Productions | CD 441

Fun Time
Count Basie And His Orchestra | Basie-Straight Ahead | Dot | DLP 25902
Warren Bernhardt Quintet | Handsn | dmp Digital Music Productions | CD 457

Funambule
Bobby Watson & Open Form Trio | Appointment In Milano | Red Records | VPA 184

Functional
Thelonious Monk | Thelonious Himself | Original Jazz Classics | OJCCD 254-2
Thelonious Monk-The Complete Riverside Recordings | Riverside | 15 RCD 022-2

Functional(alt.take)
Thelonious Monk-The Complete Riverside Recordings | Riverside | 15 RCD 022-2
Pure Monk | Milestone | M 47004

Funcused Blues
Ax Genrich Group | Wave Cut | ATM Records | ATM 3813-AH

Fundador
Art Ensemble Of Chicago And The Amabutho Male Chorus | Art Ensemble Of (Chicago) Soweto | DIW | DIW 837 CD

Funebre
Christian Willisohn New Band | Heart Broken Man | Blues Beacon | BLU-1026 2

Funeral
Moscow Art Trio | Music | JA & RO | JARO 4214-2
Pau Brasil | La Vem A Tribo | GHA Records | CD 126.005

Funeral Dance(Dar Kpee)
Uri Caine Group | Urlicht/Primal Light | Winter&Winter | 910004-2

Funeral March(from Symphny No.5)
Kamikaze Ground Crew | The Scenic Route | New World Records | 80400-2

Funeral Procession
The Scenic Route | New World Records | 80400-2

Funeral Song
Sebastian Gramss Underkarl | Jazzscene | TCB Records | TCB 99102

Fünfunddreissig
Rüdiger Carl-Sven-Ake Johansson | Fünfunddreißigvierzig | FMP | 1080

Fünfundsiebzig
Christopher Dell D.R.A. | Future Of The Smallest Form | Jazz 4 Ever Records:Jazz Network | J4E 4754

Fünfundvierzig
Stephan Froleyks | Fine Music With New Instruments | Jazz Haus Musik | JHM 0094 CD

Fünfzig Messer
Pekka's Tube Factory | Pekka's Tube Factory | Naxos Jazz | 86028-2

Funji Mama
Monty Alexander Trio | Live In Holland | Verve | 835627-2 PMS

Funk Dem Dudu
Finküberthurm | Fink Über Thurm | Jazz Haus Musik | JHM 44 CD

Funk In Deep Freeze
Chet Baker Quartet | Last Recording As Quartet(Live in Rosenheim '88) | Timeless | CD SJP 233
John Zorn-George Lewis-Bill Frisell | News For Lulu | Hat Art | CD 6005
Philip Catherine Trio | I Remember You | Criss Cross | Criss 1048

Funk In Spain
Mike Clark-Paul Jackson Quartet | The Funk Stops Here | TipToe | TIP-888811 2

Funk Is...Bill Doggett
King Pleasure With The Quincy Jones Band | Annie Ross & King Pleasure Sings | Original Jazz Classics | OJC 217(P 7128)

Funk Underneath
Roland Kirk-Jack McDuff Quartet | Pre-Rahsan | Prestige | P 24080

Funkallero
Bud Shank Quartet | Bud Shank Plays The Music Of Bill Evans | Fresh Sound Records | FSR-CD 5012
David Benoit Group | Waiting For Spring | GRP | GRP 95952
Stan Getz With The Bill Evans Trio | The Chick Corea-Bill Evans Sessions | Verve | 2610036
But Beautiful | Jazz Door | JD 1208
Ultimate Bill Evans selected by Herbie Hancock | Verve | 557536-2
Stan Getz-Bill Evans Quartet | Stan Getz & Bill Evans | Verve | 833802-2
Stan Getz With The Bill Evans Trio | The Complete Bill Evans On Verve | Verve | 527953-2

Funkallero(rehersal fragments)
Babamadu | Babamadu | Enja | 9093-2

Funkorific
Nguyen Le Group | Maghreb And Friends | ACT | 9261-2

FunkRai
Jimmy Smith Sextet | A Date With Jimmy Smith Vol.1 | Blue Note | 300148(1547)

Funky 94
Jimmy McGriff Orchestra | City Lights | JAM | 002 IMS

Funky AECO
Memphis Slim | Boogie Woogie | Accord | 402472

Funky Blues
Norman Granz Jam Session | Bird: The Complete Charlie Parker On Verve | Verve | 837141-2
Charlie Parker:The Best Of The Verve Years | Verve | 527815-2
Charlie Parker Jam Session | Verve | 833564-2 PMS

Funky Bob
Chris McGregor's Brotherhood Of Breath | Liv At Willisau | Ogun | OGCD 001

Funky Broadway
Jimmy Smith Quartet | Jimmy Smith-Talkin' Verve | Verve | 531563-2
Jimmy Smith:Best Of The Verve Years | Verve | 527950-2
Poncho Sanchez And His Orchestra | A Night At Kimball's East | Concord | CCD 4472

Funky Donkey
Luther Thomas Creative Ensemble | Funky Donkey | Circle Records | RK 15-1977/15 IMS

Funky Eaeco
Gadzho | Caffe Freddo | Meilton | 1617

Funky Flamenco
Eddie Lockjaw Davis Quartet | All Of Me | Steeplechase | SCCD 31186

Funky Fluke
Johnny Griffin-Eddie Lockjaw Davis Quintet | Tough Tenors | Original Jazz Classics | OJCCD 1094-2(JLP 931)
Gunter Hampel Quartet | Time Is Now-Live At The Eldena Jazz Festival 1992 | Birth | CD 042

Funky Get Down
Gunter Hampel Trio | Companion | Birth | 0036
Reunion | Flight Charts And Plans | Blue Flame | 40242(2132481-2)

Funky Good Time-
Maceo Parker Group | Maceo(Soundtrack) | Minor Music | 801046
The Jeff Lorber Fusion | Fusion | Inner City | IC 1026 IMS

Funky Hotel Blues
Gottfried Böttger-Reiner Regel Duo | Reedin' Piano | L+R Records | CDLR 40034

Funky London
James Blood Ulmer-George Adams Phalanx | Got Something Good For You | Moers Music | 02046 CD
Funky Mama
Florian Poser | Winds | Edition Collage | EC 500-2
Funky Marimba
Pata Horns | New Archaic Music | Pata Musik | PATA 4(JHM 42) CD
Funky Rabbits
Soul Rebels | Let Your Mind Be Free | Mardi Gras Records | MG 1020
Funky Sea, Funky Dew
Howard McGhee-Benny Bailey Sextet | Home Run | Storyville | SLP 4082
Funky Stuff
Heiner Franz & Friends | Let's Have A Ball | Jardis Records | JRCD 20030
Funky Sweet
Sultans Of Swing | This Joint Is Jumping | Mons Records | MR 874319
Funky Tonk
James Rivers Groups | The Best Of New Orleans Rhythm & Blues Vol.3 | Mardi Gras Records | MG 9009
Funky Waltz
Larry Coryell Quintet | The Coryells | Chesky | JD 192
Funny
Marcus Miller Group | Live & More | Dreyfus Jazz Line | FDM 36585-2
Marie Bergman And The Danish Radio Big Band | But Beautiful | Stunt Records | STUCD 19404
Nat King Cole And His Trio With Pete Rugolo's Orchestra | Lush Life | Capitol | 780595-2
Funny Blues
Bill Watrous And His West Coast Friends | Art Pepper:The Hollywood All-Star Sessions | Galaxy | 5GCD 4431-2
Funny Blues(alt.take)
Robert Lockwood Jr. | Contrasts | Trix Records | TRIX 3307
Funny Face
Ella Fitzgerald With The Nelson Riddle Orchestra | Ella Sings Gershwin-Vol. 1 | Metro | 2682004 IMS
Funny Feathers Man
Blind Boy Fuller | Truckin' My Blues Away | Yazoo | YAZ 1060
Funny Funny
James Mason Group | Rhythm Of Life | Chiaroscuro | CR 189
Funny Glasses & A Moustache
Mal Waldron Quartet feat.Jim Pepper | Quadrologue At Utopia Vol.1 | Tutu Records | 888118-2*
Cowws Quintet plus Guests | Book/Virtual Cowws | FMP | OWN-90007/9
Funny How
Stanley Clarke Group | If This Bass Could Only Talk | CBS | 460883-2
Funny How Time Flies(When You're Having Fun)
Ernestine Anderson With The Johnnie Scott Orchestra | Miss Ernestine Anderson | Pathe | 1566121(Columbia SX 6145)
Funny How Time Slips Away
Bill Evans | The Complete Bill Evans On Verve | Verve | 527953-2
Funny Man
Further Conversations With Myself | Verve | 559832-2
Mongo Santamaria Orchestra | The Watermelon Man | Milestone | M 47012
Funny Story
Dinah Washington With Orchestra | In Tribute... | Fresh Sound Records | FSR 628(Roulette R 25244)
Funny Thing
Michele Hendricks And Her Trio | Me And My Shadow | Muse | MCD 5404
Funny(All She Needs Is Love)
Diane Schuur And Her Band | Talkin' 'Bout You | GRP | GRP 95672
Funnybird Song
Carla Bley Group | Tropic Appetites | Watt | 1
Freddie King Group | Freddie King Gives You A Bonanza Of Instrumentals | Crosscut | CCR 1010
Funqui's Blues
Magma Trio | Urgente | yvp music | CD 3045
Fupsi
Naßler & Schneider feat. Jörg Ritter | Triologe | Acoustic Music Records | 319.1137.2
Für Den Vater
Peter Finger | Niemandsland | Acoustic Music Records | AMC 1001
Für Eine Nacht Voller Seligkeit
Jenny Evans And Her Quintet | Gonna Go Fishin' | ESM Records | ESM 9307
Gonna Go Fishin' | Enja | ENJ-9403 2
Jan Zemen | Boogie Woogie And Ragtime Piano Contest | Gold Records | 11034 AS
Für Elise
Kenny Werner | Meditations | Steeplechase | SCCD 31327
Für Glenn Gould
Martin Theurer | Moon Mood | FMP | 0700
Für Immer Steif(1)
Kölner Saxophon Mafia | Licence To Thrill | Jazz Haus Musik | JHM 0100 CD
Für Immer Steif(2)
Licence To Thrill | Jazz Haus Musik | JHM 0100 CD
Für Immer Steif(3)
Licence To Thrill | Jazz Haus Musik | JHM 0100 CD
Für Immer Steif(4)
Licence To Thrill | Jazz Haus Musik | JHM 0100 CD
Für Immer Steif(5)
Licence To Thrill | Jazz Haus Musik | JHM 0100 CD
Für Immer Steif(6)
Percussion Duo | Percussion Duo-First Of April | Moers Music | 01050
Für Meine Söhne
Evelyn Huber-Mulo Franzl | Rendezvous | Edition Collage | EC 512-2
Für Mich Soll's Rote Rosen Regnen
Ingolf Burkhardt-Ludwig Nuß Quintet | Jazzed Friends | Mons Records | MR 874780
Furry Sings The Blues
Furry Lewis | In His Prime 1927-1928 | Yazoo | YAZ 1050
Furs On Ice
John Abercrombie-Marc Johnson-Peter Erskine | John Abercrombie/Marc Johnson/Peter Erskine | ECM | 1390(837756-2)
Alfred 23 Harth-Lindsey Cooper | Plan Eden | Creative Works Records | CW LP 1008
Further Away
Jane Ira Bloom Sextet | Art And Aviation | Arabesque Recordings | AJ 0107
Furthermore
Herbie Nichols Trio | Herbie Nichols:The Complete Blue Note Recordings | Blue Note | 859352-2
Furthermore(alt.take 1)
Herbie Nichols:The Complete Blue Note Recordings | Blue Note | 859352-2
Furthermore(alt.take 2)
8 Bold Souls | Ant Farm | Arabesque Recordings | AJ 0114
Fuse Blues
Alex Gunia's Groove Cut | Alex Gunia's Groove Cut | ITM Records | ITM 1463
Fusion De Souvenirs
Eddie Harris Quartet | Listen Here! | Enja | 7079-2
Futile Frustration
Count Basie And His Orchestra | Masters Of Jazz Vol.5 | RCA | NL 89530 DP
Future Child
Wayne Darling Group | The Art Of The Bass Vol.1 | Laika Records | 35101652
Niels-Henning Orsted-Pedersen And The Danish Radio Big Band | Ambiance | dacapo | DCCD 9417
Future Child-
Tim Hagans With Norrbotten Big Band | Future Miles | ACT | 9235-2
Future Cool
Christian Elsässer Trio | Future Days | Organic Music | ORGM 9721
Future Days
Vince Jones Group | Future Girl | Intuition Records | INT 3109-2
Future Girl
Trilok Gurtu Group | The Glimpse | CMP Records | CMP CD 85
Future Plans
Joe McPhee Po Music | Oleo & A Future Retrospective | Hat Art | 3514
Futurism 1
Hans Lüdemann Rism 7 | FutuRISM | Jazz Haus Musik | JHM 0092/93 CD
Futurism 10(Malawi)
FutuRISM | Jazz Haus Musik | JHM 0092/93 CD
Futurism 2(Mysterious Call)
FutuRISM | Jazz Haus Musik | JHM 0092/93 CD
Futurism 3(The Mism Rism)
FutuRISM | Jazz Haus Musik | JHM 0092/93 CD
Futurism 4(No Hau)
FutuRISM | Jazz Haus Musik | JHM 0092/93 CD
Futurism 5(Das Wahre Clavier)
FutuRISM | Jazz Haus Musik | JHM 0092/93 CD
Futurism 6(Schöne Neue Welt)
FutuRISM | Jazz Haus Musik | JHM 0092/93 CD
Futurism 7(Wilde Augen)
Wilton Crawley And His Orchestra | The Complete Jelly Roll Morton-Vol.5/6 | RCA | 2126410-2
Fuzz
Ornette Coleman Trio | Who's Crazy? | Affinity | AFF 102 D
Fuzz Junk
George Duke Group | Night After Night | Elektra | 7559-60778-2
Fuzzy Blues(take 1)
Paul Bley | Synth Thesis | Postcards | POST 1001
G And B
Pete Johnson | Boogie Woogie Trio | Storyville | SLP 4094
G Flat Theme
Joe Van Enkhuizen Quartet | Ellington My Way | Timeless | CD SJP 419
G Minor Complex
Irene Schweizer Trio | Messer | FMP | 0290
G Waltz
Bill Evans Trio | The Complete Bill Evans On Verve | Verve | 527953-2
The Complete Bill Evans On Verve | Verve | 527953-2
G Waltz(2)
The Complete Bill Evans On Verve | Verve | 527953-2
G Waltz(3)
The Complete Bill Evans On Verve | Verve | 527953-2
G Waltz(4)
Anthony Ortega Trio | New Dance! | Hat Art | CD 6065
G.I.Jive
Woody Herman And His Orchestra | Old Gold Rehearsals 1944 | Jazz Unlimited | JUCD 2079
The Radio Years: Woody Herman And His First Herd 1944 | Hindsight | HSR 134
G.S.S.
Ron Carter Orchestra | Parade | Original Jazz Classics | OJCCD 1047-2(M 9088)
G.T J.
Earl Hines And His Orchestra | Planet Jazz:Earl Hines | Planet Jazz | 2159973-2
G.T. Stomp
Jazz Drumming Vol.4(1939) | Fenn Music | FJD 2704
G.T.B.
Moments Quartet | Original Moments | Fresh Sound Records | FSNT 052 CD
Air | Air Time | Nessa | N 12
G.W.
Eric Dolphy Quintet | Dash One | Prestige | MPP 2517
Berlin Concerts | Enja | 3007/9-2
Eric Dophy Quintet | Live At Gaslight Inn | Ingo | 14
G/Soxx
Charlie Barnet Band | The Small Groups | Laserlight | 15764
Ga Gang Gang Gong
Marilyn Mazur With Ars Nova And The Copenhagen Art Ensemble | Jordsange | dacapo | DCCD 9454
Ga!(Go!)
Duo/Trio/Quartet/Quintet | Canaille-International Women's Festival Of Improvised Music | Intakt Records | 002
Gabriel Kondor
Erskine Hawkins And His Orchestra | From Alabama To Harlem | Black & Blue | BLE 59.236 2
Gaby
Urszula Dudziak | Heritage | MPS | 68182
Gaderne(My Mystery)
Avishai Cohen Group | Adama | Stretch Records | SCD 9015-2
Gage Flips
Italian Vocal Ensemble | The Razor's Edge | SPLASC(H) Records | H 163
Gaia
Sandor Szabo | Gaia And Aries | Acoustic Music Records | 319.1146.2
Gal From Joe's
Charlie Barnet And His Orchestra | Dance Bash | Verve | 2304541 IMS
Gal In Calico
Oscar Peterson Trio | Verve Jazz Masters 16:Oscar Peterson | Verve | 516320-2
Art Ensemble Of Chicago | Naked | DIW | DIW 818 CD
Galactic Landscape
Pete York-Wolfgang Schmid-Lenny MacDowell | Wireless | BELL Records | BLR 84032
Galata Bridge
Cootie Williams And His Orchestra | Duke Ellington's Trumpets | Black & Blue | BLE 59.231 2
Galaxia
Gunter Hampel Trio | Waltz For 3 Universes In A Corridor | Birth | 0010
Galerie Des Princes
Philip Catherine Trio With Guests | Transparence | Inak | 8701
Gallop's Gallop
Steve Lacy | Interpertations Of Monk | DIW | DIW 395/8 CD
Ulf Adaker Quartet | Reflections | Touché Music | TMcCD 016
Kid Thomas And His Algiers Stompers | New Orleans-The Living Legends:Kid Thomas And His Algier Stompers | Original Jazz Classics | OJCCD 1833-2
Galopera
Paul Quinichette And His Orchestra | The Vice Pres | Verve | 543750-2
Gamalong
Tony Scott & The Indonesian All Stars | Jazz Meets Asia:Sakura Sakura-Jazz Meets India-Djanger Bali | MPS | 533132-2
Gambler's Blues(St.James Infirmary)
Hociel Thomas With Mutt Carey | Mutt Carey And Lee Collins | American Music | AMCD-72
Gambler's Dream
Helmut Kagerer 4 & Roman Schwaller | Gamblin' | Jardis Records | JRCD 9714
Gamblin'
Eddie Playboy Taylor & The Blueshounds | Ready For Eddie | Big Bear | 146407
Gamblin' Man
Staple Singers | Great Day | Milestone | MCD 47027-2
Game
Peter Bolte Trio | Trio | Jazz Haus Musik | JHM 0095 CD
Woody Shaw Quintet | Lotus Flower | Enja | 4018-2
Games
Chick Corea Trio | A.R.C. | ECM | 1009
Dave Holland Trio | Triplicate | ECM | 1373
David Kikoski Trio | Almost Twilight | Criss Cross | Criss 1190
Stanley Cowell Trio | Games | Steeplechase | SCCD 31293
Gamla Stan-The Old Town By Night
Arild Andersen Sextet | Sagn | ECM | 1435
Gamlestev
Robert Norman In Different Groups | The Best Of Robert Norman(1941-1989) | Hot Club Records | HCRCD 085
Gamsi
Nils Wogram Sextet | Odd And Awkward | Enja | ENJ-9416-2
Ganamurti
Randy Weston Quartet | Randy Weston:Self Portraits | Verve | 841314-2
Gancini Horo
Don Cherry Group | Don Cherry-The Sonet Recordings:Eternal Now/Live Ankara | Verve | 533049-2
Gandalf's Travels
Hot Club De Norvege With The Vertavo String Quartet | Vertavo | Hot Club Records | HCRCD 095
Ganesha's Jubilee Dance
Oscar Brown Jr. And His Group | Movin' On | Rhino | 8122-73678-2
Gang Bang
Sonny Clay | Sonny Clay 1922-1960 | Harlequin | HQ 2007 IMS
Ganges Gang
Trio Asab | Coast To Coast | Aho-Recording | AHO CD 1028(CD 380)
Ganges Groove
Jon Balke w/Magnetic North Orchestra | Kyanos | ECM | 1822(017278-2)
Ganglion
Susan Weinert Band | Mysterious Stories | VeraBra Records | CDVBR 2111-2
Gangster Groove
Jimmy Johnson Band | Heap See | Blue Phoenix | BLP 233720
Gangsterism On A Lunchtable
Jason Moean Group | Soundtrack To Human Motion | Blue Note | 497431-2
Gangsterism On Irons
Jason Moran Trio | The Bandwagon | Blue Note | 591893-2
Gangsterism On Stages
Peetie Wheatstraw | Peetie Wheatstraw(1930-1941) | Story Of Blues | CD 3541-2
Gankino Horo
Tommy Smith Sextet | Beasts Of Scottland | Linn Records | AKD 054
Ganz Bestimmt Vielleicht
Ulli Bögershausen | Best Of Ulli Bögershausen | Laika Records | LK 93-045
Meinert & Kropp | Innocence Is Gone | Wonderland Records | 319.9005-2
Ganz Schön Heiss Man
Jon Hiseman With The United Jazz & Rock Ensemble And Babara Thompson's Paraphernalia | About Time Too! | VeraBra Records | CDVBR 2014-2
Ganz Schön Heiss Man-2
Thomas Karl Fuchs | Piano Meditation I | Edition Collage | EC 481-2
Garagenjazz
Muddy Waters Blues Band | Live In Antibes 1974 | France's Concert | FCD 116
Garbato Con Sordina
Bob Howard And His Band | Jazz Museum-Bunny Berigan 1936 | MCA | 52067 (801842)
Gärdebylaten
Nils Landgren-Esbjörn Svensson | Swedish Folk Modern | ACT | 9428-2
Henning Berg & John Taylor With 'Tango' | Tango & Company | Jazz Haus Musik | JHM 0085 CD
Garden
William Ackerman Groups | Past Light-Visiting | Windham Hill | 34 11028-2
Garden Floor
Jim Black Quartet | Alasnoaxis | Winter&Winter | 910061-2
Garden Frequency
Blue Barron And His Orchestra | The Uncollected: Blue Barron | Hindsight | HSR 110
Garden In The Rain
Paul Desmond Quartet With The Bill Bates Singers | Desmond | Original Jazz Classics | OJCCD 712-2(F 3235/8082)
Mahalia Jackson With Choir And Orchestra | Starportrait | CBS | 67265
Garden Of Devotion
Passport | Garden Of Eden | Atlantic | 2292-44147-2
Garden Of Eden:
Dixieland Jug Blowers | Louisville Stomp-The Complete Sessions Of The Dixieland Jug Blowers | Frog | DGF 6
Garden Of Prayer(for My Mother And Father)
Blue Barron And His Orchestra | The Uncollected: Blue Barron, Vol.2 | Hindsight | HSR 137
Garden Wall
Andy LaVerne Trio | Between Mars & Earth | Steeplechase | SCCD 31478
Gardenia
Kenny Barron Quintet | Sambao | EmArCy | 512736-2
Gardenias For Gerdenis
David Newton Quartet | DNA | Candid | CCD 79742
Gardens Of Dreams
Bill Evans Group | The Alternative Man | Blue Note | BT 85111
Gardsjenta
Arild Andersen Sextet | Sagn | ECM | 1435
Carlo Actis Dato Quartet | Bagdad Boogie | SPLASC(H) Records | CD H 380-2
Garland Of Flowers (Alap And Jod In Raga Mala)
Tristan Honsinger | Live Performances | FMP | SAJ 10
Garmoochie
Claude Bolling Trio | Jazz A La Francaise | CBS | FM 39244
Garota De Ipanema -> The Girl From Ipanema
Gartman's
Horacio Molina With Band | Tango Cancion | Messidor | 15910
Garua
Leipziger Saxophon Quartet + Rolf Von Nordenskjöld | Passages: Leipziger Saxophon Quartet Plays Rolf Von Nordenskjöld | BIT | 11158
Garufa
Joe McPhee Trio | Sweet Freedom-Now What? | Hat Art | CD 6162
Gary
Stephane Grappelli Quartet | I Hear Music | RCA | 2179624-2
Thomas Clausen Trio With Gary Burton | Café Noir | M.A Music | INTCD 004
Curlew | Bee | Open Minds | OM 2408-2
Gary's Notebook
Lee Morgan Quintet | Joe Henderson-The Blue Note Years | Blue Note | 789287-2
Gary's Theme
Bill Evans Trio | Bill Evans Trio In Buenos Aires Vol.2 | Jazz Lab | JLCD 2(889054)
Cal Tjader Sextet | Here | Galaxy | GXY 5121
Gaslight
Duke Pearson Sextet | Joe Henderson-The Blue Note Years | Blue Note | 789287-2
Gasoline My Beloved
All Star Orchestra | Black California | Savoy | SJL 2215 (801191)
Gate Walks To Board
Clarence Gatemouth Brown Band | Alright Again! | Edsel | Fiend 2
Gatemouth
Chris Barber's Jazz Band | The Chris Barber Jubilee Album-Vol. 1 | Intercord | 157008
Dutch Swing College Band | Digital Dutch | Philips | 814068-2 PMS
Pete Allen's Jazz Band | North Sea Festival Vol.2 | Jazz Colours | 874759-2
Gates Of Fire
Eddie Kirkland Group | Lonely Street | Telarc Digital | CD 83424
Gates Of Paradise
Gil Evans And The Monday Night Orchestra | Bud And Bird-Live At The Sweet Basil | Electric Bird | K 19P 6455/6
Gathering-
Farlanders | The Farlander | JA & RO | JARO 4222-2
Gathering Grass
Brennan-Cline-Patumi-Voirnl-Theissing | Shooting Stars & Traffic Lights | L+R Records | CDLR 45090
Gato Gato
Rinus Groeneveld Trio | Dare To Be Different | Timeless | CD SJP 321
'Gator Swing

TITELVERZEICHNIS

Earl Hines And His Orchestra | The Indispensable Earl Hines Vol.1/2 | RCA | 2126407-2

Gattito
Ahmed El-Salamouny/Gilson De Assis | Tango Brasileiro | FSM | FCD 97725

Gauner Sind Sie Alle
Planet Blow | Alien Lunatic | Jazz Haus Musik | JHM 0071 CD

Gautamas Dream
Jan Garbarek Group | Twelve Moons | ECM | 1500(519500-2)

Gautes-Margjit
Rabih Abou-Khalil Group | Nafas | ECM | 1359(835781-2)

Gaval Dance
Clare Fischer Group | Machaca | MPS | 68254

Gavotte
Pierre Michelot Band | Jazz In Paris:Pierre Michelot-Round About The Bass | EmArCy | 832309-2 PMS

Gavotte from Partita No.3 In E Major(BWV 1006)
Jacques Loussier Trio | The Bach Book:40th Anniversary Album | Telarc Digital | CD 83474

Gaya
Hank Mobley Sextet | Thinking Of Home | Blue Note | LT 1045 (GXK 8188)

Gazelle
Joe Henderson Sextet | In Pursuit Of Blackness | Milestone | M 9034
Shelly Manne And His Men | Jimmy Giuffre:The Complete 1947-1953 Small Group Sessions,Vol.2 | Blue Moon | BMCD 1047
Joe Chambers Quintet | The Almoravid | 32 Jazz | 32099

Gazzelloni
Jay Hoggard Quintet | In The Spirit | Muse | MCD 5476
Harald Hearter Quartet With Michael Brecker | Cosmic | TCB Records | TCB 21162

GCCJ
Kip Hanrahan Groups | Exotica | American Clave | AMCL 1027-2

Geamparale
Joelle Leandre-Rüdiger Carl | Blue Goo Park | FMP | CD 52

Gedichtmachen
Charles Brown Quintet | Honey Dripper | Verve | 529848-2

Gee Baby Ain't I Good To You
Barbara Lea With The Johnny Windhurst Quartet | Barbara Lea | Original Jazz Classics | OJCCD 1713-2(PR 7065)
Billie Holiday And Her Orchestra | Body And Soul | Verve | 2304340 IMS
Billie Holiday With The JATP All Stars | Billie Holiday Story Vol.1:Jazz At The Philharmonic | Verve | 521642-2
Buck Clayton And His Orchestra | Cat Meets Chick | Fresh Sound Records | FSR 1001(CBS CL 778)
Carol Sloane And Clark Terry With The Bill Charlap Trio | The Songs Ella & Louis Sang | Concord | CCD 4787
Chu Berry And His Jazz Ensemble | The Big Sound Of Coleman Hawkins And Chu Berry | London | HMC 5006 AN
Count Basie And His Orchestra | Jazz In V.Discs Vol.2 | Collection Hugues Panassié | CTPL 002
Donald Brown Quartet | The Sweetest Sounds | Jazz City | 660.53.008
Ella Fitzgerald And Louis Armstrong With The Oscar Peterson Quartet | Ella And Louis Again,Vol.1 | Verve | 2304501 IMS
Ella And Louis Again | Verve | 825374-2
Compact Jazz: Ella Fitzgerald/Louis Armstrong | Verve | 835313-2
Ella Fitzgerald-Joe Pass Duo | Joe Pass:A Man And His Guitar | Original Jazz Classics | OJCCD 8806-2
Etta Jones And Her Band | Lonely And Blue | Original Jazz Classics | OJCCD 702-2(P 7241)
Henri Chaix Trio | Jive At Five | Sackville | SKCD2-2035
Jay McShann Quintet | What A Wonderful World | Groove Note | GRV 1005-2
Jeanie Lambe And The Danny Moss Quartet | Three Great Concerts:Live In Hamburg 1993-1995 | Nagel-Heyer | CD 019
Jimmy Knepper Quintet | Idol Of The Flies | Affinity | AFF 89
Jimmy Witherspoon And His Quartet | Jimmy Witherspoon Live | Kingdom Jazz | CDGATE 7023(882990)
Joe Pass Quartet | Apassionato | Pablo | 2310946-2
Joe Williams With The Ellis Larkin Trio | The Best Of The Blues Singers Vol.2 | LRC Records | CDC 9007
Kustbandet | On Revival Day | Stomp Off Records | CD 1294
Lorraine Geller Trio | Lorraine Geller Memorial | Fresh Sound Records | FSR-CD 0195
McKinney's Cotton Pickers | The Complete McKinney's Cotton Pickers Vol.1/2(1928-1929) | RCA | 2135550-2
Monty Alexander Sextet | To Nat, With Love From Monty Alexander | Master Mix | CHECD 12
Nat King Cole Trio | Nat King Cole:Route 66 | Dreyfus Jazz Line | FDM 36716-2
Nat King Cole Trio 1943-49-The Vocal Sides | Laserlight | 15718
Welcome To Jazz: Nat King Cole | Koch Records | 321 981 D1
Oliver Jones Trio | Northern Summit | Enja | ENJ-6086 2
Oscar Peterson-Harry Edison Duo | Oscar Peterson & Harry Edison | Original Jazz Classics | OJCCD 738-2(2310741)
Paolo Tomelleri-Fritz Hartschuh Quintet | Milan Swing | L+R Records | CDLR 45070
Ray Bryant | Ray Bryant Plays Blues And Ballads | Jazz Connaisseur | JCCD 9107-2
Richard Wyands Trio | Get Out Of Town | Steeplechase | SCCD 31401
Shirley Scott Trio | Like Cozy | Prestige | PCD 24258-2
Sir Charles Thompson Trio | Stardust | Paddle Wheel | KICJ 225
Stanley Turrentine With The Three Sounds | Blue Hour | Blue Note | 524586-2
Stefan Scaggiari Trio | That's Ska-jär-é | Concord | CCD 4510
Takashi Ohi With The Junior Mance Trio | Time Stream | Denon Compact Disc | CY-78898
Three Of A Kind | Drip Some Grease | Minor Music | 801056
Vanessa Rubin With Band | Girl Talk | Telarc Digital | CD 83480

Gee Baby Ain't I Good To You (alt.take)
Stanley Turrentine With The Three Sounds | Blue Hour | Blue Note | 524586-2
Chu Berry And His Jazz Ensemble | Commodore Classics In Swing | Commodore | 9031-72723-2

Gee Gee
John Patton Quintet | Along Came John | Blue Note | 831915-2
Zeather | Chen Yu Lips | Discovery | DS 867 IMS

Gee!
Yusef Lateef Quartet | 1984 | MCA | AS 84

Geeta's Shuffle
Gunther Klatt And Elephantrombones | Live At Leverkusen | Enja | 5069-2

Gegen Die Zeit
Christof Thewes Little Big Band | Greyhound | Jazz Haus Musik | JHM 0133 CD

Gegen K.
Ralph R.Hübner-Christoph Lauer | Mondspinner | free flow music | ffm 0796

Geh' Dahin-Weiß Nicht Wohin
Charly Antolini Orchestra | Special Delivery | MPS | 68256

Gehe Ein In Deinen Frieden
Peter Finger | Niemandsland | Acoustic Music Records | AMC 1001

Gehst Du Mit Mir Die Strassen Entlang
Wolfgang Haffner Group | Movin' On | Jazz 4 Ever Records:Jazz Network | J4E 4716

Geiereier
Göbels-Harth Group | Es Herrscht Uhu Im Land | Japo | 60037 (2360037)

Geisha
Das Böse Ding | Cleanhappydirty | Acoustic Music Records | 319.1090.2

Gelbsucht
Okay Temiz Group | Magnet Dance | TipToe | TIP-888819 2

Gelo,E Poi Sento
Keith Foley | Music For Christmas | dmp Digital Music Productions | CD 452

Gelobt Seist Du,Jesu Christ
Wittek/Kaiser/Manderscheid | Jazz...Oder Was? | Jazz Haus Musik | JHM 27

Gemini
Cannonball Adderley Sextet | Live On Planet Earth | West Wind | WW 2088
Chick Corea Trio | Circling In | Blue Note | 84555
Eric Kloss Quartet | About Time | Prestige | PRCD 24268-2
Erroll Garner Quartet | Gemini | RCA | NL 89975(809171)
Miles Davis Group | Live In Paris 1969 | Jazz Door | JD 1201
The Riverside Reunion Band | Mostly Monk | Milestone | MCD 9216-2

Gemini-
Claudio Roditi Group | Gemini Man | Milestone | M 9158

Gemischtes Wetter
Charly Antolini Orchestra | In The Groove | Inak | 806

Genarek's Tango
Möslang-Guhl Duo | Deep Voices | FMP | 0510

Gendai
Kusuma Sari(Sading) | Gamelan Batel Wayang Ramayana | CMP Records | CMP CD 3003

General Assembly
George Gruntz Concert Jazz Band | Blues 'N Dues Et Cetera | Enja | ENJ-6072 2

General Cluster
Shorty Rogers And His Giants | Collaboration-Shorty Rogers And Andre Previn | Fresh Sound Records | ND 74398

General Mojo's Well-Laid Plan
Gary Burton Quartet | Jazz:For Absolute Beginners | RCA | NL 89874 AG
Louis Stewart | Out On His Own | Jardis Records | JRCD 9612
Gary Burton Quartet | Green Apple | Moon Records | MCD 013-2

Generalife-
Hal Russell NRG Ensemble | Generation | Chief Records | CD 5

Generique
Alain Goraguer Orchestra | Jazz In Paris | EmArCy | 548793-2
Art Blakey And The Jazz Messengers | Des Femmes Disparaissent/Les Tricheurs(Original Soundtracks) | Fontana | 834752-2 PMS
Vince Guaraldi Trio | Cast Your Fate To The Wind | Original Jazz Classics | OJCCD 437-2(F 8089)
Marty Ehrlich Quintet | New York Child | Enja | ENJ-9025 2

Generosity
Marty Ehrlich Trio | Marty Ehrlich:The Welcome | Sound Aspects | sas CD 002

Gene's Blues
Gene Krupa And His Orchestra | Lionel Hampton/Gene Krupa | Forlane | UCD 19008

Genevieve
Lionel Hampton Sextet | Le Jazz En France-Vol.6 | Pathe | 1727301

Genie
Slim Gaillard | Slim Gailard Laughing In Rhythm-The Best Of The Verve Years | Verve | 521651-2

Geno
Wes Montgomery Trio | Wes Montgomery-The Complete Riverside Recordings | Riverside | 12 RCD 4408-2
Jaki Byard | Duet! | MPS | 68063

Gentil Coquelicot
Flavio Ambrosetti Quintet | Flavio Ambrosetti Anniversary | Enja | ENJ-9027 2

Gentle
Thomas Faist Sextet | Gentle | Village | VILCD 1020-2
Papa Bue's Viking Jazzband | The Golden Years Of Revival Jazz,Vol.11 | Storyville | STCD 5516

Gentle Annie
Jugendjazzorchester NW | Turning Around | Jugendjazzorchester NW | JJ 005

Gentle Ben
European Jazz Trio | Orange City | Timeless | CD SJP 336

Gentle Breeze
Art Farmer With Orchestra | Gentle Eyes | Mainstream | MD CDO 716

Gentle Eyes-
Bill Lowe/Philippe Crettien Quintet | Sunday Train | Konnex Records | KCD 5051

Gentle Force
Josep Maria Balanyà | Elements Of Development | Laika Records | 8695070

Gentle Ghost & Ganso
Greg Marvin Quintet | Workout! | Criss Cross | Criss 1037 (835629)

Gentle Mental Journey
Jazz Gala Big Band With Guest Soloists | Jazz Special-Gala Concert | RCA | CL 30069 DP

Gentle Piece
Kenny Wheeler Ensemble | Muisc For Large & Small Ensembles | ECM | 1415/16
Kenny Wheeler-Sonny Greenwich Quintet | Kenny And Sonny Live At The Montreal Bistro | Justin Time | JUST 114-2

Gentle Rain
Art Farmer With Orchestra | Gentle Eyes | Mainstream | MD CDO 716
Duo Brazil | Carioca | M.A Music | A 808-2
John Hicks Trio | Gentle Rain | Sound Hills | SSCD 8062
Lou Levy Trio | My Old Flame | Fresh Sound Records | FSR-CD 0312
Sarah Vaughan With Band | Copacabana | Pablo | 2312125
Uptown Express | Uptown Express | Palo Alto | PA 8048

Gentle Shifts South
Jason Moran Trio | The Bandwagon | Blue Note | 591893-2
Joe Pass | Joe Pass:Guitar Virtuoso | Pablo | 4 PACD 4423-2

Gentle Tears
Oscar Peterson Trio | The Paris Concert | Pablo | 2PACD 2620112
David Digs Orchestra | Realworld | Palo Alto | PA 8037

Gentle Wind And Falling Tear
Ray Walker-John Pisano Trio | Affinity | Jardis Records | JRCD 20032

Gentlefolk
Asian American Jazz Trio,The | Sound Circle | Paddle Wheel | KICJ 105

Gently Rocking The Boat
Gary Peacock | Partners | Owl Records | 014730-2

Gently,Gently
Tete Montoliu | Music For Perla | Steeplechase | SCCD 31021

Gentofte 4349
Ken Colyer's Jazzmen | The Golden Years Of Revival Jazz,Vol.13 | Storyville | STCD 5518

Gentofte Blues
Michael Sell Contemporary Music Ensemble | Innovationen Für 10 Instrumente | Misp Records | MISP 506

Geo J Lo
Tony Williams Quintet | Civilization | Blue Note | BT 85138

Geometry
Ulrich P. Lask Group | Indéan Poa | CMP Records | CMP CD 62

George M.
Mario Pavone Septet | Song For (Septet) | New World Records | 80452-2

Georgeiana
George Shearing Quintet | So Rare | Savoy | 650141(882497)

George's Dilemma
Clifford Brown-Max Roach Quintet | Brownie-The Complete EmArCy Recordings Of Clifford Brown | EmArCy | 838306-2
George Wein And The Newport All Stars | Swing That Music | CBS | CK 53317

Georgia
Dee Daniels With The Trio Johan Clement | Close Encounter Of The Swingin' Kind | Timeless | CD SJP 312

Georgia Blue
World Saxophone Quartet | Live At Brooklyn Academy Of Music | Black Saint | 120096-2

Georgia Cabin
Sidney Bechet And His New Orleans Feetwarmers | Sidney Bechet:Summertime | Dreyfus Jazz Line | FDM 36712-2
Sidney Bechet 1932-1943: The Bluebird Sessions | Bluebird | ND 90317

Georgia Camp Meeting
George Lewis And His New Orleans Jazzband | George Lewis In Japan | Storyville | SLP 514

Georgia Grind
Chris Barber's Jazz Band | The Chris Barber Concerts | Lake | LACD 55/56

Georgia On My Mind
Alvino Rey And His Orchestra With The King Sisters | The Uncollected:Alvino Rey,Vol.3 | Hindsight | HSR 196
Anson Weeks And His Orchestra | The Radio Years: Anson Weeks And His Hotel Mark Hopkins Orchestra 193 | Hindsight | HSR 146
Benny Carter And His Orchestra | Benny Carter(1928-1952) | RCA | ND 89761
Bill Ramsey With Orchestra | Gettin' Back To Swing | Bear Family Records | BCD 15813 AH
Billie Holiday With Eddie Heywood And His Orchestra | Billie Holiday:The Quintessential Vol.8/9(1939-1942) | CBS | 477837-2
Chris Barber Jazz And Blues Band feat. Wendell Brunious | Panama! | Timeless | CD TTD 568
Clark Terry Orchestra | Free And Oozy | Blue Moon | BMCD 3076
Clark Terry With Orchestra & Strings | Clark After Dark | MPS | 529088-2
Dave Brubeck Quartet | Gone With The Wind | CBS | SRCS 9362
Deborah Henson-Conant Trio | 'Round The Corner | Laika Records | LK 87-203
Digby Fairweather Quartet | Ballads For Trumpet | Jazz Colours | 874708-2
Dogs Don't Sing In The Rain | Vocal Moments | Take Twelve On CD | TT 008-2
Don Byas Et Ses Rythmes | Don Byas Complete 1946-1951 European Small Group Master Takes | Definitive Records | DRCD 11214
Earl Hines | Four Jazz Giants:Earl Hines Plays Tributes To W.C.Handy,Hoagy Carmichael And Louis Armstrong | Solo Art | SACD-111/112
Ella Fitzgerald With Joe Pass | Speak Love | Pablo | 2310888
Elmo Hope-Frank Foster Quartet | Hope Meets Foster | Original Jazz Classics | OJCCD 1703-2(P 7021)
George Melly With Arthur Greenslade's Orchestra | Melly Sings Hoagy | Ronnie Scott's Jazz House | NSPL 18557
Great Jazz Trio | Standard Collection Vol.1 | Limetree | MCD 0031
Itzak Perlman With The Oscar Peterson Quartet | Side By Side | Telarc Digital | CD 83341
Joe Beck Trio | Relaxin' | dmp Digital Music Productions | CD 444
Kay Starr With The Hal Mooney Orchestra | The One-The Only | Fresh Sound Records | NL 46052(RCA LPM 1149)
Lady Bass & The Real Gone Guys | Lady Be Good | L+R Records | CDLR 40029
Louis Armstrong With Sy Oliver And His Orchestra | Louis Armstrong:The New And Revisited Musical Autobiography Vol.3 | Jazz Unlimited | JUCD 2005
Mal Waldron Trio | You And The Night And The Muisc | Paddle Wheel | K 28P 6272
Oscar Peterson Trio | Night Train | Verve | 821724-2
Ray Brown Trio With Ernestine Anderson | Live At The Concord Jazz-Festival 1979 | Concord | CCD 4102
Ray Bryant | The Montreux '77 Collection | Pablo | 2620107
Roy Fox And His Band | Hello Ladies And Gentleman. This Is Roy Fox Speaking | Ace Of Club | ACL 1172
Shirley Horn Trio | Light Out Of Darkness(A Tribute To Ray Charles) | Verve | 519703-2
Sidney Bechet With Humphrey Lyttleton And His Band | Giants Of Traditional Jazz | Savoy | SV 0277
Toots Thielemans With The Tsuyoshi Yamamoto Trio | Toots Thielemans In Tokyo | Denon Compact Disc | DC-8551
Wycliffe Gordon Group | The Search | Nagel-Heyer | CD 2007
Zoot Sims Quartet | I Wish I Were Twins | Original Jazz Classics | OJCCD 976-2(2310868)

Georgia On My Mind-
Simon Schott | Bar Piano: Simon Schott Plays Your Favorite Evergreens Vol.1 | Organic Music | ORGM 9733
Trumpet Spectacular | The Progressive Records All Star Trumpet Spectacular | Progressive | PRO 7015 IMS

Georgia Rose
Anna Lee Chisholm | Female Country Blues Vol.1-The Twenties(1924-1926) | Story Of Blues | CD 3529-2

Georgia Swing
Jelly Roll Morton's Red Hot Peppers | The Jelly Roll Morton Centennial-His Complete Victor Recordings | Bluebird | ND 82361
Didn't He Ramble | Black & Blue | BLE 59.228 2

Georgian Bay
Count Basie And His Orchestra | The Best Of Count Basie | MCA | 82038 (801922)

Georgina
Werner Müller Mit Dem Rias-Tanzorchester | Swing Tanzen Gestattet | Vagabond | 6.28415 DP

Geo's Tune
Ralph Simon Sextet | AS | Postcards | POST 1004

Geppetto
Urs Blöchlinger Quartet | Cinema Invisible | Plainisphare | PL 1267-24/25

Geraldine
Lee Konitz Quartet | Haiku | Nabel Records:Jazz Network | CD 4664

Geraldo
Joelle Leandre | Palimpseste | Hat Art | CD 6103

Gerkin' For Perkin
Clifford Brown-Max Roach Quintet | Brownie-The Complete EmArCy Recordings Of Clifford Brown | EmArCy | 838306-2
James Spaulding Quintet | Blues Nexus | Muse | MCD 5467

German Measles
Blasnost | Anything Blows | Acoustic Music Records | 319.1049.2

Gerne Will Ich Mich Bequemen-
Hans Reichel-Rüdiger Carl Duo | Buben...Plus | FMP | CD 78

Gerra
Out Of The Blue | Spiral Staircase | Blue Note | 793006-2

Gerri's Blues
Andy Lumpp | Dreamin' Man | Nabel Records:Jazz Network | CD 4662

Gerrit's Broken Silence
Gene Ammons Quintet | Brother Jug! | Prestige | PR20 7792-2

Ger-Ru
Gerry Mulligan Septet | Gerry Mulligan:Gerry Meets Hamp | Memo Music | HDJ 4009

Gerry Mulligan Singing Off
The Birdlanders | The Birdlanders | Fresh Sound Records | FSR-CD 0170

Gerry Walks
Dave Brubeck/Jon Hendricks | Young Lions & Old Tigers | Telarc Digital | CD 83349

Gershwin Medley:
Modern Jazz Quartet | Concorde | Original Jazz Classics | OJC20 002-2
The Complete Modern Jazz Quartet Prestige & Pablo Recordings | Prestige | 4PRCD 4438-2
The MJQ Box | Prestige | 7711-2

Gershwin-Wagner Triptychon
Joan Abril Quintet | Insomnio | Fresh Sound Records | FSNT 034 CD

Gerson & Julia
Thad Jones Quartet | The Fabulous Thad Jones | Prestige | MPP 2506

Gertrude's Bounce
Clifford Brown-Max Roach Quintet | Clifford Brown-Max Roach:Alone Together-The Best Of The Mercury Years | Verve | 526373-2
Jazz Gallery:Clifford Brown | RCA | 2114176-2
Brownie-The Complete EmArCy Recordings Of Clifford Brown | EmArCy | 838306-2
The Houdini's | Headlines-The Houdini's In New York | Timeless | CD SJP 382

Geru's Blues
Sigi Schwab | Meditation | Melos Music | CDGS 701

Geschichte(His Story)
Ulrich Gumpert Quintet | Markowitz' Blues(Soundtrack) | Basic | 50002

Gestalt
Frank Gratkowski Trio | Gestalten | Jazz Haus Musik | JHM 0083 CD

Gesti

Peter Delano Group | Peter Delano | Verve | 519602-2

Gesture

Paul Bley-Hans Lüdemann | Moving Hearts | West Wind | WW 2085

Get Away Jordan

Big Bill Broonzy | Remembering Big Bill Broonzy | BGO Records | BGOCD 91

Get Back

Sarah Vaughan With Orchestra | Song Of The Beatles | Atlantic | SD 16037

Get Down

Hans Theessink Group | Crazy Moon | Minor Music | 801052

Get Down 'N Play The Blues

Buddy Johnson And His Orchestra | Buddy And Ella Johnson 1953-1964 | Bear Family Records | BCD 15479 DH

Get Down On The Road

Go Ahead & Rock Rock Rock | Official | 6011

Get Happy

Art Tatum | Decca Presents Art Tatum | MCA | MCAD 42327(872084)
Art Tatum:Complete Original American Decca Recordings | Definitive Records | DRCD 11200
Benny Goodman And His Orchestra | The Hits Of Benny Goodman | Capitol | 791212-2
Bud Powell Trio | Bud Powell Paris Sessions | Pablo | PACD 2310972-2
The Genius Of Bud Powell | Verve | 821690-1
The Legacy | Jazz Door | JD 1204
Dizzy Gillespie Jam | Montreux '77-The Art Of The Jam Session | Pablo | 2620106
Eddie Costa-Vinnie Burke Trio | Eddie Costa-Vinnie Burke Trio | Fresh Sound Records | LP 1025(Jubilee)
Ella Fitzgerald With The Billy May Orchestra | Ella Fitzgerald Sings The Harold Arlen Song Book | Verve | 589108-2
The Harold Arlen Songbook | Verve | 817526-1 IMS
Harry Edison Sextet | Sunset Swing | Black Lion | BLCD 760171
J.J.Johnson Sextet | The Best Of Clifford Brown:The Blue Note Years | Blue Note | 823373-2
June Christy With The Johnny Guarnieri Quintet | June Christy And The Johnny Guarnieri Quintet (1949) | Jazz Unlimited | JUCD 2084
June Christy With The Kentones | The Uncollected:June Christy With The Kentones | Hindsight | HSR 219
Oscar Peterson-Austin Roberts | Oscar Peterson 1951 | Just A Memory | JAS 9501-2
Oscar Peterson-Major Holley Duo | Keyboard Music By Oscar Peterson | Verve | MV 2666 IMS
Randy Sandke Quintet | Get Happy | Concord | CCD 4598
Rosemary Clooney And Her Band | Sings The Music Of Harold Arlen | Concord | MC CJ 210C
Sonny Rollins Trio | A Night At The Village Gate Vol.3 | Blue Note | 300204(BNJ 61015)
Soprano Summit | Chalumeau Blue | Chiaroscuro | CR 148

Get Happy(alt.take)

Jay Jay Johnson Sextet | Clifford Brown:The Complete Blue Note And Pacific Recordings | Blue Note | 834195-2

Get Happy(short version)

Sonny Rollins Trio | Sonny Rollins:The Blue Note Recordings | Blue Note | 821371-2
Red Norvo And His Selected Sextet | Red Norvo's Fabulous Ja Session | Spotlite | SPJ 127

Get In The Basement

Roland Kirk Quartet | Talkin' Verve-Roots Of Acid Jazz:Roland Kirk | Verve | 533101-2
Bud Powell Trio | Planet Jazz:Bud Powell | Planet Jazz | 2152064-2

Get It

Time Was | Bluebird | ND 86367
Clarence Williams' Blue Five | Big Charlie Thomas 1925-1927 | Timeless | CBC 1-030

Get It On

Kid Rena's Jazz Band | Prelude To The Revival Vol.2 | American Music | AMCD-41

Get It Straight(Straight No Chaser)

Carmen McRae And Her Quartet | Carmen Sings Monk | RCA | 2663841-2
Bill Connors Trio | Assembler | Line Records | COCD 9.00519 O

Get It To Go

Steps Ahead | Tempo Jazz Edition Vol.1-Talkin' Loud | Talkin' Loud | 848362-2

Get Loose

Chu Berry/Charlie Ventura Band | Tenor Triumvirate:Bean & Prez & Chu | Queen-Disc | 051

Get Lucky

Joe Henderson Septet feat.Terumasa Hino | Sunrise In Tokyo | Jazz Door | JD 12120

Get Me To The Church On Time

Al Porcino Big Band | Al Porcino Big Band Live! | Organic Music | ORGM 9717
Barney Kessel With The Monty Alexander Trio | Spontaneous Combustion | Contemporary | C 14033
Shelly Manne And His Friends | My Fair Lady | Mobile Fidelity | MFCD 809
Bobby Jaspar Quartet | Bobby Jaspar With Friends | Fresh Sound Records | FSR-CD 0166

Get On Board

Bob Crosby And His Orchestra | Suddely It's 1939-Bob Crosby | Giants Of Jazz | GOJ 1032

Get Open

Percy Mayfield With The Phillip Walker Blues Band | Hit The Road Again | Timeless | CD SJP 170

Get Out If You Can

Stefan Karlsson Quintet | Room 292 | Justice Records | JR 0701-2

Get Out Of Here

Keith Smith With George Lewis' Jazz Band | A Portrait Of Keith Smith 'Mr.Hefty Jazz' | Lake | LACD 67

Get Out Of Town

Artie Shaw And His Orchestra | Mixed Bag | Musicmasters | 65119-2
Chris Connor With Band | Chris Connor | Atlantic | 7567-80769-2
Coleman Hawkins Quartet | Good Old Broadway | Prestige | 0902114(Moodsville MV 23)
Ella Fitzgerald With The Buddy Bregman Orchestra | The Complete Ella Fitzgerald Song Books of Harold Arlen, Irving Berlin, Duke Ellington, George & Ira Gershwin, Jerome Kern, Johnny Mercer, Cole Porter And Rogers & Hart | Verve | 519832-2
George Shearing And His Quintet With Peggy Lee | Beauty And The Beat | Pathe | EMS 1158(Capitol ST 1219)
Holly Cole And Her Quartet | It Happened One Night | Metro Blue | 852699-0
Janet Blair With The Lou Busch Orchestra | Janet Blair Flame Out! | Fresh Sound Records | DICO D 1301 CD
Kai Winding Quartet | Duo Bones | Red Records | VPA 143
Manfred Junker Quartet | Cole Porter-Live! | Edition Collage | EC 531-2
Martha Hayes And Her Quartet | A Hayes Named Martha | Fresh Sound Records | FSR 582(Jubilee 1023)
Peter Guidi Quartet | Beautiful Friendship | Timeless | CD SJP 352
Rene Thomas Quintet | The 1954 Paris Sessions | Vogue | 21622912
Roland Kirk Quartet | Domino | Verve | 543833-2
Rosemary Clooney And Her Band | Rosemary Clooney Sings The Music Of Cole Porter | Concord | CCD 4185
Stan Kenton And His Orchestra | Back To Balbao | Creative World | ST 1031
Steve Wolfe Quintet Feat.Nancy King | First Date | Inner City | IC 1049 IMS
The Yamaha International Allstar Band | Hapy Birthday Jazzwelle Plus | Nagel-Heyer | CD 005
Tomas Franck With The Mulgrew Miller Trio | Tomas Franck In New York | Criss Cross | Criss 1052

Get Out Of Town-

Jack Sheldon Quartet | Stand By For The Jack Sheldon Quartet | Concord | CJ 229

Get Outta Yo Seat

Yusef Lateef Orchestra | The Blue Yusef Lateef | Rhino | 8122-73717-2

Get Over Get Off And Get On

Ella Fitzgerald With Orchestra | Ella/Things Ain't What They Used To Be | Warner | 9362-47875-2

Get Ready

Barrelhouse Jazzband | Showboat | L+R Records | CDLR 40032

Get Right Church

John Hammond | The Best Of John Hammond | Vanguard | VCD 11/12
Flora Molton And The Truth Band | Living Country Blues USA, Vol. 3 | L+R Records | LR 42033

Get Set For The Blues

John Slaughter Band | All That Stuff Ain't Real | Timeless | CD SJP 430

Get That Geet

James Moody Quartet with Dizzy Gillespie | Sweet And Lovely | Novus | PD 83063

Get Thee Behind Me Satan

Ella Fitzgerald With Paul Weston And His Orchestra | The Complete Ella Fitzgerald Song Books of Harold Arlen, Irving Berlin, Duke Ellington, George & Ira Gershwin, Jerome Kern, Johnny Mercer, Cole Porter And Rogers & Hart | Verve | 519832-2

Get Up

Richard 'Groove' Holmes Quintet | Blues Groove | Prestige | PCD 24133-2

Get Up Bessie

Joachim Kühn-Walter Quintus | Get Up Early | Ambiance(CMP) | AMB-CD 2

Get Your Kicks On Route 66

Eddie Locke Group | Jivin' With The Refuges From Hastings Street | Chiaroscuro | CR 2007
Jenny Evans And The Rudi Martini Quartet | At Loyd's | BELL Records | BLR 90004
Jump'n Jive | We The Cats Shall Hep Ya | Timeless | CD SJP 378
Nat King Cole Trio | Nat King Cole:Route 66 | Dreyfus Jazz Line | FDM 36716-2
Welcome To Jazz: Nat King Cole | Koch Records | 321 981 D1
Oscar Peterson Quartet With The Manhattan Transfer | A Tribute To Oscar Peterson | Telarc Digital | CD 83401
Greetje Kauffeld With Jerry Van Rooyen And Jiggs Whigham And The Rias Big Band | Greetje Kauffeld Meets Jerry Van Rooyen And Jiggs Whigham With The Rias Big Band | Mons Records | MR 874786

Get Your Ticket Here

Duke Ellington And His Famous Orchestra | The Complete Duke Ellington-Vol. 5 | CBS | CBS 88082

Get Yourself A Second Passport

Lee Morgan Sextet | Taru | Blue Note | 522670-2

Get Yourself Together

Les McCann Quartet With Rahsaan Roland Kirk | Live At Montreux | Atlantic | ATL 60051

Gettin' Back To Swing

The Young Blues Thrillers | American Folk Blues Festival Live '85 | L+R Records | CDLR 42065

Gettin' It Togetha'

Gunter Hampel Duo | Escape | Birth | 006

Gettin' Sassy

Blue Mitchell Quintet | Last Dance | JAM | 5002 IMS

Gettin' To It

Eddy Palermo Group | My Latin Feeling | Inak | 8806

Gettin' Together

Art Pepper Quintet | Gettin' Together | Contemporary | COP 023
Mezzrow-Ladnier Quintet | The Complete Sidney Bechet-Vol.5 | RCA | 2115519-2

Gettin' Up

Black Note | Nothin' But Swing | Impulse(MCA) | IMP 11772

Getting Dark

The Atlantic String Trio | First Meeting | Factory Outlet Records | FOR 2501-1 CD

Getting Even With Autumn Leaves

First Meeting | Factory Outlet Records | 2001-1 CD

Getting On My Nerves

Brian Buchanan Quintet | Avenues | Jazz Focus | JFCD 002

Getting Sentimental Over You

Carol Sloane With The Art Farmer Sextet | Love You Madly | Contemporary | CCD 14049-2

Getting Some Fun Out Of Life

Tommy Dorsey And His Orchestra | The Indispensable Tommy Dorsey Vol.2/4(1937.1938) | RCA | 2126406-2

Getting Started

John Abercrombie Quartet | Getting There | ECM | 1321(833494-2)

Getting There

Karl Berger-Dave Holland-Ed Blackwell | Crystal Fire | Enja | 7029-2
Gerals Wiggins Trio | The King And I | Fresh Sound Records | FSR-CD 0053

Gettysburg March

George Lewis And His New Orleans Stompers | George Lewis And His New Orleans Stompers | Blue Note | 821261-2
George Lewis Ragtime Jazz Band Of New Orleans | The Oxford Series Vol.6 | American Music | AMCD-26

Gettysburg March(alt.take)

Kid Rena's Jazz Band | Prelude To The Revival Vol.2 | American Music | AMCD-41

Get-With-Itness-

Brötzmann-Mengelberg-Bennink Trio | 3 Points And A Mountain...Plus | FMP | CD 107

Geysir

Terje Rypdal Trio | Chaser | ECM | 1303
Kodo VS Yosuke Yamashity | Kodo VS Yosuke Yamashita In Live | Denon Compact Disc | C38-7900

GG Train

Charles Mingus Orchestra | Nostalgia In Times Square/The Immortal 1959 Sessions | CBS | 88337
Hans Koch/Martin Schütz/Marco Käppeli | Accélération | ECM | 1357

GG-U-GG-U-RR-U-GG

New Art Saxophone Quartet | Songs And Dances | Enja | ENJ-9420 2

Ghana

Harry Verbeke-Rob Agerbeek Quartet | Seven Steps | Timeless | SJP 173

Ghana Song

Daniele Patumi | Ten Zentences | L+R Records | CDLR 45066

Ghantous

Renaud Garcia-Fons Group | Oriental Bass | Enja | ENJ-9334 2

Ghazali

Gil Melle Septet | Gil's Guests | Original Jazz Classics | OJCCD 1753-2

Ghetto Horn

Carlos Garnett Orchestra | Let This Melody Ring On | Muse | MR 5079

Ghetto Lights

Michael Riessler Group | Heloise | Wergo | WER 8008-2

Ghigo

George Gruntz Jazz Group feat. Jean-Luc Ponty & The Bedouins | Jazz Meets Africa:Noon In Tunisia-El Babaku | MPS | 531720-2

Ghost Busters

John Abercrombie | Characters | ECM | 1117

Ghost Dance

Max Roach With The So What Brass Quintet | Max Roach | Blue Note | 834813-2

Ghost Dance(part 1)

Max Roach Chorus & Orchestra | To The Max! | Enja | ENJ-7021 22

Ghost Dance(part 2)

M'Boom | To The Max! | Enja | ENJ-7021 22

Ghost Dance(part 3)

The Vivino Brothers Band | Chitlins Parmigiana | dmp Digital Music Productions | CD 492

Ghost Guests

Nils Landgren Group | Sentimental Journey | ACT | 9409-2

Ghost In This House

$$hide$$ | $$Titelverweise | |

Ghost Of A Chance -> I Don't Stand A Ghost Of A Chance With You

Ghost Of The Past

Billie Holiday And Her Orchestra | Billie Holiday:The Quintessential Vol.8/9(1939-1942) | CBS | 477837-2

Ghost Of Yesterday

Michael Kanan Trio | The Gentleman Is A Dope | Fresh Sound Records | FSNT 147 CD
Bob James Trio | Bold Conceptions | Verve | 557454-2

Ghost Riders In The Sky

Neal Kirkwood Octet | Neal Kirkwood Octet | Timescrapper | TSCR 9612

Ghost Shadows

Ken Colyer's Jazzmen | Ken Colyer's Jazzmen On Tour | GHB Records | BCD 16

Ghost Town

Steve Coleman And Five Elements | Black Science | Novus | PD 83119

Ghost Town-

Morris Lane And His Band | Tenor Saxation | Official | 6022

Giant Steps

Christian Rover Trio | New York Impressions | Organic Music | GWR 280595
Clementine And The Johnny Griffin Quartet | Continent Bleu | Orange Blue | OB 004 CD
Frank Marocco-Ray Pizzi Duo | Jazz Accordeon | Discovery | DS 797 IMS
Gonzalo Rubalcaba Trio | Images-Live At Mt. Fuji | Blue Note | 799492-2
Jerry Bergonzi Trio | Just Within | Double Time Records | DTRCD-127
Joe Pass | Virtuoso No.2 | Pablo | 2310788-2
John Coltrane Quartet | John Coltrane-The Heavyweight Champion:The Complete Atlantic Recordings | Atlantic | 8122-71984-2
John Coltrane-The Heavyweight Champion:The Complete Atlantic Recordings | Atlantic | 8122-71984-2
Jazz Gallery:John Coltrane Vol.2 | RCA | 2127276-2
The Art Of John Coltrane - The Atlantic Years | Atlantic | SD 2-313
Giant Steps | Atlantic | 8122-75203-2
The Best Of John Coltrane | Atlantic | 7567-81366-2
Atlantic Saxophones | Rhino | 8122-71256-2
Countdown | Atlantic | 90462-1 TIS
Lee Konitz Nonet | The Lee Konitz Nonet | Chiaroscuro | CR 186
Meredith D'Ambrosio With Harold Danko And Kevin Eubanks | It's Your Dance | Sunnyside | SSC 1011 D
New York Voices | Hearts Of Fire | GRP | GRP 96532
Nueva Manteca | Varadero Blues | Timeless | CD SJP 318
Pat Metheny Trio | Trio 99-00 | Warner | 9362-47632-2
Paul Robertson Quintet | Old Friends, New Friends | Palo Alto | PA 8013
Saxes Machine | Nouami | EdiPan | NPG 802
Sonny Sharrock Band | Highlife | Enemy | EMCD 119(03519)
Tete Montoliu Trio | Hot House | Steeplechase | SCCD 37027/28
Tito Puente And His Latin Ensemble | El Rey | Concord | CJ 250
Uwe Kropinski | Faces | ITM Records | ITM 14100
Vladimir Shafranov Trio | White Nights | The Jazz Alliance | TJA 10018

Giant Steps(alt.take)

John Coltrane Quartet | John Coltrane-The Heavyweight Champion:The Complete Atlantic Recordings | Atlantic | 8122-71984-2
John Coltrane-The Heavyweight Champion:The Complete Atlantic Recordings | Atlantic | 8122-71984-2

Giant Steps(false start 1)

John Coltrane-The Heavyweight Champion:The Complete Atlantic Recordings | Atlantic | 8122-71984-2

Giant Steps(false start 2)

John Coltrane-The Heavyweight Champion:The Complete Atlantic Recordings | Atlantic | 8122-71984-2

Giant Steps(incomplete take 1)

John Coltrane-The Heavyweight Champion:The Complete Atlantic Recordings | Atlantic | 8122-71984-2

Giant Steps(incomplete take 2)

John Coltrane-The Heavyweight Champion:The Complete Atlantic Recordings | Atlantic | 8122-71984-2

Giant Steps(incomplete take 3)

John Coltrane-The Heavyweight Champion:The Complete Atlantic Recordings | Atlantic | 8122-71984-2

Giant Steps(incomplete take 4)

John Coltrane-The Heavyweight Champion:The Complete Atlantic Recordings | Atlantic | 8122-71984-2

Giant Steps(incomplete take)

Art Blakey And The Jazz Messengers | Like Someone In Love | Blue Note | 784245-2

Giantis

Jerry Granelli Group | Music Has Its Way With Me | Traumton Records | 4451-2

Giants

Barre Phillips | Call Me When You Get There | ECM | 1257

Giblet Gravy

George Benson With Orchestra | The Silver Collection: George Benson | Verve | 823450-2 PMS

Gibraltar

Harry Verbeke-Rob Agerbeek Quartet | Gibraltar | Timeless | SJP 144
Tal Farlow Quartet | The Tal Farlow Album | Verve | MV 2584 IMS

Gide Gide

David Torn Group | What Means Solid,Traveler? | CMP Records | CMP CD 1012

Giffe

Henry Threadgill Sextet | Rag Bush And All | RCA | PD 83052(874077)

Gifts And Messages

Roland Kirk With The Stan Tracy Trio | Gifts And Messages | Ronnie Scott's Jazz House | JHAS 606

Giga from Cello Suite No.1 in F Minor(BWV 1009)

Elliott Sharp Carbon | Datacide | Enemy | EMCD 116(03516)

Gigante

The Jazz Giants '56 | Jazz Gallery:Lester Young Vol.2(1946-59) | RCA | 2119541-2

Gigantic Blues

Oscar Klein European All Stars Featuring Sammy Price | Oscar Klein European All Stars Featuring Sammy Price | Koch Records | 322 418

Giggin

Avishai Cohen Quartet | The Trumpet Player | Fresh Sound Records | FSNT 161 CD

Giggin'

The Bugs Henderson Group | At Last | Taxim Records | TX 1002-2 TA

Giggles

André Previn Trio | Gigi | Original Jazz Classics | OJCCD 407-2(C 7548)

Gigi

Dave Pike Sextet | On A Gentle Note | Muse | MR 5168

Gigolo

Tiziana Simona With The Kenny Wheeler Quartet | Gigolo | ITM Records | 0014
Jacques Loussier Trio | Play Bach No.2 | Decca | 157562-2

Gigue

Tomasz Gaworek-Schodrok | Found In The Flurry Of The World | Acoustic Music Records | 319.1073.2

Gigue-

Rolf Römer-Bill Dobbins Quartet | A Tribute To B.A.C.H. | Edition Collage | EC 520-2

Gigue Aus Der Partita Nr.3 A-Moll

Swingle Singers | Swingling Telemann | Philips | 586735-2

Gigue from Suite For Strings 'La Lyra'

Michiel Borstlap Sextet | Michiel Borstlap:The Sextet Live! | Challenge | CHR 70030

Gilbet Gravy

Clare Fischer Group | Lembrancas | Concord | CCD 4404

Gilles Et Mirona

Dizzy Gillespie And His Orchestra | Gillespiana And Carnegie Hall Concert | Verve | 519809-2

Gillespiana:

Dizzy Gillespie Quintet | En Concert Avec Europe 1 | Laserlight | 710705

TITELVERZEICHNIS

Kip Hanrahan Groups | Tenderness | American Clave | AMCL 1016-2

Gil's Pills

Mose Allison Quintet | Gimeracs And Gewgaws | Blue Note | 823211-2

Gimeracks And Gewgaws

Steve Grossman Quartet | Born At The Same Time | Owl Records | 010 CD

Gimme A Pigfoot

Juanita Hall With The Claude Hopkins All Stars | Sings The Blues | Fresh Sound Records | FSR 507(Counterpoint CPST 556)

LaVerne Baker And Her All Stars | That's Jazz Vol.11: LaVerne Baker Sings Bessie Smith | Atlantic | 790080-2

Gimme Five

John Abercrombie Sextet | Open Land | ECM | 1683(557652-2)

David Moss-Michael Rodach | Fragmentary Blues | Traumton Records | 4432-2

Gimme Gimme Blues

Louis Jordan And His Tympany Five | Louis Jordan-Let The Good Times Roll: The Complete Decca Recordings 1938-1954 | Bear Family Records | BCD 15557 IH

The Fabulous New Jimmy Dorsey Orchestra | Dorsey Then And Now | Atlantic | 81801-1 TIS

Gimme Some

Nina Simone With Orchestra | Nina Simone-The 60s Vol.1: Ne Me Quitte Pas | Mercury | 838543-2 PMS

Gimme Some Lovin'

Lambert, Hendricks And Bavan | At Newport '63 | RCA | 2125757-2

Gimmes Never Get

Bill Ware And The Club Bird All-Stars | Long And Skinny | Knitting Factory Works | KFWCD 131

Gin House Blues

Nina Simone Groups | You Can Have Him | Memo Music | HDJ 4087

Gin Mill Blues

Bob Crosby And His Orchestra | Big Band Bounce And Boogie-Bob Crosby:Mournin' Blues/Accent On The Bobcats | Affinity | AFS 1014

Ginette

Christoph Thewes-Rudi Mahall Quartet | Quartetto Pazzo | Jazz Haus Musik | JHM 0122 CD

Ging Ganz

Caito Marcondes Group With The Turtle Island String Quartet | Porta Do Templo | ACT | 5016-2

Ginger & Jack

James Spaulding Sextet | Gotstabe A Better Way | Muse | MCD 5413

Ginger Plant

Herb Geller-Brian Kellock | Hollywood Portraits | Hep | CD 2078

Ginger Rogers

Joseph Jarman-Don Moye Trio | Black Paladins | Black Saint | BSR 0042

Gingerbread Boy

John Abercrombie-Jarek Smietana Quartet | Speak Easy | PAO Records | PAO 10610

Lafayette Harris Jr. Quintet | Lafayette Is Here | Muse | MCD 5507

Miles Davis Quintet | Miles Davis Quintet 1965-1968 | CBS | C6K 67398

Milton Jackson Quintet | Jazz 'N' Samba | Impulse(MCA) | IMP 12932

Vital Information | Show 'Em Where You Live | Intuition Records | INT 3306-2

African Force | Palanquin's Pole | ITM Records | ITM 1433

Gingo Biloba

Dave Pike Sextet | Carnavals | Prestige | PCD 24248-2

Ginha

Eddie Gomez Quartet | Gomez | Denon Compact Disc | DC-8562

Gin's Beguine

Carlo Actis Dato Quartet | Noblesse Oblige | SPLASC(H) Records | H 118

Ginseng People

Bill Evans Group | Let The Juice Loose-Bill Evans Group Live at The Blue Note,Tokyo | Jazz City | 660.53.001

Ginza

Ron Crotty Trio | Modern Jazz From San Francisco | Original Jazz Classics | OJC 272(F 3213)

Vince Guaraldi-Bola Sete Quartet | From All Sides | Original Jazz Classics | OJCCD 989-2(F 3-362)

Gio

Ostelli-Apuzzo-Lalla Quintet | Plaything For Soul | SPLASC(H) Records | H 149

Giocoso

John Zorn Group | Cobra | Hat Art | CD 6040(2)

Giovanni

Hilton Ruiz Orchestra | Manhattan Mambo | Telarc Digital | CD 83322

Gipsy

Wynton Marsalis With Art Blakey And His Jazz Messengers | Wynton Marsalis | Jazz Classics | CD CA 36018

Gira Girou(Round 'N' Round)

Paul Desmond Quartet With The Don Sebesby Orchestra | From The Hot Afternoon | Verve | 543487-2

Gira Girou(Round 'N' Round-alt.take)

Pierre Dorge's New Jungle Orchestra | Giraf | dacapo | DCCD 9440

Giraffe

Ronald Shannon Jackson And The Decoding Society | Mandance | Antilles | ???

Girasol

Franco D'Andrea Trio | Airegin | Red Records | 123252-2

Giravolta

CTI All Stars | CTI Summer Jazz At The Hollywood Bowl-Live Two | CTI | 63027

Girimella

Remember Shakti | Saturday Night In Bombay | Verve | 014184-2

Giriraj Sudha

Arnold Ross Trio | Just You & He & Me | Fresh Sound Records | FSR-CD 313

Girl

Dice Of Dixie Crew | Second Sight | Inak | 822 Direct Cut

Girl From Ipanema(Garota De Ipanema)

Al Cohn Quartet | Nonpareil | Concord | CCD 4155

Antonio Carlos Jobim With The Claus Ogerman Orchestra | Quiet Nights | CTI Records | PDCTI 1106-2

Archie Shepp Quartet | Archie Shepp | The Rising Sun Collection | RSC 0005

Archie Shepp Sextet | Standards On Impulse! | Impulse(MCA) | IMP 12032

Astrud Gilberto With The New Stan Getz Quartet | Verve Jazz Masters 9:Astrud Gilberto | Verve | 519824-2

Baden Powell | Berlin Festival-Guitar Workshop | MPS | 68159

Billy Ross Quintet | The Sound:A Tribute To Stan Getz | Milestone | MCD 9227-2

Ella Fitzgerald With The Tommy Flanagan Trio | Compact Jazz: Ella Fitzgerald | Verve | 831367-2

Ella-At The Montreux Jazz Festival 1975 | Original Jazz Classics | OJC20 789-2(2310751)

Ella Fitzgerald In Budapest | Pablo | PACD 5308-2

Erroll Garner Quartet And The Brass Bed | Now Playing:A Night At The Movies & Up In Erroll's Room | Telarc Digital | CD 83378

Getz-Gilberto Quintet | Getz/Gilberto | Polydor | 521414-2

Getz/Gilberto No.2 | Verve | 519800-2

Getz/Gilberto:The Girl From Ipanema | CTI Records | PDCTI 1105-2

Jerry Van Rooyen With The WDR Big Band | Swing & Balladen | WDR | 2141013-2

Laurindo Almeida Trio | Outra Vez | Concord | CCD 4497

Oscar Peterson Trio | We Get Request | Verve | 521442-2

Red Norvo Quintet | Swing That Music | Affinity | AFF 776

Stan Getz Quintet Feat. Astrud Gilberto | Getz/Gilberto | Verve | 589595-2 SACD

Verve Jazz Masters 8:Stan Getz | Verve | 519823-2

Stan Getz Quintet With The Boston Pops Orchestra | Stan Getz And Arthur Fiedler At Tanglewood | RCA | 2136406-2

Stan Getz-Joao Gilberto Quintet | Compact Jazz: Antonio Carlos Jobim | Verve | 843273-2

Steffen Kamper Trio | Delight | Dr.Jazz Records | 8612-2

Zoot Sims With Bill Holman And His Orchestra | Hawthorne Nights | Pablo | 2310783

Regina Büchner's Jazz 4 Fun | Jazz 4 Fun | Satin Doll Productions | SDP 1017-1 CD

Girl From Ipanema(Garota De Ipanema)-

Getz-Gilberto Quintet | Getz/Gilberto | Polydor | 521414-2

Girl From Ipanema(Garota De Ipanema,45 rpm issue)

Kevin O'Donnell's Quality Six | Heretic Blues | Delmark | DE 513

Girl Of My Dreams

Conte Candoli-Carl Fontana Quintet | The Complete Phoenix Recordings Vol.2 | Woofy Productions | WPCD 122

The Complete Phoenix Recordings Vol.4 | Woofy Productions | WPCD 124

Dan Barrett Sextet | Reunion With Al | Arbors Records | ARCD 19124

Dizzy Gillespie Jam | Montreux '77-The Art Of The Jam Session | Pablo | 2620106

Dizzy Gillespie Sextet | The Giant | America | AM 6133

Dizzy Gillespie-Stan Getz Sextet | Welcome To Jazz: Dizzy Gillespie | Koch Records | 321 972 D1

Orexis | Orexis | Intercord | 160075

HR Big Band | The American Songs Of Kurt Weill | hr music.de | hrmj 006-01 CD

Girl Of The Moment

Ada Montellanico With The Jimmy Cobb Trio | The Encounter | Philology | W 66.2

Girl Talk

Buddy Greco Group | MacArthur Park | Celebrity | CYCD 71911

Gene Bertoncici Trio | Acoustic Romance | Paddle Wheel | KICJ 155

Jenny Evans And Band | Girl Talk | ESM Records | ESM 9306

Girl Talk | Enja | ENJ-9363 2

Live At The Allotria | BELL Records | BLR 90003

John C. Marshall Group | Same Old Story | Traditional Line | TL 1317

Julie London With The Gerald Wilson Big Band | Julie London Feeling Good | EMI Records | 1599361

Kenny Burrell Quartet | The Tender Gender | Chess | 515001

Mark Whitfield Group | True Blue | Verve | 523591-2

Singers Unlimited | A Capella 2 | MPS | 821860-2

Count Basie And His Orchestra | Basie Meets Bond | Capitol | 538225-2

Girl Trouble

Third Person | Third Person-The Bends | Enemy | EMCD 124(03524)

Girl With A Secret

Palle Mikkelborg Trio | Heart To Heart | Storyville | STCD 4114

Girl,I Really Love You So

Kenny Dorham Quintet | Zodiac:The Music Of Cecil Payne | Strata East Records | 660.51.021

Girls Evening

Mound City Blue Blowers | Eddie Condon 1928-1931 | Timeless | CBC 1-024

Girls Of My Dreams

Ralph Sutton-Jay McShann Quartet | The Last Of The Whorehouse Piano Players | Chaz Jazz | CJ 103

Giro

Christoph Stiefel Group | Ancient Longing | Jazzline | JL 11141-2

Girotondo

Mona Larsen And The Danish Radio Big Band Plus Soloists | Michael Mantler:Cerco Un Paese Innocente | ECM | 1556

Girovago-

Ragtime Specht Groove Quartet | Ragtime Specht Groove, Vol. 3 | Intercord | 130003

Giselle

Richard Galliano Group | Laurita | Dreyfus Jazz Line | FDM 36572-9

Richard Galliano Quartet | Gallianissimo! The Best Of Richard Galliano | Dreyfus Jazz Line | FDM 36616-2

New Musette | Label Bleu | LBLC 6547(889728)

Git It

Shirley Horn Trio | All Night Long | Steeplechase | SCCD 31157

Git Up From There

Hazel Scott Trio | Hazel Scott Relaxed Piano Moods | Original Jazz Classics | OJCCD 1702-2(DLP 16)

Git Up From There(alt.take)

Mahavishnu Orchestra | Inner Worlds | CBS | CBS 69216

Gitane

Laurindo Almeida-Charlie Byrd Quartet | Latin Odyssey | Concord | MC CJ 211C

Gitanerias

The Rosenberg Trio | Suenos Gitanos | Polydor | 549581-2

Gitano

Jean-Pierre Catoul Sextet | Modern Gardens | B.Sharp Records | CDS 076

GitMa

Sonny Greenwich-Ed Bickert Quartet | Days Gone By | Sackville | SKCD2-2052

Giu La Testa

A Tipico Trio | Where The Reeds Are | SPLASC(H) Records | CD H 312-2

Giudecca

Gunther Klatt & New York Razzmatazz | Volume One:Fa Mozzo | Tutu Records | 888158-2*

Günther Klatt-Tizian Jost | Art Of The Duo:Live In Mexico City | Tutu Records | 888184-2*

Paolo Fresu Quintet | Night On The City | Owl Records | 013425-2

Giuletta Degli Spiriti(to F.Fellini)

Jan Garbarek Group | Visible World | ECM | 1585(529086-2)

Giulietta

George Gruntz Concert Jazz Band | Blues 'N Dues Et Cetera | Enja | ENJ-6072 2

Giuseppi

George Gruntz Trio | Mock-Lo-Motion | TCB Records | TCB 95552

Giv Meg Ej Glans

Alex Möller-Lena Willemark Group | Hästen Och Tranan | ACT | 9244-2

Give A Little Whistle

Dave Brubeck Quartet | Dave Digs Disney | CBS | 21060

Give A Little, Get A Little

Shankar/Caroline | The Epidemics | ECM | 1308

Give An Inch

John Lindberg Trio | Give And Take | Black Saint | BSR 0072

Give Him The Ooh-La-La

Blossom Dearie Quartet | Give Him The Ooh-La-La | Verve | 517067-2

Give Him The Ooh-La-La | Verve | 517067-2

Give Him The Ooh-La-La(alt.take)

Till Brönner Quintet | My Secret Love | Minor Music | 801051

Give Him What He Wants

Herbie Hancock Group | Lite Me Up | CBS | SRCS 9507

Give It Back To The Indians

Ella Fitzgerald With The Buddy Bregman Orchestra | The Complete Ella Fitzgerald Song Books of Harold Arlen, Irving Berlin, Duke Ellington, George & Ira Gershwin, Jerome Kern, Johnny Mercer, Cole Porter And Rogers & Hart | Verve | 519832-2

Meredith d'Ambrosio Quartet | Beware Of Spring! | Sunnyside | SSC 1069 D

Give It Up

Cootie Williams And His Orchestra | Duke Ellington's Trumpets | Black & Blue | BLE 59.231 2

Give It Up Or Turn It A Loose

Count Basie And His Orchestra | Basie Big Band | Pablo | 2310756-2

Give Me A Little More Lovin'

June Christy With Orchestra | The Best Of June Christy | Capitol | 792588-2

Give Me Five Minutes More

Carol Grimes And Her Quintet | Alive At Ronnie Scott's | Ronnie Scott's Jazz House | JHCD 034

Give Me One More Chance

J.B.Lenoir Blues Band | J. B. Lenoir | Chess | 427003

Give Me The Night

George Benson Group/Orchestra | George Benson Anthology | Warner | 8122-79934-2

Give Me The Night(single version)

Annie Ross With The Gerry Mulligan Quartet | Annie Ross Sings A Song With Mulligan | Fresh Sound Records | 054 2602321(World Pacific WP 1253)

Give Me The Simple Life

Ella Fitzgerald With The Lou Levy Quartet | Ella Returns To Berlin | Verve | 837758-2

Georgia Carr With The Nelson Riddle Orchestra | Softly Baby | Pathe | 1566241(Capitol)

Sammy Kaye And His Orchestra | The Uncollected:Sammy Kaye, Vol.2 | Hindsight | HSR 163

Stan Getz Quintet | Stan Getz:The Complete 1952-1954 Small Group Sessions(Master Takes),Vol.3 | Blue Moon | BMCD 1036

Benny Goodman Septet | Benny Goodman:The Complete 1947-1949 Small Group Sessions Vol.2(1947-1949) | Blue Moon | BMCD 1043

Give Me Your Kisses

Funk Inc. | Jazzin' With The Soul Brothers | Fantasy | FANCD 6086-2

Give Me Your Love

Bob Helm's Jazz Band | Hotter Than That | Stomp Off Records | CD 1310

Give Me Your Telephone Number

Luis Russell And His Orchestra | Luis Russell | CBS | CBS 88039

Give Peace A Chance

Stefan Karlsson Quartet | Below Zero | Justice Records | JR 0703-2

Givin' In To Love

Patti Austin And Her Band | Carry On | GRP | GRP 96602

Gjesten(The Visitor)

Ketil Bjornstad Group | Water Stories | ECM | 1503(519076-2)

Glacial Reconstruction

Pat Metheny Group | Quartet | Geffen Records | GED 24978

Glacier

Paul Bley | Alone Again | DIW | DIW 319 CD

Glad 'A See Ya'

Lennie Tristano | Live At Birdland 1949 | Jazz Records | JR-1 CD

Glad Day

Lionel Hampton & His Giants Of Jazz 1979 | Hamp In Haarlem | Timeless | CD SJP 133

Glad Rag Doll

Kay Starr With The Hal Mooney Orchestra | The One-The Only | Fresh Sound Records | NL 46052(RCA LPM 1149)

Glad To Be Unhappy

Audrey Morris With The Marty Paich Orchestra | The Voice Of Audrey Morris | Fresh Sound Records | FSR 2016(Bethlehem BCP 6010)

Chris Connor With The Ralph Sharon Orchestra | Sings Ballad Of The Sad Cafe | Atlantic | AMCY 1067

Eric Dolphy With Erik Moseholm's Trio | Eric Dolphy in Europe, Vol.1 | Original Jazz Classics | OJC 413(P 7304)

Eric Dolphy:The Complete Prestige Recordings | Prestige | 9 PRCD-4418-2

Janet Blair With The Lou Busch Orchestra | Janet Blair Flame Out! | Fresh Sound Records | DICO D 1301 CD

Lee Wiley With The Ruby Braff Quartet | Duologue | Black Lion | BLP 60911

Glad To See You

Some Other Trio | A Tale Of Three Ducks | L+R Records | CDLR 45109

Gladiolus Rag

Joshua Rifkin | Scott Joplin Piano Rags | Nonesuch | 7559-79159-2

Mr.Acker Bilk And His Paramount Jazz Band | The Golden Years Of Revibal Jazz,Vol.15 | Storyville | STCD 5520

Golden Hour Of Acker Bilk And His Paramount Jazz Band | Golden Hour | 88 368 XAT

Gladys

Rein De Graaff-Koos Serierse | Duo | Timeless | SJP 213

Stan Getz-Lionel Hampton Quintet | Hamp And Getz | Verve | 831672-2

Stan Getz-Lionel Hampton Sextet | Hamp And Getz | Verve | 831672-2

Fats Waller | Piano Solos | RCA | ND 89741

Glänzender Lügner

Hans Koch/Martin Schütz/Marco Käppeli | Accélération | ECM | 1357

Glas(s)no(s)t

Rene Toledo Group | The Dreamer | GRP | GRP 96772

Glasrosen

Leni Stern Group | Ten Songs | Lipstick Records | LIP 890092

Glass Enclosure

Cliffird Jordan Quartet | Half Note | Steeplechase | SCCD 31198

Glass Culture

Andy LaVerne | In The Mood For A Classic-Andy LaVerne Plays Bud Powell | Steeplechase | SCCD 31342

Glass Enclosure

Steve Tibbetts Group | Steve Tibbetts | ECM | 1814(017068-2)

Glass Everywhere

Walt Weiskopf Nonet | Siren | Criss Cross | Criss 1187

Glass Mystery

Diedre Murray-Fred Hopkins Quartet | Stringology | Black Saint | 120143-2

Glasshouse In The Desert

Byron Stripling Sextet | Striplingnow! | Nagel-Heyer | CD 2002

Glasstronic

Greetje Bijma Trio | Barefoot | Enja | ENJ-8038 2

Glazed Frost

Stefano Battaglia Trio | Auryn | SPLASC(H) Records | CD H 162-2

Glebe Ascending

Horst Grabosch Quartet | Alltage | Jazz Haus Musik | JHM 80 CD

Gleißender Ruhm

Sputnik 27 | But Where's The Moon? | dml-records | CD 011

Gleiten Auf Dem Eis

Nils Landgren Funk Unit With Guests | 5000 Miles | ACT | 9271-2

Glen & Steve

Don Pender Quartet | Sandra Jean | Sandon Records | SD 1001

Glen Island Special

Glenn Miller And His Orchestra | The Original Sounds Of The Swing Era Vol. 5 | RCA | CL 05514 DP

The Swinging Mr. Miller | RCA | 2115522-2

Glide

Tony Rémy Groups | Boof! | GRP | GRP 97362

Glidin' Along

Alvin Queen & Junior Mance With Martin Rivera | Watch What Happens | Divox | CDX 48702

Glimpse

Los Angeles Jazz Quartet | Conversation Piece | Naxos Jazz | 86045-2

Glipse

Polo De Haas Quartet | Soolmaan | Timeless | CD SJP 384

Gloaming

Peter Brötzmann | No Nothing: Brötzmann Solo | FMP | CD 32

Global Citizen

Lars Duppler Quartet | Palindrome | Jazz Haus Musik | JHM 0108 CD

Global Player

Al Di Meola Groups | Guitar Heroes Vol.1:Al Di Meola | Zounds | CD 2700044001

Global Safari

The Al Di Meola Project | Kiss My Axe | Inak | 700782

Global Warming

Sonny Rollins Sextet | Global Warming | Milestone | MCD 9280-2

Franco D'Andrea Quartet | No Idea Of Time | Red Records | NS 202

Globetrotter

Beaver Harris | African Drums | Owl Records | 018356-2

Glo-Billy-Vee Vee

African Drums | Owl Records | 09

Globus

Woody Herman And His Orchestra | Sonny Berman:Woodshopper's Holiday 1946 | Cool & Blue | C&B-CD 111

Gloomy Sunday

Jack Walrath And The Masters Of Supense | Serious Hang | Muse | MCD 5475

Mel Tormé With The Marty Paich Orchestra | Torme 1 | Verve | 2304500 IMS

Gloomy Sunday-

Bobby Naughton Unit | Understanding | Japo | 60006 IMS

Gloria
Don Byas-Tyree Glenn Orchestra | Don Byas Complete 1946-1951
European Small Group Master Takes | Definitive Records | DRCD 11214
J.J.Johnson Quartet | Proof Positive | Impulse(MCA) | GRP 11452
Kenny Clarke-Francy Boland And Co. | The Golden 8 | Blue Note | 869935-9
Mary Lou Williams Group | Mary Lou's Mass | Mary Records | M 102

Gloria Et Tarantella
Joe Masters Orchestra & Choir | The Jazz Mass By John Masters | Discovery | DS 785 IMS

Gloria Swanson
Keith Nichols Cotton Club Orchestra With Claus Jacobi & Bent Persson | Syncopated Jamboree | Stomp Off Records | CD 1234

Gloria's Step
Bill Evans Trio | My Romance | Zeta | ZET 702
Live In Europe Vol.1 | EPM Musique | FDC 5712
The Complete Fantasy Recordings | Fantasy | 9FCD 1012-2
Live In Paris 1972 Vol.1 | France's Concert | FCD 107
Bill Evans:The Secret Sessions | Milestone | 8MCD 4421-2
Bill Evans Live In Tokyo | CBS | 481265-2
More From The Vanguard | Milestone | M 9125
Bireli Lagrene Group | Bireli Lagrene & Special Guests | Inak | 8610
Joe Lovano-Gonzalo Rubalcaba | Flying Colors | Blue Note | 856092-2
Larry Willis Trio | How Do You Keep The Music Playing? | Steeplechase | SCCD 31312
Ray Drummond Orchestra | Continuum | Arabesque Recordings | AJ 0111
Vic Juris Trio | Songbook 2 | Steeplechase | SCCD 31516
Bill Evans Trio | Sunday At The Village Vanguard | Original Jazz Classics | OJC20 140-2

Gloria's Step(alt.take)
Bill Evans:The Complete Live At The Village Vanguard 1961 | Riverside | 3RCD 1961-2

Gloria's Step(alt.take-1)
Bill Evans:The Complete Live At The Village Vanguard 1961 | Riverside | 3RCD 1961-2

Gloria's Step(alt.take-2)
Steve Kuhn Trio | Years Later | Concord | CCD 4554

Gloria's Theme(from Butterfield Eight)
Larry Coryell Quartet | Comin' Home | Muse | MCD 5303

Glory
Wayne Horvitz-Butch Morris-Robert Previte | Nine Below Zero | Sound Aspects | sas CD 014

Glory Glory
Tuck And Patti | Love Warriors | Windham Hill | 34 10116-2
First Revolution Singers | First Revolution Gospel Singers:A Capella | Laserlight | 24338

Glory Glory Hallelujah
A Cappella Gospel Anthology | Tight Harmony Records | TH 199404

Glory Hallelujah
Golden Gate Quartet | Spirituals To Swing 1955-69 | EMI Records | 791569-2
Mississippi Fred McDowell with Jo Ann Kelly | Standing At The Burying Ground | Red Lightnin' | RL 0053

Glory Of Love
Magnificant Seventh's with Milton Batiste And Alton Carson | Best Of New Orleans:Bourbon Street Jazz After Dark | Mardi Gras Records | MG 1022

Glory Of Love(alt.take)
Heikki Sarmanto Ensemble And Gregg Smith Vocal Quartet | New Hope Jazz Mass | Finlandia | FA 201

Gloryland -> Over In The Gloryland

Glow Worm
The Mills Brothers With Orchestra | The Golden Years Of The Mills Brothers | Ember | NR 5090

Glowin'
Paul Eßer-Gerd Dudek-Ali Haurand-Jiri Strivin | Jazz Und Lyrik:Schinderkarren Mit Buffet | Konnex Records | KCD 5108

Glück-
Willem Breuker Kollektief | Deadly Sin/Twice A Woman(Sountracks) | BVHAAST | CD 9708

Glucklich
Alfred 23 Harth-Bob Degen Duo | Melchior | Biber Records | BI 6240

Glühwi
Fred Van Hove | Fred Van Hove-Church Organ | FMP | SAJ 25

Gnashing
Chet Baker Quintet | Chet Baker:The Most Important Jazz Album Of 1964/65 | Roulette | 581829-2

Gnid
Chet Baker Plays & Sings | West Wind | WW 2108
Don Sickler Orchestra | Dameronia | Soul Note | 121202-2
Junior Cook Quartet | The Place To Be | Steeplechase | SCCD 31240
Pili-Pili | Nomans Land | JA & RO | JARO 4209-2

Gno Hon Mouna(No Time To Live)
Wollie Kaiser Timeghost | Post Art Core | Jazz Haus Musik | JHM 0077 CD

Gnocci In Germania
Cornelius Claudio Kreusch | The Vision | Enja | 8082-2

Gnosis
Marc Cary Quintet | The Antidote | Arabesque Recordings | AJ 0140

Gnossienne(No.1)
Jacques Loussier Trio | Erik Satie:Gymnopedies-Gnossiennes | Telarc Digital | CD 83431

Gnossienne(No.6)
Grachan Moncur III Quintet | A Blue Conception | Blue Note | 534254-2

Gnostic
Peter Sonntag Sextet | Words Written In Stone | amf records | maj 1011

Gnou-Gnou Valse
Ronald Muldrow Trio | Gnowing You | L+R Records | CDLR 45047

Gnu Suite
Kenny Wheeler Quartet | Gnu High | ECM | 1069(825591-2)
Hamiet Bluiett Group | Same Space | Justin Time | JUST 109-2

Go
Joey Baron Trio | Tongue In Groove | JMT Edition | 849158-2
Rissi-Mazzola-Geisser | Fuego | Creative Works Records | CW CD 1029-2
Seamus Blake-Marc Miralta Trio | Sun Sol | Fresh Sound Records | FSNT 087 CD
Wayne Shorter Quartet | Footprints Live! | Verve | 589679-2
Wayne Shorter Sextet | Schizophrenia | Blue Note | 84292

Go Ahead And Rock
Buddy Johnson And His Orchestra | Go Ahead & Rock Rock Rock | Official | 6011

Go Away Little Boy
Al Jarreau With Band | Tenderness | i.e. Music | 557853-2

Go Away Little Girl
Joe Pass Group | Guitar Interludes | Discovery | DS 776 IMS

Go Down Moses
Archie Shepp-Horace Parlan Duo | Swing Low | Plainisphare | PL 1267-73 CD
Charles Lloyd Quintet | Lift Every Voice | ECM | 1832/33(018783-2)
Charlie Haden-Hank Jones | Steal Away | Verve | 527249-2
Fats Waller | London Sessions 1938-39 | Jazztime(EMI) | 251271-2
Grant Green Quintet | The Blue Testament | Blue Note | 780703-2
Hampton Hawes Trio | The Sermon | Original Jazz Classics | OJCCD 1067-2(C 7653)
Jimmy Witherspoon With The Randy van Horne Choir | Feelin' The Spirit | Fresh Sound Records | FSR 578(HiFiRecords R422)
Louis Armstrong With Sy Oliver's Choir And Orchestra | Louis And The Good Book | Verve | 940130-0
Louis And The Good Book | Verve | 549593-2
Mark Whitfield Group | Patrice | Warner | 7599-26659-2
Mavis Staples-Lucky Peterson | Spirituals&Gospel:Dedicated To Mahalia Jackson | Verve | 533562-2

Go Down Sunshine
Woody Herman And His Orchestra | The Third Herd, Vol.1 | Discovery | DS 815 IMS

Go Fly A Kite
Billy Cobham Band | Billy's Best Hits | GRP | GRP 95752

Go For It
Jens Bunge Group | With All My Heart | yvp music | CD 3060

Go From Here
Pat Metheny Trio | Trio 99-00 | Warner | 9362-47632-2

Go Get It - (Go) Get It
Jimmy Rushing And His All Stars | Jack Dupree-Jimmy Rushing-Muddy Waters | Laserlight | 17062

Go Ghana
Mongo Santamaria Orchestra | The Watermelon Man | Milestone | M 47012

Go Home
Gerry Mulligan Concert Jazz Band | The Complete Verve Gerry Mulligan Concert Band | Verve | 9860613
En Concert Avec Europe 1 | Laserlight | 710382/83
Herbie Mann Group | Deep Pocket | Kokopelli Records | KOKO 1296

Go Home(alt.take)
Gerry Mulligan-Ben Webster Quintet | The Complete Gerry Mulligan Meets Ben Webster Sessions | Verve | 539055-2

Go Home(incompl.take 1)
The Complete Gerry Mulligan Meets Ben Webster Sessions | Verve | 539055-2

Go Home(incompl.take 2)
Roger Hanschel/Gabriele Hasler | Go In Green | Jazz Haus Musik | JHM 0073 CD

Go In Green
Leo Smith & New Dalta Ahkri | Go In Numbers | Black Saint | 120053-2

Go Kicks
Coleman Hawkins Quartet | Today And Now | Impulse(MCA) | 951184-2

Go Lil' Liza
The Roots Of Acid Jazz | Impulse(MCA) | IMP 12042
Today And Now | MCA | AS 34

Go Limp
Nina Simone Trio/Quartet/Orchestra | Moon Of Alabama | Jazz Door | JD 1214
André Previn | André Previn Plays Songs by Jerome Kern | Original Jazz Classics | OJCCD 1787-2(S 7567)

Go Little Boat
Fletcher Henderson And His Orchestra | Jazz:The Essential Collection Vol.1 | IN+OUT Records | 78011-2

Go Long Mule
Walter Horton Band | Mumbles Walter Horton:Mouth Harp Maestro | Ace Records | CDCH 252

Go 'N' Git It!
Les McCann Group | Another Beginning | Atlantic | 7567-80790-2

Go On And Cry
Red Richards Quartet | Swingtime | Jazzpoint | JP 1041 CD

Go Red
Arnett Cobb & His Orchestra | The Complete Apollo Sessions | Vogue | 500116

Go Red Go
New Orleans Collective | New Orleans Collective | Paddle Wheel | KICJ 165

Go Tell It On The Mountain
Henrik Johansen's Jazzband | The Golden Years Of Revival Jazz,Vol 1 | Storyville | STCD 5506
Jan Harrington Sextet | Jan Harrington's Christmas In New Orleans | Nagel-Heyer | NHR SP 4
Mahalia Jackson | In Memoriam Mahalia Jackson | CBS | 66501
Marcus Roberts | Prayer For Peace | Novus | ND 90585(847064)

Go Tenor
Larry Garner Group | Baton Rouge | Verve | 529467-2

Go To Hell
High Steppers Brass Band | New Orleans Jazz Greatest Hits | Sound Of New Orleans | SONO 1032

Go To Use You Head
Chris Connor With Band | The Best Of Chris Connor | Atlantic | AMCY 1078

Go With Your Heart
Zbigniew Namyslowski-Remy Filipovitch Quintet | Go! | Album | AS 66919 CD

Go!
Ax Genrich Group | Wave Cut | ATM Records | ATM 3813-AH

Go! Lemgo
Don Lanphere Quintet | Prestige First Sessions, Vol.1 | Prestige | PCD 24114-2

Go,Crystal Tears
Martin Schrack Trio | Catplay | yvp music | CD 3037

Goal In Mind
The Pugh-Taylor Project | The Pugh-Taylor Project | dmp Digital Music Productions | CD 448

God And The Devil In The Land Of The Sun
Johnny Thompson & The Pennsylvania District Choir | Live At Lausanne | Bellaphon | BCH 33007

God Bless America
Les McCann Group | On The Soul Side | Musicmasters | 65112-2

God Bless The Child
Angela Brown | The Voice Of Blues | Schubert Records | SCH- 105
Billie Holiday | My Greatest Songs | MCA | MCD 18767
Billie Holiday And Her All Stars | Billie Holiday Story Vol.4:Lady Sings The Blues | Verve | 521429-2
Verve Jazz Masters 12:Billie Holiday | Verve | 519825-2
The Billie Holiday Song Book | Verve | 823246-2
4 By 4:Ella Fitzgerald/Sarah Vaughan/Billie Holiday/Dinah Washington | Verve | 559693-2
Billie Holiday And Her Band | Billie Holiday Radio & TV Broadcast(1953-56) | ESP Disk | ESP 3003-2
Chris Connor With The Al Cohn Orchestra | Free Spirits | Atlantic | AMCY 1077
Clark Terry Quartet | OW | Storyville | STCD 8378
Clark Terry With The John Lewis Quartet | Jazz Monterey 1958-1980 | Palo Alto | PA 8080-2
Dick Whittington Trio | In New York | Concord | CCD 4498
Engelbert Wrobel's Swing Society | A Heartful(l) Of Swing | NCC Jazz | NCC 8502
Eric Dolphy | Copenhagen Concert | Prestige | P 24027
Berlin Concerts | Enja | 3007/9-2
The Illinois Concert | Blue Note | 499826-2
Eric Dolphy Quartet | The Illinois Concert | Blue Note | 499826-2
Eric Dolphy Quintet | Stockholm Sessions | Enja | 3055 (807503)
Eric Lugosch | Black Key Blues | Acoustic Music Records | 319.1148.2
Gene Ammons Quintet | Fine And Mellow | Prestige | PRCD 24281-2
George Adams-Don Pullen Quartet | More Funk | Palcoscenico | PAL 15003
Guy Lafitte Quartet | The Things We Did Last Summer | Black & Blue | BLE 59.192 2
Jesper Thilo Quartet | Jesper Thilo Quartet | Music Mecca | CD 1009-2
Joe Pass-Jimmy Rowles Duo | Joe Pass:A Man And His Guitar | Original Jazz Classics | OJCCD 8806-2
Joe Van Enkhuizen With The Horace Parlan Trio | Joe Meets The Rhythm Section | Timeless | CD SJP 249
Kenny Burrell With Orchestra | God Bless The Child | CTI | 6011
Lee Morgan Orchestra | Standards | Blue Note | 823213-2
Lester Bowie's Brass Fantasy | My Way | DIW | DIW 835 CD
Lou Rawls With Les McCann Ltd. | Blue Velvet: Crooners, Swooners And Velvet Vocals | Blue Note | 521153-2
Mal Waldron Trio With Abbey Lincoln | Soul Eyes | RCA | 2153887-2
Ran Blake | The Blue Potato And Other Outrages | Milestone | M 9021
Sonny Rollins Quartet | The Complete Sonny Rollins RCA Victor Recordings | RCA | 2668675-2
Sonny Rollins-The Quartets | Bluebird | ND 85643
Sonny Rollins Sextet | Horn Culture | Original Jazz Classics | OJC 314(M 9051)
Stephane Grappelli Quartet | Stephane Grappelli & Friends In Paris | Accord | 500762
Thilo Wolf Big Band | Gospel Faces:Thilo Wolf & Band Meets Joan Faulkner | MDL-Jazz | CD 1927(CD 054)
Ellis Larkins | Maybeck Recital Hall Series Volume Twenty-Two | Concord | CCD 4533

God Bless The Child(alt.take)
Billie Holiday And Her All Stars | Billie Holiday Story Vol.4:Lady Sings The Blues | Verve | 521429-2

God Bless The Child(Rehersal)
Wes Montgomery With Orchestra | Pretty Blue | Milestone | M 47030

God Don't Never Change
Leroy Carr | Leroy Carr-Singin' The Blues | Biograph | BLP C 9

God Give Me Strength
Cyrus Chestnut Trio | You Are My Sunshine | Warner | 9362-48445-2

God Has Smiled On Me
George Adams-Don Pullen Duo | Melodic Excursion | Timeless | CD SJP 166

God Is A She
Dorothy Wilson Gospel Express | O How Beautiful | L+R Records | CDLR 44019

God Is Real
Martha Bass-Fontella Bass-David Peaston Gospel Group | From The Root To The Source | Soul Note | 121006-2

God Moves On The Water
Blind Willie Johnson | Praise God I'm Satisfied | Yazoo | YAZ 1058

God Rest Ye Merry Gentlemen
George Shearing Quintet | Reflections:The Best Of George Shearing(1992-1998) | Telarc Digital | CD 83513
Mark Soskin | Jazz City Christmas Vol.2 | Jazz City | 660.53.029
Keith Foley | Music For Christmas | dmp Digital Music Productions | CD 452

Godchild
Miles Davis And His Orchestra | The Complete Birth Of The Cool | Capitol | 494550-2
The Complete Birth Of The Cool | Capitol | 494550-2
Birth Of The Cool | Capitol | 530117-2
Miles Davis:The Blue Note And Capitol Recordings | Blue Note | 827475-2
Miles Davis Nonet | The Real Birth Of The Cool | Bandstand | BDCD 1512

Goddess
Witzel's Venue | Perceptions | Lipstick Records | LIP 8963-2

Godson Song
David S. Ware Quartet | Davis S.Ware Quartet | DIW | DIW 916 CD

Godumaduma
Beaver Harris | African Drums | Owl Records | 018356-2

Godvin
African Drums | Owl Records | 09

Gofor
Roy Eldridge 4 | The Montreux '77 Collection | Pablo | 2620107

Gog(for Emil Schumacher)
Magog | Magog | Japo | 60011 IMS

Go-Getter
Chet Baker Quintet | Boppin' With The Chet Baker Quintet | Prestige | PR20 7512-2

Go-Go
Leandro Braga Group | E Por Que Nao?(And Why Not?) | Arabesque Recordings | AJ 0104
Miles Davis Quintet | The Complete Concert 1964:My Funny Valentine+Four & More | CBS | 471246-2

Go-Go(Theme And Announcement)
The Complete Concert 1964:My Funny Valentine+Four & More | CBS | 471246-2
The Complete Concert 1964:My Funny Valentine+Four & More | CBS | 471246-2

Go-Go(Theme And Re-Introduction)
Franck Band | Looser | Jazz Haus Musik | JHM 43 CD

Goin' Ahead
Pat Metheny Quintet | 80/81 | ECM | 1180/81 (843169-2)
Ella Fitzgerald And Her Orchestra | Live From The Roseland Ballroom New York 1940 | Jazz Anthology | 550032

Goin' Away
Pete Johnson-Joe Turner | The Boogie Woogie Boys | Storyville | SLP 229

Goin' Back Home
Sonny Boy Williamson Group | The Blues | Storyville | 4960323
T-Bone Walker And The Blues Band | American Folk Blues Festival '72 | L+R Records | CDLS 42018

Goin' Down Slow
Billy Wright Band | Goin' Down Slow | Savoy | SV 0257
Honeyboy Edwards | White Windows | Evidence | ECD 26039-2
Sonny Stitt Quartet | The Prestige Collection:Sonny Stitt Soul Classics | Original Jazz Classics | OJCCD 6003-2
Sonny Terry & Brownie McGhee | Home Town Blues | BGO Records | BGOCD 75
Clifton Chenier And His Band | Frenchin' The Boogie | Verve | 519724-2

Goin' Down Swingin'
Papa George Lightfoot Band | Natchez Trace | Crosscut | CCR 1001

Goin' Down To Muskogee
Jim Pepper Group | Comin' And Goin' | Bellaphon | 290.31.029

Goin' Down To The River
Memphis Slim | Alone With My Friends | Original Blues Classics | OBCCD 581-2(Battle 6118)

Goin' Home
Art Hodes | Art Hodes-The Final Sessions | Music & Arts | CD 782
Art Pepper-George Cables Duo | Goin' Home | Original Jazz Classics | GXY 5143
Art Tatum | Art Tatum:Complete Capitol Recordings | Definitive Records | DRCD 11192
Ken Colyer's Jazzmen | The Best Of Dixieland-1953/54 | London | 820879-2
Monty Sunshine's Jazz Band | Gotta Travel On | Timeless | CD TTD 570
The Three Sounds | Introducing The Three Sounds | Blue Note | 300234(1600)

Goin' Home-
Glenn Miller And The Army Air Force Band | I Sustain The Wings Vol.3(September 1943) | Magic | DAWE 78

Goin' Home Blues
Keith Smith's All Stars | A Portrait Of Keith Smith 'Mr.Hefty Jazz' | Lake | LACD 67

Goin' Nowhere
The Six Jolly Jesters | Duke Ellington:Complete Original American Decca Recordings | Definitive Records | DRCD 11196

Goin' Out Of My Head
Ella Fitzgerald With The Jimmy Jones Trio | Ella Fitzgerald And Duke Ellington:Cote D'Azure Concerts on Verve | Verve | 539033-2
Ella Fitzgerald And Duke Ellington:Cote D'Azure Concerts on Verve | Verve | 539033-2
Great Guitars | Great Guitars | Concord | CCD 4023
Wes Montgomery With The Johnny Pate Orchestra | Compact Jazz: The Sampler | Verve | 831376-2
Wes Montgomery With The Oliver Nelson Orchestra | Goin' Out Of My Head | CTI Records | PDCTI 1107-2

Goin' Through The Motions
Pharoah Sanders Group | Heart Is A Melody | Evidence | ECD 22063-2

Goin' To Alabama
Walter Brown | Living Country Blues USA Vol.5: Mississippi Delta Blues | L+R Records | LR 42035

Goin' To Chicago
Basie's Bad Boys | Lester Young:The Complete1936-1951 Group Sessions(Studio Recordings-Master Takes),Vol.1 | Blue Moon | BMCD 1001
Buck Clayton All Stars feat.Jimmy Rushing | Copenhagen Concert | Steeplechase | SCC 6006/7
Memphis Piano Red | Living Country Blues USA Vol.4:Tennessee Blues | L+R Records | LR 42034

Steve Freund Quartet/Sextet | Romance Without Finance | Steeplechase | SCB 9011

Goin' To Chicago Blues
Jimmy Witherspoon And His Quartet | Blues Around The Clock | Original Blues Classics | OBCCD 576-2(P 7314)

Goin' To Chicago(Intro)
Sonny Stitt Quintet | The Prestige Collection:Sonny Stitt Soul Classics | Original Jazz Classics | OJCCD 6003-2

Goin' To Mintons
Dave Stryker Quartet | Guitar On Top | Ken Music | 660.56.019

Goin' To Town-
Chris Barber's Jazz And Blues Band | 40 Years Jubilee | Timeless | CD TTD 589

Goin' Under
Duke Ellington And His Orchestra | At The Hurricane:Original 1943 Broadcasts | Storyville | STCD 8359

Goin' Up
Carnegie Hall Concert January 1943 | Prestige | 2PCD 34004-2
Duke Ellington:Complete Prestige Carnegie Hall 1943-1944 Concerts | Definitive Records | DRCD 11210

Goin' Up The River
Chris Barber's Jazz And Blues Band | 40 Years Jubilee | Timeless | CD TTD 589
Stars Of Faith | Live At The Montreux Jazz Festival | Black & Blue | BLE 59.186 2

Goin' Wess
Katie Kern | Still Young | Jazzpoint | JP 1070 CD

Goin' Where The Moonon Crosses The Yellow Dog
Sammy Price-J.C.Heard | Boogie And Jazz Classics | Black & Blue | BLE 59.111 2

Going Alone
Julian Dash And His Orchestra | Julian Dash:The Complete Recordings 1950-1953 | Blue Moon | BMCD 1050

Going Back To Iuka
Memphis Slim | Boogie For All My Friends | Black & Blue | BLE 59.741 2

Going Blues
Katie Webster | Pounds Of Blues | Charly | CRB 1087

Going Down Slow
Otis Spann | Walking The Blues | Candid | CCD 79025
Otis Spann Band | Blues Giants In Concert-More American Folk Blues Festival 1963 | ACT | 9205-2

Going For A Walk
Kenny Wheeler Brass Ensemble | A Long Time Ago | ECM | 1691

Going For Baroque
The Metro Stompers | The Metro Stompers | Sackville | 4002

Going Home
Dave Stryker Octet | Blue To The Bone III | Steeplechase | SCCD 31524
Dave Stryker Quintet | Strike Zone | Steeplechase | SCCD 31277
Gary Burton Group | GRP Live At The North Sea Festival | GRP | GRP 88792
Louisiana Red | The Blues Purity Of Louisiana Red | Blue Labor | BL 104

Going Jungle
Clifton Chenier And His Band | King Of The Bayous | Arhoolie | CD 339

Going Places
Tord Gustavsen Trio | Changing Places | ECM | 1834(016397-2)
Steve Tibbetts Group | Bye Bye Safe Journey | ECM | 1270

Going Somewhere
Bennie Green's Band | Juggin' Around | Atlantis | ATS 1

Going To Brownsville
Basie's Bad Boys | The Count And The President-Vol.1 1936 & 1939 | CBS | CBS 88667

Going To Chicago Blues
Peggy Lee With The Quincy Jones Orchestra | Blues Cross Country | Capitol | 520088-2
Wayne Bartlett With The Thomas Hufschmidt Trio And Wolfgang Engstfeld | Senor Blues | Laika Records | LK 95-066
Joe Williams With The Cannonball Adderley Septet | Joe Williams Live | Original Jazz Classics | OJCCD 438-2(F 9441)

Going To New York
Buddy Johnson And His Orchestra | Go Ahead & Rock Rock Rock | Official | 6011
Oscar Klein Band | Pick-A-Blues Live | Jazzpoint | JP 1071
The Icebreakers | At The New Morning Blues Festival | Spiegelei | 170600

Going To School
Louis Armstrong And The Lyn Murray Choir | Louis Armstrong Vol.3-Louis With Guest Stars | MCA | 1306

Going To Shout All Over God's Heaven
Mose Allison Quartet | The Mose Chronicles-Live In London,Vol.2 | Blue Note | 529748-2

Going To The City
Rebirth Jazz Band | Here To Stay | Arhoolie | 1092

Going To Who Owns Me- - (Going To) Who Owns Me-
Stan Getz With The Eddie Sauter Orchestra | Stan Getz Plays The Music Of Mickey One | Verve | 531232-2
Marie Knight And Her Group | Today | Blue Labor | BL 106

Going Up
Duke Ellington-Johnny Hodges All Stars | Verve Jazz Masters 4:Duke Ellington | Verve | 516338-2
Duke Ellington And Johnny Hodges Plus Others | Verve | 2304417 IMS

Going Up Town
Ron Ringwood's Gospel Messengers | You Can Lean On Me | Inak | 9040

Going West
Night Ark | In Wonderland | EmArCy | 534471-2

Going, Going, Gong!
Philip Aaberg | High Plains | Windham Hill | WD 1037

Gold-
Franz Koglmann Tentet | Ich | Hat Art | CD 6033

Gold Fish
Kenny Clarke And His Orchestra | Kenny Clarke | Swing | SW 8411 IMS

Gold Mine
Jon Jang & The Pan-Asian Arkestra | Tiananmen! | Soul Note | 121223-2

Gold Rush
Gerry Mulligan Quartet | My Funny Valentine | Jazz Society(Vogue) | 670511
Herbie Mann Group | Astral Island | Atlantic | 78-0077-1
Stan Getz And His Orchestra | Stan The Man | Verve | 815239-1 IMS
Brew Moore Septet | Brothers And Other Mothers, Vol. 2 | Savoy | SJL 2236 (801212)

Gold Sun
Louisiana Red & His Chicago Blues Friends | American Folk Blues Festival Live '83 | L+R Records | LR 42063

Golden Arches
Red Sun | Samul Nori | Amadeo | 841222-2

Golden Daze
John Stowell Sextet | Golden Delicious | Inner City | IC 1030 IMS

Golden Earrings
Charlie Byrd Quintet | Du Hot Club De Concord | Concord | CCD 4674
Geoff Keezer Quartet | Curveball | Sunnyside | SSC 1045 D
Hal Galper | Hal Galper At Café Des Copains | Philology | W 35.2
Kenny Drew Trio | Recollections | Timeless | CDSJP 333
Ray Bryant Trio | Ray Bryant Trio | Original Jazz Classics | OJCCD 793-2(P 7098)
The Mastersounds | The Mastersounds | Prestige | PRCD 24770-2
Swinging With The Mastersounds | Original Jazz Classics | OJC 280(F 8050)
Wes Montgomery With The Oliver Nelson Orchestra | Compact Jazz: Wes Montgomery | Verve | 831372-2
Goin' Out Of My Head | CTI Records | PDCTI 1107-2

Golden Era
Duke Ellington And His Orchestra | The Best Of Duke Ellington-Original Sessions 1942/1946 | Festival | 401301

Golden Green
Don Cherry Quartet | Complete Communion | Blue Note | 522673-2

Golden Heart-
James Emery Quartet | Fourth World | Between The Lines | btl 020(Efa 10190-2)

Golden Horn
Abbey Lincoln With The Archie Shepp Quintet | Painted Lady | ITM Records | ITM 1422

Golden Penciled Paradise
Pete Berryman & Adrian O'Reilly | Duet | Acoustic Music Records | 319.1163.2

Golden Rain
Charlie Shavers Quartet | Swing Along With Charlie Shavers | Fresh Sound Records | FSR-CD 327

Golden Slippers
The Minstrel Stars | The Minstrel Stars | Upbeat Jazz | URCD 105

Golden Slumbers
Orquestra Mahatma | A Young Person's Guide | Babel | BDV 9612

Golden Sunset
Volker Schlott & Reinmar Henschke | Influence | Acoustic Music Records | 319.1043.2

Goldfinger
Dave Douglas Quartet | A Thousand Evenings | RCA | 2663698-2
Earl Klugh Trio With The Royal Philharmonic Orchestra | Sounds And Visions | Warner | 9362-45158-2
Jimmy Smith Trio | En Concert Avec Europe 1 | Laserlight | 710379/80
Connie Francis With Orchestra | The Swinging Connie Francis | Audiophile | ACD-286

Goldfischgesänge(II)
Sieverts-Mahall-Elgart | Goldfischgesänge | Jazz Haus Musik | JHM 0076 CD

Goldfischgesänge(III)
Goldfischgesänge | Jazz Haus Musik | JHM 0076 CD

Goldfischgesänge(IV)
Art Blakey And The Jazz Messengers | Au Theatre Des Champs-Elysees | RCA | 2119252-2

Goldie
John Coltrane Trio | Bahia | Original Jazz Classics | OJCCD 415-2

Goldsboro Express
John Coltrane-The Prestige Recordings | Prestige | 16 PCD 4405-2
Lionel Hampton And His Orchestra | Lionel Hampton Vol.3-Sweatin' With Hamp | MCA | 1331

Gomez
Markus Stockhausen Quartet | Joyosa | Enja | ENJ-9468 2

Gommé
Ferenc Snétberger-Markus Stockhausen | For My People | Enja | ENJ-9387 2

Gond Nelkül
Victory Of The Better Man | L'Utopiste | CMP Records | CMP CD 44

Gondwana
Miles Davis Group | Pangaea | CBS | 467087-2

Gondwana(part 1&2)
George Benson Group | George Benson In Concert-Carnegie Hall | CTI | ZK 44167

Gone
Kendra Shank Group | Wish | Jazz Focus | JFCD 028
Miles Davis With Gil Evans & His Orchestra | The Miles Davis Selection | CBS | 465699-2
Reggie Workman Quintet | Summit Conference | Postcards | POST 1003
Tatsuya Takahashi & Tokyo Union | Plays Miles & Gil | Paddle Wheel | K32Y 6268

Gone Again
Teddy Charles Trio | Flyin' Home-Teddy Charles Salutes Lionel Hampton | Fresh Sound Records | FSR 2004(Bethlehem BCP 6032)

Gone Are The Days
Lainie Kazan With Band | In The Groove | Musicmasters | 65168-2

Gone But Not Forgotten
Machito And His Afro-Cuban Salseros | Mucho Macho | Pablo | 2625712-2

Gone For Nothing But Love
David Newton | Return Journey | Linn Records | AKD 025

Gone Gone Gone
Miles Davis With Gil Evans & His Orchestra | The Miles Davis Selection | CBS | 465699-2
Orquestra De Cambra Teatre Lliure | Porgy And Bess | Fresh Sound Records | FSNT 066 CD
Paolo Fresu Quintet | Kind Of Porgy & Bess | RCA | 21951952
Philly Joe Jones Septet | Mo' Joe | Black Lion | BLCD 760154

Gone Gone Gone-
Chas Burchell Quintet | Unsong Hero:The Undiscovered Genius Of Chas Burchell | IN+OUT Records | 7026-2

Gone Into It
Art Hodes | Pagin' Mr.Jelly | Candid | CS 9037

Gone To The Dogs
Quintet For A Day | What We Live | New World Records | 80553-2

Gone Walkin'
Buddy Johnson And His Orchestra | Walkin' | Official | 6008

Gone With The Wind
Art Blakey And The Jazz Messengers | At The Cafe Bohemia Vol.3 | Blue Note | 300193(BNJ 61007)
Art Pepper Quartet | Intensity | Original Jazz Classics | OJCCD 387-2
Intensity | Original Jazz Classics | OJCCD 387-2
Art Tatum | Art Tatum-The Complete Pablo Solo Masterpieces | Pablo | 7 PACD 4404-2
Jazz:The Essential Collection Vol.2 | IN+OUT Records | 78012-2
Handful Of Keys | ASV | AJA 5073
Art Tatum-Ben Webster Quartet | Art Tatum-The Complete Pablo Group Masterpieces | Pablo | 6 PACD 4401-2
The Tatum Group Masterpieces | Pablo | 2625706
Art Van Damme Group | State Of Art | MPS | 841413-2
Art Van Damme Quintet | Keep Going/Blue World | MPS | 529093-2
Ben Webster Quartet | Live At The Jazzhus Montmartre,Vol.1 | Jazz Colours | 874710-2
Ben Webster With The Junior Mance Trio | Tenor Giants | Enja | 2038-2
Bill Evans Trio | The Complete Bill Evans On Verve | Verve | 527953-2
Jazz-Club: Drums | Verve | 840033-2
Bill Evans-Eddie Gomez Duo | Eloquence | Fantasy | F 9618
Bill Evans:Piano Player | CBS | CK 65361
Billie Holiday And Her Orchestra | Billie Holiday Story Vol.5:Music for Torching | Verve | MV 2595 IMS
Bobby Short With The Alden-Barrett Quintet | Swing That Music | Telarc Digital | CD 83317
Charlie Ventura Orchestra With Jackie & Roy | Euphoria | Savoy | SJL 2243 (801889)
Chris Connor With The Vinnie Burke Quartet+Art Mardigan | Lullabys Of Birdland | Bethlehem | BTM 6823
Earl Hines And His Orchestra | Fatha Vol.1 | Zeta | ZET 710
Ella Fitzgerald With Joe Pass | Speak Love | Pablo | 2310888
Ella Fitzgerald With Orchestra | Forever Ella | Verve | 529387-2
Ella Fitzgerald With The Frank DeVol Orchestra | Ella Fitzgerald Sings Sweet Songs For Swingers | Verve | 9860417
Ella Fitzgerald With The Paul Smith Quartet | Mack The Knife-Ella In Berlin | Verve | 825670-2
Ernie Henry Quintet | Presenting Ernie Henry | Original Jazz Classics | OJC 102(RLP 222)
Gene Bertoncici Trio | Acoustic Romance | Paddle Wheel | KICJ 155
Herb Steward Quintet | One Brother | Mobile Fidelity | MFCD 884
Joe Bonner | Devotion | Steeplechase | SCCD 31182
Johnny Hodges Orchestra | The Soul Of Ben Webster | Verve | 527475-2
Jon Weber | Live In Concert:Jon Weber Flying Keys | Jazz Connaisseur | JCCD 9726-2
Jutta Hipp Quintet | Deutsches Jazz Fesival 1954/1955 | Bear Family Records | BCD 15430
Jutta Hipp Trio | Jutta Hipp At The Hickory House Vol.2 | Blue Note | 0677179
Kenny 'Pancho' Hagood With The Al Haig Trio | Cool Whalin' - Bebop Vocals | Spotlite | SPJ 135
Lee Konitz-Matt Wilson | Gone With The Wind | Steeplechase | SCCD 31528
Lightnin' Hopkins | Houston's King Of The Blues | Blues Classics | BC 30
Lyambiko And Her Trio | Out Of This Mood | Nagel-Heyer | CD 2021
Marian McPartland Trio feat. Chris Potter | In My Life | Concord | CCD 4561
Stan Getz Quartet | Stan Getz-The Complete Roost Sessions | EMI Records | 859622-2
Stan Getz:Imagination | Dreyfus Jazz Line | FDM 36733-2
Stan Getz-The Best Of The Roost Years | Roulette | 7981442
Steve Allen Sextet | Steve Allen Plays Jazz Tonight | Concord | CCD 4548
Ted Rosenthal | Maybeck Recital Hall Series Volume Thirty-Eight | Concord | CCD 4648
The Mitchell-Marsh Big Two | Hot House | Storyville | SLP 4092
Wes Montgomery Quartet | Wes Montgomery-The Complete Riverside Recordings | Riverside | 12 RCD 4408-2
Wild Bill Davis Group | Americans Swinging In Paris:Wild Bill Davis | EMI Records | 539665-2
Wynton Kelly Trio | Wynton Kelly! | Vee Jay Recordings | VJ 011

Gone With The Wind-
Willie Cook&Paul Gonsalves With The Enrque Villegas Trio | Encuentro | Fresh Sound Records | FSR-CD 0072

Gone With The Wind(2)
Bill Evans Trio | The Complete Bill Evans On Verve | Verve | 527953-2

Gone With The Wind(3)
Art Tatum-Ben Webster Quartet | The Tatum Group Masterpieces Vol.8 | Pablo | PACD20 431-2

Gone With The Wind(alt.take 1)
The Art Tatum Group Masterpieces Vol.8 | Pablo | 2405431-2
The Tatum Group Masterpieces Vol.8 | Pablo | PACD20 431-2

Gone With The Wind(alt.take 2)
Art Tatum-The Complete Pablo Group Masterpieces | Pablo | 6 PACD 4401-2

Gone With The Wind(alt.take)
Benny Carter Quintet | Cosmopolite | Verve | 521673-2
Art Tatum-Ben Webster Quartet | Art Tatum-The Complete Pablo Group Masterpieces | Pablo | 6 PACD 4401-2

Gone With The Wind(alt.take-2)
The Art Tatum Group Masterpieces Vol.8 | Pablo | 2405431-2
Bill Evans Trio | Bill Evans:From The 70's | Original Jazz Classics | OJCCD 1069-2(F 9630)

Gone With The Wind(take 3)
Alan Dean's Beboppers | Bebop In Britain | Esquire | CD ESQ 100-4

Gone(alt.take)
Duke Ellington And His Orchestra | The Afro-Eurasian Eclipse-A Suite In Eight Parts | Original Jazz Classics | OJCCD 645-2(F 9498)

Gong
Ira Sullivan Quintet | Peace | Galaxy | GXY 5114

Gonga Din
Andreas Lonardoni Group | Snooze | Lipstick Records | LIP 8956-2

Góngo
Chico Hamilton Quintet | Gongs East | Discovery | DS 831 IMS

Gonna Use My Rod
Peter Brötzmann/Alfred 23 Harth | Go-No-Go | FMP | 1150

Good Addiction
J.B.Lenoir | Alabama Blues | L+R Records | CDLR 42001

Good Bait
Art Pepper With The Duke Jordan Trio | Art Pepper With Duke Jordan In Copenhagen 1981 | Galaxy | 2GCD 8201-2
Bobby Hutcherson Quintet | Good Bait | Landmark | LCD 1501-2
Dizzy Gillespie All Stars | Dizzy Gillespie:Night In Tunisia | Dreyfus Jazz Line | FDM 36734-2
Groovin' High | Naxos Jazz | 8.120582 CD
Dizzy Gillespie And His Orchestra | Dizzier And Dizzier | RCA | 26685172
The Greatest Of Dizzy Gillespie | RCA | 2113164-2
Dizzy Gillespie (1946-1949) | RCA | ND 89763
Dizzy Gillespie Quintet | Dizzy Gillespie:Pleyel 53 | Vogue | 2115466-2
Dizzy Gillespie Sextet | Jazz Gallery:Dizzy Gillespie | RCA | 2114165-2
Don Sickler Orchestra | Dameronia | Soul Note | 121202-2
Frank Collett Trio | Perfectly Frank | Fresh Sound Records | FSR-CD 5024
Hank Crawford Quartet | The World Of Hank Crawford | Milestone | MCD 9304-2
Hank Crawford Septet | The World Of Hank Crawford | Milestone | MCD 9304-2
Jay Hoggard Quartet | Love Is The Answer | Muse | MCD 5527
Joe Pass Quartet | Live At Yoshi's | Pablo | 2310951-2
John Coltrane Quartet | John Coltrane-The Prestige Recordings | Prestige | 16 PCD 4405-2
John Coltrane | Prestige | P 24003
Max Roach Quartet | In The Light | Soul Note | 121053-2
Miles Davis/Tadd Dameron Quintet | Paris Festival International De Jazz, May 1949 | CBS | 485527-2
Steve Grossman With The McCoy Tyner Trio | In New York | Dreyfus Jazz Line | FDM 36555-2

Good Bye
Ahmad Jamal Trio | I Remember Duke,Hoagy & Strayhorn | Telarc Digital | CD 83339
Art Pepper Quartet | Art Pepper:The Complete Village Vanguard Sessions | Contemporary | 9CCD-4417-2
Art Pepper:The Complete Village Vanguard Sessions | Contemporary | 9CCD-4417-2
Art Van Damme & The Singers Unlimited | Invitation | MPS | 68107
Benny Goodman And His Orchestra | More Camel Caravans | Phontastic | NCD 8843/4
More Camel Caravans | Phontastic | NCD 8843/4
More Camel Caravans | Phontastic | NCD 8843/4
More Camel Caravans | Phontastic | NCD 8843/4
More Camel Caravans | Phontastic | NCD 8845/6
More Camel Caravans | Phontastic | NCD 8845/6
More Camel Caravans | Phontastic | NCD 8841/2
Camel Caravan Broadcast 1939 Vol.1 | Phontastic | NCD 8817
More Camel Caravans | Phontastic | NCD 8845/6
Camel Caravan Broadcast 1939 Vol.2 | Phontastic | NCD 8818
More Camel Caravans | Phontastic | NCD 8841/2
Camel Caravan Broadcast 1939 Vol.3 | Phontastic | NCD 8819
More Camel Caravans | Phontastic | NCD 8841/2
More Camel Caravans | Phontastic | NCD 8841/2
Planet Jazz:Benny Goodman | Planet Jazz | 2152054-2
The Benny Goodman Story | Capitol | 833569-2
This Is Benny Goodman Vol. 2 | RCA | NL 89410 DP
Bill Evans Trio | Empathy+A Simple Matter Of Conviction | Verve | 837757-2 PMS
Bucky Pizzarelli-John Pizzarelli Duo | The Complete Guitar Duos(The Stash Sessions) | Stash Records | ST-CD 536(889114)
Charlie Mariano With The Don Sebesky Orchestra | A Jazz Portrait Of Charlie Mariano | Fresh Sound Records | FSR-CD 0176
Chris Connor With The Hank Jones Trio | As Time Goes By | Enja | ENJ-7061 2
Chris Connor With The Ronnie Ball Quartet | Chris Connor At The Village Gate:Early Show | Roulette | 300008(TOCJ 6122)
Erroll Garner Trio | Relaxin' | Vogue | 500117
Jimmy Giuffre 3 | Flight, Bremen 1961 | Hat Art | CD 6071
Jimmy Knepper Quintet | Dream Dancing | Criss Cross | Criss 1024
Lars Moller Quartet | Kaleidoscope | Naxos Jazz | 86022-2
Maynard Ferguson And His Orchestra | Maynard '61 | Fresh Sound Records | R 52064(Roulette)
Oscar Peterson Trio With The Nelson Riddle Orchestra | The Silver Collection: Oscar Peterson | Verve | 823447-2 PMS
Pat Metheny Group | Travels | ECM | 1252/53
Paul Bley Trio | Indian Summer | Steeplechase | SCCD 31286
Ron Eschete Trio | Rain Or Shine | Concord | CCD 4665
Stan Getz Quartet | Stan Getz Highlights | Verve | 847430-2
Stan Getz At Large Plus!,Vol.1 | Jazz Unlimited | JUCD 2001

Good Bye-
Bill Frisell Trio | Live | Gramavision | GCD 79504

Good Bye, Good Bye, Good Bye
Gary Burton Quartet | Gary Burton/Larry Coryell | RCA | FXL 17101

Good Earth Smile
Bill O'Connell Group | Voices | CTI Records | CTI 1011-2
Good Enough To Keep(aka Airmail Special)
Position Alpha | Don't Bring Your Dog! | Dragon | DRLP 50
Good For Nothin'(But Love)
Chuck Foster And His Orchestra | The Uncollected:Chuck Foster, Vol.2 | Hindsight | HSR 171(835576)
Good For The Soul
Roy Haynes Quintet | Te-Vou! | Dreyfus Jazz Line | FDM 36569-2
Good Gracious
The Brecker Brothers | Return Of The Brecker Brothers | GRP | GRP 96842
Billy May And His Orchestra Plus Guests | The Capitol Years | EMI Records | EMS 1275
Good Groove
Jean-Luc Ponty Sextet | Civilized Evil | Atlantic | SD 16020
Good Humour Man
Joe Lovano Trio | One Time Out | Soul Note | SN 1224
Good King Wenceslas
Singers Unlimited | Christmas | MPS | 821859-2
Good Lord I Have Done
Bobby McFerrin | Simple Pleasures | Manhattan | 748059-2
Good Lovin'
Jugendjazzorchester NW | Turning Around | Jugendjazzorchester NW | JJ 005
Good Luck
Lucky Thompson Quintet | Tricotism | Impulse(MCA) | GRP 11352
Washboard Sam | Washboard Sam 1935-1947 | Story Of Blues | CD 3502-2
Good Message
Count Basie And His Orchestra | Digital III At Montreux | Original Jazz Classics | OJCCD 996-2(2308223)
Good Mileage
Shakey Horton Band | The Soul Of Blues Harmonica | Chess | CH 9268
Good Mornin' Blues
Kansas City Six | From Spiritual To Swing | Vanguard | VCD 169/71
Leadbelly[Huddie Ledbetter] | Alabamy Bound | Memo Music | HDJ 4073
Good Mornin' Lil' School Girl
Taj Mahal And The International Rhythm Band | Taj Mahal | The Rising Sun Collection | RSC 0003
Good Morning Bill
Big Joe Turner With The Count Basie Orchestra | Flip Flop And Fly | Original Jazz Classics | OJCCD 1053-2(2310937)
Good Morning Blues
Bunk Johnson's Jazz Band | Bunk & Leadbelly At New York Town Hall 1947 | American Music | AMCD-46
Good Morning Heartache
Billie Holiday And Her All Stars | Billie Holiday Story Vol.4:Lady Sings The Blues | Verve | 521429-2
Verve Jazz Masters 12:Billie Holiday | Verve | 519825-2
The Billie Holiday Song Book | Verve | 823246-2
4 By 4:Ella Fitzgerald/Sarah Vaughan/Billie Holiday/Dinah Washington | Verve | 559693-2
Billie Holiday With Red Norvo And His Orchestra | Masters Of Jazz Vol.3:Billie Holiday | Storyville | STCD 4103
Donald 'Duck' Harrison Quintet | Full Circle | Sweet Basil | 660.55.003
Ella Fitzgerald With The Lou Levy Quartet | Clap Hands,Here Comes Charlie! | Verve | 835646-2
Ella Fitzgerald With The Tommy Flanagan Quartet | Ella Fitzgerald:Newport Jazz Festival-Live at Carnegie Hall | CBS | C2K 66809
Jimmy Jones Trio | The Piano Collection Vol.2 | Vogue | 21610222
Joe Williams With The Jimmy Jones Orchestra | Me And The Blues | RCA | 2121823-2
Kenia And The Jay Ashby Quintet | Live At Warsaw Jazz Festival 1991 | Jazzmen Records | 660.50.006
Lee Konitz With Strings | Strings For Holiday:A Tribute To Billie Holiday | Enja | ENJ-9304 2
Lester Bowie's Brass Fantasy | Live at The 6th Tokyo Muisc Joy '90 | DIW | DIW 842 CD
McCoy Tyner Trio | Remembering John | Enja | ENJ-6080 2
McCoy Tyner Trio With Michael Brecker | Infinity | Impulse(MCA) | IMP 11712
Ray Bryant | Inimitable | Jazz Connaisseur | JCCD 9430-2
Ray Bryant Trio | Blue Moods | EmArCy | 842438-2 PMS
Good Morning Little School Girl
Muddy Waters Quartet | Folk Singer | Chess | CH 9261
Good Morning Susie Soho
Steve Beresford Orchestra | Signals For Tea | Avant | AVAN 039
Good Morning,Freedom Fighter
Trummy Young And His Lucky Seven | Buck Clayton Rarities Vol.1 | Swingtime(Contact) | ST 1024
Good News
Golden Gate Quartet With The Martial Solal Orchestra | From Sprintual To Swing Vol.2 | EMI Records | 780573-2
Jan Harrington And Friends | I Feel The Spirit | Nagel-Heyer | NHR SP 7
Jeff Palmer Quartet | Ease On | audioquest Music | AQCD 1014
Herb Ellis-Joe Pass Quartet | Jazz/Concord | Concord | CCD 6001
Good News Blues
Dollar Brand-Johnny Dyani Duo | Good News From Africa | Enja | 2048-2
Good Night
Kosh | Groovy Strings | Elite Special | 73325
Good Night Vienna
Roy Fox And His Orchestra | The Bands That Matter | Eclipse | ECM 2045
Good Night(dedicated to Seamus Heaney)
Johnny 'Hammond' Smith Quartet | Good 'Nuff | Prestige | PRCD 24282-2
Good 'Nuff
Eric Vloeiman Quartet | Bitches And Fairy Tales | Challenge | CHR 70061
Good Old Days
Jenny Evans And Her Quintet | Shiny Stockings | Enja | ENJ-9317 2
John Zorn Group | Spy Vs. Spy-The Music Of Ornette Coleman | Nonesuch | 7559-60844-2
Ornette Coleman Trio | The Best Of Ornette Coleman:The Blue Note Years | Blue Note | 823372-2
Good Queen Bess
Johnny Hodges Orchestra | Jazz Special-The 40's & 60's | RCA | CL 43236 AF
Johnny Hodges-Wild Bill Davis Sextet | In A Mellotone | RCA | ND 82305(847146)
The Swingcats | Face To Face:The Swingcats Live | Nagel-Heyer | CD 072
Johnny Hodges Orchestra | Passion Flower 1940-46 | Bluebird | 63 66616-2
Good Question
Odean Pope Trio | Almost Like Me | Moers Music | 01092 CD
Good Thing
St.Louis Kings Of Rhythm | Rhythm And Blues Showtime | Timeless | CD SJP 231/2
Good Time
Count Basie And His Orchestra | Fun Time | Pablo | 2310945-2
Good Time Blues
Jazz At The Santa Monica Civic '72 | Pablo | 2625701-2
The Count Basie Orchestra | Long Live The Chief | Denon Compact Disc | CY-1018
Good Times
Lightnin' Hopkins | The Blues Vol. 5 | Big Bear | 156042
Good To Go
Red Holloway Quintet | Coast To Coast | Milestone | MCD 9335-2
Klaus König Orchestra | The Heart Project | Enja | ENJ-9338 2
Good To Know
Joe Daniels And His Hot Shots | Steppin' Out To Swing | Saville Records | SVL 167 IMS
Good View
Clyde Bernhardt And His Blue Bazers | Clyde Bernhardt:The Complete Recordings Vol.1 (1945-1948) | Blue Moon | BMCD 6016

Good Wood
Josep Maria Balanyà | Sonateskas | Laika Records | 35101102
Good Works For Bad Pianos
Brad Goode Quartet | By Myself | Steeplechase | SCCD 31506
Goodbye
Cal Tjader Quintet | Concerts In The Sun | Fantasy | FCD 9688-2
Concerts In The Sun | Fantasy | FCD 9688-2
Concerts In The Sun | Fantasy | FCD 9688-2
Chuck Wayne Trio | Morning Mist | Original Jazz Classics | OJCCD 1097-2(P-7367)
Ed Kröger Quartet plus Guests | Movin' On | Laika Records | 35101332
Elek Bacsik Trio | Jazz In Paris:Elek Baczik | EmArCy | 542231-2
Gene Ammons Septet | Goodbye | Original Jazz Classics | OJCCD 1081-2(P 100939)
Kenny Drew Jr. Trio | Remembrance | TCB Records | TCB 20202
Tony Purrone Trio | The Tonester | Steeplechase | SCCD 31495
Goodbye Again
Art Pepper Quartet | One September Afternoon | Original Jazz Classics | OJCCD 678-2(GXY 5141)
Mike Stern Group | Upside-Downside | Atlantic | 7567-81656-1
Art Pepper Quartet | Art Pepper:The Complete Galaxy Recordings | Galaxy | 16GCD 1016-2
Goodbye Again(alt.take)
One September Afternoon | Original Jazz Classics | OJCCD 678-2(GXY 5141)
Goodbye Baby Here I Go
Buddy Johnson And His Orchestra | Buddy And Ella Johnson 1953-1964 | Bear Family Records | BCD 15479 DH
Wails | Official | 6010
Goodbye Blues
Dorothy Donegan | Makin' Whoopee | Black & Blue | BLE 59.146 2
Goodbye For Now
Seamus Blake Quintet | The Bloomdaddies | Criss Cross | Criss 1110
Goodbye J.D.
Carmen McRae With The Dixie Flyers | Just A Little Lovin' | Atlantic | AMCY 1079
Goodbye Little Godfather
Blind Blake | Blind Blake-Rope Stretchin' Blues | Biograph | BLP 12037
Goodbye Mister Froggie
The Original Five Blind Boys Of Mississippi | Oh Lord-Stand By Me/Marching Up To Zion | Ace Records | CDCHD 341
Goodbye Old Friend
Oscar Peterson And His Trio | Encore At The Blue Note | Telarc Digital | CD 83356
Goodbye Paris
Aki Takase | Shima Shoka | Enja | 6062-2
Goodbye Pork Pie Hat
Charles McPherson Quintet | First Flight Out | Arabesque Recordings | AJ 0113
Charles Mingus Jazz Workshop | Thirteen Pictures:The Charles Mingus Anthology | Rhino | R2 71402
Charles Mingus Orchestra | Charles Mingus -Passions Of A Man | Atlantic | ATL 60143
Danny Richmond Quintet | Danny Richmond Plays Charles Mingus | Timeless | CD SJP 148
Georges Arvanitas Trio | Rencontre | CBS | 491232-2
Horace Parlan | Jazzbühne Berlin '79/'83 | Repertoire Records | REPCD 4918-WZ
Jeanne Lee-Mal Waldron | After Hours | Owl Records | 013426-2
Jeff Beck Quartet | Wired | Epic | ???
Larry Coryell Quintet | The Coryells | Chesky | JD 192
Mark Murphy And His Sextet | Bop For Kerouac | Muse | MCD 5253
Mingus Dynasty | Chair In The Sky | Warner | 99081
Norbert Gottschalk-Frank Haunschild | The Art Of The Duo:Favorite Songs | Mons Records | MR 874813
Ralph Towner-Gary Burton | Matchbook | ECM | 1056(835014-2)
Sandy Lomax With The Martin Schrack Trio | Songs From The Jazz Age | Workshop Records | WOR 201(CD 583)
Tony Reedus Quintet | Minor Thang | Criss Cross | Criss 1117
Goodbye Pork Pie Hat-
Wolfgang Schmiedt | 4 Guitars | KlangRäume | 30010
Goodbye Pork Pie Hat(dedicated to Jaco Pastorius & Gil Evans)
D.D.Jackson | ...So Far | RCA | 2663549-2
Goodbye Sadness(Tristeza)
Hamiet Bluiett Quartet | Ballads & Blues:Live At The Village Vanguard | Soul Note | 121288-2
Goodbye Storyteller(for Fred Myrow)
Charles Sullivan Orchestra | Genesis | Inner City | IC 1012 IMS
Goodbye To A Friend
Ari Ambrose Quartet | Cylic Episode | Steeplechase | SCCD 31472
Goodbye To Childhood
Herbie Hancock Sextet | The Best Of Herbie Hancock | Blue Note | 89907
Herbie Hancock:The Complete Blue Note Sixties Sessions | Blue Note | 495569-2
Goodbye To Childhood(alt.take)
Greta Keller With Band | Jazz In Paris:Louis Armstrong And Friends | EmArCy | 013979-2
Goodjinns
Houston Person Sextet | Goodness! | Original Jazz Classics | OJC20 332-2(P 7678)
Goodness
George Wallington | The Symphony Of A Jazz Piano | Denon Compact Disc | 33C38-7825
Goodnight
Dick Robertson And His Orchestra | The New York Session Man | Timeless | CBC 1-008
Goodnight Angel
Louis Armstrong With Sy Oliver's Choir And Orchestra | Louis Armstrong-Heavenly Music | Ambassador | CLA 1916
Goodnight Blues
Hound Dog Taylor & The House Rockers | Natural Boogie | Sonet | 198044(SNTF 678)
Goodnight Irene
Huddie Ledbetter | Blues Roots Vol.1 | Storyville | 6.23700 AG
Goodnight My Love
Benny Goodman And His Orchestra | Camel Caravan Broadcast 1939 Vol.3 | Phontastic | NCD 8819
Planet Jazz:Benny Goodman | Planet Jazz | 2152054-2
The Birth Of Swing | Bluebird | ND 90601(3)
A-Tisket, A-Tasket | Naxos Jazz | 8.120540 CD
Urbie Green And His Orchestra | The Message | Fresh Sound Records | NL 46033(RCA)
Goodnight My Love-
Simon Schott | Bar Piano: Simon Schott Plays Your Favorite Evergreens Vol.2 | Organic Music | ORGM 9735
Sarah Vaughan With The Jimmy Jones Orchestra | Sarah Vaughan In Hi-Fi | CBS | CK 65117
Goodnight Sweet Prince
Mr.Acker Bilk And His Paramount Jazz Band | New Orleans Days | Lake | LACD 36
Goodnight Sweetheart-
Rene Thomas Quintet | Jazz In Paris:René Thomas-The Real Cat | EmArCy | 549400-2 PMS
Goodnight,Wherever You Are
Cab Calloway And His Orchestra | The Cab Calloway Show | Zounds | CD 697110
Goodtime Charlie At The Big Washdown
Bobby Bland And His Band | Bobby Bland The Voice: Duke Recordings 1959-1969 | Ace Records | CDCHD 323
Good-Time Man
Big Bill Broonzy | Big Bill Broonzy 1934-1947 | Story Of Blues | CD 3504-2
Goody Goody
Charlie Byrd Trio | I've Got The World On A String(Charlie Byrd Sings Again) | Timeless | CD SJP 427

Della Reese With The Neal Hefti Orchestra | Della | RCA | 2663912-2
Ella Fitzgerald With Frank De Vol And His Orchestra | Get Happy | Verve | 813391-1 IMS
Ella Fitzgerald With Sy Oliver And His Orchestra | Ella Fitzgerald 75th Birthday Celebration:The Original Decca Recordings | GRP | GRP 26192
Ella Fitzgerald With The Oscar Peterson Quartet | Ella Fitzgerald At The Opera House | Verve | 831269-2 PMS
Helmut Kagerer/Helmut Nieberle | Wes Trane | Edition Collage | EC 453-2
Inge Brandenburg mit Werner Müller und seinem Orchester | Why Don't You Take All Of Me | Bear Family Records | BCD 15614 AH
Jack Montrose And All-Stars | The Horn's Full | RCA | NL 45956(RCA LPM 1572)
Rosemary Clooney With The Buddy Cole Trio | Swing Around Rosie | Coral | 589485-2
Teddy Stauffer Und Seine Original Teddies | Das Schönste Von Damals | Vagabond | 6.28039 DP
Goofin Each Other
Illinois Jacquet And His Orchestra | Illinois Jacquet:All Stars Studio Recordings 1945-1947(Master Takes) | Blue Moon | BMCD 1011
Goofy
G.Q.Williams & Dave Collett | Back To The Boogie | Jazz Colours | 874735-2
Goofy's Waltz
Barrelhouse Jazzband & Carrie Smith | Barrelhouse Jazzband & Carrie Smith | Intercord | 145017
Goon
Andy Jaffe Sextet | Manhattan Projections | Stash Records | ST-CD 549(875045)
Goose Pimples
Bix Beiderbecke And His Gang | Riverboat Shuffle | Naxos Jazz | 8.120584 CD
Goosey Gander
Stephane Furic Quartet | The Twitter-Machine | Soul Note | 121225-2
Gordion's Flashes
Armand Gordon & Son Jazz Clan | Gordon's Back In Town | GIC | GD 5.1221
Gorizia
Joanne Grauer Trio | Joanne Grauer Indtroducing Lorraine Feather | MPS | 68198
Gornjak
Dino Saluzzi Trio | Cité De La Musique | ECM | 1616(533316-2)
Gorrion
Juan Serrano Group | Sabor Flamenco | Concord | CCD 4490
Goshakabuchi
Gebhard Ullmann Trio | Essencia | Between The Lines | btl 017(Efa 10187-2)
Gospel
Mike Richmond Quartet | Dance For Andy | Steeplechase | SCCD 31267
New York Unit | Tribute To George Adams | Paddle Wheel | KICJ 156
Gospel News
Jimmy McGriff Quartet | Charles Earland's Jazz Organ Summit | Cannonball Records | CBD 27102
Gospel Train
Max Collie And His Rhythm Aces | Dixie From The Island Vol.1 | Jazz Colours | 874702-2
Alice Coltrane Trio | A Monastic Trio | Impulse(MCA) | 951267-2
Gospel Trane
Herbie Mann Sextet | Just Wailin' | Original Jazz Classics | OJCCD 900-2(NJ 8211)
Gospel Truth
Tiziana Ghiglioni And Her Band | SONB-Something Old Something New Something Borrowed Something Blue | SPLASC(H) Records | CD H 370-2
Gossip Song
Bud Shank Septet | Brasamba | Pacific Jazz | LN 10092
Got A Match?
Richard Todd Quintet | Rickter Scale | GM Recordings | GM 3015 CD(882952)
Nick Woodland Quartet | Live Fireworks | Blues Beacon | BLU-1027 2
Got A Mind To Give Up Living
Albert Collins & The Ice Breakers | Frozen Alive | Sonet | 147129
Got A New Woman
Eddie Miller And His Orchestra | The Uncollected:Eddie Miller | Hindsight | HSR 225 (835033)
Got A Ticket
Ikey Robinson & His Band | Jabbo Smith 1929-1938 | Retrieval | RTR 79013
Got Love
Lonnie Brooks Blues Band | Wound Up Tight | Sonet | SNTF 974(941974)
Got My Mojo Working
Jimmy Smith Trio | Paris Jazz Concert:Jimmy Smith And The Trio | Laserlight | 36159
Jimmy Smith With The Oliver Nelson Orchestra | Compact Jazz: Jimmy Smith | Verve | 831374-2
Monty Alexander Trio | Reunion In Europe | Concord | CCD 4231
Muddy Waters Blues Band | Live In Antibes 1974 | France's Concert | FCD 116
Got No Blues
Fats Waller And His Rhythm | The Middle Years Part 2(1938-40) | RCA | 6366552-2
Got Somethin' Good For You
Carl Ravazza And His Orchestra | The Uncollected: Carl Ravazza | Hindsight | HSR 117
Got That Feeling
Blind Lemon Jefferson | Blind Lemon Jefferson | Biograph | BLP 12000
Got The Blues So Bad
Don Redman And His Orchestra | Shakin' The Africann | Hep | 1001
Got To Be Some Changes Made
Albert King Blues Band | Blues At Sunset(Live at Wattstax And Montreux) | Stax | SCD 8581-2
Got To Get You Into My Life
Peter Herbolzheimer Rhythm Combination & Brass | Bandfire | Koala Records | CD P 1
Got To Go
Rabih Abou-Khalil Group | The Cactus Of Knowledge | Enja | ENJ-9401 2
Got To Go Home
Joe Thomas And His Orchestra | Joe Thomas:The Complete Recordings 1945-1950 | Blue Moon | BMCD 1051
Got To Move Your Baby
Jazz Gillum Group | Harmonica And Washboard Blues | Black & Blue | BLE 59.252 2
Gotcha
Steve Lane's Famour Red Hot Peppers | Easy Come-Easy Go:A Jazz Cocktail | AZURE Compact Disc | AZ-CD-14
Gothic
Marvin 'Smitty' Smith Group | The Road Less Traveled | Concord | CCD 4379
Gotland
Dr. Umezu Band | Dr. Umezu Band-Live At Moers Festival | Moers Music | 02012
Gott Ist Gegenwärtig
Tilman Jäger Tape 4 | Abendlieder | Satin Doll Productions | SDP 1043-1 CD
Stan Kenton And His Orchestra | By Request Vol.3 | Creative World | ST 1062
Gotta Be This Or That
Ernst Höllerhagen Quartet | Ernst Höllerhagen 1942-1948 | Elite Special | 9522001
Gotta Dance
Jimmy Giuffre 3 | The Jimmy Giuffre 3-Hollywood & Newport 1957-1958 | Fresh Sound Records | FSCD 1026
Philippe Brun And His Swing Band | Django Reinhardt:Djangology | EMI Records | 780659-2

Gotta Go Upside Your Head - (Gotta Go) Upside Your Head
Larry Garner Group | Baton Rouge | Verve | 529467-2
Gotta Move
Lightnin' Hopkins | Blues Train | Mainstream | MD CDO 901
Gotta Move(alt.take)
Louis Prima Group | Jack Pot! | Pathe | 1566231
Gotta Travel On
Ray Bryant | Inimitable | Jazz Connaisseur | JCCD 9430-2
Alone At Montreux | 32 Jazz | 32128
Gouache
Farafina | Bolomakote | VeraBra Records | CDVBR 2026-2
Goutelas-
Sleepy John Estes-Hammie Nixon | Sleepy John Estes 1935-1938 | Black & Blue | BLE 59.254 2
Gowanus
Charly Antolini Quartet | Menue/Finale | BELL Records | BLR 84068
GP
Sorry.It's Jazz | Sorry,It's Jazz! | Satin Doll Productions | SDP 1040-1 CD
GQFS
Willis Jackson Sextet | Gravy | Prestige | PCD 24254-2
Gra-a-a-vy
Marty Cook Group feat. Jim Pepper | Red,White,Black & Blue | Tutu Records | 888174-2*
Grab Bag
Marty Cook Quintet | Red, White, Black And Blue | Enja | 5067-2
Grab The World
Johnny Griffin Quintet | Grab This! | Original Jazz Classics | OJCCD 1941-2(RLP 9437)
Grab This!
Kai Winding's New Jazz Group | Loaded:Vido Musso/Stan Getz | Savoy | SV 0227(MG 12074)
Grabschrift
Günter Sommer | Hörmusik III:Sächsische Schatulle | Intakt Records | CD 027
Grace
Leni Stern Group | Words | Lipstick Records | LIP 890282
Eddie Condon And His Orchestra | Big Band Bounce And Boogie:At The Jazz Band Ball-Eddie Condon | Affinity | AFS 1021
Grace Valse
Clarence Penn Quintet | Play-Penn | Criss Cross | Criss 1201
Graceful Touch
Tord Gustavsen Trio | Changing Places | ECM | 1834(016397-2)
Graceful Touch(Variation)
John Tchicai Trio | Real Tchicai | Steeplechase | SCS 1075
Gracey
Anders Jormin | Xieyi | ECM | 1762(013998-2)
Gracias A La Vida
Jimmy Smith Quartet | Home Cookin' | Blue Note | 853360-2
Gracie
Time Unit | Time Unit | Dragon | DRLP 69
Gracy Kelly
Takeo Moriyama Quartet | Green River | Enja | 4080
Grade 'A' Gravy
Lan Xang | Hidden Gardens | Naxos Jazz | 86046-2
Graffiti
The Errol Parker Experience | Graffiti | Sahara | 1011
Graffiti Express
Dave Soldier Group With Voices | Smut | Avant | AVAN 019
Gra'Ma's Hands
First House | Erendira | ECM | 1307
Grammenos
Elmo Hope Trio | Last Sessions | Inner City | IC 1018 IMS
Granada
Karol Adam Ensemble | Gipsy Fascination | G&J Records | GJ 2001
Reid Anderson Quartet | Abolish Bad Architecture | Fresh Sound Records | FSNT 062 CD
Stan Kenton And His Orchestra | The Exciting Stan Kenton Orchestra | Creative World | ST 1080
Granadas
Bill Evans Trio With The Claus Ogerman Orchestra | The Complete Bill Evans On Verve | Verve | 527953-2
Granados
Compact Jazz: Bill Evans | Verve | 831366-2 PMS
Grand Bazar
Michael Formanek Quartet | Nature Of The Beast | Enja | ENJ-9308 2
Grand Central
Dave Ellis Quintet | State Of Mind | Milestone | MCD 9328-2
Harold Danko | After The Rain | Steeplechase | SCCD 31356
Jimmy Dorsey And His Orchestra | The Uncollected:Jimmy Dorsey, Vol.2 | Hindsight | HSR 153
Grand Collie Dam
Jelly Jaw Short | Going Away Blues 1926-1935 | Yazoo | YAZ 1018
Grand Piano Blues
Lou Blackburn-Freddie Hill Quintet | Perception | Fresh Sound Records | FSR-CD 0307
Grand Prolog
Flip Phillips Quintet | Swing Is The Thing | Verve | 543477-2
Grand Rosé
Aera | Too Much | Spiegelei | 145625
Grand Street
Sonny Rollins Orchestra | Sonny Rollins And The Big Brass | Verve | 557545-2
Sonny Rollins And The Big Brass | Verve | 557545-2
Grand Street(mono LP ending)
Kenny Dorham Sextet | Osmosis | Black Lion | BLCD 760146
Grand Street(verve LP ending)
Cassandra Wilson Group | Jumpworld | JMT Edition | 834434-2
Grand Terrace Shuffle
Earl Hines And His Orchestra | Earl Hines-Piano Man | Bluebird | NK 86750
Grandeur Et Cadence
Tristan Honsinger Quintet | Map Of Moods | FMP | CD 76
Grandfather's Funk
Joe Haider Trio | Grandfather's Garden | JHM Records | JHM 3619
Grandfather's Garden
Slide Hampton-Joe Haider Jazz Orchestra | Give Me A Double | JHM Records | JHM 3627
Harry Verbeke/Carlo de Wijs Quartet | Mo De Bo | Timeless | SJP 246
Grandfather's Waltz
Stan Getz With The Bill Evans Trio | The Complete Bill Evans On Verve | Verve | 527953-2
The Chick Corea-Bill Evans Sessions | Verve | 2610036
Stan Getz-Bill Evans Quartet | Stan Getz & Bill Evans | Verve | 833802-2
Stan Getz With The Bill Evans Trio | The Complete Bill Evans On Verve | Verve | 527953-2
Grandfather's Waltz(alt.take)
Stan Getz-Bill Evans Quartet | Stan Getz & Bill Evans | Verve | 833802-2
Stan Getz With The Bill Evans Trio | The Complete Bill Evans On Verve | Verve | 527953-2
Grandfather's Waltz(incomplete take 1)
The Complete Bill Evans On Verve | Verve | 527953-2
Grandfather's Waltz(incomplete take 2)
Sweetman With His South Side Groove Kings | Austin Backalley Blue | Mapleshade | 02752
Grandmama's Blues
The Chicago Footwarmers | Jazz Classics In Digital Stereo: Johnny Dodds | CDS Records Ltd. | RPCD 622(CD 603)
Grandma's Hands
Dotsero And Guest Musicians | Jubilee | Nova | NOVA 9136-2
Grandma's Shoes
Friedemann Graef Group | Daily New Paradox | FMP | 0450
Grandmother's Teaching
Johnny Dyani Septet | Afrika | Steeplechase | SCS 1186(Audiophile Pressing)
Grandmother's Teaching(take 1)
Jacques Stotzem | Connections | Acoustic Music Records | 319.1194.2
Grandola Vila Morena
Chick Corea Group | Tap Step | Stretch Records | SCD 9006-2
Grandpappy's Barn Dance Death Dance(For Daddy Ben Besson)
Gene Harris Group | In His Hands | Concord | CCD 4758
Grandpa's Spells
Jelly Roll Morton's Red Hot Peppers | Doctor Jazz | Black & Blue | BLE 59.227 2
Grant
Victoria Spivey | American Folk Blues Festival '63 | L+R Records | CDLR 42023
Granted
Grant Green Trio | Green Street | Blue Note | 540032-2
Grant's Dimensions
Charles Earland Quartet | In The Pocket... | Muse | MR 5240
Grant's Stand
Grant Green Sextet | Solid | Blue Note | 833580-2
Grantstand
Leroy Vinnegar Quartet | Walkin' The Basses | Contemporary | CCD 14068-2
Grap(The Giggling Rapsids)
Art Ensemble Of Chicago | Coming Home Jamaica | Dreyfus Jazz Line | FDM 37003-2
Grape Escape
Albert Collins Blues Band | Ice Cold Blues | Charly | CRB 1119
Grapevine
Klaus Treuheit Trio | Sprengwerk | Klaus Treuheit Production | KTMP 9911(CD 164)
Grass Roots
Robert Hohner Persussion Ensemble | The Gamut | dmp Digital Music Productions | CD 505
Grasshopper
Joe Gordon Quintet | Blakey | Verve | 538634-2
Mae Glover Group | Lillians Glinn-Mae Glover(1929-1931) | Story Of Blues | CD 3537-2
Grasshoppers
Huddie Ledbetter | Classics In Jazz-Leadbelly | Pathe | 2C 068-80701(Capitol)
Grateful Parting
Chris Potter Quartet | Gratitude | Verve | 549433-2
Gratitude
Don Pullen | Plays Monk | Paddle Wheel | K 28P 6368
Frank Morgan | Mood Indigo | Antilles | 791320-2(881863)
Gratuliere-
Ralph R.Hübner-Christoph Lauer | Mondspinner | free flow music | ffm 0796
Graugänse Ins Exil
Ahmed El-Salamouny/Gilson De Assis | Tango Brasileiro | FSM | FCD 97725
Grave Train-
Magic Slim And The Teardrops | Gravel Road | Crosscut | CCD 11027
Gravel Road Blues
Christof Lauer Trio | Evidence | CMP Records | CMP CD 70
Graveyard Blues
Teddy Grace with The Charlie Shavers All Stars | Teddy Grace 1937-1940 | Timeless | CBC 1-016
Graveyard Shift
Albion Jazz Band | They're All Nice Tunes | Stomp Off Records | CD 1249
Gravier Street Blues
Johnny Dodds And His Orchestra | New Orleans Jazz Giants 1936-1940 | JSP Records | JSPCD 336
Gravy Train
Lou Donaldson Quintet | Gravy Train | Blue Note | 853357-2
Gravy Train(alt.take)
Bill Henderson With The Oscar Peterson Trio | Vocal Classics | Verve | 837937-2
Gravy Waltz
Joe Williams And Friends | At Newport '63 | RCA | 2663919-2
Junior Mance Trio | Junior's Blues | Original Jazz Classics | OJCCD 1000-2(RLP 9447)
Oscar Peterson Trio | Exclusively For My Friends-The Lost Tapes | MPS | 529096-2
Sam Yahel Trio | Trio | Criss Cross | Criss 1158
Gray And Visceral
John Scofield Quartet | Live | Enja | 3013-2
Gray Days
George Mraz Quartet | Morava | Milestone | MCD 9309-2
Gray Falcon
Lou Levy Quartet | Jazz In Four Colors | Fresh Sound Records | ND 74401
Gray Pigeon
Wardell Gray Quartet | Wardell Gray:Light Gray 1948-1950 | Cool & Blue | C&B-CD 116
Grazing Dreams
Oregon | The Essential Oregon | Vanguard | VSD 109/110
Grease
Jack McDuff Quartet | Jack McDuff:The Prestige Years | Prestige | PRCD 24387-2
Grease Monkey
Bobby Jaspar Quartet | Bobby Jaspar With Friends | Fresh Sound Records | FSR-CD 0166
Greasin Easy
Sonny Criss Quartet | This Is Criss | Original Jazz Classics | OJCCD 430-2(P 7511)
Greasy
Clark Terry Quartet | Shades Of Blues | Challenge | CHR 70007
Greasy Drums
Lionel Hampton & His Giants Of Jazz 1979 | Hamp In Haarlem | Timeless | CD SJP 133
Greasy Greens
Lionel Hampton Big Band | Newport Uproar! | RCA | NL 89590
Greasy Livin'
Trombone Red & His Blue Six | Jazz Archives Vol.77:Jabbo Smith-The Complete 1929-1938 Sessions | EPM Musique | 158112
Greasy Spoon
The Crusaders | The Best Of The Crusaders | MCA | 2292-50536-1
Great Day
Sarah Vaughan With Mundell Lowe And George Duvivier | After Hours | Roulette | 855468-2
The Roulette Years Vol. One/Two | Roulette | CDP 794983-2
Great Googa Mooga
Antonio Hart Quintet With Guests And Strings | It's All Good | Novus | 4163183-2
Great Guns
Maynard Ferguson With The Birdland Dreamband | The Birdland Dream Band Vol.1 | Fresh Sound Records | 58110 CD(RCA)
Great Is Thy Faithfulness
Otis Spann | Otis Spann Is The Blues | Crosscut | CCR 1003(Candid)
Great Northern Stomp
Abe Lyman And His Californians | The Uncollected:Abe Lyman | Hindsight | HSR 184
Great Pumpkin Waltz
Jackie McLean-Gary Bartz Quintet | Ode To Super | Steeplechase | SCCD 31009
Great Scot
Flip Phillips-Scott Hamilton Sextet | A Sound Investment | Concord | CCD 4334
Great Times
Stan Tracey With Roy Babbington | Plays Duke Ellington | Mole Jazz | Mole 10
Greater Kalesh No.48
John Patitucci Group | Sketchbook | GRP | GRP 96172
Greatest Gift
Third Person | Third Person-The Bends | Enemy | EMCD 124(03524)
Greek Triangle
Bendik Hofseth Quintet | Colours | Verve | 537627-2
Green
Tony Williams Lifetime | Lifetime | Blue Note | 499004-2
Green-
David Earle Johnson With Jan Hammer | Hip Address | CMP Records | CMP 14
Green And Gold
Oregon | Beyond Words | Chesky | JD 130
Green And Golden
Tampa Red Band | Midnight Blues | Swingtime(Contact) | BT 2003
Green Beans
Teddy Charles Tentet | The Teddy Charles Tentet | Atlantic | 790983-2
Green Chimneys
Kenny Barron Trio | Green Chimneys | Criss Cross | Criss 1008
Roy Haynes Quartet | Fountain Of Youth | Dreyfus Jazz Line | FDM 36663-2
Roy Haynes Trio | The Roy Haynes Trio | Verve | 543534-2
Tony Reedus Quartet | Incognito | Enja | ENJ-6058 2
Wynton Marsalis Group | Standard Time Vol.4:Marsalis Plays Monk | CBS | CK 67503
Giorgio Gaslini New Quartet | Skies Of China | Dischi Della Quercia | Q 28019
Green Dolphy Suite
Johnny Young | Blues Roots: Give Me The Blues-The Living Tradition | Storyville | 6.28470 DP
Green Dumplings
Woody Herman Band | Chick Donald Walter & Woodrow | Century Records | CR 1110
Green Eyes
Benny Green | Green's Blues | Telarc Digital | CD 83539
Thomas Clausen-Pyysalo Severi | Turn Out The Stars | Storyville | STCD 4215
Green Glasses
Thomas Clausen 3 | Rain | Matrix | MTX 29202 IMS
Green Grass
Big Bill Broonzy | Big Bill Broonzy 1934-1947 | Story Of Blues | CD 3504-2
Green Green Rocky Road
Cannonball Adderley Quartet | Cannonball Adderley Birthday Celebration | Fantasy | FANCD 6087-2
Green Green Rocky Road-
John Benson Brooks Ensemble | Alabama/Africa | Milestone | M 47059
Green Grow The Rushes
Miles Davis Quartet | The Musings Of Miles | Original Jazz Classics | OJCCD 004-2
Green Haze
Green Haze | Prestige | P 24064
Green House Fables
Paul Quinichette Quintet | 6 Classic Tenors | EPM Musique | FDC 5170
Green Lagoon
Bennie Green Quintet | Walkin' And Talkin' | Blue Note | 868296-2
Green Mountains-
Richard Grossman Trio | Where The Sky Ended | HatOLOGY | 541
Green Paradise
Leavin' The City | Jazz Aus Der Schweiz | GOL | GOL 11117
Green Pepper-
Wes Montgomery With The Don Sebesky Orchestra | Talkin' Jazz:Roots Of Acid Jazz | Verve | 529580-2
Green Peppers
California Dreaming | Verve | 827842-2
Andy LaVerne Trio | Glass Ceiling | Steeplechase | SCCD 31352
Green Piece
Maria Schneider Jazz Orchestra | Evanescence | Enja | ENJ-8048 2
Green Room
Ed Staginski | Just A Dream-A Collection For Easy Listening | yvp music | CD 3025
Green Sky
Herbie Mann Sextet | The Jazz We Heard Last Summer | Savoy | SV 0228(MG 12112)
Green Table Speech
John Scofield Quartet | A Go Go | Verve | 539979-2
Green Tea
Travis 'Moonchild' Haddix And The Travis Haddix Band | Shootum Up | Elite Special | 73613
Green With Envy
Grant Green Trio | Green Street | Blue Note | 540032-2
Green With Envy(alt.take)
Shirley Horn | Light Out Of Darkness(A Tribute To Ray Charles) | Verve | 519703-2
Green(It's Not Easy Being Green)
Duke Ellington And His Orchestra | Duke Ellington | Laserlight | 15753
Greenhouse Wife
Michael Bisio Quartet | Michael Bisio Quartet In Seattle | Silkheart | SHCD 107
Greens At The Chicken Shack
Benny Green | Green's Blues | Telarc Digital | CD 83539
Green's Greenery
Joshua Breakstone Trio | Remembering Grant Green | Paddle Wheel | KICJ 169
Greensleeves
Coleman Hawkins Quintet | The Real Thing | Prestige | P 24083
In A Mellow Tone | Original Jazz Classics | OJCCD 6001-2
Jim Brent-Bruce Kaminsky Duo | Greensleeves | Steeplechase | SCS 4003
Jimmy Smith Trio | Christmas Cookin' | Verve | 513711-2
John Coltrane And His Orchestra | Jazz Gallery:John Coltrane Vol.2 | RCA | 2127276-2
John Coltrane Quartet | John Coltrane:The Complete 1961 Village Vanguard Recordings | Impulse(MCA) | 954322-2
John Coltrane:The Complete 1961 Village Vanguard Recordings | Impulse(MCA) | 954322-2
The Other Village Vanguard Tapes | Impulse(MCA) | MCD 04137
Ballads | Impulse(MCA) | 589548-2
John Coltrane:The Classic Quartet-Complete Impulse Studio Recordings | Impulse(MCA) | 951280-2
John Coltrane Quartet With Brass | Africa/Brass | Impulse(MCA) | JAS 8 (AS 6)
Africa/Brass | Impulse(MCA) | GRJ 80042
Kenny Burrell With The Gil Evans Orchestra | Verve Jazz Masters 23:Gil Evans | Verve | 521860-2
Guitar Forms | Verve | 521403-2
Lisa Wahlandt & Mulo Francel And Their Fabulous Bossa Band | Bossa Nova Affair | Edition Collage | EC 534-2
Marc Copland Trio | Haunted Heart & Other Ballads | HatOLOGY | 581
Paul Desmond And The Modern Jazz Quartet | Paul Demond With The Modern Jazz Quartet | CBS | JK 57337
Paul Desmond Quartet | East Of The Sun | Discovery | DS 840 (807432)
Ray Bryant | Alone At Montreux | 32 Jazz | 32128
Shorty Rogers Big Band | Jazz Waltz | Discovery | DS 843 IMS
Oscar Klein | Oscar Klein Pickin' The Blues-Vol. 1 | Intercord | 150005
Greensleeves(45-rpm take)
John Coltrane Quartet | Ballads | Impulse(MCA) | 589548-2
Greensleeves(alt.take 1)
Ballads | Impulse(MCA) | 589548-2
Greensleeves(alt.take 2)
Ballads | Impulse(MCA) | 589548-2
Greensleeves(alt.take 3)
John Coltrane Quartet With Brass | The Complete Africa/Brass Sessions | Impulse(MCA) | 952168-2
Greensleeves(alt.take)
John Coltrane Quintet | The Mastery Of John Coltrane Vol.4:Trane's Mood | MCA | 2292-54650-2
Green-Up Time
Peter Kowald/Keiki Midorikawa | Duos: Japan | FMP | 1280
Greenwich
Billy Jenkins And Fun Horns | Mayfest '94 | Babel | BDV 9502
Greenwich Village
Werner Baumgart's Big Band Baden Baden | Jazz Rock & Sweet | MPS | 68252

Greg Leisz
Harold Danko Quartet | Next Age | Steeplechase | SCCD 31350
Gregor Is My Friend
Fred Böhler And His Orchestra | Jazz In Switzerland 1930-1975 | Elite Special | 9544002/1-4
Gregory Is Here
Pierre Boussaguet Trio | Charme | EmArCy | 538468-2
Grenadine
Tim Berne Group | Tim Berne EmpireThe Five Years Plan/Spectres/Songs And Rituals In Real Time | Screwgun | SC 70009
Greta Garbo
Joe Pass | Joe Pass At The Montreux Jazz Festival 1975 | Original Jazz Classics | OJC20 934-2(2310752)
Grete
Bud Powell Trio | The Amazing Bud Powell-The Scene Changes | Blue Note | BNJ 71004 (BST 84009)
Grey Blue
Michael Musillami Group | GlassArt | Evidence | ECD 22060-2
Grey Eyes
Dave Pell Octet | A Pell Of A Time | Fresh Sound Records | ND 74408
Grey Van Livelihood
Amos Milburn And Band | Chicken Shack Boogie | Pathe | 1561411(Aladdin)
Gridlock
Dave Grusin Ensemble | Harlequin | GRP | GRP 95222
Grievin'
Pete Franklin | Guitar Pete's Blues | Original Blues Classics | OBCCD 560-2(BV 1068)
Griffin' Leroy
The Kenny Clarke-Francy Boland Big Band | Two Originals:Sax No End/All Blues | MPS | 523525-2
Grille
Joey DeFrancesco Quartet | All About My Girl | Muse | MCD 5528
Grillitos
Tiny Grimes Swingtet | Callin' The Blues | Original Jazz Classics | OJC 191(P 7144)
Griot Song
Jean-Paul Bourelly Group | Boom Bop | PAO Records | PAO 10640
Gris
Gustavo Bergalli Group | Tango In Jazz | Touché Music | TMcCD 007
Grisel
Horacio Molina With Band | Tango Cancion | Messidor | 15910
Grisilla
Samba Trio | Tristeza | Timeless | CD SJP 169
Grits,Gravy And Groove
Barney Wilen Quintet | Wild Dogs Of The Ruwenzori | IDA Record | 020 CD
Grizzly
Down Home Jazz Band | Back To Bodega | Stomp Off Records | CD 1273
Groanin'
Jimmy Smith Trio | Home Cookin' | Blue Note | 853360-2
Günter Sommer | Hörmusik III:Sächsische Schatulle | Intakt Records | CD 027
Groofta
Simon Nabatov-Nils Wogram | Starting A Story | ACT | 9402-2
Michael Formanek Septet | Low Profile | Enja | ENJ-8050 2
Groombridge 34
Deep Creek Jazzuits | Again | Jazz Pure Collection | AU 31615 CD
Groove Blues
Gene Ammons And His All Stars | The Prestige Legacy Vol.2:Battles Of Saxes | Prestige | PCD 24252-2
John Coltrane-The Prestige Recordings | Prestige | 16 PCD 4405-2
Louie Bellson And His Orchestra | The Louis Bellson Explosion | Original Jazz Classics | OJCCD 728-2(2310755)
Groove Bone(part 1)
Rodney Jones Group | Soul Manifesto | Blue Note | 530499-2
Groove Bone(part 2)
Torsten Kamps | Groove Booster | Blackbird Records | BD 40510
Groove Drops
Jimmy Smith With The Johnny Pate Orchestra | Jimmy Smith:Best Of The Verve Years | Verve | 527950-2
John Scofield Groups | Groove Elation | Blue Note | 832801-2
Groove Elation
Jimmy McGriff Quintet | Swingin' The Blues-Jumpin' The Blues | Laserlight | 24654
Groove Fly
Jimmy McGriff-Funkiest Little Band In The Kand | LRC Records | CDC 9046(874379)
Groove Machine
First Class Blues Band | The First Class Blues Band Proudly Presents Mr. Frank Biner | Acoustic Music Records | 319.1062.2
Groove Merchant
Svend Asmussen Quartet | Fit As A Fiddle | dacapo | DCCD 9429
Thad Jones-Mel Lewis Orchestra | Swiss Radio Days Jazz Series Vol.4:Thad Jones-Mel Lewis Orchestra | TCB Records | TCB 02042
Ulf Meyer & Martin Wind Group | Kinnings | Storyville | STCD 8374
Panaudium | Stadtgarten Series Vol.5 | Jazz Haus Musik | JHM 1005 SER
Groove Move
Cedar Walton Sextet | Cedar Walton:Composer | Astor Place | TCD 4001
Groove Passion
Eugen Apostolidis Quartet | Imaginary Directions | Edition Collage | EC 503-2
Groove Positive
Art Blakey And The Jazz Messengers | New Sounds | Blue Note | 784436-2
Groove Therapy
Rolf Kühn Group | Internal Eyes | Intuition Records | INT 3328-2
Groove Town
Whisper Not | Lauter Leise Leute | Blue Concept | BCCD 94/02
Groove Waltz
Jamaaladeen Tacuma Group | Dreamscape | DIW | DIW 904 CD
Groove With Me
Joshua Redman Quartet | Joshua Redman | Warner | 9362-45242-2
Groove X(By Any Means Necessary)
| Remember When | Master Mix | CHECD 11
Groove Yard
Marian McPartland Trio | In My Life | Concord | CCD 4561
Phineas Newborn Jr. Trio | The Newborn Touch | Original Jazz Classics | OJCCD 270-2
The Trio | The Trio:Rediscovered | String Jazz | SJRCD 1007
Bill Perkins Quintet | Quietly There | Original Jazz Classics | OJCCD 1776-2
Groove's Groove
Cowws Quintet | Grooves 'N' Loops | FMP | CD 59
Groovin'
George Benson And His Orchestra | Giblet Gravy | Verve | 543754-2
George Benson Orchestra | Talkin' Verve:George Benson | Verve | 553780-2
George Benson With Orchestra | The Silver Collection: George Benson | Verve | 823450-2 PMS
Kenny Burrell Quintet | Moonglow | Prestige | P 24106
Ed Kröger Quartet plus Guests | Movin' On | Laika Records | 35101332
Groovin' At Chico's
Jimmy Smith Quintet | Cool Blues | Blue Note | 535587-2
Groovin' At Small's
Jimmy McGriff Quartet | Charles Earland's Jazz Organ Summit | Cannonball Records | CBD 27102
Groovin' For Mr.G
Dizzy Gillespie And His Orchestra | Dizzy In Greece | Verve | MV 2630 IMS
Groovin' For Nat
Dizzy Gillespie Big Band | Groovin' High | Bandstand | BDCD 1513
Groovin' Hard
Harald Rüschenbaum Orchestra | Live | Swingtime | 8203
Groovin' High
Alex Gunia's Groove Cut | Alex Gunia's Groove Cut | ITM Records | ITM 1463
Art Pepper Plus Eleven | Modern Jazz Classics | Original Jazz Classics | OJC20 341-2
A Treasury Of Modern Jazz Classics | Mobile Fidelity | MFCD 805
Bud Powell Quartet | The Legacy | Jazz Door | JD 1204
Carlo Atti With The Hal Galper Trio | Sweet Beat Blues | Red Records | 123277-2
Charlie Parker Quintet | Broadcast Performances Vol.2 | ESP Disk | ESP 3001-2
Dizzy Gillespie All Star Sextet | Groovin' High | Naxos Jazz | 8.120582 CD
Dizzy Gillespie And His Orchestra | Dizzy Gillespie 1948-1952 | Queen-Disc | 045
Dizzy Gillespie Quintet | Live | Jazz Door | JD 1277
Erroll Garner Quartet And The Brass Bed | Now Playing:A Night At The Movies & Up In Erroll's Room | Telarc Digital | CD 83378
Lou Donaldson Quartet | Live In Bologna | Timeless | CD SJP 202
Pucho & His Latin Soul Brothers | Groovin' High | Cannonball Records | CBD 27103
Sonny Stitt Quartet | Tune Up | Muse | MCD 5334
Tommy Flanagan Trio | Something Borrowed Something Blue | Original Jazz Classics | OJCCD 473-2
Dick Wellstood | Live at The Sticky Wicket | Arbors Records | ARCD 19188
Groovin' High(alttake)
Charlie Parker Quintet | Bird's Eyes-Last Unissued Vol.2+3 | Philology | W 12/15.2
Grooving With Mr.G.
Jean-Paul Bourelly Group | Vibe Music | PAO Records | PAO 10500
Groovy Samba
Rickey Woodard Quartet | The Tokyo Express | Candid | CCD 79527
Groschenotto
Dim Sum Clip Job | Harmolodic Jeopardy | Avant | AVAN 051
Grotta(for Martin)
Noctett | Heroes' Trilogy | Cain | CL 5824
Ground Control
Don Rendell Nine | Earth Music | Spotlite | SPJ 515
Ground Hog
John Lee Hooker | House Of The Blues | Chess | CHD 9258(872282)
Ground Hog Blues
Blues Roots Vol. 13: John Lee Hooker | Chess | 6.24803 AG
Groundwork
Charles Mingus Orchestra | The Black Saint And The Sinner Lady | Impulse(MCA) | 951174-2
Group And Solo Dance
Charles Mingus And His Orchestra | Great Moments With Charles Mingus | MCA | MCA 2-4128 (802130)
Group Dancers
Great Moments With Charles Mingus | MCA | MCA 2-4128 (802130)
Group Shot
Spyro Gyra & Guests | Love & Other Obsessions | GRP | GRP 98112
Group Therapy
Sam Rivers Trio | Essence | Circle Records | RK 1-2976/1 IMS
Grover Washington Jr.
Jasper Van't Hof | Un Mondo Illusorio | Challenge | CHR 70059
Grow Your Own
John Patitucci Group | John Patitucci | GRP | GRP 95602
Grüblein
Vollmond | Vollmond Jazz | Jazz Haus Musik | JHM 02
Grün
Peter Kowald/Keiki Midorikawa | Duos: Europa-America-Japan | FMP | CD 21
Gry(Dawn)
Benny Bailey Quintet | No Refil | TCB Records | TCB 94202
G-Spot
Koch-Schütz-Studer & Musicos Cubanos | Fidel | Intakt Records | CD 056
Guachi Guaro(Soul Sauce)
Paul Nero Sound | Doldinger's Best | ACT | 9224-2
Bluesy Toosy | ACT | 9200-2
Guadeloupe
Ornette Coleman & Prime Time | Tone Dialing | Verve | 527483-2
Guaganco
Nicos Jaritz Unidad | Viva Cuba | Lyraphon Music Production | LY 640001(807440)
Guaguanco Mania
The Conga Kings | The Conga Kings | Chesky | JD 193
Guamba
Eddie Lockjaw Davis Orchestra | Afro-Jaws | Original Jazz Classics | OJCCD 403-2(RLP 9373)
Guanco Lament
Juan Garcia Esquivel Orchestra | Juan's Again | RCA | 2168206-2
Guantanamera
Les McCann Group | Talkin' Verve:Les McCann | Verve | 557351-2
José Maria Vitier-Frank Emilio Flynn | Jane Bunnett And The Cuban Piano Masters | Pacific Jazz | 832695-2
Guarabe
New Generation Cuban All Stars | The New Generation Cuban All Stars Vol.1:Antes De Nuestro Tiempo | Messidor | 15941
Guaracha Potpourri:
Cal Tjader Quintet | Tjader Plays Mambo | Original Jazz Classics | OJCCD 274-2(F 3221)
Guarachi Guaro
Dizzy Gillespie And His Orchestra | Dizzy Gillspie-The Complete RCA Victor Recordings | Bluebird | 63 66528-2
Guarda Li
Sfogliare Albi | Tempo Per | yvp music | CD 3029
Guardian Angel
Tim Ries Quintet | Universal Spirits | Criss Cross | Criss 1144
Guardians Of The Deep
Donald Harrison-Terence Blanchard Quintet | Nascence | CBS | BFC 40335
Guataca City
Herbie Mann Group | Discotheque | Atlantic | SD 1670
Guch
Gary Lucas | Skeleton On The Feast | Enemy | EMCD 126(03526)
Guess What
Stan Kenton | Solo:Stan Kenton | Creative World | ST 1071
Guess Where It's Coming From
B.B. King And His Orchestra | Live In Concert | Kingdom Jazz | Gate 7017
Guess Who I Saw Today
Janis Siegel Group | I Wish You Love | Telarc Digital | CD 83551
Lezlie Anders And Her Band | With Love,Lezlie | Celebrity | CYCD 74801
Maynard Ferguson Orchestra With Chris Connor | Two's Company | Roulette | 837201-2
Bobby Short And His Orchestra | Celebrating 30 Years At The Cafe Carlyle | Telarc Digital | CD 83428
Guest In A Nest
Count Basie And His Orchestra | The Indispensable Count Basie | RCA | ND 89758
Guetteur D'Inapercu
Jimmie Lunceford And His Orchestra | The Original Jimmy Lunceford Orchestra | Jazz Anthology | JA 5224
Gugging
Vienna Art Choir | Five Old Songs | Moers Music | 02036 CD
Guided Tour
Kenny Burrel Quartet | Guiding Spirit | Contemporary | CCD 14058-2
Guijira
(Little)Jimmy Scott With The Howard Biggs Quintet | Very Truly Yours-Jimmy Scott | Savoy | SV 0239(MG 12027)
Guilty
Karrin Allyson Trio | I Didn't Know About You | Concord | CCD 4543
Orange Kellin Trio | The Orange Kellin Trio | Big Easy Records | BIG CD-004
The Bad Plus | These Are The Vistas | CBS | 510666-2
Mel Tormé And Cleo Laine With The John Dankworth Orchestra | Nothing Without You | Concord | CCD 4515
Guilty Of Not Beeing Innocent-
Niels-Henning Orsted-Pedersen Trio | Those Who Were | Verve | 533232-2
Guilty,Your Honour
Bachi Attar/Elliott Sharp Group | In New York | Enemy | EMCD 114(03514)
Guinbre
Bola Sete And His New Brazilian Trio | Autentico | Original Jazz Classics | OJC 290(F 8375)
Guinea
Stuttgarter Gitarren Trio | Stuttgarter Gitarren Trio Vol.2 | Edition Musikat | EDM 034
Guinea Fowl
Radu Malfatti-Harry Miller Duo | Zwecknagel | FMP | SAJ 34
Guinia
Miles Davis Group | Circle In The Round | CBS | 467898-2
Guinnevere
Circle In The Round | CBS | 467898-2
Tome XX | Third Degree | Jazz Haus Musik | JHM 0063 CD
Guiro
Jerry Gonzalez & Fort Apache Band | The River Is Deep | Enja | ENJ-4040 2
Guiro Apache
Marvin Stamm Sextet | Mystery Man | Musicmasters | 65085-2
Guitar Blues No.1
Big Bill Broonzy | The Blues | Storyville | 4960323
Guitar Blues No.2
The Rosenberg Trio With Frits Landesbergen | Gypsy Swing | Verve | 527806-2
Guitar Boogie
Memphis Slim And His Orchestra | Rockin' The Blues | Charly | CRB 1030
Guitar Groove
Uwe Kropinski | Guitar Guitar | ITM Records | ITM 1452
Guitarra Picante
La Vienta | Forgotten Romance | Telarc Digital | CD 83380
Guitars Of The Exotic Isle-
Khalil Chanine Group | Mektoub | AH Records | AH 40509
Gula Gula
Nils Landgren-Tomasz Stanko | Gotland | ACT | 9226-2
Guldrupe
Ed Thigpen Rhythm Features | It's Entertainment | Stunt Records | STUCD 19816
Gulf Coast Blues
Phil Mason's New Orleans All-Stars | You Do Something To Me! | Lake | LACD 33
Gülhan
Okay Temiz Group | Magnet Dance | TipToe | TIP-888819 2
Gull In A Gulch
Lars Gullin Quartet | Made In Sweden Vol.1: 1949 to March 1951 | Magnetic Records | MRCD 106
Gullharpan
Fourplay | Between The Sheets | Warner | 9362-45340-2
Gulliver
Claudio Lodati Dac'Corda | Chance | SPLASC(H) Records | CD H 306-2
Gulls
Buddy Guy Blues Band | Buddy Guy-The Complete Chess Studio Recordings | MCA | MCD 09337
Gully Hully
Buddy Guy Chicago Blues Band | Blues Rarities | Chess | 6.28601 DP
Gully Low Blues
John Gill's Dixieland Serenaders | Take Me To The Midnight Cake Walk Ball | Stomp Off Records | CD 1304
Gully Low Blues-
Lew Stone And His Band | Lew Stone And His Band | Decca | DDV 5005/6 DT
Gumbo Man
Jerome Richardson Group | Jazz Station Runaway | TCB Records | TCB 97402
Gumboot
Eric St-Laurent-Thomy Jordi-Thomas Alkier feat. Helge Schneider | Rock,Jazz & Music:Laut! | BIT | 11212
Gummy Dummy
Courtney Williams Sextet | The Changing Face Of Harlem, Vol. 2 | Savoy | SJL 2224 (801200)
Guna Guna
Passport | Iguacu | Atlantic | 2292-46031-2
Ikue Mori Trio | Painted Desert | Avant | AVAN 030
Gundula
Lee Konitz With Alan Broadbent | Live-Lee | Milestone | MCD 9329-2
Woody Herman And His Orchestra | Sonny Berman:Woodshopper's Holiday 1946 | Cool & Blue | C&B-CD 111
Gunn 2001
Russell Gunn Septet | Gunn Fu | HighNote Records | HCD 7003
Gunslinging Bird
Charles Mingus Orchestra | Nostalgia In Times Square/The Immortal 1959 Sessions | CBS | 88337
Mingus Big Band | Gunslinging Birds | Dreyfus Jazz Line | FDM 36575-2
Gurjari Todi
Toto Blanke-Diego Jasca | Sur | ALISO Records | AL 1035
Gürteltierblues
Kenny Werner | Maybeck Recital Hall Series Volume Thirty-Four | Concord | CCD 4622
Gush
Jon Gordon Quintet | Ask Me Now | Criss Cross | Criss 1099
Gus's Smile
Dave Bargeron Quartet | Barge Burns...Slide Flies | Mapleshade | 02832
Gussie's Great Escape
Eye Of The Hurricane | Eye Of The Hurricane | Aho-Recording | AHO CD 1007(CD 662)
Gut Bucket Steepy
Möslang-Guhl Duo | Deep Voices | FMP | 0510
Guten Aben
Dieter Ilg Trio | Fieldwork | Jazzline | JL 11155-2
Guten Abend,Gute Nacht
Amina Claudine Myers Trio | Jumping In The Sugarbowl | Minor Music | 8002
Guter Mond Du Gehst So Stille
Tilman Jäger Tape 4 | Abendlieder | Satin Doll Productions | SDP 1043-1 CD
Charly Antolini Septet | Wow!!! | Verve | 833796-2
Guybrush Reggae N'Blues
Joachim Kühn Trio | Easy To Read | Owl Records | 014802-2
Guyléne
Kühn/Humair/Jenny-Clark | Live-Théatre de la Ville, Paris 1989 | CMP Records | CMP CD 43
Guys And Dolls
Ella Fitzgerald With The Marty Paich Orchestra | Ella Sings Broadway | Verve | 549373-2
Rosemary Clooney With The Scott Hamilton Quintet | Show Tunes | Concord | CCD 4364
Guy's Got To Go
Minton's Playhouse All Stars | Charlie Christian:Swing To Bop | Dreyfus Jazz Line | FDM 36715-2
Jazz Legacy 64: Charlie Christian-1941 Live Sessions | Vogue | 500114
Guzzi
Joey Baron Trio | Tongue In Groove | JMT Edition | 849158-2
GVK 1 alt
Eric Dolphy Quintet | Eric Dolphy:The Complete Prestige Recordings | Prestige | 9 PRCD-4418-2
GW(alt.take)
Sonny Rollins Group | Nucleus | Original Jazz Classics | OJCCD 620-2(M 9064)

G'wan Train
Abdullah Ibrahim-Carlos Ward Duo | Live At Sweet Basil Vol.1 | Black-Hawk | BKH 50204

Gwarir
Clark Terry Sextet | Clark Terry-Remember The Time | Mons Records | MR 874762

Gwidza
Abdullah Ibrahim | Fats Duke And Monk | Sackville | SKCD2-3048

G'won Train
Rich Perry Quartet | Hearsay | Steeplechase | SCCD 31515

Gymel
Tal Farlow Trio | Tal Farlow '78 | Concord | CJ 57

Gymnopedie
Herbie Mann-Bill Evans Quartet | That's Jazz Vol.8: Nirvana | Atlantic | ATL 50238

Gymnopedie No.1
Michael Chertock | Cinematic Piano-Solo Piano Music From The Movies | Telarc Digital | CD 80357

Gypsy
Holger Mantey | Calaufa | L+R Records | CDLR 45058
The Herdsmen | Nat Pierce-Dick Collins-Ralph Burns & The Herdsmen Play Paris | Fantasy | FCD 24759-2
The Herdsmen Play Paris | Original Jazz Classics | OJC 116(F 3201)

Gypsy-
Jimmy Stewart Quartet | The Touch | Black-Hawk | BKH 50301

Gypsy Blue
James Spaulding Quintet | Blues Nexus | Muse | MCD 5467

Gypsy Blue(alt.take)
John Gill's Novelty Orchestra Of New Orleans | Headin' For Better Times | Stomp Off Records | CD 1270

Gypsy Eyes
NDR Big Band feat. Inga Rumpf | The Spirit Of Jimi Hendrix | Extra Records & Tapes | 11542

Gypsy Eyes(alt.take)
Jermaine Landsberger Trio With Bireli Lagrene | Gypsy Feeling | Edition Collage | EC 516-2

Gypsy Feeling
Art Blakey And The Jazz Messengers | Jazzbühne Berlin '80 | Repertoire Records | REPCD 4909-CC

Gypsy In My Soul
Bobby Troup Quartet | The Distinctive Style Of Bobby Troup | Fresh Sound Records | FSR 2024(Bethlehem BCP 35)
Ella Fitzgerald With Frank De Vol And His Orchestra | Get Happy | Verve | 813391-1 IMS
Joe Williams With The Frank Hunter Orchestra | Planet Jazz:Joe Williams | Planet Jazz | 2165370-2
Johnny Smith Quartet | The Sound Of The Johnny Smith Guitar | Roulette | 531792-2
The Sound Of Johnny Smith Guitar | Fresh Sound Records | FSR 583(Roost 2246)
Marion McPartland Trio | Great Britain's | Savoy | SV 0160(MG 12016)
Oscar Peterson-Austin Roberts | Oscar Peterson 1951 | Just A Memory | JAS 9501-2

Gypsy Love Song
Benny Goodman And His Orchestra | Camel Caravan Broadcast 1939 Vol.1 | Phontastic | NCD 8817
Duke Ellington And His Orchestra | At The Bal Masque | CBS | 21144

Gypsy Moth
Count Basie And His Orchestra | Jazz Special-Afrique | RCA | CL 42784 DP

Gypsy Queen
Larry Coryell Quintet | Barefoot Boy | RCA | CL 13961 DP

Gypsy Song
The Rosenberg Trio | The Rosenberg Trio:The Collection | Verve | 537152-2

Gypsy Summer
Zoot Sims-Jimmy Rowles Quartet | If I'm Lucky | Original Jazz Classics | OJCCD 683-2(2310803)

Gypsy Sweetheart
Django Reinhardt And The Quintet Du Hot Club De France | Peche Á La Mode-The Great Blue Star Sessions 1947/1953 | Verve | 835418-2

Gypsy With A Song
Django Reinhardt Portrait | Barclay | DALP 2/1939
Peche Á La Mode-The Great Blue Star Sessions 1947/1953 | Verve | 835418-2

Gypsy With A Song(alt.take)
McCoy Tyner Trio | McCoy Tyner Plays Ellington | Impulse(MCA) | 951216-2
Django Reinhardt And The Quintet Du Hot Club De France | Jazz In Paris:Django Reinhardt-Django's Blues | EmArCy | 013545-2

Gypsy With A Song(take 1)
Jazz In Paris:Django Reinhardt-Django's Blues | EmArCy | 013545-2

Gypsy With A Song(take 2)
McCoy Tyner Trio | McCoy Tyner Plays Ellington | MCA | MCAD 33124(872200)

Gypsy Woman
The Mick Clarke Band | Tell The Truth | Taxim Records | TX 1001-2 TA

Gyrate-
Greg Osby And Sound Theatre | Greg Osby And Sound Theatre | JMT Edition | 834411-2

H. D. 2
Mick Goodrick Trio | Biorhythms | CMP Records | CMP CD 46

H.B.V.
Quintet Du Hot Club De France | Verve Jazz Masters 38:Django Reinhardt | Verve | 516931-2

H.C.Q. Strut
Django Reinhardt-Un Géant Sur Son Image | Melodie | 400052

H.J. Meets M.A.H.
The New Stan Tracy Quartet | For Heaven's Sake | Cadillac | SGCCD 04

H.R.H.
Count Basie And His Orchestra | Count On The Coast Vol.2 | Phontastic | NCD 7575
En Concert Avec Europe 1 | Laserlight | 710411/12
Billy Kyle's Big Eight | Giants Of Small-Band Swing Vol.1 | Original Jazz Classics | OJC- 1723(RLP 143)

H.S.
Charlie Ventura And His Orchestra | It's All Bop To Me | Fresh Sound Records | LPM 1135(RCA)

Ha! Ha! Baby The Last Laugh's On You - (Ha! Ha! Baby) The Last Laugh's On You
L.A.4 | Live At Montreux | Concord | CJ 100

Hab' Oft Im Kreise Der Lieben Im Duftigen Grase Geruht
Paquito D'Rivera Group | The Clarinetist Vol.1 | Peregrina Music | PM 50221

Habanera
Carlo Actis Dato Quartet | Oltremare | SPLASC(H) Records | H 153

Habanerando
Victor Feldman Quartet | Suite Sixteen | Original Jazz Classics | OJCCD 1768-2C 3541)

Habar N-Am
Habarigani | Habarigani | Hat Art | CD 6007

Habe Vertrau'n(Stol Pa Mig)
Peter Herbolzheimer Orchestra | Music For Swinging Dancers Vol.4: Close To You | Koala Records | CD P 12

Habiba
Kirk Lightsey | Lightsey Live | Sunnyside | SSC 1014 D

Habits
Unit X | Rated X | Timescrapper | TSCR 9618

Hablo
Eddie Lockjaw Davis Quartet | The Cookbook | Prestige | P 24039

Hace Rato
Manfred Schoof With The Yosuke Yamashita Trio | Distant Thunder | Enja | 2066 (807601)

Haciendo Camino
Charlie Shavers Quintet | Live! | Black & Blue | 33307

Hackensack
Engstfeld-Plümer-Weiss | Drivin' | Nabel Records:Jazz Network | CD 4618
Gary Bartz Quintet | Reflections Of Monk | Steeplechase | SCCD 31248
Irene Schweizer/Han Bennink | Irene Schweizer & Han Bennink | Intakt Records | CD 010
Ronnie Mathews Trio | Shades Of Monk | Sound Hills | SSCD 8064
Sebastian Gramss-Lömsch Lehmann | knoM.T | Jazz Haus Musik | JHM 0107 CD
Steve Khan Trio | Headline | Polydor | 517690-2
Thelonious Monk | Thelonious Monk Piano Solo | Vogue | 21409362
Thelonious Monk Quartet | Monk At Newport 1963 & 1965 | CBS | C2K 63905
Live In Paris 1964 | France's Concert | FCD 132x2
Live At The Jazz Workshop-Complete | CBS | C2K 65189
Monk In France | Original Jazz Classics | OJCCD 670-2
Thelonious Monk-The Complete Riverside Recordings | Riverside | 15 RCD 022-2
Thelonious Monk Quintet | Thelonious Monk:85th Birthday Celebration | zyx records | FANCD 6076-2
The Prestige Legacy Vol.1:The High Priests | Prestige | PCD 24251-2
Thelonious Monk:The Complete Prestige Recordings | Prestige | 3 PRCD 4428-2
Thelonious Monk Trio | The London Collection Vol.2 | Black Lion | BLCD 760116
Wynton Marsalis Group | Standard Time Vol.4:Marsalis Plays Monk | CBS | CK 67503
Barney Wilen Quartet | Tilt | Vogue | 21559492

Hackenzack
Galden-Sonnenschein | Boiling Point | Aho-Recording | CD 1004

Hackin' Around
Trombone Scene | Trombone Scene | Fresh Sound Records | NL 45925(RCA LPM 1087)

Hacksack-Serenade
Mani Neumeir-Peter Hollinger | Monsters Of Drums-Live | ATM Records | ATM 3821-AH

Häckselmaschine
Mathias Demoulin-Claude Buri Group | Minging | Jazz Pure Collection | AU 31607 CD

Haden
Edward Vesala Nordic Gallery | Sound & Fury | ECM | 1541

Hadenas
Peter Herbolzheimer Rhythm Combination & Brass | Colors Of A Band | Mons Records | MR 874799

Hadja Fadima
Marty Ehrlich Quintet | Side By Side | Enja | ENJ-6092 2

Hadulangdan
Mark Egan-Danny Gottlieb Quartet | Elements | Antilles | AN 1017(802738)

Haeschen
Charles Lloyd Quintet | Lift Every Voice | ECM | 1832/33(018783-2)

Hafez,Shattered Heart
John Zorn Group | Masada Five | DIW | DIW 899 CD

Hag-
Bob Haggart's Swing Three | Hag Leaps In | Arbors Records | ARCD 19156

Haghia Sophia
New And Used | Souvenir | Knitting Factory Works | KFWCD 125

Haiku
Jerry Granelli Sextet | Koputai | ITM-Pacific | ITMP 970058

Hail Hail The Herd's All Here
Red Rodney Quintet | The Red Rodney Quintets | Fantasy | FCD 24758-2

Hail To Dale
Jazznost-The Soviet/American Jazz Quartet | Joint Venture | Timeless | CD SJP 310

Hailing
Claudio Fasoli Quartet | Bodies | Nueva Records | IN 815

Hair Male-
Gary Campbell Quintet | Intersection | Milestone | MCD 9236-2

Hairache
Phillip Johnston's Big Trouble | Flood At The Ant Farm | Black Saint | 120182-2

Hairy Canary
Lee Konitz-Harold Danko Duo | Wild As Springtime | G.F.M. Records | 8002

Hairy Canary(alt.take)
Eliane Cueni Septet | Septett | Elite Special | 73614

Haitarma
Terra Brazil | Café Com Leite | art-mode-records | AMR 2101

Haiti Acredite Ou Nao
JoAnne Brackeen Duo | Trinkets And Things | Timeless | SJP 123

Haitian Fight Song
Charles Mingus Quintet | Charles Mingus-Passion Of A Man:The Complete Atlantic Recordings 1956-1961 | Atlantic | 8122-72871-2
The Very Best Of Charles Mingus | Rhino | 8122-79988-2
The Charles Mingus Quintet+Max Roach | Original Jazz Classics | OJC20 440-2(F 6009)
Charles Mingus-The Complete Debut Recordings | Debut | 12 DCD 4402-2
Charles Mingus -Passions Of A Man | Atlantic | ATL 60143

Haitian Fight Song(alt take)
Andrew Cyrille And Maono | Celebration | IPS Records | 002

Haitian Lady
Harper Brothers | The Harper Brothers | Verve | 835025-2

Hajime!(Dedicated to Jimi Hendrix, John Coltrane And Edgar Varese)
Dollar Brand Orchestra | The Journey | Chiaroscuro | CR 187

Hajnal
Unit X | Rated X | Timescrapper | TSCR 9618

Hakuin
Jan Klare/Tom Lorenz Quartett | Das Böse Ding | Acoustic Music Records | 319.1060.2

Hal The Weenie
Dicke Luft | Halb So Wild-Wie Schlimm | Riskant | 568-722416

Halba
Klaus Treuheit Trio | Steinway Afternoon | clearaudio | 42016 CD

Hale-Bop
Wayne Shorter-Herbie Hancock | 1+1:Herbie Hancock-Wayne Shorter | Verve | 537564-2

Hale-Bopp,Hip-Hop
Chet Baker Quintet | Cool's Out | Contemporary | BOP 13

Half A Million
Crash | Every Day A Trial | JA & RO | 005(08-4105)

Half A Triple
Otis Spann | Walking The Blues | Candid | CCD 79025

Half Ain't Been Told
Otis Spann And His Piano | Crosscut | CCR 1003(Candid)

Half And Half
Paul Horn Quintet | Something Blue | Original Jazz Classics | OJCCD 1778-2(J 615)

Half Life Of Absolution
Osie Johnson And His Orchestra | A Bit Of The Blues | Fresh Sound Records | NL 45989(RCA LPM 1369)

Half Minor
Stéphane Mercier Group | Flor De Luna | Fresh Sound Records | FSNT 097 CD

Half Moon
David Lahm Group | Real Jazz For The Folks Who Feel Jazz | Palo Alto | PA 8027

Half Moon Street
Count Basie And His Orchestra | Basie On Roulette, Vol. 7: Chairman Of The Board | Vogue | 500007

Half Nelson
Bill Smith With The Enrico Pieranunzi Trio | Sonorities | EdiPan | NPG 801
Gerry Mulligan Quartet | My Funny Valentine | Jazz Society(Vogue) | 670511
Jam Session | Bird's Eyes-Last Unissued Vol.12 | Philology | W 842.2
Miles Davis All Stars | The Savoy Recordings 2 | Savoy | 650108(881908)
Miles Davis New Quintet | Workin' With The Miles Davis Qoartet | Original Jazz Classics | OJC 296(P 7166)
Sam Most Sextet | Sam Most Plays Bird, Bud, Monk And Miles | Fresh Sound Records | FSR 2039(Bethlehem BCP 75)

Half Past Late
Ralph Towner-John Abercrombie | Five Years Later | ECM | 1207

Half Step Down Please
Coleman Hawkins And His All Stars | Jazz:The Essential Collection Vol.3 | IN+OUT Records | 78013-2
The Indispensable Coleman Hawkins 1927-1956:Body And Soul | RCA | ND 89277
Duke Ellington And His Orchestra | Such Sweet Thunder | CBS | CK 65568

Half The Fun
Passion Flower | Moon Records | MCD 074-2
Ella Fitzgerald And Duke Ellington:Cote D'Azure Concerts on Verve | Verve | 539033-2
Ella Fitzgerald And Duke Ellington:Cote D'Azure Concerts on Verve | Verve | 539033-2
Such Sweet Thunder | CBS | CK 65568

Half The Fun(alt.take)
Soul Immigrants Plus Guests | A Healty Vibe | Lipstick Records | LIP 8947-2 HOT

Half-,Whole-,Tritone-Funk
Anouar Brahem Trio | Astrakan Café | ECM | 1718(159494-2)

Halfaoine
Bajazzo | Harlequin Galaxy | Edition Collage | EC 519-2

Half-Bopp Waltz
Chet Baker-Stan Getz Quintet | Stan Meets Chet | Verve | 837436-2

Halfbreed Apache
Compact Jazz: Chet Baker | Verve | 840632-2 PMS

Half-Mast Inhibition
Leni Stern Group | Words | Lipstick Records | LIP 890282

Half-Time
Georg Hofmann-Lucas Niggli Duo | Mute Songs & Drumscapes | Creative Works Records | CW CD 1022-2

Halfway Bakossi
Billy Strayhorn | The Jazz Scene | Verve | 521661-2

Hall Mark
Room | Hall Of Mirrors | Music & Arts | CD 700

Hall Russell Story,The
Armand Gordon & Son Jazz Clan | Jazz Pure | Jazz Pure Collection | AU 31618 CD

Halle Hallelujah
Sidney Bechet With Claude Luter And His Orchestra | In Concert | Vogue | 655625

Hallelujah
Bud Powell Trio | Inner Fries-The Genius Of Bud Powell | Discovery | 71007-2
Claude Williamson Trio | Have Piano..Can't Travel | Fresh Sound Records | FSR 2048(Bethlehem BCP 54)
Coleman Hawkins Quartet | Ultimate Coleman Hawkins selected by Sonny Rollins | Verve | 557538-2
Django Reinhardt And The Quintet Du Hot Club De France | Planet Jazz:Stephane Grappelli | RCA | 2165366-2
Django Reinhardt Quintet | Djangology 49 | Bluebird | NL 90448
Ella Fitzgerald And Her Orchestra | Jazz Collection:Ella Fitzgerald | Laserlight | 24397
Ella Fitzgerald With The Chick Webb Orchestra | Ella Fitzgerald-The Early Years-Part 1 | GRP | GRP 26182
Fats Waller | Fats Waller:The Complete Associated Transcription Sessions 1935-1939 | Jazz Unlimited | JUCD 2076
Louis Armstrong In The Thirties/Fats Waller Last Testament | Forlane | UCD 19005
Lionel Hampton With The Oscar Peterson Trio | Verve Jazz Masters 26:Lionel Hampton with Oscar Peterson | Verve | 521853-2
Louis Mazetier | A Friendly Chat | Jazz Connaisseur | JCCD 9932-2
Marian McPartland Trio | Marion McPartland At The Hickory House | Savoy | SJL 2248 (801856)
Red Garland Quintet | Soul Junction | Original Jazz Classics | OJCCD 481-2
Red Garland Quintet feat.John Coltrane | Jazz Junction | Prestige | P 24023
Tatum-Hampton-Rich Trio | Art Tatum-The Complete Pablo Group Masterpieces | Pablo | 6 PACD 4401-2
The Tatum Group Masterpieces | Pablo | 2625706
Tommy Dorsey And His Orchestra | Tommy Dorsey In Concert | RCA | NL 89780 DP
Wolfhound | Halleluja | BELL Records | BLR 84024
Fats Waller | Jazz In V.Discs Vol.1 | Collection Hugues Panassié | CTPL 001

Hallelujah I Love Her So
Count Basie And His Orchestra | Breakfast Dance And Barbecue | Roulette | 531791-2
Basie On Roulette, Vol. 9: Breakfast Dance And Barbecue | Vogue | 500009
Monday Night Big Band | Thanks To Thad:Monday Night Big Band Plays The Music Of Thad Jones | TCB Records | TCB 97902
Ray Charles-Milt Jackson Quintet | Soul Meeting | Atlantic | SD 1360

Hallelujah I Love Him So
Lous Dassen With Holger Clausen/Atlanta Jazzband | Let's Do It... | Dr.Jazz Records | 8606-2

Hallelujah Time
Woody Herman And His Orchestra | Live In Antibes 1965 | France's Concert | FCD 117

Hallelujah Time-
Oscar Peterson Trio | En Concert Avec Europe 1 | Laserlight | 710443/48

Hallelujah(alt.take)
Tatum-Hampton-Rich Trio | The Tatum-Hampton-Rich Trio Vol.3 | Pablo | 2405426-2

Halley's Comet
Al Cohn-Zoot Sims Quintet | Hot Stuff From Brazil | West Wind | WW 0015
Louis Scherr-Tommy Cecil Duo | The Song Is You | Limetree | MLP 0026

Hallgató
Nils Landgren-Esbjörn Svensson | Swedish Folk Modern | ACT | 9428-2

Halling
Volker Kriegel Group | Topical Harvest | MPS | 821279

Hallo Heino
Klaus Lenz Band | Aufbruch | View | VS 002 IMS

Hallo!
Freddie Brocksieper Und Seine Solisten | Shot Gun Boogie | Bear Family Records | BCD 16277 AH

Hallo,Baby,Mademoiselle(Get Up On Those Stars)
Das Saxophonorchester Frankfurt | Das Saxophonorchester Frankfurt-Live | FMP | SAJ 40

Hallucinations
John Campbell Trio | After Hours | Contemporary | CCD 14053-2
Michael Cochrane Trio | Gesture Of Faith | Steeplechase | SCCD 31459

Halt The Battle
Emile Barnes-Peter Bocage Big Five | Barnes-Bocage Big Five 1954 | American Music | AMCD-84

Halucinations
Vienna Art Orchestra | Suite For The Green Eighties | Hat Art | CD 6054

Hamba Jam
Gato Barbieri-Dollar Brand | Hamba Khale | Charly | CD 79

Hamba Khale
Abdullah Ibrahim | Fats Duke And Monk | Sackville | SKCD2-3048

Hamba Nami
Cannonball Adderley Quintet With Brass Reeds And Voices | Accent On Africa | Affinity | AFF 148
Archie Shepp Group | The New Wave In Jazz | Impulse(MCA) | GRP 11372

Hambone
Bob Stewart First Line Band | First Line | JMT Edition | 919014-2
Bob Stewart Groups | Then & Now | Postcards | POST 1014
Hamburg'n
Bebop Preservation Society | Pied Piper Of Hamelin Suite | Spotlite | SPJ 500
Hamlet-
Javon Jackson Group | A Look Within | Blue Note | 836490-2
Hammer Head
Mongo Santamaria Orchestra | Skins | Milestone | MCD 47038-2
Hammock Soliloquy
Claus Raible Trio | Introducing The Exciting Claus Raible Trio | Organic Music | ORGM 9714
Hammon Dex
Ray Anderson Lapis Lazuli Band | Funkorific | Enja | ENJ-9340 2
Hammond Eggs
Lionel Hampton And His Orchestra | The Lionel Hampton Big Band | West Wind Orchestra Series | 2404 CD
Hamp Swings The Bells(Ring Dem Bells)
Lionel Hampton Sextet | Le Jazz En France-Vol.6 | Pathe | 1727301
Hamp's Blues
Hampton Hawes Trio | Hampton Hawes Trio Vol.1 | Original Jazz Classics | OJC20 316-2(C 3505)
Oscar Peterson Trio With Herb Ellis | Hello Herbie | MPS | 821846-2
Three Originals:Motion&Emotions/Tristeza On Piano/Hello Herbie | MPS | 521059-2
The European Jazz Guitar Orchestra | The European Jazz Guitar Orchestra | Jardis Records | JRCD 9307
Axel Zwingenberger With The Lionel Hampton Big Band | The Boogie Woogie Album | Vagabond | VRCD 8.88008
Hamp's Boogie Woogie
Lionel Hampton Allstar Big Band feat.Woody Herman | Aurex Jazz Festival '81 | Eastworld | EWJ 80207
Lionel Hampton And His Giants | Live In Emmen/Holland | Timeless | CD SJP 120
Milt Buckner Trio | Milt Buckner Masterpieces | MPS | 529094-2
Lionel Hampton And His Orchestra | En Concert Avec Europe 1 | Laserlight | 710462
Hamp's Boogie Woogie(78rpm master take)
Lionel Hampton Quintet | The Complete Lionel Hampton Quartets And Quintets With Oscar Peterson On Verve | Verve | 559797-2
Hamp's Boogie Woogie(LP master take)
Lionel Hampton And His Orchestra | Big Band Bounce & Boogie-Lionel Hampton:Leapin' With Lionel | Affinity | AFS 1000
Hamp's Gumbo
Lionel Hampton Vol.3-Sweatin' With Hamp | MCA | 1331
Hamp's Thing
Big Band Bounce & Boogie-Lionel Hampton:Leapin' With Lionel | Affinity | AFS 1000
Hamsin
Main Stream Power Band | Mcmories In Swing | MWM Records | MWM 002
Hand Bags And Glad Rags
David Friedman | Air Sculpture | Traumton Records | 2406-2
Hand Dance
Paul Bley Quartet | Fragments | ECM | 1320
Mitch Watkins Quartet | Curves | Enja | ENJ-6054 2
Hand In Hand
Paul Bley-Gary Peacock Duet | Partners | Owl Records | 014730-2
Sonny Terry & Brownie McGhee | Bluesville: Sonny Terry & Brownie McGhee | Prestige | 61142
Hand Jive
Miles Davis Quintet | Miles Davis Quintet 1965-1968 | CBS | C6K 67398
Nefertiti | CBS | CK 65681
Hand Jive(alt.take 1)
Miles Davis Quintet 1965-1968 | CBS | C6K 67398
Nefertiti | CBS | CK 65681
Hand Jive(alt.take 2)
Miles Davis Quintet 1965-1968 | CBS | C6K 67398
Elliot Lawrence And His Orchestra | The Elliot Lawrence Big Band Swings Cohn & Kahn | Fantasy | FCD 24761-2
Hand Made
Passport | Handmade | Atlantic | 2292-42172-2
Passport And Guests | Doldinger Jubilee Concert | Atlantic | 2292-44175-2
Paul Weeden Quintet | Clear Sight | Timeless | JC 11012
Hand Me Down My Walkin' Cane
Fats Waller | Fine Arabian Stuff | Deluxe | DE 601
Handful Of
A Band Of Friends | Teatime Vol.2 | Poise | Poise 06/2
Handful Of Keys
Benny Goodman Quartet | Avalon-The Small Band Vol.2 (1937-1939) | Bluebird | ND 82273
Clark Terry Quintet | Ain't Misbehavin' | Pablo | 2312105
Fats Waller | Fats Waller:The Complete Associated Transcription Sessions 1935-1939 | Jazz Unlimited | JUCD 2076
Fats Waller-The Joint Is Jumpin' | RCA | ND 86288(874182)
Judy Carmichael Quintet | Two-Handed Stride | Progressive | PRO 7065 IMS
Ralph Sutton | Easy Street | Sackville | SKCD2-2040
Thomas Waller | The Indispensable Fats Waller Vol.1/2 | RCA | 2122616-2
Handful Of Stars
Monty Budwig Septet | Dig | Concord | CJ 79
Handic Apped Rabbits
Christopher Dell Quartet | Where We Belong | L+R Records | CDLR 45060
Hands
Wolfgang Muthspiel Group | Loaded, Like New | Amadeo | 527727-2
Hands Across The Table
Tatum-Carter-Bellson Trio | The Tatum Group Masterpieces | Pablo | 2625706
Hands And Feet
Karl Ratzer Quartet | Waltz For Ann | L+R Records | CDLR 45078
Hands Off The Wheel
Kuniyoshi-Kuhn/Mattos/Prevost | Handscapes | LEO | LR 143
Handwork
Don Cherry Group | Old And New Dreams | Black Saint | 120013-2
Handy
John Handy Group | Handy Dandy Man | Inak | 8618
Haneen Wa Hanaan
Bernd Köppen | Hanek ppen | Senti | SE 01
Hang Up Your Hangups
Herbie Hancock Septet | V.S.O.P. Herbie Hancock-Live At The City Center N.Y. | CBS | 486569-2
Bob Crosby's Bobcats | Bob Crosby And His Orchestra Vol.9(1939):Them There Eyes | Halcyon | DHDL 128
Hangdog
Ben van den Dungen/Jarmo Hoogendijk Quintet | Heart Of The Matter | Timeless | CD SJP 269
Hangin' Around Boudon
Dicky Wells And His Orchestra | Django Reinhardt And His American Friends:Paris 1935-1937 | Memo Music | HDJ 4124
Hanging Loose
Derrick James & Wesley 'G' Quintet | Two Sides To Every Story | Jardis Records | JRCD 20137
Hanging On Sunday
Bob Hall Trio | Alone With The Blues | Lake | LACD 44
Hanging Out
Michael Sagmeister Quartet | Motions And Emotions | BELL Records | BLR 84054
Hangover Blues
Alix Combelle Et Son Orchestre | Le Jazz En France Vol.11:Bill Coleman 1935-1937(Tome 1) | Pathe | 1552571
Hangover In Hannover
Ray McKinley & His Orchestra | Borderline | Savoy | SV 0203(MG 12024)
Hangover Triangle
Herbie Nichols Trio | Herbie Nichols Trio | Blue Note | 300098(1519)
Hanid
Coleman Hawkins-Roy Eldridge Quintet | The Essential Coleman Hawkins | Verve | 2304537 IMS
George Wettling Jazz Band | George Wettling Jazz Band | JSP Records | 1103
Hanin
Crystal | Clear | Black-Hawk | BKH 51501
Hank Miri
Paul Rutherford | Old Moers Almanach | Ring | 01014
Hank's Other Tune(aka The Late Show)
Cozy Cole All Stars | The Changing Face Of Harlem, Vol. 2 | Savoy | SJL 2224 (801200)
Hank's Symphony
Art Blakey And The Jazz Messengers | At The Cafe Bohemia Vol.3 | Blue Note | 300193(BNJ 61007)
Art Blakey/The Jazz Messengers | CBS | CK 62255
Hank's Tune
Horace Silver Quintet | Silver's Blue | Epic | ESCA 7762
Hank's Waltz
Hank Mobley Quintet | Straight No Filter | Blue Note | BST 84435
Hannah's Song
Muthspiel-Peacock-Muthspiel-Motian | Muthspiel-Peacock-Muthspiel-Motian | Amadeo | 519676-2
Hanni And Her Cat
Aparis | Despite The Fire Fighters' Efforts... | ECM | 1496(517717-2)
Hannibal
Dirty Dozen Brass Band | The New Orleans Album | CBS | CK 45414
Miles Davis Group | Miles In Montreux | Jazz Door | JD 1287/88
Hannibal's Carnivals
Andy Narell Group | The Hammer | Windham Hill | 34 10107-2
Hannie's Dream
Flemming Agerskov Quintet | Face To Face | dacapo | DCCD 9445
Hannya Plain
Vertrauensbildende Maßnahmen | Stadtgarten Series Vol.7 | Jazz Haus Musik | JHM 1007 SER
Hapnin's
Greg Abate Quintet | Bop Lives! | Blue Chip Jazz | 878401-2
Happenstance
Allen Toussaint Group | Motion | Warner | WPCP 4416
Happiness
Eric Reed Orchestra | Happiness | Nagel-Heyer | CD 2010
Leroy Jenkins-Muhal Richard Abrams Duo | Lifelong Ambitions | Black Saint | 120033-2
Tania Maria Ensemble | Outragous | Concord | CCD 4563
Happiness Is
Joseph Jarman-Don Moye Quartet | Earth Passage-Density | Black Saint | BSR 0052
Happiness Is A Thing Called Joe
Abbey Lincoln With Her Quintet | Sonny Rollins-The Freelance Years:The Complete Riverside & Contemporary Recordings | Riverside | 5 RCD 4427-2
Ann Richards With The Bill Marx Trio | Live At The Losers/We Remember Mildred Bailey | Vee Jay Recordings | VJ 018
Cal Tjader Quartet | Cal Tjader Plays Harold Arlen & West Side Story | Fantasy | FCD 24775-2
Plays Harold Arlen | Original Jazz Classics | OJC 285(F 8072)
Ella Fitzgerald With The Billy May Orchestra | The Harold Arlen Songbook | Verve | 817526-1 IMS
George Shearing | Piano | Concord | CCD 4400
Oscar Peterson Trio | Oscar Peterson Plays The Harold Arlen Song Book | Verve | 589103-2
Red Holloway/Clark Terry Sextet | Locksmith Blues | Concord | CCD 4390
Woody Herman And His Orchestra | The V-Disc Years 1944-45 Vol.1 | Hep | 34
Happiness Is A Warm Gun
Shakti | Natural Elements | CBS | 82329
Happiness Is Now
Herb Ellis-Joe Pass Quartet | Jazz/Concord | Concord | CCD 6001
Happy
Joanne Grauer Trio | Joanne Grauer Indtroducing Lorraine Feather | MPS | 68198
Mickey Tucker Sextet | Hang In There | Steeplechase | SCCD 31302
Happy Anatomy
Duke Ellington And His Orchestra | Anatomy Of A Murder | CBS | CK 65569
Anatomy Of A Murder | CBS | CK 65569
Happy Anatomy(II)
Roy Fox & His Band | This Is Romance | Saville Records | SVL 166 IMS
Happy Birthday
Liam Noble | Close Your Eyes | FMR | FMR CD 25
Happy Birthday-
The Yamaha International Allstar Band | Hapy Birthday Jazzwelle Plus | Nagel-Heyer | CD 005
Roy Gaines Quartet | Feeling The Blues | Black & Blue | BLE 59.552 2
Happy Birthday Boogie
Louis Scherr-Tommy Cecil Duo | The Song Is You | Limetree | MLP 0026
Happy Birthday Stéphane
Punch Miller's New Orleans Band | The Larry Borenstein Collection Vol.5:Punch Miller's New Orleans Band | 504 Records | 504CD 34
Happy Blues
Ella Fitzgerald With The Tommy Flanagan Quartet | Ella In London | Original Jazz Classics | OJCCD 974-2(2310711)
Poncho Sanchez And His Orchestra | Para Todos | Concord | CCD 4600
Lightnin' Hopkins | Bluesville: Lightnin' Hopkins | Prestige | 61141
Happy Coincidence
Claude Bolling And The Show Biz Band | Swing Party | Decca | 6.22983 AO
Happy Days Are Here Again
The Dutch Swing College Band | The Dutch Swing College Band Meets Teddy Wilson | Timeless | TTD 525
Happy Feet
Art Tatum | Standards | Black Lion | CD 877646-2
Happy Harvest
Esbjörn Svensson Trio(E.S.T.) | E.S.T. Live | ACT | 9295-2
Happy Heads And Crazy Feds
Mel Tormé And His Trio With The Cincinnati Sinfonietta | Christmas Songs- | Telarc Digital | CD 83315
Happy Hour
Elmo Hope Trio | Trio And Quartet | Blue Note | 784438-2
Happy House
Charlie Haden Trio | The Montreal Tapes Vol.1 | Verve | 523260-2
Cindy Blackman Quartet | In The Now | HighNote Records | HCD 7024
Old And New Dreams | Playing | ECM | 1205
Ornette Coleman Septet | Broken Shadows | CBS | SRCS 7098
Vital Information | Live Around The World Where We Come From Tour '98-'99 | Intuition Records | INT 3296-2
Kenny Drew Trio | Jazz Impressions Of Pal Joey | Original Jazz Classics | SMJ 6106
Happy Landing
Chico Hamilton | With Strings Attached/The Three Faces Of Chico | Warner | 9362-47874-2
Happy Little Dance
Barney Kessel | Solo | Concord | CJ 221
Happy Little Sunbeam
Monty Alexander Quintet | Ivory & Steel | Concord | CCD 4124
Happy Madness
Fraser MacPherson Quintet | Jazz Prose | Concord | CJ 269
Happy Man
The Jimmy Giuffre 3 | 7 Pieces | Verve | 2304438 IMS
Happy People
Schlothauer's Maniacs | Maniakisses | Timescrapper | TSCR 9811
James Zitro Sextet | James Zitro | ESP Disk | ESP 1052-2
Happy Reunion
Jean-Luc Ponty Sextet | Civilized Evil | Atlantic | SD 16020
Happy Times
The Griffith Park Collection | The Griffith Park Collection | Elektra | MUS K 52361
Howard Rumsey's Lighthouse All-Stars | Oboe/Flute | Original Jazz Classics | OJCCD 154-2(C 3520)
Happy Town
Bob Smith Group | Bob's Diner | dmp Digital Music Productions | CD 471
Happy With Friends
Hubert Sumlin Group | My Guitar And Me | Black & Blue | BLE 59.548 2
Happy With The Blues
Joseph Berardi-Kira Vollman | Happy Wretched Family | Victo | CD 033
Happy-Go-Lucky Local
Duke Ellington And His Orchestra | The Best Of Duke Ellington | Capitol | 831501-2
All Star Road Band Vol.2 | Doctor Jazz | ZL 70969(2) (809319)
The Uncollected: Duke Ellington, Vol.4 | Hindsight | HSR 128
Ellington '55 | Capitol | 520135-2
Duke Ellington:Complete Studio Transcriptions | Definitive Records | DRCD 11199
Happy Birthday Duke Vol.1 | Laserlight | 15783
Duke Ellington Orchestra | The Golden Duke | Prestige | P 24029
Happy-Go-Lucky Local(aka 'Night Train' alt.take)
Oscar Peterson Trio | Night Train | Verve | 521440-2
Happy-Go-Lucky Local(aka 'Night Train')
Duke Ellington And His Orchestra | Duke Ellington | Laserlight | 15753
Happy-Go-Lucky Local(part 1)
Duke Ellington | Laserlight | 15753
Happy-Go-Lucky Local(part 2)
Mark Murphy And His Septet | I'll Close My Eyes | Muse | MCD 5436
Harbinger
Alice Day With The Andy Scherrer Quartet | CoJazz Plus | TCB Records | TCB 96052
Harcab
Greg Gisbert Quintet | Harcology | Criss Cross | Criss 1084
Hard Bottom-
John Thomas Quartet | Serious Business | Nabel Records:Jazz Network | LP 4626
Hard But It's Fair
Alan Lomax And The Ramblers | Kings Of Skiffle | Decca | 6.28132 DP
Hard Eights
Lyle Mays Trio | Fictionary | Geffen Records | GED 24521
Hard Groove
Ricky Ford Quintet | Hard Groovin' | Muse | MCD 5373
Hard Hearted Hannah
Sigler's Birmingham Merrymakers | Jack Linx And Maurice Sigler | Jazz Oracle | BDW 8018
Hard Lovin' Blues
Louis Jordan And His Tympany Five | Louis Jordan Vol.1-Hoodoo Man | Swingtime(Contact) | ST 1011
Hard Oh Lord
Errol Parker | My Own Bag No.2 | Sahara | 1002
Hard Plains Drifter
Blind Blake | Blind Blake-That Lovin' I Crave | Biograph | BLP 12050
Hard Road Blues
The Quincy Jones-Sammy Nestico Orchestra | Basie & Beyond | Warner | 9362-47792-2
Hard Rock Dance
Last Exit | Köln | ITM Records | ITM 1446
Hard Sock Dance
Frank Foster-Frank Wess Orchestra | 2 Franks Please | Savoy | SJL 2249 (801857)
Quincy Jones And His Orchestra | The Quintessential Charts | MCA | IA 9342/2
Big Jay McNeely Band | Big Jay In 3-D | Sing | 650
Hard Times
Cab Calloway And His Orchestra | Duke Ellington/Cab Calloway | Forlane | UCD 19004
David Fathead Newman Sextet | Rhino Presents The Atlantic Jazz Gallery | Atlantic | 8122-71257-2
Houston Person Sextet | Goodness! | Original Jazz Classics | OJC20 332-2(P 7678)
Jimmy McGriff Sextet | Feelin' It | Milestone | MCD 9313-2
Johnny Fuller | California Blues | Anthology of the Blues | AB 5603
Hard To Love A Woman
Clifton Chenier And His Band | King Of The Bayous | Arhoolie | CD 339
Hard To Say Goodbye
Toots Thielemans Quartet | Toots Thielemans:The Live Takes Vol.1 | IN+OUT Records | 77041-2
Percfect Trouble | Perfect Trouble | Moers Music | 02070 CD
Hard Way
T-Bone Walker With Dave Bartholomew's Band | Hot Leftovers | Pathe | 1561451(Imperial)
Hard Working Man Blues
Count Basie-Zoot Sims Quartet | Basie & Zoot | Original Jazz Classics | OJCCD 822-2(2310745)
Hardav
Bermuda Viereck | Noblesse Galvanisee | Plainisphare | PL 1267-20/21
Hardee's Partee
Rahsaan Roland Kirk Group | Natural Black Inventions:Roots Strata | Atlantic | ATL 40185(SD 1578)
Hard-Waich-Spyler
John Lindberg-Albert Mangelsdorff-Eric Watson | Dodging Bullets | Black Saint | 120108-2
Hard-Wired
Circo Del Arca | Dies Irae | Hat Art | 3507
Hare Krishna-Hail Krishna
Champion Jack Dupree Group | Jack Dupree-Jimmy Rushing-Muddy Waters | Laserlight | 17062
Harem Dance
Armen Donelian | A Reverie | Sunnyside | SSC 1019(952119)
Harem Shuffle
Live Recordings From The Streets | Fun Horns Live In South America-Natural Music | KlangRäume | 30060
Hark
Duke Ellington And His Orchestra | Live At The 1956 Stratford Festival | Music & Arts | CD 616
Hark! The Herald Angels Sing
Mark Shane's X-Mas Allstars | Christmas Jazz! | Nagel-Heyer | NH 1008
What Would Santa Say? | Nagel-Heyer | CD 055
Mark Soskin | Jazz City Christmas,Vol.1 | Jazz City | 660.53.006
Ulli Bögershausen | Christmas Carols | Laika Records | 35101622
Vince Guaraldi Trio | A Charlie Brown Christmas | Fantasy | FSA 8431-6
Keith Foley | Music For Christmas | dmp Digital Music Productions | CD 452
Harlem
Hans Koller Big Band | New York City | MPS | 68235
Paul Howard's Quality Serenaders | Early Hamp | Affinity | CD AFS 1011
Harlem-
Mills Blue Rhythm Band | Rhythm Spasm | Hep | CD 1015
Harlem Air Shaft
Duke Ellington And His Famous Orchestra | Duke Ellington:Ko-Ko | Dreyfus Jazz Line | FDM 36717-2
Victor Jazz History Vol.8:Swing Big Bands | RCA | 2128562-2
Duke Ellington And His Orchestra | The Best Of Duke Ellington | Capitol | 831501-2
Jazz In V.Discs Vol.1 | Collection Hugues Panassié | CTPL 001
Duke Ellington At Tanglewood Vol.1 | Queen-Disc | 049
Jay Hoggard Quartet | Love Is The Answer | Muse | MCD 5527
Harlem Air Shaft(Rumpus In Richmond)
Eddie Edinborough And His New Orleans Wild Cats | The New Orleans Wild Cats | VJM | VLP 38 IMS
Harlem Bound
The Storyville Jassband | Trad Tavern | Timeless | CD TTD 577
Harlem Boys
Kai Winding All Stars | Kai Winding All Stars | Fresh Sound Records | FSR 627(Roost RLP 408)

Harlem Camp Meeting
Cab Calloway And His Orchestra | Victor Jazz History Vol.6:Harlem Jazz(1928-33) | RCA | 2128560-2

Harlem Nocturne
Fat Boogie Horns | Fat Boogie Horns(Rhythm And Soul Big Band) | Paul Records | PP 4002
Johnny Otis And His Orchestra | Spirit Of The Black Territory Bands | Arhoolie | CD 384
Lalo Schifrin And His Orchestra | Tin Tin Deo | Fresh Sound Records | FSR-CD 319
Les Misérables Brass Band | Manic Tradition | Popular Arts | NR 5004 CD
Mel Tormé With Orchestra | Comin' Home Baby!/Sings Sunday In New York | Warner | 8122-75438-2
Northern Jazz Orchestra | Good News | Lake | LACD 38
Eric Reed Trio | Manhattan Melodies | Verve | 050294-2

Harlem On Parade
Ronald Shannon Jackson And The Decoding Society | Barbeque Dog | Antilles | AN 1015(802757)

Harlem Rag
Ken Colyer's Jazzmen | Live At The Dancing Slipper 1969 | AZURE Compact Disc | AZ-CD-25

Harlem Rhythm-
Black Bottom Stompers | Ace In The Hole | Elite Special | 73357

Harlem River Drive
Bobbi Humphrey Group | Blacks And Blues | Blue Note | 498542-2

Harlem Speaks
The Nagel-Heyer Allstars | Uptown Lowdown:A Jazz Salute To The Big Apple | Nagel-Heyer | CD 2004
Gregor Hilden-Hans D. Riesop Group | Compared To What...? | Wonderland Records | 319.9014.2

Harlem Strut
Neville Dickie-Louis Mazetier | Dickie-Mazetier:Harlem Strut | Stomp Off Records | CD 1302

Harlem Sundown
Chip White Sextet | Harlem Sunset | Postcards | POST 1006

Harlem's Disciples-
Art Blakey And The Jazz Messengers | Moanin' | Blue Note | 300321

Harlem's Manhattan
Alfred Lauer Bigband | Just Music | Mons Records | MR 874819

Harlequin
Woody Mann | Stairwell Serenade | Acoustic Music Records | 319.1072.2

Harlequin Galaxy
Doctor Ross | Jivin' The Blues | Big Bear | 146409

Harmofuncalodia
Onix | Stress | Fresh Sound Records | FSR 104 (835273)

Harmonic Bearing
Marilyn Crispell Trio | Story Teller | ECM | 1847(0381192)

Harmonic Line
Sonny Terry Trio | Whoopin' The Blues | Charly | CRB 1120

Harmonica Boogie
Chris Barber's Jazz And Blues Band | Live In Munich | Timeless | CD TTD 600

Harmonie
Aera | Aera Live | Erlkönig | 148415

Harmonique
John Coltrane Quartet | Coltrane Jazz | Atlantic | 7567-81344-2
Wynton Marsalis Quintet | Soul Gestures In Southern Blue Vol.2: Uptown Ruler | CBS | 468660-2

Harmony
Johnn Mercer With The Nat King Cole Trio | Havin' Fun With(Rare Duets) | Official | 12003

Harmony In Harlem
Johnny Hodges-Wild Bill Davis Sextet | Compact Jazz: Johnny Hodges-Wild Bill Davis | Verve | 839288-2

Harolds Land
Al Cohn And His Orchestra | The Jazz Workshop:Four Brass One Tenor | RCA | PM 45164

Harpoon
Axel Zwingenberger | Powerhouse Boogie | Vagabond | 6.24210 AS-Digital

Harpsichord Concerto No.1 In D Minor(BWV 1052):
Powerhouse Boogie | Vagabond | 6.24210 AS-Digital

Harry
Klaus König Orchestra | Reviews | Enja | ENJ-9061 2

Harry Laughs
Reviews | Enja | ENJ-9061 2

Harry Laughs Still
Harry James And His Orchestra | Compact Jazz | Verve | 833285-2 PMS

Harry's Kleiner Ball-Salon
Wayne Shorter Quintet | Introducing Wayne Shorter | Vee Jay Recordings | VJ 007

Harvard Blues
Count Basie And His Orchestra | Prez's Hat Vol.4 | Philology | 214 W 9

Harvest
Duck Baker | The Clear Blue Sky | Acoustic Music Records | 319.1065.2

Has Anybody Seen My Corine
The Minstrel Stars | The Minstrel Stars | Upbeat Jazz | URCD 105

Has Anyone Here Seen Kelly?
Albert Ammons | The Boogie Woogie Boys | Storyville | 6.28469 DP

Hassan's Dream
Dadisi Komolafe Quintet | Hassan's Walk | Nimbus | NS 3035

Hasta Manana
Mind Games With Claudio Roditi | Live | Edition Collage | EC 501-2

Hasta Pronto
Jan Garbarek-Bobo Stenson Quartet | Witchi-Tai-To | ECM | 1041(833330-2)

Hasta Siempre
Ekkehard Jost & Chromatic Alarm | Von Zeit Zu Zeit | Fish Music | FM 005 CD

Haste Gesagt
Ekkehard Jost Quintet | Carambolage | View | VS 0028 IMS

Hasting Street Bounce
Charlie Spand-Blind Blake | Paramounth Piano Blues Vol.1(1928-1932) | Black Swan Records | HCD-12011

Hat And Beard
Eric Dolphy Quintet | Out To Lunch | Blue Note | 498793-2
James Newton Quartet | One Night With Blue Note Vol.1 | Blue Note | BT 85113 Digital

Hat And Cane
Ignaz Netzer-Dirk Sommer Quartet | Schnappschuss | Jazz Classics | AU 11082

Hat Trick
Jam Session | Jam Session Vol.3 | Steeplechase | SCCD 31526
Dave Grusin Orchestra | Two For The Road:The Music Of Henry Mancini | GRP | GRP 98652

Hatari
Scapes | Changes In Time | Timeless | CD SJP 361

Hatha-Sun And Moon
Didier Lockwood Group | 'Round About Silence | Dreyfus Jazz Line | FDM 36595-2

Hattara Hääraa(para mi nina)
Big Bill Broonzy | Big Bill Broonzy-1930's Blues | Biograph | BLP C 15

Hattie Wall
World Saxophone Quartet | W.S.Q. | Black Saint | 120046-2

Haulita
Sarah Jane Morris Group | A Night At Ronnie Scott's Vol.6:The Vocal Album | Ronnie Scott's Jazz House | NARCD 6

Haunted
George Shearing Quintet & The Robert Farnon Orchestra | How Beautiful Is The Night | Telarc Digital | CD 83325

Haunted Heart
Bill Evans Trio | Bill Evans Trio:The Last Waltz | Milestone | 8MCD 4430-2
Bill Evans:The Secret Sessions | Milestone | 8MCD 4421-2
Charlie Haden Quartet West | Haunted Heart | Verve | 513078-2
Fred Hersch | Maybeck Recital Hall Series Volume Thirty-One | Concord | CCD 4596
Jonathan Schwartz & Quintet | Anyone Would Love You | Muse | MCD 5325
Marc Copland Trio | Haunted Heart & Other Ballads | HatOLOGY | 581

Haunted House
Bessie Smith With Don Redman And Fletcher Henderson | Bessie Smith-The Complete Recordings Vol.1 | CBS | 467895-2

Hausmann
Oliver Augst-Rüdiger Carl-Christoph Korn | Blank | FMP | OWN-90013

Havana
Paquito D'Rivera Sextet | Live At Keystone Korner | CBS | FC 38899

Havana Manana
The Sextet Of Orchestra USA | Mack The Knife And Other Berlin Theatre Songs Of Kurt Weill | RCA | 2159162-2

Havanera
Orquestra De Cambra Teatre Lliure feat. Dave Liebman | Orquestra De Cambra Teatre Lliure and Lluis Vidal Trio feat.Dave Liebman | Fresh Sound Records | FSNT 027 CD
Mats Eden-Jonas Simonson With The Cikada String Quartet | Milvus | ECM | 1660

Haväng
Olaf Kübler Quartet | Midnight Soul | Village | VILCD 1024-2

Havanna Drive
Q4 Orchester Project | Yavapai | Creative Works Records | CW CD 1028-2

Havasupai
Joe Houston Orchestra | Screaming Saxophones Vol.1 | Swingtime(Contact) | ST 1002

Have A Good Time
Gene DiNovi Trio | Renaissance Of A Jazz Master | Candid | CCD 79708

Have A Heart
Jesse Van Ruller Trio | Trio | EmArCy | 017513-2
Keith Ingham-Harry Allen Septet | The Back Room Romp | Sackville | SKCD2-3059

Have A Talk With God
John Pizzarelli Trio With The Don Sebesky Orchestra | Our Love Is Here To Stay | RCA | 6367501-2

Have Blues Will Play'Em
Maxine Sullivan With The Keith Ingham Trio | Maxine Sullivan Sings The Music Of Burton Lane | Mobile Fidelity | MFCD 773

Have Horn, Will Blow
Eddie Lockjaw Davis Quintet | The Eddie Lockjaw Davis Cookbook Vol.1 | Original Jazz Classics | OJCCD 652-2(P 7141)

Have Mercy On A Fool
Eddie 'Blues Man' Kirkland Band | It's The Blues Man! | Original Blues Classics | OBCCD 513-2(Tru 15010)

Have The Stones Been Here?
Just Fun | Just Fun | MPS | 68286

Have You Changed
Freddy Martin And His Orchestra | The Uncollected:Freddy Martin | Hindsight | HSR 151

Have You Got The Gumption
King Curtis Quintet | I Remember King Curtis | Prestige | P 24033

Have You Heard
Pat Metheny Group | Letter From Home | Geffen Records | GED 24245
In Concert | Jazz Door | JD 1231
Ben Sidran Quartet feat. Johnny Griffin | Have You Met...Barcelona? | Orange Blue | OB 002 CD

Have You Met Chet?
| Big Band Swing | Fresh Sound Records | LSP 15624(Epic LN 3663)

Have You Met Miss Jones
Adam Makowicz Trio | My Favorite Things-The Music Of Richard Rodgers | Concord | CCD 4631
Art Farmer Quintet | You Make Me Smile | Soul Note | 121076-2
Art Tatum | The Art Tatum Solo Masterpieces | Pablo | 2625703
Art Tatum-Ben Webster Quartet | Art Tatum-The Complete Pablo Group Masterpieces | Pablo | 6 PACD 4401-2
The Tatum Group Masterpieces | Pablo | 2625706
Ben Sidran Quartet feat. Johnny Griffin | Have You Met...Barcelona? | Orange Blue | OB 002 CD
Bill O'Connell Group | Love For Sale | Jazz City | 660.53.019
Carmen McRae And Her Quintet | Any Old Time | Denon Compact Disc | CY-1216
Chet Baker Quintet | The Jazz Giants Play Rodgers & Hart:Blue Moon | Prestige | PCD 24205-2
Smokin' With The Chet Baker Quintet | Prestige | PR20 7749-2
Chuck Wayne Trio | Traveling | Progressive | PRO 7008 IMS
Count Basie And His Orchestra | Basie's Timing | MPS | 88016-2
Ella Fitzgerald With The Buddy Bregman Orchestra | Ella Fitzgerald Sings The Rodgers And Hart Song Book | Verve | 537258-2
The Rodgers And Hart Song Book, Vol.1 | Verve | 821579-2 PMS
Ethan Iverson Trio | Deconstruction Zone(Originals) | Fresh Sound Records | FSNT 047 CD
Gene Ammons-James Moody Quintet | Chicago Concert | Original Jazz Classics | OJCCD 1091-2(PR 10065)
George Coleman Quartet | I Could Write A Book:The Music Of Richard Rodgers | Telarc Digital | CD 83439
George Shearing Trio | So Rare | Savoy | 650141(882497)
Henri Crolla/Stephane Grappelli Quartet | Special Stephane Grappelli | Jazztime(EMI) | 251286-2
Jerry Wiggins Trio | The Piano Collection Vol.1 | Vogue | 21610242
Jimmy Raney Sextet | Jimmy Raney Visits Paris | Fresh Sound Records | FSR 561(Dawn DLP 1120)
Joe Pass | Virtuoso | Pablo | 2310708-2
Joe Pass:A Man And His Guitar | Original Jazz Classics | OJCCD 8806-2
Joe Pass With Red Mitchell | Finally | EmArCy | 512603-2 PMS
Joe Williams With The Harry 'Sweets' Edison Quintet | Live! A Swingin' Night At Birdland | Fresh Sound Records | FSR-CD 22(882187)
Kenny Barron Trio | Lemuria-Seascape | Candid | CCD 79508
Louis Armstrong With The Russell Garcia Orchestra | I've Got The World On A String/Louis Under The Stars | Verve | 2304428 IMS
Lucky Thompson Sextet | Lucky In Paris | HighNote Records | HCD 7045
Marcus Pintrup Quartet | Nocturnal Traces | Blue Note | 493676-2
Oscar Peterson Trio | At Zardis' | Pablo | 2CD 2620118
Paul Smith Sextet | Cool And Sparkling | Capitol | 300011(TOCJ 6125)
Sarah Vaughan And Her Band | The Devine One | Fresh Sound Records | FSR 659(Roulette R 52060)
Tony Bennett With The Stan Getz Quartet | Singin' Till The Girls Come Home | CBS | FC 38508

Have You Met Miss Jones(alt.take 1)
Coleman Hawkins With Billy Byers And His Orchestra | The Hawk In Hi-Fi | RCA | 2663842-2

Have You Met Miss Jones(alt.take 2)
Art Tatum-Ben Webster Quartet | The Tatum Group Masterpieces Vol.8 | Pablo | PACD20 431-2

Have You Met Miss Jones(alt.take)
Art Tatum-The Complete Pablo Group Masterpieces | Pablo | 6 PACD 4401-2
The Art Tatum Group Masterpieces Vol.8 | Pablo | 2405431-2
Coleman Hawkins With Billy Byers And His Orchestra | The Hawk In Hi-Fi | RCA | 2663842-2

Have You Met Miss Jones(incomplet)
Harry Beckett-Marilyn Mazur-Chris McGregor Group | Grandmother's Teaching | ITM Records | 0028

Have You Seen Elveen?
Rusty Bryant Sextet | Friday Night Funk For Saturday Night Brothers | Prestige | PCD 10054-2

Have You Seen My Baby?
Swim Two Birds | Apsion | VeraBra Records | CDVBR 2101-2

Have Yourself A Merry Little Christmas
Ella Fitzgerald With The Frank DeVol Orchestra | Ella With You A Swinging Christmas | Verve | 2304445 IMS
Kevin Gibbs Trio | Christmas Presence | Concord | CCD 4432

Haven
Louis Dumaine's Jazzola Eight | The Music Of New Orleans | RCA | NL 89724 DP

Haven't Got Anything Better To Do
Jack Payne And His BBC Dance Orchestra | Radio Nights | Saville Records | SVL 152 IMS

Haven't I Loved You Somewhere
Engelbert Wrobel-Chris Hopkins-Dan Barrett Sextet | Harlem 2000 | Nagel-Heyer | CD 082

Haven't Named It Yet
Lionel Hampton And His Orchestra | The Complete Lionel Hampton Vol.3/4(1939) | RCA | 2122614-2

Havets Herrer(Master Of the Sea)
Blues Comany And Guests | Invitation To The Blues | Inak | 9064

Having A Party
Calvin Boze And His All-Stars | Calvin Boze:The Complete Recordings 1945-1952 | Blue Moon | BMCD 6014

Having At It-
Memphis Slim Group | The Real Folk Blues | Chess | CHD 9270(872290)

Havona
Pete Berryman & Adrian O'Reilly | Duet | Acoustic Music Records | 319.1163.2

Hawaiian Hospitality
Glen Moore Group | Introducing Glen Moore | Elektra | ELK K 52151

Hawaiian War Chant
Kenny Ball And His Jazzmen | Kenny Ball And His Jazzmen 1960-1961 | Lake | LACD 76

Hawk Eyes
Joe Lee Wilson With Orchestra | Without A Song | Inner City | IC 1064 IMS

Hawkeye
Horace Silver Septet | Horace Silver-The Hardbop Grandpop | Impulse(MCA) | IMP 11922

Hawkm Meets Sun Ra
Art Blakey And The Jazz Messengers | In My Prime Vol.2 | Timeless | SJP 118

Hawk's Variation
Zoot Sims With Bill Holman And His Orchestra | Hawthorne Nights | Pablo | 2310783

Hay Ro
Duke Ellington And His Famous Orchestra | Duke Ellington:The Blanton-Webster Band | Bluebird | 21 13181-2

Hayfoot Strawfoot
Duke Ellington And His Orchestra | At The Hurricane:Original 1943 Broadcasts | Storyville | STCD 8359
Goin' Up | Duke Records | D 1011

Hayseed
Laurindo Almeida Quartet | Brazilliance Vol.1 | Pacific Jazz | 796339-2

Haze On The Danube
Doctor Ross | The Blues Vol.4 | Big Bear | 156401

Hazel's Hip
Louis Hayes Quintet | Budy DeFranco/Louis Hayes | Vee Jay Recordings | VJ 010

Hazy Hues
Booker Little Sextet | Candid Dolphy | Candid | CCD 79033

Hazy Hues(take 5)
Amstel Octet | Hazy Hugs | Limetree | MLP 198601

Hdiye
Susannah McCorkle With The Allen Farnham Orchestra | From Broadway To Bebop | Concord | CCD 4615

he Aftermanth-
Nina Simone And Orchestra | Compact Jazz: Nina Simone | Mercury | 838007-2

He Cares
Jan Garbarek Group | Legend Of The Seven Dreams | ECM | 1381(837344-2)

He Comes From The North
Benny Carter Quintet With Nancy Marano | Benny Carter Songbook Vol.2 | Musicmasters | 65155-2

He Don't Love Me Anymore
Helen Humes And Her All Stars | Lester Young:The Complete 1936-1951 Small Group Sessions(Studio Recordings-Master Takes),Vol.6 Rare Items | Blue Moon | BMCD 1006

He Goes On A Trip
Dr.Feelgood | Dr.Feelgood | Blues Classics(L+R) | CDLR 82009

He Huffed And Puffed
Joe Turner And His Memphis Men | The Complete Duke Ellington-Vol. 2 | CBS | CBS 68275

He Left The Planet
Nate Morgan Quartet | Journey Into Nigritia | Nimbus | NS 3257

He Looked Beyond My Fault
Wycliffe Gordon Group | The Search | Nagel-Heyer | CD 2007

He Looked Beyond My Fault(Danny Boy)
Wycliffe Gordon-Eric Reid | We | Nagel-Heyer | CD 2023
Miles Davis Group | Get Up With It | CBS | 485256-2

He Loved Him Madly
Allan Vaché Sextette | Swing And Other Things | Arbors Records | ARCD 19171

He Loves And She Loves
Ella Fitzgerald With The Nelson Riddle Orchestra | Ella Sings Gershwin-Vol. 2 | Metro | 2682023 IMS
Spike Robinson-Gene DiNovi Quartet | Gene DiNovi Meets Spike Robinson-At The Stables | Hep | CD 2071
Warren Vaché Quartet With The Beaux-Arts String Quartet | Warm Evening | Concord | CCD 4392

He Never Sleeps
Buddy Rich Big Band | Keep The Customer Satisfied | EMI Records | 523999-2

He Quit Me-
First Revolution Singers | First Revolution Gospel Singers:A Capella | Laserlight | 24338

He Really Cares
A Cappella Gospel Anthology | Tight Harmony Records | TH 199404

He Said
Willis Jackson Quintet | At Large | Prestige | PCD 24243-2

He Said,She Said,I Said
Kevin Eubanks Group | Shadow Prophet | GRP | GRP 95652

He Speaks To Me Often In Dreams
Ketil Bjornstad Group | Seafarer's Song | EmArCy | 9865777

He Struggled To The Surface
Jack Wilson Trio | Margo's Theme | Discovery | DS 805 IMS

He Touched Me
Lillian Boutté And Her Music Friends | Music Is My Life | Timeless | CD JC 11002

He Was Too Good For Me
Julie Wilson With The Phil Moore Orchestra | Love | Fresh Sound Records | Dolphin 6

He Was Too Good To Me
Cees Smal Quintet feat. Letty de Jong | Just Friends | Limetree | MLP 198607
Joe Newman/Joe Wilder Quintet | Hangin' Out | Concord | CCD 4262

He Who Lives In Fear
Herbie Hancock Orchestra | The Best Of Herbie Hancock | Blue Note | 89907
Duck Baker | Ms.Right | Acoustic Music Records | 319.1130.2

Head Heart And 'Hands
Chubby Jackson Quintet | Chubby Jackson-The Happy Monster:Small Groups 1944-1947 | Cool & Blue | C&B-CD 109

Head Hunters
Black Bottom Stompers | Ace In The Hole | Elite Special | 73357

Head In The Sand
The Fringe | The Return Of The Neanderthal Man | Popular Arts | NR 5006 CD

Head Peeper
Chubby Jackson Quintet | Chubby Jackson-The Happy Monster:Small Groups 1944-1947 | Cool & Blue | C&B-CD 109

Head Shakin'
Bobby Hutcherson Quartet | Happenings | Blue Note | 300285
Headache
Geoff Keezer Quartet | Here And Now | Blue Note | 796691-2
Headfake
Dick de Graaf Septet | Polder | Timeless | CD SJP 376
Headin' Home
Martin Schrack Quintet feat.Tom Harrell | Headin' Home | Storyville | STCD 4253
Eric Kloss Quintet | Bodies' Warmth | Muse | MR 5077
Heading Home
Woody Mann-Bob Brozman | Get Together | Acoustic Music Records | 319.1187.2
Headline
Chet Baker Quartet | Jazz At Ann Arbor | Fresh Sound Records | 054 2602311(Pacific Jazz PJ 1203) (835282)
Headline Suite:Lovers Shot On Bosnian Bridge
The Houdini's | Live at Kiama Jazz Festival,Australia | Challenge | CHR 70060
Heads-
Ray Anderson Alligatory Band | Heads And Tales | Enja | ENJ-9055 2
Heads And Tales
Walt Weiskopf Quartet | A World Away | Criss Cross | Criss 1100
Heads Up
David Moss Duets | Full House | Moers Music | 02010
Tony Purrone Trio | Set 'Em Up | Steeplechase | SCCD 31389
Healing Hands
Carla Bley Band | Fleur Carnivore | Watt | 21
Healing Power
Carla Bley Sextet | Sextet | Watt | 17
Lew Soloff Septet | Little Wing | Sweet Basil | 660.55.015
Healing Song For Mother Earth
Ornette Coleman & Prime Time | Virgin Beauty | CBS | 489433-2
Health And Poverty
Jimmy Johnson Band | Heap See | Blue Phoenix | BLP 233720
Hear Me Talkin' To Ya
Ella Fitzgerald And Her Quintet | Verve Jazz Masters 46:Ella Fitzgerald-The Jazz Sides | Verve | 527655-2
Horace Silver Sextet | The Story Of Jazz Piano | Laserlight | 24653
Johnny Dodds And His Orchestra | Victor Jazz History Vol.2:Black Chicago | RCA | 2128556-2
Louis Armstrong And His Orchestra | Heebie Jeebies | Naxos Jazz | 8.120351 CD
Louis Armstrong And His Big Band Vol.1-The Maturity | Black & Blue | BLE 59.225 2
Ma Rainey With The Tub Jug Washboard Band | Ma Rainey | Milestone | MCD 47021-2
Johnny Dodds' Hot Six | Blue Clarinet Stomp | RCA | ND 82293(847121)
Hear Them Say
Walter Lang Quintet | Tales Of 2 Cities | double moon | CHRDM 71016
Hear What I Mean
Sonny Rollins Quintet | Easy Living | Original Jazz Classics | OJCCD 893-2
Hear What I'm Saying
Easy Living | Milestone | M 9080
Hearsay
Bill Bickford's Bigfoot | Semi-Precious Metal | Tutu Records | 888114-2
Heart And Soul
Hank Jones | Have You Met Hank Jones ? | Savoy | WL 70544 (809329)
Heart Game
Pharoah Sanders Group | Heart Is A Melody | Evidence | ECD 22063-2
Heart Of Glass
Ellis Marsalis Trio | Heart Of Gold | CBS | CK 47509
Heart Of Mine
Firehouse Five Plus Two | Crashes A Party | Good Time Jazz | GTCD 10038-2
Heart Of My Heart
Storyville Jassband | Mallorca | Timeless | CD TTD 604
Heart On My Sleeve
Kip Hanrahan Groups | Coup De Tete | American Clave | AMCL 1007-2
Heart Still Alive
Milt Jackson Group | Soul Believer-Milt Jackson Sings And Plays | Original Jazz Classics | OJCCD 686-2(2310832)
Heart Strings
Montgomery Brothers | Groove Brothers | Milestone | M 47051
Oscar Peterson Trio With Milt Jackson | Very Tall | Verve | 559830-2
Very Tall | Verve | 827821-2
The Montgomery Brothers | Wes Montgomery-The Complete Riverside Recordings | Riverside | 12 RCD 4408-2
Wes Montgomery Quartet | Wes Montgomery:Complete Live At Jorgies | Definitive Records | DRCD 11247
Heartache Caravan
Johnny Otis Show(Johnny Otis Band/Dee Williams Band/James Von Streeter Band) | The Original Johnny Otis Show Vol.2 | Savoy | WL 70810(2) (809332)
Heartaches
Dexter Gordon Quintet | Gettin' Around | Blue Note | 300284
Ruby Braff And His New England Songhounds | Ruby Braff And His New England Songhounds Vol.2 | Concord | CCD 4504
Heartbeat
The Meeting | Update | Hip Bop | HIBD 8008
Heartbeat Stories
Dakota Staton With The Many Albam Big Band | Dakota Staton | LRC Records | CDC 9017
Heart-Broken Man
Christian Willisohn-Boris Vanderlek | Blues News | Blues Beacon | BLU-1019 2
Vince Guaraldi Group | Charlie Brown's Holiday Hits | Fantasy | FCD 9682-2
Heartburn Waltz
Peter Delano Group | Bite Of The Apple | Verve | 521869-2
Heartland
Keith Jarrett | Concerts(Bregenz/München) | ECM | 1227/9
Kenny Blake Group | A Lifetime After | Inak | 30372
Heartland-2
Eddie Daniels Quartet With String Quartet | Memos From Paradise | GRP | GRP 95612
Hearts And Numbers
Carol Sloane And Her Trio | Heart's Desire | Concord | CCD 4503
Heart's Horizon
Keith Jarrett Trio | Always Let Me Go | ECM | 1800/01(018766-2)
Hearts In Space
Charles Gayle Trio | Spirits Before | Silkheart | SHCD 117
Heat
Olaf Rupp | Life Science | FMP | CD 109
Irene Schweizer | Many And One Direction | Intakt Records | CD 044
Heat Wave
Art Tatum | The Tatum Solo Masterpieces Vol. 2 | Pablo | 2310729
Ella Fitzgerald With Paul Weston And His Orchestra | Ella Fitzgerald Sings The Irving Berlin Song Book | Verve | 543830-2
Verve Jazz Masters 6:Ella Fitzgerald | Verve | 519822-2
The Complete Ella Fitzgerald Song Books of Harold Arlen, Irving Berlin, Duke Ellington, George & Ira Gershwin, Jerome Kern, Johnny Mercer, Cole Porter And Rogers & Hart | Verve | 519832-2
Jimmy Rowles Septet | Weather In A Jazz Vane | Fresh Sound Records | FSR 502(Andex S-3007)
Heatbeat
Fourplay | Heartfelt | RCA | 2663916-2
Heatfelt
Zahara | Flight Of The Spirit | Antilles | AN 1011(802688)
Heatin' It Up
Walter 'Wolfman' Washington Group | Wolf At The Door | Rounder Records | CDRR 2098
Heaven
Dick de Graaf Septet | Polder | Timeless | CD SJP 376
Nguyen Le Trio With Guests | Bakida | ACT | 9275-2
Phil Woods Quintet | Heaven | Black-Hawk | BKH 50401 CD
Al Jarreau With Band | Heaven And Earth | i.e. Music | 557852-2
Heaven And Earth
Hazy Osterawld And His Orchestra | Rare And Historical Jazz Recordings | Elite Special | 73414
Heaven Dance
The LeadersTrio | Heaven Dance | Sunnyside | SSC 1034 D
Heaven Has Created
Eliane Cueni Septet | Septett | Elite Special | 73614
Heaven No.2.5
Ullmann-Wille-Haynes | Trad Corrosion | Nabel Records:Jazz Network | CD 4673
Heaven No.2.6
Larry Young Quintet | Heaven On Earth | Blue Note | BNJ 71040(BST 84304)
Heavenly
The Saxophone Choir | The Saxophone Choir | Soul Note | 121129-2
Heavenly Bodiesy
Albert Ayler Group | Albert Ayler Live In Greenwich Village:The Complete Impulse Recordings | Impulse(MCA) | IMP 22732
Heavenly Home
Albert Ayler Septet | The Village Concerts | MCA | IA 9336/2
Heavy Artillery(Artillery Lourde)
Joachim Kühn Group | Joachim Kühn | CMP Records | CMP 22
Heavy Cairo Trafic(dedicated to Sun Ra)
Herbert Joos Trio | Ballade Noire | free flow music | ffm 0392
Heavy Chicken
Ballade Noire | free flow music | ffm 0392
Heavy Chicken(alt.take)
Lee Morgan Quintet | The Cooker | Blue Note | 300187(1578)
Heavy Drama
Dicky Wells And His Orchestra | Trombone Four-In-Hand | Affinity | AFF 168
Heavy Heart
Chris Barber's Jazz And Blues Band | Class Of '78 | Black Lion | 187001
Heavy Hour
Houston Person Quartet | Heavy Juice | Muse | MR 5260
Heavy Mädel
Dark | Dark | CMP Records | CMP CD 28
Heavy Metal
Billy Jenkins And Fun Horns | Mayfest '94 | Babel | BDV 9502
Heavy Nights
Ronnie Laws With Strings And Voices | Solid Ground | Blue Note | 498544-2
Heavy Rotation
Kent Sangster Quartet | Adventures | Jazz Focus | JFCD 006
Heavy Snow
Wild Bill Moore Quintet | Bottom Groove | Milestone | MCD 47098-2
Heavy Soul
Bakmak | Foreward Flight | Strand | 6.23628 AO
Heavy Tango
Jan Akkerman | Can't Stand Noise | Inak | 11001
Heavy Weight
Passport | Iguacu | Atlantic | 2292-46031-2
Bertrand Gallaz | Sweet And Sour | Plainisphare | PL 1267-104 CD
Heavyweights
Manny Albam And His Orchestra | Jazz Horizons | Fresh Sound Records | DLP 9004(Dot)
Hebuwuba
Bruce Dunlap Trio | The Rhythm Of Wings | Chesky | JD 92
Hector's Dance
Bud Freeman All Stars | The Bud Freeman All Stars | Original Jazz Classics | OJC 183(SV 2012)
Hecuba
Rüdiger Carl | Rüdiger Carl Solo | FMP | CD 86
Heebie Jeebies
George Lewis Band | The George Lewis Band At Herbert Otto's Party | American Music | AMCD-74
Heed My Warning
Dianne Reeves With Orchestra | For Every Heart | Palo Alto | TB 203
Heel To Toe
Paris Jazz Quintet | The Paris Jazz Quintet | TCB Records | TCB 21112
Hefegründe
Harold Harris Trio | At The Playboy Club | Vee Jay Recordings | VJR 502
Hegel's Fantasy
Hugo Strasser Tanz-Orchester | Swing Tanzen Gestattet | Vagabond | 6.28415 DP
Heidiology
Eugen Cicero-Decebal Badila | Swinging Piano Classics | IN+OUT Records | 77047-2
Heidschi Bumbeidschi
Masquálero | Re-Enter | ECM | 1437(847939-2)
Heiemo Gardsjenta
Will Ezell | Paramounth Piano Blues Vol.1(1928-1932) | Black Swan Records | HCD-12011
Heifer Dust
Pitchin' Boogie | Oldie Blues | OL 2830
Heimaterde
Hans Lüdemann | The Natural Piano | Jazz Haus Musik | JHM 0075 CD
Heimkehr
Hans Lüdemann Rism | Aph-o-Rism's | Jazz Haus Musik | JHM 0049 CD
Heimkehr(Homecoming)
Lutz Häfner Quintet | Things & Thoughts | Mons Records | MR 874309
Heino Und Hannelore
Paul Eßer-Gerd Dudek-Ali Haurand-Jiri Strivin | Jazz Und Lyrik:Schinderkarren Mit Buffet | Konnex Records | KCD 5108
Heinrich Böll
Härte 10 | Härte 10 | Moers Music | 02006
Heitzmann's Delight
Charles Lloyd Quartet | Charles Lloyd In Europe | Atlantic | 7567-80788-2
Hej Da!
John Zorn Group | Massada Tree | DIW | DIW 890 CD
Hekkto Tekkno
Steve Lampert Group | Venus Perplexed | Steeplechase | SCCD 31557
Held In Reflection
Elmore James Band | Got To Move | Charly | CRB 1017
Helden
Bettina Born-Wolfram Born | Schattenspiel | Born&Bellmann | 993004 CD
Heleen
Miles Davis Group | On The Corner | CBS | CK 63980
Helen Butte
JoAnne Brackeen Trio | Where Legends Dwell | Ken Music | 660.56.021
Helena
Philly Joe Jones Septet | Advance | Galaxy | GXY 5122
Helena's Theme
Harry Sweets Edison And The Golden Horns | Live At The Iridium | Telarc Digital | CD 83425
Helen's Ritual
Bruce Forman Quartet | Full Circle | Concord | CJ 251
Helicopters
Elliott Sharp Groups | Monster Curve | Ear-Rational | ECD 1031
Helikon
Sun Ra And His Solar Arkestra | Heliocentric World Vol.1 | ESP Disk | ESP 1014-2
Helios Suite:
Butch Thompson | Thompson Pays Joplin | Daring Records | CD 3033
Heliotrope Bouquet-
Eero Koivistoinen Quintet | Dialog | L+R Records | CDLR 45094
Hell On Earth
Samm Bennett And Chunk | Knitting Factory Tours Europe Way 23-June 15,1991 | Enemy | EMCD 121(03521)
Hellas
Kenny Barron | Lucifer | Muse | MR 5070
Hellbound Train
Vienna Art Orchestra | All That Strauss | TCB Records | TCB 20052
Hellhound On My Trail
Cassandra Wilson Group | Blue Light 'Til Dawn | Blue Note | 781357-2
Robert Johnson | Robert Johnson-King Of The Delta Blues | CBS | 493006-2
Roy Rogers Group | Blues On The Range | Crosscut | CCD 11026
Hello Birdie
Louisiana Repertory Jazz Ensemble Of New Orleans | Uptown Jazz | Stomp Off Records | CD 1055
Hello Brother
CeDell 'Big G' Davis | Living Country Blues USA Vol.5: Mississippi Delta Blues | L+R Records | LR 42035
Hello Dolly
Eugen Cicero Trio | Eugen Cicero Highlights | MPS | 88028-2
Jeanette MacLeod With The Frieder Berlin Swing Project | The Voice Of Swing | Satin Doll Productions | SDP 1001-1 CD
Louis Armstrong And His All Stars | Jazz In Paris:Louis Armstrong:The Best Live Concer Vol.1 | EmArCy | 013030-2
The Legendary Berlin Concert Part 2 | Jazzpoint | JP 1063 CD
Live In Berlin/Friedrichstadtpalast | Jazzpoint | JP 1062 CD
The Great Performer | Traditional Line | TL 1304
Louis Armstrong And His All Stars With A Studio Orchestra | Louis Armstrong-All Time Greatest Hits | MCA | MCD 11032
Tom Talbert Septet | Things As They Are | Seabreeze | CDSB 2038(881572)
Hello Frisco
Florian Poser | Winds | Edition Collage | EC 500-2
Hello G.
Philip Catherine Quartet | Guitar Groove | Dreyfus Jazz Line | FDM 36599-2
Hello George
Willis Jackson Sextet | The Gator Horn | Muse | MR 5146
Hello Jeff
Paris Washboard | California Here We Come | Stomp Off Records | CD 1280
Hello Little Girl
Otis 'Smokey' Smothers And His Ice Cream Men | Got My Eyes On You | Steeplechase | SCB 9009
Hello Lola
Mound City Blue Blowers | Eddie Condon 1928-1931 | Timeless | CBC 1-024
Hello Love
Ella Fitzgerald And Her Famous Orchestra | Ella Fitzgerald Vol.2-Forever Young | Swingtime(Contact) | ST 1007
Hello My Lovely
Bob James Groups | The Genie:Themes & Variations From The TV Series Taxi | CBS | 25446
Hello Nellie
Bill Frisell Trio | Live | Gramavision | GCD 79504
Hello There Universe
Joachim Raffel Quintet And Large Ensemble | Another Blue | Acoustic Music Records | 319.1145.2
Hello Young Lovers
Eric Reed Trio | Pure Imagination | Impulse(MCA) | 951259-2
Everett Greene With The Houston Person Quartet | My Foolish Heart | Savant Records | SCD 2014
Gerals Wiggins Trio | The King And I | Fresh Sound Records | FSR-CD 0053
Hell's Gate
Yuri Honig Quartet | Seven | Jazz In Motion Records | JIM 75086
Hellzapoppin'
Slim And Slam | Slim Gaillard & Slam Stewart:Complete Columbia Master Takes | Definitive Records | DRCD 11190
Help
Isaac Scott Blues Band | Big Time Blues Man | Red Lightnin' | RL 0046
Music Revelation Ensemble | In The Name Of... | DIW | DIW 885 CD
Help Me
Klaus Doldinger's Passport | Running In Real Time | Warner | 2292-40633-2
Little McSimmons | Dansez-Vous Le Bop? | Black & Blue | BLE 233095
Help Me-
Johnny Otis Show(Johnny Otis Band/Dee Williams Band/James Von Streeter Band) | The Original Johnny Otis Show Vol.2 | Savoy | WL 70810(2) (809332)
Help Yourself
Larry Garner Group | Baton Rouge | Verve | 529467-2
Help!
Scenario | Jazz The Beatles | Organic Music | ORGM 9729
Pep O'Callaghan Grup | Port O'Clock | Fresh Sound Records | FSNT 069 CD
Help,Support!!
Louis Jordan Quintet | Great Rhyhtm & Blues-Vol.1 | Bulldog | BDL 1000
Helter Skelter
Derek Watkins Group | Increased Demand | M.A Music | A 707-2
Hemdendienst Blues Minue One
Der Rote Bereich | Zwei | Jazz 4 Ever Records:Jazz Network | J4E 4727
Hemlines
Shannon Jackson & The Decoding Society | Street Priest | Moers Music | 01096
Hemvändaren
Nguyen Le Group | Tales From Viet-Nam | ACT | 9225-2
Hen Ho(Promise Of A Date)
K.C. Douglas | K.C.'s Blues | Original Blues Classics | OBCCD 533-2(BV 1023)
Henad Aften(Towards Evening)
Alexander von Schlippenbach And Tony Oxley | Digger's Harvest | FMP | CD 103
Hence The Real Reason
Ray Anderson-Han Bennink-Christy Doran | Cheer Up | Hat Art | CD 6175
Henderson Stomp
Benny Goodman And His Orchestra | Jazz Collection:Benny Goodman | Laserlight | 24396
The Benny Goodman Selection | CBS | 467280-2
Henpecked Old Man
Peter Giger Trio | Jazzz... | B&W Present | BW 029
Henry Brown Blues
Roosevelt Sykes | Blues Roots Vol.7 | Storyville | 6.23706 AG
Her
Stan Getz With The Eddie Sauter Orchestra | Focus | Verve | 521419-2
Her He's World
Walt Dickerson/Richard Davis | Divine Gemini | Steeplechase | SCS 1089
Her Majesty
Tok Tok Tok | 50 Ways To Leave Your Lover | Einstein Music | EM 91051
Marc Johnson-Eric Longsworth | If Trees Could Fly | Intuition Records | INT 3228-2
Her Majesty(The Turtle)
Becker/Sclavis/Lindberg | Transition | FMP | 1170
Her Melancholy Piano
Bruce Forman Quintet | Coast To Coast | Candid | CRS 1026 IMS
Her Point Of View
Paul Russo Orchestra | Delicioso | TBA Records | TBCD 244(881844)
Her Voice
Ron McClure Sextet | Sunburst | Steeplechase | SCCD 31306
Her Wild Ways
Peggy Stern Trio | Pleiades | Philology | W 82.2
Heraldry
Carlos Bica & Azul | Look What They've Done To My Song | Enja | ENJ-9458 2
Herancas
Weather Report | Black Market | CBS | 468210-2
Herandnu
Dave Ballou Quartet | Rothko | Steeplechase | SCCD 31525
Herb
Jimmy Giuffre 3 | Jimmy Giuffre 3, 1961 | ECM | 1438/39(849644-2)
Herb & Ictus
Dave Holland Quintet | Point Of View | ECM | 1663(557020-2)
Herbaceous
Mal Waldron Quartet | One Entrance, Many Exits | Palo Alto | PA 8014

Herbal Turkey Breast
Gerardo Iacoucci Modern Big Band | Great News From Italy | yvp music | CD 3030

Herbie Nichols
Kenny Werner Trio | Introducing The Trio | Sunnyside | SSC 1038 D

Herbie's Tune
Hugh Fraser Quintet | In The Mean Time | Jazz Focus | JFCD 020

Herbob
Gianlugi Trovesi Quartet With The WDR Big Band | Dedalo | Enja | ENJ-9419 2

Herbop(fragment)
The Washington Guitar Quintet | Aquarelle | Concord | CCD 42016

Herbs And Roots
David Schnitter Sextet | Thundering | Muse | MR 5197

Herbst
Ulli Bögershausen | Private Stories | Laika Records | 35101542

Herbstallee
Best Of Ulli Bögershausen | Laika Records | LK 93-045
String Thing | String Thing:Alles Wird Gut | MicNic Records | MN 2

Herbstkristalle
Klaus Treuheit Trio | Steinway Afternoon | clearaudio | 42016 CD

Herbstone
Herbie Harper Quintet | Jazz In Hollywood:Herbie Harper | Original Jazz Classics | OJCCD 1887-2(Nocturne NLP-1/NLP-7)
Herbie Harper Feat.Bud Shank And Bob Gordon | Fresh Sound Records | 054 2600581(Liberty LJH 6003)

Herbstschleife
Johannes Rediske Quintet | Re-Disc Bounce | Bear Family Records | BCD 16119 AH

Herbst-Serenade
Aera | Hand Und Fu | Erlkönig | 148401

Hercab(live version)
Esbjörn Svensson Trio(E.S.T.) | Winter In Venice | ACT | 9007-2

Hercules Jonssons Lat
Cal Tjader Group | Solar Heat | Memo Music | HDJ 4078

Here Am I
Jimmy Johnson Band | Heap See | Blue Phoenix | BLP 233720

Here And Now
Zoot Sims Quintet | Zoot! | Original Jazz Classics | OJCCD 228-2(RLP 228)

Here And There
John Stubblefield Quartet | Morning Song | Enja | ENJ-8036 2
Kenny Barron Quintet | Quickstep | Enja | ENJ-6084 2
Claus Boesser-Ferrari | Welcome | Acoustic Music Records | 319.1117.2

Here Comes Charlie
Henry Busse And His Orchestra | Sentimental Journey-Golden Age Of Swing And Sweet | Vagabond | 6.28523 DP

Here Comes De Honey Man
Miles Davis With Gil Evans & His Orchestra | The Miles Davis Selection | CBS | 465699-2
Orquestra De Cambra Teatre Lliure | Porgy And Bess | Fresh Sound Records | FSNT 066 CD
Oscar Peterson Trio | Porgy And Bess | Verve | 519807-2
Ray Charles-Cleo Laine With The Frank DeVol Orchestra & Chorus | Porgy And Bess | London | 6.30110 EM
Bill Potts And His Orchestra | The Jazz Soul Of Porgy And Bess | Capitol | 795132-2

Here Comes De Honey Man-
Louis Armstrong And Ella Fitzgerald With Russell Garcia's Orchestra | Porgy And Bess | Verve | 2-2507 IMS
The Complete Ella Fitzgerald And Louis Armstrong On Verve | Verve | 537284-2
Paolo Fresu Quintet | Kind Of Porgy & Bess | RCA | 21951952
Shirley Horn Trio | I Loe You, Paris | Verve | 523486-2

Here Comes Mikey
Rosa Henderson With The Three Hot Eskimos | Rosa Henderson 1923-1931 | Retrieval | RTR 79016

Here Comes The Band
Willie 'The Lion' Smith Duo | Willie 'The Lion ' Smith:The Lion's In Town | Vogue | 2111506-2

Here Comes The Sphexes
Mike Westbrook Band | Off Abbey Road | TipToe | TIP-888805 2

Here Comes The Sun
Rahsaan Roland Kirk Quartet | Here Comes The Whistleman | Atlantic | ATL 40389(SD 3007)

Here I Am
Urbanator | Urbanator | Hip Bop | HIBD 8001

Here I'll Stay
Dee Dee Bridgewater With Band | Dee Dee Bridgewater Sings Kurt Weil | EmArCy | 9809601
Howard Alden Trio | Misterioso | Concord | CCD 4487
Weslia Whitefield Trio | Live In San Francisco | Landmark | LCD 1531-2

Here In My Arms
T-Bone Walker And His Band | I Get So Weary | Pathe | 1561441(Imperial)

Here In The Sun-
Louis Armstrong And His Friends | Louis Armstrong And His Friends | Bluebird | 2663961-2

Here Is My Heart For Christmas
Rinus Groeneveld Trio | Dare To Be Different | Timeless | CD SJP 321

Here Lies Love
Clifton Chenier Group | Live At Montreux | Charly | CDX 2

Here On Earth
Niels Lan Doky Trio | Here Or There | Storyville | STCD 4117

Here The Moon
Dizzy Gillespie Jam | Montreux '77-The Art Of The Jam Session | Pablo | 2620106

Here To Be
Robin Williamson Group | Skirting The River Road | ECM | 1785(016372-2

Here To Burn
Jaki Byard Trio | Giant Steps | Prestige | P 24086

Here To Stay
Rebirth Jazz Band | Here To Stay | Arhoolie | 1092

Here Today
Quintet For A Day | What We Live | New World Records | 80553-2

Here We All Are
Jan Somers Band | Here We Are | Timeless | CD SJP 397

Here We Go Again
Glenn Miller And His Orchestra | The Glenn Miller Story Vol. 2 | RCA | ND 89221
Jazz Collection:Glenn Miller | Laserlight | 24367
The Swinging Mr. Miller | RCA | 2115522-2
Sonny Rollins Quintet | No Problem | Original Jazz Classics | OJCCD 1014-2(M 9104)

Here You Come Again
Ted Lewis And His Band | The Jazzworthy Ted Lewis | Retrieval | RTR 79014

Here, There And Anywhere
Mal Waldron | Mingus Lives | Enja | 3075

Here, There And Everywhere
Mal Waldron Trio | A Touch Of The Blues | Enja | 2062
Sarah Vaughan With Orchestra | Song Of The Beatles | Atlantic | SD 16037
Singers Unlimited | A Capella | MPS | 815671-1
Stephane Grappelli Quartet | Live In San Francisco | Black-Hawk | BKH 51601
Martin Taylor | Martin Taylor Artistry | Linn Records | AKD 020

Here's Looking At You!
Shirley Horn Trio | The Main Ingredient | Verve | 529555-2
Benny Goodman And His Orchestra | The Birth Of Swing | Bluebird | ND 90601(3)

Here's One
Pete Rugolo And His Orchestra | Adventures In Rhythm | Fresh Sound Records | LSP 15560(CBS CL 604) (835208)

Here's That Rainy Day
Al Haig | Solitaire | Spotlite | SPJ LP 14
Art Pepper Quartet | San Francisco Samba | Contemporary | CCD 14086-2
Renascene | Galaxy | GCD 4202-2
Art Pepper Quintet | Art Pepper:Tokyo Debut | Galaxy | GCD 4201-2
Art Pepper Quintet With Strings | Art Pepper:The Complete Galaxy Recordings | Galaxy | 16GCD 1016-2
Art Van Damme Group | State Of Art | MPS | 841413-2
Astrud Gilberto With The Walter Wanderley Quartet | A Certain Smile A Certain Sadness | Verve | 557449-2
Attila Zoller | Attila Zoller:The Last Recordings | Enja | ENJ-9349 2
Benny Carter 4 | The Montreux '77 Collection | Pablo | 2620107
Bill Evans | The Complete Bill Evans On Verve | Verve | 527953-2
Alone | Verve | 598319-2
Verve Jazz Masters 5:Bill Evans | Verve | 519821-2
Bill Ramsey With The Toots Thielemans Quartet | When I See You | BELL Records | BLR 84022
Bobby Shew-Chuck Findley Quintet | Trumpets No End | Delos | DE 4003(882204)
Bud Shank And The Sax Section | Bud Shank And The Sax Section | Pacific Jazz | LN 10091
Buddy DeFranco Quartet | Waterbed | Candid | CRS 1017 IMS
Chet Baker-Enrico Pieranunzi | The Heart Of The Ballad | Philology | W 20.2
Diane Schuur With Orchestra | Love Songs | GRP | GRP 97032
Dick Hyman | There Will Never Be Another You | Jazz Connaisseur | JCCD 9831-2
Dolf De Vries Trio | Where's That Rainy Day | Limetree | MLP 0019
Elvin Jones-Richard Davis Quartet | Heavy Sounds | Impulse(MCA) | 547959-2
Eric Alexander Quintet | New York Calling | Criss Cross | Criss 1077
Gary Burton-Stephane Grappelli Quartet | Paris Encounter | Atlantic | 7567-80763-2
George Shearing Trio | 500 Miles High | MPS | 68219
Guy Lafitte Trio feat. Wild Bill Davis | Lotus Blossom | Black & Blue | BLE 59.188 2
Herb Ellis-Ross Tompkins Duo | A Pair To Draw To | Concord | CJ 17
Jenny Evans And Her Quintet | Whisper Not | ESM Records | Panda 16(941336)
Joe Newman/Joe Wilder Quintet | Hangin' Out | Concord | CCD 4262
Joe Pass | Virtuoso | Pablo | 2310708-2
Joe Pass:A Man And His Guitar | Original Jazz Classics | OJCCD 8806-2
Joe Pass:A Man And His Guitar | Original Jazz Classics | OJCCD 8806-2
Live At Long Beach City College | Pablo | 2308239-2
Kenny Drew Trio | In Concert | Steeplechase | SCCD 31106
Milt Jackson And His Orchestra | Reverence And Compassion | Reprise | 9362-45204-2
Monty Alexander Trio | Echoes Of Jilly's | Concord | CCD 4769
Norris Turney Quartet | Big Sweet N' Blue | Mapleshade | 02632
Oscar Peterson And His Trio | Encore At The Blue Note | Telarc Digital | CD 83356
Paul Desmond Quartet | Masters Of Jazz Vol.13 | RCA | CL 42790 AG
Paul Horn Group | 500 Miles High | West Wind | WW 2043
Phil Upchurch Quintet With Walt Fowler | L.A.Jazz Quintet | Paddle Wheel | K 28P 6440
Philly Joe Jones Septet | Mo' Joe | Black Lion | BLCD 760154
Singers Unlimited + The Oscar Peterson Trio | In Tune | MPS | 68085
Stan Kenton And His Orchestra | Hits In Concert | Creative World | ST 1074
The New Stan Getz Quartet | Getz Au Go Go | CTI Records | PDCTI 1124-2
Tomas Franck With The Mulgrew Miller Trio | Tomas Franck In New York | Criss Cross | Criss 1052
Wynton Kelly-George Coleman Quartet | Live at The Left Bank Jazz Society,Baltimore,1968 | Fresh Sound Records | FSCD 1032
Live In Baltimore | Affinity | AFF 108

Here's That Rainy Day-
André Previn Trio | Triple Play:André Previn | Telarc Digital | CD 83457
Dizzy Gillespie Jam | Montreux '77-The Art Of The Jam Session | Pablo | 2620106
Don Lamond And His Big Swing Band | Extraordinary | Progressive | PRO 7067 IMS
Louie Bellson's 7 | Live At The Concord Summer Festival | Concord | CCD 4026

Here's That Rainy Day(alt.take)
Bill Evans | Alone | Verve | 598319-2
Modern Jazz Quartet | Space | EMI Records | 8538162

Here's The Beat
Tad Shull Quartet | In The Land Of The Tenor | Criss Cross | Criss 1071

Here's 'Tis
Phil Woods Quintet | Full House | Milestone | MCD 9196-2

Here's To Joy
Irene Redfield With The Charles Earland Quintet | Million Dollar Secret | Savant Records | SCD 2007

Here's To Life
Sue Raney-Dick Shreve | Autumn In The Air | Fresh Sound Records | FSR-CD 5017

Here's To The Miracles
Sonny Rollins Sextet | Here's To The People | Milestone | MCD 9194-2

Here's To The People
Jens Thomas | Jens Thomas Plays Ennio Morricone | ACT | 9273-2

Here's To You
Bobby Watson Group | Urban Renewal | Kokopelli Records | KOKO 1309

Here's To... You Baby
Oscar Peterson-Milt Jackson Duo | Two Of The Few | Original Jazz Classics | OJCCD 689-2(2310881)

Here's Two Of The Few
Herb Geller Sextet | That Geller Feller(Fire In The West) | Fresh Sound Records | FSR CD 91(882417)

Hermann Und Dorothea(Schauspielhaus Bochum)
Marc's-Boogie | Boogie Woogie & Blues | Elite Special | 73434

Hermitage
Pat Metheny | New Chautauqua | ECM | 1131(825471-2)
Sandor Szabo | Gaia And Aries | Acoustic Music Records | 319.1146.2

Hermosa Summer
Ella Fitzgerald And Her Trio | Jazz At The Philharmonic:The Ella Fitzgerald Set | Verve | 815147-1 IMS

Hernando's Hideaway
Ella Fitzgerald With The Marty Paich Orchestra | Ella Sings Broadway | Verve | 549373-2
Laurindo Almeida/Charlie Byrd Quartet | Tango | Concord | CCD 4290

Hero To Zero
Peter Erskine Group | Motion Poet | Denon Compact Disc | CY-72582

Heroes
Donald Harrison Trio | Heroes | Nagel-Heyer | CD 2041
John Hicks | Maybeck Recital Hall Series Volume Seven | Concord | CCD 4442

Herr Geh' Nicht Ins Gericht,Arie(Bach)
Karl Scharnweber Trio | Choral Concert | Nabel Records:Jazz Network | CD 4642

Herr Jesus, Gnadensonne
Helmut 'Joe' Sachse | Solo | FMP | 1070

Herr Martin Skripinski
Clark Terry Quintet | Herr Ober | Nagel-Heyer | CD 068

Herr Ober(I)
Herr Ober | Nagel-Heyer | CD 068

Herr Ober(II)
Baron Mingus And His Symphonic Airs | Charles Mingus-The Young Rebel | Swingtime(Contact) | ST 1010

Hershey Bar
Stan Getz Quartet | Stan Getz:Imagination | Dreyfus Jazz Line | FDM 36733-2
Stan Getz-The Complete Roost Sessions | EMI Records | 859622-2
Stan Getz-The Best Of The Roost Years | Roulette | 7981442
Stan Getz Quintet | Jazz At Storyville Vol.1 | Fresh Sound Records | FSR 629(Roost RLP 407)

Heru(Redemption)
Viktoria Tabatchnikowa-Eugenij Belov | Troika | ALISO Records | AL 1036

Herzensring-
Kodexx Sentimental | Das Digitale Herz | Poise | Poise 02

Herzleid
Bobby Hutcherson Quintet | Total Eclipse | Blue Note | 784291-2

Herzog
Vienna Art Orchestra | Concerto Piccolo | Hat Art | CD 6038

He's A Carioca
Washboard Sam | Washboard Sam 1935-1947 | Story Of Blues | CD 3502-2

He's A Devil In His Own Home Town
Tommy Dorsey And His Clambake Seven | The Best Of Tommy Dorsey And His Clambake Seven | Retrieval | RTR 79012

He's A Real Gone Guy
Jack McDuff Quartet | Jack McDuff:The Prestige Years | Prestige | PRCD 24387-2
Screamin' | Original Jazz Classics | OJCCD 875-2(P 7259)
Phineas Newborn Jr. Trio | Please Send Me Someone To Love | Contemporary | C 7622
Louis Armstrong And His Orchestra | Louis Armstrong:A 100th Birthday Celebration | RCA | 2663694-2

He's A Son Of The South
Louis Armstrong-The Complete RCA Victor Recordings | RCA | 2668682-2

He's Fine
Anita Boyer & Her Tomboyers | Nat King Cole Trio:The MacGregor Years 1941/45 | Music & Arts | CD 911

He's Funny That Way
Billie Holiday And Her Band | Billie Holiday Broadcast Performances Vol.1 | ESP Disk | ESP 3002-2
Billie Holiday With Eddie Heywood And His Orchestra | Billie Holiday:The Complete Commodore Recordings | GRP | AFS 1019-8
Billie Holiday With The JATP All Stars | The Complete Jazz At The Philharmonic On Verve 1944-1949 | Verve | 523893-2
Billie Holiday Story Vol.1:Jazz At The Philharmonic | Verve | 521642-2
Billie Holiday Story Vol.1:Jazz At The Philharmonic | Verve | 521642-2
Billie Holiday With Trio/Orchestra | Billie Holiday At Her Extra Special Vol.Two | Avenue | AVINT 1020 (800971)
Rosemary Clooney With The Scott Hamilton-Warren Vache Sextet | Tribute To Billie Holiday | Concord | CCD 4081
Stan Kenton And His Orchestra | Stan Kenton Encores | Creative World | ST 1034

He's Gone
Nancy Harrow Group | Lost Lady | Soul Note | 121263-2

He's Gone Again
Shirley Horn Trio | The Garden Of The Blues | Steeplechase | SCS 1203

He's Gone Away
Marie Knight And Her Group | Today | Blue Labor | BL 106

He's Got The Whole World In His Hands
Gene Harris Group | In His Hands | Concord | CCD 4758
Jeanne Lee | The Newest Sound Around | RCA | 2122112-2

He's My Guy
Monica Zetterlund With The Zoot Sims Quartet | Monica Zetterlund-The Lost Tapes | RCA | 2136332-2
Sarah Vaughan With The Clifford Brown All Stars | Sarah Vaughan | Verve | 543305-2
Brownie-The Complete EmArCy Recordings Of Clifford Brown | EmArCy | 838306-2
Sarah Vaughan With The Ernie Wilkins Orchestra | Jazz-Club: Vocal | Verve | 840029-2

He's Okay
First Revolution Singers | A Cappella Gospel Anthology | Tight Harmony Records | TH 199404

He's Younger Than You Are
Till Martin Quintet | On The Trail | Nabel Records:Jazz Network | CD 4676

Hesitation
Wynton Marsalis Quartet | Wynton Marsalis | CBS | 468708-2
Cat Anderson And His All Stars | Plays W.C. Handy | Black & Blue | BLE 59.163 2

Hesitation Blues
Louis Armstrong And His All Stars | The Louis Armstrong Selection | CBS | 467278-2

Hesitation Blues(rehersal sequence)
Mary Lou Williams Trio | Victor Jazz History Vol.10:Kansas City(1935-71) | RCA | 2128564-2

Heute Jedoch Nicht
Fritz Hauser | Pensieri Bianchi | Hat Art | CD 6067

Hexensabbat
Art Ensemble Of Chicago | Vol.1:Ancient To The Future | DIW | DIW 8014

Hey Ba-Ba-Re-Bop
Thurston Harris With Band | Little Bitty Pretty One | Pathe | 1546651(Aladdin)

Hey Baby
John Henry Barbee | Blues Masters Vol.3 | Storyville | STCD 8003
Orchestra | Duke Ellington's Sophisticated Ladies | RCA | BL 04053 DX
Shakey Jake Quintet | American Folk Blues Festival | Polydor | 2310296 IMS

Hey Boogie
John Lee Hooker | Blues Roots Vol. 13: John Lee Hooker | Chess | 6.24803 AG

Hey Da Ba Doom
Muggsy Spanier And His Band | This Is Jazz Vol.1 | Jazzology | JCD 1025/26

Hey Driver
Lux Orchester | Lux Orchester | VeraBra Records | ???

Hey Good Lookin'
Doctor Feelgood-The Original Piano Red | Music Is Medicine | L+R Records | LR 42019

Hey Hey Beautiful Girl
Blind Blake | Blind Blake-Bootleg Rum Dum Blues | Biograph | BLP 12003

Hey Jim
Errol Dixon with Mickey Baker & The Alex Sanders Funk Time Band | Fighting The Boogie | Bellaphon | BCH 33021

Hey Jude
Joshua Breakstone Quartet | The Compositions Of The Beatles Vol.2: Oh! Darling | Paddle Wheel | KICJ 123
Lanfranco Malaguti/Enzo Pietropaoli/Fabrizio Sferra | Something | Nueva Records | NC 1010
Sarah Vaughan With Orchestra | Song Of The Beatles | Atlantic | SD 16037

Hey Lawdy Mama
June Richmond With Orchestra | Harlem Roots-Jazz On Film:Jivin' Time | Storyville | SLP 6003
Louisiana Red | New York Blues | L+R Records | LR 42002

Hey Lock
Eddie Lockjaw Davis-Johnny Griffin Quintet | Tough Tenors Back Again! | Storyville | STCD 8298
Joe Lee Wilson With Orchestra | Without A Song | Inner City | IC 1064 IMS

Hey Look Me Over
Revival Jassband | Jass, I Like It | Timeless | CD TTD 587

Hey Lordy Mama
Andy Kirk And His Twelve Clouds Of Joy | The Uncollected:Andy Kirk | Hindsight | HSR 227 (835032)

Hey Mr. Mumbles,What Did You Say?
Dutch Swing College Band | Souvenirs From Holland, Vol. 3 | DSC Production | PA 005 (801062)

Hey New Day
Ron McClure Quintet | Never Forget | Steeplechase | SCCD 31279

Hey Now
Red Garland Trio | Red Garland Revisited! | Original Jazz Classics | OJCCD 985-2(P 7658)

Tiny Grimes' Orchestra | Tiny Grimes:The Complete 1950-1954,Vol.5 | Blue Moon | BMCD 6009
Hey Pete
Dizzy Gillespie And His Orchestra | Dizzy Gillspie-The Complete RCA Victor Recordings | Bluebird | 63 66528-2
Hey Porter
Henning Berg & John Taylor With 'Tango' | Tango & Company | Jazz Haus Musik | JHM 0085 CD
Hey Presto!
Count Basie And His Orchestra | Planet Jazz:Count Basie | Planet Jazz | 2152068-2
Hey Pretty Baby
Planet Jazz:Big Bands | Planet Jazz | 2169649-2
100 Ans De Jazz:Count Basie | RCA | 2177831-2
The Indispensable Count Basie | RCA | ND 89758
Hey Raymond
Kenny Werner Trio | Press Enter | Sunnyside | SSC 1056 D
Hey Sinner
First Revolution Singers | A Cappella Gospel Anthology | Tight Harmony Records | TH 199404
Hey Sonny Red
Centrifugal Funk | Centrifugal Funk | Legato | 652508
Hey There
Bill Evans | Conversations With Myself | Verve | 521409-2
Bob Keene Quintet | The Bob Keene Quintet | Fresh Sound Records | FSR 586(Del-Fi DFLP 1202)
Fran Warren With The Marty Paich Orchestra | Hey There! Here's Fran Warren | Fresh Sound Records | Tops T 1585 CD
Jack Van Poll Trio | Tree-Oh In One | September | CD 5102
Hey Western Union Man
Jonas Hellborg Group | Jonas Hellborg Group | Day Eight Music | DEMCD 025
Hey! Mama!
Rose Murphy Trio | Rose Murphy(The Chee-Chee Girl) | RCA | 2153222-2
Hey! Now Let's Jive
Fats Waller And His Rhythm | The Last Years 1940-1943 | Bluebird | ND 90411(3)
Hey! Stop Kissin' My Sister
Milt Jackson-Kenny Clarke Sextet | Roll Em Bags | Savoy | SV 0110(MG 12042)
Hey, It's Me You're Talkin' To
Victor Lewis Quintet | Know It Today, Know It Tomorrow | Red Records | 123255-2
Hey,Lee!
Rich Corpolongo Quartet | Just Found Joy | Delmark | DE 489
Heycigany
Ian Carr's Nucleos | In Flagranty Delicto | CMP Records | CMP 1
Heymann's Alea
| Kenny Wheeler-Norma Winstone-John Taylor With The Maritime Jazz Orchestra | Justin Time | JTR 8465-2
Heyoke
Ronnie Scott's Quintet | Serious Gold | Ronnie Scott's Jazz House | NSPL 18542
Hi
André Previn Trio | Jazz At The Musikverein | Verve | 537704-2
Hi Fly
Al Grey And His Allstars | Snap Your Fingers | Verve | 9860307
Art Blakey And The Jazz Messengers | At The Jazz Corner Of The World Vol. 2 | Blue Note | 868365-5
Cannonball Adderley Quintet | Live In San Francisco | Riverside | RISA 1157-6
Cannonball Adderley Birthday Celebration | Fantasy | FANCD 6087-2
Charles Davis Quartet | Super 80 | Nilva | NQ 3410 IMS
Eric Dolphy Trio | Berlin Concerts | Enja | 3007/9-2
Eric Dolphy-Chuck Israels | Eric Dolphy:The Complete Prestige Recordings | Prestige | 9 PRCD-4418-2
Ernie Wilkins' Almost Big Band | Montreux | Steeplechase | SCCD 31190
Horace Parlan Trio | No Blues | Steeplechase | SCS 1056
Joe Beck Group | Back To Beck | dmp Digital Music Productions | CD 464
Monty Alexander Trio | Full Steam Ahead | Concord | CCD 4287
Richie Coles Sextet With Eddie Jefferson | Hollywood Madness | Muse | MCD 5207
The Riverside Reunion Band | Hi-Fly | Milestone | MCD 9228-2
Hi Hat
Earl Hines And His Orchestra | Earl Hines: His Piano 1928-His Orchestra 1938 | Swing Classics | ET 5
Hi Ho Silver
Danny Richmond Quintet | Dionysius | Red Records | VPA 161
Hi Lili Hi Lo
Bill Evans-Eddie Gomez Duo | The Complete Fantasy Recordings | Fantasy | 9FCD 1012-2
Bobby Scott Quartet | Slowly | Musicmasters | 5053-2
Martin Taylor Quintet With Guests | Spirit Of Django:Years Apart | Linn Records | AKD 058
Paul Desmond Quartet | Planet Jazz:Paul Desmond | Planet Jazz | 2152061-2
Paul Desmond-Greatest Hits | RCA | CL 89809 SF
Hi Lili Hi Lo(take 6)
Gene Ammons Quintet | The Black Cat | Prestige | P 10006
Hi 'Ya
Johnny Hodges Orchestra | Ellingtonia '56 | Verve | 2304431 IMS
Hi, Mr.Wess
Festa Group | Strings | Nueva Records | NC 3009
Hi,Little Goats
Duke Ellington And His Orchestra | Jazz:The Essential Collection Vol.2 | IN+OUT Records | 78012-2
Hiawatha
Duke Ellington Orchestra | The Golden Duke | Prestige | P 24029
Hiawatha Rag
Chris Barber's Jazz Band | Chris Barber-40 Years Jubilee(1954-1956) | Timeless | CD TTD 586
Hibble And Hydes
Lee Konitz Quartet | Jazz At Storyville | Black Lion | BLP 60901
Hi-Beck
Lee Konitz Quintet | The Lee Konitz Quintet | Chiaroscuro | CR 166
Lee Konitz-Harold Danko Duo | Once Upon A Live | Accord | 500162
Hick
Seamus Blake Quintet | The Bloomdaddies | Criss Cross | Criss 1110
Hico Killer-
Jazz Fresh | Jazz Fresh | GGG-Verlag:GGG Verlag und Mailorder | CD 01.03
Hicup
Sandor Szabo | Gaia And Aries | Acoustic Music Records | 319.1146.2
Hidden Enemies
Lan Xang | Hidden Gardens | Naxos Jazz | 86046-2
Hidden Joy
Michel Petrucciani | Michel Petrucciani:Concert Inédits | Dreyfus Jazz Line | FDM 36607-2
John Surman Quartet | Stranger Than Fiction | ECM | 1534
Hidden Orchid-
Chad Wackerman Quartet | Forty Reasons | CMP Records | CMP CD 48
Hidden Pulse
Tim Sund Trio | Trialogue | Nabel Records:Jazz Network | CD 4692
Hidden Rhapody
Kick | Wolfhound's Kick | BELL Records | BLR 84041
Hidden Sevens-Thinking Backwards
Herbie Hancock Group | Sextant | CBS | SRCS 9338
Hidden Shadows
Jorgen Emborg Group | Keyword | Stunt Records | 18904
Hide And Seek
Big Joe Turner With Axel Zwingenberger | Boogie Woogie Jubilee | Vagabond | VRCD 8.81010
Hide And Seek Boogie
King Curtis Band | King Curtis-Blow Man Blow | Bear Family Records | BCD 15670 CI
Hide Away
Blind Willie McTell | Blind Willie McTell-Trying To Get Home | Biograph | BLP 12008
Hide Out
Buddy Guy & Junior Wells With The Chicago Blues All Stars '78 | Live In Montreux | Black & Blue | BLE 59.530 2
Hideaway
Freddie King Band | Texas Cannonball-Live At The Texas Opry House | Magnum Music Group | CDBM 062
Hielan' Laddie
Gina Sbu/Etienne Brunet Group | Aller Simple | ITM Records | ITM 1458
Hi-Fi Fo Fums
Count Basie And His Orchestra | Fancy Pants | Original Jazz Classics | OJCCD 1038-2(2310920)
Hi-Five
Riccardo Ballerini Group | Blue Mesa | yvp music | CD 3048
Higga Boom
Sonny Berman Jam Session | Jazz Immortal 1946 | Fresh Sound Records | FSR 533(Esoteric ES 532)
High
Steve Lacy-Maarten Altena | High,Low And Order | Hat Art | CD 6069
High And Dry
Keith Nichols Cotton Club Gang And Janice Day With Guy Barker | I Like To Do Things For You | Stomp Off Records | CD 1242
High Crime
Al Jarreau With Band | High Crime | i.e. Music | 557848-2
Volker Kottenhahn Trio | Out Of Print | Nabel Records:Jazz Network | CD 4680
High Dee
Joe Sullivan Quintet | The Piano Artistry Of Joe Sullivan | Jazz Unlimited | JUCD 2051
High Fly
Duane Eubanks Sextet | My Shining Hour | TCB Records | TCB 99202
High Heel Blues
Antje Uhle Trio | Majazztic Steps | Mons Records | MR 874824
High In The Sky
Hampton Hawes Trio | High In The Sky | Fresh Sound Records | FSR-CD 0059
High Jingo
Mose Allison Trio | High Jinks! The Mose Allison Trilogy | CBS | J3K 64275
High Modes
James Spaulding Quintet | Escapade | HighNote Records | HCD 7039
High Noon
Ken McIntyre Trio | Chasing The Sun | Steeplechase | SCCD 31114
Van Alexander Orchestra | Home Of Happy Feet/Swing! Staged For Sound! | Capitol | 535211-2
Walt Weiskopf Nonet | Song For My Mother | Criss Cross | Criss 1127
High On An Open Mike(Intro)
Charlie Ventura Quintet | The New Charlie Ventura In Hi-Fi | Harlequin | HQ 2009(Baton BL 1202) IMS
High On The Windy Hill
Herbie Mann Quartet With Strings | Love And The Weather | Bethlehem | BET 6009-2(BCP 63)
High On You
Lonnie Liston Smith Orchestra | Lonnie Smith | America | AM 6145
David Friesen | Through The Listening Glass | Inner City | IC 1061 IMS
High Price Boogie
John Lee Hooker | House Of The Blues | Chess | CHD 9258(872282)
High Priced Woman
Andrew Cyrille Quartet | Special People | Soul Note | SN 1012
High Priest
McCoy Tyner Big Band | The Turning Point | Birdology | 513163-2
High School Cadets
George Wallington Trio | The Modern Jazz Piano Album | Savoy | WL 70510(2)(SJL 2247) DP
High Society
Chris Barber's Jazz Band | Dixieland Jubilee-Vol. 3 | Intercord | 155013
Firehouse Five Plus Two | Twenty Years Later | Good Time Jazz | 10054
George Lewis Band | The George Lewis Band At Herbert Otto's Party | American Music | AMCD-74
Jack Teagarden And His Orchestra | Jazz Original | Charly | CD 80
Jelly Roll Morton's New Orleans Jazzmen | The Jelly Roll Morton Centennial-His Complete Victor Recordings | Bluebird | ND 82361
Victor Jazz History Vol.1:New Orleans & Dixieland | RCA | 2128555-2
Louis Armstrong And His All Stars | On The Road | Laserlight | 15798
Louis Armstrong And His All Stars/Orchestra | Welcome To Jazz: Louis Armstrong | Koch Records | 321 971 D1
Louis Armstrong And His Orchestra | Louis Armstrong-Satchmo's Greatest Hits | RCA | CL 89799
Young Louis Armstrong | RCA | 2115517-2
Sidney Bechet Groups | The Collection-Sidney Bechet | Bluebird | ND 90687
Sidney Bechet's Blue Note Jazzmen | Hot Jazz On Blue Note | Blue Note | 835811-2
Turk Murphy And His Jazz Band | Turk Murphy's Jazz Band At The Italien Village San Francisco | Merry Makers Record | MMRC-CD-11
High Society Calypso
Louis Armstrong And His All Stars | Masters Of Jazz Vol.1:Louis Armstrong | Storyville | STCD 4101
High Society(take 1)
Wild Bill Davison And His Commodores | Commodore Classics-George Brunies/Wild Bill Davison: Tin Roof Blues | Commodore | 6.24294 AG
High Society(take 2)
George Lewis And His Band | George Lewis With Kid Shots | American Music | AMCD-2
High Speed Spirit
Johannes Enders Quartet | Home Ground | Enja | 9105-2
High Tide
Boyd Raeburn And His Orchestra | Boyd Raeburn:The Transcription Performances 1946 | Hep | CD 42
Matt Penman Quartet | Flipside | Naxos Jazz | 86013-2
High Wire
Dave Holland Quintet | Prime Directive | ECM | 1698(547950-2)
David Newton Quartet | DNA | Candid | CCD 79742
Ed Kröger Quartet plus Guests | Movin' On | Laika Records | 35101332
Flim & The BB's | TriCycle | dmp Digital Music Productions | CD 443
Higher Grounds
Henry Threadgill Sextet | Subject To Change | About Time | AT 1007
Highest Mountain
Klaus Weiss Quintet feat. Clifford Jordan | Live At Opus 1 | Jazzline | ???
High-Heel Sneakers
Magic Sam's Blues Band | Magic Sam | Blues Classics(L+R) | CDLR 82008
High-Heels
Jesse Van Ruller Trio | Trio | EmArCy | 017513-2
High-Higher-Her
Joe McBride | Keys To Your Heart | Inak | 30352
Highlife
Duke Ellington And His Orchestra | The Indispensable Duke Ellington Vol.1/2 | RCA | NL 89749 (809154)
Highly Artifical Blues
Wynton Marsalis Septet | Live In Swingtown | Jazz Door | JD 1290
Highway
Blind Joe Hill One-Man-Blues Band | First Chance | L+R Records | LR 42059
Highway 49-
Homesick James Quartet | Got To Move | Trix Records | TRIX 3320
Highway One
McCoy Tyner Octet | Together | Milestone | M 9087
Hi-Heel Sneakers
John Lee Hooker | Get Back Home | Black & Blue | BLE 59.023 2
Hijacked
Anouar Brahem Trio | Astrakan Café | ECM | 1718(159494-2)
Hijaz Pechref
Leo Cuypers Trio | Theatre Music | BVHAAST | 017
Hi-Lee
Ulrich Gumpert Workshop Band/DDR | Echos Von Karolinenhof | FMP | 0710
Hills
Michael Naura Quintet | Vanessa | ECM | 1053
Hills Edge
Kenny Dorham Sextet | Round Midnight At The Cafe Bohemia | Blue Note | 300105(1524)
Hillside
Connie Crothers Trio | Perception | Steeplechase | SCCD 31022
Himmel Und Hölle
Jens Skou Olsen Group | September Veje | dacapo | DCCD 9451
Himmelgrunden(Star Field)
Lito Vitale Quartet | Lito Vitale Cuarteto | Messidor | 15995 CD
Hindered On His Way To Heaven
Spencer Barefield-Anthony Holland-Tani Tabbal | Live At Nickelsdorf Konfrontation | Sound Aspects | sas CD 007
Hindsight
Phil Woods & Space Jazz Trio | Live At The Corridonia Jazz Festival 1991 | Philology | W 211.2
Hindsight And Forethought
Junior Cook Quartet | Something's Cookin' | Muse | MCD 5470
Hindustan
Alex Welsh And His Jazz Band | Compact Jazz: Best Of Dixieland | Verve | 831375-2
Bob Crosby's Bobcats | Jazz Drumming Vol.3(1938-1939) | Fenn Music | FJD 2703
Dee Dee Pierce And His New Orleans Stompers | In Binghampton,N.Y. Vol.Three | American Music | AMCD-81
Emile Barnes' Louisiana Joymakers | The Louisiana Joymakers
Introducing DeDe & Billie Pierce | American Music | AMCD-13
Jack Teagarden And His Orchestra | Jack Teagarden Plays The Blues And Dixie | Ember | CJS 803
Hindustan-
George Brunis And His Jazzband | Commodore Classics-George Brunis:King Of Tailgate Trombone | Commodore | 6.25896 AG
Hine And Seek
Earl Hines | Hine's Tune | France's Concert | FCD 101
Hip And Hop
J.J.Johnson-Kai Winding Quintet (Jay&Kai) | Early Bones | Prestige | P 24067
Hip Chops
Roland Kirk Quartet | Talkin' Verve-Roots Of Acid Jazz:Roland Kirk | Verve | 533101-2
Arthur Blythe Quartet | Calling Card | Enja | ENJ-9051 2
Hip Dripper
Joachim Kühn Sextett | Hip Elegy | MPS | 68066
Hip Hip Hora
Bob Mintzer Big Band | Carmouflage | dmp Digital Music Productions | CD 456
Hip Hop Hammer
Torsten Zwingenberger | Drumkid | AH Records | RR 40213
Hip Hop Swing, A Love Supreme
Elvin Jones Quintet | Very Rare & Love And Peace | Konnex Records | KCD 5036
Hip Knees An' Legs
Bill Perkins Quartet | Peaceful Moments | Fresh Sound Records | FSR 115(835316)
Hip Pockets
Steve Williamson Septet | Rhyme Time-That Fuss Was Us! | Verve | 511235-2
Hip Shake
Grover Mitchell & His All-Star Orchestra | Hip Shakin' | Ken Music | 660.56.005
Hip Tip
Blue Mitchell And His Orchestra | A Sure Thing | Original Jazz Classics | OJCCD 837-2
Hip To It
Christian Rover Trio | New York Impressions | Organic Music | GWR 280595
Hip Vibrations
Bernt Rosengren Big Band | Jazz In Sweden | Caprice | CAP 1214
Hipmotism
Archie Shepp Sextet | A Sea Of Faces | Black Saint | 120002-2
Hipnotism
Jesse Davis Sextet | As We Speak | Concord | CCD 4512
Hippityville
Jutta Hipp Quintet | Deutsches Jazz Fesival 1954/1955 | Bear Family Records | BCD 15430
Hipp-Noses
Pili-Pili | Stolen Moments | JA & RO | JARO 4159-2
Hippo Hips
Johnny Smith Quartet | The Sound Of The Johnny Smith Guitar | Roulette | 531792-2
Hippo The Sentimental Hippy
Cannonball Adderley Quintet | Mercy Mercy Mercy | Capitol | 829915-2
Hippodelphia
Nat Adderley Quintet | That's Jazz Vol.16: Sayin' Somethin' | Atlantic | ATL 50246
Hippukrene
Jack McDuff Quartet | The Soulful Drums | Prestige | PCD 24256-2
Hippy Dip
The Magic Triangle | The Magic Triangle | Black Saint | BSR 0038
Hipsters In The Zone
McCoy Tyner Trio | McCoy Tyner Live | Jazz Classics | AU 36006 CD
His Blessing
Charles Gayle Trio | Kingdom Come | Knitting Factory Works | KFWCD 157
His Dreams
Joe Lovano Quintet | Village Rhythm | Soul Note | 121182-2
His Eye Is On The Sparrow
Carol Leigh & The Dumoustiers Stompers | Back Water Blues | Black & Blue | BLE 59.219 2
Terrie Richard Alden And The Warren Vaché Quartet | Voice With Heart | Nagel-Heyer | CD 048
The Bemiss Brothers | The Moment I Believed | Sound Of New Orleans | SONO 6011
His Eyes Were Suns
Louis Armstrong And His Friends | Jazz Special-His Last Recordings | RCA | ND 89527
His Father Wore Long Hair
Louis Armstrong With Orchestra | Satchmo | Verve | 835895-2
His Last Journey
Joe Zawinul Group | Concerto Retitled | Atlantic | SD 1694
His Last Wish
Robin Kenyatta Quartet | Ghost Stories | ITM-Pacific | ITMP 970060
His Master's Voice
Tony Fruscella Quintet | Tony Fruscella | Atlantic | 90463-1 TIS
His Very Own Blues
Raphael Fays Group | Voyages | Acoustic Music Records | AMC 1015
Historia De Amor (Love Story)
Eddie Harris Quartet | There Was A Time-Echo Of Harlem | Enja | ENJ-6068 2
Historia De Un Amor
Häns'che Weiss-Vali Mayer Duo | Just Play | MMM Records | CD 1298
Jack Sheldon & His West Coast Friends | Angel Wings | Eastworld | CP 32-5424
Larry Vuckovich Quintet | Tres Palabras | Concord | CCD 4416
History
Kip Hanrahan Groups | Tenderness | American Clave | AMCL 1016-2
History Of The Balloon
Steve Lacy Sextet | Moon | Affinity | AFF 23
Hit And Run
Maynard Ferguson Orchestra | Storm | ARG Jazz | 21374872
Hit It
Soren Lee Trio | Soren Lee Trio | L+R Records | CDLR 45072

Hit It(alt.take)
Lars Danielsson Trio | Continuation | L+R Records | CDLR 45085
Hit That Jive Jack
Eddie Locke Group | Jivin' With The Refuges From Hastings Street | Chiaroscuro | CR 2007
Hit The Desert
Jimmy Dorsey And His Orchestra | The Uncollected:Jimmy Dorsey, Vol.2 | Hindsight | HSR 153
Hit The Road Jack
Nancy Harrow With The Clark Terry Quartet | Secrets | Soul Note | 121233-2
Stephane Grappell-Toots Thielemans Quintet | Bringing It Together | Cymekob | CYK 801-2
Hitch Hike On The Possum Trot Line
Casey Bill Weldon | Bottleneck Guitar Trendsetters Of The 1930's | Yazoo | YAZ 1049
Hittin' 12
Count Basie Big Band | The Montreux '77 Collection | Pablo | 2620107
Hittin' It
Tony Williams Quartet | The Joy Of Flying | CBS | SRCS 5825
Hittin' On Me
Etta Jones With The Houston Person Quartet | My Buddy | HighNote Records | HCD 7026
Hittin' The Jug
Gene Ammons-Richard Groove Holmes Quartet | Groovin' With Jug | Pacific Jazz | 792930-2
Hitzeplanscher
John Scofield Quintet | Works For Me | Verve | 549281-2
Hive
Francois Houle 5 | Cryptology | Between The Lines | btl 012(Efa 10182-2)
Hive-Mind
Michel Wintsch & Road Movie | Michel Wintsch & Road Movie featuring Gerry Hemingway | Between The Lines | btl 002(Efa 10172-2)
Hiver(part 1)
Michel Wintsch & Road Movie featuring Gerry Hemingway | Between The Lines | btl 002(Efa 10172-2)
Hiver(part 2)
Jacky Terrasson-Emmanuel Pahud Quartet | Into The Blue | Blue Note | 557257-2
Hiver(Vivaldi)
Mahmoud Turkmani | Fayka | Enja | ENJ-9447 2
Hkékét Jidde
Joki Freund Sextet | Yogi Jazz | L+R Records | LR 41008
Hob Nail Boogie
Dizzy Gillespie And His Orchestra | Diz Big Band | Verve | MV 2671 IMS
Hobo Flats
DRS Big Band | Jazz Aus Der Schweiz | GOL | GOL 11098
Jimmy Smith With The Oliver Nelson Orchestra | Compact Jazz: Jimmy Smith Plays The Blues | Verve | 829537-2
Jimmy Smith:Best Of The Verve Years | Verve | 527950-2
Joe Williams With The Jimmy Jones Orchestra | Me And The Blues | RCA | 2121823-2
Tony Lakatos Quintet | Different Moods | Lipstick Records | LIP 890112
Hobo Joe
Red Garland Trio | Equinox | Galaxy | GXY 5115
Hobo You Can't Ride This Train
Louis Armstrong With Sy Oliver And His Orchestra | Louis Armstrong:The New And Revisited Musical Autobiography Vol.3 | Jazz Unlimited | JUCD 2005
Ho-Cake
Peter Rühmkorf Mit Dem Michael Naura Trio | Kein Apolloprogramm Für Lyrik | ECM | 801 SP
Hocus Pocus
Fletcher Henderson And His Orchestra | The Indispensable Fletcher Henderson(1927-1936) | RCA | 2122618-2
Hocus-Pocus
Lee Morgan Quintet | Memorial Album | Blue Note | 84446
Hod O'Brien Trio | Have Piano...Will Swing! | Fresh Sound Records | FSR-CD 5030
Hodge Podge
Claude Hopkins And His Orchestra | Harlem 1935 | Jazz Anthology | JA 5156
Hodge Podge-
Bob Dorough Trio | Right On My Way Home | Blue Note | 857729-2
Hoe Down
Oliver Nelson & His Sextet | Three Dimensions | MCA | IA 9335/2
Oliver Nelson And His Orchestra | Blues And The Abstract Truth | CTI Records | PDCTI 1122-2
Hog Callin' Blues
Charles Mingus Quintet With Roland Kirk | Oh Yeah | Atlantic | 90667-1 TIS
Hog Wash
Odetta With The Buck Clayton Sextet | Odetta And The Blues | Original Blues Classics | OBCCD 509-2(RLP 9417)
Hogan's Alley
Stan Kenton And His Orchestra | Fire Fury And Fun | Creative World | STD 1073
Hogtown Blues
Oscar Peterson | Oscar Peterson In Russia | Pablo | 2CD 2625711
Solo | Pablo | 2310975-2
Oscar Peterson Trio | Paris Jazz Concert:Oscar Peterson | Laserlight | 36155
En Concert Avec Europe 1 | Laserlight | 710443/48
Stötter's Nevertheless | But, Where Is The Exit? | L+R Records | CDLR 45099
Hola, Gustavo(dedicated to G.Mahler)
Ray Bryant Trio | Here's Ray Bryant | Pablo | 2310764
Hold 'Em Joe
Sonny Rollins Quartet | The Roots Of Acid Jazz | Impulse(MCA) | IMP 12042
Sonny Rollins On Impulse | MCA | 2292-54613-2
Hold Hard,These Ancient Minutes In The Cuckoo's Month
Angela Brown | The Voice Of Blues | Schubert Records | SCH- 105
Hold It
Eddie Cleanhead Vinson With The Cannonball Adderley Quintet | Cannonball Adderley Birthday Celebration | Fantasy | FANCD 6087-2
Cleanhead & Cannonball | Landmark | LCD 1309-2(882857)
Steve Swallow Group | Carla | Watt | XtraWatt/2
Hold It Against Me
Clarence M.Jones And His Sock Four | Alexander Where's That Band?-Paramount Recordings 1926-1928 | Frog | DGF 13
Hold It Right There
Donald 'Duck' Harrison Quintet | Full Circle | Sweet Basil | 660.55.003
Hold Me
Blossom Dearie Quartet | Blossom Dearie Sings Comden And Green | Verve | 589102-2
Hold Me Hold Me Hold Me
Dick Collins And His Orchestra | King Richard The Swing Hearted | Fresh Sound Records | LJM 1027(RCA)
Hold Me Tight And Don't Let Go
Al Bowlly With The Ray Noble Orchestra | The Classic Years In Digital Stereo: Al Bowlly With Ray Noble | CDS Records Ltd. | REB 649
Hold My Hand
Don Byas Quintet | Lover Man | Vogue | 2115470-2
Hold On
Rudy Rotta Quartet | Live In Kansas City | Acoustic Music Records | 319.1138.2
Hold On I'm Coming
Herbie Mann Group | That's Jazz Vol.37: Memphis Underground | Atlantic | ATL 50520
Alex Bradford Trio | Hot Gospel | Lake | LACD 39
Hold On,I'm Waiting For You
Diane Schuur And Her Band | Pure Schuur | GRP | GRP 96282
Hold Out, Hold Up And Hold On
John Patitucci Group | Another World | GRP | GRP 97252
Hold That Thought
Peter Ehwald Trio | Away With Words:The Music Of John Scofield | Jazz Haus Musik | JHM 0128 CD
Juanita Hall With The Claude Hopkins All Stars | Sings The Blues | Fresh Sound Records | FSR 507(Counterpoint CPST 556)
Hold That Train
Doctor Clayton Band | Gotta Find My Baby | Swingtime(Contact) | BT 2005
Hold The Tiger
Benny Goodman And His Orchestra | Camel Caravan Broadcast 1939 Vol.1 | Phontastic | NCD 8817
Hold Tight
All Of Me | Black Lion | 127034
Reverend Blind Gary Davis | Say No To The Devil | Original Blues Classics | OBC 519
Holding Pattern 1
John Surman | Withholding Pattern | ECM | 1295(825407-2)
Holding Pattern 2
Oliver Lake Quartet | Holding Together | Black Saint | BSR 0009
Holey Moley
Benny Goodman And His Orchestra | Benny Goodman's 1934 Dodge All-Star Recordings(Complete) | Circle | CCD-111
Holiday
Machito And His Afro Cuban Jazz Ensemble | Machito And His Afro Cuban Jazz Ensemble | Caliente | Hot 120
Holiday For Strings
Richie Cole Quintet | Keeper Of The Flame | Muse | MR 5192
Holiday Scenes
Chris Barber's Jazz Band | 30 Years Chris Barber:Can't We Get Together | Timeless | CD TTD 517/8
Holidays
Slawterhaus | Slawterhaus Live | Victo | CD 013
Holidays In Skopje
Salvatore Bonafede Trio | Plays | Ken Music | 660.56.017
Holland
Alan Clare With Lenny Bush | Alan Clare's Holland Park:Love Music To Unwind | Master Mix | CHECD 00108
Höllenhund
John Lindberg Orchestra | Trilogy Of Works For Eleven Instrumentalists | Black Saint | BSR 0082
Holler
Phil Haynes' 4 Horns & What | 4 Horn Lore | Open Minds | OM 2413-2
Holler Stomp
Pete Johnson | Boogie Woggie Classics | Blue Note | BLP 1209
Hollis Stomp-
Georg Gräwe Quintet | Pink Pong | FMP | 0480
Hollyhocks
Dave Bargeron Quartet | Barge Burns...Slide Flies | Mapleshade | 02832
Hollywood Jam Blues
Count Basie And His Orchestra | Lester Leaps In-Vol.2 1939/1940 | CBS | CBS 88668
Hollywood Special
The Widespread Depression Orchestra | Downtown Uproar | Stash Records | ST 203 IMS
Holunderkuchen
Glenn Ferris Trio | Chrominance | Enja | 9132-2
Holy
Ok Nok...Kongo | Moonstone Journey | dacapo | DCCD 9444
Holy Coordinator
Abbey Lincoln With The Rodney Kendrick Trio | Abbey Lincoln Live-Music Is The Magic | ITM Records | ITM 1489
Holy Ghost
Mary Lou Williams Duo | Zoning | Mary Records | M 103
Holy Holy
Dave Brubeck Quartet With Chorus And Orchestra | To Hope! A Celebration | Telarc Digital | CD 80430
Holy Land
Cedar Walton Trio | The Trio | Red Records | VPA 192
Milt Jackson Sextet | The Harem | Musicmasters | 5061-2
Holy Spring
Mike Westbrook Brass Band | Glad Day:Settings Of William Blake | Enja | ENJ-9376 2
Holy Thursday
Viktoria Tolstoy With The Esbjörn Svensson Trio | Viktoria Tolstoy:White Russian | Blue Note | 821220-2
Holy Water
Marty Ehrlich-Peter Erskine-Michael Formanek | Relativity | Enja | ENJ-9341 2
Holy Waters
Monty Alexander Trio | The River | Concord | CCD 4422
Holzfällermedley:
Roger Girod-Peter A.Schmid | Windschief | Creative Works Records | CW CD 1027-2
Holzwurm II
Charles Lloyd Quartet | Voice In The Night | ECM | 1674(559445-2)
Homage
John McLaughlin With The Aighette Quartet And Yan Marez | Time Remembered:John McLaughlin Plays Bill Evans | Verve | 519861-2
Mike LeDonne Sextet | Soulmates | Criss Cross | Criss 1074
Tim Berne Quartet | Mutant Variations | Soul Note | 121091-2
Homage A Lili Boulanger
Véronique Gillet And Fernando Freitez With Carlos Franco | Terracota | Acoustic Music Records | 319.1056.2
Homage A Villa-Lobos
Kamikaze Ground Crew | Madam Marie's Temple Of Knowledge | New World Records | 80438-2
Homage To Lord Krishna
Ron Affif Quartet | Vierd Blues | Pablo | 2310954-2
Homage To O.P.
Attila Zoller-Wolfgang Lackerschmid | Live Highlights '92 | Bhakti Jazz | BR 28
Sebastian Whittaker Septet | First Outing | Justice Records | JR 0202-2
Hombre
Gumpert & Sommer Duo | Vers umnisse - Gumpert & Sommer/DDR | FMP | 0740
Home
Bob Scobey's Frisco Band | Scobey And Clancy | Good Time Jazz | GTCD 12009-2
Céline Rudolph And Her Trio | Paintings | Nabel Records:Jazz Network | CD 4661
Chick Corea & Origin | Change | Stretch Records | SCD 9023-2
Dino Saluzzi Group | If | Enja | ENJ-9451 2
Dirk Strakhof & Batoru | Arabesque | Nabel Records:Jazz Network | CD 4696
Eero Koivistoinen Quintet | Dialog | L+R Records | CDLR 45094
John Stevens Quartet | Touching On | View | VS 105 IMS
Louis Armstrong With The Russell Garcia Orchestra | Verve Jazz Masters 1:Louis Armstrong | Verve | 519818-2
Louis Armstrong With Zilmer Randolph's Orchestra | Louis Armstrong V.S.O.P. Vol. 7/8 | CBS | CBS 88004
Michel Petrucciani Group | Playground | Blue Note | 795480-2
Michel Petrucciani:The Blue Note Years | Blue Note | 789916-2
Michel Petrucciani Trio | Trio In Tokyo | Dreyfus Jazz Line | FDM 36605-2
Mike Westbrook Concert Band | Marching Songs Vol.1&2 | Deram | 844853-2
Nat King Cole And His Trio | Nat King Cole:The Snader Telescriptions | Storyville | 4960103
Combo USA | Affinity | CD AFS 1002
Niels Lan Doky Trio | The Target | Storyville | SLP 4140
Sam Jones Sextet | The Soul Society | Original Jazz Classics | OJCCD 1789-2(RLP 1172)
The Alex Welsh Legacy Band | The Sound Of Alex Vol.1 | Nagel-Heyer | CD 070
The Catholics | Simple | Laika Records | 35100802
Tom Saunders' 'Wild Bill Davison Band' & Guests | Exactly Like You | Nagel-Heyer | CD 023
The Second Sampler | Nagel-Heyer | NHR SP 6
Changes | Home Again | EGO | 4015
Home Away From Home
Bob Mintzer Big Band | Homage To Count Basie | dmp Digital Music Productions | CD 529
Home Boy
Hot Lips Page With Simon Brehms Kvintett | Americans In Sweden: Hot Lips Page 1951-Rex Stewart 1947 | Jazz Society | AA 513
Home Comin'
Horace Silver Quintet | Stylings Of Silver | Blue Note | 540034-2
Annie Ross & PonyPoindexter With The Berlin All Stars | Annie Ross & Pony Poindexter with The Berlin All Stars | MPS | 9811257
Home Cookin'
Eddie Bert Sextet | Let's Dig Bert(Eddie That Is) | Fresh Sound Records | FSR 540(Trans-World TWLP 208)
Horace Silver Quintet | The Stylings Of Silver | Blue Note | 300168(1562)
Home Cooking
Charlie Parker With The Russ Freeman Trio | Charlie Parker On Dial, Vol.3 | Spotlite | SPJ 103
Home Fries
David Newton | Return Journey | Linn Records | AKD 025
Home Grown
John Colianni Quintet | John Colianni | Concord | CCD 4309
Home In Your Arms Again
Horace Parlan Sextet | Afro Blue | Blue Note | 780701-2
Home James
Stan Kenton And His Orchestra | At The Las Legas Tropicana | Capitol | 835245-2
Home On The Range
Oscar Klein Band | Oscar Klein Jazzshow | Koch Records | 321 704
Home Run
Marco Volpe Band | Exacting Work | SPLASC(H) Records | H 193
Home Stretch
Neil Swainson Quintet | 49th Parallel | Concord | CCD 4396
Home Universe
John Stevens Orchestra | A Luta Continua | Konnex Records | KCD 5056
Home(When The Shadows Fall)
Gerry Mulligan Quartet | Triple Play:Gerry Mulligan | Telarc Digital | CD 83453
Homecoming
Claus Boesser-Ferrari | Blue Footprint | Acoustic Music Records | 319.1066.2
Eddie Daniels Quartet With String Quartet | Memos From Paradise | GRP | GRP 95612
Marion Brown Quartet | Why Not? | ESP Disk | ESP 1040-2
Ralph Peterson Quartet | Ralph Peterson Presents The Fo'tet | Blue Note | 795475-2
Homegoing
Bernie Senensky Quartet | Homeland | Timeless | CD SJP 426
Homeless
Bessie Smith And Her Band | Jazz:The Essential Collection Vol.1 | IN+OUT Records | 78011-2
Homeless Blues
Philadelphia Jerry Ricks | True Blues | Traditional Line | TL 1314
Homenaje
Joan Monné Septet | Son Song | Fresh Sound Records | FSNT 010 CD
Homére S'Arrange
The Heath Brothers | Brotherly Love | Antilles | ???
Homesick Blues
Homesick James & Snooky Prior | The Blues Vol. 5 | Big Bear | 156042
Homesick Shuffle
Homesick James Quartet | Windy City Blues | Stax | SCD 8612-2
Homesick Shuffle(alt.take)
Homesick James | Got To Move | Trix Records | TRIX 3320
Homesick That's All
Homesick James Quartet | Got To Move | Trix Records | TRIX 3320
Homesick's Blues
Travis Haddix Band With The Kala Horns | Winners Never Quit | Elite Special | 73432
Hometown
Hal Singer Orchestra | Rent Party | Savoy | SV 0258(SJL 1147)
Hometown Blues
Dave Brubeck Quartet | Back Home | Concord | CCD 4103
Homeward Bound
Jeannie And Jimmy Cheatham & The Sweet Baby Blues Band | Homeward Bound | Concord | CCD 4321
Hommage
Joseph Jarman-Don Moye Quartet | Earth Passage-Density | Black Saint | BSR 0052
Hommage A Enelram Atsenig
Trio Terracota | Savia | Acoustic Music Records | 319.1193.2
Hommage À Hojok
NuNu! | Ocean | TipToe | TIP-888837 2
Hommage A Jacques Tati
Shin-Ichi Fukuda | Guitar Legends:Homage To Great Popular Guitarists | Denon Compact Disc | CO-18048
Hommage À Lounès Matoub
Schmid-Hübner-Krill | Time Makes The Tune | Mons Records | MR 874825
Hommage A Ostad
Raphael Fays Group | Voyages | Acoustic Music Records | AMC 1015
Hommage Boris Vian
Hans-Günther Wauer/Günter Baby Sommer | Dedication | FMP | 0900
Hommage To Paul Bowles:
Reid Anderson Quartet | Abolish Bad Architecture | Fresh Sound Records | FSNT 062 CD
Hommage:Mahler
Martial Solal Big Band | Martial Solal Big Band | Dreyfus Jazz Line | FDM 36512-2
Homunculus
Elvira Plenar Trio | I Was Just... | free flow music | ffm 0191
Klaus Doldinger's Passport | Atlantic Jazz: Fusion | Atlantic | 7567-81711-2
Passport | Cross-Collateral | Atlantic | 2292-44145-2
The Real Group | The Real Group:Original | ACT | 9256-2
Honest I Do
Monty Alexander Trio | Steamin' | Concord | CCD 4636
Honest Love
Uschi Brüning/Ernst-Ludwig Petrowsky | Features Of Usel | FMP | OWN-90001
Honestly
Jaco Pastorius Trio | Heavy'n Jazz | Jazzpoint | JP 1036 CD
Jaco Pastorius | Jaco Pastorius Honestly | Jazzpoint | JP 1032 CD
Honestly(part 1-10)
Jaco Pastorius Groups | Another Side Of Jaco Pastorius | Jazzpoint | JP 1064 CD
Honestly(part 2)
George Russell Sextet | Outer Thoughts | Milestone | M 47027
Honesty
Eric Dolphy Birthday Celebration | Fantasy | FANCD 6085-2
Toots Thielemans With Orchestra | Apple Dimple | Denon Compact Disc | DC-8563
Honey Babe
Nat Pierce/Dick Collins Nonet | Nat Pierce-Dick Collins Nonet/Charlie Mariano Sextet | Original Jazz Classics | OJC 118(F 3224)
Honey Bee
Muddy Waters Blues Band | Feathers And Sons | Chess | CHD 92522(872344)
Honey Boy
Ruth Brown With The Howard Briggs Orchestra | I'll Wait For You | Official | 6004
Honey Chile
Louis Jordan And His Tympany Five | Harlem Roots-Jazz On Film:The Headliners | Storyville | SLP 6001
Honey Do
Louis Armstrong And His Orchestra | Louis Armstrong-The Complete RCA Victor Recordings | RCA | 2668682-2

Honey Don't You Love Me Anymore
Louis Armstrong-The Complete RCA Victor Recordings | RCA | 2668682-2

Honey Dripper
Oscar Peterson Trio | Masters Of Jazz Vol.7 | RCA | NL 89721 DP
Sam Montgomery | East Coast Blues In The Thirties(1934-1939) | Story Of Blues | CD 3528-2

Honey Finger
Coleman Hawkins And Confreres | Coleman Hawkins And Confreres | Verve | 835255-2 PMS

Honey Flower
Coleman Hawkins And Confreres | Verve | 835255-2 PMS

Honey Flower(alt.take)
Herbie Hancock Group | Feet's Don't Fail Me Now | CBS | SRCS 9504

Honey Hill
Johnny Hodges Orchestra | The Soul Of Ben Webster | Verve | 527475-2
Roy Eldridge 'Littel Jazz'-The Best Of The Verve Years | Verve | 523338-2

Honey Hush
Big Joe Turner And His Band | Big Joe Turner Greatest Hits | Sequel Records | RSA CD 809
Big Joe Turner With The Count Basie Band | The Bosses | Original Jazz Classics | OJCCD 821-2(2310709)
Joe Turner With Band | Great Rhythm & Blues-Vol.4 | Bulldog | BDL 1003
Clarence Gatemouth Brown Band | Alright Again! | Edsel | Fiend 2

Honey In The Bee Ball
Louis Jordan's Elks Rendez-Vous Band | Louis Jordan Vol.1-Hoodoo Man | Swingtime(Contact) | ST 1011

Honey Love
John Pizzarelli Trio With The Don Sebesky Orchestra | Our Love Is Here To Stay | RCA | 6367501-2

Honey Pie
Charles Brown Band | Drifting Blues | Pathe | 1546611(Score SLP 4011)

Honey,Wenn Du Geburtstag Hast
Septer Bourbon | Septer Bourbon-The Smile Of The Honeycakehorse | Jazzline | JL 11151-2

Honeymoon Blues
Kölner Saxophon Mafia | Place For Lovers | Jazz Haus Musik | JHM 0082 CD

Honeymoon For Two Elephants
Jack Hylton And His Orchestra | The Bands That Matter | Eclipse | ECM 2046

Honeysuckle Rose
A Jam Session At Victor | Fats Waller-The Joint Is Jumpin' | RCA | ND 86288(874182)
Jazz Drumming Vol.1(1927-1937) | Fenn Music | FJD 2701
Al Casey Quintet | Buck Jumpin' | Original Jazz Classics | OJCCD 675-2(SV 2007)
Art Tatum Trio | Art Tatum:Over The Rainbow | Dreyfus Jazz Line | FDM 36727-2
Benny Goodman And His All Star Sextet | Verve Jazz Masters 33:Benny Goodman | Verve | 844410-2
On Stage | Decca | 6.28101 DP
Benny Goodman And His Orchestra | Benny Goodman's 1934 Dodge All-Star Recordings(Complete) | Circle | CCD-111
Benny Goodman Sextet | The Benny Goodman Selection | CBS | 467280-2
Bob Brookmeyer Quintet | Traditionalism Revisited | Affinity | AFF 127
Chris Barber's Jazz And Blues Band | Live In Munich | Timeless | CD TTD 600
Coleman Hawkins And His All Star Jam Band | Django Reinhardt All Star Sessions | Capitol | 531577-2
Jazz:The Essential Collection Vol.3 | IN+OUT Records | 78013-2
Django Reinhardt 1910-1953 | Jazztime(EMI) | 790560-2
Cozy Cole's Big Seven | Body And Soul Revisited | GRP | GRP 16272
Dee Daniels With The Jack Van Poll Trio | All Of Me | September | CD 5101
Django Reinhardt And The Quintet Du Hot Club De France | The Indispensable Django Reinhardt | RCA | ND 70929
Duke Ellington And His Orchestra | Carnegie Hall 1943 | Jazz Anthology | JA 5117
Happy Birthday Duke Vol.4 | Laserlight | 15786
Duke Ellington Quartet | Jazz Live & Rare: The First And Second Esquire Concert | Jazzline | ???
Earl Hines Quartet | The Earl | Naxos Jazz | 8.120581 CD
Ella Fitzgerald With Count Basie And His Orchestra | A Perfect Match-Basie And Ella | Pablo | 2312110-2
Ella Fitzgerald With The Count Basie Orchestra | Ella And Basie | Verve | 539059-2
A Classy Pair | Pablo | 2312132-2
Erroll Garner Trio | The Erroll Garner Selection | CBS | 471624-2
Fats Waller | Fats Waller-The Joint Is Jumpin' | RCA | ND 86288(874182)
Fats Waller And His Rhythm | The Classic Years In Digital Stereo: Fats Waller And His Rhythm | CDS Records Ltd. | RPCD 315(CD 684)
Frankfurt Swing All Stars | Jive At Five | L+R Records | CDLR 40025
Harry James And His Orchestra | The Radio Years: Harry James And His Orchestra 1943-46, Vol.3 | Hindsight | HSR 141
Herb Ellis-Joe Pass Quartet | Jazz/Concord | Concord | CCD 6001
Horace Henderson And His Orchestra | Fletcher Henderson Vol.1-The End Of An Era | Swingtime(Contact) | ST 1008
Jam Session At Victor | A String Of Swingin' Pearls | RCA | 2113035-2
Jay McShann | A Tribute To Fats Waller | Sackville | 3019
Jenny Evans And Her Quintet | Shiny Stockings | ESM Records | ESM 9305
Shiny Stockings | Enja | ENJ-9317 2
Jimmie Noone Quartet | Kings Of New Orleans | Avenue | AVINT 1010
Joe Pass | Live At Long Beach City College | Pablo | 2308239-2
Joe Turner-Albert Nicholas Quartet | The Giant Of Stride Piano In Switzerland | Jazz Connaisseur | JCCD 9106-2
Joe Williams With The Count Basie Orchestra | Joe Williams:Triple Play | Telarc Digital | CD 83461
Johnny Lytle Septet | Possum Grease | Muse | MCD 5482
Jonah Jones With Dave Pochonet & His All Stars | Jonah Jones | Swing | SW 8408 IMS
Lionel Hampton Sextet | Americans Swinging In Paris:Lionel Hampton | EMI Records | 539649-2
Le Jazz En France-Vol.6 | Pathe | 1727301
Louis Armstrong And His All Stars | The Louis Armstrong Selection | CBS | 467278-2
Martin Taylor Quartet | Spirit Of Django | Linn Records | AKD 030
Nat King Cole Trio | The Great Nat King Cole | Laserlight | 15733
Vocal Classics & Instrumental Classics | Capitol | 300014(TOCJ 6128)
Oscar Peterson | Tracks | MPS | 68084
Oscar Peterson And His Trio | Live At The Blue Note | Telarc Digital | CD 83304
Oscar Peterson-Joe Pass Duo | Oscar Pterson Et Joe Pass A La Salle Pleyel | Pablo | 2CD 2625705
Live At Salle Pleyel, Paris | Pablo | 2625705
Quintet Du Hot Club De France | Verve Jazz Masters 38:Django Reinhardt | Verve | 516931-2
Welcome To Jazz: Django Reinhardt | Koch Records | 322 074 D1
Ranee Lee And Her Band | Dark Divas-Highlights | Justin Time | JUST 144-2
Sammy Price And His Bluesicians | 1944 World Jam Session | Progressive | PCD 7074
Sidney Bechet Quintet | Introducing Jazz Colours | Jazz Colours | 874720-2
Sir Charles Thompson Quartet | Key One Up | Vanguard | VCD 79612-2
Slim Gaillard Group | Anytime Anyplace Anywhere | Hep | CD 2020
Stan Getz And The Swedish All Stars | Stockholm Sessions '58 | Dragon | DRLP 157/158
Stephane Grappelli Quartet | Stephane Grappelli:I Got Rhythm | Black Lion | BLCD 7613-2
Teddy Wilson Trio | The Impeccable Mr. Wilson | Verve | 2304513 IMS
The Tremble Kids | 25 Jahre The Tremble Kids | Intercord | 180036
Thelonious Monk Trio | Thelonious Monk:85th Birthday Celebration | zyx records | FANCD 6076-2
Thelonious Monk-The Complete Riverside Recordings | Riverside | 15 RCD 022-2
Toots Thielemans-Louis van Dijk Duo | Toots & Louis | Polydor | 2925136 IMS
Wild Bill Davis Quartet | Live At Swiss Radio Studio Zürich | Jazz Connaisseur | JCCD 8701-2
Willie Humphrey Jazz Band | New Orleans Traditional Jazz Legends:Willie Humphrey | Mardi Gras Records | MG 9002

Honeysuckle Rose-
Benny Carter Big Band | On The Air | Nueva Records | JU 327
Dollar Brand | Sangoma | Sackville | 3006
Fats Waller And His Rhythm | The Joint Is Jumpin' | Ember | CJS 839
Jimmy Rowles Trio | Paws That Refresh | Candid | CRS 1023 IMS
Mel Tormé And Cleo Laine With The John Dankworth Orchestra | Nothing Without You | Concord | CCD 4515

Honeysuckle Rose(2)
| Jazz Classics In Digital Stereo: Coleman Hawkins 1927-1939 | CDS Records Ltd. | RPCD 600(CD 698)

Honeysuckle Rose(alt.take)
McKinney's Cotton Pickers | The Complete McKinney's Cotton Pickers Vol.3/4 | RCA | NL 89738(2) DP

Honeysuckle Rose(short version)
Earl Hines Trio | Earl Hines:Fine & Dandy | Vogue | 2111508-2

Hong Kong
Harry Betts And His Orchestra | The Jazz Soul Of Doctor Kildare | Fresh Sound Records | FSR 634(Choreo/Ava AS 6)

Hong Kong Blues
Keith Ingham Trio | A Star Dust Melody | Sackville | SKCD2-2051

Honi Coles
Michael Riessler Group | Honig Und Asche | Enja | ENJ-9303 2

Honky Tonk
Bobby Jaspar And His Modern Jazz | Bobby Jaspar & His Modern Jazz | Vogue | 21559512
Magnus' Trio | Dangerous Game | Mikado Records | MK 94-209

Honky Tonk-
Miles Davis Group | Another Bitches Brew | Jazz Door | JD 1284/85

Honky Tonk Blues
Jan Jankeje's Party And Swingband | Mobil | Jazzpoint | JP 1068 CD
Les Haricots Rouges + Sam Lee | En Concert | Black & Blue | BLE 59215 2

Honky Tonk Train Blues
Axel Zwingenberger | Boogie Woogie Breakdown | Vagabond | VRCD 8.78013
Bob Crosby And His Orchestra | Swing Legens:Bob Crosby | Nimbus Records | NI 2011
Bob Zurke | The Best Of Boogie Woogie | Zeta | ZET 740
Meade Lux Lewis | 1939-1949, Blue Note's Three Decades Of Jazz, Vol. 1 | Blue Note | 89902
Meade Lux Lewis 1939-1054 | Story Of Blues | CD 3506-2
The Complete Jazz At The Philharmonic On Verve 1944-1949 | Verve | 523893-2
The Story Of Boogie Woogie | Memo Music | HDJ 4089
Oscar Klein Band | Pick-A-Blues Live | Jazzpoint | JP 1071
Ralph Sutton-Jay McShann Quartet | The Last Of The Whorehouse Piano Players | Chaz Jazz | CJ 103

Honky Tonk Woman
Bill Doggett And His Orchestra | Organ Boogie Woogie | CBS | 21079

Honolulu
Miff Mole's Molers | That's A Plenty | Memo Music | HDJ 4112

Hoochie Coochie Man
Muddy Waters Band | The Blues:A Collection Of Classic Blues Singers | Black Lion | BLCD 7605-2
Muddy Waters Blues Band | Live In Switzerland 1976 | Jazz Helvet | JH 02-2
The Blues Shouters | Live At Kultur-Karussell R ssli St fa | Bellaphon | BCH 33005

Hoodoo Man
Buddy Guy-Junior Wells Band | Drinkin' TNT 'N' Smokin' Dynamite | Sequel Records | NEM CD 687

Hook Up
John Balke Group | Saturation | EmArCy | 538160-2

Hooked On A Feling-
Albert Collins Blues Band | Cold Snap | Sonet | SNTF 969(941969)

Hoomba-Hoomba
| Playing To The Moon | Ronnie Scott's Jazz House | JHCD 047

Hooray For Love
Ella Fitzgerald With The Billy May Orchestra | The Complete Ella Fitzgerald Song Books of Harold Arlen, Irving Berlin, Duke Ellington, George & Ira Gershwin, Jerome Kern, Johnny Mercer, Cole Porter And Rogers & Hart | Verve | 519832-2
Ella Fitzgerald Sings The Harold Arlen Song Book | Verve | 589108-2
The Harold Arlen Songbook | Verve | 817526-1 IMS

Hooray, Hooray, This Woman Is Killing Me
Steve Lacy-Mal Waldron | Live at Dreher Paris 1981 Vol.2 | Hat Art | CD 6186(2)

Hootie Blues
Jay McShann | Vine Street Boogie | Black Lion | BLCD 760187
Jay McShann And His Orchestra | Big Band Bounce & Boogie:Hootie's K.C.Blues | Affinity | AFS 1006
Jay McShann Quartet | Roll' Em | Black & Blue | BLE 233022

Hootie's Blues
Sonny Criss With The George Arvanitas Trio | Live In Italy | Fresh Sound Records | FSR-CD 67(881947)

Hootin' 'N' Tootin'
Sonny Terry & Brownie McGhee | American Folk Blues Festival '70 | L+R Records | LS 42021

Hooveling
RMS | Centennial Park | MMC | CDP 7900102

Hop Hip Bip Bir Rip
Fletcher Henderson And His Orchestra | Fletcher Henderson Vol.1-First Impressions | MCA | 1310'

Hop Off
Lillian Boutté And Her American Band | Live In Tivoli | Music Mecca | CD 1030-2

Hop Skip And Jump
Peter Wölpl Group | Mr. Wölps & Dr. Fudge | Blue Flame | 40422(3984042-2)

Hop!
Louis Sclavis | Clarinettes | IDA Record | 004 CD

Hope
David Azarian | Hope | Enja | ENJ-9354 2
Jean-Paul Bourelly Group | Vibe Music | PAO Records | PAO 10500
Jenny Evans And Her Quintet | Gonna Go Fishin' | Enja | ENJ-9403 2
Mahavishnu Orchestra | Birds Of Fire | CBS | 468224-2
McCoy Tyner Sextet | Asante | Blue Note | 493384-2
Mick Goodrick-David Liebman-Wolfgang Muthspiel | In The Same Breath | CMP Records | CMP CD 71

Hope And Fear
Kurt Rosenwinkel Quintet | The Enemies Of Energy | Verve | 543042-2
Billy Taylor Trio | Homage | GRP | GRP 98062

Hope No.2
Jacques Stotzem | Fingerprint | Acoustic Music Records | 319.1129.2

Hope Song
Tom Harrell Quintet | Sail Away | Original Jazz Classics | OJCCD 1095-2(C- 14054-2)

Hope St.
Die Dozenten | Take It Easy | L+R Records | CDLR 45054

Hope You Find Your Way
Oleo | Hope You Get It | Nabel Records:Jazz Network | LP 4603

Hopes
Sonny Stitt With The Zimbo Trio | Sonny Stitt In Brazil | Fresh Sound Records | FSR-CD 0118

Hoppin' John
Cannonball Adderley Quintet | Cannonball Adderley:Sophisticated Swing-The EmArCy Small Group Sessions | Verve | 528408-2
Paul Williams Sextet | Paul Williams:The Complete Recordings Vol.1 (1947-1949) | Blue Moon | BMCD 6020

Hoppoh
Manhattan New Music Project | Mood Swing | Soul Note | 121207-2

Höpsi
Uri Caine Ensemble | Love Fugue-Robert Schumann | Winter&Winter | 910049-2

Hör' Ich Das Liedchen Klingen
God Is My Co-Pilot | Mir Shlufn Nisht | Avant | AVAN 032

Horace
J.J.Johnson-Nat Adderley Quintet | The Yokohama Concert | Pablo | 2620109

Horace Silver Medley:
Horace Silver Quintet | Horace-Scope | Blue Note | 784042-2

Horacio
The New Roman Schwaller Jazzquartet | Welcome Back From Outer Space | JHM Records | JHM 3605

Horacio Hieronymus
Achim Reichel | Strapse | FMP | 0580

Horcht(John Trudell)
Georg Gräwe Quintet | Pink Pong | FMP | 0480

Hören Sie Nicht?
Baden Powell Trio | Melancholie | Festival | ???

Horizon
Marion Brown-Gunter Hampel Duo | Gemini | Birth | CD 037
Milan Swoboda Quartet | Dedication | P&J Music | P&J 001 CD

Horizon Beyond
Ellery Eskelin Quintet | Vanishing Point | HatOLOGY | 577

Horizons
Borah Bergman | Bursts Of Joy | Chiaroscuro | CR 158

Horizon's Edge
Barbara Thompson Group | Heavenly Bodies | VeraBra Records | CDVBR 2015-2

Horizons New
Wal-Berg Et Son Jazz Francais | Jazz In Paris:Django Reinhardt-Django Et Compagnie | EmArCy | 549241-2 PMS

Horizons Nouveaux
Silke Gonska-Frieder W.Bergner Group | Entdeckung Der Langsamkeit | Born&Bellmann | 970909 CD

Horizontal Shower
Jon Balke w/Magnetic North Orchestra | Further | ECM | 1517

Horizontal Song
ATonALL | ATonALL | Creative Works Records | CW CD 1024-2

Horizonte
Eliane Elias Group | A Long Story | Manhattan | CDP 795476-2

Hormony
Günter Sommer | Hörmusik | FMP | 0790

Horn O'Plenty
J.J.Johnson With The Brass Orchestra | The Brass Orchestra | Verve | 537321-2

Hornacopia
Nexus | Urban Shout | SPLASC(H) Records | H 170

Hornets
Milt Jackson Sextet | Goodbye | CTI | 6038

Hornette And The Drum Thing
Big Bill Broonzy | Big Bill Broonzy-1930's Blues | Biograph | BLP C 15

Hornin' In
Teddy Edwards Quintet | Teddy Edwards:Steady With Teddy 1946-1948 | Cool & Blue | C&B-CD 115
Thelonious Monk Sextet | Thelonious Monk:The Complete Blue Note Recordings | Blue Note | 830363-2

Hornin' In(alt.take)
More Genius Of Thelonious Monk | Blue Note | 300194(BNJ 61011)

Hornlat
Nils Landgren-Esbjörn Svensson | Swedish Folk Modern | ACT | 9428-2
Pete Rugolo And His Orchestra | Rugolomania | Fresh Sound Records | LSP 15826(CBS CL 689)

Horns-
Köln Big Band | Update | Jazzline | ???

Horn's Street
Horns | Horns | FMP | 0660

Horoscope
Sun Ra And His Arkestra | Jazz In Silhouette | Evidence | ECD 22012-2

Hors Les Murs
Bob Magnusson Quartet | Road Work Ahead | Discovery | DS 824 IMS

Horse With A Broken Leg
Slickaphonics | Modern Life | Enja | ENJ-4062 2

Horses In Rain
Rahsaan Roland Kirk Orchestra | Rahsaan Roland Kirk-Yusef Lateef:Seperate But Equal | 32 Jazz | 32111

Hospitality Creek
Vaughn Monroe And His Orchestra | Vaughn Monroe And His Orchestra 1943 | Circle | CCD-45

Hostel Psychiatrique
Glenn Spearman Double Trio | The Fields | Black Saint | 120197-2

Hot And Anxious
Clarence Profit Trio | Big Band Bounce & Boogie-Piano Portraits Vol.1 | Affinity | AFS 1022

Hot And Bothered
Mills' Ten Black Berries | The Complete Duke Ellington-Vol. 3 | CBS | CBS 88000

Hot Barbeque
Jack McDuff Quartet | The Soulful Drums | Prestige | PCD 24256-2
Pucho & His Latin Soul Brothers | Rip A Dip | Milestone | MCD 9247-2
Danilo Perez Quartet | Panamonk | Impulse(MCA) | 951190-2

Hot Bean Strut
Jay McShann And His Orchestra | Jimmy Witherspoon & Jay McShann | Black Lion | BLCD 760173

Hot Biscuits
Jay McShann Quintet | What A Wonderful World | Groove Note | GRV 1005-2
Jay McShann-Milt Buckner Sextet | Kansas City Memories | Black & Blue | BLE 59.057 2

Hot Canary
Griff Williams And His Orchestra | The Uncollected:Griff Williams | Hindsight | HSR 175

Hot Club Blues
Dicky Wells Sextet | Dicky Wells & Bill Coleman In Paris | Affinity | CD AFS 1004

Hot Club Boogie
Sammy Price Trio | Le Jazz En France Vol.14:Boogie Woogie A La Parisienne | Pathe | 1552601

Hot Club Madrid Serenade
Lionel Hampton And His Orchestra | Reunion At Newport | Bluebird | 63 66157-2

Hot Club Of 13th Street
Jazz Flamenco | RCA | 2136400-2

Hot Couscous,Cool Night And A Dog Barking
Andreas Lonardoni Group | Snooze | Lipstick Records | LIP 8956-2

Hot Dog
Lou Donaldson Quintet | Caracas | Milestone | MCD 9217-2

Hot Fun
Stanley Clarke Groups | I Wanna Play For You | Epic | 88331

Hot House
Barry Ulanov's All Star Modern Jazz Musicians | Bird's Eyes Last Unissued Vol.17 | Philology | W 847.2
Charlie Parker Quintet | Charlie Parker Live Sessions Vol.2 | Zeta | ZET 712
Dizzy Gillespie All Star Quintet | In The Beginning | Prestige | P 24030
Dizzy Gillespie And His All Star Quintet | Charlie Parker:The Complete 1944-1948 Small Group Sessions(Studio Recordings-Master Takes),Vol.1 | Blue Moon | BMCD 1007
Herb Geller Quartet | Hot House | Circle Records | RK 30-241184/30
Joe Van Enkhuizen Trio | Blues Ahead | Timeless | CD SJP 356

Johnny Griffin With The Bud Powell Trio | Salt Peanuts | Black Lion | BLCD 760121
Quintet Of The Year | The Quintet-Jazz At Massey Hall | Debut | DSA 124-6
Jazz Gallery:Dizzy Gillespie | RCA | 2114165-2
Reykjavik Jazz Quartet with Guy Barker | Hot House | Ronnie Scott's Jazz House | JHCD 032
Tete Montoliu | Boston Concert | Steeplechase | SCS 1152/3
Tete Montoliu Trio | Hot House | Steeplechase | SCCD 37027/28

Hot House Flowers
Chris Barber's Jazz Band | The Traditional Jazz Scene Vol.2 | Teldec | 2292-43997-2

Hot Jazz Biscuits
George Carter | The Georgia Blues 1927-1933 | Yazoo | YAZ 1012

Hot Lips
Henry Busse And His Orchestra | The Radio Years: Henry Busse And His Orchestra 1935 | Hindsight | HSR 122

Hot Pants
Toots Thielemans-Eugen Cicero Quintet | Nice To Meet You | Intercord | 145034

Hot Rod
Ray Charles Sextet With The Raylets | Newport Jazz Festival 1958,July 3rd-6th Vol.4:Blues In The Night No.2 | Phontastic | NCD 8816
Reuben Wilson Quintet | Reuben Wilson:Blue Breakbeats | Blue Note | 494707-2

Hot Stuff
Gene Ammons Quartet | The Gene Ammons Story: The 78 Era | Prestige | P 24058

Hot Time In The Old Town Tonight
Louis Armstrong And His All Stars | Snake Rag | Chiaroscuro | CR 2002

Hot Toddy
Julie London With Howard Roberts And Red Mitchell | Julie Is Her Name Vol.2 | Pathe | 1566201(Liberty LRP 3100)
Freddie King Orchestra | Blues Power No.6:Freddie King Is A Blues Master | Atlantic | 40496

Hot Turbes
Ray Bryant Trio | Hot Turkey | Black & Blue | BB 881.2

Hot Type
Clifford Jordan Quartet | Spellbound | Original Jazz Classics | OJCCD 766-2(RLP 9340)

Hot Water
Buster Bailey Quartet | All About Memphis | Limelight | 820598-2 IMS

Hotel 49
Pili-Pili | Hotel Babo | JA & RO | JARO 4147-2

Hotel Babo
Dance Jazz Live 1995 | JA & RO | JARO 4189-2
Nils Wogram Quartet | Speed Life | Enja | ENJ-9346 2

Hotel Blues
Roberto Perera Group | Harp And Soul | Inak | 30362

Hotel Danubio
Jasper Van't Hof Quartet | Live In Montreux | MPS | 68247

Hotel Dead End
Mike Clark-Paul Jackson Quartet | The Funk Stops Here | TipToe | TIP-888811 2

Hotel Domingo
Jimmy Smith Trio | I'm Movin' On | Blue Note | 832750-2

Hotel Happiness
Kenny Wheeler Quintet | The Widow In The Window | ECM | 1417(843198-2)

Hotel Le Hot
Tana Reid Quintet | Passing Thoughts | Concord | CCD 4505

Hotel Me
Gary Burton-Steve Swallow | Hotel Hello | ECM | 1055(835586-2)

Hotel Overture + Vamp
Olaf Kübler Quartet | When I'm 64 | Village | VILCD 1016-2

Hotel Ravel
David Pritchard Quintet | Light-Year | Inner City | IC 1047 IMS

Hotel Strandlust
Reinhard Glöder Quartet | The Glass Flower | Trion | 3201

Hottentot
The Whoopee Makers | The Complete Duke Ellington-Vol. 2 | CBS | CBS 68275

Hotter Than That
Wild Bill Davison All Stars | The Eddie Condon Floor Show Vol.1 | Queen-Disc | 030

Hou
Salvatore Bonafede Trio | Plays | Ken Music | 660.56.017

Houdouth
Angela Brown | The Voice Of Blues | Schubert Records | SCH- 105

Hourglases
David Moss Duos | Time Stories | Intakt Records | CD 054

House Arrest
Grant Calvin Weston Group | Dance Romance | IN+OUT Records | 7002-2

House Blues
James Blood Ulmer Group | Jazz Unlimited | IN+OUT Records | 7017-2
Clifford Jordan Quartet | Repetition | Soul Note | 121084-2

House Hop
Benny Goodman And His Orchestra | Swing Vol.1 | Storyville | 4960343
The Original Sounds Of The Swing Era Vol. 6 | RCA | NL 85515 DP

House In The Country
Frank Ricotti Quartet | Our Point Of View | CBS | 494440-2

House Of Davis
Chico Freeman Group | You'll Know When You Get There | Black Saint | 120128-2

House Of Jade
Laurent De Wilde Trio | Odd And Blue | IDA Record | 023 CD
Wayne Shorter Quartet | Juju | Blue Note | 837644-2

House Of Jade(alt.take)
Cootie Williams And His Orchestra | Rhythm And Jazz In The Mid Forties | Official | 3014

House Of Mirrors
Jon Gordon Sextet | Witness | Criss Cross | Criss 1121

House Of The Rising Sun
Donald Byrd Orchestra With Brass & Voices | His Majesty King Funk/Up With Donald Byrd | Verve | 527474-2

House Party
Maceo Parker Group | Maceo(Soundtrack) | Minor Music | 801046
Mezzrow-Bechet Septet | The King Jazz Story Vol. 7+8 | Storyville | SLP 820/21

House Party Starting
Herbie Nichols Trio | Herbie Nichols Trio | Blue Note | 300098(1519)
String Trio Of New York | Intermobility | Arabesque Recordings | AJ 0108

House Rent Boogie
Count Basie And His Orchestra | Masters Of Jazz Vol. 11-29 Original Boogie Woogie Hits | RCA | NL 89773 DP
Sammy Price And His Bluesicians | 1944 World Jam Session | Progressive | PCD 7074

House Rent Stomp
Big Bill Broonzy | Blues Legacy 10: Big Bill Broonzy-Feelin' Low Down | Vogue | 512510

Housed From Edward
Charles Tolliver Quartet & Big Band | Music Inc. | Strata East Records | 660.51.009

Houses And People
Sweetman With His South Side Groove Kings | Austin Backalley Blue | Mapleshade | 02752

Houston Calling
John Marshall Quintet | Keep On Keepin' On | Mons Records | MR 874774

Hout(1)
Stephan Froleyks | Fine Music With New Instruments | Jazz Haus Musik | JHM 0094 CD

Hout(2)
Fine Music With New Instruments | Jazz Haus Musik | JHM 0094 CD

Hout(3)
Fine Music With New Instruments | Jazz Haus Musik | JHM 0094 CD

Hout(4)
Sainkho Namtchylak | Lost Rivers | FMP | CD 42

How About It
Ella Fitzgerald With Paul Weston And His Orchestra | Ella Fitzgerald Sings The Irving Berlin Song Book | Verve | 543830-2

How About Me
The Complete Ella Fitzgerald Song Books of Harold Arlen, Irving Berlin, Duke Ellington, George & Ira Gershwin, Jerome Kern, Johnny Mercer, Cole Porter And Rogers & Hart | Verve | 519832-2
Rosemary Clooney And The Concord All Stars | Sings The Music Of Irving Berlin | Concord | CCD 4255

How About That
Annie Ross With The Gerry Mulligan Quartet | Annie Ross Sings A Song With Mulligan | Fresh Sound Records | 054 2602321(World Pacific WP 1253)

How About You
Bill Evans | Compact Jazz: Bill Evans | Verve | 831366-2 PMS
Bing Crosby And Rosemarie Clooney With The Billy May Orchestra | Fancy Meeting You Here | RCA | 2663859-2
Bobby Broom Quartet | No Hype Blues | Criss Cross | Criss 1109
Bud Shank Quartet | Live At The Haig | Concept | VL 2 IMS
Charlie Mariano Quintet | Boston Days | Fresh Sound Records | FSR-CD 0207
Ernie Krivda-Bill Dobbins | The Art Of The Ballad | Koch Jazz | KOC 3-7806-2
Frank Socolow Sextet | Sounds By Socolow | Fresh Sound Records | FSR 2001(Bethlehem BCP 70)
Jack Sheldon-Ross Tompkins | On My Own | Concord | CCD 4529
Keith Jarrett Trio | Standards In Norway | ECM | 1542(521717-2)
Kenny Burrell Quintet | Kenny Burrell-Vol. 2 | Blue Note | 300143(1543)
Martial Solal | Jazz 'n (e)motion:Martial Solal | RCA | 2155932-2
Oscar Peterson Trio | A Jazz Portrait Of Frank Sinatra | Verve | 825769-2
Paul Smith Quartet | I Just Love Jazz Piano | Savoy | SV 0117(MG 12100)
Ronny Lang And His All-Stars | Basie Street | Fresh Sound Records | FSR-CD 0501
Sister Rosetta Tharpe And Her Group | Gospel Train | Mercury | 841134-2
Stan Getz Quartet | The Steamer | Verve | 547771-2
Best Of The West Coast Sessions | Verve | 537084-2
Stan Getz:East Of The Sun-The West Coast Sessions | Verve | 531935-2
Stephane Grappelli Quintet | Feeling + Finesse = Jazz | Atlantic | 7567-90140-2
Tal Farlow Trio | Tal | Verve | MV 2565 IMS
Ulf Adaker Quartet | Reflections | Touché Music | TMcCD 016
George Coleman Quartet | Manhattan Panorama | Evidence | ECD 22019-2

How About You-
Michael Feinstein With Burton Lane | Michael Feinstein Sings The Burton Lane Songbook Vol.1 | Nonesuch | 7559-79243-2

How About You(2 false starts)
Stan Getz Quartet | Stan Getz:East Of The Sun-The West Coast Sessions | Verve | 531935-2

How About You(alt.take)
The Steamer | Verve | 547771-2

How About You(incomplete take)
Silje Nergard Group with Strings | Nightwatch | EmArCy | 9865648

How Am I Supposed To See The Stars
Allan Vaché-Antti Sarpila Quintet | Swing Is Here | Nagel-Heyer | CD 026

How Am I To Know?
Benny Goodman Sextet | Benny Goodman Sextet | CBS | 450411-2
Billie Holiday With Eddie Heywood And His Orchestra | Billie Holiday:The Complete Commodore Recordings | GRP | 543272-2
The Commodore Series | Decca | 180008 AG
Hatchett's Swingtette | In The Mood | Decca | RFL 11
Shirley Scott Quintet | A Wakin' Thing | Candid | CCD 79719
Stan Kenton And His Orchestra | The Ballad Style Of Stan Kenton | Blue Note | 856688-2
The Royal Air Force HQ Bomber Command Sextet | RAF HQ Bomber Command Sextet | Celebrity | CYCD 74508
Tommy Dorsey And His Orchestra | Tommy Dorsey In Concert | RCA | NL 89780 DP

How Am I To Know?-
Billie Holiday With Eddie Heywood And His Orchestra | Billie Holiday:The Complete Commodore Recordings | GRP | AFS 1019-8

How Are Things In Glocca Morra
Sonny Rollins Quintet | Sonny Rollins | Blue Note | 84508
Sonny Rollins:The Blue Note Recordings | Blue Note | 821371-2
Ballads | Blue Note | 537562-2
Tommy Dorsey And His Orchestra | The Post-War Era | Bluebird | 63 66156-2

How Are You
George Shearing Quintet & The Robert Farnon Orchestra | How Beautiful Is The Night | Telarc Digital | CD 83325

How Beautiful Is Night
Cab Calloway And His Orchestra | Cab Calloway: Jumpin' Jive 1938/1946 | Zeta | ZET 732

How Blue Can You Get
Chubby Kemp With The Ellingtonians | Jazz Legacy 62: Johnny Hodges-Jumpin' | Vogue | 500112
Bobby Sherwood And His Orchestra | Bobby Sherwood And His Orchestra:More 1944-1946 | Circle | CCD-115

How 'Bout That
Louis Jordan And His Tympany Five | Louis Jordan Vol.2: Knock Me Out | Swingtime(Contact) | ST 1012

How 'Bout You
Al Grey And The Basie Wing | The Last Of The Big Plungers/The Thinking Man's Trombone | Vogue | 655017

How Came You Do Me Like You Do
Papa Bue's Viking Jazzband With Wingy Manone | A Tribute To Wingy Manone | Storyville | SLP 210

How Can I Be Sure
Eddie Harris Quartet | Listen Here! | Enja | 7079-2

How Can I Live At The Top Of A Mountain
Washboard Sam & His Washboard Band | Harmonica And Washboard Blues | Black & Blue | BLE 59.252 2

How Can I Tell You
Gabriele Hasler-Roger Hanschel Duo | Pigeon | Jazz Haus Musik | JHM 0120 CD

How Can I Thank You
Buddy Guy-Junior Wells Band | Drinkin' TNT 'N' Smokin' Dynamite | Sequel Records | NEM CD 687

How Can You Believe
John Lee Hooker | The Great Blues Sounds Of John Lee Hooker | America | AM 6077

How Can You Do It
Fats Waller And His Rhythm | Breakin' The Ice-The Early Years Part 1(1934-1935) | Bluebird | 63 66618-2

How Can You Face Me?
Kenny Baker And His Band | Kenny Baker Presents:The Half Dozen...After Hours | Lake | LACD 88
Maxine Sullivan And Her Band | Maxine Sullivan Sings | Fresh Sound Records | FSR-CD 0178

How Can You Face Me?-
Kansas City Kitty With Georgia Tom | Come On Mama Do That Dance | Yazoo | YAZ 1041

How Can You Lose
Benny Carter Sextet | Jazz Giant | Original Jazz Classics | OJC20 167-2(C 7555)
Pee Wee Ellis Quintet With Guests | A New Shift | Minor Music | 801060

How Can You Mend A Broken Heart
Henry Hall And The BBC Dance Orchestra | Help Yourself To Happiness | Saville Records | SVL 156 IMS

How Come U Don't Call Me Anymore
| Jazz Classics In Digital Stereo: Coleman Hawkins 1927-1939 | CDS Records Ltd. | RPCD 600(CD 698)

How Could I Happen To A Dream
The Ravens | The Greatest Group Of Them All:The Ravens | Savoy | SV 0270

How Deep Are The Roots
Carl Anderson Group | Pieces Of A Heart | GRP | GRP 96122

How Deep Is The Ocean
Ahmad Jamal Quartet | Ahmad Jamal Á L'Olympia | Dreyfus Jazz Line | FDM 36629-2
Allan Holdsworth Group | None Too Soon | Cream Records | CR 400-2
Allen Farnham Quartet | The Common Ground | Concord | CCD 4634
Archie Shepp-Chet Baker Quintet | In Memory Of: First And Last Meeting In Frankfurt And Paris 1988 | L+R Records | CDLR 45006
Barry Ulanov's All Star Modern Jazz Musicians | Bird's Eyes Last Unissued Vol.17 | Philology | W 847.2
Ben Webster With The Oscar Peterson Trio | Ben Webster Meets Oscar Peterson | Verve | 829167-2
Bill Evans Trio | Spring Leaves | Milestone | M 47034
Paris 1965 | Royal Jazz | RJD 503
How Deep Is The Ocean | West Wind | WW 2055
Bill Evans/Jazzhouse | Milestone | MCD 9151-2
Chet Baker Quartet | In Paris Vol.2 | West Wind | WW 2059
Chet Baker Trio | Chet's Choice | Criss Cross | Criss 1016
Chet Baker-Paul Bley | Diane | Steeplechase | SCM 51207
Clusone 3 | Soft Lights And Sweet Music | Hat Art | CD 6153
Coleman Hawkins Sextet | Classic Tenors | CBS | AK 38446
Dinah Washington With The Teddy Stewart Orchestra | The Complete Dinah Washington Vol.4 | Official | 3008
Ella Fitzgerald With Paul Weston And His Orchestra | Ella Fitzgerald Sings The Irving Berlin Song Book | Verve | 543830-2
The Complete Ella Fitzgerald Song Books of Harold Arlen, Irving Berlin, Duke Ellington, George & Ira Gershwin, Jerome Kern, Johnny Mercer, Cole Porter And Rogers & Hart | Verve | 519832-2
Harry James And His Orchestra | Harry James & His Orchestra | Laserlight | 15732
Joe Magnarelli Quintet | Why Not | Criss Cross | Criss 1104
Joe Pass | Resonance | Pablo | 2310968-2
Joe Pass:Guitar Virtuoso | Pablo | 4 PACD 4423-2
Solo Guitar | Pablo | 2310974-2
Joe Pass Duo | Northsea Nights | Pablo | 2308221
Joe Williams With The Norman Simmons Quartet | In Good Company | Verve | 837932-2
John Gross-Putter Smith-Larry Koonse | Three Play | Nine Winds Records | NWCD 0133
John Taylor Trio | Rosslyn | ECM | 1751(159924-2)
Joshua Redman Quartet | Timeless Tales | Warner | 9362-47052-2
Keith Jarrett Trio | Keith Jarrett At The Blue Note-The Complete Recordings | ECM | 1575/80(527638-2)
Ken Peplowski Quintet | The Natural Touch | Concord | CCD 4517
McCoy Tyner | Revelations | Blue Note | 791651-2
Miles Davis All Stars | Blue Berlin | Blue Note | 799095-2
Miles Davis Sextet | Miles Davis:The Blue Note And Capitol Recordings | Blue Note | 827475-2
Miles Davis Vol.1 | Blue Note | 300081(1501)
Pete Malinverni Trio | This Time | Reservoir | RSR CD 147
Prestige All Stars | Tenor Conclave | Original Jazz Classics | OJCCD 127-2
Ralph Flanagan And His Orchestra | Dance Again Part 2 | Magic | DAWE 75
Rich Perry Trio | Doxy | Steeplechase | SCCD 31473
Stan Kenton And His Orchestra | The Ballad Style Of Stan Kenton | Blue Note | 856688-2
Steve LaSpina Quintet | The Bounce | Steeplechase | SCCD 31502
Terrie Richard Alden-Howard Alden | Love | Nagel-Heyer | CD 071
The Houdini's | The Houdini's Play The Big Five | Challenge | CHR 70027

How Deep Is The Ocean-
Roots | Saying Something | IN+OUT Records | 77031-2
Charlie Parker Sextet | Charlie Parker Story On Dial Vol.2:New York Days | Capitol | 300010(TOCJ 6124)

How Deep Is The Ocean(alt.take)
Mike Garson | Avant Garson | Contemporary | C 14003

How Did It Happen
Arthur Prysock With The Red Prysock Band | Today's Love Songs, Tomorrow's Blues | Milestone | MCD 9157-2

How Did She Look
Mel Tormé With The Marty Paich Orchestra | Torme 1 | Verve | 2304500 IMS

How Did You Know
Audrey Morris With The Marty Paich Orchestra | The Voice Of Audrey Morris | Fresh Sound Records | FSR 2016(Bethlehem BCP 6010)

How Do You Do
Victoria Spivey With Louis Armstrong And His Orchestra | Louis Armstrong And The Blues Singers 1924-1930 | Affinity | AFS 1018(6)

How Do You Keep The Music Playing
Gary Bartz Quintet | Shadows | Timeless | CD SJP 379
Marcus Pintrup Quartet | Nocturnal Traces | Blue Note | 493676-2
Patti Austin And Her Band | Patti Austin Live | GRP | GRP 96822

How Do You Like Your Eggs In The Morning?
Blossom Dearie | I'm Hip | CBS | 489123-2

How Does It Feel
Mose Allison Sextet | Middle Class White Boy | Discovery | 71011-2

How Doo's
(Little)Jimmy Scott With Orchestra | Little Jimmy Scott-All Over Again | Savoy | SV 0263

How Great Thou Art
Monty Alexander Trio | The River | Concord | CCD 4422

How High Am I
Louis Jordan And His Tympany Five | Jazz In V.Discs Vol.3 | Collection Hugues Panassié | CTPL 003

How High The Mood
Abbey Lincoln And Her All Stars | The World Is Falling Down | Verve | 843476-2

How High The Moon
Abbey Lincoln With The Rodney Kendrick Trio | Abbey Lincoln Live-Music Is The Magic | ITM Records | ITM 1489
Art Tatum | Art Tatum:Complete Capitol Recordings | Definitive Records | DRCD 11192
Benny Carter Big Band | Harlem Renaissance | Limelight | 844299-2 IMS
Benny Goodman And His Orchestra | Big City Swing | Decca | TAB 5
Billy Taylor Trio | The Billy Taylor Trio At Town Hall | Prestige | VIJ 5020
Bireli Lagrene Ensemble | Bireli Swing '81 | Jazzpoint | JP 1009 CD
Routes To Django & Bireli Swing '81 | Jazzpoint | JP 1055 CD
Bo Thorpe And His Orchestra | Live At The Omni | Hindsight | HSR 231
Bud Powell Quintet | The Legacy | Jazz Door | JD 1204
California Jam Sessions | Chet Baker:California Jam Sessions | Definitive Records | DRCD 11232
Claude Williams Quintet | Call For The Fiddler | Steeplechase | SCCD 31051
Count Basie And His Orchestra | Americans In Sweden: Roy Eldridge 1957-Count Basie 1954 | Jazz Society | AA 514
Dave Brubeck Quartet | Jazz At The College Of The Pacific Vol.2 | Original Jazz Classics | OJCCD 1076-2
Jazz At Oberlin | Original Jazz Classics | OJCCD 046-2
The Best Live Sessions | Festival | Album 254
Dee Dee Bridgewater With Her Trio | Live In Paris | Verve | 014317-2
Diane Schuur With Orchestra | In Tribute | GRP | GRP 20062
Dianne Reeves With Band | I Remember | Blue Note | 790264-2
Dianne Reeves With The Mulgrew Miller Trio | Blue Moon-Blue Note The Night And The Music | Blue Note | 789910-2
Django Reinhardt And The Quintet Du Hot Club De France | Django Reinhardt:Djangology | EMI Records | 780659-2
Ella Fitzgerald With The Hank Jones Trio | Ella Fitzgerald:The Royal Roost Sessions | Cool & Blue | C&B-CD 112
Ella Fitzgerald With The Paul Smith Quartet | Verve Jazz Masters 6:Ella Fitzgerald | Verve | 519822-2

Compact Jazz: Ella Fitzgerald | Verve | 831367-2
4 By 4:Ella Fitzgerald/Sarah Vaughan/Billie Holiday/Dinah Washington | Verve | 559693-2
Mack The Knife-The Complete Ella In Berlin | Verve | 519564-2
Ella Fitzgerald With The Ray Brown Quintet And The Lester Young Quartet | Ella Fitzgerald:The Royal Roost Sessions | Cool & Blue | C&B-CD 112
Erroll Garner Quartet | Gemini | RCA | NL 89975(809171)
George Shearing Quintet | Verve Jazz Masters 57:George Shearing | Verve | 529900-2
Hank Jones Quartet | Bluebird | Savoy | 650140(882496)
Herman Chittison Trio | Piano Genius | Musicraft | MVS 506
Jaki Byard Sextet | Jaki Byard:Solo/Strings | Prestige | PCD 24246-2
Jam Session | Miles Davis | Royal Jazz | RJD 514
JATP All Stars | JATP-1940's | Verve | MV 9070/72 IMS
Bird: The Complete Charlie Parker On Verve | Verve | 837141-2
Charlie Parker:The Best Of The Verve Years | Verve | 527815-2
JATP In Tokyo | Pablo | 2620104-2
Jazz At The Philharmonic-Frankfurt 1952 | Pablo | PACD 5305-2
The Complete Jazz At The Philharmonic On Verve 1944-1949 | Verve | 523893-2
The Complete Jazz At The Philharmonic On Verve 1944-1949 | Verve | 523893-2
The Complete Jazz At The Philharmonic On Verve 1944-1949 | Verve | 523893-2
Jazz At The Philharmonic:Best Of The 1940's Concerts | Verve | 557534-2
Charlie Parker Jazz At The Philharmonic 1949 | Verve | 519803-2
Jenny Evans And The Rudi Martini Quartet | At Loyd's | BELL Records | BLR 90004
Joe Pass | The Best Of Joe Pass | Pablo | 2405419-2
Joe Turner-Claude Dunson | The Giant Of Stride Piano In Switzerland | Jazz Connaisseur | JCCD 9106-2
Jubilee All Stars | Start To Jump Because It's Jubilee | Swingtime(Contact) | ST 1009
June Christy With The Johnny Guarnieri Quintet | June Christy And The Johnny Guarnieri Quintet (1949) | Jazz Unlimited | JUCD 2084
June Christy With The Pete Rugolo Orchestra | June Christy Recalls Those Kenton Days | EMI Records | 1599311
Les Brown And His Band Of Renown | Digital Swing | Fantasy | FCD 9650-2
Lionel Hampton And His Orchestra | Chicago Jazz Concert | CBS | 21107
Lionel Hampton Quintet | Jazz Gallery:Lionel Hampton Vol.1 | RCA | 2114170-2
Louis Armstrong And His All Stars | At The Pasadena Civic Auditorium | GNP Crescendo | GNP 11001
In Concert At The Pasadena Civic Auditorium | Vogue | 655601
Milt Jackson And His Gold Medal Winners | Brother Jim | Pablo | 2310916-2
Nat King Cole Trio | The Instrumental Classics | Capitol | 798288-2
The Legendary 1941-44 Broadcast Transcriptions | Music & Arts | CD 808
Oscar Peterson Trio | At Zardis' | Pablo | 2CD 2620118
Oscar Peterson-Ray Brown Duo | An Evening With Oscar Peterson | Verve | MV 2691 IMS
Schnuckenack Reinhardt Quintet | Live | Intercord | 160035
Slim Gaillard Group | Anytime Anyplace Anywhere | Hep | CD 2020
Sonny Rollins And The Contemporary Leaders | Sonny Rollins-The Freelance Years:The Complete Riverside & Contemporary Recordings | Riverside | 5 RCD 4427-2
Sonny Rollins Trio | St.Thomas:Sonny Rollins In Stockhom 1959 | Dragon | DRCD 229
Sonny Stitt And His West Coast Friends | Groovin' High | Eastworld | CP 32-5423
Sonny Stitt Quartet | Live At The Hi-Hat Boston | Fresh Sound Records | FSCD 1002
Stan Kenton And His Orchestra | Stan Kenton In Berlin 1953 | Duke Records | D 1022
Stephane Grappelli Quartet | Stephane Grappelli | LRC Records | CDC 9014
Stuff Smith With The Joe Turner Trio | Live In Paris 1965 | France's Concert | FCD 120
Tatum-Hampton-Rich Trio | The Tatum Group Masterpieces | Pablo | 2625706
Tommy Flanagan Trio | Lady Be Good...For Ella | Groovin' High | 521617-2
Warne Marsh Quartet | A Ballad Album | Criss Cross | Criss 1007

How High The Moon-
Bireli Lagrene Group | A Tribute To Django Reinhardt | Jazzpoint | JP 1061 CD
Bireli Lagrene Trio | Live At The Carnegie Hall: A Tribute To Django Reinhardt | Jazzpoint | JP 1040 CD
Charlie Parker Jam Session | Complete Bird In Sweden | Definitive Records | DRCD 11216
Greetje Kauffeld With Jerry Van Rooyen And Jiggs Whigham And The Rias Big Band | Greetje Kauffeld Meets Jerry Van Rooyen And Jiggs Whigham With The Rias Big Band | Mons Records | MR 874786

How I Got Over
Jan Harrington And Friends | I Feel The Spirit | Nagel-Heyer | NHR SP 7
Mahalia Jackson And Her Trio | Live In Antibes 1968 | France's Concert | FCD 122

How I Miss You
Percy Humphrey-Louis Nelson Jazz Band | A Portrait Of Percy Humphrey | Storyville | SLP 231

How I Wish
Wendi Slaton Group | Back Here Again | Justice Records | JR 0602-2

How I Wish(Ask Me Now)
Glenn Miller And His Orchestra | Glenn Miller:The Complete Studio Recordings Vol.1: King Porter Stomp | Memo Music | HDJ 4114

How Insensitive(Insensatez)
Astrud Gilberto With The Marty Paich Orchestra | Silver Collection: The Astrud Gilberto Album | Verve | 823451-2 PMS
Boel-Emborg-Vinding-Riel | Shadow Of Love | Stunt Records | 18803
Charlie Byrd Quartet With Ken Peplowski | The Bossa Nova Years | Concord | CCD 4468
Dexter Gordon And His Orchestra | Sophisticated Giant | CBS | 450316-1
Emily Remler-Larry Coryell | Retrospective Volume One: Standards | Concord | CCD 4453
Jodie Christian Trio | Blues Holiday | Steeplechase | SCCD 31337
Maximilian Geller Quartet feat. Melanie Bong | Vocal Moments | Take Twelve On CD | TT 008-2
Michele Hendricks And Her Band | Keepin' Me Satisfied | Muse | MCD 5363
Modern Walkin' | Modern Walkin'-Live In Japan | Satin Doll Productions | SDP 1009-1 CD
Pat Martino Quartet | Footprints | Muse | MR 5096
Ute Kannenberg Quartet | Kannenberg On Purpose | Jazz Haus Musik | JHM 0109 CD
Wes Montgomery Quartet With The Claus Ogerman Orchestra | Tequila | Verve | 547769-2
Wes Montgomery Quintet With The Claus Ogerman Orchestra | Tequila | CTI Records | PDCTI 1118-2

How It Was Then
Azimuth | How It Was Then...Never Again | ECM | 1538
Jelly Roll Morton | The Library Of Congress Recordings | Affinity | CD AFS 1010-3

How Late Is It In Your Life?
Carol Kidd With The David Newton Trio | The Night We Called It A Day | Linn Records | AKD 007

How Little We Know
Freddy Cole With Band | A Circle Of Love | Fantasy | FCD 9674-2
Ian Shaw With Band | Soho Stories | Milestone | MCD 9316-2
Jackie Cain/Roy Kral Quartet | Bogie | Fantasy | F 9643
Jimmy Dorsey And His Orchestra | Perfidia | Laserlight | 15768
Mose Allison Trio | High Jinks! The Mose Allison Trilogy | CBS | J3K 64275

How Long
Christian Willisohn Group | Blues On The World | Blues Beacon | BLU-1025 2
Frank Stokes | The Greatest In Country Blues Vol.1(1927-1930) | Story Of Blues | CD 3521-2

How Long Are Our Nights
Albert Nicholas With The Henri Chaix Trio | Kornhaus Theater Baden 1969 | Sackville | SKCD2-2045

How Long Blues
Archie Shepp-Horace Parlan Duo | 1rst Set | 52e Rue Est | RECD 015
Charles Lloyd Quartet | One Night With Blue Note Vol.4 | Blue Note | BT 85116 Digital
Jesse Fuller One Man Band | Brother Lowdown | Fantasy | F 24707
Ken Colyer And His Jazz Band | Ken Colyer In New Orleans:The Complete 1953 Recordings | 504 Records | 504CD 53
Ray Bush And The Avon Cities Skiffle | Kings Of Skiffle | Decca | 6.28132 DP
Sammy Price | The Blues:A Collection Of Classic Blues Singers | Black Lion | BLCD 7605-2
Sippie Wallace With Axel Zwingenberger | Sippie Wallace/Axel Zwingenberger And The Friends Of Boogie Woogie Vol.1 | Vagabond | VRCD 8.84002
Smiley Lewis Band | Ooh La La | Pathe | 1561391(Imperial)
The Varsity Seven | Boogie Woogie And More | Official | 6028

How Long Can This Go On?
Uli Beckerhoff Quintet | Dedication | Fusion | 8009

How Long Has That Train Been Gone
Lena Horne With The Phil Moore Four | Planet Jazz:Lena Horne | Planet Jazz | 2165373-2
Paul Kuhn Orchestra feat. Gustl Mayer | Street Of Dreams | Mons Records | MR 874800
Professor Longhair And His Band | Best Of Blues | Polydor | 839393-2

How Long Has This Been Going On
Al Cohn Quartet | The Progressive Al Cohn | Savoy | SV 0249
Ben Webster Quartet | Live At The Haarlemse Jazzclub | Limetree | MCD 0040
Cal Collins Trio | Cal Collins In San Francisco | Concord | CJ 71
Chet Baker Quartet | Sings/It Could Happen To You | Original Jazz Classics | OJC20 303-2
Chet Baker Trio | Embraceable You | Pacific Jazz | 831676-2
Chet Baker-Stan Getz Quintet | The Stockholm Concerts | Verve | 537555-2
Chris Connor With The Vinnie Burke Quartet | Out Of This World | Affinity | AFF 122
Cy Touff Quintet | Touff Assignement | Fresh Sound Records | LP 641(Argo)
Ella Fitzgerald With Ellis Larkins | Ella:The Legendary American Decca Recordings | GRP | GRP 46482
Ella Fitzgerald With Frank De Vol And His Orchestra | Like Someone In Love | Verve | 511524-2
Ella Fitzgerald With The Jimmy Jones Trio | Ella & Duke At The Cote D'Azur | Verve | 539030-2
Ella Fitzgerald And Duke Ellington:Cote D'Azure Concerts on Verve | Verve | 539033-2
Ella Fitzgerald With The Nelson Riddle Orchestra | Oh Lady Be Good:The Best Of The Gershwin Songbook | Verve | 529581-2
Ella Sings Gershwin-Vol. 1 | Metro | 2682004 IMS
The Complete Ella Fitzgerald Song Books of Harold Arlen, Irving Berlin, Duke Ellington, George & Ira Gershwin, Jerome Kern, Johnny Mercer, Cole Porter And Rogers & Hart | Verve | 519832-2
Ella Fitzgerald-Oscar Peterson Duo | Ella And Oscar | Pablo | 2310759-2
Fraser MacPherson Quartet | Honey And Spice | Justin Time | Just 23
Jo Ann Strazzeri With The Frank Strazzeri Quartet | Presenting Jo Ann Strazzeri | Fresh Sound Records | FSR 109
Joe Pass Quartet | Ira George And Joe-Joe Pass Loves Gershwin | Original Jazz Classics | OJCCD 828-2(2312133)
John Lewis Trio | Improvised Meditations & Excursions | Atlantic | AMCY 1104
Julie London With Howard Roberts And Red Mitchell | Julie Is Her Name Vol.2 | Pathe | 1566201(Liberty LRP 3100)
Louis Armstrong With The Oscar Peterson Quartet | Louis Armstrong Meets Oscar Peterson | Verve | 825713-2
Mose Allison Trio | Creek Bank | Prestige | PCD 24055-2
Pete Yellin Quartet | Pete Yellin's European Connection:Live! | Jazz 4 Ever Records:Jazz Network | J4E 4722
Ray Charles With Orchestra | True To Life | London | 6.23291 AO
Roy Eldridge With The Russell Garcia Orchestra | Roy Eldridge 'Littel Jazz'-The Best Of The Verve Years | Verve | 523338-2
Sarah Vaughan With The Oscar Peterson Quartet | Sarah Vaughan Birthday Celebration | Fantasy | FANCD 6090-2
How Long Has This Been Going On? | Pablo | 2310821-2
Shirley Horn Trio | Light Out Of Darkness(A Tribute To Ray Charles) | Verve | 519703-2
Sir Roland Hanna | Maybeck Recital Hall Series Volume Thirty-Two | Concord | CCD 4604
Tommy Flanagan Trio | The Cats | Original Jazz Classics | OJCCD 079-2(NJ 8217)
Tony Perkins With The Marty Paich Orchestra | Tony Perkins | Fresh Sound Records | LN 3394(Epic)
Zoot Sims Quintet | Zoot Sims And The Gershwin Brothers | Original Jazz Classics | OJC20 444-2(2310744)
Zoot Sims-Bob Brookmeyer Quintet | To Nite's Music Today | Black Lion | BLP 60907

How Long Has This Been Going On-
The Tremble Kids | The Great Jazz Tunes Of George Gershwin | BELL Records | BLR 89089

How Long How Long Blues
Ella Fitzgerald And Her All Stars | These Are The Blues | Verve | 829536-2 PMS

How Long Must I Wait For You
Louis Jordan And His Tympany Five | Five Guys Named Moe | Bandstand | BDCD 1531

How Long 'Til The Sun
Jimmy McGriff Band | Jimmy McGriff featuring Hank Crawford | LRC Records | CDC 9001(874373)

How Long Will It Be
Jimmy Witherspoon And His All Stars | Blues For Easy Livers | Original Blues Classics | OBCCD 585-2(PR 7475)

How Long Will It Take To Be A Man?
Memphis Slim With Willie Dixon | Jazz In Paris:Memphis Slim/Willie Dixon Aux Trois Mailletz | EmArCy | 658148 IMS

How Many Clouds Can You See
Art Kassel And His 'Kassels-In-The-Air' Orchestra | The Uncollected:Art Kassel | Hindsight | HSR 162

How Many More Times
Big John Wrencher With Eddie Playboy Taylor & The Blueshounds | Big John's Boogie | Big Bear | 146402

How Much Does Matter Really Matter
J.B.Lenoir | J.B.Lenoir | Blues Classics(L+R) | CDLR 82001

How Much Truth
Andy LaVerne Trio | Liquid Silver | dmp Digital Music Productions | CD 449

How My Heart Sings
Bill Evans Trio | The Complete Bill Evans On Verve | Verve | 527953-2
The Second Trio | Milestone | M 47046
My Romance | Zeta | ZET 702
Bill Evans:The Secret Sessions | Milestone | 8MCD 4421-2
Bill Evans-Montreux II | CBS | 481264-2
Eddie Daniels Quartet | Eddie Daniels...This Is Now | GRP | GRP 96352
Kim Parker With The Tommy Flanagan Trio | Good Girl | Soul Note | SN 1063
Thomas Brendgens-Mönkemeyer & Jochen Voss | Jazz Guitar Highlights 1 | Jardis Records | JRCD 20141
Tommy Campbell Trio/Quartet | My Heart | Jazz City | 660.53.003

How Short Is The Time For Love
Jörg Kaufmann Trio | Sketches | Blue Concept | BCCD 95/01

How Soon?
Chuck Foster And His Orchestra | The Uncollected:Chuck Foster, Vol.2 | Hindsight | HSR 171(835576)

How Strange
Coleman Hawkins And His All Stars | Fats Navarro:The 1946-1949 Small Group Sessions(Studio Recordings-Master Takes),Vol.2 | Blue Moon | BMCD 1017
Phil Sunkel's Jazz Band | Every Morning I Listen To..Phil Sunkel's Jazz Band | Fresh Sound Records | 252279-1(ABC-Paramount 136)

How Sweet
Count Basie And His Orchestra | Warm Breeze | Pablo | 2312131-2

How Sweet It Is
Merl Saunders Quartet | Live At Keystone | Fantasy | FCD 7703-2
Johnny Hartman And His Quintet | I Just Dropped By To Say Hello | MCA | 951176-2

How Sweet It Is To Be In Love
Joe Williams With The Thad Jones-Mel Lewis Orchestra | Joe Williams | LRC Records | CDC 9005874375)

How Sweet It Is(To Be Loved By You)
Ketil Bjornstad Group | Seafarer's Song | EmArCy | 9865777

How Sweet The Moonlight Sleeps Upon This Bank
Nick Brignola With Kenny Barron And Dave Holland | It's Time | Reservoir | RSR CD 123

How Time Flies
Don Ellis Quartet | How Time Passes | Candid | CS 9004

How Will He Know
Lorez Alexandria And Her Quintet | How Will I Remember You | Discovery | DS 782 IMS

How You Held It
Lionel Hampton And His Orchestra | Wes Montgomery:Complete Recordings With Lionel Hampton | Definitive Records | DRCD 11242

How'd You Like To Spoon With Me?
Ensemble Modern | Ensemble Modern-Fred Frith:Traffic Continues | Winter&Winter | 910044-2

Howdwhoola
Bik Bent Braam | Howdy | Timeless | CD SJP 388

Howdy Doody Time
Robert Lockwood Jr. | Contrasts | Trix Records | TRIX 3307

How's Chances
Ella Fitzgerald With Paul Weston And His Orchestra | Cheek To Cheek-The Irving Berlin Song Book | Verve | 533829-2

How's Never
Sleepy John Estes-Hammie Nixon | Sleepy John Estes 1935-1938 | Black & Blue | BLE 59.254 2

Huaino-
Ull Möck Trio | How High The Moon | Satin Doll Productions | SDP 1006-1 CD

Hub Cup
Tim Hagans-Marcus Printup Septet | Hub Songs | Blue Note | 859509-2
Gary Burton Sextet | Gary Burton Collection | GRP | GRP 98512

Hubble Bubble-
Bobby Previte's Weather Clear, Track Fast | Hue And Cry | Enja | ENJ-8064 2

Hubcaps & Taillights
Irene Schweizer | Many And One Direction | Intakt Records | CD 044

Hubris
Richard Beirach | Hubris | ECM | 1104

Hub's Nub
Freddie Hubbard Quintet | Hub-Tones | Blue Note | 499008-2

Hub-Tones
The Blue Note Years-The Best Of Freddie Hubbard | Blue Note | 793202-2

Hub-Tones(alt.take)
Perception | Another Perception Of Jazz | Aho-Recording | AHO CD 1012(CD 663)

Huchette Blues
Memphis Slim Trio | Americans Swinging In Paris:Memphis Slim | EMI Records | 539666-2

Huchette Boogie Woogie
Raymond Scott And His Orchestra | The Uncollected:Raymond Scott | Hindsight | HSR 201

Huckleberry Friend
Paul Williams Orchestra | Paul Williams:The Complete Recordings Vol.2 (1949-1952) | Blue Moon | BMCD 6021

Huck's Delight
Khan Jamal Quartet | Dark Warrior | Steeplechase | SCCD 31196

Hudi The Witch
Harry Connick Jr. Trio | Lofty's Roach Soufflé | CBS | 466949-2

Hué Is Hué?
Caoutchouc | Caoutchouc Plays Garcia Lorca | Timeless | CD SJP 399

Huffin' And Puffin'
John Lee Hooker | Half A Stranger | Mainstream | MD CDO 903

Hugo
Arnulf Ochs Group | In The Mean Time | Jazz 'n' Arts Records | JNA 1202
Piludu Quattro | Room 626 | Jazz 4 Ever Records:Jazz Network | J4E 4721
Chet Baker Quartet | Quartet | Pacific Jazz | 855453-2

Hugo Hurwey
Naylor's Seven Aces | Oliver Naylor 1924-25 | Retrieval | RTR 79008

Huh What He Say
Jan Garbarek Group | Twelve Moons | ECM | 1500(519500-2)

Huhai
Uwe Oberg Quartet | Dedicated | Jazz 'n' Arts Records | JNA 1603

Huhcks
Titi Winterstein Sextet | Djinee Tu Kowa Ziro | Boulevard | BLD 501 CD

Huit
Phil Woods Quintet | Bop Stew | Concord | CCD 4345

Huldofólk I,II
Claudio Puntin/Gerdur Gunnarsdóttir | Ýlir | ECM | 1749(158570-2)

Huldofólk III
Bert Ambrose And His Orchestra | The Bands That Matter | Eclipse | ECM 2044

Hullabaloo
McKinney's Cotton Pickers | McKinney's Cotton Pickers 1928/1930 | Zeta | ZET 743

Hullo Bolinas
Bill Evans Trio | The Tokyo Concert | Original Jazz Classics | OJCCD 345-2
Bill Evans Live In Tokyo | CBS | 481265-2
Chick Corea-Gary Burton | In Concert, Zürich, October 28, 1979 | ECM | 1182/83

Hullo Bolinas-
Buddy Guy Band | Buddy Guy | Chess | 427006

Hulmu Rabia
Clark Terry-Bob Brookmeyer Quintet | Clark Terry-Bobby Brookmeyer Quintet | Mainstream | MD CDO 728

Humaira
Pharoah Sanders Orchestra | The Best Of Pharoah Sanders | MCA | AS 9229

Hum-Allah-Hum-Allah-Hum-Allah
Ornette Coleman-Charlie Haden Duo | Soapsuds | Verve | 531917-2

Human Bites
Take 6 | So Much To Say | Reprise | 7599-25892-2

Human Body
Richard Teitelbaum Group | Concerto Grosso(1985) | Hat Art | CD 6004

Human Voice
Lee Ritenour Group | Festival | GRP | GRP 95702

Humana
Jerry Chardonnens Trio | Humanimal | Hat Art | 8 (1R08)

Humbold Street
Unternehmen Kobra | Central Europe Suite | G.N.U. Records | CD A 94.007

Hummin'

TITELVERZEICHNIS

Deep Creek Jazzuits | At Night | Jazz Pure Collection | AU 31620 CD

Humoresque

Art Tatum | Art Tatum-The Complete Pablo Solo Masterpieces | Pablo | 7 PACD 4404-2

Standards | Black Lion | CD 877646-2

The Art Tatum Solo Masterpieces | Pablo | 2625703

Joe Venuti Quartet | The Best Of The Jazz Violins | LRC Records | CDC 8532

Oscar Peterson Quartet | Masters Of Jazz Vol.7 | RCA | NL 89721 DP

Hump In Your Back

Jesse Fuller One Man Band | Brother Lowdown | Fantasy | F 24707

Humph

Randy Sandke Sextet | Get Happy | Concord | CCD 4598

Thelonious Monk Sextet | Thelonious Monk:The Complete Blue Note Recordings | Blue Note | 830363-2

Thelonious Monk:Complete 1947-1952 Blue Note Recordings | The Jazz Factory | JFCD 22838

Humphrey Bogart

Uri Caine Trio | Bedrock | Winter&Winter | 910068-2

Humphrey Pass My Way

| Moonlight On The Ganges | Red Records | 123264-2

Humpty Dumpty

Jimmy Greene Group | Brand New World | RCA | 2663564-2

Ornette Coleman Quartet | Beauty Is A Rare Thing:Ornette Coleman-The Complete Atlantic Recordings | Atlantic | 8122-71410-2

Pat Metheny Trio | Rejoicing | ECM | 1271(817795-2)

Paul Quinichette And His Orchestra | The Chase And The Steeplechase | MCA | 1336

Hundtage

Lowell Fulsom Band | Lowell Fulson | Chess | 427007

Hung Over

King Curtis Band | King Curtis-Blow Man Blow | Bear Family Records | BCD 15670 CI

Mark Helias Group | Loopin' The Cool | Enja | ENJ-9049 2

Hung Over Easy

King Curtis Band | King Curtis-Blow Man Blow | Bear Family Records | BCD 15670 CI

Hung Over(alt.take)

Andre Ekyan With The Django Reinhardt Quartet | Django Reinhardt:Djangology | EMI Records | 780659-2

Hungaria

Quintet Du Hot Club De France | Django Reinhardt Vol. 5 | Decca | 180024 AG

Jazz In Paris:Django Reinhardt-Swing From Paris | EmArCy | 159853-2 PMS

Hungaria(take 1)

Django Reinhardt Vol. 3 | Decca | 180022 AG

Hungaria(take 2)

Django Reinhardt Vol. 3 | Decca | 180022 AG

Hungarian Jazz Rhapsody

Mitch Seidman Quartet | How 'Bout It? | Jardis Records | JRCD 20135

Wheelz With Ingrid Jensen | Around The World I | ACT | 9247-2

Hungarian Stew

Rüdiger Carl | Rüdiger Carl Solo | FMP | CD 86

Hunger

Stu Williamson Septet | Stu Williamson | Fresh Sound Records | FSR 2003(Bethlehem BCP 55)

Hungry Howl

Louis Jordan And His Tympany Five | Louis Jordan-Let The Good Times Roll: The Complete Decca Recordings 1938-1954 | Bear Family Records | BCD 15557 IH

Hungry Man

Bianca Ciccu With The Randy Brecker Quintet | The Gusch | ITM Records | ITM 1440

Hunter's Song:Ibrumankuman

Ray Anderson Alligatory Band | Heads And Tales | Enja | ENJ-9055 2

Hunting And Gathering

Joel Frahm Quintet | The Rains From A Cloud Do Not Wet The Sky | Nabel Records:Jazz Network | CD 4686

Hunting Shadows

French Frith Kaiser Thompson | Invisible Means | Demon Records | Fiend CD 199

Hunzenbach

Norbert Stein Pata Orchester | Ritual Life | Pata Musik | PATA 5(JHM 50) CD

Huomaamaton

Albert Mangelsdorff Trio | Three Originals:Never Let It End-A Jazz Tune I Hope-Triple Entente | MPS | 529090-2

Hupfdohlen Im Gleißenden Neonlicht

Der Rote Bereich | Love Me Tender | ACT | 9286-2

Hüpfer

Matthias Nadolny-Gunnar Plümer | You'll Never Walk Alone | Nabel Records:Jazz Network | CD 4667

Hüppekästchen

Rabih Abou-Khalil Quartet | Bitter Harvest | MMP-Records | 170884

Hurly Burly-

Steve Morse Band | The Introduction | Elektra | 960369-1

Hurricane Connie

Cannonball Adderley Quintet | At Newport | Pablo | PACD 5315-2

Nick Brignola Quartet | Raincheck | Reservoir | RSR CD 108(882632)

Hurrle

Chet Baker Quintet | Cool Burnin' With The Chet Baker Quintet | Prestige | PR20 7496-2

Hurry

U3 Klang | U3 Klang-Jazz Goes Underground | West Wind | WW 2021

Hurry Home

Benny Goodman And His Orchestra | The Benny Goodman Caravans-Ciribiribin | Giants Of Jazz | GOJ 1030

Louis Jordan And His Tympany Five | Go Blow Your Horn-Part 2 | Pathe | 1546680(Aladdin)

Hurry On Down

Joe Williams With The Count Basie Orchestra | Joe Williams With The Count Basie Orchestra | Telarc Digital | CD 83329

Hurry Up!

Jugend-Jazzorchester Des Saarlandes | Chops & Fingers | Blue Concept | BCCD 94/04

Hurt

Ramsey Lewis Trio With Orchestra | Ramsey Lewis | Chess | 6.24473 AL

Hush-A-Bye

Chris Barber's Jazz Band | The Great Re-Union Concert | Intercord | 157011

40 Years Jubilee At The Opera House Nürnberg | Timeless | CD TTD 590

Johnny Griffin Quartet | Introducing Jazz Colours | Jazz Colours | 874720-2

Papa Bue's Viking Jazzband | The 25th Anniversary Session | V-King Records | VLP 101

Stan Kenton And His Orchestra | By Request Vol.5 | Creative World | ST 1066

Hushabye Mountain

David Moss Duets | Full House | Moers Music | 02010

Hustle With Russell

Lowell Fulsom Band | Tramp/Soul | Ace Records | CDCHD 339

Hustlin' And Bustlin' For Baby

Louis Armstrong And His Orchestra | Louis Armstrong-The Complete RCA Victor Recordings | RCA | 2668682-2

Hverdag

A Band Of Friends | Teatime Vol.1 | Poise | Poise 01

Hvert Örstutt Spor

Claudio Puntin/Gerdur Gunnarsdóttir | Ýlir | ECM | 1749(158570-2)

Hvert Östrutt Spor

Toshinori Kondo & Ima plus Guests | Human Market | JA & RO | JARO 4146-2

H-Woman

Duke Ellington And His Orchestra | The Rare Broadcast Recordings 1953 | Jazz Anthology | JA 5220

Hy' A Sue

Live At Click Restaurant Philadelphia 1948-Vol.1 | Raretone | 5000 FC

Hyacinth Rag

Turk Murphy And His Jazz Band | Turk Murphy's Jazz Band At The Italien Village San Francisco | Merry Makers Record | MMRC-CD-11

Hydrama Woman

Red Whale | Queekegg | Maracatu | MAC 940002

Hymn

Jonas Knutsson Group | Flower In The Sky | ACT | 9248-2

Keith Jarrett | Dark Intervals | ECM | 1379(837342-2)

Lars Danielsson Trio | Continuation | L+R Records | CDLR 45085

Peter Weniger-Hubert Nuss | Private Concert | Mons Records | CD 1878

Hymn Book,Holy Book And Pocket Book

David Benoit Group | This Side Up | GRP | GRP 95412

Hymn For Christine

Dennis Gonzales New Dallas Quartet | Stefan | Silkheart | SHCD 101

Hymn For Good Friday

The End | Matter Of Fact | Stunt Records | STUCD 19103

Hymn For Her

Peter Giger | Family Of Percussion | Nagara | MIX 1010-N

Hymn For Joshua

Dennis Gonzales New Dallasangels | The Desert Wind | Silkheart | SHCD 124

Hymn Medley:

Mynta | Hot Madras | Blue Flame | 40382(2132161-2)

Hymn Of Release

Keith Jarrett | Hymns/Spheres | ECM | 1086/7

Hymn Of Remembrance

Charlie Haden And The Liberation Music Orchestra | Dream Keeper | Polydor | 847876-2

Hymn Of The Orient

Stan Getz Quintet | A Life In Jazz:A Musical Biography | Verve | 535119-2

Stan Getz:The Complete 1952-1954 Small Group Sessions(Master Takes),Vol.1 | Blue Moon | BMCD 1034

Clifford Brown Sextet | More Memorable Tracks | Blue Note | 300195(BNJ 61001)

Hymn Of The Orient(alt.take)

Clifford Brown-Gigi Gryce Sextet | Alternate Takes | Blue Note | BST 84428

Hymn Of The River Brown

Chick Corea's Return To Forever | Hymn Of The Seventh Galaxy | Polydor | 2310283

Hymn Of The Seventh Galaxy

Return To Forever | Return To The 7th Galaxy-Return To Forever:The Anthology | Verve | 533108-2

Thomas Clausen | Pianomusic | M.A Music | A 801-2

Hymn To A Better World

Jack Walrath-Miles Griffith With The WDR Big Band | Get Hit In Your Soul | ACT | 9246-2

Hymn To Freedom

Gene Harris-The Three Sounds | Yesterday Today And Tomorrow | Blue Note | 84441

Oscar Peterson Trio | En Concert Avec Europe 1 | Laserlight | 710443/48

Hymn To Freedom-

Patrick Tompert Trio | Patrick Tompert Trio Live | Satin Doll Productions | SDP 1029-1 CD

Maynard Ferguson Band | Verve Jazz Masters 52:Maynard Ferguson | Verve | 529905-2

Hymn To Her

The Four Freshman With Stan Kenton And His Orchestra | Live At Butler University | Creative World | STD 1059

Hymn To Him

Duke Jordan | Duke Jordan Solo Masterpieces Vol.1 | Steeplechase | SCCD 31299

Hymn To The Mother

Benny Golson Sextet | Blues On Down | Milestone | M 47048

Hymn To The Orient

The Modern Touch | Original Jazz Classics | OJCCD 1797-2(RLP 12-256)

Hymn:Morgon Mellan Fjällen

Elements | Illumination | RCA | PD 83031(874013)

Hymne

Andre Jaume 3 | Musique Pour 3 & 8:Errance | Hat Art | 2003 Digital

Hymne A L'Amour

Guy Cabay Quartet | The Ghost Of McCoy's Castle | B.Sharp Records | CDS 101

Hymne To The Mother

McCoy Tyner Trio | Super Trios | Milestone | M 55003

Hyped

Steve Coleman And Metrics | Steve Coleman's Music Live In Paris | Novus | 2131691-2

Hyperballad

Hugh Fraser-Jean Toussaint Quartet | Back To Back | Jazz Focus | JFCD 025

Hyperborean

Charles Lloyd Quintet | Hyperion With Higgins | ECM | 1784(014000-2)

Hyperion With Higgins

Marilyn Crispell-Peter Brötzmann-Hamid Drake | Hyperion | Music & Arts | CD 852

Hyperion's Song Of Destiny

Gary Thomas Group | Found On Sordid Street | Winter&Winter | 910002-2

Hyperspace

Jan Hammer Group | Melodies | Epic | 82405

Hypnotized

Eric Dolphy Quartet | Last Date | EmArCy | 510124-2 PMS

Hypopotamus

Eje Thelin Group | Hypothesis | MRC | 066-45421

Hypothesis

Jasper Van't Hof Quintet | Eyeball | Limetree | FCD 0002

Hysterie

Jimmy Lyons Quartet | Riffs | Hat Art | 3503

I Ain't Gonna Be Worried No More

Sonny Terry Quartet | Sonny's Story | Original Blues Classics | OBC-503(BV 1025)

I Ain't Gonna Give Nobody None Of My Jelly Roll

Henrik Johansen's Jazzband | The Golden Years Of Revival Jazz,Vol.2 | Storyville | STCD 5507

International Chicago-Jazz Orchestra | That's A Plenty | JHM Records | JHM 3621

Ken Colyer's Jazzmen | Ken Colyer Very Very Live At The 100 Club | Upbeat Jazz | URCD 130

Punch Miller's New Orleans Band | The Larry Borenstein Collection Vol.5:Punch Miller's New Orleans Band | 504 Records | 504CD 34

I Ain't Gonna Give Nobody None Of My Jelly Roll(alt.take 1)

Sidney Bechet's Blue Note Jazzmen | Runnin' Wild | Blue Note | 821259-2

I Ain't Gonna Give Nobody None Of My Jelly Roll(alt.take 2)

Mezzrow-Ladnier Quintet | The Complete Sidney Bechet-Vol.5 | RCA | 2115519-2

I Ain't Gonna Play No Second Fiddle

LaVerne Baker And Her All Stars | That's Jazz Vol.11: LaVerne Baker Sings Bessie Smith | Atlantic | 790080-2

I Ain't Gonna Tell You

Woody Herman And His Orchestra | Woody Herman:Complete 1948-1950 Capitol Sessions | Definitive Records | DRCD 11195

I Ain't Got Nobody

Art Tatum | Art Tatum:Complete Original American Decca Recordings | Definitive Records | DRCD 11200

Bill Coleman And His Orchestra | Django Reinhardt:Djangology | EMI Records | 780659-2

Bill Coleman Orchestra | Bill Coleman | Swing | SW 8402 IMS

Dave Nelson And The King's Men | Thumpin' & Bumpin'-New York Vol.2 | Frog | DGF 11

Earl Hines | The Earl | Naxos Jazz | 8.120581 CD

Eddie Condon And His Band With Johnny Windhurst | The Doctor Jazz Series,Vol.1:Eddie Condon | Storyville | STCD 6041

Fats Waller | Fats Waller-The Joint Is Jumpin' | RCA | ND 86288(874182)

Miff Mole's Molers | That's A Plenty | Memo Music | HDJ 4112

Tiny Hill And His Orchestra | The Uncollected:Tiny Hill | Hindsight | HSR 181 (835574)

Wooden Joe's New Orleans Band | Wooden Joe Nicholas | American Music | AMCD-5

I Ain't Got Nothin' But The Blues

Ella Fitzgerald With The Duke Ellington Orchestra | Verve Jazz Masters 6:Ella Fitzgerald | Verve | 519822-2

The Complete Ella Fitzgerald Song Books of Harold Arlen, Irving Berlin, Duke Ellington, George & Ira Gershwin, Jerome Kern, Johnny Mercer, Cole Porter And Rogers & Hart | Verve | 519832-2

Ella Fitzgerald With The Tommy Flanagan Trio | The Montreux '77 Collection | Pablo | 2620107

Georgie Fame Group | The Blues And Me | VeraBra Records | CDVBR 2104-2

Lyambiko And Her Trio | Out Of This Mood | Nagel-Heyer | CD 2021

Mose Allison Trio | Mose In Your Ear | Atlantic | SD 1627

Sarah Vaughan | A Celebration Of Duke | Original Jazz Classics | OJC 605(2312119)

Sarah Vaughan With Joe Pass And Mike Wofford | Sarah Vaughan Birthday Celebration | Fantasy | FANCD 6090-2

Soesja Citroen Group | Songs For Lovers And Losers | Challenge | CHR 70034

I Ain't Mad At You

Count Basie And His Orchestra | The Indispensable Count Basie | RCA | ND 89758

I Ain't Nothin' But The Blues

Woody Herman And His Orchestra | Big Band Bounce & Boogie-Woody Herman:Pre-Herds | Affinity | AFS 1027

I Ain't Superstitious

Lonnie Brooks Blues Band | Bayou Lightning | Sonet | 147108

I Almost Lost My Mind

Milt Buckner Trio | Organ | Jazz Anthology | JA 5166

Jack Jackson And His Orchestra | The Classic Years In Digital Stereo: Dance Bands U.K. | CDS Records Ltd. | RPCD 303(CD 681)

I Am Going Home

Manfredo Fest Quintet | Braziliana | dmp Digital Music Productions | CD 459

I Am In Love

Bobby Hutcherson Quartet | Mirage | Landmark | LCD 1529-2

Ella Fitzgerald With The Buddy Bregman Orchestra | The Complete Ella Fitzgerald Song Books of Harold Arlen, Irving Berlin, Duke Ellington, George & Ira Gershwin, Jerome Kern, Johnny Mercer, Cole Porter And Rogers & Hart | Verve | 519832-2

Shelly Manne And His Men | At The Blackhawk Vol.3 | Contemporary | C 7579

I Am Singing

Roberto Perera Group | Seduction | Inak | 30302

I Am The Walrus

Fred Houn & The Afro-Asian Music Ensemble | We Refused To Be Used And Abused | Soul Note | 121167-2

I Am Waiting

Stanley Cowell | Maybeck Recital Hall Series Volume Five | Concord | CCD 4431

I Am Who I Am

Leon Lee Dorsey Quintet | The Watcher | Landmark | LCD 1540-2

I Apologize

Billy Eckstine With The Billy May Orchestra | Billy Eckstine | Laserlight | 17070

Larry Carlton Group | Larry Carlton | MCA | MCD 42245

I Asked The Lord

Mahalia Jackson With Choir/Orchestra/Falls-Jones Ensemble | This Is Mahalia Jackson | CBS | 66241

I Barval Pudela

Lou Donaldson Quartet | Caracas | Milestone | MCD 9217-2

I Believe

Lee Gree With Lafayette Leake | Somebody's Praying,Lord | L+R Records | LR 44013

The New Orleans Spiritualettes | I Believe | Sound Of New Orleans | SONO 6012

I Believe I Dust My Broom

Big Bill Broonzy Group | Good Time Tonight | CBS | 467247-2

I Believe I'll Go Back Home

John Lee Hooker Quartet | Sad And Lonesome | Muse | MCD 6009

I Believe I'll Settle Down

Memphis Slim Trio | Blue This Evening | Black Lion | BLCD 760155

I Believe In Miracles

Fats Waller And His Rhythm | Breakin' The Ice-The Early Years Part 1(1934-1935) | Bluebird | 63 66618-2

Louis Jordan Quintet | I Believe In Music | Black & Blue | BB 876.2

I Believe In You

Bill Evans Trio | The Complete Bill Evans On Verve | Verve | 527953-2

Empathy+A Simple Matter Of Conviction | Verve | 837757-2 PMS

Empathy | CTI Records | PDCTI 1126-2

Frankie Randall With The Marty Paich Orchestra | A Swingin' Touch | Fresh Sound Records | NL 45978(RCA)

Roland Kirk Quartet | Domino | Verve | 543833-2

Sam Yahel Trio | The The Blink Of An Eye | Naxos Jazz | 86043-2

Thomas Shaw | Do Lord Remember Me | Blues Beacon | BLU-1001 2

I Betcha A Rainbow

Howlin' Wolf Band | Blues Rarities | Chess | 6.28601 DP

I Bow To The Light With You-

James 'Sugarboy' Crawford Band | Sugarboy Crawford | Chess | 427017

I Called And No One Answered-

Archie Edwards | Living Country Blues USA Vol.6: The Road Is Rough And Rocky | L+R Records | LR 42036

I Can Dream Can't I

Digby Fairweather/Stan Barker | A Portrait Of Digby Fairweather | Black Lion | BLCD 760505

Frank Strazzeri Trio | Make Me Rainbows | Fresh Sound Records | FSR 107 (835209)

Lorez Alexandria With The Houston Person Sextet | May I Come In | Muse | MCD 5420

Ruth Brown With The Richard Wess Orchestra | Late Date With Ruth Brown | Atlantic | AMCY 1055

I Can Only Let You Feel It...

Red McKenzie & His Band | Jazz Museum-Bunny Berigan 1936 | MCA | 52067 (801842)

I Can See The Bright Islands

Willie 'The Lion' Smith And His Cubs | Willie The Lion Smith And His Cubs | Timeless | CBC 1-012

I Can See Your Dreams

John Scofield-Pat Metheny Quartet | I Can See Your House From Here | Blue Note | 827765-2

I Can See Your House From Here

Grant Calvin Weston Group | Dance Romance | IN+OUT Records | 7002-2

I Can Tell

John Handy Group | Handy Dandy Man | Inak | 8618

Tony O'Malley Quintet | Naked Flame | Ronnie Scott's Jazz House | JHCD 040

I Cannot Sleep

Artie Shaw And His Orchestra | The Indispensable Artie Shaw Vol.1/2(1938-1939) | RCA | 2126413-2

I Can't Afford To Miss This Dream

Louis Armstrong With The Commanders | Ambassador Louis Armstrong Vol.17:Moments To Remember(1952-1956) | Ambassador | CLA 1917

Sonny Boy Williamson Blues Band | Sonny Boy Williamson | Chess | 427004

I Can't Be Bothered Now

Teddi King With Dave McKenna | Teddi King Sings Ira Gershwin | Inner City | IC 1044 IMS

I Can't Be Satisfied
Big Bill Broonzy (as 'Sammy Sampson') | The Young Big Bill Broonzy | Yazoo | YAZ 1011
Muddy Waters Blues Band | Blues, Roots Vol. 11: Muddy Waters | Chess | 6.24801 AG

I Can't Believe That You're In Love With Me
Art Pepper Quartet | Intensity | Original Jazz Classics | OJCCD 387-2
Art In L.A. | West Wind | WW 2064
Artie Shaw And His Orchestra | The Indispensable Artie Shaw Vol.1/2(1938-1939) | RCA | 2126413-2
Benny Goodman And His Orchestra | Benny Goodman:Bangkok 1956/Basel 1959/Santiago De Chile 1961/Berlin 1980 | TCB Records | TCB 43012
Buck Clayton Quintet | Jazz Legacy 56: Buck Clayton-A La Buck | Vogue | 500106
Carol Sloane With The Phil Woods Quartet | The Real Thing | Contemporary | CCD 14060-2
Herb Ellis Group | Texas Swings | Justice Records | JR 1002-2
June Christy And Her Orchestra | Early June | Fresh Sound Records | FSCD 1011
June Christy With The Kentones | The Uncollected:June Christy With The Kentones | Hindsight | HSR 219
Lennie Niehaus Quintet | Lennie Niehaus Vol.1:The Quintets | Original Jazz Classics | OJCCD 1933-2(C 3518)
Les Brown And His Orchestra | The Uncollected: Les Brown | Hindsight | HSR 103
Stan Getz Quartet | Stan Getz In Stockholm | Verve | MV 2614 IMS
Eddie Condon And His Jazz Band | Eddie Condon Days | CBS | CBS 88032

I Can't Believe That You're In Love With Me(alt.take)
Edmond Hall's Swingtet | Edmond Hall Profoundly Blue | Blue Note | 821260-2

I Can't Dance With You
Emile Barnes-Peter Bocage Big Five | Barnes-Bocage Big Five 1954 | American Music | AMCD-84

I Can't Escape From You
Keith Smith With George Lewis' Jazz Band | A Portrait Of Keith Smith 'Mr.Hefty Jazz' | Lake | LACD 67
Ken Colyers's Jazzmen | Colyer's Pleasure | Lake | LACD 34

I Can't Face The Music
Oscar Peterson Quintet | A Tribute To Oscar Peterson | Telarc Digital | CD 83401

I Can't Get Next To You
Jimmy Smith Quartet | Jimmy Smith-Talkin' Verve | Verve | 531563-2

I Can't Get No Satisfaction
Monty Alexander Trio | Full Steam Ahead | Concord | CCD 4287

I Can't Get Started
Al Hirt And His Band | Cherry Pink And Apple Blossom White | Memo Music | HDJ 4085
Arrigo Cappelletti Trio | Reflections | SPLASC(H) Records | H 134
Ben Webster Quartet | Live At The Jazzhus Montmartre,Vol.2 | Jazz Colours | 874712-2
Bireli Lagrene Group | Foreign Affairs | Blue Note | 790967-2
Blue Mitchell Orchestra | A Blue Time | Milestone | M 47055
Bobby Short And His Orchestra | Celebrating 30 Years At The Cafe Carlyle | Telarc Digital | CD 83428
Bruce Williams Quintet | Brotherhood | Savant Records | SCD 2004
Buddy Tate Trio | Midnight Slows Vol.4 | Black & Blue | BLE 194682
Cannonball Adderley Quartet | Ballads | Blue Note | 537563-2
Cannonball Adderley Quintet | Nancy Wilson/The Cannonball Adderley Quintet | Capitol | 781204-2
Charles Mingus Trio | Mingus Three | Fresh Sound Records | 857155-2
Charlie Parker at 'Bob Reisner presents Bird' | Bird's Eyes Last Unissued Vol.25 | Philology | W 855.2
Charlie Parker With The Joe Lipman Orchestra | Charlie Parker Big Band | Verve | 559835-2
Chet Baker Quartet | Sings Again | Timeless | CD SJP 238
Coleman Hawkins-Roy Eldridge Quintet | Coleman Hawkins And Roy Eldridge At The Opera House | Verve | 2304432 IMS
Conte Candoli's Quartet | West Coasting | Fresh Sound Records | FSR 2005(Bethlehem BCP 9)
Curtis Counce Group | Carl's Blues | Original Jazz Classics | OJC 423(C 7574)
Dave McKenna | Teddi King Sings Ira Gershwin | Inner City | IC 1044 IMS
Dinah Washington With The Gus Chappell Orchestra | The Complete Dinah Washington On Mercury Vol.1 | Mercury | 832444-2
Dizzy Gillespie All Stars | Groovin' High | Naxos Jazz | 8.120582 CD
Dizzy Gillespie And His Orchestra | Dizzy Gillespie:Pleyel Jazz Concert 1948 + Max Roach Quintet 1949 | Vogue | 21409412
Dizzy Gillespie Big Band | Bird's Eyes-Last Unissued Vol.13 | Philology | W 843.2
Dizzy Gillespie-Roy Eldridge Sextet | Diz And Roy | Verve | 2-2524 IMS
Eddie Lockjaw Davis Quartet | Eddie 'Lockjaw' Davis/Sonny Stitt | LRC Records | CDC 9028
Ella Fitzgerald With The Nelson Riddle Orchestra | Compact Jazz: Ella Fitzgerald | Verve | 831367-2
Enrico Pieranunzi Trio | Trilogues Vol.3 | yvp music | CD 3026
Erroll Garner Trio | 1945 | Zeta | ZET 713
Hazy Osterawld And His Orchestra | Rare And Historical Jazz Recordings | Elite Special | 73414
Jam Session | Coleman Hawkins-Rare Broadcasts Area 1950 | Jazz Anthology | JA 5217
James Moody Quartet | Honey | Novus | PD 83111
JATP All Stars | Early Modern | Milestone | M 9035
Verve Jazz Masters 15:Charlie Parker | Verve | 519827-2
J.A.T.P. In London 1969 | Pablo | 2CD 2620119
The Complete Jazz At The Philharmonic On Verve 1944-1949 | Verve | 523893-2
The Complete Jazz At The Philharmonic On Verve 1944-1949 | Verve | 523893-2
JATP Jam Session | Return To Happiness-JATP At Yoyogi National Stadium,Tokyo | Pablo | 2620117-2
Jimmy Raney-Doug Raney | Nardis | Steeplechase | SCCD 31184
Joe Newman With The Ove Lind Quintet | Joe Newman At The Atlantic | Phontastic | NCD 8810
Joe Turner | I Understand | Black & Blue | BLE 59.153 2
Kenny Ball And His Jazzmen | The Very Best Of Kenny Ball | Timeless | CD TTD 598
Lee Konitz-Warne Marsh Quintet | Lee Konitz With Warne Marsh | Atlantic | 8122-75356-2
That's Jazz Vol.21: Lee Konitz & Warne Marsh | Atlantic | ATL 50298
Lester Young With The Oscar Peterson Quartet | The Pres-ident Plays | Verve | 831670-2 PMS
Lester Young-Nat Cole Trio | Lester Young 'Rarities' | Moon Records | MCD 048-2
Lester Young:The Complete Aladdin Sessions | Blue Note | 832787-2
Jazz Gallery:Lester Young Vol.1(1936-46) | RCA | 2114171-2
Lionel Hampton Allstar Big Band feat.Woody Herman | Aurex Jazz Festival '81 | Eastworld | EWJ 80207
Lionel Hampton Quartet | The Complete Lionel Hampton Quartets And Quintets With Oscar Peterson On Verve | Verve | 559797-2
Lorez Alexandria With The Jack Wilson | A Woman Knows | Discovery | DS 800 IMS
Mal Waldron Quartet | Mal Waldron In Retrospect | Eastwind | EWIND 705
Mary Lou Williams-Cecil Taylor Quartet | Embraced | Pablo | 2620108
New York Second Line | New York Second Line | Concord | CCD 43002
Paul Bley Trio | My Standard | Steeplechase | SCCD 31214
Paul Kuhn And The SDR Big Band | Swingtime-The Original Arrangements-2 | L+R Records | CDLR 40031
Ray Drummond Quintet | Susanita | Nilva | NQ 3409 IMS
Richie Cole Quintet | Keeper Of The Flame | Muse | MR 5192
Roy Eldridge Quartet | Happy Time | Original Jazz Classics | OJCCD 628-2(2310746)
Roy Eldridge-Dizzy Gillespie With The Oscar Peterson Quartet | The Complete Verve Roy Eldridge Studio Sessions | Verve | 9861278
Roy And Diz | Verve | 521647-2
Sonny Rollins Trio | Sonny Rollins:The Blue Note Recordings | Blue Note | 821371-2
Ballads | Blue Note | 537562-2
Blue Eyes-Sinatra Songs The Blue Note Way | Blue Note | 789914-2
Stan Getz Quartet | Stan Getz Cafe Montmartre | EmArCy | 586755-2
Stan Getz Quintet | Birdland Sessions 1952 | Fresh Sound Records | FSR-CD 0149
Stephane Grappelli-Barney Kessel Quintet | Stephane Grappelli:I Got Rhythm | Black Lion | BLCD 7613-2
Steve Allen Sextet | Steve Allen Plays Jazz Tonight | Concord | CCD 4548
The All Star Sextet | Bebop In Britain | Esquire | CD ESQ 100-4
Tommy Flanagan/Kenny Barron | Together | Denon Compact Disc | DC-8573
Zoot Sims Quartet | Suddenly It's Spring | Original Jazz Classics | OJCCD 742-2(2310898)
Zoot Sims-Bob Brookmeyer Quintet | Morning Fun | Black Lion | BLCD 760914

I Can't Get Started-
Dizzy Gillespie Quintet | Verve Jazz Masters 10:Dizzy Gillespie | Verve | 516319-2
Something Old Something New | Verve | 558079-2
Dorothy Donegan Trio | Live At The Widder Bar 1986 | Timeless | CD SJP 247
Roy Eldridge-Coleman Hawkins Quintet | Just You Just Me-Live In 1959! | Stash Records | ST-CD 531(882689)
Stan Getz-Lionel Hampton Quintet | Hamp And Getz | Verve | 831672-2
Lennie Tristano Trio | The Essential Keynote Collection:The Complete Lennie Tristano | Verve | 830921-2

I Can't Get Started(false start)
Enrico Pieranunzi-Bert Van Den Brink | Daedalus' Wings | Challenge | CHR 70069

I Can't Get Started(instrumental)
Charlie Parker Quintet | Bird's Eyes-Last Unissued Vol.2+3 | Philology | W 12/15.2

I Can't Give You Anything But Love
Adelaide Hall With Fats Waller | London Sessions 1938-39 | Jazztime(EMI) | 251271-2
Art Tatum | The Tatum Solo Masterpieces Vol.10 | Pablo | 2310862
Bireli Lagrene Ensemble | Bireli Swing '81 | Jazzpoint | JP 1009 CD
Live | Inak | 865
Live | Jazzpoint | JP 1047 CD
Bireli Lagrene Group | A Tribute To Django Reinhardt | Jazzpoint | JP 1061 CD
Bobby Hackett Quintet | Melody Is A Must-Live At The Roosevelt Grill Vol.1 | Phontastic | PHONT 7571
Charlie Kennedy Quintet | The Crazy Rhythms | Savoy | SV 0195(MG 6047)
Dice Of Dixie Crew | 1st Throw | Inak | 811 Direct Cut
Duke Ellington And His Orchestra | Jazz Live & Rare: The First And Second Esquire Concert | Jazzline | ???
Earl Hines | Le Jazz En France Vol.15:Earl Hunes Paris Session 1965 | Pathe | 1552611
Eartha Kitt With The Doc Cheatham Trio | Eartha Kitt-Doc Cheatham-Bill Coleman | Swing | SW 8410 IMS
Ella Fitzgerald And The Paul Smith Quartet | Compact Jazz: Ella Fitzgerald Live | Verve | 833294-2
Ella Fitzgerald With The Don Abney Trio | Ella Fitzgerald, Billie Holiday And Carmen McRae At Newport | Verve | 559809-2
Ellis Marsalis Trio | Heart Of Gold | CBS | CK 47509
JATP All Stars | Jazz At The Philharmonic 1957 | Tax | CD 3703-2
Jimmy Bruno Trio | Live At Birdland-II | Concord | CCD 4810
Jimmy Smith Trio | Groovin' At Smalls' Paradise | Blue Note | 499777-2
Joe Sullivan And His Cafe Society Orchestra | Start To Jump Because It's Jubilee | Swingtime(Contact) | ST 1009
Lillie Delk Christian With The Louis Armstrong Quartet | Louis Armstrong And The Blues Singers 1924-1930 | Affinity | AFS 1018(6)
Louis Armstrong And His Orchestra | Luis Russell And His Orchestra 1927-29 | Village(Jazz Archive) | VILCD 018-2
Lucky Thompson With Gerard Pochonet And His Orchestra | Lullaby In Rhythm | Biograph | BLP 12061
Monica Zetterlund With The Jimmy Jones Trio | Monica Zetterlund-The Lost Tapes | RCA | 2136332-2
Paul Quinichette And His Orchestra | The Chase And The Steeplechase | MCA | 1336
Red Richards Quintet | Echoes Of Spring | Sackville | SKCD2-2049
Sarah Vaughan With The Benny Carter Orchestra | The Roulette Years Vol. One/Two | Roulette | CDP 794983-2
Sonny Criss Septet | The Sonny Criss Memorial Album | DIW | DIW 302 CD
Thad Jones And His Orchestra | Eclipse | Storyville | SLP 4089
The Tremble Kids | Dixieland Jubilee Vol.4 | Intercord | 155024
Willie Humphrey Jazz Band | New Orleans Traditional Jazz Legends:Willie Humphrey | Mardi Gras Records | MG 9002

I Can't Give You Anything But Love-
Count Basie All Stars | Count Basie Get Together | Pablo | 2310924-2

I Can't Hardly See
Staple Singers | Great Day | Milestone | MCD 47027-2

I Can't Help It
Joe Pass Sextet | Whitestone | Pablo | 2310912-2

I Can't Make It By Myself
Barry Finnerty Quintet | Straight Ahead | Arabesque Recordings | AJ 0116

I Can't Quit You Baby
Cash McCall And The Young Blues Thrillers | American Folk Blues Festival Live '85 | L+R Records | CDLR 42065

I Can't See The Beautiful Codillo
Big Joe Williams | Big Joe Williams At Folk City | Original Blues Classics | OBCCD 580-2(BV 1067)

I Can't Stand It-
Albert King Blues Band | The Blues Don't Change | Stax | SCD 8570-2(STX 4101)

I Can't Stand The Rain
Robben Ford Band | Tiger Walk | Blue Thumb | BTR 70122

I Can't Stop Loving You
Count Basie And His Orchestra | Basie Bounce | Affinity | CD AFS 1001
A True Collectors Item | Jazz Archive | 90.106-2
Gene Harris Quartet | Like A Lover | Concord | CCD 4526

I Ching Das Aguas
Jerry Bergonzi And Joachim Kühn | Signed By | Adda | ZZ 84104

I Come From A Musical Family
Louis Armstrong With The Luis Russell Orchestra | Louis Armstrong Vol.6-Satchmo's Collectors Items | MCA | 1322

I Concentrate On You
Bobby Wellins Quartet | Don't Worry 'Bout Me | Cadillac | SGCCD 05
Cal Tjader's Orchestra | Tjader Plays Mambo | Original Jazz Classics | OJC 274(F 3221)
Ella Fitzgerald With The Buddy Bregman Orchestra | Ella Fitzgerald Sings The Cole Porter Songbook Vol.2 | Verve | 821990-2
The Complete Ella Fitzgerald Song Books of Harold Arlen, Irving Berlin, Duke Ellington, George & Ira Gershwin, Jerome Kern, Johnny Mercer, Cole Porter And Rogers & Hart | Verve | 519832-2
Ella Fitzgerald With The Tommy Flanagan Trio | Jazz Collection:Ella Fitzgerald | Laserlight | 24397
Frances Wayne With Neal Hefti And His Orchestra | Songs For My Man | Fresh Sound Records | LSP 15822(Epic LN 3222)
J.J.Johnson Quintet | J.J. Johnson | MCA | ???
Joe Pass | What Is There To Say | Pablo | 2310971-2
Blues For Fred | Pablo | 2310931-2
Lainie Kazan With Band | Body And Soul | Musicmasters | 65126-2
Oscar Peterson Trio | En Concert Avec Europe 1 | Laserlight | 710443/48
Peter Fessler Quartet | Foot Prints | Minor Music | 801058
Peter Leitch Quartet | Colors & Dimensions | Reservoir | RSR CD 140
Richie Kamuca Quartet | Richie | Concord | CJ 41

I Concentrate On You-
Mel Torme With The Great American Song Book Orchestra | The Great American Song Book | Telarc Digital | CD 83328
Oscar Peterson Trio | Paris Jazz Concert:Oscar Peterson | Laserlight | 36155
Girl Talk | MPS | 68074

I Concentrate On You(alt.take)
Buddy Bolden's Blues | Buddy Bolden's Blues | ITM Records | ITM 14101

I Could Have Danced All Night
Chet Baker Septet | Chet Baker Plays The Best Of Lerner And Loewe | Original Jazz Classics | OJC20 137-2
Ella Fitzgerald With The Marty Paich Orchestra | Ella Sings Broadway | Verve | 549373-2
Etta Jones With The Houston Person Sextet | Reserve The Charges | Muse | MCD 5474
Helen O'Connel With Irv Orton's Orchestra | The Uncollected:Helen O'Connell | Hindsight | HSR 217
Shelly Manne And His Friends | My Fair Lady | Mobile Fidelity | MFCD 809

I Could Have Done More
Junior Wells Blues Band | Southside Blues Jam | Delmark | 900204 AO

I Could Make You Love Me
George Adams,Hanibal & Friends | More Sightings | Enja | 4084-2

I Could Sing It For A Song
Hal Kemp And His Orchestra | The Uncollected:Hal Kemp, Vol.2 | Hindsight | HSR 161

I Could Write A Book
Charlie Byrd Trio | Isn't It Romantic | Concord | CCD 4252
Dinah Washington With The Quincy Jones Orchestra | Compact Jazz: Dinah Washington | Mercury | 830700-2 PMS
Ella Fitzgerald With The Buddy Bregman Orchestra | The Rodgers And Hart Songbook | Verve | 821693-1
The Complete Ella Fitzgerald Song Books of Harold Arlen, Irving Berlin, Duke Ellington, George & Ira Gershwin, Jerome Kern, Johnny Mercer, Cole Porter And Rogers & Hart | Verve | 519832-2
Jimmy Raney Trio | Wistraria | Criss Cross | Criss 1019 (835607)
Miles Davis Quintet | Relaxin' | Original Jazz Classics | OJC20 190-2
Relaxin' | Prestige | PRSA 7129-6
Oscar Peterson Trio | En Concert Avec Europe 1 | Laserlight | 710443/48
Sal Marquez Group | One For Dewey | GRP | GRP 96782
Shorty Rogers And His Orchestra | Shorty Rogers Plays Richard Rodgers | Fresh Sound Records | NL 45645(RCA LPM 1428)
The Mastersounds | Swinging With The Mastersounds | Original Jazz Classics | OJC 280(F 8050)
Toni Harper With The Oscar Peterson Quartet | Toni | Verve | MV 2684 IMS

I Couldn't Sleep A Wink Last Night
The Two Charles | Memphis Jamboree 1927-1936 | Yazoo | YAZ 1021

I Cover The Waterfront
Al Porcino Big Band | In Oblivion | Jazz Mark | 106 Digital
Art Tatum | Art Tatum:Complete Capitol Recordings | Capitol | 821325-2
Art Tatum-The Complete Pablo Solo Masterpieces | Pablo | 7 PACD 4404-2
Art Tatum:Complete Capitol Recordings | Definitive Records | DRCD 11192
The Art Tatum Solo Masterpieces | Pablo | 2625703
Artie Shaw And His Orchestra | The Uncollected:Artie Shaw, Vol.5 | Hindsight | HSR 176
Billie Holiday And Her Band | Jazz Live & Rare: Billie Holiday Live 1937/56 | Jazzline | ???
Billie Holiday With Bobby Tucker | Billie Holiday Story Vol.1:Jazz At The Philharmonic | Verve | 521642-2
Billie Holiday With Eddie Heywood And His Orchestra | Billie Holiday:The Complete Commodore Recordings | GRP | 543272-2
The Commodore Series | Decca | 180008 AG
Billie Holiday With The Carl Drinkard Trio | Billie Holiday At Storyville | Black Lion | CD 877625-2
Bud Powell Trio | Planet Jazz:Bud Powell | Planet Jazz | 2152064-2
Strictly Powell | RCA | 6351423-2
Charlie Shavers With Orchestra | The Most Intimate Charlie Shavers | Bethlehem | BET 6019-2(BCP 27)
Django Reinhardt Quintet | Django Reinhardt | Forlane | UCD 19001
Duke Ellington And His Orchestra | Jazz Live & Rare: The First And Second Esquire Concert | Jazzline | ???
Earl Hines | Le Jazz En France Vol.15:Earl Hunes Paris Session 1965 | Pathe | 1552611
Erroll Garner Trio | Gems | CBS | 21062
Jack McDuff Quartet | Another Real Good'Un | 32 Jazz | 32169
James Moody Quintet | James Moody/Frank Foster:Sax Talk | Vogue | 2113410-2
Jimmy Smith Trio | A New Sound A New Star:Jimmy Smith At The Organ | Blue Note | 857191-2
Incredible Jimmy Smith Vol.3 | Blue Note | 300106(1525)
Joe Pass | Digital III At Montreux | Original Jazz Classics | OJCCD 996-2(2308223)
Joe Pass Trio | Intercontinental | MPS | 68121
Lester Young Quartet | Live At The Royal Roost | Jazz Anthology | JA 5214
Lionel Hampton And His Orchestra | Jay Bird | Black Lion | 127032
Paolo Tomelleri-Fritz Hartschuh Quintet | Milan Swing | L+R Records | CDLR 45070
Paul Gonsalves/Roy Eldridge Quintet | Mexican Bandit Meets Pittsburg Pirate | Original Jazz Classics | OJCCD 751-2(F 9646)
Sonny Stitt Quartet | Saxophone Supremacy | Verve | MV 2687 IMS

I Cover The Waterfront-
Lester Young's JAPT Quintet | Prez's Hat Vol.1 | Philology | 214 W 6

I Cover The Waterfront(take 2)
Blind Boy Fuller | Truckin' My Blues Away | Yazoo | YAZ 1060

I Cried For You(Now It's Your Turn To Cry Over Me)
Benny Goodman Quartet | Camel Caravan Broadcast 1939 Vol.2 | Phontastic | NCD 8818
Benny Goodman Quintet | Avalon-The Small Band Vol.2 (1937-1939) | Bluebird | ND 82273
Billie Holiday And Her Orchestra | Billie Holiday: The First Verve Sessions | Verve | 2610027
Billie Holiday With The JATP All Stars | The Complete Jazz At The Philharmonic On Verve 1944-1949 | Verve | 523893-2
Billie Holiday Story Vol.1:Jazz At The Philharmonic | Verve | 521642-2
Buddy Tate-Harry Sweets Edison Quintet | After Dark | Progressive | PCD 7028
Ella Fitzgerald With Jackie Davis And Louis Bellson | Lady Time | Original Jazz Classics | OJCCD 864-2(2310825)
Engelbert Wrobel's Swing Society | A Heartful(l) Of Swing | NCC Jazz | NCC 8502
Lillian Boutté And Her Music Friends | Music Is My Life | Timeless | CD JC 11002
Sarah Vaughan And Her Trio | Verve Jazz Masters 42:Sarah Vaughan-The Jazz Sides | Verve | 526817-2
Swingin' Easy | EmArCy | 514072-2
The Complete Sarah Vaughan Live In Japan | Mobile Fidelity | MFCD 844-2
Sarah Vaughan With The Count Basie Band | The Roulette Years Vol. One/Two | Roulette | CDP 794983-2
Sarah Vaughan With The Hugo Winterhalter Orchestra | Ella,Billie,Sarah,Aretha,Mahalia | CBS | 473733-2
Zoot Sims Quartet | Down Home | Charly | CD 59

I Cried For You(Now It's Your Turn To Cry Over Me)-
Rosemary Clooney With Les Brown & His Band Of Renown | Aurex Jazz Festival '83 | Eastworld | EWJ 80268

I Cry
Buddy Johnson And His Orchestra | Wails | Official | 6010

I Cry And Sing The Blues
Charlie Elgart Group | Signs Of Life | RCA | PD 83045

I Denna Ljuva Sommartid
Lonnie Johnson Trio | He's A Jelly Roll Baker | Bluebird | 63 66064 2

I Didn't
Miles Davis Quartet | Green Haze | Prestige | P 24064

I Didn't Know
Erroll Garner Trio | Body & Soul | CBS | 467916-2
The Erroll Garner Selection | CBS | 471624-2
Abbey Lincoln With Orchestra | Abbey Lincoln's Affair-A Story Of A Girl In Love | Blue Note | 781199-2

I Didn't Know About You
Ella Fitzgerald With The Duke Ellington Orchestra | Ella Fitzgerald Sings The Duke Ellington Songbook | Verve | 559248-2
The Complete Ella Fitzgerald Song Books of Harold Arlen, Irving Berlin, Duke Ellington, George & Ira Gershwin, Jerome Kern, Johnny Mercer, Cole Porter And Rogers & Hart | Verve | 519832-2
Frank Morgan Quartet | Listen To The Dawn | Verve | 518979-2
Herb Geller-Hod O'Brien | To Benny & Johnny | Hep | CD 2084
Howard Alden-Dan Barrett Quintet | Swing Street | Concord | CCD 4349
James Williams Trio | The Arioso Touch | Concord | CJ 192
June Christy And Her Orchestra | The Misty Miss Christy | Pathe | 1566141(Capitol T 725)
Maxine Sullivan And Her Band | Maxine Sullivan Sings | Fresh Sound Records | FSR-CD 0178
Sarah Vaughan With Orchestra | Sweet 'N' Sassy | Roulette | 531793-2
Sarah Vaughan With Small Group & Orchestra | Duke Ellington Song Book One | Pablo | CD 2312111
Sonny Clark Trio | Sonny Clark Trio | Blue Note | 533774-2
Stacey Kent And Her Quintet | The Tender Trap | Candid | CCD 79751
The Newport Jazz Festival All-Stars | The Newport Jazz Festival All-Stars | Concord | CJ 260

I Didn't Know About You Sentimental Lady
Johnny Littlejohn Group | When Your Best Friend Turns Your Back On You | JSP Records | JSPCD 246

I Didn't Know My Mother(She Suits Me To A Tee-alt.take)
Tete Montoliu | Words Of Love | Steeplechase | SCCD 31084

I Didn't Know Until You Told Me
Jessica Williams | The Next Step | Hep | CD 2054

I Didn't Know What Time It Was
Art Blakey And The Jazz Messengers | Paris Jazz Concert:Art Blakey & The Jazz Messengers | Laserlight | 36158
En Concert Avec Europe 1 | Laserlight | 710373/74
Art Tatum | The Art Tatum Solo Masterpieces | Pablo | 2625703
Betty Carter And Her Trio | Betty Carter | Bet-Car | MK 1001
Billie Holiday And Her Orchestra | Embraceable You | Verve | 817359-1 IMS
Brad Mehldau Trio | The Art Of The Trio Vol.1 | Warner | 9362-46260-2
Bud Powell Trio | The Genius Of Bud Powell-Vol.2 | Verve | 2-2526 IMS
Carme Canela With The Joan Monné Trio | Introducing Carme Canela | Fresh Sound Records | FSNT 014 CD
Carmen Cavallaro And His Orchestra | The Uncollected: Carmen Cavallaro | Hindsight | HSR 112
Cedar Walton | Maybeck Recital Hall Series Volume Twenty-Five | Concord | CCD 4546
Charlie Byrd Trio | Au Courant | Concord | CCD 4779
Charlie Parker With Strings | Charlie Parker:April In Paris | Dreyfus Jazz Line | FDM 36737-2
Charlie Parker: The Verve Years (1948-50) | Verve | 2-2501 IMS
Charlie Parker With Strings:The Master Takes | Verve | 523984-2
Charlie Parker:The Best Of The Verve Years | Verve | 527815-2
Chick Corea | Expressions | GRP | GRP 97732
Claus Raible Sextet | Loopin' With Lea | Organic Music | ORGM 9724
Count Basie And His Orchestra | Compact Jazz: Count Basie-The Standards | Verve | 841197-2
Dave Brubeck Trio | The Dave Brubeck Trio | Fantasy | FCD 24726-2
Ella Fitzgerald With The Buddy Bregman Orchestra | The Complete Ella Fitzgerald Song Books of Harold Arlen, Irving Berlin, Duke Ellington, George & Ira Gershwin, Jerome Kern, Johnny Mercer, Cole Porter And Rogers & Hart | Verve | 519832-2
George Van Eps | Legends | Concord | CCD 4616
JoAnne Brackeen Trio | Six Ate | Choice | CHCD 71009
Joe Turner | Stride By Stride | Solo Art | SACD-106
Karrin Allyson And Her Trio | I Didn't Know About You | Concord | CCD 4543
Manhattan New Music Project | Mood Swing | Soul Note | 121207-2
Michael Cochrane Trio | Gesture Of Faith | Steeplechase | SCCD 31459
Oscar Peterson Trio | Walking The Line | MPS | 68082
Roland Kirk Quartet | Domino | Verve | 543833-2
Ruby Braff-Ellis Larkins | Duets Vol.2 | Vanguard | VCD 79611-2
Sarah Vaughan With Her Quartet | Crazy And Mixed Up | Pablo | 2312137-2
Sarah Vaughan With The Joe Pass Quartet | Joe Pass:Guitar Virtuoso | Pablo | 4 PACD 4423-2
Sarah Vaughan With The Roland Hanna Quartet | Sarah Vaughan Birthday Celebration | Fantasy | FANCD 6090-2
Shirley Horn Trio | Violets For Your Furs | Steeplechase | SCCD 31164
Shirley Scott Trio | Like Cozy | Prestige | PCD 24258-2
Shorty Baker-Doc Cheatham Quintet | Shorty & Doc | Original Jazz Classics | OJCCD 839-2(SV 2021)
Sonny Clark Trio | Sonny Clark | Blue Note | 533774-2
Sonny Stitt Quartet | The Bop Rebells | Jazz Door | JD 1218
Stan Getz-Gerry Mulligan Quintet | Getz Meets Mulligan In Hi-Fi | Verve | 849392-2
Stephane Grappelli Group | Satin Doll | Accord | 440162
Stephane Grappelli-McCoy Tyner Duo | One On One | Milestone | MCD 9181-2
Weslia Whitefield With The Mike Greensill Quartet | High Standards | HighNote Records | HCD 7025

I Didn't Know What Time It Was (alt.take)
Sonny Clark Trio | The Art Of The Trio | Blue Note | GXK 8157

I Didn't Know What Time It Was (alt.take-1)
Roland Kirk Quartet | Domino | Verve | 543833-2

I Didn't Know What Time It Was (alt.take-2)
Julia Lee And Her Boy Friends | Julia Lee's Party Time | Pathe | 2C 068-86524(Capitol)

I Didn't Mean To Love You
Winck-Büning-Schoenefeld | Truth And The Abstract Blues | Acoustic Music Records | 319.1061.2

I Dig Fig
Conte Candoli Quartet | Portrait Of A Count | Fresh Sound Records | FSR-CD 5015

I Dig It, You Dig It
Kenny Clarke-Ernie Wilkins Septet | Kenny Clarke & Ernie Wilkins | Savoy | SV 0222(MG 12007)

I Dig Your Wig
Terje Rypdal And The Chasers | Blue | ECM | 1346(831516-2)

I Disremember Quite Well
Al Jarreau With Band | All Fly Home | Warner | 7599-27362-2

I Do
Dinah Washington And Brook Benton With The Belford Hendricks Orchestra | Brook Benton-Dinah Washington:The Two Of Us | Verve | 526467-2

I Do Believe In Spring
Robert Wilkins | Memphis Blues 1928-1930 | RCA | 2126409-2

I Do Care
Billy Eckstine And His Orchestra | Billy Eckstine Sings | Savoy | SJL 1127 (801176)

I Do It For You
Barbara Thompson's Paraphernalia | Lady Saxophone | VeraBra Records | CDVBR 2166-2

I Do It For Your Love
Bill Evans Trio | Live At Balboa Jazz Club Vol.1 | Jazz Lab | JLCD 4(889363)
Bill Evans Trio:The Last Waltz | Milestone | 8MCD 4430-2

The Jazz Festivals In Latin America | West Wind | WW 2062
Claire Martin With The Gareth Williams Trio | Off Beat | Linn Records | AKD 046
Toots Thielemans Quintet | Toots Thielemans Live-Vol. 2 | Polydor | 2441063 IMS
Red Mitchell | When I'm Singing | Enja | 4058 (807658)

I Don't Belong
Ruth Brown With The Rodney Forrester Orchestra | Blues On Broadway | Fantasy | FCD 9662-2

I Don't Care Who Knows
Buddy Johnson And His Orchestra | Wails | Official | 6010

I Don't Deny It
Joe Turner With Pete Johnson And His Orchestra | Tell Me Pretty Baby | Arhoolie | CD 333

I Don't Hear Anything
Dinah Washington With The Hal Mooney Orchestra | A Slick Chick(On The Mellow Side)-The Rhythm&Blues Years | EmArCy | 814184-1 IMS

I Don't Know
Hubert Sumlin Group | Blues Anytime | L+R Records | CDLR 72010
Roy Eldridge-Alvin Stoller | The Urban Sessions/New Jazz Sound | Verve | 531637-2

I Don't Know About You
Oliver Jackson Quintet | Billie´s Bounce | Black & Blue | BLE 59.183 2

I Don't Know Enough About You
Jeanie Bryson And Her Band | Som Cats Know-Jeannie Bryson Sings Songs Of Peggy Lee | Telarc Digital | CD 83391

I Don't Know How To Turn
Billie Holiday And Her Orchestra | Billie Holiday:The Quintessential Vol.4(1937) | CBS | 463333-2

I Don't Know What Kind Of Blues I Got
Duke Ellington And His Orchestra | At The Hurricane:Original 1943 Broadcasts | Storyville | STCD 8359
Duke Ellington And His Famous Orchestra | In A Mellow Tone | RCA | 2113029-2

I Don't Know What Kind Of Blues I've Got
Singers Unlimited | The Singers Unlimited:Magic Voices | MPS | 539130-2

I Don't Know Where I Stand
A Capella 2 | MPS | 821860-2

I Don't Know Where To Turn
Dizzy Gillespie-Roy Eldridge Sextet | Diz And Roy | Verve | 2-2524 IMS

I Don't Know Why(I Just Do)
Claude Thornhill And His Orchestra | Snowfall | Fresh Sound Records | NL 46030(RCA)
John Pizzarelli Group | Let There Be Love | Telarc Digital | CD 83518
The New Orleans Spiritualettes | I Believe | Sound Of New Orleans | SONO 6012

I Don't Know Why(I Just Do)-
Roy Eldridge-Dizzy Gillespie With The Oscar Peterson Quartet | Roy And Diz | Verve | 521647-2
Count Basie Big Band | Farmers Market Barbecue | Original Jazz Classics | OJCCD 732-2(2310874)

I Don't Know Yet
John Clayton Big Band | Tribute To... | Timeless | JC 11005
Wayne Bartlett With The Thomas Hufschmidt Trio And Wolfgang Engstfeld | Senor Blues | Laika Records | LK 95-066

I Don't Know You
Dinah Washington With The Don Costa Orchestra | Drinking Again | M&M Records | R 25183(Roulette)

I Don't Like You No More
Phil Baxter And His Orchestra | Texas & Tennessee Territory Bands | Retrieval | RTR 79006

I Don't Mind
Duke Ellington And His Orchestra | The Indispensable Duke Ellington,Vol.7/8 | RCA | ND 89274

I Don't Miss You Anymore
Woody Herman And His Orchestra | Woody Herman:Complete 1948-1950 Capitol Sessions | Definitive Records | DRCD 11195

I Don't Need Anymore
Roseanna Vitro With The Ken Werner Group | Catchin' Some Rays-The Music Of Ray Charles | Telarc Digital | CD 83419

I Don't Need No Steam Heat
James 'Sugar Boy' Crawford With Dave Bartholomew's Orchestra | New Orleans Classics | Pathe | 1561351(Imperial)

I Don't Stand A Ghost Of A Chance With You
Ari Ambrose Quartet | Chainsaw | Steeplechase | SCCD 31481
Arnett Cobb Quintet | Movin' Right Along | Original Jazz Classics | OJCCD 1074-2(P 7216)
Art Tatum | Art Tatum-The Complete Pablo Solo Masterpieces | Pablo | 7 PACD 4404-2
The Tatum Solo Masterpieces Vol. 2 | Pablo | 2310729
Count Basie And His Orchestra | Compact Jazz: Count Basie-The Standards | Verve | 841197-2
Dizzy Gillespie Orchestra And The Operatic String Orchestra | Jazz In Paris:Dizzy Gillespie And His Operatic Strings Orchestra | EmArCy | 018420-2
Duke Ellington And His Orchestra | Duke Ellington:The Complete RCA-Victor Mid-Forties Recordings(1944-1946) | RCA | 2663394-2
Erroll Garner Trio | Erroll Garner:Trio | Dreyfus Jazz Line | FDM 36719-2
The Complete Savoy Sessions Vol.2 | Savoy | WL 70542 (809296)
Harry Carney And His Orchestra With Strings | Music For Loving:Ben Webster With Strings | Verve | 527774-2
Harry Sweets Edison With The Ken Peplowski Quintet | Live At Ambassador Auditorium | Concord | CCD 4610
Howard McGhee Sextet | Sunset Swing | Black Lion | BLCD 760171
Jesper Thilo Quintet Plus One | Don't Count' Him Out | Music Mecca | CD 1035-2
Joe Pass Quintet | One For My Baby | Pablo | 2310936-2
Lennie Tristano | Victor Jazz History Vol.13:Modern Jazz-Cool & West Coast | RCA | 2135732-2
Lennie Tristano Quartet | Requiem | Atlantic | 7567-80804-2
That's Jazz Vol.15: Lennie Tristano | Atlantic | ATL 50245
Lester Young Quartet | Lester Young | Blue Moon | BMCD 1506
Lester Young Quintet | The Master Touch | Savoy | SV 0113(MG 12071)
Lou Colombo Quintet | I Remember Bobby | Concord | CCD 4435
Milt Buckner Quintet | Play Milt Play | France's Concert | FCD 103
Oscar Peterson Trio | Masters Of Jazz Vol.7 | RCA | NL 89721 DP
Oscar Peterson-Austin Roberts | Oscar Peterson 1951 | Just A Memory | JAS 9501-2
Slim Gaillard Quartet | Opera In Vout | Verve | 2304554 IMS
Thelonious Monk | Thelonious Monk-The Complete Riverside Recordings | Riverside | 15 RCD 022-2
Wes Montgomery Quartet | Wes Montgomery-The Complete Riverside Recordings | Riverside | 12 RCD 4408-2
Wild Bill Davison And His Commodores | Wild Bill Davison:The Commodore Master Takes | Commodore | CMD 14052
Zoot Sims Quartet | Soprano Sax | Pablo | 2310770-2

I Don't Stand A Ghost Of A Chance With You-
Modern Jazz Quartet | The Modern Jazz Quartet | Atlantic | 7567-81331-2

I Don't Stand A Ghost Of A Chance With You(alt.take)
Dexter Gordon Quartet | Dexter:The Dial Sessions | Storyville | SLP 814
Oscar Peterson Trio | This Is Oscar Peterson | RCA | 2663990-2
Thelonious Monk | Thelonious Monk-The Complete Riverside Recordings | Riverside | 15 RCD 022-2

I Don't Wanna Be Kissed
Miles Davis + 19 | The Miles Davis Selection | CBS | 465699-2

I Don't Want Anybody At All
David Murray Sextet | Jug-A-Lug | DIW | DIW 894 CD

I Don't Want It Second Hand
Howard McGhee Quartet With Joe Carroll | Cool Whalin' - Bebop Vocals | Spotlite | SPJ 135

I Don't Want No Woman If Her Hair Ain't No Longer Than Mine(Short-Haired Woman)
John Lee Hooker Band | John Lee Hooker-The 1965 London Sessions | Sequel Records | NEB CD 657

I Don't Want Nobody(To Have My Love But You)
Maynard Ferguson And His Big Bop Nouveau Band | These Cats Can Swing! | Concord | CCD 4669

I Don't Want To Be Alone Again
Trigger Alpert's All Stars | Trigger Happy! | Fresh Sound Records | RLP 12-225(Riverside)

I Don't Want To Miss Mississippi
The Halfway House Dance Orchestra | The Halfway House Orchestra-The Complete Recordings In Chronological Order | Jazz Oracle | BDW 8001

I Don't Want To See You Cry
Chris Cheek Quartet | I Wish I Knew | Fresh Sound Records | FSNT 022 CD

I Don't Want To Set The World On Fire
Dick Garcia Quartet | A Message From Garcia | Dawn | DCD 108
Glenn Miller And His Orchestra | Glenn Miller On The Air | RCA | NL 89714(3) DX
Ella Fitzgerald With Sy Oliver And His Orchestra | Ella Fitzgerald:The Decca Years 1949-1954 | Decca | 050668-2

I Don't Want To Take A Chance
Ann Phillips And The Kermit Leslie Orchestra | Born To Be Blue | M&M Records | R 25090(Roulette)

I Don't Want Your Money
Steve Lacy Sextet | Songs | Hat Art | CD 6045

I Don't Worry About A Thing
Alex Welsh & His Band With Guests | Salute To Satchmo | Black Lion | 157005

I Double Dare You
Dan Barrett Septet | Dan Barrett's International Swing Party | Nagel-Heyer | CD 067
Eddie Brunner And His Orchestra | Americans Swinging In Paris:Bill Coleman-The Elegance | EMI Records | 539662-2
Larry Clinton And His Orchestra | The Uncollected: Larry Clinton | Hindsight | HSR 109
Louis Armstrong With Luis Russell And His Orchestra | Louis Armstrong Vol.4-Swing That Music | MCA | 1312
The Vaché-Allred-Metz Family Jazz Band | Side By Side | Nagel-Heyer | CD 042
Weslia Whitefield With The Mike Greensill Quartet | Teach Me Tonight | HighNote Records | HCD 7009

I Dreamt I Dwelt In Harlem
The Berlin Workshop Orchestra | Sib Langis | FMP | SAJ 30

I Et Skrin(In A Jewelry Box)
Joshua Breakstone Quartet | Self-Portrait In Swing | Contemporary | CCD 14050-2

I Expressed My Opinion
Agneta Baumann And Her Quintet | A Time For Love | Touché Music | TMcCD 006

I Fall In Love Too Easily
Akio Sasajima-Ron Carter | Akioustically Sound | Muse | MCD 5448
Bill Evans Trio | Bill Evans:The Secret Sessions | Milestone | 8MCD 4421-2
Bill Goodwin Trio | No Method | Fresh Sound Records | FSR-CD 136(882880)
Buster Williams Trio | Heartbeat | Muse | MR 5171
Chet Baker Quartet | Chet Baker Sings | Pacific Jazz | 300067(PJ 1222)
Chet Baker With The Radio Orchestra Hannover(NDR) | The Last Concert Vol.I+II | Enja | ENJ-6074 22
Dave Stryker Quintet | Passage | Steeplechase | SCCD 31330
Doug Raney Quartet | Rainey '96 | Steeplechase | SCCD 31397
Enrico Pieranunzi Trio | New Lands | Timeless | CD SJP 211
Jackie Terrasson Trio | Jacky Terrasson | Blue Note | 829351-2
Jacques Pelzer Open Sky Unit | Never Let Me Go | Igloo | IGL 084
Joe Magnarelli Sextet | Always There | Criss Cross | Criss 1141
Louis Stewart-Heiner Franz | I Wished On The Moon | Jardis Records | JRCD 20027
Manuel Rocheman Trio | Come Shine | CBS | 491869-2
Mehldau & Rossy Trio | When I Fall In Love | Fresh Sound Records | FSNT 007 CD
Meredith d'Ambrosio Quartet | Beware Of Spring! | Sunnyside | SSC 1069 D
Miles Davis Group | Live At The Fillmore East | CBS | C2K 65139
Miles Davis Quintet | Seven Steps To Heaven | CBS | CK 48827
Ballads | CBS | 461099-2
Niels-Henning Orsted-Pedersen/Philip Catherine Duo | The Viking | Pablo | 2310894-2
Paolo Fresu Quartet | Angel | RCA | 2155864-2
Pat LaBarbera Quartet | Virgo Dance | Justin Time | Just 24
Philip Catherine Quartet | Live | Dreyfus Jazz Line | FDM 36587-2
Randy Sandke Quintet | Cliffhanger | Nagel-Heyer | CD 2037
Rich Perry Trio | Beautiful Love | Steeplechase | SCCD 31360
Sarah Vaughan With The Don Costa Orchestra | The Roulette Years Vol. One/Two | Roulette | CDP 794983-2
Steve Grossman Trio | Reflections | Accord | 500212
Till Brönner Group | Love | Verve | 559058-2
Tommy Flanagan Trio | The Magnificent Tommy Flanagan | Progressive | PCD 7059
Warren Vaché Quintet With Special Guest Allan Vaché | Jazz Im Amerikahaus,Vol.2 | Nagel-Heyer | CD 012
Weslia Whitefield With The Mike Greensill Quartet | Teach Me Tonight | HighNote Records | HCD 7009

I Fall In Love Too Easily-
Keith Jarrett Trio | Keith Jarrett At The Blue Note-The Complete Recordings | ECM | 1575/80(527638-2)
Masabumi 'Poo' Kikuchi Trio | Tethered Moon/Triangle | Paddle Wheel | KICJ 130
Frank Sinatra With Orchestra | Frank Sinatra | Koch Records | 321 942 D1

I Feel A Song Coming On
Sonny Rollins Plus Four | Sonny Rollins Plus 4 | Original Jazz Classics | OJC20 243-2(P 7038)
Sonny Rollins Quintet | Saxophone Colossus And More | Prestige | P 24050

I Feel Airlight Again
Tete Montoliu | Music For Perla | Steeplechase | SCCD 31021

I Feel Alright-
Clarence Gatemouth Brown Band | Alright Again! | Edsel | Fiend 2

I Feel Alright Now
Barbara Lea With The Johnny Windhurst Quintet | Barbara Lea | Original Jazz Classics | OJCCD 1713-2(PR 7065)

I Feel Free
The Motherhood | Bluesy Toosy | ACT | 9200-2

I Feel Good
Big Band De Lausanne & Charles Papasoff | Astor | TCB Records | TCB 95502
John Lee Hooker Trio | I Feel Good | Memo Music | HDJ 4038
Peter Lehel Quartet | Heavy Rotation | Satin Doll Productions | SDP 1024-1 CD
Sippie Wallace With Louis Armstrong And Hersal Thomas | Louis Armstrong And The Blues Singers 1924-1930 | Affinity | AFS 1018(6)

I Feel Like A New Man
Joe Newman And His Band | I Feel Like A New Man | Black Lion | BLCD 760905

I Feel Like Going Home
Muddy Waters Group | Back In His Early Days, Vol.1+2 | Red Lightnin' | SC 001/2

I Feel Pretty
Sarah Vaughan And Her Trio | Verve Jazz Masters 42:Sarah Vaughan-The Jazz Sides | Verve | 526817-2
Stan Kenton And His Orchestra | West Side Story | Capitol | 829914-2

I Feel Pretty-
Little Milton | Heavy Heads | Chess | 6.24835 AS

I Feel So Good
Mose Allison Trio | Your Mind Is In Vacation | Atlantic | SD 1691

I Feel So Smoochie

Kurt Elling Group | This Time Its Love | Blue Note | 493543-2
Nat King Cole Trio | Love Songs | Nimbus Records | NI 2010
Urbie Green His Trombone And Rhythm | The Best Of New Broadway Show Hits | Fresh Sound Records | NL 45907(RCA LPM 1969)

I Feel The Ocean But She's On The Other Side
Jon Jang & The Pan-Asian Arkestra | Tiananmen! | Soul Note | 121223-2

I Feel Your Vibes
Miss Rhapsody With June Cole's Orchestra | Roots Of Rock 'N' Roll, Vol. 5: Ladies Sing The Blues | Savoy | SJL 2233

I Found A Dream
Teddy Wilson | Piano Solos | Affinity | CD AFS 1016

I Found A New Baby
Albert Nicholas With The Henri Chaix Trio | Kornhaus Theater Baden 1969 | Sackville | SKCD2-2045
Benny Goodman And His Orchestra | Compact Jazz: Benny Goodman | Verve | 820543-2
Benny Goodman Sextet | The Yale University Music Library Vol.5 | Limelight | 820827-2 IMS
Count Basie And His Orchestra | Count Basie And His Orchestra-1944 | Circle | CCD-60
Dexter Gordon Sextet | Midnight Dream | West Wind | WW 2040
Eddie Condon All Stars | Town Hall Concerts Vol.11 | Jazzology | JCD 1021/23
Frank Newton And His Uptown Serenaders | Frankie's Jump | Affinity | CD AFS 1014
Kid Ory's Creole Jazz Band | Kid Ory's Creole Jazz Band 1954 | Good Time Jazz | GTCD 12004-2
Papa Bue's Viking Jazzband | Live At Slukefter,Tivoli | Music Mecca | CD 1028-2
Ron Holloway Group | Struttin' | Milestone | MCD 9238-2
Stephane Grappelli-Barney Kessel Quintet | Stephane Grappelli:I Got Rhythm | Black Lion | BLCD 7613-2
Wild Bill Davison All Stars | Wild Bill At Bull Run | Jazzology | JCD-30

I Found A True Love
Albert King Blues Band | Crosscut Saw:Albert King In San Francisco | Stax | SCD 8571-2(F 9627)

I Found The Key
Al Bowlly With Roy Fox And His Band | On The Sentimental Side | Decca | DDV 5009/10

I Found You
Jackie McLean & The Macband | Fire & Love | Blue Note | 493254-2

I Get A Kick Out Of You
Artie Shaw And His Orchestra | Artie Shaw And His Orchestra 1949 | Limelight | 820817-2 IMS
Benny Carter Quintet | Cosmopolite | Verve | 521673-2
Billie Holiday And Her All Stars | Billie Holiday:The Great American Songbook | Verve | 523003-2
Charlie Parker Groups | Welcome To Jazz: Charlie Parker | Koch Records | 322 075 D1
Charlie Parker Quintet | The Cole Porter Song Book | Verve | 823250-1
Chris Connor With The Ronnie Ball Trio | At The American Jazz Festival In Latin America | West Wind | WW 2025
Dinah Washington And Her Orchestra | For Those In Love | EmArCy | 514073-2
Ella Fitzgerald And Louis Armstrong With The Oscar Peterson Quartet | The Complete Ella Fitzgerald And Louis Armstrong On Verve | Verve | 537284-2
Ella Fitzgerald With Orchestra | Forever Ella | Verve | 529387-2
Ella Fitzgerald With The Buddy Bregman Orchestra | The Cole Porter Song Book | Verve | 2683044 IMS
The Complete Ella Fitzgerald Song Books of Harold Arlen, Irving Berlin, Duke Ellington, George & Ira Gershwin, Jerome Kern, Johnny Mercer, Cole Porter And Rogers & Hart | Verve | 519832-2
Ernie Henry Quartet | Seven Standards And A Blues | Original Jazz Classics | OJCCD 1722-2(RLP 248)
Freddy Martin And His Orchestra | The Uncollected:Freddy Martin, Vol.2 | Hindsight | HSR 169
Jerry Wiggins Trio | The Piano Collection Vol.1 | Vogue | 21610242
Lisa Ekdahl With The Peter Nordahl Trio | Back To Earth | RCA | 2161463-2
Louis Armstrong With The Oscar Peterson Quartet | Louis Armstrong Meets Oscar Peterson | Verve | 539060-2
Satchmo-When The Saints Go Marching In | Verve | 711051 IMS
Max Roach Quintet | Kenny Dorham | Royal Jazz | RJD 515
Nat King Cole With The Nelson Riddle Orchestra | The Piano Style Of Nat King Cole | Capitol | 781203-2
Oscar Peterson-Ray Brown Duo | An Evening With Oscar Peterson | Verve | MV 2691 IMS
Paul Desmond Quartet | East Of The Sun | Discovery | DS 840 (807432)
Ray Anthony And His Orchestra | Ray Anthony's Houseparty Hop | Capitol | 1565471
Stephane Grappelli Trio | Live At The Blue Note | Telarc Digital | CD 83397

I Get A Kick Out Of You(alt.take)
Max Roach-Clifford Brown Quintet | Daahoud | Mobile Fidelity | MFCD 826

I Get A Kick Out Of You(take 1-7)
Cleo Laine With The Johnny Dankworth Quintet | Cleo At Carnegie Hall-The 10th Anniversary Concert | DRG | DARC 2-2101 IMS

I Get Along With You Very Well
Chet Baker Quintet/NDR Big Band/Radio Orchestra Hannover | Straight From The Heart-The Last Concert Vol.2 | Enja | ENJ-6020 2
The Last Concert Vol.I+II | Enja | ENJ-6074 22
Jane Jarvis Quartet | Jane Jarvis Jams | Arbors Records | ARCD 19152

I Get Along Without You Very Well
Ann Burton And Her Quartet | Am I Blue | Keytone | KYT 711
Billie Holiday With The Ray Ellis Orchestra | Ella,Billie,Sarah,Aretha,Mahalia | CBS | 473733-2
Chet Baker Quartet | Chet Baker Sings | Pacific Jazz | 300067(PJ 1222)
Lew Stone And His Band | Lew Stone And His Band | Decca | DDV 5005/6 DT
Oscar Peterson Trio | The London Concert | Pablo | 2CD 2620111
Pee Wee Ellis & NDR Bigband | What You Like | Minor Music | 801064
Rosemary Clooney And Her Sextet | Do You Miss New York? | Concord | CCD 4537
Singers Unlimited With The Robert Farnon Orchestra | Sentimental Journey | MPS | 68102
Stan Kenton And His Orchestra | Standards In Silhouette | Capitol | ST 1049
Vince Jones With Orchestra | Come In Spinner | Intuition Records | INT 3052-2
Kurt Elling Group | Flirting With Twilight | Blue Note | 531113-2

I Get Along Without You Very Well-
Nina Simone | Jazz:For Absolute Beginners | RCA | NL 89874 AG

I Get Evil
Louis Armstrong And His All Stars | In Concert At The Pasadena Civic Auditorium | Vogue | 655601

I Get Ideas
Louis Armstrong With The Les Brown Band | Louis And His Friends | GNP Crescendo | GNPD 11002

I Go My Way
John Lee Hooker | Live At Sugar Hill | America | AM 6094

I Got A Crush On You
Bobby Hackett And His All Stars | The Eddie Condon Floor Show Vol.1 | Queen-Disc | 030

I Got A Feeling
Lottie Murrell | Living Country Blues USA Vol.4:Tennessee Blues | L+R Records | LR 42034

I Got A Good 'Un - (I Got) A Good 'Un
Ella Fitzgerald With The Chick Webb Orchestra | Ella Fitzgerald-The Early Years-Part 1 | GRP | GRP 26182

I Got A Guy
John Lee Hooker Band | Burnin' | Joy | 124

I Got A Little Girl
American Folk Blues Festival | American Folk Blues Festival '80 | L+R Records | CDLS 42013

I Got A Man
Nick Woodland And The Magnets | Big Heart | Blues Beacon | BLU-1013 2

I Got A Mind To Give Up Living
Alberta Hunter With Buster Bailey's Blues Blasters | Songs We Taught Your Mother | Original Blues Classics | OBCCD 520-2

I Got A Mind To Ramble
Jeannie Cheatham And Jimmy Cheatham Band | Sweet Baby Blues | Concord | CCD 4258

I Got A Right To Sing The Blues
Cal Tjader Quartet | Plays Harold Arlen | Original Jazz Classics | OJC 285(F 8072)
Louis Armstrong And His Orchestra | Jazz:The Essential Collection Vol.2 | IN+OUT Records | 78012-2
Louis Armstrong With The Russell Garcia Orchestra | Verve Jazz Masters 1:Louis Armstrong | Verve | 519818-2
Maxine Sullivan With The Scott Hamilton Quintet | Swingin' Sweet | Concord | CCD 4351

I Got A Strange Feeling
Bobby Sherwood And His Orchestra | Bobby Sherwood And His Orchestra:More 1944-1946 | Circle | CCD-115

I Got A Woman
Jimmy Smith Trio | Jimmy Smith Trio: Salle Pleyel, May 28th, 1965 | Laserlight | 36135
Papa John De Francesco Quartet | Comin' Home | Muse | MCD 5531
Rockin' Dopsie And The Zydeco Twisters | Rockin' Dopsie And The Zydeco Twister | Storyville | 4960423
Snooks Eaglin | That's All Right | Original Blues Classics | OBCCD 568-2(BV 1046)

I Got A Woman-
Zoot Sims Quintet | The Swinger | Pablo | 2310861

I Got Changes
Bill Watrous Big Band | Space Available | Double Time Records | DTRCD-124

I Got It Bad And That Ain't Good
André Previn Trio | After Hours | Telarc Digital | CD 83302
Benny Carter And His Strings With The Oscar Peterson Quartet | Alone Together | Verve | 2304512 IMS
Benny Green | Green's Blues | Telarc Digital | CD 83539
Bill Perkins Big Band | Our Man Woody | Jazz Mark | 110 CD(889466)
Bobby Hackett Quintet | Live At The Roosevelt Grill-Vol. 4 | Chiaroscuro | CR 179
Cal Collins-Herb Ellis Quartet | Interplay | Concord | CJ 137
Cannonball Adderley With The Bill Russo Orchestra | Julian Cannonball Adderley And Strings/Jump For Joy | Verve | 528699-2
Charlie Byrd Trio With Sott Hamilton | It's A Wonderful World | Concord | CCD 4374
Claire Austin And Don Ewell | Memories Of You | Audiophile | ACD-143
Concord Festival All Stars | The 20th Concord Festival All Stars | Concord | CCD 4366
Count Basie And His Orchestra | Basie On Roulette, Vol. 22: Back With Basie | Vogue | 500022
Dee Daniels With The Jack Van Poll Trio | All Of Me | September | CD 5101
Duke Ellington And His Famous Orchestra | Duke Ellington:The Blanton-Webster Band | Bluebird | 21 13181-2
Passion Flower 1940-46 | Bluebird | 63 66616-2
Sophisticated Lady | RCA | 26685162
Duke Ellington And His Orchestra | Live At The 1956 Stratford Festival | Music & Arts | CD 616
Highlights From The Duke Ellington Centennial Edition | RCA | 2663672-2
All Star Road Band Vol.2 | Doctor Jazz | ZL 70969(2) (809319)
Duke Ellington In Europe | Jazz Anthology | JA 5189
Ellington At Newport 1956(Complete) | CBS | CK 64932
Ella Fitzgerald And Duke Ellington:Cote D'Azure Concerts on Verve | Verve | 539033-2
Hot Summer Dance | Red Baron | 469285-2
Earl Hines And His Orchestra | The Indispensable Earl Hines Vol.3/4(1939-1945) | RCA | 2126408-2
Ella Fitzgerald And Her Famous Orchestra | Ella Fitzgerald:The Early Years-Part 2 | GRP | GRP 26232
Ella Fitzgerald With The Duke Ellington Orchestra | The Best Of The Song Books | Verve | 519804-2
The Complete Ella Fitzgerald Song Books of Harold Arlen, Irving Berlin, Duke Ellington, George & Ira Gershwin, Jerome Kern, Johnny Mercer, Cole Porter And Rogers & Hart | Verve | 519832-2
Freddie Hubbard Orchestra | The Body And The Soul | Impulse(MCA) | 951183-2
Great Jazz Trio With String Quartet | N.Y. Sophisticate-A Tribute To Duke Ellington | Denon Compact Disc | DC-8575
Harry Allen Quintet | A Night At Birdland Vol. 1 | Nagel-Heyer | CD 5002
Harry Carney And His Orchestra With Strings | Compact Jazz: Duke Ellington And Friends | Verve | 833291-2
Helen Humes And Her All Stars | On The Sunny Side Of The Street | Black Lion | BLCD 760185
Helen Shapiro & Humphrey Lyttelton And His Band | Echoes Of The Duke | Calligraph | CLG LP 002 IMS
Jean-Michel Pilc Trio | Welcome Home | Dreyfus Jazz Line | FDM 36630-2
Jerri Winters With The Al Belletto Sextet | Somebody Loves Me | Fresh Sound Records | FSR 600(Bethlehem BCP 76)
Jimmy Witherspoon And His All Stars | Blues For Easy Livers | Original Blues Classics | OBCCD 585-2(PR 7475)
Joe Pass Trio | Portraits Of Duke Ellington | Pablo | 2310716-2
Johnny Hodges With The Al Waslon Trio | A Man And His Music | Storyville | SLP 4073
Junior Mance | Junior Mance Special | Sackville | SKCD2-3043
Kenny Burrell Quartet | Stormy Monday Blues | Fantasy | FCD 24767-2
Kenny Burrell Trio | Stormy Monday | Fantasy | F 9558
Lee Konitz With Strings | Lee Konitz Meets Jimmy Giuffre | Verve | 527780-2
Louis Armstrong And His All Stars With Duke Ellington | The Beautiful American | Jazz Society(Vogue) | 670501
McCoy Tyner Trio | The Early Trios | MCA | IA 9338/2
Oscar Peterson | Oscar Peterson In Russia | Pablo | 2CD 2625711
Oscar Peterson Trio | Night Train | Verve | 521440-2
Night Train | Verve | 821724-2
Oscar Peterson Plays The Duke Ellington Song Book | Verve | 559785-2
Oscar Peterson Plays The Duke Ellington Song Book | Verve | 559785-2
Paolo Tomelleri-Fritz Hartschuh Quintet | Milan Swing | L+R Records | CDLR 45070
Pete Jolly Quartet | Pete Jolly Duo/Trio/Quartet | Fresh Sound Records | ND 42133
Rainer Tempel Big Band | Album 03 | Jazz 'n' Arts Records | JNA 1102
Red Garland Quintet | Soul Junction | Original Jazz Classics | OJCCD 481-2
The Jazz Giants Play Duke Ellington:Caravan | Prestige | PCD 24227-2
John Coltrane-The Prestige Recordings | Prestige | 16 PCD 4405-2
Red Garland Quintet feat.John Coltrane | Jazz Junction | Prestige | P 24023
Red Holloway/Clark Terry Sextet | Locksmith Blues | Concord | CCD 4390
Rosemary Clooney With The Duke Ellington Orchestra | Blue Rose | CBS | CK 65506
Ross Tompkins-Joe Venuti Quintet | Live At Concord '77 | Concord | CJ 51
Sarah Vaughan And Her Band | Duke Ellington Song Book Two | Pablo | CD 2312116
Sarah Vaughan With Band | Linger Awhile | Pablo | 2312144-2
Sathima Bea Benjamin Group | A Morning In Paris | Enja | ENJ-9309 2
Sir Roland Hanna | A Tribute To Duke Ellington Vol.2 | Jazz Colours | 874719-2
Sonny Criss Quintet | At The Crossroad | Fresh Sound Records | 252962-1(Peacock PLP 91)
Stan Getz With The Duke Ellington Orchestra | Stan Getz:The Golden Years Vol.1(1952-1958) | Moon Records | MCD 039-2
Stephane Grappelli Quintet | Le Toit De Paris | RCA | 2119250-2
Thelonious Monk Trio | Thelonious Monk-The Complete Riverside Recordings | Riverside | 15 RCD 022-2
Zoot Sims With Bill Holman And His Orchestra | Hawthorne Nights | Pablo | 2310783
Zoot Sims-Bucky Pizzarelli Duo | Elegiac | Storyville | STCD 8238
All Star Trumpet Spectacular | The Second Progressive Records All Star Trumpet Spectacular | Progressive | PRO 7017 IMS

I Got It Bad And That Ain't Good-
Dixie-O-Naires | Strike Up The Band | Timeless | CD TTD 576
Ella Fitzgerald With Joe Pass | Sophisticated Lady | Pablo | PACD 5310-2
Ernestine Anderson With The John Horler Trio | Live From Concord To London | Concord | CCD 4054
Pearl & The Jazz's | Hear We Go! | Satin Doll Productions | SDP 1004-1 CD
Rex Allen's Swing Express | Ellington For Lovers | Nagel-Heyer | NH 1009
Benny Carter Quintet | Cosmopolite | Verve | 521673-2

I Got It Good
Thad Jones Quintet | First Recordings | Jazz Anthology | 550142

I Got Lost In Her Arms
Billy Eckstine With Bobby Tucker And His Orchestra | Billy Eckstine:Billy's Best! | Verve | 526440-2

I Got My Eyes On You
Bill Ramsey & The Ron Wilson Trio | Singin' & Swingin' | zyx records | 22001

I Got My Mojo Working
Muddy Waters Blues Band | Muddy Waters | Chess | 427005

I Got Myself A Workin' Man
Big Band Ulm | All Of Us | yvp music | 3014

I Got Plenty O'Nuttin'
Ella Fitzgerald And Louis Armstrong With The Russell Garcia Orchestra | Porgy And Bess | Verve | ???
Kenny Ball And His Jazzmen | Kenny Ball And His Jazzmen 1960-1961 | Lake | LACD 76
Louis Armstrong And Ella Fitzgerald With Russell Garcia's Orchestra | The Complete Ella Fitzgerald And Louis Armstrong On Verve | Verve | 537284-2
Louis Armstrong And His Orchestra | Armed Forces Radio Service 1943/1944 | Duke Records | D 1021
Mundell Lowe's Jazzmen | Porgy And Bess | RCA | PL 43552
Oscar Peterson Trio | Porgy And Bess | Verve | 519807-2
Oscar Peterson-Joe Pass Duo | Porgy And Bess | Original Jazz Classics | OJCCD 829-2(2310779)
Paolo Fresu Trio | Kind Of Porgy & Bess | RCA | 21951952
Pearl Bailey With The Don Redman Orchestra | Pearl Bailey-The Best Of The Roulette Years | Roulette | CDP 796483-2

I Got Rambling On My Mind
Otis Spann/Robert Lockwood Jr. | Otis Spann Is The Blues | Crosscut | CCR 1003(Candid)

I Got Rhythm
Art Tatum Trio | The Complete Trio Sessions Vol.1 | Official | 3001
Ben Webster Quartet | Live In Paris 1972 | France's Concert | FCD 131
Benny Goodman Sextet | I Got Rhythm-Benny Goodman Plays Gershwin | CBS | 21064
Slipped Disc, 1945-1946 | CBS | 463337-2
Dicky Wells And His Orchestra | Jazz Gallery:Lester Young Vol.1(1936-46) | RCA | 2114171-2
Django Reinhardt And His American Friends:Paris 1935-1937 | Memo Music | HDJ 4124
Django Reinhardt And The Quintet Du Hot Club De France | The Indispensable Django Reinhardt | RCA | ND 70929
Don Byas/Slam Stewart | Don Byas:Laura | Dreyfus Jazz Line | FDM 36714-2
Classics In Swing:Town Hall Concert | Commodore | 9031-72739-2
Ella Fitzgerald And Her Orchestra | Live From The Roseland Ballroom New York 1940 | Jazz Anthology | 550032
Ella Fitzgerald With The Nelson Riddle Orchestra | Ella Sings Gershwin-Vol. 2 | Metro | 2682023 IMS
Sings The Ira And George Gershwin Songbook | Verve | 825024-2
Erroll Garner Quartet | Magician & Gershwin And Kern | Telarc Digital | CD 83337
Gerry Mulligan Quartet | Reunion With Chet Baker | Blue Note | 746857-2
Glenn Miller And His Orchestra | His Original Recordings | RCA | NL 89026 DP
Gordon Brisker Quintet | The Gift | Naxos Jazz | 86001-2
Hampton Hawes Trio | Hampton Hawes Trio Vol.1 | Original Jazz Classics | OJC20 316-2(C 3505)
Hatchett's Swingtette | In The Mood | Decca | RFL 11
Hot Lips Page Band | After Hours In Harlem | HighNote Records | HCD 7031
JATP All Stars | JATP-1940's | Verve | MV 9070/72 IMS
The Complete Jazz At The Philharmonic On Verve 1944-1949 | Verve | 523893-2
The Complete Jazz At The Philharmonic On Verve 1944-1949 | Verve | 523893-2
Jenny Evans And The Rudi Martini Quartet | At Lloyd's | ESM Records | ESM 9302
At Loyd's | BELL Records | BLR 90004
Kansas City Six | Lester Young:The Complete 1936-1951 Small Group Sessions(Studio Recordings-Master Takes),Vol.2 | Blue Moon | BMCD 1002
Martial Solal Trio | Martial Solal At Newport '63 | RCA | 2174803-2
Martin Schrack Trio | Martin Schrack Trio Plays George Gershwin | yvp music | CD 3049
Minton's Playhouse All Stars | Thelonious Monk:After Hours At Minton's | Definitive Records | DRCD 11197
Oscar Peterson Trio | The George Gershwin Songbook | Verve | 823249-1
Masters Of Jazz Vol.7 | RCA | NL 89721 DP
Quintet Du Hot Club De France | Jazz In Paris:Django Reinhardt-Swing From Paris | EmArCy | 159853-2 PMS
Djangology Vol.1 | Naxos Jazz | 8.120515 CD
Schnuckenack Reinhardt Quintet | Live | Intercord | 160035
Singers Unlimited With The Patrick Williams Orchestra | Compact Disc:The Singers Unlimited | MPS | 831373-2 PMS
Stan Kenton And His Orchestra | Two Much | Creative World | ST 1067
Steve Allen All Stars | At The Roundtable | Fresh Sound Records | FSR 571(Roulette R 25053)
Tenor Tribute | Tenor Tribute | Soul Note | SN 1184
The Five Cousins | Spirit Of Rhythm 1932-34 | Retrieval | RTR 79004
The Moscow Sax Quintet | The Jazznost Tour | Arkadia Jazz | 71161
Willie 'The Lion' Smith Trio | Willie 'The Lion' Smith | Collection Hugues Panassié | CTPL 004/005
Zoot Sims Quintet | Zoot Sims And The Gershwin Brothers | Original Jazz Classics | OJC20 444-2(2310744)
Barry Harris Trio | Live At Dug | Enja | 9097-2

I Got Rhythm-
Sir Charles Thompson | Playing My Way | Jazz Connaisseur | JCCD 9313-2
Stefan Scaggiari Trio | That's Ska-jär-é | Concord | CCD 4510
Stephane Grappelli Trio | Live At The Blue Note | Telarc Digital | CD 83397

I Got Rhythm(alt.take 1)
Martial Solal Trio | Martial Solal At Newport '63 | RCA | 2174803-2

I Got Rhythm(alt.take 2)
Benny Goodman Sextet | Slipped Disc, 1945-1946 | CBS | 463337-2

I Got The Blues
Big Maceo Merriweather | Big Maceo Vol.1 | Blues Classics | BC 28

TITELVERZEICHNIS

I Got The Feelin'
Cold Sweat | Cold Sweat Plays J.B. | JMT Edition | 919025-2

I Got The Feelin'-
John Lee Hooker | Boogie Chillun | Fantasy | FCD 24706-2

I Got Thunder(And It Rings)
Lightnin' Hopkins Trio | Double Blues | Fantasy | FCD 24702-2

I Got To Know
Eugene Holmes | Spirituals | Schubert Records | SCH- 102

I Got What It Takes-
Luther Allison Quintet | Power Wire Blues | Charly | CRB 1105

I Got You (I Feel Good)
Mezzrow-Bechet Quintet | The Prodigious Bechet-Mezzrow Quintet & Septet | Festival | Album 117

I Gotta Be Your Man
B.B.King And His Band | B. B. King, 1949-1950 | Anthology of the Blues | AB 5611

I Gotta Move
Mose Allison Trio | Mose Allison Sings The 7th Son | Prestige | PR20 7279-2

I Gotta Right To Cry
Vic Dickenson-Red Richards All Stars | Yacht Club Swing | Harlequin | HQ 2045 IMS

I Gotta Right To Sing The Blues
Art Tatum | The Standard Sessions: Art Tatum 1935-1943 Transcriptions | Music & Arts | CD 673
Pure Genius | Atlantis | ATS 3
Art Tatum:Complete Capitol Recordings | Definitive Records | DRCD 11192
Benny Goodman And His Orchestra | Benny Goodman's 1934 Dodge All-Star Recordings(Complete) | Circle | CCD-111
Billie Holiday With Frankie Newton And His Orchestra | Fine And Mellow | Naxos Jazz | 8.120583 CD
Bob Wilber And Friends | Blues Of Summer | Nagel-Heyer | NH 1011
Chris Connor With The Jimmy Jones Quintet | A Portrait Of Chris | Atlantic | AMCY 1073
Ella Fitzgerald With The Billy May Orchestra | The Harold Arlen Songbook | Verve | 817526-1 IMS
June Richmond With The Quincy Jones Orchestra | Jazz In Paris:Harold Nicholas-June Richmond-Andy Bey | EmArCy | 013036-2
Loren Schoenberg And His Jazz Orchestra | Just A-Settin' And A-Rockin' | Musicmasters | 5039-2
Louis Armstrong And His Orchestra | Louis Armstrong-Satchmo's Greatest Hits | RCA | CL 89799
Marion Montgomery And Her Quartet | I Gotta Right To Sing... | Ronnie Scott's Jazz House | JHCD 003
Oscar Peterson Trio | Oscar Peterson Plays The Harold Arlen Song Book | Verve | 589103-2
The Song Is You-The Best Of The Verve Songbooks | Verve | 531558-2
Oscar Peterson-Joe Pass Duo | Oscar Pterson Et Joe Pass A La Salle Pleyel | Pablo | 2CD 2625705
Live At Salle Pleyel, Paris | Pablo | 2625705
Rex Stewart-Cootie Williams Orchestra | Together 1957 | Jazz Anthology | JA 5201
Sarah Vaughan And The Count Basie Orchestra | Send In The Clowns | Pablo | 2312130-2
The Big Challenge | Cootie & Rex In The Big Challenge | Fresh Sound Records | FSR-CD 0077

I Gotta Talk To Somebody
Memphis Slim Group | The Real Folk Blues | Chess | CHD 9270(872290)

I Guess I'll Hang My Tears Out To Dry
Audrey Morris Band | Bistro Ballads | Fresh Sound Records | ND 74407
Cannonball Adderley Quartet | Ballads | Blue Note | 537563-2
Dexter Gordon Quartet | Lions Abroad Volume One:Tenor Titans | Black Lion | BLCD 7620-2
Live At The Montmartre Jazzhus | Black Lion | BLCD 7606-2
Dexter Gordon:Ballads | Blue Note | 796579-2
Diane Schuur Trio With Orchestra And Strings | In Tribute | GRP | GRP 20062
Don Menza & Frank Strazzeri | Ballads | Fresh Sound Records | FSR 103 (807728)
Mel Tormé And His All-Star Quintet | Sing, Sing, Sing | Concord | CCD 4542
Tete Montoliu | Boston Concert | Steeplechase | SCS 1152/3

I Guess I'll Have To Change My Plans
Anson Weeks And His Orchestra | The Radio Years: Anson Weeks And His Hotel Mark Hopkins Orchestra 193 | Hindsight | HSR 146
Art Tatum Trio | The Tatum Group Masterpieces | Pablo | 2625706
Mundell Lowe Quartet | Exciting Modern Guitar | Original Jazz Classics | SMJ 6089
Tony Bennett With The Count Basie Orchestra | Tony Bennett In Concert With Count Basie | Laserlight | 15722
Blue Barron And His Orchestra | The Uncollected: Blue Barron | Hindsight | HSR 110

I Guess I'll Have To Dream The Rest
Glenn Miller And His Orchestra | The Glenn Miller Story Vol.4 | RCA | NL 89223 AG
Tommy Dorsey And His Orchestra | Forever | RCA | NL 89859 DP

I Guess I'll Take The Papers And Go Home
Fergus Read | Easy Come-Easy Go:A Jazz Cocktail | AZURE Compact Disc | AZ-CD-14

I Had A Ball
Blind John Davis | Blind John Davis | L+R Records | CDLR 72002

I Had A Dream
The Staple Singers | Uncloudy Day | Joy | 5019

I Had A King
Horace Silver Sextet | Deep Blue-The United States Of Mind | Blue Note | 521152-2

I Had A Little Talk
Ketil Bjornstad Group | Seafarer's Song | EmArCy | 9865777

I Had Been Hungry All The Years
Walter 'Wolfman' Washington Group | Wolf At The Door | Rounder Records | CDRR 2098

I Had It But It's All Gone Now
Sidney Bechet With Bob Wilber's Wildcats | Spreadin Joy (Original Recordings 1940-50) | Naxos Jazz | 8.120531 CD

I Had The Craziest Dream
Lou Donaldson Quintet | Play The Right Thing | Milestone | MCD 9190-2
Meredith d'Ambrosio Quartet | Beware Of Spring! | Sunnyside | SSC 1069 D
George Shearing-Mel Torme | An Elegant Evening | Concord | CCD 4294

I Hadn't Anyone 'Til You
Allan Vaché Swingtet | Jazz Im Amerikahaus,Vol.3 | Nagel-Heyer | CD 013

I Hadn't Anyone 'Till Now
Billie Holiday And Her Orchestra | Billie Holiday Story Vol.5:Music for Torching | Verve | MV 2595 IMS
George Van Eps | Legends | Concord | CCD 4616
Jimmy Cleveland And His All Stars | Introducing Jimmy Cleveland | Verve | 543752-2
Thelonious Monk | Solo Monk | CBS | 471248-2

I Hadn't Anyone 'Till You
Art Tatum | The Art Tatum Solo Masterpieces | Pablo | 2625703
Cal Tjader Sextet | A Night At The Blackhawk | Original Jazz Classics | OJC 278(F 8026)
Dinah Shore With Orchestra | The Best Of Dinah Shore | Capitol | 792895-2
Francine Griffin With Band | Francine Griffin:The Song Bird | Delmark | DE 512
Max Bennett Septet | Max Bennett | Fresh Sound Records | FSR 2002(Bethlehem BCP 48)
Mose Allison Trio | Mose Allison Sings The 7th Son | Prestige | PR20 7279-2
Phil Woods Quintet | Young Woods | Fresh Sound Records | FSR-CD 0182
The King Sisters With The Alvino Rey Orchestra | Warm And Wonderful | EMI Records | 1599351

I Hadn't Anyone 'Till You(alt.take)
Chris Barber's Jazz Band | The Best Of Dixieland-Live in 1954/55 | London | 820878-2

I Hate A Man Like You
Barber 's Best | Decca | 6.28128 DP

I Hate Money
The Halfway House Dance Orchestra | The Halfway House Orchestra-The Complete Recordings In Chronological Order | Jazz Oracle | BDW 8001

I Hate To Be Alone
Roosevelt Sykes Quintet | The Honeydripper | Original Blues Classics | OBCCD 557-2(BV 1014)

I Hate To Sing
Tete Montoliu | Yellow Dolphin Street/Catalonian Folk Songs | Timeless | CD SJP 107/116

I Hate You Baby
Herbie Hancock Orchestra | The Best Of Herbie Hancock | Blue Note | 89907

I Have A Dream
Herbie Hancock:The Complete Blue Note Sixties Sessions | Blue Note | 495569-2
Miles Davis Quintet | Miles Davis Quintet 1965-1968 | CBS | C6K 67398

I Have A Dream(rehersal)
James 'Sugar Boy' Crawford With Dave Bartholomew's Orchestra | New Orleans Classics | Pathe | 1561351(Imperial)

I Have A Love-
Five Blind Boys Of Alabama | The Five Blind Boys Of Alabama | Heritage Records | HT 315 IMS

I Have Dreamed
Gerals Wiggins Trio | The King And I | Fresh Sound Records | FSR-CD 0053

I Have Eyes
Artie Shaw And His Orchestra | The Original Sounds Of The Swing Era Vol.7 | RCA | CL 05517 DP

I Have Nothing To Say
Peggy Connelly With The Marty Paich Orchestra | Peggy Connelly Sings | Fresh Sound Records | FSR 607(835386)

I Have The Feeling I've Been Here Before
Kendra Shank With The Larry Willis Trio | Afterglow | Mapleshade | 02132

I Have To Say No
King Curtis Band | Trouble In Mind | Original Blues Classics | OBCCD 512-2(Tru 15001)

I Haven't Got Anything Better To Do
Meredith d'Ambrosio Quartet | Beware Of Spring! | Sunnyside | SSC 1069 D

I Hear A Rhapsody
Bart Van Lier With The Metropole Orchestra | Twilight | Koch Jazz | 3-6908-2
Billy Eckstine With The Billy May Orchestra | Once More With Feeling | Roulette | 581862-2
Billy Eckstine | Laserlight | 17070
Bob Mintzer Big Band | Spectrum | dmp Digital Music Productions | CD 461
Bruce Forman Quartet | Pardon Me | Concord | CCD 4368
Christian Scheuber Quartet | Clara's Smile | double moon | DMCHR 71025
Christof Sänger & Cuban Fantasy | Moliendo Café | Mons Records | MR 874302
Dave Brubeck Quartet | Paper Moon | Concord | CCD 4178
Don Friedman | Maybeck Recital Hall Series Volume Thirty-Three | Concord | CCD 4608
Freddy Martin And His Orchestra | The Uncollected: Freddy Martin, Vol.3 | Hindsight | HSR 190
Heiner Franz Trio | Jazz Guitar Highlights 1 | Jardis Records | JRCD 20141
Jackie McLean Quartet | Makin' The Changes | Original Jazz Classics | OJCCD 197-2(NJ 8231)
John Coltrane Quartet | Lush Life | Original Jazz Classics | OJC20 131-2
John Harrison Trio | Going Places | TCB Records | TCB 95702
Keith Jarrett Trio | Standards In Norway | ECM | 1542(521717-2)
Kenny Werner Trio | Introducing The Trio | Sunnyside | SSC 1038 D
Louie Bellson Quartet | Live At Joe Segal's Jazz Showcase | Concord | CJ 350
Steve Nelson Quartet | Communications | Criss Cross | Criss 1034
Enrico Pieranunzi Trio | Trilogues Vol.3 | yvp music | CD 3026

I Hear Music
Bruce Barth Quintet | In Focus | Enja | 8010-2
Ella Fitzgerald-Oscar Peterson Trio | Ella And Oscar | Pablo | 2310759-2
Hampton Hawes Trio | California Cool | Blue Note | 780707-2
Johnny Dankworth Seven | Bebop In Britain | Esquire | CD ESQ 100-4
Stan Kenton And His Orchestra | At The Rendezvous Vol.1 | Status | CD 102(882198)
Stephane Grappelli Quartet | Planet Jazz:Stephane Grappelli | RCA | 2165366-2
Stephane Grappelli Trio | How High The Moon | Memo Music | HDJ 4020
The Swingcats | Face To Face:The Swingcats Live | Nagel-Heyer | CD 072
Billie Holiday And Her Orchestra | Billie Holiday 'Control Booth' Series,Vol.1(1940-41) | Jazz Unlimited | JUCD 2014

I Hear Ya Talkin'
Frank Wess Septet | Opus De Blues | Savoy | SV 0137(MG 12142)

I Hear You
Walt Dickerson Trio | I Hear You John | Steeplechase | SCCD 31146

I Heard It Over The Radio
Ornette Coleman Quartet | Beauty Is A Rare Thing:Ornette Coleman-The Complete Atlantic Recordings | Atlantic | 8122-71410-2
Paul Plimley Trio | Density Of The Lovestruck Demons | Music & Arts | CD 906

I Heard It Through The Grapevine
Harold Mabern Quintet | Rakin' And Scrapin' | Original Jazz Classics | OJC 330(P 7624)

I Heard You
Benny Carter And His Orchestra | Coleman Hawkins/Benny Carter | Forlane | UCD 19011

I Heard You Cried Last Night
Red Garland Trio | Prestige Moodsville Vol.1 | Original Jazz Classics | OJCCD 360-2(MV 1)
Vic Juris Quartet | Night Tripper | Steeplechase | SCCD 31353

I Hela Naturen-
Elmore James Group | The Legend Of Elmore James | Anthology of the Blues | AB 5601

I Hold No Grudge
Nina Simone With Orchestra | Nina Simone-The 60s Vol.3:Work Song | Mercury | 838545-2 PMS

I Hope Gabriel Likes My Music
Louis Armstrong With Luis Russell And His Orchestra | Ambassador Louis Armstrong Vol.1(1935) | Ambassador | CLA 1901

I Hope I Don't Fall In Love With You
Tom Van Der Geld Quartet | Out Patients | Japo | 60035

I Just Can't See For Looking
Red Garland Quartet | Solar | Original Jazz Classics | VIJ 5046

I Just Dropped By To Say Hello
Diane Schuur With Orchestra | Three Ladies Of Jazz:Live In New York | Jazz Door | JD 12102

I Just Found Out About Love
Ethel Waters With Eddie Mallory And His Orchestra | Benny Carter(1928-1952) | RCA | ND 89761

I Just Landed In Your Town
Michel Petrucciani Trio | Estate | Riviera | RVR 1

I Just Telephon Upstairs
Magic Sam's Blues Band | Black Magic | Delmark | 900200 AO

I Just Want To Celebrate
The Clarke/Duke Project | The Clarke/Duke Project | Epic | 468223-2

I Just Want To Make Love To You
Big Moose Walker Group | The Rising Sun Collection | The Rising Sun Collection | RSC 0008
Etta James With The Red Holloway Quartet | Blues In The Night-Volume One:The Early Show | Fantasy | FCD 9647-2
Jeanne Carroll & Christian Christl With Band | Tribute To Willie Dixon | Acoustic Music Records | AMC 1014
Junior Wells Blues Band | Southside Blues Jam | Delmark | 900204 AO
Muddy Waters Groups | Muddy Waters-In Memoriam | Chess | 2292-44614-2
Tommy Tucker Band | The Rocks Is My Pillow-The Cold Ground Is My Bed | Red Lightnin' | RL 0037

I Just Want To Sing
Dorothy Donegan Trio | The Explosive Dorothy Donegan | Progressive | PRO 7056 IMS

I Keep Goin' Back To Joe's
Mark Murphy-Gary Schunk | Mark Murphy Sings Nat Cing Cole,Volumes 1&2 | Muse | MCD 6001

I Knew It Was You
Mississippi Sheiks | Chicago:The Living Legends-South Side Blues | Original Blues Classics | OBCCD 508-2(RLP 9403)

I Know
Freddie Roach Quartet | Mo' Greens Please | Blue Note | 869698-3
Sonny Rollins Quartet | Sonny Rollins:Complete 1949-1951 Prestige Studio Recordings | Definitive Records | DRCD 11240
Wanda Rouzan With Band | It's What I Do | Huckle-Buck Records | WR 22590

I Know A Place-
June Christy With The Bob Cooper Orchestra | Do Re Mi | Fresh Sound Records | 054 2607961(Capitol T 1586)

I Know Don't Know How
Gerry Mulligan Concert Jazz Band | The Complete Verve Gerry Mulligan Concert Band | Verve | 9860613
Maurice Meunier Quintet | Jazz In Paris:Clarinettes À Saint-Germain Des Prés | EmArCy | 013543-2

I Know It's You
Staple Singers | Great Day | Milestone | MCD 47027-2

I Know Prez
First Class Blues Band | The First Class Blues Band Proudly Presents Mr. Frank Biner | Acoustic Music Records | 319.1062.2

I Know That You Know
Art Hodes Quartet | Art Hodes Trios & Quartete | Jazzology | JCD-113
Art Tatum | Solos 1937 & Classic Piano Solos | Forlane | UCD 19010
Earl Hines Quintet | Earl's Pearl | Memo Music | HDJ 4043
Gillespie-Rollins-Stitt Sextet | The Sonny Rollins/Sonny Stitt Sessions | Verve | 2-2505 IMS
Kansas City Five | Jazz Drumming Vol.3(1938-1939) | Fenn Music | FJD 2703
Kitty White With The Benny Carter All Stars | Sweet Talk | Fresh Sound Records | FSR 557(Roulette R 52020)
Red Norvo And His Orchestra | Jivin The Jeep | Hep | CD 1019
Rex Stewart And His Feetwarmers | Django Reinhardt:Djangology | EMI Records | 780659-2

I Know What I've Got, Don't Know What I'm Getting
Sonny Boy Williamson Band | One Way Out | Chess | CHD 9116(872271)

I Know What You're Puttin' Down
Odetta | The Tin Angel | Original Blues Classics | OBCCD 565-2(F 3252)

I Know Why
Joshua Breakstone Quintet | Evening Star | Contemporary | CCD 14040-2
Ruth Brown And Her Band | The Songs Of My Life | Fantasy | FCD 9665-2

I Know You Love Me Baby
Louis Jordan And His Tympany Five | Louis Jordan-Let The Good Times Roll: The Complete Decca Recordings 1938-1954 | Bear Family Records | BCD 15557 IH

I Know You(I Know What You Wanna Do)
Louis Jordan Vol.2-Knock Me Out | Swingtime(Contact) | ST 1012

I Know,You Know
Franco Morone | Melodies Of Memories | Acoustic Music Records | 319.1153.2

I Laughed At Love
Russell Garcia Orchestra | I Lead A Charmed Life | Discovery | DS 814 IMS

I Left My Baby
John Lee Hooker | Solid Sender | Charly | CRB 1081

I Left My Heart In San Francisco
Booker Ervin Orchestra | Booker 'N' Brass | Pacific Jazz | 494509-2
Charlie Byrd Trio With Voices | Byrd Song | Original Jazz Classics | OJCCD 1092-2(RS 9481)
Count Basie And His Orchestra | This Time By Basie | Reprise | 9362-45162-2
Louis Armstrong And His All Stars | The Legendary Berlin Concert Part 2 | Jazzpoint | JP 1063 CD
Mr. Acker Bilk With The Leon Young String Chorale | Stranger On The Shore | Philips | 830779-2
Singers Unlimited | A Special Blend | MPS | 841412-2
Willis Jackson Group | At Large | Prestige | PCD 24243-2
Simon Schott | Bar Piano: Simon Schott Plays Your Favorite Evergreens Vol.1 | Organic Music | ORGM 9733

I Left My Heart In San Francisco-
The Two-Bone-Big-Band | The Retum Of The Hornplayers | Mons Records | MR 874314

I Left My Mother
The Goofus Five | The Goofus Five feat. Adrian Rollini | Timeless | CBC 1-017

I Left This Space For You
Rodney Jones Group | The Unspoken Heart | Minor Music | 801021

I Let A Song Go Out Of My Heart
Benny Goodman And His Orchestra | This Is Benny Goodman | RCA | NL 89224 DP
Bud Freeman All Stars | The Bud Freeman All Stars | Original Jazz Classics | OJC 183(SV 2012)
Dizzy Gillespie-Stan Getz Sextet | Diz And Getz | Verve | 2-2521 IMS
Welcome To Jazz: Dizzy Gillespie | Koch Records | 321 972 D1
Eddie Lockjaw Davis Quartet | Eddie Lockjaw Davis With Shirley Scott | Original Jazz Classics | OJC 218(P 7154)
Ella Fitzgerald And Her All Stars | Love Songs:The Best Of The Song Books | Verve | 531762-2
The Complete Ella Fitzgerald Song Books of Harold Arlen, Irving Berlin, Duke Ellington, George & Ira Gershwin, Jerome Kern, Johnny Mercer, Cole Porter And Rogers & Hart | Verve | 519832-2
Ellis Larkins | Maybeck Recital Hall Series Volume Twenty-Two | Concord | CCD 4533
Heinz Sauer-Bob Degen Duo | Ellingtonia Revisited | L+R Records | LR 40007 Direct To Disc
Jimmy Smith Sextet | A Date With Jimmy Smith Vol.2 | Blue Note | 300149(1548)
Johnny Hodges Orchestra | The Complete Duke Ellington-Vol. 10 | CBS | CBS 88220
Ray Bryant Trio | Ray Bryant Plays Basie & Ellington | EmArCy | 832235-2 PMS
Rosemary Clooney With The Duke Ellington Orchestra | Swing | Stereoplay-CD | CD 697042
Sarah Vaughan With Small Group & Orchestra | Duke Ellington Song Book One | Pablo | CD 2312111
Sathima Bea Benjamin With The Kenny Barron Trio | Southern Touch | Enja | ENJ-7015 2
The Danish-German Slide Combination | Fugue For Tinhorns | L+R Records | LR 45011
Thelonious Monk Trio | Thelonious Monk-The Complete Riverside Recordings | Riverside | 15 RCD 022-2
Zoot Sims With Orchestra | Passion Flower | Original Jazz Classics | OJCCD 939-2(2312120)

Allotria Jazz Band | Swing That Music | Elite Special | 73232

I Let A Song Go Out Of My Heart-
Duke Ellington And His Orchestra | Duke Ellington In Hamilton | Radiex Music | RDX-1000
Jonah Jones Quartet | Harry 'Sweets' Edison/Jonah Jones | LRC Records | CDC 9030

I Let A Song Go Out Of My Heart(alt.take)
Sarah Vaughan With Orchestra | Sarah Vaughan Birthday Celebration | Fantasy | FANCD 6090-2
Duke Ellington And His Famous Orchestra | The Complete Duke Ellington-Vol. 10 | CBS | CBS 88220

I Like 'Em Fat Like That
Louis Jordan And His Tympany Five | Louis Jordan Greatest Hits-Vol.2 | MCA | 1337

I Like Fish
Al Cohn-Zoot Sims Quintet | Either Way | Evidence | ECD 22007-2

I Like Jersey Best
Fletcher Henderson And His Orchestra | Fletcher Henderson Vol.1-The End Of An Era | Swingtime(Contact) | ST 1008

I Like Myself
Frankie Trumbauer And His Orchestra | Jazz Classics In Digital Stereo: Bix Beiderbecke | CDS Records Ltd. | RPCD 620(CD 601)

I Like That
Steve Laury Trio | Passion | Denon Compact Disc | CY-79043

I Like The Likes Of You
Trigger Alpert's Absolutely All Star Seven | East Coast Sound | Original Jazz Classics | OJCCD 1012-2(JLP 11)
Trigger Alpert's All Stars | Trigger Happy! | Fresh Sound Records | RLP 12-225(Riverside)

I Like The Sunrise
Lincoln Center Jazz Orchestra | Portraits By Ellington | CBS | 472814-2

I Like To Recognize The Tune
Stan Getz Quartet | Stan Getz At Large Plus!,Vol.1 | Jazz Unlimited | JUCD 2001

I Like To See You More Around In My Life
John Lee Hooker | Boogie Chillun | Fantasy | FCD 24706-2

I Like You You're Nice
Michael Bolivar Group | Hangin' Out | Clarity Recordings | CCD-1009

I Live To Love You
Horace Heidt And His Musical Knights | The Uncollected:Horace Heidt | Hindsight | HSR 194

I Lost My Heart In Moscow-
Big Maceo Merriweather | Big Maceo Vol.2 | Blues Classics | BC 29

I Lost My Sugar In Salt Lake City
Peggy Lee With The Quincy Jones Orchestra | Blues Cross Country | Capitol | 520088 2
Stan Kenton And His Orchestra | The Kenton Era | Creative World | ST 1030

I Love A Piano
Benny Goodman And His Orchestra | Live At Carnegie Hall-40th Anniversary Concert | Decca | 6.28451 DP

I Love Annie's Fanny
Nick Woodland Quartet | Live Fireworks | Blues Beacon | BLU-1027 2

I Love Another Woman
Gunter Hampel And His Galaxie Dream Band | I Love Beeing With You | Birth | 0012

I Love Christmas
Duke Ellington And His Orchestra | Way Low | Duke Records | D 1015

I Love Jazz
Louis Armstrong And His Orchestra | I Love Jazz | Verve | 543747-2

I Love Jazz(alt.take)
Harry Allen And Randy Sandke Meets The RIAS Big Band Berlin | The Music Of The Trumpet Kings | Nagel-Heyer | CD 037

I Love Louis
Randy Sandke Quintet | I Hear Music | Concord | CCD 4566

I Love Music
Amiri Baraka with David and Steve McCall | New Music-New Poetry | India Navigation | IN 1048
Axel Zwingenberger With Big Joe Duskin | Kansas City Boogie Jam | Vagabond | VRCD 8.00027

I Love My Baby
Charleston Chasers | Steaming South | Stomp Off Records | CD 1314

I Love New York In June
Barrett Deems Septet | Deemus | Delmark | DE 492

I Love Paris
Cal Tjader Sextet | Cal Tjader's Latin Kick | Original Jazz Classics | OJCCD 642-2(F 8033)
Black Hawk Nights | Fantasy | FCD 24755-2
A Night At The Blackhawk | Original Jazz Classics | OJC 278(F 8026)
Charlie Parker Quintet | Verve Jazz Masters 28:Charlie Parker Plays Standards | Verve | 521854-2
The Verve Years(1952-54) | Verve | 2-2523 IMS
The Cole Porter Song Book | Verve | 823250-1
Coleman Hawkins With Many Albam And His Orchestra | RCA Victor 80th Anniversary Vol.4:1950-1959 | RCA | 2668780-2
Ella Fitzgerald With Orchestra | Forever Ella | Verve | 529387-2
Ella Fitzgerald With The Buddy Bregman Orchestra | The Cole Porter Song Book | Verve | 2683044 IMS
Ella Fitzgerald Sings The Cole Porter Songbook | Verve | 537257-2
Ella Fitzgerald Sings The Cole Porter Songbook Vol.2 | Verve | 821990-2
Humphrey Lyttelton And His Band | Jazz At The Royal Festival Hall/Jazz At The Conway Hall | Dormouse | DM 22 CD
Jesse Davis Quintet | Young At Art | Concord | CCD 4565
Johnny Frigo Sextet | Debut Of A Legend | Chesky | JD 119
Louis Armstrong And His All Stars | Freddie Hubbard/Louis Armstrong | LRC Records | CDC 9044
Marty Paich Big Band | The New York Scene | Discovery | DS 844 IMS
Neil Richardson Singers With The Metropole Orchestra | A Beautiful Friendship | Koch Jazz | 3-6909-2
Oscar Peterson Trio | Night Train Vol. 3 | Verve | 711071 IMS

I Love Paris Too
Cal Tjader Sextet | A Night At The Blackhawk | Original Jazz Classics | OJC 278(F 8026)

I Love Paris(take 2)
Charlie Parker Quintet | Bird: The Complete Charlie Parker On Verve | Verve | 837141-2

I Love Paris(take 3)
Harlem Mamfats | I'm So Glad | Queen-Disc | 062

I Love That Kinda Carryin' On
Lillian Glinn Group | Lillians Glinn-Mae Glover(1929-1931) | Story Of Blues | CD 3537-2

I Love The Life I Live
Mose Allison Trio | Mose Alife!/Wild Man On The Loose | Warner | 8122-75439-2
High Jinks! The Mose Allison Trilogy | CBS | J3K 64275
The Go Jazz All Stars | Live In Japan | VeraBra Records | CDVBR 2086-2

I Love The Rhythm In A Riff
Big Joe Turner And Roomful Of Blues | Blues Train | Muse | MCD 5293

I L-o-v-e U
John Lee Hooker | Half A Stranger | Mainstream | MD CDO 903

I Love You
Akio Sasajima-Ron Carter | Akioustically Sound | Muse | MCD 5448
Art Pepper Quartet | Intensity | Original Jazz Classics | OJCCD 387-2
Art Pepper:The Complete Galaxy Recordings | Galaxy | 16GCD 1016-2
Attila Zoller Trio | Attila Zoller:The Last Recordings | Enja | ENJ-9349 2
Bill Evans | The Complete Fantasy Recordings | Fantasy | 9FCD 1012-2
Bill Evans Quartet | Modern Days & Night:Music Of Cole Porter | Double Time Records | DTRCD-120
Bill Evans Trio | New Jazz Conceptions | Original Jazz Classics | OJC20 025-2(RLP 223)
Getting Sentimental | Milestone | MCD 9346-2
Bill Evans:The Secret Sessions | Milestone | 8MCD 4421-2
Bill Evans-Eddie Gomez Duo | Montreux III | Original Jazz Classics | OJC20 644-2(F 9510)
The Complete Fantasy Recordings | Fantasy | 9FCD 1012-2
Billy Bean-Dennis Budimir | West Coast Sessions | String Jazz | SJRCD 1006
Billy Eckstine With The Billy May Orchestra | Once More With Feeling | Roulette | 581862-2
Billy Ross Quartet | The Sound:A Tribute To Stan Getz | Milestone | MCD 9227-2
Dave Liebman Trio | Plays The Music Of Cole Porter | Red Records | 123236-2
Django Reinhardt And The Quintet Du Hot Club De France | Peche À La Mode-The Great Blue Star Sessions 1947/1953 | Verve | 835418-2
Django Reinhardt Portrait | Barclay | DALP 2/1939
Dorothy Donegan Trio | The Many Faces Of Dorothy Donegan | Storyville | STCD 8362
Doug Raney Quartet | Blue And White | Steeplechase | SCCD 31191
Herbie Mann-Bill Evans Quartet | That's Jazz Vol.8: Nirvana | Atlantic | ATL 50238
J.J.Johnson Quintet | Vivian | Concord | CCD 4523
Jimmy Greene Sextet | Introducing Jimmy Greene | Criss Cross | Criss 1181
Joe Albany-Warne Marsh Trio | The Right Combination | Original Jazz Classics | OJCCD 1749-2
John Coltrane Trio | John Coltrane-The Prestige Recordings | Prestige | 16 PCD 4405-2
Lush Life | Original Jazz Classics | OJC20 131-2
John Crocker Quartet | All Of Me | Timeless | CD TTD 585
Keith Smith Hefty Jazz All Stars | Swing Is Here Again | Lake | LACD 80
Milt Jackson Orchestra | Big Mouth | Original Jazz Classics | OJCCD 865-2(2310867)
Oscar Peterson Trio | Walking The Line | MPS | 68082
Remy Filipovitch-Will Boulware | Alone Together | Album | AS 55417 CD
Rick Laird Quartet | Soft Focus | Timeless | CD SJP 104/112
Stan Getz Quartet | Serenity | EmArCy | 838770-2
Tal Farlow Trio | The Swinging Guitar Of Tal Farlow | Verve | 559515-2
Teddy Wilson | Solo:Teddy Wilson Plays Cole Porter And Fat Waller | Jazz Colours | 874715-2

I Love You-
Jimmy Rowles Trio | Grandpaws | Candid | CRS 1014 IMS
Trumpet Spectacular | The Progressive Records All Star Trumpet Spectacular | Progressive | PRO 7015 IMS

I Love You And Don't You Forget It - (I Love You) And Don't You Forget It
Sarah Vaughan With Orchestra | Sarah Vaughan Sings The Mancini Songbook | Verve | 558401-2
Magic Slim Band | Highway Is My Home | Black & Blue | BLE 59.525 2

I Love You For Sentimental Reasons
Django Reinhardt And The Quintet Du Hot Club De France | Peche À La Mode-The Great Blue Star Sessions 1947/1953 | Verve | 835418-2
Django Reinhardt Portrait | Barclay | DALP 2/1939
John Pizzarelli Trio | P.S. Mr.Cole | RCA | 2663563-2
Kurt Elling Group With Guests | Live In Chicago | Blue Note | 522211-2
Laura Fygi With Band | Bewitched | Verve | 514724-2
Mildred Bailey And Her Orchestra | Squeeze Me | Affinity | CD AFS 1013
Nat King Cole Trio | Nat King Cole:For Sentimental Reasons | Dreyfus Jazz Line | FDM 36740-2
Love Songs | Nimbus Records | NI 2010
Straighten Up And Fly Right | Pro-Arte | CDD 558
Patricia Covair With The Willie Metcalf Jr. Jazz Quartet | New Orleans After Dark | Challenger Productions | AE 1000-2
Smiley Lewis Band | Ooh La La | Pathe | 1561391(Imperial)

I Love You Madly
John Klemmer Group | Hush | Elektra | 5E-527

I Love You Samantha
James Chirillo Quartet with Vera Mara | Sultry Serenade | Nagel-Heyer | CD 061
Ruby Braff Trio | As Time Goes By... | Candid | CCD 79741

I Love You Samantha-
Bill Doggett Quintet | I Don't Know Much About Love | Black & Blue | BLE 59.029 2

I Love You Sweetheart Of All My Dreams
Thelonious Monk | Monk Alone:The Complete Columbia Solo Studio Recordings | CBS | C2K 65495
Monk Alone:The Complete Columbia Solo Studio Recordings | CBS | C2K 65495

I Love You Sweetheart Of All My Dreams(alt.take)
Med Flory and his Orchestra | Modern Jazz Gallery | Fresh Sound Records | KXL 5001(252282-1 Kapp)

I Love You Too Much
The Andrew Sisters | The Andrew Sisters | ASV | AJA 5096

I Love You Yes I Do
Rahsaan Roland Kirk And His Orchestra | Blacknuss | Rhino | 8122-71408-2
Red Garland Trio | Red Garland Trio | Original Jazz Classics | OJC 224(MV 6)

I Love You(take 1)
Kenny Dorham Quintet | Kenny Dorham Quintet | Original Jazz Classics | OJCCD 113-2(DLP 9)

I Love You(take 2)
Kenny Dorham Quintet | Original Jazz Classics | OJCCD 113-2(DLP 9)

I Loved
Carol Kidd With The David Newton Trio | The Night We Called It A Day | Linn Records | AKD 007

I Loved You
Singers Unlimited | Eventide | MPS | 68196
Freddy Cole Septet | This Is The Life | Muse | MCD 5503

I Loves You Porgy
Bill Evans | The Complete Bill Evans On Verve | Verve | 527953-2
At The Montreux Jazz Festival | Verve | 539758-2
The Best Of Bill Evans Live | Verve | 533825-2
The Gershwin Songbook(The Instrumentals) | Verve | 525361-2
Bill Evans Trio | Waltz For Debby | Original Jazz Classics | OJC20 210-2
Live In Buenos Aires 1979 | West Wind | WW 2061
The Paris Concert-Edition One | Blue Note | MUS 96.0164-1
Billie Holiday And Her Trio | Lady Day-The Storyville Concerts | Jazz Door | JD 1215
Clare Teal And Her Band | Orsino's Songs | Candid | CCD 79783
Dave Valentine Group | Jungle Garden | GRP | GRP 95232
Ella Fitzgerald With The Lou Levy Trio | For The Love Of Ella Fitzgerald | Verve | 841765-2
Ella In Rome-The Birthday Concert | Verve | 835454-2
Guido Manusardi Trio | So That | SPLASC(H) Records | CD H 328-2
Itzak Perlman With The Oscar Peterson Quartet | Side By Side | Telarc Digital | CD 83341
John Bunch Trio | The Best Thing For You | Concord | CJ 328
Lynne Arriale Trio | With Words Unspoken | dmp Digital Music Productions | CD 518
McCoy Tyner-Bobby Hutcherson Duo | Manhattan Moods | Blue Note | 828423-2
Miles Davis With Gil Evans & His Orchestra | Porgy And Bess | CBS | CK 65141
The Miles Davis Selection | CBS | 465699-2
Nina Simone Quartet | Nina Simone-The 60s Vol.1: Ne Me Quitte Pas | Mercury | 838543-2 PMS
In Concert/I Put A Spell On You | Mercury | 846543-2
Nina Simone Trio | My Baby Just Cares For Me | Charly | CR 30217
Little Girl Blue | Bethlehem | BET 6021-2(BCP 6003)
Oscar Peterson Trio | Gitanes Jazz 'Round Midnight: Oscar Peterson | Verve | 511036-2 PMS
Oscar Peterson-Joe Pass Duo | Porgy And Bess | Original Jazz Classics | OJCCD 829-2(2310779)
Paolo Fresu Quartet | Kind Of Porgy & Bess | RCA | 21951952
Pearl & The Jazz's | Hear We Go! | Satin Doll Productions | SDP 1004-1 CD
Tito Puente's Golden Latin Jazz All Stars | Live At The Village Gate | RMM Records | 660.58.021

I Loves You Porgy-
Christoph Sänger | Live At The Montreal Jazz Festival | Laika Records | 35100822
Dave Grusin Band With Orchestra | The Orchestral Album | GRP | GRP 97972
Oliver Jones Trio | Requestfully Yours | Justin Time | Just 11
Oscar Peterson Trio | At Zardis' | Pablo | 2CD 2620118
Shirley Horn Trio | I Loe You, Paris | Verve | 523486-2
Miles Davis With Gil Evans & His Orchestra | Porgy And Bess | CBS | CK 65141

I Loves You Porgy(alt.take)
Bob Cooper/Snooky Young Sextet | In A Mellotone | Contemporary | C 14017

I Made Up My Mind
Mary Lou Williams Group | Jazz In Paris:Mary Lou Williams-I Made You Love Paris | EmArCy | 013141-2

I Mani(Faith)
Lonnie Liston Smith & His Cosmic Echoes | Astral Travelling | RCA | 2663878-2

I Mani(Faith-alt.take)
Ketil Bjornstad Group | Seafarer's Song | EmArCy | 9865777

I Many Times Thought Peace Had Come
Bobby Scott Trio | The Jazz Keyboards of Joe Bushkin/Marian McPartland/Bobby Scott/Lennie Tristano | Savoy | SV 0224(MG 12043)

I Married An Angel
Kenny Clarke Quintet | The Modern Jazz Piano Album | Savoy | SV 0272
Louis Armstrong With Sy Oliver's Choir And Orchestra | Louis Armstrong-Heavenly Music | Ambassador | CLA 1916
Shelly Manne Quintet | Perk Up | Concord | CCD 4021

I May Be Wrong(But I Think You're Wonderful)
Allotria Jazz Band | Once Upon A Time | Elite Special | 73433
Clarinet Jazz Quartet | Live At Birdland Neuburg | Birdland | BN 003
Engelbert Wrobel-Chris Hopkins-Dan Barrett Sextet | Harlem 2000 | Nagel-Heyer | CD 082
Engelbert Wrobel's Swing Society | Live At Sägewerk | Timeless | CD TTD 588
Gerry Mulligan Quartet | Gerry Mulligan Quartet | Pacific Jazz | 300001(PJ 1)
Gerry Mulligan With Chubby Jackson's Orchestra | Ezz-Thetic | Original Jazz Classics | OJCCD 1726-2(P 7827)
WDR Big Band | Harlem Story | Koala Records | CD P 7

I Mean You
Astral Project | Astral Project | Astral Project | no No.
Coleman Hawkins All Stars | Fats Navarro:The 1946-1949 Small Group Sessions(Studio Recordings-Master Takes),Vol.1 | Blue Moon | BMCD 1016
Esbjörn Svensson Trio(E.S.T.) | EST Plays Monk | RCA | 2137680-2
Great Jazz Trio With Terumasa Hino | Monk's Mood | Denon Compact Disc | 38C38-7323
James Clay Quartet | I Let A Song Go Out Of My Heart | Antilles | 848279-2(889265)
Johnny Griffin Quartet | Call It Whachawana | Galaxy | GXY 5146
Ray Barretto Orchestra | Portraits In Jazz And Clave | RCA | 2168452-2
Ronnie Mathews Trio | So Sorry Please... | Nilva | NQ 3414 IMS
Ted Rosenthal Sextet | Images Of Monk | The Jazz Alliance | TJA 10023
Thelonious Monk And His Orchestra | Who's Afraid Of The Big Band Monk? | CBS | CBS 88034
Thelonious Monk Quartet | Genius Of Modern Music,Vol.1 | Blue Note | 300403
Wizard Of The Vibes | Blue Note | 532140-2
The Blue Note Years-The Best Of Thelonious Monk | Blue Note | 796636-2
April In Paris | Milestone | M 47060
Thelonious Monk:Complete 1947-1952 Blue Note Recordings | The Jazz Factory | JFCD 22838
Live at The Five Spot,NYC | Blue Note | 799786-2
Thelonious Monk Trio | The London Collection Vol.2 | Black Lion | BLCD 760116
Thelonious Monk-Gerry Mulligan Quartet | Thelonious Monk-The Complete Riverside Recordings | Riverside | 15 RCD 022-2

I Mean You-
Gerry Mulligan-Thelonious Monk Quartet | Mulligan Meets Monk | Original Jazz Classics | OJC20 301-2(RLP 1106)

I Mean You(alt.take)
Thelonious Monk-Gerry Mulligan Quartet | Thelonious Monk-The Complete Riverside Recordings | Riverside | 15 RCD 022-2

I Mean!
Johnny Hodges Orchestra | Johnny Hodges:The Complete 1941-1954 Small Group Sessions(Master Takes),Vol.2 | Blue Moon | BMCD 1029

I Miss You
T-Bone Walker And His Band | I Get So Weary | Pathe | 1561441(Imperial)

I Miss You So
Dusko Goykovich Quartet | In My Dreams | Enja | ENJ-9408 2
Etta Jones And Her Band | Lonely And Blue | Original Jazz Classics | OJCCD 702-2(P 7241)
Memphis Slim | So Long | America | AM 6130

I Miss You, My Love
Duke Ellington And His Orchestra | Live Sessions 1943/1945 | Jazz Anthology | JA 5124

I Missed My Hat
Roy Eldridge-Benny Carter Quintet | The Urban Sessions/New Jazz Sound | Verve | 531637-2

I Missed My Hat(alt.take)
The Urban Sessions/New Jazz Sound | Verve | 531637-2

I Mo' Take You To To My Hospital And Cut Your Liver Out
Jeanne Lee Group | Natural Affinities | Owl Records | 018352-2

I Move And Set The Ways-
Joe Venuti And His New Yorkers | The Big Bands Of Joe Venuti Vol.1 (1928-30) | JSP Records | 1111

I Must Have Been A Fool
Barrelhouse Jazzband | Talking Hot | L+R Records | CDLR 70002

I Must Have That Man
Abbey Lincoln With Her Quintet | Sonny Rollins-The Freelance Years:The Complete Riverside & Contemporary Recordings | Riverside | 5 RCD 4427-2
Benny Goodman Trio | Avalon-The Small Band Vol.2 (1937-1939) | Bluebird | ND 82273
Billie Holiday With Teddy Wilson And His Orchestra | This Is Jazz:Lester Young | CBS | CK 65042
Maxine Sullivan With The New Friends Of Rhythm | Maxine Sullivan 1944 to 1948 | Legend | CD 6004(875358)
Bill Perkins With The Jan Lundgren Trio | Bill Perkins Recreates The Historic Solos Of Lester Young | Fresh Sound Records | FSR-CD 5010

I Must Have That Man(alt.take)
Miff Mole And His Nicksielanders | Commodore Classics-Bobby Hackett/Miff Mole | Commodore | 6.26171 AG

I Must Know
Russ Morgan And His Orchestra | The Uncollected:Russ Morgan | Hindsight | HSR 145

I Nan Djole
Lionel Hampton And His Sextet | Lionel Hampton-Historical Recording Sessions 1939-1941 | RCA | PM 42417

I Need Some Money
Bud Freeman And His Summa Cum Laude Orchestra | It's Got To Be The Eel, A Tribute To Bud Freeman | Affinity | CD AFS 1008

I Need To Be Bee'd With
Count Basie And His Orchestra | Count Basie: Salle Pleyel, April 17th, 1972 | Laserlight | 36127
Robert Pete Williams | Blues Masters Vol.1-Robert Pete Williams | Storyville | STCD 8001

I Need You Here
Makoto Ozone | Makoto Ozone | CBS | 26198

I Need You Now
Larry O'Neill With The Houston Person Quintet | You Got Me Runnin' | Muse | MCD 5426

I Need Your Kind Of Lovin'-
Duke Jordan Trio | Kiss Of Spain | EmArCy | 510307-2 PMS
I Need's To Bee'd With
Count Basie Big Band | The Montreux '77 Collection | Pablo | 2620107
I Never Felt This Way Before
Anita O'Day With The Buddy Bregman Orchestra | Pick Yourself Up | Verve | 517329-2
I Never Had A Chance
Cheek To Cheek-The Irving Berlin Song Book | Verve | 533829-2
Ella Fitzgerald With Frank De Vol And His Orchestra | Like Someone In Love | Verve | 511524-2
Verve Jazz Masters 6:Ella Fitzgerald | Verve | 519822-2
Ella Fitzgerald With Jackie Davis And Louis Bellson | Lady Time | Original Jazz Classics | OJCCD 864-2(2310825)
Punch Miller With Emanuel Sayles | Punch Miller/Louis Gallaud | American Music | AMCD-68
I Never Had A Chance(alt.take)
Buddy Johnson And His Orchestra | Buddy And Ella Johnson 1953-1964 | Bear Family Records | BCD 15479 DH
I Never Had It So Good
Beverly Kenney With The Basie-Ites | Beverly Kenney | Fresh Sound Records | FSR-CD 33(882158)
I Never Knew
Benny Goodman-Count Basie All Star Octet | Jazz Gallery:Lester Young Vol.1(1936-46) | RCA | 2114171-2
Charleston Chasers | Steaming South | Stomp Off Records | CD 1314
Count Basie And His Orchestra | 100 Ans De Jazz:Count Basie | RCA | 2177831-2
Count Basie-Basie's Basement | RCA | ???
Courtney Williams Sextet | The Changing Face Of Harlem, Vol. 2 | Savoy | SJL 2224 (801200)
Erroll Garner Trio | The Erroll Garner Selection | CBS | 471624-2
Kansas City Five | From Spiritual To Swing | Vanguard | VCD 169/71
Kenny Burrell Quintet | John Coltrane-The Prestige Recordings | Prestige | 16 PCD 4405-2
Kenny Burrell Septet | Swingin' | Blue Note | GXK 8155
Kenny Burrell-John Coltrane Quintet | Kenny Burrell & John Coltrane | New Jazz | NJSA 8276-2
Lester Young Quartet | Verve Jazz Masters 30:Lester Young | Verve | 521859-2
Lester Young:Blue Lester | Dreyfus Jazz Line | FDM 36729-2
Lester Young:The Complete 1936-1951 Small Group Sessions(Studio Recordings-Master Takes),Vol.2 | Blue Moon | BMCD 1002
Mildred Bailey With Paul Baron's Orchestra | The Radio Years: Mildred Bailey With Paul Baron's Orchestra 1944 | Hindsight | HSR 133
Nat King Cole With The Nelson Riddle Orchestra | The Piano Style Of Nat King Cole | Capitol | 781203-2
Tommy Dorsey And His Orchestra | Tommy Dorsey In Concert | RCA | NL 89780 DP
Warne Marsh Quintet | Jazz Of Two Cities | Fresh Sound Records | FSR-CD 342
Intuition | Capitol | 852771-2
I Never Knew-
Daryl Sherman With Orchestra | Look What I Found | Arbors Records | ARCD 19154
I Never Knew Just What A Girl Could Do
Chris Barber's Jazz Band | Chris Barber's Jazz Band | Ace Of Club | ACL 1163
I Never Knew(alt.take)
Warne Marsh Quintet | Jazz Of Two Cities | Fresh Sound Records | FSR-CD 342
Eddie Condon And His Band With Johnny Windhurst | The Doctor Jazz Series,Vol.1:Eddie Condon | Storyville | STCD 6041
I Never Knew(I Could Love Anybody Like I´m Loving You)
Earl Hines | Tour De Force | Black Lion | BLCD 760140
I Never Saw A Better Day
Louis Armstrong With The Hal Mooney Orchestra | Louis Armstrong-The Complete RCA Victor Recordings | RCA | 2668682-2
I Never Told You
June Christy And Her Orchestra | The Misty Miss Christy | Pathe | 1566141(Capitol T 725)
I Never Want To Look Into Those Eyes
Vinny Golia Quintet | Out For Blood | Nine Winds Records | NW 0127
I Never Went Away
John McLaughlin's Free Spirits | Tokyo Live | Verve | 521870-2
I Often Think They Have Merely Gon Out!(from Song of The Death Children)
The Ford Blues Band | Hotshots | Crosscut | CCD 11041
I Only Feel Good With You
Jean-Luc Ponty Quartet | Cosmic Messenger | Atlantic | 7567-81550-2
Abbey Lincoln With The Harold Vick Quartet | A Tribute To Billie Holiday | Enja | 6012-2
I Only Have Eyes For You
Art Tatum | The Tatum Solo Masterpieces Vol.11 | Pablo | 2310864
Benny Goodman Quintet | Seven Come Eleven | CBS | FC 38265
Billie Holiday And Her Trio | Lady Day-The Storyville Concerts | Jazz Door | JD 1215
Bobby Jaspar With The Henri Renaud Quartet | Bobby Jaspar/Henri Renaud | Vogue | 21409372
Claire Austin And Don Ewell | Memories Of You | Audiophile | ACD-143
Coleman Hawkins Quintet | Verve Jazz Masters 43:Coleman Hawkins | Verve | 521856-2
Body And Soul | Naxos Jazz | 8.120532 CD
Dinah Shore With Orchestra | The Best Of Dinah Shore | Capitol | 792895-2
Ella Fitzgerald With Orchestra | Forever Ella | Verve | 529387-2
Erroll Garner | The Erroll Garner Collection Vol.4&5 | EmArCy | 511821-2 PMS
Frank Sinatra With The Count Basie Orchestra | Sinatra-Basie:An Historic Musical First | Reprise | 7599-27023-2
Harold Nicholas And His Orchestra | Jazz In Paris:Harold Nicholas-June Richmond-Andy Bey | EmArCy | 013036-2
Jim Galloway Trio | Music Is My Life | Sackville | SK2CD-5006
Kay Starr With Orchestra | The Uncollected:Kay Star In The 1940's | Hindsight | HSR 214
Lena Horne With The Marty Paich Orchestra | Lena Lovely & Alive | Fresh Sound Records | NL 45988(RCA LSP 2587)
Lionel Hampton And His Orchestra | European Tour 1953 | Royal Jazz | RJD 517
Lionel Hampton Trio | Lionel Hampton:Real Crazy | Vogue | 2113409-2
Louis Armstrong With The Russell Garcia Orchestra | Compact Jazz: Louis Armstrong | Verve | 833293-2
New Jazz Group Hannover | Deutsches Jazz Fesival 1954/1955 | Bear Family Records | BCD 15430
Oscar Peterson Trio | The Song Is You-The Best Of The Verve Songbooks | Verve | 531558-2
Oscar Peterson-Ray Brown Duo | Oscar Peterson:Get Happy | Dreyfus Jazz Line | FDM 36738-2
The Complete Jazz At The Philharmonic On Verve 1944-1949 | Verve | 523893-2
Paul Smith Trio | By The Fireside | Savoy | SV 0225(MG 12094)
Spike Jones And His Other Orchestra | The Uncollected:Spike Jones | Hindsight | HSR 185(835797)
Stan Kenton And His Orchestra | Innovations-Live 1951 | Bandstand | BDCD 1519
Warren Vaché Sextet | Jillian | Concord | CJ 87
Wolfgang Lauth Quartet | Lauther | Bear Family Records | BCD 15717 AH
Simon Schott | Bar Piano: Simon Schott Plays Your Favorite Evergreens Vol.1 | Organic Music | ORGM 9733
I Only Have Eyes For You-
Coleman Hawkins Quintet | Ultimate Coleman Hawkins selected by Sonny Rollins | Verve | 557538-2
I Only Have Eyes For You(alt.take)
Sandy Lomax With Band | Trance Jazz | clearaudio | WOR 171 CD
I Only Miss Her When I Think Of Her
Meredith d´Ambrosia Group | Little Jazz Bird | Sunnyside | SSC 1040 D
I Piaceri D'Amore
Tommy Dorsey And His Orchestra | The Original Sounds Of The Swing Era Vol. 8 | RCA | CL 05521 DP
I Pitched My Tend
Marty Ehrlich Quartet | Song | Enja | ENJ-9396 2
I Pity The Door Immigrant
Bobby Bland And His Band | Bobby Bland The Voice: Duke Recordings 1959-1969 | Ace Records | CDCHD 323
I Put A Spell On You
Nina Simone With Hal Mooney's Orchestra | Verve Jazz Masters 17:Nina Simone | Verve | 518198-2
In Concert/I Put A Spell On You | Mercury | 846543-2
Nina Simone With Orchestra | Nina Simone-The 60s Vol.1: Ne Me Quitte Pas | Mercury | 838543-2 PMS
Jerry Granelli Sextet | A Song I Thought I Heard Buddy Sing | ITM-Pacific | ITMP 970066
I Put My Live In Your Hands-
John Lee Hooker | The Real Folk Blues | Chess | CHD 9271(872291)
I Realize Now
Nat King Cole Trio | The Early Forties | Fresh Sound Records | FSR-CD 0139
Nat King Cole Trio:The MacGregor Years 1941/45 | Music & Arts | CD 911
I Remember
Ferenc Snétberger Trio | Obsession | TipToe | TIP-888834 2
Joel Futterman-Robert Adkins | Vision In Time | Silkheart | SHCD 125
I Remember April
Duke Jordan Trio | Tivoli One | Steeplechase | SCCD 31189
Susannah McCorkle With The Allen Farnham Orchestra | From Broadway To Bebop | Concord | CCD 4615
I Remember Bird
Lou Colombo Quintet | I Remember Bobby | Concord | CCD 4435
I Remember Britt
Lee Morgan Quintet | We Remember You | Fresh Sound Records | FSCD 1024
I Remember Clifford
Art Blakey And The Jazz Messengers | Jazz Gallery:Lee Morgan Vol.1 | RCA | 2127281-2
Benny Golson Quartet | Up Jumped Benny | Arkadia Jazz | 70741
Benny Golson Sextet With Curtis Fuller | California Message | Timeless | CD SJP 177
Bud Powell Trio | The Return Of Bud Powell | Fresh Sound Records | FSR 545(Roulette R 52115)
Court-Candiotto Quintet | Live In Montreux | Plainisphare | PAV 811
Dizzy Gillespie Band | Dizzy Gillespie At Newport | Verve | 513754-2 PMS
Don Lanphere/Marc Seales | Don Loves Midge | Hep | 2027
Lajos Dudas Quintet | Some Great Songs | double moon | DMCD 1005-2
Lee Morgan Sextet | Lee Morgan Vol.3 | Blue Note | 300159(1557)
Modern Jazz Quartet | European Concert | Atlantic | SD 2-603
Oscar Peterson Quartet | The Very Tall Band | Telarc Digital | CD 83443
Oscar Pettiford And His Birdland Band | Jazz On The Air Vol.6: Oscar Pettiford And His Birdland Band | Spotlite | SPJ 153
Roger Guerin Quintet | Roger Guerin(Prix Django Reinhardt 1959) | Fresh Sound Records | 054 2611291(Columbia FP 1117)
Stan Getz Quartet | Stan Getz In Denmark1958-59 | Olufsen Records | DOCD 6011
Stan Getz With The Eddie Louiss Trio | Dynasty | Verve | 839117-2
Stan Getz-Kenny Barron | Stan Getz Cafe Montmartre | EmArCy | 586755-2
Superblue | Superblue | Blue Note | 791731-2
Tete Montoliu Trio | Hot House | Steeplechase | SCCD 37027/28
Louie Bellson Septet | Prime Time | Concord | CCD 4064
I Remember Dexter
Paquito D'Rivera Orchestra | A Night In Englewood | Messidor | 15829 CD
I Remember Eric Dolphy
Chuck Flores Quintet | Drum Flower | Concord | CJ 49
I Remember Harlem
Roy Eldridge Quartet | Rare Broadcasts | Duke Records | D 1010
I Remember Love
Bill Hardman Septet | Home | Muse | MR 5152
I Remember Sky
Philippe LeJeune Trio | At Blue Moon,Houston Texas | Black & Blue | BLE 59.218 2
I Remember Wes
George Benson And His Orchestra | Blue Benson | Polydor | 2391242 IMS
George Benson With Orchestra | The Silver Collection: George Benson | Verve | 823450-2 PMS
I Remember Wolfred
Adonis Rose Quintet | The Unity | Criss Cross | Criss 1173
I Remember You
Bud Freeman Quartet | Stop Look And Listen To Bud Freeman | Affinity | AFF 112
Charlie Parker at 'Bob Reisner presents Bird' | Bird's Eyes Last Unissued Vol.25 | Philology | W 855.2
Charlie Parker Quartet | The Verve Years(1952-54) | Verve | 2-2523 IMS
Charlie Parker | Verve | 539757-2
Chet Baker Quartet | Let's Get Lost: The Best Of Chet Baker Sings | Pacific Jazz | 792932-2
Chet Baker Quintet | I Remember You | Circle Records | RK 28-23581/28 IMS
Dave Brubeck Quartet | Jazz At The College Of The Pacific | Original Jazz Classics | OJC20 047-2(F 3223)
The Dave Brubeck Quartet feat. Paul Desmond In Concert | Fantasy | FCD 60-013
The Art Of Dave Brubeck - The Fantasy Years:Jazz At Oberlin/College OPacific | Atlantic | SD 2-317
Doug Raney Quartet | Introducing Doug Raney | Steeplechase | SCS 1082
Ella Fitzgerald With The Nelson Riddle Orchestra | Love Songs:The Best Of The Song Books | Verve | 531762-2
The Johnny Mercer Songbook | Verve | 823247-2 PMS
Hampton Hawes Trio | Everybody Likes Hampton Hawes | Original Jazz Classics | OJCCD 421-2
Holly Slater Quartet | The Mood Was There | Ronnie Scott's Jazz House | JHCD 053
Ian McDougall Quartet | The Warmth Of The Horn | Concord | CCD 4652
Joe Pass Quartet | Nuages | Pablo | 2310961-2
Joe Pass Quintet | One For My Baby | Pablo | 2310936-2
Johnny Griffin Quartet | Blue Trails-The Rare Tracks | Blue Note | 300191
June Christy With The Pete Rugolo Orchestra | The Song Is June | Capitol | 855455-2
Kenny Burrell Trio | Tin Tin Deo | Concord | CCD 4045
Lee Konitz Trio | Motion | Verve | 065510-2
Motion | Verve | 557107-2
Lennie Niehaus Quintet | Vol.1:The Quintets | Original Jazz Classics | OJC 319(C 3518)
Philip Catherine Trio | I Remember You | Criss Cross | Criss 1048
Stan Kenton And His Orchestra | At The Rendezvous Vol.1 | Status | CD 102(882198)
Tal Farlow Trio | Tal Farlow Complete 1956 Private Recordings | Definitive Records | DRCD 11263
The Hi-Lo's | The Hi-Lo's! Back Again | MPS | 68217
I Remember You-
Roy Eldridge-Benny Carter Quintet | The Urban Sessions/New Jazz Sound | Verve | 531637-2
Warren Vaché Quintet | Warren Plays Warrey | Nagel-Heyer | CD 033
I Remember You From Somewhere
Lee Konitz Trio | Motion | Verve | 557107-2
I Remember You(alt.take)
Roy Eldridge-Benny Carter Quintet | The Complete Verve Roy Eldridge Studio Sessions | Verve | 9861278
I Remember You(alt.take)-
Lee Konitz Trio | Motion | Verve | 557107-2
I Repeat Myself II-
Fats Waller And His Rhythm | The Last Years 1940-1943 | Bluebird | ND 90411(3)
I Rolled And Turned And Cried The Whole Night Long
Ronnie Cuber Quintet | Cubism | Fresh Sound Records | FSR-CD 0188
I Rowed A Little Boat
Alberto Barattini Quartet | Panta Rei | SPLASC(H) Records | H 175
I Said I Wasn't Gonna Tell Nobody
Montreal Jubilation Gospel Choir | Jubilatio III-Glory Train | Blues Beacon | BLU-1008 2
I Said No
Art Studio & Tiziana Ghiglioni | Onde | SPLASC(H) Records | CD H 133-2
I Saw Stars
Carroll Gibbons And The Savoy Hotel Orpheans | Brighter Than The Sun | Saville Records | SVL 174 IMS
Stephane Grappelli Quintet | Hommage A Django Reinhardt | Festival | Album 120
I Saw The Sky
David Bowne Trio | One Way Elevator | DIW | DIW 920 CD
I Say A Little Prayer
Mikesch Van Grümmer | Bar-Piano | Timeless | CD SJP 362
Urbie Green His Trombone And Rhythm | The Best Of New Broadway Show Hits | Fresh Sound Records | NL 45907(RCA LPM 1969)
I See A Million People
Una Mae Carlisle With John Kirby And His Orchestra | TheComplete Una Mae Carlisle(1940-1942) And John Kirby(1941-1942) | RCA | ND 89484
I See Everybody's Baby
Roy Eldridge With The George Williams Orchestra | Rockin' Chair | Verve | MV 2686 IMS
I See Thy Form
Tubby Hayes And The All Stars | Rahsaan/The Complete Mercury Recordings Of Roland Kirk | Mercury | 846630-2
I See With My Third 'I'
Louie Bellson Sextet | Side Track | Concord | CJ 141
I See You Again-
Gary Wiggins Group | Time For Saxin' | Acoustic Music Records | AMC 1012
I See You Now
Ed Schuller Quartet feat. Dewey Redman | Mu-Point | Tutu Records | 888154-2*
I See You Now(for Jim Pepper)
Mal Waldron Quartet | Mal,Verve,Black & Blue | Tutu Records | 888170-2*
John Lee Hooker Band | Moanin' The Blues | Charly | CRB 1029
I See Your Face Before Me
Dave McKenna | Dancing In The Dark And Other Music Of Arthur Schwartz | Concord | CCD 4292
John Coltrane With The Red Garland Trio | Settin' The Pace | Original Jazz Classics | OJC20 078-2
Johnny Hartman And His Sextet | Once In Every Life | Bee Hive | BH 7012
Miles Davis Quartet | Green Haze | Prestige | P 24064
Stan Kenton And His Orchestra | Rendezvous With Kenton | Creative World | ST 1057
I Shall Be Released
Dorothy Love Coates And The Original Gospel Harmonettes | The Best Of Dorothy Love Coates And The Original Gospel Harmonettes | Ace Records | CDCHD 343
I Shall Know Him
First Revolution Singers | First Revolution Gospel Singers:A Capella | Laserlight | 24338
I Shall Not Be Moved
George Lewis Trio | George Lewis Plays Hymns | Milneburg Records | MCD 1
The Zion Harmonizers With Rhyhtm And The Olympia Brass Band | Best Of New Orleans Gospel Vol.2 | Mardi Gras Records | MG 1018
I Shot The Sheriff
Jaco Pastorius Trio | Live In Italy & Honestly | Jazzpoint | JP 1059 CD
Jaco Pastorius In New York | Jazz Door | JD 1232/33
I Should Care
Bill Evans Trio | The Second Trio | Milestone | M 47046
Paris 1965 | Royal Jazz | RJD 503
How Deep Is The Ocean | West Wind | WW 2055
Bill Evans:The Secret Sessions | Milestone | 8MCD 4421-2
Bill Evans:The Secret Sessions | Milestone | 8MCD 4421-2
Bill Evans At Town Hall | Verve | 831271-2
Ultimate Bill Evans selected by Herbie Hancock | Verve | 557536-2
Bill Hardman Sextet | What's Up' | Steeplechase | SCS 1254
Bud Powell Trio | The Genius Of Bud Powell-Vol.2 | Verve | 2-2526 IMS
Charles McPherson Sextet | Horizons | Original Jazz Classics | OJCCD 1912-2(P 7603)
Claude Williamson Trio | Tribute To Bud | Eastworld | EWJ 90009
Clifford Jordan And The Magic Triangle | On Stage Vol.2 | Steeplechase | SCCD 31092
Conte Candoli-Carl Fontana Quintet | The Complete Phoenix Recordings Vol.6 | Woofy Productions | WPCD 126
Danny Moss Quartet | Keeper Of The Flame | Nagel-Heyer | CD 064
Dave Ballou Quartet | Rothko | Steeplechase | SCCD 31525
Dexter Gordon Quartet | Hot & Cool | West Wind | WW 2066
Dexter Gordon With The Lionel Hampton Sextet | Dexter Gordon | Jazz Classics | CD CA 36002
Ed Thigpen Ensemble | Young Men & Old | Timeless | CD SJP 330
Ernestine Anderson With Frank Wess And The Gene Harris Quartet | Live At The 1990 Concord Jazz Festival-Third Set | Concord | CCD 4454
Hank Crawford And His Orchestra | South-Central | Milestone | MCD 9201-2
Herman Chittison Trio | Piano Genius | Musicraft | MVS 506
Jay Jay Johnson Quintet | Live At Cafe Bohemia 1957 | Fresh Sound Records | FSR-CD 0143
Joe Pass | Unforgettable | Pablo | 2310964-2
Joe Zawinul Quartet | The Beginning | Fresh Sound Records | FSR-CD 142(882885)
John Abercrombie-John Scofield | Solar | Palo Alto | PA 8031
June Christy With Orchestra | The Best Of June Christy | Capitol | 792588-2
June Christy With The Pete Rugolo Orchestra | Something Cool(The Complete Mono & Stereo Versions) | Capitol | 534069-2
Knud Jorgensen-Bengt Hanson | Skiss | Touché Music | TMcCD 001
Lee Konitz-Hein Van De Geyn | Hein Van De Geyn Meets Lee Konitz | September | CD 5110
Lorez Alexandria And Her Quintet | I'll Never Stop Loving You | Muse | MCD 5457
Lucky Thompson With The Gerard Pochonet All-Stars | Paris 1956 | Jazz Anthology | JA 5215
Milt Jackson Quartet | Opus De Funk | Prestige | P 24048
More Genius Of Thelonious Monk | Blue Note | 300194(BNJ 61011)
Neil Richardson Singers With The Metropole Orchestra | A Beautiful Friendship | Koch Jazz | 3-6909-2
Paul Desmond With Strings | Desmond Blue | RCA | 2663898-2
Pee Wee Ellis Quartet | Sepia Tonality | Minor Music | 801040
Philip Catherine/Niels-Henning Orsted-Pedersen | Art Of The Duo | Enja | 8016-2
Rick Hollander Quartet | Accidental Fortune | Concord | CCD 4550
Saxophone Connection | Saxophone Connection | L+R Records | CDLR 45046
Shorty Rogers And The West Coast Giants | Aurex Jazz Festival '83 | Eastworld | EWJ 80269
Steve Wilson Quintet | Blues For Marcus | Criss Cross | Criss 1073
Thelonious Monk | Thelonious Himself | Original Jazz Classics | OJCCD 254-2
Thelonious Monk-The Complete Riverside Recordings | Riverside | 15 RCD 022-2

Solo Monk | CBS | 471248-2
Thelonious Monk Quartet | Monk's Mood | Naxos Jazz | 8.120588 CD
Warren Bernhardt Trio | So Real | dmp Digital Music Productions | CD 532
Weslia Whitefield With The Mike Greensill Quartet | Teach Me Tonight | HighNote Records | HCD 7009

I Should Care(alt.take)
Thelonious Monk Quartet | Thelonious Monk:Complete 1947-1952 Blue Note Recordings | The Jazz Factory | JFCD 22838

I Should Have Known
Junior Cook Quartet | The Place To Be | Steeplechase | SCCD 31240
Wolfgang Haffner International Jazz Quintet | I Should Have Known | Jazz 4 Ever Records:Jazz Network | J4E 4712

I Shouldn't Be Singing
Cal Tjader Quintet | At Grace Cathedral | Fantasy | F 9521

I Sing A Song
Vincent Herring Quintet | Evidence | Landmark | LCD 1527-2

I Sing The Blues
Red Norvo And His Orchestra | Victor Jazz History Vol.20:Jazz & The Blues | RCA | 2135739-2

I Sing,You Sing
Buddy Guy Blues Band | The Blues Giant | Black & Blue | BLE 59.900 2

I Still Do
Stuttgarter Gitarren Trio | Stuttgarter Gitarren Trio Vol.2 | Edition Musikat | EDM 034
Ella Fitzgerald And The Ink Spots | Ella:The Legendary American Decca Recordings | GRP | GRP 46482

I Still Love Him So
Roy Eldridge-Benny Carter Quintet | The Urban Sessions/New Jazz Sound | Verve | 531637-2

I Still Love You
Ella Johnson With Orchestra | Swing Me | Official | 6009

I Still Miss You
Bobby Troup Quartet | The Distinctive Style Of Bobby Troup | Fresh Sound Records | FSR 2024(Bethlehem BCP 35)

I Still Want You-
David Bowne Trio | One Way Elevator | DIW | DIW 920 CD

I Suffer With The Blues
The Zion Harmonizers | Traditional Negro Spirituals | Mardi Gras Records | MG 1013

I Surrender Dear
Art Tatum | The Art Tatum Solo Masterpieces | Pablo | 2625703
Art Tatum Quartet | The Tatum Group Masterpieces | Pablo | 2310734
Ben Webster Quintet | Trav'lin Light | Milestone | M 47056
Bernard Peiffer Trio | Jazz In Paris:The Bernard Peiffer Trio Plays Standards | EmArCy | 018425-2
Bernd Lhotzky | Stridewalk | Jazz Connaisseur | JCCD 0029-2
Bill Harris And Friends | Bill Harris And Friends | Original Jazz Classics | OJC 083(F 3263)
Buck Clayton Quintet | Jazz Legacy 56: Buck Clayton-A La Buck | Vogue | 500106
Claire Austin And Don Ewell | Memories Of You | Audiophile | ACD-143
Coleman Hawkins And The Chocolate Dandies | Commodore Classics In Swing | Commodore | 9031-72723-2
Count Basie Kansas City 3 | For The Second Time | Original Jazz Classics | OJC 600(2310878)
Count Basie-Roy Eldridge Septet | Loose Walk | Pablo | 2310928
Dan Barrett And His Extra-Celestials | Moon Song | Arbors Records | ARCD 19158
Django Reinhardt And The Quintet Du Hot Club De France | The Indispensable Django Reinhardt | RCA | ND 70929
Dutch Swing College Band | 40 Years Dutch Swing College Band:At Its Best | Timeless | TTD 516
Earl Hines | Le Jazz En France Vol.15:Earl Hunes Paris Session 1965 | Pathe | 1552611
Erroll Garner Trio | The Complete Savoy Sessions Vol.2 | Savoy | WL 70542 (809296)
Illinois Jacquet Quintet | Illinois Jacquet:All Stars Studio Recordings 1945-1947(Master Takes) | Blue Moon | BMCD 1011
JATP All Stars | The Complete Jazz At The Philharmonic On Verve 1944-1949 | Verve | 523893-2
Jimmy Rushing/Dave Frishberg | The You And Me That Used To Be | RCA | ND 86460
Joe Venuti-Zoot Sims Quintet | Joe Venuti And Zoot Sims | Chiaroscuro | CR 142
Newport All Stars | Buddy Tate With Humphrey Lyttelton And Ruby Braff | Jazz Colours | 874713-2
Oscar Peterson Trio | Masters Of Jazz Vol.7 | RCA | NL 89721 DP
Paul Bley Trio | Reality Check | Steeplechase | SCCD 31379
Pete Jolly And His West Coast Friends | Strike Up The Band | Eastworld | CP 32-5427
Quintet Du Hot Club De France | Djangology | Bluebird | 2663957-2
Rainer Sander Swing Wing | Shine | Elite Special | 73611
Ruby Braff-Buddy Tate With The Newport All Stars | Ruby Braff-Buddy Tate With The Newport All Stars | Black Lion | BLCD 760138
Thelonious Monk | Monk Alone:The Complete Columbia Solo Studio Recordings | CBS | C2K 65495
Solo Monk | CBS | 471248-2
Wild Bill Davison All Stars | Wild Bill Davison All Stars | Timeless | CD TTD 545
Wrobel-Roberscheuten-Hopkins Jam Session | Jammin' At The IAJRC Convention Hamburg 1999 | Nagel-Heyer | CD 066
All Star Trombone Spectacular | The Progressive Records All Star Trombone Spectacular | Progressive | PRO 7018 IMS

I Surrender Dear-
JATP All Stars | JATP In Tokyo | Pablo | 2620104-2
Ray Bryant | Ray Bryant Plays Blues And Ballads | Jazz Connaisseur | JCCD 9107-2
Lennie Tristano Trio | The Essential Keynote Collection:The Complete Lennie Tristano | Verve | 830921-2

I Surrender Dear(alt.take)
Oscar Peterson Trio | This Is Oscar Peterson | RCA | 2663990-2
Red Norvo And His Swing Septet | Knock On Wood | Affinity | CD AFS 1017

I Talk To The Trees
Coleman Hawkins Quartet | Good Old Broadway | Prestige | 0902114(Moodsville MV 23)

I Talk With The Spirits
Roland Kirk Quintet | Rahsaan/The Complete Mercury Recordings Of Roland Kirk | Mercury | 846630-2
Franz De Byl | Franz De Byl-Solo | FMP | SAJ 27

I Think A Lot Of How To Be Smart
Niels Lan Doky Trio | Here Or There | Storyville | STCD 4117

I Think I Got It
Betty Carter And Her Trio | The Audience With Betty Carter | Bet-Car | MK 1003

I Think It's Going To Rain Today
Kenny Burrel Quartet | 'Round Midnight | Original Jazz Classics | OJCCD 990-2(F 9417)
Sidsel Endresen-Bugge Wesseltoft | Nightsong | ACT | 9004-2
Stanley Cowell Trio | Sienna | Steeplechase | SCCD 31253

I Think I've Met You Before
Steve Swallow Group | Deconstructed | Watt | XtraWatt/9(537119-2)

I Think My Wife Is A Hat
Billy Taylor Quartet | Where've You Been? | Concord | CJ 145

I Think Of You
Sammy Kaye And His Orchestra | The Uncollected:Sammy Kaye | Hindsight | HSR 158
Dino Saluzzi Group | If | Enja | ENJ-9451 2

I Think On It
Mundell Lowe | Souvenirs-A Tribute To Nick Ceroli | The Jazz Alliance | TJA 10011

I Thought
Doug Raney Trio | Guitar Guitar Guitar | Steeplechase | SCCD 31212

I Thought About You
Benny Goodman And His Orchestra | Roll 'Em, Vol.1 | CBS | 460062-2
Bob Berg Quintet | In The Shadows | Denon Compact Disc | CY-76210
Charlie Byrd Trio | Isn't It Romantic | Concord | CCD 4252
Dave Brubeck Quartet | Paper Moon | Concord | CCD 4178
Dinah Washington With The Belford Hendricks Orchestra | What A Diff'rence A Day Makes! | Verve | 543300-2
Dinah Washington With The Walter Rodell Orchestra | The Complete Dinah Washington On Mercury Vol.2 | Mercury | 832448-2
Ellis Marsalis Trio | Ellis Marsalis Trio | Blue Note | 796107-2
Gloria Lynne And Her Band | A Time For Love | Muse | MCD 5381
Harold Danko | This Isn't Maybe... | Steeplechase | SCCD 31471
J.J.Johnson Quintet | Vivian | Concord | CCD 4523
Jeff Jerolamon Trio | Introducing Jeff Jerolamon | Candid | CCD 79522
Joe Pass Quartet | Live At Yoshi's | Pablo | 2310951-2
Keith Jarrett Trio | Bye Bye Blackbird | ECM | 1467(513074-2)
Ken Peplowski Quintet | The Natural Touch | Concord | CCD 4517
Larry Schneider Quintet | Ali Girl | Steeplechase | SCCD 31429
Maxine Sullivan With The Doc Cheatham Quintet | We Just Couldn't Say Goodbye | Audiophile | ACD-128
Miles Davis Quartet | Someday My Prince Will Come | Mobile Fidelity | MFCD 828
Miles Davis Quintet | Miles Davis With John Coltrane | CBS | CBS 88029
Miles Davis In Person-Friday Night At The Blackhawk,San Francisco,Vol.1 | CBS | C4K 87106
Miles Davis With Gil Evans & His Orchestra | Live Miles-More From The Legendary Carnegie Hall Concert | CBS | 460064-2
Mose Allison Trio | Back Country Suite | Original Jazz Classics | OJC 075(P 7091)
Nancy Wilson With The Art Farmer-Benny Golson Quintet | In Performance At The Playboy Jazz Festival | Elektra | MUS 96.0298-1
Paolo Fresu Quintet | Ballads | SPLASC(H) Records | CD H 366-2
Ralph Sutton | More At Cafe Des Copains | Sackville | SKCD2-2036
Stan Getz Quartet | Voyage | Black-Hawk | BKH 51101
Stephane Grappelli Trio | Live | Justin Time | JTR 8469-2
Trudy Desmond With The Roger Kellaway Quartet | Tailor Made | The Jazz Alliance | TJA 10015
Walter Bishop Jr. Group | Summertime | Fresh Sound Records | FSR-CD 0011

I Thought About You(alt.take)
Özay With Band | Antiquared Love | Basic | 50004

I Thought I Heard Buddy Bolden Say
Jelly Roll Morton's New Orleans Jazzmen | Jazz Special-The Best Of Jelly Roll Morton | RCA | CL 43291 AF
Morton Gunnar Larsen | Maple Leaf Rag | Herman Records | HJCD 1009

I Thought I Knew You
Carmen McRae With The Dixie Flyers | Just A Little Lovin' | Atlantic | AMCY 1079

I Thought I'd Let You Know
Herbie Hancock Group | Directstep | CBS | SRCS 9503

I Thought It Was You
James Clay Quartet | Lorraine Geller Memorial | Fresh Sound Records | FSR-CD 0195

I Thought You Knew
Nat King Cole Trio | Nat King Cole Vol.3 | Laserlight | 15748

I Threw A Kiss In The Ocean
Warren Vaché Trio | Midtown Jazz | Concord | CJ 203

I Told You So
Frank Morgan-George Cables Duo | Double Image | Contemporary | CCD 14035-2

I Took Up The Runes
Mani Neumeir Group | Privat | ATM Records | ATM 3803-AH

I TouchYour Skin
Anita Moore And Her All Stars | The Lady | Zeus Records | Z 1000

I Tought About You
Jeremy Davenport Quartet | Maybe In A Dream | Telarc Digital | CD 83409

I Used To Be Colour Blind
Anita O'Day And Her Combo | Pick Yourself Up | Official | 3015
Benny Goodman And His Orchestra | More Camel Caravans | Phontastic | NCD 8843/4
Dave Pell Octet | The Dave Pell Octet Plays Irving Berlin | Fresh Sound Records | 252963-1(Kapp KL 1036) (835207)
Ella Fitzgerald With Paul Weston And His Orchestra | The Complete Ella Fitzgerald Song Books of Harold Arlen, Irving Berlin, Duke Ellington, George & Ira Gershwin, Jerome Kern, Johnny Mercer, Cole Porter And Rogers & Hart | Verve | 519832-2

I Used To Love You
Nat King Cole Trio | Great Capitol Masters | Pathe | 1566251(Capitol)

I Used To Love You(But It's All Over Now)
George Brunis And His Jazzband | The Davison-Brunis Sessions Vol. 3 | London | HMC 5013 AN

I Waited For You
Art Farmer Quartet | Sing Me Softly Of The Blues | Atlantic | 7567-80773-2
Brian Lynch Quintet | Back Room Blues | Criss Cross | Criss 1042
Chet Baker Trio | The Touch Of Your Lips | Steeplechase | SCCD 31122
Clifford Jordan Big Band | Play What You Feel | Mapleshade | 03232
Dizzy Gillespie Quintet | Jazz In Paris:Dizzy Gillespie-The Giant | EmArCy | 159734-2 PMS
Dizzy Gillespie Sextet | The Giant | America | AM 6133
Miles Davis All Stars | Miles Davis Vol.2 | Blue Note | 532611-2
Miles Davis Quartet | Ballads & Blues | Blue Note | 836633-2
Miles Davis Sextet | Miles Davis:The Blue Note And Capitol Recordings | Blue Note | 827475-2
Dizzy Gillespie And His Orchestra | Bebop Enters Sweden | Dragon | DRCD 318

I Walk A Little Faster
Bill Charlap Trio | Stardust | Blue Note | 535985-2

I Walk With Music
Wayne Bartlett With The Thomas Hufschmidt Trio And Wolfgang Engstfeld | Senor Blues | Laika Records | LK 95-066
Michael Mantler Group | Silence | Watt | 5 (2313105)

I Walk With My Girl
Michael Mantler: No Answer/Silence | Watt | 2/5(543374-2)
Benny Goodman And His Orchestra | The King Of Swing 1958-1967 Era | Festival | ???

I Wanna Be Around
Peggy Lee With Lou Levy's Orchestra | Pass Me By/Big Spender | Capitol | 535210-2
Tony Bennett With The Marty Manning Orchestra | I Wanna Be Around | CBS | CK 66504

I Wanna Be Good
John Swana Sextet | In The Moment | Criss Cross | Criss 1119

I Wanna Be Loved
Jimmy Reed | The Blues Vol.2 | Intercord | 158601

I Wanna Be Near To You
Jenny Evans And Band | Girl Talk | ESM Records | ESM 9306
Girl Talk | Enja | ENJ-9363 2
Live At The Allotria | BELL Records | BLR 90003

I Wanna Be Your Man
John Lee Hooker Group | Lonesome Mood | Chess | MCD 01365

I Wanna Blow Blow Blow(alt.take)
Illinois Jacquet Trio | The Comeback | Black Lion | BLCD 760160

I Wanna Have Fun
Bob Florence And His Orchestra | Name Band:1959 | Fresh Sound Records | FSCD 2008

I Wanna Hear Swing Songs
George Williams And His Orchestra | Rhythm Was His Business-A Salute To Jimmie Lunceford | Fresh Sound Records | ND 42128

I Wanna Know
Doc Cheatham Sextet | A' Portrait Of Jan Jankeje | Jazzpoint | JP 1054 CD

I Wanna Little Girl Like Mama
Guitar Slim And His Band | The Things That I Used To Do | Ace Records | CDCHD 318

I Wanna Ride You
American Folk Blues Festival | American Folk Blues Festival '62 | L+R Records | LR 42017

I Wanna Smell That Thing
Bobby Hutcherson Quartet | In The Vanguard | 32 Jazz | 32170

I Wanna Testify
Eddie Guitar Burns With The Blueshounds | The Blues Vol.3 | Big Bear | 156400

I Wanne Be Around My Baby All The Time
Ambrose And His Orchestra | The Classic Years In Digital Stereo: Dance Bands U.K. | CDS Records Ltd. | RPCD 303(CD 681)

I Want A Big Butter And Egg Man
Chilton/Fawkes Feetwarmers | Melody Maker Tribute To Louis Armstrong Vol.2 | Jazz Colours | 874768-2
Rod Mason Sextet | Great Having You Around | Black Lion | 147011

I Want A Girl
Tiny Hill And His Orchestra | The Uncollected:Tiny Hill | Hindsight | HSR 159

I Want A Girl Just Like The Girl That Married Dear Old Dad
Jesse Fuller One Man Band | Brother Lowdown | Fantasy | F 24707

I Want A Little Boy
Kay Starr With The Hal Mooney Orchestra | The One-The Only | Fresh Sound Records | NL 46052(RCA LPM 1149)

I Want A Little Girl
Buck Clayton All Stars | Baden Switzerland 1966 | Sackville | SKCD2-2028
Clark Terry With The Summit Jazz Orchestra | Clark | Edition Collage | EC 530-2
Clark Terry-Bob Brookmeyer Quintet | Gingerbread | Mainstream | MD CDO 711
Count Basie Kansas City Septem | Mostly Blues...And Some Others | Pablo | 2310919-2
Jack McDuff Quartet | Honeydripper | Original Jazz Classics | OJC 222(P 7199)
Louis Armstrong And His Hot Seven | Louis Armstrong-The Complete RCA Victor Recordings | RCA | 2668682-2
Oscar Klein Quartet | Early Oscar Klein(1954-1964) | RST-Records | 91564-2
Roy Eldridge Quartet | The Best Of Roy Eldridge | Pablo | 2310857
T-Bone Walker And His Band | Feeling The Blues | Black & Blue | BLE 59.552 2
The Vaché-Allred-Metz Family Jazz Band | Side By Side | Nagel-Heyer | CD 042
Wild Bill Davis Quartet | Organ 1959 | Jazz Anthology | JA 5132
Lester Young Septet | Laughin' To Keep From Cryin' | Verve | 543301-2

I Want A Little Girl-
Buck Clayton Quintet | Jazz Legacy 56: Buck Clayton-A La Buck | Vogue | 500106

I Want A Little Sugar In My Bowl
Earl Hines And His Orchestra | Deep Forest | Hep | 1003

I Want A Roof Over My Head
Lucky Millinder And His Orchestra | Big Band Bounce & Boogie:Apollo Jump | Affinity | AFS 1004

I Want Dance
Clyde Hart All Stars | Charlie Parker:The Complete 1944-1948 Small Group Sessions(Studio Recordings-Master Takes),Vol.1 | Blue Moon | BMCD 1007

I Want The Waiter With The Water
Ella Fitzgerald And Her Famous Orchestra | Ella Fitzgerald:The Early Years-Part 2 | GRP | GRP 26232

I Want To Be A Popstar
Rosemary Clooney With The Count Basie Orchestra | At Long Last | Concord | CCD 4795

I Want To Be Happy
Art Van Damme Quintet | Keep Going/Blue World | MPS | 529093-2
Benny Goodman And His Jazz Group | Benny Goodman:Bangkok 1956/Basel 1959/Santiago De Chile 1961/Berlin 1980 | TCB Records | TCB 43012
Bob Wilber Quintet | A Man And His Music | J&M Records | J&MCD 503
Bud Powell Trio | The Legacy | Jazz Door | JD 1204
Cal Tjader Quartet | Cool California | Savoy | WL 70511(2)(SJL 2254) DP
Chico Hamilton Quintet | Chico Hamilton Quintet | Pacific Jazz | 300002(PJ 1209)
Joe Venuti-George Barnes Quintet | Gems | Concord | CJ 14
Lester Young Trio | Lester Young Trio | Verve | 521650-2
Oscar Peterson Trio | The History Of An Artist | Pablo | 2625702-2
Pete York & His All Star Group | It's You Or No One | Mons Records | MR 874772
Sonny Rollins Quartet | The Thelonious Monk Memorial Album | Milestone | MCD 47064-2
Sonny Stitt Quartet | Sonny Stitt | Original Jazz Classics | OJCCD 009-2
Sonny Stitt With The Bud Powell Trio | Genesis | Prestige | P 24044
Stan Kenton And His Orchestra | Road Show Vol.1 | Creative World | ST 1019
Stephane Grappelli Quartet | Grapelli Story | Verve | 515807-2
Super Trio | Brotherhood Of Man | L+R Records | CDLR 45095
Thelonious Monk Quartet | Thelonious Monk:85th Birthday Celebration | zyx records | FANCD 6076-2
Till Brönner-Gregoire Peters Quintet | Generations Of Jazz | Minor Music | 801037
Toshiko Akiyoshi Quartet | Amazing Toshiko Akiyoshi | Verve | MV 2579 IMS
Edmond Hall Quartet With Teddy Wilson | Commodore Classics In Swing | Commodore | 9031-72723-2

I Want To Be Loved
Cootie Williams And His Orchestra | Cootie Williams-Typhoon | Swingtime(Contact) | ST 1003
Muddy Waters Group | Muddy Waters-Hard Again | CBS | PZ 34449

I Want To Go Home
Gary McFarland Orchestra | Soft Samba | Verve | MV 2102 IMS

I Want To Live
Nappy Brown And His Orchestra | Don't Be Angry! | Savoy | SV 0259(SJL 1149)

I Want To Play For Ya
Montreal Jubilation Gospel Choir | Jubilation VI 'Looking Back'-Special 20th Anniversary Compilation | Blues Beacon | BLU-1022 22

I Want To See You
Peppermint Harris With Band | Sittin' In With Peppermint Harris | Mainstream | MD CDO 907

I Want To Sing A Song
Alvin Batiste Ensemble | Bayou Magic | India Navigation | IN 1069 CD

I Want To Talk About You
Ella Fitzgerald-Joe Pass Duo | Joe Pass:A Man And His Guitar | Original Jazz Classics | OJCCD 8806-2
Everett Greene With The Houston Person Quartet | My Foolish Heart | Savant Records | SCD 2014
Jerry Bergonzi Quartet | Jerry On Red | Red Records | 123224-2
John Coltrane Quartet | Visit To Scandinavia | Jazz Door | JD 1210
John Coltrane-Live Trane:The European Tours | Pablo | 7PACD 4433-2
The Complete Graz Concert Vol.2 | Magnetic Records | MRCD 105
The European Tour | Pablo | 2308222-2
Live In Stockholm 1963 | Charly | CD 33
The Mastery Of John Coltrane/Vol. 2: To The Beat Of A Different Drum | MCA | IZ 9346/2
Coltrane Live At Birdland | MCA | 2292-54654-2
The Copenhagen Concerts | Ingo | 4
LeeAnn Ledgerwood | Compassion | Steeplechase | SCCD 31477
Pharoah Sanders Quartet | Welcome To Love | Timeless | CD SJP 358

I Want You (She's So Heavy)
Sarah Vaughan And Her Band | Songs Of The Beatles | Atlantic | 16037-2
Sarah Vaughan With Orchestra | Song Of The Beatles | Atlantic | SD 16037

I Want You So Bad
Louis Jordan With The Nelson Riddle Orchestra | Louis Jordan-Let The Good Times Roll: The Complete Decca Recordings 1938-1954 | Bear Family Records | BCD 15557 IH

I Want You To Be My Baby
Sister O.M. Terrell | The Voice Of The Blues-Bottleneck Guitar Masterpieces | Yazoo | YAZ 1046

I Wanted To Say
Stan Getz Quartet | Live In Paris | Dreyfus Jazz Line | FDM 36577-9

I Wants To Stay Here
Louis Armstrong And Ella Fitzgerald With Russell Garcia's Orchestra | Porgy And Bess | Verve | 2-2507 IMS
The Complete Ella Fitzgerald And Louis Armstrong On Verve | Verve | 537284-2
Oscar Peterson Trio | Porgy And Bess | Verve | 519807-2

I Wants To Stay Here(aka I Loves You Porgy)
Buddy DeFranco With The Oscar Peterson Trio And The Russell Garcia Orchestra | Buddy DeFranco And Oscar Peterson Play Gershwin | Verve | 557099-2

I Warn You
Jackie Allen With The Bill Cunlife Sextet | Which? | Naxos Jazz | 86042-2

I Was A Little Too Lonely
Nat King Cole Quintet | After Midnight | Capitol | 520087-2
Wilie Smith With The Nat King Cole Quartet | The Complete After Midnight Sessions | Capitol | 748328-2

I Was Born To Love You
Brownie McGhee & Sonny Terry | Blues Is My Companion | Aves | 146508

I Was Doing Alright
Dexter Gordon Quintet | Doin' Allright | Blue Note | 784077-2
Dexter Gordon:The Complete Blue Note Sixties Sessions | Blue Note | 834200-2
Ella Fitzgerald And Her Savoy Eight | Ella Fitzgerald-The Early Years-Part 1 | GRP | GRP 26182
Louis Armstrong With The Oscar Peterson Quartet | Compact Jazz: Louis Armstrong | Verve | 833293-2
Meredith d'Ambrosio | Another Time | Sunnyside | SSC 1017 D
Oscar Peterson Trio | Oscar Peterson:The Gershwin Songbooks | Verve | 529698-2
At Zardis' | Pablo | 2CD 2620118
Stan Getz And The Oscar Peterson Trio | Stan Getz And The Oscar Peterson Trio | Verve | 2304440 IMS
Sergey Strarostin's Vocal Family | Journey | JA & RO | JARO 4226-2

I Was Fooling The Turkish-
Louis Prima And His Orchestra | Remember | Magic | DAWE 12(882656)

I Watch The Clouds
Michael Mantler Group | Michael Mantler: No Answer/Silence | Watt | 2/5(543374-2)
Christian Rover Trio | New York Impressions | Organic Music | GWR 280595

I Went On Your Wing
Joe Williams With The Jimmy Jones Orchestra | Jump For Joy | Bluebird | 63 52713-2

I Went Out This Morning Over The Countryside(from Songs of A Wayfarer)-
David Benoit Group | Shaken Not Stirred | GRP | GRP 97872

I Werde Jede Nacht Von Ihnen Träumen
Dirty Butter | Memphis Jug Band Vol.2 | Frog | DGF 16

I Will Be Blessed
Al Jarreau With Band | Jarreau | i.e. Music | 557847-2

I Will Be Here For You(Nitakungodea Milele)
Al Jarreau In London | i.e. Music | 557849-2
Golden Gate Quartet | Golden Gate Quartet | CBS | 471559-2

I Will Be There
Pat Metheny | One Quiet Night | Warner | 9362-48473-2

I Will Find The Way
Pink Anderson | The Blues Of Pink Anderson:Ballad & Folksinger Vol.3 | Original Blues Classics | OBCCD 577-2(BV 1071)

I Will Say Goodbye
Bill Evans Trio | I Will Say Goodbye | Original Jazz Classics | OJCCD 761-2(F 9593)
Carmen McRae With The Shirley Horn Trio | Sarah-Dedicated To You | Novus | PD 90546
Rein De Graaff-Koos Serierse | Duo | Timeless | SJP 213

I Will Say Goodbye(alt.take)
Bill Evans Trio | I Will Say Goodbye | Original Jazz Classics | OJCCD 761-2(F 9593)
Nils Landgren Group | Sentimental Journey | ACT | 9409-2

I Will Survive
Miroslav Vitous Quintet | Mountain In The Clouds | Atlantic | SD 1622

I Will Wait For You
Barney Kessel Trio | Autumn Leaves | Black Lion | CD 877634-2
Laura Fygi Meets Michel Legrand | Watch What Happens | Mercury | 534598-2
Laura Fygi With Band | Laura Fygi Live At The North Sea Jazz | Spectra | 9811207
McCoy Tyner Quartet | Prelude And Sonata | Milestone | MCD 9244-2
Michel Legrand Big Band | Michel Legrand Big Band | Verve | 538937-2
Rigmor Gustafsson With The Nils Landgren Quartet And The Fleshquartet | I Will Wait For You | ACT | 9418-2
Toots Thielemans-Kenny Werner Duo | Toots Thielemans & Kenny Werner | EmArCy | 014722-2

I Will Wait For You-
Anglo Italian Quartet | Put It Right Mr.Smoothie | SPLASC(H) Records | CD H 313-2

I Wish
Tok Tok Tok | 50 Ways To Leave Your Lover | Einstein Music | EM 91051
Tuck And Patti | Dream | Windham Hill | 34 10130-2
Urbie Green & Groover Washington Jr.With Davis Matthews Big Band | Senor Blues | CTI | 63029

I Wish I Could Be Free
Amos White's Band | Frank 'Big Boy' Goudie With Amos White | American Music | AMCD-50

I Wish I Could Shimmy Like My Sister Kate
Bill Coleman Quintet | Dicky Wells & Bill Coleman In Paris | Affinity | CD AFS 1004
Dutch Swing College Band | Souvenirs From Holland, Vol. 1 | DSC Production | PA 003 (801060)
Franz Jackson's Original Jass All-Stars feat. Bob Shoffner | Chicago-The Living Legends:Franz Jackson | Original Jazz Classics | OJCCD 1824-2(RLP 9406)
Muggsy Spanier And His Ragtime Band | Jazz Classics In Digital Stereo: Muggsy Spanier 1931 & 1939 | CDS Records Ltd. | REB 687
Paris Washboard | Love Nest | Stomp Off Records | CD 1308
Sonny Clay | Sonny Clay 1922-1960 | Harlequin | HQ 2007 IMS

I Wish I Didn't Love You So
Carl Ravazza And His Orchestra | The Uncollected: Carl Ravazza | Hindsight | HSR 117

I Wish I Knew
Al Casey Sextet | Jumpin' With Al | Black & Blue | BB 873.2
Bill Evans Trio | The Jazz Giants Play Harry Warren:Lullaby Of Broadway | Prestige | PCD 24204-2
Bill Mays | Maybeck Recital Hall Series Volume Twenty-Six | Concord | CCD 4567
Concord Festival All Stars | The 20th Concord Festival All Stars | Concord | CCD 4366
John Coltrane Quartet | John Coltrane:The Classic Quartet-Complete Impulse Studio Recordings | Impulse(MCA) | 951280-2
Karin Krog With The Dexter Gordon Quartet | Some Other Spring | Storyville | STCD 4045
Lorez Alexandria With The Houston Person Sextet | May I Come In | Muse | MCD 5420
Sonny Rollins Quintet | Here's To The People | Milestone | MCD 9194-2
Spike Robinson Quartet | Music Of Harry Warren | Discovery | DS 870 IMS
Wes Montgomery Quintet | So Much Guitar! | Original Jazz Classics | OJC20 233-2
Winston Mankunku Band | Crossroads | ITM Records | ITM 1441

I Wish I Were A Child Again-
Braff/Barnes Quartet | Salutes Rodgers And Hart | Concord | CCD 6007

I Wish I Were In Love Again
Ella Fitzgerald With The Buddy Bregman Orchestra | The Rodgers And Hart Song Book, Vol.1 | Verve | 821579-2 PMS
Rosemary Clooney With The Scott Hamilton Quintet | Show Tunes | Concord | CCD 4364
Stacy Kent With The Jim Tomlinson Quintet | In Love Again | Candid | CCD 79786
Tony Bennett With The Ruby Braff-George Barnes Quartet | My Funny Valentine-The Rogers & Hart Songbook | Verve | 526448-2
Trigger Alpert's All Stars | Trigger Happy! | Fresh Sound Records | RLP 12-225(Riverside)

I Wish You Love
Chet Baker Quartet | Compact Jazz: Chet Baker | Verve | 840632-2 PMS
Frant Green Quartet | Street Of Dreams | Blue Note | 821290-2
Janis Siegel Group | I Wish You Love | Telarc Digital | CD 83551
Rosemary Clooney And Her Sextet | Do You Miss New York? | Concord | CCD 4537
Singers Unlimited | A Capella III | MPS | 68245
Alan Clare With Lenny Bush | Alan Clare's Holland Park:Love Music To Unwind | Master Mix | CHECD 00108

I Wish You Love(alt.take)
Earl Hines | Dinah | RCA | NL 70577

I Wished On The Moon
Art Pepper Quartet | Intensity | Original Jazz Classics | OJCCD 387-2
Bill Perkins With The Metropole Orchestra | I Wished On The Moon | Candid | CCD 79524
Billie Holiday And Her All Stars | Stay With Me | Verve | 511523-2
Billie Holiday And Her Orchestra | Embraceable You | Verve | 817359-1 IMS
Billie Holiday With Teddy Wilson And His Orchestra | Billie Holiday:The Quintessential Vol.1(1933-1935) | CBS | 450987-2
Coleman Hawkins With The Oscar Peterson Quartet | Verve Jazz Masters 43:Coleman Hawkins | Verve | 521856-2
The Genuis Of Coleman Hawkins | Verve | 825673-2 PMS
Dave McKenna | McKenna | Chiaroscuro | CR 202
George Shearing Trio | 500 Miles High | MPS | 68219
Ian Shaw With Band | Soho Stories | Milestone | MCD 9316-2
June Christy With The Pete Rugolo Orchestra | The Song Is June | Capitol | 855455-2
Lennie Niehaus Sextet | Lennie Niehaus Vol.5:The Sextet | Original Jazz Classics | OJCCD 1944-2(C 3524)
Lew Tabackin Quartet | What A Little Moonlight Can Do | Concord | CCD 4617
Lynne Arriale Trio | A Long Road Home | TCB Records | TCB 97952
Morgana King With Orchestra | Looking Through The Eyes Of Love | Muse | MR 5257
Rosemary Clooney With The Scott Hamilton Quintet | Rosie Sings Bing | Concord | CJ 60

I Wished On The Moon-
Ruby Braff-Scott Hamilton Sextet | A First | Concord | CJ 274

I Wished On The Moon(alt.take)
New Dalta Ahk | Reflectativity | Kabell | 2

I Wonder
Clarence Gatemouth Brown Band | One More Mile | Rounder Records | CDRR 2034
Louis Armstrong And His Orchestra | Louis Armstrong Radio Days | Moon Records | MCD 056-2

I Wonder Where My Baby Is Tonight
Quintet Du Hot Club De France | Welcome To Jazz: Django Reinhardt | Koch Records | 322 074 D1

I Wonder Where My Baby Is Tonight(take 1)
Django Reinhardt Vol. 4 | Decca | 180023 AG

I Wonder Where My Baby Is Tonight(take 2)
Django Reinhardt Vol. 4 | Decca | 180023 AG

I Wonder Where Our Love Has Gone
Buddy Johnson And His Orchestra | Wails | Official | 6010
Etta Jones With The Houston Person Quartet | My Buddy | HighNote Records | HCD 7026
American Folk Blues Festival | American Folk Blues Festival '80 | L+R Records | CDLS 42013

I Wonder Who
Zoot Sims Quartet | Zoot Sims:The Complete 1944-1954 Small Group Sessions(Master Takes),Vol.2 | Blue Moon | BMCD 1039

I Wonder Who My Daddy Is
Louisiana Red Group | The Lowdown Back Porch Blues | Sequel Records | NEX CD 213

I Wonder Who's In Love With Me
Helmut Kagerer/Helmut Nieberle | Guitar Moments | Take Twelve On CD | TT 006-2

I Wonder Who's Kissing Her Now
Louis Nelson Big Four | Louis Nelson Big Four Vol.2 | GHB Records | BCD-26

I Wonder Who's Kissing Her Now-
Duke Ellington And His Orchestra | Way Low | Duke Records | D 1015

I Wonder Why
Freddie King Orchestra | My Feeling For The Blues | Repertoire Records | REPCD 4170-WZ
Otis Rush Quartet | Live In Europe | Isabel | BLE 59.921 2

I Won't Be Back
Bull City Red | Bull City Red(1935-1939) | Story Of Blues | CD 3527-2

I Won't Cry Anymore
Dinah Washington With The Jimmy Carroll Orchestra | A Slick Chick(On The Mellow Side)-The Rhythm&Blues Years | EmArCy | 814184-1 IMS
Lou Donaldson Quintet | Swing And Soul | Blue Note | 300172(1566)

I Won't Dance
Anita O'Day With The Buddy Bregman Orchestra | Pick Yourself Up | Official | 3015
Art Tatum | The Tatum Solo Masterpieces Vol.8 | Pablo | 2310793
Art Tatum Quartet | The Tatum Group Masterpieces | Pablo | 2310734
Ella Fitzgerald And Louis Armstrong With The Oscar Peterson Quartet | Ella And Louis Again | Verve | 825374-2
Compact Jazz: Ella Fitzgerald/Louis Armstrong | Verve | 835313-2
Ella Fitzgerald With Orchestra | Forever Ella | Verve | 529387-2
Ernestine Anderson With The George Shearing Trio | A Perfect Match | Concord | CCD 4357
Fred Astaire With The Oscar Peterson Sextet | Fred Astaire Steppin' Out:Astaire Sings | Verve | 523006-2
Marian McPartland Quartet | Portrait Of Marian McPartland | Concord | CCD 4101
Peter Herbolzheimer Orchestra | Music For Swinging Dancers,Vol.2:I Won't Dance | Koala Records | CD P 9
Stephane Grappelli Group | Plays Jerome Kern | GRP | GRP 95422
Vic Juris Trio | Songbook | Steeplechase | SCCD 31843
Lew Stone And His Band | Lew Stone And His Band | Decca | DDV 5005/6 DT

I Won't Dance(alt.take)
Art Tatum-Roy Eldridge Quartet | The Tatum Group Masterpieces Vol.2 | Pablo | 2405425-2

I Won't Say I Will
Sarah Vaughan With The Hal Mooney Orchestra | Sarah Vaughan Sings Gershwin | Verve | 557567-2

I Won't Say I Will(alt.take)
Sarah Vaughan Sings Gershwin | Verve | 557567-2

I Won't Say I Will(rehersal)
Spike Robinson-Gene DiNovi Quartet | Gene DiNovi Meets Spike Robinson-At The Stables | Hep | CD 2071

I Worship You
The Prestige All Stars | Earthy | Original Jazz Classics | OJCCD 1707-2(P 7102)

I Would Do Anything For You
Art Tatum Trio | Art Tatum:Over The Rainbow | Dreyfus Jazz Line | FDM 36727-2
Cap'n John Handy With The Claude Hopkins Band | Introducing Cap'n John Handy | RCA | NL 89503
MOKAVE | MOKAVE Vol.2 | audioquest Music | AQCD 1007
Wild Bill Davison And The Jazz Giants | The Jazz Giants | Sackville | SKCD2-3002

I Would Do Most Anything For You
Art Hodes-Jim Galloway | Live From Toronto's Cafe Des Copains | Music & Arts | CD 610
Rex Stewart Sextet | Trumpet Jive! | Prestige | PCD 24119-2(P 7812/SV 2006)

I Wouldn't Be Where I Am
Jimmy Rowles Trio | The Complete Nocturne Recordings:Jazz In Hollywood Series Vol.1 | Fresh Sound Records | NR 3CD-101

I Wouldn't Change You For The World-
Percy Mayfield With The Phillip Walker Blues Band | Hit The Road Again | Timeless | CD SJP 170

I Wouldn't Tread A Dog
Gregor Hilden-Hans D. Riesop Group | Compared To What...? | Wonderland Records | 319.9014.2

I.C.
Big Bill Broonzy Group | Big Bill Broonzy 1935-1940 | Black & Blue | BLE 59.253 2

I.D.M.A.T.(It Don't Mean A Thing)
Dirk Berger Quartet | Garagenjazz | Jazz Haus Musik | JHM 0090 CD

I.G.
Frank Tannehill | Frank Tannehill(1932-1941) | Story Of Blues | CD 3526-2

I.Q.Blues
Ike Quebec Quintet | The Tenor Sax Album-The Savoy Sessions | Savoy | WL 70812(2) (809331)

Ianicum
Ben Waltzer Trio | For Good | Fresh Sound Records | FSNT 013 CD

Ian's Move
Lazaro Ros Con Mezcla | Cantos | Intuition Records | INT 3080-2

Ibanlayé
R.Angus-J.Greinke | Crossing Ngoli | Ear-Rational | ECD 1033

Icaro
Jamie Findlay | Wings Of Light | Acoustic Music Records | 319.1076.2

Icarus
Ralph Towner-Gary Burton | Matchbook | ECM | 1056(835014-2)
Stefan Scaggiari Trio | Stefanitely | Concord | CCD 4570
Dimitrios Vassilakis Daedalus Project | Labyrinth | Candid | CCD 79776

Icarus In Flight
Jasper Van't Hof Group | Blue Corner | ACT | 9228-2

Icarus(for Henri Matisse)
Marilyn Crispell-Gerry Hemingway Duo | Marilyn Crispell And Gerry Hemingway Duo | Knitting Factory Works | KFWCD 117

Ice Cream
Chris Barber's American Jazz Band | Chris Barber Starportrait | Aves | 156502
Chris Barber's Jazz Band | The Golden Years Of Revibal Jazz,Vol.15 | Storyville | STCD 5520
The Golden Years Of Revival Jazz,Vol 1 | Storyville | STCD 5506
The Very Best Of Dixieland Jazz | Verve | 535529-2
The Best Of Dixieland-Live in 1954/55 | London | 820878-2
40 Years Jubilee At The Opera House Nürnberg | Timeless | CD TTD 590
Punch Miller's Band | Punch Miller 1960 | American Music | AMCD-52
Sweet Emma Barrett And Herr Bell Boys | Mardi Grax Day 1960-Live | 504 Records | 504CD 67

Ice Cream Freezer
Lee Konitz Quintet | Subconcious-Lee | Original Jazz Classics | OJCCD 186-2(P 7004)

Ice Cream Konitz
Trinity | Trinity | Steeplechase | SCCD 31171

Ice Cream(Reprise)
Chris Barber's Jazzband & das Große Rundfunkorchester Berlin,DDR | Jazz Zounds: Chris Barber | Zounds | CD 2720007

Ice Dream
Chris Cheek Quintet | Vine | Fresh Sound Records | FSNT 086 CD

Ice Fall
Horst Grabosch DDT | Die Kälte Des Weltraums | Jazz Haus Musik | JHM 48 CD

Ice Freezes Red
Danny Gatton Septet | New York Stories Volume One | Blue Note | 798959-2

Icebird Song
Thomas Karl Fuchs | Piano Meditation I | Edition Collage | EC 481-2

Iced Tea
Pat Metheny Quartet | Watercolors | ECM | 1097(827409-2)

Icefire
Thomas Heidepriem Quartet | Brooklyn Shuffle | L+R Records | CDLR 45084

Icey
Franz Koglmann Tentet | Ich | Hat Art | CD 6033

Ich Bin Da...
Ekkehard Jost Quartet | Deep | Fish Music | FM 007 CD

Ich Bin Ein Freier Bauernknecht
Ekkehard Jost Quintet | Some Other Tapes | Fish Music | FM 009/10 CD
Kodexx Sentimental | Das Digitale Herz | Poise | Poise 02

Ich Bin Hi-Fi
Heinz Sauer Quintet | Lost Ends:Live at Alte Oper Frankfurt | free flow music | ffm 0594

Ich Bin Kein Held,Das Ist Nicht Mein Job(to whom it may concern)
Uwe Werner-Mick Baumeister Duo | Oh Brother | Chaos | CACD 8067-2

Ich Bin Von Kopf Bis Fuß Auf Liebe Eingestellt
Hartmut Kracht | Kontrabass Pur | Jazz Haus Musik | JHM 0103 CD
Joe Kienemann Trio | All That Jazz Special | Blue Flame | 40742(2132446-2)
Matthias Bröde Quartet | European Faces | Edition Collage | EC 517-2
Max Neissendorfer Trio | Staubfrei | EGO | 95100
Till Brönner Quartet & Deutsches Symphonieorchester Berlin | German Songs | Minor Music | 801057
Lisa Wahland And Her Trio | Marlene | Fine Music | FM 108-2

Ich Bin Von Kopf Bis Fuß Auf Liebe Eingestellt(alt.take)
Werner Lüdi-Burhan Öcal | Grand Bazar | Creative Works Records | CW LP 1012

Ich Brech' Die Herzen Der Stolzesten Frau'n
Der Rote Bereich | Risky Business | ACT | 9407-2

Ich Geh' Zur Polizei
Heiner Goebbels-Alfred Harth Duo | Vom Sprengen Des Gartens | FMP | SAJ 20

Ich Grolle Nicht
Karl Scharnweber Trio | Choral Concert | Nabel Records:Jazz Network | CD 4642

Ich Grüße Dich Am Kreuzesstamm
Ekkehard Jost Quartet | Deep | Fish Music | FM 007 CD

Ich Hab' Des Nachts Geträumet
Uri Caine Ensemble | Love Fugue-Robert Schumann | Winter&Winter | 910049-2

Ich Hab Im Traum Geweint
Till Brönner Group | Love | Verve | 559058-2

Ich Hab Noch Einen Koffer In Berlin
Lyrik-Performance | Ich Brenne Und Ich Werde Immer Brennen | Born&Bellmann | 973110 CD

Ich Habe Rhythmus(I Got Rhythm)
Ulli Bögershausen | Best Of Ulli Bögershausen | Laika Records | LK 93-045

Ich Kann Nicht Länger Warten
Helmut Zacharias Quintet | Ich Habe Rhythmus | Bear Family Records | BCD 15642 AH

Ich Küsse Ihre Hand Madame
Vladimir Estragon | Three Quarks For Muster Mark | TipToe | TIP-888803 2

Ich Liebe Ihn
Franck Band | Looser | Jazz Haus Musik | JHM 43 CD

Ich Nenne Alle Frauen Baby
Göbels-Harth Group | Es Herrscht Uhu Im Land | Japo | 60037 (2360037)

Ich Seh' Die Welt So Gern Durch Meine Sonnenbrille

Brocksi-Quartett | Globetrotter | Bear Family Records | BCD 15912 AH

Ich Sing' Mir Eins
Fun Horns | Choral Concert(Weihnachtsoratorium/Choräle) | KlangRäume | 30090

Ich Warte,Ich Warte
Ekkehard Jost Nonet | Out Of Jost's Songbook | Fish Music | FM 006 CD

Ich Weiß Auch Nicht,Was Los Ist
Max Neissendorfer Trio | Staubfrei | EGO | 95100

Ich Weiß Nicht Was Soll Es Bedeuten
Ulli Bögershausen | Sologuitar | Laika Records | 35101132

Ich Weiß Nicht,Woran In Bin
Best Of Ulli Bögershausen | Laika Records | LK 93-045
Grosses Tanzorchester Vom Palace-Hotel St.Moritz | International Schlager & In Mood mit Teddy Stauffer's Original Teddies | Elite Special | 9522003

Ich Weiß,Es Wird Einmal Ein Wunder Gescheh'n
Mikesch Van Grümmer | Bar-Piano | Timeless | CD SJP 362

Ich Werde Jede Nacht Von Ihnen Träumen
Fun Horns | Choral Concert(Weihnachtsoratorium/Choräle) | KlangRäume | 30090

Ich Will Meine Seele Tauchen
Brocksi-Quartett | Globetrotter | Bear Family Records | BCD 15912 AH

Ich Wüsst' So Gern
Heiner Goebbels/Alfred Harth | Berold Brecht:Zeit wird knapp | Riskant | 568-72414

Ichano
Yuko Gulda Trio | Mellow Sky | Alpha Music | 198805

Ichi-Ban
Ronnie Mathews Quintet | Legacy | Bee Hive | BH 7011

Icing What Comes After
Jim Black Quartet | Alasnoaxis | Winter&Winter | 910061-2

Icon
Jim Black Alasnoaxis | Splay | Winter&Winter | 910076-2

Icratic
Stefania Tallini Trio With Guests | New Life | yvp music | CD 3114

Ics Dance
Attila Zoller Quartet | The Horizon Beyond | ACT | 9211-2

Ictus
Jimmy Giuffre Trio | Paris Jazz Concert:Jimmy Giuffre | Laserlight | 17249
Live In Europe Vol.1 | Raretone | 5018 FC
Paul Bley Quartet | Rejoicing | Steeplechase | SCCD 31274

Ictus-
Albert Collins Blues Band | The Master Of The Telecaster | Crosscut | CCR 1011

Icy Desert
Dinah Washington With Orchestra | In Tribute... | Fresh Sound Records | FSR 628(Roulette R 25244)

I'd Climb The Highest Mountain
Pee Wee Russell Quintet | Portrait Of Pee Wee | Fresh Sound Records | FSR-CD 126(882874)

I'd Love It
Chris Barber's Jazz Band | Barber 's Best | Decca | 6.28128 DP

I'd Rather Drink Muddy Water
Ron Ringwood's Crosscut Bluesband | Earth Tones | Organic Music | ORGM 9722
Sweet Miss Coffy With Band | Mississippi Burnin' Blues | Mardi Gras Records | MG 1017

I'd Rather Go Blind
Etta James & The Roots Band | Burnin' Down he House | RCA | 3411633-2
Etta James With Band | The Late Show-Recorded Live At Marla's Memory Lane Supper Club Vol.2 | Fantasy | FCD 9655-2
Etta James With Orchestra | Peaches | Chess | 427014

I'd Rather Have A Memory Than A Dream
Soesja Citroen Group | Songs For Lovers And Losers | Challenge | CHR 70034

I'd Rather Ride An Elephant
Mark Kramer Trio | Evita En Jazz | Telarc Digital | CD 83422

I'd Take Her To Chicago
Svend Asmussen Sextet | Svend Asmussen Collection Vol.14 | Swan Music | CD 2514-2

Ida Lupino
Charlie Haden Trio | The Montreal Tapes | Verve | 523295-2
Joe Sachse | Ballade Für Jimi Metag | Born&Bellmann | 991503 CD
Paul Bley | Open, To Love | ECM | 1023
Paul Bley Quartet | New Music: Second Wave | Savoy | SJL 2235 (801211)
Yuko Gulda Trio | Mellow Sky | Alpha Music | 198805

Idaho
Avishai Cohen Quartet | The Trumpet Player | Fresh Sound Records | FSNT 161 CD
Benny Carter All Stars | Aurex Jazz Festival '80:Gentlemen Of Swing | Eastworld | EWJ 80188
Count Basie And His Orchestra | Compact Jazz: Count Basie-The Standards | Verve | 841197-2
Gene Krupa Trio | The Drum Battle:Gene Krupa And Buddy Rich At JATP | Verve | 559810-2
The Complete Jazz At The Philharmonic On Verve 1944-1949 | Verve | 523893-2
Jazz At The Philharmonic:Best Of The 1940's Concerts | Verve | 557534-2
Great British Jazz Band | The Great British Jazz Band:Jubilee | Candid | CCD 79720
Harry Edison Sextet | Swing Summit | Candid | CCD 79050
Harry Sweets Edison & His West Coast Friends | Blues For Lovers | Eastworld | CP 32-5430
June Christy With The Johnny Guarnieri Quintet | June Christy And The Johnny Guarnieri Quintet (1949) | Jazz Unlimited | JUCD 2084
Lionel Hampton And His Orchestra | A True Collectors Item | Jazz Archive | 90.506-2
Red Richards-George Kelly Sextet With Doc Cheatham | Groove Move | Jazzpoint | JP 1045 CD
Sonny Stitt Quartet | Tune Up | Muse | MCD 5334
Tatum-Carter-Bellson Trio | The Tatum Group Masterpieces | Pablo | 2625706

Idas Sommarvisa
Thomas Chapin Trio | Third Force | Knitting Factory Works | KFWCD 103

Iddy Bitty
Flavio Boltro-Furio di Castri-Manhu Roche | Immagini | Red Records | NS 210

Identity Crisis
Trombone Summit | Trombone Summit | MPS | 68272

Idgo Now
The Herbie Nichols Project | Dr. Cyclops' Dream | Soul Note | 121333-2

Idicatif
Vienna Art Orchestra | Serapionsmuisc | Moers Music | 02050

Idiom
Duke Ellington And His Orchestra | Duke Ellington Live ! | EmArCy | 842071-2

Idle Moments
Joshua Breakstone Trio | Remembering Grant Green | Paddle Wheel | KICJ 169

Idle While
Christopher Hollyday Quartet | The Natural Moment | Novus | PD 83118

Idole
Jean Goldkette And His Orchestra | The Indispensable Bix Beiderbecke(1924-1930) | RCA | ND 89572

Idoma
Friedeman Graef-Achim Goettert | Saxoridoo | FMP | OWN-90010

Idris
Cecil Taylor Jazz Unit | Cecil Taylor | New World Records | 80201-2

Idyll
Adam Makowicz | From My Window | Candid | CRS 1028 IMS

If
Art Tatum Trio | The Tatum Group Masterpieces | Pablo | 2310735-2
Eliane Cueni Septet | Septett | Elite Special | 73614
George Shearing Trio | Light,Airy And Swinging | MPS | 68094
Joe Pass | Virtuoso No.2 | Pablo | 2310788-2
Larry Young Quartet | Joe Henderson-The Blue Note Years | Blue Note | 789287-2
Mark Murphy And His Septet | I'll Close My Eyes | Muse | MCD 5436
Oscar Peterson-Joe Pass Duo | Live At Salle Pleyel, Paris | Pablo | 2625705
Singers Unlimited | Four Of Us | MPS | 68106

If-
Dave Stryker Octet | Blue To The Bone III | Steeplechase | SCCD 31524

If 6 Was 9
Nguyen Le Trio With Guests | Purple:Celebrating Jimi Hendrix | ACT | 9410-2
Spanish Fly | Rags To Britches | Knitting Factory Works | KFWCD 114

If Dreams Come True
Benny Goodman And His Orchestra | Jazz Giants:Benny Goodman | RCA | NL 89731 SI
The Indispensable Benny Goodman Vol.3/4 | RCA | 2115520-2
Paris Washboard | 10'eme Anniversaire:Love For Sale | Stomp Off Records | CD 1326
Ralph Sutton Trio | Pocketful Of Dreams | Sackville | SKCD2-3062
Summit Reunion | Jazz Im Amerikahaus,Vol.5 | Nagel-Heyer | CD 015
Teddy Wilson Sextet | Everytime We Say Goodbye | Musicraft | MSVCD-59
Warren Vaché-Allen Vaché Sextet | Mrs.Vaché's Boys | Nagel-Heyer | CD 050
Excelsior New Orleans Brass Band | Excelsior New Orleans Brass Band | Bartrax | BARX 051 CD

If Ever I Would Leave You
Lester Lanin And His Orchestra | The Uncollected:Lester Lanin | Hindsight | HSR 210
Sonny Rollins Septet | Masters Of Jazz Vol.14 | RCA | CL 42874 AG
Mildred Bailey And Her Orchestra | Squeeze Me | Affinity | CD AFS 1013

If I Break
G.Q.Williams & Dave Collett | Back To The Boogie | Jazz Colours | 874735-2

If I Can Just Make It Into Heaven
Ruth Brown With The Rodney Forrester Orchestra | Blues On Broadway | Fantasy | FCD 9662-2

If I Could
Roy Haynes Quintet | Te-Vou! | Dreyfus Jazz Line | FDM 36569-2

If I Could Be With You One Hour Tonight
Benny Goodman And His Orchestra | The Birth Of Swing | Bluebird | ND 90601(3)
Buck Clayton And His Orchestra | Cat Meets Chick | Fresh Sound Records | FSR 1001(CBS CL 778)
Carmen McRae With Orchestra | Woman Talk | Mainstream | MD CDO 706
Cootie Williams And His Orchestra | Cootie In Hi-Fi | RCA | NL 89811
Count Basie Kansas City 7 | Count Basie Kansas City 7 | Pablo | 2310908-2
Della Reese With The Neal Hefti Orchestra | Della | RCA | 2663912-2
Della | RCA | 2663912-2
Dinah Washington With The Eddie Chamblee Orchestra | Dinah Sings Bessie Smith | Verve | 538635-2
Doc Cheatham Sextet | Hey Doc! | Black & Blue | BLE 59.090 2
Dutch Swing College Band With Johnny Meyer | Johnny Goes Dixie | DSC Production | PA 1014 (801069)
Eddie Condon And His Band With Johnny Windhurst | The Doctor Jazz Series,Vol.1:Eddie Condon | Storyville | STCD 6041
Erroll Garner | The Erroll Garner Collection Vol.4&5 | EmArCy | 511821-2 PMS
Helen Humes With Roy Milton's Band | E-Baba-Le-Ba The Rhythm And Blues Years | Savoy | WL 70824 (809326)
Jack Teagarden And His Orchestra | Varsity Sides | Savoy | WL 70827 (809324)) SF
Marcus Roberts | If I Could Be With You | Novus | 4163149-2
McKinney's Cotton Pickers | McKinney's Cotton Pickers 1928/1930 | Zeta | ZET 743
Oscar Peterson Quartet | Masters Of Jazz Vol.7 | RCA | NL 89721 DP
The New York Allstars | We Love You,Louis! | Nagel-Heyer | CD 029
Tom Saunders' 'Wild Bill Davison Band' & Guests | Exactly Like You | Nagel-Heyer | CD 023
Trevor Richards New Orleans Trio | The Trevor Richards New Orleans Trio | Stomp Off Records | CD 1222
V-Disc All Stars | Texas Tea Party | Naxos Jazz | 8.120585 CD

If I Could Be With You One Hour Tonight(incomplete)
Jay McShann-Buddy Tate Duo | Crazy Legs & Friday Strut | Sackville | 3011

If I Could Hear My Mother Pray Again
The Staple Singers | Uncloudy Day | Joy | 5019

If I Didn't Care
Count Basie And His Orchestra | Count Basie And His Great Vocalists | CBS | CK 66374
Singers Unlimited With The Robert Farnon Orchestra | Sentimental Journey | MPS | 68102

If I Did-Would You
Duke Jordan Trio | Tivoli One | Steeplechase | SCCD 31189

If I Ever Cease To Love You
Ken Colyers's Jazzmen | Sensation!:The Decca Years 1955-59 | Lake | LACD 1

If I Fell
Joshua Breakstone Quartet | The Composition Of The Beatles Vol.1: I Want To Hold Your Hand | Paddle Wheel | KICJ 122

If I Find You Again
Ahmad Jamal Quartet | Nature(The Essence Part III) | Atlantic | 3984-23105-2
Ahmad Jamal-Othello Molineaux | Nature(The Essence Part III) | Atlantic | 3984-23105-2
Claude Thornhill And His Orchestra | Snowfall | Fresh Sound Records | NL 46030(RCA)

If I Gave My Heart To You-
J.B.Lenoir | J.B.Lenoir | Blues Classics(L+R) | CDLR 82001

If I Had A Talking Picture Of You
Les Brown And His Orchestra | Les Brown And His Orchestra 1944 & 1946 | Circle | CCD-90

If I Had Known
Stan Kenton And His Orchestra | The Complete MacGregor Transcriptions Vol.2 | Naxos Jazz | 8.120518 CD

If I Had My Druthers
Billy Wright Band | Goin' Down Slow | Savoy | SV 0257

If I Had Possession Over Judgement Day
Robert Johnson | Classic Blues | Zounds | CD 2700048
Al Fairweather Band | Fairweather Friends Made To Measure | Lake | LACD 75

If I Had You
Art Blakey And The Jazz Messengers(Art Blakey Quintet) | Clifford Brown:The Complete Blue Note And Pacific Recordings | Blue Note | 834195-2
Art Tatum | Art Tatum:Over The Rainbow | Dreyfus Jazz Line | FDM 36727-2
The Art Tatum Solo Masterpieces | Pablo | 2625703
Bernard Peiffer Trio | Jazz In Paris:The Bernard Peiffer Trio Plays Standards | EmArCy | 018425-2
Bob Haggart's Swing Three | Hag Leaps In | Arbors Records | ARCD 19156
Cal Collins Trio | Cincinnati To L.A. | Concord | CJ 59
Count Basie And His Orchestra | En Concert Avec Europe 1 | Laserlight | 710706/07
Dick Hyman Orchestra | Swing Is Here | Reference Recordings | RR-72 CD
Django Reinhardt-Stephane Grappelli Duo | The One And The Only | Decca | 6.28589 DP
Eddie Lockjaw Davis Quartet | Eddie 'Lockjaw' Davis | Divox | CDX 48701
Ernst Höllerhagen Quartet | Ernst Höllerhagen 1942-1948 | Elite Special | 9522001
Freddy Martin And His Orchestra | The Uncollected:Freddy Martin, Vol.2 | Hindsight | HSR 169
Guy Lafitte Sextet | Jazz In Paris:Guy Lafitte-Blue And Sentimental | EmArCy | 159852-2 PMS
Harry James And His Orchestra | The Uncollected:Harry James, Vol.5 | Hindsight | HSR 142
Henri Renaud All Stars | Jazz Legacy 30: J.J.Johnson/Milt Jackson-A Date In New York Vol.1 | Vogue | 500080
Jackie And Roy With The Charlie Ventura Band | Jackie And Roy:Jazz Classics By Charlie Ventura's Band | Savoy | SV 0218(MG 6057)
Joe Pass Quartet | Nuages | Pablo | 2310961-2
Joe Turner Trio | Joe Turner | Black & Blue | BLE 233031
Lee Konitz Quartet | Lee Konitz In Harvard Square | Black Lion | BLCD 760928
Lennie Tristano Quartet | That's Jazz Vol.15: Lennie Tristano | Atlantic | ATL 50245
Merseysippi Jazz Band 1954-1957 | Mersey Tunnel Jazz | Lake | LACD 85
Muggsy Spanier And His Dixieland All Stars | Muggsy Spanier At Club Hangover 1953/54 | Storyville | STCD 6033
At Club Hangover-Vol. 2 | Storyville | SLP 249
Nat King Cole Trio | Nat King Cole:For Sentimental Reasons | Dreyfus Jazz Line | FDM 36740-2
Nat King Cole Trio 1943-49-The Vocal Sides | Laserlight | 15718
Oscar Peterson-Milt Jackson Duo | Two Of The Few | Original Jazz Classics | OJCCD 689-2(2310881)
Oscar Peterson-Stephane Grappelli Quartet | Jazz In Paris:Oscar Peterson-Stephane Grappelli Quartet Vol.2 | EmArCy | 013029-2
Peanuts Hucko Quintet | Tribute To Louis Armstrong And Benny Goodman | Timeless | TTD 541/42
Roy Eldridge And His Orchestra | The Complete Verve Roy Eldridge Studio Sessions | Verve | 9861278
Roy Eldridge Quartet | Frenchie Roy | Vogue | 655009
Sheila Jordan With Te Alan Broadbent Trio And The Hiraga String Quartet | Heart Strings | Muse | MCD 5468
Stephane Grappelli-Django Reinhard | A Swinging Affair | Decca | 6.24725 AO

If I Had You-
Dizzy Gillespie-Roy Eldridge Sextet | Diz And Roy | Verve | 2-2524 IMS
Norman Granz Jam Session | Jam Session No. 3 | Verve | 2304421 IMS
Roy Eldridge-Dizzy Gillespie With The Oscar Peterson Quartet | Roy And Diz | Verve | 521647-2
Art Tatum Trio | The Complete Trio Sessions Vol.2 | Official | 3002

If I Had You(alt.take)
Henri Renaud All Stars | Jazz Legacy 46: Jay Jay Johnson/Al Cohn-A Date In New York Vol.2 | Vogue | 500096

If I Knew Then(What I Know Now)
Joe Farrell Quintet | Sonic Text | Contemporary | C 14002

If I Lose
Maggie Jones With Louis Armstrong And Fletcher Henderson | Louis Armstrong And The Blues Singers 1924-1930 | Affinity | AFS 1018(6)

If I Love Again
Cannonball Adderley Quintet | Cannonball's Sharpshooters | Mercury | 826986-2 PMS
Charlie Parker And His Orchestra | Bird On Verve-Vol.7:Charlie Parker Big Band | Verve | 817448-1 IMS
Charlie Parker With Orchestra | Charlie Parker Big Band | Verve | 559835-2
Charlie Parker With Orchestra & The Dave Lambert Singers | The Verve Years(1952-54) | Verve | 2-2523 IMS
Clifford Brown-Max Roach Quintet | Brownie-The Complete EmArCy Recordings Of Clifford Brown | EmArCy | 838306-2
Domenic Landolf Quartet | Levitation | JHM Records | JHM 3616
Donald Byrd Quartet | Donald Byrd & Doug Watkins:The Tradition Sessions | Blue Note | 540528-2
Donald Byrd Quintet | Long Green | Muse | 650137(882380)

If I Love You
Bud Powell Trio | The Return Of Bud Powell | Fresh Sound Records | FSR 545(Roulette R 52115)

If I Loved You
Charles McPherson Quintet | Bebop Revisited! | Original Jazz Classics | OJCCD 710-2(P 7359)
Fred Hersch | Maybeck Recital Hall Series Volume Thirty-One | Concord | CCD 4596
Paul Bley/Jesper Lundgaard | Live Again | Steeplechase | SCCD 31230
Rahsaan Roland Kirk Sextet | Bright Moments | Rhino | 8122-71409-2

If I Only Had A Brain
Philip DeGruy | Innuendo Out The Other | NYC-Records | NYC 6013-2

If I Perish
Artie Shaw And His Orchestra | Original Recordings 1937/1938 | Festival | Album 248

If I Should Lose You
Benny Golson Orchestra | Walkin' | Fresh Sound Records | FSR-CD 0302
Booker Little Sextet | Booker Little And Friends | Bethlehem | BTM 6821
Charlie Parker With Strings | Charlie Parker:April In Paris | Dreyfus Jazz Line | FDM 36737-2
Charlie Parker: The Verve Years (1948-50) | Verve | 2-2501 IMS
Charlie Parker With Strings:The Master Takes | Verve | 523984-2
Chet Baker Group | My Funny Valentine-Live At The Salt Peanuts Club, K In | Circle Records | RK 24-23581/24 IMS
Haze Greenfield Group | All About You | Black-Hawk | BKH 535 CD
Herb Ellis Quartet | Soft & Mellow | Concord | CCD 4077
James Zollar Quintet | Soaring With Bird | Naxos Jazz | 86008-2
Jesse Davis Quintet | From Within | Concord | CCD 4727
Joe Bonner Trio | New Life | Steeplechase | SCCD 31239
Joe Pisano And Friends | Joe Pisano:Among Friends | Pablo | 2310956-2
Ken Peplowski/Howard Alden | Concord Duo Series Volume Three | Concord | CCD 4556
Milt Jackson Quartet | Ain't But A Few Of Us Left | Pablo | 2310873-2
Montgomery Brothers | Groove Brothers | Milestone | M 47051
Monty Alexander-Ernest Ranglin Duo | Monty Alexander - Ernest Ranglin | MPS | 68269
Nina Simone Quintet | Nina Simone-The 60s Vol.3:Work Song | Mercury | 838545-2 PMS
Oscar Peterson | Tracks | MPS | 68084
Paul Bley | Solo Piano | Steeplechase | SCCD 31236
Pete York & His All Star Group | It's You Or No One | Mons Records | MR 874772
Phineas Newborn Jr. With Dennis Farnon And His Orchestra | While My Lady Sleeps | RCA | 2185157-2
Rickey Woodard With The Frank Capp Trio | The Frank Capp Trio Presents Rickey Woodard | Concord | CCD 4469
Sadao Watanabe Quartet | Dedicated To Charlie Parker | Denon Compact Disc | DC 8558
The Oscar Peterson Four | If You Could Se Me Now | Pablo | 2310918-2
Walt Dickerson Quartet | A Sense Of Direction | Original Jazz Classics | OJCCD 1794-2(NJ 8268)
Wynton Kelly Trio | New Faces-New Sounds:Piano Interpretations | Blue Note | 784456-2

If I Should Lose You-
Silvia Droste & New Wings | Seize The Day | BELL Records | BLR 84055

If I Should Lose You(alt.take)
The Montgomery Brothers | Encores | Milestone | M 9110

If I Were A Bell
Ella Fitzgerald With Marty Paich's Dektette | Ella Swings Lightly | Verve | 517535-2
Ella Fitzgerald With The Marty Paich Orchestra | Ella Sings Broadway | Verve | 549373-2
Everett Greene With The Houston Person Quartet | My Foolish Heart | Savant Records | SCD 2014

Francine Griffin With Band | Francine Griffin:The Song Bird | Delmark | DE 512
James McMillan Group | Up All Day All Night | Savoy | CY 78899
Johnny 'Hammond' Smith Quartet | The Soulful Blues | Prestige | PCD 24244-2
Keith Jarrett Trio | Keith Jarrett At The Blue Note-The Complete Recordings | ECM | 1575/80(527638-2)
Lem Winchester Quintet | Winchester Special | Original Jazz Classics | OJCCD 1719-2(NJ 8223)
Marty Paich Big Band | The New York Scene | Discovery | DS 844 IMS
Miles Davis Quintet | Miles Davis In Person-Friday Night At The Blackhawk,San Francisco,Vol.1 | CBS | C4K 87106
Relaxin' | Prestige | PRSA 7129-6
Live In Stockholm | Dragon | DRCD 228
En Concert Avec Europe 1 | Laserlight | 710455/58
Oliver Jones Trio | Cookin' At Sweet Basil | Justin Time | JUST 25
Oscar Peterson Jam | Montreux '77-The Art Of The Jam Session | Pablo | 2620106
Roger Kellaway/Red Mitchell | Concord Duo Series Volume One | Concord | CCD 4551
Stan Kenton And His Orchestra | Adventures In Standards | Creative World | ST 1025
Woody Shaw Quintet | Imagination | 32 Jazz | 32090

If I Were A Bell(alt.take)
Louie Bellson And His Jazz Orchestra | Air Mail Special-A Salute To The Big Band Masters | Limelight | 820824-2 IMS

If I Were A Carpenter
Lou Rawls And His Orchestra | At Last | Blue Note | 791937-2

If I Where A Bell
Chuck Loeb Group | My Shing Hour | Jazz City | 660.53.009
Herb Geller Quartet | Jazz-Club: Bass | Verve | 840037-2
Miles Davis Quintet | Jazz At The Plaza | CBS | SRCS 5700
Mel Tormé And His Trio | Night At The Concord Pavillion | Concord | CCD 4433

If I'm Lucky
Julie London With Howard Roberts And Red Mitchell | Julie Is Her Name Vol.2 | Pathe | 1566201(Liberty LRP 3100)
Winner's Circle | Winner's Circle(Various Artists) | Bethlehem | BET 6027-2(BCP 6066)

If It Didn't Hurt So Much
Leon Thomas With Orchestra | Spirits Known And Unknown | RCA | 2663876-2

If It Didn't Hurt So Much(alt.take)
The Jackson Singers | Gospel Emotions | L+R Records | CDLR 44016

If It's Love You Want Baby, That's Me
Michele Hendricks And Her Band | Keepin' Me Satisfied | Muse | MCD 5363

If It's Magic
Little Ester With Band | Roots Of Rock 'N' Roll, Vol. 5: Ladies Sing The Blues | Savoy | SJL 2233

If It's The Last Thing I Do
Dinah Washington With Orchestra | Ballads | Roulette | 537559-2
Dinah Washington With The Don Costa Orchestra | In Love | Roulette | CDP 797273-2
Paula Haliday With Orchestra | Haliday Sings Holiday | Fresh Sound Records | FSR 709(835321)

If It's True
Red Richards | Dreamy | Sackville | SKCD2-3053

If Love Is Good To Me
Sarah Vaughan With Mundell Lowe And George Duvivier | After Hours | Roulette | 855468-2
Buddy Stewart Quintet | Al Haig Meets The Master Saxes Vol.2 | Spotlite | SPJ 140

If Mountains Could Sing
Billie Holiday And Her Orchestra | Billie Holiday:The Quintessential Vol.3(1936-1937) | CBS | 460820-2

If Not Now
Billy Harper Quintet | Live On Tour In The Far East Vol.1 | Steeplechase | SCCD 31311

If Only I Had Known
John Handy Quintet | Live At Yoshi's Nightspot | Boulevard | BLD 531 CD

If Only We Knew & T.S. Monk, Sir
Lonnie Plaxico Group | Plaxico | Muse | MCD 5389

If Six Was Nine
Pinguin Moschner-Joe Sachse | If 69 Was 96/The Music Of Jimi Hendrix | Aho-Recording | CD 1016

If The Misfits (Wear It) - (If The) Misfits (Wear It)
Anita O'Day With The Johnny Mandel Orchestra | Trav'lin Light | Verve | 2304584 IMS

If The Moon Turns Green
Carmen McRae And Her Sextet | Carmen McRae Sings Lover Man | CBS | CK 65115

If There Is Someone Lovelier Than You
Enrico Pieranunzi Trio | New Lands | Timeless | CD SJP 211
John Coltrane With The Red Garland Trio | Settin' The Pace | Original Jazz Classics | OJC20 078-2
Johnny Coates Jr. Trio | Portrait | Savoy | SV 0234(MG 12082)

If This Bass Could Only Talk
Duke Robillard Group | Rockin' Blues | Rounder Records | CDRR 11548

If This Isn't Love
Gary Bartz Quartet | Episode One Children Of Harlem | Challenge | CHR 70001
Sarah Vaughan And Her Trio | Sarah Vaughan At Mister Kelly's | EmArCy | 832791-2 PMS
Sarah Vaughan With The Jimmy Jones Trio | Linger Awhile | Pablo | 2312144-2
The Clayton Brothers Quintet | Siblingity | Warner | 9362-47813-2
Cold Sweat | 4 Play | JMT Edition | 834444-2

If We Ever
Teddy Edwards Quartet With Christian Escoudé And Strings | La Villa-Live In Paris | Verve | 523495-2

If We Never Meet Again
Louis Armstrong And His Orchestra | Louis Armstrong Vol.2 | Ambassador | CLA 1902

If We Never Needed The Lord Before
Lillian Boutté And Her Group & The Soulful Heavenly Stars | The Gospel Book | Blues Beacon | BLU-1017 2
Take 6 | Tonight Take 6 | Warner | 9362-47611-2
Der Rote Bereich | Der Rote Bereich | Jazz 4 Ever Records:Jazz Network | J4E 4715

If You Ain´t Got It(I Got To Get It Somewhere)
Al Casey Sextet | Jumpin´ With Al | Black & Blue | BB 873.2

If You Are But A Dream
Red Rodney Quintet | Prestige First Sessions, Vol.3 | Prestige | PCD 24116-2

If You Build A Better Moustrap
Sun Ra Arkestra | Cosmo Omnibus Imagiable Illusion/Live At Pit-Inn,Tokyo | DIW | DIW 824 CD

If You Can See Me Now
Chris Barber's Jazz Band | Trad Tavern | Philips | 838397-2 PMS

If You Can't Beat 'Em,Beat 'Em!
Elevyn Preer With The Duke Ellington Orchestra | Not Notes-New York Vol.1 | Frog | DGF 8

If You Can't Know If You Mustn't Ask,Why Look?
Dixieland Jug Blowers | Louisville Stomp-The Complete Sessions Of The Dixieland Jug Blowers | Frog | DGF 6

If You Can't Sing It, You'll Have To Swing It -> Mr.Paganini

If You Can't Smile And Say Yes
Nat King Cole Trio | Love Songs | Nimbus Records | NI 2010
Any Old Time | Giants Of Jazz | GOJ 1031
Live At The Circle Room | Capitol | 521859-2
The Forgotten Years | Giants Of Jazz | GOJ 1013

If You Could See Me Now
Al Haig Trio | Invitation | Spotlite | SPJ LP 4 (AH 4)
Bertha Hope Trio | Between Two Kings | Minor Music | 801025
Bill Evans Trio | The Complete Bill Evans On Verve | Verve | 527953-2
The Second Trio | Milestone | M 47046
Bill Evans Trio:The Last Waltz | Milestone | 8MCD 4430-2
Bill Evans:The Secret Sessions | Milestone | 8MCD 4421-2
Live In Buenos Aires 1979 | West Wind | WW 2061
Moonbeams | Original Jazz Classics | OJC20 434-2(RLP 9428)
Bill Evans:The Secret Sessions | Milestone | 8MCD 4421-2
Billy Higgins Quartet | The Soldier | Timeless | CD SJP 145
Chet Baker-Enrico Pieranunzi | The Heart Of The Ballad | Philology | W 20.2
Dexter Gordon Quartet | The Jumpin' Blues | Original Jazz Classics | OJCCD 899-2(PR 10020)
Diane Schuur And Her Band | Music Is My Life | Atlantic | 7567-83150-2
Dick Katz Quintet | The Line Forms Here | Reservoir | RSR CD 141
Doug Raney Quintet | Cuttin' Loose | Steeplechase | SCS 1105
Gil Evans And Ten | Gil Evans And Ten | Prestige | PRSA 7120-6
Great Jazz Trio | Threesome | Eastworld | EWJ 90015
Irene Kral With Alan Broadbent | Gentle Rain | Candid | CRS 1020 IMS
Jaco Pastorius Group | Live In New York City Volume Three | Big World | BW 1003
Jan Lundgren Trio | Cooking! At The Jazz Bakery | Fresh Sound Records | FSR-CD 5019
Lee Konitz With The Bert Van Den Brink Trio | Dialogues | Challenge | CHR 70053
LeeAnn Ledgerwood Trio | Walkin' Up | Steeplechase | SCCD 31541
Lou Levy Trio | My Old Flame | Fresh Sound Records | FSR-CD 312
My Old Flame | Fresh Sound Records | FSR-CD 0312
Milt Jackson Orchestra | To Bags...With Love:Memorial Album | Pablo | 2310967-2
Morgana King And Her Sextet | Portraits | Muse | MR 5301(952107)
Peter Leitch Sextet | From Another Perspective | Concord | CCD 4535
Ranee Lee And Her Band | Dark Divas-Highlights | Justin Time | JUST 144-2
Sarah Vaughan And The Count Basie Orchestra | Send In The Clowns | Pablo | 2312130-2
Wynton Kelly Trio With Wes Montgomery | Smokin' At The Half Note | CTI Records | PDCTI 1117-2

If You Dig Me
Lester Bowie's Brass Fantasy | The Odysse Of Funk & Popular Music | Dreyfus Jazz Line | FDM 37004-2

If You Don't Know Me By Now
John Patitucci Group | Sketchbook | GRP | GRP 96172

If You Don't Mind
The Pilgrim Jubilee Singers | Walk On/The Old Ship Of Zion | Mobile Fidelity | MFCD 756

If You Ever Come To Me
Vanessa Rubin With Band | Girl Talk | Telarc Digital | CD 83480

If You Ever Need Me-
Stan Getz With The Eddie Sauter Orchestra | Stan Getz Plays The Music Of Mickey One | Verve | 531232-2
Ella Fitzgerald And Her Savoy Eight | Ella Fitzgerald-The Early Years-Part 1 | GRP | GRP 26182

If You Go
Helen Merrill With The Stan Getz Quartet | Just Friends | EmArCy | 842007-2 PMS

If You Go Away
Shirley Horn And Her Trio | May The Music Never End | Verve | 076028-2
Lou Rawls And His Orchestra | It's Suposed To Be Fun | Blue Note | 793841-2

If You Hadn't Gone Away
Art Tatum | Art Tatum-The Complete Pablo Solo Masterpieces | Pablo | 7 PACD 4404-2
The Art Tatum Solo Masterpieces | Pablo | 2625703

If You Have Nothing To Say
Hamiet Bluiett Group | ...You Don't Need To Know...If You Have To Ask | Tutu Records | 888128-2*

If You Have To Ask, You Don't Need To Know
Nehemiah 'Skip' James | Skip James-King Of The Delta Blues Singers | Biograph | BLP 12029

If You Knew-
Tiny Hill And His Orchestra | The Uncollected:Tiny Hill | Hindsight | HSR 159

If You Leave Them Cats Alone,They'll Play Nothin' But Shit
Stanley Cowell Ensemble | Talkin' 'Bout Love | Galaxy | GXY 5111

If You Live
Mose Allison Trio | Mose Allison Sings The 7th Son | Prestige | PR20 7279-2
The Stephen Barry Band | Blues Under A Full Moon | Blues Beacon | BLU-1009 2

If You Look
Tomasz Stanko Trio | Bluish | Power Bros | 00113

If You Look Far Enough
Agneta Baumann And Her Quintet | A Time For Love | Touché Music | TMcCD 006

If You Love Me
J.B.Lenoir Blues Band | J. B. Lenoir | Chess | 427003
Albert Collins & The Ice Breakers | Frostbite | Sonet | 147110

If You Never Came To Me
Harry Allen Sextet | Eu Nao Quero Dancar-I Won't Dance | Novus | 2158126-2
Ray Walker-John Pisano | Affinity | Jardis Records | JRCD 20032
Rob McConnell And The Boss Brass | Don't Get Around Much Anymore | Concord | CCD 4661

If You Never Come To Me
Carmen McRae With The Norman Simmons Trio | Live At Century Plaza | Atlantic | AMCY 1075

If You Only Knew
John Stubblefield Sextet | Prelude | Storyville | SLP 1018
Oscar Peterson Quartet | Oscar Peterson:The Composer | Pablo | 2310970-2
Oscar Peterson Quintet | A Tribute To Oscar Peterson | Telarc Digital | CD 83401

If You Pray Right
Nina Simone Trio | Let It Be Me | Verve | 831437-1

If You Pray Right(Heaven Belongs To You)
Rusty Bryant Quintet | Jazzin' With The Soul Brothers | Fantasy | FANCD 6086-2

If You Really Love Me
Bola Sete Quintet | Tour De Force:The Bola Sete Trios | Fantasy | FCD 24766-2

If You Return
Bossa Nova | Original Jazz Classics | OJC 286(F 8349)

If You Say So
Memphis Slim | All Kinds Of Blues | Original Blues Classics | OBC-507(BV 1053)

If You See Kay
Brian Blade Group | Fellowship | Blue Note | 859417-2

If You See Lurah
Humphrey Lyttelton And His Band | Delving Back With Humph:Humphrey Lyttelton 1948-1949 | Lake | LACD 72

If You See My Baby
Georgia Tom Dorsey | Come On Mama Do That Dance | Yazoo | YAZ 1041

If You See My Saviour
Eric Person Sextet | More Tales To Tell | Soul Note | 121307-2

If You So Smart, How Come You Ain't Rich
Diederik Wissels Quintet | Kamook | B.Sharp Records | CDS 083

If You Want To Write Me
Freddy Cole With Band | Merry-Go-Round | Telarc Digital | CD 83493

If You Went Away
Milt Jackson With Strings | Feelings | Original Jazz Classics | OJC 448(2310774)
Bud Powell Trio | Budism | Steeplechase | SCCD 30007/9

If You Were In My Place (What Would You Do)
Duke Ellington And His Famous Orchestra | The Complete Duke Ellington-Vol. 10 | CBS | CBS 88220

If You Were Mine
Nancy Harrow With The Clark Terry Quartet | Secrets | Soul Note | 121233-2
Tony Bennett With The Marty Manning Orchestra | I Wanna Be Around | CBS | CK 66504

If You Were Mine-
Johnny Hodges Orchestra | The Rabbit's Work On Verve In Chronological Order, Vol.4 | Verve | 2304450 IMS
Ruby Braff-Scott Hamilton Sextet | A First | Concord | CJ 274

If You Were The Only Girl In The World
Rene Thomas Quintet | Meeting Mister Thomas | Fresh Sound Records | FSR 554(Barclay 84091)
Soprano Summit | Crazy Rhythm | Chiaroscuro | CR 178

If You Would Only Say You're Sorry
Ella Johnson With Orchestra | Swing Me | Official | 6009

If You'd Know Me
Buddy Johnson And His Orchestra | Buddy And Ella Johnson 1953-1964 | Bear Family Records | BCD 15479 DH

If You'd Say Yes
Ella Johnson With Orchestra | Swing Me | Official | 6009

If You're Goin' To The City
Annie Laurie And Her Orchestra | It Hurts To Be In Love | Sing | 1155

If You're Not Part Of The Solution, You're Part Of The Problem
Joe Henderson Sextet | At The Lighthouse | Milestone | M 9028

If You've Got Some Place To Go
Tom Scott Group | Keep This Love Alive | GRP | GRP 96462

Ife-
Miles Davis Group | Paris Jazz Concert:Miles Davis | Laserlight | 17445
Art Blakey And The Afro Drum Ensemble | The African Beat | Blue Note | 522666-2

Ife L'ayo
Elliott Lawrence Orchestra | Jazz Goes Broadway | Fresh Sound Records | NL 45905(RCA Vik LX 1113)

Ifrikyia
Baden Powell Ensemble | Apaixonado | MPS | 68090

Igarape
Das Böse Ding | Cleanhappydirty | Acoustic Music Records | 319.1090.2

Igloo
Kai Winding All Stars | Kai Winding-Bop City:Small Groups 1949-1951 | Cool & Blue | C&B-CD 110
Tord Gustavsen Trio | Changing Places | ECM | 1834(016397-2)

IGN
Klaus Ignatzek Quintet | All Systems Go | Candid | CCD 79738

Igneous Ejaculation
Les McCann Group | On The Soul Side | Musicmasters | 65112-2

Ignunt Oil
Milt Jackson Sextet | That's Jazz Vol.22: Plenty Plenty Soul | Atlantic | ATL 50299

Iguacu
Loren Schoenberg And His Jazz Orchestra | Out Of This World | TCB Records | TCB 98902

Ihr Kinderlein Kommet
Jimmy Lyons Quartet | Riffs | Hat Art | 3503

Il B.S.
Buddy Moreno And His Orchestra | Buddy Moreno And His Orchestra 1947 and 1949 | Circle | CCD-49

II-V-I
Gilbert Paeffgen Trio | Pedestrian Tales | Edition Musikat | EDM 061

Ijri
Louie Bellson's Big Band Explosion | The Art Of The Chart | Concord | CCD 4800

Ikiri Adda
Robert Norman In Different Groups | The Best Of Robert Norman(1941-1989) | Hot Club Records | HCRCD 085

Iko-Iko
Chris Barber's Jazz And Blues Band With Dr.John | On A Mardy Gras Day | Great Southern Records | GS 11024
Lovie Lee And Band | American Folk Blues Festival Live '83 | L+R Records | LR 42063

Il Camino
Franco D'Andrea Trio | Volte | Owl Records | 052 CD

Il Campo
Mario Fragiacomo Orchestra | Trieste Ieri Un Secolo Fa | SPLASC(H) Records | HP 08

Il Canto Della Sierra
Cassandra | Enten Eller | SPLASC(H) Records | H 176

Il Disegno Smangiato D'Un Uomo
Speakers And Singers On Radio Spot | Radio Suite | Red Records | 123280-2

Il Est Grand Temps (Perdu?)
Claude Bernhard-Raymond Bo | Pot-Pouri Pour Parce Que | Hat Art | G

Il Est Né Le Divin Enfant
Cécile Verny Quartet | Métisse | double moon | CHRDM 71010

Il Est Trop Tarde
Pino Distaso/Roberto Gotta/Beto Cutillo | Tell Her It's All Right | Edition Collage | EC 463-2

Il Fiume
Paolo Fresu Quartet | Angel | RCA | 2155864-2

Il Gatto E La Volpe
Enrico Rava Quartet | Il Giro Del Giorno In 80 Mondi | Black Saint | BSR 0011

Il Grande Fave
Asita Hamidi & Arcobaleno | Mosaic | Laika Records | 8695067

Il Khan
Giannantonio De Vincenzo Quintet | Soft Landing | SPLASC(H) Records | H 137

Il Lungo Addio
Italian Instabile Orchestra | Skies Of Europe | ECM | 1543

Il Maestro Muratore-
Skies Of Europe | ECM | 1543

Il Maestro Muratore(reprise)-
Skies Of Europe | ECM | 1543

Il Maestro Muratore:
Toast Man Quartet Plus Friends | One For Leonardo | SPLASC(H) Records | CD H 379-2

Il Manto Porpora
One For Leonardo | SPLASC(H) Records | CD H 379-2

Il Monstro Saltando After Having Eaten The Turkish Dancer
Marion Brown Sextet | Marion Brown In Sommerhausen | Calig | 30605

Il Passo Pesante
Daniel Schnyder Group | Words Within Music | Enja | ENJ-9369 2

Il Pastor Fido
Aldo Romano Duo | Il Piacere | Owl Records | 013575-2

Il Piacere
Henri Texier Quintet | Colonel Skopje | Label Bleu | LBLC 6523(881998)

Il Postino
Massimo Colombo Trio | Alexander | SPLASC(H) Records | H 177

Il Sogno Del Pescecane
Günter Sommer | Hörmusik III:Sächsische Schatulle | Intakt Records | CD 027

Il Suono Giallo-
Arrigo Cappelletti New Latin Ensemble | Pianure | SPLASC(H) Records | CD H 308-2

Ila
Dollar Brand | Ancient Africa | Japo | 60005(2360005)

Ilé
Pili-Pili | Pili-Pili Live 88 | JA & RO | JARO 4139-2
Pili-Pili | JA & RO | JARO 4141-2
Peter Schärli Quintet With Glenn Ferris | Drei Seelen/Three Souls | Creative Works Records | MIWI 1014-2

Il'e 'Ak'e
Ramon Valle Trio | No Escape | ACT | 9424-2

Ilegal
Benny Goodman And His Orchestra | The Indispensable Benny Goodman(Big Band) Vol.5/6(1938-1939) | RCA | 2122621-2

I'll Always Be In Love With You

Count Basie Kansas City Septem | Mostly Blues...And Some Others | Pablo | 2310919-2
Fletcher Henderson And His Orchestra | The Indispensable Fletcher Henderson(1927-1936) | RCA | 2122618-2
Mickey Baker | The Blues Vol.3 | Big Bear | 156400
Paul Quinichette And His Orchestra | The Vice Pres | Verve | 543750-2

I'll Always Be With You
Rodney Jones Sextet | When You Feel The Love | Timeless | CD SJP 152

I'll Always Love You
Tiny Grimes Quintet | Charlie Parker:The Complete 1944-1948 Small Group Sessions(Studio Recordings-Master Takes),Vol.1 | Blue Moon | BMCD 1007

I'll Be A Friend With Pleasure
Eric Lugosch | Kind Heroes | Acoustic Music Records | 319.1188.2

I'll Be Around
Anita Boyer & Her Tomboyers | Nat King Cole Trio:The MacGregor Years 1941/45 | Music & Arts | CD 911
Billy Taylor Trio | Cross-Section | Original Jazz Classics | OJCCD 1730-2
George Shearing And His Quintet | Combo USA | Affinity | CD AFS 1002
Gerry Mulligan Quartet | Triple Play:Gerry Mulligan | Telarc Digital | CD 83453
John Hicks-Ray Drummond | Two Of A Kind | Evidence | ECD 22017-2
Johnny Smith Quintet | Zoot Sims:The Complete 1944-1954 Small Group Sessions(Master Takes),Vol.3 | Blue Moon | BMCD 1040
Ronny Lang And His All-Stars | Basie Street | Fresh Sound Records | FSR-CD 0501

I'll Be Around(Slow En Ré Majeur)
Herb Geller Quartet | You're Looking At Me | Fresh Sound Records | FSR-CD 5018

I'll Be Back
Marshall Royal Quintet | Royal Blue | Concord | CJ 125

I'll Be Glad
Adrian Bentzon's Jazzband | The Golden Years Of Revival Jazz,Vol.14 | Storyville | STCD 5519

I'll Be Glad When You're Dead You Rascal You
Barrelhouse Jazzband | You Are Driving Me Crazy | L+R Records | CDLR 70005
Louis Armstrong And His All Stars | Satchmo-A Musical Autobiography Vol.2 | MCA | 2-4174
Louis Armstrong And His Orchestra | Harlem Roots-Jazz On Film:The Headliners | Storyville | SLP 6001
Louis Armstrong With Orchestra | Louis Armstrong & Duke Ellington | Avenue | AVINT 1006
Luis Russell And His Orchestra | Harlem Big Bands | Timeless | CBC 1-010

I'll Be Glad When You're Dead You Rascal You-
Louis Armstrong And His Orchestra | Laughin' Louie | RCA | ND 90404
Louis Armstrong-Satchmo's Greatest Hits | RCA | CL 89799
Fletcher Henderson And His Orchestra | The Crown King Of Swing | Savoy | SV 0254(SJL 1152)

I'll Be Home
Bob Mover Trio | Jazz City Christmas Vol.2 | Jazz City | 660.53.029

I'll Be Satisfied
Abbey Lincoln With The Harold Vick Quartet | A Tribute To Billie Holiday | Enja | 6012-2

I'll Be Seeing You
Billie Holiday With Eddie Heywood And His Orchestra | The Commodore Series | Decca | 180008 AG
Bud Powell Orchestra | Bebop | Pablo | PACD 2310978-2
Bud Shank Quartet | This Bud's For You | Muse | MR 5309(952106)
George Shearing-Mel Torme | An Elegant Evening | Concord | CCD 4294
Jimmy Slyde With The Milt Buckner Trio | Special Tap Dance-Four Dancing Masters | Black & Blue | BLE 191652
Sonny Stitt Quartet | The Last Stitt Sessions Vol. One And Two | 32 Jazz | 32127
Tommy Dorsey And His Orchestra | This Is Tommy Dorsey | RCA | PL 89536 DP

I'll Be Seing You
Ruth Brown With Mike Renzi | The Songs Of My Life | Fantasy | FCD 9665-2

I'll Be Somewhere Listening For My Name
Cash McCall And The Young Blues Thrillers | Cash McCall | Blues Classics(L+R) | CDLR 82010

I'll Be There -> (Reach Out) I'll Be There

I'll Be There When The Time Is Right
Amos Milburn Quintet | 13 Unreleased Masters | Pathe | 1546701(Aladdin)

I'll Be Your Baby Tonight
Dave McKenna | The Key Man | Concord | CJ 261

I'll Bet You Thought I'd Never Find You
Lanin's Jazz Band | Le Jazz En France Vol.1:Premiers Jazz Bands | Pathe | 1727251

I'll Build A Stairway To Paradise
Eddie Miller And His Orchestra | The Uncollected:Eddie Miller | Hindsight | HSR 225 (835033)

I'll Buy You A Star
Jerry Gray And His Orchestra | The Sound Of Jerry Gray And His Orchestra | Magic | DAWE 73

I'll Catch You
Peter Ehwald Trio | Away With Words:The Music Of John Scofield | Jazz Haus Musik | JHM 0128 CD
Ella Fitzgerald With Chick Webb And His Orchestra | Ella Fitzgerald Vol.1-Forever Young | Swingtime(Contact) | ST 1006

I'll Close My Eyes
Barrett Deems Big Band | Groovin' Hard | Delmark | DE 505
Dinah Washington With The Don Costa Orchestra | In Love | Roulette | CDP 797273-2
Doug Raney Quintet | I'll Close My Eyes | Steeplechase | SCCD 31166
Gary Foster Quartet | Make Your Own Fun | Concord | CCD 4459
Harry Allen Duo/Trio | I'll Never Be The Same | Master Mix | CHECD 00106
Jimmy Smith Trio | Verve Jazz Masters 29:Jimmy Smith | Verve | 521855-2
Organ Grinder Swing | Verve | 543831-2
Joe Bawelino Quartet | Happy Birthday Stéphane | Edition Collage | EC 458-2
John Critchinson-Art Themen Quartet | First Moves | Ronnie Scott's Jazz House | JHCD 052
Ken Peplowski Quintet | The Natural Touch | Concord | CCD 4517
Mark Murphy And His Septet | I'll Close My Eyes | Muse | MCD 5436
Seldon Powell Sextet | Seldon Powell Sextet | Fresh Sound Records | FSR 588(Roost 2220)

I'll Dearly Love You
Jon Hendricks & Company | Love | Muse | MCD 5258

I'll Dream Of You Again
Teddy Wilson And His Orchestra | The Rarest 1937-42 | Everybody's | 1003

I'll Drown In My Own Tears
Dinah Washington With Orchestra | Dinah '63 | Roulette | 7945762

I'll Drown In My Tears
Sugar Chile Robinson Trio | Go Boy Go | Oldie Blues | OL 2828

I'll Finally Answer
Tampa Red Band | Midnight Blues | Swingtime(Contact) | BT 2003

I'll Fly Away
Reverend Blind Gary Davis | When I Die I 'll Live Again | Fantasy | F 24704

I'll Follow My Secret Heart
Nancy Harrow With The Clark Terry Quartet | Secrets | Soul Note | 121233-2

I'll Follow The Sun
Joshua Breakstone Quartet | The Composition Of The Beatles Vol.1: I Want To Hold Your Hand | Paddle Wheel | KICJ 122

I'll Follow You
Thelonious Monk Sextet | More Genius Of Thelonious Monk | Blue Note | 300194(BNJ 61011)

I'll Get Along
Jazz Gillum Group | Harmonica And Washboard Blues | Black & Blue | BLE 59.252 2

I'll Get Along Somehow
Billie Holiday With Eddie Heywood And His Orchestra | Billie Holiday:The Complete Commodore Recordings | GRP | AFS 1019-8

I'll Get By(As Long As I Have You)
Billie Holiday:The Complete Commodore Recordings | GRP | 543272-2
The Commodore Series | Decca | 180008 AG
Billie Holiday With Teddy Wilson And His Orchestra | Rare And Unissued Recordings From The Golden Years Vol.4 | Queen-Disc | 068
Della Reese With The Neal Hefti Orchestra | Della | RCA | 2663912-2
Della | RCA | 2663912-2
Dick Hyman Orchestra | Swing Is Here | Reference Recordings | RR-72 CD
John Coltrane Quintet | John Coltrane-The Prestige Recordings | Prestige | 16 PCD 4405-2
Johnny Hodges Orchestra | Johnny Hodges At The Sportpalast, Berlin | Pablo | 2CD 2620102
Leonard Feather's Esquire All Stars | Metropolitan Opera House Jam Session | Jazz Anthology | 550212
Anson Weeks And His Orchestra | The Radio Years: Anson Weeks And His Hotel Mark Hopkins Orchestra 193 | Hindsight | HSR 146

I'll Get By(As Long As I Have You)-
Norman Granz Jam Session | Charlie Parker Jam Session | Verve | 833564-2 PMS

I'll Get Mine Bye And Bye
Louisiana Red & Gerhard Engbarth | Anti-Nuclear Blues | L+R Records | LR 42045

I'll Get You Let
Five Blind Boys Of Alabama | Negro Spirituals,Gospel & Jubilee Songs | Vogue | 655015

I'll Go My Way By Myself
Jimmy Witherspoon And His Band | Baby, Baby, Baby | Original Blues Classics | OBCCD 527-2(P 7290)

I'll Go On Living
Horace Tapscott | The Tapscott Sessions Vol.5 | Nimbus | NS 1925

I'll Keep Loving You
Bud Powell Trio | Bud Powell:Bouncing With Bud | Dreyfus Jazz Line | FDM 36725-2
The Genius Of Bud Powell | Verve | 821690-1
Hugh Lawson Trio | Prime Time | Storyville | 3 IMA
Mulgrew Miller Trio | Time And Again | Landmark | LCD 1532-2
Steve Grossman Quartet | Do It | Dreyfus Jazz Line | FDM 36550-2

I'll Keep The Lovelight Burning(In My Heart)
Patti Austin And Her Band | Patti Austin:The Ultimate Collection | GRP | GRP 98212

I'll Keep Your Dreams Alive
Bill Evans-Don Elliott | Tenderly | Milestone | MCD 9317-2

I'll Know
Cal Tjader Quartet | Cal Tjader Plays Jazz | Original Jazz Classics | OJCCD 986-2(F 3-211)
Coleman Hawkins And His Quartet | Hawk Variation | Swingtime(Contact) | ST 1004
Horace Silver Quintet | Silver's Blue | Epic | ESCA 7762
Klaus Weiss Quintet | A Taste Of Jazz | ATM Records | ATM 3810-AH
Beverly Kenney With The Johnny Smith Quartet | Sings For Johnny Smith | Fresh Sound Records | FSR-CD 79(882164)

I'll Live Another Day
Louis Moholo's Viva-La-Black | Freedom Tour-Live In South Afrika 1993 | Ogun | OGCD 006

I'll Love You
Marvin 'Smitty' Smith Group | The Road Less Traveled | Concord | CCD 4379

I'll Make Love To You
Good Fellas | Good Fellas 2 | Paddle Wheel | KICJ 115

I'll Never Be Free
John Patton Quintet | Along Came John | Blue Note | 0675614
Lionel Hampton And His Orchestra | Wes Montgomery:Complete Recordings With Lionel Hampton | Definitive Records | DRCD 11242
Mose Allison Trio | Local Color | Original Jazz Classics | OJCCD 457-2
Sal Salvador Quartet | Stop Smoking Or Else Blues | Fresh Sound Records | FSR 556(Roulette SR 25262)

I'll Never Be The Same
Art Tatum | The Standard Sessions: Art Tatum 1935-1943 Transcriptions | Music & Arts | CD 673
In Private | Fresh Sound Records | FSR-CD 0127
Art Tatum Trio | The Tatum Group Masterpieces | Pablo | 2625706
Billie Holiday With Teddy Wilson And His Orchestra | Billie Holiday:The Quintessential Vol.4(1937) | CBS | 463333-2
Coleman Hawkins With The Oscar Peterson Quartet | Compact Jazz: Coleman Hawkins/Ben Webster | Verve | 833296-2
Dave Bartholomew With The Todd Rhodes Orchestra | My Ding-A-Ling | Sing | 1158
Django Reinhardt And The Quintet Du Hot Club De France | The Indispensable Django Reinhardt | RCA | ND 70929
Eddie Lockjaw Davis Quartet | Eddie Lockjaw Davis With Shirley Scott | Original Jazz Classics | OJC 218(P 7154)
Ernestine Anderson With Orchestra | My Kinda Swing | Mercury | 842409-2
Flip Phillips Quintet | Flip Phillips Flip Wails-The Best Of The Verve Years | Verve | 521645-2
Jeri Southern With The Lennie Hayton Orchestra | Coffee Cigarettes And Memories | Fresh Sound Records | FSR-CD 29(882157)
Joe Venuti-George Barnes Quintet | Gems | Concord | CJ 14
Louis Armstrong With The Oscar Peterson Quartet | Louis Armstrong Meets Oscar Peterson | Verve | 539060-2
Louis Armstrong Meets Oscar Peterson | Verve | 825713-2
Mildred Bailey With Paul Baron's Orchestra | The Radio Years: Mildred Bailey With Paul Baron's Orchestra 1944 | Hindsight | HSR 133
Nat King Cole With The Sunset All Stars | Music At Sunset | Jazz Colours | 874738-2
Nat Pierce/Dick Collins Nonet | Nat Pierce-Dick Collins Nonet/Charlie Mariano Sextet | Original Jazz Classics | OJC 118(F 3224)
Red Mitchell Quintet | Red Mitchell | Bethlehem | BTM 6825
Sarah Vaughan With The Benny Carter Orchestra | The Roulette Years Vol. One/Two | Roulette | CDP 794983-2
Spike Jones And His Other Orchestra | The Uncollected:Spike Jones | Hindsight | HSR 185(835797)
Tatum-Hampton-Rich Trio | The Tatum-Hampton-Rich Trio Vol.3 | Pablo | 2405426-2

I'll Never Be The Same(alt.take)
Nat King Cole Quintet | Anatomy Of A Jam Session | Black Lion | BLCD 760137

I'll Never Do You Wrong
Big Bill Broonzy | Big Bill Broonzy 1934-1947 | Story Of Blues | CD 3504-2

I'll Never Fall In Love Again
Ella Fitzgerald With The Tommy Flanagan Trio | Ella Fitzgerald In Budapest | Pablo | PACD 5308-2
Grant Green Orchestra | Green Is Beautiful | Blue Note | 300275(4342)
Tok Tok Tok | 50 Ways To Leave Your Lover | Einstein Music | EM 91051
Matthias Bätzel Trio | Green Dumplings | JHM Records | JHM 3618

I'll Never Forget That
La Vienta | Forgotten Romance | Telarc Digital | CD 83380

I'll Never Let You Go
Big Jay McNeely And His Orchestra | Deacon Rides Again | Pathe | 1546691(Imperial)

I'll Never Say Goodbye(The Promise)
Warren Vaché Quartet | What Is There To Say? | Nagel-Heyer | CD 056

I'll Never See Maggie Alone
Bill Evans Quintet | The 'Interplay' Sessions | Milestone | M 47066

I'll Never Smile Again
Billie Holiday With The Ray Ellis Orchestra | Last Recordings | Verve | 835370-2 PMS
Dave Brubeck Quartet | The Dave Brubeck Quartet feat. Paul Desmond In Concert | Fantasy | FCD 60-013
The Art Of Dave Brubeck - The Fantasy Years:Jazz At Oberlin/College OPacific | Atlantic | SD 2-317
Erroll Garner | Compact Jazz:Erroll Garner | Mercury | 830695-2 PMS
Frank Sinatra With The Tommy Dorsey Orchestra | The Popular Sinatra Vol.1 | RCA | 2668711-2
Oscar Peterson Quintet With Orchestra | The Personal Touch | Pablo | 2312135-2
Tommy Dorsey And His Orchestra | Planet Jazz:Big Bands | Planet Jazz | 2169649-2
Frank Sinatra And The Tommy Dorsey Orchestra | RCA | 2668701-2
This Is Tommy Dorsey | RCA | PL 89536 DP

I'll Never Smile Again(take 1)
Django Reinhardt And The Quintet Du Hot Club De France | Jazz In Paris:Django Reinhardt-Django's Blues | EmArCy | 013545-2

I'll Never Smile Again(take 2)
Big Joe Turner And His Band | Big Joe Turner Greatest Hits | Sequel Records | RSA CD 809

I'll Only Miss Her When I Think Of Her
Jiggs Whigham With The Netherlands Metropole Orchestra | Love Walked In | Koch Jazz | 3-6920-2

I'll Only Miss Him When I Think Of Him
Hip Linkchain Group | Airbusters | Evidence | ECD 26038-2

I'll Provide The Thrills
Brownie McGhee | Blues Is My Companion | Aves | 146508

I'll Remember April
André Previn' s Jazz Trio | King Size! | Original Jazz Classics | OJCCD 691-2(S 7570)
Andy Bey Group | Tuesdays In Chinatown | Minor Music | 801099
Anita Boyer & Her Tomboyers | Nat King Cole Trio:The MacGregor Years 1941/45 | Music & Arts | CD 911
Art Pepper Quartet | Among Friends | Discovery | DSCD 837
Benny Golson Sextet | Time Speaks-Dedicated To The Memory Of Clifford Brown | Timeless | CD SJP 187
Billy Taylor Trio | The Billy Taylor Trio At Town Hall | Prestige | VIJ 5020
Bob Florence And His Orchestra | Name Band:1959 | Fresh Sound Records | FSCD 2008
Bud Powell Trio | Bud Powell:Bouncing With Bud | Dreyfus Jazz Line | FDM 36725-2
Bud Powell:Complete 1947-1951 Blue Note,Verve & Roost Recordings | The Jazz Factory | JFCD 22837
Cal Tjader's Modern Mambo Quintet(Sextet) | Mambo With Tjader | Original Jazz Classics | OJCCD 271-2(F 3202)
California Jam Sessions | Chet Baker:California Jam Sessions | Definitive Records | DRCD 11232
Carla White And Her Trio | Orient Express | Milestone | M 9147
Charles Mingus Quintet | Charles Mingus-The Complete Debut Recordings | Debut | 12 DCD 4402-2
Charles Mingus Quintet Plus Max Roach | The Charlie Mingus Quintet Plus Max Roach | Debut | VIJ 5011 IMS
Charles Mingus Quintet With Bud Powell | Charles Minus-Live | Affinity | CD AFS 778
Charlie Parker at 'Bob Reisner presents Bird' | Bird's Eyes Last Unissued Vol.25 | Philology | W 855.2
Charlie Parker With Strings | The Verve Years (1950-51) | Verve | 2-2512 IMS
Chet Baker And The Lighthouse All Stars | Witch Doctor | Original Jazz Classics | OJCCD 609-2
Chet Baker Quartet | Jazz In Paris:Chet Baker Quartet Plays Standards | EmArCy | 014378-2 PMS
Chet Baker-Stan Getz Quintet | Stan Meets Chet | Verve | 837436-2
The Stockholm Concerts | Verve | 537555-2
Chet Baket Quartet | Chet Baker In Paris | Fresh Sound Records | FSR Box 1(Barclay)
Clifford Brown All Stars With Dinah Washington | Verve Jazz Masters 40:Dinah Washington | Verve | 522055-2
Clifford Brown-Max Roach Quintet | Clifford Brown And Max Roach At Basin Street | Verve | 589826-2
Hot Tracks For Cool Cats Vol.3 | Polydor | 816411-2
Pure Genius | Elektra | MUS K 52388
Dizzy Gillespie All Stars | Highlights Of The Montreux Jazz Festival 1975 | Pablo | 2625707
Don Byas Quartet | A Night In Tunisia | Black Lion | BLCD 760136
Dorothy Donegan Trio | Donnybrook With Donegan | Capitol | 300217
Eddie Lockjaw Davis Quartet | Jazz Till Midnight | Storyville | STCD 4123
Eddy Howard And His Orchestra | The Uncollected: Eddy Howard | Hindsight | HSR 119
Four Trombones | Four Trombones Vol.1 | Debut | VIJ 5003 IMS
Frank Morgan Septet | Frank Morgan | Vogue | 655018
George Wallington Trio | The Modern Jazz Piano Album | Savoy | SV 0272
Great Jazz Trio | Threesome | Eastworld | EWJ 90015
Hank Jones Trio | The Trio | Chiaroscuro | CR 188
Joe Maini Sextet | Bird's Eyes-Last Unissued Vol.13 | Philology | W 843.2
John Harrison Trio | Going Places | TCB Records | TCB 95702
John Lewis | Afternoon In Paris | Dreyfus Jazz Line | FDM 36507-2
John Lewis-Hank Jones Duo | An Evening With Two Grand Pianos | Little David | LD 59657
June Christy With Orchestra | This Is June Christy/June Christy Recalls Those Kenton Days | Capitol | 535209-2
Jutta Hipp Trio | Jutta Hipp At The Hickory House Vol.1 | Blue Note | 300094(1515)
Kenny 'Pancho' Hagood With The Al Haig Trio | Cool Whalin' - Bebop Vocals | Spotlite | SPJ 135
Kenny Dorham Quintet | Sonny Rollins-The Freelance Years:The Complete Riverside & Contemporary Recordings | Riverside | 5 RCD 4427-2
Lajos Dudas Quartet | Nightlight | double moon | DMCHR 71030
Lanfranco Malaguti/Enzo Pietropaoli/Fabrizio Sferra | Sound Investigations | SPLASC(H) Records | H 143
Lars Gullin Quintet | Lars Gullin 1951/52 Vol.5:First Walk | Dragon | DRCD 380
Lee Konitz & The Gerry Mulligan Quartet | Konitz Meets Mulligan | Pacific Jazz | 746847-2
Lee Konitz Quartet | The Saxophon Collection | Vogue | 21610232
Lee Konitz Trio | Motion | Verve | 557107-2
Lee Konitz-Enrico Rava Quartet | L'Age Mür | Philology | W 123.2
Marian McPartland Trio feat. Chris Potter | Silver Anniversary Set | Concord | CCD 7002
Miles Davis Quintet | Tune Up | Prestige | P 24077
Welcome To Jazz: Miles Davis Vol.2 | Koch Records | 321 975 D1
Modern Jazz Quartet | Concorde | Original Jazz Classics | OJC20 002-2
The Complete Modern Jazz Quartet Prestige & Pablo Recordings | Prestige | 4PRCD 4438-2
Modern Jazz Quartet | Prestige | P 24005
Neil Richardson Singers With The Metropole Orchestra | A Beautiful Friendship | Koch Jazz | 3-6909-2
Phineas Newborn Jr. Trio | Tivoli Encounter | Storyville | STCD 8221
Putte Wickman And The Hal Galper trio | Time To Remember | Dragon | DRCD 378
Red Garland Trio | Live Under The Sky-Galaxy All Stars In Tokyo | Galaxy | GXY 95001
Sarah Vaughan And Her Trio | The Complete Sarah Vaughan Live In Japan | Mobile Fidelity | MFCD 844-2
Singers Unlimited With The Robert Farnon Orchestra | Sentimental Journey | MPS | 68102
Sonny Clark Trio | Sonny Clark Trio | Blue Note | 533774-2
Sonny Rollins Trio | More From The Vanguard | Blue Note | 84556
Sonny Rollins:The Blue Note Recordings | Blue Note | 821371-2
Sonny Stitt With The Oscar Peterson Trio | Sits In With The Oscar Peterson Trio | Verve | 849396-2 PMS
Stan Kenton And His Orchestra | The Kenton Era | Creative World | ST 1030

Stephane Grappelli-Bucky Pizzarelli Duo | Duet | Ahead | 33755
Teddy Wilson Trio | Masters Of Jazz Vol.11:Teddy Wilson | Storyville | STCD 4111
The Birdlanders | The Birdlanders | Fresh Sound Records | FSR-CD 0170
Toshiko Akiyoshi Trio | Amazing Toshiko Akiyoshi | Verve | MV 2579 IMS
Werner Pöhlert Combo | Something Cool:Werner Pöhlert Combo Recordings 1985-1009 | Hohner Records | ohne Nummer(2)
Zoot Sims Quartet | On The Korner | Pablo | 2310953-2

I'll Remember April(alt.take 1)
Clifford Brown-Max Roach Quintet | Brownie-The Complete EmArCy Recordings Of Clifford Brown | EmArCy | 838306-2

I'll Remember April(alt.take 2)
Charles Mingus Quintet | Charles Mingus-The Complete Debut Recordings | Debut | 12 DCD 4402-2

I'll Remember April(alt.take)
Clifford Brown-Max Roach Quintet | Clifford Brown And Max Roach At Basin Street | Verve | 589826-2
Clifford Brown And Max Roach At Basin Street | Verve | 589826-2

I'll Remember April(breakdown)
Charlie Parker With Strings | Bird: The Complete Charlie Parker On Verve | Verve | 837141-2

I'll Remember April(take 1)
Lee Konitz Quintet | Lee Konitz/Bob Brookmeyer:Quintets | Vogue | 2111503-2

I'll Remember April(take 2)
Lee Konitz/Bob Brookmeyer:Quintets | Vogue | 2111503-2

I'll Remember April(take 3)
Lee Konitz Quartet | Konitz | Black Lion | BLCD 760922

I'll Remember August
Greg Abate Quintet | Dr. Jeckyll & Mr. Hyde | Candid | CCD 79715

I'll Remember Murph
Jackie McLean Quartet | Swing Swang Swingin' | Blue Note | BOP 2

I'll See You Again
Art Tatum | The Art Tatum Solo Masterpieces | Pablo | 2625703
Bill Evans Trio | Trio (Motian Peacock)-Duo(Hall) | Verve | 2-2509 IMS
Joe Diorio/Ira Sullivan | The Breeze And I | RAM Records | RMCD 4508
Sonny Rollins Quintet | Sunny Days Stary Nights | Milestone | M 9122

I'll See You Again(alt.take)
Bill Evans Trio | Trio 64 | Verve | 539058-2
The Complete Bill Evans On Verve | Verve | 527953-2

I'll See You Again(incompl.take)
Trio 64 | Verve | 539058-2
Alberta Hunter With The Charlie Shavers Quartet | Charlie Shavers And The Blues Singers 1938-1939 | Timeless | CBC 1-025

I'll See You In My Dreams
Art Tatum | The Art Tatum Solo Masterpieces | Pablo | 2625703
Django Reinhardt Trio | Django Reinhardt:Djangology | EMI Records | 780659-2
Kenny Davern Quartet | I'll See You In My Dreams | Musicmasters | 5020-2
The Swingcats | Face To Face:The Swingcats Live | Nagel-Heyer | CD 072
Willie Humphrey With The Maryland Jazz Band | Willie Humphrey Meets Maryland Jazz Band Of Cologne | DuBat Music | BMI 41991
Joe Robichaux-Alfred Williams | Peter Bocage | American Music | AMCD-93

I'll String Along With You
Coleman Hawkins All Stars | Accent On Tenor Sax | Fresh Sound Records | FSR-CD 0039
Leroy Vinnegar Quintet | Leroy Walks Again | Original Jazz Classics | OJCCD 454-2
Louis Armstrong With Sy Oliver's Choir And Orchestra | Louis Armstrong-Heavenly Music | Ambassador | CLA 1916
Nat King Cole Trio | Vocal Classics & Instrumental Classics | Capitol | 300014(TOCJ 6128)
Ronnie Earl & The Broadcasters | Deep Blues | Black Top | BT 1033 CD

I'll Take Les
Art Farmer Quintet | Farmer 's Market | Prestige | P 24032

I'll Take Romance
Bill Evans-Don Elliott | Tenderly | Milestone | MCD 9317-2
Bob Florence Trio | Bob Florence Trio | Fresh Sound Records | FSR-CD 0303
June Christy With The Pete Rugolo Orchestra | Something Cool(The Complete Mono & Stereo Versions) | Capitol | 534069-2
Lennie Niehaus Quintet | Lennie Niehaus Vol.1:The Quintets | Original Jazz Classics | OJCCD 1933-2(C 3518)
Vol.1:The Quintets | Original Jazz Classics | OJC 319(C 3518)
Marion McPartland | Marion McPartland's Piano Jazz With Rosemarie Clooney | The Jazz Alliance | TJA 12003
The Westcoasters | The West Coasters Feat. Jimmy Giuffre | Bethlehem | BTM 6826

I'll Wait And Pray
John Coltrane Quartet | Coltrane Jazz | Atlantic | 7567-81344-2
Countdown | Atlantic | 90462-1 TIS

I'll Wait And Pray(alt.take)
Coltrane Jazz | Atlantic | 7567-81344-2
Giants Of Jazz | Giants Of Jazz | George Wein Collection | AU 36100

I'll Walk Alone
Art Farmer Quartet | The Jazz Giants Play Sammy Cahn:It's Magic | Prestige | PCD 24226-2
Art Kassel And His 'Kassels-In-The-Air' Orchestra | The Uncollected:Art Kassel | Hindsight | HSR 162
CoJazz feat. Gianni Basso | All Those Melodies | TCB Records | TCB 20402
Louis Prima And His Orchestra | Remember | Magic | DAWE 12(882656)

Ill Wind
Art Blakey And The Jazz Messengers | Art Blakey/The Jazz Messengers | CBS | CK 62265
Art Tatum | The Tatum Solo Masterpieces Vol.4 | Pablo | 2310789
Ben Webster Quintet | Soulville | Verve | 521449-2
Benny Carter And His Orchestra | Three Great Swing Saxophones | RCA | NL 90405
Earl Hines | One For My Baby | Black Lion | BLCD 760198
Ella Fitzgerald With The Billy May Orchestra | The Best Of The Song Books:The Ballads | Verve | 521867-2
The Complete Ella Fitzgerald Song Books of Harold Arlen, Irving Berlin, Duke Ellington, George & Ira Gershwin, Jerome Kern, Johnny Mercer, Cole Porter And Rogers & Hart | Verve | 519832-2
Helen Merrill And Her Band | You And The Night And The Music | Verve | 537087-2
Larry Coryell-Emily Remler Duo | Together | Concord | CJ 289
Lee Morgan Sextet | Cornbread | Blue Note | 784222-2
Louis Hayes Quintet | The Candy Man | TCB Records | TCB 20972
Oscar Peterson Trio | En Concert Avec Europe 1 | Laserlight | 710443/48
Paul Desmond With Strings | Desmond Blue | RCA | 2663898-2
Phineas Newborn Jr. Trio | Back Home | Original Jazz Classics | OJCCD 971-2(C 7648)
Sarah Vaughan With Orchestra | The Best Of Sarah Vaughan | Pablo | 2405416-2
Stan Kenton And His Orchestra | Standards In Silhouette | Capitol | ST 1049
Terrie Richard Alden And The Warren Vaché Quartet | Voice With Heart | Nagel-Heyer | CD 048
Thad Jones Sextet | Magnificent Thad Jones Vol.3 | Blue Note | 300147(1546)
Zoot Sims Quartet | The Big Stampede | Biograph | BLP 12064

Ill Wind(alt. take)
Horace Parlan | The Maestro | Steeplechase | SCCD 31167

Ill Wind(You're Blowin' Me No Good)
Coleman Hawkins With The Oscar Peterson Quartet | Verve Jazz Masters 43:Coleman Hawkins | Verve | 521856-2
Ella Fitzgerald With The Billy May Orchestra | Ella Fitzgerald Sings The Harold Arlen Song Book | Verve | 589108-2
Lennie Niehaus Sextet | Lennie Niehaus Vol.5:The Sextet | Original Jazz Classics | OJCCD 1944-2(C 3524)
Milt Jackson Quartet | The Jazz Giants Play Harold Arlen:Blues In The Night | Prestige | PCD 24201-2
Oscar Peterson | Oscar Peterson Plays The Harold Arlen Song Book | Verve | 589103-2
Chico Freeman Group | The Emissary | Clarity Recordings | CCD-1015

I'll Write A Song For You
Chico Freeman Septet | The Search | India Navigation | IN 1059

Illinoise
Art Ensemble Of Chicago | Fanfare For The Warriors | Atlantic | 90046-1 TIS

Illumination
Walter Davis Jr. Quartet | Illumination | Jazz City | 660.53.004

Illusion
Nat King Cole With The Ralph Carmichael Orchestra | The Touch Of Your Lips | Capitol | EMS 1111
Zollsounds 4 feat. Lee Konitz | Open Hearts | Enja | 9123-2

Illusions
Arthur Blythe Quintet | Illusions | CBS | SRCS 7188
Curtis Amy Group | Peace For Love | Fresh Sound Records | FSR CD 5004
Eliane Elias Trio | The Best Of Eliane Elias On Denon Years | Denon Compact Disc | DC-8592
Ron McClure Quintet | Never Forget | Steeplechase | SCCD 31279

Ils Vagants-Senza Patria(Homeless)
Markus Stockhausen Orchestra | Sol Mestizo:Markus Stockhausen Plays The Music Of Enrique Diaz | ACT | 9222-2

Ilumination
Joan Abril Sextet | Eric | Fresh Sound Records | FSNT 092 CD

Ilúsiao
Jorge Sylvester Quintet | Musicollage | Postcards | POST 1011

I'm A Comin' On Home
Eddie Playboy Taylor | The Blues Vol. 5 | Big Bear | 156042

I'm A Ding Dong Daddy
Benny Goodman Quartet | Benny Goodman:The Complete Small Combinations Vol.3/4 | RCA | ND 89754

I'm A Dreamer Aren't We All
John Marshall Quintet | Dreamin' On The Hudson | Organic Music | ORGM 9713
Keith Ingham & Marty Grosz And Their Hot Cosmopolites | Just Imagine..Songs Of DeSylva, Brown And Henderson | Stomp Off Records | CD 1285

I'm A Fool To Want You
Billie Holiday With The Ray Ellis Orchestra | This Is Jazz:Billie Holiday Sings Standards | CBS | CK 65048
Chet Baker Quartet | Last Recording As Quartet(Live in Rosenheim '88) | Timeless | CD SJP 233
Dinah Washington With The Ike Carpenter Orchestra | The Complete Dinah Washington Vol.7 | Official | 3018
Hank Mobley Quartet | Complete 'The Jazz Message Sessions With Kenny Clarke' | The Jazz Factory | JFCD 22858
Lisa Ekdahl With The Peter Nordahl Trio | When Did You Leave Heaven | RCA | 2143175-2
Mark Nightingale Quartet | What I Wanted To Say | Mons Records | MR 874763

I'm A Fool To Want You-
Richie Vitale Quintet | The Richie Vitaleo Quintet feat.Ralph Lalama | TCB Records | TCB 96402

I'm A Fool To Want You(alt.take 1)
Lee Morgan Quintet | Here's Lee Morgan | Vee Jay Recordings | VJ 005

I'm A Fool To Want You(alt.take 2)
Here's Lee Morgan | Vee Jay Recordings | VJ 005

I'm A Little Blackbird Looking For A Little Bluebird
Eva Taylor With Clarence Williams' Blue Five | Louis Armstrong And The Blues Singers 1924-1930 | Affinity | AFS 1018(6)

I'm A Loser
Vince Guaraldi-Bola Sete Quartet | Live At El Matador | Original Jazz Classics | OJC 289(F 8371)

I'm A Old Cowhand
Nat King Cole Trio With Maxine Johnson | Nat King Cole | Savoy | 650120(881920)

I'm A Poor Boy
Eddie Boyd Blues Band | Blues Roots Vol. 20: Eddie Boyd | Chess | 6.24810 AG

I'm A Rattlesnakin' Daddy
Victoria Spivey | Bawdy Blues | Original Blues Classics | OBCCD 544-2(BV 1055)

I'm A Red Hot Mama
Victoria Spivey With Lonnie Johnson | Woman Blues! | Original Blues Classics | OBCCD 566-2(BV 1054)

I'm A Salty Dog - (I'm A) Salty Dog
Cannonball Adderley Group | Cannonball Adderley-Lovers... | Fantasy | F 9505
George Lewis Band Of New Orleans | Jazz At Preservation Hall, Vol.4 | Atlantic | SD 1411

I'm A Sentimental Tango
Toto Blanke-Rudolf Dasek | Two Much Guitar! | ALISO Records | AL 1022
Nat King Cole Trio | The Small Black Groups | Storyville | 4960523

I'm A Shy Guy
The Best Of The Nat King Cole Trio:The Vocal Classics(1942-1946) | Blue Note | 833571-2
Annie Laurie With Andy Gibson's Orchestra | It Hurts To Be In Love | Sing | 1155

I'm A Steady Rollin' Man
Robert Lockwood Jr. | Robert Lockwood Jr. Plays Robert(Johnson) & Robert(Lockwood) | Black & Blue | BLE 59.740 2

I'm A Stranger Here Myself
Dee Dee Bridgewater With Band | Dee Dee Bridgewater Sings Kurt Weil | EmArCy | 9809601
American Folk Blues Festival | American Folk Blues Festival 1964 | L+R Records | CDLR 42024

I'm A Woman Locked Inside A Man's Body
T-Bone Walker And His Band | Classics Of Modern Blues | Blue Note | 84550

I'm Afraid
Charles Lloyd Quintet | Lift Every Voice | ECM | 1832/33(018783-2)
The Mills Brothers With Orchestra | The Golden Years Of The Mills Brothers | Ember | NR 5090

I'm Afraid The Masquerade Is Over - (I'm Afraid) The Masquerade Is Over
Alice Day With The Andy Scherrer Quartet | CoJazz Plus | TCB Records | TCB 96052
Ann Richards With The Jack Sheldon Quartet | Ann,Man! | Atlantic | AMCY 1071
Cannonball Adderley With Richard Hayman's Orchestra | Julian Cannonball Adderley And Strings/Jump For Joy | Verve | 528699-2
Eliane Elias | Eliane Elias | Blue Note | 832073-2
Gene Harris And The All Star Big Band | Tribute To Count Basie | Concord | CCD 4337
Johnny Griffin Quartet | The Man I Love | Black Lion | BLP 60107
Kenny Burrell Quartet | Stormy Monday | Fantasy | F 9558
Lou Colombo Quintet | I Remember Bobby | Concord | CCD 4435
Nancy Wilson With The Joe Zawinul Trio | Nancy Wilson/The Cannonball Adderley Quintet | Capitol | 781204-2
Ron Crotty Trio | The Jazz Scene:San Francisco | Fantasy | FCD 24760-2
Modern Jazz From San Francisco | Original Jazz Classics | OJC 272(F 3213)
Sarah Vaughan With The Jimmy Jones Trio | Linger Awhile | Pablo | 2312144-2
Sonny Criss Quartet | The Sonny Criss Memorial Album | DIW | DIW 302 CD
Torsten Goods Group | Manhattan Walls | Jardis Records | JRCD 20139
Uschi Brüning And Ernst-Ludwig Petrowsky With The Günter Bartel Trio | Enfant | Aho-Recording | CD 1017

I'm Alabamy Bound -> Alabamy Bound

I'm All For You
Etta Jones And Her Band | Ms. Jones To You | Muse | MR 5099

I'm All Smiles
Bill Evans Quartet With Orchestra | From Left To Right | Verve | 557451-2
Carol Kidd With The Sandy Taylor Trio And String Quartet | All My Tomorrows | Linn Records | AKD 005
Kenny Drew Jr. Trio | Third Phase | Jazz City | 660.53.002
Phil Woods Quartet With Orchestra & Strings | Round Trip | Verve | 559804-2
Steve Rochinski Quartet | Otherwise | Jardis Records | JRCD 20133
Jenny Evans And Her Quintet | Nuages | Enja | ENJ-9467 2

I'm Alone After All
Nuages | ESM Records | ESM 9308
Marlene And Her Band | Elemental Soul | Concord | CCD 4774

I'm Always Chasing Butterflies
Bud Powell Trio | Ups 'N Downs | Mainstream | MD CDO 724

I'm Always Chasing Rainbows
Reuben Brown | Blue And Brown | Steeplechase | SCCD 31445

I'm Always Drunk In San Francisco
Mike Campbell And His Band | Secret Fantasy | Palo Alto | PA 8020

I'm An Errand Boy For Rhythm
Nat King Cole Trio | Nat King Cole:For Sentimental Reasons | Dreyfus Jazz Line | FDM 36740-2
Great Capitol Masters | Pathe | 1566251(Capitol)

I'm An Errand Girl For Rhythm
Clusone 3 | I Am An Indian | Gramavision | GCD 79505

I'm An Old Cowhand
Jimmy Smith Trio | Bashin' | Verve | 2304481 IMS
Sonny Rollins Trio | Contemporary Sonny Rollins-Alternate Takes | Contemporary | C 7651
Jazz Gallerie:Sonny Rollins Vol.1 | RCA | 2127283-2

I'm An Old Cowhand(alt.take)
Sonny Rollins-The Freelance Years:The Complete Riverside & Contemporary Recordings | Riverside | 5 RCD 4427-2
Duke Pearson Trio | Bag's Groove | Black Lion | BLCD 760149

Im August
Horace Silver Quintet/Sextet With Vocals | Total Response | Blue Note | 300212

I'm Be Boppin' Too
Dizzy Gillespie And His Orchestra | Planet Jazz:Male Jazz Vocalists | Planet Jazz | 2169657-2
Dizzier And Dizzier | RCA | 26685172

I'm Beginning To See The Light
Al Casey Quartet | Jumpin' With Al | Black & Blue | BB 873.2
Art Tatum | Art Tatum:Memories Of You | Black Lion | BLCD 7608-2
Benny Carter Quintet | All That Jazz-Live At Princeton | Limelight | 820841-2 IMS
Bill Ramsey With Orchestra | Gettin' Back To Swing | Bear Family Records | BCD 15813 AH
Billy Eckstine With The Billy May Orchestra | Once More With Feeling | Roulette | 581862-2
Billy Eckstine | Laserlight | 17070
Clare Fischer Orchestra | America The Beautiful | Discovery | DS 786 IMS
Cootie Williams And His Orchestra | Cootie Williams-Typhoon | Swingtime(Contact) | ST 1003
Della Reese With The Neal Hefti Orchestra | Della | RCA | 2663912-2
Diane Schuur With The Dave Grusin Orchestra | Deedles | GRP | GRP 91010-1(808702)
Don Byas Quartet | Don Byas Complete 1946-1951 European Small Group Master Takes | Definitive Records | DRCD 11214
Duke Ellington And His Orchestra | Duke Ellington:The Complete RCA-Victor Mid-Forties Recordings(1944-1946) | RCA | 2663394-2
Duke Ellington | Bluebird | ND 86641(3)
Earl Hines | Earl Hine Plays Duke Ellington | New World Records | 80361/362-2
Ella Fitzgerald With The Count Basie Orchestra | Ella And Basie | Verve | 539059-2
Ella & Basie-On The Sunny Side Of The Street | Verve | 821576-2
Ella Fitzgerald With The Duke Ellington Orchestra | Love Songs:The Best Of The Song Books | Verve | 531762-2
The Complete Ella Fitzgerald Song Books of Harold Arlen, Irving Berlin, Duke Ellington, George & Ira Gershwin, Jerome Kern, Johnny Mercer, Cole Porter And Rogers & Hart | Verve | 519832-2
Harry James And His Orchestra | Trumpet Blues:The Best Of Harry James | Capitol | 521224-2
Jack Sharpe Big Band | Roarin' | Ronnie Scott's Jazz House | JHCD 016
Johnny Hodges-Wild Bill Davis Sextet | Johnny Hodges-Wild Bill Davis, Vol.1-2(1965-1966) | RCA | ND 89765
Louis Armstrong-Duke Ellington Group | The Complete Louis Armstrong & Duke Ellington Sessions | Roulette | 793844-2
Mary Osborne Quintet | Now And Then | Stash Records | ST 215 IMS
Peter Nero Trio | Now | Concord | CCD 4048

I'm Beginning To See The Light-
Billy Eckstine With Bobby Tucker And His Orchestra | No Cover No Minimum | Blue Note | 798583-2
Duke Ellington | Masters Of Jazz Vol.6:Duke Ellington | Storyville | STCD 4106
Duke Ellington And His Orchestra | Duke Ellington:The Complete RCA-Victor Mid-Forties Recordings(1944-1946) | RCA | 2663394-2

I'm Beginning To See The Light(alt.take)
First Class Blues Band | The First Class Blues Band Proudly Presents Mr. Frank Biner | Acoustic Music Records | 319.1062.2

I'm Burnin' Up(Fire Theme)
Steve Coleman And Five Elements | Steve Coleman's Music Live In Paris | Novus | 2131691-2

I'm Calling You
Nat Pierce Quintet | Crosby-Bennett-Çlooney-Herman:A Tribute To Duke | Concord | CCD 4050

I'm Checking Out Goodbye
Bob Wilber Big Band | Bufadora Blow-up | Arbors Records | ARCD 19187

I'm Coming Home
Clifton Chenier And His Band | King Of The Bayous | Arhoolie | CD 339

I'm Coming Through
Edwin Hawkins Singers | The Best Of The Edwin Hawkins Singers | Warner | 252213-1

I'm Coming Virginia
Art Tatum | Art Tatum At The Piano Vol.2 | GNP Crescendo | GNP 9026
Benny Carter And His Orchestra | Django Reinhardt All Star Sessions | Capitol | 531577-2
L'Essentiel Django Reinhardt | EMI Records | 780671-2
Benny Goodman And His Orchestra | Live At The International World Exhibition,Brussels 1958: The Unissued Recordings | Magic | DAWE 36(881849)
Benny Goodman Septet | 1938 Carnegie Hall Concert | CBS | 450983-2
Dinah Shore With Orchestra | The Best Of Dinah Shore | Capitol | 792895-2
Ed Hall And The All Star Stompers | This Is Jazz Vol.3 | Storyville | SLP 4069
Gene Krupa Septet | The Exciting Gene Krupa | Enoch's Music | 57271033
Stephane Grappelli With The George Shearing Trio | Compact Jazz:Stephane Grappelli | MPS | 831370-2 PMS

I'm Coming Virginia-
Sidney Bechet And His New Orleans Feetwarmers | Sidney Bechet 1932-1943: The Bluebird Sessions | Bluebird | ND 90317

I'm Confessin'(That I Love You)
Cat Anderson & The Ellington All-Stars | Cat Anderson | Swing | SW 8412 IMS
Django Reinhardt And The Quintet Du Hot Club De France | Django Reinhardt Portrait | Barclay | DALP 2/1939
Eric Lugosch | Kind Heroes | Acoustic Music Records | 319.1188.2
Jo Ann Strazzeri With The Frank Strazzeri Quartet | Presenting Jo Ann Strazzeri | Fresh Sound Records | FSR 109

Kenny Burrell Quartet | The Tender Gender | Cadet | 515001
Lester Young And His Band | Lester Young:The Complete Aladdin Sessions | Blue Note | 832787-2
Lester Young Quartet | Live At The Royal Roost | Jazz Anthology | JA 5214
Lester Young With The Oscar Peterson Quartet | Lester Swings Again | Verve | MV 2680 IMS
Liller & Papa Bue's Viking Jazzband | En Buttet Og En Skaeg Mand | Storyville | SLP 279
Thelonious Monk | Solo Monk | CBS | 471248-2
Urbie Green And His Orchestra | The Message | Fresh Sound Records | NL 46033(RCA)
Veterinary Street Jazz Band | Everybody Stomp | Elite Special | 730220
Benny Carter And His Orchestra | Benny Carter-Live And Well In Japan! | Pablo | 2308216

I'm Confessin'(That I Love You)(alt.take)
V-Disc All Star Jam Session | Louis Armstrong-Jack Teagarden-Woody Herman:Midnights At V-Disc | Jazz Unlimited | JUCD 2048
Cousin Joe | The Blues Vol.3 | Big Bear | 156400

I'm Crazy 'Bout My Baby
Fats Waller | Jazz Classics In Digital Stereo: Fats Waller | CDS Records Ltd. | RPCD 619(CD 598)
Fats Waller And His Rhythm | Planet Jazz Sampler | Planet Jazz | 2152326-2
Fats Waller:The Complete Associated Transcription Sessions 1935-1939 | Jazz Unlimited | JUCD 2076
Fats Waller-The Joint Is Jumpin' | RCA | ND 86288(874182)
Joe Turner | I Understand | Black & Blue | BLE 59.153 2
Louis Armstrong And His All Stars | Satch Plays Fats(Complete) | CBS | CK 64927
The Louis Armstrong Selection | CBS | 467278-2
Tom Saunders' 'Wild Bill Davison Band' & Guests | Exactly Like You | Nagel-Heyer | CD 023
Weslia Whitefield With The Mike Greensill Duo | Nice Work... | Landmark | LCD 1544-2

I'm Crazy 'Bout My Baby(alt.take)
Louis Armstrong And His All Stars | Satch Plays Fats(Complete) | CBS | CK 64927
Clyde Bernhardt And His Blue Bazers | Clyde Bernhardt:The Complete Recordings Vol.1 (1945-1948) | Blue Moon | BMCD 6016

I'm Delirium
Blueslady Toni Spearman + Wetsox | Rock With Mama ! | Star Club | SWX 186

I'm Dreamer Aren't We All
$$hide$$ | $$Titelverweise | |

I'm Dreaming Of A White Christmas -> WhiteChristmas

I'm Drifter
Earl Hines And His Orchestra | The Indispensable Earl Hines Vol.1/2 | RCA | 2126407-2

I'm Getting Sentimental Over You
Anthony Braxton | Wesleyan(12 Altosolos) 1992 | Hat Art | CD 6128
Bill Evans Trio | The Complete Bill Evans On Verve | Verve | 527953-2
A Simple Matter Of Conviction | Verve | 23MJ 3040 IMS
Bill Evans:The Secret Sessions | Milestone | 8MCD 4421-2
Bill Evans-Jim Hall | Undercurrent | Blue Note | 538228-2
Bill Harris And Friends | Bill Harris And Friends | Original Jazz Classics | OJC 083(F 3263)
Conrad Herwig Quartet | New York Hardball | Ken Music | 660.56.002
Count Basie And His Orchestra | Basie's Timing | MPS | 88016-2
Ella Fitzgerald With The Count Basie Orchestra | A Classy Pair | Pablo | 2312132-2
Fraser MacPherson Trio | Live At The Planetarium | Concord | CJ 92
John Abercrombie-Don Thompson | Witch Craft | Justin Time | Just 16
Roy Williams With The Eddie Thompson Trio | Something Wonderful | Hep | 2015
Schnuckenack Reinhardt Quintet | Live | Intercord | 160035
Sir Charles Thompson Trio | Stardust | Paddle Wheel | KICJ 225
The Dorsey Brothers Orchestra | Mood Hollywood | Hep | 1005
Thelonious Monk | Thelonious Monk-The Complete Riverside Recordings | Riverside | 15 RCD 022-2
Thelonious Monk Quartet | En Concert Avec Europe 1 | Laserlight | 710377/78
April In Paris | Milestone | M 47060
Live At Monterey Jazz Festival,1963 | Jazz Unlimited | JUCD 2045/2046
Thelonious Monk Sextet | In Person | Milestone | M 47033
Tommy Dorsey And His Orchestra | This Is Tommy Dorsey | RCA | PL 89536 DP

I'm Getting Sentimental Over You(alt.take)
Zoot Sims Quartet | Getting Sentimental | Choice | CHCD 71006
Lee Konitz Trio | Motion | Verve | 557107-2

I'm Glad There Is You
Barney Kessel Quintet | Red Hot And Blues | Contemporary | CCD 14044-2
Carmen McRae And Her Quintet | Any Old Time | Denon Compact Disc | CY-1216
Danny Moss Quartet | The Second Sampler | Nagel-Heyer | NHR SP 6
David Sills Quintet | Bigs | Naxos Jazz | 86070-2
Eric Alexander Quartet | The First Milestone | Milestone | MCD 9302-2
Eric Kloss Quartet | About Time | Prestige | PRCD 24268-2
Ethel Azama With The Marty Paich Orchestra | Cool Heat | Fresh Sound Records | 054 2600411(Liberty LRP 3142)
Hal McKusick Quintet | Triple Exposure | Original Jazz Classics | OJCCD 1811-2(P 7135)
Jimmy Rowles-Red Mitchell Quartet | I'm Glad There Is You | Contemporary | CCD 14032-2
Johnny Griffin Quartet | The Congregation | Blue Note | 300189(1580)
Kenny Burrell Trio | Handcrafted | Muse | MR 5144
Kenny Clarke-Francy Boland Big Band | En Concert Avec Europe 1 | Laserlight | 710413/14
Russ Garcia And His Orchestra | Jazz City Presents... | Fresh Sound Records | FSR 2017(Bethlehem BCP 80)
Sarah Vaughan With The Clifford Brown All Stars | Sarah Vaughan | Verve | 543305-2
Brownie-The Complete EmArCy Recordings Of Clifford Brown | EmArCy | 838306-2
Sathima Bea Benjamin Group | A Morning In Paris | Enja | ENJ-9309 2
Sathima Bea Benjamin With The Kenny Barron Trio | Southern Touch | Enja | ENJ-7015 2
Stan Kenton And His Orchestra | By Request Vol.5 | Creative World | ST 1066
The Fabulous New Jimmy Dorsey Orchestra | Dorsey Then And Now | Atlantic | 81801-1 TIS

I'm Glad You're Glad
Mezzrow-Bechet Quintet | The King Jazz Story Vol. 7+8 | Storyville | SLP 820/21

I'm Goin' To Jackson
Eddie 'Blues Man' Kirkland Band | It's The Blues Man! | Original Blues Classics | OBCCD 513-2(Tru 15010)

I'm Going Back Home
Nina Simone With Hal Mooney's Orchestra | Verve Jazz Masters Vol.58:Nina Simone Sings Nina | Verve | 529867-2
Nina Simone With Orchestra | Nina Simone-The 60s Vol.3:Work Song | Mercury | 838545-2 PMS

I'm Going To Shout
Taj Mahal And The International Rhythm Band | Taj Mahal | The Rising Sun Collection | RSC 0003

I'm Going Way Down Home
Ella Mae Morse With Orchestra | Sensational Ella Mae Morse | Pathe | 1566211

I'm Gonna Charleston
Gene Krupa And His Swing Band | The Original Sounds Of The Swing Era Vol. 6 | RCA | NL 85515 DP

I'm Gonna Go Fishin'
Gerry Mulligan Concert Jazz Band | En Concert Avec Europe 1 | Laserlight | 710382/83
Jenny Evans And Her Quintet | Gonna Go Fishin' | Enja | ENJ-9403 2
Singers Unlimited With The Patrick Williams Orchestra | Compact Disc:The Singers Unlimited | MPS | 831373-2 PMS

I'm Gonna Laugh You Out Of My Life
Dinah Washington With The Don Costa Orchestra | Drinking Again | M&M Records | R 25183(Roulette)
Larry Willis Trio | Serenade | Sound Hills | SSCD 8063
Sarah Vaughan And Her Band | The Devine One | Fresh Sound Records | FSR 659(Roulette R 52060)

I'm Gonna Leave You
Nina Simone With Orchestra | Nina Simone-The 60s Vol.3:Work Song | Mercury | 838545-2 PMS

I'm Gonna Leave You On The Outskirts Of Town
Jenny Evans And Her Quintet | Gonna Go Fishin' | ESM Records | ESM 9307

I'm Gonna Live 'Till I Die
Gonna Go Fishin' | Enja | ENJ-9403 2

I'm Gonna Meet My Sweety Now
The Back Bay Ramblers | My Mamma's In Town! | Stomp Off Records | CD 1279

I'm Gonna Move To The Outskirts Of Town
Geoff Bradford Group | Tribute To Fats Waller | Jazz Colours | 874730-2
Louis Jordan And His Tympany Five | Louis Jordan-Let The Good Times Roll: The Complete Decca Recordings 1938-1954 | Bear Family Records | BCD 15557 IH
Louis Jordan Vol.2-Knock Me Out | Swingtime(Contact) | ST 1012

I'm Gonna Serve The Lord
Big Bill Broonzy | Trouble In Mind | Spotlite | SPJ 900

I'm Gonna Sit Right Down And Write Myself A Letter
Art Tatum | Art Tatum-The Standard Transcriptions | Music & Arts | CD 919
Bill Ramsey With Orchestra | Gettin' Back To Swing | Bear Family Records | BCD 15813 AH
Charlie Byrd Trio | I've Got The World On A String(Charlie Byrd Sings Again) | Timeless | CD SJP 427
Dutch Swing College Band With Johnny Meyer | Johnny Goes Dixie | DSC Production | PA 1014 (801069)
Ella Fitzgerald With The Don Abney Trio | Ella Fitzgerald, Billie Holiday And Carmen McRae At Newport | Verve | 559809-2
Fats Waller And His Rhythm | I'm Gonna Sit Right Down...The Early Years-Part 2(1935-1936) | Bluebird | 63 66640-2
George Brunis And His Jazzband | The Davison-Brunis Sessions Vol. 3 | London | HMC 5013 AN
Madeline Bell With The Metropole Orchestra | Beat Out That Rhythm On A Drum | Koch Jazz | 3-6910-2
Ralph Sutton Quartet | The Ralph Sutton Quartet With Ruby Braff,Vol.2 | Storyville | STCD 8246
Live At Sunnie's Rendezvous Vol.1 | Storyville | STCD 8280
Ralph Sutton-Bernd Lhotzky | Stridin' High | Jazz Connaisseur | JCCD 9728-2
Ralph Sutton-Ruby Braff Duo | Ralph Sutton & Ruby Braff | Chaz Jazz | CJ 101

I'm Gonna Sit Right Down And Write Myself A Letter-
WDR Big Band | Harlem Story | Koala Records | CD P 7

I'm Gonna Stomp Mr.Henry Lee
Eddie Miller And His Orchestra | Swinging Tenors | Affinity | AFF 64
Jack Teagarden And His Band | The Club Hangover Broadcast | Arbors Records | ARCD 19150/51

I'm Gonna Wash That Man Right Outa My Hair
Chris Barber's Jazz Band | Barber's Choice | Vagabond | 6.28491 DP

I'm Grätenwald
Fats Waller And His Rhythm | The Classic Years In Digital Stereo: Fats Waller And His Rhythm | CDS Records Ltd. | RPCD 315(CD 684)

I'm Hip
Dave Frishberg Trio | Classics | Concord | CCD 4462

I'm His Boss
Al Jarreau With Band | All Fly Home | Warner | 7599-27362-2

I'm Home
Fats Waller And His Rhythm | The Indispensable Fats Waller Vol.1/2 | RCA | 2122616-2

I'm In A Dancing Mood
Putney Dandridge Band | Putney Dandridge 1935-1936 | Timeless | CBC 1-023

I'm In Love
Abbey Lincoln With The Stan Getz Quartet | You Gotta Pay The Band | Verve | 511110-2
American Folk Blues Festival | American Folk Blues Festival '62 | L+R Records | LR 42017
Memphis Slim/T-Bone Walker Quartet | American Folk Blues Festival | Polydor | 2310296 IMS
The Halfway House Dance Orchestra | The Halfway House Orchestra-The Complete Recordings In Chronological Order | Jazz Oracle | BDW 8001

I'm In Love With Miss Logan
Anita Boyer & Her Tomboyers | Nat King Cole Trio:The MacGregor Years 1941/45 | Music & Arts | CD 911

I'm In Love(alt.take)
Al Jolson With Orchestra | Al Jolson-Great Original Performances(1926-1932) | CDS Records Ltd. | RPCD 300

I'm In The Mood For Love
Art Tatum | The Art Tatum Solo Masterpieces | Pablo | 2625703
Bill Coleman Trio | Bill Coleman | Swing | SW 8402 IMS
Charlie Parker Quartet | Charlie Parker: The Verve Years (1948-50) | Verve | 2-2501 IMS
Charlie Parker | Verve | 539757-2
Charlie Parker With Strings | Charlie Parker:April In Paris | Dreyfus Jazz Line | FDM 36737-2
The Verve Years (1950-51) | Verve | 2-2512 IMS
Coleman Hawkins Quintet | Ultimate Coleman Hawkins selected by Sonny Rollins | Verve | 557538-2
David Murray-George Arvanitas | Tea For Two | Fresh Sound Records | FSR-CD 0164
Ella Fitzgerald With The Tommy Flanagan Quartet | Ella Fitzgerald:Newport Jazz Festival-Live at Carnegie Hall | CBS | C2K 66809
Erroll Garner Trio | The Complete Savoy Sessions Vol.2 | Savoy | WL 70542 (809296)
Lester Young And His Orchestra | It Don't Mean A Thing (If It Ain't Got That Swing) | Verve | MV 2685 IMS
Louis Armstrong With Luis Russell And His Orchestra | Ambassador Louis Armstrong Vol.1(1935) | Ambassador | CLA 1901
Marc Ribot | Don't Blame Me | DIW | DIW 902 CD
Nat King Cole Trio | The Legendary 1941-44 Broadcast Transcriptions | Music & Arts | CD 808
Oscar Peterson Trio | Girl Talk | MPS | 68074
Putney Dandridge Band | Putney Dandridge 1935-1936 | Timeless | CBC 1-023
Shirley Horn With The Quincy Jones Orchestra | Loads Of Love + Shirley Horn With Horns | Mercury | 843454-2
Sonny Stitt Quartet | Live At The Hi-Hat Boston | Fresh Sound Records | FSCD 1002
Zoot Sims Quartet | Zoot Sims:The Complete 1944-1954 Small Group Sessions(Master Takes),Vol.4 | Blue Moon | BMCD 1041

I'm In The Mood For Love(take 2)
Charlie Parker With Strings | Bird: The Complete Charlie Parker On Verve | Verve | 837141-2

I'm In The Mood For Love(take 3)
Benny Carter Big Band | On The Air | Nueva Records | JU 327

I'm In The Mood For Swing
Lionel Hampton And His Orchestra | Planet Jazz:Jazz Saxophone | Planet Jazz | 2169653-2
The Complete Lionel Hampton Vol.1/2(1937-1938) | RCA | 2115525-2

Im Internet
Ella Fitzgerald With The Chick Webb Orchestra | Ella Fitzgerald-The Early Years-Part 1 | GRP | GRP 26182

I'm Just A Lucky So-And-So
Annie Ross With Her Quintet | A Gasser | Pacific Jazz | 746854-2
Bill Mays Trio | An Ellington Affair | Concord | CCD 4651
Chico Hamilton Quintet | The Original Ellington Suite | Pacific Jazz | 524567-2
Dakota Staton With Her Quartet | Darling Please Save Your Love For Me | Muse | MCD 5462
Duke Ellington And His Orchestra | Duke Ellington | Bluebird | ND 86641(3)
Ella Fitzgerald With The Duke Ellington Orchestra | The Complete Ella Fitzgerald Song Books of Harold Arlen, Irving Berlin, Duke Ellington, George & Ira Gershwin, Jerome Kern, Johnny Mercer, Cole Porter And Rogers & Hart | Verve | 519832-2
Ella Fitzgerald With The Hank Jones Trio | The Complete Jazz At The Philharmonic On Verve 1944-1949 | Verve | 523893-2
Ernestine Anderson And Her Quartet | When The Sun Goes Down | Concord | CCD 4263
Jimmy Smith Trio | Standards | Blue Note | 821282-2
Kenny Burrell Quintet | Soul Call | Original Jazz Classics | OJCCD 846-2(P 7315)
Ellington Is Forever Vol.2 | Fantasy | F 79008
Louis Armstrong-Duke Ellington Group | The Complete Louis Armstrong & Duke Ellington Sessions | Roulette | 793844-2
Marilyn Moore With Don Abney And His Orchestra | Moody | Affinity | AFF 157
Mose Allison Sextet | Middle Class White Boy | Discovery | 71011-2
Soesja Citroen And Her Trio | Here And Now | Challenge | CHR 70003
The Chris White Project | The Chris White Project | Muse | MCD 5494
Wes Montgomery Quintet | Wes Montgomery-The Complete Riverside Recordings | Riverside | 12 RCD 4408-2
Wild Bill Davis Super Trio | That's All | Jazz Connaisseur | JCCD 9005-2
Yusef Lateef Quintet | The Many Faces Of Yusef Lateef | Milestone | M 47009

I'm Just A Lucky So-And-So(alt.take)
Duffy Jackson Orchestra | Swing! Swing! Swing! | Milestone | MCD 9233-2

I'm Just Wild About Harry
Slam Stewart Quartet | Fish Scales | Black & Blue | BLE 233109

I'm Just Your Fool
Jimmy Witherspoon And His Quartet | Jimmy Witherspoon Live | Kingdom Jazz | CDGATE 7023(882990)

I'm Late, I'm Late
Stan Getz With The Eddie Sauter Orchestra | Stan Getz:Focus | CTI Records | PDCTI 1111-2

I'm Left With The Blues In My Heart
Tatum-Carter-Bellson Trio | The Tatum Group Masterpieces | Pablo | 2625706

Im Lichthaus
Benny Goodman And His Orchestra | Jazz Giants:Benny Goodman | RCA | NL 89731 SI

I'm Looking Over A Four Leaf Clover
Jean Goldkette And His Orchestra | The Indispensable Bix Beiderbecke(1924-1930) | RCA | ND 89572

I'm Lost
The Heath Brothers Orchestra | Jazz Family | Concord | CCD 4846

I'm Lost Without
Les Blue Stars | Jazz In Paris:Les Blue Stars-Pardon My English/Henri Salvador-Plays The Blues | EmArCy | 013035-2

I'm Movin' On
Jimmy Smith Trio | I'm Movin' On | Blue Note | 832750-2
King Curtis Band | King Curtis-Blow Man Blow | Bear Family Records | BCD 15670 CI
Charlie Mariano-Gregor Josephs Quartet | Lustinseln | L+R Records | CDLR 45097

Im Nebel Nach Brüssel
Lightnin' Hopkins | Really The Blues | America | AM 6080

I'm Never Happy Anymore
Per Husby Orchestra | Dedications | Affinity | AFF 136

I'm Nobody
Vocal Summit | Conference Of The Birds | ITM-Pacific | ITMP 970070

I'm Not A Spy
Anima Claudine Myers Duo | Song For Nother E | LEO | LR 100

I'm Not Ashamed To Sing The Blues
Ella Fitzgerald And Her Famous Orchestra | Ella Fitzgerald Vol.2-Forever Young | Swingtime(Contact) | ST 1007

I'm Not Lonely
Freddy Cole Trio | I'm Not My Brother,I'm Me | Sunnyside | SSC 1054 D

I'm Not Rough
Bob Scobey's Frisco Band | Victor Jazz History Vol.19:Dixieland Revival | RCA | 2135738-2

I'm Not So Sure
Cedar Walton Quintet | As Long As There's Music | Muse | MCD 5405

I'm Not Such A Bad Guy
Anita O'Day With The Cal Tjader Quartet | Time For 2 | Verve | 559808-2

I'm Not Supposed To Be Blue Blues
Abbey Lincoln And Her Trio With Guests | Over The Years | Verve | 549101-2

I'm Not Supposed To Know
Nicki Leighton-Thomas Group | Forbidden Games | Candid | CCD 79778

I'm Not Taking Any Chances
Mose Allison Trio | The Mose Chronicles-Live In London,Vol.1 | Blue Note | 529747-2

I'm Not Talkin'
The Word From Mose | Atlantic | 8122-72394-2
Bianca Ciccu With The Randy Brecker Quintet | The Gusch | ITM Records | ITM 1440

I'm Okay
Stan Getz-Kenny Barron | Stan Getz Cafe Montmartre | EmArCy | 586755-2
Adam Makowicz Trio | The Music Of Jerome Kern | Concord | CCD 4575

I'm Old Fashioned
Cassandra Wilson With The Mulgrew Miller Trio | A Fine Romance | Verve | 523827-2
Cedar Walton | Maybeck Recital Hall Series Volume Twenty-Five | Concord | CCD 4546
Chet Baker Trio | Someday My Prince Will Come | Steeplechase | SCS 1180(Audiophile Pressing)
Derek Smith Trio | Derek Smith Trio Plays Jerome Kern | Progressive | PRO 7055 IMS
Ella Fitzgerald With The Nelson Riddle Orchestra | The Best Of The Song Books:The Ballads | Verve | 521867-2
The Complete Ella Fitzgerald Song Books of Harold Arlen, Irving Berlin, Duke Ellington, George & Ira Gershwin, Jerome Kern, Johnny Mercer, Cole Porter And Rogers & Hart | Verve | 519832-2
John Coltrane Sextet | Blue Train | Mobile Fidelity | MFCD 547(UDCD)
Johnny Frigo Sextet | Debut Of A Legend | Chesky | JD 119
Kenny Burrell Quintet | Sunup To Sundown | Contemporary | CCD 14065-2
Larry Schneider Quartet | Ali Girl | Steeplechase | SCCD 31429
Margaret Whiting With Russel Garcia And His Orchestra | Margaret Whiting Sings The Jerome Kern Song Book | Verve | 559553-2
Trav'lin' Light:The Johnny Mercer Songbook | Verve | 555402-2
Mike Wofford Trio | Plays Jerome Kern, Vol. 1 | Discovery | DS 808 IMS
Oscar Peterson Trio With The All Star Big Band | Bursting Out/Swinging Brass | Verve | 529699-2
Richard Davis Trio | Way Out West | Muse | MR 5180
Russ Freeman-Shelly Manne | One On One | Contemporary | CCD 14090-2
Ryan Kisor Quartet | Battle Cry | Criss Cross | Criss 1145
Sonny Rollins Quintet | Sunny Days,Starry Nights | Milestone | MCD 9122-2
Just Once | Jazz Door | JD 12121
Stan Getz Quartet | Spring Is Here | Concord | CCD 4500
Tom McKinley/Ed Schuller Group | Life Cycle | GM Recordings | GM 3001(807786)

Buck Clayton All Stars | Jammin' At 'Eddie Condon' | Moon Records | MCD 067-2

I'm Old Fashioned-
Morgana King With Orchestra | Looking Through The Eyes Of Love | Muse | MR 5257

I'm On My Way
Lillian Boutté And Her Group | The Gospel Book | Blues Beacon | BLU-1017 2
Take 6 | Tonight Take 6 | Warner | 9362-47611-2
So Much To Say | Reprise | 7599-25892-2
Fernest Arceneaux And The Zydeco All Stars feat. Rockin' Dopsie Jr. | Zydeco Blues Party | Mardi Gras Records | MG 1019

I'm On My Way From You
Lionel Hampton And His Orchestra | The Complete Lionel Hampton Vol.3/4(1939) | RCA | 2122614-2

I'm On My Way(intro)
Joe Venuti And His New Yorkers | The Big Bands Of Joe Venuti Vol.1 (1928-30) | JSP Records | 1111

I'm Only Trying
Ann Hampton Callaway And Her Band | Songbirds Special | Blue Flame | 40562(2132444-2)

Im Paradies
Don Redman And His Orchestra | The Complete McKinney's Cotton Pickers Vol.5 Plus Don Redman & His Orchestra | RCA | NL 89161 (809233)

I'm Prison Bound
Sonny Terry & Brownie McGhee | Back To New Orleans | Fantasy | FCD 24708-2

I'm Pulling Through
Diana Krall Group | The Girl In The Other Room | Verve | 9862246
Etta Jones And Her Band | Lonely And Blue | Original Jazz Classics | OJCCD 702-2(P 7241)

I'm Putting All My Eggs In One Basket
Dave Pell Octet | The Dave Pell Octet Plays Irving Berlin | Fresh Sound Records | 252963-1(Kapp KL 1036) (835207)
Ella Fitzgerald And Louis Armstrong With The Oscar Peterson Quartet | The Best Of Ella Fitzgerald And Louis Armstrong On Verve | Verve | 537909-2
Ella And Louis Again, Vol.2 | Verve | 711122 IMS
The Complete Ella Fitzgerald And Louis Armstrong On Verve | Verve | 537284-2
Cheek To Cheek-The Irving Berlin Song Book | Verve | 533829-2
Ella Fitzgerald With Paul Weston And His Orchestra | Ella Fitzgerald Sings The Irving Berlin Song Book | Verve | 543830-2
The Complete Ella Fitzgerald Song Books of Harold Arlen, Irving Berlin, Duke Ellington, George & Ira Gershwin, Jerome Kern, Johnny Mercer, Cole Porter And Rogers & Hart | Verve | 519832-2
Stuff Smith And The Onyx Club Boys | Jivin' At The Onyx | Affinity | CD AFS 1005

I'm Ready
Muddy Waters Blues Band | Jack Dupree-Jimmy Rushing-Muddy Waters | Laserlight | 17062
The Rockets | Out Of The Blue | L+R Records | CDLR 42077

Im Rheim,Im Heiligen Strome
Fletcher Henderson And His Orchestra | Jazz:The Essential Collection Vol.1 | IN+OUT Records | 78011-2

I'm Rhythm Crazy Now
Don Neely's Royal Society Jazz Orchestra | Don't Bring Lulu | Stomp Off Records | CD 1250

I'm Scared
Sarah Vaughan With John Kirby And His Orchestra | Sarah Vaughan Birthday Celebration | Fantasy | FANCD 6090-2
Schmid-Hübner-Krill | Time Makes The Tune | Mons Records | MR 874825

I'm Shadowing You
Singers Unlimited With The Pat Williams Orchestra | Feeling Free | MPS | 68103

I'm Shooting
Ann Richards With Orchestra | I'm Shooting High | Jasmine | JAS 310

I'm Shooting High
Kai Winding Quintet | Kai Winding-Bop City:Small Groups 1949-1951 | Cool & Blue | C&B-CD 110
Louis Armstrong With Luis Russell And His Orchestra | Ambassador Louis Armstrong Vol.1(1935) | Ambassador | CLA 1901

I'm So Lonesome I Could Cry
Jack Walrath Group | Master Of Suspense | Blue Note | BLJ 46905 Digital

I'm So Tired Of Being Alone
Big Maceo Merriweather | Big Maceo Vol.2 | Blues Classics | BC 29

I'm Sorry I Made You Cry
Nick's Dixieland Band | Muggsy Spanier | Storyville | SLP 4020
Trevor Richards New Orleans Trio | The Trevor Richards New Orleans Trio | Stomp Off Records | CD 1222

I'm St.Louis Bound
Robert Lockwood Jr. | Robert Lockwood Jr. Plays Robert (Johnson) & Robert (Lockwood) | Black & Blue | 33740

I'm The Knife-Thrower's Partner
Ella Fitzgerald And Her Famous Orchestra | A-Tisket, A-Tasket | Naxos Jazz | 8.120540 CD

I'm Thrilled
June Christy With The Pete Rugolo Orchestra | Something Cool(The Complete Mono & Stereo Versions) | Capitol | 534069-2
Something Cool(The Complete Mono & Stereo Versions) | Capitol | 534069-2
Clarence Williams And His Orchestra | King Oliver 1928-29 | Village(Jazz Archive) | VILCD 005-2

I'm Through With Love-
Roy Eldridge-Dizzy Gillespie With The Oscar Peterson Quartet | The Complete Verve Roy Eldridge Studio Sessions | Verve | 9861278
David Klein Quintet | My Marilyn | Enja | ENJ-9422 2

I'm Through With You
Keith Jarrett | The Melody At Night,With You | ECM | 1675(547949-2)
Sam Montgomery | East Coast Blues In The Thirties(1934-1939) | Story Of Blues | CD 3528-2

I'm Thru With Love
Dinah Washington With The Belford Hendricks Orchestra | What A Diff'rence A Day Makes! | Verve | 543300-2
Donald Brown | Piano Short Stories | Space Time Records | BG 9601
Julie Wilson With The Phil Moore Orchestra | Love | Fresh Sound Records | Dolphin 6
Lena Horne With Marty Gold And His Orchestra | Lena Horne:Love Songs | RCA | 2663604-2
Nat King Cole Trio | Nat King Cole Trio 1943-49-The Vocal Sides | Laserlight | 15718
Live At The Circle Room | Capitol | 521859-2
Per Henrik Wallin Trio | Per Henrik Wallin Trio | Caprice | CAP 1185

I'm Tired Of Crying Over You
Buddy Johnson And His Orchestra | Go Ahead & Rock Rock Rock | Official | 6011

I'm Waiting
Ann Cole With Band | Got My Mojo Working | Krazy Kat | KK 782 IMS

Im Wald
Keith Nichols Cotton Club Gang And Janice Day With Guy Barker | I Like To Do Things For You | Stomp Off Records | CD 1242

I'm Walkin'
Ella Fitzgerald With Jackie Davis And Louis Bellson | Lady Time | Original Jazz Classics | OJCCD 864-2(2310825)
Ernestine Anderson With The Monty Alexander Trio | Sunshine | Concord | CCD 4109

I'm Walking Through Heaven With You
Joe Turner | Walking Through Heaven | Swingtime | 8205

I'm Wanderin'
King Oliver And His Dixie Syncopators | Papa Joe | MCA | 1309

Im 'Weissen Rössl' Am Wolfgang See
Jim Jackson | Memphis Blues 1928-1930 | RCA | 2126409-2

I'm Wit' It
Anita O'Day With The Buddy Bregman Orchestra | Pick Yourself Up | Verve | 517329-2

I'm With You
Bobby Troup Quintet | Bobby Troup Sings Johnny Mercer | Fresh Sound Records | FSR 2008(Bethlehem BCP 19)

I'm Wondering
Bix Beiderbecke Orchestra/Gang | The Golden Age Of Bix Beiderbecke | EMI Records | CD MFP 6046

Im Wunderschönen Monat Mai
Jack Hylton And His Orchestra | The Talk Of The Town | Saville Records | SVL 164 IMS

I'm Your Pal
Chick Corea-Gary Burton | In Concert, Zürich, October 28, 1979 | ECM | 1182/83

I'm Your Pal-
First Class Blues Band | The First Class Blues Band Proudly Presents Mr. Frank Biner | Acoustic Music Records | 319.1062.2

I'm Yours
Billie Holiday With Eddie Heywood And His Orchestra | The Commodore Series | Decca | 180008 AG
Mel Tormé And His Band | Torme-A New Album | Memo Music | HDJ 4086

Image In Atom
Eddy Palermo Trio | The Way I See | EdiPan | NPG 806

Imagen
Baden Powell Ensemble | Samba Triste | Accord | 102772

Imagenes
Mosalini/Beytelmann/Caratini | Imagenes | Riskant | ???

Images
Nina Simone | Nina Simone After Hours | Verve | 526702-2
Verve Jazz Masters Vol.58:Nina Simone Sings Nina | Verve | 529867-2
Nina Simone Quartet | Nina Simone-The 60s Vol.2:Mood Indigo | Mercury | 838544-2 PMS
Oliver Nelson Quintet | Images | Prestige | P 24060
Eric Dolphy:The Complete Prestige Recordings | Prestige | 9 PRCD-4418-2
Sam Rivers Quartet | Contrasts | ECM | 1162
Sonny Red (Kyner) Quintet | Images:Sonny Red | Original Jazz Classics | OJC 148(J 974)
Toots Thielemans Quartet | Images | Choice | CHCD 71007
Toots Thielemans Quintet | Toots Thielemans Live-Vol. 2 | Polydor | 2441063 IMS

Images 4,2,3
Sergey Kuryokhin-Anatoly Vapirov Quartet | Sentenced To Silence | LEO | LR 110

Images Unseen
Terje Rypdal Trio | Chaser | ECM | 1303

Imagi(Theme)
Pat Metheny Group | Imaginary Day | Warner | 9362-46791-2

Imaginary Day
Art Ensemble Of Chicago | The Alternatetive Express | DIW | DIW 8033

Imaginary Time
Jean-Luc Ponty Quintet | Imaginary Voyage | Atlantic | SD 19136

Imagination
(Little)Jimmy Scott With The Howard Biggs Sextet | Little Jimmy Scott-All Over Again | Savoy | SV 0263
Ann Gilbert With The Elliot Lawrence Orchestra | In A Swingin' Mood | Fresh Sound Records | NL 45997(RCA LX 1090)
Artie Shaw And His Gramercy Five | I Can't Get Started | Verve | MV 2559 IMS
Carmen McRae And Her Quintet | The Best Of The Jazz Singers | LRC Records | CDC 8517(874388)
Chet Baker Quintet | Blues For A Reason | Criss Cross | Criss 1010
Clark Terry Quintet | Having Fun | Delos | DE 4021(882677)
Dave Pell Octet feat. Lucy Ann Polk | Plays Burke And Van Heusen | Fresh Sound Records | KL 1034(Kapp)
Elmo Hope Trio | The All Star Sessions | Milestone | M 47037
Hal Schaefer And His Orchestra | The RCA Victor Jazz Workshop | Fresh Sound Records | NL 45975(RCA LPM 1199)
Jesse Belvin With Marty Paich And His Orchestra | Mr. Easy | Fresh Sound Records | ND 74402
Jimmy Raney Quintet | Too Marvelous For Words | Biograph | BLP 12060
Jimmy Smith Trio | Groovin' At Smalls' Paradise Vol.2 | Blue Note | 300222(1586)
Joshua Redman Trio | Choices | Enja | 7073-2
Ken Peplowski Quintet | Double Exposure | Concord | CJ 344
Lou Levy Quartet | Jazz In Four Colors | Fresh Sound Records | ND 74401
Paul Desmond With Strings | Desmond Blue | RCA | 2663898-2
Ray Brown Trio With Marlena Shaw | Some Of My Best Friends Are Singers | Telarc Digital | CD 83441
Sonny Stitt Quartet | Genesis | Prestige | P 24044
Prestige First Sessions, Vol.2 | Prestige | PCD 24115-2
Stan Getz Quartet | Stan Getz-The Complete Roost Sessions | EMI Records | 859622-2
Stan Getz-The Best Of The Roost Years | Roulette | 7981442
Tommy Dorsey And His Orchestra | Forever | RCA | NL 89859 DP

Imagination Is Important
Paul Desmond With Strings | Desmond Blue | RCA | 2663898-2

Imagination(alt.take)
Stan Getz Quartet | The Complete Roost Session Vol.1 | Roulette | 300005(TOCJ 6118)
Stan Getz-The Complete Roost Sessions | The Jazz Factory | JFCD 22839

Imaginationen
Gonzalo Rubalcaba | Imagine | Blue Note | 830491-2

Imagine
Gonzalo Rubalcaba Trio | Images-Live At Mt. Fuji | Blue Note | 799492-2
Michael Mantler Group With The Danish Concert Radio Orchestra | Many Have No Speech | Watt | 19(835580-2)
Muhal Richard Abrams Octet | Song For All | Black Saint | 120161-2

Imagine My Frustration
Ella Fitzgerald With The Duke Ellington Orchestra | The Stockholm Concert 1966 | Pablo | 2308242-2
Orchestra | Duke Ellington's Sophisticated Ladies | RCA | BL 04053 DX
Fats Waller And His Rhythm | The Middle Years Part 2(1938-40) | RCA | 6366552-2

Imala Maika
Dollar Brand Quartet | Africa Tears And Laugher | Enja | ENJ-3039 2

Imam
Dewey Redman Group | The Ear Of The Behearer | Impulse(MCA) | IMP 12712

Imani's Dance
Mongo Santamaria And His Rhythm Afro-Cubanos | Afro Roots | Prestige | PCD 24018-2(F 8012/8032)

Imari's Lullaby
Cornelius Claudio Kreusch Group | Scoop | ACT | 9255-2

Imbao
Lazaro Ros Con Mezcla | Cantos | Intuition Records | INT 3080-2

Imbe Imbé
Torbjorn Sunde Group | Meridians | ACT | 9263-2

Imi
Don Ellis Quintet | New Ideas | Original Jazz Classics | OJCCD 431-2(NJ 8257)

Imke
Joe Barnikel-Norbert Nagel Group | Zero Gravity | Mons Records | MR 874808

Immaculate Deception
Mark Whitfield Group | True Blue | Verve | 523591-2

Immigrant-
Chris Barber's Jazz And Blues Band | Class Of '78 | Black Lion | 187001

Immigration Blues
Duke Ellington And His Kentucky Club Orchestra | Vol.1: Early Recordings Of Ellington Classics | MCA | MCAD 42325(872082)

Imminent Journey
Bobby Hutcherson Quintet | Cruisin' The Bird | Landmark | LCD 1517-2

Immm
The London Jazz Orchestra | Stonhenge/Carousel Suite | GM Recordings | GM 3014 CD(882949)

Impending Bloom
The Philly Groove | Roots & Fruits | EmArCy | 537495-2

Impossible
Singers Unlimited With The Roger Kellaway Cello Quartet | The Singers Unlimited:Magic Voices | MPS | 539130-2
Sue Raney With The Billy May Orchestra | Songs For A Raney Day | Capitol | 300015(TOCJ 6129)

Impossible Waltz
Slide Hampton Quartet | Le Jazz En France Vol.16:The Fabulous Slide Hampton Quartet | Pathe | 1552621

Impressario
Ran Blake Quartet | Short Life Of Barbara Monk | Soul Note | SN 1127

Impression-
Slide Hampton Octet | Two Sides Of Slide | Fresh Sound Records | FSR-CD 0206

Impression(No.1-4)
Friedemann Graef Group | Orlando Fragments | Nabel Records:Jazz Network | CD 4681

Impressione Impreciso
Richard Beirach Trio | Round About Federico Mompou | ACT | 9296-2

Impressiones Intimas No.1
Stan Kenton And His Orchestra | A Concert In Progressive Jazz | Creative World | ST 1037

Impressionistic
Anthony Braxton-Chick Corea Quartet | Woodstock Jazz Festival Vol.2 | Douglas Music | DM 10009

Impressions
Erroll Garner Trio | The Greatest Garner | Rhino | SD 1227
Gary Bartz Candid All Stars | There Goes The Neighborhood! | Candid | CCD 79506
John Coltrane Quartet | John Coltrane:The Complete 1961 Village Vanguard Recordings | Impulse(MCA) | 954322-2
On Stage 1962 | Accord | 556632
John Coltrane-Live Trane:The European Tours | Pablo | 7PACD 4433-2
The Complete 1962 Stockholm Concert Vol.2 | Magnetic Records | MRCD 109
Live In Paris | Charly | CD 87
Coltrane | Impulse(MCA) | 589567-2
The Mastery Of John Coltrane/Vol. 2: To The Beat Of A Different Drum | MCA | IZ 9346/2
John Coltrane Quartet With Eric Dolphy | John Coltrane:The Complete 1961 Village Vanguard Recordings | Impulse(MCA) | 954322-2
The Complete Copenhagen Concert | Magnetic Records | MRCD 116
José Luis Gámez Quartet | Dr.Jeckyl | Fresh Sound Records | FSNT 006 CD
Larry Coryell Quartet | Air Dancing | Jazzpoint | JP 1025 CD
McCoy Tyner Trio | Reflections | Milestone | M 47062
McCoy Tyner Trio With Michael Brecker | Infinity | Impulse(MCA) | IMP 11712
Milt Jackson Quartet | A London Bridge | Pablo | 2310932-2
Pat Martino Quartet | Consciousness | Muse | MCD 5039
Sebastian Whittaker Septet | First Outing | Justice Records | JR 0202-2
Stanley Jordan Trio | Stolen Moments | Blue Note | 797159-2
Wes Montgomery Quartet | Talkin' Jazz:Roots Of Acid Jazz | Verve | 529580-2
The Small Group Recordings | Verve | 2-2513 IMS
Wes Montgomery Quartet With The Claus Ogerman Orchestra | Willow Weep For Me | Verve | 589486-2
Willy Vande Walle Quartet | Midnight | Jazz Pure Collection | AU 31617 CD
Zachary Breaux Group | Groovin' | Ronnie Scott's Jazz House | JHCD 023

Impressions-
Directions In Music | Live at Massey Hall:Celebrating Miles Davis & John Coltrane | Verve | 589654-2
Jaki Byard And The Apollo Stompers | Phantasies | Soul Note | 121075-2

Impressions Of Cadiz
Joseph Bonner Trio And Strings | Impressions Of Copenhagen | Evidence | ECD 22024-2

Impressions Of Turkey
Dollar(Abdullah Ibrahim) Brand | Ode To Duke Ellington | West Wind | WW 0020

Impressions(alt.take)
John Coltrane Quintet | The Mastery Of John Coltrane, Vol. 4: Tranes Modes | MCA | 82711 (801449)

Impromede
Stephan Oliva Trio | Novembre | Owl Time Line | 3819092

Impromptu
Dizzy Gillespie-Stan Getz Sextet | Welcome To Jazz: Dizzy Gillespie | Koch Records | 321 972 D1
Gary Burton-Steve Swallow | Hotel Hello | ECM | 1055(835586-2)
Jimmie Lunceford And His Orchestra | Jimmi Lunceford Vol.6-The Last Sparks | MCA | 1321

Impromptu Ensemble
Eddie Condon And His Orchestra | Big Band Bounce And Boogie:At The Jazz Band Ball-Eddie Condon | Affinity | AFS 1021

Impromptu Ensemble(No.1)
Danilo Perez Group | Central Avenue | Impulse(MCA) | 951281-2

Impromptu(Conversations)
Misha Mengelberg | Impromptus | FMP | CD 7

Impromptune
Josep Maria Balanyà | Elements Of Development | Laika Records | 8695070

Impromptus Interruptus
Ben Webster With The Rhythm Section | No Fool No Fun | Spotlite | SPJ 142

Improvisation
Dave Brubeck Quartet | Koto Song | Memo Music | HDJ 4023
James Newton | 7.Zelt-Musik-Festival:Jazz Events | Zounds | CD 2730001
John Coltrane Quartet With Eric Dolphy | Two Giants Together | Jazz Anthology | JA 5184

Improvisation-
Jeff Beal | Contemplations | Triloka Records | 320204-2

Improvisation For Two Unaccompanied Saxophones
Wuppertaler Free Jazz Workshop Orchestra | Wuppertaler Free Jazz Workshop 1980 | FMP | 0940

Improvisation In G Minor
Eric Person Trio | Prophecy | Soul Note | 121287-2

Improvisation IV für Klavier(Teil 1-3)
Leroy Jenkins | Leroy Jenkins Solo Concert | India Navigation | IN 1028

Improvisation No.1
Sonny Clark | Sonny Clark 1954 Memorial Album | The Jazz Factory | JFCD 22834

Improvisation No.1-
Christian Escoude Quartet With Strings | Plays Django Reinhardt | EmArCy | 510132-2

Improvisation No.2
Sonny Clark | Sonny Clark 1954 Memorial Album | The Jazz Factory | JFCD 22834

Improvisation On Pathétique(Andante)
Stephane Grappelli With The Roland Hanna Trio | Parisian Thoroughfare | Black Lion | BLCD 760132

Improvisation Sur Le Theme Libertango
Quintet Du Hot Club De France | Jazz Legacy 58: Django Reinhardt-Rythme Futur-Radio Sessions 1947 Vol | Vogue | 500108

Improvisation(Improvisasjon)
John Coltrane Quintet | Live 1962 | Festival | ???

Improvisationen(1-4)
Makoto Ozone Group | Makoto Ozone | CBS | FC 39624

Improvised Songs(1-20)
Whisper Not | Lauter Leise Leute | Blue Concept | BCCD 94/02
Impulse(1)
Elise Einarsdottir-Olle Steinholz | Sketches Of Roses | Touché Music | TMcCD 008
Impulse(2)
Adam Rudolph's Moving Pictures | Skyway | Soul Note | 121269-2
Imre,The Gambler
Frank Wess And His Orchestra | Fujitsu-Concord Jazz Festival In Japan '90: Entre Nous | Concord | CCD 4456
In
Paolo Fresu Sextet | Mamut: Music For A Mime | SPLASC(H) Records | CD H 127-2
In & Out Underground
Elvin Jones Jazz Machine | Going Home | Enja | ENJ-7095 2
In 3-4 Thee
Bengt Berger & Bitter Funeral Beer Band | Praise Drumming | Dragon | DRLP 142
In A Blue Summer Garden
Noble Sissle And His Sizzling Syncopators | Tropical Mood | Swingtime(Contact) | ST 1014
In A Capricornian Way
Joyful | New Orleans Gospel | Mardi Gras Records | MG 5009
I'n A Child's Eyes
Cecil Scott And His Bright Boys | Harlem Big Bands | Timeless | CBC 1-010
In A Dream
Tabasco | Live Music | Jazz Classics | AU 11160
In A Flat Minor
Duke Ellington And His Orchestra | Such Sweet Thunder | CBS | CK 65568
In A Flat Minor(rehersal)
Nils Landgren Funk Unit With Guests | 5000 Miles | ACT | 9271-2
In A Fonky Mood
Jason Moran | Modernistic | Blue Note | 539838-2
In A Fortress-
Gijs Hendriks-Beaver Harris Quartet | Second Compound | yvp music | CDX 48804
In A Funky Groove
Charlie Rouse Band | Two Is One | Strata East Records | 660.51.012
In A Hurry
Duke Ellington And His Orchestra | The Complete Duke Ellington-Vol. 7 | CBS | CBS 88140
In A Little Spanish Town
Erroll Garner | The Erroll Garner Collection Vol.4&5 | EmArCy | 511821-2 PMS
Lester Young Quartet | Lester Swings | Verve | 833554-1
Oscar Peterson Trio | Masters Of Jazz Vol.7 | RCA | NL 89721 DP
Sonny Thompson Quintet/Sharps And Flats | Sonny Thompson:The Complete Recordings Vol.1 (1946-1948) | Blue Moon | BMCD 6024
Oscar Peterson Trio | This Is Oscar Peterson | RCA | 2663990-2
In A Little Spanish Town(alt.take)
Jack Teagarden And His Orchestra | Think Well Of Me | Verve | 557101-2
In A Maze
Hans Kumpf Trio | On A Baltic Trip | LEO | LR 122
In A Melancholy Way
Archie Shepp Quartet | On Green Dolphin Street | Denon Compact Disc | DC-8587
In A Mellow Tone
Albert Nicholas And His New Orleans Friends | Jazz In Paris:Classic Jazz At Saint-Germain-Des-Prés | EmArCy | 013045-2
Art Pepper Trio | Art Pepper:The Complete Galaxy Recordings | Galaxy | 16GCD 1016-2
Art Pepper-George Cables Duo | Art Pepper:The Complete Galaxy Recordings | Galaxy | 16GCD 1016-2
Goin' Home | Original Jazz Classics | GXY 5143
Ben Webster Quartet | Live At The Haarlemse Jazzclub | Limetree | MCD 0040
Benny Carter All Stars | Aurex Jazz Festival '80:Gentlemen Of Swing | Eastworld | EWJ 80188
Buddy Rich And His Orchestra | Buddy Rich In London | RCA | PL 43695
Charlie Shavers Quintet | Live! | Black & Blue | 33307
Chris Barber's Jazz And Blues Band With Special Guests | Echoes Of Harlem | Black Lion | 187000
Clark Terry And His All Stars | Duke With A Difference | Original Jazz Classics | OJCCD 229-2
Clark Terry Sextet | Clark Terry | Swing | SW 8406 IMS
Coleman Hawkins With The Oscar Peterson Quartet | The Genius Of Coleman Hawkins | Verve | 825673-2 PMS
Coleman Hawkins-Eddie Lockjaw Davis Quintet | In A Mellow Tone | Original Jazz Classics | OJCCD 6001-2
Count Basie And His Orchestra | En Concert Avec Europe 1 | Laserlight | 710411/12
I Got Rhythm | Affinity | AFF 48
David 'Bubba' Brooks With The Kenny Drew Jr. Quartet | Smooth Sailing | TCB Records | TCB 97702
Duke Ellington And His Famous Orchestra | Duke Ellington:The Blanton-Webster Band | Bluebird | 21 13181-2
Passion Flower 1940-46 | Bluebird | 63 66616-2
Victor Jazz History Vol.12:Ellingtonia | RCA | 2135731-2
Duke Ellington And His Orchestra | Duke Ellington:Complete Prestige Carnegie Hall 1946-1947 Concerts | Definitive Records | DRCD 11211
Ella Fitzgerald And Her All Stars | The Complete Ella Fitzgerald Song Books of Harold Arlen, Irving Berlin, Duke Ellington, George & Ira Gershwin, Jerome Kern, Johnny Mercer, Cole Porter And Rogers & Hart | Verve | 519832-2
Ella Fitzgerald With The Hank Jones Trio | Ella Fitzgerald:Mr.Paganini | Dreyfus Jazz Line | FDM 36741-2
Ella Fitzgerald:The Royal Roost Sessions | Cool & Blue | C&B-CD 112
Ernestine Anderson And Her All Stars | Be Mine Tonight | Concord | CJ 319
Flip Phillips-Christian McBride | Swing Is The Thing | Verve | 543477-2
Fraser MacPherson Trio | Ellington '87 | Sackville | SKCD2-2043
George Masso-Ken Peplowski Quintet | Just Friends | Nagel-Heyer | CD 5001
Gerry Mulligan-Ben Webster Quintet | Gerry Mulligan Meets Ben Webster | Verve | 841661-2 PMS
Grover Mitchell & His All-Star Orchestra | Hip Shakin' | Ken Music | 660.56.005
Jack Van Poll Trio | Cats Groove | September | CD 5107
JATP All Stars | Jazz At The Santa Monica Civic '72 | Pablo | 2625701-2
Jenny Evans And Her Quintet | Shiny Stockings | Enja | ENJ-9317 2
Jimmy Ponder Sextet | Jump | Muse | MCD 5347
Louis Armstrong-Duke Ellington Group | The Complete Louis Armstrong & Duke Ellington Sessions | Roulette | 793844-2
Marcus Roberts Quintet | The Truth Is Spoken Here | Novus | PD 83051
Monty Alexander/John Clayton | The Duke Ellington Song Book | MPS | 821151-1
Oscar Peterson Trio | En Concert Avec Europe 1 | Laserlight | 710443/48
Oscar Peterson Plays The Duke Ellington Song Book | Verve | 559785-2
Panama Francis And The Savoy Sultans | Grooving | Stash Records | ST 218 IMS
Sarah Vaughan With Small Group & Orchestra | Duke Ellington Song Book One | Pablo | CD 2312111
Stan Tracey With Roy Babbington | Plays Duke Ellington | Mole Jazz | Mole 10
Van Alexander Orchestra | Home Of Happy Feet/Swing! Staged For Sound! | Capitol | 535211-2
Victor Goines Quintet | Genesis | AFO Records | AFO 92-0428-2
Wild Bill Davis Quartet | The Swinging Organ Of Wild Bill Davis:In The Mellow Tone | Fresh Sound Records | FSR-CD 0309
Zoot Sims With Orchestra | Passion Flower | Original Jazz Classics | OJCCD 939-2(2312120)
Zoot Sims-Bucky Pizzarelli Duo | Elegiac | Storyville | STCD 8238
Ellis Marsalis | Duke In Blue | CBS | CK 63631
In A Mellow Tone(aka Finale)
Coleman Hawkins With The Oscar Peterson Quartet | The Genius Of Coleman Hawkins | Verve | 539065-2
In A Mellow Tone(alt.take)
Gerry Mulligan-Ben Webster Quintet | The Complete Gerry Mulligan Meets Ben Webster Sessions | Verve | 539055-2
Louis Armstrong And His All Stars With Duke Ellington | Louis Armstrong-Duke Ellington:The Great Summit-Complete Session | Roulette | 524546-2
Roberto Ottaviano Quintet feat. Ray Anderson | The Leap | Red Records | NS 213
In A Mist
Benny Goodman And His Orchestra | More Camel Caravans | Phontastic | NCD 8843/4
Bix Beiderbecke | The Studio Groups 1927 | EMI Records | EG 2605271
Riverboat Shuffle | Naxos Jazz | 8.120584 CD
Helmut Nieberle-Helmut Kagerer | Flashes | Jardis Records | JRCD 20031
Manny Albam And His Orchestra | Jazz Horizons | Fresh Sound Records | DLP 9004(Dot)
Ralph Sutton | Commodore Classics-Ralph Sutton | Commodore | 6.25525 AG
In A Mist-
Morton Gunnar Larsen | Maple Leaf Rag | Herman Records | HJCD 1009
In A Misty Night
Joe Henderson Sextet | In A Modal Way | Jazz Door | JD 1267
In A Mountain Greenery -> Mountain Greenery
In A Natural Way
Jenny Evans And Her Quintet | Gonna Go Fishin' | Enja | ENJ-9403 2
In A New York Minute
Nicki Leighton-Thomas Group | Forbidden Games | Candid | CCD 79778
Ronnie Cuber Quartet | In A New York Minute | Steeplechase | SCCD 31372
In A Pinch
Wardell Gray Quintet | Wardell Gray:Light Gray 1948-1950 | Cool & Blue | C&B-CD 116
In A Quiet Place
Enzo Scoppa Quartet & Guests | Enzo Scoppa Quartet & Guests | Penta Flowers | CDPIA 011
In A Rush
Lutz Häfner Quartet | Way In Way Out | Jazz 4 Ever Records:Jazz Network | J4E 4757
James Emery Quartet | Fourth World | Between The Lines | btl 020(Efa 10190-2)
In A Secret Place
Standing On A Whale... | Enja | ENJ-9312 2
Silje Nergard Group with Strings | Nightwatch | EmArCy | 9865648
In A Sentence
MOKAVE | MOKAVE Vol.1 | audioquest Music | AQCD 1006
In A Sentimental Mood
Ahmad Jamal Trio | I Remember Duke,Hoagy & Strayhorn | Telarc Digital | CD 83339
Art Tatum | Art Tatum-The Complete Jazz Chronicle Solo Session | Storyville | STCD 8253
The Standard Sessions: Art Tatum 1935-1943 Transcriptions | Music & Arts | CD 673
Standards | Black Lion | CD 877646-2
In Private | Fresh Sound Records | FSR-CD 0127
Art Tatum Quartet | The Tatum Group Masterpieces | Pablo | 2310734
Benny Goodman And His Orchestra | The Birth Of Swing | Bluebird | ND 90601(3)
Bill Evans Trio | The Complete Bill Evans On Verve | Verve | 527953-2
Bill Evans:The Secret Sessions | Milestone | 8MCD 4421-2
Bill Evans:The Secret Sessions | Milestone | 8MCD 4421-2
Bill Evans/Hank Jones/Red Mitchell | Moods Unlimited | Paddle Wheel | KICJ 65
Bill Evans-Eddie Gomez Duo | Eloquence | Fantasy | F 9618
Bill Holman And His Orchestra | Great Big Band | Fresh Sound Records | T 1464(Capitol)
Chris Potter Quartet | This Will Be | Storyville | STCD 4245
Chris Potter Quintet | Concentric Circle | Concord | CCD 4595
Claudio Roditi Quintet | Samba Manhattan Style | Reservoir | RSR CD 139
David Matthews & The Manhattan Jazz Orchestra | Hey Duke! | Milestone | MCD 9320-2
David Murray & Pierre Dorge's New Jungle Orchestra | The Jazzpar Price | Enja | 7031-2
Dexter Gordon Quartet | Stable Mable | Steeplechase | SCS 1040
Dianne Reeves With Orchestra | Three Ladies Of Jazz:Live In New York | Jazz Door | JD 12102
Dieter Fischer Trio | Trio Music | Jardis Records | JRCD 9925
Dollar(Abdullah Ibrahim) Brand | Ode To Duke Ellington | West Wind | WW 0020
Duke Ellington And His Orchestra | The Complets Duke Ellington-Vol. 6 | CBS | CBS 88137
Ella Fitzgerald-Barney Kessel | The Complete Ella Fitzgerald Song Books of Harold Arlen, Irving Berlin, Duke Ellington, George & Ira Gershwin, Jerome Kern, Johnny Mercer, Cole Porter And Rogers & Hart | Verve | 519832-2
George Cables | Person To Person | Steeplechase | SCCD 31369
Georges Arvanitas Trio | Rencontre | CBS | 491232-2
Grace Knight With Orchestra | Come In Spinner | Intuition Records | INT 3052-2
Great Jazz Trio With String Quartet | N.Y. Sophisticate-A Tribute To Duke Ellington | Denon Compact Disc | DC-8575
Günther Klatt-Tizian Jost | Art Of The Duo:Live In Mexico City | Tutu Records | 888184-2*
Hal Schaefer | Solo, Duo, Trio | Discovery | DSCD 975(889499)
Jerome Richardson Group | Jazz Station Runaway | TCB Records | TCB 97402
Jim Hall-Bob Brookmeyer | Live At The North Sea Jazz Festival | Challenge | CHR 70063
John Coltrane-Duke Ellington Quartet | Duke Ellington & John Coltrane | Impulse(MCA) | 951166-2
John Hicks | Steadfast | Strata East Records | 660.51.010
Johnny Frigo Quintet | Live From Studio A In New York City | Chesky | JD 1
Khan Jamal Group | Thinking Of You | Storyville | STCD 4138
Lucky Thompson Quartet | Lucky Strikes | Original Jazz Classics | OJCCD 194-2
Mark Whitfield Quartet | The Marksman | Warner | 7599-26321-2
Martial Solal Dodecaband | Martial Solal Dodecaband Play Ellington | Dreyfus Jazz Line | FDM 36613-2
McCoy Tyner Big Band | The Turning Point | Birdology | 513163-2
Michel Petrucciani | Michel Petrucciani:Concert Inédits | Dreyfus Jazz Line | FDM 36607-2
Mike Richmond Trio | On The Edge | Steeplechase | SCCD 31237
Oliver Jackson Quintet | Billie's Bounce | Black & Blue | BLE 59.183 2
Oscar Peterson Trio | The History Of An Artist | Pablo | 2625702-2
Pete Magadini Quintet | Night Dreamers | Timeless | CD SJP 317
Phil Abraham Quartet | Phil Abraham-At The Sugar Village | Jazz Pure Collection | AU 31604 CD
Quintet Du Hot Club De France | Django/Django In Rome 1949-1050 | BGO Records | BGOCD 366
Django Reinhardt:Djangology | EMI Records | 780659-2
Ray Blue Quartet | Always With A Purpose | Ray Blue Music | JN 007(RMB 01)
Ray Brown Trio With Ulf Wakenius | Seven Steps To Heaven | Telarc Digital | CD 83384
Roman Schwaller Jazz Quartet | Some Changes In Life | JHM Records | JHM 3612
Ronnie Cuber Quintet | Cubism | Fresh Sound Records | FSR-CD 0188
Ruby Braff-Marshall Brown Sextet | The Ruby Braff/Marshall Brown Sextet | Fresh Sound Records | UAS 5093(United Artists)
Sarah Vaughan With Mundell Lowe And George Duvivier | The Man I Love | Jazz Society(Vogue) | 670504
Sarah Vaughan With Orchestra | Sarah Vaughan Birthday Celebration | Fantasy | FANCD 6090-2
The Best Of Sarah Vaughan | Pablo | 2405416-2
Schlosser/Weber/Böhm/Huber/Binder | L 14,16 | Jazz 4 Ever Records:Jazz Network | J4E 4760
Scott Hamilton Quintet | Plays Ballads | Concord | CCD 4386
Sonny Rollins With The Modern Jazz Quartet | The Jazz Giants Play Duke Ellington:Caravan | Prestige | PCD 24227-2
Welcome To Jazz: Sonny Rollins | Koch Records | 322 079 D1
Sonny Rollins With The Modern Jazz Quintet | Vintage Sessions | Prestige | P 24096
Steve Kuhn Trio | Years Later | Concord | CCD 4554
Tenor Saxes | Frankfurt Workshop '78:Tenor Saxes | Circle Records | RK 31-24978/31 IMS
Tommy Flanagan Trio | Communication-Live At Fat Tuesday's New York | Paddle Wheel | KICJ 73
Vanessa Rubin With Orchestra | Pastiche | Novus | 4163152-2
World Saxophone Quartet | Plays Duke Ellington | Nonesuch | 7559-79137-2
Zoot Sims Trio | In A Sentimental Mood | Sonet | SNTF 932(941396)
In A Sentimental Mood-
Duke Ellington | The Complete Duke Ellington-Vol. 7 | CBS | CBS 88140
George Shearing-Neil Swainson Duo | Dexterity | Concord | CCD 4346
Oscar Peterson-Joe Pass Duo | Live At Salle Pleyel, Paris | Pablo | 2625705
Roots | Saying Something | IN+OUT Records | 77031-2
Satchmo Legacy Band | Salute To Pops-Vol.1 | Soul Note | 121116-2
Bill Evans Trio | The Complete Bill Evans On Verve | Verve | 527953-2
In A Sentimental Mood(2)
Art Tatum Quartet | Art Tatum-The Complete Pablo Group Masterpieces | Pablo | 6 PACD 4401-2
In A Sentimental Mood(alt.take)
Art Tatum-Roy Eldridge Quartet | The Tatum Group Masterpieces Vol.2 | Pablo | 2405425-2
In A Silent Way
Joe Zawinul Group | Concerto Retitled | Atlantic | SD 1694
In A Silent Way-
Miles Davis Group | The Miles Davis Selection | CBS | 471623-2
In A While There Will Be...
Norbert Stein Pata Orchester | The Secret Act Of Painting | Pata Musik | PATA 7 CD
In A Woman's Mood
Wolfgang Muthspiel Group | Loaded, Like New | Amadeo | 527727-2
In And Out
Joe Chambers Quintet | Phantom Of The City | Candid | CCD 79517
Wes Montgomery With The Johnny Pate Orchestra | Talkin' Jazz:Roots Of Acid Jazz | Verve | 529580-2
Trevor Coleman Group | Kiwi Love | Fiala Music | JFJ 90005
In Between The Heartaches
Stan Getz With The Richard Evans Orchestra | What The World Needs Now-Stan Getz Plays Bacharach And David | Verve | 557450-2
In Between The Heartaches(alt.take)
Rainer Pusch-Horace Parlan | In Between Those Changes | yvp music | CD 3046
In Case Of Emergency
Slide Hampton Quartet | Phil Woods/Slide Hampton 1968 Jazz | Jazztime(EMI) | 781253-2
In Cerca Di Cibo
Wolfgang Fuchs-Jean Marc Montera | Solos & Duets | FMP | OWN-90004
In Common
DIX | Percussion & Voice | Born&Bellmann | 980504 CD
In De Back Room
Ray Bryant | The Best Of Ray Bryant | Pablo | 2310846
In Der Fremde
Günter Sommer | Hörmusik III:Sächsische Schatulle | Intakt Records | CD 027
In Dulci Jubilo
Keith Foley | Music For Christmas | dmp Digital Music Productions | CD 452
In Einem Fernen Land(dedicated to Gary McFarland)
Victory Of The Better Man | L'Utopiste | CMP Records | CMP CD 44
In Flight
Ron McClure Sextet | Double Triangle | Naxos Jazz | 86044-2
In Fragranti
Billy Usselton Sextet | Modern Jazz Gallery | Fresh Sound Records | KXL 5001(252282-1 Kapp)
In Front
Joe Maneri Quartet | In Full Cry | ECM | 1617(537048-2)
In Full Cry
Henri Chaix Trio | Just Friends | Sackville | SKCD2-2048
In Germany Before The War
Eddie Pierson's Band | Recorded In New Orleans Vol. 2 | Good Time Jazz | GTCD 12020-2
In Good Spirits
Bourbon Street | Jazzpuzzle | GIC | GD 4.1411
In India
Michel Benita Quartet | Preferences | Label Bleu | LBLC 6532(882935)
In Justspring
Leo Smith Trio | Touch The Earth | FMP | 0730
In Line
Gregor Hübner Quintet | Januschke's Time | Satin Doll Productions | SDP 1034-1 CD
In Line Again
Marilyn Crispell | The Woodstock Concert | Music & Arts | CD 929
In Love In L.A.
Hal Galper Quintet | Let's Call This That | Double Time Records | DTRCD-157
In Love In Vain
Alan Broadbent Trio | Pacific Standard Time | Concord | CCD 4664
Charlie Haden Quartet West With Strings | The Art Of The Song | Verve | 547403-2
Dave McKenna Quartet | Piano Mover | Concord | CJ 146
Keith Jarrett Trio | Standards Vol.2 | ECM | 1289(825015-2)
Louis Scherr-Tommy Cecil Duo | The Song Is You | Limetree | MLP 0026
Stefan Karlsson Quartet | Below Zero | Justice Records | JR 0703-2
In Martinique
Billy May & His Orchestra | I Believe In You | Bainbridge | BT 1001
In Memoriam
Ethan Iverson Trio | Contruction Zone(Originals) | Fresh Sound Records | FSNT 046 CD
Modern Jazz Quartet | The Complete Last Concert | Atlantic | 81976-2
In Memoriam Of Stan Getz
Don Byron-Reggie Workman | Tuskegee Experiments | Nonesuch | 7559-79280-2
In Memoriam: Uncle Dan
Barbara Thompson's Paraphernalia | Lady Saxophone | VeraBra Records | CDVBR 2166-2
In Memory
Bruce Gertz Quintet | Third Eye | RAM Records | RMCD 4509
In Memory Of My Father:
Bill Evans | Bill Evans At Town Hall | Verve | 831271-2
Joseph Jarman-Don Moye Trio | Black Paladins | Black Saint | BSR 0042
In Motion-
Robin Williamson | The Seed-At-Zero | ECM | 1732(543819-2)
In My Craft Or Sullen Art
Glenn Ferris Trio | Chrominance | Enja | 9132-2
In My Dream
Dusko Goykovich Quartet | In My Dreams | Enja | ENJ-9408 2
In My Dreams
Steve Laury Trio | Passion | Denon Compact Disc | CY-79043
In My Garage
Eunice Davis And Her Blues Band | Eunice Davis Sings The Classic Blues Of Victoria Spivey | L+R Records | LR 42016

In My Heart
Mahalia Jackson | In Memoriam Mahalia Jackson | CBS | 66501

In My Live(Walt's Walz)
Jean Goldkette And His Orchestra | The Indispensable Bix Beiderbecke(1924-1930) | RCA | ND 89572

In My Own Walkman
Jon Burr Quartet | In My Own Words | Cymekob | CYK 804-2

In My Rays
Directors | Stadtgarten Series Vol.2 | Jazz Haus Musik | JHM 1002 SER

In My Solitude
Billie Holiday And Her Orchestra | Billie Holiday: The First Verve Sessions | Verve | 2610027
Billie Holiday With Bob Haggart And His Orchestra | Jazz Gallery:Billie Holiday Vol.1(1933-49) | RCA | 2119542-2
Buck Hill Quartet | Impulse | Muse | MCD 5483
Duke Ellington And His Orchestra | Jazz Group 1964 | Jazz Anthology | 550192
Original Sessions 1943 / 1945 | Jazz Anthology | JA 5103
Duke Ellington-Coleman Hawkins Orchestra | Duke Ellington Meets Coleman Hawkins | MCA | MCAD 5650
Ella Fitzgerald-Barney Kessel | Ella Fitzgerald Sings The Duke Ellington Songbook | Verve | 559248-2
The Complete Ella Fitzgerald Song Books of Harold Arlen, Irving Berlin, Duke Ellington, George & Ira Gershwin, Jerome Kern, Johnny Mercer, Cole Porter And Rogers & Hart | Verve | 519832-2
Ellington/Mingus/Roach Trio | Money Jungle | Blue Note | 538227-2
Fats Waller-Cedric Wallace | Fats Waller:The Complete Associated Transcription Sessions 1935-1939 | Jazz Unlimited | JUCD 2076
George Adams-Don Pullen Quartet | Live At Village Vanguard | Soul Note | 121094-2
Great Jazz Trio With String Quartet | N.Y. Sophisticate-A Tribute To Duke Ellington | Denon Compact Disc | DC-8575
Jimmy Hamilton And The New York Jazz Quintet | Jimmy Hamilton And The New York Jazz Quintet | Fresh Sound Records | FSCD 2002
Jon Weber | Live In Concert:Jon Weber Flying Keys | Jazz Connaisseur | JCCD 9726-2
Karin Krog-Archie Shepp | Karin Krog Jubilee-The Best Of 30 Years | Verve | 523716-2
Morgana King And Her Quintet | Another Time Another Space | Muse | MCD 5339
Rebecca Parris With The Gary Burton Group | It's Another Day | GRP | GRP 97382
Red Garland Quintet feat.John Coltrane | High Pressure | Original Jazz Classics | OJCCD 349-2(P 7209)
Red Holloway Quartet | In The Red | HighNote Records | HCD 7022
Sarah Vaughan With The Benny Carter Orchestra | The Man I Love | Jazz Society(Vogue) | 670504
Stan Kenton And His Orchestra | The Uncollected:Stan Kenton, Vol.5 | Hindsight | HSR 157
Stephane Grappelli With The Diz Disley Trio | Violinspiration | MPS | 68058
Thelonious Monk | Pure Monk | Milestone | M 47004
Toshiko Akiyoshi Trio | Interlude | Concord | CCD 4324

In My Solitude-
Duke Ellington | The Complete Duke Ellington-Vol. 7 | CBS | CBS 88140
Lew Stone And His Band | Lew Stone And His Band | Decca | DDV 5005/6 DT
Rex Allen's Swing Express | Ellington For Lovers | Nagel-Heyer | NH 1009
Teddy Wilson | Jazz Piano Masters | Chiaroscuro | CR 170

In My Solitude(alt.take)
Duke Ellington | Solos, Duets And Trios | RCA | ND 82178(847130)

In November
Christmann-Schönenberg Duo | Topic | Ring | 01020

In Orbit
John Campbell Quartet | Turning Point | Contemporary | CCD 14061-2

In Our Pasture-
Michael Feinstein With Burton Lane | Michael Feinstein Sings The Burton Lane Songbook Vol.1 | Nonesuch | 7559-79243-2

In Parallel
Paolo Fresu Quintet | Live In Montpellier | SPLASC(H) Records | CD H 301-2

In Passing
Oliver Nelson Sextet | Soul Battle | Original Jazz Classics | OJC 325(P 7223)

In Praise
Mick Goodrick Trio | Biorhythms | CMP Records | CMP CD 46

In Pursuit Of Happiness
Horace Silver Quartet | In Pursuit Of The 27th Man | Blue Note | 84433

In Pursuit Of The 27th Man
Bruno Tommaso Orchestra | Su Un Tema Di Jerome Kern | SPLASC(H) Records | HP 18

In Re:Nude Orbit
Barry Guy-Howard Riley-John Stevens-Trevor Watts | Endgame | Japo | 60028

In Rillievo
Louie Bellson And His Jazz Orchestra | Air Mail Special-A Salute To The Big Band Masters | Limelight | 820824-2 IMS

In Salah
The Couriers Of Jazz | The Couries Of Jazz-England's Greatest Combo | Fresh Sound Records | Carlton STCD 116

In San Francisco
George Sams Quintet | Nomadic Winds | Hat Art | 3506

In Search Of A Theme
David Milne Group | Berlin Connection | BIT | 11254

In Search Of The Well
Ron McClure Quartet | Match Point | Steeplechase | SCCD 31517

In Search Of Times Lost
Jimmy Smith With Orchestra | The Big Brawl | Milan | CD CH 128(883460)

In Search Of Truth
Lonnie Liston Smith & His Cosmic Echoes | Astral Travelling | RCA | 2663878-2

In Search Of Truth(alt.take)
Ahmad Jamal Trio | In Search Of Momentum (1-10) | Dreyfus Jazz Line | FDM 36644-2

In Search Of...
Bertha Hope Trio | In Search Of.. | Steeplechase | SCCD 31276

In So Many Wordls(for Jaki Byard):
Stan Red Fox | Stan Red Fox | ITM Records | ITM 1436

In Spite Of Everything
A Band Of Friends | René Wohlhauser Werkauswahl 1978-1993 | Creative Works Records | CW CD 1026-2

In Statu Mutandi für Orchester
Peter Erskine Orchestra | Peter Erskine | Original Jazz Classics | OJC 610(C 14010)

In Statu Nascendi
Peter Erskine | Contemporary | CCD 14010-2

In Suspense
Earl Hines And His Orchestra | The Indispensable Earl Hines Vol.1/2 | RCA | 2126407-2

In The Anna(Indiana)
Cannonball Adderley-Nat Adderley Sextet | The Adderley Brothers In New Orleans | Milestone | M 9030

In The Bag
Harold Land Quintet | Damisi | Mainstream | MD CDO 714

In The Beginning
Nicholas Payton Quintet | From This Moment... | Verve | 527073-2

In The Beginning There Was Africa
Don Pullen | Evidence Of Things Unseen | Black Saint | 120080-2

In The Blue Of The Evening
Tommy Dorsey And His Orchestra | Planet Jazz:Tommy Dorsey | Planet Jazz | 2159972-2
Forever | RCA | NL 89859 DP

In The Blues (1-2-3)
Eric Dolphy With Erik Moseholm's Trio | Eric Dolphy:The Complete Prestige Recordings | Prestige | 9 PRCD-4418-2
Clarence Williams And His Novelty Four | Jazz Classics In Digital Stereo: King Oliver Volume Two 1927 To 1930 | CDS Records Ltd. | ZCF 788

In The Cave In The Light
Palo Alto | Crash Test | Jazz 'n' Arts Records | JNA 1803

In The Cave Of Pan
André Previn-Russ Freeman | Double Play! | Original Jazz Classics | OJC 157(C 7537)

In The Chapel In The Moonlight
Sonny Rollins And The Contemporary Leaders | Sonny Rollins-The Freelance Years:The Complete Riverside & Contemporary Recordings | Riverside | 5 RCD 4427-2
Will Osborne And His Orchestra | The Uncollected:Will Osborne | Hindsight | HSR 197

In The City
Muddy Waters Band | Blues Giants In Concert-More American Folk Blues Festival 1963 | ACT | 9205-2

In The Dark
Ralph Sutton | Stridin' High | Jazz Connaisseur | JCCD 9728-2
Maybeck Recital Hall Series Volume Thirty | Concord | CCD 4586
The Washington Guitar Quintet | Aquarelle | Concord | CCD 42016

In The End
Albert Wynn And His Gutbucket Seven | Chicago-The Living Legends:Albert Wynn | Original Jazz Classics | OJCCD 1826-2(RLP 9426)

In The Evening
Count Basie And His Orchestra | En Concert Avec Europe 1 | Laserlight | 710706/07
Dave Bartholomew And His Orchestra | The Monkey | Pathe | 1561331(Imperial)
Junior Mance Trio | Junior's Blues | Original Jazz Classics | OJCCD 1000-2(RLP 9447)
Ken Colyer's Jazzmen | Ken Colyer's Jazzmen Serenading Auntie-BBC Recordings 1955-1960 | Upbeat Jazz | URCD 111

In The Evening When The Sun Goes Down
Ella Fitzgerald And Her All Stars | These Are The Blues | Verve | 829536-2 PMS
Ella Fitzgerald With Sy Oliver And His Orchestra | Ella:The Legendary American Decca Recordings | GRP | GRP 46482
Ella Fitzgerald 75th Birthday Celebration:The Original Decca Recordings | GRP | GRP 26192
Joe Williams With The Red Saunders Orchestra | Joe Williams Sings Everyday | Savoy | SV 0199(MG 6002)
Woody Allen Trio | Wild Man Blues | RCA | 2663353-2
Big Bill Broonzy | Black Brown And White | Mercury | 842743-2

In The Eye Of The Storm
Esbjörn Svensson Trio(E.S.T.) | Est-From Gagarin's Point Of View | ACT | 9005-2

In The Face Of Day
Sebastian Weiss Trio | Polaroid Memory | Fresh Sound Records | FSNT 085 CD

In The Fading Light
Steve Swallow Group | Home | ECM | 1160(513424-2)

In The Fall
Esbjörn Svensson Trio(E.S.T.) | Winter In Venice | ACT | 9007-2

In The Fall Of Things
David Torn/Geoffrey Gordon | Best Laid Plans | ECM | 1284

In The Fifth Direction
Bengt-Arne Wallin Orchestra | The Birth+Rebirth Of Swedish Folk Jazz | ACT | 9254-2

In The Firmament-
Sonny Sharrock/Nicky Skopelitis | Faith Moves | CMP Records | CMP CD 52

In The Folk Tune
Jo Jones Sextet | Jo Jones Sextet | Fresh Sound Records | FSR-CD 0144

In The Garden
Don Lanphere Quintet Feat. Jon Pugh Plus Two | Into Somewhere | Hep | 2022

In The Garden Of Eden(Thinking Inside Of You)
Barney Kessel | Yesterday | Black Lion | BLCD 760183

In The Gate Of Another Gate
Buster Benton Blues Band | Blues At The Top | Black & Blue | BLE 59.001 2

In The Good Old Summertime
Dee Dee Pierce And His New Orleans Stompers | A Portrait Of George Lewis | Lake | LACD 50
Frederica von Stade With The Chris Brubeck-Bill Crofut Ensemble | Across Your Dreams: Frederica von Stade Sings Brubeck | Telarc Digital | CD 80467

In The Hall
Duke Ellington And His Orchestra | Three Suites | CBS | 467913-2

In The Heat
Bill Evans Group | Let The Juice Loose-Bill Evans Group Live at The Blue Note,Tokyo | Jazz City | 660.53.001

In The High Valleys
Frank Vignola Sextet | Off Broadway | Nagel-Heyer | CD 2006

In The Hills
John Goldsby Sextet | Viewpoint | Nagel-Heyer | CD 2014
Ben Pollack And His Park Central Orchestra | Ben Pollack Vol.3 | Jazz Oracle | BDW 8017

In The Jazzclub
Landes Jugend Jazz Orchester Hessen | Touch Of Lips | hr music.de | hrmj 004-01 CD

In The Jungle
Jean-Luc Ponty | Fables | Atlantic | 781276-2

In The Kitchen
Eddie Lockjaw Davis Quintet | The Eddie Lockjaw Davis Cookbook Vol.1 | Original Jazz Classics | OJCCD 652-2(P 7141)
Henri Texier Quintet | Colonel Skopje | Label Bleu | LBLC 6523(881998)

In The Land Of Ephesus
| Marian McPartland Plays The Music Of Mary Lou Williams | Concord | CCD 4605

In The Land Of Oo-Bla-Dee
Dizzy Gillespie And His Orchestra | Groovin' High | Naxos Jazz | 8.120582 CD

In The Meantime
Christian Rover Trio | New York Impressions | Organic Music | GWR 280595

In The Middle
Nicola Puglielli Group | Jazz Guitar Highlights 1 | Jardis Records | JRCD 20141
Pee Wee Ellis Trio | Twelve And More Blues | Minor Music | 801034
Art Tatum | Art Tatum-The Standard Transcriptions | Music & Arts | CD 919

In The Middle Of A Kiss
Oscar Peterson-Major Holley Duo | Oscar Peterson:Get Happy | Dreyfus Jazz Line | FDM 36738-2
Tenderly | Verve | MV 2662 IMS
Zoot Sims Quartet | Zoot At Easy | Mobile Fidelity | MFCD 842
NRG Ensemble | This Is My House | Delmark | DE 485

In The Middle Of The Night
Frans Bak & Jazz Group 90 | Hymn To The Rainbow | L+R Records | CDLR 45055

In The Midst Of Change
John Hicks Quartet | In The Mix | Landmark | LCD 1542-2

In The Moment
Charlie Haden Trio | Quartet West | Verve | 831673-2
Gateway | In The Moment | ECM | 1574(529346-2)
Jerry Granelli Sextet | Koputai | ITM-Pacific | ITMP 970058

In The Mood
Erich Kunzel Cincinnati Pops Big Band Orchestra | Big Band Hit Parade | Telarc Digital | CD 80177
Glenn Miller And His Orchestra | Planet Jazz:Glenn Miller | Planet Jazz | 2152056-2
In The Mood | Intercord | 125403
The Unforgettable Glenn Miller | RCA | PD 89260
Planet Jazz:Swing | Planet Jazz | 2169651-2
Planet Jazz:Big Bands | Planet Jazz | 2169649-2
Glenn Miller-The Great Instrumentals 1938-1942 | Retrieval | RTR 79001
The Ultimate Glenn Miller-22 Original Hits From The King Of Swing | RCA | 2113137-2
The Carnegie Hall Concert | Bluebird | 63 66147-2
Glenn Miller Revival Orchestra | Forever-From The Forties To The... | Timeless | CD JC 11013
Dorothy Donegan Trio | Live At The Widder Bar 1986 | Timeless | CD SJP 247

In The Morning Light
Geri Allen Trio | Twenty One | Blue Note | 830028-2

In The Mornings Out There
Christoph Mudrich Trio feat. Sir Henry | Christmas In Blue | Blue Concept | BCCD 93/03

In The Mud
Jenny Evans And Her Quintet | Whisper Not | ESM Records | Panda 16(941336)

In The Park
Steve Coleman And Five Elements | World Expansion | JMT Edition | 834410-2

In The Pocket
Grafitti | Good Groove | Lipstick Records | LIP 890202

In The Racket
Billy Eckstine With Hal Mooney And His Orchestra | Billy Eckstine:Billy's Best! | Verve | 526440-2

In The Red(A Xmas Carol)
Max Roach Quintet | Drums Unlimited | Atlantic | AMCY 1043

In The Shade
Bob Crosby And His Orchestra | Bob Crosby And His Orchestra-1938 | Circle | CCD-1

In The Shade Of The Old Apple Tree
Bob Crosby And His Orchestra-1938 | Circle | CCD-1
Louis Armstrong And His All Stars/Orchestra | The Wonderful World Of Louis Armstrong | MCA | 2292-57202-2
Rod Mason-Ray Foxley | Six For Two | BELL Records | BLR 84035

In The Shadow
Vincent Herring Quintet | Don't Let It Go | Musicmasters | 65121-2

In The Shadow Of The Moon
Bob Berg Sextet | The Best Of Bob Berg On Denon | Denon Compact Disc | DC-8593

In The Speed Mode
David Murray Quartet | Shakill's Warrior | DIW | DIW 850 CD

In The Still Of The Night
Charlie Parker And His Orchestra | Bird On Verve-Vol.7:Charlie Parker Big Band | Verve | 817448-1 IMS
Compact Jazz: Charlie Parker | Verve | 833288-2
Charlie Parker With Orchestra | Compact Jazz: Charlie Parker | Verve | 833268-2
Charlie Parker With Orchestra & The Dave Lambert Singers | The Verve Years(1952-54) | Verve | 2-2523 IMS
Dave Liebman Trio | Plays The Music Of Cole Porter | Red Records | 123236-2
Ella Fitzgerald With The Buddy Bregman Orchestra | The Complete Ella Fitzgerald Song Books of Harold Arlen, Irving Berlin, Duke Ellington, George & Ira Gershwin, Jerome Kern, Johnny Mercer, Cole Porter And Rogers & Hart | Verve | 519832-2
Gabe Baltazar Quartet | Birdology | Fresh Sound Records | FSR-CD 5001
George Shearing & Barry Tuckwell With Orchestra | Plays The Music Of Cole Porter | Concord | CCD 42010
Mel Tormé With Rob McConnell And The Boss Brass | Velvet & Brass | Concord | CCD 4667
Ozzie Nelson And His Orchestra | The Uncollected:Ozzie Nelson,Vol.3 | Hindsight | HSR 208
Rosemary Clooney And Her Band | Rosemary Clooney Sings The Music Of Cole Porter | Concord | CCD 4185
Stacey Kent And Her Quintet | The Tender Trap | Candid | CCD 79751
Stephane Grappelli Sextet | Jazz In Paris:Stephane Grappelli Plays Cole Porter | EmArCy | 014061-2

In The Still Of The Night(3 false starts)
Charlie Parker With Orchestra | Charlie Parker Big Band | Verve | 559835-2

In The Still Of The Night(alt.take 1)
Charlie Parker Big Band | Verve | 559835-2

In The Still Of The Night(alt.take 2)
Charlie Parker Big Band | Verve | 559835-2

In The Still Of The Night(alt.take 3)
Charlie Parker And His Orchestra | Bird: The Complete Charlie Parker On Verve | Verve | 837141-2

In The Still Of The Night(take 1-7)
Kenny Drew/Niels-Henning Orsted-Pedersen Duo | Duo | Steeplechase | SCS 1002

In The Tavern Of Ruin
Niels Jensen Trio | Nude But Still Stripping | ITM Records | 0038

In The Theatre
Bruce Dunlap Trio | The Rhythm Of Wings | Chesky | JD 92

In The Tradition
McCoy Tyner Trio | McCoy Tyner With Stanley Clarke And Al Foster | Telarc Digital | CD 83488

In The Tradition Of Switzerland
Amiri Baraka with David and Steve McCall | New Music-New Poetry | India Navigation | IN 1048

In The Traffic(Song For The Modern World)
Billy Higgins Trio With Harold Land | 3/4 For Peace | Red Records | 123258-2

In The Wee Small Hours Of The Morning
Ben Webster With The Oscar Peterson Trio | Ben Webster Meets Oscar Peterson | Verve | 521448-2
Ben Webster Meets Oscar Peterson | Verve | 829167-2
David Newton | A Jazz Portrait Of Frank Sinatra | Candid | CCD 79728
Dieter Ilg-Marc Copeland-Jeff Hirshfield | What's Goin' On | Jazzline | JL 11138-2
Joe Pass | Virtuoso Live! | Pablo | 2310948-2
Johnny Lytle Trio(Quartet) | Got That Feeling/Moon Child | Milestone | MCD 47093-2
Keith Jarrett Trio | Keith Jarrett At The Blue Note-The Complete Recordings | ECM | 1575/80(527638-2)
Lex Jasper Trio With Orchestra | Lexpression | Limetree | MCD 0016
Lynne Arriale Trio | When You Listen | dmp Digital Music Productions | CD 511
Monty Alexander Trio | Triple Treat III | Concord | CCD 4394
Oscar Peterson Trio | The Trio-Live From Chicago | Verve | 823008-2
Stacey Kent And Her Quintet | The Tender Trap | Candid | CCD 79751
Teresa Brewer With The David Murray Quartet | Softly I Swing | Red Baron | 471575-2

In The Year Of The Dragon
Geri Allen Trio | Live At The Village Vanguard | DIW | DIW 847 CD
Paul Motian Trio | It Should've Happened A Long Time Ago | ECM | 1283
Charlie Barnet And His Orchestra | Little Jazz Special | Queen-Disc | 066

In Thought...
Ellery Eskelin Trio | Forms | Open Minds | OM 2403-2

In Time
Music Revelation Ensemble | In The Name Of... | DIW | DIW 885 CD

In Times Like These
Vaughn Monroe And His Orchestra | Vaughn Monroe And His Orchestra 1943 | Circle | CCD-45

In Touch
Yves Robert Trio | In Touch | ECM | 1787(016375-2)

In Touch(variation I)
In Touch | ECM | 1787(016375-2)

In Touch(variation II)
Sandy Lomax With Band | Trance Jazz | Workshop Records | WOR 171(CD 581 Maxi)

In Vitro
Cannonball Adderley Sextet | En Concert Avec Europe 1 | Laserlight | 710466

In Walked Bud
Bobby Hutcherson Quintet | Good Bait | Landmark | LCD 1501-2
Don Pullen | Plays Monk | Paddle Wheel | K 28P 6368
Esbjörn Svensson Trio(E.S.T.) | EST Plays Monk | RCA | 2137680-2
Milt Jackson Quartet | Milt Jackson Birthday Celebration | Fantasy | FANCD 6079-2
Memories Of Thelonious Sphere Monk | Pablo | 2308235
Ron Holloway Group | Slanted | Milestone | MCD 9219-2
Stanley Cowell Trio | Live At Copenhagen Jazz House | Steeplechase | SCCD 31359
Thelonious Monk Quartet | Misterioso | Original Jazz Classics | OJC20 206-2
San Francisco Holiday | Milestone | MCD 9199-2
Thelonious Monk Quintet | The Complete Genius | Blue Note | LA 579
Monk's Mood | Naxos Jazz | 8.120588 CD
Thelonious Monk:Complete 1947-1952 Blue Note Recordings | The Jazz Factory | JFCD 22838
Thelonious Monk With Art Blakey's Jazz Messengers | Art Blakey's Jazz Messengers With Thelonious Monk | Atlantic | SD 1278
Giacomo Gates With The Harold Danko Quartet | Blue Skies | dmp Digital Music Productions | CD 3001

In Walked Horace
J.J.Johnson Sextet | J.J.Inc. | CBS | CK 65296

In Walked Ray
Billy Pierce Quartet | Rolling Monk | Paddle Wheel | KICJ 154

In Weiter Entfernung
Lee Morgan Orchestra | Lee Morgan | Blue Note | 84901

In What Direction Are You Headed
Kuniyoshi-Kuhn/Mattos/Prevost | Handscapes | LEO | LR 143

In Your Arms
John Abercrombie Trio | Gateway | ECM | 1562(527637-2)
Karin Krog With The Don Ellis Orchestra | Karin Krog Jubilee-The Best Of 30 Years | Verve | 523716-2
Thom Rotella Group | Without Words | dmp Digital Music Productions | CD 476

In Your Eyes
Just Friends | Jazz Unlimited | IN+OUT Records | 7017-2
University Six | University Six Vol.One 1925-26 | Harlequin | HQ 2036 IMS

In Your Mind
Al Haig | Solitaire | Spotlite | SPJ LP 14

In Your Own Sweet Way
Base Line | Baseline:Standards | Challenge | CHR 70023
Bill Evans | The Complete Fantasy Recordings | Fantasy | 9FCD 1012-2
The Complete Fantasy Recordings | Fantasy | 9FCD 1012-2
Bill Evans Trio | The Second Trio | Milestone | M 47046
In His Own Way | West Wind | WW 2028
How My Heart Sings! | Original Jazz Classics | OJCCD 369-2
Bobby Wellins Quartet | Don't Worry 'Bout Me | Cadillac | SGCCD 05
Chet Baker Quintet | Stella By Starlight | West Wind | WW 0033
Chet Baker Trio | Someday My Prince Will Come | Steeplechase | SCS 1180(Audiophile Pressing)
Conrad Herwig-Andy LaVerne | Shades Of Light | Steeplechase | SCCD 31520
Daniel Küffer Quartet | Daniel Küffer Quartet | Satin Doll Productions | SDP 1010-1 CD
Dave Brubeck Quartet | All The Things We Are | Atlantic | 7567-81399-2
Dave Brubeck Quartet With Orchestra | Brandenburg Gate:Revisited | CBS | CK 65725
Dave Brubeck Quintet | The Quartet | LRC Records | CDC 7681(974377)
Emily Remler Quartet | Take Two | Concord | CCD 4195
Franck Avitabile Trio | Right Time | Dreyfus Jazz Line | FDM 36608-2
Jeanfracois Prins Trio | All Around Town | TCB Records | TCB 99402
Jochen Rueckert Group | Introduction | Jazzline | JL 11152-2
Joe Pass/Niels-Henning Orsted-Pedersen Duo | Chops | Original Jazz Classics | OJCCD 786-2(2310830)
John Abercrombie Trio | Straight Flight | JAM | 5001 IMS
Jon Faddis With The Carlos Franzetti Orchestra | Rememberances | Chesky | JD 166
Kenn Drew Trio | Kenny Drew Trio At The Brewhouse | Storyville | 4960633
Kenny Barron/Michael Moore | 1+1+1 | Black-Hawk | BKH 50601
Lina Nyberg-Esbjörn Svensson | Close | Touché Music | TMcCD 004
Louis Hayes & Company | The Super Quartet | Timeless | CD SJP 424
McCoy Tyner Trio | Chick Corea-Herbie Hancock-Keith Jarrett-McCoy Tyner | Atlantic | ATL 50326
Michal Urbaniak Quartet | Live In New York | L+R Records | CDLR 45041
Miles Davis New Quintet | Workin' With The Miles Davis Qoartet | Original Jazz Classics | OJC 296(P 7166)
Nick Brignola Quartet | New York Bound | Interplay | IP 7719
Sal Marquez Group | One For Dewey | GRP | GRP 96782
Tal Farlow Trio | A Sign Of The Times | Concord | CCD 4026
Wes Montgomery Quartet | Wes Montgomery-The Complete Riverside Recordings | Riverside | 12 RCD 4408-2
Woody Shaw Quartet | In My Own Sweet Way | IN+OUT Records | 7003-2
Kenny Werner | Maybeck Recital Hall Series Volume Thirty-Four | Concord | CCD 4622

In Your Own Sweet Way(alt.take)
Ron McClure Trio | Never Always | Steeplechase | SCCD 31355

In Your Quiet Place-
Gary Burton-Keith Jarrett Quintet | Gary Burton & Keith Jarrett | Atlantic | 7567-81374-2
David Murray/Fred Hopkins/Jack DeJohnette | In Our Style | DIW | DIW 819 CD

Inadvertent Introduction
Milt Jackson Quartet | In A New Setting | Verve | 538620-2

Inaffable
Chet Baker & The Boto Brasilian Quartet | Chet Baker & The Boto Brasilian Quartet | Dreyfus Jazz Line | FDM 36511-9

Inaia
Miles Davis Group | Live-Evil | CBS | 485255-2

Inamorata And Narration
Akira Sakata Trio | Dance | Enja | 4002 Digital

Inanga
Frank Lowe & The Saxemple | Inappropriate Choices | ITM-Pacific | ITMP 970062

Inarticulate Spech Of The Heart
Indiscreet | Difficult To Contribute Silence | Nabel Records:Jazz Network | LP 4620

Incandescene
Bill Smith | Colours | EdiPan | NPG 807

Incantation
Elisabeth Kontomanou & Jean-Michel Pilc | Hands & Incantation | Steeplechase | SCCD 31484
Rabih Abou-Khalil Group | Nafas | ECM | 1359(835781-2)
Henri Guédon Et L'Orchestre D'Harmonie Du Havre | L'Opera Triangulaire | Messidor | 15997 CD

Incantation For An Alto Player
Ali Ryerson Quintet | Brasil:Quiet Devotion | Concord | CCD 4762

Inception
Emily Remler Quartet | Firefly | Concord | CJ 162
McCoy Tyner Trio | The Early Trios | MCA | IA 9338/2

Inception-
Bruno Tommaso Orchestra | Su Un Tema Di Jerome Kern | SPLASC(H) Records | HP 18

Incident At Harpham Flat
Stan Kenton And His Orchestra | Innovations In Modern Music | Creative World | ST 1009

Incoherent Blues
Northern Jazz Orchestra | Good News | Lake | LACD 38

Increasing Silence
Pili-Pili | Ballads Of Timbuktu | JA & RO | JARO 4240-2

Incredible Astonishment(Ka Ba Ko)
Bob Mintzer Big Band | Incredible Journey | dmp Digital Music Productions | CD 451

Incurably Romantic
Ulrich P. Lask Group | Indéan Poa | CMP Records | CMP CD 62

Indecisione
Tim Ries Quintet | Universal Spirits | Criss Cross | Criss 1144

Indefinite Expansion
Sunny Murray Quartet | Indelicacy | West Wind | WW 2005

Independence Blues
Michele Rosewoman Trio | Spirit | Blue Note | 836777-2

Independent Blues
Der Rote Bereich | Risky Business | ACT | 9407-2

Independent Swing
Peter Giger | Family Of Percussion | Nagara | MIX 1010-N

Index
John Wolf Brennan | Flügel | Creative Works Records | CW CD 1037-2

Index-E Pi? Lo Go,Lipel-?S...Is Pony S?
Dave Liebman Quintet | Homage To John Coltrane | Owl Records | 018357-2

India
Dave Liebman With Gunnar Mossblad And The James Madison University Jazz Esemble | The Music Of John Coltrane | Candid | CCD 79531
Jack DeJohnette Quartet | Special Edition | ECM | 1152
Joe Diorio | We Will Meet Again | RAM Records | RMCD 4501
John Coltrane Quintet With Eric Dolphy | Jazz Gallery:John Coltrane Vol.2 | RCA | 2127276-2
John Coltrane Septet With Eric Dolphy | John Coltrane:The Complete 1961 Village Vanguard Recordings | Impulse(MCA) | 954322-2
The Other Village Vanguard Tapes | Impulse(MCA) | MCD 04137
John Coltrane Sextet | John Coltrane:The Complete 1961 Village Vanguard Recordings | Impulse(MCA) | 954322-2
Impressions | Impulse(MCA) | 543416-2
Live At The Village Vanguard:The Master Takes | Impulse(MCA) | 951251-2
The Best Of John Coltrane-His Greatest Years, Vol. 2 | MCA | AS 9223
Paul Motian Trio | It Should've Happened A Long Time Ago | ECM | 1283
Robert Dick Group With The Soldier String Quartet | Jazz Standard On Mars | Enja | ENJ-9327 2
Shakti | A Handful Of Beauty | CBS | 81664
Paul Bollenback Quintet | Original Visions | Challenge | CHR 70022

India Town
Joe Puma Sextet | Wild Kitten | Dawn | DCD 109

Indian Blues
Donald Harrison With The Guardians Of The Flame And The Mardi Gras Indians | Indian Blues | Candid | CCD 79514

Indian Boogie Shoes
Woody Herman And His Orchestra | Boogie Woogie-Great Original Performances 1928-1941 | CDS Records Ltd. | RPCD 601

Indian Club
Shorty Rogers And His Giants | Short Stops | RCA | NL 85917(2)

Indian Cods
Louis Armstrong And His Orchestra | Louis Armstrong-St.Louis Blues Vol.6 | CBS | 467919-2

Indian Lady
Don Ellis Orchestra | Electric Bath | CBS | CK 65522

Indian Lady(single-version)
Artie Shaw And His Orchestra | The Indispensable Artie Shaw Vol.1/2(1938-1939) | RCA | 2126413-2

Indian Love Call
This Is Artie Shaw | RCA | NL 89411 DP
Peter Bocage And His Band | Peter Bocage | American Music | AMCD-93

Indian Morning
Anca Parghel With The Klaus Ignatzek Trio | Indian Princess | Blue Flame | 40262(2132488-2)

Indian River
Charlie Love Jazz Band | Kid Sheik With Charlie Love And His Cado Jazz Band | 504 Records | 504CD 21

Indian Summer
Bernard Berkhout '5' | Royal Flush | Timeless | CD SJP 425
Coleman Hawkins And Friends | Bean Stalkin' | Pablo | 2310933-2
Coleman Hawkins-Lou Levy | Coleman Hawkins | West Wind | WW 2034
Count Basie And His Orchestra | Live! | Laserlight | 15797
Count Basie & His Orchestra:Fresno,California April 24,1959 | Jazz Unlimited | JUCD 2039
Dave Hancock Trio | Out Of Nowhere | Timeless | CD SJP 303
Fraser MacPherson Quartet | Indian Summer | Concord | CJ 224
Glenn Miller And His Orchestra | Candlelight Miller | RCA | 2668716-2
Live At Meadowbrook Ballroom 1939 | Magic | DAWE 34(881864)
Jam Session | Coleman Hawkins-Rare Broadcasts Area 1950 | Jazz Anthology | JA 5217
Joe Pass | Virtuoso No.4 | Pablo | 2640102
Joe Puma Quartet | Jazz | Fresh Sound Records | JLP 1070(Jubilee)
Keith Ingham Manhattan Swingtet | We're In The Money | Sackville | SKCD2-2055
Klaus Kreuzeder & Henry Sincigno | Saxappeal | Trick Music | TM 9013 MC
Lee Konitz With The Metropole Orchestra | Saxophone Dreams | Koch Jazz | 3-6900-2
Red Holloway Quintet | Coast To Coast | Milestone | MCD 9335-2
Rinde Eckert Group | Story In,Story Out | Intuition Records | INT 3507-2
Ron Carter-Jim Hall Duo | Telephone | Concord | CCD 4270
Sidney Bechet And His New Orleans Feetwarmers | Sidney Bechet 1932-1943: The Bluebird Sessions | Bluebird | ND 90317
Masters Of Jazz Vol.3 | RCA | NL 89719 DP
Singers Unlimited | A Capella 2 | MPS | 821860-2
Stan Getz Quartet | Stan Getz:The Complete 1946-1951 Quartet Sessions(Master Takes),Vol.1 | Blue Moon | BMCD 1013
Sue Raney With The Alan Broadbent Sextet | In Good Company | Discovery | DSCD 974(889498)
The Rippingtons | Weekend In Monaco | GRP | GRP 96812
Thomas Schiedel | All Alone | AH Records | AH 404001-13
Wheelz With Ingrid Jensen | Around The World | ACT | 9247-2
Zoot Sims Four | The Innocent Years | Pablo | 2310872

Indian Summer-
Nancy Marano With The Nederlands Metropole Orchestra | If You Could See Me Now | Koch Jazz | 3-6918-2

Indian Summer Boogie
Paul Desmond Orchestra | Skylark | CTI | ZK 65133

Indian Summer(alt.take)
Matalex | Wild Indian Summer | Lipstick Records | LIP 890192

Indian Water
Mal Waldron & Jim Pepper | Art Of The Duo | Tutu Records | 888106-2*
Ran Blake-Houston Person Duo | Suffield Gothic | Soul Note | 121077-2

Indiana -> Back Home Again In Indiana

Indiana Indian
Original Memphis Five | Original Memphis Five Groups | Village(Jazz Archive) | VILCD 016-2

Indicatif(2)
Dietrich Jeske Groups | Strings And Things | Jazz Classics | AU 11205

Indifference
New York Jazz Collective | I Don't Know This World Without Don Cherry | Naxos Jazz | 86003-2

Indigo
Jan Schaffer Group | Electric Graffiti | VeraBra Records | CDVBR 2027-2
Hank Crawford Orchestra | Indigo Blue | Milestone | MCD 9119-2

Indikativ
Jackie McLean Quintet | Contour | Prestige | P 24076

Individual Choice
Jon Gordon Sextet | Witness | Criss Cross | Criss 1121

Indomitable
Mark Nauseef Group | Sura | CMP Records | CMP 21

Indonesian Dock Sucking Supreme
Frank Vaganee 5 | Picture A View | B.Sharp Records | CDS 080

Indo-Serenade
Stan Kenton And His Orchestra | Live At Butler University | Creative World | ST 1058

Industrial Suite
Bob Cooper Quartet | Tenor Sax Jazz Impressions | Trend | TR 518 Direct-to-Disc

Ineffable
Joachim Kühn | Distance | CMP Records | CMP CD 26

Ineo Op.29 for Choir And Chamber Orchestra
Kevin Bruce Harris Quartet | Folk Songs-Folk Tales | TipToe | TIP-888807 2

Inevitability Of You
Alte Leidenschaften | Alte Leidenschaften | Carsten Hormes Musikverlag | 807446

Infancia
Egberto Gismonti Group | Infancia | ECM | 1428
Enrico Rava 4uartet | Animals | Inak | 8801

Infant Eyes
Charles Earland Sextet | Infant Eyes | Muse | MR 5181
Fred Hersch Quartet | Point In Time | Enja | ENJ-9035 2
Jazzerie Feat. Roberto Ottaviano | Another Day | SPLASC(H) Records | H 156
Judy Niemack With The Fred Hersch Trio | Long As You're Living | Freelance | FRL-CD 014
Stan Getz Quartet | Montreux Summit Vol.1 | CBS | 478607-2
Wayne Shorter Quintet | Wayne Shorter:The Classic Blue Note Recordings | Blue Note | 540856-2
Don Cherry Septet | Symphony For Improvisers | Blue Note | 828976-2

Infant Joy
Karl Ratzer Quartet | Waltz For Ann | L+R Records | CDLR 45078

Infatuation
Don Lanphere Quintet | Fats Navarro:The 1946-1949 Small Group Sessions(Studio Recordings-Master Takes),Vol.3 | Blue Moon | BMCD 1018
Frank Kimbrough Quintet | The Herbie Nichols Project | Soul Note | 121313-2

Infection
Marilyn Crispell-Tim Berne | Inference | Music & Arts | CD 851

Inferno
Don Byas With Bernard Hilda Y Su Orquesta | Don Byas-George Johnson:Those Barcelona Days 1947-1948 | Fresh Sound Records | FSR-CD 3001

Infinite Distance
Edward Vesala Ensemble | Ode Of The Death Of Jazz | ECM | 1413(843196-2)

Infinite Express
Billy Cobham Group | Art Of Five | IN+OUT Records | 77063-2

Infinite Heart
Donald 'Duck' Harrison Quintet | Full Circle | Sweet Basil | 660.55.003

Infinite Pursuit
Jean-Luc Ponty Quartet | Fables | Atlantic | 781276-2

Infinite Spirit
Albert Ayler Septet | The Village Concerts | MCA | IA 9336/2

Infinity
Khan Jamal Septet | Infinity | Stash Records | ST 278(807425)

Infinity Machine
Miles Davis And The Lighthouse All Stars | At Last! | Original Jazz Classics | OJCCD 480-2

Infinity Promenade
Shorty Rogers And His Giants | The Big Shorty Rogers Express | RCA | 2118519-2
Shorty Rogers And His Orchestra Feat. The Giants | Short Stops | RCA | NL 85917(2)

Inflation Blues
Jimmy Witherspoon With Orchestra | Spoonful | Blue Note | 84545
Ernest Ranglin Group | Modern Answers To Old Problems | Telarc Digital | CD 83526

Influence
Marvin Stamm Sextet | Mystery Man | Musicmasters | 65085-2

Information
Clarence Gatemouth Brown Band | One More Mile | Rounder Records | CDRR 2034

Information,Please:
Alguimia | Alguimia:Standards | Fresh Sound Records | FSNT 049 CD

Informia
Jason Moran Trio | The Bandwagon | Blue Note | 591893-2

Infospace
Art Blakey And The Jazz Messengers | Art Blakey-The Jazz Messenger | CBS | 467920-2

Infra-Rae
Art Blakey/The Jazz Messengers | CBS | CK 62265

Infrared
Clifford Jordan Quartet | Firm Roots | Steeplechase | SCCD 31033

Inga
Dusko Goykovich Quartet | Celebration | DIW | DIW 806 CD
Peter Gullin Trio | Untold Story | Dragon | DRCD 315

Ingen Vinner Frem Til Den Evige Ro
Susanne Lundeng Quartet | Waltz For The Red Fiddle | Laika Records | 35101402

Ingenting Sakralt(Sanctimonious)
Mose Allison Trio | Ol' Devil Mose | Prestige | P 24089

Ingredience Of The Blues
Herb Geller-Brian Kellock | Hollywood Portraits | Hep | CD 2078

Ingrid Bergman
Barre Phillips Quartet | Three Day Moon | ECM | 1123

Inhaling You
Plimley/Ellis/Cyrille | When Silence Pulls | Music & Arts | CD 692

Inizio(1)-
Mona Larsen And The Danish Radio Big Band Plus Soloists | Michael Mantler:Cerco Un Paese Innocente | ECM | 1556

Inizio(2)-
Buddy Banks Sextet | Buddy Banks:The Complete Recordings 1945-1949 | Blue Moon | BMCD 6015

Inky
Jay Clayton And Her Quintet | Circle Dancing | Sunnyside | SSC 1076 D

Inner Child
Andy McKee And NEXT with Hamiet Bluiett | Sound Root | Mapleshade | 04432

Inner Circle
Marion McPartland-Michael Moore | Marion McPartland Plays The Music Of Alec Wilder | The Jazz Alliance | TJA 10016
Tome XX | The Red Snapper | Jazz Haus Musik | JHM 0047 CD
Bobby Hutcherson Orchestra | Deep Blue-The United States Of Mind | Blue Note | 521152-2

Inner City Blues
Jim Kahr Group | Burnin' The Blues | Acoustic Music Records | 319.1044.2
Larry Coryell Group | Fallen Angel | CTI Records | CTI 1014-2

Inner Glimpse
McCoy Tyner Quartet | Four Times Four | Milestone | M 55007

Inner Journey
Toots Thielemans/Philip Catherine And Friends | Two Generations | Limetree | FCD 0003

Inner Logic
Walt Weiskopf Sextet | Sleepless Nights | Criss Cross | Criss 1147

Inner Organs
Lee Morgan Orchestra | Lee Morgan | Blue Note | 84901

Inner Passions-Out
Miroslav Vitous Group | Miroslav Vitous Group | ECM | 1185

Inner Space
Joe Locke Quartet | Inner Space | Steeplechase | SCCD 31380
Shorty Rogers And His Orchestra Feat. The Giants | An Invisible Orchard | Fresh Sound Records | 49560 CD(RCA)

Inner Trust
Ahmad Mansour Quartet | Is Really This It ? | Plainisphare | PAV 805

Inner Urge
Barry Finnerty Quintet | Straight Ahead | Arabesque Recordings | AJ 0116

TITELVERZEICHNIS

George Gruntz Concert Jazz Band | Happening Now | Hat Art | CD 6008
Inner Vibes Of Love
Walt Dickerson Trio | Serendipity | Steeplechase | SCCD 31070
Inner Voice
Larry Schneider Quartet | Jazz | Steeplechase | SCCD 31505
Innerfern
Muhal Richard Abrams Ensemble | Spihumonesty | Black Saint | 120032-2
Innerplay
Agnes Buen Garnas-Jan Garbarek | Rosensfole-Medieval Songs From Norway | ECM | 1402(839293-2)
Innferd
Stan Kenton And His Orchestra | National Anthems Of The World | Creative World | ST 1060
Innocence
Keith Jarrett Quartet | Personal Mountains | ECM | 1382(837361-2)
Meinert & Kropp | Innocence Is Gone | Wonderland Records | 319.9005-2
Innocent Erendira
Michael Hornstein Quartet | Innocent Green | Enja | 9099-2
Innocente
Ralph Towner-Gary Burton | Slide Show | ECM | 1306
Innocenti
Thomas Horstmann-Martin Wiedmann Group | Decade | Factory Outlet Records | WO 95001
Terje Rypdal Trio | Descendre | ECM | 1144
Innseiling
Works | ECM | 825428-1
Inot
Out Of The Blue | Spiral Staircase | Blue Note | 793006-2
Inscenes
Robin Kenyatta Orchestra | Take The Heat Off Me | ITM-Pacific | ITMP 970069
Insects
Joachim Kühn-Walter Quintus | Dark | Ambiance(Blue Flame) | AMB 1
Insects(part 1)
Anliker-Parker-Schmid-Senn-Solothurnmann | September Winds | Creative Works Records | CW CD 1038/39
Insects(part 2)
Das Böse Ding | Germ Germ | Acoustic Music Records | 319.1160.2
Insensatez(How Insensitive)
Antonio Carlos Jobim With The Claus Ogerman Orchestra | Compact Jazz: Best Of Bossa Nova | Verve | 833269-2
Banda Mantiqueira | Aldeia | ACT | 5008-2
Earl Klugh Trio | The Earl Klugh Trio Volume One | Warner | 7599-26750-2
Franco D'Andrea New Quartet | Jobim | Philology | W 125.2
Stan Getz-Luiz Bonfa Orchestra | Compact Jazz: Antonio Carlos Jobim | Verve | 843273-2
Jazz Samba Encore! | CTI Records | PDCTI 1125-2
Django Reinhardt And His Rhythm | Peche Á La Mode-The Great Blue Star Sessions 1947/1953 | Verve | 835418-2
Insensiblement
Django Reinhardt And The Quintet Du Hot Club De France | Peche Á La Mode-The Great Blue Star Sessions 1947/1953 | Verve | 835418-2
Django Reinhardt Portrait | Barclay | DALP 2/1939
Django Reinhardt Quartet | Jazz In Paris:Django Reinhardt-Nuages | EmArCy | 018428-2
Stephane Grappelli With The Michel Legrand Orchestra | Verve Jazz Masters 11:Stéphane Grappelli | Verve | 516758-2
Joe Pass Quartet | For Django | Pacific Jazz | 300007(PJ 85)
Inside
Paul Bley-Paul Motian Duo | Notes | Soul Note | 121190-2
Inside Chella
Marc Johnson Trio | Right Brain Patrol | JMT Edition | 849153-2
Inside In
Rush Hour | Pall Mall Export Swing Award: Swing Night | EMI Records | CDP 748910-2
Inside Inside
Boogaloo Joe Jones Sextet | Discovery:Grover Washington Jr.-The First Recordings | Prestige | PCD 11020-2
Inside Job
Antonio Scarano Octet | Hot Blend | SPLASC(H) Records | H 183
Inside Moves
Black Swan Quartet | Black Swan Quartet | Minor Music | 009
Inside Out
Jerry Bergonzi Quartet | Inside Out | Red Records | 123230-2
Klaus Suonsaari Quintet | True Colours | L+R Records | CDLR 45080
Lennie Niehaus Quintet | Vol.1:The Quintets | Original Jazz Classics | OJC 319(C 3518)
Unit X | Rated X | Timescrapper | TSCR 9618
Victor Feldman's Generation Band | Smooth | TBA Records | TB 215
In-Side Out
Prince Lasha Quartet | Inside Story | Enja | 3073
Inside Straight
Cannonball Adderley Septet | Inside Straight | Original Jazz Classics | OJCCD 750-2(F 9435)
Cannonball Adderley Sextet | Cannonball Adderley Birthday Celebration | Fantasy | FANCD 6087-2
Dirty Dozen Brass Band | The New Orleans Album | CBS | CK 45414
Tim Berne/Bill Frisell Duo | Theoretically | Empire | EPC 72 K
Inside The Whale
Generation Band | Call Of The Wild | Palo Alto | PA 202
Insight
Cedar Walton Quintet | Cedar's Blues-Live | Red Records | VPA 179
Insomnia
Peter Brötzmann | No Nothing: Brötzmann Solo | FMP | CD 32
Insomnio
The Fraterman | Spielerlaubnis | Aho-Recording | CD 1014
Inspiration
Ron McClure Trio | Inspiration | Ken Music | 660.56.015
Uli Gutscher Quintet | Inspiration | Edition Collage | EC 462-2
Inspiration 2
Paul Motian Quartet | Conception Vessel | ECM | 1028(519279-2)
Inspiration From A Vietnamese Lullaby
Tony Williams Lifetime | Tony Williams Lifetime-The Collection | CBS | 468924-2
Instance
Bruno Castellucci Groups | Bim Bam | Koala Records | CD P 19
Instand Judgement
Zoot Sims And His Orchestra | Recado Bossa Nova | Fresh Sound Records | FSR-CD 0189
Instru (For The) Mental
Louis Jordan And His Tympany Five | Look Out Sisters-Unissued Film Soundtracks 1944-1948 | Krazy Kat | KK 7415 IMS
Intangible Waltz
Minas Alexiades | Integra | Praxis | GM 1001
Integration
Urs Leimgruber/John Wolf Brennan | M.A.P. | L+R Records | CDLR 45021
Intente
Trio M.G.M. | Jazz In Switzerland 1930-1975 | Elite Special | 9544002/1-4
Inter Tribal(I)
Gunther Schuller With The WDR Radio Orchestra & Rememberance Band | Witchi Tia To, The Music Of Jim Pepper | Tutu Records | 888204-2*
Inter Tribal(II)
European Trumpet Summit | European Trumpet Summit | Konnex Records | KCD 5064
Interaction
Free Fair + 8 | Free Fair + 8 | Limetree | MLP 198127
Peter Sonntag Sextet | Words Written In Stone | amf records | maj 1011
Interception
Heikki Sarmanto Ensemble And Gregg Smith Vocal Quartet | New Hope Jazz Mass | Finlandia | FA 201
Interface
Ronnie Scott's Quintet | Serious Gold | Ronnie Scott's Jazz House | NSPL 18542
Interieur Jour
Hal McKusick Quintet | Bird Feathers | Original Jazz Classics | OJCCD 1735-2
Interlude
Allen Farnham | The Common Ground | Concord | CCD 4634
Florian Trübsbach Quintet | Manson & Dixon | Jazz 4 Ever Records:Jazz Network | J4E 4759
Gary Smulyan Quartet And Brass | Blue Suite | Criss Cross | Criss 1189
Joachim Raffel Quintet | Circlesongs | Acoustic Music Records | 312.1093.2
Lorry Raine With The Russ Garcia Orchestra | Interlude With Lorry Raine | Fresh Sound Records | Advance CD 714
Milt Jackson Sextet | Goodbye | CTI | 6038
Steve Tibbetts | Steve Tibbetts | ECM | bzz- 77
Toshiko Akiyoshi Trio | Interlude | Concord | CCD 4324
Interlude-
John Taylor Group | Pause, And Think Again | FMR | FMR CD 24
New York Voices | What's Inside | GRP | GRP 97002
Interlude 1
Rodney Jones Orchestra | Articulation | Timeless | CD SJP 125
Roger Hanschel/Gabriele Hasler | Go In Green | Jazz Haus Musik | JHM 0073 CD
Vienna Art Orchestra | The Original Charts Of Duke Ellington & Charles Mingus | Verve | 521998-2
Interlude 1 B
Ben Wolfe Sextet | Bagdad Theater | Mons Records | MR 874827
Interlude 2
Roger Hanschel/Gabriele Hasler | Go In Green | Jazz Haus Musik | JHM 0073 CD
Vienna Art Orchestra | The Original Charts Of Duke Ellington & Charles Mingus | Verve | 521998-2
Interlude 2-
Karl Berger | Interludes | FMP | 0460
Interlude 3
Vienna Art Orchestra | The Original Charts Of Duke Ellington & Charles Mingus | Verve | 521998-2
Interlude 4
Karl Berger | Interludes | FMP | 0460
Interlude No.1
Lares | Lares | yvp music | 3017
Interlude No.1(Turn Up The Funk)
Joe Pass Group | Guitar Interludes | Discovery | DS 776 IMS
Interlude No.2
Lares | Lares | yvp music | 3017
Nicholas Payton Quintet | Nick@Night | Verve | 547598-2
Interlude No.2(Turn Out The Burn Out)
Joe Pass Group | Guitar Interludes | Discovery | DS 776 IMS
Interlude No.3
Lares | Lares | yvp music | 3017
Interlude No.4
Joe Pass Group | Guitar Interludes | Discovery | DS 776 IMS
Interlude With Spasms-
Perry Robinson Quartet | Perry Robinson Quartet | Timescrapper | TSCR 9613
Interlude(1)
Stephen Scott Trio | Vision Quest | Enja | ENJ-9347 2
Perry Robinson Quartet | Perry Robinson Quartet | Timescrapper | TSCR 9613
Interlude(2)
Stephen Scott Quartet | Vision Quest | Enja | ENJ-9347 2
Interlude(3)
Stephen Scott Trio | Vision Quest | Enja | ENJ-9347 2
Boyd Raeburn And His Orchestra | Groovin' High | Naxos Jazz | 8.120582 CD
Interlude(A Night In Tunisia)
Lennie Tristano Trio | Jazz-Club: Guitar | Verve | 840035-2
Interlude:Blue
The Atlantic String Trio | First Meeting | Factory Outlet Records | 2001-1 CD
Interlude:Green
First Meeting | Factory Outlet Records | 2001-1 CD
Interlude:Lament-Intermission Music-
First Meeting | Factory Outlet Records | FOR 2501-1 CD
Interlude:Not All Blues
First Meeting | Factory Outlet Records | 2001-1 CD
Interlude:Shovels-
Rova Saxophone Quartet | Rova:The Works Vol.1 | Black Saint | 120176-2
Interludium
Christian Griese Group | Affinities:My Berlin Phone Book | BIT | 11216
Gilles Torrent Jazztet | Terre Engloutie | Plainisphare | PL 1267-22
Intermezzo
Oliver Lake/Donal Leonellis Fox | Boston Duets | Music & Arts | CD 732
Pete Rugolo And His Orchestra incl.The Rugolettes(eight-man-combo) | Rugolomania | Fresh Sound Records | LSP 15826(CBS CL 689)
Urs Leimgruber/John Wolf Brennan | Polyphyllum | L+R Records | CDLR 45013
Intermezzo No.1
World Quintet With The London Mozart Players | World Quintet | TipToe | TIP-888843 2
Intermezzo No.3
Jason Moran Trio | The Bandwagon | Blue Note | 591893-2
Intermezzo Op.118, No.2
Ensemble Pago Libre | Ensemble Pago Libre | SPLASC(H) Records | CD H 314-2
Intermezzo(1)-
Mona Larsen And The Danish Radio Big Band Plus Soloists | Michael Mantler:Cerco Un Paese Innocente | ECM | 1556
Intermezzo(2)-
Michael Mantler:Cerco Un Paese Innocente | ECM | 1556
Intermezzo(3)-
Michael Mantler:Cerco Un Paese Innocente | ECM | 1556
Intermezzo(4)-
Michael Mantler:Cerco Un Paese Innocente | ECM | 1556
Intermezzo(5)-
Duke Ellington And His Orchestra | Duke Ellington In Hamilton | Radiex Music | RDX-1000
Intermission Music
Cab Calloway And His Orchestra | The Cab Calloway Show | Zounds | CD 697110
Intermission Riff
Eddie Lockjaw Davis-Johnny Griffin Quintet | Tough Tenors Back Again! | Storyville | STCD 8298
Glen Gray And The Casa Loma Orchestra | Swingin' Decade! Sounds Of The Great Bands Of The 40's | Pathe | 1566171(Capitol ST 1289)
Stan Kenton And His Orchestra | The Early Years | Capitol | 166219-2
Return To Biloxi | Magic | DAWE 35(881848)
Stan Kenton Orchestra | Rhapsody In Blue | Moon Records | MCD 012-2
Intermitencia
Wild Bill Davis Trio | Impulsions | Black & Blue | BLE 233037
Internal Affairs
Glen Velez-Layne Redmond | Internal Combustion | CMP Records | CMP CD 23
Interplay
Bill Mays/Ray Drummond | One To One | dmp Digital Music Productions | CD 473
Chick Corea-Stanley Clarke | Verve Jazz Masters 3:Chick Corea | Verve | 519820-2
Jiri Stivin-Ali Haurand | Just The Two Of Us | Konnex Records | KCD 5095
Klaus Treuheit-Andreas Hansl | Sprengwerk | Klaus Treuheit Production | KTMP 9911(CD 164)
Prestige All Stars | Interplay For Two Trumpets And Two Tenors | Prestige | VIJ 5028
Interplay | Original Jazz Classics | OJCCD 292-2(P 7112)
Interview
Roy Eldridge Quartet | Rare Broadcasts | Duke Records | D 1010
Charlie Parker Quintet | Bird At The High-Hat | Blue Note | 799787-2
Interview-
Charlie Parker 1950-1951:The Complete Bird At Birdland Vol.1 | Fat Boy Jazz | FBB 901
Interview I
Fritz Münzer Quintet | Jazz für junge Leute:Live im HR 1962 | Jazz 'n' Arts Records | C 01
Interview II
Jazz für junge Leute:Live im HR 1962 | Jazz 'n' Arts Records | C 01
Interview III
Jazz für junge Leute:Live im HR 1962 | Jazz 'n' Arts Records | C 01
Interview IV
Johannes Rediske Sextet | Re-Disc Bounce | Bear Family Records | BCD 16119 AH
Interview mit Eberhard Kruppa-
Fritz Münzer Quintet | Jazz für junge Leute:Live im HR 1962 | Jazz 'n' Arts Records | C 01
Interview V
Art Tatum Trio | Art Tatum:Complete Capitol Recordings | Capitol | 821325-2
Interview with Art Tatum and Paul Weston
Art Tatum:Complete Capitol Recordings | Definitive Records | DRCD 11192
Interview(12:49) with Art Blakey by Mike Hennessey
Charlie Parker Quintet | Bird's Eyes Last Unissued Vol.18 | Philology | W 848.2
Interview(18:03) by Charles Schwartz
Louis Armstrong And His All Stars | Louis Armstrong Plays W.C.Handy | CBS | CK 64925
Interview(2:44) with W.C.Handy by George Avakian
Dizzy Gillespie/Max Roach | Max+Dizzy | A&M Records | 396404-2
Interview(6:00) With Bill Evans by Rod Starns
James Blood Ulmer | After Dark | DIW | DIW 855 CD
Interview(76:26) by Nesuhi Ertegun
Klaus Treuheit-Andreas Hansl | Sprengwerk | Klaus Treuheit Production | KTMP 9911(CD 164)
Intimacy Of The Blues
The Dave Glasser/Clark Terry/Barry Harris Project | Blues Of Summer | Nagel-Heyer | NH 1011
Toshiko Akiyoshi Trio | A Tribute To Billy Strayhorn | JAM | 5003 IMS
Intimate Desire
Kip Hanrahan Group | Vertical's Currency | American Clave | AMCL 1010-2
Into A Dream
Cecil McBee Quintet | Flying Out | India Navigation | IN 1053
Into Darkness
Ralph Moore Quintet | Furthermore | Landmark | LCD 1526-2
Into Each Life Some Rain Must Fall
Ella Fitzgerald With The Count Basie Orchestra | Ella & Basie-On The Sunny Side Of The Street | Verve | 821576-2
Into Eternal Silence
Mani Neumeir | Privat | ATM Records | ATM 3803-AH
Into Gagaku
Joe Douglas Trio | Visage | Spotlite | SPJ 514
Into Somewhere
Anthony Wonsey Quintet | Open The Gates | Criss Cross | Criss 1162
Into The Dream
Terumasa Hino Quartet | Vibrations | Enja | 2010
Into The Light
Ellis=Ochs=Robinson | What We Live | DIW | DIW 909 CD
Into The Night
Paul Bley | Blues For Red | Red Records | 123238 2
Matthias Daneck's N.O.W. | Seven Portraits Of Obviously Unpredictable Mood Swings And Subsequent Behaviour | Satin Doll Productions | SDP 1012-1 CD
Into The Pocket
Alexander von Schlippenbach | The Living Music | FMP | 0100
Into The Wilderness
Terje Rypdal Group | Skywards | ECM | 1608(533768-2)
Richie Hart | Remembering Wes | Blue Flame | 40222
Intolerance
Positive Knowledge | Another Day's Journey | Music & Arts | CD 842
Intro
Dizzy Gillespie Quintet | Dizzy Gillespie:Pleyel 53 | Vogue | 2115466-2
Duke Ellington And His Orchestra | Ellington At Basin Street:The Complete Concert | Music & Arts | CD 908
George Lewis Ragtime Jazz Band Of New Orleans | The Oxford Series Vol.2 | American Music | AMCD-22
Jessica Williams | The Victoria Concert | Jazz Focus | JFCD 015
Matzeit-Daerr | September | Jazz Haus Musik | JHM 0125 CD
Miles Davis With The Danish Radio Big Band | Aura | CBS | CK 63962
New Jazz Trio | Three Trees | Elite Special | 73410
Ray Barretto And His Orchestra | Tomorrow | Messidor | 15948
Thomas Heidepriem Quartet | Brooklyn Shuffle | L+R Records | CDLR 45084
Voices | Voices:Live In Rome | Nueva Records | IN 806
Duke Ellington And His Orchestra | Live Recording At The Cotton Club-Vol. 1 | Jazz Anthology | JA 5168
Intro-
Tadd Dameron Tentet | Bird's Eyes-Last Unissued Vol.20 | Philology | W 850.2
Intro & Fanfare-
Kelm 3 | Per Anno | dml-records | CD 013
Intro <143
Kenny Burrell Quartet | Midnight At The Village Vanguard | Paddle Wheel | KICJ 178
Intro Per Stella
Paolo Fresu-Furio Di Castri | Evening Song | Owl Records | 014733-2
Intro Per Un Basso Nel Buio
Jaki Byard | Blues For Smoke | Candid | CCD 79018
Intro To Byard's Favorite Medleys
Julian Argüelles-Steve Argüelles | Scapes | Babel | BDV 9614
Intro To Song For...
Scapes | Babel | BDV 9614
Intro(ABR)
Tiziana Ghiglioni And Her Band | Tiziana Ghiglioni Canta Luigi Tenco | Philology | W 60.2
Introduccion Y Milonga Del Ausente
Klaus König Orchestra | Hommage A Douglas Adams | Enja | ENJ-6078 2
Introducing Arthur Dent(Overture)
John Gill's Novelty Orchestra Of New Orleans | Headin' For Better Times | Stomp Off Records | CD 1270
Introducing The Band
The Rippingtons | Live In L.A. | GRP | GRP 97182
Introducing the Tunes(3:30)
Soesja Citroen And Her Quartet | Song For Ma | Challenge | CHR 70056
Introduction
Benny Carter Quintet | All That Jazz-Live At Princeton | Limelight | 820841-2 IMS
Cannonball Adderley Sextet | Live On Planet Earth | West Wind | WW 2088
Charlie Haden Quartet West | Haunted Heart | Verve | 513078-2
Chet Baker Quartet | Chet Baker Quartet Live Vol.1:This Time The Dreams's On Me | Pacific Jazz | 525248-2
Chicago Blues All Stars | American Folk Blues Festival '70 | L+R Records | LS 42021
Clarinet Summit | Clarinet Summit In Concert At The Public Theater | India Navigation | IN 1062 CD
Count Basie And His Orchestra | Live at The Sands | Reprise | 9362-45946-2
Crusaders | Live In Japan | GRP | GRP 97462
Dave Liebman Ensemble | John Coltrane's Medetation | Arkadia Jazz | 71042
Duke Ellington And His Orchestra | Carnegie Hall Concert December 1944 | Prestige | 2PCD 24073-2

Duke Ellington:Complete Prestige Carnegie Hall 1943-1944 Concerts | Definitive Records | DRCD 11210
Ed Blackwell Project | Vol.1:What It Is? | Enja | ENJ-7089 2
Ella Fitzgerald With The Lou Levy Trio | Ella In Rome-The Birthday Concert | Verve | 835454-2
Franck Band | Franckband Live | Jazz Haus Musik | JHM 64 CD
Frank Carlberg Group | Variations On A Summer Day | Fresh Sound Records | FSNT 083 CD
Franz Koglmann Group With Voices | O Moon My Pin-Up | HatOLOGY | 566
Guido Manusardi | Contrasti | Penta Flowers | CDPIA 012
International Commission For The Prevention Of Musical Border Control,The | The International Commission For The Prevention Of Musical Border Control | VeraBra Records | CDVBR 2093-2
Irvin Rochlin Trio | Quirine | Limetree | MLP 198036
Jan Lundgren Trio | Cooking! At The Jazz Bakery | Fresh Sound Records | FSR-CD 5019
Michael Mantler Group With The Danish Radio Concert Orchestra Strings | The School Of Understanding(Sort-Of-An-Opera) | ECM | 1648/49(537963-2)
Michel Godard Ensemble | Castel Del Monte II | Enja | ENJ-9431 2
Mike Westbrook Concert Band | Marching Songs Vol.1&2 | Deram | 844853-2
Miles Davis Sextet | Miles Davis All Stars Live in 1958-59 | Jazz Band Records | EBCD 2101-2(882858)
Norbert Gottschalk With The Matthias Bröde Quintet | Norbert Gottschalk:Two Sessions | Dr.Jazz Records | 8605-2
Oscar Peterson Trio | Oscar Peterson-The London House Sessions | Verve | 531766-2
Pata Music Meets Arfi | News Of Roi Ubu | Pata Musik | PATA 10 CD
Patrick Karlhuber Group | So What | Edition Collage | EC 480-2
Rahsaan Roland Kirk & The Vibration Society | Rahsaan Rahsaan | Atlantic | ATL 40127(SD 1575)
The Heath Brothers With Pat Metheny | Live In Concert | Kingdom Jazz | Gate 7017

Introduction-
Gato Barbieri Sextet | Gato Barbieri:The Complete Flying Dutchman Recordings 1969-1973 | RCA | 2154555-2
Karoline Höfler Quartet | Charly Haigl's Festival Band | Satin Doll Productions | SDP 1007-1 CD

Introduction & Kalina
Leonard Feather's Esquire All Stars | Metropolitan Opera House Jam Session | Jazz Anthology | 550212

Introduction And Dance In 7-4
Charles Mingus Quintet | The Great Concert,Paris 1964 | Accord | 500072

Introduction by Al Jarvis
Albert Ayler Quartet | My Name Is Albert Ayler | Black Lion | BLCD 760211

Introduction by André Francis
André Previn Trio | Jazz At The Musikverein | Verve | 537704-2

Introduction by Billy Taylor
Paul Moer Trio | Live At The Pour House | Fresh Sound Records | FSCD 1025

Introduction by Bob Shad
Cannonball Adderley Sextet | Jazz Workshop Revisited | Capitol | 529441-2

Introduction by Cannonball Adderley
Coast To Coast | Milestone | M 47039
Cedar Walton Quartet | First Set | Steeplechase | SCCD 31085

Introduction by Cedar Walton
Chet Baker Quartet | In You Own Sweet Way | Circle Records | RK 26-22380/26 IMS

Introduction by Claude Nobbs
Miles Davis With Gil Evans Orchestra, The George Gruntz Concert Jazz Band And Guests | Miles & Quincy Live At Montreux | Warner | 9362-45221-2

Introduction by Claude Nobbs And Quincy Jones
Birdland Stars | Birdland Stars 1956 | Bluebird | 63 66159-2

Introduction by Dannie Richmond
GRP All-Star Big Band | GRP All-Star Big Band:Live! | GRP | GRP 97402

Introduction by Dave Grusin
Dexter Gordon Quartet | I Want More | Steeplechase | SCC 6015

Introduction by Dexter Gordon
Dexter Gordon With The Kenny Drew Trio | Loose Walk | Steeplechase | SCCD 36032
Loose Walk | Steeplechase | SCCD 36032
Jam Session | Miscellaneous Davis 1955-1957 | Jazz Unlimited | JUCD 2050

Introduction by Ed Williams
Ella Fitzgerald With Joe Pass | Sophisticated Lady | Pablo | PACD 5310-2

Introduction by Ella Fitzgerald
Dave Brubeck Quartet With Gerry Mulligan | The Last Set At Newport | Atlantic | 7567-81382-2

Introduction by Father Norman O'Connor
Louis Armstrong And His All Stars | Louis Armstrong:Wintergarden 1947/Blue Note 1948 | Storyville | STCD 8242

Introduction by Fred Murray
The Complete Town Hall Concert 17.May 1947 | RCA | ND 89746

Introduction by Hank Stewart
Alex Welsh And His Band | Melody Maker Tribute To Louis Armstrong Vol.1 | Jazz Colours | 874767-2

Introduction by Jerry Gonzalez
Randy Weston Sextet With Booker Ervin | Monterey '66 | Verve | 519698-2

Introduction by John Hammond
Count Basie Trio | From Spiritual To Swing | Vanguard | VCD 169/71
Helen Humes With The Kansas City Five | From Spiritual To Swing | Vanguard | VCD 169/71
Jimmy Rushing With Count Basie And His Orchestra | From Spiritual To Swing | Vanguard | VCD 169/71
Lee Konitz Quartet | Jazz At Storyville | Black Lion | BLP 60901

Introduction by John Sinclair
June Christy With The Johnny Guarnieri Quintet | June Christy And The Johnny Guarnieri Quintet (1949) | Jazz Unlimited | JUCD 2084

Introduction by Johnny Guarnieri
Return To The Wide Open Spaces | Live At The Caravan Of Dreams | Amazing Records | AMCD 1021

Introduction by Lee Morgan
Bud Powell Orchestra | Bebop | Pablo | PACD 2310978-2

Introduction by Leonard Feather
Duke Ellington And His Orchestra | Jazz In V.Discs Vol.2 | Collection Hugues Panassié | CTPL 002

Introduction by Mark Morganelli
Ricky Ford Quartet | Ebony Rhapsody | Candid | CCD 79053
Heads Up Super Band | Live at The Berks Jazz Fest | Inak | 30462

Introduction by Mort Fega
Muhal Richard Abrams Septet | Interpertations Of Monk | DIW | DIW 395/8 CD

Introduction by Norman Granz
Coleman Hawkins Quartet | The Complete Jazz At The Philharmonic On Verve 1944-1949 | Verve | 523893-2
Ella Fitzgerald With The Hank Jones Trio | The Complete Jazz At The Philharmonic On Verve 1944-1949 | Verve | 523893-2
The Complete Jazz At The Philharmonic On Verve 1944-1949 | Verve | 523893-2
Ella Fitzgerald With The Lou Levy Quartet | Ella Returns To Berlin | Verve | 837758-2
Gerry Mulligan Quartet | Jazz At The Philharmonic: The Gerry Mulligan Quartets In Concert | Pablo | PACD 5309-2
Hank Jones Trio | The Complete Jazz At The Philharmonic On Verve 1944-1949 | Verve | 523893-2
JATP All Stars | The Drum Battle:Gene Krupa And Buddy Rich At JATP | Verve | 559810-2
Welcome To Jazz At The Philharmonic | Fantasy | FANCD 6081-2
Bird: The Complete Charlie Parker On Verve | Verve | 837141-2
Bird: The Complete Charlie Parker On Verve | Verve | 837141-2
JATP In Tokyo | Pablo | 2620104-2
Jazz At The Philharmonic-Frankfurt 1952 | Pablo | PACD 5305-2
The Complete Jazz At The Philharmonic On Verve 1944-1949 | Verve | 523893-2
Norman Granz' JATP: Carnegie Hall 1949 | Pablo | PACD 5311-2
Norman Granz' JATP: Carnegie Hall 1949 | Pablo | PACD 5311-2
John Coltrane Quartet | John Coltrane-Live Trane:The European Tours | Pablo | 7PACD 4433-2
Oscar Peterson-Ray Brown Duo | The Complete Jazz At The Philharmonic On Verve 1944-1949 | Verve | 523893-2
Horace Silver Quintet | Paris Blues | Pablo | PACD 5316-2

Introduction by Norman Granz And Horace Silver
Art Blakey And The Jazz Messengers | Meet You At The Jazz Corner Of The World Vol. 1 | Blue Note | 84054

Introduction by Pee-Wee Marquette
Aretha Franklin With Choir And Soloists | One Lord One Faith One Baptism | Arista | 393178-2

Introduction by Sterling A.Brown
Alex Welsh And His Band | Melody Maker Tribute To Louis Armstrong Vol.2 | Jazz Colours | 874768-2

Introduction by 'Symphony Sid Torin'
Mongo Santamaria And His Band | Mongo At The Village Gate | Original Jazz Classics | OJCCD 490-2(RLP 9529)
Mongo Santamaria Orchestra | The Watermelon Man | Milestone | M 47012

Introduction by Ted O'Reilly
Maria Joao/Aki Takase/Niels-Henning Orsted-Pedersen | Alice | Enja | 6096-2

Introduction by Woody Herman
Woody Herman And The Herd | Woody Herman (And The Herd) At Carnegie Hall | Verve | 559833-2
Sax Mal Anders | Kontraste | Chaos | CACD 8185

Introduction Et Variations Sur Une Ronde Populaire
Willem Breuker Kollektief With Strings And Choir | Psalm 122 | BVHAAST | CD 9803

Introduction in Swedish
Eartha Kitt And A 100 Voices Gospel Choir | My Way:A Musical Tribute To Rev.Martin Luther King Jr. | Basic | 50015

Introduction No.1
Stan Kenton And His Orchestra | Festival Of Modern American Jazz | Status | CD 101(882197)

Introduction Of Players
Giants Of Jazz | Giants Of Jazz In Berlin '71 | EmArCy | 834567-2

Introduction To 'My Favorite Things'
Charlie Parker With Machito And His Orchestra | Charlie Parker-South Of The Border | Verve | 527779-2

Introduction To Hag'Houge And String Bass
Duke Ellington And His Orchestra | Live At Carnegie Hall 1964 Vol.1 | Nueva Records | JU 322

Introduction To Miles Ahead Medley
Michael Brecker Group | Tales From The Hudson | Impulse(MCA) | 951191-2

Introduction To Naked Soul
Charlie Haden Orchestra | The Ballad Of The Fallen | ECM | 1248(811546-2)

Introduction To People
Ray Run No Star Band | I Got Gershwin | Jazzline | ???

Introduction To Porgy And Bess Medley
Spyro Gyra | Three Wishes | GRP | GRP 96742

Introduction Y Danca(Nr.1)
René Marino Rivero | Che Bandoneon | ALISO Records | AL 1020

Introduction Y Danca(Nr.2)
Lightnin' Hopkins | Lightnin' Strikes Back | Charly | CRB 1031

Introduction:Limbo
Grant Green Septet | Live | Blue Note | 84431

Introductions
Ellis Larkins | Maybeck Recital Hall Series Volume Twenty-Two | Concord | CCD 4533

Introduzione-
Slim Gaillard-Bam Brown | Opera In Vout | Verve | 2304554 IMS

Introduzione Pianissimo(Softly Most Softly)-
Gary Peacock Quartet | Guamba | ECM | 1352

Introending
Butch Morris Orchestra | Homeing | Sound Aspects | sas CD 4015

Introitus
Manfred Zepf Meets Andrew Cyrille | Paintings | West Wind | 003

Introspecciò Stomacal
Jim Snidero Sextet | San Juan | Red Records | 123265-2

Introspection
Mike DiRubbo Quintet | Keep Steppin' | Criss Cross | Criss 1205
Ralph Burns And His Orchestra | The Jazz Scene | Verve | 521661-2
Thelonious Monk | Solo Monk | CBS | 471248-2
Thelonious Monk Trio | The Complete Genius | Blue Note | LA 579
Thelonious Monk:The Complete Blue Note Recordings | Blue Note | 830363-2

Introspection(alt.take)
Thelonious Monk | The London Collection Vol.3 | Black Lion | BLCD 760142

Introvert Blues
Gary Burton Quintet With Eberhard Weber | Ring | ECM | 1051

Intrude
Jessica Williams | Maybeck Recital Hall Series Volume Twenty-One | Concord | CCD 4525

Intruders
Art Pepper Quintet | Art Pepper:Tokyo Debut | Galaxy | GCD 4201-2

Intruduction
Claude Williamson Trio | Live! At The Jazz Bakery | Fresh Sound Records | FSR-CD 5014
Kenny Dorham Quintet | Last But Not Least 1966 Vol.2 | Raretone | 5022 FC

Intruduction:
Tommy Smith Sextet | Misty Morning And No Time | Linn Records | AKD 040

Intuition
Babamadu | Babamadu | Enja | 9093-2

Inuit Erzählung-
Ana Caram Group | Blue Bossa | Chesky | JD 219

Inutil Paisagem(Useless Landscape)
Nicola Puglielli Group | In The Middle | Jardis Records | JRCD 9924
Zona Sul | Pure Love | Nagel-Heyer | CD 3039
Herbie Hancock | Antonio Carlos Jobim And Friends | Verve | 531556-2

Inutil Paisagem(Useless Landscape)-
Alfred 23 Harth Group | Sweet Paris | free flow music | ffm 0291

Invalides-
Evan Parker/Barry Guy/Paul Lytton | Imaginary Values | MAYA Recordings | MCD 9401

Invasion Of The Forest
Ruud Jan Bos-Francois Van Bemmel Quartet | Bos & Van Bemmel | Timeless | CD SJP 363

Invencao Em 7 1
Dave Brubeck Quartet feat. Bill Smith | Brubeck A La Mode | Original Jazz Classics | OJCCD 200-2

Invention
Francis Coletta Trio + One | Cris De Balaines | IN+OUT Records | 77030-2
Eugen Cicero Quartet | Jazz Bach | Timeless | CD SJP 216

Invention In D-Moll
Shin-Ichi Fukuda | Guitar Legends:Homage To Great Popular Guitarists | Denon Compact Disc | CO-18048

Invention No.4
Jacques Loussier Trio | Play Bach No.2 | Accord | 500182

Invention Nr.9-
Les Brown And His Orchestra | The Uncollected: Les Brown | Hindsight | HSR 103

Invierno Porteno
Richard Galliano Septet | Piazzolla Forever | Dreyfus Jazz Line | FDM 36642-2
Per Carsten Quintet | Via | dacapo | DCCD 9462

Invinisible Turtle
Geri Allen/Charlie Haden/Paul Motian | In The Year Of The Dragon | JMT Edition | 919027-2

Invisible
Joe Morris Trio | Symbolic Gesture | Soul Note | 121204-2
Ornette Coleman Quintet | Something Else | Contemporary | C 7551
Lenni-Kalle Taipale Quartet | Nothing To Hide | Naxos Jazz | 86035-2

Invisible Changes
Richard Beirach | Hubris | ECM | 1104

Invisible Hands
Jean-Paul Bourelly Group | Boom Bop | PAO Records | PAO 10640

Invisible Lady
Charles Mingus Quintet With Roland Kirk | Charles Mingus-Passion Of A Man:The Complete Atlantic Recordings 1956-1961 | Atlantic | 8122-72871-2
Tonight At Noon | Atlantic | 7567-80793-2
Mingus Big Band 93 | Nostalgia In Times Square | Dreyfus Jazz Line | FDM 36559-2
Alex Riel Sextet | Unriel | Stunt Records | STUCD 19707

Invisible Man
Conrad Herwig Quintet | The Amulet | Ken Music | 660.56.016

Invisible Sideman
Kenny Wheeler Quartet | Welcome | Soul Note | 121171-2

Invitation
Anthony Wonsey Trio | Open The Gates | Criss Cross | Criss 1162
Art Van Damme & The Singers Unlimited | Invitation | MPS | 68107
Bill Evans-Eddie Gomez Duo | The Complete Fantasy Recordings | Fantasy | 9FCD 1012-2
Bill Mays/Ray Drummond | One To One 2 | dmp Digital Music Productions | CD 482
Brad Goode Quintet | Toy Trumpet | Steeplechase | SCCD 31491
Carmen Lundy With Band | Moment To Moment | Arabesque Recordings | AJ 0102
Dick Hyman-Derek Smith Duo | Dick(Hyman) And Derek(Smith) At The Movies | Arbors Records | ARCD 19197
Jack Wilkins Sextet | You Can't Live Without It | Chiaroscuro | CR 185
Jaco Pastorius Trio | Live In New York City Volume One | Big World | BW 1001
Jaco Pastorius In New York | Jazz Door | JD 1232/33
Jaco Pastorius' Word Of Mouth Big Band | Invitation | Warner | 92-3876-1
Jam Session | Jam Session Vol.4 | Steeplechase | SCCD 31527
James Williams-Dennis Irwin | Focus | Red Records | VPA 132
Jimmy Gourley-Richard Galliano 4 | Flyin' The Coop | 52e Rue Est | RECD 020
Joe Henderson Quartet | Joe Henderson:The Milestone Years | Milestone | 8MCD 4413-2
Joe Henderson Quintet | In Pursuit Of Blackness | Milestone | M 9034
Joe Lovano With The Junko Onishi Trio | Tenor Time | somethin'else | 300230(TOCJ 5584)
John Campbell | Maybeck Recital Hall Series Volume Twenty-Nine | Concord | CCD 4581
John Coltrane Quintet | John Coltrane-The Prestige Recordings | Prestige | 16 PCD 4405-2
Johnny Thompson & The Pennsylvania District Choir | Live At Lausanne | Bellaphon | BCH 33007
Julia Hülsmann Trio | Julia Hülsmann-Marc Muellbauer-Rainer Winch Trio | BIT | 11218
Kenny Barron Quartet | Invitation | Criss Cross | Criss 1044
Louis Stewart-Heiner Franz | I Wished On The Moon | Jardis Records | JRCD 20027
Lucky Thompson Quartet | Lucky Strikes | Original Jazz Classics | OJCCD 194-2
Ray Drummond Sextet | Excursion | Arabesque Recordings | AJ 0106
Stan Getz Quartet | The Master | CBS | 467138-2

Invitation To The Blues
Nova Bossa Nove | Jazz Influence | Arkadia Jazz | 71241

Invocation
Markus Stockhausen Quartet | Karta | ECM | 1704(543035-2)
Sotto In Su | Vanitas | Poise | Poise 04
Positive Knowledge | Invocation No.9 | Music & Arts | CD 909

Invocations:
Michael Marcus And The Jaki Byard Trio | Involution | Justin Time | JUST 116-2

Involved
Positive Knowledge | Another Day's Journey | Music & Arts | CD 842

Ionic Velocity
Thomas Chapin Trio Plus Brass | Insomnia | Knitting Factory Works | KFWCD 132

Ipanema Sol
Ronnie Foster | The Racer | Electric Bird | K 28P 6441

IPCA
Ed Schuller Quartet feat. Dewey Redman | Mu-Point | Tutu Records | 888154-2*

I-Pimp
T.A.O. | Amaremandorle | yvp music | CD 3041

Iqbal
Max Bennett Septet | Max Bennett | Fresh Sound Records | FSR 2002(Bethlehem BCP 48)

Irate Blues
Luis Bonilla Latin Jazz All Stars | Pasos Gigantes | Candid | CCD 79507

Irene Goodnight
Thomas Heberer | Mouth | Poise | Poise 09

Irene(2002)
Peg Leg Sam | Medicine Show Man | Trix Records | TRIX 3302

Iris
Horn Knox | The Song Is You | JHM Records | JHM 3625
JoAnne Brackeen Trio | Invitation | Black Lion | BLCD 760218
Kirk Lightsey-Harold Danko | Shorter By Two-The Music Of Wayne Shorter Played On Two Pianos | Sunnyside | SSC 1004 D
Perico Sambeat Quartet | Friendship | ACT | 9421-2
Ralph Peterson's Fo'tet | Ornettology | Blue Note | 798290-2

Iris In The Rain
Manfred Christl Farnbach-Oliver Spieß Group | Bilder | clearaudio | 180492 CD

Irish
Peter O'Mara Sextet | Stairway | Enja | 7077-2

Irish Black Bottom
Art Connection | Stolen Moments | Acoustic Music Records | 319.1035.2

Iron Fist And Velvet Gloves
John McNeil-Mike Hyman Duo | Faun | Steeplechase | SCCD 31117

Iron Man
Jerome Harris Septet | Hidden In Plain View | New World Records | 80472-2
Woody Shaw Quintet | The Iron Man | Muse | MR 5160

Iron Painting
Daniel Schnyder Septet | The City | Enja | ENJ-6002 2

Ironical Evening
Misha Alperin Quintet | North Story | ECM | 1596
Unternehmen Kobra | Central Europe Suite | G.N.U. Records | CD A 94.007

Irr
Irene Schweizer | Piano Solo Vol.1 | Intakt Records | CD 020

Irreplacable
Gunter Hampel And His Galaxie Dream Band | Out From Under | Birth | 0016

Is
Dewey Redman-Cecil Taylor-Elvin Jones | Momentum Space | Verve | 559944-2
Bazillus | The Regulator | ACT | 9206-2

Is Everybody Sees I'm Oldfashioned
Gary Thomas Quartet | Pariah's Pariah | Winter&Winter | 910033-2

Is Everything Relative?

TITELVERZEICHNIS

George Wettling Jazz Band | George Wettling Jazz Band | JSP Records | 1103

Is It A Crime
Mitch Watkins Quartet | Curves | Enja | ENJ-6054 2

Is It In
Eddie Harris Quartet | Is It In | Atlantic | 780240-1

Is It True What They Say About Dixie
Clyde McCoy And His Orchestra | The Uncollected:Clyde McCoy | Hindsight | HSR 180
Eddy Howard And His Orchestra | The Uncollected:Eddy Howard, Vol.2 | Hindsight | HSR 156
Kenny Dorham Quartet | But Beautiful | Milestone | M 47036
Stan Getz Quartet | Stan Getz:The Golden Years Vol.1(1952-1958) | Moon Records | MCD 039-2

Is My Pop In There?
Tony Scott Trio | Music For Zen Meditation | Verve | 521444-2

Is Not All One
Andy Laverne Quartet | Frozen Music | Steeplechase | SCCD 31244

Is Nothing Near?
Renee Manning And Her Orchestra | As Is | Ken Music | 660.56.013

Is Once Enough
Jean-Luc Ponty Quintet | Aurora | Atlantic | SD 19158

Is Something I Don't Understand Yet
Sidsel Endresen-Bugge Wesseltoft | Nightsong | ACT | 9004-2

Is Somewhere Out There
Elliot Lawrence Band | Plays Tiny Kahn And Johnny Mandel Arrangements | Fantasy | 0902109(F 3219)

Is That My Bizness?
Sammy Kaye And His Orchestra | The Uncollected:Sammy Kaye | Hindsight | HSR 158

Is That You,Santa Claus?
Bill Frisell Band | Is That You? | Nonesuch | 7559-60956-2

Is That You?
Dave Brubeck With The Erich Kunzel Orchestra | Truth Is Fallen | Atlantic | 7567-80761-2

Is The Lord's Hand Shortened?
Mark Dresser Trio | The Cabinet Of Dr. Caligari(Music For The Silent Film) | Knitting Factory Works | KFWCD 155

Is There A Beauty In The Beast
Mike Clark Quartet | Give The Drummer Some | Stash Records | ST-CD 22(881997)

Is There Any Word From The Lord?-
Stan Getz With The Eddie Sauter Orchestra | Stan Getz Plays The Music Of Mickey One | Verve | 531232-2
Stan Getz Plays The Music Of Mickey One | Verve | 531232-2

Is There Any Word? So This Is The Word
Stan Getz Plays The Music Of Mickey One | Verve | 531232-2
Ray Charles And His Orchestra | Love & Peace | London | 6.23662 AO

Is This The Same Place I'm In?
Matthias Daneck's N.O.W. | Seven Portraits Of Obviously Unpredictable Mood Swings And Subsequent Behaviour | Satin Doll Productions | SDP 1012-1 CD

Is This True(dedicated to Jimi Hendrix)
Thomas Schmidt Trio | For Good Reasons | Jazz 4 Ever Records:Jazz Network | J4E 4742

Is You Is Or Is You Ain't My Baby
Dutch Swing College Band With Johnny Meyer | Johnny Goes Dixie | DSC Production | PA 1014 (801069)
Erroll Garner Quartet | The Fascinating Erroll Garner | Fontana | 6430135
Joe Williams And Marlena Shaw With The Norman Simmons Quintet | In Good Company | Verve | 837932-2
Leonardo Pedersen's Jazzkapel | Harry Sweets Edison-Eddie Lockjaw Davis-Richard Boone | Storyville | SLP 271
Louis Jordan And His Tympany Five | Louis Jordan Greatest Hits-Vol.2 | MCA | 1337
Nat King Cole Trio | The Early Forties | Fresh Sound Records | FSR-CD 0139
Raymond Scott And His Orchestra | The Uncollected:Raymond Scott Vol.2 | Hindsight | HSR 211
The Widespread Depression Orchestra | Time To Jump And Shout | Stash Records | ST 212 IMS
Woody Herman And His Orchestra | The Radio Years: Woody Herman And His First Herd 1944 | Hindsight | HSR 134

Isabelle
Dave Ellis Quintet | State Of Mind | Milestone | MCD 9328-2

IsabelleBlue
Claus Boesser-Ferrari | Blue Footprint | Acoustic Music Records | 319.1066.2

I'se A Muggin'
Paul Whiteman's Three T's | The Indispensable Jack Teagerden(1928-1957) | RCA | ND 89613

Isfahan
Donny McCaslin Quartet | Exile And Discovery | Naxos Jazz | 86014-2
Duke Ellington And His Orchestra | Highlights From The Duke Ellington Centennial Edition | RCA | 2663672-2
All Star Road Band Vol.2 | Doctor Jazz | ZL 70969(2) (809319)
Gabriele Mirabassi Trio | Latakia Blend | Enja | ENJ-9441 2
Gary Burton Quartet | Easy As Pie | ECM | 1184
Jimmy Rowles Trio | Jimmy Rowles/Subtle Legend Vol.1 | Storyville | STCD 8287
Joe Henderson/Christian McBride | Lush Life-The Music Of Billy Strayhorn | Verve | 511779-2
Joe Van Enkhuizen Quartet | Ellington My Way | Timeless | CD SJP 419
Lew Tabackin Quartet | I'll Be Seeing You | Concord | CCD 4528
Marian McPartland Quartet | Plays The Music Of Billy Strayhorn | Concord | CCD 4326
Scott Hamilton Quartet | Organic Duke | Concord | CCD 4623
Warren Vaché Quintet With Special Guest Allan Vaché | Jazz Im Amerikahaus,Vol.2 | Nagel-Heyer | CD 012
Joe Pass | University Of Akron Concert | Pablo | 2308249-2

Isfahan(alt.take)
Chick Corea Electric Band II | Paint The World | GRP | GRP 97412

Ishmael
Abdullah Ibrahim Trio With The Munich Radio Symphony Orchestra | African Symphony | Enja | ENJ-9410 2
Abdullah Ibrahim(Dollar Brand) | Autobiography | Plainisphare | PL 1267-68 CD
Dollar Brand Quintet | Montreux '80 | Enja | 3079-2
Art Farmer With The Enrico Pieranunzi Quintet | Isis | Soul Note | SN 1021

Isis And Osiris
Landes Jugend Jazz Orchester Hessen | Touch Of Lips | hr music.de | hrmj 004-01 CD

Isi's Choice
Jan Garbarek-Kjell Johnsen Duo | Aftenland | ECM | 1169(839304-2)

Iskirken
Ralph Towner-John Abercrombie | Five Years Later | ECM | 1207

Island Anthem
Steps Ahead | Steps Ahead:Copenhagen Live | Storyville | 4960363
Elvin Jones Jazz Machine | In Europe | Enja | ENJ-7009 2

Island Birdie
McCoy Tyner Trio | Live At The Musicians Exchange Cafe Ft.Lauderdale,USA | Kingdom Jazz | Gate 7021(805830)

Island Blues-
Richie Cole Septet | Alto Madness | Muse | MCD 5155

Island Fantasy
Ahmad Jamal Trio | In Search Of Momentum (1-10) | Dreyfus Jazz Line | FDM 36644-2

Island Fever
Eric Reed Orchestra | Happiness | Nagel-Heyer | CD 2010

Island Grind-
Albert Ayler Group | Music Is The Healing Force Of The Universe | Impulse(MCA) | AS 9191

Island Holiday
Spyro Gyra | Access All Areas | MCA | 2292-51215-1

Island Lady
Dave Weckl Group | Master Plan | GRP | GRP 96192

Island Magic
Howard McGhee Sextet | Jazzbrothers | Storyville | SLP 4077

Island Virgin
Duke Ellington And His Orchestra | Concert In The Virgin Islands | Discovery | DS 841 (807431)

Islands
Thomas Kessler Group | Untitled | Laika Records | LK 92-027
Phil Nimmons 'N' Nine Plus Six | The Atlantic Suite | Sackville | 2008

Islands Everywhere
Spyro Gyra | City Kids | MCA | 2292-50456-1

Islands Smiling
Al Bowlly With Monia Liter | On The Sentimental Side | Decca | DDV 5009/10

Isle Of Capri
Chris Barber Original Jazzband Of 1954 | Chris Barber:40 Years Jubilee Concert | Storyville | 4990013
Chris Barber's Jazz And Blues Band | 30 Years Chris Barber:Can't We Get Together | Timeless | CD TTD 517/8
Duke Ellington And His Orchestra | Happy Birthday Duke Vol.5 | Laserlight | 15787
Ken Colyer's Jazzmen | The Best Of Dixieland-1953/54 | London | 820879-2

Islero
Ahmed Abdul-Malik Orchestra | East Meets West | RCA | 2125723-2

Isma'a(Listen)
Beaver Harris Quartet | Beaver Is My Name | Timeless | SJP 196

Ismenor
Chris McGregor's Brotherhood Of Breath | Liv At Willisau | Ogun | OGCD 001

Isn't It A Lovely Day
Billie Holiday And Her Orchestra | Billie Holiday Story Vol.5:Music for Torching | Verve | MV 2595 IMS
Ella Fitzgerald And Louis Armstrong With The Oscar Peterson Quartet | Ella And Louis | Verve | 543304-2
The Complete Ella Fitzgerald And Louis Armstrong On Verve | Verve | 537284-2
Ella & Louis | Verve | 825373-2
Harry Allen Quintet | A Night At Birdland | Nagel-Heyer | CD 010
Mel Tormé | Mel Torme | Glendale | GLS 6007 IMS

Isn't It A Lovely Day-
Ruby Braff Trio | Calling Berlin Vol.1 | Arbors Records | ARCD 19139

Isn't It A Pity
Carme Canela With The Joan Monné Trio | Introducing Carme Canela | Fresh Sound Records | FSNT 014 CD
Ella Fitzgerald With The Nelson Riddle Orchestra | Ella Sings Gershwin-Vol. 2 | Metro | 2682023 IMS
LaVerne Butler With Band | No Looking Back | Chesky | JD 91
Shirley Horn With Strings | Here's To Life | Verve | 511879-2
Stacey Kent With The Jim Tomlison Quintet | Dreamsville | Candid | CCD 79775
Teddi King With Dave McKenna | Teddi King Sings Ira Gershwin | Inner City | IC 1044 IMS
Zoot Sims Quintet | Zoot Sims And The Gershwin Brothers | Original Jazz Classics | OJC20 444-2(2310744)
Members Only...Too! | The Way You Make Me Feel | Muse | MCD 5348

Isn't It Romantic
Art Tatum | The Art Tatum Solo Masterpieces | Pablo | 2625703
Art Tatum Trio | Art Tatum-The Complete Pablo Group Masterpieces | Pablo | 6 PACD 4401-2
The Tatum Group Masterpieces | Pablo | 2310735-2
Bill Mays/Ray Drummond | One To One 2 | dmp Digital Music Productions | CD 482
Danny Moss-Roy Williams Quintet | Steamers! | Nagel-Heyer | CD 049
Ella Fitzgerald With The Buddy Bregman Orchestra | The Rodgers And Hart Songbook | Verve | 821693-1
My Funny Valentine-The Rogers & Hart Songbook | Verve | 526448-2
Great Jazz Trio | The Club New Yorker | Denon Compact Disc | DC-8567
Jeri Southern With The Johnny Smith Quartet | Jeri Southern Meets Johnny Smith | Fresh Sound Records | FSR-CD 28(882156)
Joe Turner | The Giant Of Stride Piano In Switzerland | Jazz Connaisseur | JCCD 9106-2
Johnny Hartman And His Orchestra | Unforgettable | Impulse(MCA) | IMP 11522
Jugendjazzorchester NW | Turning Around | Jugendjazzorchester NW | JJ 005
Kenny Drew Trio | Morning | Steeplechase | SCCD 31048
Teddy Wilson | Teddy Wilson Revamps Rodgers & Hart | Chiaroscuro | CR 168
Bill Evans | The Complete Fantasy Recordings | Fantasy | 9FCD 1012-2

Isn't It Romantic-
Eloquence | Fantasy | F 9618
Joe Albany | Live In Paris | Fresh Sound Records | FSCD 1010
Norman Granz Jam Session | Charlie Parker Jam Session | Verve | 833564-2 PMS
New York Second Line | New York Second Line | Concord | CCD 43002

Isn't She Lovely
Art Pepper-George Cables Duo | Art Pepper:The Complete Galaxy Recordings | Galaxy | 16GCD 1016-2
Goin' Home | Original Jazz Classics | GXY 5143
Jacky Terrasson Trio | Smile | Blue Note | 542413-2
Joe Beck Trio | Relaxin' | dmp Digital Music Productions | CD 444
Monty Alexander Quartet | Three Originals:Love And Sunshine/Estade/Cobilimbo | MPS | 523526-2
Sonny Rollins Sextet | Easy Living | Original Jazz Classics | OJCCD 893-2
Easy Living | Milestone | M 9080
Stephane Grappelli Quartet | Vintage 1981 | Concord | CCD 4169
Terry Smith With The Tony Lee Trio | British Jazz Artists Vol. 2 | Lee Lambert | LAM 002
Winard Harper Sextet | Winard | Savant Records | SCD 2021

Isn't That The Thing To Do
Wingy Mannone And His Club Royal Orchestra | Muggsy,Tesch And The Chicagoans Vol.2 | Village(Jazz Archive) | VILCD 014-2

Isn't This A Lovely Day
Ella Fitzgerald With Paul Weston And His Orchestra | The Complete Ella Fitzgerald Song Books of Harold Arlen, Irving Berlin, Duke Ellington, George & Ira Gershwin, Jerome Kern, Johnny Mercer, Cole Porter And Rogers & Hart | Verve | 519832-2
Woody Herman And His Orchestra | Songs For Hip Lovers | Verve | 559872-2
McCoy Tyner-Bobby Hutcherson Duo | Manhattan Moods | Blue Note | 828423-2

Isomnia
Eddy Louiss Trio & Fanfare | Sentimental Feeling | Dreyfus Jazz Line | FDM 36600-2

Isotope
Craig Handy Trio | Three For All + One | Arabesque Recordings | AJ 0109
Joe Henderson Quartet | Joe Henderson-The Blue Note Years | Blue Note | 789287-2
Joe Henderson Trio | Power To The People | Milestone | M 9024
Joe Henderson-The Blue Note Years | Blue Note | 789287-2

Israel
Bill Evans Trio | The Complete Bill Evans On Verve | Verve | 527953-2
The Complete Bill Evans On Verve | Verve | 527953-2
Spring Leaves | Milestone | M 47034
Trio '65 | Verve | 2304517 IMS
Bill Evans-Montreux II | CBS | 481264-2
Franz Koglmann Quintet | Orte Der Geometrie | Hat Art | CD 6018
Gerry Mulligan Concert Jazz Band | Verve Jazz Masters 36:Gerry Mulligan | Verve | 523342-2
Gerry Mulligan Orchestra | Re-Birth Of The Cool | GRP | GRP 96792
Joe Roccisano Orchestra | The Shape I'm In | Landmark | LCD 1535-2

Masahiko Sato Trio | As If... | Denon Compact Disc | 33C38-7455
Miles Davis And His Orchestra | Birth Of The Cool | Capitol | 530117-2
Miles Davis:The Blue Note And Capitol Recordings | Blue Note | 827475-2
Nat Adderley Sextet | Much Brass | Original Jazz Classics | OJCCD 848-2(R 1143)
Peter Herbolzheimer Rhythm Combination & Brass | Bigband Bebop | Koala Records | CD P 5

Israel Adventi
Tubby Hayes Orchestra | Tubbs' Tours | Mole Jazz | MOLE 4

Ist Das Ansteckend?
Ekkehard Jost Quartet | Deep | Fish Music | FM 007 CD

Ist Ein Bauer In' Brunnen Gefall'n
Karl Scharnweber Trio | Coral Concert II/Another View | Nabel Records:Jazz Network | CD 4650

Ist Gott Für Mich
Conrad Bauer Trio | Was Ist Denn Nun? | FMP | 0780

Istambul
Lew Soloff Quartet | With A Song In My Heart | Milestone | MCD 9290-2

Istanbul
Özay With Band | Antiquared Love | Basic | 50004

Istics
Otis Spann/Robert Lockwood Jr. | Otis Spann Is The Blues | Crosscut | CCR 1003(Candid)

Isus Mirror
Jack Teagarden And His Orchestra | Masters Of Jazz Vol.10:Jack Teagarden | Storyville | STCD 4110

It
Dewey Redman-Cecil Taylor-Elvin Jones | Momentum Space | Verve | 559944-2
Joe McPhee Po Music | Oleo & A Future Retrospective | Hat Art | 3514

It Ain't Easy
Frankie Laine With Carl Fischer's Orchesrtra | The Uncollected:Frankie Lane Vol.2 | Hindsight | HSR 216 (835570)

It Ain't Necessarily So
Bernard Zacharias Et Ses Solistes | Jazz In Paris:Modern Jazz At Saint-Germain-De-Prés | EmArCy | 013042-2
Cab Calloway And His Orchestra | Planet Jazz:Cab Calloway | Planet Jazz | 2161237-2
Hi-De-Hi-Di-Ho | RCA | 2118524-2
Cal Tjader's Orchestra | Tjader Plays Mambo | Original Jazz Classics | OJC 274(F 3221)
Conrad Herwig Quintet | Osteology | Criss Cross | Criss 1176
Ella Fitzgerald And Louis Armstrong With The Russell Garcia Orchestra | Porgy And Bess | Verve | ???
Grant Green Quartet | Nigeria | Blue Note | LT 1032 (GXK 8180)
Herbie Mann Sextet | Herbie Mann At The Village Gate | Atlantic | 7567-81350-2
Jamie Cullum Group | Pointless Nostalgic | Candid | CCD 79782
Joe Henderson Group | Porgy And Bess | Verve | 539048-2
Joe Pass Quartet | Joe Pass:Guitar Virtuoso | Pablo | 4 PACD 4423-2
Ira George And Joe-Joe Pass Loves Gershwin | Original Jazz Classics | OJCCD 828-2(2312133)
Johnny Lytle Trio(Quartet) | Got That Feeling/Moon Child | Milestone | MCD 47093-2
Jon Weber | Live In Concert:Jon Weber Flying Keys | Jazz Connaisseur | JCCD 9726-2
Klaus Ignatzek | Piano Solo | Nabel Records:Jazz Network | CD 4691
Gershwin Songs | Nabel Records:Jazz Network | CD 4631
Larry Goldings Trio | Intimacy Of The Blues | Minor Music | 801017
Louis Armstrong And Ella Fitzgerald With Russell Garcia's Orchestra | The Complete Ella Fitzgerald And Louis Armstrong On Verve | Verve | 537284-2
Louis Armstrong And His Orchestra | Armed Forces Radio Service 1943/1944 | Duke Records | D 1021
Miles Davis With Gil Evans & His Orchestra | The Miles Davis Selection | CBS | 465699-2
Oscar Peterson Trio | Oscar Peterson:The Gershwin Songbooks | Verve | 529698-2
The Song Is You-The Best Of The Verve Songbooks | Verve | 531558-2
Gitanes Jazz 'Round Midnight: Oscar Peterson | Verve | 511036-2 PMS
Porgy And Bess | Verve | 519807-2
Oscar Peterson-Joe Pass Duo | Porgy And Bess | Original Jazz Classics | OJCCD 829-2(2310779)
Ran Blake-Steve Lacy | That Certain Feeling(George Gershwin Songbook) | Hat Art | CD 6077

It Ain't Necessarily So-
Gene Harris And The Philip Morris Superband | Live At Town Hall N.Y.C. | Concord | CCD 4397

It All Belongs To Me
Keith Nichols Cotton Club Gang And Janice Day With Guy Barker | I Like To Do Things For You | Stomp Off Records | CD 1242

It All Comes Round
Carl Ravazza And His Orchestra | The Uncollected: Carl Ravazza | Hindsight | HSR 117

It All Depends On You
Lester Young Quartet | Lester Swings | Verve | 833554-1
Harry Edison-Buck Clayton Orchestra | Swing Trumpet Kings:Harry Edison Swings Buck Clayton And Vice Versa/Red Allen Plays King Oliver/Swing Goes Dixie | Verve | 533263-2

It All Ends Up In Tears
Sheila Jordan-Mark Murphy Group | One For Junior | Muse | MCD 5489

It All Has To End Sometime
Ahmad Jamal Trio | Picture Perfect-70th Anniversary | Warner | 8573-85268-2

It Always Happens
Tom Harrell Quintet | Sail Away | Original Jazz Classics | OJCCD 1095-2(C- 14054-2)

It Always Is
Bill Evans | Eloquence | Fantasy | F 9618

It Amazes Me
Bill Evans Trio | The Complete Fantasy Recordings | Fantasy | 9FCD 1012-2
George Shearing | Favorite Things | Telarc Digital | CD 83398
Bill Connors Trio | Assembler | Line Records | COCD 9.00519 O

It Can't Be Wrong
Harry James And His Orchestra | The Radio Years: Harry James And His Orchestra 1943-46, Vol.3 | Hindsight | HSR 141

It Could Be
Karin Krog With John Surman | Karin Krog Jubilee-The Best Of 30 Years | Verve | 523716-2

It Could Be You
Buddy DeFranco Quartet | Mr. Clarinet | Verve | POCJ 1943 PMS

It Could Happen To Me
Count Basie And His Orchestra | En Concert Avec Europe 1 | Laserlight | 710706/07
Pat Thomas With Band | Jazz Patterns | Fresh Sound Records | Strand SLS CD 1015
Akio Sasajima Trio | Time Remembered | Muse | MCD 5417

It Could Happen To You
Anita O'Day With The Bill Holman Orchestra | Incomparable! Anita O'Day | Verve | 589516-2
Ann Phillips And The Kermit Leslie Orchestra | Born To Be Blue | M&M Records | R 25090(Roulette)
Barry Harris | Maybeck Recital Hall Series Volume Twelve | Concord | CCD 4476
Bob Dorough Quintet | Devil May Care | Affinity | AFF 176
Bud Powell | Bud Powell:The Complete Blue Note And Roost Recordings | Blue Note | 830083-2
Bud Powell Trio | From 'Birdland' New York City 1956 | Jazz Anthology | 550202
Chick Corea | Expressions | GRP | GRP 97732
Standards | Stretch Records | SCD 9028-2
Dorothy Donegan Trio | I Just Want To Sing | Audiophile | ACD-281
Erroll Garner Quartet | Gemini | RCA | NL 89975(809171)

Hampten Hawes | The Challenge | Storyville | SLP 1013
Herb Ellis Trio | Herb Mix | Concord | CJ 181
HUM | HUM(Humair-Urtreger-Michelot) | Sketch | SKE 333006
Jack Millman Sextet | Shades Of Things To Come | Fresh Sound Records | 054 2600571(Liberty LJH 6007)
Joe Reichman And His Orchestra | The Uncollected:Joe Reichman | Hindsight | HSR 166
June Christy With The Pete Rugolo Orchestra | Something Cool(The Complete Mono & Stereo Versions) | Capitol | 534069-2
Keith Jarrett Trio | Tokyo '96 | ECM | 1666(539955-2)
Kenny Burrell Trio | Handcrafted | Muse | MR 5144
Louis Stewart-Heiner Franz Quartet | Jazz Guitar Highlights 1 | Jardis Records | JRCD 20141
Mat Mathews Orchestra | The Gentle Art Of Love | Dawn | DCD 111
Miles Davis Quintet | Relaxin' | Original Jazz Classics | OJC20 190-2
Relaxin' | Prestige | PRSA 7129-6
Miles Davis Sextet | Miles Davis:Quintet & Sextet | Fresh Sound Records | FSCD 1000
Monica Zetterlund With The Bill Evans Trio | Bill Evans-Monica Zetterlund | West Wind | WW 2073
Nancy Wright With Caesar Giovannini +6 | You Make Me Feel So Young! | Fresh Sound Records | Concert-Disc CD 43 CD
Nicholas Payton Quintet | From This Moment... | Verve | 527073-2
Red Richards | Lullaby In Rhythm | Sackville | SKCD2-3044
Singers Unlimited | The Singers Unlimited:Magic Voices | MPS | 539130-2
Four Of Us | MPS | 68106
Sonny Rollins | Sonny Rollins-The Freelance Years:The Complete Riverside & Contemporary Recordings | Riverside | 5 RCD 4427-2
Sonny Rollins Quartet | The Freedom Suite Plus | Milestone | M 47007
Sonny Rollins-All The Things You Are (1963-1964) | Bluebird | ND 82179
The Mastersounds | The Mastersounds | Prestige | PRCD 24770-2
A Date With The Mastersounds | Original Jazz Classics | OJC 282(F 8062)
Thomas Brendgens-Mönkemeyer | Beauty | Jardis Records | JRCD 20138
Thomas Brendgens-Mönkemeyer & Jochen Voss | Textures | Jardis Records | JRCD 9920
Tony Perkins With Orchestra | On A Rainy Afternoon | Fresh Sound Records | ND 42123

It Could Happen To You-
The Tenor Triangle & The Melvin Rhyne Trio | Aztec Blues | Criss Cross | Criss 1143

It Could Happen To You(alt.take 1)
Monica Zetterlund With The Bill Evans Trio | The Complete Bill Evans On Verve | Verve | 527953-2

It Could Happen To You(alt.take 2)
Bud Powell | Bud Powell:The Complete Blue Note And Roost Recordings | Blue Note | 830083-2

It Could Happen To You(alt.take)
Bud Powell Trio | Bud Powell:Complete 1947-1951 Blue Note,Verve & Roost Recordings | The Jazz Factory | JFCD 22837

It Could Have Been A Lovely Night
Saheb Sarbib Quintet | It Couldn't Happen Without You | Soul Note | 121098-2

It Didn't End(Nao Se Acabou)
Herbie Nichols Trio | The Third World | Blue Note | 84552

It Didn't Happen
The Herbie Nichols Project | Dr. Cyclops' Dream | Soul Note | 121333-2

It Didn't Happen(alt.take)
Mose Allison Trio | I Don't Worry About A Thing | Rhino | 8122-71417-2

It Didn't Turn Out That Way
Spyro Gyra | Morning Dance | MCA | ???

It Doesn't Matter
Walter 'Wolfman' Washington Group | Wolf At The Door | Rounder Records | CDRR 2098

It Don't Mean A Thing If It Ain't Got That Swing
Al Casey Quartet | A' Portrait Of Jan Jankeje | Jazzpoint | JP 1054 CD
Alex Welsh And His Jazz Band | At Home With... | Dormouse | DM 16 IMS
Carmen McRae-Betty Carter With Trio | The Carmen McRae-Betty Carter Duets | Verve | 529579-2
Chris Barber's Jazz And Blues Band feat. Russell Procope & Wild Bill Davis | Echoes Of Ellington Vol.2 | Timeless | CD TTD 556
Claude Bolling And His Orchestra With Joe Williams | Jazz Gala 79 | America | AM 015/16
Deborah Brown With The Horace Parlan Trio | Jazz 4 Jazz | Reckless Records | RR 9901 CD
Dizzy Gillespie-Stan Getz Sextet | Diz And Getz | Verve | 2-2521 IMS
Welcome To Jazz: Dizzy Gillespie | Koch Records | 321 972 D1
Duffy Jackson Orchestra | Swing! Swing! Swing! | Milestone | MCD 9233-2
Duke Ellington And His Orchestra | Carnegie Hall Concert December 1944 | Prestige | 2PCD 24073-2
The Best Of Duke Ellington | Capitol | 831501-2
Duke Ellington:The Complete RCA-Victor Mid-Forties Recordings(1944-1946) | RCA | 2663394-2
It Don't Mean A Thing(If It Ain't Got That Swing) | Naxos Jazz | 8.120526 CD
Hot Summer Dance | Red Baron | 469285-2
Ella Fitzgerald And Her All Stars | The Complete Ella Fitzgerald Song Books of Harold Arlen, Irving Berlin, Duke Ellington, George & Ira Gershwin, Jerome Kern, Johnny Mercer, Cole Porter And Rogers & Hart | Verve | 519832-2
Ella Fitzgerald With The Duke Ellington Orchestra | Ella Fitzgerald-First Lady Of Song | Verve | 517898-2
Ella Fitzgerald And Duke Ellington:Cote D'Azure Concerts on Verve | Verve | 539033-2
Ella Fitzgerald With The Tommy Flanagan Quartet | Ella In London | Original Jazz Classics | OJCCD 974-2(2310711)
Elmer Snowden Quartet | Harlem Banjo | Original Jazz Classics | OJCCD 1756-2
Ernestine Anderson With The Hank Jones Trio | Hello Like Before | Concord | CCD 4031
George Shearing Trio With Stephane Grappelli | The Reunion | MPS | 821868-1
Gérard Badini Quartet | Jazz In Paris:Gérard Badini-The Swing Machine | EmArCy | 018417-2
Gerry Mulligan Sextet | California Concerts Vol.2 | Pacific Jazz | 746864-2
Helen Merrill With The Stan Getz Quartet | Just Friends | EmArCy | 842007-2 PMS
James Spaulding And His Orchestra | James Spaulding Plays The Legacy Of Duke Ellington | Storyville | SLP 4034
Kenny Burrell All Stars | Ellington Is Forever | Fantasy | F 79005
Louis Armstrong And His All Stars With Duke Ellington | The Beautiful American | Jazz Society(Vogue) | 670501
McCoy Tyner Trio | The Early Trios | MCA | IA 9338/2
Modern Jazz Quartet | For Ellington | East-West | 7567-90926-2
Muneer B.Fennell & The Rhythm String Band | An Encounter With Higher Forces | double moon | CHRDM 71019
Nat Pierce Quintet | Crosby-Bennett-Clooney-Herman:A Tribute To Duke | Concord | CCD 4050
Orchestra | Duke Ellington's Sophisticated Ladies | RCA | BL 04053 DX
Paul Gonsalves-Earld Hines Quartet | It Don't Mean A Thing If It Ain't Got That Swing | Jazz Colours | 874766-2
Ralph Sharon Sextet | Mr.& Mrs. Jazz | Fresh Sound Records | FSR 2028(Bethlehem BCP 13)
Roy Eldridge And His Friends | Americans In Sweden: Roy Eldridge 1957-Count Basie 1954 | Jazz Society | AA 514
Sarah Vaughan With Orchestra | Sarah Vaughan Birthday Celebration | Fantasy | FANCD 6090-2
Sheila Jordan/Harvie Swartz | Old Time Feeling | Muse | MCD 5366
Sonny Rollins Trio | In Sweden 1959 | Ingo | 9
Stanley Cowell Quartet | Back To The Beautiful | Concord | CCD 4398
Stephane Grappelli And His Hot Four | Djangology Vol.1 | Naxos Jazz | 8.120515 CD
The Rosenberg Trio | Gypsy Swing | Verve | 527806-2
The Steamboat Rats | ...Got That Swing | Elite Special | 73435
Thelonious Monk Trio | The Riverside Trios | Milestone | M 47052
Thelonious Monk-The Complete Riverside Recordings | Riverside | 15 RCD 022-2
Zoot Sims With Orchestra | Passion Flower | Original Jazz Classics | OJCCD 939-2(2312120)
Allotria Jazz Band | Swing That Music | Elite Special | 73232

It Don't Mean A Thing If It Ain't Got That Swing-
Enrico Pieranunzi-Bert Van Den Brink | Daedalus' Wings | Challenge | CHR 70069

It Don't Mean A Thing If It Ain't Got That Swing(alt.take)
King David And His Little Jazz | Little Jazz Special | Queen-Disc | 066

It Had Better Be Tonight
Fantasy Band | Sweet Dreams | dmp Digital Music Productions | CD 508

It Had To Be You
Billie Holiday And Her Band | Verve Jazz Masters 47:Billie Holiday Sings Standards | Verve | 527650-2
Billie Holiday And Her Orchestra | Billie Holiday Story Vol.5:Music for Torching | Verve | MV 2595 IMS
Chris Flory Quartet | For All We Know | Concord | CCD 4403
Heiner Franz & Friends | Let's Have A Ball | Jardis Records | JRCD 20030
Helmut Nieberle & Cordes Sauvages | Salut To Django | Jardis Records | JRCD 9926
Herb Ellis And Freddie Green Quintet | Rhythm Willie | Concord | CCD 6010
Jo Ann Strazzeri With The Frank Strazzeri Quartet | Presenting Jo Ann Strazzeri | Fresh Sound Records | FSR 109
Mildred Bailey With Paul Baron's Orchestra | The Radio Years: Mildred Bailey With Paul Baron's Orchestra 1944 | Hindsight | HSR 133
Sidney Bechet And His Feetwarmers | Jazz In Paris:Sidney Bechet Et Claude Luther | EmArCy | 159821-2 PMS
Singers Unlimited With The Roger Kellaway Cello Quartet | The Singers Unlimited:Magic Voices | MPS | 539130-2
Stephane Grappelli Quartet | Stephane Grappelli | LRC Records | CDC 9014
Sterling Young And His Orchestra | The Uncollected: Sterling Young | Hindsight | HSR 113
The Johnes Brothers | Keepin' Up With The Jones | Verve | 538633-2
Zoot Sims Quartet | Zoot Sims:The Complete 1944-1954 Small Group Sessions(Master Takes),Vol.2 | Blue Moon | BMCD 1039
Edmond Hall Quartet With Teddy Wilson | Commodore Classics In Swing | Commodore | 9031-72723-2

It Happened In Monterey
Firehouse Five Plus Two | Around The World | Good Time Jazz | GTCD 10044-2
Mel Tormé With The Mel-Tones | Back In Town | Verve | MV 2675 IMS
Oscar Peterson Trio | Oscar Peterson-The London House Sessions | Verve | 531766-2
Woody Mann-Bob Brozman | Get Together | Acoustic Music Records | 319.1187.2

It Happened In Monterey-
Ella Fitzgerald With The Tommy Flanagan Trio | Jazz Collection:Ella Fitzgerald | Laserlight | 24397
Glenn Miller And His Orchestra | Glenn Miller In Hollyqood:Sun Valley Serenade-Orchestra Wives | Mercury | 826635-2 PMS

It Happens Everyday
Lonnie Plaxico Group | Iridescence | Muse | MCD 5427

It Happens To Be Me
Earl Hines | Earl Hines At Home | Delmark | 900240 AO

It Has Happened To Me
Bennie Wallace Quartet | The Talk Of The Town | Enja | ENJ-7091 2
Ruby Braff Quintet | Cornet Chop Suey | Concord | CCD 4606

It Hurts Me Too
Elmore James | The Blues Vol.1 | Intercord | 158600

It Is
Paul Motian Trio | Motian In Tokyo | JMT Edition | 849154-2

It Is Curiously Hot
Michael Mantler Group | Michael Mantler: No Answer/Silence | Watt | 2/5(543374-2)
Walt Dickerson Trio | To My Son | Steeplechase | SCS 1130

It Is Time
Montreal Jubilation Gospel Choir | Jubilation VI 'Looking Back'-Special 20th Anniversary Compilation | Blues Beacon | BLU-1022 22

It Is Written
Paul Bley Trio | Reality Check | Steeplechase | SCCD 31379

It It
Third Kind Of Blue | Third Kind Of Blue | Minor Music | 006

It Just So Happens
Bill Holman And His Orchestra | Satin Nights | Black-Hawk | BKH 536

It Makes No Difference To Me
When Granny Sleeps | Welcome | dacapo | DCCD 9447

It Matters,JR.
Coleman Hawkins With The Berries | Coleman Hawkins In Europe | Timeless | CBC 1-006

It Might As Well Be Spring
Bill Evans Trio | Moonbeams | Original Jazz Classics | OJC20 434-2(RLP 9428)
Bill Harris And Friends | Bill Harris And Friends | Original Jazz Classics | OJC 083(F 3263)
Billy Eckstine With Bobby Tucker And His Orchestra | No Cover/No Minimum | M&M Records | R 52052(Roulette)
Brad Mehldau Trio | Introducing Brad Mehldau | Warner | 9362-45997-2
Charles Mingus And His Orchestra | Charlie Mingus:Duke Ellington's Sound Of Love | Memo Music | HDJ 4008
Clifford Brown-Max Roach Quartet | Verve Jazz Masters 44:Clifford Brown and Max Roach | Verve | 528109-2
Dave Hancock Trio | Out Of Nowhere | Timeless | CD SJP 303
Gene Ammons And His All Stars | John Coltrane-The Prestige Recordings | Prestige | 16 PCD 4405-2
Gene Harris Quartet | Black And Blue | Concord | CCD 4482
George Young Quartet | Spring Fever | Sweet Basil | 660.55.009
Grady Tate And His Trio | Body & Soul | Milestone | MCD 9208-2
Joe Zawinul Trio | The Beginning | Fresh Sound Records | FSR-CD 142(882885)
John Hart | Bridges | Concord | CCD 4746
Joshua Redman Quartet | Timeless Tales | Warner | 9362-47052-2
Julian Priester Sextet | Out Of This World | Milestone | MCD 47087-2
Karl Schloz Quartet | A Mooth One | Nagel-Heyer | CD 2012
Karrin Allyson And Her Quintet | I Didn't Know About You | Concord | CCD 4543
Lionel Hampton Quartet | Mostly Ballads | Limelight | 820834-2 IMS
Ralph Moore Quintet | Rejuvenate! | Criss Cross | Criss 1035
Sarah Vaughan With John Kirby And His Orchestra | Sarah Vaughan Birthday Celebration | Fantasy | FANCD 6090-2
Sarah Vaughan With The Jimmy Jones Orchestra | Sarah Vaughan In Hi-Fi | CBS | CK 65117
Singers Unlimited With Rob McConnell And The Boss Brass | The Singers Unlimited With Rob McConnell And The Boss Brass | MPS | 817486-1
Stan Getz Quartet | Stan Getz-The Complete Roost Sessions | EMI Records | 859622-2
Unearthed Masters-Vol.2: Stan Getz | JAM | 5007 IMS
Stan Kenton And His Orchestra | Sophisticated Approach | Creative World | ST 1018
The New Stan Getz Quintet Feat. Astrud Gilberto | Getz Au Go Go | CTI Records | PDCTI 1124-2
Virgil Gonsalves Sextet | Jazz In Hollywood:Virgil Gonsalves/Steve White | Original Jazz Classics | OJCCD 1889-2(Nocturne NLP-8/NLP-9)
Woody Shaw Quartet | Solid | 32 Jazz | 32153

It Might As Well Be Spring-
Louie Bellson's 7 | Live At The Concord Summer Festival | Concord | CCD 4026

It Might As Well Be Spring(alt.take)
Stan Getz Quartet | Stan Getz-The Complete Roost Sessions | The Jazz Factory | JFCD 22839

It Might As Well Be Swing
Charlie Haden Quartet With Orchestra | American Dreams | Verve | 064096-2

It Might Be You
Dave Grusin Band With The London Symphony Orchestra | Cinemagic | GRP | GRP 91037-1(808732)

It Must Be Jelly(alt.take 1)
Bill Evans Quartet | The Complete Bill Evans On Verve | Verve | 527953-2

It Must Be Jelly(alt.take 2)
Woody Herman And His Orchestra | Old Gold Rehearsals 1944 | Jazz Unlimited | JUCD 2079

It Must Be Jelly('Cause Jam Don't Shake Like That)
Big Band Bounce & Boogie-Woody Herman:Pre-Herds | Affinity | AFS 1027

It Must Be Love
Harry Dial's Blusicians | That's My Stuff | Frog | DGF 7

It Must Have Been Love-
Otis Spann | Walking The Blues | Candid | CCD 79025

It Must Have Been The Devil
Blues Roots Vol.9 | Storyville | 6.23708 AG

It Never Entered My Mind
Agneta Baumann And Her Quartet | Comes Love... | Touché Music | TMcCD 011
Benny Goodman And His Orchestra | Benny Goodman Vol.2: Clarinet A La King | CBS | 460829-2
Bud Powell Trio | The Genius Of Bud Powell-Vol.2 | Verve | 2-2526 IMS
Carl Burnett Quintet | Carl Burnett Plays Music Of Richard Rodgers | Discovery | DS 819 IMS
Chico Freeman Quartet | Spirit Sensitive | India Navigation | IN 1045 CD
Concord All Stars | Concord All Stars On Cape Cod | Concord | CCD 4530
Ella Fitzgerald With The Buddy Bregman Orchestra | The Rodgers And Hart Song Book, Vol.1 | Verve | 821579-2 PMS
Gene Harris-Scott Hamilton Quintet | At Last | Concord | CCD 4434
George Shearing | Grand Piano | Concord | CCD 4281
Hal McKusick Quintet | Now's The Time(1957-58) | GRP | GRP 16512
John Colianni | Maybeck Recital Hall Series Volume Thirty-Seven | Concord | CCD 4643
Ken Peplowski & Friends | It's A Lonesome Old Town' | Concord | CCD 4673
Miles Davis New Quintet | Workin' With The Miles Davis Qoartet | Original Jazz Classics | OJC 296(P 7166)
Miles Davis Quartet | Miles Davis:The Blue Note And Capitol Recordings | Blue Note | 827475-2
Miles Davis:The Best Of The Capitol/Blue Note Years | Blue Note | 798287-2
Miles Davis Vol.2 | Blue Note | 300082(1502)
Morgana King With The Bill Mays Quartet | Simply Eloquent | Muse | MCD 5326
Oscar Peterson-Joe Pass Duo | Oscar Pterson Et Joe Pass A La Salle Pleyel | Pablo | 2CD 2625705
Live At Salle Pleyel, Paris | Pablo | 2625705
Peggy Connelly With The Russ Garcia 'Wigville' Band | Peggy Connelly | Fresh Sound Records | FSR 2018(Bethlehem BCP 53)
Rob Schneiderman Trio | Smooth Sailing | Reservoir | RSR CD 114(882903)
Ruth Price With The Johnny Smith Quartet | Ruth Price Sings With The Johnny Smith Quartet | Fresh Sound Records | FSR 596(Roost 2217)
Singers Unlimited + The Oscar Peterson Trio | In Tune | MPS | 68085
Stan Getz And J.J. Johnson With The Oscar Peterson Quartet | Stan Getz And J.J. Johnson At The Opera House | Verve | 831272-2 PMS
Stan Getz With The Oscar Peterson Quartet | Ultimate Stan Getz selected by Joe Henderson | Verve | 557532-2
Susannah McCorkle With The Frank Wess Quintet | I'll Take Romance | Concord | CCD 4491
Barry Harris | Maybeck Recital Hall Series Volume Twelve | Concord | CCD 4476

It Only Happens Every Time
Frankie Laine With Carl Fischer And His Orchestra | The Uncollected:Frankie Laine | Hindsight | HSR 198 (835569)

It Only Happens When I Dance With You
Morgana King And Her Band | I Just Can't Stop Loving You | Muse | MCD 5408

It Should Be You
Henry Allen Jr. And His New York Orchestra | Victor Jazz History Vol.6:Harlem Jazz(1928-33) | RCA | 2128560-2

It Should Have Been Me
The Go Jazz All Stars | Live In Japan | VeraBra Records | CDVBR 2086-2

It Shouldn't Happen To A Dream
Carmen McRae With Orchestra | The Ultimate Carmen McRae | Mainstream | MD CDO 705
Johnny Hodges Orchestra | Jazz Legacy 62: Johnny Hodges-Jumpin' | Vogue | 500112

It Should've Happened A Long Time Ago
Stephan Oliva Trio | Fantasm | RCA | 2173925-2
Enrico Pieranunzi Quintet | Don't Forget The Poet | Challenge | CHR 70065

It Started All Over Again
Tommy Dorsey And His Orchestra | Tommy Dorsey And His Orchestra With Frank Sinatra | RCA | 2115518-2

It Takes A Village
Carmen McRae And Her Quintet | Velvet Soul | LRC Records | CDC 7970

It Took So Long
Buddy Johnson And His Orchestra | Buddy And Ella Johnson 1953-1964 | Bear Family Records | BCD 15479 DH

It Used To Hurt Me
Ella Johnson With Orchestra | Swing Me | Official | 6009

It Was Just A Dream
Phillip Johnston's Big Trouble | The Unknown | Avant | AVAN 037

It Was So Beautiful
Kitty White With The Benny Carter All Stars | Sweet Talk | Fresh Sound Records | FSR 557(Roulette R 52020)
Stephane Grappelli And His Hot Four | Django Reinhardt Vol. 1 | Decca | 180020 AG

It Was The Lark
Stan Kenton And His Orchestra | Two Much | Creative World | ST 1067

It Was Written In The Stars
Ella Fitzgerald With The Billy May Orchestra | The Complete Ella Fitzgerald Song Books of Harold Arlen, Irving Berlin, Duke Ellington, George & Ira Gershwin, Jerome Kern, Johnny Mercer, Cole Porter And Rogers & Hart | Verve | 519832-2
The Harold Arlen Songbook | Verve | 817526-1 IMS

It Was You
Johnny Lytle Sextet | Everything Must Change | Muse | MR 5158

Italien Concerto In F Major(BWV 971):
Jacques Loussier Trio | Play Bach No.3 | Decca | 157892-2
The Best Of Play Bach | Philips | 824664-2

Italien Concerto:
Play Bach | Decca | 6.30006 DX

Italik(part 1)
Michel Wintsch & Road Movie | Michel Wintsch & Road Movie featuring Gerry Hemingway | Between The Lines | btl 002(Efa 10172-2)

Italik(part 2)
Franco & Lorenzo Petrocca | Italy | Edition Musikat | EDM 062

Italy
Joe Diorio | Italy | MGI Records | MGR CD 1010

Itchycoo Park

Steve Swallow Trio | Damaged In Transit | Watt | XtraWatt/11(067792-2)

Item 1,D.I.T.
Damaged In Transit | Watt | XtraWatt/11(067792-2)

Item 2,D.I.T.
Damaged In Transit | Watt | XtraWatt/11(067792-2)

Item 3,D.I.T.
Damaged In Transit | Watt | XtraWatt/11(067792-2)

Item 4,D.I.T.
Damaged In Transit | Watt | XtraWatt/11(067792-2)

Item 5,D.I.T.
Damaged In Transit | Watt | XtraWatt/11(067792-2)

Item 6,D.I.T.
Damaged In Transit | Watt | XtraWatt/11(067792-2)

Item 7,D.I.T.
Damaged In Transit | Watt | XtraWatt/11(067792-2)

Item 8,D.I.T.
Damaged In Transit | Watt | XtraWatt/11(067792-2)

Item 9,D.I.T.
Johnny Dyani-Clifford Jarvis Duo | African Bass | Red Records | VPA 149

Itinéraires-
Steve Lacy + 16 | Itinerary | Hat Art | CD 6079

It's A Blue World
Barney Kessel Quartet | Yesterday | Black Lion | BLCD 760183
Ella Fitzgerald And Her Orchestra | Live From The Roseland Ballroom New York 1940 | Jazz Anthology | 550032
Glenn Miller And His Orchestra | Glenn Miller:The Complete Studio Recordings Vol.2:In The Mood | Memo Music | HDJ 4115
Red Garland Trio | It's A Blue World | Original Jazz Classics | OJCCD 1028-2(P 7838)
Sterling Young And His Orchestra | The Uncollected: Sterling Young | Hindsight | HSR 113
Zim Zemarel And His Orchestra | Live At The Hyatt Regency | Hindsight | HSR 230

It's A Blue World(78rpm master take)
Lionel Hampton Quartet | The Complete Lionel Hampton Quartets And Quintets With Oscar Peterson On Verve | Verve | 559797-2

It's A Blue World(alt.take)
The Complete Lionel Hampton Quartets And Quintets With Oscar Peterson On Verve | Verve | 559797-2

It's A Blue World(false start)
The Complete Lionel Hampton Quartets And Quintets With Oscar Peterson On Verve | Verve | 559797-2

It's A Blue World(LP master take)
André Previn Trio | Gigi | Original Jazz Classics | OJCCD 407-2(C 7548)

It's A Dance
Garth Webber-Mark Ford Band | On The Edge | Crosscut | CCD 11045

It's A Funky Thing
Jon Burr Quartet | In My Own Words | Cymekob | CYK 804-2

It's A Good Good Night
Blind Willie McTell | 1927-1935 | Yazoo | YAZ 1037

It's A Grand Night For Swingin'
Mundell Lowe Quartet | A Grand Night For Swinging | Original Jazz Classics | OJCCD 1940-(RLP 238)
Ernie Royal Sextet | Accent On Trumpet | Fresh Sound Records | FSR 645(Urania UJLP 1203)

It's A Great, Great Pleasure
Grosses Tanzorchester Vom Palace-Hotel St.Moritz | Hot Jazz & Swing Mit Teddy Stauffer's Original Teddies | Elite Special | 9522002

It's A Jungle Out There
George Shearing Trio | Windows | MPS | 68200

It's A Little Thing
Gene McDaniels And His Band | Another Tear Falls | Charly | CRB 1136

It's A Lonesome Old Town When You're Not Around
McKinney's Cotton Pickers | The Complete McKinney's Cotton Pickers Vol.5 Plus Don Redman & His Orchestra | RCA | NL 89161 (809233)

It's A Lonesome Old World
Lowell Fulsom Band | Lowell Fulson | Chess | 427007

It's A Lovely Day Today
Astrud Gilberto With The Walter Wanderley Trio | This Is Astrud Gilberto | Verve | 825064-2
Cleo Laine With The Johnny Dankworth Quintet | Cleo At Carnegie Hall-The 10th Anniversary Concert | DRG | DARC 2-2101 IMS
Ella Fitzgerald With Paul Weston And His Orchestra | The Complete Ella Fitzgerald Song Books of Harold Arlen, Irving Berlin, Duke Ellington, George & Ira Gershwin, Jerome Kern, Johnny Mercer, Cole Porter And Rogers & Hart | Verve | 519832-2

It's A Low Down Dirty Shame
Louis Jordan And His Tympany Five | Louis Jordan Vol.2-Knock Me Out | Swingtime(Contact) | ST 1012

It's A Man's World
Inga Rumpf With The NDR Big Band | It's A Man's World | Extra Records & Tapes | 800860

It's A Marshmallow World
Dinah Washington With The Fred Norman Orchestra | Back To The Blues | Roulette | 8543342

It's A Pitty To Say Goodnight
June Christy With The Pete Rugolo Orchestra | June Christy Recalls Those Kenton Days | EMI Records | 1599311

It's A Raggy Waltz
Dave Brubeck Quartet | Dave Brubeck's All-Time Greatest Hits | CBS | 68288

It's A Samba
Margie Evans Group | Mistreated Woman | L+R Records | LR 42050

It's A Sin To Tell A Lie
Willie Humphrey With The Maryland Jazz Band | Willie Humphrey Meets Maryland Jazz Band Of Cologne | DuBat Music | BMI 41991

It's A Wonderful World
Benny Carter With The Oscar Peterson Trio | Benny Carter Meets Oscar Peterson | Original Jazz Classics | 2310926
Gust! Mayer's Jazz Stampede | Yellow Cab | L+R Records | LR 40004
Oscar Peterson Trio | The London Concert | Pablo | 2CD 2620111
Peggy Lee With Jack Marshall's Music | Things Are Swingin' | Capitol | 597072-2
Peggy Lee With The Bill Holman Orchestra | Pass Me By/Big Spender | Capitol | 535210-2
Roger Kellaway/Red Mitchell | Alone Together | Dragon | DRCD 168
Stan Kenton And His Orchestra | Two Much | Creative World | ST 1067

It's A Wonderful World-
Ella Fitzgerald With The Tommy Flanagan Trio | Jazz Collection:Ella Fitzgerald | Laserlight | 24397
Gene Roland Orchestra feat. Charlie Parker | Bird's Eyes:Last Unissued Vol.15 | Philology | W 845.2

It's About That Time
Miles Davis Group | Live At The Fillmore East | CBS | C2K 65139
Live At The Fillmore East | CBS | C2K 65139
Live At The Fillmore East | CBS | C2K 65139
Teodross Avery Quartet | My Generation | Impulse(MCA) | 951181-2
Miles Davis Sextet | Black Beauty-Miles Davis At Filmore West | CBS | C2K 65138

It's About That Time-
Buddy Rich And His Orchestra | Live Sessions At The Palladium, Hollywood | Jazz Anthology | JA 5206

It's About Time
Space Jazz Trio | Space Jazz Trio Vol.1 | yvp music | CD 3007
Miles Davis Group | In A Silent Way | CBS | 86556-2

It's About Time-
The Miles Davis Selection | CBS | 471623-2

It's After The End Of The World-
Ozie Ware With The Whoopee Makers | The Complete Duke Ellington-Vol. 2 | CBS | CBS 68275

It's All In The Game
Patricia Covair With Satin Blues And The Larks Of New Orleans | New Orleans After Dark | Challenger Productions | AE 1000-2
Joe Pass | What Is There To Say | Pablo | 2310971-2

It's All In The Game-
Fleurine With Band And Horn Section | Meant To Be! | EmArCy | 159085-2

It's All In The Mind
Sarah Vaughan With Orchestra | Sarah Vaughan In Hi-Fi | CBS | CK 65117

It's All In Your Mind
Michael Mantler Orchestra | Hide And Seek | ECM | 1738(549612-2)

It's All Just Words
Cecil Gant | Cecil Gant:The Complete Recordings Vol.1 (1944) | Blue Moon | BMCD 6022

It's All Right Baby
8 1/2 Souvenirs | Happy Feet | RCA | 2663226-2

It's All Right With Me
Bireli Lagrene Quartet | Blue Eyes | Dreyfus Jazz Line | FDM 36591-2
Bob Keene Quintet | The Bob Keene Quintet | Fresh Sound Records | FSR 586(Del-Fi DFLP 1202)
Buddy Rich And His Sextet | Buddy Rich Just Sings | Verve | MV 2689 IMS
Danny Moss-Roy Williams Quintet | Steamers! | Nagel-Heyer | CD 049
Dardanelle Quintet | The Colors Of My Life | Stash Records | ST 217 IMS
Ella Fitzgerald With Orchestra | Essential Ella | Verve | 523990-2
Ella Fitzgerald With The Buddy Bregman Orchestra | The Cole Porter Song Book | Verve | 2683044 IMS
The Complete Ella Fitzgerald Song Books of Harold Arlen, Irving Berlin, Duke Ellington, George & Ira Gershwin, Jerome Kern, Johnny Mercer, Cole Porter And Rogers & Hart | Verve | 519832-2
Erroll Garner Trio | Concert By The Sea | CBS | 451042-2
George Masso Sextet | C'Est Magnifique! | Nagel-Heyer | CD 060
Grant Stewart Quartet | Buen Rollo | Fresh Sound Records | FSNT 053 CD
Greg Abate Quintet | Straight Ahead | Candid | CCD 79530
Igor Brill Quartet & The All-Star Soviet Jazz Band | Live At The Village Gate | Mobile Fidelity | MFCD 861
Ike Quebec Quartet | Jazz Hot & Blue-Blue Note Plays The Music Of Cole Porter | Blue Note | 795591-2
Johnny Griffin Quartet | Jazz Hot & Blue-Blue Note Plays The Music Of Cole Porter | Blue Note | 795591-2
Lena Horne With The Lennie Hayton Orchestra | Planet Jazz:Lena Horne | Planet Jazz | 2165373-2
Les Arbuckle Quartet | No More No Les | audioquest Music | AQCD 1019
Oscar Peterson-Joe Pass Duo | Oscar Pterson Et Joe Pass A La Salle Pleyel | Pablo | 2CD 2625705
Live At Salle Pleyel, Paris | Pablo | 2625705
Sonny Rollins Quartet | Taking Care Of Business | Prestige | P 24082
The New York Allstars | Broadway | Nagel-Heyer | CD 003
The Original Benny Goodman Quartet | The Yale University Music Library:Benny Goodman Vol.10 | Musicmasters | 65129-2
Thilo Wolf Big Band | Mr. Grooverix | MDL-Jazz | CD 1925(CD 053)
Allotria Jazz Band | Cleared For Take Off | Elite Special | 73331

It's All There
Niels-Henning Orsted-Pedersen/Kenneth Knudsen Duo | Pictures | Steeplechase | SCCD 31068

It's Allright
Wynton Kelly Quintet | It's All Right! | Verve | 537750-2

It's Alvin Again
Claire Martin With The Jim Mullen Quartet | The Waiting Game | Linn Records | AKD 018

It's Always Some Kind Of A Freak
Olivier Peters Quartet Feat.Joan Johnson | Wings Of Spring | Village Music | VM 1002

It's Always You
Chet Baker Quartet | Chet Baker Sings | Pacific Jazz | 300067(PJ 1222)
Glenn Miller And His Orchestra | The Glenn Miller Story Vol.4 | RCA | NL 89223 AG
Julian Argüelles-Steve Argüelles | Scapes | Babel | BDV 9614

It's April Again
Count Basie And His Orchestra | Basie On Roulette, Vol. 2: Basie Plays Hefti | Vogue | 500002

It's Been A Long Long Time
Jonathan Butler Group | Personality | Zounds | CD 697100
Stan Kenton And His Orchestra | The Christy Years | Creative World | ST 1035

It's Been So Long
Edmond Hall's Swingtet | Edmond Hall Profoundly Blue | Blue Note | 821260-2
Harry James And His Orchestra | The Uncollected: Harry James | Hindsight | HSR 102

It's Been Too Long
Eric Marienthal Group | Round Trip | GRP | GRP 95862

It's Better To Be By Yourself
Helen Humes And Her All Stars | Lester Young:The Complete Aladdin Sessions | Blue Note | 832787-2

It's Better To Give Than To Receive
Lester Young:The Complete 1936-1951 Small Group Sessions(Studio Recordings-Master Takes),Vol.6 Rare Items | Blue Moon | BMCD 1006

It's Better Wait For Love
Loft Line | Visitors | Acoustic Music Records | 319.1085.2

It's 'Bout To Break My Heart In Two
Max Roach Quartet | It's Christmas Again | Soul Note | 121153-2

It's Crazy
Lightnin' Hopkins | The Swartmore Concert | Original Blues Classics | OBCCD 563-2
Sarah Vaughan With The Clifford Brown All Stars | Jazz Gallery:Clifford Brown | RCA | 2114176-2
Compact Jazz: Clifford Brown | EmArCy | 842933-2 PMS
Clifton Chenier And His Band | King Of The Bayous | Arhoolie | CD 339

It's De-Lovely
Ella Fitzgerald With The Buddy Bregman Orchestra | Ella Fitzgerald Sings The Cole Porter Songbook Vol.2 | Verve | 821990-2
Eugen Cicero Trio | Eugen Cicero Highlights | MPS | 88028-2
Oscar Peterson Trio | Oscar Peterson Plays The Cole Porter Song Book | Verve | 821987-2
Peter Fessler Quartet | Colours Of My Mind | Minor Music | 801063
Rosemary Clooney And Her Band | Rosemary Clooney Sings The Music Of Cole Porter | Concord | CCD 4185
Tommy Dorsey And His Orchestra | This Is Tommy Dorsey Vol. 2 | RCA | 26.28041 DP
Will Osborne And His Orchestra | The Uncollected:Will Osborne | Hindsight | HSR 197

It's D'Lovely
Mel Tormé With Band/Orchestra | Mel Torme | Musicraft | MVS 508 IMS

It's Easy To Remember
Ben Webster With Strings | The Warm Mood | Discovery | DS 818 IMS
Benny Goodman Band | Aurex Jazz Festival '80:Live Special | Eastworld | EWJ 80253
Carl Burnett Quintet | Carl Burnett Plays Music Of Richard Rodgers | Discovery | DS 819 IMS
George Hall And His Orchestra | The Uncollected:George Hall | Hindsight | HSR 144
John Coltrane Quartet | John Coltrane:The Classic Quartet-Complete Impulse Studio Recordings | Impulse(MCA) | 951280-2
Joshua Breakstone Quintet | Echoes | Contemporary | C 14025
Keith Jarrett Trio | At The Deer Head Inn | ECM | 1531(517720-2)
Louis Armstrong And His All Stars | Jazz In Paris:Louis Armstrong-The Best Live Concert Vol.2 | EmArCy | 013031-2
Pharoah Sanders Group | Journey To The One | Evidence | ECD 22016-2
Rosemary Clooney With The Scott Hamilton Quintet | Rosie Sings Bing | Concord | CJ 60
Sadao Watanabe Quintet With Strings | Plays Ballads | Denon Compact Disc | DC-8555
We Three | The Drivin' Beat | Organic Music | ORGM 9707
| A Tribute To Bing Crosby-Paramount's Greatest Singer | Concord | CCD 4614

It's Easy To Remember-
George Hall And His Orchestra | The Uncollected:George Hall | Hindsight | HSR 144

It's For You
Pat Metheny Group | Works | ECM | 823270-2

It's Funny
Bob Crosby And His Orchestra | The Summer Of '39-Bob Crosby's Camel Caravan | Giants Of Jazz | GOJ 1037

It's Glory
Johnny Hodges And Leon Thomas With The Oliver Nelson Orchestra | 3 Shades Of Blues | RCA | 2147787-2

It's Gonna Rain
Buster Benton Blues Band | Blues At The Top | Black & Blue | BLE 59.001 2

It's Got To Be Love
Sarah Vaughan And Her Trio | Sarah Vaughan At Mister Kelly's | EmArCy | 832791-2 PMS

It's Hard
Joe Stone | St. Louis Town 1927-1932 | Yazoo | YAZ 1003

It's Hard To Be Good
Eunice Davis And Her Blues Band | Eunice Davis Sings The Classic Blues Of Victoria Spivey | L+R Records | LR 42016

It's High Time
The Ford Blues Band | Hotshots | Crosscut | CCD 11041

It's Impossible
Red Garland Trio | Red Alert | Original Jazz Classics | OJCCD 647-2(GXY 5109)
Stella Levitt With The Jacques Pelzer Quartet | Stella Levitt | Adda | 590066

It's In The Air
Celestin's Original Tuxedo Jazz Orchestra | New Orleans Classics:Papa Celestin And Sam Morgan | AZURE Compact Disc | AZ-CD-12

It's Just A Flesh Wound
Ruth Brown With Orchestra | Fine And Mellow | Fantasy | FCD 9663-2

It's Just A Matter Of Time
New York Jazz Quartet | Oasis | Enja | ENJ-3083 2

It's Just Gotta Be That Way
Barbecue Bob | Chocolate To The Bone | Yazoo | YAZ 2005

It's Like Reaching For The Moon-
Blossom Dearie Quartet | Blossom Dearie Sings Comden And Green | Verve | 589102-2

It's Love
Dick Collins And His Orchestra | King Richard The Swing Hearted | Fresh Sound Records | LJM 1027(RCA)
Melvin Rhyne Quintet | Stick To The Kick | Criss Cross | Criss 1137
Stan Kenton And His Orchestra | Artistry In Voices And Brass | Creative World | ST 1038

It's Lovely Once You're In
Abbey Lincoln With The Benny Golson Quintet | It's Magic | Original Jazz Classics | OJCCD 205-2

It's Magic
Carmen McRae With The Shirley Horn Trio | The Collected Carmen McRae | RCA | 2668713-2
Sarah-Dedicated To You | Novus | PD 90546
Eric Dolphy Quintet | Magic | Prestige | P 24053
Eric Dolphy-Booker Little Quintet | Eric Dolphy:The Complete Prestige Recordings | Prestige | 9 PRCD-4418-2
Etta Jones And Her Band | Love Shout | Original Jazz Classics | OJCCD 941-2(P 7272)
All The Way:Etta Jones Sings Sammy Cahn | HighNote Records | HCD 7047
Lous Dassen With Holger Clausen | Welcome To Dr. Jazz | Dr.Jazz Records | 8600-2

It's Me Oh Lord
Hank Jones | Tiptoe Tapdance | Original Jazz Classics | OJCCD 719-2(GXY 5108)

It's My Own Fault
John Lee Hooker | Blues Roots Vol. 13: John Lee Hooker | Chess | 6.24803 AG

It's Name Is Secret Road
Tee Carson & The Basie Bandsmen | Basically Count | Palo Alto | PA 8005

It's Never Too Late For The Blues
The Three Sounds | Introducing The Three Sounds | Blue Note | 300234(1600)

It's Nice To Go Trav'ling
Dan Rose Quartet | The Water's Rising | Enja | 9116-2

It's No Sin - (It's No) Sin
Coleman Hawkins And His Orchestra | The Hawk Talks | Affinity | AFF 139

It's Not Going That Way
Al Jarreau With Band | Heaven And Earth | i.e. Music | 557852-2

It's Not Hard To Love You
Terje Rypdal Group | Skywards | ECM | 1608(533768-2)

It's Not Over Until The Fat Lady Sings!
Steckar Tubapack | Tubakoustik | IDA Record | 024 CD

It's Now Or Never
Buddy Johnson And His Orchestra | Buddy And Ella Johnson 1953-1964 | Bear Family Records | BCD 15479 DH

It's Obdacious
Oscar Brown Jr. And His Group | Live Every Minute | Minor Music | 801071

It's October
Count Basie And His Orchestra | Basie-Straight Ahead | Dot | DLP 25902

It's OK To Listen To The Gray Voice
Jan Garbarek Group | Rites | ECM | 1685/86(559006-2)
It's OK To Listen To The Gray Voice | ECM | 1294(825406-2)

It's OK To Phone Island That Is A Mirage
Oscar Peterson With Orchestra | A Royal Wedding Suite | Original Jazz Classics | OJCCD 973-2(2312129)

It's On
Ahmad Jamal Trio | Picture Perfect-70th Anniversary | Warner | 8573-85268-2

It's Only A Flower
Art Blakey And The Jazz Messengers | Paris Jazz Concert:Art Blakey & The Jazz Messengers | Laserlight | 36158

It's Only A Paper Moon
Lee Morgan More Birdland Sessions | Fresh Sound Records | FSCD 1029
Art Tatum | Art Tatum-The Standard Transcriptions | Music & Arts | CD 919
Pure Genius | Atlantis | ATS 3
Bill Allred-Roy Williams Quintet | Absolutely | Nagel-Heyer | CD 024
Bob Wilber-Dick Hyman Sextet | A Perfect Match:A Tribute To Johnny Hodges & Wild Bill Davis | Arbors Records | ARCD 19193
Buddy Rich And His Orchestra | Live Sessions At The Palladium, Hollywood | Jazz Anthology | JA 5206
Coleman Hawkins And His Orchestra | Coleman Hawkins Vol.1-Hawk Variation | Swingtime(Contact) | ST 1004
Count Basie-Zoot Sims Quartet | Basie & Zoot | Original Jazz Classics | OJCCD 822-2(2310745)
Dave Brubeck Quartet | Paper Moon | Concord | CCD 4178
Ella Fitzgerald With The Billy May Orchestra | The Silver Collection: Ella Fitzgerald-The Songbooks | Verve | 823445-2 PMS
The Complete Ella Fitzgerald Song Books of Harold Arlen, Irving Berlin, Duke Ellington, George & Ira Gershwin, Jerome Kern, Johnny Mercer, Cole Porter And Rogers & Hart | Verve | 519832-2
The Harold Arlen Songbook | Verve | 817526-1 IMS
J.J. Johnson-Al Grey Sextet | Things Are Getting Better All The Time | Pablo | 2312141
John Kirby And His Orchestra | TheComplete Una Mae Carlisle(1940-1942) And John Kirby(1941-1942) | RCA | ND 89484
Johnny Hodges-Wild Bill Davis Sextet | Planet Jazz:Johnny Hodges | Planet Jazz | 2152065-2
In A Mellotone | RCA | ND 82305(847146)
Les Brown And His Orchestra | The Uncollected: Les Brown | Hindsight | HSR 103
Lester Young And His Band | Jazz Gallery:Lester Young Vol.2(1946-59) | RCA | 2119541-2

Lester Young:The Complete 1936-1951 Small Group Sessions(Studio Recordings-Master Takes),Vol.3 | Blue Moon | BMCD 1003
Lionel Hampton Quintet | The Lional Hampton Quintet | Verve | 589100-2
Marian McPartland Trio | Marion McPartland At The Hickory House | Savoy | SJL 2248 (801856)
Miles Davis Sextet | The Jazz Giants Play Harold Arlen:Blues In The Night | Prestige | PCD 24201-2
Monty Alexander Sextet | To Nat, With Love From Monty Alexander | Master Mix | CHECD 12
Nat King Cole Quintet | After Midnight | Capitol | 520087-2
Nat King Cole Trio | Nat King Cole:For Sentimental Reasons | Dreyfus Jazz Line | FDM 36740-2
The Great Nat King Cole | Laserlight | 15733
Live At The Circle Room | Capitol | 521859-2
The Forgotten Years | Giants Of Jazz | GOJ 1013
Oscar Peterson Trio | With Respect To Nat | Verve | 557486-2
Peter Bocage With His Creole Serenaders | Peter Bocage | American Music | AMCD-93
Ray Brown Trio With Ulf Wakenius | Summertime | Telarc Digital | CD 83430
Sammy Kaye And His Orchestra | The Uncollected:Sammy Kaye, Vol.2 | Hindsight | HSR 163
Stephane Grappelli Quintet | Steff And Slam | Black & Blue | BLE 233076
Stephane Grappelli-Barney Kessel Quintet | Stephane Grappelli:I Got Rhythm | Black Lion | BLCD 7613-2
Buddy Greco Quartet | Route 66-A Personal Tribute To Nat King Cole | Celebrity | CYCD 71901

It's Over
James 'Sugar Boy' Crawford With Dave Bartholomew's Orchestra | New Orleans Classics | Pathe | 1561351(Imperial)

It's Over Because We're Through
Carmen McRae And Her Quartet | Carmen Sings Monk | RCA | 2663841-2

It's Over Now(Well You Needn't)
Judy Niemack With The Kenny Werner Quartet | ...Night And The Music | Freelance | FRL-CD 026

It's Played Slowly-
Marco Piludu International Quartet | New York Travels | Jazz 4 Ever Records:Jazz Network | J4E 4733

It's Probably Me
Secret Agent Men | Secret Agent Men | Paddle Wheel | KICJ 135

It's Right Here For You
Georgia Strutters | Jazz Archives Vol.77:Jabbo Smith-The Complete 1929-1938 Sessions | EPM Musique | 158112

It's Sand Man
Frank Capp-Nat Pierce Orchestra | Juggernaut | Concord | CCD 4040
Lambert, Hendricks And Ross | Lambert,Hendricks & Ross:Sing A Song Of Basie | CTI Records | PDCTI 1115-2

It's Sandy At The Beach
Bourbon Street | Jazzpuzzle | GIC | GD 4.1411

It's Snowing On My Piano
Tom Scott Group | Blow It Out | CBS | EK 46108

It's So Easy
Dinah Shore With Orchestra | The Best Of Dinah Shore | Capitol | 792895-2

It's Still Quite Dark,But There Are Some Signs Of Light
John Pizzarelli Trio With The Don Sebesky Orchestra | Our Love Is Here To Stay | RCA | 6367501-2

It's The Sentimental Thing To Do
Jim Snidero Quartet With Strings | Strings | Milestone | MCD 9326-2

It's The Talk Of The T
Al Haig Sextet(Quintet) | Al Haig Trio And Sextets | Original Jazz Classics | OJCCD 1929-2(SPL 1118)

It's The Talk Of The Town
Art Tatum | Art Tatum:Complete Capitol Recordings | Capitol | 821325-2
Art Tatum:Over The Rainbow | Dreyfus Jazz Line | FDM 36727-2
Art Tatum-The Complete Jazz Chronicle Solo Session | Storyville | STCD 8253
Art Tatum-The Complete Pablo Solo Masterpieces | Pablo | 7 PACD 4404-2
Art Tatum:Complete Capitol Recordings | Definitive Records | DRCD 11192
Claus Raible Trio | Introducing The Exciting Claus Raible Trio | Organic Music | ORGM 9714
Coleman Hawkins Quartet | Swiss Radio Days Jazz Series Vol.13:Coleman Hawkins | TCB Records | TCB 02132
Coleman Hawkins With Leo Mathisen And His Band | Hawk Variation | Swingtime(Contact) | ST 1004
Concord Jazz All Stars | At The Northsea Jazz Festival | Concord | CJ 182
Dexter Gordon Quartet | Dexter Gordon:Dexter's Mood 1945-1947 | Cool & Blue | C&B-CD 114
Dizzy Gillespie-Stan Getz Sextet | Verve Jazz Masters 25:Stan Getz & Dizzy Gillespie | Verve | 521852-2
Diz And Getz | Verve | 2-2521 IMS
Welcome To Jazz: Dizzy Gillespie | Koch Records | 321 972 D1
Erroll Garner Trio | The Erroll Garner Selection | CBS | 471624-2
Giacomo Gates With The Harold Danko Quartet | Blue Skies | dmp Digital Music Productions | CD 3001
Maxine Sullivan With The Art Hodes Sextet | We Just Couldn't Say Goodbye | Audiophile | ACD-128
Stephane Grappelli-Alan Clare Duo | Stardust | Black Lion | CD 877630-2
Teddy Edwards Quintet | Teddy Edwards:Steady With Teddy 1946-1948 | Cool & Blue | C&B-CD 115
Wardell Gray Quintet | Wardell Gray:Light Gray 1948-1950 | Cool & Blue | C&B-CD 116

It's The Talk Of The Town(alt.take)
Geoff Keezer Quintet | Here And Now | Blue Note | 796691-2

It's Tight Like That
Chris Barber's Jazz Band | The Chris Barber Jubilee Album, Vol. 3 | Intercord | 157010
The Best Of Dixieland-Live in 1954/55 | London | 820878-2
40 Years Jubilee At The Opera House Nürnberg | Timeless | CD TTD 590

It's Time
Ed Bickert Quartet | Bye Bye Baby | Concord | CJ 232
Max Roach Sextet With Choir | It's Time | Impulse(MCA) | 951185-2
M'Boom | Collage | Soul Note | SN 1059

It's Time For A Change
Dizzy Gillespie And His Orchestra | Closer To The Source | Atlantic | 7567-80776-2

It's Time For Love
Jack Teagarden And His Orchestra | Masters Of Jazz Vol.10:Jack Teagarden | Storyville | STCD 4110

It's Time To Sing
Jack DeJohnette Special Edition | Earth Walk | Blue Note | 796690-2

It's To You
Chicago Rhythm Kings | The Memphis Night Hawks & Chicago Rhythm Kings | Cygnet | CYG 1001

It's Too Good To Talk About Now
Billie Holiday With Teddy Wilson And His Orchestra | Billie Holiday:The Quintessential Vol.1(1933-1935) | CBS | 450987-2

It's Too Late
Dave Spencer & The Bluebirds | Live In Europe | Crosscut | CCD 11047

It's You
Lee Konitz-Frank Wunsch | The Frankfurt Concert | West Wind | WW 2106
Lee Konitz-Martial Solal Duo | Star Eyes,Hamburg 1983 | HatOLOGY | 518

It's You-
Jimmy McGriff Quintet | Georgia On My Mind | LRC Records | CDC 8513

It's You Or No One
Art Blakey And The Jazz Messengers | Art Blakey/The Jazz Messengers | CBS | CK 62265
Dexter Gordon Quartet | Nights At The Keystone | Blue Note | BT 85112
Dexter Gordon Quintet | Dexter Gordon:The Complete Blue Note Sixties Sessions | Blue Note | 834200-2
Etta Jones And Her Band | All The Way:Etta Jones Sings Sammy Cahn | HighNote Records | HCD 7047
Henning Berg Quartet | Minnola | Jazz Haus Musik | JHM 0127 CD
Holly Slater Quartet | The Mood Was There | Ronnie Scott's Jazz House | JHCD 053
J.J.Johnson Quintet | Let's Hang Out | EmArCy | 514454-2
Jeff Hamilton Quintet | Indiana | Concord | CJ 187
Kenny Drew Quintet | This Is New | Original Jazz Classics | OJCCD 483-2
Marian McPartland | Maybeck Recital Hall Series Volume Nine | Concord | CCD 4460
Max Roach Quintet | Deeds Not Words | Original Jazz Classics | OJC20 304-2(RLP 1122)
McCoy Tyner Quartet | Four Times Four | Milestone | M 55007
Stephane Grappelli Trio | Live | Justin Time | JTR 8469-2
Tal Farlow Quartet | Poppin' And Burnin' | Verve | 815236-1 IMS

It's You Or No One-
Lee Konitz Trio | Motion | Verve | 557107-2

It's Your Thing
Lou Donaldson Quintet | Hot Dog | Blue Note | 828267-2

It's Your Turn
Page One | Page One | Storyville | STCD 4171

Itsbynne Reel
Albert Ayler Group | New York Eye And Ear Control | ESP Disk | ESP 1016-2

Ittle Onk Usik
Ray Brown Trio With Clark Terry | Some Of My Best Friends Are The Trumpet Players | Telarc Digital | CD 83495

Ivan Illych
Michel Portal-Richard Galliano | Concerts | Dreyfus Jazz Line | FDM 36661-2

Ivan Ivanovitch Kossiakof
Richard Galliano-Michel Portal | Concert Inédits | Dreyfus Jazz Line | FDM 36606-2

Ivanushka Durachok
The Moscow Chambers Jazz Ensemble | Kadans | Mobile Fidelity | MFCD 916

I've Been A Fool(Thinking You Cared)
Lionel Hampton And His Orchestra | Wes Montgomery:Complete Recordings With Lionel Hampton | Definitive Records | DRCD 11242

I've Been There Before
Benny Goodman And His Orchestra | Roll 'Em, Vol.1 | CBS | 460062-2

I've Been Used
Big Bill Broonzy | Trouble In Mind | Spotlite | SPJ 900

I've Been Working On The Railroad
The Bourbon Street Stompers | I Like Dixieland | Bainbridge | BT 1019

I've Changed My Adress
Errol Dixon Trio | In The Groove | Bellaphon | BCH 33001

I've Found A New Baby
Benny Goodman And His All Star Sextet | On Stage | Decca | 6.28101 DP
Benny Goodman Quartet | The Benny Goodman Caravans-The Small Groups Vol.1 | Giants Of Jazz | GOJ 1034
Bireli Lagrene Ensemble | Routes To Django & Bireli Swing '81 | Jazzpoint | JP 1055 CD
Bobby Hackett-Jack Teagarden All Stars | Coast Concert/Jazz Ultimate | Dormouse | DMI CDX 02(882984)
Dave McKenna | Giant Strides | Concord | CCD 4099
Dizzy Gillespie-Roy Eldridge Sextet | Diz And Roy | Verve | 2-2524 IMS
JATP All Stars | The Complete Jazz At The Philharmonic On Verve 1944-1949 | Verve | 523893-2
The Complete Jazz At The Philharmonic On Verve 1944-1949 | Verve | 523893-2
Jay McShann And His Orchestra | Early Bird | Spotlite | SPJ 120
Lester Young Trio | Verve Jazz Masters 30:Lester Young | Verve | 521859-2
Lester Young Trio | Verve | 521650-2
Lionel Hampton And His Orchestra | Planet Jazz Sampler | Planet Jazz | 2152326-2
Lionel Hampton Orchestra | Lionel Hampton Story Vol.2 | Black & Blue | BLE 59.238 2
McKinney's Cotton Pickers | The Complete McKinney's Cotton Pickers Vol.1/2(1928-1929) | RCA | 2135550-2
Quintet Du Hot Club De France | Django/Django In Rome 1949-1050 | BGO Records | BGOCD 366
Swing '35 -'39 | Eclipse | ECM 2051
Roy Eldridge-Dizzy Gillespie With The Oscar Peterson Quartet | Roy And Diz | Verve | 521647-2
Sonny Rollins And The Contemporary Leaders | Jazz Gallerie:Sonny Rollins Vol.1 | RCA | 2127283-2
Stephane Grappelli And His Hot Four | Jazz In Paris:Django Reinhardt-Swing From Paris | EmArCy | 159853-2 PMS
Django Reinhardt Vol. 1 | Decca | 180020 AG
Teddy Buckner And His Dixieland Band | Crescendo-Gene Norman Presents | Dixieland Jubilee | DJ 516
The Chicago All Stars | Newport Jazz Festival | RCA | 2121829-2
The New Orleans Feetwarmers | The Legendary Sidney Bechet | RCA | ND 86590(874092)

I've Found A New Baby(alt.take)
DeParis Brothers Orchestra | Commodore Classics-De Paris Brothers/Edmond Hall: Jimmy Ryans/Uptown Soc. | Commodore | 6.24296 AG

I've Got A Crush On You
Art Tatum | The Tatum Solo Masterpieces Vol.6 | Pablo | 2310791
Carol Kidd With Band And String Quartet | Crazy For Gershwin | Linn Records | AKD 026
Ella Fitzgerald With The Don Abney Trio | Compact Jazz: Ella Fitzgerald Live | Verve | 833294-2
Ella Fitzgerald With The Nelson Riddle Orchestra | Ella Sings Gershwin-Vol. 2 | Metro | 2682023 IMS
George Van Eps-Howard Alden Quartet | Hand-Crafted Swing | Concord | CCD 4513
Ike Quebec Quartet | Easy Living | Blue Note | 869478-1
Kenny Burrell And The Jazz Heritage All-Stars | Live At The Blue Note | Concord | CCD 4731
Nat Adderley Trio | Wes Montgomery-The Complete Riverside Recordings | Riverside | 12 RCD 4408-2
Nicole Metzger With The Christoph Mudrich Trio | Nicole Metzger Sings Gershwin | Blue Concept | BCCD 97/01
Oscar Peterson Trio | Oscar Peterson:Exclusively For My Friends | MPS | 513830-2
Ruby Braff-Gene DiNovi | Ruby Braff-The Canadian Sessions | Sackville | SK2CD-5005
Stacey Kent With The Jim Tomlison Quintet | Dreamsville | Candid | CCD 79775
Thad Jones Quartet | Magnificent Thad Jones Vol.3 | Blue Note | 300147(1546)
Zoot Sims Quintet | Zoot Sims And The Gershwin Brothers | Original Jazz Classics | OJC20 444-2(2310744)
Ella Fitzgerald With Andre Previn | Nice Work If You Can Get It-Ella Fitzgerald And Andre Previn Do Gershwin | Pablo | 2312140-2

I've Got A Crush On You-
Ralph Sutton | More At Cafe Des Copains | Sackville | SKCD2-2036

I've Got A Date With A Dream
Billie Holiday And Her Orchestra | Billie Holiday:The Quintessential Vol.6(1938) | CBS | 466313-2

I've Got A Feeling I'm Falling
Buck Clayton And His Orchestra | Cat Meets Chick | Fresh Sound Records | FSR 1001(CBS CL 778)
Fats Waller | Piano Solos | RCA | ND 89741
Louis Armstrong And His All Stars | The Louis Armstrong Selection | CBS | 467278-2

I've Got A Feeling I'm Falling(alt.take)
Fats Waller | Turn On The Heat-The Fats Waller Piano Solos | Bluebird | ND 82482

I've Got A Feeling You're Fooling
Willie Lewis And His Entertainers | Le Jazz En France Vol.3 | Pathe | 1727271

I've Got A Feeling You're Fooling-
Count Basie And His Orchestra | Count On The Coast Vol.2 | Phontastic | NCD 7575

I've Got A Girl
DMP Big Band | Glenn Miller Project | dmp Digital Music Productions | CD 519

I've Got A Girl In Kalamazoo
Glenn Miller And His Orchestra | In The Mood | Intercord | 125403
The Ultimate Glenn Miller-22 Original Hits From The King Of Swing | RCA | 2113137-2
Play Selections From The Glenn Miller Story And Other Hits | RCA | NL 89073

I've Got A Great Idea
June Christy And Her Orchestra | Early June | Fresh Sound Records | FSCD 1011

I've Got A Heart Full Of Rhythm
Louis Armstrong With Luis Russell And His Orchestra | Louis Armstrong Vol.7-Satchmo's Discoveries | MCA | 1326

I've Got A Heartful Of Music
Stuff Smith And The Onyx Club Boys | Jivin' At The Onyx | Affinity | CD AFS 1005

I've Got A Pocket Full Of Dreams
Dick Jurgens And His Orchestra | The Uncollected: Dick Jurgens | Hindsight | HSR 111

I've Got A Pocket Full Of Money
Big Joe Turner With The Milt Buckner Trio | Texas Style | Black & Blue | BLE 59.547 2

I've Got A Right To Sing The Blues
Louis Armstrong And His Orchestra | Best Of The Complete RCA Victor Recordings | RCA | 2663636-2
Paula Haliday With Orchestra | Haliday Sings Holiday | Fresh Sound Records | FSR 709(835321)

I've Got A Robe, You Got A Robe(Goin' To Shout All Over God's Heaven)
Yvonne Walter With Band | Thrills | Mons Records | MR 874805

I've Got A Way With Women
Nat King Cole Trio | Great Capitol Masters | Pathe | 1566251(Capitol)

I've Got Another Rhythm
Ella Fitzgerald With The Nelson Riddle Orchestra | Ella Sings Gershwin-Vol. 1 | Metro | 2682004 IMS

I've Got Dreams To Remember
Bing Crosby With Buddy Bregman's Orchestra | Bing Sings Whilst Bregman Swings | Verve | MV 2663 IMS

I've Got Five Dollars
Ella Fitzgerald With The Buddy Bregman Orchestra | The Rodgers And Hart Song Book, Vol.1 | Verve | 821579-2 PMS

I've Got Just About Everything
Lorraine Feather And Her Quintet | Sweet Lorraine | Concord | CJ 78
Take 6 | Tonight Take 6 | Warner | 9362-47611-2

I've Got Life-
Errol Dixon Trio | In The Groove | Bellaphon | BCH 33001

I've Got My Fingers Crossed
Louis Armstrong With Luis Russell And His Orchestra | Ambassador Louis Armstrong Vol.1(1935) | Ambassador | CLA 1901

I've Got My Love To Keep Me Warm
Art Tatum And His Swingsters | Big Band Bounce & Boogie-Piano Portraits Vol.1 | Affinity | AFS 1022
Billie Holiday And Her All Stars | Stay With Me | Verve | 511523-2
Ella Fitzgerald And Louis Armstrong With The Oscar Peterson Quartet | The Best Of Ella Fitzgerald And Louis Armstrong On Verve | Verve | 537909-2
Ella And Louis Again, Vol.2 | Verve | 711122 IMS
The Complete Ella Fitzgerald And Louis Armstrong On Verve | Verve | 537284-2
Ella And Louis Again | Verve | 825374-2
Ella Fitzgerald With Orchestra | Forever Ella | Verve | 529387-2
Ella Fitzgerald With Paul Weston And His Orchestra | Ella Fitzgerald Sings The Irving Berlin Song Book | Verve | 543830-2
The Best Of The Song Books | Verve | 519804-2
The Complete Ella Fitzgerald Song Books of Harold Arlen, Irving Berlin, Duke Ellington, George & Ira Gershwin, Jerome Kern, Johnny Mercer, Cole Porter And Rogers & Hart | Verve | 519832-2
Les Brown And His Orchestra | The Uncollected: Les Brown | Hindsight | HSR 103
Reinhardt-Grappelli Duo | Django Reinhardt Vol. 3 | Decca | 180022 AG

I've Got No Strings
Ann Cole With Band | Got My Mojo Working | Krazy Kat | KK 782 IMS

I've Got Plenty Of Nothin'
Art Tatum | Art Tatum:Memories Of You | Black Lion | BLCD 7608-2

I've Got Rhythm
Steven King | Acoustic Swing | Acoustic Music Records | 319.1107.2

I've Got The World On A String
Art Tatum | Art Tatum At The Piano Vol.2 | GNP Crescendo | GNP 9026
Billy Butterfield And His Modern Dixie Stompers | Soft Strut | Fresh Sound Records | FSR-CD 318
Bob Cooper Quartet | Tenor Sax Jazz Impressions | Trend | TR 518 Direct-to-Disc
Dee Daniels With The Jack Van Poll Trio | All Of Me | September | CD 5101
Ella Fitzgerald And Her Quintet | Ella In Hollywood-Recorded Live At The Crescendo | Verve | V 6-4052 IMS
Ella Fitzgerald With Sy Oliver And His Orchestra | Ella Fitzgerald 75th Birthday Celebration:The Original Decca Recordings | GRP | GRP 26192
Ella Fitzgerald With The Billy May Orchestra | The Complete Ella Fitzgerald Song Books of Harold Arlen, Irving Berlin, Duke Ellington, George & Ira Gershwin, Jerome Kern, Johnny Mercer, Cole Porter And Rogers & Hart | Verve | 519832-2
The Harold Arlen Songbook | Verve | 817526-1 IMS
Ernestine Anderson With The Monty Alexander Trio | Sunshine | Concord | CCD 4109
Erroll Garner Trio | Erroll Garner | Verve | 846191-2 PMS
Glenn Miller Revival Orchestra | Forever-From The Forties To The... | Timeless | CD JC 11013
Helen O'Connell With The Page Cavanaugh Trio | The Uncollected:Helen O'Connell | Hindsight | HSR 228
Henry Red Allen's All Stars | World On A String | RCA | ND 82497847084)
Louis Armstrong And His Orchestra | Louis Armstrong-The Complete RCA Victor Recordings | RCA | 2668682-2
Young Louis Armstrong | RCA | 2115517-2
Louis Armstrong With The Russell Garcia Orchestra | Verve Jazz Masters 1:Louis Armstrong | Verve | 519818-2
Louis Mazetier | In Concert:What A Treat! | Jazz Connaisseur | JCCD 9522-2
Good Vibrations | Jazz Connaisseur | JCCD 9521-2
Marian McPartland Trio | Marion McPartland At The Hickory House | Savoy | SJL 2248 (801856)
Oscar Peterson Trio | Oscar Peterson Plays The Harold Arlen Song Book | Verve | 589103-2
The Oscar Peterson Trio At The Concertgebouw | Verve | 521649-2
Oscar Peterson Plays The Harold Arlen Song Book | Verve | 589103-2
Panama Francis And The Savoy Sultans | Grooving | Stash Records | ST 218 IMS
Ruth Brown And Her Band | The Songs Of My Life | Fantasy | FCD 9665-2
Sarah Vaughan With The Oscar Peterson Quartet | How Long Has This Been Going On? | Pablo | 2310821-2
Serge Chaloff Quartet | Blue Serge | Capitol | 494505-2
Spike Jones And His Other Orchestra | The Uncollected:Spike Jones | Hindsight | HSR 185(835797)
Teresa Brewer & Friends | Memories Of Louis | Red Baron | 469283-2

Woody Herman And His Orchestra | The V-Disc Years 1944-45 Vol.1 | Hep | 34

I've Got The World On A String-

Benny Carter Quintet | Cosmopolite | Verve | 521673-2

I've Got The World On A String(alt.take)-

Eva Taylor With Clarence Williams' Blue Five | The Complete 1923-1926 Clarence Williams Sessions Vol.1 | EPM Musique | FDC 5107

I've Got To Be A Rug Cutter

Duke Ellington And His Orchestra | Duke Ellington And His Orchestra 1929-1943 | Storyville | 4960333
Erroll Garner Quartet | Verve Jazz Masters 7:Erroll Garner | Verve | 518197-2
Erroll Garner Trio | Contrasts | Verve | 558077-2
Orchestra | Duke Ellington's Sophisticated Ladies | RCA | BL 04053 DX

I've Got To Move

Ann Phillips And The Kermit Leslie Orchestra | Born To Be Blue | M&M Records | R 25090(Roulette)

I've Got To Sing A Torch Song

Thursday Diva | Folow Me | dmp Digital Music Productions | CD 509

I've Got You Under My Skin

Andy LaVerne Trio | Modern Days & Night:Music Of Cole Porter | Double Time Records | DTRCD-120
Bill Evans-Jim Hall | Trio (Motian Peacock)-Duo(Hall) | Verve | 2-2509 IMS
Bob Wilber-Dick Wellstood | The Duet | Progressive | PCD 7080
Bud Powell Trio | The Legacy | Jazz Door | JD 1204
Live At Birdland | Queen-Disc | 024
Charlie Parker Quintet | The Verve Years(1952-54) | Verve | 2-2523 IMS
Bird: The Complete Charlie Parker On Verve | Verve | 837141-2
The Cole Porter Song Book | Verve | 823250-1
Chet Baker Quintet | All Blues | Arco | 3 ARC 102
Dinah Washington All Star Jam Session | Compact Jazz: Clifford Brown | EmArCy | 842933-2 PMS
Dinah Washington With The Clifford Brown All Stars | Compact Jazz: Dinah Washington | Mercury | 830700-2 PMS
Dorothy Donegan Trio | Donnybrook With Donegan | Capitol | 300217
Ella Fitzgerald With The Buddy Bregman Orchestra | Ella Fitzgerald Sings The Cole Porter Songbook Vol.2 | Verve | 821990-2
Erroll Garner | Erroll Garner | Verve | 846191-2 PMS
George Shearing & Barry Tuckwell With Orchestra | Plays The Music Of Cole Porter | Concord | CCD 42010
Horst Jankowski Quartet | Jankowskinetik | MPS | 9808189
Jane Jarvis Quartet | Jane Jarvis Jams | Arbors Records | ARCD 19152
Jenny Evans And The Rudi Martini Quartet | At Loyd's | BELL Records | BLR 90004
Joe Henderson Quartet | The Jazz Giants Play Cole Porter:Night And Day | Prestige | PCD 24203-2
Joe Henderson:The Milestone Years | Milestone | 8MCD 4413-2
Larry Schneider Quartet | Just Cole Porter | Steeplechase | SCCD 31291
Oscar Peterson Trio | At Zardis' | Pablo | 2CD 2620118
At Zardis' | Pablo | 2CD 2620118
Paul Desmond Orchestra | Late Lament | Bluebird | ND 90207
Paul Desmond With Different Groups | 100 Ans De Jazz:Paul Desmond | RCA | 2177830-2
Paul Desmond With Strings | Desmond Blue | RCA | 2663898-2
Pete Jolly Trio | Jolly Jumps In | Fresh Sound Records | 12582 CD(RCA)
Red Norvo Trio | Move! | Savoy | SV 0168(MG 12088)
Sonny Rollins Trio | A Night At The Village Vanguard Vol.2 | Blue Note | 300203(BNJ 61014)
Stan Getz Quartet | Stan Getz:Imagination | Dreyfus Jazz Line | FDM 36733-2
Early Getz | Prestige | P 24088
Stan Kenton And His Orchestra | Portraits On Standards | Creative World | ST 1042
Contemporary Concepts | Creative World | ST 1003
Vince Jones With Orchestra | Come In Spinner | Intuition Records | INT 3052-2
Will Osborne And His Orchestra | The Uncollected:Will Osborne | Hindsight | HSR 197

I've Got Your Number

Jackie & Roy | We've Got It-The Music Of Cy Coleman | Discovery | DSCD 907(881988)
Thomas Chapin Quartet | I've Got Your Number | Arabesque Recordings | AJ 0110

I've Gotta Crush On You-

Lorry Raine With The Nelson Riddle Orchestra | Interlude With Lorry Raine | Fresh Sound Records | Advance CD 714

I've Gotta Right To Cry

Doris Day With Orchestra | The Uncollected:Doris Day | Hindsight | HSR 200

I've Grown Accustomed To Her Face

Billy Eckstine With Bobby Tucker And His Orchestra | No Cover/No Minimum | M&M Records | R 52052(Roulette)
Brecker-Engstfeld-Plümer-Weiss | ToGether | Nabel Records:Jazz Network | CD 4648
Buck Hill Quintet | The Buck Stops Here | Muse | MCD 5416
Coleman Hawkins Meets The Big Sax Section | Coleman Hawkins Meets The Big Sax Sextion | Savoy | SV 0248(SJL 1123)
Jesse Davis Quartet | Second Nature | Concord | CCD 4883
Paul Desmond Quartet | Easy Living | RCA | 2174796-2
Jazz:For Absolute Beginners | RCA | NL 89874 AG
Rick Hollander Quartet | Accidental Fortune | Concord | CCD 4550
Ruby Braff Trio | Bravura Eloquence | Concord | CCD 4423
Shelly Manne And His Friends | My Fair Lady | Mobile Fidelity | MFCD 809
Stan Getz-Bob Brookmeyer Quintet | Hollywood Jazz | CBS | 474373-2
Stan Kenton And His Orchestra | Adventures In Standards | Creative World | ST 1025
Wes Montgomery Quintet | Full House | Original Jazz Classics | OJC20 106-2
Wes Montgomery Trio | Movin' | Milestone | M 47040
Bobby Jaspar Quartet | Bobby Jaspar With Friends | Fresh Sound Records | FSR-CD 0166

I've Grown Accustomed To His Face

Lena Horne With The Marty Paich Orchestra | Lena Lovely & Alive | Fresh Sound Records | NL 45988(RCA LSP 2587)

I've Grown Accustomed To Your Face

Carol Kidd With The Sandy Taylor Trio | Carol Kidd | Linn Records | AKD 003

I've Heard It All Before

Benny Green | Green's Blues | Telarc Digital | CD 83539

I've Heard That Song Before

Harry James And His Orchestra | Trumpet Blues:The Best Of Harry James | Capitol | 521224-2
Jazz-Club: Big Band | Verve | 840030-2

I've Known Rivers

Gary Bartz Ntu Troop | I 've Known Rivers And Other Bodies | Prestige | P 66001

I've Lost My Love(take 1)

Bob Benton With The Charles Mingus Quintet | Charles Mingus-The Complete Debut Recordings | Debut | 12 DCD 4402-2

I've Lost My Love(take 2)

Kenny Clarke All Stars | Meet Milt Jackson | Savoy | SV 0172(MG 12061)

I've Lost Your Love

Milt Jackson Quintet | The MJQ Box | Prestige | 7711-2

I've Never Been Blue Before

Tim Warfield Sextet | A Whisper In The Midnight | Criss Cross | Criss 1122

I've Never Been In Love Before

Ahmad Jamal Trio | Ahmad Jamal:Waltz For Debby | Memo Music | HDJ 4018
Andy Martin With The Metropole Orchestra | Andy Martin & Metropole Orchestra | Mons Records | MR 874802
Barney Kessel Trio | Jellybeans | Concord | CJ 164
Cal Tjader Quartet | Cal Tjader Plays Jazz | Original Jazz Classics | OJCCD 986-2(F 3-211)
Cannonball Adderley With Richard Hayman's Orchestra | Julian Cannonball Adderley And Strings/Jump For Joy | Verve | 528699-2
Chet Baker Quartet | Chet Baker Sings | Pacific Jazz | 300067(PJ 1222)
Frank Capp Quartet | Quality Time | Concord | CCD 4677
Lou Levy Trio | My Old Flame | Fresh Sound Records | FSR-CD 0312
Mel Tormé With The Mel-Tones | Back In Town | Verve | MV 2675 IMS
Oscar Peterson Trio | The Trio-Live From Chicago | Verve | 823008-2
Stan Kenton And His Orchestra | The Stage Door Swings | Capitol | EMS 1159
Vladimir Shafranov Trio | White Nights | The Jazz Alliance | TJA 10018

I've Never Been In Love Before-

Sonny Terry/Brownie McGhee Quintet | The Rising Sun Collection:Louisiana Red/Sonny Terry&Brownie McGhee/Lightnin' Hopkins | The Rising Sun Collection | RSC 0011

I've Never Seen Anything Like You

Peppermint Harris With Band | Sittin' In With Peppermint Harris | Mainstream | MD CDO 907

I've Only Myself To Blame

Dinah Washington With Orchestra | In Tribute... | Fresh Sound Records | FSR 628(Roulette R 25244)

I've Started All Over Again

Hociel Thomas With The Louis Armstrong Quartet | Louis Armstrong And The Blues Singers 1924-1930 | Affinity | AFS 1018(6)

I've Surrendered

Jimmy Johnson Band | Heap See | Blue Phoenix | BLP 233720

I've Told Every Little Star

Bud Shank Quartet | That Old Feeling | Contemporary | C 14019
Charlie Mariano Sextet | Nat Pierce-Dick Collins Nonet/Charlie Mariano Sextet | Original Jazz Classics | OJC 118(F 3224)
Sonny Rollins And The Contemporary Leaders | Sonny Rollins-The Freelance Years:The Complete Riverside & Contemporary Recordings | Riverside | 5 RCD 4427-2
Sonny Rollins Trio | Sonnymoon For Two | Moon Records | MCD 015-2
In Sweden 1959 | Ingo | 9

I'ver Got Another Rhythm

Quartett & Brass | Culloo | Line Records | COCD 9.00919 O

Iverson's Odyssey

Kenny Werner Trio | A Delicate Ballace | RCA | 2151694-2

Ivoronics

Tiziana Ghiglioni Quartet | Spellbound | yvp music | CD 3058

Ivory Cliffs

Remy Filipovitch-Gediminas Laurinavicius | Open Your Eyes | Album | AS 331108 CD

Ivory Coast-

John Patitucci Group | Another World | GRP | GRP 97252

Ivory Dance

Hal Galper Quartet | Ivory Forest | Enja | ENJ-3053 2

Ivy

Rick Hollander Quartet | Once Upon A Time-The Music Of Hoagy Carmichael | Concord | CCD 4666

IX Love

Rahsaan Roland Kirk And His Orchestra | Left & Right | Atlantic | ATL 40235(SD 1518)

Iya Maasé Lobi Shango

The Hawks | Dave Bartholomew Presents The Hawks | Pathe | 1561371(Imperial)

J & B

Michel Legrand Sextet | Legrand 'Live' Jazz | Novus | ND 83103(847033)

J And B Blues

Guy Barker Quintet | Into The Blue | Verve | 527656-2

J.& B's Bag

Gary Campbell Quartet | Intersection | Milestone | MCD 9236-2

J.B.Blues

Modern Jazz Quartet | Compact Jazz: The Modern Jazz Quartet Plus | Verve | 833290-2

J.C.

Mark Dresser Quintet | Force Green | Soul Note | 121273-2

J.C. Blues

Mike Nock Quartet | Almanac | Improvising Artists Inc. | 123851-2

J.C.Heard Drum Solo

Beaver Harris 360 Degrees Experience | Safe | Red Records | VPA 151

J.E.V.

Uri Caine Trio | Bedrock | Winter&Winter | 910068-2

J.Edgar Hoover In A Dress

Michel Portal-Richard Galliano | Concerts | Dreyfus Jazz Line | FDM 36661-2

J.F.

Richard Galliano Group | French Touch | Dreyfus Jazz Line | FDM 36596-2
Richard Galliano Quartet | Gallianissimo! The Best Of Richard Galliano | Dreyfus Jazz Line | FDM 36616-2
Richard Galliano-Michel Portal | Concert Inédits | Dreyfus Jazz Line | FDM 36606-2

J.G.'s Dance

George Benson Quartet | It's Uptown | CBS | 502469-2

J.H. Bossa Nova

Jonah Jones Sextet | Harlem Jump And Swing | Affinity | AFF 96

J.M.'s Dream Doll

Mal Waldron Trio | Mal/4 | Original Jazz Classics | SMJ 6512

J.S.

Badiane | Flavours | Acoustic Music Records | 319.1071.2

Ja

Gust Williams Tsilis Quintet | Wood Music | Enja | ENJ-7093 2

Ja Ja Ja

Marilyn Mazur With Ars Nova And The Copenhagen Art Ensemble | Jordsange | dacapo | DCCD 9454

Ja Ja Ja(Yes Yes Yes)

Mongo Santamaria And His Band | Sabroso | Original Jazz Classics | OJCCD 281-2

Ja Ja-Ja

Stan Red Fox | Stan Red Fox | ITM Records | ITM 1436

Jab Blues

Drumming Birds | East Side | ITM Records | ITM 1415

Jabulani-

Dollar Brand Orchestra | The Journey | Chiaroscuro | CR 187

Jabulani-Easter Joy

Dollar Brand And His Orchestra | African Space Program | Enja | 2032-2

Jaca

Mike Nock | Piano Solos | Timeless | SJP 134

Jack And Betty

Count Basie And His Orchestra | The Count | Verve | MV 2644 IMS

Jack Hits The Road

Bud Freeman And His Summa Cum Laude Orchestra | Planet Jazz:Jack Teagarden | Planet Jazz | 2161236-2
Chicago/Austin High School Jazz In Hi-Fi | RCA | 2113031-2

Jack In

Peter Brötzmann | Brötzmann/Solo | FMP | 0360

Jack O'Diamonds

Paul Motian Quintet | Jack Of Clubs | Soul Note | 121124-2

Jack Rabbit

Herb Pomeroy Orchestra | Life Is A Many Splendored Gig | Fresh Sound Records | FSR-CD 84(882191)

Jack The Bear

Duke Ellington And His Famous Orchestra | Jazz:The Essential Collection Vol.2 | IN+OUT Records | 78012-2
Duke Ellington:Ko-Ko | Dreyfus Jazz Line | FDM 36717-2
Victor Jazz History Vol.12:Ellingtonia | RCA | 2135731-2
Duke Ellington And His Orchestra | Highlights From The Duke Ellington Centennial Edition | RCA | 2663672-2
Duke Elliongton:Complete Prestige Carnegie Hall 1943-1944 Concerts | Definitive Records | DRCD 11210

Jack The Bellboy

Nat King Cole Trio | Straighten Up And Fly Right | Pro-Arte | CDD 558

Jack The Fieldstalker

The New Oscar Pettiford Sextet | The New Oscar Pettiford Sextet | Original Jazz Classics | OJC 112(DLP 8)

Jack You're Dead

Louis Jordan And His Tympany Five | Look Out Sisters-Unissued Film Soundtracks 1944-1948 | Krazy Kat | KK 7415 IMS

Jack-Armstrong Blues

Louis Armstrong And His All Stars | Best Of The Complete RCA Victor Recordings | RCA | 2663636-2
Planet Jazz:Male Jazz Vocalists | Planet Jazz | 2169657-2
Planet Jazz:Jack Teagarden | Planet Jazz | 2161236-2
Louis Armstrong-The Complete RCA Victor Recordings | RCA | 2668682-2
The Complete Town Hall Concert 17.May 1947 | RCA | ND 89746
Louis Armstrong And His Orchestra | Swing Legends:Louis Armstrong | Nimbus Records | NI 2012
Louis Armstrong-Satchmo's Greatest Hits | RCA | CL 89799
V-Disc All Stars | Jazz Gallery:Jack Teagerden | RCA | 2114175-2
V-Disc All Star Jam Session | Louis Armstrong-Jack Teagarden-Woody Herman:Midnights At V-Disc | Jazz Unlimited | JUCD 2048

Jack-Armstrong Blues(alt.take)

Chris Barber's Jazz Band | The Great Re-Union Concert | Intercord | 157011

Jacket Town

Berlin Contemporary Jazz Orchestra | The Morlocks And Other Pieces | FMP | CD 61

Jackie

Jimmie Lunceford And His Orchestra | The Original Jimmy Lunceford Orchestra | Jazz Anthology | JA 5224
Wardell Gray Quintet | Live At The Haig 1952 | Fresh Sound Records | FSR-CD 0157

Jackie My Little Cat

Kenny Clarke 8 | Americans Swinging In Paris:Kenny Clarke | EMI Records | 539652-2
Kenny Clarke And His Orchestra | Kenny Clarke | Swing | SW 8411 IMS

Jackie My Little Cat(alt.take)

Buell Neidlinger's String Jazz | Locomotive | Soul Note | 121161-2

Jackie-Ing

Der Rote Bereich | Der Rote Bereich | Jazz 4 Ever Records:Jazz Network | J4E 4715
Thelonious Monk Quartet | Thelonious Monk In Copenhagen | Storyville | STCD 8283
1961 European Tour Vol.1 | Ingo | 5
Thelonious Monk Quintet | The Thelonious Monk Memorial Album | Milestone | MCD 47064-2
Tiny Grimes And His Rockin' Highlanders | Rockin' And Sockin' | Oldie Blues | OL 8009

Jackie's Dolly

Jackie McLean Sextet | Makin' The Changes | Original Jazz Classics | OJCCD 197-2(NJ 8231)

Jackleg

Jackie McLean Quintet | Jacknife | Blue Note | 540535-2

Jacknife

The Brecker Brothers | RCA Victor 80th Anniversary Vol.7:1980-1989 | RCA | 2668783-2

Jackpot

Lars Danielsson Group | Fresh Enough | L+R Records | CDLR 45051

Jack's Back

George Russell Smalltet | Victor Jazz History Vol.15:Progressive Jazz | RCA | 2135734-2

Jack's Blues

Henri Chaix Trio | Jumpin' Punkins | Sackville | SKCD2-2020
Hot Mallets | Hot Mallets...Live | Jazzcharge | JC 8302
Steve Lacy Group | Nine Futurities-Part 1 | Hat Art | CD 6031

Jack's Boogie Woogie

Toshinori Kondo/Tristan Honsinger Group | This That And The Other | ITM Records | 0021

Jack's Theme

Phil Sunkel's Jazz Band | Every Morning I Listen To..Phil Sunkel's Jazz Band | Fresh Sound Records | 252279-1(ABC-Paramount 136)

Jackson,Tennessee

29th Street Saxophone Quartet | Underground | Antilles | 848415-2(889151)

Jacky's Place

Marc's-Boogie | Boogie Woogie & Blues | Elite Special | 73434

Jaco

Brodmann-Pausch Percussion Duo | Percussion Duo | Fiala Music | JFJ 92002
Pat Metheny Group | Unity Village | Jazz Door | JD 1246

Jaco Past

Bireli Lagrene & Jaco Pastorius | Stuttgart Aria | Jazzpoint | JP 1019 LP

Jaco Reggae

Jaco Pastorius Groups | Another Side Of Jaco Pastorius | Jazzpoint | JP 1064 CD
Jaco Pastorius Trio | Jaco Pastorius Heavy'n Jazz & Stuttgart Aria | Jazzpoint | JP 1058 CD
Jaco Pastorius Heavy'n Jazz & Stuttgart Aria | Jazzpoint | JP 1058 CD
Jaco Pastorius Broadway Blues & Theresa | Jazzpoint | JP 1053 CD
Heavy'n Jazz | Jazzpoint | JP 1036 CD
Steve Slagle Quartet | Alto Blue | Steeplechase | SCCD 31416

Jacob

Kenny Wheeler Sextet | Uncovered Heart | Sunnyside | SSC 1048 D

Jacqueline's Chimes

Billy Cobham Group | Art Of Five | IN+OUT Records | 77063-2

Jacquelyne

Mark Helias Quintet | Attack The Future | Enja | ENJ-7019 2

Jacqui

Clifford Brown-Max Roach Quintet | Brownie-The Complete EmArCy Recordings Of Clifford Brown | EmArCy | 838306-2
Dino Saluzzi-Anthony Cox-David Friedman | Rios | VeraBra Records | CDVBR 2156-2

Jad

| Max And Pee Wee At The Copley Terrace 1945 | Jazzology | JCD-15

Ja-Da

Erroll Garner Trio | The Erroll Garner Selection | CBS | 471624-2
Oscar Peterson Quartet | The Very Tall Band | Telarc Digital | CD 83443
Roy Eldridge And His Central Plaza Dixielanders | The Very Best Of Dixieland Jazz | Verve | 535529-2
Roy Eldridge 'Littel Jazz'-The Best Of The Verve Years | Verve | 523338-2
Singers Unlimited With The Pat Williams Orchestra | Feeling Free | MPS | 68103
Terry Gibbs Big Band | The Exciting Terry Gibbs Big Band-Recorded Live | Verve | 2304441 IMS
The Arkansas Travelers | Red Nichols And Miff Mole 1927 | Village(Jazz Archive) | VILCD 015-2

Jade Et Melody

Human Factor | Forbidden City | Nabel Records:Jazz Network | CD 4635

Jade Green

Franklin Kiermyer & Jericho | Break Down The Walls | Konnex Records | KCD 5044

Jade Visions

Bill Evans Trio | Sunday At The Village Vanguard | Original Jazz Classics | OJC20 140-2
More From The Vanguard | Milestone | M 9125
Bill Evans:The Complete Live At The Village Vanguard 1961 | Riverside | 3RCD 1961-2

Jade Visions(alt.take)

Sunday At The Village Vanguard | Original Jazz Classics | OJC20 140-2
Andrew Rathbun Group | Jade | Fresh Sound Records | FSNT 076 CD

Jade(part I-VI)

Eugen Cicero Trio | Swings Tschaikowsky & Liszt | MPS | 88039-2

Jadoo

Passport | Cross-Collateral | Atlantic | 2292-44145-2
The Atlantic All Stars | The Atlantic Family Live At Montreux | Atlantic | ATL 60136

Jafro

Monica Zetterlund With The Bill Evans Trio | The Complete Bill Evans On Verve | Verve | 527953-2

Jag Vet En Deglig Rosa(A Beautiful Rose)
The Real Group | The Real Group:Original | ACT | 9256-2
Jaguar
Howard Alden-Jimmy Bruno Quartet | Full Circle | Concord | CCD 4788(2)-2
Johnny Smith Quintet | Moonlight In Vermont | Roulette | 300016
Johnny Smith-Stan Getz Quintet | Stan Getz-The Complete Roost Sessions | The Jazz Factory | JFCD 22839
Jaguar(alt.take)
Marc Ribot Y Los Cubanos Postizos | Nuy Divertido(Very Entertaining) | Atlantic | 7567-83293-2
Jaguey
Frank Kirchner Group | Frank Kirchner | Laika Records | LK 93-036
Jah Man
Tadd Dameron Septet | Fats Navarro/Tadd Dameron:Complete Blue Note & Capitol Sessions | Definitive Records | DRCD 11191
Jahbero
The Fabulous Fats Navarro Vol.2 | Blue Note | 0677208
Jahbero(alt.master)
Fats Navarro/Tadd Dameron:Complete Blue Note & Capitol Sessions | Definitive Records | DRCD 11191
J'ai Ta Main
Joelle Leandre | Contrebasse & Voix/Double Bass & Voice | Adda | 581043
Jailbreaker's Nightmare
Amina Claudine Myers Trio | Salutes Bessie Smith | LEO | LR 103
Jailhouse Blues
Ella Fitzgerald And Her All Stars | These Are The Blues | Verve | 829536-2 PMS
Jaimi's Birthday Song
Krakatau | Matinale | ECM | 1529
Jai-Ping
Bill Bickford's Bigfoot | Semi-Precious Metal | Tutu Records | 888114-2
Jake What A Snake
Louis Jordan And His Tympany Five | Louis Jordan Vol.1-Hoodoo Man | Swingtime(Contact) | ST 1011
Jaki
Jaki Byard Quartet | The Last From Lennie's | Prestige | PRCD 11029-2
Jaki Byard's Ballad Medley:
Donald Harrison With The Guardians Of The Flame And The Mardi Gras Indians & Dr. John | Indian Blues | Candid | CCD 79514
Jakko Jakko
Drümmele Maa | Villa Rhododendron | Jazz Haus Musik | JHM 25
Jakubu's Dance
Sonny Phillips Sextet | My Black Flower | Muse | MR 5118
Jalousie
Eckart Runge-Jacques Ammon | Cello Tango | Edition Musikat | EDM 053
Laurindo Almeida/Charlie Byrd Quartet | Tango | Concord | CCD 4290
Jalousie-Cha-Cha
Willem Breuker Kollektief | Willem Breuker Kollektief Live In Berlin | FMP | SAJ 06
Jam & Ham
All Stars | Bird's Eyes Last Unissued Vol.21:Bird On TV/Bird On Bandbox | Philology | W 851.2
Jam Blues
Norman Granz Jam Session | Talkin' Bird | Verve | 559859-2
Verve Jazz Masters Vol.60:The Collection | Verve | 529866-2
Charlie Parker Jam Session | Verve | 833564-2 PMS
Renaud Garcia-Fons Group | Oriental Bass | Enja | ENJ-9334 2
Jam Buleria
Jimmy Rowles Trio | Grandpaws | Candid | CRS 1014 IMS
Jam Fo' Real
Tom Browne Groups | Mo' Jamaica Funk | Hip Bop | HIBD 8002
Benny Golson Quintet | Gone With Golson | Original Jazz Classics | OJCCD 1850-2
Jam For Brigitte
Lionel Hampton Sextet | Le Jazz En France-Vol.6 | Pathe | 1727301
Jam Session
JATP All Stars | Jam Session 1955 | Moon Records | MCD 029-2
Jam Session Blues
Johnny Otis And His Orchestra & The Jubilee All Stars | Start To Jump Because It's Jubilee | Swingtime(Contact) | ST 1009
Jam With Sam
Duke Ellington And His Orchestra | Duke Ellington In Hamilton | Radiex Music | RDX-1000
Duke Ellington Live ! | EmArCy | 842071-2
Live | Affinity | AFF 28
Soul Call | Verve | 539785-2
Duke Ellington: The Champs-Elysees Theater January 29-30th,1965 | Laserlight | 36131
Duke Ellington At The Alhambra | Pablo | PACD 5313-2
Happy Birthday Duke Vol.5 | Laserlight | 15787
Jazz Festival Vol.2 | Storyville | 4960743
Jam With Sam-
Masters Of Jazz Vol.6:Duke Ellington | Storyville | STCD 4106
Jamabiko
The Legends Of Swing | Laserlight | 24659
Jam-A-Ditty
The Uncollected: Duke Ellington, Vol.4 | Hindsight | HSR 128
Jam-A-Ditty-
Duke Ellington:Complete Prestige Carnegie Hall 1946-1947 Concerts | Definitive Records | DRCD 11211
Jamaica Farewell
Bob James And His Orchestra | The Best Of Bob James | CTI | 63034
Earl Klugh-Dr.Gibbs | Late Night Guitar | Blue Note | 498573-2
Henry Butler | Blues & More Vol.1 | Windham Hill | 34 10138-2
Jamaica Shout
Ralph Towner Quintet | City Of Eyes | ECM | 1388
Jamaica Stopover
Duke Ellington And His Orchestra | Jazz Legacy 11: Duke Ellington-Ellington Moods | Vogue | 500061
Jamaican Farewell
M'Boom | Collage | Soul Note | SN 1059
Jamala
John Abercrombie Trio | Gateway | ECM | 1061(829192-2)
Chick Corea Septet | The Complete 'Is' Sessions | Blue Note | 540532-2
Jamala(alt.take)
Jack Wilkins Quintet | Mexico | CTI Records | CTI 1004-2
Jambalaya(On The Bayou)
Franz Koglmann Tentet | A White Line | Hat Art | CD 6048
Jambangle
Gil Evans And Ten | Gil Evans And Ten | Prestige | PRSA 7120-6
Hal McKusick Ninetet | Victor Jazz History Vol.15:Progressive Jazz | RCA | 2135734-2
Jambo
Dizzy Gillespie Sextet | Dizzy's Diamonds-Best Of The Verve Years | Verve | 513875-2
Stan Kenton And His Orchestra | One Night Stand | Choice | CHCD 71051
Innovations-Live 1951 | Bandstand | BDCD 1519
Jamboree
Dave Samuels Group | Del Sol | GRP | GRP 96962
Don Byas All Star Quintet | Don Byas Complete American Small Group Recordings | Definitive Records | DRCD 11213
James
Pat Metheny Group | Works | ECM | 823270-2
Roy Haynes Quintet | Te-Vou! | Dreyfus Jazz Line | FDM 36569-2
James And Wes
Jimmy Smith-Wes Montgomery Quartet | Jimmy & Wes-The Dynamic Duo | Verve | 521445-2
Jimmy Smith-Wes Montgomery Trio | Compact Jazz: Wes Montgomery Plays The Blues | Verve | 835318-2 PMS
James' Bounce
Positive Knowledge | Invocation No.9 | Music & Arts | CD 909
Jamey
Big Band Ulm | All Of Us | yvp music | 3014
Jamie
Stephane Grappelli Quartet | Vintage 1981 | Concord | CCD 4169
Jamie My Boy
Hank Roberts Group | Black Pastels | JMT Edition | 919016-2
Jamil(For Jane)
Sahib Shihab Sextet | Jazz Sahib | Savoy | SV 0141(MG 12124)
Jamilah
Manfred Zepf Meets Andrew Cyrille | Paintings | West Wind | 003
Jammin'
Charly Antolini Trio | Knock Out 2000 | Inak | 9053
Tommy Dorsey And His Orchestra | The Indispensable Tommy Dorsey Vol.1/2 | RCA | 2126405-2
Jammin' At Duffield
Malachi Thompson's Freebop Band | Freebop Now!(20th Anniversary Of The Freebop Band) | Delmark | DE 506
Jammin E. Cricket
Plas Johnson-Red Holloway Quintet | Keep That Groove Going! | Milestone | MCD 9319-2
Jammin' For Mr. Lee
Sammy Price Sextet | Sammy Price In Europe | Jazz Anthology | JA 5192
Jammin' With Gene
James Moody And His Band | James Moody | Prestige | P 24015
Jammin' With Jimmy
Lester Young And His Band | Lester Young:The Complete Aladdin Sessions | Blue Note | 832787-2
Jammin' With Lester
Lester Young:The Complete 1936-1951 Small Group Sessions(Studio Recordings-Master Takes),Vol.3 | Blue Moon | BMCD 1003
Jamph
Monday Night At Birdland | Another Monday Night At Birdland | Fresh Sound Records | FSR-CD 32(882176)
Jams And Jellies
Charlie Mariano Quintet | Boston Days | Fresh Sound Records | FSR-CD 0207
Jan Jan
Jonas Hellborg | Elegant Punk | Day Eight Music | DEMCD 004
Jan Lukas
Ullmann-Wille-Haynes | Trad Corrosion | Nabel Records:Jazz Network | CD 4673
Leo Cuypers Quartet | Theatre Music | BVHAAST | 017
Jana's Delight
Don Pullen Trio | New Beginnings | Blue Note | 791785-2
Jandor
Jim Hall Quartet | All Across The City | Concord | CCD 4384
Jane-O
Zoot Sims Quartet | Zoot Sims:The Complete 1944-1954 Small Group Sessions(Master Takes),Vol.2 | Blue Moon | BMCD 1039
Janeology
Allen Eager Quintet | Brothers And Other Mothers, Vol. 2 | Savoy | SJL 2236 (801212)
Janet
Philip Catherine/Niels-Henning Orsted-Pedersen | Art Of The Duo | Enja | 8016-2
Louis Scherr-Tommy Cecil Duo | The Song Is You | Limetree | MLP 0026
Jangled Nerves
Fletcher Henderson And His Orchestra | Hocus Pocus | RCA | ND 90413(847143)
Janine
Sammy Price And His Bluesicians | Sammy Price:Blues & Boogie | Vogue | 2111509-2
Janine(alt.take)
Bob Smith Band | Radio Face | dmp Digital Music Productions | CD 483
January-
Avery Sharpe Sextet | Unspoken Words | Sunnyside | SSC 1029 D
January Sring
George Winston | Winter Into Spring | Windham Hill | 34 11019-2
Japan
Linda Sharrock With The Wolfgang Puschnig Trio | Linda Sharrock & The Three Man Band | Moers Music | 02078 CD
Tito Puente And His Ensemble | Mambo Of The Times | Concord | CCD 4499
Japan Smiles
Paul Bley Trio | Japan Suite | Improvising Artists Inc. | 123849-2
Japan(take 2)
Roland Kirk Quartet | Rahsaan/The Complete Mercury Recordings Of Roland Kirk | Mercury | 846630-2
Japan(take 3)
Max Roach Quartet | Pictures In A Frame | Soul Note | 121003-2
Japanese Flute & Raindrops
Jessica Williams | Arrival | Jazz Focus | JFCD 001
Japanese Folk Song
Sebastian Gramss-Lömsch Lehmann | knoM.T | Jazz Haus Musik | JHM 0107 CD
Lotte Anker-Marilyn Crispell-Marilyn Mazur | Poetic Justice | dacapo | DCCD 9460
Japanese Gong Piece
Simon Jeffes | Piano Music | Peregrina Music | PM 50262
Japanese Sandman
Art Tatum | The Art Tatum Solo Masterpieces | Pablo | 2625703
Dicky Wells And His Orchestra | Django Reinhardt And His American Friends:Paris 1935-1937 | Memo Music | HDJ 4124
Quintet Du Hot Club De France | Jazz In Paris:Django Reinhardt-Swing 39 | EmArCy | 159854-2 PMS
Django Reinhardt Vol. 4 | Decca | 180023 AG
Mickey Tucker Octet | Sweet Lotus Lips | Denon Compact Disc | DC-8552
Jar Of Hair
Maynard Ferguson Orchestra | Storm | ARG Jazz | 21374872
Jardin De Chine
Ali Ryerson Quartet | Portrait In Silver | Concord | CCD 4638
Jardins D'Enfance
Heiner Franz Trio | Gouache | Jardis Records | JRCD 8904
Jardis Blues
Joe Sachse/David Moss/George Lewis | Berlin Tango | ITM Records | ITM 1448
Jarue
Orquestra De Cambra Teatre Lliure | Porgy And Bess | Fresh Sound Records | FSNT 066 CD
Jasbo Brown Blues
Joe Henderson Group | Porgy And Bess | Verve | 539048-2
Jasbo Brown Blues-
European Jazz Ensemble & The Khan Family feat. Joachim Kühn | European Jazz Ensemble Meets The Khan Family | M.A Music | A 807-2
Jashad
Max Roach With String Quartet | Survivors | Soul Note | 121093-2
Jasmin
Bob Degen Trio With Zbigniew Namyslowski | Joy | Dr.Jazz Records | 8611-2
Jasmine
Bud Shank Quintet | Jazz In Hollywood:Bud Shank/Lou Levy | Original Jazz Classics | OJCCD 1890-2(Nocturne NLP-2/NLP-10)
Jasper
Steps&Jumps | JazzNord | KlangRäume | 30100
Jasper Country Man
Original Washboard Band | Get Easy Blues | Frog | DGF 9
Jassfriends
David Murray Octet | Ming | Black Saint | 120045-2
JATP Blues
JATP All Stars | The Complete Jazz At The Philharmonic On Verve 1944-1949 | Verve | 523893-2
Martial Solal | Jazz 'n (e)motion:Martial Solal | RCA | 2155932-2
Jaunty
Al Hirt And His Band | Cherry Pink And Apple Blossom White | Memo Music | HDJ 4085
Java
Claude Bernhard-Raymond Bo | Pot-Pouri Pour Parce Que | Hat Art | G
Java Indigo
Henry Kaiser Group | Marrying For Money | Minor Music | 1010
Jave And A Nail
Walfredo De Los Reyes-Louis Bellson Group | Ecue Ritmos Cubanos | Original Jazz Classics | 2310807
Jaw
Joseph Jarman-Don Moye Quartet | Earth Passage-Density | Black Saint | BSR 0052
Jaws
Eddie Lockjaw Davis-Sonny Stitt Quartet | Jaws & Stitt At Birdland | Roulette | CDP 797507-2
Jay
Jay McShann Quartet | Goin' To Kansas City | Stony Plain | SPCD 1286
Jay And Johnnie Conversation
Goin' To Kansas City | Stony Plain | SPCD 1286
Jay at home and at his Piano(Interview 19:51)
Al King And His Kingsmen | Thunderbold-Honkin' R&B Sax Instrumentals 1952-1956 | Krazy Kat | KK 778 IMS
Jay Hawk Talk
J.J.Johnson Quintet | J.J. Johnson's Jazz Quintets | Savoy | SV 0151(MG 12106)
Jay Jay's Blues
The Birdlanders | The Birdlanders | Fresh Sound Records | FSR-CD 0170
Jaycee
Joey Seller's Jazz Aggregation | Something For Nothing | Nine Winds Records | NWCD 0136
Jaylock
Kansas City Seven | The J.J.Johnson Memorial Album | Prestige | PRCD 11025-2
Aldo Romano Quartet | To Be Ornette To Be | Owl Records | 057 CD
Jayne
Steve Wilson Quintet | Blues For Marcus | Criss Cross | Criss 1073
Jay-Tee
Laurent Coq Quartet | Jaywalker | Enja | 9111-2
Jaywalkin'
Niels-Henning Orsted-Pedersen Quartet | Jaywalkin' | Steeplechase | SCCD 31041
Jazmin
Bobby Hutcherson-Harold Land Quintet | San Francisco | Blue Note | 828268-2
Jazz 55
Barney Bigard And His Jazzopators | The Complete Duke Ellington-Vol. 8 | CBS | CBS 88185
Jazz In The House
Fabien Degryse Group | Quadruplex | B.Sharp Records | CDS 077
Jazz Is
Terri Lyne Carrington Group | Jazz Is A Spirit | ACT | 9408-2
Jazz Is A Spirit
James Blood Ulmer Quartet | Blues Preacher | DIW | DIW 869 CD
Jazz Jump
John McLaughlin Group | The Promise | Verve | 529828-2
Jazz Jungle
Niko Schäuble Quintet | On The Other Hand | Naxos Jazz | 86011-2
Jazz Life
NColor | NColor | clearaudio | 220391 LP
Jazz Like
Barrelhouse Jazzband | Barrelhouse Jazzband & Carrie Smith | Intercord | 145017
Jazz Lips
Duke Ellington And His Orchestra | The Indispensable Duke Ellington Vol.1/2 | RCA | NL 89749 (809154)
Jazz Lullaby
Pete Daily's Rhythm Kings | Jazz Band Ball | Good Time Jazz | GTCD 12005-2
Jazz Me Blues
Beryl Bryden And The Louisiana Dandies | Beryl Bryden:Queen Of Bues And Washboard | Elite Special | 72430
Bob Crosby's Bobcats | Big Band Bounce And Boogie-Bob Crosby:Mournin' Blues/Accent On The Bobcats | Affinity | AFS 1014
Danny Polo And His Swing Stars | Swingin' Britain-The Thirties | Decca | DDV 5013/14
Dutch Swing College Band | Souvenirs From Holland, Vol. 2 | DSC Production | PA 004 (801061)
Frank Teschemacher's Chicagoans | Jazz From Windy City | Timeless | CBC 1-021
Harry Gold And His Pieces Of Eight | Best Of British Jazz From The BBC Jazz Club Vol.6 | Upbeat Jazz | URCD 127
Jack Teagarden And His Band | The Club Hangover Broadcast | Arbors Records | ARCD 19150/51
Original Dixieland Jazz Band | Victor Jazz History Vol.4:New York Jazz | RCA | 2128558-2
Rusty Dedrick Quintet | Salute To Bunny | Fresh Sound Records | FSR 534(Counterpoint CPT 552)
The Legendary Lawson-Haggart Jazz Band | Jazz At His Best | Jazzology | JCD-183
Woody Herman And His Orchestra | The Formative Years Of 'The Band That PLays The Blues' | Circle | CCD-95
Jazz Oder Später
Warne Marsh Quintet | Jazz Of Two Cities | Fresh Sound Records | FSR-CD 342
Jazz Of Two Cities
Intuition | Capitol | 852771-2
Jazz Of Two Cities(alt.take)
Intuition | Capitol | 852771-2
Jazz Ostinato
John Graas Nonet | Jazzmantics | Fresh Sound Records | 252283-1(Decca DL 8677)
Jazz Roost
Charlie Ventura Quintet | The New Charlie Ventura In Hi-Fi | Harlequin | HQ 2009(Baton BL 1202) IMS
Jazz Samba
Bill Evans-Jim Hall | Intermodulation | Verve | 833771-2 PMS
Ella Fitzgerald With The Jimmy Jones Trio | Ella & Duke At The Cote D'Azur | Verve | 539030-2
Ella Fitzgerald-First Lady Of Song | Verve | 517898-2
Antonio Carlos Jobim With The Claus Ogerman Orchestra | Quiet Nights | CTI Records | PDCTI 1106-2
Jazz Stars News
Jerome Richardson Group | Jazz Station Runaway | TCB Records | TCB 97402
Jazz Time Riff
Uli Binetsch's Own Bone | Boone Up Blues | Rockwerk Records | CD 011001
Jazz Tools
Alguimia | Alguimia 'U' | Fresh Sound Records | FSNT 023 CD
Jazz Total 1
Peter Eigenmann Trio | Something Special | TCB Records | TCB 20102
Jazz+ Afrika - (Jazz+) Afrika
Paul Desmond Quartet | Desmond | Original Jazz Classics | OJCCD 712-2(F 3235/8082)
Jazzabelle
Paul Desmond Quartet Featuring Don Elliott | Original Jazz Classics | OJC 119(F 3235)
Jazz-A-Samba
Carol Leigh & The Dumoustiers Stompers | Back Water Blues | Black & Blue | BLE 59.219 2
Jazzhousing
Delta Blues Band | Delta Blues Band | Red Records | VPA 135
Jazzin' Babies Blues
King Oliver's Jazz Band | Louis Armstrong With King Oliver Vol.2 | Village(Jazz Archive) | VILCD 012-2
Jazzland Blues
Oscar Klein Band | Oscar Klein Jazzshow | Koch Records | 321 704
Jazzman

TITELVERZEICHNIS

Wayne Horvitz Group | Pigpen-V As In Victim | Avant | AVAN 027
Jazzmine
Orexis | Inspiration | Intercord | 160108
Jazzpar Suite:
Joachim Kühn And The Radio Philharmonie Hannover NDR With Jazz Soloists | Europeana | ACT | 9220-2
Jazzpony No.1:
Duke Ellington And His Orchestra | Duke Ellington's Masterpieces Vol.1: 1938-1940 | Black & Blue | BLE 59.233 2
Je
Yves Teicher Quartet | Fiddler On The Groove | RCA | 2147489-2
Je Cherche Aprés Titine
Clifton Chenier And His Band | Boogie & Zydeco | Sonet | 147109
Je Me Souviens
Michael Riessler Group | Honig Und Asche | Enja | ENJ-9303 2
Je Ne Sais Pas
Lionel Hampton Quintet | The Lional Hampton Quintet | Verve | 589100-2
Lionel Hampton With Buddy DeFranco And The Oscar Peterson Trio | Verve Jazz Masters 26:Lionel Hampton with Oscar Peterson | Verve | 521853-2
Robert Jeanne Quartet | Quartets | B.Sharp Records | CDS 084
Je Ne Veux Pas Mentir
Bireli Lagrene Group | Gipsy Project | Dreyfus Jazz Line | FDM 36626-2
Je Tire Ma Révérence
Al Rapone & The Zydeco Express | New Orleans Louisiana | Traditional Line | TL 1319
Jealjon
Jimmie Lunceford And His Orchestra | Jimmy Lunceford - Rythm Is Our Business | MCA | 1302
Jealous Blues
Duke Jordan Trio | Tivoli Two | Steeplechase | SCCD 31193
Jean
Grant Green Sextet | Idle Moments | Blue Note | 499003-2
Jean De Fleur
Vic Juris Trio | While My Guitar Gently Weeps | Steeplechase | SCCD 31553
Grant Green Sextet | Idle Moments | Blue Note | 499003-2
Jean De Fleur(alt.take)
Joe Kienemann Trio | All That Jazz Special | Blue Flame | 40742(2132446-2)
Jean Pierre
Miles Davis Group | We Want Miles | CBS | 469402-2
| Modern Walkin':Greatest Hits Volume 1 | Satin Doll Productions | SDP 1008-1 CD
Jean Pierre(short)
Rainer Pusch-Horace Parlan | In Between Those Changes | yvp music | CD 3046
Jeanie Lambe Talkin'
Allan Botschinsky/Niels-Henning Orsted-Pedersen | Duologue | M.A Music | NU 206-3
Jeanie With The Light Brown Hair
Singers Unlimited | The Singers Unlimited:Magic Voices | MPS | 539130-2
A Capella III | MPS | 68245
Jeanie-Weenie
Cannonball Adderley Quintet | Them Dirty Blues | Blue Note | 495447-2
Jeanine
George Robert Quartet | Voyage | TCB Records | TCB 95102
Jeanine I Dream Of Lilac Time
Stephane Metraux/Bemard Ogay | Oxymore | Plainisphare | PAV 803
Jeannie
Cannonball Adderley Quintet | Cannonball Adderley:Sophisticated Swing-The EmArCy Small Group Sessions | Verve | 528408-2
Flip Phillips Quartet | Spanish Eyes | Choice | CRS 1013 IMS
Jeannie With The Light Brown Hair
Phil Haynes Quartet | Phil Haynes & Free Country | Premonition | 790744-2
Jeannine
Cannonball Adderley Quintet | En Concert Avec Europe 1 | Laserlight | 710466
Julian Cannonball Adderly: Salle Pleyel/Olympia | Laserlight | 36126
The Cannonball Adderley Collection Vol.1:Them Dirty Blues | Landmark | CAC 1301-2(882341)
Donald Byrd Quintet | Blue Bop! | Blue Note | BNSLP 2
Eddie Jefferson With Orchestra | The Main Man | Inner City | IC 1033 IMS
Gene Harris Quartet | Like A Lover | Concord | CCD 4526
James Weiman Trio | People Music | TCB Records | TCB 96302
Melvin Rhyne Quartet | Boss Organ | Criss Cross | Criss 1080
Montgomery Brothers | Groove Brothers | Milestone | M 47051
Richard 'Groove' Holmes Trio | After Hours | Blue Note | 837986-2
Torsten Goods Group | Manhattan Walls | Jardis Records | JRCD 20139
Wolfgang Haffner International Jazz Quintet | I Should Have Known | Jazz 4 Ever Records:Jazz Network | J4E 4712
Jean-Paul
Kenny Clarke And His Orchestra | Kenny Clarke | Swing | SW 8411 IMS
Jeb
Trio Da Paz With Special Guests | Brazil From The Inside | Concord | CCD 4524
Jeep Is Jumpin'-
Glenn Miller And His Orchestra | 15 Rare Broadcast-Performances From 1943-1944 | RCA | NL 89499 AG
Jeep Jockey Jump
Glenn Miller And The Army Air Force Band | Glenn Miller And The Army Air Force Band | RCA | ND 89767
Jeep On 35
Jimmie Lunceford And His Harlem Express | The Uncollected:Jimmie Lunceford | Hindsight | HSR 221 (835573)
Jeepers Creepers
Bernard Peiffer Trio | Jazz In Paris:Bernard Peiffer-La Vie En Rose | EmArCy | 013980-2
Count Basie And His Orchestra With Tony Bennett | Basie-Bennett | Roulette | 7938992
Digby Fairweather Band | Wonderful Dixieland Vol.2 | Sonia | CD 77269
Elliot Lawrence Band | Plays Tiny Kahn And Johnny Mandel Arrangements | Fantasy | 0902109(F 3219)
Henri Crolla Sextet | Jazz In Paris:Henri Crolla-Notre Ami Django | EmArCy | 014062-2
Les McCann Trio | In San Francisco | Pacific Jazz | LN 10077
Lester Young With The Bill Potts Trio | Lester Young In Washington,DC 1956:Vol.1 | Original Jazz Classics | OJCCD 782-2(2308219)
Louis Armstrong And His All Stars | Ambassador Louis Armstrong Vol.15:When You And I Were Young Maggie(1946-1951) | Ambassador | CLA 1915
Louis Armstrong And His Orchestra | Big Band Bounce & Boogie-Louis Armstrong:Struttin' With Some Barbecue | Affinity | AFS 1024
Ralph Sutton-Cliff Leeman | Big Band Bounce & Boogie:Stacy 'N' Sutton | Affinity | AFS 1020
Ruby Braff-Dick Hyman | Manhattan Jazz | Musicmasters | 5031-2
Warren Vaché Quintet | Warren Plays Warrey | Nagel-Heyer | CD 033
Sonny Clark | Sonny Clark 1954 Memorial Album | The Jazz Factory | JFCD 22834
Jeepers Creepers(take 1)
Quintet Du Hot Club De France | Django Reinhardt Vol. 3 | Decca | 180022 AG
Jazz In Paris:Django Reinhardt-Swing 39 | EmArCy | 159854-2 PMS
Jeepers Creepers(take 2)
Django Reinhardt Vol. 3 | Decca | 180022 AG
Bob Gordon Quintet | Bob Gordon Memorial | Fresh Sound Records | FSR-CD 0180
Jeepers Leapers
Herbie Harper Quintet | The Complete Nocturne Recordings:Jazz In Hollywood Series Vol.1 | Fresh Sound Records | NR 3CD-101
Herbie Harper Feat.Bud Shank And Bob Gordon | Fresh Sound Records | 054 2600581(Liberty LJH 6003)
Jeep's Blues
Billy Strayhorn Orchestra | Johnny Hodges With Billy Strayhorn And The Orchestra | Verve | 557543-2
C.I.Williams Quintet | When Alto Was King | Mapleshade | 04532
Duke Ellington And His Orchestra | Ellington At Newport 1956(Complete) | CBS | CK 64932
Duke Ellington At The Alhambra | Pablo | PACD 5313-2
Duke Ellington: The Champs-Elysees Theater January 29-30th,1965 | Laserlight | 36131
Jazz Sax | CBS | 474186-2
Eric Felten Group | Gratitude | Soul Note | 121296-2
Johnny Hodges Orchestra | Johnny Hodges-Hodge Podge | CBS | EK 66972
Jeep's Blues-
Duke Ellington And His Orchestra | Duke Ellington:Complete Prestige Carnegie Hall 1946-1947 Concerts | Definitive Records | DRCD 11211
Jeez
Sam Butler | Guitar Wizards 1926-1935 | Yazoo | YAZ 1016
Jeffie
Giorgio Rosciglione Quartet | Giorgio Rosciglione Quartet | Penta Flowers | CDPIA 013
Jeg Elsker Dig
Moscow Art Trio | Music | JA & RO | JARO 4214-2
Jeg Er Norsk I Dag(Today,I'm Norwegian)
Kenny Drew Trio | Afternoon In Europe | RCA | PL 45373
Jeg Gik Mig Ud En Sommerdag
Niels-Henning Orsted-Pedersen Trio | The Eternal Traveller | Pablo | 2310910
Jeg Gik Mig Ud Spadserende
Christina Nielsen-Carsten Dahl Duo | Lys Pa Himlen | dacapo | DCCD 9458
Jeg Har En Angst
Lys Pa Himlen | dacapo | DCCD 9458
Jeg Ved En Dejlig Rose
Niels-Henning Orsted-Pedersen Trio | The Eternal Traveller | Pablo | 2310910
Jeg Vil Ga Tur Langs Maelkevejen
Ruud Jan Bos-Francois Van Bemmel Quartet | Bos & Van Bemmel | Timeless | CD SJP 363
Jelly Jelly
Earl Hines And His Orchestra | The Indispensable Earl Hines Vol.3/4(1939-1945) | RCA | 2126408-2
Earl Hines-Piano Man | Bluebird | NK 86750
Jelly Jelly Blues
Joe Turner With Orchestra | Things That I Used To Do | Pablo | 2310800
Jelly Man
Sammy Price Septet | Barrelhouse And Blues | Black Lion | BLCD 760159
Jelly Roll
Charles Mingus Orchestra | Nostalgia In Times Square/The Immortal 1959 Sessions | CBS | 88337
Don Wilkerson Quintet | The Texas Twister | Original Jazz Classics | OJCCD 1950-2(RLP 1186)
Donald Byrd Quintet | Donald Byrd:Blue Breakbeats | Blue Note | 494708-2
Furry Lewis | In His Prime 1927-1928 | Yazoo | YAZ 1050
Jelly Roll-
Guitar Frank | Living Country Blues USA, Vol.8 | L+R Records | LR 42038
Jelly Roll Baker
Lonnie Johnson With Elmer Snowden | Blues And Ballads | Original Blues Classics | OBCCD 531-2(BV 1011)
Otis Spann | Blues Roots Vol.9 | Storyville | 6.23708 AG
Jelly Roll Blues
Sidney Bechet And His New Orleans Feetwarmers | Commodore Claasics-Sidney Bechet/Bob Wilber:New Orleans Style Old & New | Commodore | 6.25492 AG
Jelly Roll Junior Blues
Sammy Price | Le Jazz En France Vol.14:Boogie Woogie A La Parisienne | Pathe | 1552601
Jelly Roll(alt.take)
Gil Evans Orchestra | Live At The Public Theater Vol.1(New York 1980) | Black-Hawk | BKH 525 CD
Jelly Whipping Blues
Barney Kessel | Solo | Concord | CJ 221
Jemsken
Mitchell's Jazz Kings | Le Jazz En France Vol.1:Premiers Jazz Bands | Pathe | 1727251
Jennie's Ball
Mike Garson | Avant Garson | Contemporary | C 14003
Jennifer Marie
Christmann-Schönenberg Duo | We Play | FMP | 0120
Jennifer's Rabbit
Singers Unlimited | Four Of Us | MPS | 68106
Jenny Lou
Buddy Tate Quintet | Broadway | Black & Blue | BLE 233054
Jenny's Dream
Jenny Evans And Band | Live At The Allotria | ESM Records | ESM 9301
Jenny's Place
Girl Talk | ESM Records | ESM 9306
Girl Talk | Enja | ENJ-9363 2
Live At The Allotria | BELL Records | BLR 90003
Jero
Joe Albany | Live In Paris | Fresh Sound Records | FSCD 1010
Jerry
Frank Wright Trio | Frank Wright Trio | ESP Disk | ESP 1023-2
The Vivino Brothers Band | Chitlins Parmigiana | dmp Digital Music Productions | CD 492
Jerry's Mood
Milt Jackson Sextet | The Birdlanders Vol.1 | Original Jazz Classics | OJCCD 1930-2
Jerry's Old Man
Lonnie Johnson With Joshua Altheimer | He's A Jelly Roll Baker | Bluebird | 63 66064 2
Jersey Bounce
Benny Goodman And His Orchestra | Big City Swing | Decca | TAB 5
Ella Fitzgerald With The Lou Levy Quartet | Verve Jazz Masters 46:Ella Fitzgerald-The Jazz Sides | Verve | 527655-2
Clap Hands,Here Comes Charlie! | Verve | 835646-2
Gerry Mulligan Quartet | Reunion With Chet Baker | Blue Note | 746857-2
Joe Reisman And His Orchestra | Party Night At Joe's | Fresh Sound Records | NL 46027(RCA LPM 1476)
Les & Larry Elgart Orchestra | Swing | Stereoplay-CD | CD 697042
Jeru
Gerry Mulligan Orchestra | Re-Birth Of The Cool | GRP | GRP 96792
Gerry Mulligan Quartet | The Best Of The Jazz Saxophone | LRC Records | CDC 8520
Miles Davis And His Orchestra | Miles Davis:Milestones | Dreyfus Jazz Line | FDM 36731-2
The Complete Birth Of The Cool | Capitol | 494550-2
Birth Of The Cool | Capitol | 530117-2
Miles Davis:The Blue Note And Capitol Recordings | Blue Note | 827475-2
Jerusalem Blues
Doc Houlind & His Copenhagen Ragtime Band | What A Wonderful World | Timeless | CD TTD 591
Jeruvian
Tommy Flanagan Trio | The Tommy Flanagan Trio | Original Jazz Classics | OJC 182(MV 9)
Jesaja 40(Wer Mißt Das Meer Mit Der Hohlen Hand)
The International Jazz Group | The International Jazz Group Vol.2 | Swing | SW 8416
Jespers Vuggevise
Johnny Copeland Group | Texas Twister | Edsel | 66.23401 AS
Jessica
Gerd Baumann-Alessandro Ricciarelli Quartet | Say No More | Edition Collage | EC 489-2
Greg Abate Quintet | Straight Ahead | Candid | CCD 79530
Jessica's Birthday
Cannonball Adderley Sextet | Swiss Radio Days Jazz Series Vol.3:Cannonball Adderley Sextet | TCB Records | TCB 02032
Jessica's Day
Dizzy Gillespie Big Band | Groovin' High | Bandstand | BDCD 1513
Jessica's Sunwheel
Jean Evans Orchestra | Keep It A Secret | B.Sharp Records | 1004
Jesu Meine
Singers Unlimited | Christmas | MPS | 821859-2
Jesus Hits Like The Atom Bomb
The Pilgrim Travelers | The Best Of The Pilgrim Travelers | Ace Records | CDCHD 342
Jesus' Last Ballad
Wiregrass Sacred Harp Singers | The Colored Sacred Harp | New World Records | 80433-2
Jesus Maria
Jimmy Giuffre 3 | Jimmy Giuffre 3, 1961 | ECM | 1438/39(849644-2)
Emphasis,Stuttgart 1961 | Hat Art | CD 6072
Carla Bley Band | Musique Mecanique | Watt | 9
Jesus Maria And Other Spanish Strains
Mahalia Jackson | In Memoriam Mahalia Jackson | CBS | 66501
Jesus Un St.Johänneken
Dorothy Wilson Gospel Express | O How Beautiful | L+R Records | CDLR 44019
Jet Black Blues
Blind Willie Dunn's Gin Bottle Four | King Oliver 1928-29 | Village(Jazz Archive) | VILCD 005-2
Jet Propulsion
The Errol Parker Experience | Graffiti | Sahara | 1011
Jet Song
Grover Washington Jr. Orchestra | Inside Moves | Elektra | 7559-60318-2
Jet Stream
Jason Seizer Quartet | Serenity | Acoustic Music Records | 319.1152.2
Peter Bernstein Quartet | Signs Of Life | Criss Cross | Criss 1095
Jet(take 1)
Spaulding Givens Trio | Debut Rarities Vol.2 | Original Jazz Classics | OJCCD 1808-2
Jet(take 2)
David Doucet Group | Quand Jai Parti | Rounder Records | CDRR 6040
Jette
Vince Jones Group | It All Ends Up In Tears | Intuition Records | INT 3069-2
Jettison
Charlie Mariano-Gregor Josephs Quartet | Lustinseln | L+R Records | CDLR 45097
Jetzt Oder Nie
Dieter Ilg Trio | Fieldwork | Jazzline | JL 11155-2
Jeux De Quartes
Bobby Jaspar Quintet | Jazz In Paris:Bobby Jaspar-Jeux De Quartes | EmArCy | 018423-2
Jeux De Quartes(alt.take)
J.J.Johnson-Nat Adderley Quintet | The Yokohama Concert | Pablo | 2620109
Jewel Ornament
Mark Isaacs/Dave Holland/Roy Haynes | Encounters | VeraBra Records | CDVBR 2076-2
Jewelette
Gregory James Quartet | Alicia | Inner City | IC 1050 IMS
Jewels Of Love
Booker Little 4 & Max Roach | Booker Little 4 & Max Roach | Blue Note | 784457-2
Jewish Dance
Dizzy Gillespie With The Mitchell/Ruff Duo | Enduring Magic | Black-Hawk | BKH 51801
Jhana
Les Misérables Brass Band | Manic Tradition | Popular Arts | NR 5004 CD
Jig
Dorothy Dandridge With Orchestra | Harlem Roots-Jazz On Film:Jivin' Time | Storyville | SLP 6003
Jig-A-Jug
Marty Ehrlich-Peter Erskine-Michael Formanek | Relativity | Enja | ENJ-9341 2
Jiggle The Handle
Melvin Sparks Group | I'm A 'Gittar' Player | Cannonball Records | CBD 27101
Jigsaw
Joe Chambers Quintet | The Almoravid | 32 Jazz | 32099
Jil
George Lewis-Douglas Ewart | George Lewis-Douglas Ewart | Black Saint | BSR 0026
Jilli
Miles Davis Group | Time After Time | Jazz Door | JD 1256/57
Jim
Betty Roche And Her Quartet | Lightly And Politely | Original Jazz Classics | OJCCD 1802-2(P 7198)
Dakota Staton With The Dave Berkman Trio | Dakota Staton | Muse | MCD 5401
Houston Person Sextet | Ain't She Sweet(Save Your Love For Me/I'll Be Seeing You) | 32 Jazz | 32120
Oscar Peterson Trio | Oscar Peterson-The London House Sessions | Verve | 531766-2
Sarah Vaughan With The Clifford Brown All Stars | Sarah Vaughan | Verve | 543305-2
Brownie-The Complete EmArCy Recordings Of Clifford Brown | EmArCy | 838306-2
Sarah Vaughan With The Hal Mooney Orchestra | It's A Man's World | Mercury | 589487-2
Tanzorchester Der Original Teddies | International Schlager & In Mood mit Teddy Stauffer's Original Teddies | Elite Special | 9522003
Jim Jam
Duke Robillard Group | Swing | Demon Records | Fiend CD 191
Glenn Miller And His Orchestra | The Glenn Miller Carnegie Hall Concert | RCA | NL 81506
Jimane's Creation
Mandingo Griot Society | Mandingo Griot Society | Flying Fish | FF 70076
Jimbo's Lullaby(Debussy)
Jukka Tolonen Group | Impressions | Sonet | 147126
Jim-Jam-Jug
Chico Hamilton Quartet | The Dealer | Impulse(MCA) | 547958-2
Jim-Jeannie
Diana Krall Trio | Stepping Out | Enja | ENJ-8042 2
Jimmy
Temperance Seven | Pasadena & The Lost Cylinders-Music From The Archives | Lake | LACD 77
Jimmy And The Duck-
Big Bill Broonzy | Black Brown And White | Mercury | 842743-2
Jimmy Van Heusen Medley:
Django's Music | Django Reinhardt:Djangology | EMI Records | 780659-2
Jimmy's Mode
Jimmy McGriff Orchestra | City Lights | JAM | 002 IMS
Jim's Ballad
Kevin Mahogany With Orchestra | Songs And Moments | Enja | ENJ-8072 2
Herb Ellis Quartet | Softly ... But With That Feeling | Verve | MV 2674 IMS
Jim's Jam
Philly Joe Jones Quartet | Philly Mignon | Original Jazz Classics | GXY 5112
Jingle Bells
Jan Harrington Sextet | Jan Harrington's Christmas In New Orleans | Nagel-Heyer | NHR SP 4
Jimmy Smith Trio | Christmas Cookin' | Verve | 513711-2
Maryland Jazzband Of Cologne feat. Papa Don Vappie And Erny Elly | Christmas In New Orleans | Maryland Records | MJCD 0895
Charlie Parker All Stars | Bird At The Roost Vol.2 | Savoy | 650125(882115)

Jingles
Milt Jackson-Wes Montgomery Quintet | Wes Montgomery-The Complete Riverside Recordings | Riverside | 12 RCD 4408-2
Montgomery Brothers | Wes'Best | America | AM 6092
Unknown Group | Lenox School Of Jazz Concert | Royal Jazz | RJD 513
Wes Montgomery Trio | Wes Montgomery-The Complete Riverside Recordings | Riverside | 12 RCD 4408-2
Bernard Peiffer Trio | Jazz In Paris:Bernard Peiffer-La Vie En Rose | EmArCy | 013980-2

Jingles(alt.take)
Wes Montgomery-Milt Jackson Quintet | The Alternative Wes Montgomery | Milestone | MCD 47065-2

Jinrikisha
Big Joe Williams | Classic Delta Blues | Original Blues Classics | OBCCD 545-2

Jinx Blues
Blues Masters Vol.2 | Storyville | STCD 8002

Jit It
Al Casey Quartet | A' Portrait Of Jan Jankeje | Jazzpoint | JP 1054 CD
Buddy Johnson And His Orchestra | Buddy And Ella Johnson 1953-1964 | Bear Family Records | BCD 15479 DH

Jit Jit
Cecil Taylor | Silent Tongues | Black Lion | CD 877633-2

Jitterbug
Amos Milburn Quintet | Chicken Shack Boogie | Pathe | 1561411(Aladdin)

Jitterbug Waltz
Art Tatum | Art Tatum-The Complete Pablo Solo Masterpieces | Pablo | 7 PACD 4404-2
Art Tatum:20th Century Piano Genius | Verve | 531763-2
The Tatum Solo Masterpieces Vol. 3 | Pablo | 2310730
Barry Altschul Quartet | Irina | Soul Note | SN 1065
Bucky Pizzarelli-John Pizzarelli Duo | Live at The Vineyard | Challenge | CHR 70025
David Grisman Quintet Feat. Swend Asmussen | Svingin' With Svend | Zebra Acoustic Records | ???
Dick Johnson-Dave McKenna Duo | Spider's Blues | Concord | CJ 135
Eddie Henderson Quintet | Phantoms | Steeplechase | SCCD 31250
Frank Marocco-Ray Pizzi Duo | New Colors | Trend | TR 516 Direct-to-Disc
Herb Geller Sextet | That Geller Feller(Fire In The West) | Fresh Sound Records | FSR CD 91(882417)
Joe Albany | Joe Albany At Home | Spotlite | SPJ LP 1 (JA 1)
Pepper Adams Quartet | Epherma | Spotlite | SPJ LP 6 (PA 6)
Zoot Sims Quartet | Warm Tenor | Pablo | 2310831-2

Jitterbug Waltz-
Horace Parlan | Musically Yours | Steeplechase | SCCD 31141

Jive At Five
Art Pepper-Shorty Rogers Quintet | Art Pepper & Shorty Rogers:Complete Lighthouse Sessions | The Jazz Factory | JFCD 22836
Count Basie And His Orchestra | Basie On Roulette, Vol. 14: The Best Of Basie-Vol. 1 | Vogue | 500014
Count Basie's Kansas City Five | Count Basie: Kansas City 5 | Pablo | 2312126
Herbie Harper Quintet | The Complete Nocturne Recordings:Jazz In Hollywood Series Vol.1 | Fresh Sound Records | NR 3CD-101
Jazz In Hollywood:Herbie Harper | Original Jazz Classics | OJCCD 1887-2(Nocturne NLP-1/NLP-7)
Martial Solal And The Kentonians | Martial Solal:The Complete Vogue Recordings Vol.3 | Vogue | 21606372
Paul Quinichette Quartet | The International Jazz Group Vol.2 | Swing | SW 8416
Zoot Sims Quartet | Down Home | Charly | CD 59

Jive At Six
The Tremble Kids All Stars | Dixieland At Its Best | BELL Records | BLR 89091

Jive Bomber
Stephane Grappelli Quartet | Grapelli Story | Verve | 515807-2
Larry Goldings Trio | Intimacy Of The Blues | Minor Music | 801017

Jive Elephant
Roland Kirk Quartet | Talkin' Verve-Roots Of Acid Jazz:Roland Kirk | Verve | 533101-2
Axel Zwingenberger-Torsten Zwingenberger | Boogie Woogie Bros. | Vagabond | VRCD 8.88015

Jive For Johnson
Louis Stewart-Heiner Franz | In A Mellow Tone | Jardis Records | JRCD 9206

Jive Hot
Duke Ellington And His Orchestra | Ella & Duke At The Cote D'Azur | Verve | 539030-2

Jive Jam
Sammy Price Sextet | Roots Of Rock 'N' Roll, Vol. 7: Rib Joint | Savoy | SJL 2240 (801886)

Jive Samba
Cannonball Adderley Quintet | Cannonball In Japan | Capitol | 793560-2
Cannonball Adderley Sextet | Swiss Radio Days Jazz Series Vol.3:Cannonball Adderley Sextet | TCB Records | TCB 02032
Essence Of Funk | Essence Of Funk | Hip Bop | HIBD 8007
Jazz Gala Big Band With Guest Soloists | Jazz Special-Gala Concert | RCA | CL 30069 DP
Thad Jones-Mel Lewis Orchestra | Thad Jones-Mel Lewis | Blue Note | 84498
The Riverside Reunion Band | Hi-Fly | Milestone | MCD 9228-2
Dim Sum Clip Job | Harmolodic Jeopardy | Avant | AVAN 051

Jivin' In Jazzland
Duke Robillard-Herb Ellis Quintet | Conversation In Swing Guitar | Stony Plain | SPCD 1260

Jivin' In Rhythm
Count Basie And His Orchestra | Count Basie And His Great Vocalists | CBS | CK 66374

Jivin' With Jarvis
Lionel Hampton With Nat King Cole And His Trio | Hot Mallets Vol.1 | Bluebird | ND 86458

Jiwa
Keshavan Maslak With Charles Moffett | Blaster Master | Black Saint | BSR 0079

JJ Jump
Andrew Cyrille Trio | Nuba | Black Saint | 120030-2

JL's Wish
Lionel Hampton All Stars | Lionel Hampton And His Jazz Giants | Black & Blue | BLE 59.107 2

Jo Mo
Tete Montoliu Trio | I Wanna Talk About You | Steeplechase | SCS 1137

Joab
SHQ | SHQ | ESP Disk | ESP 1080-2

Joachim's B Part
George Robert Quartet With Clark Terry | Live At The Q-4 Rheinfelden | TCB Records | TCB 9080

Joan
John Patitucci Group | Imprint | Concord | CCD 4881

Joan Crawford
Helmut Kagerer/Helmut Nieberle | Wes Trane | Edition Collage | EC 453-2

Joana
Badi Assad | Solo | Chesky | JD 99

Joana's Dance,Epilog
Lee Konitz-Frank Wunsch | The Frankfurt Concert | West Wind | WW 2106

Joan-Capetown Flower
Abdullah Ibrahim Trio | African Magic | TipToe | TIP-888845 2
Dollar(Abdullah Ibrahim) Brand Group | African River | Enja | ENJ-6018 2
Michel Godard-Dave Bargeron Quartet | Tuba Tuba | Enja | 9133-2

Joanna's Theme
Al Haig | Solitaire | Spotlite | SPJ LP 14

Joanne Julia
Stan Getz Quartet | The Lost Sessions | Verve | 9801098
David Murray & Low Class Conspiracy | Vol. 1: Penthouse Jazz | Circle Records | RK 4-18877/4 IMS

Joao
Jim Hall | Dedications & Inspirations | Telarc Digital | CD 83365

Job
Ornette Coleman & Prime Time Band | Of Human Feelings | Antilles | AN 2001(802385)

Job's Red Wagon-
John Benson Brooks Ensemble | Alabama/Africa | Milestone | M 47059

Jockey-Bounce
James 'Sugarboy' Crawford Band | Sugarboy Crawford | Chess | 427017

Jodi
Dexter Gordon Quartet | Dexter Gordon:The Complete Blue Note Sixties Sessions | Blue Note | 834200-2

Jodie Man
Max Roach Quintet | Conversations | Milestone | M 47061

Jodie's Cha-Cha
Stanley Turrentine Sextet | In Memory Of | Blue Note | LT 1037

Joe Avery's Blues
Eureka Brass Band | Jazz At Preservation Hall, Vol.1 | Atlantic | SD 1408

Joe Brown
Kid Thoams Valentine Jazz Band | The Dance Hall Years | American Music | AMCD-48

Joe Cool
Jeff Berlin Group | Crossroads | Denon Compact Disc | CY-18077

Joe Is Watching You
Joe Lutcher's Jump Band | Joe Joe Jump | Charly | CRB 1038

Joelle
David Qualey | Talking Hands:Live | ALISO Records | AL 1021

Joel's Song
Joe Maneri Quartet | Coming Down The Mountain | HatOLOGY | 501

Joe's Blues
The Capp/Pierce Juggernaut | Live At The Century Plaza | Concord | CCD 4072

Joe's Lonesome Blues
Son House-Woody Mann | Been Here And Gone | Acoustic Music Records | 319.1174.2

Joey
René Pretschner Quartet | Floating Pictures | Green House Music | CD 1001

Joey & Jerry
Vinny Golia Quintet | Out For Blood | Nine Winds Records | NW 0127

Johann Brown(Hommage à James Brown)
Pata Horns | New Archaic Music | Pata Musik | PATA 4(JHM 42) CD

Johanna's Waltz
Johannes Enders Group | Reflections Of South Africa | Jazz 4 Ever Records:Jazz Network | J4E 4729

Johannesburg
Woody Herman And His Orchestra | Woody Herman:Complete 1948-1950 Capitol Sessions | Definitive Records | DRCD 11195

Johann's Step
Hamiet Bluiett Quartet | Sankofa/Rear Garde | Soul Note | 121238-2

John And Mary
Jaki Byard Quartet | Family Man | 32 Jazz | 32171

John Brown's Body
Harry Happel Trio | Intrioduction | Timeless | SJP 149
Jimmy Smith With Orchestra | Who's Afraid Of Virginia Woolf? | Verve | 823309-2 PMS
Oscar Peterson Trio With Milt Jackson | Very Tall | Verve | 559830-2
Very Tall | Verve | 827821-2
The Banjo Crackers | Dixieland Jubilee-Vol. 2 | Intercord | 155005

John Hardy's Wife
Duke Ellington And His Famous Orchestra | Duke Ellington & His Famous Orchestra | Forlane | UCD 19003
Oscar Peterson Trio | Oscar Peterson Plays The Duke Ellington Song Book | Verve | 559785-2
Oscar Peterson Plays The Duke Ellington Song Book | Verve | 559785-2
Woody Herman And His Orchestra | The V Disc Years Vol.1&2 | Hep | CD 2/3435
Big Bill Broonzy | Blues Legacy 1: Big Bill Broonzy-Lonesome Road Blues | Vogue | 512501

John Henry
Big Bill Blues | Vogue | 655501
Brownie McGhee & Sonny Terry | You Hear Me Talkin' | Muse | MR 5131
Furry Lewis | Shake 'Em On Down | Fantasy | F 24703
Memphis Slim With Willie Dixon | The Blues Every Which Way | Verve | 2304505 IMS
Shakey Horton Band | The Soul Of Blues Harmonica | Chess | CH 9268

John Henry(alt.take)
American Folk Blues Festival | American Folk Blues Festival 1969 | L+R Records | CDLR 42071

John Lennnon's Assassination
Chuck Loeb Group | Life Colors | dmp Digital Music Productions | CD 475

John McLaughlin
Eric Alexander Quartet | The Second Milestone | Milestone | MCD 9315-2

John Neely Beautiful People
George Shearing | Piano | Concord | CCD 4400

John S.
Duke Ellington Trio | Duke Ellington-New York Concert | Musicmasters | 65122-2

John Silver
Count Basie And His Orchestra | Live In Japan '78 | Pablo | 2308246-2

John, Stop Teasing Me
John Carter | A Suite Of Early American Folk Pieces For Solo-Clarinet | Moers Music | 02014

Johnnie Walker
Benny Carter Group | Wonderland | Pablo | 2310922-2

Johnny Be Gay If You Can Be
Chuck Berry With The Blues Band | Newport Jazz Festival 1958,July 3rd-6th Vol.3:Blues In The Night No.1 | Phontastic | NCD 8815

Johnny Be Good
Lee Konitz Trio | Three Guys | Enja | ENJ-9351 2

Johnny Broken Wing
Paul Motian Quintet | Misterioso | Soul Note | 121174-2

Johnny Cat
Art Farmer Quintet | Something To Live For | Contemporary | CCD 14029-2

Johnny Comes Lately
Dizzy Gillespie And His Orchestra | A Portrait Of Duke Ellington | Verve | 817107-1 IMS
Duke Ellington And His Orchestra | At The Hurricane:Original 1943 Broadcasts | Storyville | STCD 8359
100 Years Duke | Laserlight | 24906
Jazz Giants:Duke Ellington | RCA | NL 45179 SI
The Indispensable Duke Ellington,Vol.7/8 | RCA | ND 89274
Eddie Lockjaw Davis Trio | Eddie 'Lockjaw' Davis His Tenor Saxophone And Trio | Sing | 506
Jimmy Smith With The Oliver Nelson Orchestra | Verve Jazz Masters 29:Jimmy Smith | Verve | 521855-2
Joe Henderson Quintet | Lush Life-The Music Of Billy Strayhorn | Verve | 511779-2
Johnny Hodges And The Ellington Men | The Big Sound | Verve | MV 2525 IMS
Roman Schwaller Jazz Quartet | Some Changes In Life | JHM Records | JHM 3612
Live At The Nachtcafé Munich | Bassic-Sound | CD 019

Johnny Hodges Medley:
Duke Ellington And His Orchestra | Duke Ellington:Complete Prestige Carnegie Hall 1946-1947 Concerts | Definitive Records | DRCD 11211

Johnny Hornet
Acoustic Guitars | Acoustic Guitars | Stunt Records | 18703

Johnny Mae
Woody Herman And His Orchestra | Jazz Legacy 18: Woody Herman-The Fourth Herd | Vogue | 500068

Johnny One Note
Art Farmer Sextet | The Meaning Of Art | Arabesque Recordings | AJ 0118
Ella Fitzgerald With The Buddy Bregman Orchestra | The Rodgers And Hart Song Book, Vol.1 | Verve | 821579-2 PMS
Ronnell Bright Trio | The Ronnell Bright Trio | Fresh Sound Records | FSR 559(Polydor 46106)

Johnny Ramsay
Christopher Hollyday Quartet | The Natural Moment | Novus | PD 83118

Johnny,Wenn Du Geburtstag Hast
Dennis Gonzales New Dallas Sextet | Namesake | Silkheart | SHCD 106

Johnny's Blues
Elliot Lawrence Band | Plays Tiny Kahn And Johnny Mandel Arrangements | Fantasy | 0902109(F 3219)

Johnology
Bob Mover Trio Feat. Paul Bley And John Abercrombie | The Night Bathers | Justin Time | Just 14

John's Abbey
Bud Powell Trio | Duke Jordan New York/Bud Powell Paris | Vogue | 21457272
The Legacy | Jazz Door | JD 1204
The Essen Jazz Festival Concert | Black Lion | CD 877638-2
Mel Lewis Quintet | Mellifous | Landmark | LCD 1543-2
Walter Davis Trio | Live Au Dreher | Harmonia Mundi | PJC 222005

John's Abbey(alt.take)
Big Joe Turner With Axel Zwingenberger | Let's Boogie Woogie All Night Long | Vagabond | VRCD 8.79012

John's And Louis' Blues
Charles Mingus Quintet | Stormy & Funky Blues | Moon Records | MCD 064-2

John's Groove
Basie Reunion | Basie Reunion | Prestige | P 24109

John's Waltz
John Abercrombie-Andy LaVerne | Where We Were | Double Time Records | DTRCD-110

Johnson Rag
Glenn Miller And His Orchestra | Glenn Miller | Koch Records | 321 941 D1
Glenn Miller:The Complete Studio Recordings Vol.2:In The Mood | Memo Music | HDJ 4115

Joie De Roy
Dewey Redman Group | The Ear Of The Behearer | Impulse(MCA) | IMP 12712

Joie De Vivre
Panama Francis And The Savoy Sultans | Grooving | Stash Records | ST 218 IMS

Jo-Jo
Miles Davis Group | Miles In Montreux | Jazz Door | JD 1287/88
Lester Young And The Kansas City Six | Commodore Classics In Swing | Commodore | 9031-72723-2

Jöklabaen
Charles Mingus Workshop | Charles Mingus-The Complete Debut Recordings | Debut | 12 DCD 4402-2

Joldi(take 4)
Charles Mingus-The Complete Debut Recordings | Debut | 12 DCD 4402-2

Joldi(take 5)
Elefanten | Faust | KlangRäume | 30150

Jolly Jume Jumey
Pete Jolly Sextet | Jolly Jumps In | Fresh Sound Records | 12582 CD(RCA)

Jonah
Sister Rosetta Tharpe With The Sammy Price Trio | Gospel Train | MCA | 1317

Jonah And The Whale
Louis Armstrong With Sy Oliver's Choir And Orchestra | Louis And The Good Book | Verve | 549593-2
Louis Armstrong With The Lyn Murray Chorus | Louis Armstrong:Hallelujah(Gospel 1930-1941) | Fremeaux | FA 001
Med Flory and his Orchestra | Jazz Wave | Fresh Sound Records | JLP 1066(Jubilee)

JonBenet
Firma Kischke | Nix Als The Blues-Live Im Allgäu | Jazz Classics | AU 11126 Digital

Jones Beachhead
Woody Herman And His Orchestra | The Radio Years: Woody Herman And His First Herd 1944 | Hindsight | HSR 134

Jones Street
Tony Lakatos Quintet | Generation X | Jazzline | JL 11149-2

Jongo
Yosuke Yamashita New York Trio | Dazzling Days | Verve | 521303-2

Jonona
Lee Konitz Quartet | Tranquility | Verve | MV 2508 IMS

Joogie Boogie
Lil Armstrong | The Club Hangover Broadcast | Arbors Records | ARCD 19150/51

Joom Jooms
Bill Lowe/Philippe Crettien Quintet | Sunday Train | Konnex Records | KCD 5051

Joone
Clark Terry & Chico O Farril Orchestra | Spanish Rice | Verve | 9861050

Joonji
Clark Terry Quintet | The Second Set-Recorded Live At The Village Gate | Chesky | JD 127

Joram
Alex Möller-Lena Willemark Group | Hästen Och Tranan | ACT | 9244-2

Jordan For President
Louis Jordan And His Tympany Five | The Small Black Groups | Storyville | 4960523

Jordan Jive
The Jumping Notes Dixieland-Band | C'Est Si Bon | Elite Special | 73444

Jordan's Mood
Oliver Jones Trio | Northern Summit | Enja | ENJ-6086 2

Jordsang(Earth Song)
Andre Hodeir And His Jazz Group De Paris | The Historic Donaueschingen Jazz Concert | MPS | 68161

Jordu
Andy LaVerne Trio | Glass Ceiling | Steeplechase | SCCD 31352
Benny Golson Sextet | Time Speaks-Dedicated To The Memory Of Clifford Brown | Timeless | CD SJP 187
Chet Baker-Stan Getz Quintet | Stan Meets Chet | Verve | 837436-2
Clifford Brown-Max Roach Quintet | Clifford Brown-Max Roach:Alone Together-The Best Of The Mercury Years | Verve | 526373-2
Jazz-Club: Drums | Verve | 840033-2
Compact Jazz: Clifford Brown | EmArCy | 842933-2 PMS
More Study In Brown | EmArCy | 814637-2
Conte Candoli Quintet | West Coast Wailers | Fresh Sound Records | 1268(Atlantic)
Duke Jordan Trio | Live In Japan | Steeplechase | SCCD 31063+31064
Tivoli Two | Steeplechase | SCCD 31193
Oscar Peterson Trio | En Concert Avec Europe 1 | Laserlight | 710443/48
Stan Getz Quartet | Live At The Village Vanguard | Ingo | 1
Tommy Flanagan And Hank Jones | Our Delights | Original Jazz Classics | GXY 5113

Joren's Dance
Badi Assad Group | Echoes Of Brazil | Chesky | JD 154

Jorge's Bolero
Donald Byrd Quintet | Royal Flush | Blue Note | 869476-7

Jorjana (No.2)
Roger Kellaway Cello Quartet With The A&M Symphony Orchestra | Roger Kellaway Cello Quartet | A&M Records | 9861062

Jorjana(No.8)
Jan Garbarek Trio | Madar | ECM | 1515(519075-2)

Joron
Piirpauke | Birgi Bühtüi | JA & RO | 004(08-4104)

Joropo Llandero

TITELVERZEICHNIS

Jo Mikowich Group | Storm Thunder Lighning | yvp music | 3008

Joschke Fort Avek
Hilton Ruiz Group | A Moment's Notice | Novus | PD 83123

Jose Valeria Matias
Norbert Stein Pata Orchester | Ritual Life | Pata Musik | PATA 5(JHM 50) CD

Josebas Traum
Pata Trio | Lucy Und Der Ball | Jazz Haus Musik | JHM 34

Josef Fran Arimatea
Kol Simcha | Contemporary Klezmer | Laika Records | LK 93-048

Josef's Freilach
Alan Shorter Quartet | Orgasm | Verve | 557094-2

Joseph 'n His Brudders
Louis Armstrong And His Orchestra | Louis Armstrong-The Complete RCA Victor Recordings | RCA | 2668682-2

Joseph,Lieber Joseph Mein
Gerald Wilson Big Band | Moment Of The Truth | Pacific Jazz | 792928-2

Josephine
Mark Isaacs Quintet | Closer | Naxos Jazz | 86065-2

Joshua
Miles Davis Quintet | The Complete Concert 1964:My Funny Valentine+Four & More | CBS | 471246-2
Four & More | CBS | SRCS 5145
Miles In Antibes | CBS | 462960-2

Joshua C.
Golden Gate Quartet | Golden Gate Quartet | CBS | 471559-2

Joshua Fit The Battle Of Jericho
Spirituals To Swing 1955-69 | EMI Records | 791569-2
Best Of Golden Gate Quartet | Sonia | CD 77285
Hampton Hawes Trio | The Sermon | Original Jazz Classics | OJCCD 1067-2(C 7653)
Joe Turner | Walking Through Heaven | Swingtime | 8205
Louisiana Red | The Blues Purity Of Louisiana Red | Blue Labor | BL 104
Sister Rosetta Tharpe And Her Group | Gospel Train | Mercury | 841134-2
Sister Rosetta Tharpe With The Original Tuxedo Jazz Band | Live In Paris 1964 | France's Concert | FCD 118

Joshua(for Rev.Charles Koen And The People Of Cairo,Ill.
Joe Lovano Septet | Universal Language | Blue Note | 799830-2

Jot Biscuits
Tom Van Der Geld Trio | Path | ECM | 1134

Jour De Fete-Avant
Albrecht Maurer Trio Works | Movietalks | Jazz Haus Musik | JHM 0119 CD

Jour De Fete-Passe
Didier Lockwood Group | 'Round About Silence | Dreyfus Jazz Line | FDM 36595-2

Journal Violone II(part 1-4)
Barre Phillips Trio | Journal Violone II | ECM | 1149

Journal Violone II(part 5:to Aquirax Aida)
Journal Violone II | ECM | 1149

Journal Violone II(part 6)
Christoph Spendel | Park Street No 92 | EGO | 4009

Journey
Jan Akkerman | Can't Stand Noise | Inak | 11001

Journey-
Jaki Byard | Empirical | Muse | MCD 6010

Journey Agent
Martial Solal/Joachim Kühn | Duo In Paris | Dreyfus Jazz Line | FDM 36503-2

Journey East From West
Roosevelt Sykes | Roosevelt Sykes(1929-1941) | Story Of Blues | CD 3542-2

Journey In Satchidananda
Stan Kenton And His Orchestra | Journey Into Capricorn | Creative World | STD 1077

Journey Of
Carlo Mombelli Quartet | Abstractions | West Wind | WW 2024

Journey Of Now
Sun Ra And His Intergalactic Research Arkestra | Black Myth/Out In Space | MPS | 557656-2

Journey Through The Outer Darkness
Sun Ra Arkestra | Concert For The Comet Kohoutek | ESP Disk | ESP 3033-2

Journey To Edaneres
Jesse Davis Quintet | From Within | Concord | CCD 4727

Journey To Recife
Erich Bachträgl Quartet | Gollum | Bellaphon | 270.31.004

Journey To The Sky
Count Basie And His Orchestra | Prez's Hat Vol.1 | Philology | 214 W 6

Journey To The Twin Planet
Prince Lasha Quintet | Journey To Zoar | Enja | 4008

Journey Towards Freedom
Sun Ra And His Arkestra | Purple Night | A&M Records | 395324-2

Jovane Mori Jovane
Mara! | Ruino Vino | Laika Records | 35100792

Jove
Elaine Delmar With Band | 'S Wonderful | Ronnie Scott's Jazz House | JHCD 027

Joy
Jimmy Smith Trio | Jimmy Smith At The Organ | Blue Note | 300154(1512)
John Coltrane Quintet | The Mastery Of John Coltrane/Vol. 1: Feelin' Good | MCA | 2292-54641-2
Stephane Grappelli With The Diz Disley Trio | Violinspiration | MPS | 68058
Wayne Shorter Orchestra | Odyssey Of Iska | Blue Note | 784363-2

Joy-
Dave Liebman With Gunnar Mossblad And The James Madison University Jazz Esemble | The Music Of John Coltrane | Candid | CCD 79531
Los Angeles Neophonic Orchestra | Stan Kenton Conducts The Los Angeles Neophonic Orchestra | Capitol | 494502-2

Joy For Joy
Helmut Kagerer-Peter Bernstein Quartet | April In New York | Jardis Records | JRCD 9818
Lee Konitz Trio | Thingin | Hat Art | CD 6174

Joy In A Scene From Sadness
Bob Degen Trio With Zbigniew Namyslowski | Joy | Dr.Jazz Records | 8611-2

Joy Is Better
Kenny Barron Group | Things Unsee | Verve | 537315-2

Joy Juice
Sam Morrison Group | Natural Layers | Chiaroscuro | CR 184

Joy Mentin'
Ornette Coleman Quartet | Beauty Is A Rare Thing:Ornette Coleman-The Complete Atlantic Recordings | Atlantic | 8122-71410-2

Joy Of A Toy
Steve Houben-Michel Herr Quartet | Steve Houben & Michel Herr Meets Curtis Lundy & Kenny Washington | B.Sharp Records | CDS 094

Joy Of Life
Ornette Coleman Quartet | Twins | Atlantic | SD 8810

Joy Ride
Bobby Timmons Trio | This Here Is Bobby Timmons | Original Jazz Classics | OJC20 104-2(RLP 1164)
Ray Charles And His Orchestra | The Genius After Hours | Atlantic | 50916(SD 1369)

Joy Riding
Hod O'Brien Quintet | Opalessence | Criss Cross | Criss 1012

Joy Spring
Barney Kessel Quartet | Barney Kessel's Swingin' Party At Contemporary | Original Jazz Classics | OJCCD 1066-2(S 7613)
Billy Taylor | Ten Fingers-One Voice | Arkadia Jazz | 71602
Clifford Brown All Stars | Zoot Sims:The Featured Sessions With Great Leaders 1949-1954 | Blue Moon | BMCD 1037
Clifford Brown-Max Roach Quintet | Clifford Brown And Max Roach | Verve | 543306-2
Compact Jazz: Clifford Brown | EmArCy | 842933-2 PMS
Brownie-The Complete EmArCy Recordings Of Clifford Brown | EmArCy | 838306-2
Daniel Küffer Quartet | Daniel Küffer Quartet | Satin Doll Productions | SDP 1010-1 CD
Freddie Hubbard Sextet | The Best Of Freddie Hubbard | Pablo | 2405415-2
George Shearing Quintet | Back To Birdland | Telarc Digital | CD 83524
Helen Merrill And Her Band | Brownie:Homage To Clifford Brown | Verve | 522363-2
John Park Quartet | If Winter Comes | Jazz Mark | 105
Larry Coryell Quartet | Equipoise | Muse | MCD 5319
Max Roach-Clifford Brown Quintet | Daahoud | Mobile Fidelity | MFCD 826
Oscar Peterson Trio | Compact Jazz: Oscar Peterson Plays Jazz Standards | Verve | 833283-2
Paul Robertson Quintet | Old Friends, New Friends | Palo Alto | PA 8013
Sigi Finkel's Powerstation | Voyeur,Voyeur | Open Minds | OM 2404-2

Joy To The World
Mark Shane's X-Mas Allstars | What Would Santa Say? | Nagel-Heyer | CD 055
Singers Unlimited | Christmas | MPS | 821859-2

Joy To The World-
Keith Foley | Music For Christmas | dmp Digital Music Productions | CD 452

Joyce's Samba
Peter Schärli Quintet | Ballads And Brazil | TCB Records | TCB 98952

Joyeses Farces
Alix Combelle Et Son Orchestre | Django Reinhardt:Djangology | EMI Records | 780659-2

Joyful Departure
Ralph Towner | Ana | ECM | 1611(537023-2)
Fritz Pauer Trio | Water Plants | EGO | 4007

Joyful Noise
Louis Moholo's Viva-La-Black | Freedom Tour-Live In South Afrika 1993 | Ogun | OGCD 006
Don Sebesky Orchestra | Joyful Noise:A Tribute To Duke Ellington | RCA | 2663552-2

Joyful Sorrow
Markus Stockhausen Quartet | Joyosa | Enja | ENJ-9468 2

Joyosa
Pat Martino Quintet | Stone Blue | Blue Note | 830822-2

Joyous Lake
Jay Clayton-Jerry Granelli | Sound Songs | JMT Edition | 919006-2

Joyous March
Ken McIntyre-Thierry Bruneau 5tet feat. Richard Davis | Tribute | Serene Records | SER 02

Joys And Sorrows
Tom Van Der Geld Trio | Path | ECM | 1134

Joyspring(alt.take)
Clifford Brown-Max Roach Quintet | Brownie-The Complete EmArCy Recordings Of Clifford Brown | EmArCy | 838306-2
Max Roach-Clifford Brown Quintet | Daahoud | Mobile Fidelity | MFCD 826

J'rai Cracher Sur Vos Tombes
Jesse Davis Quintet | First Insight | Concord | CCD 4796

Juan E Il Cinque
Mongo Santamaria And His Orchestra | Live At Jazz Alley | Concord | CCD 4427

Juana Azurduy
Fritz Pauer Trio | City Blues | RST-Records | 91545-2

Juanita
Tino Tracanna Sextet | Mr. Frankenstein Blues | SPLASC(H) Records | H 158

Juarez
Barney Kessel Trio | Jellybeans | Concord | CJ 164

Juba Juba
John Carter Quintet | Night Fire | Black Saint | BSR 0047

Jubilation
Cannonball Adderley Quintet | Cannonball's Sharpshooters | Mercury | 826986-2 PMS
Edwin Hawkins Singers | The Best Of The Edwin Hawkins Singers | Warner | 252213-1
Oscar Peterson With Orchestra | A Royal Wedding Suite | Original Jazz Classics | OJCCD 973-2(2312129)
Randy Johnston Quintet | Jubilation | Muse | MCD 5495
Helmut Kagerer/Helmut Nieberle | Wes Trane | Edition Collage | EC 453-2

Jubilation-
Elliott Lawrence Orchestra | Jazz Goes Broadway | Fresh Sound Records | NL 45905(RCA Vik LX 1113)

Jubilation T. Cornepone
Allan Vaché's Florida Jazz Allstars | Allan Vaché's Floridy Jazz Allstars | Nagel-Heyer | CD 032

Jubilee
Bill Charlap Trio | Stardust | Blue Note | 535985-2
Bobby McFerrin Group | Bobby McFerrin | Elektra | 7559-60023-2
Bud Powell Trio | The Bud Powell Trio | Debut | VIJ 5002 IMS
Butch Miles-Howard Alden Sextet | Cookin' | Nagel-Heyer | CD 5003
Charlie Byrd Quintet | Du Hot Club De Concord | Concord | CCD 4674
Hank Crawford And His Orchestra | Roadhouse Symphony | Original Jazz Classics | OJCCD 1048-2(M 9140)
Harry James And His Orchestra | Harry James.His Orchestra And The Boogie Woogie Trio | Affinity | CD AFS 1009
Original Indiana Five | Original Indiana Five Vol.1 | Jazz Oracle | BDW 8019

Jubilee Stomp
Duke Ellington And His Orchestra | The Complete Duke Ellington-Vol. 1 | CBS | CBS 67264

Judo Mambo
Jimmy Smith Trio | Incredible Jimmy Smith Vol.3 | Blue Note | 300106(1525)

Judy
Art Tatum | Standards | Black Lion | CD 877646-2
Keith Ingham Sextet | A Star Dust Melody | Sackville | SKCD2-2051
Lew Stone And His Band | Lew Stone And His Band | Decca | DDV 5005/6 DT

Judy Full Grown
Herb Geller-Brian Kellock | Hollywood Portraits | Hep | CD 2078

Judy Garland
Hollywood Portraits | Hep | CD 2078

Judy Holliday
Keshavan Maslak With Charles Moffett | Blaster Master | Black Saint | BSR 0079

Jug Handle
Gene Ammons And His All Stars | The Big Sound | Prestige | P 24098

Jugandträume
Das Böse Ding | Germ Germ | Acoustic Music Records | 319.1160.2

Jugglers Parade
Dave Holland Quintet | Prime Directive | ECM | 1698(547950-2)
Steve Lacy Group | Nine Futurities-Part 1 | Hat Art | CD 6031

Jug's Jug
Babamadu | Babamadu | Enja | 9093-2

Juice A-Plenty
Paul Williams Orchestra | Paul Williams:The Complete Recordings Vol.2 (1949-1952) | Blue Moon | BMCD 6021

Juicy
Willie Bobo Group | Juicy | Verve | 519857-2
Fritz Münzer Tentet | Blue Ideas | Jazz 'n' Arts Records | 0200

Juicy Blues
Coleman Hawkins All Stars | The Hawk Flies High | Original Jazz Classics | OJC 027(R 12-223)

Juicy Lucy
Horace Silver Quintet | Finger Poppin' | Blue Note | 542304-2
Horace Silver Retrospective | Blue Note | 495576-2
Jeff Hamilton Trio | Hands On | Mons Records | MR 874812

Juicy(alt.take)
Fourplay | Heartfelt | RCA | 2663916-2

Juju
Jam Session | Jam Session Vol.4 | Steeplechase | SCCD 31527
Marcus Miller Group | The Sun Don't Lie | Dreyfus Jazz Line | FDM 36560-2
String Trio Of New York | Intermobility | Arabesque Recordings | AJ 0108
Wayne Shorter Quartet | Juju | Blue Note | 499005-2
Juju | Blue Note | 837644-2

Juju(alt.take)
Jay Leonhart-Mike Renzi | Salamander Pie | dmp Digital Music Productions | CD 442

Ju-Ju-Man
Little Walter | Heavy Heads | Chess | 6.24835 AS

Juke
The Stephen Barry Band | Blues Under A Full Moon | Blues Beacon | BLU-1009 2

Julia
Earl Hines And His Orchestra | The Indispensable Earl Hines Vol.3/4(1939-1945) | RCA | 2126408-2
Tommy Smith Quartet | Standards | Blue Note | 796452-2

Julian
Pepper Adams Quartet | Julian | Enja | 9115-2

Juliano
Julian Priester Quartet | Keep Swingin' | Original Jazz Classics | SMJ 6081

Julie
Leadbelly[Huddie Ledbetter] | Huddie Ledbetter | Fantasy | F 24715

Julie Is Her Name
Jack Sheldon And His Exciting All-Star Big Band | Jack's Groove | Fresh Sound Records | FSR 624(GNP 60)

Julien Dans L'Ascenseur
Barney Wilen With The Mal Waldron Trio | Movie Themes From France | Timeless | CD SJP 335

Julinho
Gebhard Ullmann-Andreas Willers | Playful '93 | Nabel Records:Jazz Network | CD 4659

Juliusstraße 25
Ullmann-Wille-Haynes | Trad Corrosion | Nabel Records:Jazz Network | CD 4673
Byron Stripling Sextet | Striplingnow! | Nagel-Heyer | CD 2002

Julliette's Holiday
Renaud Garcia-Fons Group | Oriental Bass | Enja | ENJ-9334 2

Jullundur
Al Di Meola Group | Soaring Through A Dream | Manhattan | CDP 7463372

July First
Nina Simone With Orchestra | Nina Simone-The 60s Vol.1: Ne Me Quitte Pas | Mercury | 838543-2 PMS

Jumbo The Elephant
Roy Eldridge Quintet | Rockin' Chair | Verve | MV 2686 IMS

Jump
Snooky Prior Group | Shake Your Boogie | Big Bear | 146406

Jump And Jive
Cozy Cole All Stars | Concerto For Cozy | Jazz Anthology | JA 5161

Jump City
Bud Powell Trio | Strictly Powell | RCA | 6351423-2

Jump Did-Le-Ba
Dizzy Gillespie And His Orchestra | Jazz Special-The Best Of Dizzy Gillespie | RCA | NL 89727 AG

Jump For Joy
Duke Ellington And His Orchestra | Duke Ellington Private Collection/Studio Sessions-Chicago 1956 | Music De Luxe Special | MSCD 22
Duke Ellington:Complete Studio Transcriptions | Definitive Records | DRCD 11199
Eddie Chamblee And His Orchestra | Eddie Chamblee:The Complete Recordings 1947-1952 | Blue Moon | BMCD 1049
Joe Williams,With The Oliver Nelson Orchestra | Jump For Joy | Bluebird | 63 52713-2

Jump For Joy-
Tommy Flanagan 3 | The Montreux '77 Collection | Pablo | 2620107

Jump Lester J
Lester Young Quintet | The Art Of Saxophone | Laserlight | 24652

Jump Lester Jump
Lester Young:The Complete 1936-1951 Small Group Sessions(Studio Recordings-Master Takes),Vol.3 | Blue Moon | BMCD 1003
Lester Young With The Count Basie Quartet | Lester Young Master Takes | Savoy | SV 0250(SJL 1133)

Jump Monk
Charles Mingus Quintet | Charles Mingus-The Complete Debut Recordings | Debut | 12 DCD 4402-2
Thirteen Pictures:The Charles Mingus Anthology | Rhino | R2 71402

Jump Monk(alt.take)
Charles Mingus-The Complete Debut Recordings | Debut | 12 DCD 4402-2
Wingy Mannone And His Orchestra | Chu Berry: Berry Story | Zeta | ZET 738

Jump Over! And Join The Party
Charlie Barnet And His Orchestra | The Indispensable Charlie Barnet Vol.1/2 | RCA | 2135554-2

Jump That's All
Jay McShann And His Orchestra | Early Bird | Spotlite | SPJ 120

Jump The Blues Away
Luke Jones With Joe Alexander's Highlanders | Luke Jones:The Complete Recordings 1946-1949 | Blue Moon | BMCD 6012

Jump To Dive
Jimmy Lyons/Sunny Murray Trio | Jump Up | Hat Art | CD 6139

Jumper
Jo Jo Jackson & His Jumpin' Jivers | Lem Johnson-Doc Sausage-Jo Jo Jackson | Blue Moon | BMCD 6004

Jumpin' At Capitol
Nat King Cole Trio | The Great Nat King Cole | Laserlight | 15733
Papa Bue's Viking Jazzband | At The CCP Main Theater Manila, Philippines | V-King Records | VLP 100

Jumpin' At Mesners
Lester Young And His Band | Lester Young:The Complete 1936-1951 Small Group Sessions(Studio Recordings-Master Takes),Vol.3 | Blue Moon | BMCD 1003

Jumpin' At The Badewanne
Erroll Garner Quartet | Yesterdays | Savoy | SV 0244(SJL 1118)

Jumpin' At The Lochness
Paul Kuhn Quintet | Deutsches Jazz Fesival 1954/1955 | Bear Family Records | BCD 15430

Jumpin' At The Rosengarten
Al Cooper And His Savoy Sultans | Big Band Bounce & Boogie:Jump Steady | Affinity | AFS 1009

Jumpin' At The Woodside
Arnett Cobb Quartet | Funky Butt | Progressive | PRO 7054 IMS
Benny Goodman And His Orchestra | The Hits Of Benny Goodman | Capitol | 791212-2
Great Swing Classics In Hi-Fi | Capitol | 521223-2
Benny Waters Sextet | When You're Smiling | Hep | CD 2010
Buddy Tate With The Torsten Zwingenberger Trio | Buddy Tate Meets Torsten Zwingenberger | Moustache Music | 120159
Concord All Stars | Tour De Force | Concord | CCD 4172
Count Basie And His Orchestra | Americans In Sweden: Roy Eldridge 1957-Count Basie 1954 | Jazz Society | AA 514
Live! | Laserlight | 15797
Birdland All Stars At Carnegie Hall | Roulette | CDP 798660-2
Count Basie Big Band | Farmers Market Barbecue | Original Jazz Classics | OJCCD 732-2(2310874)
The Montreux '77 Collection | Pablo | 2620107
Count Basie Jam | Montreux '77-The Art Of The Jam Session | Pablo | 2620106

Count Basie-Oscar Peterson Quintet | Jazz Dance | Original Jazz Classics | OJCCD 1002-2(1210890)
Duke Ellington And Count Basie With Their Orchestras | First Time! | CBS | CK 65571
Earl Bostic And His Orchestra | Bostic Rocks Hits Of The Swing Age | Swingtime(Contact) | ST 1022
Hot Mallets | Hot Mallets...Live | Jazzcharge | JC 8302
Jay McShann And His Orchestra | Atlantic Jazz: Kansas City | Atlantic | 7567-81701-2
Jay McShann Orchestra | The Last Of The Blue Devils | Atlantic | 7567-80791-2
Jay McShann Quartet | The Man From Muskogee | Sackville | SKCD2-3005
Lambert, Hendricks And Bavan | Havin' A Ball-Live At The Village Gate | RCA | 2122111-2
Lester Young Quintet | Lester Swings | Verve | 2683066 IMS
Paul Kuhn And The SDR Big Band | Swingtime-The Original Arrangements-2 | L+R Records | CDLR 40031
Ted Heath And His Orchestra | Swing Is King | Decca | 6.28129 DP
Terry Lightfoot And His Band | Stardust | Upbeat Jazz | URCD 104
The Buck Clayton Legacy | All The Cats Join In(Buck Clayton Remembered) | Nagel-Heyer | CD 006
Encore Live | Nagel-Heyer | CD 018
The Dave Glasser/Clark Terry/Barry Harris Project | Uh! Oh! | Nagel-Heyer | CD 2003
The Sunshine Terrace Swing Band | Swinging In A New Mood | Vagabond | 6.22997 AS
The Yamaha International Allstar Band | Hapy Birthday Jazzwelle Plus | Nagel-Heyer | CD 005
Warren Vaché And The New York City All-Star Big Band | Swingtime! | Nagel-Heyer | CD 059
WDR Big Band | Harlem Story | Koala Records | CD P 7

Jumpin' At The Woodside(alt.take)
Dexter Gordon Quartet | Dexter Gordon:Atlanta Georgia May 5,1981 | Storyville | STCD 8363

Jumpin' Blues
American Classic | Discovery | 71009-2

Jumpin' Gemini
Gordon Lee Quartet feat. Jim Pepper | Landwhales In New York | Tutu Records | 888136-2*
Jim Pepper Quartet | Dakota Song | Enja | 5043-2

Jumpin' In
Jimi Sumen Group | Paintbrush,Rock Penstemon | CMP Records | CMP CD 61

Jumpin' Jane
Count Basie And His Orchestra | Los Angeles 1945/New York 1946 | Jazz Anthology | JA 5147

Jumpin' Kalushary
Leo Parker Sextet | Rollin' With Leo | Blue Note | LT 1076

Jumpin' Off
Chet Baker Quintet | Chet Baker & Crew | Pacific Jazz | 582671-2

Jumpin' Off A Clef
Chet Baker Sextet | The Best Of Chet Baker Plays | Pacific Jazz | 797161-2
Chet Baker Quintet | Cools Out | Ace Records | CDBOP 013

Jumpin' Punkins
Dick Wellstood | Diane | Swingtime | 8207
Duke Ellington And His Famous Orchestra | Duke Ellington & His Famous Orchestra | Forlane | UCD 19003
Duke Ellington And His Orchestra | Big Band Bounce And Boogie:Classic Transcriptions-Duke Ellington | Affinity | AFS 1032
Dick Wellstood | Live at The Sticky Wicket | Arbors Records | ARCD 19188

Jumpin' The Blues
Jay McShann Orchestra | The Big Apple Bash | Atlantic | 90047-1 TIS
Jimmy McGriff Orchestra | Jimmy McGriff-Funkiest Little Band In The Kand | LRC Records | CDC 9046(874379)
Ray Brown All Stars | Don't Forget The Blues | Concord | MC CJ 293C

Jumpin' With Symphony Sid
Benny Harris Orchestra | New York All Star Sessions | Bandstand | BDCD 1507
Buddy Tate Quintet | Broadway | Black & Blue | BLE 233054
Dizzy Gillespie And His Orchestra | Dizzier And Dizzier | RCA | 26685172
Dizzy Gillespie (1946-1949) | RCA | ND 89763
George Benson Quartet + Guests | The George Benson Cookbook | CBS | 502470-2
George Shearing Quintet | Jazz-Club: Vibraphone | Verve | 840034-2
George Shearing Quintet/With Strings/Latin Mood | The Best Of George Shearing-All Time Shearing Favorites | Capitol | SM 2104
Jam Session | Coleman Hawkins-Rare Broadcasts Area 1950 | Jazz Anthology | JA 5217
Jubilee All Stars | Jazz Gallery:Lester Young Vol.2(1946-59) | RCA | 2119541-2
King Pleasure And His Band | Annie Ross & King Pleasure Sings | Original Jazz Classics | OJC 217(P 7128)
Lester Young And His Band | Lester Young:The Complete Aladdin Sessions | Blue Note | 832787-2
Lester Young:The Complete 1936-1951 Small Group Sessions(Studio Recordings-Master Takes),Vol.4 | Blue Moon | BMCD 1004
Lester Young Quartet | Live Recordings In New York City | Jazz Anthology | JA 5174
Oscar Peterson-Major Holley Duo | Keyboard Music By Oscar Peterson | Verve | MV 2666 IMS
Stan Getz Quintet | Jazz At Storyville Vol.2 | Fresh Sound Records | FSR 630(Roost RLP 411)
Wild Bill Davis Group | Americans Swinging In Paris:Wild Bill Davis | EMI Records | 539665-2
Willis Jackson Quintet | Soul Night Live! | Prestige | PRCD 24273-2
Charlie Parker All Stars | Charlie Parker 1950-1951:The Complete Bird At Birdland Vol.1 | Fat Boy Jazz | FBB 901

Jumping Jack
Inga Rumpf With The NDR Big Band | It's A Man's World | Extra Records & Tapes | 800860

Jump'n Jive,Still Alive
Copenhagen Art Ensemble | Angels' Share | dacapo | DCCD 9452

Jumps
Franco D'Andrea Trio | Airegin | Red Records | 123252-2

Jumpstart
Gunter Hampel And His Galaxie Dream Band | A Place To Be With Us | Birth | 0032

Jumpy Nerves
Piano Connection | Boogie Woogie & Blues | Elite Special | 73434

Junco Partner
Professor Longhair Group | Rock'n Roll Gumbo | Verve | 519746-2

Junction:
Gerry Hemingway Quintet | Outerbridge Crossing | Sound Aspects | sas CD 017

June In January
Benny Carter Trio | 3,4,5 The Verve Small Group Sessions | Verve | 849395-2 PMS
Montgomery Brothers | Groove Brothers | Milestone | M 47051

June Is Busting Out All Over
Bill Holman And His Orchestra | Great Big Band | Fresh Sound Records | T 1464(Capitol)

June Is Busting Out All Over(alt.take)
Allan Vaché Sextette | Swing And Other Things | Arbors Records | ARCD 19171

June Spleen
Louis Jordan And His Tympany Five | Louis Jordan-Let The Good Times Roll: The Complete Decca Recordings 1938-1954 | Bear Family Records | BCD 15557 IH

June Tenth Jamboree
David Newton Trio | In Good Company | Candid | CCD 79714

June(2002)
Andy Lumpp | Andy Lump Piano Solo | Nabel Records:Jazz Network | LP 4608(Audiophile)

Jungle
Five + Jazz Comfort | Brazz | Memo Music | MM 6061

Jungle-
Irene Schweizer | Many And One Direction | Intakt Records | CD 044

Jungle Blues
Jelly Roll Morton | The Library Of Congress Recordings | Affinity | CD AFS 1010-3
Jelly Roll Morton's Red Hot Peppers | Doctor Jazz | Black & Blue | BLE 59.227 2
The Complete Jelly Roll Morton-Vol.1/2 | RCA | ND 89768

Jungle Cowboy
Jimmy Giuffre-Paul Bley-Steve Swallow | Conversations With A Goose | Soul Note | 121258-2

Jungle Drums
Yusef Lateef Orchestra | The Centaur And The Phoenix | Original Jazz Classics | OJCCD 721-2(RLP 9337)

Jungle Fantasy
Yusef Lateef Sextet With Voices | The Many Faces Of Yusef Lateef | Milestone | M 47009

Jungle Groove
Laurent De Wilde Sextet | Time Change | Warner | 8573-84315-2

Jungle Hard Bop
The Harlem Footwarmers | The Complete Duke Ellington-Vol. 2 | CBS | CBS 68275

Jungle Kitty
Gene Krupa And His Orchestra | Jazz Drumming Vol.5(1940) | Fenn Music | FJD 2705

Jungle Night
Duke Ellington And His Cotton Club Orchestra | Victor Jazz History Vol.6:Harlem Jazz(1928-33) | RCA | 2128560-2

Jungle Nights In Harlem
Duke Ellington And His Orchestra | Jazz Giants:Duke Ellington | RCA | NL 45179 SI
Browning And Starr | Curtis Mosby And Henry Star | Jazz Oracle | BDW 8003

Jungle Of My Life
Buddy Collette Quintet | Man Of Many Parts | Original Jazz Classics | OJCCD 239-2(C 3522)

Jungle Song
Gene Ammons Quintet | Greatest Hits | Prestige | P 10084

Jungle Strut
Ron Holloway Group | Struttin' | Milestone | MCD 9238-2

Jungle Town Jubilee
Ray Bryant | Montreux '77 | Original Jazz Classics | OJC 371(2308201)

Jungoso
Sonny Rollins Quintet | Sonny Rollins & Co.Vol.3:What's New/Vol.4:Our Man In Jazz | RCA | 741091/92

Junifl
Clark Terry With Bob Lark And The DePaul University Big Band | Clark Terry Express | Reference Recordings | RR-73 CD

Junimond
Bob Berg Group | Short Stories | Denon Compact Disc | CY-1768

Junior
Louis Jordan And His Tympany Five | Louis Jordan And His Tympany Five 1944-1945 | Circle | CCD-53

Junior Hop-
Duke Ellington And His Orchestra | Duke Ellington:Complete Prestige Carnegie Hall 1946-1947 Concerts | Definitive Records | DRCD 11211

Junk Blues
Joe Henderson Quartet | Joe Henderson:The Milestone Years | Milestone | 8MCD 4413-2
Steve Lacy Sextet | Songs | Hat Art | CD 6045

Junk Man
The Spirits Of Rhythm | Spirit Of Rhythm 1932-34 | Retrieval | RTR 79004

Junka
Sonny Clark Trio | Blues Mambo | West Wind | WW 2103

Junkanoo
Champion Jack Dupree Quintet | Blues Power No.8:Champion Jack Dupree - Blues From The Gutter | Atlantic | 40526

Jupiter
Jerry Bergonzi Quartet | Inside Out | Red Records | 123230-2
The Errol Parker Experience | Baobab | Sahara | 1008

Jupiter-
Paul Horn Group | Jupiter 8 | Golden Flute Records | GFR 2004

Jupiter(Variation)
John Coltrane-Rashied Ali Duo | The Mastery Of John Coltrane Vol.3:Jupiter Variations | MCA | 2292-54649-2

Jupiter's Child
Hein Känzig Quartet | Awakening | L+R Records | CDLR 45067

Jurasic Park
George Mraz Quartet | Morava | Milestone | MCD 9309-2

Jurenko,Jurenko
Kixx | Kixx | ITM Records | 0013

Juriki
Peter Leitch-Heiner Franz | At First Sight | Jardis Records | JRCD 9611

Juris Blues
Joe Gilman Trio | Treasure Chest | Timeless | CD SJP 346

Just 40 Bars
The Herdsmen | The Herdsmen Play Paris | Original Jazz Classics | OJC 116(F 3201)

Just A Ballad For Woody
Art Kassel And His 'Kassels-In-The-Air' Orchestra | The Uncollected:Art Kassel, Vol.2 | Hindsight | HSR 170

Just A Blues
Lee Konitz-Martial Solal Duo | Live At The Berlin Jazz Days 1980 | MPS | 68289
Harry Connick Jr. Quartet | We Are In Love | CBS | 466736-2

Just A Boy
String Thing | String Thing:Alles Wird Gut | MicNic Records | MN 2

Just A Cappuccino
Bill Perkins Quintet | Quietly There | Original Jazz Classics | OJCCD 1776-2

Just A Child
Stan Getz Quartet | Stan Getz At Large Plus!,Vol.2 | Jazz Unlimited | JUCD 2002

Just A Closer Walk With Thee
Art Hodes-Jim Galloway | Live From Toronto's Cafe Des Copains | Music & Arts | CD 610
Dejan's Olympia Brass Band | Here Come Da Great Olympia Band | Preservation Hall | VPS-4
Earl Hines And His Band | A Monday Date | Original Jazz Classics | OJCCD 1740-2(RLP 9398)
George Lewis And His New Orleans Stompers | George Lewis And His New Orleans Stompers-Vol. 2 | Blue Note | 81206
Hampton Hawes Trio | The Sermon | Original Jazz Classics | OJCCD 1067-2(C 7653)
Henry Red Allen Sextet | Swing Trumpet Kings:Harry Edison Swings Buck Clayton And Vice Versa/Red Allen Plays King Oliver/Swing Goes Dixie | Verve | 533263-2
Jim Beebe's Chicago Jazz | A Sultry Serenade | Delmark | DE 230
John Handy's Louisiana Shakers | John Handy-The Very First Recordings | American Music | AMCD-51
Ken Colyer's Omega Brass Band | Marching Back To New Orleans | Lake | LACD 21
Magnificant Seventh's Brass Band | Authentic New Orleans Jazz Funeral | Mardi Gras Records | MG 1012
Stars Of Jazz | Stars Of Jazz Vol.1 | Jazzology | JCD-62

Just A Day
Alex Merck & Painted Birds | Minds And Bodies | yvp music | 3003(Demon)

Just A Dream
Jimmy Witherspoon With The Ben Webster Quintet | That's Jazz Vol.30: Jimmy Witherspoon & Ben Webster | Warner | WB 56295

Just A Few
Bud Shank Quintet | Jazz In Hollywood:Bud Shank/Lou Levy | Original Jazz Classics | OJCCD 1890-2(Nocturne NLP-2/NLP-10)

Just A Gigolo
Coleman Hawkins Quintet | The Hawk Relaxes | Original Jazz Classics | OJCCD 709-2(MV 15)
Connie Francis With Orchestra | The Swinging Connie Francis | Audiophile | ACD-286
Oscar Peterson | Gitanes Jazz 'Round Midnight: Oscar Peterson | Verve | 511036-2 PMS
Papa Bue's Viking Jazzband | The Golden Years Of Revival Jazz,Vol.14 | Storyville | STCD 5519
Ralph Flanagan And His Orchestra | Dance Again Part 2 | Magic | DAWE 75
Thelonious Monk | Monk's Dream | CBS | CK 63536
Thelonious Monk:85th Birthday Celebration | zyx records | FANCD 6076-2
Live In Stockholm 1961 | Dragon | DRLP 151/152
Thelonious Monk:The Complete Prestige Recordings | Prestige | 3 PRCD 4428-2
The Prestige Legacy Vol.1:The High Priests | Prestige | PCD 24251-2
Thelonious Monk-The Complete Riverside Recordings | Riverside | 15 RCD 022-2
April In Paris | Milestone | M 47060
Thelonious Monk Quartet | The Paris Concert | Charly | CD 74

Just A Little
Little Milton And His Band | Little Milton | Chess | 427013

Just A Little Bit
The Ford Blues Band | Hotshots | Crosscut | CCD 11041

Just A Little Bit North Of South Carolina
Freddy Martin And His Orchestra | The Uncollected:Freddy Martin | Hindsight | HSR 151

Just A Little Kiss
B.B.King And His Band | Completely Live And Well | Charly | CDX 14

Just A Little Lovin'
Belgian All Stars Big Band feat. Benny Bailey & 'Toots' Thielemans | Changing Moods-The Music Of Gastry Meyer | B.Sharp Records | CDS 091

Just A Little While To Stay Here
Sweet Emma Barrett Jazz Band | Sweet Emma Barrett And Her New Orleans Music | GHB Records | BCD 141

Just A Memory
Mike Melillo | Live And Well | Red Records | VPA 188

Just A Minute
Count Basie And His Orchestra | Count Basie-Basie's Basement | RCA | ???
Jazz:The Essential Collection Vol.3 | IN+OUT Records | 78013-2
David Qualey | Talking Hands:Live | ALISO Records | AL 1021

Just A Moment
Eberhard Weber | Orchestra | ECM | 1374
Joe Gallardo's Latino Blue | A Latin Shade Of Blue | Enja | ENJ-9421 2
Roman Schwaller-Mel Lewis Sextet | Roman Schwaller-Mel Lewis | Bassic-Sound | CD 005

Just A Mood
Willie Lewis And His Entertainers | Le Jazz En France Vol.3 | Pathe | 1727271

Just A Piece Of Cake
Ganelin Trio | Con Fuoco | LEO | LR 106

Just A Quickie
Henk De Jonge Trio With Willem Breuker | Henk De Jonge Trio | BVHAAST | 058

Just A Riff
Big Sid Catlett Quartet With Ben Webster | Sax Scene | London | HMC 5004 AN

Just A Second To Catch My Breath
McKinney's Cotton Pickers | McKinney's Cotton Pickers (1928-1930)-The Band Don Redman Built | RCA | ND 90517(874152)

Just A Tune
Dave Holland - Barre Phillips | Music For Two Basses | ECM | 1011

Just About Crazy
Gregorio-Gustafsson-Nordeson | Background Music | HatOLOGY | 526

Just An Illusion
Clark Terry Quartet | OW | Storyville | STCD 8378

Just An Old Manuscript
Clark Terry-Bob Brookmeyer Quintet | The Power Of Positive Swinging | Mainstream | JK 57117
Count Basie And His Orchestra | The Indispensable Count Basie | RCA | ND 89758
Rosemary Galloway's Swing Sisters | You're A Sweetheart | Sackville | SKCD2-2038

Just Another Blues
Nat King Cole Trio | The Early Forties | Fresh Sound Records | FSR-CD 0139

Just Another Lullaby
Ella Fitzgerald With The Nelson Riddle Orchestra | Ella Sings Gershwin-Vol. 1 | Metro | 2682004 IMS

Just Another Sunday
Alex Gunia's Groove Cut | Alex Gunia's Groove Cut | ITM Records | ITM 1463

Just Arrived
Henry Kaiser-Jim O'Rourke | Tomorrow Knows Where You Live | Victo | CD 014

Just As I Am
Mahalia Jackson | Welcome To Europe | CBS | SPR 32

Just As I Am Without One Plea-
Claude Hopkins And His Orchestra | Harlem 1935 | Jazz Anthology | JA 5156

Just As Someone
Cousin Joe And His Quintet | Cousin Joe From New Orleans In His Prime | Oldie Blues | OL 8008

Just As Though You Were Here
Tommy Dorsey And His Orchestra | Frank Sinatra And The Tommy Dorsey Orchestra | RCA | 2668701-2
Forever | RCA | NL 89859 DP

Just A-Sittin' And A-Rockin'
Art Tatum | The Tatum Solo Masterpieces Vol. 1 | Pablo | 2310723
Chris Barber's Jazz Band | The Great Re-Union Concert | Intercord | 157011
Duke Ellington And His Famous Orchestra | Victor Jazz History Vol.12:Ellingtonia | RCA | 2135731-2
Duke Ellington And His Orchestra | The Best Of Duke Ellington | Capitol | 831501-2
The Jazz Giants Play Duke Ellington:Caravan | Prestige | PCD 24227-2
En Concert Avec Europe 1 | Laserlight | 710433/34
A True Collectors Item | Jazz Archive | 90.105-2
Duke Ellington Trio | Legends Of The 20th Century | EMI Records | 522048-2
Ella Fitzgerald And Her All Stars | The Complete Ella Fitzgerald Song Books of Harold Arlen, Irving Berlin, Duke Ellington, George & Ira Gershwin, Jerome Kern, Johnny Mercer, Cole Porter And Rogers & Hart | Verve | 519832-2
Ella Fitzgerald With The Count Basie Orchestra | A Classy Pair | Pablo | 2312132-2
Joe Williams With The Jimmy Jones Orchestra | Planet Jazz:Joe Williams | Planet Jazz | 2165370-2
Jump For Joy | Bluebird | 63 52713-2
June Christy With The Pete Rugolo Orchestra | June Christy Recalls Those Kenton Days | EMI Records | 1599311
Kenny Burrell | Night Song | Verve | 2304539 IMS
Oscar Peterson Trio | Oscar Peterson Plays The Duke Ellington Song Book | Verve | 559785-2
Oscar Peterson Plays The Duke Ellington Song Book | Verve | 559785-2
Paul Gonsalves Quintet | Three Tenors | Jazz Colours | 874706-2
Scott Hamilton Quartet | Organic Duke | Concord | CCD 4623
Stan Kenton And His Orchestra | Artistry In Rhythm | Creative World | ST 1043

Just Because
Ray Charles With Orchestra | Ain't It So | London | 6.23864 AP

Just Before Dawn
Marion Meadows Group | For Lovers Only | Novus | PD 83097

Just Before Daybreak
Jesse Price And His Jump Jivers | Swingin' Small Combos Kansas City Style Vol.1 | Blue Moon | BMCD 6019

Just Before The Breath Of Day
Christina Nielsen Quintet | From This Time Forward | Stunt Records | STUCD 19503

Just Buddy's
Mark Soskin Trio | Views From Here | Paddle Wheel | KICJ 126

Just By Myself
Benny Golson Band | Benny Golson's New York Scene | Contemporary | C 3552

Just Comming Home
Art Blakey And The Jazz Messengers | At The Jazz Corner Of The World Vol. 1 | Blue Note | 868364-8

Just Cooling
Lester Young Sextet | Lester Young:The Complete 1936-1951 Small Group Sessions(Studio Recordings-Master Takes),Vol.4 | Blue Moon | BMCD 1004

Just Don't
Lightnin' Hopkins | Lightnin' Hopkins Strums The Blues | Pathe | 2C 068-83076(Score)

Just Don't Go
Marlena Shaw With Orchestra | From The Depths Of My Soul | Blue Note | 84443

Just Dropped By
Kenwood Dennard Quintet | Just Advance | Big World | BW 2006

Just For A Thrill
Keith Ingham Sextet | A Mellow Bit Of Rhythm | Sackville | SKCD2-3063
Lou Donaldson Quintet | Pretty Things | Blue Note | 789794-2
Peggy Lee With Orchestra | The Basin Street Proudly Presents Peggy Lee | Capitol | 832744-2

Just For Fun
Jay McShann Quintet | What A Wonderful World | Groove Note | GRV 1005-2
Pierre Guyonnet Onzetetes | Joue | Plainisphare | PAV 809

Just For Fun-K
John Handy Group | Musical Dreamland | Boulevard | BLD 515 CD

Just For Me
Junior Wells Blues Band | Pleading The Blues | Black & Blue | BLE 59.901 2

Just For Now
Joe Locke Quartet | Longing | Steeplechase | SCCD 31281
Montgomery Brothers | Groove Brothers | Milestone | M 47051
The Montgomery Brothers | Wes Montgomery-The Complete Riverside Recordings | Riverside | 12 RCD 4408-2
Urbie Green His Trombone And Rhythm | The Best Of New Broadway Show Hits | Fresh Sound Records | NL 45907(RCA LPM 1969)

Just For The Love
Pat Martino Quartet | Interchange | Muse | MCD 5529

Just For You
Deborah Henson-Conant Trio | Just For You | Laika Records | LK 95-063
Dolf De Vries Trio | Where's That Rainy Day | Limetree | MLP 0019
Jay McShann Quartet | Goin' To Kansas City | Stony Plain | SPCD 1286
Ornette Coleman Quartet | Beauty Is A Rare Thing:Ornette Coleman-The Complete Atlantic Recordings | Atlantic | 8122-71410-2
Pete Johnson | Boogie Woogie Mood | MCA | 1333

Just Friends
Anthony Braxton | Wesleyan(12 Altosolos) 1992 | Hat Art | CD 6128
Billie Holiday With Jimmy Rowles | Billie Holiday In Rehersal | Mobile Fidelity | MFCD 840
Buddy DeFranco Quartet Feat. Martin Taylor | On Tour-UK | Hep | 2023
Charlie Parker With Strings | Bird With Strings-Live At The Apollo, Carnegie Hall & Birdland | CBS | CBS 82292
Compact Jazz: Charlie Parker | Verve | 833268-2
Charlie Parker:The Best Of The Verve Years | Verve | 527815-2
Bird's Eyes-Last Unissued Vol.1 | Philology | 214 W 5
Chet Baker Quartet | Let's Get Lost: The Best Of Chet Baker Sings | Pacific Jazz | 792932-2
Chet Baker | Carlyne | 695015
Chet Baker-Stan Getz Quintet | The Stockholm Concerts | Verve | 537555-2
Clark Terry With The Summit Jazz Orchestra | Clark | Edition Collage | EC 530-2
Claude Tissendier Saxomania | Saxomania | OMD | CD 1522
Dee Dee Bridgewater With Her Trio | Dee Dee Bridgewater In Montreux | Polydor | 847913-2
Dexter Gordon Quartet | Stable Mable | Steeplechase | SCS 1040
Eddie Lockjaw Davis Quartet | Eddie 'Lockjaw' Davis/Sonny Stitt | LRC Records | CDC 9028
George Cables Trio | Cables Fables | Steeplechase | SCCD 31287
Harry Edison Sextet | Swing Summit | Candid | CCD 79050
Harry Edison-Eddie Lockjaw Davis Quintet | Light And Lovely | Black & Blue | BB 883.2
Jimmy Smith All Stars | House Party | Blue Note | 524542-2
Jimmy Smith Trio | Groovin' At Smalls' Paradise | Blue Note | 499777-2
Groovin' At Smalls' Paradise Vol.2 | Blue Note | 300222(1586)
Joe Pass | I Remember Charlie Parker | Original Jazz Classics | OJC 602(2312109)
Joe Pass Quartet | The Complete 'Catch Me' Sessions | Blue Note | LT 1053
Joe Williams With The Norman Simmons Quartet And Supersax | In Good Company | Verve | 837932-2
Kenny Dorham Sextet | Soul Support | Jazz Colours | 874756-2
Mary Osborne Trio | Now And Then | Stash Records | ST 215 IMS
Nat Pierce-Irving Stokes | My Pal Basie | Jazz Connaisseur | JCCD 8904-2
Nueva Manteca | Varadero Blues | Timeless | CD SJP 318
Oscar Peterson Trio | Walking The Line | MPS | 68082
Paul Chambers Quintet | Paul Chambers/Go | Vee Jay Recordings | VJ 017
Phil Woods Quartet | Ornithology:Phil Salutes Bird | Philology | W 69.2
Sam Jones Septet | The Soul Society | Original Jazz Classics | OJCCD 1789-2(RLP 1172)
Sarah Vaughan And The Count Basie Orchestra | Send In The Clowns | Pablo | 2312130-2
Singers Unlimited With Orchestra | Friends | MPS | 821286-1
Sonny Rollins & Co. | Sonny Rollins-All The Things You Are (1963-1964) | Bluebird | ND 82179
Sonny Rollins-Coleman Hawkins Quintet | The Complete Sonny Rollins RCA Victor Recordings | RCA | 2668675-2
Sonny Stitt Quartet | Saxophone Supremacy | Verve | MV 2687 IMS
Sonny Stitt-Red Holloway Quintet | Just Friends | Affinity | AFF 51
The New Stan Tracy Quartet | For Heaven's Sake | Cadillac | SGCCD 04
The Trumpet Summit With The Oscar Peterson Big 4 | The Trumpet Summit Meets The Oscar Peterson Big 4 | Original Jazz Classics | OJCCD 603-2
Tony Bennett With The Stan Getz Quartet | Singin' Till The Girls Come Home | CBS | FC 38508
Werner Lener Quartet | My Own | Satin Doll Productions | SDP 1013-1 CD
Wes Montgomery Quintet | Straight No Chaser | Bandstand | BDCD 1504

Just Friends-
Sonny Rollins Quintet | Sonny Rollins Plays For Bird | Original Jazz Classics | OJCCD 214-2
Chet Baker-Stan Getz Quintet | The Stockholm Concerts | Verve | 537555-2

Just Friends(2)
Charlie Parker Quintet | Charlie Parker At Birdland And Cafe Society | Cool & Blue | C&B-CD 108

Just Going On
Barrelhouse Jazzband | The Barrelhouse Jazzband Plays King Oliver | L+R Records | CDLR 40028

Just In Time
Antonio Farao Trio | Black Inside | Enja | ENJ-9345 2
Azymuth feat. Jürgen Seefelder | Volta á Turma | West Wind Latina | 2206 CD
Booker Ervin Quintet | Exultation! | Original Jazz Classics | OJCCD 835-2(P 7293)
Carmel Jones Quintet | Jay Hawk Talk | Original Jazz Classics | OJCCD 1938-2(P7401)
Cedar Walton | Blues For Myself | Red Records | NS 205
Eddie Higgins Trio | Portrait In Black And White | Sunnyside | SSC 1072 D
Gene Ammons-Sonny Stitt Quintet | Left Bank Encores | Prestige | PRCD 11022-2
George Van Eps-Howard Alden Quartet | Hand-Crafted Swing | Concord | CCD 4513
Jimmy Slyde With The Milt Buckner Trio | Special Tap Dance-Four Dancing Masters | Black & Blue | BLE 191652
Keith Jarrett Trio | Standards In Norway | ECM | 1542(521717-2)
Kenny Clarke-Francy Boland Big Band | More Smiles | MPS | 9814789
Kevin Mahogany With The James Williams Trio And Benny Golson | You Got What It Takes | Enja | ENJ-9039 2
Lucie Arnaz And Her Orchestra | Just In Time | Concord | CCD 4573
Oscar Peterson Trio | Verve Jazz Masters 37:Oscar Peterson Plays Broadway | Verve | 516893-2
A Jazz Portrait Of Frank Sinatra | Verve | 825769-2
Patty Peterson Group | The More I See You | Jazz Pure Collection | AU 31614 CD
Slide Hampton Quintet | Roots | Criss Cross | Criss 1015
Sonny Rollins Quartet | Sonny Rollins-The Freelance Years:The Complete Riverside & Contemporary Recordings | Riverside | 5 RCD 4427-2
Sonny Rollins:Brown Skin Girl | Memo Music | HDJ 4041
Tommy Flanagan Trio | The Magnificent Tommy Flanagan | Progressive | PCD 7059

Just In Time(long take)
Michiel Borstlap Sextet | Michiel Borstlap:The Sextet Live! | Challenge | CHR 70030

Just In Tune
John Abercrombie-Jarek Smietana Quartet | Speak Easy | PAO Records | PAO 10610

Just Jivin' Around
Horace Parlan Quintet | Arrival | Steeplechase | SCCD 31012

Just Kiddin'
Artie Shaw And His Orchestra | The Indispensable Artie Shaw Vol.3/4 | RCA | 2126414-2

Just Knock On My Door
Memphis Slim | Memphis Slim USA | Candid | CCD 79024

Just Let Me Be
Ian Shaw With Band | The Echo Of A Song | Ronnie Scott's Jazz House | JHCD 048

Just Like A Butterfly
Art Tatum | Art Tatum:20th Century Piano Genius | Verve | 531763-2
The Tatum Solo Masterpieces Vol.12 | Pablo | 2310870
Teddy Wilson | Everytime We Say Goodbye | Musicraft | MSVCD-59

Just Like Livin'
Alvin Batiste Ensemble | Musique D'Afrique Nouvelle Orleans | India Navigation | IN 1064

Just Like That
Fred Wesley Group | Comme Ca | Minor Music | 801020

Just Like The Day
Betty Carter And Her Quartet | Look What I Got! | Verve | 835661-2 PMS

Just Married Today
Max Bennett Quintet | Max Bennett Plays | Fresh Sound Records | FSR 2015(Bethlehem BCP 50)

Just Me And My Telefone
John Lee Hooker | Blues Roots Vol. 13: John Lee Hooker | Chess | 6.24803 AG

Just Missed The 'A'-Train
Luther Allison Blues Band | Let's Try It Again-Live 89 | TIS | LACD 1989-2

Just My Imagination
Larry Carlton Group | Kid Gloves | GRP | GRP 96832

Just One Hour
Dixie Hummingbirds | Live | Mobile Fidelity | MFCD 771

Just One More Chance
Dinah Washington With The Ike Carpenter Orchestra | The Complete Dinah Washington Vol.7 | Official | 3018

Just One Of Those Things
Al Haig Trio | The Piano Collection Vol.2 | Vogue | 21610222
Andy LaVerne Trio | Standard Eyes | Steeplechase | SCCD 31280
Art Blakey And The Jazz Messengers | The Jazz Messengers At The Cafe Bohemia Vol. 2 | Blue Note | 300088(1508)
At The Cafe Bohemia Vol.3 | Blue Note | 300193(BNJ 61007)
Art Tatum Trio | Art Tatum:Complete Capitol Recordings | Definitive Records | DRCD 11192
The Tatum Group Masterpieces | Pablo | 2310735-2
Bernd Lhotzky-Colin Dawson | Sophisticated | ART BY HEART | ABH 2003 2
Bill Evans Quartet | Modern Days & Night:Music Of Cole Porter | Double Time Records | DTRCD-120
Billie Holiday And Her Orchestra | Embraceable You | Verve | 817359-1 IMS
Bob Mover Quintet | You Go To My Head | Jazz City | 660.53.013
Branford Marsalis Quartet | Renaissance | CBS | 460229-2
Bud Powell | The Genius Of Bud Powell | Verve | 827901-2 PMS
Bud Powell Trio | The Return Of Bud Powell | Fresh Sound Records | FSR 545(Roulette R 52115)
Cannonball Adderley Quintet | Cannonball And Eight Giants | Milestone | M 47001
Cannonball Adderley-Milt Jackson Quintet | Cannonball Adderley Birthday Celebration | Fantasy | FANCD 6087-2
Carmen Cavallaro And His Orchestra | The Uncollected: Carmen Cavallaro | Hindsight | HSR 112
Charlie Parker Quintet | The Cole Porter Song Book | Verve | 823250-1
Chet Baker Meets Space Jazz Trio | Little Girl Blue | Philology | W 21.2
Coleman Hawkins Quartet | Ultimate Coleman Hawkins selected by Sonny Rollins | Verve | 557538-2
Dave Brubeck Quartet | Stardust | Fantasy | FCD 24728-2
Dizzy Gillespie All Stars | Dizzy's Diamonds-Best Of The Verve Years | Verve | 513875-2
Duke Jordan Trio | Duke Jordan New York/Bud Powell Paris | Vogue | 21457272
Ella Fitzgerald With The Buddy Bregman Orchestra | The Cole Porter Song Book | Verve | 2683044 IMS
Love Songs:The Best Of The Song Books | Verve | 531762-2
The Complete Ella Fitzgerald Song Books of Harold Arlen, Irving Berlin, Duke Ellington, George & Ira Gershwin, Jerome Kern, Johnny Mercer, Cole Porter And Rogers & Hart | Verve | 519832-2
Ella Fitzgerald With The Paul Smith Quartet | Mack The Knife-The Complete Ella In Berlin | Verve | 519564-2
Ella Fitzgerald With The Tommy Flanagan Trio | Jazz Collection:Ella Fitzgerald | Laserlight | 24397
Ernest Ranglin Trio | Soul D'Ern | Ronnie Scott's Jazz House | JHAS 611
Frank Sinatra With The Red Norvo Quintet(Sextet!) | Live In Australia,1959 | Blue Note | 837513-2
Freddie Hubbard Quintet | Jazz-Club: Trumpet | Verve | 840038-2
Gil Evans And Ten | Gil Evans And Ten | Prestige | PRSA 7120-6
The Jazz Giants Play Cole Porter:Night And Day | Prestige | PCD 24203-2
Hampten Hawes | The Challenge | Storyville | SLP 1013
Hank Mobley Quartet | Complete 'The Jazz Message Sessions With Kenny Clarke' | The Jazz Factory | JFCD 22858
Helmut Nieberle-Helmut Kagerer | Skyliner | ART BY HEART | ABH 2001 2
Herbie Hancock Quartet | The Herbie Hancock Quartet Live | Jazz Door | JD 1270
James Spaulding Quartet | Escapade | HighNote Records | HCD 7039
Jesper Thilo Quartet | Swingin' Friends | Storyville | SLP 4065
Laura Fygi With Band | Bewitched | Verve | 514724-2
Lawrence Brown With The Ralph Burns Orchestra | Slide Trombone | Verve | 559930-2
Lee Konitz-Red Mitchell Duo | I Concentrate On You | Steeplechase | SCCD 31018
Lionel Hampton Quartet | The Complete Lionel Hampton Quartets And Quintets With Oscar Peterson On Verve | Verve | 559797-2
Lisa Ekdahl With The Peter Nordahl Trio | When Did You Leave Heaven | RCA | 2143175-2
Louis Armstrong With The Oscar Peterson Quartet | Verve Jazz Masters 20:Introducing | Verve | 519853-2
Louis Armstrong Meets Oscar Peterson | Verve | 539060-2
Satchmo-When The Saints Go Marching In | Verve | 711051 IMS
Louis Mazetier | Good Vibrations | Jazz Connaisseur | JCCD 9521-2
Lous Dassen With Holger Clausen/Atlanta Jazzband | Let's Do It... | Dr.Jazz Records | 8606-2
Max Roach Plus Four | Max Roach + 4 | EmArCy | 822673-2 PMS
Paul Motian Quartet With Lee Konitz | Paul Motian On Broadway, Vol.3 | JMT Edition | 849157-2
Peter Sprague Quintet | Musica Del Mar | Concord | CJ 237
Quintet Du Hot Club De France | Welcome To Jazz: Django Reinhardt | Koch Records | 322 074 D1
Ranee Lee And Her Band | Dark Divas-Highlights | Justin Time | JUST 144-2
Stephane Grappelli Quartet | Grapelli Story | Verve | 515807-2
Stephane Grappelli Trio With Marcel Azzola | Stephane Grappelli In Toky | Denon Compact Disc | CY-77130
Teddy Wilson | Solo:Teddy Wilson Plays Cole Porter And Fat Waller | Jazz Colours | 874715-2
Terry Gibbs-Buddy DeFranco-Herb Ellis Sextet | Kings Of Swing | Contemporary | CCD 14067-2
Tony Ortega Octet | Jazz For Young Moderns | Fresh Sound Records | FSR 2006(Bethlehem BCP 79)
Walter Davis Jr. | Illuminations | Denon Compact Disc | DC-8553
Weslia Whitefield Trio | Live In San Francisco | Landmark | LCD 1531-2

Just One Of Those Things(take 5)
Don Ellis Trio | Out Of Nowhere | Candid | CCD 79032

Just One Of Those Things(take 8)
Barry Harris Trio | Magnificent! | Original Jazz Classics | OJCCD 1026-2(P 7733)

Just Open Your Heart
Joshua Breakstone Quintet | Evening Star | Contemporary | CCD 14040-2

Just Passing
Denny Zeitlin | Maybeck Recital Hall Series Volume Twenty-Seven | Concord | CCD 4572

Just Plain Meyer
Terry Gibbs Dream Band | Terry Gibbs Dream Band Vol.3:Flying Home | Contemporary | CCD 7654-2
Al Cohn And His Orchestra | The Jazz Workshop:Four Brass One Tenor | RCA | PM 45164

Just Play
Barbara Dennerlein Quintet | Bebab | Bebab Records | 250964(880159)

Just Rave In A Bin Bar
Ralph Bowen Quintet | Movin' On | Criss Cross | Criss 1066

Just Relax
Ben van den Dungen/Jarmo Hoogendijk Quintet | Heart Of The Matter | Timeless | CD SJP 269

Just Right Mama-
Big Bill Broonzy | Big Bill Broonzy 1934-1947 | Story Of Blues | CD 3504-2

Just Say
Benny Moten's Kansas City Orchestra | Bennie Moten Vol.1 | Zeta | ZET 750

Just Squeeze Me(But Don't Tease Me)
Albert Burbank With Kid Ory And His Creole Jazzband | Sounds Of New Orleans Vol.3 | Storyville | STCD 6010
Bechet-Spanier Big Four | The Best Original Sessions Of Sidney Bechet | Festival | Album 139
Bob Crosby And His Orchestra | Big Band Bounce And Boogie-Bob Crosby:Mournin' Blues/Accent On The Bobcats | Affinity | AFS 1014
Charly Antolini-Dick Morrissey Quartet | Charly Antolini Meets Dick Morrissey | BELL Records | BLR 84045
Clark Terry Quintet | Cruising | Milestone | M 47032
Ain't Misbehavin' | Pablo | 2312105
Duke Ellington And His Orchestra | Duke Ellington | Bluebird | ND 86641(3)
Hot Summer Dance | Red Baron | 469285-2
Dutch Swing College Band | The Joint Is Jumpin'! | Timeless | CD TTD 594
Ella Fitzgerald And Her All Stars | The Complete Ella Fitzgerald Song Books of Harold Arlen, Irving Berlin, Duke Ellington, George & Ira Gershwin, Jerome Kern, Johnny Mercer, Cole Porter And Rogers & Hart | Verve | 519832-2
Ella Fitzgerald With The Duke Ellington Orchestra | Compact Jazz: Ella Fitzgerald Live | Verve | 833294-2
Ella Fitzgerald With The Lou Levy Trio | Ella In Rome-The Birthday Concert | Verve | 835454-2
George Shearing Trio | Breakin' Out | Concord | CJ 335
Gerald Wiggins Trio | Relax And Enjoy It | Original Jazz Classics | OJC 173(C 7595)
Hank Jones | Handful Of Keys-The Music Of Thomas 'Fats' Waller | EmArCy | 512737-2 PMS
Henri Chaix Trio | Just Friends | Sackville | SKCD2-2048
Jeff Hamilton Trio | Hamilton House | Mons Records | MR 874316
Jimmy Smith Trio | Jimmy Smith Plays Fats Waller | Blue Note | 869943-4
Joe Sullivan | The Piano Artistry Of Joe Sullivan | Jazz Unlimited | JUCD 2051
Johnny Hodges And The Ellington All-Stars Without Duke | Duke's In Bed | Verve | 2304383 IMS
Johnny Hodges-Wild Bill Davis Sextet | In A Mellotone | RCA | ND 82305(847146)
Louis Armstrong-Duke Ellington Group | The Complete Louis Armstrong & Duke Ellington Sessions | Roulette | 793844-2
Marian McPartland Trio | Marion McPartland At The Hickory House | Savoy | SJL 2248 (801856)
Milt Jackson Quartet | Mostly Duke | Pablo | 2310944-2
Muggsy Spanier And His Dixieland All Stars | At Club Hangover-Vol. 2 | Storyville | SLP 249
Orchestra | Duke Ellington's Sophisticated Ladies | RCA | BL 04053 DX
Paul Desmond Quartet | Pure Desmond | CTI | EPC 450572-2
Shelly Manne And His Men | At The Blackhawk Vol.4 | Contemporary | C 7580
The Three Sounds | Here We Come | Blue Note | BNJ 71009(BST 84088)
Tierney Sutton And Her Trio | Blue In Green | Telarc Digital | CD 83522
Woody Herman And His Orchestra | The Formative Years Of 'The Band That PLays The Blues' | Circle | CCD-95

Just Squeeze Me(But Don't Tease Me)-
George Shearing-Neil Swainson Duo | Dexterity | Concord | CCD 4346

Just Squeeze Me(But Don't Tease Me) Intro
Art Hodes' Blue Note Jazzmen | Hot Jazz On Blue Note | Blue Note | 835811-2

Just The Blues
Count Basie And His Orchestra | En Concert Avec Europe 1 | Laserlight | 710706/07
Little Brother Montgomery & Ken Colyer | Little Brother Montgomery | Aves | 146502

Just The Way I Am

Stan Kenton-June Christy | Duet | Capitol | 789285-2

Just The Way You Are
Grant Green With Orchestra | Last Session | Atlantis | ATS 9
Zim Zemarel And His Orchestra | Live At The Hyatt Regency | Hindsight | HSR 230

Just Think It Over
Anne Morre | Anne Morre | Bellaphon | BCH 33008

Just To Keep You Satisfied
Eric Marienthal Group | Oasis | GRP | GRP 96552

Just Too Soon
Henry Threadgill Sextet | Subject To Change | About Time | AT 1007

Just Waiting
Billy Mitchell Quintet | This Is Billy Mitchell | Smash | 065507-2
Milt Jackson And Big Brass | For Someone I Love | Original Jazz Classics | OJCCD404-2(RLP 9478)

Just Walkin'
Wes Montgomery With The Don Sebesky Orchestra | Bumpin' | Verve | 539062-2

Just Walkin'(alt.take)
Big Joe Williams | Big Joe Williams At Folk City | Original Blues Classics | OBCCD 580-2(BV 1067)

Just Wen We're Falling In Love(Robbin's Nest)
Karl Ratzer Quintet | Saturn Returning | Enja | ENJ-9315 2

Just You & He & Me
Memphis Slim With Willie Dixon | Jazz In Paris:Memphis Slim/Willie Dixon Aux Trois Mailletz | EmArCy | 658148 IMS

Just You Just Me
Al Haig Trio | Al Haig Trio And Sextets | Original Jazz Classics | OJCCD 1929-2(SPL 1118)
The Piano Collection Vol.2 | Vogue | 21610222
Bill Evans | The Complete Bill Evans On Verve | Verve | 527953-2
Verve Jazz Masters 5:Bill Evans | Verve | 519821-2
Conversations With Myself | Verve | 521409-2
Bill Jennings-Leo Parker Quintet | Billy In The Lion's Den | Swingtime(Contact) | ST 1025
Brad Goode-Von Freeman Sextet | Inside Chicago Vol.3 | Steeplechase | SCCD 31531
Buddy Rich And His Orchestra | Live Sessions At The Palladium, Hollywood | Jazz Anthology | JA 5206
Dave Brubeck | Just You, Just Me | Telarc Digital | CD 83363
Don Ewell/Willie The Lion Smith | Grand Piano Duets | Sackville | 2004
Eddie Heywood Sextet | Commodore Classics-Eddie Heywood:The Biggest Little Band In The Forties | Commodore | 6.25493 AG
Ella Fitzgerald With The Marty Paich Dek-tette | Verve Jazz Masters 6:Ella Fitzgerald | Verve | 519822-2
Ernst Höllerhagen Quartet | Jazz In Switzerland 1930-1975 | Elite Special | 9544002/1-4
Gene Krupa Quartet | Compact Jazz: Gene Krupa | Verve | 833286-2 PMS
Harry Edison Quartet | The Inventive Mr. Edison | Fresh Sound Records | 054 2402661(Pacific Jazz PJ 11)
Helmut Nieberle-Helmut Kagerer | Skyliner | ART BY HEART | ABH 2001 2
Howard Alden-George Van Eps Quartet | 13 Strings | Concord | CCD 4464
Jay McShann Quintet | Roll´ Em | Black & Blue | BLE 233022
Lester Young Quartet | Verve Jazz Masters 30:Lester Young | Verve | 521859-2
Lester Young:Blue Lester | Dreyfus Jazz Line | FDM 36729-2
Lester Young:The Complete 1936-1951 Small Group Sessions(Studio Recordings-Master Takes),Vol.2 | Blue Moon | BMCD 1002
Lionel Hampton All Stars | Jazz In Paris:Lionel Hampton Mai 1956 | EmArCy | 013880-2
Nat King Cole Quintet | After Midnight | Capitol | 520087-2
Olaf Polziehn Trio | American Songbook | Satin Doll Productions | SDP 1032-1 CD
Oscar Peterson-Joe Pass Duo | Oscar Pterson Et Joe Pass A La Salle Pleyel | Pablo | 2CD 2625705
Live At Salle Pleyel, Paris | Pablo | 2625705
Prestige All Stars | Tenor Conclave | Prestige | SMJ 6539
Tenor Conclave | Original Jazz Classics | OJCCD 127-2
Quartet Der Kurt Edelhagen All Stars | Deutsches Jazz Fesival 1954/1955 | Bear Family Records | BCD 15430
Ralph Flanagan And His Orchestra | Dance Again Part 2 | Magic | DAWE 75
Schlüter-Nabatov-Antolini | Swing Kings | ACT | 9298-2
Scott Hamilton-Bucky Pizzarelli | ...Remember Zoot Sims:The Red Door | Concord | CCD 4799
Thelonious Monk Quartet | Live At The Jazz Workshop-Complete | CBS | C2K 65189
Live At The It Club:Complete | CBS | C2K 65288
Thelonious Monk Sextet | Thelonious Monk-The Complete Riverside Recordings | Riverside | 15 RCD 022-2
Thelonious Monk Trio | Thelonious Monk-The Complete Riverside Recordings | Riverside | 15 RCD 022-2
Willie Smith With The Nat King Cole Quartet | The Complete After Midnight Sessions | Capitol | 748328-2
JATP All Stars | The Complete Jazz At The Philharmonic On Verve 1944-1949 | Verve | 523893-2

Just You Just Me-
Jeff Jerolamon Quartet | Jeff Jerolamon's Swing Thing! | Candid | CCD 79538
Little Walter Blues Band | Little Walter | Chess | 427001

Juste Un Moment
Salsaya Big Band | Live | Timeless | CD SJP 209

Justice
Art Blakey And The Jazz Messengers | At The Jazz Corner Of The World | Blue Note | 828888-2
Kenwood Dennard Quintet | Just Advance | Big World | BW 2006

Justice And Honor
Bill Frisell Trio | Bill Frisell With Dave Hollnad And Elvin Jones | Nonesuch | 7559-79624-2
Clarence Gatemouth Brown Quintet | Cold Storage | Black & Blue | BLE 59.096 2

Justice(Evidence)
Stanley Clarke Groups | Stanley Clarke Best | Zounds | CD 2700020089

Justice's Groove
Black Swan Quartet | Black Swan Quartet | Minor Music | 009

Justin Time
Art Farmer/Benny Golson Jazztet | Here And Now | Verve | 558052-2
Everette DeVan Quartet | East Of The Sun | Organic Music | ED 2
Lee Morgan Quintet | Expoobident | Vee Jay Recordings | VJ 008
Orrin Evans Ortet | Justin Time | Criss Cross | Criss 1125
Terrie Richard Alden-Heyer Alden | Love | Nagel-Heyer | CD 071
The Sauter-Finegan Orchestra | That's All | Magic | DAWE 80

Jutta
Teddy Edwards Quartet With Christian Escoudé | La Villa-Live In Paris | Verve | 523495-2

Juzto Na 3 Juz Na 4
Norbert Stein Pata Masters meets Djaduk Ferianto Kua Etnika | Pata Java | Pata Musik | PATA 16 CD

Juzzla Juzzli
Alan Skidmore Quartet | El Skid | View | VS 103 IMS

K Twist
Kenny Burrell Sextet | Freedom | Blue Note | GXK 8170

K&K
Raum-Zeit-Klang-Project | Dimensionale X H2O Memory | Born&Bellmann | 970612 CD

K.C.Blues
Charlie Parker Quintet | The Verve Years (1950-51) | Verve | 2-2512 IMS
Charlie Parker:The Best Of The Verve Years | Verve | 527815-2
Swedish Schnapps + | Verve | 849393-2
Count Basie And His Orchestra | En Concert Avec Europe 1 | Laserlight | 710706/07
Frank Morgan With The Rodney Kendrick Trio | Bop! | Telarc Digital | CD 83413

Massimo Urbani Quintet | The Urbisaglia Concert | Philology | W 70.2

K.C.Organ Blues
Count Basie Sextet | The Swinging Count | Verve | MV 2646 IMS

K.D.'s Blues
Kenny Dorham Sextet | Round About Midnight At The Cafe Bohemia Vol.3 | Blue Note | 300197(BNJ 61004)

K.D.'s Blues(alt.take)
Blue Trails-The Rare Tracks | Blue Note | 300191

K.D.'s Motion
Kenny Dorham Octet | Afro-Cuban | Blue Note | 746815-2

K.High
Alexander von Schlippenbach Trio | Elf Bagatellen | FMP | CD 27

K.T.
John Tchicai & Strange Brothers | Darktown Highlights | Storyville | SLP 1015

K-4 Pacific
Gerry Mulligan Quartet With The Houston Symphony | Symphonic Dreams | Sion | Sion 18130

Kaba Nestra
Brennan-Cline-Patumi-Voirol-Theissing | Shooting Stars & Traffic Lights | L+R Records | CDLR 45090

Kabbelige See
Dennis Warren's Full Metal Revolutionary Jazz Ensemble | Watch Out! | Accurate | AC 5017

Kadota's Blues
Oscar Peterson Trio | Oscar Peterson-The London House Sessions | Verve | 531766-2

Kaffeepause
Barbara Thompson's Paraphernalia | Pure Fantasy | VeraBra Records | No. 8

Kafka
Tristan Honsinger Quintet | Map Of Moods | FMP | CD 76

Kahlil The Prophet
Strata Institute | Transmigration | DIW | DIW 860 CD

Kaira
dAs prOjekT | dAs prOjekT | Foolish Music | FM 211288

Kairo
Norbert Gottschalk With The Matthias Bröde Quartet | Norbert Gottschalk:Two Sessions | Dr.Jazz Records | 8605-2
Charles Mingus Jazz Workshop | Autobiography In Jazz | Original Jazz Classics | OJC 115(DEB 198)

Kai's Day
Kai Winding All Stars | Kai Winding-Bop City:Small Groups 1949-1951 | Cool & Blue | C&B-CD 110

Kakonita
Art Blakey And The Jazz Messengers | Art Blakey And The Jazz Messengers Vol.1:Child's Dance | Prestige | PCD 24130-2

Kalahari Lives
Noma Kosazana & Uli Lenz | Art Of The Duo: Trouble In Paradise | Tutu Records | 888144-2*

Kalahari Song
David Valentine Group | Kalahari | GRP | GRP 95082

Kalamazoo
John Pizzarelli Trio With The Don Sebesky Orchestra | Our Love Is Here To Stay | RCA | 6367501-2

Kale Yaka
Human Feel | Welcome To Malpesta | New World Records | 80450-2

Kaleidoscope
Ornette Coleman Quartet | Beauty Is A Rare Thing:Ornette Coleman-The Complete Atlantic Recordings | Atlantic | 8122-71410-2
Scott Wendholt Quintet | Through The Shadows | Criss Cross | Criss 1101

Kaleidoscope(theme)
Luca Flores-Michelle Bobko | For Those I Never Knews | SPLASC(H) Records | CD H 439-2

Kali Dance
Kenny Werner | Meditations | Steeplechase | SCCD 31327

Kali La Nuit
Andy Laverne Quartet | Stan Getz Live(The Great Jazz Gala '80) | Jazz Classics | CD CA 36005

Kalifactors
Sven Ake Johansson-Alexander von Schlippenbach Duo | Kalfaktor A.Falke Und Andere Lieder | FMP | 0970

Kalimba
Bob Berg Group | Short Stories | Denon Compact Disc | CY-1768
Egberto Gismonti Group | Sol Do Meio Dia | ECM | 1116(829117-2)
Jamenco | Conversations | Trick Music | TM 9202 CD
Jasper Van't Hof Quartet | Live In Montreux | MPS | 68247

Kalimba I
Triocolor | Colours Of Ghana | ACT | 9285-2

Kalimba II
David Moss Duos | Time Stories | Intakt Records | CD 054

Kalimba Theme
Johannes Barthelmes Group | Blues For George | L+R Records | CDLR 45113

Kalina
Andy Narell Group | Down The Road | Windham Hill | 34 10139-2

Kalligrafil Dance
Stephan Noel Lang Trio | Echoes | Nagel-Heyer | CD 2033

Kallipygos
French Frith Kaiser Thompson | Invisible Means | Demon Records | Fiend CD 199

Kalungu Talks
Pili-Pili | Pili-Pili | JA & RO | JARO 4141-2
Paul Motian Trio | Dance | ECM | 1108

Kamara River
Winterschladen-Krämer-Manderscheid | Unroll | Sound Aspects | sas CD 043

Kammerflirren
Claudio Fasoli/Kenny Wheeler/J.F. Jenny-Clark | Land | Nueva Records | IN 802

Kampala
Dirk Raulf-Frank Shulte | Theater III(Bühnenmusik) | Poise | Poise 11

Kampfhunde
Foday Musa Suso | The Dreamtime | CMP Records | CMP CD 3001

Kanga-
Hank Jones | Have You Met Hank Jones ? | Savoy | WL 70544 (809329)

Kännsch Högg?
Hans Koller Groups | Out Of The Rim | IN+OUT Records | 7014-2

Kanon
KontaSax | KontraSax Plays Getrude Stein | Jazz Haus Musik | JHM 0096 CD

Kanon Á Deux
Montreux Summit | Montreux Summit Vol.2 | CBS | CBS 88286

Kansas City
Booker Ervin Orchestra | Booker 'N' Brass | Pacific Jazz | 494509-2
Golden Gate Quartet | Best Of Golden Gate Quartet | Sonia | CD 77285
Jay McShann Quartet | Goin' To Kansas City | Stony Plain | SPCD 1286
Jay McShann Trio | Roll´ Em | Black & Blue | BLE 233022
Joe Williams With The Jimmy Jones Orchestra | Me And The Blues | RCA | 2121823-2
Washboard Willie | The Blues Vol.3 | Big Bear | 156400

Kansas City Blues
Tampa Red | Don't Tampa With The Blues | Original Blues Classics | OBCCD 516-2

Kansas City Boogie Jam
Sammy Price Quintet | Roots Of Rock 'N' Roll, Vol. 7: Rib Joint | Savoy | SJL 2240 (801886)

Kansas City Kitty
Count Basie Band | Basie Jam No. 2 | Original Jazz Classics | OJCCD 631-2(2310786)

Kansas City Line
Julius Hemphill | Bluy Boyé | Screwgun | SC 70008

Kansas City Man Blues
Sidney Bechet With Bob Wilber's Wildcats | New Orleans Jazz | CBS | 462954-2

Kansas City Moan
Ronnie Earl & The Broadcasters | Blues Masters | audioquest Music | AQCD 1034

Kansas City Nights
Wee Big Band | Kansas City Nights | Sackville | SKCD2-3057

Kansas City Shout
Count Basie And His Orchestra | Basie On Roulette, Vol. 7: Chairman Of The Board | Vogue | 500007

Kansas City Stomps
Jelly Roll Morton's Red Hot Peppers | The Jelly Roll Morton Centennial-His Complete Victor Recordings | Bluebird | ND 82361
Didn't He Ramble | Black & Blue | BLE 59.228 2
Lu Watters' Yerba Buena Jazz Band | Lu Watters' Yerba Buena Jazz Band At Hambone Kelly's 1949-50 | Merry Makers Record | MMRC-CD-10

Kansas City Wrinkles
Count Basie And His Orchestra | Li'l Ol' Groovemaker...Basie | Verve | 821799-2 PMS

Kansas City(revisited)
Tom Beckham Quartet | Suspicions | Fresh Sound Records | FSNT 075 CD

Kansas Tale
Hans Reichel-Rüdiger Carl Duo | Buben...Plus | FMP | CD 78

Kapazunder
Gerry Mulligan All Stars | Mulligan Plays Mulligan | Original Jazz Classics | OJCCD 003-2

Kaputt For Keeps
Don Cherry Group | Don Cherry-The Sonet Recordings:Eternal Now/Live Ankara | Verve | 533049-2

Kara Deniz(turkish folk material)
Per Gudmundson-Ale Möller-Lene Willemark | Frifot | ECM | 1690(557653-2)

Kära Sol-
Herbie Hancock Group | Sound-System | CBS | SRCS 9509

Karabenemdusi
Das Pferd | The World Of 'Das Pferd' | ITM Records | ITM 1488

Karakoum
Sven Ake Johansson-Alexander von Schlippenbach Duo | Kalfaktor A.Falke Und Andere Lieder | FMP | 0970

Karandila
Trio Töykeät | [Sisu] | EmArCy | 536580-2

Karatschan
Max Roach Quintet | Again | Affinity | AFF 32

Karen
Mack Goldsbury And The New York Connection | Songs I Love To Play | Timesarapper | TSCR 9615
Matthew Fries Quintet | Song For Today | TCB Records | TCB 20752

Karen(Intro)
Don Menza And The Joe Haider Trio | Bilein | JHM Records | JHM 3608

Karen's Birthday Waltz
Henning Wolter Trio With Guests | Years Of A Trilogy | double moon | DMCHR 71021

Karen's Call
Rick Margitza Septet | Color | Blue Note | 792279-2

Karin
Peter Bolte Trio | Trio | Jazz Haus Musik | JHM 0095 CD
Thomas Stabenow-Lothar Schmitz | Swet Peanuts | Bassic-Sound | CD 007

Karita
Robert Watson/Curtis Lundy Quartet | Beatitudes | New Note Records | KM 11867

Karma
Fourplay | Heartfelt | RCA | 2663916-2
Robin Eubanks Group | Tempo Jazz Edition Vol.2-Playin' Now | Polydor | 847903-2

Karma Shadub
Ronnie Laws With Strings And Voices | Fever | Blue Note | 84557

Karmic Ramifications:
Motus Quartett | Grimson Flames | Creative Works Records | CW CD 1023-2

Karminrote Flammen(Streichquartett Nr.2, 1991):
Jürgen Seefelder Trio | Straight Horn | Enja | 9120-2

Karrusel(Roundabout)
Nat Su Quartet | The J.Way | Fresh Sound Records | FSNT 038 CD

Karry's Trance
Orquestra Mahatma | A Young Person's Guide | Babel | BDV 9612

Kartik
Charlie Mariano & The Karnataka College Of Percussion | Live | VeraBra Records | CDVBR 2034-2
John Handy-Ali Akbar Khan Group | Karuna Supreme | MPS | 821295-1

Karuna Supreme
Antje Uhle Trio | Majazztic Steps | Mons Records | MR 874824

Karussell
Jon Balke w/Magnetic North Orchestra | Kyanos | ECM | 1822(017278-2)

Karyon
Lee Konitz Quartet | Inside Hi-Fi | Rhino | 790669-1

Kary's Trance
Lee Konitz-Sal Mosca Duo | Spirits | Milestone | M 9038
Warne Marsh Quintet | Jazz Exchange Volume One | Storyville | SLP 4001

Kasbah Tadla
Michal Urbaniak Quintet | Music For Violin & Jazz Quartet | JAM | 001 IMS

Kashf
Carl Ludwig Hübsch | Der Erste Bericht | IN+OUT Records | 77035-2

Kashmir
Josh Roseman Unit | Cherry | Enja | ENJ-9392 2
Jan Garber And His Orchestra | The Uncollected:Jan Garber, Vol.2 | Hindsight | HSR 155

Kaspar Hauser
Ullmann-Willers-Schäuble-Lorenz | Out To Lunch | Nabel Records:Jazz Network | CD 4623
Jeff 'Tain' Watts Trio | MegaWatts | Sunnyside | SSC 1055 D

Kastanie
Bill Perkins Quartet | Peaceful Moments | Fresh Sound Records | FSR 115(835316)

Kata
Jon Balke w/Magnetic North Orchestra | Kyanos | ECM | 1822(017278-2)

Katabolic
Robert Zollitsch Group | Zanskar | KlangRäume | 30130

Kathedrale Im Dunkeln(Hans Koller gewidmet)
James Emery Septet | Spectral Domains | Enja | ENJ-9344 2

Kathelin Gray
Ornette Coleman & Prime Time | Tone Dialing | Verve | 527483-2
Paul Motian Trio | Motian In Tokyo | JMT Edition | 849154-2

Kathleen's Theme
Les McCann-Eddie Harris Quintet | Swiss Movements | Atlantic | 7567-81365-2

Kathy's Waltz
Dave Brubeck Quartet | The Dave Brubeck Selection | CBS | 467279-2
David Benoit Group | Letter To Evan | GRP | GRP 96872

Katie Mae
Lightnin' Hopkins Trio | The Rising Sun Collection: Lightnin' Hopkins | The Rising Sun Collection | RSC 0009

Katinka's Ballad
Gary Burton-Makoto Ozone | Face To Face | GRP | GRP 98052

Katsijma
Marco Ballanti Trio | Ballanti's Organic Unity | Philology | W 126.2

Katut
Anthony Braxton Quartet | Four Compositions(Quartet) 1984 | Black Saint | 120086-2

Katy (Dizzier and Dizzier)
Dizzy Gillespie And His Orchestra | Jazz Special-The Best Of Dizzy Gillespie | RCA | NL 89727 AG

Katzenjammer
Kelm 3 | Per Anno | dml-records | CD 013

Katzenmusik I
Per Anno | dml-records | CD 013

Katzenmusik II
Joe Haider Trio | Katzenvilla | EGO | 4013

Katzenvilla
Pharoah Sanders Group | Journey To The One | Evidence | ECD 22016-2

Kauf Dir Einen Bunten Luftballon
Jazzensemble Des Hessischen Rundfunks | Atmosphering Conditions Permitting | ECM | 1549/50
Wolfgang Lauth Quartet | Lauther | Bear Family Records | BCD 15717 AH
Nils Landgren-Esbjörn Svensson | Layers Of Light | ACT | 9281-2

Kauk
Hugo Siegmeth Quintet | Live At The Jazzclub Unterfahrt | Edition Collage | EC 533-2

Kaul
Jazzensemble Des Hessischen Rundfunks | Atmosphering Conditions Permitting | ECM | 1549/50

Käuze Und Käuzchen
Gilad Atzmon Group | Spiel | Ohne Label | CD 19862

Kayak
Head Heart & Hands | The Best Of Head Heart & Hands | Blue Flame | 40061

Kazochock
Thomas Heberer-Dieter Manderscheid | What A Wonderful World | Jazz Haus Musik | JHM 0118 CD

Kazue
Pharoah Sanders Group | Save Our Children | Verve | 557297-2

Kazuko
Jazz Orchester Rheinland-Pfalz | Kazzou | Jazz Haus Musik | LJBB 9104

Kazzou
Blues & Boogie Explosion | Blues & Boogie Explosion | BELL Records | BLR 84003

Ke Mo Ki Mo(The Magic Song)
Darius And Dan Brubeck Group | Gathering Forces 1 | B&W Present | BW 022

Keen And Peachy
Woody Herman's 2nd Herd | This Is Jazz:Woody Herman | CBS | CK 65040

Keep A Song In Your Soul
Warren Vaché With The Howard Alden Trio | The Howard Alden Trio Plus Special Guests | Concord | CCD 4378

Keep A-Knockin'
Rockin' Dopsie And The Zydeco Twisters | Rockin' Dopsie And The Zydeco Twister | Storyville | 4960423
Vince Weber | Blues 'N Boogie | Rüssl Räckords | 064-32295

Keep A-Knockin'(But You Can't Come In)
Jean-Paul Bourelly & The BluWave Bandits | Rock The Cathartic Spirits:Vibe Music And The Blues! | DIW | DIW 911 CD

Keep Cool
Silvan Koopmann Bigband | Silvan Koopmann Big Band | Workshop Records | WR 051

Keep Dein Heart Richtig
Stan Getz Quintet | Another World | CBS | 466445-2

Keep Going
Jutta Gruber & The Martin Schrack Trio | Keep Hanging On | yvp music | CD 3043

Keep Hold Of Yourself
Patrick Bebelaar Quartet | You Never Lose An Island | dml-records | CD 015

Keep Holding-
Joe Haider Jazz Orchestra featuring Mel Lewis | Mel Lewis Meets The Joe Haider Jazz Orchestra | JHM Records | JHM 3604

Keep It Like That-Tight
Red Norvo's Orchestra | Red's 'X' Sessions | Fresh Sound Records | NL 46034(RCA)

Keep It Moving
Wynton Kelly Sextet | Kelly Blue | Riverside | RISA 1142-6
Kelly Blue | Original Jazz Classics | OJC20 033-2(RLP 1142)

Keep It Moving(alt.take)
Kelly Blue | Riverside | RISA 1142-6
Buddy Guy Blues Band | Buddy Guy-The Complete Chess Studio Recordings | MCA | MCD 09337

Keep It To Myself(aka Keep It To Yourself)
Buddy Guy-The Complete Chess Studio Recordings | MCA | MCD 09337

Keep It To Myself(aka Keep It To Yourself-alt.take)
Bessie Smith And Her Band | Jazz Classics In Digital Stereo: Bessie Smith | CDS Records Ltd. | REB 602

Keep Loose
Jimmy Heath Orchestra | New Picture | Landmark | LCD 1506-2

Keep Me In Mind
The Atlantic Jazz Trio | Some Other Time | Factory Outlet Records | FOR 2002-1 CD
Swan Silvertones | My Rock/Love Lifted Me | Ace Records | CDCHD 340

Keep On
Willis Jackson Sextet | Cool Gator | Original Jazz Classics | OJC 220(P 7172)

Keep On Jumpin'
Louis Armstrong And His Orchestra | Armed Forces Radio Service 1943/1944 | Duke Records | D 1021

Keep On Kicking
Amina Claudine Myers Group | Amina | RCA | PD 83030

Keep On Loving You
Maceo Parker Group | Southern Exposure | Minor Music | 801033

Keep On Marching
Kölner Saxophon Mafia With Irene Lorenz | Kölner Saxophon Mafia Proudly Presents | Jazz Haus Musik | JHM 0046 CD

Keep On Moving
Ray Brown Quintet | Brown's Bag | Concord | CCD 6019

Keep On Rainin'
Billie Holiday And Her Band | Jazz Live & Rare: Billie Holiday Live 1937/56 | Jazzline | ???

Keep On Walkin'
Walter Brown | Living Country Blues USA, Vol. 2: Blues On Highway 61 | L+R Records | LR 42032

Keep Silent
Darol Anger-Barbara Higbie Duo | Tideline | Windham Hill | WD 1021

Keep Smiling At Trouble
Bud Freeman Trio | Commodore Classics -Bud Freeman: Three's No Crowd | Commodore | 6.24061 AG

Keep That Groove Going
The Crusaders | The Best Of The Crusaders | MCA | 2292-50536-1

Keep The Bugs Off Your Glass And The Bears Off Your Ass
Steve Lacy Sextet | Songs | Hat Art | CD 6045

Keep The Customer Satisfied
David Fathead Newman Septet | Back To Basics | Milestone | MCD 9188-2

Keep The Faith Baby
Incognito | Positivity | Talkin' Loud | 518260-2

Keep The Heavens Beautiful
Firehouse Five Plus Two | Goes To A Fire | Good Time Jazz | GTCD 10052-2

Keep The Home Fires Burning
Louis Armstrong And His Orchestra | Ambassador Louis Armstrong Vol.7(1940-1941) | Ambassador | CLA 1907

Keep Them Chords Comin'
Glenn Miller And His Orchestra | Glenn Miller Forever | RCA | NL 89214 DP

Keep Your Arms Around Me
Monty Waters' Hot Rhythm Junction | Jazzoerty | Tutu Records | 888196-2*

Keep Your Beat Alive
Carol Leigh & The Dumoustiers Stompers | Back Water Blues | Black & Blue | BLE 59.219 2

Keep Your Hands Off Her
Martin Schmitt | Handful Of Blues | AH Records | ESM 9303

Keep Your Heart Right
Blind Willie Johnson | Praise God I'm Satisfied | Yazoo | YAZ 1058

Keep Your Lamp Trimmed And Burning
Reverend Blind Gary Davis | Gospel, Blues And Street Songs | Original Blues Classics | OBCCD 524-2(RLP 148)

Keep Your Temper
Ralph Sutton | The Other Side Of Ralph Sutton | Chaz Jazz | CJ 107

Keeper Of The Flame
Nina Simone With Orchestra | Nina Simone-The 60s Vol.3:Work Song | Mercury | 838545-2 PMS

Keepin' In The Groove
Rob Schneiderman Trio | Keepin' In The Groove | Reservoir | RSR CD 144

Keepin' Out Of Mischief Now
Barbara Sutton Curtis-Ralph Sutton | Solos & Duets | Sackville | SKCD2-2027
Charleston Chasers | Steaming South | Stomp Off Records | CD 1314
Dave McKenna-Hal Overton Quartet | Dual Piano Jazz | Fresh Sound Records | FSR 2036(Bethlehem BCP 6049)
Dick Wellstood | This Is The One...Dig! | Solo Art | SACD-119
Eddie Condon All Stars | Ringside At Condons | Savoy | SV 0231(MG 12055)
Engelbert Wrobel's Swing Society | Live At Sägewerk | Timeless | CD TTD 588
Fats Waller | Piano Solos | RCA | ND 89741
Hank Jones | Handful Of Keys-The Music Of Thomas 'Fats' Waller | EmArCy | 512737-2 PMS
Louis Armstrong And His All Stars | The Louis Armstrong Selection | CBS | 467278-2
Louis Armstrong With Zilmer Randolph's Orchestra | Louis Armstrong V.S.O.P. Vol. 7/8 | CBS | CBS 88004
Nat Pierce/Dick Collins Nonet | Nat Pierce-Dick Collins Nonet/Charlie Mariano Sextet | Original Jazz Classics | OJC 118(F 3224)
Ralph Sutton-Bernd Lhotzky | Stridin' High | Jazz Connaisseur | JCCD 9728-2
Ralph Sutton-Ruby Braff Duo | Ralph Sutton & Ruby Braff | Chaz Jazz | CJ 101
Sammy Price Septet | Barrelhouse And Blues | Black Lion | BLCD 760159
Teddi King With Orchestra | All The Kings' Song | M&M Records | CRL 57278(Coral)

Keepin' Out Of Mischief Now-
Steve Laury Trio | Keepin' The Faith | Denon Compact Disc | CY-75283

Keepin' The News
The Johnes Brothers | Keepin' Up With The Jones | Verve | 538633-2

Keeping My Love For You
Ed Bickert Quartet | Bye Bye Baby | Concord | CJ 232

Keeping Still-
Jason Rebello Group | Keeping Time | Novus | 2112904-2

Kein Problem
Habarigani | Habarigani Two | Hat Art | CD 6064

Keine-Keiner
Paul Eßer-Gerd Dudek-Ali Haurand-Jiri Strivin | Jazz Und Lyrik:Schinderkarren Mit Buffet | Konnex Records | KCD 5108

KeinOrt:
David Benoit Group | The Best Of David Benoit 1987-1995 | GRP | GRP 98312

Kei's Song
Keith Tippett Group | Warm Spirits-Cool Spirits | View | VS 101 IMS

Kekeli
Attilio Zanchi Group | Early Spring | SPLASC(H) Records | H 129

Kel Enkle O Pender
Don Pullen' s African-Brazilian Connection | Live...Again | Blue Note | 830271-2

Kelley's Line
Rüdiger Carl | Vorn:Lieder Und Improvisationen Für Akkordeon, Bandoneon Und Ziehharmonika | FMP | 1110

Kelly Blue
Wynton Kelly Sextet | Kelly Blue | Riverside | RISA 1142-6
John Surman | Road To Saint Ives | ECM | 1418(843849-2)

Kelly Bray
Dick Johnson Quartet | Dick Johnson Plays | Concord | CCD 4107

Kelly's Blues
Mike LeDonne Quintet | 'Bout Time | Criss Cross | Criss 1033

Kelo
Miles Davis Sextet | Miles Davis:The Blue Note And Capitol Recordings | Blue Note | 827475-2
Miles Davis Vol.1 | Blue Note | 300081(1501)
Miles Davis All Stars | Miles Davis Vol.2 | Blue Note | 532611-2

Kelo(alt.take)
Miles Davis Sextet | Miles Davis:The Blue Note And Capitol Recordings | Blue Note | 827475-2

Kelvin & Sophia
Trio Asab | Coast To Coast | Aho-Recording | AHO CD 1028(CD 380)

Kennedy In Napoli
Erika Rojo & Tim Sund | Das Lied | Nabel Records:Jazz Network | CD 4684

Kennst Du Das Land
Oliver Augst-Rüdiger Carl-Christoph Korn | Blank | FMP | OWN-90013

Kenny
Kenny Clarke-Milford Graves-Famoudou Don Moye-Andrew Cyrille | Pieces Of Time | Soul Note | 121078-2

Kenny G
Conrad Herwig Quintet | Osteology | Criss Cross | Criss 1176

Kenny's Pennies
Jimmy Smith Quartet | Jimmy Smith:Best Of The Verve Years | Verve | 527950-2

Kenny's Sound
Kenny Burrell Quintet | Midnight Blue | Blue Note | 495335-2
Kenny Burrell-Jimmy Smith Trio | Blue Bash | Verve | 557453-2
Blue Bash | Verve | 557453-2

Kenny's Sound(alt.take)
Blue Bash | Verve | 557453-2

Kenny's Sound(alt.take-2)
Kenny Clarke-Martial Solal Sextet | Roy Haynes/Kenny Clarke:Transatlantic Meetings | Vogue | 2111512-2

Kenny's Theme
Duffy Jackson Orchestra | Swing! Swing! Swing! | Milestone | MCD 9233-2

Kentish Hunting (Lady Margaret's Air)
Paul Cacia And The Stan Kenton Alumni | The Alumni Tribute To Stan Kenton | Happy Hour Music | HH 6001-2(886370)

Kentucky Avenue,A.C.
The Bourbon Street Stompers | I Like Dixieland | Bainbridge | BT 1019

Kentucky Man Blues
George Russell Sextet | Stratusphunk | Original Jazz Classics | OJC 232(RLP 9341)

Kerava
Piirpauke | Zerenade | JA & RO | JARO 4142-2

Kerelele
Anouar Brahem Trio | Barzakh | ECM | 1432(847540-2)

Kerkenah
Erhard Hirt | Guitar Solo | FMP | OWN-90003

Kernow
Charlie Christian All Stars | Charlie Christian-Jazz Immortal/Dizzy Gillespie 1944 | Original Jazz Classics | OJCCD 1932-2(ES 548)

Kerouac
Dizzy Gillespie Quintet | Jazz Gallery:Dizzy Gillespie | RCA | 2114165-2

Kerry Dance
Gigi Gryce And His Orchestra | Nica's Tempo | Savoy | SV 0126(MG 12137)

Keshan
Dave Belany And Her Trio | Motivations | Sahara | 1005

Keter's Dirty Blues
George Wettling Jazz Band | George Wettling Jazz Band | JSP Records | 1103

Kevin
Fernand Englebert Group | Fantasmatic | B.Sharp Records | CDS 078

Kevin Devin
First Class Blues Band | First Class Blues | Acoustic Music Records | 319.1031.2

Key Largo
Jackie Cain/Roy Kral Quartet | Bogie | Fantasy | F 9643
Manfred Dierkes | It's About Time | Acoustic Music Records | 319.1176.2
Sarah Vaughan Plus Two | Sarah + 2 | Fresh Sound Records | FSR 605(Roulette R 52118)
Benny Carter And His Strings With The Oscar Peterson Quartet | The Urban Sessions/New Jazz Sound | Verve | 531637-2

Key To The Highway
Frank Edwards | Done Some Travelin' | Trix Records | TRIX 3303
John Lee Hooker | Burning Hell | Original Blues Classics | OBCCD 555-2(RLP 008)
K.C. Douglas | Big Road Blues | Original Blues Classics | OBCCD 569-2(BV 1050)

Keyhole Blues
Graham Stewart Seven | Best Of British Jazz From The BBC Jazz Club Vol.5 | Upbeat Jazz | URCD 125

Keys
Al Rapone & The Zydeco Express | New Orleans Louisiana | Traditional Line | TL 1319

Keystream Mystery
Jorgen Emborg Group | Keyword | Stunt Records | 18904

Kharma
Charlie Mariano's Nassim | Charlie Mariano's Nassim | Off The Wall Records | OTW 9801-CD

Khmer
Abdullah Ibrahim(Dollar Brand) | Autobiography | Plainisphare | PL 1267-68 CD

Khormiloi
Anouar Brahem Trio | Astrakan Café | ECM | 1718(159494-2)

Khotan
Alexander von Schlippenbach And Sunny Murray | Smoke | FMP | CD 23

Kiba
Pili-Pili | Hoomba-Hoomba | JA & RO | JARO 4192-2
Pili-Pili Live 88 | JA & RO | JARO 4139-2

Kibassa
Rabih Abou-Khalil Group | Bukra | Enja | ENJ-9372 2

Kibbe
Krzyaztof Scieranski Trio | No Radio | ITM Records | ITM 001 JP

Kick Hit 4 Hit Kix U(Blues For Jimi And Janis)
Bud Freeman Trio | The Joy Of Sax | Chiaroscuro | CR 135

Kick It!
Carey & Lurrie Bell Band | Son Of A Gun | Rooster | R 2617

Kickapoo Joy Juice
Duke Ellington And His Orchestra | Duke Ellington:Complete Prestige Carnegie Hall 1946-1947 Concerts | Definitive Records | DRCD 11211

Kickass
Chick Corea Electric Band | Inside Out | GRP | GRP 96012

Kicker
Hans Reichel-Rüdiger Carl Duo | Buben...Plus | FMP | CD 78

Kickin' The Gong Around
Cab Calloway And His Orchestra | Hi-De-Hi-Di-Ho | RCA | 2118524-2

Kicking Monster And The Vagina Girls
June Christy And Her Orchestra | The Misty Miss Christy | Pathe | 1566141(Capitol T 725)

Kicks
Nat King Cole Quintet | Anatomy Of A Jam Session | Black Lion | BLCD 760137

Kicks In Love
Buddy Bregman And His Orchestra | Swinging Kicks | Verve | 559514-2

Kicks Swings
Hans Koller & The International Brass Company | The Horses | L+R Records | LR 40008

Kid From Red Bank
Count Basie And His Orchestra | The Complete Atomic Basie | Roulette | 828635-2
Larry Carlton Group | Kid Gloves | GRP | GRP 96832

Kid Song
George Young Quartet | Spring Fever | Sweet Basil | 660.55.009

Kidnapped
Herbie Mann Orchestra | Yellow Fever | Atlantic | SD 19252

Kidnapping Kissinger
Clark Terry Sextet | Yes The Blues | Pablo | 2312127

Kidney Stew
Count Basie Jam | Montreux '77-The Art Of The Jam Session | Pablo | 2620106
Eddie Cleanhead Vinson With The Red Holloway Quartet | Blues In The Night-Volume One:The Early Show | Fantasy | FCD 9647-2
Lionel Hampton And His Orchestra | Hamp's Big Band | RCA | 2121821-2

Kids Know
Sonny Rollins Quintet | Saxophone Colossus And More | Prestige | P 24050

Kierlighed Pa Prove-
Heinz Sauer Trio | Exchange | free flow music | ffm 0695

Kieser's Exchange
Jerry Coker Orchestra | Modern Music From Indiana University | Fantasy | 0902116(F 3214)

Kiki's Last Farewell
Urs Leimgruber/John Wolf Brennan | Mountain Hymn | L+R Records | CDLR 45002

Kilauea
Jan Garbarek-Kjell Johnsen Duo | Aftenland | ECM | 1169(839304-2)

Kilden
Asita Hamidi & Arcobaleno | Mosaic | Laika Records | 8695067

Kilele
Mosaic | Laika Records | 8695067

Kilele(Intro)
Sonny Rollins Quintet | Sunny Days Stary Nights | Milestone | M 9122

Kilimandjaro Cookout
Brubeck-Ntoni Group | Afro Cool Concept | B&W Present | BW 024

Kilimanjaro
Red Sun/SamulNori | Then Comes The White Tiger | ECM | 1499

Kil-Kun-Ak
Blind Willie McTell | Last Session | Original Blues Classics | OBCCD 517-2

Kill It Kid
Last Session | Original Blues Classics | OBCCD 517-2
Kölner Saxophon Mafia | Go Commercial... | Jazz Haus Musik | JHM 0065 CD

Kill Your Darlings
Dave Bartholomew And His Orchestra | The Monkey | Pathe | 1561331(Imperial)

Killer Joe
Bill Perkins Quartet | Killer Joe | Fresh Sound Records | FSR 106 (807739)
Buddy Childers Big Band | It's What Happening Now! | Candid | CCD 79749
Charles Persip And Superband(II) | In Case You Missed It | Soul Note | 121079-2
Monty Alexander's Ivory & Steel | To The Ends Of The Earth | Concord | CCD 4721
Tito Puente's Latin Ensemble And Orchestra | Un Poco Loco | Concord | CCD 4329
Walter Bishop Jr. Trio | Valley Land | Muse | MR 5060

Killer Love
Peter Kowald Group | When The Is Out You Don't See Stars | FMP | CD 38

Killing Me Softly With His Song
Nils Landgren Group | Ballads | ACT | 9268-2
Roland Hanna | Sir Elf | Candid | CRS 1003 IMS

Singers Unlimited | Compact Disc:The Singers Unlimited | MPS | 831373-2 PMS
A Capella 2 | MPS | 821860-2

Killing Time
Gunter Hampel Next Generation | Next Generation | Birth | CD 043

Killing Time,Till Time Kills Me
Wayne Peet's Doppler Funk | Plasto! | Nine Winds Records | NW 0126

Kim
Charlie Parker Quartet | Charlie Parker | Verve | 539757-2
Charlie Parker:Bird's Best Bop On Verve | Verve | 527452-2
Lanny Morgan Quartet | A Suite For Yardbird | Fresh Sound Records | FSR-CD 5023

Kim(alt.take)
Charlie Parker Quartet | Bird: The Complete Charlie Parker On Verve | Verve | 837141-2

Kim(take 2)
Bird: The Complete Charlie Parker On Verve | Verve | 837141-2

Kim(take 4)
The Visitors | Motherland | Muse | MR 5094

Kimbaran Pa Nico
Kenny Burrell Quintet | Sky Street | Fantasy | F 9514

Kim-Den-Strut
Bugge Wesseltoft | It's Snowing On My Piano | ACT | 9260-2

Kimer,I Klokker
Stan Kenton And His Orchestra | National Anthems Of The World | Creative World | ST 1060

Kind Folk
Lee Konitz-Kenny Wheeler Quartet | Live At Birdland Neuburg | double moon | CHRDM 71014
Tiziana Simona With The Kenny Wheeler Quartet | Gigolo | ITM Records | 0014

Kind Hearted Woman
Robert Lockwood Jr. | Robert Lockwood Jr. Plays Robert(Johnson) & Robert(Lockwood) | Black & Blue | BLE 59.740 2

Kind Hearted Woman(alt.take)
Eric Lugosch | Kind Heroes | Acoustic Music Records | 319.1188.2

Kind Of Blue Period
Warren Bernhardt Trio | Handsn | dmp Digital Music Productions | CD 457

Kind Of Gentle
Jerri Winters With The Al Belletto Sextet | Somebody Loves Me | Fresh Sound Records | FSR 600(Bethlehem BCP 76)

Kind Of New
Johannes Enders Quartet | Sandsee | Organic Music | ORGM 9720

Kind Of Now
Zbigniew Seifert | Solo Violin | MRC | 066-45088

Kinda Dukish
Duke Ellington And His Orchestra | Duke Ellington-Count Basie | CBS | 473753-2

Kinda Dukish-
Ella Fitzgerald And Duke Ellington:Cote D'Azure Concerts on Verve | Verve | 539033-2
Soul Call | Verve | 539785-2
The Echoes Of Ellington Orchestra | Rockin' In Ronnie's | Ronnie Scott's Jazz House | JHCD 050

Kinda Kanonic
The Prestige All Stars | Four Altos | Original Jazz Classics | OJC- 1734(P 7116)

Kindercountry
Derek Watkins Group | Increased Demand | M.A Music | A 707-2

Kinderhund
Matthias Spillmann Septet | Something About Water | JHM Records | JHM 3620

Kinderlied No.1
Cadavre Exquis | Cadavre Exquis | Creative Works Records | CW CD 1014-1

Kinderlieder Nach A.Wölfli
Bik Bent Braam | Howdy | Timeless | CD SJP 388

Kinderprogramm
Live Recordings From The Streets | Fun Horns Live In South America-Natural Music | KlangRäume | 30060

Kinderspiel
Viktoria Tabatchnikowa-Eugenij Belov | Troika | ALISO Records | AL 1036

Kindersuite:
Erich Bachträgl Quartet | Gollum | Bellaphon | 270.31.004

Kindertraum
Family Of Percussion | Message To The Enemies Of Time | Nagara | MIX 1016-N

King Baby
Rich Perry Quartet | Hearsay | Steeplechase | SCCD 31515

King Cobra
Herbie Hancock Sextet | Herbie Hancock:The Complete Blue Note Sixties Sessions | Blue Note | 495569-2
Larry Willis Sextet | A Tribute To Someone | audioquest Music | AQCD 1022
Chick Corea Electric Band | The Chick Corea Electric Band | GRP | GRP 95352

King Cockroach
Bob Crosby And His Orchestra | The Uncollected:Bob Crosby Vol.2 | Hindsight | HSR 209

King David
King David And His Little Jazz | Zoot Sims:The Complete 1944-1954 Small Group Sessions(Master Takes),Vol.1 | Blue Moon | BMCD 1038

King Font
Artie Shaw And His Orchestra | The Indispensable Artie Shaw Vol.3/4 | RCA | 2126414-2

King Freddie Of Hubbard
Thilo Wolf Big Band | Sternstunden Des Swing | MDL-Jazz | CD 27768

King Joe
Mr.Acker Bilk And His Paramount Jazz Band | The Golden Years Of Revival Jazz,Vol.10 | Storyville | STCD 5515

King Joe(alt.take)
Young People With Faces | Uncle Festive | Denon Compact Disc | CY-2135

King Kong
Riccardo Fassi Tankio Band | Riccardo Fassi Tankio Band Pays The Music Of Frank Zappa | SPLASC(H) Records | CD H 428-2

King Kong-
Joseph Robechaux And His New Orleans Boys | Joe Robichaux And His New Orleans Boys | Folklyric | 9032

King Korn
Jaco Pastorius Quartet | Jaco | DIW | DIW 312 CD
Paul Bley Trio | Footoose | Savoy | SV 0140(MG 12182)

King Of Harts
Chris Kase Sextet | Starting Now | Mons Records | MR 874659

King Of The Lobby
Gambit Jazzmen With Tim Laughlin | King Of The Mardi Gras | Lake | LACD 54

King Of The Zulus
Dixie Washboard Band | Big Charlie Thomas 1925-1927 | Timeless | CBC 1-030
Louis Armstrong And His All Stars | Satchmo-A Musical Autobiography Vol.1 | MCA | 2-4173
Stuttgarter Dixieland All Stars | Dixieland Jubilee-Vol. 3 | Intercord | 155013

King Of Trash
Ronnie Scott And The Band | Live At Ronnie Scott's | CBS | 494439-2

King Pete
King Oliver-Jelly Roll Morton Duo | Jelly Roll Morton | Milestone | MCD 47018-2

King Porter Stomp
Benny Goodman And His Orchestra | The Benny Goodman Story | Capitol | 833569-2
The Birth Of Swing | Bluebird | ND 90601(3)
The Best Of The Big Dance Bands | LRC Records | CDC9010
This Is Benny Goodman | RCA | NL 89224 DP
Claude Hopkins And His Orchestra | Big Bands Uptown 1931-40 | MCA | 1323
Glenn Miller And His Orchestra | Glenn Miller And His Orchestra-Swinging Instrumentals | Bluebird | 63 66529-2
The Genius Of Glenn Miller Vol.1 | RCA | ND 90090
Glenn Miller In Concert | RCA | NL 89216 DP
Jack Teagarden And His Orchestra | Jazz Original | Charly | CD 80
Jelly Roll Morton | Doctor Jazz | Black & Blue | BLE 59.227 2
Trevor Richards New Orleans Trio | The Trevor Richards New Orleans Trio | Stomp Off Records | CD 1222
Zutty Singleton And His Orchestra | Jazz Drumming Vol.5(1940) | Fenn Music | FJD 2705

King Precious
Gene Ammons And His All Stars | Funky | Original Jazz Classics | OJCCD 244(P 7083)

King's Riff
Quincy Jones All Stars | Quincy Jones:This Is How I Feel About Jazz | Impulse(MCA) | GRP 11152

Kingston Calypso
Great Guitars | Great Guitars/Straight Tracks | Concord | CCD 4421

Kingston Lounge
Tony Kinsey Orchestra | Thames Suite | Spotlite | SPJ 504

Kinnings
Stefan Bauer Quintet | Best Of Two Worlds | Jazzline | JL 11147-2

Kin's
Scott Cossu Quintet | Wind Dance | Windham Hill | TA-C- 1016

Kinsey Report
Naked Jazz | Takes Off | Savoy | CY 18040

Kinshasa Im Boté
Pili-Pili | Pili-Pili | JA & RO | JARO 4141-2
Erich Bachträgl Quartet | Gollum | Bellaphon | 270.31.004

Kippieology
Elliott Sharp Carbon | Datacide | Enemy | EMCD 116(03516)

Kippy
Ben Waltzer Quintet | In Metropolitan Motion | Fresh Sound Records | FSNT 082 CD

Kira Da Anshi(I)
In Metropolitan Motion | Fresh Sound Records | FSNT 082 CD

Kira Da Anshi(II)
Deborah Henson-Conant | The Celtic Album | Laika Records | 35101022

Kira's Lullabye-
Willem Breuker & Leo Cuypers | ...Superstars | FMP | SAJ 17

Kirk's Work
Roland Kirk-Jack McDuff Quartet | Pre-Rahsan | Prestige | P 24080

Kirsten
Jack Walrath-Larry Willis-Steve Novosel | Portraits In Ivory & Brass | Mapleshade | 02032

Kiruna
Toshiko Mariano And Her Big Band | Recorded In Tokyo | Vee Jay Recordings | VJ 023

Kismet
Hank Mobley Quartet | Complete 'The Jazz Message Sessions With Kenny Clarke' | The Jazz Factory | JFCD 22858

Kiss
Mike Nock Trio | Not We But One | Naxos Jazz | 86006-2
Niels Lan Doky Trio | Niels Lan Doky | Verve | 559087-2

Kiss & Fly
Gary Smulyan Quintet | The Lure Of Beauty | Criss Cross | Criss 1049

Kiss And Run
Larry Vuckovich Sextet | City Sounds,Village Voices | Palo Alto | PA 8012
Sonny Rollins Plus Four | Sonny Rollins Plus 4 | Original Jazz Classics | OJC20 243-2(P 7038)
Sonny Rollins Quintet | Saxophone Colossus And More | Prestige | P 24050

Kiss My Axe
The Al Di Meola Project | Kiss My Axe | Inak | 700782

Kiss Of Fire
Louis Armstrong And His Orchestra | Louis Armstrong-All Time Greatest Hits | MCA | MCD 11032

Kiss The Night,Huntin' Santa Claus
Dizzy Gillespie Trio | Dizzy Gillespie Digital At Montreux, 1980 | Original Jazz Classics | OJCCD 882-2(2308226)

Kisses In The Moonlight(single version)
John Pizzarelli Trio | Kisses In The Rain | Telarc Digital | CD 83491

Kissing Joy(As It Flies)
Pago Libre | Cinémagique | TCB Records | TCB 01112

Kit-
Mark Feldman Quartet | Book Of Tells | Enja | ENJ-9385 2

Kit Suite:
Dave Grusin Group | Night-Lines | GRP | GRP 95042

Kite
Jan Garbarek Quartet | Paths, Prints | ECM | 1223(829377-2)

Kite Dance
Claudio Fasoli/Kenny Wheeler/J.F. Jenny-Clark | Land | Nueva Records | IN 802

Kitt's Kiss
Ben Webster-Harry Sweets Edison Quintet | Ben And Sweets | CBS | CK 40853

Kitty's Dream
Trevor Coleman Group | Kiwi Love | Fiala Music | JFJ 90005

Kix
Duke Ellington Trio | Duke Ellington Live At The Whitney | Impulse(MCA) | 951173-2

Kixx
Ensemble FisFüz | SimSim | Peregrina Music | PM 50211

Klact-Oveedseds-Tene
Ira Sullivan And His Chicago Jazz Quintet | Bird Lives | Affinity | AFF 71
Lanny Morgan Quartet | A Suite For Yardbird | Fresh Sound Records | FSR-CD 5023
Charlie Parker Quintet | Charlie Parker On Dial, Vol.5 | Spotlite | SPJ 105

Klagita
Björn Alke Quartet | Jazz Sverige 1974 | Caprice | CAP 1072

Klarinettentrio Metamusil für drei B-Klarinettes
Teddy Kleindin-Trio | Swing tanzen verboten | Vagabond | 6.28360 DP

Klavierkonzert in C-Dur,2.Satz(Mozart)
La Gaia Scienza | Love Fugue-Robert Schumann | Winter&Winter | 910049-2

Klavier-Quartett(Robert Schumann op.47)
Chris Potter Quintet | Concentric Circle | Concord | CCD 4595

Kleine Serenade Für HeHe
Ekkehard Jost Quintet | Carambolage | View | VS 0028 IMS

Kleiner Trommler-
Larry Garner Group | Too Blues | JSP Records | JSPCD 249

Klezmer In Black
Urszula Dudziak-Michal Urbaniak | Urszula-Future Talk | Inner City | IC 1066 IMS

Kline
Kölner Saxophon Mafia | Space Player | Jazz Haus Musik | JHM 0132 CD

Klingonenträume
Peter Giger Group | Illigitimate Music | Nagara | MIX 1014-N

Klop-
Anirahtak und die Jürgen Sturm Band | Das Kurt Weill Programm | Nabel Records:Jazz Network | CD 4638

Klops Lied
Thomasz Stanko Quartet | Matka Joanna | ECM | 1544(523986-2)

Klostergeist
Ketil Bjornstad Group | Early Years | EmArCy | 013271-2

Klovnen Synger(The Clown Wings)
Elliott Sharp + Guitarists | 'Dyners Club | Intakt Records | CD 036

Kluski Theory
Gabriele Hasler-Elvira Plenar-Andreas Willers | Sonetburger-Nach Texten Von Oskar Pastior | Foolish Music | FM 211793

Knabe Mit Dem Bildnusch
Amani A.W.-Murray Quintet | Amani A.W.-Murray | GRP | GRP 96332

Knee Deep
Maynard Ferguson And His Big Bop Nouveau Band | Brass Attitude | Concord | CCD 4848

Kneedrops
Ted Heath And His Orchestra | Ted Heath And His Music-It's Swing Time | Magic | DAWE 82

Knights Of The Steamtable
Bill Evans Trio | His Last Concert In Germany | West Wind | WW 2022

Knit For Mary F
Bill Evans Trio:The Last Waltz | Milestone | 8MCD 4430-2
David Benoit Group | Letter To Evan | GRP | GRP 96872

Knitting Harmonix
Mark Helias Quintet | Attack The Future | Enja | ENJ-7019 2

Knock Me A Kiss
Ella Fitzgerald With The Marty Paich Dek-tette | Verve Jazz Masters 46:Ella Fitzgerald-The Jazz Sides | Verve | 527655-2
Ida James With The Nat King Cole Trio | Nat King Cole Trio:The MacGregor Years 1941/45 | Music & Arts | CD 911
Louis Jordan And His Tympany Five | Five Guys Named Moe | Bandstand | BDCD 1531
Roosevelt Sykes | The Honeydripper | Queen-Disc | 055

Knock On Wood
Herbie Mann Group | Deep Pocket | Kokopelli Records | KOKO 1296
Maceo Parker Group | Maceo(Soundtrack) | Minor Music | 801046
Red Norvo Quintet | Knock On Wood | Affinity | CD AFS 1017
Travis 'Moonchild' Haddix And The Travis Haddix Band | Shootum Up | Elite Special | 73613
Willie Mabon & His Combo | Blues Roots Vol. 16: Willie Mabon | Chess | 6.24806 AG

Knockin' A Jug
Louis Armstrong With Sy Oliver And His Orchestra | Louis Armstrong:The New And Revisited Musical Autobiography Vol.2 | Jazz Unlimited | JUCD 2004

Know Not One
Jack Bruce-Bernie Worrell | Monkjack | CMP Records | CMP CD 1010

Know What I Mean
Roy Williams Quartet | When You're Smiling | Hep | CD 2010

Know What I Mean (alt.take)
Kenny Wheeler Ensemble | Muisc For Large & Small Ensembles | ECM | 1415/16

Know Where You Are
Billy Bang | Bangception | HatOLOGY | 517

Knowing Me Knowing
Triocolor | Colours Of Ghana | ACT | 9285-2

Knowing Sowah
Leroy Jenkins Quartet | Space Minds,New Worlds,Survival America | Tomato | 2606512

Knowledge Box
Ran Blake Trio | Horace Is Blue:A Silver Noir | HatOLOGY | 550

Knubbel Blues
Bobby Hutcherson Orchestra | Knucklebean | Blue Note | LA 789

Knut Hauling
Sergey Kuryokhin/Boris Grebenshchikov | Subway Culture:The Third Russian Opera | LEO | LR 402/403

Ko
Lee Konitz-Harold Danko Duo | Wild As Springtime | G.F.M. Records | 8002

Ko Ko Mo(I Love You So)
Louis Armstrong And His All Stars | Historic Barcelona Concerts At Windsor Palace 1955 | Fresh Sound Records | FSR-CD 3004
Rare Performances Of The 50's And The 60's | CBS | CBS 88669
Louis Armstrong And His All Stars With Sonny Burke's Orchestra | Ambassador Louis Armstrong Vol.17:Moments To Remember(1952-1956) | Ambassador | CLA 1917
Andy Lumpp | Andy Lump Piano Solo | Nabel Records:Jazz Network | LP 4608(Audiophile)

Koan(part 1-5)
Good Fellas | Good Fellas 3 | Paddle Wheel | KICJ 166

Köcekce(turkish folk material)
Oliver Augst-Rüdiger Carl-Christoph Korn | Blank | FMP | OWN-90013

Koch's Curve
Farafina | Bolomakote | VeraBra Records | CDVBR 2026-2

Koen(da kaze ga dandan tsuyoku ni naru yo ni...)
Kelm 3 | Per Anno | dml-records | CD 013

Koengskreis
Stephan-Max Wirth Quartet | Jazzchanson 20th Century Suite | double moon | DMCD 1008-2

Koffer In Berlin
Abdullah Ibrahim | Knysna Blue | TipToe | TIP-888816 2

Kofifi Blue
Untemehmen Kobra | Central Europe Suite | G.N.U. Records | CD A 94.007

Ko-Kee
Mills Blue Rhythm Band | Rhythm Spasm | Hep | CD 1015

Kökler-Die Wurzeln
Anthony Braxton Group | Anthony Braxton's Charlie Parker Project 1993 | Hat Art | CD 6160(2)

Ko-Ko
Dizzy Gillespie Quintet | The Bird Flies Deep | Atlantis | ATS 12
Duke Ellington And His Famous Orchestra | Jazz:The Essential Collection Vol.2 | IN+OUT Records | 78012-2
Duke Ellington:Ko-Ko | Dreyfus Jazz Line | FDM 36717-2
Duke Ellington And His Orchestra | Carnegie Hall Concert January 1943 | Prestige | 2PCD 34004-2
Duke Ellington:Complete Prestige Carnegie Hall 1943-1944 Concerts | Definitive Records | DRCD 11210
Duke Ellington's Masterpieces Vol.1: 1938-1940 | Black & Blue | BLE 59.233 2
Grant Stewart Quintet | Downtown Sounds | Criss Cross | Criss 1085
Super Sax | Supersax Plays Bird | Blue Note | 796264-2

Koko's Tune
Art Blakey And The Jazz Messengers | Lee Morgan More Birdland Sessions | Fresh Sound Records | FSCD 1029

Kolarpolskan
Jugendjazzorchester NW | Back From The States | Jugendjazzorchester NW | JJO 004

Kollerland
Charles Fambrough Group | Keeper Of The Spirit | audioquest Music | AQCD 1033

Köln Blues
Keith Jarrett | The Köln Concert | ECM | 1064/65(810067-2)

Köln, January 24, 1975(part 1)
The Köln Concert | ECM | 1064/65(810067-2)

Köln, January 24, 1975(part 2)
Uwe Kropinski | So Oder So | ITM Records | 0025

Kom Helga Ande
Edward Vesala Ensemble | Satu | ECM | 1088

Komet Ihr Hirten
Hank Jones Meets Cheik-Tidiana Seck | Sarala | Verve | 528783-2

Komidiara
Jo Ambros Group | Wanderlust | dml-records | CD 016

Komite
Das Pferd | Das Pferd | ITM Records | ITM 1416

Komm Auf Die Schaukel,Luise
Joe Kienemann Trio | Liedgut:Amsel,Drossel,Swing & Funk | yvp music | CD 3095

Komm Lieber Mai Und Mache
Willem Breuker & Leo Cuypers | ...Superstars | FMP | SAJ 17

Komm,Gott Schöpfer,Heiliger Geist
Martin Theurer | Moon Mood | FMP | 0700

Kommet Ihr Hirten
David Gazarov Trio | Let's Have A Merry Christmas With The David Gazarov Trio! | Organic Music | ORGM 9712
Jan Von Klewitz-Markus Burger | Spiritual Standards | Jazzline | JL 11156-2

Komungo
Der Rote Bereich | Der Rote Bereich 3 | Jazz 4 Ever Records:Jazz Network | J4E 4740

Konäsörs
Robin Eubanks/Steve Turre Group | Dedication | JMT Edition | 834433-2

Konevitsan Kirkonkellot
Klaus Treuheit | Solo | Klaus Treuheit Production | A+P 9304(CD 161)

Kongolela
Tomatic 7 | Haupstrom | Jazz Haus Musik | JHM 0101 CD

König Der Gemeinheiten
Fun Horns | Surprise | Jazzpoint | JP 1029 CD

Königin Der Nacht-Oder Eine Kleine Horn-Musik
Norbert Stein Pata Orchester | The Secret Act Of Painting | Pata Musik | PATA 7 CD

Königskinder
Ulrich Gumpert Workshop Band/DDR | Unter Anderem: 'N Tango Für Gitti | FMP | 0600

Könn't Ich Sie Trinken,Ich Wollt' An Ihr Ersticken
Jemeel Moondoc-Quartet Muntu | The Athens Concert | Praxis | CM 107

Kon-Tiki
Dabiré Gabin | Kontômé | Nueva Records | IN 816

Konya
Carlo Actis Dato Quartet | Noblesse Oblige | SPLASC(H) Records | H 118

Kool
Albert Collins Blues Band | The Master Of The Telecaster | Crosscut | CCR 1011

Kool Kitty
| Marian McPartland Plays The Music Of Mary Lou Williams | Concord | CCD 4605

Korako
Arild Andersen Quartet | A Molde Concert | ECM | 1236

Korall
Brennan-Cline-Patumi-Voirol-Theissing | Shooting Stars & Traffic Lights | L+R Records | CDLR 45090

Kosacken-Patrouille
Max Greger Und Sein Orchester | Swing Tanzen Gestattet | Vagabond | 6.28415 DP

Kosende Hände
Brocksi-Quintett | Drums Boogie | Bear Family Records | BCD 15988 AH
Drums Boogie | Bear Family Records | BCD 15988 AH

Kosende Hände(false-start)
Steve Tibbetts Group | Steve Tibbetts | ECM | 1814(017068-2)

Koshala
Steve Coleman And Five Elements | World Expansion | JMT Edition | 834410-2

Kosmuus
Peter Fulda Trio With Céline Rudolph | Silent Dances | Jazz 4 Ever Records:Jazz Network | J4E 4731

Kotekan
Dave Brubeck Quartet | Concord On A Summer Night | Concord | CCD 4198

Koto Song
Triple Play:Dave Brubeck | Telarc Digital | CD 83449
Dave Brubeck Quartet With The Montreal International Jazz Festival Orchestra | New Wine | Limelight | 820830-2
Joe Lovano-Aldo Romano | Ten Tales | Owl Records | 018350-2

Koua 1
Bensusan & Malherbe | Live Au New Morning | Acoustic Music Records | 319.1142.2

Kozo's Waltz
Art Blakey And The Jazz Messengers | A Night In Tunisia | Blue Note | 784049-2
Heiner Goebbels-Alfred Harth Duo | Vom Sprengen Des Gartens | FMP | SAJ 20

Kraine
Frank Strozier Sextet | Remember Me | Steeplechase | SCCD 31066

Kramat
Dollar Brand Quartet | Zimbabwe | Enja | 4056-2

Kramim
Hans Reichel | Wichlinghauser Blues | FMP | 0150

Kraniche Im Zweireiher
Allan Vaché's Florida Jazz Allstars | Allan Vaché's Floridy Jazz Allstars | Nagel-Heyer | CD 032

Krazy Kapers
Chocolate Dandies | The Various Facets Of A Genius 1929-1940 | Black & Blue | BLE 59.230 2

Krazy Kat
Frankie Trumbauer And His Orchestra | Riverboat Shuffle | Naxos Jazz | 8.120584 CD

Kreise I
Adelhard Roidinger Trio | Computer & Jazz Project I | Thein | TH 100384

Kreta
Association Urbanetique | Don't Look Back | Enja | ENJ-6056 2

Kristallen
Art Farmer Quartet Feat Jim Hall | To Sweden With Love | Atlantic | AMCY 1016

Kristi-Blodsdaper(Fucsia)
Frank Tusa Duo | Father Time | Enja | 2056

Kriv Sadosko
Unternehmen Kobra | Central Europe Suite | G.N.U. Records | CD A 94.007

Kronach Waltz
King Oliver's Creole Jazz Band | King Oliver's Creole Jazzband-The Complete Set | Retrieval | RTR 79007

Krötenbalz
Dollar Brand | African Sketch Book | Enja | 2026-2

Krukma
Guy Lafitte Sextet | Jazz In Paris:Guy Lafitte-Blue And Sentimental | EmArCy | 159852-2 PMS

Krum Elbow Blues
Johnny Hodges Orchestra | Johnny Hodges-Hodge Podge | CBS | EK 66972

Krupa-
Jan Garbarek-Ralph Towner | Dis | ECM | 1093(827408-2)

Krusning
Klaus Treuheit | Solo | Klaus Treuheit Production | A+P 9304(CD 161)

KSM
Anthony Braxton | 8KN-(B-12)IR10(for string quartet) | Sound Aspects | sas CD 009

Kubismus 502
Glen Moore -Rabih Abou-Khalil | Nude Bass Ascending... | Intuition Records | INT 3192-2

Kubla Khan
John Scofield Quartet | A Go Go | Verve | 539979-2

Kubrick
Horace Parlan Sextet | Happy Frame Of Mind | Blue Note | 869784-7

Ku'Damm 1:30 A.M.
Willem Breuker Kollektief | In Holland | BVHAAST | 041/42 (807118)

Kudu
Naßler & Schneider feat. Jörg Ritter | Triologe | Acoustic Music Records | 319.1137.2

Kuka
The Robert Hohner Percussion Ensemble | Different Strokes | dmp Digital Music Productions | CD 485

Kultrum Pampa
Paul Eßer-Gerd Dudek-Ali Haurand-Jiri Strivin | Jazz Und Lyrik:Schinderkarren Mit Buffet | Konnex Records | KCD 5108

Kulturaustausch
Gary Thomas Quintet | Exile's Gate | JMT Edition | 514009-2

Kulture Of Jazz
Nana | Schwarze Nana | Jazz Haus Musik | JHM 23

Kulu Se Mama
John Coltrane And His Orchestra | The Best Of John Coltrane-His Greatest Years | MCA | AS 9200-2

Kum Ba Ya
Pharoah Sanders Orchestra | Message From Home | Verve | 529578-2

Kumba
Miki N'Doye Orchestra | Joko | ACT | 9403-2

Kümmel's Traum Oder Die Rheinische Republik
Eddie Henderson Orchestra | Blue Breaks Beats Vol.2 | Blue Note | 789907-2

Kumquat Kids
SheshBesh | SheshBesh | TipToe | TIP-888830 2

Kumran
Tony Scott | Music For Yoga Meditation And Other Joys | Verve | 2304471 IMS

Kundalina-Serpent Power
Perry Robinson-Badal Roy | Kundalini | Improvising Artists Inc. | 123856-2

Kundarra
Ernest Ranglin Group | Modern Answers To Old Problems | Telarc Digital | CD 83526

Kunst Der Fuge(Contrapunctus)
Hans Koller Quintet | Kunstkopfindianer | MPS | 9813439

Kunstkopfindianer
Globe Unity Orchestra And Guests | Pearls | FMP | 0380

Kupala
Thomas Chapin Quintet | You Don't Know Me | Arabesque Recordings | AJ 0115

Kurhadanadur
Giorgio Gaslini Trio | Schumann Reflections | Soul Note | SN 1120

Kuriosita
Joelle Leandre-Rüdiger Carl | Blue Goo Park | FMP | CD 52

Kurita Sensei
Herbie Mann & The Family Of Mann With Minoru Muraoka,Shomyo & Gagaku | Gagaku & Beyond | Finnadar | SR 9014

Kurz Vor Zein
Thomas Stiffling Group | Stories | Jazz 4 Ever Records:Jazz Network | J4E 4756

Kurzer Ausbruch
Joos-Czelusta-Konrad Trio | Blow!!! | FMP | 0370

Kush
Dizzy Gillespie And His Orchestra | Gillespiana And Carnegie Hall Concert | Verve | 519809-2
Dizzy Gillespie And The United Nation Orchestra | Live At The Royal Festival Hall | Enja | ENJ-6044 2
Dizzy Gillespie Quintet | Swing Low, Sweet Cadillac | Impulse(MCA) | 951178-2
Do Pop A Da | Affinity | AFF 142
Lalo Schifrin Sextet | Tin Tin Deo | Fresh Sound Records | FSR-CD 319
Heinz Sauer Trio | Exchange | free flow music | ffm 0695

Küss' Die Hand,Madame
Rüdiger Carl | Vorn:Lieder Und Improvisationen Für Akkordeon, Bandoneon Und Ziehharmonika | FMP | 1110

Kwa Heri
Louis Moholo's Viva-La-Black | Exile | Ogun | OGCD 003

Kwa-Blaney
Prince Lasha Quartet | Inside Story | Enja | 3073

Kwaedid Um Fuglana
Bobby Scott Octet | The Compositions Of Bobby Scott | Fresh Sound Records | FSR 2020(Bethlehem BCP 8)

Kwirk
Bill Evans Group | Let The Juice Loose-Bill Evans Group Live at The Blue Note,Tokyo | Jazz City | 660.53.001

Kyanos
Stan Kenton And His Orchestra | National Anthems Of The World | Creative World | ST 1060

Kymenlaakson Laulu
John Wolf Brennan-Daniele Patumi | Ten Zentences | L+R Records | CDLR 45066

Kyoto
John Wolf Brennan | Flügel | Creative Works Records | CW CD 1037-2
Steven Halpern-Dalles Smith | Threshold | Gramavision | 18-7301-1

Kyoto(part 1&2)
Dave Douglas Group | Soul On Soul | RCA | 2663603-2

Kyrie
David Matthews & The Manhattan Jazz Orchestra | Back To Bach | Milestone | MCD 9312-2
Jazzensemble Des Hessischen Rundfunks | Jazz Messe-Messe Für Unsere Zeit | hr music.de | hrmj 003-01 CD
Joe Masters Orchestra & Choir | The Jazz Mass By John Masters | Discovery | DS 785 IMS
Paul Giger Trio | Vindonissa | ECM | 1836(066069-2)
Gianluigi Trovesi With The Orchestra Da Camera Di Nembro Enea Salmeggia | Around Small Fairy Tales | Soul Note | 121341-2

Kyser Sozée
Ed Schuller Group feat. Dewey Redman | The Force | Tutu Records | 888166-2*

Kyyoi
Pheeroan akLaff Group | Fits Like A Glove | Gramavision | GR 8207-2

L
Lowell Davidson Trio | Lowell Davidson Trio | ESP Disk | ESP 1012-2

L & A Groove
Bill Coleman-Guy Lafitte Quintet | Bill Coleman Meets Guy Lafitte | Black Lion | BLCD 760182

L Bird
Al Jarreau With Band | L Is For Lover | i.e. Music | 557850-2

L Is For Lover
Walter Davis Group | Let Me In Your Saddle | Swingtime(Contact) | BT 2004

L&J
Philadelphia Jerry Ricks & Oscar Klein | Low Light Blues | L+R Records | LR 42007

L.A. Calling
Eckinger/Manning Quintet | L.A. Calling | TCB Records | TCB 9090

L.B. And Me
Johnny Hodges-Wild Bill Davis Sextet | In A Mellotone | RCA | ND 82305(847146)

L.Eave's Dropping On Higgledy Piggledy
Jaki Byard Quartet | Family Man | 32 Jazz | 32171

L.O.V.E.
Teddy Wilson Trio | J.A.T.P. In London 1969 | Pablo | 2CD 2620119
Soul Rebels | Let Your Mind Be Free | Mardi Gras Records | MG 1020

La Ballade Irlandaise
Roman Schwaller Jazz Quartet | Live In Vienna | Bassic-Sound | 002

La Ballade Pour Pipette
Roman Schwaller-Mel Lewis Sextet | Roman Schwaller-Mel Lewis | Bassic-Sound | CD 005

La Bamba
Dave Pike Sextet | Carnavals | Prestige | PCD 24248-2
Kenny Garrett Sextet | Garrett 5 | Paddle Wheel | K32Y 6280

La Belle Afrique
Cadavre Exquis | Cadavre Exquis | Creative Works Records | CW CD 1014-1

La Belle Et La Bete
Elmo Hope Trio | The All Star Sessions | Milestone | M 47037

La Boe La Boe
Francis Coletta Trio + One | Cris De Balaines | IN+OUT Records | 77030-2

La Boheme
Antoine Hervé Quintet | Invention Is You | Enja | ENJ-9398 2

La Boite A Musique
Gianluigi Trovesi Trio | Les Boites A Musique | SPLASC(H) Records | CD H 152-2

La Brea
Bernard Vitet Quintet | Jazz In Paris:Jazz & Cinéma Vol.2 | EmArCy | 013044-2

La Broma
Karlheinz Miklin Quintet & KUG Big Band | KH Miklin Quinteto Argentina & KUG Big Band | TCB Records | TCB 21232

La Camorra
Astor Piazzolla Group | Piazzolla | American Clave | AMCL 1021-2

La Cantatrice
Italian String Trio | From Groningen To Mulhouse | SPLASC(H) Records | CD H 416-2

La Carezza
Lindemann/Santa Maria Quartet | Piano Duo Plus | Plainisphare | PL 1267-8

La Casa Sin Luz
Gustavo Bergalli Group | Tango In Jazz | Touché Music | TMcCD 007

La Casita De Mis Viejos
Charlie Mariano's Nassim | Charlie Mariano's Nassim | Off The Wall Records | OTW 9801-CD

La Chambelona-
Mulgrew Miller Trio | From Day To Day | Landmark | LCD 1525-2

La Champagne
Michel Petrucciani Trio | Michel Petrucciani:The Blue Note Years | Blue Note | 789916-2
TSF+Daniel Huck | Drolement Vocal! | IDA Record | 013 CD

La Chanson Des Rues
Judy Niemack With The Kenny Werner Quintet | ...Night And The Music | Freelance | FRL-CD 026

La Chapelle-
Claude Luter With Orchestra | La Nuit Es Une Sorciere | Vogue | 21134142

La Charanga
Michael Riessler Group | Tentations D'Abélard | Wergo | WER 8009-2

La Chasse
Jean Pierre Mas Trio | Jamais 2 Sans 3 | Owl Records | 06

La China Leonica Arreo La Correntinada Trajo Entre La Muchachada

La Flor De La Juvuntud
Gato Barbieri Orchestra | Latino America | Impulse(MCA) | 952236-2
Gato Barbieri Septet | Gato Chapter Four: Alive In New York | Impulse(MCA) | JAS 54(AS 9303)

La Chipaca
Coleman Hawkins With Many Albam And His Orchestra | The Hawk In Paris | Bluebird | 63 51059-2

La Cigale Ivre S'Envoie El L'Air
Jorge Pardo Band | Cicadas | ACT | 9209-2

La Cita
Eladio Reinon Quintet | Es La Historia De Un Amor | Fresh Sound Records | FSNT 004 CD
Ruben Blades Y Seis Del Solar | Agua De Luna | Messidor | 15964 CD

La Ciudad Habana
Conexion Latina | La Conexión | Enja | ENJ-9065 2

La Clave
Mario Bauzá And The Afro-Cuban Jazz Orchestra | 944 Columbus | Messidor | 15828 CD

La Comparsa
Michel Camilo Trio | Triangulo | Telarc Digital | CD 83549
Santos Chillemi Group | Trinidad | Maracatu | MAC 940001
Mike Westbrook Trio | Love For Sale | Hat Art | CD 6061

La Conexión
Ramon Valle Quintet | Ramon Valle Plays Ernesto Lecuona | ACT | 9404-2

La Conga De Medianoche
Markus Stockhausen Orchestra | Sol Mestizo:Markus Stockhausen Plays The Music Of Enrique Diaz | ACT | 9222-2

La Conquista
Gerald Wiggins Trio | Around The World In 80 Days | Original Jazz Classics | OJCCD 1761-2(SP 2101)

La Couperin from Pieces For Harpsichord, Book 4(Francois Couperin)
McCoy Tyner Orchestra | Sama Layuca | Original Jazz Classics | OJCCD 1071-2(M 9056)

La Cubana
Benny Goodman And His Orchestra | More Camel Caravans | Phontastic | NCD 8841/2

La Cucaracha
Charlie Parker And His Orchestra | Bird On Verve-Vol.6:South Of The Border | Verve | 817447-1 IMS
Charlie Parker Septet | The Latin Bird | Memo Music | HDJ 4076
Louis Armstrong With Luis Russell And His Orchestra | Ambassador Louis Armstrong Vol.1(1935) | Ambassador | CLA 1901

La Cucaracha(take 1-4)
Ana Caram Group | Rio After Dark | Chesky | JD 28

La Cumparsita
Laurindo Almeida/Charlie Byrd Quartet | Tango | Concord | CCD 4290
Stan Kenton And His Orchestra | The Kenton Era | Creative World | ST 1030
Tango Orkestret | Tango Orkestret | Stunt Records | STUCD 19303

La Curda
Tete Montoliu Trio | Tete Montoliu Interpreta A Serrat | Fresh Sound Records | FSR 4004(835319)

La Danse Du Coeur
Magma Trio | Urgente | yvp music | CD 3045

La Danza Delle Ombre
Cosmo Intini & The Jazz Set | Seeing The Cosmic | SPLASC(H) Records | H 121

La Dernière Bergére(The Last Shepherdess)
Aldo Romano Group | AlmaLatina | Owl Records | 018364-2

La Derniere Chanson
Willie Bobo Group | Juicy | Verve | 519857-2

La Descargo Del Bobo
Bill Evans Group | Escape | Escape | ESC 03650-2

La Divetta
Art Blakey And The Jazz Messengers | Des Femmes Disparaissent/Les Tricheurs(Original Soundtracks) | Fontana | 834752-2 PMS

La Donna
Banda Cittá Ruvo Di Puglia | La Banda/Banda And Jazz | Enja | ENJ-9326 2

La Donna E Mobile & Quaretteo(Rigoletto)
Randy Weston Orchestra | The Spirits Of Our Ancestors | Verve | 511857-2

La Estiba
Irakere | Yemayá | Blue Note | 498239-2

La Explosion
Poncho Sanchez And His Orchestra | A Night With Poncho Sanchez Live:Bailar | Concord | CCD 4558

La Félure
Ernie Krivda Quintet | Satanic | Inner City | IC 1031 IMS

La Fete Surreale
Sidney Bechet With Orchestra | La Nuit Es Une Sorciere | Vogue | 21134142

La Fiesta
Chick Corea's Return To Forever | Works | ECM | 825426-2
Herbie Hancock & Chick Corea | An Evening With Herbie Hancock & Chick Corea In Concert | CBS | SRCS 9346-2
Maynard Ferguson And His Orchestra | Chameleon | CBS | 467091-2
Stan Getz Quartet | The Lyrical Stan Getz | CBS | 460819-2
Stan Getz Quintet | Captain Marvel | CBS | 468412-2
Woody Herman And His Orchestra | La Fiesta | West Wind Orchestra Series | 2400 CD

La Fille Bleue
Vincent Courtois Quartet | Translucide | Enja | ENJ-9380 2

La Fille Et L'Affiche
Sfogliare Albi | Tempo Per | yvp music | CD 3029

La Fruite De Jazz
Bill Watrous With The Patrick Williams Orchestra | Someplace Else | Soundwings | SW 2100(807411)

La Fuerza Del Viento
Louis Sclavis Group | Dans La Nuit | ECM | 1805(589524-2)

La Fuite
Riccardo Fassi Tankio Band | Riccardo Fassi Tankio Band | SPLASC(H) Records | H 107

La Galinette
Juraj Galan-Norbert Dömling | Playing For Love | BELL Records | BLR 84026

La Gitana(Hevi Bülbül)
Banda Cittá Ruvo Di Puglia | La Banda/Banda And Jazz | Enja | ENJ-9326 2
La Gitana(Il Trovatore)
Mal Waldron Trio | Black Glory | Enja | 2004
La Goualante De L'Idiot
Joelle Leandre-Carlos Zingaro | Ecritures | Adda | 590038
La Guarapachanga
Stan Kenton And His Orchestra | Cuban Fire | Capitol | 796260-2
La Guitare A King Kong
McCoy Tyner And The Latin All-Stars | McCoy Tyner And The Latin All-Stars | Telarc Digital | CD 83462
La Ibkey
Ahmed Abdul-Malik Orchestra | East Meets West | RCA | 2125723-2
La Intrigosa
Didier Lockwood Group | 'Round About Silence | Dreyfus Jazz Line | FDM 36595-2
La Javanaise
Richard Galliano Trio | Gallianissimo! The Best Of Richard Galliano | Dreyfus Jazz Line | FDM 36616-2
Jimmy Lunceford And His Orchestra | Jimmy Lunceford And His Orchestra Vol.1 | Black & Blue | BLE 59.241 2
La Joaquina
Gregor Hübner Quintet | Januschko's Time | Satin Doll Productions | SDP 1034-1 CD
La Juana
Eddie Chamblee Quintet | Eddie Chamblee/Julian Dash/Joe Thomas:The Complete Recordings 1951-1955 | Blue Moon | BMCD 1052
La Ladra Di Cuori
Winanda Del Sur | Luny Y Mar | Challenge | CHR 70037
La Legenda Del Pescatore
Les Blue Stars | Jazz In Paris:Blossom Dearie-The Pianist/Les Blue Stars | EmArCy | 064784-2
La Legende Du Pays Des Oiseaux(Lullaby Of Birdland)
Caoutchouc | Caoutchouc Plays Garcia Lorca | Timeless | CD SJP 399
La Liberte Est Un Fleur
Eddy Louiss Orchestra | Multicolor Feeling-Fanfare | Nocturne Productions | NTCD 105
La Lugubre Gondola
Piirpauke | Zerenade | JA & RO | JARO 4142-2
La Luna
Mario Piacentini Trio | Canto Atavico | SPLASC(H) Records | H 146
La Macarena(La Virchin De La Macarena)
I.C.P.Tentet | I.C.P.-Tentet In Berlin | FMP | SAJ 23
La Madre Di Tutte Le Guerre
Doudou Gouirand Quartet | La Nuit De Wounded Knee | Blue Line | VB 055 CD
La Malaura(The Tempest)
Corina Curschellas-John Wolf Brennan | Willisau And More Live | Creative Works Records | CW CD 1020-2
Ulf Adaker Quartet | Reflections | Touché Music | TMcCD 016
La Mano
Didier Lockwood Duo | New World | MPS | 68237
La Mar Esta Enferma
| Son Song | Fresh Sound Records | FSNT 010 CD
La Mariposa
George Lewis Quartet | George Lewis:Trios & Bands | American Music | AMCD-4
La Mémoire Du Silence
Ana Caram Group | Maracana | Chesky | JD 104
La Mere De La Mer-
Sidney Bechet With Orchestra | La Nuit Es Une Sorciere | Vogue | 21134142
La Mesha
Roman Schwaller Jazz Quartet | Clubdate | Jazz 4 Ever Records:Jazz Network | J4E 4713
Wolfgang Haffner International Jazz Quintet | Whatever It Is | Jazz 4 Ever Records:Jazz Network | J4E 4714
Lluis Vidal Trio | Milikituli | Fresh Sound Records | FSNT 009 CD
La Meva Enamorada
Myra Melford Extended Ensemble | Even The Sounds Shine | Hat Art | CD 6161
La Mort C'est La Vie(Hommage á Jean Tinguely)
René Pretschner & Melo Mafali | The Piano Duo:El Latino | Green House Music | CD 1006
La Morte Douce
Steve Lacy Quintet | The Gap | America | AM 6125
La Muerta Del Angel
Gary Burton Group | Tango | Concord | CCD 4793
La Muerte Del Angel
Pablo Ziegler And His Quintet For New Tango | Asfalto-Street Tango | RCA | 2663266-2
La Muntagnella
Bruce Forman Quintet | 20/20 | Muse | MR 5273
La Negra
Mario Piacentini Trio | Canto Atavico | SPLASC(H) Records | H 146
La Nevada
Gil Evans Orchestra | Out Of The Cool | CTI Records | PDCTI 1114-2
La Noche De Lemuria
Riccardo Fassi Septet | Toast Man | SPLASC(H) Records | CD H 307-2
La Nostalgie De La Boue
Horacio Molina With Band | Tango Cancion | Messidor | 15910
La Nuit Des Yeux
Sidney Bechet With Orchestra | La Nuit Es Une Sorciere | Vogue | 21134142
La Nuit Ravie
Dhafer Youssef Group | Electric Sufi | Enja | ENJ-9412 2
La Nuit Sacrée
Trio Terracota | Savia | Acoustic Music Records | 319.1193.2
La Palazzina Americana
Barre Phillips Group | For All It Is | Japo | 60003 IMS
La Paloma
Charlie Parker Septet | Charlie Parker-South Of The Border | Verve | 527779-2
The Latin Bird | Memo Music | HDJ 4076
Jelly Roll Morton | The Library Of Congress Recordings | Affinity | CD AFS 1010-3
Dave Brubeck Sextet | Bravo! Brubeck! | CBS | CK 65723
La Paloma Azul
Frederica von Stade With The Chris Brubeck-Bill Crofut Ensemble | Across Your Dreams: Frederica von Stade Sings Brubeck | Telarc Digital | CD 80467
La Paloma Revisited
Zollsounds 4 feat. Lee Konitz | Open Hearts | Enja | 9123-2
La Palomeinding
Aldo Romano Trio | Il Piacere | Owl Records | 013575-2
La Panna
Nguyen Le Trio | Nguyen Le:3 Trios | ACT | 9245-2
La Parfum
John Fedchock New York Big Band | John Fedchock New York Big Band | Reservoir | RSR CD 138
La Pasionara
Charlie Haden Orchestra | The Ballad Of The Fallen | ECM | 1248(811546-2)
La Pasionaria
Charlie Haden Trio | The Montreal Tapes | Verve | 537670-2
Geri Allen Trio | Segments | DIW | DIW 833 CD
La Pendaison
Dino Saluzzi Trio | Responsorium | ECM | 1816(017069-2)
La Pequena Historia De...!
Christian Escoudé Group | A Suite For Gypsies | EmArCy | 558403-2
La Peur Du Noir
Lionel Hampton Quintet | Americans Swinging In Paris:Lionel Hampton | EMI Records | 539649-2
La Piege
Lionel Hampton Sextet | Recorded In Paris 1956 | Swing | SW 8415 IMS
La Place Street
Stanley Turrentine Group | La Place | Blue Note | 790261-2
La Plus Belle Africaine
Duke Ellington And His Orchestra | Antibes Concert-Vol.2 | Verve | 2304065 IMS
Ella Fitzgerald And Duke Ellington:Cote D'Azure Concerts on Verve | Verve | 539033-2
Ella Fitzgerald And Duke Ellington:Cote D'Azure Concerts on Verve | Verve | 539033-2
Soul Call | Verve | 539785-2
Steve Kuhn Trio | Oceans In The Sky | Owl Records | 013428-2
La PlusQue Lente-
Gato Barbieri Orchestra | Chapter Three:Viva Emiliano Zapata | Impulse(MCA) | 2292-52001-1
La Podrida
Dhafer Youssef Group | Electric Sufi | Enja | ENJ-9412 2
La Prière De L'Absent
Charlie Byrd Trio With Strings & Brass | Crystal Silence | Fantasy | F 9429
La Prima Vera-
The Rosenberg Trio With Frits Landesbergen | Caravan | Verve | 523030-2
La Puerta
Hector Martignon Group | Portrait In White And Black | Candid | CCD 79727
Paquito D'Rivera Orchestra | A Night In Englewood | Messidor | 15829 CD
La Rage
Eugenio Colombo | Summertime | SPLASC(H) Records | H 122
La Rateta Que Escombrava L'Escaleta
Maxim Saury And His New Orleans Sound | Homage A Sidney Bechet | Jazztime(EMI) | 792406-2
La Resureccion Del Angel
Claude Luter With Orchestra | La Nuit Es Une Sorciere | Vogue | 21134142
La Rive Gauche
Thierry Lang Trio with Toots Thielemans & Carine Sarrasin | The Blue Peach | TCB Records | TCB 95302
La Romance De Maitre Pathelin
Raymond Boni | L'Homme Etoile | Hat Art | 3510
La Ronde
Modern Jazz Quartet | Modern Jazz Quartet | Prestige | P 24005
The MJQ Box | Prestige | 7711-2
La Ronde Suite
MJQ 40 | Atlantic | 7567-82330-2
Modern Jazz Quartet | Prestige | P 24005
La Ronde Suite:
The Modern Jazz Quartet | Atlantic | 7567-81331-2
La Rosita
Coleman Hawkins Sextet | Hawk Eyes | Original Jazz Classics | OJCCD 294-2
Conrad Gozzo And His Orchestra | GOZ The Great | Fresh Sound Records | LPM 1124(RCA)
Laurindo Almeida/Charlie Byrd Quartet | Tango | Concord | CCD 4290
La Route Enchantée
Elek Bacsik Quartet | Jazz In Paris:Elek Baczik | EmArCy | 542231-2
La Saison Des Pluies
John Wright Trio | South Side Soul | Original Jazz Classics | OJC-1743(P 7190)
La Santa Espina
Giessen-Köln-Nonett | Some Other Tapes | Fish Music | FM 009/10 CD
Grumpff | Wetterau | FMP | SAJ 16
La Scala
Keith Jarrett | La Scala | ECM | 1640(537268-2)
La Scala(part 1)
La Scala | ECM | 1640(537268-2)
La Scala(part 2)
Eddy Louiss Trio & Fanfare | Sentimental Feeling | Dreyfus Jazz Line | FDM 36600-2
La Seduction:
Palatino | Palationo Chap.3 | EmArCy | 013610-2
La Sevigliana
Andre Jaume 8 | Musique Pour 3 & 8:Errance | Hat Art | 2003 Digital
La Spuda(The Slope)
Herbert Distel | La Stazione | Hat Art | CD 6060
La Suerte De Los Tontos(Fortune Of Fools)
Blasnost | Blasnost | Acoustic Music Records | AMC 1023
La Tendresse
Conjunto Clave Y Guaguanco | Dejala En La Puntica | TipToe | TIP-888829 2
La Terigonza
Red Whale | Queekegg | Maracatu | MAC 940002
La Torture D'Alphise
Barbara Thompson's Paraphernalia | Barbara Thompson's Paraphernalia | MCA | 2292-50577-1
La Ultima Curda
Soledad Bravo With Band | Volando Voy | Messidor | 15966 CD
La Valse A Margaux
Richard Galliano Quartet | New Musette | Label Bleu | LBLC 6547(889728)
Keith Jarrett Trio | Keith Jarrett At The Blue Note-The Complete Recordings | ECM | 1575/80(527638-2)
La Valse Bleue
Clifton Chenier And His Band | Frenchin' The Boogie | Verve | 519724-2
La Valse Des Fromages Blancs
Lee Konitz-Kenny Werner | Unleemited | Owl Records | 014727-2
La Valse Qui Rit
Christoph Haberer Group | Pulsation | Jazz Haus Musik | JHM 0066 CD
La Valse Virgin
David Doucet Group | Quand Jai Parti | Rounder Records | CDRR 6040
La Vida Del Senor Lorenzo
Candela | La Maquina | BELL Records | BLR 84031
La Vida Es Un Sueno
Mario Bauzá And His Afro-Cuban Jazz Orchestra | My Time Is Now | Messidor | 15842 CD
La Vie En Rose
David Murray-George Arvanitas | Tea For Two | Fresh Sound Records | FSR-CD 0164
Louis Armstrong And His All Stars | Masters Of Jazz Vol.1:Louis Armstrong | Storyville | STCD 4101
Louis Armstrong With Sy Oliver And His Orchestra | Ambassador Louis Armstrong Vol.18:Because Of You(1950-1953) | Ambassador | CLA 1918
Louis Armstrong-All Time Greatest Hits | MCA | MCD 11032
Masha Bijlsma Band With Bob Malach | Lebo | Jazzline | JL 11145-2
New Orleans All Stars | At The Dixieland Jubilee | Dixieland Jubilee | DJ 502
Skinnay Ennis And His Orchestra | The Uncollected:Skinnay Ennis | Hindsight | HSR 164 (835575)
Shelly Manne Trio | In Zürich | Contemporary | C 14018
La Vie En Rose-
Buddy Collette Quintet | Jazz For Lovers | Original Jazz Classics | OJCCD 1764-2(SP 5002)
La Vie N'est Qu'une Lutte
Ricardo Moyano-Juan Falù | Internationales Guitarren Festival '94 | ALISO Records | AL 1030
La Vieja
Gabriel Pérez Group | La Chipaca | Green House Music | CD 1011
La Viejita Clotilde
David Murray Octet | Picasso | DIW | DIW 879 CD
La Villa
Kenny Dorham Quintet | Sonny Rollins-The Freelance Years:The Complete Riverside & Contemporary Recordings | Riverside | 5 RCD 4427-2
Max Roach Plus Four | Clifford Brown-Max Roach:Alone Together-The Best Of The Mercury Years | Verve | 526373-2
Michael Weiss Quintet | Presenting Michael Weiss | Criss Cross | 1022
La Ville Blanche
Ben Waltzer Quintet | In Metropolitan Motion | Fresh Sound Records | FSNT 082 CD
La Ville Tentaculaire
Duke Ellington And His Orchestra | Live At The 1956 Stratford Festival | Music & Arts | CD 616
La Vita
Véronique Gillet And Fernando Freitez With Carlos Franco | Terracota | Acoustic Music Records | 319.1056.2
La Voce
Urs Leimgruber/John Wolf Brennan | M.A.P. | L+R Records | CDLR 45021
La Voz Del Centro
Conjunto Clave Y Guaguanco | Dejala En La Puntica | TipToe | TIP-888829 2
La Voz Del Congo
Tomatito Group | Soleá: A Flamenco-Jazz Fantasy | ACT | 9208-2
LA,Case Study House
Baden Powell And His Orchestra | Canta Vinicius De Moraes E Paolo Cesar Pinheiro | Festival | 114911
Labour Day
John Abercrombie-Andy LaVerne Quartet | Now It Can Be Played | Steeplechase | SCCD 31314
Labyrinth
Art Pepper Quartet | Art Pepper:The Complete Village Vanguard Sessions | Contemporary | 9CCD-4417-2
Connie Crothers Trio | Perception | Steeplechase | SCCD 31022
Fritz Hauser | Solodrumming | Hat Art | CD 6023(2)
Steve Lacy | Outings | Nueva Records | NC 1012
Tom Harrell Quintet | RCA Victor 80th Anniversary Vol.8:1990-1997 | RCA | 2668784-2
Labyrinths
Dominique Pifarély-Francois Couturier | Poros | ECM | 1647
Labyrintus
Davide Petrocca Quartet | Move | Edition Musikat | EDM 026
Lac Lamand
Carl Ludwig Hübsch | Der Erste Bericht | IN+OUT Records | 77035-2
Lacaille 8760
Bobby Naughton Unit | Nauxtagram | Otic | 1009
L'Accident(part 1)
Louis Sclavis Group | Dans La Nuit | ECM | 1805(589524-2)
L'Accident(part 2)
Tethered Moon | Chansons D'Edith Piaf | Winter&Winter | 910048-2
L'Accordeoniste
Sonny Boy Williamson Group | Sonny Boy Williamson(1937-1947) | RCA | 2126418-2
Lacis Ou C'Est Dans Le Lac!
Clifford Jordan Quintet | Cliff Craft | Blue Note | BLP 1582
Ladenball
Harry Verbeke-Rob Agerbeek Quartet | Seven Steps | Timeless | SJP 173
Ladies Choice
Carla Bley-Steve Swallow | Duets | Watt | 20(837345-2)
Ladies In Mercedes
Gary Burton Quartet | Real Life Hits | ECM | 1293
Jasper Van't Hof-Charlie Mariano-Steve Swallow | Brutto Tempo | Intuition Records | INT 3309-2
Steve Kuhn Trio | Years Later | Concord | CCD 4554
Ladie's Waders
Eugen Cicero Trio | Rokoko Jazz | MPS | 68127
Lady
Hugh Masekela Group | Hope | Triloka Records | 320203-2
Lady Be Good -> Oh! Lady Be Good
Lady Bird
Art Blakey And The Jazz Messengers | At The Cafe Bohemia Vol.3 | Blue Note | 300193(BNJ 61007)
Bud Powell Trio | The Best Of Bud Powell On Verve | Verve | 523392-2
Charles Mingus Quintet | The Charles Mingus Quintet+Max Roach | Original Jazz Classics | OJC20 440-2(F 6009)
Charles Mingus-The Complete Debut Recordings | Debut | 12 DCD 4402-2
Charles Mingus Quintet Plus Max Roach | The Charlie Mingus Quintet Plus Max Roach | Debut | VIJ 5011 IMS
Continuum | Mad About Tadd | Palo Alto | PA 8029
Don Byas Quartet | A Night In Tunisia | Black Lion | BLCD 760136
Gerry Mulligan Quartet | My Funny Valentine | Jazz Society(Vogue) | 670511
Horace Parlan Trio | Movin' And Groovin' | Blue Note | 0677187
Jam Session | Jam Session Vol.9 | Steeplechase | SCCD 31554
Jan Lundgren Trio | Cooking! At The Jazz Bakery | Fresh Sound Records | FSR-CD 5019
Stan Getz Quintet | Stan Getz With European Friends | LRC Records | CDC 7679(874365)
Tadd Dameron Septet | Fats Navarro/Tadd Dameron:Complete Blue Note & Capitol Sessions | Definitive Records | DRCD 11191
Tete Montoliu Trio | Catalonian Nights | Steeplechase | SCCD 31148
Lady Bird(alt.master)
Charles Mingus Quintet | Charles Mingus-The Complete Debut Recordings | Debut | 12 DCD 4402-2
Lady Bird(alt.take)
Tadd Dameron Septet | Fats Navarro/Tadd Dameron:Complete Blue Note & Capitol Sessions | Definitive Records | DRCD 11191
Lady Bug
Maynard Ferguson With The Birdland Dreamband | The Birdland Dream Band Vol.1 | Fresh Sound Records | 58110 CD(RCA)
Lady Bug(alt.take)
Birdland Dream Band | Birdland Dream Band | RCA | 2663873-2
Lady Bug(incompl.take)
Dexter Gordon-James Moody Quintet | Power! | Prestige | P 24087
Lady Chatterley's Mother
Gerry Mulligan Concert Jazz Band | The Complete Verve Gerry Mulligan Concert Band | Verve | 9860613
Verve Jazz Masters 36:Gerry Mulligan | Verve | 523342-2
Compact Jazz: Gerry Mulligan Concert Jazz Band | Verve | 838933-2
Lady Day
Lem Winchester Sextet | Lem's Beat | Original Jazz Classics | OJCCD 1785-2(NJ 8239)
Lady Day's Lament
Vienna Art Orchestra | Perpetuum Mobile | Hat Art | 2024 Digital
Lady Di's Waltz
Oscar Peterson With Orchestra | A Royal Wedding Suite | Original Jazz Classics | OJCCD 973-2(2312129)
Balthasar Thomass-Tony Pagano Quartet | Double Mind | ACT | 9213-2
Lady 'E'
Billy Bauer Quartet | Billy Bauer Plectrist | Verve | MV 2678 IMS
Lady Eve
Trio Larose | Debut | Jazz 'n' Arts Records | JNA 0802
Lady Face
Oscar Peterson-Count Basie Quartet | Satch And Josh...Again | Pablo | 2310802-2
Lady G's Delight
Helmut Nieberle & Cordes Sauvages | Jazz Guitar Highlights 1 | Jardis Records | JRCD 20141
Joe Gallardo Group | Latino Blue | Inak | 853
Lady In Lace
Joe Chambers Trio | Mirrors | Blue Note | 496685-2
Lady In My Life
Stanley Jordan Trio | Festival International De Jazz De Montreal | Spectra | 9811660
Stolen Moments | Blue Note | 797159-2
Lady In The Lake
Hal Russell NRG Ensemble | The Hal Russell Story | ECM | 1498
Lady In The Lake-
Lowell Fulsom Band | Man Of Motion | Charly | CRB 1018
Lady Lover
Billy Eckstine With Bobby Tucker And His Orchestra | No Cover/No Minimum | M&M Records | R 52052(Roulette)

Lady Luck
Elvin Jones Sextet | The Big Beat | Milestone | MCD 47016-2
Bessie Smith With Fletcher Henderson | Bessie Smith-The Complete Recordings Vol.1 | CBS | 467895-2

Lady Lynda
Uli Beckerhoff Quartet | Secret Obsession | Nabel Records:Jazz Network | CD 4647

Lady M.
Duke Ellington And His Orchestra | Such Sweet Thunder | CBS | CK 65568

Lady Mac(Lady Macbeth)
Johnny King Septet | The Meltdown | Enja | ENJ-9329 2

Lady Macbeth
Cal Tjader Quintet | Solar Heat | Memo Music | HDJ 4078

Lady Madonna
Gene Ammons Quintet | Fine And Mellow | Prestige | PRCD 24281-2

Lady Mama
Herbie Mann Group | Discotheque | Atlantic | SD 1670

Lady McGowans Dream(pert 1 2)
Thärichens Tentett | Lady Moon | Minor Music | 801094

Lady Moon
Cecil Payne Septet | Scotch And Milk | Delmark | DE 494

Lady Of Chet
James Blood Ulmer Quartet | Black And Blues | DIW | DIW 845 CD

Lady Of Rome Sister Of Brazil
Al Bowlly With The Ray Noble Orchestra | The Classic Years In Digital Stereo: Al Bowlly With Ray Noble | CDS Records Ltd. | REB 649

Lady Of Spain
Victor Feldman Orchestra | Latinsville | Contemporary | CCD 9005-2
Latinsville | Contemporary | CCD 9005-2
Mark Whitfield Group | Patrice | Warner | 7599-26659-2

Lady Of The Day
Dick Hyman | Dick Hyman Plays The Great American Songbook | Musicmasters | 65120-2

Lady Of The Lavender Mist
Oscar Peterson | The History Of An Artist | Pablo | 2625702-2

Lady Of The Lavender Mist-
Oscar Peterson-Joe Pass Duo | Live At Salle Pleyel, Paris | Pablo | 2625705

Lady Red
Jerome Richardson Group | Jazz Station Runaway | TCB Records | TCB 97402

Lady S.
Archie Shepp Quintet | Live In San Francisco | Impulse(MCA) | JAS 68(AS 9162)

Lady Sings The Blues
Billie Holiday And Her All Stars | The Billie Holiday Song Book | Verve | 823246-2
Billie Holiday And Her Band | Tempo Jazz Edition Vol.3-Stayin' Cool | Verve | 847902-2
Billie Holiday With The Mal Waldron Trio | Ella Fitzgerald, Billie Holiday And Carmen McRae At Newport | Verve | 559809-2
Gioconda Cilio With The Stefano Maltese Band | Deep Inside | SPLASC(H) Records | H 138
Stan Getz Quartet | Live At Montmartre(CD=Stan's Party) | Steeplechase | SCCD 37021/22
Terence Blanchard Quartet | The Billie Holiday Songbook | CBS | 475926-2

Lady Sophie
Lee Ritenour Sextet | Sugar Loaf Express | JVC | JVC 2008-2

Ladyfingers
Stanley Turrentine Quintet | Hustlin' | Blue Note | 540036-2
Harry Verbeke-Rob Agerbeek Quartet | Stardust | Timeless | CD SJP 334

Lafayette
Benny Moten's Kansas City Orchestra | RCA Victor 80th Anniversary Vol.2:1930-1939 | RCA | 2668778-2

Lager Och Jon
Joel Palsson Group | Prim | Naxos Jazz | 86049-2

Laguna
Trio Asab | Coast To Coast | Aho-Recording | AHO CD 1028(CD 380)

Lagwood Walk
David Paquette Trio | Mood Swings | ART BY HEART | ABH 2004 2

Lahaina Cake Glide
Piirpauke | Zerenade | JA & RO | JARO 4142-2

Lähtetään Kulkemaan(Vamonos)
Elvin Jones Trio | Puttin' It Together | Blue Note | 784282-2

Laica
Pete York-Wolfgang Schmid-Lenny MacDowell | Wireless | BELL Records | BLR 84032

Laila
Anouar Brahem Trio | Le Pas Du Chat Noir | ECM | 1792(016373-2)

Laila Au Pays Du Carrousel
Le Pas Du Chat Noir | ECM | 1792(016373-2)

Laila Au Pays Du Carrousel(variations)
Geri Allen Group | Maroons | Blue Note | 799493-2

L'Air De Rien
Yves Robert Trio | In Touch | ECM | 1787(016375-2)

L'Air D'y Toucher
Charlie Parker Groups | Welcome To Jazz: Charlie Parker | Koch Records | 322 075 D1

Laird Baird
Charlie Parker Quartet | Charlie Parker:The Best Of The Verve Years | Verve | 527815-2
Charlie Parker | Verve | 539757-2
Charlie Parker:Bird's Best Bop On Verve | Verve | 527452-2
Ray Anderson Quartet | Old Bottles-New Wine | Enja | ENJ-4098 2
Charlie Parker Quartet | Bird On Verve-Vol.7:Charlie Parker Big Band | Verve | 817448-1 IMS

Laird Turner Meteor
Michael Riessler Group | Heloise | Wergo | WER 8008-2

Lais
Clifton Chenier And His Band | Frenchin' The Boogie | Verve | 519724-2

Laissez-Moi Tranquille
Muhal Richard Abrams Octet | View From Within | Black Saint | 120081-2

Lake Ponchartrain Blues
Harlem Hamfats | Hot Chicago Jazz Blues And Jive 1936-1937 | Folklyric | 9029

Lake Taco
Mike Zwerin Trio | Not Much Noise | Spotlite | SPJ LP 19

Lakes
Tom Harrell Sextet | Passages | Chesky | JD 64

Lakk
Gunther Schuller With The WDR Radio Orchestra & Rememberance Band | Witchi Tia To, The Music Of Jim Pepper | Tutu Records | 888204-2*

Lakoda Song
Jim Pepper Group | Comin' And Goin' | Bellaphon | 290.31.029

Lakutshonilanga(When The Sun Sets)
Africa Djole | Percussion Music From Africa | FMP | SAJ 50

Lalene
Yusef Lateef Ensemble | Yusef Lateef In Nigeria | Landmark | LLP 502

Lalla Mira
Randy Weston African Rhythm Quintet and The Gnawa Master Musicians of Marocco | Spirit! The Power Of Music | Verve | 543256-2

Lalla Mira(part 2)
Quincy Jones And His Orchestra | Big Band Bossa Nova | Verve | 557913-2

Lalo Bossa Nova
Rolf Zielke Trio Feat. Mustafa Boztüy | Rolf Zielke Trio Feat. Mustafa Boztüy | Jazz 'n' Arts Records | JNA 0602
Arnold Ross Trio | The Piano Collection Vol.1 | Vogue | 21610242

Lam Earth
Jukka Tolonen Band | Montreux Boogie | Sonet | 147121

Lamb Kurma
Modern Jazz Quartet | Lonely Woman | Atlantic | 7567-90665-2

Lamb Leopard
Dave Brubeck Quartet With Chorus And Orchestra | To Hope! A Celebration | Telarc Digital | CD 80430

Lambda
Jukka Tolonen Quintet | Tasavallan Presidentti-Lambert Land | Sonet | 147116

Lambert's Point
Artie Shaw And His Orchestra | The Uncollected:Artie Shaw And His Orchestra, Vol.1 | Hindsight | HSR 139

Lambkin
Piirpauke | Piirpauke-Global Servisi | JA & RO | JARO 4150-2

Lamb's Polka
George Russell Sextet | Stratusphunk | Original Jazz Classics | OJC 232(RLP 9341)

Lament
Ahmad Jamal Trio | At The Top-Poinciana Revisited | Impulse(MCA) | JAS 15 (AS 9176)
Dezsö Lakatos With The Super Trio | Elliptic Dance | Timeless | CD SJP 298
Hugh Fraser-Jean Toussaint Quartet | Back To Back | Jazz Focus | JFCD 025
Jerry Gonzalez & Fort Apache Band | Crossroads | Milestone | MCD 9225-2
John Clark Quartet | Faces | ECM | 1176
Ken Peplowski Quartet | Lost In The Stars | Nagel-Heyer | CD 2020
Kenny Dorham Quartet | Kenny Dorham | Royal Jazz | RJD 515
Mark Murphy With The Marc Seales Trio & Background Voices | Song For The Geese | RCA | 2144865-2
Milt Jackson Sextet | Jackson, Johnson, Brown And Company | Pablo | 2310897-2
Pat Martino-Gil Goldstein Duo | We'll Be Together Again | Muse | MR 5090
Roland Kirk Quartet | Rahsaan/The Complete Mercury Recordings Of Roland Kirk | Mercury | 846630-2
Domino | Verve | 543833-2
Shirley Scott Quintet | Oasis | Muse | MCD 5388
Slide Hampton Quartet | Phil Woods/Slide Hampton 1968 Jazz | Jazztime(EMI) | 781253-2
Dennis Rowland Group | A Vocal Celebration Of Miles Davis | Concord | CCD 4751

Lament-
Miles Davis + 19 | Miles Ahead | CBS | CK 65121
Miles Davis With Gil Evans & His Orchestra | Miles Davis At Carnegie Hall | CBS | CK 65027
Soprano Summit | Soprano Summit Live At Concord '77 | Concord | CCD 4052

Lament For Booker
Freddie Hubbard/Woody Shaw Sextet | Double Take | Blue Note | 746294-2
Horace Parlan | Lament For Booker Ervin | Enja | 2054-2

Lament For Javanette
Barney Bigard And His Orchestra | The Indispensable Duke Ellington And The Small Groups,Vol.9/10 | RCA | NL 89582 (809207)

Lament For Lester
Buddy Rich And His Orchestra | Big Swing Face | Pacific Jazz | 837989-2
Woody Herman And His Orchestra | Jazz Legacy 18: Woody Herman-The Fourth Herd | Vogue | 500068

Lament For Linus
Brad Mehldau Trio | The Art Of The Trio Vol.1 | Warner | 9362-46260-2
Ron McClure Quintet | Never Forget | Steeplechase | SCCD 31279

Lament For Love
Toshiko Akiyoshi-Lew Tabackin Big Band | Tanuki's Night Out | JAM | 006 IMS

Lament For The Living
Tadd Dameron And His Orchestra | The Lost Sessions | Blue Note | 521484-2

Lament For Thelonious
Eckinger/Manning Quintet | L.A. Calling | TCB Records | TCB 9090

Lament Of The Old Man
Abe Lyman And His Californians | The Uncollected:Abe Lyman | Hindsight | HSR 184

Lament(alt.take)
Marty Ehrlich Trio | Marty Ehrlich:The Welcome | Sound Aspects | sas CD 002

Lamentation
Rabih Abou-Khalil Group | The Sultan's Picnic | Enja | ENJ-8078 2
Malachi Thompson Sextet With Voices | 47th Street | Delmark | DE 497

Lamenting
Carlos Barbosa-Lima | Music Of The Americas | Concord | CCD 4461

Lamento
Joaquin Chacón Group | San | Fresh Sound Records | FSNT 015 CD
Nelson Riddle And His Orchestra | Changing Colors | MPS | 9814794
String Band Featuring Isao Suzuki | String Band Featuring Isao Suzuki | Flying Disk | VIDC 601 Direct Disc

Lamento Borincano
Bebo Valdés Trio | El Arte Del Sabor | Blue Note | 535193-2

Lamento Cubano
Bola Sete Quintet | The Incomparable Bola Sete | Original Jazz Classics | OJC 288(F 8364)

Lamento Gitano
Stan Kenton And His Orchestra | The Formative Years(1941-1942) | Creative World | ST 1061

L'Amour De Moy
Kendra Shank Group | Wish | Jazz Focus | JFCD 028

Lampoon
Bjarne Roupe Group | Passion Play | Stunt Records | 18801

Lana Turner
Drümmele Maa | Villa Rhododendron | Jazz Haus Musik | JHM 25

Land Of 1000 Dancers
John Graas Nonet | Coup De Graas | EmArCy | EJD 3083 PMS

Land Of Desolation,Land Of Mist
Axis | Axis | Jazz 4 Ever Records:Jazz Network | J4E 4735

Land Of Desolation,Land Of Mist(part 1&2)
| Pete Fountain And His Basin Street Six | 504 Records | 504CD 16

Land Of Dreams
Harry Edison-Eddie Lockjaw Davis Quintet | Light And Lovely | Black & Blue | BB 883.2
Jay McShann Quintet | What A Wonderful World | Groove Note | GRV 1005-2
Paul Mares And His Friars Society Orchestra | Chicago 1935 | Gannet | CJR 1001

Land Of Make Believe
L.A.4 | Watch What Happens | Concord | CCD 4063

Land Of Me
Dizzy Gillespie Sextet | Dizzy's Party | Original Jazz Classics | OJCCD 823-2(2310784)

Land Of Peace
Toshiko Akiyoshi Quintet | Recorded In Tokyo | Vee Jay Recordings | VJ 023

Land Of The Lonely
Mike Nock Trio | Ondas | ECM | 1220

Land Of The Long White Cloud
David Benoit Group | This Side Up | GRP | GRP 95412

Land Of The Midnight Sun
Al Di Meola Groups | Guitar Heroes Vol.1:Al Di Meola | Zounds | CD 2700044001
Wolfgang Schmid's Kick | No Filters | TipToe | TIP-888809 2

Land Of The Morning Sun
Don Pullen Quartet | Warriors | Black Saint | 120019-2

Land Preserved
Gordon Lee Quartet feat. Jim Pepper | Landwhales In New York | Tutu Records | 888136-2*

Land Whales
Enrico Pieranunzi/Enrico Rava | Nausicaa | Quadrivium | SCA 037

Ländler
Fischbacher Group & Modern String Quartet | Fischbacher Group & Modern String Quartet | Dr.Jazz Records | 8608-2

Landmark
Joe Lovano Quintet | Landmarks | Blue Note | 796108-2

Landpartie
Cal Tjader Quartet | Jazz At The Blackhawk | Original Jazz Classics | OJCCD 436-2(F 8096)

Lands End
Clifford Brown-Max Roach Quintet | Jazz Gallery:Clifford Brown | RCA | 2114176-2
Brownie-The Complete EmArCy Recordings Of Clifford Brown | EmArCy | 838306-2
Mark Helias Quintet | Split Image | Enja | 4086 (807528)
Clifford Brown-Max Roach Quintet | More Study In Brown | EmArCy | 814637-2

Lands End(alt.take)
Art Pepper Quartet | Art Pepper:The Complete Galaxy Recordings | Galaxy | 16GCD 1016-2

Landscape
Art Pepper:The Complete Galaxy Recordings | Galaxy | 16GCD 1016-2
Art Pepper:The Complete Galaxy Recordings | Galaxy | 16GCD 1016-2
Art Pepper:The Complete Galaxy Recordings | Galaxy | 16GCD 1016-2
Art Pepper:The Complete Galaxy Recordings | Galaxy | 16GCD 1016-2
Landscape | Original Jazz Classics | OJCCD 676-2(GXY 5128)
Keith Jarrett | Facing You | ECM | 1017(827132-2)

Landscape For Future Earth
Matthew Shipp-Mat Maneri Duo | Gravitational Systems | HatOLOGY | 530

Landscape I Heavy Weather
Frank Kroll Quintet | Landscape | dml-records | CD 014

Landscape II Rain
Landscape | dml-records | CD 014

Landscape III Silence And Storm
Landscape | dml-records | CD 014

Landscape IV Ice And Sun
Arndt/Kussatz Duo | Working | FMP | 0750

Landscapes
David Benoit | This Side Up | GRP | GRP 95412
Bill Frisell-Vernon Reid Duo | Smash & Scatteration | Minor Music | 005

Language Of Time
Gunter Hampel And His Galaxie Dream Band | Out From Under | Birth | 0016

Langue Muette
Jimmy Knepper Quintet | Cunningbird | Steeplechase | SCCD 31061

Lap
George Van Eps-Howard Alden Quartet | Hand-Crafted Swing | Concord | CCD 4513

L'Apolide
Nils Landgren-Esbjörn Svensson | Swedish Folk Modern | ACT | 9428-2

Lapp Nils Polska
Arnulf Ochs Group | In The Mean Time | Jazz 'n' Arts Records | JNA 1202

L'Apres Midi
Nels Cline Trio | Silencer | Enja | ENJ-6098 2

Laranga
Anouar Brahem Trio | Le Pas Du Chat Noir | ECM | 1792(016373-2)

L'arbre Qui Voit
Cousin Joe With Band | Cousin Joe:The Complete 1945-1947 Vol.1 (1945-1946) | Blue Moon | BMCD 6001

Larghetto from Concerto In A Major For Oboe D'Amore And Strings
Booker Ervin Quartet | The Book Cooks | Fresh Sound Records | FSR 2050(Bethlehem BCP 6048)(835051)

Largo
Uwe Kropinski | Faces | ITM Records | ITM 14100

Largo-
Raymond Fol Big Band | Jazz In Paris:Raymond Fol-Les 4 Saisons | EmArCy | 548791-2
Viktoria Tabatchnikowa-Eugenij Belov | Troika | ALISO Records | AL 1036
Troika | ALISO Records | AL 1036
Banda Cittá Ruvo Di Puglia | La Banda/Banda And Jazz | Enja | ENJ-9326 2

Largo Al Factotum(Il Barbiere Di Siviglia)
Swingle Singers | Swingle Singers Going Baroque | Philips | 546746-2

Largo from Harpsichord Concerto in F Minor(BWV 1056)
Jacques Loussier Trio | Baroque Favorites | Telarc Digital | CD 83516

Lark
Robin Holcomb Sextet | Larks,They Crazy | Sound Aspects | sas CD 026

Larry Larue
Chico Hamilton Quintet | The Dealer | Impulse(MCA) | 547958-2

Larry Of Arabia
Max Roach Quintet | The Big Beat | Milestone | MCD 47016-2

Larry's Delight
Paul Weeden Quintet | Clear Sight | Timeless | JC 11012

L'Arte Mistica Del Vasaio-
Hal McKusick Septet | Now's The Time(1957-58) | GRP | GRP 16512

Larve
Tom Harrell Group | The Art Of Rhythm | RCA | 2668924-2

Las Bolleras(Adios Mama)-
Christoph Sänger Trio | Imagination | Laika Records | 35100752

Las Brisas
Art Pepper Quartet | Friday Night At The Village Vanguard | Original Jazz Classics | OJCCD 695-2(C 7643)

Las Cuevas De Mario
Art Pepper:The Complete Village Vanguard Sessions | Contemporary | 9CCD-4417-2
Art Pepper:The Complete Village Vanguard Sessions | Contemporary | 9CCD-4417-2
Art Pepper Quintet | Smack Up | Contemporary | C 7602
Camaron | Soleá: A Flamenco-Jazz Fantasy | ACT | 9208-2

Las Lomas De New Jersey
Michael Gerber Group | This Is Michael Gerber | Big World | BW 2007

Las Palmas
Kenny Drew Jr. Quartet | The Flame Within | Jazz City | 660.53.017

Las Ramblas
Julian Argüelles-Steve Argüelles | Scapes | Babel | BDV 9614

Las Tijeras
Arny Kay Band With Guests | Hang On Jimi | L+R Records | CDLR 42078

Las Vegas Tango
Gil Evans Orchestra | The Individualism Of Gil Evans | Verve | 833804-2 PMS
Michael Shrieve Group | Stiletto | RCA | PL 83050

Laser
Spyro Gyra | Catching The Sun | MCA | ???

L'Assassinat De Carala
Oregon | Northwest Passage | Intuition Records | INT 3191-2

L'Assassino Che Suona(The Musical Assassin)
Per Husby Orchestra | Dedications | Affinity | AFF 136

Last Ballad
Joe Sachse | Ballade Für Jimi Metag | Born&Bellmann | 991503 CD

Last Breath
Nat King Cole Trio | Rare Live Performences | Jazz Anthology | JA 5175

Last Call
Greg Marvin Sextet | Taking Off! | Timeless | CD SJP 348
The Crusaders | Rhapsody And Blues | MCA | 2292-50535-1

Last Call At Jimmy Ryan's
Roy Eldridge And The Jimmy Ryan All Stars | Little Jazz And The Jimmy Ryan All-Stars | Original Jazz Classics | OJCCD 1058-2(DRE 1001)

Last Call At Jimmy Ryan's(alt.take)
Eddie Locke Group | Jivin' With The Refuges From Hastings Street | Chiaroscuro | CR 2007

Last Chance
Changes | Some More Changes | EGO | 4022

Last Day In May
Ran Blake-Jeanne Lee | You Stepped Out Of A Cloud | Owl Records | 055 CD

Last Dream
Fun Horns & Baticun | Live And Latin | KlangRäume | 30110

Last Escape
Roland Dahinden/Christian Muthspiel | Trombone Performance | Amadeo | 841330-1

Last Exit To Brooklyn
Bowling Green John Cephas & Harmonica Phil Wiggins | American Folk Blues Festival '81 | L+R Records | CDLS 42022

Last Fair Deal Gone Down
Gary Peacock Trio | Shift In The Wind | ECM | 1165

Last First
Barbara Dennerlein With The Peter Herbolzheimer Big Band | Tribute To Charlie | Koala Records | CD P 14

Last Legs Blues(part 1)
Johnny Hodges Orchestra | Jazz Legacy 9: Johnny Hodges-The Rabbit In Paris | Vogue | 500059

Last Legs Blues(part 2)
Esbjörn Svensson Trio(E.S.T.) | Good Morning Susie Soho | ACT | 9009-2

Last Letter From Lithuania
John Abercrombie Trio | Animato | ECM | 1411

Last Light
Toshinori Kondo & Ima plus Guests | Human Market | JA & RO | JARO 4146-2

Last Lost
Oscar Klein's Jazz Show | Oscar Klein's Jazz Show Vol.2 | Jazzpoint | JP 1048 CD

Last Lost Love
Cal Tjader Quintet | San Francisco Moods | Original Jazz Classics | OJC 277(F 8017)

Last Meet Jeff
Zion Harmonizers | Thank You Lord | Sound Of New Orleans | SONO 6007

Last Minute Blues
Slide Hampton Quartet | Phil Woods/Slide Hampton 1968 Jazz | Jazztime(EMI) | 781253-2

Last Night
Franz Koglmann Quintet | About Yesterdays Ezzthetics | Hat Art | CD 6003

Last Night Blues
Humphrey Lyttelton And His Band | Lay 'Em Straight! | Calligraph | CLGCD 033

Last Night On The Back Porch
Kid Sheik's Storyville Ramblers | Kid Sheik In Boston And Cleveland | American Music | AMCD-69

Last Night When We Were Young
Bucky Pizzarelli | Love Songs | Stash Records | ST 213 IMS
Cal Tjader Quartet With Strings | Plays Harold Arlen | Original Jazz Classics | OJC 285(F 8072)
Don Lanphere Quintet Feat. Jon Pugh Plus Two | Into Somewhere | Hep | 2022
Frank Morgan Quartet | Love,Lost & Found | Telarc Digital | CD 83374
Jimmy Heath Quartet | You've Changed | Steeplechase | SCCD 31292
Ken Peplowski & Friends | It's A Lonesome Old Town' | Concord | CCD 4673
Kenny Burrell With The Gil Evans Orchestra | Verve Jazz Masters 45:Kenny Burrell | Verve | 527652-2
Guitar Forms |'Verve | 521403-2
Verve Jazz Masters Vol.60:The Collection | Verve | 529866-2
Paul Motian Quartet | Paul Motian On Broadway Vol.1 | JMT Edition | 919029-2
Peter Leitch-John Hicks | Duality | Reservoir | RSR CD 134

Last Nite
Hans Koller & The International Brass Company | Live At The Jazz Festival Frankfurt | L+R Records | LR 40014

Last November
David Binney Group | The Luxury Of Guessing | audioquest Music | AQCD 1030

Last Picture Of Solaris
Gino Lattuca Quartet | My Impression | B.Sharp Records | CDS 085

Last Poem
Bill Perkins With The Metropole Orchestra | I Wished On The Moon | Candid | CCD 79524

Last Rite
Rinde Eckert Group | Story In,Story Out | Intuition Records | INT 3507-2
Gary McFarland And His Orchestra | America The Beautiful | Gryphon | 6.24452 AT

Last Rites Of Rock 'N Roll
Kenny Garrett | Black Hope | Warner | 9362-45017-2

Last Season
Rick Margitza Quartet | Work It | Steeplechase | SCCD 31358

Last Service
Humphrey Lyttelton And His Band | Best Of British Jazz From The BBC Jazz Club Vol.2 | Upbeat Jazz | URCD 119

Last Song
Peter O'Mara Trio | Spirits | Acoustic Music Records | 319.1068.2

Last Stop
Herbie Hancock Group | Death Wish | CBS | 491981-2

Last Summer
Frank Nimsgern Group | Frank Nimsgern feat. Chaka Khan/Billy Cobham | Lipstick Records | LIP 890012

Last Tango For Astor
Al Di Meola World Sinfonia | World Sinfonia | Inak | 700772

Last Thing Blues
Bobby Vega Group With The Turtle Island String Quartet | Down The Road | Lipstick Records | LIP 8955-2

Last Time Around
Ida Cox With Tommy Ladnier | Isa Cox-The Uncrowned Queen Of The Blues | Black Swan Records | BSCD-7

Last Train From Overbrook
Eddie Lockjaw Davis-Shirley Scott Sextet | Bacalao | Original Jazz Classics | OJCCD 1090-2(P 7178)
James Moody And His Band | James Moody | Prestige | P 24015

Last Train Home
Pat Metheny Group | In Concert | Jazz Door | JD 1231
Radius | Elevation | Ear-Rational | ECD 1036

Last Trane
Jessica Williams Trio | Inventions | Jazz Focus | JFCD 008

Last Waltz
John Abercrombie Trio | Tactics | ECM | 1623(533680-2)
Karlheinz Miklin Quartet | Last Waltz | Acoustic Music Records | 319.1126.2
John Scofield Trio | Out Like A Light | Enja | 4038-2

Last Xango
Roy Ayers Group | Nasté | RCA | 6366613-2

Lastuna
Berlin Jazz Composers Orchestra(JayJayBeCe) | JayJayBeCe-V-15-Twenty | BIT | 11273

Lat Scream
Gabriele Mirabassi Trio | Latakia Blend | Enja | ENJ-9441 2

Latakia Blend
Cleo Brown Quartet | Boogie Woogie | Official | 3010

Latches
Bireli Lagrene Ensemble | Routes To Django & Bireli Swing '81 | Jazzpoint | JP 1055 CD
29th Street Saxophone Quartet | Milano New York Bridge | Red Records | 123262-2

Late
Markus Stockhausen Quartet | Cosi Lontano...Quasi Dentro | ECM | 1371
Michael Sagmeister Quartet | Motions And Emotions | BELL Records | BLR 84054

Late Afternoon
Till Martin Quintet | On The Trail | Nabel Records:Jazz Network | CD 4676
Memphis Slim | Memphis Slim USA | Candid | CCD 79024

Late Afternoon Blues
Mitch Seidman-Fred Fried | This Over That | Jardis Records | JRCD 9816

Late Again
Jacques Stotzem | Fingerprint | Acoustic Music Records | 319.1129.2

Late Date
Buddy Rich Sextet | Compact Jazz: Buddy Rich | Verve | 823295-2 PMS
Count Basie And His Orchestra | Count Basie & His Orchestra:Fresno,California April 24,1959 | Jazz Unlimited | JUCD 2039

Lars Sjösten Octet Feat. Lee Konitz | Dedicated To Lee-Lars Sjösten Plays The Music Of Lars Gullin | Dragon | DRLP 66

Late Fall
Sonny Thompson Quintet/Sharps And Flats | Sonny Thompson:The Complete Recordings Vol.1 (1946-1948) | Blue Moon | BMCD 6024

Late Green
Willie 'The Lion' Smith Duo | Willie 'The Lion ' Smith:The Lion's In Town | Vogue | 2111506-2

Late Lament
Mark Turner Quartet | Ballad Session | Warner | 9362-47631-2
Paul Desmond Orchestra | Late Lament | Bluebird | ND 90207
Paul Desmond With Strings | Desmond Blue | RCA | 2663898-2
Hans Theessink Group | Call Me | Minor Music | 801022

Late Last Night
Jerry Walden-Michael Karn Quintet | Head To Head | Criss Cross | Criss 1159

Late Night
Heads Up Super Band | Live at The Berks Jazz Fest | Inak | 30462

Late Night Willie
Jazz Indeed | Under Water | Traumton Records | 2415-2

Late Nite
The Meeting | Update | Hip Bop | HIBD 8008

Late One Night
Alec Seward & Friends | Late One Saturday Evening | Blue Labor | BL 103

Late Show
Art Blakey And The Jazz Messengers | Art Blakey/The Jazz Messengers | CBS | CK 62265

Late Spring
Ketil Bjornstad | New Life | EmArCy | 017265-2

Late Summer
Lee Konitz And Lars Gullin With Hans Koller's New Jazz Stars | Lee Konitz:Move | Moon Records | MCD 057-2

Late Woman Blues
Yusef Lateef Quintet | The Many Faces Of Yusef Lateef | Milestone | M 47009

Later
Eddie Allen Quintet | Another Point Of View | Enja | 8004-2
Sonny Stitt Quartet | Prestige First Sessions, Vol.2 | Prestige | PCD 24115-2

Later In The Evening
Mat Mathews Quintet | The Modern Art Of Jazz | Dawn | DCD 110

Later Than You Think
Klaus König Orchestra | Time Fragments:Seven Studies In Time And Motion | Enja | ENJ-8076 2

Later That Night That Knight Laid Her
Grant Geissman Quintet | Good Stuff | Concord | CJ 62

Later With Them Woes
Oleo | Hope You Get It | Nabel Records:Jazz Network | LP 4603

Latin American Sunshine
Jazz Crusaders | Chile Con Soul | Pacific Jazz | 590957-2

Latin Bit
Poncho Sanchez Band | Fredom Sound | Concord | CCD 4778

Latin Bump-
Thomas Sliomis/Daunik Lazro Duo | Phonorama | Praxis | GM 1002

Latin Connection
Antonio Farao Trio | Black Inside | Enja | ENJ-9345 2

Latin Dance
Bob Mintzer Big Band | Incredible Journey | dmp Digital Music Productions | CD 451

Latin Dreaming
Ed Staginski | Just A Dream-A Collection For Easy Listening | yvp music | CD 3025

Latin Fever
Woody Herman And His Orchestra With Tito Puente's Rhythm Section | Herman's Heat & Puente's Beat | Palladium Records | PDC 156(889168)

Latin For Luca
David Chesky-Romero Lubambo Duo | The New York Chorinhos | Chesky | JD 39

Latin Genetics
Heiner Stadler Jazz Alchemy | Jazz Alchemy | Tomato | 2696702

Latin Groove
Lee Morgan Sextet | Lee Morgan | Blue Note | 300141(1541)

Latin Kaleidoscope:
Bill Heid Trio | Bop Rascal | Savant Records | SCD 2009

Latin Lovers
Greetje Kauffeld With Jerry Van Rooyen And Jiggs Whigham And The Rias Big Band | Greetje Kauffeld Meets Jerry Van Rooyen And Jiggs Whigham With The Rias Big Band | Mons Records | MR 874786

Latin Quarter
Johnny Griffin Quartet | The Congregation | Blue Note | 300189(1580)

Latin Quartet No.4
Buddy Rich Band | Buddy's Rock | Memo Music | HDJ 4042

Latin Steps
Spyro Gyra | Access All Areas | MCA | 2292-51215-1

Latino
Gato Barbieri Orchestra | Latino America | Impulse(MCA) | 952236-2

Latino Amarica
Latino America | Impulse(MCA) | 952236-2
Maynard Ferguson Orchestra | Storm | ARG Jazz | 21374872

Latona
Big John Patton Quartet | The Organization! The Best Of Big John Patton | Blue Note | 830728-2

Latscheben
Titi Winterstein Quintet plus Guests | Live! | Boulevard | BLD 508 LP

L'Attente Reste
Jimmy Knepper Quintet | Special Relationship | Hep | CD 2012

Latterday Saint
Charles Mingus-The Complete Debut Recordings | Debut | 12 DCD 4402-2

Latterday Saint(alt.take 1)
Charles Mingus-The Complete Debut Recordings | Debut | 12 DCD 4402-2

Latterday Saint(alt.take 2)
Charles Mingus-The Complete Debut Recordings | Debut | 12 DCD 4402-2

Latterday Saint(alt.take 3)
Mat Maneri | Trinity | ECM | 1719

Lattice
Stefanie Schlesiger And Her Group plus String Quartet | What Love Is | Enja | ENJ-9434 2

Laudate
Okschila Tatanka | Wounded Knee-Lyrik Und Jazz | Wergo | SM 1088-2

Lauf Indianer Lauf(John Trudell)
Georgia Carr With The Nelson Riddle Orchestra | Softly Baby | Pathe | 1566241(Capitol)

Laugh! Cool Clown
Nat King Cole Trio | Vocal Classics & Instrumental Classics | Capitol | 300014(TOCJ 6128)

Laugh, Clown, Laugh
Benny Carter Quartet | Swingin' The Twenties | Original Jazz Classics | OJCCD 339-2

Laughin' Louie
Louis Armstrong And His Orchestra | Louis Armstrong-The Complete RCA Victor Recordings | RCA | 2668682-2

Laughing At Dinosaurs
Ann Burton And Her Quartet | Am I Blue | Keytone | KYT 711

Laughing At Life
Billie Holiday And Her Orchestra | Billie Holiday:The Quintessential Vol.8/9(1939-1942) | CBS | 477837-2

Laughing Boy
Dinah Washington With Orchestra | The Complete Dinah Washington Vol.4 | Official | 3008

Laughing On The Outside(Crying On The Inside)
Dinah Shore With Orchestra | The Best Of Dinah Shore | Capitol | 792895-2

Ernst Höllerhagen Quartet | Ernst Höllerhagen 1942-1948 | Elite Special | 9522001

Laura
André Previn Trio | After Hours | Telarc Digital | CD 83302
Art Van Damme Quintet | Keep Going/Blue World | MPS | 529093-2
Association Urbanetique | Don't Look Back | Enja | ENJ-6056 2
Bill Evans Trio | Empathy+A Simple Matter Of Conviction | Verve | 837757-2 PMS
Billy Taylor | Ten Fingers-One Voice | Arkadia Jazz | 71602
Charlie Parker With Strings | Bird With Strings-Live At The Apollo, Carnegie Hall & Birdland | CBS | CBS 82292
Charlie Parker With The Joe Lipman Orchestra | Verve Jazz Masters 28:Charlie Parker Plays Standards | Verve | 521854-2
Charlie Parker With Strings:The Master Takes | Verve | 523984-2
Charlie Parker Big Band | Verve | 559835-2
Charlie Parker With The Woody Herman Orchestra | Bird's Eyees Last Unissued Vol.23 | Philology | W 853.2
Clifford Brown With Strings | Jazz Gallery:Clifford Brown | RCA | 2114176-2
Clifford Jordan-Ran Blake Groups | Masters From Different Worlds | Mapleshade | 01732
Craig Bailey Band | A New Journey | Candid | CCD 79725
Dave Brubeck Octet | The Dave Brubeck Octet | Original Jazz Classics | OJCCD 101-2(F 3239)
Dave Brubeck Quartet | Jazz At The College Of The Pacific | Original Jazz Classics | OJC20 047-2(F 3223)
The Art Of Dave Brubeck - The Fantasy Years:Jazz At Oberlin/College OPacific | Atlantic | SD 2-317
Don Byas Quartet | New York 1945 | Jazz Anthology | JA 5106
Don Byas Ree-Boppers | Jazz In Paris:Bebop | EmArCy | 014063-2
Eddie Cleanhead Vinson Sextet | Jamming The Blues | Black Lion | BLCD 760188
Ella Fitzgerald With The Nelson Riddle Orchestra | The Silver Collection: Ella Fitzgerald-The Songbooks | Verve | 823445-2 PMS
Ella Fitzgerald Sings The Johnny Mercer Songbook | Verve | 539057-2
The Best Of The Song Books:The Ballads | Verve | 521867-2
The Johnny Mercer Songbook | Verve | 823247-2 PMS
Eric Dolphy With Erik Moseholm's Trio | Eric Dolphy:The Complete Prestige Recordings | Prestige | 9 PRCD-4418-2
Erroll Garner Trio | Gems | CBS | 21062
Frank Sinatra With Orchestra | Frank Sinatra | Koch Records | 321 942 D1
Gerry Mulligan Quartet | Jazz At The Philharmonic: The Gerry Mulligan Quartets In Concert | Pablo | PACD 5309-2
My Funny Valentine | Jazz Society(Vogue) | 670511
Gerry Mulligan:Pleyel Concert Vol.2 | Vogue | 21409432
Griff Williams And His Orchestra | The Uncollected:Griff Williams | Hindsight | HSR 175
Harold Vick Orchestra Quintet | Steppin' Out | Blue Note | 852433-2
Houston Person Quartet | My Romance | HighNote Records | HCD 7033
Jimmy Smith Trio | Cherokee | Blue Note | 300246
Joe Beck-Ali Ryerson | Django | dmp Digital Music Productions | CD 530
Joe Lovano Sextet | Tenor Legacy | Blue Note | 827014-2
Joe Pass | I Remember Charlie Parker | Original Jazz Classics | OJC 602(2312109)
Johannes Rediske Quintet | Re-Disc Bounce | Bear Family Records | BCD 16119 AH
John Mehegan-Eddie Costa Trio | A Pair Of Pianos | Savoy | SV 0206(MG 12049)
Les Brown And His Band Of Renown | Les Brown And His Band Of Renown | CDS Records Ltd. | CJCD 834
Nat King Cole Trio | Straighten Up And Fly Right | Pro-Arte | CDD 558
Oscar Peterson-Ray Brown Duo | Gitanes Jazz 'Round Midnight: Oscar Peterson | Verve | 511036-2 PMS
Oscar Pettiford Orchestra | Deep Passion | Impulse(MCA) | GRP 11432
Philip Catherine Trio | Summer Night | Dreyfus Jazz Line | FDM 36637-2
Red Rodney Quintet | Modern Music From Chicago | Original Jazz Classics | OJC 048(F 3208)
Rosemary Clooney And Her Band | Sings The Lyrics Of Johnny Mercer | Concord | CCD 4333
Royce Campbell Quartet | Gentle Breeze | Timeless | CD SJP 389
Sidney Bechet With Andre Reweliotty And His Orchestra | Sidney Bechet | Vogue | 000001 GK
Singers Unlimited With Rob McConnell And The Boss Brass | The Singers Unlimited With Rob McConnell And The Boss Brass | MPS | 817486-1
Spike Jones And His Other Orchestra | The Uncollected:Spike Jones | Hindsight | HSR 185(835797)
Stan Kenton And His Orchestra | Stan Kenton In New Jersey | Status | CD 104(882200)
Teddy Edwards Quartet | Good Gravy | Original Jazz Classics | OJCCD 661-2(S 7592)
Ahmad Jamal Trio | Live In Paris 1992 | Dreyfus Jazz Line | FDM 37019-2

Laura-
Live In Paris 92 | Birdology | 849408-2
Quincy Jones All Stars | Go West Man | Fresh Sound Records | ABC 186 (Paramount)
Teddy Wilson Quintet | Air Mail Special | Black Lion | BLCD 760115

L'Aurà
Lew Soloff Group | My Romance | Paddle Wheel | K32Y 6278

Laura Et Astor
Ruben Blades Y Seis Del Solar | Agua De Luna | Messidor | 15964 CD

Laura With The Laughing Eyes
Charlie Parker With Strings | Bird: The Complete Charlie Parker On Verve | Verve | 837141-2

Laura(take 1)
Bird: The Complete Charlie Parker On Verve | Verve | 837141-2

Laura(take 2)
Astor Piazzolla-Gary Burton Sextet | The New Tango | Warner | 2292-55069-2

Laura's Dream
Gary Burton-Makoto Ozone | Face To Face | GRP | GRP 98052

Laurdagskveld
Dry Jack | Dry Jack/Magical Elements | Inner City | IC 1063 IMS

Laurita
Richard Galliano Quartet | Gallianissimo! The Best Of Richard Galliano | Dreyfus Jazz Line | FDM 36616-2
Bill Evans Trio | A Simple Matter Of Conviction | Verve | 23MJ 3040 IMS

Lausanne(part 1a)
Keith Jarrett | Solo-Concerts(Bremen-Lausanne) | ECM | 1035/7(827747-2)

Lausanne(part 1b)
Solo-Concerts(Bremen-Lausanne) | ECM | 1035/7(827747-2)

Lausanne(part 2a)
Solo-Concerts(Bremen-Lausanne) | ECM | 1035/7(827747-2)

Lausanne(part 2b)
Franco Morone | Guitarea | Acoustic Music Records | 319.1046.2

Lauthentic
Wolfgang Lauth Quartet | Lauther | Bear Family Records | BCD 15717 AH

Lauther
Ken McIntyre Quintet feat.Eric Dolphy | Fire Waltz | Prestige | P 24085

Lautir
Looking Ahead | Original Jazz Classics | OJC 252(NJ 8247)
Chuck Marohnic Quartet | Chuck Marohnic Quartet | Steeplechase | SCS 4002

Lava Coils
Terumasa Hino Sextet | From The Heart | Blue Note | 796688-2

Lavender Dreams
Grover Mitchell & His All-Star Orchestra | Hip Shakin' | Ken Music | 660.56.005

Lavender Lass Blossom
Irene Schweizer | Hexensabbat | FMP | 0500

Lavonne

Enrico Rava Quartet | Enrico Rava Quartet | ECM | 1122

Lavori Casalinghi
Steve Coleman And Five Elements | Genesis & The Opening Of The Way | RCA | 2152934-2

Law Of Ballance
Michel Petrucciani Group | Playground | Blue Note | 795480-2

Law Of Physics
Bob Stewart Groups | Then & Now | Postcards | POST 1014

Law Years
Geri Allen Trio | Segments | DIW | DIW 833 CD

Lawn Party
Eddie Taylor Blues Band | My Heart Is Bleeding | L+R Records | CDLR 72008

Lawns
Ron Carter Trio | Third Plane | Original Jazz Classics | OJCC20 754-2(M 9105)

Lawra
V.S.O.P. | The Quintet | CBS | 88273

Laxed & Warped
Steve Coleman And Metrics | Steve Coleman's Music Live In Paris | Novus | 2131691-2

Lay The Lily Low
Muddy Waters Blues Band | Blues Roots Vol. 11: Muddy Waters | Chess | 6.24801 AG

Lay Something On The Bar(Beside Your Below)
Clyde Bernhardt And His Blue Bazers | Clyde Bernhardt:The Complete Recordings Vol.1 (1945-1948) | Blue Moon | BMCD 6016

Lay-By
Hot Mallets | Hot Mallets...Live | Jazzcharge | JC 8302

Lay-By-
Ray Mantilla Space Station | Synergy | Red Records | VPA 198

Layers Of Light
Stephan Rigert's Talking Drums | Different Colours | TCB Records | TCB 03032

Layin' In The Cut
Buddy Rich Big Band | Backwoods Siseman/Pieces Of Dream | Laserlight | 24655

Layin' It Down
Cousin Joe With The Mezzrow-Bechet Septet | Cousin Joe:The Complete 1945-1947 Vol.1 (1945-1946) | Blue Moon | BMCD 6001

Layin' On Mellow
Jimmy Smith With Orchestra | The Big Brawl | Milan | CD CH 128(883460)

Layla's Dream
James Blood Ulmer Group | Are You Glad To Be In America? | DIW | DIW 400 CD

Lay-Up
Cuarteto Las D'Aida Y Su Grupo | Soy La Mulata | L+R Records | CDLR 45059

Lazeez
Stan Kenton And His Orchestra | The Jazz Compositions Of Stan Kenton | Creative World | ST 1078

Laziest Girl In Town
Sam Rivers Quartet | Lazuli | Timeless | CD SJP 291

Lazy
Benny Goodman Sextet | The Yale University Muisc Library Vol.5 | Limelight | 820827-2 IMS

Lazy Afternoon
Dave Liebman Quintet | Besame Mucho And Other Latin Jazz Standards | Red Records | 123260-2
Frant Green Quartet | Street Of Dreams | Blue Note | 821290-2
Gabriele Hasler Group | Listening To Löbering | Foolish Music | FM 211389
Hank Jones Quartet | Lazy Afternoon | Concord | CCD 4391
Joe Henderson Trio | Power To The People | Milestone | M 9024
Lucy Reed With Dick Marx And Johnny Frigo | The Singing Reed | Original Jazz Classics | OJCCD 1777-2(F 3212)
Ronnie Scott's Quintet | Serious Gold | Ronnie Scott's Jazz House | NSPL 18542
Sarah Vaughan With Orchestra | Sweet 'N' Sassy | Roulette | 531793-2
Sheila Jordan/Harvie Swartz | Old Time Feeling | Muse | MCD 5366
Stan Kenton And His Orchestra | Stan Kenton In New Jersey | Status | CD 104(882200)
Fleurine With Band And Horn Section | Meant To Be! | EmArCy | 159085-2

Lazy And Satisfied
Bob Cooper Quartet | For All We Know | Fresh Sound Records | FSR-CD 5029

Lazy Bird
John Coltrane Sextet | Blue Train | Mobile Fidelity | MFCD 547(UDCD)
Takin' Off | Blue Note | 300415
José Luis Gámez Quartet | José Luis Gámez Quattro | Fresh Sound Records | FSNT 094 CD
Kurt Rosenwinkel Trio | East Coast Love Affair | Fresh Sound Records | FSNT 016 CD
McCoy Tyner | Revelations | Blue Note | 791651-2
McCoy Tyner Trio | Chick Corea-Herbie Hancock-Keith Jarrett-McCoy Tyner | Atlantic | ATL 50326
Philip DeGruy | Innuendo Out The Other | NYC-Records | NYC 6013-2

Lazy Bird(alt.take)
John Coltrane Sextet | The Ultimate Blue Train | Blue Note | 853428-2
Maxim Saury And His New Orleans Sound | Homage A Sidney Bechet | Jazztime(EMI) | 792406-2

Lazy Bones
Juan Garcia Esquivel Orchestra | Juan's Again | RCA | 2168206-2
Keith Ingham Sextet | A Star Dust Melody | Sackville | SKCD2-2051

Lazy Daisy
Stan Kenton And His Orchestra | By Request Vol.4 | Creative World | ST 1064

Lazy Mae
Red Garland Quintet | Saying Something | Prestige | P 24090
Clarence Williams' Orchestra | Clarence Williams 1928 | Village(Jazz Archive) | VILCD 010-2

Lazy Melody
Bobby Hackett And His Jazz Band | Gotham Jazz Scene/Big T's Dixieland Band | Dormouse | DMI CDX 03(882985)

Lazy Mood
Ralph Sutton | The Other Side Of Ralph Sutton | Chaz Jazz | CJ 107

Lazy River -> Up A Lazy River

Lazy 'Sippi' Steamer
Roger Kellaway | The Art Of Interconnectedness | Challenge | CHR 70042

Lazy Snake
Tony Reedus Quartet | Incognito | Enja | ENJ-6058 2

Lazy Sunday Afternoon
Miles Davis Quartet | Miles Davis Vol.1 | Blue Note | 532610-2

Lazy Susan
Miles Davis:The Blue Note And Capitol Recordings | Blue Note | 827475-2

Lazy Things
Henri Renaud-Al Cohn Quartet | Cohn´s Delight | Vogue | 655011

Lazy Train
Makoto Ozone Trio With John Scofield | The Trio | Verve | 537503-2

Lazy we
Ella Fitzgerald With Paul Weston And His Orchestra | The Complete Ella Fitzgerald Song Books of Harold Arlen, Irving Berlin, Duke Ellington, George & Ira Gershwin, Jerome Kern, Johnny Mercer, Cole Porter And Rogers & Hart | Verve | 519832-2

Lazy, Long Hot Summer's Day
Harald Rüschenbaum Orchestra | Rondo | Swingtime | 8208

Le Ansie-
BBFC | Souvenir D'Italie | Plainisphare | PL 1267-19

Le Belvédère Assiége
Earl Hines Sextet | Swingin' Away | Black Lion | BLCD 760210

Le Binz
The Jazz Corps | The Jazz Corps | Pacific Jazz | 829101-2

Le Bricoleur De Big Sur
Enrico Rava-Dino Saluzzi Quintet | Volver | ECM | 1343

Le But Du Souffle
Renaud Garcia-Fons & Jean-Louis Matinier | Fuera | Enja | ENJ-9364 2

Le Byzantin
John Goldsby Sextet | Viewpoint | Nagel-Heyer | CD 2014

Le Cannet
John Lewis And The New Jazz Quartet | Slavic Smiles | Baystate | BVCJ 2005(889371)
Modern Jazz Quartet | Topsy-This One's For Basie | Original Jazz Classics | OJCCD 1073-2(2310917)
The Best Of The Modern Jazz Quartet | Pablo | 2405423-2

Le Chat
Pierre Boussaguet Trio | Charme | EmArCy | 538468-2

Le Chien Du Héro
Anouar Brahem Quartet | Conte De L'Incroyable Amour | ECM | 1457(511959-2)

Le Chien Sur Les Genoux De La Devineresse
Michel Portal/Leon Francioli/Pierre Favre | Arrivederci Le Chouartse | Hat Art | CD 6022

Le Concerto Improvisé(part 1-8)
Charles Davis & Captured Moments | Strange Goodbyes | L+R Records | CDLR 45101

Le Continental
Babs Gonzales Group | Properly Presenting Babs Gonzales | Fresh Sound Records | FSR 702(835422)

Le Corps Abstrait S'Abandonne À La Lumière
Galardini-Lessmann-Morena Trio | Insolitudine | SPLASC(H) Records | H 155

Le Coucou from Pieces For Harpsichórd,Book 1(Louis-Claude Daguin)
Mosalini/Beytelmann/Caratini | Imagenes | Riskant | ???

Le Decor
Urs Leimgruber-Fritz Hauser | L'Enigmatique | Hat Art | CD 6091

Le Desert
Eddy Louiss Trio & Fanfare | Sentimental Feeling | Dreyfus Jazz Line | FDM 36600-2

Le Diable Et Son Train
Christoph Stiefel Trio | Sweet Paradox | Jazzline | JL 11148-2

Le Giostre Di Piazza Savona
Piacentini/Bonati/McCandless/Moreno | Circles | Nueva Records | NC 1014

Le Grand Voyage
Claude Bernhard-Raymond Bo | Pot-Pouri Pour Parce Que | Hat Art | G

Le Jamf
Bobby Jaspar/Jymie Merritt Quartet | Bobby Jaspar | Fresh Sound Records | 84063(Barclay)

Le Jardin De Madi
Jacky Terrasson Trio | Smile | Blue Note | 542413-2

Le Jardin D'Hiver
Ketil Bjornstad-David Darling | Epigraphs | ECM | 1684(543159-2)

Le Jour S'endort
Ekkehard Jost Quartet | Deep | Fish Music | FM 007 CD

Le Lapin
Billy Cobham Group | Spectrum | Atlantic | 7567-81428-2

Le Lis
Marcel Azzola-Itaru Oki Group | Transat Rue Des Orchidées | Zoo Records | J 9001

Le Luops Dans La Bergerie
Francois Jeanneau Quartet | Techniques Douces | Owl Records | 04

Le Marchand De Poisson
Alain Everts | Terra Nueva | Acoustic Music Records | 319.1103.2

Le Mémoire Des Mains
Stephan Oliva | Jazz 'n (e)motion:Stephan Oliva | RCA | 2155936-2

Le Modulor
Ahmad Jamal Trio | Picture Perfect-70th Anniversary | Warner | 8573-85268-2

Le Moment De Vérité-The Providing Ground
Paco De Lucia-Al Di Meola-John McLaughlin | Paco De Lucia-Al Di Meola-John McLaughlin | Verve | 533215-2

Le Monastère Dans Les Montagnes
Deep Creek Jazzuits | Again | Jazz Pure Collection | AU 31615 CD

Le Moroir
Don Byas Quintet | Lover Man | Vogue | 2115470-2

Le Nez Du Sphinx
Urs Leimgruber/John Wolf Brennan | M.A.P. | L+R Records | CDLR 45021

Le Pas Du Chat Noir
Tchangodei Trio | Jeux D'Ombres | Volcanic Records | 30030

Le Petit Bal(2 takes)
Vincent Courtois Quartet | Translucide | Enja | ENJ-9380 2

Le Petit Cheval
BBFC | Souvenir D'Italie | Plainisphare | PL 1267-19

Le Petit Monsieur Triste
Pekka's Tube Factory | Pekka's Tube Factory | Naxos Jazz | 86028-2

Le Phare
Lionel Hampton Quintet | Paris Session 1956 | Jazztime(EMI) | 251274-2

Le Puits
Eddy Louiss Orchestra | Multicolor Feeling-Fanfare | Nocturne Productions | NTCD 105

Le Relief
Ivan Paduart Group | Aftertough | B.Sharp Records | CDS 079

Le Retour D'Ottomar
Joelle Leandre | Contrebasse & Voix/Double Bass & Voice | Adda | 581043

Le Rituel-The Ritual
Jacky Terrasson Group | What It Is | Blue Note | 498756-2

Le Roi Brasil
Joe Venuti-Zoot Sims Sextet | Joe Venuti And Zoot Sims | Chiaroscuro | CR 142

Le Sed
Philip Catherine-Charlie Mariano-Jasper Van't Hof | Sleep My Love | CMP Records | CMP CD 5

Le Soir
Guy Lafitte Quartet | Joue Charles Trénet | Black & Blue | BLE 59.190 2

Le Sucrier Velours
Howard Alden Trio With Monty Alexander | Snowy Morning Blues | Concord | CCD 4424

Le Sucrier Velours-
Duke Ellington And His Orchestra | The Best Of Duke Ellington | Pablo | 2405401-2
Nils Landgren Funk Unit | Fonk Da World | ACT | 9299-2

Le Sunset
Barry Altschul Quartet | Irina | Soul Note | SN 1065

Le Temps D'Après
Khalil Chanine Group | Mektoub | AH Records | AH 40509

Le Tien
Stephane Grappelli Quintet | Feeling + Finesse = Jazz | Atlantic | 7567-90140-2
Free Flight | Soaring | Palo Alto | PA 8050

Le Tombeau De Jean Nicot
Eddy Louiss Trio | Tabataba(Soundtrack) | Nocturne Productions | NTCD 106

Le Travail
BBFC | Quelle Memoire! | Plainisphare | PL 1267-9

Le Trois Carton Corton Cartoon
HUM | HUM(Humair-Urtreger-Michelot) | Sketch | SKE 333006

Le Trottoir
Enrico Pieranunzi Trio With Ada Montellancino And Enrico Rava | Ma L'Amore No | Soul Note | 121321-2

Le Vent Respire
Angelo Debarre Group | Angelo Debarre | Hot Club Records | HCRCD 116

Le Voyage
Musique De La Garde Republicaine | Le Jazz En France Vol.9:Pionniers Du Jazz Francais 1906-1931 | Pathe | 1552551

Lea
Thomas Heidepriem Quartet | Brooklyn Shuffle | L+R Records | CDLR 45084

Lead Me On
Ken Colyer's All Stars | Just A Little While To Say Here | CMJ Records | CMJ CD 012

Lead Me Saviour
Sarah Spencer's Rue Conti Jazz Band | Laisses Les Bons Temps Rouler! | Lake | LACD 22
Papa Bue's Viking Jazzband | At The CCP Main Theater Manila, Philippines | V-King Records | VLP 100

Leading Me Back To You
Brad Dutz | Brad Dutz | Nine Winds Records | NWCD 0141

Leamata
Buck Clayton Jam Session | Buck Clayton Jam Session,Vol1 | Blue Moon | BMCD 3044

Lean Baby
The Buck Clayton Legacy | Encore Live | Nagel-Heyer | CD 018
Brew Moore With Unkn.Orchestra | Afro-Cubop | Spotlite | SPJ 138 (807749)

Lean On Me
Shelly Manne Trio | Shelly Manne 2-3-4 | Impulse(MCA) | GRP 11492

Lean Years
Pat Martino Quintet | Strings! | Original Jazz Classics | OJCCD 223-2(P 7547)
Deborah Henson-Conant | The Gift:15 Weihnachtslieder der Erde | Laika Records | 35100992

Leanabh An Ai Auld Lang Syne-
Ray Drummond Quintet | Camera In A Bag | Criss Cross | Criss 1040

Leap Frog
Charlie Parker Quintet | Charlie Parker:The Best Of The Verve Years | Verve | 527815-2
Charlie Parker:Bird's Best Bop On Verve | Verve | 527452-2
Charlie Parker-Dizzy Gillespie Quintet | Dizzy's Diamonds-Best Of The Verve Years | Verve | 513875-2
Louis Armstrong With Luis Russell And His Orchestra | Louis Armstrong Vol.11-Satchmo For Ever | MCA | 1334

Leap Frog(7 incompl.takes)
Charlie Parker Quintet | Bird And Diz | Verve | 521436-2

Leap Frog(alt.take 1)
Bird And Diz | Verve | 521436-2

Leap Frog(alt.take 2)
Bird And Diz | Verve | 521436-2

Leap Frog(alt.take 3)
Charlie Parker And His Orchestra | Bird On Verve-Vol.2:Bird & Diz | Verve | 817443-1 IMS

Leap Frog(take 1-11)
Charlie Parker Quintet | Verve Jazz Masters 10:Dizzy Gillespie | Verve | 516319-2

Leap Frog(take 5)
Les Brown And His Orchestra | Les Brown And His Orchestra 1944 & 1946 | Circle | CCD-90

Leap Here
The Metronome All Stars | Nat King Cole-Jazz Encounters | Capitol | 796693-2

Leap Of Faith
Wolfgang Dauner Trio | Music Zounds | MPS | 9808190

Leap Tick
Jon Eardley Seven | The John Eardley Seven | Original Jazz Classics | OJC 123(P 7033)

Leapin' At The Lennox
Artie Shaw And His Orchestra | The Uncollected:Artie Shaw And His Orchestra, Vol.1 | Hindsight | HSR 139

Leapin' On Lenox
Reid Anderson Quartet | Dirty Show Tunes | Fresh Sound Records | FSNT 030 CD

Leaping Greenly Spirits
Gene Ammons Sextet | Red Top-The Savoy Sessions | Savoy | SJL 1103 (801179)

Learnin' The Blues
Ella Fitzgerald And Louis Armstrong With The Oscar Peterson Quartet | Ella And Louis Again, Vol.2 | Verve | 711122 IMS
Ella And Louis Again | Verve | 825374-2
Verve Jazz Masters 1:Louis Armstrong | Verve | 519818-2
Frank Sinatra With The Count Basie Orchestra | Sinatra-Basie:An Historic Musical First | Reprise | 7599-27023-2
Freddie Green And His All Stars | Mr. Rhythm | RCA | 2130072-2
Jack Dieval Trio | Jazz In Paris:Jack Diéval-Jazz Aux Champs Elysées | EmArCy | 018419-2
Jonah Jones Quartet | Jonah Jones At The Embers | RCA | 2118523-2
Peter Herbolzheimer Orchestra | Music For Swinging Dancers,Vol.3:Cheek To Cheek | Koala Records | CD P 10

Learning How To Listen
Buddy DeFranco Quintet | Free Fall | Choice | CHCD 71008

Leaster Leaps In
Ruby Braff And His Buddies | Controlled Nonchalance At The Regattabar Vol.1 | Arbors Records | ARCD 19134

Leather Cats
Oregon | Beyond Words | Chesky | JD 130

Leave Me
Warne Marsh Quintet | Back Home | Criss Cross | Criss 1023

Leave Me Paralysed
Saint Louis Creative Ensemble | I Can't Figure Out (Whatcha Doin' To Me) | Moers Music | 01052 CD

Leave My Girl Alone
Coleman Hawkins And His Orchestra | Body And Soul | Naxos Jazz | 8.120532 CD

Leave My Wife Alone
John Lee Hooker | Blues Roots Vol. 13: John Lee Hooker | Chess | 6.24803 AG

Leave Taking
First Revolution Singers | A Cappella Gospel Anthology | Tight Harmony Records | TH 199404

Leave Us Leap
Mel Lewis Septet | Got' Cha | Fresh Sound Records | FSR-CD 0073

Leaves In The Wind
Dave Liebman | The Three | Soul Note | 121195-2

Leavin' It
George 'G.P.' Jackson With The Blueshounds | The Blues Vol.4 | Big Bear | 156401

Leavin' This Mornin'
Steve Gadd Group | Gaddabout | Electric Bird | K32Y 6015

Leavin' Town
Marilyn Moore With Don Abney And His Orchestra | Moody | Affinity | AFF 157

Leaving
Chet Baker Trio | Chet Baker-Philip Catherine-Jean Louis Rassinfosse | Igloo | IGL 034
Masha Bijlsma Band With Bob Malach | Lebo | Jazzline | JL 11145-2
Piano Connection | Boogie Woogie & Blues | Elite Special | 73434

Leaving-
Leadbelly[Huddie Ledbetter] | Alabamy Bound | Memo Music | HDJ 4073

Leaving Home
Jugend-Jazzorchester Des Saarlandes | Chops & Fingers | Blue Concept | BCCD 94/04

Leaving The Sea
Charles Earland Septet | Charlie's Greatest Hits | Prestige | PCD 24250-2

Leaving This Planet
Andreas Willers Quintet | The Privat Ear | Sound Aspects | sas CD 034

Leb In Meinem Garnichts
Der Rote Bereich | Love Me Tender | ACT | 9286-2

Leba,Si?
Ernst Bier-Mack Goldsbury Quartet | At Night When You Go To Sleep | Timescrapper | TSCR 9611
John Zorn Group | Massada Tree | DIW | DIW 890 CD

Leben Und Schlafen
Alfred 23 Harth-Bob Degen Duo | Melchior | Biber Records | BI 6240

Lebenslänglich
Art Ensemble Of Chicago | Phase One | America | AM 6116

Lebnia
Masha Bijlsma Band With Bob Malach | Lebo | Jazzline | JL 11145-2

L'Écrevisse-
Gus Viseur Sextet | Gus Viseur A Bruxelles | Harmonia Mundi | PJC 222006

Lecuonerias
Jeff Beck Quintet | Wired | Epic | ???

Led Connossence
Fun Horns | Fun Horns Live In South America-Natural Music | KlangRäume | 30060

L'Education Sentimentale
Don Menza Quartet | Las Vegar Late Night Sessions:Live At Capozzoli's | Woofy Productions | WPCD 116

Lee
Jimmy Raney Quintet | Early Stan | Original Jazz Classics | OJCCD 654-2(P 7255)
Early Getz | Prestige | P 24088
Stan Getz Quintet | Stan Getz:The Complete 1952-1954 Small Group Sessions(Master Takes),Vol.1 | Blue Moon | BMCD 1034

Leeaison
Lee Morgan Quintet | The Sixth Sense | Blue Note | 522467-2

Leebop
Lee Konitz And Lars Gullin With Hans Koller's New Jazz Stars | Lee Konitz:Move | Moon Records | MCD 057-2

Lee's Lament
Art Blakey Percussion Ensemble | Drums Around The Corner | Blue Note | 521455-2

Lee's Tune
Lee Morgan Quintet | Take Twelve | Original Jazz Classics | OJCCD 310-2

Lee-Sure Time
George Young Orchestra | Chant | Electric Bird | K32Y 6033

L'Effet Que Tu Me Fais
Ulla Oster 'Beyond Janis' | Stadtgarten Series Vol.3 | Jazz Haus Musik | JHM 1003 SER

Left
Jimmy Rodgers Blues Band | Sloppy Drunk | Black & Blue | BLE 59.544 2

Left Alone
Abraham Burton Quartet | Closest To The Sun | Enja | ENJ-8074 2
Archie Shepp-Dollar Brand Duo | The Art Of Saxophone | Laserlight | 24652
Duet | Denon Compact Disc | DC-8561
Eric Dolphy Quintet | Far Cry | Original Jazz Classics | OJC20 400-2
Magic | Prestige | P 24053
Eric Dophy Quintet | Live At Gaslight Inn | Ingo | 14
Götz Tangerding Group | A La Ala - A Voice In Jazz | Bhakti Jazz | BK 22

Left Bank
John Hicks Trio | Nightwind:An Erroll Garner Songbook | HighNote Records | HCD 7035

Left Behind
Buddy DeFranco Quartet | Mr. Clarinet | Verve | POCJ 1943 PMS

Left Field
Steve Coleman And Metrics | A Tale Of 3 Cities,The EP | Novus | 2124747-2

Left Go Right
Toon Roos Quartet | Attitudes | Timeless | CD SJP 285

Left Hand Corner
Dizzy Gillespie And His Orchestra | Dizzy Gillespie:Birks Works-The Verve Big Band Sessions | Verve | 527900-2

Left Hand Corner(alt.take 1)
Dizzy Gillespie:Birks Works-The Verve Big Band Sessions | Verve | 527900-2

Left Hand Corner(alt.take 2)
Dizzy Gillespie:Birks Works-The Verve Big Band Sessions | Verve | 527900-2

Left Hand Corner(false start 1)
Dizzy Gillespie:Birks Works-The Verve Big Band Sessions | Verve | 527900-2

Left Hand Corner(false start 2)
Count Basie And His Orchestra | Live In Japan '78 | Pablo | 2308246-2

Left Hand(Fossa Sanguinis)
New On The Corner | Left Handed | Jazz 4 Ever Records:Jazz Network | J4E 4758

Left Handed
Matthias Petzold Working Band | Elements | Indigo-Records | 1005 CD

Left Handed Blues
Jimmy Reed | I'm The Man Down There | Charly | CRB 1082

Left Lane
Steve Coleman Group | Rhythm In Mind | Novus | PD 90654

Legacy
New York Jazz Collective | I Don't Know This World Without Don Cherry | Naxos Jazz | 86003-2

Legacy Of The Flying Eagle
Gunther Schuller With The WDR Radio Orchestra & Rememberance Band | Witchi Tia To, The Music Of Jim Pepper | Tutu Records | 888204-2*

Legacy Of The Flying Eagle No.3
Jim Pepper Flying Eagle | Live At New Morning,Paris | Tutu Records | 888194-2*

Legacy Of The Flying Eagle:
Sandy Brown With The Brian Lemon Trio | In The Evening | Hep | CD 2017

Legend In C Minor
Pat Metheny Quartet | Watercolors | ECM | 1097(827409-2)

Legend Of The Fountain-
Charles Tyler And Brus Trio | Autumn In Paris | Silkheart | SHCD 118

Legendary
Joe McPhee | Graphics | Hat Art | I/J

Legendes
Dave Valentine Group | Legends | GRP | GRP 95192

Legends
Philippe Macé Group | Aventures | AH Records | PAM 969

Leggiero Up
Mary Lou Williams Group | Jazz In Paris:Mary Lou Williams-I Made You Love Paris | EmArCy | 013141-2

Legs
Jack Jeffer's N.Y. Classic Big Band | New York Dreams | Mapleshade | 03632

Leicester Court
Oliver Augst-Rüdiger Carl-Christoph Korn | Blank | FMP | OWN-90013

Leinen Los!
Bernie Senensky Quartet | Homeland | Timeless | CD SJP 426

Leise Klingt's Über's Wasser(Bölgende Rytmer)
Werner Lener Trio | Colours | Satin Doll Productions | SDP 1033-1 CD

Leise Leise,Fromme Weise(from Freischütz)
Jan Von Klewitz-Markus Burger | Spiritual Standards | Jazzline | JL 11156-2

Leise Rieselt Der Schnee
New Orleans Quarter | Christmas Jazz | New Orleans Quarter Records | NOQR-V-DIV-CD 2
David Gazarov Trio | Let's Have A Merry Christmas With The David Gazarov Trio! | Organic Music | ORGM 9712

Leise Rieselt Der Schnee-
Thilo Wolf Big Band | Sternstunden Des Swing | MDL-Jazz | CD 27768

Lejos De Usted
Johnny Lytle Septet | Everything Must Change | Muse | MR 5158

Lela
Lem Winchester Sextet | Lem's Beat | Original Jazz Classics | OJCCD 1785-2(NJ 8239)

Lembrancas
Das Obertontrio Und Toto Blanke | Energy Fields | ALISO Records | AL 1029

Lemniscate
Tania Maria Quintet | Piquant | Concord | CCD 4151

Lemon Drop
Ella Fitzgerald With The Tommy Flanagan Quartet | Ella,Billie,Sarah,Aretha,Mahalia | CBS | 473733-2

Lemonade
Kenny Barron Trio | Lemuria-Seascape | Candid | CCD 79508

Lemuria's Dance
Passport And Guests | Doldinger Jubilee Concert | Atlantic | 2292-44175-2
Cecil Taylor Trio | Trance | Black Lion | BLCD 760220

Lena And Lenny
Milt Jackson With The Count Basie Orchestra | Milt Jackson Birthday Celebration | Fantasy | FANCD 6079-2
Milt Jackson + Count Basie + The Big Band Vol.2 | Pablo | 2310823
Chico Freeman And Brainstorm | Threshold | IN+OUT Records | 7022-2

Lena's Lullaby
Dreamtime | Bunny Up | Affinity | AFF 109

Lende(Homeground)
Ayibobo | Ayibobo:Freestyle | DIW | DIW 877 CD

Lennies
Furio Di Castri-Paolo Fresu | Urlo | yvp music | CD 3035

Lennie's Pennies
Clare Fischer And His Orchestra | 'T Was Only Yesterday | Discovery | DS 798 IMS
Rein de Graaff Quintet | Nostalgia | Timeless | CD SJP 429

L'Ennui
Patrick Bebelaar Quartet | Never Thought It Could Happen | dml-records | CD 007

Lenny
Herb Geller Quartet | Playing Jazz:The Musical Autobiography Of Herb Geller | Fresh Sound Records | FSR-CD 5011

Lenore
Sammy Price | Midnight Boogie | Black & Blue | BLE 59.025 2

Lenox Avenue Breakdown
Five Red Caps | Lenox Avenue Jump | Krazy Kat | KK 779 IMS

Lentement Mademoiselle
George Gruntz Concert Jazz Band | Live At The Jazz Fest Berlin | TCB Records | TCB 99452

Lento
John Zorn Group | Cobra | Hat Art | CD 6040(2)

L'Envers Du Décor
Buster Williams Quartet | Joined At The Hip | TCB Records | TCB 21202

Leo
John Coltrane-Rashied Ali Duo | The Mastery Of John Coltrane Vol.3:Jupiter Variations | MCA | 2292-54649-2
Eric Person Trio | Prophecy | Soul Note | 121287-2

Leo Rising
Charlie Parker With The Woody Herman Orchestra | Bird's Eyees Last Unissued Vol.23 | Philology | W 853.2

Leo, Estante Num Instante
Richard Galliano Group | Laurita | Dreyfus Jazz Line | FDM 36572-9
Richard Galliano-Michel Portal | Gallianissimo! The Best Of Richard Galliano | Dreyfus Jazz Line | FDM 36616-2
Concert Inédits | Dreyfus Jazz Line | FDM 36606-2

Leola
Illinois Jacquet Sextet | Illinois Jacquet Flying Home-The Best Of The Verve Years | Verve | 521644-2

Leonardo's Spoon
Enzo Scoppa Quartet & Guests | Enzo Scoppa Quartet & Guests | Penta Flowers | CDPIA 011

Leonora
Richard Wyands Trio | Then Here And Now | Storyville | STCD 8269

Leonora(alt.take)
Astor Piazzolla Group | The Rough Dancer And The Cyclical Night(Tango Apasionado) | American Clave | AMCL 1019-2

Leo's Place
Ray Anderson With The George Gruntz Concert Jazz Band | Ray Anderson Big Band Record | Gramavision | R2 79497

Leosia
Jasper Van't Hof Group | Blau | ACT | 9203-2

L'Epoque Bleue(for Ives Klein)
Dave Liebman Quintet | The Last Call | EGO | 4016

Leroy Street
Peter Erskine Orchestra | Peter Erskine | Contemporary | CCD 14010-2

Les
Eric Dolphy Quintet | Outward Bound | Original Jazz Classics | OJC 022(NJ 8236)
Eric Dolphy With Erik Moseholm's Trio | Eric Dolphy:The Complete Prestige Recordings | Prestige | 9 PRCD-4418-2
Eric Dolphy With The Kenny Drew Trio | Daniel Humair Surrounded 1964-1987 | Blue Flame | 40322(2132163-2)

Les 2 Visages
Montreal Jubilation Gospel Choir | Jubilation VI 'Looking Back'-Special 20th Anniversary Compilation | Blues Beacon | BLU-1022 22

Les Ailes Du Bourak
Sylvain Luc-Biréli Lagrène | Duet | Dreyfus Jazz Line | FDM 36604-2

Les Amoureux Des Bancs Publics
Ulli Bögershausen | Christmas Carols | Laika Records | 35101622

Les Anges Dans Nos Campagnes
Louis Sclavis Group | Napoli's Walls | ECM | 1857(038504-2)

Les Apparences
Joelle Leandre-Carlos Zingaro | Ecritures | Adda | 590038

Les Bouteilles
L'Orchestre De Contrebasses | Les Cargos | Label Bleu | LBLC 6536(889138)

Les Demoiselles D'Avignon
BBFC | Souvenir D'Italie | Plainisphare | PL 1267-19

Les Douzilles
Oregon | Beyond Words | Chesky | JD 130
Ralph Towner Quintet | City Of Eyes | ECM | 1388
Gunther Klatt & New York Razzmatazz | Volume One:Fa Mozzo | Tutu Records | 888158-2*

Les Enfants Des Dubrovnik
Günther Klatt & New York Razzmatazz | Fa Mozzo | Tutu Records | 888138-2

Les Enfants Qui S'Aiment
Habarigani Brass | Hans Kennel:Habarigani Brass | Hat Art | CD 6185

Les Fesses Au Clair De Lune
Barney Wilen With The Mal Waldron Trio | Movie Themes From France | Timeless | CD SJP 335

Les Feuilles Mortes
Häns'che Weiss-Vali Mayer Duo | The Duo Live In Concert | MMM Records | CD 1296
Hartmut Kracht | Kontrabass Pur | Jazz Haus Musik | JHM 0103 CD
Stochelo Rosenberg Trio | Seresta | Hot Club Records | HCRCD 059

Les Feuilles Mortes -> Autumn Leaves

Les III
booMbooM meets Uli Beckerhoff | Resurection Lounge | Laika Records | 35101512

Les Insecteurs
Harry Beckett/Django Bates | Les Jardins Du Casino | West Wind | WW 2080

Les Jeux Sont Faits
Tome XX | Stadtgarten Series Vol.4 | Jazz Haus Musik | JHM 1004 SER

Les Loups Dans La Bergerie(fin)
Alain Goraguer Orchestra | Jazz In Paris | EmArCy | 548793-2

Les Loups Dans La Bergerie:
Louis Sclavis & The Bernard Struber Jazztet | La Phare | Enja | ENJ-9359 2

Les Marches
Tethered Moon | Chansons D'Edith Piaf | Winter&Winter | 910048-2

Les Mois D'Amour
Quatuor De Saxophones Gabriel Pierné | Musiques De Films | Nocturne Productions | NPCD 507

Les Moutons(Su Le Lit)
Bobby Hutcherson Sextet | Dialogue | Blue Note | 535586-2

Les Noirs Marchent
A Blue Conception | Blue Note | 534254-2
Maxim Saury And His New Orleans Sound | Homage A Sidney Bechet | Jazztime(EMI) | 792406-2

Les Oignons
Sidney Bechet With Claude Luter And His Orchestra | Sidney Bechet:Summertime | Dreyfus Jazz Line | FDM 36712-2
Salle Pleyel 31 January 52 | Vogue | 655001

Les Salades De L'Oncle Francois
Jacotte Perrier With The Quintet Du Hot Club De France | Le Jazz En France Vol.5:Django Plus | Pathe | 1727291

Les Tenebrides-
Jim Pepper With The Claudine Francois Trio | Camargue | Pan Music | PMC 1106

Les Tricheurs
Oscar Peterson Quartet With Stan Getz And Roy Eldridge | Des Femmes Disparaissent/Les Tricheurs(Original Soundtracks) | Fontana | 834752-2 PMS
Susan Weinert Band | Point Of View | Intuition Records | INT 3272-2

Les Trois Arbres
Pierre Boussaguet Trio | Charme | EmArCy | 538468-2

Les Trois Lagons(D'apres Henri Matisse)
Didier Lockwood Trio | Tribute To Stépane Grappelli | Dreyfus Jazz Line | FDM 36611-2

Les Valseuses
Tacabanda | Ora Imprecisa | yvp music | CD 3055

Les Vieux Alemands
Pierre Bensusan Group | Bamboulé | Acoustic Music Records | 319.1040.2

Les Yeux Noirs
Django Reinhardt And The Quintet Du Hot Club De France | Django Reinhardt:Djangology | EMI Records | 780659-2
The Rosenberg Trio | Suenos Gitanos | Polydor | 549581-2
Yves Teicher Quartet | Fiddler On The Groove | RCA | 2147489-2

Lesmiante-The Forest Tale
Martin Classen Quartet | Cereal | Acoustic Music Records | 319.1122.2

Less Is Little
Shorty Rogers-Bud Shank And The Lighthouse All Stars | America The Beautiful | Candid | CCD 79510

Lestat's Lamento
David Murray Big Band | David Murry Big Band | CBS | CK 48964

Lester
Antonello Salis | Salis! | SPLASC(H) Records | H 136

Lester Blows Again
Lester Young And His Band | Jazz Gallery:Lester Young Vol.1(1936-46) | RCA | 2114171-2
Ari Brown Sextet | Ultimate Frontier | Delmark | DE 486

Lester Leaps Again
Kansas City Five | Lester Young:Blue Lester | Dreyfus Jazz Line | FDM 36729-2
Lester Young Sextet | Live At The Royal Roost 1948 | Jazz Anthology | 550092

Lester Leaps In
Conte Candoli-Carl Fontana Quintet | The Complete Phoenix Recordings Vol.6 | Woofy Productions | WPCD 126
Count Basie And His Orchestra | Count Basie At Newport | Verve | 9861761
Count Basie At Newport | Verve | 2304414 IMS
Swingin' The Blues | Arco | 3 ARC 111
Count Basie Jam Session | Count Basie Jam Session At The Montreux Jazz Festival 1975 | Original Jazz Classics | OJC20 933-2(2310750)
Count Basie Septet | Prez's Hat Vol.1 | Philology | 214 W 6
Count Basie's Kansas City Seven | This Is Jazz:Lester Young | CBS | CK 65042
David Murray Quartet | David Murray-Saxmen | Red Baron | JK 57758
Erwin Lehn Und Sein Südfunk-Tanzorchester | Deutsches Jazz Fesival 1954/1955 | Bear Family Records | BCD 15430
Gil Evans Orchestra | Pacific Standart Time | Blue Note | 84494
JATP All Stars | Jazz At The Philharmonic:Bird & Pres-Carnegie Hall 1949 | Verve | 815150-1 IMS
Talkin' Bird | Verve | 559859-2
Jazz At The Philharmonic-The First Concert | Verve | 521646-2
The Complete Jazz At The Philharmonic On Verve 1944-1949 | Verve | 523893-2
Charlie Parker Jazz At The Philharmonic 1949 | Verve | 519803-2
Lee Konitz Quintet | Peacemeal | Milestone | M 9025
Roots | Salutes The Saxophone: Tributes To John Coltrane, Dexter Gordon, Sonny Rollins, Ben Webster And Lester Young | IN+OUT Records | 7016-1
Jazz Unlimited | IN+OUT Records | 7017-2
Saying Something | IN+OUT Records | 77031-2
Slide Hampton Orchestra | World Of Trombones | Black Lion | CD 877641-2
Sonny Stitt Quartet | Salt And Pepper/Now! | Impulse(MCA) | 951210-2
The New York Allstars | Count Basie Remembered | Nagel-Heyer | CD 031
The Newport All Stars | That Newport Jazz | CBS | 21139
Very Saxy | Very Saxy | Original Jazz Classics | OJCCD 458-2
Von Freeman Quartet | Lester Leaps In | Steeplechase | SCCD 31320
Zoot Sims Quintet | Zoot Sims | Storyville | STCD 8367
Zoot Sims-Bucky Pizzarelli Duo | Elegiac | Storyville | STCD 8238
Lester Young's JAPT Quintet | Prez's Hat Vol.1 | Philology | 214 W 6

Lester Left Town
Art Blakey And The Jazz Messengers | The Art Of Jazz | IN+OUT Records | 77028-2
Live In Stockholm 1959 | DIW | DIW 313 CD
Live In Stockholm 1959 | Dragon | DRCD 182
Stan Getz Quartet | Live At Montmartre(CD=Stan's Party) | Steeplechase | SCCD 37021/22
Lover Man | Moon Records | MCD 020-2
Stan Getz Sextet | Jazzbühne Berlin '78 | Repertoire Records | REPCD 4915-WZ
Vladimir Shafranov Trio | White Nights | The Jazz Alliance | TJA 10018

Lester Smooths It Out
Lester Young And His Band | Lester Young:The Complete Aladdin Sessions | Blue Note | 832787-2
Lester Young Sextet | Lester Young:The Complete 1936-1951 Small Group Sessions(Studio Recordings-Master Takes),Vol.4 | Blue Moon | BMCD 1004

Lester's Be-Bop Boogie
Lester Young And His Band | Lester Young:The Complete 1936-1951 Small Group Sessions(Studio Recordings-Master Takes),Vol.4 | Blue Moon | BMCD 1004

Lester's Blues
Lester Young Quintet | Jazz Immortal Series Vol.2: The Pres | Savoy | SV 0180(MG 12155)

Let Her Go
Hubert Laws And His Orchestra | Flute By - Laws | Atlantic | SD 1452

Let Him Beat Me
Lew Stone And His Band | Lew Stone And His Band | Decca | DDV 5005/6 DT

Let It Be Me
Nina Simone Quartet | Nina Simone | The Rising Sun Collection | RSC 0004

Let It Be Me-
Gene Ammons Quintet | Gentle Jug Vol.3 | Prestige | PCD 24249-2

Let It Be You
'Jug' | Original Jazz Classics | OJCCD 701-2(P 7192)

Let It Go
McCoy Tyner Big Band | The Turning Point | Birdology | 513163-2

Let It Loose
Patricia Barber Group | Modern Cool | Blue Note | 521811-2

Let It Rain
Modern Cool | Blue Note | 521811-2

Let It Rain-Vamp
Patti Austin And Her Band | Live At The Bottom Line | CBS | 467922-2
Let It Shine
Christoph Mudrich Trio feat. Sir Henry | Christmas In Blue | Blue Concept | BCCD 93/03
Let It Snow, Let It Snow, Let It Snow
Ernst Höllerhagen Quartet | Ernst Höllerhagen 1942-1948 | Elite Special | 9522001
Jimmy Rowles Septet | Weather In A Jazz Vane | Fresh Sound Records | FSR 502(Andex S-3007)
Let It Stand
Staple Singers | Great Day | Milestone | MCD 47027-2
Let Me Count My Ways
Victor Feldman Orchestra | Secret Of The Andes | Palo Alto | PA 8053
Let Me In
Champion Jack Dupree Group | Chamion Jack Dupree | EPM Musique | FDC 5504
Let Me Love You
Blossom Dearie Quartet | Give Him The Ooh-La-La | Verve | 517067-2
Duke Robillard Group | Rockin' Blues | Rounder Records | CDRR 11548
Pam Purvis/Bob Ackerman Quintet | Heart Song | Black-Hawk | BKH 51201
Buddy Guy Band | Buddy Guy | Chess | 427006
Let Me Love You Baby
Eddie Taylor Blues Band | Stormy Monday | Blues Beacon | BLU-1004 2
Let Me Off Uptown
Dakota Staton With The Groove Holmes Sextet | Dakota Staton | LRC Records | CDC 9017
Roy Eldridge Quintet | Happy Time | Original Jazz Classics | OJCCD 628-2(2310746)
Let Me Play With Your Poodle
Tampa Red | Don't Tampa With The Blues | Original Blues Classics | OBCCD 516-2
Let Me See
J.J. Johnson-Al Grey Sextet | Things Are Getting Better All The Time | Pablo | 2312141
Red Garland Trio | At The Prelude Vol.1 | Prestige | PCD 24132-2
Let Me Take You Home
James Blood Ulmer Quartet | Blues Preacher | DIW | DIW 869 CD
Let Me Tell You
Graef-Schippa-Moritz | Orlando Frames | Nabel Records:Jazz Network | CD 4690
Let Me Tell You A Xmas Night Farewell
Leo Parker Sextet | Let Me Tell You 'Bout It | Blue Note | 869956-4
Let Me Tell You Why
Johnny Griffin Quartet | NYC Underground | Galaxy | GXY 5132
Let My People Be
Gerry Mulligan Concert Jazz Band | The Complete Verve Gerry Mulligan Concert Band | Verve | 9860613
Compact Jazz: Gerry Mulligan Concert Jazz Band | Verve | 838933-2
Let My People Go(for Patrice E.Lumuba)
Benny Goodman And His Orchestra | The Indispensable Benny Goodman Vol.3/4 | RCA | 2115520-2
Let The Cat Out
Mahalia Jackson With Choir/Orchestra/Falls-Jones Ensemble | This Is Mahalia Jackson | CBS | 66241
Let The Good Times Roll
Allotria Jazz Band | Cleared For Take Off | Elite Special | 73331
Big Allanbik | Batuque Y Blues | Blues Beacon | BLU-1031 2
Clarence Gatemouth Brown Quartet | Cold Storage | Black & Blue | BLE 59.096 2
Louis Jordan And His Tympany Five | Five Guys Named Moe | Bandstand | BDCD 1531
Jaki Byard | Jaki Byard:Solo/Strings | Prestige | PCD 24246-2
Let The Good Times Roll-
Memphis Slim Group | I'll Just Keep On Singin' The Blues | Muse | MR 5219
Let The Music Take Your Mind
Erskine Hawkins And His Orchestra | The Complete Erskine Hawkins Vol.1/2 | RCA | 2135552-2
Let The Rain Fall On Me
Bob Schulz And His Frisco Jazz Band | Travelin' Shoes | Stomp Off Records | CD 1315
Let The Slave Incorporating The Prince Of Experience
Charles Brown | Great Rhythm & Blues-Vol.1 | Bulldog | BDL 1001
Let The Words
Oscar Peterson With Orchestra | A Royal Wedding Suite | Original Jazz Classics | OJCCD 973-2(2312129)
Let The World Sing
Duke Ellington And His Orchestra | Live Sessions 1943/1945 | Jazz Anthology | JA 5124
Let Them Talk
George Benson Quartet + Guests | The George Benson Cookbook | CBS | 502470-2
James Booker | Boogie Woogie And Ragtime Piano Contest | Gold Records | 11035 AS
Let There Be Love
Laura Fygi With Band | Bewitched | Verve | 514724-2
Nat King Cole With The George Shearing Quintet Plus String Choir | Net King Cole Sings/George Shearing Plays | Capitol | EMS 1113
Mahalia Jackson With Choir And Orchestra | Starportrait | CBS | 67265
Let Up
Melanie Bong With Band | Fantasia | Jazz 4 Ever Records:Jazz Network | J4E 4755
Let Us
David & Roselyn Group | Gospel From The Streets Of New Orleans | Sound Of New Orleans | SONO 1033
Let Us Go Into The House Of The Lord
Mahavishnu Orchestra With Carlos Santana | Love Devotion Surrender | CBS | 69037
Monnette Sudler Quartet | Time For A Change | Steeplechase | SCCD 31062
Let Your Hair Down Blues
Denise Lawrence & Storeyville Tickle | Let It Shine | Lake | LACD 37
Let Yourself Down
Bunny Berigan | I Can't Get Started | Pro-Arte | CDD 554
Let Yourself Go
Ella Fitzgerald With Paul Weston And His Orchestra | The Complete Ella Fitzgerald Song Books of Harold Arlen, Irving Berlin, Duke Ellington, George & Ira Gershwin, Jerome Kern, Johnny Mercer, Cole Porter And Rogers & Hart | Verve | 519832-2
Stacey Kent And Her Quintet | Let Yourself Go-Celebrating Fred Astaire | Candid | CCD 79764
Serge Chaloff All Stars | The Fable Of Mabel | Black Lion | CD 877627-2
L'Etang
Blossom Dearie Quartet | My Gentleman Friend | Verve | 519905-2
Erwin Lehn Und Sein Südfunk-Tanzorchester | Swing Tanzen Gestattet | Vagabond | 6.28415 DP
Lethargend
Clint Houston Quartet | Inside The Plain Of The Elliptic | Timeless | SJP 132
L'Étranger
Tommy Flanagan Trio | Sunset And The Mockingbird-The Birthday Concert | Blue Note | 493155-2
Let's
Let's Play The Muisc Of Thad Jones | Enja | ENJ-8040 2
Let's Begin
Anita O'Day With The Buddy Bregman Orchestra | Pick Yourself Up | Official | 3015
Ella Fitzgerald With The Nelson Riddle Orchestra | The Complete Ella Fitzgerald Song Books of Harold Arlen, Irving Berlin, Duke Ellington, George & Ira Gershwin, Jerome Kern, Johnny Mercer, Cole Porter And Rogers & Hart | Verve | 519832-2
Margaret Whiting With Russel Garcia And His Orchestra | A Fine Romance | Verve | 523827-2
Let's Burn Down The Cornfield
Billie Holiday And Her Orchestra | Billie Holiday:The Quintessential Vol.2(1936) | CBS | 460060-2
Let's Call It A Day
Peggy Lee With Orchestra | All Aglow Again | Capitol | 1565541
Let's Call The Whole Thing Off
Billie Holiday And Her Orchestra | Billie Holiday:The Quintessential Vol.4(1937) | CBS | 463333-2
Ella Fitzgerald And Louis Armstrong With The Oscar Peterson Quartet | Ella And Louis Again, Vol.2 | Verve | 711122 IMS
Compact Jazz: Ella Fitzgerald/Louis Armstrong | Verve | 835313-2
Ella Fitzgerald With Andre Previn | Nice Work If You Can Get It-Ella Fitzgerald And Andre Previn Do Gershwin | Pablo | 2312140-2
Ella Fitzgerald With The Nelson Riddle Orchestra | Ella Sings Gershwin-Vol. 1 | Metro | 2682004 IMS
Marian McPartland Trio | At The Hickory House | Jasmine | JAS 312
Rex Stewart-Dickie Wells Quintet | Chatter Jazz | RCA | 2118525-2
Sir Roland Hanna | Maybeck Recital Hall Series Volume Thirty-Two | Concord | CCD 4604
Let's Call This
Roland Kirk Quartet | Rahsaan/The Complete Mercury Recordings Of Roland Kirk | Mercury | 846630-2
Steve Grossman Quartet | Do It | Dreyfus Jazz Line | FDM 36550-2
Steve Lacy-Mal Waldron | Vol.1:Round Midnight | Hat Art | CD 6172(2)
Thelonious Monk Quintet | MONK | Original Jazz Classics | OJCCD 016-2
Thelonious Monk:The Complete Prestige Recordings | Prestige | 3 PRCD 4428-2
The Prestige Legacy Vol.1:The High Priests | Prestige | PCD 24251-2
Thelonious Monk Sextet | In Person | Milestone | M 47033
Roland Kirk Quartet | Verve Jazz Masters 27:Roland Kirk | Verve | 522062-2
Let's Call This-
Hal Galper Quintet | Let's Call This That | Double Time Records | DTRCD-157
Let's Call This(Walkin' The Blues)
Randy Weston | Marrakech In The Cool Of The Evening | Verve | 521588-2
Let's Cool One
Clark Terry-Thelonious Monk Quartet | In Orbit | Original Jazz Classics | OJC 302(R 12-271)
Ellery Eskelin + Han Bennink | Dissonant Characters | HatOLOGY | 534
Thelonious Monk Quartet | Thelonious Monk-The Complete Riverside Recordings | Riverside | 15 RCD 022-2
Thelonious Monk Sextet | Thelonious Monk:The Complete Blue Note Recordings | Blue Note | 830363-2
Genius Of Modern Music,Vol.1 | Blue Note | 781510-2
Clark Terry-Max Roach Quartet | Friednship | CBS | 510886-2
Let's Cool One(Come With Me)
Soesja Citroen And Her All Stars | Sings Thelonious Monk | Turning Point | 30001
Let's Dance
Benny Goodman And His Orchestra | The Benny Goodman Story | Capitol | 833569-2
The Best Of The Big Dance Bands | LRC Records | CDC9010
Let's Dance (Theme)
More Camel Caravans | Phontastic | NCD 8841/2
More Camel Caravans | Phontastic | NCD 8845/6
More Camel Caravans | Phontastic | NCD 8843/4
More Camel Caravans | Phontastic | NCD 8841/2
Camel Caravan Broadcast 1939 Vol.1 | Phontastic | NCD 8817
More Camel Caravans | Phontastic | NCD 8843/4
More Camel Caravans | Phontastic | NCD 8845/6
More Camel Caravans | Phontastic | NCD 8843/4
More Camel Caravans | Phontastic | NCD 8845/6
More Camel Caravans | Phontastic | NCD 8845/6
More Camel Caravans | Phontastic | NCD 8843/4
More Camel Caravans | Phontastic | NCD 8841/2
Camel Caravan Broadcast 1939 Vol.2 | Phontastic | NCD 8818
More Camel Caravans | Phontastic | NCD 8841/2
Birth Of A Band | Giants Of Jazz | GOJ 1038
Recorded Live In Stockholm-1970 | Verve | 820471-2
Let's Do It
Dee Dee Bridgewater With Orchestra | Dear Ella | Verve | 539102-2
Ella Fitzgerald And Louis Armstrong With The Oscar Peterson Quartet | The Complete Ella Fitzgerald And Louis Armstrong On Verve | Verve | 537284-2
Ella Fitzgerald With The Duke Ellington Orchestra And Jimmy Jones Trio | Ella Fitzgerald And Duke Ellington:Cote D'Azure Concerts on Verve | Verve | 539033-2
Ella Fitzgerald And Duke Ellington:Cote D'Azure Concerts on Verve | Verve | 539033-2
Ella Fitzgerald And Duke Ellington:Cote D'Azure Concerts on Verve | Verve | 539033-2
Gérard Badini Quartet | Jazz In Paris:Gérard Badini-The Swing Machine | EmArCy | 018417-2
Peggy Lee With The Benny Goodman Orchestra | Peggy Lee & Benny Goodman:The Complete Recordings 1941-1947 | CBS | C2K 65686
Tal Farlow Trio | Tal Farlow Complete 1956 Private Recordings | Definitive Records | DRCD 11263
Let's Do It Again(single version)
Louis Jordan And His Tympany Five | Rock 'N Roll Call | Bluebird | 63 66145-2
Let's Do It(Let's Fall In Love)
Eddie Costa-Vinnie Burke Trio | Eddie Costa-Vinnie Burke Trio | Fresh Sound Records | LP 1025(Jubilee)
Ella Fitzgerald With Orchestra | Essential Ella | Verve | 523990-2
Ella Fitzgerald With The Buddy Bregman Orchestra | The Cole Porter Song Book | Verve | 2683044 IMS
The Complete Ella Fitzgerald Song Books of Harold Arlen, Irving Berlin, Duke Ellington, George & Ira Gershwin, Jerome Kern, Johnny Mercer, Cole Porter And Rogers & Hart | Verve | 519832-2
Ella Fitzgerald With The Tommy Flanagan Trio | Ella-At The Montreux Jazz Festival 1975 | Original Jazz Classics | OJC20 789-2(2310751)
Louis Armstrong With The Oscar Peterson Quartet | Louis Armstrong Meets Oscar Peterson | Verve | 539060-2
Compact Jazz: Louis Armstrong | Verve | 833293-2
Lous Dassen With Holger Clausen/Atlanta Jazzband | Let's Do It... | Dr.Jazz Records | 8606-2
Rex Stewart-Dickie Wells Quintet | Chatter Jazz | RCA | 2118525-2
Let's Do It(Let's Fall In Love-alt.take)
The Human Arts Ensemble | The Human Arts Ensemble Live, Vol.1 | Circle Records | RK 9-23578/9 IMS
Let's Dream In The Moonlight
Teddy Wilson And His Orchestra | Rare And Unissued Recordings From The Golden Years,Vol.2 | Queen-Disc | 065
Let's Eat
Dave Frishberg Quintet | Let's Eat Home | Concord | CCD 4402
Let's Face The Music And Dance
Anita O'Day And Her Combo | Pick Yourself Up | Verve | 517329-2
Pick Yourself Up | Official | 3015
Ella Fitzgerald With Orchestra | Essential Ella | Verve | 523990-2
Ella Fitzgerald With Paul Weston And His Orchestra | Ella Fitzgerald Sings The Irving Berlin Song Book | Verve | 543830-2
The Complete Ella Fitzgerald Song Books of Harold Arlen, Irving Berlin, Duke Ellington, George & Ira Gershwin, Jerome Kern, Johnny Mercer, Cole Porter And Rogers & Hart | Verve | 519832-2
Mel Tormé With The Marty Paich Dek-Tette | Mel Torme Sings Fred Astaire | Charly | CD 96
Rosemary Clooney And The Concord All Stars | Sings The Music Of Irving Berlin | Concord | CCD 4255
Anita O'Day And Her Combo | Pick Yourself Up | Verve | 517329-2
Let's Face The Music And Dance(alt.take)
Ella Fitzgerald With The Frank DeVol Orchestra | Ella Fitzgerald Sings Sweet Songs For Swingers | Verve | 9860417
Let's Fall In
| Remember When | Master Mix | CHECD 11
Let's Fall In Love
Dave Brubeck Quartet | Jazz At The College Of The Pacific Vol.2 | Original Jazz Classics | OJCCD 1076-2
The Best Live Sessions | Festival | Album 254
Don Elliott Orchestra | Don Elliott Sings | Fresh Sound Records | FSR 2049(Bethlehem BCP 15)
Ella Fitzgerald With The Billy May Orchestra | The Harold Arlen Songbook | Verve | 817526-1 IMS
John Graas Nonet | Jazzmantics | Fresh Sound Records | 252283-1(Decca DL 8677)
Johnny Smith Quartet | The Sound Of The Johnny Smith Guitar | Roulette | 531792-2
Lester Young Quartet | Lester Swings | Verve | 833554-1
Louis Armstrong With The Oscar Peterson Quartet | Louis Armstrong Meets Oscar Peterson | Verve | 825713-2
Oscar Peterson Trio | Exclusively For My Friends-The Lost Tapes | MPS | 529096-2
Compact Jazz:Oscar Peterson | Mercury | 830698-2
En Concert Avec Europe 1 | Laserlight | 710443/48
Peggy Lee With The Bill Holman Orchestra | Pass Me By/Big Spender | Capitol | 535210-2
Shorty Rogers And His Orchestra | Swings | Bluebird | ND 83012
Stephane Grappelli Quartet | At The Winery | Concord | CCD 4139
Live In San Francisco | Black-Hawk | BKH 51601
Tal Farlow Trio | Guitar Player | Prestige | P 24042
Let's Fall In Love(alt.take)
Ingrid Sertso And Her Sextet | Dance With Me | Enja | 8024-2
Let's Get Away From It All
Charlie Mariano Sextet | Nat Pierce-Dick Collins Nonet/Charlie Mariano Sextet | Original Jazz Classics | OJC 118(F 3224)
Della Reese With The Neal Hefti Orchestra | Della | RCA | 2663912-2
Ernestine Anderson With The Johnnie Scott Orchestra | Miss Ernestine Anderson | Pathe | 1566121(Columbia SX 6145)
Paul Desmond Quartet | Paul Desmond Quartet Featuring Don Elliott | Original Jazz Classics | OJC 119(F 3235)
Let's Get Down
B.B.King And His Band | Completely Live And Well | Charly | CDX 14
Let's Get Drunk(And Be Somebody)
Billy Cotton And His Band | Sing A New Song | Saville Records | SVL 160 IMS
Let's Get It On
Red Norvo And His Orchestra | Live From The Blue Gardens | Musicmasters | 65090-2
Let's Get Lost
Christian Josi With The Harry Allen Quartet | I Walk With My Feet Off The Ground | Master Mix | CHECD 00111
Vince Jones With The Benny Green Quartet | One Day Spent | Intuition Records | INT 3087-8(CD-Single)
Let's Get Medieval
Joelle Leandre | Sincerely | Plainisphare | PL 1267-92 CD
Let's Get To The Nitty Gritty
Duke Ellington And His Orchestra | Recollections Of The Big Band Era | Atlantic | 90043-2
Let's Get Together
Ella Fitzgerald With The Chick Webb Orchestra | Let's Get Together | Laserlight | 17003
Let's Get Together(Theme)
Ella Fitzgerald With Chick Webb And His Orchestra | Ella Fitzgerald Vol.1-Forever Young | Swingtime(Contact) | ST 1006
Let's Go Back To The Waltz
Bill Evans Trio | Empathy+A Simple Matter Of Conviction | Verve | 837757-2 PMS
Empathy | CTI Records | PDCTI 1126-2
Let's Go Get Stoned
Martin Schmitt | Handful Of Blues | AH Records | ESM 9303
Let's Go Home
Cab Calloway And His Orchestra | Cab Calloway: Jumpin' Jive 1938/1946 | Zeta | ZET 732
Let's Go Together
Paulinho Da Costa Orchestra | Happy People | Original Jazz Classics | OJCCD 783-2(2312102)
Helmut Kagerer 4 & Roman Schwaller | Gamblin' | Jardis Records | JRCD 9714
Let's Go Wes
Blossom Dearie Trio | Sweet Blossom Dearie | Philips | PHCE 1019 PMS
Let's Groove
Stanley Turrentine Quartet | Stan 'The Man' | Bainbridge | BT 1038
Let's Have A Baby
Clyde Bernhardt And His Blue Bazers | Clyde Bernhardt:The Complete Recordings Vol.1 (1945-1948) | Blue Moon | BMCD 6016
Let's Have A Party
Count Basie And His Orchestra | Breakfast Dance And Barbecue | Roulette | 531791-2
Let's Have A Taste
Count Basie & His Orchestra:Fresno,California April 24,1959 | Jazz Unlimited | JUCD 2039
Let's Have Another Cigarette
Dave Pell Octet | The Dave Pell Octet Plays Irving Berlin | Fresh Sound Records | 252963-1(Kapp KL 1036) (835207)
Let's Jump
Count Basie And His Orchestra | Prez's Hat Vol.2 | Philology | 214 W 7
Let's Lay Down
Jeremy Davenport Quartet | Maybe In A Dream | Telarc Digital | CD 83409
Let's Live Again
The Three Sounds | Bottoms Up | Blue Note | 0675629
Let's Love
You Cindy Lou | Confessin' The Blues | Affinity | AFF 66
Let's Make Love
Fourplay | Heartfelt | RCA | 2663916-2
John Klemmer Group | Hush | Elektra | 5E-527
Let's Make Rhythm:
Riccardo Fassi Tankio Band | Riccardo Fassi Tankio Band Pays The Music Of Frank Zappa | SPLASC(H) Records | CD H 428-2
Let's March
Steve Grossman Quartet | Do It | Dreyfus Jazz Line | FDM 36550-2
Let's Not Take A Raincheck
Tim Sund Trio | Trialogue | Nabel Records:Jazz Network | CD 4692
Let's Open The Year!
Eddie C. Campbell & Tip On In | Let's Pick It | Black Saint | 9007
Let's Pretend
Al Jarreau With Band | High Crime | i.e. Music | 557848-2
Bill Evans Group | Let The Juice Loose-Bill Evans Group Live at The Blue Note,Tokyo | Jazz City | 660.53.001
Let's Roll It
Dick Robertson And His Orchestra | The New York Session Man | Timeless | CBC 1-008
Let's Say A Prayer
Spyro Gyra & Guests | Love & Other Obsessions | GRP | GRP 98112
Let's Say Goodbye
John Scofield Quartet | Time On My Hands | Blue Note | 792894-2
Let's Say We Did
Volker Kriegel Group | Topical Harvest | MPS | 821279
Let's See
Jimmie Grier And His Orchestra | The Uncollected:Jimmie Grier | Hindsight | HSR 177
Let's Sing Like A Dixieland Band
Ben Pollack And His Park Central Orchestra | Ben Pollack Vol.2 | Jazz Oracle | BDW 8016
Let's Split
Nat King Cole Trio | Nat King Cole | Savoy | 650120(881920)
Let's Start All Over Again(Down On Bended Knee)
Mel Tormé And His Trio With The Cincinnati Sinfonietta | Christmas Songs- | Telarc Digital | CD 83315

Let's Stay Together
Herbie Mann Group | Sunbelt | Atlantic | ATL 50536
Sweet Miss Coffy With The Mississippi Burnin' Blues Revue | Sweet Miss Coffy | Mardi Gras Records | MG 1021
Artie Shaw And His Orchestra | The Uncollected: Artie Shaw, Vol.2 | Hindsight | HSR 140

Let's Take 16 Bars
Klaus Ignatzek Group | Jacaranda | Timeless | CD SJP 292

Let's Take A Walk Around The Block
Ella Fitzgerald With The Billy May Orchestra | Ella Fitzgerald Sings The Harold Arlen Song Book | Verve | 589108-2
The Harold Arlen Songbook | Verve | 817526-1 IMS

Let's Take An Old Fashioned Walk
Sarah Vaughan With Hal Mooney's Orchestra | Sarah Vaughan Sings Broadway:Grat Songs From Hit Shows | Verve | 526464-2

Let's Talk About Jazz
Benny Waters & Jan Jankeje | Let's Talk About Jazz | G&J Records | GJ 2009 Maxi-CD

Let's Talk About Jazz(instrumental version)
Rosa Henderson With Rex Stewart And Louis Hooper | Rosa Henderson 1923-1931 | Retrieval | RTR 79016

Let's Twist Again
Nelson Rangell Group | Playing For Keeps | GRP | GRP 95932

Letter From Home
Pat Metheny Group | The Road To You | Geffen Records | GED 24601
Paco De Lucia-Al Di Meola-John McLaughlin | Paco De Lucia-Al Di Meola-John McLaughlin | Verve | 533215-2

Letter From India
J.B.Hutto Quartet | Slidewinder | Delmark | 900208 AO

Letter From My Mother
Lowell Fulsom Band | Man Of Motion | Charly | CRB 1018

Letter Perfect
Dave Soldier Group With Voices | Smut | Avant | AVAN 019

Letter To Evan
Bill Evans Trio | Bill Evans Trio:The Last Waltz | Milestone | 8MCD 4430-2
Bill Evans Trio:The Last Waltz | Milestone | 8MCD 4430-2
The Jazz Festivals In Latin America | West Wind | WW 2062
David Benoit Group | Letter To Evan | GRP | GRP 96872

Lettre Á Louis
Les Blue Stars | Jazz In Paris:Blossom Dearie-The Pianist/Les Blue Stars | EmArCy | 064784-2

Lettre A Virginie
Bettina Born-Wolfram Born | Irgenwo Zwischen Tango,Musette Und Jazz | Born&Bellmann | 972708 CD

Letzten Wille
Paul Eßer-Gerd Dudek-Ali Haurand-Jiri Strivin | Jazz Und Lyrik:Schinderkarren Mit Buffet | Konnex Records | KCD 5108

Letzter Trip-
Attila Zoller Quartet | Overcome | Enja | 5053 (807556)

Levando A Vida
Sammy Price Quintet | Roots Of Rock 'N' Roll, Vol. 7: Rib Joint | Savoy | SJL 2240 (801886)

Levels And Degrees
Babatunde And Phenomena | Levels Of Conciousness | Evidence | TR 107

Levitate
Domenic Landolf Quartet | Levitation | JHM Records | JHM 3616

Levitation
John Surman | Private City | ECM | 1366
Andrew Cyrille And Maono | Celebration | IPS Records | 002

Levrette
Larry Sonn And His Orchestra | Jazz Band Having A Ball | Fresh Sound Records | DLP 9005(Dot)

Lew's Piece
Jimmy McGriff-Hank Crawford Quartet | Blues Groove | Telarc Digital | CD 83381

Lex
Dick Meldonian And The Jersey Swingers | Some Of These Days | Progressive | PRO 7033 IMS

L'extreme Jonction
Claudio Puntin/Gerdur Gunnarsdóttir | Ýlir | ECM | 1749(158570-2)

Leysing
Cal Tjader's Orchestra | Verve Jazz Masters 39:Cal Tjader | Verve | 521858-2

Leyte
Cal Tjader/Soul Sauce | Verve | 521668-2

L'Harka Li Jeya
Franz Koglmann Monoblue Quartet | L'Heure Bleue | Hat Art | CD 6093

L'Homme De Berlin
Raymond Boni | L'Homme Etoile | Hat Art | 3510

Libed
Pili-Pili | Stolen Moments | JA & RO | JARO 4159-2

Liberata
Horace Silver Quintet | In Pursuit Of The 27th Man | Blue Note | 84433

Liberation
The Jazz Corps | The Jazz Corps | Pacific Jazz | 829101-2
Vincent Herring Quintet | Don't Let It Go | Musicmasters | 65121-2

Liberation Dance (When Tarzan Meets The African Freedom Figh
Abdullah Ibrahim(Dollar Brand) | Jazzbühne Berlin '82 | Repertoire Records | REPCD 4907-CC

Liberia
John Coltrane Quartet | Coltrane's Sound | Atlantic | 7567-81358-2
Ian Wheeler Jazz Band | Ian Wheeler At Farnham Maltings | Lake | LACD 32

Liberian Suite:
Duke Ellington And His Orchestra | Duke Ellington:Complete Prestige Carnegie Hall 1946-1947 Concerts | Definitive Records | DRCD 11211

Libertad(Freedom)
Astor Piazzolla Group | Live at Cine Teatro Gran Rex De Buenos Aires | West Wind Latina | 2212 CD

Libertango
Galliano-Portal | Blow Up | Dreyfus Jazz Line | FDM 36589-2
HR Big Band | Libertango:Homage An Astor Piazolla | hr music.de | hrmj 014-02 CD
Inga Lühning With Trio | Lühning | Jazz Haus Musik | JHM 0111 CD
Michel Portal-Richard Galliano | Concerts | Dreyfus Jazz Line | FDM 36661-2
Mulo Francel-Evelyn Huber | Tango Lyrico | Fine Music | FM 102-2
Richard Galliano Trio | Concert Inédits | Dreyfus Jazz Line | FDM 36606-2

Liberté
Stan Kenton And His Orchestra | National Anthems Of The World | Creative World | ST 1060

Liberty Belle
Lindsay Cooper Group | Oh Moscow | Victo | CD 015

Liberty City
Jaco Pastorius' Word Of Mouth Big Band | Invitation | Warner | 92-3876-1
The Danish-German Slide Combination | Fugue For Tinhorns | L+R Records | LR 45011

Libra
Khaliq Al-Rouf & Salaam | The Elephant Trop Dance | Nilva | NQ 3404 IMS

Libra Me,Domine
Monnette Sudler Quartet | Live In Europe | Steeplechase | SCS 1102

Lichen
Das Obertontrio Und Toto Blanke | Energy Fields | ALISO Records | AL 1029

Lichtbogen
Max Neissendorfer Trio | Staubfrei | EGO | 95100

Lichter Der Venus
Gunter Hampel Trio | Companion | Birth | 0036

Lichtung(Clearing)
Keshavan Maslak Trio | Humanplexity | LEO | LR 101

Licking Stick-
Dirty Dozen Brass Band | Live:Mardi Gras In Montreux | Rounder Records | CDRR 2052

Licorice Stick
Lem Winchester Quintet | Another Opus | Original Jazz Classics | OJCCD 1816-2(NJ 8244)

Liebeslaunen(Milostne Nalady)
Bob Wilber Quintet | Bob Wilbur:Nostalgia | Arbors Records | ARCD 19145

Liebeslied(Love Song)
Uri Caine Ensemble | Wagner E Venezia | Winter&Winter | 910013-2

Liebestod(Tristan und Isolde)
Eugen Cicero Trio | Classics In Rhythm(Bach-Mozart-Chopin-Liszt-Tchaikovsky-Scarlatti) | MPS | 817924-2

Liebestraum
Sammy Kaye And His Orchestra | The Uncollected:Sammy Kaye | Hindsight | HSR 158

Liebling Kreuzberg
Susan Weinert Band | Point Of View | Intuition Records | INT 3272-2

Liebman
Michael Moore-Bill Charlap | Concord Duo Series Volume Nine | Concord | CCD 4678

Lied Der Mignon
Gabriele Hasler-Elvira Plenar-Andreas Willers | Sonetburger-Nach Texten Von Oskar Pastior | Foolish Music | FM 211793

Lied Der Seemaid
Trio KoKoKo | Good Night | Creative Works Records | CW LP 1002

Lied Des 20. Novembers
Rade Soric Trio | Nahend | Edition Collage | EC 455-2

Lied Ohne Worte
Willem Breuker Kollektief | Driesbergen-Zeist | BVHAAST | 050 (807052)

Lied Vom Achten Elefanten
Habarigani | Habarigani | Hat Art | CD 6007

Lieder Ohne Sorte
Deep Creek Jazzuits | Again | Jazz Pure Collection | AU 31615 CD

Life
James Booker | The Piano Prince From New Orleans | Aves | 146509

Life-
Billy Cobham Group | Life & Times | Atlantic | ATL 50253

Life As
Vienna Art Orchestra | A Notion In Perpetual Motion | Hat Art | CD 6096

Life Circle
Chuck Loeb Group | Life Colors | dmp Digital Music Productions | CD 475

Life Connects
Lisle Ellis Group | Elevations | Victo | CD 027

Life Cycle:
Hubert Laws Group | Storm Then The Calm | Musicmasters | 65118-2

Life Flight
Kenneth Knudsen Trio | Bombay Hotel | Stunt Records | 18903

Life Goes To A Party
Benny Goodman And His Orchestra | Benny Goodman At Carnegie Hall 1938(Complete) | CBS | C2K 65143
The Indispensable Benny Goodman Vol.3/4 | RCA | 2115520-2
Harry James And His Orchestra | Harry James.His Orchestra And The Boogie Woogie Trio | Affinity | CD AFS 1009

Life Is For Livin'
Sibongile Khumalo Group | Live At The Market Theatre | CBS | 491322-2

Life Is So Peculiar
Mose Allison Trio | High Jinks! The Mose Allison Trilogy | CBS | J3K 64275

Life On Mars
David Xirgu Quartet | Idolents | Fresh Sound Records | FSNT 077 CD
Jukka Tolonen | Mountain Stream | Sonet | 147122

Life Plans
Yusef Lateef Ensemble | Nocturnes | Atlantic | 7567-81977-2

Life Property
Walt Dickerson Trio | Life Rays | Soul Note | SN 1028

Life Road
Pili-Pili | Be In Two Minds | JA & RO | JARO 4134-2

Life Size
Bud Freeman And His Gang | Commodore Classics-Bud Freeman/George Wettling:Commodore Style | Commodore | 6.25894 AG

Life,Liberty And The Prosciutto Happiness
Brian Blade Group | Fellowship | Blue Note | 859417-2

Lifeline
Darol Anger-Barbara Higbie Duo | Tideline | Windham Hill | WD 1021
Keith Jarrett Trio | Changeless | ECM | 1392(839618-2)
Jackie McLean Quintet | New And Old Gospel | Blue Note | 853356-2

Lifelines
Booker Little Quartet | Booker Little | Bainbridge | BT 1041

Life's A Very Funny Proposition After All
Steve Kuhn | Ecstasy | ECM | 1058

Life's Backward Glance
Steve Kuhn With Strings | Promises Kept | ECM | 1815(0675222)
Steve Kuhn/Sheila Jordan Band | Playground | ECM | 1159

Life's Too Short To Be Unhappy Without You
The Vivino Brothers Band | Chitlins Parmigiana | dmp Digital Music Productions | CD 492

Lifescape
Howard McGhee And His Band | Dexter Gordon: Move! | Spotlite | SPJ 133 (835055)

Lifetime
Clint Houston Quintet | Watership Down | Storyville | STCD 4150

Lift
Gutbucket | Dry Humping The American Dream | Enja | ENJ-9466 2

Lift Cover,Pull Cord
2nd Nature | What Comes Natural | Inak | 41232

Lift Every Voice And Sing
Dorothy Donegan Trio | The Many Faces Of Dorothy Donegan | Storyville | STCD 8362
Hank Crawford-Jimmy McGriff Quintet | Steppin' Up | Milestone | M 9153

Lift It
Andy Narell Group | Light In Your Eyes | HipPocket | TA-HP 103

Lift Off
Paul Wertico Trio | Don't Be Scared Anymore | Premonition | 790748-2

Light
Misha Alperin | At Home | ECM | 1768(549610-2)
Stephane Grappelli Quintet | Le Toit De Paris | RCA | 2119250-2

Light-
Duke Ellington And His Orchestra | Duke Ellington: The Champs-Elysees Theater January 29-30th,1965 | Laserlight | 36131
Louie Bellson And His All-Star Orchestra | Duke Ellington:Black, Brown & Beige | Musicmasters | 65096-2

Light And Lovely
Eddie Lockjaw Davis Quartet | Jaws Strikes Again | Black & Blue | BLE 233101
Bart Van Lier With The Metropole Orchestra | Twilight | Koch Jazz | 3-6908-2

Light As A Feather
Chick Corea's Return To Forever | Verve Jazz Masters 3:Chick Corea | Verve | 519820-2
Flora Purim And Her Sextet | Butterfly Dreams | Original Jazz Classics | OJCCD 315-2
Joe Henderson:The Milestone Years | Milestone | 8MCD 4413-2
Return To Forever | Return To The 7th Galaxy-Return To Forever:The Anthology | Verve | 533108-2
Chick Corea And Return To Forever | Light As A Feather | Polydor | 557115-2

Light As A Feather(alt.take)
Billy Cobham Group | A Funky Thide Of Sings | Atlantic | ATL 50189

Light Beam
Arthur Blythe Quartet | Retroflection | Enja | ENJ-8046 2

Light Blue
Barry Harris Septet | Interpertations Of Monk | DIW | DIW 395/8 CD
Jessica Williams Trio | Jazz In The Afternoon | Candid | CCD 79750
Monk By Five | Monk By Five | Touché Music | TMcCD 012
Paul Motian Electric Bebop Band | Flight Of The Blue Jay | Winter&Winter | 910009-2
Prestige All Stars | Interplay For Two Trumpets And Two Tenors | Prestige | VIJ 5028
Interplay | Original Jazz Classics | OJCCD 292-2(P 7112)
Thelonious Monk Quartet | Monk At Newport 1963 & 1965 | CBS | C2K 63905
Live In Switzerland 1966 | Jazz Helvet | JH 06
Andy Summers Group | Green Chimneys:The Music Of Thelonious Monk | RCA | 2663472-2

Light Blues
Stephan Schmolck Quartet | Rites Of Passage | L+R Records | CDLR 45064

Light Green
Passport | Garden Of Eden | Atlantic | 2292-44147-2

Light I-
Garden Of Eden | Atlantic | 2292-44147-2

Light II-
Albert Ayler Group | Albert Ayler Live In Greenwich Village:The Complete Impulse Recordings | Impulse(MCA) | IMP 22732

Light In Darkness
Albert Ayler Septet | The Village Concerts | MCA | IA 9336/2

Light My Fire
Joe Reisman And His Orchestra | Party Night At Joe's | Fresh Sound Records | NL 46027(RCA LPM 1476)

Light Oer Darkness
Charles Lloyd-Billy Higgins | Which Way Is East | ECM | 1878/79(9811796)

Light Of Love
Zipflo Reinhardt Group | Light Of The Future | MPS | 68274

Light Or Dark
Pete Johnson | Big Band Bounce And Boogie:Rockin' In Rhythm-Piano Portraits Vol.2 | Affinity | AFS 1028

Light Out Of Darkness
Curlew | North America | Moers Music | 02042

Light Shadows
Gary Campbell Quartet | Thick & Thin | Double Time Records | DTRCD-115

Light Stuff
David Moss-Michael Rodach | Fragmentary Blues | Traumton Records | 4432-2

Light Sweet Crude
Larry Coryell | Twelve Frets To One Octave | Koch Records | 322 657

Light Years
David Murray Quartet | Recording NYC 1986 | DIW | DIW 8009
Doris Day With The Page Cavanaugh Trio | The Uncollected:Doris Day | Hindsight | HSR 226

Light(alt.take)
Duke Ellington And His Orchestra | Duke Ellington -Carnegie Hall Concert | Ember | 800851-370(EMBD 2001)

Lighthearted Intelligence
Erskine Butterfield | Part-Time Boogie | Harlequin | HQ 2050

Lighthouse
Gerald Wilson And His Orchestra | On Stage | Pacific Jazz | LN 10100

Light'n Up
Gene Ammons Quartet | The Mal Waldron Memorial Album:Soul Eyes | Prestige | PRCD 11024-2
Glenn Ferris Trio | Chrominance | Enja | 9132-2

Lightnin'
Sun Ra Arkestra | Sunrise In Different Dimensions | HatOLOGY | 568

Lightning Bugs And Frogs-
Duke Ellington And His Orchestra | The Best Of Duke Ellington | Pablo | 2405401-2
Lyle Mays | Improvisations For Expanded Piano | Warner | 9362-47284-2

Lightning Fields
Cousin Joe With Band | Cousin Joe:The Complete 1945-1947 Vol.2(1946-1947) | Blue Moon | BMCD 6002

Lightnin's Stroke
Maurizio Picchio Quartet | Biri San | SPLASC(H) Records | H 172

Lights On A Satelite
Sun Ra & His Arkestra | Live At Montreux | Inner City | IC 1039 IMS

Lights,Receding
Norbert Gottschalk With The Peter Weniger Quartet | Light Weight Sight | Dr.Jazz Records | 8603-2

Ligia
Jim Tomlinson Quartet | Brazilian Sketches | Candid | CCD 79769
Joe Henderson Group | Double Rainbow | Verve | 527222-2
Manfredo Fest Quartet | Just Jobim | dmp Digital Music Productions | CD 524
Simon Nabatov | Ten Piano Players,Vol.1 | Green House Music | CD 1002

Ligibul
Frieder Berlin Trio | Soul Fingers | Satin Doll Productions | SDP 1039-1 CD

Lignano
Vincent Courtois Quartet | Translucide | Enja | ENJ-9380 2

Ligne Droite
Nils Petter Molvaer Group | Solid Ether | ECM | 1722(543365-2)

Ligotage
Ike Quebec Quintet | Blue And Sentimental | Blue Note | 784098-2

Like
Andy Lumpp-Hugo Read-Michael Küttner | Lonely Passengers | Nabel Records:Jazz Network | LP 4625(Audiophile)

Like A Blues
Benny Goodman And His Orchestra | Breakfast Ball | Saville Records | SVL 172 IMS

Like A Child At PLay
Terje Rypdal | After The Rain | ECM | 1083

Like A Lover
Dianne Reeves With Band | Blue Valentines | Blue Note | 781331-2
Elaine Delmar With Band | 'S Wonderful | Ronnie Scott's Jazz House | JHCD 027
Mel Tormé With Band And Symphony Orchestra | A New Album | Paddle Wheel | KICJ 128

Like A Lover(Cantador)
Sarah Vaughan With Orchestra | I Love Brazil | Pablo | 2312101-2
Vince Guaraldi Trio | A Flower Is A Lovesome Thing | Original Jazz Classics | OJC 235(F 3257)

Like A Quiet Storm
Linda Sharrock Trio | Live In Vitoria-Gasteiz | Amadeo | 537693-2

Like A Road Leading Home
Merl Saunders Quartet | Live At Keystone Vol.2 | Fantasy | FCD 7702-2

Like A Samba
European Jazz Youth Orchestra | Swinging Europe 3 | dacapo | DCCD 9461

Like A Secret
Inga Rumpf With The NDR Big Band | It's A Man's World | Extra Records & Tapes | 800860

Like A Star In The Clear Sky
Jorge Sylvester Quintet | Musicollage | Postcards | POST 1011

Like A Virgin
Chris Connor With The Richard Wess Orchestra | Witchcraft | Atlantic | AMCY 1068

Like Cozy
Bill Frisell Band | Blues Dream | Nonesuch | 7559-79615-2

Like Dreamers Do(part 1)
Blues Dream | Nonesuch | 7559-79615-2

Like Dreamers Do(part 2)
Cafe Du Sport Jazzquartett | Cafe Du Sport Jazzquartett | Minor Music | 801096

Like Eddie
Richard Grossman Trio | Where The Sky Ended | HatOLOGY | 541

Like It Is
Al Casey Quartet | A Tribute To Fats | Jazzpoint | JP 1044 CD

Like It Ji's
Count Basie All Stars | Count Basie Get Together | Pablo | 2310924-2

Like Life
Red Richards-George Kelly Sextet With Doc Cheatham | Groove Move | Jazzpoint | JP 1045 CD

Like Mama
Skip Martin Orchestra | The Music From Mickey Spillane's Mike Hammer | Fresh Sound Records | ND 42124

Like Music From The Skies
Antonio Hart Group | Here I Stand | Impulse(MCA) | 951208-2

Like My Own
Shorty Rogers And The Big Band | The Swingin' Nutcracker | Fresh Sound Records | ND 42121

Like Someone In Love
Ahmad Jamal Quartet | Nature(The Essence Part III) | Atlantic | 3984-23105-2
Ahmad Jamal Trio | At The Blackhawk | Chess | 515002
Art Blakey And The Jazz Messengers | At The Club St.Germain | RCA | ND 74897(2)
Live In Stockholm 1959 | Dragon | DRCD 182
Bill Evans Quartet With Orchestra | From Left To Right | Verve | 557451-2
Bill Evans Trio | Live At Balboa Jazz Club Vol.2 | Jazz Lab | JLCD 5(889364)
Bill Evans Trio:The Last Waltz | Milestone | 8MCD 4430-2
Consecration 2 | Timeless | CD SJP 332
Bill Hardman Sextet | What's Up' | Steeplechase | SCS 1254
Bob Howard With The Hank Jones Trio | In A Sentimental Mood | Stash Records | ST 266 IMS
Bud Powell Trio | At The Golden Circle, Vol.2 | Steeplechase | SCCD 36002
Chet Baker Quartet | Chet Baker Sings | Pacific Jazz | 300067(PJ 1222)
Coleman Hawkins With The Oscar Peterson Quartet | Ultimate Coleman Hawkins selected by Sonny Rollins | Verve | 557538-2
Dave Brubeck Quartet | Tritonis | Concord | CJ 129
The Dave Brubeck Selection | CBS | 467279-2
The Dave Brubeck Selection | CBS | 474769-2
Denny Zeitlin-David Friesen Duo | In Concert | ITM-Pacific | ITMP 970068
Dexter Gordon Quartet | Body And Soul | Black Lion | CD 877628-2
Ella Fitzgerald With Frank De Vol And His Orchestra | Like Someone In Love | Verve | 511524-2
Elmo Hope Trio | HiFiJazz | Fresh Sound Records | FSR-CD 0074
Eric Dolphy-Booker Little Quintet | The Great Concert Of Eric Dolphy | Prestige | P 34002
Ernie Henry Quartet | Seven Standards And A Blues | Original Jazz Classics | OJCCD 1722-2(RLP 248)
Ethel Azama With The Marty Paich Orchestra | Cool Heat | Fresh Sound Records | 054 2600411(Liberty LRP 3142)
Franco Ambrosetti Quartet | A Jazz Portrait Of Franco Ambrosetti | Sound Hills | SSCD 8071(RTCL 812 SH)
Gary Thomas Quintet | Exile's Gate | JMT Edition | 514009-2
Hank Jones Trio | I Remember You | Black & Blue | BLE 233122
Herb Ellis Quartet | Softly ... But With That Feeling | Verve | MV 2674 IMS
Jesper Thilo Quintet feat. Harry Edison | Jesper Thilo Quintet feat. Harry Edison | Storyville | STCD 4120
John Coltrane Quintet | Coltrane Time | Blue Note | 784461-2
John Coltrane Trio | Lush Life | Original Jazz Classics | OJC20 131-2
Kenny Dorham Sextet | Soul Support | Jazz Colours | 874756-2
Lee Morgan-Clifford Jordan Quintet | Live In Baltimore 1968 | Fresh Sound Records | FSCD 1037
Lou Levy Trio | Jazz In Hollywood:Bud Shank/Lou Levy | Original Jazz Classics | OJCCD 1890-2(Nocturne NLP-2/NLP-10)
Mal Waldron Trio | Mal/4 | Original Jazz Classics | SMJ 6512
Michael Weiss Trio | Milestones | Steeplechase | SCCD 31449
Milt Jackson Big 4 | Milt Jackson At The Montreux Jazz Festival 1975 | Original Jazz Classics | OJC20 884-2(2310753)
Milt Jackson-Ray Brown Quintet | Fuji Mama | West Wind | WW 2054
Paul Bley Trio | Charles Mingus-The Complete Debut Recordings | Debut | 12 DCD 4402-2
Paul Desmond Orchestra | Late Lament | Bluebird | ND 90207
Paul Desmond With Strings | Desmond Blue | RCA | 2663898-2
Pete Minger Quartet | Look To The Sky | Concord | CCD 4555
Renaud Garcia-Fons | Légendes | Enja | ENJ-9314 2
Rene Thomas Quartet | Guitar Groove | Original Jazz Classics | OJCCD 1725-2(JLP 27)
Saxophone Connection | Saxophone Connection | L+R Records | CDLR 45046
Singers Unlimited | A Capella 2 | MPS | 821860-2
Sonny Rollins Quintet | The Bop Rebells | Jazz Door | JD 1218
Stan Getz Quartet | Stan Getz:East Of The Sun-The West Coast Sessions | Verve | 531935-2
Stan Kenton And His Orchestra | Sophisticated Approach | Creative World | ST 1018
Steve Grossman Quartet | Hold The Line | DIW | DIW 912 CD
Tete Montoliu Trio | A Spanish Treasure | Concord | CCD 4493

Like Someone In Love-
Dorothy Donegan Trio | Live At The Widder Bar 1986 | Timeless | CD SJP 247
Coleman Hawkins With The Oscar Peterson Quartet | The Genius Of Coleman Hawkins | Verve | 539065-2

Like Someone In Love(alt.take)
Ernie Henry Quartet | Last Chorus | Original Jazz Classics | OJC 086(R 12-266)

Like Someone In Love(incomplete take)
Franco Ambrosetti Quartet | A Jazz Portrait Of Franco Ambrosetti | Sound Hills | SSCD 8071(RTCL 812 SH)

Like Sonny
Joe Lovano With The Junko Onishi Trio | Tenor Time | somethin'else | 300230(TOCJ 5584)
John Coltrane Quartet | John Coltrane-The Heavyweight Champion:The Complete Atlantic Recordings | Atlantic | 8122-71984-2
The Very Best Of John Coltrane | Rhino | 8122-79778-2
The Art Of John Coltrane - The Atlantic Years | Atlantic | SD 2-313
Countdown | Atlantic | 90462-1 TIS
Luis Agudo With The Pierro Bassini Quartet | Afrorera | Red Records | VPA 185
Melvin Rhyne Quintet | Classmasters | Criss Cross | Criss 1183
John Coltrane Quartet | John Coltrane-The Heavyweight Champion:The Complete Atlantic Recordings | Atlantic | 8122-71984-2

Like Sonny(alt.take)
Coltrane Jazz | Atlantic | 7567-81344-2
John Coltrane-The Heavyweight Champion:The Complete Atlantic Recordings | Atlantic | 8122-71984-2

Like Sonny(false start 1)
John Coltrane-The Heavyweight Champion:The Complete Atlantic Recordings | Atlantic | 8122-71984-2

Like Sonny(false start 2)
John Coltrane-The Heavyweight Champion:The Complete Atlantic Recordings | Atlantic | 8122-71984-2

Like Sonny(incomplete take 1)
John Coltrane-The Heavyweight Champion:The Complete Atlantic Recordings | Atlantic | 8122-71984-2

Like Sonny(incomplete take 2)
John Coltrane-The Heavyweight Champion:The Complete Atlantic Recordings | Atlantic | 8122-71984-2

Like Sonny(incomplete take 3)
John Coltrane-The Heavyweight Champion:The Complete Atlantic Recordings | Atlantic | 8122-71984-2

Like Sonny(incomplete take 4)
John Coltrane-The Heavyweight Champion:The Complete Atlantic Recordings | Atlantic | 8122-71984-2

Like Sonny(rehersal 1-false start)
John Coltrane-The Heavyweight Champion:The Complete Atlantic Recordings | Atlantic | 8122-71984-2

Like Sonny(rehersal 2-incomplete take)
Shorty Rogers And His Orchestra Feat. The Giants | An Invisible Orchard | Fresh Sound Records | 49560 CD(RCA)

Like That
Don Cherry/Nana Vasconcelos/Collin Walcott | Codona | ECM | 1132(829371-2)

Like That Of Sky
Gracie Fields With Studio Orchestra | Amazing Gracie-The Incomparable Gracie Fields | Saville Records | SVL 170 IMS

Like The Morning Sunrise
Thärichens Tentett | Lady Moon | Minor Music | 801094

Like The Touch Of Rain
Kevin Eubanks Group | Spiritalk 2 | Blue Note | 830132-2

Like There's No Place Like...
Crazy Art Quintet | Looking Up Looking Down | yvp music | CD 3040

Like Warriors Everywhere(Courage) - (Like) Warriors Everywhere(Courage)
Esbjörn Svensson Trio(E.S.T.) | E.S.T. Live | ACT | 9295-2

Like Wash It Or Something
John Barnes-Roy Williams Group | Like We Do | Lake | LACD 69

Like Wow
Melvin Rhyne Trio | Mel's Spell | Criss Cross | Criss 1118

Like You Do
Gunter Hampel Duo | Escape | Birth | 006

Like Young
Illinois Jacquet Septet | Illinois Flies Again | Argo | ARC 503 D
Wild Bill Davis Quartet | The Swinging Organ Of Wild Bill Davis:In The Groove! | Fresh Sound Records | FSR-CD 0308

Lil' Darlin'
Chuck Wayne Trio | Morning Mist | Original Jazz Classics | OJCCD 1097-2(P-7367)
Clark Terry And Frank Wess With Bob Lark And The DePaul University Jazz Ensemble I | Big Band Basie | Reference Recordings | RR-63 CD
Cootie Williams Quintet | Jazz In Paris:Joe Newman-Jazz At Midnight-Cootie Williams | EmArCy | 018446-2
Count Basie And His Orchestra | Live In Antibes 1968 | France's Concert | FCD 112
Breakfast Dance And Barbecue | Roulette | 531791-2
En Concert Avec Europe 1 | Laserlight | 710411/12
Fun Time | Pablo | 2310945-2
The Great Concert Of Count Basie | Festival | 402311
A True Collectors Item | Jazz Archive | 90.106-2
Basie On Roulette, Vol. 3: Sing Along With Basie | Vogue | 500003
Craig Bailey Band | A New Journey | Candid | CCD 79725
Danny Moss-Roy Williams Quintet | Steamers! | Nagel-Heyer | CD 049
DMP Big Band | Carved In Stone | dmp Digital Music Productions | CD 512
Frank Wess-Harry Edison Orchestra | Dear Mr. Basie | Concord | CCD 4420
Horst Gmeinwieser 'One Cue Big Band' | Bigband-Fieber | Media Arte | CD 06569209(BRW)
Jimmy Smith Sextet | Angel Eyes-Ballads & Slow Jams | Verve | 527632-2
Joe Newman Quintet | Good 'N' Groovy | Original Jazz Classics | OJCCD 185-2(SV 2019)
Joe Pass | Digital III At Montreux | Original Jazz Classics | OJCCD 996-2(2308223)
Joe Pass At The Montreux Jazz Festival 1975 | Original Jazz Classics | OJC20 934-2(2310752)
Joe Pass Quartet | Apassionato | Pablo | 2310946-2
Joe Pass Trio | Jazz-Club: Guitar | Verve | 840035-2
Lambert, Hendricks And Ross With Count Basie And His Orchestra | The Best Of The Jazz Singers Vol.2 | LRC Records | CDC 9008
Marshall Royal Quintet | First Chair | Concord | CJ 88
Nat Pierce Trio | My Pal Basie | Jazz Connaisseur | JCCD 8904-2
Oscar Peterson Trio | The Oscar Peterson Trio Plays | Verve | POCJ 1827 PMS
Red Garland Trio | Bright And Breezy | Original Jazz Classics | OJC 265(JLP 948)
Richie Cole Quintet | Profile | Inak | 30222
The Poll Winners | Exploring The Scene | Original Jazz Classics | OJCCD 969-2(C 7581)
The Real Group | Jazz:Live | ACT | 9258-2
Vince Jones With Orchestra | Come In Spinner | Intuition Records | INT 3052-2
Werner Bühler Quartet | At The Swinging Organ | MWM Records | MWM 005
WDR Big Band | Harlem Story | Koala Records | CD P 7

Lil' Dog
Buddy Johnson And His Orchestra | Wails | Official | 6010

Lil' Duke's Strut
Kenny Burrell Septet | All Day Long And All Night Long | Prestige | P 24025

Lil' Lisa
Chris Barber's Jazz And Blues Band With Dr.John | On A Mardy Gras Day | Great Southern Records | GS 11024

Lil' Liza Jane
Nina Simone Groups | You Can Have Him | Memo Music | HDJ 4087
Papa Bue's Viking Jazzband | Greatest Hits | Storyville | 6.23336 AF

Lil' Max
Clark Terry And Frank Wess With Bob Lark And The DePaul University Jazz Ensemble I | Big Band Basie | Reference Recordings | RR-63 CD

Lil' Sherry
Art Blakey And The Jazz Messengers | Originally | CBS | FC 38036

Lila
Gregor Van Buggenum Trio With Rolf Römer | Springtime | Open Minds | OM 2407-2

Lila Lullaby
Fats Waller And His Rhythm | Fifty Thousand Killer Watts Of Jive | Ember | CJS 842

Lilac Wine
Nina Simone Quartet | Nina Simone-The 60s Vol.3:Work Song | Mercury | 838545-2 PMS

Lilacs In The Rain
Jimmy Rowles-Red Mitchell Trio | The Jimmy Rowles/Red Mitchell Trio | Contemporary | C 14016

Lila's Dance
Ralph Burns And His Orchestra | Ralph Burns Conducts Ralph Burns | Raretone | 5017 FC

Lili Marlene
Old Merrytale Jazz Band | 25 Jahre Old Merrytale Jazzband Hamburg | Intercord | 155043

Lilian
BLU | Rhythm & Blu. | Gramavision | 18-8606-1

Liliana
Clark Terry Orchestra | Free And Oozy | Blue Moon | BMCD 3076

Lillebroer Og Storebroer
Jan Garbarek Trio | Eventyr | ECM | 1200

Lillekort
Dioko | Potosi | Jazz Haus Musik | JHM 20

Lilli Goes To Town
Cannonball Adderley Sextet | Jazz Workshop Revisited | Capitol | 529441-2

Lillie
Milt Jackson Quintet | Milt Jackson | Blue Note | 81509
Frank Tannehill | Frank Tannehill(1932-1941) | Story Of Blues | CD 3526-2

Lillie Stomp
Milt Jackson Quintet | Wizard Of The Vibes | Blue Note | 532140-2

Lillie(alt.take)
David Fiuczynski-John Medeski Group | Lunar Crush | Gramavision | R2 79498

L'illuminata Rugiada-
Dejan's Olympia Brass Band | The Best Of New Orleans Jazz, Vol.2 | Mardi Gras Records | MG 1008

Lil's Blues
Randy Sandke And The New York Allstars | The Re-Discovered Louis And Bix | Nagel-Heyer | CD 058

Lily
Sonny Greenwich-Ed Bickert Quartet | Days Gone By | Sackville | SKCD2-2052

Lily Of The Valley
Butch Thompson | Thompson Pays Joplin | Daring Records | CD 3033

L'Imbécile
Andrew Hill Orchestra | Compulsion | Blue Note | 84217

Limbo
M.T.B. | Consenting Adults | Criss Cross | Criss 1177
Michel Petrucciani feat. Jim Hall and Wayne Shorter | Power Of Three-Live At Montreux | Blue Note | 746427-2
Wayne Shorter:The Classic Blue Note Recordings | Blue Note | 540856-2
Miles Davis Quintet | Sorcerer | CBS | CBS PC 9532
Miles Davis Quintet 1965-1968 | CBS | C6K 67398
Miles Davis Quintet 1965-1968 | CBS | C6K 67398
Ray Anderson Trio | Right Down Your Alley | Soul Note | 121087-2

Limbo Boat
Roland Kirk Sextet | Talkin' Verve-Roots Of Acid Jazz:Roland Kirk | Verve | 533101-2
Bob Wilber-Dick Hyman Sextet | A Perfect Match:A Tribute To Johnny Hodges & Wild Bill Davis | Arbors Records | ARCD 19193

Limbo Jazz
Duke Ellington-Coleman Hawkins Orchestra | Duke Ellington Meets Coleman Hawkins | MCA | MCAD 5650

Limbo Rock
Miles Davis Quintet | Sorcerer | CBS | CK 65680

Limbo(alt.take)
Mauricio Einhorn Sextet | Me | MPS | 68257

Limehouse Blues
Benny Goodman Octet | Seven Come Eleven | CBS | FC 38265
Bireli Lagrene Ensemble | Routes To Django & Bireli Swing '81 | Jazzpoint | JP 1055 CD
Bireli Lagrene Group | Gipsy Project | Dreyfus Jazz Line | FDM 36626-2
Cannonball Adderley Quintet | Compact Jazz: Cannonball Adderley | EmArCy | 842930-2 PMS
Carmen McRae With Orchestra | The Ultimate Carmen McRae | Mainstream | MD CDO 705
Charlie Ventura Quartet | Charlie Ventura Complete 1951-1952 Verve Studio Recordings | Definitive Records | DRCD 11202
Ellis Marsalis Trio | Ellis Marsalis Trio | Blue Note | 796107-2
Fletcher Henderson And His Orchestra | Wild Party | Hep | 1009
Harry Allen Quartet | Jazz Im Amerika Haus,Vol.1 | Nagel-Heyer | CD 011
Harry Allen With The John Pizzarelli Trio | Harry Allen Meets The John Pizzarelli Trio | Novus | 2137397-2
J.J.Johnson-Joe Pass | We'll Be Together Again | Pablo | 2310911-2
Joe Ascione Octet | My Buddy:A Tribute To Buddy Rich | Nagel-Heyer | CD 036
Joe Henderson With The Wynton Kelly Trio | Straight No Chaser | Verve | 531561-2
Mary Lou Williams Trio | Mary Lou Williams Trio-Roll 'Em(1944) | Solo Art | SACD-43
Paolo Tomelleri-Fritz Hartschuh Quintet | Milan Swing | L+R Records | CDLR 45070
Quintet Du Hot Club De France | Jazz In Paris:Django Reinhardt-Swing From Paris | EmArCy | 159853-2 PMS
Django Reinhardt:Nuages | Arkadia Jazz | 71431
Randy Sandke Quintet | Cliffhanger | Nagel-Heyer | CD 2037
Roy Eldridge-Dizzy Gillespie With The Oscar Peterson Quartet | The Complete Verve Roy Eldridge Studio Sessions | Verve | 9861278
Roy And Diz | Verve | 521647-2
Sidney Bechet And His New Orleans Feetwarmers | Sidney Bechet 1932-1943: The Bluebird Sessions | Bluebird | ND 90317
Stan Kenton With The Danish Radio Big Band | Stan Kenton With The Danish Radio Big Band | Storyville | STCD 8340
Stephane Grappelli And His Hot Four | Django Reinhardt Vol. 1 | Decca | 180020 AG
The Great British Jazz Band | A British Jazz Odyssey | Candid | CCD 79740
The Oscar Peterson Four | If You Could Se Me Now | Pablo | 2310918-2
Sam Pilafian & Friends | Travelin' Light | Telarc Digital | CD 80281

Limelight
Gerry Mulligan Quartet | Gerry Mulligan:Pleyel Concert Vol.2 | Vogue | 21409432
Gerry Mulligan Septet | Gerry Mulligan:Gerry Meets Hamp | Memo Music | HDJ 4009

Limerick
Terry Gibbs Big Band | The Exciting Terry Gibbs Big Band-Recorded Live | Verve | 2304441 IMS

Limerick Waltz
Art Tatum | Art Tatum-The Standard Transcriptions | Music & Arts | CD 919

Liminipse
Olga Konkova | Her Point Of View | Candid | CCD 79757

Limited
St.Louis Kings Of Rhythm | Rhythm And Blues Showtime | Timeless | CD SJP 231/2

Limoges,The Market from Pictures At An Exhibition(Mussorsky)
Frank Vignola Sextet | Off Broadway | Nagel-Heyer | CD 2006

Limone's Blues
Christoph Spendel Group | Limousine | Trion | 3001

L'Impossible
The Oscar Peterson Four | If You Could Se Me Now | Pablo | 2310918-2

Lina's Waltz
Bob Mintzer Big Band | Urban Contours | dmp Digital Music Productions | CD 467

Lincoln Reviews His Notes
Lyle Mays Trio | Fictionary | Geffen Records | GED 24521

Linda
Frank Rosolino Sextet | Kenton Presents: Frank Rosolino | Affinity | AFF 61
Linda Sharrock With The Wolfgang Puschnig Trio | Linda Sharrock & The Three Man Band | Moers Music | 02078 CD

Linda's Rock Vamp
Memphis Jug Band | Memphis Jug Band Vol.2 | Frog | DGF 16

Linden Boulevard
Laurent Coq Quartet | Jaywalker | Enja | 9111-2

Line Down
Leadbelly[Huddie Ledbetter] | Huddie Ledbetter | Fantasy | F 24715

Line For Lyons
Chet Baker Quartet | Chet Baker Quartet Live Vol.1:This Time The Dreams's On Me | Pacific Jazz | 525248-2
Chet Baker Quartet Live Vol.3: May Old Flame | Pacific Jazz | 531573-2
Jazz At Ann Arbor | Fresh Sound Records | 054 2602311(Pacific Jazz PJ 1203) (835282)
Chet Baker Sextet | Chet Baker In Milan | Original Jazz Classics | OJC20 370-2(JLP 18)
Chet Baker-Gerry Mulligan Group | Carnegie Hall Concert Vol. 1/2 | CTI | EPC 450554-2
Chet Baker-Stan Getz Quintet | The Stockholm Concerts | Verve | 537555-2
Clarinet Jazz Trio | Live At Birdland Neuburg | Birdland | BN 003
Gerry Mulligan Quartet | Gerry Mulligan:Pleyel Concert Vol.2 | Vogue | 21409432
Gerry Mulligan Septet | Gerry Mulligan:Gerry Meets Hamp | Memo Music | HDJ 4009
Harold Danko Quartet | Stable Mates | Steeplechase | SCCD 31451
John Basile Quartet | The Desmond Project | Chesky | JD 156
Paul Desmond Quartet | Live | Verve | 543501-2
Paul Desmond Quartet Featuring Don Elliott | Original Jazz Classics | OJC 119(F 3235)

Line Up
Lennie Tristano Trio | That's Jazz Vol.15: Lennie Tristano | Atlantic | ATL 50245
Joe Koinzer Group | Percussive Music | Sesam Jazz | 1002

Lineage
Simon Nabatov | Loco Motion | ASP Records | 11988

Lined With A Groove
Oscar Peterson Trio | En Concert Avec Europe 1 | Laserlight | 710443/48

Lines
Jorge Sylvester Quintet | Musicollage | Postcards | POST 1011
Lines & Spaces
Jochen Feucht | Signs On Lines | Satin Doll Productions | SDP 1019-1 CD
Lines 1
Karl Berger-Paul Shigihara | Karl Berger + Paul Shigihara | L+R Records | CDLR 45045
Lines In The Sky
Sergey Kuryokhin-Anatoly Vapirov Trio | Sentenced To Silence | LEO | LR 110
L'Infanta Arcibizzarra
Alan Pasqua Group | Milargo | Postcards | POST 1002
L'Infini Un Vent De Sable
Al Cohn And His Orchestra | The Jazz Workshop:Four Brass One Tenor | RCA | PM 45164
Linger Awhile
Dickie Wells And His Orchestra | Lester Young:The Complete 1936-1951 Small Group Sessions(Studio Recordings-Master Takes),Vol.2 | Blue Moon | BMCD 1002
Johnny Wiggs Jam Session | Sounds Of New Orleans Vol.10-New Orleans Trumpets | Storyville | STCD 6017
Rex Stewart And His Orchestra | The Great Ellington Units | RCA | ND 86751
Sarah Vaughan And Her Trio | Swingin' Easy | EmArCy | 514072-2
Verve Jazz Masters 18:Sarah Vaughan | Verve | 518199-2
Sarah Vaughan With The Jimmy Jones Trio | Linger Awhile | Pablo | 2312144-2
Scott Hamilton Trio | Major League | Concord | CCD 4305
Linger In My Arms A Little Longer Baby
Louis Armstrong And His Orchestra | Louis Armstrong-The Complete RCA Victor Recordings | RCA | 2668682-2
Lingus
Raiz De Pedra | Diario De Bordo | TipToe | TIP-888822 2
Linha Azul
Banda Mantiqueira | Aldeia | ACT | 5008-2
Linje
Aldo Romano Quintet | Dreams & Waters | Owl Records | 063 CD
Link
Henrichs-Kuchenbuch-Rilling | Ohpsst | FMP | SAJ 22
Links Und Rechts Vom Bahnhof
Ronnie Foster | The Racer | Electric Bird | K 28P 6441
Linus And Lucy
David Benoit Group | This Side Up | GRP | GRP 95412
Vince Guaraldi Group | Charlie Brown's Holiday Hits | Fantasy | FCD 9682-2
Vince Guaraldi Trio | A Charlie Brown Christmas | Fantasy | FSA 8431-6
Art Blakey And The Messengers Big Band | Live At Montreux And Northsea | Timeless | CD SJP 150
Lip Lap Louie
Albert Collins Blues Band | Ice Cold Blues | Charly | CRB 1119
Lip Tone Galaxy
New Winds | Traction | Sound Aspects | sas CD 044
Lips Apart
Ray Anderson With The George Gruntz Concert Jazz Band | Ray Anderson Big Band Record | Gramavision | R2 79497
Lips Flips
Minton's Playhouse All Stars | Charlie Christian:Swing To Bop | Dreyfus Jazz Line | FDM 36715-2
Lips Flips(On With Charlie Christian)
Jazz Legacy 64: Charlie Christian-1941 Live Sessions | Vogue | 500114
Liquid Bird
Norbert Stein Pata Orchester | The Secret Act Of Painting | Pata Musik | PATA 7 CD
Nornert Stein Pata Masters | Live In Australia | Pata Musik | PATA 15 CD
Kazumi Watanabe Group | To Chi Ka | Denon Compact Disc | DC-8568
Liquid Stone
Jack DeSalvo-Arthur Lipner | Liquide Stones | Tutu Records | 888132-2
Lisa
George Coleman-Tete Montoliu Duo | Meditation | Timeless | CD SJP 110
Night Ark | In Wonderland | EmArCy | 534471-2
Lisa Marie
Lüdi-Öcal | The Bird Who Makes The Cloud Sing As He Drums It-Live At The Montreux Jazz Festival | Creative Works Records | CW CD 1019-1
Lisa Mona Overdrive
Gust Williams Tsilis Quintet | Sequestered Days | Enja | ENJ-6094 2
Lisa's Love
Rena Rama | Inside-Outside | Caprice | CAP 1182
Lisbon Antiqua
Bob Cooper Quintet | Group Activity | Affinity | AFF 65
Lisette
Barry Altschul Trio | Brahma | Sackville | 3023
Listen Here
Eric Reed Trio | Eric Reed:The Swing And I | MoJazz | 530468-2
Gene Harris Group | Alley Cats | Concord | CCD 4859
Listen To Me
Bunk Johnson And His New Orleans Band | Baby Dodds | American Music | AMCD-17
Listen To Monk(Rhythm-A-Ning)
Jon Hendricks And Friends | Freddie Freeloader | Denon Compact Disc | CY-76302
Listen To Monk(Rhythm-A-Ning-alt.take)
Chuck Foster And His Orchestra | The Uncollected: Chuck Foster | Hindsight | HSR 115
Listen To The Mockingbird
Don Pullen's African-Brazilian Connection | Kele Mou Bana | Blue Note | 798166-2
Listen To The Plants
Barbara Thompson's Paraphernalia | Pure Fantasy | VeraBra Records | No. 8
Listen To The Rain
Cécile Verny Quartet | Got A Ticket | double moon | DMCD 1002-2
Listen To The Rainbow
George Russell's New York Big Band | New York Big Band | Soul Note | 121039-2
Listen To The Wind
Zbigniew Namyslowski-Remy Filipovitch Quintet | Go! | Album | AS 66919 CD
Dave Stryker And The Bill Warfield Big Band | Nomad | Steeplechase | SCCD 31371
Listen Up!
Vital Information | Live Around The World Where We Come From Tour '98-'99 | Intuition Records | INT 3296-2
Gerry Mulligan Quartet With Brassensemble and Guests | Dragonfly | Telarc Digital | CD 83377
Listening To Löbering
Carol Emanuel Group | Tops Of Trees | Koch Jazz | KOC 3-7802-2
L'Italiana
Tomasz Stanko Sextet | Litania | ECM | 1636(537551-2)
Litania
From The Green Hill | ECM | 1680(547336-2)
Italian Instabile Orchestra | Litania Sibilante | Enja | ENJ-9405 2
Litania(2)
Lars Moller Quartet | Kaleidoscope | Naxos Jazz | 86022-2
Lite Hit
John Patton Quartet | Minor Swing | DIW | DIW 896 CD
Lite Hit)alt.take)
Herbie Hancock Group | Lite Me Up | CBS | SRCS 9507
Liten Visa Till Karin
Andy LaVerne Trio | Glass Ceiling | Steeplechase | SCCD 31352
Litha
Chick Corea Quintet | That's Jazz Vol.25: Tones For Joan's Bones | Atlantic | ATL 50302
John Swana Quintet | The Feeling's Mutual | Criss Cross | Criss 1090
Stan Getz Quartet | A Life In Jazz:A Musical Biography | Verve | 535119-2

Sweet Rain | Verve | 815054-2 PMS
Lithe Dream
Ed Blackwell Project | Vol.2:What It Be Like? | Enja | ENJ-8054 2
Lito(part 1)
Vol.2:What It Be Like? | Enja | ENJ-8054 2
Lito(part 2)
Vol.2:What It Be Like? | Enja | ENJ-8054 2
Lito(part 3)
Ahmad Mansour Quartet | Oxiana | Timeless | CD SJP 344
Little 'B'
Masabumi 'Poo' Kikuchi Trio | Tethered Moon/Triangle | Paddle Wheel | KICJ 130
Little Angel
Christian Willisohn Group | Blues On The World | Blues Beacon | BLU-1025 2
David Hazeltine Quintet | How It Is | Criss Cross | Criss 1142
Little Angel(for Christopher)
Philip Catherine/Niels-Henning Orsted-Pedersen With The Royal Copenhagen Chamber Orchestra | Spanish Nights | Enja | ENJ-7023 2
Little Anna
Barbara Thompson's Paraphernalia | Barbara Thompson's Special Edition | VeraBra Records | CDVBR 2017-2
Little Annie-Ooh
Live In Concert | MCA | 2292-50425-1
Little Banjo Man
Gene Quill All Stars | 3 Bones And A Quill | Fresh Sound Records | FSR-CD 105(882183)
Little Ben Blues
Wild Bill Davison With The Eddie Condon All Stars | Wild Bill Davison | Storyville | SLP 4005
Little Big Horn
Nat Adderley Quintet | Natural Soul | Milestone | M 9009
Pago Libre | Cinémagique | TCB Records | TCB 01112
Little Big Horns
The LeadersTrio | Heaven Dance | Sunnyside | SSC 1034 D
Little Bigger
Ernestine Anderson And Her All Stars | Be Mine Tonight | Concord | CJ 319
Little Bird
Jessica Williams Trio | Inventions | Jazz Focus | JFCD 008
Little Black Coot
Brownie McGhee Trio | Brownie's Blues | Original Blues Classics | OBCCD 505-2(BV 1042)
Little Black Swallow
Jesse Fuller | San Francisco Bay Blues | Good Time Jazz | 10051
Little Boat
$$hide$$ | $$Titelverweise | |
Little Boat -> O Barquinho(Little Boat)
Little Booboo
John Abercrombie Sextet | Open Land | ECM | 1683(557652-2)
Little Booker
Rebecka Gordon Quartet | Yiddish'n Jazz | Touché Music | TMcCD 014
Little Boots
John Tchicai Group | Put Up The Flight | Storyville | SLP 4141
Little Bossa
Johannes Herrlich Quintet | Thinking Of You | Edition Collage | EC 499-2
Royce Campbell-Adrian Ingram Group | Hands Across The Water | String Jazz | SJRCD 1002
Abdullah Ibrahim(Dollar Brand) | Autobiography | Plainisphare | PL 1267-68 CD
Little Boy Blue
Otis Spann/Robert Lockwood Jr. | Otis Spann Is The Blues | Crosscut | CCR 1003(Candid)
Robert Lockwood Jr. | Robert Lockwood Jr. Plays Robert (Johnson) & Robert (Lockwood) | Black & Blue | 33740
Little Brother Bobby
King Curtis Quintet | I Remember King Curtis | Prestige | P 24033
Little Brother Soul
Albert King Blues Band | Blues At Sunrise | Stax | SCD 8546-2
Little Brown Jug
Glenn Miller And His Orchestra | In The Mood | Intercord | 125403
Glenn Miller-The Great Instrumentals 1938-1942 | Retrieval | RTR 79001
The Ultimate Glenn Miller-22 Original Hits From The King Of Swing | RCA | 2113137-2
The Carnegie Hall Concert | Bluebird | 63 66147-2
Glenn Miller Revival Orchestra | Forever-From The Forties To The... | Timeless | CD JC 11013
Peter Herbolzheimer Orchestra | Music For Swinging Dancers Vol.4: Close To You | Koala Records | CD P 12
Little B's Poem
Bobby Hutcherson Orchestra | Knucklebean | Blue Note | LA 789
Little Butterfly(Pannonica)
Kevin Mahogany With The Kenny Barron Trio And Ralph Moore | Double Rainbow | Enja | ENJ-7097 2
Little Camila
Fernando Tarrés And The Arida Conta Group With Guests | Secret Rhythm | Muse | MCD 5516
Little Child(Daddy Dear)
Marilyn Crispell | Contrasts: Live At Yoshi's | Music & Arts | CD 930
Little Chris
Thom Rotella Band | Thom Rotella Band | dmp Digital Music Productions | CD 460
Little Church
Miles Davis Group | This Is Jazz:Miles Davis Electric | CBS | CK 65449
Little Dave
JATP All Stars | Welcome To Jazz At The Philharmonic | Fantasy | FANCD 6081-2
Little David
The Exciting Battle-JATP Stockholm '55 | Pablo | 2310713-2
Little David's Fugue
The Swingle Singers With The Modern Jazz Quartet | Compact Jazz:The Swingle Singers | Mercury | 830701-2 PMS
Little Digi's Strut
Bennie Green's Band | Juggin' Around | Atlantis | ATS 1
Little Drummer Boy
Take 6 | He Is Christmas | Reprise | 7599-26665-2
Gary Lucas | Skeleton On The Feast | Enemy | EMCD 126(03526)
Little Eva's Dance
Paul Smith Sextet | Cool And Sparkling | Capitol | 300011(TOCJ 6125)
Little Fantasy
Chubby Newsom With Orchestra | The Original Hip Shakin' Mama | Official | 6020
Little Flowers
Jesse Davis Quintet | Young At Art | Concord | CCD 4565
Little Freak
Giancarlo Nicolai Trio | The Giancarlo Nicolai Trio | LEO | LR 134
Little Giant
Barbara Thompson Group | Ghosts | MCA | 2292-50484-1
Little Girl
John Pizzarelli Trio | Dear Mr.Cole | Novus | 4163182-2
John Pizzarelli Trio With The Don Sebesky Orchestra | Our Love Is Here To Stay | RCA | 6367501-2
Nat King Cole And His Trio | Combo USA | Affinity | CD AFS 1002
Nat King Cole Trio | Nat King Cole:Route 66 | Dreyfus Jazz Line | FDM 36716-2
Vocal Classics & Instrumental Classics | Capitol | 300014(TOCJ 6128)
Rocky Cole With Al Cohn And His Orchestra | Smooth & Rocky | M&M Records | R 25113(Roulette)
Warren Vaché Sextet | Easy Going | Concord | CCD 4323
Little Girl Blue
Ann Richards With The Bill Marx Trio | Live At The Losers/We Remember Mildred Bailey | Vee Jay Recordings | VJ 018
Bud Shank-Laurindo Almeida Quartet | Braziliance Vol.2 | Pacific Jazz | 796102-2
Carol Sloane And Her Band | Out Of The Blue | Fresh Sound Records | LSP 15823(CBS CS 8566)

Chet Baker-Paul Bley | Diane | Steeplechase | SCM 51207
Dave Brubeck Quartet | Jazz:Ted Hot And Cool | CBS | CK 61468
My Favorite Things | CBS | SRCS 9369
Eddie Henderson Quintet | Phantoms | Steeplechase | SCCD 31250
Ella Fitzgerald With The Buddy Bregman Orchestra | The Rodgers And Hart Song Book, Vol.1 | Verve | 821579-2 PMS
George Duke Quartet | Presented By The Jazz Workshop 1966 In San Francisco | MPS | 68233
Hank Jones Trio | Urbanity | Verve | 537749-2
Jimmy Jones Trio | The Piano Collection Vol.2 | Vogue | 21610222
John Lewis Trio | The John Lewis Piano | Atlantic | AMCY 1035
Jutta Glaser & Bernhard Sperrfechter | Little Girl Blue | Jazz 'n' Arts Records | JNA 0502
Katia Labeque | Little Girl Blue | Dreyfus Jazz Line | FDM 36186-2
Keith Jarrett Trio | Tribute | ECM | 1420/21
Standards In Norway | ECM | 1542(521717-2)
LaVerne Butler With The Rob Bargad Band | Day Dreamin' | Chesky | JD 117
Marshall Royal Quintet | First Chair | Concord | CJ 88
Milt Jackson Quintet | At The Village Gate | Original Jazz Classics | OJCCD 309-2
Nancy Wright With Caesar Giovannini +6 | You Make Me Feel So Young! | Fresh Sound Records | Concert-Disc CD 43 CD
Nina Simone Trio | My Baby Just Cares For Me | Charly | CR 30217
Little Girl Blue | Bethlehem | BET 6021-2(BCP 6003)
Ray Brown Trio | Something For Lester | Original Jazz Classics | OJCCD 412-2
Rosemary Clooney And Her Sextet & The L.A. Jazz Choir | Sings Rodgers,Hart & Hammerstein | Concord | CCD 4405
Sadao Watanabe Quintet With Strings | Plays Ballads | Denon Compact Disc | DC-8555
Sonny Rollins Quartet | Falling In Love With Jazz | Milestone | M 9179
Stan Getz Quartet | Nobody Else But Me | Verve | 521660-2
Thad Jones Sextet | Detroit-New York Junction | Blue Note | 300092(1513)
Little Girl Blue-
Coleman Hawkins With Billy Byers And His Orchestra | The Hawk In Hi-Fi | RCA | 2663842-2
Little Girl Blue(alt.take)
Louis Armstrong With The Russell Garcia Orchestra | I've Got The World On A String/Louis Under The Stars | Verve | 2304428 IMS
Little Girl Blue(vocal-version)
Axel Zwingenberger With Big Joe Duskin | Kansas City Boogie Jam | Vagabond | VRCD 8.00027
Little Girl Boogie
Michael Feinstein With Jule Styne | Michael Feinstein Sings The Jule Styne Songbook | Nonesuch | 7559-79274-2
Little Girl In Blue
Birdland Dream Band | Birdland Dream Band | RCA | 2663873-2
Little Girl Kimbi
Birdland Dream Band | RCA | 2663873-2
Maynard Ferguson With The Birdland Dreamband | The Birdland Dream Band Vol.1 | Fresh Sound Records | 58110 CD(RCA)
Little Girl Kimbi(alt.take)
Dave Bartholomew And His Orchestra | Jump Children | Pathe | 1546601(Imperial)
Little Girl Your Daddy Is Calling You
Charlie Byrd Quartet | Moments Like This | Concord | CCD 4627
Little Island
Astor Piazzolla-Gary Burton Sextet | The New Tango | Warner | 2292-55069-2
Little Italy 1930
The Jazz Passengers | Implement Yourself | New World Records | 80398-2
Little Jazz
Artie Shaw And His Orchestra | The Indispensable Artie Shaw Vol.5/6(1944-1945) | RCA | ND 89914
Ella Fitzgerald With Marty Paich's Dektette | Ella Swings Lightly | Verve | 517535-2
Jon Faddis Quintet | Legacy | Concord | CCD 4291
Roy Eldridge And His Orchestra | At The Arcadia Ballroom New York | Jazz Anthology | JA 5149
Roy Eldridge Quintet | Roy Eldridge 'Littel Jazz'-The Best Of The Verve Years | Verve | 523338-2
Little Jazz Bird
Blossom Dearie Quartet | My Gentleman Friend | Verve | 519905-2
Carol Kidd With Band And String Quartet | Crazy For Gershwin | Linn Records | AKD 026
Meredith d'Ambrosia Group | Little Jazz Bird | Sunnyside | SSC 1040 D
Little Jazz Boogie
Roy Eldridge & His Orchestra | Big Band Bounce And Boogie:Tippin' Out | Affinity | AFS 1016
Little Jazz(alt.take)
Illinois Jacquet And His Orchestra | Groovin' | Verve | 2304511 IMS
Little Jimmy Scott With The Paul Gayten Band
Nat Adderley Quintet | Introducing Nat Adderley | Verve | 543828-2
Little Joanie Walks
Frank Socolow Sextet | Sounds By Socolow | Fresh Sound Records | FSR 2001(Bethlehem BCP 70)
Little John Special
Zoot Sims Quintet | Zoot Sims | Swing | SW 8417
Little Jump
Quincy Jones And His Orchestra | The Quintessence | Impulse(MCA) | 951222-2
Little Karen
Benny Golson Band | Benny Golson:Free | GRP | 951816-2
Little Karin
Jim Rotondi Sextet | Excursions | Criss Cross | Criss 1184
Little Lady
Tony Scott Quartet | Tony Scott Plays Gypsy | Fresh Sound Records | FSR 574(Signature SS 6001)
Little Lees
Kxutrio | Riff-ifi | Sound Aspects | sas CD 032
Little Leo
Lu Watters' Yerba Buena Jazz Band | Lu Watters' Yerba Buena Jazz Band At Hambone Kelly's 1949-50 | Merry Makers Record | MMRC-CD-10
Little Lulu
Bill Evans | Further Conversations With Myself | Verve | 559832-2
Bill Evans Trio | The Complete Bill Evans On Verve | Verve | 527953-2
The Complete Bill Evans On Verve | Verve | 527953-2
Trio (Motian Peacock)-Duo(Hall) | Verve | 2-2509 IMS
Trio 64 | Verve | 539058-2
The Complete Bill Evans On Verve | Verve | 527953-2
Little Lulu(alt.take 1)
Trio 64 | Verve | 539058-2
The Complete Bill Evans On Verve | Verve | 527953-2
Little Lulu(alt.take 2)
Trio 64 | Verve | 539058-2
John Lindberg Ensemble | A Tree Frog Tonality | Between The Lines | btl 008(Efa 10178-2)
Little m And Big M
Thomas Chapin Trio | Anima | Knitting Factory Works | KFWCD 121
Little Malonae
John Coltrane With The Red Garland Trio | Settin' The Pace | Original Jazz Classics | OJC20 078-2
Kenny Garrett Sextet | Garrett 5 | Paddle Wheel | K32Y 6280
Little Man
Dave Brubeck Quartet | Angel Eyes | CBS | SRCS 9368
Little Man You've Had A Busy Day
Bert Ambrose And His Orchestra | Saturday Night | Decca | DDV 5003/4 DT
The Mel Lewis Jazz Orchestra | Soft Lights And Hot Music | Limelight | 820813-2 IMS
Little Marie And The Wolf

Washboard Doc, Luckey & Flash | Early Morning Bluus | L+R Records | LR 42010

Little Me

Abraham Burton Quartet | The Magician | Enja | ENJ-9037 2

Little Melonae

Andy Fusco Quintet | Big Man's Blues | Double Time Records | DTRCD-116

Frank Morgan Quintet | Bebop Lives! | Contemporary | C 14026

Little Miss

Rob Agerbeek Trio | Miss Dee | Limetree | MLP 198100

Little Movements

Richard Galliano Quartet | Viaggio | Dreyfus Jazz Line | FDM 36562-9

Little Muse

Ellis=Ochs=Robinson | What We Live | DIW | DIW 909 CD

Little Niles

Bill Stewart Qaurtet | Think Before You Think | Jazz City | 660.53.024

James Spaulding Quintet | Gotstabe A Better Way | Muse | MCD 5413

Kenny Barron | Spiral | Eastwind | EWIND 709

The Danish-German Slide Combination | Fugue For Tinhorns | L+R Records | LR 45011

Uwe Kropinski | Faces | ITM Records | ITM 14100

Little Old Lady

John Coltrane Quartet | Coltrane Jazz | Atlantic | 7567-81344-2

Kirk Lightsey Trio | From Kirk To Nat | Criss Cross | Criss 1050

Little One

Herbie Hancock Quintet | Maiden Voyage | Blue Note | 495331-2

Herbie Hancock:The Complete Blue Note Sixties Sessions | Blue Note | 495569-2

Katie Webster | Pounds Of Blues | Charly | CRB 1087

Miles Davis Quintet | E.S.P. | CBS | CK65683

Miles Davis Quintet 1965-1968 | CBS | C6K 67398

Rob Van Den Broeck-Wiro Mahieu | Departures | Green House Music | CD 1004

Ruby Braff All Stars | Being With You:Ruby Braff Remembers Louis Armstrong | Arbors Records | ARCD 19163

Little One I'll Miss You

Tony Fruscella Quintet | Pernod | The Jazz Factory | JFCD 22804

Little Outsider

Al Jolson With Orchestra | Al Jolson-Great Original Performances(1926-1932) | CDS Records Ltd. | RPCD 300

Little Peace

Heinz Von Hermann Quintet | Jazz Ahead | Mons Records | MR 874810

Little Peace In C For U

Stephane Grappelli-Michel Petrucciani Quartet | Flamingo | Dreyfus Jazz Line | FDM 36580-2

Dave Liebman Group | Songs For My Daughter | Soul Note | 121295-2

Little Piece In C For U

Joe McPhee Po Music | Linear B | Hat Art | CD 6057

Little Pixie

The Mel Lewis Jazz Orchestra | The Definitive Thad Jones-Live At The Village Vanguard Vol.1 | Musicmasters | 5024-2

Little Pony

Count Basie And His Orchestra | Basie In Sweden | Roulette | CDP 759974-2

Lambert, Hendricks And Ross | Lambert,Hendricks & Ross:Sing A Song Of Basie | CTI Records | PDCTI 1115-2

Little Poolie

Duke Ellington And His Orchestra | From Southland Cafe Boston 1940 | Jazz Anthology | 550022

Little Pugie

Ronnie Ball Quintet | All About Ronnie | Savoy | SV 0174(MG 12075)

Little Queen Of Spades

Robert Lockwood Jr. | Robert Lockwood Jr. Plays Robert (Johnson) & Robert (Lockwood) | Black & Blue | 33740

Little Queen Of Spades(alt.take)

Luther Johnson Blues Band | Lonesome In My Bedroom | Black & Blue | BLE 233515

Little Rabbit Blues

John Lee Hooker | Get Back Home | Black & Blue | BLE 59.023 2

Little Red Ribbon

Slim Gaillard And His Band | Cement Mixer Put-Ti Put-Ti | Folklyric | 9038

Little Red Rooster

Howlin' Wolf | Black & White Blues-The Little Red Rooster | Chess | 2292-44598-1

Little Right Foot

Larry Davis Quintet | I Ain't Beggin' Nobody | Evidence | ECD 26016-2

Little Rock

Bob Crosby And His Orchestra | Bob Crosby And His Orchestra-1938 | Circle | CCD-1

Little Rock Getaway

Dutch Swing College Band | Ain't Nobody's Business | DSC Production | PA 002 (801059)

Great Guitars | Great Guitars/Straight Tracks | Concord | CCD 4421

Little Rocks Of Aruanda

Bruce Forman Quartet With Bobby Hutcherson | There Are Times | Concord | CCD 4332

Little Rootie Tootie

Chick Corea Trio | Trio Music | ECM | 1232/33(159454-2)

Esbjörn Svensson Trio(E.S.T.) | EST Plays Monk | ACT | 9010-2

EST Plays Monk | RCA | 2137680-2

Sebastian Gramss Underkarl | 20th Century Jazz Cover-Live | TCB Records | TCB 96202

Sonny Fortune Quartet | Monk's Mood | Konnex Records | KCD 5048

Steve Lacy | Only Monk | Soul Note | SN 1160

Thelonious Monk Trio | Thelonious Monk | Original Jazz Classics | OJC20 010-2(P 7027)

Thelonious Monk:85th Birthday Celebration | zyx records | FANCD 6076-2

Thelonious Monk:The Complete Prestige Recordings | Prestige | 3 PRCD 4428-2

The Prestige Legacy Vol.1:The High Priests | Prestige | PCD 24251-2

The Thelonious Monk Memorial Album | Milestone | MCD 47064-2

Little Rootie Tootie-

Steve Khan | Evidence | Novus | ND 83074

Little Sheri

Kevin Mahogany With The James Williams Trio And Benny Golson | You Got What It Takes | Enja | ENJ-9039 2

Little Sister's Boogie

Charles Lloyd Quartet | Voice In The Night | ECM | 1674(559445-2)

Little Sister's Dance-

Chuck Foster And His Orchestra | The Uncollected:Chuck Foster, Vol.2 | Hindsight | HSR 171(835576)

Little Song

Michel Grailler-Michel Petrucciani | Dream Drops | Owl Records | 013434-2

Sonny Clark Quintet | My Conception | Blue Note | 522674-2

Little Sonny

Lee Morgan Quintet | Take Twelve | Original Jazz Classics | OJCCD 310-2

Little Spain

Robert Lockwood Jr. | Robert Lockwood Jr. Plays Robert(Johnson) & Robert(Lockwood) | Black & Blue | BLE 59.740 2

Little Spirit

Stephane Grappelli Quintet | The Best Of Stephane Grappelli | Black Lion | 147013

Little Suede Shoes

Joe Albany Trio | Bird Lives! | Interplay | IP 7723

Little Sunflower

Freddie Hubbard Sextet | Backlash | Atlantic | SD 1477

Ray Blue Quartet | Always With A Purpose | Ray Blue Music | JN 007(RMB 01)

Sam Yahel Quartet | The The Blink Of An Eye | Naxos Jazz | 86043-2

Little Susie

Ragtime Specht Groove Trio | Stuttgart Jazz Society E. V. Dixieland Hall Live | Intercord | 130002

Ray Bryant | Alone At Montreux | 32 Jazz | 32128

The Hudson Project | The Hudson Project | Stretch Records | SCD 9024-2

Little Symphony

Art Blakey And The Jazz Messengers | Once Upon A Groove | Blue Note | LT 1065

Little T

Galliano-Portal | Blow Up | Dreyfus Jazz Line | FDM 36589-2

Little Tango

Michel Portal-Richard Galliano | Concerts | Dreyfus Jazz Line | FDM 36661-2

Richard Galliano | Concert Inédits | Dreyfus Jazz Line | FDM 36606-2

Little Taste

Lucky Thompson Trio | Tricotism | Impulse(MCA) | GRP 11352

Little Theo

Dodo Greene With The Ike Quebec Quintet | My Hour Of Need | Blue Note | 852442-2

Little ThingsThat Count

Michael Sagmeister Trio | Sagmeister Trio/Ganshy | BELL Records | BLR 83753

Little Tin Box

Oscar Peterson Trio | Oscar Peterson Plays My Fair Lady And The Music From Fiorello! | Verve | 521677-2

Little Town Gal

Buddy Rich And His Orchestra | The Amazing Buddy Rich: Time Being | RCA | ND 86459(847168)

Little Train

Masabumi Kikuchi Trio | Feel You | Paddle Wheel | KICJ 141

Little Unhappy Boy

Nancy Wilson With The Cannonball Adderley Quintet | Nancy Wilson/The Cannonball Adderley Quintet | Capitol | 781204-2

Little Voodoo Baby

Charles Lloyd Quartet | Charles Lloyd In Europe | Atlantic | 7567-80788-2

Little Wahid's Day

John Scofield Quartet | What We Do | Blue Note | 799586-2

Little Walk

Walter Horton Band | Joe Hill Louis: The Be-Bop Boy | Bear Family Records | BCD 15524 AH

Little Walter's Boogie(take 1)

Joe Hill Louis: The Be-Bop Boy | Bear Family Records | BCD 15524 AH

Little Walter's Boogie(take 2)

Changes | Home Again | EGO | 4015

Little Waltz

Helen Merrill + Ron Carter | Duets | Mercury | 838097-2 PMS

Joscho Stephan Group | Swinging Strings | Acoustic Music Records | 319.1195.2

Rich Perry Quartet | So In Love | Steeplechase | SCCD 31447

Steve Kuhn Trio | The Vanguard Date | Owl Time Line | 3819062

Little White Lies

George Shearing Quintet/With Strings/Latin Mood | The Best Of George Shearing-All Time Shearing Favorites | Capitol | SM 2104

Julie London With Howard Roberts And Red Mitchell | Julie Is Her Name Vol.2 | Pathe | 1566201(Liberty LRP 3100)

Louis Armstrong And His All Stars | Louis Armstrong In Philadelphia | Jazz Anthology | JA 5190

Oscar Peterson-Major Holley Duo | Tenderly | Verve | MV 2662 IMS

Thilo Wolf Trio With Randy Brecker,Chuck Loeb & New York Strings | A Swinging Hour In New York | Mons Records | MR 874801

Tommy Dorsey And His Orchestra | Let There Be Jazz | RCA | NL 45175 AG

Little Willie Leaps

Miles Davis All Stars | Miles Davis:Milestones | Dreyfus Jazz Line | FDM 36731-2

The Savoy Recordings 2 | Savoy | 650108(881908)

Red Rodney Quintet | One For Bird | Steeplechase | SCCD 31238

Warne Marsh-Lee Konitz Quintet | Warne Marsh-Lee Konitz,Vol.3 | Storyville | SLP 4096

Little Wing

Gil Evans Orchestra | Little Wing | West Wind | WW 2042

Jonas Hellborg | Elegant Punk | Day Eight Music | DEMCD 004

Pinguin Moschner-Joe Sachse | If 69 Was 96/The Music Of Jimi Hendrix | Aho-Recording | CD 1016

Tuck And Patti | Love Warriors | Windham Hill | 34 10116-2

Little Wing-

Claus Boesser-Ferrari | Ten | Acoustic Music Records | 319.1168.2

Littlle One

Christian Wallumrod Ensemble | Sofienberg Variations | ECM | 1809(017067-2)

Liturgia

Gary Burton Quartet | Duster | RCA | 2125730-2

Liv(2001)

Intergalactic Maiden Ballet,The | Gulf | TipToe | TIP-888817 2

Live And Learn

Stan Kenton And His Orchestra | 7,5 On The Richter Scale | Creative World | STD 1070

Live At The Vanguard

Zion Harmonizers | Thank You Lord | Sound Of New Orleans | SONO 6007

Live For Life

Robert Conti | Solo Guitar | Trend | TR 519 Direct-to-Disc

Live For Love

Peter Herborn's Acute Insights | Peter Herborn's Acute Insights | JMT Edition | 919017-2

Live Force-

Taylor Hawkins Group | Wake Up Call | Fresh Sound Records | FSCD 145 CD

Live Free Or Die

Benny Goodman And His Orchestra | Jazz Giants:Benny Goodman | RCA | NL 89731 SI

Live Is Lonely

Pili-Pili | Boogaloo | JA & RO | JARO 4174-2

Live Is Not A Video

Billy Taylor Trio | Billy Taylor Trio | Prestige | PRCD 24285-2

Live It Up

Rudy Linka Quartet | Live It Up | Timeless | CD SJP 407

Live Pulse

Eddie Harris Group | The Best Of Eddie Harris | Atlantic | 7567-81370-2

Live Right Now

The Gospelaire Of Dayton,Ohio | Can I Get A Witness/Bones In The Valley | Mobile Fidelity | MFCD 763

Live Steps

Billy Wright Band | Goin' Down Slow | Savoy | SV 0257

Live Your Dreams

Medeski Martin & Wood With Guests | It's A Jungle In Here | Gramavision | R2 79495

Livery Stable Blues

Muggsy Spanier And His Ragtime Band | Jazz Classics In Digital Stereo: Muggsy Spanier 1931 & 1939 | CDS Records Ltd. | REB 687

Living Bicycles

Oscar Brown Jr. With The Floyd Morris Quartet | Mr.Oscar Brown Jr. Goes To Washington | Verve | 557452-2

Living In A Dream World

Ull Möck Trio | Drilling | Satin Doll Productions | SDP 1023-1 CD

Living In Chelsea

David Azarian Trio | Hope | Enja | ENJ-9354 2

Living In Overdrive

Roy Fox And His Orchestra | The Bands That Matter | Eclipse | ECM 2045

Living Room

John Coltrane And His Orchestra | John Coltrane-His Greatest Years, Vol. 3 | MCA | AS 9278

Living Space

John Coltrane Quartet | John Coltrane:The Classic Quartet-Complete Impulse Studio Recordings | Impulse(MCA) | 951280-2

John Coltrane Quintet | The Mastery Of John Coltrane/Vol. 1: Feelin' Good | MCA | 2292-54641-2

Living Space(breakdown and alt.take)

Acoustic Jazz Quartet | Acoustic Jazz Quartet | Naxos Jazz | 86033-2

Living Without You

Peter Herborn's Acute Insights | Peter Herborn's Acute Insights | JMT Edition | 919017-2

Living Yet-

Joe Newman Septet | The Complete Joe Newman RCA-Victor Recordings(1955-1956):The Basie Days | RCA | 2122613-2

Livingo

George Russell Smalltet | The RCA Victor Jazz Workshop | RCA | 2159144-2

Livingstone I Presume

Art Lande And Rubisa Patrol | Desert Marauders | ECM | 1106

Liza

Art Hodes | Someone To Watch Over Me-Live At Hanratty's | Muse | MR 5252

Art Tatum | Art Tatum:Complete Original American Decca Recordings | Definitive Records | DRCD 11200

Benny Goodman Original Quartet | Benny Goodman:The King Of Swing | Musicmasters | 65130-2

Benny Goodman Quartet | Avalon-The Small Band Vol.2 (1937-1939) | Bluebird | ND 82273

Duke Ellington And His Orchestra | The Rare Broadcast Recordings 1953 | Jazz Anthology | JA 5220

Harald Rüschenbaum Orchestra | Double Faces | Swingtime | 8206

James P.Johnson | The Story Of Jazz Piano | Laserlight | 24653

Jo Jones Sextet | Jo Jones Sextet | Fresh Sound Records | FSR-CD 0144

Klaus Ignatzek | Gershwin Songs | Nabel Records:Jazz Network | CD 4631

Lars Gullin Septet | Lars Gullin 1951/52 Vol.5:First Walk | Dragon | DRCD 380

Laurindo Almeida Trio | Artistry In Rhythm | Concord | CCD 4238

Quintet Du Hot Club De France | Welcome To Jazz: Django Reinhardt | Koch Records | 322 074 D1

Ruby Braff Trio | Ruby Braff Trio:In Concert | Storyville | 4960543

Ruby Braff-George Barnes Quartet | Plays Gershwin | Concord | CCD 6005

Stan Kenton And His Orchestra | The Kenton Era | Creative World | ST 1030

Thomas Clausen | Pianomusic | M.A Music | A 801-2

Warren Vaché Quintet | Horn Of Plenty | Muse | MCD 5524

Liza(All The Clouds'll Roll Away)

Duke Ellington And His Orchestra | Happy Birthday Duke Vol.1 | Laserlight | 15783

Fletcher Henderson And His Orchestra | Wild Party | Hep | 1009

Quintet Du Hot Club De France | The Very Best Of Django Reinhardt | Decca | 6.28441 DP

The Big 18 | Live Echoes Of The Swinging Bands | RCA | 2113032-2

Thelonious Monk Trio | Thelonious Monk-The Complete Riverside Recordings | Riverside | 15 RCD 022-2

Liza(All The Clouds'll Roll Away)-

Teddy Wilson | Piano Solos | Affinity | CD AFS 1016

Liz-Anne

Der Rote Bereich | Love Me Tender | ACT | 9286-2

Lizard

Mark Nauseef/Miroslav Tadic Group | The Snake Music | CMP Records | CMP CD 60

Lizbet

George Zack-George Wettling Duo | Commodore Classics-George Zack/George Wettling:Barrelhouse Piano | Commodore | 6.25895 AG

Llegué A La Cima

Mara! | Ruino Vino | Laika Records | 35100792

Llew's Blues

Tete Montoliu Trio | Lliure Jazz | Fresh Sound Records | FSR 4005(835330)

Llonio's Song

Machito And His Afro-Cuban Salseros | Mucho Macho | Pablo | 2625712-2

Llovisna(Light Rain)

Bennie Wallace Trio & Chick Corea | Mystic Bridge | Enja | 4028 (807516)

Lluna

Gato Barbieri Group | Gato Chapter Four: Alive In New York | MCA | AS 9303

Lo Bess Goin' To The Picnic?

Joan Abril Quintet | Eric | Fresh Sound Records | FSNT 092 CD

Lo De Siempre

Afrocuba | Electicism | Ronnie Scott's Jazz House | JHCD 039

Lo Pass

Guillermo Klein & Big Van | El Minotauro | Candid | CCD 79706

Lo Que Todos Sabemos

Irakere | The Legendary 'Irakere' In London | Ronnie Scott's Jazz House | JHCD 005

Lo Ultimo

Diego Carraresi Quartet | Attrezzo | SPLASC(H) Records | H 140

Loaded

Kai Winding's New Jazz Group | Loaded:Vido Musso/Stan Getz | Savoy | SV 0227(MG 12074)

Loads Of Love

Fats Waller And His Rhythm | I'm Gonna Sit Right Down...The Early Years-Part 2(1935-1936) | Bluebird | 63 66640-2

Lobby Daze

Eddy Louiss Orchestra | Multicolor Feeling-Fanfare | Nocturne Productions | NTCD 105

Lobster

Shin-Ichi Fukuda | Guitar Legends:Homage To Great Popular Guitarists | Denon Compact Disc | CO-18048

Loch Lomond

Benny Goodman And His Orchestra | 40th Anniversary Concert-Live At Carnegie Hall | London | 820349-2

Benny Goodman At Carnegie Hall 1938(Complete) | CBS | C2K 65143

The Indispensable Benny Goodman Vol.3/4 | RCA | 2115520-2

Deborah Henson-Conant | The Celtic Album | Laika Records | 35101022

Dick Hyman | Maybeck Recital Hall Series Volume Three | Concord | CCD 4415

Lochana

David Murray Quintet | Remembrances | DIW | DIW 849 CD

Lock All The Gates

Bessie Smith With James P. Johnson | Jazz:The Essential Collection Vol.1 | IN+OUT Records | 78011-2

Lock And Key

Charles Mingus Orchestra | Mingus | Candid | CCD 79021

Lock 'Em Up

Blind Lemon Jefferson | Blind Lemon Jefferson | Milestone | MCD 47022-2

Lock Up And Bow Out

Dick Verbeeck-Michael De Bruin Sextet | 12th Jazz Hoeilaart International Europ' Jazz Contest 90 | B.Sharp Records | CDS 081

Locked In Amber

Louis Jordan With The Nelson Riddle Orchestra | Louis Jordan-Let The Good Times Roll: The Complete Decca Recordings 1938-1954 | Bear Family Records | BCD 15557 IH

Locked Up

Sergio Salvatore Quintet | Tune Up | GRP | GRP 97632

Loco Madi-

Buell Neidlinger's String Jazz | Locomotive | Soul Note | 121161-2

Loco Motif

Leo Smith & New Dalta Ahkri | New York City Jazz-2 | Polydor | 815111-1 IMS

Locomonktion

Bill Holman Octet | Group Activity | Affinity | AFF 65

Locomotion

John Coltrane Sextet | Blue Train | Mobile Fidelity | MFCD 547(UDCD)

The Ultimate Blue Train | Blue Note | 853428-2

Takin' Off | Blue Note | 300415

Locomotive
Thelonious Monk Quintet | Thelonious Monk:The Complete Prestige Recordings | Prestige | 3 PRCD 4428-2
Vic Juris Trio | Songbook 2 | Steeplechase | SCCD 31516
Lenny MacDowell Quintet | Magic Flute | BELL Records | BLR 84027
Locos De La Opera
Loren Stillman Quartet | Cosmos | Soul Note | 121310-2
Locus Amoenus-
Hans Reichel | Coco Bolo Nights | FMP | CD 10
Loie
Ike Quebec Quintet | Bossa Nova Soul Samba | Blue Note | 300052(4114)
Bossa Nova Soul Samba | Blue Note | 852443-2
Loin Du Brésil
George Shearing With The Montgomery Brothers | George Shearing And The Montgomery Brothers | Original Jazz Classics | OJCCD 040-2
Lois Ann
Wes Montgomery-The Complete Riverside Recordings | Riverside | 12 RCD 4408-2
Wes Montgomery Quintet | Fingerpickin' | Pacific Jazz | 837987-2
Loisaida
Hans Koch/Martin Schütz/Marco Käppeli | Accélération | ECM | 1357
Anouar Brahem Quartet | Conte De L'Incroyable Amour | ECM | 1457(511959-2)
L'Oiseau De Bois
I Compani | Rota-Music To The Films Of Fellini | ITM Records | ITM 1426
Loki
Donald Byrd Sextet | Blackjack | Blue Note | 784466-2
Lokk(Etter Thorvald Tronsgard)
Lee Konitz Quartet | Lee Konitz/Rhapsody | Paddle Wheel | KICJ 174
Lola
Albrecht Maurer Trio Works | Movietalks | Jazz Haus Musik | JHM 0119 CD
Lola Rennt...Nicht Immer
Joe Bawelino Quartet | Happy Birthday Stéphane | Edition Collage | EC 458-2
Lola Swing
Barney Wilen Quintet | La Note Bleue | IDA Record | 010 CD
Lolita
Cannonball Adderley Quintet | Wes Montgomery-The Complete Riverside Recordings | Riverside | 12 RCD 4408-2
Kirk Lightsey Quintet feat. Marcus Belgrave | Kirk 'N Marcus | Criss Cross | Criss 1030
Wes Montgomery Trio | Wes Montgomery-The Complete Riverside Recordings | Riverside | 12 RCD 4408-2
Buddy DeFranco Quintet | Mr.Lucky | Pablo | 2310906
Lollypop
Stephane Metraux/Bernard Ogay | Oxymore | Plainisphare | PAV 803
Lombardy
Palo Alto | Crash Test | Jazz 'n' Arts Records | JNA 1803
L'Ombra Di Frisell
Vincent Courtois Quartet | Translucide | Enja | ENJ-9380 2
L'Ombre Sout Le Lit
Gerald Wilson Orchestra Of The 80's | Lomelin | Discovery | DS 833 IMS
Lon Lon
Kevin Bruce Harris Quartet | Folk Songs-Folk Tales | TipToe | TIP-888807 2
Lonconao
Joe Turner/Tommy Bedford | Jazz Piano Vol.1 | Jazztime(EMI) | 251282-2
London Blues
Brad Mehldau Trio | Introducing Brad Mehldau | Warner | 9362-45997-2
Chris Barber's Jazz Band | Ice Cream | Black Lion | 127029
London By Night
Singers Unlimited | A Capella | MPS | 815671-1
King Oliver's Creole Jazz Band | King Oliver's Creole Jazzband-The Complete Set | Retrieval | RTR 79007
London Cafe Blues(A New Orleans Stomp)
King Oliver's Jazz Band | New Orleans Stomp | VJM | VLP 35 IMS
London Duty Free
Oscar Peterson With Orchestra | A Royal Wedding Suite | Original Jazz Classics | OJCCD 973-2(2312129)
London Gets Ready
Bill Evans & Push | Live In Europe | Lipstick Records | LIP 890292
London Song
Fats Waller | London Sessions 1938-39 | Jazztime(EMI) | 251271-2
Londonderry Air -> Danny Boy
Lone Jack
Pat Metheny Trio | Trio 99-00 | Warner | 9362-47632-2
Unknown Group | Lenox School Of Jazz Concert | Royal Jazz | RJD 513
Loneliness
Niels Lan Doky Trio | Dreams | Milestone | MCD 9178-2
Lonely
Swim Two Birds | Sweet Relief | Laika Records | 35101182
Reuben Brown Trio | Ice Shape | Steeplechase | SCCD 31423
Lonely At The Top
Longstreet Jazzband | New York,New York | Elite Special | 73436
Lonely Avenue
Grady Tate Quintet | TNT/Grady Tate Sings | Milestone | MCD 9193-2
Lonely Boy Blues
Jay McShann Quintet | What A Wonderful World | Groove Note | GRV 1005-2
Jimmy Witherspoon And His Band | Baby, Baby, Baby | Original Blues Classics | OBCCD 527-2(P 7290)
John Lee Hooker | John Lee Hooker Plays And Sings The Blues | Chess | MCD 09199
Bob Florence Big Band | Concerts By The Sea | Trend | TR 523 Digital
Lonely Dancer
Lowell Fulsom Band | Tramp/Soul | Ace Records | CDCHD 339
Lonely Days And Lonely Nights
Cannonball Adderley With Richard Hayman's Orchestra | Julian Cannonball Adderley And Strings/Jump For Joy | Verve | 528699-2
Lonely Frog
Kölner Saxophon Mafia | Saxfiguren | Jazz Haus Musik | JHM 0036 CD
Lonely From Sky It's A Home For Benefit Within Sixty Lovely Good Hearts A Day
Stadtgarten Series Vol.1 | Jazz Haus Musik | JHM 1001 SER
Lonely Girl
Tony Bennett-Bill Evans | Together Again | DRG | MRS 901 IMS
Lonely Hours
Lowell Fulsom Band | Lowell Fulson | Chess | 427007
Martin Schmitt | Handful Of Blues | AH Records | ESM 9303
Abbey Lincoln With The Kenny Dorham Quintet | Abbey Is Blue | Original Jazz Classics | OJC20 069-2(RLP 1153)
Lonely House
HR Big Band | The American Songs Of Kurt Weill | hr music.de | hrmj 006-01 CD
Jane Ira Bloom Quartet | The Nearness | Arabesque Recordings | AJ 0120
June Christy With The Pete Rugolo Orchestra | Something Cool(The Complete Mono & Stereo Versions) | Capitol | 534069-2
Ran Blake-Christine Correa | Round About | Music & Arts | CD 807
Lonely In The Lakeside
Xu Feng Xia | Difference And Similarity | FMP | CD 96
Lonely Lady
Ekkehard Jost Quintet | Some Other Tapes | Fish Music | FM 009/10 CD
Lonely Langgöns
Carambolage | View | VS 0028 IMS
Lonely Melody
Paul Whiteman And His Orchestra | The Indispensable Bix Beiderbecke(1924-1930) | RCA | ND 89572
The Famous Paul Whiteman:Jazz A La King | RCA | 2135547-2
Lonely Moments
Benny Goodman And His Orchestra | Undercurrent Blues | Capitol | 832086-2
George Shearing/Hank Jones | The Spirit Of 176 | Concord | CCD 4371

Ruby Braff Trio | Ruby Braff Trio:In Concert | Storyville | 4960543
Bravura Eloquence | Concord | CCD 4423
Lonely One
Clark Terry And His Orchestra | Clark Terry And His Orchestra Feat. Paul Gonsalves | Storyville | STCD 8322
Johnny Griffin Trio | The Little Giant | Original Jazz Classics | OJCCD 136-2(R 1149)
Mississippi Sheiks | Stop And Listen | Yazoo | YAZ 2006
Lonely Star
Count Basie And His Orchestra | Basie-Straight Ahead | Dot | DLP 25902
Lonely Street
Everyman Band | Everyman Band | ECM | 1234
Lonely Streets
Coleman Hawkins With The Frank Hunter Orchestra | Hawk Talk | Fresh Sound Records | FSR-CD 0130
Lonely Town
Charlie Haden Quartet West With Strings | The Art Of The Song | Verve | 547403-2
Chris Connor With The Ralph Sharon Sextet | A Jazz Date With Chris Connor | Atlantic | AMCY 1072
Lonely Voyager
Greetje Bijma Trio | Barefoot | Enja | ENJ-8038 2
Lonely Walk
Leith Stevens All Stars | Jazz Themes From The Wild One(Soundtrack) | Fresh Sound Records | 252280-1(Decca DL 8349)
Lonely Woman
Andy Summers Trio | The Last Dance Of Mr.X | RCA | 2668937-2
Billy Bang | Bangception | HatOLOGY | 517
Charlie Haden Trio | The Montreal Tapes Vol.1 | Verve | 523260-2
Charlie Haden-Paul Motian Trio Feat.Geri Allen | Etudes | Soul Note | 121162-2
Gary Bartz-Sonny Fortune Quintet | Alto Memories | Verve | 523268-2
Herb Geller Quartet | To Benny & Johnny | Hep | CD 2084
Horace Silver Quintet | Song For My Father | Blue Note | 499002-2
Hugh Ragin Trio | Metaphysical Question | Cecma | 1007
Kevin Hays Quintet | Sweetear | Steeplechase | SCCD 31282
Nancy Marano With The Benny Carter Band | Benny Carter Songbook | Musicmasters | 65134-2
Ornette Coleman Quartet | Beauty Is A Rare Thing:Ornette Coleman-The Complete Atlantic Recordings | Atlantic | 8122-71410-2
Atlantic Jazz: The Avant-Garde | Atlantic | 7567-81709-2
Pat Dahl With Orchestra | We Dig Pat Dahl | Fresh Sound Records | Audio Fidelity AF 6157 CD
Paul Shigihara-Charlie Mariano Quartet | Tears Of Sound | Nabel Records:Jazz Network | CD 4616
Peter Brötzmann | 14 Love Poems | FMP | 1060
Sarah Vaughan With Hal Mooney's Orchestra | Verve Jazz Masters 18:Sarah Vaughan | Verve | 518199-2
Lonely Woman-
Jaki Byard And The Apollo Stompers | Phantasies | Soul Note | 121075-2
Laurie Altman | For Now At Least | Progressive | PRO 7066 IMS
Lonesome
The Real Ambassadors | The Real Ambassadors | CBS | 467140-2
Lonesome August Child
Champion Jack Dupree Group | Back Home In New Orleans | Rounder Records | BB 9502
Lonesome Blues
Henry Williams And Eddie Anzhony | Georgia String Bands(1928-1930) | Story Of Blues | CD 3516-2
John King Trio | Electric World | Ear-Rational | ECD 1016
Lonesome Guitar
Smiley Lewis Band | Ooh La La | Pathe | 1561391(Imperial)
Lonesome Lover
Stanley Turrentine And His Orchestra | The Blue Note Years-The Best Of Stanley Turrentine | Blue Note | 793201-2
Billy Eckstine And His Orchestra | Mister B. And The Band/Billy Eckstine | Savoy | SV 0264(SJL 2214)
Lonesome Man
Cousin Joe With Band | Cousin Joe:The Complete 1945-1947 Vol.1 (1945-1946) | Blue Moon | BMCD 6001
Lonesome Me
Fats Waller And His Rhythm | Private Acetates And Film Soundtracks | Jazz Anthology | JA 5148
Lonesome Me-
Count Basie And His Orchestra | The Count And The President-Vol.1 1936 & 1939 | CBS | CBS 88667
Lonesome Reverie
Anita O'Day With The Nat King Cole Trio | Nat King Cole Trio:The MacGregor Years 1941/45 | Music & Arts | CD 911
Lonesome Road
Huub Janssen's Amazing Jazzband | Huub Janssen's Amazing Jazzband | Timeless | CD TTD 536
Jimmy Smith Trio | Lonesome Road | Blue Note | 300205
Lonesome Road Blues
Sam Collins | 15 Years In The Mississippi Delta 1926-1941 | Yazoo | YAZ 1038
Lonesome Sundown
Eddie Condon And His Band | Commodore Classics In Swing | Commodore | 9031-72723-2
Lonesome Wells(Gwendy Trio)
Tony Williams Lifetime | Spectrum:The Anthology | Verve | 537075-2
Long About Midnight
Cab Calloway And His Orchestra | Victor Jazz History Vol.8:Swing Big Bands | RCA | 2128562-2
Long Ago And Far Away
Arrigo Cappelletti Trio | Open Spaces | SPLASC(H) Records | HP 16
Art Pepper Quartet | Intensity | Original Jazz Classics | OJCCD 387-2
The Jazz Giants Play Jerome Kern:Yesterdays | Prestige | PCD 24202-2
Art In L.A. | West Wind | WW 2064
Benny Carter And His Strings With The Oscar Peterson Quartet | Alone Together | Verve | 2304512 IMS
Charlie Lewis Trio | JazzIn Paris:Harlem Piano In Montmartre | EmArCy | 018447-2
Chet Baker Quartet | Let's Get Lost: The Best Of Chet Baker Sings | Pacific Jazz | 792932-2
When Sunny Gets Blue | Steeplechase | SCS 1221
Dave Brubeck Quartet | Paper Moon | Concord | CCD 4178
George Shearing-Neil Swainson Duo | Dexterity | Concord | CCD 4346
Jeanie Lambe And The Danny Moss Quartet | The Blue Noise Session | Nagel-Heyer | CD 052
Jeff Hamilton Trio With Frits Landesbergen | Dynavibes | Mons Records | MR 874794
John Colianni | John Colianni | Concord | CCD 4309
Johnny Richards And His Orchestra | Something Else By Johnny Richards | Affinity | AFF 155
Les Brown And His Orchestra | From The Cafe Rouge | Giants Of Jazz | GOJ 1027
Marian McPartland | Willow Creek And Other Ballads | Concord | CCD 4272
Paul Bley Trio | Indian Summer | Steeplechase | SCCD 31286
Rob McConnell Trio | Trio Sketches | Concord | CCD 4591
Sonny Rollins Quintet | Here's To The People | Milestone | MCD 9194-2
Stan Kenton And His Orchestra | Mellophonium Magic | Status | CD 103(882199)
Warren Vaché Quartet | Horn Of Plenty | Muse | MCD 5524
Long Ago And Far Away-
Benny Carter Quintet | Cosmopolite | Verve | 521673-2
Long Ago And Far Away(take 2)
Jimmy Raney Trio | But Beautiful | Criss Cross | Criss 1065
Long Ago And Far Away(take 4)
Charles Mingus Workshop | Charles Mingus-The Complete Debut Recordings | Debut | 12 DCD 4402-2
Long Ago And Far Away(take 5)
Mark Murphy And His Orchestra | The Artistry Of Mark Murphy | Muse | MR 5286

Long As You Know
Joe Sachse | Ballade Für Jimi Metag | Born&Bellmann | 991503 CD
Long As You're Living
Judy Niemack With The Fred Hersch Quartet | Long As You're Living | Freelance | FRL-CD 014
Ran Blake-Christine Correa | Round About | Music & Arts | CD 807
Long Daddy Green
Jack McDuff Sextet | Another Real Good'Un | 32 Jazz | 32169
Long Days Journey
Black Eagle Jazz Band | Black Eagle Jazz Band | Stomp Off Records | CD 1224
Long Deep And Wide
Clarence Williams And His Orchestra | King Oliver 1928-29 | Village(Jazz Archive) | VILCD 005-2
Long Distance
Muddy Waters Quartet | Folk Singer | Chess | CH 9261
Long Fade-
Urs Leimgruber-Fritz Hauser | L'Enigmatique | Hat Art | CD 6091
Long Gone
Louis Armstrong And His All Stars | The Louis Armstrong Selection | CBS | 467278-2
Billie Holiday And Her Orchestra | Billie Holiday:The Quintessential Vol.7(1938-1939) | CBS | CK 46180
Long Gone(rehersal sequence)
Butch Morris Orchestra | Homeing | Sound Aspects | sas CD 4015
Long Hair Woman
Ugetsu | Ugetsu-Live In Athens | Mons Records | MR 874779
Long Island Sound
Stan Getz Quartet | Stan Getz:The Complete 1946-1951 Quartet Sessions(Master Takes),Vol.1 | Blue Moon | BMCD 1013
Stan Getz Quintet | Birdland Sessions 1952 | Fresh Sound Records | FSR-CD 0149
Long Johns Brown And Little Mary Bell
Paul Wertico Trio | Don't Be Scared Anymore | Premonition | 790748-2
Long Life
Paul Smith Quartet | Softly Baby | Jasmine | JAS 311
Long Live The Nigun
Blind Lemon Jefferson | Blind Lemon Jefferson | Biograph | BLP 12000
Long Long Journey
Esquire All-American Award Winners | Esquire's All-American Hot Jazz Sessions | RCA | ND 86757
Victor Jazz History Vol.7:Swing Groups | RCA | 2128561-2
Town Hall Concert Plus | RCA | 2113036-2
Leonard Feather's Esquire All-Americans | Jazz Giants:Louis Armstrong | RCA | NL 89823 SI
Long Lost Love
Oscar Klein Band | Pick-A-Blues Live | Jazzpoint | JP 1071
T-Bone Walker And His Band | Good Feelin' | Verve | 519723-2
Long Mile To Houston-
Julian Dash And His Orchestra | Julian Dash:The Complete Recordings 1950-1953 | Blue Moon | BMCD 1050
Long Night
Tom Varner Group | Long Night Big Day | New World Records | 80410-2
Long Nite
Heinz Sauer Quintet | Lost Ends:Live at Alte Oper Frankfurt | free flow music | ffm 0594
Long Note
Lost Ends:Live at Alte Oper Frankfurt | free flow music | ffm 0594
Long Note(reprise)
Rova Saxophone Quartet | Long On Logic | Sound Aspects | sas CD 037
Long Space
Wolfgang Haffner Project | Back Home | Jazz 4 Ever Records:Jazz Network | J4E 4730
Long Stories
John Patitucci Group | Mistura Fina | GRP | GRP 98022
Long Story
Duke Ellington And His Famous Orchestra | Duke Ellington:The Complete RCA-Victor Mid-Forties Recordings(1944-1946) | RCA | 2663394-2
Long Time Ago
Little Brother Montgomery's Quintet | New Orleans To Chicago:The Forties | Gannet | CJR 1002
Long Time No See
Paul Plimley-Lisle Ellis | Kaleidoscopes(Ornette Coleman Songbook) | Hat Art | CD 6117
Long Tom
David Friesen | Long Trip Home | ITM-Pacific | ITMP 970073
Long Wharf
Toshiko Mariano Quartet | Toshiko Mariano Quartet | Candid | CCD 79012
Long Yellow Road
Abdu Dagir Group | Malik At-Taqasim | Enja | 8012-2
Longa Yurgo
Pat Metheny | New Chautauqua | ECM | 1131(825471-2)
Long-Ago Child
Professor Longhair And His New Orleans Boys | New Orleans Piano | Sequel Records | RSA CD 808
Longhair's Rhumba
Bebop And Beyond | Bebop And Beyond | Concord | CJ 244
Longing
David Linx With The Jack Van Poll Trio | Where Rivers Join | September | CD 5109
Ed Neumeister Trio | The Mohican And The Great Spirit | TCB Records | TCB 01072
International Jazz Consensus | Beak To Beak | Nabel Records:Jazz Network | LP 4602
Peter Ponzol Trio | Prism | View | VS 114 IMS
Longing-
George Winston | Autumn | Windham Hill | 34 11012-2
Longworld
Lonnie Pitchford | Living Country Blues USA Vol.7: Afro-American Blues Roots | L+R Records | LR 42037
Lonnie's Blues
Chico Freeman Quartet | Spirit Sensitive | India Navigation | IN 1045 CD
Lonnie's Lament
Harold Danko | After The Rain | Steeplechase | SCCD 31356
John Coltrane Quartet | John Coltrane-Live Trane:The European Tours | Pablo | 7PACD 4433-2
Afro Blue Impressions | Pablo | 2PACD 2620101
Crescent | Impulse(MCA) | 951200-2
John Coltrane:The Classic Quartet-Complete Impulse Studio Recordings | Impulse(MCA) | 951280-2
LeeAnn Ledgerwood Trio | Walkin' Up | Steeplechase | SCCD 31541
Marty Ehrlich Quartet | The Traveller's Tale | Enja | ENJ-6024 2
Lontano
Mona Larsen And The Danish Radio Big Band Plus Soloists | Michael Mantler:Cerco Un Paese Innocente | ECM | 1556
Lontano-
Terje Rypdal Sextet | Terje Rypdal | ECM | 1016(527645-2)
Lontano II
Tiziana Ghiglioni And Her Band | Tiziana Ghiglioni Canta Luigi Tenco | Philology | W 60.2
Loodle-Lot
Jonas Hellborg Group | Jonas Hellborg Group | Day Eight Music | DEMCD 025
Look A-Here Andy
Phalanx | In Touch | DIW | DIW 8026
Look Around
Singers Unlimited | The Singers Unlimited:Magic Voices | MPS | 539130-2
Four Of Us | MPS | 68106
Look At The Birdie
J.B.Hutto Quartet | Slideslinger | Black & Blue | BLE 59.540 2
Look For The Silver Lining
Ahmad Jamal Trio | Live In Paris 92 | Birdology | 849408-2
Benny Goodman Sextet | Benny Goodman:The King Of Swing | Musicmasters | 65130-2

Chet Baker Quartet | Chet Baker Sings | Pacific Jazz | 300067(PJ 1222)
Chet Baker Quintet/NDR Big Band/Radio Orchestra Hannover | The Last Concert Vol.I+II | Enja | ENJ-6074 22
Chet Baker Sextet | Chet Baker In Milan | Original Jazz Classics | OJC20 370-2(JLP 18)
Chet Baker With The NDR-Bigband | Chet Baker-The Legacy Vol.1 | Enja | ENJ-9021 2
Dave Brubeck Quartet | Stardust | Fantasy | FCD 24728-2
Luca Flores | For Those I Never Knews | SPLASC(H) Records | CD H 439-2
Paul Desmond Quartet | The Jazz Giants Play Jerome Kern:Yesterdays | Prestige | PCD 24202-2
Desmond | Original Jazz Classics | OJCCD 712-2(F 3235/8082)
Paul Desmond Quartet Featuring Don Elliott | Original Jazz Classics | OJC 119(F 3235)

Look Here
Uncle Bud Walker | Going Away Blues 1926-1935 | Yazoo | YAZ 1018

Look It Up
Elliot Lawrence And His Orchestra | Big Band Sound | Fresh Sound Records | FSCD 2003

Look Of Love
Harold Mabern Trio | Lookin' On The Bright Side | DIW | DIW 614 CD

Look On Yonder Wall
The Rockets | Out Of The Blue | L+R Records | CDLR 42077

Look Out
Sam 'The Man' Taylor Orchestra | Back Beat-The Rhythm Of The Blues Vol.5 | Mercury | 511270-2 PMS

Look Out Up There
Louis Mazetier | Good Vibrations | Jazz Connaisseur | JCCD 9521-2

Look Out,Lion,I've Got You
In Concert:What A Treat! | Jazz Connaisseur | JCCD 9522-2
Okeh Melody Stars | Big Charlie Thomas 1925-1927 | Timeless | CBC 1-030

Look To The Black Wall
Paul Motian Quintet | The Story Of Maryam | Soul Note | 121074-2

Look To The Rainbow
Astrud Gilberto With The Al Cohn Orchestra | Verve Jazz Masters 9:Astrud Gilberto | Verve | 519824-2
Paul Motian Quartet | Paul Motian On Broadway Vol.2 | JMT Edition | 834440-2

Look To The Sky -> Olha Pro Céu

Look To The Stars
Duke Ellington Orchestra | Only God Can Make A Tree | Musicmasters | 65117-2

Look To Your Heart
Les McCann Group | On The Soul Side | Musicmasters | 65112-2

Look To Your Heart(alt.take)
Chico Freeman Orchestra | Peaceful Heart Gentle Spirit | Contemporary | C 14005

Look What They've Done To My Song(What have They Done To My Song,Ma)
American Blues Legends 79 | American Blues Legends 79 | Big Bear | 146410

Look Who's Here
The Golden Gate Orchestra | The California Ramblers With Adrian Rollini | Village(Jazz Archive) | VILCD 011-2

Lookin' Good
Sweetman With His South Side Groove Kings | Austin Backalley Blue | Mapleshade | 02752

Looking At The World Thru Rose Colored Glassas
Barbara Sutton Curtis | Old Fashioned Love | Sackville | SKCD2-2042

Looking At You
Mel Tormé And His Trio | Mel Tormé In New York | Jazz Door | JD 12103
Trigger Alpert's Absolutely All Star Seven | East Coast Sound | Original Jazz Classics | OJCCD 1012-2(JLP 11)
Trigger Alpert's All Stars | Trigger Happy! | Fresh Sound Records | RLP 12-225(Riverside)
Mel Tormé And His Band | Fujitsu-Concord Jazz Festival In Japan '90 | Concord | CCD 4481

Looking Back
Carl Saunders-Lanny Morgan Quintet | Las Vegar Late Night Sessions:Live At Capozzoli's | Woofy Productions | WPCD 109
David Benoit Group | Urban Daydreams | GRP | GRP 95872
Harvie Swartz Septet | Smart Moves | Gramavision | GR 8607-2
Northern Jazz Orchestra | Good News | Lake | LACD 38

Looking Back(Reflections)
Adelaide Robbins Trio | Looking For A Boy | Savoy | SV 0226(MG 12097)

Looking For A Boy
Ella Fitzgerald With The Nelson Riddle Orchestra | Ella Sings Gershwin-Vol. 1 | Metro | 2682004 IMS
Vince Guaraldi Trio | A Flower Is A Lovesome Thing | Original Jazz Classics | OJC 235(F 3257)

Looking For Jon
Charles Sullivan Quintet | Kamau | Arabesque Recordings | AJ 0121

Looking Glass
American Folk Blues Festival | American Folk Blues Festival 1969 | L+R Records | CDLR 42071

Looking' Good But Feelin' Bad
Chet Baker Quintet | Blues For A Reason | Criss Cross | Criss 1010

Looking On
Gracie Fields With Studio Orchestra | Amazing Gracie-The Incomparable Gracie Fields | Saville Records | SVL 170 IMS

Looking Out
Sun Ra And His Arkestra | The Futuristic Sounds Of Sun Ra | Savoy | SV 0213(MG 12169)

Looking Through The Eyes Of Love
Passport | Looking Thru | Atlantic | 2292-44144-2

Looking Thru
Thilo Wolf Big Band | Swing It! Vol.2 | Mons Records | MR 874315

Looking Up
Dreyfus All Stars | Dreyfus Night In Paris | Dreyfus Jazz Line | FDM 36652-2
Michel Petrucciani | Live In Germany | Dreyfus Jazz Line | FDM 36597-2
Michel Petrucciani Group | Music | Blue Note | 792563-2
Michel Petrucciani:The Blue Note Years | Blue Note | 789916-2
Michel Petrucciani Quintet | Michel Petrucciani Live | Blue Note | 780589-2
Sylvain Luc-Biréli Lagrène | Duet | Dreyfus Jazz Line | FDM 36604-2
Buddy Childers Big Band | Just Buddy's | Candid | CCD 79761

Looking Up Old Friends
Bheki Mseleku Group | Timelessness | Verve | 521306-2

Looking-Glass Man
Theo Bleckman & Kirk Nurock | Looking-Glass River | Traumton Records | 2412-2

Looking-Glass River
New Orchestra Workshop | The Future Is N.O.W. | Nine Winds Records | NWCD 0131

Lookout Farm
Dave Liebman Ensemble | Lookout Farm | ECM | 1039

Lookout For Hope
Steve Smith & Vital Information | Vitalive! | VeraBra Records | CDVBR 2051-2

Looks Bad Feels Good
Steve Smith Quintet | Vital Information | CBS | 25682

Loom
Bruce Dunlap Trio | The Rhythm Of Wings | Chesky | JD 92

Loop De Loop
Jeff Palmer Quartet | Island Universe | Soul Note | 121301-2

Loop The Cool
Tony Fruscella Septet | Tony's Blues | The Jazz Factory | JFCD 22805

Loop-D-Loop
Calvin Boze And His All-Stars | Calvin Boze:The Complete Recordings 1945-1952 | Blue Moon | BMCD 6014

Loopin' With Lea
Norbert Scholly Quartet | Norbert Scholly Quartet | Jazz Haus Musik | JHM 0086 CD

Loopline
World Saxophone Quartet | Rhythm And Blues | Nonesuch | 7559-60864-2

Loopy
Buddy Rich And His Orchestra | Big Swing Face | Pacific Jazz | 837989-2

Loose
Wallace Roney Trio | The Standard Bearer | Muse | MCD 5372

Loose As A Goose
Russ Freeman-Shelly Manne | One On One | Contemporary | CCD 14090-2

Loose As A Goose(alt.take)
Bill Evans Quintet | The 'Interplay' Sessions | Milestone | M 47066

Loose Bloose
Loose Blues | Milestone | MCD 9200-2

Loose Blues
Lutz Wichert Trio | Ambiguous | Edition Musikat | EDM 068

Loose But Cues
Eddie Harris Quartet | A Study In Jazz/Breakfast At Tiffany's | Vee Jay Recordings | VJ 020

Loose Calypso
John Scofield Quintet | Works For Me | Verve | 549281-2

Loose Canon
Dizzy Gillespie With The Phil Woods Quintet | Dizzy Gillespie Meets Phil Woods Quintet | Timeless | CD SJP 250

Loose Change
Melvin Rhyne Quartet | Kojo | Criss Cross | Criss 1164

Loose Changes
Dejan Terzic Quartet | Four For One | Naxos Jazz | 86036-2

Loose Ends
Mike Stern Group | Jigsaw | Atlantic | 7567-82027-2
Michael Beck Trio | Michael Beck Trio | JHM Records | JHM 3623

Loose Ends(alt.take)
Original Memphis Five | Original Memphis Five Groups | Village(Jazz Archive) | VILCD 016-2

Loose Foot
Tommy Dorsey And His Orchestra | Let There Be Jazz | RCA | NL 45175 AG

Loose Lips
Erroll Garner | Erroll Garner:Trio | Dreyfus Jazz Line | FDM 36719-2

Loose Nut
Play Piano Play | Spotlite | SPJ 129

Loose Trade
Count Basie-Roy Eldridge Septet | Loose Walk | Pablo | 2310928

Loose Walk
JATP All Stars | Jazz At The Santa Monica Civic '72 | Pablo | 2625701-2

Loose Wig
Lionel Hampton And His Orchestra | Lionel Hampton Vol.1-Steppin' Out | MCA | 1315

Loot To Boot
Erroll Garner | Yesterdays | Naxos Jazz | 8.120528 CD

Lopa Tola
J.J.Johnson-Kai Winding Quintet (Jay&Kai) | Kai Winding And Jay Jay Johnson | Bethlehem | BET 6026-2(BCP 76)

Lopin'
Count Basie And His Orchestra | The Indispensable Count Basie | RCA | ND 89758

Lord Ananea
Jimmy Dorsey And His Orchestra | The Uncollected:Jimmy Dorsey, Vol.2 | Hindsight | HSR 153

Lord Help Me To Be
Montreal Jubilation Gospel Choir | Jubilation II | Blues Beacon | BLU-1006 2

Lord I Want To Be A Christian
First Revolution Singers | A Cappella Gospel Anthology | Tight Harmony Records | TH 199404

Lord Lord Lord
Chris Barber's Jazz Band With Alex Bradford | Hot Gospel | Lake | LACD 39
Joe Zawinul Group | The Rise & Fall Of The Third Stream | 32 Jazz | 32133

Lord Lord Lord You've Sure Been Good To Me
George Lewis And His New Orleans Stompers | George Lewis And His New Orleans Stompers-Vol. 1 | Blue Note | 81205
George Lewis And His Original New Orleans Jazzmen | George Lewis In Stockholm,1959 | Dragon | DRCD 221
George Lewis And His Ragtime Band | Jazz At Vesper | Original Jazz Classics | OJCCD 1721-2(RLP 230)

Lord Of The Reedy River
Niels Lan Doky Trio | The Target | Storyville | SLP 4140

Lord, Let Me In The Lifeboat
Bunk Johnson-Sidney Bechet Sextet | Jazz Classics Vol.2 | Blue Note | 789385-2

Lord,Lord Am I Ever Gonna Know
The Feel Trio | Celebrated Blazons | FMP | CD 58

Lords Of The Low Frequencies
Don Lanphere Quintet Feat. Jon Pugh | From Out Of Nowhere | Hep | 2019

Lorelei
Sarah Vaughan With The Hal Mooney Orchestra | Sarah Vaughan Sings Gershwin | Verve | 557567-2
The Jazz Age Quintet And The Kammerorchester Schloß Werneck | Happy Birthday,Mr.Gershwin! | Balthasar Records | Balthasar 001(CD 584)

Lorelei's Lament
NAD | Ghosts | ITM Records | ITM 1454

Lorenzo's Soul
Don Patterson Quartet | The Genius Of The B-3 | Muse | MCD 5443

L'Orient Est Grand
The Enja Band | The Enja Band-Live At Sweet Basil | Enja | ENJ-8034 2

Loriken(Polska Altributed To Lorns Anders Ersson)
Tal Farlow Sextet | A Recital By Tal Farlow | Verve | MV 2586 IMS

Lorinesque
Louie Bellson Quintet | Skin Deep | Verve | 559825-2

Loro
Duo Brazil | Carioca | M.A Music | A 808-2
Egberto Gismonti Group | Works | ECM | 823269-2

Lorraine
Ornette Coleman Quartet | Tomorrow Is The Question | Original Jazz Classics | OJC20 342-2(S 7569)
Paul Bley Trio | Notes On Ornette | Steeplechase | SCCD 31437
Gust Williams Tsilis Quartet | Wood Music | Enja | ENJ-7093 2

Los Angeles
Brad Mehldau Trio | Places | Warner | 9362-47693-2
Ran Blake-Christine Correa | Round About | Music & Arts | CD 807

Los Angeles Blues
Peggy Lee With The Quincy Jones Orchestra | Blues Cross Country | Capitol | 520088-2
Russell Garcia And His Orchestra | Modern Jazz Gallery | Fresh Sound Records | KXL 5001(252282-1 Kapp)

Los Angeles(reprise)
Winanda Del Sur | Luny Y Mar | Challenge | CHR 70037

Los Bandidos
Heiner Goebbels-Alfred Harth Duo | Vom Sprengen Des Gartens | FMP | SAJ 20

Los Carnavales
Mongo Santamaria And His Rhythm Afro-Cubanos | Afro Roots | Prestige | PCD 24018-2(F 8012/8032)

Los Cuatro Generales(The Four Generales)
Ray Barretto And His Orchestra | Carnaval | Fantasy | FCD 24713-2

Los Dandy-
Essence All Stars | Afro Cubano Chant | Hip Bop | HIBD 8009

Los Dos Lorettas
Mike Mainieri Group | An American Diary:The Dreaming | NYC-Records | NYC 6026-2

Los Ejas De Mi Carreta
Arturo Sandoval And His Cuban Jazz Masters | Tumbaito | Inak | 2003

Los Feliz
Cal Tjader & Eddie Palmieri Orchestra | El Sonido Nuevo | Verve | 519812-2

Los Jibaros
Arrigo Cappelletti New Latin Ensemble | Pianure | SPLASC(H) Records | CD H 308-2

Los Mareados
Jacinte/Juan-José Mosalini Trio | Tango, Mi Corazón | Messidor | 15911 CD

Los Mariachis(The Street Musicians)
Charles Mingus Orchestra | New Tijuana Moods | Bluebird | ND 85644

Los Mariachis(The Street Musicians-alt.take)
New Tijuana Moods | Bluebird | ND 85644

Los Mariachis(The Street Musicians-alt.take-2)
Tijuana Moods(The Complete Edition) | RCA | 2663840-2

Los Mariachis(The Street Musicians-alt.take-3)
Tijuana Moods(The Complete Edition) | RCA | 2663840-2

Los Mariachis(The Street Musicians-short-take)
Gabor Szabo Quintet | The Sorcerer | Impulse(MCA) | IMP 12112

Los Matodoros
Gerald Wilson And His Orchestra | On Stage | Pacific Jazz | LN 10100

Los Olvidados
Winanda Del Sur | Luny Y Mar | Challenge | CHR 70037

Los Teenagers Bailan Changui
Dino Saluzzi-Anthony Cox-David Friedman | Rios | VeraBra Records | CDVBR 2156-2

Los Them
Mind Games | Pretty Fonky | Edition Collage | EC 482-2

Los Uncoolos
Wind Moments | Take Twelve On CD | TT 009-2
Mind Games With Claudio Roditi | Live | Edition Collage | EC 501-2
Rumbata | Canto Al Caribe | Timeless | CD JC 11019

Losing Hand
Holly Cole And Her Quartet | It Happened One Night | Metro Blue | 852699-0

Losing My Mind
Jack Sheldon-Ross Tompkins | On My Own | Concord | CCD 4529

Losing Temple
Thomas Horstmann-Martin Wiedmann Group | Decade | Factory Outlet Records | WO 95001

Losing You
Eric Dolphy Quartet | Stockholm Sessions | Enja | 3055 (807503)

Loss Of Love
Christoph Sänger Trio | Caprice | Laika Records | LK 94-057

Lost
Harvey Wainapel Quartet | At Home On The Road | Bassic-Sound | CD 011
Nelson Carlson Septet | R&B Guitars 1950-1954 | Blue Moon | BMCD 6018

Lost-
John Lee Hooker Band | Burnin' | Joy | 124

Lost A t Last
Phillip Wilson-Olu Dara Duo | Esoteric | Hat Art | Q

Lost And Found
Art Blakey And The Jazz Messengers | Art Blakey & The Jazz Messengers: Olympia, May 13th, 1961 | Laserlight | 36128
Dave Holland Quintet | Not For Nothin' | ECM | 1758(014004-2)
Enrico Rava Quintet | Andanada | Soul Note | SN 1064
Submedia | Submedia | Nine Winds Records | NWCD 0137
Tony Purrone Quartet | Electric Poetry | B&W Present | BW 028

Lost And Lookin'
Bev Kelly With The Jimmy Jones Quintet | Love Locked Out | Original Jazz Classics | OJCCD 1798-2(RLP 1182)

Lost April
Red Garland Trio | The P.C. Blues | Original Jazz Classics | OJCCD 898-2(PR 7752)

Lost Centuries
George Cables Quartet | Beyond Forever | Steeplechase | SCCD 31305

Lost Ends
John Lee Hooker Band | John Lee Hooker-The 1965 London Sessions | Sequel Records | NEB CD 657

Lost Forest
Jean-Luc Ponty Quintet | Aurora | Atlantic | SD 19158

Lost Generations
Pierre Favre Singing Drums | Souffles | Intakt Records | CD 049

Lost Hills Road(Song Of The Seeker)
Ned Rothenberg Trio | Port Of Entry | Intuition Records | INT 3249-2

Lost In A Blue Forest
Avery Sharpe Sextet | Unspoken Words | Sunnyside | SSC 1029 D

Lost In A Fog
Coleman Hawkins-Stanley Black | Coleman Hawkins In Europe | Timeless | CBC 1-006
Tommy Dorsey And His Orchestra | 1946 / 1947 | Jazz Anthology | JA 5118

Lost In Boston
Jens Bunge Group | With All My Heart | yvp music | CD 3060

Lost In Loving You
Miles Davis-Marcus Miller Group | Siesta(Soundtrack) | Warner | 7599-25655-2

Lost In Madrid(part 1-5)
Thomas Kessler Group | Untitled | Laika Records | LK 92-027

Lost In Main Street
Duke Ellington And His Famous Orchestra | The Complete Duke Ellington-Vol. 10 | CBS | CBS 88220

Lost In Meditation
Ella Fitzgerald With The Duke Ellington Orchestra | The Complete Ella Fitzgerald Song Books of Harold Arlen, Irving Berlin, Duke Ellington, George & Ira Gershwin, Jerome Kern, Johnny Mercer, Cole Porter And Rogers & Hart | Verve | 519832-2

Lost In The Abyss
Longineu Parsons Group | Work Song | TCB Records | TCB 94302

Lost In The Hours
Chico Hamilton Quintet | Chico Hamilton Quintet feat. Eric Dolphy | Fresh Sound Records | FSCD 1004

Lost In The Stars
Anita O'Day And Her Orchestra | Mello'day | GNP Crescendo | GNP 2126
Dave McKenna | A Handful Of Stars | Concord | CCD 4580
Dee Dee Bridgewater With Band | Dee Dee Bridgewater Sings Kurt Weil | EmArCy | 9809601
Dick Hyman | Dick Hyman In Recital | Reference Recordings | RR-84 CD
Günther Klatt-Tizian Jost | Art Of The Duo:Live In Mexico City | Tutu Records | 888184-2*
HR Big Band | The American Songs Of Kurt Weill | hr music.de | hrmj 006-01 CD
Jack Nimitz Quartet | Confirmation | Fresh Sound Records | FSR CD 5006
Roberta Piket Trio | Speak,Memory | Fresh Sound Records | FSNT 088 CD
Ross Tompkins Trio | Lost In The Stars | Concord | CJ 46
Singers Unlimited | A Capella 2 | MPS | 821860-2
Weslia Whitefield Trio | Live In San Francisco | Landmark | LCD 1531-2

Lost In The Stars-
Jane Ira Bloom | Art And Aviation | Arabesque Recordings | AJ 0107

Lost Keys
John Horler Duo/Trio | Lost Keys | Master Mix | CHECD 00109

Lost Life
Blasnost | Anything Blows | Acoustic Music Records | 319.1049.2

Lost Mind
Mose Allison Trio | Mose Allison:Greatest Hits | Original Jazz Classics | OJCCD 6004-2
The Word From Mose | Atlantic | 8122-72394-2
Mose Allison Sings The 7th Son | Prestige | PR20 7279-2
Local Color | Original Jazz Classics | OJCCD 457-2
Joe Lovano Septet | Universal Language | Blue Note | 799830-2

Lost Ocean
Lonnie Johnson | Another Night To Cry | Original Blues Classics | OBCCD 550-2(BV 1062)

Lost One
James Blood Ulmer With The Quartet Indigo | Harmolodic Guitar With Strings | DIW | DIW 878 CD
Lost Song
Azimuth | Azimuth '85 | ECM | 1298
Lost Song-
Dwayne Dolphin Quintet | Portrait Of Adrian | Minor Music | 801042
Lost Souls-
Terri Lyne Carrington Group | Jazz Is A Spirit | ACT | 9408-2
Lost Star
Vienna Art Orchestra | Inside Out | Moers Music | 02062/3 CD
Lost Time
Mike Stern Group | Standards(And Other Songs) | Atlantic | 7567-82419-2
Phil Minton | The Berlin Station | FMP | SAJ 57
Lost Woltz
John Surman | Road To Saint Ives | ECM | 1418(843849-2)
Lostwithiel
Paul Eßer-Gerd Dudek-Ali Haurand-Jiri Strivin | Jazz Und Lyrik:Schinderkarren Mit Buffet | Konnex Records | KCD 5108
Lösung-
Chris Connor With The Ronnie Ball Quartet | Late Show-At The Village Gate | Fresh Sound Records | FSR 705(FM 3035)(835430)
Lothlorien
Rein De Graaff-Dick Vennik Quartet | Cloud People | Timeless | SJP 191
Lotrecht In Die Tiefe
Roy Ayers Quintet | Hot | Ronnie Scott's Jazz House | JHCD 021
Lots Of Lovely Love
Curtis Jones | Americans In Europe Vol.2 | Impulse(MCA) | JAS 65(AS 37)
Lotta Colada
Ekkehard Jost Quartet | Deep | Fish Music | FM 007 CD
Lotta Libera
Andy Kirk And His Twelve Clouds Of Joy | Big Band Bounce & Boogie-Andy Kirk And His Clouds Of Joy:Walkin' & Swingin' | Affinity | AFS 1011
Lotto Graf Lambsdorff
Claudio Puntin Quartet | Mondo | Jazz Haus Musik | JHM 0134 CD
Lotus
Marcel Zanini Quintet | Lotus | Black & Blue | 33213
Phil Woods/Jim McNeely | Flowers For Hodges | Concord | CCD 4485
Lotus Blossom
Charles Lloyd Quintet | The Water Is Wide | ECM | 1734(549043-2)
Conexion Latina | Mambo Nights | Enja | ENJ-9402 2
Dado Moroni | The Way I Am | Jazz Connaisseur | JCCD 9518-2
Dave Frishberg Quintet | Getting Some Fun Out Of Life | Concord | CJ 37
Duke Ellington | And His Mother Called Him Bill | RCA | 2125762-2
Duke Ellington Trio | And His Mother Called Him Bill | RCA | 2125762-2
Guy Lafitte Trio feat. Wild Bill Davis | Lotus Blossom | Black & Blue | BLE 59.188 2
Jimmy Witherspoon With The Dutch Swing College Band | The Dutch Swing College Band Vol.1 | Philips | 839771-2
John Zorn-George Lewis-Bill Frisell | News For Lulu | Hat Art | CD 6005
Louis Mazetier | In Concert:What A Treat! | Jazz Connaisseur | JCCD 9522-2
Marian McPartland Quartet | Plays The Music Of Billy Strayhorn | Concord | CCD 4326
Max Roach Quintet | Drum Conversation | Enja | 4074-2
The Ritz feat.Clark Terry | Almost Blue | Denon Compact Disc | CY-77999
Dave Frishberg Quintet | Let's Eat Home | Concord | CCD 4402
Lotus Bud
Bud Shank Quintet | Jazz In Hollywood:Bud Shank/Lou Levy | Original Jazz Classics | OJCCD 1890-2(Nocturne NLP-2/NLP-10)
Lotus Feet
Remember Shakti | The Believer | Verve | 549044-2
George Winston | An Evening With Windham Hill:Live | Windham Hill | TA-C- 1026
Lotus Flower
Kenny Dorham Octet | Afro-Cuban | Blue Note | 746815-2
Lotus Land
Kenny Burrell With The Gil Evans Orchestra | Guitar Forms | Verve | 521403-2
Tito Puente Orchestra | Planet Jazz:Tito Puente | Planet Jazz | 2165369-2
Charles Lloyd Quartet | A Night In Copenhagen | Blue Note | 785104-2
Lou Easy
Patrick Williams Orchestra | Come On And Shine | MPS | 68199
Louanges
Le Petit Chien | Woof | Enja | 9122-2
Lou-Easy-An-I-A
Joe Darensbourg And His Dixie Fliers | Petite Fleur | Dixieland Jubilee | DJ 515
Loughin' To Keep From Cryin'
Louie Bellson And His Big Band | Live From New York | Telarc Digital | CD 83334
Louie B.
The Clarke/Duke Project | The Clarke/Duke Project | Epic | 468223-2
Louis Armstrong Counter-Pointing
Mississippi John Hurt | Today! | Vanguard | VMD 79220
Louis' Oldsmobile Song
Allen Lowe-Roswell Rudd Sextet | Dark Was The Night-Cold Was The Ground | Music & Arts | CD 811
Louise
Art Tatum | Masters Of Jazz Vol.8:Art Tatum | Storyville | SLP 4108
The Tatum Solo Masterpieces Vol.5 | Pablo | 2310790
Django Reinhardt-Stephane Grappelli Duo | The One And The Only | Decca | 6.28589 DP
Keith Ingham & Marty Grosz And Their Hot Cosmopolites | Going Hollywood | Stomp Off Records | CD 1323
Oscar Peterson Trio | Masters Of Jazz Vol.7 | RCA | NL 89721 DP
Stephane Grappelli Quintet | London Meeting | String | BLE 233852
Gabor Szabo Quintet | The Sorcerer | Impulse(MCA) | IMP 12112
Lou-ise
Kxutrio | Riff-ifi | Sound Aspects | sas CD 032
Louise Louise
Lem Johnson And His Washboard Band | Lem Johnson-Doc Sausage-Jo Jo Jackson | Blue Moon | BMCD 6004
Louise Louise Blues
John Hammond | The Best Of John Hammond | Vanguard | VCD 11/12
Louise(alt.take)
Benny Goodman And His Orchestra | Wrappin' It Up-The Harry James Years Part 2 | Bluebird | 63 66549-2
Louisiana
Andy J. Forest Band | Shuffle City | L+R Records | CDLR 42068
Bix Beiderbecke And His Gang | Riverboat Shuffle | Naxos Jazz | 8.120584 CD
Paul Whiteman And His Orchestra | The Indispensable Bix Beiderbecke(1924-1930) | RCA | ND 89572
Rob McConnell & The Boss Brass | Live In Digital | Seabreeze | CDSB 106(881884)
Louisiana 1927
Big Bill Broonzy | Blues Roots Vol.4 | Storyville | 6.23703 AG
Louisiana Fairytale
Barry Martyn's Down Home Boys | Barry Martyn's Down Home Boys | Sackville | SKCD2-3056
Louisiana Glide
Lew Stone And His Orchestra | The Bands The Matter | Eclipse | ECM 2047
Louisiana Man
Mino Cinelu-Kenny Barron | Swamp Sally | Verve | 532268-2
Louisiana Sunset
London Ragtime Orchestra | Easy Winners | LRO Records | LRO CD 501
Louisville Lodge Meeting
Louis Jordan And His Tympany Five | Louis Jordan-Let The Good Times Roll: The Complete Decca Recordings 1938-1954 | Bear Family Records | BCD 15557 IH
Arthur Gibbs And His Gang | Victor Jazz History Vol.5:Harlem Jazz(1921-28) | RCA | 2128559-2
Louizalaan
Louis Sclavis Group | Chine | IDA Record | 012 CD
Lounging At The Waldorf
Conjure | Cab Calloway Stands In For The Moon | American Clave | AMCL 1015-2
Lourdement Gai
Mario Bauzá And The Afro-Cuban Jazz Orchestra | 944 Columbus | Messidor | 15828 CD
Lou's Blues
Art Blakey And The Jazz Messengers | A Night At Birdland Vol. 3 | Blue Note | 300192(BNJ 61002)
Lou's Tune
Jimmy Patrick Quintet | You Are My Audience | BELL Records | BLR 84036
Love
Berry Lipman Orchestra | Easy Listening Vol.1 | Sonia | CD 77280
Chet Baker Quintet And Strings | Chet Baker And Strings | CBS | 21142
Ernestine Anderson With The Monty Alexander Trio | Sunshine | Concord | CCD 4109
George Duke Group | George Duke & Feel | MPS | 68023
John Coltrane Quartet | First Meditation | Impulse(MCA) | GRP 11182
Ray Brown-Jimmy Rowles | As Good As It Gets | Concord | CCD 4066
Sandro Cerino Action Quartet | Che Fine Fanno I Personaggi Dei Sogni | SPLASC(H) Records | H 190
Susannah McCorkle With The Allen Farnham Orchestra | From Bessie To Brazil | Concord | CCD 4547
Love-
Leroy Jenkins Quartet | Space Minds,New Worlds,Survival America | Tomato | 2696512
Love Affair-Forever And Never
Barbara Dennerlein Quintet | That's Me | Enja | ENJ-7043 2
Love Affair-The Ballad
Tok Tok Tok | Love Again | Einstein Music | EM 01081
Love Again
Wal-Berg Et Son Jazz Francais | Jazz In Paris:Django Reinhardt-Django Et Compagnie | EmArCy | 549241-2 PMS
Junior Parker Group | The Best Of The Blues Singers Vol.2 | LRC Records | CDC 9007
Love All The Hurt Away
Nils Landgren Funk Unit | Paint It Blue:A Tribute To Cannonball Adderley | ACT | 9243-2
Love All,Serve All
Dick Griffin Quintet | A Dream For Rahsaan & More | Konnex Records | KCD 5062
Love And Deception
Etta James & The Roots Band | Burnin' Down he House | RCA | 3411633-2
Love And Happiness
Larry Coryell Quintet | The Coryells | Chesky | JD 192
Love And Hate
Jackie McLean Quintet | Destination Out | Blue Note | 870171-7
Love And Kisses
Ella Fitzgerald With Chick Webb And His Orchestra | Ella Fitzgerald Vol.1-Forever Young | Swingtime(Contact) | ST 1006
Love And Laughter
Niels Lan Doky Quartet | The Truth | Storyville | STCD 4144
Love And The Weather
Charlie Ventura Quintet | The New Charlie Ventura In Hi-Fi | Harlequin | HQ 2009(Baton BL 1202) IMS
Love Ballad(single version)
Oscar Peterson Quartet | Oscar In Paris | Telarc Digital | CD 83414(2)
Love Ballade
A Summer Night In Munich | Telarc Digital | CD 83450
Love Begins
Dannie Richmond Quartet | Ode To Mingus | Soul Note | 121005-2
Love Blues
John Lee Hooker Band | House Of The Blues | Chess | CHD 9258(872282)
Love Calculator
Al Sears And His Orchestra | Sear-iously | Bear Family Records | BCD 15668 AH
Love Call
Jimmy Ponder Sextet | Soul Eyes | Muse | MCD 5514
Love Castle
Chick Corea Quartet | Compact Jazz: Chick Corea | Polydor | 831365-2
Chick Corea-Gary Burton | Native Sense-The New Duets | Stretch Records | SCD 9014-2
Love Channel
Andreas Maile Quartet | Mailensteine | Satin Doll Productions | SDP 1022-1 CD
Love Chant
Anthony Braxton | Four Pieces | Dischi Della Quercia | Q 28015
Charles Mingus Jazz Workshop | Pithecanthropus Erectus | Atlantic | 7567-81456-2
Charles Mingus Quintet | Charles Mingus-The Complete Debut Recordings | Debut | 12 DCD 4402-2
Charles Mingus Quintet Plus Max Roach | The Charlie Mingus Quintet Plus Max Roach | Debut | VIJ 5011 IMS
Love Chant(alt.take)
Fred Wesley Group | Comme Ca | Minor Music | 801020
Love Choir
Lee Konitz-Charlie Mariano-Jackie McLean-Gary Bartz Group | Altissimo | West Wind | WW 2019
Love Come Back To Me
Makoto Ozone Trio | Nature Boys | Verve | 531270-2
Irene Kral With Alan Broadbent | Where Is Love? | Choice | CHCD 71012
Love Come On Stealthy Fingers
Bob Wilber And Friends | What Swing Is All About | Nagel-Heyer | CD 035
Love Comes Along Once In A Lifetime
Vince Jones Group | Here's To The Miracles | Intuition Records | INT 3198-2
Love Comes Back
Steve Lacy Group | Nine Futurities-Part 1 | Hat Art | CD 6031
Love Continues
Coleman Hawkins With The Berries | Coleman Hawkins In Europe | Timeless | CBC 1-006
Love Cry New York
Bill O'Connell Group | Love For Sale | Jazz City | 660.53.019
Love Dance
James Blood Ulmer Trio | Odyssey | CBS | 25602
Woody Shaw And His Orchestra | Love Dance | Muse | MR 5074
Love Dong From Apache
J.B.Lenoir Blues Band | J. B. Lenoir | Chess | 427003
Love Dreams
Louis Bellson And His Big Band | 150 MPH | Concord | CCD 4036
Love Ends
Jack Walrath And The Masters Of Supense | Hip Gnosis | TCB Records | TCB 01062
Love Eyes
Albert Ayler Sextet | Love Cry | Impulse(MCA) | GRP 11082
Love Flower
Yusef Lateef With Eternal Wind And The 'Kölner Rundfunk Orchester' | The African American Epic Suite:Music For Quintet And Orchestra | ACT | 9214-2
Love For All-
La Vienta | Night Dance | Telarc Digital | CD 83359
Love For Living
Dexter Gordon Quartet | Live At The Montmartre Jazzhus | Black Lion | BLCD 7606-2
Love For Sale
Andy Martin With The Metropole Orchestra | Andy Martin & Metropole Orchestra | Mons Records | MR 874802
Art Tatum | Art Tatum-The Complete Pablo Solo Masterpieces | Pablo | 7 PACD 4404-2
Art Tatum:20th Century Piano Genius | Verve | 531763-2
Art Tatum:20th Century Piano Genius | Verve | 531763-2
The Art Tatum Solo Masterpieces | Pablo | 2625703
Art Tatum Trio | The Best Of Art Tatum | Pablo | 2405418-2
Big Band Ulm | All Of Us | yvp music | 3014
Billy Taylor Trio With Candido | The Billy Taylor Trio With Candido | Original Jazz Classics | OJCCD 015-2(P 7051)
Cal Tjader Quartet | Our Blues | Fantasy | FCD 24771-2
Cal Tjader Quintet | Concerts In The Sun | Fantasy | FCD 9688-2
Concerts In The Sun | Fantasy | FCD 9688-2
Concerts In The Sun | Fantasy | FCD 9688-2
Concert On The Campus | Original Jazz Classics | OJC 279(F 8044)
Cannonball Adderley Quintet | Miles Davis:The Blue Note And Capitol Recordings | Blue Note | 827475-2
Carlos Barbosa-Lima | Plays The Music Of Luiz Bonfa And Cole Porter | Concord | CCD 42008
Charlie Parker Quintet | Verve Jazz Masters 28:Charlie Parker Plays Standards | Verve | 521854-2
The Verve Years(1952-54) | Verve | 2-2523 IMS
The Cole Porter Song Book | Verve | 823250-1
Chet Baker Quartet | Live In Chateauvallon 1978 | France's Concert | FCD 128
Chet Baker Trio | Candy | Sonet | SNTF 946(941424)
Chet's Choice | Criss Cross | Criss 1016
Denny Zeitlin | Maybeck Recital Hall Series Volume Twenty-Seven | Concord | CCD 4572
Derek Smith Trio | Love For Sale | Progressive | PRO 7002 IMS
Dexter Gordon Quartet | Dexter Gordon:The Complete Blue Note Sixties Sessions | Blue Note | 834200-2
Diane Schuur With Orchestra | In Tribute | GRP | GRP 20062
Dianne Reeves With Band | I Remember | Blue Note | 790264-2
Dianne Reeves With Orchestra | Three Ladies Of Jazz:Live In New York | Jazz Door | JD 12102
Dinah Washington And Her Band | Verve Jazz Masters 40:Dinah Washington | Verve | 522055-2
Dinah Washington With Orchestra | Mad About The Boy-The Best Of Dinah Washington | Mercury | 512214-2
Dizzy Gillespie Quintet | The Great Modern Jazz Trumpet | Festival | 402151
Ella Fitzgerald With The Buddy Bregman Orchestra | The Cole Porter Song Book | Verve | 2683044 IMS
Ella Fitzgerald Sings The Cole Porter Songbook | Verve | 537257-2
Ella Fitzgerald Sings The Cole Porter Songbook Vol.2 | Verve | 821990-2
Ella Fitzgerald With The Paul Smith Quartet | Mack The Knife-The Complete Ella In Berlin | Verve | 519564-2
Ellis Marsalis Trio | Heart Of Gold | CBS | CK 47509
Ernestine Allen With The King Curtis Group | Let It Roll | Original Blues Classics | OBCCD 539-2(TRU 15004)
Erroll Garner | Relaxin' With Erroll | Vogue | 655008
George Shearing With The Montgomery Brothers | Wes Montgomery-The Complete Riverside Recordings | Riverside | 12 RCD 4408-2
George Shearing-Brian Torff Duo | On A Clear Day | Concord | CCD 4132
Guido Manusardi | Concerto | SPLASC(H) Records | CD H 437-2
Hank Jones Trio | Hank Jones Favors | Verve | 537316-2
Herb Ellis-Joe Pass | The Jazz Giants Play Cole Porter:Night And Day | Prestige | PCD 24203-2
Two For The Road | Original Jazz Classics | 2310714
JATP All Stars | Jazz At The Philharmonic 1957 | Tax | CD 3703-2
Jeffery Smith Group | A Little Sweeter | Verve | 537790-2
Jenny Evans And Band | Girl Talk | ESM Records | ESM 9306
Girl Talk | Enja | ENJ-9363 2
Live At The Allotria | BELL Records | BLR 90003
Jimmy Raney Sextet | Too Marvelous For Words | Biograph | BLP 12060
Joe Pass | Virtuoso Live! | Pablo | 2310948-2
Joe Pass With The NDR Big Band | Joe Pass In Hamburg | ACT | 9100-2
Joe Zawinul Quartet | The Beginning | Fresh Sound Records | FSR-CD 142(882885)
Johannes Rediske Quintet | Jumpin' At The Badewanne | Bear Family Records | BCD 16172 AH
Re-Disc Bounce | Bear Family Records | BCD 16119 AH
Johnny Lytle Septet | Possum Grease | Muse | MCD 5482
Jude Swift Group | Music For Your Neighborhood | Nova | NOVA 8917-2
Kurt Weil Sextet | Jazz In Switzerland 1930-1975 | Elite Special | 9544002/1-4
Lisa Ekdahl With The Peter Nordahl Trio | When Did You Leave Heaven | RCA | 2143175-2
Lloyd Glenn Trio | After Hours | Pathe | 1546641(Aladdin)
Lorenzo Petrocca Organ Trio | Milan In Minor | Jardis Records | JRCD 20136
Lucy Reed With Orchestra | This Is Lucy Reed | Original Jazz Classics | OJCCD 1943-2(F 3243)
Manfred Junker Quartet | Cole Porter-Live! | Edition Collage | EC 531-2
Manhattan Jazz Quintet | Bed Time Eyes-Original Soundtrack Recording | Paddle Wheel | K 28P 6451
Miles Davis Sextet | Circle In The Round | CBS | 467898-2
'58 Miles | CBS | 467918-2
MJT+3 | MJT+3 | Vee Jay Recordings | VJ 002
Mose Allison Trio | High Jinks! The Mose Allison Trilogy | CBS | J3K 64275
NDR Big Band With Guests | 50 Years Of NDR Big Band:Bravissimo II | ACT | 9259-2
Oscar Peterson Trio | Oscar Peterson Plays The Cole Porter Song Book | Verve | 821987-2
The Song Is You-The Best Of The Verve Songbooks | Verve | 531558-2
Verve Jazz Masters 16:Oscar Peterson | Verve | 516320-2
At Zardis' | Pablo | 2CD 2620118
Paris Washboard | 10'eme Anniversaire:Love For Sale | Stomp Off Records | CD 1326
Ruby Braff-Ellis Larkins | Duets Vol.1 | Vanguard | VCD 79609-2
Sammy Price Trio | Americans Swinging In Paris:Sammy Price | EMI Records | 539650-2
Scott Wendholt Quintet | The Scheme Of Things | Criss Cross | Criss 1078
Shelly Manne Trio | Gemini Three | Eastworld | CP 32-5426
Soesja Citroen Group | Songs For Lovers And Losers | Challenge | CHR 70034
Stan Greig Trio | Blues Every Time | Calligraph | CLG LP 004 IMS
Stan Kenton And His Orchestra | By Request Vol.1 | Creative World | ST 1036
Stanley Turrentine Quintet | Up At Minton's | Blue Note | 828885-2
Love For Sale (Concept 1)
Art Tatum Trio | Tatum-Hampton-Rich...Again | Pablo | 2310775
Love For Sale (Concept 2)
Charlie Parker Quintet | Bird On Verve-Vol.8:Charlie Parker | Verve | 817449-1 IMS
Love For Sale(take 1-5)
Gunter Hampel-Christian Weider Duo | Solid Fun | Birth | CD 044
Love For Two
Don Bennett Quintet | Chicago Calling | Candid | CCD 79713
Love Has Gone Away
Ruth Brown With Orchestra | I'll Wait For You | Official | 6004
Love In 5-
| A Tribute To Bing Crosby-Paramount's Greatest Singer | Concord | CCD 4614
Love In Bloom
Fred Wesley Group | Comme Ca | Minor Music | 801020
Love In New Orleans
Gerry Mulligan Quartet | Swiss Radio Days Jazz Series:Gerry Mulligan | TCB Records | TCB 02092
Love In Outer Space
Sun Ra And His Arkestra | Calling Planet Earth | Freedom | FCD 741071
Love In Silent Amber
Johnny Hodges Orchestra | The Complete Duke Ellington-Vol.11 | CBS | CBS 88242
Love In The Open

TITELVERZEICHNIS

Peter Herborn's Acute Insights | Peter Herborn's Acute Insights | JMT Edition | 919017-2

Love In Tune(For B.A. part 1-4)

Peter Herborn's Acute Insights | JMT Edition | 919017-2

Love In Tune(For B.A.)

Robert Johnson | Robert Johnson-King Of The Delta Blues | CBS | 493006-2

Love In Vain

Sammy Vomacka | Easy Rider | BELL Records | BLR 84019

Love In Vain(alt.take)

Dee Daniels With The Metropole Orchestra | Wish Me Love | Mons Records | MR 874769

Love Irgendwie

Baker Gurvitz Army | Live In London 1975 | Traditional Line | TL 1311

Love Is

Joyful | New Orleans Gospel | Mardi Gras Records | MG 5009

Love Is A Dangerous Necessity

Blind Gilbert Trio | Percy Humphrey | American Music | AMCD-88

Love Is A Many-Splendored Thing

Clifford Brown-Max Roach Quintet | Jazz Gallery:Clifford Brown | RCA | 2114176-2
Gray Sargent Trio | Shades Of Gray | Concord | CCD 4571
Keith Jarrett Trio | Standards In Norway | ECM | 1542(521717-2)
Kirk Lightsey And His Trio With Freddy Hubbard | Temptation | Timeless | CD SJP 257
Clifford Brown-Max Roach Quintet | Brownie-The Complete EmArCy Recordings Of Clifford Brown | EmArCy | 838306-2

Love Is A Many-Splendored Thing(alt.take 1)

Brownie-The Complete EmArCy Recordings Of Clifford Brown | EmArCy | 838306-2

Love Is A Many-Splendored Thing(alt.take 2)

Clifford Brown And Max Roach At Basin Street | Verve | 589826-2

Love Is A Many-Splendored Thing(alt.take)

Clifford Brown And Max Roach At Basin Street | Verve | 589826-2

Love Is A Many-Splendored Thing(breakdown)

Artie Shaw And His Orchestra | Original Recordings 1937/1938 | Festival | Album 248

Love Is A Simple Thing

Herbie Mann Quartet | Flamingo Vol.2 | Bethlehem | BET 6007-2(BCP 24)
Lorenzo Petrocca Quartet Feat. Bruno De Filippi | Insieme | Edition Musikat | EDM 002

Love Is A Splendored Thing

Johnny Mars & The Oakland Boogie | Johnny Mars & The Oakland Boogie | Big Bear | 146405

Love Is Blue

Bill Ware And The Club Bird All-Stars | Long And Skinny | Knitting Factory Works | KFWCD 131

Love Is For The Very Young

Sandy Mosse Quartet With Strings | Relaxin' With... | Fresh Sound Records | LP 639(Argo)

Love Is Gonna Getcha

Patti Austin And Her Band | Patti Austin Live | GRP | GRP 96822

Love Is Just Around The Corner

Eddie Condon All Stars | That Toodlin' Town-Chicago Jazz Revisited | Atlantic | 90461-1 TIS
Firehouse Five Plus Two | Plays For Lovers | Good Time Jazz | GTCD 12014-2
Hampton Hawes Quartet | Hampton Hawes:Four! | Contemporary | COP 022
Harry Roy And His Orchestra | May Fair Nights | Saville Records | SVL 171 IMS
Mel Tormé With The George Shearing Trio | An Evening At Charlie's | Concord | CCD 4248
Wild Bill Davison With The Alex Welsh Band | Memories | Jazzology | JCD-201

Love Is Just Around The Corner-

Eddie Condon And His Windy City Seven | Commodore Classics In Swing | Commodore | 9031-72723-2

Love Is More Thicker Than Forget

Weslia Whitefield Trio | Live In San Francisco | Landmark | LCD 1531-2

Love Is Never Out Of Season

James Spaulding Quartet | The Smile Of The Snake | HighNote Records | HCD 7006

Love Is On Your Side

Frank Kimbrough Quintet | The Herbie Nichols Project | Soul Note | 121313-2

Love Is Real

Dave Bartholomew And His Band | Shrimp And Gumbo | Pathe | 1566311

Love Is Stronger Than Pride

Ella Fitzgerald With The Nelson Riddle Orchestra | Ella Sings Gershwin-Vol. 2 | Metro | 2682023 IMS

Love Is The Answer

Jenny Evans And Her Quintet | Gonna Go Fishin' | Enja | ENJ-9403 2
Michael Carvin | Drum Concerto At Dawn | Mapleshade | 03732

Love Is The Key

Aretha Franklin With The Ray Bryant Combo | Ella,Billie,Sarah,Aretha,Mahalia | CBS | 473733-2

Love Is The Sweetest Thing

Ziggy Elman And His Orchestra | Zaggin' With Ziggy | Affinity | CD AFS 1006

Love Is The Tender Trap - (Love Is) The Tender Trap

Jimmy Dorsey And His Orchestra | Perfidia | Laserlight | 15768

Love Is The Tender Trap -> The Tender Trap

Love Is The Thing

Etta Jones And Her Quartet | Something Nice | Original Jazz Classics | OJCCD 221-2(P 7194)
Lena Horne With The Lennie Hayton Orchestra | Lena Horne:Love Songs | RCA | 2663604-2
Annabelle Wilson With The Jerry Granelli-Jane Ira Bloom Group | On Music | ITM-Pacific | ITMP 970071

Love Is Waiting

Nancy King-Steve Christofferson With The Metropole Orchestra | Straight Into Your Heart | Mons Records | MR 874778

Love I've Found You

Wynton Kelly Trio | Wrinkles-Wynton Kelly & Friends | Affinity | AFF 151

Love I've Found You(alt.take)

Bheki Mseleku Group | Beauty Of Sunrise | Verve | 531868-2

Love Joy

David Murray Big Band | David Murry Big Band | CBS | CK 48964

Love Just Took A Bow

Abbey Lincoln With Her Band | Who Used To Dance | Verve | 533559-2

Love Lament

Cornell Dupree Group | Bop 'N' Blues | Kokopelli Records | KOKO 1302

Love Letter

Westbrook & Company | Platterback | PAO Records | PAO 10530

Love Letters

Bobby Hutcherson Quartet | Mirage | Landmark | LCD 1529-2
Dave McKenna | Giant Strides | Concord | CCD 4099
Gogi Grant With The Dennis Farnon Orchestra | Welcome To My Heart | Fresh Sound Records | ND 42126
Johnny Smith Quartet | The Johnny Smith Foursome | Fresh Sound Records | FSR 581(Roost 2223)
Julie London With Orchestra | Blue Valentines | Blue Note | 781331-2
MJT+3 | Walter Perkins' MJT+3/Make Everybody Happy | Vee Jay Recordings | VJ 009
Nat Pierce And His Orchestra | Big Band At The Savoy Ballroom | RCA | 2130073-2
Rob Schneiderman Trio | Standards | Reservoir | RSR CD 126
Sonny Rollins Trio | St.Thomas:Sonny Rollins In Stockhom 1959 | Dragon | DRCD 229
In Sweden 1959 | Ingo | 9
Steve Gibbons Band | Birmingham To Memphis | Linn Records | AKD 019

Love Lies

Ralph Sutton | Stridin' High | Jazz Connaisseur | JCCD 9728-2
Maybeck Recital Hall Series Volume Thirty | Concord | CCD 4586

Love Life

Marty Cook Quintet | Red, White, Black And Blue | Enja | 5067-2

Love Like Ours

Duke Ellington And His Famous Orchestra | Duke Ellington & His Famous Orchestra | Forlane | UCD 19003

Love Line

Lennie Tristano | The New Tristano | Atlantic | 7567-80475-2

Love Lines

Ed Schuller & Band | The Eleventh Hour | Tutu Records | 888124-2*

Love Lite

Al Bowlly With The Ray Noble Orchestra | The Classic Years In Digital Stereo: Al Bowlly With Ray Noble | CDS Records Ltd. | REB 649

Love Lost

Julian Priester Group | Love Love | ECM | 1044

Love Machine

Roland Kirk Quintet | Live In Paris 1970 Vol.1 | France's Concert | FCD 109

Love Makes The Change

Freddy Cole With The Cedar Walton Trio And Grover Washington Jr. | Love Makes The Changes | Fantasy | FCD 9681-2
Lambert, Hendricks And Ross | The Swingers | Blue Note | AFF 131

Love Me

Joe Venuti-Zoot Sims Sextet | Joe Venuti And Zoot Sims | Chiaroscuro | CR 142
Zoot Sims Quartet | Getting Sentimental | Choice | CHCD 71006
Anita Carmichael Quintet | Anita Carmichael | Lipstick Records | LIP 8944-2

Love Me Like A Man

Sarah Jane Morris Group | Blue Valentine | Ronnie Scott's Jazz House | JHCD 038

Love Me Or Leave Me

Art Tatum | Art Tatum-The Complete Pablo Solo Masterpieces | Pablo | 7 PACD 4404-2
The Art Tatum Solo Masterpieces | Pablo | 2625703
Benny Goodman And His Orchestra | Benny Goodman's 1934 Dodge All-Star Recordings(Complete) | Circle | CCD-111
Bert Ambrose And His Orchestra | Happy Days | Saville Records | SVL 147 IMS
Bud Freeman All Stars | The Bud Freeman All Stars | Original Jazz Classics | OJC 183(SV 2012)
Fats Waller | Piano Solos | RCA | ND 89741
Gerry Mulligan Quartet | Planet Jazz:Gerry Mulligan | Planet Jazz | 2152070-2
Gene Norman Presents The Original Gerry Mulligan Tentet And Quartet | GNP Crescendo | GNPD 56
Gerry Mulligan Quartet | Pacific Jazz | 300001(PJ 1)
Gerry Mulligan:Pleyel Concert Vol.2 | Vogue | 21409432
Helen Humes With The Marty Paich Orchestra | Songs I Like To Sing | Original Jazz Classics | OJCCD 171-2
Kenny Clarke And His Orchestra | Kenny Clarke | Swing | SW 8411 IMS
Lena Horne With The Lennie Hayton Orchestra | Lena Horne:Love Songs | RCA | 2663604-2
Lester Young Quartet | Pres And Teddy And Oscar | Verve | 2-2502 IMS
Miles Davis Quintet | Tune Up | Prestige | P 24077
Mundell Lowe Quintet | A Grand Night For Swinging | Original Jazz Classics | OJCCD 1940-(RLP 238)
Nana Mouskouri With The Berlin Radio Big Band | Nana Swings | Mercury | 074394-2
Newport Jazz Festival All-Stars | European Tour | Concord | CCD 4343
Nina Simone Quartet | Verve Jazz Masters 20:Introducing | Verve | 519853-2
Nina Simone-The 60s Vol.2:Mood Indigo | Mercury | 838544-2 PMS
Nina Simone Trio | My Baby Just Cares For Me | Charly | CR 30217
Ruby Braff And His Buddies | Controlled Nonchalance At The Regattabar Vol.1 | Arbors Records | ARCD 19134
Ruby Braff Trio | Cornet Chop Suey | Concord | CCD 4606
Wild Bill Davis Super Trio | That's All | Jazz Connaisseur | JCCD 9005-2
Mel Tormé With The George Shearing Trio | A Vintage Year | Concord | CJ 341

Love Me Tender

Houston Person Quintet | The Party | Muse | MCD 5451

Love Me To Death

Koko Taylor With The Jimmy Rogers Blues Band | South Side Lady | Black & Blue | BLE 59.542 2

Love Me Tomorrow

Trigger Alpert's All Stars | Trigger Happy! | Fresh Sound Records | RLP 12-225(Riverside)

Love Me Tonight

Michael Bolivar Group | Hangin' Out | Clarity Recordings | CCD-1009

Love Motel-

Eric Felten-Jimmy Knepper Group | T-Bop | Soul Note | 121196-2

Love Nest

Jo Jones-Milt Hinton | Percussion And Bass | Fresh Sound Records | FSR-CD 0204
Tal Farlow Quartet | The Tal Farlow Album | Verve | MV 2584 IMS

Love No.1

Keith Jarrett Trio | Chick Corea-Herbie Hancock-Keith Jarrett-McCoy Tyner | Atlantic | ATL 50326

Love Nocturne

Betty Carter With The Geri Allen Trio | Feed The Fire | Verve | 523600-2

Love Of My Life

Artie Shaw And His Orchestra | Mixed Bag | Musicmasters | 65119-2

Love On My Mind

Ray Charles-Milt Jackson Quintet | Soul Meeting | Atlantic | SD 1360

Love On The Edge Of Life

George Shearing-Mel Torme | An Elegant Evening | Concord | CCD 4294

Love Or Infatuation

Jo Swan And Her Quartet | Primal Schmaltz | Timbre | TRCD 004

Love Poem For Donna

Peter Brötzmann | 14 Love Poems | FMP | 1060

Love Power

Thomas Karl Fuchs | Piano Meditation I | Edition Collage | EC 481-2

Love Reborn

Flora Purim And Her Sextet | Butterfly Dreams | Original Jazz Classics | OJCCD 315-2
Sonny Rollins And His Orchestra | The Way I Feel | Original Jazz Classics | OJCCD 666-2(M 9074)

Love Remembered

Willie 'The Lion' Smith | The Memoirs Of Willie 'The Lion' Smith | RCA | 2126415-2

Love Samba

McCoy Tyner Quintet | Atlantis | Milestone | MCD 55002-2

Love Saves The Day

Lonnie Plaxico Group | Iridescence | Muse | MCD 5427

Love Someone You

Lutz Häfner Quartet | Lutz Häfner | Mons Records | MR 874804

Love Someone You Like

Anthony Williams Quintet | Spring | Blue Note | 746135-2

Love Song

Bobby Lyle Group | Pianomagic | Atlantic | 7567-82346-2
Carl Kress | Pioneers Of Jazz Guitar 1927-1939 | Retrieval | RTR 79015
Klaus Kreuzeder & Franz Benton | Big little Gigs: First Takes Live | Trick Music | TM 0112 CD
Morgana King And Her Quintet | Everything Must Change | Muse | MCD 5190
The Vee-Jays | Harbour Blues | Crosscut | CCR 1017

Love Song For The Dead Che

Gunther Klatt & New York Razzmatazz | Volume One:Fa Mozzo | Tutu Records | 888158-2*

Love Song From A Movie Never Made

Günther Klatt & New York Razzmatazz | Fa Mozzo | Tutu Records | 888138-2

Love Speaks Louder Than Words

Branford Marsalis Quartet | Renaissance | CBS | 460229-2

Love Stone

Buddy Rich And His Orchestra | Buddy Rich In London | RCA | PL 43695

Love Streams

John Coltrane Quartet | A Love Supreme | France's Concert | FCD 106

Love Supreme(for John Coltrane)

McCoy Tyner Big Band | Uptown/Downtown-Recorded Live At The Blue Note | Milestone | MCD 9167-2

Love Takes Changes

Boyd Raeburn And His Orchestra | Man With The Horns | Savoy | WL 70534 (809300)

Love That Boy

Ella Fitzgerald With The Hank Jones Trio | Ella Fitzgerald:The Royal Roost Sessions | Cool & Blue | C&B-CD 112

Love Theme From Farewell To Maria

Dizzy Gillespie Quintet | The Cool World/Dizzy Goes Hollywood | Verve | 531230-2

Love Theme From Pictures Of The Sea

Bill Evans | Compact Jazz: Bill Evans | Verve | 831366-2 PMS

Love Theme From Spartacus

Eddie Gomez Trio | Live In Moscow | B&W Present | BW 038
Barrett Deems Big Band | Groovin' Hard | Delmark | DE 505

Love Theme From Superman(Can You Read My Mind)

Earl Klugh Trio With The Royal Philharmonic Orchestra | Sounds And Visions | Warner | 9362-45158-2

Love Theme From The Robe

Astrud Gilberto With Orchestra | The Shadow Of Your Smile | Verve | 2304540

Love Thy Neighbor

John Coltrane Quintet | John Coltrane-The Prestige Recordings | Prestige | 16 PCD 4405-2
Paulinho Da Costa Orchestra | Happy People | Original Jazz Classics | OJCCD 783-2(2312102)

Love Till The End Of Time

Doris Day With Orchestra | The Uncollected:Doris Day | Hindsight | HSR 200

Love Train

Duke Jordan Trio | Lover Man | Steeplechase | SCS 1127
Bill Gaither | Bill Gaither(Leroy's Buddy) 1935-1941 | Story Of Blues | CD 3503-2

Love Utopia

Dee Dee Bridgewater With Her Trio | Keeping Tradition | Verve | 519607-2

Love Vibrations

Frank Catalano Quintet | Cut It Out!?! | Delmark | DE 501

Love Walked In

Bob Rockwell Trio | The Bob Rockwell Trio | Steeplechase | SCS 1242
Dave Brubeck Quartet | Jazz At The College Of The Pacific Vol.2 | Original Jazz Classics | OJCCD 1076-2
Interchanges '54 | CBS | 467917-2
Live | Bandstand | BDCD 1538
Freddy Cole With Band | To The End Of The Earth | Fantasy | FCD 9675-2
George Benson Quartet | Love Walked In | Magnum Music Group | CDTB 088
George Shearing With The Montgomery Brothers | Wes Montgomery-The Complete Riverside Recordings | Riverside | 12 RCD 4408-2
Gogi Grant With The Dennis Farnon Orchestra | Welcome To My Heart | Fresh Sound Records | ND 42126
Hank Jones Trio | Essence | dmp Digital Music Productions | CD 480
Jack McDuff Quartet | The Concert McDuff | Prestige | PRCD 24270-2
Jiggs Whigham With The Netherlands Metropole Orchestra | Love Walked In | Koch Jazz | 3-6920-2
Loren Schoenberg And His Jazz Orchestra | Out Of This World | TCB Records | TCB 98902
Lou Levy Trio | My Old Flame | Fresh Sound Records | FSR-CD 312
My Old Flame | Fresh Sound Records | FSR-CD 0312
Martial Solal Quartet | Martial Solal-The Vogue Recordings Vol.1:Trios & Quartet | Vogue | 21115142(875744)
Oscar Peterson Trio | Oscar Peterson:The Gershwin Songbooks | Verve | 529698-2
Pierre Boussaguet Trio | Charme | EmArCy | 538468-2
Ray Brown Trio | Some Of My Best Friends Are The Piano Players | Telarc Digital | CD 83373
Sir Roland Hanna | Maybeck Recital Hall Series Volume Thirty-Two | Concord | CCD 4604
Sonny Clark Trio | Dial S For Sonny | Blue Note | 0675621
Stan Getz Quartet | Stan Getz:The Golden Years Vol.2(1958-1961) | Moon Records | MCD 040-2
Toots Thielemans With Orchestra | Bluesette | Polydor | 2482218 IMS

Love Walked In-

Modern Jazz Quartet | The Complete Modern Jazz Quartet Prestige & Pablo Recordings | Prestige | 4PRCD 4438-2
The MJQ Box | Prestige | 7711-2

Love Walked In(alt.take)

Allan Botschinsky/Niels-Henning Orsted-Pedersen | Duologue | M.A Music | NU 206-3

Love Waltz

First Brass | First Brass | M.A Music | NU 158-3
Torsten Zwingenberger & Band With Guests | Open Sunroof | Blackbird Records | BD 41012

Love Warriors

Jan Somers Band | Here We Are | Timeless | CD SJP 397

Love What You Doin'

Roy Ayers Group | Roy Ayers-The Essential Groove:Live | Ronnie Scott's Jazz House | JHCD 035

Love Won't Let Me Wait

Bing Crosby And Rosemarie Clooney With The Billy May Orchestra | Fancy Meeting You Here | RCA | 2663859-2

Love Won't Let You Get Away

Rosemary Clooney And Her Sextet | Sings The Music Of Jimmy Van Heusen | Concord | CCD 4308

Love Won't Let You Get Away(alt.take 1)

Bing Crosby And Rosemarie Clooney With The Billy May Orchestra | Fancy Meeting You Here | RCA | 2663859-2

Love Won't Let You Get Away(alt.take 2)

Ornette Coleman & Prime Time Band | Of Human Feelings | Antilles | AN 2001(802385)

Love You Like Mad

John Scofield Quintet | Works For Me | Verve | 549281-2

Love You Long Time

Anders Lindskog Trio | Fine Together | Touché Music | TMcCD 010

Love You Madly

Barbara Sutton Curtis | Old Fashioned Love | Sackville | SKCD2-2042
Ella Fitzgerald And Her All Stars | Love Songs:The Best Of The Song Books | Verve | 531762-2
The Complete Ella Fitzgerald Song Books of Harold Arlen, Irving Berlin, Duke Ellington, George & Ira Gershwin, Jerome Kern, Johnny Mercer, Cole Porter And Rogers & Hart | Verve | 519832-2
Ella Fitzgerald With The Oscar Peterson Quartet And Ben Webster | Ella Fitzgerald Sings The Duke Ellington Song Book Vol.2 | Verve | 2615033 IMS
Hal Galper Trio | Tippin' | Concord | CCD 4540
Kenny Burrell With The Don Sebesky Orchestra | Night Song | Verve | 2304539 IMS
Oscar Peterson Trio | Compact Jazz: Oscar Peterson Plays Jazz Standards | Verve | 833283-2
Ray Brown Trio | Live At Starbucks | Telarc Digital | CD 83502

Love You Madly-

Kenny Burrell Trio | Live At The Village Vanguard | Muse | 600623(882378)

Love You 'Til You're Money's Gone Blues

The Legendary Blues Band | Life Of Ease | Edsel | 6.25170 AP

Love, The Mystery Of

Curtis Fuller Quintet | Blues-ette | Savoy | SV 0127(ST 13006)

Love,Put On Your Faces

Art Blakey And The Jazz Messengers | Anthenagin | Prestige | P 10076

Loved One

Albert King Blues Band | Lovejoy | Stax | SCD 8517-2(STS 2040)

Lovejoy,Ill.

Adelhard Roidinger Septet | Schattseite | ECM | 1221

Lovelee

Art Hodes Trio | Art Hodes Trios & Quartete | Jazzology | JCD-113

Loveless Love

Duke Ellington-Johnny Hodges All Stars | Back To Back | Verve | 521404-2
Earl Hines | Four Jazz Giants:Earl Hines Plays Tributes To W.C.Handy,Hoagy Carmichael And Louis Armstrong | Solo Art | SACD-111/112
Jack Teagarden And His Orchestra | Jazz Gallery:Jack Teagerden | RCA | 2114175-2
Louis Armstrong And His All Stars | The Louis Armstrong Selection | CBS | 467278-2

Loveless Love(rehersal sequence)

Roland Kirk Quartet | The Inflated Tear | Atlantic | 8122-75207-2

Lovellevelliloqui

The Inflated Tear | Atlantic | 7567-90045-2
Chuck Wayne Trio | Morning Mist | Original Jazz Classics | OJCCD 1097-2(P-7367)

Lovely

Green Cosmos | Abendmusiken | amf records | amf 1018
Joe Puma Trio | Shining Hour | Reservoir | RSR 102

Lovely How I Let My Mind Float

Tommy Dorsey And His Orchestra | The Original Sounds Of The Swing Era Vol. 8 | RCA | CL 05521 DP

Lovely Sky Boat

Bert Ambrose And His Orchestra | Saturday Night | Decca | DDV 5003/4 DT

Lovely Weather We're Having

Louis Armstrong And His All Stars | Louis Armstrong-The Complete RCA Victor Recordings | RCA | 2668682-2

Lovemachine

| Big Band Swing | Fresh Sound Records | LSP 15624(Epic LN 3663)

Lover

Art Tatum | Art Tatum:Memories Of You | Black Lion | BLCD 7608-2
Art Tatum Trio | Art Tatum:Complete Capitol Recordings | Definitive Records | DRCD 11192
Bernd Lhotzky-Colin Dawson | Sophisticated | ART BY HEART | ABH 2003 2
Braff/Barnes Quartet | Salutes Rodgers And Hart | Concord | CCD 6007
Charlie Parker With The Joe Lipman Orchestra | Charlie Parker With Strings:The Master Takes | Verve | 523984-2
Charlie Parker Big Band | Verve | 559835-2
Charlie Ventura Quartet | Charlie Ventura Complete 1951-1952 Verve Studio Recordings | Definitive Records | DRCD 11202
Dan Faulk Quartet | Focusing In | Criss Cross | Criss 1076
Dick Hyman | Dick Hyman In Recital | Reference Recordings | RR-84 CD
Ella Fitzgerald With The Buddy Bregman Orchestra | The Complete Ella Fitzgerald Song Books of Harold Arlen, Irving Berlin, Duke Ellington, George & Ira Gershwin, Jerome Kern, Johnny Mercer, Cole Porter And Rogers & Hart | Verve | 519832-2
Erroll Garner Trio | The Erroll Garner Selection | CBS | 471624-2
Great Guitars | Great Guitars | Concord | CCD 4023
John Coltrane Quintet | The Last Trane | Original Jazz Classics | OJC 394(P 7378)
John Coltrane-The Prestige Recordings | Prestige | 16 PCD 4405-2
John Eaton | It Seems Like Old Times | Chiaroscuro | CR 174
Louis Armstrong And His All Stars | Rockin' Chair | Topline Records | TOP 119
Oscar Peterson Trio | The Song Is You-The Best Of The Verve Songbooks | Verve | 531558-2
Paul Smith Trio | Intensive Care | Pausa | PR 7167(952078)
Ray Brown Trio | Some Of My Best Friends Are The Piano Players | Telarc Digital | CD 83373
Red Garland Quartet | Rediscovered Masters, Vol.1 | Original Jazz Classics | OJCCD 768-2
Sonny Clark Quintet | Blue Valentines | Blue Note | 781331-2

Lover-

Rahsaan Roland Kirk & The Vibration Society | Rahsaan Rahsaan | Atlantic | ATL 40127(SD 1575)

Lover Bird

| Sound Sun Pleasure | Evidence | ECD 22014-2

Lover Come Back To Me

Al Porcino Big Band | In Oblivion | Jazz Mark | 106 Digital
Allan Vaché-Harry Allen Quintet | Allan And Allan | Nagel-Heyer | CD 074
Anita O'Day With The Johnny Mandel Orchestra | Trav'lin Light | Verve | 2304584 IMS
Art Pepper Quartet | Today | Original Jazz Classics | OJCCD 474-2
Art Pepper Quintet | Art Pepper Quintet Live At Donte's 1968 | Fresh Sound Records | FSCD 1039/2
Art Tatum | The Tatum Solo Masterpieces Vol. 2 | Pablo | 2310729
Artie Shaw And His Orchestra | This Is Artie Shaw Vol. 2 | RCA | NL 89411 DP
Benny Golson Group | Tenor Legacy | Arkadia Jazz | 70742
Billie Holiday And Her All Stars | Recital By Billie Holiday | Verve | 521868-2
Billie Holiday And Her Band | Jazz Live & Rare: Billie Holiday Live 1937/56 | Jazzline | ???
Billie Holiday With Eddie Heywood And His Orchestra | Billie Holiday:The Complete Commodore Recordings | GRP | AFS 1019-8
Billie Holiday With The Mal Waldron Trio | Ella Fitzgerald, Billie Holiday And Carmen McRae At Newport | Verve | 559809-2
Cal Tjader Sextet | Cal Tjader's Latin Kick | Original Jazz Classics | OJCCD 642-2(F 8033)
Charles McPherson Quartet | Siku Ya Bibi | Mainstream | MD CDO 713
Clifford Brown And Art Farmer With The Swedish All Stars | Jazz Gallery:Clifford Brown | RCA | 2114176-2
Dennis Farnon And His Orchestra | Caution! Men Swinging | Fresh Sound Records | LPM 1495(RCA)
Dizzy Gillespie And His Orchestra | Groovin' High | Naxos Jazz | 8.120582 CD
Dizzy Gillespie Sextet | Live At The Village Vanguard | Blue Note | 780507-2
Eddie Metz And His Gang | Tough Assignment:A Tribute To Dave Tough | Nagel-Heyer | CD 053
Ella Fitzgerald And Barney Kessel | Jazz Collection:Ella Fitzgerald | Laserlight | 24397
Ella Fitzgerald And Her Orchestra | Live From The Roseland Ballroom New York 1940 | Jazz Anthology | 550032
Gillespie-Stitt-Getz Septet | Diz And Getz | Verve | 2-2521 IMS
Hal & Peggy Serra With Oscar Pettiford | Jazzville | Dawn | DCD 114
Harry James And His Orchestra | The Uncollected:Harry James, Vol.6 | Hindsight | HSR 150
Henri Chaix Trio | Jive At Five | Sackville | SKCD2-2035
Jeff Jerolamon Quartet | Jeff Jerolamon's Swing Thing! | Candid | CCD 79538
Jimmy Smith Trio | Incredible Jimmy Smith Vol.3 | Blue Note | 300106(1525)
John Coltrane Quintet | Black Pearls | Original Jazz Classics | OJC 352(P 7316)
Black Pearls | Prestige | P 24037
Kenny Davern Trio | Strechin' Out | Jazzology | JCD-187
Lester Young And His Band | Lester Young:The Complete 1936-1951 Small Group Sessions(Studio Recordings-Master Takes),Vol.3 | Blue Moon | BMCD 1003
Louis Armstrong And His All Stars | New Orleans Louisiana | Traditional Line | TL 1319
The Best Live Concert | Festival | ???
Oscar Peterson-Ray Brown Duo | Tenderly | Verve | MV 2662 IMS
Ralph Burns And His Ensemble | Bijou | Fresh Sound Records | FSR 2014(Bethlehem BCP 68)
Stan Getz Quintet | Stan Getz Plays | Verve | 2304387 IMS
Stephane Grappelli With The Diz Disley Trio | Violinspiration | MPS | 68058
The Concord All Stars | Take 8-Jazz Festival Japan '87 | Concord | CJ 347
Al Bowlly With The Novelty Group | On The Sentimental Side | Decca | DDV 5009/10

Lover Come Back To Me-

Billie Holiday With Eddie Heywood And His Orchestra | Billie Holiday:The Complete Commodore Recordings | GRP | AFS 1019-8

Lover Man Express

Giants Of Jazz | Live | Jazz Door | JD 1277

Lover Man(dedicated to Mario Schiano)

Duke Ellington And His Orchestra | Duke Ellington:The Complete RCA-Victor Mid-Forties Recordings(1944-1946) | RCA | 2663394-2

Lover Man(Oh,Where Can You Be?)

Albert Dailey Trio | That Old Feeling | Steeplechase | SCCD 31107
Allotria Jazz Band | Swing That Music | Elite Special | 73232
Archie Shepp Quartet feat. Annette Lowman | Lover Man | Timeless | CD SJP 287
Arnie Lawrence Quartet | Reneval | Palo Alto | PA 8033
Art Pepper | New York Album | Galaxy | GXY 5154
Art Pepper-George Cables Duo | Goin' Home | Original Jazz Classics | GXY 5143
Art Tatum-Buddy DeFranco Quartet | The Tatum Group Masterpieces | Pablo | 2625706
Base Line | Baseline:Standards | Challenge | CHR 70023
Bill Coleman Quintet | Americans Swinging In Paris:Don Byas | EMI Records | 539655-2
Bill Evans Trio | Live In Europe Vol.1 | EPM Musique | FDC 5712
Bill Evans Trio With Jeremy Steig | What's New | Enoch's Music | 57271053
Billie Holiday And Her All Stars | The Billie Holiday Song Book | Verve | 823246-2
Billie Holiday And Her Band | Billie Holiday Broadcast Performances Vol.1 | ESP Disk | ESP 3002-2
Billie Holiday With Orchestra | Billie Holiday Radio & TV Broadcast(1953-56) | ESP Disk | ESP 3003-2
Billie Holiday With Toots Camarata And His Orchestra | Lover Man | MCA | 2292-52317-1
Bud Shank Quartet | Live At The Haig | Concept | VL 2 IMS
C.I.Williams Quintet | When Alto Was King | Mapleshade | 04532
Cannonball Adderley Quintet | Cannonball Adderley:Sophisticated Swing-The EmArCy Small Group Sessions | Verve | 528408-2
Carmen McRae And Her Sextet | Carmen McRae Sings Lover Man | CBS | CK 65115
Cecil Payne Sextet | Payne's Window | Delmark | DE 509
Charlie Parker And The Swedish All Stars | Complete Bird In Sweden | Definitive Records | DRCD 11216
Charlie Parker Quintet | Bird's Eyes-Last Unissued Vol.11(Bird In France 1949) | Philology | W 622.2
Chet Baker Quartet | Jazz In Paris:Chet Baker Quartet Plays Standards | EmArCy | 014378-2 PMS
Jazz At Ann Arbor | Fresh Sound Records | 054 2602311(Pacific Jazz PJ 1203) (835282)
Coleman Hawkins Quartet | Masters Of Jazz Vol.12:Coleman Hawkins | Storyville | STCD 4112
Conte Candoli Quintet | West Coast Wailers | Fresh Sound Records | 1268(Atlantic)
Count Basie And His Orchestra With Sarah Vaughan | Count Basie-Sarah Vaughan | Roulette | 8372412
Dinah Washington With The Don Costa Orchestra | Drinking Again | M&M Records | R 25183(Roulette)
Don Byas Quartet | Lover Man | Vogue | 2115470-2
Duke Ellington And His Orchestra | Duke Ellington:The Complete RCA-Victor Mid-Forties Recordings(1944-1946) | RCA | 2663394-2
Live At Click Restaurant Philadelphia 1948-Vol.2 | Raretone | 5003 FC
Eddie Harris Group | A Tale Of Two Cities | Night Records | VNCD 3(887046)
Ella Fitzgerald With The Duke Ellington Orchestra | The Stockholm Concert 1966 | Pablo | 2308242-2
Ella Fitzgerald With The Marty Paich Orchestra | Whisper Not | Verve | 589947-2
Eric Gale Quintet | In A Jazz Tradition | Mercury | 836369-2
Franco D'Andrea Trio | Airegin | Red Records | 123252-2
Gerry Mulligan Quartet With Lee Konitz | Complete 1953 The Haig Performances | The Jazz Factory | JFCD 22861
Guido Manusardi/Red Mitchell | Together Again | Soul Note | 121181-2
Herbie Mann-Bill Evans Quartet | That's Jazz Vol.8: Nirvana | Atlantic | ATL 50238
Hot Mallets | Hot Mallets...Live | Jazzcharge | JC 8302
Italian Instabile Orchestra | Litania Sibilante | Enja | ENJ-9405 2
J.J.Johnson's All Stars | The Be Bop Legends | Moon Records | MCD 072-2
Jimmy Bruno Trio With Scott Hamilton | Live At Birdland-II | Concord | CCD 4810
Jimmy Smith All Stars | House Party | Blue Note | 524542-2
Jimmy Smith Trio | Groovin' At Smalls' Paradise | Blue Note | 499777-2
Groovin' At Smalls' Paradise Vol.2 | Blue Note | 300222(1586)
Joe Newman And His Orchestra | Joe Newman With Woodwinds | Fresh Sound Records | FSR 663(Roulette R 52014)
Joe Pass | Virtuoso No.4 | Pablo | 2640102
Joe Pass/Niels-Henning Orsted-Pedersen Duo | Chops | Original Jazz Classics | OJCCD 786-2(2310830)
Joe Sachse/David Moss/George Lewis | Berlin Tango | ITM Records | ITM 1448
Karl Berger-Paul Shigihara | Karl Berger + Paul Shigihara | L+R Records | CDLR 45045
Kenny Burrell & The Jazz Guitar Band | Generation | Blue Note | BT 85137
Kurt Edelhagen All Stars | Deutsches Jazz Fesival 1954/1955 | Bear Family Records | BCD 15430
Landes Jugend Jazz Orchester Hessen | Magic Morning | Mons Records | CD 1905
Lawrence Marable Quartet | Tenorman | Fresh Sound Records | 054 2608851(Jazz West JWLP 8)
Lee Konitz & The Gerry Mulligan Quartet | Konitz Meets Mulligan | Pacific Jazz | 746847-2
Lee Konitz Quartet | Round & Round | Musicmasters | 65140-2
Lee Konitz With Strings | Strings For Holiday:A Tribute To Billie Holiday | Enja | ENJ-9304 2
Lee Konitz With The Bert Van Den Brink Trio | Dialogues | Challenge | CHR 70053
Lee Konitz-Gerry Mulligan Quintet | California Cool | Blue Note | 780707-2
Lee Morgan Quintet | The Cooker | Blue Note | 300187(1578)
McCoy Tyner Quartet | Double Trios | Denon Compact Disc | CY-1128
New Jazz Group Hannover | Deutsches Jazz Festival 1954/1955 | Bear Family Records | BCD 15430
Niels Lan Doky Quartet | Paris By Night | Soul Note | 121206-2
Oliver Jones Trio | Just In Time | Justin Time | JUST 120/1-2
Paul Bley Trio | My Standard | Steeplechase | SCCD 31214
Phil Woods & Space Jazz Trio | Live At The Corridonia Jazz Festival 1991 | Philology | W 211.2
Randy Brecker-Wolfgang Engstfeld Quartet | Mr. Max! | Nabel Records:Jazz Network | CD 4637
Ray Bryant | Alone With The Blues | Original Jazz Classics | OJC 249(NJ 8213)
Rickey Woodard Quartet | California Cooking No.2 | Candid | CCD 79762
Rob Mullins Quartet | Jazz Jazz | Nova | NOVA 8918-2
Rolf Kühn Group | Internal Eyes | Intuition Records | INT 3328-2
Rosemary Clooney With The Scott Hamilton-Warren Vache Sextet | Tribute To Billie Holiday | Concord | CCD 4081
Sandy Lomax With The Martin Schrack Trio | Songs From The Jazz Age | Workshop Records | WOR 201(CD 583)
Sarah Vaughan And Her Trio | Compact Jazz:Sarah Vaughan Live! | Mercury | 832572-2 PMS
Sarah Vaughan And The Count Basie Orchestra | Ballads | Roulette | 537561-2
Sarah Vaughan With Dizzy Gillespie And His All Star Quintet | Sarah Vaughan:Lover Man | Dreyfus Jazz Line | FDM 36739-2
Sarah Vaughan With Her Trio | Compact Jazz: Sarah Vaughan | Mercury | 830699-2
Shirley Horn Trio | Violets For Your Furs | Steeplechase | SCCD 31164
Shirley Scott Trio | Like Cozy | Prestige | PCD 24258-2
Slide Hampton & The Jazz Masters | Dedicated To Diz | Telarc Digital | CD 83323
Sonny Stitt And His West Coast Friends | Atlas Blues Blow And Ballade | Eastworld | CP 32-5428
Stan Getz With The Bill Evans Trio | But Beautiful | Jazz Door | JD 1208
Stephane Grappelli-Michel Petrucciani Quartet | Flamingo | Dreyfus Jazz Line | FDM 36580-2
Steve Davis Quartet | Songs We Know | dmp Digital Music Productions | CD 3005
Ted Brown Quartet | Preservation | Steeplechase | SCCD 31539
Teddy Edwards Quartet | La Villa-Live In Paris | Verve | 523495-2
Tete Montoliu Trio | Tootie's Tempo | Steeplechase | SCCD 31108
Thelonious Monk | Thelonious Monk Collection | Black Lion | BLCD 7601-2
Wardell Gray Quintet | Wardell Gray Memorial Vol.2 | Original Jazz Classics | OJCCD 051-2(P 7009)
Warne Marsh Quintet | Jazz Of Two Cities | Fresh Sound Records | FSR-CD 342
Intuition | Capitol | 852771-2

Lover Man(Oh,Where Can You Be?)-

Cecil Payne Quintet | Bright Moments | Spotlite | SPJ LP 21
Modern Jazz Quartet | The Modern Jazz Quartet At Music Inn With Sonny Rollins,Vol.2 | Atlantic | 7567-80794-2
Warne Marsh Quintet | Intuition | Capitol | 852771-2

Lover(Mono Version)

Ella Fitzgerald With The Buddy Bregman Orchestra | Ella Fitzgerald Sings The Rodgers And Hart Song Book | Verve | 537258-2

Lover(Stereo Version)

The Legendary Blues Band With Guests | Red Hot 'N' Blue | Edsel | RounderRAS 2035

Lovers

Lindsay Cooper Group | Oh Moscow | Victo | CD 015

Lover's Infinteness

Cadence All Stars | Lee's Keys Please | Timeless | CD SJP 284

Lover's X-Dream

Toshinori Kondo & Ima | Red City Smoke | JA & RO | JARO 4173-2

Lovers,Hold Up

Kölner Saxophon Mafia | Place For Lovers | Jazz Haus Musik | JHM 0082 CD

Loverwoman

Brownie McGhee & Sonny Terry Sextet | Climbin' Up | Savoy | SV 0256(MG 12118)

Love's Away

Ben Webster With The Teddy Wilson Trio | Music For Loving:Ben Webster With Strings | Verve | 527774-2
Nighthawks | CitizenWayne | Call It Anything | CIA 4004-2

Love's Eyes

Mingus Big Band | Tonight At Noon...Three Or Four Shades Of Love | Dreyfus Jazz Line | FDM 36633-2

Love's Fury

Barbara Lea And The Legendary Lawson-Haggart Jazz Band | You're The Cats! | Audiophile | ACD-252

Love's Growth

Lonnie Plaxico Group | Plaxico | Muse | MCD 5389

Love's Melody(Melodie Au Crepuscule)

George Robert-Dado Moroni | Youngbloods | Mons Records | CD 1897

Love's Mood

Django Reinhardt And The Quintet Du Hot Club De France | Django Reinhardt Portrait | Barclay | DALP 2/1939
Don Friedman Trio | Circle Waltz | Original Jazz Classics | SMJ 6082

Love's So Far Away

Donald Byrd Orchestra | Donald Byrd:Blue Breakbeats | Blue Note | 494708-2

Love's Usury

Bertha 'Chippie' Hill With Louis Armstrong And Richard M. Jones | Louis Armstrong And The Blues Singers 1924-1930 | Affinity | AFS 1018(6)

Lovesong No.1

Centrifugal Funk | Centrifugal Funk | Legato | 652508

Lovethings

Peter Herborn Group With The WDR Big Band | Traces Of Trane | JMT Edition | 514002-2

Lovie Joe

Lightnin' Hopkins | The Great Electric Show And Dance | America | AM 013/014

Lovin' Man

Muddy Waters Group | Back In His Early Days, Vol.1+2 | Red Lightnin' | SC 001/2

Lovin' Sam(The Sheik Of Alabam')

Syncopated Six | Le Jazz En France Vol.1:Premiers Jazz Bands | Pathe | 1727251

Loving Mother For You

Brian Blade Group | Fellowship | Blue Note | 859417-2

Loving Without Asking

Jackie And Roy | High Standards | Concord | CJ 186

Loving You

Tom Schuman Group | Extremities | GRP | GRP 96252
Vanessa Rubin With Band | Girl Talk | Telarc Digital | CD 83480

Low And Behold

The New Oscar Pettiford Sextet | The New Oscar Pettiford Sextet | Original Jazz Classics | OJC 112(DLP 8)

Low And Inside

Rüdiger Carl | Rüdiger Carl Solo | FMP | CD 86

Low Bottom

Stan Kenton And His Orchestra | The Radio Years: Stan Kenton And His Orchestra 1941-Vol.2 | Hindsight | HSR 124

Low Brown

Rex Stewart And His Feetwarmers | Django Reinhardt All Star Sessions | Capitol | 531577-2

Low Cotton

Django Reinhardt:Djangology | EMI Records | 780659-2

Low Down

Masha Bijlsma Band With Bob Malach | Lebo | Jazzline | JL 11145-2

Low Down & Dirty

George Benson Quintet | Blue Benson | Polydor | 2391242 IMS

Low Down And Dirty

George Benson Sextet | Talkin' Verve:George Benson | Verve | 553780-2

Low Down And Dirty Blues

Big Bill Broonzy | Blues Legacy 1: Big Bill Broonzy-Lonesome Road Blues | Vogue | 512501

Low Down Dirty Shame

Jimmy Witherspoon With The Robben Ford Quartet | Live:Jimmy Witherspoon & Robben Ford | ARG Jazz | 2133292-2

Low Down Dog

Big Joe Turner And His Band | Have No Fear Big Joe Turner Is Here | Savoy | WL 70822 (809333)
Big Joe Turner With Pete Johnson's All Stars | Roots Of Rock And Roll Vol. 2: Big Joe Turner | Savoy | SJL 2223 (801199)

Low Flame

Bruce Dunlap Trio | The Rhythm Of Wings | Chesky | JD 92

Low Gravy

Oscar Pettiford Septet | Jazz Legacy Baden Baden Unreleased Radio Tapes | Jazzline | ???

Low Key Lightly

Charlie Haden Quartet West | Always Say Goodbye | Verve | 521501-2

Low Key Lightly(Variation On The Theme Of Here To Zero)

Bud Shank And Trombones | Cool Fool | Fresh Sound Records | FSR CD 507

Low Life
Count Basie And His Orchestra | Hall Of Fame | Verve | MV 2645 IMS
Donald Byrd Quintet | Fuego | Blue Note | 300376
Zoot Sims Quintet | Quietly There-Zoot Sims Plays Johnny Mandel | Original Jazz Classics | OJCCD 787-2(2310903)
Bud Shank And Trombones | Cool Fool | Fresh Sound Records | FSR CD 507

Low Life(alt.take)
Philadelphia Jerry Ricks & Oscar Klein | Low Light Blues | L+R Records | LR 42007

Low Pressure Liquid Colorado-
Lloyd Glenn Quartet | Old Time Shuffle | Black & Blue | BLE 59.077 2

Lowdown And Flyin' High
Art Hodes' Back Room Boys | Hot Jazz On Blue Note | Blue Note | 835811-2

Low-Down Thing Or Two
First House | Cantilena | ECM | 1393

Low-Down(Toytown)
Joe Morris Trio | Symbolic Gesture | Soul Note | 121204-2

Lowena
Trio KoKoKo | Good Night | Creative Works Records | CW LP 1002

Lower East Side
Jeanfracois Prins Trio With Lee Konitz | All Around Town | TCB Records | TCB 99402

Lower East Side Story
John Wolf Brennan | The Beauty Of Fractals | Creative Works Records | CW CD 1017-1
Howard Johnson's Nubia | Arrival | Verve | 523985-2

Lowered
Bertha 'Chippie' Hill With Louis Armstrong And Richard M. Jones | Louis Armstrong And The Blues Singers 1924-1930 | Affinity | AFS 1018(6)

Low-Liness-
Big Joe Turner With Axel Zwingenberger | Let's Boogie Woogie All Night Long | Vagabond | VRCD 8.79012

Lown Down Dog
Hanno Giulini-Eva Mayerhofer | Anyone | Acoustic Music Records | 319.1171.2

Loxodrome
Steps Ahead | Steps Ahead | Elektra | 7559-60168-2
Andy Middleton Group | Nomad's Notebook | Intuition Records | INT 3264-2

Loyalsock
Roscoe Mitchell Trio | Roscoe Mitchell | Nessa | N 14/15

Lu
Nguyen Le Trio With Guests | Bakida | ACT | 9275-2

Lü
Attila Zoller Quintet | When It's Time | Enja | ENJ-9031 2

Lu And Shu
Frank Vignola Trio With Davis Grisman | Let It Happen | Concord | CCD 4625

Luana
John Zorn Naked City | Naked City-Grand Guignol | Avant | AVAN 002

Luanna's Theme
Grant Green With Orchestra | The Final Comedown(Soundtrack) | Blue Note | 581678-2
Flute Force Four | Flutistry | Black Saint | 120164-2

Luau
Bobo Stenson Trio | Underwear | ECM | 1012

Lucero
Cal Tjader's Modern Mambo Quintet(Sextet) | Mambo With Tjader | Original Jazz Classics | OJCCD 271-2(F 3202)
Galardini-Lessmann-Morena Trio | Insolitudine | SPLASC(H) Records | H 155

Lucid
Art Erios | Thebe Stofar Terios | Nueva Records | NC 3010

Lucien's Blues
Henning Wolter Trio With Guests | Years Of A Trilogy | double moon | DMCHR 71021

Lucien's Sweet Suite
Kenny Barron Orchestra | Lucifer | Muse | MR 5070

Lucignolo
Nels Cline Trio | Silencer | Enja | ENJ-6098 2

Lucille
Joe Turner With The Pee Wee Crayton-Sonny Stitt Quintet | Everyday I Have The Blues | Original Jazz Classics | OJCCD 634-2(2310818)
Sonny Rollins Group | Nucleus | Original Jazz Classics | OJCCD 620-2(M 9064)

Lucinda
William Galison-Mulo Franzl Group | Midnight Sun | Edition Collage | EC 508-2

Lucita
Chet Baker Quartet | Cools Out | Ace Records | CDBOP 013

Lucius Lou
Bireli Lagrene Quartet | Blue Eyes | Dreyfus Jazz Line | FDM 36591-2

Luck Be A Lady
Eddie Costa Quartet | Guys And Dolls Like Vives | Verve | 549366-2
Ken Peplowski Quartet | A Good Reed | Concord | CCD 4767

Lucky
Vladimir Estragon | Three Quarks For Muster Mark | TipToe | TIP-888803 2

Lucky Day
Teddy Stauffer Und Seine Original Teddies | Hot Jazz & Swing Mit Teddy Stauffer's Original Teddies | Elite Special | 9522002

Lucky Dog
Tummy Young's Big Seven | The Classic Swing Of Buck Clayton | Original Jazz Classics | OJCCD 1709-2(RLP 142)

Lucky In Love
Sarah Vaughan And Her Trio | Sarah Vaughan At Mister Kelly's | EmArCy | 832791-2 PMS

Lucky Life
Miff Mole's Molers | That's A Plenty | Memo Music | HDJ 4112

Lucky Loser
Vienna Art Orchestra | Artistry In Rhythm-A European Suite | TCB Records | TCB 01102

Lucky Number
Mr.Acker Bilk And His Paramount Jazz Band | The Traditional Jazz Scene Vol.1 | Teldec | 2292-43996-2

Lucky Strikes
Lucky Thompson-Sammy Price Quintet | Jazz In Paris:Sammy Price And Lucky Thompson-Paris Blues | EmArCy | 013038-2

Lucky To Be Me
Bill Evans | Peace Piece And Other Pieces | Milestone | M 47024
Blossom Dearie Trio | Blossom Dearie Sings Comden And Green | Verve | 589102-2
Buddy DeFranco Trio | Do Nothing Till You Hear From Us! | Concord | CCD 4851
Matthew Fries Quintet | Song For Today | TCB Records | TCB 20752
Trudy Desmond With The Roger Kellaway Trio | Tailor Made | The Jazz Alliance | TJA 10015

Lucky To Be Me-
Monica Zetterlund With The Bill Evans Trio | The Complete Bill Evans On Verve | Verve | 527953-2

Lucky To Be Me(alt.take)
Muggsy Spanier And His Band | Muggsy Spanier | Storyville | SLP 4020

Lucky You'r Right, I'm Wrong -> You'r Right, I'm Wrong

Lucky's Lament
Klaus Ignatzek | Plays Beatles Songs | Nabel Records:Jazz Network | CD 4643

Lucy In The Sky With Diamonds
Scenario | Jazz The Beatles | Organic Music | ORGM 9729
Joe Lutcher's Jump Band | Joe Joe Jump | Charly | CRB 1038

Lucy Lou
Perry Bradford's Jazz Phools | Louis Armstrong Vol.1-Young Louis 'The Side Man' | MCA | 1301

Lucyna
Don Byron Quartet | Romance With The Unseen | Blue Note | 499545-2

'Lude
Jimmy Rodgers Blues Band | Sloppy Drunk | Black & Blue | BLE 59.544 2

Ludens Ludentis
Frank Kroll Quintet | Landscape | dml-records | CD 014

Ludi Garden
Humphrey Lyttelton-Acker Bilk Band | More Humph & Acker | Calligraph | CLGCD 030

Lueurs Perdues
Gumpert-Malfatti-Oxley Trio | Ach Was!? | FMP | 0870

Lugar Comun I
Michael Riessler & Singer Pur with Vincent Courtois | Ahi Vita | ACT | 9417-2

Lugebat
Andreas Willers | Hie & Als Auch | FMP | 0880

Lugubre
Artie Shaw And His Gramercy Five | I Can't Get Started | Verve | MV 2559 IMS

Luhsbluhs
Hilaria Kramer 6 | Trigon | SPLASC(H) Records | H 191

Luigi
Manfredo Fest Quartet | Just Jobim | dmp Digital Music Productions | CD 524

Luiza
Carlos Barbosa-Lima/Sharon Isbin Duo | Brazil With Love | Concord | CCD 4320
Maximilian Geller Quartet feat. Melanie Bong | Maimilian Geller Goes Bossa Encore | Edition Collage | EC 505-2
Nicola Stilo Quartet | Errata Corrige | SPLASC(H) Records | CD H 440-2
Vic Juris Trio | Songbook | Steeplechase | SCCD 31843

Luki
Benny Carter And His Orchestra | Opening Blues | Prestige | MPP 2513

Lulajze Jezuniu
Hans Reichel | Shamghaied On Tor Road | FMP | CD 46

Lullababy
Bill Bickford's Bigfoot | Semi-Precious Metal | Tutu Records | 888114-2
Jiggs Whigham With The Netherlands Metropole Orchestra | Love Walked In | Koch Jazz | 3-6920-2
Steve Kuhn Trio | Remembering Tomorrow | ECM | 1573(529035-2)
Tomasz Gaworek-Schodrok | Found In The Flurry Of The World | Acoustic Music Records | 319.1073.2

Lullaby
Ethan Iverson Trio | The Minor Passions | Fresh Sound Records | FSNT 064 CD
Farlanders | The Farlander | JA & RO | JARO 4222-2
Frank Morgan Quartet | A Lovesome Thing | Antilles | 848213-2(882988)
Impetus | Down To Earth | Plainisphare | PL 1267-5
Kenny Drew/Niels-Henning Orsted-Pedersen Duo | Duo | Steeplechase | SCS 1002
Marc Johnson-Eric Longsworth | If Trees Could Fly | Intuition Records | INT 3228-2
Max Collie Sextet | Gospel Train | Black Lion | 147007
Mike Westbrook Brass Band | Glad Day:Settings Of William Blake | Enja | ENJ-9376 2
Nils Landgren-Esbjörn Svensson | Layers Of Light | ACT | 9281-2
Orchestra | Piano Music | Peregrina Music | PM 50262
Piirpauke | The Wild East | JA & RO | JARO 4128-2
Ray Bryant | Solo Flight | Pablo | 2310798
Singers Unlimited | A Capella | MPS | 815671-1
The Houdini's | Headlines-The Houdini's In New York | Timeless | CD SJP 382
Toots Thielemans Group | Live | Polydor | 831694-2 PMS

Lullaby For Carol
Free Flight | Beyond The Clouds | Palo Alto | PA 8075

Lullaby For Helene
Bill Evans Quartet | From Left To Right | Verve | 557451-2
Bill Evans Trio | The Complete Bill Evans On Verve | Verve | 527953-2
Bill Evans With Orchestra | The Complete Bill Evans On Verve | Verve | 527953-2
From Left To Right | Verve | 557451-2
Bill Evans Quartet | The Complete Bill Evans On Verve | Verve | 527953-2

Lullaby For Helene(alt.take)
Carlos Barbosa-Lima | Music Of The Americas | Concord | CCD 4461

Lullaby For Jule
Special EFX | Peace Of The World | GRP | GRP 96402

Lullaby For Rabbit
Sun Ra And His Arkestra | Sun Song | Delmark | DE 411

Lullaby For Tchicai
Freddie Bryant Group | Brazilian Rosewood | Fresh Sound Records | FSNT 035 CD

Lullaby For The Newborn
Night Ark | In Wonderland | EmArCy | 534471-2

Lullaby In Rhythm
Art Pepper-Shorty Rogers Quintet | Art Pepper & Shorty Rogers:Complete Lighthouse Sessions | The Jazz Factory | JFCD 22836
Benny Goodman And His Orchestra | Wrappin' It Up-The Harry James Years Part 2 | Bluebird | 63 66549-2
Dave Brubeck Quartet | The Dave Brubeck Quartet feat. Paul Desmond In Concert | Fantasy | FCD 60-013
The Art Of Dave Brubeck - The Fantasy Years:Jazz At Oberlin/College OPacific | Atlantic | SD 2-317
June Christy With The Kentones | The Uncollected:June Christy With The Kentones | Hindsight | HSR 219
Mike Wofford | Maybeck Recital Hall Series Volume Eighteen | Concord | CCD 4514
Red Richards | Lullaby In Rhythm | Sackville | SKCD2-3044
Ronny Lang Quartet | Basie Street | Fresh Sound Records | FSR-CD 0501
Stan Kenton And His Orchestra | One Night Stand | Choice | CHCD 71051
Innovations-Live 1951 | Bandstand | BDCD 1519

Lullaby Of Birdland
Bernard Peiffer Trio | Jazz In Paris:The Bernard Peiffer Trio Plays Standards | EmArCy | 018425-2
Bill Ramsey & The Ron Wilson Trio | Singin' & Swingin' | zyx records | 22001
Bud Powell Trio | Inner Fries-The Genius Of Bud Powell | Discovery | 71007-2
Coleman Hawkins All Stars | Timeless Jazz-A Jazztone Society Classic | Fresh Sound Records | FSR-CD 0088
Count Basie And His Orchestra | Live At Birdland | Jazz Anthology | JA 5225
Dexter Gordon Septet | Seven Come Eleven | Memo Music | HDJ 4054
Duke Ellington And His Orchestra | The Legends Of Swing | Laserlight | 24659
Concert At Carnegie Hall | Atlantis | ATS 2 D
Duke 56/62 Vol.1 | CBS | 88653
Ella Fitzgerald With Orchestra | Welcome To Jazz: Ella Fitzgerald | Koch Records | 322 078 D1
Ella Fitzgerald With Sy Oliver And His Orchestra | Ella Fitzgerald 75th Birthday Celebration:The Original Decca Recordings | GRP | GRP 26192
Ella Fitzgerald With The Jimmy Jones Trio | Ella & Duke At The Cote D'Azur | Verve | 539030-2
Ella Fitzgerald And Duke Ellington:Cote D'Azure Concerts on Verve | Verve | 539033-2
Ella Fitzgerald And Duke Ellington:Cote D'Azure Concerts on Verve | Verve | 539033-2
Erroll Garner Trio | This Is Erroll Garner 2 | CBS | 68219
Frieder Berlin Trio | Soul Fingers | Satin Doll Productions | SDP 1039-1 CD
George Shearing And His Quintet | The Swingin's Mutual | Capitol | 799190-2
George Shearing Group | Two Originals:Light,Airy And Swinging/Continental Experience/On Target | MPS | 523522-2
George Shearing Quintet | Back To Birdland | Telarc Digital | CD 83524
Howard Alden-George Van Eps | Seven And Seven | Concord | CCD 4584
Jenny Evans And The Rudi Martini Quartet | At Loyd's | BELL Records | BLR 90004
John Mehegan-Kenny Clarke | Johnny Mehegan's Reflections | Savoy | SV 0204(MG 12028)
Jonah Jones Quartet | Jonah Jones At The Embers | RCA | 2118523-2
Lester Young And Earl Swope With The Bill Potts Trio | Lester Young In Washington,DC 1956:Vol.5 | Original Jazz Classics | OJCCD 993-2
Lester Young Quintet | Lester Young In Paris | Verve | 2304489 IMS
Mel Tormé With The George Shearing Duo | An Evening With George Shearing & Mel Torme | Concord | CCD 4190
Sarah Vaughan With The Clifford Brown All Stars | Sarah Vaughan | EmArCy | 9860779
Sarah Vaughan | Verve | 543305-2
4 By 4:Ella Fitzgerald/Sarah Vaughan/Billie Holiday/Dinah Washington | Verve | 559693-2
Brownie-The Complete EmArCy Recordings Of Clifford Brown | EmArCy | 838306-2
Verve Jazz Masters 18:Sarah Vaughan | Verve | 518199-2
Stan Getz Quintet | Stan Getz-The Complete Roost Sessions | EMI Records | 859622-2
Unearthed Masters-Vol.2: Stan Getz | JAM | 5007 IMS
Tito Puente And His Latin Ensemble feat. George Shearing | Mambo Diablo | Concord | CJ 283
Willy Bischof Jazztet | Swiss Air | Jazz Connaisseur | JCCD 9523-2
Earl Hines | Live In Milano 1966 | Nueva Records | JU 315

Lullaby Of Birdland-
Johannes Rediske Sextet | Re-Disc Bounce | Bear Family Records | BCD 16119 AH
Keely Smith And Her Band | I'm In Love Again | Fantasy | F 9639

Lullaby Of Birdland(alt.take)
Sarah Vaughan With The Clifford Brown All Stars | Sarah Vaughan | Verve | 543305-2
Brownie-The Complete EmArCy Recordings Of Clifford Brown | EmArCy | 838306-2
Count Basie And His Orchestra | The Birdland Era Vol.2 | Duke Records | D 1018

Lullaby Of Broadway
Ernestine Allen With The King Curtis Group | Let It Roll | Original Blues Classics | OBCCD 539-2(TRU 15004)
Randy Sandke Septet | The Chase | Concord | CCD 4642

Lullaby Of Love
Art Tatum | Art Tatum-The Complete Pablo Solo Masterpieces | Pablo | 7 PACD 4404-2

Lullaby Of Rhythm
The Art Tatum Solo Masterpieces | Pablo | 2625703

Lullaby Of The Doomed
Babs Gonzales Group | Properly Presenting Babs Gonzales | Fresh Sound Records | FSR 702(835422)

Lullaby Of The Leaves
Art Tatum | Art Tatum:Complete Original American Decca Recordings | Definitive Records | DRCD 11200
Charlie Ventura And His Orchestra | It's All Bop To Me | Fresh Sound Records | LPM 1135(RCA)
Chris Flory Quartet | For All We Know | Concord | CCD 4403
Gerry Mulligan Quintet | Live In Stockholm-Vol.2 | Ingo | 6
Hank Jones Trio | The Trio | Chiaroscuro | CR 188
Joe Pass With The NDR Big Band | Joe Pass In Hamburg | ACT | 9100-2
Joe Turner | Stride By Stride | Solo Art | SACD-106
Kenny Davern And The Rhythm Men | Kenny Davern And The Rhythm Men | Arbors Records | ARCD 19147
Lucky Thompson With The Gerard Pochonet All-Stars | Paris 1956 | Jazz Anthology | JA 5215
Milt Jackson And His Gold Medal Winners | Brother Jim | Pablo | 2310916-2
Milt Jackson Trio | Jazz Legacy 30: J.J.Johnson/Milt Jackson-A Date In New York Vol.1 | Vogue | 500080
Monty Alexander-Ernest Ranglin Duo | Monty Alexander - Ernest Ranglin | MPS | 68269
Original Motion Picture Soundtrack | Kansas City | Verve | 529554-2
Singers Unlimited With Rob McConnell And The Boss Brass | The Singers Unlimited:Magic Voices | MPS | 539130-2
The Singers Unlimited With Rob McConnell And The Boss Brass | MPS | 817486-1

Lullaby Of The Leaves(alt.take)
Duke Jordan | Duke Jordan-Solo Masterpieces Vol.2 | Steeplechase | SCCD 31300

Lullaby Petite
Ben Webster-Don Byas Quintet | Ben Webster/Don Byas | Jazz Magazine | 48018

Lull-A-Bye
The Houdini's | Kickin' In The Frontwindows | Timeless | CD SJP 405

L'Ultimo Abbraccio
Schorn-Puntin Duo | Elephant's Love Affair | NCC Jazz | NCC 8002

Lulubelle
J.B.Hutto Quartet | Slideslinger | Black & Blue | BLE 59.540 2

Lulu's Back In Town
Bob Enevoldsen Quintet | Jazz In Hollywood:Harry Babasin/Bob Enevoldsen | Original Jazz Classics | OJCCD 1888-2(Nocturne NLP3/NLP-6)
Dutch Swing College Band | Digital Date | Philips | 834087-2
Earl Hines Quartet | Another Monday Date | Prestige | P 24043
Fats Waller And His Rhythm | The Classic Years In Digital Stereo: Fats Waller And His Rhythm | CDS Records Ltd. | RPCD 315(CD 684)
Henri Chaix Trio | Just Friends | Sackville | SKCD2-2048
Johnny Mercer With Paul Weston's Orchestra | The Uncollected:Johnny Mercer | Hindsight | HSR 152
Lyke Ritz Trio | How About Uke? | Verve | 0760942
Mel Tormé And His All-Star Quintet | Sing, Sing, Sing | Concord | CCD 4542
Roy Gerson Quartet | The Gerson Person | The Jazz Alliance | TJA 10012
Thelonious Monk Quartet | It's Monk's Time | CBS | 468405-2
Vinnie Burke All-Stars | Vinnie Burke All-Stars | Fresh Sound Records | ABC 139(Paramount)
Earl Hines Trio | The Lengendary Little Theater Concert of 1964 | Savoy | 650139(882495)

Lumi
Pekka Pylkkännen's Tube Factory | Opaque | Naxos Jazz | 86068-2

Lumiere Du Silence
A Band Of Friends | René Wohlhauser Werkauswahl 1978-1993 | Creative Works Records | CW CD 1026-2

Lumière(s) für Orgel
Winterschladen-Krämer-Manderscheid | Unroll | Sound Aspects | sas CD 043

Luminessence
Chico Freeman-Arthur Blythe Sextet | Luminous | Ronnie Scott's Jazz House | JHCD 010

Luminous Cycles
Marty Fogel Quartet | Many Bobbing Heads, At Last... | CMP Records | CMP CD 37

Luminous Energy
Sam Rivers Quartet | Fuchsia Swing Song | Blue Note | 593874-2

Luminous Monolith
Ed Hamilton Group | Path To The Heartland | Telarc Digital | CD 83404

Lumpy
Mani Neumeir-Peter Hollinger | Monsters Of Drums-Live | ATM Records | ATM 3821-AH

Lumumba
Ed Neumeister Trio | The Mohican And The Great Spirit | TCB Records | TCB 01072

Luna
The Leaders | Out Here Like This... | Black Saint | 120119-2
Luna En New York
Eric Alexander Quintet | The Second Milestone | Milestone | MCD 9315-2
Luna Naranja
Bertha Hope Quintet | Elmo's Fire | Steeplechase | SCCD 31289
Luna, Luna, Luna
Joey Calderazzo Trio | The Traveler | Blue Note | 780902-2
Lunacy
Shpere | Four For All | Verve | 831674-2
Lunar Oder Solar?
Claus Raible Trio | Introducing The Exciting Claus Raible Trio | Organic Music | ORGM 9714
Lunar Web
Billy Cobham Group | Total Eclipse | Atlantic | ATL 50098
Lunatic
Enrico Rava-Dino Saluzzi Quintet | Volver | ECM | 1343
Luna-Volver
Les Brown And His Band Of Renown | Ridin' High | Blue Moon | BMCD 3058
Lunch With Pancho Villa
Dino Saluzzi-Anthony Cox-David Friedman | Rios | VeraBra Records | CDVBR 2156-2
Vince Jones Group | Here's To The Miracles | Intuition Records | INT 3198-2
Luncheon With The President
Takabanda | La Leggenda Del Pescatore | Jazz 4 Ever Records:Jazz Network | J4E 4752
Lundi Au Lit
Egberto Gismonti | Danca Dos Escravos | ECM | 1387(837753-2)
Lundu(Azul)
Egberto Gismonti Group | Musica De Sobrevivencia | ECM | 1509(519706-2)
Lundu(No.2)
Gianni Basso European Quartet | Lunet | SPLASC(H) Records | H 101
Lungs
Irene Schweizer Trio | Live At Taktlos | Intakt Records | 001
Luny Tune
Grant Green Trio | Talkin' About | Blue Note | 521958-2
Vittorino Curci/Pino Minafra/Carlos Actis Dato Group | L'Invenzione Del Verso Sfuso | SPLASC(H) Records | HP 21
Lupita-
Steve Tibbetts Group | Steve Tibbetts | ECM | 1814(017068-2)
Lupra
Hans Reichel | Bonobo | FMP | 0280
Luriecal
David Binney Group | Balance | ACT | 9411-2
Lurker
Gene Harris | Maybeck Recital Hall Series Volume Twenty-Three | Concord | CCD 4536
Lush Life
Anita O'Day And Her Trio | Anita And The Rhythm Section | Glendale | GLS 6001 IMS
Bernd Lhotzky-Colin Dawson | Sophisticated | ART BY HEART | ABH 2003 2
Bill Holman And His Orchestra | Great Big Band | Fresh Sound Records | T 1464(Capitol)
Bucky Pizzarelli-John Pizzarelli Duo | The Complete Guitar Duos(The Stash Sessions) | Stash Records | ST-CD 536(889114)
Buddy DeFranco Quartet | Lush Life | Choice | CHCD 71017
Waterbed | Candid | CRS 1017 IMS
Carmen McRae With The Jimmy Mundy Orchestra | Blue Moon | Verve | 543829-2
Carol Grimes And Her Sextet | Alive At Ronnie Scott's | Ronnie Scott's Jazz House | JHCD 034
Chris Connor With The Vinnie Burke Quartet | Out Of This World | Affinity | AFF 122
Clifford Jordan Quartet | Live At Ethell's | Mapleshade | 56292
Court-Candiotto Quintet | Live In Montreux | Plainisphare | PAV 811
Dave Burrell | Plays Ellington & Monk | Denon Compact Disc | DC-8550
Don Braden Quintet | The Open Road | Double Time Records | DTRCD-114
Ella Fitzgerald And Her All Stars | The Complete Ella Fitzgerald Song Books of Harold Arlen, Irving Berlin, Duke Ellington, George & Ira Gershwin, Jerome Kern, Johnny Mercer, Cole Porter And Rogers & Hart | Verve | 519832-2
Ella Fitzgerald-Joe Pass Duo | Take Love Easy | Pablo | 2310702
Joe Pass:A Man And His Guitar | Original Jazz Classics | OJCCD 8806-2
Ella Fitzgerald-Oscar Peterson Duo | Compact Jazz: Oscar Peterson & Friends | Verve | 835315-2
Geoff Keezer | Turn Up The Quiet | CBS | 488830-2
Hans Koller Groups | Out Of The Rim | IN+OUT Records | 7014-2
Harold Ousley Sextet | Harold Ousley | Fresh Sound Records | FSR 2027(Bethlehem BCP 6059)
Heinz Sauer 4tet | Exchange 2 | free flow music | ffm 0998
Heinz Sauer Quartet | Cherry Bat | Enja | ENJ-5083 2
James Chirillo Sextet | Sultry Serenade | Nagel-Heyer | CD 061
Jay Hoggard Quintet | Riverside Dance | India Navigation | IN 1068
Joe Henderson | Lush Life-The Music Of Billy Strayhorn | Verve | 511779-2
Joe Pass | Joe Pass:Guitar Virtuoso | Pablo | 4 PACD 4423-2
What Is There To Say | Pablo | 2310971-2
Virtuoso No.4 | Pablo | 2640102
Johannes Mössinger | Spring In Versailles | double moon | DMCD 1004-2
John Coltrane Quartet With Johnny Hartman | The Gentle Side Of John Coltrane | Impulse(MCA) | 951107-2
John Coltrane Quintet | John Coltrane-The Prestige Recordings | Prestige | 16 PCD 4405-2
Lush Life | Original Jazz Classics | OJC20 131-2
John Coltrane Sextet | Jazz Gallery:John Coltrane Vol.1 | RCA | 2119540-2
Johnny Hartman With The John Coltrane Quartet | John Coltrane And Johnny Hartman | Impulse(MCA) | 951157-2
Joint Venture | Joint Venture | Enja | ENJ-5049 2
Klaus Weiss Quintet feat. Clifford Jordan | Live At Opus 1 | Jazzline | ???
Lisle Atkinson Quartet | Bass Contra Bass | Storyville | STCD 8270
Major Holley Trio | Two Big Mice | Black & Blue | BLE 59.124 2
Mickey Tucker | Gettin' There | Steeplechase | SCCD 31365
Petra Straue & The Moonmen | Voices Around My House | Satin Doll Productions | SDP 1016-1 CD
René Pretschner | Story Of A Jazz Piano Vol.1 | Green House Music | CD 1013
Return To The Wide Open Spaces | Live At The Caravan Of Dreams | Amazing Records | AMCD 1021
Sarah Vaughan With Hal Mooney's Orchestra | Compact Jazz: Sarah Vaughan | Mercury | 830699-2
Sarah Vaughan With The Hal Mooney Orchestra | 4 By 4:Ella Fitzgerald/Sarah Vaughan/Billie Holiday/Dinah Washington | Verve | 559693-2
Sathima Bea Benjamin With The Kenny Barron Trio | Southern Touch | Enja | ENJ-7015 2
Stan Getz Quintet | Captain Marvel | CBS | 468412-2
Tito Puente And His Latin Ensemble | Mambo Diablo | Concord | CJ 283
World Saxophone Quartet | Plays Duke Ellington | Nonesuch | 7559-79137-2
Duke Jordan Trio | Jazz Legends:Clark Terry-Duke Jordan | Storyville | 4960283
Lush Life-
When You're Smiling | Steeplechase | SCCD 37023/24
Jimmy Rowles Trio | Grandpaws | Candid | CRS 1014 IMS
Oscar Peterson Trio | The London Concert | Pablo | 2CD 2620111
Peter Leitch | Red Zone | Reservoir | RSR CD 103(882905)
Tony Scott Trio | Lush Life Vol.2 | Line Records | COCD 9.00667 O
Lush Life Variations:
Doug Hammond Trio | Perspicuity | L+R Records | CDLR 45031
Lush Life(R.Ringwood)
Stan Kenton | Solo:Stan Kenton | Creative World | ST 1071
Lussi
Steps Ahead | N.Y.C. | Intuition Records | INT 3007-2
Lust For Life
Thad Jones Quintet | The Bop Rebells | Jazz Door | JD 1218
Lustiger Tiroler
Charlie Mariano-Gregor Josephs Quartet | Lustinseln | L+R Records | CDLR 45097
Lustrin
Al Di Meola World Sinfonia | World Sinfonia | Inak | 700772
Luteous Pangolin
Luther Allison Blues Band | Luther's Blues | Motown | 523030
Luv
Lee Konitz Quartet | Round & Round | Musicmasters | 65140-2
Lux Aeterna:
David Murray-Milford Graves | Real Deal | DIW | DIW 867 CD
Luxuriate
Cecil Taylor Quartet | Looking Ahead | Original Jazz Classics | OJC 452(C 7562)
Luz Do Sol
Fernando Tarrés And The Arida Conta Group With Guests | The Outsider | Savant Records | SCD 2002
LWS
Bluiett-Jackson-Thiam | Join Us | Justin Time | JUST 124-2
Lyasata
Vera Guimaraes Group | Stirring The Forest | West Wind Latina | 2202 CD
Lydia
George Russell And His Sextet | At Beethoven Hall | MPS | 539084-2
Lydian Waltz
Klaus Treuheit Trio | Steinway Afternoon | clearaudio | 42016 CD
Lydia's Crush
Harold Land Quintet | Groove Yard | Original Jazz Classics | OJCCD 162-2
Lydiot
The United Women's Orchestra | The Blue One | Jazz Haus Musik | JHM 0099 CD
Lydisch Blau
Louis Armstrong And His Orchestra | Big Band Bounce & Boogie-Louis Armstrong:Struttin' With Some Barbecue | Affinity | AFS 1024
Lykief
Riccardo Fassi Trio | Riccardo Fassi New York Trio | yvp music | CD 3036
Lynxpaw
John Lewis Sextet | John Lewis:Kansas City Breaks | Red Baron | JK 57759
Lyon's Brood
Dave Brubeck Quartet | Stardust | Fantasy | FCD 24728-2
Lyon's Head
David Murray Quartet | Ballads For Bass Clarinet | DIW | DIW 880 CD
Lyresto
Kenny Burrell-John Coltrane Quintet | Kenny Burrell & John Coltrane | Original Jazz Classics | OJC20 300-2
Kenny Burrell & John Coltrane | New Jazz | NJSA 8276-2
Artie Shaw And His Gramercy Five | I Can't Get Started | Verve | MV 2559 IMS
Lyric
Julius Hemphill Sextet | 'Coon Bid'Ness | Freedom | CD 741028
Lyric Collection-
Chick Corea And Gary Burton With A String Quartet | Lyric Suite For Sextet | ECM | 1260
Lyriste
Christina Nielsen-Carsten Dahl Duo | Lys Pa Himlen | dacapo | DCCD 9458
Lys Pa Himlen
Jens Skou Olsen Group | September Veje | dacapo | DCCD 9451
Lyse Dage(Bright Days)
Billy Cobham Group | Art Of Five | IN+OUT Records | 77063-2
Lzatso
KontaSax | KontraSax Plays Getrude Stein | Jazz Haus Musik | JHM 0096 CD
Lzw(1)
KontraSax Plays Getrude Stein | Jazz Haus Musik | JHM 0096 CD
Lzw(2)
Charles Lloyd Quartet | Canto | ECM | 1635(537345-2)
M
Greg Osby Quartet With String Quartet | Symbols Of Light(A Solution) | Blue Note | 531395-2
Joey Baron Quartet | We'll Soon Find Out | Intuition Records | INT 3515-2
John Abercrombie Quartet | M | ECM | 1191
Art Blakey And The Jazz Messengers | At The Jazz Corner Of The World Vol. 2 | Blue Note | 868365-5
M IV
Jim Black Quartet | Alasnoaxis | Winter&Winter | 910061-2
M m
Count Basie And His Orchestra | Ain't Misbehavin' | Laserlight | 15778
M Squad
Stanley Wilson And His Orchestra | The Music From M Squad | Fresh Sound Records | PL 45929(RCA LPM 2062)
M V
Peter Kleindienst Group | Zeitwärts:Reime Vor Pisin | double moon | DMCD 1001-2
M VI
Manel Camp & Matthew Simon Acustic Jazz Quintet | Rosebud | Fresh Sound Records | FSNT 011 CD
M x M
Kölner Saxophon Mafia | Place For Lovers | Jazz Haus Musik | JHM 0082 CD
M&F PNZ(Männer & Frauen passen nicht zusammen)
Tim Berne/Bill Frisell Duo | Theoretically | Empire | EPC 72 K
M.B.
Machiel S. Sextet | For Flora | Limetree | MLP 198506
M.E.
Marilyn Crispell-Gary Peacock-Paul Motian | Amaryllis | ECM | 1742(013400-2)
Francois Magnin Trio | M.J. | Plainisphare | PAV 806
M.F.
Pierre Favre Trio | Santana | FMP | 0630
M.J.
Jazz Crusaders | Freedom Sound | Pacific Jazz | 796864-2
M.T.
Rene Thomas Quintet | Guitar Groove | Original Jazz Classics | OJCCD 1725-2(JLP 27)
M.W.A.(Musicians With Attitude)
David Benoit Group With Symphony Orchestra | Inner Motion | GRP | GRP 96212
M1
Carl Ludwig Hübsch | Der Erste Bericht | IN+OUT Records | 77035-2
M2
Der Erste Bericht | IN+OUT Records | 77035-2
M3
Der Erste Bericht | IN+OUT Records | 77035-2
M4
Der Erste Bericht | IN+OUT Records | 77035-2
M5
Der Erste Bericht | IN+OUT Records | 77035-2
M6
Lars Gullin Octet | Lars Gullin 1955/56 Vol.1 | Dragon | DRCD 224
Ma
Ray Charles With Orchestra | 20 Superhits | London | 6.22554 AP
Ma Bel
Kenny Wheeler Quintet | Double, Double You | ECM | 1262(815675-2)
Jasper Van't Hof Trio | Tomorrowland | Challenge | CHR 70040
Ma Belle Hélène
Phil Grenadier Quintet | Sweet Transients | Fresh Sound Records | FSNT 093 CD
Lightnin' Hopkins | Lightnin' Hopkins Strums The Blues | Pathe | 2C 068-83076(Score)
Ma Cheuse
Count Basie And His Orchestra | Basie's Timing | MPS | 88016-2
Ma Jolie
Enrico Pieranunzi Trio With Ada Montellancino And Enrico Rava | Ma L'Amore No | Soul Note | 121321-2
Ma Muse M'amuse
Masters | Masters | Carlyne | 695011
Ma Perché
Marc Ducret | Detail | Winter&Winter | 910003-2
Ma Plus Belle Histoire D'Amour
Häns'che Weiss Quintet & Guests | Fünf Jahre Musik Deutscher Zigeuner | Intercord | 160088
Ma Risparmia Un Innocente!
The Voodoo Gang | Return Of The Turtle-Old And New Songs From Africa | Enja | 9112-2
Maalfri Mi Fruve
Piirpauke | Piirpauke-Global Servisi | JA & RO | JARO 4150-2
Maam Bamba
Peter Brötzmann-Willi Kellers Duo | Maar Helaas! | FMP | 0800
Maasai
Akili | Maasai Mara | M.A Music | A 802-2
Maasai Mara
Jeff Gardner-Gary Peacock | Alchemy | fnac Muisc | 662016
Maat
Django Reinhardt And The Quintet Du Hot Club De France | Django Reinhardt:Djangology | EMI Records | 780659-2
Mabellene
Acker Bilk With Ken Colyer's Jazzmen | Together Again | Lake | LACD 53
Mabel's Dream
King Oliver's Jazz Band | Louis Armstrong With King Oliver Vol.1 | Village(Jazz Archive) | VILCD 003-2
Theis/Nyegaard Jazzband | The Golden Years Of Revibal Jazz,Vol.15 | Storyville | STCD 5520
The New York Allstars | We Love You,Louis! | Nagel-Heyer | CD 029
Mabel's Dream-
Barrelhouse Jazzband | The King Oliver Heritage Jazz Band | L+R Records | CDLR 40033
Mabuse
Michael Hornstein Trio | Langsames Blau | Enja | 8028-2
Mac Attack
Pat Martino Trio | Live At Yoshi's | Blue Note | 499749-2
Mac Tough
Josep Maria Balanyà | Elements Of Development | Laika Records | 8695070
Macaccos Macaccos
Maynard Ferguson And His Orchestra | Dues | Mainstream | MD CDO 725
Macedonia
Dusko Goykovich Sextet | Swinging Macedonia | Enja | 4048-2
MacGuffie's Blues
Brodmann-Pausch Percussion Duo | Are You Serious? | Jazz 4 Ever Records:Jazz Network | J4E 4718
Mach 1
Franck Band | Liebeslieder | Jazz Haus Musik | JHM 35 CD
Machajo
Blasnost | Anything Blows | Acoustic Music Records | 319.1049.2
Mache Dich,Mein Herze,Rein-
Rabih Abou-Khalil Quartet | Bitter Harvest | MMP-Records | 170884
Machine
Buddy Rich Big Band | The New One! | Pacific Jazz | 494507-2
Joachim Kühn | Wandlungen-Transformations | CMP Records | CMP CD 29
Machine Gun
Jean-Paul Bourelly Group | Tribute To Jimi | DIW | DIW 893 CD
Machines-A-Sons
Sylvie Courvoisier Group | Ocre | Enja | ENJ-9323 2
Karl Ratzer | Dancing On A String | CMP Records | CMP 13
Macho Man
Ornette Coleman Quartet | Sound Museum | Verve | 531657-2
Macho(Dedicated To Machito)
Dollar Brand | African Sketch Book | Enja | 2026-2
Machopi-
Johnny Smith | Legends | Concord | CCD 4616
Machribinia 4 5
Double You | Menschbilder | Jazz Haus Musik | JHM 0062 CD
Machtspiele
Enrique Diaz Quintet | Sin Tempo | Acoustic Music Records | 319.1121.2
Mack 'N' Duff
Alfred Lauer Bigband | Just Music | Mons Records | MR 874819
Mack The Knife(Moritat)
Clark Terry Quartet | OW | Storyville | STCD 8378
Clark Terry With The Oscar Peterson Trio | Compact Jazz:Oscar Peterson | Mercury | 830698-2
Dee Dee Bridgewater With Her Trio | Dear Ella | Verve | 539102-2
Dorothy Donegan Trio | The Many Faces Of Dorothy Donegan | Storyville | STCD 8362
Ella Fitzgerald With Jackie Davis And Louis Bellson | Lady Time | Original Jazz Classics | OJCCD 864-2(2310825)
Ella Fitzgerald With Orchestra | Essential Ella | Verve | 523990-2
Ella Fitzgerald With The Duke Ellington Orchestra And Jimmy Jones Trio | Ella & Duke At The Cote D'Azur | Verve | 539030-2
Ella Fitzgerald And Duke Ellington:Cote D'Azure Concerts on Verve | Verve | 539033-2
Ella Fitzgerald And Duke Ellington:Cote D'Azure Concerts on Verve | Verve | 539033-2
Ella Fitzgerald With The Lou Levy Quartet | Ella Returns To Berlin | Verve | 837758-2
Ella Fitzgerald With The Paul Smith Quartet | Verve Jazz Masters 6:Ella Fitzgerald | Verve | 519822-2
Compact Jazz: Ella Fitzgerald | Verve | 831367-2
4 By 4:Ella Fitzgerald/Sarah Vaughan/Billie Holiday/Dinah Washington | Verve | 559693-2
Mack The Knife-The Complete Ella In Berlin | Verve | 519564-2
Ella Fitzgerald With The Paul Smith Trio | Compact Jazz: The Sampler | Verve | 831376-2
Elliott Lawrence Orchestra | Jazz Goes Broadway | Fresh Sound Records | NL 45905(RCA Vik LX 1113)
Jimmy Giuffre Trio | Paris Jazz Concert:Jimmy Giuffre | Laserlight | 17249
Jimmy McGriff Quintet | Georgia On My Mind | LRC Records | CDC 8513
Joe Pass | Virtuoso Live! | Pablo | 2310948-2
Lou Donaldson Sextet | The Best Of Lou Donaldson Vol.1(1957-1967) | Blue Note | 827298-2
Louis Armstrong And His All Stars | Live In Berlin/Friedrichstadtpalast | Jazzpoint | JP 1062 CD
The Great Performer | Traditional Line | TL 1304
Louis Armstrong And His All Stars/Orchestra | Welcome To Jazz: Louis Armstrong | Koch Records | 321 971 D1
Milt Buckner Trio | Them There Eyes | Black & Blue | BLE 233013
NDR Big Band | The Theatre Of Kurt Weill | ACT | 9234-2
New York Unit | Tribute To George Adams | Paddle Wheel | KICJ 156
Oscar Klein's Anniversary Band | Moonglow | Nagel-Heyer | CD 021
Oscar Peterson Jam | Montreux '77 | Original Jazz Classics | OJC 385(2620105)
Montreux '77-The Art Of The Jam Session | Pablo | 2620106
Papa Bue's Viking Jazzband | Everybody Loves Saturday Night | Timeless | CD TTD 580
Sonny Rollins Quartet | Saxophone Colossus And More | Prestige | P 24050
Stephane Grappelli Group | Satin Doll | Accord | 440162
The Poll Winners | Poll Winners Three | Original Jazz Classics | OJCCD 692-2(C 7576)
The Sextet Of Orchestra USA | Mack The Knife And Other Berlin Theatre Songs Of Kurt Weill | RCA | 2159162-2

Wayne Shorter Quintet | Introducing Wayne Shorter | Vee Jay Recordings | VJ 007

Mack The Knife(Moritat)-
Lennie Felix Trio | Melody Maker Tribute To Louis Armstrong Vol.1 | Jazz Colours | 874767-2
NDR Big Band | The Theatre Of Kurt Weil | ACT | 9234-2

Mack The Knife(Moritat,alt-take))
The Sextet Of Orchestra USA | Mack The Knife And Other Berlin Theatre Songs Of Kurt Weill | RCA | 2159162-2

Mack The Knife(Moritat-deutsch gesungen)
Earl Hines | Tour De Force Encore | Black Lion | BLCD 760157

Macondo
The Quartet | Loaded | Leo Records | 010

Macumba
Pocket Change | Random Axis | Passport Jazz | ???

Mad About The Boy
Dinah Washington With Orchestra | Mad About The Boy-The Best Of Dinah Washington | Mercury | 512214-2
Dinah Washington With The Quincy Jones Orchestra |'4 By 4:Ella Fitzgerald/Sarah Vaughan/Billie Holiday/Dinah Washington | Verve | 559693-2
Dinah Washington With The Walter Rodell Orchestra | The Complete Dinah Washington On Mercury Vol.2 | Mercury | 832448-2
Jenny Evans And Her Quintet | Nuages | ESM Records | ESM 9308
Joe Wilder Quartet | Wilder' N' Wilder | Savoy | SV 0131(MG 12063)
Lena Horne With The Lennie Hayton Orchestra | Lena Horne:Love Songs | RCA | 2663604-2

Mad About The Boys
Jutta Hipp Trio | Jutta Hipp At The Hickory House Vol.1 | Blue Note | 300094(1515)

Mad Africa
Lightnin' Hopkins | Blues Train | Mainstream | MD CDO 901

Mad At The World
J.J.Johnson Quintet | J.J. Johnson's Jazz Quintets | Savoy | SV 0151(MG 12106)

Mad Bird
Big Joe Turner And His All Stars | Roots Of Rock And Roll Vol. 2: Big Joe Turner | Savoy | SJL 2223 (801199)

Mad House
Leo Parker Quartet | Prestige First Sessions, Vol.1 | Prestige | PCD 24114-2

Mad Mad Me
John Lee Hooker | John Lee Hooker Plays And Sings The Blues | Chess | MCD 09199

Mad Man Blues
Sigi Finkel's Powerstation | Voyeur,Voyeur | Open Minds | OM 2404-2

Mad Quasar
Tom White With Band | Keep It Under Your Hat | Ronnie Scott's Jazz House | JHCD 018

Madagascar
Nguyen Le Trio With Guests | Bakida | ACT | 9275-2

Madal
Don Grusin Group | Native Land | GRP | GRP 97192

Madalena
Ella Fitzgerald With The Tommy Flanagan Trio | Jazz At The Santa Monica Civic '72 | Pablo | 2625701-2
Steve Gut & The RTB Big Band | Steve Gut & RTB Big Band | Timeless | CD SJP 293

Madame
Makoto Kuriya Quintet | X-Based Music | Paddle Wheel | KICJ 171

Madame Toulouse
Meade Lux Lewis | The Blues Piano Artistry Of Meade Lux Lewis | Original Jazz Classics | OJCCD 1759-2

Madar
Ray Pizzi Quintet | I Hear You | Bhakti Jazz | BR 27

Made In France
Tiziana Ghiglioni Sextet | Streams | SPLASC(H) Records | CD H 104-2

Made In New York
Jack McDuff Quartet With Orchestra | Moon Rappin' | Blue Note | 538697-2

Made In Sweden
Pierre Guyonnet And His Orchestra | Joue | Plainisphare | PAV 809

Madeleine After Prayer
Hank Mobley Quartet | Complete 'The Jazz Message Sessions With Kenny Clarke' | The Jazz Factory | JFCD 22858

Madelyn
Jean Tranchant Trio | Le Jazz En France Vol.5:Django Plus | Pathe | 1727291

Mademoiselle Mabry
Four For Jazz | The Best Of Four For Jazz & Benny Bailey | JHM Records | JHM 3615

Mademoiselle Martine
Gordon Beck | The French Connection | Owl Records | 11

Madhawi
Benny Goodman And His Orchestra | More Camel Caravans | Phontastic | NCD 8843/4

Madhouse
Camel Caravan Broadcast 1939 Vol.3 | Phontastic | NCD 8819
The Indispensable Benny Goodman Vol.1/2:Birth Of A Big Band | RCA | NL 89755 (809180)

Madhouse Jam
Passport | 2 Originals Of Passport(Passport-Second Passport) | Atlantic | ATL 60117

Madison Avenue
David Chesky-Romero Lubambo Duo | The New York Chorinhos | Chesky | JD 39

Madness
Miles Davis Quintet | Miles Davis Quintet 1965-1968 | CBS | C6K 67398
Steve LaSpina Quintet | Remember When | Steeplechase | SCCD 31540
Duke Ellington And His Orchestra | Passion Flower | Moon Records | MCD 074-2

Madness In Great Ones
Ella Fitzgerald And Duke Ellington:Cote D'Azure Concerts on Verve | Verve | 539033-2
Ella Fitzgerald And Duke Ellington:Cote D'Azure Concerts on Verve | Verve | 539033-2
Ella Fitzgerald And Duke Ellington:Cote D'Azure Concerts on Verve | Verve | 539033-2
Soul Call | Verve | 539785-2
Vienna Art Orchestra | The Original Charts Of Duke Ellington & Charles Mingus | Verve | 521998-2

Madness In Great Ones(Hamlet)
Miles Davis Quintet | Nefertiti | CBS | CK 65681

Madness(alt.take)
Miles Davis Quintet 1965-1968 | CBS | C6K 67398
Miles Davis Quintet 1965-1968 | CBS | C6K 67398

Madness(rehersal)
Jim Nolet Group | With You | Knitting Factory Works | KFWCD 150

Madrid
Dick Griffin Orchestra | A Dream For Rahsaan & More | Konnex Records | KCD 5062

Madrugada
Tamia | Senza Tempo | T-Records | T 1002 CD

Maduna
Ana Caram Group | Amazonia | Chesky | JD 45

Mae West
Maria Joao/Aki Takase/Niels-Henning Orsted-Pedersen | Alice | Enja | 6096-2

Maelstrom
Victor Feldman Big Band | Suite Sixteen | Original Jazz Classics | OJCCD 1768-2C 3541)

Mafia Blues
Kölner Saxophon Mafia | Saxfiguren | Jazz Haus Musik | JHM 0036 CD

Mafia Indikativ
Saxfiguren | Jazz Haus Musik | JHM 0036 CD

Mafia Indikativ(alt.take)
Gebbia/Kowald/Sommer | Cappuccini Klang | SPLASC(H) Records | CD H 383-2

Magdalena-
Andreas Heuser | Unknown Places | Acoustic Music Records | 319.1191.2

Magenta
Duke Ellington And His Orchestra | Carnegie Hall Concert January 1946 | Prestige | 2PCD 24074-2

Magenta Haze
Duke Ellington:Complete Studio Transcriptions | Definitive Records | DRCD 11199

Magg Zelma
Kahlil El' Zabar Trio | The Ritual | Sound Aspects | sas CD 011

Maggie And Milly And Molly And May
Susanne Abbuehl Group | April | ECM | 1766(013999-2)
Boogie Bill Webb | Living Country Blues USA,Vol.9:Mississippi Moan | L+R Records | LR 42039

Magic
Grover Mitchell & His All-Star Orchestra | Hip Shakin' | Ken Music | 660.56.005
Urbanator | Urbanator II | Hip Bop | HIBD 8012
Hot Jazz Bisquits | Hip Bop | HIBD 8801
Max Roach-Anthony Braxton | Birth And Rebirth | Black Saint | 120024-2

Magic Box
Philip Catherine Quartet | Blue Prince | Dreyfus Jazz Line | FDM 36614-2
Chick Corea Group | Tap Step | Stretch Records | SCD 9006-2

Magic Carpet
Armando Bertozzi Trio | Armando Bertozzi Trioz | Penta Flowers | CDPIA 014

Magic Horn
Sidney Bechet And His Haitian Orchestra | Tropical Mood | Swingtime(Contact) | ST 1014

Magic Lake
Per Carsten Quintet | Via | dacapo | DCCD 9462

Magic Man
Shorty Rogers-Bud Shank And The Lighthouse All Stars | Eight Brothers | Candid | CCD 79521

Magic Number
Aldo Romano Quartet | Ritual | Owl Records | 050 CD

Magic Pouch
Philip Catherine Group | Babel | Elektra | ELK K 52244

Magic Squares
Rolf Von Nordenskjöld-Marc Muellbauer | Sleep Walk | BIT | 11109

Magic Strings
Christoph Spendel Group | Radio Exotic | L+R Records | CDLR 70001

Magic Walk
Count Basie And His Orchestra | April In Paris | Verve | 521402-2

Magic(alt.take 1)
April In Paris | Verve | 521402-2

Magic(alt.take 2)
Francesca Simone Trio | Guardia Li | Minor Music | 801093

Magica
Sarah Vaughan With The Ernie Wilkins Orchestra | A Time In My Life | Mobile Fidelity | MFCD 855

Magico
Charlie Haden Trio | Works | ECM | 823269-2

Magnetic Rag
London Ragtime Orchestra | Easy Winners | LRO Records | LRO CD 501

Magnificat
Michel Godard Ensemble | Castel Del Monte II | Enja | ENJ-9431 2
Walt Dickerson Trio | Serendipity | Steeplechase | SCCD 31070

Magnolia Island
Scott Wendholt Sextet | From Now On | Criss Cross | Criss 1123

Magrouni
Nels Cline Trio | Silencer | Enja | ENJ-6098 2

Mag's Alley
Toba Multijazz | Meridiana | SPLASC(H) Records | H 132

Mahaba
Max Collie And His Rhythm Aces | Frintline/Backline | Timeless | CD TTD 504/508

Mahat
Austria Drei | Austria Drei | EGO | 4019

Mahfouz
George Gruntz Jazz Group feat. Jean-Luc Ponty & The Bedouins | Jazz Meets Africa:Noon In Tunisia-El Babaku | MPS | 531720-2

Mahjong
Wayne Shorter Quartet | Juju | Blue Note | 837644-2

Mahogany Hall Stomp
Buck Clayton And His Band | The Doctor Jazz Series Vol.3:Buck Clayton | Storyville | STCD 6043
George Lewis And His New Orleans Jazzband | Sounds Of New Orleans Vol.7 | Storyville | STCD 6014
George Lewis And His Original New Orleans Jazzmen | George Lewis In Stockholm,1959 | Dragon | DRCD 221
George Lewis And The Barry Martyn Band | For Dancers Only | GHB Records | BCD 37
Louis Armstrong And His All Stars/Orchestra | St.Louis Blues | Black Lion | 127035
Louis Armstrong And His Dixieland Seven | Planet Jazz:Jazz Trumpet | Planet Jazz | 2169654-2
Victor Jazz History Vol.1:New Orleans & Dixieland | RCA | 2128555-2
Louis Armstrong And His Orchestra | Louis Armstrong-Satchmo's Greatest Hits | RCA | CL 89799
Best Of The Complete RCA Victor Recordings | RCA | 2663636-2
Luis Russell And His Orchestra 1927-29 | Village(Jazz Archive) | VILCD 018-2
Louis Armstrong And His Savoy Ballroom Five | Louis Armstrong Plays And Sings The Great Standards, Vol.1 | Black & Blue | BLE 59.226 2
The Crossover Ensemble | The River:Image Of Time And Life | dacapo | DCCD 9434

Mahogni
Tal Farlow Trio | Tal Farlow '78 | Concord | CJ 57

Mahoor
John Zorn Group | Masada Seven | DIW | DIW 915 CD

Mahzel
Conexion Latina | Mambo 2000 | Enja | ENJ-7055 2

Mai Gel
David Sills Quintet | Journey Together | Naxos Jazz | 86023-2

Mai Tai
Kenny Wheeler Sextet | Around 6 | ECM | 1156

Mai We Go Round
Some Other Trio | A Tale Of Three Ducks | L+R Records | CDLR 45109

Maid In Mexico
Chet Baker Quartet | Chet Baker Quartet Live Vol.1:This Time The Dreams's On Me | Pacific Jazz | 525248-2
Jazz At Ann Arbor | Fresh Sound Records | 054 2602311(Pacific Jazz PJ 1203) (835282)

Maiden Voyage
Carl Anderson Group | Pieces Of A Heart | GRP | GRP 96122
Chuck Marohnic Trio | Now Alone | ITM-Pacific | ITMP 970076
GRP All-Star Big Band | GRP 10th Anniversary | GRP | GRP 96722
Herbie Hancock Quintet | The Best Of Herbie Hancock | Blue Note | 89907
The Best Of Herbie Hancock | Blue Note | 791142-2
Herbie Hancock:The Complete Blue Note Sixties Sessions | Blue Note | 495569-2
Cantaloupe Island | Blue Note | 829331-2
Herbie Hancock Trio | Live In New York | Jazz Door | JD 1274
Nnenna Freelon And Her Band | Maiden Voyage | Concord | CCD 4794

Maidens Of Cadiz
Bob Rockwell Quartet | Shades Of Blue | Steeplechase | SCCD 31378

Maids Of Cadiz
Monty Budwig Septet | Dig | Concord | CJ 79

Maienlied
Dieter Ilg Trio With Wolfgang Muthspiel | Folk Songs | Jazzline | JL 11146-2

Maigret's Letzter Fall
Volker Schlott | First Catalogue | KlangRäume | 30170

Mailensteine
David Murray Group | The Tip | DIW | DIW 891 CD

Main Man
Trio Trabant A Roma | State Of Volgograd | FMP | CD 57

Main Stem
Don Byron Quartet | Tuskegee Experiments | Nonesuch | 7559-79280-2
Duke Ellington And His Famous Orchestra | Duke Ellington:The Blanton-Webster Band | Bluebird | 21 13181-2
Ben Webster-Cotton Tail | RCA | 63667902
Duke Ellington And His Orchestra | At The Hurricane:Original 1943 Broadcasts | Storyville | STCD 8359
Duke Ellington And His Orchestra 1943,Vol.1 | Circle | CCD-101
Soul Call | Verve | 539785-2
The Indispensable Duke Ellington,Vol.7/8 | RCA | ND 89274
Jimmy Smith Quartet | Fourmost | Milestone | MCD 9184-2
Oscar Peterson Trio | The History Of An Artist | Pablo | 2625702-2
Quadrant | All Too Soon-Quadrant Toasts Duke Ellington | Original Jazz Classics | OJCCD 450-2
The Echoes Of Ellington Orchestra | Rockin' In Ronnie's | Ronnie Scott's Jazz House | JHCD 050
Zoot Sims And His Orchestra | The Best Of Zoot Sims | Pablo | 2405406-2

Main Street
Jane Bunnett-Don Pullen | New York Duets | Music & Arts | CD 629

Main Title From 'The Carpetbaggers'
Billy May And His Orchestra | California Cool | Blue Note | 780707-2

Main Title Of Anatomy Of A Murder
Dave Grusin Orchestra | The Fabulous Baker Boys(Soundtrack) | GRP | GRP 20022

Mainstay
Alfred 23 Harth Group | Sweet Paris | free flow music | ffm 0291

Mairie Des Lilas
Phil Haynes Quartet | Phil Haynes & Free Country | Premonition | 790744-2

Maison Á Bordeau
Charles Davis & Captured Moments | Strange Goodbyes | L+R Records | CDLR 45101

Maitre Baboma
Pata Music Meets Arfi | News Of Roi Ubu | Pata Musik | PATA 10 CD

Maitre De Plaisir
William Hooker Quartet | Lifeline | Silkheart | SHCD 119

Maiysha
Miles Davis Group | Get Up With It | CBS | 485256-2

Majestic
Return To Forever | Romantic Warrior | CBS | SRCS 9348

Majon
Carla Bley-Steve Swallow | Are We There Yet? | Watt | 29(547297)

Major
Gary Dial-Dick Oatts Quartet With Strings | Dial And Oatts | dmp Digital Music Productions | CD 465

Major-
Larry Young-Eddie Gladden | The Art Of Larry Young | Blue Note | 799177-2

Major Love
Ricky Ford Sextet | Saxotic Stomp | Muse | MCD 5349

Major Major
Jonas Hellborg Group | Adfa | Demon Records | DEM 020

Majority
Antonio Hart Quintet | For The First Time | Novus | PD 83120

Major's Minor
Robert Lockwood Jr. | Contrasts | Trix Records | TRIX 3307

Makana
Joe McPhee Po Music | Linear B | Hat Art | CD 6057

Make A List Make A Wish
Art Pepper Quintet | Art Pepper:The Complete Galaxy Recordings | Galaxy | 16GCD 1016-2
Milcho Leviev Quartet | Blues For The Fisherman | Mole Jazz | MOLE 1

Make Believe
Dave Holland Quintet | Prime Directive | ECM | 1698(547950-2)
Earl Hines Trio | Boogie Woogie On St.Louis Blues | Prestige | MPP 2515
Glenn Miller And His Orchestra | Glenn Miller In Concert | RCA | NL 89216 DP
Jim Rotondi Quintet | Introducing Jim Rotondi | Criss Cross | Criss 1128

Make Haste
John Handy Group | Carnival | MCA | 28691 XOT

Make It Funky-
Duke Pearson Big Band | Introducing Duke Pearson's Big Band | Blue Note | 494508-2

Make It Right
James Blood Ulmer Quartet | Black And Blues | DIW | DIW 845 CD

Make It So
Spark Plug Smith | Country Blues Collector Items Vol.2(1931-1937) | Story Of Blues | CD 3540-2

Make It With You
Gunter Hampel Group | Music From Europe | ESP Disk | ESP 1042-2

Make Me A Pallet On The Floor
Angela Brown | The Voice Of Blues | Schubert Records | SCH- 105
Archie Shepp-Horace Parlan Duo | Swing Low | Plainisphare | PL 1267-73 CD
Chris Barber's Jazz Band | Ottilie Patterson With Chris Barber's Jazzband 1955-1958 | Lake | LACD 30
Jimmy Yancey | The Yancey-Lofton Sessions Vol. 2 | Storyville | SLP 239
Philadelphia Jerry Ricks & Oscar Klein | Jazz Roots | L+R Records | LR 40011

Make Me Call California
J.D.Short | The Blues, Vol. 6 | Sonet | 157102

Make My Love Stay Warm
Ruby Braff Trio | Bravura Eloquence | Concord | CCD 4423

Make Someone Happy
Bill Evans | The Complete Fantasy Recordings | Fantasy | 9FCD 1012-2
Bill Evans Trio | The Complete Bill Evans On Verve | Verve | 527953-2
The Complete Bill Evans On Verve | Verve | 527953-2
The Complete Bill Evans On Verve | Verve | 527953-2
The Best Of Bill Evans Live | Verve | 533825-2
Bill Evans At Town Hall | Verve | 831271-2
Brad Goode Quintet | Toy Trumpet | Steeplechase | SCCD 31491
Jane Bunnett-Don Pullen | New York Duets | Music & Arts | CD 629
Lorez Alexandria And Her Quintet | How Will I Remember You | Discovery | DS 782 IMS
Lucie Arnaz And Her Orchestra | Just In Time | Concord | CCD 4573

Make Sure You're Sure
Junior Cook Quartet | On A Misty Night | Steeplechase | SCCD 31266

Make The Man Love Me
Dinah Washington And Her Orchestra | Compact Jazz:Dinah Washington Sings The Blues | Mercury | 832573-2 PMS

Make The World Your Own
Billy Ver Planck And His Orchestra | Dancing Jazz | Savoy | SV 0235(MG 12101)

Make Your Own Temple
Jack Payne And His BBC Dance Orchestra | Radio Nights | Saville Records | SVL 152 IMS

Make!
Kenny Wheeler Sextet | Uncovered Heart | Sunnyside | SSC 1048 D

Makes Her Move
Bob Robinson And His Bob Cats | Piano Blues Vol.2-The Thirties(1930-1939) | Story Of Blues | CD 3512-2

Makin' Brownies
Ben Pollack-Irving Mills Unit/Kentucky Grasshoppers | Jazz Gallery:Jack Teagarden | RCA | 2114175-2

Makin' Whoopee
Alan Clare With Lenny Bush | Alan Clare's Holland Park:Love Music To Unwind | Master Mix | CHECD 00108
Art Tatum | Art Tatum:Complete Capitol Recordings | Capitol | 821325-2
Art Tatum-The Complete Pablo Solo Masterpieces | Pablo | 7 PACD 4404-2

Art Tatum:Complete Capitol Recordings | Definitive Records | DRCD 11192
The Tatum Solo Masterpieces Vol.5 | Pablo | 2310790
Art Tatum-Buddy DeFranco Quartet | The Tatum Group Masterpieces | Pablo | 2625706
Benny Goodman And His Orchestra | Artie Shaw/Benny Goodman | Forlane | UCD 19006
Billy May And His Orchestra | Bacchanalia | Capitol | ED 2604201
Bud Shank-Shorty Rogers Quintet | California Concert | Contemporary | CCD 14012-2
Clark Terry-Max Roach Quartet | Friednship | CBS | 510886-2
Count Basie And His Orchestra | En Concert Avec Europe 1 | Laserlight | 710706/07
Basie On Roulette, Vol. 11: Dance Along With Basie | Vogue | 500011
Dinah Washington With The Quincy Jones Orchestra | The Swingin' Miss 'D' | Verve | 558074-2
Don Bennett Quintet | Chicago Calling | Candid | CCD 79713
Don Senay With Strings | Autobiography In Jazz | Original Jazz Classics | OJC 115(DEB 198)
Ella Fitzgerald And Louis Armstrong With The Oscar Peterson Quartet | Ella And Louis Again,Vol.1 | Verve | 2304501 IMS
Ella Fitzgerald With Ellis Larkins | Ella:The Legendary American Decca Recordings | GRP | GRP 46482
Ella Fitzgerald With The Frank DeVol Orchestra | Ella Fitzgerald Sings Sweet Songs For Swingers | Verve | 9860417
Ella Fitzgerald-First Lady Of Song | Verve | 517898-2
Ernie Wilkins And His Orchestra | Here Comes The Swingin' Mr.Wilkins | Fresh Sound Records | FSR 511(Everest LPBR 5077)
Gerry Mulligan Quartet | Planet Jazz Sampler | Planet Jazz | 2152326-2
California Concerts Vol.1 | Pacific Jazz | 746860-2
Gerry Mulligan:Pleyel Concert Vol.2 | Vogue | 21409432
Gerry Mulligan Sextet | Compact Jazz:Gerry Mulligan | Mercury | 830697-2 PMS
JATP All Stars | Jazz At The Santa Monica Civic '72 | Pablo | 2625701-2
Louis Armstrong With The Oscar Peterson Quartet | Satchmo-When The Saints Go Marching In | Verve | 711051 IMS
Nat King Cole Trio | Nat King Cole:Route 66 | Dreyfus Jazz Line | FDM 36716-2
Love Songs | Nimbus Records | NI 2010
Vocal Classics & Instrumental Classics | Capitol | 300014(TOCJ 6128)
Oscar Peterson Quintet | Skol | Original Jazz Classics | OJC20 496-2
Oscar Peterson-Clark Terry Duo | Oscar Peterson & Clark Terry | Original Jazz Classics | OJCCD 806-2(2310742)
Oscar Peterson-Harry Edison Duo | Jousts | Pablo | 2310817
Peter Madsen Trio | Three Of A Kind | Minor Music | 801039
Rigmor Gustafsson With The Nils Landgren Quartet And The Fleshquartet | I Will Wait For You | ACT | 9418-2
Roland Kirk With The Jack McDuff Trio | Kirk's Work | Original Jazz Classics | OJC20 459-2(P 7210)
Roland Kirk-Jack McDuff Quartet | Pre-Rahsan | Prestige | P 24080
Stacy Kent With The Jim Tomlinson Quintet | The Boy Next Door | Candid | CCD 79797
Stephane Grappelli Quartet | Jazz In Paris:Stephane Grappelli-Django | EmArCy | 018421-1
Stephane Grappelli Quintet | Grapelli Story | Verve | 515807-2
Feeling + Finesse = Jazz | Atlantic | 7567-90140-2
Stephane Grappelli Trio | Live | Justin Time | JTR 8469-2
Tatum-Carter-Bellson Trio | The Tatum Group Masterpieces | Pablo | 2625706
Tatum-Hampton-Rich Trio | The Tatum Group Masterpieces | Pablo | 2625706
The Three Sounds | Standards | Blue Note | 821281-2
Woody Herman And His Sextet | Compact Jazz: Woody Herman | Verve | 835319-2 PMS

Makin' Whoopee-
Dorothy Donegan Trio | Live At The Widder Bar 1986 | Timeless | CD SJP 247
Wild Bill Davison All Stars | The Idividualism Of Wild Bill Davison | Savoy | SJL 2229 (801205)

Makin' Whoopee(reprise)
Dorothy Donegan | Makin' Whoopee | Black & Blue | BLE 59.146 2

Making The Scene(Love Scenes)
Karl Denson Group | Herbal Turkey Breast | Minor Music | 801032

Making Love
Rahsaan Roland Kirk Quartet | Here Comes The Whistleman | Atlantic | ATL 40389(SD 3007)

Making Music
Matthias Stich Sevensenses | ...mehrschichtig | Satin Doll Productions | SDP 1038-1 CD

Making Sense
Fourplay | Heartfelt | RCA | 2663916-2

Making Up
Mombasa | African Rhythm & Blues | Intercord | 160020

Makondi
Don Grusin Group | No Borders | GRP | GRP 96762

Mal Menor
Ton-Art | Mal Vu. Mal Dit. | Hat Art | CD 6088

Malachi(The Messenger)
Ramsey Lewis Quintet | Ivory Pyramid | GRP | GRP 96882

Malafemmena
Stan Kenton And His Orchestra | Hits In Concert | Creative World | ST 1074

Malaguena
Mel Tormé With The Billy May Orchestra | Mel Tormé Goes South Of The Border With Billy May | Verve | 589517-2
Pete LaRoca Quartet | Basra | Blue Note | 300262
Ray Brown & Laurindo Almeida | Moonlight Serenade | Jeton | JET 60005
Stan Kenton And His Orchestra | Stan Kenton Today | Decca | 6.28097 DP
Harry James And His Music Makers | Live At Cleareater Florida,Vol.2 | Magic | DAWE 77

Malaib Schina-
Sadao Watanabe Group | My Dear Life | Flying Disk | VIJ 6001

Malak 'Uqabe
Jacques Pirotton Trio | Soty | B.Sharp Records | CDS 087

Malambo
Roberto Perera Group | Harp And Soul | Inak | 30362

Malcolm Malcolm-Semper Malcolm
Khaliq Al-Rouf & Salaam | The Elephant Trop Dance | Nilva | NQ 3404 IMS

Malcolm's Gone
Bruce Cox Quartet With Guests | Stick To It | Minor Music | 801055

Malcolm's Mood
Peter Madsen Trio With Stanley Turrentine | Three Of A Kind Meets Mister T. | Minor Music | 801043

Maldoror's War Song
Wollie Kaiser Timeghost | Tust Du Fühlen Gut | Jazz Haus Musik | JHM 0060 CD

Male Couple
Les McCann Trio | Les Is More | Night Records | VNCD 4(887048)

Maleva
Jali Nyama Suso | Jali Nyama-Kora Music From Gambia | FMP | SAJ 51

Malice Towards None
Das Pferd | Kisses | ITM Records | ITM 1430

Malika
Matthias Schubert Quartet | Blue And Grey Suite | Enja | ENJ-9045 2

Malinconie
Fletcher Henderson And His Orchestra | The Indispensable Fletcher Henderson(1927-1936) | RCA | 2122618-2

Malinye
Jan Garbarek Group | Rites | ECM | 1685/86(559006-2)
Gunther Schuller With The WDR Radio Orchestra & Rememberance Band | Witchi Tia To, The Music Of Jim Pepper | Tutu Records | 888204-2*

Malinyea
Jim Pepper & Eagle Wing | Rerembrance-Live At The International Jazzfestival Münster | Tutu Records | 888152-2*
Jim Pepper Group | Comin' And Goin' | Bellaphon | 290.31.029

Mallet Man
Ed Blackwell Project | Vol.1:What It Is? | Enja | ENJ-7089 2

Mallet Song
Dennis Warren's Full Metal Revolutionary Jazz Ensemble | Watch Out! | Accurate | AC 5017

Mallorca
Storyville Jassband | Mallorca | Timeless | CD TTD 604

Maloma
New England Ragtime Ensemble | The Art Of The Rag | GM Recordings | GM 3018 CD(882950)

Malted Milk
Blind Lemon Jefferson | Blind Lemon Jefferson-Master Of The Blues | Biograph | BLP 12015

Maltese Chicken Farm
Wolfgang Lauth Quartet | Noch Lauther | Bear Family Records | BCD 15942 AH

Malu
Count Basie And His Orchestra | Broadway Basie's...Way | Command | CQD 40004

Mama Don't Allow
Mark Shane-Terry Blaine Group | With Thee I Swing! | Nagel-Heyer | CD 040
Mick Mulligan's Magnolia Jazz Band With George Melly | Great British Traditional Bands Vol.7:Mick Mulligan & George Melly | Lake | LACD 66

Mama Don't Wear No Drawers
Snooks Eaglin | That's All Right | Original Blues Classics | OBCCD 568-2(BV 1046)

Mama I'll Be Home Someday
Barney Wilen Quintet | Wild Dogs Of The Ruwenzori | IDA Record | 020 CD

Mama Inez
Charlie Parker Septet | Charlie Parker-South Of The Border | Verve | 527779-2
Grant Green Sextet | The Latin Bit | Blue Note | 300051(4111)
Wrobel-Roberscheuten-Hopkins Jam Session | Jammin' At The IAJRC Convention Hamburg 1999 | Nagel-Heyer | CD 066
Ragtime Specht Groove Trio | Ragtime Specht Groove Vol. 4: Little Susie | Intercord | 145032

Mama Lou
Oliver Nelson Quintet | Eric Dolphy:The Complete Prestige Recordings | Prestige | 9 PRCD-4418-2
The Georgians | The Georgians 1922-23 | Retrieval | RTR 79003

Mama Mama Blues(Rusty Dusty Blues)
Louis Jordan And His Tympany Five | Louis Jordan Vol.2-Knock Me Out | Swingtime(Contact) | ST 1012

Mama Rose
Archie Shepp Quartet | Devil Blues-The Essential Archie Shepp | Circle Records | RK 33-7884/33 IMS

Mama That Moon Is Here Again
Dan Barrett And His Extra-Celestials | Moon Song | Arbors Records | ARCD 19158

Mama Told Me Not To Come
Archie Shepp Orchestra | Mama Too Tight | Impulse(MCA) | 951248-2

Mama Too Tight
Art Ensemble Of Chicago | Coming Home Jamaica | Dreyfus Jazz Line | FDM 37003-2

Mama Wants You
J.B.Lenoir Blues Band | J. B. Lenoir | Chess | 427003

Mama Yo Quiero
John Lee Hooker Band | Moanin' The Blues | Charly | CRB 1029

Mamacita
Joe Henderson Sextet | The Kicker | Original Jazz Classics | OJCCD 465-2
Foresight | Milestone | M 47058
Kenny Dorham Quintet | Trompeta Toccata | Blue Note | BST 84181

Mamaita..What You've Got
Mandingo Griot Society | Mandingo Griot Society | Flying Fish | FF 70076

Mamamita
David Thomas Roberts | Ragtime Piano | Mardi Gras Records | MG 1002

Mama's Bitter Sweet
James P.Johnson | Rare Piano Rags | Jazz Anthology | JA 5120

Mama's Gone Goodbye
Bob Crosby's Bobcats | So Far So Good | Halcyon | DHDL 132
Peter Bocage With His Creole Serenaders | New Orleans-The Living Legends:Peter Bocage | Original Jazz Classics | OJCCD 1835-2

Mama's In The Groove
Christian Griese Group | Affinities:My Berlin Phone Book | BIT | 11216

Mambeando
Vince Guaraldi-Bola Sete Quartet | From All Sides | Original Jazz Classics | OJCCD 989-2(F 3-362)

Mamblue
Cal Tjader's Modern Mambo Quintet(Sextet) | Mambo With Tjader | Original Jazz Classics | OJCCD 271-2(F 3202)

Mamblues
Cal Tjader's Orchestra | Cal Tjader/Soul Sauce | Verve | 521668-2

Mambo 2000
Erroll Garner Trio | The Best Of Erroll Garner | CBS | CBS 52706

Mambo A La Mintzer
Poncho Sanchez With The Clare Fischer Septet | Straight Ahead (Pa'lante) | Discovery | DS 813 IMS

Mambo Bounce
Sonny Rollins Quartet | Sonny Rollins:Complete 1949-1951 Prestige Studio Recordings | Definitive Records | DRCD 11240
Welcome To Jazz: Sonny Rollins | Koch Records | 322 079 D1
Erroll Garner Trio | Concert By The Sea | CBS | 451042-2

Mambo Cuco
Art Blakey And The Jazz Messengers | Des Femmes Disparaissent/Les Tricheurs(Original Soundtracks) | Fontana | 834752-2 PMS

Mambo De La Pinta
Art Pepper Quartet | No Limit | Contemporary | COP 019
Art Pepper:The Complete Galaxy Recordings | Galaxy | 16GCD 1016-2
Landscape | Original Jazz Classics | OJCCD 676-2(GXY 5128)

Mambo Del Crow
Shorty Rogers And His Giants | Short Stops | RCA | NL 85917(2)

Mambo DeLas Brujas-
Al Porcino Big Band | Al Cohn Meets Al Porcino | Organic Music | ORGM 9730

Mambo Di Paulo
Tito Puente And His Latin Ensemble | Mambo Diablo | Concord | CJ 283

Mambo For Roy
Tito Puente Orchestra | Royal T | Concord | CCD 4553

Mambo Gumbo
Woody Herman And His Orchestra | Woody Herman 1954 And 1959 | Status | DSTS 1021

Mambo In Chimes
George Shearing With The Montgomery Brothers | Wes Montgomery-The Complete Riverside Recordings | Riverside | 12 RCD 4408-2
Wes Montgomery Sextet | Wes And Friends | Milestone | M 47013

Mambo In Chimes(alt.take)
Cal Tjader Sextet | Talkin Verve/Roots Of Acid Jazz:Cal Tjader | Verve | 531562-2

Mambo In Miami
George Shearing And His Quintet | Beauty And The Beat | Pathe | EMS 1158(Capitol ST 1219)
Jesus Chucho Valdes | Lucumi | Messidor | 15976 CD

Mambo Influenciado
Paquito D'Rivera Group feat. Arturo Sandoval | Reunion | Messidor | 15805 CD

Mambo Inn
Count Basie And His Orchestra | Live In Basel 1956 | Jazz Helvet | JH 05
Grant Green Sextet | The Latin Bit | Blue Note | 300051(4111)
Hendrik Meurkens Sextet | The Clear Of Clouds | Concord | CCD 4531
Poncho Sanchez Group | La Familia | Concord | CCD 4369

Mambo Jambo
Freddie Brocksieper Trio | Shot Gun Boogie | Bear Family Records | BCD 16277 AH
Machito And His Afro-Cuban Salseros | Mucho Macho | Pablo | 2625712-2

Mambo Jazz Opus No.7
Tito Puente And His Ensemble | Mambo Of The Times | Concord | CCD 4499

Mambo Koyama
Art Pepper Quartet | Art Pepper:The Complete Galaxy Recordings | Galaxy | 16GCD 1016-2
Art Pepper:The Complete Galaxy Recordings | Galaxy | 16GCD 1016-2
Art Pepper:The Complete Galaxy Recordings | Galaxy | 16GCD 1016-2
APQ-The Maiden Voyage Sessions,Vol.3 | Galaxy | GXY 5151
Maynard Ferguson And His Orchestra | Straightaway Jazz Themes | Fresh Sound Records | FSR 656(Roulette R 52076)

Mambo Macumba
Cal Tjader's Orchestra | Tjader Plays Mambo | Original Jazz Classics | OJC 274(F 3221)

Mambo Mongo
Conexion Latina | Mambo Nights | Enja | ENJ-9402 2

Mambo Nights
Freddie Brocksieper Orchester | Shot Gun Boogie | Bear Family Records | BCD 16277 AH

Mambo No.8
Hilton Ruiz Orchestra | Manhattan Mambo | Telarc Digital | CD 83322

Mambo Ricci
Mario Bauzá And His Afro-Cuban Jazz Orchestra | Tanga | Messidor | 15819 CD

Mambo Terrifico
Poncho Sanchez And His Orchestra | Poncho | Discovery | DS 799 IMS

Mambo With Me
James Moody And His Band | James Moody | Prestige | P 24015

Mambossa
Andres Boiarsky Quartet | Into The Light | Reservoir | RSR CD 149

Mamie's Blues
Jelly Roll Morton | The Commodore Story | Commodore | CMD 24002

Mam'selle
Grant-Lyttelton Paseo Jazz Band | A Tribute To Humph-Vol.4 | Dormouse | DM 4 IMS

Man Alone
Jimmy Giuffre Three | Free Fall | CBS | CK 65446
Carey Bell's Blues Harp Band | Goin' On Main Street | L+R Records | CDLR 72006

Man In The Mirror
Tuck Andress | Reckless Precision | Windham Hill | 34 10124-2

Man Of Considerable Taste
Cecil Payne Quintet | Patterns Of Jazz | Savoy | SV 0135(MG 12147)

Man Of Wool
Booker Little Sextet | Out Front | Candid | CCD 79027

Man Of Words
Anthony Davis | For Deborah-Lady Of The Mirrors | India Navigation | IN 1047

Man On Mars-
J.R. Monterose Sextet | Jaywalkin' | Fresh Sound Records | FSR-CD 320

Man On The Couch
Don Cherry Group | Don Cherry-The Sonet Recordings:Eternal Now/Live Ankara | Verve | 533049-2

Man On The Moon
George Russell Sextet | Trip to Prillarguri | Soul Note | 121029-2

Man On Water
Cassiber | Man Or Monkey | Riskant | 6.28624

Man With A Broken Heart
Boyd Raeburn And His Orchestra | Man With The Horns | Savoy | WL 70534 (809300)

Man With A Horn
John Hardee Quartet | 6 Classic Tenors | EPM Musique | FDC 5170

Man With The Horn
Anita O'Day With The Buddy Bregman Orchestra | Pick Yourself Up | Official | 3015

Man,That Was A Dream(Monk's Dream)
Karen Francis With The Mark Turner Quintet | Little Sunflower | Steeplechase | SCCD 31431

Man,That Was A Dream(Monk's Dream-alt.take)
Freddie Hubbard Quintet | Bolivia | Limelight | 820837-2

Manana Iguana
Mr.Acker Bilk And His Paramount Jazz Band | White Cliffs Of Dover | Intercord | 125408

Manaus Fever
Wanderlust + Guests | Full Bronte | Laika Records | 35101412

Manchao
Gus Viseur Sextet | Gus Viseur A Bruxelles | Harmonia Mundi | PJC 222006

Manchmal, Manchmal Lieber Nicht
Guido Manusardi Quartet | Bra Session | SPLASC(H) Records | H 125

Mandakini
Elements | Illumination | RCA | PD 83031(874013)

Mandala
Ray Russell Octet | Dragon Hill | CBS | 494435-2

Mandalay Express
Peter Materna Quartet | Aquarius | Jazzline | JL 11142-2

Mandela
Chico Freeman Group | The Emissary | Clarity Recordings | CCD-1015
Lee Ritenour Group | Banded Together | Elektra | 960358-1

Mandeville
Zipflo Reinhardt Quintet | Oceana | Intercord | 160114

Mandragora
Chico Hamilton And Euphoria | My Panamanian Friend-The Music Of Eric Dolphy | Soul Note | 121265-2

Mandrake
Thierry Bruneau 4tet feat. Mal Waldron | Live At De Kave | Serene Records | SER 01

Mandy Lee Blues
King Oliver's Creole Jazz Band | King Oliver's Creole Jazzband-The Complete Set | Retrieval | RTR 79007

Mandy Make Up Your Mind
Bud Freeman With The Dutch Swing College Band | The Dutch Swing College Band Vol.1 | Philips | 839771-2
Dixie-O-Naires | Strike Up The Band | Timeless | CD TTD 576
Sonny Morris And The Delta Jazz Band | The Spirit Lives On | Lake | LACD 46

Mane Na
Sahib Shihab Quartet | Sentiments | Storyville | SLP 1008

Maneklar
Vigleik Storaas Trio | Bilder | Curling Legs Prod. | C.L.P. CD 018

Manenat(Moon Night)
Abdullah Ibrahim And Ekaya | Water From An Ancient Well | TipToe | TIP-888812 2

Manenberg Revisited(Cape Town Fringe)
Kip Hanrahan Group | A Fre Short Notes From The End Run | American Clave | AMCL 1011 EP

Mangalam-
Eric Lugosch | Black Key Blues | Acoustic Music Records | 319.1148.2

Mango
Nguyen Le Trio | Million Waves | ACT | 9221-2

Mango Blues
Zbigniew Namyslowski Quartet | Namyslovski | Inner City | IC 1048 IMS

Mango Mangue
Charlie Parker With Machito And His Orchestra | Charlie Parker:The Best Of The Verve Years | Verve | 527815-2
The Latin Bird | Memo Music | HDJ 4076

Mango On The Rocks
Monty Alexander 7 | Jamento | Pablo | 2310826

Mango Tango
Carlos Garnett Quintet | Under Nubian Skies | HighNote Records | HCD 7023

Mangoes
Sonny Rollins Quartet | Sonny Rollins-The Freelance Years:The Complete Riverside & Contemporary Recordings | Riverside | 5 RCD 4427-2
Sonny Rollins:Brown Skin Girl | Memo Music | HDJ 4041

Mangrove
Lee-Askill-Atherton | Shoalhaven Rise | Black Sun Music | 15019-2

Mangustao(part 1)
Nguyen Le Group | Tales From Viet-Nam | ACT | 9225-2

Mangustao(part 2)
Art Pepper Septet | Art Pepper:Tokyo Debut | Galaxy | GCD 4201-2

Manha De Carnaval(Morning Of The Carnival)
Barney Kessel | Solo | Concord | CJ 221
Bola Sete Quintet | Tour De Force:The Bola Sete Trios | Fantasy | FCD 24766-2
Carlos Barbosa-Lima | Plays The Music Of Luiz Bonfa And Cole Porter | Concord | CCD 42008
Charlie Mariano With The Tete Montoliu Trio | It's Standard Time Vol.1 | Fresh Sound Records | FSR-CD 5021
Frank Morgan Quartet | Easy Living | Original Jazz Classics | OJCCD 833-2(C 14013)
Freddy Cole With Band | A Circle Of Love | Fantasy | FCD 9674-2
George Cables Trio | Skylark | Steeplechase | SCCD 31381
Hampton Hawes Trio | I'm All Smiles | Original Jazz Classics | OJCCD 796-2(C 7631)
Jimmy Bruno Trio With The Edgardo Cintron Orchestra | Sleight Of Hand | Concord | CCD 4532
Lou Blackburn-Freddie Hill Quintet | Perception | Fresh Sound Records | FSR-CD 0307
McCoy Tyner Quartet | Just Feelin' | Palo Alto | PA 8083
Paco De Lucia-Al Di Meola-John McLaughlin | Paco De Lucia-Al Di Meola-John McLaughlin | Verve | 533215-2
Patricia Barber Quartet | Café Blue | Blue Note | 521810-2
Patrick Tompert Trio | Patrick Tompert Trio Live | Satin Doll Productions | SDP 1029-1 CD
Paul Desmond Quartet | Live | Verve | 543501-2
Quincy Jones And His Orchestra | Big Band Bossa Nova | Verve | 557913-2
Ray Barretto And His Orchestra | Carnaval | Fantasy | FCD 24713-2
Ron Eschete | A Closer Look | Concord | CCD 4607
Stan Getz With The Gary McFarland Orchestra | Stan Getz Highlights | Verve | 847430-2
Compact Jazz | Verve | 831368-2
Stanley Turrentine Orchestra | New Time Shuffle | Blue Note | LT 993 (GXK 8189)
Barney Kessel | Berlin Festival-Guitar Workshop | MPS | 68159

Manha De Carnaval(Morning Of The Carnival)-
Trio Da Paz With Special Guests | Black Orpheus | Kokopelli Records | KOKO 1299

Manhattan
Bobby Short Sextet | Songs Of New York | Telarc Digital | CD 83346
Dinah Washington With The Belford Hendricks Orchestra | Compact Jazz: Dinah Washington | Mercury | 830700-2 PMS
Earl Hines Trio | Boogie Woogie On St.Louis Blues | Prestige | MPP 2515
Ella Fitzgerald With The Buddy Bregman Orchestra | The Rodgers And Hart Songbook | Verve | 821693-1
Ella Fitzgerald Sings The Rodgers And Hart Song Book | Verve | 537258-2
The Rodgers And Hart Song Book, Vol.1 | Verve | 821579-2 PMS
Grant Stewart Quartet | Buen Rollo | Fresh Sound Records | FSNT 053 CD
Great Jazz Trio | The Club New Yorker | Denon Compact Disc | DC-8567
Hans Koller Big Band | New York City | MPS | 68235
J.R. Monterose Sextet | Jaywalkin' | Fresh Sound Records | FSR-CD 320
Jake Hanna Quintet | Jake Takes Manhattan | Concord | CJ 35
Marian McPartland Trio | Marion McPartland At The Hickory House | Savoy | SJL 2248 (801856)
Michel Petrucciani Trio | Michel Petrucciani:Concert Inédits | Dreyfus Jazz Line | FDM 36607-2
Olaf Polziehn Trio | American Songbook | Satin Doll Productions | SDP 1032-1 CD
Paul Kuhn Orchestra feat. Gustl Mayer | Street Of Dreams | Mons Records | MR 874800
Rosemary Clooney With The Scott Hamilton Quintet | Show Tunes | Concord | CCD 4364
Stacy Kent With The Jim Tomlinson Quintet | In Love Again | Candid | CCD 79786
Stephane Grappelli & Earl Hines | Lions Abroad Vol.3:Le Lion Á Paris | Black Lion | BLCD 7622-2
George Coleman Quartet | Manhattan Panorama | Evidence | ECD 22019-2

Manhattan-
Simon Schott | Bar Piano: Simon Schott Plays Your Favorite Evergreens Vol.2 | Organic Music | ORGM 9735
Walton Ornato | Magic Mountain | Black Sun Music | 15016-2

Manhattan Blues
Sammy Price All Stars | New York 1955 | Jazz Anthology | JA 5211

Manhattan Carousel
Don Cherry Septet | Symphony For Improvisers | Blue Note | 828976-2

Manhattan Lorelei
Freddie Brocksieper Orchester | Shot Gun Boogie | Bear Family Records | BCD 16277 AH

Manhattan Mambo
Eric Reed Trio | Manhattan Melodies | Verve | 050294-2

Manhattan Mood
McCoy Tyner-Bobby Hutcherson Duo | Manhattan Moods | Blue Note | 828423-2

Manhattan Reflections
Ahmad Jamal Trio | Freeflight | Impulse(MCA) | GRP 11332

Manhattan,3 A.M.
George Russell And His Orchestra | Geogre Russell New York N.Y. | Impulse(MCA) | 951278-2

Manhattan-Rico
Freddie King Group | Freddie King Gives You A Bonanza Of Instrumentals | Crosscut | CCR 1010

Mania De Maria
Stan Getz-Luiz Bonfa Quartet | Jazz Samba Encore! | CTI Records | PDCTI 1125-2

Manic Depression
Defunkt | Defunkt/Heroes | DIW | DIW 838 CD
Nguyen Le Trio With Guests | Purple:Celebrating Jimi Hendrix | ACT | 9410-2
String Trio Of New York & Jay Clayton | String Trio Of New York & Jay Clayton | West Wind | WW 2008

Manic Musical Depression
Machito and His Salsa Big Band | Machito | Timeless | CD SJP 161

Maningafoly
Trilok Gurtu Group | Crazy Saints | CMP Records | CMP CD 66

Manipulation
Jerry Bergonzi And Joachim Kühn | Signed By | Adda | ZZ 84104

Mank De Monk
Beverly Kenney With The Basie-Ites | Beverly Kenney | Fresh Sound Records | FSR-CD 33(882158)

Manneling
Abdullah Ibrahim Trio | Yarona | TipToe | TIP-888820 2

Mannenberg
Abdullah Ibrahim(Dollar Brand) | Autobiography | Plainisphare | PL 1267-68 CD

Mannix
Brew Moore Quartet | I Should Care | Steeplechase | SCCD 36019

Manny's Tune
Django Reinhardt And The Quintet Du Hot Club De France | Peche Á La Mode-The Great Blue Star Sessions 1947/1953 | Verve | 835418-2

Mano
Django Reinhardt Portrait | Barclay | DALP 2/1939
Louis Sclavis & The Bernard Struber Jazztet | La Phare | Enja | ENJ-9359 2

Manoir
Häns'che Weiss-Vali Mayer Duo | Just Play II | MMM Records | CD 1303

Manoir-
André Villeger Connection | André Villeger Connection | Black & Blue | BLE 59.641 2

Manoir De Mes Reves
Christian Escoude Quartet With Strings | Plays Django Reinhardt | EmArCy | 510132-2
Django Reinhardt And The Quintet Du Hot Club De France | Swing De Paris | Arco | 3 ARC 110
Hagood Hardy Septet | Morocco | Sackville | SKCD2-2018
Martin Taylor Quintet With Guests | Spirit Of Django:Years Apart | Linn Records | AKD 058

Manoir De Mes Reves-
Gerry Mulligan Concert Jazz Band | Verve Jazz Masters 36:Gerry Mulligan | Verve | 523342-2

Manoir De Mes Reves(aka Django's Castle)
James Carter Group | Chasin' The Gypsy | Atlantic | 7567-83304-2
Gerry Mulligan Concert Jazz Band | The Complete Verve Gerry Mulligan Concert Band | Verve | 9860613

Manoir De Mes Reves(aka Django's Castle)[remake]
Henri Crolla/Stephane Grappelli Quartet | Special Stephane Grappelli | Jazztime(EMI) | 251286-2

Manolete
Tuck Andress | Reckless Precision | Windham Hill | 34 10124-2

Mansali
Eric St-Laurent-Thomy Jordi-Thomas Alkier feat. Helge Schneider | Rock,Jazz & Music:Laut! | BIT | 11212

Manson & Dixon
Chuz Alfred Quintet | Jazz Youn Blood | Savoy | SV 0211(MG 12030)

Manteca
Bob Cunningham Quartet | Walking Bass | Nilva | NQ 3411 IMS
Cal Tjader's Orchestra | Soul Burst | Verve | 557446-2
Cedar Walton Sextet | Eastern Rebellion 4 | Timeless | SJP 184
Dizzy Gillespie And His Orchestra | Bebop Enters Sweden | Dragon | DRCD 318
Dizzy Gillespie-Diz Delights | RCA | CL 89804 SF
Gillespiana And Carnegie Hall Concert | Verve | 519809-2
The Greatest Of Dizzy Gillespie | RCA | 2113164-2
Dizzy Gillespie Quintet | On The Sunny Side Of The Street | Moon Records | MCD 077-2
Ella Fitzgerald With The Paul Smith Trio | Return To Happiness-JATP At Yoyogi National Stadium,Tokyo | Pablo | 2620117-2
GRP All-Star Big Band | GRP 10th Anniversary | GRP | GRP 96722
Sal Salvador Quartet | A Tribute To The Greats | Fresh Sound Records | FSR 2019(Bethlehem BCP 74)
Woody Herman And The Young Thundering Herd With Friends | Woody And Friends At Monterey Jazz Festival 1979 | Concord | CCD 4170

Mantes
Ray Mantilla Space Station | Hands Of Fire | Red Records | 123174-2

Mantis
Alice Coltrane Quintet | Ptah The El Daoud | Impulse(MCA) | 951201-2

Mantra
Stephan Dietz Quartet | Mirrors | EGO | 4008
Abdullah Ibrahim Group | Mantra Mode | TipToe | TIP-888810 2

Manu
Eduardo M.Kohan Trio | Dies Irae | Hat Art | 3507

Manu Pombo
Joaquin Chacón Group | San | Fresh Sound Records | FSNT 015 CD

Manuel
Tete Montoliu | Yellow Dolphin Street/Catalonian Folk Songs | Timeless | CD SJP 107/116

Manuel Deeghit
Joe Bonner Quartet | The Lost Melody | Steeplechase | SCCD 31227

Manuel's Mambo
Delle Haensch Jump Combo | Deutsches Jazz Fesival 1954/1955 | Bear Family Records | BCD 15430

Manuscript Blues
Organic Music Society | Organic Music | Caprice | CAP 2001 (1-2)

Many Blessings
Roland Kirk Quartet | The Inflated Tear | Atlantic | 7567-90045-2
Art Lande Quartet | Rubisa Patrol | ECM | 1081

Many Chinas
Mark Isham-Peter Van Hooke Duo | Vapor Drawings | Windham Hill | TA-C- 1027

Many Kochanas
Sonny Sharrock Quartet | Ask The Ages | Antilles | 848957-2(889515)

Mapa
Ornette Coleman Quartet | Beauty Is A Rare Thing:Ornette Coleman-The Complete Atlantic Recordings | Atlantic | 8122-71410-2
Ornette On Tenor | Atlantic | 8122-71455-2
Kölner Saxophon Mafia-Drümmele Maa-Elima | Baboma | Jazz Haus Musik | JHM 33

Maple Leaf Rag
Earl Hines And His Orchestra | Earl Hines Vol.1-South Side Swing | MCA | 1311
Kid Ory's Creole Jazz Band | The Legendary Crescent Recording Sessions | GHB Records | BCD 10
New Orleans Feetwarmers | Victor Jazz History Vol.1:New Orleans & Dixieland | RCA | 2128555-2
New Orleans Rhythm Kings | New Orleans Rhythm Kings | Milestone | MCD 47020-2
Turk Murphy And His Jazz Band | The Many Faces Of Ragtime | Atlantic | SD 1613
Yerba Buena Jazz Band | Bunk & Lu | Good Time Jazz | GTCD 12024-2
Willie 'The Lion' Smith Duo | Willie 'The Lion ' Smith:The Lion's In Town | Vogue | 2111506-2

Maputo
Marcus Miller Group | Live & More | Dreyfus Jazz Line | FDM 36585-2
Michael Sagmeister Quartet | Motions And Emotions | BELL Records | BLR 84054

Maputo Introduction
Dave Douglas Trio | Constellations | Hat Art | CD 6173

Mar
Josep Maria Balanyà | Elements Of Development | Laika Records | 8695070
The Doug Sides Ensemble | Perseverance | No Name | CD-001

Mara Pooh
Al Di Meola Group | Tiramisu | Manhattan | CDP 7469952

Maraba Blue
The Brazz Brothers | Ngoma | Laika Records | 35101562
Cannonball Adderley Quintet With Brass Reeds And Voices | Accent On Africa | Affinity | AFF 148

Marable's Parade
Pili-Pili | Nomans Land | JA & RO | JARO 4209-2

Marabout
Ana Caram Group | Maracana | Chesky | JD 104

Maracatu
Egberto Gismonti & Academia De Dancas | Sanfona | ECM | 1203/04(829391-2)
Egberto Gismonti Group | Works | ECM | 823269-2

Maracatu-Too
Memphis Slim Group | The Real Folk Blues | Chess | CHD 9270(872290)

Maramoor Mambo
Cal Tjader's Orchestra | Cal Tjader/Soul Sauce | Verve | 521668-2

Maramu
Norbert Stein Pata Masters | Pata Maroc | Pata Musik | PATA 12(AMF 1063)

Marasouks
Alex Gunia's Groove Cut | Alex Gunia's Groove Cut | ITM Records | ITM 1463

Marathon
Peter Finger Und Gäste | InnenLeben | Acoustic Music Records | AMC 1019

Marathon Man
Eef Albers Group | Pyramids | Cris Crazz | CCR 017 IMS

Maravilla De Son
John Surman | Road To Saint Ives | ECM | 1418(843849-2)

Marazion
Dave Brubeck Quartet | Jazz Impressions Of Eurasia | CBS | SRCS 9360

Marcel Le Fourreur
Bobby Jaspar Group | Bobby Jaspar/Henri Renaud | Vogue | 21409372

Marcel The Furrier
Oscar Pettiford Sextet | Oscar Pettiford Sextet | Vogue | 21409452

March
Art Ensemble Of Chicago | Urban Bushmen | ECM | 1211/12

March-
Roscoe Mitchell-Muhal Richard Abrams | Duets And Solos | Black Saint | 120133-2

March For My Friend Blam
Tom Varner Group | Long Night Big Day | New World Records | 80410-2

March Hare
Richard Zimmerman | The Complete Works Of Scott Joplin | Laserlight | 15945

March Of Destiny
Michael Shrieve Group | The Leaving Time | RCA | PD 83032

March Of The Bob Cats
Jack Teagarden And His Band | The Club Hangover Broadcast | Arbors Records | ARCD 19150/51

March Of The Indians
Trombone Summit | Trombone Summit | MPS | 68272

March Of The Siamese Children
Gerals Wiggins Trio | The King And I | Fresh Sound Records | FSR-CD 0053

March On March On
Bud Freeman All Stars | The Bud Freeman All Stars | Original Jazz Classics | OJC 183(SV 2012)
Oliver Nelson Sextet | Eric Dolphy:The Complete Prestige Recordings | Prestige | 9 PRCD-4418-2
Blue Mitchell Quintet | Down With It | Blue Note | 854327-2

March On Selma
Roland Kirk Quartet | Verve Jazz Masters 27:Roland Kirk | Verve | 522062-2

March On Swan Lake
Verve Jazz Masters Vol.60:The Collection | Verve | 529866-2
Oscar Peterson And His Trio | At The Blue Note: Last Call | Telarc Digital | CD 83314

March Wind
Paolo Fresu Sextet | Mamut: Music For A Mime | SPLASC(H) Records | CD H 127-2

Marche
Jacky Terrasson-Emmanuel Pahud Quartet | Into The Blue | Blue Note | 557257-2

Marche À La Turque(Mozart)
Gianluigi Trovesi Octet | Les Hommes Armés | Soul Note | 121311-2

Märchenstunde
Clifton Chenier Group | Live At Montreux | Charly | CDX 2

Marchin' For Abilene-
John Lewis | Afternoon In Paris | Dreyfus Jazz Line | FDM 36507-2

Marching Aunts
John Tchicai-Hartmut Geerken | Continent | Praxis | CM 102

Marchons
Dan Rose Trio | Conversations | Enja | 8006-2

Mar-cia
Carlo Actis Dato Quartet | Noblesse Oblige | SPLASC(H) Records | H 118

Mare Mosso
Alberto Nacci Alma Quartet | Isola Lontana | SPLASC(H) Records | CD H 310-2

Maree
Flautissimo | Flautissimo | Edition Collage | EC 445-2

Margaret
Perry Robinson 4 | Funk Dumpling | Savoy | SV 0255(MG 12177)

Margerine
Chet Baker Quintet | Chet Baker Plays & Sings | West Wind | WW 2108

Margie
Benny Goodman And His Orchestra | More Camel Caravans | Phontastic | NCD 8843/4
Benny Goodman Forever | RCA | NL 89955(2) DP
Billy May And His Orchestra With Members Of The Jimmy Lunceford Orchestra | Great Swing Classics In Hi-Fi | Capitol | 521223-2
Bob Hall | Pianissimo-Barpiano | BELL Records | BLR 89063
Chris Barber-Barry Martin Band | Collaboration | GHB Records | BCD 40
Dave Brubeck Quartet | Double Live From The USA & UK | Telarc Digital | CD 83400(2)
Ernst Höllerhagen Quintet | Ernst Höllerhagen 1942-1948 | Elite Special | 9522001
Henrik Johansen's Jazzband | The Golden Years Of Revibal Jazz,Vol.15 | Storyville | STCD 5520
Jay McShann-Major Holley | Havin' Fun | Sackville | SKCD2-2047
Jimmy Lunceford And His Orchestra | Jimmy Lunceford And His Orchestra Vol.1 | Black & Blue | BLE 59.241 2
Louis Armstrong And His All Stars | Louis Armstrong:The Great Chicago Concert 1956 | CBS | C2K 65119
Old Favorites | MCA | 1335
Oscar Peterson Trio | Masters Of Jazz Vol.7 | RCA | NL 89721 DP
Prowizorka Jazz Band | Prowizorka Jazz Band | Timeless | CD TTD 558
Sidney Bechet And His Feetwarmers | Jazz In Paris:Sidney Bechet Et Claude Luther | EmArCy | 159821-2 PMS
Stephane Grappelli And His Quintet | Stephane's Tune | Naxos Jazz | 8.120570 CD

Margie(alt.take)
Joe Morris Trio | Symbolic Gesture | Soul Note | 121204-2

Margjit Og Targjei Risvollo
Teddy Charles Quintet | Jimmy Giuffre:The Complete 1947-1953 Small Group Sessions Vol.3 | Blue Moon | BMCD 1048

Margot
Keith Jarrett Trio | Chick Corea-Herbie Hancock-Keith Jarrett-McCoy Tyner | Atlantic | ATL 50326

Margueritte
Oregon | Winter Light | Vanguard | VMD 79350

Maria
Coleman Hawkins And Ben Webster With The Oscar Peterson Quartet | Tenor Giants | Verve | 2610046
Dave Brubeck Quartet | Brubeck Plays Music From West Side Story And... | CBS | 450410-2
Horn Knox | The Song Is You | JHM Records | JHM 3625
Joan Monné Trio | Mireia | Fresh Sound Records | FSNT 100 CD
Junior Mance Trio & Orchestra | That Lovin' Feelin' | Milestone | MCD 47097-2
Martial Solal | Jazz 'n (e)motion:Martial Solal | RCA | 2155932-2
Oscar Peterson Trio | Verve Jazz Masters 37:Oscar Peterson Plays Broadway | Verve | 516893-2
West Side Story | Verve | 539753-2
Sarah Vaughan With The Quincy Jones Orchestra | You're Mine You | Fresh Sound Records | 857157-2

Maria Cardona
Tito Puente And His Ensemble | On Broadway | Concord | CCD 4207

Maria Domingas
Gato Barbieri Group | Gato Barbieri:The Complete Flying Dutchman Recordings 1969-1973 | RCA | 2154555-2

Maria Durch Den Dornwald Ging
Christoph Lauer & Norwegian Brass | Heaven | ACT | 9420-2

Maria Durch Einen Dornwald Ging
Jan Von Klewitz-Markus Burger | Spiritual Standards | Jazzline | JL 11156-2

Maria Fumaca
Claudio Lodati Dac'Corda | Voci | SPLASC(H) Records | H 154

Maria Interlude
Kenny Barron Trio | Lemuria-Seascape | Candid | CCD 79508

Maria Moca
Artie Shaw And His Orchestra | In The Blue Room/In The Café Rouge | RCA | 2118527-2
Mariaaa
Louis Sclavis | Clarinettes | IDA Record | 004 CD
Mariama
Dave Brubeck Quartet | Double Live From The USA & UK | Telarc Digital | CD 83400(2)
Marianne
Niels Lan Doky Trio | Close Encounter | Storyville | STCD 4173
Marianne-
Friedemann Graef-Albrecht Riermeier Duo | Exit | FMP | 0820
Maria's Folly
Nicholas Payton Quintet | From This Moment... | Verve | 527073-2
Marie
Kid Thomas And His Algiers Stompers | The Original 1951 Session | American Music | AMCD-10
Ray Stokes | Jazz Piano Vol.1 | Jazztime(EMI) | 251282-2
Ruby Braff And His Men | Hi-Fi Salute To Bunny | RCA | 2118520-2
Tommy Dorsey And His Orchestra | Tommy Dorsey In Concert | RCA | NL 89780 DP
Marie Antoinette
Kirk Lightsey-Harold Danko | Shorter By Two-The Music Of Wayne Shorter Played On Two Pianos | Sunnyside | SSC 1004 D
Marie-Line
Becker/Sclavis/Lindberg | Transition | FMP | 1170
Marilyn Monroe
Shelly Manne Double Piano Jazz Quartet | In Concert At Carmelo's | Trend | TR 526 Digital
Marilyn(Requiem For An Actress)
Jackie McLean Quintet | Vertigo | Blue Note | 522669-2
Marilyn's Dilemma
Louis Hayes Sextet | The Real Thing | 32 Jazz | 32119
Marimbula
Al Di Meola Group | Soaring Through A Dream | Manhattan | CDP 7463372
Marina
Clark Terry Sextet | Yes The Blues | Pablo | 2312127
Mariona
Joan Monné Trio | Mireia | Fresh Sound Records | FSNT 100 CD
Mariona,Maria,Mare-
Charlie Haden-Carlos Paredes | Dialogues | Polydor | 843445-2 PMS
Mariposa
Ray Mantilla Quintet | Mantilla | Inner City | IC 1052 IMS
Mari's Soul
Five For Jazz | Live In Sanremo | SPLASC(H) Records | HP 01
Marissea
Piirpauke | Tuku Tuku | JA & RO | JARO 4158-2
Marita
Raum-Zeit-Klang-Project | Dimensionale X H2O Memory | Born&Bellmann | 970612 CD
Maritirine
Dizzy Reece Quintet | Mose The Mooche | Discovery | DS 839 IMS
Mark
Red Rodney Quintet | Prestige First Sessions, Vol.3 | Prestige | PCD 24116-2
Mark One
Albert Mangelsdorff | Tromboneliness | MPS | 68129
Mark Time-
Norma Winstone With Group | Live At Roccella Jonica | SPLASC(H) Records | CD H 508-2
Mark,Nothing Appears-
Fernando Tarrés And The Arida Conta Group With Guests | On The Edges Of White | Muse | MCD 5463
Marlene Dietrich
Italian Instabile Orchestra | Skies Of Europe | ECM | 1543
Marlene E Gli Ospiti Misterioso-
Hans Lüdemann Rism | Unitarism | Jazz Haus Musik | JHM 0067 CD
Marlene(Ich Bin Von Kopf Bis Fuß Auf Liebe Eingestellt)
Singers Unlimited | The Singers Unlimited:Magic Voices | MPS | 539130-2
Marlies
Eventide | MPS | 68196
Marmaduke
Charlie Parker All Stars | Charlie Parker:The Complete 1944-1948 Small Group Sessions(Studio Recordings-Master Takes),Vol.4 | Blue Moon | BMCD 1010
The Charlie Parker Memorial Band | Bird Still Lives! Vol.1 | Timeless | CD SJP 373
Marmalade
Bud Powell Trio | The Amazing Bud Powell Vol.4 | Blue Note | BLP 1598
Marmasita
Nick Brignola Sextet | Baritone Madness | Bee Hive | BH 7000
Marmor I
Susanne Lundeng Quartet | Waltz For The Red Fiddle | Laika Records | 35101402
Marmor II
Waltz For The Red Fiddle | Laika Records | 35101402
Marmor III
Brew Moore Quintet | Brew Moore | Original Jazz Classics | OJC 049(F 3208)
Marney
Cannonball Adderley Sextet | The Cannonball Adderley Collection Vol.3:Jazz Workshop Revisited | Landmark | CAC 1303-2(882343)
Gato Barbieri Group | The Third World Revisited | Bluebird | ND 86995
Marnie
Gato Barbieri Septet | Gato Barbieri:The Complete Flying Dutchman Recordings 1969-1973 | RCA | 2154555-2
Marquese De Villamagna
Lalo Schifrin Quintet | Marquis De Sade | Verve | 537751-2
Marquita
Joe Pass-Jimmy Rowles Duo | Joe Pass:A Man And His Guitar | Original Jazz Classics | OJCCD 8806-2
Graham Haynes & No Image | What Time It Be | Muse | MCD 5402
Marriage Is For Old Folks
Nina Simone With Orchestra | Nina Simone-The 60s Vol.1: Ne Me Quitte Pas | Mercury | 838543-2 PMS
Married Alive
Big Bill Broonzy Group | Big Bill Broonzy 1935-1940 | Black & Blue | BLE 59.253 2
Mars
International Commission For The Prevention Of Musical Border Control,The | The International Commission For The Prevention Of Musical Border Control | VeraBra Records | CDVBR 2093-2
James Hurt Group | Dark Grooves-Mystcal Rhythms | Blue Note | 495104-2
John Coltrane-Rashied Ali Duo | Interstellar Space | Impulse(MCA) | 543415-2
Sun Ra And His Intergalactic Research Arkestra | Black Myth/Out In Space | MPS | 557656-2
Mars-
Schmilz | Schmilz | Creative Works Records | CW CD 1041
Mars And Milky Way
Michael Musillami Group | GlassArt | Evidence | ECD 22060-2
Mars Theme
Graham Haynes Group | Transition | Verve | 529039-2
Marsch Der Ketzer
Das Saxophonorchester Frankfurt | Das Saxophonorchester Frankfurt-Live | FMP | SAJ 40
Marsh Bars
Ingrid Jensen Sextet | Vernal Fields | Enja | ENJ-9013 2
Marsh Blues
Paul Bley/Evan Parker/Barre Phillips | Time Will Tell | ECM | 1537
Marsh Tides
Bruce Forman Quartet | Full Circle | Concord | CJ 251
Marshmallow
National Youth Jazz Orchestra | A View From The Hill | Ronnie Scott's Jazz House | JHCD 044
Marsyas
Franco D'Andrea Trio | Volte | Owl Records | 052 CD
Marte Belona
Dick Jurgens And His Orchestra | The Uncollected:Dick Jurgens,Vol.3 | Hindsight | HSR 191
Martha & Romao
Woody Allen Trio | Wild Man Blues | RCA | 2663353-2
Martha(aka Mazie)
Cedar Walton Sextet | Cedar Walton:Composer | Astor Place | TCD 4001
Martina
Bill Evans Quintet | The Complete Fantasy Recordings | Fantasy | 9FCD 1012-2
David Azarian Trio | Stairway To Seventh Heaven | Mobile Fidelity | MFCD 902
Martina(Les Enfants Qui Pleurent)
Joachim Raffel Quintet | Thinkin' Of Trane | Acoustic Music Records | 319.1059.2
Martini Time
Barrelhouse Jazzband | The New Orleans Renaissance | L+R Records | CDLR 40022
Martinique
Stuttgarter Dixieland All Stars | It's The Talk Of The Town | Jazzpoint | JP 1069 CD
Teddy Buckner And His Dixieland Band | Frank Bull And Gene Norman Present | Dixieland Jubilee | DJ 504
Marutcha
Francesco D'Errico Quartet | Tartana | yvp music | CD 3032
Marvellous Pig Stories
Superblue | Superblue | Blue Note | 791731-2
Marvin Gaye
Stan Kenton And His Orchestra | The Complete MacGregor Transcriptions Vol.2 | Naxos Jazz | 8.120518 CD
Marvin's Song
Stanley Turrentine Group | If I Could | Limelight | 518444-2
Mary
Take 6 | Goldmine | Reprise | 7599-25670-2
Temperance Seven | 33 Not Out | Upbeat Jazz | URCD 103
Maryke
Mr.Acker Bilk And His Paramount Jazz Band | Dixieland Collection | Aves | 146534
Maryland My Maryland
Bunk Johnson And His New Orleans Band | Baby Dodds | American Music | AMCD-17
Chris Barber's Jazz Band | Ice Cream | Storyville | 6.23326 AF
Sidney Bechet With Claude Luter And His Orchestra | Salle Pleyel 31 January 52 | Vogue | 655001
Mary's Blues
Mary Osborne Quintet | Now And Then | Stash Records | ST 215 IMS
Andy Kirk And His Twelve Clouds Of Joy | Big Band Bounce & Boogie-Andy Kirk And His Clouds Of Joy:Walkin' & Swingin' | Affinity | AFS 1011
Mary's Idea
Oregon | Our First Record | Vanguard | 62162
Mary's Traum(Mary's Dröm)
| Marian McPartland Plays The Music Of Mary Lou Williams | Concord | CCD 4605
Mas Alla(Beyond)
Joe Haider Quintet | Reconciliation | EGO | 4001
Mas Que Nada
De Novo | L.A. Transit | Denon Compact Disc | CY-1004
Hank Jones With Oliver Nelson's Orchestra | Happenings | Impulse(MCA) | JAS 61(AS 9132)
Tamba Trio | Tamba Trio Classics | EmArCy | 536958-2
Mas que nada (Pow, Pow, Pow)
Dizzy Gillespie Quintet | Latin On Impulse! Various Artists | Impulse(MCA) | IMP 12762
Maschinenherz
Savoy Havanah Band | The Classic Years In Digital Stereo: Dance Bands U.K. | CDS Records Ltd. | RPCD 303(CD 681)
Maseru
Hugh Masekela Quintet | The African Connection | MCA | IA 9343/2
Mason Changes
Lucky Millinder And His Orchestra | Big Band Bounce & Boogie:Apollo Jump | Affinity | AFS 1004
Masqualero
Miles Davis Quintet | Sorcerer | CBS | CBS PC 9532
Miles Davis Quintet 1965-1968 | CBS | C6K 67398
Steve Khan Trio | Let's Call This | Polydor | 849563-2
Miles Davis Sextet | Black Beauty-Miles Davis At Filmore West | CBS | C2K 65138
Masqualero-
Miles Davis Quintet | Sorcerer | CBS | CK 65680
Masqualero(alt.take)
Miles Davis Quintet 1965-1968 | CBS | C6K 67398
Marvin Stamm Orchestra | Stampede | Palo Alto | PA 8022
Masque(Strehgth)
Carmen McRae And Her Quintet | Velvet Soul | LRC Records | CDC 7970
Masquerade
Joe Pass | The Montreux '77 Collection | Pablo | 2620107
Masquerade(in 3 parts):
Dirk Raulf Group | Theater I (Bühnenmusik) | Poise | Poise 07
Maß Für Maß(Schauspielhaus Zürich)
Nate Morgan Quintet | Retribution Reparation | Nimbus | NS 3479 (835528)
Mass Ritual
Anita O'Day With Gene Krupa And His Orchestra | Let Me Off Uptown:Anita O'Day With Gene Krupa | CBS | CK 65625
Massachusetts
Maxine Sullivan And Her Band | Maxine Sullivan Sings | Fresh Sound Records | FSR-CD 0178
Masse D'Urto(a Michelangelo Antonioni)-
X-Communication | X-Communication | FMP | CD 33
Master Mind
Art Blakey And The Jazz Messengers | Roots And Herbs | Blue Note | 521956-2
Roots And Herbs | Blue Note | 521956-2
Dave Liebman Quartet | Trio + One | Owl Records | 051 CD
Master Of TheWar
Dave Weckl Group | Master Plan | GRP | GRP 96192
Master Plan
Clifford Adams Quintet | The Master Power | Naxos Jazz | 86015-2
Masters Of The Midiverse
Wolfgang Puschnig Group With Ernst Jandl | Mixed Metaphors | Amadeo | 527266-2
Match
Albert King Blues Band | Blues At Sunset(Live at Wattstax And Montreux) | Stax | SCD 8581-2
Match Point
Gary Burton-Ralph Towner | Works | ECM | 823267-2
Matchbook
John Lee Hooker | Boogie Chillun | Fantasy | FCD 24706-2
Matches In Bermuda
Marty Hall Band | Who's Been Talkin'?s | Blues Beacon | BLU 1033 2
Matching Pair
Ella Fitzgerald With The Marty Paich Orchestra | Whisper Not | Verve | 589947-2
Matchmaker Matchmaker
Eric Alexander Quartet | The Second Milestone | Milestone | MCD 9315-2
Vanessa Rubin With Band | Girl Talk | Telarc Digital | CD 83480
Gato Barbieri Orchestra | Latino America | Impulse(MCA) | 952236-2
Maté
Peter Giger's Family Of Percussion & Friends And Gripo Timbila Eduardo Durao | Mozambique Meets Europe | B&W Present | BW 031
Mater Aurea
European Tuba Quartet | Low And Behold | Jazz Haus Musik | JHM 0110 CD
Material Girls
Future Shock | It's Great | BVHAAST | 067(807058)
Maternal Love(N'unga)
| In The Beginning...Bebop | Savoy | SV 0169(MG 12119)
Mathar
Perico Sambeat Quartet | Friendship | ACT | 9421-2
Mathilda
Dave Pike Sextet | Carnavals | Prestige | PCD 24248-2
Mathilda,Mathilda
Jimmy Smith Quintet | Rockin' the Boat | Blue Note | 576755-2
Didier Lockwood Quartet | Storyboard | Dreyfus Jazz Line | FDM 36582-2
Matie's Trophies(Motystrophe)
Jimmy Forrest Quintet | Most Much! | Original Jazz Classics | OJCCD 350-2(P 7218)
Matinale
Sergey Kuryokhin | Sentenced To Silence | LEO | LR 110
Mating Call
Chet Baker Quintet | Chet Baker Plays & Sings | West Wind | WW 2108
Tadd Dameron Quartet | On A Misty Night | Prestige | P 24084
Willie Bobo Group | Juicy | Verve | 519857-2
Paul Bley/Niels-Henning Orsted-Pedersen Duo | Paul Bley-NHOP | Steeplechase | SCCD 31005
Matka Joanna From The Angels
Orrin Evans Sextet | Listen To The Band | Criss Cross | Criss 1195
Matrimonial Stomp
Bobby Hutcherson Quintet | Total Eclipse | Blue Note | 784291-2
Matrix
Chick Corea Trio | Chick Corea | Blue Note | 84504
Matrosen Tango
Lena Willemark-Ale Möller Group | Nordan | ECM | 1536(523161-2)
Mats Hansu Polskan-
Norbert Gottschalk With The Peter Weniger Quartet | Light Weight Sight | Dr.Jazz Records | 8603-2
Matter And Spirit-
Sonny Stitt Quintet | Autumn In New York | Black Lion | CD 877642-2
Matter Of Fact
Jimmy Smith All Stars | Prime Time | Milestone | MCD 9176-2
Matters Of The Heart
Daniel Schnyder Group | Words Within Music | Enja | ENJ-9369 2
Matthäus Passion Suite(Johann Sebastian Bach):
Eugen Cicero Quartet | Jazz Bach | Timeless | CD SJP 216
Mattmar
American Folk Blues Festival | American Folk Blues Festival '63 | L+R Records | CDLR 42023
Mau Mau
John Lee Hooker | Blues Before Sunrise | Bulldog | BDL 1011
Maud's Mood
Michael Session Quintet | Michael Session 'N Session | ITM-Pacific | ITMP 970074
Maulbeerbaumbeerblues
Lew Stone And His Band | Lew Stone And His Band | Decca | DDV 5005/6 DT
Maurizio
Eberhard Weber Quintet | Later That Evening | ECM | 1231(829382-2)
Maurizius
Franco Morone | Guitarea | Acoustic Music Records | 319.1046.2
Maus,Raus,Aus
Louis Sclavis Group | Dans La Nuit | ECM | 1805(589524-2)
Mauvais Reve
Marc Ducret Group | Gris | Label Bleu | LBLC 6531(882934)
Mave Mave
Chuck Marohnic Quartet | Chuck Marohnic Quartet | Steeplechase | SCS 4002
Mawdo
Helmut Forsthoff Trio | Four Together | Aho-Recording | CD 1011
Max
Loope | Red & Yellow | Aho-Recording | CD 1003
Max Blues
Herb Geller Quartet | Playing Jazz:The Musical Autobiography Of Herb Geller | Fresh Sound Records | FSR-CD 5011
Max Tango
Jesse Davis Quartet | Second Nature | Concord | CCD 4883
Max-A-Man
Vital Information | Ray Of Hope | VeraBra Records | CDVBR 2161-2
Maxed Out
Bruno Tommaso Orchestra | Barga Jazz | SPLASC(H) Records | HP 06
Maximum
Andy Laverne Quartet | True Colors | Jazz City | 660.53.015
Maxixe
Juanjo Dominguez | Internationales Guitarren Festival '94 | ALISO Records | AL 1030
Massimo Urbani Quintet | The Urbisaglia Concert | Philology | W 70.2
Max's Variations
Gary Thomas And Seventh Quadrant | Code Violations | Enja | 5085
Maxwell's Silver Hammer
Woody Shaw With The Tone Jansa Quartet | Woody Shaw With Tone Jansa Quartet | Timeless | CD SJP 221
May Be
Dave Holland - Barre Phillips | Music For Two Basses | ECM | 1011
May Dance
Irene Schweizer | Many And One Direction | Intakt Records | CD 044
May Every Day Be Christmas
Klaus König Orchestra & Guests | The Song Of Songs:Oratorio For Two Solo Voices,Choir And Orchestra | Enja | ENJ-7057 2
May He Smother Me With Kisses
| A Tribute To Bing Crosby-Paramount's Greatest Singer | Concord | CCD 4614
May I Come In?
Lina Nyberg-Esbjörn Svensson | Close | Touché Music | TMcCD 004
Lorez Alexandria With The Houston Person Sextet | May I Come In | Muse | MCD 5420
May I Dance
J.J.Johnson Quintet | Let's Hang Out | EmArCy | 514454-2
May Ride
Ahmad Mansour Quartet | Oxiana | Timeless | CD SJP 344
May The Fourth Be With You
Lars Duppler Quartet | Palindrome | Jazz Haus Musik | JHM 0108 CD
Houston Person Quartet | Person-ified | HighNote Records | HCD 7004
May The Music Never End
Jill Seifers And Her Quartet | The Waiting | Fresh Sound Records | FSNT 072 CD
May This Be Love
Jay Hoggard | Solo Vibraphone | India Navigation | IN 1040 CD
Maya
David Gibson Sextet | Maya | Nagel-Heyer | CD 2018
James Blood Ulmer With The Quartet Indigo | Harmolodic Guitar With Strings | DIW | DIW 878 CD
Thierry Maillard Trio | Paris New York | EmArCy | 558041-2
Mayamalaragaula
Antoine Roney Sextet | The Traveler | Muse | MCD 5469
Maybe
Elliot Lawrence And His Orchestra | The Elliot Lawrence Big Band Swings Cohn & Kahn | Fantasy | FCD 24761-2
Glen Gray And The Casa Loma Orchestra | The Radio Years: Glen Gray And The Casa Loma Orchestra 1943-46 | London | HM-A 5050 AN
Leni Stern Group | Secrets | Enja | ENJ-5093 2
Ruby Braff-Gene DiNovi | Ruby Braff-The Canadian Sessions | Sackville | SK2CD-5005
Teddy Stauffer Und Seine Original Teddies | Hot Jazz & Swing Mit Teddy Stauffer's Original Teddies | Elite Special | 9522002
Maybe-
John Mooney And Bluesiana | Travelin' On | Crosscut | CCD 11032
Maybe It's Beacause
Jeri Southern With The Lennie Hayton Orchestra | Coffee Cigarettes And Memories | Fresh Sound Records | FSR-CD 29(882157)

TITELVERZEICHNIS

Maybe Next Year
Future Shock | Handclaps | Timeless | CD SJP 374

Maybe September
Jimmy Smith-Wes Montgomery Quartet | Further Adventures Of Jimmy And Wes | Verve | 519802-2
Stanley Turrentine Group | If I Could | Limelight | 518444-2
Tommy Flanagan | Alone Too Long | Denon Compact Disc | DC-8572
Tony Bennett-Bill Evans | Together Again | DRG | MRS 901 IMS

Maybe Tomorrow
Jürgen Sturm's Ballstars | Tango Subversivo | Nabel Records:Jazz Network | CD 4613

Maybe We Should'nt
Michel Petrucciani Trio | Estate | Riviera | RVR 1

Maybe You'll Come Back
Raymond Burke's Big Three | Raymond Burke And Cie Frazier With Butch Thompson In New Orleans | 504 Records | 504CD 27

Mayday
Evan Parker Quartet | London Air Lift | FMP | CD 89
Jaco Pastorius/Brian Melvin Group | Jazz Street | Timeless | CD SJP 258

Mayday Hymn
Eric St.Laurent & Osmose | Eric St-Laurent & Osmose | BIT | 11190

Mayflower Rock
Dizzy Gillespie And His Orchestra | Dizzy Gillespie:Birks Works-The Verve Big Band Sessions | Verve | 527900-2

Mayflower Rock(alt.take)
Jack Sharpe Big Band | Roarin' | Ronnie Scott's Jazz House | JHCD 016

Maynard The Fox
Maynard Ferguson With The Birdland Dreamband | The Birdland Dream Band Vol.1 | Fresh Sound Records | 58110 CD(RCA)

Mayreh
Art Blakey And The Jazz Messengers | Blue Moon | Zounds | CD 2720010
Helmut Kagerer/Helmut Nieberle | Wes Trane | Edition Collage | EC 453-2
Woody Schabata Quintet | May-Rimba | Amadeo | 829324-2

Maytanca
Bob Berg Quintet | Cycles | Denon Compact Disc | CY 72745

Mazad
Paul Bley Trio | Ramblin' | Affinity | AFF 37

Mazééj,Wahdi Trikni
New Orleans Klezmer Allstars | Manichalfwitz | Gert Town Records | GT-1117

Mazu
Jan Fryderyk | Piano Works: Live Recordings | Jazzline | ???

Mbizo
World Saxophone Quartet | B'Bizo | Justin Time | Just 123-2

M'Bogne Mou Ra Fanhe M'Ma(I Am Sad)
Peter Herbolzheimer All Star Big Band | Jazz Gala Concert '79 | Rare Bid | BID 156501

MC
Joachim Raffel Quintet And Large Ensemble | Another Blue | Acoustic Music Records | 319.1145.2

McGhee And Me
Andy Kirk And His Orchestra | A Mellow Bit Of Rhythm | RCA | 2113028-2

McGriff Avenue
Jimmy McGriff Sextet | McGriff's House Party | Milestone | MCD 9300-2

McGriff's House Party
Ron McClure Quartet | McJolt | Steeplechase | SCCD 31262

McPherson's Mood
Jay McShann Quartet | Nobody's Business | Jazz Colours | 874721-2

McSplivens
Benny Green Trio | Testifyin'!-Live at The Village Vanguard | Blue Note | 798171-2

MDM
Ben Selvin And His Orchestra | Cheerful Little Earful | Saville Records | SVL 165 IMS

Me & Groove
Joe Henderson And His Orchestra | Joe Henderson:The Milestone Years | Milestone | 8MCD 4413-2

Me Among Others
Chris Barber's Jazz And Blues Band | Sideways | Black Lion | 147009

Me And Brother Bill
Earl Hines And His Orchestra | The Indispensable Earl Hines Vol.1/2 | RCA | 2126407-2

Me And Mrs.Jones
Benny Green Trio | That's Right! | Blue Note | 784467-2

Me And My Baby
Lee Konitz Orchestra | Chicago'n All That Jazz | LRC Records | CDC 7971

Me And My Gin
Dinah Washington With The Fred Norman Orchestra | Back To The Blues | Roulette | 8543342
Jimmie Gordon Band | Jimmie Gordon 1934-1941 | Story Of Blues | CD 3510-2

Me And My Guitar
Oscar Klein's Jazz Show | Oscar Klein's Jazz Show | Jazzpoint | JP 1043 CD
Tanzorchester Der Original Teddies | International Schlager & In Mood mit Teddy Stauffer's Original Teddies | Elite Special | 9522003

Me And Ornette C.
Little Walter Blues Band | Blues Roots Vol. 15: Little Walter | Chess | 6.24805 AG

Me And The Devil Blues
Robert Johnson | Robert Johnson-King Of The Delta Blues | CBS | 493006-2

Me And The Devil Blues(alt.take)
Lanigiro Syncopating Melody Kings | Jazz In Switzerland 1930-1975 | Elite Special | 9544002/1-4

Me And Tony
Julius Hemphill-Abdul K.Wadud | Oakland Duets | Music & Arts | CD 791

Me And You
Duke Ellington And His Orchestra | Jazz Giants:Duke Ellington | RCA | NL 45179 SI
Jo Jones-Milt Hinton | Percussion And Bass | Fresh Sound Records | FSR-CD 0204
Vic Lewis West Coast All Stars | Me And You! | Candid | CCD 79739
Miles Davis Group | Miles Davis Live From His Last Concert In Avignon | Laserlight | 24327

Me And You-
Charles Mingus Group | Mysterious Blues | Candid | CCD 79042

Me And You Blues
Ran Blake | Duke Dreams/The Legacy Of Strayhorn-Ellington | Soul Note | SN 1027

Me Myself And I(Are All In Love With You)
Billie Holiday And Her Orchestra | Billie Holiday:The Quintessential Vol.4(1937) | CBS | 463333-2

Me 'n You
Ike Quebec Quintet | Bossa Nova Soul Samba | Blue Note | 852443-2

Me Spelled M-E Me
Babs Gonzales Group | Properly Presenting Babs Gonzales | Fresh Sound Records | FSR 702(835422)

Me Too
Irazu | La Fiesta Del Timbalero | L+R Records | CDLR 45039

Me, Among Others
Carlo Mombelli's Abstractions | Dancing In A Museum | ITM-Pacific | ITMP 970078

Mea Culpa
Artie Shaw And His Orchestra | Original Recordings 1937/1938 | Festival | Album 248

Meadow Bells
Darius Brubeck And The Nu Jazz Connection | African Tributes | B&W Present | BW 023

Meal Time-
Eddie Bums Group | Treat Me Like I Treat You | Moonshine | BLP 106

Mean As A Swan
Jimmy Dawkins Chicago Blues Band | Tribute To Orange | Black & Blue | BLE 59.556 2

Mean Blues
Varsity Eight | The Complete Sessions 1923-24 Vol.1 | Harlequin | HQ 2055 IMS

Mean MC Mudda
Original Indiana Five | Original Indiana Five Vol.1 | Jazz Oracle | BDW 8019

Mean Mistreater
Chris Barber's Jazz Band | The Chris Barber Concerts | Lake | LACD 55/56

Mean Mr.Mustard
Adam Holzman Group | Overdrive | Lipstick Records | LIP 890252

Mean Old Bed Bug Blues
Furry Lewis | In His Prime 1927-1928 | Yazoo | YAZ 1050

Mean Old Frisco
Junior Mance Quartet | That Lovin' Feelin' | Milestone | MCD 47097-2
Lightnin' Hopkins | The Swartmore Concert | Original Blues Classics | OBCCD 563-2
Lil' Ed Williams And The Blues Imperials | Roughhousin' | Sonet | SNTF 966(941966)

Mean Old Lone Train
Lester Bowie Ensemble | Jazzbühne Berlin '82 | Repertoire Records | REPCD 4911-CC

Mean Streak
Tommy Flanagan Trio | Jazz Poet | Timeless | CD SJP 301

Mean To Be
Alex Riel Quartet | D.S.B. Kino | Stunt Records | STUCD 19811

Mean To Me
Art Tatum | Pure Genius | Atlantis | ATS 3
Benny Goodman-Jimmy Rowles | Benny Goodman:The Complete 1947-1949 Small Group Sessions Vol.1(1947) | Blue Moon | BMCD 1042
Clark Terry Quintet | Ain't Misbehavin' | Pablo | 2312105
Curtis Counce Group | You Get More Bounce With Curtis Counce | Original Jazz Classics | OJCCD 159-2
Dick Meldonian And The Jersey Swingers | Some Of These Days | Progressive | PRO 7033 IMS
Erroll Garner Trio | Gems | CBS | 21062
Jack McDuff Quartet With Orchestra | Prelude:Jack McDuff Big Band | Prestige | PRCD 24283-2
Jackie McLean Quintet | McLean's Scene | Original Jazz Classics | OJCCD 098-2(NJ 8212)
Johnny King Quintet | Notes From The Underground | Enja | ENJ-9067 2
June Christy And Her Orchestra | Early June | Fresh Sound Records | FSCD 1011
Lars Gullin Quartet | Lars Gullin 1951/52 Vol.5:First Walk | Dragon | DRCD 380
Made In Sweden Vol.2: 24.3.1951-12.12.1952 | Magnetic Records | MRCD 113
Lester Young Sextet | Lester Leaps Again | Affinity | AFF 80
Lester Young Trio | Lester Young Trio | Verve | 521650-2
Mal Waldron | Blues For Lady Day | Black Lion | BLCD 760193
Milt Jackson-Ray Brown Jam | Montreux '77-The Art Of The Jam Session | Pablo | 2620106
Modern Jazz Sextet | The Modern Jazz Sextet | Verve | 559834-2
Nat Adderley Quartet | Work Songs | Milestone | M 47047
Wes Montgomery-The Complete Riverside Recordings | Riverside | 12 RCD 4408-2
Nat Pierce | My Pal Basie | Jazz Connaisseur | JCCD 8904-2
Newport All Stars | Buddy Tate With Humphrey Lyttelton And Ruby Braff | Jazz Colours | 874713-2
Pat Thomas With Band | Jazz Patterns | Fresh Sound Records | Strand SLS CD 1015
Sarah Vaughan With Her Quartet | One Night Stand-The Town Hall Concert 1947 | Blue Note | 832139-2
Woody Herman And His Orchestra | The V-Disc Years 1944-46 Vol.2 | Hep | 35
Simon Schott | Bar Piano: Simon Schott Plays Your Favorite Evergreens Vol.2 | Organic Music | ORGM 9735

Mean To Me-
Sarah Vaughan With The Jimmy Jones Orchestra | Sarah Vaughan In Hi-Fi | CBS | CK 65117

Mean What You Say
Thad Jones-Mel Lewis Orchestra | Thad Jones-Mel Lewis | Blue Note | 84498

Mean Wile
John Lee Hooker | I Wanna Dance All Night | America | AM 6101

Meaning Of The Blues
Julie London With Russ Garcia And His Orchestra | About The Blues/London By Night | Capitol | 535208-2
Keith Jarrett Trio | Standarts Vol.1 | ECM | 1255(811966-2)
Michael Bocian | Premonition:Solo Debut For Nylon String Guitar | Enja | 9118-2

Meant To Be
Helmut Kagerer/Helmut Nieberle | Wes Trane | Edition Collage | EC 453-2
John Scofield Quartet | Meant To Be | Blue Note | 795479-2
Fleurine With Band And Horn Section | Meant To Be! | EmArCy | 159085-2

Meant To Be!
Jimi Sumen Group | Paintbrush,Rock Penstemon | CMP Records | CMP CD 61

Meanville
Art Lande-Jan Garbarek | Red Lanta | ECM | 1038(829383-2)

Meanwhile
The Jazz Corps | The Jazz Corps | Pacific Jazz | 829101-2

Measure For Measure
Ax Genrich Group | Wave Cut | ATM Records | ATM 3813-AH

Meat
Jack Walrath Group | Master Of Suspense | Blue Note | BLJ 46905 Digital
Pete Christlieb Quartet | Conversations With Warne Vol.1 | Criss Cross | Criss 1043

Meat Snake
Edward Vesala Orchestra | Heavy Life | Leo Records | 009

Meatwave
La Vienta | Jazzmenco | Telarc Digital | CD 83353

Mecca Flat
Frank 'Big Boy' Goudie With Burt Bales | Frank 'Big Boy' Goudie With Amos White | American Music | AMCD-50

Mechanical Accordeon-
BBFC | Quelle Memoire! | Plainisphare | PL 1267-9

Meci Bon Dieu
David Binney Group | The Luxury Of Guessing | audioquest Music | AQCD 1030

Medea
The Reggie Workman Ensemble | Images | Music & Arts | CD 634

Medgar Evers Blues
The Jazz Futures | Live In Concert | Novus | 4163158-2

Media
Andy Lumpp Trio | Ostara | Nabel Records:Jazz Network | CD 4682

Mediane
Ellery Eskelin With Andrea Parkins & Jim Black | The Secret Museum | HatOLOGY | 552

Medicine Man
Herbie Steward Quintet | Al Haig Meets The Master Saxes Vol.3 | Spotlite | SPJ 143

Medieval Dance-
Return To Forever | Romantic Warrior | CBS | SRCS 9348

Meditacao(Meditation)
Maximilian Geller Quartet feat. Melanie Bong | Maimilian Geller Goes Bossa Encore | Edition Collage | EC 505-2
Oscar Peterson Sextet | Soul Espanol | Limelight | 510439-2
Stan Getz With The Joao Gilberto Trio & Orchestra | The Carnegie Hall Concert | Jazz Door | JD 1221

Meditarranean Bossa
Chris Jarrett | Short Stories For Piano | Edition Musikat | EDM 056

Meditatio Carthage
A Band Of Friends | Art Of The Improviser | Naxos Jazz | 86026-2

Meditation
Astrud Gilberto With Antonio Carlos Jobim And The Marty Paich Orchestra | The Astrud Gilberto Album | Verve | 823009-1
Dexter Gordon Quartet | Power! | Prestige | P 24087
More Power | Original Jazz Classics | OJC20 815-2(P 7680)
Duke Ellington | Duke Ellington Live At The Whitney | Impulse(MCA) | 951173-2
Second Sacred Concert | America | AM 006/007
Eddie Lockjaw Davis Quartet | Eddie 'Lockjaw' Davis | Divox | CDX 48701
Joao Gilberto Trio | Compact Jazz: Best Of Bossa Nova | Verve | 833269-2
Joe Diorio | To Jobim With Love | RAM Records | RMCD 4529
Joe Pass Trio | Intercontinental | MPS | 68121
Lena Horne With The Lennie Hayton Orchestra | Lena Goes Latin | DRG | MRS 510 IMS
Shirley Horn Trio | All Night Long | Steeplechase | SCCD 31157

Meditation Carthage
Mingus Big Band | Blues & Politics | Dreyfus Jazz Line | FDM 36603-2

Meditation For Christie
Joe Venuti Quartet | Hooray For Joe | Chiaroscuro | CR 153

Meditation I
Abdullah Ibrahim Septet | No Fear, No Die(S'en Fout La Mort):Original Soundtrack | TipToe | TIP-888815 2

Meditation II
Friedrich Gulda-Klaus Weiss Duo | It 's All One | MPS | 68059

Meditation On A Pair Of Wire Cutters
Charles Mingus Sextet | Concertgebouw Amsterdam April 10th 1964 | Ulysse | ???

Meditation On Two Medieval Songs:
Jimmie Lunceford And His Orchestra | Live Sessions 1944-1945 | Jazz Anthology | JA 5200

Meditations
Tony Dagradi Trio | Live At The Columns | Turnipseed | TMCD 07

Meditations For Moses
Charles Mingus | Great Moments With Charles Mingus | MCA | MCA 2-4128 (802130)

Meditations(Suite):
Chuck Loeb Groups | Mediterranean | dmp Digital Music Productions | CD 494

Mediterranean Nights
The Benoit/Freeman Project | The Benoit/Freeman Project | GRP | GRP 97392

Mediterranean Sundance
Al Di Meola Groups | Guitar Heroes Vol.1:Al Di Meola | Zounds | CD 2700044001
Al Di Meola-Paco De Lucia | Soleá: A Flamenco-Jazz Fantasy | ACT | 9208-2
Chris Kase Sextet | Starting Now | Mons Records | MR 874659

Medium
Volker Schlott & Reinmar Henschke | Influence | Acoustic Music Records | 319.1043.2

Medium-
Meade Lux Lewis | Meade Lux Lewis 1939-1054 | Story Of Blues | CD 3506-2

Medium Rare
Dusko Goykovich-Gianni Basso Quintet | Live At Birdland Neuburg | Birdland | BN 004
Chet Baker Quintet | Chet Baker & Crew | Pacific Jazz | 582671-2

Medium Rock
Cinzia Gizzi Sextet | Trio & Sextet | Penta Flowers | CDPIA 017

Medley
Blossom Dearie | I'm Hip | CBS | 489123-2
Jaco Pastorius Trio | Jaco Pastorius Broadway Blues & Theresa | Jazzpoint | JP 1053 CD
Willis Jackson Quintet | Together Again: Willis Jackson With Jack McDuff | Prestige | PRCD 24284-2
Art Blakey And The Jazz Messengers | Wynton | Inak | 2002

Medley Blues
Greetje Kauffeld With Jerry Van Rooyen And Jiggs Whigham And The Rias Big Band | Greetje Kauffeld Meets Jerry Van Rooyen And Jiggs Whigham With The Rias Big Band | Mons Records | MR 874786

Medley Of Armstrong's Hits:
Louis Armstrong And His Orchestra | The Cotton Club Legend | RCA | NL 89506 AG
The Young Tuxedo Brass Band | That's Jazz Vol.32: Jazz Begins | Atlantic | ATL 50404

Medley Of My Favorite Songs
Red Rodney & The New Danish Jazzarmy | Society Red | Music Mecca | CD 1003-2

Medley Paco De Lucia:
Scott Hamilton-Buddy Tate Quintet | Back To Back | Concord | CJ 85

Medley:
Dakota Staton With Her Sextet | Isn't It A Lovely Day | Muse | MCD 5502
Dick Johnson Quartet | Dick Johnson Plays | Concord | CCD 4107
Duke Ellington | Masters Of Jazz Vol.6:Duke Ellington | Storyville | STCD 4106
Earl Hines Trio | Boogie Woogie On St.Louis Blues | Prestige | MPP 2515
Ella Fitzgerald With Benny Carter's Magnificent Seven | 30 By Ella | Capitol | 520090-2
30 By Ella | Capitol | 520090-2
30 By Ella | Capitol | 520090-2
30 By Ella | Capitol | 520090-2
30 By Ella | Capitol | 520090-2
Ella Fitzgerald With The Jazz At Carnegie All-Stars | Newport Jazz Festival - Live At Carnegie Hall | CBS | CBS 68279
Jaco Pastorius Trio | Live In New York City Volume Four | Big World | BW 1004
Heavy'n Jazz | Jazzpoint | JP 1036 CD
JATP All Stars | The Complete Jazz At The Philharmonic On Verve 1944-1949 | Verve | 523893-2
Jazz At Carnegie Hall All Stars | Ella Fitzgerald:Newport Jazz Festival-Live at Carnegie Hall | CBS | C2K 66809
Joe Roccisano Orchestra | Leave Your Mind Behind | Landmark | LCD 1541-2
Mary Lou Williams Trio | Mary Lou Williams Trio-Roll 'Em(1944) | Solo Art | SACD-43
Miles Davis Group | Live-Evil | CBS | 485255-2
Montreal Jubilation Gospel Choir | Jubilatio III-Glory Train | Blues Beacon | BLU-1008 2
Oscar Peterson-Joe Pass Duo | Oscar Pterson Et Joe Pass A La Salle Pleyel | Pablo | 2CD 2625705
Ray Brown | The Very Tall Band | Telarc Digital | CD 83443
Ray Bryant Trio | Ray Bryant Plays Basie & Ellington | EmArCy | 832235-2 PMS
Sheila Jordan With Te Alan Broadbent Trio And The Hiraga String Quartet | Heart Strings | Muse | MCD 5468
Sonny Rollins With The Kenny Drew Trio | Sonny Rollins In Denmark Vol.2 | Moon Records | MCD 038-2
Stephane Grappelli Quartet | Live At The Blue Note | Telarc Digital | CD 83397
Thelonious Monk Quartet | Sweet And Lovely | Moon Records | MCD 079-2
Weather Report | Weathe Report Live In Tokyo | CBS | 489208-2
Weathe Report Live In Tokyo | CBS | 489208-2
Wild Bill Davison All Stars | The Idividualism Of Wild Bill Davison | Savoy | SJL 2229 (801205)

Medley: Open Return-Cancion Del Momento
Weather Report | I Sing The Body Electric | CBS | 468207-2

Medor Sadness
Peter Fulda | Fin De Siècle | Jazz 4 Ever Records:Jazz Network | J4E 4724

Meduse

Ronnie Burrage Septet | Shuttle | Sound Hills | SSCD 8052
Meet Benny Bailey
Lionel Hampton Big Band | Newport Uproar! | RCA | NL 89590
Meet Doctor Foo
Robert Pete Williams | Blues Masters Vol.1-Robert Pete Williams | Storyville | STCD 8001
Meet Me At No Special Place
Mose Allison Trio | The Mose Chronicles-Live In London,Vol.1 | Blue Note | 529747-2
I Don't Worry About A Thing | Rhino | 8122-71417-2
Nat King Cole Trio | Love Songs | Nimbus Records | NI 2010
Drümmele Maa | Stadtgarten Series Vol.5 | Jazz Haus Musik | JHM 1005 SER
Meet Me In St.Louis,Louis
Big Joe Williams | Big Joe Williams-The Final Years | Verve | 519943-2
Meet Me Tonight In Dreamland
Allan Vaché's Florida Jazz Allstars | Allan Vaché's Floridy Jazz Allstars | Nagel-Heyer | CD 032
Barry Martyn's Down Home Boys | Barry Martyn's Down Home Boys | Sackville | SKCD2-3056
Meet Me Where They Play The Blues
Jack Teagarden And His Orchestra | Jazz Gallery:Jack Teagerden | RCA | 2114175-2
Meet Quincy Jones
Page One | Beating Bop Live | Stunt Records | 18808
Meet The Fog
Hendrik Meurkens Band | A View From Manhattan | Concord | CCD 4585
Meet You In Chicago
Bud Freeman Quartet | Lions Abroad Volume One:Tenor Titans | Black Lion | BLCD 7620-2
Meeting
Lou Bennett Trio | Jazz In Paris | EmArCy | 548790-2
Mitch Seidman Quartet | How 'Bout It? | Jardis Records | JRCD 20135
Monika Linges Quartet | Songing | Nabel Records:Jazz Network | LP 4615
Rene Thomas Quintet | Meeting Mister Thomas | Fresh Sound Records | FSR 554(Barclay 84091)
Erich Bachträgl Quartet | Gollum | Bellaphon | 270.31.004
Meeting Of The Spirits
Roland Kirk Quartet | Verve Jazz Masters 27:Roland Kirk | Verve | 522062-2
Meeting On Termini's Corner
Domino | Verve | 543833-2
Andre Ceccarelli 4tet | 61:32 00 | RCA | 2165773-2
Meetings
Mahavishnu Orchestra | The Inner Mounting Flame | CBS | CK 65523
Meetings In The Spirit
Andy Emler Mega Octet | Mega Octet | Label Bleu | LBLC 6533(882936)
Megaera
Tomasz Stanko Quartet | Almost Green | Leo Records | 008
Megalopolis
Friedeman Graef-Achim Goettert | Saxoridoo | FMP | OWN-90010
Mehir 1-
Stephan-Max Wirth Quartet | Jazzchanson 20th Century Suite | double moon | DMCD 1008-2
Mehir 2-
Jazzchanson 20th Century Suite | double moon | DMCD 1008-2
Mehir 3-
Ernst-Ludwig Petrowsky Quartet | Synopsis/DDR | FMP | 0240
Mehr Licht
Matthias Stich Sevensenses | ...mehrschichtig | Satin Doll Productions | SDP 1038-1 CD
Mehrschichtig...Mehrschichtig...Mehrschichtig
A Band Of Friends | Teatime Vol.1 | Poise | Poise 01
Mei
Eberhard Blum | Kazuo Fukushima: Works For Flute, Piano And Flute & Piano | Hat Art | CD 6114
Mein Automobil
Norbert Stein Pata Masters | Blue Slit | Pata Musik | PATA 8 CD
Mein Halblächelnder Freund
Kodexx Sentimental | Das Digitale Herz | Poise | Poise 02
Mein Herz
Wolfgang Lauth Quartet | Lauther | Bear Family Records | BCD 15717 AH
Mein Herz Hat Heut' Premiere
Inge Brandenburg mit Werner Müller und seinem Orchester | Why Don't You Take All Of Me | Bear Family Records | BCD 15614 AH
Mein Herz Schlägt Für Jacky(A-Tisket, A-Tasket)
Wütrio | Free And Easy | Blütenstaub | 1
Mein Mann Ist Verhindert
Karl Scharnweber Trio | Coral Concert II/Another View | Nabel Records:Jazz Network | CD 4650
Mein Schönste Zier Und Kleinod
Paul Brody's Tango Toy | Klezmer Stories | Laika Records | 35101222
Mein Sohn,Was Immer Aus Dir Werde
Der Rote Bereich | Risky Business | ACT | 9407-2
Mein Sportheim
Heinz Becker/Karl-Heinz Stegman/Isabel Zeumer | Else Lasker-Schüler: Ich Träume So Leise Von Dir | ITM Records | ITM 1418
Meje
Omar Belmonte's Latin Lover | Vamos A Ver | EGO | 96170
Mejor Me Pongo A Bailar
Joe Zawinul And The Austrian All Stars | His Majesty Swinging Nephews 1954-1957 | RST-Records | 91549-2
Mekong
Khalil Chanine Group | Mektoub | AH Records | AH 40509
Melancholia
Duke Ellington And His Orchestra | Welcome To Jazz: Duke Ellington | Koch Records | 321 943 D1
Wynton Marsalis Quintet | Think Of One | CBS | 468709-2
Peter Rühmkorf Mit Dem Michael Naura Trio | Phönix Voran | ECM | 802 SP
Melancholy
Louis Armstrong And His Hot Seven | Louis Armstrong-The Hot Fives & Hot Sevens Vol.2 | CBS | 463052-2
Melancholy Blues-
Al King And His Kingsmen | Thunderbold-Honkin' R&B Sax Instrumentals 1952-1956 | Krazy Kat | KK 778 IMS
Melancholy Me
Bob Crosby And His Orchestra | Bob Crosby And His Orchestra Vol.9(1939):Them There Eyes | Halcyon | DHDL 128
Melancholy Mood
Horace Silver Quintet | Further Explorations By The Horace Silver Quintet | Blue Note | 300044(1589)
Melancholy Rhapsody
Harry James And His Orchestra | More Harry James In Hi-Fi | Capitol | EMS 1148
Melancholy Serenade
Irene Schweizer | Piano Solo Vol.1 | Intakt Records | CD 020
Melancolico
Madrid Jazz Group | Unreleased Madrid Jazz Sessions 1964-1981 | Fresh Sound Records | FSR-CD 3003
Melanga Raikiki
Häns'che Weiss-Vali Mayer Duo | Just Play II | MMM Records | CD 1303
Melange
Heinrich Von Kalnein Group | New Directions | Nabel Records:Jazz Network | CD 4670
Jimmy Dorsey And His Orchestra | Jimmy Dorsey And His Orchestra | Jazz Anthology | JA 5221
Melba's Minor
Bennie Green Quintet | Back On The Scene | Blue Note | BLP 1587
Melinda
Stan Getz With The Bill Evans Trio | The Chick Corea-Bill Evans Sessions | Verve | 2610036
Stan Getz-Bill Evans Quartet | Stan Getz & Bill Evans | Verve | 833802-2
Gabriele Hasler-Elvira Plenar-Andreas Willers | Sonetburger-Nach Texten Von Oskar Pastior | Foolish Music | FM 211793
Melisme
Laurindo Almeida Trio | Chamber Jazz | Concord | CCD 4084
Melize
Lee Konitz Trio | It's You | Steeplechase | SCCD 31398
Mella Brava
Duke Ellington And His Orchestra | Duke Ellington:Complete Prestige Carnegie Hall 1946-1947 Concerts | Definitive Records | DRCD 11211
Mellenthin
Carnegie Hall Concert January 1946 | Prestige | 2PCD 24074-2
Mello-Ditti-
Duke Ellington:Complete Prestige Carnegie Hall 1946-1947 Concerts | Definitive Records | DRCD 11211
Mellow Acid
Philip Harper Sextet | Soulful Sin | Muse | MCD 5505
Mellow Alto
Sonny Thompson And His Orchestra | Cat On The Keys | Swingtime(Contact) | ST 1027
Mellow Buno
Cannonball Adderley Sextet | The Cannonball Adderley Collection Vol.3:Jazz Workshop Revisited | Landmark | CAC 1303-2(882343)
Mellow D
Kenneth Knudsen Trio | Bombay Hotel | Stunt Records | 18903
Mellow Gravy
Jack McDuff Quintet | Jack McDuff:The Prestige Years | Prestige | PRCD 24387-2
Dinah Washington With Lucky Thompson And His All Stars | The Complete Dinah Washington Vol.1 | Official | 3004
Mellow Mood
Jimmy Smith-Wes Montgomery Quartet | Wes Montgomery:The Verve Jazz Sides | Verve | 521690-2
Further Adventures Of Jimmy And Wes | Verve | 519802-2
Mellow T.-
Herbie Mann Group | London Underground | Atlantic | SD 1648
Mellowdrama
Joe Beck Trio | Relaxin' | dmp Digital Music Productions | CD 444
Mellstock Quire
Trio Neue Deutsche Blasmusik | Vier Stücke Für Das Trio Neue Deutsche Blasmusik | Misp Records | CD 512
Melodica
Toba Multijazz | Meridiana | SPLASC(H) Records | H 132
Melodicelli
Brocksieper-Solisten-Orchester | Globetrotter | Bear Family Records | BCD 15912 AH
Melodie
Christofer Varner | Christofer Varner-Solo | G.N.U. Records | CD A 96.010
Melodie Au Crepuscule
Django Reinhardt And The Quintet Du Hot Club De France | Swing De Paris | Arco | 3 ARC 110
Quintet Du Hot Club De France | Jazz Legacy 58: Django Reinhardt-Rythme Futur-Radio Sessions 1947 Vol | Vogue | 500108
Melodie In Es
Thilo Wolf Quartet With Strings | I Got Rhythm | MDL-Jazz | CD 1911(CD 050)
Melodie Pour Les Radio-Taxis
Teddy Stauffer Und Seine Original Teddies | International Schlager & In Mood mit Teddy Stauffer's Original Teddies | Elite Special | 9522003
Melodies Of 1997
Rainer Tempel Big Band | Melodies Of '98 | Jazz 4 Ever Records:Jazz Network | J4E 4744
Melodies Of '98
Crusaders | Live In Japan | GRP | GRP 97462
Melody
George Wallington | Virtuoso | Denon Compact Disc | 35C38-7248
Stan Getz Quintet | Stan Getz-The Complete Roost Sessions | EMI Records | 859622-2
Melody Express
Chamber Music | Fresh Sound Records | FSR-CD 78(882177)
Melody For Jack
David Torkanowsky Group | Steppin' Out | Line Records | COCD 9.00900 O
Melody For Melonae
Jackie McLean Quartet | Dr. Jackle | Steeplechase | SCCD 36005
Melody For Thelma
Opposite Corner | Jazz I Sverige '76 | Caprice | CAP 1117
Melody From The Drums
Michael Feinstein With Jule Styne | Michael Feinstein Sings The Jule Styne Songbook | Nonesuch | 7559-79274-2
Melody In F, Opus 3 No.1
Art Tatum Trio | Art Tatum:Complete Capitol Recordings | Definitive Records | DRCD 11192
Melody Lane
Jack Hylton And His Orchestra | Swing | Saville Records | SVL 158 IMS
Melody Room
Buddy Bregman And His Orchestra | Swinging Kicks | Verve | 559514-2
Melodyville
Art Pepper Quartet | Art Pepper:The Complete Galaxy Recordings | Galaxy | 16GCD 1016-2
Melolev
One September Afternoon | Original Jazz Classics | OJCCD 678-2(GXY 5141)
Melolev(alt.take)
One September Afternoon | Original Jazz Classics | OJCCD 678-2(GXY 5141)
Meloman
Jackie McLean Sextet | Jackie's Bag | Blue Note | BST 84051
Melos(Variazione Nove)
The Dance Band | Pierides | Line Records | COCD 9.00377 0
Melted Matter
Gebhard Ullmann Quartet | Kreuzberg Park East | Soul Note | 121371-2
Melting
Schmilz | Schmilz | Creative Works Records | CW CD 1041
Melting Point
Glenn Spearman Double Trio | The Fields | Black Saint | 120197-2
Melvalita
Steve Marcus Quartet | Green Line | Storyville | SLP 1011
Memo To My Son
Forward Motion | Reminiscence | Linn Records | AKD 024
Memoir
Daniel Schnyder Group | Words Within Music | Enja | ENJ-9369 2
Memoires
Daniel Schnyder Orchestra | Decoding The Message | Enja | ENJ-6036 2
Memor
Christian Wallumrod Ensemble | Sofienberg Variations | ECM | 1809(017067-2)
Memor Variation
David Chevallier Quintet | Migration | Adda | 590094
Memoria A Fado(Marrom)
Perico Sambeat Quintet | Friendship | ACT | 9421-2
Memoria De Un Sueno
Dylan Fowler Group | Portrait | Acoustic Music Records | 319.1185.2
Memorial Song
Sadao Watanabe Group | In Tempo | Verve | 527221-2
Memories
Antonio Farao Trio | Black Inside | Enja | ENJ-9345 2
Beaver | Friends | I-Records | IR 119304-M
Dino Saluzzi | Andina | ECM | 1375(837186-2)
Earl Bostic And His Orchestra | For You | Sing | 503
Johannes Mössinger-Wolfgang Lackerschmid | Joana's Dance | double moon | CHRDM 71017
Klaus Ignatzek-Florian Poser Duo | Music For Grandpiano And Vibraphone | Fusion | 8021 Digital
Paul Bley Quartet | Fragments | ECM | 1320
Preservation Hall Jazz Band | Preservation Hall Jazz Band New Orleans Vol.1 | CBS | MK 34594
Stivin-Van Den Broeck-Haurand | Bordertalk | Konnex Records | KCD 5068
Taragota Hot Seven | Bavarian Jazz Live | Calig | 30620/21
Überfall | Next To Silence | GIC | DL 4.1871
Memories Of A Pure Spring
Oscar Klein | Pickin' The Blues Vol. 2 | Intercord | 150006
Memories Of Paris
Ernest Ranglin Group | Modern Answers To Old Problems | Telarc Digital | CD 83526
Memories Of Spring
Peter Herbolzheimer Rhythm Combination & Brass | Colors Of A Band | Mons Records | MR 874799
Memories Of Tomorrow
Jochen Voss/Thomas Brendgens-Mönkemeyer | Alterations | Acoustic Music Records | 319.1029.2
Memories Of You
Art Tatum | Art Tatum:Memories Of You | Black Lion | BLCD 7608-2
Art Tatum:20th Century Piano Genius | Verve | 531763-2
Solos 1937 & Classic Piano Solos | Forlane | UCD 19010
Art Tatum-Buddy DeFranco Quartet | The Tatum Group Masterpieces | Pablo | 2625706
Benny Goodman And His Orchestra | The Yale University Muisc Library Vol.5 | Limelight | 820827-2 IMS
Benny Goodman Sextet | From Spiritual To Swing | Vanguard | VCD 169/71
Benny Goodman:Bangkok 1956/Basel 1959/Santiago De Chile 1961/Berlin 1980 | TCB Records | TCB 43012
Charles Mingus | Great Moments With Charles Mingus | MCA | MCA 2-4128 (802130)
Clifford Brown With Strings | Brownie-The Complete EmArCy Recordings Of Clifford Brown | EmArCy | 838306-2
Coleman Hawkins All Stars | 6 Classic Tenors | EPM Musique | FDC 5170
Erroll Garner Trio | Erroll Garner | Verve | 846191-2 PMS
Gerry Hayes-Charlie Antolini Quintet | Swing Explosion | BELL Records | BLR 84061
Golden Gate Quartet | Spirituals To Swing 1955-69 | EMI Records | 791569-2
Hank Jones | Tiptoe Tapdance | Original Jazz Classics | OJCCD 719-2(GXY 5108)
Joe Sullivan | The Piano Artistry Of Joe Sullivan | Jazz Unlimited | JUCD 2051
Lou Colombo Quintet | I Remember Bobby | Concord | CCD 4435
Louis Armstrong And His Sebastian New Cotton Club Orchestra | This Is Jazz:Louis Armstrong Sings | CBS | CK 65039
Marcus Roberts | Marsalis Standard Time Vol.1 | CBS | 451039-2
Rainer Sander Swing Wing | Shine | Elite Special | 73611
Sir Charles Thompson | Portrait Of A Piano | Sackville | 3037
Sweet Basil Trio | My Funny Valentine | Sweet Basil | 660.55.010
Thelonious Monk | Live At The Jazz Workshop-Complete | CBS | C2K 65189
Thelonious Monk-The Complete Riverside Recordings | Riverside | 15 RCD 022-2
Thelonious Monk Trio | The Riverside Trios | Milestone | M 47052
Zoot Sims Quartet | Zoot Sims:The Complete 1944-1954 Small Group Sessions(Master Takes),Vol.2 | Blue Moon | BMCD 1039
Zoot Sims-Bucky Pizzarelli Duo | A Summer Thing | Laserlight | 15754
Memories Of You-
Lennie Felix Trio | Melody Maker Tribute To Louis Armstrong Vol.1 | Jazz Colours | 874767-2
Sammy Price | Doc Cheattam&Sammy Price:Duos And Solos | Sackville | SK2CD-5002
The Tenor Triangle & The Melvin Rhyne Trio | Tell It Like It Is | Criss Cross | Criss 1089
Memory
Simon Schott | Bar Piano: Simon Schott Plays Your Favorite Evergreens Vol.1 | Organic Music | ORGM 9733
Memory-
Stanley Clarke-Al DiMeola-Jean Luc Ponty | The Rite Of Strings | Gai Saber | 834167-2
Memory Of A Dream
Bobby Jaspar All Stars | The Bobby Jaspar All Stars | Fresh Sound Records | FSR 549(Barclay 84023)
Memory Of Dick
Wayne Shorter-Herbie Hancock | 1+1:Herbie Hancock-Wayne Shorter | Verve | 537564-2
Memory Of Enchantment
Tony Scott | Dedications | Line Records | COCD 9.00803
Memory Of Scotty
Don Friedman Quartet | My Foolish Heart | Steeplechase | SCCD 31534
Don Friedman-Don Thompson | Opus D'Amour | Sackville | SKCD2-3058
Memory's Tricks
Evan Parker Electro-Acoustic Ensemble | Memory/Vision | ECM | 1852(0381172)
Memory-Vision(Staring Into The Time Cone)
Eddie Daniels Quintet With String Quartet | Memos From Paradise | GRP | GRP 95612
Memphis
Muddy Waters Groups | Muddy Waters-In Memoriam | Chess | 2292-44614-2
Memphis Blues
Louis Armstrong And His All Stars | The Louis Armstrong Selection | CBS | 467278-2
Monty Sunshine's Jazz Band | New Orleans Hula | Lake | LACD 47
Muggsy Spanier And His Ragtimers | The Commodore Story | Commodore | CMD 24002
Wild Bill Davison All Stars | The Idividualism Of Wild Bill Davison | Savoy | SJL 2229 (801205)
Earl Hines | Live In Milano 1966 | Nueva Records | JU 315
Memphis Blues-
Fletcher Henderson And His Orchestra | Wild Party | Hep | 1009
Memphis Slim U.S.A.
Memphis Slim And His Band | Memphis Slim:Born To Boogie | Memo Music | HDJ 4007
Memphis Underground
Herbie Mann Group | Memphis Underground | Atlantic | 7567-81364-2
Memphis Underground | Atlantic | ATL 40038
Men At Work
Mark Isham-Peter Van Hooke Duo | Vapor Drawings | Windham Hill | TA-C- 1027
Men Hunters
Leonard Feather All Star Jam Band | Hickory House Jazz | Affinity | CD AFS 1012
Men Of Mystery
Peter Gullin Trio | Untold Story | Dragon | DRCD 315
Men Suffer Too
Dizzy Gillespie Septet | The Great Modern Jazz Trumpet | Festival | 402151
Menage A Trois
Joe McPhee Trio | Sweet Freedom-Now What? | Hat Art | CD 6162
Menelaos(King of Sparta)
Rex Stewart And His Orchestra | The Great Ellington Units | RCA | ND 86751
Menilmontant
Django Reinhardt And The Quintet Du Hot Club De France | The Indispensable Django Reinhardt | RCA | ND 70929
Charlie Byrd Group | My Inspiration:Music Of Brazil | Concord | CCD 4850
Menina Flor
Stan Getz-Luiz Bonfa Quartet | Jazz Samba Encore! | Verve | 823613-2
Jazz Samba Encore! | CTI Records | PDCTI 1125-2
Menina Moca(Young Lady)
Stan Getz-Laurindo Almeida Orchestra | Verve Jazz Masters 53:Stan Getz-Bossa Nova | Verve | 529904-2
Egberto Gismonti Group | Infancia | ECM | 1428
Meninas
Charlie Byrd Trio | Sugarloaf Suite | Concord | CCD 4114

TITELVERZEICHNIS

Mensajero
Frank Castenier Group | For You,For Me For Evermore | EmArCy | 9814976
Mensch
Jan Von Klewitz-Markus Burger | Spiritual Standards | Jazzline | JL 11156-2
Mental Phrasing
Allen Lowe-Roswell Rudd Sextet | Dark Was The Night-Cold Was The Ground | Music & Arts | CD 811
Mental Surf
| Playing To The Moon | Ronnie Scott's Jazz House | JHCD 047
Mentor's Praise
Billy Oskay/Michael O'Domhnaill | Nightnoise | Windham Hill | WD 1031
Menuet
Viktoria Tabatchnikowa-Eugenij Belov | Troika | ALISO Records | AL 1036
Jacques Loussier Trio | Play Bach No.2 | Decca | 157562-2
Menuet 1
Play Bach No.2 | Decca | 157562-2
Menuet 2
Eugen Cicero Trio | Rococo Jazz 2 | Timeless | CD SJP 255
Menuetto-
Lee Morgan Quintet | Live At the Lighthouse '70 | Fresh Sound Records | FSR-CD 0140(2)
Meow
Duke Ellington And His Orchestra | Two Great Concerts | Festival | ???
Mephisto
Zipflo Reinhardt Group | Light Of The Future | MPS | 68274
Mer Blanche
Hot Club The Zigan | Adagio | Jazz Pure Collection | AU 31601 CD
Mer Loss D'r Dom In Kölle
David Friedman Trio | Ternaire | Deux Z | ZZ 84107
Mercé
Ken McIntyre Quartet | Hindsight | Steeplechase | SCCD 31014
Mercedes Benz(take 1)
Pee Wee Ellis-Horace Parlan | Gentle Men Blue | Minor Music | 801073
Mercedes Benz(take 2)
Danilo Perez Quartet | Panamonk | Impulse(MCA) | 951190-2
Mercedes Mood
Gabriel Pérez Group | Alfonsina | Jazz 4 Ever Records:Jazz Network | J4E 4751
Merceditas
Gato Barbieri Group | Bolivia | RCA | FD 10158
Merci Afrique
BBFC | Live | Plainisphare | PL 1267-14
Merciful 1
Nils Petter Molvaer Group | Solid Ether | ECM | 1722(543365-2)
Merciful 2
Dave Brubeck With The Erich Kunzel Orchestra | Truth Is Fallen | Atlantic | 7567-80761-2
Merciful Men Are Taken Away
Mark Nauseef Group | Dark | CMP Records | CMP CD 36
Mercury-
Larry Schneider Trio | Freedom Jazz Dance | Steeplechase | SCCD 31390
Mercy Mercy Me
Al Di Meola Group | Winter Nights | Telarc Digital | CD 83458
Mercy Street
Alberto Marsico Quintet | Them That's Got | Organic Music | ORGM 9705
Mercy Train
Chico Freeman Group | You'll Know When You Get There | Black Saint | 120128-2
Mercy, Mercy Me(The Ecology)-
Albert Louis Jazzband | Live Im Neumeyer Dr. Flotte | Jazz Classics | AU 11089
Mercy, Mercy, Mercy
Cannonball Adderley Quintet | Julian Cannonball Adderlry: Salle Pleyel/Olympia | Laserlight | 36126
Live On Planet Earth | West Wind | WW 2088
Charles Earland Quintet | The Groove Masters Series | Savant Records | SCD 2008
Ernestine Anderson And Her Quartet | When The Sun Goes Down | Concord | CCD 4263
Maceo Parker With The Rebirth Brass Band | Southern Exposure | Minor Music | 801033
Manhattan Jazz Quintet | Funky Strut | Sweet Basil | 660.55.006
Nils Landgren Funk Unit | Live In Montreux | ACT | 9265-2
Orquestra Mahatma | A Young Person's Guide | Babel | BDV 9612
Cannonball Adderley Group | Phenix | Fantasy | FCD 79004-2
Mercy, Mercy, Mercy-
Cannonball Adderley Sextet | Cannonball Adderley Birthday Celebration | Fantasy | FANCD 6087-2
Babatunde And Phenomena | Levels Of Conciousness | Evidence | TR 107
Merge Song
Chico Freeman Quintet | Chico | India Navigation | IN 1031 CD
Meridian
Don Rendell Nine | Earth Music | Spotlite | SPJ 515
Meridianne-A Wood Sylph
Michael Mantler Group With The Danish Concert Radio Orchestra | Many Have No Speech | Watt | 19(835580-2)
Merk, Jetzt
The Splendid Master Gnawa Musicians Of Morocco | The Splendid Master Gnawa Musicians Of Morocco | Verve | 521587-2
Merry Christmas Baby
Sonny Parker With The Lionel Hampton Orchestra | Sonny Parker:The Complete 1948-1953 | Blue Moon | BMCD 6003
Merry Pranks (The Jester's Song)
Chris Barber's Jazz Band | The Best Of Dixieland-Live in 1954/55 | London | 820878-2
Merrydown Blues
Chris Barber-40 Years Jubilee(1954-1956) | Timeless | CD TTD 586
Merry-Go-Round
Charlie Parker All Stars | The Savoy Recordings 2 | Savoy | 650108(881908)
Meru Lo Snob-
André Ricros-Louis Sclavis Group | Le Partage Des Eaux | Silex | Y 225003 IMS
Mes Trois Fils
Turk Murphy And His Jazz Band | Turk Murphy's San Francisco Jazz-Vol.2 | Good Time Jazz | 12027
Mesa Verde
Lee Morgan Sextet | Jazz Gallery:Lee Morgan Vol.1 | RCA | 2127281-2
Mescalin
Sonny Sharrock/Nicky Skopelitis | Faith Moves | CMP Records | CMP CD 52
Mesolithic Tomtomfool
Tony Purrone Trio | Electric Poetry | B&W Present | BW 028
Mess Around
Professor Longhair Group | Rock'n Roll Gumbo | Verve | 519746-2
Message Du Dylph
Albert Ayler Group | New Grass | MCA | AS 9175
Message From Kenia
Joe Chambers-Larry Young | Double Exposure | Muse | MR 5165
Message From Milan
Bent Axen Quintet(Jazz Quintet '60) | Axen | Steeplechase | SCCD 36003
Message From The Nile
Rex Stewart All-Stars | Hollywood Jam | Duke Records | D 1017
Message To A Friend
Lena Horne And Gabor Szabo | Lena & Gabor | Gryphon | 6.24451 AT
Message To My Friend
Bunk Johnson | Prelude To The Revival Vol.2 | American Music | AMCD-41
Messin' Around
Joe Turner With Pete Johnson And His Orchestra | Tell Me Pretty Baby | Arhoolie | CD 333

Messing
Buddy Guy & Junior Wells With The Chicago Blues All Stars '78 | Live In Montreux | Black & Blue | BLE 59.530 2
Messy Bessie
Louis Jordan And His Tympany Five | Go Blow Your Horn-Part 2 | Pathe | 1546680(Aladdin)
Mestico & Caboclo
Brötzmann-Mengelberg-Bennink Trio | 3 Points And A Mountain...Plus | FMP | CD 107
Meta
Fonolite Group | Gland | SPLASC(H) Records | H 151
Metal Beauty
Pierre Favre Ensemble | Singing Drums | ECM | 1274
Metal Birds
Heinz Sauer Quartet | Metal Blossoms | L+R Records | LR 40019
Metal Summer
Georg Hofmann-Lucas Niggli Duo | Mute Songs & Drumscapes | Creative Works Records | CW CD 1022-2
Metal Winds
Richard Carr Trio | Coast To Coast | Nabel Records:Jazz Network | CD 4675
String Thing | String Thing:Turtifix | MicNic Records | MN 4
Metall
Georg Ruby Group | Stange Loops | Jazz Haus Musik | JHM 0057 CD
Metalog 1
Stange Loops | Jazz Haus Musik | JHM 0057 CD
Metalog 2
Stange Loops | Jazz Haus Musik | JHM 0057 CD
Metalog 3
Stange Loops | Jazz Haus Musik | JHM 0057 CD
Metalog 4
Stange Loops | Jazz Haus Musik | JHM 0057 CD
Metalog 5
Jazz Orchester Rheinland-Pfalz | Last Season | Jazz Haus Musik | LJBB 9706
John Zorn Naked City | Naked City:Radio | Avant | AVAN 003
Metamorfose
Massimo Ciolli Quartet | Cronopios | SPLASC(H) Records | H 171
Metamorfosi
Paul Bley | Moving Hearts | West Wind | WW 2085
Metamorphos
Dave Holland Quintet | Point Of View | ECM | 1663(557020-2)
Arthur Blythe Quintet & Guests | Elaborations | CBS | FC 38163
Metamorphosis
Dizzy Gillespie/Max Roach | Max+Dizzy | A&M Records | 396404-2
Horace Silver Quintet | The Stylings Of Silver | Blue Note | 300168(1562)
Lennie Niehaus Quintet | Patterns | Fresh Sound Records | FSR-CD 5013
Metanois
Yusef Lateef Sextet | Morning-The Savoy Sessions | Savoy | SJL 2205 (801181)
Metaphor Of Travel
Steve Coleman And Five Elements | On The Edge Of Tomorrow | JMT Edition | 919005-2
Metaphysical Phunktion
Hugh Ragin Trio | Metaphysical Question | Cecma | 1007
Metaren
Franklin Kiermyer & Jericho | Break Down The Walls | Konnex Records | KCD 5044
Meta-Waltz
ATonALL | ATonALL | Creative Works Records | CW CD 1024-2
Metazoen
Reggie Workman Quintet | Summit Conference | Postcards | POST 1003
Meteor
Tal Farlow Trio | Verve Jazz Masters 41:Tal Farlow | Verve | 527365-2
Bob Florence Trio | Bob Florence Trio | Fresh Sound Records | FSR-CD 0303
Métisse
Jo Jones Orchestra | The Main Man | Pablo | 2310799
Metropol
Bernhard Arndt | Insight Insight | FMP | OWN-90005
Meu Jardim
Eddie Daniels Quartet | Under The Influence | GRP | GRP 97172
Mevagissey
Ralph Towner | Blue Sun | ECM | 1250(829162-2)
Mevlana Etude
Gary Burton Quintet With Eberhard Weber | Ring | ECM | 1051
Mevlevia
Chubby 'Hip Shakin" Newsom And Her Band | The Original Hip Shakin' Mama | Official | 6020
Mex
Loverly | Play World Wild Music | ITM Records | ITM 1419
Mexicali Nose
Dave Bargeron Quartet | Barge Burns...Slide Flies | Mapleshade | 02832
Mexican Hat Dance
Les Brown And His Orchestra | The Les Brown Story | Capitol | 791226-2
Mexican Hip Dance
Jim Brent-Bruce Kaminsky Duo | Greensleeves | Steeplechase | SCS 4003
Mexican Song No.1
Charlie Byrd | Latin Byrd | Milestone | MCD 47005-2
Mexican Song No.2
Rebirth Brass Band | Feel Like Funkin' It Up | Rounder Records | CDRR 2093
Mexico City
Kenny Burrell Sextet | Kenny Burrell-Vol. 2 | Blue Note | 300143(1543)
Kenny Dorham Sextet | Round Midnight At The Cafe Bohemia | Blue Note | 300105(1524)
Mexico City(alt.take)
Nat King Cole Trio | The Early Forties | Fresh Sound Records | FSR-CD 0139
Mi Amigo Carlos
Robert Jeanne Quartet | Quartets | B.Sharp Records | CDS 084
Mi Ardillita
Jan Hengmith Group | Fusion Flamenca | Acoustic Music Records | 319.1048.2
Mi Cosa
Wes Montgomery With The Don Sebesky Orchestra | Bumpin' | Verve | 539062-2
Sergio Vesely With Band | Personas | Messidor | 15914
Mi Fas Y Recordar
Gonzalo Rubalcaba Group | Mi Gran Pasion | Messidor | 15999 CD
Mi Guaquanco
Mongo Santamaria And His Rhythm Afro-Cubanos | Yambu | Original Jazz Classics | OJC 276(F 8012)
Mi Querido Monk...
Gary Burton Group | Tango | Concord | CCD 4793
Mi Saeta
Tiziana Ghiglioni And Her Band | Tiziana Ghiglioni Canta Luigi Tenco | Philology | W 60.2
Mi Tristeza
Guillermo Marchena Y El Grupo Irazu | Boleros | L+R Records | CDLR 45068
Mi Vida Contigo
Bud Shank-Shorty Rogers Quintet | California Concert | Contemporary | CCD 14012-2
Mial
Katrina Krimsky-Trevor Watts | Stella Malu | ECM | 1199
Paul Williams Orchestra | Paul Williams:The Complete Recordings Vol.2 (1949-1952) | Blue Moon | BMCD 6021
Mia's Proof
Michael Riessler Group | What A Time | Label Bleu | LBLC 6537(889280)
Michaela Sofia
Changes | Jazz Changes? | Jazz 'n' Arts Records | 0100
Michael's Blues
Hilton Ruiz Orchestra | Manhattan Mambo | Telarc Digital | CD 83322

Michelangelo
Pablo Ziegler And His Quintet For New Tango | Asfalto-Street Tango | RCA | 2663266-2
Astor Piazzolla Group | Tango: Zero Hour | American Clave | AMCL 1013-2
Michelle
Gato Barbieri Quartet | In Search Of The Mystery | ESP Disk | ESP 1049-2
Johnny Smith Quartet | Johnny Smith | Verve | 537752-2
Singers Unlimited | The Singers Unlimited:Magic Voices | MPS | 539130-2
A Capella | MPS | 815671-1
Michelle (alt.take 1)
Terry Gibbs Septet | Early Stan | Original Jazz Classics | OJCCD 654-2(P 7255)
Michelle (alt.take 2)
Early Getz | Prestige | P 24088
Michelle(part 1&2)
Gato Barbieri Group | Bolivia | RCA | FD 10158
Michellina
Gato Barbieri:The Complete Flying Dutchman Recordings 1969-1973 | RCA | 2154555-2
Michelone
Jermaine Landsberger Trio | Gypsy Feeling | Edition Collage | EC 516-2
Michels Tune
Michel And Tony Petrucciani | Conversations | Dreyfus Jazz Line | FDM 36617-2
Manhattan Project,The | The Manhattan Project | Blue Note | 794204-2
Mickey Polka
Michael Sagmeister Quartet | A Certain Gift | MGI Records | MGR CD 1014
Mickey's Flight
Stan Getz With The Eddie Sauter Orchestra | Stan Getz Plays The Music Of Mickey One | Verve | 531232-2
Mickey's Flight-
Stan Getz Plays The Music Of Mickey One | Verve | 531232-2
Stan Getz Plays The Music Of Mickey One | Verve | 531232-2
Mickey's Theme
Mickey Tucker Sextet | Hang In There | Steeplechase | SCCD 31302
Mickey's Tune
Ull Möck Trio | How High The Moon | Satin Doll Productions | SDP 1006-1 CD
Micro
Quintet Du Hot Club De France | Django/Django In Rome 1949-1050 | BGO Records | BGOCD 366
Tino Tracanna Group | '292' | SPLASC(H) Records | CD H 322-2
Micro-Orka
Wolfgang Puschnig Group With Ernst Jandl | Mixed Metaphors | Amadeo | 527266-2
Mic's Jump
Oscar Peterson Quartet With Dizzy Gillespie | Des Femmes Disparaissent/Les Tricheurs(Original Soundtracks) | Fontana | 834752-2 PMS
Middag(Noon)
Don Friedman Trio | A Day In The City:Six Variations On A Theme | Original Jazz Classics | OJCCD 1775-2(RLP 9384)
Midday Riser
Flora Purim & Airto | The Sun Is Out | Concord | CCD 45003
Middle Class White Boy
String Trio Of New York | Time Never Lies | Stash Records | ST-CD 544(889796)
Middle Way
Chet Baker Quartet | Chet Baker In Paris-The Complete Barclay Recordings Vol.1 | EmArCy | 837474-2 PMS
Midgets
Count Basie And His Orchestra | The Basie Band 1952-1957 | Jazz Magazine | 40200
Harry Sweets Edison And The Golden Horns | Live At The Iridium | Telarc Digital | CD 83425
Midgets(alt.take)
Woody Shaw With The Tone Jansa Quartet | Woody Shaw With Tone Jansa Quartet | Timeless | CD SJP 221
Midlife
Benny Carter And His Orchestra | Coleman Hawkins/Benny Carter | Forlane | UCD 19011
Midnight
Hal Singer-Charlie Shavers Quintet | Blue Stompin' | Original Jazz Classics | OJCCD 834-2(P 7153)
Phil Minton And Veryan Weston | Ways Past | ITM Records | ITM 1468
George Winston | December | Windham Hill | 34 11025-2
Midnight And You
Eddie Lockjaw Davis-Johnny Griffin Quintet | Blues Up And Down | Milestone | MCD 47084-2
Midnight At Mintons
Howard McGhee Sextet | Teddy Edwards:Steady With Teddy 1946-1948 | Cool & Blue | C&B-CD 115
Midnight Blue
Oliver Nelson And His Orchestra | More Blues And The Abstract Truth | Impulse(MCA) | 951212-2
See You At The Fair | MCA | AS 65
Midnight Blue...Red Shift
Benny Moten's Kansas City Orchestra | The Complete Bennie Moten Vol.1/2 | RCA | NL 89881(2) DP
Midnight Cowboy-
Buddy Rich Big Band | Keep The Customer Satisfied | EMI Records | 523999-2
Midnight Cowboy Medley:
Humphrey Lyttelton And His Band | ...It Seems Like Yesterday | Calligraph | CLG LP 001 IMS
Midnight Creeper
Lou Donaldson Quintet | Lou Donaldson:The Righteous Reed! The Best Of Poppa Lou | Blue Note | 830721-2
Midnight Hour Blues
Bob Hall Trio | Alone With The Blues | Lake | LACD 44
Ken Colyer's Skiffle Group | The Decca Skiffle Sessions 1954-57 | Lake | LACD 7
Midnight In Berkeley Square
Wayne Shorter Orchestra | High Life | Verve | 529224-2
Midnight Indigo
Hal Singer Orchestra | Roots Of Rock 'N' Roll, Vol. 6: Honkers & Screamers | Savoy | SJL 2234 (801210)
Midnight Mood
Bill Evans | Alone | Verve | 598319-2
Alone | Verve | 598319-2
Bill Evans Trio | Since We Met | Original Jazz Classics | OJC 622(F 9501)
Live In Europe Vol.2 | EPM Musique | FDC 5713
Homecoming | Milestone | MCD 9291-2
Bill Evans:The Secret Sessions | Milestone | 8MCD 4421-2
Cannonball Adderley Quintet | Radio Nights | Night Records | VNCD 2(887045)
Peter Finger | Solo | Acoustic Music Records | 319.1032.2
Wes Montgomery Quintet With The Claus Ogerman Orchestra | Tequila | CTI Records | PDCTI 1118-2
Midnight Mood-
Bill Evans | Alone | Verve | 598319-2
The Complete Bill Evans On Verve | Verve | 527953-2
Midnight Mood(alt.take)
Duke Jordan | Midnight Moonlight | Steeplechase | SCCD 31143
Midnight Plea
Hank Crawford Orchestra | Midnight Ramble | Milestone | MCD 9112-2
Midnight Ride
Lil' Ed Williams And The Blues Imperials | Roughhousin' | Sonet | SNTF 966(941966)
Midnight Sevilla

Lowell Fulsom Band | San Francisco Blues | Black Lion | BLCD 760176

Midnight Soul
Big Bill Broonzy | An Evening With Big Bill Broonzy,Vol.2 | Storyville | STCD 8017

Midnight Special
Jesse Fuller One Man Band | Brother Lowdown | Fantasy | F 24707

Midnight Standoff-
Big Bill Broonzy Group | Midnight Steppers | Swingtime(Contact) | BT 2001

Midnight Stroll
O'Bryant's Washboard Band | Chicago South Side Jazz | Village(Jazz Archive) | VILCD 019-2

Midnight Sun
Ahmad Jamal Quartet | Digital Works | Atlantic | 781258-2
Bill Doggett And His Orchestra | Bill's Honky Tonk | Memo Music | HDJ 4048
Carmen McRae With The Norman Simmons Trio | Live At Century Plaza | Atlantic | AMCY 1075
Dee Dee Bridgewater With Her Trio | Live At Yoshi's | Verve | 543354-2
Dee Dee Bridgewater With Orchestra | Dear Ella | Verve | 539102-2
Eddie Lockjaw Davis Sextet | Lock,The Fox | RCA | NL 89584(809143)
Ella Fitzgerald With The Lou Levy Trio | Ella In Rome-The Birthday Concert | Verve | 835454-2
Ella Fitzgerald With The Nelson Riddle Orchestra | The Best Of The Song Books | Verve | 519804-2
Ella Fitzgerald Sings The Johnny Mercer Songbook | Verve | 539057-2
The Johnny Mercer Songbook | Verve | 823247-2 PMS
Glen Gray And The Casa Loma Orchestra | Swingin' Decade! Sounds Of The Great Bands Of The 40's | Pathe | 1566171(Capitol ST 1289)
Jeff Hamilton Trio With Frits Landesbergen | Dynavibes | Mons Records | MR 874794
Jimmy Smith Trio | A New Sound A New Star:Jimmy Smith At The Organ | Blue Note | 857191-2
Jimmy Smith At The Organ | Blue Note | 300154(1512)
John Graas Nonet | Jazzmantics | Fresh Sound Records | 252283-1(Decca DL 8677)
June Christy With The Pete Rugolo Orchestra | Something Cool(The Complete Mono & Stereo Versions) | Capitol | 534069-2
Kenny Drew Trio | Afternoon In Europe | RCA | PL 45373
Lionel Hampton And His Orchestra | Lionel Hampton:Flying Home | Dreyfus Jazz Line | FDM 36735-2
The Lionel Hampton Big Band | West Wind Orchestra Series | 2404 CD
Lionel Hampton Quartet | The Complete Lionel Hampton Quartets And Quintets With Oscar Peterson On Verve | Verve | 559797-2
Lionel Hampton With Milt Buckner And The All Stars | Alive & Jumping | MPS | 821283-1
Mark Whitfield Group | Patrice | Warner | 7599-26659-2
Milt Buckner Trio | Midnight Slows No.1 | Black & Blue | BLE 233026
Sarah Vaughan With The Oscar Peterson Quartet | How Long Has This Been Going On? | Pablo | 2310821-2
Stan Kenton And His Orchestra | Road Show Vol.1 | Creative World | ST 1019
Toni Jannotta Group | Jazz At The Ranch | TCB Records | TCB 21182

Midnight Swinger
Lester Young And His Orchestra | Jammin The Blues | Jazz Anthology | JA 5110

Midnight Tango
Frank Emilio Flynn | Jane Bunnett And The Cuban Piano Masters | Pacific Jazz | 832695-2

Midnight Voyage
Al Sears And His Orchestra | Sear-iously | Bear Family Records | BCD 15668 AH

Midnight Wail
Billy Higgins Quartet | The Soldier | Timeless | CD SJP 145

Midnight Waltz
Milt Jackson Quartet | Milt Jackson Birthday Celebration | Fantasy | FANCD 6079-2
Milt Jackson-Ray Brown Quartet | It Don't Mean A Thing If You Can't Tap Your Foot To It | Original Jazz Classics | OJCCD 601-2
Philly Joe Jones Septet | Drum Song | Milestone | GXY 5153

Midnite
Count Basie And His Orchestra | The Complete Atomic Basie | Roulette | 828635-2

Midnite Blue
Basie On Roulette, Vol. 1: E : MC 2 : Count Basie Orchestra+Neal HeftArrangeme | Roulette | CDP 793273-2

Midori
Richie Beirach | Common Heart | Owl Records | 048 CD

Midriff
Duke Ellington And His Orchestra | Duke Ellington:The Complete RCA-Victor Mid-Forties Recordings(1944-1946) | RCA | 2663394-2
Duke Ellington: The Champs-Elysees Theater January 29-30th,1965 | Laserlight | 36131
Jimmie Lunceford And His Orchestra | The Original Jimmy Lunceford Orchestra | Jazz Anthology | JA 5224

Midsommarvaka From Svedish Rhapsody No.1(Hugo Alfven)
Modern Jazz Quartet | MJQ 40 | Atlantic | 7567-82330-2

Midsömmer
The Modern Jazz Quartet At Music Inn With Sonny Rollins,Vol.2 | Atlantic | 7567-80794-2
The Modern Jazz Society | A Concert Of Contemporary Music | Verve | 559827-2
A Concert Of Contemporary Music | Verve | 559827-2

Midsömmer(rehersal take)
Eero Koivistoinen Quintet | Dialog | L+R Records | CDLR 45094

Midsummer Night
Paco De Lucia-Al Di Meola-John McLaughlin | Paco De Lucia-Al Di Meola-John McLaughlin | Verve | 533215-2
Jim Snidero Quintet | Vertigo | Criss Cross | Criss 1112

Midway
Bud Powell Trio | Time Was | Bluebird | ND 86367

Midwestern Nights Dream
Al Di Meola Group | Winter Nights | Telarc Digital | CD 83458

Miff's Blues
Makoto Ozone Group | Treasure | Verve | 021906-2

Might As Well
Arnold Ross Trio | Just You & He & Me | Fresh Sound Records | FSR-CD 313

Might Be
Lightnin' Hopkins | Lightnin' In New York | Candid | CS 9010

Mighty Denn-
The New York Saxophone Quartet | An American Experience | Stash Records | ST 220 IMS

Mighty Lak A Rose -> Mighty Like A Rose

Mighty Like A Rose
Al Haig Trio | The Piano Collection Vol.2 | Vogue | 21610222
Art Tatum | Art Tatum:20th Century Piano Genius | Verve | 531763-2
The Tatum Solo Masterpieces Vol.7 | Pablo | 2310792
Jack Teagarden All Stars | Giants Of Traditional Jazz | Savoy | SV 0277
Duke Ellington And His Orchestra | Unknown Session | CBS | 467180-2

Mighty Low
Sonny Criss Quintet | Blues Pour Flirter | Polydor | 2445034 IMS

Mighty Spirit
Mills Blue Rhythm Band | Rhythm Spasm | Hep | CD 1015

Mighty Tight Woman
Sippie Wallace With Jim Dapogny's Chicago Jazz Band | Sippie | Atlantic | SD 19350

Mignon's Song
Don Ewell | Jazz Greats | Chiaroscuro | CR 204

Migrations
Charles Davis & Captured Moments | Strange Goodbyes | L+R Records | CDLR 45101

Miguel's Party
Art Blakey And The Jazz Messengers | Jazz-Club: Trumpet | Verve | 840038-2

Bud Powell Quintet | The Story Of Jazz Piano | Laserlight | 24653
The Best Of The Jazz Pianos | LRC Records | CDC 8519

Mihiyo Ha Bohimara(Nomansland)
Boulou Ferre-Elios Ferre Duo | Gypsy Dreams | Steeplechase | SCCD 31140

Mikail's Dream
Django Reinhardt And The Quintet Du Hot Club De France | Django Reinhardt:Djangology | EMI Records | 780659-2

Mikesh
Willem Breuker Kollektief | To Remain | BVHAAST | CD 8904

Mi-La
John McLaughlin Trio | Que Alegria | Verve | 837280-2

Mila Repa
European Jazz Ensemble & The Khan Family feat. Joachim Kühn | European Jazz Ensemble Meets The Khan Family | M.A Music | A 807-2

Milab
Great Jazz Trio | Re-Visited:At The Village Vanguard Vol.1 | Eastworld | EWJ 90002

Milan In Minor
Bruce Forman Quartet With Bobby Hutcherson | There Are Times | Concord | CCD 4332

Milan To Lyon-
Brötzmann-Mengelberg-Bennink Trio | 3 Points And A Mountain...Plus | FMP | CD 107

Milano
Bill Evans-Eddie Gomez Duo | Montreux III | Original Jazz Classics | OJC20 644-2(F 9510)
The Complete Fantasy Recordings | Fantasy | 9FCD 1012-2
Chris Connor With The Al Cohn Orchestra | Free Spirits | Atlantic | AMCY 1077
John Lewis | Private Concert | EmArCy | 848267-2
Modern Jazz Quartet | The Complete Modern Jazz Quartet Prestige & Pablo Recordings | Prestige | 4PRCD 4438-2
The Complete Modern Jazz Quartet Prestige & Pablo Recordings | Prestige | 4PRCD 4438-2
Topsy-This One's For Basie | Original Jazz Classics | OJCCD 1073-2(2310917)
MJQ 40 | Atlantic | 7567-82330-2
Modern Jazz Quartet | Prestige | P 24005

Milarepa
Alan Pasqua Group | Milargo | Postcards | POST 1002

Milargo-
Adelhard Roidinger Trio | Computer & Jazz Project I | Thein | TH 100384

Mildama
Clifford Brown-Max Roach Quintet | More Study In Brown | EmArCy | 814637-2
Max Roach-Clifford Brown Quintet | Daahoud | Mobile Fidelity | MFCD 826

Mildama(alt.take 1)
Clifford Brown-Max Roach Quintet | Brownio The Complete EmArCy Recordings Of Clifford Brown | EmArCy | 838306-2

Mildama(alt.take 2)
Brownie-The Complete EmArCy Recordings Of Clifford Brown | EmArCy | 838306-2

Mildama(alt.take 3)
Brownie-The Complete EmArCy Recordings Of Clifford Brown | EmArCy | 838306-2

Mildama(alt.take 4)
Brownie-The Complete EmArCy Recordings Of Clifford Brown | EmArCy | 838306-2

Mildama(alt.take 5)
Brownie-The Complete EmArCy Recordings Of Clifford Brown | EmArCy | 838306-2

Mildama(alt.take 6)
Johnny Griffin Quartet | Introducing Johnny Griffin | Blue Note | 746536-2

Mildred-
Steve Tibbetts Group | Big Map Idea | ECM | 1380

Mile 234
John Wolf Brennan | The Well-Prepared Clavier/Das Wohlpräparierte Klavier | Creative Works Records | CW CD 1032-2

Mile End
Chris Barber's Jazz And Blues Band | 40 Years Jubilee At The Opera House Nürnberg | Timeless | CD TTD 590

Milen
Anderson-Harris-Lewis-Valente | Slideride | Hat Art | CD 6165

Miles Ahead
Miles Davis + 19 | The Miles Davis Selection | CBS | 465699-2
Miles Davis Quartet | Welcome To Jazz: Miles Davis | Koch Records | 321 944 D1
Pat LaBarbera Quartet | Virgo Dance | Justin Time | Just 24

Miles Away
Simon Phillips-Jeff Babko Group | Vantage Point | Jazzline | JL 11159-2

Miles Behind
Clare Fischer And His Orchestra | 'T Was Only Yesterday | Discovery | DS 798 IMS

Miles Davis' Licks
Michel Petrucciani Group | Michel Petrucciani:The Blue Note Years | Blue Note | 789916-2
Michel Petrucciani Quintet | Michel Petrucciani Live | Blue Note | 780589-2
Lester Bowie | All The Magic! | ECM | 1246/47

Miles Magic
Clark Terry With The Summit Jazz Orchestra | Clark | Edition Collage | EC 530-2

Miles' Mode
Helmut Forsthoff Trio | Four Together | Aho-Recording | CD 1011
Jaco Pastorius/Brian Melvin Group | Jazz Street | Timeless | CD SJP 258
John Coltrane Quartet | John Coltrane:The Classic Quartet-Complete Impulse Studio Recordings | Impulse(MCA) | 951280-2
John Coltrane Quartet With Eric Dolphy | John Coltrane:The Complete 1961 Village Vanguard Recordings | Impulse(MCA) | 954322-2
Two Giants Together | Jazz Anthology | JA 5184
John Coltrane Quintet With Eric Dolphy | John Coltrane-Live Trane:The European Tours | Pablo | 7PACD 4433-2
Peter Delano Group | Peter Delano | Verve | 519602-2

Miles Mode(alt.take)
Bill Bickford's Bigfoot | Semi-Precious Metal | Tutu Records | 888114-2

Miles Of The Blues
Charles Davis & Captured Moments | Strange Goodbyes | L+R Records | CDLR 45101

Miles Runs The Voodoo Down
Miles Davis Quintet | Paraphernalia | JMY(Jazz Music Yesterdays) | JMY 1013-2

Miles Runs The Voodoo Down-
Winard Harper Sextet | Winard | Savant Records | SCD 2021

Miles Sign-Off
Michael Bocian Quartet | Reverence | Enja | 8096-2

Miles' Theme
Jane Ira Bloom-Kent McLagan Duo | We Are Outline | Outline | OTL 137

Miles To Go
Miles Davis All Stars | Miles Davis:Early Milestones 1945-1949 | Naxos Jazz | 8.120607 CD

Milestones
Bill Evans Trio | Waltz For Debby | Original Jazz Classics | OJC20 210-2
Bobby Jaspar All Stars | The Bobby Jaspar All Stars | Fresh Sound Records | FSR 549(Barclay 84023)
Booker Little 4 & Max Roach | Booker Little 4 & Max Roach | Blue Note | 784457-2
Charlie Parker All Stars | Charlie Parker:The Complete 1944-1948 Small Group Sessions(Studio Recordings-Master Takes),Vol.3 | Blue Moon | BMCD 1009
Claudio Roditi Quintet | Milestones | Candid | CCD 79515
Dexter Gordon Quintet | The Jazz Giants Play Miles Davis:Milestones | Prestige | PCD 24225-2
Eddie Henderson Quintet | Phantoms | Steeplechase | SCCD 31250

Fred Hersch Trio | The Fred Hersch Trio Plays | Chesky | JD 116
Jimmy Smith And Wes Montgomery With The Oliver Nelson Orchestra | Jimmy Smith:Best Of The Verve Years | Verve | 527950-2
Joe Pass Trio | Live At Donte's | Pablo | 2620114-2
Johnny Lytle Septet | Possum Grease | Muse | MCD 5482
Maynard Ferguson And His Big Bop Nouveau Band | One More Trip To Birdland | Concord | CCD 4729
Miles Davis All Stars | The Savoy Recordings 2 | Savoy | 650108(881908)
Miles Davis Quintet | Live In New York | Bandstand | BDCD 1501
Ray Brown Trio | Bassface | Telarc Digital | CD 83340
The Jazz Crusaders | Live At The Lighthouse '66 | Pacific Jazz | 837988-2
Vic Juris Trio | Songbook | Steeplechase | SCCD 31843
Charlie Parker Quintet | The Complete Savoy Sessions Vol.3 | Savoy | WL 70548 (809291)

Milestones(alt.take)
First Miles | Savoy | SV 0159(SJL 1196)

Milestrane
Defunkt | Defunkt/Heroes | DIW | DIW 838 CD

Milikituli
Orquestra De Cambra Teatre Lliure | Orquestra De Cambra Teatre Lliure and Lluis Vidal Trio feat.Dave Liebman | Fresh Sound Records | FSNT 027 CD
No Nett | Wenn Der Weiße Flieder Wieder Blüht | Jazz Haus Musik | JHM 14

Milk
Big Joe Turner | Roots Of Rock And Roll Vol. 2: Big Joe Turner | Savoy | SJL 2223 (801199)

Milk Cow Blues
Fred McDowell | Mississippi Blues | Black Lion | BLCD 760179

Milk Cow's Calf Blues
Robert Johnson | Country Bottleneck Guitar Classics | Yazoo | YAZ 1026

Milk Cow's Calf Blues(alt.take)
Salvatore Bonafede Trio | Plays | Ken Music | 660.56.017

Milky White Way
Billy Bird | Guitar Wizards 1926-1935 | Yazoo | YAZ 1016

Millard Mottker
Axel Fischbacher Group | Moods | Blue Flame | 40082(2132484-2)

Mille Vagues
Bensusan & Malherbe | Live Au New Morning | Acoustic Music Records | 319.1142.2

Millenium
Ron Eschete Quintet | To Let You Know I Care | Muse | MR 5186

Millie's Delight
Jackie McLean Sextet | Fat Jazz | Fresh Sound Records | FSR-CD 18(882155)

Million Dollar Secret
Lionel Hampton And His Orchestra | Lionel Hampton:Flying Home | Dreyfus Jazz Line | FDM 36735-2

Million Dollar Smile
The Mess Is Here | Magic | AWE 18(807364)

Millionaire's Daughter Blues
| Pete Fountain And His Basin Street Six | 504 Records | 504CD 16

Milneberg Joys
Bunk Johnson-Sidney Bechet Sextet | Jazz Classics Vol.1 | Blue Note | 789384-2
Fletcher Henderson And His Orchestra | The Crown King Of Swing | Savoy | SV 0254(SJL 1152)
George Lewis Ragtime Jazz Band Of New Orleans | The Oxford Series Vol.2 | American Music | AMCD-22
Jack Teagarden And His Orchestra | Jazz Original | Charly | CD 80
Kid Rena's Jazz Band | Prelude To The Revival Vol.2 | American Music | AMCD-41
New Orleans Rhythm Kings | New Orleans Rhythm Kings Vol.2 | Village(Jazz Archive) | VILCD 013-2
Tommy Dorsey And His Orchestra | This Is Tommy Dorsey Vol. 2 | RCA | 26.28041 DP

Milonga
T.A.O. | Amaremandorle | yvp music | CD 3041

Milonga Del 900
Al Di Meola World Sinfonia | Heart Of The Immigrants | Inak | 700792

Milonga Del Angel
HR Big Band | Libertango:Homage An Astor Piazolla | hr music.de | hrmj 014-02 CD
Phil Woods Quintet | Astor& Elis | Chesky | JD 146
Richard Galliano Septet | Piazzolla Forever | Dreyfus Jazz Line | FDM 36642-2
Pablo Ziegler And His Quintet For New Tango | Asfalto-Street Tango | RCA | 2663266-2

Milonga Is Coming
Astor Piazzolla Group | Tango: Zero Hour | American Clave | AMCL 1013-2

Milonga Para Grela
Paquito D'Rivera Orchestra | A Night In Englewood | Messidor | 15829 CD

Milonga Sentimental
Jacinte/Juan-José Mosalini Trio | Tango, Mi Corazón | Messidor | 15911 CD

Milonga(La Punalado)
Rumbata | Canto Al Caribe | Timeless | CD JC 11019

Milz
Gonzalo Rubalcaba | Imagine | Blue Note | 830491-2

Mima
Gonzalo Rubalcaba Trio | The Blessing | Blue Note | 797197-2
Images-Live At Mt. Fuji | Blue Note | 799492-2

Mime
Till Brönner Quartet & Deutsches Symphonieorchester Berlin | German Songs | Minor Music | 801057
Dom Salvador Quintet | Brazilian Adventure | Muse | MCD 6006

Mimmi's Interlude
George Benson Group/Orchestra | George Benson Anthology | Warner | 8122-79934-2

Mimosa
Herbie Hancock Quartet | Invetions And Dimensions | Blue Note | 781147-2
James Williams-Dennis Irwin | Focus | Red Records | VPA 132

Mimosa(alt.take)
Steve Gut & The RTB Big Band | Steve Gut & RTB Big Band | Timeless | CD SJP 293

Min Verden(My World)
Ivo Perlman Group | Children Of Ibeji | Enja | ENJ-7005 2

Mina Do Sante
Don Rendell Five | Just Music | Spotlite | SPJ 502

Minaret
Soviet Jazz Ensemble | Boomerang | Mobile Fidelity | MFCD 908

Mina's Song
Toninho Horta Trio | Once I Loved | Verve | 513561-2

Mina's Waltz
Hugh Masekela Quintet | The African Connection | MCA | IA 9343/2

Mind And Time
Francois Carrier Trio | Compassion | Naxos Jazz | 86062-2

Mind Over Matter
Nils Gessinger Orchestra | Ducks 'N' Cookies | GRP | GRP 98302

Mind Reader
Santi Debriano Quintet | Obeah | Freelance | FRL-CD 008

Mind Spaces
Berlin Jazz Composers Orchestra(JayJayBeCe) | JayJayBeCe-V-15-Twenty | BIT | 11273

Mind The Step
David S. Ware Quartet | Great Bliss Vol.1 | Silkheart | SHCD 127

Mindful Intent
Greg Osby Quintet | Mindgames | JMT Edition | 919021-2

Mindgames
Sonic Fiction | Changing With The Times | Naxos Jazz | 86034-2

Mindiatyr

Bobo Stenson Trio | Reflections | ECM | 1516(523160-2)
Abdullah Ibrahim Sextet | Mindif | Enja | ENJ-5073 2

Mindif
Abdullah Ibrahim Trio And A String Orchestra | African Suite | TipToe | TIP-888832 2
Abdullah Ibrahim Trio With The Munich Radio Symphony Orchestra | African Symphony | Enja | ENJ-9410 2
Abdullah Ibrahim With The NDR Big Band | Ekapa Lodumo | TipToe | TIP-888840 2
Big Bill Broonzy | Last Session-Vol.1/The Big Bill Broonzy Story | Verve | 2304559 IMS

Mindoro
Walt Weiskopf Sextet | Sleepless Nights | Criss Cross | Criss 1147

Mine
Buddy DeFranco Quartet | The Gershwin Songbook(The Instrumentals) | Verve | 525361-2
Herbie Nichols Trio | Blue Note Plays Gershwin | Blue Note | 520808-2
Herbie Nichols Trio | Blue Note | 300098(1519)

Mine Too
Count Basie And His Orchestra | The Indispensable Count Basie | RCA | ND 89758

Mine(alt.take)
Carbonell Austin 'Bola' Group | Carmen | Messidor | 15814 CD

Minesan's Dream
Cal Tjader's Orchestra | Cal Tjader/Soul Sauce | Verve | 521668-2

Ming Blue
Andy Middleton Quartet | 13th Jazz Hoeilaart International Europ' Jazz Contest 91 | B.Sharp Records | CDS 086

Mingle In The Mincing-Machine
Cannōn's Jug Stompers | The Greatest In Country Blues Vol.1(1927-1930) | Story Of Blues | CD 3521-2

Minglin'
Buddy Johnson And His Orchestra | Wails | Official | 6010

Minguito
Enrico Rava-Dino Saluzzi Quintet | Volver | ECM | 1343
Charles Mingus And His Orchestra | Charles Mingus And Friends In Concert | CBS | C2K 64975

Mingus
Paul Smoker Trio | Alone | Sound Aspects | sas CD 018(32018)

Mingus Fingers
Charles Mingus Orchestra | Charles Mingus:Pre-Bird(Mingus Revisited) | Verve | 538636-2

Mingus Fingus No.2
Philip Catherine Quartet | Moods Vol.II | Criss Cross | Criss 1061

Mingus Meditations
Kevin Mahogany With The WDR Big Band And Guests | Pussy Cat Dues:The Music Of Charles Mingus | Enja | ENJ-9316 2

Mingus Medley
Tiziana Ghiglioni And The Strings Ensemble | Tiziana Ghiglioni Sings Gaslini | Soul Note | 121297-2

Mingus-Griff Song
Ralph Towner-Gary Peacock | A Closer View | ECM | 1602(531623-2)

Mingusiana
Denny Christianson Big Band | Suite Mingus | Justin Time | Just 15

Minha Saudade
Hendrik Meurkens Octet | Sambahia | Concord | CCD 4474

Minha(All Mine)
Bill Evans Trio | Homecoming | Milestone | MCD 9291-2
Bill Evans-Eddie Gomez Duo | Montreux III | Original Jazz Classics | OJC20 644-2(F 9510)
The Complete Fantasy Recordings | Fantasy | 9FCD 1012-2
Kenny Burrell | Lotus Blossom | Concord | CCD 4668

Mini Skirt
Sigi Schwab | Meditation Vol.2 | Melos Music | CDGS 705

Miniatura(6)
Mikhail Alperin/Arkady Shilkloper | Wave Over Sorrow | ECM | 1396

Miniature
Schlosser/Weber/Böhm/Huber/Binder | L 14,16 | Jazz 4 Ever Records:Jazz Network | J4E 4760

Miniature 1-Blauer Jatz
L 14,16 | Jazz 4 Ever Records:Jazz Network | J4E 4760

Miniature 2-Masha
L 14,16 | Jazz 4 Ever Records:Jazz Network | J4E 4760

Miniature 3-Blues For Hub
Peter Schärli Special Sextet feat.Glenn Ferris and Tom Varner | Blues For The Beast | Enja | 9103-2

Miniaturen I&II
ATonALL | ATonALL | Creative Works Records | CW CD 1024-2

Miniaturen III
Südpool Jazz Project IV | Südpol Jazz Project IV-Quartet | L+R Records | CDLR 45091

MiniRock
Howard Alden-Dan Barrett Quintet | The A.B.Q Salutes Buck Clayton | Concord | CCD 4395

Minnehaha
Duke Ellington Orchestra | The Golden Duke | Prestige | P 24029

Minnesota
Hans Theessink | Hans Theessink:Solo | Minor Music | 801047

Minnibelle
Tanzorchester Der Original Teddies | International Schlager & In Mood mit Teddy Stauffer's Original Teddies | Elite Special | 9522003

Minnie The Moocher
Cab Calloway And His Orchestra | The Jazz Collector Edition: Cotton Club Days | Laserlight | 15707
Hi-De-Hi-Di-Ho | RCA | 2118524-2

Minnie The Moocher's Wedding Day
Benny Goodman And His Orchestra | Jazz Giants:Benny Goodman | RCA | NL 89731 SI
Mills Blue Rhythm Band | Rhythm Spasm | Hep | CD 1015

Minnola
Robin Eubanks Group | Karma | JMT Edition | 834446-2

Minoat
Yosuke Yamashita Trio | A Tribute To Mal Waldron | Enja | 3057-2

Minor Affairs
Lou Donaldson Quintet | Blue Breakbeats:Lou Donaldson | Blue Note | 494709-2

Minor Billy
Louis Smith Quintet | Just Friends | Steeplechase | SCCD 31096

Minor Blues
Elvin Jones Quartet | Familiar Ground | West Wind | WW 2104
Lucky Thompson-Sammy Price Quintet | Jazz In Paris:Sammy Price And Lucky Thompson-Paris Blues | EmArCy | 013038-2
Victor Feldman Quartet | Your Smile | Candid | CRS 1005 IMS

Minor Changes
Peter Bernstein Quartet | Signs Of Life | Criss Cross | Criss 1095

Minor Chant
Jimmy Smith Quartet | Back At The Chicken Shack | Blue Note | 746402-2
Heinz Sauer Quartet | Isolation Row | MRC | 066-45423

Minor Circles-
George Gruntz Quintet | Jazz In Switzerland 1930-1975 | Elite Special | 9544002/1-4

Minor Dance
Joe Pass | Virtuoso No.3 | Original Jazz Classics | OJC20 684-2(2310805)

Minor Detail
Hank Mobley Quintet | Mobley's Message | Prestige | VIJ 5040

Minor Drag
Cy Laurie's New Orleans Septet | The Golden Years Of Revival Jazz,Vol 1 | Storyville | STCD 5506
Fats Waller And His Buddies | Fats Waller-The Joint Is Jumpin' | RCA | ND 86288(874182)

Minor Drop
Bobby Jaspar Quintet | Bobby Jaspar | Swing | SW 8413 IMS

Minor Escamp(aka Jordu)
Roy Haynes Sextet | The 1954 Paris Sessions | Vogue | 21622912

Minor Groove
Peter Hertmans Quartet | Waiting | Timeless | CD SJP 418

Minor Importance
Don Friedman | Themes And Variations | EGO | 4014

Minor Impulse
John Stubblefield Sextet | Prelude | Storyville | SLP 1018

Minor Jazz Waltz
Frankie Newton And His Orchestra | Frankie's Jump | Affinity | CD AFS 1014

Minor Journey
Klaus Doldinger Quartet | Doldinger's Best | ACT | 9224-2

Minor Kick
Joe Van Enkhuizen Quartet | Back On The Scene | Criss Cross | Criss 1013 (835601)

Minor March
George Wallington Quintet | Life! At The Cafe Bohemia | Original Jazz Classics | OJCCD 1813-2(P 7820)
Life! At The Cafe Bohemia | Original Jazz Classics | OJCCD 1813-2(P 7820)

Minor Meeting
Sonny Clark Quintet | My Conception | Blue Note | 522674-2
Sonny Clark Trio | Blues Mambo | West Wind | WW 2103

Minor Mind
Freddie Hubbard Quintet | Breaking Point! | Blue Note | 781172-2

Minor Mishap
J.J.Johnson-Kai Winding All Stars | Aurex Jazz Festival '82:All Star Jam | Eastworld | EWJ 80238
Prestige All Stars | John Coltrane-The Prestige Recordings | Prestige | 16 PCD 4405-2
Freddie Hubbard Sextet | Minor Mishap | Black Lion | BLP 60122

Minor Mode For Majors
Alvin Queen Quartet | Introducing:RTB Big Band | Plainisphare | PL 1267-23

Minor Mood
Furio Di Castri | Solo | SPLASC(H) Records | HP 04
Tina Brooks Quintet | Minor Move | Blue Note | 522671-2

Minor Move
Minor Move | Blue Note | 522671-2

Minor Mystery
Earl Hines | Earl Hines At Home | Delmark | 900240 AO

Minor On Top
Jacob Young Quintet | Evening Falls | ECM | 1876(9811780)

Minor Peace
Tommy Flanagan Trio | Super-Session | Enja | 3059-2

Minor Reggae
Jim Snidero Quintet | Mixed Bag | Criss Cross | Criss 1032

Minor Seconds
Hal McKusick Octet | In A Twentieth-Century Drawing Room | Fresh Sound Records | ND 12584

Minor Swing
Bireli Lagrene Ensemble | Live | Inak | 865
Bireli Lagrene Group | A Tribute To Django Reinhardt | Jazzpoint | JP 1061 CD
Bireli Lagrene Trio | Live At The Carnegie Hall: A Tribute To Django Reinhardt | Jazzpoint | JP 1040 CD
Didier Lockwood Trio | Tribute To Stépane Grappelli | Dreyfus Jazz Line | FDM 36611-2
Django Reinhardt And The Quintet Du Hot Club De France | Planet Jazz:Django Reinhardt | Planet Jazz | 2152071-2
Planet Jazz:Stephane Grappelli | RCA | 2165366-2
The Indispensable Django Reinhardt | RCA | ND 70929
Henri Crolla Orchestra | Jazz In Paris:Henri Crolla-Notre Ami Django | EmArCy | 014062-2
Quintet Du Hot Club De France | Djangology | Bluebird | 2663957-2
Django Reinhardt-Un Géant Sur Son Image | Melodie | 400052
Django Reinhardt:Nuages | Arkadia Jazz | 71431
Schnuckenack Reinhardt Quintet | 15.3.1973 | Intercord | 160031
Stephane Grappelli Group | Giants | MPS | 68265
Stephane Grappelli Quartet | Stephane Grappelli 1992 Live | Dreyfus Jazz Line | FDM 37006-2
Django Reinhardt | Black-Hawk | BKH 51601
Stephane Grappelli Quintet | Hommage A Django Reinhardt | Festival | Album 120
Live In San Francisco | Black-Hawk | BKH 51601
The Rosenberg Trio | Tribute To Django Reinhardt | EmArCy | 9811568
Titi Winterstein Quintet plus Guests | Live! | Boulevard | BLD 508 LP

Minor Vamp
Curtis Fuller Quintet | Blues-ette | Savoy | SV 0127(ST 13006)

Minor Walk
Dizzy Gillespie And His Orchestra | Dizzier And Dizzier | RCA | 26685172

Minor With A Bridge(part I fast)
Milton Mezz Mezzrow Sextet | Americans Swinging In Paris:Mezz Mezzrow | EMI Records | 539660-2

Minor With A Bridge(part I slow)
Americans Swinging In Paris:Mezz Mezzrow | EMI Records | 539660-2

Minor With A Bridge(part II fast)
Americans Swinging In Paris:Mezz Mezzrow | EMI Records | 539660-2

Minor With A Bridge(part II slow)
Erroll Garner Trio | Relaxin' | Vogue | 500117

Minor Yours
Chet Baker-Art Pepper Sextet | The Route | Pacific Jazz | 792931-2
Jerome Richardson Sextet | Midnight Oil | Original Jazz Classics | OJCCD 1815-2(NJ 8205)

Minority
Cal Tjader Quartet | Cool California | Savoy | WL 70511(2)(SJL 2254) DP
Jack DeJohnette Trio | The Jack DeJohnette Piano Album | Landmark | LCD 1504-2
Jacques Pelzer Quartet | Salute To The Band Box | Igloo | IGL 106
Ricky Ford Quintet | Hard Groovin' | Muse | MCD 5373
Franco Ambrosetti Quartet | A Jazz Portrait Of Franco Ambrosetti | Sound Hills | SSCD 8071(RTCL 812 SH)

Minority(take 1)
Gigi Gryce-Clifford Brown Sextet | Clifford Brown:The Complete Paris Sessions Vol.2 | Vogue | 21457292

Minority(take 2)
Clifford Brown:The Complete Paris Sessions Vol.2 | Vogue | 21457292

Minority(take 3)
Clifford Brown:The Complete Paris Sessions Vol.2 | Vogue | 21457292

Minor's Holiday
Art Blakey And The Jazz Messengers | The History Of Art Blakey And The Jazz Messengers | Blue Note | 797190-2
Kenny Dorham Octet | Afro-Cuban | Blue Note | 746815-2

Minstrale Again
Barrelhouse Jazzband | Barrelhouse Jazzband & Carrie Smith | Intercord | 145017

Minuet In G
Eddie Palmieri Group | Vortex | RMM Records | 660.58.116

Minuet(A Lover's Concerto)
Glen Gray And The Casa Loma Orchestra | Shall We Swing? | Creative World | ST 1055

Minuetto I-
Jacques Loussier Trio | Play Bach Aux Champs-Élyssées | Decca | 159203-2

Minuetto II-
Herbie Hancock/Bobby Hutcherson | Round Midnight(Soundtrack) | CBS | 70300

Minus One
Jesper Thilo Quartet | Jesper Thilo Quartet | Music Mecca | CD 1009-2

Minute Steak
Diedre Murray-Fred Hopkins Quartet | Stringology | Black Saint | 120143-2

Mir Ist's So Leicht(Letter Sagt Enn Gjort)
Christoph Haberer | Mir Was Dir Was | Jazz Haus Musik | JHM 15

Mira
Andrew Hill Quintet | Grass Roots | Blue Note | 522672-2
Blue Bossa | Blue Note | 795590-2

Mirabellla
Perico Sambeat Quartet | Friendship | ACT | 9421-2

Miracel
Larry Porter/Allan Praskin Quartet With Sal Nistico | Sonnet For Sal | Enja | 8026-2

Miracle
Urban Knights | Urban Knights | GRP | GRP 98152

Miracle Steps
Alan Braufman Quintet | Valley Of Search | India Navigation | IN 1024

Miracles
Paul Bley-Franz Koglmann-Gary Peacock | Anette | HatOLOGY | 564

Mirage
Bireli Lagrene Ensemble | Bireli Lagrene 15 | Antilles | 802503
Bireli Lagrene Group | A Tribute To Django Reinhardt | Jazzpoint | JP 1061 CD
Bireli Lagrene Trio | Live At The Carnegie Hall: A Tribute To Django Reinhardt | Jazzpoint | JP 1040 CD
Bob Crosby And His Orchestra | The Uncollected:Bob Crosby | Hindsight | HSR 192
Jean-Luc Ponty Sextet | Enigmatic Ocean | Atlantic | 19110-2
Jorge Strunz-Ardeshir Farah Group | Guitars | Milestone | MCD 9136-2
Oscar Peterson-Joe Pass Duo | Oscar Pterson Et Joe Pass A La Salle Pleyel | Pablo | 2CD 2625705
Live At Salle Pleyel, Paris | Pablo | 2625705
The Benoit/Freeman Project | The Benoit/Freeman Project | GRP | GRP 97392

Mirages(Chasing Shadows)
Bebo Valdés Trio | El Arte Del Sabor | Blue Note | 535193-2

Mirala Que Linda Viene-
Irene Schweizer/Pierre Favre | Irene Schweizer & Pierre Favre | Intakt Records | CD 009

Mirante Do Vale
Stephane Grappelli-Martin Taylor | Reunion | Linn Records | AKD 022

Mireia-
Silent Circus | Silent Circus | SPLASC(H) Records | H 166

Miriama
David Kikoski Trio | Inner Trust | Criss Cross | Criss 1148

Miro
Jane Ira Bloom Quintet | Art And Aviation | Arabesque Recordings | AJ 0107

Miro Bop
The Rosenberg Trio With Frits Landesbergen | Gypsy Swing | Verve | 527806-2

Miro Tat Mimer(For My Dad Mimer)
Stefano Maltese Open Music Orchestra | Hanging In The Sky | SPLASC(H) Records | H 139

Miroirs
Gilad Atzmon & The Orient House Ensemble | Gilad Atzmon & The Orient House Ensemble | TipToe | TIP-888839 2

Miron Dance
Kurt Weil & Vibes Revisited | Moving Foreward-Reaching Back | TCB Records | TCB 20302

Mirovisions
Charles Lloyd Quartet | Fish Out Of Water | ECM | 1398

Mirror
Chuck Israels International Trio | Meeting On Hvar | Anima Records | DV-CD 001
Sam Rivers | Portrait Sam Rivers Live | FMP | CD 82

Mirror Act
Cecil Taylor | For Olim | Soul Note | 121150-2

Mirror Image
Sidsel Endresen Quartet | So I Write | ECM | 1408(841776-2)
Horace Parlan Quintet | Frank-ly Speaking | Steeplechase | SCS 1076

Mirror Man
Ari Ambrose Quartet | Cylic Episode | Steeplechase | SCCD 31472

Mirror Mirror
Greg Osby Quintet | Mindgames | JMT Edition | 919021-2
Joe Henderson Quartet | Mirror Mirror | MPS | 519092-2
Roy Haynes Group | Praise | Dreyfus Jazz Line | FDM 36598-2

Mirror On Yourself
Jan Garbarek Group | Legend Of The Seven Dreams | ECM | 1381(837344-2)

Mirror Stone(I)
Legend Of The Seven Dreams | ECM | 1381(837344-2)

Mirror Stone(II)
Dewey Redman Quartet | Living On The Edge | Black Saint | 120123-2

Mirror-Mind Rose
Bobby Hutcherson Quintet | The Kicker | Blue Note | 521437-2

Mirrors
John Abercrombie Trio | While We're Young | ECM | 1489
Joint Venture | Mirrors | Enja | ENJ-7049 2
Mario Neunkirchen Quintet | Long Distance | Laika Records | LK 94-060
Nada | Panta Rei | Naxos Jazz | 86069-2

Misbehavin'
John Lee Hooker | Blues Power No.1:John Lee Hooker-Don't Turn Me From Your Door | Atlantic | 40507

Mischief
Greg Osby Group | Season Of Reneval | JMT Edition | 834435-2

Misdemeanor
Robben Ford & The Blue Line | Mystic Line | Stretch Records | GRS 00082

Misericordia
Paul Dunmall Trio | Ghostly Thoughts | HatOLOGY | 503

Miserlou
Lynn Hope Band | Lynn Hope And His Tenor Sax | Pathe | 1546661(Aladdin)

Misery Loves Company
Woody Herman And His Orchestra | Jazz Legacy 18: Woody Herman-The Fourth Herd | Vogue | 500068

Misfit Blues-
Vienna Art Orchestra | Vienna Art Orchestra Plays For Jean Cocteau | Amadeo | 529290-2

Mish-Mash-Bash
Steve Elson's Lips & Fingers Ensemble | Lips & Fingers | Open Minds | OM 2406-2

Misionerita
Marty Paich Piano Quartet | Lush Latin & Cool | Fresh Sound Records | 58058 CD(RCA)

Misplaced Cowpoke
Maynard Ferguson And His Big Bop Nouveau Band | Brass Attitude | Concord | CCD 4848

Mis'ry And The Blues
Jack Teagarden And His Orchestra | Jazz Original | Charly | CD 80
Jack Teagarden And His Sextet | Jazz-Club: Vocal | Verve | 840029-2

Miss 'B'
Knut Kiesewetter With Orchestra | Jazz Again | Polydor | 2372016

Miss Ann
Eric Dolphy Quintet | Magic | Prestige | P 24053
Eric Dophy Quintet | Live At Gaslight Inn | Ingo | 14

Miss Ann,Lisa,Sue And Sadie
Charlie Barnet And His Orchestra | The Indispensable Charlie Barnet Vol.1/2 | RCA | 2135554-2

Miss Ann's Tempo
Ray Crawford Sextet | I Know Pres | Candid | SMJ 6196

Miss April
Dick de Graaf Septet | Polder | Timeless | CD SJP 376

Miss Bliss
Joe Newman Sextet | Jazz For Playboys | Savoy | SV 0191(MG 12095)

Miss Bo
Gianni Basso Quartet | Gianni Basso Quartet | Penta Flowers | CDPIA 005

Miss Brown To
Anita O'Day With The Barney Kessel Sextet | Trav'lin Light | Verve | 2304584 IMS

Miss Celie's Blues
Angela Brown With Christian Christl | Wild Turkey | Acoustic Music Records | AMC 1017
Miss Cool
Johnny Harris | Blues From The Deep South | Anthology of the Blues | AB 5604
Miss Etna
Arthur Blythe Group | Hipmotism | Enja | ENJ-6088 2
Miss Eugie
Oliver Nelson And His Orchestra | Verve Jazz Masters 48:Oliver Nelson | Verve | 527654-2
Miss Fortune
Tino Tracanna Sextet | Mr. Frankenstein Blues | SPLASC(H) Records | H 158
Miss Hannah
McKinney's Cotton Pickers | McKinney's Cotton Pickers (1928-1930)-The Band Don Redman Built | RCA | ND 90517(874152)
Miss J.
Cannonball Adderley Quintet | Compact Jazz: Cannonball Adderley | EmArCy | 842930-2 PMS
Miss Jackie's Delight
Jerry Dodgion Quartet | The Jazz Scene:San Francisco | Fantasy | FCD 24760-2
Miss Jackie's Dish
Modern Jazz From San Francisco | Original Jazz Classics | OJC 272(F 3213)
Miss Jennie's Ball
Charles Lloyd Quintet | Hyperion With Higgins | ECM | 1784(014000-2)
Miss Jessye
Larry Coryell-Michael Urbaniak Trio | A Quiet Day In Spring | Steeplechase | SCCD 31187
Miss M
Asgard | Songs Of G. | Acoustic Music Records | 319.1042.2
Miss Martingale
V-Disc All Star Jam Session | Louis Armstrong-Jack Teagarden-Woody Herman:Midnights At V-Disc | Jazz Unlimited | JUCD 2048
Miss Martingale(incomplete)
Bukka White | Baton Rouge Mosby Street | Blues Beacon | BLU-1003 2
Miss Mayenne
Barney Kessel Quartet | Barney Kessel's Swingin' Party At Contemporary | Original Jazz Classics | OJCCD 1066-2(S 7613)
Miss Menphis
Count Basie And His Orchestra | Kansas City Suite-The Music Of Benny Cater | Roulette | CDP 794575-2
Miss Morgan
Chico Hamilton And Euphoria | My Panamanian Friend-The Music Of Eric Dolphy | Soul Note | 121265-2
Miss Movement
Chico Hamilton Quintet | That's Jazz Vol.20: Chico Hamilton | Warner | WB 56239
Miss Oidipus
Art Hodes-Milt Hinton Duo | Just The Two Of Us | Muse | MR 5279
Miss Otis Regrets
Ella Fitzgerald And The Paul Smith Quartet | The Best Of The Song Books | Verve | 519804-2
Ella Fitzgerald With The Buddy Bregman Orchestra | The Cole Porter Song Book | Verve | 2683044 IMS
The Complete Ella Fitzgerald Song Books of Harold Arlen, Irving Berlin, Duke Ellington, George & Ira Gershwin, Jerome Kern, Johnny Mercer, Cole Porter And Rogers & Hart | Verve | 519832-2
Ella Fitzgerald With The Tommy Flanagan Quartet | Newport Jazz Festival - Live At Carnegie Hall | CBS | CBS 68279
Herman Chittison | JazzIn Paris:Harlem Piano In Montmartre | EmArCy | 018447-2
Jenny Evans And Band | Live At The Allotria | ESM Records | ESM 9301
Girl Talk | ESM Records | ESM 9306
Girl Talk | Enja | ENJ-9363 2
Live At The Allotria | BELL Records | BLR 90003
The King Sisters With Frank DeVol's Orchestra | The Uncollected:The King Sisters | Hindsight | HSR 168
Miss Thing
Count Basie And His Orchestra | The Count And The President-Vol.1 1936 & 1939 | CBS | CBS 88667
Hubert Laws Quartet | The Laws Of Jazz | Atlantic | 8122-71636-2
Nat King Cole Trio | The Legendary 1941-44 Broadcast Transcriptions | Music & Arts | CD 808
Miss Toni
Dave Valentine Group | Light Struck | GRP | GRP 95372
Miss Who
New Emily Jazz Orchestra | Neanthropus Retractus | SPLASC(H) Records | HP 10
Missile Blues
Wes Montgomery Trio | Guitar On The Go | Original Jazz Classics | OJCCD 489-2(RLP 9494)
Wes Montgomery-The Complete Riverside Recordings | Riverside | 12 RCD 4408-2
Wes Montgomery-The Complete Riverside Recordings | Riverside | 12 RCD 4408-2
Missile Blues(alt.take)
Antonio Hart Quintet With Guests And Strings | It's All Good | Novus | 4163183-2
Missing A Page
European Jazz Ensemble | European Jazz Ensemble 25th Anniversary | Konnex Records | KCD 5100
Missing A Page-
Vienna Art Orchestra | Two Little Animals | Moers Music | 02066 CD
Missing You
Cindy Blackman Quartet | Cindy Blackman Telepathy | Muse | MCD 5437
Larry Willis Trio | How Do You Keep The Music Playing? | Steeplechase | SCCD 31312
Mission
Unternehmen Kobra | Central Europe Suite | G.N.U. Records | CD A 94.007
Mission To Moscow
Benny Goodman And His Orchestra | Jazz Collection:Benny Goodman | Laserlight | 24396
The Benny Goodman Selection | CBS | 467280-2
Mission To Stars
Stan Kenton And His Orchestra | Viva Kenton | Creative World | ST 1063
Mission: To Be Where I Am
David Murray Group | Speaking In Togues | Enja | ENJ-9370 2
Missionary
Jorge Cardoso | Talking Hands:Live | ALISO Records | AL 1021
Missionerita-
Miltiades Papastamou-Marcos Alexiou | Dialogue Blue | CCn'C Records | 01102
Mississippi Delta Sunrise(for Bobbie)
Duke Pearson Big Band | Introducing Duke Pearson's Big Band | Blue Note | 494508-2
Mississippi Goddam
Nina Simone Quartet | Nina Simone-The 60s Vol.1: Ne Me Quitte Pas | Mercury | 838543-2 PMS
In Concert/I Put A Spell On You | Mercury | 846543-2
Nina Simone | The Rising Sun Collection | RSC 0004
Nina Simone Trio/Quartet/Orchestra | Moon Of Alabama | Jazz Door | JD 1214
Mississippi Mud
Trombone Summit | Trombone Summit | MPS | 68272
Heads Up Super Band | Live at The Berks Jazz Fest | Inak | 30462
Missouri Uncompromised
George Girard And His Dixieland All Stars | Sounds Of New Orleans Vol.6 | Storyville | STCD 6013
Misstery
Richard Tee Group | The Bottom Line | Electric Bird | K32Y 6035
Mist
Chico Freeman Group | You'll Know When You Get There | Black Saint | 120128-2
The Leaders | Slipping And Sliding | Sound Hills | SSCD 8054
Mister B
Johnny Coles Quartet | New Morning | Criss Cross | Criss 1005
Mister B.C.
Oscar Peterson-Milt Jackson Duo | To Bags...With Love:Memorial Album | Pablo | 2310967-2
Mister Basie
Two Of The Few | Original Jazz Classics | OJCCD 689-2(2310881)
Golden Gate Quartet With The Martial Solal Orchestra | From Spriritual To Swing Vol.2 | EMI Records | 780573-2
Mister Blue
Americans Swinging In Paris:Golden Gate Quartet | EMI Records | 539659-2
Jim Hall Sextet | Subsequently | Limelight | 844278-2 IMS
Mister Broadway
Irakere | Yemayá | Blue Note | 498239-2
Mister Bruce
Charly Antolini Orchestra | Special Delivery | MPS | 68256
Mister Dave
Sonny Boy Williamson & The Yardbirds | 1963 Live In London | L+R Records | CDLR 42020
Mister E
Nathan Davis Quintet | Two Originals:Happy Girl/The Hip Walk | MPS | 539082-2
Mister Ed
Jimmy Rushing And His Orchestra | Jimmy Rushing And The Big Brass/Rushing Lullabies | CBS | CK 65118
Mister Joe
Chris Tyle's Silver Leaf Jazz Band | Here Comes The Hot Tamale Man | Stomp Off Records | CD 1311
Mister Lovingood
Louis Jordan And His Tympany Five | Louis Jordan Vol.2-Knock Me Out | Swingtime(Contact) | ST 1012
Mister M
Lucky Thompson Trio | Tricotism | Impulse(MCA) | GRP 11352
Mister New Orleans Blues
Giorgio Gaslini Jazz Orchestra | Mister O(Jazz Opera) | Soul Note | 121300-2
Mister Tarzan
Keith Nichols Cotton Club Gang And Janice Day With Guy Barker | I Like To Do Things For You | Stomp Off Records | CD 1242
Mister Walker
Booker Ervin Quintet | Down In The Dumps | Savoy | SV 0245(SJL 1119)
Misterioso
Artie Shaw And His Gramercy Five | The Complete Gramercy Five Sessions | Bluebird | ND 87637
Bobby Watson | This Little Light Of Mine-The Bobby Watson Solo Album | Red Records | 123250-2
Cowws Quintet plus Guests | Book/Virtual Cowws | FMP | OWN-90007/9
Kenny Barron-Regina Carter | Freefall | Verve | 549706-2
Kronos Quartet | Monk Suite | Landmark | LCD 1505-2
Masabumi 'Poo' Kikuchi Trio | Tethered Moon | Paddle Wheel | KICJ 93
Peter Herborn Orchestra | Large One | Jazzline | JL 11174-2
Sonny Rollins Quintet | Sonny Rollins | Blue Note | 84508
Jazz Gallerie:Sonny Rollins Vol.1 | RCA | 2127283-2
Sonny Rollins Sextet | Sonny Rollins:The Blue Note Recordings | Blue Note | 821371-2
Thelonious Monk:The Complete Blue Note Recordings | Blue Note | 830363-2
Thelonious Monk Quartet | Greatest Hits | CBS | CK 65422
The Complete Genius | Blue Note | LA 579
The Blue Note Years-The Best Of Thelonious Monk | Blue Note | 796636-2
Live At The Jazz Workshop-Complete | CBS | C2K 65189
Thelonious Monk-The Complete Riverside Recordings | Riverside | 15 RCD 022-2
Thelonious Monk:Complete 1947-1952 Blue Note Recordings | The Jazz Factory | JFCD 22838
Thelonious Monk Trio | The London Collection Vol.2 | Black Lion | BLCD 760116
Misterioso-
Rahsaan Roland Kirk Group | Rahsaan Rolnd Kirk:Dog Years In The Fourth Ring | 32 Jazz | 32032
Misterioso(alt.take)
Thelonious Monk Quartet | Thelonious Monk:Complete 1947-1952 Blue Note Recordings | The Jazz Factory | JFCD 22838
Misterioso(slow)-
Chinese Compass | Chinese Compass | dacapo | DCCD 9443
Mistero
Matalex | Wild Indian Summer | Lipstick Records | LIP 890192
Mistery Song
Wild Indian Summer | Lipstick Records | LIP 890192
Mistral
Peter Giger | Family Of Percussion | Nagara | MIX 1010-N
Memphis Slim | Boogie Woogie | Accord | 402472
Mistral Breeze No. One
Mal Waldron Quartet feat. Jim Pepper | The Git-Go At Utopia,Volume Two | Tutu Records | 888148-2*
Mistral Breeze No. Two
Jesse Price And His Orchestra | Swingin' Small Combos Kansas City Style Vol.1 | Blue Moon | BMCD 6019
Mistreatin' Boogie
Furry Lewis | In His Prime 1927-1928 | Yazoo | YAZ 1050
Mistura Fina
Orquestra Mahatma | A Young Person's Guide | Babel | BDV 9612
Misty
Bill Ramsey With Orchestra | Gettin' Back To Swing | Bear Family Records | BCD 15813 AH
Billy Eckstine With Bobby Tucker And His Orchestra | No Cover/No Minimum | M&M Records | R 52052(Roulette)
Bob Brookmeyer Sextet | The Lyrical Stan Getz | CBS | 460819-2
Bobby Enriquez Trio | The Wildman Returns | Paddle Wheel | KICJ 127
Carmen McRae With The Shirley Horn Trio | Sarah-Dedicated To You | Novus | PD 90546
Derek Smith Trio | Dark Eyes | Eastwind | EWIND 711 Digital
Dexter Gordon Quartet | Both Sides Of Midnight | Black Lion | BLP 60103
Didier Lockwood Trio | Tribute To Stépane Grappelli | Dreyfus Jazz Line | FDM 36611-2
Don Rader Quintet | A Foreign Affair | L+R Records | CDLR 45034
Duke Jordan Trio | Flight To Norway | Steeplechase | SCCD 31543
Wait And See | Steeplechase | SCCD 31211
Ella Fitzgerald With Orchestra | Forever Ella | Verve | 529387-2
Ella Fitzgerald With The Jimmy Jones Trio | Ella & Duke At The Cote D'Azur | Verve | 539030-2
Ella Fitzgerald And Duke Ellington:Cote D'Azure Concerts on Verve | Verve | 539033-2
Ella Fitzgerald With The Lou Levy Quartet | Ella Returns To Berlin | Verve | 837758-2
Ella Fitzgerald With The Paul Smith Quartet | Mack The Knife-Ella In Berlin | Verve | 825670-2
Ella Fitzgerald-Paul Smith | Compact Jazz: Ella Fitzgerald | Verve | 831367-2
Erroll Garner Quartet | Plays Misty | Fresh Sound Records | FSR-CD 0158
Erroll Garner Trio | Erroll Garner | Verve | 846191-2 PMS
Etta James With The Red Holloway Quartet | Blues In The Night-Volume One:The Early Show | Fantasy | FCD 9647-2
Etta Jones With The Houston Person Quintet | The Melody Lingers On | HighNote Records | HCD 7005
Hannibal And The Sunrise Orchestra | Hannibal | MPS | 68061
JATP Jam Session | Return To Happiness-JATP At Yoyogi National Stadium,Tokyo | Pablo | 2620117-2
Jimmy Witherspoon With Groove Holmes | Wonderful World | Memo Music | HDJ 4006
Joe Pass | Joe Pass:Guitar Virtuoso | Pablo | 4 PACD 4423-2
Virtuoso No.2 | Pablo | 2310788-2
Joe Turner | Walking Through Heaven | Swingtime | 8205
Johnny Smith Quartet | The Sound Of Johnny Smith Guitar | Fresh Sound Records | FSR 583(Roost 2246)
King Curtis Band | King Curtis-Blow Man Blow | Bear Family Records | BCD 15670 CI
L.A.4 | Watch What Happens | Concord | CCD 4063
Melvin Sparks Quartet | Sparkling | Muse | MR 5248
Richard 'Groove' Holmes Trio | Misty | Original Jazz Classics | OJCCD 724-2(P 7485)
Roy Eldridge Quartet | Swingin' On The Town | Verve | 559828-2
Sarah Vaughan And Her Trio | Verve Jazz Masters 42:Sarah Vaughan-The Jazz Sides | Verve | 526817-2
The Complete Sarah Vaughan Live In Japan | Mobile Fidelity | MFCD 844-2
Sarah Vaughan With The Quincy Jones Orchestra | Compact Jazz: Sarah Vaughan | Mercury | 830699-2
Verve Jazz Masters 18:Sarah Vaughan | Verve | 518199-2
Stephane Grappelli Quartet | Stephane Grappelli | Jazz Colours | 874717-2
Compact Jazz:Stephane Grappelli | MPS | 831370-2 PMS
Steve White Quartet | In The Spur Of The Moment | Telarc Digital | CD 83484
Teresa Brewer With The David Murray Quartet | Softly I Swing | Red Baron | 471575-2
Tony Lakatos With The Martin Sasse Trio | Feel Alright | Edition Collage | EC 494-2
Tony Lee Trio | British Jazz Artists Vol. 1 | Lee Lambert | LYN 3416
Wes Montgomery With The Don Sebesky Orchestra | Bumpin' | Verve | 539062-2
Wild Bill Davis | Greatest Organ Solos Ever! | Jazz Connaisseur | JCCD 8702-2
Wild Bill Davis-Eddie Lockjaw Davis Quartet | Live! | Black & Blue | 33308
Buck Clayton All Stars | Jammin' At 'Eddie Condon' | Moon Records | MCD 067-2
Misty-
Earl Hines | Live In Milano 1966 | Nueva Records | JU 315
Eugen Cicero-Decebal Badila | Swinging Piano Classics | IN+OUT Records | 77047-2
Oscar Peterson Trio | Nigerian Marketplace | Pablo | 2308231-2
Sammy Price | Doc Cheattam&Sammy Price:Duos And Solos | Sackville | SK2CD-5002
Ella Fitzgerald With Orchestra | Misty Blue:Sweet Sisters Swing Songs Of Sorrow And Sadness | Blue Note | 521151-2
Misty Blue
Billy Taylor Quintet | Separate Keyboards:Erroll Garner/Billy Taylor | Savoy | SV0223(MG 12008)
Misty Cat
Joanne Grauer Trio | Joanne Grauer Indtroducing Lorraine Feather | MPS | 68198
Misty Roses
Modern Jazz Quartet | The Legendary Profile | Atlantic | AMCY 1103
Misty Window
Eugene Chadbourne | End To Slavery | Intakt Records | CD 047
Mistytorway
Udo Schild Group | Morning | Jazz Haus Musik | ohne Nummer
Misunderstood
Count Basie And His Orchestra | Basie On Roulette, Vol. 19: Basie Easin' It | Vogue | 500019
Mit Dabei Sein
Nana | Über Leben | Jazz Haus Musik | JHM 17
Mit Erhobenem Zeigefinger, Ein Grauer Flanellzwerg-
Vienna Art Orchestra | All That Strauss | TCB Records | TCB 20052
Mitt Hjerte Alltid Vanker
Christoph Lauer & Norwegian Brass | Heaven | ACT | 9420-2
We Three | We See | TCB Records | TCB 21142
Mitti
Peter Materna Quartet | Full Moon Party | Village | VILCD 1021-2
Mittwoch Morgen
Buck Hill Quartet | I'm Beginning To See The Light | Muse | MCD 5449
Mixed
Dave Liebman Trio | Spirit Renewed | Owl Time Line | 3819112
Miyako
Malachi Thompson Sextet | 47th Street | Delmark | DE 497
Miyan Ki Malhar
Steve Williamson Septet | Rhyme Time-That Fuss Was Us! | Verve | 511235-2
Mizrab
Lonnie Plaxico Group | Plaxico | Muse | MCD 5389
Mizu-Water
Free Kick | Natural Desire | Timeless | CD SJP 408
MJA Jr.
Uralsky All Stars | Russian Roulette | Timeless | CD TTD 597
Mjukfoten-
Allen Farnham Quartet | Play-Cation | Concord | CCD 4521
Mkis(Soul Soothing Beach)
Orquestra Mahatma | A Young Person's Guide | Babel | BDV 9612
Mmball
Anthony Braxton | Saxophone Improvisations Series F | America | AM 011/012
M-M-M-M-Milkers
Bobby Broom Trio | Waitin' And Waitin' | Criss Cross | Criss 1135
Mo' Better Blues
The Steamboat Rats | ...Got That Swing | Elite Special | 73435
Jack McDuff Quintet | Color Me Blue | Concord | CCD 4516
Mo' Joe
Joe Henderson Sextet | The Kicker | Original Jazz Classics | OJCCD 465-2
Loose Tubes | Jazzbühne Berlin '87 | Repertoire Records | REPCD 4916-WZ
Mo Stuff
Clifton Chenier And His Band | King Of The Bayous | Arhoolie | CD 339
Moana I
Eberhard Weber With Orchestra | The Following Morning | ECM | 1084(829116-2)
Moana II
Jesus Chucho Valdes | Lucumi | Messidor | 15976 CD
Moanin'
Art Blakey And The Jazz Messengers | Live At Bubba's | Toledo | 147529
Standards | Paddle Wheel | 292 E 6026
Night In Tunisia | Philips | 800064-2
Paris Jazz Concert:Art Blakey & The Jazz Messengers | Laserlight | 36158
Jazz Gallery:Lee Morgan Vol.1 | RCA | 2127281-2
The Blue Note Years-The Best Of Art Blakey And The Jazz Messengers | Blue Note | 793205-2
Bernard Purdie's Soul To Jazz | Bernard Purdie's Soul To Jazz | ACT | 9242-2
Bill Cosby All Stars | Bill Cosby-Hello,Friend:To Ennis With Love | Verve | 539171-2
Bobby Timmons Trio | Moanin' | Milestone | M 47031
From The Bottom | Original Jazz Classics | OJCCD 1032-2(RS 3053)
Buddy Guy Band | Buddy Guy | Chess | 427006
Buddy Guy Chicago Blues Band | Blues Rarities | Chess | 6.28601 DP
Charles Mingus And His Orchestra | Charles Mingus-Passion Of A Man:The Complete Atlantic Recordings 1956-1961 | Atlantic | 8122-72871-2
Charles Mingus Jazz Workshop | Blues & Roots | Atlantic | 8122-75205-2
Blues & Roots | Atlantic | 8122-81336-2
Charly Antolini-Charly Augschöll Quartet | Charlie Antolini-40 Years Jubilee Drumfire | BELL Records | BLR 86001
Fat Boogie Horns | Fat Boogie Horns(Rhythm And Soul Big Band) | Paul Records | PP 4002

Herbie Mann Group | Deep Pocket | Kokopelli Records | KOKO 1296
Manhattan Jazz Quintet | Face To Face | Paddle Wheel | 292 E 6032
Message | The Art Of Blakey | Paddle Wheel | KICJ 162
Monty Alexander-Sly Dunbar-Robbie Shakespeare Group | Monty Meets Sly And Robbie | Telarc Digital | CD 83494
Oscar Peterson Trio | En Concert Avec Europe 1 | Laserlight | 710443/48
Ray Bryant | Solo Flight | Pablo | 2310798
Roger Guerin Quintet | Roger Guerin(Prix Django Reinhardt 1959) | Fresh Sound Records | 054 2611291(Columbia FP 1117)
Tito Puente Orchestra | Royal T | Concord | CCD 4553
Wes Montgomery Trio | Wes Montgomery-The Complete Riverside Recordings | Riverside | 12 RCD 4408-2
Uli Wewelsiep-Thomas Brill | Live At The Forum | Aho-Recording | CD 1010

Moanin' Bench
John Lee Hooker Band | Moanin' The Blues | Charly | CRB 1029

Moanin' Low
Harry James And His Orchestra | Harry James And His Orchestra Feat. Buddy Rich | CBS | CBS 21105
Lena Horne With The Lou Bring Orchestra | Planet Jazz:Lena Horne | Planet Jazz | 2165373-2
Marilyn Middleton Pollock With The Lake Records All-Star Jazzband | Marilyn Middleton Pollock With The Lake Records All-Star Jazzband | Lake | LACD 35

Moanin' With Hazel
Art Blakey And The Jazz Messengers | Victor Jazz History:From Bebop To Fusion | RCA | 2135740-2
Moanin' | Blue Note | 495324-2

Moanin'(alt.take)
Bernard Purdie's Soul To Jazz | Bernard Purdie's Soul To Jazz | ACT | 9242-2
Wes Montgomery Trio | Wes Montgomery-The Complete Riverside Recordings | Riverside | 12 RCD 4408-2
Encores | Milestone | M 9110

Mob Job
Ornette Coleman Quartet | Sound Museum | Verve | 531914-2
Helmut Zacharias Quintet | Ich Habe Rhythmus | Bear Family Records | BCD 15642 AH

Mob Mob
Chris Fagan Quartet | Lost Bohemia | Open Minds | OM 2411-2

Mobibobi-
Aki Takase Quintet | St.Louis Blues | Enja | 9130-2

Mobile
Charlie Mariano Quartet | Warum Bist Du Traurig(Why Are You So Sad) | B&W Present | BW 019

Mobile Für Katharina
Louisiana Repertory Jazz Ensemble Of New Orleans | Hot & Sweet Sounds Of Lost New Orleans | Stomp Off Records | CD 1140

Mobius 3
Rodney Jones Quintet | Rodney Jones-The 'X' Field | Musicmasters | 65147-2

Moby Dick
Vital Information | Live Around The World Where We Come From Tour '98-'99 | Intuition Records | INT 3296-2
Roman Schwaller-Mel Lewis Sextet | Roman Schwaller-Mel Lewis | Bassic-Sound | CD 005

Moca Flor
Declam | Declam | Blue Flame | 40232(2132482-2

Moche!
Chick Corea Trio | Trio Music,Live In Europe | ECM | 1310(827769-2)

Mock Up
Mose Allison Quintet | Gimeracs And Gewgaws | Blue Note | 823211-2

Mockingbird
F | Schwarzwaldmädel | Jazz Haus Musik | JHM 24

Modaji
Pekka Pöyry With Band/Orchestra | Happy Peter | Leo Records | 016

Modal Forces-
Fritz Pauer Trio | Live At The Berlin Jazz Galerie | MPS | 9811263

Modal Forces(Suite In Three Movements:
Dexter Gordon Quartet | Dexter Gordon | Blue Note | 84502

Mode For Dulcimer
Jackie McLean Quartet | A Ghetto Lullaby | Steeplechase | SCCD 31013

Mode For Joe
Joe Henderson Septet | Mode For Joe | Blue Note | 591894-2
The Blue Note Years-The Best Of Joe Henderson | Blue Note | 795627-2
Joe Henderson-The Blue Note Years | Blue Note | 789287-2

Mode For Martin-
Teodross Avery Quartet | My Generation | Impulse(MCA) | 951181-2

Mode For My Father
Billy Gault Quintet | When Destiny Calls | Steeplechase | SCCD 31027

Modeidi's Modalities
Dieter Köhnlein-Uwe Kropinski | In Und Um C | Aho-Recording | AHO CD 1015(CD 661)

Moderato-
Astor Piazzolla With Orchestra Of St. Luke's | Concierto Para Bandoneon-Tres Tangos | Nonesuch | 7559-79174-2

Moderato Mistico-
The Robert Hohner Percussion Ensemble | Different Strokes | dmp Digital Music Productions | CD 485

Modern Memory 1(Improvisation for John Coltrane)
Rez Abbasi Group | Modern Memory | String Jazz | SJRCD 102

Modern Memory 2(Improvisation For Jim Hall)
Modern Memory | String Jazz | SJRCD 102

Modern Memory 3(Improvisation for Keith Jarrett)
Stan Kenton And His Orchestra | The Kenton Era | Creative World | ST 1030

Modern Times
Steps Ahead | Modern Times | Elektra | 7559-60351-2
Steve Khan Quartet | Blades | Passport Jazz | PJ 88001

Moderne
Boury | Moderne Zeiten-Musik Und Tanz | Jazz Haus Musik | JHM 11

Modes
Peter Leitch Quintet | Portraits And Dedications | Criss Cross | Criss 1039

Modette
Joe Henderson Group | Double Rainbow | Verve | 527222-2

Modinha
Laurindo Almeida/Carlos Barbosa-Lima/Charlie Byrd Quintet | Music Of The Brazilian Masters | Concord | CCD 4389
Chris Hunter And His Orchestra | I Want You | Sweet Basil | 660.55.004

Modmood
Jean-Luc Ponty Quintet | Jazz In Paris:Jean-Luc Ponty-Jazz Long Playing | EmArCy | 548150-2 PMS

Modo Azul
Gunter Hampel Group | Music From Europe | ESP Disk | ESP 1042-2

Modus Operandy
Vinding/Norris/Herman | 2nd Trio | Koala Records | CD P 23

Moe' Joe
Philly Joe Jones Septet | Mo' Joe | Black Lion | BLCD 760154

Moeshoeshoe The First
The Dedication Orchestra | Ixesha(Time) | Ogun | OGCD 102/103

Mogigrafisch Einerlei
Rudi Neuwirth Group | Sand | Traumton Records | 2413-2

Mogli
Rade Soric Quartet | Mixturiosities | Edition Collage | EC 502-2

Mohabbat
Dean Magraw | Broken Silence | Acoustic Music Records | 319.1054.2

Mohave
Anthony Braxton Group | Anthony Braxton's Charlie Parker Project 1993 | Hat Art | CD 6160(2)

Mohawk
Charlie Parker-Dizzy Gillespie Quintet | Thelonious Monk:Misterioso | Dreyfus Jazz Line | FDM 36743-2
Ira Sullivan And His Chicago Jazz Quintet | Bird Lives | Affinity | AFF 71
Larry Schneider Quartet | Mohawk | Steeplechase | SCCD 31347

Mohawk(alt.take)
Charlie Parker And His Orchestra | Bird: The Complete Charlie Parker On Verve | Verve | 837141-2

Mohawk(take 3)
Bird: The Complete Charlie Parker On Verve | Verve | 837141-2

Mohawk(take 6)
Guillermo Gregorio Group | Ellipsis | HatOLOGY | 511

Moin,Moin
Klaus Ignatzek Quintet | Is That So? | Koala Records | CD P 24

Moist Windows
Gene Ammons Septet | Bad! Bossa Nova | Original Jazz Classics | OJC20 351-2(P 7257)

Moito Mato Grosso
Gene Ammons Bossa Nova | Original Jazz Classics | OJCCD 351-2(PR 7257)

Moja(part 1)
Miles Davis Group | Dark Magus | CBS | C2K 65137

Moja(part 2)
Ikue Mori Trio | Painted Desert | Avant | AVAN 030

Mojave
Lionel Hampton All Stars | For The Love Of Music | MoJazz | 530554-2

Mojo
Booker Ervin Quartet | The Space Book | Original Jazz Classics | OJCCD 896-2(PR 7386)
Sylvain Luc-André Ceccarelli-Jean Marc Jafet | SUD | Dreyfus Jazz Line | FDM 36612-2
Armand Gordon & Son Jazz Clan | Jazz Pure | Jazz Pure Collection | AU 31618 CD

Mojo Clinton
Lightnin' Hopkins | The Blues Vol.1 | Intercord | 158600

Mojo Highway
Joe Lutcher's Jump Band | Joe Joe Jump | Charly | CRB 1038

Mojo Woman
Dino Saluzzi Group | Mojotoro | ECM | 1447

Mojotoro
The Rippingtons | Weekend In Monaco | GRP | GRP 96812

Moksha
John Tchicai Trio | Real Tchicai | Steeplechase | SCS 1075

Mo-Lasses
Woody Herman And His Orchestra | Woody Herman-1963 | Philips | 589490-2
Weather Report | Procession | CBS | 25241

Moldau
Jan Garbarek Group | I Took Up The Runes | ECM | 1419(843850-2)

Molde Canticle(part 1-5)
Victory Of The Better Man | L'Utopiste | CMP Records | CMP CD 44

Molecular Structure
Mark Helias' Open Loose | New School | Enja | ENJ-9413 2

Molecule
Chick Corea And Origin | A Week At The Blue Note | Stretch Records | SCD 9020-2

Moliendo Cafe
Trio Terracota | Savia | Acoustic Music Records | 319.1193.2

Moll-Blues
Bireli Lagrene Group | A Tribute To Django Reinhardt | Jazzpoint | JP 1061 CD
Bireli Lagrene Trio | A' Portrait Of Jan Jankeje | Jazzpoint | JP 1054 CD
Anthony Cox Quartet | Dark Metals | Minor Music | 801019

Molly
Dancing Hands | Jaguar At Halfmoon Lake | Acoustic Music Records | 319.1151.2

Mom
Phil Woods Quintet | Bouquet/Fujitsu-Concord Jazz Festival In Japan '87 | Concord | CCD 4377

Mom And Dad
Tony Williams Lifetime | Spectrum:The Anthology | Verve | 537075-2

Moment
Louis Sclavis Quintet | Rouge | ECM | 1458

Moment Donné
Cal Tjader Quartet | Our Blues | Fantasy | FCD 24771-2

Moment In Madrid
David Binney Group | South | ACT | 9279-2

Moment In Memory
Charlie Haden Quartet West With Strings | The Art Of The Song | Verve | 547403-2

Moment Musical Opus 16 No.3 In B Minor
Peter Finger | Solo | Acoustic Music Records | 319.1032.2

Moment Of Truth
Gerald Wilson Big Band | Moment Of The Truth | Pacific Jazz | 792928-2
Benny Golson Quintet | Domingo | Dreyfus Jazz Line | FDM 36557-2

Moment To Moment
Dave Young-Cyrus Chestnut | Two By Two Vol.2 | Justin Time | JUST 81-2
Freddie Hubbard Orchestra | First Light | CTI | EPC 450562-2
Matthieu Michel Quintet feat. Richard Galliano | Estate | TCB Records | TCB 95802

Momentos Dificiles
Axel Zinowsky Quartet | Mindwalk | Acoustic Music Records | 319.1064.2

Moments
Stivin-Van Den Broeck-Haurand | Bordertalk | Konnex Records | KCD 5068
Cal Tjader Quintet | Concert On The Campus | Original Jazz Classics | OJC 279(F 8044)

Moment's Notice
John Coltrane Sextet | Blue Train | Mobile Fidelity | MFCD 547(UDCD)
Takin' Off | Blue Note | 300415
McCoy Tyner Trio | Super Trios | Milestone | M 55003
Moncef Genoud Trio | Waiting For Birth | Nilva | NQ 3420 CD

Moments Of Love
The Ethnic Heritage Ensemble | Ethnic Heritage Ensemble | Leo Records | 014

Moments To Remember
Louis Armstrong With Benny Carter's Orchestra | Louis Armstrong-My Greatest Songs | MCA | MCD 18347
Chico Freeman-Cecil McBee | Chico | India Navigation | IN 1031 CD

Mon Amour
Roland Kirk Quintet | Live In Paris 1970 Vol.1 | France's Concert | FCD 109

Mon Coer Est Rouge
Nitta Rette Et Son Trio Hot | Jazz In Paris:Django Reinhardt-Django Et Compagnie | EmArCy | 549241-2 PMS

Mon Coer Reste De Toi
Caterina Zapponi With The Monty Alexander Quartet | Universal Lovesongs | Inak | 9062

Mon Enfant
Ralph Towner Quartet | Lost And Found | ECM | 1563(529347-2)
Claus Stötter's Nevertheless | Die Entdeckung Der Banane | Jazz 'n' Arts Records | JNA 1403

Mon Four
Coleman Hawkins With Many Albam And His Orchestra | The Hawk In Paris | Bluebird | 63 51059-2

Mon Homme
Dizzy Gillespie Sextet | Pleyel Jazz Concert 1953 | Vogue | 21409392

Mon Homme(My Man)
Sidney Bechet And His All Stars | Sidney Bechet:Summertime | Dreyfus Jazz Line | FDM 36712-2
Sidney Bechet Quartet | Planet Jazz:Sidney Bechet | Planet Jazz | 2152063-2
Poncho Sanchez Group | Conga Blue | Concord | CCD 4726

Mona
Joe Bawelino Quartet | Guitar Moments | Take Twelve On CD | TT 006-2
Stan Getz With The Eddie Louiss Trio | Dynasty | Verve | 839117-2

Mona Lisa
Guy Barker With The London Metropolitan Orchestra | What Love Is | EmArCy | 558331-2
Keith Jarrett Trio | Tokyo '96 | ECM | 1666(539955-2)
L.A.4 | Watch What Happens | Concord | CCD 4063
Ray Anderson Quintet | Blues Bred In The Bone | Enja | ENJ-5081 2
Ray Brown Trio | Summerwind-Live At The Loa | Concord | CCD 4426
Sonny Rollins Plus 3 | Sonny Rollins + 3 | Milestone | MCD 9250-2
Toto Blanke-Rudolf Dasek | Mona Lisa | ALISO Records | AL 1037
Freddy Cole Trio | I'm Not My Brother,I'm Me | Sunnyside | SSC 1054 D

Monaco
Kenny Dorham Sextet | Round Midnight At The Cafe Bohemia | Blue Note | 300105(1524)

Monaco(alt.take)
Taku Sugimoto | Oposite | HatNOIR | 802

Monajat(Le Temps Ne Revient Pas)
Rodney Kendrick Trio | We Don't Die We Multiply | Verve | 537447-2

Monastery In The Dark
Trio Friedrich-Hebert-Moreno | Surfacing | Naxos Jazz | 86060-2

Monday
Les Brown And His Band Of Renown | Ridin' High | Blue Moon | BMCD 3058

Monday Blues
Earl Hines And His Band | A Monday Date | Original Jazz Classics | OJCCD 1740-2(RLP 9398)

Monday Date-
Jo Mikowich Group | Just A Dream-A Collection For Easy Listening | yvp music | CD 3025

Monday Night
Frank Wess Quintet | Jazz Is Busting Out All Over | Savoy | SV 0178(12123)

Monday's Child
Ira Sullivan Quintet | Ira Sullivan | Flying Fish | FF 075

Mondom
Ray Brown & Laurindo Almeida | Moonlight Serenade | Jeton | JET 60005

Mondspinner
Lumpp-Read-Küttner Trio | Midnight Sun | Nabel Records:Jazz Network | CD 4612

Mondstein
Jim Hall | Dedications & Inspirations | Telarc Digital | CD 83365

Money
Clifton Chenier Group | Live At Montreux | Charly | CDX 2
John Lee Hooker | It Serve You Right To Suffer | Impulse(MCA) | MCD 18186

Money Blues
Keith Nichols And The Cotton Club Orchestra | Henderson Stomp | Stomp Off Records | CD 1275

Money Is Honey
Count Basie And His Orchestra | The Indispensable Count Basie | RCA | ND 89758

Money Jungle
Albert King Blues Band | The Lost Session | Stax | SCD 8534-2

Money Lovin' Women
Paul Millns-Olf Kübler | Finally Falls The Rain | BELL Records | BLR 84707

Money, Money
Jimmy Witherspoon And His Band | Evenin' Blues | Original Blues Classics | OBCCD 511-2

Mongo's Groove
Mongo Santamaria Orchestra | The Watermelon Man | Milestone | M 47012

Monica
Lee Konitz-Kenny Werner | Unleemited | Owl Records | 014727-2
Mal Waldron/Doudou Gouirand/Michel Marre | Space | Vent Du Sud | VSCD 107

Monica Jane
Monica Zetterlund With The Bill Evans Trio | The Complete Bill Evans On Verve | Verve | 527953-2

Monica Vals(aka Waltz For Debby)
Hal Russell NRG Ensemble | The Finnish/Swiss Tour | ECM | 1455

Monica's Having A Baby
Abdullah Ibrahim(Dollar Brand) | Autobiography | Plainisphare | PL 1267-68 CD

Monique
Mino Cinelu-Kenny Barron | Swamp Sally | Verve | 532268-2
John Gordon's Trombones Unlimited | Live In Concert | Mons Records | CD 1890

Monitor
Oscar Peterson Trio With Roy Eldridge,Sonny Stitt & Jones | The Oscar Peterson Trio,Roy Eldridge,Sonny Stitt And Jo Jones At Newp | Verve | MV 2618 IMS

Monitor Theme
Enrico Pieranunzi | What's What | yvp music | CDX 48704

Monk And The Nun
Ornette Coleman Quartet | Twins | Atlantic | SD 8810

Monk In Cage
Abdullah Ibrahim Trio | Cape Town Flowers | TipToe | TIP-888826 2

Monk In Harlem
Charles Lloyd Quartet | Notes From Big Sur | ECM | 1465(511999-2)

Monk In Paris
Mario Pavone Group | Toulon Days | New World Records | 80420-2

Monk Me
Helmut Nieberle-Helmut Kagerer | Skyliner | ART BY HEART | ABH 2001 2

Monk Medley:
Jack Walrath Group | Master Of Suspense | Blue Note | BLJ 46905 Digital

Monk Up And Down
Carmen McRae And Her Quartet | Carmen Sings Monk | RCA | 2663841-2

Monkery's The Blues(Blue Monk)
Tom Coster Groups | From The Street | JVC | JVC 2053-2

Monkey
Jazz Circle | Sun Games | Timeless | CD SJP 167

Monkey Face Woman
Pierre Dorge & New Jungle Orchestra | Live In Chicago | Olufsen Records | DOCD 5122

Monkey Lens Dipthong String
Mama Estella Yancey With Erwin Helfer | Maybe I'll Cry | Steeplechase | SCB 9001

Monkey Monkey Do
Houston Boines Band | Mississippi Blues | Anthology of the Blues | AB 5609

Monkey See Monkey Do
Ray Anderson Lapis Lazuli Band | Funkorific | Enja | ENJ-9340 2

Monkey Talk
Sophisticated Jimmy La Rue | Country Blues Collector Items Vol.2(1931-1937) | Story Of Blues | CD 3540-2

Monkey Woman
Estella Mama Yancey With Axel Zwingenberger | Axel Zwingenberger And The Friends Of Boogie Woogie Vol.4: The Blues Of Mama Yancey | Vagabond | VRCD 8.88009

Monkey Woman Blues
Peter Madsen Group | Snuggling Snakes | Minor Music | 801030

Monkish Business
Karlheinz Miklin Quartet | Last Waltz | Acoustic Music Records | 319.1126.2

Monkology
Nornert Stein Pata Masters | Live In Australia | Pata Musik | PATA 15 CD

Monks
Young People With Faces | Uncle Festive | Denon Compact Disc | CY-2135

Monk's Blues
McCoy Tyner Trio | McCoy Tyner-Reevaluation | MCA | AS 9235-2

Monk's Dream
Chick Corea | Standards | Stretch Records | SCD 9028-2
Jessica Williams | Intuition | Jazz Focus | JFCD 010
John Nugent Quartet | Taurus People | Jazz Focus | JFCD 030
Larry Young-Elvin Jones | The Art Of Larry Young | Blue Note | 799177-2
McCoy Tyner | Monk's Dream | Memo Music | HDJ 4019
Pete York & His All Star Group | It's You Or No One | Mons Records | MR 874772

Steve Lacy-Roswell Rudd Quartet | School Days | Hat Art | CD 6140
T.S. Monk Sextet | Changing Of The Guard | Blue Note | 789050-2
Thelonious Monk Trio | Thelonious Monk | Original Jazz Classics | OJC20 010-2(P 7027)
Thelonious Monk:85th Birthday Celebration | zyx records | FANCD 6076-2
Thelonious Monk:The Complete Prestige Recordings | Prestige | 3 PRCD 4428-2
Travelin' Light | Cookin' With Frank And Sam | Concord | CCD 4647

Monk's Dream(alt.take)
Soesja Citroen And Her All Stars | Sings Thelonious Monk | Turning Point | 30001

Monk's Food & Feet
Teo Macero And His Orchestra | Impressions Of Charles Mingus | Palo Alto | PA 8046

Monk's Mood
Chris Cody Coalition | Oasis | Naxos Jazz | 86018-2
Dave Liebman Trio | Monk's Mood | Double Time Records | DTRCD-154
Dollar Brand | Reflections | Black Lion | BLCD 760127
Jerry Gonzales Quintet | Rumba Para Monk | Sunnyside | SSC 1036 D
Joe Lovano Trio | One Time Out | Soul Note | SN 1224
Johannes Mössinger | Spring In Versailles | double moon | DMCD 1004-2
Johannes Mössinger New York Trio | Monk's Corner | double moon | DMCHR 71032
John Coltrane-Thelonious Monk Quartet | Monk & Trane | Milestone | M 47011
Michael Rabinowitz Quartet | Gabrielle's Balloon | Jazz Focus | JFCD 011
Paolo Fresu Quintet | Ballads | SPLASC(H) Records | CD H 366-2
Roswell Rudd Quintet | Regeneration | Soul Note | 121054-2
Steve Grossman With The Cedar Walton Trio | A Small Hotel | Dreyfus Jazz Line | FDM 36561-2
Thelonious Monk Quartet | Thelonious Himself | Original Jazz Classics | OJCCD 254-2
On Tour In Europe | Charly | CD 122
Thelonious Monk Quintet | Thelonious Monk:The Complete Blue Note Recordings | Blue Note | 830363-2
Genius Of Modern Music,Vol.1 | Blue Note | 781510-2
Thelonious Monk Trio | Thelonious Monk:85th Birthday Celebration | zyx records | FANCD 6076-2
Jazz Gallery:John Coltrane Vol.1 | RCA | 2119540-2
Joshua Breakstone | 9 By 3 | Contemporary | CCD 14062-2

Monk's Mood(reprise)
Soesja Citroen And Her All Stars | Sings Thelonious Monk | Turning Point | 30001

Monk's Point
Thelonious Monk | Solo Monk | CBS | 471248-2

Monk's Visit
Klaus Ignatzek Group | Monk's Visit | Hep | 2036

Monky Tonky
Jimmy Smith With The Oliver Nelson Orchestra | Jimmy Smith:Best Of The Verve Years | Verve | 527950-2

Monlope
Franz Koglmann Monoblue Quartet | L'Heure Bleue | Hat Art | CD 6093

Monolithic Attidude
Robert Norman In Different Groups | The Best Of Robert Norman(1941-1989) | Hot Club Records | HCRCD 085

Monollith
Conrad Bauer-Johannes Bauer | Bauer Bauer | Intakt Records | CD 040

Monologue
Enrico Pieranunzi | Autumn Song | Enja | 4094

Monologue by Louis Armstrong
Louis Armstrong And His All Stars | The Louis Armstrong Selection | CBS | 467278-2

Monologue For Two
Duke Ellington And His Orchestra | Duke Ellington In Hamilton | Radiex Music | RDX-1000

Monologue(Un Mondo De Dire)
Bud Powell Trio | The Blue Note Years:The Best Of Bud Powell | Blue Note | 793204-2

Monopoly
Sticks & Strings | Uru | Timeless | CD SJP 411

Monotonous
Stan Kenton And His Orchestra | A Concert In Progressive Jazz | Creative World | ST 1037

Monroe
Bennie Wallace Quintet | The Art Of The Saxophone | Denon Compact Disc | CY-1648

Monsieur Hulot
Tomé XX | The Red Snapper | Jazz Haus Musik | JHM 0047 CD

Monsieur Loyal
Chico Freeman & Franco Ambrosetti Meet Reto Weber Percussion Orchestra | Face To Face | double moon | CHRDM 71018

Monsieur Sel
Tommy Tedesco Quintet | My Desire | Discovery | DS 851 IMS

Monster
Polyphonix | Alarm | Jazz 'n' Arts Records | 0300
Schlothauer's Maniacs | Maniakisses | Timescrapper | TSCR 9811

Monster Mobbin'
Klaus Ignatzek Group | New Surprise | Timeless | CD SJP 324

Monsun Afterthoughts
Malcolm Goldstein-Peter Niklas Wilson | Goldstein-Wilson | true muze | TUMU CD 9801

Monsun Vibrations I
Goldstein-Wilson | true muze | TUMU CD 9801

Monsun Vibrations II
Walter Norris Trio | Lush Life | Concord | CCD 4457

Montage
Johnny Smith Quartet | Johnny Smith And His New Quartet | Fresh Sound Records | FSR-CD 80(882190)

Montara
John Stubblefield Quintet | Countin' The Blues | Enja | ENJ-5051 2

Montbéliard Trio
Mongo Santamaria And His Rhythm Afro-Cubanos | Afro Roots | Prestige | PCD 24018-2(F 8012/8032)

Monte Azul
Andres Boiarsky Sextet | Into The Light | Reservoir | RSR CD 149

Montego
Danny Gottlieb Group | Aquamarine | Atlantic | 781806-1

Monterey
George Winston | Linus & Lucy-The Music Of Vince Guaraldi | Windham Hill | 34 11187-2
Jeff Linsky Quintet | Up Late | Concord | CCD 4363

Monterey Mist
Modern Jazz Quartet | MJQ 40 | Atlantic | 7567-82330-2
Together Again | Pablo | PACD20 244-2(2308244)
Ray Brown-Milt Jackson Orchestra | Much In Common | Verve | 533259-2

Montevideo
Pete Rugolo And His Orchestra incl.The Rugolettes(eight-man-combo) | Rugolomania | Fresh Sound Records | LSP 15826(CBS CL 689)
Duke Ellington Quartet | Piano Reflections | Capitol | 792863-2

Monteville No.2
Bobby Hutcherson Quintet | Good Bait | Landmark | LCD 1501-2

Monti Chardas
Alex Welsh And His Jazz Band | The Best Of British Traditional Jazz | Philips | 818651-2

Montmartre
Dexter Gordon Quintet | Tower Of Power | Original Jazz Classics | OJCCD 299-2(P 7623)
Dexter Gordon-Benny Bailey Quintet | The Rainbow People | Steeplechase | SCCD 31521
Dexter Gordon-James Moody Quintet | Power! | Prestige | P 24087

Montmartre Blues
Oscar Pettiford Sextet | Montmartre Blues | Black Lion | BLP 60124

Montmartre loan
Joelle Leandre-Rüdiger Carl | Blue Goo Park | FMP | CD 52

Montmartre(Django's Jump)
Rex Stewart And His Feetwarmers | L'Essentiel Django Reinhardt | EMI Records | 780671-2

Montpellier
Ulli Bögershausen | Best Of Ulli Bögershausen | Laika Records | LK 93-045
Stu Goldberg Group | Eye Of The Beholder | MPS | 68282

Montville No. One
Monty Alexander-Sly Dunbar-Robbie Shakespeare Group | Monty Meets Sly And Robbie | Telarc Digital | CD 83494

Monty's Mood
Thierry Maillard Trio | Paris New York | EmArCy | 558041-2

Mooche Mooche
Dave Stryker Octet | Blue To The Bone II | Steeplechase | SCCD 31465

Mood
Miles Davis Quintet | E.S.P. | CBS | CK65683
Miles Davis Quintet 1965-1968 | CBS | C6K 67398
Oscar Peterson Trio | 1953 Live | Jazz Band Records | EBCD 2111-2(875389)

Mood Azur
Ricky Ford Septet | Hot Brass | Candid | CCD 79518

Mood For Milt
Toots Thielemans-Eugen Cicero Quintet | Nice To Meet You | Intercord | 145034

Mood Indigo
(Little)Jimmy Scott And His Band | Mood Indigo | Milestone | MCD 9305-2
Al Cohn Meets The Jazz Seven | Keeper Of The Flame | Ronnie Scott's Jazz House | JHCD 022
Albert Mangelsdorff With The NDR Big Band | NDR Big Band-Bravissimo | ACT | 9232-2
Albert Nicholas With Alan Elsdon's Band | Albert Nicholas With Alan Elsdon's Band Vol.2 | Jazzology | JCD-269
Charles Mingus Orchestra | Charles Mingus:The Complete 1959 Columbia Recordings | CBS | C3K 65145
Charlie Byrd | Solo Flight | Original Jazz Classics | OJCCD 1093-2(RS 9498)
Charlie Byrd Trio With Sott Hamilton | It's A Wonderful World | Concord | CCD 4374
Clarinet Summit | Clarinet Summit In Concert At The Public Theater | India Navigation | IN 1062 CD
Clark Terry Quintet | The Hymn | Candid | CCD 79770
Cruising | Milestone | M 47032
Danny Moss-Roy Williams Quintet | Steamers! | Nagel-Heyer | CD 049
Ellington For Lovers | Nagel-Heyer | NH 1009
David Matthews & The Manhattan Jazz Orchestra | Hey Duke! | Milestone | MCD 9320-2
Digby Fairweather/Stan Barker | Ballads For Trumpet | Jazz Colours | 874708-2
Duke Ellington And His Cotton Club Orchestra | Victor Jazz History Vol.6:Harlem Jazz(1928-33) | RCA | 2128560-2
Duke Ellington And His Orchestra | Greatest Hits | CBS | 462959-2
Unknown Session | CBS | 467180-2
Duke Ellington And His Orchestra 1943,Vol.1 | Circle | CCD-101
The Big Bands Vol.1:The Snader Telescriptions | Storyville | 4960043
Duke Ellington:The Complete RCA-Victor Mid-Forties Recordings(1944-1946) | RCA | 2663394-2
100 Years Duke | Laserlight | 24906
All Star Road Band Vol.2 | Doctor Jazz | ZL 70969(2) (809319)
From The Blue Note, Chicago | Jazz Anthology | JA 5197
The Best Of Early Ellington | GRP | GRP 16602
Happy Birthday Duke Vol.3 | Laserlight | 15785
Duke Ellington-Coleman Hawkins Orchestra | Duke Ellington Meets Coleman Hawkins | Impulse(MCA) | 951162-2
Duke Ellington Meets Coleman Hawkins | MCA | MCAD 5650
Dutch Swing College Band | Dutch Swing College Band Live In 1960 | Philips | 838765-2
Souvenirs From Holland, Vol. 3 | DSC Production | PA 005 (801062)
Ella Fitzgerald And Her All Stars | For The Love Of Ella Fitzgerald | Verve | 841765-2
Ella Fitzgerald Sings The Duke Ellington Songbook | Verve | 559248-2
The Complete Ella Fitzgerald Song Books of Harold Arlen, Irving Berlin, Duke Ellington, George & Ira Gershwin, Jerome Kern, Johnny Mercer, Cole Porter And Rogers & Hart | Verve | 519832-2
Ella Fitzgerald With The Oscar Peterson Quartet | Ella Fitzgerald Sings The Duke Ellington Song Book Vol.2 | Verve | 2615033 IMS
Erroll Garner Solo/Trio/Quartet | Inedits 1946-1947 | Festival | 402791
George Mraz Trio | Duke's Place | Milestone | MCD 9292-2
Gianluigi Trovesi Octet | Les Hommes Armés | Soul Note | 121311-2
Jerry Tilitz Sextet | Trombone Tangents | Limetree | MLP 0025
Jimmy Smith Quartet | Fourmost Return | Milestone | MCD 9311-2
Jimmy Smith Trio | Standards | Blue Note | 821282-2
Jodie Christian Sextet | Front Line | Delmark | DE 490
Joe Pass Quartet | The Complete 'Catch Me' Sessions | Blue Note | LT 1053
Johnny Hodges Orchestra | Jazz Legacy 9: Johnny Hodges-The Rabbit In Paris | Vogue | 500059
Johnny Hodges Septet | Compact Jazz: Duke Ellington And Friends | Verve | 833291-2
Louis Armstrong And His Friends | Planet Jazz:Louis Armstrong | Planet Jazz | 2152052-2
Jazz Special-His Last Recordings | RCA | ND 89527
Louis Armstrong With Orchestra | Satchmo | Verve | 835895-2
Marcus Roberts | Alone With Three Giants | Novus | PD 83109
Metronome Quintet | Just Friends | Gold Records | 11047
New Winds | The Cliff | Sound Aspects | sas CD 025
Nina Simone Quartet | Nina Simone-The 60s Vol.2:Mood Indigo | Mercury | 838544-2 PMS
Oscar Pettiford Nonet | Oscar Rides Again | Affinity | AFF 160
Ran Blake | Something To Live For | HatOLOGY | 527
Roland Kirk Quintet | Rahsaan/The Complete Mercury Recordings Of Roland Kirk | Mercury | 846630-2
Rosemary Clooney With The Duke Ellington Orchestra | Blue Rose | CBS | CK 65506
Sarah Vaughan And Her Band | Duke Ellington Song Book Two | Pablo | CD 2312116
Sidney Bechet And His New Orleans Feetwarmers | Sidney Bechet 1932-1943: The Bluebird Sessions | Bluebird | ND 90317
SLC(The Swing Limited Corporation) | The Swing Limited Corporation Story | Nocturne Productions | NTCD 107
Thelonious Monk Trio | Thelonious Monk:85th Birthday Celebration | zyx records | FANCD 6076-2
Thelonious Monk-The Complete Riverside Recordings | Riverside | 15 RCD 022-2
Wild Bill Davis | Greatest Organ Solos Ever! | Jazz Connaisseur | JCCD 8702-2
Wild Bill Davison Quintet | Plays The Greatest Of The Greats | Dixieland Jubilee | DJ 508
Wycliffe Gordon Quintet | What You Dealin' With | Criss Cross | Criss 1212

Mood Indigo-
Eric Reed Trio | Soldier's Hymn-Dedicated To Art Blakey | Candid | CCD 79511
Johnny Hodges Orchestra | Johnny Hodges At The Sportpalast, Berlin | Pablo | 2CD 2620102
Jonah Jones Quartet | Harry 'Sweets' Edison/Jonah Jones | LRC Records | CDC 9030
Rex Allen's Swing Express | Ellington For Lovers | Nagel-Heyer | NH 1009
Svend Asmussen Sextet | Svend Asmussen Collection Vol.14 | Swan Music | CD 2514-2
The Tremble Kids | 25 Jahre The Tremble Kids | Intercord | 180036

Mood Midnight
Manhattan Jazz Quintet | Bed Time Eyes-Original Soundtrack Recording | Paddle Wheel | K 28P 6451

Moods
Oscar Klein Band | Pick-A-Blues Live | Jazzpoint | JP 1071
Philip Catherine Trio | Moods Vol.1 | Criss Cross | Criss 1060

Moods For Mitch
Booker Little Sextet | Out Front | Candid | CCD 79027

Moods In Free Time
Dave Douglas Sextet | In Our Lifetime | New World Records | 80471-2

Moods In Free Time(take 5)
Mingus Big Band | Que Viva Mingus! | Dreyfus Jazz Line | FDM 36593-2

Moody's Mood
James Moody Quintet | James Moody/Frank Foster:Sax Talk | Vogue | 2113410-2

Moody's Mood For Love
Eddie Jefferson And His Orchestra | The Jazz Singer | Inner City | IC 1016 IMS
World Bass Violin Ensemble | BASSically Yours | Black Saint | 120063-2

Moohah The D.J.
Jack McDuff Group | Bringin' It Home | Concord | CCD 4855

Moon
George Winston | Autumn | Windham Hill | 34 11012-2

Moon And Sand
Kenny Burrell Quartet | Moon And Sand | Concord | CCD 4121
Kenny Burrell With The Gil Evans Orchestra | Guitar Forms | Verve | 521403-2
Marian McPartland Trio feat. Chris Potter | In My Life | Concord | CCD 4561

Moon Child
Dan Barrett Octet | Strictly Instrumental | Concord | CJ 331

Moon Cup
Mino Cinelu-Kenny Barron | Swamp Sally | Verve | 532268-2

Moon Dance(1)
Paquito D'Rivera Group With The Absolute Ensemble | Habanera | Enja | ENJ-9395 2

Moon Dance(2)
Karl Ratzer Group | Moon Dancer | Enja | ENJ-9357 2

Moon Dream
Flavio Ambrosetti Quartet | Flavio Ambrosetti Anniversary | Enja | ENJ-9027 2

Moon Dreams
Franz Koglmann Monoblue Quartet | L'Heure Bleue | Hat Art | CD 6093
Miles Davis And His Orchestra | The Complete Birth Of The Cool | Capitol | 494550-2
The Complete Birth Of The Cool | Capitol | 494550-2
Miles Davis:Milestones | Dreyfus Jazz Line | FDM 36731-2
Birth Of The Cool | Capitol | 530117-2
Miles Davis:The Blue Note And Capitol Recordings | Blue Note | 827475-2
Miles Davis Nonet | The Real Birth Of The Cool | Bandstand | BDCD 1512

Moon Flower
Fabio Jegher Trio | Time Zone-Fabio Jegher Boston & L.A.Trios | Red Records | VPA 175

Moon Germs
Joe Farrell Quartet | Moon Germs | CTI | 6023

Moon In The West
Henry Mancini And His Orchestra | The Blues And The Beat | Fresh Sound Records | ND 74409

Moon Inhabitants
Paul Plimley-Lisle Ellis | Kaleidoscopes(Ornette Coleman Songbook) | Hat Art | CD 6117

Moon Lake
Curlew | North America | Moers Music | 02042

Moon Love
Glenn Miller And His Orchestra | The Genius Of Glenn Miller Vol.2 | RCA | ND 90205
Harry James And His Orchestra | Harry James & His Orchestra Feat.Frank Sinatra | CBS | CK 66377

Moon Mist
Duke Ellington And His Famous Orchestra | Passion Flower 1940-46 | Bluebird | 63 66616-2
Duke Ellington & His Famous Orchestra | Forlane | UCD 19003
Duke Ellington And His Orchestra | Carnegie Hall Concert January 1943 | Prestige | 2PCD 34004-2
Jazz Live & Rare: The Immortal Duke Ellington | Jazzline | ???

Moon Mist(theme)
Martin Theurer | Moon Mood | FMP | 0700

Moon Moth
Chris Jarrett | Live In Tübingen | Edition Collage | EC 490-2

Moon Music
Wolfgang Fuhr Quartet | Song Of India:Music For Quartet | Mons Records | MR 874776

Moon Noom
Nina Simone Trio/Quartet/Orchestra | Moon Of Alabama | Jazz Door | JD 1214

Moon Of Manakoora
Wayne Shorter Quintet | Wayning Moments | Vee Jay Recordings | VJ 014

Moon Over Bourbon Street
Lester Bowie/Nobuyoshi Ino | Duet | Paddle Wheel | K 28P 6367

Moon Over Cuba
Loren Schoenberg And His Jazz Orchestra | Out Of This World | TCB Records | TCB 98902

Moon Over Miami
Sarah Vaughan With The Jimmy Jones Orchestra | Dreamy | Fresh Sound Records | SR 52046(Roulette)

Moon Rappin'
Adam Makowicz Quintet | Moonray | RCA | PL 83003

Moon Ray
Milt Jackson Quartet | Milt Jackson | Original Jazz Classics | OJC20 001-2(P 7003)
Opus De Funk | Prestige | P 24048
Roy Haynes Quartet | Out Of The Afternoon | Impulse(MCA) | 951180-2
Thomas Chapin Quartet | I've Got Your Number | Arabesque Recordings | AJ 0110

Moon Ray-
Horace Silver Quintet | Further Explorations By The Horace Silver Quintet | Blue Note | 300044(1589)

Moon Rays
Enrico Rava 4uartet | Animals | Inak | 8801

Moon River
Billy Eckstine With Bobby Tucker And His Orchestra | Billy Eckstine Now Singing In 12 Great Movies | Verve | 589307-2
Bob Dorough Trio With Joe Lovano | Right On My Way Home | Blue Note | 857729-2
Brad Mehldau Trio | The Art Of The Trio Vol.2 | Warner | 9362-46848-2
Charlie Byrd Quartet | Du Hot Club De Concord | Concord | CCD 4674
George Adams Quartet | Nightingale | Blue Note | 791984-2
Larry Coryell | Privat Concert | Acoustic Music Records | 319.1159.2
Sarah Vaughan With Orchestra | Sarah Vaughan Sings The Mancini Songbook | Verve | 558401-2
Sarah Vaughan With The Quincy Jones Orchestra | Trav'lin' Light:The Johnny Mercer Songbook | Verve | 555402-2
Stanley Jordan | Standards Vol.1 | Blue Note | 746333-2
Thomas Clausen Trio | She Touched Me | M.A Music | A 628-2
Vince Guaraldi Trio | Cast Your Fate To The Wind | Original Jazz Classics | OJCCD 437-2(F 8089)
Oscar Peterson | Oscar Peterson:Exclusively For My Friends | MPS | 513830-2

Moon River-
Oscar Peterson Trio | Girl Talk | MPS | 68074
Art Blakey And The Jazz Messengers | Buhaina's Delight | Blue Note | 784104-2

Moon Song
Art Tatum | Art Tatum:20th Century Piano Genius | Verve | 531763-2
The Art Tatum Solo Masterpieces | Pablo | 2625703
Art Tatum Quartet | The Tatum Group Masterpieces | Pablo | 2310734
Louis Armstrong With The Oscar Peterson Quartet | Louis Armstrong Meets Oscar Peterson | Verve | 825713-2

Roland Kirk Quartet | Rahsaan/The Complete Mercury Recordings Of Roland Kirk | Mercury | 846630-2
Sarah Jane Cion Quartet | Moon Song | Naxos Jazz | 86054-2
Warren Vaché Sextet | Easy Going | Concord | CCD 4323

Moon Story(1-2)
A Band Of Friends | Teatime Vol.2 | Poise | Poise 06/2

Moon Story(3)
Gil Evans Orchestra | Into The Hot | Impulse(MCA) | IMP 12922

Moon-A-Tic
Elmo Hope | Hope-Full | Original Jazz Classics | VIJ 5050

Moonbeams
Katrina Krimsky-Trevor Watts | Stella Malu | ECM | 1199
Alexander von Schlippenbach Trio | Pakistani Pomade | FMP | 0110

Moonbow
Michael Bocian | Premonition:Solo Debut For Nylon String Guitar | Enja | 9118-2

Moonchild-
Gary Burton-Keith Jarrett Quintet | Gary Burton & Keith Jarrett | Atlantic | 7567-81374-2
Stephan Kurmann Strings | Alive | TCB Records | TCB 96152

Moondance
Four For The Blues | Four For The Blues | Elite Special | 73623
Lorraine Feather And Her Quintet | Sweet Lorraine | Concord | CJ 78
Nana Mouskouri With The Berlin Radio Big Band | Nana Swings | Mercury | 074394-2
Norbert Gottschalk-Frank Haunschild | The Art Of The Duo:Favorite Songs | Mons Records | MR 874813

Moondance In Tajikistan
Joelle Leandre-Rüdiger Carl | Blue Goo Park | FMP | CD 52

Moon-Faced,Star-Eyed
Teddy Wilson Quartet | I Want To Be Happy | Naxos Jazz | 8.120538 CD

Moonglow
Art Tatum | Decca Presents Art Tatum | MCA | MCAD 42327(872084)
Artie Shaw And His Orchestra | This Is Artie Shaw | RCA | NL 89411 DP
Benny Goodman And His Orchestra | Breakfast Ball | Saville Records | SVL 172 IMS
Benny Goodman Quartet | Jazz Live & Rare: Benny Goodman & His Group/Orchestra | Jazzline | ???
Bob Florence Trio | Bob Florence Trio | Fresh Sound Records | FSR-CD 0303
Coleman Hawkins All Stars | Moonglow | Prestige | P 24106
Coleman Hawkins With The Oscar Peterson Trio | The Greatest Jazz Concert In The World | Pablo | 2625704-2
Erroll Garner Trio | Welcome To Jazz: Erroll Garner | Koch Records | 322 077 D1
Joe Venuti And His New Yorkers | The Big Bands Of Joe Venuti Vol.2 (1930-1933) | JSP Records | 1112
Krupa-Hampton-Wilson Quartet | This Is Jazz | Verve | 2615040 IMS
Lionel Hampton Quartet | Compact Jazz: Lionel Hampton | Verve | 833287-2
Ridin' On The L&N | Affinity | AFS 1037
Nat Gonella And His Georgians | Mister Rhythm Man | EMI Records | EG 2601881
Oscar Klein's Anniversary Band | Moonglow | Nagel-Heyer | CD 021
Peanuts Hucko Quintet | Tribute To Louis Armstrong And Benny Goodman | Timeless | TTD 541/42
Salut! | Green & Orange | Edition Collage | EC 488-2
Sarah Vaughan With The Quincy Jones Orchestra | You're Mine You | Fresh Sound Records | 857157-2
Stephane Grappelli And His Hot Four | Jazz In Paris:Django Reinhardt-Swing From Paris | EmArCy | 159853-2 PMS
Django Reinhardt Vol. 1 | Decca | 180020 AG
The Big Three | The Big Three | Original Jazz Classics | OJCCD 805-2(2310757)
The Fabulous New Jimmy Dorsey Orchestra | Dorsey Then And Now | Atlantic | 81801-1 TIS
The Ravens | The Greatest Group Of Them All:The Ravens | Savoy | SV 0270
Wynton Kelly Trio | New Faces-New Sounds:Piano Interpretations | Blue Note | 784456-2

Moonglow-
Lionel Hampton And His Orchestra | Made In Japan | Timeless | CD SJP 175

Moonjogger
Ralph Towner Quartet | Lost And Found | ECM | 1563(529347-2)

Moonless
John Surman With String Quartet | Coruscating | ECM | 1702(543033-2)

Moonless Midnight
Randy Brecker-Wolfgang Engstfeld Quartet | Mr. Max! | Nabel Records:Jazz Network | CD 4637

Moonlift
Ingrid Sertso/Karl Berger Group | Jazz Dance | ITM Records | ITM 1427

Moonlight
Jimmy Giuffre-André Jaume | Momentum,Willisay 1988 | HatOLOGY | 508
Jimmie Lunceford And His Orchestra | The King Of Big Band Jazz | Festival | Album 146

Moonlight And Shadows
Ernie Watts Trio | The Long Road Home | JVC | JVC 2058-2

Moonlight Bay
Kid Thomas' Dixieland Band | New Orleans Traditional Jazz Legends:Kid Thomas | Mardi Gras Records | MG 9004

Moonlight Becomes You
Booker Little 4 & Max Roach | Booker Little 4 & Max Roach | Blue Note | 784457-2
Chet Baker Septet | Chet Baker-Grey December | Pacific Jazz | 797160-2
Glenn Miller And His Orchestra | Candelight Miller | RCA | 2668716-2
Original Recordings From 1938 to 1942,Vol.2 | RCA | 2118549-2
Paul Motian Quartet | Paul Motian On Broadway Vol.2 | JMT Edition | 834440-2
Chet Baker Septet | Chet Baker-Grey December | Pacific Jazz | 797160-2

Moonlight Cello Rivers
Glenn Miller And His Orchestra | The Very Best Of Glenn Miller | RCA | PL 89009 AO

Moonlight Cocktail
A Legendary Performer-Previously Unreleased Live Recordings | RCA | NL 89212 DP
Mel Tormé With The Russell Garcia Orchestra | Swingin' On The Moon | Verve | 511385-2
Ozzie Nelson And His Orchestra | The Uncollected: Ozzie Nelson | Hindsight | HSR 107

Moonlight Elephants
Clark Terry-Thelonious Monk Quartet | In Orbit | Original Jazz Classics | OJC 302(R 12-271)

Moonlight Fiesta
Duke Ellington And His Orchestra | The Rare Broadcast Recordings 1952 | Jazz Anthology | JA 5213

Moonlight In Vermont
Ahmad Jamal Trio | At The Pershing | Affinity | CD AFS 780
Andy LaVerne | Maybeck Recital Hall Series Volume Twenty-Eight | Concord | CCD 4577
Billie Holiday And Her Orchestra | Body And Soul | Verve | 2304340 IMS
Carol Sloane And Clark Terry With The Bill Charlap Trio | The Songs Ella & Louis Sang | Concord | CCD 4787
Chris Connor With The Stan Free Quartet | Chris Craft | Atlantic | AMCY 1062
Eddie Lockjaw Davis Trio | Eddie 'Lockjaw' Davis His Tenor Saxophone And Trio | Sing | 506
Ella Fitzgerald And Louis Armstrong With The Oscar Peterson Quartet | Ella And Louis | Verve | 543304-2
The Jazz Collector Edition: Ella & Louis | Laserlight | 15706
Welcome To Jazz: Ella Fitzgerald | Koch Records | 322 078 D1
Ella Fitzgerald With The Oscar Peterson Quartet | Ella Fitzgerald At The Opera House | Verve | 831269-2 PMS
Frank Rosolino Quintet | Frankly Speaking | Affinity | AFF 69
George Garzone Group | Alone | NYC-Records | NYC 6018-2
Gerry Mulligan Quartet | Live In Stockholm 1957 | Nueva Records | JU 324
Walkin' Shoes | Bandstand | BDCD 1536
Live In Stockholm-Vol.1 | Ingo | 3
Gil Melle Quintet | Patterns In Jazz | Blue Note | 300096(1517)
Heiner Franz & Friends | Let's Have A Ball | Jardis Records | JRCD 20030
Herb Ellis Trio | Herb Mix | Concord | CJ 181
Jimmy Smith Trio | The Champ-Jimmy Smith At The Organ Vol.2 | Blue Note | 300093(1514)
Joe Pass | Unforgettable | Pablo | 2310964-2
Joe Williams With The Harry 'Sweets' Edison Band | Together/Have A Good Time | Roulette | 531790-2
Joe Zawinul And The Austrian All Stars | His Majesty Swinging Nephews 1954-1957 | RST-Records | 91549-2
John Colianni | Prime Cuts | Jazz Connaisseur | JCCD 9935-2
John Stein Quintet | Portraits And Landscapes | Jardis Records | JRCD 20029
Johnny Lytle Quartet | Got That Feeling/Moon Child | Milestone | MCD 47093-2
Johnny Smith Quintet | Moonlight In Vermont | Roulette | 596593-2
Blue Moon-Blue Note The Night And The Music | Blue Note | 789910-2
Johnny Smith-Stan Getz Quintet | Stan Getz-The Complete Roost Sessions | The Jazz Factory | JFCD 22839
Lee Konitz With The Bert Van Den Brink Trio | Dialogues | Challenge | CHR 70053
Marcus Roberts | If I Could Be With You | Novus | 4163149-2
Mel Tormé With The Russell Garcia Orchestra | Swingin' On The Moon | Verve | 511385-2
Michel Leeb And Gérard Badini 'Super Swing Machine' | Certains Leeb Jazz | Dreyfus Jazz Line | FDM 36586-2
Oscar Moore Quartet | Oscar Moore And Friends | Fresh Sound Records | FSR-CD 0202
Pedro Iturralde Quartet | Pedro Iturralde Quartet feat. Hampton Hawes | Fresh Sound Records | FSR 546(Hispavox 550-4020411)
Richie Beirach & Andy LaVerne | Too Grand | Steeplechase | SCCD 31335
Stan Getz With The Claus Ogerman Orchestra | Compact Jazz | Verve | 831368-2
Tete Montoliu-Mundell Lowe | Sweet'n Lovely Vol.1 | Fresh Sound Records | FSR-CD 0161
Wynton Kelly Trio | New Faces-New Sounds:Piano Interpretations | Blue Note | 784456-2

Moonlight In Vermont-
Gillespie-Eldridge-Edison Septet | Tour De Force | Verve | MV 2524 IMS

Moonlight Mississippi
Rosemary Clooney With The John Oddo Big Band | Still On The Road | Concord | CCD 4590

Moonlight On The Ganges
Art Tatum | The Art Tatum Solo Masterpieces | Pablo | 2625703
Glenn Miller And His Orchestra | The Glenn Miller Orchestra:The Early Years | Halcyon | DHDL 129
Jimmy Dorsey And His Orchestra | The Uncollected:Jimmy Dorsey, Vol.2 | Hindsight | HSR 153

Moonlight Saving Time
Jack Payne And His BBC Dance Orchestra | Radio Nights | Saville Records | SVL 152 IMS

Moonlight Serenade
Bob Mintzer Big Band | Art Of The Big Band | dmp Digital Music Productions | CD 479
Count Basie And His Orchestra | Lester Leaps In-Vol.2 1939/1940 | CBS | CBS 88668
Glenn Miller And His Orchestra | In The Mood | Intercord | 125403
Candelight Miller | RCA | 2668716-2
Glenn Miller-The Great Instrumentals 1938-1942 | Retrieval | RTR 79001
Glenn Miller | Koch Records | 321 941 D1
The Ultimate Glenn Miller-22 Original Hits From The King Of Swing | RCA | 2113137-2
Play Selections From The Glenn Miller Story And Other Hits | RCA | NL 89073
Kurt Elling Group | Flirting With Twilight | Blue Note | 531113-2
Olaf Polziehn Trio | American Songbook | Satin Doll Productions | SDP 1032-1 CD
Peter Herbolzheimer Orchestra | Music For Swinging Dancers Vol.4: Close To You | Koala Records | CD P 12
The Universal-International Orchestra | The Glenn Miller Story | MCA | ???

Moonlight Serenade-
Glenn Miller And His Orchestra | Live At Meadowbrook Ballroom 1939 | Magic | DAWE 34(881864)

Moonlow
Art Tatum Trio | The Complete Trio Sessions Vol.1 | Official | 3001

Moonpower
Bobby Watson Sextet | No Question About It | Blue Note | 790262-2

Moons
Jugend-Jazzorchester Des Saarlandes | Chops & Fingers | Blue Concept | BCCD 94/04

Moonshine
Gertrude 'Ma' Rainey With Lovie Austin And Her Blues Serenaders | Gertrude 'Ma' Rainey-Queen Of The Blues | Biograph | BLP 12032

Moonshine Dancer
Barbara Lea And The Legendary Lawson-Haggart Jazz Band | You're The Cats! | Audiophile | ACD-252

Moonspell For Pleasure
Alex Sipiagin Quintet | Steppin' Zone | Criss Cross | Criss 1202

Moonstone Journey
Jack Hylton And His Orchestra | The Bands That Matter | Eclipse | ECM 2046

Moontide
Dave Liebman Quintet | If They Only Knew | Timeless | CD SJP 151

Moonwaltz
Südpool Jazz Project II | Moon Dance Suite(Karl Berger) | L+R Records | CDLR 45062

Moor
Hans Reichel | Bonobo | FMP | 0280
Ralph Towner-Gary Peacock | A Closer View | ECM | 1602(531623-2)
Ron McClure Trio | Never Always | Steeplechase | SCCD 31355

Moose March
Crane River Jazz Band | The Legendary Crane River Jazz Band | Lake | LACD 57

Moose The Mooche
Art Blakey Percussion Ensemble | Drums Around The Corner | Blue Note | 521455-2
Art Farmer Quartet | Warm Valley | Concord | CCD 4212
Bud Powell Trio | At The Golden Circle, Vol.4 | Steeplechase | SCCD 36014
Charlie Parker Quintet | Charlie Parker Live Sessions Vol.2 | Zeta | ZET 712
Charlie Parker Sextet | Jazz Gallery:Charlie Parker Vol.1 | RCA | 2114174-2
Fred Wesley Group | Comme Ca | Minor Music | 801020
Larry Schneider Quartet | Mohawk | Steeplechase | SCCD 31347
Roots | For Diz & Bird | IN+OUT Records | 77039-2
Roy Haynes Quintet | Birds Of A Feather:A Tribute To Charlie Parker | Dreyfus Jazz Line | FDM 36625-2
Shelly Manne And His Men | More Swinging Sounds | Contemporary | COP 036
Sphere | Bird Songs | Verve | 837032-2

Moot
Ben Webster Quintet | At The Renaissance | Original Jazz Classics | OJC 390(C 7646)

Mop Mop
Ben Webster Sextet | Perdido | Moon Records | MCD 070-2
Esquire Metropolitan Opera House Jam Session | Jazz Live & Rare: The First And Second Esquire Concert | Jazzline | ???
Louis Armstrong And His All Stars | Historic Barcelona Concerts At Windsor Palace 1955 | Fresh Sound Records | FSR-CD 3004
The Legendary Berlin Concert Part 2 | Jazzpoint | JP 1063 CD
Louis Armstrong And His Orchestra | The Immortal Live Sessions 1944 / 1947 | Jazz Anthology | JA 5102
Max Roach Quartet | Again | Affinity | AFF 32
Victor Feldman Quartet | Bebop In Britain | Esquire | CD ESQ 100-4

Moppin' And Boppin'
Fats Waller And His Rhythm | The Indispensable Fats Waller Vol.9/10 | RCA | 2115526-2
Hot Stuff | Hot Stuff! Celebrating Early Jazz | Lake | LACD 40
Fats Waller And His Orchestra | The Last Years 1940-1943 | Bluebird | ND 90411(3)

Moppin' The Bride
Django Reinhardt And The Quintet Du Hot Club De France | Django Reinhardt Portrait | Barclay | DALP 2/1939
Peche Á La Mode-The Great Blue Star Sessions 1947/1953 | Verve | 835418-2

Moppin' The Bride(Micro)
Jazz In Paris:Django Reinhardt-Django's Blues | EmArCy | 013545-2
Mani Neumeir | Privat | ATM Records | ATM 3803-AH

Mopsa Mopsa
Michael Gibbs Orchestra | Great European Jazz Orchestras Vol.1:Big Music | ACT | 9231-2

Mopti
Cornelius Claudio Kreusch Quintet | Black Mud Sound | Enja | 9087-2
Sebastian Gramss Underkarl | Jazzscene | TCB Records | TCB 99102

Mor M-
Joachim Kühn-Walter Quintus | Dark | Ambiance(Blue Flame) | AMB 1

Morals In The Mud
Jason Moran | Modernistic | Blue Note | 539838-2

Moran Tonk Circa 1936
System Tandem | System Tandem | Japo | 60008 IMS

Mordido
David Friedman-Jasper Van't Hof | Birds Of A Feather | Traumton Records | 2428-2

Mordogan Köj
Noel Akchoté Trio | Rien | Winter&Winter | 910057-2

Mords
Aretha Franklin Quartet | In Person With Her Quartet | CBS | 21066

More
Dizzy Gillespie Quintet | The Cool World/Dizzy Goes Hollywood | Verve | 531230-2
Erroll Garner Quintet | That's My Kick | RCA | NL 89433
Frankie Randall With The Marty Paich Orchestra | A Swingin' Touch | Fresh Sound Records | NL 45978(RCA)
Lena Horne With The Lennie Hayton Orchestra | Lena Goes Latin | DRG | MRS 510 IMS
Stephane Grappelli And Friends | Grapelli Story | Verve | 515807-2
Stephane Grappelli Quartet | Stephane Grappelli | Jazz Colours | 874717-2

More (Theme From Mondo Cane)
Charlie Byrd Quartet | Charlie Byrd In Greenwich Village | Milestone | M 47049
Vince Guaraldi-Bola Sete Quartet | Vince & Bola | Fantasy | FCD 24756-2
Volker Kriegel Quintet | Spectrum | MPS | 9808699

More About D
Joe Derisi With The Australian Jazz Quintet | Joe Derisi | Fresh Sound Records | FSR 2044(Bethlehem BCP 51)

More And More Crazy
Lionel Hampton And His Orchestra | Lionel Hampton:Real Crazy | Vogue | 2113409-2

More Bells
James Blood Ulmer Group | Black Rock | CBS | 25064

More Blues
Project G-7 | Tribute To Wes Montgomery, Vol.2 | Paddle Wheel | KICJ 131

More Bounce To The Vonce
Carla Bley Sextet | Sextet | Watt | 17

More Brahms
Al Cohn-Zoot Sims Sextet | From A To Z | RCA | 2147790-2

More Colours
Eberhard Weber With The Südfunk Symphony Orchestra | Works | ECM | 825429-2

More Crazy
Lionel Hampton And His Orchestra | Lionel Hampton:Real Crazy | Vogue | 2113409-2

More Cymbals
Harry Pepl/Herbert Joos/Jon Christensen | Cracked Mirrors | ECM | 1356

More Far Out Than East
George Adams-Don Pullen Quartet | Earth Beams | Timeless | CD SJP 147

More For Less
Art Pepper Quartet | More For Less At The Village Vanguard Vol.4 | Original Jazz Classics | OJCCD 697-2(C 7650)

More For Less(alt.take)
Frank Marocco-Ray Pizzi Duo | New Colors | Trend | TR 516 Direct-to-Disc

More Gravy
Singers Unlimited | The Singers Unlimited:Magic Voices | MPS | 539130-2

More I Can Not Wish You
A Capella | MPS | 815671-1

More Love
Denise Jannah And Her Band | A Heart Full Of Music | Timeless | CD SJP 414

More Love Than Your Love
Thad Jones Quartet | Thad Jones | Original Jazz Classics | OJCCD 625-2(DEB 127)

More Moon
Woody Herman And His Orchestra | Woody Herman:Complete 1948-1950 Capitol Sessions | Definitive Records | DRCD 11195

More Of The Same
Thad Jones Quartet | The Fabulous Thad Jones | Prestige | MPP 2506
Donald Byrd Quintet | The Best Of The Jazz Trumpet | LRC Records | CDC 8516

More Pointing
Fats Waller And His Rhythm | The Indispensable Fats Waller Vol.5/6 | RCA | 2126416-2

More Power To You
Jim McNeely Quartet And The WDR Big Band | East Coast Blow Out | Lipstick Records | LIP 890072

More Soul
King Curtis Band | King Curtis-Blow Man Blow | Bear Family Records | BCD 15670 CI
Thomas Stabenow Quartet | Chiara | UJQ Production | 515201

More Streetprayers
Gerry Hemingway Quintet | Demon Chaser | Hat Art | CD 6137

More Than You Ever Know
Dexter Gordon With Orchestra | Strings & Things | Steeplechase | SCCD 31145
Hubert Nuss Trio | The Shimmering Colours Of The Stained Glass | Green House Music | CD 1008
Rosemary Clooney With The John Oddo Big Band | Girl Singer | Concord | CCD 4496

More Than You Know
Archie Shepp Quartet | Doodlin' | Inner City | IC 1001 IMS
Art Tatum Trio | The Tatum Group Masterpieces | Pablo | 2310735-2
Billy Taylor And His Orchestra | Solo | Taylor Made Records | T 1002
Dave Brubeck | Just You, Just Me | Telarc Digital | CD 83363
Ella Fitzgerald With The Frank DeVol Orchestra feat. Stan Getz | Ella Fitzgerald-First Lady Of Song | Verve | 517898-2
Elliot Lawrence And His Orchestra | The Uncollected:Elliot Lawrence | Hindsight | HSR 182
George Shearing Quintet & The Robert Farnon Orchestra | How Beautiful Is The Night | Telarc Digital | CD 83325

Jo Ann Strazzeri With The Frank Strazzeri Quartet | Presenting Jo Ann Strazzeri | Fresh Sound Records | FSR 109
Joe Pass | Solo Guitar | Pablo | 2310974-2
Joe Pass With The NDR Big Band | Joe Pass In Hamburg | ACT | 9100-2
Joe Venuti-Dave McKenna Duo | Alone At The Palace | Chiaroscuro | CR 160
Mel Tormé With The Marty Paich Dek-Tette | In Concert Tokyo | Concord | CCD 4382
Ove Lind Quintet feat. Lars Erstand | Joe Newman At The Atlantic | Phontastic | NCD 8810
Sarah Vaughan With The Lalo Schifrin Orchestra | Jazz Profile | Blue Note | 823517-2
Sarah Vaughan With The Oscar Peterson Quartet | How Long Has This Been Going On? | Pablo | 2310821-2
Schlüter-Nabatov-Antolini | Swing Kings | ACT | 9298-2
Shirley Horn Trio | Violets For Your Furs | Steeplechase | SCCD 31164
Shirley Scott Trio | Like Cozy | Prestige | PCD 24258-2
Sonny Criss Quintet | Jazz-U.S.A. | Blue Note | 300013(TOCJ 6127)
Stacey Kent And Her Quintet | Close Your Eyes | Candid | CCD 79737
Stan Kenton And His Orchestra | The Ballad Style Of Stan Kenton | Blue Note | 856688-2
Tatum-Hampton-Rich Trio | The Tatum Group Masterpieces | Pablo | 2625706
Teddy Wilson And His Orchestra | Rare And Unissued Recordings From The Golden Years,Vol.2 | Queen-Disc | 065

More Today Then Yesterday
Charles Earland Sextet | Charlie's Greatest Hits | Prestige | PCD 24250-2
Charlie's Greatest Hits | Prestige | PCD 24250-2
Leni Stern Group | Ten Songs | Lipstick Records | LIP 890092

More Tuna
Birdland Dream Band | Birdland Dream Band | RCA | 2663873-2

More West
Maynard Ferguson With The Birdland Dreamband | The Birdland Dream Band Vol.1 | Fresh Sound Records | 58110 CD(RCA)

More(Theme From Mondo Cane)
Wes Montgomery With The Don Sebesky Orchestra | California Dreaming | Verve | 827842-2

More, More, Amor
Toshinori Kondo/Tristan Honsinger Group | This That And The Other | ITM Records | 0021

Morenito
Renaud Garcia-Fons | Légendes | Enja | ENJ-9314 2

Moreno
Charles Earland Orchestra | Charlie's Greatest Hits | Prestige | PCD 24250-2

Morgan
Charles Earland Sextet | Charles Earland In Concert | Prestige | PRCD 24267-2
Howard Rumsey's Lighthouse All-Stars | Sunday Jazz A La Lighthouse,Vol.1 | Original Jazz Classics | OJC 151(C 3501)

Morgan The Pirate
Lee Morgan Sextet | Search For The New Land | Blue Note | 84169

Morgen
Ulli Bögershausen | Ageless Guitar Solos | Laika Records | 8695071

Morgen Ist Alles Wieder Gut
Christmas Carols | Laika Records | 35101622

Morgen Kinder Wird's Was Geben
New Orleans Quarter | Christmas Jazz | New Orleans Quarter Records | NOQR-V-DIV-CD 2

Morgen Nehme Ich Dein Foto Von Der Wand
Brass Attack | Brecht Songs | Tutu Records | 888190-2*

Morgenchoral Des Peachum
Erdmann 2000 | Recovering From y2k | Jazz 4 Ever Records:Jazz Network | J4E 4750

Morgengrauen In Hafen Von Piräus
Blue Collar | Diary Of A Working Band | Jazz Haus Musik | JHM 0089 CD

Morgenlied
Heiner Goebbels/Alfred Harth | Berold Brecht:Zeit wird knapp | Riskant | 568-72414

Morgenstern
Charly Antolini Jazz Power | Bop Dance | BELL Records | BLR 84043

Morgonlat
Rein De Graaff-Dick Vennik Sextet | Jubilee | Timeless | CD SJP 294

Moriba Ka Foly
$$hide$$ | $$Titelverweise | |

Moritat(Mack The Knife) -> Mack The Knife(Moritat)

Mormorio
Al Jarreau With Band | Jarreau | i.e. Music | 557847-2

Mornin'
Bill Evans Trio | Bill Evans Trio:The Last Waltz | Milestone | 8MCD 4430-2

Mornin' Glory
Bill Evans Live In Tokyo | CBS | 481265-2

Mornin', Noon And Night
Bill Dixon Sextet | Bill Dixon In Italy-Volume One | Soul Note | 121008-2

Morning
Clare Fischer Septet | Salsa Picante | MPS | 68209
Poncho Sanchez And His Orchestra | Poncho | Discovery | DS 799 IMS

Morning Air
Claude Bolling | Jazz In Paris:Claude Bolling Plays Original Piano Greats | EmArCy | 548151-2 PMS
Louis Mazetier | The Piano Starts Talking | Jazz Connaisseur | JCCD 0243-2
Morton Gunnar Larsen | Maple Leaf Rag | Herman Records | HJCD 1009

Morning Bird Call
Jesse Fuller | San Francisco Bay Blues | Good Time Jazz | 10051

Morning Blues
Stephan Micus | Towards The Wind | ECM | 1804(159453-2)

Morning Breeze
James Blood Ulmer Quartet | Tales Of Captain Black | DIW | DIW 403 CD

Morning Coffee
Spyro Gyra | Access All Areas | MCA | 2292-51215-1

Morning Dew
Larry Carlton Group | The Gift | GRP | GRP 98542

Morning Dove
Peggy Stern Trio | Pleiades | Philology | W 82.2

Morning Dove Blues
Stan Getz With The Eddie Sauter Orchestra | Stan Getz Plays The Music Of Mickey One | Verve | 531232-2

Morning Ecstasy(Under The Scaffold)
Stan Getz Plays The Music Of Mickey One | Verve | 531232-2
The Hot Club Swing Stars | Le Jazz En France Vol.13:Alix Combelle 1937-1940(Tome 1) | Pathe | 1552591

Morning Fire-
Andrew Hill Trio | Invitation | Steeplechase | SCCD 31026

Morning Fun
Zoot Sims-Bob Brookmeyer Quintet | Morning Fun | Black Lion | BLCD 760914

Morning Glory
Bill Evans Trio | The Tokyo Concert | Original Jazz Classics | OJCCD 345-2
Bill Evans:The Secret Sessions | Milestone | 8MCD 4421-2
Bill Evans-Eddie Gomez Duo | Bill Evans:Piano Player | CBS | CK 65361
Bob Brookmeyer With The Metropole Orchestra | Out Of This World | Koch Jazz | 3-6913-2
Duke Ellington And His Famous Orchestra | Duke Ellington:Ko-Ko | Dreyfus Jazz Line | FDM 36717-2
Duke Ellington And His Orchestra | Duke Ellington's Masterpieces Vol.1: 1938-1940 | Black & Blue | BLE 59.233 2
James Moody Quartet | Feelin' It Together | Muse | MCD 5020

Morning Heavy Song
Myriam Alter Quintet | Silent Walk | Challenge | CHR 70035

Morning Lake
Weather Report | Weather Report | CBS | 468212-2

Morning Lake Forever
Foday Musa Suso | The Dreamtime | CMP Records | CMP CD 3001

Morning Light
Patrick Bebelaar Quartet | You Never Lose An Island | dml-records | CD 015

Morning Light-
Jimmy Rowles-Eric Von Essen | Lilac Time | Kokopelli Records | KOKO 1297

Morning Of The Carnival
Rodney Jones/Tommy Flanagan Quartet | My Funny Valentine | Timeless | CD SJP 162

Morning Prayer
Rebecka Gordon Quartet | Yiddish'n Jazz | Touché Music | TMcCD 014
Tom Harrell Group | Paradise | RCA | 2663738-2

Morning Prayer(part)
Paradise | RCA | 2663738-2

Morning Prayer(part 1)
LeeAnn Ledgerwood Trio | Transition | Steeplechase | SCCD 31468

Morning Rain
Tom Scott Group | Steamline | GRP | GRP 95552

Morning Song
David Murray Quartet | I Want To Talk About You | Black Saint | 120105-2
George Cables Sextet | Cables Vision | Original Jazz Classics | C 14001
Jens Bunge Group | Meet You In Chicago | Jazz 4 Ever Records:Jazz Network | J4E 4749
John G. Smith Quartet | Roadside Picnic | RCA | PD 74002
Klaus Weiss Big Band | Lightnin' | Jeton | ???
The Brecker Brothers | Score | Jazz Door | JD 1211

Morning Sprite
Aki Takase Quintet | St.Louis Blues | Enja | 9130-2

Morning Star
Stanley Cowell | Angel Eyes | Steeplechase | SCCD 31339

Morning Sun
Klaus Doldinger & Passport | Lifelike | Warner | 2292-46478-2
Passport | Infinity Machine | Atlantic | 2292-44146-2
Mary Johnson | St.Louis Girls(1929-1937) | Story Of Blues | CD 3536-2

Morning Talk
Christoph Oeding Trio | Pictures | Mons Records | MR 874829

Morning(part 1)
Gary Burton Quartet | Gary Burton/Larry Coryell | RCA | FXL 17101

Morning(part 2)
Temperance Seven | The Writing On The Wall | Upbeat Jazz | URCD 108

Moro Lasso
La Vienta | Jazzmenco | Telarc Digital | CD 83353

Morpheus
Miles Davis Sextet | Welcome To Jazz: Miles Davis | Koch Records | 321 944 D1

Morphing
Shorty Rogers And His Giants | Shorty Rogers-Shorty's Greatest Hits | RCA | ???

Morpho
Short Stops | RCA | NL 85917(2)

Morpion
Paul Motian And The E.B.B.B. | Holiday For Strings | Winter&Winter | 910069-2
Caterina Zapponi With The Monty Alexander Quartet | Universal Lovesongs | Inak | 9062

Mortal Stone
A.Spencer Barefield Group | After The End | Sound Aspects | sas CD 030

Mortgage Stomp
Members Of The Basie Band | Lester Young:The Complete 1936-1951 Small Group Sessions(Studio Recordings-Master Takes),Vol.6 Rare Items | Blue Moon | BMCD 1006

Mort's Report
Fode Youla And African Djole | Basikolo | FMP | SAJ 48

Mosaic
Clifford Jordan Quintet | Mosaic | Milestone | MCD 47092-2
Starting Time | Original Jazz Classics | OJC 147(J 952)

Mosher
Jimmy Giuffre Trio | Night Dance | Choice | CHCD 71001

Mosquito Dance
The Jimmy Giuffre 3 | Music For People,Birds,Butterflies & Mosquitoes | Candid | CRS 1001 IMS

Mosquito Knees
Stan Getz Quintet | Jazz At Storyville Vol.1 | Fresh Sound Records | FSR 629(Roost RLP 407)

Most Beautiful Girl
| Moonlight On The Ganges | Red Records | 123264-2

Most Wanted
Der Rote Bereich | Der Rote Bereich 3 | Jazz 4 Ever Records:Jazz Network | J4E 4740

Most Wanted Marathon Weekend
Larry Vuckovich Quintet | Blues For Red | Hot House Records | HH 1001 IMS

Motel
Gerry Mulligan Concert Jazz Band | Swiss Radio Days Jatt Sries Vol.12:Gerry Mulligan And The Concert Jazz Big Band | TCB Records | TCB 02122
Miles Davis Quintet | Ascenseur Pour LÉchafaud | Fontana | 836305-2
Gerry Mulligan Quartet | Gerry Mulligan:Pleyel Concert Vol.2 | Vogue | 21409432

Motel-
Larry Coryell | Bolero | String | BLE 233850

Motel(alt.take)
Benny Moten's Kansas City Orchestra | Bennie Moten Vol.1 | Zeta | ZET 750

Moten Shake
Bennie Moten Vol.1 | Zeta | ZET 750

Moten Swing
Andy Kirk And His Twelve Clouds Of Joy | Big Band Bounce & Boogie-Andy Kirk And His Clouds Of Joy:Walkin' & Swingin' | Affinity | AFS 1011
Barrett Deems Big Band | Groovin' Hard | Delmark | DE 505
Benny Goodman And His Orchestra | All Of Me | Black Lion | 127034
Benny Moten's Kansas City Orchestra | Victor Jazz History Vol.9:Kansas City(1926-32) | RCA | 2128563-2
The Complete Bennie Moten Vol.5/6 | RCA | PM 45688
Charly Antolini Jazz Power | Recorded At The BBC Studio London | BELL Records | BLR 84042
Claude Williams Quintet | Call For The Fiddler | Steeplechase | SCCD 31051
Count Basie And His Orchestra | Count On The Coast Vol.1 | Phontastic | NCD 7555
Breakfast Dance And Barbecue | Roulette | 531791-2
Atomic Swing | Roulette | 497871-2
Me And You | Pablo | 2310891-2
Danny Moss Quartet | Keeper Of The Flame | Nagel-Heyer | CD 064
Dick Hafer Quartet | Prez Impressions-Dedicated To The Memory Of Lester Young | Fresh Sound Records | FSR-CD 5002
Elliot Lawrence And His Orchestra | The Elliot Lawrence Big Band Swings Cohn & Kahn | Fantasy | FCD 24761-2
Frank Capp-Nat Pierce Orchestra | Juggernaut | Concord | CCD 4040
Harry James And His Orchestra | Sounds Familiar | Saville Records | SVL 151 IMS
James Morrison-Ray Brown Quartet | Two The Max | East-West | 9031-77125-2
Jay McShann And His Orchestra | Early Bird | Spotlite | SPJ 120
Oscar Peterson Trio | Night Train | Verve | 821724-2
The International Jazz Group | The International Jazz Group | Swing | SW 8407 IMS
The New York Allstars | Broadway | Nagel-Heyer | CD 003
The Newport Jazz Festival All-Stars | The Newport Jazz Festival All-Stars | Concord | CJ 260

Moten Swing(rehersal take)
Robben Ford & The Blue Line | Mystic Line | Stretch Records | GRS 00082

Mother Earth
Memphis Slim | All Kinds Of Blues | Original Blues Classics | OBC-507(BV 1053)
Norbert Stein Pata Orchester | Ritual Life | Pata Musik | PATA 5(JHM 50) CD
Pianekdrum(The Accoustic Trio) | The Rainbow Suite-Live | Edition Collage | EC 473-2

Mother Fonk
Natraj | The Goat Also Gallops | Dorian Discovery | DIS 80124

Mother Goose Marches On
Mongo Santamaria Orchestra | Olé Ola | Concord | CCD 4387

Mother Nature
Things | Mother Nature | Jazzpoint | JP 1028 CD
Uli Harmssen/Jochen Voss Duo | Mother Nature Father Harmony | Inak | 863

Mother Nature's Blues
Pete York Group | String Time In New York | BELL Records | BLR 84015

Mother Of Earl
Bill Evans Trio | At The Montreux Jazz Festival | Verve | 539758-2
Bill Evans Trio:The Last Waltz | Milestone | 8MCD 4430-2
Verve Jazz Masters 5:Bill Evans | Verve | 519821-2
Ultimate Bill Evans selected by Herbie Hancock | Verve | 557536-2
Diederik Wissels-Steve Houben Quartet | Juvia | Timeless | SJP 218

Mother Of Light
Al Jolson With Orchestra | Al Jolson-Great Original Performances(1926-1932) | CDS Records Ltd. | RPCD 300

Mother Of The Dead Man
Gary Burton Quartet | Gary Burton/Larry Coryell | RCA | FXL 17101

Mother Of The Dead Man-
Charles Davis Quartet | Super 80 | Nilva | NQ 3410 IMS

Mother Song
Kazumi Watanabe Groups | Kylyn | Denon Compact Disc | 35C38-7135

Mother Tongues
John McLaughlin Trio | Live At The Royal Festival Hall | JMT Edition | 834436-2

Mother: Sarah Brown-Smith-Wallace
Roy Hargrove Quintet | Of Kindred Souls:Live | Novus | 4163154-2

Mother-In-Law Blues
Memphis Piano Red | Living Country Blues USA Vol.4:Tennessee Blues | L+R Records | LR 42034

Motherland Pulse
Steve Coleman Quintet | Jump On It | Enja | 4094

Motherless Child
Memphis Slim | Raining The Blues | Fantasy | FCD 24705-2

Motherless Child -> Sometimes I Feel Like A Motherless Child

Mother's Blues
Leadbelly[Huddie Ledbetter] | Alabamy Bound | Memo Music | HDJ 4073

Mother's Day Blues
Henk De Jonge Trio With Willem Breuker | Henk De Jonge Trio | BVHAAST | 058

Mother's Eyes
Hannibal Marvin Peterson Group | The Angels Of Atlanta | Enja | 3085-2

Motion
Howard Riley Trio | Flight | FMR | FMR CD 26
Klaus Suonsaari Quartet | True Colours | L+R Records | CDLR 45080

Motion Suspended
Fritz Hauser Duo | Zwei | Hat Art | CD 6010

Motivation
Peter Brötzmann/Alfred 23 Harth | Go-No-Go | FMP | 1150

Motive For Its Use
Jack Walrath-Miles Griffith With The WDR Big Band | Get Hit In Your Soul | ACT | 9246-2

Moto Perpetuo(Paganini)
Mark Helias/Gerry Hemingway/Ray Anderson | Bassdrumbone(Hence The Reason) | Enja | ENJ-9322 2

Moto Proto
Charly Antolini Quintet | Crash | BELL Records | BLR 84002

Motorin' Along
Jimmy Smith Trio | Home Cookin' | Blue Note | 853360-2

Motorin' Along(alt.take)
James Carter Group | Layin' In The Cut | Atlantic | 7567-83305-2

Motown Mash
Elisabet Raspall Grup | Lila | Fresh Sound Records | FSNT 058 CD

Mots Muts
Jean-Marc Montera | Hang Around Shout | FMP | CD 71

Moulin Rouge
Dan Barrett And His Extra-Celestials | Moon Song | Arbors Records | ARCD 19158

Mound Bayou
Humphrey Lyttelton-Acker Bilk Band | More Humph & Acker | Calligraph | CLGCD 030

Mount Everest
Duke Ellington And His Orchestra | Duke Ellington's Far East Suite | RCA | 2174797-2

Mount Harissa
Eric Vloeiman Quartet | Bitches And Fairy Tales | Challenge | CHR 70061

Mount Olive
Andy Middleton Group | Nomad's Notebook | Intuition Records | INT 3264-2

Mount Rundle
Ed Schuller & Band | The Eleventh Hour | Tutu Records | 888124-2*

Mountain-
Sandy Williams' Big Eight | Giants Of Small-Band Swing Vol.2 | Original Jazz Classics | OJCCD 1724-2

Mountain Blues
Washboard Sam & His Washboard Band | Harmonica And Washboard Blues | Black & Blue | BLE 59.252 2

Mountain Dance
Peter Herbolzheimer Rhythm Combination & Brass | Friends And Sihouettes | Koala Records | CD P 25

Mountain Greenery
Betty Bennett And Her Orchestra | Nobody Else But Me-Betty Bennett Sings The Arrangements Of Shorty Rogers & André Previn | Atlantic | AMCY 1065
Dave Pell Octet | The Dave Pell Octet Plays Again | Fresh Sound Records | FSR-CD 5009
Ella Fitzgerald With The Buddy Bregman Orchestra | The Rodgers And Hart Songbook | Verve | 821693-1
The Complete Ella Fitzgerald Song Books of Harold Arlen, Irving Berlin, Duke Ellington, George & Ira Gershwin, Jerome Kern, Johnny Mercer, Cole Porter And Rogers & Hart | Verve | 519832-2
Henri Renaud-Al Cohn Quartet | Cohn's Delight | Vogue | 655011
Shorty Rogers And His Orchestra | Shorty Rogers Plays Richard Rodgers | Fresh Sound Records | NL 45645(RCA LPM 1428)
Sylvia Syms With The Barbara Carroll Trio | Sylvia Syms Sings | Atlantic | AMCY 1076

Mountain In The Clouds
Abdullah Ibrahim Trio With The Munich Radio Symphony Orchestra | African Symphony | Enja | ENJ-9410 2

Mountain In The Night
Ma Rainey With Jimmy Blythe | Ma Rainey | Milestone | MCD 47021-2

Mountain Morning
Lynne Arriale Trio | Inspiration | TCB Records | TCB 22102

Mountain Speaks
David Friesen Quartet/Trio/Duo/Solo | Star Dance | Inner City | IC 1019 IMS

Mountain Talk
Steve Morse Band | The Introduction | Elektra | 960369-1

Mountains Polka
Barre Phillips Quartet | Mountainscapes | ECM | 1076

Mountainscape I
Mountainscapes | ECM | 1076

Mountainscape II
Mountainscapes | ECM | 1076

Mountainscape III
Mountainscapes | ECM | 1076

Mountainscape IV
Mountainscapes | ECM | 1076

Mountainscape V
Mountainscapes | ECM | 1076

Mountainscape VI
Mountainscapes | ECM | 1076

Mountainscape VII
Barre Phillips Quintet | Mountainscapes | ECM | 1076

Mountainscape VIII
Lu Watters' Yerba Buena Jazz Band | Lu Watters' Yerba Buena Jazz Band At Hambone Kelly's 1949-50 | Merry Makers Record | MMRC-CD-10

Mour
Booker Ervin Quintet | The In Between | Blue Note | 859379-2

Mournful
Jelly Roll Morton Quartet | The Jelly Roll Morton Centennial-His Complete Victor Recordings | Bluebird | ND 82361

Mourning Grace
John Hicks Trio | East Side Blues | DIW | DIW 828 CD

Mouse
Stivin-Van Den Broeck-Haurand | Bordertalk | Konnex Records | KCD 5068
Directors | Directors | Jazz Haus Musik | JHM 0040 CD

Mouse In History
Ensemble FisFüz | SimSim | Peregrina Music | PM 50211

Mousing-
Marilyn Crispell Trio | Highlights From The Summer Of 1992 American Tour | Music & Arts | CD 758

Mouwasha Arjii Ya Alfa Layla
Mahmoud Turkmani Group | Zakira | Enja | ENJ-9475 2

Mouwasha Aytatouhou Ma Sala
Zakira | Enja | ENJ-9475 2

Mouwasha Imlalil Aqdaha
Mahmoud Turkmani | Fayka | Enja | ENJ-9447 2

Mouwasha Lamma Bada
Mahmoud Turkmani Group | Zakira | Enja | ENJ-9475 2

Mouwasha Nozuhatoul Arwah
Zakira | Enja | ENJ-9475 2

Mouwasha Zanalil Mahboub
All Star Live Jam Session | Brownie-The Complete EmArCy Recordings Of Clifford Brown | EmArCy | 838306-2

Move
Antonio Petrocca Trio | But Not For Me | Edition Musikat | EDM 047
Art Pepper Plus Eleven | Art Pepper + Eleven | Contemporary | CSA 7568-6
Modern Jazz Classics | Original Jazz Classics | OJC20 341-2
A Treasury Of Modern Jazz Classics | Mobile Fidelity | MFCD 805
Charlie Parker Quintet | One Night At Birdland | CBS | CBS 88250
Earl Coleman-Fats Navarro Quintet | Fats Navarro:The 1946-1949 Small Group Sessions(Studio Recordings-Master Takes),Vol.3 | Blue Moon | BMCD 1018
George Shearing And His Quintet | Combo USA | Affinity | CD AFS 1002
Jeff Hamilton Trio | Hands On | Mons Records | MR 874812
Klaus Doldinger's Passport | Klaus Doldinger Passport Live | Warner | 8573-84132-2
Lee Konitz-Warne Marsh Septet | Lee Konitz:Move | Moon Records | MCD 057-2
Miles Davis And His Orchestra | New York All Star Sessions | Bandstand | BDCD 1507
The Complete Birth Of The Cool | Capitol | 494550-2
The Complete Birth Of The Cool | Capitol | 494550-2
Birth Of The Cool | Capitol | 530117-2
Miles Davis:The Blue Note And Capitol Recordings | Blue Note | 827475-2
Miles Davis Nonet | Cool Boppin' | Fresh Sound Records | FSCD 1008
Stan Getz Quintet | Jazz At Storyville Vol.1 | Fresh Sound Records | FSR 629(Roost RLP 407)
Wardell Gray's Los Angeles All Stars | Dexter Gordon Birthday Celebration | Fantasy | FANCD 6082-2
Charlie Parker Quintet | Charlie Parker 1950-1951:The Complete Bird At Birdland Vol.1 | Fat Boy Jazz | FBB 901

Move Me
Jean-Paul Bourelly Group | Vibe Music | PAO Records | PAO 10500

Move The Body Over
Sammy Rimington With Ken Pye's Creole Serenaders | The Whitewater Session | p.e.k.Sound | PKCD 071

Move Toward The Light
Savannah Jazz Band | It's Only A Beautiful Picture | Lake | LACD 51

Move(für Ina)
Marty Ehrlich Group | The Long View | Enja | ENJ-9452 2

Movemenet IV
Bobby Hutcherson Sextet | Components | Blue Note | 829027-2

Movement
Misha Alperin Group With The Brazz Brothers | Portrait | JA & RO | JARO 4227-2
Max Roach With The New Orchestra Of Boston | Max Roach | Blue Note | 834813-2

Movement I
Marty Ehrlich Group | The Long View | Enja | ENJ-9452 2

Movement II
The Long View | Enja | ENJ-9452 2

Movement III
The Long View | Enja | ENJ-9452 2

Movement V
The Long View | Enja | ENJ-9452 2

Movement VI
Frank Gratkowski Trio | Gestalten | Jazz Haus Musik | JHM 0083 CD

Movements
Thomas Stiffling Group | Stories | Jazz 4 Ever Records:Jazz Network | J4E 4756
Stories | Jazz 4 Ever Records:Jazz Network | J4E 4756

Movements(pocket radio edition)
Jasper Van't Hof | Un Mondo Illusorio | Challenge | CHR 70059

Movie Eight
Michael Mantler Group | Movies/More Movies | Watt | 7/10(543377-2)
Michael Mantler Sextet | More Movies | Watt | 10 (2313110)

Movie Eleven
More Movies | Watt | 10 (2313110)

Movie Fifteen
Michael Mantler Group | Movies | Watt | 7 (2313107)

Movie Five
Movies/More Movies | Watt | 7/10(543377-2)
Movies | Watt | 7 (2313107)

Movie Four
Movies/More Movies | Watt | 7/10(543377-2)
Michael Mantler Sextet | More Movies | Watt | 10 (2313110)

Movie Fourteen
More Movies | Watt | 10 (2313110)

Movie Nine
Michael Mantler Group | Movies | Watt | 7 (2313107)

Movie One
Movies/More Movies | Watt | 7/10(543377-2)
Movies | Watt | 7 (2313107)

Movie Seven
Movies/More Movies | Watt | 7/10(543377-2)
Movies | Watt | 7 (2313107)

Movie Six
Movies/More Movies | Watt | 7/10(543377-2)
Miles Davis Group | Miles Davis Live From His Last Concert In Avignon | Laserlight | 24327

Movie Star
Michael Mantler Sextet | More Movies | Watt | 10 (2313110)

Movie Ten
More Movies | Watt | 10 (2313110)

Movie Thirteen
Michael Mantler Group | Movies | Watt | 7 (2313107)

Movie Three
Movies/More Movies | Watt | 7/10(543377-2)
Michael Mantler Sextet | More Movies | Watt | 10 (2313110)

Movie Twelve
Michael Mantler Group | Movies | Watt | 7 (2313107)

Movie Two
Movies/More Movies | Watt | 7/10(543377-2)
Andres Boiarsky Septet | Into The Light | Reservoir | RSR CD 149

Movin' Along
Wes Montgomery Quintet | Wes Montgomery-The Complete Riverside Recordings | Riverside | 12 RCD 4408-2
Wes Montgomery Trio | Portrait Of Wes | Original Jazz Classics | OJCCD 144-2
Wes Montgomery-The Complete Riverside Recordings | Riverside | 12 RCD 4408-2
Wes Montgomery Quintet | Wes Montgomery-The Complete Riverside Recordings | Riverside | 12 RCD 4408-2

Movin' Along(alt.take)
The Alternative Wes Montgomery | Milestone | MCD 47065-2

Movin' And Groovin'
Babs Gonzales Group | Properly Presenting Babs Gonzales | Fresh Sound Records | FSR 702(835422)

Movin' On
Jimmy McGriff Quintet | The Starting Five | Milestone | MCD 9148-2

Movin' On Out
Luther Allison Blues Band | South Side Safari | Red Lightnin' | RL 0036

Movin' Out
Brownie McGhee & Sticks McGhee | Circle Blues Session | Southland | SCD 9

Movin' Up
The Ritz | Movin' Up | Denon Compact Disc | CY-72526

Movin' Wes(part 1)
Wes Montgomery With The Johnny Pate Orchestra | Talkin' Jazz:Roots Of Acid Jazz | Verve | 529580-2
Compact Jazz: Wes Montgomery | Verve | 831372-2

Movin' Wes(part 2)
Talkin' Jazz:Roots Of Acid Jazz | Verve | 529580-2
Compact Jazz: Wes Montgomery | Verve | 831372-2

Movin' With Lester
Lester Young Sextet | Lester Young:The Complete 1936-1951 Small Group Sessions(Studio Recordings-Master Takes),Vol.4 | Blue Moon | BMCD 1004

Moving
Thomas Francke Group | Rabiator | G.N.U. Records | CD A 96.086

Moving Beauty
Jon Balke w/Magnetic North Orchestra | Further | ECM | 1517

Moving Carpet
European Tuba Quartet | Low And Behold | Jazz Haus Musik | JHM 0110 CD

Moving Clusters
Ronnie Taheny Group | Briefcase | Laika Records | 35101152

Moving Door
Hans Lüdemann | The Natural Piano | Jazz Haus Musik | JHM 0075 CD

Moving Hearts
Moving Hearts | West Wind | WW 2085

Moving Out
Barney Wilen Quintet | Barney Wilen Quintet | Fresh Sound Records | FSR-CD 0048
Joe Haider Trio | A Magyar-The Hungarian-Die Ungarische | JHM Records | JHM 3626
Sonny Rollins Quintet | Moving Out | Original Jazz Classics | OJC 058(P 7058)

Moving Pictures For The Ear
Foday Musa Suso | The Dreamtime | CMP Records | CMP CD 3001

Moving Somewhere
Keith Jarrett Trio | Somewhere Before | Atlantic | 7567-81455-2

Moving Soon
The Ethnic Heritage Ensemble | Three Gentleman From Chicago | Moers Music | 01076

Mozaik
Drumming Birds | East Side | ITM Records | ITM 1415

Mozambique
Michel Portal-Richard Galliano | Concerts | Dreyfus Jazz Line | FDM 36661-2
Never Been There | Ambience | VeraBra Records | CDVBR 2030-2

Mozart Matriculates
Cannonball Adderley-Nat Adderley Sextet | The Adderley Brothers In New Orleans | Milestone | M 9030

Mozart-In'
Ellis Marsalis Quartet | Whistle Stop | CBS | 474555-2

Mozy's Land
Eric St.Laurent & Osmose | Eric St-Laurent & Osmose | BIT | 11190

Mr. 4,5 Volt
Lee Konitz Quintet | Sound Of Surprise | RCA | 2169309-2

Mr. 88
Larry Garner Group | Too Blues | JSP Records | JSPCD 249

Mr. And Mrs. People
Ralph Abelein Group | Mr. B's Time Machine | Satin Doll Productions | SDP 1042-1 CD

Mr. B's Time Machine
Michel Camilo Trio | Triangulo | Telarc Digital | CD 83549

Mr. G's Stepping Shoes
Funky Groove | Funky Groove | EmArCy | 536043-2

Mr. Omaha
Jazz Pistols | Special Treatment | Lipstick Records | LIP 8971-2

Mr. Smithers
Vital Information | Show 'Em Where You Live | Intuition Records | INT 3306-2

Mr. T.C.
Jeff Gardner Trio | The Music Must Change:Jazz Compositions Inspired By The Works Of Paul Auster | Naive | 225079

Mr. Wu
Willie Rodriguez Jazz Quartet | Flatjacks | Milestone | MCD 9331-2

Mr. Yosso
Tania Maria Trio | Live | Accord | 112552

Mr.& Mrs. Hankerchief
Taylor's Wailers | Mr. A.T. | Enja | ENJ-7017 2

Mr.A.T.
Art Taylor's Wailers | Wailin' At The Vanguard | Verve | 519677-2

Mr.A.T.(alt.take)
Peter Herbolzheimer Orchestra | Music For Swinging Dancers,Vol.1:You Make Me Feel So Young | Koala Records | CD P 8

Mr.B
Kent Sangster Quartet | Adventures | Jazz Focus | JFCD 006

Mr.Big Falls His J.G. Hand
Art Pepper Quintet | One September Afternoon | Original Jazz Classics | OJCCD 678-2(GXY 5141)

Mr.Blakey
The Hi-Lo's | Now | MPS | 68264

Mr.Blues
Lil' Son Jackson With Band | Rockin' And Rollin' | Pathe | 1546671(Imperial)

Mr.Bojangles
Jenny Evans And Band | Girl Talk | ESM Records | ESM 9306
Girl Talk | Enja | ENJ-9363 2
Live At The Allotria | BELL Records | BLR 90003
Defunkt | Defunkt/Heroes | DIW | DIW 838 CD

Mr.Broadway
Dave Brubeck Quartet | Collection Dave Brubeck | Atlantic | ATL 20269

Mr.Bruce
Larry Coryell-Alphonse Mouzon Quartet | Back Together Again | Atlantic | ATL 50382

Mr.Callahan
Steve Kuhn Trio | Life's Magic | Black-Hawk | BKH 522

Mr.Clean
Jack McDuff Quartet With Gene Ammons | Brother Jack Meets The Boss | Original Jazz Classics | OJCCD 326-2(P 7228)
Peter Herbolzheimer Rhythm Combination & Brass | Scejes | MPS | 68041
Richard Galliano Group | Laurita | Dreyfus Jazz Line | FDM 36572-9

Mr.Clifton
David Friedman Quartet | Of The Wind's Eye | Enja | ENJ-3089 2

Mr.Cool
Donald Harrison Sextet | Free To Be | Impulse(MCA) | 951283-2

Mr.Cool Breeze
Eddie Daniels Quartet | Under The Influence | GRP | GRP 97172

Mr.D.C.
John McLaughlin Group | The Heart Of Things | Verve | 539153-2
Marty Cook Group feat. Jim Pepper | Red,White,Black & Blue | Tutu Records | 888174-2*
Marty Cook Quartet | Red, White, Black And Blue | Enja | 5067-2

Mr.Day
Dave Liebman Quintet | Homage To John Coltrane | Owl Records | 018357-2
Harold Danko | After The Rain | Steeplechase | SCCD 31356
John Coltrane Quartet | Coltrane Plays The Blues | Rhino | 8122-79966-2
Coltrane Plays The Blues | Atlantic | 7567-81351-2
McCoy Tyner Trio | McCoy Tyner Plays John Coltrane | Impulse(MCA) | 589183-2
Scott Colley Trio | This Place | Steeplechase | SCCD 31443

Mr.Freddie Blues
Axel Zwingenberger | Boogie Woogie Classics | Vagabond | VRCD 8.92023
Axel Zwingenberger With The Lionel Hampton Big Band | The Boogie Woogie Album | Vagabond | VRCD 8.88008
Bob Hall Quartet | At The Window | Lake | LACD 23
Mary Lou Williams | Big Band Bounce & Boogie-The Boogie Woogie Masters | Affinity | AFS 1005
Axel Zwingenberger-Sam Price | Kansas City Boogie Jam | Vagabond | VRCD 8.00027

Mr.Freddie Boogie
Memphis Slim | Steady Rolling Blues | Original Blues Classics | OBCCD 523-2(BV 1075)

Mr.Freedom X
Henry Starr | Curtis Mosby And Henry Starr | Jazz Oracle | BDW 8003

Mr.Gentle And Mr.Cool
Ken Peplowski Quintet | Mr.Gentle And Mr.Cool | Concord | CCD 4419
McCoy Tyner Trio | The Early Trios | MCA | IA 9338/2

Mr.George
Dave Frishberg Quintet | Let's Eat Home | Concord | CCD 4402

Mr.Glime-Glide
Weather Report | Mr. Gone | CBS | 468208-2

Mr.Gone
Jimmy Hamilton Sextet | It's About Time | Prestige | 0902123(Swingville 2022)

Mr.Guitar Man
Eric Alexander Quartet | Two Of A Kind | Criss Cross | Criss 1133

Mr.Heine's Blues
Eladio Reinon Quintet | Es La Historia De Un Amor | Fresh Sound Records | FSNT 004 CD

Mr.Henderson
Das Böse Ding | Germ Germ | Acoustic Music Records | 319.1160.2

Mr.Hurt
Joe Lovano-Gonzalo Rubalcaba | Flying Colors | Blue Note | 856092-2

Mr.Hyde
Winard Harper Sextet | Winard | Savant Records | SCD 2021

Mr.J.D.(..sic!)
Peter Möltgen Quartet | Mellow Acid | Edition Collage | EC 495-2

Mr.J.L.M.
Zoot Sims Quintet | The Swinger | Pablo | 2310861

Mr.Jackson From Jacksonville
Art Hodes | Pagin' Mr.Jelly | Candid | CS 9037

Mr.Jelly Lord
Jelly Roll Morton Trio | Doctor Jazz | Black & Blue | BLE 59.227 2

Mr.Joe
Terri Lyne Carrington Group | Jazz Is A Spirit | ACT | 9408-2

Mr.Joe Jones
Lionel Hampton And His Orchestra | Lionel Hampton | Laserlight | 17068

Mr.Johnson
Lee Morgan Sextet | Sonic Boom | Blue Note | 590414-2
Elvin Jones Quartet | Live At The Village Vanguard | Enja | 2036-2

Mr.K.
Tony Lakatos With The Martin Sasse Trio | Feel Alright | Edition Collage | EC 494-2
Michel Petrucciani Trio | Michel Plays Petrucciani | Blue Note | 748679-2

Mr.K.J.
Hilton Ruiz Sextet | Live At Birdland | Candid | CCD 79532

Mr.Kenyatta
Peter Bernstein Quartet | Somethin's Burnin' | Criss Cross | Criss 1079

Mr.Kicks
John Coltrane Quartet | John Coltrane-The Heavyweight Champion:The Complete Atlantic Recordings | Atlantic | 8122-71984-2

Mr.Knight
Coltrane Plays The Blues | Rhino | 8122-79966-2
The Art Of John Coltrane - The Atlantic Years | Atlantic | SD 2-313
Curtis Fuller Sextet | Boss Of The Soul-Stream Trombone | Fresh Sound Records | FSR-CD 0209

Mr.Lampshade
Buddy DeFranco Quintet | Mr.Lucky | Pablo | 2310906

Mr.Lucky
Donald Byrd-Pepper Adams Quintet | Out Of This World-The Complete Warwick Sessions | Fresh Sound Records | FSR-CD 0137
Jack McDuff Quartet | Honeydripper | Original Jazz Classics | OJC 222(P 7199)
Strata Institute | Transmigration | DIW | DIW 860 CD

Mr.M
Nils Landgren First Unit And Guests | Nils Landgren-The First Unit | ACT | 9292-2
Bernard Purdie's Soul To Jazz | Bernard Purdie's Soul To Jazz II | ACT | 9253-2

Mr.Magic
Charles Earland Sextet | The Groove Masters Series | Savant Records | SCD 2008

Mr.Magoo
Charlie Mariano & The Karnataka College Of Percussion | Live | VeraBra Records | CDVBR 2034-2

Mr.Mani
Philippe Petit/Miroslav Vitous | Impressions Of Paris | EPM Musique | FDC 5524

Mr.Max
Nicolas Simion Group | Black Sea | Tutu Records | 888134-2*

Mr.McCoy
The Upper Manhattan Jazz Society | The Upper Manhattan Jazz Society | Enja | ENJ-4090 2

Mr.McGee
John Goldsby Sextet | Viewpoint | Nagel-Heyer | CD 2014

Mr.McGregor
Jimmy Greene Group | Brand New World | RCA | 2663564-2

Mr.Meadowlark
Fred Wesley And The Horny Horns | Say Blow By Blow Backwards | Sequel Records | NED CD 269

Mr.Mule
Martin Keller Quintet/Octet | Quintett/Oktett | yvp music | CD 3038

Mr.Music
Herb Geller Quartet | Playing Jazz:The Musical Autobiography Of Herb Geller | Fresh Sound Records | FSR-CD 5011

Mr.Mystery
John Tchicai-Pierre Dorge | Ball At Louisiana | Steeplechase | SCCD 31174

Mr.P
Bobby Watson Quartet | Perpetual Groove-Live In Europe | Red Records | VPA 173

Mr.P.C.

Doug Raney Quartet | Introducing Doug Raney | Steeplechase | SCS 1082
John Coltrane Quartet | Visit To Scandinavia | Jazz Door | JD 1210
John Coltrane-Live Trane:The European Tours | Pablo | 7PACD 4433-2
John Coltrane-Live Trane:The European Tours | Pablo | 7PACD 4433-2
The Complete 1962 Stockholm Concert Vol.1 | Magnetic Records | MRCD 108
Live In Stockholm 1963 | Charly | CD 33
The Copenhagen Concerts | Ingo | 4
Junior Cook Quintet | You Leave Me Breathless | Steeplechase | SCCD 31304
Von Freeman-Ed Petersen Quintet | Von & Ed | Delmark | DE 508
Wynton Kelly-George Coleman Quartet | Live In Baltimore | Affinity | AFF 108

Mr.P.C.(2)
Peter Weniger-Hubert Nuss | Private Concert | Mons Records | CD 1878

Mr.Paganini
Ella Fitzgerald And Her Quintet | Ella In Hollywood-Recorded Live At The Crescendo | Verve | V 6-4052 IMS
Ella Fitzgerald With The Hank Jones Trio | Ella Fitzgerald:The Royal Roost Sessions | Cool & Blue | C&B-CD 112
Ella Fitzgerald With The Lou Levy Quartet | Compact Jazz: Ella Fitzgerald | Verve | 831367-2
4 By 4:Ella Fitzgerald/Sarah Vaughan/Billie Holiday/Dinah Washington | Verve | 559693-2
Ella Fitzgerald With The Tommy Flanagan Trio | Jazz Collection:Ella Fitzgerald | Laserlight | 24397
Ella Fitzgerald In Budapest | Pablo | PACD 5308-2
Sandy Lomax With The Martin Schrack Trio | Songs From The Jazz Age | Workshop Records | WOR 201(CD 583)

Mr.Pastorius
Marcus Miller Group | The Sun Don't Lie | Dreyfus Jazz Line | FDM 36560-2
Miles Davis Group | Amandla | Warner | 7599-25873-2
Time After Time | Jazz Door | JD 1256/57

Mr.R.B.
Stephan Noel Lang Trio | Echoes | Nagel-Heyer | CD 2033

Mr.R.M.
Ambrose & His Orchestra | Champagne Cocktail | Ace Of Club | ACL 1246

Mr.Right
Count Basie And His Orchestra | Planet Jazz:Count Basie | Planet Jazz | 2152068-2

Mr.Roberts' Roost
Wayne Horvitz Group | Pigpen-V As In Victim | Avant | AVAN 027

Mr.Sandman
Joscho Stephan Group | Swinging Strings | Acoustic Music Records | 319.1195.2

Mr.Spirit
Tony Williams Lifetime | Tony Williams Lifetime-The Collection | CBS | 468924-2

Mr.Steepee
Olivier Peters Quartet Feat.Joan Johnson | Wings Of Spring | Village Music | VM 1002

Mr.Stinky's Blues
Harold Mabern Trio | Straight Street | DIW | DIW 608 CD

Mr.Syms
Billy Bang Quartet | Bang On! | Justin Time | JUST 105-2
Jessica Williams | The Victoria Concert | Jazz Focus | JFCD 015
John Coltrane Quartet | Coltrane Plays The Blues | Rhino | 8122-79966-2
The Very Best Of John Coltrane | Rhino | 8122-79778-2
Coltrane Plays The Blues | Atlantic | 7567-81351-2
Mark Whitfield Group | True Blue | Verve | 523591-2

Mr.Tambourine Man
David Matthews Trio With Gary Burton | American Pie | Sweet Basil | 660.55.005

Mr.Thomas
Alice Day With The Andy Scherrer Quartet | CoJazz Plus | TCB Records | TCB 96052

Mr.Unison
Roni Ben-Hur Trio | Sofia's Butterfly | TCB Records | TCB 98802

Mr.Walker
Wes Montgomery With The Don Sebesky Orchestra | Talkin' Jazz:Roots Of Acid Jazz | Verve | 529580-2
California Dreaming | Verve | 827842-2
Randy Burns-Emery Fletcher | Of Love And War | ESP Disk | ESP 1039-2

Mr.Wonderful
Red Garland Quartet | Rojo | Original Jazz Classics | OJCCD 772-2(P 7193)

Mr.Wonsey
Ragtime Specht Groove Trio | Mr. Woodpeckers Special | Intercord | 130001

Mr.Yohe
Eddie Harris Sextet | A Study In Jazz/Breakfast At Tiffany's | Vee Jay Recordings | VJ 020

Mrs. Scofield's Waltz
Robert Zollitsch Group | First Catalogue | KlangRäume | 30170

Mrs.D.P.-
Greg Tardy Band | Crazy Love | DuBat Music | CD 26293

Mrs.Miniver
Keith Smith With George Lewis' Jazz Band | A Portrait Of Keith Smith 'Mr.Hefty Jazz' | Lake | LACD 67

Mrs.Parker Of K.C.
Eric Dolphy-Booker Little Quintet | Eric Dolphy:The Complete Prestige Recordings | Prestige | 9 PRCD-4418-2
Harold Danko Trio | Fantasy Exit | Steeplechase | SCCD 31530
David Xirgu Quartet | Idolents | Fresh Sound Records | FSNT 077 CD

Mrs.PC
Buddy Collette Quintet | Everybody's Buddy | Fresh Sound Records | FSR 506(Challenge CHL 603)

Ms. Raymona's House
Steve Wilson Quintet | Blues For Marcus | Criss Cross | Criss 1073

Ms.Shirley Scott
Craig Handy Quintet | Split Second Timing | Arabesque Recordings | AJ 0101

M-Squad Theme
Dollar Brand-Johnny Dyani Duo | Good News From Africa | Enja | 2048-2

Mt. Zion
George Benson Group/Orchestra | George Benson Anthology | Warner | 8122-79934-2

Mt.Airy Road
Miles Davis Group | Get Up With It | CBS | 485256-2

MTV-Revolution Handmade Version
Wollie Kaiser Timeghost | Post Art Core | Jazz Haus Musik | JHM 0077 CD

MTV-Revolution Nomal Version
Alex De Grassi Quintet | Altiplano | RCA | PL 83016

Mu
Sun Ra And His Astro-Infinity Arkestra | Atlantis | Evidence | ECD 22067-2

Much More
Bob Howard And His Band | Jazz Museum-Bunny Berigan 1936 | MCA | 52067 (801842)

Much Too Late
National Youth Jazz Orchestra | These Are The Jokes | Ronnie Scott's Jazz House | JHCD 024

Mucha Muchacha
Four For Jazz | Joe Haider And His Friends | Calig | 30618

Muchacho Azul
Lionel Hampton And His Orchestra | Lionel Hampton Vol.3-Sweatin' With Hamp | MCA | 1331

Mucho Dinero
Erroll Garner Sextet | Magician & Gershwin And Kern | Telarc Digital | CD 83337

Mücken Im Wald-
Baecastuff | Out Of This World | Naxos Jazz | 86063-2

Mud Island-
Graef-Schippa-Moritz | Orlando Frames | Nabel Records:Jazz Network | CD 4690

Mud On Face
Dave Weckl Band | Rhythm In My Soul | Stretch Records | SCD 9016-2

Mud Turtle
Kai Winding All Stars | Kai Winding-Bop City:Small Groups 1949-1951 | Cool & Blue | C&B-CD 110

Muddy In The Bank
Muddy Waters Group | Back In His Early Days, Vol.1+2 | Red Lightnin' | SC 001/2

Muddy Water(A Mississippi Moan)
Jimmie Lunceford And His Orchestra | Jimmie Lunceford Vol.5-Jimmie's Legacy | MCA | 1320

Muddy Waters Blues
Eddie Clearwater Group | The Ralph Bass Sessions Vol.2:Jimmy Johnson/Eddie Clearwater | Red Lightnin' | RL 0051

Muezzin-
Crazy Art Quintet | Looking Up Looking Down | yvp music | CD 3040

Muffin
Hampton Hawes Trio | High In The Sky | Fresh Sound Records | FSR-CD 0059

Mug Shots:
Guy Klucevsek-Alan Bern | Accordance | Winter&Winter | 910058-2
Martin Taylor Quartet | Don't Fret | Linn Records | AKD 014

Muggin' Lightly
Luis Russell And His Orchestra | Luis Russell | CBS | CBS 88039

Muggles
Louis Armstrong And His Orchestra | Heebie Jeebies | Naxos Jazz | 8.120351 CD
Russell Malone Quintet | Sweet Georgia Peach | Impulse(MCA) | 951282-2

Mugshot
Creative Construction Company | CCC | Muse | MR 5071

Muhammed
Essence All Stars | Afro Cubano Chant | Hip Bop | HIBD 8009

Mui Tarde Amor
David Kikoski Trio | Surf's Up | Criss Cross | Criss 1208

Muko
Lionel Hampton And His All Stars | Masters Of Jazz Vol.8 | RCA | NL 89540 DP

Mukti
Cuarteto Las D'Aida Y Su Grupo | Soy La Mulata | L+R Records | CDLR 45059

Muldoon In June-
Kenny Burrell Quintet | Midnight Blue | Blue Note | 746399-2

Mule
Mose Allison Trio | Creek Bank | Prestige | PCD 24055-2

Mule Walk
James P.Johnson | 1939-1949, Blue Note's Three Decades Of Jazz, Vol. 1 | Blue Note | 89902

Mullenium
Gerry Mulligan New Stars | Gerry Mulligan:Complete 1950-1952 Prestige Studio Recordings | Definitive Records | DRCD 11227

Mulliganville
John Mayer's Indio-Jazz Fusions | Ragatal | Nimbus Records | NI 5569

Multani
Terje Rypdal | After The Rain | ECM | 1083

Multibluetonic Blues
Pata Horns | New Archaic Music | Pata Musik | PATA 4(JHM 42) CD

Multichronik
Billy Strayhorn | The Peaceful Side Of Billy Strayhorn | Capitol | 852563-2

Multikulti Soothsayer
Don Cherry | Multi Kulti | A&M Records | 395323-2

Multikulti Soothsayer Player
Ira Sullivan Quintet | Multimedia | Galaxy | GXY 5137

Multimedia Bonus Track
Peter Finger | Solo | Acoustic Music Records | 319.1032.2

Multiphone Blues
Odean Pope Trio | Almost Like Me | Moers Music | 01092 CD

Multiple Choice
John Lindberg Revolving Ensemble | Relative Reliability | West Wind | WW 2014

Multiples
Giorgio Gaslini Quintet | Multipli | Soul Note | 121220-2

Multiplicity Of Approaches(The African Way Of Knowing)
Twice A Week & Steve Elson | Play Of Colours | Edition Collage | EC 511-2

Multiply
Jack DeJohnette New Directions | In Europe | ECM | 1157

Multo Spiliagio
Lucky Thompson Quartet | Lucky Strikes | Original Jazz Classics | OJCCD 194-2

Mumbles
Clark Terry With The Summit Jazz Orchestra | Clark | Edition Collage | EC 530-2
George Robert Quartet With Clark Terry | Live At The Q-4 Rheinfelden | TCB Records | TCB 9080

Mumbo Jumbo
Paul Motian Trio | Motian In Tokyo | JMT Edition | 849154-2
Abdullah Ibrahim-Carlos Ward Duo | Live At Sweet Basil Vol.1 | Black-Hawk | BKH 50204

Mumuki
Aldo Romano Quartet | Canzoni | Enja | 9102-2

München(part 1)
Keith Jarrett | Concerts(Bregenz/München) | ECM | 1227/9

München(part 2)
Concerts(Bregenz/München) | ECM | 1227/9

München(part 3)
Concerts(Bregenz/München) | ECM | 1227/9

München(part 4)
Ernie Krivda Quintet | Satanic | Inner City | IC 1031 IMS

Munchkins
Andreas Schnerman Quartet | 4 In One | Edition Collage | EC 526-2

Munchquell
Franck Band | Looser | Jazz Haus Musik | JHM 43 CD

Mundos(Exposicion-Desarrollo-Cadensia-Imitacion-Marcha-Recapitulacion)
Christof Sänger & Cuban Fantasy | Moliendo Café | Mons Records | MR 874302

Munecas Aminadas
Schlaier-Hirt Duo | Don't Walk Outside Thos Area | Chaos | CACD 8186

Mungo Park
Volker Kriegel & Mild Maniac Orchestra | Live In Bayern | MPS | 68270

Munique
Chicago Underground Trio | Possible Cube | Delmark | DE 511

Mu-Point
Larry Coryell | Twelve Frets To One Octave | Koch Records | 322 657

Murder
Charlie Barnet And His Orchestra | Clap Hands,Here Comes Charlie! | Bluebird | ND 86273

Murder On Heaven Seven
Henry Kaiser Group | Marrying For Money | Minor Music | 1010

Murder One
The Mick Clarke Band | Tell The Truth | Taxim Records | TX 1001-2 TA

Murmeltanz
Mark Feldman Quartet | Book Of Tells | Enja | ENJ-9385 2

Murmur-
Michel Godard Ensemble | Castel Del Monte | Enja | ENJ-9362 2

Murmures
Edward Vesala Sound And Fury | Invisible Strom | ECM | 1461

Murmuring Morning
Ekkehard Jost Quartet | Deep | Fish Music | FM 007 CD

Murphy
Grumpff | Wetterau | FMP | SAJ 16

Murphy's Law
Paul Smith Sextet | Cool And Sparkling | Capitol | 300011(TOCJ 6125)

Mursiya
Okay Temiz Group | Magnet Dance | TipToe | TIP-888819 2

Muschel Von Margate(Petroleum Song)
Benny Moten's Kansas City Orchestra | Bennie Moten Vol.1 | Zeta | ZET 750

Musenkuss
Thomas Heidepriem Quartet | Brooklyn Shuffle | L+R Records | CDLR 45084

Mush Mouth
Buddy Johnson And His Orchestra | Buddy And Ella Johnson 1953-1964 | Bear Family Records | BCD 15479 DH

Mush Mouth(alt.take)
John Tchicai Quartet | Timo's Message | Black Saint | 120094-2

Mushrooms
Joachim Kühn | Snow In The Desert | Atlantic | ATL 50718 Digital

Music & Interviews-Documentation
Herb Geller Quartet | Playing Jazz:The Musical Autobiography Of Herb Geller | Fresh Sound Records | FSR-CD 5011

Music 4 Food
Ornette Coleman Quartet | Beauty Is A Rare Thing:Ornette Coleman-The Complete Atlantic Recordings | Atlantic | 8122-71410-2

Music Always
Andrew Rathbun Group | Jade | Fresh Sound Records | FSNT 076 CD

Music Based On A Poem By Cathy Song
Steve Lampert Group | Venus Perplexed | Steeplechase | SCCD 31557

Music Box
Takashi Yoshimatsu | Tender Toys:Shin-Ichi Fukuda | Denon Compact Disc | CO-18053

Music Box/I'm Alone
Sadao Watanabe Group | My Dear Life | Flying Disk | VIJ 6001

Music For 'Todo Modo'
Steve Reich And Musicians | Music For 18 Musicians | ECM | 1129(821417-2)

Music For A Quintet
Ralph Burns And His Orchestra | The Complete Verve Roy Eldridge Studio Sessions | Verve | 9861278

Music For A Stripteaser
Flip Phillips Flip Wails-The Best Of The Verve Years | Verve | 521645-2

Music For A While
Lee Konitz With Strings | Lee Konitz Meets Jimmy Giuffre | Verve | 527780-2

Music For Eyes:
Peter Herborn Group With The Auryn String Quartet | Something Personal | JMT Edition | 849156-2

Music For Lovers
Hans Koller Groups And Orchestra | Hans Koller Masterpieces | MPS | 529078-2

Music For Pablo(I)
Hans Koller Masterpieces | MPS | 529078-2

Music For Pablo(II)
Robert Hohner Persussion Ensemble | The Gamut | dmp Digital Music Productions | CD 505

Music For Swinging Dancers
Gary Lucas/Walter Horn | Skeleton On The Feast | Enemy | EMCD 126(03526)

Music For Two Pianos(part 1-17)
Cornelius Claudio Kreusch/Hans Poppel | Piano Moments | Take Twelve On CD | TT 007-2

Music For Two Pianos(part 3+9)
Jude Swift Group | Music For Your Neighborhood | Nova | NOVA 8917-2

Music Forever
Freddie Redd Quartet | The Music From The Connection | Blue Note | 84027

Music From Planet Earth
Chris Barber's Jazzband & das Große Rundfunkorchester Berlin,DDR | Jazz Zounds: Chris Barber | Zounds | CD 2720007

Music From The Land Of Dreams
Kenny Werner Group | Beauty Secrets | RCA | 2169904-2

Music Goes 'Round And 'Round
Jimmie Grier And His Orchestra | The Uncollected:Jimmie Grier | Hindsight | HSR 177

Music Has Its Way With Me
Joe Roland Quartet | Joltin' Joe | Savoy | SV 0215(MG 12039)

Music I Heard
James Blood Ulmer Group | Music Speaks Louder Than Words:James Blood Ulmer Plays The Music Of Ornette Coleman | DIW | DIW 910 CD

Music Is My Life
Lillian Boutté And Her Group | Lipstick Traces(A New Orleans R&B Session) | Blues Beacon | BLU-1011 2

Music Maestro Please
Al Bowlly With Lew Stone And His Band | On The Sentimental Side | Decca | DDV 5009/10
Jeri Southern With The Johnny Smith Quartet | Jeri Southern Meets Johnny Smith | Fresh Sound Records | FSR-CD 28(882156)

Music Makers
Harry James And His Orchestra | Welcome To Jazz: Harry James | Koch Records | 321 983 D1

Music On My Mind
Peter Erskine Group | Transition | Denon Compact Disc | CY-1484

Music Reaches Places
Albert Dailey Trio | That Old Feeling | Steeplechase | SCCD 31107

Music To Dance By
Al Porcino Big Band | Al Cohn Meets Al Porcino | Organic Music | ORGM 9730

Music To Dance To
In Oblivion | Jazz Mark | 106 Digital

Music To Love By
Jack Teagarden And His Orchestra | Jazz Original | Charly | CD 80

Music To Watch Girls By
Willie Bobo Group | Juicy | Verve | 519857-2
Juicy | Verve | 519857-2

Music To Watch Girls By(alt.take)
Hugo Read Group | Songs Of A Wayfarer | Nabel Records:Jazz Network | CD 4653

Music,After Stories From The 'Thousand And One Nights':
Martial Solal/Joachim Kühn | Duo In Paris | Dreyfus Jazz Line | FDM 36503-2

Musica Callada No.1
Richard Beirach Trio | Round About Federico Mompou | ACT | 9296-2

Musica Callada No.10
Round About Federico Mompou | ACT | 9296-2

Musica Callada No.15
Round About Federico Mompou | ACT | 9296-2

Musica Callada No.18
Round About Federico Mompou | ACT | 9296-2

Musica Callada No.19
Round About Federico Mompou | ACT | 9296-2

Musica Callada No.22
Round About Federico Mompou | ACT | 9296-2

Musica Callada No.27
Round About Federico Mompou | ACT | 9296-2

Musica Callada No.6
Martin Joseph-Eugenio Colombo | Duets And Solos | Red Records | VPA 139

Musica De Sobrevivencia
Peter Sprague Quartet | Musica Del Mar | Concord | CJ 237

Musica Ex Spiritu Sancto(part 1-8)
Egberto Gismonti With The Lithuanian State Symphony Orchestra | Meeting Point | ECM | 1586(533681-2)

Musica Para Cordas
Chris Jarrett | Live In Tübingen | Edition Collage | EC 490-2

Musica Satirica
Fess Williams And His Orchestra | Fess Williams-The Complete Sessions 1929 Vol.1 | Harlequin | HQ 2039 IMS

Musical Silence

Ensemble Indigo | Reflection | Enja | ENJ-9417 2

Musical Toys:

Horace Parlan | Musically Yours | Steeplechase | SCCD 31141

Musician's Musician

Return To Forever | Sony Jazz Collection:Return To Forever | CBS | 488631-2

Musique Mecanique(I)

Carla Bley-Steve Swallow | Are We There Yet? | Watt | 29(547297)
Carla Bley Band | Musique Mecanique | Watt | 9

Musique Mecanique(II-At Midnight)

Carla Bley-Steve Swallow | Are We There Yet? | Watt | 29(547297)
Carla Bley Band | Musique Mecanique | Watt | 9

Musique Mecanique(III)

Carla Bley-Steve Swallow | Are We There Yet? | Watt | 29(547297)
Francioli-Bovard Orchestra | Musique | Plainisphare | PL 1267-11/12

Muskrat Ramble

Cat Anderson And His All Stars | Ellingtonians In Paris | Jazztime(EMI) | 251275-2
Dr. Henry Levine's Barefoot Dixieland Philharmonic feat.Prof. Sidney Bechet | Planet Jazz | Planet Jazz | 2169652-2
Dutch Swing College Band | Still Blowing Strong - 34 Years | DSC Production | PA 1022 (801071)
Ed Hall And The All Star Stompers | This Is Jazz Vol.3 | Storyville | SLP 4069
Eddie Condon All Stars | Eddie Condon Town Hall Concerts Vol.1 | Jazzology | JCECD-1001
Firehouse Five Plus Two | At Disneyland | Good Time Jazz | GTCD 10049-2
George Lewis And His New Orleans All Stars | King Of New Orleans | Vagabond | 6.28053 DP
Isidore 'Tuts' Washington | The Larry Borenstein Collection Vol.3:Isidore 'Tuts' Washington-New Orleans Piano | 504 Records | 504CD 32
Louis Armstrong And His All Stars | New Orleans Louisiana | Traditional Line | TL 1319
Louis Armstrong:Wintergarden 1947/Blue Note 1948 | Storyville | STCD 8242
Louis Armstrong:Wintergarden 1947/Blue Note 1948 | Storyville | STCD 8242
Jazz Collection:Louis Armstrong | Laserlight | 24366
The Complete Town Hall Concert 17.May 1947 | RCA | ND 89746
Munich Saxophon Family | Family Life | Bassic-Sound | CD 006
Sidney Bechet Groups | The Collection-Sidney Bechet | Bluebird | ND 90687
The New York Allstars | We Love You,Louis! | Nagel-Heyer | CD 029
The Royal Air Force HQ Bomber Command Sextet | RAF HQ Bomber Command Sextet | Celebrity | CYCD 74508
Toots Thielemans Quintet | Toots Thielemans Live-Vol. 2 | Polydor | 2441063 IMS
Earl Hines Trio | Jazz In Paris:Earl Hines-Paris One Night Stand | EmArCy | 548207-2 PMS

Muskrat Ramble(alt.take)

Lu Watters' Yerba Buena Jazz Band | Lu Watters' Yerba Buena Jazz Band-1942 Series | Good Time Jazz | GTCD 12007-2

Muss I Denn Zum Städtele Hinaus

Ronaldo Folegatti Groups | Sound Of Watercolors | AH Records | AH 403001-11

Must Have Been The Devil

Otis Spann Band | The Blues Never Die! | Original Blues Classics | OBCCD 530-2(P 7391)
Bumble Bee Slim(Amos Easton) | Bumble Bee Slim(Amos Easton) 1931-1937 | Story Of Blues | CD 3501-2

Must I,Miss Sophie?

Lonnie Brooks Blues Band | Wound Up Tight | Sonet | SNTF 974(941974)

Mustache-

Donald Byrd Sextet | Mustang! | Blue Note | 300269(4238)

Mutab Ali

Sylvie Courvoisier Group | Y2K | Enja | ENJ-9383 2

Mutant

Mike Clark Sextet | Give The Drummer Some | Stash Records | ST-CD 22(881997)

Mutatio

Stefan Bauer-Claudio Puntin-Marcio Doctor | Lingo | Jazz Haus Musik | JHM 0116 CD

Mutation

Christy Doran Group | Cor Por Ate Art | JMT Edition | 849155-2

Mutazione

Harald Hearter Quartet With Dewey Redman | Mostly Live | TipToe | TIP-888825 2

Mute

Don Cherry/Ed Blackwell | El Corazon | ECM | 1230

Mutron

Boots Mussuli Quartet | Little Man | Affinity | AFF 67

Mutt And Jeff

Count Basie And His Orchestra | Basie On Roulette, Vol. 7: Chairman Of The Board | Vogue | 500007

Mutterliebe

Tex Allen Quintet | Late Night | Muse | MCD 5492

Muttnik

Count Basie And His Orchestra | Duke Ellington-Count Basie | CBS | 473753-2

Mwalimu

Odean Pope Trio | Almost Like Me | Moers Music | 01092 CD

Mweya

Art Blakey And The Jazz Messengers | Jazz Life Vol.2:From Seventh At Avenue South | Storyville | 4960763

MX'B,C.

Lowell Fulsom Band | Tramp/Soul | Ace Records | CDCHD 339

My All

Archie Shepp Group | Blase | Charly | CD 77

My April Heart

Juan Martin Group | Through The Moving Window | RCA | PD 83036(874035)

My Babe

Bunky Green Sextet | Step High | Fresh Sound Records | FSR-CD 0301
Hubert Sumlin Group | Blues Anytime | L+R Records | CDLR 72010
Matchbox Bluesband | Live Recordings Extravaganza! | L+R Records | CDLR 42074
Willie Dixon Blues Band | Blues Roots Vol. 12: Willie Dixon | Chess | 6.24802 AG

My Baby Comes To Me

Tiny Grimes And His Rockin' Highlanders | Tiny Grimes:The Complete 1950-1954,Vol.3 | Blue Moon | BMCD 6007

My Baby Just Cares For Me

Nina Simone Trio | Tempo Jazz Edition Vol.3-Stayin' Cool | Verve | 847902-2
Let It Be Me | Verve | 831437-1

My Baby Said Yes(Yip, Yip De Hootie)

Ted Heath And His Orchestra | Ted Heath And His Music-It's Swing Time | Magic | DAWE 82

My Baby Said Yes(Yip, Yip De Hootie-alt.take)

Buddy Guy-Junior Wells Band | Blues Power No.9: Buddy Guy & Junior Wells Play The Blues | Atlantic | 40240

My Baby Upsets Me

Joe Williams With The Count Basie Orchestra | Joe Williams:Triple Play | Telarc Digital | CD 83461

My Back Pages

Irene Scruggs | Country Bottleneck Guitar Classics | Yazoo | YAZ 1026

My Beautiful

Michel Petrucciani Group | Music | Blue Note | 792563-2

My Bebop Tune

The RH Factor feat. Reuben Hoch | Live In New York | L+R Records | CDLR 45074

My Bells

Bill Evans Trio With The Claus Ogerman Orchestra | The Complete Bill Evans On Verve | Verve | 527953-2
Bud Shank Quartet | Bud Shank Plays The Music Of Bill Evans | Fresh Sound Records | FSR-CD 5012
Philip DeGruy | Innuendo Out The Other | NYC-Records | NYC 6013-2

My Blue Heaven

Coleman Hawkins All Star Octet | The Indispensable Coleman Hawkins 1927-1956:Body And Soul | RCA | ND 89277
Cozy Cole's Big Seven | Body And Soul Revisited | GRP | GRP 16272
Doris Day With Orchestra | The Uncollected:Doris Day | Hindsight | HSR 200
Glenn Miller And His Orchestra | Glenn Miller | Memo Music | HDJ 4116
The Swinging Mr. Miller | RCA | 2115522-2
Ken Colyer's Jazzmen | Ken Colyer's Jazzmen Serenading Auntie-BBC Recordings 1955-1960 | Upbeat Jazz | URCD 111
Oscar Peterson Trio | Masters Of Jazz Vol.7 | RCA | NL 89721 DP
Slam Stewart/Major Holley Quartet | Shut Yo' Mouth | Delos | DE 1024
Stephane Grappelli Quartet | Stephane Grappelli | LRC Records | CDC 9014
Tatum-Carter-Bellson Trio | The Tatum Group Masterpieces | Pablo | 2625706

My Blue Heaven-

The Minstrel Stars | The Minstrel Stars | Upbeat Jazz | URCD 105

My Blue House

Benny Golson Quintet | Domingo | Dreyfus Jazz Line | FDM 36557-2

My Blues

John Klemmer Quartet | Involvement | Chess | 076139-2
Martin Schrack Quartet | Headin' Home | Storyville | STCD 4253
Ray Bryant | Alone With The Blues | Original Jazz Classics | OJC 249(NJ 8213)

My Brother

Hugh Marsh Duo/Quartet/Orchestra | The Bear Walks | VeraBra Records | CDVBR 2011-2
Nat King Cole Trio With Pete Rugolo's Orchestra | Lush Life | Capitol | 780595-2

My Bucket's Got A Hole In It

Jim Robinson's New Orleans Band | Jazz At Preservation Hall, Vol.2 | Atlantic | SD 1409
Kid Ory's Creole Jazz Band | Sounds Of New Orleans Vol.9 | Storyville | STCD 6016
Kid Thomas' Dixieland Band | The Larry Borenstein Collection Vol.2:Willie Pajeaud/Kid Thomas | 504 Records | 504CD 31

My Buddy

Chet Baker Quartet | Chet Baker Sings | Pacific Jazz | 300067(PJ 1222)
Count Basie And His Orchestra | The Indispensable Count Basie | RCA | ND 89758
Doc Cheatham/Jim Galloway Sextet | At The Bern Festival | Sackville | SKCD2-3045
Joey & 'Papa' John DeFrancesco Group | All In The Family | HighNote Records | HCD 7021
Susannah McCorkle With The Allen Farnham Orchestra | From Broadway To Bebop | Concord | CCD 4615

My Cabin Of Dreams

Muddy Waters Quartet | Folk Singer | Chess | CH 9261

My Cat Arnold

Sabine&Markus Setzer | Between The Words | Lipstick Records | LIP 8970

My Celtic Heart

Mel Lewis And The Jazz Orchestra | Naturally! | Telarc Digital | CD 83301

My Cherie Amour

Charles McPherson Quartet | Jazzin' Vol.2: The Music Of Stevie Wonder | Fantasy | FANCD 6088-2
McPherson's Mood | Original Jazz Classics | OJCCD 1947-2(PR 7743)
Charlie Byrd-Cal Tjader Orchestra | Tambu | Fantasy | FCD 9453-2
Joe Henderson Group | Jazzin' Vol.2: The Music Of Stevie Wonder | Fantasy | FANCD 6088-2
Rahsaan Roland Kirk Sextet | Volunteered Slavery | Rhino | 8122-71407-2
Roland Kirk Quintet | Roller Coaster | Bandstand | BDCD 1539

My Childhood Years

Ray Anderson-Han Bennink-Christy Doran | Cheer Up | Hat Art | CD 6175

My Chile

Jay McShann Quartet | Goin' To Kansas City | Stony Plain | SPCD 1286
The Man From Muskogee | Affinity | AFF 147

My Conception

Sonny Clark Quintet | My Conception | Blue Note | 522674-2
Sonny Clark Trio | Blues Mambo | West Wind | WW 2103

My Corner Of The Sky

Sadao Watanabe Orchestra & Strings | California Shower | Flying Disk | VIJ 6012

My Daddy Rocks Me

Ralph Sutton-Kenny Davern Trio | Ralph Sutton & Kenny Davern Vol. 2 | Chaz Jazz | CJ 106

My Daily Wish

Moscow Art Trio | Once Upon A Time | JA & RO | JARO 4238-2

My Dance

Billy May Big Band | The Girls And Boys On Broadway | Fresh Sound Records | T 1418(Capitol)

My Darling Nellie Gray

Louis Armstrong With The Mills Brothers | Louis Armstrong Vol.6-Satchmo's Collectors Items | MCA | 1322

My Delight

La Vienta | Jazzmenco | Telarc Digital | CD 83353

My Diane

Bola Sete Quintet | Tour De Force:The Bola Sete Trios | Fantasy | FCD 24766-2

My Different World

Bossa Nova | Original Jazz Classics | OJC 286(F 8349)

My Discontent

Piccadilly Six | Fans' Favourites | Elite Special | 73319

My Fantasy

Barbara Sutton Curtis | Old Fashioned Love | Sackville | SKCD2-2042

My Fate Is In Your Hands

Fats Waller | Turn On The Heat-The Fats Waller Piano Solos | Bluebird | ND 82482

My Fate Is In Your Hands-

Gordon Beck/Rowanne Mark | Dreams | JMS | 049-2

My Father

Hamiet Bluiett | Birthright-A Solo Blues Concert | India Navigation | IN 1030

My Favorite Fantasy

Rabih Abou-Khalil | Il Sospiro | Enja | ENJ-9440 2

My Favorite Feet

Bill Evans Group | Let The Juice Loose-Bill Evans Group Live at The Blue Note,Tokyo | Jazz City | 660.53.001

My Favorite Things

Antonio Scarano Octet | Hot Blend | SPLASC(H) Records | H 183
Betty Carter And The John Hicks Trio | The Audience With Betty Carter | Verve | 835684-2 PMS
Chuck Wayne/Joe Puma Duo | Interactions | Candid | CRS 1004 IMS
Datevik With The Larry Willis Quartet | Ballads From The Black Sea | Mapleshade | 04332
John Coltrane Group | The Olatunji Concert:The Last Live Recording | Impulse(MCA) | 589120-2
John Coltrane Quartet | The Promise | Moon Records | MCD 058-2
Visit To Scandinavia | Jazz Door | JD 1210
John Coltrane-Live Trane:The European Tours | Pablo | 7PACD 4433-2
John Coltrane-Live Trane:The European Tours | Pablo | 7PACD 4433-2
John Coltrane-Live Trane:The European Tours | Pablo | 7PACD 4433-2
The Complete Graz Concert Vol.2 | Magnetic Records | MRCD 105
Afro Blue Impressions | Pablo | 2PACD 2620101
My Favorite Things | Atlantic | 8122-75204-2
The Art Of John Coltrane - The Atlantic Years | Atlantic | SD 2-313
The Mastery Of John Coltrane/Vol. 1: Feelin' Good | MCA | 2292-54641-2
John Coltrane Quintet | Live At Birdland | Charly | CD 68
John Coltrane Quintet With Eric Dolphy | European Impressions | Bandstand | BDLP 1514
John Coltrane-Live Trane:The European Tours | Pablo | 7PACD 4433-2
John Coltrane-Live Trane:The European Tours | Pablo | 7PACD 4433-2
John McLaughlin Trio | After The Rain | Verve | 527467-2
Johnny Hartman With The Masahiko Kikuchi Trio | For Trane | Blue Note | 835346-2
Louis Hayes Group | Variety Is The Spice | Gryphon | 6.23952 AT
Maria Joao Quintet | Cem Caminhos | Nabel Records:Jazz Network | LP 4622
McCoy Tyner | The Jazz Giants Play Rodgers & Hammerstein:My Favorite Things | Prestige | PCD 24223-2
Peter Herborn Group With The WDR Big Band | Traces Of Trane | JMT Edition | 514002-2
Robin Kenyatta Quartet | Ghost Stories | ITM-Pacific | ITMP 970060
Sarah Vaughan With Mundell Lowe And George Duvivier | Jazz Profile | Blue Note | 823517-2
Sheila Jordan And Her Quartet | Confirmation | East Wind | EW 8024 IMS
Weslia Whitefield With The Mike Greensill Quartet | High Standards | HighNote Records | HCD 7025

My Foolish Dream?

(Little)Jimmy Scott And His Quintet | All The Way | Warner | 7599-26955-2

My Foolish Heart

Adonis Rose Quintet | Song For Donise | Criss Cross | Criss 1146
Allen Farnham With The Rias Big Band | Allen Farnham Meets The Rias Big Band | Concord | CCD 4789
Bill Evans Trio | The Village Vanguard Sessions | Milestone | M 47002
My Romance | Zeta | ZET 702
Bill Evans Trio:The Last Waltz | Milestone | 8MCD 4430-2
Bill Evans Trio:The Last Waltz | Milestone | 8MCD 4430-2
Bill Evans Trio:The Last Waltz | Milestone | 8MCD 4430-2
Bill Evans:The Secret Sessions | Milestone | 8MCD 4421-2
Consecration 2 | Timeless | CD SJP 332
Bill Evans:The Secret Sessions | Milestone | 8MCD 4421-2
Bill Evans At Town Hall | Verve | 831271-2
Bill Watrous Big Band | Space Available | Double Time Records | DTRCD-124
Cedar Walton Trio With Bobby Hutcherson | Among Friends | Evidence | ECD 22023-2
Chet Baker And The Mike Melillo Trio With Orchestra | Symphonically | Soul Note | 121134-2
Christian Elsässer Trio | Future Days | Organic Music | ORGM 9721
Chucho Valdes Quartet | Chucho Veldes Solo Piano | Blue Note | 780597-2
David Hazeltine Quartet | A World For Her | Criss Cross | Criss 1170
Don Friedman Quartet | My Foolish Heart | Steeplechase | SCCD 31534
Don Menza & Frank Strazzeri | Ballads | Fresh Sound Records | FSR 103 (807728)
Eddie Daniels Quartet | Real Time | Chesky | JD 118
Etta Jones With The Houston Person Sextet | Fine And Mellow/Save Your Love For Me | Muse | MCD 6002
Gary Burton | Country Roads & Other Places | RCA | PL 45139
Gene Ammons-Sonny Stitt Quintet | Gene Ammons-Greatest Hits Vol.1:The Sixties | Original Jazz Classics | OJCCD 6005-2
Herb Ellis-Remo Palmier Quartet | Windflower | Concord | CJ 56
Kurt Elling Group | This Time Its Love | Blue Note | 493543-2
Kurt Elling Group With Guests | Live In Chicago | Blue Note | 522211-2
Lenny Hambro Quintet | The Nature Of Things | Fresh Sound Records | LSP 15821(Epic LN 3361)
Mark Nightingale With The RIAS Big Band | Destiny | Mons Records | MR 874793
Mitchel Forman Trio | Now And Then-A Tribute To Bill Evans | Novus | 4163165-2
Olaf Kübler Quartet | When I'm 64 | Village | VILCD 1016-2
Oscar Peterson Quintet | Oscar Peterson Meets Roy Hargrove And Ralph Moore | Telarc Digital | CD 83399
Patty Waters-Jessica Williams | Love Songs | Jazz Focus | JFCD 012
Peter Herbolzheimer Rhythm Combination & Brass | Colors Of A Band | Mons Records | MR 874799
Scott Hamilton Quartet | Tenorshoes | Concord | CCD 4127
Stefon Harris-Jacky Terrasson Group | Kindred | Blue Note | 531868-2
Stephane Grappelli-Marc Fosset Duo | Stephanova | Concord | CJ 225
Tony Bennett-Bill Evans | The Tony Bennett-Bill Evans Album | Original Jazz Classics | OJC20 439-2(F 9489)
Torsten Zwingenberger & Band With Guests | Open Sunroof | Blackbird Records | BD 41012

My Friend

Wiregrass Sacred Harp Singers | The Colored Sacred Harp | New World Records | 80433-2

My Friend Ethyl

Charlie Mariano Sextet | Nat Pierce-Dick Collins Nonet/Charlie Mariano Sextet | Original Jazz Classics | OJC 118(F 3224)

My Friend From Rio

Yoshiaki Masuo Group | A Subtle One | Jazz City | 660.53.030

My Friend John

Art Pepper Quartet | Art Pepper:The Complete Galaxy Recordings | Galaxy | 16GCD 1016-2
Art Pepper:The Complete Galaxy Recordings | Galaxy | 16GCD 1016-2
Art Pepper:The Complete Village Vanguard Sessions | Contemporary | 9CCD-4417-2
Art Pepper:The Complete Village Vanguard Sessions | Contemporary | 9CCD-4417-2
Art Pepper:The Complete Village Vanguard Sessions | Contemporary | 9CCD-4417-2
New York Album | Galaxy | GXY 5154

My Friend John(alt.take)

Art Pepper:The Complete Village Vanguard Sessions | Contemporary | 9CCD-4417-2
Andrew Cyrille Quintet | My Friend Louis | DIW | DIW 858 CD

My Friends

Axel Petry Quintet | Live At Salt Peanuts | amf records | amf 1016

My Funny Valentine

Adam Makowicz Trio | My Favorite Things-The Music Of Richard Rodgers | Concord | CCD 4631
Art Blakey And The Jazz Messengers | Blakey's Theme | West Wind | WW 2045
Benny Goodman And His All Star Sextet | On Stage | Decca | 6.28101 DP
Bill Perkins Big Band | Our Man Woody | Jazz Mark | 110 CD(889466)
Brian Bromberg Group | A New Day | Black-Hawk | BKH 524
Carmen McRae With Her Trio | Carmen McRae:New York State Of Mind | Memo Music | HDJ 4024
Charles McPherson Orchestra | Siku Ya Bibi | Mainstream | MD CDO 713
Chet Baker Quartet | Chet Baker-The Legacy Vol.4:Oh You Crazy Moon | Enja | ENJ-9453 2
Chet Baker | Carlyne | 695015
Chet Baker Quartet Live Vol.1:This Time The Dreams's On Me | Pacific Jazz | 525248-2
Chet Baker In Paris | West Wind | WW 2109
Chet Baker Quintet/NDR Big Band/Radio Orchestra Hannover | The Last Concert Vol.I+II | Enja | ENJ-6074 22
Chet Baker Trio | Chet Baker In Bologna | Dreyfus Jazz Line | FDM 36558-9
Chet Baker With The Radio Orchestra Hannover(NDR) | My Favourite Songs: The Last Great Concert Vol.1 | Enja | ENJ-5097 2
The Last Concert Vol.I+II | Enja | ENJ-6074 22
Chet Baker-Enrico Pieranunzi | Soft Journey | EdiPan | NGP 805
Chet Baker-Stan Getz Quintet | The Stockholm Concerts | Verve | 537555-2
Chico Hamilton Quintet | Chico Hamilton Quintet | Pacific Jazz | 300002(PJ 1209)
David Friesen/Clark Terry/Bud Shank | Three To Get Ready | ITM-Pacific | ITMP 970084
Don Friedman | My Romance | Steeplechase | SCCD 31403
Duke Ellington And His Orchestra | Duke Ellington Presents... | Bethlehem | BET 6004-2(BCP 6005)

My Funny Valentine
Bielefelder Katalog 217 Jazz • Ausgabe 2004
My Little Strayhorn

Eartha Kitt With The Joachim Kühn Quartet | Standards/Live | ITM Records | ITM 1484
Ella Fitzgerald With Orchestra | Essential Ella | Verve | 523990-2
Ella Fitzgerald With The Buddy Bregman Orchestra | The Rodgers And Hart Songbook | Verve | 821693-1
The Rodgers And Hart Songbook Vol.2 | Verve | 821580-2 PMS
The Complete Ella Fitzgerald Song Books of Harold Arlen, Irving Berlin, Duke Ellington, George & Ira Gershwin, Jerome Kern, Johnny Mercer, Cole Porter And Rogers & Hart | Verve | 519832-2
Ernestine Anderson And Her Trio | Late At Night | Paddle Wheel | KICJ 113
European Jazz Trio | Nowegian Wood | Timeless | CD SJP 322
Franco Ambrosetti Quintet | Heart Bop | Enja | 3087 (807508)
Gary Burton Quintet | Gary Burton Collection | GRP | GRP 98512
Gerry Mulligan All-StarTribute Band | Thank You,Gerry! Our Tribute To Gerry Mulligan | Arkadia Jazz | 71191
Gerry Mulligan Concert Jazz Band | En Concert Avec Europe 1 | Laserlight | 710382/83
Gerry Mulligan Quartet | Live In Stockholm-Vol.2 | Ingo | 6
Gerry Mulligan-Bill Mays | Triple Play:Gerry Mulligan | Telarc Digital | CD 83453
Grant Green Quartet | Ballads | Blue Note | 537560-2
Guido Manusardi | Concerto | SPLASC(H) Records | CD H 437-2
Helen Ward With The Peanuts Hucko Quartet | The Eddie Condon Floor Show Vol.1 | Queen-Disc | 030
J.J.Johnson Quartet | Proof Positive | Impulse(MCA) | GRP 11452
Jacky Terrasson Trio | Smile | Blue Note | 542413-2
JATP All Stars | JATP In Tokyo | Pablo | 2620104-2
Jeanie Lambe And The Danny Moss Quartet | Three Great Concerts:Live In Hamburg 1993-1995 | Nagel-Heyer | CD 019
Jim Hall Trio | These Roots | Denon Compact Disc | CY-30002
Jimmy Jones Trio | The Piano Collection Vol.2 | Vogue | 21610222
Jimmy Smith Trio | Groovin' At Smalls' Paradise | Blue Note | 499777-2
Joe Turner | I Understand | Black & Blue | BLE 59.153 2
John Basile Quartet | The Desmond Project | Chesky | JD 156
Johnny Smith Quintet | Zoot Sims:The Complete 1944-1954 Small Group Sessions(Master Takes),Vol.3 | Blue Moon | BMCD 1040
Keith Jarrett Trio | Still Live | ECM | 1360/61(835008-2
Tokyo '96 | ECM | 1666(539955-2)
Kenny Dorham Quintet | Short Story | Steeplechase | SCCD 36010
L.A.4 | Executive Suite | Concord | CCD 4215
Mat Maneri Quintet | Acceptance | HatOLOGY | 512
Merl Saunders Quartet | Live At Keystone | Fantasy | F 79002
Michel And Tony Petrucciani | Conversations | Dreyfus Jazz Line | FDM 36617-2
Michel Legrand Orchestra | Compact Jazz: Michel Legrand | Philips | 840944-2
Miles Davis Quartet | Miles Davis Classics | CBS | CBS 88138
Miles Davis Quintet | Miles Davis-Heard 'Round The World | CBS | 88626
Greatest Hits | CBS | CK 65418
Milt Jackson Quartet | Milt Jackson | Original Jazz Classics | OJC20 001-2(P 7003)
Opus De Funk | Prestige | P 24048
Nancy Wilson With The Great Jazz Trio | What's New | Eastworld | EWJ 90014
Niels-Henning Orsted-Pedersen/Philip Catherine Duo | The Viking | Pablo | 2310894-2
Paul Desmond Orchestra | Planet Jazz:Jazz Saxophone | Planet Jazz | 2169653-2
Late Lament | Bluebird | ND 90207
Paul Desmond With Different Groups | 100 Ans De Jazz:Paul Desmond | RCA | 2177830-2
Paul Desmond With Strings | Desmond Blue | RCA | 2663898-2
Paul Quinichette Septet | On The Sunny Side | Original Jazz Classics | OJCCD 076-2(P 7103)
Ray Anthony And His Orchestra | Dancing Alone Together | Capitol | EMS 1156
Sam Jones Quintet | Visitation | Steeplechase | SCS 1097
Shirley Horn Trio | I Remember Miles | Verve | 557109-2
Sonny Stitt With The Hank Jones Trio | Good Life | Black-Hawk | BKH 528 CD
Stan Getz With Ib Glindemann And His Orchestra | Stan Getz | Laserlight | 15761
Thierry Lang Trio with Toots Thielemans & Carine Sarrasin | The Blue Peach | TCB Records | TCB 95302
Thomas Jäger | Orgel Ist Mehr...In Bamberg Vol.2 | Orgel ist mehr! | OIM/BA/1999-2 CD
Till Brönner Group | Chattin' With Chet | Verve | 157534-2
Tiziana Ghiglioni With The Kenny Drew Trio | Sounds Of Love | Soul Note | SN 1056
Tony Scott Quartet | Both Sides Of Tony Scott | Fresh Sound Records | 61120 CD(RCA)
Warren Bernhardt Quintet | Reflections | dmp Digital Music Productions | CD 489

My Funny Valentine-
Bill Henderson And His Quintet | Street Of Dreams | Discovery | DS 802 IMS

My Funny Valentine(2)
Bill Evans-Jim Hall | Undercurrent | Blue Note | 538228-2

My Funny Valentine(alt.take)
Chet Baker With The Don Sebesky Orchestra | She Was Too Good To Me | Epic | 450954-2

My Future Just Passed
The Boswell Sisters | It's The Girls | ASV | AJA 5014

My Gal
Clark Terry-Bob Brookmeyer Quintet | Gingerbread | Mainstream | MD CDO 711

My Gal Sal
Tiny Hill And His Orchestra | The Uncollected:Tiny Hill | Hindsight | HSR 159

My Gal Sal-
Anita Boyer & Her Tomboyers | Nat King Cole Trio:The MacGregor Years 1941/45 | Music & Arts | CD 911

My Garden
Viktoria Tolstoy With The Esbjörn Svensson Trio | Viktoria Tolstoy:White Russian | Blue Note | 821220-2
Chuck Thomas And His Dixieland Band | Woody Herman:Complete 1948-1950 Capitol Sessions | Definitive Records | DRCD 11195

My Generation
Blossom Dearie Quartet | My Gentleman Friend | Verve | 519905-2

My Gentleman Friend
Carol Sloane With The Art Farmer Sextet | Love You Madly | Contemporary | CCD 14049-2
Louis Hayes Sextet | The Real Thing | 32 Jazz | 32119

My Girl
The Storry-tellers | Frankie Rose And The Story-Tellers | Jazz Pure Collection | AU 31603 CD

My Girl Is Just Enough Woman For Me
Donald Byrd Quintet | Byrd In Flight | Blue Note | 852435-2

My God
Rova Saxophone Quartet | Rova:The Works Vol.2 | Black Saint | 120186-2

My Gongoma
Pili-Pili | Pili-Pili | JA & RO | JARO 4141-2
The Lousiville Jug Band | Blue Yodelers | Retrieval | RTR 79020

My Greatest Mistake
Duke Ellington And His Famous Orchestra | Duke Ellington:The Blanton-Webster Band | Bluebird | 21 13181-2
Ben Webster-Cotton Tail | RCA | 63667902

My Groove Your Moove
Jim Kahr | My Guitar And I Have Travelled | L+R Records | LR 42064

My Guy
Perry Robinson Quartet | Perry Robinson Quartet | Timescrapper | TSCR 9613

My Gypsy Baby
Carmen McRae With The Red Holloway Quintet | Fine And Mellow | Concord | CCD 4342

My Haven
Chico Freeman And Brainstorm | Sweet Explosion | IN+OUT Records | 7010-2

My Heart
Louis Armstrong And His Hot Five | Louis Armstrong-The Hot Fives Vol.1 | CBS | 460821-2

My Heart At Thy Sweet Voice
Vaughn Monroe And His Orchestra | Vaughn Monroe And His Orchestra 1943 | Circle | CCD-45

My Heart Belongs To Daddy
Anita O'Day With Orchestra | Cool Heat | Verve | MV 2679 IMS
Benny Goodman And His Orchestra | Camel Caravan Broadcast 1939 Vol.1 | Phontastic | NCD 8817
Bobby Burgess Big Band Explosion | Butters Idea | BELL Records | BLR 84069
Charlie Parker Quintet | The Cole Porter Song Book | Verve | 823250-1
Dee Dee Bridgewater With Orchestra | Dear Ella | Verve | 539102-2
Dizzy Gillespie Quintet | Have Trumpet Will Exite | Verve | MV 2696 IMS
Ella Fitzgerald With The Chick Webb Orchestra | Jazz Collection:Ella Fitzgerald | Laserlight | 24397
Let's Get Together | Laserlight | 17003
Gerry Mulligan Quartet | Reunion With Chet Baker | Blue Note | 746857 2
John Haley Sims-Harry Sweets Edison Quintet | Just Friends | Original Jazz Classics | OJCCD 499-2
Kenny Clarke-Francy Boland Big Band | More Smiles | MPS | 9814789
Lisa Bassenge Trio With Guests | A Sight, A Song | Minor Music | 801100
Lisa Ekdahl With The Peter Nordahl Trio | When Did You Leave Heaven | RCA | 2143175-2
Max Bennett Septet | Max Bennett | Fresh Sound Records | FSR 2002(Bethlehem BCP 48)
Mr.Acker Bilk And His Paramount Jazz Band | Dixieland Collection | Aves | 146534
Paul Motian Quartet | Paul Motian On Broadway Vol.1 | JMT Edition | 919029-2
Rosemary Clooney And Her Band | Rosemary Clooney Sings The Music Of Cole Porter | Concord | CCD 4185
Ruby Braff-Dick Hyman | Ruby Braff And Dick Hyman Play Nice Tunes | Arbors Records | ARCD 19141

My Heart Belongs To Daddy(take 1)
Charlie Parker Quintet | Bird: The Complete Charlie Parker On Verve | Verve | 837141-2

My Heart Belongs To Daddy(take 2)
Clyde Bernhardt And His Blue Bazers | Clyde Bernhardt:The Complete Recordings Vol.1 (1945-1948) | Blue Moon | BMCD 6016

My Heart Is A n Open Book
J.B.Hutto Quartet | Slideslinger | Black & Blue | BLE 59.510 2

My Heart Is An Open Book
Eddie Taylor Blues Band | My Heart Is Bleeding | L+R Records | CDLR 72008

My Heart Is Dancing
Little Johnny Taylor With Band | The Galaxy Years | Ace Records | CDCHD 967

My Heart Is Loaded With Trouble
Charles Brown Band | Drifting Blues | Pathe | 1546611(Score SLP 4011)

My Heart Skips A Beat
Duke Jordan Trio | Tivoli One | Steeplechase | SCCD 31189

My Heart Stood Still
Art Tatum | Art Tatum:Complete Capitol Recordings | Definitive Records | DRCD 11192
Artie Shaw And His Orchestra | The Indispensable Artie Shaw Vol.1/2(1938-1939) | RCA | 2126413-2
Bill Evans Trio | Peace Piece And Other Pieces | Milestone | M 47024
The Jazz Giants Play Rodgers & Hart:Blue Moon | Prestige | PCD 24205-2
Trio 64 | Verve | 539058-2
Billy Taylor | Ten Fingers-One Voice | Arkadia Jazz | 71602
Claude Williamson Trio | Keys West | Affinity | AFF 62
Ella Fitzgerald With The Buddy Bregman Orchestra | The Complete Ella Fitzgerald Song Books of Harold Arlen, Irving Berlin, Duke Ellington, George & Ira Gershwin, Jerome Kern, Johnny Mercer, Cole Porter And Rogers & Hart | Verve | 519832-2
Elliot Lawrence Band | Plays Tiny Kahn And Johnny Mandel Arrangements | Fantasy | 0902109(F 3219)
Harry Allen Quintet | A Night At Birdland Vol. 1 | Nagel-Heyer | CD 5002
Joe Wilder Quartet | Wilder' N' Wilder | Savoy | SV 0131(MG 12063)
Kenny Burrell Quintet | Swingin' | Blue Note | GXK 8155
Knud Jorgensen-Bengt Hanson | Bojangles | Touché Music | TMcCD 002
Lee Wiley With The Ruby Braff Quartet | Duologue | Black Lion | BLP 60911
Nat Adderley Quintet | Wes Montgomery-The Complete Riverside Recordings | Riverside | 12 RCD 4408-2
Nat King Cole With The Nelson Riddle Orchestra | The Piano Style Of Nat King Cole | Capitol | 781203-2
Oscar Peterson Trio | The Jazz Soul Of Oscar Peterson | Verve | MV 2098 IMS
The Jazz Soul Of Oscar Peterson/Affinity | Verve | 533100-2
RCA Victor 80th Anniversary Vol.3:1940-1949 | RCA | 2668779-2
Paul Smith Trio | Intensive Care | Pausa | PR 7167(952078)
Ross Tompkins Quartet | Ross Tompkins And Good Friends | Concord | CJ 65
Shorty Rogers And His Giants | The Swinging Mr.Rogers | Atlantic | 90042-1 TIS
Stan Getz With The Bill Evans Trio | The Complete Bill Evans On Verve | Verve | 527953-2
The Chick Corea-Bill Evans Sessions | Verve | 2610036
Stan Getz-Bill Evans Quartet | Stan Getz & Bill Evans | Verve | 833802-2
Stephane Grappelli With The Diz Disley Trio | Compact Jazz:Stephane Grappelli | MPS | 831370-2 PMS

My Heart Stood Still(alt.take)
Nat King Cole With The Nelson Riddle Orchestra | The Piano Style Of Nat King Cole | Capitol | 781203-2
Stan Getz-Bill Evans Quartet | Stan Getz & Bill Evans | Verve | 833802-2
Bill Evans Trio | Trio 64 | Verve | 539058-2

My Heart Stood Still(incompl.take)
Stan Getz With The Bill Evans Trio | The Complete Bill Evans On Verve | Verve | 527953-2
The Complete Bill Evans On Verve | Verve | 527953-2

My Heart Stood Still(rehersal fragments)
Charlie Parker | The Complete 'Bird Of The Bebop' | Stash Records | ST-CD 535(889113)

My Heart Tells Me
Ida James With The Nat King Cole Trio | Nat King Cole Trio:The MacGregor Years 1941/45 | Music & Arts | CD 911

My Hearts Escapade
The Bemiss Brothers | The Moment I Believed | Sound Of New Orleans | SONO 6011

My Home In Louisiana
Ronnie Earl & The Broadcasters | Deep Blues | Black Top | BT 1033 CD

My Home Is In The Delta
Otis Spann/Robert Lockwood Jr. | Otis Spann And His Piano | Crosscut | CCR 1003(Candid)

My Honey's Lovin' Arms
Barbara Lea With The Johnny Windhurst Quintet | Barbara Lea | Original Jazz Classics | OJCCD 1713-2(PR 7065)
Bud Freeman Trio | Commodore Classics -Bud Freeman: Three's No Crowd | Commodore | 6.24061 AG
Pee Wee Russell And His Orchestra | Muggsy Spanier | Storyville | SLP 4020

My Idea
Luca Flores | For Those I Never Knews | SPLASC(H) Records | CD H 439-2

My Ideal
Andy Middleton Quintet | Acid Rain | Owl Time Line | 3819082
Art Blakey And The Jazz Messengers | Art Blakey | Jazz Classics | AU 36019 CD
Art Tatum-Ben Webster Quartet | Art Tatum-The Complete Pablo Group Masterpieces | Pablo | 6 PACD 4401-2
The Tatum Group Masterpieces | Pablo | 2310737-2
Bennie Wallace With Yosuke Yamashita | Brilliant Corners | Denon Compact Disc | CY-30003
Chet Baker Quartet | Chet Baker Sings | Pacific Jazz | 300067(PJ 1222)
Ernie Henry Quartet | Seven Standards And A Blues | Original Jazz Classics | OJCCD 1722-2(RLP 248)
John Coltrane Quintet | The Stardust Sessions | Prestige | P 24056
Lee Wiley With The Raph Burns Orchestra | As Time Goes By | RCA | ND 83138(847185)
Lew Tabackin Quartet | Nature | Inner City | IC 1028 IMS
Sonny Rollins-Larry Coryell Duo | Don't Ask | Original Jazz Classics | OJCCD 915-2(M 9090)
Stan Getz Quartet With Chet Baker | Stan Getz-Chet Baker:Quintessece Vol.1 | Concord | CCD 4807
Vince Jones Septet | On The Brink Of It | Intuition Records | INT 3068-2
Wild Bill Davis Super Trio | That's All | Jazz Connaisseur | JCCD 9005-2
Wynton Marsalis Quintet | Think Of One | CBS | 460709-2

My Inspiration
Bob Crosby And His Orchestra | The Uncollected:Bob Crosby Vol.2 | Hindsight | HSR 209

My Invitation
Gino Lattuca Quartet | My Impression | B.Sharp Records | CDS 085

My Jelly Roll Soul
Charles Mingus Jazz Workshop | Blues & Roots | Atlantic | 8122-75205-2
Blues & Roots | Atlantic | 7567-81336-2

My Jelly Roll Soul(alt.take)
Blues & Roots | Atlantic | 8122-75205-2
Vido Musso's All Stars | Loaded:Vido Musso/Stan Getz | Savoy | SV 0227(MG 12074)

My Kind A (Of) Love
Albert Mangelsdorff-John Surman Quintet | Room 1220 | Konnex Records | KCD 5037

My Kind Of Beauty
Frank Sinatra With The Count Basie Orchestra | Sinatra-Basie:An Historic Musical First | Reprise | 7599-27023-2

My Kind Of Girl
Les Brown And His Band Of Renown | Today | MPS | 68118

My Kind Of Jazz
Beverly Kenney With The Basie-Ites | Beverly Kenney | Fresh Sound Records | FSR-CD 33(882158)

My Kind Of Time
Bireli Lagrene Quartet | Blue Eyes | Dreyfus Jazz Line | FDM 36591-2

My Kind Of Town
Count Basie And His Orchestra | Frankly Basie-Count Basie Plays The Hits Of Frank Sinatra | Verve | 519849-2

My Kind Of Town(Chicago Is)
Benny Carter Quintet | My Kind Of Trouble | Pablo | 2310935-2

My Kinda Love
Ben Pollack And His Park Central Orchestra | Ben Pollack Vol.3 | Jazz Oracle | BDW 8017
Futuristic Rhythm | Saville Records | SVL 154 IMS
Ernestine Anderson With Orchestra | My Kinda Swing | Mercury | 842409-2
Gerry Mulligan Concert Jazz Band | The Complete Verve Gerry Mulligan Concert Band | Verve | 9860613
Lurlean Hunter And Her All Stars | Blue & Sentimantel | Atlantic | AMCY 1081

My Ladies Waltz
Buster Benton Blues Band | Blues At The Top | Black & Blue | BLE 59.001 2

My Lady
Lutz Häfner Quartet | Way In Way Out | Jazz 4 Ever Records:Jazz Network | J4E 4757
Stan Kenton And His Orchestra | New Concepts | Capitol | 792865-2

My Lament
Maria Schneider Jazz Orchestra | Evanescence | Enja | ENJ-8048 2

My Last Affair
Art Tatum | The Tatum Solo Masterpieces Vol. 1 | Pablo | 2310723
Ella Fitzgerald And Her Savoy Eight | Ella Fitzgerald-The Early Years-Part 1 | GRP | GRP 26182
Ella Fitzgerald With The Count Basie Orchestra | Ella And Basie | Verve | 539059-2
Ella & Basie-On The Sunny Side Of The Street | Verve | 821576-2
Jo Jones Quartet | Our Man Papa Jo! | Denon Compact Disc | 38C38-7047

My Last Affair(alt.take)
Lionel Hampton And His Orchestra | The Complete Lionel Hampton Vol.1/2(1937-1938) | RCA | 2115525-2

My Last Chance
King Curtis Band | King Curtis-Blow Man Blow | Bear Family Records | BCD 15670 CI

My Last Date
Paquito D'Rivera Group | Why Not | CBS | 467137-2

My Late Coming Out
Ahmad Jamal Trio | Picture Perfect-70th Anniversary | Warner | 8573-85268-2

My Latin
Ray Barretto & New World Spirit | Ancestral Messages | Concord | CCD 4549

My Laurie
Art Pepper Quartet | No Limit | Contemporary | COP 019

My Lazy Uncle
Bill Ramsey With The Toots Thielemans Quartet | When I See You | BELL Records | BLR 84022

My Life
The Chris White Project | The Chris White Project | Muse | MCD 5494

My Life Is Hell
Muddy Waters Blues Band | Muddy Waters | Chess | 427005

My Little Bimbo
Papa Bue's Viking Jazzband | Live In Dresden | Storyville | SLP 815/16

My Little Boat
Steve Gadd Group | Gaddabout | Electric Bird | K32Y 6015

My Little Brown Book
Duke Ellington And His Orchestra | And His Mother Called Him Bill | RCA | 2125762-2
John Coltrane-Duke Ellington Quartet | The Gentle Side Of John Coltrane | Impulse(MCA) | 951107-2
Duke Ellington & John Coltrane | Impulse(MCA) | 951166-2
Mario Raja Big Band | Ellington | SPLASC(H) Records | CD H 427-2
Roman Schwaller Jazz Quartet | The Bizarre Is Open | Jazz Publications | JPV 8505

My Little Brown Book-
Oscar Pettiford Sextet | Montmartre Blues | Black Lion | BLP 60124

My Little Cousin
Joe Haider Trio | Katzenvilla | EGO | 4013

My Little Darling
Jelly Roll Morton Trio | The Jelly Roll Morton Centennial-His Complete Victor Recordings | Bluebird | ND 82361

My Little Drum(Little Drummer Boy)
Art Kassel And His 'Kassels-In-The-Air' Orchestra | The Uncollected:Art Kassel | Hindsight | HSR 162

My Little Girl
Willie Humphrey With The Maryland Jazz Band | Willie Humphrey Meets Maryland Jazz Band Of Cologne | DuBat Music | BMI 41991

My Little Sad Lucie
Stanley Cowell Trio | We Three | DIW | DIW 8017

My Little Strayhorn
Allan Botschinsky Quartet | I've Got Another Rhythm | M.A Music | A 916-2

TITELVERZEICHNIS

My Little Suede Shoes

Billy May And His Orchestra | Billy May's Big Fat Brass/Bill's Bag | Capitol | 535206-2
Charlie Parker All Stars | Bird's Eyes Last Unissued Vol.24 | Philology | W 854.2
Charlie Parker Sextet | Charlie Parker:The Best Of The Verve Years | Verve | 527815-2
Charlie Parker's Jazzers | Bird On Verve-Vol.5:The Magnificent Charlie Parker | Verve | 817446-1 IMS
Charly Antolini-Charly Augschöll Quartet | Charlie Antolini-40 Years Jubilee Drumfire | BELL Records | BLR 86001
Cornell Dupree Group | Bop 'N' Blues | Kokopelli Records | KOKO 1302
Donald 'Duck' Harrison Quintet | Full Circle | Sweet Basil | 660.55.003
J.J.Johnson And His Orchestra | Planet Jazz:J.J.Johnson | Planet Jazz | 2159974-2
J.J.! | RCA | 2125727-2
James Zollar Quintet | Soaring With Bird | Naxos Jazz | 86008-2
Red Rodney Quintet | One For Bird | Steeplechase | SCCD 31238
Walter Bishop Jr.Orchestra | Cubicle | Muse | MR 5151

My Little Suede Shoes-

Steve Grossman Trio | Bouncing With Mr. A.T. | Dreyfus Jazz Line | FDM 36579-2

My Lonely Room

Sammy Price | Doc Cheattam&Sammy Price:Duos And Solos | Sackville | SK2CD-5002

My Lord What A Morning

Charlie Haden-Hank Jones | Steal Away | Verve | 527249-2
Arturo Sandoval Sextet | Just Music | Ronnie Scott's Jazz House | JHCD 008

My Love

Charlie Haden Quartet West | Always Say Goodbye | Verve | 521501-2

My Love And I(Love Song From Apache)

Cousin Joe With Band | Cousin Joe:The Complete 1945-1947 Vol.1 (1945-1946) | Blue Moon | BMCD 6001

My Love Has Gone

Mose Vinson Band | Joe Hill Louis: The Be-Bop Boy | Bear Family Records | BCD 15524 AH
Diana Krall Trio | Love Scenes | Impulse(MCA) | 951234-2

My Love Is

Mat Mathews Orchestra | The Gentle Art Of Love | Dawn | DCD 111

My Love Is An April Song

Bill Evans Trio | The Complete Bill Evans On Verve | Verve | 527953-2
Deborah Henson-Conant | The Celtic Album | Laika Records | 35101022

My Love Is Like A Red, Red Rose

Buddy Guy Blues Band | Buddy Guy-The Complete Chess Studio Recordings | MCA | MCD 09337

My Love Is Real

Buddy Guy Chicago Blues Band | Blues Rarities | Chess | 6.28601 DP

My Love Is You

Lorry Raine With The Dennis Farnon Orchestra | Interlude With Lorry Raine | Fresh Sound Records | Advance CD 714

My Love Supreme

Duke Pearson Orchestra | The Right Touch | Blue Note | 828269-2

My Love(from Candide)

Kurt Elling Group | Blue Velvet: Crooners, Swooners And Velvet Vocals | Blue Note | 521153-2

My Love,Effendi

This Time Its Love | Blue Note | 493543-2
Peggy Lee With Lou Levy's Orchestra | Pass Me By/Big Spender | Capitol | 535210-2

My Love,Forgive Me

Dinah Washington With Lucky Thompson And His All Stars | The Complete Dinah Washington Vol.1 | Official | 3004

My Mama Rocks Me

Kenny Davers/Humphrey Lyttelton Sextet | This Old Gang Of Ours | Calligraph | CLG LP 012 IMS

My Man

Abbey Lincoln With Her Quintet | Sonny Rollins-The Freelance Years:The Complete Riverside & Contemporary Recordings | Riverside | 5 RCD 4427-2
Archie Shepp Quartet | Passport To Paradise-Archie Shepp Play Sidney Bechet | West Wind | WW 0002
Billie Holiday And Her All Stars | The Essential Billie Holiday:Carnegie Hall Concert | Verve | 833767-2
Billie Holiday And Her Orchestra | Billie Holiday: The First Verve Sessions | Verve | 2610027
Billie Holiday With The Bobby Tucker Quartet | Lover Man | MCA | 2292-52317-1
Billie Holiday With The Count Basie Orchestra | Birdland All Stars At Carnegie Hall | Roulette | CDP 798660-2
Billie Holiday With The Mal Waldron Trio | Billie Holiday Radio & TV Broadcast(1953-56) | ESP Disk | ESP 3003-2
Ella Fitzgerald With The Tommy Flanagan Trio | The Montreux '77 Collection | Pablo | 2620107
Louis Armstrong And His All Stars | The Legendary Berlin Concert Part 2 | Jazzpoint | JP 1063 CD
The Best Live Concert | Festival | ???
Shirley Horn Trio | Violets For Your Furs | Steeplechase | SCCD 31164
Teddy Wilson And His Orchestra | Jazz Gallery:Billie Holiday Vol.1(1933-49) | RCA | 2119542-2

My Man In Sidney

Svend Asmussen Quartet | Still Fiddling | Storyville | STCD 4252

My Man Is Gone Now

Rosetta Howard And Her Hep Cats | The 30's Girls | Timeless | CBC 1-026

My Man's In Trouble

Sippie Wallace With Axel Zwingenberger | Sippie Wallace/Axel Zwingenberger And The Friends Of Boogie Woogie Vol.1 | Vagabond | VRCD 8.84002
Count Basie And His Orchestra | Count Basie 1954 | Jazz Society | AA 526/527

My Man's Gone Now

Adam Makowicz Trio | Naughty Baby | RCA | 3022-1-N(809279)
Bill Evans Trio | Bill Evans Trio:The Last Waltz | Milestone | 8MCD 4430-2
Bill Evans Trio:The Last Waltz | Milestone | 8MCD 4430-2
Bill Evans Trio:The Last Waltz | Milestone | 8MCD 4430-2
Letter To Evan | Dreyfus Jazz Line | FDM 36554-2
Bill Evans:The Secret Sessions | Milestone | 8MCD 4421-2
Sunday At The Village Vanguard | Original Jazz Classics | OJC20 140-2
Bill Evans-Jim Hall | The Complete Bill Evans On Verve | Verve | 527953-2
Trio (Motian Peacock)-Duo(Hall) | Verve | 2-2509 IMS
Bill Mays Group | Kaleidoscope | The Jazz Alliance | TJA 10013
Buddy Rich And His Orchestra | Swingin' New Big Band | Pacific Jazz | 835232-2
Dave Grusin Group | The Gershwin Connection | GRP | GRP 20052
GRP All-Star Big Band | GRP All-Star Big Band:Live! | GRP | GRP 97402
Hal Galper | Hal Galper At Café Des Copains | Philology | W 35.2
Julie London With Pete King And His Orchestra | About The Blues/London By Night | Capitol | 535208-2
Karin Krog With The Egil Kapstad Quartet | Gershwin With Karin Krog | Polydor | 2382045 IMS
Louis Armstrong And Ella Fitzgerald With Russell Garcia's Orchestra | The Complete Ella Fitzgerald And Louis Armstrong On Verve | Verve | 537284-2
Lynne Arriale Trio | The Eyes Have It | dmp Digital Music Productions | CD 502
Miles Davis With Gil Evans & His Orchestra | Porgy And Bess | CBS | CK 65141
The Miles Davis Selection | CBS | 465699-2
Mundell Lowe's Jazzmen | Porgy And Bess | RCA | PL 43552
Nina Simone-Bob Bushnell | Planet Jazz:Female Jazz Vocalists | Planet Jazz | 2169656-2
Orquestra De Cambra Teatre Lliure | Porgy And Bess | Fresh Sound Records | FSNT 066 CD
Oscar Peterson-Joe Pass Duo | Porgy And Bess | Original Jazz Classics | OJCCD 829-2(2310779)
Paolo Fresu Quintet | Kind Of Porgy & Bess | RCA | 21951952
Peter King Quintet | Speed Trap | Ronnie Scott's Jazz House | JHCD 041
Shirley Horn Trio with Roy Hargrove | I Remember Miles | Verve | 557109-2

My Man's Gone Now-

Mani Neumeir Group | Privat | ATM Records | ATM 3803-AH

My Master

John Zorn Naked City | Heretic-Jeux Des Dames Cruelles | Avant | AVAN 001

My Melancholy Baby

Benny Goodman Quartet | Benny Goodman:The Complete Small Combinations Vol.1/2(1935-1937) | RCA | ND 89753
Bill Evans Trio | Empathy+A Simple Matter Of Conviction | Verve | 837757-2 PMS
Bireli Lagrene Ensemble | Routes To Django & Bireli Swing '81 | Jazzpoint | JP 1055 CD
Bireli Lagrene Quartet | A' Portrait Of Jan Jankeje | Jazzpoint | JP 1054 CD
Cal Collins Quartet | Blues On My Mind | Concord | CJ 95
Charlie Parker And His Orchestra | Bird On Verve-Vol.2:Bird & Diz | Verve | 817443-1 IMS
Charlie Parker Quintet | Verve Jazz Masters 15:Charlie Parker | Verve | 519827-2
Dave McKenna | Dave Fingers McKenna | Chiaroscuro | CR 175
Don Redman And His Orchestra | For Europeans Only | Steeplechase | SCC 6020/21
Earl Hines | The Earl | Naxos Jazz | 8.120581 CD
Ella Fitzgerald With Teddy Wilson And His Orchestra | Ella Fitzgerald Vol.1-Forever Young | Swingtime(Contact) | ST 1006
Frankfurt Swing All Stars | Can't We Be Friends | Joke Records | JLP 219
Glenn Miller And His Orchestra | Original Recordings From 1938 to 1942,Vol.2 | RCA | 2118549-2
Original Recordings From 1938 To 1942 Vol. 2 | RCA | NL 89218
John McNeil Quartet | I've Got The World On A String | Steeplechase | SCCD 31183
Quintet Du Hot Club De France | Welcome To Jazz: Django Reinhardt | Koch Records | 322 074 D1
Sonny Stitt Quartet | Live At The Hi-Hat Boston | Fresh Sound Records | FSCD 1002
Thelonious Monk | Thelonious Monk Collection | Black Lion | BLCD 7601-2

My Melancholy Baby-

Charlie Parker Quintet | Bird And Diz | Verve | 521436-2

My Melancholy Baby(alt.take)

Earl Hines | The Indispensable Earl Hines Vol.3/4(1939-1945) | RCA | 2126408-2

My Melancholy Baby(coda rehearsal)

Charlie Parker And His Orchestra | Bird: The Complete Charlie Parker On Verve | Verve | 837141-2

My Melancholy Baby(take 1)

Quintet Du Hot Club De France | Jazz In Paris:Django Reinhardt-Swing 39 | EmArCy | 159854-2 PMS
Charlie Parker And His Orchestra | Bird: The Complete Charlie Parker On Verve | Verve | 837141-2

My Melancholy Baby(take 2)

Quintet Du Hot Club De France | Jazz In Paris:Django Reinhardt-Swing 39 | EmArCy | 159854-2 PMS
Didier Lockwood Trio | New World | MPS | 68237

My Mind's Eye

Mulgrew Miller Trio | Time And Again | Landmark | LCD 1532-2

My Mommie Sent Me To The Store

Dick Sudhalter Band | Melodies Heard,Melodies Sweet... | Challenge | CHR 70055

My Monday Date

Earl Hines-Muggsy Spanier All Stars | The Essential Earl Hine With Guest Star Muggsy Spanier | Ember | CJS 851
Harry James And His Orchestra With The Dixieland Five | Compact Jazz | Verve | 833285-2 PMS

My Mother

Flora Molton And The Truth Band | Living Country Blues USA, Vol. 3 | L+R Records | LR 42033

My Mother's Eyes-

Wiregrass Sacred Harp Singers | The Colored Sacred Harp | New World Records | 80433-2

My Neighbourhood

Pee Wee Ellis Trio | Twelve And More Blues | Minor Music | 801034
George Wallington Trio | Our Delight | Prestige | P 24093

My Old Flame

Al Haig | Jazz Will O'-The -Wisp | Fresh Sound Records | FSR-CD 0038
Billie Holiday With Eddie Heywood And His Orchestra | Jazz Gallery:Billie Holiday Vol.1(1933-49) | RCA | 2119542-2
Bob Enevoldsen Quintet | The Complete Nocturne Recordings:Jazz In Hollywood Series Vol.1 | Fresh Sound Records | NR 3CD-101
Jazz In Hollywood:Harry Babasin/Bob Enevoldsen | Original Jazz Classics | OJCCD 1888-2(Nocturne NLP3/NLP-6)
Cathy Hayes With The Barney Kessel Orchestra | It's All Right With Me | Fresh Sound Records | FSR 531(HiFiJazz R 416)
Chet Baker Quartet | Chet Baker Quartet Live Vol.1:This Time The Dream's On Me | Pacific Jazz | 525248-2
Chet Baker In Milan | Original Jazz Classics | OJC20 370-2(JLP 18)
Jazz At Ann Arbor | Fresh Sound Records | 054 2602311(Pacific Jazz PJ 1203) (835282)
Dizzy Gillespie And His Operatic Strings | Dizzy In Paris | Ember | CJS 841
Dizzy Gillespie Orchestra And The Operatic String Orchestra | Jazz In Paris:Dizzy Gillespie And His Operatic Strings Orchestra | EmArCy | 018420-2
Dorothy Carless With The Barney Kessel Trio | The Carless Torch | Fresh Sound Records | HIFI R 403 CD
Duke Ellington And His Orchestra | Reminiscing In Tempo | Naxos Jazz | 8.120589 CD
Ella Fitzgerald-Joe Pass Duo | Fitzgerald & Pass... Again | Original Jazz Classics | OJCCD 1052-2(2310772)
Flip Phillips-Howard McGhee Boptet | Flip Phillips Complete 1947-1951 Verve Master Takes | Definitive Records | DRCD 11201
Gene DiNovi Trio | Renaissance Of A Jazz Master | Candid | CCD 79708
Greg Marvin Quintet | Taking Off! | Timeless | CD SJP 348
Jackie McLean Quintet | Consequence | Blue Note | LT 994 (GXK 8172)
Joe Pass | Joe Pass:A Man And His Guitar | Original Jazz Classics | OJCCD 8806-2
John Pisano-Billy Bean-Dennis Budimir | West Coast Sessions | String Jazz | SJRCD 1006
Jon Eardley/Mick Pyne | Two Of A Kind | Spotlite | SPJ LP 16
Kenny Dorham Sextet | But Beautiful | Milestone | M 47036
Lee Konitz Quartet | Lee Konitz In Harvard Square | Black Lion | BLCD 760928
Lou Levy Trio | My Old Flame | Fresh Sound Records | FSR-CD 0312
Martial Solal Trio | Balade Du 10 Mars | Soul Note | 121340-2
Peggy Lee With The Benny Goodman Orchestra | Peggy Lee & Benny Goodman:The Complete Recordings 1941-1947 | CBS | C2K 65686
Pete Jolly Trio | Take The 'A' Train | Fresh Sound Records | FSR-CD 0306
Phil Woods Quartet | Birds Of A Feather | Antilles | AN 1006(802505)
Rick Hollander Quartet | Accidental Fortune | Concord | CCD 4550
Sal Salvador Quartet | Stop Smoking Or Else Blues | Fresh Sound Records | FSR 556(Roulette SR 25262)
Sarah Vaughan With The Oscar Peterson Quartet | How Long Has This Been Going On? | Pablo | 2310821-2
Sarah Vaughan-Joe Pass | Sarah Vaughan Birthday Celebration | Fantasy | FANCD 6090-2
Scott Hamilton Quintet | Live At Brecon Jazz Festival | Concord | CCD 4649
Stan Getz Quartet | Stan Getz:Imagination | Dreyfus Jazz Line | FDM 36733-2
Early Getz | Prestige | P 24088
Stan Getz Quintet | Birdland Sessions 1952 | Fresh Sound Records | FSR-CD 0149
Zoot Sims Quintet | Zoot Sims | Swing | SW 8417
All Star Trumpet Spectacular | The Second Progressive Records All Star Trumpet Spectacular | Progressive | PRO 7017 IMS

My Old Kentucky Home(Epilogue)

Andrew Adair Group | States | Fresh Sound Records | FSNT 061 CD

My Old Kentucky Home(Prologue)

Phil Haynes Quartet | Phil Haynes & Free Country | Premonition | 790744-2

My Old Kentucky Home,Good Night

Otis Rush And His Band | Blues Power No.3:Otis Rush - Mourning In The Morning | Atlantic | 40495

My Old Man

Peter Bolte Trio | Trio | Jazz Haus Musik | JHM 0095 CD
The Five Cousins | Spirit Of Rhythm 1932-34 | Retrieval | RTR 79004

My Old Town

Akio With Joe Henderson | Akio | Muse | 600617(882118)

My One And Only

Dick Hyman | The Gershwin Songbook:Jazz Variations | Musicmasters | 65094-2
Ella Fitzgerald With The Nelson Riddle Orchestra | Oh Lady Be Good:The Best Of The Gershwin Songbook | Verve | 529581-2
Sings The Ira And George Gershwin Songbook | Verve | 825024-2
Joe Zawinul | Concerto Retitled | Atlantic | SD 1694
Silvia Droste And Her Quartet | Audiophile Voicings | BELL Records | BLR 84004
Trudy Desmond Band | My One And Only Love | Justin Time | JTR 8468-2

My One And Only Love

Allen Harris With The Metropole Orchestra | Here Comes Allen Harris... | Mons Records | MR 874771
Art Tatum-Ben Webster Quartet | The Tatum Group Masterpieces Vol.8 | Pablo | PACD20 431-2
Art Tatum-The Complete Pablo Group Masterpieces | Pablo | 6 PACD 4401-2
The Tatum Group Masterpieces | Pablo | 2310737-2
Art Van Damme & The Singers Unlimited | Invitation | MPS | 68107
Carlos Garnett Quartet | Under Nubian Skies | HighNote Records | HCD 7023
Chet Baker Trio | Let's Get Lost | RCA | PL 83054
Chico Freeman Quintet | Beyond The Rain | Original Jazz Classics | OJCCD 479-2
Diane Schuur With Orchestra | Love Songs | GRP | GRP 97032
Dick Collins And The Runaway Heard | Horn Of Plenty | Fresh Sound Records | NL 45632(RCA LJM 1019)
Dino Saluzzi-Anthony Cox-David Friedman | Rios | VeraBra Records | CDVBR 2156-2
Dominik Grimm-Thomas Wallisch Trio | A Brighter Day | Edition Collage | EC 510-2
Don Thompson Quartet | Beautiful Friendship | Concord | CJ 243
Frank Marocco-Ray Pizzi Duo | New Colors | Trend | TR 516 Direct-to-Disc
George Shearing Trio | Walkin'-Live At The Blue Note | Telarc Digital | CD 83333
Gerald Albright Group | Live At Birdland West | Atlantic | 7567-82334-2
Grant Green Quintet | Born To Be Blue | Blue Note | 784432-2
Horace Silver Quintet | The Stylings Of Silver | Blue Note | 300168(1562)
James Williams Quartet | Everything I Love | Concord | CJ 104
Jimmy Bruno Trio With Bobby Watson | Live At Birdland | Concord | CCD 4768
Joe Zawinul Quartet | The Beginning | Fresh Sound Records | FSR-CD 142(882885)
Joel Weiskopf Trio | The Search | Criss Cross | Criss 1174
John Hicks | Steadfast | Strata East Records | 660.51.010
Joshua Redman Quartet | Spirit Of The Moment:Live At The Village Vanguard | Warner | 9362-45923-2
June Christy With Bob Cooper's Orchestra | June's Got Rhythm | Fresh Sound Records | 054 1867331(Capitol T 1076)
Louis Armstrong And His Friends | Jazz Special-His Last Recordings | RCA | ND 89527
Louis Armstrong With Orchestra | Satchmo | Verve | 835895-2
Michael Urbaniak Trio | My One And Only Love | Steeplechase | SCCD 31159
Nelson Riddle And His Orchestra | Changing Colors | MPS | 9814794
New York Unit | Tribute To Great Tenors | Paddle Wheel | KICJ 68
Oscar Peterson Trio | We Get Request | Verve | 521442-2
En Concert Avec Europe 1 | Laserlight | 710443/48
Pat Thomas With Band | Jazz Patterns | Fresh Sound Records | Strand SLS CD 1015
Ray Bryant Trio | Potpouri | Pablo | 2310860
Rickey Woodard Quartet | California Cooking | Candid | CCD 79509
Ron Holloway Group | Slanted | Milestone | MCD 9219-2
Sir Charles Thompson Trio | Robbin's Nest | Paddle Wheel | KICJ 181
Sonny Rollins Quartet | Masters Of Jazz Vol.14 | RCA | CL 42874 AG
Sonny Rollins Quintet | Easy Living | Original Jazz Classics | OJCCD 893-2
Easy Living | Milestone | M 9080
Tom Lellis Group | Taken To Heart | Concord | CCD 4574
Wes Montgomery With The Don Sebesky Orchestra | Bumpin' | Verve | 539062-2
Verve Jazz Masters 14:Wes Montgomery | Verve | 519826-2
Wolfgang Haffner Jazz Quintet | Live Im Leibnitz-Gymnasium Altdorf | Jazz 4 Ever Records:Jazz Network | J4E 4711

My One And Only Love-

Sarah Vaughan With The Hal Mooney Orchestra | Sarah Vaughan Sings Gershwin | Verve | 557567-2

My One And Only(alt.take 1)

Sarah Vaughan Sings Gershwin | Verve | 557567-2

My One And Only(alt.take 2)

Sarah Vaughan Sings Gershwin | Verve | 557567-2

My One And Only(rehersal)

Dave Brubeck Group | In Their Own Sweet Way | Telarc Digital | CD 83355

My Organ

Werner Lener Quartet | My Own | Satin Doll Productions | SDP 1013-1 CD

My Own

Werner Lener Trio | Colours | Satin Doll Productions | SDP 1033-1 CD
Personal Moments | Satin Doll Productions | SDP 1026-1 CD
Lee Konitz Orchestra | The Best Of The Jazz Saxophones Vol.3 | LRC Records | CDC 9009

My Own True Love

Stan Getz With The Claus Ogerman Orchestra | What The World Needs Now-Stan Getz Plays Bacharach And David | Verve | 557450-2
Nat Pierce Trio | My Pal Basie | Jazz Connaisseur | JCCD 8904-2

My Pal Basie

Woody Herman And His Orchestra | Hollywood Paladium 1948 | Jazz Anthology | JA 5237

My Pet

Paul Whiteman And His Orchestra | The Indispensable Bix Beiderbecke(1924-1930) | RCA | ND 89572

My Pleasure

Mitchell's Christian Singers | From Spiritual To Swing | Vanguard | VCD 169/71

My Poor Mother Died A'Shoutin'

Roberto Ottaviano Quintet feat. Ray Anderson | The Leap | Red Records | NS 213

My Prayer

Sue Raney With The Billy May Orchestra | Songs For A Raney Day | Capitol | 300015(TOCJ 6129)

My Prayer(ballad)

Dee Dee Bridgewater With Band | Dee Dee Bridgewater | Atlantic | 7567-80760-2

My Prayer(fast)
Charleston Chasers | Steaming South | Stomp Off Records | CD 1314

My Pretty Girl
Charly Antolini Jazz Power | Bop Dance | BELL Records | BLR 84043

My Reverie
Don Elliott Octet | Don Elliott:Mellophone | Fresh Sound Records | FSR 2009(Bethlehem BCP 12)
Glenn Miller And His Orchestra | Original Recordings From 1938 to 1942,Vol.2 | RCA | 2118549-2
Sonny Rollins Quartet | Tenor Madness | Original Jazz Classics | OJC20 124-2
Stan Kenton And His Orchestra | Stan Kenton Portraits On Standards | Capitol | 531571-2
Teddy Stauffer Und Seine Original Teddies | Teddy Stauffer:Rare And Historical Jazz Recordings | Elite Special | 9522009
Johnny Hodges Orchestra | The Rabbit's Work On Verve In Chronological Order Vol. 1: 1951 | Verve | 2304447 IMS

My Romance
Bill Evans | New Jazz Conceptions | Original Jazz Classics | OJC20 025-2(RLP 223)
Bill Evans Trio | The Village Vanguard Sessions | Milestone | M 47002
My Romance | Zeta | ZET 702
Bill Evans Trio:The Last Waltz | Milestone | 8MCD 4430-2
The Brilliant | West Wind | WW 2058
The Tokyo Concert | Original Jazz Classics | OJCCD 345-2
Bill Evans Live In Tokyo | CBS | 481265-2
Buck Clayton All Stars feat.Ben Webster | Ben And Buck | Sackville | SKCD2-2037
Cal Tjader Quintet | Concerts In The Sun | Fantasy | FCD 9688-2
Concerts In The Sun | Fantasy | FCD 9688-2
Concerts In The Sun | Fantasy | FCD 9688-2
Charlie Byrd Trio | Au Courant | Concord | CCD 4779
Claude Williamson Trio | Live! The Sermon | Fresh Sound Records | FSR 105
Darji With The Hank Jones Quartet | Darji Meets Hank Jones | Timeless | SJP 171
Ella Fitzgerald With The Buddy Bregman Orchestra | The Complete Ella Fitzgerald Song Books of Harold Arlen, Irving Berlin, Duke Ellington, George & Ira Gershwin, Jerome Kern, Johnny Mercer, Cole Porter And Rogers & Hart | Verve | 519832-2
Ernestine Anderson With The John Horler Trio | Live From Concord To London | Concord | CCD 4054
Gary Burton-Makoto Ozone | Face To Face | GRP | GRP 98052
George Coleman Quartet | My Horns Of Plenty | Dreyfus Jazz Line | FDM 37005-2
Jimmy Smith Trio | The Master II | Blue Note | 855466-2
Johnny Griffin Quintet | Johnny Griffin:Chicago-New York-Paris | Verve | 527367-2
Junior Mance Quartet | At Town Hall Vol.2 | Enja | 9095-2
Kenny Werner | Copenhagen Calypso | Steeplechase | SCCD 31346
L.A.4 | Montage | Concord | CJ 156
Lee Wiley With The Ruby Braff Quartet | Duologue | Black Lion | BLP 60911
Mitchel Forman Trio | Now And Then-A Tribute To Bill Evans | Novus | 4163165-2
Paul Kuhn Trio | Blame It On My Youth | Timbre | TRCD 003
Ray Brown Trio | 3 Dimensional | Concord | CCD 4520
Red Richards | My Romance | Jazzpoint | JP 1042 CD
Ron Carter Trio | Jazz,My Romance | Blue Note | 830492-2
Ruby Braff-Ellis Larkins | Duets Vol.1 | Vanguard | VCD 79609-2
Sadao Watanabe Quintet With Strings | Plays Ballads | Denon Compact Disc | DC-8555
Singers Unlimited | A Capella 2 | MPS | 821860-2
Tal Farlow-Red Norvo Quintet | On Stage | Concord | CJ 143
The Atlantic String Trio | First Meeting | Factory Outlet Records | 2001-1 CD
Thomas Brendgens-Mönkemeyer | Beauty | Jardis Records | JRCD 20138
Thomas Stabenow-Lothar Schmitz | Swet Peanuts | Bassic-Sound | CD 007
Warne Marsh Quartet | A Ballad Album | Criss Cross | Criss 1007
Wes Montgomery With Orchestra | Pretty Blue | Milestone | M 47030
Wes Montgomery With The Jimmy Jones Orchestra | Wes Montgomery-The Complete Riverside Recordings | Riverside | 12 RCD 4408-2
Ian Shaw With Band | Taking It To Hart | Ronnie Scott's Jazz House | JHCD 036

My Romance(alt.take)
Bill Evans Trio | Waltz For Debby | Original Jazz Classics | OJC20 210-2
Charles Mingus And His Orchestra | The Complete Town Hall Concert | Blue Note | 828353-2

My Search
Andreas Schnerman Quintet | Welcome To My Backyard | Edition Collage | EC 535-2

My Secret Friends
Till Brönner Quintet | My Secret Love | Minor Music | 801051

My Secret Love
Tommy Smith Quartet | Standards | Blue Note | 796452-2

My Shing Hour
Baptiste Trotignon Trio | Fluide | Naive | 225099

My Shining Hour
Ella Fitzgerald With The Billy May Orchestra | The Harold Arlen Songbook | Verve | 817526-1 IMS
Ernestine Anderson With The Monty Alexander Trio | Never Make your Move Too Soon | Concord | CCD 4147
Guido Manusardi/Red Mitchell | Together Again | Soul Note | 121181-2
Joe Pass | Virtuoso No.4 | Pablo | 2640102
John Coltrane Quartet | The Very Best Of John Coltrane | Rhino | 8122-79778-2
Coltrane Jazz | Atlantic | 7567-81344-2
The Art Of John Coltrane - The Atlantic Years | Atlantic | SD 2-313
Karl Ratzer Quartet | Waltz For Ann | L+R Records | CDLR 45078
Meredith d'Ambrosio Quintet | South To A Warmer Place | Sunnyside | SSC 1039 D
Norman Simmons Quartet | Ramira The Dancer | Spotlite | SPJ LP 13
Shorty Rogers And His Orchestra | Swings | Bluebird | ND 83012
Warren Vaché Quintet With Special Guest Allan Vaché | Jazz Im Amerikahaus,Vol.2 | Nagel-Heyer | CD 012
Weslia Whitefield With The Mike Greensill Trio And Warren Vaché | My Shining Hour | HighNote Records | HCD 7012

My Ship
Andrew Cyrille And Maono | Metamusicians' Stomp | Black Saint | BSR 0025
Art Blakey And The Jazz Messengers | Jazz Life Vol.2:From Seventh At Avenue South | Storyville | 4960763
Bev Kelly With The Jimmy Jones Quintet | Love Locked Out | Original Jazz Classics | OJCCD 1798-2(RLP 1182)
Cal Tjader's Orchestra | Soul Burst | Verve | 557446-2
Carmen Lundy With The Cedar Walton Trio | Carmen Lundy:Self Portrait | JVC | JVC 2047-2
Cindy Blackman Quartet | Works On Canvas | HighNote Records | HCD 7038
Dennis Rowland Group | A Vocal Celebration Of Miles Davis | Concord | CCD 4751
Eden Atwood Group | Cat On A Hot Tin Roof | Concord | CCD 4599
Joe Venuti-Zoot Sims Sextet | Joe Venuti And Zoot Sims | Chiaroscuro | CR 142
Kenny Burrell Quartet | Moon And Sand | Concord | CCD 4121
Miles Davis + 19 | Miles Ahead | CBS | CK 65121
The Miles Davis Selection | CBS | 465699-2
Miles Davis With Gil Evans Orchestra, The George Gruntz Concert Jazz Band And Guests | Miles & Quincy Live At Montreux | Warner | 9362-45221-2

NDR Big Band | The Theatre Of Kurt Weil | ACT | 9234-2
Nick Brignola Quartet | Raincheck | Reservoir | RSR CD 108(882632)
Pearl & The Jazz's | Hear We Go! | Satin Doll Productions | SDP 1004-1 CD
Peter Erskine Orchestra | Peter Erskine | Contemporary | CCD 14010-2
Roland Kirk Quintet | Rahsaan/The Complete Mercury Recordings Of Roland Kirk | Mercury | 846630-2
Roland Kirk With The Stan Tracy Trio | Gifts And Messages | Ronnie Scott's Jazz House | JHAS 606
Rosemary Clooney With The Scott Hamilton Quintet | Show Tunes | Concord | CCD 4364
Singers Unlimited | Four Of Us | MPS | 68106
Sören Fischer Quartet | Don't Change Your Hair For Me | Edition Collage | EC 513-2
Stanley Turrentine Sextet | Jubilee Shout | Blue Note | 869692-1

My Silent Love
Zoot Sims Quartet | Zoot Sims:The Complete 1944-1954 Small Group Sessions(Master Takes),Vol.2 | Blue Moon | BMCD 1039

My Sin
Patti Page With Pete Rugolo And HisOrchestra | Patti Page In The Land Of Hi-Fi | Verve | 538320-2

My Socks
Gordon Brisker Quintet | My Son John | Naxos Jazz | 86064-2

My Son M'Ball Jo(M'Ball Jo)
Arthur Blythe Group | Hipmotism | Enja | ENJ-6088 2

My Son Ra
Arthur Blythe Quartet | Illusions | CBS | SRCS 7188

My Song
Pat Metheny | One Quiet Night | Warner | 9362-48473-2
Re-Birth Jazz Band | Do Whatcha Wanna | Mardi Gras Records | MG 1003

My Song In The Night
Fred Houn & The Afro-Asian Music Ensemble | We Refused To Be Used And Abused | Soul Note | 121167-2

My Songs Remain In Darkness Hidden
Les McCann Group | Another Beginning | Atlantic | 7567-80790-2

My Soul Lies Deep
Fleurine With Band And Horn Section | Meant To Be! | EmArCy | 159085-2

My Souldance With You
Mongo Santamaria And His Band | Mongo At The Village Gate | Original Jazz Classics | OJCCD 490-2(RLP 9529)

My Sound
Mongo Santamaria Orchestra | The Watermelon Man | Milestone | M 47012

My Spanish Heart
Chick Corea Group | Verve Jazz Masters 3:Chick Corea | Verve | 519820-2
Khan Jamal Trio | Three | Steeplechase | SCCD 31201

My Stove
Casey Bill Weldon | Masters Of Jazz Vol. 15-Blues Giants | RCA | NL 89728 DP

My Style
Nat King Cole Trio | Live At The Circle Room | Capitol | 521859-2

My Sugar Is So Refined
Live At The Circle Room | Capitol | 521859-2
Westbrook & Company | Platterback | PAO Records | PAO 10530

My Sweert Lord
Louis Armstrong And His Orchestra | Louis Armstrong-St.Louis Blues Vol.6 | CBS | 467919-2

My Sweet
Quintet Du Hot Club De France | Grapelli Story | Verve | 515807-2
Django Reinhardt-Stephane Grappelli | Ace Of Club | ACL 1158

My Sweet Hank O'Trash
Louis Armstrong And His All Stars/Orchestra | The Wonderful World Of Louis Armstrong | MCA | 2292-57202-2

My Temple
Stuff Smith And His Orchestra | The Varsity Session Vol.2 | Storyville | SLP 703

My Thoughts Are Wing'd With Hopes
Jim Nolet Group | With You | Knitting Factory Works | KFWCD 150

My Three Sons
Jack McDuff Quartet | The Soulful Drums | Prestige | PCD 24256-2
Cousin Joe With Band | Cousin Joe:The Complete 1945-1947 Vol.2(1946-1947) | Blue Moon | BMCD 6002

My Time After A While
Buddy Guy Blues Band | Buddy Guy-The Complete Chess Studio Recordings | MCA | MCD 09337

My Time After A While(alt.take)
Clarence Gatemouth Brown Quartet | Cold Storage | Black & Blue | BLE 59.096 2

My Time Of Day
Mel Tormé And His Trio | Night At The Concord Pavillion | Concord | CCD 4433

My Verse
Shorty Rogers And His Orchestra | Swings | Bluebird | ND 83012

My Very Good Friend The Milkman
Fats Waller And His Rhythm | I'm Gonna Sit Right Down...The Early Years-Part 2(1935-1936) | Bluebird | 63 66640-2

My Walking Stick
Ruby Braff And His Men | Easy Now | RCA | 2118522-2

My Way-
HR Big Band | The American Songs Of Kurt Weill | hr music.de | hrmj 006-01 CD

My Week
Count Basie And His Orchestra | Prez's Hat Vol.3 | Philology | 214 W 8

My Wife My Friend(As Each Day Goes By)
Charlie Shavers Quartet | Swing Along With Charlie Shavers | Fresh Sound Records | FSR-CD 327

My Wild Irish Rose
Muggsy Spanier And His Jazz Band | Big Band Bounce & Boogie-Muggsy Spanier:Hesitatin' Blues | Affinity | AFS 1030

My Wild Irish Rose-
Buddy Childers Quintet | Sam Songs | Fresh Sound Records | LJH 6009(Liberty)

My Yiddish Momma
Terry Gibbs Octet | Jewis Melodies In Jazztime | Mercury | 589673-2
Jimmy Lyons | Other Afternoons | Affinity | AFF 34

Myjava
George Benson Quartet | It's Uptown | CBS | 502469-2

Myna Bird Blues
Zoot Sims-Bucky Pizzarelli Duo | Summum | Ahead | 33752

Mynah Lament
Ralph Sharon Sextet | Mr.& Mrs. Jazz | Fresh Sound Records | FSR 2028(Bethlehem BCP 13)

Myndir Now
Johnny Dankworth Seven | Bebop In Britain | Esquire | CD ESQ 100-4

Myriam
Mark Turner Quartet | Dharma Days | Warner | 9362-47998-2

Myron's World
Herlin Riley Quintet | Watch What You're Doing | Criss Cross | Criss 1179

Myself When I Am Real
Charles Mingus | Thirteen Pictures:The Charles Mingus Anthology | Rhino | R2 71402

Mysteries Unfolding
Aki Takase-Alexander von Schlippenbach | Piano Duets-Live In Berlin 93/94 | FMP | OWN-90002

Mysterioso-
John Zorn Group | Cobra | Hat Art | CD 6040(2)

Mysterious Blues
Jazz Artists Guild | Newport Rebels-Jazz Artists Guild | Candid | CCD 79022
Duke Ellington And His Orchestra | Afro-Bossa | Reprise | 9362-47876-2

Mysterious Chick
Concert In The Virgin Islands | Discovery | DS 841 (807431)

Mysterious Dream
Dieter Köhnlein | Three Faces(At Least) | Aho-Recording | CD 1022

Mysterious Phonecall(dedicated to Klaus Kinski)
Fischbacher Group feat. Adam Nussbaum | Mysterious Princess | Acoustic Music Records | AMC 1025

Mysterious Traveler(part 1)
Ron Marvin & Remy Filipovitch | Mysterious Traveler | Album | AS 44677 CD

Mysterious Traveler(part 2)
Wolfgang Fuhr Quartet | Song Of India:Music For Quartet | Mons Records | MR 874776

Mysterium
David S.Ware Trio | Passage To Music | Silkheart | SHCD 113

Mystery
Miles Davis Group | Doo-Bop | Warner | 7599-26938-2
Myriam Alter Quintet | Reminiscence | B.Sharp Records | CDS 098

Mystery Girl
Gerard Pansanel Quintet | Voices | Owl Time Line | 3819102

Mystery Man
Wolfgang Lackerschmid Group | Mallet Connection | Bhakti Jazz | BR 33

Mystery Movie
Carlos Garnett Orchestra | Cosmos Nucleus | Muse | MR 5104

Mystery Of Green And Black
Malachi Thompson Sextet With Voices | 47th Street | Delmark | DE 497

Mystery Of Love
Randy Weston Orchestra | Volcano Blues | Verve | 519269-2

Mystery Train
Merl Saunders Quartet | Live At Keystone Vol.2 | Fantasy | FCD 7702-2

Mystery Trip
Miles Davis Group | Doo-Bop | Warner | 7599-26938-2

Mystery(reprise)
Vassilis Tsabropoulos Trio | Achirana | ECM | 1728(157462-2)

Mystic
Osman Ismen Project | Jazz Eastern | CBS | 489840-2

Mystic Dreams
Steve Coleman And The Mystic Rhythm Society | Myths, Modes And Means | Novus | 2131692-2

Mystical Adventures Suite(part 1-5)
Roland Kirk Quartet | Rahsaan/The Complete Mercury Recordings Of Roland Kirk | Mercury | 846630-2

Mystical Dream
Rip Rig And Panic/Now Please Don't You Cry Beautiful Edith | EmArCy | 832164-2 PMS

Mystifying
Eric Kloss Quintet | Bodies' Warmth | Muse | MR 5077

Mystique
Don Byas-Bud Powell Quintet | A Tribute To Cannonball | CBS | CK 65186

Myth
Jean-Paul Bourelly Trance Atlantic | Boom Bop II | Double moon | CHRDM 71023

Myth And Diffusion
Sun Ra And His Intergalactic Research Arkestra | Black Myth/Out In Space | MPS | 557656-2

Myth Versus Reality
The Contemporary Alphorn Orchestra | Mytha | Hat Art | CD 6110

Mythos Berlin
Erhard Hirt | Guitar Solo | FMP | OWN-90003

N 2.21
Thomas Kessler & Group | Thomas Kessler & Group | Laika Records | LK 190-015

N 2.21(reprise)
Möslang-Guhl Duo | Deep Voices | FMP | 0510

N S A
Ulrich Gumpert Workshop Band/DDR | Unter Anderem: 'N Tango Für Gitti | FMP | 0600

N.C. Blues
Joe Pass Trio | Resonance | Pablo | 2310968-2

N.E.C. Blues
Mary Lou Williams | The Best Of Mary Lou Williams | Pablo | 2310856

N.O.Blues
Milestone Jazz Stars | Milestone Jazz Stars in Concert | Milestone | MCD 55006-2
Gary Peacock-Bill Frisell | Just So Happens | Postcards | POST 1005

N.Y. Flat Top Box
The Brecker Brothers | The Brecker Brothers Live | Jazz Door | JD 1248

N.Y.C.
Jaco Pastorius Group | Live In New York City Volume One | Big World | BW 1001

N.Y.C.'s No Lark
Bill Evans | Verve Jazz Masters 5:Bill Evans | Verve | 519821-2
Ultimate Bill Evans selected by Herbie Hancock | Verve | 557536-2
Conversations With Myself | Verve | 521409-2
Bachi Attar/Elliott Sharp Group | In New York | Enemy | EMCD 114(03514)

N.Y.Slick
Kenny Dorham Sextet | Round About Midnight At The Cafe Bohemia Vol.3 | Blue Note | 300197(BNJ 61004)

N.Y.Theme
Derek Bailey Group | Guitar Drums 'N' Bass | Avant | AVAN 060

Na Francisca
Michele Hendricks And Her Trio | Me And My Shadow | Muse | MCD 5404

Na Uskrs Sam Se Rodila
Slawterhaus | Slawterhaus Live | Victo | CD 013

Naakkurat Na
Michael Leonhart Quartet | Aardvark Poses | Sunnyside | SSC 1070 D

Nabob
Gary Burton Quartet With Eberhard Weber | Passengers | ECM | 1092(835016-2)

Nacada
David Hazeltine Quartet | Blues Quarters Vol.1 | Criss Cross | Criss 1188

Nachiketa's Lament
Andy Lutter Trio | Nichtendende Geschichten | Extra Records & Tapes | 57230463

Nachspiel
Alan Skidmore-Gerd Dudek Quartet | Morning Rise | EGO | 4006

Nacht
Christoph Spendel Group | Radio Exotic | L+R Records | CDLR 70001

Nacht Eines Fauns
Blueprint Stage | Puzzle | Mons Records | MR 874817

Nachwort
Joelle Leandre | Contrebasse & Voix/Double Bass & Voice | Adda | 581043

Nacogdoches Gumbo-
Tino Tracanna Group | '292' | SPLASC(H) Records | CD H 322-2

Nada
Freddie Roach Quartet | Mo' Greens Please | Blue Note | 869698-3

Nadim
Franco D'Andrea Quartet | Live | Red Records | VPA 195

Nadja
Thomas Heberer | Mouth | Poise | Poise 09

Nadja(2001)
Shankar Group | Nobody Told Me | ECM | 1397

Nadru Dri Dhom-Tilana
Ahmed Abdul-Malik Orchestra | Jazz Sounds Of Africa | Prestige | PRCD 24279-2

Nadusilma
Ketil Bjornstad Group | Early Years | EmArCy | 013271-2

Naermere(Closer)
Erdmann 2000 | Recovering From y2k | Jazz 4 Ever Records:Jazz Network | J4E 4750

Naf Naf Naf
New Orleans Klezmer Allstars | Manichalfwitz | Gert Town Records | GT-1117

Nafas
Dhafer Youssef Group | Electric Sufi | Enja | ENJ-9412 2

Nafha

TITELVERZEICHNIS

Andrew Cyrille-Milford Graves Duo | Dialogue Of The Drums | IPS Records | 001

Nagaraja

Al Cohn-Zoot Sims Quintet | Either Way | Evidence | ECD 22007-2

Nagasaki

Benny Goodman Quartet | Welcome To Jazz: Benny Goodman | Koch Records | 321 973 D1
Fats Waller And His Rhythm | Private Acetates And Film Soundtracks | Jazz Anthology | JA 5148
Jesse Price And His Orchestra | Swingin' Small Combos Kansas City Style Vol.1 | Blue Moon | BMCD 6019
The Poll Winners | The Poll Winners | Original Jazz Classics | OJC 156(C 7535)
Willie Lewis And His Entertainers | Le Jazz En France Vol.3 | Pathe | 1727271

Nagoya(part 1&2)

Keith Jarrett | Works | ECM | 825425-1

Nahend

Clark Terry Orchestra | Color Changes | Candid | CCD 79009

Nahstye Blues

Donald Byrd Quintet | Free Form | Blue Note | 595961-2

Nai Nai

Krakatau | Volition | ECM | 1466

Naiads

Oregon | The Essential Oregon | Vanguard | VSD 109/110

Nails

Ahmed El-Salamouny/Claudio Menandro | Aquarela | FSM | FCD 97770

Naima

Archie Shepp-Jasper Van't Hof | The Fifth Of May | L+R Records | LR 45004
Bernt Rosengren Big Band | Jazz In Sweden | Caprice | CAP 1214
Corinne Chatel Quintet | Ma Vie En Rose | Edition Collage | EC 525-2
Curtis Fuller And The Roma Jazz Trio | Curtis Fuller Meets Roma Jazz Trio | Timeless | CD SJP 204
Eddie Henderson Quintet | Phantoms | Steeplechase | SCCD 31250
Hendrik Meurkens Band | A View From Manhattan | Concord | CCD 4585
Jaco Pastorius Group | Jaco Pastorius In New York | Jazz Door | JD 1232/33
Janice Borla With Band | Lunar Octave | dmp Digital Music Productions | CD 3004
Jean Toussaint Quartet | Impressions Of Coltrane | September | CD 5104
John Coltrane Quartet | John Coltrane-The Heavyweight Champion:The Complete Atlantic Recordings | Atlantic | 8122-71984-2
Visit To Scandinavia | Jazz Door | JD 1210
John Coltrane-Live Trane:The European Tours | Pablo | 7PACD 4433-2
John Coltrane-Live Trane:The European Tours | Pablo | 7PACD 4433-2
John Coltrane-Live Trane:The European Tours | Pablo | 7PACD 4433-2
The Complete 1962 Stockholm Concert Vol.1 | Magnetic Records | MRCD 108
Giant Steps | Atlantic | 8122-75203-2
Live In Paris | Charly | CD 87
Live In Antibes, 1965 | France's Concert | FCD 119
Countdown | Atlantic | 90462-1 TIS
John Coltrane Quartet With Eric Dolphy | John Coltrane:The Complete 1961 Village Vanguard Recordings | Impulse(MCA) | 954322-2
The Complete Copenhagen Concert | Magnetic Records | MRCD 116
John Coltrane Quintet | The Mastery Of John Coltrane Vol.4:Trane's Mood | MCA | 2292-54650-2
John Coltrane Sextet | The Best Of John Coltrane-His Greatest Years | MCA | AS 9200-2
John McLaughlin-Carlos Santana Group | John McLaughlin-Carlos Santana | Jazz Door | JD 1250
Matthew Shipp-Mat Maneri Duo | Gravitational Systems | HatOLOGY | 530
McCoy Tyner | Monk's Dream | Memo Music | HDJ 4019
Melissa Walker And Her Band | Moment Of Truth | Enja | ENJ-9365 2
Tommy Flanagan Trio | Giant Steps - In Memoriam Of John Coltrane | Enja | 4022-2
Woody Herman And The New Thundering Herd | Woody Herman:Thundering Herd | Original Jazz Classics | OJCCD 841-2
Gunter Hampel | Dances | Birth | 002

Naima(alt.take 1)

John Coltrane Quartet | John Coltrane-The Heavyweight Champion:The Complete Atlantic Recordings | Atlantic | 8122-71984-2

Naima(alt.take 2)

David Murray-Dave Burrell | Windward Passages | Black Saint | 120165-2

Naima(false start)

John Coltrane Quartet | John Coltrane-The Heavyweight Champion:The Complete Atlantic Recordings | Atlantic | 8122-71984-2

Naima(incomplete take 1)

John Coltrane-The Heavyweight Champion:The Complete Atlantic Recordings | Atlantic | 8122-71984-2

Naima(incomplete take 2)

Alvin Queen Sextet | Ashanti | Nilva | NQ 3402 IMS

Naima's Love Song

Betty Carter And The John Hicks Quartet | It's Not About The Melody | Verve | 513870-2
The Upper Manhattan Jazz Society | The Upper Manhattan Jazz Society | Enja | ENJ-4090 2
Najma & Her Group | Atish | VeraBra Records | ???

Najat(2002 Reprise)

Thomas Heberer | Mouth | Poise | Poise 09

Najat(2002)

John Coltrane Quintet | The Believer | Original Jazz Classics | OJCCD 876-2(P 7292)

Nakatini Serenade

Black Pearls | Prestige | P 24037
Larry Nocella/Dannie Richmond Quartet | Everything Happens To Me | Red Records | VPA 167

Naked

Ketil Bjornstad Group | Grace | EmArCy | 013622-2
J.J.Johnson-Joe Pass | We'll Be Together Again | Pablo | 2310911-2

Naked City Theme

Mike Wofford | Afterthoughts | Discovery | DS 784 IMS

Naked Eye

Tony O'Malley Quintet | Naked Flame | Ronnie Scott's Jazz House | JHCD 040

Naked In The Jungle-

Billy May & His Orchestra | I Believe In You | Bainbridge | BT 1001

Naked Moon

Arcado String Trio With The Kölner Rundfunkorchester | For Three Strings And Orchestra | JMT Edition | 849152-2

Naked Soul

Wheelz With Ingrid Jensen | Around The World I | ACT | 9247-2

Namasté-

Peter Erskine Trio | Juni | ECM | 1657(539726-2)

Namasti

Erdmann 2000 | Recovering From y2k | Jazz 4 Ever Records:Jazz Network | J4E 4750

Namderyew,ed!

Steve Lacy | Remains | Hat Art | CD 6102

Name Everything

Randy Brecker Quintet | Score | Blue Note | 781202-2

Name That Tune

Russ Freeman-Shelly Manne | One On One | Contemporary | CCD 14090-2
Steve Swallow Group | Deconstructed | Watt | XtraWatt/9(537119-2)
Marion Brown Sextet | Marion Brown In Sommerhausen | Calig | 30605

Nameless

Oscar Peterson-Major Holley Duo | Tenderly | Verve | MV 2662 IMS

Namely You

Conte Candoli Quartet | Portrait Of A Count | Fresh Sound Records | FSR-CD 5015
P.J. Perry Quartet | Worth Waiting For | The Jazz Alliance | TJA 10007
Sonny Rollins Quartet | Sonny Rollins | Blue Note | 84508
Ballads | Blue Note | 537562-2
Newk's Time | Blue Note | 576752-2
Pata Trio | Lucy Und Der Ball | Jazz Haus Musik | JHM 34

Namesake

Milt Jackson Orchestra | Big Bags | Original Jazz Classics | OJCCD 366-2(RLP 9429)
Dollar Brand-Johnny Dyani Duo | Echoes From Africa | Enja | ENJ-3047 2

Namhanje(Today)

Johnny Mbizo Dyani Group | Born Under The Heat | Dragon | DRLP 68

NamNamSuri

Okay Temiz Group | Magnet Dance | TipToe | TIP-888819 2

Namu

Thierry Lang Quintet | Nan | Blue Note | 498492-2

Nan Madol

Erika Rojo & Tim Sund | Das Lied | Nabel Records:Jazz Network | CD 4684

Nana

Jimmie Lunceford And His Orchestra | Jimmie Lunceford Vol.5-Jimmie's Legacy | MCA | 1320

Nancy

Paul Desmond Quartet | Live | Verve | 543501-2
Take Ten | RCA | 63661462
Paul Kuhn Orchestra feat. Gustl Mayer | Street Of Dreams | Mons Records | MR 874800

Nancy And The Colonel

Jay McShann Quartet | The Man From Muskogee | Sackville | SKCD2-3005

Nancy(With The Laughing Face)

Brew Moore Quintet | Brew Moore | Original Jazz Classics | OJC 049(F 3208)
Cannonball Adderley Quartet | Cannonball Adderley Birthday Celebration | Fantasy | FANCD 6087-2
Claude Williamson Trio | The Fabulous Claude Williamson Trio | Fresh Sound Records | FSR-CD 0051
Flip Phillips Quartet | Spanish Eyes | Choice | CRS 1013 IMS
Grant Green Quartet | Ballads | Blue Note | 537560-2
Henry Mancini And His Orchestra | Experiment In Terror(Sountrack) | Fresh Sound Records | NL 45964(RCA LSP 2442)
John Coltrane Quartet | The Gentle Side Of John Coltrane | Impulse(MCA) | 951107-2
John Coltrane:The Classic Quartet-Complete Impulse Studio Recordings | Impulse(MCA) | 951280-2
Ken Peplowski Quintet | Illumination | Concord | CCD 4449
Paul Desmond Quartet | Masters Of Jazz Vol.13 | RCA | CL 42790 AG
Tete Montoliu | The Music I Like To Play Vol.4: Let's Call This | Soul Note | 121250-2

Nandi

Mynta | Nandu's Dance | Blue Flame | 40782(2132162-2)

Nanigo Soul

Red Sun/SamulNori | Then Comes The White Tiger | ECM | 1499

Nanjang(The Meeting Place)

Ernst Reijseger & Tenore E Cuncordu De Orosei | Colla Voche | Winter&Winter | 910037-2

Nanneddu Meu

Jon Balke w/Magnetic North Orchestra | Kyanos | ECM | 1822(017278-2)

Nano

Aldo Romano Duo | Il Piacere | Owl Records | 013575-2

Nano Nano

John Wolf Brennan | The Beauty Of Fractals | Creative Works Records | CW CD 1017-1

Nantucket

The Beauty Of Fractals | Creative Works Records | CW CD 1017-1

Nantucket Took It

Dwight Andrews Trio | Dwight Andrews | Otic | 1007

Naomi

World Music Meeting | World Music Meeting | Eigelstein | 568-72224

Naphtule Is Having A Bad Boy

Tete Montoliu | Yellow Dolphin Street/Catalonian Folk Songs | Timeless | CD SJP 107/116

Napoli's Wall

Steve Lacy Sextet | The Gleam | Silkheart | SHCD 102

Naptown Blues

Buddy Rich Big Band | The New One! | Pacific Jazz | 494507-2
Herb Ellis Quintet | Roll Call | Justice Records | JR 1001-2
Oscar Peterson Trio With Herb Ellis | Three Originals:Motion&Emotions/Tristeza On Piano/Hello Herbie | MPS | 521059-2
Project G-5 | Tribute To Wes Montgomery | Paddle Wheel | KICJ 146
Wes Montgomery With The Oliver Nelson Orchestra | Compact Jazz: Wes Montgomery Plays The Blues | Verve | 835318-2 PMS

Naranja

Enrico Rava Group | Quotation Marks | Japo | 60010 IMS (2360010)

Naranjo En Flor

Joe Diorio-Hal Crook 4et | Narayani | RAM Records | RMCD 4522

Nardis

Bill Evans Trio | The Complete Bill Evans On Verve | Verve | 527953-2
Spring Leaves | Milestone | M 47034
Live At Balboa Jazz Club Vol.2 | Jazz Lab | JLCD 5(889364)
Paris 1965 | Royal Jazz | RJD 503
Bill Evans Trio:The Last Waltz | Milestone | 8MCD 4430-2
Bill Evans Trio:The Last Waltz | Milestone | 8MCD 4430-2
Bill Evans Trio:The Last Waltz | Milestone | 8MCD 4430-2
Bill Evans Trio:The Last Waltz | Milestone | 8MCD 4430-2
Bill Evans Trio:The Last Waltz | Milestone | 8MCD 4430-2
The Best Of Bill Evans Live | Verve | 533825-2
Bill Evans:The Secret Sessions | Milestone | 8MCD 4421-2
How Deep Is The Ocean | West Wind | WW 2055
Bill Evans:The Secret Sessions | Milestone | 8MCD 4421-2
The Legendary Bill Evans Trio-The Legendary 1960 Birdland Sessions | Cool & Blue | C&B-CD 106
Candid Jazz Masters | The Candid Jazz Masters:For Miles | Candid | CCD 79710
Cannonball Adderley Quintet | Cannonball And Eight Giants | Milestone | M 47001
Portrait Of Cannonball | Original Jazz Classics | OJCCD 361-2(RLP 269)
Chet Baker Quartet | Chet Baker-The Legacy Vol.2:I Remember You | Enja | ENJ-9077 2
Chet Baker Trio | Candy | Sonet | SNTF 946(941424)
David Matthews Big Band | Live at The Five Spot,NYC | Muse | MR 5073
Eddie Gomez Trio | Live In Moscow | B&W Present | BW 038
Engstfeld-Plümer-Weiss | Drivin' | Nabel Records:Jazz Network | CD 4618
Frank Haunschild & Tom Van Der Geld | Getting Closer | Acoustic Music Records | 319.1170.2
George Russell Sextet | The Jazz Giants Play Miles Davis:Milestones | Prestige | PCD 24225-2
Horace Parlan | The Maestro | Steeplechase | SCCD 31167
Jam Session | Jam Session Vol.10 | Steeplechase | SCCD 31555
Jan Verwey Quartet | You Must Believe In Spring | Timeless | CD SJP 369
Joe Beck-Ali Ryerson | Django | dmp Digital Music Productions | CD 530
Joe Henderson Sextet | Foresight | Milestone | M 47058
John Abercrombie Trio | Straight Flight | JAM | 5001 IMS
Larry Willis Trio | Let's Play | Steeplechase | SCCD 31283
Masahiko Sato Trio | As If... | Denon Compact Disc | 33C38-7455
Michel Petrucciani Trio | Live At The Village Vanguard | Blue Note | 540382-2
Mick Goodrick-David Liebman-Wolfgang Muthspiel | In The Same Breath | CMP Records | CMP CD 71
Mitchel Forman Trio | Now And Then-A Tribute To Bill Evans | Novus | 4163165-2
Patricia Barber Quartet | Café Blue | Blue Note | 521810-2
Peter Weniger Quartet | Key Of The Moment | Mons Records | CD 1901
Ray Drummond Quintet | Susanita | Nilva | NQ 3409 IMS
The Atlantic String Trio | First Meeting | Factory Outlet Records | 2001-1 CD
Trio Wolf-Sperl-Bräuer | Polar Bear Express | Polar Bear Express | 609001

Nardis(alt.take)

Horace Parlan | Musically Yours | Steeplechase | SCCD 31141

Nard-ish

Carsten Daerr Trio | PurpleCoolCarSleep | Traumton Records | 4472-2

Nardism

Sadao Watanabe Group | Go Straight Ahead 'N Make A Left | Verve | 537944-2

Narrow Bolero

Roland Kirk Quintet | Rahsaan/The Complete Mercury Recordings Of Roland Kirk | Mercury | 846630-2
Rahsaan/The Complete Mercury Recordings Of Roland Kirk | Mercury | 846630-2

Narrow Bolero(alt.take)

Diana Krall Group | The Girl In The Other Room | Verve | 9862246

Narrow Daylight

Washboard Walter And His Band | John Byrd & Walter Taylor(1929-1931) | Story Of Blues | CD 3517-2

Nasce La Pena Mia

Michael Riessler & Singer Pur with Vincent Courtois | Ahi Vita | ACT | 9417-2

Nasce La Pena Mia-Introduktion

Cannonball Adderley Group | Cannonball Adderley-Lovers... | Fantasy | F 9505

Nascente

Al Grey And His Allstars | Centerpiece | Telarc Digital | CD 83379

Nashville Woman's Blues

Bessie Smith With The Louis Armstrong Trio | Louis Armstrong And The Blues Singers 1924-1930 | Affinity | AFS 1018(6)

Nashwa

Orchestra International | Sim-Sim | Plainisphare | Zone Z- 4

Nasty

Johnny 'Hammond' Smith Quartet | The Soulful Blues | Prestige | PCD 24244-2
Nils Landgren Funk Unit With Guests | 5000 Miles | ACT | 9271-2
Shannon Jackson & The Decoding Society | Nasty | Moers Music | 01086

Nasty Attitude

You Cindy Lou | Confessin' The Blues | Affinity | AFF 66

Nat(Night)

Dani Perez Quartet | Buenos Aires-Barcelona Connections | Fresh Sound Records | FSNT 144 CD

Nata

Mike Nock Quartet | Dark & Curious | VeraBra Records | CDVBR 2074-2

Nata Lagal

New York Jazz Collective | Everybody Wants To Go To Heaven | Naxos Jazz | 86073-2

Natacha's Blues

Barry Altschul Quintet | You Can't Name Your Own Tune | Muse | MR 5124

Natalia

Deborah Henson-Conant | Naked Music | Laika Records | LK 94-051

Nataliana

Good Fellas | Good Fellas 3 | Paddle Wheel | KICJ 166

Natalie

Thomas Heberer | Stella | Poise | Poise 08
Memphis Slim | Boogie Woogie | Accord | 402472

Natchez Fire(Burnin')

Andy Goodrich Quintet | Motherless Child | Delmark | DE 495

Natgo

Hod O'Brien Trio | Ridin' High | Reservoir | RSR CD 116(881745)

Nationalfeiertag

Jim Pepper & Eagle Wing | Rerembrance-Live At The International Jazzfestival Münster | Tutu Records | 888152-2*

Native American Visions: Remembrance-Ya Na Ho-Four Winds

Mel Lewis And His Sextet | The Lost Art | Limelight | 820815-2 IMS

Native Song

McCoy Tyner Septet | Reflections | Milestone | M 47062

Native Tongue

Anthony Braxton | 8KN-(B-12)IR10(for string quartet) | Sound Aspects | sas CD 009

Nat's Everglade

Ippe Kätkä Band | Ippe Kätkä Band | Leo Records | 018

Natt

Masqualero | Bande A Part | ECM | 1319
Niels-Henning Orsted-Pedersen And The Danish Radio Big Band | Ambiance | dacapo | DCCD 9417

Natura, Festa Do Interior

Niels Lan Doky Quartet | Daybreak | Storyville | STCD 4160

Natural Accurance

John Lewis Quartet | Mirjana | Ahead | 33750

Natural Sounds

Michael Sagmeister Trio | Sagmeister Trio/Ganshy | BELL Records | BLR 83753

Nature Boy

Annie Ross With The Johnny Spence Orchestra | Annie Ross Sings A Handful Of Songs | Fresh Sound Records | FSR-CD 0061
Art Pepper Quartet | Art Pepper:The Complete Galaxy Recordings | Galaxy | 16GCD 1016-2
Barney Wilen Quartet | Tilt | Vogue | 21559492
Clark Terry With Orchestra & Strings | Clark After Dark | MPS | 529088-2
Enrico Rava-Ran Blake | Duo En Noir | Between The Lines | btl 004(Efa 10174-2)
Etta Jones With The Jerome Richardson Sextet | Hollar! | Original Jazz Classics | OJCCD 1061(PR 7284)
Evelyn Huber-Mulo Franzl | Rendezvous | Edition Collage | EC 512-2
Five + Jazz Comfort | Brazz | Memo Music | MM 6061
George Benson Group/Orchestra | George Benson Anthology | Warner | 8122-79934-2
George Garzone Group | Alone | NYC-Records | NYC 6018-2
Harold Land With Orchestra | A Lazy Afternoon | Postcards | POST 1008
J.J.Johnson-Joe Pass | We'll Be Together Again | Pablo | 2310911-2
John Collins | The Incredible John Collins | Nilva | NQ 3412 IMS
John Coltrane Quartet | The Coltrane Quartet Plays | Impulse(MCA) | 951214-2
John Coltrane:The Classic Quartet-Complete Impulse Studio Recordings | Impulse(MCA) | 951280-2
John Haley Sims-Harry Sweets Edison Quintet | Just Friends | Original Jazz Classics | OJCCD 499-2
Johnny Hartman With The Masahiko Kikuchi Trio | For Trane | Blue Note | 835346-2
Jörg Seidel Group | I Feel So Smoochie: A Tribute To Nat King Cole | Edition Collage | EC 532-2
Junko Onishi Trio | Wow | somethin'else | 300032(TOCJ 5547)
Karrin Allyson And Her Quartet | I Didn't Know About You | Concord | CCD 4543
Makoto Ozone Trio | Nature Boys | Verve | 531270-2
Mike Nock Quartet | Dark & Curious | VeraBra Records | CDVBR 2074-2
Miles Davis Quintet | Blue Moods | Debut | VIJ 5009 IMS
Charles Mingus-The Complete Debut Recordings | Debut | 12 DCD 4402-2
Milt Jackson Big 4 | Milt Jackson At The Montreux Jazz Festival 1975 | Original Jazz Classics | OJC20 884-2(2310753)
Modern Jazz Quartet | Milt Jackson Birthday Celebration | Fantasy | FANCD 6079-2
The Complete Modern Jazz Quartet Prestige & Pablo Recordings | Prestige | 4PRCD 4438-2
Topsy-This One's For Basie | Original Jazz Classics | OJCCD 1073-2(2310917)
The Best Of The Modern Jazz Quartet | Pablo | 2405423-2
Nat King Cole And His Trio | Nat King Cole:The Snader Telescriptions | Storyville | 4960103
Combo USA | Affinity | CD AFS 1002
Nat King Cole Trio | Love Songs | Nimbus Records | NI 2010
Nat King Cole Trio With Frank DeVol's Orchestra | Nat King Cole:Route 66 | Dreyfus Jazz Line | FDM 36716-2

Nat King Cole With Orchestra | Welcome To Jazz: Nat King Cole | Koch Records | 321 981 D1
Oscar Peterson Quartet | The Very Tall Band | Telarc Digital | CD 83443
Red Garland Trio | Equinox | Galaxy | GXY 5115
Singers Unlimited | A Capella 2 | MPS | 821860-2
The Three Sounds | Black Orchid | Blue Note | 821289-2
Vince Jones Septet | On The Brink Of It | Intuition Records | INT 3068-2
Woody Herman's 2nd Herd | Woody Herman's 2nd Herd Live 1948-Vol.2 | Raretone | 5002 FC
Freddy Cole Trio | I'm Not My Brother,I'm Me | Sunnyside | SSC 1054 D

Nature Boy(alt.take)
Barney Wilen Quartet | Tilt | Vogue | 21559492

Nature Boy(first version)
John Coltrane Quartet | John Coltrane:The Classic Quartet-Complete Impulse Studio Recordings | Impulse(MCA) | 951280-2
Chico Hamilton Quintet | Gongs East | Discovery | DS 831 IMS

Nature Girl
Deborah Henson-Conant Group | Budapest | Laika Records | LK 93-039
Uli Beckerhoff Quartet | New York Meeting | L+R Records | CDLR 45082

Nature Of Power
Bob Berg Quartet | Enter The Spirit | Stretch Records | SCD 9004-2

Naturgeschichte
Nat Adderley Quartet | Naturally! | Original Jazz Classics | OJCCD 1088-2(JLP 947)

Naturly
Richie Cole Quintet | Side By Side | Muse | MCD 6016

Navigatore
Renaud Garcia-Fons Group | Navigatore | Enja | ENJ-9418 2
Robert Norman In Different Groups | The Best Of Robert Norman(1941-1989) | Hot Club Records | HCRCD 085

Navratil
Keith Ingham & Marty Grosz And Their Hot Cosmopolites | Going Hollywood | Stomp Off Records | CD 1323

Navy Blues
Stan Getz Quartet | Stan Getz-The Complete Roost Sessions | The Jazz Factory | JFCD 22839

Naxotique
Horace Tapscott Trio | The Dark Tree 2 | Hat Art | CD 6083

Nayla
Anouar Brahem Quartet | Conte De L'Incroyable Amour | ECM | 1457(511959-2)

Nayzak
Maria Joao-Mario Laginha Group | Cor | Verve | 557456-2

N'Diaraby(Friendship)
Stefan Bauer-Claudio Puntin-Marcio Doctor | Lingo | Jazz Haus Musik | JHM 0116 CD

N'diaye
Leni Stern Group | Words | Lipstick Records | LIP 890282

'Ne Handvoll Duos:
Elisabeth Kontomanou & Jean-Michel Pilc | Hands & Incantation | Steeplechase | SCCD 31484

Ne Me Quitte Pas
Nina Simone With Hal Mooney's Orchestra | Verve Jazz Masters 17:Nina Simone | Verve | 518198-2
In Concert/I Put A Spell On You | Mercury | 846543-2
Nina Simone With Orchestra | Nina Simone-The 60s Vol.1: Ne Me Quitte Pas | Mercury | 838543-2 PMS
Yves Teicher Quartet | Fiddler On The Groove | RCA | 2147489-2

Ne-Afterglow
Count Basie And His Orchestra | Duke Ellington-Count Basie | CBS | 473753-2

Neapolitan Nights
Jamenco | Conversations | Trick Music | TM 9202 CD

Neapolitaner
Eugen Cicero Trio | Swings Tschaikowsky & Liszt | MPS | 88039-2

Near North
Charlie Love Jazz Band | Kid Sheik With Charlie Love And His Cado Jazz Band | 504 Records | 504CD 21

Near The Grapes
Chris Hirson-Geoff Goodman | Human Lives | Acoustic Music Records | 319.1112.2

Near-in
Norman Burns Quintet | Bebop In Britain | Esquire | CD ESQ 100-4

Nearly
Jane Ira Bloom Sextet | The Nearness | Arabesque Recordings | AJ 0120

Nearly The Blues
Continuum | Mad About Tadd | Palo Alto | PA 8029

Nearness Of You
Jimmy Dorsey And His Orchestra | The Uncollected: Jimmy Dorsey | Hindsight | HSR 101

Neath(take 1)
James Moody Quartet | Americans Swinging In Paris:James Moody | EMI Records | 539653-2

Neath(take 2)
Henri Texier Quintet | La Companera | Label Bleu | LBLC 6525(882052)

Nebbiolo
Max Neissendorfer Trio | Staubfrei | EGO | 95100

Nebenan
Robert Marcus Octet | The Collected Robert Marcus | RCA | 2668720-2

Nebula
McCoy Tyner Quartet | Reflections | Milestone | M 47062

Nebulosity
Beaver Harris Quartet | Beaver Is My Name | Timeless | SJP 196

Necessary Evil
Elvin Jones Quartet | Familiar Ground | West Wind | WW 2104

Neck Bones
Slickaphonics | Slickaphonics | Enja | ENJ-4024 2

Neckan's Reel-
Jesse Clayton | Piano Blues Vol.1-The Twenties(1923-1930) | Story Of Blues | CD 3511-2

Neckbones À La Carte
Florian Ross Quintet | Seasons And Places | Naxos Jazz | 86029-2

Need More Mamma
Charles Musselwhite Band | Mellow-Dee | Crosscut | CCD 11013

Needle Children
Diane Schuur And Her Band | Schuur Thing | GRP | GRP 91022-1(808721)

Neenah
Lester Young Quartet | Lester Young:The Complete 1936-1951 Small Group Session(Studio Recordings-Master Takes),Vol.5 | Blue Moon | BMCD 1005

Nefertiti
Andrew Hill | Live At Montreux | Freedom | FCD 741023
Chick Corea Trio | The Song Of Singing | Blue Note | 784353-2
Cold Sweat | 4 Play | JMT Edition | 834444-2
Dioko | Potosi | Jazz Haus Musik | JHM 20
J.J.Johnson Quintet | Live At The Village Vanguard | EmArCy | 848327-2
Jerry Gonzalez & Fort Apache Band | Obatala | Enja | ENJ-5095 2
Manhattan Project,The | Wayne Shorter:The Classic Blue Note Recordings | Blue Note | 540856-2
Marc Copland & Tim Hagans | Between The Lines | Steeplechase | SCCD 31488
Miles Davis Quintet | Nefertiti | CBS | CK 65681
Miles Davis Quintet 1965-1968 | CBS | C6K 67398
Peter Herbolzheimer Rhythm Combination & Brass | Colors Of A Band | Mons Records | MR 874799
Phil Woods Quartet | Musique Du Bois | Muse | MCD 5037

Nega Do Cabelo Duro
John McLaughlin Group | Music Spoken Here | Warner | 99254

Neger Karl
Kol Simcha | Contemporary Klezmer | Laika Records | LK 93-048

Negev
Fats Waller And His Rhythm | The Indispensable Fats Waller Vol.5/6 | RCA | 2126416-2

Negrin
Santos Chillemi Group | Trinidad | Maracatu | MAC 940001

Negro De Sociedad
Steve Williamson Sextet | Rhyme Time-That Fuss Was Us! | Verve | 511235-2

Neither Fire Nor Place-
Mulgrew Miller Septet | Hand In Hand | Novus | 4163153-2

Nelgat
Stefano Di Battista Quintet | A Prima Vista | Blue Note | 497945-2

Nella
Dusko Goykovich Quartet | Celebration | DIW | DIW 806 CD

Nelson
Kenny Drew Jr. Quartet | The Rainbow Connection | Jazz City | 660.53.010

Nem Um Talvez
Miles Davis Group | Live-Evil | CBS | 485255-2
Philip Catherine Quartet | Live | Dreyfus Jazz Line | FDM 36587-2

Nemesis
Eric Alexander Quartet | Nightlife In Tokyo | Milestone | MCD 9330-2
Ralph Peterson's Fo'tet | Ornettology | Blue Note | 798290-2

Nenaliina
Armand Gordon & Son Jazz Clan | Jazz Pure | Jazz Pure Collection | AU 31618 CD

Neo
Miles Davis Quintet | Miles Davis In Person-Friday Night At The Blackhawk,San Francisco,Vol.1 | CBS | C4K 87106

Neo(alt.take)
Jean-Paul Bourelly & The BluWave Bandits | Rock The Cathartic Spirits:Vibe Music And The Blues! | DIW | DIW 911 CD

Neon
Flim & The BB's | Neon | dmp Digital Music Productions | CD 458

Neophilia
Peter Herbolzheimer All Star Big Band | Jazz Gala Concert '79 | Rare Bid | BID 156501

Neothis And Neothat
Björn Alke Quartet | Jazz Sverige 1974 | Caprice | CAP 1072

Neptun-
Billy Higgins Quartet | Soweto | Red Records | VPA 141

Neptune
John Abercrombie Quartet | Arcade | ECM | 1133

Nergiz
Robert Zollitsch Group | Zanskar | KlangRäume | 30130

Nervous Blues
Luther Thomas & Dizzazz | Yo' Momma | Moers Music | 01088

Nesraf
Karim Ziad Groups | Ifrikya | ACT | 9282-2

Nesrafet
Banda Città Ruvo Di Puglia | La Banda/Banda And Jazz | Enja | ENJ-9326 2

Nessun Dorma(Turandot)
Lester Bowie's Brass Fantasy | The Odyssey Of Funk & Popular Music | Dreyfus Jazz Line | FDM 37004-2
Elliott Sharp Carbon | Datacide | Enemy | EMCD 116(03516)

Nestor's Saga (The Tale Of The Ancient)
Lee Konitz Quartet | Inside Hi-Fi | Rhino | 790669-1

Netsuke
Bob Stewart Groups | Then & Now | Postcards | POST 1014

'Nette
Cowws Quintet plus Guests | Book/Virtual Cowws | FMP | OWN-90007/9

Network Of Sparks(The Delicate Code)
Kodexx Sentimental | Das Digitale Herz | Poise | Poise 02

Neue Stadt
Matthias Petzold Septett | Ulysses | Indigo-Records | 1003 CD

Neujahrslied
Andy Lumpp | Piano Solo | Nabel Records:Jazz Network | CD 4646

Neuland
Piano Solo | Nabel Records:Jazz Network | CD 4646

Neuland(for Garcia Morales)
Michael Riessler Group | Heloise | Wergo | WER 8008-2

Neulich
Andreas Hansl | Dualism | UAK | UAK 1

Neunundsiebzig
Glenn Ferris Trio | Flesh & Stone | Enja | 8088-2

Nevada
David Murray Quartet | Live At The Lower Manhattan Ocean Club Vol.1&2 | India Navigation | IN 1032 CD

Never
Clark Terry Quintet | Having Fun | Delos | DE 4021(882677)
Jimmy Lyons Quintet | Give It Up | Black Saint | BSR 0087

Never Again
Johnny Parker With Pete Rugolo And His Orchestra | Way To The West | Fresh Sound Records | 054 2602131(Capitol)
Vincent Courtois Quartet | Cello News | Nocturne Productions | NPCD 508

Never Alone
Michael Brecker Quindectet | Wide Angles | Verve | 076142-2
Ron McClure Trio | Never Always | Steeplechase | SCCD 31355

Never Broken(ESP)
Anton Fier Group | Dreamspeed | Avant | AVAN 009

Never Can Say Goodbye
Karoline Höfler Quartet | Charly Haigl's Festival Band | Satin Doll Productions | SDP 1007-1 CD

Never Did It
Nils Petter Molvaer Group | Elegy For Africa | Nabel Records:Jazz Network | CD 4678

Never Disturb A Ballaphon Player At Work
Frank Rehak Sextet | Jazzville Vol.2 | Fresh Sound Records | FSR 601(Dawn DLP 1107)

Never Ending Blues
Wolfgang Engstfeld Quartet | Songs And Ballads | Nabel Records:Jazz Network | CD 4658

Never Ending Nights
Ray Charles With Orchestra | Ray Charles | London | 6.24034 AL

Never Felt This Way Before
Cees Slinger Octet | Live At The Northsea Jazz Festival | Limetree | MLP 198244

Never Give Up
Robin Eubanks Group | Karma | JMT Edition | 834446-2

Never Had A Reason To Believe In You
Wingy Mannone And His Orchestra | The Classic Years In Digital Stereo: Swing-Small Groups | CDS Records Ltd. | REB 666

Never In A Single Year
Mal Waldron Quartet feat.Jim Pepper | Quadrologue At Utopia Vol.1 | Tutu Records | 888118-2*

Never In Hurry
The Clarke/Duke Project | The Clarke/Duke Project | Epic | 468223-2

Never Leave Me
Albert Mangelsdorff Quartet | Three Originals:Never Let It End-A Jazz Tune I Hope-Triple Entente | MPS | 529090-2

Never Let Me Go
Bill Evans | Alone | Verve | 598319-2
Bob Howard With The Hank Jones Trio | In A Sentimental Mood | Stash Records | ST 266 IMS
Dinah Washington With The Quincy Jones Orchestra | The Swingin' Miss 'D' | Verve | 558074-2
Don Bagley Quintet | The Soft Sell | Blue Moon | BMCD 1603
George Coleman Quintet | Blues Inside Out | Ronnie Scott's Jazz House | JHCD 046
J.R. Monterose-Tommy Flanagan | A Little Pleasure | Reservoir | RSR CD 109(882633)
Keith Jarrett Trio | Standards Vol.2 | ECM | 1289(825015-2)
Kirk Lightsey Trio | From Kirk To Nat | Criss Cross | Criss 1050
Mark Murphy-Gary Schunk | Mark Murphy Sings Nat Cing Cole,Volumes 1&2 | Muse | MCD 6001
Red Garland Trio | Crossings | Original Jazz Classics | OJCCD 472-2
Roni Ben-Hur With The Barry Harris Trio | Backyard | TCB Records | TCB 95902
Stanley Turrentine Quartet | Never Let Me Go | Blue Note | 576750-2
Stefon Harris-Jacky Terrasson Group | Kindred | Blue Note | 531868-2
Tierney Sutton And Her Trio | Blue In Green | Telarc Digital | CD 83522
Vince Jones With The Benny Green Quartet | One Day Spent | Intuition Records | INT 3087-2
Von Freeman Quartet | Never Let Me Go | Steeplechase | SCCD 31310
Bill Mays | Maybeck Recital Hall Series Volume Twenty-Six | Concord | CCD 4567

Never Let Me Go(alt.take)
Houston Person Quartet | Heavy Juice | Muse | MR 5260

Never Let Your Left Hand Know What Your Right Hand's Doin'
Louis Jordan And His Tympany Five | Louis Jordan Vol.1-Hoodoo Man | Swingtime(Contact) | ST 1011

Never Looking Back
Lem Johnson And His Band | Lem Johnson-Doc Sausage-Jo Jo Jackson | Blue Moon | BMCD 6004

Never Make A Move Too Soon
The Crusaders With The Royal Philharmonic Orchestra Feat. B.B.King | Royal Jam | MCA | ???

Never Make Your Move Too Soon
Dee Daniels With The Trio Johan Clement | Close Encounter Of The Swingin' Kind | Timeless | CD SJP 312

Never More
Cal Tjader Group | Solar Heat | Memo Music | HDJ 4078

Never Never
Larry Coryell Group | Fallen Angel | CTI Records | CTI 1014-2

Never Never Land
Michele Hendricks Trio | Me And My Shadow | Muse | MCD 5404
Vince Guaraldi Trio | Vince Guaraldi Trio | Original Jazz Classics | OJC20 149-2(F 3225)
William Galison-Mulo Franzl Group | Midnight Sun | Edition Collage | EC 508-2
Carol Sloane And Her Trio | Heart's Desire | Concord | CCD 4503

Never No Lament
Duke Ellington And His Famous Orchestra | Duke Ellington:Ko-Ko | Dreyfus Jazz Line | FDM 36717-2
Sophisticated Lady | RCA | 26685162
Duke Ellington And His Orchestra | Crystal Ballroom, Fargo Concert | Jazz Anthology | JA 5229/30
The Indispensable Duke Ellington Vol.5/6 | RCA | ND 89750

Never No Lament(Don't Get Around Much Anymore)
Duke Ellington And His Famous Orchestra | Passion Flower 1940-46 | Bluebird | 63 66616-2

Never On Sunday
Dizzy Gillespie Quintet | The Cool World/Dizzy Goes Hollywood | Verve | 531230-2
Ran Blake | The Blue Potato And Other Outrages | Milestone | M 9021

Never Said A Mumblin' Word
Marty Fogel Quartet | Many Bobbing Heads, At Last... | CMP Records | CMP CD 37

Never Say Yes
Cannonball Adderley Sextet | Dizzy's Business-Live In Concert | Milestone | MCD 47069-2
Oscar Peterson Trio | Exclusively For My Friends-The Lost Tapes | MPS | 529096-2
Benny Goodman And His Orchestra | This Is Benny Goodman | RCA | NL 89224 DP

Never Take No For An Answer
Archie Shepp Quintet | Passion | 52e Rue Est | RECD 018

Never Thought It Could Happen
Willem Breuker Kollektief | Deadly Sin/Twice A Woman(Sountracks) | BVHAAST | CD 9708

Never Trust A Woman
Montreal Jubilation Gospel Choir | Highway To Heaven | Blues Beacon | BLU-1005 2

Never Will I Marry
Cannonball Adderley And The Poll Winners | The Cannonball Adderley Collection Vol.4:C.Adderley And The Poll Winners | Landmark | CAC 1304-2(882340)
Cannonball Adderley Quintet | Wes Montgomery-The Complete Riverside Recordings | Riverside | 12 RCD 4408-2
Carmen McRae With The Norman Simmons Trio | Live At Century Plaza | Atlantic | AMCY 1075
Elke Reiff Quartett | There Is More | Laika Records | 35101112
Helen Merrill With The Dick Katz Group | A Shade Of Difference | EmArCy | 558851-2
Nancy Wilson With The Cannonball Adderley Quintet | Nancy Wilson/The Cannonball Adderley Quintet | Capitol | 781204-2
Juez | There's A Room | Stunt Records | 18806

Never You Mind
Full Faith & Credit Big Band | Debut | Palo Alto | PA 8001

Neverend
Joshua Redman Quartet | Spirit Of The Moment:Live At The Village Vanguard | Warner | 9362-45923-2
Charlie Mariano Group | Helen 12 Trees | MPS | 68112

Nevertheless
Thomas Hufschmidt & Tyron Park | Pepila | Acoustic Music Records | 319.1034.2

New & Average
Tristan Honsinger Quintet | Map Of Moods | FMP | CD 76

New Africa
Grachan Moncur III Quintet | New Africa | Affinity | AFF 38

New Amsterdam
| La Voce-Music For Voices,Trumpet And Bass | JA & RO | JARO 4208-2

New And Again And Again
Cannonball Adderley-Nat Adderley Sextet | The Adderley Brothers In New Orleans | Milestone | M 9030

New Arrival
Tito Puente's Golden Latin Jazz All Stars | Live At The Village Gate | RMM Records | 660.58.021

New Arrivals
Harold Danko Quartet | New Autumn | Steeplechase | SCCD 31377

New Awlins'
The Pilgrim Jubilee Singers | Walk On/The Old Ship Of Zion | Mobile Fidelity | MFCD 756

New Beginning
Charlie Haden Trio | The Montreal Tapes | Verve | 523295-2

New Block For The Kids
Simon Phillips-Jeff Babko Group | Vantage Point | Jazzline | JL 11159-2

New Blues
Buddy Rich Big Band | The New One! | Pacific Jazz | 494507-2
Chris Barber's Jazz Band | The Chris Barber Concerts | Lake | LACD 55/56
Joey DeFrancesco Group | Reboppin' | CBS | CK 48624
Miles Davis Group | Miles In Montreux | Jazz Door | JD 1287/88

New Blues On The Dark Side
Gene Ammons-Sonny Stitt All Stars | Gene Ammons All Star Sessions | Original Jazz Classics | OJCCD 014-2(P 7050)

New Box
The Kenny Clarke-Francy Boland Big Band | Two Originals:Sax No End/All Blues | MPS | 523525-2

New Chances
Pat Metheny | New Chautauqua | ECM | 1131(825471-2)

New Chautauqua
Ethan Iverson Trio | Contruction Zone(Originals) | Fresh Sound Records | FSNT 046 CD

New Chimes Blues
Walter Davis | Let Me In Your Saddle | Swingtime(Contact) | BT 2004

New Country
Jean-Luc Ponty Quintet | Imaginary Voyage | Atlantic | SD 19136

New Dance
Keith Jarrett Quartet | Nude Ants | ECM | 1171/72(829119-2)
King Curtis Band | King Curtis-Blow Man Blow | Bear Family Records | BCD 15670 CI
King Curtis-Blow Man Blow | Bear Family Records | BCD 15670 CI

New Dance(alt.take)
Anthony Ortega Trio | New Dance! | Hat Art | CD 6065
New Day
Jeff Jarvis Group | When It Rains | Jazz Pure Collection | AU 31612 CD
New Delhi
Cannonball Adderley Quintet Plus | Cannonball Adderley Quintet Plus | Original Jazz Classics | OJC20 306-2
Cannonball Adderley Sextet | What I Mean | Milestone | M 47053
James Clay Quintet | A Double Dose Of Soul | Original Jazz Classics | OJCCD 1790-2(RLP 9349)
New Delhi, New Delhi
Willie Trice | Blue & Rag'd | Trix Records | TRIX 3305
New Dream
Shorty Rogers-Bud Shank And The Lighthouse All Stars | America The Beautiful | Candid | CCD 79510
New East St.Louis Toodle Oo
Louis Hayes Sextet | Blue Lou | Steeplechase | SCCD 31340
New Fables
David Moss Dense Band | Dense Band | Moers Music | 02040
New Friends
Lou Blackburn-Freddie Hill Quintet | Perception | Fresh Sound Records | FSR-CD 0307
New Girl
Big Joe Turner With Axel Zwingenberger | Let's Boogie Woogie All Night Long | Vagabond | VRCD 8.79012
New Goin' Away Blues
Benny Moten's Kansas City Orchestra | Bennie Moten Vol.1 | Zeta | ZET 750
New Ground-
Ray Anderson-Han Bennink-Christy Doran | Cheer Up | Hat Art | CD 6175
New Harmonica Breakdown
Christoph Oeding Trio | Taking A Chance | Mons Records | MR 874784
New Hope
Nova Bossa Nove | Jazz Influence | Arkadia Jazz | 71241
New Horizons
Engstfeld-Herr Quartet | Short Stories | Nabel Records:Jazz Network | LP 4609
New Key To The Highway
Paul Howard's Quality Serenaders | Early Hamp | Affinity | CD AFS 1011
New King Porter Stomp
Paul Brody's Tango Toy | Klezmer Stories | Laika Records | 35101222
New Klezmer Band
Enrico Pieranunzi Trio | New Lands | Timeless | CD SJP 211
New Lester Leaps In
Lester Young And His Band | Lester Young:The Complete 1936-1951 Small Group Sessions(Studio Recordings-Master Takes),Vol.4 | Blue Moon | BMCD 1004
New Level
Bernt Rosengren Big Band | Jazz In Sweden | Caprice | CAP 1214
New Life
Stefania Tallini Trio | New Life | yvp music | CD 3114
Steve LaSpina Quartet | Eclipse | Steeplechase | SCCD 31343
New Line
David Friedman Trio | Other Worlds | Intuition Records | INT 3210-2
New Los Them
Billy Barron Quintet | Jazz Caper | Muse | MR 5235
New Monastory
Andrew Hill Sextet | Point Of Departure | Blue Note | 499007-2
New Monastory(alt.take)
Karl Berger Woodstock Workshop Orchestra | Live At The Donaueschingen Music Festival | MPS | 68250
New Moon
Maceo Parker Group | Maceo(Soundtrack) | Minor Music | 801046
Nana Simopoulos Group | Wings And Air | Enja | 5031-2
Pee Wee Ellis Quintet With Guests | A New Shift | Minor Music | 801060
Ralph Towner Group | Works | ECM | 823268-1
Sandor Szabo | Gaia And Aries | Acoustic Music Records | 319.1146.2
New Morning
David Darling | Dark Wood | ECM | 1519(523750-2)
New Morning-
New York Jazz Collective | I Don't Know This World Without Don Cherry | Naxos Jazz | 86003-2
New Neighbour
Huey Simmons Quartet | Burning Spirits | Contemporary | C 7625/6
New Now Know How
Charles Mingus Orchestra | Nostalgia In Times Square/The Immortal 1959 Sessions | CBS | 88337
Charles Mingus Group | Charles Mingus:Alternate Takes | CBS | CK 65514
New Now Know How(alt.take)
Harlem Mamfats | I'm So Glad | Queen-Disc | 062
New Old Age
Gerardo Iacoucci Modern Big Band | Great News From Italy | yvp music | CD 3030
New Orleans
Benny Moten's Kansas City Orchestra | The Complete Bennie Moten Vol.5/6 | RCA | PM 45688
Deep Creek Jazzuits | Dixie | Jazz Pure Collection | AU 31600 CD
Herbie Mann Group | The Evolution Of Mann | Atlantic | SD 2-300
That's Jazz Vol.37: Memphis Underground | Atlantic | ATL 50520
New Orleans Function-
Louis Armstrong And His All Stars | Louis Armstrong:C'est Si Bon | Dreyfus Jazz Line | FDM 36730-2
New Orleans Function:
Louis Armstrong-My Greatest Songs | MCA | MCD 18347
Satchmo-A Musical Autobiography Vol.1 | MCA | 2-4173
New Orleans Hop Scop Blues
Henrik Johansen's Jazzband | The Golden Years Of Revival Jazz,Vol.7 | Storyville | STCD 5512
Jimmie Noone And His Orchestra | New Orleans Jazz Giants 1936-1940 | JSP Records | JSPCD 336
New Orleans Stomp
Humphrey Lyttelton And His Band | Jazz At The Royal Festival Hall/Jazz At The Conway Hall | Dormouse | DM 22 CD
Bumble Bee Slim(Amos Easton) | Favorite Country Blues Guitar-Piano Duets | Yazoo | YAZ 1015
New Orleans Strut
Cannonball Adderley Group | Cannonball Adderley-Lovers... | Fantasy | F 9505
Jaki Byard | Jaki Byard:Solo/Strings | Prestige | PCD 24246-2
Lincoln Center Jazz Orchestra | Portraits By Ellington | CBS | 472814-2
New Orleans Twist
Gene Gifford And His Orchestra | Jazz Drumming Vol.1(1927-1937) | Fenn Music | FJD 2701
New Parchman
Mose Allison Trio | That's Jazz Vol.19: Mose Allison | Atlantic | ATL 50249
New Place
Joe McPhee | Glasses | Hat Art | P
New Rag
Jack DeJohnette's Directions | New Rags | ECM | 1103
New Rhumba
Bop City | Bop City:Hip Strut | Hip Bop | HIBD 8013
Miles Davis + 19 | The Miles Davis Selection | CBS | 465699-2
Bob Mintzer Big Band | Latin From Manhattan | dmp Digital Music Productions | CD 523
New Shoes
Sammy Price Sextet | Sammy Price In Europe | Jazz Anthology | JA 5192
New Skies
Moscow Art Trio And The Bulgarian Voices Angelite | Portrait | JARO | JARO 4227-2
New Skomorohi
Bill Dixon Sextet | Bill Dixon In Italy-Volume One | Soul Note | 121008-2
New Song
Mario Rusca Trio | Up And Down | Red Records | NS 209
New Spanish Boots
Jack DeJohnette Group | Sorcery | Prestige | P 10081
New Start
Horace Parlan Quintet | Arrival | Steeplechase | SCCD 31012
New Surprise
Klaus Ignatzek Group | New Surprise | Timeless | CD SJP 324
New Three And One Boogie
Louis Armstrong With Zilmer Randolph's Orchestra | Louis Armstrong V.S.O.P. Vol. 7/8 | CBS | CBS 88004
New Waltz
Karl Ratzer Group | Fingerprints | CMP Records | CMP 7
Ron Carter-Jim Hall Duo | Live At Village West | Concord | CJ 245
New Warrior
James Emery Quartet | Standing On A Whale... | Enja | ENJ-9312 2
New Water
Lucille Bogan | Lucille Bogan(Bessie Jackson) | Story Of Blues | CD 3535-2
New World
Didier Lockwood Quartet | New World | MPS | 68237
New World A-Coming
Duke Ellington | Duke Ellington Live At The Whitney | Impulse(MCA) | 951173-2
Masters Of Jazz Vol.6:Duke Ellington | Storyville | STCD 4106
Duke Ellington And His Orchestra | Duke Ellington -Carnegie Hall Concert | Ember | 800851-370(EMBD 2001)
New York
David Chesky-Romero Lubambo Duo | The New York Chorinhos | Chesky | JD 39
Ornette Coleman Quartet | Languages | Moon Records | MCD 044-2
New York 19
Modern Jazz Quartet | Lonely Woman | Atlantic | 7567-90665-2
Billy Bang Quintet | Rainbow Gladiator | Soul Note | 121016-2
New York Chicago And Rhythm Burrage
Marty Ehrlich Quintet | New York Child | Enja | ENJ-9025 2
New York Child
Abdullah Ibrahim | South African Sunshine | Pläne | CD 88778
New York City
Django Reinhardt And The Quintet Du Hot Club De France | Peche À La Mode-The Great Blue Star Sessions 1947/1953 | Verve | 835418-2
Django Reinhardt Portrait | Barclay | DALP 2/1939
Leadbelly[Huddie Ledbetter] | Alabama Bound | RCA | ND 90321(847151)
Snowball | Cold Heat | Atlantic | ATL 58036
New York City Blues
Duke Ellington And His Orchestra | Duke Ellington:Complete Prestige Carnegie Hall 1946-1947 Concerts | Definitive Records | DRCD 11211
Suzanne Dean Group | I Wonder | Nova | NOVA 9028-2
New York City(Radio Edit)
Harris Simen Group | New York Connection | Eastwind | EWIND 701
New York Fascination
Miles Davis Group | On The Corner | CBS | CK 63980
New York Girl
Hilton Ruiz Trio | New York Hilton | Steeplechase | SCCD 31094
New York Is Full Of Lonely People
Jack Sheldon-Ross Tompkins | On My Own | Concord | CCD 4529
New York Minute
David Binney Group | South | ACT | 9279-2
New York Nature
Bo Thorpe And His Orchestra | Live At The Omni | Hindsight | HSR 231
New York New York
Mickey Baker Quartet | The Blues Vol.4 | Big Bear | 156401
New York Shuffle
The Capp/Pierce Orchestra | Juggernaut Strikes Again | Concord | CCD 4183
New York State Of Mind
Diane Schuur With The Dave Grusin Orchestra | Deedles | GRP | GRP 91010-1(808702)
Greetje Kauffeld With Jerry Van Rooyen And Jiggs Whigham And The Rias Big Band | Greetje Kauffeld Meets Jerry Van Rooyen And Jiggs Whigham With The Rias Big Band | Mons Records | MR 874786
New York Sunday Afternoon
Richard Galliano Quartet | Gallianissimo! The Best Of Richard Galliano | Dreyfus Jazz Line | FDM 36616-2
New York Tango
New York Tango | Dreyfus Jazz Line | FDM 36581-2
Tango Five feat. Raul Jaurena | Obsecion | Satin Doll Productions | SDP 1027-1 CD
Ken Colyer's Skiffle Group | Wandering | Lake | LACD 68
New York-Brazil
Urbanator | Urbanator II | Hip Bop | HIBD 8012
New Yorker
Maynard Ferguson Orchestra With Chris Connor | Two's Company | Roulette | 837201-2
New York's My Home
Shirley Horn Trio | A Lazy Afternoon | Steeplechase | SCCD 31111
Hank Crawford And His Orchestra | Cajun Sunrise | Kudu | 63048
Newark Experience
Ed Kelly & Friends | Ed Kelly & Pharoah Sanders | Evidence | ECD 22056-2
Newest Blues
Ralph Lalama Quartet | Music For Grown-Ups | Criss Cross | Criss 1165
Newk's Fadeway
Jessica Williams Trio | ...And Then,There's This! | Timeless | CD SJP 345
New-One
Slide Hampton Octet | Two Sides Of Slide | Fresh Sound Records | FSR-CD 0206
Newport Festival Suite:
Duke Ellington And His Orchestra | Ellington At Newport 1956(Complete) | CBS | CK 64932
Peter Herbolzheimer Orchestra | Music For Swinging Dancers,Vol.1:You Make Me Feel So Young | Koala Records | CD P 8
Newport News
Chico Hamilton Quintet | That's Jazz Vol.20: Chico Hamilton | Warner | WB 56239
Newport Romp
Duke Ellington And His Orchestra | Live In Paris 1959 | Affinity | CD AFS 777
Newport Up
The Duke Live In Santa Monica Vol.1 | Queen-Disc | 069
Newport Up-
Ellington At Newport 1956(Complete) | CBS | CK 64932
Dave Brubeck | Just You, Just Me | Telarc Digital | CD 83363
News
Michael Mantler Quintet With The Balanescu Quartet | Folly Seeing All This | ECM | 1485
Mose Allison Trio | High Jinks! The Mose Allison Trilogy | CBS | J3K 64275
News From Blueport
Yakou Tribe | Red & Blue Days | Traumton Records | 4474-2
News From Home
Rudy Linka Quartet | News From Home | ARTA Records | F 1 0026-2511
Newsed
Entra Live | Live Lights | Timeless | CD SJP 320
Next
A.D.D.Trio | Instinct | L+R Records | CDLR 45104
Next Love
Eric Person Trio | Prophecy | Soul Note | 121287-2
Next Please!
Barbara Thompson's Paraphernalia | Barbara Thompson's Paraphernalia | MCA | 2292-50577-1
Next Stories
I.C.P. Orchestra | Jubilee Varia | HatOLOGY | 528
Next Time I Fall In Love-
Festival All Stars | American Folk Blues Festival '81 | L+R Records | CDLS 42022
Next Time You See Me
Mel Rhyne Trio | The Legend | Criss Cross | Criss 1059
Monoblue Quartet | An Affair With Strauss | Between The Lines | btl 006(Efa 10176-2)
Next To Nothing-A Non Affair
Überfall | Next To Silence | GIC | DL 4.1871
Next Year
Albert Mangelsdorff | Albert Mangelsdorff-Solo | MPS | 68287
Nexus
Passport | 2 Originals Of Passport(Passport-Second Passport) | Atlantic | ATL 60117
Nexux
Art Ensemble Of Chicago | Bap-Tizum | Atlantic | 7567-80757-2
N'Famoudou Boudougou
Live In Berlin | West Wind | WW 2051
N'Ga Bohe(Motherland)
Hanschel-Hübsch-Schipper | Planet Blow Chill | Jazz Haus Musik | JHM 0087 CD
NGC 221
Planet Blow Chill | Jazz Haus Musik | JHM 0087 CD
NGC 4755
Carl Ludwig Hübsch Trio | Carl Ludwig Hübsch's Longrun Development Of The Universe | Jazz Haus Musik | JHM 0112 CD
NGC 7541
Hanschel-Hübsch-Schipper | Planet Blow Chill | Jazz Haus Musik | JHM 0087 CD
Nomakozasana-Uli Lenz | Tenderness | Tutu Records | 888198-2*
Ngekengiye Kwazulu
Sibongile Khumalo Group | Live At The Market Theatre | CBS | 491322-2
N'hi Ha Un Altre
Maria Joao-Mario Laginha Group | Cor | Verve | 557456-2
Ni Deklaw Evol
Warren Bernhardt Quintet | Heat Of The Moment | dmp Digital Music Productions | CD 468
Niahnie's Dance
Willis Jackson Group | In The Alley | Muse | MR 5100
Nica
Sonny Clark Trio | Blues Mambo | West Wind | WW 2103
Nicaragua
Emil Mangelsdorff Quartet | This Side Up | L+R Records | CDLR 45065
Gil Evans And The Monday Night Orchestra | Bud And Bird-Live At The Sweet Basil | Electric Bird | K 19P 6455/6
Nica's Dream
Art Blakey And The Jazz Messengers | Art Blakey/The Jazz Messengers | CBS | CK 62265
Bud Shank Quartet | This Bud's For You | Muse | MR 5309(952106)
Buddy Rich Septet | Tuff Dude | Denon Compact Disc | 33CJ8-7972
Ellis Marsalis | Solo Piano | Line Records | COCD 9.01022 0
Gary Foster Quartet | Make Your Own Fun | Concord | CCD 4459
Jazz Cussion/Marion Brown | Native Land | ITM Records | ITM 1471
Joe Beck Trio | Relaxin' | dmp Digital Music Productions | CD 444
Joe Sample Group | Invitation | Warner | 9362-45209.2
Johnny 'Hammond' Smith Quartet | Open House | Milestone | MCD 47089-2
Jugendjazzorchester NW | Back From The States | Jugendjazzorchester NW | JJO 004
Mel Tormé With The George Shearing Trio | An Evening At Charlie's | Concord | CCD 4248
Red Holloway Quartet | Nica's Dream | Steeplechase | SCCD 31192
Sal Salvador Sextet | Starfingers | Bee Hive | BH 7002
Nica's Tempo
Danny D'Imperio Group | The Outlaw | Sackville | SKCD2-3060
Oscar Pettiford And His Birdland Band | Jazz On The Air Vol.6: Oscar Pettiford And His Birdland Band | Spotlite | SPJ 153
Nice And Easy
Frank Strozier Quartet | Cloudy And Cool | Vee Jay Recordings | VJ 013
Nice And Warm
Robert Cray Band | The Robert Cray Band | Charly | ???
Nice Day
Abe Lyman And His Californians | The Uncollected:Abe Lyman | Hindsight | HSR 184
Nice Eyes
Denise Lawrence & Storeyville Tickle | Let It Shine | Lake | LACD 37
Nice Guys
The Bob Thiele Collective | Louis Satchmo | Red Baron | 471578-2
Nice Lines Man
Chet Baker Quintet | Albert's House | Repertoire Records | REPCD 4167-WZ
Nice 'N' Easy
Rosemary Clooney With The John Oddo Big Band | Girl Singer | Concord | CCD 4496
Lou Donaldson Quintet | The Natural Soul | Blue Note | 542307-2
Nice 'N Greasy
The Natural Soul | Blue Note | 542307-2
Benny Green Trio | The Place To Be | Blue Note | 829268-2
Nice Pants For Everybody
Brad Mehldau Trio | Art Of The Trio Vol.4: Back At The Vanguard | Warner | 9362-47463-2
Nice Pass
Jimmy Heath Sextet | The Riverside Collection: Jimmy Heath-Nice People | Original Jazz Classics | OJCCD 6006-2
Nice Talking To You
Toots Thielemans Group | Live | Polydor | 831694-2 PMS
Nice To Be Around(Nice To Have Around)
Albert King Blues Band | The Blues Don't Change | Stax | SCD 8570-2(STX 4101)
Nice Work If You Can Get It
Art Tatum | Art Tatum:Complete Capitol Recordings | Capitol | 821325-2
Art Tatum:Complete Capitol Recordings | Definitive Records | DRCD 11192
Billie Holiday And Her Orchestra | Billie Holiday Story Vol.5:Music for Torching | Verve | MV 2595 IMS
Bing Crosby With Buddy Bregman's Orchestra | Bing Sings Whilst Bregman Swings | Verve | MV 2663 IMS
Bud Powell Trio | Bud Powell:Complete 1947-1951 Blue Note,Verve & Roost Recordings | The Jazz Factory | JFCD 22837
Carmen McRae And Her Quintet | The Best Of The Jazz Singers Vol.2 | LRC Records | CDC 9008
Eddy Howard And His Orchestra | The Uncollected:Eddy Howard, Vol.2 | Hindsight | HSR 156
Ella Fitzgerald With The Nelson Riddle Orchestra | Oh Lady Be Good:The Best Of The Gershwin Songbook | Verve | 529581-2
Ella Sings Gershwin-Vol. 1 | Metro | 2682004 IMS
The Complete Ella Fitzgerald Song Books of Harold Arlen, Irving Berlin, Duke Ellington, George & Ira Gershwin, Jerome Kern, Johnny Mercer, Cole Porter And Rogers & Hart | Verve | 519832-2
Erroll Garner Trio | Erroll Garner Plays Gershwin & Kern | EmArCy | 826224-2 PMS
Fred Astaire With The Oscar Peterson Sextet | Fred Astaire Steppin' Out:Astaire Sings | Verve | 523006-2
Jessica Williams | Maybeck Recital Hall Series Volume Twenty-One | Concord | CCD 4525
John Mehegan-Kenny Clarke | Johnny Mehegan's Reflections | Savoy | SV 0204(MG 12028)
Johnny Smith-Stan Getz Quintet | Stan Getz-The Complete Roost Sessions | EMI Records | 859622-2
Stan Getz-The Complete Roost Sessions | The Jazz Factory | JFCD 22839
Karin Krog Quintet | Karin Krog Jubilee-The Best Of 30 Years | Verve | 523716-2
Paul Motian Quartet | Paul Motian On Broadway Vol.2 | JMT Edition | 834440-2
Sarah Vaughan With The Jimmy Jones Orchestra | Sarah Vaughan In Hi-Fi | CBS | CK 65117
Teddy Wilson | Jazz Piano Masters | Chiaroscuro | CR 170
Thelonious Monk | Nice Work In London | Freedom | 147307

Thelonious Monk Collection | Black Lion | BLCD 7601-2
Thelonious Monk Trio | Thelonious Monk:Misterioso | Dreyfus Jazz Line | FDM 36743-2
Genius Of Modern Music,Vol.2 | Blue Note | 300404
Thelonious Monk:The Complete Blue Note Recordings | Blue Note | 830363-2
Tiziana Ghiglioni And Her Quartet | Lonely Woman | Dischi Della Quercia | Q 28014
Weslia Whitefield With The Mike Greensill Duo | Nice Work... | Landmark | LCD 1544-2

Nice Work If You Can Get It-
Marion Montgomery And Her Quintet | Nice And Easy | Ronnie Scott's Jazz House | JHCD 011
Uli Wewelsiep-Thomas Brill | Live At The Forum | Aho-Recording | CD 1010

Nice Work If You Can Get It(alt.take)
Thelonious Monk Trio | More Genius Of Thelonious Monk | Blue Note | 300194(BNJ 61011)

Nice!
Vesna Skorija Band | Niceland | Satin Doll Productions | SDP 1037-1 CD

Niceland
Jackie McLean Quintet | Tippin' The Scales | Blue Note | 784427-2

Nicholas 3-4
Herbie Nichols Quartet | M+N Thelonious Monk/Herbie Nichols | Savoy | 650112(881912)

Nicht So Schnell,Mit Viel Ton Zu Spielen
Andy Lutter Trio | Nichtendende Geschichten | Extra Records & Tapes | 57230463

Nichts Muss,Alles Kann
Helmut 'Joe' Sachse | Solo | FMP | 1070

Nici's Blues
Andreas Georgiou | Spatial Trembling | Praxis | GM 1008

Nick At T's
Amsterdam Jazz Quintet | Portraits | Challenge | CHR 70048

Nick@Night
Amos Milburn Quintet | 13 Unreleased Masters | Pathe | 1546701(Aladdin)

Nick's Dilemma
Nick Travis Quintet | The Panic Is On | Fresh Sound Records | NL 45846(RCA LPM 1010)

Nicolas-
Louis Mazetier | Good Vibrations | Jazz Connaisseur | JCCD 9521-2
Hans Koller Free Sound | Phoenix | MPS | 9813438

Nicolas 1-2
Nicolas Simion Quartet feat. Tomasz Stanko | Dinner For Don Carlos | Tutu Records | 888146-2*

Nicolas' Blues
Pep O'Callaghan Grup | Port O'Clock | Fresh Sound Records | FSNT 069 CD

Nicolas El Valiente
Antonio Petrocca Trio | But Not For Me | Edition Musikat | EDM 047

Nicole
Howard McGhee Sextet | Jazz In Paris:Bebop | EmArCy | 014063-2

Nicolette
Duo Brazil | Carioca | M.A Music | A 808-2

Nida
Abdu Dagir Group | Malik At-Taqasim | Enja | 8012-2

Niding Summer
Boogie Junction | I Wake You Up | Jazz Pure Collection | AU 31602 CD

Niebla Del Riachuelo
Yakou Tribe | Red & Blue Days | Traumton Records | 4474-2

Niebo
Paul Eßer-Gerd Dudek-Ali Haurand-Jiri Strivin | Jazz Und Lyrik:Schinderkarren Mit Buffet | Konnex Records | KCD 5108

Niederrheinsonntag
Jaco Pastorius Group | Live In New York City Volume Three | Big World | BW 1003

Niemandsland
Lothar Müller Trio | Müller Q[kju] | JA & RO | JARO 4251-2
Peter Finger Und Gäste | Niemandsland | Acoustic Music Records | AMC 1001

Niet Pivo Niet Blues
Bertha Hope Trio | In Search Of... | Steeplechase | SCCD 31276

Nieves
Roy Smeck | Roy Smeck Plays Hawaiian Guitar, Banjo, Ukelele And Guitar | Yazoo | YAZ 1052

Niger Mambo
Stanley Turrentine Sextet | In Memory Of | Blue Note | LT 1037

Nigerian Marketplace
Bobby McFerrin Group | The Young Lions | Elektra | MUS 96.0196-1

Night
John Abercrombie Quartet | Night | ECM | 1272(823212-2)
Mario Neunkirchen Quintet | Long Distance | Laika Records | LK 94-060
Misha Alperin Trio | Night After Night | ECM | 1769(014431-2)
Stan Kenton And His Orchestra | The Complete MacGregor Transcriptions Vol.1 | Naxos Jazz | 8.120517 CD
Thomas Clausen Trio With Gary Burton | Café Noir | M.A Music | INTCD 004
Tommy Tedesco Quartet | When Do We Start | Discovery | DS 789 IMS

Night After Night
Roy Fox & His Band | This Is Romance | Saville Records | SVL 166 IMS

Night Again
Jeff Jarvis Group | When It Rains | Jazz Pure Collection | AU 31612 CD

Night And Day
Art Tatum | Art Tatum-The Complete Pablo Solo Masterpieces | Pablo | 7 PACD 4404-2
Masters Of Jazz Vol.8:Art Tatum | Storyville | SLP 4108
Art Tatum Quartet | The Tatum Group Masterpieces | Pablo | 2310734
Art Tatum-Ben Webster Quartet | Art Tatum-The Complete Pablo Group Masterpieces | Pablo | 6 PACD 4401-2
The Tatum Group Masterpieces | Pablo | 2310737-2
Art Tatum-Roy Eldridge Quartet | The Tatum Group Masterpieces | Pablo | 2625706
Bill Evans Trio | Peace Piece And Other Pieces | Milestone | M 47024
The Jazz Giants Play Cole Porter:Night And Day | Prestige | PCD 24203-2
Bill Evans Trio With Lee Konitz & Warne Marsh | Crosscurrents | Original Jazz Classics | OJCCD 718-2(F 9568)
Billie Holiday And Her Orchestra | Billie Holiday:The Quintessential Vol.8/9(1939-1942) | CBS | 477837-2
This Is Jazz:Billie Holiday Sings Standards | CBS | CK 65048
Bireli Lagrene Ensemble | Routes To Django & Bireli Swing '81 | Jazzpoint | JP 1055 CD
Bobby Short Trio | Late Night At The Cafe Carlyle | Telarc Digital | CD 83311
Charlie Parker And His Orchestra | Compact Jazz: Charlie Parker | Verve | 833288-2
Charlie Parker Big Band | Bird On Verve-Vol.7:Charlie Parker Big Band | Verve | 817448-1 IMS
Chick Corea Trio | Trio Music,Live In Europe | ECM | 1310(827769-2)
Claude Thornhill And His Orchestra | Tapestries | Affinity | ???
Coleman Hawkins Quartet | Body And Soul | Naxos Jazz | 8.120532 CD
Dave Brubeck Quartet | Dave Brubeck's All-Time Greatest Hits | CBS | 68288
Dizzy Gillespie And His Operatic Strings | Dizzy In Paris | Ember | CJS 841
Dizzy Gillespie Orchestra And The Operatic String Orchestra | Jazz In Paris:Dizzy Gillespie And His Operatic Strings Orchestra | EmArCy | 018420-2
Django Reinhardt And His Rhythm | Verve Jazz Masters 38:Django Reinhardt | Verve | 516931-2
Peche À La Mode-The Great Blue Star Sessions 1947/1953 | Verve | 835418-2
Django Reinhardt And The Quintet Du Hot Club De France | Django Reinhardt Portrait | Barclay | DALP 2/1939
Don Byas Et Ses Rythmes | Don Byas Complete 1946-1951 European Small Group Master Takes | Definitive Records | DRCD 11214
Duke Ellington And His Orchestra | Duke 56/62 Vol.1 | CBS | 88653
Eartha Kitt With The Joachim Kühn Quartet | Standards/Live | ITM Records | ITM 1484
Ella Fitzgerald With The Buddy Bregman Orchestra | The Complete Ella Fitzgerald Song Books of Harold Arlen, Irving Berlin, Duke Ellington, George & Ira Gershwin, Jerome Kern, Johnny Mercer, Cole Porter And Rogers & Hart | Verve | 519832-2
Ernie Watts-Chick Corea Quartet | 4Tune | West Wind | WW 2105
Frank Sinatra With Orchestra | Frank Sinatra | Koch Records | 321 942 D1
Franz Koglmann Monoblue Quartet | L'Heure Bleue | Hat Art | CD 6093
Helen Merrill With The Piero Umilliani Group | Parole E Musica | RCA | 2174798-2
Henri Crolla Sextet | Jazz In Paris:Henri Crolla-Notre Ami Django | EmArCy | 014062-2
Jenny Evans And The Rudi Martini Quartet | At Loyd's | BELL Records | BLR 90004
Jimmy Raney Quintet | Too Marvelous For Words | Biograph | BLP 12060
Joe Henderson Quartet | Inner Urge | Blue Note | 784189-2
Joe Pass | Virtuoso | Pablo | 2310708-2
Blues For Fred | Pablo | 2310931-2
Joe Pass Quartet | For Django | Pacific Jazz | 300007(PJ 85)
Joe Sullivan Quintet | The Piano Artistry Of Joe Sullivan | Jazz Unlimited | JUCD 2051
Kent Sangster Quartet | Adventures | Jazz Focus | JFCD 006
Lee Konitz-Red Mitchell Duo | I Concentrate On You | Steeplechase | SCCD 31018
Lisa Ekdahl With The Peter Nordahl Trio | Back To Earth | RCA | 2161463-2
Loren Schoenberg And His Jazz Orchestra | Just A-Settin' And A-Rockin' | Musicmasters | 5039-2
Martin Taylor Quartet | Spirit Of Django | Linn Records | AKD 030
Oscar Peterson Trio | Oscar Peterson Plays The Cole Porter Song Book | Verve | 821987-2
The Song Is You-The Best Of The Verve Songbooks | Verve | 531558-2
Oscar Peterson-Austin Roberts | Oscar Peterson 1951 | Just A Memory | JAS 9501-2
Peter Fessler Quartet | Foot Prints | Minor Music | 801058
Phil Woods Quartet | Ornithology:Phil Salutes Bird | Philology | W 69.2
Red Norvo Trio | Red Norvo Trio | Savoy | SV 0267
Rex Stewart Quintet | Peche À La Mode-The Great Blue Star Sessions 1947/1953 | Verve | 835418-2
Jazz In Paris:Django Reinhardt-Swing 48 | EmArCy | 013544-2
Sonny Rollins Trio | Live In Europe '65 | Magnetic Records | MRCD 118
Stan Getz And The Swedish All Stars | Stan Getz:The Complete 1946-1951 Quartet Sessions(Master Takes),Vol.2 | Blue Moon | BMCD 1014
Stan Getz With The Bill Evans Trio | The Chick Corea-Bill Evans Sessions | Verve | 2610036
Stan Getz-Bill Evans Quartet | Compact Jazz: Stan Getz & Friends | Verve | 835317-2
Stan Getz-Kenny Barron | People Time | EmArCy | 510134-2
Stephane Grappelli Trio | Live | Justin Time | JTR 8469-2
The Brass Connection | Standards | The Jazz Alliance | TJA 10014
Tommy Dorsey And His Orchestra | This Is Tommy Dorsey Vol. 2 | RCA | 26.28041 DP
Werner Pöhlert Combo | Something Cool:Werner Pöhlert Combo Recordings 1985-1009 | Hohner Records | ohne Nummer(2)

Night And Day-
Mihaly Tabany Orchestra | Jubilee Edition | double moon | CHRDM 71020
Simon Schott | Bar Piano: Simon Schott Plays Your Favorite Evergreens Vol.1 | Organic Music | ORGM 9733
Stan Getz With The Bill Evans Trio | The Complete Bill Evans On Verve | Verve | 527953-2

Night And Day(alt.take 1)
Zoot Sims Quartet | Zoot Sims:Quartet&Sextet | Vogue | 21511522

Night And Day(alt.take 2)
Zoot Sims:Quartet&Sextet | Vogue | 21511522

Night And Day(alt.take)
Bill Evans Trio With Lee Konitz & Warne Marsh | Crosscurrents | Original Jazz Classics | OJCCD 718-2(F 9568)
Edmond Hall Quartet With Teddy Wilson | Commodore Classics In Swing | Commodore | 9031-72723-2

Night And Day(This Cloudy World)
Leon Monosson With Alain Romans Et Son Orchestra Du Poste Parisien | Le Jazz En France Vol.5:Django Plus | Pathe | 1727291

Night At Ghandi's
Stefan Karlsson Quintet | The Road Not Taken | Justice Records | JR 0702-2

Night At The Circus
Stan Kenton And His Orchestra | Adventures In Blues | Capitol | 520089-2

Night At The Gold Nugget
Adventures In Blues | Capitol | 520089-2

Night At The Gold Nugget(alt.take)
Michael Naura Quintet | Jazz In Deutschland 1957-1958/Kühl Und Modern | Vagabond | 6.22563 AG

Night Bird
Chet Baker Quintet | Live In Paris | Circle Records | RK 22-25680/22 IMS

Night Breed
Steve Coleman And Metrics | Steve Coleman's Music Live In Paris | Novus | 2131691-2

Night Bus
Charlie Parker With The Cootie Williams Orchestra | Bird's Eyes Last Unissued Vol.22:Don't Blame Me | Philology | W 852.2

Night Child
Oscar Peterson Quartet | Night Child | Original Jazz Classics | OJCCD 1030-2(2312108)
Freedom Song | Pablo | 2640101-2

Night Circles
Borah Bergman | A New Frontier | Soul Note | 121030-2

Night Crawler
Sonny Stitt Trio | The Prestige Collection:Sonny Stitt Soul Classics | Original Jazz Classics | OJCCD 6003-2

Night Dance
The Jimmy Giuffre 3 | Music For People,Birds,Butterflies & Mosquitoes | Candid | CRS 1001 IMS

Night Delighter
Aldo Romano Quartet | Night Diary | Owl Records | 018

Night Dream
Dwight Dickerson Trio | Sooner Or Later | Discovery | DS 792 IMS

Night Dreamer
Wayne Shorter Quintet | Night Dreamer | Blue Note | 784173-2
Tom Scott Group | Flashpoint | GRP | GRP 95712

Night Flight
Conte Candoli Quartet | Fine & Dandy | Affinity | AFF 173
Louie Bellson Big Band | London Scene | Concord | CJ 157
The Frank Capp Juggernaut | Play It Again Sam | Concord | CCD 4747

Night Flower
Michael Naura Quintet | Michael Naura Quintet | Brunswick | 543128-2

Night Glider
Richard 'Groove' Holmes Orchestra | The Best Of The Jazz Organs | LRC Records | CDC 9006

Night Has Come
Charly Antolini-Charly Augschöll Quartet | Charlie Antolini-40 Years Jubilee Drumfire | BELL Records | BLR 86001

Night Hawk
Kenny Burrell Quartet | Night Song | Verve | 2304539 IMS

Night Images
Walt Weiskopf Nonet | Siren | Criss Cross | Criss 1187

Night In The City
$$hide$$ | $$Titelverweise | |

Night In Tunisia -> A Night In Tunisia

Night Jessamine
Canoneo | Canodeo | Passport Jazz | ???

Night Life
Ronnie Foster | The Racer | Electric Bird | K 28P 6441

Night Lights
Gerry Mulligan Sextet | Compact Jazz:Gerry Mulligan | Mercury | 830697-2 PMS
Christoph Spendel Group | City Kids | TCB Records | TCB 01052

Night Meandering
Howard McGhee Sextet | Trumpet At Tempo | Spotlite | SPJ 131

Night Mist Blues
Thad Jones Quartet | Three And One | Steeplechase | SCCD 31197

Night Movements
Bob Berg Quartet | Enter The Spirit | Stretch Records | SCD 9004-2

Night Moves(Fear)
Eric Dolphy Quintet | Vintage Dolphy | Enja | ENJ-5045 2

Night Must Fall
Jan Savitt And His Top Hatters | The Uncollected:Jan Svitt | Hindsight | HSR 213

Night Of My Love(A Noite Do Meu Bem)
Geri Allen Sextet | The Nurturer | Blue Note | 795139-2

Night Out
Michael Logan Quartet | Night Out | Muse | MCD 5458

Night Passage
Allen Toussaint Group | Motion | Warner | WPCP 4416

Night Rhythms
Lee Ritenour Sextet | Alive In L.A. | GRP | GRP 98822
Lee Ritenour With Special Guests | Festival International De Jazz De Montreal | Spectra | 9811661
Bert Ambrose And His Orchestra | Saturday Night | Decca | DDV 5003/4 DT

Night Ride Home
Bob Rockwell Quartet | On The Natch | Steeplechase | SCCD 31229

Night Rider
Stan Getz With The Eddie Sauter Orchestra | Focus | Verve | 521419-2

Night Shift Blues
Edmond Hall's Blue Note Jazzmen | Hot Jazz On Blue Note | Blue Note | 835811-2

Night Shift Blues(alt.take)
Imre Köszegi Trio | Drummer's Dream | yvp music | CD 3044

Night Song
Bernd Köppen | Hanek ppen | Senti | SE 01
Frank Foster Sextet | Soul Outing! | Original Jazz Classics | OJCCD 984-2(7479)
Kenny Burrell With The Don Sebesky Orchestra | Night Song | Verve | 2304539 IMS
Nina Simone With Hal Mooney's Orchestra | Broadway-Blues-Ballads | Verve | 518190-2
Sarah Vaughan With Orchestra | !Viva! Vaughan | Mercury | 549374-2
Stan Kenton And His Orchestra | Artistry In Voices And Brass | Creative World | ST 1038

Night Sound
Harry James And His Orchestra | Harry James:Concerto For Orchestra 1939-1941 | Naxos Jazz | 8.120618

Night Speed Chase
Henry Threadgill-Craig Harris Group | Hip Hop Be Bop | ITM Records | ITM 1480

Night Street
Chick Corea Group | Verve Jazz Masters 3:Chick Corea | Verve | 519820-2
Bob Cooper Orchestra | COOP! The Music Of Bob Cooper | Original Jazz Classics | OJCCD 161-2

Night Sun In Blois
Free Kick | Natural Desire | Timeless | CD SJP 408

Night Time Is The Right Time
Al Smith With The Eddie Lockjaw Davis Quartet | Hear My Blues | Original Blues Classics | OBC 514
Count Basie And His Orchestra With Joe Williams | Basie On Roulette, Vol. 17: Just The Blues | Vogue | 500017
Ray Charles Sextet With The Raylets | Newport Jazz Festival 1958,July 3rd-6th Vol.4:Blues In The Night No.2 | Phontastic | NCD 8816
Roosevelt Sykes Quintet | Urban Blues | Fantasy | F 24717

Night Time Was My Mother
Blues & Boogie Explosion | Blues & Boogie Explosion | BELL Records | BLR 84003

Night Train
Cootie Williams Quintet | Jazz In Paris:Joe Newman-Jazz At Midnight-Cootie Williams | EmArCy | 018446-2
Dirty Dozen Brass Band | Live:Mardi Gras In Montreux | Rounder Records | CDRR 2052
Jimmy Smith And Wes Montgomery With The Oliver Nelson Orchestra | Talkin' Jazz:Roots Of Acid Jazz | Verve | 529580-2
Compact Jazz: Jimmy Smith | Verve | 831374-2
Lincoln Center Jazz Orchestra | Big Train | CBS | CK 69860
Lionel Hampton And His Orchestra | Hamp's Big Band | RCA | 2121821-2
Max Greger Quintet | Night Train | Polydor | 543393-2
Maynard Ferguson And His Orchestra | The Blues Roar | Mainstream | MD CDO 717
Oscar Peterson Trio | Hot Tracks For Cool Cats Vol.3 | Polydor | 816411-2
Rahsaan Roland Kirk Group | The Man Who Cried Fire | Night Records | VNCD 1(887047)
Roots | Stablemates | IN+OUT Records | 7021-2
Shorty Baker-Doc Cheatham Quintet | Shorty & Doc | Original Jazz Classics | OJCCD 839-2(SV 2021)
Sweetman With His South Side Groove Kings | Austin Backalley Blue | Mapleshade | 02752
Wild Bill Davis Trio | Organ Boogie Woogie | CBS | 21079

Night Train To Memphis
Duke Jordan Quartet | Misty Thursday | Steeplechase | SCCD 31053

Night Turns Into Day
Jimmy Knepper Quintet | Dream Dancing | Criss Cross | Criss 1024

Night Watch
Barbara Thompson's Paraphernalia | Pure Fantasy | VeraBra Records | No. 8
Roy Hargrove Quintet | Public Eye | Novus | PD 83113

Night Whistler
Ella Fitzgerald With Frank De Vol And His Orchestra | Like Someone In Love | Verve | 511524-2

Night Wind
Erroll Garner Sextet | Magician & Gershwin And Kern | Telarc Digital | CD 83337
Fats Waller And His Rhythm | Breakin' The Ice-The Early Years Part 1(1934-1935) | Bluebird | 63 66618-2

Nightclubbing With Hatschepsud(dedicated to Grace Jones)
Jack DeSalvo-Arthur Lipner | Liquide Stones | Tutu Records | 888132-2

Nightfall
Elliot Lawrence And His Orchestra | The Elliot Lawrence Big Band Swings Cohn & Kahn | Fantasy | FCD 24761-2
Giko Pavan Quartet | Gino Pavan | SPLASC(H) Records | H 128
Lajos Dudas Quartet | Urban Blues | Konnex Records | KCD 5050
Oregon | Northwest Passage | Intuition Records | INT 3191-2
Rabih Abou-Khalil Quintet | Between Dusk And Dawn | Enja | ENJ-9771 2
Ralph Towner-Peter Erskine | Open Letter | ECM | 1462(511980-2)
Rob McConnell And The Boss Brass | Our 25th Year | Concord | CCD 4559

Nightgarden
Eddie Kirkland Group | Lonely Street | Telarc Digital | CD 83424

Night-Glo
George Baquet Band | The John Reid Collection 1940-1944 | American Music | AMCD-44

Nightingale
Earl Coleman With Unkn.Trio | Cool Whalin' - Bebop Vocals | Spotlite | SPJ 135

Meredith d'Ambrosio Quintet | South To A Warmer Place | Sunnyside | SSC 1039 D
Oscar Peterson Trio | Oscar Peterson Trio: Olympia/Theatre Des Champs-Elysees | Laserlight | 36134
Three Originals:Motion&Emotions/Tristeza On Piano/Hello Herbie | MPS | 521059-2
Oscar Peterson Trio With The Nelson Riddle Orchestra | The Silver Collection: Oscar Peterson | Verve | 823447-2 PMS
Shelly Manne And His Men | West Coast Jazz In England | Jazz Groove | JG 006 IMS
At The Blackhawk Vol.4 | Contemporary | C 7580

Nightlee Vienna
Oliver Strauch Group With Lee Konitz | City Lights | Blue Concept | BCCD 94/03

Nightlife In Tokyo
Don Braden Quartet | Landing Zone | Landmark | LCD 1539-2

Nightly
John LaPorta Octet | Theme And Variations | Fantasy | FCD 24776-2

Nightly Vigil
Tomasz Stanko | Music From Thaj Mahal And Karla Caves | Leo Records | 011

Nightmare
Artie Shaw And His Orchestra | The Original Sounds Of The Swing Era Vol.7 | RCA | CL 05517 DP

Nightmare Of A White Elephant
The Uncollected:Artie Shaw And His Orchestra, Vol.3 | Hindsight | HSR 148

Nightowls
Vienna Art Orchestra | Nightride Of A Lonely Saxophoneplayer | Moers Music | 02054/5 CD

Nights At The Turntable
Gerry Mulligan Quartet | Chet Baker:Complete 1952 Fantasy & Pacific Jazz Sessions | Definitive Records | DRCD 11233

Nights Of Skopje
Dusko Goykovich Quintet | Balkan Blues | Enja | ENJ-9320 2
Ahmed Abdullah Sextet | Jazz Sounds Of Africa | Prestige | PRCD 24279-2

Nights On Saturn
Dejan Terzic Quartet | Four For One | Naxos Jazz | 86036-2

Nightshade Rounds
John Fedchock New York Big Band | John Fedchock New York Big Band | Reservoir | RSR CD 138

Nightsong
Bob Nell Quintet | Why I Like Coffee | New World Records | 80419-2

Nighttime
Royce Campbell Quintet | Nighttime Daydreams | Timeless | CD SJP 337

Nighttime In The City
Tomasz Stanko Sextet | Litania | ECM | 1636(537551-2)

Night-Time,Daytime Requiem
Don Grolnick Septet | Nighttown | Blue Note | 798689-2

Nigun
Anouar Brahem Trio | Astrakan Café | ECM | 1718(159494-2)

Nihawend Lunga
Schmilz | Schmilz | Creative Works Records | CW CD 1041

Nihil
Art Blakey And The Jazz Messengers | Kyoto | Original Jazz Classics | OJCCD 145-2

Nii Voi Naa
Willem Breuker Kollektief | To Remain | BVHAAST | CD 8904

Nik-Nik
Landes Jugend Jazz Orchester Hessen | Magic Morning | Mons Records | CD 1905

Nil
Unternehmen Kobra | Central Europe Suite | G.N.U. Records | CD A 94.007

Niles
Louie Bellson & The 'Explosion' Orchestra | Sunshine Rock | Pablo | 2310813

Nils Walksong
Dick Oatts Quartet | Standard Issue | Steeplechase | SCCD 31439

Nimbus
Alexander von Schlippenbach | Payan | Enja | 2012

Nimm Zwei
Franck Band | Dufte | Jazz Haus Musik | JHM 0054 CD

Nimmich
Mike Wofford Trio | Bird Of Paradise | Discovery | DS 778 IMS

Nina
Thomas Faist Jazzquartet | Visionary | JHM Records | JHM 3609
Wooding's Grand Central Red Caps | Thumpin' & Bumpin'-New York Vol.2 | Frog | DGF 11

Nina Never Knew
Curtis Peagler Quartet | I'll Be Around | Pablo | 2310930
The King Sisters With The Alvino Rey Orchestra | Warm And Wonderful | EMI Records | 1599351

Nina Valeria
Joe Pass-John Pisano | Joe Pass-John Pisano:Duets | Pablo | 2310959-2

Nina's Birthday Song
Joe Pass | Virtuoso No.3 | Original Jazz Classics | OJC20 684-2(2310805)

Nina's Blues
Frederic Rabold Crew | Funky Tango | MPS | 68242

Nina's Dance
Yosuke Yamashita Trio | Clay | Enja | 2052 (807597)

Nine
Big Daddy Kinsey Group | Big Daddy Kinsey:I Am The Blues | Verve | 519175-2

Nine Doors
Mehmet Ergin Group | Beyond The Seven Hills | MCA | MCD 70020

Nine The Five
Roscoe Mitchell And The Note Factory | Nine To Get Ready | ECM | 1651(539725-2)

Nine To Get Ready
Jazzartrio | From Time To Time | SPLASC(H) Records | H 148

Nineteen
Horace Silver Quintet | Silver's Serenade | Blue Note | 821288-2

Nineteen Bars
Sylvie Courvoisier Group | Abaton | ECM | 1838/39(157628-2)

Nineteen Improvisations
Leroy Carr | Leroy Carr & Scapper Blackwell(1930-1958) | Story Of Blues | CD 3538-2

Nineteeneightyfour
Fabien Degryse Quintet | Medor Sadness | Edition Collage | EC 454-2

Nineties
Joachim Raffel Quintet | Thinkin' Of Trane | Acoustic Music Records | 319.1059.2

Ninety-Nine And A Half A Won't Do
Ingrid Jensen Quintet | Here On Earth | Enja | ENJ-9313 2

Ninety-One
Odean Pope Trio | Ninety-Six | Enja | 9091-2

Ninja
Threeo | Racing Time | L+R Records | CDLR 45103

Ninna Nanna Per Vale
Cecil Payne Quintet | Bird Gets The Worm | Muse | MR 5061

Ninths
Bluiett-Pullen Duo | Hamiet Bluiett | Chiaroscuro | CR 182

Nion
Warren Vaché And Bill Charlap | 2Gether | Nagel-Heyer | CD 2011

Nip-Hoc Waltz(Homage To Chopin)
Johnny Richards And His Orchestra | Wide Range | Creative World | ST 1052

Nippon Soul
Cannonball Adderley Sextet | Nippon Soul | Original Jazz Classics | OJC20 435-2(RLP 9477)

Nippon Soul(Nihon No Soul)
Modern Walkin' | Modern Walkin'-Live In Japan | Satin Doll Productions | SDP 1009-1 CD

Nirgendwohin,Hartnäckig
Herbie Mann Group | The Evolution Of Mann | Atlantic | SD 2-300

Nirvana
Herbie Mann-Bill Evans Quartet | That's Jazz Vol.8: Nirvana | Atlantic | ATL 50238

Nisa
Abdullah Ibrahim Trio | Yarona | TipToe | TIP-888820 2
Music Revelation Ensemble | Music Revelation Ensemble | DIW | DIW 825 CD

Nishijski Chochek-Joe-Jack
DIX | Percussion & Voice | Born&Bellmann | 980504 CD

Nissen Hut
Benny Goodman And His Orchestra | Breakfast Ball | Saville Records | SVL 172 IMS

Nite Mist Blues
Trio Hein Van Der Gaag | To The Point | Limetree | MLP 0018

Nite Sprite
Brian Lynch Sextet | At The Main Event | Criss Cross | Criss 1070

Nitetime Street
Andy Laverne Quartet | Frozen Music | Steeplechase | SCCD 31244

Nitrams Rock
Jimmy Hamilton Sextet | It's About Time | Prestige | 0902123(Swingville 2022)

Nitty Gritty
Jan Klare/Tom Lorenz Quartett | Das Böse Ding | Acoustic Music Records | 319.1060.2

Nix It Mix It
Hannes Clauss Quartett | Walk | Acoustic Music Records | 319.1074.2

Njeto
Anthony Braxton Quartet | Four Compositions(Quartet) 1984 | Black Saint | 120086-2

Nne(part 1)
Miles Davis Group | Dark Magus | CBS | C2K 65137

Nne(part 2)
Anthony Braxton | Live At Moers Festival | Moers Music | 01002 CD

No
Trio Neue Deutsche Blasmusik | Vier Stücke Für Das Trio Neue Deutsche Blasmusik | Misp Records | CD 512

No Agenda
Odean Pope Trio | Almost Like Me | Moers Music | 01092 CD

No Baby Nobody But You
Stan Kenton And His Orchestra | The Uncollected:Stan Kenton, Vol.5 | Hindsight | HSR 157

No Bass Trio
Eric Watson Trio | Conspiracy | Owl Records | 027

No Beguis Mai Got
Kim Kristensen | Pulse Of Time | dacapo | DCCD 9435

No Belonging
Booker Ervin Quintet | The Blues Book | Original Jazz Classics | OJCCD 780-2(P 7340)

No Blooze Blooze
Brad Mehldau With The Rossy Trio | New York-Barcelona Crossing Vol.2 | Fresh Sound Records | FSNT 037 CD

No Blues
Dexter Gordon Quintet | After Midnight | Steeplechase | SCCD 31226
Miles Davis Quintet | Miles Davis In Person-Friday Night At The Blackhawk,San Francisco,Vol.1 | CBS | C4K 87106
Miles Davis In Person-Friday Night At The Blackhawk,San Francisco,Vol.1 | CBS | C4K 87106
Live In Stockholm | Dragon | DRCD 228
En Concert Avec Europe 1 | Laserlight | 710455/58
Wynton Kelly Trio With Wes Montgomery | Smokin' At The Half Note | Verve | 2304480 IMS
Smokin' At The Half Note | CTI Records | PDCTI 1117-2

No Blues-
John Kirby And His Orchestra | TheComplete Una Mae Carlisle(1940-1942) And John Kirby(1941-1942) | RCA | ND 89484

No Blues(alt.take)
Eddie Cleanhead Vinson & Roomful Of Blues | Eddie Cleanhead Vinson & Roomful Of Blues | Muse | MCD 5282

No Calypso Tonight
Eddie Brunner Und Die Original Teddies | Teddy Stauffer:Rare And Historical Jazz Recordings | Elite Special | 9522009

No Computer Aid
Steve Coleman And Five Elements | Rhythm People | Novus | PL 83092

No Contract
Ensemble Modern | Ensemble Modern-Fred Frith:Traffic Continues | Winter&Winter | 910044-2

No Convenient Time
Bill Evans Trio | New Jazz Conceptions | Original Jazz Classics | OJC20 025-2(RLP 223)

No Cover No Minimum
Bud Shank Quartet | Bud Shank Plays The Music Of Bill Evans | Fresh Sound Records | FSR-CD 5012

No Crooks
Shankar/Caroline | The Epidemics | ECM | 1308

No Cure
Benny Golson Sextet | Time Speaks-Dedicated To The Memory Of Clifford Brown | Timeless | CD SJP 187

No Dinner
Trilok Gurtu Group | Crazy Saints | CMP Records | CMP CD 66

No Dispareu Contra El Baixista
Clifton Chenier Group | On Tour | EPM Musique | FDC 5505

No Dog No More
Jimmy Greene Sextet | Introducing Jimmy Greene | Criss Cross | Criss 1181

No Else Thank You
Frank Wright Quintet | Your Prayer | ESP Disk | ESP 1053-2

No Eyes Blues
Lester Young And His Band | Lester Young:The Complete 1936-1951 Small Group Sessions(Studio Recordings-Master Takes),Vol.4 | Blue Moon | BMCD 1004

No Fair Lady
Ron McClure Sextet | Sunburst | Steeplechase | SCCD 31306

No Fear
John Stevens Quartet | Re-Touch & Quartet | Konnex Records | KCD 5027
John Stevens Trio | No Fear | Spotlite | SPJ 508

No Fi
Tony Ortega Octet | Jazz For Young Moderns | Fresh Sound Records | FSR 2006(Bethlehem BCP 79)

No Filters
Five Red Caps | Lenox Avenue Jump | Krazy Kat | KK 779 IMS

No Flower Please
Oscar Peterson-Clark Terry Duo | Oscar Peterson & Clark Terry | Original Jazz Classics | OJCCD 806-2(2310742)

No Flugel Blues
Chuck Foster And His Orchestra | The Uncollected: Chuck Foster | Hindsight | HSR 115

No Future
Rebecca Coupe Franks Group | Suit Of Amor | Justice Records | JR 0901-2

No Good Man
Billie Holiday With Tony Scott And His Orchestra | Lady Sings The Blues | Enoch's Music | 57271013

No Goodtime Fairies
Steve Coleman Quintet | Jump On It | Enja | 4094

No Greater Lunch
Wolfgang Lackerschmid Quartet | One More Life | Bhakti Jazz | BR 29
Wolfgang Lackerschmid & Lynne Arriale Trio | You Are Here | Bhakti Jazz | BR 43

No Greater Lunch-
Manhattan Jazz Quintet | My Favorite Things | Paddle Wheel | K32Y 6210

No Happiness For Slater
Dinah Washington With The Fred Norman Orchestra | Back To The Blues | Roulette | 8543342

No Hard Feelings
George Shearing With The Montgomery Brothers | Wes Montgomery-The Complete Riverside Recordings | Riverside | 12 RCD 4408-2
Lowell Fulsom Band | Tramp/Soul | Ace Records | CDCHD 339

No Hau
Art Blakey And The Afrocuban Boys | Les Liaisons Dangereuses(Original Soundtrack) | Fontana | 812017-2

No Hay Problema
Ray Barretto + New World Spirit | My Summertime | Owl Records | 835830-2

No Hay Problema(take 2)
Terry Gibbs Dream Band | Terry Gibbs Dream Band Vol.2:The Sundown Sessions | Contemporary | CCD 7652-2

No Heat
Dorothy Love Coates And The Original Gospel Harmonettes | The Best Of Dorothy Love Coates And The Original Gospel Harmonettes | Ace Records | CDCHD 343

No Hip Hop
Tiny Grimes Quintet | Tiny Grimes:The Complete 1950-1954,Vol.4 | Blue Moon | BMCD 6008

No Idea
Fabio Jegher Italian Vocal Ensemble | Chiaroscuri | Red Records | NS 203
Franco D'Andrea Quartet | No Idea Of Time | Red Records | NS 202

No Ill Wind
Don 'Sugar Cane' Harris Quartet | Fiddler On The Rock | MPS | 68028

No Jungle?
Steve Laury Trio | Passion | Denon Compact Disc | CY-79043

No Lic
Buddy Guy Band | Buddy Guy | Chess | 427006

No Limit
Art Pepper Quartet | More For Less At The Village Vanguard Vol.4 | Original Jazz Classics | OJCCD 697-2(C 7650)

No Line
Les DeMarle Sextet | On Fire | Palo Alto | PA 8008

No Lonely Nights
Keith Jarrett Trio | Keith Jarrett At The Blue Note-The Complete Recordings | ECM | 1575/80(527638-2)
Keith Jarrett At The Blue Note-The Complete Recordings | ECM | 1575/80(527638-2)
Gerry Niewood Group | Share My Dream | dmp Digital Music Productions | CD 450

No Love Without Tears
Jenny Evans And Her Quintet | Nuages | ESM Records | ESM 9308
New Orleans Rhythm Kings | Big Band Bounce & Boogie-Muggsy Spanier:Hesitatin' Blues | Affinity | AFS 1030

No Man Is An Island
Ketil Bjornstad Group | Grace | EmArCy | 013622-2

No Man Is An Island(Finale)
Bill Frisell Band | Is That You? | Nonesuch | 7559-60956-2

No Man's Land
Billy Sheehan-John Novello-Dennis Chambers | Niacin | Stretch Records | SCD 9011-2
Enrico Pieranunzi Trio | No Man's Land | Soul Note | 121221-2

No Man's Land(long take)
Jack Jeffer's N.Y. Classic Big Band | New York Dreams | Mapleshade | 03632

No Matter What
Benny Golson Orchestra | Tune In,Turn On | Verve | 559793-2

No Matter What They Say
Trio Asab | Coast To Coast | Aho-Recording | AHO CD 1028(CD 380)

No Me Esqueca
Lionel Hampton And His Giants | Live In Emmen/Holland | Timeless | CD SJP 120

No Me Llored Mas
Herbie Hancock Group | Sunlight | CBS | 486570-2

No Means Yes
Gary Thomas Sextet | Exile's Gate | JMT Edition | 514009-2

No Mission But You
Benny Bailey Quintet | Live At Grabenhalle, St.Gallen | TCB Records | TCB 8940

No Moe
Sonny Rollins With The Modern Jazz Quartet | Welcome To Jazz: Sonny Rollins | Koch Records | 322 079 D1
Sonny Rollins With The Modern Jazz Quintet | Vintage Sessions | Prestige | P 24096
Bill Frisell Trio | Live | Gramavision | GCD 79504

No Money Down
John Hammond Band | The Best Of John Hammond | Vanguard | VCD 11/12

No Money No Tolerance
Pili-Pili | Hotel Babo | JA & RO | JARO 4147-2
Joachim Kühn Trio And The WDR Big Band | Carambolage | CMP Records | CMP CD 58(EFA 03058)

No Moon At All
Count Basie And His Orchestra | Breakfast Dance And Barbecue | Roulette | 531791-2
Dunstan Coulber Quartet | Standards For A New Century | Nagel-Heyer | CD 081
Ella Fitzgerald With The Bill Doggett Orchestra | Rhythm Is My Business | Verve | 559513-2
George Shearing Trio | Windows | MPS | 68200
Joe Newman Septet | The Complete Joe Newman RCA-Victor Recordings(1955-1956):The Basie Days | RCA | 2122613-2
Mary Ann McCall With The Teddy Charles Quintet | Detour To The Moon | Fresh Sound Records | FSR 584(Jubilee JLP 1078)
Memphis Convention | Memphis Convention | DIW | DIW 874 CD
Nana Mouskouri With The Berlin Radio Big Band | Nana Swings | Mercury | 074394-2
Paul Quinichette Sextet | The Kid From Denver:Paul Quinichette Complete Dawn Sessions | Dawn | DCD 106
Phineas Newborn Jr. Trio | Back Home | Original Jazz Classics | OJCCD 971-2(C 7648)
Stan Kenton And His Orchestra | Two Much | Creative World | ST 1067

No Moon At All-
Erroll Garner Trio | Erroll Garner | Verve | 846191-2 PMS

No More
Bill Perkins With The Metropole Orchestra | I Wished On The Moon | Candid | CCD 79524
Carmen McRae And Her Sextet | Woman Talk | Mainstream | MD CDO 706
Marty Paich Band | I Get A Boot Out Of You | Discovery | DS 829 IMS
Zoot Sims Quartet | For Lady Day | Pablo | 2310942-2

No More Blues
Joe Diorio | To Jobim With Love | RAM Records | RMCD 4529
$$hide$$ | $$Titelverweise | |

No More Blues -> Chega De Saudade

No More Brew
Klaus Ignatzek Group Feat.Dave Liebman | Tender Mercies | Nabel Records:Jazz Network | LP 4621

No More Chains
Mariano-Humair-Haurand | Frontier Traffic | Konnex Records | KCD 5110
Stivin-Van Den Broeck-Haurand | Bordertalk | Konnex Records | KCD 5068
Ronnie Earl & The Broadcasters | Deep Blues | Black Top | BT 1033 CD

No More Doggin'
Yoshiaki Masuo Group | A Subtle One | Jazz City | 660.53.030

No More Jogging
The Ravens | The Greatest Group Of Them All:The Ravens | Savoy | SV 0270

No More Lonely Nights
Willie Nix And His Combo | Combination Blues | Charly | CRB 1042

No More Misunderstanding
Geri Allen | Home Grown | Minor Music | 8004

No More Mr. Nice Guy

Guy Klucevsek-Phillip Johnston | Tales From The Cryptic | Winter&Winter | 910088-2
Takashi Kazamaki & Kalle Laar Group | Floating Frames | Ear-Rational | ECD 1038

No More Princess
Thursday Diva | Folow Me | dmp Digital Music Productions | CD 509

No More Quarrels -> Brigas, Nunca Mais

No More Stress
Sadik Hakim Trio | Witches Gobelins etc. | Steeplechase | SCCD 31091

No More Troubles
Tim Whitehead Quartet | Authentic | Ronnie Scott's Jazz House | JHCD 017

No Motion Picture
Al Di Meola World Sinfonia | World Sinfonia | Inak | 700772

No Name
Barry Harris Trio | Live At Dug | Enja | 9097-2

No Name Samba
Peter Herbolzheimer Rhythm Combination & Brass | Friends And Sihouettes | Koala Records | CD P 25

No Ni No
Mark Zubeck Quintet | Horse With A Broken Leg | Fresh Sound Records | FSNT 078 CD

No No
Smiley Lewis And His Orchestra | No No | Pathe | 1566321

No Noise(part 1&2)
Charlie Parker With Machito And His Orchestra | The Latin Bird | Memo Music | HDJ 4076

No Noise(part 2)
Bob Keene Quintet | The Bob Keene Quintet | Fresh Sound Records | FSR 586(Del-Fi DFLP 1202)

No Olvides
Boyd Senter And His Senterpedes | Boyd Senter:Jazzologist Supreme | Timeless | CBC 1-032

No One
Eddie Harris Quintet | A Study In Jazz/Breakfast At Tiffany's | Vee Jay Recordings | VJ 020
Johnny Hodges-Wild Bill Davis Sextet | Johnny Hodges-Wild Bill Davis, Vol.1-2(1965-1966) | RCA | ND 89765

No One Can Explain It
Bob Barnard Quintet | New York Notes | Sackville | SKCD2-3061

No One Else But You
Louis Armstrong And His Savoy Ballroom Five | Jazz:The Essential Collection Vol.2 | IN+OUT Records | 78012-2
Red Richards | Dreamy | Sackville | SKCD2-3053
Eden Atwood Group | No One Ever Tells You | Concord | CCD 4560

No One Ever Tells You
Ruth Brown With The Richard Wess Orchestra | Late Date With Ruth Brown | Atlantic | AMCY 1055

No One Knows What It's All About
Mind Games | Mind Games Plays The Music Of Stan Getz & Astrud Gilberto | Edition Collage | EC 515-2

No One Like You(for Ursula)
Dinah Washington With The Fred Norman Orchestra | Back To The Blues | Roulette | 8543342

No Opera
Gary Dial-Dick Oatts Quartet With Strings | Dial And Oatts | dmp Digital Music Productions | CD 465

No Ordinary Romance
Ella Fitzgerald With The Marty Paich Orchestra | Ella Sings Broadway | Verve | 549373-2

No Other Love
The Sauter-Finegan Orchestra | That's All | Magic | DAWE 80

No Pain For Cakes
Lily White Group | Somewhere Between Truth & Fiction | Knitting Factory Works | KFWCD 153

No Panama
Duke Ellington And His Cotton Club Orchestra | Duke Ellington Playing The Blues 1927-1939 | Black & Blue | BLE 59.232 2

No Place Nowhere
Louis Conte Group | La Cocina Caliente | Denon Compact Disc | CY-30001

No PLace To Be Somebody
Howlin' Wolf Band | Howlin' Wolf | Chess | 427016

No Problem
Barney Wilen Quintet | La Note Bleue | IDA Record | 010 CD
Bud Powell Quintet | The Best Of The Jazz Pianos | LRC Records | CDC 8519
Clark Terry Sextet | Clark Terry | Swing | SW 8406 IMS
Tommy Chase Quartet | Hard! | Contemporary | BOP 5

No Problem(take 2)
Duke Jordan Trio | Flight To Denmark | Steeplechase | SCCD 31011

No Puedo Prenar
Paul Bley-Gary Peacock Duet | Partners | Owl Records | 014730-2

No Pun Intended
Flemming Agerskov Quintet | Face To Face | dacapo | DCCD 9445

No Purpose
Ellery Eskelin + Han Bennink | Dissonant Characters | HatOLOGY | 534

No Questions
Krzyaztof Scieranski Trio | No Radio | ITM Records | ITM 001 JP

No Rags
Richard Tee Group | The Bottom Line | Electric Bird | K32Y 6035

No Regerts
Das Pferd | Blue Turns To Grey | VeraBra Records | CDVBR 2065-2

No Regrets-
Ella Fitzgerald With The Tommy Flanagan Trio | Jazz Collection:Ella Fitzgerald | Laserlight | 24397
Marty Cook Quartet | Red, White, Black And Blue | Enja | 5067-2

No Resolution
Marty Hall Band | Tried & True | Blues Beacon | BLU-1030 2

No Respect
Daniel Guggenheim Group | Daniel Guggenheim Group feat. Jasper van't Hof | Laika Records | LK 990-018

No Rest
Daniel Guggenheim Quartet | Melancholy | Edition Collage | EC 493-2

No Rest InTainan
Golden Gate Quartet | Golden Gate Quartet | CBS | 471559-2

No Return
Ray Anderson-Han Bennink-Christy Doran | Cheer Up | Hat Art | CD 6175

No Room For Squares
Hank Mobley Quintet | True Blue | Blue Note | 534032-2
Trombonefire | Sliding Affairs | Laika Records | 35101462

No Rules Allowed
Bob Rockwell Quartet | No Rush | Steeplechase | SCCD 31219

No Sadness No Pain
Louis Jordan And His Tympany Five | Louis Jordan-Let The Good Times Roll: The Complete Decca Recordings 1938-1954 | Bear Family Records | BCD 15557 IH

No Sale
Clifton Chenier Group | Live At Montreux | Charly | CDX 2

No Samba
Randy Brecker Quintet | In The Idiom | Denon Compact Disc | CY-1483

No Shit
John Lee Hooker | Solid Sender | Charly | CRB 1081

No Smoke Blues
Archie Shepp Quartet | Live At Totem Vol.1:Things Have Got To Change | EPM Musique | 152172

No Smokin'
Horace Silver Quintet | The Stylings Of Silver | Blue Note | 300168(1562)

No Smoking
Sputnik 27 | But Where's The Moon? | dml-records | CD 011

No Snow Here
Zoot Sims Quintet | The Modern Art Of Jazz | Dawn | DCD 101

No Soap
Dick Collins And The Runaway Heard | Horn Of Plenty | Fresh Sound Records | NL 45632(RCA LJM 1019)

No Soap, No Hope Blues
Meredith d'Ambrosia-Gene Bertoncini | Silent Passion | Sunnyside | SSC 1075 D

No Song
Shelly Manne Quartet | Rex-From The Broadway Musical oRex o | Discovery | DS 783 IMS

No Speak No English,Man
Little Brother Montgomery | Paramounth Piano Blues Vol.1(1928-1932) | Black Swan Records | HCD-12011

No Start No End
Gigi Gryce-Clifford Brown Octet | Clifford Brown:The Complete Paris Sessions Vol.2 | Vogue | 2115462-2

No Strings (I'm Fancy Free)
Ella Fitzgerald With Paul Weston And His Orchestra | The Complete Ella Fitzgerald Song Books of Harold Arlen, Irving Berlin, Duke Ellington, George & Ira Gershwin, Jerome Kern, Johnny Mercer, Cole Porter And Rogers & Hart | Verve | 519832-2

No Strings Attached
Jean-Luc Ponty | Jean-Luc Ponty: Live | Atlantic | ATL 50594

No Talk
Lajos Dudas Quartet | Maydance | Pannon Jazz/Classic | PJ 1003

No Te Imaginas
Paquito D'Rivera Orchestra | Portraits Of Cuba | Chesky | JD 145

No Tears For Me
Candela | La Maquina | BELL Records | BLR 84031

No Thanks
Al Porcino Big Band | In Oblivion | Jazz Mark | 106 Digital

No Time Like The Present
Duffy Jackson Orchestra | Swing! Swing! Swing! | Milestone | MCD 9233-2

No Time To Share
Paul Quinichette Sextet | The Vice Pres | Verve | 543750-2

No Title
Al Foster Quartet | Brandyn | Laika Records | 35100832
Mary Lou Williams Duo | My Mama Pinned A Rose On Me | Pablo | 2310819

No Title No.1
Bobby Previte-John Zorn | Euclid's Nightmare | Depth Of Field | DOF1-2

No Title No.3-
Elke Reiff Quartett | There Is More | Laika Records | 35101112

No Tomorrow
Roland Kirk Quartet | Rahsaan/The Complete Mercury Recordings Of Roland Kirk | Mercury | 846630-2

No Tonic Press
Rip Rig And Panic/Now Please Don't You Cry Beautiful Edith | EmArCy | 832164-2 PMS

'No Trees?' He Said
John Gordon Sextet | Step By Step | Strata East Records | 660.51.005

No Trouble Livin'
Mose Allison Trio | Mose Alife!/Wild Man On The Loose | Warner | 8122-75439-2
Horst Jankowski Quartet | Jankowskinetik | MPS | 9808189

No Troubles At All
Woody Herman And His Orchestra | The Third Herd, Vol.1 | Discovery | DS 815 IMS

No Twilight
Johnny Hodges Orchestra | The Rabbit's Work On Verve In Chronological Order, Vol. 6 | Verve | 2304446 IMS

No Visa
Dinah Washington With Lucky Thompson And His All Stars | The Complete Dinah Washington Vol.1 | Official | 3004

No Walls
Badiane | Flavours | Acoustic Music Records | 319.1071.2

No Warm-Ups
Stefano D'Anna Trio | Leapin' In | SPLASC(H) Records | CD H 374-2

No Way
Jutta Gruber & The Martin Schrack Trio | Keep Hanging On | yvp music | CD 3043
John Scofield-Pat Metheny Quartet | I Can See Your House From Here | Blue Note | 827765-2

No Way Jose
Drei Vom Rhein | Drei Vom Rhein | Mons Records | CD 1896

No Way,Ohhh!
Doctor Clayton's Buddy | Doctor Clayton And His Buddy(1935-1947) | Story Of Blues | CD 3539-2

No Zone
Chick Corea Electric Band | GRP Super Live In Concert | GRP | GRP 16502

No!
Buddy Johnson And His Orchestra | Buddy And Ella Johnson 1953-1964 | Bear Family Records | BCD 15479 DH

No! I Ain't Gonna Let You Go
Louis Armstrong And His Orchestra | Louis Armstrong:Fireworks | Dreyfus Jazz Line | FDM 36710-2

No(No,Papa,No)
Milton Batiste With The Rue Conti Jazz Band | Milton Batiste With The Rue Conti Jazz Band | Lake | LACD 31

No.0
Air | New Air:Live At Montreal International Jazz Festival | Black Saint | 120084-2

No.1 Green Street
Sandy Lomax With Band | Trance Jazz | clearaudio | WOR 171 CD

No.11
Kenny Clarke-Milford Graves-Famoudou Don Moye-Andrew Cyrille | Pieces Of Time | Soul Note | 121078-2

No.12
Das Pferd | Das Pferd | ITM Records | ITM 1416

No.13 Haviland Street
Anthony Braxton-Ted Reichman | Duo(Leipzig) 1993 | Music & Arts | CD 848

No.16753
Duo(Leipzig) 1993 | Music & Arts | CD 848

No.17
Hans Kennel Group feat. Mark Soskin | Stella | TCB Records | TCB 97102

No.2
Buddy Tate Quintet feat.Clark Terry | Tate-A-Tate | Original Jazz Classics | OJC 184(SV 2014)

No.29
Geri Allen Sextet | The Nurturer | Blue Note | 795139-2

No.34 Was Sweetness(for Walter Payton)
Kalaparusha Maurice McIntyre Quartet | Peace And Blessing | Black Saint | BSR 0037

No.5
Hildegard Kleeb | Anthony Braxton Piano Music(Notated) 1968-1988 | Hat Art | CD 6141/4

No.8
Anthony Braxton-Ted Reichman | Duo(Leipzig) 1993 | Music & Arts | CD 848

Noa Noa
Nathalie Lorriers Quartet | Dance Or Die | Igloo | IGL 105

Noadi
Donald Byrd Orchestra With Brass & Voices | I'm Tryin'To Get Home | Blue Note | 84188

Noah
Woody Herman And His Orchestra | Old Gold Rehearsals 1944 | Jazz Unlimited | JUCD 2079
Big Band Bounce & Boogie-Woody Herman:Pre-Herds | Affinity | AFS 1027

Nobody
Nina Simone With Hal Mooney's Orchestra | Broadway-Blues-Ballads | Verve | 518190-2
Sputnik 27 | But Where's The Moon? | dml-records | CD 011

Nobody At Home
Ann Cole With Band | Got My Mojo Working | Krazy Kat | KK 782 IMS

Nobody Else
Vince Guaraldi-Bola Sete Quartet | Live At El Matador | Original Jazz Classics | OJC 289(F 8371)

Nobody Else But Me
Bill Evans Quintet | The Jazz Giants Play Jerome Kern:Yesterdays | Prestige | PCD 24202-2
The Complete Fantasy Recordings | Fantasy | 9FCD 1012-2
Bill Evans Trio | Bill Evans:From The 70's | Fantasy | F 9630
I Will Say Goodbye | Original Jazz Classics | OJCCD 761-2(F 9593)
Bob Rockwell/Jesper Lundgaard | Light Blue | Steeplechase | SCCD 31326
Bud Shank And Bob Cooper With The Metropole Orchestra | A Flower Is A Lovesome Thing | Koch Jazz | 3-6912-2
John Marshall Quintet | Keep On Keepin' On | Mons Records | MR 874774
Mike Wofford Trio | Plays Jerome Kern, Vol. 1 | Discovery | DS 808 IMS
Peter Bernstein Quartet | Signs Of Life | Criss Cross | Criss 1095
Ray Linn And The Chicago Stompers | Empty Suit Blues | Discovery | DS 823 IMS
Soesja Citroen Group | Songs For Lovers And Losers | Challenge | CHR 70034
Stan Getz Quartet | Stan Getz And The 'Cool' Sounds | Verve | 547317-2
Stan Getz:The Complete 1952-1954 Small Group Sessions(Master Takes),Vol.3 | Blue Moon | BMCD 1036
Nobody Else But Me | Verve | 521660-2
Vinding/Norris/Herman | 2nd Trio | Koala Records | CD P 23

Nobody Got The Blues But Me
Deborah Henson-Conant | Alter Ego | Laikà Records | 35100852

Nobody Half As Strong
Alterd Ego | Laika Records | 35100962
Ku-umba Frank Lacy & The Poker Bigband | Songs From The Musical 'Poker' | Tutu Records | 888150-2*

Nobody Helps You-
Johnny Hartman With Al Gafa | Once In Every Life | Bee Hive | BH 7012

Nobody Knows
Dizzy Gillespie Quintet | School Days | Savoy | SV 0157(MG 6043)
Otis Spann Band | The Bottom Of The Blues | BGO Records | BGOCD 92
Sippie Wallace With Axel Zwingenberger | Sippie Wallace/Axel Zwingenberger And The Friends Of Boogie Woogie Vol.1 | Vagabond | VRCD 8.84002
Strange Meeting | Stadtgarten Series Vol.3 | Jazz Haus Musik | JHM 1003 SER

Nobody Knows The Trouble I've Seen
Benny Carter-Dizzy Gillespie Inc. | Carter Gillespie Inc. | Original Jazz Classics | OJCCD 682-2(2310781)
Big Bill Broonzy | Blues Legacy 11: Big Bill Broonzy-Hollerin' And Cryin' The Blues | Vogue | 512511
Bobby Timmons Trio | Bobby Timmons:The Prestige Trio Sessions | Prestige | PRCD 24277-2
Charlie Haden-Hank Jones | Steal Away | Verve | 527249-2
Clyde Wright With Orchestra | Golden Great Gospel Songs | Sonia | CD 77284
Frankie Passions With Quintet | Cool Whalin' - Bebop Vocals | Spotlite | SPJ 135
Grant Green Quintet | Feelin' The Spirit | Blue Note | 746822-2
Hampton Hawes Trio | The Sermon | Original Jazz Classics | OJCCD 1067-2(C 7653)
Horace Silver Quintet | That Healin' Feelin' | Blue Note | 84352
Jimmie Gordon Band | Jimmie Gordon 1934-1941 | Story Of Blues | CD 3510-2
Kay Starr With Orchestra | The Uncollected:Kay Starr Vol.2 | Hindsight | HSR 229
Louis Armstrong And His All Stars | En Concert Avec Europe 1 | Laserlight | 710415
Louis Armstrong With Sy Oliver's Choir And Orchestra | Louis And The Good Book | Verve | 549593-2
Louis Armstrong With The Dukes Of Dixieland | Sweetheart-Definite Alternatives | Chiaroscuro | CR 2006
Louis Armstrong With The Russell Garcia Orchestra | I've Got The World On A String/Louis Under The Stars | Verve | 2304428 IMS
Mahalia Jackson | Amazing Grace | Intercord | 125402
Mavis Staples-Lucky Peterson | Spirituals&Gospel:Dedicated To Mahalia Jackson | Verve | 533562-2
David Murray Quartet | Spirituals | DIW | DIW 841 CD

Nobody Knows The Trouble I've Seen(alt.take)
Alberta Hunter With The Red Onion Jazz Babies | Louis Armstrong And The Blues Singers 1924-1930 | Affinity | AFS 1018(6)

Nobody Knows The Way I Feel This Morning
George Lewis And His Original New Orleans Jazzmen | George Lewis In Stockholm,1959 | Dragon | DRCD 221
George Lewis Trio | George Lewis Bands, Trios & Quartets | American Music | AMCD-83
Punch Miller's Bunch & George Lewis | Atlantic Jazz: New Orleans | Atlantic | 7567-81700-2
Jazz At Preservation Hall, Vol.3 | Atlantic | SD 1410

Nobody Knows You When You're Down And Out
Archie Shepp-Horace Parlan Duo | 2nd Set | 52e Rue Est | RECD 016
Clarence 'Pinetop' Smith | Big Band Bounce & Boogie-Piano Portraits Vol.1 | Affinity | AFS 1022
Jimmy Witherspoon With The Ben Webster Quintet | That's Jazz Vol.30: Jimmy Witherspoon & Ben Webster | Warner | WB 56295
Lous Dassen With Holger Clausen/Atlanta Jazzband | Let's Do It... | Dr.Jazz Records | 8606-2
Nina Simone Quintet | Nina Simone-The 60s Vol.2:Mood Indigo | Mercury | 838544-2 PMS
Old Merrytale Jazz Band | Hot Time | Intercord | 160002
The Jumping Notes Dixieland-Band | C'Est Si Bon | Elite Special | 73444

Nobody Loves Me But My Mother
Esther Phillips With Band | The Rising Sun Collection: Esther Phillips | The Rising Sun Collection | RSC 0007

Nobody Loves Me Like You Do
Jon Burr Trio | 3 For All | Cymekob | CYK 806-2

Nobody Wants You When You're Down And Out
King Curtis Band | Trouble In Mind | Original Blues Classics | OBCCD 512-2(Tru 15001)

Nobody's Afraid Of Howard Monster
Annie Ross With Her Quartet | A Gasser | Pacific Jazz | 746854-2

Nobody's Blues But My Own
Dicky Wells Septet | Dicky Wells & Bill Coleman In Paris | Affinity | CD AFS 1004

Nobody's Fault But Mine
Ken Colyer's All Stars | Just A Little While To Say Here | CMJ Records | CMJ CD 012
Walter 'Wolfman' Washington And The Roadmasters | Out Of The Dark | Rounder Records | CDRR 2068

Nobody's Heart
Gil Evans And Ten | Gil Evans And Ten | Prestige | PRSA 7120-6
J.J.Johnson's All Stars | J.J.'s Broadway | Verve | 9860308
Jackie And Roy | High Standards | Concord | CJ 186
Julie London With Pete King And His Orchestra | About The Blues/London By Night | Capitol | 535208-2
June Christy With The Pete Rugolo Orchestra | The Song Is June | Capitol | 855455-2
Mel Tormé And His Band | Live At The Crescendo | Charly | CD 60
Teddy Charles Quartet | The Duale Roll Of Bob Brookmeyer | Original Jazz Classics | OJCCD 1729-2

Nobody's Heat Belongs To Me
Big Joe Turner And His Band | Jumpin' Tonight | Pathe | 1561431(Imperial)

Nobody's Name
Litschie Hrdlicka Group | Falling Lovers | EGO | 93020
Jack Linx And His Birmingham Society Serenaders | Jack Linx And Maurice Sigler | Jazz Oracle | BDW 8018

Nobody's Something
Seamus Blake Quintet | The Call | Criss Cross | Criss 1088

Nobody's Sweetheart
Bud Freeman And His Summa Cum Laude Orchestra | Victor Jazz History Vol.18:Chicago Jazz(1934-64) | RCA | 2135737-2
Eddie Condon All Stars | That Toddlin' Town-Chicago Jazz Revisited | Atlantic | 90461-1 TIS
Fred Elizalde And His Orchestra | Fred Elizalde And His Anglo American Band | Retrieval | RTR 79011
McKenzie And Condon's Chicagoans | Eddie Condon-Chicago Style | VJM | VLP 55 IMS
Paul Whiteman And His Orchestra | The Famous Paul Whiteman:Jazz A La King | RCA | 2135547-2

Nobody's Sweetheart-
Louis Armstrong And His Orchestra | Laughin' Louie | RCA | ND 90404
Louis Armstrong-Satchmo's Greatest Hits | RCA | CL 89799
Max Collie And His Rhythm Aces | Sensation | Timeless | CD TTD 530

Nobs
Philip Catherine Trio | Guitars | Atlantic | ATL 50193

Noch Einmal
Deborah Henson-Conant | Naked Music | Laika Records | LK 94-051

Noche
Nguyen Le Trio | Bakida | ACT | 9275-2

Noche Y Luz
Juanjo Dominguez | Che Guitarra | ALISO Records | AL 1025

Noche Carioca
Astor Piazzolla Y Su Orquesta | Pulsacion | West Wind Latina | 2220 CD

Noche De Tormenta(Sevillanas)
Jimmy Knepper Quintet | Cunningbird | Steeplechase | SCCD 31061

Noches Calientes
Hermann Martlreiter Quartet | Live at Birdland Neuburg | Birdland | BN 005

Noctuary
Ernie Krivda Quintet | The Alchemist | Inner City | IC 1043 IMS

Nocturn
Claudio Roditi With The Metropole Orchestra | Metropole Orchestra | Mons Records | MR 874767

Nocturnal
Quest | Natural Selection | Line Records | COCD 9.00748 O

Nocturnal Transmission
Al Ryerson Quintet | Blue Flute | Red Baron | 471576-2

Nocturne
Charles Lloyd Sextet | Lift Every Voice | ECM | 1832/33(018783-2)
Charlie Byrd | Solo Flight | Original Jazz Classics | OJCCD 1093-2(RS 9498)
Django Reinhardt-Stephane Grappelli Duo | Stephane's Tune | Naxos Jazz | 8.120570 CD
Jürgen Seefelder Trio | Straight Horn | Enja | 9120-2
Night Ark | Moments | RCA | PD 83028(874049)
Teddy Charles Quartet | Ezz-Thetic | Prestige | P 7827
Toots Thielemans With Gals And Pals | Verve Jazz Masters Vol.59:Toots Thielemans | Verve | 535271-2
Rabih Abou-Khalil Group | The Sultan's Picnic | Enja | ENJ-8078 2

Nocturne Au Villaret
Jan Fryderyk Trio | tri-o (tri-ou) Trio n. | Jazzline | ???

Nocturne Premier(Erik Satie)
Gary Burton Quartet With Chamber Orchestra | Seven Songs For Quartet And Chamber Orchestra | ECM | 1040

Noddin Ya Head Blues
Danny Richmond Quintet | Danny Richmond Plays Charles Mingus | Timeless | CD SJP 148

Nods(2000)
Vigleik Storaas Trio | Bilder | Curling Legs Prod. | C.L.P. CD 018

Noelle's Theme-
Christoph Haberer Group | Pulsation | Jazz Haus Musik | JHM 0066 CD

Noget Om Helte-
Anthony Braxton Quartet | Anthony Braxton | Affinity | AFF 15

Noise In The Attic
Art Blakey And The Jazz Messengers | Lee Morgan More Birdland Sessions | Fresh Sound Records | FSCD 1029

Noise Of The World
Thurston Moore Trio | Lost In The City | Intakt Records | CD 055

Noisy Silence-Gentle Noise
Nathan Davis Quintet | London By Night | DIW | DIW 813 CD

Noite Triste
Bryan Lee Group | Crawfish Lady | Blues Beacon | BLU-1035 2

Noldes Himmel
Chucho Valdes Quartet | Chucho Veldes Solo Piano | Blue Note | 780597-2

Nom
Léon Francioli | Jazz In Switzerland 1930-1975 | Elite Special | 9544002/1-4

Nomad
Dave Brubeck Quartet | St.Louis Blues | Moon Records | MCD 028-2
Louis Armstrong-Dave Brubeck Orchestra | Rare Performances Of The 50's And The 60's | CBS | CBS 88669

Nomad Song
George Sams Quintet | Nomadic Winds | Hat Art | 3506

Nomads
Taylor Hawkins Group | Wake Up Call | Fresh Sound Records | FSCD 145 CD
Hugh Masekela Group | Hope | Triloka Records | 320203-2

Nomen Est Omen
Urs Voerkel Group | Propinquity Zwischenszeitstück Aria | Intakt Records | CD 057

Nommo
Max Roach Quintet | Drums Unlimited | Atlantic | AMCY 1043

Non Ci Resta Che...Chorar!
Joe Gilman Trio With Joe Henderson & Tom Peron | Treasure Chest | Timeless | CD SJP 346

Non Gridate Più-
New Art Saxophone Quartet | Songs And Dances | Enja | ENJ-9420 2

Non Stop City
Ada Montellanico With The Jimmy Cobb Trio | The Encounter | Philology | W 66.2

Non,Je Ne Regrette Rien-
The Oom Maw Maw | Roger's Living Room | Timeless | CD SJP 353

Nona's Blues
Music Revelation Ensemble | In The Name Of... | DIW | DIW 885 CD

Non-Brewed Condiment
Clifton Chenier And His Band | Boogie & Zydeco | Sonet | 147109

Non-Cents
Ralph Lalama Quartet | Music For Grown-Ups | Criss Cross | Criss 1165

None Too Soon(part 1)
Allan Holdsworth Group | None Too Soon | Cream Records | CR 400-2

None Too Soon(part 2)
Carsten Daerr Trio | PurpleCoolCarSleep | Traumton Records | 4472-2

Nonen Est Omen
Bob Stewart First Line Band | First Line | JMT Edition | 919014-2

Nonet
Christoph Lauer-Wolfgang Puschnig-Bob Stewart-Thomas Alkier | Bluebells | CMP Records | CMP CD 56(EFA 03056)
Kenny Wheeler/Lee Konitz/Dave Holland/Bill Frisell | Angel Song | ECM | 1607(533098-2)

Nonetheless
Marilyn Crispell | The Woodstock Concert | Music & Arts | CD 929

NongQongQo
Uli Lenz | Love Channel | L+R Records | CDLR 45100

Nonom
Scott Joplin | Piano Rags-Vol. 1 | Jazz Anthology | JA 5134

Nonsense Conversation
Gary Burton Quartet | The New Quartet | ECM | 1030

Nonsequence
Heartbop | Wednesday Night | yvp music | CD 3033

Non-Stop Home
Astrud Gilberto With Orchestra | The Shadow Of Your Smile | Verve | 2304540

Non-Viennese Waltz Blues
Noodband | Shiver | Moers Music | 01094

Nooks And Crannies
Christopher Dell Quartet | Other Voices, Other Rooms | L+R Records | CDLR 45093

Noon Morning
Charles Mingus Orchestra | Tonight At Noon...Three Or Four Shades Of Love | Dreyfus Jazz Line | FDM 36633-2

Noon Night
Mingus Big Band | Gunslinging Birds | Dreyfus Jazz Line | FDM 36575-2

Noon Song
Chick Corea | Works | ECM | 825426-2

Noon Tide
Biosintes | The First Take | FMP | CD 80

Noon Train
Bunk Johnson's Jazz Band | Bunk Johnson 1944/45 | American Music | AMCD-12

Noosphere
Stan Greig Trio | Blues Every Time | Calligraph | CLG LP 004 IMS

Nor Night,Nor Day,No Rest
Eddie Kirkland | Front And Center | Trix Records | TRIX 3301

Nora
Warren Bernhardt Quintet | Family Album | dmp Digital Music Productions | CD 499

Noray Rai
Jon Balke w/Oslo 13 | Nonsentration | ECM | 1445

Nord
Jonas Hellborg Group | Jonas Hellborg Group | Day Eight Music | DEMCD 025

Nordafjalls-Efter Torleiv Björgum
Joachim Kühn | Distance | CMP Records | CMP CD 26

Norden
Pata Trio | Lucy Und Der Ball | Jazz Haus Musik | JHM 34

Nordlicht
Bernd Konrad Sextet | Traumtänzer | Hat Art | 3509
Helmut Brandt Combo | Jazz Made In Germany | MPS | 88053-2

Nordsee-Mordsee(The Unanswered Call)
Alexander von Schlippenbach And Sven-Ake Johansson | Live 1976/77 | FMP | CD 111

Noreen's Nocturne
Oscar Peterson Trio | The Way I Really Play | MPS | 821287-1
At Zardis' | Pablo | 2CD 2620118
The Mastersounds | A Date With The Mastersounds | Original Jazz Classics | OJC 282(F 8062)

Normandie
Count Basie And His Orchestra | Masters Of Jazz Vol.5 | RCA | NL 89530 DP

Normania
The Indispensable Count Basie | RCA | ND 89758

North
Karl Berger-James Blood Ulmer Duo | Conversations | IN+OUT Records | 77027-2
Jimmy Gourley Trio | Jimmy Gourley And The Paris Heavyweights | 52e Rue Est | RECD 002

North Express
Torsten Zwingenberger's Swingburger | Groovy At The Movie | Moustache Music | 02 03 37 72 86

North Of The Sunset
Thelonious Monk | Solo Monk | CBS | 471248-2
Karl Berger-Dave Holland-Ed Blackwell | Crystal Fire | Enja | 7029-2

North Print
Sharkey Bonano And His Band | Sounds Of New Orleans Vol.8 | Storyville | STCD 6015

North Star Street
Benny Bailey With The Bernhard Pichl Trio | On The Corner | Jazz 4 Ever Records:Jazz Network | J4E 4726
Harris Simen Group | New York Connection | Eastwind | EWIND 701

North Story
Pat Metheny | One Quiet Night | Warner | 9362-48473-2

North To South,East To West
Oscar Peterson Quintet | Oscar Peterson Meets Roy Hargrove And Ralph Moore | Telarc Digital | CD 83399

Northbound
Lincoln Center Jazz Orchestra | Big Train | CBS | CK 69860

Northbound-Southbound
Dick Collins And His Orchestra | King Richard The Swing Hearted | Fresh Sound Records | LJM 1027(RCA)

Northern Cross
Steps Ahead | Steps Ahead | Elektra | 7559-60168-2
Olga Konkova-Per Mathisen Quartet | Northern Crossing | Candid | CCD 79766

Northern Crossing
Heikki Sarmanto Ensemble And Gregg Smith Vocal Quartet | New Hope Jazz Mass | Finlandia | FA 201

Northern Dances
Jan Gunnar Hoff Trio | Moving | Curling Legs Prod. | C.L.P. CD 016

Northern Light
Jukka Tolonen Group | Crossection | Sonet | 147119

Northern Lights-
Ralph Schweizer Big Band | DAY Dream | Chaos | CACD 8177
Hans Reichel | Dix Improvisations, Victoriaville 1989 | Victo | CD 009

Northern Tribes
Jonas Hellborg | Elegant Punk | Day Eight Music | DEMCD 004

Northwest Passage
Chubby Jackson And His Orchestra | Chubby Jackson-The Happy Monster:Small Groups 1944-1947 | Cool & Blue | C&B-CD 109
Woody Herman And His Orchestra | Woody's Winners | CBS | CBS 21110
The Best Of The Big Bands | LRC Records | CDC 8518
Woody Herman's 2nd Herd | The Herd Rides Again...In Stereo | Evidence | ECD 22010-2

Norton Utilities
Red Norvo And His Orchestra | Live From The Blue Gardens | Musicmasters | 65090-2

Norwegian Fox Trot
Joachim Kühn And The Radio Philharmonie Hannover NDR With Jazz Soloists | Europeana | ACT | 9220-2

Norwegian Psalm
John Patitucci Group | Another World | GRP | GRP 97252

Norwegian Wood
Buddy Rich And His Orchestra | Big Swing Face | Pacific Jazz | 837989-2
Carol Sloane With The Art Farmer Sextet | Love You Madly | Contemporary | CCD 14049-2
Johannes Enders Quintet | Quiet Fire | Enja | ENJ-9390 2
Klaus Ignatzek | Piano Solo | Nabel Records:Jazz Network | CD 4691
Plays Beatles Songs | Nabel Records:Jazz Network | CD 4643
Maurizio Rolli-Diana Torto Group | Norwegian Mood | Philology | W 124.2
Theo Bleckman & Kirk Nurock | Looking-Glass River | Traumton Records | 2412-2
Tony Purrone Quartet | Electric Poetry | B&W Present | BW 028

Nos Da
Astrud Gilberto With The Shigeharu Mukai Group And Strings | Mukai Meets Gilberto | Denon Compact Disc | DC-8569

Nose At Nose
New Orleans Saxophone Ensemble | New New Orleans Music: New Music Jazz | Line Records | COCD 9.00917 O

Nose Cone
Heorge Handy And His Orchestra | Handyland U.S.A. | Fresh Sound Records | LXA 1004('X' Records)

Nostalgia
Fats Navarro All Stars | Nostalgia | Savoy | SV 0123(MG 12133)
Fats Navarro Quintet | Fats Navarro:The 1946-1949 Small Group Sessions(Studio Recordings-Master Takes),Vol.2 | Blue Moon | BMCD 1017
Frank Strazzeri Trio | I Remember You(Chet Baker) | Fresh Sound Records | FSR 118(835299)
Mahavishnu | Mahavishnu | Warner | 251351-1
Misha Alperin | Portrait | JA & RO | JARO 4227-2
At Home | ECM | 1768(549610-2)
Oliver Pospiech's Small Big Band | Cool Blue | Mons Records | MR 874809
Passport | 2 Originals Of Passport(Passport-Second Passport) | Atlantic | ATL 60117
Rein De Graaff-Barry Harris Quartet | Nostalgia | Timeless | CD SJP 429
Salsaya Big Band | Live | Timeless | CD SJP 209
The Heath Brothers | As We Were Saying... | Concord | CCD 4777

Nostalgia De Mexico
Sandro Cerino Action Quartet | Tom Thumb In The Magic Castle | SPLASC(H) Records | HP 03

Nostalgia In Time Square
Orage Then Blue Orchestra | Orange Then Blue | GM Recordings | GM 3006(807787)
Tito Puente And His Latin Jazz All Stars | Master Timbalero | Concord | CCD 4594

Nostalgia Soul Ship
Vladimir Chekasin Quartet | Nostalgia | LEO | LR 119

Nostalgias
Jacinte/Juan-José Mosalini Trio | Tango, Mi Corazón | Messidor | 15911 CD

Nostalgias Santiagueras
Jean-Luc Ponty Sextet | Enigmatic Ocean | Atlantic | 19110-2

Nostalgic Lady
Louis Mazetier | Barrel Of Keys | Jazz Connaisseur | JCCD 0140-2

Nostalgic Walk
American Jazz Philharmonic(The New American Orchestra) | American Jazz Philharmonic | GRP | GRP 97302

Not A Care In The World
Leandro Braga Group | E Por Que Nao?(And Why Not?) | Arabesque Recordings | AJ 0104

Not A Rondo
Chris Cheek Quintet | Vine | Fresh Sound Records | FSNT 086 CD

Not A Samba
Peter Erskine Group | Motion Poet | Denon Compact Disc | CY-72582

Not Again?
Olivier Peters Quartet | What Is New | NCC Jazz | NCC 8503

Not Consciously Written About
Bazillus | The Regulator | ACT | 9206-2

Not Enough Mama-
Frank Gambale-Allan Holdsworth Group | Truth In Shredding | Legato | HW 652507

Not For Nothin'
Bill Connors Quartet | Of Mist And Melting | ECM | 1120(847324-2)

Not Forgetting
Miles Donahue Quintet | The Good Listener | RAM Records | RMCD 4510

Not If I See You First
Cedar Walton Quartet With Abbey Lincoln | The Maestro | Muse | MCD 6008

Not Like This
Helen Merrill With The Roger Kellaway Trio | Clear Oot Of This World | EmArCy | 510691-2 PMS
John Surman | Private City | ECM | 1366

Not Love Perhaps
Cassiber | Man Or Monkey | Riskant | 6.28624

Not Mine
Fred Astaire With The Oscar Peterson Sextet | The Astaire Story | Verve | 835649-2 PMS

Not Quiet A Ballad
Coleman Hawkins With The Frank Hunter Orchestra | Hawk Talk | Fresh Sound Records | FSR-CD 0130

Not Quite That
Junior Cook Quartet | Pressure Cooker | Affinity | AFF 53

Not Really Sorry
Gene Ammons And His All Stars | Juganthology | Prestige | P 24036

Not Really The Blues
Henri Renaud Trio With Jimmy Gourley | Henri Reanaud Trio,Sextet & All Stars | Vogue | 21606382
Woody Herman And His Orchestra | Woody Herman:Complete 1948-1950 Capitol Sessions | Definitive Records | DRCD 11195

Not Sentimental
Roger Guerin Quintet | Roger Guerin(Prix Django Reinhardt 1959) | Fresh Sound Records | 054 2611291(Columbia FP 1117)

Not So Dukish
Johnny Hodges Orchestra | Not So Dukish | Verve | 2304510 IMS

Not That You Asked
Sergey Starostin's Vocal Family | Journey | JA & RO | JARO 4226-2

Not The Last One-
Fats Waller-Johnny Marks | London Sessions 1938-39 | Jazztime(EMI) | 251271-2

Not To Be Forgotten(Our Final Hour)
James McMillan Group | Up All Day All Night | Savoy | CY 78899

Not To Worry
Rose Murphy Trio | Rose Murphy(The Chee-Chee Girl) | RCA | 2153222-2

Not Too Tough
Annie Laurie With Andy Gibson's Orchestra | It Hurts To Be In Love | Sing | 1155

Not What It Seems
Eden Atwood Group | Cat On A Hot Tin Roof | Concord | CCD 4599

Not While I'm Around
Sonny Greenwich Quartet | Bird Of Paradise | Justin Time | Just 22

Not Without You
James Newton Octet | Luella | Gramavision | GR 8304-2

Not Yet
Javon Jackson-Billy Pierce Quintet | Burnin' | Criss Cross | Criss 1139
Johnny Griffin Quartet | Johnny Griffin:Chicago-New York-Paris | Verve | 527367-2
Rajesh Metha | Orka | HatOLOGY | 524
George Shearing | Favorite Things | Telarc Digital | CD 83398

Not You Again
Paul Bley Trio | Not Two, Not One | ECM | 1670(559447-2)

Not Zero:In One Part
Not Two, Not One | ECM | 1670(559447-2)

Not Zero:In Three Parts
Häns'che Weiss Quintet & Guests | Fünf Jahre Musik Deutscher Zigeuner | Intercord | 160088

Nota Cambiata
Lee Konitz-Kenny Werner | Unleemited | Owl Records | 014727-2

Nota Della Notte
Lewis Trio With Guests | Battangó | Intuition Records | INN 1101-2

Notas Da Habana
Steve Lacy Sextet | Moon | Affinity | AFF 23

Note Di Un Libretto Per Un'Opera Mai Scitta
Paul Bley Quartet | In The Evenings Out There | ECM | 1488

Note Police
Barone-Burghardt Orchestra | Maiden Switzerland | Discovery | DS 790 IMS

Note(I)
Gabriele Hasler Group | Gabriele Hasler's Personal Notebook | Foolish Music | FM 211490

Note(II)
Gabriele Hasler's Personal Notebook | Foolish Music | FM 211490

Note(III)
Gabriele Hasler's Personal Notebook | Foolish Music | FM 211490

Note(IV)
Sarah Vaughan With Orchestra | The Best Of Sarah Vaughan | Pablo | 2405416-2

Notes After An Evening
Sonny Rollins Sextet | Horn Culture | Original Jazz Classics | OJC 314(M 9051)

Notes From The Underground
Risto Toppola Trio | Europ' Jazz Contest '95 | B.Sharp Records | CDS 107

'Nother Fu'ther

The Tenor Triangle & The Melvin Rhyne Trio | Aztec Blues | Criss Cross | Criss 1143

Nothin'
Luckey Roberts | Luckey & The Lion:Harlem Piano | Good Time Jazz | GTCD 10035-2

Nothin" But De Best
Jack McVea Quintet | Nothin' But Jazz | Harlequin | HQ 2046 IMS

Nothin' But The Blues
Lazy Lester Band | Rides Again | Line Records | STLP 400396 J

Nothin' But The Soul
Lucky Thompson Quartet | Lucky Thompson | Swing | SW 8404 IMS

Nothin' But The Truth
Jessica Williams Trio | Nothin' But The Truth | Black-Hawk | BKH 51301 CD

Nothin' I Do Is Right
Marcus Roberts Trio | In Honor Of Duke | CBS | CK 63630

Nothing
Milford Graves-Sunny Morgan | Milford Graves Percussion Ensemble | ESP Disk | ESP 1015-2
John Stevens Quartet | Re-Touch & Quartet | Konnex Records | KCD 5027

Nothing-
Milford Graves-Sunny Morgan | Milford Graves Percussion Ensemble | ESP Disk | ESP 1015-2

Nothing Blues
The Georgians | The Georgians 1922-23 | Retrieval | RTR 79003

Nothing But The Soul
Peter Fessler Quintet | Colours Of My Mind | Minor Music | 801063

Nothing But The Truth
Roland Kirk And His Orchestra | Rahsaan/The Complete Mercury Recordings Of Roland Kirk | Mercury | 846630-2
Homesick James & Snooky Prior With The Bob Hall Trio | Homesick James And Snooky Prior | Big Bear | 146404

Nothing Comes From Fighting This Way
Alex Smith Quintet | Jazzville Vol.2 | Fresh Sound Records | FSR 601(Dawn DLP 1107)

Nothing Ever Changes For You My Love
Barbara Morrison With The Lafayette Harris Jr.Trio | Doing All Right | Mons Records | CD 1895

Nothing Ever Changes My Love For You
Tina Brooks Quintet | True Blue | Blue Note | 868846-9

Nothing Ever Was, Anyway
Paul Bley Quartet | Fragments | ECM | 1320
Marilyn Crispell Trio | Nothing Ever Was,Anyway.Music Of Annette Peacock | ECM | 1626/27(537222-2)

Nothing Ever Was, Anyway(Version 1)
Nothing Ever Was,Anyway.Music Of Annette Peacock | ECM | 1626/27(537222-2)

Nothing Ever Was, Anyway(Version 2)
Paul Bley Synthesizer Show | The Paul Bley Synthesizer Show | Milestone | M 9033

Nothing For Nothing
Mongo Santamaria Orchestra | The Watermelon Man | Milestone | M 47012

Nothing In The World(Could Make Me Love You More Than I Do)
Trio Friedrich-Hebert-Moreno | Surfacing | Naxos Jazz | 86060-2

Nothing Like This
Ann Malcom With The Kenny Barron Quartet | Incident'ly | Sound Hills | SSCD 8053

Nothing Like You
Miles Davis Sextet | Sorcerer | CBS | CBS PC 9532
Roseanna Vitro With The Fred Hersh Quartet | Softly | Concord | CCD 4587

Nothing More-
Betty Carter With Orchestra | 'Round Midnight | Atlantic | AMCY 1060

Nothing Of All
Peter Brötzmann | No Nothing: Brötzmann Solo | FMP | CD 32

Nothing Personal
Michael Brecker Group | The Cost Of Living | Jazz Door | JD 1260

Nothing Stays The Same
Ruth Brown With Orchestra | Fine And Mellow | Fantasy | FCD 9663-2

Nothing Takes The Place Of You
Wolfgang Dauner Trio | Output | ECM | 1006 (2301006)

Notiz I
Gabriele Hasler Group | Gabriele Hasler's Rosensrücke | Foolish Music | FM 211096

Notiz II
Gabriele Hasler's Rosensrücke | Foolish Music | FM 211096

Notiz III
Vittorino Curci | Notizie Del Sole Vero | SPLASC(H) Records | HP 12

Notorious Thugs
Ton-Art | Zu | Hat Art | CD 6034

Notti Eluse E Attese Deluse
Tino Tracanna Group | '292' | SPLASC(H) Records | CD H 322-2

Nouba
Gilad Atzmon Group | Spiel | Ohne Label | CD 19862

Nouveau Odeur
Donald Harrison Quartet | Nouveau Swing | Impulse(MCA) | 951209-2

Nouveau Swing
Donald Harrison Sextet | Free To Be | Impulse(MCA) | 951283-2

Nouveau Swing(reprise)
Acoustic Alchemy | Against The Grain | GRP | GRP 97832

Nouveau Tango
Raphael Fays Group | Voyages | Acoustic Music Records | AMC 1015

Nouvelle Vague
Badiane | Flavours | Acoustic Music Records | 319.1071.2

Nova
Walt Barr Quintet | Artful Dancer | Muse | MR 5238

Novalis 24(Christian Henking)
Modern Jazz Quartet | Live At The Lighthouse | Mobile Fidelity | MFCD 827

Novamo
Naßler & Schneider feat. Jörg Ritter | Triologe | Acoustic Music Records | 319.1137.2

Novel Pets
The Rosenberg Trio With Orchestra | Noches Calientes | Verve | 557022-2

Noveleo
George Gruntz Concert Jazz Band | Happening Now | Hat Art | CD 6008

Novelty Accordion
Richard M. Jones' Jazz Wizzards | Victor Jazz History Vol.2:Black Chicago | RCA | 2128556-2

November
John Abercrombie Quartet | November | ECM | 1502(519073-2)
Lotte Anker-Marilyn Crispell-Marilyn Mazur | Poetic Justice | dacapo | DCCD 9460
Michael Kiedaisch-Eberhard Hahn Group | Terra Incognita | Peregrina Music | PM 50051

November 1st
Joe Farrell Quintet | Outback | CTI | 6014

November Afternoon
Dizzy Gillespie Quintet | Verve Jazz Masters 10:Dizzy Gillespie | Verve | 516319-2
Something Old Something New | Verve | 558079-2
James Moody Quintet | Moving Forward | Novus | PD 83026

November Girl
Mark Murphy With The Bill Mays Trio | Kerouac, Then And Now | Muse | MCD 5359

November Song
Shin-Ichi Fukuda | Guitar Legends:Homage To Great Popular Guitarists | Denon Compact Disc | CO-18048

November/December 1993
Leipziger Saxophon Quartet + Rolf Von Nordenskjöld | Passages: Leipziger Saxophon Quartet Plays Rolf Von Nordenskjöld | BIT | 11158

Novitango
Andrew Cyrille Trio | X Man | Soul Note | 121262-2

Novo Skopje
Chet Baker & The Boto Brasilian Quartet | Chet Baker & The Boto Brasilian Quartet | Dreyfus Jazz Line | FDM 36511-9

Novos Tempos
Dave Liebman | Time Immemorial | Enja | ENJ-9389 2

Now
Diederik Wissels Quintet | Kamook | B.Sharp Records | CDS 083
Freddie Redd Sextet | Redd's Blues | Blue Note | 540537-2
John Patitucci Quartet | Now | Concord | CCD 4806
Ray Noble And His Orchestra | The Radio Years | London | HMG 5019 AN

Now And Again
Bill Smith/Enrico Pieranunzi Duo | Colours | EdiPan | NPG 807

Now And Here
Irene Schweizer Quintet | The Storming Of The Winter Palace | Intakt Records | CD 003

Now He Tells Me
Kenny Clarke-Francy Boland Big Band | En Concert Avec Europe 1 | Laserlight | 710413/14

Now Hear My Meaning
Ray Brown-Milt Jackson Orchestra | Much In Common | Verve | 533259-2

Now Here(Nowhere)
Nat Simpkins Quartet | Cookin' With Some Barbeque | Muse | MCD 5510

Now I Can
Cannonball Adderley Sextet | Ballads | Blue Note | 537563-2

Now I Have Everything
Cootie Williams And His Orchestra | Big Band Bounce And Boogie:Echoes Of Harlem-Cootie Williams | Affinity | AFS 1031

Now Is The Hour(Haere Ra-Maori Farewell Song)
Dick Griffin Septet | The Eighth Wonder & More | Konnex Records | KCD 5059

Now Is The Time
John Abercrombie-Andy LaVerne Quartet | Now It Can Be Played | Steeplechase | SCCD 31314

Now It Can Be Told
Ella Fitzgerald With Paul Weston And His Orchestra | The Complete Ella Fitzgerald Song Books of Harold Arlen, Irving Berlin, Duke Ellington, George & Ira Gershwin, Jerome Kern, Johnny Mercer, Cole Porter And Rogers & Hart | Verve | 519832-2
Harry Arnold Big Band | Big Band Classics 1957-58 | Dragon | DRLP 139/140

Now Or Never
JoAnne Brackeen | Mythical Magic | MPS | 68211
New York Voices | New York Voices | GRP | GRP 95892
Terrie Richard With The Harry Allen Quartet | I Cried For You | Master Mix | CHECD 00107

Now Playing
Herbie Harper Quintet | Herbie Harper Feat.Bud Shank And Bob Gordon | Fresh Sound Records | 054 2600581(Liberty LJH 6003)

Now That You Are Gone
Lionel Hampton And His Orchestra | Lionel Hampton-Historical Recording Sessions 1939-1941 | RCA | PM 42417

Now That You'r Gone
Cootie Williams And His Savoy Ballroom Orchestra | Cootie Williams | Fresh Sound Records | NL 46032(RCA)

Now Will The Sun Rise As Brightly(from Songs of The Death Children)
Jimmy Rushing With The Count Basie Orchestra | Big Band Bounce And Boogie Woogie:Good Mornin' Blues-Jimmy Rushing | Affinity | AFS 1002

Now You Know
The Westcoasters | The West Coasters Feat. Jimmy Giuffre | Bethlehem | BTM 6826

Now,And Now Again
Carmen McRae With The Tadd Dameron Orchestra | Blue Moon | Verve | 543829-2

Nowhere
Marilyn Crispell | Live At Mills College, 1995 | Music & Arts | CD 899
Schlaier-Hirt Duo | Don't Walk Outside Thos Area | Chaos | CACD 8186
Butch Morris Orchestra | Homeing | Sound Aspects | sas CD 4015

Nowhere One
Steve Lacy Sextet | Songs | Hat Art | CD 6045

Now's The Time
Art Blakey And The Jazz Messengers | At The Club St.Germain | RCA | ND 74897(2)
Swiss Radio Days Jazz Series Vol.2:Art Blakey's Jazz Messengers | TCB Records | TCB 02022
Benny Carter Quintet | All That Jazz-Live At Princeton | Limelight | 820841-2 IMS
Budd Johnson Quartet | In Memory Of A Very Dear Friend | Dragon | DRLP 94
Charlie Parker All Stars | More Unissued Vol.1 | Royal Jazz | RJD 505
Charlie Parker Quartet | Talkin' Bird | Verve | 559859-2
Charlie Parker:The Best Of The Verve Years | Verve | 527815-2
Charlie Parker | Verve | 539757-2
Charlie Parker:Bird's Best Bop On Verve | Verve | 527452-2
Charlie Parker Quintet | Bird At St. Nick's | Original Jazz Classics | OJC20 041-2(JWS 500)
Live At Carnegie Hall | Bandstand | BDCD 1518
Bird-The Savoy Recordings(Master Takes) | Savoy | ZD 70737 (886420)
Charlie Parker's Beboppers | The Savoy Recordings 1 | Savoy | 650107(881907)
Eddie Cleanhead Vinson Sextet | Jamming The Blues | Black Lion | BLCD 760188
Four Trombones | Four Trombones Vol.2 | Debut | VIJ 5004 IMS
Frank Morgan Quartet | Bird Lives! | Milestone | MCD 9166-2
Hal McKusick Septet | Now's The Time(1957-58) | GRP | GRP 16512
Houston Person-Ron Carter | Now's The Time | Muse | MCD 5421
Jodie Christian Quintet | Soul Fountain | Delmark | DE 498
Keith Jarrett Trio | Keith Jarrett At The Blue Note-The Complete Recordings | ECM | 1575/80(527638-2)
Ken McIntyre Sextet | Introducing The Vibrations | Steeplechase | SCCD 31065
Kenny Clarke-Ernie Wilkins Septet | Kenny Clarke & Ernie Wilkins | Savoy | SV 0222(MG 12007)
Monty Sunshine Quartet | Love And Sunshine-Monty Alexander In Concert | MPS | 68043
Patrick Tompert Trio | Hallelujah Time | Satin Doll Productions | SDP 1020-1 CD
Paul Bley Trio | BeBopBeBopBeBopBeBop | Steeplechase | SCCD 31259
Richard Davis Quintet | Epistrophy & Now's The Time | Muse | MR 5002
Sonny Rollins & Co. | Sonny Rollins & Co-1964 | RCA | 2125767-2
Sonny Rollins Quartet | The Complete Sonny Rollins RCA Victor Recordings | RCA | 2668675-2

Nozipho
Tim Sund & Tom Christensen Quartet | Americana | Nabel Records:Jazz Network | CD 4697

Nozomi(The Secret Garden)
Lucky Thompson Quintet | Tricotism | Impulse(MCA) | GRP 11352

Nr. 74(to Morton Feldman)
Roger Hanschel | Stadtgarten Series Vol.1 | Jazz Haus Musik | JHM 1001 SER

Nr.2
Stadtgarten Series Vol.1 | Jazz Haus Musik | JHM 1001 SER

Ntyilo Ntyilo
Johnny Dyani Sextet feat.John Tchicai & Dudu Pukwana | Witchdoctor's Son | Steeplechase | SCCD 31098

Nu Mess
Philipp Wachsmann-Paul Lytton | Some Other Season | ECM | 1662

Nu Shu
Hamiet Bluiett Quartet | EBU | Soul Note | 121088-2

Nuages
Allan Vaché-Antti Sarpila & 1 Sextet | Summit Meeting | Nagel-Heyer | CD 027
Angelo Debarre Group | Angelo Debarre | Hot Club Records | HCRCD 116
Bireli Lagrene Ensemble | Bireli Swing '81 | Jazzpoint | JP 1009 CD
Routes To Django & Bireli Swing '81 | Jazzpoint | JP 1055 CD
Bireli Lagrene Quartet | Standards | Blue Note | 780251-2
My Favorite Django | Dreyfus Jazz Line | FDM 36574-2
Bireli Lagrene Trio | Live In Marciac | Dreyfus Jazz Line | FDM 36567-2
Christian Escoude Quartet With Strings | Plays Django Reinhardt | EmArCy | 510132-2
Django Reinhardt And His Rhythm | Peche Á La Mode-The Great Blue Star Sessions 1947/1953 | Verve | 835418-2
Django Reinhardt And The Quintet Du Hot Club De France | Planet Jazz:Django Reinhardt | Planet Jazz | 2152071-2
Swing De Paris | Arco | 3 ARC 110
Georges Arvanitas Trio | Rencontre | CBS | 491232-2
Helen Merrill-Gordon Beck with Stephane Grappelli & Steve Lacy | Music Makers | Owl Records | 044
Jenny Evans And Her Quintet | Nuages | ESM Records | ESM 9308
Nuages | Enja | ENJ-9467 2
Joe Kienemann Trio | All That Jazz Special | Blue Flame | 40742(2132446-2)
Joe Pass Quartet | For Django | Pacific Jazz | 300007(PJ 85)
John Purcell Orchestra | Naturally | Novus | 4163151-2
Michel Legrand Orchestra | Compact Jazz: Michel Legrand | Philips | 840944-2
Oscar Peterson Quintet | Skol | Original Jazz Classics | OJC20 496-2
Oscar Peterson Trio | At The Stratford Shakespearean Festival | Verve | 513752-2
Panama Francis And His Savoy Sultans | Gettin' In The Groove | Black & Blue | BLE 233320
Quintet Du Hot Club De France | Le Jazz En France Vol.5:Django Plus | Pathe | 1727291
Verve Jazz Masters 38:Django Reinhardt | Verve | 516931-2
Django Reinhardt:Nuages | Arkadia Jazz | 71431
Stephane Grappelli Group | Golden Hour Of Stephane Grappelli | Golden Hour | GH 650
Stephane Grappelli Quintet | Hommage A Django Reinhardt | Festival | Album 120
Stephane Grappelli Trio | Live | Justin Time | JTR 8469-2
Stephane Grappelli-Martial Solal Duo | Happy Reunion | Owl Records | 013430 2
Stochelo Rosenberg Trio | Seresta | Hot Club Records | HCRCD 059
The Rosenberg Trio | Tribute To Django Reinhardt | EmArCy | 9811568
The Rosenberg Trio:The Collection | Verve | 537152-2
The Tango Kings | The Tango Kings | Big World | BW 2016
Travelin' Light | Cookin' With Frank And Sam | Concord | CCD 4647
George Wein And The Newport All Stars | Swing That Music | CBS | CK 53317

Nuances
Jimmy Lyons-Andrew Cyrille Duo | Something In Return | Black Saint | 120125-2

Nubian Bonus Track
Stephen Scott Sextet | Something To Consider | Verve | 849557-2

Nubian Lady
Cornelius Claudio Kreusch Quartet | Black Mud Sound | Enja | 9087-2

Nu-Bouk
Peter Weniger Quartet | Tiptap | Mons Records | MR 874768

Nuclear Suite
Matt Penman Quartet | Flipside | Naxos Jazz | 86013-2

Nude Bass Descending
Cowws Quintet plus Guests | Book/Virtual Cowws | FMP | OWN-90007/9

Nuevo Tango
Thomas Heberer | Stella | Poise | Poise 08

Nuggets
Eberhard Weber Group | Endless Days | ECM | 1748(013420-2)

Nuit Blanthe
Boulou & Elios Ferre Quintet | New York,N.Y. | Steeplechase | SCCD 31404

Nuit Sur Les Champs-Elysees(4 takes)
Bireli Lagrene Group | A Tribute To Django Reinhardt | Jazzpoint | JP 1061 CD

Nuits De St.Germain-Des-Pres
Bireli Lagrene Quartet | My Favorite Django | Dreyfus Jazz Line | FDM 36574-2
Christian Escoude Quartet With Strings | Plays Django Reinhardt | EmArCy | 510132-2
Jermaine Landsberger Trio | Gypsy Feeling | Edition Collage | EC 516-2
Organ Jazztrio & Martin Weiss | Hommage | Edition Collage | EC 492-2
Quintet Du Hot Club De France | Welcome To Jazz: Django Reinhardt | Koch Records | 322 074 D1

Num
Badi Assad | Solo | Chesky | JD 99

Number 19
Earl Hines And His Orchestra | The Earl | Naxos Jazz | 8.120581 CD

Number Eight
Eric Dophy Quintet | Eric Dolphy:The Complete Prestige Recordings | Prestige | 9 PRCD-4418-2
Harold Danko Quintet | Prestigious-A Tribute To Eric Dolphy | Steeplechase | SCCD 31508

Number Eleven
Herbie Mann Group | Opalescence | Kokopelli Records | KOKO 1298

Number Five(aka Miss Bertha D.Blues)
Freddie Hubbard Sextet | Minor Mishap | Black Lion | BLP 60122

Number One
John Coltrane Quartet | The Mastery Of John Coltrane Vol.3:Jupiter Variations | MCA | 2292-54649-2
Russ Spiegel Group | Twilight | double moon | CHRDM 71026
Steve Lacy Group | Anthem | Novus | PD 83079

Number One(take 1)
Cecil Taylor Quartet | Cecil Taylor: Air | Candid | CCD 79046

Number One(take 2)
Jelly Roll Morton | The Library Of Congress Recordings | Affinity | CD AFS 1010-3

Number Six(part 1-4)
Kurt Rosenwinkel Quintet | The Enemies Of Energy | Verve | 543042-2

Number Ten
Harry James And His Orchestra | Broadcasts From The Southerland Cafe & Hotel Loncoln New York | Jazz Anthology | JA 5150

Number Twelve(part 1-4)
Booker Ervin Quartet | The Freedom And Space Sessions | Prestige | P 24091

Number Two
Peter Hertmans Quartet | Waiting | Timeless | CD SJP 418

Numbers On Paper
John Zorn Naked City | Naked City-Grand Guignol | Avant | AVAN 002

Numinor
Habarigani | Habarigani Two | Hat Art | CD 6064

Nun Bitten Wir Den Heiligen Geist
Conrad Bauer Trio | Was Ist Denn Nun? | FMP | 0780

Nun Komm Der Heiden Heiland
Karl Scharnweber Trio With Timbre | Choral Concert(Passion) | KlangRäume | 30160

Nun Laube,Lindlein,Laube
Andreas Hansl | Dualism | UAK | UAK 1

Nun Ruhen Alle Wälder
Transalpin Express Orchestra | Some Other Tapes | Fish Music | FM 009/10 CD
Lauren Newton Quintet | Kindertotenlieder | KlangRäume | 30140

Nun Seh's Mood
Dieter Ilg Trio | Fieldwork | Jazzline | JL 11155-2

Nunca Mas
Gato Barbieri Quartet | Latin On Impulse! Various Artists | Impulse(MCA) | IMP 12762

Nunca Mas(alt.take)
Juanjo Dominguez | Che Guitarra | ALISO Records | AL 1025

Nunca Tuvo Novia
Gustavo Bergalli Group | Tango In Jazz | Touché Music | TMcCD 007

Nunca Tuvo Novio

Diego Ruvidotti Quartet | Maestrale | SPLASC(H) Records | H 135

Nuqta
Aki Takase Quintet | St.Louis Blues | Enja | 9130-2

Nur Ein Schatten
Kurt Hohenberger Orchester | Swing tanzen verboten | Vagabond | 6.28360 DP

Nusia's Poem
Donald Harrison Quintet | For Art's Sake | Candid | CCD 79501

Nut Is Wahn
Loren Stilllman Quartet | Cosmos | Soul Note | 121310-2

Nuther'n Like Thuther'n
Paul Whiteman And His Orchestra | The Famous Paul Whiteman:Jazz A La King | RCA | 2135547-2

Nutman's Invention
Cyrus Chestnut Trio | Earth Stories | Atlantic | 7567-82876-2

Nutman's Invention No.1
Art Pepper Quintet | Complete Discovery-Savoy Master Takes | Definitive Records | DRCD 11218

Nuts
Roy Eldridge Quartet | Frenchie Roy | Vogue | 655009

Nuttville
Charlie Rouse Quartet | Epistrophy | Landmark | LCD 1521-2

Nutty
Stan Tracey Trio | Laughin' And Scratchin' | Ronnie Scott's Jazz House | JHAS 608
Thelonious Monk Quartet | Thelonious Monk:85th Birthday Celebration | zyx records | FANCD 6076-2
Jazz Gallery:John Coltrane Vol.1 | RCA | 2119540-2
Live At The Jazz Workshop-Complete | CBS | C2K 65189
Pianology | Moon Records | MCD 055-2
Thelonious Monk With John Coltrane | Original Jazz Classics | OJC20 039-2
Thelonious Monk Quartet With Pee Wee Russell | Miles & Monk At Newport | CBS | SRCS 5698
Thelonious Monk Trio | Thelonious Monk/Sonny Rollins | Original Jazz Classics | OJCCD 059-2
The London Collection Vol.2 | Black Lion | BLCD 760116
Thelonious Monk Collection | Black Lion | BLCD 7601-2
Jimmy Giuffre Four Brothers Septet | Four Brothers | Affinity | AFF 70

Nutville
Horace Silver Sextet | The Blue Note Years-The Best Of Horace Silver Vol.2 | Blue Note | 793206-2
Monday Night At Birdland | Another Monday Night At Birdland | Fresh Sound Records | FSR-CD 32(882176)

Nuzzolese Blues
Zoot Sims Quintet | Zoot Sims | Swing | SW 8417

Ny Little Grass Shack-
The Crossover Ensemble With The Zapolski Quartet | Helios Suite | dacapo | DCCD 9459

Ny Nat(New Night)
Ron Carter Sextet | New York Slick | Original Jazz Classics | OJCCD 916-2(M 9096)

Ny Slik
Al Cohn Quartet | The Birdlanders Vol.2 | Original Jazz Classics | OJCCD 1931-2

Ny´s Idea
Henri Renaud-Al Cohn Quartet | Cohn´s Delight | Vogue | 655011

Ny´s Idea(alt.take)
Cohn´s Delight | Vogue | 655011

NY-1
God Is My Co-Pilot | Mir Shlufn Nisht | Avant | AVAN 032

Nyah Shore
Papa Bue's Viking Jazzband | The Golden Years Of Revival Jazz,Vol.3 | Storyville | STCD 5508

Nyboder's Pris
Storyville Jassband | Mallorca | Timeless | CD TTD 604

NYC
Freddy Cole With Band | To The End Of The Earth | Fantasy | FCD 9675-2
Gary Burton Quartet | Duster | RCA | 2125730-2
John Tropea Group | NYC Cats Direct | dmp Digital Music Productions | CD 453

Nyemma
Francois Carrier Trio + 1 | Compassion | Naxos Jazz | 86062-2

Nyl
Mark Levin Quintet | Social Sketches | Enja | 2058

Nymanebla(Interlude)
Ellery Eskelin With Andrea Parkins & Jim Black | The Secret Museum | HatOLOGY | 552

Nympheas
Jacques Loussier Trio | Ravel's Bolero | Telarc Digital | CD 83466

Nymphomania
Holger Mantey | Piano Total | NCC Jazz | NCC 8506

Nystev
Darius Brubeck And The Nu Jazz Connection | African Tributes | B&W Present | BW 023

O
John Stevens Orchestra | Folkus-The Life Of Riley | Affinity | AFF 130

O Amor En Paz(Once I Loved)
Cannonball Adderley With Sergio Mendes And The Bossa Rio Sextet | Cannonball's Bossa Nova | Blue Note | 522667-2
Chet Baker-Steve Houben Sextet | Chet Baker-Steve Houben | 52e Rue Est | RECD 019
Ella Fitzgerald-Joe Pass Duo | Joe Pass:A Man And His Guitar | Original Jazz Classics | OJCCD 8806-2
Florian Poser Group | Say Yes! | Edition Collage | EC 452-2
Franco D'Andrea New Quartet | Jobim | Philology | W 125.2
Joe Henderson Quartet | In A Modal Way | Jazz Door | JD 1267
Larry Goldings Quartet | Caminhos Cruzados | Novus | 4163184-2
Michael Cochrane Trio | Song Of Change | Soul Note | 121252-2
Milt Jackson With The Monty Alexander Trio | The Best Of Milt Jackson | Pablo | 2405405-2
Ronnie Mathews Quintet | Legacy | Bee Hive | BH 7011

O Astronauta
Charlie Byrd Trio | Great Guitars | Concord | CCD 6004

O Barquinho(Little Boat)
Gabor Szabo Quintet | Latin On Impulse! Various Artists | Impulse(MCA) | IMP 12762
L.A.4 | Zaca | Concord | CCD 4130

O Berimbau
Gerry Mulligan Group With Jane Duboc | Triple Play:Gerry Mulligan | Telarc Digital | CD 83453

O Cantador
Lee Konitz Sextet | Lee Konitz In Rio | M.A Music | A 737-1

O Circe,Guide Me
Harold Danko Trio | Alone But Not Forgotten | Sunnyside | SSC 1033 D

O Come All Ye Faithful
Marcus Roberts | Prayer For Peace | Novus | ND 90585(847064)
Keith Foley | Music For Christmas | dmp Digital Music Productions | CD 452

O Coreto
Joao Bosco | Montreux Jazz Festival | ACT | 9001-2

O Dia A Noite
Michael Riessler & Singer Pur with Vincent Courtois | Ahi Vita | ACT | 9417-2

O Dolorosa Gioia
Dieter Ilg Trio | Fieldwork | Jazzline | JL 11155-2

O Gato
Paul Desmond Quartet | Planet Jazz:Paul Desmond | Planet Jazz | 2152061-2
Paul Desmond-Greatest Hits | RCA | CL 89809 SF
Bossa Antigua | RCA | 2174795-2

O Gato(alt.take)
Al Cohn Quartet | Standards Of Excellence | Concord | CJ 241

O Grande Amor
Chet Baker-Stan Getz Quintet | The Stockholm Concerts | Verve | 537555-2
David Friedman Trio | Other Worlds | Intuition Records | INT 3210-2
Double Image | Open Hand | dmp Digital Music Productions | CD 503
Gary Burton-Makoto Ozone | Face To Face | GRP | GRP 98052
Getz-Gilberto Quintet | Verve Jazz Masters 13:Antonio Carlos Jobim | Verve | 516409-2
Getz/Gilberto:The Girl From Ipanema | CTI Records | PDCTI 1105-2
Jack Wilkins Quintet | Mexico | CTI Records | CTI 1004-2
John McNeil Quartet | I've Got The World On A String | Steeplechase | SCCD 31183
Peter Guidi Meets Michael Herr And Riccardo Del Fra | A Weaver Of Dreams | Timeless | CD SJP 401
Stan Getz Quartet | The Stan Getz Quartet In Paris | Enoch's Music | 57271043
Stan Getz Sextet | Jazzbühne Berlin '78 | Repertoire Records | REPCD 4915-WZ
Thomas Stabenow Trio | Human Spirit | Bassic-Sound | CD 009
Arnold Klos Trio | Crinkle's Garden | Limetree | MLP 198537

O Little Town Of Bethlehem
Mahalia Jackson With Choir And Orchestra | Stille Nacht | CBS | COLCD 62130
Oscar Peterson Sextet With Strings | An Oscar Peterson Christmas | Telarc Digital | CD 83372

O Meu Amor
Luis Agudo | Afrorera | Red Records | VPA 185

O Milho Verde-
Antonio Carlos Jobim With The Claus Ogerman Orchestra | Quiet Nights | CTI Records | PDCTI 1106-2

O Morro Nao Tem Vez(One I Loved)
Astrud Gilberto With Antonio Carlos Jobim And The Marty Paich Orchestra | The Astrud Gilberto Album | Verve | 823009-1
Manfredo Fest Quintet | Jungle Cat | dmp Digital Music Productions | CD 470
Stan Getz-Luiz Bonfa Group | Compact Jazz: Best Of Bossa Nova | Verve | 833269-2
Stan Getz-Luiz Bonfa Orchestra | Jazz Samba Encore! | Verve | 823613-2
Jazz Samba Encore! | CTI Records | PDCTI 1125-2

O Morro Nao Tem(Somewhere In The Hills)
Michael Formanek Quintet | Extented Animation | Enja | ENJ-7041 2

O My Seh Yeh
Roy Hargrove's Crisol | Habana | Verve | 537563-2

O My Seh Yeh(reprise)
Michel Petrucciani Group | Music | Blue Note | 792563-2

O Nana Oye
Michel Petrucciani:The Blue Note Years | Blue Note | 789916-2
Serge Forté-Michel Petrucciani | Vaina | Laika Records | LK 90-021
Raiz De Pedra | Diario De Bordo | TipToe | TIP-888822 2

O Navio
Charlie Byrd Quartet With Ken Peplowski | The Bossa Nova Years | Concord | CCD 4468

O Nosso Amor
Ella Fitzgerald With The Tommy Flanagan Trio | Ella A Nice | Original Jazz Classics | OJC20 442-2

O Nosso Amor-
Folklore E Bossa Nova Do Brasil | Jazz Meets Brasil | MPS | 533133-2

O Pato(The Duck)
Charlie Byrd Trio With Ken Peplowski | The Bossa Nova Years | Concord | CCD 4468
Harry Allen Sextet | Eu Nao Quero Dancar-I Won't Dance | Novus | 2158126-2
Michele Hendricks With The David Leonhadt Quintet | Carryin' On | Muse | MCD 5336
Patrick Karlhuber Group | So What | Edition Collage | EC 480-2
Stan Getz-Charlie Byrd Sextet | Stan Getz/Charlie Byrd:Jazz Samba | CTI Records | PDCTI 1104-2
Clusone 3 | An Hour With... | HatOLOGY | 554

O Pen,To Be
Jorge Degas-Wolfgang Loos | Cantar A Vida | Traumton Records | 4446-2

O Poeta Beija Flor
Carlos Bica & Azul | Twist | Enja | ENJ-9386 2

O Profeta II
Tania Maria Trio | Live | Accord | 112552

O Quem Tai!
Howard Johnson & Gravity | Right Now! | Verve | 537801-2

O Ronco Cuica-
Tamba Trio | Tamba Trio Classics | EmArCy | 536958-2

O Si No Que?
Chicago Underground Trio | Possible Cube | Delmark | DE 511

O Sole Mio
Franco & Lorenzo Petrocca | Italy | Edition Musikat | EDM 062
Oscar Klein's Jazz Show | Oscar Klein's Jazz Show | Jazzpoint | JP 1043 CD
Papa Bue's Viking Jazzband | The Golden Years Of Revival Jazz,Vol.9 | Storyville | STCD 5514
Schlafe Mein Prinzchen | Storyville | 6.23327 AF
Wingy Mannone Septet | Trumpet Jive! | Prestige | PCD 24119-2(P 7812/SV 2006)

O Tannenbaum
Marcus Roberts | Prayer For Peace | Novus | ND 90585(847064)
Vince Guaraldi Trio | A Charlie Brown Christmas | Fantasy | FSA 8431-6
Ana Caram Group | Rio After Dark | Chesky | JD 28

O Tempo Passou
Enrico Pieranunzi-Bert Van Den Brink | Daedalus' Wings | Challenge | CHR 70069

O Vos Omnis
Schnuckenack Reinhardt Quintet | Live | Intercord | 160035

O wie schön ist die Karibik
Peter Bolte Trio | Trio | Jazz Haus Musik | JHM 0095 CD

O Willow Waly
Trio | Jazz Haus Musik | JHM 0095 CD

O Willow Waly(2)
Fode Youla And African Djole | Basikolo | FMP | SAJ 48

O&B-
Brocksi-Quartett | Globetrotter | Bear Family Records | BCD 15912 AH

O,La La Madame!
Rockin' Dopsie And The Zydeco Twisters | Rockin' Dopsie And The Zydeco Twister | Storyville | 4960423

O,O,Ba,Ba
Niels-Henning Orsted-Pedersen And The Danish Radio Big Band | Ambiance | dacapo | DCCD 9417

O,Tysta Ensamhet
Archie Shepp & The New York Contemporary Five | Archie Shepp & The New York Contemporary Five | Storyville | SLP 1010

O.C.
Ekkehard Jost & Chromatic Alarm | Von Zeit Zu Zeit | Fish Music | FM 005 CD
Marty Cook Group feat. Monty Waters | Borderlines | Tutu Records | 888122-2*

O.C. & Montville
Big Three Trio | Willie Dixon-The Big Three Trio | CBS | 467248-2

O.D.
Joachim Kühn | Live! | Elektra | ELK K 52232

O.D.R.I.P.
Tony Dagradi Trio | Images From The Floating World | Line Records | COCD 9.00727 O

O.G.D.(alt.take)
Jimmy Smith-Wes Montgomery Quartet | Jimmy & Wes-The Dynamic Duo | Verve | 521445-2
Yoron Israel Connection | A Gift For You | Freelance | FRL-CD 024

O.J. Bin Laden
Frank Morgan All Stars | Reflections | Original Jazz Classics | OJCCD 1046-2(C 14052)

O.K.
Reflections | Contemporary | CCD 14052-2
Benny Carter And His Orchestra | Big Bands Uptown 1931-40 | MCA | 1323

O.P.
Charles Mingus Group With Orchestra | Charles Mingus | Denon Compact Disc | DC-8565
Oscar Pettiford Quartet | Jazz Legacy Baden Baden Unreleased Radio Tapes | Jazzline | ???

O.T.
Out Of The Blue | O.T.B. | Blue Note | BT 85118 Digital

Oaf
JoAnne Brackeen Trio | Where Legends Dwell | Ken Music | 660.56.021

Oak Bluffs
Oscar Peterson-Jon Faddis Duo | Jousts | Pablo | 2310817

Oakmoss-
Thomas Hufschmidt & Tyron Park | Pepila | Acoustic Music Records | 319.1034.2

Oas
Klaus Ignatzek-Florian Poser Duo | Music For Grandpiano And Vibraphone | Fusion | 8021 Digital

Oasis
Keith Jarrett Quartet | Nude Ants | ECM | 1171/72(829119-2)
Personal Mountains | ECM | 1382(837361-2)
Kenny Blake Group | Interior Design | Heads Up Records | 889010
Robben Ford Band | Tiger Walk | Blue Thumb | BTR 70122
Hamiet Bluiett | Walkin' & Talkin' | Tutu Records | 888172-2*

Oasis-
Sandy Lomax With Band | Trance Jazz | clearaudio | WOR 171 CD

Ob Ich Spartacus Kenne?
Jere Laukkanen's Finnish Afro-Cuban Jazz Orchestra | Jere Laukkanen's Finnish Afro-Cuban Jazz Orchestra | Naxos Jazz | 86056-2

Obatala
Milton Cardona With The Eya Arania Ensemble | Bembe | American Clave | AMCL 1004

Obba-In
The Houdini's | Cooee | Challenge | CHR 70045

Obeah
Santi Debriano Quintet | Obeah | Freelance | FRL-CD 008

Obeah Man
John Surman Quintet | John Surman | Deram | 844883-2

Obecni Dum
Ed Blackwell Trio | Walls-Bridges | Black Saint | 120153-2

Oben
BBFC | Cherchez L'Erreur | Plainisphare | PL 1267-1

Oberkampf
Gianluigi Trovesi Nonet | Round About A Midsummer's Dream | Enja | ENJ-9384 2

Oberon
Gebhard Ullmann Quartet | Basement Research | Soul Note | 121271-2

Oberschöneweide
Dewey Redman Trio | Choices | Enja | 7073-2

Obirin African
Sorgen/Rust/Windbiel Trio | Outlet | ESP Disk | ESP 3029-2

Oblighetto
Eddie Palmieri Group | Arbete | RMM Records | 660.58.087

Oblique
Andy LaVerne | In The Mood For A Classic-Andy LaVerne Plays Bud Powell | Steeplechase | SCCD 31342

Oblivion
Bud Powell Trio | The Genius Of Bud Powell | Verve | 2304112
Chick Corea | Standards | Stretch Records | SCD 9028-2
Geri Allen/Charlie Haden/Paul Motian | In The Year Of The Dragon | JMT Edition | 919027-2
Horace Parlan Quintet | Glad I Found You | Steeplechase | SCCD 31194
Mike Wofford | Afterthoughts | Discovery | DS 784 IMS
Richard Galliano Quartet | New Musette | Label Bleu | LBLC 6547(889728)
Richard Galliano-Michel Portal | Concert Inédits | Dreyfus Jazz Line | FDM 36606-2

Obrigado
Klaus Ignatzek-Martin Wind Duo | Obrigado | Acoustic Music Records | 319.1113.2

Obscure
Tango Five feat. Raul Jaurena | Obsecion | Satin Doll Productions | SDP 1027-1 CD

Obsecion
Woody Shaw And His Orchestra | Love Dance | Muse | MR 5074

Observation Car
Stefano Battaglia | Baptism | SPLASC(H) Records | CD H 417-2

Obsesion
Art Blakey And The Jazz Messengers | Feeling Good | Delos | DE 4007

Obsession
Ferenc Snétberger Quartet | Signature | Enja | ENJ-9017 2
Ferenc Snétberger Trio | Obsession | TipToe | TIP-888834 2
Herbie Hancock Group | Perfect Machine | CBS | SRCS 9510
Malta And His Orchestra | Obsession | JVC | ???

Obstinate Isles
Tome XX | The Red Snapper | Jazz Haus Musik | JHM 0047 CD

Obstinate Isles(No.2)
Jack DeJohnette Group | Sorcery | Prestige | P 10081

Obvious
Maria Joao & Grupo Cal Viva | Sol | Enja | ENJ-7001 2

Occasion To Rise
Michele Rosewoman Trio | Occasion To Rise | Evidence | ECD 22042-2

OC-DC
Gato Barbieri Quintet | The Best Of The Jazz Saxophones Vol.2 | LRC Records | CDC 8529

Ocean
Christoph Spendel Group | City Kids | TCB Records | TCB 01052

Ocean Drive Talk
Steve Kuhn Trio | Oceans In The Sky | Owl Records | 013428-2

Ocean In The Sky
Leonard Feather All Star Jam Band | Hickory House Jazz | Affinity | CD AFS 1012

Ocean Song
John Blake Group | Twinkling Of An Eye | Gramavision | GR 8501-2

Ocean Waves
George Winston | Winter Into Spring | Windham Hill | 34 11019-2

Ocean(part 1-4)
Zipflo Reinhardt Quintet | Oceana | Intercord | 160114

Oceania
Alice Coltrane Trio | A Monastic Trio | Impulse(MCA) | 951267-2

Oceanic Beloved
Klaus Doldinger's Passport | Oceanliner | Warner | 2292-46479-2

Oceanliner
Walt Weiskopf Quartet | A World Away | Criss Cross | Criss 1100

Oceans In The Sky
Steve Kuhn With Strings | Promises Kept | ECM | 1815(0675222)
Carroll Gibbons And The Savoy Hotel Orpheans | Brighter Than The Sun | Saville Records | SVL 174 IMS

Oceanus
Ralph Towner Group | Works | ECM | 823268-1

Och Kanske Är Det Natt
Tango Five feat. Raul Jaurena | Obsecion | Satin Doll Productions | SDP 1027-1 CD

Ochiata
Jo Jones-Milt Hinton | Percussion And Bass | Fresh Sound Records | FSR-CD 0204

Ochosi
Milton Cardona With The Eya Arania Ensemble | Bembe | American Clave | AMCL 1004

Oclupaca
Ray Barretto Orchestra | Portraits In Jazz And Clave | RCA | 2168452-2
Riccardo Fassi-Antonello Salis Duo | Joining | SPLASC(H) Records | H 113

Ocre
Lluis Vidal | Lluis Vidal Piano Solo | Fresh Sound Records | FSNT 001 CD
Lluis Vidal Trio | Tren Nocturn | Fresh Sound Records | FSNT 003 CD
Intergalactic Maiden Ballet,The | Gulf | TipToe | TIP-888817 2

Octavon

Volker Kriegel & Mild Maniac Orchestra | Octember Variations | MPS | 68147

October 17, 1988

Blue Collar | Diary Of A Working Band | Jazz Haus Musik | JHM 0089 CD

October 21th

The Griffith Park Collection | The Griffith Park Collection | Elektra | MUS K 52361

October Morning

Jim Hall Group With Strings | By Arrangement | Telarc Digital | CD 83436

October Sunshine

Claire Martin With The Jim Mullen Quartet And Special Guests | Devil May Care | Linn Records | AKD 021

October Walk

George Winston | Autumn | Windham Hill | 34 11012-2

Octopus's Garden

George Benson With The Don Sebesky Orchestra | Verve Jazz Masters 21:George Benson | Verve | 521861-2

Octopus's Garden-

Jack Teagarden And His Orchestra | Birth Of A Band | Giants Of Jazz | GOJ 1038

Ocult

John Tchicai-Pierre Dorge | Ball At Louisiana | Steeplechase | SCCD 31174

Odalisque

Dave Soldier Group With Voices | Smut | Avant | AVAN 019

Odd

Arnold Dreyblatt & The Orchestra Of Excited Strings | Propellers In Love | Hat Art | CD 6011

Odd And Awkward

Barbara Dennerlein Group | Outhipped | Verve | 547503-2

Odd Blues

Jazz Pistols | Special Treatment | Lipstick Records | LIP 8971-2

Kölner Saxophon Mafia | Go Commercial... | Jazz Haus Musik | JHM 0065 CD

Odd Job

Hank Jones Trio | The Jazz Trio Of Hank Jones | Savoy | SV 0184(MG 12023)

Oddi Lobbe

Furio Di Castri-Paolo Fresu | Urlo | yvp music | CD 3035

Odds Against Tomorrow

John Lewis-Hank Jones Duo | An Evening With Two Grand Pianos | Little David | LD 59657

Modern Jazz Quartet | The Complete Modern Jazz Quartet Prestige & Pablo Recordings | Prestige | 4PRCD 4438-2

Odds Against Tomorrow | Blue Note | 793415-2

European Concert | Atlantic | SD 2-603

The Modern Jazz Quartet | Reunion At Budokan 1981 | Atlantic | 251210-1 TIS

Odds Or Evens

Frank Minion With The Tommy Flanagan Quartet | The Soft Land Of Make Believe | Fresh Sound Records | FSR 2013(Bethlehem BCP 6052)

Ode

Lee Konitz-Michel Petrucciani Duo | Toot Sweet | Owl Records | 013432-2

Pata Masters | Pata-Bahia | Pata Musik | PATA 11 CD

Kölner Saxophon Mafia | Licence To Thrill | Jazz Haus Musik | JHM 0100 CD

Ode An Erik

Zentralquartet | Plie | Intakt Records | CD 037

Ode For Tomten

Max Roach Quartet | Pictures In A Frame | Soul Note | 121003-2

Ode To An Oud

Billy Drummond Quartet | The Gift | Criss Cross | Criss 1083

Ode To Billy Joe

Jimmy Smith With The Johnny Pate Orchestra | Jimmy Smith-Talkin' Verve | Verve | 531563-2

Joe Beck-Ali Ryerson-Steve Davis | Alto | dmp Digital Music Productions | CD 521

Oscar Peterson Trio With The Claus Ogermann Orchestra | Three Originals:Motion&Emotions/Tristeza On Piano/Hello Herbie | MPS | 521059-2

Oscar Peterson With Orchestra | Motions & Emotions | MPS | 821289-2 PMS

Sonny Criss Quartet | The Beat Goes On! | Original Jazz Classics | OJCCD 1051-2(P 7558)

The Charlie Parker Memorial Band | Bird Still Lives! Vol.1 | Timeless | CD SJP 373

Ode To Charlie Parker

Eric Dolphy Group | Naima | West Wind | WW 2063

Eric Dolphy-Booker Little Quintet | Eric Dolphy:The Complete Prestige Recordings | Prestige | 9 PRCD-4418-2

Marty Ehrlich Quartet | Can You Hear A Motion? | Enja | ENJ-8052 2

Ode To Cleavage Or The Camel

Bob Degen-Harvie Swartz Duo | Chartreuse | Enja | 3015

Ode To Crispus Attucks

Fritz Münzer Tentet | Blue Ideas | Jazz 'n' Arts Records | 0200

Ode To D

Dollar(Abdullah Ibrahim) Brand | Ode To Duke Ellington | West Wind | WW 0020

Ode To Mariann

Marilyn Crispell | A Concert In Berlin-Summer '83 | FMP | SAJ 46

Ode To Sammy Davis Jr.

Wolfgang Engstfeld Quartet | Songs And Ballads | Nabel Records:Jazz Network | CD 4658

Toshiyuki Honda With The Chick Corea Trio | Dream | Eastworld | EWJ 90027

Ode To The Doo Da Day

Bobby Bradford/John Carter Quintet | Comin' On | Hat Art | CD 6016

Ode(an einen Rittmeister der Tonkunst)

Ahmed El-Salamouny/Gilson De Assis | Tango Brasileiro | FSM | FCD 97725

Oderbruch

Arthur Blythe Group | Lenox Avenue Breakdown | CBS | SRCS 7187

Odessa

Aschaffenburger Jazzbigband | Bigband-Fieber | Media Arte | CD 06569209(BRW)

Odile Odila

Art Studio & Tiziana Ghiglioni | Onde | SPLASC(H) Records | CD H 133-2

Odje Ayne

Lee Konitz Sextet | Ezz-Thetic | Prestige | P 7827

Odwalla

Art Ensemble Of Chicago | Bap-Tizum | Atlantic | 7567-80757-2

Live In Berlin | West Wind | WW 2051

Complete Live In Japan-April 22, 1984 Tokyo | DIW | DIW 815/16 CD

Odwalla Theme

Live In Japan | DIW | DIW 8005

Odyssey

James Blood Ulmer Trio | Odyssey | CBS | 25602

Of My Conceit

Quest | Of One Mind | CMP Records | CMP CD 47

Of Ours

Thierry Péala Group | Inner Traces:A Kenny Wheeler Songbook | Naive | 226102

Of Thee I Sing

Stan Getz Quartet | West Coast Jazz | Verve | 557549-2

Stan Getz And The 'Cool' Sounds | Verve | 547317-2

Best Of The West Coast Sessions | Verve | 537084-2

Stan Getz:East Of The Sun-The West Coast Sessions | Verve | 531935-2

Of Thee I Sing(alt.take 1)

Stan Getz:East Of The Sun-The West Coast Sessions | Verve | 531935-2

Of Thee I Sing(alt.take 2)

Stan Getz:East Of The Sun-The West Coast Sessions | Verve | 531935-2

Of Thee I Sing(alt.take 3)

Stan Getz:East Of The Sun-The West Coast Sessions | Verve | 531935-2

Of Thee I Sing(alt.take 4)

Stan Getz:East Of The Sun-The West Coast Sessions | Verve | 531935-2

Of Thee I Sing(alt.take 5)

Stan Getz:East Of The Sun-The West Coast Sessions | Verve | 531935-2

Of Thee I Sing(alt.take)

Ella Fitzgerald With The Nelson Riddle Orchestra | Sings The Ira And George Gershwin Songbook | Verve | 825024-2

Of Thee I Sing(stereo)

Tommy Tedesco Quintet | My Desire | Discovery | DS 851 IMS

Of Things To Come

Dave Ballou Quintet | On This Day | Steeplechase | SCCD 31504

Of Winter

Sun Ra And His Arkestra | The Futuristic Sounds Of Sun Ra | Savoy | SV 0213(MG 12169)

O-Fayces

Manfredo Fest Quintet | Oferenda | Concord | CCD 4539

Off A Bird

Meredith D'Ambrosio With Harold Danko And Kevin Eubanks | It's Your Dance | Sunnyside | SSC 1011 D

Off Beat

Vienna Art Orchestra | Artistry In Rhythm-A European Suite | TCB Records | TCB 01102

Off Broadway

Frank Vignola Sextet | Off Broadway | Nagel-Heyer | CD 2006

George Benson Group/Orchestra | George Benson Anthology | Warner | 8122-79934-2

Jimmy Dawkins Chicago Blues Band | Tribute To Orange | Black & Blue | BLE 59.556 2

Off Limit

Abdullah Ibrahim | South African Sunshine | Pläne | CD 88778

Off Minor

Beboppin' | Beboppin' | Limetree | MLP 198403

Bill Carrothers-Bill Stewart | Bill Carrothers Duets With Bill Stewart | Dreyfus Jazz Line | FDM 37002-2

Bud Powell Trio | Bud Powell:Complete 1947-1951 Blue Note,Verve & Roost Recordings | The Jazz Factory | JFCD 22837

Cedar Walton Trio | Among Friends | Evidence | ECD 22023-2

Michael Marcus And The Jaki Byard Trio | Involution | Justin Time | JUST 116-2

Peter Leitch Quartet | Red Zone | Reservoir | RSR CD 103(882905)

Steve Lacy-Misha Mangelberg | Five Facings | FMP | CD 85

Thelonious Monk And His Orchestra | In Person | Milestone | M 47033

Thelonious Monk Quartet | Monk At Newport 1963 & 1965 | CBS | C2K 63905

Live In Switzerland 1966 | Jazz Helvet | JH 06

April In Paris | Milestone | M 47060

Thelonious Monk Septet | Thelonious Monk | Jazz Classics | AU 36008 CD

Thelonious Monk:85th Birthday Celebration | zyx records | FANCD 6076-2

Thelonious Monk-The Complete Riverside Recordings | Riverside | 15 RCD 022-2

Thelonious Monk Trio | Thelonious Monk:The Complete Blue Note Recordings | Blue Note | 830363-2

Thelonious Monk:Complete 1947-1952 Blue Note Recordings | The Jazz Factory | JFCD 22838

Vienna Art Orchestra | Inside Out | Moers Music | 02062/3 CD

Wolfgang Puschnig-Jamaladeen Tacuma Trio | Gemini Gemini-The Flavors Of Thelonious Monk | ITM-Pacific | ITMP 970082

Off Minor(alt.take)

Thelonious Monk Septet | Thelonious Monk With John Coltrane | Jazzland | JZSA 946-6

Thelonious Monk-The Complete Riverside Recordings | Riverside | 15 RCD 022-2

Barry Harris Sextet | Bull's Eye! | Original Jazz Classics | OJCCD 1082-2(P 7600)

Off Monk

Max Roach Trio | The Max Roach Trio Featuring The Legendary Hasaan | Atlantic | 7567-82273-2

Off Range, No Hands

John Lindberg Ensemble | Bounce | Black Saint | 120192-2

Off Road

David Murray Quartet | Fast Life | DIW | DIW 861 CD

Off She Hoes & She's Gone

Frank Strozier-Booker Little Quintet | Waltz Of The Demons | Atlantis | ATS 5

Off The Table

Harry Verbeke-Rob Agerbeek Quartet | Seven Steps | Timeless | SJP 173

Off The Wagon

Tubby Hayes Quartet | Live 1969 | Harlequin | HQ 3006 IMS

Off The Wall

Jim Kahr Group | Back To Chicago | Acoustic Music Records | AMC 1027

Off The Wall(alt.take)

Yoshi Wada Group | Off The Wall | FMP | SAJ 49

Off Time Blues

Fletcher Henderson And His Orchestra | Fletcher Henderson Vol.2(1927) | Village(Jazz Archive) | VILCD 020-2

Off We Go Into The Wild Blue Yonder

Joe Pass | Virtuoso No.3 | Original Jazz Classics | OJC20 684-2(2310805)

Offbeat

John Coltrane Quartet | Expression | MCA | 2292-54646-2

Offering

Expression | Impulse(MCA) | GRP 11312

Offering-

Barondown | Crackshot | Avant | AVAN 059

Offering Time

Glen Velez Group | Assyrian Rose | CMP Records | CMP CD 42

Offramp

National Youth Jazz Orchestra | In Control | Ronnie Scott's Jazz House | JHCD 037

Offshore Piper

Jackie McLean Quintet | New And Old Gospel | Blue Note | 853356-2

Often Annie

Laurie Altman Quintet | For Now At Least | Progressive | PRO 7066 IMS

Often In The Open

Terje Rypdal And The Chasers | Blue | ECM | 1346(831516-2)

Og Hva Synes Vi Om Det

Jimmy Smith-Wes Montgomery Quartet | Talkin' Jazz:Roots Of Acid Jazz | Verve | 529580-2

OGD(Road Song)

Compact Jazz: Wes Montgomery | Verve | 831372-2

Further Adventures Of Jimmy And Wes | Verve | 519802-2

OGD(Road Song-alt.take)

Oregon | Roots In The Sky | Elektra | ELK K 52169

Ogden Road

Terry Gibbs Quartet | Take It From Me | Impulse(MCA) | JAS 60 (AS 58)

Ogeda

Dieter Reith Quintet | Join Us | Intercord | 145025

Ogguere

Lazaro Ros Ensemble | Ori Batá (Cuban Yoruba Music) | Enja | ENJ-9381 2

Oggun

Ulrich Gumpert | Satie: Trois Gymnopédies | ITM Records | ITM 1451

OGM

Brennan-Cline-Patumi-Voirol-Theissing | Shooting Stars & Traffic Lights | L+R Records | CDLR 45090

Ogunde

John Coltrane Quartet | The Best Of John Coltrane-His Greatest Years, Vol. 2 | MCA | AS 9223

Expression | Impulse(MCA) | GRP 11312

Oh Babe! Maybe Someday

Duke Ellington And His Orchestra | Crystal Ballroom, Fargo Concert | Jazz Anthology | JA 5229/30

Humphrey Lyttelton And His Band | Take It From The Top-A Dedication To Duke Ellington | Black Lion | BLCD 760516

Oh Baby Don't You Know

Buddy Johnson And His Orchestra | Walkin' | Official | 6008

Oh Baby, Watcha Doing To Me

Peter Herbolzheimer Orchestra | Music For Swinging Dancers Vol.4: Close To You | Koala Records | CD P 12

Oh Bess Where's My Bess

Joe Henderson Group | Porgy And Bess | Verve | 539048-2

Louis Armstrong And Ella Fitzgerald With Russell Garcia's Orchestra | Porgy And Bess | Verve | 2-2507 IMS

Oscar Peterson-Joe Pass Duo | Porgy And Bess | Original Jazz Classics | OJCCD 829-2(2310779)

Paolo Fresu Quartet | Kind Of Porgy & Bess | RCA | 21951952

Ray Charles-Cleo Laine With The Frank DeVol Orchestra & Chorus | Porgy And Bess | London | 6.30110 EM

Oh Boy I'm In The Groove

Louis Jordan And His Tympany Five | Louis Jordan Vol.1-Hoodoo Man | Swingtime(Contact) | ST 1011

Oh But I Do

Nat King Cole Trio | Live At The Circle Room | Capitol | 521859-2

Billy May And His Orchestra | Sorta Dixie | Creative World | ST 1054

Oh Christmas Tree(O Tannenbaum)

Mark Shane's X-Mas Allstars | What Would Santa Say? | Nagel-Heyer | CD 055

Oscar Peterson Sextet With Strings | An Oscar Peterson Christmas | Telarc Digital | CD 83372

Oh Daddy

Johnny Dodds With Tiny Parham | Johnny Dodds Vol.2 | Village(Jazz Archive) | VILCD 017-2

Raymond Burke's Big Three | Raymond Burke And Cie Frazier With Butch Thompson In New Orleans | 504 Records | 504CD 27

Turk Murphy And His Jazz Band | Turk Murphy's San Francisco Jazz-Vol.2 | Good Time Jazz | 12027

Oh Darling

Terry Callier Duo | The New Folk Sound Of Terry Callier | Prestige | PRCD 11026-2

Oh Dear,What Can The Matter Be

Fats Waller | Fine Arabian Stuff | Deluxe | DE 601

Oh Dey's So Fresh An' Fine (Strawberry Woman)

Ella Fitzgerald And Louis Armstrong With The Russell Garcia Orchestra | Porgy And Bess | Verve | ???

Oh Dey's So Fresh An' Fine (Strawberry Woman)-

Louis Armstrong And Ella Fitzgerald With Russell Garcia's Orchestra | The Complete Ella Fitzgerald And Louis Armstrong On Verve | Verve | 537284-2

Porgy And Bess | Verve | 2-2507 IMS

Oh Dey's So Fresh And Fine-

Adrian Bentzon's Jazzband | The Golden Years Of Revival Jazz,Vol.4 | Storyville | STCD 5509

Oh Didn't He Ramble

Algiers Brass Band | Lord Lord Lord | Sound Of New Orleans | SONO 1030

Chris Barber's Jazz Band | Chris Barber's Jazz Band | Ace Of Club | ACL 1163

Oh Didn't He Ramble-

Louis Armstrong And His All Stars | Louis Armstrong-My Greatest Songs | MCA | MCD 18347

Satchmo-A Musical Autobiography Vol.1 | MCA | 2-4173

Louis Armstrong:The New And Revisited Musical Autobiography Vol.1 | Jazz Unlimited | JUCD 2003

Oh Doctor Jesus

Louis Armstrong And Ella Fitzgerald With Russell Garcia's Orchestra | The Complete Ella Fitzgerald And Louis Armstrong On Verve | Verve | 537284-2

Ray Charles-Cleo Laine With The Frank DeVol Orchestra & Chorus | Porgy And Bess | London | 6.30110 EM

Oh Du Fröhliche-

Benny Moten's Kansas City Orchestra | Basie Beginnings | Bluebird | ND 90403

Oh Gee

Eddie Lockjaw Davis Quartet | Jazz Till Midnight | Storyville | STCD 4123

Eddie Lockjaw Davis-Johnny Griffin Quintet | Tough Tenors Back Again! | Storyville | STCD 8298

Eddie Lockjaw Davis Sextet | Save Your Love For Me | RCA | ND 86463

Oh Hangelstein-

Aretha Franklin With Choir And Soloists | One Lord One Faith One Baptism | Arista | 393178-2

Oh Happy Day

Golden Gate Quartet | Spirituals To Swing 1955-69 | EMI Records | 791569-2

Joyful Gospel Singers,USA | Take Me,Use Me | Rampart Street Music | RS-100-003

The Heavenly Stars | Old Time Religion | Sound Of New Orleans | SONO 6009

Oh Haupt Voll Blut Und Wunden

Joe Venuti-Zoot Sims Sextet | Joe Venuti And Zoot Sims | Chiaroscuro | CR 142

Oh Henry

Sheila Jordan With The Steve Kuhn Trio | Jazz Child | HighNote Records | HCD 7029

Oh Horn

Harry Edison-Buck Clayton Orchestra | Swing Trumpet Kings:Harry Edison Swings Buck Clayton And Vice Versa/Red Allen Plays King Oliver/Swing Goes Dixie | Verve | 533263-2

Oh How The Ghost Sings

Mitch Watkins Group | Strings With Wings | TipToe | TIP-888814 2

Oh I See

Una Mae Carlisle With John Kirby And His Orchestra | TheComplete Una Mae Carlisle(1940-1942) And John Kirby(1941-1942) | RCA | ND 89484

Oh Joe

Joe Newman -Zoot Sims Quintet | Locking Horns | Fresh Sound Records | FSR 657(Rama RLP 1003)

Oh Johnny Oh Johnny

Ella Fitzgerald And Her Orchestra | Jazz Collection:Ella Fitzgerald | Laserlight | 24397

Glenn Miller And His Orchestra | The Very Best Of Glenn Miller | RCA | PL 89009 AO

Naylor's Seven Aces | Oliver Naylor 1924-25 | Retrieval | RTR 79008

Oh Kickeroony

September Band | The Vandoeuvre Concert | FMP | CD 72

Oh Lawd I'm On My Way

Louis Armstrong And Ella Fitzgerald With Russell Garcia's Orchestra | The Complete Ella Fitzgerald And Louis Armstrong On Verve | Verve | 537284-2

Oscar Peterson Trio | Porgy And Bess | Verve | 519807-2

Rex Stewart And His Orchestra | Porgy And Bess Revisited | Swing | SW 8414 IMS

Oh Look At Me Now

Dick Sudhalter Band | Melodies Heard,Melodies Sweet... | Challenge | CHR 70055

Gene Harris Quartet | Like A Lover | Concord | CCD 4526

George Shearing/Hank Jones | The Spirit Of 176 | Concord | CCD 4371

Sammy Kaye And His Orchestra | The Uncollected:Sammy Kaye | Hindsight | HSR 158

Oh Lord Don't Let Them Drop That Atomic Bomb On Me

Charles Mingus Quintet With Roland Kirk | Oh Yeah | Atlantic | 90667-1 TIS

Oh Lord Don't Let Them Drop That Atomic Bomb On Me-

Boyd Rivers | Living Country Blues USA Vol.11:Country Gospel Rock | L+R Records | LR 42041

Oh Lord,Give Me A Cigarette

Change Of Mind | Change Of Mind | Aho-Recording | CD 1006

Oh Me, Oh My, Oh Gosh

Nat Gonella And His Jazz Band | The Best Of British Traditional Jazz | Philips | 818651-2

TITELVERZEICHNIS

Oh My Babe
Kurt Elling Group With Guests | Live In Chicago | Blue Note | 522211-2

Oh My God
Richard Davis Sextet | With Understanding | Muse | MR 5083

Oh My Stars
Mikhail Alperin's Moscow Art Trio With The Russkaja Pesnja Folk Choir | Folk Dreams | JA & RO | JARO 4187-2

Oh Ne Budite
David Kikoski Trio | Surf's Up | Criss Cross | Criss 1208

Oh No Babe
ULG | Spring | Laika Records | 35101382

Oh No Not I
Johnny Griffin Quartet | The Kerry Dancers | Original Jazz Classics | OJCCD 1952-2(RLP 9420)

Oh Now I See
Herbie Hancock Sextet | That's Jazz Vol.28: Fat Albert Rotunda | Warner | WB 56293

Oh Papa
Ma Rainey And Her Band | Ma Rainey | Milestone | MCD 47021-2

Oh Sister Ain't That Hot
Firehouse Five Plus Two | Goes To A Fire | Good Time Jazz | GTCD 10052-2
Hot Stuff | Hot Stuff! Celebrating Early Jazz | Lake | LACD 40

Oh So Basal
Horace Parlan Quintet | Speakin' My Piece | Blue Note | 868848-3

Oh Sonho
Count Basie And His Orchestra | This Time By Basie | Reprise | 9362-45162-2

Oh Tannenbaum
David Gazarov Trio | Let's Have A Merry Christmas With The David Gazarov Trio! | Organic Music | ORGM 9712
Jan Harrington Sextet | Jan Harrington's Christmas In New Orleans | Nagel-Heyer | NHR SP 4
Billy Cotton And His Band | Sing A New Song | Saville Records | SVL 160 IMS

Oh Well-
Five Blind Boys Of Mississippi | My Desire/There's A God Somewhere | Mobile Fidelity | MFCD 769

Oh Well,Oh Well
Glen Gray And The Casa Loma Orchestra | Swingin' Decade! Sounds Of The Great Bands Of The 40's | Pathe | 1566171(Capitol ST 1289)

Oh What A Beautiful Mornin'
Peggy Lee With The David Barbour And Billy May Bands | The Uncollected:Peggy Lee | Hindsight | HSR 220

Oh What A Night
Lou Rawls And His Orchestra | At Last | Blue Note | 791937-2

Oh What A Night For Love(long version)
Ella Fitzgerald With Marty Paich's Dektette | Ella Swings Lightly | Verve | 517535-2

Oh What A Night For Love(single version)
Otis Blackwell With Band | Listen To Dr. Jive | Krazy Kat | KK 780 IMS

Oh Yeah,Oh Yeah
Big Bill Broonzy Group | Big Bill Broonzy 1935-1940 | Black & Blue | BLE 59.253 2

Oh You Beautiful Vermland
Willie 'The Lion' Smith Duo | Willie 'The Lion ' Smith:The Lion's In Town | Vogue | 2111506-2

Oh!
Scolohofo | Oh! | Blue Note | 542081-2
The Sauter-Finegan Orchestra | That's All | Magic | DAWE 80

Oh! Baby
Edmond Hall-Bobby Hackett Band | Edmond Hall's Last Concert | Jazzology | JCD-223
Serge Chaloff Quintet | The Fable Of Mabel | Black Lion | CD 877627-2
The Tremble Kids | 25 Jahre The Tremble Kids | Intercord | 180036

Oh! Freedom
First Revolution Singers | A Cappella Gospel Anthology | Tight Harmony Records | TH 199404

Oh! He Is Christmas
The Goofus Five | Adrian Rollini Groups 1924-27 | Village(Jazz Archive) | VILCD 023-2

Oh! Lady Be Good
Artie Shaw And His Orchestra | Planet JazzArtie Shaw | Planet Jazz | 2152057-2
The Legends Of Swing | Laserlight | 24659
Begin The Beguine | RCA | ND 86274(847176)
Benny Goodman And His All Star Sextet | On Stage | Decca | 6.28101 DP
Benny Goodman And His Orchestra | 40th Anniversary Concert-Live At Carnegie Hall | London | 820349-2
The Benny Goodman Caravans Vol.3-One O'Clock Jump | Giants Of Jazz | GOJ 1036
Benny Goodman Trio | Benny Goodman:The Complete Small Combinations Vol.1/2(1935-1937) | RCA | ND 89753
Bernard Peiffer Trio | Jazz In Paris:Bernard Peiffer-La Vie En Rose | EmArCy | 013980-2
Bireli Lagrene Ensemble | Routes To Django & Bireli Swing '81 | Jazzpoint | JP 1055 CD
Bob Hall | Pianissimo-Barpiano | BELL Records | BLR 89063
Charlie Ventura Orchestra With Jackie & Roy | Euphoria | Savoy | SJL 2243 (801889)
Coleman Hawkins Quartet | Coleman Hawkins In Europe | Timeless | CBC 1-006
Count Basie And His Orchestra | Count Basie Vol.2(1938-1940) | CDS Records Ltd. | RPCD 603
Count Basie Jam Session | Count Basie-Jam Session | Jazz Magazine | 40196
Dexter Gordon-Sonny Stitt Quintet | Dexter Gordon:The Complete Blue Note Sixties Sessions | Blue Note | 834200-2
Dicky Wells Quartet | Dicky Wells & Bill Coleman In Paris | Affinity | CD AFS 1004
Dizzy Gillespie Quartet | School Days | Savoy | SV 0157(MG 6043)
Django Reinhardt And The Quintet Du Hot Club De France | Django Reinhardt:Djangology | EMI Records | 780659-2
Don Byas/Dizzy Gillespie All Stars | Yesterdays-Don Byas Meets Dizzy Gillespie | Moon Records | MCD 009-2
Ella Fitzgerald With Bob Haggart And His Orchestra | Ella:The Legendary American Decca Recordings | GRP | GRP 46482
Ella Fitzgerald With The JATP All Stars | For The Love Of Ella Fitzgerald | Verve | 841765-2
Compact Jazz: Ella Fitzgerald Live | Verve | 833294-2
Ella Fitzgerald With The Nelson Riddle Orchestra | Oh Lady Be Good:The Best Of The Gershwin Songbook | Verve | 529581-2
Ella Sings Gershwin-Vol. 1 | Metro | 2682004 IMS
The Best Of The Song Books:The Ballads | Verve | 521867-2
The Complete Ella Fitzgerald Song Books of Harold Arlen, Irving Berlin, Duke Ellington, George & Ira Gershwin, Jerome Kern, Johnny Mercer, Cole Porter And Rogers & Hart | Verve | 519832-2
Erroll Garner Solo/Trio/Quartet | Inedits 1946-1947 | Festival | 402791
Fred Astaire With The Oscar Peterson Sextet | The Astaire Story | Verve | 835649-2 PMS
George Shearing Quintet & The Robert Farnon Orchestra | How Beautiful Is The Night | Telarc Digital | CD 83325
JATP All Stars | Hot Tracks For Cool Cats Vol.3 | Polydor | 816411-2
JATP In Tokyo | Pablo | 2620104-2
The Complete Jazz At The Philharmonic On Verve 1944-1949 | Verve | 523893-2
The Complete Jazz At The Philharmonic On Verve 1944-1949 | Verve | 523893-2
The Complete Jazz At The Philharmonic On Verve 1944-1949 | Verve | 523893-2
The Complete Jazz At The Philharmonic On Verve 1944-1949 | Verve | 523893-2
Jazz At The Philharmonic:Best Of The 1940's Concerts | Verve | 557534-2
Jay McShann And His Orchestra | Jazz Gallery:Charlie Parker Vol.1 | RCA | 2114174-2
Jimmy Smith Trio | A New Sound A New Star:Jimmy Smith At The Organ | Blue Note | 857191-2
Jimmy Smith At The Organ | Blue Note | 300154(1512)
Joe Venuti Duo | The Joe Venuti Blue Four | Chiaroscuro | CR 134
Joscho Stephan Group | Swinging Strings | Acoustic Music Records | 319.1195.2
Jubilee All Stars | The Great Tenors | Jazz Anthology | JA 5205
Keith Ingham | Out Of The Past | Sackville | SKCD2-3047
Klaus Ignatzek | Gershwin Songs | Nabel Records:Jazz Network | CD 4631
Lee Konitz & The Gerry Mulligan Quartet | Konitz Meets Mulligan | Pacific Jazz | 746847-2
Lee Konitz-Franco D'Andrea | 12 Gershwin In 12 Keys | Philology | W 312.2
Lester Young And His Orchestra | Jammin The Blues | Jazz Anthology | JA 5110
Oscar Peterson Quartet | Oscar Peterson | Jazz Magazine | 40198
Oscar Peterson Trio | Oscar Peterson:The Gershwin Songbooks | Verve | 529698-2
Oscar Peterson-Milt Jackson Duo | Two Of The Few | Original Jazz Classics | OJCCD 689-2(2310881)
Pete Fountain With Orchestra | The Best Of Pete Fountain | MCA | MCD 4032
Quadrant | Quadrant | Original Jazz Classics | OJCCD 498-2
Ranee Lee And Her Band | Dark Divas-Highlights | Justin Time | JUST 144-2
Red Richards-George Kelly Sextet With Doc Cheatham | Groove Move | Jazzpoint | JP 1045 CD
Roy Eldridge-Coleman Hawkins Quintet | Just You Just Me-Live In 1959! | Stash Records | ST-CD 531(882689)
Schnuckenack Reinhardt Quintet | Swing Session | Intercord | 160010
Snooky Young Quintet | Horn Of Plenty | Concord | CJ 91
Stephane Grappelli Trio | Live | Justin Time | JTR 8469-2
Stuff Smith With The Henri Chaix Trio | Late Woman Blues | Storyville | STCD 8328
Stuff Smith-Svend Asmussen Quintet | Hot Violins | Storyville | STCD 4170
Super Sax | Supersax Plays Bird | Blue Note | 796264-2
Teddy Wilson And His Orchestra | The Radio Years | London | HMG 5020 AN
Teddy Wilson Sextet | Take It Edmond Hall With Your Clarinet That Ballet | Queen-Disc | 020
Zoot Sims Quintet | Zoot Sims And The Gershwin Brothers | Original Jazz Classics | OJC20 444-2(2310744)
Benny Goodman Quintet | I Got Rhythm-Benny Goodman Plays Gershwin | CBS | 21064

Oh! Lady Be Good-
Simon Schott | Bar Piano: Simon Schott Plays Your Favorite Evergreens Vol.1 | Organic Music | ORGM 9733
New York Voices | What's Inside | GRP | GRP 97002

Oh! Lady Be Good(alt.take)
Sidney Bechet And His New Orleans Feetwarmers | Sidney Bechet 1932-1943: The Bluebird Sessions | Bluebird | ND 90317

Oh! Lady Be Good(Fanfare with announcements)
Billie Holiday With The Mal Waldron Trio | Billie Holiday Story Vol.1:Jazz At The Philharmonic | Verve | 521642-2

Oh! Lady Be Good(Fanfare)
Count Basie And His Orchestra | From Spiritual To Swing | Vanguard | VCD 169/71

Oh! Lady Be Good(Jam Session)
Joe Bushkin Sextet | Commodore Classics In Swing | Commodore | 9031-72723-2

Oh! Que Noite Tao Bonita
Bertrand Gallaz | Sweet And Sour | Plainisphare | PL 1267-104 CD

Oh! Why?(Mon Amour Oublié)
Golden Gate Quartet With The Martial Solal Orchestra | Americans Swinging In Paris:Golden Gate Quartet | EMI Records | 539659-2
Art Tatum | Art Tatum-The Standard Transcriptions | Music & Arts | CD 919

Oh! You Crazy Moon
Chet Baker Quartet | Jazz In Paris:Chet Baker-Broken Wing | EmArCy | 013043-2
In Paris Vol.2 | West Wind | WW 2059
Russ Morgan And His Orchestra | The Uncollected:Russ Morgan | Hindsight | HSR 145
Wes Montgomery With The Don Sebesky Orchestra | Verve Jazz Masters 14:Wes Montgomery | Verve | 519826-2
California Dreaming | Verve | 827842-2
Wynton Kelly Trio With Wes Montgomery | Wes Montgomery:The Verve Jazz Sides | Verve | 521690-2
George Shearing-Mel Torme | An Elegant Evening | Concord | CCD 4294

Oh, De Lawd Shake De Heavens-
Paolo Fresu Trio | Kind Of Porgy & Bess | RCA | 21951952

Oh, Doctor Jesus-
Peppermint Harris With Band | Sittin' In With Peppermint Harris | Mainstream | MD CDO 907

Oh, Miss Hannah
Randy Sandke Sextet | The Chase | Concord | CCD 4642

Oh,Good Grief(vocal)
Swan Silvertones | My Rock/Love Lifted Me | Ace Records | CDCHD 340

Oh,Lady Be-Bop
Rhoda Scott | Rhoda Scott:Alone | Verve | 537635-2

Oh,Mountain
Trio Raphiphi | Trio Raphiphi | ITM Records | ITM 1465

Oh,Qual Traspare Orribile
Dave Brubeck With The Erich Kunzel Orchestra | Truth Is Fallen | Atlantic | 7567-80761-2

Oh,That My Head Were Waters
Lee Konitz-Kenny Werner | Unleemited | Owl Records | 014727-2

Ohad
American Jazz Quintet | AJQ-In The Beginning | AFO Records | AFO 91-1028-2

Ohadi
Zbigniew Namyslowski Quartet | Namyslovski | Inner City | IC 1048 IMS

Ohne Titel
Unternehmen Kobra | Central Europe Suite | G.N.U. Records | CD A 94.007

Ohne Worte
Ull Möck Trio | How High The Moon | Satin Doll Productions | SDP 1006-1 CD

Ohne Worte(I)
Rainer Tempel Big Band | Melodies Of '98 | Jazz 4 Ever Records:Jazz Network | J4E 4744

Ohne Worte(II)
Alice Coltrane Quartet | A Monastic Trio | Impulse(MCA) | 951267-2

Ohnedaruth
Art Ensemble Of Chicago | Dreaming Of The Masters Suite | DIW | DIW 854 CD
Phase One | America | AM 6116

Ohrid
Luigi Archetti | Das Ohr | ATM Records | ATM 3804-AH

Oif'n Pripitchik
Cannonball Adderley Quintet | Country Preacher | Capitol | 830452-2

Oil On Water
Jelly Roll Morton's Red Hot Peppers | The Complete Jelly Roll Morton-Vol.5/6 | RCA | 2126410-2

Oil Well, Texas
Richard Carr Trio | Along The Edge | Nabel Records:Jazz Network | CD 4683

Oilator
Hans Koch | Uluru | Intakt Records | CD 014

Oissa
Vasilic Nenad Balkan Band | Joe-Jack | Nabel Records:Jazz Network | CD 4693

Oj Kceri Moja
Jay Hoggard Quintet | Riverside Dance | India Navigation | IN 1068

Ojos Chinos De Santa Ana
Paul Bley | Alone Again | DIW | DIW 319 CD

Ojos De Rojo
John Hicks-Elise Wood Quartet | Luminous | Evidence | ECD 22033-2
Cedar Walton Quartet | Bluesville Time | Criss Cross | Criss 1017

Okam
Stephan Kurmann Strings | Olan Layé | TCB Records | TCB 03052

Okay Now
Pension Winnetou | Pension Winnetou | Moers Music | 02028

Okevi
Jan Klare/Tom Lorenz Quartett | Das Böse Ding | Acoustic Music Records | 319.1060.2

Okidoki
Oscar Peterson Trio | The History Of An Artist | Pablo | 2625702-2

Okiedoke
Charlie Parker With Machito And His Orchestra | Bird On Verve-Vol.1:Charlie Parker With Strings | Verve | 817442-1 IMS
The Latin Bird | Memo Music | HDJ 4076

Okinawa
John Stevens Sextet | Freebop | Affinity | AFF 101

Okonkolé Y Trompa
Lester Bowie | All The Magic! | ECM | 1246/47

Okuka Lokole
Francois Jeanneau Quartet | Techniques Douces | Owl Records | 04

Ol' 55
Dave Brubeck Quartet | Live In Concert | Kingdom Jazz | Gate 7017

Ol' Man Rebop
Dizzy Gillespie And His Orchestra | Jazz Gallery:Dizzy Gillespie | RCA | 2114165-2

Ol' Man River
Art Pepper Quintet With Strings | Art Pepper:The Complete Galaxy Recordings | Galaxy | 16GCD 1016-2
Bill Holman And His Orchestra | Great Big Band | Fresh Sound Records | T 1464(Capitol)
Bix Beiderbecke And His Gang | Riverboat Shuffle | Naxos Jazz | 8.120584 CD
Django Reinhardt And The Quintet Du Hot Club De France | Django Reinhardt:Djangology | EMI Records | 780659-2
Earl Hines Trio | Boogie Woogie On St.Louis Blues | Prestige | MPP 2515
Gene Ammons Quintet | 'Jug' | Original Jazz Classics | OJCCD 701-2(P 7192)
Harry James And His Orchestra | Harry James:Concerto For Orchestra 1939-1941 | Naxos Jazz | 8.120618
Ran Blake | Suffield Gothic | Soul Note | 121077-2
Van Alexander Orchestra | Home Of Happy Feet/Swing! Staged For Sound! | Capitol | 535211-2
Willie Lewis And His Entertainers | Le Jazz En France Vol.3 | Pathe | 1727271

Ol' Rockin' Chair -> Rockin' Chair

Old Acquaintance
Ed Sarath Quintet | Last Day In May | Konnex Records | KCD 5042

Old Age
Don Cherry Group | Old And New Dreams | Black Saint | 120013-2

Old Apple Tree -> In The Shade Of The Old Apple Tree

Old Blues For Walt's Torin
Charles Mingus Quintet With Roland Kirk | Tonight At Noon | Atlantic | 7567-80793-2
Clifford Jordan Big Band | Play What You Feel | Mapleshade | 03232

Old Bones
Ernie Carson And The Castle Jazz Band | Old Bones | Stomp Off Records | CD 1283

Old Bowl, New Grits
Frank Morgan All Stars | Reflections | Contemporary | CCD 14052-2

Old Cape Cod
H.P.Salentin Group | It's Up To You | Mons Records | MR 874787

Old Clothes
Wynton Kelly Trio | Kelly Blue | Riverside | RISA 1142-6
Odetta | The Tin Angel | Original Blues Classics | OBCCD 565-2(F 3252)

Old Devil Moon
Andrew Hill Trio | So In Love | Fresh Sound Records | FSR 653(Warwick W 2002)
Anita O'Day With The Bill Holman Orchestra | Incomparable! Anita O'Day | Verve | 589516-2
Ann Hampton Callaway And Her Band | After Hours | Denon Compact Disc | CY-18042
Doug Raney Quartet | Blue And White | Steeplechase | SCCD 31191
Eddie Lockjaw Davis Quartet | Eddie Lockjaw Davis With Shirley Scott | Original Jazz Classics | OJC 218(P 7154)
George Benson Group | Star Edition-George Benson | CTI | 83002
Gloria Lynne And Her Band | No Detour Ahead | Muse | MCD 5414
Jay Jay Johnson Quintet | Live At Cafe Bohemia 1957 | Fresh Sound Records | FSR-CD 0143
Lou Levy Trio | My Old Flame | Fresh Sound Records | FSR-CD 0312
Milt Jackson Quintet | Goodbye | CTI | 6038
Pete Magadini Quartet | Bones Blues | Sackville | 4004
Sonny Rollins Trio | Sonny Rollins:The Blue Note Recordings | Blue Note | 821371-2
Stan Getz Quartet | Spring Is Here | Concord | CCD 4500

Old Diary
Gene Harris Quartet | A Little Piece Of Heaven | Concord | CCD 4578

Old Dogs
Joe McPhee Group | Old Eyes | Hat Art | CD 6047

Old Fashioned Love
Benny Goodman Quintet | The Benny Goodman Caravans Vol.5:Jumpin' At The Woodside | Giants Of Jazz | GOJ 1042
Doc Cheatham And Sammy Price | Doc Cheattam&Sammy Price:Duos And Solos | Sackville | SK2CD-5002
Herb Hall Quartet | Old Time Modern | Sackville | 3003
Tatum-Carter-Bellson Trio | The Tatum Group Masterpieces | Pablo | 2625706
Vic Dickenson Septet With Ruby Braff | Nice Work | Vanguard | VCD 79610-2
Wild Bill Davison & Papa Bue | Wild Bill Davison & Papa Bue | Storyville | SLP 250

Old Folks
Art Blakey And The Jazz Messengers | Live At Kimball's | Concord | CCD 4307
Ben Webster Quartet | Live In Paris 1972 | France's Concert | FCD 131
Ben Webster With The Denmark Radio Big Band | No Fool No Fun | Spotlite | SPJ 142
Charles Earland Quartet | Mama Roots | Muse | MR 5156
Charlie Parker Groups | Welcome To Jazz: Charlie Parker | Koch Records | 322 075 D1
Charlie Parker With Orchestra & The Dave Lambert Singers | Verve Jazz Masters 28:Charlie Parker Plays Standards | Verve | 521854-2
The Verve Years(1952-54) | Verve | 2-2523 IMS
Denny Zeitlin-David Friesen Duo | Concord Duo Series Volume Eight | Concord | CCD 4639
Don Byas Quartet | Don Byas:Laura | Dreyfus Jazz Line | FDM 36714-2
Don Byas Complete American Small Group Recordings | Definitive Records | DRCD 11213
Dusko Goykovich Quintet | It's About Blues Time | Fresh Sound Records | FSR-CD 0305
Eddie Condon All Stars | Town Hall Concerts Vol.11 | Jazzology | JCD 1021/23
Ernestine Anderson With Orchestra | Three Ladies Of Jazz:Live In New York | Jazz Door | JD 12102
Frank Collett Trio | Perfectly Frank | Fresh Sound Records | FSR-CD 5024
Grant Green Quartet | Grantstand | Blue Note | 591723-2
Great Guitars | Great Guitars At Charlie's Georgetown | Concord | CCD 4209
James Williams Sextet | James Williams Meets The Saxophone Masters | DIW | DIW 868 CD

Joaquin Chacón Group | San | Fresh Sound Records | FSNT 015 CD
Joe Pass | What Is There To Say | Pablo | 2310971-2
Sophisticated Lady | Pablo | PACD 5310-2
Joe Pass/Niels-Henning Orsted-Pedersen Duo | Chops | Original Jazz Classics | OJCCD 786-2(2310830)
Joe Williams With The Harry 'Sweets' Edison Band | Together/Have A Good Time | Roulette | 531790-2
Johnny Griffin Quartet | Live At The Jazzhus Montmartre,Copenhagen Vol.2 | Jazz Colours | 874724-2
Keith Jarrett Trio | The Cure | ECM | 1440(849650-2)
Kenny Ball And His Jazzmen | Greensleeves | Timeless | CD TTD 505
Larry Schneider Quartet | Jazz | Steeplechase | SCCD 31505
Miles Davis Quintet | Miles Davis With John Coltrane | CBS | CBS 88029
Someday My Prince Will Come | Mobile Fidelity | MFCD 828
Pee Wee Ellis-Horace Parlan | Gentle Men Blue | Minor Music | 801073
Pete York & His All Star Group | It's You Or No One | Mons Records | MR 874772
Sadao Watanabe Quintet With Strings | Plays Ballads | Denon Compact Disc | DC-8555
Stan Getz With The Danish Radio Big Band | Stan Getz | Laserlight | 15761

Old Folks-
Jam Session | Jam Session Vol.1 | Steeplechase | SCCD 31522
Joe Henderson With The Wynton Kelly Trio | Four! | Verve | 523657-2
Ralph Sutton | Eye Opener | Solo Art | SACD-122
Steve Kuhn Quartet | Last Year's Waltz | ECM | 1213

Old Folks At Home
Grand Dominion Jazz Band | Half And Half | Stomp Off Records | CD 3989

Old Folks Not At Home
Cl.W. Jacobi's Bottomland Orchestra | A Tribute To Clarence Williams | Stomp Off Records | CD 1266

Old Folks(5 false starts)
Charlie Parker With Orchestra | Charlie Parker Big Band | Verve | 559835-2

Old Folks(alt.take 1)
Charlie Parker Big Band | Verve | 559835-2

Old Folks(alt.take 2)
Charlie Parker Big Band | Verve | 559835-2

Old Folks(alt.take 3)
Charlie Parker And His Orchestra | Bird: The Complete Charlie Parker On Verve | Verve | 837141-2

Old Folks(take 1-9)
Vince Jones Group | For All Colours | Intuition Records | INT 3071-2

Old For The New
Eugen Cicero Trio | Classics In Rhythm(Bach-Mozart-Chopin-Liszt-Tchaikovsky-Scarlatti) | MPS | 817924-2

Old Friend
Toots Thielemans-Louis van Dijk Duo | Toots & Louis | Polydor | 2925136 IMS

Old Friends
Lloyd Jones Blues Band | Trouble Monkey | audioquest Music | AQCD 1037

Old Friends Blues
Gene Harris Quartet | Funky Gene's | Concord | CCD 4609

Old Jim Crow
Nina Simone Trio | Verve Jazz Masters Vol.58:Nina Simone Sings Nina | Verve | 529867-2
Nina Simone Trio/Quartet/Orchestra | Moon Of Alabama | Jazz Door | JD 1214

Old King Dooji
Duke Ellington And His Orchestra | Duke Ellington/Cab Calloway | Forlane | UCD 19004

Old Lovers Song
Eddie Cleanhead Vinson Septet | The 'Clean' Machine | Muse | MR 5116

Old Maid Boogie
Fred Van Hove | Verloren Maandag | FMP | SAJ 11

Old Man Blues
Mose Allison Quintet | Gimeracs And Gewgaws | Blue Note | 823211-2
New Orleans Feetwarmers | Jazz:The Essential Collection Vol.1 | IN+OUT Records | 78011-2
Sidney Bechet And His New Orleans Feetwarmers | Sidney Bechet 1932-1943: The Bluebird Sessions | Bluebird | ND 90317

Old Man Mose
Lillian Boutté And Her Group | You've Gotta Love Pops:Lillian Bouté Sings Louis Armstrong | ART BY HEART | ABH 2005 2
Louis Armstrong And His Orchestra | Louis Armstrong:Hallelujah(Gospel 1930-1941) | Fremeaux | FA 001
Louis Armstrong With Luis Russell And His Orchestra | Ambassador Louis Armstrong Vol.1(1935) | Ambassador | CLA 1901
Taragota Hot Seven | Bavarian Jazz Live | Calig | 30620/21

Old Man On The Farm
Don Bagley Quintet | Jazz On The Rocks | Blue Moon | BMCD 1602

Old Man-Old Country
Elsie Jones With Smilin' Joe's Sextet | Cousin Joe:The Complete Recordings Vol.3(1947-1955) | Blue Moon | BMCD 6013

Old McDonald
Paquito D'Rivera Orchestra | Tropicana Nights | Chesky | JD 186

Old Mother Hubbard
Horace Silver Quintet/Sextet With Vocals | Total Response | Blue Note | 300212

Old Mother Nature Calls
Diedre Murray-Fred Hopkins Quartet | Stringology | Black Saint | 120143-2

Old Orleans,New Orleans
Karin Krog With The Steve Kuhn Trio | We Could Be Flying | Polydor | 2382051 IMS

Old Portrait
Charles Mingus Quintet | Portrait | Prestige | P 24092

Old Rag
Lucky Thompson Quintet | Tricotism | Impulse(MCA) | GRP 11352

Old Slippers
Christian Stock International Jazz Quartet | Back Home | yvp music | CD 3031

Old Soul
Freddie Redd Sextet | Redd's Blues | Blue Note | 540537-2

Old Spice
Ken Colyer's Jazzmen | When I Leave The World Behind | Lake | LACD 19

Old Spinning Wheel
Cy Laurie's New Orleans Septet | The Golden Years Of Revival Jazz,Vol.8 | Storyville | STCD 5513

Old Stack O'Lee Blues
Monty Sunshine's Jazz Band | Just A Little While To Stay Here | Lake | LACD 70

Old Style
Memphis Slim | Masters Of Jazz Vol. 11-29 Original Boogie Woogie Hits | RCA | NL 89773 DP

Old Time Religion
Lillian Boutté And Her Music Friends | I Sing Because I'm Happy | Timeless | CD JC 11003

Old Time Southside Street Dance
Paul Smoker Trio | Come Rain Or Come Shine | Sound Aspects | sas CD 024

Old Timey
Buddy Rich Big Band | The New One! | Pacific Jazz | 494507-2
Jimmy Haslip Group | ARC | GRP | GRP 97262

Old Town
Bill McHenry Quartet | Graphic | Fresh Sound Records | FSNT 056 CD

Old Tune
Meyer-Fleck-Marshall | Unconnon Ritual | CBS | SK 62891

Old World, New Imports
Cab Calloway And His Orchestra | Cab Calloway Vol.1-Jumping And Jiving | Swingtime(Contact) | ST 1001

Olden Times
David Newton Trio | In Good Company | Candid | CCD 79714

Olé
John Coltrane Group | Olé Coltrane | Atlantic | 7567-81349-2
John Coltrane: The Legend 'Ole' | Atlantic | ATL 40286
John Coltrane Sextet With Eric Dolphy | Soleá: A Flamenco-Jazz Fantasy | ACT | 9208-2
Maynard Ferguson And His Orchestra | Maynard '61 | Fresh Sound Records | R 52064(Roulette)

Ole Miss
Louis Armstrong And His All Stars | Historic Barcelona Concerts At Windsor Palace 1955 | Fresh Sound Records | FSR-CD 3004
Masters Of Jazz Vol.1:Louis Armstrong | Storyville | STCD 4101

Ole Miss-
Rare Performances Of The 50's And The 60's | CBS | CBS 88669
Ben Webster Quintet | At The Renaissance | Contemporary | COP 026

Ole Miss Blues
Louis Armstrong And His All Stars | On The Road | Laserlight | 15798

Oleander
Wolfgang Lackerschmid Group | Mallet Connection | Bhakti Jazz | BR 33

Olenka
Alan Broadbent | Maybeck Recital Hall Series Volume Fourteen | Concord | CCD 4488

Oleo
Bobby Jaspar Quartet | At Ronnie Scott's 1962 | Mole Jazz | Mole 11
Buck Hill Quartet | This Is Buck Hill | Steeplechase | SCCD 31095
Cody Moffett Septet | Evidence | Telarc Digital | CD 83343
Eric Dolphy With Erik Moseholm's Trio | Eric Dolphy:The Complete Prestige Recordings | Prestige | 9 PRCD-4418-2
Ernie Watts-Chick Corea Quartet | 4Tune | West Wind | WW 2105
Hampton Hawes Trio | The Seance | Original Jazz Classics | OJCCD 455-2
Joe Pass Quartet | Live At Yoshi's | Pablo | 2310951-2
Joe Pass/Niels-Henning Orsted-Pedersen Duo | Chops | Original Jazz Classics | OJCCD 786-2(2310830)
John Swana Sextet | John Swana And Friends | Criss Cross | Criss 1055
Kenn Drew Trio | Kenny Drew Trio At The Brewhouse | Storyville | 4960633
Kenny Barron Orchestra | Lucifer | Muse | MR 5070
Michel Petrucciani/Niels-Henning Orsted-Pedersen | Michel Petrucciani:Concert Inédits | Dreyfus Jazz Line | FDM 36607-2
Mikio Masuda Trio | Black Daffodils | JVC | JVC 9030-2
Miles Davis Quintet | Miles Davis At Carnegie Hall | CBS | CK 65027
Miles Davis Classics | CBS | CBS 88138
Relaxin' | Original Jazz Classics | OJC20 190-2
Miles Davis In Person-Friday Night At The Blackhawk,San Francisco,Vol.1 | CBS | C4K 87106
Relaxin' | Prestige | PR3A 7129-6
En Concert Avec Europe 1 | Laserlight | 710455/58
Miles Davis Sextet | Jazz At The Plaza | CBS | SRCS 5700
Norman Simmons Quartet | Ramira The Dancer | Spotlite | SPJ LP 13
Pat Martino Trio | Live At Yoshi's | Blue Note | 499749-2
Pedro Iturralde Quartet | Pedro Iturralde Quartet feat. Hampton Hawes | Fresh Sound Records | FSR 546(Hispavox 550-4020411)
Phineas Newborn Jr. Trio | A World Of Piano | Original Jazz Classics | OJC 175(C 7600)
Sonny Rollins Trio | In Sweden 1959 | Ingo | 9

Oleo-
Live In Europe '65 | Magnetic Records | MRCD 118

Oleo De Mujer Con Sombrero
Joe McPhee Po Music | Oleo & A Future Retrospective | Hat Art | 3514

Olga's Dream
Ana Caram Group | Bossa Nova | Chesky | JD 129

Olhos De Gato
Gary Burton Quartet | Works | ECM | 823267-2
Paul Bley Trio | Paul Plays Carla | Steeplechase | SCCD 31303

Olhos Negros-
Peter Kowald/Han Bennink | Duos: Europa | FMP | 1260

Ololiqui Valley
Herbie Hancock Quartet | Empyrean Isles | Blue Note | 498796-2
Herbie Hancock:The Complete Blue Note Sixties Sessions | Blue Note | 495569-2
Empyrean Isles | Blue Note | 498796-2

Ololiqui Valley(alt.take)
Herbie Hancock:The Complete Blue Note Sixties Sessions | Blue Note | 495569-2
Cecil Taylor | For Olim | Soul Note | 121150-2

Oliver
Rodney Jones Group | The Undiscoverd Few | Blue Note | 496902-2

Oliver's Twist
New York Second Line | New York Second Line | Concord | CCD 43002

Olives In The Ashtray
Glen Moore -Rabih Abou-Khalil | Nude Bass Ascending... | Intuition Records | INT 3192-2

Olivewood
Flora Purim & Airto | The Sun Is Out | Concord | CCD 45003

Ollie Mention
Carl Ravazza And His Orchestra | The Uncollected: Carl Ravazza | Hindsight | HSR 117

Olor De Lavanda
Ellery Eskelin + Han Bennink | Dissonant Characters | HatOLOGY | 534

Olu
Cecil Taylor Quartet | Olu Iwa | Soul Note | 121139-2

Olympus
Jimmy Giuffre Trio | The Train And The River | Choice | CHCD 71011

_Om_
John Coltrane Septet | The Best Of John Coltrane-His Greatest Years | MCA | AS 9200-2

Om Bare
Kenny Werner | Meditations | Steeplechase | SCCD 31327

Om Stenen-
John Coltrane And His Orchestra | Om | Impulse(MCA) | IMP 12912

Omaha Celebration
Marilyn Crispell | Live At Mills College, 1995 | Music & Arts | CD 899

Ombrellino
Ulli Bögershausen | Best Of Ulli Bögershausen | Laika Records | LK 93-045
Albert Ayler Sextet | Love Cry | Impulse(MCA) | GRP 11082

Omega
John Wolf Brennan | Irisations | Creative Works Records | CW CD 1021-2
Manfred Christl Farnbach-Oliver Spieß Group | Groovin' | clearaudio | 42021 CD
Albert Ayler Group | Albert Ayler Live In Greenwich Village:The Complete Impulse Recordings | Impulse(MCA) | IMP 22732

Omega Is The Alpha
Albert Ayler Septet | The Village Concerts | MCA | IA 9336/2

Omega Jive-
Alfred 23 Harth | Plan Eden | Creative Works Records | CW LP 1008

Omenaldi(Hommage)
Uli Beckerhoff Septet | Private Life | Nabel Records:Jazz Network | CD 4657

Omerta
Bill McHenry Quartet | Graphic | Fresh Sound Records | FSNT 056 CD

Omi-
Bud Powell Quartet | Parisian Thoroughfare | Pablo | CD 2310976-2

Omicron
Paul Chambers Quintet | Whims Of Chambers | Blue Note | 300122(1534)

Omikron
Stan Tracey-John Surman | Stan Tracey Duets(Sonatinas/TNT) | Blue Note | 789450-2

Omvendt
Louis Sclavis-Ernst Reijseger | Et On Ne Parle Pas Du Temps | FMP | CD 66

On A Bus
Huddie Ledbetter | Classics In Jazz-Leadbelly | Pathe | 2C 068-80701(Capitol)

On A Clear Day You Can See Forever
Bill Evans | Alone | Verve | 598319-2
Blossom Dearie Trio | Sweet Blossom Dearie | Philips | PHCE 1019 PMS
Dee Dee Bridgewater With Her Trio | Live In Paris | Verve | 014317-2
Eddie Lockjaw Davis Quartet | The Best Of Eddie 'Lockjaw' Davis | Pablo | 2405414-2
Illinois Jacquet Trio | Illinois Flies Again | Argo | ARC 503 D
Johnny Smith Quartet | Johnny Smith | Verve | 537752-2
Maxine Sullivan With The Keith Ingham Trio | Maxine Sullivan Sings The Music Of Burton Lane | Mobile Fidelity | MFCD 773
Monty Sunshine Quartet | Love And Sunshine-Monty Alexander In Concert | MPS | 68043
Oscar Peterson Trio | En Concert Avec Europe 1 | Laserlight | 710443/48
Paul Kuhn Trio | Blame It On My Youth | Timbre | TRCD 003
Singers Unlimited With The Pat Williams Orchestra | Feeling Free | MPS | 68103
Traubeli Weiß Ensemble | Dreaming Of You | Edition Collage | EC 468-2
Trio Karel Boehlee | Switch | Timeless | CD SJP 206
Vesna Skorija Band | Niceland | Satin Doll Productions | SDP 1037-1 CD
Wynton Kelly Trio | Full View | Original Jazz Classics | OJCCD 912-2(M 9004)
Wynton Kelly Trio With Hank Mobley | Live at The Left Bank Jazz Society,Baltimore,1967 | Fresh Sound Records | FSCD 1031
Wynton Kelly-George Coleman Quartet | Live at The Left Bank Jazz Society,Baltimore,1968 | Fresh Sound Records | FSCD 1032
In Concert | Affinity | AFF 54

On A Clear Day You Can See Forever(alt.take)
Dee Dee Pierce And His New Orleans Stompers | A Portrait Of George Lewis | Lake | LACD 50

On A Little Bamboo Bridge
Billy May And His Orchestra | Billy May's Big Fat Brass | Capitol | EMS 1155

On A Little Street In Singapore
Dave Brubeck Quartet | Dave Brubeck-Paul Desmond | Fantasy | FCD 24727-2

On A Misty Night
Don Menza-Pete Magadini Quartet | Live At Claudios | Sackville | SKCD2-3052
Gary Bartz Candid All Stars | There Goes The Neighborhood! | Candid | CCD 79506
Junior Cook Quartet | On A Misty Night | Steeplechase | SCCD 31266
Tadd Dameron Orchestra | The Magic Touch | Original Jazz Classics | OJCCD 143-2(RLP 9419)

On A Riff
Dave Burrell | Windward Passages | Hat Art | CD 6138

On A Scale
Andre Hodeir And His Jazz Group De Paris | Andre Hodeir:The Vogue Sessions | Vogue | 21610202

On A Summer's Evening
Ray Barretto & New World Spirit | Ancestral Messages | Concord | CCD 4549

On A Turquoise Cloud
Duke Ellington And His Orchestra | Duke Ellington:Complete Prestige Carnegie Hall 1946-1947 Concerts | Definitive Records | DRCD 11211

On And On
Silje Nergard Group with Strings | Nightwatch | EmArCy | 9865648
Cécile Verny Quintet | Kekeli | double moon | CHRDM 71028

On Another's Sorrow
Radius | Elevation | Ear-Rational | ECD 1036

On Bleeker Street
Tome XX | The Red Snapper | Jazz Haus Musik | JHM 0047 CD

On Borrowed Time
Stadtgarten Series Vol.4 | Jazz Haus Musik | JHM 1004 SER

On Both Sides Of The Fence
Blossom Dearie Trio | At Ronnie Scott's:Blossom Time | EmArCy | 558683-2

On Broadway
Ernie Andrews With Orchestra | From The Heart | Discovery | DS 825 IMS

On Children
European Tuba Quartet | Heavy Metal-Light Industry | FMP | 1200

On Clouds,Danced
Kjell Jansson Quartet | Back From Where We Came | Touché Music | TMcCD 009

On Crutches
Seamus Blake Quintet | The Call | Criss Cross | Criss 1088

On Danish Shore
The Oscar Peterson Four | If You Could Se Me Now | Pablo | 2310918-2

On Est Ensemble Sans Se Parler-L.O.V.E.
Katia Labeque-Marielle Labeque | Little Girl Blue | Dreyfus Jazz Line | FDM 36186-2

On Fire
Willie Rodriguez Jazz Quartet | Flatjacks | Milestone | MCD 9331-2

On Foot In The Gutter
Lindsay Cooper Group | Oh Moscow | Victo | CD 015

On Good Evening
Michael Mantler Group | Michael Mantler: No Answer/Silence | Watt | 2/5(543374-2)
| Modern Walkin':Greatest Hits Volume 1 | Satin Doll Productions | SDP 1008-1 CD

On Green Dolphin Street
Albert Ayler Quartet | My Name Is Albert Ayler | Black Lion | BLCD 760211
Andy LaVerne Trio | Between Mars & Earth | Steeplechase | SCCD 31478
Barbara Long With The Billy Howell Quintet | Soul-The Voice Of Babara Long | Savoy | SV 0216(MG 12161)
Benny Carter 4 | The Montreux '77 Collection | Pablo | 2620107
Bill Evans Trio | The Complete Bill Evans On Verve | Verve | 527953-2
The Complete Bill Evans On Verve | Verve | 527953-2
Peace Piece And Other Pieces | Milestone | M 47024
The Brilliant | West Wind | WW 2058
The Tokyo Concert | Original Jazz Classics | OJCCD 345-2
Verve Jazz Masters 5:Bill Evans | Verve | 519821-2
Bill Evans:The Secret Sessions | Milestone | 8MCD 4421-2
Bill Evans:The Secret Sessions | Milestone | 8MCD 4421-2
Bill Evans Live In Tokyo | CBS | 481265-2
Billy Jenkins | In The Nude | West Wind | ???
Charles Bell Trio | In Concert | Fresh Sound Records | FSR 544(Gateway LP 7012)
Chick Corea Akoustic Band | Alive | GRP | GRP 96272
David Friedman | Air Sculpture | Traumton Records | 2406-2
David Gazarov | David Gazarov's Jazz Time | VIST | MK 437055
Dutch Swing College Band | Digital Dixie | Philips | 800065-2 PMS
Eric Dolphy Quintet | Eric Dolphy:The Complete Prestige Recordings | Prestige | 9 PRCD-4418-2
Father Tom Vaughn Trio | Joyful Jazz | Concord | CJ 16
Fred Wesley Group | Comme Ca | Minor Music | 801020
Grant Green Quartet | Gooden's Corner | Blue Note | GXK 8168
Herb Ellis-Ray Brown Quintet | Soft Shoe | Concord | CCD 6003
Jack Sheldon And His Exciting All-Star Big Band | Jack's Groove | Fresh Sound Records | FSR 624(GNP 60)
Jimmy Heath Orchestra | Really Big! | Original Jazz Classics | OJCCD 1799-2(RLP 1188)
Joe Pass | Virtuoso No.2 | Pablo | 2310788-2
Junior Mance Trio & Orchestra | That Lovin' Feelin' | Milestone | MCD 47097-2
Kai Winding Quintet | Duo Bones | Red Records | VPA 143
Kenny Drew Jr. | This One's For Bill | TCB Records | TCB 99352
Marc Copland & Tim Hagans | Between The Lines | Steeplechase | SCCD 31488
Michael Cochrane Trio | Song Of Change | Soul Note | 121252-2
Miles Davis Quintet | Copenhagen 1960 | Royal Jazz | RJD 501
En Concert Avec Europe 1 | Laserlight | 710455/58

TITELVERZEICHNIS

Miles Davis In Stockholm Complete | Dragon | DRCD 228
Olga Konkova | Her Point Of View | Candid | CCD 79757
Oliver Jones Trio | Requestfully Yours | Justin Time | Just 11
Oscar Peterson Trio | The Sound Of The Trio | Verve | 543321-2
En Concert Avec Europe 1 | Laserlight | 710443/48
Oscar Peterson Trio With Milt Jackson | Very Tall | Verve | 559830-2
Very Tall | Verve | 827821-2
Patrick Tompert Trio | Moche! | Satin Doll Productions | SDP 1035-1 CD
Pedro Iturralde Quartet | Pedro Iturralde Quartet feat. Hampton Hawes | Fresh Sound Records | FSR 546(Hispavox 550-4020411)
Ran Blake-Jaki Byard Duo | Improvisations | Soul Note | 121022-2
Ray Charles With Orchestra | Hollywood Jazz | CBS | 474373-2
Rich Perry Quartet | O Grande Amor | Steeplechase | SCCD 31492
Sarah Vaughan And Her Trio | Compact Jazz:Sarah Vaughan Live! | Mercury | 832572-2 PMS
Shelly Manne Trio | Gemini Three | Eastworld | CP 32-5426
Singers Unlimited With The Pat Williams Orchestra | Feeling Free | MPS | 68103
Sonny Rollins Quartet | Rollins Meets Cherry Vol.1 | Moon Records | MCD 053-2
Stuttgart 1963 | Jazz Anthology | JA 5235
Stefan Karlsson Quintet | Room 292 | Justice Records | JR 0701-2
Thomas Stabenow Trio | Chutney | Bassic-Sound | 001
Wynton Kelly Trio | Keep It Moving | Milestone | M 47026
Kelly Blue | Riverside | RISA 1142-6
Wynton Kelly Trio With Hank Mobley | Live at The Left Bank Jazz Society,Baltimore,1967 | Fresh Sound Records | FSCD 1031
Yoshiko Kishino Trio | Photograph | GRP | GRP 98842

On Green Dolphin Street-
Mel Tormé With The George Shearing Trio | An Evening At Charlie's | Concord | CCD 4248

On Green Dolphin Street(alt.take)
Russ Freeman-Shelly Manne | One On One | Contemporary | CCD 14090-2
Berliner Saxophon Quartet | 12 Notes 4 Musicians And The Blues | BIT | 11150

On Hubbard's Hill
Cafe Du Sport Jazzquartett | Cafe Du Sport Jazzquartett | Minor Music | 801096

On Ice
Sonny Rollins Orchestra | Alfie | Impulse(MCA) | 951224-2

On Impulse
Elmo Hope Sextet | The All Star Sessions | Milestone | M 47037

On It
Franco D'Andrea Trio | Volte | Owl Records | 052 CD

On Liberty Road(For South Africa)
Joe Sachse | Ballade Für Jimi Metag | Born&Bellmann | 991503 CD

On Mediterian Waves
Phil Minton | The Berlin Station | FMP | SAJ 57

On Mike
Lee Konitz-Kenny Wheeler Quartet | Live At Birdland Neuburg | double moon | CHRDM 71014

On Mo
Rolf Kühn Group | Cucu Ear | MPS | 68259

On Morning In May
Carol Sloane And Her Trio feat. Frank Wess | Sweet And Slow | Concord | CCD 4564

On My Own
Charnett Moffett-Kenny Kirkland | Nettwork | Manhattan | CDP 796109-2

On My Way
Louis Armstrong With Sy Oliver's Choir And Orchestra | Louis And The Good Book | Verve | 549593-2
U.P. Wilson Band | On My Way | Red Lightnin' | RL 0078

On My Way To You
Freddy Cole With The Cedar Walton Trio | Love Makes The Changes | Fantasy | FCD 9681-2
Monica Zetterlund With The Bill Evans Trio | The Complete Bill Evans On Verve | Verve | 527953-2

On Natten(In The Night)
Robin Williamson | The Seed-At-Zero | ECM | 1732(543819-2)

On No Work Of Words
Dave Douglas Quartet | A Thousand Evenings | RCA | 2663698-2

On Our Way Home
Betty Carter And Her Trio | Betty Carter Album | Bet-Car | MK 1002

On Our Way Up (Sister Candy)
Richie Beirach/John Abercrombie | Emerald City | Line Records | COCD 9.00522 O

On Second Line
Bob Berg Sextet | Virtual Reality | Denon Compact Disc | CY-75369

On Stage(I'm A Polack Noel Coeard)-
Paul Grabowsky Sextet | Tee Vee | VeraBra Records | CDVBR 2050-2

On Stream
The Rippingtons | Live In L.A. | GRP | GRP 97182

On The Air
Al Cohn-Zoot Sims Quintet | You 'N' Me | Verve | 589318-2

On The Alamo
Al Haig Trio | Jazz Will O'-The -Wisp | Fresh Sound Records | FSR-CD 0038
Benny Carter And His Orchestra | Coleman Hawkins/Benny Carter | Forlane | UCD 19011
Conte Candoli Quartet | Fine & Dandy | Affinity | AFF 173
George Masso-Ken Peplowski Quintet | Just Friends | Nagel-Heyer | CD 5001
Gerry Hayes-Charlie Antolini Quintet | Swing Explosion | BELL Records | BLR 84061
Louis Armstrong And His All Stars | Bird's Eyes-Last Unissued Vol.16 | Philology | W 846.2
Stan Getz Quartet | Stan Getz:Imagination | Dreyfus Jazz Line | FDM 36733-2
Unearthed Masters-Vol.2: Stan Getz | JAM | 5007 IMS
Zoot Sims Quintet | The Swinger | Pablo | 2310861

On The Alamo(alt.take)
Stan Getz Quartet | Stan Getz-The Complete Roost Sessions | The Jazz Factory | JFCD 22839

On The Backside
Jim Snidero Quartet With Strings | Strings | Milestone | MCD 9326-2

On The Bank
Dollar Brand | Pre Abdullah Ibrahim | Jazz Colours | 874711-2

On The Bayou
George Lewis And The Barry Martyn Band | For Dancers Only | GHB Records | BCD 37
Illinois Jacquet And His All Stars | Illinois Jacquet Birthday Party | Groove Note | GRV 1003-2

On The Bean
Coleman Hawkins Quartet | Monk's Mood | Naxos Jazz | 8.120588 CD
Bean And The Boys | Prestige | PCD 24124-2

On The Bill
Ernie Watts Quartet | Ernie Watts Quartet | JVC | ???

On The Brink Of It
Dick Hyman Orchestra | Swing Is Here | Reference Recordings | RR-72 CD

On The Corner
Roman Bunka Group | Dein Kopf Ist Ein Schlafendes Auto | ATM Records | ATM 3818-AH
Roland Kirk Quintet | Rahsaan/The Complete Mercury Recordings Of Roland Kirk | Mercury | 846630-2

On The Corner Of King And Scott Streets
Roscoe Mitchell | Sound Songs | Delmark | DE 493(2)

On The Edge
Wolfgang Muthspiel Quintet | Timezones | Amadeo | 839013-2

On The Ginza
Art Blakey And The Jazz Messengers | Feeling Good | Delos | DE 4007

On The Green Grass A Cup Of Cottage Cheese
Michael Schiefel | I Don't Belong | Traumton Records | 4433-2

On The Highway
Patrick Tompert Trio | Moche! | Satin Doll Productions | SDP 1035-1 CD
David Newton | Return Journey | Linn Records | AKD 025

On The Lake
Warren Bernhardt Trio | So Real | dmp Digital Music Productions | CD 532

On The Lee Side-
Lee Ritenour Group | On The Line | GRP | GRP 95252

On The Lion
Joe Turner Trio | Joe Turner | Black & Blue | BLE 233031

On The Loose
Denny Zeitlin-David Friesen Duo | In Concert | ITM-Pacific | ITMP 970068

On The Move
Bob Rockwell Quartet | On The Natch | Steeplechase | SCCD 31229

On The Nile
Charles Tolliver Quartet | Live In Berlin-At The Quasimodo Vol.1 | Strata East Records | 660.51.001
Horace Tapscott | The Tapscott Sessions Vol.7 | Nimbus | NS 2147
Forward Motion | Reminiscence | Linn Records | AKD 024

On The Other Hand
Lyle Mays Trio | Fictionary | Geffen Records | GED 24521

On The Que-Tee
Urban Knights | Urban Knights | GRP | GRP 98152

On The Red Side Of The Street
Alvin Queen Quartet With The RTB Big Band | Introducing:RTB Big Band | Plainisphare | PL 1267-23

On The Road
David Newton | Return Journey | Linn Records | AKD 025

On The Road Again
Isaac Scott Blues Band | Big Time Blues Man | Red Lightnin' | RL 0046

On The Road To Mandalay
Jan Savitt And His Top Hatters | The Uncollected:Jan Svitt | Hindsight | HSR 213

On The Scene
Peter Herbolzheimer Rhythm Combination & Brass | Bigband Bebop | Koala Records | CD P 5

On The Shady Side Of Forty
Clark Terry Sextet | Clark Terry-Remember The Time | Mons Records | MR 874762

On The Spot
Matthieu Michel Quintet feat. Richard Galliano | Estate | TCB Records | TCB 95802

On The Stage In Cages
Pat Martino Quartet | Consciousness | Muse | MCD 5039

On The Street Where You Live
Art Blakey And The Jazz Messengers | Planet Jazz:Art Blakey | Planet Jazz | 2152066-2
Second Edition | Bluebird | 63 66661-2
Cootie Williams And His Orchestra | Cootie In Hi-Fi | RCA | NL 89811
John Harrison Trio | Going Places | TCB Records | TCB 95702
Richard 'Groove' Holmes Trio | Misty | Original Jazz Classics | OJCCD 724-2(P 7485)
Shelly Manne And His Friends | My Fair Lady | Mobile Fidelity | MFCD 809
Stan Kenton And His Orchestra | The Stage Door Swings | Capitol | EMS 1159

On The Street Where You Live-
Pucho & His Latin Soul Brothers | Groovin' High | Cannonball Records | CBD 27103

On The Sunny Side Of The Street
Art Tatum | Art Tatum At The Piano Vol.1 | GNP Crescendo | GNPD 9025
Bernard Berkhout '5' | Royal Flush | Timeless | CD SJP 425
Billie Holiday With Eddie Heywood And His Orchestra | Billie Holiday:The Complete Commodore Recordings | GRP | AFS 1019-8
Chris Barber's Jazz And Blues Band | Class Of '78 | Black Lion | 187001
Coleman Hawkins And His Sax Ensemble | Rare Dates Without The Duke 1944/49 | Raretone | 5011 FC
Cozy Cole All Stars | Concerto For Cozy | Jazz Anthology | JA 5161
Dizzy Gillespie Sextet | The Champ | Jazz Anthology | JA 5183
Dizzy Gillespie 1948-1952 | Queen-Disc | 045
Django Reinhardt And The Quintet Du Hot Club De France | Django Reinhardt:Djangology | EMI Records | 780659-2
Duke Ellington And His Orchestra | Duke Ellington All Star Road Band | Doctor Jazz | ZL 70968(2) (809318)
Earl Hines | Jazz:The Essential Collection Vol.2 | IN+OUT Records | 78012-2
The Earl | Naxos Jazz | 8.120581 CD
Ella Fitzgerald With The Count Basie Orchestra | For The Love Of Ella Fitzgerald | Verve | 841765-2
Ella And Basie | Verve | 539059-2
Ella & Basie-On The Sunny Side Of The Street | Verve | 821576-2
Erroll Garner Trio | Yesterdays | Savoy | SV 0244(SJL 1118)
Gillespie-Rollins-Stitt Sextet | The Sonny Rollins/Sonny Stitt Sessions | Verve | 2-2505 IMS
Golden Gate Quartet | Spirituals To Swing 1955-69 | EMI Records | 791569-2
Best Of Golden Gate Quartet | Sonia | CD 77285
Jesse Davis Quartet | Second Nature | Concord | CCD 4883
John Pizzarelli Trio | Dear Mr.Cole | Novus | 4163182-2
Johnny Hodges Orchestra | The Rabbit's Work On Verve In Chronological Order, Vol.4 | Verve | 2304450 IMS
Johnny Hodges Septet | Masters Of Jazz Vol.9:Johnny Hodges | Storyville | STCD 4109
Johnny Hodges-Wild Bill Davis Sextet | Jazz Special-The 40's & 60's | RCA | CL 43236 AF
Ken Colyer's All Stars | The Sunny Side Of Ken Colyer | Upbeat Jazz | URCD 113
Lester Young And His Band | Lester Young:The Complete 1936-1951 Small Group Sessions(Studio Recordings-Master Takes),Vol.4 | Blue Moon | BMCD 1004
Lester Young With The Oscar Peterson Quartet | The Pres-ident Plays | Verve | 831670-2 PMS
Lionel Hampton All Star Band | At Newport '78 | Timeless | CD SJP 142
Lionel Hampton And His All Star Jazz Inner Circle | En Concert Avec Europe 1 | Laserlight | 710375/76
Lionel Hampton And His All Stars | Masters Of Jazz Vol.8 | RCA | NL 89540 DP
Lionel Hampton And His Orchestra | En Concert Avec Europe 1 | Laserlight | 710462
Lionel Hampton Quintet | The Lional Hampton Quintet | Verve | 589100-2
Lonnie Johnson With Elmer Snowden | Lonnie Johnson With Elmer Snowden Vol.2:Blues Ballads And Jumpin' Jazz | Original Blues Classics | OBCCD 570-2
Louis Armstrong And His All Stars | Satchmo-A Musical Autobiography Vol.2 | MCA | 2-4174
Jazz-Club: Vocal | Verve | 840029-2
The Complete Town Hall Concert 17.May 1947 | RCA | ND 89746
Louis Armstrong And His Orchestra | Louis Armstrong In The Thirties/Fats Waller Last Testament | Forlane | UCD 19005
Louis Armstrong With Orchestra | Satchmo | Verve | 835895-2
Magnificant Seventh's with Milton Batiste And Alton Carson | Best Of New Orleans:Bourbon Street Jazz After Dark | Mardi Gras Records | MG 1022
Nancy Harrow And The Buck Clayton All Stars | Wild Women Don't Have The Blues | Candid | CCD 79008
Nat King Cole Quartet | The Changing Face Of Harlem, Vol. 2 | Savoy | SJL 2224 (801200)
Nat King Cole Trio | Nat King Cole | Savoy | 650120(881920)
Paul Quinichette Septet | On The Sunny Side | Original Jazz Classics | OJCCD 076-2(P 7103)
Peter Herbolzheimer Orchestra | Music For Swinging Dancers Vol.4: Close To You | Koala Records | CD P 12
Si Zentner And His Orchestra With The Johnny Mann Singers | Great Band With Great Voices | Capitol | EMS 1164
Sidney Bechet Quintet | Clarinet/Soprano | Jazz Colours | 874714-2
Svend Asmussen Sextet | Svend Asmussen Collection Vol.14 | Swan Music | CD 2514-2
The New York Allstars | Oh,Yeah! The New York Allstars Play More Music Of Louis Armstrong | Nagel-Heyer | CD 046
The Tremble Kids All Stars | Dixieland Forever Vol.2 | BELL Records | BLR 89046
Tommy Dorsey And His Orchestra | This Is Tommy Dorsey | RCA | PL 89536 DP
Willis Jackson Quintet | Cool Gator | Original Jazz Classics | OJC 220(P 7172)

On The Sunny Side Of The Street-
Louis Armstrong And His Orchestra | Louis Armstrong Radio Days | Moon Records | MCD 056-2
Earl Hines | The Indispensable Earl Hines Vol.3/4(1939-1945) | RCA | 2126408-2

On The Trail(From The Grand Canyon Suite)
Clark Terry-Chris Woods Quintet | Swiss Radio Days Jazz Series Vol.8:Clark Terry-Chris Woods | TCB Records | TCB 02082
Dizzy Gillespie Sextet | Village Vanguard Live Sessions No.2 | LRC Records | CDC 9012
Itzak Perlman With The Oscar Peterson Quartet | Side By Side | Telarc Digital | CD 83341
Oscar Peterson Quartet | Time After Time | Pablo | 2310947-2
Oscar Peterson Trio | Swinging Cooperations:Reunion Blues/Great Connection | MPS | 539085-2
Peter Leitch-Heiner Franz | At First Sight | Jardis Records | JRCD 9611
Peter Madsen Trio With Stanley Turrentine | Three Of A Kind Meets Mister T. | Minor Music | 801043
Wynton Kelly Quintet | It's All Right! | Verve | 537750-2
Wynton Kelly-George Coleman Quartet | In Concert | Affinity | AFF 54

On The Up And Up
Stan Getz Quartet | Pure Getz | Concord | CCD 4188

On The Way
Uli Gutscher Quintet | Inspiration | Edition Collage | EC 462-2

On The Way Back
Mahavishnu Orchestra | Visions Of The Emerald Beyond | CBS | 467904-2

On The Way Home To Earth
Johnny Hodges Orchestra | Triple Play | RCA | ND 90208(847147)

On The Wing Again
Steve Coleman And Five Elements | Black Science | Novus | PD 83119

On This
Steve Coleman Quintet | Jump On It | Enja | 4094

On This Day(Just Like Any Other)
Billy Taylor Quartet | Homage | GRP | GRP 98062

On Time
Lucky Thompson Quartet | Lucky Meets Tommy | Fresh Sound Records | FSR-CD 0199

On Ton
Billy Ver Planck And His Orchestra | Dancing Jazz | Savoy | SV 0235(MG 12101)

On Top Of The Roof
Ulli Bögershausen | Private Stories | Laika Records | 35101542

On Tour
Steve Elson's Lips & Fingers Ensemble | Lips & Fingers | Open Minds | OM 2406-2

On Your Daddy's Knee
Roger Kellaway Cello Quartet With The A&M Symphony Orchestra | Roger Kellaway Cello Quartet | A&M Records | 9861062

On Your Mark,Get Set-Blues
Illinois Jacquet And His Orchestra | Groovin' | Verve | 2304511 IMS

Once
Jean-Luc Ponty Quintet | Civilized Evil | Atlantic | SD 16020

Once Again
Franz Weyerer Quartet | For You | Bassic-Sound | CD 012
Macrino-Rovagna Ensemble | New Age Jazz | Penta Flowers | CDPIA 003
Uwe Werner-Mick Baumeister Duo | Oh Brother | Chaos | CACD 8067-2

Once Again & Far Away
Marlene And Her Band | Elemental Soul | Concord | CCD 4774

Once Again(Outra Vez)
Thad Jones-Mel Lewis Orchestra | Paris 1969-Vol.1 | Royal Jazz | RJD 511

Once Around The Park
Paul Motian Quintet | Misterioso | Soul Note | 121174-2
Pat LaBarbera Quartet | Virgo Dance | Justin Time | Just 24

Once Forgotten
Superblue | Superblue | Blue Note | 791731-2

Once I Loved
Eda Zari With The Mark Joggerst Trio | The Art Of Time | Laika Records | 35100902
Harry Allen Quintet | Love Songs Live! | Nagel-Heyer | NH 1014
Harry Allen Sextet | Eu Nao Quero Dancar-I Won't Dance | Novus | 2158126-2
Joe Diorio | To Jobim With Love | RAM Records | RMCD 4529
Keith Copeland Trio | The Irish Connection | Steeplechase | SCCD 31395
Maximilian Geller Quartet feat. Susan Tobocman | Maimilian Geller Goes Bossa Encore | Edition Collage | EC 505-2
Mikio Masuda Trio | Black Daffodils | JVC | JVC 9030-2
Shirley Horn Trio | The Antonio Carlos Jobim Songbook | Verve | 525472-2
Tony Williams Lifetime | Turn It Over | Verve | 539118-2

Once I Loved -> O Amor En Paz

Once In A Blue Mood
Jimmy Rowles Quartet | Fiorello-Uptown/Mary Sunshine-Downtown | Fresh Sound Records | FSR 587(Signature SM 6011)

Once In A Blue Moon
Joe Derisi With The Australian Jazz Quintet | Joe Derisi | Fresh Sound Records | FSR 2044(Bethlehem BCP 51)

Once In A Lifetime
Mel Tormé With Orchestra | That's All Mel Tormé | CBS | CK 65165

Once In A While
Art Blakey And The Jazz Messengers | A Night At Birdland Vol. 1 | Blue Note | 532146-2
Jazz Gallery:Clifford Brown | RCA | 2114176-2
Art Tatum-Buddy DeFranco Quartet | The Tatum Group Masterpieces | Pablo | 2625706
Earl Hines | Earl Hines Piano Solos's | Laserlight | 15790
Jimmy Smith Trio | Cool Blues | Blue Note | 535587-2
Johannes Rediske Quintet | Re-Disc Bounce | Bear Family Records | BCD 16119 AH
John Barnes-Roy Williams Group | Like We Do | Lake | LACD 69
Julian Priester Quintet | Keep Swingin' | Original Jazz Classics | SMJ 6081
Red Richards Quartet | Swingtime | Jazzpoint | JP 1041 CD
Roland Kirk Quartet | Rahsaan/The Complete Mercury Recordings Of Roland Kirk | Mercury | 846630-2
Rip Rig And Panic/Now Please Don't You Cry Beautiful Edith | EmArCy | 832164-2 PMS
Sonny Criss Quintet | Blues Pour Flirter | Polydor | 2445034 IMS
Stan Kenton And His Orchestra | The Romantic Approach | Creative World | ST 1017
The Ravens | Old Man River | Savoy | SV 0260
Tommy Dorsey And His Orchestra | Planet Jazz:Tommy Dorsey | Planet Jazz | 2159972-2
This Is Tommy Dorsey | RCA | PL 89536 DP

Once In A While-
Ella Fitzgerald With Benny Carter's Magnificent Seven | 30 By Ella | Capitol | 520090-2
Art Tatum-Buddy DeFranco Quartet | Art Tatum-The Complete Pablo Group Masterpieces | Pablo | 6 PACD 4401-2

Once In A While(alt.take)
Karl Denson Group | The Red Snapper | Minor Music | 801024

Once In Th A.M.
Lex Jasper Trio With Orchestra | Lexpression | Limetree | MCD 0016

Once More With Feeling
Trombonefire | Sliding Affairs | Laika Records | 35101462

Once Or Twice
Lucky Thompson Trio | Tricotism | Impulse(MCA) | GRP 11352
Once Upon A Love
Red Rodney & The New Danish Jazzarmy | Society Red | Music Mecca | CD 1003-2
Once Upon A Summertime
Astrud Gilberto With The Gil Evans Orchestra | Trav'lin' Light:The Johnny Mercer Songbook | Verve | 555402-2
Blossom Dearie Trio | At Ronnie Scott's:Blossom Time | EmArCy | 558683-2
Carmen McRae With Orchestra | The Ultimate Carmen McRae | Mainstream | MD CDO 705
Chet Baker Quartet | Live In Chateauvallon 1978 | France's Concert | FCD 128
David Kikoski Trio | Inner Trust | Criss Cross | Criss 1148
George Shearing Trio | Light,Airy And Swinging | MPS | 68094
Michel Legrand Sextet | Legrand 'Live' Jazz | Novus | ND 83103(847033)
Miles Davis With Gil Evans & His Orchestra | Ballads | CBS | 461099-2
Monica Zetterlund With The Bill Evans Trio | The Complete Bill Evans On Verve | Verve | 527953-2
Bill Evans-Monica Zetterlund | West Wind | WW 2073
Oscar Peterson Trio | Two Originals:Walking The Line/Another Day | MPS | 533549-2
Walking The Line | MPS | 68082
Singers Unlimited + The Oscar Peterson Trio | The Singers Unlimited:Magic Voices | MPS | 539130-2
In Tune | MPS | 68085
Helen Merrill With The Gary Peacock Trio | Sposin' | Storyville | SLP 1014
Once Upon A Time
Jay McShann Quartet | Just A Lucky So And So | Sackville | SKCD2-3035
Klaus König Orchestra | Time Fragments:Seven Studies In Time And Motion | Enja | ENJ-8076 2
Lucky Thompson And His Orchestra | Lucky Thompson/Gigi Gryce:Street Scenes | Vogue | 2115467-2
Myriam Alter Quintet | Silent Walk | Challenge | CHR 70035
Ruby Braff-Dick Hyman | Ruby Braff And Dick Hyman Play Nice Tunes | Arbors Records | ARCD 19141
Stan Getz With The Eddie Sauter Orchestra | Stan Getz Plays The Music Of Mickey One | Verve | 531232-2
Ultimate Stan Getz selected by Joe Henderson | Verve | 557532-2
Stan Getz:Focus | CTI Records | PDCTI 1111-2
Zoom | Three Ways | Bhakti Jazz | BR 101
Once Upon A Time In America
Jens Thomas | Jens Thomas Plays Ennio Morricone | ACT | 9273-2
Once Upon A Time In The West
Hendrik Meurkens Quintet | Slidin' | Concord | CCD 4628
Once We Were Young
Albert Mangelsdorff Duo | A Jazz Tune I Hope | MPS | 68212
Once You've Been In Love
Freddy Cole With Band | To The End Of The Earth | Fantasy | FCD 9675-2
Sarah Vaughan With The Michel Legrand Orchestra | Sarah Vaughan With Michel Legrand | Mainstream | MD CDO 703
Ondas
NuNu! | Ocean | TipToe | TIP-888837 2
Ondas Do Mar-
Nana Vasconcelos/Antonello Salis | Lester | Soul Note | 121157-2
Ondas(Na Ohlos De Petronila)
Don Grusin Group | Native Land | GRP | GRP 97192
Ondine
Oscar Pettiford Sextet | Oscar Pettiford Sextet | Vogue | 21409452
One
Louis Sclavis Quintet | Rouge | ECM | 1458
Mary Lou Williams Group | Mary Lou's Mass | Mary Records | M 102
One Alone
Ralph Flanagan And His Orchestra | Dance Again Part 2 | Magic | DAWE 75
One And Four
Jack Wilson Quartet | Something Personal | Blue Note | 852436-2
One And Four(aka Mr.Day)
Miles Davis Group | On The Corner | CBS | CK 63980
One And One
David Newton Trio | Victim Of The Circumstance | Linn Records | AKD 013
One At A Time
Keely Smith And Her Band | I'm In Love Again | Fantasy | F 9639
One Bass Hit
Modern Jazz Quartet | The Complete Modern Jazz Quartet Prestige & Pablo Recordings | Prestige | 4PRCD 4438-2
Modern Jazz Quartet | Prestige | P 24005
One Bass Rag
Michael Karn Quintet | In Focus | Criss Cross | Criss 1191
One Big Yes
The Lounge Lizards | Voice Of Chunk | VeraBra Records | CDVBR 2025-2
One Bird, One Stone
Don Grolnick Septet | Nighttown | Blue Note | 798689-2
One By One
Art Blakey And The Jazz Messengers | Dr. Jeckyle | Paddle Wheel | K32Y 6183
Michael Cochrane Trio | Footprints | Steeplechase | SCCD 31476
One Chance At Life
Lucky Thompson Quintet | Americans Swinging In Paris:Lucky Thompson | EMI Records | 539651-2
One Cool Night
Lucky Thompson-Emmett Berry Quintet | Lucky Thompson | Swing | SW 8404 IMS
One Cool Night(alt.take)
Sabine&Markus Setzer | Between The Words | Lipstick Records | LIP 8970
One Couple-Two Heads
Lou Donaldson Quintet | Blue Breakbeats:Lou Donaldson | Blue Note | 494709-2
One Day
Steve Tibbetts Group | Yr | ECM | 1355(835245-2)
Tom Scott And His Orchestra | One Night/One Day | Soundwings | SW 2102(807410)
One Day In March I Go Down To The Sea And Listen
Dollar Brand | Anthem For The New Nations | Denon Compact Disc | DC-8588
One Day With You
Cats & Camels | Face To Face | L+R Records | CDLR 45038
One Down
Freddie Redd Sextet | Everybody Loves A Winner | Milestone | MCD 9187-2
John Coltrane Quartet | Dear Old Stockholm | Impulse(MCA) | GRP 11202
One Down, One Up
McCoy Tyner Quartet | McCoy Tyner-Reevaluation | MCA | AS 9235-2
One Dream Come
Marty Cook Group | Theory Of Strange | Enja | 9107-2
One Fine Day In May
Betty Carter And Her Trio | Jazzbühne Berlin '85 | Repertoire Records | REPCD 4901-CC
One Finger Snap
Fred Hersch Trio | Horizons | Concord | CJ 267
Herbie Hancock Quartet | Herbie Hancock:The Complete Blue Note Sixties Sessions | Blue Note | 495569-2
Herbie Hancock Trio | Live In New York | Jazz Door | JD 1274
One Finger Snap(alt.take)
Herbie Hancock Quartet | Herbie Hancock:The Complete Blue Note Sixties Sessions | Blue Note | 495569-2
Vienna Art Orchestra | Chapter II | Amadeo | 849066-2
One Flight Down
Steve Smith & Vital Information | Vitalive! | VeraBra Records | CDVBR 2051-2
One Flight Up
Artie Shaw And His Orchestra | The Indispensable Artie Shaw Vol.1/2(1938-1939) | RCA | 2126413-2
One Foot In The Gutter
Dave Bailey Sextet | One Foot In The Gutter | Epic | ESCA 7759
One For Amos
Clifford Jordan Quartet | Night Of The Mark VII | 32 Jazz | 32118
One For Bill
Billy Barron Quintet | Jazz Caper | Muse | MR 5235
One For Bob
Oliver Nelson And His Orchestra | More Blues And The Abstract Truth | MCA | 2292-54643-2
One For Brahms
Humphrey Lyttelton And His Band | Movin' And Groovin' | Black Lion | BLCD 760504
One For Daddy-O
Cannonball Adderley Quintet | Somethin' Else | Blue Note | 495329-2
Miles Davis:The Blue Note And Capitol Recordings | Blue Note | 827475-2
Cannonball Adderley-Nat Adderley Quintet | What Is This Thing Called Soul:In Europe-Live! | Original Jazz Classics | OJCCD 801-2(2308238)
Longineu Parsons Group | Work Song | TCB Records | TCB 94302
Nat Adderley Quintet | The Old Country | Enja | ENJ-7027 2
McCoy Tyner Quintet | Dimensions | Elektra | 960350-1
One For Duke
The Jazz Interactions Orchestra | Verve Jazz Masters 48:Oliver Nelson | Verve | 527654-2
One For Eddie
Grant Green Quintet | Reaching Out | Black Lion | BLCD 760129
One For Emily
Jack DeJohnette Quartet | Special Edition | ECM | 1152
One For Eric
Jack DeJohnette Special Edition | Works | ECM | 825427-2
One For Five
Billy Taylor And The Turtle Island String Quartet | Homage | GRP | GRP 98062
One For Helen
Bill Evans Trio | The Complete Bill Evans On Verve | Verve | 527953-2
At The Montreux Jazz Festival | Verve | 539758-2
Bill Evans:The Secret Sessions | Milestone | 8MCD 4421-2
Blue In Green | Milestone | MCD 9185-2
Bill Evans At Town Hall | Verve | 831271-2
Pete Jolly Duo | Pete Jolly Duo/Trio/Quartet | Fresh Sound Records | ND 42133
One For Joan
Wynton Kelly Quintet | It's All Right! | Verve | 537750-2
One For Joe
Guido Manusardi Trio | Introduction | Penta Flowers | CDPIA 009
One For Kirk
Nicolas Simion Group | Balkan Jazz | Intuition Records | INT 3339-2
One For Kisser
Dusko Goykovich Quintet | Dusko Goykovich Portrait | Enja | ENJ-9427 2
One For Majid
Fra-Fra Sound | Third Life Stream | Jazz Pure Collection | AU 31608 CD
One For Michael(No.1)
Nicolas Simion Quartet feat. Tomasz Stanko | Dinner For Don Carlos | Tutu Records | 888146-2*
One For Michael(No.2)
Barbara Dennerlein Quintet | That's Me | Enja | ENJ-7043 2
One For Miss D.
Saheb Sarbib Quartet | Seasons | Soul Note | 121048-2
One For Mort
Jan Verwey Quartet | You Must Believe In Spring | Timeless | CD SJP 369
One For Mulgrew
Billie Holiday And Her All Stars | Billie Holiday:The Great American Songbook | Verve | 523003-2
One For My Baby(And One More For The Road)
Billie Holiday And Her Orchestra | Embraceable You | Verve | 817359-1 IMS
Ella Fitzgerald And Paul Smith | The Intimate Ella | Verve | 839838-2
Ella Fitzgerald With Orchestra | Forever Ella | Verve | 529387-2
Ella Fitzgerald With The Billy May Orchestra | The Complete Ella Fitzgerald Song Books of Harold Arlen, Irving Berlin, Duke Ellington, George & Ira Gershwin, Jerome Kern, Johnny Mercer, Cole Porter And Rogers & Hart | Verve | 519832-2
The Harold Arlen Songbook | Verve | 817526-1 IMS
George Cables Trio | One For My Baby | Steeplechase | SCCD 31487
Lena Horne With The Horace Henderson Orchestra | Planet Jazz:Lena Horne | Planet Jazz | 2165373-2
Mel Tormé With The Marty Paich Quintet | Live At The Crescendo | Charly | CD 60
Roland Kirk Quintet | Rahsaan/The Complete Mercury Recordings Of Roland Kirk | Mercury | 846630-2
Rosemary Clooney And Her Band | Sings The Music Of Harold Arlen | Concord | MC CJ 210C
Tal Farlow Trio | Chromatic Palette | Concord | CCD 4154
Wes Montgomery Quintet | So Much Guitar! | Original Jazz Classics | OJC20 233-2
Wes Montgomery-The Complete Riverside Recordings | Riverside | 12 RCD 4408-2
Weslia Whitefield With The Mike Greensill Trio And Warren Vaché | My Shining Hour | HighNote Records | HCD 7012
One For Myrtle
Robert Hurst Trio | One For Namesake | DIW | DIW 617 CD
One For Paulo
Muhal Richard Abrams-Amina Claudine Myer | Duet | Black Saint | 120051-2
One For Phil
Ron Eschete | A Closer Look | Concord | CCD 4607
One For Rose
Carlo Atti Quartet | Straight Ahead | Timeless | CD SJP 316
One For Sonny
Vic Juris Quartet | Roadsong | Muse | MR 5150
One For The Kids
Wolfhound | Wolfhound Live | BELL Records | BLR 84047
One For The Roadrunner
Geoffrey McCabe Quartet | Teseract Complicity | Timeless | SJP 212
One For Trule
Eddie Bert Quartet | Encore | Savoy | SV 0229(MG 12019)
One For Us
Billy Drummond Quintet | Native Colours | Criss Cross | Criss 1057
One Full Moon Night
Erroll Garner Sextet | Magician & Gershwin And Kern | Telarc Digital | CD 83337
One Hand One Heart
Dave Grusin Orchestra | David Grusin Presents West Side Story | N2K | 43062
Rhein Brass And Friends | Kant Park | Mons Records | MR 874318
One Handed Woman
Nelson Rangell Groups | Yes, Then Yes | GRP | GRP 97552
One Horse Town
| Jazz Classics In Digital Stereo: Coleman Hawkins 1927-1939 | CDS Records Ltd. | RPCD 600(CD 698)
One Hour
Coleman Hawkins With Different Bands | 100 Ans De Jazz:Coleman Hawkins | RCA | 2177832-2
Count Basie And His Orchestra | Count Basie 1940/44 | Jazz Society | AA 512
Mound City Blue Blowers | The Indispensable Coleman Hawkins 1927-1956:Body And Soul | RCA | ND 89277
One I Held A Moon
Vital Information | Where We Come From | Intuition Records | INT 3218 2
One In A Lifetime
Anita Carmichael Quintet | Anita Carmichael | Lipstick Records | LIP 8944-2
One In Four
Ginger Baker Group | No Material | ITM Records | 0035
One In Three
Max Roach-Anthony Braxton | One In Two-Two In One | Hat Art | CD 6030
One Kind Of Favor
Lightnin' Hopkins | Really The Blues | America | AM 6080
One Last Goodbye
Lucky Thompson Quartet | Lucky Thompson | Swing | SW 8404 IMS
One Less Bell To Answer
Frankfurt Jazz Big Band | El Carpincho | L+R Records | CDLR 45027
One Line(Is Enough)
Muhal Richard Abrams Orchestra | One Line, Two Views | New World Records | 80469-2
One Liners
Yusef Lateef Quartet | 1984 | MCA | AS 84
One Look,One Touch
Mitch Watkins Group | Strings With Wings | TipToe | TIP-888814 2
One Love
Marjorie Lee With The John T.Williams Quintet | Remembering With Marjorie Lee | Fresh Sound Records | Beaumonde BR 100 CD
One Milestone
Klaus Ignatzek Quintet | The Answer! | Candid | CCD 79534
One Mind
Rahsaan Roland Kirk Group | Rahsaan Rolnd Kirk:Dog Years In The Fourth Ring | 32 Jazz | 32032
One Mint Julep
Charles Musselwhite Band | Charles Musselwhite Memphis,Tennessee | Crosscut | CCR 1008
Ernestine Anderson With The Clayton-Hamilton Jazz Orchestra | Boogie Down | Concord | CCD 4407
Freddie Hubbard Quintet | Cordon Blue | Blue Note | 789915-2
Jimmy Smith With The Oliver Nelson Orchestra | Jimmy Smith-Talkin' Verve | Verve | 531563-2
Kenny Burrell Quartet | Kenny Burrell-Bluesin' Around | CBS | FC 38507
Ray Charles With Orchestra | Portrait In Music | London | 6.28338 DP
One Minute Of Flamenco For Three Minutes
Rochester/Veasley Band | One Minute Of Love | Gramavision | GR 8505-2
One More
John Patitucci Group | One More Angel | Concord | CCD 4753
One More Life
Wolfgang Lackerschmid Group | Gently But Deep | Lady Hamilton Productions | BR 39
Wolfgang Lackerschmid-Donald Johnston Group | New Singers-New Songs | Bhakti Jazz | BR 31
Benny Golson Quintet | One More Mem'ry | Timeless | SJP 180
One More Mile
Clarence Gatemouth Brown Band | The Blues Of Clarence 'Gatemouth Brown | Storyville | 4960563
One More Mile | Rounder Records | CDRR 2034
One More Mile To Go
Dave Douglas Group | Witness | RCA | 2663763-2
One More News
Patti Austin And Her Band | Live At The Bottom Line | CBS | 467922-2
One More Once
Duke Ellington And His Orchestra | The Duke Live In Santa Monica Vol.1 | Queen-Disc | 069
Avantgarden Party | Into The Blue | Stunt Records | 18906
One More String
Babik Reinhardt Group | All Love | Melodie | 400012
One More Time
Duke Robillard Group | Rockin' Blues | Rounder Records | CDRR 11548
One More Time Chuck Corea
Singers Unlimited | A Capella III | MPS | 68245
One More(alt.take)
The Trio Electric Child | The Trio Electric Child | Penta Flowers | CDPIA 010
One Morning In May
Bucky Pizzarelli | Love Songs | Stash Records | ST 213 IMS
Frank Foster-Frank Wess Quintet | Frankly Speaking | Concord | CCD 4276
One Nation
Michael Shrieve Trio | Fascination | CMP Records | CMP CD 67
One Never Knows
Modern Jazz Quartet And The All-Star Jazz Band | Jazz Dialogue | Philips | PHCE 3018 PMS
One Never Knows Do One-
Bluiett-Jackson-Thiam | Join Us | Justin Time | JUST 124-2
One Night At Ken And Jessica's
Ronnie Scott Quartet | When I Want You Opinion,I'll Give It To You | Ronnie Scott's Jazz House | JHAS 610
One Night In The Hotel
Earl Hines Quartet | Earl's Pearl | Memo Music | HDJ 4043
One Note
Tobias Langguth Band | One Note Bossa | Jardis Records | JRCD 9510
One Note Bossa
Red Norvo And His Orchestra | Commodore Classics-Red Norvo:Town Hall Concert 1945 | Commodore | 6.26168 AG
One Note Samba
$$hide$$ | $$Titelverweise | |
One Note Samba -> Samba Da Una Nota
One Note Samba 'Waltz'
Jaki Byard And The Apollo Stompers | Phantasies | Soul Note | 121075-2
One Ocean Way
Stuff Smith With The Eddie Bernard Trio | Live In Paris 1965 | France's Concert | FCD 120
One O'Clock Boogie
Count Basie And His Orchestra | 100 Ans De Jazz:Count Basie | RCA | 2177831-2
Boogie Woogie Hits-Various Artists | RCA | CL 89803 SF
One O'Clock Jump
Benny Goodman And His Orchestra | The Benny Goodman Story | Capitol | 833569-2
Jazz Collection:Benny Goodman | Laserlight | 24396
The Best Of The Big Dance Bands | LRC Records | CDC9010
Benny Goodman Bangkok 1956 | TCB Records | TCB 43042
Cootie Williams And His Orchestra | Bird's Eyes Last Unissued Vol.24 | Philology | W 854.2
Count Basie And His Orchestra | Basie Boogie | CBS | 21063
One O'Clock Jump | Black Lion | 127033
Compact Jazz: Count Basie | Verve | 831364-2
Breakfast Dance And Barbecue | Roulette | 531791-2
En Concert Avec Europe 1 | Laserlight | 710411/12
Live In Basel 1956 | Jazz Helvet | JH 05
The Great Concert Of Count Basie | Festival | 402311
Jazz:The Essential Collection Vol.3 | IN+OUT Records | 78013-2
Live! | Laserlight | 15797
Jazz Collection:Count Basie | Laserlight | 24368
The Legendary Count Basie | CBS | 26033
Count Basie Sextet | Combo USA | Affinity | CD AFS 1002
Duke Ellington And His Orchestra | Recollections Of The Big Band Era | Atlantic | 90043-2
Glenn Miller And His Orchestra | The Glenn Miller Story Vol. 2 | RCA | ND 89221
The Glenn Miller Carnegie Hall Concert | RCA | NL 81506
JATP All Stars | Jazz At The Philharmonic:One O'Clock Jump 1953 | Verve | 815153-1 IMS
Jesper Thilo Quintet Plus One | Don't Count' Him Out | Music Mecca | CD 1035-2
Just Jazz All Stars | Way Out Wardell | Ace Records | CDBOP 014
Lambert, Hendricks And Bavan | At Newport '63 | RCA | 2125757-2
Lambert, Hendricks And Ross | Lambert,Hendricks & Ross:Sing A Song Of Basie | CTI Records | PDCTI 1115-2

TITELVERZEICHNIS

Lester Young And His Band | Tenor Triumvirate:Bean & Prez & Chu | Queen-Disc | 051
Nat King Cole Trio | Live At The Circle Room | Capitol | 521859-2
Peter Herbolzheimer Rhythm Combination & Brass | Fat Man Boogie | Koala Records | CD P 2
The Royal Air Force HQ Bomber Command Sextet | RAF HQ Bomber Command Sextet | Celebrity | CYCD 74508

One O'Clock Jump(alt.take)
Harry James And His Orchestra | Harry James.His Orchestra And The Boogie Woogie Trio | Affinity | CD AFS 1009

One O'Clock Jump(EP version)
Harry James And His Music Makers | Live At Cleareater Florida,Vol.2 | Magic | DAWE 77

One Of A Kind
Freddie Hubbard All Stars | MMTC(Monk,Miles,Trane And Cannon) | Musicmasters | 65132-2
Freddie Hubbard Sextet | The Best Of Freddie Hubbard | Pablo | 2405415-2
V.S.O.P. | The Quintet | CBS | 88273

One OF A Kinf
Benny Green Trio | The Place To Be | Blue Note | 829268-2

One Of Another Kind
Freddie Hubbard Quintet | Rollin' | MPS | 68284
Freddie Hubbard Sextet | Keystone Bop | Fantasy | F 9615

One Of These Days
Mose Allison Quartet | The Mose Chronicles-Live In London,Vol.2 | Blue Note | 529748-2
Mose Allison Sextet | Your Mind Is In Vacation | Atlantic | SD 1691
Ray Charles With Orchestra | Ain't It So | London | 6.23864 AP

One Of Those Days
Benny Bailey Quartet | Islands | Enja | ENJ-2082 2

One Of Two
Ed Mann Group | Perfect World | CMP Records | CMP MC 45

One Of Us Is Over
Thärichens Tentett | Lady Moon | Minor Music | 801094

One Of Us Two
Sigrid Meyer And Her Quartet | Serene | Metronome | 60544

One On One
Gerald Wilson Orchestra | Feelin' Kinda Blues | Pacific Jazz | CDP 79-2

One Phone Call-
Kenny Wheeler Brass Ensemble | A Long Time Ago | ECM | 1691

One Plus Three(version 1)
A Long Time Ago | ECM | 1691

One Plus Three(version 2)
Coryell/Catherine | Splendid | Elektra | ELK K 52086

One Quiet Night
James Emery Sextet | Luminous Cycles | Between The Lines | btl 015(Efa 10185-2)

One Red Thread
George Benson With The David Matthews Orchestra | Georg Benson | Jazz Magazine | 43002

One Room
Blood,Sweat And Tears | Monterey Jazz Festival 1975 | Storyville | 4960213

One Room Country Shack
Buddy Guy & Junior Wells With The Chicago Blues All Stars '78 | Live In Montreux | Black & Blue | BLE 59.530 2
Mose Allison Trio | Mose Allison:Greatest Hits | Original Jazz Classics | OJCCD 6004-2
Mose Allison Sings The 7th Son | Prestige | PR20 7279-2
Sunny Blake Group | The Devil's Music:Mississippi And Memphis/Chicago Blues | Red Lightnin' | RL 0033

One Scotch One Bourbon One Beer
Snooks Eaglin | Blues From New Orleans Vol.1 | Storyville | SLP 119

One Second After Death
Grant Green With Orchestra | The Final Comedown(Soundtrack) | Blue Note | 581678-2
Harold Land Quintet | The Fox | Original Jazz Classics | OJCCD 343-2

One Second Please
Paul Moer Trio | Paul Moer Trio Plays The Music Of Elmo Hope | Fresh Sound Records | FSR-CD 5008

One September Day
Nina Simone With Orchestra | Nina Simone-The 60s Vol.1: Ne Me Quitte Pas | Mercury | 838543-2 PMS

One Shining Soul
Blue Mitchell Quintet | Down With It | Blue Note | 854327-2

One Shirt
Dave Douglas Tiny Bell Trio | Wandering Souls | Winter&Winter | 910042-2

One Shot
Chick Webb And His Orchestra | Chick Webb Vol.4-Ella Swings The Band | MCA | 1327

One Small Day
John Tchicai-Albert Mangelsdorff Duo | John Tchicai Solo Plus Albert Mangelsdorff | FMP | SAJ 12

One Sparrow
Dave Samuels Group | Del Sol | GRP | GRP 96962

One Summer
The Rippingtons | Tourist In Paradise | GRP | GRP 95882

One Summer Night In Brazil
Joe McBride And Friends | Double Take | Inak | 30442

One Sweet Letter From You
Keith Ingham-Harry Allen Septet | The Back Room Romp | Sackville | SKCD2-3059

One Symphony(part 1-4)
Five Blind Boys Of Alabama | Negro Spirituals,Gospel & Jubilee Songs | Vogue | 655015

One Thousand Years Of Peace
Anglo Italian Quartet | Put It Right Mr.Smoothie | SPLASC(H) Records | CD H 313-2

One Time Only
Joe Lovano Trio | One Time Out | Soul Note | SN 1224

One Time Swing
Zoot Sims-Bob Brookmeyer Quintet | One To Blow On | Biograph | BLP 12062

One True Friend
AM 4 | ...And She Answered | ECM | 1394

One T'une
Rodney Jones Group | Soul Manifesto | Blue Note | 530499-2

One Turnip Green
Stan Kenton And His Orchestra | The Kenton Era | Creative World | ST 1030

One Way
Carla Bley Big Band | The Carla Bley Big Band Goes To Church | Watt | 27(533682-2)
Enrico Pieranunzi | What's What | yvp music | CD 3006(Demon)

One Way In Harlem
Cornelius Claudio Kreusch | Piano Moments | Take Twelve On CD | TT 007-2
Dave McMurdo Jazz Orchestra | Different Paths | Sackville | SKCD2-2034

One Way Out
Sonny Boy Williamson Band | The Real Folk Blues | Chess | CHD 9272(872292)

One Way To Be
Montreal Jubilation Gospel Choir | Jubilatio III-Glory Train | Blues Beacon | BLU-1008 2

One With One
Ben Pollack And His Park Central Orchestra | Futuristic Rhythm | Saville Records | SVL 154 IMS

One Woman's Man
Sonny Terry Trio | Robbin' The Grave | Blue Labor | BL 101

One Ying For Every Yang
Craig Handy Trio | Three For All + One | Arabesque Recordings | AJ 0109

One! Of Parker's Moods
John Stevens Quartet | Re-Touch & Quartet | Konnex Records | KCD 5027

One, Two-
Gary Burton Quartet | Duster | RCA | 2125730-2

One, Two, 1-2-3-4
Victor Jazz History Vol.16:Jazz-Rock & Fusion | RCA | 2135735-2

One-Eyed Jack
Brian Barley Trio | Brian Barley Trio 1970 | Just A Memory | JAS 9502-2

Oneness
Illinois Jacquet And His Orchestra | Groovin' | Verve | 2304511 IMS

One-Two-Three Or Four-Five-Six
Mal Waldron Quintet | One-Upmanship | Enja | 2092 (807490)

Onion
Ernie Carson And The Castle Jazz Band | Old Bones | Stomp Off Records | CD 1283

Onion Field
Herb Ellis-Ray Brown Sextet | Hot Tracks | Concord | CCD 6012

Onion Straw
Duke Ellington And His Orchestra | The Greatest Jazz Concert In The World | Pablo | 2625704-2

Only A Blues
George Robert-Phil Woods Quintet | The Summit | Mons Records | MR 874304

Only A Rose
Zoot Sims With Bill Holman And His Orchestra | Hawthorne Nights | Pablo | 2310783

Only 'Cause I Don't Have You
Bill Evans Quintet | We Will Meet Again | Warner | 7599-27504-2

Only Child
Bill Evans Trio | Empathy+A Simple Matter Of Conviction | Verve | 837757-2 PMS
Stefano Battaglia Trio | Bill Evans Compositions Vol.2 | SPLASC(H) Records | CD H 410-2

Only Forever
Nat King Cole With The Ralph Carmichael Orchestra | The Touch Of Your Lips | Capitol | EMS 1111
Gary Thomas Quartet | Pariah's Pariah | Winter&Winter | 910033-2

Only Hearsay
Hal Crook Trio | Only Human | RAM Records | RMCD 4506

Only In It For The Money
Members Only...Too! | The Way You Make Me Feel | Muse | MCD 5348

Only One
Belgian All Stars Big Band feat. Benny Bailey & 'Toots' Thielemans | Changing Moods-The Music Of Gastry Meyer | B.Sharp Records | CDS 091

Only The Lonely
Jim Tomlinson Quintet | Only Trust Your Heart | Candid | CCD 79758
Roman Schwaller Jazz Quartet | Live At The Nachtcafé Munich | Bassic-Sound | CD 019
Mel Tormé With Orchestra | That's All Mel Tormé | CBS | CK 65165

Only Trees
Agneta Baumann Group | Sentimental Lady | Touché Music | TMcCD 017

Only Trust You Heart
Dick Sudhalter Band | Melodies Heard,Melodies Sweet... | Challenge | CHR 70055
Maximilian Geller Quartet feat. Susan Tobocman | Maimilian Geller Goes Bossa Encore | Edition Collage | EC 505-2
Benny Carter Quintet | My Kind Of Trouble | Pablo | 2310935-2

Only Trust Your Heart
Herb Geller Quartet | To Benny & Johnny | Hep | CD 2084
Houston Person Sextet | The Talk Of The Town | Muse | MCD 5331
Marian McPartland Trio feat. Benny Carter | Plays The Benny Carter Songbook | Concord | CCD 4412
Steve LaSpina Quintet | When I'm Alone | Steeplechase | SCCD 31376
The New Stan Getz Quartet Feat. Astrud Gilberto | Getz Au Go Go | CTI Records | PDCTI 1124-2

Only We Know
Mahalia Jackson With Orchestra | In Memoriam Mahalia Jackson | CBS | 66501

Only Why No More
Johnny Hodges And Shorty Baker And Their Orchestra | Ellingtonians In Paris | Jazztime(EMI) | 251275-2

Only Women Bleed
Paolo Fresu Quintet | Qvatro | SPLASC(H) Records | CD H 160-2

Only Yesterday
Louis Jordan With The Nelson Riddle Orchestra | Louis Jordan-Let The Good Times Roll: The Complete Decca Recordings 1938-1954 | Bear Family Records | BCD 15557 IH
Peppino D'Agostino | A Glimpse Of Times Past | Acoustic Music Records | 319.1157.2

Only You
Louis Armstrong And His All Stars With Benny Carter's Orchestra | Ambassador Louis Armstrong Vol.17:Moments To Remember(1952-1956) | Ambassador | CLA 1917
Mr. Acker Bilk With The Leon Young String Chorale | Stranger On The Shore | Philips | 830779-2

Ontem A Note
Steve Khan Trio | Headline | Polydor | 517690-2

Ontet
Gerry Mulligan Tentette | The Birth Of The Cool Vol.2 | Capitol | 798935-2

Ontology
Eric Felten-Jimmy Knepper Group | T-Bop | Soul Note | 121196-2

Onward
Sun Ra And His Solar Arkestra | Sun Ra Visit Planet Earth/Interstellar Low Ways | Evidence | ECD 22039-2

Oo Wheel!! Hidewe
Jon Rose Group | Violin Music In The Age Of Shopping | Intakt Records | CD 038

Oodles Of Noodles
Harry Edison-Eddie Lockjaw Davis Quintet | Jawbreakers | Original Jazz Classics | OJCCD 487-2(RLP 9430)

Oooeh Train
Franz Koglmann Tentet | A White Line | Hat Art | CD 6048

Ooga Booga
Coleman Hawkins Meets The Big Sax Section | Coleman Hawkins Meets The Big Sax Sextion | Savoy | SV 0248(SJL 1123)

Oogoogajoo
Diamond, Angel & Crooks | More Where That Came From | Intuition Records | INT 3061-2

Ooh Wee Baby
Glenn Miller And His Orchestra | Glenn Miller:The Complete Studio Recordings Vol.2:In The Mood | Memo Music | HDJ 4115

Ooh! Boogie!
Charlie Parker Quintet | Charlie Parker Live Sessions Vol.2 | Zeta | ZET 712

Ooh-Shoo-Be-Doo-Bee
First Class Blues Band | The First Class Blues Band Proudly Presents Mr. Frank Biner | Acoustic Music Records | 319.1062.2

Ool-Ya-Koo
Dizzy Gillespie And His Orchestra | Bebop Enters Sweden | Dragon | DRCD 318
Dizzy's Diamonds-Best Of The Verve Years | Verve | 513875-2
Dizzy Gillespie:Pleyel Jazz Concert 1948 + Max Roach Quintet 1949 | Vogue | 21409412
Dizzy Gillespie (1946-1949) | RCA | ND 89763
Ella Fitzgerald With The Hank Jones Trio | Ella Fitzgerald:The Royal Roost Sessions | Cool & Blue | C&B-CD 112

Ooo Baby Baby
Louis Jordan And His Tympany Five | Go Blow Your Horn-Part 2 | Pathe | 1546680(Aladdin)

Oooh! Look-A-There Ain't She Pretty
Benny Goodman And His Orchestra | The Indispensable Benny Goodman(Big Band) Vol.5/6(1938-1939) | RCA | 2122621-2

Oop-Bop-Sh-Bam
Dizzy Gillespie Sextet | In The Beginning | Prestige | P 24030
Kenny Clarke And His 52nd Street Boys | Fats Navarro:The 1946-1949 Small Group Sessions(Studio Recordings-Master Takes),Vol.1 | Blue Moon | BMCD 1016
Oscar Peterson Quartet | Victor Jazz History Vol.11:Bebop | RCA | 2135730-2
Oscar Peterson Trio | The Complete Young Oscar Peterson(1945-1949) | RCA | 2122612-2
Masters Of Jazz Vol.7 | RCA | NL 89721 DP

Oop-Pap-A-Da
Bill Doggett And His Orchestra | Organ Boogie Woogie | CBS | 21079

Oops!
Joey Baron Trio | Tongue In Groove | JMT Edition | 849158-2
Teo Macero And His Orchestra | Impressions Of Charles Mingus | Palo Alto | PA 8046

Oo-Shoo-Be-Doo-Bee
Jeri Brown With Band feat. Leon Thomas | Zaius | Justin Time | JUST 117-2

Oouffnoon
[Deacon] Lem Johnson And His Band | Lem Johnson-Doc Sausage-Jo Jo Jackson | Blue Moon | BMCD 6004

Opal
Jeff 'Tain' Watts Trio | MegaWatts | Sunnyside | SSC 1055 D

Opale Concerto In Three Movements(for Accordeon And Orchestra)
Charles McPherson Quartet | McPherson's Mood | Original Jazz Classics | OJCCD 1947-2(PR 7743)

Opalescence
James Emery | Exo Eso | FMP | SAJ 59

Opalesque
Hod O'Brien Quintet | Opalessence | Criss Cross | Criss 1012

Opaling
Bill Perkins With The Metropole Orchestra | I Wished On The Moon | Candid | CCD 79524

Open
Gerd Dudek-Buschi Niebergall-Edward Vesala | Open | FMP | 0570
Urs Leimgruber-Adelhard Roidinger-Fritz Hauser | Lines | Hat Art | CD 6149

Open 12
Michel Herr Quintet | Solis Lacus | B.Sharp Records | 1001

Open Beauty
Teo Macero And His Orchestra | Impressions Of Charles Mingus | Palo Alto | PA 8046

Open Country
Gerry Mulligan Quartet | Gerry Mulligan Quartet At Storyville | Pacific Jazz | 794472-2

Open De Trio
Zoot Sims Septet | The Concert 23.6.1958 | Jazzline | ???

Open Doors
Rudy Linka Quartet | Jazz Collection | ARTA Records | N 1 0007-2311

Open Drive
Dudek-Van Den Broek-Haurand | Pulque | Konnex Records | KCD 5055

Open End
Frey-Tiepold-Thierfelder-Lang | Colibry | VeraBra Records | No. 2

Open Eyes
Markus Becker Quartet | Lacuna | L+R Records | CDLR 45043

Open House
Lionel Hampton And His Sextet | Lionel Hampton-Historical Recording Sessions 1939-1941 | RCA | PM 42417

Open Jaw
John Abercrombie Sextet | Open Land | ECM | 1683(557652-2)

Open Land
Loose Tubes | Jazzbühne Berlin '87 | Repertoire Records | REPCD 4916-WZ

Open Letter To Duke
Charles Mingus Orchestra | Nostalgia In Times Square/The Immortal 1959 Sessions | CBS | 88337
Mingus Big Band 93 | Nostalgia In Times Square | Dreyfus Jazz Line | FDM 36559-2
Orquestra De Cambra Teatre Lliure | Tributes To Duke Ellington | Fresh Sound Records | FSNT 084 CD
David Torn/Mick Karn/Terry Bozzio | Polytown | CMP Records | CMP CD 1008

Open Noisy
Tarheel Slim | No Time At All | Trix Records | TRIX 3310

Open Or Close
Doneda-Rogers-Le Quan | Open Paper Tree | FMP | CD 68

Open Sea
Spyro Gyra & Guests | Love & Other Obsessions | GRP | GRP 98112

Open Season
Ginger Baker/Jens Johansson/Jonas Hellborg | Unseen Rain | Day Eight Music | DEMCD 028

Open Sesame
Freddie Hubbard Quintet | The Blue Note Years-The Best Of Freddie Hubbard | Blue Note | 793202-2
Superblue | Superblue | Blue Note | 791731-2

Open Sesame(alt.take)
Simon Cato Spang-Hansen Quartet | Identified | dacapo | DCCD 9448

Open Sky Blue
Albert Mangelsdorff Quartet | Live In Tokyo | Enja | 2006-2

Open Spaces
Jean-Luc Ponty Experience | Open Strings | MPS | 68088

Open The Door Richard
Louis Jordan And His Tympany Five | Louis Jordan-Let The Good Times Roll: The Complete Decca Recordings 1938-1954 | Bear Family Records | BCD 15557 IH
Louis Jordan-Let The Good Times Roll: The Complete Decca Recordings 1938-1954 | Bear Family Records | BCD 15557 IH
Louis Jordan Greatest Hits-Vol.2 | MCA | 1337

Open The Gates(Out Of The Way Of The People)
Peter Weniger Quartet | Weirdoes | Mons Records | MR 874826

Open To Love
Paul Bley | Open, To Love | ECM | 1023
Masabumi Kikuchi Trio | Tethered Moon-First Meeting | Winter&Winter | 910016-2

Open Trio
Joachim Kühn | Solo's Duo's And Trio's | Keytone | KYT 718

Open Up The Pearly Gates
Julian Dash And His Orchestra | Julian Dash:The Complete Recordings 1950-1953 | Blue Moon | BMCD 1050

Open Window
Stefano Maltese Open Music Orchestra | Hanging In The Sky | SPLASC(H) Records | H 139

Open Windows
Nicolas Simion Quartet feat. Tomasz Stanko | Dinner For Don Carlos | Tutu Records | 888146-2*
Bruce Williamson Sextet | Big City Magic | Timeless | CD SJP 413

Open Your Eyes
Gary Burton Quartet | The New Quartet | ECM | 1030

Open Your Eyes, You Can Fly
Eva Taylor & Lawrence Lomax With Clarence Williams' Band | The Complete 1923-1926 Clarence Williams Sessions Vol.1 | EPM Musique | FDC 5107

Open Your Window
Ella Fitzgerald With The Tommy Flanagan Trio | Ella Fitzgerald In Budapest | Pablo | PACD 5308-2
Louie Bellson And His Orchestra | The Louis Bellson Explosion | Original Jazz Classics | OJCCD 728-2(2310755)

Opener
Lionel Hampton And His Orchestra | En Concert Avec Europe 1 | Laserlight | 710462

Opening
Hans Koller Big Band | New York City | MPS | 9813437
New York City | MPS | 68235
John Abercrombie Trio | Gateway 2 | ECM | 1105(847323-2)
John Zorn Group | Cobra | Hat Art | CD 6040(2)
Martin Kolbe-Ralf Illenberger | Waves/Colouring The Leaves | BELL Records | BLR 83751

Opening-
Kenny Wheeler Ensemble | Muisc For Large & Small Ensembles | ECM | 1415/16
Michael Mantler Group | Songs And One Symphony | ECM | 1721
Richie Cole Group | Jazz Life Vol.1:From Village Vanguard | Storyville | 4960753
Eddie Condon All Stars | Town Hall Concerts Vol.11 | Jazzology | JCD 1021/23

Opening Gambit
Anthony Braxton Orchestra | Composition No. 173 | Black Saint | 120166-2

Opening Remarks
John Coltrane And His Orchestra | The Best Of John Coltrane-His Greatest Years, Vol. 2 | MCA | AS 9223

Opening Theme
Nat King Cole Trio | Live At The Circle Room | Capitol | 521859-2
Raymond Scott And His Orchestra | The Uncollected:Raymond Scott | Hindsight | HSR 201

Opera In Vout(Groove Juice Symphony)
Claudio Puntin Quartet | Mondo | Jazz Haus Musik | JHM 0134 CD

Opera Meditativa
Moscow Art Trio | Once Upon A Time | JA & RO | JARO 4238-2

Opera Rap
Glenn Spearman Double Trio | Smokehouse | Black Saint | 120157-2

Operation Tango
Gene Harris Group | In His Hands | Concord | CCD 4758

Ophelia
Mike Santiago/Entity | White Trees | Chiaroscuro | CR 193

Ophelia's Arrival
Eddie Bert Quartet | Encore | Savoy | SV 0229(MG 12019)

Opium-
Marilyn Crispell-Doug James Duo | And Your Ivory Voice Sings | LEO | LR 126

Opportunity
David Kikoski Trio | Almost Twilight | Criss Cross | Criss 1190

Opposite World
Christoph Stiefel Trio | Dream Of The Camel | Enja | 9135-2

Optical
Kenny Dorham Quintet | New Blue Horns | Original Jazz Classics | OJC 256(RLP 294)

Opus
Jerry Coker Orchestra | Modern Music From Indiana University | Fantasy | 0902116(F 3214)

Opus 1
Mundell Lowe Quintet | Mundell's Moods | Nagel-Heyer | CD 065
Paul Bley Trio | Introducing Paul Bley-| Original Jazz Classics | OJCCD 201-2(DEB 7)
Charles Mingus-The Complete Debut Recordings | Debut | 12 DCD 4402-2
Rex Allen's Swing Express | Keep Swingin' | Nagel-Heyer | CD 016
Robert Hohner Persussion Ensemble | The Gamut | dmp Digital Music Productions | CD 505
Tommy Dorsey And His Orchestra | Planet Jazz:Jazz Greatest Hits | Planet Jazz | 2169648-2
Werner Müller Mit Dem Rias-Tanzorchester | Swing Tanzen Gestattet | Vagabond | 6.28415 DP

Opus 1(alt.take)
Paul Bley Trio | Charles Mingus-The Complete Debut Recordings | Debut | 12 DCD 4402-2
Mark Morganelli And The Jazz Forum All Stars | Speak Low | Candid | CCD 79054

Opus 1,5
Benny Goodman Quartet | Avalon-The Small Band Vol.2 (1937-1939) | Bluebird | ND 82273

Opus 2
Ulli Bögershausen | Ageless Guitar Solos | Laika Records | 8695071

Opus 20
Benny Goodman Quartet | Jazz Giants:Benny Goodman | RCA | NL 89731 SI

Opus 3-4
Avalon-The Small Band Vol.2 (1937-1939) | Bluebird | ND 82273

Opus 5
Adam Makowicz Trio With The Wilanow Quartet | 7.Zelt-Musik-Festival:Jazz Events | Zounds | CD 2730001

Opus 57
Fernand Englebert Group | Fantasmatic | B.Sharp Records | CDS 078

Opus De Don
J.J.Johnson-Chris Laurence | Tangerine | Verve | 526588-2

Opus De Funk
Art Pepper Plus Eleven | Modern Jazz Classics | Original Jazz Classics | OJC20 341-2
A Treasury Of Modern Jazz Classics | Mobile Fidelity | MFCD 805
Horace Silver Trio | Horace Silver Trio And Spotlight On Drums:Art Blakey-Sabu | Blue Note | 591725-2
Jack McDuff Quartet | Jack McDuff:The Prestige Years | Prestige | PRCD 24387-2
Milt Jackson Quintet | Opus De Funk | Prestige | P 24048
Goodbye | CTI | 6038
From Opus De Jazz To Jazz Skyline | Savoy | ???

Opus In Barock
Johannes Rediske Quintet | Re-Disc Bounce | Bear Family Records | BCD 16119 AH
Stan Kenton And His Orchestra | The Kenton Touch | Creative World | ST 1033

Opus On B.A.C.H.
Alex Welsh And His Band | If I Had A Talking Picture | Black Lion | BLCD 760521

Opus One
DMP Big Band | Carved In Stone | dmp Digital Music Productions | CD 512
The Four Freshmen | Stars In Your Eyes | Capitol | EMS 1152
Tommy Dorsey And His Orchestra | This Is Tommy Dorsey | RCA | PL 89536 DP

Opus One-Point-Five
Joe Henderson Trio | Power To The People | Milestone | M 9024

Opus Six
Harry Edison-Eddie Lockjaw Davis Quintet | Simple Sweets | Pablo | 2310806-2

Or So You Thought - ...Or So You Thought
The Doug Sides Ensemble | Perseverance | No Name | CD-001

Oracle
Dimitrios Vassilakis Daedalus Project | Labyrinth | Candid | CCD 79776

Oracle Of The Wise One
Michel Petrucciani | Oracle's Destiny | Owl Records | 032 CD

Oran
Charlie Mariano's Nassim | Charlie Mariano's Nassim | Off The Wall Records | OTW 9801-CD

Orange
Bendik Hofseth Quintet | Colours | Verve | 537627-2
Miles Davis With The Danish Radio Big Band | Aura | CBS | CK 63962
Ruby Braff Quartet | Live At The Regattabar | Arbors Records | ARCD 19131

Orange Ashtray
Ronald Shannon Jackson And The Decoding Society | Eye On You | About Time | AT 1003

Orange Blossom In Summertime
Munich Saxophon Family | Survival Song | JHM Records | JHM 3613

Orange Blue
Herb Ellis And Freddie Green Quintet | Rhythm Willie | Concord | CCD 6010

Orange Coloured Sky
Oscar Peterson With Orchestra | With Respect To Nat | Verve | 557486-2
Ray Gelato Giants | The Full Flavour | Linn Records | AKD 034

Orange Fields
Jimmy Haslip Group | ARC | GRP | GRP 97262

Orange Lady
Gil Evans Orchestra | Tokyo Concert | West Wind | WW 2056

Orange Peel
Count Basie And His Orchestra | Basie Big Band | Pablo | 2310756-2

Orange Was The Colour Of Her Dress Then Blue Silk
Charles Mingus | Great Moments With Charles Mingus | MCA | MCA 2-4128 (802130)
Charles Mingus Sextet | Meditations On Integration | Bandstand | BDCD 1524
Borah Bergman | Bursts Of Joy | Chiaroscuro | CR 158

Oranges Améres
Chris Barber's Jazz And Blues Band | 30 Years Chris Barber:Can't We Get Together | Timeless | CD TTD 517/8

Orava(Squirrel)
Ricky Ford Quartet | Tenor For The Times | Muse | MR 5250

Orb
Comité Imaginaire | Holz Für Europa | FMP | CD 84

Orbis
Andy LaVerne | Buy One, Get One Free | Steeplechase | SCCD 31319

Orbit of LA-BA
Bill Evans Trio | The Complete Bill Evans On Verve | Verve | 527953-2

Orbit(Unless It's You)
Empathy+A Simple Matter Of Conviction | Verve | 837757-2 PMS

Orbital Excursion
Mori-Frith-Dresser | Live At Knitting Factory Vol.2 | Enemy | EMY 112(03512)

Orbits
Miles Davis Quintet | Miles Davis Quintet 1965-1968 | CBS | C6K 67398
Jam Session | Jam Session Vol.10 | Steeplechase | SCCD 31555

Orchids
Thomas Kessler & Group | Thomas Kessler & Group | Laika Records | LK 190-015
Walter Norris-George Mraz Duo | Hues Of Blues | Concord | CCD 4671

Orders To Take Out
Bobby Naughton Unit | The Haunt | Otic | 1005

Ordinary Fool
Mel Tormé With Band And Symphony Orchestra | A New Album | Paddle Wheel | KICJ 128

Oréade
Dick Griffin Orchestra | A Dream For Rahsaan & More | Konnex Records | KCD 5062

Oree Me(alt.take)
Jerry Hahn Quartet | Time Changes | Enja | ENJ-9007 2

Oregon
Chris Barber's Jazz Band | The Outstanding Album | BELL Records | BLR 89300

Oren
Position Alpha | Don't Bring Your Dog! | Dragon | DRLP 50

Orfeo Negro
Marc Moulin Group | Top Secret | Blue Note | 536034-2

Organ Grinder's Blues
Andy Kirk And His Twelve Clouds Of Joy | Live Sessions 1937 | Jazz Anthology | JA 5133

Organ Grinder's Swing
Darji With The Hank Jones Quartet | Darji Meets Hank Jones | Timeless | SJP 171
Jack McDuff Quartet | Brother Jack | Prestige | PR20 7174-2
Jimmie Lunceford And His Orchestra | Big Band Bounce & Boogie:Strictly Lunceford | Affinity | AFS 1003
Jimmy Smith Trio | En Concert Avec Europe 1 | Laserlight | 710379/80
Verve Jazz Masters Vol.60:The Collection | Verve | 529866-2
Jimmy Smith:Best Of The Verve Years | Verve | 527950-2
Organ Grinder Swing | Verve | 543831-2
Jimmy Smith Trio: Salle Pleyel, May 28th, 1965 | Laserlight | 36135
Johnny Otis Band | Creepin' With The Cats: The Legendary DIG Masters Vol.1 | Ace Records | CDCHD 325
Wild Bill Davis Quartet | The Swinging Organ Of Wild Bill Davis:In The Mellow Tone | Fresh Sound Records | FSR-CD 0309

Organic Greenery
George Russell And The Living Time Orchestra | The African Game | Blue Note | 746335-2

Organic Movement
Stu Goldberg Trio | Fancy Glance | Inak | 8614

Organismus Vitalis
Michael Riessler Group | Heloise | Wergo | WER 8008-2

Organistrum
Jane Jarvis Quartet | Jane Jarvis Jams | Arbors Records | ARCD 19152

Orgelpunkt 34 Grad F
A Band Of Friends | René Wohlhauser Werkauswahl 1978-1993 | Creative Works Records | CW CD 1026-2

Orgelstück für Orgel
Lew Soloff Group | My Romance | Paddle Wheel | K32Y 6278

Orgone
The Al Di Meola Project | Kiss My Axe | Inak | 700782

Orient House
Don Cherry Trio | Orient | Affinity | CD AFS 769

Oriental Bass
Aki Takase Septet | Oriental Express | Enja | 9101-2

Oriental Folk Song
Brian Bromberg Group | A New Day | Black-Hawk | BKH 524

Oriental Line
Henrik Johansen's Jazzband | The Golden Years Of Revival Jazz,Vol.13 | Storyville | STCD 5518

Oriental Man
Jacques Gauthé-Alain Marquet Clarinet Serenaders | Paris Blues | Stomp Off Records | CD 1216

Oriental Shuffle
Kristian Jorgensen Quartet With Monty Alexander | Meeting Monty | Stunt Records | STUCD 01212
Quintet Du Hot Club De France | Django Reinhardt:Echoes Of France | Dreyfus Jazz Line | FDM 36726-2
Django Reinhardt-Un Géant Sur Son Image | Melodie | 400052
Marvin Stamm Orchestra | Stampede | Palo Alto | PA 8022

Oriental Spices
Osman Ismen Project | Jazz Eastern | CBS | 489840-2

Oriental Spring
| Soprano Summit At Thatchers | J&M Records | J&MCD 501

Oriental Strut
Turk Murphy And His Jazz Band | Concert In The Park | Merry Makers Record | MMRC-CD-12

Origami
Cliff Habian Group | Tonal Paintings | Milestone | MCD 9161-2

Original Blues
Lil Armstrong | Chicago And All That Jazz! | Verve | MV 2535 IMS

Original Dixieland One Step
Alvin Alcorn Jam Session | Sounds Of New Orleans Vol.5 | Storyville | STCD 6012
Eddie Condon All Stars | Ringside At Condons | Savoy | SV 0231(MG 12055)
Five A Slide | Strike Up The Band! | Black Lion | BLCD 760509
Irving Fazola's Dixielanders | The Music Of New Orleans | RCA | NL 89724 DP
Jack Teagarden And His Orchestra | Jazz Original | Charly | CD 80
Jack Teagarden-Earl Hines All Stars | In England 1957 | Jazz Groove | JG 001 IMS
Miff Mole And His Molers | Jazz Classics In Digital Stereo: Red Nichols And Miff Mole | CDS Records Ltd. | RPCD 627(CD 664)

Original Faubus Fables
Sidney Bechet And His Haitian Orchestra | Tropical Mood | Swingtime(Contact) | ST 1014

Original Jelly Roll Blues
Jelly Roll Morton's Red Hot Peppers | Jelly Roll Morton-Doctor Jazz | RCA | CL 89808 SF
Doctor Jazz | Black & Blue | BLE 59.227 2
The Complete Jelly Roll Morton-Vol.1/2 | RCA | ND 89768

Original Rays
Columbia Dance Orchestra | Le Jazz En France Vol.9:Pionniers Du Jazz Francais 1906-1931 | Pathe | 1552551

Original Untitled Ballad(To Her Ladyship)
Phil Woods Quartet | Here's To My Lady | Chesky | JD 3

Orion
Steps Ahead With Guests | Yin-Yang | NYC-Records | NYC 6001-2

Orion Nebula-
Guillermo Gregorio Group | Ellipsis | HatOLOGY | 511

Orion's View
Billy Brooks' El Babaku | Jazz Meets Africa:Noon In Tunisia-El Babaku | MPS | 531720-2

Orixás
Rajesh Metha | Orka | HatOLOGY | 524

Orlando Di Lata
Graef-Schippa-Moritz | Orlando Frames | Nabel Records:Jazz Network | CD 4690

Orlando's Endless Silver Wake
Orlando Frames | Nabel Records:Jazz Network | CD 4690

Orlando's Evening Prayer
Orlando Frames | Nabel Records:Jazz Network | CD 4690

Orlando's Midtown Anthem
Danielsson-Liebman-Christensen-Stenson | Far North | Curling Legs Prod. | C.L.P. CD 013

Ornaments
Zagreb Jazz Quartet | Animal Dance | Atlantic | AMCY 1100

Ornen
Bright Moments | Return Of The Lost Tribe | Delmark | DE 507

Ornette
Nicolas Simion Quartet feat. Tomasz Stanko | Dinner For Don Carlos | Tutu Records | 888146-2*
Rolf Kühn Group | Inside Out | Intuition Records | INT 3276-2
The Ethnic Heritage Ensemble | The Continuum | Delmark | DE 496

Ornette Never Sleeps
Rabih Abou-Khalil Group | Al-Jadida | Enja | ENJ-6090 2
Brian Trainor Quintet | Brian Trainor:Portraits | Candid | CCD 79731

Ornette's Concept
Albert Sarko Quintet | Blues And Views(Bagdad Christmas) | Enja | 8018-2

Ornette's Tune
Gianni Gebbia Group | Arabesques | SPLASC(H) Records | H 147

Ornithology
Babs Gonzales And His Band | The Bebop Boys | Savoy | WL 70547 (809278)
Bireli Lagrene Group | A Tribute To Django Reinhardt | Jazzpoint | JP 1061 CD
Bud Powell Orchestra | Bebop | Pablo | PACD 2310978-2
Bud Powell Quintet | The Amazing Bud Powell Vol.1 | Blue Note | 532136-2
Bud Powell Trio | Bud Powell:Bouncing With Bud | Dreyfus Jazz Line | FDM 36725-2
The Amazing Bud Powell Vol.1 | Blue Note | 300366
Charlie Parker Quintet | One Night At Birdland | CBS | CBS 88250
Live At Carnegie Hall | Bandstand | BDCD 1518
Charlie Parker Septet | Charlie Parker:The Complete 1944-1948 Small Group Sessions(Studio Recordings-Master Takes),Vol.2 | Blue Moon | BMCD 1008
Eddie Jefferson And His Band | Godfather Of Vocalese | Muse | MCD 6013
Oscar Peterson Trio | The Paris Concert | Pablo | 2PACD 2620112
Paul Bley Trio | BeBopBeBopBeBopBeBop | Steeplechase | SCCD 31259
Bill Ramsey & Juraj Galan | Caldonia And More... | Bear Family Records | BCD 16151 AH

Ornithology-
Bireli Lagrene Group | A Tribute To Django Reinhardt | Jazzpoint | JP 1061 CD
Bireli Lagrene Trio | Live At The Carnegie Hall: A Tribute To Django Reinhardt | Jazzpoint | JP 1040 CD
Charlie Parker Jam Session | Complete Bird In Sweden | Definitive Records | DRCD 11216

Ornithology(alt.take)
Bud Powell Trio | Bud Powell:Complete 1947-1951 Blue Note,Verve & Roost Recordings | The Jazz Factory | JFCD 22847

Ornothoids
Chris Barber's Jazz Band | The Chris Barber Jubilee Album, Vol. 3 | Intercord | 157010

Oro Incienso Y Mirra
Gianluigi Trovesi Nonet | Round About A Midsummer's Dream | Enja | ENJ-9384 2

Orobop
Sylvie Courvoisier Group | Abaton | ECM | 1838/39(157628-2)

Orodruin
Slim Gaillard Trio | The Small Black Groups | Storyville | 4960523

O'Rooney's Overture Hoboken Bounce
Peter A. Schmid Trio With Guests | Profound Sounds In An Empty Reservoir | Creative Works Records | CW CD 1033

Oropendula
Anita O'Day With Orchestra | Cool Heat | Verve | MV 2679 IMS

Orpheo Negro
Donald Byrd Sextet | Star Eyes | Savoy | SJL 1114 (801190)

'Orse At Safari
Herb Geller Quartet | You're Looking At Me | Fresh Sound Records | FSR-CD 5018

Orson's Theme
Bill Evans Trio | I Will Say Goodbye | Original Jazz Classics | OJCCD 761-2(F 9593)
Michel Legrand Orchestra | After The Rain | Original Jazz Classics | 2312139

Orthodox Hymn From Asia Minor
Gulf Stream | Gulf Stream | B.Sharp Records | 1005

Orula
The Houdini's | Headlines-The Houdini's In New York | Timeless | CD SJP 382

Ory's Creole Trombone
Castle Jazz Band | The Famous Castle Jazz Band In Stereo | Good Time Jazz | GTCD 10030-2
Five A Slide | The Music Of King Oliver And Kid Ory | Jazz Colours | 874729-2
Theis/Nyegaard Jazzband | The Golden Years Of Revival Jazz,Sampler | Storyville | 109 1001
Turk Murphy And His Jazz Band | Turk Murphy's San Francisco Jazz-Vol.2 | Good Time Jazz | 12027

Oryssa
Maria Joao & Grupo Cal Viva | Sol | Enja | ENJ-7001 2

Osaka Cool
Jim Hall-Red Mitchell Duo | Jim Hall/Red Mitchell | Artists House | AH 5 IMS

Osaka(part 1&2)
Thelonious Monk And His Orchestra | Who's Afraid Of The Big Band Monk? | CBS | CBS 88034

Oscalypso
Oscar Pettiford All Stars | Oscar Pettiford | Polydor | MP 2346 IMS

Oscar
Stephane Grappelli Quartet | Tribut To | Blue Silver | BS 3007

Oscar's Arrangement
Oscar Klein | Blues Of Summer | Nagel-Heyer | NH 1011

Oscar's Blues
Oscar Klein Quartet | Early Oscar Klein(1954-1964) | RST-Records | 91564-2
Oscar Peterson-Ray Brown Duo | Oscar Peterson:Get Happy | Dreyfus Jazz Line | FDM 36738-2
Tenderly | Verve | MV 2662 IMS

Oscar's Boogie
Oscar Peterson Trio | Masters Of Jazz Vol.7 | RCA | NL 89721 DP
This Is Oscar Peterson | RCA | 2663990-2

Oscar's Boogie(alt.take)
Havana Flute Summit | Havana Flute Summit | Naxos Jazz | 86005-2

TITELVERZEICHNIS

Oscar's Theme
Duke Ellington Orchestra | Only God Can Make A Tree | Musicmasters | 65117-2
Osho Ibi
Adam Rudolph's Moving Pictures | Skyway | Soul Note | 121269-2
Osie Mae
Larry Ridley & The Jazz Legacy Ensemble | Live At Rutgers University | Strata East Records | 660.51.020
Oska-T
Association Urbanetique | Don't Look Back | Enja | ENJ-6056 2
Oslo Sun
Jaki Byard Trio | Foolin' Myself | Soul Note | 121125-2
Osmosis
Zoot Sims Quintet | Zoot! | Original Jazz Classics | OJCCD 228-2(RLP 228)
Osmotin
Cesc Miralta Quartet | Sol De Nit | Fresh Sound Records | FSNT 098 CD
Ossa Nova
Paolo Fresu Quintet | Night On The City | Owl Records | 013425-2
Ossi Di Seppia
Paolo Fresu Sextet | Ossi Di Seppia | SPLASC(H) Records | CD H 350-2
Naked Ear | Acoustik Guitar Duolog | Acoustic Music Records | AMC 1022
Ossobucco
Andy Lumpp Trio | Ostara | Nabel Records:Jazz Network | CD 4682
Ostara
Humphrey Lyttelton And His Band | Lay 'Em Straight! | Calligraph | CLGCD 033
Osteria
Tony Lakatos Quintet | Different Moods | Lipstick Records | LIP 890112
Ostinato
Klaus Doldinger & Passport | Lifelike | Warner | 2292-46478-2
Liam Noble | Close Your Eyes | FMR | FMR CD 25
Paolo Fresu Quintet | Live In Montpellier | SPLASC(H) Records | CD H 301-2
Paul Bley | Tears | Owl Records | 034 CD
Ostinato II
Paolo Fresu Quintet | Ostinato | SPLASC(H) Records | H 106
Ostrich Walk
Alex Welsh And His Jazz Band | Dixieland To Duke-The Melrose Folio | Dormouse | DM 7 IMS
Harry Gold And His Famous Pieces Of Eight | Dixie! | Harlequin | HQ 3001 IMS
Ost-West
Jesus Chucho Valdes | Lucumi | Messidor | 15976 CD
Oszillato
Avishai Cohen Group | Devotion | Stretch Records | SCD 9021-2
Otchi-Tchor-Ni-Ya
Louis Armstrong And His All Stars | Louis Armstrong-My Greatest Songs | MCA | MCD 18347
Otchi-Tchor-Ni-Ya[Dark Eyes]
Yusef Lateef Orchestra | The Blue Yusef Lateef | Rhino | 8122-73717-2
Othelia
Bobby Lyle Group | The Journey | Atlantic | 7567-82138-2
Othello
Chicago Underground Trio | Possible Cube | Delmark | DE 511
Other Roses
Red Rodney & The New Danish Jazzarmy | Society Red | Music Mecca | CD 1003-2
Other Times,Other Places
Christopher Dell Quartet | Other Voices, Other Rooms | L+R Records | CDLR 45093
Otherlands
Les McCann Quartet | Straight Ahead | Blue Note | 064 240331-1(BT 85105)
O'Thy Beautiful
Art Blakey Percussion Ensemble | Afro Blue | Blue Note | 780701-2
Otis Blues
Otis Spann | Otis Spann And His Piano | Crosscut | CCR 1003(Candid)
Otis In The Dark
Günther Klatt & New York Razzmatazz | Fa Mozzo | Tutu Records | 888138-2
Otok Is Around
Joaquin Chacón Group | San | Fresh Sound Records | FSNT 015 CD
Otono
Astor Piazzolla Group | Live at Cine Teatro Gran Rex De Buenos Aires | West Wind Latina | 2212 CD
Otono Porteno
José Luis Gámez Quartet | Colores | Fresh Sound Records | FSNT 028 CD
Otra De Piratas
Gabriel Pérez Group | Alfonsina | Jazz 4 Ever Records:Jazz Network | J4E 4751
Otra Dia
Joachim Kühn And The Radio Philharmonie Hannover NDR With Jazz Soloists | Europeana | ACT | 9220-2
Otra Jazzpana
Gonzalo Rubalcaba Trio | Supernova | Blue Note | 531172-2
Otra Mirada
Joaquin Chacón Group | San | Fresh Sound Records | FSNT 015 CD
Otro Comienzo
Helmut Brandt's Mainstream Orchestra | Chez Pep | BIT | 10599
Otublohu
Heiner Goebbels Group | Ou Bien Le Debarquement Desastreux | ECM | 1552
Ou Bien Le Débarquement Désastreux(part 1-31)
Häns'che Weiss-Vali Mayer Duo | Just Play II | MMM Records | CD 1303
Ou Es Tu...?
Charlie Haden Quartet West | Always Say Goodbye | Verve | 521501-2
Ou Es-Tu Mon Amour
Django Reinhardt Quintet | Djangology 49 | Bluebird | NL 90448
Stochelo Rosenberg Trio | Seresta | Hot Club Records | HCRCD 059
Ouch!
Nils Landgren First Unit And Guests | Nils Landgren-The First Unit | ACT | 9292-2
Ahmed Abdullah Sextet | Jazz Sounds Of Africa | Prestige | PRCD 24279-2
Oud Blues
Diz Disley And His String Quartet | Best Of British Jazz From The BBC Jazz Club Vol.4 | Upbeat Jazz | URCD 122
Oui Sait?(Quizas)
Vaughn Monroe And His Orchestra | Vaughn Monroe And His Orchestra 1943 | Circle | CCD-45
Oum Said
Africa Djole | The Concert In Berlin '78 | FMP | CD 1
Ounce To The Bounce
Dave Soldier Group With Voices | Smut | Avant | AVAN 019
Our Blues
Enrico Pieranunzi | The Day After The Silence | EdiPan | NPG 800
Sadik Hakim Trio | Witches Gobelins etc. | Steeplechase | SCCD 31091
Our Cow Pat Pride(Mi Si Bo Kolo Kagele)
Alfred 23 Harth Group | Gestalt Et Jive | Moers Music | 02038
Our Day Will Come
Houston Person Sextet | The Lion And His Pride | Muse | MCD 5480
Our Delight
Bill Evans Trio | The Legendary Bill Evans Trio-The Legendary 1960 Birdland Sessions | Cool & Blue | C&B-CD 106
Cannonball Adderley Quintet | The Cannonball Adderley Collection Vol.5:At The Lighthouse | Landmark | CAC 1305-2(882344)
Dizzy Gillespie And His Orchestra | Bebop Enters Sweden | Dragon | DRCD 318
Eddie Lockjaw Davis-Johnny Griffin Quintet | Live At Minton's | Prestige | P 24099
Red Garland Quintet | John Coltrane-The Prestige Recordings | Prestige | 16 PCD 4405-2
Red Garland Quintet feat.John Coltrane | Jazz Junction | Prestige | P 24023
Scott Hamilton Quartet | Tenorshoes | Concord | CCD 4127
Shelly Manne And His Men | At The Blackhawk Vol.1 | Contemporary | C 7577
Tadd Dameron-Fats Navarro Quintet | Live At The Birdland | Jazz Anthology | JA 5176
Tadd Dameron-Fats Navarro Sextet | Fats Navarro/Tadd Dameron:Complete Blue Note & Capitol Sessions | Definitive Records | DRCD 11191
Our Delight(alt.master)
Tadd Dameron Orchestra | The Magic Touch | Original Jazz Classics | OJCCD 143-2(RLP 9419)
Our Father
Mary Lou Williams Group | Mary Lou's Mass | Mary Records | M 102
Our Father Abraham
Charles Fambrough Group | The Proper Angle | CTI Records | CTI 1002-2
Our Feelings-
Houston Person Quartet | Christmas With Houston Person And Friends | Muse | MCD 5530
Our Game
Geri Allen Sextet | The Nurturer | Blue Note | 795139-2
Our Hour
Matthew Shipp-Joe Morris | Thesis | HatOLOGY | 506
Our Kind Of Sabi
Stan Getz Quartet | Stan Getz With European Friends | LRC Records | CDC 7679(874365)
Our Love
Frank Sinatra With The Tommy Dorsey Orchestra | The Popular Sinatra Vol.1 | RCA | 2668711-2
Our Love Is Here To Stay
Ben Webster Quartet | Live At The Jazzhus Montmartre,Vol.1 | Jazz Colours | 874710-2
Benny Carter Quartet | 3,4,5 The Verve Small Group Sessions | Verve | 849395-2 PMS
Bill Evans Trio | The Complete Bill Evans On Verve | Verve | 527953-2
The Complete Bill Evans On Verve | Verve | 527953-2
Trio '65 | Verve | 2304517 IMS
Live In Stockholm 1965 | Royal Jazz | RJD 519
Billie Holiday And Her All Stars | Billie Holiday:The Great American Songbook | Verve | 523003-2
Billie Holiday And Her Band | Verve Jazz Masters 47:Billie Holiday Sings Standards | Verve | 527650-2
Billie Holiday And Her Orchestra | Billie Holiday:The Quintessential Vol.7(1938-1939) | CBS | CK 46180
Bud Powell Quartet | Alternate Takes | Blue Note | BST 84430
Dave Brubeck | Dave Brubeck Plays And Plays And Plays... | Original Jazz Classics | OJCCD 716-2(F 3259)
Dave Grusin Group | The Gershwin Connection | GRP | GRP 20052
Dexter Gordon Quartet | Blue Note Plays Gershwin | Blue Note | 520808-2
Dexter Gordon:The Complete Blue Note Sixties Sessions | Blue Note | 834200-2
Dinah Shore With Orchestra | The Best Of Dinah Shore | Capitol | 792895-2
Dinah Washington With Orchestra | Mad About The Boy-The Best Of Dinah Washington | Mercury | 512214-2
Dinah Washington With The Hal Mooney Orchestra | Verve Jazz Masters 19:Dinah Washington | Verve | 518200-2
Ella Fitzgerald And Louis Armstrong With The Oscar Peterson Quartet | The Best Of Ella Fitzgerald And Louis Armstrong On Verve | Verve | 537909-2
Ella And Louis Again, Vol.2 | Verve | 711122 IMS
Ella And Louis Again | Verve | 825374-2
Ella Fitzgerald With Orchestra | Essential Ella | Verve | 523990-2
Ella Fitzgerald With The Nelson Riddle Orchestra | Ella Sings Gershwin-Vol. 2 | Metro | 2682023 IMS
Sings The Ira And George Gershwin Songbook | Verve | 825024-2
Erroll Garner Trio | The Erroll Garner Collection Vol.2: Dancing On The Ceiling | EmArCy | 834935-2 PMS
Four Freshmen And 5 Trombones | Four Freshmen And 5 Trombones | Capitol | 300004(TOCJ 6117)
Herb Geller Trio | Birdland Stomp | Enja | 5019 (807540)
Jackie McLean Quartet | McLean's Scene | Original Jazz Classics | OJCCD 098-2(NJ 8212)
John Pizzarelli Trio With The Don Sebesky Orchestra | Our Love Is Here To Stay | RCA | 6367501-2
Johnny Lytle Trio(Quartet) | Got That Feeling/Moon Child | Milestone | MCD 47093-2
Karin Krog With The Egil Kapstad Quartet | Gershwin With Karin Krog | Polydor | 2382045 IMS
Lucky Thompson With Gerard Pochonet And His Orchestra | Lullaby In Rhythm | Biograph | BLP 12061
Marcus Roberts Trio | Gershwin For Lovers | CBS | 477752-2
Nat Simpkins Quartet | Cookin' With Some Barbeque | Muse | MCD 5510
Oliver Jones With Orchestra | From Lush To Lively | Justin Time | JUST 73-2
Oscar Peterson Trio | Oscar Peterson:The Gershwin Songbooks | Verve | 529698-2
The Way I Really Play | MPS | 821287-1
Red Norvo Trio | The Red Norvo Trios | Prestige | P 24108
Saxophone Connection | Saxophone Connection | L+R Records | CDLR 45046
Singers Unlimited | The Singers Unlimited:Magic Voices | MPS | 539130-2
A Capella III | MPS | 68245
Stan Getz Quartet | Stan Getz And The 'Cool' Sounds | Verve | 547317-2
Stan Getz:East Of The Sun-The West Coast Sessions | Verve | 531935-2
Our Love Is Here To Stay-
Modern Jazz Quartet | The Complete Modern Jazz Quartet Prestige & Pablo Recordings | Prestige | 4PRCD 4438-2
The MJQ Box | Prestige | 7711-2
Our Love Is Here To Stay(alt.take 1)
Ben Webster With Orchestra And Strings | Music For Loving:Ben Webster With Strings | Verve | 527774-2
Our Love Is Here To Stay(alt.take 2)
Stan Getz Quartet | West Coast Jazz | Verve | 557549-2
Our Love Is Here To Stay(alt.take)
Stan Getz:East Of The Sun-The West Coast Sessions | Verve | 531935-2
Our Love Will Never Die
Tuey Connell Group | Songs For Joy And Sadness | Minor Music | 801095
Our Love Will Never End
Nina Simone With Horace Ott's Orchestra | Broadway-Blues-Ballads | Verve | 518190-2
Our Man In Louisiana
Leni Stern Group | Ten Songs | Lipstick Records | LIP 890092
Our Minuet
Fred Houn & The Afro-Asian Music Ensemble | We Refused To Be Used And Abused | Soul Note | 121167-2
Our Monday Date
Louis Armstrong And His Orchestra | Louis Armstrong And His Big Band Vol.1-The Maturity | Black & Blue | BLE 59.225 2
Our Neighbours Party
Guitar Slim And His Band | The Things That I Used To Do | Ace Records | CDCHD 318
Our Prayer
Dixie Hummingbirds | Live | Mobile Fidelity | MFCD 771
Our Revels Now Are Ended
Jenny Evans And Her Quintet | Nuages | ESM Records | ESM 9308
Enrico Pieranunzi Trio | Deep Down | Soul Note | 121121-2
Our Roots(Began In Africa)
Charles Tolliver Quartet | Grand Max | Black Lion | BLCD 760145
Our Song
Art Pepper Quintet With Strings | Art Pepper:The Complete Galaxy Recordings | Galaxy | 16GCD 1016-2
Carmen McRae With The Johnny Keating Orchestra | For Once In My Life | Atlantic | AMCY 1064
Our Song(alt.take)
Art Pepper Quintet With Strings | Art Pepper:The Complete Galaxy Recordings | Galaxy | 16GCD 1016-2
Charlie Haden Quartet West | Always Say Goodbye | Verve | 521501-2
Our Spanish Love Song
Charlie Haden-Pat Metheny | Beyond The Missouri Sky | Verve | 537130-2
Gonzalo Rubalcaba Group | Suite 4 y 20 | Blue Note | 780054-2
Teodross Avery Quartet | In Other Words | GRP | GRP 97982
Our Thing
Joe Henderson Quintet | The Blue Note Years-The Best Of Joe Henderson | Blue Note | 795627-2
Our Thing | Blue Note | 525647-2
Joe Henderson-The Blue Note Years | Blue Note | 789287-2
Our Time
Teodross Avery Quartet | In Other Words | GRP | GRP 97982
Our Tune
Michel Petrucciani Trio | Michel Petrucciani:The Blue Note Years | Blue Note | 789916-2
Sonny Stitt Band | Stitt's Bits | Prestige | VIJ 5037
Our Waltz
Frankie Randall With The Marty Paich Orchestra | A Swingin' Touch | Fresh Sound Records | NL 45978(RCA)
Kent Carter String Trio | The Willisau Suites | ITM-Pacific | ITMP 970077
Ourb
Adam Rudolph's Moving Pictures | Skyway | Soul Note | 121269-2
Out
Willie Williams Quartet | Spirit Willie | Enja | ENJ-7045 2
Out Beyond Ideas
Jimmy Witherspoon With Groove Holmes | Cry The Blues | Bulldog | BDL 1012
Out Coming Voices
Sunny Murray Trio | 13 Steps On Glass | Enja | 8094-2
Out For A Walk
Odean Pope Trio | Out For A Walkf Happiness | Moers Music | 02072 CD
Out Front
Rick Hollander Quartet | Out Here | Timeless | CD SJP 309
Out In Cold Again
Jukkis Uotila Band | Live | Stunt Records | STUCD 18909
Out In Space
Dave Douglas Sextet | In Our Lifetime | New World Records | 80471-2
Out In The Fields
Christoph Oeding Trio | Taking A Chance | Mons Records | MR 874784
Out 'N In
Joe Henderson Quartet | Joe Henderson:The Milestone Years | Milestone | 8MCD 4413-2
Dogs Don't Sing In The Rain | Bones For Breakfast | Edition Collage | EC 472-2
Out Of A Bandbox
Wind Moments | Take Twelve On CD | TT 009-2
Erik Truffaz Quartet Quintet | Out Of A Dream | Blue Note | 855855-2
Out Of A Dream
David Friedman Quartet | Shades Of Change | Enja | ENJ-5017 2
Out Of Body
Dave Stryker Quartet | Blue Degrees | Steeplechase | SCCD 31315
Out Of Habit
Gary Thomas And Seventh Quadrant | By Any Means Necessary | JMT Edition | 834432-2
Out Of June
Kermit Ruffins Septet | The Big Butter & Egg Man | Justice Records | JR 1102-2
Out Of Many People, One
Edward Vesala Trio With Orchestra | Bad Luck Good Luck | Leo Records | 015
Out Of My Mind
Gabriele Hasler Group | Listening To Löbering | Foolish Music | FM 211389
Listening To Löbering | Foolish Music | FM 211389
Out Of My Mind(2)
Benny Carter And His Chocolate Dandies | Coleman Hawkins & Benny Carter | Swing | SW 8403 IMS
Out Of Nowhere
Al Porcino Big Band | Al Porcino Big Band Live! | Organic Music | ORGM 9717
Al Sears Quintet | Swing's The Thing | Original Jazz Classics | OJCCD 838-2(SV 2018)
Art Tatum | Art Tatum-The Complete Pablo Solo Masterpieces | Pablo | 7 PACD 4404-2
RCA Victor 80th Anniversary Vol.3:1940-1949 | RCA | 2668779-2
Art Tatum Trio | Art Tatum:Complete Capitol Recordings | Capitol | 821325-2
Art Tatum:Complete Capitol Recordings | Definitive Records | DRCD 11192
Buddy DeFranco Trio | Do Nothing Till You Hear From Us! | Concord | CCD 4851
California Jam Sessions | Chet Baker:California Jam Sessions | Definitive Records | DRCD 11232
Charlie Parker Quintet | Charlie Parker:Now's The Time | Dreyfus Jazz Line | FDM 36724-2
One Night At Birdland | CBS | CBS 88250
Charlie Parker Sessions Live Vol.1 | Zeta | ZET 703
Charlie Parker With Strings | The Verve Years (1950-51) | Verve | 2-2512 IMS
Charlie Parker The Immortal Sessions Vol.2:1949-1953 | SAGA Jazz Classics | EC 3319-2
Charlie Shavers With Orchestra | The Most Intimate Charlie Shavers | Bethlehem | BET 6019-2(BCP 27)
Coleman Hawkins And His All Star Jam Band | Django Reinhardt All Star Sessions | Capitol | 531577-2
Django Reinhardt:Djangology | EMI Records | 780659-2
Don Byas All Star Quintet | Don Byas Complete American Small Group Recordings | Definitive Records | DRCD 11213
Don Lanphere Quintet Feat. Jon Pugh | From Out Of Nowhere | Hep | 2019
Eddie Lockjaw Davis Quartet | That's All | Kingdom Jazz | Gate 7019
Eric Dolphy Quartet | The Complete Uppsala Concert | Jazz Door | JD 1253/54
Harry James And His Orchestra | Harry James.His Orchestra And The Boogie Woogie Trio | Affinity | CD AFS 1009
Henri Renaud All Stars | Jazz Legacy 30: J.J.Johnson/Milt Jackson-A Date In New York Vol.1 | Vogue | 500080
Jack Teagarden And His Orchestra | A Standard Library Of Jazz Vol. 2 | Storyville | SLP 704
Joe Newman And His Orchestra | Joe Newman With Woodwinds | Fresh Sound Records | FSR 663(Roulette R 52014)
Johnnes Rediske Quintet | Deutsches Jazz Fesival 1954/1955 | Bear Family Records | BCD 15430
Johnny Smith Quartet | The Sound Of The Johnny Smith Guitar | Roulette | 531792-2
Kenny Davern And The Rhythm Men | Kenny Davern And The Rhythm Men | Arbors Records | ARCD 19147
Milt Jackson Septet | The Birdlanders Vol.1 | Original Jazz Classics | OJCCD 1930-2
Morgana King And Her Quintet | Everything Must Change | Muse | MCD 5190
Paquito D'Rivera Group | Who's Smooking?! | Candid | CCD 79523
Paul Desmond-Gerry Mulligan Quartet | Two Of A Mind | RCA | 2179620-2
Jazz Special-Two Of A Mind | RCA | CL 42788 AG
Phil Woods Quartet | The Best Of The Jazz Saxophones Vol.2 | LRC Records | CDC 8529
Prestige All Stars | Two Guitars | Original Jazz Classics | OJCCD 216-2(P 7119)

Richard 'Groove' Holmes-Jimmy McGriff Sextet | The Best Of The Jazz Organs | LRC Records | CDC 9006
Stan Getz Quartet | Stan Getz:Imagination | Dreyfus Jazz Line | FDM 36733-2
Unearthed Masters-Vol.2: Stan Getz | JAM | 5007 IMS
Tal Farlow Sextet | A Recital By Tal Farlow | Verve | MV 2586 IMS
Tal Farlow Trio | Tal Farlow Complete 1956 Private Recordings | Definitive Records | DRCD 11263
Tenor Conclave With The Rein De Graaff Trio | Tenor Conclave | Timeless | CD SJP 306
Walter Blanding Quintet | The Olive Tree | Criss Cross | Criss 1186

Out Of Nowhere (Concept 1)
Joe Pass | I Remember Charlie Parker | Original Jazz Classics | OJC 602(2312109)

Out Of Nowhere (Concept 2)
Charlie Parker Quintet | Charlie Parker Story On Dial Vol.2:New York Days | Capitol | 300010(TOCJ 6124)

Out Of Silence
Howard Rumsey's Lighthouse All-Stars | Jimmy Giuffre:Complete 1947-1952 Master Takes | Definitive Records | DRCD 11212

Out Of Strauss
Philip DeGruy | Innuendo Out The Other | NYC-Records | NYC 6013-2

Out Of The Blue
Miles Davis Sextet | Sonny Rollins:Complete 1949-1951 Prestige Studio Recordings | Definitive Records | DRCD 11240
Miles Davis:Quintet & Sextet | Fresh Sound Records | FSCD 1000
Toon Roos Quartet | The Human Feel | September | CD 5114

Out Of The City
Allen Toussaint Group | Life, Love And Faith | Warner | WPCP 4414

Out Of The Gallion
Humphrey Lyttelton And His Band | Jazz At The Royal Festival Hall/Jazz At The Conway Hall | Dormouse | DM 22 CD

Out Of The Mesa
Stefano Battaglia Trio | Confession | SPLASC(H) Records | CD H 344-2

Out Of The Night
Ted Weems And His Orchestra | Here's That Band Again | Naxos Jazz | 8.120619 CD
Zeather | Chen Yu Lips | Discovery | DS 867 IMS

Out Of The Past
Art Blakey And The Jazz Messengers | At The Club St.Germain | RCA | ND 74897(2)
Benny Golson Quintet | One More Mem'ry | Timeless | SJP 180

Out Of The Rim(1)
Hans Koller Groups | Out Of The Rim | IN+OUT Records | 7014-2

Out Of The Rim(2)
Out Of The Rim | IN+OUT Records | 7014-2

Out Of The Rim(3)
Out Of The Rim | IN+OUT Records | 7014-2

Out Of The Rim(4)
Out Of The Rim | IN+OUT Records | 7014-2

Out Of The Rim(5)
Out Of The Rim | IN+OUT Records | 7014-2

Out Of The Rim(6)
Out Of The Rim | IN+OUT Records | 7014-2

Out Of The Rim(7)
June Christy With The Pete Rugolo Orchestra | The Song Is June | Capitol | 855455-2

Out Of The Shadow
Sumi Tonooka Quartet | Taking Time | Candid | CCD 79502

Out Of This World
Bill Perkins-Bud Shank Quintet | Serious Swingers | Contemporary | CCD 14031-2
Bud Shank Quartet | Live At The Haig | Choice | CHCD 71030
Live At The Haig | Concept | VL 2 IMS
Cal Tjader Quartet With Strings | Plays Harold Arlen | Original Jazz Classics | OJC 285(F 8072)
Ella Fitzgerald With The Billy May Orchestra | The Complete Ella Fitzgerald Song Books of Harold Arlen, Irving Berlin, Duke Ellington, George & Ira Gershwin, Jerome Kern, Johnny Mercer, Cole Porter And Rogers & Hart | Verve | 519832-2
Frank Strazzeri Trio | Make Me Rainbows | Fresh Sound Records | FSR 107 (835209)
Gerry Mulligan Concert Jazz Band | En Concert Avec Europe 1 | Laserlight | 710382/83
John Coltrane Quartet | John Coltrane:The Classic Quartet-Complete Impulse Studio Recordings | Impulse(MCA) | 951280-2
John Coltrane:Standards | Impulse(MCA) | 549914-2
John Coltrane Sextet | Live In Seatle | Impulse(MCA) | GRP 21462
Kai Winding-J.J.Johnson Quintet | Kai & Jay! | Affinity | AFF 161
LeeAnn Ledgerwood Trio | Walkin' Up | Steeplechase | SCCD 31541
Lew Tabackin Quartet | Nature | Inner City | IC 1028 IMS
Mel Tormé With The George Shearing Trio | A Vintage Year | Concord | CJ 341
Pepper Adams-Donald Byrd Quintet | Out Of This World Vol.2 | Fresh Sound Records | FSR 669(Warwick W 2041-2)
Weslia Whitefield With The Mike Greensill Trio And Warren Vaché | My Shining Hour | HighNote Records | HCD 7012

Out Of This World(remake)
Terje Rypdal Group | Skywards | ECM | 1608(533768-2)

Out Of This World(Sinfonietta)
David Moss Duos | Time Stories | Intakt Records | CD 054

Out Of Weimar-
Joyce Cooling Group | Keeping Cool | Inak | 30532

Out On A Limb
Lennie Tristano Trio | The Essential Keynote Collection:The Complete Lennie Tristano | Verve | 830921-2

Out Pours(Kongo)
Maneri/Morris/Maneri | Out Right Now | HatOLOGY | 561

Out South
Junior Mance Quartet | That Lovin' Feelin' | Milestone | MCD 47097-2
Junior Mance Trio | Happy Time | Original Jazz Classics | VIJ 5049

Out The Window
Count Basie And His Orchestra | Big Band Bounce & Boggie:Swingin' The Blues | Affinity | AFS 1010

Out There
Eric Dolphy Quartet | Out There | New Jazz | NJSA 8252-6
Eric Dolphy:The Complete Prestige Recordings | Prestige | 9 PRCD-4418-2
Kenny Burrell Quintet | Sunup To Sundown | Contemporary | CCD 14065-2

Out There Alone
Karl Berger-Dave Holland-Ed Blackwell | Transit | Black Saint | 120092-2

Out To Lunch
Barbara Thompson's Paraphernalia | A Cry From The Heart | VeraBra Records | CDVBR 2021-2
Buddy DeFranco Quintet | Chip Off The Old Bop | Concord | CCD 4527
Jerome Harris Sextet | Hidden In Plain View | New World Records | 80472-2

Outa Town
David Becker Tribune | In Motion | Bluemoon | R 27-7916-2

Outback Spirits
Michal Urbaniak Quartet | Live In New York | L+R Records | CDLR 45041

Outer Space Were I Cam From(recitation)
Wolfgang Puschnig-Jamaladeen Tacuma Group With Guests | Journey Into The Gemini Territory | ITM-Pacific | ITMP 970091

Outfits
Freddie Hubbard Septet | Blue Spirits | Blue Note | 870674-3

Outhipped
Arild Andersen Quartet | Clouds In My Mind | ECM | 1059

Outlaw
Radius | Sightseeing | Ear-Rational | ECD 1017

Outlaws
Jeremy Steig-Eddie Gomez | Outlaws | Enja | ENJ-2098 2

Outlook
Horst Jankowski Quartet | Jankowskinetik | MPS | 9808189

Out'n Ground
Barry Finnerty Quintet | Straight Ahead | Arabesque Recordings | AJ 0116

Outono
Albert Mangelsdorff-Karl Berger | Albert Mangelsdorff And His Friends | MPS | 067375-2

Outox
Out Of The Blue | O.T.B. | Blue Note | BT 85118 Digital

Outra Vez
Clementine With The Johnny Griffin Quartet | Continent Bleu | Orange Blue | OB 004 CD

Outrance
Jack Dieval And The J.A.C.E. All-Stars | Jazz In Paris:Jack Diéval-Jazz Aux Champs Elysées | EmArCy | 018419-2

Outro
Heiner Stadler Jazz Alchemy | Jazz Alchemy | Tomato | 2696702

Outro-Guiding Light
Heiri Känzig Quartet | Grace Of Gravity | Plainisphare | PL 1267-102 CD

Outside
George Braith Quartet | Soul Stream | Blue Note | 870167-0

Outside Balimba
Hank Crawford Orchestra | The Best Of The Jazz Saxophone | LRC Records | CDC 8520

Outside The Dance Hall
Kjell Jansson Quartet | Back From Where We Came | Touché Music | TMcCD 009

Outside The Grotto
Joe Maneri-Mat Maneri | Blessed | ECM | 1661(557365-2)

Outside The Whole Thing
Enrico Rava Quartet | AH | ECM | 1166

Outskirts Of Town
Buddy Guy Blues Band | The Blues Giant | Black & Blue | BLE 59.900 2
Brötzmann, van Hove, Bennink + Albert Mangelsdorff | Outspan Nr. 1 | FMP | 0180

Outubro (October)
Ketil Bjornstad Group | The Sea II | ECM | 1633(537341-2)

Outward Bound
Eric Kloss Quintet | Eric Kloss & The Rhythm Section | Prestige | PCD 24125-2(P 7689/7793)

Over
The Trio Electric Child | The Trio Electric Child | Ponta Flowers | CDPIA 010

Over And Gone
Flim & The BB's | The Further Adventures | dmp Digital Music Productions | CD 462

Over And Out
Vital Information | Live Around The World Where We Come From Tour '98-'99 | Intuition Records | INT 3296-2
Bill Saxton Quartet | Atymony | Jazzline | JL 11136-2

Over And Over
Thurston Harris With Band | Little Bitty Pretty One | Pathe | 1546651(Aladdin)

Over Big Top
Terje Rypdal Group | Odyssey | ECM | 1067/8

Over Birkerot
Enrico Pieranunzi/Enrico Rava | Nausicaa | Quadrivium | SCA 037

Over Crimson Stones
Bob Smith Group | Bob's Diner | dmp Digital Music Productions | CD 471

Over Heat
Mani Neumeir Group | Privat | ATM Records | ATM 3803-AH
Fred Van Hove | Verloren Maandag | FMP | SAJ 11

Over In The Burying Ground
Arne Birger's Jazzsjak | The Golden Years Of Revival Jazz,Vol.8 | Storyville | STCD 5513

Over In The Gloryland
Bunk's Brass Band | Bunk's Brass Band And Dance Band | American Music | AMCD-6
Chris Barber's Jazz Band | In The Beginning... | Black Lion | BLCD 760520

Over in The New Burying Ground
Jan Harrington And Friends | I Feel The Spirit | Nagel-Heyer | NHR SP 7

Over My Head
Montreal Jubilation Gospel Choir | Jubilation VI 'Looking Back'-Special 20th Anniversary Compilation | Blues Beacon | BLU-1022 22

Over On 4th Street
Peter Bolte-Marcio Doctor | Zeitraum | Jazz Haus Musik | JHM 0113 CD

Over Silence And Secrecy
Charly Augschöll Quartet | Bus Stop | Koch Records | 322 424

Over The Hill Is Home
Take 6 | Tonight Take 6 | Warner | 9362-47611-2

Over The Hill Is Home(Intro)
Cool Blue | House In The Country | Foolish Music | FM 211591

Over The Hills
Michael Chertock | Cinematic Piano-Solo Piano Music From The Movies | Telarc Digital | CD 80357

Over The Rainbow
André Previn Trio | Uptown | Telarc Digital | CD 83303
Art Pepper Quartet | Art & Zoot | West Wind | WW 2071
Art Pepper:The Complete Galaxy Recordings | Galaxy | 16GCD 1016-2
Art Pepper:The Complete Galaxy Recordings | Galaxy | 16GCD 1016-2
Art Pepper:The Complete Galaxy Recordings | Galaxy | 16GCD 1016-2
Art Pepper:The Complete Galaxy Recordings | Galaxy | 16GCD 1016-2
Landscape | Original Jazz Classics | OJCCD 676-2(GXY 5128)
Tokyo Encore | Dreyfus Jazz Line | FDM 36551-2
Art Pepper-George Cables Duo | Tete-A-Tete | Original Jazz Classics | OJCCD 843-2(GXY 5147)
Art Pepper:The Complete Galaxy Recordings | Galaxy | 16GCD 1016-2
Art Tatum | Art Tatum-The Standard Transcriptions | Music & Arts | CD 919
Art Tatum:Over The Rainbow | Dreyfus Jazz Line | FDM 36727-2
Art Tatum-The Complete Jazz Chronicle Solo Session | Storyville | STCD 8253
The Standard Sessions: Art Tatum 1935-1943 Transcriptions | Music & Arts | CD 673
Standards | Black Lion | CD 877646-2
In Private | Fresh Sound Records | FSR-CD 0127
Bob Crosby And His Orchestra | Bob Crosby And His Orchestra Vol.9(1939):Them There Eyes | Halcyon | DHDL 128
Cal Tjader Quartet With Strings | Plays Harold Arlen | Original Jazz Classics | OJC 285(F 8072)
Dick Hyman | Dick Hyman Plays The Great American Songbook | Musicmasters | 65120-2
Don Byas Et Ses Rythmes | Don Byas Complete 1946-1951 European Small Group Master Takes | Definitive Records | DRCD 11214
Don Menza & Frank Strazzeri | Ballads | Fresh Sound Records | FSR 103 (807728)
Ella Fitzgerald With The Billy May Orchestra | The Silver Collection: Ella Fitzgerald-The Songbooks | Verve | 823445-2 PMS
The Complete Ella Fitzgerald Song Books of Harold Arlen, Irving Berlin, Duke Ellington, George & Ira Gershwin, Jerome Kern, Johnny Mercer, Cole Porter And Rogers & Hart | Verve | 519832-2
The Harold Arlen Songbook | Verve | 817526-1 IMS
Erroll Garner Trio | Penthouse Serenade | Savoy | SV 0162(MG 12002)
George Cables | Maybeck Recital Hall Series Volume Thirty-Five | Concord | CCD 4630
Joe Lee Wilson Quintet | Secrets From The Sun | Inner City | IC 1042 IMS
Junior Cook Quartet | The Place To Be | Steeplechase | SCCD 31240
Karol Adam Ensemble | Gipsy Fascination | G&J Records | GJ 2001
Keith Jarrett | La Scala | ECM | 1640(537268-2)
Kenia And The Jay Ashby Quintet With Michal Urbaniak | Live At Warsaw Jazz Festival 1991 | Jazzmen Records | 660.50.006
Louis Smith Quartet | Once In A While | Steeplechase | SCCD 31464
Martial Solal | Jazz 'n (e)motion:Martial Solal | RCA | 2155932-2
Mr.Acker Bilk And His Paramount Jazz Band | The Golden Years Of Revival Jazz,Vol.2 | Storyville | STCD 5507
Nana Mouskouri With The Berlin Radio Big Band | Nana Swings | Mercury | 074394-2
New York Unit | Over The Rainbow | Paddle Wheel | KICJ 136
Oscar Peterson Trio | Oscar Peterson Plays The Harold Arlen Song Book | Verve | 589103-2
Paul Gonsalves-Earld Hines Quartet | Classic Ballads | Jazz Colours | 874741-2
Richard Williams Quintet | New Horn In Town | Candid | CCD 79003
Rita Reys With The Lars Gullin Quartet | Lars Gullin 1953,Vol.2:Moden Sounds | Dragon | DRCD 234
Rob Parton's Jazztech Big Band | The Count Is In | Seabreeze | CDSB 2047(874256)
Ronnie Mathews | Ronnie Matthews At Cafe Des Copains | Sackville | SKCD2-2026
Sarah Vaughan And Her Trio | The Complete Sarah Vaughan Live In Japan | Mobile Fidelity | MFCD 844-2
Stan Kenton And His Orchestra | Sketches On Standards | Creative World |
Stanley Jordan Trio | Stolen Moments | Blue Note | 797159-2
Weslia Whitefield With The Mike Greensill Trio And Warren Vaché | My Shining Hour | HighNote Records | HCD 7012
Zoot Sims With The Nederlands Metropole Orchestra | Only A Rose | Koch Jazz | 3-6916-2

Over The Rainbow-
Sonny Clark | Sonny Clark 1954 Memorial Album | The Jazz Factory | JFCD 22834

Over The Rainbow(alt.take)
Art Pepper-George Cables Duo | Art Pepper:The Complete Galaxy Recordings | Galaxy | 16GCD 1016-2
Art Tatum | Art Tatum-The Complete Jazz Chronicle Solo Session | Storyville | STCD 8253
Dizzy Atmosphere | Dizzy Atmosphere | Original Jazz Classics | OJCCD 1762-2

Over The Waves
Brunies Brothers Dixieland Jazz Band | Brunies Brothers | American Music | AMCD-77
George Lewis Quartet | George Lewis:Trios & Bands | American Music | AMCD-4

Over There
Glenn Miller And The Army Air Force Band | Glenn Miller And The Army Air Force Band | RCA | ND 89767
Golden Gate Quartet | Spirituals To Swing 1955-69 | EMI Records | 791569-2
World Trio | World Trio | VeraBra Records | CDVBR 2052-2
David Murray Quartet | Tenors | DIW | DIW 881 CD

Over Your Shoulder
Walter Roland | Sonny Scott(1933) | Story Of Blues | CD 3525-2

Overdose
J.J.Johnson Quintet | Mr.Jay Jay Johnson-Live | Queen-Disc | 046

Overdrive
Keshavan Maslak Trio | Humanplexity | LEO | LR 101

Overlap
Jon Lloyd Quartet | By Confusion | Hat Art | CD 6198

Overmade Fullt Av Nade
Art Farmer Quartet | Art Farmer In Europe | Enja | 9113-2

Overnight
Wayne Horvitz Trio | Todos Santos | Sound Aspects | sas CD 019

Overtime
Gene Krupa Sextet | The Exciting Gene Krupa | Enoch's Music | 57271033
James Blood Ulmer Quartet | Jazz Unlimited | IN+OUT Records | 7017-2
Jeff Jerolamon Quintet | Jeff Jerolamon's Swing Thing! | Candid | CCD 79538

Overtoned
Sun Ra And His Solar Arkestra | Sun Ra Visit Planet Earth/Interstellar Low Ways | Evidence | ECD 22039-2

Overtones Song-
A Tipico Trio | Where The Reeds Are | SPLASC(H) Records | CD H 312-2

Overture
Herb Geller Quartet | Playing Jazz:The Musical Autobiography Of Herb Geller | Fresh Sound Records | FSR-CD 5011
Ku-umba Frank Lacy & The Poker Bigband | Songs From The Musical 'Poker' | Tutu Records | 888150-2*
Louis Armstrong And Ella Fitzgerald With Russell Garcia's Orchestra | Porgy And Bess | Verve | 2-2507 IMS
The Complete Ella Fitzgerald And Louis Armstrong On Verve | Verve | 537284-2
Mark Dresser Trio | The Cabinet Of Dr. Caligari(Music For The Silent Film) | Knitting Factory Works | KFWCD 155
Misha Alperin Group With John Surman | First Impression | ECM | 1664(557650-2)
Odean Pope Trio | Ninety-Six | Enja | 9091-2
Urs Leimgruber/John Wolf Brennan | M.A.P. | L+R Records | CDLR 45021

Overture-
Chick Corea And Gary Burton With A String Quartet | Lyric Suite For Sextet | ECM | 1260

Overture En Re
Shorty Rogers And His Sax Quintet | The Swingin' Nutcracker | Fresh Sound Records | ND 42121

Overture To You Can't Keep A Good Cowboy Down
Jacques Loussier Trio | Play Bach | Decca | 6.24015 AL

Overtüre(Die Meistersinger von Nürnberg)
Ran Blake | That Certain Feeling(George Gershwin Songbook) | Hat Art | CD 6077

Overtüre(Lohengrin,1.Akt)
Uri Caine Ensemble | Wagner E Venezia | Winter&Winter | 910013-2

Overtüre(Lohengrin,3.Akt)
Natascha Majevskaja-Thomas Jäger | Orgel Ist Mehr!...In Bamberg,Vol.1 | Orgel ist mehr! | OIM/BA/1999-1 CD

Overtüre(Mozart:Cosi fan tutte)
Orgel Ist Mehr...In Bamberg Vol.2 | Orgel ist mehr! | OIM/BA/1999-2 CD

Overtüre(Mozart:Titus)
Orgel Ist Mehr!...In Bamberg,Vol.1 | Orgel ist mehr! | OIM/BA/1999-1 CD

Overtüre(Rossini:Il Barbiere di Seviglia)
Uri Caine Ensemble | Wagner E Venezia | Winter&Winter | 910013-2

Overtüre(Tannhäuser)
Orchestra | Duke Ellington's Sophisticated Ladies | RCA | BL 04053 DX

Overture:
WDR Big Band | Harlem Story | Koala Records | CD P 7

Overture-Communion
Jay Hoggard Quartet | Overview | Muse | MCD 5383

Ovulus
Blue Mitchell Quintet | Last Dance | JAM | 5002 IMS

Ow!
Clark Terry Quintet | The Hymn | Candid | CCD 79770
Coleman Hawkins Quartet | Supreme | Enja | ENJ-9009 2
Conte Candoli-Carl Fontana Quintet | The Complete Phoenix Recordings Vol.2 | Woofy Productions | WPCD 122
Dizzy Gillespie And His Orchestra | Dizzy Gillspie-The Complete RCA Victor Recordings | Bluebird | 63 66528-2
Dizzy Gillespie (1946-1949) | RCA | ND 89763
Don Byas With The Mary Lou Williams Trio | Don Byas Featuring Mary Lou Williams Trio & Beryl Booker Trio | Vogue | 21610212
George Wallington Quintet | Jazz Editions Presents: Jazz At Hotchkiss | Savoy | SV 0119(MG 12122)
JATP All Stars | J.A.T.P. In London 1969 | Pablo | 2CD 2620119
OW! All Star Jam Session | Moon Records | MCD 075-2
Charlie Parker Jazz At The Philharmonic 1949 | Verve | 519803-2

Owl Blues
Paul Bley | The Life Of A Trio:Saturday | Owl Records | 014731-2

Owl Eyes
Randy Sandke Sextet | Get Happy | Concord | CCD 4598

Oxeye

TITELVERZEICHNIS

Toast Man Quartet Plus Friends | One For Leonardo | SPLASC(H) Records | CD H 379-2

Oxymoron
Baba Jam Band | Kayada | Acoustic Music Records | 319.1036.2

Oye Como Va
The Conga Kings | Jazz Descargas | Chesky | JD 217

Oye Negra
Candela | La Maquina | BELL Records | BLR 84031

Oz Blu
Pat Metheny & Lyle Mays | As Falls Wichita, So Falls Wichita Falls | ECM | 1190(821416-2)

Ozark
Barrelhouse Jazzband | Travellin' Blues | L+R Records | CDLR 70004

Ozark Mountain Railroad
Mike Nock Quintet | Ozboppin' | Naxos Jazz | 86019-2

Ozone
Philip Catherine Trio With Guests | Transparence | Inak | 8701

O-Zone
Dizzy Gillespie With The Lalo Schifrin Orchestra | Free Ride | Pablo | 2310794

Ozone Madness
Butch Morris-Le Quan Ninh-J.A. Deane | Burning Cloud | FMP | CD 77

P.O.B.
Georg Ruby Group | Stange Loops | Jazz Haus Musik | JHM 0057 CD

P.O.B. 499
Georg Ruby-Wollie Kaiser | Ruby Domesticus Vugaris | Jazz Haus Musik | JHM 26

P.S.
Masabumi 'Poo' Kikuchi Trio | Tethered Moon | Paddle Wheel | KICJ 93

P.S. Unless One Has(Blues Connotation No.2)
Pete Berryman & Adrian O'Reilly | Duet | Acoustic Music Records | 319.1163.2

P.S.I Love You
Billie Holiday And Her All Stars | Recital By Billie Holiday | Verve | 521868-2
Jimmy Witherspoon And His All Stars | Blues For Easy Livers | Original Blues Classics | OBCCD 585-2(PR 7475)
Lionel Hampton Quartet | Mostly Ballads | Limelight | 820834-2 IMS
Sonny Stitt Quartet | Genesis | Prestige | P 24044

P.T.1
Willem Breuker Kollektief | To Remain | BVHAAST | CD 8904

Pa 'Delante Como Sea
Bebo Valdés Group | Bebo Rides Again | Messidor | 15834 CD

Pablo
Paul Bley Trio | Touching | Black Lion | BLCD 760195

Pablo(Lady Z)
Dave Liebman Ensemble | Lookout Farm | ECM | 1039

Pablo's Story
Hubert Laws All Stars | Aurex Jazz Festival '81:Fusion Super Jam | Eastworld | EWJ 80210

Pace
Apaturia Quintet | Apaturia | yvp music | CD 3054

Pacemaker
Eddie Louiss Orchestra | Flomela | Dreyfus Jazz Line | FDM 36578-2

Pacha Nadai Pallavi
Ray Barretto And His Orchestra | Carnaval | Fantasy | FCD 24713-2

Pachanga Pa'ti
Carnaval | Fantasy | FCD 24713-2

Pacic
Bunk Johnson's Jazz Band | Bunk Johnson In San Francisco | American Music | AMCD-16

Pacific Breeze
Dinah Washington With Lucky Thompson And His All Stars | The Complete Dinah Washington Vol.1 | Official | 3004

Pacific Coast Highway
Mahavishnu | Mahavishnu | Warner | 251351-1

Pacific Nights
Peter Herbolzheimer Rhythm Combination & Brass | Bandfire | Koala Records | CD P 1

Pacific Rim
Spyro Gyra | Freetime | MCA | 2292-50417-1

Pacific View Drive
Flautissimo | Flautissimo | Edition Collage | EC 445-2

Pacifica(I,II & III)
First Class Blues Band | The First Class Blues Band Proudly Presents Mr. Frank Biner | Acoustic Music Records | 319.1062.2

Packing Up
The Caribbean Jazz Project | The Caribbean Jazz Project | Inak | 9038

Paco De Lucia
Dirk Raulf Group | Theater I (Bühnenmusik) | Poise | Poise 07

Paco Und Die Tiere(Schauspielhaus Bochum)
La Vienta | Jazzmenco | Telarc Digital | CD 83353

Padma
Eric St-Laurent-Thomy Jordi-Thomas Alkier feat. Helge Schneider | Rock,Jazz & Music:Laut! | BIT | 11212

Padre
Gary Thomas And Seventh Quadrant | Code Violations | Enja | 5085

Paff, Der Zauberdrachen
Deborah Henson-Conant | The Gift:15 Weihnachtslieder der Erde | Laika Records | 35100992

Pag A-Tao
Rissi-Mazzola-Geisser | Fuego | Creative Works Records | CW CD 1029-2

Pagago
Benny Goodman Quartet | The Benny Goodman Caravans Vol.3-One O'Clock Jump | Giants Of Jazz | GOJ 1036

Pagan Love Song
Gene Ammons Septet | Gene Ammons Bossa Nova | Original Jazz Classics | OJCCD 351-2(PR 7257)
Glenn Miller And His Orchestra | Original Recordings From 1938 to 1942,Vol.2 | RCA | 2118549-2

Page 1
Benny Golson Quintet | This Is For You, John | Timeless | CD SJP 235

Page 172
Oliver Lake Quintet | Dedicated To Dolphy | Black Saint | 120144-2

Page Two
Oregon | 45th Parallel | VeraBra Records | CDVBR 2048-2

Pageant
45th Parallel | VeraBra Records | CDVBR 2048-2

Pageant(Epilogue)
Anne Morre | Anne Morre | Bellaphon | BCH 33008

Pagin' The Devil
Kansas City Six | Jazz Gallery:Lester Young Vol.1(1936-46) | RCA | 2114171-2
Lester Young:The Complete1936-1951 Group Sessions(Studio Recordings-Master Takes),Vol.1 | Blue Moon | BMCD 1001

Pagode
Scott Henderson-Gary Willis Quartet | Illicit | Bluemoon | R 27-9180-2

Pain In My Heart
Don Pullen | Healing Force | Black Saint | BSR 0010

Paint The Town
Chick Corea Electric Band II | Paint The World | GRP | GRP 97412

Paint Up House
Marlene And Her Band | Elemental Soul | Concord | CCD 4774

Painted Rhythm
Stan Kenton And His Orchestra | The Early Years | Capitol | 166219-2

Painter At Work
Hans Koller Groups And Orchestra | Hans Koller Masterpieces | MPS | 529078-2

Painter's Lament
Hans Koller Quartet | Multiple Koller | L+R Records | LR 41003

Paixao
Curtis Fuller-Slide Hampton Quintet | Two Bones | Blue Note | GXK 8166

Pajaro Canter
Clare Fischer With The Metropole Orchestra | The Latin Side | Koch Jazz | 3-6907-2

Pajaros Choiques-
Dino Saluzzi | Kultrum | ECM | 1251(821407-2)

Pajaros Y Ceibos
Furio Romano Quartet | What Colour For A Tale | SPLASC(H) Records | CD H 351-2

Pal Of Mine
Blind Willie McTell | Blind Willie McTell/Memphis Minnie-Love Changin' Blues | Biograph | BLP 12035

Palacio De Pintures
Harry James And His New Jazz Band | Saturday Night Swing | Giants Of Jazz | GOJ 1016

Palestrina
Ekkehard Jost Nonet | Out Of Jost's Songbook | Fish Music | FM 006 CD

Palestrinas Reise Nach Cadiz
Ekkehard Jost Quintet | Carambolage | View | VS 0028 IMS

Palhaco
Charlie Haden-Egberto Gismonti | In Montreal | ECM | 1746(543813-2)
Madmo(Two Guitars & Percussion) | Cicles | Acoustic Music Records | 319.1053.2

Palindrome
Richard Beirach | Breathing Of Status | CMP Records | CMP 17

Palinodia I
Francois Houle 5 | Cryptology | Between The Lines | btl 012(Efa 10182-2)

Palinodia II
Ken Peplowski Quartet | Grenadilla | Concord | CCD 4809

Palladium
Weather Report | Heavy Weather | CBS | CK 65108
Harry James And His Orchestra | Harry James And His Orchestra Feat. Buddy Rich | CBS | CBS 21105

Palle's Headache
Matthias Müller Quartet | Bhavam | Jazz Haus Musik | JHM 0126 CD

Palm
The Herdsmen | Nat Pierce-Dick Collins-Ralph Burns & The Herdsmen Play Paris | Fantasy | FCD 24759-2

Palm Cafe
The Herdsmen Play Paris | Original Jazz Classics | OJC 116(F 3201)

Palm Grease
Dominique Cornil | Scott Joplin Ragtimes | GHA Records | CD 126.004

Palm Tree
Klaus Doldinger's Passport | Earthborn | Atlantic | 2292-46477-2

Palm Tree Song
Raphael Fays Group | Voyages | Acoustic Music Records | AMC 1015

Palma Latex Tuteflum
Family Of Percussion | Message To The Enemies Of Time | Nagara | MIX 1016-N

Palmira
The Far East Side Band | Caverns | New World Records | 80458-2

Palo Alto
Lee Konitz Quintet | Parallels | Chesky | JD 213
Lee Konitz-Jimmy Giuffre Octet | Lee Konitz Meets Jimmy Giuffre | Verve | 2304381 IMS

Palomita
Toto Blanke-Rudolf Dasek | Talking Hands:Live | ALISO Records | AL 1021
Mosalini/Beytelmann/Caratini | Inspiration Del Tango | Eigelstein | 568-72223

Palomita(dedicated to Rose)
Mark Soskin Sextet | 17(Seventeen) | TCB Records | TCB 20652

Palude
Elmo Hope Trio | Last Sessions | Inner City | IC 1018 IMS

Pam Ain't Blue
Eje Thelin Group | Ejs Thelin 1966 With Barney Wilen | Dragon | DRCD 366

Pam Kan
Boi Akih | Uwa I | Enja | ENJ-9472 2

Pamamurolo
29th Street Saxophone Quartet | Your Move | Antilles | 314512524(875360)

Pamela
Larry Karush-Glen Moore Duo | May 24, 1976 | Japo | 60014(2360014)

Pamela's Passion
Chet Baker Sextet | Compact Jazz: Chet Baker | Verve | 840632-2 PMS

Pammie Dear
Larry Carlton Group | The Gift | GRP | GRP 98542
Stan Getz Quartet | Stan Getz At Large Plus!,Vol.1 | Jazz Unlimited | JUCD 2001

Pamoeana 'Mapu'
David Friedman-Jasper Van't Hof | Birds Of A Feather | Traumton Records | 2428-2

Pampas Fugue
Scheer Music | Rappin' It Up | Palo Alto | PA 8025

Pam's Waltz
Randy Weston Trio With The Orchestre Du Festival De Monreal | Earth Birth | Verve | 537088-2

Pan
Ray Warleigh Quartet | Reverie | View | VS 106 IMS

Pan Con Pan
Bebo Valdés Group | Bebo Rides Again | Messidor | 15834 CD

Pan Pan
Louis Jordan And His Tympany Five | Louis Jordan-Let The Good Times Roll: The Complete Decca Recordings 1938-1954 | Bear Family Records | BCD 15557 IH
Louis Jordan Vol.2-Knock Me Out | Swingtime(Contact) | ST 1012

Panacea
Woody Herman And The Herd | Woody Herman (And The Herd) At Carnegie Hall | Verve | 559833-2
Herb Robertson Group | The Little Trumpet | JMT Edition | 919007-2

Panacoustica
The Little Trumpet | JMT Edition | 919007-2

Panacoustica(Overture)
Juan Serrano Group | Sabor Flamenco | Concord | CCD 4490

Panama
Alvin Alcorn' 'Gay Paree' Stompers | Alvin Alcorn/Harrison Verret | American Music | AMCD-65
Bunk Johnson's Jazz Band | Bunk & Leadbelly At New York Town Hall 1947 | American Music | AMCD-46
David Ostwald's Gully Low Jazz Band | Blues In Your Heart | Nagel-Heyer | CD 051
Dee Dee Pierce And His New Orleans Stompers | In Binghampton,N.Y. Vol.Three | American Music | AMCD-81
Lionel Hampton Sextet | Le Jazz En France-Vol.6 | Pathe | 1727301
Louisiana Repertory Jazz Ensemble Of New Orleans | Marching, Ragging And Mourning:Brass Band Music Of New Orleans 1900-1920 | Stomp Off Records | CD 1197
Wild Bill Davison And His Commodores | Wild Bill Davison:The Commodore Master Takes | Commodore | CMD 14052
Louis Armstrong And His Orchestra | Louis Armstrong Vol.8:1941-1942 | Ambassador | CLA 1908

Panama Blues
Danilo Perez Quintet | Danilo Perez | Novus | 4163148-2

Panama Rag
Chris Barber's Jazz Band | Barber-Bue Concerts | Storyville | 671196

Panamericana
Dizzy Gillespie And His Orchestra | Gillespiana And Carnegie Hall Concert | Verve | 519809-2

Panamericana-
Dizzy Gillespie Quintet | En Concert Avec Europe 1 | Laserlight | 710705

Panamonk
Horace Parlan Quartet | One For Wilton | EGO | 4018

Pancho
George Russell Septet | Outer Thoughts | Milestone | M 47027

Pandemonium
Diederik Wissels Trio | Tender Is The Night | Jazz Pure Collection | AU 31616 CD

Pandora
Makoto Ozone Trio | Pandora | Verve | 549629-2
Wayne Shorter Orchestra | High Life | Verve | 529224-2

Pandora's Box
Niels Lan Doky Quartet | The Truth | Storyville | STCD 4144

Pangäa:
Dave Brubeck Quartet | For Iola | Concord | CCD 4259

Panhalder
Aydin Esen Group | Pictures | Jazz City | 660.53.007

Pannonia
Kurt Rosenwinkel Trio | East Coast Love Affair | Fresh Sound Records | FSNT 016 CD
Steve Lacy-Roswell Rudd Quartet | Monk's Dream | Verve | 543090-2
Thelonious Monk Quartet | MONK. | CBS | CK 86564
Thelonious Monk Quintet | Thelonious Monk:85th Birthday Celebration | zyx records | FANCD 6076-2
Sonny Rollins-The Freelance Years:The Complete Riverside & Contemporary Recordings | Riverside | 5 RCD 4427-2
Aki Takase-Alexander von Schlippenbach | Piano Duets-Live In Berlin 93/94 | FMP | OWN-90002

Pannonica
Anthony Braxton Quartet | Antony Braxton Piano Quartet,Yoshi 1994 | Music & Arts | CD 849
Chick Corea Trio | Circling In | Blue Note | 84555
Clifford Jordan Quartet | Royal Ballads | Criss Cross | Criss 1025 (835613)
Dudek-Van Den Broek-Haurand | Pulque | Konnex Records | KCD 5055
Flavio Boltro-Furio di Castri-Manhu Roche | Immagini | Red Records | NS 210
Horace Parlan Trio | Pannonica | Enja | ENJ-4076 2
McCoy Tyner Quartet | Four Times Four | Milestone | M 55007
Monk By Five | Monk By Five | Touché Music | TMcCD 012
Nueva Manteca | Afrodisia | Timeless | CD SJP 355
Paul Motian Quintet | Misterioso | Soul Note | 121174-2
Thelonious Monk | Thelonious Monk-The Complete Riverside Recordings | Riverside | 15 RCD 022-2
Thelonious Monk Quintet | Thelonious Monk-The Complete Riverside Recordings | Riverside | 15 RCD 022-2
Trio Impossible | Trio Impossible | Jazz 4 Ever Records:Jazz Network | J4E 4738

Pannonica-
Joshua Breakstone Trio | 9 By 3 | Contemporary | CCD 14062-2

Pannonica No.2
Thelonious Monk Quartet | MONK. | CBS | CK 86564

Pannonica(alt.take)
Thelonious Monk Quintet | Thelonious Monk-The Complete Riverside Recordings | Riverside | 15 RCD 022-2

Panonien
Donald Johnston Quartet | There's No Forgetting You | Bhakti Jazz | BR 30

Pansies
Jack DeJohnette's Directions | Untitled | ECM | 1074

Panta Rhei
Sieverts-Enders-Salfellner Trio | Brooklyn Blue | Jazz 4 Ever Records:Jazz Network | J4E 4732

Panther
Marcus Miller Group | Live & More | Dreyfus Jazz Line | FDM 36585-2
Sidney Bechet With Claude Luter And His Orchestra | In The Groove | Jazz Society(Vogue) | 670506

Panther Rag
Blind Blake | Blind Blake-No Dough Blues | Biograph | BLP 12031

Pantin' In The Panther Room
Joshua Redman Quintet | Freedom In The Goove | Warner | 9362-46330-2

Pantomime
Slickaphonics | Modern Life | Enja | ENJ-4062 2

Pantronic
Christy Doran's New Bag With Muthuswamy Balasubramoniam | Black Box | double moon | CHRDM 71022

Pantrova
Becker/Sclavis/Lindberg | Transition | FMP | 1170

Papa
Fats Waller | Jazz Live & Rare: Fats Waller-Rare Early Piano Solos 1923-27 | Jazzline | ???

Papa Groove
Rosa Henderson With The Big Charlie Thomas Band | Big Charlie Thomas 1925-1927 | Timeless | CBC 1-030

Papa N'as Pas Voulu
Louis Conte Group | La Cocina Caliente | Denon Compact Disc | CY-30001

Papa Wants To Knock A Jug
Gene Ammons Quintet | Fine And Mellow | Prestige | PRCD 24281-2

Papa Was A Rolling Stone
Herbie Mann Group | Deep Pocket | Kokopelli Records | KOKO 1296

Papa What Are You Trying To Do To Me I've Been Doing It For Years
Mongo Santamaria Orchestra | Olé Ola | Concord | CCD 4387

Papa Willy Rhumba
Margaret Johnson With Clarence Williams' Blue Five | Louis Armstrong And The Blues Singers 1924-1930 | Affinity | AFS 1018(6)

Papa-Daddy And Me
Claudio Roditi Group | Slow Fire | Milestone | MCD 9175-2

Papagaio Louro-
Woody Herman And His Orchestra | Sonny Berman:Woodshopper's Holiday 1946 | Cool & Blue | C&B-CD 111

Papalongi
Sandro Satta-Antonello Salis Duo | Live In Come | SPLASC(H) Records | CD H 432-2

Papaya
Urszula Dudziak With Orchestra | Ulla | Pop-Eye | PE 101

Paper Boy
Carl Ravazza And His Orchestra | The Uncollected: Carl Ravazza | Hindsight | HSR 117

Paper Doll
The Mills Brothers | Harlem Roots-Jazz On Film:Rhythm In Harmony | Storyville | SLP 6002

Paper Nut
Jan Savitt And His Top Hatters | The Uncollected:Jan Svitt | Hindsight | HSR 213

Paperballs
$$hide$$ | $$Titelverweise | |

Papermoon -> It's Only A Papermoon

Papillon
Dwayne Dolphin Quintet | Portrait Of Adrian | Minor Music | 801042

Papirossen
NuNu! | Ocean | TipToe | TIP-888837 2

Papirossn
Luis Agudo | Afrosamba | Red Records | VPA 172

Papp Joe
Medeski Martin & Wood | Univisible | Blue Note | 535870-2

Pappy Check
Woody Allen And His New Orleans Jazz Band | Wild Man Blues | RCA | 2663353-2

Pappy's B Flat Blues
Chris Jarrett | Fire | Edition Collage | EC 443-2

Paprika Lady
Piano Moments | Take Twelve On CD | TT 007-2
Herb Ellis Quintet | Nothing But The Blues | Verve | 521674-2

Pap's Blues
Louis Sclavis-Ernst Reijseger | Et On Ne Parle Pas Du Temps | FMP | CD 66

Par Les Gouffres
Ben Waltzer Quintet | In Metropolitan Motion | Fresh Sound Records | FSNT 082 CD

Par(nas)se
Cornelius Claudio Kreusch | The Vision | Enja | 8082-2

Para
Joachim Kühn Trio And The WDR Big Band | Carambolage | CMP Records | CMP CD 58(EFA 03058)

Para Camagüey Se Va Panchita-

Conjunto Clave Y Guaguanco | Dejala En La Puntica | TipToe | TIP-888829 2

Para Clave Y Guaguando
Victor Mendoza Group | If Only You Knew | L+R Records | CDLR 45019

Para Machucar Meu Coracao
Getz-Gilberto Quintet | Getz/Gilberto | Polydor | 521414-2

Para Machuchar Meu Conancao
Getz/Gilberto:The Girl From Ipanema | CTI Records | PDCTI 1105-2

Para Mi Nina(para angeles)
Gato Barbieri Group | Chapter Two-Hasta Siempre | MCA | 28675 XOT

Para Nosotros
Acoustic Guitars | Acoustic Guitars | Stunt Records | 18703

Para Petra
Conjunto Clave Y Guaguanco | Dejala En La Puntica | TipToe | TIP-888829 2

Para Rita Montaner
Phil Minton | A Doughnut In One Hand | FMP | CD 91

Para Ti
Mongo Santamaria And His Band | Mongo At The Village Gate | Original Jazz Classics | OJCCD 490-2(RLP 9529)
Sabroso | Original Jazz Classics | OJCCD 281-2
Mongo Santamaria And His Orchestra | Live At Jazz Alley | Concord | CCD 4427
Bebo Valdés Trio | El Arte Del Sabor | Blue Note | 535193-2

Para Vigo Me Voy-
Cuarteto Las D'Aida Y Su Grupo | Soy La Mulata | L+R Records | CDLR 45059

Para.ph(r)ase
Branford Marsalis Quartet | Scenes In The City | CBS | 468458-2

Parable
MOKAVE | Afrique | audioquest Music | AQCD 1024

Parablue
Alan Shorter Quartet | Orgasm | Verve | 557094-2

Parade
Herbie Hancock Quartet | Herbie Hancock Quartet | CBS | SRCS 9343
Joe Bonner Trio | Parade | Steeplechase | SCCD 31116
Ron Carter Trio | The Golden Striker | Blue Note | 590831-2
Jimmy Smith With The Oliver Nelson Orchestra | Peter & The Wolf | Verve | 547264-2

Parade-
The London Gabrieli Brass Ensemble feat. Chris Barber | Under The Influence Of Jazz | Timeless | CD TTD 569

Parade Of The Wooden Soldiers
Cab Calloway And His Orchestra | Jazz Drumming Vol.5(1940) | Fenn Music | FJD 2705

Paradigm
Tony Dagradi Quintet | Dreams Of Love | Line Records | COCD 9.00798 O

Paradise
Herbie Hancock Group | Lite Me Up | CBS | SRCS 9507

Paradise-
David Murray Quartet | David Murray:Ballads | DIW | DIW 840 CD

Paradise Of The Have's And Hell Of The Have Not's
Michael Formanek Septet | Low Profile | Enja | ENJ-8050 2

Paradise Squat
Count Basie And His Orchestra | The Count | Verve | MV 2644 IMS

Paradise Sring
Paul Williams Sextet | Paul Williams:The Complete Recordings Vol.1 (1947-1949) | Blue Moon | BMCD 6020

Paradiso
Steps Ahead | N.Y.C. | Intuition Records | INT 3007-2
Sylvie Courvoisier Group | Ocre | Enja | ENJ-9323 2

Paradiso Perduto
Bruce Eskovitz Quintet | One For Newk | Koch Jazz | KOC 3-7801-2

Paradox
Jack Montrose Quintet | Atlantic Jazz: West Coast | Atlantic | 7567-81703-2
LeeAnn Ledgerwood Trio | Paradox | Steeplechase | SCCD 31497
McCoy Tyner Quartet | Four Times Four | Milestone | M 55007
Tok | Paradox | Japo | 60029

Paradoxe I
Bobby Jaspar And His Modern Jazz | Bobby Jaspar & His Modern Jazz | Vogue | 21559512

Paradoxical Conversation
Ernst Bier-Mack Goldsbury Quartet | At Night When You Go To Sleep | Timescrapper | TSCR 9611
European Jazz Youth Orchestra | Swinging Europe 1 | dacapo | DCCD 9449

Paradoxy
Joshua Rifkin | Scott Joplin Piano Rags | Nonesuch | 7559-79159-2

Paragon Rag
Richard Zimmerman | The Complete Works Of Scott Joplin | Laserlight | 15945

Para-Graffiti
Peter Leitch-Heiner Franz | At First Sight | Jardis Records | JRCD 9611
Miroslav Vitous Group | Journey's End | ECM | 1242(843171-2)

Paragraph Jay
Gerry Mulligan Group With Jane Duboc | Triple Play:Gerry Mulligan | Telarc Digital | CD 83453

Parakeet Prowl
Michael Riessler Group | Heloise | Wergo | WER 8008-2

Paraklet
Dirk Schreurs-Walter Baeken Group | Beyond Ballads | B.Sharp Records | CDS 100

Parallel
Joe Harriott Quintet | Free Form | EmArCy | 538184-2
Lennie Tristano Trio | The Rarest Trio/Quartet Sessions 1946/47 | Raretone | 5008 FC

Parallels
The Lizard Brothers | Saxophone Animals | Nine Winds Records | NWCD 0139

Paramount Stomp
Quintet Du Hot Club De France | Django Reinhardt:Djangology | EMI Records | 780659-2

Paramour
John Abercrombie Quartet | Arcade | ECM | 1133

Paraphernalia
Miles Davis Sextet | Miles In The Sky | CBS | CK 65684
Nicholas Payton Quintet | Payton's Place | Verve | 557327-2
Wittek/Kaiser/Manderscheid | Trotzdem | Jazz Haus Musik | JHM 09

Parasol
Franco Morone | Melodies Of Memories | Acoustic Music Records | 319.1153.2

Paratactic Paths-
Mauro Negri Quartet | Patarau | SPLASC(H) Records | H 185

Paraty
Tete Montoliu | Tete Montoliu Interpreta A Serrat | Fresh Sound Records | FSR 4004(835319)

Parazula
Eliane De Creus & Jean Sablon | Le Jazz En France Vol.5:Django Plus | Pathe | 1727291

Parchman Farm
Mose Allison Trio | Mose Allison Sings The 7th Son | Prestige | PR20 7279-2
Local Color | Original Jazz Classics | OJCCD 457-2
Mose Alife!/Wild Man On The Loose | Warner | 8122-75439-2
Bukka White | Classic Blues | Zounds | CD 2700048

Parchman Farm Blues
Olaf Tarenskeen | Decisions | Acoustic Music Records | 319.1144.2

Pardon My Rags
Jack Sheldon Quintet | Hollywood Heroes | Concord | CCD 4339

Pardon,Ist Da Noch Frei?(I Wanne Be Loved By You)
Gilad Atzmon & The Orient House Ensemble | Gilad Atzmon & The Orient House Ensemble | TipToe | TIP-888839 2

Pardonnez Nous
Willem Breuker Kollektief | Sensemayá | BVHAAST | CD 9509

Pare Cochero
Ron Carter Quartet | Parfait | Milestone | M 9107

Parfait
Django Reinhardt | Django Reinhardt-Un Géant Sur Son Image | Melodie | 400052

Parfum De Gitane
Anouar Brahem Trio | Barzakh | ECM | 1432(847540-2)
Gary Thomas Quartet | Pariah's Pariah | Winter&Winter | 910033-2

Pariah's Pariah
Lisle Ellis Group | What We Live Fo(u)r | Black Saint | 120156-2

Paris
Bireli Lagrene Group | A Tribute To Django Reinhardt | Jazzpoint | JP 1061 CD
A Tribute To Django Reinhardt | Jazzpoint | JP 1061 CD
A' Portrait Of Jan Jankeje | Jazzpoint | JP 1054 CD
Down In Town | Island | 205863-320
Brad Mehldau | Places | Warner | 9362-47693-2
Jan Jankeje Quintet | Zum Trotz | Jazzpoint | JP 1016 CD
Lily White Group | Somewhere Between Truth & Fiction | Knitting Factory Works | KFWCD 153
Taku Sugimoto | Oposite | HatNOIR | 802

Paris Blues
Duke Ellington And His Orchestra | In The Uncommon Market | Pablo | 2308247-2
Joe Turner Trio | Joe Turner | Black & Blue | BLE 233031
Wycliffe Gordon-Eric Reid | We | Nagel-Heyer | CD 2023
Kendra Shank With The Larry Willis Quartet Plus Gary Bartz | Afterglow | Mapleshade | 02132

Paris Canaille
Cowws Quintet plus Guests | Book/Virtual Cowws | FMP | OWN-90007/9

Paris In Blue
Jackie Paris With The Charles Mingus Quintet | Autobiography In Jazz | Original Jazz Classics | OJC 115(DEB 198)

Paris In The Rain
Bob Florence Trio | Bob Florence Trio | Fresh Sound Records | FSR-CD 0303

Paris In The Spring
Beryl Booker Trio | Don Byas Featuring Mary Lou Williams Trio & Beryl Booker Trio | Vogue | 21610212

Paris Je T'Aime
Martial Solal-Sadi Quartet | Martial Solal:The Complete Vogue Recordings Vol.2 | Vogue | 21409332

Paris Nostalgie
Memphis Slim | Boogie Woogie | Accord | 402472

Paris-Dakar(Banjot 2)
Oliver Augst-Rüdiger Carl-Christoph Korn | Blank | FMP | OWN-90013

Parisian Sketches:
Alan Broadbent | Maybeck Recital Hall Series Volume Fourteen | Concord | CCD 4488

Parisian Thoroughfare
Andy LaVerne | In The Mood For A Classic-Andy LaVerne Plays Bud Powell | Steeplechase | SCCD 31342
Bud Powell | The Genius Of Bud Powell | Verve | 821690-1
The Genius Of Bud Powell | Verve | 827901-2 PMS
Bud Powell Trio | The Blue Note Years:The Best Of Bud Powell | Blue Note | 793204-2
Clifford Brown-Max Roach Quintet | Clifford Brown And Max Roach | Verve | 543306-2
Compact Jazz: Clifford Brown | EmArCy | 842933-2 PMS
Donald Byrd Quartet With Bobby Jaspar | Au Chat Qui Peche 1958 | Fresh Sound Records | FSCD 1028
Jaki Byard Experience | Pre-Rahsan | Prestige | P 24080
Joe Morello Quartet | Going Places | dmp Digital Music Productions | CD 497
OTB Out Of The Blue | Live At Mt. Fuji | Blue Note | 746784-2
René Urtreger Trio | Jazz In Paris:René Urtreger Joue Bud Powell | EmArCy | 014182-2
Super Sax | Supersax Dynamite | MPS | 68210

Parisian Welcome
Dave Soldier Group With Voices | Smut | Avant | AVAN 019

Park Avenue Petite
Pat Martino Trio | East! | Original Jazz Classics | OJCCD 248-2

Parker 51
Stan Getz Quintet | Jazz At Storyville Vol.1 | Fresh Sound Records | FSR 629(Roost RLP 407)
Charles Mingus Quintet | The Great Concert,Paris 1964 | Accord | 500072

Parker's Mood
Charlie Parker All Stars | The Savoy Recordings 2 | Savoy | 650108(881908)
James Moody Quartet | Moody's Party | Telarc Digital | CD 83382
Judy Niemack With The Cedar Walton Trio | Blue Bop | Freelance | FRL-CD 009
Roots | Salutes The Saxophones: Tributes To Gene Ammons, Eric Dolphy, Coleman Hawkins And Charlie Parker | IN+OUT Records | 7016-3
Salutes The Saxophone | IN+OUT Records | 7016-2
Roy Hargrove Trio | Parker's Mood | Verve | 527907-2
Sadao Watanabe Quartet | Dedicated To Charlie Parker | Denon Compact Disc | DC 8558

Parking Lot Blues
Milt Jackson-Sonny Stitt Quintet | Loose Walk | Palcoscenico | PAL 15009

Parking Lots
Peter Herbolzheimer Rhythm Combination & Brass | Friends And Sihouettes | Koala Records | CD P 25

Parks
Paul Bley Synthesizer Show | The Paul Bley Synthesizer Show | Milestone | M 9033

Parlay 2
Charlie Ventura Quintet | The New Charlie Ventura In Hi-Fi | Harlequin | HQ 2009(Baton BL 1202) IMS

Parlaying
Noel Akchoté Trio | Rien | Winter&Winter | 910057-2

Parle
Steckar Tubapack | Tubakoustik | IDA Record | 024 CD

Parliament Of Music
Nornert Stein Pata Masters | Live In Australia | Pata Musik | PATA 15 CD
Erik Truffaz Quartet | Mantis | Blue Note | 535101-2

Parlophone
Don Ewell | Free 'N' Easy | Good Time Jazz | GTCD 10046-2

Parlor Social
Duke Ellington's Washingtonians | The Complete Duke Ellington-Vol. 1 | CBS | CBS 67264

Parody
Xanadu All Stars | Xanadu At Montreux Vol.4 | Vogue | 506617

Parody No.Two
Mauro Negri Quartet | Patarau | SPLASC(H) Records | H 185

Parole,Parole
Evan Parker | Process And Reality | FMP | CD 37

Parrhesia
Bob Scobey's Frisco Band | Bob Scobey's Frisco Band | Good Time Jazz | GTCD 12006-2

Part 1
Florian Ross Quartet With The Event String Ensemble | Suite For Soprano Sax And String Orchestra | Naxos Jazz | 86037-2

Part 1(alt.take)
Bigband Der Musikschule Der Stadt Brühl Mit Gastsolisten | Pangäa | Indigo-Records | 1004 CD

Part 1(Featherdance)
Irakere | Misa Negra | Messidor | 15972 CD

Part 1:Dünung
Jaco Pastorius Trio | Live In Italy & Honestly | Jazzpoint | JP 1059 CD

Part 1-10
Ben Wolfe Sextet | Bagdad Theater | Mons Records | MR 874827

Part 1-5
Stephan Micus | Wings Over Water | Japo | 60038(831058-2)

part 1-6
Duke Ellington And His Orchestra | Black Brown And Beige | CBS | CK 65566

Part 2
Florian Ross Quartet With The Event String Ensemble | Suite For Soprano Sax And String Orchestra | Naxos Jazz | 86037-2

Part 2(alt.take)
Bigband Der Musikschule Der Stadt Brühl Mit Gastsolisten | Pangäa | Indigo-Records | 1004 CD

Part 2(What Passes,Passes Like Clouds)
Irakere | Misa Negra | Messidor | 15972 CD

Part 2:Treppenhaus
Phil Woods Orchestra | Rights Of Swing | Candid | CS 9016

Part 3(Mulanga)
Paquito D'Rivera Group feat. Arturo Sandoval | Reunion | Messidor | 15805 CD

Part 3:Wahnfried
Phil Woods Orchestra | Rights Of Swing | Candid | CS 9016

Part 4(Millenium Blues)
Irakere | Misa Negra | Messidor | 15972 CD

Part 4:Tirolerhut
Phil Woods Orchestra | Rights Of Swing | Candid | CS 9016

Part 5(Roma Termini)
Rights Of Swing | Candid | CS 9016

Part Five
Alex De Grassi | Clockwork | Windham Hill | WD 1018

Part Five-The Birth Of The Free:
Gerard Presencer Group | Chasing Reality | ACT | 9422-2

Part Four
Hal Russell NRG Ensemble | The Hal Russell Story | ECM | 1498

Part Four-Fast Company:
Willem Breuker Kollektief With Strings And Choir | Psalm 122 | BVHAAST | CD 9803

Part I-III
Geir Lysne Listening Ensemble | Aurora Borealis-Nordic Lights | ACT | 9406-2

Part IV(coda)
Billy Bang | Distinction Without A Difference | Hat Art | 4 (1Ro4)

Part Of Life
Sweet Miss Coffy With The Mississippi Burnin' Blues Revue | Sweet Miss Coffy | Mardi Gras Records | MG 1021

Part One
LSM | Live At The ZMF Freiburg | B&W Present | BW 027

Part One:Blue Ice(The Glacier):
George Winston | Winter Into Spring | Windham Hill | 34 11019-2

Part One-Family Jam:
Gerard Presencer Group | Chasing Reality | ACT | 9422-2

Part Six
Hal Russell NRG Ensemble | The Hal Russell Story | ECM | 1498

Part Six-NRG Rising:
Gerard Presencer Group | Chasing Reality | ACT | 9422-2

Part Three
Joelle Leandre | Urban Bass | Adda | 581254

Part Three-Hit The Road,Hal:
Erroll Garner Quartet | Plays Misty | Fresh Sound Records | FSR-CD 0158

Part Time Blues
Erroll Garner Trio | Erroll Garner | Verve | 846191-2 PMS

Part Two
Joelle Leandre | Urban Bass | Adda | 581254

Part Two:Approaching The Sea:
Joel Futterman Trio | Berlin Images | Silkheart | SHCD 131

Part Two-Scholar And Fan:
Rajesh Metha-Paul Lovens | Orka | HatOLOGY | 524

Parthenope
John Handy's Louisiana Shakers | John Handy-The Very First Recordings | American Music | AMCD-51

Partido Alto
Azimuth | Light As A Feather | Milestone | M 9089
Terra Brazil | Café Com Leite | art-mode-records | AMR 2101
Armen Donelian Sextet | Secrets | Sunnyside | SSC 1031 D

Parting
Stephan Noel Lang Trio | Echoes | Nagel-Heyer | CD 2033
Wolfgang Engstfeld Quartet | Songs And Ballads | Nabel Records:Jazz Network | CD 4658
Lan Xang | Hidden Gardens | Naxos Jazz | 86046-2

Partita
Jacques Loussier Trio | Play Bach | Accord | 500372

Partita No.1 In B Flat Major(BWV 825):
Play Bach No.2 | Decca | 157562-2
Portrait | Decca | 6.28511 DO

Parti-Time Blues
Andrew Hill Quintet | Dance With Death | Blue Note | LT 1030 (GXK 8184)

Partly Raggy
Keith Jarrett Trio | Keith Jarrett At The Blue Note-The Complete Recordings | ECM | 1575/80(527638-2)

Partners
Keith Jarrett At The Blue Note-The Complete Recordings | ECM | 1575/80(527638-2)
Claire Martin With Band | Old Boyfriends | Linn Records | AKD 028

Parto
Cats & Camels | Face To Face | L+R Records | CDLR 45038

Party Blues
Ella Fitzgerald And Joe Williams With The Count Basie Octet | Compact Jazz: Count Basie & Joe Williams | Verve | 835329-2 PMS

Party In The Ghetto
Frank Eberle Septet | Scarlet Sunrise | Satin Doll Productions | SDP 1041-1 CD

Party In The Pentagon
Joe McPhee | As Serious As Your Life | HatOLOGY | 514

Party Song
Alex Merck Group | Dog Days | Jazzline | ???

Party Time
Vince Jones Group | For All Colours | Intuition Records | INT 3071-2
Oscar Peterson Septet | The Silent Partner | Pablo | 2312103

Pas A Pas
Vario 12 | Vario | Moers Music | 02048

Pas De Deux
Bob Belden Ensemble | Treasure Island | Sunnyside | SSC 1041 D
Jasper Van't Hof Groups | The Selfkicker | MPS | 68164
Jasper Van't Hof | Flowers Allover lf675 | MPS | 68207

Pas De Nuit
Radtke/Bauer/Basmann | A Contrast Music | Edition Collage | EC 491-2

Pas De Nuit-
Bertha Hope Trio | In Search Of.. | Steeplechase | SCCD 31276

Pas De Trois
John Hicks Trio | John Hicks | Evidence | TR 119

Pas Si Belle
Guy Cabay Quartet | The Ghost Of McCoy's Castle | B.Sharp Records | CDS 101

Pas(s)ing Moments
Rod Mason's Savannah Orchestra/Hot Five | Rod Mason's Hot Music | Timeless | TTD 550/51

Pasilo Costaricense Pirre,Vals Venecolano Alp
Dimitrios Vassilakis Daedalus Project | Labyrinth | Candid | CCD 79776

Pasiphae's Dance
Bennie Wallace Quartet | The Free Will | Enja | ENJ-3063 2

Pasos Que Quedan
Art Blakey And The Jazz Messengers | Des Femmes Disparaissent/Les Tricheurs(Original Soundtracks) | Fontana | 834752-2 PMS

Pass Me By
The Jackson Singers | Gospel Emotions | L+R Records | CDLR 44016

Pass Me Not O Gentle Savior
Benny Moten's Kansas City Orchestra | Victor Jazz History Vol.9:Kansas City(1926-32) | RCA | 2128563-2

TITELVERZEICHNIS

Pass Out Lightly
Shorty Rogers And The Big Band | The Swingin' Nutcracker | Fresh Sound Records | ND 42121

Pass The Gravy
Lou Stein Duo | Stompin' 'Em Down | Chiaroscuro | CR 173

Passacaglia In C Minor(BWV 582)
Jacques Loussier Trio | Reflections Of Bach | Teldec | 2292-44431-2

Passacaille
Play Bach No.2 | Accord | 500182

Passage
Cindy Blackman Quartet | In The Now | HighNote Records | HCD 7024
William Ackerman Group | Passage | Windham Hill | TA-C- 1014

Passage-
European Jazz Trio | Orange City | Timeless | CD SJP 336

Passage To The Ear(part 1)
Reiner Witzel Group | Passage To The Ear | Nabel Records:Jazz Network | CD 4668

Passage To The Ear(part 2)
Benny Aronov Quintet | Shadow Box | Candid | CRS 1021 IMS

Passages
Leipziger Saxophon Quartett + Rolf Von Nordenskjöld | Passages: Leipziger Saxophon Quartet Plays Rolf Von Nordenskjöld | BIT | 11158

Passaggio
Jean-Paul Céléa-Francois Couturier Quintet | Passagio | Nocturne Productions | NPCD 509

Passanova
Joe Pass | Virtuoso No.3 | Original Jazz Classics | OJC20 684-2(2310805)
Caito Marcondes Group With The Turtle Island String Quartet | Porta Do Templo | ACT | 5016-2

Passarim
Manfredo Fest Quintet | Oferenda | Concord | CCD 4539

Passarinho
Chicago Underground Trio | Possible Cube | Delmark | DE 511

Passe
Günter Christmann/Torsten Müller | Carte Blanche | FMP | 1100

Passege D.E.
Draft | Traveling Birds | Jazz Haus Musik | JHM 68 CD

Passenger Of The Dark
Jean-Luc Ponty Quintet | Aurora | Atlantic | SD 19158

Passing
Jan Garbarek Quartet | Works | ECM | 823266-2

Passing Cloud
Thilo von Westernhagen Group | Forgotten Gardens | Acoustic Music Records | AMC 1011

Passing Ships
Masters | Masters | Carlyne | 695011

Passing Time
Archie Shepp Sextet | Passion | 52e Rue Est | RECD 018

Passion
Karl Scharnweber Trio With Timbre | Choral Concert(Passion) | KlangRäume | 30160

Passion Dance
Kenny Barron | Spiral | Eastwind | EWIND 709
LeeAnn Ledgerwood Trio | Walkin' Up | Steeplechase | SCCD 31541
McCoy Tyner Big Band | The Best Of McCoy Tyner Big Band | Dreyfus Jazz Line | FDM 37012-2
The Turning Point | Birdology | 513163-2
Rahsaan Roland Kirk Group | Rahsaan Rolnd Kirk:Dog Years In The Fourth Ring | 32 Jazz | 32032

Passion Flower
Chico Hamilton Quintet | Gongs East | Discovery | DS 831 IMS
Duke Ellington And His Orchestra | Duke Ellington: The Champs-Elysees Theater January 29-30th,1965 | Laserlight | 36131
The Duke Live In Santa Monica Vol.2 | Queen-Disc | 070
Ella Fitzgerald With The Duke Ellington Orchestra | Ella At Duke's Place | Verve | 529700-2
Elvin Jones Quartet | Very Rare & Love And Peace | Konnex Records | KCD 5036
Johnny Hodges Orchestra | Planet Jazz:Johnny Hodges | Planet Jazz | 2152065-2
Highlights From The Duke Ellington Centennial Edition | RCA | 2663672-2
Passion Flower 1940-46 | Bluebird | 63 66616-2
Kenny Barron Trio | Wanton Spirit | Verve | 522364-2
Oliver Nelson Quintet | Oliver Nelson Feat. Kenny Dorham | Original Jazz Classics | OJCCD 227-2(NJ 8224)
Peter Appleyard Quintet | Barbados Cool | Concord | CCD 4475
SLC(The Swing Limited Corporation) | The Swing Limited Corporation Story | Nocturne Productions | NTCD 107
Zoot Sims With Orchestra | Passion Flower | Original Jazz Classics | OJCCD 939-2(2312120)
Bill Mays Trio | An Ellington Affair | Concord | CCD 4651

Passion Flower-
Johnny Hodges Orchestra | The Rabbit's Work On Verve In Chronological Order, Vol. 6 | Verve | 2304446 IMS
The Pugh-Taylor Project | The Pugh-Taylor Project | dmp Digital Music Productions | CD 448

Passion Flower(aka A Flower Is A Lovesome Thing)
John Klemmer Quartet | Involvement | Chess | 076139-2

Passion Food
Steve Turre Group | Lotus Flower | Verve | 559787-2

Passionnova
Charles Mingus Quintet With Roland Kirk | Charles Mingus-Passion Of A Man:The Complete Atlantic Recordings 1956-1961 | Atlantic | 8122-72871-2

Passions Of A Man
The Very Best Of Charles Mingus | Rhino | 8122-79988-2
Oh Yeah | Atlantic | 90667-1 TIS

Passions Of A Woman Loved
Charles Mingus Quintet | Charles Mingus-Passion Of A Man:The Complete Atlantic Recordings 1956-1961 | Atlantic | 8122-72871-2
Charles Mingus -Passions Of A Man | Atlantic | ATL 60143
Johannes Barthelmes-Uli Lenz | Trane's Tree | Konnex Records | KCD 5057

Passport
Charlie Haden-Joe Henderson-Al Foster | The Montreal Tapes | Verve | 9813132
Charlie Parker Quintet | Charlie Parker: The Verve Years (1948-50) | Verve | 2-2501 IMS
Eddie Daniels Group | To Bird With Love | GRP | GRP 95442

Passport To Paradise
Herbie Steward Quintet | Al Haig Meets The Master Saxes Vol.3 | Spotlite | SPJ 143

Passport Tune Y(rare)
Charlie Parker Quintet | Swedish Schnapps + | Verve | 849393-2

Passport Tune Z(common)
Swedish Schnapps + | Verve | 849393-2

Passport's In The House
Carlos Bica & Azul | Look What They've Done To My Song | Enja | ENJ-9458 2

Password
Bennie Maupin Ensemble | The Jewel In The Lotus | ECM | 1043

Past Carin'
B.B.King And His Band | Singin' The Blues/The Blues | Ace Records | CDCHD 320

Past In The Present
Bennie Maupin Ensemble | The Jewel In The Lotus | ECM | 1043

Past Mistakes
Shelly Manne Trio | Li'l Abner | Original Jazz Classics | OJCCD 1087-2(S 7533)

Past My Prime
Christoph Schweizer Sextet | Normal Garden | Mons Records | MR 874660

Past Present(2)
Eddie Cleanhead Vinson & Roomful Of Blues | Eddie Cleanhead Vinson & Roomful Of Blues | Muse | MCD 5282

Past Time
James Blood Ulmer-George Adams Phalanx | Got Something Good For You | Moers Music | 02046 CD

Past,Present & Future
Grant Green With Orchestra | The Final Comedown(Soundtrack) | Blue Note | 581678-2
Joe Pass | Virtuoso No.3 | Original Jazz Classics | OJC20 684-2(2310805)

Pasta Blues
Phil Minton And Veryan Weston | Ways Past | ITM Records | ITM 1468

Pastel
Illinois Jacquet Quintet | Illinois Jacquet Flying Home-The Best Of The Verve Years | Verve | 521644-2

Pastel Morning
David Murray/Jack DeJohnette | In Our Style | DIW | DIW 819 CD

Pastels
Stan Kenton And His Orchestra | Swing Vol.1 | Storyville | 4960343
Wolfgang Lauth Quartet | Lauther | Bear Family Records | BCD 15717 AH
Bill Evans & Push | Live In Europe | Lipstick Records | LIP 890292

Pastilja Elastica
Paul Lingle | They Tore My Playhouse Down...But I've Still Got My Bales & Lingle Records | Good Time Jazz | GTCD 12025-2

Pastoral
Bobby Hutcherson Sextet | Components | Blue Note | 829027-2
Mike Westbrook Concert Band | Celebration | Deram | 844852-2

Pastorale
Jacques Loussier Trio | Jacques Loussier Plays Bach | Telarc Digital | CD 83411

Pas-Vous?
Fats Waller And His Rhythm | The Classic Years In Digital Stereo: Swing-Small Groups | CDS Records Ltd. | REB 666

Pat 'n Chat
Guido Manusardi Quartet | Bra Session | SPLASC(H) Records | H 125

Pata In Rouen
Volker Schlott Quartet | Akribik | Acoustic Music Records | 319.1165.2

Patch Of Light(I)
Arild Andersen Quintet With The Cikada String Quartet | Hyperborean | ECM | 1631(537342-2)

Patch Of Light(II)
The Colson Unity Troup | No Reservation | Black Saint | BSR 0043

Patches
Ron Carter Group | Peg Leg | Original Jazz Classics | OJCCD 621-2

Patchouli
Freddie Bryant Group | Brazilian Rosewood | Fresh Sound Records | FSNT 035 CD

Patchwork In D
Sweet Honey In The Rock | In This Land | FMS-Records | 2054 CD

Pateiros
Joe Masters Orchestra & Choir | The Jazz Mass By John Masters | Discovery | DS 785 IMS

Path Of The Heart
Vinny Valentino & Here No Evil | Now And Again | dmp Digital Music Productions | CD 3003

Path To The Shore
Shelly Manne And His Men | Swinging Sounds | Original Jazz Classics | OJCCD 267-2(C 3516)

Pathways
Frederic Rabold Crew | Funky Tango | MPS | 68242

Patmos
Juraj Galan-Norbert Dömling And Friends | Playing For Love | BELL Records | BLR 84026

Patrice
Pepper Adams Quartet | Epherma | Spotlite | SPJ LP 6 (PA 6)

Patricia
Art Pepper Quartet | Art Pepper:The Complete Galaxy Recordings | Galaxy | 16GCD 1016-2
Art Pepper Quintet | The Return Of Art Pepper -The Complete Art Pepper Aladdin Recordings Vol.1 | Blue Note | 870601-9

Patrick's Mood
Harmut Geerken/Famoudou Don Moye/John Tchicai | Cassava Balls | Praxis | CM 111

Pat's Blues
Frank Nimsgern Group | Frank Nimsgern feat. Chaka Khan/Billy Cobham | Lipstick Records | LIP 890012

Patterns
Bobby Hutcherson Quintet | Patterns | Blue Note | 833583-2

Patterns Which Connect
Herb Ellis Quintet | Jazz-Club: Guitar | Verve | 840035-2

Patti Cake
Thom Rotella Band | Thom Rotella Band | dmp Digital Music Productions | CD 460

Pattin' And Pokin'
Fats Waller And His Rhythm | The Last Years 1940-1943 | Bluebird | ND 90411(3)

Patting
Tony Ortega Octet | Jazz For Young Moderns | Fresh Sound Records | FSR 2006(Bethlehem BCP 79)

Patty
Herbie Harper Quartet | Jazz In Hollywood:Herbie Harper | Original Jazz Classics | OJCCD 1887-2(Nocturne NLP-1/NLP-7)

Pau Rolov(dedicated to Nana Vasconcelos)
Ray Anderson Trio | Right Down Your Alley | Soul Note | 121087-2

Pauline's Blues
Terry Gibbs Quartet | Take It From Me | Impulse(MCA) | JAS 60 (AS 58)

Paul's Abschied
Don Bagley Quintet | The Soft Sell | Blue Moon | BMCD 1603

Paul's Cause
Paul Kuhn Quintet | Deutsches Jazz Fesival 1954/1955 | Bear Family Records | BCD 15430

Paul's Festival Blues
Eric Felten Group | Gratitude | Soul Note | 121296-2

Paul's Pal
Herb Pomeroy Ensemble | Lenox School Of Jazz Concert | Royal Jazz | RJD 513
John Hicks Quintet | In Concert | Evidence | TRCD 123
Red Mitchell Quartet | Presenting Red Mitchell | Original Jazz Classics | OJCCD 158-2(C 7538)
Sonny Rollins Quartet | Tenor Madness | Original Jazz Classics | OJC20 124-2
Sonny Rollins Trio | St.Thomas:Sonny Rollins In Stockholm 1959 | Dragon | DRCD 229
St.Thomas:Sonny Rollins In Stockhom 1959 | Dragon | DRCD 229
In Sweden 1959 | Ingo | 9
Buddy Rich And His Orchestra | The Amazing Buddy Rich: Time Being | RCA | ND 86459(847168)

Pause
John Taylor Group | Pause, And Think Again | FMR | FMR CD 24
Joey Baron | Live At Knitting Factory Vol.2 | Enemy | EMY 112(03512)

Pauvre Terre
Ferenc Snétberger Trio | Obsession | TipToe | TIP-888834 2

Pava
Deborah Henson-Conant Group | Deborah Henson-Conant:Best Of Instrumental Music | Laika Records | 35101322

Pava Diablo
Budapest | Laika Records | LK 93-039
Arild Andersen Trio | The Triangle | ECM | 1752(0381212)

Pavane
Bill Evans Trio With Symphony Orchestra | Bach-Chopin-Scriabin-Granados-Faure-Evans | Verve | 2304525 IMS
Bill Evans Trio With The Claus Ogerman Orchestra | The Complete Bill Evans On Verve | Verve | 527953-2
Compact Jazz: Bill Evans | Verve | 831366-2 PMS
Erroll Garner Trio | That's Jazz Vol.13: The Greatest Garner | Atlantic | ATL 50243
Glenn Miller And His Orchestra | The Original Sounds Of The Swing Era Vol. 3 | RCA | 26.28131 DP
Louis Stewart Quintet | Milesian Source | Ronnie Scott's Jazz House | NSPL 18555
Peter Fulda Trio With Céline Rudolph | Silent Dances | Jazz 4 Ever Records:Jazz Network | J4E 4731
Vince Mendoza With The WDR Big Band And Guests | Sketches | ACT | 9215-2
Woody Herman And His Orchestra | La Fiesta | West Wind Orchestra Series | 2400 CD

Pavane 'Thoughts Of A Septuagenarian'
Christoph Stiefel Trio | Sweet Paradox | Jazzline | JL 11148-2

Pavane(Pour Une Infante Defunte)
Jacky Terrasson-Emmanuel Pahud Quartet | Into The Blue | Blue Note | 557257-2

Pavane(Ravel)
Erroll Garner Trio | The Greatest Garner | Rhino | SD 1227

Pawn Ticket
George Shearing Quintet | At Newport | Pablo | PACD 5315-2
Johnny Smith Quartet | Johnny Smith And His New Quartet | Fresh Sound Records | FSR-CD 80(882190)

Pawnee Junction
Cowws Quintet | Grooves 'N' Loops | FMP | CD 59

Paws
Carla Bley Band | Night-Glo | Watt | 16

Paws Without Claws-
Andrew Hill Quintet | Joe Henderson-The Blue Note Years | Blue Note | 789287-2

Payhouse
The Robert Cray Band | False Accusations | Crosscut | CCD 11012

Pays Lointain(Schumann)
Mario Bauzá And His Afro-Cuban Jazz Orchestra | My Time Is Now | Messidor | 15842 CD

Pazmuerte
Phineas Newborn Jr. Trio | The Newborn Touch | Original Jazz Classics | OJCCD 270-2

Pazuzu
Rob Brown Trio | Breath Rhyme | Silkheart | SHCD 122

P-Bouk
Yusef Lateef Quintet | Live at Pep's Vol.2 | Impulse(MCA) | 547961-2
Axel Zwingenberger | Kansas City Boogie Jam | Vagabond | VRCD 8.00027

PC Bounce
Dean Magraw Group | Kitchen Man | Acoustic Music Records | 319.1133.2

Pea Vine Special
John Lee Hooker | John Lee Hooker | Original Jazz Classics | 61140
Abdullah Ibrahim | Knysna Blue | TipToe | TIP-888816 2

Peace
Ashley Alexander Big Band | Power Slide | Pausa | PR 7178(952087)
Borah Bergman-Hamid Drake | Reflections On Ornette Coleman And The Stone House | Soul Note | 121280-2
Chet Baker Quartet | Echoes of Enja | Enja | 4000
Chico Freeman Quartet | Spirit Sensitive | India Navigation | IN 1045 CD
Dick de Graaf-Tony Lakatos Quintet | New York Straight Ahead | Challenge | CHR 70033
Horace Silver Quintet | Horace Silver | Blue Note | 84510
Horace Silver Retrospective | Blue Note | 495576-2
Ira Sullivan Quintet | Peace | Galaxy | GXY 5114
Joe Diorio | Italy | MGI Records | MGR CD 1010
Larry Schneider Quartet | Ornettology | Steeplechase | SCCD 31461
Mike Zwerin Trio | Not Much Noise | Spotlite | SPJ LP 19
Ornette Coleman Quartet | The Shape Of Jazz To Come | Atlantic | 7567-81339-2
Shirley Scott Trio | Skylark | Candid | CCD 79705
Stefan Pelzl's Juju feat. Idris Muhammad | Juju | L+R Records | CDLR 45026
The Atlantic String Trio | First Meeting | Factory Outlet Records | 2001-1 CD
Viktoria Tolstoy With The Jacob Karlzon Trio | Blame It On My Youth | Kaza(EMI) | 536620-2
Abdullah Ibrahim | Fats Duke And Monk | Sackville | SKCD2-3048

Peace-
Peter Kowald/Vincent Chancey | Duos: America | FMP | 1270

Peace Above
James Blood Ulmer's Black Rock Revival | Knitting Factory Tours Europe Way 23-June 15,1991 | Enemy | EMCD 121(03521)

Peace Chorale-
Jeanne Lee Group | Natural Affinities | Owl Records | 018352-2

Peace Chorale(II)-
Jean-Luc Ponty Quintet | Civilized Evil | Atlantic | SD 16020

Peace For Kabul
The Fringe | It's Time For The Fringe | Soul Note | 121205-2

Peace Fugue
Gil Scott-Heron/Brian Jackson Group | Winter In America | Strata East Records | 660.51.015

Peace In Our Time
John Lee Hooker | The Real Folk Blues | Chess | CHD 9271(872291)

Peace Memory
D.D.Jackson-David Murray | Paired Down,Vol.2 | Justin Time | JUST 104-2

Peace Of Mind
Lonnie Smith Septet | Live At Club Mozambique | Blue Note | 831880-2

Peace Of The Korridor
Special EFX | Peace Of The World | GRP | GRP 96402

Peace Piece
Bill Evans Trio | Paris 1965 | Royal Jazz | RJD 503
Kronos Quartet | Music Of Bill Evans | Landmark | LCD 1510-2

Peace Pipe
Diederik Wissels Quintet | Kamook | B.Sharp Records | CDS 083

Peace Power
John Patitucci Group | Another World | GRP | GRP 97252

Peace To
B.B.King And His Band | Live At San Quentin | MCA | MCD 06103

Peace To The World
B.B.King With The Philip Morris Super Band | Live At The Apollo | MCA | MCA 09637

Peace Tongues
Attila Zoller | Lasting Love | Acoustic Music Records | 319.1131.2

Peace Waltz
Dianne Mower And Her Group | A Song For You | Jazz City | 660.53.023

Peace Warriors
Noel Akchoté-Marc Ribot-Eugene Chadbourne | Lust Corner | Winter&Winter | 910019-2
Ornette Coleman & Prime Time | In All Languages | Harmolodic | 531915-2

Peace,Love And Light
Dave Young-Renee Rosnes | Two By Two Vol.2 | Justin Time | JUST 81-2

Peaceful
Miles Davis Group | In A Silent Way | CBS | 86556-2

Peaceful-
The Miles Davis Selection | CBS | 471623-2

Peaceful Heart
Chico Freeman Orchestra | Peaceful Heart Gentle Spirit | Contemporary | C 14005

Peaceful Question
Naked Jazz | Takes Off | Savoy | CY 18040

Peaceful Valley
Toshiko Akiyoshi-Lew Tabackin Big Band | Insights | RCA | PL 43363

Peacemaker
Chico Freeman Quintet | Focus | Contemporary | CCD 14073-2

Peach
Yutaka Yokokura Group | Yutaka | GRP | GRP 95572

Peach Tree
Sonny Boy Williamson Band | The Real Folk Blues | Chess | CHD 9272(872292)

Peaches

The Young Lions | The Young Lions | Vee Jay Recordings | VJ 001

Peaches En Regalia
Memphis Jug Band | Memphis Blues 1928-1930 | RCA | 2126409-2

Pea-Eye
Thelonious Monk Quartet | Thelonious Monk-The Complete Riverside Recordings | Riverside | 15 RCD 022-2

Pea-Eyes
Greg Abate Quartet | Bop City-Live At Birdland | Candid | CCD 79513

Peanut Butter Blues
John Hicks Trio | Some Other Time | Evidence | TR 115

Peanut Vendor
Jack Costanzo Group | Latin Fever:The Wild Rhythms Of Jack Costanza | Capitol | 590955-2
Ken Colyer's Jazzmen | Ken Colyer's Jazzmen In Concert 1959 | Dine-A-Mite Jazz | DJCD-001

Peasant Flute Song Round About Underground No.One
Bill Evans Trio | Bill Evans Trio:The Last Waltz | Milestone | 8MCD 4430-2

Peau Douce
Turn Out The Stars | Dreyfus Jazz Line | FDM 36553-2
I Will Say Goodbye | Original Jazz Classics | OJCCD 761-2(F 9593)
Carla Bley-Steve Swallow | Go Together | Watt | 24(517673-2)
Ed Bickert-Lorne Lofsky Quartet | This Is New | Concord | CCD 4414
Philipp Van Endert Group | Philipp Van Endert Group | L+R Records | CDLR 45107

Peche A La Mouche
Django Reinhardt And The Quintet Du Hot Club De France | Django Reinhardt Portrait | Barclay | DALP 2/1939

Peckin'
Benny Goodman And His Orchestra | The Indispensable Benny Goodman Vol.3/4 | RCA | 2115520-2

Peculiar
Michael Cain-Ralph Alessi-Peter Epstein | Circa | ECM | 1622

Ped Cruc
Horacio Molina With Band | Tango Cancion | Messidor | 15910

Pedal Point Blues
Charles Mingus Orchestra | Nostalgia In Times Square/The Immortal 1959 Sessions | CBS | 88337
Howard Riley | For Four On Two Two | Affinity | AFF 110

Pedalin'
Mick Goodrick Quartet | In Pas(s)ing | ECM | 1139

Pedalpusher
Emily Remler Quartet | Catwalk | Concord | CCD 4265

Pedestrian Tales
George Colligan & Jesper Bodilsen | A Wish | Steeplechase | SCCD 31507

Pedro Strodder
Joe Henderson Quintet | Our Thing | Blue Note | 525647-2

Pedro's Time
Tubby Hayes Orchestra | Tubbs' Tours | Mole Jazz | MOLF 4

Pee Wee
Herbie Hancock Quartet | Herbie Hancock Quartet | CBS | SRCS 9343
Miles Davis Quintet | Miles Davis Quintet 1965-1968 | CBS | C6K 67398
Tony Williams Quintet | Angel Street | Blue Note | 748494-2
Pee Wee Russell And His Orchestra | Portrait Of Pee Wee | Fresh Sound Records | FSR-CD 126(882874)

Pee Wee Speaks
Eddie Condon All Stars | Eddie Condon In Japan | Chiaroscuro | CR 154

Peel Me A Grape
Blossom Dearie Trio | Sweet Blossom Dearie | Philips | PHCE 1019 PMS
Kristin Korb With The Ray Brown Trio And Guests | Introducing Kristin Korb | Telarc Digital | CD 83386
Soesja Citroen And Her Quartet | Here And Now | Challenge | CHR 70003

Peepin'
Lou Donaldson Quintet | Blue Note's Three Decade Of Jazz 1959-1969, Vol. 1 | Blue Note | 89904

Peepnyv
Dave Binney Quintet | Point Game | Owl Time Line | 3819032

Pefidia
Gust Williams Tsilis Quartet | Possibilities | Ken Music | 660.56.009

Peg Leg
Hermann Martlreiter Quartet | Live at Birdland Neuburg | Birdland | BN 005

Peg O' My Heart
Lester Young-Buddy Rich Trio | Lester Swings | Verve | 833554-1
Lester Young-Nat King Cole | Lester Young:The Complete 1936-1951 Small Group Sessions(Studio Recordings-Master Takes),Vol.3 | Blue Moon | BMCD 1003
Miff Mole And His Nicksieland Band | The Commodore Story | Commodore | CMD 24002

Pega Joso
Ugly White Belly | South Of No North | Timeless | CD SJP 415

Pegasos
Jack Walrath-Ralph Reichert Sextet | Solidarity | ACT | 9241-2

Pegasus
Stan Kenton And His Orchestra | Journey Into Capricorn | Creative World | STD 1077

Peggy The Pin Up Girl
Charles Mingus And His Orchestra | Charlie Mingus:Duke Ellington's Sound Of Love | Memo Music | HDJ 4008

Peggy's Blue Skylight
Charles Mingus Group | Live In Stockholm 1964 | Royal Jazz | RJD 518
Charles Mingus Quintet With Roland Kirk | Tonight At Noon | Atlantic | 7567-80793-2
Charles Mingus Sextet | Meditations On Integration | Bandstand | BDCD 1524
Jaki Byard | Live At The Royal Festival Hall | LEO | LR 133
Richie Cole Quintet | Signature | Milestone | MCD 9162-2

Peinlich(Desverre)
Henning Wolter Trio With Guests | Years Of A Trilogy | double moon | DMCHR 71021

Peja
Duke Ellington And His Orchestra | Togo Brava Swuite | Storyville | STCD 8323

Peke
Heiner Goebbels/Alfred Harth | Frankfurt-Peking | Riskant | 568-72411

Pekkos-Per's Wedding March
Amsterdam Jazz Quintet | Portraits | Challenge | CHR 70048

Penance
Conexion Latina | Mambo 2000 | Enja | ENJ-7055 2

Penar
William Winant-Julie Steinberg | Nana+Victorio | Avant | AVAN 012

Pendulum
Jan Garbarek Quartet | Wayfarer | ECM | 1259(811968-2)
Richard Beirach Trio | ELM | ECM | 1142

Penelope
Harold Danko/Rufus Reid | Mirth Song | Sunnyside | SSC 1001 D

Pénétration(El Nino)
Okay Temiz Group | Drummer Of Two Worlds | Warner | 58186

Penitas De Amor
Bessie Tucker | Better Boot That Thing-Great Women Blues Singers Of The 1920's | Bluebird | 63 66065 2

Pennies From Heaven
Al Haig Sextet | Stan Getz:The Complete 1948-1952 Quintet Sessions(Master Takes) | Blue Moon | BMCD 1015
Ben Webster And His Orchestra | Verve Jazz Masters 43:Ben Webster | Verve | 525431-2
Ben Webster With The Junior Mance Trio | Tenor Giants | Enja | 2038-2
Bennie Green Septet | Trombone By Three | Original Jazz Classics | OJCCD 091-2(P 7023)
Benny Goodman And His Orchestra | The Benny Goodman Yale Archives Vol.3 | Limelight | 820814-2
Dave Brubeck Quartet | Interchanges '54 | CBS | 467917-2
David 'Bubba' Brooks With The Kenny Drew Jr. Quartet | Smooth Sailing | TCB Records | TCB 97702
Dinah Washington With Her All Stars | Verve Jazz Masters 19:Dinah Washington | Verve | 518200-2
Django Reinhardt-André Ekyan | Django Reinhardt:Djangology | EMI Records | 780659-2
Gene Ammons And His All Stars | Juganthology | Prestige | P 24036
Harry Edison Quartet | The Inventive Mr. Edison | Fresh Sound Records | 054 2402661(Pacific Jazz PJ 11)
J.J.Johnson Quintet | The Eminent J.J.Johnson Vol.1 | Blue Note | BLP 1505 (CDP 7815052)
Jacintha And Her Band | Jacintha | Groove Note | GRV 1001-2(Gold CD 2001-2)
Jimmy Rushing With The Count Basie Orchestra | Big Band Bounce And Boogie Woogie:Good Mornin' Blues-Jimmy Rushing | Affinity | AFS 1002
Joe Newman And His Orchestra | The Complete Joe Newman RCA-Victor Recordings(1955-1956):The Basie Days | RCA | 2122613-2
Lester Young With The Bill Potts Trio | Lester Young In Washington,DC 1956:Vol.4 | Pablo | 2308230
Lester Young-Harry Edison With The Oscar Peterson Quartet | Pres & Sweets | Verve | 849391-2 PMS
Oscar Peterson Trio | The London Concert | Pablo | 2CD 2620111
Oscar Peterson-Austin Roberts | Oscar Peterson 1951 | Just A Memory | JAS 9501-2
Sarah Vaughan And Her Trio | Swingin' Easy | EmArCy | 514072-2
Schnuckenack Reinhardt Quintet | 15.3.1973 | Intercord | 160031
Stan Getz Quartet | Stan Getz In Denmark1958-59 | Olufsen Records | DOCD 6011
Stan Getz Quintet | Jazz At Storyville Vol.2 | Fresh Sound Records | FSR 630(Roost RLP 411)
Sy Oliver Orchestra | Yes Indeed | Black & Blue | BLE 59.049 2
Thilo Wagner Trio | Wagner,Mörike.Beck,Finally. | Nagel-Heyer | CD 078
Vince Giordano's Nighthawks | Qualty Shout | Stomp Off Records | CD 1260
Zoot Sims/Bob Brookmeyer Octet | Stretching Out | Fresh Sound Records | 054 2602761(United Artists UAL 4023)

Pennies From Heaven-
J.J.Johnson Quintet | The Eminent J.J.Johnson Vol.2 | Blue Note | 532144-2

Pennies From Heaven(alt.take)
Rolf Römer-Bill Dobbins Quartet | A Tribute To B.A.C.H. | Edition Collage | EC 520-2

Pennies In D(for J.S.B.)
Walter Roland | Lucille Bogan & Walter Roland 1927-1935 | Yazoo | YAZ 1017

Pennillium
Clarence Penn Quartet | Penn's Landing | Criss Cross | Criss 1134

Pennsylvania Six Five Thousand
Glenn Miller And His Orchestra | The Unforgettable Glenn Miller | RCA | PD 89260
Glenn Miller-The Great Instrumentals 1938-1942 | Retrieval | RTR 79001
Glenn Miller | Koch Records | 321 941 D1
The Very Best Of Glenn Miller | RCA | PL 89009 AO
Horst Gmeinwieser 'One Cue Big Band' | Bigband-Fieber | Media Arte | CD 06569209(BRW)

Penny
Stan Getz Quartet | Stan Getz-The Complete Roost Sessions | The Jazz Factory | JFCD 22839

Penny Lane
Klaus Ignatzek | Plays Beatles Songs | Nabel Records:Jazz Network | CD 4643
Randy Weston Orchestra | Volcano Blues | Verve | 519269-2

Penny Saved
Sidsel Endresen-Bugge Wesseltoft | Duplex Ride | ACT | 9000-2

Pensativa
Bill Evans Trio With Lee Konitz & Warne Marsh | Crosscurrents | Original Jazz Classics | OJCCD 718-2(F 9568)
Clare Fischer With The Metropole Orchestra | The Latin Side | Koch Jazz | 3-6907-2
Hubert Laws And His Orchestra | Wild Flower | Atlantic | SD 1624

Pensativa-
Bengt Hallberg Quartet | Hallberg's Hot Accordion In The Foreground | Phontastic | NCD 7532

Penséer,Waltz
EOS | Mosaico | yvp music | CD 3056

Pension Lotterman
Pension Winnetou | Pension Winnetou | Moers Music | 02028

Pensive
Great Guitars | Great Guitars At Charlie's Georgetown | Concord | CCD 4209
Julius Hemphill Quintet | New York City Jazz-4 | Polydor | 815109-1 IMS
Count Basie And His Orchestra | Count On The Coast Vol.2 | Phontastic | NCD 7575

Pensive Miss
Jazz Collection:Count Basie | Laserlight | 24368
Basie On Roulette, Vol. 2: Basie Plays Hefti | Vogue | 500002

Penta
Rolf Römer Trio | Tesoro | Jazz 4 Ever Records:Jazz Network | J4E 4743

Penta Chang
Dino Saluzzi-Anthony Cox-David Friedman | Rios | VeraBra Records | CDVBR 2156-2

Penta Y Uno
Silvano Chimenti Quartet & Guests | Soft Impressions | Penta Flowers | CDPIA 018

Pentacostal Feeling
Robin Eubanks Group | Karma | JMT Edition | 834446-2

Pentahouve
Mark Helias Group | Loopin' The Cool | Enja | ENJ-9049 2
Ray Drummond Sextet | Excursion | Arabesque Recordings | AJ 0106

Pentatonic
Donald Byrd Sextet | Blackjack | Blue Note | 784466-2

Pentecostal Feeling
Donald Byrd Quintet | The Blue Testament | Blue Note | 780703-2

Penthés(il)ée
Bill Dixon Quartet | November 1981 | Soul Note | 121038-2

Penthouse In The Basement
Louis Jordan And His Tympany Five | Louis Jordan Vol.1-Hoodoo Man | Swingtime(Contact) | ST 1011

Penthouse Serenade
Erroll Garner Trio | Gems | CBS | 21062
Stan Getz With Strings And Voices | Reflections | Verve | 523322-2
Toots Thielemans With Orchestra | Bluesette | Polydor | 2482218 IMS

Penthouse Serenade-
Eric Alexander Quartet | Two Of A Kind | Criss Cross | Criss 1133

Pentimento
Jürgen Knieper Quintet | State Of Things | Jazz Haus Musik | JHM 0104 CD

Pentium
Bluiett-Jackson-Thiam | Join Us | Justin Time | JUST 124-2

Pentonville
29th Street Saxophone Quartet | Milano New York Bridge | Red Records | 123262-2

Pent-Up House
Chet Baker Sextet | Chet Is Back | RCA | NL 70578 AG
Chet Baker-Paul Bley | Diane | Steeplechase | SCM 51207
Hank Jones Trio | A Jazz Par 91 Project | Storyville | STCD 4180
Sonny Rollins Quintet | Saxophone Colossus And More | Prestige | P 24050
Stephane Grappelli Quintet | Grapelli Story | Verve | 515807-2
Stephane Grappelli Trio With Marcel Azzola | Stephane Grappelli In Toky | Denon Compact Disc | CY-77130
Ted Curson Trio | The Trio | Interplay | IP 7722

People
Bill Evans | The Complete Fantasy Recordings | Fantasy | 9FCD 1012-2
Charlie Hunter & Pound For Pound | Return Of The Candyman | Blue Note | 823108-2
Ella Fitzgerald With The Tommy Flanagan Quartet | Ella Fitzgerald:Newport Jazz Festival-Live at Carnegie Hall | CBS | C2K 66809
Esther Phillips With The Ray Ellis Orchestra | And I Love Him! | Atlantic | AMCY 1061
George Shearing | More Grand Piano | Concord | CCD 4318
Gunter Hampel Quartet | Time Is Now-Live At The Eldena Jazz Festival 1992 | Birth | CD 042
Hampton Hawes Trio | Here And Now | Original Jazz Classics | OJCCD 178-2(C 7616)
Maynard Ferguson And His Orchestra | Dues | Mainstream | MD CDO 725
Oscar Peterson And The Bassists | Montreux '77-The Art Of The Jam Session | Pablo | 2620106
Oscar Peterson Trio | The London Concert | Pablo | 2CD 2620111
Pata Horns | New Archaic Music | Pata Musik | PATA 4(JHM 42) CD
The American Jazz Orchestra | Central City Sketches | Limelight | 820819-2 IMS
Vince Guaraldi-Bola Sete Quartet | Live At El Matador | Original Jazz Classics | OJC 289(F 8371)
Michael Feinstein With Jule Styne | Michael Feinstein Sings The Jule Styne Songbook | Nonesuch | 7559-79274-2

People-
Herbie Hancock Group | Sound-System | CBS | SRCS 9509

People Die
Roland Kirk Quintet | Rahsaan/The Complete Mercury Recordings Of Roland Kirk | Mercury | 846630-2

People From Funny Girl-
Eddie Harris Quartet | People Get Funny... | Timeless | CD SJP 228

People Get Ready
J.C. Dook Quartet | Travelin' Man | Organic Music | ORGM 9734
James Booker | Blues & Ragtime From New Orleans | Aves | 146530
The Guest Stars | Live In Berlin | Riskant | 568-72233

People In Sorrow(part 1&2)
Art Ensemble Of Chicago | People In Sorrow | Nessa | N 3

People In Time
Mary Lou Williams Group | Mary Lou's Mass | Mary Records | M 102

People Makes The World Go Round
Milt Jackson And His Orchestra | Sunflower | CTI | ZK 65131
Monty Alexander Trio | The Way It Is | MPS | 68223
Ramsey Lewis Quintet | Ivory Pyramid | GRP | GRP 96882

People Time
Stan Getz-Kenny Barron | Stan Getz Cafe Montmartre | EmArCy | 586755-2
Third Person | Third Person-The Bends | Enemy | EMCD 124(03524)

People Will Say We're In Love
Cannonball Adderley Quintet | Portrait Of Cannonball | Original Jazz Classics | OJCCD 361-2(RLP 269)
Doug Watkins Trio | Donald Byrd & Doug Watkins:The Tradition Sessions | Blue Note | 540528-2
Eddie Lockjaw Davis And His Orchestra | The Fox And The Hounds | RCA | NL 70120
Eric Alexander Sextet | Full Range | Criss Cross | Criss 1098
Kenny Burrell Quartet | Kenny Burrell-Bluesin' Around | CBS | FC 38507
Lou Donaldson Quintet | The Natural Soul | Blue Note | 542307-2
Marion Montgomery And Her Quartet | I Gotta Right To Sing... | Ronnie Scott's Jazz House | JHCD 003
Ted Brown Quintet | In Good Company | Criss Cross | Criss 1020 (835608)
The Mastersounds | Swinging With The Mastersounds | Original Jazz Classics | OJC 280(F 8050)

People(radio edit)
Peter Weniger Quartet | Weirdoes | Mons Records | MR 874826

Pep
Jelly Roll Morton | Didn't He Ramble | Black & Blue | BLE 59.228 2

Pepe Linque
Paul Quinichette Quartet | The International Jazz Group Vol.2 | Swing | SW 8416

Peping
Marcos Valle With Orchestra | Samba '68 | Verve | 559516-2

Pepino Beach
Cecil McBee Sextet | Compassion-Music From The Source Vol.2 | Enja | 3041 (807498)

Pepit
The Rosenberg Trio | Suenos Gitanos | Polydor | 549581-2

Pepito
Irvin Rochlin Trio | Quirine | Limetree | MLP 198036

Pepper Con Salsa
Nat Pierce And His Orchestra | Big Band At The Savoy Ballroom | RCA | 2130073-2

Pepper Pot
Stan Kenton And His Orchestra | Stan Kenton On The Air | Status | DSTS 1022

Peppermint Party
Count Basie And His Orchestra | Basie On Roulette, Vol. 22: Back With Basie | Vogue | 500022

Pequeno Passeio
Heiner Franz Trio | Gouache | Jardis Records | JRCD 8904
Tony Purrone Trio | Set 'Em Up | Steeplechase | SCCD 31389

Per Andsu Lietjin
Bruno Tommaso Orchestra | Su Un Tema Di Jerome Kern | SPLASC(H) Records | HP 18

Per Toda Minha Vida
Terje Rypdal Quartet | Waves | ECM | 1110(827419-2)

Per Ulv
Mitchel Forman Trio | Now And Then-A Tribute To Bill Evans | Novus | 4163165-2

Perception
Connie Crothers Trio | Perception | Steeplechase | SCCD 31022
Kenny Burrell Quintet | Kenny Burrell | Original Jazz Classics | OJCCD 019-2(P 7088)
Lou Blackburn-Freddie Hill Quintet | Perception | Fresh Sound Records | FSR-CD 0307

Perché?-
Crystal | Clear | Black-Hawk | BKH 51501

Percussion Discussion
Charles Mingus-Max Roach | Mingus At The Bohemia | Debut | VIJ 5010 IMS
Franco Ambrosetti Quintet | Light Breeze | Enja | ENJ-9331 2

Percussion Dreams
Ray Mantilla Quintet | Mantilla | Inner City | IC 1052 IMS

Perdendosi
Aki Takase | Perdido | Enja | 4034-2

Perdido
Ben Webster Quartet | Live At The Jazzhus Montmartre,Vol.2 | Jazz Colours | 874712-2
Bud Powell Trio | Bud Powell Paris Sessions | Pablo | PACD 2310972-2
Cap'n John Handy With The Claude Hopkins Band | Introducing Cap'n John Handy | RCA | NL 89503
Danny Moss Quartet | Keeper Of The Flame | Nagel-Heyer | CD 064
Datevik With The Larry Willis Quartet | Ballads From The Black Sea | Mapleshade | 04332
Dave Brubeck Quartet | The Dave Brubeck Quartet feat. Paul Desmond In Concert | Fantasy | FCD 60-013
Newport '58:Brubeck Plays Ellington | CBS | 450317-1
Dinah Washington With The Quincy Jones Orchestra | The Swingin' Miss 'D' | Verve | 558074-2
Dizzy Gillespie And His Orchestra | A Portrait Of Duke Ellington | Verve | 817107-1 IMS
Duke Ellington And His Famous Orchestra | Duke Ellington:The Blanton-Webster Band | Bluebird | 21 13181-2
Ben Webster-Cotton Tail | RCA | 63667902
Duke Ellington And His Orchestra | Duke Ellington's 70th Birthday Concert | Blue Note | 837746-2
The Jazz Collector Edition: Duke Ellington | Laserlight | 15710
Highlights From The Duke Ellington Centennial Edition | RCA | 2663672-2
Duke Ellington:Complete Studio Transcriptions | Definitive Records | DRCD 11199

TITELVERZEICHNIS

Duke Ellington All Star Road Band | Doctor Jazz | ZL 70968(2) (809318)
Togo Brava Swuite | Storyville | STCD 8323
Duke Ellington: The Champs-Elysees Theater January 29-30th,1965 | Laserlight | 36131
Happy Birthday Duke Vol.2 | Laserlight | 15784
Jazz Collection:Duke Ellington | Laserlight | 24369
Way Low | Duke Records | D 1015
Dutch Swing College Band | Digital Dutch | Philips | 814068-2 PMS
Earl Hines Trio | Earl Hines Live! | Storyville | STCD 8222
Eddie Allen Quintet | Another Point Of View | Enja | 8004-2
Ella Fitzgerald With The Duke Ellington Orchestra | The Complete Ella Fitzgerald Song Books of Harold Arlen, Irving Berlin, Duke Ellington, George & Ira Gershwin, Jerome Kern, Johnny Mercer, Cole Porter And Rogers & Hart | Verve | 519832-2
Erroll Garner | Historical First Recording 1944 | Jazz Anthology | 550042
Gebhard Ullmann Quartet | Per-Dee-Doo | Nabel Records:Jazz Network | CD 4640
George Robert-Phil Woods Quintet | The Summit | Mons Records | MR 874304
JATP All Stars | This Is Jazz | Verve | 2615040 IMS
JATP In Tokyo | Pablo | 2620104-2
The Complete Jazz At The Philharmonic On Verve 1944-1949 | Verve | 523893-2
The Complete Jazz At The Philharmonic On Verve 1944-1949 | Verve | 523893-2
Jazz At The Philharmonic:Best Of The 1940's Concerts | Verve | 557534-2
Charlie Parker Jazz At The Philharmonic 1949 | Verve | 519803-2
Johnny Hodges Orchestra | Jazz Legacy 9: Johnny Hodges-The Rabbit In Paris | Vogue | 500059
Coleman Hawkins/Johnny Hodges:The Vogue Recordings | Vogue | 21559712
Johnny Hodges With The Al Waslon Trio | A Man And His Music | Storyville | SLP 4073
Louis Armstrong And His All Stars | Jazz In Paris:Louis Armstrong:The Best Live Concer Vol.1 | EmArCy | 013030-2
New Orleans Louisiana | Traditional Line | TL 1319
The Best Live Concert | Festival | ???
Luis 'Perico' Ortiz And His Orchestra | In Tradition | Messidor | 15947
Max Roach Quartet | Jazzbühne Berlin '84 | Repertoire Records | REPCD 4902-CC
Oscar Pettiford And His Birdland Band | Jazz On The Air Vol.6: Oscar Pettiford And His Birdland Band | Spotlite | SPJ 153
Quintet Of The Year | The Quintet-Jazz At Massey Hall | Debut | DSA 124-6
Charlie Parker The Immortal Sessions Vol.2:1949-1953 | SAGA Jazz Classics | EC 3319-2
Randy Weston Trio | Berhshire Blues | Black Lion | BLCD 760205
Rias Big Band | The Music Of Duke Ellington | Mons Records | MR 874306
Roy Eldridge 4 | The Montreux '77 Collection | Pablo | 2620107
Sarah Vaughan With The Count Basie Band | The Roulette Years Vol. One/Two | Roulette | CDP 794983-2
Sonny Criss With The JATP All Stars | Intermission Riff | Pablo | 2310929
Swiss All Stars | Jazz In Switzerland 1930-1975 | Elite Special | 9544002/1-4
Tatum-Hampton-Rich Trio | The Tatum Group Masterpieces | Pablo | 2625706

Perdido-
Oscar Peterson Quartet | Oscar Peterson Live! | Pablo | 2310940-2
Tenor Conclave With The Rein De Graaff Trio | Tenor Conclave | Timeless | CD SJP 306

Perdido Street Blues
Barrelhouse Jazzband | Barrelhouse Jazzband & Angi Domdey | L+R Records | CDLR 70003
Louis Armstrong And His Orchestra | Louis Armstrong Vol.3-Louis With Guest Stars | MCA | 1306

Perdido(part 1&2)
Don Byron Quartet | Romance With The Unseen | Blue Note | 499545-2

Perdido(Pegao)
Charlie Parker Quintet | Bird's Eyes-Last Unissued Vol.2+3 | Philology | W 12/15.2

Perenne
Benny Green Quintet | Prelude | Criss Cross | Criss 1036

Peresina
McCoy Tyner Big Band | Journey | Birdology | 519941-2

Perfect Time
Benni Chaves-Laszlo Gardony | Human Bass | Laika Records | 35101042

Perfect Touch
Steve Coleman And Five Elements | On The Edge Of Tomorrow | JMT Edition | 919005-2

Perfect Union
Miles Davis Group | Miles Davis Live From His Last Concert In Avignon | Laserlight | 24327

Perfect Way
Tutu | Warner | 7599-25490-2
Time After Time | Jazz Door | JD 1256/57

Perfidia
Ahmad Jamal's Three Strings | Latin Jazz | CBS | 472683-2
Glenn Miller And His Orchestra | Glenn Miller In Concert | RCA | NL 89216 DP
The Ultimate Glenn Miller-22 Original Hits From The King Of Swing | RCA | 2113137-2
Gonzalo Rubalcaba Group | Suite 4 y 20 | Blue Note | 780054-2
Harold Harris Trio | Here's Harold | Vee Jay Recordings | VJR 501

Perfido
John Balke Group | Saturation | EmArCy | 538160-2

Perfume Light:
Ellis Larkins | Maybeck Recital Hall Series Volume Twenty-Two | Concord | CCD 4533

Perfume River
Duke Ellington And His Orchestra | Carnegie Hall Concert December 1944 | Prestige | 2PCD 24073-2

Perfume Suite:
Duke Ellington | Bluebird | ND 86641(3)

Perfume Worlds-
Horace Tapscott | The Tapscott Sessions Vol.5 | Nimbus | NS 1925

Perhaps
The Modern Jazz Disciples | Disciples Blues | Prestige | PCD 24263-2
Thomas Brendgens-Mönkemeyer & Jochen Voss | Textures | Jardis Records | JRCD 9920
Charlie Parker All Stars | The Complete Savoy Studio Sessions | Savoy | 886421

Perhaps One Touch Of
Charlie Parker Quintet | Bird/Encores Vol. 2 | Savoy | SJL 1129 (801883)

Perico-Lo
Gary Bartz Quartet | Another Earth | Milestone | M 9018

Perihelion And Aphelion
Kenny Werner | Beyond The Forest Of Mirkwood | Enja | 9121-2

Peripheral Vision
Phil Woods Quintet & The Festival Orchestra | Celebration! | Concord | CCD 4770

Peri's Scope
Bill Evans Trio | Bill Evans-Montreux II | CBS | 481264-2
Bill Perkins Quartet | Peaceful Moments | Fresh Sound Records | FSR 115(835316)

Perk
Shelly Manne Quintet | Perk Up | Concord | CCD 4021

Perking Lot Blues-
Bud Shank Sextet | New Gold! | Candid | CCD 79707

Perkolater
Emily Remler Quartet | Firefly | Concord | CJ 162

Perle
Blueprint Stage | Puzzle | Mons Records | MR 874817

Perlon Sweet
Ken McIntyre Trio With Strings | Ken McIntyre:The Complete United Artists Sessions | Blue Note | 857200-2

Permanent Way
Fun Horns | Fun Horns Live In South America-Natural Music | KlangRäume | 30060

Permit Me To Introduce You To Yourself
Horace Silver Quintet | That Healin' Feelin' | Blue Note | 84352

Perntz
Lars Sjösten Octet Feat. Lee Konitz | Dedicated To Lee-Lars Sjösten Plays The Music Of Lars Gullin | Dragon | DRLP 66

Perpetua
Al Di Meola Groups | Guitar Heroes Vol.1:Al Di Meola | Zounds | CD 2700044001

Perpetual Emotion
Al Di Meola World Sinfonia | World Sinfonia | Inak | 700772

Perpetuum
Indiscreet | Difficult To Contribute Silence | Nabel Records:Jazz Network | LP 4620

Perranporth
Joan Abril Quintet | Eric | Fresh Sound Records | FSNT 092 CD

Perry Mason
Mundell Lowe And His All Stars | TV Action Jazz! | RCA | 2159154-2

Persepolis
Anthony Davis-Jay Hoggard Duo | Under The Double Moon | MPS | 68267

Person To Person
Curlew | North America | Moers Music | 02042
Elmore James Band | One Way Out | Charly | CRB 1008
Oregon | The Essential Oregon | Vanguard | VSD 109/110
Joe Williams With The Norman Simmons Quartet | Ballad And Blues Master | Verve | 511354-2 PMS

Personal Extenz(for Ornette)
Albert King Blues Band | Wednesday Night In San Francisco | Stax | SCD 8556-2

Personal Manager
Blues Power No.4: Albert King-King Of The Blues Guitar | Atlantic | 40494

Personal Mountains
Kick | Wolfhound's Kick | BELL Records | BLR 84041

Perspicuity
Doug Hammond Trio | Perspicuity | L+R Records | CDLR 45031

Persuance-
Cindy Blackman Quartet | Cindy Blackman Telepathy | Muse | MCD 5437

Perugia
Roland Hanna | Perugia | Freedom | FLP 41010

Peruvian Nights
Benny Bailey Quartet With Strings | I Remember Love | Laika Records | 35101752
Benny Bailey Quintet | Live At Grabenhalle, St.Gallen | TCB Records | TCB 8940

Pesadilla
Enrico Rava Quartet | The Pilgrim And The Stars | ECM | 1063(847322-2)

Pesce Naufrago
Anouar Brahem Quartet | Conte De L'Incroyable Amour | ECM | 1457(511959-2)

Peshrev Hidjaz Homayoun
Ted Pilzecker Group | Destinations | Mons Records | CD 1885

Pet Shop
James Weiman Trio | People Music | TCB Records | TCB 96302

Petaluma
Bill Holman Band | A View From The Side | JVC | JVC 2050-2

Pete And Repete
Pete Brown Quintet | The Changing Face Of Harlem-The Savoy Sessions | Savoy | SJL 2208 (801184)

Pete Kelly's Blues
June Christy And Her Orchestra | The Misty Miss Christy | Pathe | 1566141(Capitol T 725)

Pete The Poet
Jimmy Smith With The Oliver Nelson Orchestra | Peter & The Wolf | Verve | 547264-2

Peter-
Art Ensemble Of Chicago | Urban Bushmen | ECM | 1211/12

Peter And Judith
Cannonball Adderley Sextet | THE Sextet | Milestone | M 9106

Peter And The Goats
Piccadilly Six | Fans' Favourites | Elite Special | 73319

Peter Gunn
King Curtis Band | King Curtis-Blow Man Blow | Bear Family Records | BCD 15670 CI
Mundell Lowe And His All Stars | TV Action Jazz! | RCA | 2159154-2
Sarah Vaughan With Orchestra | Sarah Vaughan Sings The Mancini Songbook | Verve | 558401-2
Shelly Manne And His Men | Jazz Gunn | Atlantic | 7567-82271-2

Peter Lorre
Lee Konitz With The Lars Sjösten Quartet | Dedicated To Lee-Lars Sjösten Plays The Music Of Lars Gullin | Dragon | DRLP 66

Peter Plays Some Blues
Horst Faigle's Jazzkrement | Gans Normal | Jazz 4 Ever Records:Jazz Network | J4E 4748

Peter Und Der Golf
Hans Reichel | Bonobo | FMP | 0280

Peter,The Genius And The Revolution
Doctor Clayton | Doctor Clayton And His Buddy(1935-1947) | Story Of Blues | CD 3539-2

Peter's Theme-
Jimmy Gourley-Richard Galliano 4 | Flyin' The Coop | 52e Rue Est | RECD 020

Peter's Waltz
The Kenny Clarke-Francy Boland Big Band | Two Originals:Sax No End/All Blues | MPS | 523525-2

Pete's Feet
Pete Johnson All Stars | All Star Swing Groups-The Savoy Sessions | Savoy | WL 70533 (809316)

Pete's Repeat
Brötzmann, van Hove, Bennink | Tschüs | FMP | 0230

Petit Déjeuner
Archie Shepp Quartet | Passport To Paradise-Archie Shepp Play Sidney Bechet | West Wind | WW 0002

Petit Machins(Little Stuff)
Pierto Tonolo Quartet | Quartet-Quintet-Sextet | SPLASC(H) Records | H 105

Petite Bel
Art Farmer Quartet | Sing Me Softly Of The Blues | Atlantic | 7567-80773-2

Petite Belle
Phil Woods Quartet | Birds Of A Feather | Antilles | AN 1006(802505)

Petite Fleur
Buck Clayton Quintet | Jazz Legacy 56: Buck Clayton-A La Buck | Vogue | 500106
Don Friedman Quartet | My Foolish Heart | Steeplechase | SCCD 31545
My Foolish Heart | Steeplechase | SCCD 31534
Firehouse Five Plus Two | Twenty Years Later | Good Time Jazz | 10054
Heritage Hall Jazz Band | New Orleans | Dixieland Jubilee | DJ 512
Jan Jankeje's Party And Swingband | Mobil | Jazzpoint | JP 1068 CD
Joe Darensbourg And His Dixie Fliers | Petite Fleur | Dixieland Jubilee | DJ 515
Roland Kirk Quintet | Live In Paris 1970 Vol.1 | France's Concert | FCD 109
Sidney Bechet All Stars | Planet Jazz:Sidney Bechet | Planet Jazz | 2152063-2
Sidney Bechet With Andre Reweliotty And His Orchestra | En Concert Avec Europe 1 | Laserlight | 710440

Petite Fleur-
Earl Hines-Roy Eldridge Duo | Hine's Tune | France's Concert | FCD 101

Petite Louise
Floyd Smith Trio | Relaxin' With Floyd | Black & Blue | BB 875.2

Petite Marché
Guy Klucevsek-Phillip Johnston | Tales From The Cryptic | Winter&Winter | 910088-2

Petite Overture A Danser(Erik Satie)
Johannes Cernota | Sparta | JA & RO | JARO 4136-2
TSF+Daniel Huck | Drolement Vocal! | IDA Record | 013 CD

Petite Phrases
John Graas Nonet | Jazzmantics | Fresh Sound Records | 252283-1(Decca DL 8677)

Petite Rosalie
Andreas Willers Quintet | The Privat Ear | Sound Aspects | sas CD 034

Petite Valse
Ulli Bögershausen | Ageless Guitar Solos | Laika Records | 8695071
Joelle Leandre-Carlos Zingaro | Ecritures | Adda | 590038

Petits Machines
Tony Purrone Trio | Rascality | Steeplechase | SCCD 31514
Django Reinhardt And The Quintet Du Hot Club De France | Django Reinhardt:Djangology | EMI Records | 780659-2

Petootie Pie
Louis Jordan And His Tympany Five | Louis Jordan-Let The Good Times Roll: The Complete Decca Recordings 1938-1954 | Bear Family Records | BCD 15557 IH
Louis Sclavis Septet | Chamber Music | IDA Record | 022 CD

Petra Vom Finanzamt
The Intergalactic Maiden Ballet feat. John Zorn | Square Dance | TipToe | TIP-888804 2

Petruschka
Buddy Charles | Jive's Alive | Steeplechase | SCB 9006

Pettiford Bridge
Ed Blackwell Project | Vol.1:What It Is? | Enja | ENJ-7089 2
Dick Powell And His Orchestra | Jazz Goes To The Movies | Timeless | CBC 1-020

Peyote
Lee Morgan Quintet | Live At the Lighthouse '70 | Fresh Sound Records | FSR-CD 0140(2)

Peysireid
Schiaffini-Iannaccone-Colombo/S.I.C. | 29.9.78 Pezzo | Red Records | VPA 136

Pfeifender Berg
Sven Ake Johansson-Alexander von Schlippenbach Duo | Kalfaktor A.Falke Und Andere Lieder | FMP | 0970

Pfrancing
Miles Davis Quintet | Someday My Prince Will Come | CBS | CK 65919
Miles Davis With John Coltrane | CBS | CBS 88029

Phanai
Matthias Stich Sevensenses | ...mehrschichtig | Satin Doll Productions | SDP 1038-1 CD

Phanta
Petra Straue & The Moonmen | Voices Around My House | Satin Doll Productions | SDP 1016-1 CD

Phantasiereise
Joe Lovano-Gonzalo Rubalcaba | Flying Colors | Blue Note | 856092-2

Phantasm
M.T.B. | Consenting Adults | Criss Cross | Criss 1177

Phantoms
Kenny Barron Quintet | What If | Enja | ENJ-5013 2
Kenny Barron-Regina Carter | Freefall | Verve | 549706-2
Phil Haynes' 4 Horns & What | 4 Horn Lore | Open Minds | OM 2413-2

Pharao
Flim & The BB's | The Further Adventures | dmp Digital Music Productions | CD 462

Pharoah's Dance
Leon Thomas With The Oliver Nelson Quintet | Leon Thomas In Berlin | RCA | 2663877-2

Pharoah's Tune-
Pharoah Sanders Quartet | Live | Evidence | TR 116

Phase Dance
Pat Metheny Group | Pat Metheny Group | ECM | 1114(825593-2)
Unity Village | Jazz Door | JD 1246

Phase I-
Craig Harris And Tailgater's Tales | Blackout In The Square Root Of Soul | JMT Edition | 919015-2

Phase II-
Cassandra Wilson Group | Jumpworld | JMT Edition | 834434-2

Phase One
Christoph Schweizer Sextet | Normal Garden | Mons Records | MR 874660

Phases Of The Moon
Christoph Spendel Group | City Kids | TCB Records | TCB 01052

Phatsha-Phatsha(Hurry-Hurry)
Cozy Cole Septet | Earl's Backroom And Cozy's Caravan | Affinity | AFF 167

Phenil Isopropil Amin
John McLaughlin Duo | Electric Guitarist | CBS | 467093-2

Phenomena
George Lewis | The George Lewis Solo Trombone Record | Sackville | 3012

Pheromonical
John Wolf Brennan | Irisations | Creative Works Records | CW CD 1021-2

Phi
John Stevens Away | Mutual Benefit | Konnex Records | KCD 5061

Phil T. McNasty's Blues
Kenny Baker And His Orchestra | Date With The Dozen | Dormouse | DM 9 IMS

Philharmonis Blues(Carnegie Blues)
JATP All Stars | Jazz At The Philharmonic:Best Of The 1940's Concerts | Verve | 557534-2
Christoph Oeding Trio | Taking A Chance | Mons Records | MR 874784

Philipp's Pavilion
Eugen Cicero Trio | Rococo Jazz 2 | Timeless | CD SJP 255

Philips Hymn
Horace Silver Quintet | Jazz Has... A Sense Of Humor | Verve | 050293-2

Philley Millie
Nelson's Paramount Serenaders | Alexander Where's That Band?-Paramount Recordings 1926-1928 | Frog | DGF 13

Philly Dog
St.Louis Kings Of Rhythm | Rhythm And Blues Showtime | Timeless | CD SJP 231/2

Philly J.J.
Philly Joe Jones Big Band | Drums Around The World | Original Jazz Classics | VIJ 5055
Freddie Hubbard Quintet | Here To Stay | Blue Note | 869788-1

'Philly' Twist
Tom Browne Quintet | Another Shade Of Browne | Hip Bop | HIBD 8011
John Swana-Joe Magnarelli Sextet | Philly-New York Junction | Criss Cross | Criss 1150

Philly's Blount
Jack Walrath And The Masters Of Supense | Hip Gnosis | TCB Records | TCB 01062

Phil's Tune
Oscar Peterson Quartet With Roy Eldridge | Des Femmes Disparaissent/Les Tricheurs(Original Soundtracks) | Fontana | 834752-2 PMS
Pepper Adams-Donald Byrd Sextet | Pepper Adams&Donald Byrd:Stardust | Bethlehem | BET 6000-2(BCP 6029)

Philumba
Donald Brown Quintet | Sources Of Inspiration | Muse | MCD 5385

Phinupi
Kenny Burrell Septet | Blue Lights-Vol. 2 | Blue Note | 300231(1597)
Mario Piacentini Trio | Frozen Pool | SPLASC(H) Records | H 181

Phloy In The Frame
Simon Nabatov Trio | For All The Marbles Suite | ASP Records | 31990

Phoena

Dogslyde | Hair Of The Dog | Intuition Records | INT 3223-2

Phoena Intro
Hair Of The Dog | Intuition Records | INT 3223-2

Phoena Reprise
Burkhard Beins-Martin Pfleiderer-Peter Niklas Wilson | Yarbles | HatOLOGY | 510

Phoenix
Jimmy Giuffre Trio | Night Dance | Choice | CHCD 71001
Joe Sample Group | Ashes To Ashes | Warner | 7599-26318-2
Kölner Saxophon Mafia | Saxfiguren | Jazz Haus Musik | JHM 0036 CD
Leni Stern Group | Closer To The Light | Enja | ENJ-6034 2
Martin Krusche Quintet | Friendship Pagoda | Naxos Jazz | 86057-2

Phoenix And The Fire
Russell Garcia Orchestra | I Lead A Charmed Life | Discovery | DS 814 IMS

Phonograph Blues
Robert Johnson | Robert Johnson-King Of The Delta Blues | CBS | 493006-2

Phonograph Blues(alt.take)
Bernd Konrad Sextet | Traumtänzer | Hat Art | 3509

Phosphor Colors
Ladonna Smith-Davey Williams | Dix Improvisations, Victoriaville 1989 | Victo | CD 009

Photogallery
Antonio Carlos Jobim With Orchestra | A Certain Mr. Jobim | Discovery | DSCD 848(881790)

Photograph
Kendra Shank With The Larry Willis Quartet | Afterglow | Mapleshade | 02132

Photographs Of You
Weslia Whitefield Trio | Live In San Francisco | Landmark | LCD 1531-2

Phrasen
Tommy Smith Sextet | Paris | Blue Note | 780612-2

Phum
Quiet Now | Inside The Waltz | Blue Concept | BCCD 94/01

Pi
Stanley Turrentine Quartet | That's Where It's At | Blue Note | 869939-7

Piano-
Gerry Mulligan Quartet | California Concerts Vol.1 | Pacific Jazz | 746860-2

Piano Bossa
Erskine Butterfield | Part-Time Boogie | Harlequin | HQ 2050

Piano Groove
Philip Catherine Quartet | Live | Dreyfus Jazz Line | FDM 36587-2

Piano Interlude
Wynton Kelly-George Coleman Quartet | In Concert | Affinity | AFF 54

Piano Introduction
Rob Van Den Broeck Quintet | Free Fair | Timeless | SJP 122

Piano Man
Earl Hines And His Esquire All Stars | Earl Hines And His Esquire All Stars | Storyville | SLP 4071
Earl Hines And His Orchestra | The Earl | Naxos Jazz | 8.120581 CD

Piano Play The Man
Ben Sidran Group | Old Songs For New The Depression | Antilles | 846132-2(889648)

Piano Sonata No.15 in C Major(KV 545):
McCoy Tyner Quartet | Prelude And Sonata | Milestone | MCD 9244-2

Piano Sonata No.8 In C Minor
Lionel Hampton And His Orchestra | Hot Mallets Vol.1 | Bluebird | ND 86458

Pianofighter Rag
Fate Marable's Society Syncopators | New Orleans In The '20s | Timeless | CBC 1-014

Pianomagic
Elmar Kräling | Pianomusic | FMP | 0560

Piano-Trumpet
Modern Jazz Quartet & Guests | Plastic Dreams | Atlantic | AMCY 1099

Pic Du Midi D'Ossau
Toninho Horta Trio | Once I Loved | Verve | 513561-2

Picadillo
Zachary Breaux Group | Groovin' | Ronnie Scott's Jazz House | JHCD 023

Picasso
Coleman Hawkins | The Jazz Scene | Verve | 521661-2
Tenor Triumvirate:Bean & Prez & Chu | Queen-Disc | 051

Piccolo Blues
Ted Weems And His Orchestra | The Clasic Years In Digital Stereo: Dance Bands USA | CDS Records Ltd. | RPCD 302(CD 650)

Piccoloco
Larry Coryell Group | Difference | EGG | 66048

Pick And Roll
Bull City Red | Bull City Red(1935-1939) | Story Of Blues | CD 3527-2

Pick 'Em
John Scofield Quintet | Electric Outlet | Gramavision | GR 8405-2

Pick Pocket
Bessie Smith And Her Band | Jazz:The Essential Collection Vol.1 | IN+OUT Records | 78011-2

Pick Pocket Blues
Geechie Wiley And Elvie Thomas | Mississippi Girls(1928-1931) | Story Of Blues | CD 3515-2

Pick That Thing(dedicated to Albert Lee)
Oscar Klein Band | Pick-A-Blues Live | Jazzpoint | JP 1071
Dave Brubeck Quartet | Time Out/Time Further Out | CBS | CBS 22013

Pick Up Sticks
The Dave Brubeck Selection | CBS | 467279-2

Pick Yourself Up
Anita O'Day And Her Combo | A Fine Romance | Verve | 523827-2
Billy May And His Orchestra | Bacchanalia | Capitol | ED 2604201
George Barnes Quartet | Blues Going Up | Concord | CJ 43
Jackie Coon Sextet | Jazzin' With Jackie | Arbors Records | ARCD 19110
John Colianni | John Colianni | Concord | CCD 4309
Mark Murphy With The Ralph Burns Orchestra | Crazy Rhythm:His Debut Recordings | Decca | 050670-2
Mel Tormé With The Mike Renzi Trio | An Evening With Mel Tormé | Concord | CCD 4736

Pick-A.Boo
Viktoria Tabatchnikowa-Eugenij Belov | Troika | ALISO Records | AL 1036

Pickaninny:
Benny Goodman And His Orchestra | The Indispensable Benny Goodman(Big Band) Vol.5/6(1938-1939) | RCA | 2122621-2

Pick-A-Rib
Camel Caravan Broadcast 1939 Vol.3 | Phontastic | NCD 8819
Benny Goodman Quintet | Jazz Gallery:Lionel Hampton Vol.1 | RCA | 2114170-2

Picnic At The Mozarteum
Boyd Raeburn And His Orchestra | Boyd Raeburn:The Transcription Performances 1946 | Hep | CD 42

Picnickin'
Accroche Note | Live In Berlin | FMP | CD 83

Picture 1
Jack DeJohnette | Pictures | ECM | 1079

Picture 2
Jack DeJohnette-John Abercrombie Duo | Pictures | ECM | 1079

Picture 3
Pictures | ECM | 1079

Picture 4
Pictures | ECM | 1079

Picture 5
Jack DeJohnette | Pictures | ECM | 1079

Picture 6
Uwe Kropinski & John Stowell | Picture In Black And White | Acoustic Music Records | 319.1134.2

Picture Of Heath
Joe Van Enkhuizen Quartet | Back On The Scene | Criss Cross | Criss 1013 (835601)

Picture Of Kerstin
Lightnin' Hopkins | Lightnin' Hopkins Sings The Blues | Pathe | 2C 068-83075(Imperial)

Picture Perfect
Bruce Forman Quartet | Pardon Me | Concord | CCD 4368

Pie Eye
Clark Terry/Barney Wilen With The Bud Powell Trio | More Unissued Vol.1 | Royal Jazz | RJD 507

Piec
Horace Silver Quintet | The Best Of Horace Silver | Blue Note | 791143-2

Piece For Guitar Quartet
Stephen Horenstein Ensemble | Collages Jerusalem '85 | Soul Note | SN 1099

Piece For Ornette(long version)
Keith Jarrett Quartet | El Juicio(The Judgement) | Atlantic | 7567-80783-2

Piece For Ornette(short version)
Cornelius Claudio Kreusch | Talking To A Goblin | Edition Collage | EC 441-2

Piece For Paul Bley
Phil Woods Quintet | Astor& Elis | Chesky | JD 146

Piece For Rock Orchestra
Dewey Redman Trio | Soundsigns | Galaxy | GXY 5130

Piece No.8 From Benny's Gig
Idris Muhammad Groups | My Turn | Lipstick Records | LIP 890022

Piece Of Heart
Hans Lüdemann | The Natural Piano | Jazz Haus Musik | JHM 0075 CD

Piece Of Mind
Jukka Tolonen Quintet | Tasavallan Presidentti-Milky Way Moses | Sonet | 147118

Piece Of One:
Hans Lüdemann | The Natural Piano | Jazz Haus Musik | JHM 0075 CD

Piece Of Soul
Five Up High | Five Up High | Timeless | CD SJP 417

Piece O'Pisces
Martial Solal Trio And The A Piacere Saxophone Quartet | Triptyque | Adda | 590067

Pieces Of Dreams
Lee Gibson With The Metropole Orchestra | Night Songs | Koch Jazz | 3-6911-2
Singers Unlimited With Rob McConnell And The Boss Brass | The Singers Unlimited With Rob McConnell And The Boss Brass | MPS | 817486-1
Stanley Turrentine And His Orchestra | Pieces Of Dream | Original Jazz Classics | OJCCD 831-2(F 9465)

Pieces Of Dreams(alt.take)
Sandole Brothers | The Sandole Brothers | Fantasy | FCD 24763-2

Pieces Of Eight
Lotte Anker/Mette Petersen Quartet | Beyond The Mist | Stunt Records | STUCD 18908

Pieds-en-l'air
Pierre Guyonnet Onzetetes | Joue | Plainisphare | PAV 809

Piel De Toro
Bob Degen | Sandcastle | free flow music | ffm 0897

Pier 14
Marcus Pintrup Quartet | Nocturnal Traces | Blue Note | 493676-2

Piercing The Veil
Gianluigi Trovesi With The Orchestra Da Camera Di Nembro Enea Salmeggia | Around Small Fairy Tales | Soul Note | 121341-2

Pieta
Larry Coryell Group | Fallen Angel | CTI Records | CTI 1014-2

Pietre Di Luca
Tete Montoliu | Words Of Love | Steeplechase | SCCD 31084

Pigen In Rodt
Gabriele Hasler-Roger Hanschel Duo | Pigeon | Jazz Haus Musik | JHM 0120 CD

Pigeon
Don Wilkerson Quintet | Preach Brother! | Blue Note | 0677212

Pigeon Peas
JazzHorchEster | ...Du Bist Nicht Die Erste! | Elite Special | 73625

Pigfoot
John Patton Quintet | Along Came John | Blue Note | 0675614
John Surman Quartet | Adventure Playground | ECM | 1463(511981-2)
Paul Bley Trio | Closer | ESP Disk | ESP 1021-2

Pilansberg
Pili-Pili | Boogaloo | JA & RO | JARO 4174-2
Fritz Hauser & Stephan Grieder | The Mirror | Hat Art | CD 6037

Pilatus Sprach Zu Ihnen:Da Habt Ihr Die Hüter-
Eddie Costa-Vinnie Burke Trio | Eddie Costa-Vinnie Burke Trio | Fresh Sound Records | LP 1025(Jubilee)

Pilgrimage To The Mountain-Part 1:Persevere
Charles Lloyd Quartet | Notes From Big Sur | ECM | 1465(511999-2)

Pilgrimage To The Mountain-Part 2:Surrender
Stan Kenton And His Orchestra | Kenton Plays Wagner | Creative World | ST 1024

Pili Pili
Jugendjazzorchester NW | Beau Rivage | Jugendjazzorchester NW | JJO 003

Pili Pili(new version)
Jasper Van't Hof | Pili-Pili | Warner | 2292-40458-2

Pili-Pili
Woody Herman And His Orchestra | Herman's Heat & Puente's Beat | Palladium Records | PDC 156(889168)

Pillen
Dinah Washington With The Jimmy Cobb Quintet | The Complete Dinah Washington On Mercury Vol.2 | Mercury | 832448-2

Pilvetslednah
Woody Herman And His Orchestra | Woody Herman Live 1957 Featuring Bill Harris Vol.1 | Status | CD 107(882500)

Pindakaas
Allen Farnham Quintet | 5th House | Concord | CCD 4413

Pineapple Rag
Lu Watters' Yerba Buena Jazz Band | The San Francisco Style Vol.1:Dawn Club Favorites | Good Time Jazz | GTCD 12001-2

Pinetop's Blues
Clarence 'Pinetop' Smith | Boogie Woogie-Great Original Performances 1928-1941 | CDS Records Ltd. | RPCD 601

Pinetop's Boogie Woogie
Louis Mazetier | The Piano Starts Talking | Jazz Connaisseur | JCCD 0243-2
Memphis Piano Red | Living Country Blues USA Vol.10 | L+R Records | LR 42040
Pinetop Perkins Quartet | Boogie Woogie Masters | Black & Blue | BLE 59.063 2
Sammy Price | Midnight Boogie | Black & Blue | BLE 59.025 2

Piney Brown Blues
Jay McShann Quintet | What A Wonderful World | Groove Note | GN 1005(180gr-Pressung)
What A Wonderful World | Groove Note | GRV 1005-2
Jimmy Rushing With The Buck Clayton All Stars | The Jazz Odyssey Of James Rushing Esq. | Fresh Sound Records | FSR 591(CBS CL 963)
Jimmy Witherspoon With Jay McShann And His Band | Victor Jazz History Vol.10:Kansas City(1935-71) | RCA | 2128564-2
Joe Turner With Orchestra | The Boss Of The Blues | Atlantic | SD 8812

Ping Pong
Art Blakey And The Jazz Messengers | Ugetsu | Original Jazz Classics | OJC20 090-2(RLP 9464)
Three Blind Mice Vol.2 | Blue Note | 784452-2
Wayne Shorter:The Classic Blue Note Recordings | Blue Note | 540856-2
Blue N' Groovy | Blue Note | 780679-2
Bill O'Connell Group | Love For Sale | Jazz City | 660.53.019
Message | The Art Of Blakey | Paddle Wheel | KICJ 162

Ping Pong(alt.take)
Dan Moretti Quintet | Some Time Inside | Black-Hawk | BKH 51901

Pink Lady
Curtis Counce Group | Carl's Blues | Original Jazz Classics | OJC 423(C 7574)

Pink Peaches
Shelly Manne All Stars | Mannekind | Mainstream | MD CDO 727

Pink Topsy
Charles Mingus And His Orchestra | Charles Mingus-The Complete Debut Recordings | Debut | 12 DCD 4402-2

Pink Topsy(alt.take)
Earl Bostic Quintet | Alto Magic In Hi Fi | Sing | 597

Pinky
James Newton Quartet | Paseo Del Mar | India Navigation | IN 1037

Pinnacles
J.J.Johnson Sextet | Pinnacles | Original Jazz Classics | M 9093

Pinocchio
Miles Davis Quintet | Miles Davis Quintet 1965-1968 | CBS | C6K 67398
Roy Hargrove Quintet | RCA Victor 80th Anniversary Vol.8:1990-1997 | RCA | 2668784-2
Ponta Box | Ponta Box | JVC | JVC 2000-2

Pinocchio(alt.take)
Miles Davis Quintet | Miles Davis Quintet 1965-1968 | CBS | C6K 67398
Bernard Peiffer And His St.Germain Des Pres Orchestra | Jazz In Paris:Modern Jazz At Saint-Germain-De-Prés | EmArCy | 013042-2

Pinocchio:In Groppa Al Tonno
Gebhard Ullmann Trio | Essencia | Between The Lines | btl 017(Efa 10187-2)

Pinoquio
Sun Ra Arkestra | Sunrise In Different Dimensions | HatOLOGY | 568

Pint Of Blues
Gene Ammons And His All Stars | Funky | Original Jazz Classics | OJCCD 244(P 7083)

Pintoso-
Céline Rudolph And Her Trio | Paintings | Nabel Records:Jazz Network | CD 4661

Pintura Desse Mundo
Clark Terry Orchestra | Clark Terry | Swing | SW 8406 IMS

Pio Rhythm
Jens Thomas | Jens Thomas Plays Ennio Morricone | ACT | 9273-2

Pioggia
Chet Baker Sextet | At Capolinea | Red Records | NS 206

Pioggoa Sul'Pineto
Andrew Cyrille | What About? | Affinity | AFF 75

Pip, Squeak-
Bill Frisell Trio | Live | Gramavision | GCD 79504

Piper
The Fraterman | Spielerlaubnis | Aho-Recording | CD 1014

Piperspool
Bob Berg Sextet | The Best Of Bob Berg On Denon | Denon Compact Disc | DC-8593

Pipo
Jasper Van't Hof | My World Of Music | Keytone | KYT 3-100 Digital

Pipo's Walk
Odwalla | Schiuma D'Onda | SPLASC(H) Records | CD H 305-2

Pique Nique À Nagpur
John Zorn Group | Masada Two | DIW | DIW 889 CD

Piranha
Nina Simone Quartet | Nina Simone-The 60s Vol.1: Ne Me Quitte Pas | Mercury | 838543-2 PMS

Pirate Jenny
In Concert/I Put A Spell On You | Mercury | 846543-2
Nina Simone Trio/Quartet/Orchestra | Moon Of Alabama | Jazz Door | JD 1214

Piratenlied
Peter Erskine Trio | ELB | ACT | 9289-2

Pirates
Bengt Berger & Bitter Funeral Beer Band | Praise Drumming | Dragon | DRLP 142

Piri
Chet Baker And The Lighthouse All Stars | Witch Doctor | Original Jazz Classics | OJCCD 609-2

Pirouette
Lajos Dudas Quintet | Talk Of The Town | double moon | CHRDM 71012
Shorty Rogers And His Giants | Jimmy Giuffre:The Complete 1947-1953 Small Group Sessions,Vol.2 | Blue Moon | BMCD 1047
Short Stops | RCA | NL 85917(2)

Pisa Luna
Gonzalo Rubalcaba Group | Live In Havanna Vol.2 | Messidor | 15956

Piscean Dance
Art Blakey And The Jazz Messengers | Feedom Rider | Blue Note | 821287-2

Pisces
Pisces | Blue Note | GXK 8151
Naima | Vertigo | Mons Records | MR 874816

Pisces Soul
Tony Williams Lifetime | Ego | Verve | 559512-2

Piskow's Filigree
Axel Fischbacher Quartet | Coast To Coast | L+R Records | CDLR 45025

Pistachio
Joelle Leandre | Palimpseste | Hat Art | CD 6103

Pistolero-
Stanley Clarke Groups | Stanley Clarke Best | Zounds | CD 2700020089

Pit Bulls(An Endangered Species)
Ronnie Cuber Quartet | Airplay | Steeplechase | SCCD 31309

Pit Jazz
Frank Wess And His Orchestra | Fujitsu-Concord Jazz Festival In Japan '90: Entre Nous | Concord | CCD 4456

Pithecanthropus Erectus
Charles Mingus Jazz Workshop | The Very Best Of Charles Mingus | Rhino | 8122-79988-2
Pithecanthropus Erectus | Atlantic | 7567-81456-2

Pito Pito
André Ricros-Louis Sclavis Group | Le Partage Des Eaux | Silex | Y 225003 IMS

Pitt & The Pendulum
Canadian Brass | Take The A Train | RCA | 2663455-2

Pitter Panther Patter
Duke Ellington And His Orchestra | Carnegie Hall Concert December 1944 | Prestige | 2PCD 24073-2
Carnegie Hall Concert January 1946 | Prestige | 2PCD 24074-2
Duke Ellington:Complete Prestige Carnegie Hall 1946-1947 Concerts | Definitive Records | DRCD 11211
Duke Ellington/Jimmy Blanton | Jazz Giants:Duke Ellington | RCA | NL 45179 SI

Pittsburgh
Mercy Dee Walton Trio | Pity And A Shame | Original Blues Classics | OBCCD 552-2(BV 1039)

Pivot
Scott Kreitzer Group | New York State Of Mind | Jazz City | 660.53.022

Pizzicato
Jean-Luc Ponty Quintet | Sonata Erotica-Live At Montreux | Inner City | IC 1003 IMS

Place De Brouckere
Django Reinhardt And His Orchestra | Django Reinhardt:Djangology | EMI Records | 780659-2
The International Jazz Group | The International Jazz Group Vol.2 | Swing | SW 8416

Place Pigalle
Harry Happel Trio | North Sea High Lights | Timeless | SJP 156/7

Place St.Henri
Oscar Peterson | Oscar Peterson In Russia | Pablo | 2CD 2625711
Vintage Introduction | North Sea Highlights | Timeless | CD SJP 156

Places And Spaces
Dave Liebman Septet | Time Line | Owl Records | 054 CD

Plädoyer
Vienna Art Orchestra | Suite For The Green Eighties | Hat Art | CD 6054

Plage St. Henri
Mickey Tucker Septet | Mister Mysterious | Muse | MR 5174

Plaid
Art Tatum Sextet | The Tatum Group Masterpieces | Pablo | 2310731

TITELVERZEICHNIS

Plain Brown Bag
Jimmy McGriff Orchestra | The Best Of The Jazz Organs | LRC Records | CDC 9006

Plain Brown Wrapper
Academic Jazz Band | 7.Zelt-Musik-Festival:Jazz Events | Zounds | CD 2730001

Plain Dirt
McKinney's Cotton Pickers | The Complete McKinney's Cotton Pickers Vol.1/2(1928-1929) | RCA | 2135550-2

Plain Gold Ring
Nina Simone Trio | My Baby Just Cares For Me | Charly | CR 30217

Plain Jane
Sonny Rollins Quintet | Sonny Rollins:The Blue Note Recordings | Blue Note | 821371-2
Jazz Profile:Sonny Rollins | Blue Note | 823516-2
Med Flory and his Orchestra | Modern Jazz Gallery | Fresh Sound Records | KXL 5001(252282-1 Kapp)

Plain Talk
Bill Holman Octet | Group Activity | Affinity | AFF 65

Plainitude
Lisa Ekdahl With The Peter Nordahl Trio | Back To Earth | RCA | 2161463-2

Plaintive Rumba
Michael Riessler Group | Tentations D'Abélard | Wergo | WER 8009-2

Planctus-
Cannonball Adderley Sextet | Live On Planet Earth | West Wind | WW 2088

Planet Earth
Enrico Rava Quintet | Secrets | Soul Note | 121164-2

Planet Rock
Jason Moran Trio | The Bandwagon | Blue Note | 591893-2
Jason Moran | Modernistic | Blue Note | 539838-2

Planet Rock Postscript
Glenn Wilson Quintet | Blue Porpoise Avenue | Sunnyside | SSC 1074 D

Planetarian Citizen
Mahavishnu Orchestra | Inner Worlds | CBS | CBS 69216

Planetenfahrer
Cannonball Adderley Sextet | Coast To Coast | Milestone | M 47039

Planicies
Gebhard Ullmann Trio | Essencia | Between The Lines | btl 017(Efa 10187-2)
Willem Breuker Kollektief | To Remain | BVHAAST | CD 8904

Plant Dance
Big Joe Turner And His All Stars | Life Ain't Easy | Original Jazz Classics | 2310883

Plantation Bag
Luis Russell And His Orchestra | Luis Russell | CBS | CBS 88039

Plante Ris
Mike Mainieri Group | An American Diary:The Dreaming | NYC-Records | NYC 6026-2

Planxit
Franco Morone | The South Wind | Acoustic Music Records | 319.1115.2

Planxty Irwin-
Plas Johnson Band | Rockin' With The Plas | Pathe | 2C 068-86529(Capitol)

Plate XIX-
Carla Bley Band | 4X4 | Watt | 30(159547-2)

Plate XVII-
4X4 | Watt | 30(159547-2)

Plate XVIII-
Julius Hemphill Trio | Raw Materials And Residuals | Black Saint | 120015-2

Platitudes
Nils Petter Molvaer Group | Khmer | ECM | 1560(537798-2)

Platonic Years
Peter Kowald Quintett | Peter Kowald Quintett | FMP | 0070

Platzangst
Mike Stern Group | Play | Atlantic | 7567-83219-2

Play
Sakis Papadimitriou | Piano Plays | LEO | LR 111

Play Ball
Main Stream Power Band | Memories In Swing | MWM Records | MWM 002

Play Fiddle Play
Dizzy Gillespie Quintet | Dizzy Gillespie:Pleyel 53 | Vogue | 2115466-2
Milt Buckner Trio | Play Milt Play | France's Concert | FCD 103
Absolute Ensemble | Absolution | Enja | ENJ-9394 2

Play It Again Sam
Tom Kubis Big Band | Slightly Off The Ground | Seabreeze | CDSB 109(881861)

Play It Momma
Mary Lou Williams Trio | Zoning | Mary Records | M 103

Play It Red
The Little Ramblers | Adrian Rollini Groups 1924-27 | Village(Jazz Archive) | VILCD 023-2

Play It, Maestro
Punch Miller's Band | Punch Miller 1960 | American Music | AMCD-52

Play Me
Michel Petrucciani Group | Music | Blue Note | 792563-2
Michel Petrucciani:The Blue Note Years | Blue Note | 789916-2
Frank Lowe Quintet | Fresh | Black Lion | BLCD 760214

Play Of Colours
Twice A Week & Steve Elson | Play Of Colours | Edition Collage | EC 511-2
Steven Halpern-Dallas Smith | Natural Light | Gramavision | 18-7834-1

Play Out-
Erroll Garner | Giants Of The Jazz Piano | Fresh Sound Records | FSR-CD 21(882186)

Play Piano Play
Erroll Garner Trio | Relaxin' With Erroll | Vogue | 655008

Play School
Walt Dickerson/Richard Davis | Tenderness | Steeplechase | SCCD 31213

Play Time
Thomas Clausen Trio With Gary Burton | Flowers And Trees | M.A Music | A 805-2
Jack Jackson And His Orchestra | Things Are Looking Up | Saville Records | SVL 173 IMS

Play With Your Poodle
Lightnin' Hopkins | The Great Electric Show And Dance | America | AM 013/014

Play Your Own Bone
Shorty Rogers And His Giants | A Portrait Of Shorty | RCA | 2121822-2

Playboy Rag
Spanish Fly | Rags To Britches | Knitting Factory Works | KFWCD 114

Playboy's Theme
Henry Mancini And His Orchestra | Combo! | RCA | 2147794-2
Poncho Sanchez And His Orchestra | Afro-Cuban Fantasy | Concord | CCD 4847

Played Twice
Ed Jackson Group | Wake Up Call | New World Records | 80451-2
Peter Leitch Quintet | Exhilaration | Reservoir | RSR CD 118(889465)
Roy Haynes Quartet | True Or False | Freelance | FRL-CD 007

Played Twice(take 1)
Thelonious Monk Quintet | Blues Five Spot | Milestone | M 9124

Played Twice(take 2)
5 By Monk By 5 | Original Jazz Classics | OJCCD 362-2

Played Twice(take 3)
Lester Bowie's Brass Fantasy | When The Spitit Returns | Dreyfus Jazz Line | FDM 37016-2

Player Hater
Uli Trepte Group | Real Time Music | ATM Records | ATM 3820-AH

Player's Digest
Yusef Lateef Quintet | Blues For The Orient | Prestige | P 24035

Playground-
Oregon | Always,Never And Forever | Intuition Records | INT 2073-2

Playground In Nuclear Winter
George Adams-Don Pullen Duo | Melodic Excursion | Timeless | CD SJP 166

Playin' In The Yard
Sonny Rollins Quintet | Next Album | Original Jazz Classics | OJC 312 (M 9042)
Old And New Dreams | Playing | ECM | 1205

Playing
Alphonse Mouzon | In Search Of A Dream | MPS | 68192

Playing For Keeps
Nelson Rangell Group | Playing For Keeps | GRP | GRP 95932

Playing Games
Olaf Kübler Quartet | Midnight Soul | Village | VILCD 1024-2

Playing In The Yard
Herb Geller Quartet | Playing Jazz:The Musical Autobiography Of Herb Geller | Fresh Sound Records | FSR-CD 5011

Playing The Dues Blues
Les Brown And His Band Of Renown | Ridin' High | Blue Moon | BMCD 3058

Playing With The Blues
Sonny Terry Trio | Robbin' The Grave | Blue Labor | BL 101

Playing With Water
Steve Swallow Group | Swallow | Watt | XtraWatt/6
Jimmy McGriff Band | Jimmy McGriff featuring Hank Crawford | LRC Records | CDC 9001(874373)

Playland-At-The-Beach
Benny Green Trio | The Place To Be | Blue Note | 829268-2

Playmates
Rey DeMichel Orchestra | For Bloozers Only! | Fresh Sound Records | CHS 2503(Challenge)

Playtime
Meeting Point | Europ' Jazz Contest '92 Belgium | B.Sharp Records | CDS 092

Plaza De Toros
Steve Grossman Quartet | Born At The Same Time | Owl Records | 010 CD

Pleadin' For Love
Bertha 'Chippie' Hill With Louis Armstrong And Richard M. Jones | Louis Armstrong And The Blues Singers 1924-1930 | Affinity | AFS 1018(6)

Pleading The Blues
Junior Wells Blues Band | Pleading The Blues | Black & Blue | BLE 59.901 2

Pleasant Dreams
Terri Lyne Carrington Group | Real Life Story | Verve | 837697-2

Please
Taragota Hot Seven | Bavarian Jazz Live | Calig | 30620/21

Please Be Kind
Art Tatum | The Jazz Giants Play Sammy Cahn:It's Magic | Prestige | PCD 24226-2
The Art Tatum Solo Masterpieces | Pablo | 2625703
Bob Crosby And His Orchestra | Bob Crosby And His Orchestra-1938 | Circle | CCD-1
Frank Sinatra With The Count Basie Orchestra | Sinatra-Basie:An Historic Musical First | Reprise | 7599-27023-2
Ken Peplowski Quintet | Mr.Gentle And Mr.Cool | Concord | CCD 4419
Reinhardt-Grappelli Duo | Parisian Swing | Ace Of Club | ACL 1189
Stan Kenton And His Orchestra | Stan Kenton Encores | Creative World | ST 1034
Big Bill Broonzy | Big Bill Broonzy 1934-1947 | Story Of Blues | CD 3504-2

Please Be Quiet,Please
Big Bill Broonzy Group | Midnight Steppers | Swingtime(Contact) | BT 2001

Please Come Back
David Newton Trio | Victim Of The Circumstance | Linn Records | AKD 013

Please Don't Bug Me
Charles Mingus And His Orchestra | The Complete Town Hall Concert | Blue Note | 828353-2

Please Don't Come Back From The Moon
Mingus Big Band | Gunslinging Birds | Dreyfus Jazz Line | FDM 36575-2

Please Don't Go
Larry Davis Quintet | I Ain't Beggin' Nobody | Evidence | ECD 26016-2

Please Don't Leave Me
Rockin' Dopsie And The Zydeco Twisters | Rockin' Dopsie And The Zydeco Twister | Storyville | 4960423
Charlie Singleton And His Band | Screaming Saxophones Vol.1 | Swingtime(Contact) | ST 1002

Please Don't Talk About Me When I'm Gone
Benny Goodman And His Orchestra | Big City Swing | Decca | TAB 5
Billie Holiday And Her All Stars | The Essential Billie Holiday Carnegie Hall Concert | Verve | 833767-2
Billie Holiday And Her Orchestra | Billie Holiday Story Vol.5:Music for Torching | Verve | MV 2595 IMS
Dutch Swing College Band | Still Blowing Strong - 34 Years | DSC Production | PA 1022 (801071)
Erroll Garner Trio | The Erroll Garner Selection | CBS | 471624-2
Joe Williams And His Band | A Night At Count Basie's | Vanguard | VMD 8508
Louis Armstrong And His All Stars | The Jazz Collector Edition: Louis Armstrong | Laserlight | 15700
Michael White's New Orleans Music | Shake It & Breake It | 504 Records | 504CD 6
Paul Kuhn Orchestra feat. Gustl Mayer | Street Of Dreams | Mons Records | MR 874800
Sidney DeParis' Blue Note Stompers | Hot Jazz On Blue Note | Blue Note | 835811-2
Spike Robinson With The Eddie Thompson Trio | At Chesters | Hep | CD 2028
The Tremble Kids All Stars | Dixieland At Its Best | BELL Records | BLR 89091

Please Give Me A Chance
Lionel Hampton And His Orchestra | Wes Montgomery:Complete Recordings With Lionel Hampton | Definitive Records | DRCD 11242

Please Let Me Forget
Helen Humes And Her All Stars | Lester Young:The Complete 1936-1951 Small Group Sessions(Studio Recordings-Master Takes),Vol.6 Rare Items | Blue Moon | BMCD 1006

Please Let The Sun Come Out Again
B.B.King And His Band | Singin' The Blues/The Blues | Ace Records | CDCHD 320

Please Mr. Johnson
Buddy Johnson And His Orchestra | Wails | Official | 6010

Please Please Please
Joe Stanley Sextet | King Of The Honky-Tonk Sax | Mapleshade | 03852

Please Remember Me
Wild Bill Davis Super Trio | That's All | Jazz Connaisseur | JCCD 9005-2

Please Save Your Love For Me
Benny Bailey Septet | Big Brass | Candid | CCD 79011

Please Say Yes
Curtis Lundy Quintet | Trouble Blues | Original Blues Classics | OBCCD 515-2(BV 1022)

Please Send Me Someone To Love
Count Basie And His Orchestra | Compact Jazz: Count Basie & Joe Williams | Verve | 835329-2 PMS
David Fathead Newman Sextet | Still Hard Times | Muse | MCD 5283
Gene Ammons Trio | Live! In Chicago | Original Jazz Classics | OJCCD 395-2(P 7495)
James Booker | The Piano Prince From New Orleans | Aves | 146509
Jimmy Smith Quartet | Midnight Blue(The [Be]witching Hour) | Blue Note | 854365-2
Jimmy Smith Quintet | Rockin' the Boat | Blue Note | 576755-2
Jimmy Witherspoon With Groove Holmes | Cry The Blues | Bulldog | BDL 1012
Jon Weber | Live In Concert:Jon Weber Flying Keys | Jazz Connaisseur | JCCD 9726-2

Kevin Mahogany With The James Williams Trio And Benny Golson | You Got What It Takes | Enja | ENJ-9039 2
Red Garland Trio | I Left My Heart... | Muse | MR 5311(952091)

Please Stop Me Now
Louis Armstrong And His All Stars | Louis Armstrong-The Complete RCA Victor Recordings | RCA | 2668682-2

Please Tell Me Now
Billie Holiday With Gordon Jenkins And His Orchestra | Lover Man | MCA | 2292-52317-1

Pleasing Man Blues
Helen Humes And Her All Stars | Lester Young:The Complete 1936-1951 Small Group Sessions(Studio Recordings-Master Takes),Vol.6 Rare Items | Blue Moon | BMCD 1006

Pleasingly Plump
Al Jarreau With Band | L Is For Lover | i.e. Music | 557850-2

Pleasure
Directors | Directors | Jazz Haus Musik | JHM 0040 CD
Stadtgarten Series Vol.2 | Jazz Haus Musik | JHM 1002 SER

Pleasure Bent
Al Jarreau With Band | Heart's Horizon | i.e. Music | 557851-2

Pleasure Of Pain
Joachim Kühn | United Nations | Atlantic | ATL 50719

Pledging My Love
Peggy Stern Trio | Pleiades | Philology | W 82.2

Pleiades Skirt
Nathalie Lorriers Quartet | Nympheas | Igloo | IGL 088

Plenty Plenty Soul
Milt Jackson Orchestra | Plenty Plenty Soul | Atlantic | SD 8811

Pleure
Michael Riessler & Singer Pur with Vincent Courtois | Ahi Vita | ACT | 9417-2

Pleurez Mes Yeux
Ahi Vita | ACT | 9417-2

Pleurez Mes Yeux(Riesler)
Brian Barley Trio | Brian Barley Trio 1970 | Just A Memory | JAS 9502-2

Plexus
The Jazz Messengers | The Legacy Of Art Blakey | Telarc Digital | CD 83407

Plexus(alt.take)
Oscar Peterson-Joe Pass Duo | Oscar Pterson Et Joe Pass A La Salle Pleyel | Pablo | 2CD 2625705

Pleyel Bis
Live At Salle Pleyel, Paris | Pablo | 2625705

Plica
Zentralquartet | Plie | Intakt Records | CD 037

Plight
Pinguin Moschner | The Flight Of The Humble Beast | Born&Bellmann | 980205 CD

Pluies
Trygve Seim-Oyvind Braekke-Per Oddvar Johansen Orchestra | The Source And Different Cikadas | ECM | 1764(014432-2)

Plukk
George Benson Orchestra | Body Talk | CTI | 6033

Plum Island
Peter Herbolzheimer Rhythm Combination & Brass | Friends And Sihouettes | Koala Records | CD P 25

PlumbThe Bayou
Eric Person Trio | Prophecy | Soul Note | 121287-2

Plus Je T'Embrasse
Lisle Ellis Group | What We Live Fo(u)r | Black Saint | 120156-2

Plüschtier
String Thing | String Thing:Alles Wird Gut | MicNic Records | MN 2

Pluto
Sun Ra And His Intergalactic Research Arkestra | Black Myth/Out In Space | MPS | 557656-2

Pluto-
Maurice McIntyre Ensemble | Humility In The Light Of The Creator | Delmark | 900252 AO

Pluto Launge
J.R. Monterose Sextet | Jaywalkin' | Fresh Sound Records | FSR-CD 320

Plutocrat At The Automat
Charles Persip And Superband(II) | In Case You Missed It | Soul Note | 121079-2

Plymouth
Benny Carter And His Orchestra | The Various Facets Of A Genius 1929-1940 | Black & Blue | BLE 59.230 2

Plymouth Rock
Count Basie And His Orchestra | Count Basie 1954 | Jazz Society | AA 526/527

PM In The AM
Anthony Braxton-George Lewis Duo | Donaueschingen (Duo) 1976 | Hat Art | CD 6150

Po Tamtej Stronie Gory
Urszula Dudziak And Band Walk Away | Magic Lady | IN+OUT Records | 7008-2
Transition Jazz Group | Richard's Rumba | SPLASC(H) Records | H 182

Pobre Pibe
Radu Malfatti-Stephan Wittwer Duo | Thrumblin' Malfatti-Wittwer | FMP | 0350

Pocket Book
Jim Snidero Quintet | Vertigo | Criss Cross | Criss 1112

Pocket Full Of Blues:
Keith Jarrett Quartet | Bop-Be | MCA | 62734 (801427)

Pocket Full Of Dreams
Roosevelt Sykes Quintet | The Honeydripper | Original Blues Classics | OBCCD 557-2(BV 1014)

Pocket Symphony:
Emily Remler Quartet | Take Two | Concord | CCD 4195

Poco A Poco
Klaus König Orchestra | Times Of Devastation/Poco A Poco | Enja | ENJ-6014 22
Sylvie Courvoisier Group | Abaton | ECM | 1838/39(157628-2)
D.D.Jackson | ...So Far | RCA | 2663549-2

Poem
Blue Box | Blue Box 10 | TipToe | TIP-888818 2

Poem For Eva-
One For All | Live At Smoke Vol.1 | Criss Cross | Criss 1211

Poem For Paula
Uri Caine Trio | Blue Wail | Winter&Winter | 910034-2

Poem For Shulamit
Robin Williamson | The Seed-At-Zero | ECM | 1732(543819-2)

Poem On His Birthday
Eduardo Niebla-Antonio Forcione Group | Poema | Jazzpoint | JP 1035 CD

Poema
Lalo Schifrin Sextet | Brazilian Jazz | Aleph Records | 020

Poeme
Red Norvo Sextet | Muisc To Listen To Red Norvo By | Original Jazz Classics | OJC 155(C 7534)

Poemia Trois
Ferenc Snétberger Quartet | Signature | Enja | ENJ-9017 2

Poems For My People
José Maria Vitier-Frank Emilio Flynn | Jane Bunnett And The Cuban Piano Masters | Pacific Jazz | 832695-2

Poet Staggered
Kenny Dorham Septet | But Beautiful | Milestone | M 47036

Poetic Justice
Paul Bley/Evan Parker/Barre Phillips | Time Will Tell | ECM | 1537
Paul Bley | Synth Thesis | Postcards | POST 1001

Poetry And All That Jazz
James Emery Quartet | Standing On A Whale... | Enja | ENJ-9312 2

Poetry In Stillness
Helmut Nieberle-Helmut Kagerer | Skyliner | ART BY HEART | ABH 2001 2

Poevis
Claus Stötter's Nevertheless | Die Entdeckung Der Banane | Jazz 'n' Arts Records | JNA 1403

Poggibonsi
Albert Dailey Trio | Textures | Muse | MR 5256

Poinciana
Ahmad Jamal Trio | At The Pershing | Affinity | CD AFS 780
Cal Tjader's Orchestra | Several Shades Of Jade/Breeze From The East | Verve | 537083-2
Dave Brubeck Quintet | Latin Jazz | CBS | 472683-2
Dave Liebman Quintet | Besame Mucho And Other Latin Jazz Standards | Red Records | 123260-2
Keith Jarrett Trio | Whisper Not | ECM | 1724/25(543813-2)
Lennie Niehaus Quintet | Lennie Niehaus Vol.1:The Quintets | Original Jazz Classics | OJCCD 1933-2(C 3518)
Lew Tabackin Quartet | What A Little Moonlight Can Do | Concord | CCD 4617
McCoy Tyner And The Latin All-Stars | McCoy Tyner And The Latin All-Stars | Telarc Digital | CD 83462
Reg Schwager Trio | Resonance | Justin Time | Just 13
Shelly Manne And His Men | At The Black Hawk Vol.1 | Original Jazz Classics | OJCCD 656-2(S 7577)
At The Blackhawk Vol.1 | Contemporary | C 7577
Sonny Stitt Orchestra | Sonny Stitt & The Top Brass | Atlantic | 90139-1 TIS
Victor Feldman Orchestra | Latinsville | Contemporary | CCD 9005-2
Poncho Sanchez Group | Soul Sauce-Memories Of Cal Tjader | Concord | CCD 4662

Poinciana(Song Of The Tree)
Martial Solal Trio | At Newport '63 | RCA | 2125768-2

Point Falling
Dave Binney Quintet | Point Game | Owl Time Line | 3819032

Point II
Mahmoud Turkmani With The Ludus Guitar Quartet | Nuqta | TipToe | TIP-888835 2

Point III
Larry Carlton Group | Larry Carlton | MCA | MCD 42245

Point Of Time
Kurt Rosenwinkel Quintet | The Enemies Of Energy | Verve | 543042-2

Point Of View
Matthias Frey Group | Liquid Crystal | Inak | 9026

Point Of View(part 1-3
Cecil Taylor | One Night With Blue Note Vol.2 | Blue Note | BT 85114 Digital

Point Roses
Matthew Ship 'String' Trio | By The Law Of Music | Hat Art | CD 6200

Point Turnagain
Cecil Taylor | One Night With Blue Note Vol.2 | Blue Note | BT 85114 Digital

Pointe Dancing
Jimmy Owens Sextet | Heiner Stadler Retrospection | Tomato | 2696522

Pointing At The Moon
Mahmoud Turkmani With The Ludus Guitar Quartet | Nuqta | TipToe | TIP-888835 2
Rubberlegs Williams With Herbie Fields' Band | Obscure Blues Shouters Vol.2 | Blue Moon | BMCD 6011

Pointless Nostalgic
Bill Dixon Orchestra | Thoughts | Soul Note | 121111-2

Poise
Ornette Coleman Quartet | Beauty Is A Rare Thing:Ornette Coleman-The Complete Atlantic Recordings | Atlantic | 8122-71410-2
Paul Plimley-Lisle Ellis | Kaleidoscopes(Ornette Coleman Songbook) | Hat Art | CD 6117

Poison Ya' Blues
John Zorn Naked City | Naked City:Radio | Avant | AVAN 003

Poker Finale-
Blind Blake | Blind Blake-Search Warrant Blues | Biograph | BLP 12023

Polak
Freddie Hubbard Orchestra | Polar AC | CTI | 9031

Polar Lights
James Plotkin Group | The Joy Of Disease | Avant | AVAN 028

Polar Shift
Yusef Lateef Quintet | Jazz For Thinkers | Savoy | WL 70535(MG 12109)SF

Polaroid Memory
Dick de Graaf Septet | Polder | Timeless | CD SJP 376

Polina
Trio Clastrier-Riessler-Rizzo | Palude | Wergo | WER 8010-2

Poliritmia
Wiener Art Orchester | Tango From Obango | Art Record | 1002(ES 7819)

Polite Blues
Roy Eldridge-Benny Carter Quintet | The Urban Sessions/New Jazz Sound | Verve | 531637-2

Politely
Bobby Sherwood And His Orchestra | Bobby Sherwood And His Orchestra:More 1944-1946 | Circle | CCD-115

Politicos
Bruce Ditmas & D 3 | Spontaneous Combustion | Tutu Records | 888126-2

Polka Dots And Moonbeams
Betty Roche And Her Quartet | Lightly And Politely | Original Jazz Classics | OJCCD 1802-2(P 7198)
Bill Cunliffe Quintet | Bill Plays Bud | Naxos Jazz | 86024-2
Bill Evans Trio | The Second Trio | Milestone | M 47046
Bill Evans Trio:The Last Waltz | Milestone | 8MCD 4430-2
The Best Of Bill Evans Live | Verve | 533825-2
Consecration 1 | Timeless | CD SJP 331
Bill Evans:The Secret Sessions | Milestone | 8MCD 4421-2
Bill Evans:The Secret Sessions | Milestone | 8MCD 4421-2
Bill Evans:The Secret Sessions | Milestone | 8MCD 4421-2
Bill Evans/Jazzhouse | Milestone | MCD 9151-2
Bob Brookmeyer Quartet | Old Friends | Storyville | STCD 8292
Bob Brookmeyer With The Metropole Orchestra | Out Of This World | Koch Jazz | 3-6913-2
Bud Powell Trio | The Greatest Jazz Concert Ever (Massey Hall Concert) | Prestige | P 24024
Buddy Tate Trio | Midnight Slows Vol.4 | Black & Blue | BLE 194682
Charlie Byrd Quartet | Moments Like This | Concord | CCD 4627
Chris Walden Orchestra | Great European Jazz Orchestras Vol.3:Ticino | ACT | 9229-2
Count Basie And His Orchestra | Count Basie At Newport | Verve | 9861761
Count Basie At Newport | Verve | 2304414 IMS
Dave Pell Octet feat. Lucy Ann Polk | Plays Burke And Van Heusen | Fresh Sound Records | KL 1034(Kapp)
Dexter Gordon Quartet | Something Different | Steeplechase | SCS 1136
The Shadow Of Your Smile | Steeplechase | SCCD 31206
Ella Fitzgerald Jam | Fine And Mellow | Pablo | 2310829-2
Emil Mangelsdorff Swingin' Oil Drops | Emil Mangelsdorff Swinging Oildrops 1966 | L+R Records | LR 41002
Harry Allen With The John Pizzarelli Trio | Harry Allen Meets The John Pizzarelli Trio | Novus | 2137397-2
Herb Ellis Quartet | Soft & Mellow | Concord | CCD 4077
Joe Bawelino Quartet | Happy Birthday Stéphane | Edition Collage | EC 458-2
Joe Pass With The NDR Big Band | Joe Pass In Hamburg | ACT | 9100-2
Joe Puma Quartet | Wild Kitten | Dawn | DCD 109
John Bunch-Bucky Pizzarelli Quartet | NY Swing | LRC Records | CDC 9045
Karen Francis With The George Colligan Trio | Where Is Love? | Steeplechase | SCCD 31393
Lester Young Quartet | Lester Young:Blue Lester | Dreyfus Jazz Line | FDM 36729-2
Lester Swings | Verve | 833554-1
Live Recordings In New York City | Jazz Anthology | JA 5174
Lou Donaldson Quintet | Blue Moon-Blue Note The Night And The Music | Blue Note | 789910-2
Marion McPartland Trio | From This Moment On | Concord | CJ 86
Oscar Peterson Trio | Romance-The Vocal Style Of Oscar Peterson | Verve | MV 2688 IMS
Paul Desmond Quartet | Easy Living | RCA | 2174796-2
Easy Living | RCA | 2174796-2
Masters Of Jazz Vol.13 | RCA | CL 42790 AG
Pharoah Sanders Quartet | Welcome To Love | Timeless | CD SJP 358
Royce Campbell-Adrian Ingram Group | Hands Across The Water | String Jazz | SJRCD 1002
Sarah Vaughan And Her Trio | Verve Jazz Masters 42:Sarah Vaughan-The Jazz Sides | Verve | 526817-2
Swingin' Easy | EmArCy | 514072-2
Sarah Vaughan With The Jimmy Jones Trio | Birdland All Stars At Carnegie Hall | Roulette | CDP 798660-2
Stan Getz Quartet | Stan Getz:The Golden Years Vol.1(1952-1958) | Moon Records | MCD 039-2
Tommy Dorsey And His Orchestra | Frank Sinatra Sings The Standards | RCA | NL 89102 AP
Twobones | Spiral Stairway | TCB Records | TCB 99752
Wes Montgomery Quartet | Wes Montgomery-The Complete Riverside Recordings | Riverside | 12 RCD 4408-2
André Previn Trio | Triple Play:André Previn | Telarc Digital | CD 83457

Polka Dots And Moonbeams-
Dexter Gordon-Benny Bailey Quintet | Revelation | Steeplechase | SCCD 31373
Doc Cheatham/Jim Galloway Sextet | At The Bern Festival | Sackville | SKCD2-3045
Stan Getz And The Oscar Peterson Trio | Stan Getz And The Oscar Peterson Trio | Verve | 2304440 IMS
Irene Schweizer | Piano Solo Vol.1 | Intakt Records | CD 020

Polonaise Pour Pietro-
Jan Fryderyk | Piano Works: Live Recordings | Jazzline | ???

Polperro
ULG | Spring | Laika Records | 35101382

Polsk Dans-
Mats Eden-Jonas Simonson With The Cikada String Quartet | Milvus | ECM | 1660

Polska Efter Ärtbergs Kalle Karlström
Lena Willemark-Ale Möller Group | Nordan | ECM | 1536(523161-2)

Polska Efter Jones Olle
Jonas Knutsson Group | Flower In The Sky | ACT | 9248-2

Polska Efter Rolings Per
Bobo Stenson Trio | Serenity | ECM | 1740/41(543611-2)

Polska Of Despair(I)
Serenity | ECM | 1740/41(543611-2)

Polska Of Despair(II)
New Way Out | New Way Out | Jazz 4 Ever Records:Jazz Network | J4E 4725

Polyphona
Mike Westbrook Band | Off Abbey Road | TipToe | TIP-888805 2

Polythene Pam
Benny Carter And His Orchestra | Big Bands Uptown 1931-40 | MCA | 1323

Pomona
Chet Baker Quartet | Chet Baker In Paris-The Complete Barclay Recordings Vol.1 | EmArCy | 837474-2 PMS

Pompeiian Tango
Günther Klatt & New York Razzmatazz | Fa Mozzo | Tutu Records | 888138-2

Pomponio
Donald Byrd Sextet | Landmarks | 32 Jazz | 32080

Pompton Turnpike
Oscar Peterson Trio | At Zardis' | Pablo | 2CD 2620118
Wild Bill Davis Quartet | Live At Swiss Radio Studio Zürich | Jazz Connaisseur | JCCD 8701-2
Elliot Lawrence And His Orchestra | The Elliot Lawrence Big Band Swings Cohn & Kahn | Fantasy | FCD 24761-2

Ponce
Mongo Santamaria And His Orchestra | Live At Jazz Alley | Concord | CCD 4427

Pong
Peter Erskine Trio | ELB | ACT | 9289-2
Urs Leimgruber-Fritz Hauser | L'Enigmatique | Hat Art | CD 6091

Pont Neuf
JoAnne Brackeen Quartet | Take A Chance | Concord | CCD 4602

Ponteio
Chris Barber's Jazz Band | The Chris Barber Jubilee Album-Vol. 2 | Intercord | 157009

Pony Blues
Bowling Green John Cephas & Harmonica Phil Wiggins | Living Country Blues USA, Vol. 1 | L+R Records | LR 42031
Jimmy Giuffre 3 | Hollywood Live Sessions 1957-58 | Fresh Sound Records | FSR 405(835553)

Pony Express-
The Jimmy Giuffre 3-Hollywood & Newport 1957-1958 | Fresh Sound Records | FSCD 1026

Ponytail
Carlo Actis Dato Quartet | Bagdad Boogie | SPLASC(H) Records | CD H 380-2

Poobly
Shelly Manne Orchestra | Cool California | Savoy | WL 70511(2)(SJL 2254) DP

Pool Shark
Don Grolnick Group | Hearts And Numbers | VeraBra Records | CDVBR 2016-2

Pools
Steps Ahead | Steps Ahead:Copenhagen Live | Storyville | 4960363
Steps Ahead | Elektra | 7559-60168-2
Woody Herman And His Orchestra | 50th Anniversary Tour | Concord | CCD 4302

Poom-A-Loom
Bobby Vega Group | Down The Road | Lipstick Records | LIP 8955-2

Poop Deck
Al Haig Sextet | Stan Getz:The Complete 1948-1952 Quintet Sessions(Master Takes) | Blue Moon | BMCD 1015

Poor Boy
Louisiana Red | The Blues Purity Of Louisiana Red | Blue Labor | BL 104
Jude Taylor And His Burning Flames | Autentic Bayou Blues-Best Of Zydeco | Mardi Gras Records | MG 5011

Poor Boy Long Way From Home
Gus Cannon-Blind Blake | Suitcase Full Of Blues | Black Swan Records | HCD-23

Poor Butterfly
Art Tatum | Art Tatum:Memories Of You | Black Lion | BLCD 7608-2
Barney Kessel-Herb Ellis Quartet | Poor Butterfly | Concord | CJ 34
Benny Goodman Trio | Jazz Live & Rare: Benny Goodman & His Group/Orchestra | Jazzline | ???
Booker Ervin Sextet | The Book Cooks | Fresh Sound Records | FSR 2050(Bethlehem BCP 6048)(835051)
Carmen McRae And Her Trio | Live | Ronnie Scott's Jazz House | NSPL 18543
Carmen McRae With The Shirley Horn Trio | Sarah-Dedicated To You | Novus | PD 90546
Count Basie With Strings | Basie On Roulette, Vol. 13: String Along With Basie | Vogue | 500013
Dave Shepherd Quintet | Good Enough To Keep | Black Lion | BLCD 760514
Flip Phillips Sextet | A Real Swinger | Concord | CJ 358
Herman Chittison Trio | Piano Genius | Musicraft | MVS 506
Ken Colyer's Jazzmen | Watch That Dirty Tone Of Yours... | Joy | 164 (800974)
Oscar Peterson Trio | Masters Of Jazz Vol.7 | RCA | NL 89721 DP
Planet Jazz:Jazz Piano | RCA | 2169655-2
Oscar Pettiford Trio | Jazz Legacy Baden Baden Unreleased Radio Tapes | Jazzline | ???
Sarah Vaughan With The Jimmy Jones Trio | Linger Awhile | Pablo | 2312144-2
Scott Hamilton Quartet | My Romance | Concord | CCD 4710
Sonny Rollins Quintet | Sonny Rollins | Blue Note | 84508
Sonny Rollins:The Blue Note Recordings | Blue Note | 821371-2
Ballads | Blue Note | 537562-2
Spiegle Willcox Septet | Vintage '89 | Timeless | CD TTD 579
Warren Vaché Quintet With Special Guest Allan Vaché | Jazz Im Amerikahaus,Vol.2 | Nagel-Heyer | CD 012
West Coast Jazz Summit | West Coast Jazz Summit | Mons Records | MR 874773

Poor Butterfly-
Johnny Hodges Orchestra | The Rabbit's Work On Verve In Chronological Order, Vol.4 | Verve | 2304450 IMS

Poor Butterfly(alt.take)
Dick Wellstood | Dick Wellstood-Alone | Solo Art | SACD-73

Poor Child
Springback James | Favorite Country Blues Guitar-Piano Duets | Yazoo | YAZ 1015

Poor Eric
Smith And Harper | Mama Let Me Lay It On You | Yazoo | YAZ 1040

Poor Joe
Rod Mason Band | Heebie Jeebies | Jazz Colours | 874725-2

Poor Little Jesus
Nomakozasana-Uli Lenz | Tenderness | Tutu Records | 888198-2*

Poor Little Music Boy
Lester Young And His Orchestra | Lester Young Master Takes | Savoy | SV 0250(SJL 1133)

Poor Pierrot
Ahmad Jamal Quartet | Nature | Dreyfus Jazz Line | FDM 37018-2

Poor Pierrot-
Nature(The Essence Part III) | Atlantic | 3984-23105-2
Champion Jack Dupree With Tony McPhee | From New Orleans To Chicago | Crosscut | CCR 1009

Poor You
Maxine Sullivan With The Keith Ingham Quartet | Maxine Sullivan Sings The Music Of Burton Lane | Mobile Fidelity | MFCD 773

Pop
Benny Goodman And His Orchestra | The Indispensable Benny Goodman Vol.3/4 | RCA | 2115520-2

Poppin' Pop
Lambert, Hendricks And Ross With Count Basie And His Orchestra | The Best Of The Jazz Singers Vol.2 | LRC Records | CDC 9008

Poppy
Greetje Bijma Kwintet | Tales Of A Voice | TipToe | TIP-888808 2

Pops
Rüdiger Carl | Rüdiger Carl Solo | FMP | CD 86

Pop's Blues
Dizzy Gillespie Quintet | School Days | Savoy | SV 0157(MG 6043)

Popsicle Toes
Chubby Jackson Sextet | Chubby Jackson The Happy Monster:Small Groups 1944-1947 | Cool & Blue | C&B-CD 109

Popsong
Bobby Timmons Trio | In Person | Original Jazz Classics | OJC20 364-2(RLP 9391)

Popsy
Sergey Kuryokhin | Popular Zoological Elements | LEO | LR 148

Por El Sol Y Por La Lluvia
Eugen Cicero Trio | Eugen Cicero Highlights | MPS | 88028-2

Por Toda A Minha Vida
Eddie Higgins Trio | Those Quiet Days | Sunnyside | SSC 1052 D

Por Tu Culpa
Peter Fulda Trio With Céline Rudolph | Silent Dances | Jazz 4 Ever Records:Jazz Network | J4E 4731

Poravi
Theo Jörgensmann Quartet feat.John Thomas | Go Ahead Clarinet | CMP Records | CMP 4

Porch Swing
Nat King Cole And His Trio With Pete Rugolo's Orchestra | Lush Life | Capitol | 780595-2

Porgy
Abbey Lincoln With Her Quintet | Sonny Rollins-The Freelance Years:The Complete Riverside & Contemporary Recordings | Riverside | 5 RCD 4427-2
Archie Shepp-Mal Waldron | Left Alone Revisited | Enja | 9141-2
Billie Holiday With The Bobby Tucker Quartet | Lover Man | MCA | 2292-52317-1
Oscar Peterson Trio | Three Originals:Motion&Emotions/Tristeza On Piano/Hello Herbie | MPS | 521059-2
Paul Bley | Axis | Improvising Artists Inc. | 123853-2

Porgy-
Chet Baker With The Georges Arvanitas Trio | Live In Paris 1960-63 & Nice 1975 | France's Concert | FCD 123

Porgy And Bess Medley
The Trio | The Trio:Rediscovered | String Jazz | SJRCD 1007
Gene Harris And The Philip Morris Superband | Live At Town Hall N.Y.C. | Concord | CCD 4397

Porgy(alt.take)
Brötzman-Laswell-Evans-Helborg | Ode To A Tractor | Demon Records | DEM 030

Pork And Beans
Lu Watters' Jazz Band | Blues Over Bodega | Good Time Jazz | GTCD 12066-2
Lucky Roberts | Lucky Roberts & Ralph Sutton:The Circle Recordings | Solo Art | SACD-10

Pork Chops
Louis Delisle's Band | Echoes From New Orleans | Storyville | SLP 212

Pork Pie
Cannonball Adderley Quintet | Cannonball Adderley:Sophisticated Swing-The EmArCy Small Group Sessions | Verve | 528408-2

Porky
Nat Adderley Quintet | The Adderleya-That's Nat And Julian! | Savoy | 650138(882381)

Porno Hirn
Dominique Pifarély-Francois Couturier | Poros | ECM | 1647

Poros
Gabriele Mirabassi Quartet | Gabriele Mirabassi Electroacoustic Quartetto | Quadrivium | SCA 015

Porsche
McCoy Tyner Trio | Live At The Musicians Exchange Cafe Ft.Lauderdale,USA | Kingdom Jazz | Gate 7021(805830)

Port Authority
Dylan Fowler | Portrait | Acoustic Music Records | 319.1185.2

Port O'Clock
Gerry Mulligan-Scott Hamilton Quintet | Soft Light & Sweet Music | Concord | CCD 4300

Port Of Call
Cecil Taylor Quartet | Cecil Taylor: Air | Candid | CCD 79046

Port Of Call(take 3)
Ned Rothenberg Trio | Port Of Entry | Intuition Records | INT 3249-2

Port Of Entry
Weather Report | Night Passage | CBS | 468211-2
Port Of Harlem Jazzmen | 1939-1949, Blue Note's Three Decades Of Jazz, Vol. 1 | Blue Note | 89902

Port Royal
Bud Shank Sextet | New Gold! | Candid | CCD 79707

Port Townsend
Miles Davis Group | Montreux Jazz Festival | ACT | 9001-2

Porta Camollia
Perico Sambeat Group | Ademuz | Fresh Sound Records | FSNT 041 CD

Porta Do Ferro
Egberto Gismonti | Danca Das Cabecas | ECM | 1089

Porta Encantada
Louis Sclavis Group | Napoli's Walls | ECM | 1857(038504-2)

Porta Segreta
Vic Juris Quartet | Roadsong | Muse | MR 5150

Port-Au-Prince
Shorty Rogers And His Giants | Collaboration-Shorty Rogers And Andre Previn | Fresh Sound Records | ND 74398

Porter's House
Marty Cook Group | Theory Of Strange | Enja | 9107-2

Portia
Miles Davis Group | Miles In Montreux | Jazz Door | JD 1287/88

Porto Allegro
Jörg Krückel-Brad Leali Quartet | Cookin' Good | Edition Collage | EC 507-2
Django Reinhardt And The Quintet Du Hot Club De France | Bruxelles/Paris | Accord | 403222

Portrait
Charles Mingus Group With Orchestra | Charles Mingus | Denon Compact Disc | DC-8565
Dylan Fowler | Portrait | Acoustic Music Records | 319.1185.2
Kevin Mahogany With The WDR Big Band And Guests | Pussy Cat Dues:The Music Of Charles Mingus | Enja | ENJ-9316 2
Mike Westbrook Concert Band | Celebration | Deram | 844852-2
Thad Jones With Strings | Autobiography In Jazz | Original Jazz Classics | OJC 115(DEB 198)

Portrait In Black And White
Joe Henderson Group | Double Rainbow | Verve | 527222-2
Phil Grenadier Quintet | Sweet Transients | Fresh Sound Records | FSNT 093 CD
Reggio-Danko-Pejrolo | Three For Chet | Philology | W 226.2

Portrait Of A Romantic
Dutch Jazz Orchestra | Portrait Of A Silk Thread | Kokopelli Records | KOKO 1310

Portrait Of Benny
Duke Ellington And His Famous Orchestra | Duke Ellington:The Blanton-Webster Band | Bluebird | 21 13181-2

Portrait Of Bert Williams
Duke Ellington And His Orchestra | Carnegie Hall Concert January 1943 | Prestige | 2PCD 34004-2
Duke Elliongton:Complete Prestige Carnegie Hall 1943-1944 Concerts | Definitive Records | DRCD 11210

Portrait Of Bojangles
Duke Elliongton:Complete Prestige Carnegie Hall 1943-1944 Concerts | Definitive Records | DRCD 11210

Portrait Of Cheikh Anta Diop
Mike Garson | Avant Garson | Contemporary | C 14003

Portrait Of Cootie
Sadik Hakim Trio | Witches Gobelins etc. | Steeplechase | SCCD 31091

Portrait Of Ella Fitzgerald:
Ella Fitzgerald With The Duke Ellington Orchestra | The Complete Ella Fitzgerald Song Books of Harold Arlen, Irving Berlin, Duke Ellington, George & Ira Gershwin, Jerome Kern, Johnny Mercer, Cole Porter And Rogers & Hart | Verve | 519832-2

Portrait Of Florence Mills(Black Beauty)
Duke Ellington And His Orchestra | Duke Elliongton:Complete Prestige Carnegie Hall 1943-1944 Concerts | Definitive Records | DRCD 11210

Portrait Of Jenny
Clifford Brown With Strings | Brownie-The Complete EmArCy Recordings Of Clifford Brown | EmArCy | 838306-2
David Friesen Quartet | Four To Go | ITM-Pacific | ITMP 970088
George Shearing Trio & The Robert Farnon Orchestra | On Target | MPS | 68280
Joe Lovano Quartet | From The Soul | Blue Note | 798636-2
John Pizzarelli Trio | Dear Mr.Cole | Novus | 4163182-2
Jon Gordon Quartet/Quintet | Along The Way | Criss Cross | Criss 1138
Oliver Jackson Quartet | Billie's Bounce | Black & Blue | BLE 59.183 2
Ralph Peterson Quintet | The Art Of War | Criss Cross | Criss 1206
Rein De Graaff-Dick Vennik Quartet | Cloud People | Timeless | SJP 191
Scott Hamilton Quintet | Close Up | Concord | CCD 4197
Wes Montgomery Quartet | The Small Group Recordings | Verve | 2-2513 IMS
Wynton Kelly Trio | It's All Right! | Verve | 537750-2
All Star Trumpet Spectacular | The Second Progressive Records All Star Trumpet Spectacular | Progressive | PRO 7017 IMS

Portrait Of Johnny
Curtis Clark Quintet | Amsterdam Sunshine | Nimbus | NS 3691

Portrait Of Louis Armstrong
Duke Ellington And His Orchestra | That's Jazz Vol.31: New Orleans Suite | Atlantic | ATL 50403

Portrait Of Mahalia Jackson
That's Jazz Vol.31: New Orleans Suite | Atlantic | ATL 50403

Portrait Of Mingus
Ricky Ford Quartet | Flying Colors | Muse | MR 5227

Portrait Of My Mother
Randy Weston | African Nite | Owl Records | 01

Portrait Of Pony Poindexter
Tony Scott-Bill Evans Sextet | A Day In New York | Fresh Sound Records | FSR-CD 0160(2)

Portrait Of Sidney Bechet
Duke Ellington And His Orchestra | That's Jazz Vol.31: New Orleans Suite | Atlantic | ATL 50403
Paul Bley Quartet | In The Evenings Out There | ECM | 1488

Portrait Of Silence
Hod O'Brien Trio | Ridin' High | Reservoir | RSR CD 116(881745)

Portrait Of The Artist As A Small Furry Creature From Betelgeuze IV
Horace Silver Ensemble | Silver 'N Strings Play The Music Of The Spheres | Blue Note | LWB 1033

Portrait Of The Duke
Willie 'The Lion' Smith | The Memoirs Of Willie 'The Lion' Smith | RCA | 2126415-2

Portrait Of The Lion
Duke Ellington And His Orchestra | Duke Ellington's Masterpieces Vol.1: 1938-1940 | Black & Blue | BLE 59.233 2

Portrait Of The Lion(The Second)
Sun Ra And His Arkestra | Supersonic Jazz | Evidence | ECD 22015-2

Portrait Of Wellman Braud
Duke Ellington And His Orchestra | That's Jazz Vol.31: New Orleans Suite | Atlantic | ATL 50403

Portrait(take 1)
Jackie Paris With The Charles Mingus Quintet | Charles Mingus-The Complete Debut Recordings | Debut | 12 DCD 4402-2

Portrait(take 2)
Sam Rivers | Portrait Sam Rivers Live | FMP | CD 82

Portret De Iubire
Gary Burton Quartet | Green Apple | Moon Records | MCD 013-2

Portugal
Franz De Byl | Franz De Byl-Solo | FMP | SAJ 27

Portuguese Washerwoman
Patrick Bebelaar Quartet | You Never Lose An Island | dml-records | CD 015

Pos Pregatz Mi
Günter Christmann | Off | Moers Music | 01070

Pose Nude
Bill Smith/Enrico Pieranunzi Duo | Sonorities | EdiPan | NPG 801

Poseidon
Dave Douglas Group | The Infinite | RCA | 2663918-2

Poses
Jimmie Lunceford And His Orchestra | Jimmie Lunceford Vol.3-For Dancers Only | MCA | 1307

Position Konkret
Erich Bachträgl Quartet | Gollum | Bellaphon | 270.31.004

Positive
Stephen Scott Septet | Aminah's Dream | Verve | 517996-2

Positivity
Don Friedman Quartet | My Foolish Heart | Steeplechase | SCCD 31534
Harold Ousley Group | The People's Groove | Muse | MR 5107

Possibilities
Gust Williams Tsilis Quartet | Possibilities | Ken Music | 660.56.009

Possibles
Kölner Saxophon Mafia | Licence To Thrill | Jazz Haus Musik | JHM 0100 CD

Possibly A Mission Impossible
Johnny Lytle Septet | Possum Grease | Muse | MCD 5482

Post Scriptum
Cousin Joe With Band | Cousin Joe:The Complete 1945-1947 Vol.1 (1945-1946) | Blue Moon | BMCD 6001

Postamt
Jimmy Jewell Sextet | From The First Time I Met You | Affinity | AFF 5

Postcard To Salta
| Love Every Moment | Concord | CCD 4534

Postizo
Earl Klugh Trio With The Royal Philharmonic Orchestra | Sounds And Visions | Warner | 9362-45158-2

Postlude
John Carter Octet | Castles Of Ghana | Gramavision | GR 8603-2
Sam Rivers Orchestra | Crystals | Impulse(MCA) | 589760-2
Freddie Hubbard And His Quintet With Reciters,Chorus,Strings,Tape | That's Jazz Vol.5: Sing Me A Song Of Songmy | Atlantic | ATL 50235

Postlude In C
John Wolf Brennan | The Well-Prepared Clavier/Das Wohlpräparierte Klavier | Creative Works Records | CW CD 1032-2

Postlude(for two light and an invisdible reft hand[s])
Paul Smoker Trio | Alone | Sound Aspects | sas CD 018(32018)

Postludique
Lars Danielsson Trio | Continuation | L+R Records | CDLR 45085

Postman's Lament
Mr.Acker Bilk And His Paramount Jazz Band | New Orleans Days | Lake | LACD 36

Post-Mesotonique
Patricia Barber Group | Modern Cool | Blue Note | 521811-2

Postmodern Blues
Room | Room | Sound Aspects | sas CD 028

Pot Luck
Gary Peacock | Partners | Owl Records | 014730-2
Henri Renaud And His Orchestra | New Sound At The Boeuf Sur Le Toit | Fresh Sound Records | FSR 576(Blue Star BS 6831)
The Herdsmen | The Herdsmen Play Paris | Original Jazz Classics | OJC 116(F 3201)

Pot Pourri Transitions-
Michael Moore Group | Tunes For Horn Guys | Ramboy Recordings | No.08

Potato Head Blues
Louis Armstrong And His Hot Seven | Heebie Jeebies | Naxos Jazz | 8.120351 CD
Teddy Buckner And His Dixieland Band | A Salute To Louis Armstrong | Dixieland Jubilee | GNPD 505
Willem Breuker Kollektief And Djazzex | Dance Plezier-Joy Of Dance | BVHAAST | CD 9513

Potion(1)
Azimuth | Azimuth '85 | ECM | 1298

Potion(2)
John Rae Quintet | Opus De Jazz Vol.2-John Rae | Savoy | SV 0179(MG 12156)

Potpourri
Mal Waldron Sextet | John Coltrane-The Prestige Recordings | Prestige | 16 PCD 4405-2
Prestige All Stars | After Hours | Prestige | P 24107
Alexander von Schlippenbach And Sven-Ake Johansson | Live 1976/77 | FMP | CD 111

Potpourri(A.Lauro)
Juanjo Dominguez | Internationales Guitarren Festival '94 | ALISO Records | AL 1030

Potpourri(Carlos Gardel)
Wieland Kleinbub | Sirkle | Edition Musikat | EDM 071

Potpüree
Bob Brookmeyer Quartet | The Duale Roll Of Bob Brookmeyer | Original Jazz Classics | OJCCD 1729-2

Pots
Bob Mintzer Big Band | Bob Mintzer Big Band-The First Decade | dmp Digital Music Productions | CD 510

Pots On, Gas On High
Harold Danko Quintet | Prestigious-A Tribute To Eric Dolphy | Steeplechase | SCCD 31508

Potter's Luck
Stan Getz Quintet | Chamber Music | Fresh Sound Records | FSR-CD 78(882177)

Pottsville U.S.A.
Freddy Merkle Group | Jazz Under The Dome | Fresh Sound Records | NL 45957(RCA Vik LX 1114)

Potu Loto Potu
Brötzmann-Mengelberg-Bennink Trio | 3 Points And A Mountain...Plus | FMP | CD 107

Pound Underground-
Port Of Harlem Seven | Jazz Classics Vol.2 | Blue Note | 789385-2

Pour La Fille Du Soleil
Jack Dieval Trio | Jazz In Paris:Jack Diéval-Jazz Aux Champs Elysées | EmArCy | 018419-2

Pour Penser Á Toi
Francois Jeanneau Quartet | Techniques Douces | Owl Records | 04

Pour Une Femme(to Chet Baker)
Louis Sclavis Sextet | Les Violences De Rameau | ECM | 1588(533128-2)

Pour Vous...Ces Quelques Fleurs
Lucky Peterson Group | Beyond Cool | Verve | 521147-2

Pourquoi Une Valse-
Andre Pasdoc With The Orchestra Vola | Jazz In Paris:Django Reinhardt-Django Et Compagnie | EmArCy | 549241-2 PMS

Pourquoi,Pourquoi?
Stephane Grappelli Sextet | Stephane Grappelli & Friends In Paris | Accord | 500762

Pousse
Al Casey Quartet | Jumpin' With Al | Black & Blue | BB 873.2

Pousse Cafe
Jumpin' With Al | Black & Blue | BB 873.2

Pousuite Et Metro
Ben Webster Quartet | Perdido | Moon Records | MCD 070-2

Poutin'
Jimmy Blythe's Owls | South Side Chicago Jazz | MCA | MCAD 42326(872083)

Pouts' Over(And The Day's Not Through)
Dave Douglas Quartet | Charms Of The Night Sky | Winter&Winter | 910015-2

Poveri Fiori
Jens Thomas | Jens Thomas Plays Ennio Morricone | ACT | 9273-2

Poverty
Benny Golson-Freddie Hubbard Quintet | Stardust | Denon Compact Disc | CY-1838

Povo
Fourth World | Fourth World | B&W Present | BW 030

Powder Puff
Shorty Rogers And His Giants | Short Stops | RCA | NL 85917(2)

Powder Your Face With Sunshine
Steve Rochinski Solo/Duo/Trio/Quartet | Jazz Guitar Highlights 1 | Jardis Records | JRCD 20141
Clifford Brown-Max Roach Quintet | Clifford Brown And Max Roach At Basin Street | Verve | 589826-2

Powell's Prances
Brownie-The Complete EmArCy Recordings Of Clifford Brown | EmArCy | 838306-2
Mulgrew Miller Trio | Work! | Landmark | LCD 1511-2
Matthew Ship 'String' Trio | Expansion,Power,Release | HatOLOGY | 558

Power House
Axel Zwingenberger | Powerhouse Boogie | Vagabond | 6.24210 AS-Digital

Power Of Love
Mahavishnu Orchestra | Apocalypse | CBS | 467092-2
Michal Urbaniak With The Horace Parlan Trio | Take Good Care Of My Heart | Steeplechase | SCCD 31195

Power Of Nature
Jean-Paul Bourelly Group | Tribute To Jimi | DIW | DIW 893 CD

Power Spot
Johnny Griffin-Steve Grossman Quintet | Johnny Griffin & Steve Grossman | Dreyfus Jazz Line | FDM 36615-2

Power Station
Bruce Ditmas Quintet | What If | Postcards | POST 1007

Power To The People
Joe Henderson Quintet | Joe Henderson:The Milestone Years | Milestone | 8MCD 4413-2
Dave Grusin Group | Night-Lines | GRP | GRP 95042

Pow-Wow
Warren Vaché Quartet | What Is There To Say? | Nagel-Heyer | CD 056
Vladimir Estragon | Three Quarks For Muster Mark | TipToe | TIP-888803 2

Pra Dizer Adeus
Peter Herbolzheimer Rhythm Combination & Brass | Latin Groove | Koala Records | CD P 13

Präambulum from Partita No.5 in G Major(BWV 829)
Jugendjazzorchester NW | Beau Rivage | Jugendjazzorchester NW | JJO 003

Practise Makers Poifect
Frederic Rabold Inspiration Orchestra | Relaxing Walk | Fusion | 8019

Prager Schlüsselklingeln
Mikel Andueza Quintet | BCN | Fresh Sound Records | FSNT 036 CD

Pragmático
Joe Baudisch Quartet | The Meeting Of Two Tenors | Acoustic Music Records | 319.1135.2

Praha
Tony Scott | Music For Yoga Meditation And Other Joys | Verve | 2304471 IMS

Prahna-Life Force
Passport | Iguacu | Atlantic | 2292-46031-2

Praia Leme
Seger Ellis | Prairie Blues-The Music Of Seger Ellis | AZURE Compact Disc | AZ-CD-22

Praise
Steps Ahead With Guests | Yin-Yang | NYC-Records | NYC 6001-2

Prajna-Paramita-Hridaya Sutra(Sutra Chant)
William Hooker Quartet | The Firmament Fury | Silkheart | SHCD 123

Präludium Aus Der Cello-Suite Nr.2
Ali Ryerson Quintet | Brasil:Quiet Devotion | Concord | CCD 4762

Präludium in e-Moll(Bach BWV 548)
Max Neissendorfer Trio | Staubfrei | EGO | 95100

Präludium Nr.1
Jacques Loussier Trio | Portrait | Decca | 6.28511 DO

Präludium Nr.12 f-moll
Play Bach | Decca | 6.30006 DX

PräludiumIn C-Moll Ünd Dur
Juhani Aaltonen Trio | Prana-Live At Groovy | Leo Records | 013

Prancing
Bernhard Arndt | Insight Insight | FMP | OWN-90005

Präsentation
Bründl's Basslab | Aisha | L+R Records | CDLR 45036

Pratt City Blues
Rüdiger Carl | Rüdiger Carl Solo | FMP | CD 86

Prayer
Billy Taylor Trio | You Tempt Me | Taylor Made Records | T 1004
Dave Ballou Quartet | Dancing Foot | Steeplechase | SCCD 31556
David Azarian Trio | Hope | Enja | ENJ-9354 2
François Houle 5 | Cryptology | Between The Lines | btl 012(Efa 10182-2)
Fred Wesley Group | Comme Ca | Minor Music | 801020
Kamal And The Brothers | Dance | Stash Records | ST 279(807426)
Michael Urbaniak's Fusion | Heritage | MPS | 68182
Miles Davis With Gil Evans & His Orchestra | The Miles Davis Selection | CBS | 465699-2

Prayer-
Wiregrass Sacred Harp Singers | The Colored Sacred Harp | New World Records | 80433-2

Prayer And Despair
Charles Gayle Trio | Homeless | Silkheart | SHCD 116

Prayer Beads
Randy Weston African Rhythm | Khepera | Verve | 557821-2

Prayer Blues
Art Blakey And The Afro Drum Ensemble | The African Beat | Blue Note | 522666-2

Prayer by Solomon G.Ilori
Rachelle Ferrell With The Eddie Green Trio | First Instrumental | Blue Note | 827820-2

Prayer Dance
George Adams-Dannie Richmond Quintet | Gentlemen's Agreement | Soul Note | 121057-2

Prayer For Jimbo Kwesi
Father Tom Vaughn Trio | Joyful Jazz | Concord | CJ 16

Prayer For Passive Resistance
Charles Mingus Quintet | Charles Mingus-Passion Of A Man:The Complete Atlantic Recordings 1956-1961 | Atlantic | 8122-72871-2
Charles Minus-Live | Affinity | CD AFS 778
Roberto Ottaviano Six Mobiles | Mingus: Portrait In Six Colors | SPLASC(H) Records | H 169

Prayer For Peace
Marcus Roberts | Prayer For Peace | Novus | ND 90585(847064)

Prayer For Sibylle
Ray Pizzi Quartet | I Hear You | Bhakti Jazz | BR 27

Prayer For The Newborn
Tim Warfield Sextet | A Whisper In The Midnight | Criss Cross | Criss 1122

Prayer Meetin'
Pee Wee Ellis Quartet | Sepia Tonality | Minor Music | 801040

Prayer Of Love
Matrix | Harvest | Pablo | 2312121

Prayer(part 1)
Mikhail Alperin's Moscow Art Trio With The Tuva Folk & Russian Folk Ensemble | Prayer | JA & RO | JARO 4193-2

Prayer(part 2)
Charles Lloyd Quintet | Lift Every Voice | ECM | 1832/33(018783-2)

Prayer,The Crossing
Lightnin' Hopkins | Blues Train | Mainstream | MD CDO 901

Praying With Eric
Charles Mingus Sextet | Town Hall Concert | America | AM 6140

Prayoga
Duke Ellington And His Orchestra & Choir | Second Sacred Concert | America | AM 006/007

Preacher Man-
Horst Jankowski Orchestra With Voices | Jankowskeynotes | MPS | 9814806

Preacherman's Daughter
Julian Dash And His Orchestra | Julian Dash:The Complete Recordings 1950-1953 | Blue Moon | BMCD 1050

Preaching Blues[Up Jumped The Devil]
Paulus Potters Trio With Guests | The Argonauts | Timeless | CD SJP 423

Preamble
White Diamonds And Vladimir Botschakow | The White Diamonds | Jazz Pure Collection | AU 31624 CD

Preamp
Tom Varner Sextet | Martian Heartache | Soul Note | 121286-2

Precession
Benni Chaves-Laszlo Gardony | Human Bass | Laika Records | 35101042

Precious
John Serry Quartet | Enchantress | Telarc Digital | CD 83392

Precious Joy
Horace Parlan Quartet | Little Esther | Soul Note | 121145-2

Precious Lord Take My Hand
Chris Barber's Jazz Band | The Golden Years Of Revival Jazz,Vol 1 | Storyville | STCD 5506

Ice Cream | Storyville | 6.23326 AF
Cyrus Chestnut Trio | You Are My Sunshine | Warner | 9362-48445-2
Dejan's Olympia Brass Band | Here Come Da Great Olympia Band | Preservation Hall | VPS-4
Katie Webster | The Many Faces Of Katie Webster | Schubert Records | SCH- 103
The Jackson Singers | Gospel Emotions | L+R Records | CDLR 44016 AM 4 | Roots & Fruits | EmArCy | 537495-2

Precious Memories
Henrik Johansen's Jazzband | The Golden Years Of Revival Jazz,Vol 1 | Storyville | STCD 5506
Sister Rosetta Tharpe And Her Group | Gospel Train | Mercury | 841134-2
Sister Rosetta Tharpe With The Otis Spann Trio | Live In Paris 1964 | France's Concert | FCD 118

Precious One
Geoff Keezer Group | Turn Up The Quiet | CBS | 488830-2

Precious Thing(Till The Next...Somewhere)
Nick Woodland And The Magnets | Big Heart | Blues Beacon | BLU-1013 2

Precious Time
Lonely Universe | Lonely Universe | CMP Records | CMP CD 41

Précipice
Slide Hampton Quintet | Roots | Criss Cross | Criss 1015

Preface
Sidney Bechet With Orchestra | La Nuit Es Une Sorciere | Vogue | 21134142

Preface To Truth
Gunter Hampel Jazz Sextet | Gunter Hampel: The 8th Of Sept.1999 | Birth | CD 049

Preface(II)
Michel Benita Quartet | Preferences | Label Bleu | LBLC 6532(882935)

Preghiera
Keith Jarrett Quartet | El Juicio(The Judgement) | Atlantic | 7567-80783-2

Pre-Judgement Armosphere
Fabien Degryse Group | Quadruplex | B.Sharp Records | CDS 077

Prelude
Bennie Wallace Trio | Bennie Wallace Plays Monk | Enja | ENJ-3091 2
Bernard Peiffer | Jazz In Paris:Bernard Peiffer-La Vie En Rose | EmArCy | 013980-2
Charlie Byrd Quartet | Jazz Recital | Savoy | SV 0192(MG 12099)
Dave Brubeck Quintet | Reunion | Original Jazz Classics | OJCCD 150-2
Dave Brubeck With The Erich Kunzel Orchestra | Truth Is Fallen | Atlantic | 7567-80761-2
Dieter Ilg-Marc Copeland-Jeff Hirshfield | What's Goin' On | Jazzline | JL 11138-2
Dusan Bogdanovic Quartet | Early To Rise | Palo Alto | PA 8049
Jerry Granelli-Annabelle Wilson-Glenn Moore | Forces Of Flight | ITM-Pacific | ITMP 970061
John Surman-John Taylor With Chorus | Proverbs And Songs | ECM | 1639
Johnny Smith Quartet | The Sound Of The Johnny Smith Guitar | Roulette | 531792-2
The Sound Of Johnny Smith Guitar | Fresh Sound Records | FSR 583(Roost 2246)
Last Affair | Sound Movie-Suite | Blue Flame | 40312
Max Roach Quintet | Clifford Brown-Max Roach:Alone Together-The Best Of The Mercury Years | Verve | 526373-2
Drum Conversation | Enja | 4074-2
Mike Westbrook Concert Band | Marching Songs Vol.1&2 | Deram | 844853-2

Prelude-
Dizzy Gillespie And His Orchestra | Gillespiana And Carnegie Hall Concert | Verve | 519809-2
Dizzy Gillespie Quintet | En Concert Avec Europe 1 | Laserlight | 710705
Les Arbuckle Quartet | No More No Les | audioquest Music | AQCD 1019

Prelude A L'Unisson
Eugen Cicero Trio | Cicero's Chopin | MPS | 68128

Prelude And Fugue No.1 In C Major(BWV 846)
Swingle Singers | Jazz Sebastian Bach Vol.2 | Philips | 542553-2

Prelude And Fugue No.10 In E Minor(BWV 855)
Jazz Sebastian Bach Vol.2 | Philips | 542553-2

Prelude And Fugue No.3 In C Sharp Major(BWV 848)
Phil Woods Orchestra | Rights Of Swing | Candid | CS 9016

Prelude And Rustic Dance
Kölner Saxophon Mafia With Guests | Kölner Saxophon Mafia: 20 Jahre Saxuelle Befreiung | Jazz Haus Musik | JHM 0115 CD

Prelude And Scurrying
Sun Ra And His Arkestra | Spaceways | Freedom | CD 741047

Prelude En La Mineur
John Kirby Sextet | John Kirby | Atlantis | ATS 6

Prelude In B Minor
Art Blakey-Barney Wilen Quartet | Les Liaisons Dangereuses(Original Soundtrack) | Fontana | 812017-2

Prelude In Blue(A L'Esquinade)
Art Blakey And The Jazz Messengers | Les Liaisons Dangereuses(Original Soundtrack) | Fontana | 812017-2

Prelude In Blue(Chez Miguel)
Artie Shaw And His Orchestra | The Indispensable Artie Shaw Vol.3/4 | RCA | 2126414-2

Prelude In C Sharp Minor
Nat King Cole Trio | Vocal Classics & Instrumental Classics | Capitol | 300014(TOCJ 6128)

Prelude In C Sharp Minor(BWV 849)
Eddie Lang | Pioneers Of Jazz Guitar 1927-1939 | Retrieval | RTR 79015

Prelude In E Minor
Steve Kuhn | Ecstasy | ECM | 1058

Prelude Medley:
Art Farmer Quintet | You Make Me Smile | Soul Note | 121076-2

Prelude No.1
Jacques Loussier Trio | Play Bach | Accord | 500372

Prelude No.1 In C Major(BWV 846)
Play Bach Live In Concert | Decca | 6.22597 AO
Swingle Singers | Jazz Sebastian Bach | Philips | 542552-2

Prelude No.1 In C Major(BWV 870)
Jazz Sebastian Bach | Philips | 542552-2

Prelude No.11 In F Major(BWV 880)
Jacques Loussier Trio | Play Bach | Accord | 500372

Prelude No.12 In F Minor(BWV 881)
Play Bach Live In Concert | Decca | 6.22597 AO

Prelude No.16 In G Minor(BWV 861)
Swingle Singers | Swingle Singers Going Baroque | Philips | 546746-2

Prelude No.19 in A Major(BWV 864)
Chick Corea Trio | Trio Music,Live In Europe | ECM | 1310(827769-2)

Prelude No.2
Jacques Loussier Trio | The Best Of Play Bach | Philips | 824664-2
Larry Coryell | Privat Concert | Acoustic Music Records | 319.1159.2
Ray Run No Star Band | I Got Gershwin | Jazzline | ???

Prelude No.2 In C Minor(BWV 847)
Jacques Loussier Trio | Play Bach No.1 | Decca | 157561-2
Chick Corea | Originals | Stretch Records | SCD 9029-2

Prelude No.20
Lee Konitz-Gil Evans | Hereos | Verve | 511621-2 PMS

Prelude No.21 In B Flat Major(BWV 866)
Swingle Singers | Swingle Singers Going Baroque | Philips | 546746-2

Prelude No.24 in B Minor(BWV 893)
Jaki Byard And The Apollo Stompers | Phantasies | Soul Note | 121075-2

Prelude No.3
Helmut Nieberle-Helmut Kagerer | Flashes | Jardis Records | JRCD 20031
Barbara Dennerlein Quartet | Orgelspiele | Böhm Records | 65145 IMS

Prelude No.4
Chick Corea | Originals | Stretch Records | SCD 9029-2

Prelude No.5 In D Major(BWV 850)
Jacques Loussier Trio | Focus On Jacques Loussier | Decca | FOS-R 5/6

Prelude No.6 In D Minor(BWV 851)
Swingle Singers | Swingle Singers Going Baroque | Philips | 546746-2

Prelude No.7 in E Flat Major(BWV 876)
Andy LaVerne | Jazz Piano Lineage | dmp Digital Music Productions | CD 463

Prelude No.8 In E Flat Minor(BWV 853)
Swingle Singers | Jazz Sebastian Bach | Philips | 542552-2

Prelude No.9(BWV 878)
Jacques Loussier Trio | Play Bach | Decca | 6.28150 DP

Prelude Para Riccarda
Urs Leimgruber | Ungleich | Hat Art | CD 6049

Prelude To A Kiss
Archie Shepp-Michel Marre Quintet | Passion | 52e Rue Est | RECD 018
Ben Webster Quartet | For The Guv'nor | Charly | CD 15
Bennie Wallace Quartet | Bennie Wallace | audioquest Music | AQCD 1051
Benny Carter And His Orchestra | The Uncollectet:Banny Carter-Live At The Trianon Ballroom | Hindsight | HSR 218
Bill Easley Quintet | First Call | Milestone | MCD 9186-2
Brad Mehldau Trio | Introducing Brad Mehldau | Warner | 9362-45997-2
Bruce Forman Quartet With Bobby Hutcherson | There Are Times | Concord | CCD 4332
Charlie Shavers/Budd Johnson Quintet | Live | Black & Blue | BLE 59.302 2
Diane Schuur With Orchestra | Love Songs | GRP | GRP 97032
Don Friedman | Maybeck Recital Hall Series Volume Thirty-Three | Concord | CCD 4608
Duke Ellington And His Orchestra | Greatest Hits | CBS | 462959-2
Duke Ellington:The Complete RCA-Victor Mid-Forties Recordings(1944-1946) | RCA | 2663394-2
Sophisticated Lady | RCA | 26685162
The Indispensable Duke Ellington Vol.11/12 | RCA | 2115524-2
Ella Fitzgerald And Her All Stars | Love Songs:The Best Of The Song Books | Verve | 531762-2
The Complete Ella Fitzgerald Song Books of Harold Arlen, Irving Berlin, Duke Ellington, George & Ira Gershwin, Jerome Kern, Johnny Mercer, Cole Porter And Rogers & Hart | Verve | 519832-2
Great Jazz Trio | Standard Collection Vol.1 | Limetree | MCD 0031
Günther Klatt-Tizian Jost | Art Of The Duo:Live In Mexico City | Tutu Records | 888184-2*
Harold Ashby Quartet | What Am I Here For? | Criss Cross | Criss 1054
Howard Rumsey's Lighthouse All-Stars | Howard Rumsey's Lighthouse All-Stars Vol.6 | Original Jazz Classics | OJCCD 386-2(C 3504)
Jasper Van't Hof | Solo Piano | Timeless | CD SJP 286
Jimmy Rowles Trio | Shade And Light | Ahead | 33751
Joe Pass Trio | The Concord Jazz Guitar Collection Volumes 1 And 2 | Concord | CCD 4160
John Campbell Trio | Turning Point | Contemporary | CCD 14061-2
Joris Teepe Quintet | Bottom Line | Mons Records | MR 874770
Junior Mance Martin Rivera Duo | For Dancer's Only | Sackville | SKCD2-3031
Kenny Barron/Ron Carter | 1+1+1 | Black-Hawk | BKH 50601
Louie Bellson And His Jazz Orchestra | Air Mail Special-A Salute To The Big Band Masters | Limelight | 820824-2 IMS
McCoy Tyner Quintet | Dimensions | Elektra | 960350-1
Oscar Peterson Trio | Oscar Peterson Plays The Duke Ellington Song Book | Verve | 559785-2
Oscar Peterson Plays The Duke Ellington Song Book | Verve | 559785-2
Paolo Tomelleri-Fritz Hartschuh Quintet | Milan Swing | L+R Records | CDLR 45070
Pee Wee Russell Quartet | Ask Me Now! | Impulse(MCA) | 755742-2
Peter Appleyard Quintet | Barbados Cool | Concord | CCD 4475
Rob Parton's Jazztech Big Band | The Count Is In | Seabreeze | CDSB 2047(874256)
Ronnie Mathews Trio | So Sorry Please... | Nilva | NQ 3414 IMS
Russell Procope-Wild Bill Davis Quartet | Echoes Of Ellington Vol.1 | Timeless | CD TTD 555
Sarah Vaughan And Her Trio | Verve Jazz Masters 42:Sarah Vaughan-The Jazz Sides | Verve | 526817-2
Swingin' Easy | EmArCy | 514072-2
Seamus Blake Quintet | The Call | Criss Cross | Criss 1088
Sonny Rollins Quintet With Brass | Old Flames | Milestone | MCD 9215-2
Stan Getz And The Swedish All Stars | Stan Getz:The Complete 1946-1951 Quartet Sessions(Master Takes),Vol.2 | Blue Moon | BMCD 1014
Tal Farlow Quintet | The Legendary Tal Farlow | Concord | CJ 266
Terry Gibbs-Buddy DeFranco Quintet | Air Mail Special | Contemporary | CCD 14056-2
Tito Puente's Latin Ensemble And Orchestra | Un Poco Loco | Concord | CCD 4329
Wes Montgomery With Orchestra | Pretty Blue | Milestone | M 47030
Woody Herman Orchestra(The '51 Herd) | Live In New Orleans | Giants Of Jazz | GOJ 1022
André Previn Trio | Uptown | Telarc Digital | CD 83303

Prelude To A Kiss-
Billy Eckstine With Bobby Tucker And His Orchestra | No Cover No Minimum | Blue Note | 798583-2
Dick Wellstood | Dick Wellstood-Alone | Solo Art | SACD-73
Duke Ellington And His Orchestra | Duke Ellington:The 1952 Seatle Concert | Bluebird | 63 66531-2
Gene Krupa And His Orchestra | The King Of Jazz Big Band | Festival | Album 153

Prelude To A Kiss(alt.take)
Billie Holiday And Her Orchestra | Billie Holiday Story Vol.5:Music for Torching | Verve | MV 2595 IMS

Prelude To Club Vinyl
Chick Corea And His Orchestra | My Spanish Heart | Polydor | 543303-3

Prelude To El Bozo
Roberto Perera Group | Seduction | Inak | 30302

Prelude(Isle Of View)
Bill Evans Trio With The Claus Ogerman Orchestra | The Complete Bill Evans On Verve | Verve | 527953-2

Prelude(No.15 in D-Flat Major[Scriabin])
Miles Davis Group | Agharta | CBS | 467897-2

Prelude(part 1&2)
Eddie Lang | Jazz Guitar Virtuoso | Yazoo | YAZ 1059

Prelude(Tristan und Isolde)
Paul Smoker Trio | Alone | Sound Aspects | sas CD 018(32018)

Preludio
Astor Piazzolla Group | Onda Nueve | West Wind Latina | 2213 CD

Preludio Y Danca
Javier Paxarino Group With Glen Velez | Temurá | ACT | 9227-2

Preludio Y Danza
René Marino Rivero | Che Bandoneon | ALISO Records | AL 1020

Preludio Y Fuga In D-Major
Che Bandoneon | ALISO Records | AL 1020

Preludio Y Fuga In F-Major
Michael Gregory Jackson Group | Clarity | ESP Disk | ESP 3028-2

Premeditation Das L'Appartement
Archie Shepp Quartet | Passport To Paradise-Archie Shepp Play Sidney Bechet | West Wind | WW 0002

Premier Bal
Claude Luter Quartet | Saint Germain Dance | Vogue | 655013

Premonition
Paul McCandless Group | Premonition | Windham Hill | 34 10140-2

Preparation
Chick Corea | Piano Improvisations-Vol.2 | ECM | 1020(829190-2)

Preparation(1)
Piano Improvisations-Vol.2 | ECM | 1020(829190-2)

Preparation(2)
Willem Breuker Kollektief | Willem Breuker Kollektief | About Time | AT 1006

Prepare Your Shoes
George Duke Group | I Love The Blues | MPS | 817488-1

Pre-Rise: I'm On My Way
Count Basie Trio | For The First Time | Pablo | 2310712-2

Pres Returns
David Kikoski Trio | Presage | Freelance | FRL-CD 011

Presence Always Presence-
Jacob Young Quintet | Evening Falls | ECM | 1876(9811780)

Presence Of Descant
Michel Bisceglia Trio | About Stories | RCA | 2153080-2

Present Notion
Kenny Wheeler/Lee Konitz/Dave Holland/Bill Frisell | Angel Song | ECM | 1607(533098-2)

Present Past
Sebastian Whittaker And The Creators | One For Bu!! | Justice Records | JR 0203-2

Presentation Du Septet
Gerry Mulligan Quartet | Gerry Mulligan:Pleyel Concert Vol.1 | Vogue | 21409422

Presentation Of The Musicians
Michel Warlop Et Son Orchestre | Le Jazz En France Vol.4 | Pathe | 1727281

Presente De Natal
Jimmy Raney Quintet | Two Jims And Zoot | Mobile Fidelity | MFCD 833

Presently
Ted Brown Quartet | Preservation | Steeplechase | SCCD 31539

Preservation
Punch Miller's Bunch & George Lewis | Jazz At Preservation Hall, Vol.3 | Atlantic | SD 1410

President Hayes
Champion Jack Dupree Group | Chamion Jack Dupree | EPM Musique | FDC 5504

Pressure
Clarence Gatemouth Brown Band | The Blues Of Clarence 'Gatemouth Brown | Storyville | 4960563

Pressure Cooker
Clarence Gatemouth Brown Quartet | Cold Storage | Black & Blue | BLE 59.096 2

Presto
John Zorn Group | Cobra | Hat Art | CD 6040(2)
Astor Piazzolla With Orchestra Of St. Luke's | Concierto Para Bandoneon-Tres Tangos | Nonesuch | 7559-79174-2

Presto-
Eddie Daniels Quartet With The London Philharmonia Orchestra | Breakthrough | GRP | GRP 95332
Jacques Loussier Trio | Reflections Of Bach | Teldec | 2292-44431-2
Swingle Singers | Swingling Telemann | Philips | 586735-2
Slim Gaillard-Bam Brown | Opera In Vout | Verve | 2304554 IMS

Presto Con Stomp(With A Floy Floy)-
Swingle Singers | Swingling Telemann | Philips | 586735-2

Presto from Sonata No.4 For Flute And Continuo In E Minor(Benedetto Marcello)
Swingling Telemann | Philips | 586735-2

Presto from Trio Sonata In E Major
Aki Takase | Shima Shoka | Enja | 6062-2

Presto(aus der Fantasie In Be-Bop)
Clarence Penn Quintet | Play-Penn | Criss Cross | Criss 1201

Pretend You're In Love
Planet Blow | Alien Lunatic | Jazz Haus Musik | JHM 0071 CD

Pretended Alien
Memphis Slim | Memphis Slim Story | Arco | 3 ARC 108

Pretoria Three
Buddy Childers Big Band | Just Buddy's | Candid | CCD 79761

Pretty
Duke Ellington And His Orchestra | Live At The 1956 Stratford Festival | Music & Arts | CD 616

Pretty Baby
Jelly Roll Morton | The Library Of Congress Recordings | Affinity | CD AFS 1010-3

Pretty Ballad
Wes Montgomery With Orchestra | Pretty Blue | Milestone | M 47030

Pretty Blue
Terry Gibbs Dream Band | Terry Gibbs Dream Band Vol.5:The Big Cat | Contemporary | CCD 7657-2

Pretty Blue Eyes
Wes Montgomery With Strings | Fusion! | Original Jazz Classics | OJC 368(RLP 9472)

Pretty Blue(alt.take)
Blind John Davis | Blind John Davis | L+R Records | CDLR 72002

Pretty Eyed Baby
Roy Eldridge-Dizzy Gillespie With The Oscar Peterson Quartet | Roy And Diz | Verve | 521647-2

Pretty Eyes
Frank Wess Sextet | Commodore Classics-Frank Wess:Wess Of The Moon | Commodore | 6.25897 AG
Horace Silver Quintet | The Blue Note Years-The Best Of Horace Silver Vol.2 | Blue Note | 793206-2

Pretty Flowers Were Made For Blooming
Mind Games With Philip Catherine | Pretty Fonky | Edition Collage | EC 482-2

Pretty Fonky
Clark Terry-Bob Brookmeyer Quintet | Clark Terry-Bobby Brookmeyer Quintet | Mainstream | MD CDO 728

Pretty Girl
Charles McPherson Quartet | Come Play With Me | Arabesque Recordings | AJ 0117

Pretty Larceny
Eric Felten Group | Gratitude | Soul Note | 121296-2

Pretty Lil
Jelly Roll Morton And His Orchestra | Jazz Classics In Digital Stereo: Jelly Roll Morton | CDS Records Ltd. | RPCD 623(CD 604)

Pretty Little Gypsy
Dixie-O-Naires | Strike Up The Band | Timeless | CD TTD 576

Pretty Little Missy
The Tremble Kids All Stars | The Tremble Kids All Stars Play Chicago Jazz! | Nagel-Heyer | CD 043
Charlie Mariano Quintet | A Jazz Portrait Of Charlie Mariano | Fresh Sound Records | FSR-CD 0176

Pretty Memory
Nat Adderley Sextet | Wes Montgomery-The Complete Riverside Recordings | Riverside | 12 RCD 4408-2
John Scofield Quartet | Gracy Under Pressure | Blue Note | 798167-2

Pretty Scattered
Frank Nimsgern Group | Frank Nimsgern feat. Chaka Khan/Billy Cobham | Lipstick Records | LIP 890012

Pretty Stars Were Made To Shine
Johnny Coles Quartet | The Warm Sound | Koch Jazz | KOC 3-7804-2

Preview
Ella Fitzgerald With Sy Oliver And His Orchestra | Ella Fitzgerald 75th Birthday Celebration:The Original Decca Recordings | GRP | GRP 26192
Joachim Kühn Band | Sunshower | Atlantic | ATL 50472
Tim Berne/Bill Frisell Duo | Theoretically | Empire | EPC 72 K

Preview-No Answer
David Torn Quartet | Cloud About Mercury | ECM | 1322(831108-2)

Previous Man
Heinz Sauer-Bob Degen Duo | Plaza Lost And Found | L+R Records | CDLR 45044

Prez
Woody Herman And His Orchestra | Jantzen Beach Oregon 1954 | Status | DSTS 1020

Prezzo X(to Miles Davis)To M.
Mikhail Alperin's Moscow Art Trio | Folk Dreams | JA & RO | JARO 4187-2

Pri Doline
J.B.& His Hawks | Combination Blues | Charly | CRB 1042

Pride
Lil' Ed Williams And The Blues Imperials | Roughhousin' | Sonet | SNTF 966(941966)

Priestess
Jack DeJohnette Quartet | Oneness | ECM | 1637(537343-2)

Priestesses Of The Mist

TITELVERZEICHNIS

Jack DeJohnette Special Edition | Earth Walk | Blue Note | 796690-2

Prima Vista Sofa Pub
Maria Joao/Aki Takase/Niels-Henning Orsted-Pedersen | Alice | Enja | 6096-2

Primavera
Dave Liebman And The Lluis Vidal Trio | Dave Liebman And The Lluis Vidal Trio | Fresh Sound Records | FSNT 026 CD

Primavera 1986
Lluis Vidal | Lluis Vidal Piano Solo | Fresh Sound Records | FSNT 001 CD
Richard Galliano Septet | Piazzolla Forever | Dreyfus Jazz Line | FDM 36642-2

Primavera Porteno
Tango Orkestret | Tango Orkestret | Stunt Records | STUCD 19303

Primavera(II)
Piirpauke | Tuku Tuku | JA & RO | JARO 4158-2

Primavera(Kevät)
Dave Holland Quintet | Extended Play | ECM | 1864/65(038505-2)

Prime Directive
Joe Beck Quartet | The Journey | dmp Digital Music Productions | CD 481

Prime Ribs
Lennie Niehaus Quintet | Vol.1:The Quintets | Original Jazz Classics | OJC 319(C 3518)

Prime Time
Charlie Byrd Trio | Sugarloaf Suite | Concord | CCD 4114

Primitivo
Cannonball Adderley Sextet | The Japanese Concerts | Milestone | M 47029
Nils Landgren Funk Unit | Paint It Blue:A Tribute To Cannonball Adderley | ACT | 9243-2
Fun Horns | Fun Horns Live In South America-Natural Music | KlangRäume | 30060

Primordial Call
Karl Berger-Dave Holland-Ed Blackwell | Crystal Fire | Enja | 7029-2

Primpin
Duke Ellington And His Orchestra | 100 Years Duke | Laserlight | 24906

Primpin' At The Prom
The Rare Broadcast Recordings 1953 | Jazz Anthology | JA 5220

Primpin(Salif Keita)
Cleo Laine With The Johnny Dankworth Quintet | Cleo At Carnegie Hall-The 10th Anniversary Concert | DRG | DARC 2-2101 IMS

Primrose lane
Golden Gate Quartet With The Martial Solal Orchestra | Americans Swinging In Paris:Golden Gate Quartet | EMI Records | 539659-2

Primrose Lane
Bill Holman Band | Bill Holman Band | JVC | ???

Prince Albert
Jesper Thilo Quintet feat. Hank Jones | A Jazz Par 91 Project | Storyville | STCD 4178
Cecil Payne Quintet | Bird Gets The Worm | Muse | MR 5061

Prince Of Darkness
Miles Davis Quintet | Miles Davis Quintet 1965-1968 | CBS | C6K 67398
Tom Varner Group | Long Night Big Day | New World Records | 80410-2

Prince Of Peace
Tony Scott | Astral Meditation-Voyage Into A Black Hole | Line Records | LICD 9.21328

Prince Of The Night
Benny Moten's Kansas City Orchestra | The Complete Bennie Moten Vol.5/6 | RCA | PM 45688

Prince Vaillant
Billy Cobham Quartet | Flight Time | Inak | 8616

Princess
Marty Cook Conspiracy | Phases Of The Moon | Tutu Records | 888160-2*
Ralph Peterson Trio | Triangular | Blue Note | 792750-2
The Jimmy Giuffre 3 | 7 Pieces | Verve | 2304438 IMS
Sonny Sharrock | Sonny Sharrock Guitar | Enemy | EMCD 102(03502)

Princess Of Third Street
Sonny Sharrock Band | Live In New York | Enemy | EMCD 108(03508)

Princess Song
The Sextet | Jazz Workshop Presents The Sextet | somethin'else | 300252(TOCJ 5586)

Printemps(Vivaldi)
Masqualero | Aero | ECM | 1367

Printer
Clifford Jordan Quintet | Mosaic | Milestone | MCD 47092-2

Prints
Bobby Hutcherson-Harold Land Quintet | San Francisco | Blue Note | 828268-2

Printupian Prance
Kick | Wolfhound's Kick | BELL Records | BLR 84041

Prinz
Hans Lüdemann Rism | Aph-o-Rism's | Jazz Haus Musik | JHM 0049 CD
Loope | Prinz Henry | ITM Records | ITM 1447

Prioridad A La Emoción
George Barnes Octet | The Uncollected: George Barnes | Hindsight | HSR 106

Priquitin Pin Pon
Ray Walker-John Pisano Trio | Affinity | Jardis Records | JRCD 20032

Priscilla's Blues
Jazz Guitar Highlights 1 | Jardis Records | JRCD 20141
Arild Andersen Trio | The Triangle | ECM | 1752(0381212)

Prism
Bobby Hutcherson Sextet | Farewell Keystone | Evidence | TR 124
Chick Corea Electric Band | Light Years | GRP | GRP 95462
Dan Papaila Trio | Positively! | Timeless | CD SJP 403
Keith Jarrett Trio | Changes | ECM | 1276(817436-2)
Mary Lou Williams Duo | My Mama Pinned A Rose On Me | Pablo | 2310819
Szakcsi Trio | Straight Ahead | GRP | GRP 97582

Prisma-
Paul Horn Group | Jupiter 8 | Golden Flute Records | GFR 2004

Prison Blues
Louisiana Red | Louisiana Red | Blues Classics(L+R) | CDLR 82002

Prison Changes
Lightnin' Hopkins And Friends | Smokes Like Lighning | Original Blues Classics | OBCCD 551(BV 1070)

Prisoner Of Love
Art Tatum | The Art Tatum Solo Masterpieces | Pablo | 2625703
Greg Tardy Band | Serendipity | Impulse(MCA) | 951258-2
Helen Humes With The Teddy Wilson Trio | Aurex Jazz Festival '80:Live Special | Eastworld | EWJ 80253
Lester Young Quartet | Pres And Teddy And Oscar | Verve | 2-2502 IMS
Simon Schott | Bar Piano: Simon Schott Plays Your Favorite Evergreens Vol.2 | Organic Music | ORGM 9735

Prisoner Of Love-
Sarah Jane Cion Quartet | Summer Night | Naxos Jazz | 86071-2

Prisoner's Song
Michael Mantler Group With The Danish Concert Radio Orchestra | Many Have No Speech | Watt | 19(835580-2)

Prisonniers
Art Blakey And The Jazz Messengers | For Minors Only | Bethlehem | BET 6001-2(BCP 6023)

Private Eye
Terje Rypdal Group | If Mountains Could Sing | ECM | 1554(523987-2)
John Hart Quartet | Bridges | Concord | CCD 4746

Private Life
Pink Inc. | A.Deutsch's Pink Inc. | DIW | DIW 852 CD

Procession
Lyle Mays | Improvisations For Expanded Piano | Warner | 9362-47284-2
Reiner Winterschladen-Manos Tsangaris | King Kong | Jazz Haus Musik | JHM 0056 CD
Renaud Garcia-Fons | Légendes | Enja | ENJ-9314 2
Tom Harrell Sextet | Upswing | Chesky | JD 103

Procession Of The Bulls
Stan Kenton And His Orchestra | Live At Brigham Young University | Creative World | STD 1039

Processional
Don Menza And The Joe Haider Trio | Bilein | JHM Records | JHM 3608
Keith Jarrett Quartet | Nude Ants | ECM | 1171/72(829119-2)
Nude Ants | ECM | 1171/72(829119-2)
Roy Haynes Duo | Thank You Thank You | Galaxy | GXY 5103

Proclamation
Gil Evans Orchestra | The Individualism Of Gil Evans | Verve | 833804-2 PMS
Harry James And His Orchestra | The Radio Years: Harry James And His Orchestra 1948-49 | Hindsight | HSR 135
Roy Hargrove Sextet | Diamond In The Rough | Novus | PD 90471

Prodefunctus
The New York Composers Orchestra | Music By Marty Ehrlich, Robin Holcomb, Wayne Horvitz, Doug Wieselman | New World Records | 80397-2

Prof. Genessier
Cuarteto Las D'Aida Y Su Grupo | Soy La Mulata | L+R Records | CDLR 45059

Professor Boogie
Babs Gonzales And His Orchestra | Sonny Rollins | Definitive Records | DRCD 11243

Professor Jazz
The Buck Clayton Legacy | Encore Live | Nagel-Heyer | CD 018
Clark Terry & Collage | Professor Jive-A Jazz Symphony by Charles Schwartz | Inner City | IC 1015 IMS

Professor Longhair
Nils Landgren Funk Unit With Guests | 5000 Miles | ACT | 9271-2
Professor Longhair And His New Orleans Boys | New Orleans Piano | Sequel Records | RSA CD 808

Professor Mackel's Famous Ride-
Marilyn Crispell | Contrasts: Live At Yoshi's | Music & Arts | CD 930

Profile Man
New Orleans Collective | New Orleans Collective | Paddle Wheel | KICJ 165

Profile Of Jackie
Charles Mingus Jazz Workshop | The Very Best Of Charles Mingus | Rhino | 8122-79988-2
Pithecanthropus Erectus | Atlantic | 7567-81456-2
Munich Saxophon Family | Survival Song | JHM Records | JHM 3613
Ernest Ranglin Group | Modern Answers To Old Problems | Telarc Digital | CD 83526

Profundus Tremens
Bernhard Arndt | Insight Insight | FMP | OWN-90005

Progress Is The Root Of All Evil
Art Farmer Quintet | Blame It On My Youth | Contemporary | CCD 14042-2

Progression
Alex Theus Trio | Boum Boum Miaouuuu | Plainisphare | PL 1267-16

Prohibido
Barrelhouse Jazzband | 25 Jahre Barrelhouse Jazzband Frankfurt | Intercord | 155030

Projectile
Jimmy Heath Quintet | On The Trail | Original Jazz Classics | OJCCD 1854-2

Project-S
Willem Breuker Kollektief | In Holland | BVHAAST | 041/42 (807118)

Prokyon
Joe McPhee Trio | Sweet Freedom-Now What? | Hat Art | CD 6162

Prolix
A Band Of Friends | Teatime Vol.1 | Poise | Poise 01

Prolog
Teatime Vol.2 | Poise | Poise 06/2
Teatime Vol.2 | Poise | Poise 06/2
Christian Griese Group | Affinities:My Berlin Phone Book | BIT | 11216
Stephan Noel Lang Trio | Echoes | Nagel-Heyer | CD 2033
Thomas Heberer | The Heroic Millepede | ITM Records | ITM 1443

Prologo Comienzo
Orchestre National De Jazz | Charmediterranéen | ECM | 1828(018493-2)

Prologo:L'Orfeo
Dave Grusin Orchestra | David Grusin Presents West Side Story | N2K | 43062

Prologue
Julian Priester Group | Love Love | ECM | 1044
Norma Winstone Trio | Somewhere Called Home | ECM | 1337
Stan Kenton And His Orchestra | New Concepts | Capitol | 792865-2
Vienna Art Orchestra | Vienna Art Orchestra Plays For Jean Cocteau | Amadeo | 529290-2

Prologue-
Bill Evans | Bill Evans At Town Hall | Verve | 831271-2
Cal Tjader With The Clare Fischer Orchestra | Cal Tjader Plays Harold Arlen & West Side Story | Fantasy | FCD 24775-2
James Blood Ulmer With The Quartet Indigo | Harmolodic Guitar With Strings | DIW | DIW 878 CD

Prologue From Outside
Duke Ellington And His Famous Orchestra | The Complete Duke Ellington-Vol. 10 | CBS | CBS 88220

Promenade
Blue Mitchell Sextet | Blue Mitchell Big 6 | Original Jazz Classics | OJCCD 615-2(RLP 12-273)
Denny Zeitlin Quartet | Tidal Wave | Palo Alto | PA 8044
Joe Douglas Trio | Visage | Spotlite | SPJ 514

Promenade Aux Champs-Elysees
Bob Wilber's Bechet Legacy | The Hamburg Concert-Tribute To A Legend | Nagel-Heyer | CD 028
Sidney Bechet With Claude Luter And His Orchestra | Sidney Bechet | Vogue | 000001 GK

Promenade Avec Christine
Alix Combelle Et Son Orchestre | Buck Clayton:Buck Special | Vogue | 2111513-2

Promenade De Memoire
HUM | HUM(Humair-Urtreger-Michelot) | Sketch | SKE 333006

Promenade In Greed
John Lewis And The New Jazz Quartet | Slavic Smiles | Baystate | BVCJ 2005(889371)

Promenade: Cote Bamako(I)
Art Ensemble Of Chicago | Urban Bushmen | ECM | 1211/12

Promenade: Cote Bamako(II)
Salsaya Big Band | Live | Timeless | CD SJP 209

Promise
Ralph Simon Sextet | AS | Postcards | POST 1004

Promise The Sun
Herbie Hancock Orchestra | Herbie Hancock:The Complete Blue Note Sixties Sessions | Blue Note | 495569-2
Christine Tobin Band | Aililiu | Babel | BDV 9501

Promised Land-
Laurindo Almeida/Carlos Barbosa-Lima/Charlie Byrd Quintet | Music Of The Brazilian Masters | Concord | CCD 4389

Promises Kept
Joe Venuti And His New Yorkers | The Big Bands Of Joe Venuti Vol.2 (1930-1933) | JSP Records | 1112

Promising Horizons
Dick de Graaf Quartet | Hot Hazy And Humid | Limetree | MLP 0017

Promontory
Four For Jazz & Benny Bailey | The Best Of Four For Jazz & Benny Bailey | JHM Records | JHM 3615

Prompt
Pilz-Niebergall-Schmitt Trio | Celeste | Trion | 3901

Proof Readers
Arnold Dreyblatt & The Orchestra Of Excited Strings | Propellers In Love | Hat Art | CD 6011

Prophet Jennings
John Zorn Naked City | Naked City-Grand Guignol | Avant | AVAN 002

Propulsion
Katie Kern Group | Still Young | Jazzpoint | JP 1070 CD

Prosecutor
Misery Loves Company | Magia Ke Miseria | Enja | 9117-2

Prostetnic Vogon Jeltz
Bing Crosby And Rosemarie Clooney With The Billy May Orchestra | Fancy Meeting You Here | RCA | 2663859-2

Protection
George Adams-Don Pullen Quartet | Life Line | Timeless | CD SJP 154

Protee
Max Roach Group | Live In Europe 1964-Freedom Now Suite | Magnetic Records | MRCD 110

Protest-
The Jeff Lorber Fusion | Soft Space | Inner City | IC 1056 IMS

Proto-Cosmos
Tony Williams Lifetime | Tony Williams Lifetime-The Collection | CBS | 468924-2

Protoplasm
Eddy Palermo Trio | The Way I See | EdiPan | NPG 806

Protzeduren
Wanda Rouzan With Band | It's What I Do | Huckle-Buck Records | WR 22590

Proud Mary
Gijs Hendriks Quartet | Print Collection | yvp music | 3012

Proverbes(part 1-3)
Art Ensemble Of Chicago | 1969-1970 People In Sorrow/Les Stances A Sophie(Soundtrack) | Jazztime(EMI) | 795818-2

Proverbi(Uno)-
Contraband | Live At The Bimhuis | BVHAAST | CD 8906

Providence
Haze Greenfield Quaret | Providence | Owl Records | 069 CD
Wes Martin Group | 3 Pound Universe | CMP Records | CMP CD 1009

Psalm
Chick Corea Quartet | Live In Montreux | Stretch Records | SCD 9009-2
David Darling | Cello | ECM | 1464(511982-2)
Jan Garbarek Group | Twelve Moons | ECM | 1500(519500-2)
John Coltrane Quartet | The Best Of John Coltrane-His Greatest Years | MCA | AS 9200-2
A Love Supreme | Ingo | 11
Roy Haynes Quartet | True Or False | Freelance | FRL-CD 007
Wayne Horvitz-Butch Morris-William Parker Trio | Some Order Long Understood | Black Saint | BSR 0059

Psalm-
John Coltrane Quartet | A Love Supreme | Impulse(MCA) | 589945-2
John Coltrane:The Classic Quartet-Complete Impulse Studio Recordings | Impulse(MCA) | 951280-2
Pete Malinverni Trio | This Time | Reservoir | RSR CD 147

Psalm 118
Willem Breuker Kollektief With Strings And Choir | Psalm 122 | BVHAAST | CD 9803

Psalm 131
Matthias Petzold Group With Choir | Psalmen und Lobgesänge für Chor und Jazz-Enseble | Indigo-Records | 1002 CD

Psalm 139
Irene Schweizer Trio | Jazz In Switzerland 1930-1975 | Elite Special | 9544002/1-4

Psalm 24
Wynton Marsalis Trio | Soul Gestures In Southern Blue Vol.2: Uptown Ruler | CBS | 468660-2

Psalm 33
Matthias Petzold Group With Choir | Psalmen und Lobgesänge für Chor und Jazz-Enseble | Indigo-Records | 1002 CD

Psalm 42
Nat Adderley Group | Soul Of The Bible | Capitol | 358257-2

Psalm 54
Munich Saxophon Family | Family Life | Bassic-Sound | CD 006

Psalm No.1
Misha Alperin Quintet | North Story | ECM | 1596

Psalm No.2
Natascha Majevskaja | Orgel Ist Mehr!...In Bamberg,Vol.1 | Orgel ist mehr! | OIM/BA/1999-1 CD

Psalm Nr.42,Arie(Mendelssohn-Bartholdy)
Michel Godard Ensemble | Castel Del Monte II | Enja | ENJ-9431 2

Psalmodia Clarinet
Castel Del Monte II | Enja | ENJ-9431 2

Psalmodia Serpent
John Stevens Orchestra | Folkus-The Life Of Riley | Affinity | AFF 130

Psalms
Prince Lasha-Sonny Simmons Quintet | Firebirds | Original Jazz Classics | OJCCD 1822-2(C 7617)

Psi
Jürgen Seefelder-Thomas Stabenow | Visitation | Bassic-Sound | CD 008

PSP Nr.2
Bireli Lagrene Group | Bireli Lagrene & Special Guests | Inak | 8610

PSS
Lee Morgan Sextet | The Sixth Sense | Blue Note | 522467-2

Psychedelic
Lonnie Smith Quintet | Deep Blue-The United States Of Mind | Blue Note | 521152-2

Psychedelic Pi
Bitkicks | Kickbit Information | ATM Records | ATM 3823-AH

Psychedelic Review
Eddie Jefferson With The James Moody Quintet | Body And Soul | Original Jazz Classics | OJCCD 396-2(P 7619)

Psychedelic Sally
Horace Silver Quintet | Horace Silver | Blue Note | 84510
Lionel Hampton All Stars | Jazz In Paris:Lionel Hampton-Ring Dem Bells | EmArCy | 159825-2 PMS
Lionel Hampton And His Orchestra | Lionel Hampton | America | AM 6143

Psyche's Springs
Shankar Trio | Vision | ECM | 1261(811969-2)

Psychic Elephant
Sergey Kuryokhin | Popular Zoological Elements | LEO | LR 148

Psycho-Loco
Jazznost-The Soviet/American Jazz Quartet | Joint Venture | Timeless | CD SJP 310

Psychotria Nervosa(Wild Coffee)
Maurizio Picchio Quartet | Biri San | SPLASC(H) Records | H 172

Psylomobil
Alice Coltrane Quintet | Ptah The El Daoud | Impulse(MCA) | 951201-2

Ptah, The El Daoud
Michel Petrucciani Group | Playground | Blue Note | 795480-2

P'tit Louis
Al Cohn Quintet | Overtones | Concord | CJ 194

P-Town
Dave Frishberg Quintet | You're A Lucky Guy | Concord | CJ 74

Puasing Daffriek
John Scofield Quartet | East Meets West | Black-Hawk | BKH 533 CD

Public Melody Number One
Louis Armstrong And His Orchestra | Louis Armstrong:Swing That Music | Laserlight | 36056
Louis Armstrong With Luis Russell And His Orchestra | Louis Armstrong Vol.4-Swing That Music | MCA | 1312

Puccini
Jan Akkerman Group | Puccini's Cafe | Inak | 9027

Pucho's Descarga II
Gianluigi Trovesi Nonet | Round About A Midsummer's Dream | Enja | ENJ-9384 2

Puck
Illinois Jacquet And His Orchestra | Illinois Jacquet | CBS | EK 64654

Pud Wud
Ken McIntyre Trio | Chasing The Sun | Steeplechase | SCCD 31114

Puer Apuliae
Tocando La Tierra | Tocando La Tierra | Jazz Haus Musik | JHM 55 CD

Pula
Nana Simopoulos Group | Wings And Air | Enja | 5031-2

Pule

Abdullah Ibrahim With The NDR Big Band | Ekapa Lodumo | TipToe | TIP-888840 2
Abdullah Ibrahim Sextet | Mindif | Enja | ENJ-5073 2

Pule(Rain)
Tangata Rea | Tango Alla Baila | Winter&Winter | 910025-2

Pulentosa Baby
Michel Godard-Dave Bargeron Quartet | Tuba Tuba | Enja | 9133-2

Pull My Coat
Guitar Shorty | Alone In His Field | Trix Records | TRIX 3306

Pullin' Strings
Joe Maneri Quartet | In Full Cry | ECM | 1617(537048-2)

Pulling The Boat In
Ruby Braff And His Orchestra | The Mighty Braff | Affinity | AFF 757

Pulque
European Jazz Ensemble | 20th Anniversary Tour | Konnex Records | KCD 5078
European Trumpet Summit | European Trumpet Summit | Konnex Records | KCD 5064
Mariano-Humair-Haurand | Frontier Traffic | Konnex Records | KCD 5110
Astor Piazzolla Y Su Tentet | Pulsacion | West Wind Latina | 2220 CD

Pulse
Joey Baron Trio | RAIsedpleasuredot | New World Records | 80449-2

Pulse Of Time
Ray Anderson Trio | You Be | Minor Music | 8007

Pump & Circumstance
Jack McDuff Quintet | Color Me Blue | Concord | CCD 4516

Pumpa
Red Rodney Sextet | Serge Chaloff Memorial | Cool & Blue | C&B-CD 102

Pumpkinet(h)ics
Bob Florence Big Band | Westlake | Discovery | DS 832 IMS

Punic Dance
Chris Jarrett Trio | Chris Jarrett Trio Plays New World Music | Edition Musikat | EDM 067
Sonny Clay | Sonny Clay 1922-1960 | Harlequin | HQ 2007 IMS

Punishment Blues
Richie Cole Quintet | Alive! | Muse | MR 5270

Punjab
Jim Snidero Sextet | The Music Of Joe Henderson | Double Time Records | DTRCD-152
Ralph Moore Quintet | Images | Landmark | LCD 1520-2

Punk China Doll
Eric Watson Trio | Punk Circus | Freelance | FRL-CD 023

Punk Jazz
David Earle Johnson With Jan Hammer | Hip Address | CMP Records | CMP 14

Punkoholic
Jukka Tolonen Group | A Passenger To Paramaribo | Sonet | 147120

Punta Del Soul
Abraham Burton-Eric McPherson Quartet | Cause And Effect | Enja | ENJ-9377 2

Punto
Dave Liebman Group | The Blessing Of The Old Long Sound | Nueva Records | IN 810

Punto Neutro
New Generation Cuban All Stars | The New Generation Cuban All Stars Vol.1:Antes De Nuestro Tiempo | Messidor | 15941

Pupa
Rabih Abou-Khalil Group | Yara | Enja | ENJ-9360 2

Puppet Master
Gianluigi Trovesi Nonet | Round About A Midsummer's Dream | Enja | ENJ-9384 2

Puppet Theatre
Gianluigi Trovesi Trio | Les Boites A Musique | SPLASC(H) Records | CD H 152-2

Puppet's Dance
Ana Caram Group | Blue Bossa | Chesky | JD 219

Pure & Simple
Gil Goldstein Trio | Pure As Rain | Chiaroscuro | CR 201

Pure Imagination
John Swana Quintet | Tug Of War | Criss Cross | Criss 1163
Sarah Jane Cion Trio | Summer Night | Naxos Jazz | 86071-2

Pure Mode
Szakcsi | Szakcsi | GRP | GRP 95562

Pure Village(Kangaba)
Music Revelation Ensemble | In The Name Of... | DIW | DIW 885 CD

Purple
Ken Schaphorst Big Band | Purple | Naxos Jazz | 86030-2

Purple City
Yusef Lateef Quartet | Blues For The Orient | Prestige | P 24035

Purple Flower
Duke Ellington And His Orchestra | Afro-Bossa | Reprise | 9362-47876-2

Purple Gazelle
Ken Peplowski Quartet | A Good Reed | Concord | CCD 4767
Warren Vaché With The Howard Alden Trio | The Howard Alden Trio Plus Special Guests | Concord | CCD 4378

Purple Haze
Art Ensemble Of Chicago | Vol.1:Ancient To The Future | DIW | DIW 8014
NDR Big Band feat. Inga Rumpf | The Spirit Of Jimi Hendrix | Extra Records & Tapes | 11542
Robert Dick Group With The Soldier String Quartet | Third Stone From The Sun | New World Records | 80435-2

Purple Haze-
Jaco Pastorius Trio | Heavy'n Jazz | Jazzpoint | JP 1036 CD
Pinguin Moschner-Joe Sachse | If 69 Was 96/The Music Of Jimi Hendrix | Aho-Recording | CD 1016

Purple Hyazinth
Roscoe Mitchell | Songs In The Wind | Victo | CD 011

Purple Light
Jones Hellborg | The Silent Life | Demon Records | DEM 026

Purple Mood
Scott Cossu Quintet | Wind Dance | Windham Hill | TA-C- 1016

Purple On Gold
The Al Di Meola Project | Kiss My Axe | Inak | 700782

Purple Shades
Cannonball Adderley Group | Julian 'Cannonball' Adderley | EmArCy | 830381-2
Gigi Gryce-Clifford Brown Octet | Lucky Thompson/Gigi Gryce:Street Scenes | Vogue | 2115467-2

Purple Skies
Charlie Singleton And His Band | Jazz In Paris:Peanuts Holland-Buck Clayton-Charlie Singleton | EmArCy | 013032-2

PurpleCoolCarSleep
Batida | Batida | Timeless | CD SJP 200

Pursuance
John Coltrane Quartet | A Love Supreme | Ingo | 11
A Love Supreme | Impulse(MCA) | 589945-2

Pursuance-
John Coltrane:The Classic Quartet-Complete Impulse Studio Recordings | Impulse(MCA) | 951280-2
Dave Stryker Quintet | Passage | Steeplechase | SCCD 31330

Push-Ka-Pee She Pie(The Saga Of Saga Boy)
Etta James With Orchestra | Peaches | Chess | 427014

Pussy Cat Dues
Charles Mingus Orchestra | Nostalgia In Times Square/The Immortal 1959 Sessions | CBS | 88337
Kevin Mahogany With The WDR Big Band And Guests | Pussy Cat Dues:The Music Of Charles Mingus | Enja | ENJ-9316 2
Mingus Big Band | Blues & Politics | Dreyfus Jazz Line | FDM 36603-2

Pussy Willow
Duke Ellington And His Orchestra | Duke Ellington's Masterpieces Vol.1: 1938-1940 | Black & Blue | BLE 59.233 2
Tommy Dorsey And His Orchestra | The Post-War Era | Bluebird | 63 66156-2

Puszczykowo
Attila Zoller Trio | The K & K In New York | L+R Records | LR 40009

Put A Little Love In Your Heart
Jan Harrington Sextet | Jan Harrington's Christmas In New Orleans | Nagel-Heyer | NHR SP 4
Mahalia Jackson With Orchestra | In Memoriam Mahalia Jackson | CBS | 66501

Put All In There
Joe Venuti's Blue Four | Jazz Classics In Digital Stereo: Joe Venuti/Eddie Lang | CDS Records Ltd. | RPCD 626(CD 644)

Put Another Nickel In Music! Music! Muisc! - (Put Another Nickel In) Music! Music! Muisc!
Black Eagle Jazz Band | Black Eagle Jazz Band | Stomp Off Records | CD 1224

Put 'Em In A Box
Glen Moore | Dragonetti's Dream | VeraBra Records | CDVBR 2154-2

Put In A Qaurter
McKinney's Cotton Pickers | The Complete McKinney's Cotton Pickers Vol.1/2(1928-1929) | RCA | 2135550-2

Put It Right Here
Louie Bellson Big Band | The London Gig | Pablo | 2310880

Put Me In Coach, 'Cause I'm The Right Man For That Job
Charles Mingus Group | Mingus Dynasty | CBS | CK 65513

Put Me In That Dungeon
Charles Mingus Orchestra | Charles Mingus:The Complete 1959 Columbia Recordings | CBS | C3K 65145
André Previn | André Previn Plays Songs by Jerome Kern | Original Jazz Classics | OJCCD 1787-2(S 7567)

Put On A Happy Face
Jack McDuff Group | The Heatin' System | Concord | CCD 4644
Jay Hoggard Quartet | Overview | Muse | MCD 5383
Oscar Peterson Trio | Oscar Peterson-The London House Sessions | Verve | 531766-2

Put On Your Old Grey Bonnet
Coleman Hawkins Quartet | Today And Now | MCA | AS 34

Put That Down In Writing
Jan Savitt And His Top Hatters | The Uncollected:Jan Svitt | Hindsight | HSR 213

Put Your Dreams Away(For Another Day)
Golden Gate Quartet | Best Of Golden Gate Quartet | Sonia | CD 77285

Put Your Mind On Vacation
Ted Des Plantes' Washboard Wizards | Midnight Stomp | Stomp Off Records | CD 1231

Put-tin
Claude Thornhill And His Orchestra | The Real Birth Of the Cool | The Jazz Factory | JFCD 22803

Puttin' On The Ritz
Bill Carrothers-Bill Stewart | Bill Carrothers Duets With Bill Stewart | Dreyfus Jazz Line | FDM 37002-2
Ella Fitzgerald With Paul Weston And His Orchestra | The Complete Ella Fitzgerald Song Books of Harold Arlen, Irving Berlin, Duke Ellington, George & Ira Gershwin, Jerome Kern, Johnny Mercer, Cole Porter And Rogers & Hart | Verve | 519832-2
Eric Reed Quartet | Manhattan Melodies | Verve | 050294-2
Vinny Golia Quintet | Out For Blood | Nine Winds Records | NW 0127

Putting All My Eggs In One Basket
Phillip Johnston's Big Trouble | The Unknown | Avant | AVAN 037

Puzzle
Passport | Handmade | Atlantic | 2292-42172-2
Tim Sund Trio | Trialogue | Nabel Records:Jazz Network | CD 4692

Puzzle 1499
System Tandem | System Tandem | Japo | 60008 IMS

Pygmi Up!
Lotz Of Music | Puasong Daffriek | Laika Records | LK 94-054

Pygmies In The Dark
Buster Williams Sextet | Heartbeat | Muse | MR 5171

Pygmy Lullaby
Submedia | Submedia | Nine Winds Records | NWCD 0137

Pyjama-
Lito Voyatzoglou Quintet | Tili-Tili-Tili | Praxis | GM 1003

Pyramid
Duke Ellington And His Orchestra | The Great Paris Concert | Atlantic | 7567-81303-2
Glen Velez | Internal Combustion | CMP Records | CMP CD 23
John Graas Octet | Jimmy Giuffre:The Complete 1947-1953 Small Group Sessions Vol.3 | Blue Moon | BMCD 1048
Modern Jazz Quartet | European Concert | Atlantic | SD 2-603

Pyramides
Baikida Carroll Quintet | Shadows And Reflections | Soul Note | SN 1023

Q
Balance | Elements | double moon | DMCHR 71033
Bobo Stenson Trio | Reflections | ECM | 1516(523160-2)
Unternehmen Kobra | Central Europe Suite | G.N.U. Records | CD A 94.007

Q&A
Terje Rypdal With The Borealis Ensemble | Q.E.D. | ECM | 1474

Q.E.D.(Quod erat demonstrandum)
The New York Saxophone Quartet | The New York Saxophone Quartet | Stash Records | ST 210 IMS

Q1
Müller-Svoboda-Dähn-Kniel | 9Q | Edition Musikat | EDM 064

Q2
9Q | Edition Musikat | EDM 064

Q3
9Q | Edition Musikat | EDM 064

Q4
9Q | Edition Musikat | EDM 064

Q5
9Q | Edition Musikat | EDM 064

Q6
9Q | Edition Musikat | EDM 064

Q7
9Q | Edition Musikat | EDM 064

Q8
9Q | Edition Musikat | EDM 064

Q9
Winard Harper Group | Trap Dancer | Savant Records | SCD 2013

Qawarma-
Jan Garbarek Trio | Madar | ECM | 1515(519075-2)

Qaws
George Gruntz Concert Jazz Band | Blues 'N Dues Et Cetera | Enja | ENJ-6072 2

Q-Base
Marion Brown Trio | Porto Novo | Black Lion | BLCD 760200

Q's Dues Blues
Sebastian Whittaker And The Creators | One For Bu!! | Justice Records | JR 0203-2

Q-Tips
Titi Winterstein Quintet | Saitenstra en | Intercord | 160117

Quadrant 4
Billy Cobham Group | The Best Of Billy Cobham | Atlantic | 7567-81558-2
Billy Cobham Quartet | Atlantic Jazz: Fusion | Atlantic | 7567-81711-2
John Surman Quartet | Adventure Playground | ECM | 1463(511981-2)

Quadraphonic Question
Michael Marcus And The Jaki Byard Trio | Involution | Justin Time | JUST 116-2

Quadrille
Toshiko Akiyoshi | Maybeck Recital Hall Series Volume Thirty-Six | Concord | CCD 4635

Quae Moerebat
Art Blakey And The Jazz Messengers | Des Femmes Disparaissent/Les Tricheurs(Original Soundtracks) | Fontana | 834752-2 PMS

Qualify Your Funk
John Abercrombie-Andy LaVerne | Where We Were | Double Time Records | DTRCD-110

Qualude
Italian Instabile Orchestra | Skies Of Europe | ECM | 1543

Quand Duchamp Joue Du Marteau-
Eddie Barclay Et Son Grand Orchestre | Et Voila! | Fresh Sound Records | FSR 515(Barclay 82138)

Quand Les Chlamydes Sont Fatiguées
Claude Bernhard-Raymond Bo | Pot-Pouri Pour Parce Que | Hat Art | G

Quand Refleuriront Las Lilas Blancs?
Alex Theus Trio | Boum Boum Miaouuuu | Plainisphare | PL 1267-16

Quando Corpus
Pino Minafra Sud Ensemble | Sudori | Victo | CD 034

Quando Un Giorno-
Michael Riessler Group | Heloise | Wergo | WER 8008-2

Quanta Qualia
Curtis Fuller Quintet | Curtis Fuller Vol.3 | Blue Note | 300219(1583)

Quark
Salsaya Big Band | Live | Timeless | CD SJP 209

Quartenwaltzer
NDR-Workshop | Doldinger Jubilee | Atlantic | ATL 60073

Quarters And Dimes
Benny Bailey With On The Corner And The Philharmonic Orchestra,Würzburg | On The Corner feat. Benny Bailye | Mons Records | MR 874807

Quartet
Steve Nelson-Bobby Watson Quintet | Live Session Two | Red Records | 123235-2
Jim Hall Jazzpar Quartet +4 | Jazzpar 98 | Storyville | STCD 4230

Quartet + 4
Habarigani | Habarigani Two | Hat Art | CD 6064

Quartet Ghost[incl. After The Rain](to John Coltrane)
Marilyn Crispell Quartet | Quartet Improvisations-Paris 1986 | LEO | LR 144

Quartetto 1
Takabanda | La Leggenda Del Pescatore | Jazz 4 Ever Records:Jazz Network | J4E 4752

Quartetto 2
Egberto Gismonti | Danca Das Cabecas | ECM | 1089

Quarto Mundo(No.1)
Danca Das Cabecas | ECM | 1089

Quarto Mundo(No.2)
Coliseum Jazz Trio | Coliseum Jazz Trio | EdiPan | NGP 810

Quasar
Ed Schuller Quartet feat. Dewey Redman | Mu-Point | Tutu Records | 888154-2*
Globe Unity Orchestra | Intergalactic Blow | Japo | 60039(811874-1)

Quasi
Thomas Schiedel | All Alone | AH Records | AH 404001-13

Quasi Raga
Roy Eldridge-Dizzy Gillespie With The Oscar Peterson Quartet | Jazz Maturity... Where It's Coming From | Original Jazz Classics | OJCCD 807-2(2310816)

Quasi-Boogaloo
Ronald Muldrow Trio | Gnowing You | L+R Records | CDLR 45047

Quasimodo
Mark Alban Lotz/Tjitze Anne Vogel | Mostly Harmless... | Edition Collage | EC 470-2
Peter Leitch | Red Zone | Reservoir | RSR CD 103(882905)
Sphere | Bird Songs | Verve | 837032-2
Tom Varner Quintet | Jazz French Horn | New Note Records | NN 1004

Quatessence
Trevor Richards New Orleans Trio | The Trevor Richards New Orleans Trio | Stomp Off Records | CD 1222

Quatorze
Stephan Oliva Trio | Novembre | Owl Time Line | 3819092

Quatretonic
Louis Sclavis Septet | Chamber Music | IDA Record | 022 CD

Que Alegria
Pierre Favre Singing Drums | Souffles | Intakt Records | CD 049

Que Dios Te Lo Deba
Don Cherry/Nana Vasconcelos/Collin Walcott | Codona 2 | ECM | 1177(833332-2)

Que Faser
Mongo Santamaria And His Band | Sabroso | Original Jazz Classics | OJCCD 281-2

Que Maravilloso
Tethered Moon | Chansons D'Edith Piaf | Winter&Winter | 910048-2

Que Nadie Sepa Mi Sufrir
Caterina Zapponi With The Monty Alexander Quartet | Universal Lovesongs | Inak | 9062

Que Pasa
Horace Silver Quintet | Horace Silver Retrospective | Blue Note | 495576-2
Joe Henderson-The Blue Note Years | Blue Note | 789287-2
Marilyn Lerner Group | Birds Are Returning | Jazz Focus | JFCD 022
Mel Lewis And The Jazz Orchestra | Naturally! | Telarc Digital | CD 83301

Que Reste-T-Il De Nos Amours
Guy Lafitte Quartet | Joue Charles Trénet | Black & Blue | BLE 59.190 2
Stephane Grappelli Quartet | Stephane Grappelli:I Got Rhythm | Black Lion | BLCD 7613-2

Que Reste-T-Il De Nos Yorks?
Tito Puente And His Latin Ensemble | Sensacion | Concord | CCD 4301

Que Sera Sera
Holly Cole And Her Quartet | It Happened One Night | Metro Blue | 852699-0
Willis Jackson Sextet | Nuther'n Like Thuther'n | Prestige | PRCD 24265-2

Que Sera,Sweetie
Tania Maria Sextet | Taurus | Concord | CCD 4175

Queca
José Luis Gutiérrez Trio | Núcleo | Fresh Sound Records | FSNT 039 CD

Quechua
Jo Ambros Group | Wanderlust | dml-records | CD 016

Qued
Gerardo Nunez Group | Flamencos En Nueva York | VeraBra Records | CDVBR 2028-2

Quee Baby
Reiner Winterschladen-Manos Tsangaris | King Kong | Jazz Haus Musik | JHM 0056 CD

Queeker
Howard Roberts Quartet | Turning To Spring | Discovery | DS 812 IMS

Queen Of Sidney
Yusef Lateef Group | The Gentle Giant | Atlantic | 1602-2

Queen's Pawn
Christoph Spendel Group | Ready For Take Off | L+R Records | LR 45010

Queen's Suite:
Darktown Strutters Trio | Jazz In Switzerland 1930-1975 | Elite Special | 9544002/1-4

Queer Notions
Original Motion Picture Soundtrack | Kansas City | Verve | 529554-2

Quejas De Bandoneon
Montreal Jubilation Gospel Choir | Joy To The World | Blues Beacon | BLU-1018 2

Querer
Doug Raney Quartet | Rainey '96 | Steeplechase | SCCD 31397

Querido
Helmut Kagerer/Helmut Nieberle | Wes Trane | Edition Collage | EC 453-2

Querido Luis-
Tania Maria/Nils-Henning Orsted-Pederson Duo | Tania Maria & Nils-Henning Orsted-Pedersen | Accord | ACV 130010

Query
Herbie Nichols Trio | Herbie Nichols Trio | Blue Note | 300098(1519)

Query(alt.take)
Ike Quebec Quartet | The Art Of Ike Quebec | Blue Note | 799178-2

Quest
Charlie Mariano Group | Cascade | Keytone | KYT 707
Ahmad Jamal Quartet | Crystal | Atlantic | 781793-2

Questar
Joachim Kühn | Distance | CMP Records | CMP CD 26
Question And Answer
Roy Haynes Quartet | Fountain Of Youth | Dreyfus Jazz Line | FDM 36663-2
Roy Haynes Trio | The Roy Haynes Trio | Verve | 543534-2
Juan Garcia Esquivel Orchestra | Juan's Again | RCA | 2168206-2
Question Mark
Ray Anderson Trio | You Be | Minor Music | 8007
Question Time(Knitting Our Quitting-part 5)
John Lindberg Quartet | Quartet Afterstorm | Black Saint | 120162-2
Questions Without Answer
Joe Carroll With The Ray Bryant Quartet | Joe Carroll | Epic | ESCA 7766
Quetschuan
Hubert Rostaing And Aimé Barelli Et Leur Orchestre | Django Reinhardt:Djangology | EMI Records | 780659-2
Qui Parle?
Stephane Grappelli's Hot Four | Special Stephane Grappelli | Jazztime(EMI) | 251286-2
Qui S'ha Begut La Lluna?
Django Reinhardt And The Quintet Du Hot Club De France | Django Reinhardt:Djangology | EMI Records | 780659-2
Quick Sand
French Frith Kaiser Thompson | Invisible Means | Demon Records | Fiend CD 199
Quick Step
Gigi Gryce And His Orchestra | Clifford Brown:The Complete Paris Sessions Vol.2 | Vogue | 21457292
Quick Zap
Dave King Group | Wildcat | Off The Wall Records | OTW 9501-CD
Quicksilver
Art Blakey And The Jazz Messengers | The History Of Art Blakey And The Jazz Messengers | Blue Note | 797190-2
Howard Rumsey's Lighthouse All Stars Hosts Charlie Persip's Jazz Statesmen | Double Or Nothin' | Fresh Sound Records | 054 26011491(Liberty LRP 3045)
John Campbell Trio | Turning Point | Contemporary | CCD 14061-2
Quicksilver(alt.take)
Art Blakey And The Jazz Messengers(Art Blakey Quintet) | Clifford Brown:The Complete Blue Note And Pacific Recordings | Blue Note | 834195-2
Quieck!
Henry Johnson Group | Missing You | Inak | 30292
Quiero No Puedo
Mark Helias Quintet | Split Image | Enja | 4086 (807528)
Quiet Adventure
Bob Degen Trio With Zbigniew Namyslowski | Joy | Dr.Jazz Records | 8611-2
Quiet Afternoon
Stanley Clarke Groups | I Wanna Play For You | Epic | 88331
Quiet As It's Kept
Steve Nelson-Bobby Watson Quintet | Live Session One | Red Records | 123231-2
Quiet City
Jimmy Giuffre Trio | The Jimmy Giuffre Clarinet | Atlantic | 90144-1 TIS
Quiet Dawn
Joseph Bonner Trio And Strings | Impressions Of Copenhagen | Evidence | ECD 22024-2
Quiet Departures
Toots Thielemans Quartet With Orchestra | Bluesette | CBS | CDCOL 26604
Quiet Fire
Frank Morgan-Bud Shank Quintet | Quiet Fire | Contemporary | CCD 14064-2
Louis Hayes Sextet | Blue Lou | Steeplechase | SCCD 31340
Quiet I
Lothar Müller Trio | Müller Q[kju] | JA & RO | JARO 4251-2
Quiet II
Nat Adderley Orchestra | Double Expusure | Prestige | P 10090
Quiet Kinda Guy
Kenny Burrell Quintet | Sky Street | Fantasy | F 9514
Quiet Lady
Pepper Adams Quartet | Epherma | Spotlite | SPJ LP 6 (PA 6)
Quiet Light
Bill Evans Trio | I Will Say Goodbye | Original Jazz Classics | OJCCD 761-2(F 9593)
Conrad Herwig Quartet | Hieroglyphica | Criss Cross | Criss 1207
Quiet Night
Mimmo Cafiero Sextet | I Go | SPLASC(H) Records | H 157
Quiet Nights Of Quiet Stars(Corcovado)
Houston Person-Ron Carter | Now's The Time | Muse | MCD 5421
Joe Diorio | To Jobim With Love | RAM Records | RMCD 4529
Lewis Keel Sextet | Coming Out Swinging | Muse | MCD 5438
Oscar Peterson Trio | Travelin' On | MPS | 68078
Sarah Vaughan With Orchestra | !Viva! Vaughan | Mercury | 549374-2
The Hi-Lo's | Now | MPS | 68264
Quiet Now
Bill Evans | The Complete Bill Evans On Verve | Verve | 527953-2
At The Montreux Jazz Festival | Verve | 539758-2
Verve Jazz Masters 5:Bill Evans | Verve | 519821-2
Further Conversations With Myself | Verve | 559832-2
Bill Evans Trio | Bill Evans:From The 70's | Fantasy | F 9630
My Romance | Zeta | ZET 702
Quiet Now | Affinity | AFF 73
Bill Evans:From The 70's | Original Jazz Classics | OJCCD 1069-2(F 9630)
Half Moon Bay | Milestone | MCD 9282-2
The Paris Concert-Edition One | Blue Note | MUS 96.0164-1
Quiet Place
Booker Little Sextet | Out Front | Candid | CCD 79027
Quiet Please
Tommy Dorsey And His Orchestra | Jazz Drumming Vol.5(1940) | Fenn Music | FJD 2705
Quiet Please(take 1)
Shadow Vignettes | Birth Of A Notion | Open Minds | OM 2410-2
Quiet Rising
Thad Jones Sextet | Mad Thad | Fresh Sound Records | FSR-CD 0117
Quiet Times
Les Baxter And His Orchestra | Baxter's Best | Capitol | 791218-2
Quietly There
Spike Robinson-Gene DiNovi Quartet | Gene DiNovi Meets Spike Robinson-At The Stables | Hep | CD 2071
Poncho Sanchez Band With Tito Puente | Chile Con Soul | Concord | CCD 4406
Quietude
Thad Jones-Mel Lewis Orchestra | The Groove Merchant/The Second Race | Laserlight | 24656
A Touch Of Class | West Wind Orchestra Series | 2402 CD
Quilombos
Andrew Cyrille-Peter Brötzman Duo | Andrew Cyrille Meets Peter Brötzmann In Berlin | FMP | 1000
Quimbombo-
Tete Montoliu | Catalonian Folksongs | Timeless | SJP 116
Quincy Street Stomp
Dick Wellstood | I Wish I Were Twins | Swingtime | 8204
Quint
Maria Joao & Grupo Cal Viva | Sol | Enja | ENJ-7001 2
Quintennaissance
J.J.Johnson Quintet | Live At The Village Vanguard | EmArCy | 848327-2
Quintessence
Coleman Hawkins Quartet | Today And Now | MCA | AS 34
Rahsaan Roland Kirk And His Orchestra | Left & Right | Atlantic | ATL 40235(SD 1518)
Warne Marsh Quintet | Jazz Of Two Cities | Fresh Sound Records | FSR-CD 342
Intuition | Capitol | 852771-2
Quintessential
011 Jazz Sextet | Bustring | SPLASC(H) Records | H 114
Quintet's Time
Stan Kenton And His Orchestra | Adventures In Time | Capitol | 855454-2
Quirilunga
Irvin Rochlin Trio | Quirine | Limetree | MLP 198036
Quit
Bar Scott Group | Silence Is Broken | clearaudio | JSR 1011 CD
Quittin' Time
Clifford Jordan Quintet | Starting Time | Original Jazz Classics | OJC 147(J 952)
Quixotic
Frank Vignola Trio With Davis Grisman | Let It Happen | Concord | CCD 4625
Quizas Quizas Quizas
Stan Kenton And His Orchestra | Stan Kenton-Jean Turner | Creative World | ST 1046
Quizas Quizas Quizas-
Dusko Goykovich Quartet | Samba Do Mar | Enja | ENJ-9473 2
Quo Vadis
Thierry Lang-Daniel Perrin | Tusitala | Plainisphare | PL 1267-105 CD
R
Charles Mingus Group | The Jazz Life! | Candid | CCD 79019
R & R
Charles Mingus Sextet | Reincarnation Of A Love Bird | Candid | CS 9026
R U There?
Klaus Müller-Ekkehard Rössle | Auf Und Davon | Jazz Haus Musik | JHM 0091 CD
R&B
The World Saxophone Quartet | Steppin' With The World Saxophone Quartet | Black Saint | 120027-2
R.B.
Air | Air Mail | Black Saint | 120049-2
R.B.Q.
Teddy Edwards Quintet | Teddy Edwards:Steady With Teddy 1946-1948 | Cool & Blue | C&B-CD 115
R.J.
Joe Henderson Quartet | Foresight | Milestone | M 47058
Miles Davis Quintet | E.S.P. | CBS | CK65683
Miles Davis Quintet 1965-1968 | CBS | C6K 67398
Wynton Marsalis Quintet | Wynton Marsalis | CBS | 468708-2
Ornette Coleman Quartet | Beauty Is A Rare Thing:Ornette Coleman-The Complete Atlantic Recordings | Atlantic | 8122-71410-2
R.P.D.D.
Earl Hines | Another Monday Date | Prestige | P 24043
R.R.Blues
Macrino-Rovagna Ensemble | New Age Jazz | Penta Flowers | CDPIA 003
R.S.V.P.
Inno | Insonnie | SPLASC(H) Records | CD H 321-2
R2D2
Evan Parker-Paul Lytton Duo | Ra 1+2 | Ring | 01016
Rabazzo Moderne
Gary Lucas/Walter Horn | Skeleton On The Feast | Enemy | EMCD 126(03526)
Rabbi Mogen's Hideout
Rebecca Gordon Quartet | Yiddish'n Jazz | Touché Music | TMcCD 014
Rabbi Motenyu
Count Basie's Kansas City Five | Count Basie: Kansas City 5 | Pablo | 2312126
Rabo De Nube(Tail Of The Tornado)
Charlie Haden And The Liberation Music Orchestra | Dream Keeper | Polydor | 847876-2
Rabou-Abou-Kabou
Rabih Abou-Khalil Group | Odd Times | Enja | ENJ-9330 2
Cal Tjader Quartet | Black Hawk Nights | Fantasy | FCD 24755-2
Raccoons Strait
Cal Tjader Quintet | Concerts In The Sun | Fantasy | FCD 9688-2
Concerts In The Sun | Fantasy | FCD 9688-2
Concerts In The Sun | Fantasy | FCD 9688-2
San Francisco Moods | Original Jazz Classics | OJC 277(F 8017)
Race Face
Don Cherry/Nana Vasconcelos/Collin Walcott | Codona | ECM | 1132(829371-2)
Race Face-
Curtis Counce Quintet | Exploring The Future | Contemporary | BOP 7(Dootone 247)
Race In Space For Face
Scott Hamilton Quartet | Race Point | Concord | CCD 4492
Race With Devil On Spanish Highway
Al Di Meola Group | Tour De Force-Live | CBS | 25121-2
Joe Maneri-Mat Maneri | Blessed | ECM | 1661(557365-2)
Race You Home
Count Basie Kansas City 3 | For The Second Time | Original Jazz Classics | OJC 600(2310878)
Racehorse
Harmut Geerken/Famoudou Don Moye/John Tchicai | Cassava Balls | Praxis | CM 111
Rache Akt-
David Friesen Trio | The Name Of A Woman | Intuition Records | INT 3334-2
Rachel
Laura Fygi Meets Michel Legrand | Watch What Happens | Mercury | 534598-2
Nelson Riddle And His Orchestra | Communication | MPS | 9814795
Dan Barrett Sextet | Reunion With Al | Arbors Records | ARCD 19124
Rachel's Song
Eddy Louiss-Michel Petrucciani | Conference De Presse Vol.2 | Dreyfus Jazz Line | FDM 36573-2
Rachid
Michel Petrucciani Group | Playground | Blue Note | 795480-2
Michel Petrucciani Quintet | Michel Petrucciani Live | Blue Note | 780589-2
Freddy Martin And His Orchestra | The Uncollected:Freddy Martin,Vol.4 | Hindsight | HSR 205
Rachmaninoff's Prelude In C-Sharp Minor
Ran Blake | Realization Of A Dream | Owl Records | 012
Racing Heart(version 1998)
Kölner Saxophon Mafia | Licence To Thrill | Jazz Haus Musik | JHM 0100 CD
Racing Max
Threeo | Racing Time | L+R Records | CDLR 45103
Racing Waters
Gary Bartz Candid All Stars | There Goes The Neighborhood! | Candid | CCD 79506
Racquet Club
Illinois Jacquet Sextet | Loot To Boot | LRC Records | CDC 9034
Rad-At
Johnny Dyani Sextet feat.John Tchicai & Dudu Pukwana | Witchdoctor's Son | Steeplechase | SCCD 31098
Radiation
New Orleans Saxophone Ensemble | New New Orleans Music: New Music Jazz | Line Records | COCD 9.00917 O
Radiator
Tom Varner Quartet | Tom Varner Quartet | Soul Note | 121017-2
Radio
Gary Burton-Chick Corea | Duet | ECM | 1140(829941-2)
Kenny Drew Jr. | Live At The Montreux Jazz Fesival '99 | TCB Records | TCB 21152
Radio Blues
Boogie Junction | I Wake You Up | Jazz Pure Collection | AU 31602 CD
Radio Days
Michel Petrucciani | Au Theatre Des Champ-Elysees(Paris Concert) | Dreyfus Jazz Line | FDM 36570-2
Radio Dial-
Christoph Spendel Group | Radio Exotic | L+R Records | CDLR 70001
Radio Funk
Slickaphonics | Slickaphonics | Enja | ENJ-4024 2
Radio-Active
Knut Kiesewetter With Orchestra | Jazz Again | Polydor | 2372016
Radio-Activity
Billy Taylor Trio | Billy Taylor Trio | Prestige | PRCD 24285-2
Mahavishnu | Mahavishnu | Warner | 251351-1
Radspuren
Anouar Brahem Trio | Barzakh | ECM | 1432(847540-2)
Raf Raf
Maria Joao-Mario Laginha Group | Cor | Verve | 557456-2
Raffedore
Günter Christmann Group | Vario II | Moers Music | 01084
Raffish
Ralph Towner | Anthem | ECM | 1743(543814-2)
Mark Isham-Peter Van Hooke Duo | Vapor Drawings | Windham Hill | TA-C- 1027
Rag
Bill Frisell Trio | Live | Gramavision | GCD 79504
Rag Bag
Pili-Pili | Boogaloo | JA & RO | JARO 4174-2
Dink Johnson One Man Band | Dink Johnson-Charlie Thompson: The Piano Players | American Music | AMCD-11
Raga
Egberto Gismonti Group | Works | ECM | 823269-2
Patrick Bebelaar Group | Point Of View | dml-records | CD 017
Soma | Southern Cross | West Wind Latina | 2208 CD
Raga Desh
Jan Garbarek With Ustad Fateh Ali Khan & Musicians From Pakistan | Ragas And Sagas | ECM | 1442(511263-2)
Raga I
Urs Leimgruber | Statement Of An Antirider | Hat Art | CD 6013
Raga II
Statement Of An Antirider | Hat Art | CD 6013
Raga III
Pirchner-Pepl Jazzzwio | Live At Montreux '81 | Warner | 58393
Raga IV
Dave Pike Set | Dave Pike Set:Masterpieces | MPS | 531848-2
Raga Jeeva Swara
Ustad Zakir Hussain | Essence Of Rhythm | EmArCy | 536943-2
Raga Rag
Paul Horn Group | Paul Horn In India | Blue Note | 84551
Raga Up And Down(Variations On An Indian Scale)
Klaus Doldinger Quartet | Doldinger Jubilee | Atlantic | ATL 60073
Ragam Sankarabharanam
Shankar | Who's To Know | ECM | 1195
Ragam-Tanam-Pallavi
Shankar Quartet | Pancha Nadai Pallavi | ECM | 1407(841641-2)
Pancha Nadai Pallavi | ECM | 1407(841641-2)
Frank Rosolino Sextet | Kenton Presents: Frank Rosolino | Affinity | AFF 61
Ragamuffin
Ten Black Berries | The Complete Duke Ellington-Vol. 3 | CBS | CBS 88000
Ragavardhana
Loren MazzaCane Connors | A Possible Dawn | HatNOIR | 801
Ragga Muffia
Al Jarreau With Band | We Got By | Reprise | 7599-27222-2
Raggedy Ann
Lee Morgan Quintet | Take Twelve | Original Jazz Classics | OJCCD 310-2
Louis Hayes Quintet | The Candy Man | TCB Records | TCB 20972
Raging Thirst
Al Jarreau With Band | High Crime | Warner | 2292-50807-2
Raging Waters
Jim Hall With Strings | Textures | Telarc Digital | CD 83402
Rags And Old Iron
Buddy Rich And His Orchestra | Live Sessions At The Palladium, Hollywood | Jazz Anthology | JA 5206
Ragtag And Bobtail
BBFC | Quelle Memoire! | Plainisphare | PL 1267-9
Ragtime-
Eddy Howard And His Orchestra | The Uncollected:Eddy Howard, Vol.2 | Hindsight | HSR 156
Ragtime Dance
Max Collie And His Rhythm Aces | Max Collie Rhyhtm Aces Vol.3 | GHB Records | BCD-98
Ragtime(Andante)-
Dusan Bogdanovic Quartet | Early To Rise | Palo Alto | PA 8049
Rahkki Sruvvis
Rahsaan Roland Kirk Group | Natural Black Inventions:Roots Strata | Atlantic | ATL 40185(SD 1578)
Rai Print
Erskine Hawkins And His Orchestra | From Alabama To Harlem | Black & Blue | BLE 59.236 2
Railroad Porter Blues
T-Bone Walker And His Band | T-Bone Walker Sings The Blues | Pathe | 1546751(Imperial LP 9098)
Railships To Rabat
Furio Romano Quartet | What Colour For A Tale | SPLASC(H) Records | CD H 351-2
Rain
Bill Stewart Qaurtet | Think Before You Think | Jazz City | 660.53.024
Christoph Spendel Group | Ready For Take Off | L+R Records | LR 45010
Ella Fitzgerald-Joe Pass Duo | Fitzgerald & Pass... Again | Original Jazz Classics | OJCCD 1052-2(2310772)
Enrico Rava Quintet | Easy Living | ECM | 1760(9812050)
Geri Allen Trio | Segments | DIW | DIW 833 CD
Ella Fitzgerald With Benny Carter's Magnificent Seven | 30 By Ella | Capitol | 520090-2
Rain-
George Winston | Winter Into Spring | Windham Hill | 34 11019-2
Meredith Monk | Dolman Music | ECM | 1197(825459-2)
Rain Dance
Horace Silver Quintet | Serenade To A Soul Sister | Blue Note | 300271(4277)
Rain Forest
Hampton Hawes-Charlie Haden Duo | As Long As There's Music | Artists House | AH 4 IMS
Nelson Rangell Group | Nelson Rangell | GRP | GRP 96242
Tim Brady-Kenny Wheeler Duo | Visions | Justin Time | JTR 8413-2
Rain Forest Breeze
Hamiet Bluiett Quartet | Ballads & Blues:Live At The Village Vanguard | Soul Note | 121288-2
Rain Is Such A Lonesome Sound
Jay McShann Quintet | What A Wonderful World | Groove Note | GRV 1005-2
Jimmy Witherspoon With Jay McShann And His Band | Goin' To Kansas City Blues | RCA | 2113027-2
Rain Rain
Louis Armstrong With The Hal Mooney Orchestra | Louis Armstrong-The Complete RCA Victor Recordings | RCA | 2668682-2
Rain River
Joe Lovano-Aldo Romano | Ten Tales | Owl Records | 018350-2
Rain Season
Hamiet Bluiett Quintet | Dangerously Suite | Soul Note | 121018-2
Rain Village
Toots Thielemans Quartet | Only Trust Your Heart | Concord | MC CJ 355C
Rain(take 2)
Werner Lener Trio | Personal Moments | Satin Doll Productions | SDP 1026-1 CD
Rain,Sun,Grass And Flowers
Flora Purim And Fourth World | A Night At Ronnie Scott's Vol.6:The Vocal Album | Ronnie Scott's Jazz House | NARCD 6

Rainbow
Lee Ritenour Group | Rio | GRP | GRP 95242
Marion Brown Sextet | Marion Brown In Sommerhausen | Calig | 30605
Werner Bühler Quartet | At The Swinging Organ | MWM Records | MWM 005
Rainbow Birds Suite(part 1a)
Marilyn Mazur's Future Song | Marilyn Mazure's Future Song | VeraBra Records | CDVBR 2105-2
Rainbow Birds Suite(part 1b)
Marilyn Mazure's Future Song | VeraBra Records | CDVBR 2105-2
Rainbow Birds Suite(part 2b)
Vince Jones Group | It All Ends Up In Tears | Intuition Records | INT 3069-2
Rainbow Cake
Eddie Lang | Pioneers Of Jazz Guitar 1927-1939 | Retrieval | RTR 79015
Rainbow Mountain
Tiziano Tononi Group | Going For The Magic | SPLASC(H) Records | HP 13
Rainbow Serenade
Eddie Daniels Quartet | Real Time | Chesky | JD 118
Rainbow Sleeves
Ed Kelly & Friends | Ed Kelly & Pharoah Sanders | Evidence | ECD 22056-2
Rainbow Songs
Jean-Paul Bourelly & The BluWave Bandits | Rock The Cathartic Spirits:Vibe Music And The Blues! | DIW | DIW 911 CD
Rainbow's Cadillac
Makoto Ozone Group | Treasure | Verve | 021906-2
Rainbow's End
Lonnie Liston Smith Group | Dreams Of Tomorrow | Doctor Jazz | FW 38447
Raincheck
Art Blakey And The Jazz Messengers | Chippin' In | Timeless | CD SJP 340
Duke Ellington And His Famous Orchestra | Duke Ellington:The Blanton-Webster Band | Bluebird | 21 13181-2
Ben Webster-Cotton Tail | RCA | 63667902
Duke Ellington And His Orchestra | And His Mother Called Him Bill | RCA | 2125762-2
In The Sixties | RCA | PD 89565
Joe Temperley Quintet | Double Duke | Naxos Jazz | 86032-2
Sonny Rollins Quartet | Taking Care Of Business | Prestige | P 24082
Tommy Flanagan Trio | Jazz Poet | Timeless | CD SJP 301
Raindrops Keep Fallin' On My Head
Ella Fitzgerald With The Tommy Flanagan Trio | Ella Fitzgerald In Budapest | Pablo | PACD 5308-2
Roy Ayers Ubiquity | Live At The Montreux Jazz Festival | Verve | 531641-2
Rainfall
Tito Puente And His Latin Ensemble | El Rey | Concord | CJ 250
Raining Violets
MOKAVE | MOKAVE Vol.1 | audioquest Music | AQCD 1006
Rainy Day
Richard 'Groove' Holmes Quintet | Grove Holmes/Jimmy McGriff | LRC Records | CDC 9042
Erwin Helfer | Chicago Piano | Steeplechase | SCB 9010
Rainy Day Blues
Randy Burns Quartet | Evening Of The Magician | ESP Disk | ESP 1089-2
Rainy Days
Sarah Vaughan And Her Trio | The Complete Sarah Vaughan Live In Japan | Mobile Fidelity | MFCD 844-2
Rainy Mornin' Blues
Lee Morgan Sextet | Charisma | Blue Note | 300260(4312)
Rainy Night In Georgia
Red Mitchell Quartet | Presenting Red Mitchell | Original Jazz Classics | OJCCD 158-2(C 7538)
Raise Four & Monk's Point
Freddie Brown | Paramount Piano Blues Vol.2(1927-1932) | Black Swan Records | HCD-12012
Raisin' The Roof
Red Whale | Queekegg | Maracatu | MAC 940002
Rajashik-The Majesty Of Wisdom
Sadao Watanabe With Lee Ritenour & His Gentle Thought | Autumn Blow | Flying Disk | VIJ 6006
Rakin' And Scrapin'
Albert Mangelsdorff Quintet | Now Jazz Ramwong | L+R Records | CDLR 71001
Rally
Ron Carter Quintet | Eric Dolphy Birthday Celebration | Fantasy | FANCD 6085-2
Eric Dolphy:The Complete Prestige Recordings | Prestige | 9 PRCD-4418-2
Red Garland Quartet | Rojo | Original Jazz Classics | OJCCD 772-2(P 7193)
Ralph's New Blues
Modern Jazz Quartet | Blues At Carnegie Hall | Philips | PHCE 3019 PMS
The Complete Modern Jazz Quartet Prestige & Pablo Recordings | Prestige | 4PRCD 4438-2
To Bags...With Love:Memorial Album | Pablo | 2310967-2
Modern Jazz Quartet | Prestige | P 24005
Modern Jazz Quartet And The All-Star Jazz Band | Jazz Dialogue | Philips | PHCE 3018 PMS
Oliver Nelson Quintet | Eric Dolphy Birthday Celebration | Fantasy | FANCD 6085-2
Eric Dolphy:The Complete Prestige Recordings | Prestige | 9 PRCD-4418-2
Jochen Voss/Thomas Brendgens-Mönkemeyer | Alterations | Acoustic Music Records | 319.1029.2
Ralph's Piano Waltz
John Abercrombie Trio | Current Event | ECM | 1311(827770-2)
John Abercrombie With The Ansgar Striepens Quintet | Dreams And Realities | Laika Records | 35101642
Ralph Towner | Solo Concert | ECM | 1173(827268-2)
Ralph Sutton | Stridin' High | Jazz Connaisseur | JCCD 9728-2
Ralph's Very Special Bonus Track
Buck Ram All-Stars | The Black Swing Tradition | Savoy | SJL 2246 (801854)
Rambler
Bill Frisell Quintet | Rambler | ECM | 1287
Bob Stewart Groups | Then & Now | Postcards | POST 1014
Ramblin'
Ornette Coleman Quartet | Change Of The Century | Atlantic | 7567-81341-2
Beauty Is A Rare Thing:Ornette Coleman-The Complete Atlantic Recordings | Atlantic | 8122-71410-2
Paul Bley Trio | Ramblin' | Affinity | AFF 37
Ramblin' In You Dresser Drawers
Ramblin' Thomas | Suitcase Full Of Blues | Black Swan Records | HCD-23
Rambling
Paul Williams & Friends | In Memory Of Robert Johnson | Black Sun Music | 15017-2
Rambling By Myself
John Lee Hooker | Blues Roots Vol. 13: John Lee Hooker | Chess | 6.24803 AG
Rambling On My Mind
Robert Lockwood Jr.With The Aces | Steady Rollin' Man | Delmark | 900206 AO
Rambling On My Mind(alt.take)
Louis Gallaud | Punch Miller/Louis Gallaud | American Music | AMCD-68
Rambo
Dave Valentine Group | Two Amigos | GRP | GRP 96062
Rame Head
Nana Vasconcelos/Antonello Salis | Lester | Soul Note | 121157-2
Ramo Des Flores-
Les Misérables Brass Band | Manic Tradition | Popular Arts | NR 5004 CD
Ramona
Les Brown And His Orchestra | The Les Brown Story | Capitol | 791226-2
Martial Solal Trio | Martial Solal:The Complete Vogue Recordings Vol.1 | Vogue | 21409322
Rampage
Allen Eager Quartet | Brothers And Other Mothers, Vol. 1 | Savoy | SJL 2210 (801186)
Rampenlicht(I Rampelyset)
Schmilz | Schmilz | Creative Works Records | CW CD 1041
Rampid Rabbit
Nels Cline Trio | Silencer | Enja | ENJ-6098 2
Ramy
Tito Puente And His Latin Ensemble | El Rey | Concord | CJ 250
Ranalla Istrusa
Rüdiger Carl | Vorn:Lieder Und Improvisationen Für Akkordeon, Bandoneon Und Ziehharmonika | FMP | 1110
Random Abstract(Diddle-It)
Branford Marsalis Trio | Trio Jeepy | CBS | 465134-2
Random Abstract(Tain's Rampage)
Marco Cerletti Group | Random And Providence | VeraBra Records | CDVBR 2039-2
Random And Providence
Pocket Change | Random Axis | Passport Jazz | ???
Random Brande
Stan Kenton And His Orchestra | At The Las Legas Tropicana | Capitol | 835245-2
Random Vibrations
Buck Hill Quartet | Impulse | Muse | MCD 5483
Randy
Super Session | Welcome & Alive | Vagabond | 6.28604 DP
Randy's Rolls Royce
Randy Sandke Sextet | The Chase | Concord | CCD 4642
Range
Cootie Williams Septet | Cootie In Hi-Fi | RCA | NL 89811
Rank
Buddy Charles | Jive's Alive | Steeplechase | SCB 9006
Rann & Roll
Soft Head | Soft Head-Rogue Element | Ogun | OGCD 013
Raoni
Roland Kirk And His Orchestra | Rahsaan/The Complete Mercury Recordings Of Roland Kirk | Mercury | 846630-2
Raouf
Essence All Stars | Bongobop | Hip Bop | HIBD 8017
Raoul
| La Voce-Music For Voices,Trumpet And Bass | JA & RO | JARO 4208-2
Rap
Ku-umba Frank Lacy & The Poker Bigband | Songs From The Musical 'Poker' | Tutu Records | 888150-2*
Rap-
Keith Ingham-Harry Allen Septet | The Back Room Romp | Sackville | SKCD2-3059
Rap For Nap
James Blood Ulmer Group | Music Speaks Louder Than Words:James Blood Ulmer Plays The Music Of Ornette Coleman | DIW | DIW 910 CD
Rapid Rabbit
Shirley Scott Quartet | Queen Of The Organ | Impulse(MCA) | GRP 11232
Rapid Speed
Oregon | Always,Never And Forever | Intuition Records | INT 2073-2
Rapid Transit
Roscoe Mitchell | Songs In The Wind | Victo | CD 011
Rapidité(Arrivée)
Ekkehard Jost Nonet | Out Of Jost's Songbook | Fish Music | FM 006 CD
Rapidité(Départ)
Alan Shorter Quartet | Orgasm | Verve | 557094-2
Rapids
Oregon | Oregon | ECM | 1258(811711-2)
Luther Thomas & Dizzazz | Yo' Momma | Moers Music | 01088
Rapped From The Circus Tent
Roy Ayers Sextet | Good Vibrations | Ronnie Scott's Jazz House | JHCD 028
Rappell
Lotz Of Music | Puasong Daffriek | Laika Records | LK 94-054
Rappin' Donna
Scheer Music | Rappin' It Up | Palo Alto | PA 8025
Rasgido Doble-
Finküberthurm | Fink Über Thurm | Jazz Haus Musik | JHM 44 CD
Rasheed
George Duke Group | George Duke & Feel | MPS | 68023
Rashim
Christoph Spendel Group | Raspail Hotel | Trion | 3104
Rast
Kowalt-Smith-Sommer Trio | If You Want The Kernels, You Have To Break The Shells | FMP | 0920
Rat Dance
Stefon Harris-Jacky Terrasson Group | Kindred | Blue Note | 531868-2
Rat Entrance
Mal Waldron Trio | Free At Last | ECM | 1001
Rat Now
Richard Fairhurst Quartet | The Hungry Ants | Babel | BDV 9504
Rat Race
Count Basie And His Orchestra | Count Basie & His Orchestra:Fresno,California April 24,1959 | Jazz Unlimited | JUCD 2039
Stefon Harris-Jacky Terrasson Group | Kindred | Blue Note | 531868-2
Cab Calloway And His Orchestra | Jazz Drumming Vol.3(1938-1939) | Fenn Music | FJD 2703
Rated X-
Peter Brötzmann/Werner Lüdi | Wie Das Leben So Spielt | FMP | CD 22
Rather Dead
Tacuma-Puschnig Duo | Gemini-Gemini | ITM-Pacific | ITMP 970063
Ration Blues
Louis Jordan And His Tympany Five | Louis Jordan Vol.2-Knock Me Out | Swingtime(Contact) | ST 1012
Ratte
Helmut 'Joe' Sachse | Solo | FMP | 1070
Rattler's Groove
John Brim & His Gary Kings | Whose Muddy Shoes | Chess | CH 9114
Raucous Notes
Klaus Treuheit | Solo | Klaus Treuheit Production | A+P 9304(CD 161)
Raunchy
Elvin Jones-Richard Davis Quartet | Heavy Sounds | Impulse(MCA) | 547959-2
Raunchy Rita
Jeannie And Jimmy Cheatham & The Sweet Baby Blues Band | Luv In The Afternoon | Concord | CCD 4429
Rava-Tanz
John Zorn Group | Masada Two | DIW | DIW 889 CD
Raven
Bruno Tommaso Orchestra | Barga Jazz | SPLASC(H) Records | HP 06
Raven's Jolly Jump-Up
Ralph Towner | Trios/Solos | ECM | 1025(833328-2)
Raven's Wood
Stan Getz Quartet | The Master | CBS | 467138-2
Ravi
Ugetsu | Ugetsu-Live In Athens | Mons Records | MR 874779
Raw Groove
Joe Thomas And His Orchestra | Joe Thomas:The Complete Recordings 1945-1950 | Blue Moon | BMCD 1051
Ray
Geri Allen Quartet | The Gathering | Verve | 557614-2
Ray Charles' Place
Duke Ellington-Coleman Hawkins Orchestra | Duke Ellington Meets Coleman Hawkins | MCA | MCAD 5650
Ray Of Hope
George Coleman Quartet | Manhattan Panorama | Evidence | ECD 22019-2
Ray's Blues
Steve White Quartet | In The Spur Of The Moment | Telarc Digital | CD 83484
Ray's Dad's Cadillac
Allan Botschinsky Quartet | I've Got Another Rhythm | M.A Music | A 916-2
Ray's Delight
Art Blakey And The Jazz Messengers | Au Theatre Des Champs-Elysees | RCA | 2119252-2
Ray's Idea
Hampton Hawes Trio | Bird Song | Original Jazz Classics | OJCCD 1035-2
Jimmy Forrest Sextet | Live At The Barrel | Prestige | P 7858
Miles Davis All Stars | Live At The Hi-Hat Boston | Jazz Door | JD 1216
Miles Davis Sextet | Miles Davis:The Blue Note And Capitol Recordings | Blue Note | 827475-2
Miles Davis Vol.1 | Blue Note | 300081(1501)
Ray's Idea(alt.take)
Miles Davis:The Blue Note And Capitol Recordings | Blue Note | 827475-2
Razzle Dazzle
Count Basie-Oscar Peterson Quintet | Satch And Josh | Pablo | 2310722-2
RB
Anthony Braxton Quartet | At Moers Festival | Ring | 01010-11
Re
Lionel Hampton And His Orchestra | Lionel Hampton/Gene Krupa | Forlane | UCD 19008
Re:Person I Knew
Bill Evans Trio | The Second Trio | Milestone | M 47046
Bill Evans Trio:The Last Waltz | Milestone | 8MCD 4430-2
Bill Evans:The Secret Sessions | Milestone | 8MCD 4421-2
The Brilliant | West Wind | WW 2058
The Paris Concert-Edition Two | Blue Note | 60311-1
Moonbeams | Original Jazz Classics | OJC20 434-2(RLP 9428)
Homecoming | Milestone | MCD 9291-2
Bill Evans:The Secret Sessions | Milestone | 8MCD 4421-2
Carlos Denia-Uli Glaszmann | Ten Strings For Bill Evans | Edition Musikat | EDM 069
Coe,Oxley & Co. | Nutty On Willisau | Hat Art | CD 6046
Stefano Battaglia Trio | Bill Evans Compositions Vol.1 | SPLASC(H) Records | CD H 400-2
Reach
Jackie Terrasson Trio | Reach | Blue Note | 837570-2
Reach-
Reach | Blue Note | 837570-2
Toon Roos Quartet | The Human Feel | September | CD 5114
Reach For Tomorrow
Ralph Towner | Trios/Solos | ECM | 1025(833328-2)
Reach Me, Friend
John Lee Hooker Duo | Detroit Blues | Anthology of the Blues | AB 5606
Reach Out For Love
Brainstorm feat. Chico Freeman | The Mystical Dreamer | IN+OUT Records | 7006-2
Reach Out I'll Be There - (Reach Out) I'll Be There
Chico Freeman And Brainstorm | Jazz Unlimited | IN+OUT Records | 7017-2
Hal Galper Quintet | Reach Out | Steeplechase | SCCD 31067
Reaching For The Moon
Ella Fitzgerald With Paul Weston And His Orchestra | The Complete Ella Fitzgerald Song Books of Harold Arlen, Irving Berlin, Duke Ellington, George & Ira Gershwin, Jerome Kern, Johnny Mercer, Cole Porter And Rogers & Hart | Verve | 519832-2
Reactinary Tango(part 1-3)
Gary Burton Quartet | Easy As Pie | ECM | 1184
Reactionary Tango (In Three Parts)
Steve Swallow Group | Carla | Watt | XtraWatt/2
Read My Lips
Ronnie Taheny Group | Briefcase | Laika Records | 35101152
Read My Mind
Eddie Boyd Blues Band | Blues Roots Vol. 20: Eddie Boyd | Chess | 6.24810 AG
Read The Signs
Salvatore Bonafede Trio | Plays | Ken Music | 660.56.017
Reading Of Sacred Books
Marty Ehrlich Quartet | Can You Hear A Motion? | Enja | ENJ-8052 2
Ready And Able
George Benson Quartet + Guests | The George Benson Cookbook | CBS | 502470-2
Jimmy Smith Trio | A New Sound A New Star:Jimmy Smith At The Organ | Blue Note | 857191-2
Barney Bigard And His Orchestra | The Great Ellington Units | RCA | ND 86751
Ready For Love To Begin
Christoph Spendel Group | Ready For Take Off | L+R Records | LR 45010
Ready For Take Off
Jimmie Noone-Earl Hines Quintet | Jimmie Noone/Earl Hines Vol.1-At The Apex Club | MCA | 1313
Ready For The River
Joe Turner | Walking Through Heaven | Swingtime | 8205
Freddie Redd Trio | Piano:East/West | Original Jazz Classics | OJCCD 1705-2(P 7067)
Ready Go
Jasper Van't Hof + Eyeball | Jazzbühne Berlin '80 | Repertoire Records | REPCD 4908-CC
Ready Now That You Are
Herbie Hancock Group | Feet's Don't Fail Me Now | CBS | SRCS 9504
Ready Out There
Duke Pearson Sextet | Sweet Honey Bee | Blue Note | 595974-2
Ready Rudy
Mike LeDonne Quintet | The Feeling Of Jazz | Criss Cross | Criss 1041
Ready Rusty
Roman Schwaller Nonet | The Original Tunes | JHM Records | JHM 3629
Ready Set Go
Wolfgang Haffner International Jazz Quintet | Whatever It Is | Jazz 4 Ever Records:Jazz Network | J4E 4714
John Slaughter Band | All That Stuff Ain't Real | Timeless | CD SJP 430
Ready-made:Torrid Zone
Jimmy Greene Sextet | Introducing Jimmy Greene | Criss Cross | Criss 1181
Real Cool
Babs Gonzales And His Orchestra | Sonny Rollins | Definitive Records | DRCD 11243
Real Crazy
Lionel Hampton And His Orchestra | Lionel Hampton:Real Crazy | Vogue | 2113409-2
Real Fine Frame
Buddy Johnson And His Orchestra | Go Ahead & Rock Rock Rock | Official | 6011
Real Joe
John Tchicai-Pierre Dorge | Ball At Louisiana | Steeplechase | SCCD 31174
Real Life Hits
Carla Bley/Andy Sheppard/Steve Swallow | Song With Legs | Watt | 26(527069)
Gary Burton Quartet | Real Life Hits | ECM | 1293
Terri Lyne Carrington Group | Real Life Story | Verve | 837697-2
Real Real
Sonny Thompson And His Orchestra | Cat On The Keys | Swingtime(Contact) | ST 1027
Real Tight
Paolo Fresu Quartet | Angel | RCA | 2155864-2

TITELVERZEICHNIS

Real Time
Spyro Gyra | Three Wishes | GRP | GRP 96742
Reality Check
Paul Bley Trio | Reality Check | Steeplechase | SCCD 31379
Really
Tristan Honsinger Quintet | Map Of Moods | FMP | CD 76
Really Fine
Memphis Slim Group | The Real Folk Blues | Chess | CHD 9270(872290)
Really The Blues
Tommy Ladnier And His Orchestra | The Complete Sidney Bechet-Vol.1/2 | RCA | ND 89760
Really True Blues
Modern Jazz Quartet | The Complete Modern Jazz Quartet Prestige & Pablo Recordings | Prestige | 4PRCD 4438-2
Together Again | Pablo | PACD20 244-2(2308244)
The Modern Jazz Quartet | Reunion At Budokan 1981 | Atlantic | 251210-1 TIS
Really You Know
Joe Newman Septet | The Midgets | Fresh Sound Records | 60987-2(RCA)
Reanascreena
Batman | Naked City | Nonesuch | 7559-79238-2
Reanimator
Don Pullen Trio | New Beginnings | Blue Note | 791785-2
Reap What You Sow
Otis Rush And His Band | Blues Power No.3:Otis Rush - Mourning In The Morning | Atlantic | 40495
Rearin' Back
Children At Play | Children At Play | Japo | 60009 IMS
Reasons
Henning Berg Quartet | Minnola | Jazz Haus Musik | JHM 0127 CD
Reasons To Play
Tim Brady-Kenny Wheeler Duo | Visions | Justin Time | JTR 8413-2
Rebecca
Lee Konitz-Billy Bauer Duo | Subconcious-Lee | Original Jazz Classics | OJCCD 186-2(P 7004)
Milton Batiste With The Rue Conti Jazz Band | Milton Batiste With The Rue Conti Jazz Band | Lake | LACD 31
Rebellion
Massimo De Mattia Group | The Silent Drama | SPLASC(H) Records | CD H 442-2
Rebica
Conrad Herwig Sextet | Unseen Universe | Criss Cross | Criss 1194
Rebirth
Max Roach-Anthony Braxton | Birth And Rebirth | Black Saint | 120024-2
McCoy Tyner Quartet | Reflections | Milestone | M 47062
Rebop
Darrell Grant Quintet | The New Bop | Criss Cross | Criss 1106
Recado Bossa Nova
Javon Jackson Group | A Look Within | Blue Note | 836490-2
Lisa Wahlandt & Mulo Francel And Their Fabulous Bossa Band | Bossa Nova Affair | Edition Collage | EC 534-2
Major Holley Trio | Mule | Black & Blue | BLE 233074
Roy Eldridge Septet | The Best Of Roy Eldridge | Pablo | 2310857
Al Cohn-Zoot Sims Quintet | Body & Soul | Muse | MCD 5356
Receipt Please
Jim Hall-Ron Carter Duo | Alone Together | Original Jazz Classics | OJC 467(M 9045)
Red Garland Quintet | Strike Up The Band | Galaxy | GXY 5135
Randy Weston African Rhythm Quintet and The Gnawa Master Musicians of Marocco | Spirit! The Power Of Music | Verve | 543256-2
Receiving The Spirit
Charlie Hunter-Leon Parker | Duo | Blue Note | 499187-2
Recess
George Adams-James Blood Ulmer Quartet | Jazzbühne Berlin '85 | Repertoire Records | REPCD 4912-CC
Recife & O Amor Que Move O Sol E Outras Estrelas
McCoy Tyner Quintet | Blue Bossa | LRC Records | CDC 9033(874377)
Recipe For Love
Lucie Arnaz And Her Orchestra | Just In Time | Concord | CCD 4573
Recitative
Chinese Compass | Chinese Compass | dacapo | DCCD 9443
Recitativo
Slim Gaillard-Bam Brown | Opera In Vout | Verve | 2304554 IMS
Recitativo E Finale(Of Much Scat)-
Bessie Smith With Louis Armstrong And Fred Longshaw | Louis Armstrong And The Blues Singers 1924-1930 | Affinity | AFS 1018(6)
Reckless Blues
Chris Barber's Jazz Band | The Best Of Dixieland-Live in 1954/55 | London | 820878-2
Chris Barber-40 Years Jubilee(1954-1956) | Timeless | CD TTD 586
Reckon I'm In Love
Vince Benedetti Quartet | The Dwellers On The High Plateau | EGO | 4005
Recollection
Paul Bley Duo | Sonor | Soul Note | SN 1085
Recollections
Coleman Hawkins Quartet | Bean And The Boys | Prestige | PCD 24124-2
Reconciliacion
Andrew Hill Quartet | Judgment! | Blue Note | 870079-6
Reconfigurations(part 1-3)
T-Bone Walker And His Band | Good Feelin' | Verve | 519723-2
Reconversion Blues
Dinah Washington With The Cootie Williams Orchestra | A Slick Chick(On The Mellow Side)-The Rhythm&Blues Years | EmArCy | 814184-1 IMS
Record Hop
Art Farmer Quartet | Soul Eyes | Enja | ENJ-7047 2
Recorda-Me
Bobby Hutcherson Quartet | Color Schemes | Landmark | LCD 1508-2
Joe Henderson Quintet | The Blue Note Years-The Best Of Joe Henderson | Blue Note | 795627-2
Joe Henderson:The Milestone Years | Milestone | 8MCD 4413-2
Joe Henderson-The Blue Note Years | Blue Note | 789287-2
The Atlantic String Trio | First Meeting | Factory Outlet Records | FOR 2501-1 CD
First Meeting | Factory Outlet Records | 2001-1 CD
Recovered Residence
Barbara Dennerlein Quartet | Orgelspiele | Böhm Records | 65145 IMS
Recto Verso
Billy Pierce Trio | Equilateral | Sunnyside | SSC 1037 D
Recuerdo
Chuck Mangione Quintet | Jazz Brother | Milestone | M 47042
Recycle
Das Saxophonorchester Frankfurt | Das Saxophonorchester Frankfurt-Live | FMP | SAJ 40
Recycling
Jacques Pirotton Quartet | Artline | B.Sharp Records | CDS 070
Red
Nicolas Simion Group | Black Sea | Tutu Records | 888134-2*
Urs Leimgruber-Adelhard Roidinger-Fritz Hauser | Lines | Hat Art | CD 6149
Red-
Marco Ballanti Trio | Ballanti's Organic Unity | Philology | W 126.2
Red And Black
Ralph Towner Quartet | Solstice | ECM | 1060(825458-2)
John Abercrombie Trio | Timeless | ECM | 1047(829114-2)
Red And Orange
Steve White Quartet | Jazz In Hollywood:Steve White | Original Jazz Classics | OJCCD 1891-2(Nocturne unreleased)
Red Bank Shuffle
Billy Cobham Group | Spectrum | Atlantic | 7567-81428-2
Red Baron
The Best Of Billy Cobham | Atlantic | 7567-81558-2
Jazz Bomberos | Naranja | Green House Music | CD 1003(Maxi)
Billy Cobham Group | Shabazz | Atlantic | ATL 50147
Red Beans
Humphrey Lyttelton-Acker Bilk Band | Humph & Acker-Together For The Very First Time! | Calligraph | CLGCD 027
Red Black And Blue
Charles Earland Trio | Mama Roots | Muse | MR 5156
Red Black And Green
Robin Eubanks/Steve Turre Group | Dedication | JMT Edition | 834433-2
Red Cadillac
Jimmy McGriff Sextet | McGriff's House Party | Milestone | MCD 9300-2
Red Cadillac Boogaloo
Louis Armstrong With Luis Russell And His Orchestra | Louis Armstrong Vol.7-Satchmo's Discoveries | MCA | 1326
Red Car
Art Pepper Quartet | Art Pepper:The Complete Galaxy Recordings | Galaxy | 16GCD 1016-2
David Murray Quartet | Recording NYC 1986 | DIW | DIW 8009
Red City Smoke
Cody Moffett Septet | Evidence | Telarc Digital | CD 83343
Red Clay
Freddie Hubbard Quintet | Red Clay | CTI | 6001
Freddie Hubbard Sextet | Keystone Bop Vol.2:Friday/Saturday | Prestige | PCD 24163-2
The Best Of Freddie Hubbard | Pablo | 2405415-2
Red Cross
Art Farmer Quartet | A Work Of Art | Concord | CJ 179
Dexter Gordon Quartet | Stable Mable | Steeplechase | SCS 1040
Red Door
The New Jazztet | Nostalgia | Baystate | BVCJ 2010(889376)
Red Dwarf
Michel Bisceglia Trio | About Stories | RCA | 2153080-2
Red Eye
Hal Galper Quartet | Now Hear This | Enja | ENJ-2090 2
Red Haired Boogie
Henry Kaiser Group | Marrying For Money | Minor Music | 1010
Red Horn
Niels Landgren Funk Unit | Live In Stockholm | ACT | 9223-2
Nils Landgren First Unit And Guests | Nils Landgren-The First Unit | ACT | 9292-2
Duke Ellington And His Cotton Club Orchestra | The Essential Duke Ellington 29.12.1927 to 1.10.1928 | VJM | VLP 73 IMS
Red Hot Pepper
Jelly Roll Morton And His Orchestra | The Jelly Roll Morton Centennial-His Complete Victor Recordings | Bluebird | ND 82361
The Complete Jelly Roll Morton-Vol.3/4 | RCA | NL 89769(2) DP
Red Is Blue
Sotto In Su | Vanitas | Poise | Poise 04
Red Is My Blood
Herman Chittison | JazzIn Paris:Harlem Piano In Montmartre | EmArCy | 018447-2
Red Jill Rag
Jerry Coker Orchestra | Modern Music From Indiana University | Fantasy | 0902116(F 3214)
Red Label
Robben Ford Band | Tiger Walk | Blue Thumb | BTR 70122
Red Neon, Go Or Give
Louis Armstrong And His Orchestra | Louis Armstrong Vol.2 | Ambassador | CLA 1902
Red Nose
Conrad Herwig Quintet | With Every Breath | Ken Music | 660.56.008
Red On Maroon
Paquito D'Rivera Sextet | Live At Keystone Korner | CBS | FC 38899
Red Pepper Blues
Lu Watters' Yerba Buena Jazz Band | Lu Watters' Yerba Buena Jazz Band At Hambone Kelly's 1949-50 | Merry Makers Record | MMRC-CD-10
Red Planet
Marian McPartland Trio feat. Chris Potter | In My Life | Concord | CCD 4561
Red Points
Lionel Hampton All Stars | Jazz In Paris:Lionel Hampton And His French New Sound Vol.2 | EmArCy | 549406-2 PMS
Red Ribbon
Rex Stewart Sextet | Trumpet Jive! | Prestige | PCD 24119-2(P 7812/SV 2006)
Red River
Sonny Terry & Woody Guthrie | Blind Sonny Terry & Woody Guthrie | Ember | CW 136
Red River Blues
Peruna Jazzmen | Come On And Stomp, Stomp, Stomp | Stomp Off Records | CD 1003
Red River Revel
Gary Peacock-Bill Frisell | Just So Happens | Postcards | POST 1005
Red Rock Rain
Red Rodney | One Night In Washington | Elektra | MUS K 52359
Red Roof
Chubby 'Hip Shakin" Newsom And Her Hip Shakers | The Original Hip Shakin' Mama | Official | 6020
Red Roses For A Blue Lady
Valery Mysovsky Trio | Jazz From The USSR | Mobile Fidelity | MFCD 890
Red Sails
Red Norvo Sextet | Muisc To Listen To Red Norvo By | Original Jazz Classics | OJC 155(C 7534)
Red Sails In The Sunset-
Bill Evans Quintet | Summertime | Jazz City | 660.53.018
Red Sky
David Torn/Mick Karn/Terry Bozzio | Polytown | CMP Records | CMP CD 1008
Red Spaces In A Blue Field(part 1)
James Emery Septet | Spectral Domains | Enja | ENJ-9344 2
Red Spaces In A Blue Field(part 2)
Maurice Magnoni Orchestra | New York Suite | L+R Records | CDLR 45077
Red Stripe
Dave Valentine Group | Red Sun | GRP | GRP 96992
Red Temple
European Tuba Quartet | Low And Behold | Jazz Haus Musik | JHM 0110 CD
Red Thread
David Fathead Newman Quintet | Chillin' | HighNote Records | HCD 7036
Red Top
Joey DeFrancesco Group | Where Were You? | CBS | CK 45443
Kevin Mahogany With Orchestra | Songs And Moments | Enja | ENJ-8072 2
King Pleasure And His Band | Annie Ross & King Pleasure Sings | Original Jazz Classics | OJC 217(P 7128)
Lionel Hampton And His Orchestra | Big Band Bounce & Boogie-Lionel Hampton:Leapin' With Lionel | Affinity | AFS 1000
Montreux Summit | Montreux Summit Vol.2 | CBS | CBS 88286
Oscar Peterson-Milt Jackson Quartet | Reunion Blues | MPS | 817490-1
Richie Cole Quintet | Alive! | Muse | MR 5270
Roots | Salutes The Saxophone | IN+OUT Records | 7016-2
Sonny Stitt Quartet | My Buddy-Sonny Stitt Plays For Gene Ammons | Muse | MR 5091
Woody Herman And His Orchestra | The Radio Years: Woody Herman And His First Herd 1944 | Hindsight | HSR 134
Count Basie Quartet | Big Band Bounce & Boogie-Count Basie:Swingin' At The Daisy Chain | Affinity | AFS 1019
Red Wig
Red Rodney Quintet | Prestige First Sessions, Vol.3 | Prestige | PCD 24116-2
Red Wind
Chris Barber-Barry Martin Band | Collaboration | GHB Records | BCD 40
Red Wing
George Lewis Quartet | Jazz In The Classic New Orleans Tradition | Original Jazz Classics | OJCCD 1736-2(RLP 12-207)
Red,Crack And Blue
Cassandra Wilson Group | After The Beginning Again | JMT Edition | 514001-2
Redbone
Blue Light 'Til Dawn | Blue Note | 781357-2
Sonny Red (Kyner) Quintet | Two Altos | Savoy | SV 0161(MG 6069)
Redemption
Stan Getz With The Michel Legrand Orchestra | Compact Jazz: Michel Legrand | Philips | 840944-2
ReDial
Johannes Rediske Quintet | Jumpin' At The Badewanne | Bear Family Records | BCD 16172 AH
Re-Disc Boogie
Re-Disc Bounce | Bear Family Records | BCD 16119 AH
Re-Disc Bounce
Jumpin' At The Badewanne | Bear Family Records | BCD 16172 AH
Re-Disc Bounce(im Trott)
Georg Ruby-Wollie Kaiser | Ruby Domesticus Vugaris | Jazz Haus Musik | JHM 26
Redmm Saat
Stephane Grappelli Trio | Unique Piano Session | Jazz Anthology | JA 5216
Red's Good Groove
Hod O'Brien Trio | Have Piano...Will Swing! | Fresh Sound Records | FSR-CD 5030
Red's Mood
Louisiana Red & His Chicago Blues Friends | American Folk Blues Festival Live '83 | L+R Records | LR 42063
Redwood City
Jonas Hellborg | Elegant Punk | Day Eight Music | DEMCD 004
Reed Hornets
Tom Scott Groups | Reed My Lips | GRP | GRP 97592
Reed Rapture
Stan Kenton And His Orchestra | The Formative Years(1941-1942) | Creative World | ST 1061
Reeds And Deeds
Roland Kirk Sextet | Verve Jazz Masters 27:Roland Kirk | Verve | 522062-2
Reef And Kneebus
Bill Evans Quintet | Living In The Crest Of A Wave | Elektra | MUS 96.0349-1
Reefer
Mills Blue Rhythm Band | Rhythm Spasm | Hep | CD 1015
Reelin' And Rockin'
Johnny Hodges Orchestra | The Soul Of Ben Webster | Verve | 527475-2
Reelin' And Rockin'(alt.take)
Charles Kynard Quintet | Reelin' With The Feelin' | Original Jazz Classics | OJC 333(P 7688)
Reelin' With The Feelin'
Roland Kirk With The Stan Tracy Trio | Gifts And Messages | Ronnie Scott's Jazz House | JHAS 606
Re-Enter
Art Farmer Quartet | Art Farmer In Europe | Enja | 9113-2
Reet Petite And Gone
Louis Jordan And His Tympany Five | Louis Jordan Greatest Hits-Vol.2 | MCA | 1337
Reets And I
Bud Powell Trio | Bud Powell:The Complete Blue Note And Roost Recordings | Blue Note | 830083-2
Reets And I(alt.take 1)
The Amazing Bud Powell Vol.2 | Blue Note | 532137-2
Reets And I(alt.take 2)
Bud Powell:The Complete Blue Note And Roost Recordings | Blue Note | 830083-2
Reeves
Marco Volpe Band | Exacting Work | SPLASC(H) Records | H 193
Reflecting On Jimmy
Dave Liebman Quartet | The Elements:Water | Arkadia Jazz | 71043
Reflection
Low Flying Aircraft | Low Flying Aircraft | Line Records | COCD 9.00426 O
Ray Bryant Trio | All Mine All Yours | EmArCy | 510423-2 PMS
Sam Rivers | Portrait Sam Rivers Live | FMP | CD 82
Thelonious Monk Trio | Thelonious Monk | Original Jazz Classics | OJC20 010-2(P 7027)
Universal-International Orchestra | Touch Of Evil | Fresh Sound Records | FSR 610(Challenge CHL 602)
Reflections
Chris Potter Quintet | Presenting Chriss Potter | Criss Cross | Criss 1067
Dave Liebman Trio | Monk's Mood | Double Time Records | DTRCD-154
Frank Morgan All Stars | Reflections | Contemporary | CCD 14052-2
Harold Land Quintet | Take Aim | Blue Note | LT 1057 (GXK 8174)
JazzHorchEster | ...Zudem Wird Auch Jazz Komponiert | Elite Special | 73412
Joe Sullivan | The Piano Artistry Of Joe Sullivan | Jazz Unlimited | JUCD 2051
Ran Blake | Epistrophy | Soul Note | 121177-2
Sonny Rollins Quartet | Sonny Rollins:The Blue Note Recordings | Blue Note | 821371-2
Thelonious Monk:The Complete Blue Note Recordings | Blue Note | 830363-2
Sonny Rollins Quartet feat.Thelonious Monk | Ballads | Blue Note | 537562-2
Sonny Rollins Quintet | Sonny Rollins | Blue Note | 84508
Stan Kenton And His Innovations Orchestra | The Innovations In Modern Music Orchestra | Laserlight | 15770
Steve Lacy Sextet | We See(Thelonious Monk Songbook) | Hat Art | CD 6127
Thelonious Monk | Pure Monk | Milestone | M 47004
Alone In San Francisco | Original Jazz Classics | OJC 231(RLP 1158)
Thelonious Monk-The Complete Riverside Recordings | Riverside | 15 RCD 022-2
Thelonious Monk And His Orchestra | Who's Afraid Of The Big Band Monk? | CBS | CBS 88034
Tommy Flanagan Trio | Thelonica | Enja | ENJ-4052 2
Tommy Smith Sextet | Paris | Blue Note | 780612-2
Warren Bernhardt Quintet | Reflections | dmp Digital Music Productions | CD 489
Reflections-
Loren Stillman Quartet | Cosmos | Soul Note | 121310-2
Reflections In A Cracked Mirror
Harold Danko | Ink And Water | Sunnyside | SSC 1008(952101)
Reflections In D
Bobo Stenson Trio | Reflections | ECM | 1516(523160-2)
Duke Ellington And His Orchestra | Welcome To Jazz: Duke Ellington | Koch Records | 321 943 D1
Native Colours | One World | Concord | CCD 4646
Reflections In The Park
Paul Plimley-Lisle Ellis | Both Sides Of The Same Mirror | Nine Winds Records | NWCD 0135
Reflections Of South Aftica
Dave Brubeck Quartet | Reflections | Concord | CCD 4299
Reflet
David Chevallier Quintet | Migration | Adda | 590094
Reflexe:
Markus Stockhausen Orchestra | Sol Mestizo:Markus Stockhausen Plays The Music Of Enrique Diaz | ACT | 9222-2
Reflexion
Maximilian Geller Quartet feat. Melanie Bong | Smile | Edition Collage | EC 461-2
Carlos Patato Valdes Group | Master Pieces | Messidor | 15827 CD
Refractions
Bennie Wallace With The Blues Ensemble Of Biloxi | Sweeping Through The City | Enja | 4078 (807526)
Refsetufsa(Wild Child)

Andrew Hill Sextet | Point Of Departure | Blue Note | 499007-2
Refuge
Joe Henderson-The Blue Note Years | Blue Note | 789287-2
Refugees
Glenn Ferris Trio | Refugees | Enja | 9108-2
Refugees At The Rich Man's Gate
Thomas Hass Group | A Honeymoon Too Soon | Stunt Records | STUCD 19601
Refugium
The Jeff Lorber Fusion | Fusion | Inner City | IC 1026 IMS
Regard De Mounette
Dave Pike Set | Dave Pike Set:Masterpieces | MPS | 531848-2
Regards From Freddie Horowitz
Dave Pike Sextet | On A Gentle Note | Muse | MR 5168
Regards To Gershwin's Honeyman
Steve Coleman And Five Elements | Genesis & The Opening Of The Way | RCA | 2152934-2
Regeneration
Chico Freeman-Cecil McBee | Chico | India Navigation | IN 1031 CD
Regenwald
Frank Sackenheim Quartet | The Music Of Chance | Jazz 4 Ever Records:Jazz Network | J4E 4753
Reger
Barbara Thompson's Paraphernalia | Thompson's Tangos | Intuition Records | INT 3290-2
Regga Ragga
Arturo Sandoval Sextet | Just Music | Ronnie Scott's Jazz House | JHCD 008
Reggae Blues
Pep O'Callaghan Grup | Tot Just | Fresh Sound Records | FSNT 017 CD
Reggae Boats
String Thing | String Thing:Turtifix | MicNic Records | MN 4
Reggae For Donald
Future Shock | It's Great | BVHAAST | 067(807058)
Regginella
Jonas Hellborg With Glen Velez | Ars Moriende | Day Eight Music | DEMCD 034
Regime
Michel Petrucciani Trio | Pianism | Blue Note | 746295-2
Regina
Natascha Majevskaja | Orgel Ist Mehr...In Bamberg Vol.2 | Orgel ist mehr! | OIM/BA/1999-2 CD
Regina Angelorum(Mozart)
Tony Rémy Groups | Boof! | GRP | GRP 97362
Registration O
Ronnie Earl & The Broadcasters | Blues And Forgiveness | Crosscut | CCD 11042
Regret
Randy Sandke Quintet | Get Happy | Concord | CCD 4598
Regrets
Peter Kowald/Michihiro Sato | Duos: Japan | FMP | 1280
Rehcabnettul-
Ella Fitzgerald With The Duke Ellington Orchestra | The Complete Ella Fitzgerald Song Books of Harold Arlen, Irving Berlin, Duke Ellington, George & Ira Gershwin, Jerome Kern, Johnny Mercer, Cole Porter And Rogers & Hart | Verve | 519832-2
Reich Und Berühmt
David S. Ware Quartet | Great Bliss Vol.2 | Silkheart | SHCD 128
Reime Vor Pisin
John McLaughlin And Mahavishnu | Adventures In Radioland | Verve | 519397-2
Reincarnation
Paul Mares And His Friars Society Orchestra | Chicago 1935 | Gannet | CJR 1001
Re-Incarnation Of A Love Bird
Charles Mingus Group | Mysterious Blues | Candid | CCD 79042
Charles Mingus Jazz Workshop | The Clown | Atlantic | 790142-2
Charles Mingus Quintet | Charles Mingus-Passion Of A Man:The Complete Atlantic Recordings 1956-1961 | Atlantic | 8122-72871-2
The Very Best Of Charles Mingus | Rhino | 8122-79988-2
Charles Mingus -Passions Of A Man | Atlantic | ATL 60143
Lee Konitz-Gil Evans | Hereos | Verve | 511621-2 PMS
Mingus Dynasty | Reincarnation | Soul Note | 121042-2
Reinforzamento..The Healing Force
Bireli Lagrene Group | Down In Town | Island | 205863-320
Reinsburgstrasse
Steve Swallow Quintet | Always Pack Your Uniform On Top | Watt | XtraWatt/10(543506-2)
Reinventing The Wheel
Irene Schweizer-Rüdiger Carl Duo | Die V-Mann Suite | FMP | 0860
Reisefieber
Michael Sell Contemporary Music Ensemble | Innovationen Für 10 Instrumente | Misp Records | MISP 506
Rejoice
Billy Taylor Trio | You Tempt Me | Taylor Made Records | T 1004
Michael Bocian | Premonition:Solo Debut For Nylon String Guitar | Enja | 9118-2
Rejoicing
Larry Schneider Quartet | Ornettology | Steeplechase | SCCD 31461
Pat Metheny Trio | Rejoicing | ECM | 1271(817795-2)
Paul Bley Quartet | Rejoicing | Steeplechase | SCCD 31274
Rejuvenation
Lonnie Liston Smith & His Cosmic Echoes | Astral Travelling | RCA | 2663878-2
Rejuvenation(alt.take)
Dewey Redman Trio | Tarik | Affinity | AFF 42
Relation
Houston Boines Band | Mississippi Blues | Anthology of the Blues | AB 5609
Relation To Light Colour And Feeling
Norbert Dömling | Internationales Guitarren Festival '99 | ALISO Records | AL 1038
Relationes
Steve Lacy-Evan Parker | Chirps | FMP | CD 29
Relationshipping With Controlled Probalities
Cowws Quintet | Grooves 'N' Loops | FMP | CD 59
Relative Lightness
Andrew Hill | Live At Montreux | Freedom | FCD 741023
Relativo
Arturo Sandoval And His Cuban Jazz Masters | Tumbaito | Inak | 2003
Relax
Hans Koller Trio | Relax With My Horns | MPS | 9813445
Philippe Caillat Special Project | Melodic Travel | Laika Records | LK 689-012
Melodic Travel | Laika Records | LK 689-012
Alix Combelle Et Son Orchestre | Buck Clayton:Buck Special | Vogue | 2111513-2
Relax Max
Jazz Pistols | 3 On The Floor | Lipstick Records | LIP 8959-2
Relaxed Focus
Bill Perkins Quartet | Peaceful Moments | Fresh Sound Records | FSR 115(835316)
Relaxin' At Clifford's
Randy Sandke Sextet | The Sandke Brothers | Stash Records | ST-CD 575(875901)
Relaxin' At The Camarillo
Charlie Parker All Stars | Charlie Parker Anthology | Accord | 500122
Charlie Parker's New Stars | Jazz Gallery:Charlie Parker Vol.1 | RCA | 2114174-2
Geoff Keezer Trio | Trio | Sackville | SKCD2-2039
Joe Henderson Quartet | Five Birds And A Monk | Galaxy | GXY 5134
Joe Pass Quartet | Joe Pass:Guitar Virtuoso | Pablo | 4 PACD 4423-2
Apassionato | Pablo | 2310946-2
John Campbell Trio | After Hours | Contemporary | CCD 14053-2
Tommy Flanagan Trio | Eclypso | Enja | 2088-2
Relaxin' At The Grand Balcon
Allan Vaché Big Four | Revisited! | Nagel-Heyer | CD 044
Relaxin' At The Touro
Earl Hines-Muggsy Spanier All Stars | The Essential Earl Hine With Guest Star Muggsy Spanier | Ember | CJS 851
Muggsy Spanier And His Ragtime Band | Jazz Classics In Digital Stereo: Muggsy Spanier 1931 & 1939 | CDS Records Ltd. | REB 687
Relaxin' At The Touro (Theme)
Muggsy Spanier And His Dixieland All Stars | Muggsy Spanier At Club Hangover 1953/54 | Storyville | STCD 6033
At Club Hangover-Vol. 2 | Storyville | SLP 249
Relaxin' Rain
Frederic Rabold Inspiration Orchestra | Relaxing Walk | Fusion | 8019
Relaxin' With Lee
Charlie Parker Quintet | Charlie Parker:Bird's Best Bop On Verve | Verve | 527452-2
Hank Jones Trio | 'Bop Redux | Muse | MCD 5444
Relaxin' With Lee(4 incompl.takes)
Charlie Parker And His Orchestra | Bird On Verve-Vol.3:Charlie Parker With Strings | Verve | 817444-1 IMS
Relaxin' With Lee(alt.take)
Bird: The Complete Charlie Parker On Verve | Verve | 837141-2
Relaxin' With Lee(take 1-6)
Nicolas Simion Quartet feat. Tomasz Stanko | Dinner For Don Carlos | Tutu Records | 888146-2*
Relaxin' With Lonnie
Hank Garland Group | Jazz Winds From New Directions | CBS | 492532-2
Relay
Diedre Murray-Fred Hopkins Quartet | Stringology | Black Saint | 120143-2
Reliable Source
Herbert Joos-Mathias Ruegg Duo | Mel-An-Cho | Pläne | 88261 Digital
Religion
Wayne Peet's Doppler Funk | Plasto! | Nine Winds Records | NW 0126
Religious Ceremony
Carla Bley Big Band | The Carla Bley Big Band Goes To Church | Watt | 27(533682-2)
Religious Experience-
Daniel Flors Group | When Least Expected | Fresh Sound Records | FSNT 080 CD
Relocco's Blues
Jim Snidero Quartet | Storm Rising | Ken Music | 660.56.006
Rem Blues
Ellington/Mingus/Roach Trio | Money Jungle | Blue Note | 538227-2
Rem Blues(alt.take)
Soft Head | Soft Head-Rogue Element | Ogun | OGCD 013
Remanence
Vladimir Estragon | Three Quarks For Muster Mark | TipToe | TIP-888803 2
Remedios The Beauty
Willem Breuker Kollektief | Willem Breuker Kollektief Live In Berlin | FMP | SAJ 06
Remember
Anita O'Day With The Barney Kessel Sextet | Trav'lin Light | Verve | 2304584 IMS
Benny Goodman And His Orchestra | The Birth Of Swing | Bluebird | ND 90601(3)
Billie Holiday And Her Orchestra | Billie Holiday: The First Verve Sessions | Verve | 2610027
Bobby Hutcherson Quintet | Color Schemes | Landmark | LCD 1508-2
Conrad Gozzo With Strings | GOZ The Great | Fresh Sound Records | LPM 1124(RCA)
George Adams-Don Pullen Quartet | Don't Loose Control | Soul Note | 121004-2
Gil Evans And Ten | Gil Evans And Ten | Prestige | PRSA 7120-6
Greenfish | Perfume Light... | TipToe | TIP-888831 2
Hank Mobley Quartet | Soul Station | Blue Note | 495343-2
Blue Berlin | Blue Note | 799095-2
Joe Puma Trio | Shining Hour | Reservoir | RSR 102
Joshua Breakstone Quartet | Remembering Grant Green | Paddle Wheel | KICJ 169
Larry Clinton And His Orchestra | The Uncollected: Larry Clinton | Hindsight | HSR 109
Lennie Tristano Quintet | Live At Birdland 1949 | Jazz Records | JR-1 CD
Mal Waldron-Jeanne Lee-Toru Tenda | Travellin' In Soul-Time | BVHAAST | CD 9701
Mike Richmond Quartet | Blue In Green | Steeplechase | SCCD 31296
Montreal Jubilation Gospel Choir | Joy To The World | Blues Beacon | BLU-1018 2
Sarah Vaughan And Billy Eckstine With Hal Mooney And His Orchestra | The Irving Berlin Songbook | EmArCy | 822526-1 IMS
Sonic Fiction | Changing With The Times | Naxos Jazz | 86034-2
Thelonious Monk | Pure Monk | Milestone | M 47004
Thelonious Monk-The Complete Riverside Recordings | Riverside | 15 RCD 022-2
Remember Hymn
Jimmy McHugh's Bostonians | Ben Pollack Vol.1 | Jazz Oracle | BDW 8015
Remember Me
Jenny Evans And Her Quintet | Nuages | ESM Records | ESM 9308
Muddy Waters Blues Band | Mud In Your Ear | Muse | MCD 6004
Woody Herman And His Orchestra | The Formative Years Of 'The Band That PLays The Blues' | Circle | CCD-95
Remember Me-
Five Blind Boys Of Mississippi | My Desire/There's A God Somewhere | Mobile Fidelity | MFCD 769
Remember Radio Hanoi
Charles Mingus Quintet | Keystone Korner | Jazz Door | JD 1219
Remember Rockefeller At Attica
Steve Lacy-Eric Watson | Spirit Of Mingus | Freelance | FRL-CD 016
Remember The Time
Lester Bowie's Brass Fantasy | The Fire This Time | IN+OUT Records | 7019-2
James Spaulding Sextet | Gotstabe A Better Way | Muse | MCD 5413
Remember To Remember
Hot Club The Zigan | Witchcraft | Jazz Pure Collection | AU 31605 CD
Remember When
Steve LaSpina Quintet | Remember When | Steeplechase | SCCD 31540
Robin Eubanks Group | Karma | JMT Edition | 834446-2
Remember(take 1)
Thomas Stiffling Group | Stories | Jazz 4 Ever Records:Jazz Network | J4E 4756
Remember(take 2)
Rabih Abou-Khalil Group | Bukra | Enja | ENJ-9372 2
Remember...The Desert
Emborg-Larsen Group | Face The Music | Stunt Records | STUCD 19805
Remembering
Peter Fessler Group | Eastside Moments | Minor Music | 801078
Peter Weniger Quartet | Tiptap | Mons Records | MR 874768
Remembering Machghara
David Murray Quartet | Body And Soul | Black Saint | 120155-2
Remembering The Start Of A Never Ending Story
Philip Aaberg | High Plains | Windham Hill | WD 1037
Remembering Tomorrow
Project G-7 | Tribute To Wes Montgomery, Vol.1 | Paddle Wheel | KICJ 112
Remembrance
Flemming Agerskov Quintet | Face To Face | dacapo | DCCD 9445
George Winston | Linus & Lucy-The Music Of Vince Guaraldi | Windham Hill | 34 11187-2
Gunther Schuller With The WDR Radio Orchestra & Rememberance Band | Witchi Tia To, The Music Of Jim Pepper | Tutu Records | 888204-2*
Harper Brothers | Tempo Jazz Edition Vol.2-Playin' Now | Polydor | 847903-2
Kostas Konstantinou-Vassilis Tsabropoulos | Concentric Cycles | Nabel Records:Jazz Network | CD 4698
Steve Slagle Quartet | The Steve Slagle Quartet | Steeplechase | SCCD 31323
Remembrance-
Jim Pepper Flying Eagle | Live At New Morning,Paris | Tutu Records | 888194-2*
Mike Santiago/Entity | White Trees | Chiaroscuro | CR 193
Remind Me
June Christy With The Pete Rugolo Orchestra | The Song Is June | Capitol | 855455-2
Margaret Whiting With Russel Garcia And His Orchestra | Margaret Whiting Sings The Jerome Kern Song Book | Verve | 559553-2
Mike Wofford Trio | Plays Jerome Kern, Vol. 1 | Discovery | DS 808 IMS
Reminiscence
Gerry Mulligan/Astor Piazolla Group | Gerry Mulligan/Astor Piazolla 1974 | Accord | 556642
Karl Berger-Paul Shigihara | Karl Berger + Paul Shigihara | L+R Records | CDLR 45045
Reminiscence Of A Soul
Szakcsi Trio | Straight Ahead | GRP | GRP 97582
Reminiscing
Dizzy Gillespie Octet | The Greatest Trumpet Of Them All | Verve | 2304382 IMS
Reminiscing At Blue Note
Charlie Parker With Unkn.Afro-Cuban Band | Afro-Cubop | Spotlite | SPJ 138 (807749)
Remoteness
David Torn/Geoffrey Gordon | Best Laid Plans | ECM | 1284
Removable Tongue
David Murray Group | The Tip | DIW | DIW 891 CD
Renaissance
Jean-Luc Ponty Quintet | The Very Best Of Jean-Luc Ponty | Rhino | 8122-79862-2
Aurora | Atlantic | SD 19158
Renaissance Blues
Percfect Trouble | Perfect Trouble | Moers Music | 02070 CD
Renaissance Man
Narada Burton Greene | European Heritage | Circle Records | RK 18-121178/18 IMS
Renard & Les Déserteurs
Azymuth feat. Jürgen Seefelder | Volta á Turma | West Wind Latina | 2206 CD
Renascimiento
Stanley Clarke-Al DiMeola-Jean Luc Ponty | The Rite Of Strings | Gai Saber | 834167-2
Rendezvous
Organ Jazztrio & Martin Weiss | Hommage | Edition Collage | EC 492-2
Paul McCandless Group | Premonition | Windham Hill | 34 10140-2
Rene
Philip Catherine Quartet | Live | Dreyfus Jazz Line | FDM 36587-2
Rene Thomas
Groove Holmes Septet | Hot Tat | Muse | MCD 5395
Reneval
Monty Alexander Quartet | Friday Night | Limetree | MCD 0022
Reng Ding Dang Dong
Wes Montgomery Quintet | Far Wes | Pacific Jazz | 794475-2
Renita's Bounce
Chris Cheek Quintet | Vine | Fresh Sound Records | FSNT 086 CD
Reno
Wayne Horvitz-Butch Morris-Robert Previte | Nine Below Zero | Sound Aspects | sas CD 014
Rent Party
Hal Singer Quintet | Rent Party | Savoy | SV 0258(SJL 1147)
Repay In Kind
Charles Gayle Trio | Repent | Knitting Factory Works | KFWCD 122
Repepetititive
Jerry Tilitz Sextet | Trombone Tangents | Limetree | MLP 0025
Repetition
Charlie Parker With Strings | Charlie Parker With Strings:The Master Takes | Verve | 523984-2
Charlie Parker The Immortal Sessions Vol.2:1949-1953 | SAGA Jazz Classics | EC 3319-2
Charlie Parker With The Neal Hefti Orchestra | Bird: The Complete Charlie Parker On Verve | Verve | 837141-2
Charlie Parker:The Best Of The Verve Years | Verve | 527815-2
Clifford Jordan Quartet | Repetition | Soul Note | 121084-2
Lou Bennett Trio | Jazz In Paris | EmArCy | 548790-2
Phil Woods Quartet | A Tribute To Charlie Parker Vol.2 | Storyville | 4960493
At The Vanguard | Antilles | AN 1013(802736)
Steve Kuhn Trio | Porgy | Jazz City | 660.53.012
Wes Montgomery Quartet | Wes Montgomery-The Complete Riverside Recordings | Riverside | 12 RCD 4408-2
Wes Montgomery Quintet | Bird Lives! | Milestone | MCD 9166-2
John Goldsby Sextet | Viewpoint | Nagel-Heyer | CD 2014
Replaceable You
Eric Kloss-Barry Miles Duo | Together | Muse | MR 5112
Reponse
Louis Sclavis Sextet | Les Violences De Rameau | ECM | 1588(533128-2)
Reponses A Gavotte
Jeff Beal With The Metropole Orchestra | Concerto For Orchestra | Koch Jazz | 3-6904-2
Reprise
Medeski Martin & Wood | Univisible | Blue Note | 535870-2
Oregon | Out Of The Woods | Elektra | ELK K 52101
Woody Herman And His Orchestra With Duke Ellington And His Orchestra | The V Disc Years Vol.1&2 | Hep | CD 2/3435
Reprise 4755
Hanschel-Hübsch-Schipper | Planet Blow Chill | Jazz Haus Musik | JHM 0087 CD
Reprise D.o.t.F.P.
Wayne Horvitz Group | This New Generation | Nonesuch | 7559-60759-2
Reprise Stomp(Presto)-
Dino Saluzzi Trio | Responsorium | ECM | 1816(017069-2)
Reprise:Los Hijos De Fierro
Andreas Willers Group | Tin Drum Stories(inspired by the novel 'Die Blechtrommel' by Günter Grass) | Between The Lines | btl 009(Efa 10179-2)
Reprise:Shelter
Harold Land/Blue Mitchell Quintet | Mapenzi | Concord | CCD 4044
Republic Of..(II)
Jo Ambros Group | Wanderlust | dml-records | CD 016
Republic Of...
Heinz | Bavarian Back Beat | Jazz Haus Musik | JHM 41 CD
Re-Pyrrect
Wolfgang Schlüter-Christoph Spendel Duo | Dualism | MPS | 68285
Requiem
Charles Lloyd Quartet | Notes From Big Sur | ECM | 1465(511999-2)
Charlie Haden Quartet West With Strings | Now Is The Hour | Verve | 527827-2
Donald Byrd Quintet | Royal Flush | Blue Note | 869476-7
Gary Peacock Quartet | Guamba | ECM | 1352
Giovanni Mirabassi Trio | Architectures | Sketch | SKE 333010
Lennie Tristano Trio | That's Jazz Vol.15: Lennie Tristano | Atlantic | ATL 50245
Mike Westbrook Concert Band | Marching Songs Vol.1&2 | Deram | 844853-2
Sylvain Luc-André Ceccarelli-Jean Marc Jafet | SUD | Dreyfus Jazz Line | FDM 36612-2
Thierry Lang Quintet | Nan | Blue Note | 498492-2
Requiem For A Rabbit
Tommy Tedesco Quartet | When Do We Start | Discovery | DS 789 IMS
Requiem For Flying Eagle
James Carter Group | Layin' In The Cut | Atlantic | 7567-83305-2

Requiem For Hartford Ave.
Tony Scott With The Bill Evans Trio | Dedications | Line Records | COCD 9.00803
Requiem Für Ein Phänomen
Barbara Thompson Group | Heavenly Bodies | VeraBra Records | CDVBR 2015-2
Requiem Pour Deux Pilotes
Stefano Battaglia | Baptism | SPLASC(H) Records | CD H 417-2
Requiem(Number 1)
Jack DeJohnette Sextet | The DeJohnette Complex | Original Jazz Classics | OJCCD 617-2
Requiem(Number 2)
Bob Mintzer Quartet | Bob Mintzer Hymn | Owl Records | 062 CD
Re-Re
Derek Bailey Group | Guitar Drums 'N' Bass | Avant | AVAN 060
Researching Has No Limits
Lennie Tristano Quartet | The Rarest Trio/Quartet Sessions 1946/47 | Raretone | 5008 FC
Residence
Ellery Eskelin Quintet | Ramifications | HatOLOGY | 551
Resignacion
Tango Five feat. Raul Jaurena | Obsecion | Satin Doll Productions | SDP 1027-1 CD
Brad Mehldau Trio | Art Of The Trio Vol.5:Progression | Warner | 9362-48005-2
Resignation
Frank Eberle Septet | Scarlet Sunrise | Satin Doll Productions | SDP 1041-1 CD
Jon Lloyd Quartet | By Confusion | Hat Art | CD 6198
Resistor
Bill Frisell Quintet | Rambler | ECM | 1287
Resitor
2nd Nature | What Comes Natural | Inak | 41232
Resolution
Natraj | Meet Me Anywhere | Dorian Discovery | DIS-80119
Resolution-
John Coltrane Quartet | A Love Supreme | Impulse(MCA) | 589945-2
A Love Supreme | Impulse(MCA) | 589945-2
John Coltrane:The Classic Quartet-Complete Impulse Studio Recordings | Impulse(MCA) | 951280-2
Massimo De Mattia Group | The Silent Drama | SPLASC(H) Records | CD H 442-2
Resolution(alt.take)-
John Coltrane Quartet | John Coltrane:The Classic Quartet-Complete Impulse Studio Recordings | Impulse(MCA) | 951280-2
A Love Supreme | Impulse(MCA) | 589945-2
Resolution(alt.take,breakdown)-
Sonny Simmons Quintet | Music From The Spheres | ESP Disk | ESP 1043-2
Resonance
Manfred Schoof Quintet | Light Lines | Japo | 60019(2360019)
Resonant Emotions
Luigi Archetti | Das Ohr | ATM Records | ATM 3804-AH
Respects
Gary Burton Quartet | Duster | RCA | 2125730-2
Responso Por La Muerte De Cruz
Albert Mangelsdorff | Albert Mangelsdorff-Solo | MPS | 68287
Rest Enough(Song To Mother)
Shankar/Garbarek/Hussain/Gurtu | Song For Everyone | ECM | 1286(823795-2)
Rest In Peace
Tommy Dorsey And His Orchestra | The Post-War Era | Bluebird | 63 66156-2
Restless
Herb Geller Quartet | You're Looking At Me | Fresh Sound Records | FSR-CD 5018
Maxine Sullivan With Orchestra | Maxine Sullivan 1944 to 1948 | Legend | CD 6004(875358)
Riccardo Ballerini Group | Blue Mesa | yvp music | CD 3048
Billie Holiday With Jimmy Rowles | Billie Holiday In Rehersal | Mobile Fidelity | MFCD 840
Restless Moon
Horace Tapscott | The Tapscott Sessions Vol.6 | Nimbus | NS 2036
Restons En La!
Hubert Laws And His Orchestra | In The Beginning | CTI | ZK 65127
Resulution
Dennis Farnon And His Orchestra | Caution! Men Swinging | Fresh Sound Records | LPM 1495(RCA)
Resurrection
Cassandra Wilson Group | Traveling Miles | Blue Note | 854123-2
Resurrection Blues(Tutu)
HR Big Band | Libertango:Homage An Astor Piazolla | hr music.de | hrmj 014-02 CD
Resurrection Del Angel
booMbooM meets Uli Beckerhoff | Resurection Lounge | Laika Records | 35101512
Resurrection Lounge
John Lindberg Quartet | Resurrection Of A Dormant Soul | Black Saint | 120172-2
Retirement Song
John Stevens Quartet | Re-Touch & Quartet | Konnex Records | KCD 5027
Re-Touch
Louis Sclavis Group | Dans La Nuit | ECM | 1805(589524-2)
Retour De Noce
Dominique Pifarély-Francois Couturier | Poros | ECM | 1647
Retours
George Gruntz Jazz Ensemble With The Basel Tambours & Pipers | Jazz Meets Europe:Flamenco Jazz/From Sticksland With Love | MPS | 531847-2
Retrato Em Branco E Preto
Alguimia | Alguimia:Standards | Fresh Sound Records | FSNT 049 CD
Retrato En Branco E Preto
Eddie Higgins Trio | Portrait In Black And White | Sunnyside | SSC 1072 D
Rich Perry Quartet | To Start Again | Steeplechase | SCCD 31331
Retribution
Nate Morgan Quintet | Retribution Reparation | Nimbus | NS 3479 (835528)
Retro'
Four Keys | Four Keys | MPS | 68241
Retrogradus Ex Machina
Paul Chambers Sextet | Paul Chambers-1st Bassman | Vee Jay Recordings | VJ 004
Retrospection
Tim Sund Quartet | About Time | Laika Records | LK 93-043
Retrospective
Saxophon And Organ | Above The Clouds | Naxos Jazz | 86041-2
Retsim B.
Chet Baker Quintet | Chet Baker Plays & Sings | West Wind | WW 2108
Return
Sandro Cerino Action Quartet | Che Fine Fanno I Personaggi Dei Sogni | SPLASC(H) Records | H 190
Return Match
L.A.4 | Live At Montreux | Concord | CJ 100
Return Of The Prodigal Son
Joe Lee Wilson With Orchestra | Without A Song | Inner City | IC 1064 IMS
Return Of The Zombie
Richie Cole-Art Pepper Quintet | Return To Alto Acres | Palo Alto | PA 8023
Return To Copenhagen
Airto Moreira And His Orchestra | The Best Of Airto | CTI | 63044
Return To Forever
Melissa Walker And Her Band | I Saw The Sky | Enja | ENJ-9409 2
Return To Me
Dave Liebman Quartet | Trio + One | Owl Records | 051 CD
Return To Paradise
Ramsey Lewis Trio/And Orchestra | The Best Of Ramsey Lewis | Chess | 515022
Oscar Castro-Neves Orchestra | Brazilian Scandals | JVC | ???
Return To Ulster(Variations On A Scottish Theme)
Mulgrew Miller Septet | Hand In Hand | Novus | 4163153-2
Returning-
Trilok Gurtu Group | Bad Habits Die Hard | CMP Records | CMP CD 80
Reuben, Reuben
Bill Smith Quartet | Folk Jazz U.S.A. | Original Jazz Classics | OJCCD 1956-2(S 7591)
Folk Jazz U.S.A. | Original Jazz Classics | OJCCD 1956-2(S 7591)
Reuben, Reuben(alt.take)
Stan Kenton And His Orchestra | Mellophonium Magic | Status | CD 103(882199)
Reuben's Blues
The Uncollected:Stan Kenton,Vol.6 | Hindsight | HSR 195
Reunion
Andrew Hill Trio | Strange Serenade | Soul Note | SN 1013
Michael Cochrane Quintet | Elements | Soul Note | 121151-2
Reunion At Newport
Florian Bührich Quintet | endlich Jazz...? | Jazz 4 Ever Records:Jazz Network | J4E 4764
Reunion Blues
Milt Jackson With The Oscar Peterson Trio | Compact Jazz: The Modern Jazz Quartet Plus | Verve | 833290-2
Modern Jazz Quartet | Topsy-This One's For Basie | Original Jazz Classics | OJCCD 1073-2(2310917)
The Best Of The Modern Jazz Quartet | Pablo | 2405423-2
Oscar Peterson Big 6 | Oscar Peterson At The Montreux Jazz Festival 1975 | Original Jazz Classics | 2310747
Oscar Peterson Trio With Milt Jackson | Very Tall | Verve | 559830-2
Reunion Blues | MPS | 817490-2 PMS
Oscar Peterson-Milt Jackson Duo | Two Of The Few | Original Jazz Classics | OJCCD 689-2(2310881)
Oscar Peterson-Milt Jackson Quartet | Reunion Blues | MPS | 817490-1
Ray Brown Trio With Ulf Wakenius | Summertime | Telarc Digital | CD 83430
Reve
Andre Jaume 3 | Musique Pour 3 & 8:Errance | Hat Art | 2003 Digital
Reve-A-Ca
Claudio Fasoli | Egotrip | SPLASC(H) Records | H 161
Revealing
Bob Hall | No.29 | BELL Records | BLR 84038
Revelation
Dexter Gordon-Benny Bailey Quintet | Revelation | Steeplechase | SCCD 31373
Eddie Henderson Quintet | Think On Me | Steeplechase | SCCD 31264
Hannibal And The Sunrise Orchestra | Hannibal | MPS | 68061
Sam Rivers' Rivbea All-Star Orchestra | Culmination | RCA | 2168311-2
Yusef Lateef Orchestra | The Many Faces Of Yusef Lateef | Milestone | M 47009
James Blood Ulmer Group | Are You Glad To Be In America? | DIW | DIW 400 CD
Reven
Niacin | High Bias | Stretch Records | SCD 9017-2
Revenge
Dick Berk Sextet | One By One | Reservoir | RSR CD 143
Reverence
Milton Mezz Mezzrow Sextet | Bechet/Nicholas/Mezzrow:Spirits Of New Orleans | Vogue | 2113408-2
Reverie
Django Reinhardt Quintet | Django/Django In Rome 1949-1050 | BGO Records | BGOCD 366
Erroll Garner Trio | The Greatest Garner | Rhino | SD 1227
Hot Club De Norvege With Guests | Portrait Of Django | Hot Club Records | HCRCD 083
Reverse
Etta Jones And Her Quartet | Hollar! | Original Jazz Classics | OJCCD 1061(PR 7284)
Reverse The Charges
Gus Viseur Sextet | Gus Viseur A Bruxelles | Harmonia Mundi | PJC 222006
Revol
Stockholm JazzOrchestra | Tango | dmp Digital Music Productions | CD 525
Revolution II
Barrelhouse Jazzband | Showboat | L+R Records | CDLR 40032
Revolving Door
World Saxophone Quartet | Revue | Black Saint | 120056-2
Reyes Y Reinas
Baden Powell Quartet | Poema On Guitar | MPS | 68089
Reza
Bud Shank And The Sax Section | Bud Shank And The Sax Section | Pacific Jazz | LN 10091
Jaco Pastorius Groups | Another Side Of Jaco Pastorius | Jazzpoint | JP 1064 CD
Jaco Pastorius Trio | Jaco Pastorius Heavy'n Jazz & Stuttgart Aria | Jazzpoint | JP 1058 CD
Jaco Pastorius Broadway Blues & Theresa | Jazzpoint | JP 1053 CD
Heavy'n Jazz | Jazzpoint | JP 1036 CD
Larry Vuckovich Quartet With Jon Hendricks | Cast Your Fate | Palo Alto | PA 8042
Rhap.s.odie(John Wolf Brennan)
Sabu L. Martinez Group | Afro Blue | Blue Note | 780701-2
Rhapsodia Del Maravilloso
Ray Pizzi Group | Conception | Pablo | 2310795
Rhapsody In Blue
Duke Ellington And His Orchestra | Recollections Of The Big Band Era | Atlantic | 90043-2
Glenn Miller And His Orchestra | Glenn Miller-The Great Instrumentals 1938-1942 | Retrieval | RTR 79001
Glenn Miller And The Army Air Force Band | I Sustain The Wings Vol.3(September 1943) | Magic | DAWE 78
Leroy Smith And His Orchestra | Not Notes-New York Vol.1 | Frog | DGF 8
Rhapsody In Blue-
Oscar Klein | Pickin' The Blues Vol. 2 | Intercord | 150006
Rhapsody In Love
Woody Herman And His Orchestra | Woody Herman:Four Brother | Dreyfus Jazz Line | FDM 36722-2
Rhapsody In Wood
Woody Herman:Complete 1948-1950 Capitol Sessions | Definitive Records | DRCD 11195
Rhapsody Italia-
Jimmie Lunceford And His Orchestra | Jimmy Lunceford - Rythm Is Our Business | MCA | 1302
Rhinoceros
Magog | Magog | Japo | 60011 IMS
Rhode Island Is Famous For You
Weslia Whitefield Trio | Lucky To Be Me | Landmark | LCD 1524-2
Rhumba Azul
Nat King Cole Trio | Vocal Classics & Instrumental Classics | Capitol | 300014(TOCJ 6128)
Rhumba Finale
Dizzy Gillespie And His Orchestra | Afro Cuban Jazz | Verve | 833561-1
Rhumba Multikulti
Walter Davis Quintet | Davis Cup | Blue Note | 0675597
Rhumba Numba
Neal Hefti And His Orchestra | The Jazz Scene | Verve | 521661-2
Rhumblues
Oscar Pettiford Sextet | Oscar Pettiford Sextet | Vogue | 21409452
Rhyhtm And Blues No.1
Ellery Eskelin Trio | Kulak, 29 & 30 | HatOLOGY | 521
Rhymes
Chick Corea Trio | The Song Of Singing | Blue Note | 784353-2
Rhythm Circle
Katrina Krimsky-Trevor Watts | Stella Malu | ECM | 1199
King Oliver And His Orchestra | Jazz Classics In Digital Stereo: King Oliver Volume Two 1927 To 1930 | CDS Records Ltd. | ZCF 788
Rhythm Cole
Dejan's Young Olympia Brass Band | Alive And Kicken | Traditional Line | TL 1310
Rhythm For Runner
Monette Moore And Her Swing Shop Boys | The 30's Girls | Timeless | CBC 1-026
Rhythm Form
Matthias Stich & Whisper Not | Bach Lives!! | Satin Doll Productions | SDP 1018-1 CD
Rhythm Fugue
Boulou Ferre-Elios Ferre Duo | Pour Django | Steeplechase | SCCD 31120
Rhythm In Blue Suite:
Count Basie And His Orchestra | Recorded at Famous Door & Meadowbrook | Jazz Anthology | JA 5172
Rhythm Is Our Business
Nat Gonella And His Georgians | Mister Rhythm Man | EMI Records | EG 2601881
Rhythm King
Harry Strutters Hot Rhythm | Harry Strutters Hot Rhythm Orchestra | Jazz Colours | 874751-2
Rhythm Or Reason
Steve Coleman And Five Elements | Rhythm People | Novus | PL 83092
Rhythm Ride
Scott Hamilton And Friends | Blues,Bop & Ballads | Concord | CCD 4866
Rhythm Saved The World
Louis Armstrong And His Orchestra | Louis Armstrong Vol.2 | Ambassador | CLA 1902
Louis Armstrong:Swings | Memo Music | HDJ 4033
Rhythm-A-Ning
Art Pepper Quintet | Gettin' Together | Contemporary | COP 023
Art Pepper With The Duke Jordan Trio | Art Pepper With Duke Jordan In Copenhagen 1981 | Galaxy | 2GCD 8201-2
Art Taylor Quintet | Taylor's Tenors | Prestige | VIJ 5034
Cedar Walton Quartet | The Maestro | Muse | MCD 6008
Chico Freeman Quintet | Focus | Contemporary | CCD 14073-2
Dexter Gordon Quartet | The Jumpin' Blues | Original Jazz Classics | OJCCD 899-2(PR 10020)
Live At The Amsterdam Paradiso | Affinity | AFF 751
Dexter Gordon Quintet | Round Midnight(Soundtrack) | CBS | 70300
Esbjörn Svensson Trio(E.S.T.) | EST Plays Monk | RCA | 2137680-2
Gil Evans Orchestra | Live '76 | Zeta | ZET 714
Jeff Hamilton Trio | Hamilton House | Mons Records | MR 874316
Kenny Drew Jr. Quartet | The Rainbow Connection | Jazz City | 660.53.010
Larry Willis Quartet | My Funny Valentine | Jazz City | 660.53.005
Thelonious Monk Quartet | Thelonious Monk:85th Birthday Celebration | zyx records | FANCD 6076-2
Paris Jazz Concert:Theloniuos Monk And His Quartet | Laserlight | 17250
Live In Paris, Alhambra 1964 Vol.1 | France's Concert | FCD 135
The Be Bop Legends | Moon Records | MCD 072-2
Thelonious Monk In Copenhagen | Storyville | STCD 8283
Evidence | France's Concert | FCD 105
Andy Summers Group | Green Chimneys:The Music Of Thelonious Monk | RCA | 2663472-2
Rhythm-A-Ning-
Johnny Griffin Quartet | Live at The Jazzhus Montmartre,Copenhagen Vol.1 | Jazz Colours | 874723-2
Rhythmatics
Quintet Du Hot Club De France | Jazz Legacy 58: Django Reinhardt-Rythme Futur-Radio Sessions 1947 Vol'| Vogue | 500108
Rhythme Futur
Chris Jarrett | Short Stories For Piano | Edition Musikat | EDM 056
Rhythmic Battle
Joachim Kühn | The Diminished Augmented System | EmArCy | 542320-2
Rhythmic Inclinations
Mary Lou Williams Duo | My Mama Pinned A Rose On Me | Pablo | 2310819
Rhythmic Wind
Andrew Cyrille | What About? | Affinity | AFF 75
Rhythms Of Hope
Jean-Luc Ponty Sextet | The Very Best Of Jean-Luc Ponty | Rhino | 8122-79862-2
Marion Brown-Leo Smith | Porto Novo | Black Lion | BLCD 760200
Rhythmus Revue:
Freddie Brocksieper Quartett | Shot Gun Boogie | Bear Family Records | BCD 16277 AH
Kenny Burrell Quintet | Introducing Kenny Burrell | Blue Note | 300104(1523)
Ribbon In The Sky
Leny Andrade And The Fred Hersch Trio | Mayden Voyage | Chesky | JD 113
Ricardo's Dilemma
George Colligan Quintet | The Newcomer | Steeplechase | SCCD 31414
Rice Pudding
Ernst Reijseger | Colla Parta | Winter&Winter | 910012-2
Ricercare
Swingle Singers With The Modern Jazz Quartet | Place Vendome | Philips | 824545-2 PMS
Rich Girl
Dinah Washington With Lucky Thompson And His All Stars | Lucky Thompson Vol.1-Test Pilot | Swingtime(Contact) | ST 1005
Richard Diamond Theme
West Coast All Stars | TV Jazz Themes | Fresh Sound Records | FSR 517(Somerset SF 8800)
Richard Diamond's Blues
Bob Helm's Jazz Band | Hotter Than That | Stomp Off Records | CD 1310
Richie's Secret World
Mississippi John Hurt | The Best Of Mississippi John Hurt | Vanguard | VCD 19/20
Rickover's Dream
Michael Hedges | An Evening With Windham Hill:Live | Windham Hill | TA-C- 1026
Ricky's Living Room
Bud Shank Quartet | After You,Jeru | Fresh Sound Records | FSR-CD 5026
Ric's Hum
Les McCann Orchestra | Live At The Roxy | MCA | AS 9333
Riddled
John Abercrombie Quartet | Abercrombie Quartet | ECM | 1164
Riddles
Eddie Taylor Blues Band | Street Talkin' | Muse | MCD 5087
Ride Of The Headless Horseman
Stan Kenton And His Orchestra | Kenton Plays Wagner | Creative World | ST 1024
Ride On Midnight Special
Louisiana Red Group | The Lowdown Back Porch Blues | Sequel Records | NEX CD 213
Ride Red Ride
Henry Red Allen's All Stars | World On A String | RCA | ND 82497847084)
Sam 'The Man' Taylor Orchestra | Back Beat-The Rhythm Of The Blues Vol.5 | Mercury | 511270-2 PMS
Riders On The Storm
Oskar Aichinger Trio | Elelents Of Poetry | Between The Lines | btl 005(Efa 10175-2)
Ridicolosamente
Martial Solal Quartet | Martial Solal-The Vogue Recordings Vol.1:Trios & Quartet | Vogue | 21115142(875744)

Ridin' But Walkin'
Jess Stacy-Specs Powell Duo | Commodore Classics-Jess Stacy And Friends | Commodore | 6.24298 AG

Ridin' High
Ella Fitzgerald With The Buddy Bregman Orchestra | The Complete Ella Fitzgerald Song Books of Harold Arlen, Irving Berlin, Duke Ellington, George & Ira Gershwin, Jerome Kern, Johnny Mercer, Cole Porter And Rogers & Hart | Verve | 519832-2
Peggy Lee With Jack Marshall's Music | Things Are Swingin' | Capitol | 597072-2
Klaus Doldinger & Passport | Down To Earth | Warner | 4509-93207-2

Ridin' On A Rainbow
Big Bill Broonzy | See See Rider-Sixteen Tons | Jazz Anthology | JA 5127

Ridin' The Treasure
Westbrook & Company | Platterback | PAO Records | PAO 10530

Riding On A Cloud
Marie Knight And Her Group | Today | Blue Labor | BL 106

Riding On The D Train
Joe Stafford And Her Band | Nat King Cole-Jazz Encounters | Capitol | 796693-2

Rien
Michel Portal-Martial Solal | Fast Mood | RCA | 2169310-2

Rien D'un Blues
Günter Christmann/Torsten Müller | Carte Blanche | FMP | 1100

Rien Nul
Kosh | Groovy Strings | Elite Special | 73325

Riera Blanca
Göbels-Harth Group | Es Herrscht Uhu Im Land | Japo | 60037 (2360037)

Rif Hi-Fi
Bob Wilber & The Scott Hamilton Quartet | Bob Wilbur And The Scott Hamilton Quartet | Chiaroscuro | CR 171

Riff Blues
Skip Martin Orchestra | The Music From Mickey Spillane's Mike Hammer | Fresh Sound Records | ND 42124

Riff Medley
Earl Hines And His Orchestra | Jazz:The Essential Collection Vol.2 | IN+OUT Records | 78012-2
Jazz Drumming Vol.4(1939) | Fenn Music | FJD 2704

Riff Primitif
The Herbie Nichols Project | Dr. Cyclops' Dream | Soul Note | 121333-2

Riff Primitif(alt.take)
Alvin Queen-Bill Saxton Sextet | Ashanti | Divox | CDX 48703

Riff Up Them Stairs
The Capitol International Jazzmen | Nat King Cole-Jazz Encounters | Capitol | 796693-2

Riffamarole
Nat King Cole-Jazz Encounters | Capitol | 796693-2

Riffin'
Sam Rivers' Rivbea All-Star Orchestra | Culmination | RCA | 2168311-2

Riffin' And Raffin'
Illinois Jacquet And His Orchestra | The Black Velvet Band | Bluebird | ND 86571

Riffin' Drill
Duke Ellington And His Orchestra | Duke Ellington:Complete Prestige Carnegie Hall 1946-1947 Concerts | Definitive Records | DRCD 11211

Riffin' With Helen
Illinois Jacquet And His Orchestra | Illinois Jacquet:All Stars Studio Recordings 1945-1947(Master Takes) | Blue Moon | BMCD 1011

Riffs'n Changes
Al Cohn With The Rein De Graaff Trio | Rifftide | Timeless | CD SJP 259

Rifftide
Coleman Hawkins Quintet | Body And Soul | West Wind | WW 2018
Joe Gordon Quintet | Blakey | Verve | 538634-2
Miles Davis/Tadd Dameron Quintet | Paris Festival International De Jazz, May 1949 | CBS | 485527-2
Roy Eldridge & Coleman Hawkins With The Tommy Flanagan Trio | At The American Jazz Festival In Latin America | West Wind | WW 2025

Rifftide(aka Disorder At The Border)
Thilo Wolf Trio With Randy Brecker,Chuck Loeb & New York Strings | A Swinging Hour In New York | Mons Records | MR 874801

Right About Now
Benny Golson Orchestra | Tune In,Turn On | Verve | 559793-2

Right As The Rain
String Summit | One World In Eight | MPS | 68275

Right Before My Eyes
John Abercrombie Quartet | November | ECM | 1502(519073-2)

Right Brain Patrol
Marc Johnson Trio | Right Brain Patrol | JMT Edition | 849153-2

Right Down Front
Ray Anderson Trio | Right Down Your Alley | Soul Note | 121087-2

Right Here Right Now
Hank Jones Trio | The Trio | Chiaroscuro | CR 188

Right Now
Jerry Van Rooyen With The WDR Big Band | Swing & Balladen | WDR | 2141013-2
Martin Koller's Third Movement | Right Now | Traumton Records | 4430-2
Mel Tormé With The Claus Ogerman Orchestra | Comin' Home Baby!/Sings Sunday In New York | Warner | 8122-75438-2
Rodney Jones Quintet | Right Now | Minor Music | 801054

Right Now(alt.take)
Martin Koller's Third Movement | Right Now | Traumton Records | 4430-2

Right Now(Core Mix)
Al Sears And His Orchestra | Sear-iously | Bear Family Records | BCD 15668 AH

Right Now, Right Now
Alain Trudel Quartet | Jericho's Legacy | Naxos Jazz | 86021-2

Right Off
Miles Davis Group | In Concert | CBS | C2K 65140

Right Off-
Count Basie And His Orchestra | Sixteen Men Swinging | Verve | 2-2517 IMS

Right On
George Kelly Quintet | A' Portrait Of Jan Jankeje | Jazzpoint | JP 1054 CD
Red Richards-George Kelly Sextet With Doc Cheatham | Groove Move | Jazzpoint | JP 1045 CD
Tony Williams Lifetime | Spectrum:The Anthology | Verve | 537075-2

Right Shoes
Frank Paul Schubert Quartet | Der Verkauf Geht Weiter | Jazz Haus Musik | JHM 0114 CD
Steve Turre Sextet | Right There | Antilles | 510040-2(889653)

Rightousness
Hot Club The Zigan | Adagio | Jazz Pure Collection | AU 31601 CD

Rilucere Inveduto-
Jan Garbarek Trio | Triptychon | ECM | 1029(847321-2)

Rim
Hanno Giulini-Eva Mayerhofer | Anyone | Acoustic Music Records | 319.1171.2

Rimbaud Gedichte
Charly Antolini Septet | Wow!!! | Verve | 833796-2

Rincon
Clark Suprynowicz-Rinde Eckert Group | In Sleep A King | Sound Aspects | sas CD 029

Ring Dem Bells
Duke Ellington And His Orchestra | Big Band Bounce And Boogie:Classic Transcriptions-Duke Ellington | Affinity | AFS 1032
Fats Waller | Masters Of Jazz Vol. 2 | RCA | NL 89724 DP
Hot Mallets | Hot Mallets...Live | Jazzcharge | JC 8302
Lionel Hampton And His All Stars | Masters Of Jazz Vol.8 | RCA | NL 89540 DP
The Harlem Footwarmers | Hot From The Cotton Club | EMI Records | EG 2605671
Zoot Sims Quintet | Somebody Loves Me | LRC Records | CDC 8514

Ringin' In
Sonic Fiction | Changing With The Times | Naxos Jazz | 86034-2

Ringing My Phone(Straight Outa Istanbul)
Gust Williams Tsilis Quartet | Wood Music | Enja | ENJ-7093 2

Ringside
Joe Mannone's Harmony Kings | New Orleans Stomp | VJM | VLP 35 IMS

Rio
Leonard Feather All Stars | Night Blooming | Mainstream | MD CDO 719

Rio Ancho
The Rosenberg Trio With Orchestra | Noches Calientes | Verve | 557022-2

Rio Ancho-
Joe Barnikel-Norbert Nagel Group | Zero Gravity | Mons Records | MR 874808

Rio Con Brio
Jimmy Heath Quartet | You Or Me | Steeplechase | SCCD 31370

Rio De Janeiro
Frey-Tiepold-Thierfelder | Ziyada | Concept | CC 001679

Rio D'Oro
Claus Boesser-Ferrari | Blue Footprint | Acoustic Music Records | 319.1066.2

Rio Esta Hondo
GRP All Stars | GRP Live In Session | GRP | GRP 95312

Rio Funk
Lee Ritenour With Special Guests | Festival International De Jazz De Montreal | Spectra | 9811661
Alan Pasqua Group | Milargo | Postcards | POST 1002

Rio Sol
Lee Ritenour With Special Guests | Festival International De Jazz De Montreal | Spectra | 9811661
Flautissimo | Flautissimo | Edition Collage | EC 445-2

Rio-Kyoto-Blues
Vital Information | Ray Of Hope | VeraBra Records | CDVBR 2161-2

Rio-Lize
Dino Saluzzi-Anthony Cox-David Friedman | Rios | VeraBra Records | CDVBR 2156-2

Rios
Lester Bowie Quartet | The Great Pretender | ECM | 1209(829369-2)

Rios Negroes
Antonio Scarano Octet | Hot Blend | SPLASC(H) Records | H 183

Riot
Herbie Hancock Sextet | The Best Of Herbie Hancock | Blue Note | 89907
Keith Jarrett Trio | Inside Out | ECM | 1780(014005-2)
Miles Davis Quintet | Nefertiti | CBS | CK 65681
Paraphernalia | JMY(Jazz Music Yesterdays) | JMY 1013-2
Phil Woods And His European Rhythm Machine | At The Montreux Jazz Festival | Verve | 065512-2
Scott Henderson-Gary Willis Quartet | Illicit | Bluemoon | R 27-9180-2

Riot(alt.take 1)
Herbie Hancock Sextet | Herbie Hancock:The Complete Blue Note Sixties Sessions | Blue Note | 495569-2

Riot(alt.take 2)
Hank Garland Group | Jazz Winds From New Directions | CBS | 492532-2

Riots...The Voice Of The Unheard
Pucho & His Latin Soul Brothers | Rip A Dip | Milestone | MCD 9247-2

Rip A Dip
The Latin Jazz Quintet | Hot Sauce | Prestige | PCD 24128-2

Rip Off
Sidney Bechet And His New Orleans Feetwarmers | Sidney Bechet 1932-1943: The Bluebird Sessions | Bluebird | ND 90317

Rip,Rig And Panic
Roland Kirk Quartet | Rip Rig And Panic/Now Please Don't You Cry Beautiful Edith | EmArCy | 832164-2 PMS

Ripe Banana
George Adams-Dannie Richmond Quintet | Gentlemen's Agreement | Soul Note | 121057-2

Ripples Edge
Lucky Roberts | Lucky Roberts & Ralph Sutton:The Circle Recordings | Solo Art | SACD-10

Rip-Tip-Tap
Philipp Van Endert Group | Philipp Van Endert Group | L+R Records | CDLR 45107

Rise
Rez Abbasi Group | Modern Memory | String Jazz | SJRCD 102

Rise Above
Lee Gree With Lafayette Leake | Somebody's Praying,Lord | L+R Records | LR 44013

Rise And Fall
Ornette Coleman Quartet | Beauty Is A Rare Thing:Ornette Coleman-The Complete Atlantic Recordings | Atlantic | 8122-71410-2

Rise And Shine
Buck Clayton Swing Band | Swing's The Village | Nagel-Heyer | CD 5004

Rise 'N' Shine
Eddie Duran Quartet | Eddie Duran-Jazz Guitarist | Original Jazz Classics | OJC 120(F 3247)
John Coltrane With The Red Garland Trio | Settin' The Pace | Original Jazz Classics | OJC20 078-2
The Jay And Kai Trombone Octet | Jay & Kai + 6 | CBS | 480990-2

Rise Up In The Morning
Philipp Wachsmann-Paul Lytton | Some Other Season | ECM | 1662

Riser
Mario Fragiacomo Orchestra | Trieste Ieri Un Secolo Fa | SPLASC(H) Records | HP 08

Rising Star(for Wilma)
Charles Brown Band | Drifting Blues | Pathe | 1546611(Score SLP 4011)

Rising Tide
P.U.L.S.E. | Amsterdam Groove | ACT | 9262-2

Risk-
Frank Kirchner Group | Frank Kirchner | Laika Records | LK 93-036

Risk Of Electric Shock
Der Rote Bereich | Risky Business | ACT | 9407-2

Risky Business
John Abercrombie Quartet | Class Trip | ECM | 1846(0381182)
John Wolf Brennan | The Well-Prepared Clavier/Das Wohlpräparierte Klavier | Creative Works Records | CW CD 1032-2

Risoluto(an imaginary thriller)-
Count Basie And His Orchestra | Basie On Roulette, Vol. 3: Sing Along With Basie | Vogue | 500003

Rita Hayworth
Art Pepper Quartet | No Limit | Original Jazz Classics | OJCCD 411-2

Rita-San
No Limit | Contemporary | COP 019

Rite Of Passage
John Hart Quartet | Bridges | Concord | CCD 4746

Rites
Baikida Carroll | The Spoken Word | Hat Art | M/N

Rites Of Passage
Stephan Schmolck Quartet | Rites Of Passage | L+R Records | CDLR 45064
Sadao Watanabe And His Brazilian Friends | Sadao Meets Brazilian Friends | Denon Compact Disc | DC-8557

Ritmo Arauca:
Al Di Meola Groups | Guitar Heroes Vol.1:Al Di Meola | Zounds | CD 2700044001

Ritmo De La Noche
Conexion Latina | La Conexión | Enja | ENJ-9065 2

Ritmo Internacional
Pucho & His Latin Soul Brothers | Rip A Dip | Milestone | MCD 9247-2

Ritmo Nueva York
Paulinho Da Costa Orchestra | Agora | Original Jazz Classics | OJCCD 630-2(2310785)

Ritmo Number One
Poncho Sanchez And His Orchestra | Afro-Cuban Fantasy | Concord | CCD 4847

Ritooria
Keith Jarrett | Works | ECM | 825425-1

Ritornello
Flavio Boltro-Furio di Castri-Manhu Roche | Immagini | Red Records | NS 210

Ritrovarsi
Quartett & Brass | More Than Four | Line Records | COCD 9.01068 0

Ritual
Aldo Romano Quartet | Ritual | Owl Records | 050 CD
Kenny Barron Quintet | Sambao | EmArCy | 512736-2

Ritual-
Monday Night Big Band | Thanks To Thad:Monday Night Big Band Plays The Music Of Thad Jones | TCB Records | TCB 97902

Ritual Life
Jonas Hellborg With Glen Velez | Ars Moriende | Day Eight Music | DEMCD 034

Ritual Prayer
Dennis Russell Davies | Keith Jarrett: Ritual | ECM | 1112

Ritus
Lyle Ritz Quartet | How About Uke? | Verve | 0760942

Ritz Cracker
Lothar Müller Trio | Müller Q[kju] | JA & RO | JARO 4251-2

River
Monty Alexander Quartet | Friday Night | Limetree | MCD 0022

River Chant
Septer Bourbon | Septer Bourbon-The Smile Of The Honeycakehorse | Jazzline | JL 11151-2

River Edge Rock
Washboard Sam & His Washboard Band | Chicago Blues(1935-1942) | RCA | 2126404-2

River Man
Brad Mehldau Trio | Art Of The Trio Vol.5:Progression | Warner | 9362-48005-2
Art Of The Trio Vol.3: Songs | Warner | 9362-47051-2
Hamiet Bluiett Clarinet Family | The Clarinet Family | Black Saint | 120097-2

River People
Pat Metheny Quartet | Watercolors | ECM | 1097(827409-2)

River Quay
The Crusaders | Free As The Wind | MCA | 2292-50776-1

River Stay Away From My Door
The Boswell Sisters With The Dorsey Brothers' Orchestra | Everybody Loves My Baby | Pro-Arte | CDD 550

River Suite:
Tony Harper With The Marty Paich Orchestra | Lady Lonely | Fresh Sound Records | ND 42131

Riverbank Air
Joe Zawinul Group | Concerto Retitled | Atlantic | SD 1694

Riverboat Shuffle
Allotria Jazz Band | All That Jazz | Elite Special | 730217
George Girard & His New Orleans Five | Sounds Of New Orleans Vol.6 | Storyville | STCD 6013
Jack Teagarden And His Orchestra | Jazz Original | Charly | CD 80
The Riverboat Jazzband | 35th Anniversary | Timeless | CD TTD 574
The Wolverines | Bix Beiderbecke | Milestone | MCD 47019-2

Riverrun
Third Eye | Third Eye Live! | View | VS 021 IMS

Rivers Of Love
Gil Scott-Heron/Brian Jackson Group | Winter In America | Strata East Records | 660.51.015

Rivers Run
Ketil Bjornstad Group | Water Stories | ECM | 1503(519076-2)

Riverscape
Dave Binney Quintet | Point Game | Owl Time Line | 3819032

Riverside Blues
King Oliver's Jazz Band | Louis Armstrong With King Oliver Vol.1 | Village(Jazz Archive) | VILCD 003-2
Louis Armstrong With The Dukes Of Dixieland | Sweetheart-Definite Alternatives | Chiaroscuro | CR 2006
Muggsy Spanier And His Dixieland All Stars | At Club Hangover-Vol. 2 | Storyville | SLP 249

Riverside Drive
Eugen Cicero Trio | Rococo Jazz 2 | Timeless | CD SJP 255

Riverside Jump-
Jon Faddis With The Carlos Franzetti Orchestra | Rememberances | Chesky | JD 166

Riviera Blues(Blues A La Don)
Louis Sclavis Group | Chine | IDA Record | 012 CD

RM Express-
Art Ensemble Of Chicago | Naked | DIW | DIW 818 CD

Road Dogs
Kostas Konstantinou-Vassilis Tsabropoulos | Concentric Cycles | Nabel Records:Jazz Network | CD 4698

Road Ends
Misery Loves Company | Magia Ke Miseria | Enja | 9117-2

Road Runner
Yusef Lateef Quartet | The Golden Flute | MCA | AS 9125
Grant Geissman Quintet | Good Stuff | Concord | CJ 62

Road Song
Sylvain Luc-Biréli Lagrène | Duet | Dreyfus Jazz Line | FDM 36604-2
Vic Juris Quartet | Roadsong | Muse | MR 5150
Toshiko Akiyoshi/Lew Tabackin Big Band | Live At Newport '77 | RCA | NL 70579

Road To Gopala
Kim Pensyl Group | Eyes Of Wonder | GRP | GRP 97102

Road To Moroco
Rosemary Clooney With The John Oddo Big Band | Still On The Road | Concord | CCD 4590

Road Travelled,Road Veiled
Art Pepper Quartet | Roadgame | Galaxy | GXY 5142

Road Waltz
Art Pepper:The Complete Galaxy Recordings | Galaxy | 16GCD 1016-2
Art Pepper:The Complete Galaxy Recordings | Galaxy | 16GCD 1016-2
Roadgame | Original Jazz Classics | OJCCD 774-2(GXY 5142)
Roadgame | Galaxy | GXY 5142

Roadgame
Art Pepper:The Complete Galaxy Recordings | Galaxy | 16GCD 1016-2
Roadgame | Original Jazz Classics | OJCCD 774-2(GXY 5142)
Roadgame | Original Jazz Classics | OJCCD 774-2(GXY 5142)

Roadgame(alt.take)
Albert King Blues Band | Blues At Sunrise | Stax | SCD 8546-2

Roadhouse Symphony
Louis Smith Quintet | Silvering | Steeplechase | SCCD 31336

Roam And Spy
Fred Elizalde And His Orchestra | An Evening At The Savoy | Decca | DDV 5011/12

Roamin' Blues
Louis Jordan And His Tympany Five | Look Out Sisters-Unissued Film Soundtracks 1944-1948 | Krazy Kat | KK 7415 IMS

Roanugo
Günter Lenz Springtime | The First Jazz Sampler: 25 Years Of Jazz | L+R Records | LS 40012

Rob Roy
Oscar Peterson Quintet | Oscar Peterson Meets Roy Hargrove And Ralph Moore | Telarc Digital | CD 83399

Robbin's Nest
Count Basie And His Orchestra | The Indispensable Count Basie | RCA | ND 89758
Duke Robillard-Herb Ellis Quintet | More Conversations In Swing Guitar | Stony Plain | SPCD 1292
Eddie Lockjaw Davis-Johnny Griffin Quintet | Live At Minton's | Prestige | P 24099
Ella Fitzgerald With The Hank Jones Trio | Ella Fitzgerald:Mr.Paganini | Dreyfus Jazz Line | FDM 36741-2
Jazz At The Philharmonic:The Ella Fitzgerald Set | Verve | 815147-1 IMS
Erroll Garner Trio | Body & Soul | CBS | 467916-2
The Erroll Garner Selection | CBS | 471624-2
Joe Pass Trio | Eximious | Original Jazz Classics | OJCCD 1037-2(2310877)

Lionel Hampton And His All Star Jazz Inner Circle | En Concert Avec Europe 1 | Laserlight | 710375/76
Mal Waldron-John Coltrane Sextet | Wheelin' | Prestige | P 24069
Milt Buckner Trio | Milt Buckner Masterpieces | MPS | 529094-2
Oscar Peterson | Oscar Peterson:Exclusively For My Friends | MPS | 513830-2
Oscar Peterson-Major Holley Duo | Keyboard Music By Oscar Peterson | Verve | MV 2666 IMS
Prestige All Stars | John Coltrane-The Prestige Recordings | Prestige | 16 PCD 4405-2
Scott Hamilton Quintet | Close Up | Concord | CCD 4197
Sir Charles Thompson Trio | Robbin's Nest | Paddle Wheel | KICJ 181
The Buck Clayton Legacy | Encore Live | Nagel-Heyer | CD 018
The Jazz Crusaders | The Young Rabbits | Blue Note | 84553
Sir Charles Thompson | Playing My Way | Jazz Connaisseur | JCCD 9313-2

Robbin's Nest-
Plas Johnson Band | Rockin' With The Plas | Pathe | 2C 068-86529(Capitol)

Robbin's Nest(alt.take 1)
Ella Fitzgerald With The Count Basie Orchestra | Ella And Basie | Verve | 539059-2

Robbin's Nest(alt.take 2)
Illinois Jacquet And His Orchestra | Illinois Jacquet Flies Again | Roulette | CDP 797272-2

Robbin's Nest(incomplete take)
Cassiber | The Beauty And The Beast | Riskant | 528-72410

Roberto
Tim Berne Group | Tim Berne EmpireThe Five Years Plan/Spectres/Songs And Rituals In Real Time | Screwgun | SC 70009

Roberto Zucco
Gary Lucas | Skeleton On The Feast | Enemy | EMCD 126(03526)

Robins And Roses
Mellow Moods Of Jazz | Mellow Moods Of Jazz | Fresh Sound Records | LPM 1365(RCA)

Roblinga
Fourplay | Fourplay...Yes,Please! | Warner | 9362-47694-2

Robo Bop
Frank Ku-Umba Lacy Group | Tonal Weights & Blue Fire | Tutu Records | 888112-2*

Robot
Miles Davis Group | Decoy | CBS | 468702-2

Robot 415
Gyjho Frank | Aeuropa | Blue Flame | 40372

Robot Portrait
Fallen Angels-Sound Paintings | Blue Flame | 40252

Robotalk
Squeeze Me Jazzband | Salute To Uncle Bijou | Jazz Pure Collection | AU 31623 CD

Roc And Troll
Cesc Miralta Quartet | Sol De Nit | Fresh Sound Records | FSNT 098 CD

Roc Blanc
Gianluigi Trovesi Trio | Les Boites A Musique | SPLASC(H) Records | CD H 152-2

Rock And Roll Ball
Anita O'Day And Her Trio | Tea For Two | Moon Records | MLP 023-1

Rock Beat Alemania
Benny Carter And His Orchestra | Additions To Further Definitions | Impulse(MCA) | JAS 57 (AS 9116)

Rock Bottom
Pete Peterson Band | Jumping On The West Coast-Buddy Tate & Friends | Black Lion | BLCD 760175

Rock Candy
Jack McDuff Quartet | Another Real Good'Un | 32 Jazz | 32169

Rock I
Cassandra Wilson And Her Trio | Live | JMT Edition | 849149-2

Rock It
Pete Johnson | The Boogie King | MCA | 52046 (801837)

Rock It For Me
Ella Fitzgerald With The Chick Webb Orchestra | Let's Get Together | Laserlight | 17003

Rock Me
Mary Lou Williams Group | Jazz In Paris:Mary Lou Williams-I Made You Love Paris | EmArCy | 013141-2
Wolfgang Bernreither-Golly-Rudy Bayer Group | I Wonder Why | L+R Records | CDLR 42079

Rock Me Baby
Big Bill Broonzy | The Blues Vol.2 | Intercord | 158601
James Sparky Rucker | American Folk Blues Festival Live '83 | L+R Records | LR 42063
Christian Rover Trio | New York Impressions | Organic Music | GWR 280595

Rock My Soul
Lou Stein Duo | Stompin' 'Em Down | Chiaroscuro | CR 173
Louis Armstrong With Sy Oliver's Choir And Orchestra | Louis And The Good Book | Verve | 549593-2
Mal Waldron Trio | Free At Last | ECM | 1001
Black Glory | Enja | 2004

Rock Of Ages
Oscar Peterson Trio | Walking The Line | MPS | 68082
Big Joe Turner And His Band | Have No Fear Big Joe Turner Is Here | Savoy | WL 70822 (809333)

Rock On
Buddy Johnson And His Orchestra | Walkin' | Official | 6008

Rock On(alt.take)
Art Ensemble Of Chicago | A Jackson In Your House/Message To Our Folks | Affinity | AFF 752

Rock Salt
Duke Ellington And His Orchestra | And His Mother Called Him Bill | RCA | 2125762-2

Rock Skippin' At The Blue Note
Paul Williams Orchestra | Paul Williams:The Complete Recordings Vol.2 (1949-1952) | Blue Moon | BMCD 6021

Rock The Boat
Jean-Paul Bourelly & The BluWave Bandits | Rock The Cathartic Spirits:Vibe Music And The Blues! | DIW | DIW 911 CD

Rock The Joint Boogie
Eddie Boyd Blues Band | Five Long Years | L+R Records | CDLR 72009

Rock-A-Bye
Jack McDuff Quartet With Orchestra | Prelude:Jack McDuff Big Band | Prestige | PRCD 24283-2
Alix Combelle And His Swing Band | Django Reinhardt:Djangology | EMI Records | 780659-2

Rock-A-Bye Basie
Count Basie And His Orchestra | Los Angeles 1945/New York 1946 | Jazz Anthology | JA 5147
Birdland All Stars At Carnegie Hall | Roulette | CDP 798660-2
Prez's Hat Vol.4 | Philology | 214 W 9

Rock-A-Bye Basie-
Chuck Wayne And His Orchestra | String Fever | Fresh Sound Records | NL 46067(RCA LX 1098)

Rock-A-Bye Your Baby With A Dixie Melody
Sonny Rollins And The Contemporary Leaders | Sonny Rollins-The Freelance Years:The Complete Riverside & Contemporary Recordings | Riverside | 5 RCD 4427-2
Antonio Carlos Jobim Group | Tide | A&M Records | 393031-2

Rocker
Charlie Parker With Strings | Bird's Eyes Last Unissued Vol.17 | Philology | W 847.2
Elliot Lawrence And His Orchestra | Plays Gerry Mulligan Arrangements | Original Jazz Classics | OJC 117(F 3206)
Gerry Mulligan Tentette | The Birth Of The Cool Vol.2 | Capitol | 798935-2
Miles Davis And His Orchestra | The Complete Birth Of The Cool | Capitol | 494550-2
Birth Of The Cool | Capitol | 530117-2

Miles Davis:The Blue Note And Capitol Recordings | Blue Note | 827475-2
Charlie Parker With Strings | Bird On Verve-Vol.4:Machito Jazz With Flip And Bird | Verve | 817445-1 IMS

Rocket Number Nine
Sun Ra And His Solar Arkestra | Sun Ra Visit Planet Earth/Interstellar Low Ways | Evidence | ECD 22039-2

Rockin' A Heart Place
Doctor Ross | The Harmonica Boss | Big Bear | 146403

Rockin' Chair
George Melly With John Chilton's Feetwarmers | Melly Sings Hoagy | Ronnie Scott's Jazz House | NSPL 18557
Jack Teagarden And His Swingin' Gates | Jazz Gallery:Jack Teagarden | RCA | 2114175-2
Louis Armstrong And His All Stars | This Is Jazz:Louis Armstrong Sings | CBS | CK 65039
Louis Armstrong:A 100th Birthday Celebration | RCA | 2663694-2
Rare Performances Of The 50's And The 60's | CBS | CBS 88669
Louis Armstrong-The Complete RCA Victor Recordings | RCA | 2668682-2
Louis Armstrong And His Orchestra | Swing Legends:Louis Armstrong | Nimbus Records | NI 2012
Louis Armstrong:Swings | Memo Music | HDJ 4033
Mavis Rivers And Her Septet | Live At The Losers/We Remember Mildred Bailey | Vee Jay Recordings | VJ 018
Roy Eldridge Quintet | Roy Eldridge 'Littel Jazz'-The Best Of The Verve Years | Verve | 523338-2
Sir Charles Thompson Trio | Midnight Slows Vol.8 | Black & Blue | BLE 193582

Rockin' Chair-
Daryl Sherman-John Cocuzzi Orchestra | Daryl Sherman And John Cocuzzi Celebrating Mildred Bailey And Red Norvo | Audiophile | ACD-295
Joe Venuti And His Orchestra | The Radio Years | London | HMG 5023 AN
Big Bill Broonzy Group | Midnight Steppers | Swingtime(Contact) | BT 2001

Rockin' Daddy
Cozy Cole With The Henry Jerome Orchestra | It's A Cozy World | MCA | 252319-1

Rockin' In Rhythm
Aki Takase | Shima Shoka | Enja | 6062-2
Duke Ellington And His Orchestra | The Indispensable Duke Ellington Vol.3/4(1930-1934) | RCA | 2122620-2
Duke Ellington And His Orchestra 1943,Vol.1 | Circle | CCD-101
The Best Of The Big Bands | LRC Records | CDC 8518
Two Great Concerts | Festival | ???
Duke Ellington -Carnegie Hall Concert | Ember | 800851-370(EMBD 2001)
The Best Of Early Ellington | GRP | GRP 16602
Duke Ellington At The Alhambra | Pablo | PACD 5313-2
A True Collectors Item | Jazz Archive | 90.105-2
Ella Fitzgerald With The Duke Ellington Orchestra | Ella Fitzgerald Sings The Duke Ellington Songbook | Verve | 559248-2
The Complete Ella Fitzgerald Song Books of Harold Arlen, Irving Berlin, Duke Ellington, George & Ira Gershwin, Jerome Kern, Johnny Mercer, Cole Porter And Rogers & Hart | Verve | 519832-2
Hank Jones/Tommy Flanagan | Jazz-Club: Piano | Verve | 840032-2
Jones-Brown-Smith | Rockin' In Rhythm | Concord | CCD 4032
Maxine Sullivan With The Bob Wilber Quartet | Clse As Pages In A Book | Audiophile | ACD-203
Munich Saxophon Family | Family Life | Bassic-Sound | CD 006
Oscar Peterson Trio | The Complete Young Oscar Peterson(1945-1949) | RCA | 2122612-2
Night Train Vol. 3 | Verve | 711071 IMS
Oscar Peterson Plays The Duke Ellington Song Book | Verve | 559785-2
Ray Anthony And His Orchestra | Ray Anthony's Houseparty Hop | Capitol | 1565471
Terry Gibbs-Buddy DeFranco Quintet | Chicago Fire | Contemporary | CCD 14036-2
Zoot Sims Quartet | A Celebration Of Duke | Original Jazz Classics | OJC 605(2312119)

Rockin' In Rhythm-
Duke Ellington And His Orchestra | Soul Call | Verve | 539785-2
Duke-Ellington: The Champs-Elysees Theater January 29-30th,1965 | Laserlight | 36131
George Gruntz Concert Jazz Band | 25 Years George Gruntz Concert Jazz Band:The World's Greatest Unknown Hits | TCB Records | TCB 96602

Rockin' In Rhythm(alt.take)
Duke Ellington And His Orchestra | Duke Ellington And His Orchestra 1943,Vol.1 | Circle | CCD-101

Rockin' The Blues
Max [Blues] Bailey Group | Obscure Blues Shouters Vol.1 | Blue Moon | BMCD 6010

Rockin' Time
Buddy Johnson And His Orchestra | Walkin' | Official | 6008

Rock'n Roll Jelly
Johnny Copeland Band | Make My Home Where Hang My Hat | Edsel | Fiend 4

Rock'n Roll Man
Tom Shaka | Hit From The Heart | Crosscut | CCD 11025

Rockochet
Passport | Looking Thru | Atlantic | 2292-44144-2

Rockport
Passport And Guests | Doldinger Jubilee Concert | Atlantic | 2292-44175-2
Frank Gambale-Allan Holdsworth Group | Truth In Shredding | Legato | HW 652507

Rocks
Sippie Wallace With Axel Zwingenberger | Sippie Wallace/Axel Zwingenberger And The Friends Of Boogie Woogie Vol.1 | Vagabond | VRCD 8.84002

Rocks & Mountains
Betty Roche And Her Quartet | Lightly And Politely | Original Jazz Classics | OJCCD 1802-2(P 7198)

Rocks In My Bed
Duke Ellington And His Famous Orchestra | In A Mellow Tone | RCA | 2113029-2
Duke Ellington And His Orchestra | Masters Of Jazz Vol.6 | RCA | NL 89824 DP
Ella Fitzgerald And Her All Stars | The Complete Ella Fitzgerald Song Books of Harold Arlen, Irving Berlin, Duke Ellington, George & Ira Gershwin, Jerome Kern, Johnny Mercer, Cole Porter And Rogers & Hart | Verve | 519832-2
Joe Turner And His Band | Have No Fear Joe Turner Is Here | Pablo | 2310863
Joe Williams With The Jimmy Jones Orchestra | Victor Jazz History Vol.20:Jazz & The Blues | RCA | 2135739-2
Sarah Vaughan And Her Band | Duke Ellington Song Book Two | Pablo | CD 2312116
Gene Harris And The Philip Morris All-Stars | Live | Concord | CCD 4808

Rocky Mountain
Billie Holiday With The Tiny Grimes Quintet | Billie's Blues | Blue Note | 748786-2

Rocky Mountain Blues
Count Basie And His Orchestra | Shoutin' Blues:Count Basie 1949 | Bluebird | 63 66158-2

Rocky Mountains
Pete Franklin | Guitar Pete's Blues | Original Blues Classics | OBCCD 560-2(BV 1068)

Rocky Raccoon
Benny Goodman And His Orchestra | Live At Carnegie Hall-40th Anniversary Concert | Decca | 6.28451 DP

Rod Halling(Red Halling)
Pata Masters | Pata-Bahia | Pata Musik | PATA 11 CD

Roda De Sete
Rüdiger Carl | Rüdiger Carl Solo | FMP | CD 86

Rohnlief
Julius Hemphill | Roi Boye & The Gotham Minstrels | Sackville | 3014/15

RoJoJo
Roy Haynes Group | Vistalita | Galaxy | GXY 5116

Roland Alphonso
Charles Mingus | Mingus Plays Piano | Mobile Fidelity | MFCD 783

Roland Kirk's Message
Great Moments With Charles Mingus | MCA | MCA 2-4128 (802130)

Roland Speaks
Roland Kirk Quartet | Verve Jazz Masters 27:Roland Kirk | Verve | 522062-2

Rolando
Domino | Verve | 543833-2
Roland Kirk With The Stan Tracy Trio | Gifts And Messages | Ronnie Scott's Jazz House | JHAS 606

Roland's Opening Remarks
Roland Kirk Quartet | Rahsaan Roland Kirk | Bethlehem | BET 6006-2(BCP 6016)

Rolf And The Gang
Peter Ehwald Trio | Away With Words:The Music Of John Scofield | Jazz Haus Musik | JHM 0128 CD
Rolf Zielke Trio Feat. Mustafa Boztüy | Rolf Zielke Trio Feat. Mustafa Boztüy | Jazz 'n' Arts Records | JNA 0602

Rolfing
Per Gudmundson-Ale Möller-Lene Willemark | Frifot | ECM | 1690(557653-2)

Roligs Per-Latar
Hans Lüdemann Rism | Aph-o-Rism's | Jazz Haus Musik | JHM 0049 CD

Roll
Honeyboy Edwards | White Windows | Evidence | ECD 26039-2

Roll Call
Rodney Jones Group | Soul Manifesto | Blue Note | 530499-2

Roll Call(Interlude)
Ted Rosenthal Trio With Tom Harrell | New Tunes New Traditions | Ken Music | 660.56.003

Roll 'Em
Benny Goodman And His Orchestra | Camel Caravan Broadcast 1939 Vol.1 | Phontastic | NCD 8817
Roll 'Em, Vol.1 | CBS | 460062-2
The Benny Goodman Yale Archives Vol.3 | Limelight | 820814-2

Roll 'Em Boy
Joe Turner With Band | Great Rhythm & Blues-Vol.4 | Bulldog | BDL 1003

Roll 'Em Pete
Axel Zwingenberger-Vince Weber | The Boogiemeisters | Vagabond | VRCD 8.99026
Big Joe Turner And His Band | American Folk Blues Festival '66 | L+R Records | CDLR 42069
Count Basie And His Orchestra | Breakfast Dance And Barbecue | Roulette | 531791-2
En Concert Avec Europe 1 | Laserlight | 710706/07
Count Basie And The Kansas City 7 | Count Basie: Salle Pleyel, April 17th, 1972 | Laserlight | 36127
Dutch Swing College Band Meets Jimmy Witherspoon | Ain't Nobody's Business | DSC Production | PA 002 (801059)
Joe Williams With The Count Basie Orchestra | Joe Williams:Triple Play | Telarc Digital | CD 83461

Roll Jordan Roll
Jacques Gauthé's Creole Rice Yerba Buena Jazz Band | Creole Jazz | Stomp Off Records | CD 1256
Papa Bue's Viking Jazzband | Greatest Hits | Storyville | 6.23336 AF

Roll On
John Rae Quintet | Opus De Jazz Vol.2-John Rae | Savoy | SV 0179(MG 12156)

Roll On The Left Side
Big Moose Walker Group | The Rising Sun Collection | The Rising Sun Collection | RSC 0008

Roll With The Punches
Hound Dog Taylor & The House Rockers | Natural Boogie | Sonet | 198044(SNTF 678)

Rollano
Billy Barber | Lighthouse | dmp Digital Music Productions | CD 455

Roller Jubilee
Blue Barron And His Orchestra | The Uncollected: Blue Barron, Vol.2 | Hindsight | HSR 137

Rollin'
Lightnin' Hopkins | Lightnin' Strikes Back | Charly | CRB 1031

Rollin' And Tumblin'
Buddy Guy-Junior Wells Band | Alone & Acoustic | Isabel | BLE 59.910 2
Muddy Waters Blues Band | Live In Switzerland 1976 | Jazz Helvet | JH 02-2

Rollin' Stone
Mose Allison Trio | That's Jazz Vol.19: Mose Allison | Atlantic | ATL 50249

Rollin' To Killeen-
Leo Parker Sextet | Rollin' With Leo | Blue Note | LT 1076

Rolling Car
Paolo Fresu Sextet | Ossi Di Seppia | SPLASC(H) Records | CD H 350-2

Rolling On Western Ave.
Axel Zwingenberger With The Lionel Hampton Big Band | The Boogie Woogie Album | Vagabond | VRCD 8.88008

Rolling Slow
Hans Theessink Group | Crazy Moon | Minor Music | 801052

Rolling Stone
Muddy Waters Blues Band | Muddy Waters-The Collection | MCA | MCD 18961
Robert Pete Williams | Free Again | Original Blues Classics | OBCCD 553-2(BV 1026)
The Brothers | The Brothers! | RCA | 2147792-2

Rollinissimo
Wolfgang Haffner Group | Movin' On | Jazz 4 Ever Records:Jazz Network | J4E 4716

Romain
Bill Evans-Jim Hall | Undercurrent | Blue Note | 538228-2

Romain(alt.take)
Jim Hall Trio | It's Nice To Be With You -Jim Hall In Berlin | MPS | 843035-2 PMS

Romaine
Modern Jazz Quartet | Pyramid | Rhino | 812273679-2
Jones Hellborg | The Silent Life | Demon Records | DEM 026

Romance
Ed Staginski | Just A Dream-A Collection For Easy Listening | yvp music | CD 3025
SheshBesh | SheshBesh | TipToe | TIP-888830 2
Steve Kuhn Trio | Seasons Of Romance | Postcards | POST 1009

Romance-
Fats Waller And His Rhythm | The Last Years 1940-1943 | Bluebird | ND 90411(3)

Romance De Amor
Tangata Rea | Tango Alla Baila | Winter&Winter | 910025-2

Romance De Barrio
Johnny Smith | Legends | Concord | CCD 4616

Romance En La Habana
The Swingle Singers | Compact Jazz:The Swingle Singers | Mercury | 830701-2 PMS

Romance-Distance
Tom Scott And His Orchestra | One Night/One Day | Soundwings | SW 2102(807410)

Romancing You
Luther Hughes Group | Luther Hughes & Cahoots | Contemporary | CCD 14028-2

Romanesque
Hot Club The Zigan | Witchcraft | Jazz Pure Collection | AU 31605 CD

Romanichel
Giulio Granata/Christian Gilardi | Cornici & Children's Song | Nueva Records | NC 2002
Romantic But Not Blue
Terence Blanchard Quintet | Romantic Defiance | CBS | 480489-2
Romantic Descension
Jo Mikowich Quartet | Jazzin' | yvp music | CD 3039
Romantic Notion(No.4)
Carla Bley Band | Fancy Chamber Music | Watt | 28(539937-2)
Romantic Notion(No.6)
Carla Bley-Steve Swallow | Duets | Watt | 20(837345-2)
Romantic Notions(No.3)
Nelson Riddle And His Orchestra | Communication | MPS | 9814795
Romantic Places
Terence Blanchard Quintet | Romantic Defiance | CBS | 480489-2
Romantic Rag
Toots Thielemans-Eugen Cicero Quartet | Nice To Meet You | Intercord | 145034
Romany
Bob Wilber Octet | Bean:Bob Wilber's Tribute To Coleman Hawkins | Arbors Records | ARCD 19144
Romanze
Caito Marcondes Group With The Turtle Island String Quartet | Porta Do Templo | ACT | 5016-2
Romas
John Coltrane-Tadd Dameron Quartet | Mating Call | Original Jazz Classics | OJCCD 212-2(P 7070)
Tadd Dameron Quartet | On A Misty Night | Prestige | P 24084
Riccardo Fassi Quartet | Toast Man | SPLASC(H) Records | CD H 307-2
Romeno Baschepen
Matthias Petzold Working Band | Elements | Indigo-Records | 1005 CD
Romeo
MIJ | Yodeling Astrologer | ESP Disk | ESP 1098-2
Romeo & Juliet
Lionel Hampton And His All Stars | Lionel Hampton And His All Stars 1956 | Jazz Anthology | 550152
Romp
Al Grey And The Basie Wing | The Last Of The Big Plungers/The Thinking Man's Trombone | Vogue | 655017
Rompin' At Red Bank
Count Basie And His Orchestra | Kansas City Suite-The Music Of Benny Cater | Roulette | CDP 794575-2
Romping
Bill Frisell Band | Blues Dream | Nonesuch | 7559-79615-2
Ron Carter
Joelle Leandre-Rüdiger Carl | Blue Goo Park | FMP | CD 52
Ronda
Horacio Molina With Band | Tango Cancion | Messidor | 15910
Rondo
Dave Grusin Group | Mountain Dance | GRP | GRP 95072
Florian Ross Quintet | Seasons And Places | Naxos Jazz | 86029-2
Rondo-
Chris Jarrett | Fire | Edition Collage | EC 443-2
Rondo 21
Shin-Ichi Fukuda | Guitar Legends:Homage To Great Popular Guitarists | Denon Compact Disc | CO-18048
Ronnie
Hans Koller Quartet | Multiple Koller | L+R Records | LR 41003
Ronnie's Line
Lee Konitz-Warne Marsh Sextet | That's Jazz Vol.21: Lee Konitz & Warne Marsh | Atlantic | ATL 50298
Ronnie's Tune
Lee Konitz Quartet | Lee Konitz In Harvard Square | Black Lion | BLCD 760928
Ron's Place
Charlie Haden Quartet With Orchestra | American Dreams | Verve | 064096-2
Randy Burns Quartet | Evening Of The Magician | ESP Disk | ESP 1089-2
Roof Garden
European Jazz Trio | Orange City | Timeless | CD SJP 336
Room 608
George Gruntz Concert Jazz Band | 25 Years George Gruntz Concert Jazz Band:The World's Greatest Unknown Hits | TCB Records | TCB 96602
Room 626
Sherrie Maricle/John Mastroianni Quintet | Cookin' On All Burners | Stash Records | ST-CD 24(881828)
Room No.251
Rudy Linka Trio | Always Double Czech! | Enja | ENJ-9301 2
Room Rent Blues
John Gill's Novelty Orchestra Of New Orleans | Headin' For Better Times | Stomp Off Records | CD 1270
Room Upstairs
Lou Rawls And His Orchestra | At Last | Blue Note | 791937-2
Rooming House Boogie
Cab Calloway And His Cab Jivers | Cab Calloway & Co | RCA | ND 89560
Rooms
Bill Hardman Sextet | What's Up' | Steeplechase | SCS 1254
Root Canal
Doctor Clayton Band | Gotta Find My Baby | Swingtime(Contact) | BT 2005
Root Down(And Get It)
Jimmy Smith Quintet | Root Down | Verve | 559805-2
Root Down(And Get It-alt.take)
Scott Henderson-Gary Willis Quartet | Illicit | Bluemoon | R 27-9180-2
Rootie Tootie -> Little Rootie Tootie
Roots
Muhal Richard Abrams | Afrisong | India Navigation | IN 1058
Ulli Bögershausen | Sologuitar | Laika Records | 35101132
Willie Bobo Group | Juicy | Verve | 519857-2
Chris Beier | Roots | Media Arte | CD 587
Roots 6406
Manfred Schoof Quintet | Voices | L+R Records | LR 41005
Roots And Herbs
Harold Danko | Ink And Water | Sunnyside | SSC 1008(952101)
Roots In The Sky(1)
Glen Moore Group | Nude Bass Ascending... | Intuition Records | INT 3192-2
Roots In The Sky(2)
Serge Forté Trio | Vaina | Laika Records | LK 90-021
Roots Of Love
Albert Mangelsdorff Quartet | Spontaneous | Enja | 2064
Roots Woman
Wolfgang Haffner Group | Movin' On | Jazz 4 Ever Records:Jazz Network | J4E 4716
Roots(part 2)
Dave Liebman | The Three | Soul Note | 121195-2
Roppongi
Rob Mullins Group | Tokyo Nights | Nova | NOVA 9026-2
Rosa
Jeremy Steig-Eddie Gomez Group | Rain Forest | CMP Records | CMP 12
Rosa Del Desert
Onix | Stress | Fresh Sound Records | FSR 104 (835273)
Rosa Mae
Mary Lou Williams Trio | Zoning | Mary Records | M 103
Rosa Morena
Kurt Elling Group | This Time Its Love | Blue Note | 493543-2
The Haitian Orchestra | Haitin Understanding | Avenue | AVINT 1021
Rosa Takes A Stand(for Rosa Parks)
Toots Thielemans Quartet With Orchestra | Bluesette | CBS | CDCOL 26604
Ros-Al
| Earl Hines Plays Cole Porter | New World Records | 80501-2

Rosalie
Erroll Garner Trio | Separate Keyboards:Erroll Garner/Billy Taylor | Savoy | SV0223(MG 12008)
Rosanne
Jack Montrose And All-Stars | The Horn's Full | RCA | NL 45956(RCA LPM 1572)
Rosaria
Manhattan Jazz Quintet | Face To Face | Paddle Wheel | 292 E 6032
Rosati At Popolo Square-
David Murray Quartet | Flowers For Albert | India Navigation | IN 1026
Rose
Larry Nocella/Dannie Richmond Quartet | Everything Happens To Me | Red Records | VPA 167
Rose And Sad Song
Nat King Cole Trio With Pete Rugolo's Orchestra | Lush Life | Capitol | 780595-2
Rose Arco
Count Basie And His Orchestra | On My Way And Shoutin' Again | Verve | 2304385 IMS
Rose Drop
Wally Cirillo Quartet | Jazz Composers Workshop | Savoy | SV 0171(MG 12059)
Rose Of The Rio Grande
Charlie Byrd Quartet | Moments Like This | Concord | CCD 4627
Duke Ellington And His Orchestra | Ella & Duke At The Cote D'Azur | Verve | 539030-2
Big Band Bounce And Boogie:Classic Transcriptions-Duke Ellington | Affinity | AFS 1032
Crystal Ballroom, Fargo Concert | Jazz Anthology | JA 5229/30
The Duke At Fargo 1940 | Storyville | STCD 8316/17
Dutch Swing College Band | 25th Anniversary Concert | DSC Production | PA 001 (801058)
Johnny Hodges Orchestra | Johnny Hodges At The Sportpalast, Berlin | Pablo | 2CD 2620102
Johnny St.Cyr And His Hot Five | Johnny St. Cyr | American Music | AMCD-78
Marty Grosz And His Swinging Fools | The Second Sampler | Nagel-Heyer | NHR SP 6
Ring Dem Bells | Nagel-Heyer | CD 022
Mike Wofford | Maybeck Recital Hall Series Volume Eighteen | Concord | CCD 4514
Modern Jazz Quartet | MJQ | Original Jazz Classics | OJCCD 125-2
The MJQ Box | Prestige | 7711-2
Rose Of Washington Square
Bob Crosby And His Orchestra | Bob Crosby And His Orchestra Vol.9(1939):Them There Eyes | Halcyon | DHDL 128
Rose Of Washington Square-
Pee Wee Russell's Hot Four | Pee Wee Russell:Jazz Original | Commodore | CMD 14042
Rose Petals
Keith Jarrett Quintet | Shades | MCA | 62742 (801433)
Rose Room
Albert Nicholas With The Henri Chaix Trio | Kornhaus Theater Baden 1969 | Sackville | SKCD2-2045
Big Eye Louis Nelson Band | Big Eye Louis Nelson:1949 Sessions & Live At Luthjens | American Music | AMCD-7
Bill Coleman Quintet | Dicky Wells & Bill Coleman In Paris | Affinity | CD AFS 1004
Carmen Cavallaro And His Orchestra | The Uncollected: Carmen Cavallaro | Hindsight | HSR 112
Dutch Swing College Band | 25th Anniversary Concert | DSC Production | PA 001 (801058)
Earl Hines | Dinah | RCA | NL 70577
Muggsy Spanier And His Dixieland All Stars | At Club Hangover-Vol. 2 | Storyville | SLP 249
Nat King Cole Quartet | Penthouse Serenade | Capitol | 494504-2
Oscar Peterson-Austin Roberts | Oscar Peterson 1951 | Just A Memory | JAS 9501-2
Sidney Bechet And His New Orleans Feetwarmers | Sidney Bechet 1932-1943: The Bluebird Sessions | Bluebird | ND 90317
Teddy Wilson And His Orchestra | The Radio Years | London | HMG 5020 AN
Teddy Wilson Trio | Revisited The Goodman Years | Storyville | STCD 4046
The Leon Prima Gang | Jazz Live & Rare: The First And Second Esquire Concert | Jazzline | ???
The Rosenberg Trio | Tribute To Django Reinhardt | EmArCy | 9811568
Woody Herman And The Concord Jam | A Concord Jam-Vol. 1 | Concord | CCD 4142
Benny Goodman And His Orchestra | The Yale University Muisc Library Vol.5 | Limelight | 820827-2 IMS
Rose Room(alt.take-1)
Earl Hines | Americans Swinging In Paris:Earl Hines | EMI Records | 539661-2
Rose Room(alt.take-2)
Benny Carter And His Orchestra | Jazz Off The Air Vol. 3 | Spotlite | SPJ 147
Rose Waltz
KontaSax | KontraSax Plays Getrude Stein | Jazz Haus Musik | JHM 0096 CD
Rose(1)
KontraSax Plays Getrude Stein | Jazz Haus Musik | JHM 0096 CD
Rose(3)
David Kikoski Trio | Almost Twilight | Criss Cross | Criss 1190
Rosebud
Manel Camp & Matthew Simon Acustic Jazz Quintet | Rosebud | Fresh Sound Records | FSNT 011 CD
Richard Zimmerman | The Complete Works Of Scott Joplin | Laserlight | 15945
Rosebud(alt.take 1)
Birdland Dream Band | Birdland Dream Band | RCA | 2663873-2
Rosebud(alt.take 2)
Basie Reunion | Basie Reunion | Prestige | P 24109
Roseland Shuffle
Lloyd Jones Blues Band | Trouble Monkey | audioquest Music | AQCD 1037
Rosemary's Baby
Zoot Sims Quartet | Zoot At Easy | Mobile Fidelity | MFCD 842
Rosemonday Blues
Gabriele Hasler Group | Gabriele Hasler's Rosensrücke | Foolish Music | FM 211096
Rosenchor
Emil Mangelsdorff Quartet & Sebastian Norden | Allen Ginsberg: Das Geheul | Trion | 5101/2
Rosenholz
Gabriele Hasler Group | Gabriele Hasler's Rosensrücke | Foolish Music | FM 211096
Rosenrot
Agnes Buen Garnas-Jan Garbarek | Rosensfole-Medieval Songs From Norway | ECM | 1402(839293-2)
Rosensfole
Gabriele Hasler Group | Gabriele Hasler's Rosensrücke | Foolish Music | FM 211096
Rosenstück
David Murray Big Band | Live At Sweet Basil Vol.2 | Black Saint | 120095-2
Roses And
Sarah Vaughan With Orchestra | I Love Brazil | Pablo | 2312101-2
Roses And Roses
Heinz Sauer 4tet | Exchange 2 | free flow music | ffm 0998
Roses Are Black
Exchange 2 | free flow music | ffm 0998
Roses Are Black(fast version)
Sidney Bechet With Andre Rewellotty And His Orchestra | Sidney Bechet | Vogue | 000001 GK

Roses For You
Nat Adderley Quintet | Natural Soul | Milestone | M 9009
Roses For Your Pillow
Benny Carter And His Orchestra | Aspects | Capitol | 852677-2
Roses In December
Dick Robertson And His Orchestra | The New York Session Man | Timeless | CBC 1-008
Rose's Last Summer
Alvin Alcorn New Orleans Jazz Babies | Sounds Of New Orleans Vol.5 | Storyville | STCD 6012
Roses Of Picardy
Bob Wilber Quintet | Bob Wilbur:Nostalgia | Arbors Records | ARCD 19145
Frankie Laine With Carl Fischer's Orchesrtra | The Uncollected:Frankie Lane Vol.2 | Hindsight | HSR 216 (835570)
Rosetta
Art Tatum | Art Tatum:Complete Original American Decca Recordings | Definitive Records | DRCD 11200
Duke Jordan Trio | When You're Smiling | Steeplechase | SCCD 37023/24
Earl Hines | Jazz:The Essential Collection Vol.2 | IN+OUT Records | 78012-2
Hine's Tune | France's Concert | FCD 101
Garnet Clark And His Hot's Club Four | Django Reinhardt And His American Friends:Paris 1935-1937 | Memo Music | HDJ 4124
Jimmy Dorsey And His Dorseyland Band | The Uncollected:Jimmy Dorsey-Dorseyland Band | Hindsight | HSR 203
Joe Turner | Another Epoch-Stride Piano | Pablo | 2310763
Kenny Davern-Dick Wellstood | Live At The Vineyard | Challenge | CHR 70019
Magnificant Seventh's with Milton Batiste And Alton Carson | Best Of New Orleans:Bourbon Street Jazz After Dark | Mardi Gras Records | MG 1022
Muggsy Spanier And His Ragtimers | Commodore Classics-Muggsy Spanier:Hot Horn 1944 | Commodore | 6.26167 AG
Sammy Price Septet | Barrelhouse And Blues | Black Lion | BLCD 760159
Summit Reunion | Jazz Im Amerikahaus,Vol.5 | Nagel-Heyer | CD 015
Teddy Wilson | Piano Solos | Affinity | CD AFS 1016
The New York Allstars | Broadway | Nagel-Heyer | CD 003
The Newport All Stars | That Newport Jazz | CBS | 21139
The Tremble Kids | The Tremble Kids:The Of 40 Years | BELL Records | BLR 84060
Vic Lewis Jam Session | Vic Lewis:The Golden Years | Candid | CCD 79754
Wild Bill Davison All Stars | Wild Bill At Bull Run | Jazzology | JCD-30
Earl Hines | Live At The New School-Vol. 2 | Chiaroscuro | CR 180
Rosetta(alt.take)
Fats Waller And His Rhythm | Breakin' The Ice-The Early Years Part 1(1934-1935) | Bluebird | 63 66618-2
Rosita
Mel Tormé With The Billy May Orchestra | Mel Tormé Goes South Of The Border With Billy May | Verve | 589517-2
Randy Sandke Sextet | The Sandke Brothers | Stash Records | ST-CD 575(875901)
Rosiwalzer
New York Art Quartet | New York Art Quartet | ESP Disk | ESP 1004-2
Ross 780
Ray Anderson Sextet | It Just So Happens | Enja | ENJ-5037 2
Ross The Boss
Ahmad Jamal Quartet | Life At The Montreal Jazz Festival 1985 | Atlantic | 781699-2
Rosslyn
Riccardo Fassi Tankio Band | Il Principe | SPLASC(H) Records | H 180
Rostock,Wir Kommen!
Harmut Geerken/Famoudou Don Moye/John Tchicai | Cassava Balls | Praxis | CM 111
Rotarumpo
Duke Pearson Orchestra | The Right Touch | Blue Note | 828269-2
Rotation
Charly Antolini Quintet | Crash | BELL Records | BLR 84002
Rothko
Polo De Haas Quartet | Soolmaan | Timeless | CD SJP 384
Rotterdam Blues
McCoy Tyner Group With Voices | Inner Voices | Original Jazz Classics | OJCCD 1039-2(M 9079)
Rotunda
McCoy Tyner Quartet | The Story Of Jazz Piano | Laserlight | 24653
McCoy Tyner Quintet | Blue Bossa | LRC Records | CDC 9033(874377)
Rouge
Gerry Mulligan Orchestra | Re-Birth Of The Cool | GRP | GRP 96792
Miles Davis And His Orchestra | Birth Of The Cool | Capitol | 530117-2
Miles Davis:The Blue Note And Capitol Recordings | Blue Note | 827475-2
Rouge-
Joachim Raffel Quintet With Maria De Fatima | Thinkin' Of Trane | Acoustic Music Records | 319.1059.2
Rough Night
Artie Shaw Quintet | Artie Shaw:The Last Recordings | Limelight | 820847-2 IMS
Rough Ridin'
Ella Fitzgerald With The Ray Brown Orchestra | Ella Fitzgerald 75th Birthday Celebration:The Original Decca Recordings | GRP | GRP 26192
Roulette
Badiane | Flavours | Acoustic Music Records | 319.1071.2
Round About Midnight
Al Haig Trio | The Piano Collection Vol.2 | Vogue | 21610222
Andy Summers Group | Green Chimneys:The Music Of Thelonious Monk | RCA | 2663472-2
Art Blakey And The Jazz Messengers | Blakey's Theme | West Wind | WW 2045
Meet You At The Jazz Corner Of The World | Blue Note | 535565-2
Art Farmer/Benny Golson Jazztet | The Jazztet At Birdhouse | Argo | 589762-2
Art Pepper Plus Eleven | Art Pepper + Eleven | Contemporary | CSA 7568-6
Modern Jazz Classics | Original Jazz Classics | OJC20 341-2
A Treasury Of Modern Jazz Classics | Mobile Fidelity | MFCD 805
Art Pepper-George Cables Duo | Art Pepper:The Complete Galaxy Recordings | Galaxy | 16GCD 1016-2
Aurora | Aurora | Denon Compact Disc | CY-73148
Baden Powell Solo/Group | Tristeza On Guitar | MPS | 68087
Barney Kessel With The Monty Alexander Trio | Spontaneous Combustion | Contemporary | C 14033
Benny Carter And His Strings With The Oscar Peterson Quartet | Alone Together | Verve | 2304512 IMS
Bill Evans | Compact Jazz: Bill Evans | Verve | 831366-2 PMS
Conversations With Myself | Verve | 521409-2
Bill Evans Trio | The Complete Bill Evans On Verve | Verve | 527953-2
The Complete Bill Evans On Verve | Verve | 527953-2
The Complete Bill Evans On Verve | Verve | 527953-2
Trio '65 | Verve | 2304517 IMS
Bill Evans:The Secret Sessions | Milestone | 8MCD 4421-2
Live In Stockholm 1965 | Royal Jazz | RJD 519
Bill Evans:The Secret Sessions | Milestone | 8MCD 4421-2
'Round Midnight | Milestone | MCD 9144-2
Bob Cooper And His Orchestra | Shifting Winds | Affinity | AFF 59
Bobby Watson Quartet | Advance | Enja | ENJ-9075 2
Boulou Ferre Quartet | Relax And Enjoy | Steeplechase | SCS 1210
C.I.Williams Quintet | When Alto Was King | Mapleshade | 04532
Carol Kidd With The Sandy Taylor Trio And String Quartet | All My Tomorrows | Linn Records | AKD 005
Charles Brown Quartet | The Legend Charles Brown-Blues And Other Love Songs | Muse | MCD 5466
Charlie Parker All Stars | Summit Meeting At Birdland | CBS | CBS 82291

TITELVERZEICHNIS

Chris Connor And Her Quartet | Chris In Person | Atlantic | AMCY 1063
Clifford Jordan Quartet | Live At Ethell's | Mapleshade | 56292
Dave Burrell | Plays Ellington & Monk | Denon Compact Disc | DC-8550
Diane Schuur With Orchestra | The Best Of Diane Schuur | GRP | GRP 98882
Dizzy Gillespie And His Big Band | Gene Norman Presents Dizzy Gillespie And His Big Band | GNP Crescendo | GNPD 23
Dizzy Gillespie Big Band | Bird's Eyes-Last Unissued Vol.13 | Philology | W 843.2
Dollar Brand Trio | 'Round Midnight At The Montmartre | Black Lion | BLP 60111
Duo Brazil | Carioca | M.A Music | A 808-2
Ella Fitzgerald With The Lou Levy Quartet | Ella Returns To Berlin | Verve | 837758-2
Esbjörn Svensson Trio(E.S.T) With Strings | EST Plays Monk | ACT | 9010-2
Esbjörn Svensson Trio(E.S.T.) | EST Plays Monk | RCA | 2137680-2
George Russell Sextet | Eric Dolphy Birthday Celebration | Fantasy | FANCD 6085-2
Geri Allen | Home Grown | Minor Music | 8004
Giants Of Jazz | Live | Jazz Door | JD 1277
Grant Green Trio | Ballads | Blue Note | 537560-2
Great Jazz Trio With Terumasa Hino | Monk's Mood | Denon Compact Disc | 38C38-7323
Hank Jones | Maybeck Recital Hall Series Volume Sixteen | Concord | CCD 4502
Herbie Hancock | The Other Side Of Round Midnight | Blue Note | 746397-2
International All Stars | Doldinger Jubilee | Atlantic | ATL 60073
Jaki Byard Trio | Giant Steps | Prestige | P 24086
James Moody Quintet | Moving Forward | Novus | PD 83026
Jessica Williams Trio | Nothin' But The Truth | Black-Hawk | BKH 51301 CD
Jimmy Raney Quintet | Early Getz | Prestige | P 24088
Jimmy Smith And Wes Montgomery With The Oliver Nelson Orchestra | Compact Jazz: Wes Montgomery Plays The Blues | Verve | 835318-2 PMS
Joe Beck-Ali Ryerson-Steve Davis | Alto | dmp Digital Music Productions | CD 521
Joe Henderson Quartet | Keystone Bop Vol.2:Friday/Saturday | Prestige | PCD 24163-2
Joe Henderson:The Milestone Years | Milestone | 8MCD 4413-2
Joe Henderson Quintet | At The Lighthouse | Milestone | M 9028
Joe Henderson Trio | The Standard Joe | Red Records | 123248-2
Joe Pass | Virtuoso | Pablo | 2310708-2
Joe Pass:A Man And His Guitar | Original Jazz Classics | OJCCD 8806-2
Joe Pass:A Man And His Guitar | Original Jazz Classics | OJCCD 8806-2
Live At Long Beach City College | Pablo | 2308239-2
Joe Roccisano Orchestra | Leave Your Mind Behind | Landmark | LCD 1541-2
Jon Faddis Quartet | Youngblood | Pablo | 2310765
Ken McIntyre Quartet | Hindsight | Steeplechase | SCCD 31014
Kenny Burrell And The Jazz Guitar Band | Pieces Of Blue And The Blues | Blue Note | 790260-2
Kenny Dorham Quartet | Blowin' From New York 1964 Vol.1 | Raretone | 5021 FC
Kenny Dorham Sextet | Round Midnight At The Cafe Bohemia | Blue Note | 300105(1524)
Larry Coryell Quartet | Toku Do | Muse | MCD 5350
Lee Konitz With Strings | Lee Konitz Meets Jimmy Giuffre | Verve | 527780-2
Lilian Terry With The Tommy Flanagan Trio | A Dream Comes True | Soul Note | 121047-2
Martial Solal Trio | At Newport '63 | RCA | 2125768-2
Mel Tormé With The Marty Paich Orchestra | Torme 1 | Verve | 2304500 IMS
Mike Campbell And His Band | Secret Fantasy | Palo Alto | PA 8020
Miles Davis And The Lighthouse All Stars | At Last! | Original Jazz Classics | OJCCD 480-2
Miles Davis Quintet | Miles Davis Classics | CBS | CBS 88138
Miles Davis In Person-Friday Night At The Blackhawk,San Francisco,Vol.1 | CBS | C4K 87106
The Miles Davis Selection | CBS | 465699-2
Miles Davis: Olympia, March 29th,1960 | Laserlight | 36130
Miles Davis In Stockholm Complete | Dragon | DRCD 228
Milt Jackson Quartet | Memories Of Thelonious Sphere Monk | Pablo | 2308235
Modern Jazz Quartet | European Concert | Atlantic | SD 2-603
Music Inc | Live In Tokyo | Strata East Records | 660.51.016
New York Voices | New York Voices | GRP | GRP 95892
Oliver Jones Trio | Requestfully Yours | Justin Time | Just 11
Overtone | All The Things We Are | Workshop Records | WR 071
Plas Johnson Band | The Warm Sound Of Plas Johnson Tenor Sax Vol.1:Midnight Blue | Blue Moon | BMCD 3060
Red Rodney Quintet | Bird Lives! | Muse | MCD 5371
Ron Carter Quartet | 'Round Midnight | Milestone | MCD 9144-2
Sarah Vaughan With The Gerald Wilson Orchestra | The Roulette Years Vol. One/Two | Roulette | CDP 794983-2
Sir Charles Thompson | Portrait Of A Piano | Sackville | 3037
Sonny Rollins Quartet | Masters Of Jazz Vol.14 | RCA | CL 42874 AG
Stan Getz-Albert Dailey Duo | Poetry | Blue Note | 960370-1 TIS
Steve Coleman And Five Elements | Steve Coleman's Music Live In Paris | Novus | 2131691-2
Steve Kuhn | Mostly Ballads | New World Records | 80351-2
Sun Ra Arkestra | Sunrise In Different Dimensions | HatOLOGY | 568
Sweet Basil Trio | My Funny Valentine | Sweet Basil | 660.55.010
Tempo Jazzmen | Groovin' High | Naxos Jazz | 8.120582 CD
The Prestige All Stars | Two Trumpets | Original Jazz Classics | OJCCD 018-2(P 7062)
Thelonious Monk | Pure Monk | Milestone | M 47004
The Story Of Jazz Piano | Laserlight | 24653
Thelonious Himself | Original Jazz Classics | OJCCD 254-2
The Thelonious Monk Memorial Album | Milestone | MCD 47064-2
Thelonious Monk Piano Solo | Vogue | 21409362
'Round Midnight | Milestone | MCD 9144-2
Thelonious Monk Quartet | Live At The Jazz Workshop-Complete | CBS | C2K 65189
Live In Switzerland 1966 | Jazz Helvet | JH 06
Thelonious Monk In Copenhagen | Storyville | STCD 8283
Thelonious Monk In Stockholm | Duke Records | D 1020
Thelonious Monk Quintet | Thelonious Monk:Misterioso | Dreyfus Jazz Line | FDM 36743-2
The Complete Genius | Blue Note | LA 579
Monk's Mood | Naxos Jazz | 8.120588 CD
Thelonious Monk:Complete 1947-1952 Blue Note Recordings | The Jazz Factory | JFCD 22838
Thelonious Monk Sextet | In Person | Milestone | M 47033
Tito Puente And His Latin Ensemble | Sensacion | Concord | CCD 4301
Toto Blanke-Rudolf Dasek | Mona Lisa | ALISO Records | AL 1037
Vienna Art Orchestra | Perpetuum Mobile | Hat Art | 2024 Digital
Walter Davis Trio | Live Au Dreher | Harmonia Mundi | PJC 222005
Wes Montgomery Trio | 'Round Midnight | Milestone | MCD 9144-2
Wild Bill Davis Quartet | Organ 1959 | Jazz Anthology | JA 5132
Wolfgang Puschnig-Jamaladeen Tacuma Trio | Gemini Gemini-The Flavors Of Thelonious Monk | ITM-Pacific | ITMP 970082

Round About Midnight-
Charlie Parker With The Cootie Williams Orchestra | Bird's Eyes Last Unissued Vol.22:Don't Blame Me | Philology | W 852.2
Deborah Brown With The Jack Van Poll Trio | Deborah! | September | CD 5103
Dizzy Gillespie Quintet | Something Old Something New | Verve | 558079-2
Ella Fitzgerald With The Jazz At Carnegie All-Stars | Newport Jazz Festival - Live At Carnegie Hall | CBS | CBS 68279
Ray Brown & Laurindo Almeida | Moonlight Serenade | Jeton | JET 60005

Round About Midnight(alt.take)
Chet Baker Quintet | All Blues | Arco | 3 ARC 102
Thelonious Monk Quartet | Live At The Jazz Workshop-Complete | CBS | C2K 65189
Benny Carter And His Strings With The Oscar Peterson Quartet | The Urban Sessions/New Jazz Sound | Verve | 531637-2

Round And Round
J.B.Lenoir | Down In Mississippi | L+R Records | LR 42012
Louis Hayes Quintet | The Candy Man | TCB Records | TCB 20972
Lee Konitz Quartet | Round & Round | Musicmasters | 65140-2

Round 'Bout Five
Andy LaVerne/Dave Samuels | Fountainhead | Steeplechase | SCCD 31261

Round Johnny Ronde
John Schröder-Henrik Walsdorff-Uli Jenneßen | Freedom Of Speech | FMP | OWN-90011

Round Lights
Thelonious Monk | Thelonious Monk-The Complete Riverside Recordings | Riverside | 15 RCD 022-2

Round Midnight -> Round About Midnight

'Round Robin
Stan Kenton And His Orchestra | By Request Vol.1 | Creative World | ST 1036

Round She Goes
Gene Quill With The Hank Jones Quartet | Rhythm Plus One | Fresh Sound Records | LSP 15597(Epic LN 3297)

'Round The Bay Of Mexico
European Tuba Quartet | Low And Behold | Jazz Haus Musik | JHM 0110 CD

'Round The Block
Deborah Henson-Conant Trio | 'Round The Corner | Laika Records | LK 87-203

'Round The Corner
Jimmy Smith With Orchestra | Sum Serious Blues | Milestone | MCD 9207-2

'Round The Four Corners
Bob Degen Trio | Catability | Enja | ENJ-9332 2

Round Trip
Bobby Watson & Open Form Trio | Round Trip | Red Records | VPA 187
Joe Fonda-Michael Jefry Stevens Group | The Wish | Music & Arts | CD 916
Matthieu Michel Quintet feat. Richard Galliano | Estate | TCB Records | TCB 95802
Ornette Coleman Quartet | The Best Of Ornette Coleman:The Blue Note Years | Blue Note | 823372-2
Saheb Sarbib Quartet | Seasons | Soul Note | 121048-2
Tiziana Ghiglioni And Her Quartet | Yet Time | SPLASC(H) Records | CD H 150-2

Round Trip-
Joel Futterman-Robert Adkins | Vision In Time | Silkheart | SHCD 125

Roundalay
John Surman | Private City | ECM | 1366

Roundelay
Booker Little 4 & Max Roach | Booker Little 4 & Max Roach | Blue Note | 784457-2

Rounder's Mood
Charlie Parker With The Joe Timer Orchestra | Bird's Eyes Last Unissued Vol.22:Don't Blame Me | Philology | W 852.2

Rounds
Steve Allen All Stars | At The Roundtable | Fresh Sound Records | FSR 571(Roulette R 25053)

Roundtrip
Erik Truffaz Quartet | The Dawn | Blue Note | 493916-2

Round-Trip
Paul Motian And The E.B.B.B. | Holiday For Strings | Winter&Winter | 910069-2

Roundup
Stan Getz Quintet | Stan Getz Highlights:The Best Of The Verve Years Vol.2 | Verve | 517330-2

Roundup Time
Stan Getz And The 'Cool' Sounds | Verve | 547317-2
Tony Fruscella Quintet | Pernod | The Jazz Factory | JFCD 22804

Rouse's Point
Keith Jarrett Group | Expectations | CBS | C2K 65900

Roussillon
Walter Brown | Living Country Blues USA Vol.7: Afro-American Blues Roots | L+R Records | LR 42037

Route 4
Prestige All Stars | John Coltrane-The Prestige Recordings | Prestige | 16 PCD 4405-2
Teddy Charles New Directions Quartet With Booker Little And Booker Ervin | Jazz In The Garden At The Museum Of Modern Art | Fresh Sound Records | FSR-CD 0212

Route 66
Bebo Valdés Trio | El Arte Del Sabor | Blue Note | 535193-2
Bill Ramsey & Juraj Galan | Caldonia And More... | Bear Family Records | BCD 16151 AH
Buddy Greco Quartet | Route 66-A Personal Tribute To Nat King Cole | Celebrity | CYCD 71901
Katie Kern Group | Still Young | Jazzpoint | JP 1070 CD
Max Greger Quintet | Night Train | Polydor | 543393-2
Nat King Cole And His Trio | Nat King Cole:The Snader Telescriptions | Storyville | 4960103
Werner Pöhlert Combo | Something Cool:Werner Pöhlert Combo Recordings 1985-1009 | Hohner Records | ohne Nummer(2)

Row To Tow
Kid Bailey | The Greatest In Country Blues Vol.3(1929-1956) | Story Of Blues | CD 3523-2

Roxane
Gil Evans Orchestra With Sting | Sting And Gil Evans/Last Session | Jazz Door | JD 1228

Roxanne(reprise)
Norbert Emminger Quintet | In The Park | Edition Collage | EC 521-2

Roxi Music
Lee Konitz Orchestra | Chicago'n All That Jazz | LRC Records | CDC 7971

Roy Allen
Dave Brubeck/Jon Hendricks | Young Lions & Old Tigers | Telarc Digital | CD 83349

Royal
Ella Fitzgerald With The Duke Ellington Orchestra | Ella Fitzgerald Sings The Duke Ellington Song Book Vol.2 | Verve | 2615033 IMS

Royal Ancestry(First Movement)
The Complete Ella Fitzgerald Song Books of Harold Arlen, Irving Berlin, Duke Ellington, George & Ira Gershwin, Jerome Kern, Johnny Mercer, Cole Porter And Rogers & Hart | Verve | 519832-2

Royal Blue-
Rob McConnell-Ed Bickert-Don Thompson | Three For The Road | Concord | CCD 4765

Royal Flush
Sonny Clark Quintet | My Conception | Blue Note | 522674-2
Christian Wallumrod Trio | No Birch | ECM | 1628(537344-2)

Royal Garden
| Pete Fountain And His Basin Street Six | 504 Records | 504CD 16

Royal Garden Blues
Albert Nicholas With Alan Elsdon's Band | Albert Nicholas With Alan Elsdon's Band Vol.2 | Jazzology | JCD-269
Alvin Alcorn Jam Session | Sounds Of New Orleans Vol.5 | Storyville | STCD 6012
Bix Beiderbecke And His New Orleans Lucky Seven | Riverboat Shuffle | Naxos Jazz | 8.120584 CD
Count Basie Sextet | The Swinging Count | Verve | MV 2646 IMS
Dutch Swing College Band | Dixieland Jubilee-Vol. 2 | Intercord | 155005
Earl Hines Trio | Jazz In Paris:Earl Hines-Paris One Night Stand | EmArCy | 548207-2 PMS
Eddie Condon All Stars | Jazz Festival Vol.1 | Storyville | 4960733
Eddie Condon In Japan | Chiaroscuro | CR 154
Ella Fitzgerald And Her Orchestra | Live From The Roseland Ballroom New York 1940 | Jazz Anthology | 550032
Frl. Mayer's Hinterhaus Jazzer | Frl. Mayer's Hinterhaus Jazzer | Jazz Classics | AU 11097
George Lewis Ragtime Jazz Band Of New Orleans | The Oxford Series Vol.7 | American Music | AMCD-27
Humphrey Lyttelton And His Band | North Sea Festival Vol.1 | Jazz Colours | 874758-2
John Kirby And His Band | 1940 | Jazz Anthology | 550252
Louis Armstrong And His All Stars | The Legendary Berlin Concert Part 2 | Jazzpoint | JP 1063 CD
Victor Jazz History Vol.19:Dixieland Revival | RCA | 2135738-2
Louis Armstrong:Wintergarden 1947/Blue Note 1948 | Storyville | STCD 8242
Jazz Collection:Louis Armstrong | Laserlight | 24366
Rockin' Chair | Topline Records | TOP 119
Muggsy Spanier And His Dixieland All Stars | At Club Hangover-Vol. 2 | Storyville | SLP 249
National Jazz Ensemble | National Jazz Ensemble Vol. 2 | Chiaroscuro | CR 151
Paul Barbarin's Jazz Band Of New Orleans | The Oxford Series Vol.15 | American Music | AMCD-35
Ruby Braff All Stars | Being With You:Ruby Braff Remembers Louis Armstrong | Arbors Records | ARCD 19163
Sidney Bechet With Claude Luter And His Orchestra | Salle Pleyel 31 January 52 | Vogue | 655001
The Sidney Bechet Society | Jam Session Concert | Nagel-Heyer | CD 076
The Wolverines | Bix Beiderbecke | Milestone | MCD 47019-2
Chicago Jazz 1924-28 | Village(Jazz Archive) | VILCD 007-2

Royal Garden Blues-
Wild Bill Davison And His World Famous Jazz Band | Wild Bill Davison And His Jazz Band 1943 | Jazzology | JCD-103

Royal Garden Blues(alt.take)
Mezzrow-Ladnier Quintet | The Complete Sidney Bechet-Vol.5 | RCA | 2115519-2
Sidney Bechet With Claude Luter And His Orchestra | Salle Pleyel 31 January 52 | Vogue | 655001

Royal Honeymoon
Ella Fitzgerald With The Duke Ellington Orchestra | Ella Fitzgerald Sings The Duke Ellington Song Book Vol.2 | Verve | 2615033 IMS

Royal Poinciana
Marshall Royal Quintet | Royal Blue | Concord | CJ 125

Royal Roost
Charlie Parker All Stars | Bird At The Roost Vol.3 | Savoy | ???

Royal Telephone
Phil Mason's New Orleans All-Stars | West Indies Blues | Lake | LACD 93

Roy's Riff
Roy Eldridge With The Oscar Peterson Quartet | Rockin' Chair | Verve | MV 2686 IMS

Roy's Tune
Roy Haynes Hip Ensemble | Equipoise | Mainstream | MD CDO 715

Rraam
Ahmad Mansour Quartet | Oxiana | Timeless | CD SJP 344

Rub A Dub Dub
Lloyd Smith's Gut-Bucketeers | Jazz Archives Vol.77:Jabbo Smith-The Complete 1929-1938 Sessions | EPM Musique | 158112

Rub-A-Dub
Ippe Kätkä Band | Ippe Kätkä Band | Leo Records | 018

Rubato
Rade Soric Quartet | Mixturiosities | Edition Collage | EC 502-2

Rubato-
Phil Minton/Roger Turner Duo | Ammo | LEO | LR 116

Rubber Dolly
Dick Wellstood | Diane | Swingtime | 8207

Rubberneck
Frank Rosolino Quartet | The Trombone Album | Savoy | WL 70523(2)(809310)
Stan Getz Quintet | Jazz At Storyville Vol.2 | Fresh Sound Records | FSR 630(Roost RLP 411)

Rubum Allorans
Ahmad Jamal Trio | I Remember Duke,Hoagy & Strayhorn | Telarc Digital | CD 83339

Ruby
Coleman Hawkins With The Neal Hefti Orchestra | The Hawk Talks | Affinity | AFF 139
Jimmy Ponder Quartet | To Reach A Dream | Muse | MCD 5394
Jimmy Smith With The Claus Ogerman Orchestra | Any Number Can Win | Verve | 557447-2
Milt Jackson All Stars | Invitation | Original Jazz Classics | OJCCD 260-2
Mark Murphy-Gary Schunk | Mark Murphy Sings Nat Cing Cole,Volumes 1&2 | Muse | MCD 6001

Ruby Domesticus
Wollie Kaiser Timeghost | Tust Du Fühlen Gut | Jazz Haus Musik | JHM 0060 CD
European Jazz Quintet | European Jazz Quintet III | Fusion | 8010

Ruby Lapp Is Dead-
B.B.King And His Band | Singin' The Blues/The Blues | Ace Records | CDCHD 320

Ruby My Dear
Billy Drummond Quintet | Native Colours | Criss Cross | Criss 1057
Dave McKenna-Hal Overton Quartet | Dual Piano Jazz | Fresh Sound Records | FSR 2036(Bethlehem BCP 6049)
Dexter Gordon Sextet | Dexter Gordon Plays-The Bethlehem Years | Fresh Sound Records | FSR-CD 154(882891)
Henri Chaix Trio | Jumpin' Punkins | Sackville | SKCD2-2020
Kenny Drew Trio | The Riverside Collection: Kenny Drew | Original Jazz Classics | OJCCD 667-2
Mal Waldron & Jim Pepper | Art Of The Duo | Tutu Records | 888106-2*
Marilyn Crispell | Live In San Francisco | Music & Arts | CD 633
Max Roach Quartet | In The Light | Soul Note | 121053-2
Melissa Walker And Her Band | May I Feel | Enja | ENJ-9335 2
Paul Motian Quartet | Monk In Motian | JMT Edition | 919020-2
Peter Leitch Sextet | From Another Perspective | Concord | CCD 4535
Stan Levey Sextet | ...This Time The Drum's On Me | Fresh Sound Records | FSR 2045(Bethlehem BCP 37)
Thelonious Monk | Pure Monk | Milestone | M 47004
Thelonious Monk-The Complete Riverside Recordings | Riverside | 15 RCD 022-2
Solo Monk | CBS | 471248-2
Thelonious Monk Quartet | Monk At Newport 1963 & 1965 | CBS | C2K 63905
Thelonious Monk:85th Birthday Celebration | zyx records | FANCD 6076-2
Live In Paris, Alhambra 1964 Vol.1 | France's Concert | FCD 135
Thelonious Monk Septet | Thelonious Monk-The Complete Riverside Recordings | Riverside | 15 RCD 022-2
Thelonious Monk Trio | Genius Of Modern Music,Vol.1 | Blue Note | 300403
Thelonious Monk:The Complete Blue Note Recordings | Blue Note | 830363-2
Thelonious Monk Collection | Black Lion | BLCD 7601-2
Tiziana Ghiglioni Sextet | Streams | SPLASC(H) Records | CD H 104-2

Ruby My Dear-
Jaki Byard | Maybeck Recital Hall Series Volume Seventeen | Concord | CCD 4511

Ruby My Dear(alt.take)
Thelonious Monk Trio | Genius Of Modern Music,Vol.1 | Blue Note | 532138-2
More Genius Of Thelonious Monk | Blue Note | 300194(BNJ 61011)

Ruck Än Ruul
Hans Lüdemann Rism | Stadtgarten Series Vol.2 | Jazz Haus Musik | JHM 1002 SER

Rückblick
Sigrid Meyer And Her Quartet | Serene | Metronome | 60544
Ruckus
Tete Montoliu | Yellow Dolphin Street/Catalonian Folk Songs | Timeless | CD SJP 107/116
Rude Old Man
Paul Desmond Quartet | Glad To Be Unhappy | RCA | 2131311-2
Wittek/Kaiser/Manderscheid | Trotzdem | Jazz Haus Musik | JHM 09
Rudimentär
Bobo Stenson Trio | Underwear | ECM | 1012
Rudolph The Red Nosed Reindeer
HR Big Band With Marjorie Barnes And Frits Landesbergen And Strings | Swinging Christmas | hr music.de | hrmj 012-02 CD
Jim Galloway-Jay McShann Quartet | Jim & Jay's Christmas | Sackville | SKCD2-3054
Marcus Roberts | Prayer For Peace | Novus | ND 90585(847064)
Rudolphplatz 02:00
Kölner Saxophon Mafia | Unerhört-Stadtklänge | Jazz Haus Musik | JHM 21
Rudolphplatz 17:00 Uhr
Unerhört-Stadtklänge | Jazz Haus Musik | JHM 21
Rudophplatz 04:30 Uhr
Andreas Schnerman Quartet | 4 In One | Edition Collage | EC 526-2
Rudy My Beer
Jeff Beal With The Metropole Orchestra | Concerto For Orchestra | Koch Jazz | 3-6904-2
Rue Chaptal
Kenny Clarke And His 52nd Street Boys | Fats Navarro:Nostalgia | Dreyfus Jazz Line | FDM 36736-2
Jan Harrington With The Nat Adderley Quintet | Remembering Dinah-A Salute To Dinah Washington | Hot Shot Records | HSR 8313-2
Rue Chaptal-
Kenny Clarke And His 52nd Street Boys | Fats Navarro:The 1946-1949 Small Group Sessions(Studio Recordings-Master Takes),Vol.1 | Blue Moon | BMCD 1016
Rue De Buci
Bud Powell Trio | Bud Powell Paris Sessions | Pablo | PACD 2310972-2
Rue De Clichy
Anouar Brahem Trio | Le Pas Du Chat Noir | ECM | 1792(016373-2)
Rue De Départ
David Binney Group | The Luxury Of Guessing | audioquest Music | AQCD 1030
Rue De Lafayette
Ekkehard Jost Nonet | Out Of Jost's Songbook | Fish Music | FM 006 CD
Rue De Lappe
Cesarius Alvim-J.P.Mas Duo | Rue De Lourmel | Owl Records | 03
Rue De Pierre
Bireli Lagrene Group | A Tribute To Django Reinhardt | Jazzpoint | JP 1061 CD
A Tribute To Django Reinhardt | Jazzpoint | JP 1061 CD
Bireli Lagrene Trio | Live At The Carnegie Hall: A Tribute To Django Reinhardt | Jazzpoint | JP 1040 CD
Jan Jankeje Quintet | Zum Trotz | Jazzpoint | JP 1016 CD
Bireli Lagrene Group | Inferno | Blue Note | 748016-2
Rue Gregoire Du Tour
Larry Coryell-Michael Urbaniak Trio | A Quiet Day In Spring | Steeplechase | SCCD 31187
Rue Hamra
David Amram-Bobby Jaspar Quintet | Bobby Jaspar Featuring Dave Amram | Vogue | 21606392
Rue Montmarte-
Franz Koglmann Quintet | Make Believe | Between The Lines | btl 001(Efa 10171-2)
Rue Montmartre Trilogy:
Mwendo Dawa | Street Lines | Dragon | DRLP 72
Rueda Del Juglar
Brass Attack | Brecht Songs | Tutu Records | 888190-2*
Ruf Aus Der Gruft
Joachim Kühn Trio | Musik Aus Der Dreigroschenoper | Verve | 532498-2
Rufus
Ron Carter Quartet | Etudes | Discovery | 71012-2
Rufus Still Skinned
Ben Wolfe Sextet | Bagdad Theater | Mons Records | MR 874827
Rug Cutter's Swing
Glenn Miller And His Orchestra | The Glenn Miller Collection | RCA | ???
Rugged Road
Duke Ellington And His Orchestra | Carnegie Hall Concert January 1946 | Prestige | 2PCD 24074-2
Rugged Romeo
Duke Ellington:Complete Prestige Carnegie Hall 1946-1947 Concerts | Definitive Records | DRCD 11211
Ruh' Dich Mal Aus Bei Mir
Cowws Quintet plus Guests | Book/Virtual Cowws | FMP | OWN-90007/9
Ruin, Klatsch Und Tratsch
Roland Kirk Group | I Talk With The Spirits | Verve | 558076-2
Ruined Castles
Roland Kirk Quintet | Rahsaan/The Complete Mercury Recordings Of Roland Kirk | Mercury | 846630-2
Mara! | Ruino Vino | Laika Records | 35100792
Ruino Vino
Glenn Ferris Trio | Refugees | Enja | 9108-2
Ruint
Maarten Altena Octet | Rif | Hat Art | CD 6056
Rumanian Folk Song
Rena Rama | Landscapes | Japo | 60020 IMS
Rumanian Rapsody
Pata Trio | Lucy Und Der Ball | Jazz Haus Musik | JHM 34
Rumba Mama
Jürgen Sturm's Ballstars | Tango Subversivo | Nabel Records:Jazz Network | CD 4613
Rumba Meu Boi
Benny Moten's Kansas City Orchestra | Bennie Moten Vol.1 | Zeta | ZET 750
Rumba's Sunset
Cuban All Stars | Passaporte | Enja | ENJ-9019 2
Rumble
Chick Corea Electric Band | GRP Super Live In Concert | GRP | GRP 16502
Rumbo Norte
I.C.P.Tentet | I.C.P.-Tentet In Berlin | FMP | SAJ 23
Rumination,Dasein Blues
Ben Waltzer Quintet | In Metropolitan Motion | Fresh Sound Records | FSNT 082 CD
Rumination,Oranienburg Str.
In Metropolitan Motion | Fresh Sound Records | FSNT 082 CD
Rumination,Prenzlauerberg
Andre Jaume 8 | Musique Pour 3 & 8:Errance | Hat Art | 2003 Digital
Rumour
Mark Isaacs/Dave Holland/Roy Haynes | Encounters | VeraBra Records | CDVBR 2076-2
Rumours
Ralph Towner | Blue Sun | ECM | 1250(829162-2)
Rumours Of Rain
Fats Waller And His Rhythm And His Orchestra | The Last Years 1940-1943 | Bluebird | ND 90411(3)
Rump Steak Serenade
Andy Summers Trio | The Last Dance Of Mr.X | RCA | 2668937-2
Rump-L-Rumba(7-4 For 5 Hands)
Duke Ellington And His Famous Orchestra | Duke Ellington:The Blanton-Webster Band | Bluebird | 21 13181-2
Rumpus In Richmond
Duke Ellington:Ko-Ko | Dreyfus Jazz Line | FDM 36717-2
In A Mellow Tone | RCA | 2113029-2
Duke Ellington And His Orchestra | The Indispensable Duke Ellington Vol.5/6 | RCA | ND 89750
Rumpus Rag
Tome XX | Third Degree | Jazz Haus Musik | JHM 0063 CD
Rumpuvalssi(Drum Waltz)
Frank Strozier-Booker Little Quintet | The Fantastic Frank Strozier | Vee Jay Recordings | VJ 012
Run About
Mahalia Jackson | Amazing Grace | Intercord | 125402
Run And See
Hamiet Bluiett Clarinet Family | The Clarinet Family | Black Saint | 120097-2
Run Before The Sun
Mr.Acker Bilk And His Paramount Jazz Band | Acker's Choice | Vagabond | 6.28490 DP
Run Joe
Randy Weston Quintet | How High The Moon | Biograph | BLP 12065
Run Joe,A Hit When I Was A Kid
Ruth Price With The Johnny Smith Quartet | Ruth Price Sings With The Johnny Smith Quartet | Fresh Sound Records | FSR 596(Roost 2217)
Run The Human Race
Cassandra Wilson Group | Traveling Miles | Blue Note | 854123-2
Run The VooDoo Down
Rex Stewarts Orkester | Americans In Sweden: Hot Lips Page 1951-Rex Stewart 1947 | Jazz Society | AA 513
Rune
Zutty And His Band | Chicago 1935 | Gannet | CJR 1001
Runes
Frans Bak & Jazz Group 90 | Hymn To The Rainbow | L+R Records | CDLR 45055
Runferyerlife
The Hudson Project | The Hudson Project | Stretch Records | SCD 9024-2
Thurston Harris With Band | Little Bitty Pretty One | Pathe | 1546651(Aladdin)
Runnin' Away
Rahsaan Roland Kirk Group | Natural Black Inventions:Roots Strata | Atlantic | ATL 40185(SD 1578)
Runnin' Round
Roosevelt Sykes Quintet | Urban Blues | Fantasy | F 24717
Runnin' Wild
Benny Goodman Quartet | Benny Goodman:The Complete Small Combinations Vol.1/2(1935-1937) | RCA | ND 89753
Chris Barber's Jazz Band | The Chris Barber Jubilee Album-Vol. 2 | Intercord | 157009
Dutch Swing College Band | DSC Live 1974 | DSC Production | PA 1013 (801068)
Elmer Snowden Quartet | Harlem Banjo | Original Jazz Classics | OJCCD 1756-2
George Lewis Ragtime Jazz Band Of New Orleans | The Oxford Series Vol.11:George Lewis Ragtime Band | American Music | AMCD-31
Glenn Miller And His Orchestra | The Glenn Miller Carnegie Hall Concert | RCA | NL 81506
Oscar Peterson Trio | Masters Of Jazz Vol.7 | RCA | NL 89721 DP
Sidney Bechet's Blue Note Jazzmen | Hot Jazz On Blue Note | Blue Note | 835811-2
Southland Six | Original Memphis Five Groups | Village(Jazz Archive) | VILCD 016-2
Teddy Wilson | Teddy Wilson In Tokyo | Sackville | 2005
The Jungle Band | Duke Ellington:Complete Original American Decca Recordings | Definitive Records | DRCD 11196
Glenn Miller And His Orchestra | The Carnegie Hall Concert | Bluebird | 63 66147-2
Runnin' Wild(alt.take)
Sidney Bechet's Blue Note Jazzmen | Runnin' Wild | Blue Note | 821259-2
Glenn Miller And His Orchestra | Meadowbrook Ballroom Vol.2 | Magic | DAWE 81
Running
Steve Tibbetts Group | Bye Bye Safe Journey | ECM | 1270
Tim Brady | Visions | Justin Time | JTR 8413-2
Running After Dreams
Franck Amsallem-Tim Ries-Leon Parker | Is That So? | Sunnyside | SSC 1071 D
Running After This & That
Bowling Green John Cephas & Harmonica Phil Wiggins | Sweet Bitter Blues | L+R Records | CDLR 72004
Running In Real Time
Steve Swallow Group | Deconstructed | Watt | XtraWatt/9(537119-2)
Running In The Family
Festa Group | Congo Square | SPLASC(H) Records | H 142
Running Out On Me
Koch-Schütz-Studer | Hardcore Chambermusic | Intakt Records | CD 042
Running Sands
American Folk Blues Festival | American Folk Blues Festival 1969 | L+R Records | CDLR 42071
Running Through My Dreams(Interlude)
Mihaly Pocs Quintet | Waxwork | Corvus Records | CRV 001
Running Wild
Arnett Cobb & His Orchestra | The Complete Apollo Sessions | Vogue | 500116
Runway
Krakatau | Matinale | ECM | 1529
Rural
Bengt-Arne Wallin Orchestra | The Birth+Rebirth Of Swedish Folk Jazz | ACT | 9254-2
Rural Song From The District Of Karleby,Swedish Finland-
Humphrey Lyttelton And His Band | Best Of British Jazz From The BBC Jazz Club Vol.2 | Upbeat Jazz | URCD 119
Rush Over
Ulli Bögershausen | Sologuitar | Laika Records | 35101132
Rushhour
Rüdiger Carl Inc. | King Alcohol | FMP | 0060
Rushour
Chet Baker Quartet | Chet Baker Quartet Live Vol.3: May Old Flame | Pacific Jazz | 531573-2
Russ Job
Chet Baker Quartet Live Vol.1:This Time The Dreams's On Me | Pacific Jazz | 525248-2
Jazz At Ann Arbor | Fresh Sound Records | 054 2602311(Pacific Jazz PJ 1203) (835282)
Russell And Eliot
Benny Green Trio | Naturally | Telarc Digital | CD 83498
Russian Doors No.1(Pushkin)
John Wolf Brennan | The Well-Prepared Clavier/Das Wohlpräparierte Klavier | Creative Works Records | CW CD 1032-2
Russian Doors No.2(Moscow:Container Lid)
The Well-Prepared Clavier/Das Wohlpräparierte Klavier | Creative Works Records | CW CD 1032-2
Russian Doors No.3(Mos Cowboys & Shriking Hinges)
The Well-Prepared Clavier/Das Wohlpräparierte Klavier | Creative Works Records | CW CD 1032-2
Russian Doors No.4(St.Petersburg A Walk On The Riverside)
The Well-Prepared Clavier/Das Wohlpräparierte Klavier | Creative Works Records | CW CD 1032-2
Russian Doors No.5(Dubna:Steps In A Staircase
Fats Waller | Fats Waller:The Complete Associated Transcription Sessions 1935-1939 | Jazz Unlimited | JUCD 2076
Russian Fantasy
The Music Of New Orleans | RCA | NL 89724 DP
Russian Folksong No.1
Belov Duo | Internationales Guitarren Festival '99 | ALISO Records | AL 1038
Russian Folksong No.2
Internationales Guitarren Festival '99 | ALISO Records | AL 1038
Russian Folksong No.3
Gregor Hübner Quartet | Panonien | Satin Doll Productions | SDP 1015-1 CD
Russian Impressions
Mikhail Alperin's Moscow Art Trio | Hamburg Concert | JA & RO | JARO 4201-2
Russian In China
Ganelin Trio | Baltic Triangle-Live In Leningrad | LEO | LR 125
Russian Lullaby
Benny Goodman And His Orchestra | More Camel Caravans | Phontastic | NCD 8843/4
Jazz Giants:Benny Goodman | RCA | NL 89731 SI
Ella Fitzgerald With Paul Weston And His Orchestra | The Complete Ella Fitzgerald Song Books of Harold Arlen, Irving Berlin, Duke Ellington, George & Ira Gershwin, Jerome Kern, Johnny Mercer, Cole Porter And Rogers & Hart | Verve | 519832-2
John Coltrane Quartet | John Coltrane-The Prestige Recordings | Prestige | 16 PCD 4405-2
John Coltrane | Prestige | P 24003
Stan Kenton And His Orchestra | Stan Kenton And His Orchestra On AFRS 1944-1945 | Status | DSTS 1019
Russian Raga(Za Nashey Derevney)
Tubby Hayes Orchestra | Tubbs' Tours | Mole Jazz | MOLE 4
Russian Swing
Gyjho Frank | Aeuropa | Blue Flame | 40372
Russian Winter
Christof Lauer-Jens Thomas With The Cikada String Quartet | Shadows In The Rain | ACT | 9297-2
Russians
Choo Choo Light:Stammberger-Rädler-Schöne | Choo Choo Light | G.N.U. Records | CD A 92.007
Russisches Lied
Freddie Hubbard Quintet | Skagly | CBS | 84242
Rustic Hop
Gerry Mulligan Quartet | Gerry Mulligan Quartet At Storyville | Pacific Jazz | 794472-2
Stan Getz Quintet | Stan Getz And The 'Cool' Sounds | Verve | 547317-2
Stan Getz:The Complete 1952-1954 Small Group Sessions(Master Takes),Vol.1 | Blue Moon | BMCD 1034
Rut
Keith Jarrett - Jack DeJohnette | Ruta + Daitya | ECM | 1021(513776-2)
Ruta + Daitya
Bobby Hutcherson Quintet | Spiral | Blue Note | LT 996 (GXK 8178)
Ruth
Wheelz With Ingrid Jensen | Around The World I | ACT | 9247-2
Ruth Is Back To Joseph
Pata Horns | New Archaic Music | Pata Musik | PATA 4(JHM 42) CD
Ruthless
Charlie Haden Quartet West With Strings | The Art Of The Song | Verve | 547403-2
Ruth's Waltz
Christmann-Schönenberg Duo | Live At Moers Festival 76 | Ring | 01012
Ruvo(for Pablo,Solea & Gabriel)
Yusef Lateef Ensemble | Yusef Lateef In Nigeria | Landmark | LLP 502
Rydbo
Paul Williams Sextet | Paul Williams:The Complete Recordings Vol.2 (1949-1952) | Blue Moon | BMCD 6021
Ryokam
Arild Andersen Sextet | Sagn | ECM | 1435
Rysen
Amiri Baraka And His Blue Ark | Amiri Baraka:Real Song | Enja | 8098-2
S & J Blues
Dewey Redman/Ed Blackwell Duo | Redman And Blackwell In Willisau | Black Saint | 120093-2
S And S
Eric Kloss Quartet | About Time | Prestige | PRCD 24268-2
'S 'Bout Time
Stan Getz And The Swedish All Stars | Stan Getz:The Complete 1946-1951 Quartet Sessions(Master Takes),Vol.2 | Blue Moon | BMCD 1014
'S Make It
George Wallington Quintet | Jazz Editions Presents: Jazz At Hotchkiss | Savoy | SV 0119(MG 12122)
S' Posin'
Art Tatum | The Art Tatum Solo Masterpieces | Pablo | 2625703
Bill Russo And His Orchestra | Deep People | Savoy | SV 0186(MG 12045)
Bud Freeman All Stars | The Bud Freeman All Stars | Original Jazz Classics | OJC 183(SV 2012)
Fats Waller And His Rhythm | Fats Waller-The Joint Is Jumpin' | RCA | ND 86288(874182)
Helen Humes And Her All Stars | Swingin' With Helen | Original Jazz Classics | OJCCD 608-2
Johnny Hartman With The Terumasa Hino Quartet | For Trane | Blue Note | 835346-2
Ken Peplowski/Howard Alden | Concord Duo Series Volume Three | Concord | CCD 4556
The Riverside Reunion Band | Hi-Fly | Milestone | MCD 9228-2
'S Wonderful
Al Haig Trio | The Piano Collection Vol.2 | Vogue | 21610222
Bill Evans Quartet | The Complete Bill Evans On Verve | Verve | 527953-2
Bobby Hackett-Jack Teagarden All Stars | Coast Concert/Jazz Ultimate | Dormouse | DMI CDX 02(882984)
Count Basie And His Orchestra | The Greatest | Verve | MV 2650 IMS
Don Elliott Quartet | The Gershwin Songbook(The Instrumentals) | Verve | 525361-2
Eddie Condon All Stars | Town Hall Concerts Vol.11 | Jazzology | JCD 1021/23
Eddie Lockjaw Davis Quartet | Eddie 'Lockjaw' Davis | Divox | CDX 48701
Ella Fitzgerald With The Nelson Riddle Orchestra | Oh Lady Be Good:The Best Of The Gershwin Songbook | Verve | 529581-2
Ella Sings Gershwin-Vol. 1 | Metro | 2682004 IMS
Sings The Ira And George Gershwin Songbook | Verve | 825024-2
Gene Krupa Quartet | Compact Jazz: Gene Krupa | Verve | 833286-2 PMS
Gerry Mulligan Trio | Gerry Mulligan:Complete 1950-1952 Prestige Studio Recordings | Definitive Records | DRCD 11227
Guy Lafitte-Peanuts Holland And Their Orchestra | Two Great Trumpets Of Swing Era | Jazz Anthology | JA 5202
Harry Edison Quartet | Can't Get Out Of This Mood... | Orange Blue | OB 006 CD
Harry Sweets Edison Quintet | Swingin' 'Sweets' | L+R Records | CDLR 45076
Helen Merrill And Her Trio | The Best Of The Jazz Singers Vol.2 | LRC Records | CDC 9008
Helen O'Connell With The Page Cavanaugh Trio | The Uncollected:Helen O'Connell | Hindsight | HSR 228
Jenny Evans And Band | Girl Talk | ESM Records | ESM 9306
Girl Talk | Enja | ENJ-9363 2
Live At The Allotria | BELL Records | BLR 90003
Johnny Smith Quartet | Johnny Smith And His New Quartet | Fresh Sound Records | FSR-CD 80(882190)
Klaus Ignatzek Trio | Airballoon | Nabel Records:Jazz Network | CD 4651
Lee Konitz & His West Coast Friends | High Jingo | Eastworld | CP 32-5422
Lee Konitz-Franco D'Andrea | 12 Gershwin In 12 Keys | Philology | W 312.2
Lionel Hampton With The Oscar Peterson Trio | Compact Jazz: Oscar Peterson & Friends | Verve | 835315-2
Lucie Arnaz And Her Orchestra | Just In Time | Concord | CCD 4573
Paul Kuhn Orchestra feat. Gustl Mayer | Street Of Dreams | Mons Records | MR 874800
Red Richards Quintet | Echoes Of Spring | Sackville | SKCD2-2049
Stan Getz Quartet | The Complete Roost Session Vol.1 | Roulette | 300005(TOCJ 6118)
Stan Getz-The Complete Roost Sessions | EMI Records | 859622-2

TITELVERZEICHNIS

Unearthed Masters-Vol.2: Stan Getz | JAM | 5007 IMS
Stephane Grappelli Quartet | Grapelli Story | Verve | 515807-2
Steve Wilson Quintet | Step Lively | Criss Cross | Criss 1096
Sun Ra & His Omniverse Arkestra | Destination Unknown | Enja | 7071-2
Tatum-Carter-Bellson Trio | The Tatum Group Masterpieces | Pablo | 2625706
Tito Puente Orchestra | Out Of This World | Concord | CCD 4448
Zoot Sims Quintet | Zoot Sims And The Gershwin Brothers | Original Jazz Classics | OJC20 444-2(2310744)
Anita O'Day With The Oscar Peterson Quartet | Jazz-Club: Vocal | Verve | 840029-2

'S Wonderful-
Stephane Grappelli Trio | Live At The Blue Note | Telarc Digital | CD 83397

'S Wonderful(alt.take)
Scalesenders | This And More | Edition Collage | EC 498-2

S.C.O.
Glenn Spearman Double Trio | Mystery Project | Black Saint | 120147-2

S.D.F.-q.e.d.
Mel Martin Quartet | Listen-Growing | Inner City | IC 1054 IMS

S.F.K.
Dizzy Gillespie Sextet | Musician: Composer Raconteur | Pablo | 2620116

S.J.K.
Monty Alexander Quartet | Three Originals:Love And Sunshine/Estade/Cobilimbo | MPS | 523526-2
String Thing | String Thing:Turtifix | MicNic Records | MN 4

S.K.
Jimmy Witherspoon And His All Stars | Singin' The Blues | Pacific Jazz | 494108-2

S.K.J.
Jam Session | Jam Session Vol.6 | Steeplechase | SCCD 31537
James Williams Sextet feat. Clark Terry | Talkin' Trash | DIW | DIW 887 CD
Milt Jackson Sextet | Goodbye | CTI | 6038
Milt Jackson-Wes Montgomery Quintet | To Bags...With Love:Memorial Album | Pablo | 2310967-2
Wes Montgomery-The Complete Riverside Recordings | Riverside | 12 RCD 4408-2
Monty Alexander Quartet | Saturday Night | Limetree | MCD 0024

S.K.J.(alt.take)
Lester Young And His Band | Lester Young:The Complete Aladdin Sessions | Blue Note | 832787-2

S.M.Blues
Lester Young:The Complete 1936-1951 Small Group Sessions(Studio Recordings-Master Takes),Vol.4 | Blue Moon | BMCD 1004

S.M.E.
Sahib Shihab Sextet | Jazz Sahib | Savoy | SV 0141(MG 12124)

S.O.L.Blues
Louis Armstrong And His Hot Seven | Louis Armstrong-The Hot Fives & Hot Sevens Vol.3 | CBS | 465189-2

S.O.S.
Wes Montgomery Quintet | Full House | Original Jazz Classics | OJC20 106-2
Your Neighborhood Saxophone Quartet | Boogie Stop Shuffle | Coppens | CCD 3004(882623)

S.O.S. Radio-Taxis
Wes Montgomery Quintet | Wes Montgomery-The Complete Riverside Recordings | Riverside | 12 RCD 4408-2

S.O.S.(alt.take)
Full House | Original Jazz Classics | OJC20 106-2
The Alternative Wes Montgomery | Milestone | MCD 47065-2

S.S.Groove
Cal Tjader Quintet | Concert On The Campus | Original Jazz Classics | OJC 279(F 8044)

S/Catch
Lena Willemark-Ale Möller Group | Nordan | ECM | 1536(523161-2)

S:t Göran Och Draken
Padouk | Padouk | SPLASC(H) Records | H 192

Saarländer Mädel
Milt Buckner Trio | Milt Buckner Masterpieces | MPS | 529094-2

Sabah
Karl Ratzer Group | Moon Dancer | Enja | ENJ-9357 2

Sabar Dance
Special EFX | Confidential | GRP | GRP 95812

Sabe Más El Diablo Por Viejo,Que No For Diablo
Eliane Elias Group | Fantasia | Blue Note | 796146-2

Säbel
Sammy Vomacka | Easy Rider | BELL Records | BLR 84019

Säbeltanz-Boogie
Antonio Carlos Jobim With Orchestra | This Is Jazz:Bossa Nova | CBS | CK 65045

Sabika
Habarigani | Habarigani Two | Hat Art | CD 6064

Sabine's Jazz Arena
The Buck Clayton Legacy | Encore Live | Nagel-Heyer | CD 018
The Yamaha International Allstar Band | Hapy Birthday Jazzwelle Plus | Nagel-Heyer | CD 005
Mynta | Hot Madras | Blue Flame | 40382(2132161-2)

Sabiza
Dizzy Gillespie Sextet | Jazz In Paris:Dizzy Gillespie-Cognac Blues | EmArCy | 014064-2

Sables
Stephan Oliva Trio | Novembre | Owl Time Line | 3819092
L'Orchestre De Contrebasses | Les Cargos | Label Bleu | LBLC 6536(889138)

Sabrina And Joseph
Freddie Hubbard Group | Times Are Changing | Blue Note | B 1-90905

Sacha's March
Modern Jazz Quartet | MJQ 40 | Atlantic | 7567-82330-2
Echoes | Pablo | 2312142-2

Sack O'Woe
Cannonball Adderley Quintet | At The Lighthouse | Capitol | 531572-2
The Cannonball Adderley Collection Vol.5:At The Lighthouse | Landmark | CAC 1305-2(882344)
Mercy Mercy Mercy | Capitol | 829915-2
Cannonball Adderley Sextet | Cannonball Adderley Birthday Celebration | Fantasy | FANCD 6087-2
George Benson And His Orchestra | Giblet Gravy | Verve | 543754-2
George Benson Orchestra | Verve Jazz Masters 21:George Benson | Verve | 521861-2
Compact Jazz: George Benson | Verve | 833292-2 PMS
Nat Adderley Sextet | Work Songs | Milestone | M 47047
Wes Montgomery-The Complete Riverside Recordings | Riverside | 12 RCD 4408-2
Randy Johnston Quartet | Somewhere In The Night | HighNote Records | HCD 7007

Sacra Romana Rota
Musica Libera | Musica Libera:Dialog & Begegnung | Hat Art | 3513

Sacrament
Ram-lösa | Ram-lösa In Mesopotamia | Aho-Recording | AHO CD 1008(CD 665)

Sacre Blues
Renaud Garcia-Fons Quartet | Alboreá | Enja | ENJ-9057 2

Sacre Coeur
Steve Cárdenas Trio | Shebang | Fresh Sound Records | FSNT 079 CD
Martial Solal Trio | Just Friends | Dreyfus Jazz Line | FDM 36592-2

Sacred Treasure
Mark Nauseef Group | Dark | CMP Records | CMP CD 36

Sad
Milcho Leviev Quartet | Blues For The Fisherman | Mole Jazz | MOLE 1

Sad Blues
Sammy Price | Le Jazz En France Vol.14:Boogie Woogie A La Parisienne | Pathe | 1552601

Sad But True
Riot | Green And Blue | Nagara | MIX 1012-N

Sad Fate
Helen Humes With Marshall Royal And His Orchestra | E-Baba-Le-Ba The Rhythm And Blues Years | Savoy | WL 70824 (809326)

Sad Feeling
Lionel Hampton And His Orchestra | Wes Montgomery:Complete Recordings With Lionel Hampton | Definitive Records | DRCD 11242

Sad Hero
Jerry Granelli UFB | News From The Street | VeraBra Records | CDVBR 2146-2

Sad Hour
Little Walter Blues Band | Little Walter | Chess | 427001

Sad Letter
Muddy Waters Group | More Real Folk Blues | Chess | CH 9278

Sad Little Girl
Oliver Lake Quartet | Gallery | Gramavision | GR 8609-2

Sad Morning
Louisiana Red Group | The Lowdown Back Porch Blues | Sequel Records | NEX CD 213

Sad Note(Nota Triste)
Simply Red | Montreux Jazz Festival | ACT | 9001-2

Sad Sack
Muddy Waters Group | Back In His Early Days, Vol.1+2 | Red Lightnin' | SC 001/2

Sad Sap Sucker Am I
New Jazz Trio | Three Trees | Elite Special | 73410

Sad Song
Moscow Art Trio | Jazzy World | JA & RO | JARO 4200-2
Alex Merck Group | Dog Days | Jazzline | ???

Sad Twilight
Carlo Mombelli'a Abstractions | Dancing In A Museum | ITM-Pacific | ITMP 970078

Sad Was The Song
Mick Karn Group | Bestial Cluster | CMP Records | CMP CD 1002

Sadhana
Hound Dog Taylor & The House Rockers | Natural Boogie | Sonet | 198044(SNTF 678)

Sadie Green
South Frisco Jazz Band | Got Everything | Stomp Off Records | CD 1240

Sadie Hall
John Lee Hooker | Solid Sender | Charly | CRB 1081

Sadir
Martial Solal Quartet | Martial Solal-The Vogue Recordings Vol.1:Trios & Quartet | Vogue | 21115142(875744)

Saeta
Miles Davis With Gil Evans & His Orchestra | The Miles Davis Selection | CBS | 465699-2

Safa
David Benoit Group | Urban Daydreams | GRP | GRP 95872

Safari
Horace Silver Quintet | Further Explorations By The Horace Silver Quintet | Blue Note | 300044(1589)
Horace Silver Trio | Horace Silver Trio And Spotlight On Drums:Art Blakey-Sabu | Blue Note | 591725-2
Louis Hayes Quintet | The Candy Man | TCB Records | TCB 20972
Sadao Watanabe Group | My Dear Life | Flying Disk | VIJ 6001
The Trio | The Trio:Rediscovered | String Jazz | SJRCD 1007
Thomas Chapin Quintet | You Don't Know Me | Arabesque Recordings | AJ 0115

Safe
André Previn-Russ Freeman | Double Play! | Original Jazz Classics | OJC 157(C 7537)

Safe,Sane And Single
Louis Jordan And His Tympany Five | Five Guys Named Moe | Bandstand | BDCD 1531

Safely In Your Arms
Steve Cárdenas Trio | Shebang | Fresh Sound Records | FSNT 079 CD

Safer Than Heaven
Stan Kenton And His Orchestra | Artistry In Rhythm | Creative World | ST 1043

Sag Mir Wo Die Blumen Sind
Cassiber | Man Or Monkey | Riskant | 6.28624

Saga
Viktoria Tolstoy With The Jacob Karlzon Trio | Blame It On My Youth | Kaza(EMI) | 536620-2

Sage
Göbels-Harth Group | Es Herrscht Uhu Im Land | Japo | 60037 (2360037)

Sage Brush Rider
Gary McFarland Orchestra | The Great Arrangers | MCA | IA 9340/2

Sagg Shootin' His Arrow
Stephane Grappelli Quartet | Stephane Grappelli '80 | Blue Silver | BS 3002

Sagittarius
Philippe Petit/Miroslav Vitous | Impressions Of Paris | EPM Musique | FDC 5524

Sagma
Arild Andersen Sextet | Sagn | ECM | 1435

Sagn
Sagn | ECM | 1435

Sagn(II)
Jimmy Smith Sextet | Jimmy Smith:Best Of The Verve Years | Verve | 527950-2

Sags Shootin' His Arrow
Anliker-Parker-Schmid-Senn-Solothurnmann | September Winds | Creative Works Records | CW CD 1038/39

Sagssolo
Nat Adderley Quintet | A Little New York Midtown Music | Original Jazz Classics | OJCCD 1008-2(GXY 5120)

Saguaro
Joe Kienemann | Liedgut:Amsel,Drossel,Swing & Funk | yvp music | CD 3095

Sah Ein Knab' Ein Röslein Steh'n
John Zorn Group | Masada Two | DIW | DIW 889 CD

Sahara
Michel Petrucciani Trio | Michel Plays Petrucciani | Blue Note | 748679-2
Rabih Abou-Khalil Group | Blue Camel | Enja | ENJ-7053 2
Temperance Seven | Tea For Eight | Upbeat Jazz | URCD 101

Sahara-
Illinois Jacquet And His Orchestra | Illinois Jacquet:All Stars Studio Recordings 1945-1947(Master Takes) | Blue Moon | BMCD 1011

Sahara Romance
Klaus Doldinger's Passport | Klaus Doldinger Passport Live | Warner | 8573-84132-2

Sahara Sketches
Renaud Garcia-Fons Group | Navigatore | Enja | ENJ-9418 2

Sahari
Tony Scott | Music For Yoga Meditation And Other Joys | Verve | 2304471 IMS

Sahasrara-Highest Chakra
Randy Weston | Blues To Africa | Freedom | FCD 741014

Saidas Bandeiras
Paolo Fresu Quartet | Angel | RCA | 2155864-2

Saigon
Batman | Naked City | Nonesuch | 7559-79238-2

Saigon Pickup
Oregon | The Essential Oregon | Vanguard | VSD 109/110

Sail Away
Joe Lovano Quartet | Live At The Village Vanguard | Blue Note | 829125-2
Kenny Barron Trio | Wanton Spirit | Verve | 522364-2
Matthieu Michel Quintet feat. Richard Galliano | Estate | TCB Records | TCB 95802
Alexis Korner's Skiffle Group | Kings Of Skiffle | Decca | 6.28132 DP

Sail On
Klaus Weiss Orchestra | Live At The Domicile | ATM Records | ATM 3805-AH
Patrick Williams Orchestra | Come On And Shine | MPS | 68199
Memphis Slim | Memphis Slim Live! | Storyville | SLP 4058

Sail On Little Girl Sail On
Jimmy Witherspoon And His Band | Baby, Baby, Baby | Original Blues Classics | OBCCD 527-2(P 7290)
Leadbelly[Huddie Ledbetter] | Alabamy Bound | Memo Music | HDJ 4073

Sailboat In The Moonlight
Benny Goodman Trio | More Camel Caravans | Phontastic | NCD 8841/2
Dick Jurgens And His Orchestra | The Uncollected: Dick Jurgens | Hindsight | HSR 111
Ronnell Bright Trio | The Ronnell Bright Trio | Fresh Sound Records | FSR 559(Polydor 46106)

Sailing
Rob Van Den Broeck-Wiro Mahieu | Departures | Green House Music | CD 1004
Uli Wewelsiep-Thomas Brill | Live At The Forum | Aho-Recording | CD 1010

Saint Nick's Groove
Dee Dee Bridgewater With Her Quintet | Love And Peace-A Tribute To Horace Silver | Verve | 527470-2

Saint Vitus Dance
Louis Jordan And His Tympany Five | Louis Jordan-Let The Good Times Roll: The Complete Decca Recordings 1938-1954 | Bear Family Records | BCD 15557 IH
Saxophon And Organ | Above The Clouds | Naxos Jazz | 86041-2

Saints & Science
The Chamber Symphony Of Philadelphia String Quartet | The Music Of Ornette Coleman: Forms + Sounds | RCA | ND 86561(847114)

Sais
Sonny Rollins Sextet | Horn Culture | Original Jazz Classics | OJC 314(M 9051)

Saisir
Erik Truffaz Quartet Quintet | Out Of A Dream | Blue Note | 855855-2
Bennie Wallace Group | Twilight Time | Blue Note | BT 85107

Saja Terikè(My Brother Died)
Sylvester Cotton | Detroit Blues | Anthology of the Blues | AB 5606

Sakyi's Song
The Baltimore Syndicate | The Baltimore Syndicate | Paddle Wheel | KICJ 72

Salaam
Abdullah Ibrahim | Fats Duke And Monk | Sackville | SKCD2-3048

Salamander
Jay Leonhart-Mike Renzi | Salamander Pie | dmp Digital Music Productions | CD 442

Salif
Ronnie Mathews Quintet | Roots Branches & Dances | Bee Hive | BH 7008

Salima's Dance
Kühn/Humair/Jenny-Clark | Tripple Entente | EmArCy | 558690-2

Salinas
European Jazz Ensemble | European Jazz Ensemble 25th Anniversary | Konnex Records | KCD 5100

Salinas-
Billy Pierce Quartet | Rio-Ballads & Bossa Novas | Sunnyside | SSC 1065 D

S'Allota Si,Si
Alex Möller-Lena Willemark Group | Hästen Och Tranan | ACT | 9244-2

Sally
Eddie Harris Trio | Eddie Who? | Timeless | CD SJP 244

Sally's Tomato
Oscar Peterson With Orchestra | Motions & Emotions | MPS | 821289-2 PMS

Salmon Flight
The New Dave Pike Set & Grupo Baiafra De Bahia | Dave Pike Set:Masterpieces | MPS | 531848-2

Salomao
Duke Ellington And His Orchestra | Yale Concert | Fantasy | F 9433

Salome
The Greatest Jazz Concert In The World | Pablo | 2625704-2

Salomé(Sal-Owe-May)
Chris Potter Quartet | Pure | Concord | CCD 4637

Salome's Tune
Joachim Kühn Trio | Musik Aus Der Dreigroschenoper | Verve | 532498-2

Salsa Corrupti
Lionel Hampton & His Giants Of Jazz 1979 | Hamp In Haarlem | Timeless | CD SJP 133

Salsa For Eddie G.
Orquesta Conexion Latina | Un Poco Loco | Enja | ENJ-5023 2

Salsamba
Peter Schärli Quintet | Ballads And Brazil | TCB Records | TCB 98952

Salseando
Lewis Trio With Guests | Battangó | Intuition Records | INN 1101-2

Salsera
Antoine Hervé Quintet | Invention Is You | Enja | ENJ-9398 2

Salsita
Baden Powell Quartet | L'Ame De Baden Powell | Festival | 114811

Salt Peanuts
Bud Powell Trio | Birdland '53 | Fresh Sound Records | FSCD 1017
Salt Peanuts | Black Lion | BLCD 760121
Dizzy Gillespie All Stars | Groovin' High | Naxos Jazz | 8.120582 CD
Dizzy Gillespie Quintet | Charlie Parker Vol.2:Bird On The Side 1941-1947 | Naxos Jazz | 8.120622 CD
Klaus Weiss Quintet | Salt Peanuts | BELL Records | BLR 84018
Miles Davis Quintet | Steamin' | Original Jazz Classics | OJC20 391-2
Milt Jackson Septet | Bebop | East-West | ???
Quintet Of The Year | The Quintet-Jazz At Massey Hall | Debut | DSA 124-6
Charlie Parker The Immortal Sessions Vol.2:1949-1953 | SAGA Jazz Classics | EC 3319-2
Steve Coleman And Five Elements | Def Trance Beat(Modalities Of Rhythm) | Novus | 4163181-2

Salt Pork West Virginia
Louis Jordan And His Tympany Five | Louis Jordan Greatest Hits-Vol.2 | MCA | 1337

Saltpastil
Alfred Lauer Bigband | Just Music | Mons Records | MR 874819

Salty Dog
Dick Charlesworth And His City Gents | The Golden Years Of Revival Jazz,Vol.11 | Storyville | STCD 5516
Don Ewell's Hot Four | A Portrait Of George Lewis | Lake | LACD 50

Salty Dog -> I'm A Salty Dog

Salty Papa Blues
Ruth Brown With Orchestra | Fine And Mellow | Fantasy | FCD 9663-2
John Handy/Lee Ritenour Group | Where Go The Boats | Inak | 861

Salutation March
Chris Barber's Jazz Band | Barber's Best | Decca | 6.28128 DP
Excelsior New Orleans Brass Band | Excelsior New Orleans Brass Band | Bartrax | BARX 051 CD
Mr.Acker Bilk And His Paramount Jazz Band | New Orleans Days | Lake | LACD 36

Salute
Stan Kenton And His Orchestra | The Kenton Touch | Creative World | ST 1033

Salute To Benny
Art Blakey And The Jazz Messengers | Blakey | Verve | 538634-2

Salute To Charlie Christian
Monty Budwig Septet | Dig | Concord | CJ 79

Salute To Garner
Oscar Peterson-Ray Brown Duo | An Evening With Oscar Peterson | Verve | MV 2691 IMS

Salute To Gene Krupa
Max Greger Big Band | Maximum | Polydor | 825703-1 IMS

Salvador
Egberto Gismonti | Solo | ECM | 1136
Works | ECM | 823269-2
Duo Gismonti-Vasconcelos | Jazzbühne Berlin '84 | Repertoire Records | REPCD 4906-CC

Salvador Dali-
Henri Salvador Trio | Jazz In Paris:Les Blue Stars-Pardon My English/Henri Salvador-Plays The Blues | EmArCy | 013035-2
Salvador(Branco)
McCoy Tyner Trio With Woodwinds And Strings | Fly With The Wind | Original Jazz Classics | OJCCD 699-2(M 9067)
Salvese Quien Pueda
Berlin Contemporary Jazz Orchestra | Berlin Contemporary Jazz Orchestra | ECM | 1409
Salz
Riot | Riot-Black Hill | Nagara | MIX 1017-N
Sam
Rich Perry Quartet | Hearsay | Steeplechase | SCCD 31515
Sam Hill
Jim Hall-Dave Holland | Jim Hall & Basses | Telarc Digital | CD 83506
Sam Jones Done Snagged His Britches On
Jin Hi Kim Group | Sargeng | Ear-Rational | ECD 1014
Sam Sack
Milt Jackson-Wes Montgomery Quintet | Wes Montgomery-The Complete Riverside Recordings | Riverside | 12 RCD 4408-2
Tony Reedus Quartet | Minor Thang | Criss Cross | Criss 1117
Sam Sack(alt.take)
Orexis | Inspiration | Intercord | 160108
Sam Song
Michael Shrieve Trio | Fascination | CMP Records | CMP CD 67
Sam Woodyard Is Back In Town
Duke Ellington Trio | The Pianist | Original Jazz Classics | OJCCD 717-2(F 9462)
Sama Layuca
Gene Krupa And His Orchestra | Lionel Hampton/Gene Krupa | Forlane | UCD 19008
Samai Shadd Araban
Madmo(Two Guitars & Percussion) | Cicles | Acoustic Music Records | 319.1053.2
Samandhi-Ultimate Bliss
Amalgam | Samanna | View | VS 104 IMS
Samantha
Kenny Ball And His Jazzmen | The Very Best Of Kenny Ball | Timeless | CD TTD 598
Warren Vaché Quartet | What Is There To Say? | Nagel-Heyer | CD 056
Erik Truffaz Quartet Quintet | Out Of A Dream | Blue Note | 855855-2
Samara
Oliver Augst-Rüdiger Carl-Christoph Korn | Blank | FMP | OWN-90013
Samba
Johnny Smith Quartet | Johnny Smith And His New Quartet | Fresh Sound Records | FSR-CD 80(882190)
Samba An Einem Ruhigen Sonntag
Barbara Dennerlein Group | Junkanoo | Verve | 537122-2
Samba And The Drum Stick
Super Session | Welcome & Alive | Vagabond | 6.28604 DP
Samba Cantina
Baden Powell Quartet | En Concert Avec Europe 1 | Laserlight | 710703/04
Samba Cepeda
Carlos Barbosa-Lima | Music Of The Americas | Concord | CCD 4461
Samba Da Minha Terra
Archie Shepp Orchestra | There's A Trumpet In My Soul | Freedom | FCD 741016
Samba Da Sahra(Sahra's Samba)
Antonio Carlos Jobim With The Claus Ogerman Orchestra | Compact Jazz: Antonio Carlos Jobim | Verve | 843273-2
Samba Da Una Nota So(One Note Samba)
Astrud Gilberto With The New Stan Getz Quartet | Jazz-Club: Vocal | Verve | 840029-2
Charlie Byrd Trio With Ken Peplowski | The Bossa Nova Years | Concord | CCD 4468
Count Basie And His Orchestra | Basie On Roulette, Vol. 22: Back With Basie | Vogue | 500022
Dizzy Gillespie Quintet | En Concert Avec Europe 1 | Laserlight | 710465
Eliane Elias Quartet | Eliane Elias Plays Jobim | Blue Note | 793089-2
Ella Fitzgerald With The Tommy Flanagan Trio | The Montreux '77 Collection | Pablo | 2620107
Ella Fitzgerald-Joe Pass Duo | Fitzgerald & Pass... Again | Original Jazz Classics | OJCCD 1052-2(2310772)
Ernest Ranglin Trio | Jazz At Ronnie Scott's | Ronnie Scott's Jazz House | JHAS 612
Karrin Allyson And Her Sextet | Sweet Home Cookin' | Concord | CCD 4593
Quincy Jones And His Orchestra | Big Band Bossa Nova | Verve | 557913-2
Stan Getz New Quartet | Compact Jazz | Verve | 831368-2
Stan Getz With The Joao Gilberto Trio & Orchestra | The Carnegie Hall Concert | Jazz Door | JD 1221
Stan Getz-Charlie Byrd Sextet | Hot Tracks For Cool Cats Vol.2 | Polydor | 816380-2
Jazz Samba | Verve | 521413-2
Stan Getz/Charlie Byrd:Jazz Samba | CTI Records | PDCTI 1104-2
The New Stan Getz Quartet Feat. Astrud Gilberto | Getz Au Go Go | CTI Records | PDCTI 1124-2
Samba De Amor
Arturo Sandoval Group | Flight To Freedom | GRP | GRP 96342
Samba De Duas Notas
Stan Getz-Luiz Bonfa Quartet | Jazz Samba Encore! | CTI Records | PDCTI 1125-2
Samba De Orfeu
Brew Moore Quartet | No More Brew | Storyville | STCD 8275
Bud Shank Septet | Brasamba | Pacific Jazz | LN 10092
Charlie Byrd Trio With Ken Peplowski | The Bossa Nova Years | Concord | CCD 4468
Dutch Swing College Band | Dutch Samba | Timeless | CD TTD 552
Joe Pass-Herb Ellis | Joe Pass:Guitar Virtuoso | Pablo | 4 PACD 4423-2
Jon Faddis Quartet | Youngblood | Pablo | 2310765
Pablo All Star Jam | Montreux '77-The Art Of The Jam Session | Pablo | 2620106
Paul Desmond Quartet | Take Ten | RCA | 63661462
Paul Desmond-Gerry Mulligan Quartet | The Ballad Of Paul Desmond | RCA | 21429372
Paul Horn Group | 500 Miles High | West Wind | WW 2043
Cal Tjader Quintet | At Grace Cathedral | Fantasy | F 9521
Samba De Orfeu(I Want To Live)
Kenny Dorham Quintet | West 42nd Street | Black Lion | BLP 60119
Samba De Stacy
Ana Caram Group | Bossa Nova | Chesky | JD 129
Samba Dees Days
Stan Getz-Charlie Byrd Sextet | Stan Getz/Charlie Byrd:Jazz Samba | CTI Records | PDCTI 1104-2
Samba D'Esprit
Tom Harrell Group | The Art Of Rhythm | RCA | 2668924-2
Samba Do Aviao(Song Of The Jet)
Stanley Turrentine Orchestra | Stanley Turrentine | Blue Note | 84506
Samba Do Mar
Bola Sete Quintet | Tour De Force:The Bola Sete Trios | Fantasy | FCD 24766-2
Samba Do Perroquet
JoAnne Brackeen Quartet | Breath Of Brazil | Concord | CCD 4479
Samba Do Suenho
Makoto Ozone Group | Treasure | Verve | 021906-2
Samba D'Rivera
Phil Woods Quartet | Musique Du Bois | Muse | MCD 5037
Samba Em Preludio
Baden Powell Quartet | Canto On Guitar | MPS | 68157
Samba For Bob
Helmut Kagerer 4 & Roman Schwaller | Jazz Guitar Highlights 1 | Jardis Records | JRCD 20141
David Janeway Quartet | Inside Out | Timeless | CD SJP 402
Samba For Now
Grooveyard Meets Roman Schwaller | Basic Instinct | Organic Music | ORGM 9701
Samba For Pat And Billy
The Steamboat Rats | ...Got That Swing | Elite Special | 73435
Samba In June
Chick Corea Group | Tap Step | Warner | WB 56801
Samba Mom Mom
Art Pepper Quartet | Art Pepper:The Complete Galaxy Recordings | Galaxy | 16GCD 1016-2
San Francisco Samba | Contemporary | CCD 14086-2
Art Pepper-George Cables Duo | Art Pepper:The Complete Galaxy Recordings | Galaxy | 16GCD 1016-2
Art Pepper:The Complete Galaxy Recordings | Galaxy | 16GCD 1016-2
Goin' Home | Original Jazz Classics | GXY 5143
Samba Night
Traubeli Weiß Ensemble | Guitar Moments | Take Twelve On CD | TT 006-2
Samba Nights
Clarion Fracture Zone | Blue Shift | VeraBra Records | CDVBR 2075-2
Samba Nova
Baden Powell Quartet | En Concert Avec Europe 1 | Laserlight | 710703/04
Samba Novo
Bajazzo | Caminos | Edition Collage | EC 485-2
Samba Now!
Nicos Jaritz Sextet | Macumba | Amadeo | AVRS 6491
Samba Of My Country
Jay Hoggard | Solo Vibraphone | India Navigation | IN 1040 CD
Samba Para Bean
Irakere | Misa Negra | Messidor | 15972 CD
Samba Per La Gamba
Allan Botschinsky/Niels-Henning Orsted-Pedersen | Duologue | M.A Music | NU 206-3
Samba Petite
Masters | Masters | Carlyne | 695011
Samba School
Oscar Peterson Sextet | Soul Espanol | Limelight | 510439-2
Samba Sensitive
Carlos Garnett Orchestra | Let This Melody Ring On | Muse | MR 5079
Samba Tala
Paul Glasse Group | Paul Glasse | Amazing Records | AMCD 1022
Samba Triste
Baden Powell Trio | Jazz-Club: Guitar | Verve | 840035-2
Charlie Byrd Trio With Strings | Latin Byrd | Milestone | M 47005
Stan Getz-Charlie Byrd Sextet | Jazz Samba | Verve | 521413-2
Stan Getz/Charlie Byrd:Jazz Samba | CTI Records | PDCTI 1104-2
Samba Two Step
Urszula Dudziak And Band Walk Away | Magic Lady | IN+OUT Records | 7008-2
Samba Ulla
Urszula Dudziak With Orchestra | Ulla | Pop-Eye | PE 101
Sambady
Jean-Louis Matinier Quartet | Confluences | Enja | ENJ-9454 2
Sambadynos
Hendrik Meurkens Octet | Sambahia | Concord | CCD 4474
Sambalero
Stan Getz-Luiz Bonfa Orchestra | Jazz Samba Encore! | CTI Records | PDCTI 1125-2
Sambali
Charly Antolini Jazz Power | Caravan | BELL Records | BLR 84044
Sambananda
Louie Bellson Big Band | Dynamite! | Concord | CCD 4105
Sambolero
Luiz Bonfa/Cafe | Non Stop To Brazil | Chesky | JD 29
Sambop
Cannonball Adderley With Sergio Mendes And The Bossa Rio Sextet | Cannonball's Bossa Nova | Blue Note | 522667-2
Poncho Sanchez And His Orchestra | Afro-Cuban Fantasy | Concord | CCD 4847
Sambukada
Passport | Iguacu | Atlantic | 2292-46031-2
Walkaway With Urszula Dudziak | Saturation | IN+OUT Records | 77024-2
Sambula
Dick Katz Trio | 3wayPlay | Reservoir | RSR CD 127(875790)
Same As Before
John Scofield Quartet | Gracy Under Pressure | Blue Note | 798167-2
Same Girl
Max Bennett & Freeway | Images | TBA Records | TBCD 243(881845)
Same Shame
Rickey Kelly Quintet | Limited Stops Only | Nimbus | NS 3146
Same Train
Duke Ellington And His Orchestra | Louis Armstrong & Duke Ellington | Avenue | AVINT 1006
Jon Strong Trio | Follow Me | Linn Records | AKD 023
Sameeda
Fred Van Hove | Verloren Maandag | FMP | SAJ 11
Samicotico
Paul Quinichette And His Orchestra | The Vice Pres | Verve | 543750-2
Samiel
Lenni-Kalle Taipale Trio | Nothing To Hide | Naxos Jazz | 86035-2
Sammy
John Stein Quintet | Portraits And Landscapes | Jardis Records | JRCD 20029
Riccardo Fassi Tankio Band | Il Principe | SPLASC(H) Records | H 180
Sammy Plays The Blues For Mezz
Sammy Price Quintet | Le Jazz En France Vol.14:Boogie Woogie A La Parisienne | Pathe | 1552601
Samotek
Vincent Courtois Quartet | Cello News | Nocturne Productions | NPCD 508
Sams
Patrick Tompert Trio | Moche! | Satin Doll Productions | SDP 1035-1 CD
Sam's Blues
Sam 'The Man' Taylor Orchestra | Back Beat-The Rhythm Of The Blues Vol.5 | Mercury | 511270-2 PMS
Sam's Song
Art Blakey And The Jazz Messengers | Once Upon A Groove | Blue Note | LT 1065
Sam's Tune
Cannonball Adderley Quintet | Cannonball Adderley:Sophisticated Swing-The EmArCy Small Group Sessions | Verve | 528408-2
Cannonball Adderley:Sophisticated Swing-The EmArCy Small Group Sessions | Verve | 528408-2
Sam's Tune(alt.take)
Stéphane Mercier Group | Flor De Luna | Fresh Sound Records | FSNT 097 CD
Samsara
Terri Lyne Carrington Group | Jazz Is A Spirit | ACT | 9408-2
Samsara(for Wayne)
Lena Willemark-Ale Möller Group | Agram | ECM | 1610
Samsingen
David Murray Octet | Dark Star(The Music Of The Grateful Dead) | Astor Place | TCD 4002
Samurai Hee-Haw
Marc Johnson Quartet | Bass Desires | ECM | 1299(827743-2)
Marc Johnson Trio | Magic Labyrith | JMT Edition | 514018-2
San
Billie & Dee Dee Pierce | Jazz At Preservation Hall, Vol.2 | Atlantic | SD 1409
San Andrea
Lu Watters' Jazz Band | Blues Over Bodega | Good Time Jazz | GTCD 12066-2
San Andreas Fault
John Zorn Group | Spillane | Nonesuch | 7559-79172-2
San Angelo Release-
Bluesiana | Bluesiana II | Windham Hill | 34 10133-2
San Calimero
Don Grusin Group | No Borders | GRP | GRP 96762
San Domingo Night
Jürgen Wuchner's String Project | Jürgen Wuchner's String Project | Blue Flame | 40092(2132483-2)
San Felice
The Washington Guitar Quintet | Aquarelle | Concord | CCD 42016
San Francisco
Louis Armstrong And His All Stars | The Best Live Concert | Festival | ???
San Francisco-
Jesse Fuller | San Francisco Bay Blues | Good Time Jazz | 10051
San Francisco Bay Blues
Philadelphia Jerry Ricks & Oscar Klein | Low Light Blues | L+R Records | LR 42007
San Francisco Blues
Doctor Ross | The Harmonica Boss | Big Bear | 146403
San Francisco Holiday
Jessica Williams | In The Key Of Monk | Jazz Focus | JFCD 029
Steve Lacy Quartet | Evidence With Don Cherry | Prestige | MPP 2505
Thelonious Monk Sextet | Thelonious Monk-The Complete Riverside Recordings | Riverside | 15 RCD 022-2
San Ignacio
Toto Blanke-Rudolf Dasek | Mona Lisa | ALISO Records | AL 1037
George Lewis And His Band | George Lewis With Kid Shots | American Music | AMCD-2
San Juan
Keith Ingham-Harry Allen Septet | The Back Room Romp | Sackville | SKCD2-3059
San Juan Sunset
Lee Ritenour Sextet | Alive In L.A. | GRP | GRP 98822
Enrico Rava Group | Quotation Marks | Japo | 60010 IMS (2360010)
San Lorenzo
Pat Metheny Group | Travels | ECM | 1252/53
Blue Asphalt | Jazz Door | JD 1223
San Marcos
Andy Martin With The Metropole Orchestra | Andy Martin & Metropole Orchestra | Mons Records | MR 874802
San Peyre
String Trio Of New York | Common Goal | Black Saint | 120058-2
Sancta Mater
Coleman Hawkins All Stars | The Hawk Flies High | Original Jazz Classics | OJC 027(R 12-223)
Sanctified Waltz
Tiny Grimes And His Rockin' Highlanders | Tiny Grimes:The Complete 1950-1954,Vol.3 | Blue Moon | BMCD 6007
Sanctimonious Sam
Baron-Berne-Roberts Trio | Miniature | JMT Edition | 834423-2
Sanctuary
Miles Davis Group | Live At The Fillmore East | CBS | C2K 65139
Live At The Fillmore East | CBS | C2K 65139
Miles Davis Quintet | Paraphernalia | JMY(Jazz Music Yesterdays) | JMY 1013-2
Miles Davis Sextet | Circle In The Round | CBS | 467898-2
Circle In The Round | CBS | 467898-2
Wayne Shorter Quartet | Footprints Live! | Verve | 589679-2
Miles Davis Sextet | Black Beauty-Miles Davis At Filmore West | CBS | C2K 65138
Sanctuary-
Paul Bley/Steve Swallow | The Life Of A Trio:Sunday | Owl Records | 014735-2
Sanctuary Much
Joe Lovano Trio | Trio Fascination | Blue Note | 833114-2
Sanctuary Park
Mahavishnu Orchestra | Birds Of Fire | CBS | 468224-2
Sanctus-
Steve Houben Trio | 3 | B.Sharp Records | CDS 071
Sand
Keith Jarrett | Staircase | ECM | 1090/91
Medeski Martin & Wood With Guests | It's A Jungle In Here | Gramavision | R2 79495
Ralph Towner Quartet | Solstice | ECM | 1060(825458-2)
Rudi Neuwirth Group | Sand | Traumton Records | 2413-2
Mike Richmond Trio | On The Edge | Steeplechase | SCCD 31237
Sand Box
Mark Egan Group | A Touch Of Light | GRP | GRP 95722
Sand Dune
Willie 'The Lion' Smith | The Memoirs Of Willie 'The Lion' Smith | RCA | 2126415-2
Sandalia Dela
Bob Degen | Sandcastle | free flow music | ffm 0897
Sandcastle
Cesc Miralta Quartet | Carretera Austal | Fresh Sound Records | FSNT 149 CD
Sandernes
Naßler & Schneider feat. Jörg Ritter | Triologe | Acoustic Music Records | 319.1137.2
Sand-Glass
Charlie Haden-Paul Motian Trio Feat.Geri Allen | Etudes | Soul Note | 121162-2
Sandino
Gonzalo Rubalcaba Trio | The Blessing | Blue Note | 797197-2
Charlie Shoemake Sextet | Away From The Crowd | Discovery | DS 856 IMS
Sandiya
Benny Goodman And His Orchestra | The Birth Of Swing | Bluebird | ND 90601(3)
Sandman
Jonas Hellborg Group | Adfa | Demon Records | DEM 020
Sandman's Coming
Bruce Turner Quartet | The Dirty Bopper | Calligraph | CLG LP 003 IMS
Sandsee
Paul Quinichette Sextet | Paul Quinichete:All Stars Sessions 1951-1953 | Blue Moon | BMCD 1012
Sandu
Clifford Brown-Max Roach Quintet | Clifford Brown-Max Roach:Alone Together-The Best Of The Mercury Years | Verve | 526373-2
Jazz Gallery:Clifford Brown | RCA | 2114176-2
Brownie-The Complete EmArCy Recordings Of Clifford Brown | EmArCy | 838306-2
Dave Bailey Sextet | One Foot In The Gutter | Epic | ESCA 7759
Louis Smith Quartet | Once In A While | Steeplechase | SCCD 31464
Wes Montgomery Quintet | Wes Montgomery-The Complete Riverside Recordings | Riverside | 12 RCD 4408-2
Arturo Sandoval Group | Hot House | N2K | 43072
Sandy
John Carter with The Horace Tapscott Trio | The Dark Tree 2 | Hat Art | CD 6083
Sandyken
Oscar Peterson | Oscar Peterson:Exclusively For My Friends | MPS | 513830-2
Sanf Kanf
Renee Rosnes Trio | Art & Soul | Blue Note | 499997-2
Sanfona
Richard Galliano Group | French Touch | Dreyfus Jazz Line | FDM 36596-2
Egberto Gismonti & Academia De Dancas | Sanfona | ECM | 1203/04(829391-2)
Sanfona-
Jan Garbarek Trio | Triptychon | ECM | 1029(847321-2)
Sang
Randy Brecker Quintet | In The Idiom | Denon Compact Disc | CY-1483
Sangaredi
Archie Shepp With Chris McGregor And His Brotherhood Of Breath | En Concert A Banlieues Bleues | 52e Rue Est | RECD 017

TITELVERZEICHNIS

Sanguine
Herbie Harper Quintet | Herbie Harper Feat.Bud Shank And Bob Gordon | Fresh Sound Records | 054 2600581(Liberty LJH 6003)
Franklin Kiermyer & Jericho | Break Down The Walls | Konnex Records | KCD 5044
Sankofa
Hamiet Bluiett Quartet | Sankofa/Rear Garde | Soul Note | 121238-2
Sankt Gerold Variations 1-12
Renaud Garcia-Fons & Jean-Louis Matinier | Fuera | Enja | ENJ-9364 2
Sanlucar
Loek Dikker Waterland Ensemble | Tan Tango | Waterland | WM 001
Sans Chant
Eric Le Lann Group | New York | OMD | VB 053 CD
Sans Titre
Joelle Leandre | Palimpseste | Hat Art | CD 6103
Santa Amalia
Odetta | The Tin Angel | Original Blues Classics | OBCCD 565-2(F 3252)
Santa Claus Came In The Spring
Mark Shane's X-Mas Allstars | What Would Santa Say? | Nagel-Heyer | CD 055
Putney Dandridge Band | Putney Dandridge 1935-1936 | Timeless | CBC 1-023
Sackville All Stars | The Sackville All Star Christmas Records | Sackville | SKCD2-3038
Santa Claus Is Coming To Town
Bill Evans | Further Conversations With Myself | Verve | 559832-2
Bill Evans Trio | The Complete Bill Evans On Verve | Verve | 527953-2
Trio (Motian Peacock)-Duo(Hall) | Verve | 2-2509 IMS
Christoph Mudrich Trio feat. Sir Henry | Christmas In Blue | Blue Concept | BCCD 93/03
Ella Fitzgerald With The Frank DeVol Orchestra | Ella With You A Swinging Christmas | Verve | 2304445 IMS
Jan Harrington Sextet | Jan Harrington's Christmas In New Orleans | Nagel-Heyer | NHR SP 4
Jimmy Smith Trio | Christmas Cookin' | Verve | 513711-2
Mark Shane's X-Mas Allstars | What Would Santa Say? | Nagel-Heyer | CD 055
Maryland Jazzband Of Cologne feat. Papa Don Vappie And Erny Elly | Christmas In New Orleans | Maryland Records | MJCD 0895
Paul Bley Trio | My Standard | Steeplechase | SCCD 31214
Autobiography In Jazz | Original Jazz Classics | OJC 115(DEB 198)
Santa Cruz
Soul Rebels | Let Your Mind Be Free | Mardi Gras Records | MG 1020
Santa Fe Blues
The Rippingtons | Curves Ahead | GRP | GRP 96512
Santa Maria Novella
Buddy Collette Octet | Man Of Many Parts | Original Jazz Classics | OJCCD 239-2(C 3522)
Santeria Sunrise
Bajazzo | Caminos | Edition Collage | EC 485-2
Santiago
Irakere | Homenaje A Beny Moré | Messidor | 25904 CD
Santissima Trinidade
Gonzalo Rubalcaba Quartet | Rapsodia | Blue Note | 828264-2
Sanzen(Moment Of The Truth)
Acoustic Guitars | Gajos In Disguise | Stunt Records | STUCD 18901
Sao Cristovao
Fourth World | Fourth World | Ronnie Scott's Jazz House | JHCD 026
Sao Paolo
Kenny Dorham Quintet | Joe Henderson-The Blue Note Years | Blue Note | 789287-2
Sao Paulo
Nelson Riddle And His Orchestra | Changing Colors | MPS | 9814794
Tom Harrell Orchestra | Time's Mirror | RCA | 2663524-2
Peter Erskine Trio | ELB | ACT | 9289-2
Sao Sen
Raiz De Pedra | Diario De Bordo | TipToe | TIP-888822 2
Sao Sepé
Egberto Gismonti Group | Sol Do Meio Dia | ECM | 1116(829117-2)
Sapain
Charlie Byrd Trio | Sugarloaf Suite | Concord | CCD 4114
Sapore Di Sale
Palatino | Palationo Chap.3 | EmArCy | 013610-2
Sapore Di Si Minore
Elvira Plenar-Vitold Rek | Elvira Plenar-Vitold Rek | L+R Records | CDLR 45089
Sapporo(part 1&2)
David Chevallier Quintet | Migration | Adda | 590094
Saptarshi
Charlie Byrd Trio With Bud Shank | Brazilville | Concord | CCD 4173
Sara
Michael Gerber Group | This Is Michael Gerber | Big World | BW 2007
Sarabande
National Jazz Ensemble | National Jazz Ensemble Vol. 2 | Chiaroscuro | CR 151
Sarabande-
Jacques Loussier Trio | Baroque Favorites | Telarc Digital | CD 83516
Sarabande From Violin Sonata In B Minor
Christian Wallumrod Ensemble | Sofienberg Variations | ECM | 1809(017067-2)
Sarabande Nouvelle
Sofienberg Variations | ECM | 1809(017067-2)
Sarabande Nouvelle Variation 1
Sofienberg Variations | ECM | 1809(017067-2)
Sarabande Nouvelle Variation 2
Joachim Kühn | The Diminished Augmented System | EmArCy | 542320-2
Sarabande(from Partita 2)
Klaus Doldinger Quartet | Doldinger's Best | ACT | 9224-2
Saragossa
Carmen McRae With The Shirley Horn Trio | Sarah-Dedicated To You | Novus | PD 90546
Sarah
Oliver Lake/Donal Leonellis Fox | Boston Duets | Music & Arts | CD 732
Richard Zimmerman | The Complete Works Of Scott Joplin | Laserlight | 15945
Sarah's Bande
Wolfgang Lackerschmid & Lynne Arriale Trio | You Are Here | Bhakti Jazz | BR 43
Dave Burrell | Windward Passages | Hat Art | CD 6138
Sarajevo
Sylvie Courvoisier Group | Y2K | Enja | ENJ-9383 2
Hank Jones Meets Cheik-Tidiana Seck | Sarala | Verve | 528783-2
Sarala
Stephan Rigert's Talking Drums | Different Colors Vol.2 | TCB Records | TCB 03062
Saranac By Starlight
Anouar Brahem Trio | Barzakh | ECM | 1432(847540-2)
Sarandib
Stanley Turrentine Quintet | Never Let Me Go | Blue Note | 576750-2
Sara's Dance
Mike Mainieri Group | Jazz Life Vol.2:From Seventh At Avenue South | Storyville | 4960763
Sara's Touch
Mike Mainieri Orchestra | Wanderlust | NYC-Records | NYC 6002 2
Steps Ahead With Guests | Yin-Yang | NYC-Records | NYC 6001-2
Sarastus
Holger Mantey | Piano Total | NCC Jazz | NCC 8506
Saratoga Shout
Luis Russell And His Orchestra | Luis Russell | CBS | CBS 88039
Saratoga Swing
Chris Barber's Jazz Band | They All Play The Duke | Jazz Colours | 874740-2
The Riverboat Jazzband | 35th Anniversary | Timeless | CD TTD 574
Sarava
Bola Sete Quintet | The Incomparable Bola Sete | Original Jazz Classics | OJC 288(F 8364)
Sardinian Princess
Renaud Garcia-Fons Group | Entremundo | Enja | ENJ-9464 2
Sareban
Bill Evans Trio | Since We Met | Original Jazz Classics | OJC 622(F 9501)
Sareen Jurer
In His Own Way | West Wind | WW 2028
Half Moon Bay | Milestone | MCD 9282-2
John Abercrombie-Ralph Towner Duo | Sargasso Sea | ECM | 1080
Sargasso Sea
Willie Williams Quartet | Spirit Willie | Enja | ENJ-7045 2
Sarlat
John Benson Brooks' Orchestra | Folk Jazz U.S.A. | RCA | PM 43767
Sart
Papa Bue's Viking Jazzband | At The CCP Main Theater Manila, Philippines | V-King Records | VLP 100
Sasom Fagelen
Michael 'Patches' Stewart Group | Penetration | Hip Bop | HIBD 8018
Sass
Ernst-Ludwig Petrowsky Quartet | Synopsis/DDR | FMP | 0240
Sassie Lassie
Lou Donaldson Quintet | Pretty Things | Blue Note | 789794-2
Sassy
Illinois Jacquet Quartet | Bottoms Up | Original Jazz Classics | OJCCD 417-2(P 7575)
Sassy Mae
Memphis Slim | The Blues Vol.2 | Intercord | 158601
Sassy Stew
Buddy Rich And His Orchestra | The Amazing Buddy Rich: Time Being | RCA | ND 86459(847168)
Satan Takes A Holiday
Duke Ellington And His Orchestra | At The Bal Masque | CBS | 21144
Satan's Dance
Joe Venuti And His Orchestra | The Radio Years | London | HMG 5023 AN
Satchel Mouth Swing
Louis Armstrong With Luis Russell And His Orchestra | Louis Armstrong Vol.7-Satchmo's Discoveries | MCA | 1326
Satelite
John Coltrane Trio | Coltrane's Sound | Atlantic | 7567-81358-2
Denny Zeitlin-Charlie Haden Duo | Time Remembers One Time Once | ECM | 1239
Satelite-
Sun Ra & His Omniverse Arkestra | Destination Unknown | Enja | 7071-2
Satellite Village
Dollar Brand Septet | Soweto/Dollar Brand-Abdullah Ibrahim | Bellaphon | BID 155501
Satie
Paolo Fresu Quintet | Night On The City | Owl Records | 013425-2
Carla Bley-Steve Swallow | Are We There Yet? | Watt | 29(547297)
Satie For Two
Vienna Art Orchestra | The Minimalism Of Erik Satie | Hat Art | CD 6024
Satin Doll
Big Band Ulm | All Of Us | yvp music | 3014
Bill Allred-Roy Williams Quintet | Ellington For Lovers | Nagel-Heyer | NH 1009
Bill Coleman Sextet | Americans Swinging In Paris:Bill Coleman | EMI Records | 539663-2
Bill Mays Trio | An Ellington Affair | Concord | CCD 4651
Blossom Dearie | I'm Hip | CBS | 489123-2
Bobby Hackett Quintet | Melody Is A Must-Live At The Roosevelt Grill Vol.2 | Phontastic | PHONT 7572
Bud Powell Trio | Bud Powell In Paris | Discovery | DS 830 IMS
Charlie Byrd Trio | The Best Of The Jazz Guitars | LRC Records | CDC 8531(874372)
I've Got The World On A String(Charlie Byrd Sings Again) | Timeless | CD SJP 427
Clark Terry Quartet | Jazz Legends:Clark Terry-Duke Jordan | Storyville | 4960283
Count Basie And His Orchestra | Warm Breeze | Pablo | 2312131-2
David Matthews & The Manhattan Jazz Orchestra | Hey Duke! | Milestone | MCD 9320-2
Dexter Gordon Quartet | King Neptune | Steeplechase | SCCD 36012
Duke Ellington And His Orchestra | The Best Of Duke Ellington | Capitol | 831501-2
100 Years Duke | Laserlight | 24906
All Star Road Band Vol.2 | Doctor Jazz | ZL 70969(2) (809319)
This Is Jazz:Duke Ellington Play Standards | CBS | CK 65056
Carnegie Hall '64 Vol.2 | Moon Records | MCD 068-2
A True Collectors Item | Jazz Archive | 90.105-2
Duke 56/62 Vol.1 | CBS | 88653
Duke Ellington Trio | Duke Ellington-New York Concert | Musicmasters | 65122-2
Ella Fitzgerald And Her All Stars | The Complete Ella Fitzgerald Song Books of Harold Arlen, Irving Berlin, Duke Ellington, George & Ira Gershwin, Jerome Kern, Johnny Mercer, Cole Porter And Rogers & Hart | Verve | 519832-2
Ella Fitzgerald With The Count Basie Orchestra | Ella And Basie | Verve | 539059-2
Ella & Basie-On The Sunny Side Of The Street | Verve | 821576-2
Ella Fitzgerald With The Duke Ellington Orchestra And Jimmy Jones Trio | Ella Fitzgerald And Duke Ellington:Cote D'Azure Concerts on Verve | Verve | 539033-2
Ella Fitzgerald And Duke Ellington:Cote D'Azure Concerts on Verve | Verve | 539033-2
Ella Fitzgerald And Duke Ellington:Cote D'Azure Concerts on Verve | Verve | 539033-2
Ella Fitzgerald With The Tommy Flanagan Trio | Ella-At The Montreux Jazz Festival 1975 | Original Jazz Classics | OJC20 789-2(2310751)
Ella Fitzgerald In Budapest | Pablo | PACD 5308-2
Ernestine Anderson With The Monty Alexander Trio | Sunshine | Concord | CCD 4109
Gene Ammons Sextet | The Gene Ammons Story: Organ Combos | Prestige | P 24071
George Shearing And His Quintet | Beauty And The Beat | Pathe | EMS 1158(Capitol ST 1219)
Gerald Wiggins Trio | Relax And Enjoy It | Original Jazz Classics | OJC 173(C 7595)
Helmut Brandt's Mainstream Orchestra | Chez Pep | BIT | 10599
Humphrey Lyttelton And His Band | Lay 'Em Straight! | Calligraph | CLGCD 033
Jaco Pastorius Trio | Live In Italy & Honestly | Jazzpoint | JP 1059 CD
Jay McShann | Vine Street Boogie | Black Lion | BLCD 760187
Jesper Thilo Quintet feat. Harry Edison | Jesper Thilo Quintet feat. Harry Edison | Storyville | STCD 4120
Jimmy Smith Trio | Paris Jazz Concert:Jimmy Smith And The Trio | Laserlight | 36159
Compact Jazz: Jimmy Smith | Verve | 831374-2
Joe Pass Trio | The Best Of Joe Pass | Pablo | 2405419-2
Johnny Hodges Orchestra | Johnny Hodges At The Sportpalast, Berlin | Pablo | 2CD 2620102
Johnny Hodges Quartet | Compact Jazz: Duke Ellington And Friends | Verve | 833291-2
Maurice Vander Trio | Maurice Vander | Dreyfus Jazz Line | FDM 36502-2
McCoy Tyner Trio + Latin Percussion | McCoy Tyner Plays Ellington | Impulse(MCA) | 951216-2
Michael Moore-Rufus Reid | Doublebass Delights | Double Time Records | DTRCD-117
Michel Petrucciani | Promenade With Duke | Blue Note | 780590-2
Michel Sardaby Trio | Night Cap | Debs Disc | HDD 522
Nancy Wilson With Gerald Wilson's Orchestra | Yesterday's Love Songs-Today's Blues | Capitol | 796265-2
Orchestra | Duke Ellington's Sophisticated Ladies | RCA | BL 04053 DX
Oscar Peterson All Stars | Oscar Peterson+Harry Edison+Eddie 'Cleanhead' Vinson's | Pablo | 2310927-2
Oscar Peterson Trio | The Way I Really Play | MPS | 821287-1
Oscar Peterson-Clark Terry Duo | Oscar Peterson Plays Duke Ellington | Pablo | 2310966-2
Oscar Peterson & Clark Terry | Original Jazz Classics | OJCCD 806-2(2310742)
Oscar Peterson-Harry Edison Duo | Jousts | Pablo | 2310817
Red Garland Trio | At The Prelude Vol.1 | Prestige | PCD 24132-2
Rias Big Band | The Music Of Duke Ellington | Mons Records | MR 874306
Roland Kirk Quintet | Live In Paris 1970 Vol.2 | France's Concert | FCD 115
Tony Scott Group | Tony Scott | Verve | 9861063
Toots Thielemans Quartet | Jazz In Paris:Toots Thielemans-Blues Pour Flirter | EmArCy | 549403-2 PMS
Toots Thielemans/Jonny Teupen/Paul Kuhn And Friends | Just Friends | Jazzline | ???
Wes Montgomery Trio | Wes Montgomery-The Complete Riverside Recordings | Riverside | 12 RCD 4408-2
Wild Bill Davis Quartet | Organ 1959 | Jazz Anthology | JA 5132
Bill Ramsey & Juraj Galan | Caldonia And More... | Bear Family Records | BCD 16151 AH
Satin Doll-
Carmen McRae And Her Trio | Live | Jazz Door | JD 1280
Duke Ellington | Masters Of Jazz Vol.6:Duke Ellington | Storyville | STCD 4106
George Shearing-Neil Swainson Duo | Dexterity | Concord | CCD 4346
Oscar Peterson-Joe Pass Duo | Live At Salle Pleyel, Paris | Pablo | 2625705
Stephane Grappelli | 7.Zelt-Musik-Festival:Jazz Events | Zounds | CD 2730001
Stephane Grappelli Trio | Stephane Grappelli | Hot Club Records | HCRCD 101
Satin Doll(alt.take)
Jimmy Smith Trio | Jimmy Smith Trio: Salle Pleyel, May 28th, 1965 | Laserlight | 36135
Satin Doll(part 1)
Jimmy Smith Trio: Salle Pleyel, May 28th, 1965 | Laserlight | 36135
Satin Doll(part 2)
The Frank Capp Juggernaut | Play It Again Sam | Concord | CCD 4747
Satin Satie-
The Heartland Consort | The Heartland Consort | Enja | 4070 (807666)
Satisfaction
John Tchicai-Vitold Rek Duo | Art Of The Duo:Satisfaction | Enja | 7033-2
Roy Ayers Group | Nasté | RCA | 6366613-2
Rufus & Ben Quillian(Blue Harmony Boys) | Please Warm My Weiner-Old Time Hokum Blues | Yazoo | YAZ 1043
Satisfaction Guaranteed
Calvin Boze With Maxwell Davis & His Orchestra | Calvin Boze:The Complete Recordings 1945-1952 | Blue Moon | BMCD 6014
Satisfied With Love
Christoph Stiefel Trio | Dream Of The Camel | Enja | 9135-2
Satori
Tony Scott Trio | Music For Zen Meditation | Verve | 521444-2
Satori(Enlightenment)
Gyjho Frank | Aeuropa | Blue Flame | 40372
Satunalia
Walkaway With Urszula Dudziak | Saturation | IN+OUT Records | 77024-2
Saturation
Eric Watson-John Lindberg | Soundpost: Works For Piano And Double Bass | Music & Arts | CD 920
Saturday
Axel Fischbacher Quartet | Coast To Coast | L+R Records | CDLR 45025
Saturday-
The Chris White Project | The Chris White Project | Muse | MCD 5494
Saturday Afternoon Blues
Jackie McLean Quintet | One Step Beyond | Blue Note | 746821-2
Saturday Blues
Big Bill Broonzy | Big Bill Broonzy-The 1955 London Sessions | Sequel Records | NEX CD 119
Saturday Night
John Surman Trio | Such Winters Of Memory | ECM | 1254(810621-2)
Louis Armstrong And His Orchestra | Louis Armstrong Radio Days | Moon Records | MCD 056-2
Saturday Night Blues
Jimmy Giuffre 3 | Western Suite | Atlantic | 7567-80777-2
Saturday Night Dance-
Annie Ross & PonyPoindexter With The Berlin All Stars | Annie Ross & Pony Poindexter with The Berlin All Stars | MPS | 9811257
Saturday Night Fish Fry
Charlie Byrd Trio | Bluebyrd | Concord | CCD 4082
Joseph Robechaux And His New Orleans Boys | Joe Robichaux And His New Orleans Boys | Folklyric | 9032
Saturday Night Fish Fry(part 1)
Louis Jordan And His Tympany Five | Louis Jordan-Let The Good Times Roll: The Complete Decca Recordings 1938-1954 | Bear Family Records | BCD 15557 IH
Saturday Night Fish Fry(part 2)
Art Hodes | Keepin' Out Of Mischief Now | Candid | CCD 79717
Saturday Night Function
Chris Barber's Jazz Band | The Great Re-Union Concert | Intercord | 157011
Ken Colyer's Jazzmen | The Best Of Dixieland-1953/54 | London | 820879-2
Saturday Night Is The Loneliest Night Of The Week
Dutch Swing College Band | Digital Anniversary | Philips | 824585-2 PMS
Jeanie Lambe And The Danny Moss Quartet | The Blue Noise Session | Nagel-Heyer | CD 052
Oscar Peterson Trio | A Jazz Portrait Of Frank Sinatra | Verve | 825769-2
Rosemary Clooney And Her Band | For The Duration | Concord | CCD 4444
Saturday's Children
Dean Magraw Group | Broken Silence | Acoustic Music Records | 319.1054.2
Saturn
Sun Ra And His Arkestra | Sound Of Joy | Delmark | DE 414
Saturn-
Elements | Illumination | RCA | PD 83031(874013)
Saturn Returning
Karl Ratzer Quintet | Saturn Returning | Enja | ENJ-9315 2
Saturn Song
Volker Kriegel Group | Topical Harvest | MPS | 821279
Saturnia
Shorty Rogers And His Giants | A Portrait Of Shorty | RCA | 2121822-2
Saturns Child
Dave Liebman Orchestra | Drum Ode | ECM | 1046
Satyr Satire
David Amram Quintet | Amarcord Nino Rota | Hannibal | HNBL 9301
Sau
Jabbo Smith And His Rhythm Aces | Big Band Bounce & Boogie-Jabbo Smith:Sweet 'N' Low Down | Affinity | AFS 1029
Saubersinn-
Cecil Payne Quintet | Patterns Of Jazz | Savoy | SV 0135(MG 12147)
Saucer Eyes
Ron Carter Quintet | Eric Dolphy:The Complete Prestige Recordings | Prestige | 9 PRCD-4418-2
The Three Sounds | Black Orchid | Blue Note | 821289-2
The Best Of The Three Sounds | Blue Note | 827323-2
Saud(Dedicated To McCoy Tyner)
Al Haig Trio | Al Haig Today! | Fresh Sound Records | FSR-CD 0006
Saudade
Christof Sänger Trio | Chorinho | Laika Records | LK 93-033
David Benoit Group With Symphony Orchestra | Shadows | GRP | GRP 96542
Hipsters In The Zone | Into The Afro-Latin Bag | Nabel Records:Jazz Network | CD 4663

Louis Hayes Sextet | Una Max | Steeplechase | SCCD 31263
Charlie Byrd Orchestra | Latin Byrd | Milestone | M 47005

Saudade Da Bahia
Charlie Byrd Trio | Sugarloaf Suite | Concord | CCD 4114

Saudade Do Brazil
Bill Evans-Eddie Gomez Duo | Eloquence | Fantasy | F 9618
Bob Mover Sextet Feat.Tom Harrell | On The Move | Candid | CRS 1015 IMS

Saudade Vem Correndo
Stan Getz-Luiz Bonfa Quintet | Jazz Samba Encore! | CTI Records | PDCTI 1125-2

Sausalito
Kenny Burrell Quartet | Blues-The Common Ground | Verve | 589101-2

Sausalito Nights
Kenny Burrell Sextet | Up The Street 'Round The Corner, Down The Block | Fantasy | F 9458

Sauve Qui Peut(Vienne)
Mongo Santamaria Orchestra | The Watermelon Man | Milestone | M 47012

Savanna Rainbow
Adam Rudolph's Moving Pictures | Skyway | Soul Note | 121269-2

Savannah Calling
Blind Willie McTell | Blind Willie McTell-Death Cell Blues | Biograph | BLP C 14

Savant
Lenny White Group | Renderers Of Spirit | Hip Bop | HIBD 8014
Kick | Wolfhound's Kick | BELL Records | BLR 84041

Save It Pretty Mama
Adrian Bentzon's Jazzband | The Golden Years Of Revival Jazz.Vol.3 | Storyville | STCD 5508
Art Hodes | Someone To Watch Over Me-Live At Hanratty's | Muse | MR 5252
Earl Hines Trio | The Indispensable Earl Hines Vol.5/6:The Bob Thiele Sessions | RCA | ND 89618
Louis Armstrong And His All Stars | Louis Armstrong-The Complete RCA Victor Recordings | RCA | 2668682-2
Louis Armstrong And His Orchestra | Heebie Jeebies | Naxos Jazz | 8.120351 CD
Louis Armstrong And His Savoy Ballroom Five | Jazz Classics In Digital Stereo: Louis Armstrong | CDS Records Ltd. | REB 597

Save Me
Pharoah Sanders Group | Save Our Children | Verve | 557297-2

Save Our Children
Fourplay | Fourplay...Yes,Please! | Warner | 9362-47694-2

Save Some Love For Me
Charles Fambrough Group | Keeper Of The Spirit | audioquest Music | AQCD 1033

Save The Best For Last
Warren Bernhardt Quintet | Family Album | dmp Digital Music Productions | CD 499

Save The Children
Morgana King And Her Sextet | Portraits | Muse | MR 5301(952107)

Save You Love For Me
David Fathead Newman Sextet | Back To Basics | Milestone | MCD 9188-2
Klaus Weiss Quintet | A Taste Of Jazz | ATM Records | ATM 3810-AH
Mike Turk With The Alkaline Jazz Trio | A Little Taste Of Cannonball | Organic Music | ORGM 9708
Nancy Wilson With The Art Farmer-Benny Golson Quintet | In Performance At The Playboy Jazz Festival | Elektra | MUS 96.0298-1

Save Your Love For Me
Claire Martin With The Jim Mullen Quartet And Special Guests | Devil May Care | Linn Records | AKD 021
Jesper Thilo Quartet | Swingin' Friends | Storyville | SLP 4065
Mark Whitfield Group | True Blue | Verve | 523591-2
Walter 'Wolfman' Washington And The Roadmasters | Out Of The Dark | Rounder Records | CDRR 2068

Save Yourself For Me
George Lewis-Douglas Ewart | George Lewis-Douglas Ewart | Black Saint | BSR 0026

Saving All My Love For You
Larry Clinton And His Orchestra | The Uncollected: Larry Clinton | Hindsight | HSR 109

Savoy
Lucky Millinder And His Orchestra | Lucky Days | MCA | 1319

Savoy Blues
Bob Crosby And His Orchestra | The Radio Years | London | HMG 5021 AN
Dutch Swing College Band | Souvenirs From Holland, Vol. 2 | DSC Production | PA 004 (801061)
George Lewis And His New Orleans Ragtime Band | The Radio Broadcast: 1950-1951 | Folklyric | 9030
George Lewis Session | George Lewis/Paul Barbarin | Storyville | SLP 4049
Louis Armstrong And His Hot Five | Louis Armstrong-The Hot Fives & Hot Sevens Vol.3 | CBS | 465189-2
Louis Armstrong And His Orchestra | Jazz:The Essential Collection Vol.2 | IN+OUT Records | 78012-2
Jazz Drumming Vol.4(1939) | Fenn Music | FJD 2704
Louis Armstrong And His Big Band Vol.1-The Maturity | Black & Blue | BLE 59.225 2
Mr.Acker Bilk And His Paramount Jazz Band | That's My Home | Philips | 830778-2 PMS
Papa Bue's Viking Jazzband | Live In Dresden | Storyville | SLP 815/16
The New York Allstars | We Love You,Louis! | Nagel-Heyer | CD 029
The Riverboat Jazzband | 35th Anniversary | Timeless | CD TTD 574

Savoy Truffle
Carroll Dickerson's Savoyagers | Louis Armstrong:Fireworks | Dreyfus Jazz Line | FDM 36710-2

Savoyager's Stomp
Jazz Gallery:Louis Armstrong Vol.1 | RCA | 2114166-2

Sax Appeal
Klaus Kreuzeder & Willi Herzinger | Sax As Sax Can | Trick Music | TM 8712 CD

Sax As Sax Can
Jack Costanzo Group | Latin Fever:The Wild Rhythms Of Jack Costanza | Capitol | 590955-2

Sax Con Ritmo
Phil Woods-Gene Quill Sextet | Phil And Quill | RCA | 2159153-2

Sax Mambo
Kenny Clarke-Francy Boland Big Band | En Concert Avec Europe 1 | Laserlight | 710413/14

Sax No End
Oscar Peterson | Oscar Peterson:Exclusively For My Friends | MPS | 513830-2

Sax Rap
Remy Filipovitch-Gediminas Laurinavicius | Open Your Eyes | Album | AS 331108 CD
Barbara Thompson's Paraphernalia | Breathless | VeraBra Records | CDVBR 2057-2

Sax Rap(short cut)
Amos Milburn And His Aladdin Chicken-Shackers | Chicken Shack Boogie | Pathe | 1561411(Aladdin)

Saxappeal
Tom Scott Groups | Reed My Lips | GRP | GRP 97592

Saxa-Woogie
Juhani Aaltonen Trio | Prana-Live At Groovy | Leo Records | 013

Sax-O-Be-Bop
Lester Young And His Band | Lester Young:The Complete 1936-1951 Small Group Sessions(Studio Recordings-Master Takes),Vol.4 | Blue Moon | BMCD 1004
Albert Mangelsdorff Quartet | Shake,Shuttle And Blow | Enja | ENJ-9374 2

Saxobonia
Alain Monnier Trio | Tribulat | Hat Art | 3505

Saxoraga
Friedeman Graef-Achim Goettert | Saxoridoo | FMP | OWN-90010

Saxtett
Carlos Garnett Orchestra | Cosmos Nucleus | Muse | MR 5104

Say Ah
Jack Jeffer's N.Y. Classic Big Band | New York Dreams | Mapleshade | 03632

Say Goodbye
George Duke Group | Night After Night | Elektra | 7559-60778-2

Say Hello To Mr.D(To Mr.S)
John Pizzarelli Trio With The Don Sebesky Orchestra | Our Love Is Here To Stay | RCA | 6367501-2

Say It
Harry Roy And His Orchestra | May Fair Nights | Saville Records | SVL 171 IMS
Randy Sandke Quintet | I Hear Music | Concord | CCD 4566
Teddy Stauffer Und Seine Original Teddies | Hot Jazz & Swing Mit Teddy Stauffer's Original Teddies | Elite Special | 9522002
Tommy Dorsey And His Orchestra | Forever | RCA | NL 89859 DP

Say It Again And Again
Chick Corea And Origin | Live At The Blue Note | Stretch Records | SCD 9018-2

Say It In French
Adam Makowicz-George Mraz Duo | Concord Duo Series Volume Five | Concord | CCD 4597

Say It Isn't So
Billie Holiday And Her All Stars | Billie Holiday:The Great American Songbook | Verve | 523003-2
Stay With Me | Verve | 511523-2
Coleman Hawkins' Fifty-Second Street All-Stars | Body And Soul | RCA | 26685152
Dinah Washington With The Don Costa Orchestra | Drinking Again | M&M Records | R 25183(Roulette)
Jay McShann-Buddy Tate Duo | Crazy Legs & Friday Strut | Sackville | 3011
Stan Kenton And His Orchestra | Blue Berlin | Blue Note | 799095-2
Lou Donaldson Quintet | Lou Donaldson:The Righteous Reed! The Best Of Poppa Lou | Blue Note | 830721-2

Say It Over And Over Again
John Coltrane Quartet | John Coltrane:The Classic Quartet-Complete Impulse Studio Recordings | Impulse(MCA) | 951280-2
Pharoah Sanders Quartet | Welcome To Love | Timeless | CD SJP 358

Say Listen
The Prestige All Stars | All Day Long | Prestige | SMJ 6604

Say Of The Gulls
T-Bone Walker And His Band | T-Bone Walker Sings The Blues | Pathe | 1546751(Imperial LP 9098)

Say Si Si
Clark Terry & Chico O Farril Orchestra | Spanish Rice | Verve | 9861050
Don Bagley Quintet | The Soft Sell | Blue Moon | BMCD 1603
Roger Kellaway | Say That Again | Dobre | 800880-320(DR 1045)

Say The Brother's Name
John Scofield Quartet | What We Do | Blue Note | 799586-2

Say The Word
Luis Russell And His Orchestra | Harlem Big Bands | Timeless | CBC 1-010

Say When
Michele Hendricks With The David Leonhadt Quartet | Carryin' On | Muse | MCD 5336

Say Yes
Ralph Sutton | The Other Side Of Ralph Sutton | Chaz Jazz | CJ 107
Roger Wolfe Kahn And His Orchestra | Red & Miff | Saville Records | SVL 146 IMS

Say You Blues
Eric Reed Orchestra | Happiness | Nagel-Heyer | CD 2010

Say You Care
Jimmy Rushing And His All Stars | Jimmy Rushing And The Big Brass/Rushing Lullabies | CBS | CK 65118

Sayo
Kazumi Watanabe Group | To Chi Ka | Denon Compact Disc | DC-8568

Sayonara Blues
Horace Silver Quintet | Horace Silver Retrospective | Blue Note | 495576-2
The Tokyo Blues | Blue Note | 853355-2
Anthony Ortega Quintet | Rain Dance | Discovery | DS 788 IMS

Says
Ann Malcom With The Robi Szakcsi Jr. Trio | R.S.V.P. | Mons Records | MR 874301

Says My Heart
Jackie And Roy | Jackie And Roy | Black Lion | BLCD 760904

Says You
Wes Montgomery Quartet | Movin' | Milestone | M 47040
Wes Montgomery-The Complete Riverside Recordings | Riverside | 12 RCD 4408-2
Jim Hall Quartet | Textures | Telarc Digital | CD 83402

Scablemates
Sammy Stewart And His Orchestra | Get Easy Blues | Frog | DGF 9

Scam
Mose Allison Trio | Back Country Suite | Original Jazz Classics | OJC 075(P 7091)

Scamper-
Sonny Stitt Septet | In The Beginning | Original Jazz Classics | OJCCD 1771-2(G 204)

Scamperin'
Benny Carter And His Orchestra | The Various Facets Of A Genius 1929-1940 | Black & Blue | BLE 59.230 2

Scandal(I)
Eric Reed Quintet | Musicale | Impulse(MCA) | 951196-2

Scandal(II)
Musicale | Impulse(MCA) | 951196-2

Scandal(III)
Reichlich Weiblich | Live At Moers Festival '87 | Moers Music | 02064 CD

Scandinavian Shuffle
Dan Rose Quartet | The Water's Rising | Enja | 9116-2

Scarborough Fair
Jean-Michel Pilc Trio | Welcome Home | Dreyfus Jazz Line | FDM 36630-2
Klaus Doldinger Quartet | Bluesy Toosy | ACT | 9200-2

Scarborough Fair-
Joe Beck-Ali Ryerson-Steve Davis | Alto | dmp Digital Music Productions | CD 521

Scarecrow Shakedown
Jeff Berlin Group | Taking Notes | Denon Compact Disc | CY-18043

Scared Hearts
The World Saxophone Quartet | Point Of No Return | Moers Music | 01034 CD

Scared To Be Alone
Blind Willie McTell | Blind Willie McTell-Death Cell Blues | Biograph | BLP C 14

Scarlatti Fever
Italian Instabile Orchestra | Litania Sibilante | Enja | ENJ-9405 2

Scarlet Sunrise
John Benson Brooks' Orchestra | Folk Jazz U.S.A. | RCA | PM 43767

Scars
The Blues Shouters | Live At Kultur-Karussell R ssli St fa | Bellaphon | BCH 33005

SCD
Al Di Meola Group | Scenario | CBS | 25718-2

Scene
Sun Ra And His Myth Arkestra | The Solar Myth Approach | Affinity | AFF 760

Scene 1-9
Lennie Tristano | The New Tristano | Atlantic | 7567-80475-2

Scene And Variations:
Maarten Altena Ensemble | Code | Hat Art | CD 6094

Scenes From A Silver Screen
Maria Schneider Jazz Orchestra | Coming About | Enja | ENJ-9062 2

Scent Of Dream
Manfred Zepf Meets Andrew Cyrille | Paintings | West Wind | 003

Scents
Hans Lüdemann Rism | Aph-o-Rism's | Jazz Haus Musik | JHM 0049 CD

Schabertnack
Stadtgarten Series Vol.2 | Jazz Haus Musik | JHM 1002 SER

Schachriars Dream
Ralf R. Hübner Quartet | Perlboot | L+R Records | CDLR 40023

Schall Und Rauch
Percussion Summit | Percussion Summit | Moers Music | 02056 CD

Schattenfrei
Jazzensemble Des Hessischen Rundfunks | Atmosphering Conditions Permitting | ECM | 1549/50

Schattenlehre
Bettina Born-Wolfram Born | Schattenspiel | Born&Bellmann | 993004 CD

Schausteller
Mike Mainieri Group | An American Diary:The Dreaming | NYC-Records | NYC 6026-2

Scheherazade-
Irene Schweizer-Rüdiger Carl Quartett | Goose Pannée | FMP | 0190

Scherzo
Draft | Traveling Birds | Jazz Haus Musik | JHM 68 CD
The Swingle Singers | Compact Jazz:The Swingle Singers | Mercury | 830701-2 PMS

Scherzo For An Old Shoe-
Swingle Singers | Swingle Singers Getting Romantic | Philips | 586736-2

Scherzo from Sonata for Violin And Piano Op.24 In F Major(L.v.Beethoven)
Schnuckenack Reinhardt Quintet | Jak-Swing | RCA | PL 28415 AS

Schikaneder Delight
Franz Koglmann Quintet | About Yesterdays Ezzthetics | Hat Art | CD 6003

Schinderkarren Mit Büffet
Passport | 2 Originals Of Passport(Passport-Second Passport) | Atlantic | ATL 60117

Schirokko
Passport And Guests | Doldinger Jubilee Concert | Atlantic | 2292-44175-2
Rundfunk-Berlin-Tanzorchester | Swing Tanzen Gestattet | Vagabond | 6.28415 DP

Schism
Wayne Shorter Sextet | Schizophrenia | Blue Note | 84292

Schizophrenic Scherzo
Andreas Willers Octet | The Ground Music | Enja | ENJ-9368 2

Schlaf Du Mein Erquicker
Dieter Ilg Trio | Fieldwork | Jazzline | JL 11155-2

Schlafende Hunde
Claus Boesser-Ferrari | Blue Footprint | Acoustic Music Records | 319.1066.2

Schlaflose-
Mani Neumeir-Peter Hollinger | Monsters Of Drums-Live | ATM Records | ATM 3821-AH

Schlagoberst
A Band Of Friends | Renè Wohlhauser Werkauswahl 1978-1993 | Creative Works Records | CW CD 1026-2

Schlagzeugtrio für drei Schlagzeuger
KontaSax | KontraSax Plays Getrude Stein | Jazz Haus Musik | JHM 0096 CD

Schlamm
Der Rote Bereich | Zwei | Jazz 4 Ever Records:Jazz Network | J4E 4727

Schleckereien Auf Der Flucht
Double You | Menschbilder | Jazz Haus Musik | JHM 0062 CD

Schlehmil
Der Rote Bereich | Der Rote Bereich | Jazz 4 Ever Records:Jazz Network | J4E 4715

Schlof Majn Kind
Joachim Kühn Group | Joachim Kühn | CMP Records | CMP 22

Schloss Elmau
Brian Barley Trio | Brian Barley Trio 1970 | Just A Memory | JAS 9502-2

Schmalz On The Bottom
Zentralquartet | Plie | Intakt Records | CD 037

Schmetterlinge Weinen Nicht
Dieter Bihlmaier Selection | Mallet Connection | Bhakti Jazz | BR 33

Schmetterlinge(dedicated to Gerhard Ziegler)
Eric Marienthal Group | Crossroads | GRP | GRP 96102

Schnecke Turtur
Kölner Saxophon Mafia | Die Saxuelle Befreiung | Jazz Haus Musik | JHM 19

Schneeballschlacht
Ulli Bögershausen | Christmas Carols | Laika Records | 35101622

Schneeflöckchen, Weißröckchen
Klaus Ignatzek-Florian Poser Duo | Music For Grandpiano And Vibraphone | Fusion | 8021 Digital

Schnell Und Schmerzhaft-
Günther Klatt & New York Razzmatazz | Fa Mozzo | Tutu Records | 888138-2

Schnellbedienung
Sven-Ake Johansson Quintet | Six Little Pieces For Quintet | HatOLOGY | 538

Scholocho
No Nett | Zur Lage Der Nation | Jazz Haus Musik | JHM 10

Schönes Kind(für Lena-Marie)
Schnuckenack Reinhardt Quintet | Swing Session | Intercord | 160010

School Days
Chuck Berry With The Blues Band | Newport Jazz Festival 1958,July 3rd-6th Vol.3:Blues In The Night No.1 | Phontastic | NCD 8815
Dizzy Gillespie And His Orchestra | Dizzy In Greece | Verve | MV 2630 IMS
Dizzy Gillespie Band | Dizzy Gillespie At Newport | Verve | 513754-2 PMS
Don Byas/Dizzy Gillespie All Stars | Yesterdays-Don Byas Meets Dizzy Gillespie | Moon Records | MCD 009-2
Oscar Peterson Sextet | En Concert Avec Europe 1 | Laserlight | 710443/48
Roy Eldridge And His Friends | Americans In Sweden: Roy Eldridge 1957-Count Basie 1954 | Jazz Society | AA 514
Dave McKenna | Maybeck Recital Hall Series Volume Two | Concord | CCD 4410

Schroeder
Sotto In Su | Südamerika Sept. 90 | Jazz Haus Musik | JHM 0051 CD

Schrott, Charmante Erscheinungen, Fieber
Untemehmen Kobra | Central Europe Suite | G.N.U. Records | CD A 94.007

Schuga Souni
Joe Bawelino Quartet | Guitar Moments | Take Twelve On CD | TT 006-2

Schummer
Spyro Gyra | Access All Areas | MCA | 2292-51215-1

Schwarze Augen
Bireli Lagrene Ensemble | Bireli Lagrene 15 | Antilles | 802503
Bireli Lagrene Group | Bireli Lagrene 'Highlights' | Jazzpoint | JP 1027 CD
Gadzho | Caffe Freddo | Meilton | 1617
No Nett | Wenn Der Weiße Flieder Wieder Blüht | Jazz Haus Musik | JHM 14

Schweigsam
Kölner Saxophon Mafia | Space Player | Jazz Haus Musik | JHM 0132 CD

Schwein Im Weltall
Pata Horns | New Archaic Music | Pata Musik | PATA 4(JHM 42) CD

Schwesterlein,Schwesterlein,Wann Geh'n Wir Nach Haus?
Wolfgang Lauth Quartet | Noch Lauther | Bear Family Records | BCD 15942 AH

Schwetzinger Original
Luigi Archetti | Das Ohr | ATM Records | ATM 3804-AH

Schwiphti-
Helmut Zacharias mit seiner Swing-Besetzung | Ich Habe Rhythmus | Bear Family Records | BCD 15642 AH

Schwips Boogie
Fisherman's Break | Fisherman's Break | Edition Collage | EC 450-2
Schwirbel
Gunter Hampel | Solo Now | MPS | 68067
Science
SWR Big Band | Jazz In Concert | Hänssler Classics | CD 93.004
Science Fiction
Frank Giebels-Chiz Harris Trio | Sience Fiction | Jazz Pure Collection | AU 31621 CD
Scientific
Collin Walcott Quartet | Cloud Dance | ECM | 1062(825469-2)
Scimitar
Tony Oxley Sextet | 4 Compositions For Sextet | CBS | 494437-2
Scintilla
Jimmy Giuffre Quartet | Tangents In Jazz | Affinity | AFF 60
Scivolando(stretto)-
Dave Belany And Her Trio | Motivations | Sahara | 1005
Sco Cone
Future Shock | Handclaps | Timeless | CD SJP 374
Scomotion
Barbara Jungfer Trio | Vitamin B 3 | yvp music | CD 3097
Scones
Teddy Charles New Directions Quartet With Booker Little And Booker Ervin | Jazz In The Garden At The Museum Of Modern Art | Fresh Sound Records | FSR-CD 0212
Scoop
Marcus Miller Group | The Sun Don't Lie | Dreyfus Jazz Line | FDM 36560-2
Ralph Lalama Quartet | Music For Grown-Ups | Criss Cross | Criss 1165
Scoops
Earl Hines And His Orchestra | The Indispensable Earl Hines Vol.3/4(1939-1945) | RCA | 2126408-2
Scoot
Count Basie And His Orchestra | Basie On Roulette, Vol. 2: Basie Plays Hefti | Vogue | 500002
Scooter
Rolf Römer Quartet | Tesoro | Jazz 4 Ever Records:Jazz Network | J4E 4743
Aera | Aera Live | Erlkönig | 148415
Scootin' About
Jimmy Giuffre Trio | Live In Europe 1961 Vol.2 | Raretone | 5019 FC
Scope
John Patitucci Group | Sketchbook | GRP | GRP 96172
Scophile
Howard Riley Trio | The Day Will Come | CBS | 494434-2
Score
Randy Brecker Sextet | Score | Blue Note | 781202-2
Scorpio
Clifford Jordan Quartet | Firm Roots | Steeplechase | SCCD 31033
Kölner Saxophon Mafia | Die Saxuelle Befreiung | Jazz Haus Musik | JHM 19
Lou Blackburn-Freddie Hill Quintet | Perception | Fresh Sound Records | FSR-CD 0307
Scotch
Michael Blass Group | Wait And See | B.Sharp Records | CDS 089
Scotch And Water
Frank Collett Trio | Perfectly Frank | Fresh Sound Records | FSR-CD 5024
Stan Kenton And His Orchestra | The Uncollected:Stan Kenton, Vol.5 | Hindsight | HSR 157
Scotch And Women
Art Blakey And The Jazz Messengers | Once Upon A Groove | Blue Note | LT 1065
Scotch Blues
Duke Jordan Trio | Osaka Concert Vol.1 | Steeplechase | SCCD 31271
Toots Thielemans Quartet | Harmonica Jazz | CBS | CBS 21108
Scotch Thing
Nat King Cole Trio | Big Band Bounce & Boogie-Nat King Cole:Trio Days | Affinity | AFS 1001
Scotland
J.F. Jenny Clark | Unison | CMP Records | CMP CD 32
Scott Joplin's New Rag
Richard Zimmerman | The Complete Works Of Scott Joplin | Laserlight | 15945
Scram
Jack McDuff Quartet With Gene Ammons | Soul Summit | Prestige | PCD 24118-2(P 7234/7275)
Scramble
David Phillips & Fredance | David Phillips & Freedance | Naxos Jazz | 86061-2
Scrambled Eggs
Nat Adderley Sextet | Work Songs | Milestone | M 47047
Wes Montgomery-The Complete Riverside Recordings | Riverside | 12 RCD 4408-2
Paul Bley/Steve Swallow | The Life Of A Trio:Sunday | Owl Records | 014735-2
Scrambled Legs
Duke Pearson Orchestra | The Right Touch | Blue Note | 828269-2
Scrap Metal
Hound Dog Taylor Band | Blues Rarities | Chess | 6.28601 DP
Scrapple From The Apple
Art Pepper-Shorty Rogers Quintet | Art Pepper & Shorty Rogers:Complete Lighthouse Sessions | The Jazz Factory | JFCD 22836
Charlie Parker Quintet | Bird At St. Nick's | Original Jazz Classics | OJC20 041-2(JWS 500)
Bird In Boston-Live At The Hi Hat 1953/54 Vol.1 | Fresh Sound Records | FSCD 1006
Dexter Gordon Quartet | Live At The Amsterdam Paradiso | Affinity | AFF 751
Frank Morgan Quartet | Yardbird Suite | Original Jazz Classics | OJCCD 1060-2(C 14045)
Gene Ammons Trio | Live! In Chicago | Original Jazz Classics | OJCCD 395-2(P 7495)
Louis Smith Quintet | Louisville | Steeplechase | SCCD 31552
Lover Man | Loose Walk | Palcoscenico | PAL 15009
Oscar Peterson Trio | Oscar Peterson-The London House Sessions | Verve | 531766-2
Sonny Stitt Quintet | Stitt Plays Bird | Rhino | SD 1418
Stefano Benini Quintet | Fluteprints | SPLASC(H) Records | CD H 333-2
The Ritz | The Ritz | Denon Compact Disc | CY-1839
Tom Harrell Quintet | Moon Alley | Criss Cross | Criss 1018
Wardell Gray's Los Angeles All Stars | Wardell Gray Memorial Vol.2 | Original Jazz Classics | OJCCD 051-2(P 7009)
Tete Montoliu Trio | Live At Keystone Corner | Timeless | CD SJP 138
Scratch My Back
Jimmie Lunceford And His Orchestra | The Original Jimmy Lunceford Orchestra | Jazz Anthology | JA 5224
Scream
Hank Roberts And Birds Of Pray | Birds Of Pray | JMT Edition | 834437-2
Screamin'
Jack McDuff Quartet | Screamin' | Original Jazz Classics | OJCCD 875-2(P 7259)
Muddy Waters Blues Band | I'm Ready | Blue Sky | 82235
Screamin' The Blues
Oliver Nelson Sextet | Images | Prestige | P 24060
Sonny Terry Trio | Whoopin' The Blues | Charly | CRB 1120
Screwed Up
Dave Douglas Trio | Constellations | Hat Art | CD 6173
Scrimshaw
Plas Johnson Band | The Warm Sound Of Plas Johnson Tenor Sax Vol.2:The Madison Avenue Strut | Blue Moon | BMCD 3061
Scrjabin
Friedrich Gulda Septet | Friedrich Gulda At Birdland | Fresh Sound Records | ND 12587
Scruby
The Brecker Brothers | Out Of The Loop | GRP | GRP 97842
Scrunch
Ikey Robinson And His Windy City Five | Chicago 1935 | Gannet | CJR 1001
Scufflin'
Ray Brown Group | Super Bass | Telarc Digital | CD 83393
Scurry
Wollie Kaiser Timeghost | Post Art Core | Jazz Haus Musik | JHM 0077 CD
'Scuse Me
Clifford Brown And Art Farmer With The Swedish All Stars | Clifford Brown Memorial | Original Jazz Classics | OJC20 017-2(P 7055)
'Scuse These Blues
Artie Shaw And His Gramercy Five | The Complete Gramercy Five Sessions | Bluebird | ND 87637
Scylla
Ricky Ford Sextet | Interpretations | Muse | MR 5275
Se Acabo La Choricera-
Bobby Hutcherson Orchestra | Montara | Blue Note | 590956-2
Se Acabo La Malanga - (Se Acabo) La Malanga
Poncho Sanchez And His Orchestra | A Night At Kimball's East | Concord | CCD 4472
Se Efter(Look)
Ahmed El-Salamouny/Gilson De Assis | Tango Brasileiro | FSM | FCD 97725
Se Eu Quiser Falar Com Deus
Marc Ribot Y Los Cubanos Postizos | Nuy Divertido(Very Entertaining) | Atlantic | 7567-83293-2
Se Formo El Bochinche
Bebo Valdés Trio | El Arte Del Sabor | Blue Note | 535193-2
Se Fue-
Tiziana Ghiglioni And Her Band | Tiziana Ghiglioni Canta Luigi Tenco | Philology | W 60.2
Se Todos Fossem Iquais A Voce
Mona Larsen And The Danish Radio Big Band Plus Soloists | Michael Mantler:Cerco Un Paese Innocente | ECM | 1556
Se Una Tua Mano-
Duke Jordan Trio | Lover Man | Steeplechase | SCS 1127
Sea
George Winston | Autumn | Windham Hill | 34 11012-2
Sea 57
Spyro Gyra | Access All Areas | MCA | 2292-51215-1
Sea Breezes
Med Flory and his Orchestra | Jazz Wave | Fresh Sound Records | JLP 1066(Jubilee)
Sea Change
John Surman-Jack DeJohnette With The London Brass | Printed In Germany | ECM | 1802(017065-2)
Nancy Harrow With The Clark Terry Quartet | Secrets | Soul Note | 121233-2
Sea Glass
Henning Schmiedt-Volker Schlott Group | PAmagieRA | Peregrina Music | PM 50081
Sea Journey
John Campbell Trio | Workin' Out | Criss Cross | Criss 1198
Sea Lady
Norma Winstone Trio | Somewhere Called Home | ECM | 1337
Barney Kessel And Friends | Barney Plays Kessel | Concord | CCD 6009
Sea Of Sounds
Andy Narell Group | Down The Road | Windham Hill | 34 10139-2
Sea Of Swollen Hands-
Michel Herr Quintet | Solis Lacus | B.Sharp Records | 1001
Sea Shantey
The Heartland Consort | The Heartland Consort | Enja | 4070 (807666)
Sea Song
Pat Metheny Quartet | Watercolors | ECM | 1097(827409-2)
Bill Perkins Quintet | Swing Spring | Candid | CCD 79752
Sea Swirls
Ken McIntyre Quartet | Home | Steeplechase | SCCD 31039
Seafarer's Song
Bud Shank Quartet | At Jazz Alley | Contemporary | C 14027
Seafood Wally
Barney Kessel Trio | Soaring | Concord | CCD 6033
Seagulls Of Kristiansund
Tommy Smith Sextet | Beasts Of Scottland | Linn Records | AKD 054
Search-
Charlie Mariano Quartet | Warum Bist Du Traurig(Why Are You So Sad) | B&W Present | BW 019
Search For Euridice
Ornette Coleman & Prime Time | Tone Dialing | Verve | 527483-2
Search For Peace
McCoy Tyner Quartet | The Real McCoy | Blue Note | 497807-2
Melvin Rhyne Quartet | Classmasters | Criss Cross | Criss 1183
Search For The New Land
Longineu Parsons Group | Work Song | TCB Records | TCB 94302
Search For The Reason Why
The Ethnic Heritage Ensemble | Ethnic Heritage Ensemble | Leo Records | 014
Search Me Lord
Mahalia Jackson | In Memoriam Mahalia Jackson | CBS | 66501
Search Silence
Blind Blake | Blind Blake-Search Warrant Blues | Biograph | BLP 12023
Searchin'
Roy Ayers Group | Roy Ayers-The Essential Groove:Live | Ronnie Scott's Jazz House | JHCD 035
Searching-
Earl Coleman With Unkn.Trio | Cool Whalin' - Bebop Vocals | Spotlite | SPJ 135
Searching For June
Otis 'Smokey' Smothers And His Ice Cream Men | Got My Eyes On You | Steeplechase | SCB 9009
Searching For The A.M.(contains portions of Reincarnation Of A Lovebird)
Billy Cobham Group | Spectrum | Atlantic | 7567-81428-2
Searching For The Right Door
Herb Geller Quartet | Playing Jazz:The Musical Autobiography Of Herb Geller | Fresh Sound Records | FSR-CD 5011
Searching In Heavy Weather
Richard Zimmerman | The Complete Works Of Scott Joplin | Laserlight | 15945
Sear-iously
Johnny Hodges Orchestra | Jazz Legacy 62: Johnny Hodges-Jumpin' | Vogue | 500112
Seascape
Bill Evans Trio | I Will Say Goodbye | Original Jazz Classics | OJCCD 761-2(F 9593)
Kenny Barron Trio | Lemuria-Seascape | Candid | CCD 79508
Seaside
John Surman Trio | Such Winters Of Memory | ECM | 1254(810621-2)
Seaside Postcard 1951
Thomas Heberer | The Heroic Millepede | ITM Records | ITM 1443
Seasons
Saheb Sarbib Quartet | Seasons | Soul Note | 121048-2
Rahsaan Roland Kirk Group | Rahsaan Rolnd Kirk:Dog Years In The Fourth Ring | 32 Jazz | 32032
Seatic
Isaac Scott Blues Band | Big Time Blues Man | Red Lightnin' | RL 0046
Seattle Hunch
Jelly Roll Morton | Didn't He Ramble | Black & Blue | BLE 59.228 2
Sechser II
Ralph R.Hübner-Christoph Lauer | Mondspinner | free flow music | ffm 0796
Sechskant
Christopher Dell D.R.A. | Future Of The Smallest Form | Jazz 4 Ever Records:Jazz Network | J4E 4754
Sechsundvierzig
Bob Degen | Sandcastle | free flow music | ffm 0897
Secluded Branch
Leszek Zadlo Quartet | Sting | Fusion | 8001
Second (Mirages, Realities)-
Al Cooper And His Savoy Sultans | Big Band Bounce & Boogie:Jump Steady | Affinity | AFS 1009
Second Balcony Jump
Dexter Gordon Quartet | Dexter Gordon:The Complete Blue Note Sixties Sessions | Blue Note | 834200-2
Dexter Gordon Quintet | Landslide | Blue Note | LT 1051 (GXK 8175)
Earl Hines | Le Jazz En France Vol.15:Earl Hunes Paris Session 1965 | Pathe | 1552611
Earl Hines And His Orchestra | Earl Hines-Piano Man | Bluebird | NK 86750
Henri Chaix Trio | Just Friends | Sackville | SKCD2-2048
Second Chance
Paul Gonsalves Quintet | Tell The Way It Is | Impulse(MCA) | JAS 27 (AS 55)
Second Chorus:
Joachim Raffel Quintet | Circlesongs | Acoustic Music Records | 312.1093.2
Second Game
Wayne Shorter Quartet | Second Genesis | Vee Jay Recordings | VJ 016
Second Hand
Paul Motian Band | Psalm | ECM | 1222
The Mick Clarke Band | Tell The Truth | Taxim Records | TX 1001-2 TA
Second Handy Motion
Tacuma-Puschnig Duo | Gemini-Gemini | ITM-Pacific | ITMP 970063
Second Impression
Jon Jang Octet | Island: The Immigrant Suite No.1 | Soul Note | 121303-2
Second Item
Chris Barber's Jazz And Blues Band With Special Guests | Echoes Of Harlem | Black Lion | 187000
Second Line
Duke Ellington And His Orchestra | That's Jazz Vol.31: New Orleans Suite | Atlantic | ATL 50403
Second Movement
Steve Cohn Trio | Ittekemasu | ITM-Pacific | ITMP 970059
Second Movement-Brown-
Duke Ellington And His Orchestra | Duke Elliongton:Complete Prestige Carnegie Hall 1943-1944 Concerts | Definitive Records | DRCD 11210
Second Portrait Of The Lion
Ronnie Scott And The Band | Live At Ronnie Scott's | CBS | 494439-2
Second Question
Thad Jones-Mel Lewis Orchestra | Swiss Radio Days Jazz Series Vol.4:Thad Jones-Mel Lewis Orchestra | TCB Records | TCB 02042
Second Sight
Joshua Redman Quartet | Spirit Of The Moment:Live At The Village Vanguard | Warner | 9362-45923-2
Second Snow
Cannonball Adderley Septet | Inside Straight | Original Jazz Classics | OJCCD 750-2(F 9435)
Second Son
Roland Dahinden/Christian Muthspiel | Trombone Performance | Amadeo | 841330-1
Second Stop Is Jupiter-
Joachim Kühn-Chris Hinze Duo | Solo's And Duo's | Keytone | KYT 708
Second Symphony:Johannes Braun
Hans Lüdemann Rism | Unitarism | Jazz Haus Musik | JHM 0067 CD
Second Symphony:No Hau
Unitarism | Jazz Haus Musik | JHM 0067 CD
Second Symphony:No Hau(Epilog)
Unitarism | Jazz Haus Musik | JHM 0067 CD
Second Symphony:No Hau(Prolog)
Unitarism | Jazz Haus Musik | JHM 0067 CD
Second Symphony:Zerkall Bleu
Unitarism | Jazz Haus Musik | JHM 0067 CD
Second Symphony:Zerkall Bleu(Version 2)
Pat Metheny Group | Quartet | Geffen Records | GED 24978
Second Thought
Art Blakey And The Jazz Messengers | Live At Kimball's | Concord | CCD 4307
Second Thoughts
Eero Koivistoinen Sextet | Picture In Three Colours | Line Records | COCD 9.00515 O
Lee Konitz Quintet | Peacemeal | Milestone | M 9025
Second Time Around
Bill Evans Quintet | The Jazz Giants Play Sammy Cahn:It's Magic | Prestige | PCD 24226-2
The Complete Fantasy Recordings | Fantasy | 9FCD 1012-2
Etta Jones And Her Band | Ms. Jones To You | Muse | MR 5099
Sarah Vaughan With The Quincy Jones Orchestra | You're Mine You | Fresh Sound Records | 857157-2
Per Goldschmidt Quintet | Frankly:A Tribute To Sinatry | Milestone | MCD 9224-2
Second Visit
Bründl's Basslab | Aisha | L+R Records | CDLR 45036
Seconde
Gregor Hilden-Hans D. Riesop Group | Compared To What...? | Wonderland Records | 319.9014.2
Second-line Beckmann
Brennan-Cline-Patumi-Voirol-Theissing | Shooting Stars & Traffic Lights | L+R Records | CDLR 45090
Seconds
Pago Libre | Pago Libre | L+R Records | CDLR 45105
Second's Best
Louis Hayes Quintet | The Candy Man | TCB Records | TCB 20972
Seconds,Anyone?
Family Of Percussion | Message To The Enemies Of Time | Nagara | MIX 1016-N
Secret
Steve Elson's Lips & Fingers Ensemble | Lips & Fingers | Open Minds | OM 2406-2
Secret Codes
Daniel Schnyder & The Modern Art Septet | Secret Cosmos | Enja | ENJ-5055 2
Secret Heart
Charles Fambrough Group | Keeper Of The Spirit | audioquest Music | AQCD 1033
Secret Life Of The Forbidden City
Noctett | Full Score | Cain | CL 5804
Secret Love
Benny Carter Quintet | New York Nights | Musicmasters | 65154-2
Bob Howard With The Hank Jones Trio | In A Sentimental Mood | Stash Records | ST 266 IMS
Carmen McRae And Her Trio | Carmen McRae | Jazz Classics | CD CA 36004
Claudio Roditi Quartet | Two Of Swords | Candid | CCD 79504
Donald Byrd Quintet | Slow Drag | Blue Note | 535560-2
Earl Klugh Trio With The Royal Philharmonic Orchestra | Sounds And Visions | Warner | 9362-45158-2
Jimmy McGriff Orchestra | Georgia On My Mind | LRC Records | CDC 8513
John D'Earth Quartet | One Bright Glance | Enja | ENJ-6040 2
Patrick Tompert Trio | Moche! | Satin Doll Productions | SDP 1035-1 CD
Randy Johnston Quartet | Somewhere In The Night | HighNote Records | HCD 7007
Sandy Lomax With The Martin Schrack Trio | Songs From The Jazz Age | Workshop Records | WOR 201(CD 583)
Ulf Wakenius Group | Venture | L+R Records | CDLR 45052
Willis Jackson Quintet | Soul Night Live! | Prestige | PRCD 24273-2
David Friesen-John Stowell | Through The Listening Glass | Inner City | IC 1061 IMS
Secret Name
Bruce Barth Quintet | In Focus | Enja | 8010-2
Secret Obsession
Lorry Raine With The Nelson Riddle Orchestra | Interlude With Lorry Raine | Fresh Sound Records | Advance CD 714

Secret Of The Night
Conte Candoli Quartet | Portrait Of A Count | Fresh Sound Records | FSR-CD 5015
Secret Sounds
Special EFX | Confidential | GRP | GRP 95812
Secret Story
Tim Whitehead Quartet | Silence Between Waves | Ronnie Scott's Jazz House | JHCD 033
Secret Zambra
Ulrich Gumpert | The Secret Concert | ITM Records | ITM 1461
Secrets
Enrico Rava Quintet | Secrets | Soul Note | 121164-2
Eric Watson Quartet | Full Metal Quartet | Owl Records | 159572-2
Jesper Thilo Quartet | Jesper Thilo Quartet | Music Mecca | CD 1009-2
Nancy Harrow With The Clark Terry Quartet | Secrets | Soul Note | 121233-2
Secrets-
Larry Garner Group | Baton Rouge | Verve | 529467-2
Section Blues
Red Mitchell Quintet | Red Mitchell | Bethlehem | BTM 6825
Sector 51
Woody Herman And His Orchestra | The V Disc Years Vol.1&2 | Hep | CD 2/3435
Security Blues
Bobo Stenson Trio | War Orphans | ECM | 1604(539723-2)
Sediment
Joe Lovano-Aldo Romano | Ten Tales | Owl Records | 018350-2
Sediments
Joelle Leandre | Palimpseste | Hat Art | CD 6103
Seduction
Stefan Bauer-Claudio Puntin-Marcio Doctor | Lingo | Jazz Haus Musik | JHM 0116 CD
Steve LaSpina Quintet | Remember When | Steeplechase | SCCD 31540
John Capec And The Family Of Man | Indaba | Intuition Records | INT 3094-2
See
Sal Salvador Quartet | Boo Boo Be Doop | Affinity | AFF 68
See If You Can Git To That
Warren Vaché Quartet | What Is There To Say? | Nagel-Heyer | CD 056
See Jim, See Joe, C-Jam Blues
Marc Van Roon Trio With David Liebman | Falling Stones | Mons Records | MR 874730
See Line Woman
Nina Simone Quartet | Verve Jazz Masters 17:Nina Simone | Verve | 518198-2
Nina Simone | The Rising Sun Collection | RSC 0004
See Me Fel Me-
Hound Dog Taylor & The House Rockers | Natural Boogie | Sonet | 198044(SNTF 678)
See Saw
Bill Evans Trio | The Complete Fantasy Recordings | Fantasy | 9FCD 1012-2
Chico Hamilton Trio | Trio! | Soul Note | 121246-2
David Holland Quartet | Conference Of The Birds | ECM | 1027(829373-2)
Jimmy Dorsey And His Orchestra | Jimmy Dorsey And His Orchestra | Jazz Anthology | JA 5221
Steve Coleman-Dave Holland | Phase Space | DIW | DIW 865 CD
See See Rider
Archie Shepp-Horace Parlan Duo | Swing Low | Plainisphare | PL 1267-73 CD
Big Bill Broonzy | Last Session-Vol.1/The Big Bill Broonzy Story | Verve | 2304559 IMS
Chris Barber's Jazz Band | Chris Barber-40 Years Jubilee(1954-1956) | Timeless | CD TTD 586
Donald Byrd Orchestra With Brass & Voices | His Majesty King Funk/Up With Donald Byrd | Verve | 527474-2
Ella Fitzgerald And Her All Stars | For The Love Of Ella Fitzgerald | Verve | 841765-2
These Are The Blues | Verve | 829536-2 PMS
Frisco Syncopators | Firehouse Stomp | Stomp Off Records | CD 1245
George Lewis Ragtime Jazz Band Of New Orleans | The Oxford Series Vol.8 | American Music | AMCD-28
Helen Humes And Her All Stars | Lester Young:The Complete 1936-1951 Small Group Sessions(Studio Recordings-Master Takes),Vol.6 Rare Items | Blue Moon | BMCD 1006
Jimmy Smith Trio | Paris Jazz Concert:Jimmy Smith And The Trio | Laserlight | 36159
Paris Jazz Concert:Jimmy Smith And The Trio | Laserlight | 36159
Jimmy Witherspoon With The Robben Ford Quartet | Live At The Notodden Blues Festival | Crosscut | CCD 11035
Kid Howard's La Vida Band | Kid Howard's La Vida Band | American Music | AMCD-54
Louis Armstrong And His All Stars | Satchmo-A Musical Autobiography Vol.1 | MCA | 2-4173
Ma Rainey And Her Band | Ma Rainey | Milestone | MCD 47021-2
Robert Lockwood Jr. | Robert Lockwood Jr. Plays Robert (Johnson) & Robert (Lockwood) | Black & Blue | 33740
See The World
Marilyn Mazur's Future Song | Small Labyrinths | ECM | 1559(533679-2)
See There
Gunter Hampel And His Galaxie Dream Band | Life On This Planet 1981 | Birth | 004
See What I Mean
Teddy Grace with Bud Freeman And His Summa Cum Laude Orchestra | It's Got To Be The Eel, A Tribute To Bud Freeman | Affinity | CD AFS 1008
See What's Going On
Airto Moreira And The Gods Of Jazz | Killer Bees | B&W Present | BW 041
See You At Per Tutti's
Bob Smith Group | Bob's Diner | dmp Digital Music Productions | CD 471
See You In My Dreams
Philip DeGruy | Innuendo Out The Other | NYC-Records | NYC 6013-2
See You Tomorrow
Gene Ammons Quartet | Gene Ammons-Greatest Hits Vol.1:The Sixties | Original Jazz Classics | OJCCD 6005-2
Seeheim Nightlife
Paulinho Da Costa Orchestra | Happy People | Original Jazz Classics | OJCCD 783-2(2312102)
Seeing Is Believing
Rolf Kühn Group | Inside Out | Intuition Records | INT 3276-2
Seeing Salinas Again
The Three Sopranos With The HR Big Band | The Three Sopranos | hr music.de | hrmj 001-01 CD
New Winds | The Cliff | Sound Aspects | sas CD 025
Seems Like Old Times-
Rob McConnell-Ed Bickert-Don Thompson | Three For The Road | Concord | CCD 4765
'Seen A Man About A Dog
Sun Ra And His Myth Arkestra | The Solar Myth Approach | Affinity | AFF 760
Segeln In Der Wetterau-
Brian Melvin Trio | Old Voices | Timeless | CD SJP 396
Segment
Charlie Parker Quintet | Charlie Parker: The Verve Years (1948-50) | Verve | 2-2501 IMS
Dave Holland Trio | Triplicate | ECM | 1373
Geri Allen Trio | Segments | DIW | DIW 833 CD
Sax Mal Anders | Kontraste | Chaos | CACD 8185
Scott Colley Quartet | Subliminal... | Criss Cross | Criss 1157
Segment Tune X
Charlie Parker Quintet | Swedish Schnapps + | Verve | 849393-2
Segoh
Marty Ehrlich/Anthony Cox | Falling Man | Muse | MCD 5398
Segue In C
Count Basie And His Orchestra | Count Basie-The Best Of The Roulette Years | Roulette | CDP 797969-2
Duke Ellington And Count Basie With Their Orchestras | Duke Ellington-Count Basie | CBS | 473753-2
Segundo Plano
Gabriele Mirabassi Trio | Latakia Blend | Enja | ENJ-9441 2
Segura Ele
Georgie Auld Quintet | Unearthed Masters-Vol.1: Charlie Parker/Coleman Hawkins/Georgie Auld | JAM | 5006 IMS
Sehnsucht
Brad Mehldau Trio | Art Of The Trio Vol.3: Songs | Warner | 9362-47051-2
Ernst Jandl Mit Band | Bist Eulen? | Extraplatte | EX 316141
Sehnsucht Der Heringe
Eugen Cicero Trio | Rococo Jazz 2 | Timeless | CD SJP 255
Sehr Reizend
Joos-Czelusta-Konrad Trio | Blow!!! | FMP | 0370
Sei Lieb Zu Mir
Torsten Zwingenberger's Swingburger | Groovy At The Movie | Moustache Music | 02 03 37 72 86
Seidah's Eyes
Stephan-Max Wirth Quartet | Jazzchanson 20th Century Suite | double moon | DMCD 1008-2
Seidenduft-
Yosuke Yamashita-Hozan Yamamoto Duo | Yosuke Yamashita-Hozan Yamamoto | Enja | 5003/4
Seila
Erdmann 2000 | Recovering From y2k | Jazz 4 Ever Records:Jazz Network | J4E 4750
Sein AKG
Vladimir Estragon | Three Quarks For Muster Mark | TipToe | TIP-888803 2
Seinesgleichen:
Banda Mantiqueira | Aldeia | ACT | 5008-2
Seit Jahren
Kölner Saxophon Mafia | Place For Lovers | Jazz Haus Musik | JHM 0082 CD
Seitensprung(amerikanisch)
Place For Lovers | Jazz Haus Musik | JHM 0082 CD
Seitensprung(brasilianisch)
Place For Lovers | Jazz Haus Musik | JHM 0082 CD
Seitensprung(indisch)
Place For Lovers | Jazz Haus Musik | JHM 0082 CD
Seitensprung(karibisch)
Niels Lan Doky Trio | Niels Lan Doky | Verve | 559087-2
Sejours
Dudu Pukwana & Spear | In The Townships | Caroline | C 1504
Selby That The Eternal Spirit Is The Only Realty
Anthony Ortega Quintet | Rain Dance | Discovery | DS 788 IMS
Selena
Ronnie Mathews Trio | Selena's Dance | Timeless | CD SJP 304
Self Portrait
Steps Ahead | Modern Times | Elektra | 7559-60351-2
The United Women's Orchestra | The Blue One | Jazz Haus Musik | JHM 0099 CD
Lee Konitz | Lee Konitz 'Self Portrait'(In Celebration Of Lee Konitz' 70th Birthday) | Philology | W 121.2
Self Portrait In Three Colors
Sax Appeal Saxophone Quartet plus Claudio Fasoli | Giotto | Soul Note | 121309-2
The Atlantic String Trio | First Meeting | Factory Outlet Records | 2001-1 CD
Self Portrait(Of The Bean)
Duke Ellington-Coleman Hawkins Orchestra | Duke Ellington Meets Coleman Hawkins | MCA | MCAD 5650
Selffulfilling Prophecys
Ruby Smith With Blind John Davis | Blind John Davis(1938) | Story Of Blues | CD 3520-2
Selflessness
John Coltrane And His Orchestra | Selflessness | MCA | 2292-54629-2
Selflessness-
Dave Liebman With Gunnar Mossblad And The James Madison University Jazz Esemble | The Music Of John Coltrane | Candid | CCD 79531
Self-Portrait In 3 Colors
Charles Mingus Septet | Charles Mingus:The Complete 1959 Columbia Recordings | CBS | C3K 65145
Jay Collins Quintet | Reality Tonic | Reservoir | RSR CD 142
Mingus By Five | Mingus By Five | Touché Music | TMcCD 019
Richard Fairhurst Quartet | The Hungry Ants | Babel | BDV 9504
Selim
World Saxophone Quartet With Jack DeJohnette And African Drums | Selim Sivad:A Tribute To Miles Davis | Justin Time | JUST 119-2
Selim(Coda 2000)
Walt Dickerson Quartet | Impressions Of A Patch Of Blue | Verve | 559929-2
Selje
Jan Garbarek Trio | Works | ECM | 823266-2
Selva Amâzonica
Buddy Collette Septet | Jazz Heat Bongo Beat | Blue Moon | BMCD 1604
Semblance
Igor Brill Quartet & The All-Star Soviet Jazz Band | Live At The Village Gate | Mobile Fidelity | MFCD 861
Esbjörn Svensson Trio(E.S.T.) | Winter In Venice | ACT | 9007-2
Semblance(part 1-5)
Tania Maria And Her Band | Come With Me | Concord | MC CJ 200C
Sempre Notte-
Jorge Degas-Wolfgang Loos | Cantar A Vida | Traumton Records | 4446-2
Sempre Sonhei
Trygve Seim-Oyvind Braekke-Per Oddvar Johansen Orchestra | The Source And Different Cikadas | ECM | 1764(014432-2)
Sen Kjellertango
Dani Perez Quartet | Buenos Aires-Barcelona Connections | Fresh Sound Records | FSNT 144 CD
Senales
Buddy Rich Big Band | Backwoods Siseman/Pieces Of Dream | Laserlight | 24655
Senator Sam
Backwoods Siseman/Pieces Of Dream | Laserlight | 24655
Earl Hines Sextet | Swingin' Away | Black Lion | BLCD 760210
Senator Whitehead
Yosuke Yamashita-Hozan Yamamoto Duo | Yosuke Yamashita-Hozan Yamamoto | Enja | 5003/4
Sencillito Y De Alpargatas
Mel Tormé With The George Shearing Trio | A Vintage Year | Concord | CJ 341
Send For Me
The Ravens | Old Man River | Savoy | SV 0260
Send In The Clowns
Benny Goodman And His Orchestra | Live At Carnegie Hall-40th Anniversary Concert | Decca | 6.28451 DP
Eric Reed Trio | Pure Imagination | Impulse(MCA) | 951259-2
Ernestine Anderson With The Hank Jones Trio | Hello Like Before | Concord | CCD 4031
Sarah Vaughan And The Count Basie Orchestra | Send In The Clowns | Pablo | 2312130-2
Terell Stafford Quintet | Time To Let Go | Candid | CCD 79702
Zoot Sims-Bucky Pizzarelli Duo | Stan Getz/Zoot Sims | LRC Records | CDC 9041
Send In The World Quintet
Tom Varner Quintet | Martian Heartache | Soul Note | 121286-2
Send Me Some Lovin'
Ron Ringwood's Crosscut Bluesband | Earth Tones | Organic Music | ORGM 9722
Send Me Someone To Love
Dave Pike Set | Dave Pike Set:Masterpieces | MPS | 531848-2
Send Me The Yellow Guys
Bessie Smith With Her Blue Boys | Jazz Classics In Digital Stereo: Bessie Smith | CDS Records Ltd. | REB 602
Send Me To The 'Lectric Chair
Dinah Washington And Her Sextet | Newport Jazz Festival 1958,July 3rd-6th Vol.4:Blues In The Night No.2 | Phontastic | NCD 8816
Dinah Washington With The Eddie Chamblee Orchestra | Dinah Sings Bessie Smith | Verve | 538635-2
Dinah Washington With The Newport All Stars | Dinah Sings Bessie Smith | Verve | 538635-2
Nancy Wilson With Gerald Wilson's Orchestra | Yesterday's Love Songs-Today's Blues | Capitol | 796265-2
Send Out For A Bucket Of Beer
Jan Garbarek Group | Legend Of The Seven Dreams | ECM | 1381(837344-2)
Send Word
Ken McIntyre Quartet | Ken McIntyre:The Complete United Artists Sessions | Blue Note | 857200-2
Senegal-
Steps Ahead | N.Y.C. | Intuition Records | INT 3007-2
Senegal Calling
Cl.W. Jacobi's Bottomland Orchestra | A Tribute To Clarence Williams | Stomp Off Records | CD 1266
Senhor Gor
Art Blakey And The Jazz Messengers | Hard Champion | Paddle Wheel | K32Y 6209
Senor Blues
Bernard Purdie's Soul To Jazz | Bernard Purdie's Soul To Jazz | ACT | 9242-2
Bill Cosby All Stars | Bill Cosby-Hello,Friend:To Ennis With Love | Verve | 539171-2
Billy Ver Planck And His Orchestra | Jazz For Playgirls | Savoy | SV 0209(MG 12121)
Horace Silver Quintet | 1949-1959, Blue Note's Three Decades Of Jazz, Vol. 1 | Blue Note | 89903
The Best Of Blue Note Vol.2 | Blue Note | 797960-2
The Best Of Horace Silver | Blue Note | 791143-2
Blue Velvet: Crooners, Swooners And Velvet Vocals | Blue Note | 521153-2
Jimmy Jewell Sextet | I'm Amazed | Affinity | AFF 2
Urbie Green & Groover Washington Jr.With Davis Matthews Big Band | Senor Blues | CTI | 63029
Dee Dee Bridgewater With Her Trio | Dee Dee Bridgewater In Montreux | Polydor | 847913-2
Senor Blues-
Horace Silver Quintet | Blue Trails-The Rare Tracks | Blue Note | 300191
Senor Mouse
Chick Corea-Gary Burton | In Concert, Zürich, October 28, 1979 | ECM | 1182/83
Duo Fenix | Karai-Eté | IN+OUT Records | 7009-2
Hal Di Meola Group | Casino | CBS | 468215-2
Bruce Forman Quintet | Coast To Coast | Candid | CRS 1026 IMS
Sensation Rag
Adrian Bentzon's Jazzband | The Golden Years Of Revival Jazz,Vol.4 | Storyville | STCD 5509
Benny Goodman Dixieland Quintet | Benny Goodman At Carnegie Hall 1938(Complete) | CBS | C2K 65143
Benny Goodman Quintet | 1938 Carnegie Hall Concert | CBS | 450983-2
Sensible
Luiz Bonfa/Cafe | Non Stop To Brazil | Chesky | JD 29
Sensing
Teddy Edwards Quintet | Midnight Creeper | HighNote Records | HCD 7011
Sensitive Details
John Wolf Brennan-Daniele Patumi | Ten Zentences | L+R Records | CDLR 45066
Sensitivity(part 1-3)
Radius | Elevation | Ear-Rational | ECD 1036
Sent A Message-
Benny Goodman And His Orchestra | The Indispensable Benny Goodman(Big Band) Vol.5/6(1938-1939) | RCA | 2122621-2
Sent For You Yesterday And Here You Come Today
The Hits Of Benny Goodman | Capitol | 791212-2
Live At The International World Exhibition,Brussels 1958: The Unissued Recordings | Magic | DAWE 36(881849)
Count Basie And His Orchestra | Count Basie At Newport | Verve | 9861761
Basie Rides Again | Verve | MV 2643 IMS
Basie On Roulette, Vol. 14: The Best Of Basie-Vol. 1 | Vogue | 500014
Jimmy Witherspoon And Panama Francis' Savoy Sultans | Jimmy Witherspoon & Panama Francis' Savoy Sultans | Black & Blue | BLE 59.177 2
Sentimental Journey
Buck Clayton Jam Session | Buck Clayton Jam Session,Vol1 | Blue Moon | BMCD 3044
Jan Jankeje's Party And Swingband | Mobil | Jazzpoint | JP 1068 CD
Juan Garcia Esquivel Orchestra | Juan's Again | RCA | 2168206-2
Julie London And Her Band | Julie At Home | EMI Records | EMS 1186
Pee Wee Russell Sextet | Jazz At Storyville: Pee Wee Russell + Ruby Braff | Savoy | WL 70538 (2) (809317)
Rosemary Clooney And Her Band | For The Duration | Concord | CCD 4444
Singers Unlimited With The Robert Farnon Orchestra | Sentimental Journey | MPS | 68102
Sentimental Journey-
Duke Ellington And His Famous Orchestra | Duke Ellington:The Blanton-Webster Band | Bluebird | 21 13181-2
Sentimental Lady
Passion Flower 1940-46 | Bluebird | 63 66616-2
Sentimental Over Mental Food-
Stan Kenton And His Orchestra | At The Las Legas Tropicana | Capitol | 835245-2
Sentimental Walk(Theme From Diva)
Bolling-Rampal Quartet | Suite Für Flöte und Jazz Piano | Decca | 6.22610 AO
Sento Freddo
Voices | Voices:Live In Rome | Nueva Records | IN 806
Senza Fine
Ellen Christi-Claudio Lodati Duo | Dreamers | SPLASC(H) Records | CD H 311-2
Sepia Panorama
Duke Ellington And His Famous Orchestra | Duke Ellington:The Blanton-Webster Band | Bluebird | 21 13181-2
Duke Ellington:Ko-Ko | Dreyfus Jazz Line | FDM 36717-2
In A Mellow Tone | RCA | 2113029-2
Duke Ellington And His Orchestra | The Duke At Fargo 1940 | Storyville | STCD 8316/17
The Indispensable Duke Ellington Vol.5/6 | RCA | ND 89750
Sepia Panorama(Night House)
Pee Wee Ellis Quintet | Sepia Tonality | Minor Music | 801040
Sepia Tonality
Nnenna Freelon And Her Band | Maiden Voyage | Concord | CCD 4794
Sept. 21st, 1966
Karl Ratzer | Dancing On A String | CMP Records | CMP 13
September
Charly D'Inverno Trio | Following The Band | Jazz Pure Collection | AU 31622 CD
Del Ferro/Overwater/Paeffgen | Dices | Acoustic Music Records | 319.1139.2
Lothar Müller Trio | Müller Q[kju] | JA & RO | JARO 4251-2
Matzeit-Daerr | September | Jazz Haus Musik | JHM 0125 CD
Craig Harris Quintet | Black Bone | Soul Note | 121055-2
September Ballad

TITELVERZEICHNIS

Cowws Quintet plus Guests | Book/Virtual Cowws | FMP | OWN-90007/9
September Fifteenth (Dedicated To Bill Evans)
Danilo Perez Quartet | Panamonk | Impulse(MCA) | 951190-2
September In Rio
Latin On Impulse! Various Artists | Impulse(MCA) | IMP 12762
September In The Rain
Al Fairweather Band | Fairweather Friends Made To Measure | Lake | LACD 75
Anke Helfrich Trio With Mark Turner | You'll See | double moon | CHRDM 71013
Arnett Cobb Quartet | Funky Butt | Progressive | PRO 7054 IMS
Dave Brubeck Octet | The Dave Brubeck Octet | Original Jazz Classics | OJCCD 101-2(F 3239)
Diane Schuur With Orchestra | Love Songs | GRP | GRP 97032
Dinah Washington With Orchestra | Mad About The Boy-The Best Of Dinah Washington | Mercury | 512214-2
Don Byas Quartet | Don Byas Complete American Small Group Recordings | Definitive Records | DRCD 11213
Savoy Jam Party-The Savoy Sessions | Savoy | WL 70512 (809315)
George Shearing Quintet/With Strings/Latin Mood | The Best Of George Shearing-All Time Shearing Favorites | Capitol | SM 2104
Harry Edison Quartet | The Inventive Mr. Edison | Fresh Sound Records | 054 2402661(Pacific Jazz PJ 11)
Joe Williams With The Harry 'Sweets' Edison Quintet | Live! A Swingin' Night At Birdland | Fresh Sound Records | FSR-CD 22(882187)
June Christy With The Kentones | The Uncollected:June Christy With The Kentones | Hindsight | HSR 219
Lionel Hampton Trio | Lionel Hampton:Real Crazy | Vogue | 2113409-2
Red Norvo Trio | Rare 1950-51 Transcriptions | Queen-Disc | 061
The Tremble Kids | 25 Jahre The Tremble Kids | Intercord | 180036
Zoot Sims Quintet | The Modern Art Of Jazz | Dawn | DCD 101
September In The Rain-
Christoph Spendel | Thoughts | L+R Records | CDLR 45092
September Morning
Neil Richardson Singers With The Metropole Orchestra | A Beautiful Friendship | Koch Jazz | 3-6909-2
September Riff
Michel Petrucciani Group | Playground | Blue Note | 795480-2
September Second
Michel Petrucciani Trio | Trio In Tokyo | Dreyfus Jazz Line | FDM 36605-2
James Moody Quintet With Strings | James Moody/Frank Foster:Sax Talk | Vogue | 2113410-2
September Song
Art Pepper Quartet | Straight Life | Original Jazz Classics | OJCCD 475-2
Art Pepper:The Complete Galaxy Recordings | Galaxy | 16GCD 1016-2
Art Tatum | Art Tatum-The Complete Pablo Solo Masterpieces | Pablo | 7 PACD 4404-2
Art Tatum:20th Century Piano Genius | Verve | 531763-2
The Art Tatum Solo Masterpieces | Pablo | 2625703
Art Tatum Sextet | The Tatum Group Masterpieces | Pablo | 2310731
Art Tatum Trio | Art Tatum:Complete Capitol Recordings | Definitive Records | DRCD 11192
Benny Goodman Original Quartet | Benny Goodman:The King Of Swing | Musicmasters | 65130-2
Bireli Lagrene Ensemble | Routes To Django & Bireli Swing '81 | Jazzpoint | JP 1055 CD
Bireli Lagrene Group | A Tribute To Django Reinhardt | Jazzpoint | JP 1061 CD
Bireli Lagrene Trio | Live At The Carnegie Hall: A Tribute To Django Reinhardt | Jazzpoint | JP 1040 CD
Cab Calloway And His Orchestra | The Cab Calloway Show | Zounds | CD 697110
Chet Baker Quartet | Chet | Original Jazz Classics | OJC20 087-2
Clarinet Jazz Trio | Live At Birdland Neuburg | Birdland | BN 003
Dizzy Gillespie's Big 4 | Dizzy's Big 4 | Original Jazz Classics | OJC 443(2310719)
Django Reinhardt And The Quintet Du Hot Club De France | Swing De Paris | Arco | 3 ARC 110
Django Reinhardt Portrait | Barclay | DALP 2/1939
The Indispensable Django Reinhardt | RCA | ND 70929
Don Byas Quartet | Don Byas:Laura | Dreyfus Jazz Line | FDM 36714-2
Don Byas Complete American Small Group Recordings | Definitive Records | DRCD 11213
Emil Mangelsdorff/Attila Zoller | Meditation | L+R Records | CDLR 45088
HR Big Band | The American Songs Of Kurt Weill | hr music.de | hrmj 006-01 CD
Illinois Jacquet And Ben Webster Orchestra | The Kid And The Brute | Verve | 2304555 IMS
JATP All Stars | J.A.T.P. In London 1969 | Pablo | 2CD 2620119
Jimmy Ponder Quartet | James Street | HighNote Records | HCD 7017
Joe Pass Quartet | Nuages | Pablo | 2310961-2
Joe Turner | I Understand | Black & Blue | BLE 59.153 2
John Lewis Trio | Improvised Meditations & Excursions | Atlantic | AMCY 1104
Johnny Lytle Septet | Possum Grease | Muse | MCD 5482
Kikuchi-Peacock-Motian | Tethered Moon(Play Kurt Weil) | JMT Edition | 514021-2
Les Brown And His Orchestra | The Uncollected: Les Brown And His Orchestra 1949-Vol.2 | Hindsight | HSR 132
Milt Buckner Quartet | Midnight Slows Vol.6 | Black & Blue | BLE 190932
Phil Woods-Enrico Pieranunzi | Elsa | Philology | W 206.2
Ronnie Scott Quartet | Bebop In Britain | Esquire | CD ESQ 100-4
Sarah Vaughan With The Clifford Brown All Stars | Sarah Vaughan | EmArCy | 9860779
Sarah Vaughan | Verve | 543305-2
Brownie-The Complete EmArCy Recordings Of Clifford Brown | EmArCy | 838306-2
Verve Jazz Masters 18:Sarah Vaughan | Verve | 518199-2
Scott Hamilton-Buddy Tate Quintet | Back To Back | Concord | CJ 85
September Song-
Art Tatum Sextet | Art Tatum-The Complete Pablo Group Masterpieces | Pablo | 6 PACD 4401-2
September Song(alt.take)
Niels-Henning Orsted-Pedersen/Philip Catherine Duo | The Viking | Pablo | 2310894-2
September Veje(Sptember Roads)
Lee Konitz Quartet | The New York Album | Soul Note | SN 1169
Septemberljus
Charles Mingus Quintet | Mingus At The Bohemia | Debut | VIJ 5010 IMS
Septemberly
Charles Mingus-The Complete Debut Recordings | Debut | 12 DCD 4402-2
Chick Corea With String Quartet,Flute And French Horn | Septet | ECM | 1297
Septet(5 Movements)
Daniel Schnyder & The Modern Art Septet | Secret Cosmos | Enja | ENJ-5055 2
Septfamilles
Henning Wolter Trio With Guests | Years Of A Trilogy | double moon | DMCHR 71021
Septology
Muhal Richard Abrams Orchestra | Blu Blu Blu | Black Saint | 120117-2
Sequence
Human Arts Ensemble | Junk Trap | Black Saint | BSR 0021
The Human Arts Ensemble | The Human Arts Ensemble Live, Vol.2 | Circle Records | RK 12-23578/12 IMS
Sequence Voiture(2 takes)
Ellery Eskelin With Andrea Parkins & Jim Black | The Secret Museum | HatOLOGY | 552
Sequentiae
Lee Konitz With Alan Broadbent | Live-Lee | Milestone | MCD 9329-2
Sequentialee
Axis | Axis | Jazz 4 Ever Records:Jazz Network | J4E 4735
Sequenz
Orchestre National De Jazz | Charmediterranéen | ECM | 1828(018493-2)
Sequenza Prima
Charmediterranéen | ECM | 1828(018493-2)
Sequenza Quartra
Charmediterranéen | ECM | 1828(018493-2)
Sequenza Seconda
Charmediterranéen | ECM | 1828(018493-2)
Sequenza Terza
Italian Instabile Orchestra | Litania Sibilante | Enja | ENJ-9405 2
Sequenze Orfiche
Gust Williams Tsilis Quintet | Sequestered Days | Enja | ENJ-6094 2
Sequoia Song
Carlos Bica & Azul | Twist | Enja | ENJ-9386 2
Serafina
John Coltrane Quartet | Stellar Regions | Impulse(MCA) | 951169-2
Seraphic Light
Joelle Leandre | Urban Bass | Adda | 581254
Sereia
Paulo Moura Group | Rio Nocturnes | Messidor | 15816 CD
Serenade
Freddie Bryant Group | Brazilian Rosewood | Fresh Sound Records | FSNT 035 CD
Gracie Fields With Studio Orchestra | Amazing Gracie-The Incomparable Gracie Fields | Saville Records | SVL 170 IMS
Michel Warlop Et Son Orchestre | Le Jazz En France Vol.4 | Pathe | 1727281
Serenade For A Whealty Widow
Bud Shank-Laurindo Almeida Quartet | Braziliance Vol.2 | Pacific Jazz | 796102-2
Serenade For Leonie
Ronald Shannon Jackson And The Decoding Society | What Spirit Say | DIW | DIW 895 CD
Serenade For Marion Brown
Marion Brown-Gunter Hampel Duo | Gemini | Birth | CD 037
Thilo Wolf Quartet | I Got Rhythm | MDL-Jazz | CD 1911(CD 050)
Serenade For The Renegade
Al Casey Quintet | Serenade In Blue | Savoy | SV 0232(MG 12057)
Serenade In Blue
Charles Mingus Quintet | Charles Mingus-The Complete Debut Recordings | Debut | 12 DCD 4402-2
Charles Owens New York Art Ensemble | Charles Owens Plays The Music Of Harry Warren | Discovery | DS 811 IMS
Glenn Miller And His Orchestra | Glenn Miller | Koch Records | 321 941 D1
Jazz Collection:Glenn Miller | Laserlight | 24367
The Ultimate Glenn Miller-22 Original Hits From The King Of Swing | RCA | 2113137-2
Glenn Miller Orchestra | Glenn Miller Serenade | CBS | 487445-2
Jazz City Workshop | Jazz City Workshop | Fresh Sound Records | FSR 2025(Bethlehem BCP 44)
Larry Vuckovich Sextet | City Sounds,Village Voices | Palo Alto | PA 8012
Lou Levy Trio | Jazz In Hollywood:Bud Shank/Lou Levy | Original Jazz Classics | OJCCD 1890-2(Nocturne NLP-2/NLP-10)
Phil Woods Quintet | Gratitude | Denon Compact Disc | CY-1316
Randy Weston Quartet | Zulu | Milestone | M 47045
Stan Getz Quartet | West Coast Jazz | Verve | 557549-2
Stan Getz And The 'Cool' Sounds | Verve | 547317-2
Stan Getz:East Of The Sun-The West Coast Sessions | Verve | 531935-2
Serenade In Blue-
Eddie Condon All Stars | Town Hall Concerts Vol.11 | Jazzology | JCD 1021/23
Serenade No.13 in G Major 'Eine Kleine Nachtmusik'(KV 525):
Clark Terry And His Orchestra | Clark Terry And His Orchestra Feat. Paul Gonsalves | Storyville | STCD 8322
Serenade To A Bus Seat
Clark Terry Quintet | The Second Set-Recorded Live At The Village Gate | Chesky | JD 127
Serenade To A Cuckoo
Roland Kirk Quintet | Rahsaan/The Complete Mercury Recordings Of Roland Kirk | Mercury | 846630-2
Royce Campbell-Adrian Ingram Group | Hands Across The Water | String Jazz | SJRCD 1002
John Barnes-Roy Williams Group | Like We Do | Lake | LACD 69
Serenade To A Mule
Benny Bailey Quintet | No Refil | TCB Records | TCB 94202
Serenade To A Soul Sister
Kenny Dorham Quintet | The Bebop Boys | Savoy | WL 70547 (809278)
Serenade's Suite
Art Farmer/Benny Golson Jazztet | Met The Jazztet | Chess | CHD 91550(872338)
Serenata
CoJazz feat. Gianni Basso | All Those Melodies | TCB Records | TCB 20402
Joe Pass Trio | Eximious | Original Jazz Classics | OJCCD 1037-2(2310877)
Larry Goldings Quartet | Caminhos Cruzados | Novus | 4163184-2
Richard Wyands Trio | Get Out Of Town | Steeplechase | SCCD 31401
Mark Murphy-Joe Lo Duca | Mark Murphy Sings Nat Cing Cole,Volumes 1&2 | Muse | MCD 6001
Serendipity
Rebecca Coupe Franks Group | All Of A Sudden | Justice Records | JR 0902-2
Serendipity I
Schmilz | Schmilz | Creative Works Records | CW CD 1041
Serendipity II-VI
Schmilz | Creative Works Records | CW CD 1041
Serendipity IX-XIII
Schmilz | Creative Works Records | CW CD 1041
Serendipity VIII
Last Affair | Sound Movie-Suite | Blue Flame | 40312
Serendipty II-VI
Aki Takase-Rudi Mahall | Duet For Eric Dolphy | Enja | 9109-2
Serene
Chico Hamilton And Euphoria | My Panamanian Friend-The Music Of Eric Dolphy | Soul Note | 121265-2
Eric Dolphy Quartet | Out There | New Jazz | NJSA 8252-6
Eric Dolphy:The Complete Prestige Recordings | Prestige | 9 PRCD-4418-2
Eric Dolphy Quintet | Far Cry | Original Jazz Classics | OJC20 400-2
Eric Dolphy With The Kenny Drew Trio | Daniel Humair Surrounded 1964-1987 | Blue Flame | 40322(2132163-2)
Harold Danko Quintet | Prestigious-A Tribute To Eric Dolphy | Steeplechase | SCCD 31508
Robert Stewart Quartet | Judgement | Red Records | 123268-2
Serengeti
Spyro Gyra & Guests | Love & Other Obsessions | GRP | GRP 98112
Billy Cobham Group | By Design | fnac Muisc | 662144
Serengeti Plains
Geoff Keezer Group | Other Spheres | DIW | DIW 871 CD
Serenghetti Slide
Bud Shank Septet | Brasamba | Pacific Jazz | LN 10092
Serenidade
Poncho Sanchez And His Orchestra | Papa Gato | Concord | CCD 4310
Serenity
Bobo Stenson Trio | Serenity | ECM | 1740/41(543611-2)
Cannonball Adderley Quintet | En Concert Avec Europe 1 | Laserlight | 710466
Chet Baker Quintet | Smokin' With The Chet Baker Quintet | Prestige | PR20 7749-2
Clark Terry Quartet | Funk Dumplin's | Matrix | MTX 1002 IMS
Dizzy Gillespie Sextet | The Giant | America | AM 6133
Frank Marocco-Ray Pizzi Duo | Jazz Accordeon | Discovery | DS 797 IMS
John Coltrane And His Orchestra | Meditations | Impulse(MCA) | 951199-2
John Coltrane Quartet | First Meditation | Impulse(MCA) | GRP 11182
Stanley Cowell Trio | Close To You Alone | DIW | DIW 6003 CD
Serenity-
Bright Passion | Steeplechase | SCCD 31328
Sergey's Ballad-
Serge Chaloff Sextet | Boston Blow-Up! | Affinity | AFF 63
Serial Blues
Kenny Drew Jr. Trio | Secrets | TCB Records | TCB 98502
Serial Mother Blues
Didier Lockwood Quintet | Storyboard | Dreyfus Jazz Line | FDM 36582-2
Serie De Arco
Brötzmann, van Hove, Bennink + Albert Mangelsdorff | Outspan Nr. 1 | FMP | 0180
Serigraphien I-III
Piirpauke | Tuku Tuku | JA & RO | JARO 4158-2
Serimeni
Soma | Southern Cross | West Wind Latina | 2208 CD
Seriously Deep
George Adams-Don Pullen Quartet | Life Line | Timeless | CD SJP 154
Sermon For Stuff
Dave Brubeck Group | In Their Own Sweet Way | Telarc Digital | CD 83355
Sermonette
Eddie Barclay Et Son Grand Orchestre | Et Voila! | Fresh Sound Records | FSR 515(Barclay 82138)
Nat Adderley Quintet | Good Company | Challenge | CHR 70009
Sermonized
Jimmy McGriff Sextet | Feelin' It | Milestone | MCD 9313-2
Sermonizing
Michel Godard Ensemble | Castel Del Monte | Enja | ENJ-9362 2
Serpent D'Or
Spyro Gyra | Access All Areas | MCA | 2292-51215-1
Serpent In Sky
Peter Herbolzheimer Rhythm Combination & Brass | Bandfire | Koala Records | CD P 1
Sertao
Richard Galliano Trio | Concert Inédits | Dreyfus Jazz Line | FDM 36606-2
Serves Me Right
Cannonball Adderley-Milt Jackson Quintet | Cannonball Adderley Birthday Celebration | Fantasy | FANCD 6087-2
Cannonball Adderley Quintet | Cannonball And Eight Giants | Milestone | M 47001
Sesame
Maynard Ferguson Orchestra | Storm | ARG Jazz | 21374872
Sesame Street
Singers Unlimited + The Oscar Peterson Trio | In Tune | MPS | 68085
Set Call
Ben Webster Quartet | Gone With The Wind | Black Lion | CD 877644-2
Set Me As A Seal
Montreal Jubilation Gospel Choir | Jubilation VI 'Looking Back'-Special 20th Anniversary Compilation | Blues Beacon | BLU-1022 22
Set Me Free
Mal Waldron Trio | Set Me Free | Affinity | AFF 116
Set Them Free
Paul Bley Trio | Not Two, Not One | ECM | 1670(559447-2)
Set Up Set
Eddie Harris Group | Dancing By A Rainbow | Enja | 9081-2
Setembro
Donald Harrison Quartet | Nouveau Swing | Impulse(MCA) | 951209-2
Latin On Impulse! Various Artists | Impulse(MCA) | IMP 12762
Seth
Steve Coleman And Five Elements | Genesis & The Opening Of The Way | RCA | 2152934-2
Seti I
Mario Piacentini Trio | Canto Atavico | SPLASC(H) Records | H 146
Settegast Strut
Booker Ervin-Dexter Gordon Quintet | Dexter Gordon Birthday Celebration | Fantasy | FANCD 6082-2
Settin' The Pace
Settin' The Pace | Prestige | PCD 24123-2(P 7455/7462)
Dexter Gordon Quintet | Master Takes-The Savoy Recordings | Savoy | WL 70814 SF
Setting Calvin's Waltz
Chris Jones-Steve Baker | Everybody's Cryin' Mercy | Acoustic Music Records | 319.1147.2
Setting Sun Blues
Marco Cerletti Group | Random And Providence | VeraBra Records | CDVBR 2039-2
Setting The Sailes
Bob Smith Group | Bob's Diner | dmp Digital Music Productions | CD 471
Seulb
Yusef Lateef Quintet | Gong! | Savoy | SJL 2226 (801202)
Seule
Barney Wilen Quartet | French Ballads | IDA Record | 014 CD
Seulement
European Jazz Quintet | European Jazz Quintet III | Fusion | 8010
Seven
Leszek Zadlo Ensemble | Time Emit | MRC | 066-32858
Paul Bley | Homage To Carla | Owl Records | 013427-2
Paul Bley Quartet | Fragments | ECM | 1320
Paul Bley Trio | Paul Plays Carla | Steeplechase | SCCD 31303
Wallace Roney Quintet | Obsession | Muse | MCD 5423
Seven Cherries
Andy Kirk And His Twelve Clouds Of Joy | The Uncollected:Andy Kirk | Hindsight | HSR 227 (835032)
Seven Come Eleven
Benny Goodman And His Orchestra | 40th Anniversary Concert-Live At Carnegie Hall | London | 820349-2
The War Years | Jazz Anthology | JA 5226
Benny Goodman Quintet | The Benny Goodman Story | Capitol | 833569-2
Benny Goodman Sextet | Jazz Live & Rare: Benny Goodman & His Group/Orchestra | Jazzline | ???
Billy Taylor And The Jazzmobile Allstars | The Jazzmobile Allstars | Taylor Made Records | T 1003
Herb Ellis-Joe Pass | Two For The Road | Original Jazz Classics | 2310714
Jeff Jerolamon Quintet | Jeff Jerolamon's Swing Thing! | Candid | CCD 79538
Lionel Hampton All Stars | Jazz In Paris:Lionel Hampton-Ring Dem Bells | EmArCy | 159825-2 PMS
Michael Moore-Bill Charlap | Concord Duo Series Volume Nine | Concord | CCD 4678
Monty Alexander Trio | Triple Treat II | Concord | CJ 338
Oscar Peterson Trio With Herb Ellis | Three Originals:Motion&Emotions/Tristeza On Piano/Hello Herbie | MPS | 521059-2
Oscar Peterson-Austin Roberts | Oscar Peterson 1951 | Just A Memory | JAS 9501-2
The Two-Bone-Big-Band | The Return Of The Hornplayers | Mons Records | MR 874314
Seven Days
Pat Metheny Group | Quartet | Geffen Records | GED 24978
Esbjörn Svensson Trio(E.S.T.) | Seven Days Of Falling | ACT | 9012-2
Seven Days Of Falling
Red Rodney With The Bebop Preservation Society | Red Rodney With The Bebop Preservation Society | Spotlite | SPJ LP 7
Seven For Twelve
Dave Doran Group | Rhythm Voice | Plainisphare | PL 1267-109 CD
Seven Kinds Of Jewels(Cha-Cha For A Jiyu)
Charles Brown Band | Drifting Blues | Pathe | 1546611(Score SLP 4011)
Seven Moons
John Dennis Trio | Charles Mingus-The Complete Debut Recordings | Debut | 12 DCD 4402-2
Seven Moons(alt.take)
Eberhard Weber Orchestra | Orchestra | ECM | 1374
Seven Movements

Johnny Dankworth Seven | Bebop In Britain | Esquire | CD ESQ 100-4
Seven Past Midnight
Mark Turner Quartet | Dharma Days | Warner | 9362-47998-2
Seven Points
The Dolphins | Malayan Breeze | dmp Digital Music Productions | CD 474
Seven Pounds Fifty
World Trio | World Trio | VeraBra Records | CDVBR 2052-2
Seven Rings
Wadada Leo Smith | Kulture Jazz | ECM | 1507
Seven Rings Of Light In The Hola Trinity
Joachim Kühn Sextett | Hip Elegy | MPS | 68066
Seven Seas
Copenhagen Art Ensemble | Angels' Share | dacapo | DCCD 9452
Seven Secrets
Christy Doran-Hank Roberts | Christy Doran's Phoenix' | Hat Art | CD 6074
Seven Signs
John McLaughlin Group | Live In Paris | Verve | 543536-2
Seven Sisters
The Heart Of Things | Verve | 539153-2
Boogie Bill Webb | Living Country Blues USA,Vol.9:Mississippi Moan | L+R Records | LR 42039
Seven Steppes
Cassandra Wilson Group | Traveling Miles | Blue Note | 854123-2
Seven Steps
Fourth World | Fourth World | B&W Present | BW 030
Seven Steps To Heaven
Charly Antolini Jazz Power | Bop Dance | BELL Records | BLR 84043
Jürgen Seefelder Quartet | The Standard Project | West Wind | WW 2086
Miles Davis Quintet | Four & More | CBS | SRCS 5145
No (More) Blues | Jazz Door | JD 1224
Peter Herbolzheimer Rhythm Combination & Brass | More Bebop | Koala Records | CD P 6
Tamami Koyake Quartet | Tamami Koyake First New York Session | Paddle Wheel | KICJ 85
Seven Studies For Prepared Piano:
Albrecht Riermeier Quartet | Four Drummers Drumming | Riff Records | CD RIFF 902-2
Seven Thirty
Uwe Kropinski Trio | First Time In Manhattan | ITM Records | ITM 1486
Seven Up
Peter O'Mara Quartet | Wind Moments | Take Twelve On CD | TT 009-2
Sonny Stitt All Stars (Be-Bop Boys) | Fats Navarro Memorial | Jazz Anthology | JA 5129
Seven Wojos
Dannie Richmond Quintet | The Last Mingus Band A.D. | Landmark | LCD 1537-2
Seven Years Of Good Luck
Susanne Abbuehl Group | April | ECM | 1766(013999-2)
Seven,Somewhere I Have Never Travelled,Gladly Beyond
Ragtime Specht Groove Trio | Ragtime Specht Groove Vol. 4. Little Susie | Intercord | 145032
Seventeen
Udo Schild Group | Morning | Jazz Haus Musik | ohne Nummer
Seventh (Solo Voice)-
Weather Report | Weather Report | CBS | 468212-2
Seventh Arrow-
Clyde Hart All Stars | Charlie Parker:The Complete 1944-1948 Small Group Sessions(Studio Recordings-Master Takes),Vol.1 | Blue Moon | BMCD 1007
Seventh Avenue
Louis Jordan And His Tympany Five | Louis Jordan And His Tympany Five 1944-1945 | Circle | CCD-53
Seventh Avenue Express
Count Basie And His Orchestra | Planet Jazz:Count Basie | Planet Jazz | 2152068-2
Count Basie-Basie's Basement | RCA | ???
The Indispensable Count Basie | RCA | ND 89758
Seventh Dream
Oscar Pettiford And His Birdland Band | Jazz On The Air Vol.6: Oscar Pettiford And His Birdland Band | Spotlite | SPJ 153
Seventh Siga
Big Allanbik | Batuque Y Blues | Blues Beacon | BLU-1031 2
Seventh Son
Mose Allison Trio | The Mose Chronicles-Live In London,Vol.1 | Blue Note | 529747-2
Mose Alife!/Wild Man On The Loose | Warner | 8122-75439-2
That's Jazz Vol.19: Mose Allison | Atlantic | ATL 50249
Seventh Son(aka Lateef Minor Seventh)
Dizzy Gillespie With Orchestra | Stonhenge/Carousel Suite | GM Recordings | GM 3014 CD(882949)
Sevenths
Adonis Rose Quintet | Song For Donise | Criss Cross | Criss 1146
Sew It Seems
Larry Coryell Group | Coryell! | Vanguard | 662124
Sex Is For Woman
David Murray Group | The Tip | DIW | DIW 891 CD
Sex Machine
Pucho & His Latin Soul Brothers | Rip A Dip | Milestone | MCD 9247-2
Jazzin' With The Soul Brothers | Fantasy | FANCD 6086-2
Sons Of Blues | Where's My Money | Steeplechase | SCB 9004
Sex With Birds-
Gerry Mulligan And The Sax Section | The Gerry Mulligan Songbook | Pacific Jazz | 833575-2
Sextet
Gerry Mulligan Quartet With Lee Konitz | Complete 1953 The Haig Performances | The Jazz Factory | JFCD 22861
Fats Waller | Private Acetates And Film Soundtracks | Jazz Anthology | JA 5148
Sexy Dream
Pink Inc. | A.Deutsch's Pink Inc. | DIW | DIW 852 CD
Sezopen
John Stevens Away | Mutual Benefit | Konnex Records | KCD 5061
Shablool
Art Farmer Quintet | Art Farmer Quintet | Original Jazz Classics | OJCCD 241-2(P 7017)
Shade Of Jade
Toots Thielemans With The Tsuyoshi Yamamoto Trio | Toots Thielemans In Tokyo | Denon Compact Disc | DC-8551
Shade Tree-
Chico Hamilton Quartet | Man From Two Worlds | Impulse(MCA) | JAS 48 (AS 59)
Shaded Place
Bill Watrous And His Orchestra | Reflections | Soundwings | SW 2104(807408)
Shades
The Mike Hennessey Chastet | Shades Of Chas Burchell | IN+OUT Records | 7025-2
Chas Burchell Sextet | Unsong Hero:The Undiscovered Genius Of Chas Burchell | IN+OUT Records | 7026-2
Shades-
David Friedman Quartet | Shades Of Change | Enja | ENJ-5017 2
Shades Of Bu
Herb Robertson Brass Ensemble | Shades Of Bud Powell | JMT Edition | 919019-2
Shades Of Bud
Klaus Weiss Quintet | On Tour | Calig | 30623
Shades Of Gray
Billy Barber | Shades Of Gray | dmp Digital Music Productions | CD 445
Jörg Kaufmann Trio | Sketches | Blue Concept | BCCD 95/01
Shades Of Light
McCoy Tyner Octet | Together | Milestone | M 9087
Shades Of Sutton Hoo
Jeff Palmer Quartet | Shades Of The Pine | Reservoir | RSR CD 137
Shadow
George Howard Group | Do I Ever Cross Your Mind | GRP | GRP 96692
Manhattan New Music Project | Mood Swing | Soul Note | 121207-2
Shadow & Light
John Abercrombie-Andy LaVerne Quartet | Now It Can Be Played | Steeplechase | SCCD 31314
Shadow Dance
Dave Holland Quintet | Jumpin' In | ECM | 1269
Kazda | New Strategies Of Riding | ITM Records | ITM 1492
Shadow Dancer
George Benson With The Jack McDuff Quartet | The New Boss Guitar | Original Jazz Classics | OJCCD 461-2
Shadow Dancers
Bernhard Reinke Transfusion | Cabo Blanco, From A Distance | Timeless | CD SJP 377
Shadow Fountain
String Trio Of New York | Time Never Lies | Stash Records | ST-CD 544(889796)
Shadow Of A Tree On Sand-
Boel-Emborg-Vinding-Riel | Shadow Of Love | Stunt Records | 18803
Shadow OnThe Floor
Loose Tubes | Jazzbühne Berlin '87 | Repertoire Records | REPCD 4916-WZ
Shadow Waltz
Sonny Rollins Trio | The Freedom Suite Plus | Milestone | M 47007
Sonny Rollins-The Freelance Years:The Complete Riverside & Contemporary Recordings | Riverside | 5 RCD 4427-2
Stan Kenton And His Orchestra | Sketches On Standards | Creative World |
Zoot Sims-Jimmy Rowles Quartet | If I'm Lucky | Original Jazz Classics | OJCCD 683-2(2310803)
Evan Parker Electro-Acoustic Ensemble | Toward The Margins | ECM | 1612(453514-2)
Shadow Without An Object
Sun Ra And His Solar Arkestra | Nothing Is | ESP Disk | ESP 1045-2
Shadow/Landscapes With Argonauts-With Words by Edgar Allen Poe and Heiner Müller
JoAnne Brackeen Quartet | Tring-A-Ling | Candid | CRS 1016 IMS
Shadows
Arthur Blythe Quintet & Guests | Elaborations | CBS | FC 38163
Coleman Hawkins And His Orchestra | The Hawk Swings | Ace Records | CDBOP 015
Misha Alperin | At Home | ECM | 1768(549610-2)
Tom Scott Group | Blow It Out | CBS | EK 46108
Christof Lauer-Jens Thomas | Shadows In The Rain | ACT | 9297-2
Shadows In The Rain
Gil Evans Orchestra With Sting | Sting And Gil Evans/Last Session | Jazz Door | JD 1228
Shadows On The Frontier
Tommy Dorsey And His Orchestra | Tommy Dorsey And His Orchestra With Frank Sinatra | RCA | 2115518-2
Shadrack
Benny Goodman And His Orchestra | The Benny Goodman Caravans Vol.4 | Giants Of Jazz | GOJ 1039
Golden Gate Quartet | Spirituals To Swing 1955-69 | EMI Records | 791569-2
Grant Green Quartet | Gooden's Corner | Blue Note | GXK 8168
Louis Armstrong With Sy Oliver's Choir And Orchestra | Louis And The Good Book | Verve | 549593-2
Louis Armstrong With The Lyn Murray Chorus | Louis Armstrong:Hallelujah(Gospel 1930-1941) | Fremeaux | FA 001
Ruth Price With Shelly Manne & His Men | Ruth Price With Shelly Manne & His Men At The Manne Hole | Original Jazz Classics | OJCCD 1770-2(S 7590)
Toshiko Akiyoshi Quartet | Amazing Toshiko Akiyoshi | Verve | MV 2579 IMS
Shady Lady Bird
Mercy Dee Walton | Pity And A Shame | Original Blues Classics | OBCCD 552-2(BV 1039)
Shady Side
Kenny Blake Group | A Lifetime After | Inak | 30372
Shag
Sidney Bechet And His New Orleans Feetwarmers | Sidney Bechet 1932-1943: The Bluebird Sessions | Bluebird | ND 90317
Shagadelic Boogaloo
Adam Holzman Group | Overdrive | Lipstick Records | LIP 890252
Shaine Une Zees
Paul Motian Trio | Motian In Tokyo | JMT Edition | 849154-2
Shake
The Ferals | Ruff | LEO | LR 138
Shake Baby Shake
Larry Garner Group | Too Blues | JSP Records | JSPCD 249
Shake Down The Stars
Jeri Southern With The Johnny Smith Quartet | Jeri Southern Meets Johnny Smith | Fresh Sound Records | FSR-CD 28(882156)
Shake Hands
John Lee Hooker | Half A Stranger | Mainstream | MD CDO 903
Shake It And Break It
Eddie Edwards And His Original Dixieland Jazz Band | The Commodore Series | London | HMC 5014 AN
Kid Sheik's Storyville Ramblers | Kid Sheik In Boston And Cleveland | American Music | AMCD-69
Original Tenith Brass Band | George Lewis Of New Orleans | Original Jazz Classics | OJC- 1739(RLP 12-283)
Sidney Bechet And His New Orleans Feetwarmers | Sidney Bechet 1932-1943: The Bluebird Sessions | Bluebird | ND 90317
Shake It To A Jelly
Sippie Wallace With Axel Zwingenberger | An Evening With Sippie Wallace | Vagabond | VRCD 8.86006
Clifton Chenier Group | On Tour | EPM Musique | FDC 5505
Shake Rattle And Roll
Big Joe Turner With The Count Basie Orchestra | Flip Flop And Fly | Original Jazz Classics | OJCCD 1053-2(2310937)
Clifton Chenier And His Band | Frenchin' The Boogie | Verve | 519724-2
Shake That Boogie
The Mojo Bluesband | Shake That Boogie | Gold Records | 11048
Shake That Thing
Graham Stewart Seven | The Golden Years Of Revival Jazz,Vol.8 | Storyville | STCD 5513
Kid Ory's Creole Jazz Band | Kid Ory's Creole Jazz Band | Good Time Jazz | GTCD 12008-2
Big Eye Louis Nelson Band | Big Eye Louis Nelson:1949 Sessions & Live At Luthjens | American Music | AMCD-7
Shake The Cage
Lisa Bassenge Trio | A Sight, A Song | Minor Music | 801100
Shake The Disease
Satoko Fuji Trio | Toward,To West | Enja | ENJ-9382 2
Shake Your Fish
Jimmie Lunceford And His Orchestra | Jimmy Lunceford - Rythm Is Our Business | MCA | 1302
Shake,Shuttle And Blow
Steve Laury Quartet | Stepping Out | Denon Compact Disc | CY-75870
Shakehandre
Frank Carlberg Group | Variations On A Summer Day | Fresh Sound Records | FSNT 083 CD
Shaken And Shaken
David Benoit Group | Shaken Not Stirred | GRP | GRP 97872
Shakey Money
David Murray Quartet | Shakill's II | DIW | DIW 884 CD
Shakin' Mother For You
Don Redman And His Orchestra | Shakin' The Africann | Hep | 1001
Shaking Lights
Anthony Braxton Duo/Quintet | Dances & Orations | Music & Arts | CD 923
Shaky Shuffler
Stan Getz With The Eddie Sauter Orchestra | Stan Getz Plays The Music Of Mickey One | Verve | 531232-2
Shaley's Neighborhood Sewer & The Pickle Club Rock-
Stan Getz Plays The Music Of Mickey One | Verve | 531232-2
Chuck Wayne Trio | Morning Mist | Original Jazz Classics | OJCCD 1097-2(P-7367)
Shalimar
Cassandra Wilson With The Mulgrew Miller Trio | Blue Skies | JMT Edition | 919018-2
Shall We Dance?
Dan Rose Trio | Conversations | Enja | 8006-2
Soesja Citroen With The Metropole Orchestra | Yesterdays | Challenge | CHR 70049
Stacy Kent With The Jim Tomlinson Quintet | In Love Again | Candid | CCD 79786
Tommy Flanagan-Wilbur Harden Quartet | The Music Of Rodgers And Hammerstein | Savoy | 650116(881916)
Shallow Dreamers
John Zorn Naked City | Naked City-Grand Guignol | Avant | AVAN 002
Shalom
Claude Williamson Quartet | Theatre Party | Fresh Sound Records | FSR 551(Contract 15003)
Shalom Elechem
Lionel Hampton And His Orchestra | The Great Hamptologia, Vol. 1 | MGM | 2304527 IMS
Shamal
Gianni Gebbia Group | Arabesques | SPLASC(H) Records | H 147
Shame Time
Joe Newman Octet | The Complete Joe Newman RCA-Victor Recordings(1955-1956):The Basie Days | RCA | 2122613-2
Shana
David Fathead Newman Septet | Still Hard Times | Muse | MCD 5283
Shané
Martin Theurer | Moon Mood | FMP | 0700
Shanghai Shuffle
Fletcher Henderson And His Orchestra | Wild Party | Hep | 1009
Shango...The Ballad
Trilok Gurtu With Shobha Gurtu | Usfret | CMP Records | CMP CD 33
Shankar
Bud Shank Quintet | Jazz In Hollywood:Bud Shank/Lou Levy | Original Jazz Classics | OJCCD 1890-2(Nocturne NLP-2/NLP-10)
Shank's Pranks
Sonny Boy Williamson Group | Bluebird Blues | Swingtime(Contact) | BT 2006
Shanti-Peace
Mel Brown Quintet | Chicken Fat | Impulse(MCA) | 9861047
Shanty
Louis Armstrong And His Orchestra | Louis Armstrong And His Big Band Vol.1-The Maturity | Black & Blue | BLE 59.225 2
Shape Of Things(To Come)
Steve Nelson Quartet | New Beginnings | TCB Records | TCB 99302
Shape To Twelve
Jean-Luc Ponty Quintet | Civilized Evil | Atlantic | SD 16020
Shapes
David Friesen | Paths Beyond Tracing | Steeplechase | SCCD 31138
Shapes Of Light
Shelly Manne And His Men | Shelly Manne Vol.2 | Original Jazz Classics | OJCCD 1910-2(C 2511)
Share My Love
Franz De Byl | Franz De Byl-Solo | FMP | SAJ 27
Share Your Love With Me
Vienna Art Orchestra | Innocence Of Clichés | Amadeo | 841646-2
Sharing
Lucky Four | Lucky Four | Tutu Records | 888108-2
Shark Bite
George Benson Group/Orchestra | George Benson Anthology | Warner | 8122-79934-2
David Sills Quintet | Bigs | Naxos Jazz | 86070-2
Sharkey's
Uli Lenz | Love Channel | L+R Records | CDLR 45100
Sharp
Harry James And His Orchestra | James And Haymes | Circle | CCD-5
Sharper Than A Tack
Cootie Williams And His Rug Cutters | The Complete Duke Ellington-Vol.11 | CBS | CBS 88242
Sharpville
World Saxophone Quartet | Moving Right Along | Black Saint | 120127-2
Shave Trail
Hans Reichel | Wichlinghauser Blues | FMP | 0150
Shaw 'Nuff
Art Pepper Plus Eleven | Modern Jazz Classics | Original Jazz Classics | OJC20 341-2
A Treasury Of Modern Jazz Classics | Mobile Fidelity | MFCD 805
Bud Powell Trio | Parisian Thoroughfare | Pablo | CD 2310976-2
The Legacy | Jazz Door | JD 1204
'Round About Midnight At The Blue Note | Dreyfus Jazz Line | FDM 36500-2
Dizzy Gillespie And His All Star Quintet | Charlie Parker:The Complete 1944-1948 Small Group Sessions(Studio Recordings-Master Takes),Vol.1 | Blue Moon | BMCD 1007
Donald Byrd Sextet | First Flight | Delmark | DE 407
Ira Sullivan And His Chicago Jazz Quintet | Bird Lives | Affinity | AFF 71
Phil Woods Quintet | Song For Sisyphus | CDS Records Ltd. | CJCD 831
Shaw Was A Good Man,Peewee
Buddy Stewart Sextet | Al Haig Meets The Master Saxes Vol.1 | Spotlite | SPJ 139
She Acts Like A Woman Should
Roosevelt Sykes Quintet | The Honeydripper | Original Blues Classics | OBCCD 557-2(BV 1014)
She Came In Through The Bathroom Window
Mike Westbrook Band | Off Abbey Road | TipToe | TIP-888805 2
Salvatore Bonafede Trio | Nobody's Perfect | Penta Flowers | CDPIA 022
She Caught The Katy And Left A Mule To Ride
Joe Hill Louis | Joe Hill Louis: The Be-Bop Boy | Bear Family Records | BCD 15524 AH
She Comes To See Me
Roy Dunn | Know'd Them All | Trix Records | TRIX 3312
She Could Do Tothing By Halves
Lonnie Johnson Quintet | Blues By Lonnie Johnson | Original Blues Classics | OBCCD 502-2(BV 1007)
She Did It Again
Michel Petrucciani Trio | Michel Petrucciani:The Blue Note Years | Blue Note | 789916-2
Michel Petrucciani | Live In Germany | Dreyfus Jazz Line | FDM 36597-2
She Did It Again-
Live In Germany | Dreyfus Jazz Line | FDM 36597-2
Bob Cooper Sextet | Group Activity | Affinity | AFF 65
She Didn't Say Yes,She Didn't Say No
Roy Fox And His Band | Hello Ladies And Gentleman. This Is Roy Fox Speaking | Ace Of Club | ACL 1172
She Expected A Caress
Billy Boy Arnold With The Aces | The Devil's Music:Mississippi And Memphis/Chicago Blues | Red Lightnin' | RL 0033
She Got It Like That
Sonny Boy Williamson Blues Band | Sonny Boy Williamson | Chess | 427004
She Loves To Dance
Berry Lipman Orchestra | Easy Listening Vol.1 | Sonia | CD 77280
She Loves You
Gary McFarland Orchestra | Soft Samba | Verve | MV 2102 IMS
She May Be Your Woman
Duke Ellington And His Orchestra | Happy Birthday Duke Vol.3 | Laserlight | 15785
She Moved Through The Fair
Joachim Kühn And The Radio Philharmonie Hannover NDR With Jazz Soloists | Europeana | ACT | 9220-2
Louis Stewart | Out On His Own | Jardis Records | JRCD 9612
Corey Harris | Betwen Midnight And Day | Alligator Records | ALCD 4837

She Moves Me
Luther Johnson | On The Road Again | Black & Blue | BLE 59.546 2

She Never Has A Window
Al Jones Blues Band | Paying Our Dues | Dues | AJBB 01

She Opened The Door
Christian Wallumrod Trio | No Birch | ECM | 1628(537344-2)

She Passes The House Of Her Grandmother
Diamond, Angel & Crooks | More Where That Came From | Intuition Records | INT 3061-2

She Quits Me To A Tee
Charlie Parker And His Orchestra | Bird On Verve-Vol.5:The Magnificent Charlie Parker | Verve | 817446-1 IMS

She Rote
Charlie Parker Quintet | Swedish Schnapps + | Verve | 849393-2
Eddie Daniels Group | To Bird With Love | GRP | GRP 95442

She Rote(take 3)
Charlie Parker And His Orchestra | Bird: The Complete Charlie Parker On Verve | Verve | 837141-2

She Rote(take 5)
Champion Jack Dupree Group | The Blues Of Champion Jack Dupree,Vol.1 | Storyville | STCD 8019

She Sells Sea Shells
Sonny Parker With Band | Sonny Parker:The Complete 1948-1953 | Blue Moon | BMCD 6003

She Speak Her Name
Memphis Jug Band | Memphis Jug Band Vol.2 | Frog | DGF 16

She Told Me,She Told Me
Thomas Clausen Trio | She Touched Me | M.A Music | A 628-2

She Touched Me
Joe Hill Louis | Joe Hill Louis: The Be-Bop Boy | Bear Family Records | BCD 15524 AH

She Treats Me Mean And Evil
Kip Hanrahan Groups | Tenderness | American Clave | AMCL 1016-2

She Walks In A Meadow
Matchbox Bluesband | Four Of A Kind | L+R Records | CDLR 42080

She Wants To Be Free
Baecastuff | Out Of This World | Naxos Jazz | 86063-2

She Was Looking Down
Michael Mantler Group | Michael Mantler: No Answer/Silence | Watt | 2/5(543374-2)
Chet Baker With The Don Sebesky Orchestra | She Was Too Good To Me | Epic | 450954-2

She Was Too Good To Me
Till Brönner Group | Chattin' With Chet | Verve | 157534-2
Steve Swallow Group | Home | ECM | 1160(513424-2)

She Was Young
Andrew Rathbun Group | True Stories | Fresh Sound Records | FSNT 099 CD

She Who Chose(The Lies That That Daylight Told Us)
Cassandra Wilson Group | She Who Weeps | JMT Edition | 834443-2

She Won't Gimme No Lovin'
Jazz Gillum Group | Harmonica And Washboard Blues | Black & Blue | BLE 59.252 2

Shebang
Giuseppi Logan Quartet | More | ESP Disk | ESP 1013-2

Sheet
Edward Vesala Sound And Fury | Invisible Strom | ECM | 1461

Sheets And Shrouds
Wolfgang Muthspiel Group | Loaded, Like New | Amadeo | 527727-2

Sheila's Song
String Band Featuring Isao Suzuki | String Band Featuring Isao Suzuki | Flying Disk | VIDC 601 Direct Disc

Sheking
Riccardo Fassi Tankio Band | Il Principe | SPLASC(H) Records | H 180

Shell
Philipp Wachsmann-Paul Lytton | Some Other Season | ECM | 1662
Earl Hines And His Orchestra | The Indispensable Earl Hines Vol.3/4(1939-1945) | RCA | 2126408-2

Shell Blues
Michael Gerber Group | This Is Michael Gerber | Big World | BW 2007

Shelley's Eyes
Oscar Peterson Trio | En Concert Avec Europe 1 | Laserlight | 710443/48

Shelter
Mitchel Forman | Harvest Song | Jazzline | JL 11150-2

Shelter Suite:
Craig Harris And Tailgater's Tales | Shelter | JMT Edition | 919008-2

Shelter(Reprise)-
Stephan Micus | Desert Poems | ECM | 1757(159739-2)

Shen Khar Venakhi
Bill Watrous With The Patrick Williams Orchestra | Someplace Else | Soundwings | SW 2100(807411)

Shenandoah
Mr. Acker Bilk With The Leon Young String Chorale | Stranger On The Shore | Philips | 830779-2

Shepherd's Baroque
Dave Shepherd Sextet | Good Enough To Keep | Black Lion | BLCD 760514

Shepherd's Tune
Richard Carr Trio | Along The Edge | Nabel Records:Jazz Network | CD 4683

Shep's Carr-
Valentina Ponomareva With Symphony Orchestra | Fortune-Teller | LEO | LR 136

Sher
Sonny Sharrock Band | Seize The Rainbow | Enemy | EMCD 104(03504)

Sherlock Holmes Junior
Jessica Williams Trio | Momentum | Jazz Focus | JFCD 003

Sherman Shuffle
Duke Ellington And His Orchestra | The Indispensable Duke Ellington,Vol.7/8 | RCA | ND 89274

Sherry
Ray Charles Sextet With The Raylets | Newport Jazz Festival 1958,July 3rd-6th Vol.4:Blues In The Night No.2 | Phontastic | NCD 8816
Serge Chaloff All Stars | The Fable Of Mabel | Black Lion | CD 877627-2

She's A Carioca
Jim Tomlinson Quartet | Brazilian Sketches | Candid | CCD 79769
Stanley Turrentine Orchestra | Stanley Turrentine | Blue Note | 84506

She's A Great,Great Girl
Roger Wolfe Kahn And His Orchestra | The Indispensable Jack Teagerden(1928-1957) | RCA | ND 89613

She's A Lady
Bert Ambrose And His Orchestra | Saturday Night | Decca | DDV 5003/4 DT

She's A Latin From Manhattan
Bob Robinson And His Bob Cats | Piano Blues Vol.2-The Thirties(1930-1939) | Story Of Blues | CD 3512-2

She's A Wine-O
Count Basie And His Orchestra | The Indispensable Count Basie | RCA | ND 89758

She's As Wild As Springtime
Lee Konitz-Harold Danko Duo | Wild As Springtime | G.F.M. Records | 8002

She's Crying For Me
New Orleans Rhythm Kings | New Orleans In The '20s | Timeless | CBC 1-014

She's Funny That Way
Art Tatum | Art Tatum:Over The Rainbow | Dreyfus Jazz Line | FDM 36727-2
Art Tatum-The Complete Pablo Solo Masterpieces | Pablo | 7 PACD 4404-2
The V-Discs | Black Lion | BLP 60114
Bill Coleman Quintet | Really I Do | Black & Blue | BLE 59.162 2
Chubby Jackson And His Orchestra | Chubby Jackson-The Happy Monster:Small Groups 1944-1947 | Cool & Blue | C&B-CD 109
Coleman Hawkins And His Orchestra | The Indispensable Coleman Hawkins 1927-1956:Body And Soul | RCA | ND 89277
Count Basie And Friends | Basie And Friends | Pablo | 2310925
Count Basie Jam | Montreux '77-The Art Of The Jam Session | Pablo | 2620106
Harry Edison Quartet | Can't Get Out Of This Mood... | Orange Blue | OB 006 CD
Joe Turner | I Understand | Black & Blue | BLE 59.153 2
Knud Jorgensen-Bengt Hanson | Bojangles | Touché Music | TMcCD 002
Kurt Elling Group | This Time Its Love | Blue Note | 493543-2
Lee Konitz Quartet | Lee Konitz In Harvard Square | Black Lion | BLCD 760928
Lester Young And His Band | Lester Young:The Complete Aladdin Sessions | Blue Note | 832787-2
Lester Young:The Complete 1936-1951 Small Group Sessions(Studio Recordings-Master Takes),Vol.4 | Blue Moon | BMCD 1004
Pee Wee Russell Sextet | We're In The Money | Black Lion | BLCD 760909
Stuff Smith Trio | The Stuff Smith Trio 1943 | Progressive | PCD 7053

She's Funny That Way-
Ray Bryant | Ray Bryant Plays Blues And Ballads | Jazz Connaisseur | JCCD 9107-2
Sam Wooding And His Orchestra | Le Jazz En France Vol.2:Black Bands In Paris | Pathe | 1727261

She's Gone
Woody Herman And The New Thundering Herd | The 40th Anniversary Carnegie Hall Concert | RCA | 2159151-2

She's Gone Again
Dizzy Gillespie Sextet | In The Beginning | Prestige | P 24030

She's Got It
Muddy Waters Band | Good News-Muddy Waters, Vol.3 | Red Lightnin' | SC 002

She's Just Miss Popular Hybrid
Count Basie And His Orchestra | Sixteen Men Swinging | Verve | 2-2517 IMS

She's Just Perfect
Al Jarreau With Band | Tenderness | i.e. Music | 557853-2

She's Leaving Home
All Fly Home | Warner | 7599-27362-2
Jaco Pastorius Groups | Holiday For Pans | Sound Hills | SSCD 8001
Walkaway With Urszula Dudziak | Saturation | IN+OUT Records | 77024-2

She's Like A Sexmachine
Eb Davis Bluesband | Good Time Blues | Acoustic Music Records | AMC 1016

She's Long She's Tall She Weeps Like A Willow Tree
Canned Heat | Black & White Blues-The Little Red Rooster | Chess | 2292-44598-1

She's Makin' Whoopee In Hell Tonight
Jimmy Rushing And His All Stars | Jack Dupree-Jimmy Rushing-Muddy Waters | Laserlight | 17062

She's No Trouble
Das Pferd | Ao Vivo | VeraBra Records | CDVBR 2029-2

She's Not The One For Me
Martin Schmitt | Handful Of Blues | AH Records | ESM 9303

She's So Lucky
Muddy Waters Group | Back In His Early Days, Vol.1+2 | Red Lightnin' | SC 001/2

She's The Daughter Of A Planter From Havana
Louis Armstrong With Luis Russell And His Orchestra | Louis Armstrong Vol.7-Satchmo's Discoveries | MCA | 1326

She's Warm She's Willing She's Wonderful
John Zorn Group | Masada Seven | DIW | DIW 915 CD

Shhh-
Miles Davis Group | The Miles Davis Selection | CBS | 471623-2

Shift In The Wind
Steve Coleman And Five Elements | Drop Kick | Novus | 4163144-2

Shifting Down
Cecil Taylor Quintet | Coltrane Time | Contemporary | BOP 1
Chet Baker With The Amstel Octet | Hazy Hugs | Limetree | MLP 198601

Shifting Sands
Dave Holland Quintet | Not For Nothin' | ECM | 1758(014004-2)
MAX feat.Henry Scott III | Personal Note | Moers Music | 02034

Shifting Views
Herbie Hancock Group | Mr. Hands | CBS | 32362

Shim Sham Shimmy
The Dorsey Brothers Orchestra | Mood Hollywood | Hep | 1005

Shimmering
Adrian Bentzon's Jazzband | The Golden Years Of Revival Jazz,Vol 1 | Storyville | STCD 5506

Shim-Me-Sha-Wabble
Alex Welsh And His Band | Great British Jazz Bands Vol.6:Alex Welsh | Lake | LACD 62
Max Kaminsky And His Dixieland Bashers | Victor Jazz History Vol.18:Chicago Jazz(1934-64) | RCA | 2135737-2
The Wolverines | Chicago Jazz 1924-28 | Village(Jazz Archive) | VILCD 007-2

Shin Jin Rui
Artie Shaw And His New Muisc | Artie Shaw/Benny Goodman | Forlane | UCD 19006

Shine
Benny Goodman Quartet | More Camel Caravans | Phontastic | NCD 8843/4
More Camel Caravans | Phontastic | NCD 8841/2
Welcome To Jazz: Benny Goodman | Koch Records | 321 973 D1
Diz Disley And His String Quartet | Best Of British Jazz From The BBC Jazz Club Vol.4 | Upbeat Jazz | URCD 122
Frl. Mayer's Hinterhaus Jazzer | Frl. Mayer's Hinterhaus Jazzer | Jazz Classics | AU 11097
Henry Threadgill-Craig Harris Group | Hip Hop Be Bop | ITM Records | ITM 1480
Kid Ory's Creole Jazz Band | The Legendary Kid | Good Time Jazz | GTCD 12016-2
Nat Gonella's Georgia Jazz Band | Runnin' Wild | Harlequin | HQ 3003 IMS
Oliver Lake Trio | Zaki | Hat Art | CD 6113
Rene Thomas Quintet | Jazz In Paris:René Thomas-The Real Cat | EmArCy | 549400-2 PMS
Ruby Braff-Scott Hamilton Sextet | A First | Concord | CJ 274
Stan Getz Quintet | Verve Jazz Masters 8:Stan Getz | Verve | 519823-2
Stephane Grappelli Quartet | Verve Jazz Masters 11:Stéphane Grappelli | Verve | 516758-2
Stephane Grappelli With The Diz Disley Trio | Grapelli Story | Verve | 515807-2
Compact Jazz:Stephane Grappelli | MPS | 831370-2 PMS
Sweet Emma Barrett And Herr Bell Boys | Mardi Grax Day 1960-Live | 504 Records | 504CD 67
Willie 'The Lion' Smith | Jazz In Paris:Willie 'The Lion' Smith-Music On My Mind | EmArCy | 014032-2

S-h-i-n-e
Stan Getz Quintet | Stan Getz:East Of The Sun-The West Coast Sessions | Verve | 531935-2
Willie 'The Lion' Smith Duo | Willie 'The Lion ' Smith:The Lion's In Town | Vogue | 2111506-2

Shine A Light
Ben Sidran Group | Enivre D'Amour | VeraBra Records | CDVBR 2097-2

Shine Boy
Willie Trice | Blue & Rag'd | Trix Records | TRIX 3305

Shine On Harvest Moon
Coleman Hawkins And Ben Webster With The Oscar Peterson Quartet | Tenor Giants | Verve | 2610046
Count Basie & His Rhyhtm | Victor Jazz History Vol.10:Kansas City(1935-71) | RCA | 2128564-2
Count Basie Quartet | Masters Of Jazz Vol.5 | RCA | NL 89530 DP
The Indispensable Count Basie | RCA | ND 89758
Dave Brubeck Quartet | Once When I Was Very Young | Limelight | 844298-2 IMS
John Gill's Novelty Orchestra Of New Orleans | Smile, Darn Ya, Smile | Stomp Off Records | CD 1227
Jaki Byard Experience | Pre-Rahsan | Prestige | P 24080

Shing-A-Ling Baby
Willie Bobo Group | Juicy | Verve | 519857-2

Shing-A-Ling Baby(alt.take)
John Surman Orchestra | Tales Of The Algonquin | Deram | 844884-2

Shinin' Moon
Terje Rypdal Group | Skywards | ECM | 1608(533768-2)

Shining
First House | Cantilena | ECM | 1393

Shining Brightly
Lightnin' Hopkins | Lightnin' Hopkins(1946-1960) | Story Of Blues | CD 3524-2

Shining On You
Harry Allen Duo/Trio | I'll Never Be The Same | Master Mix | CHECD 00106

Shiny Stockings
Art Van Damme Group | State Of Art | MPS | 841413-2
Barney Kessel Trio | Jellybeans | Concord | CJ 164
Billy May And His Orchestra | Billy May's Big Fat Brass/Bill's Bag | Capitol | 535206-2
Bob Mintzer Big Band | Homage To Count Basie | dmp Digital Music Productions | CD 529
Brian Melvin Trio | Old Voices | Timeless | CD SJP 396
Cal Tjader Sextet | Soul Bird | Verve | 549111-2
Charlie Byrd Trio | Charlie Byrd In Greenwich Village | Milestone | M 47049
Clark Terry And Frank Wess With Bob Lark And The DePaul University Jazz Ensemble I | Big Band Basie | Reference Recordings | RR-63 CD
Count Basie And His Orchestra | Verve Jazz Masters 2:Count Basie | Verve | 519819-2
April In Paris | Verve | 521402-2
The Atomic Band Live In Europe | Bandstand | BDLP 1506
En Concert Avec Europe 1 | Laserlight | 710411/12
Eddie Lockjaw Davis Quartet | Jazz Legends:Eddie Lockjaw Davis Quartet Vol.1&2 | Storyville | 4960263
Ella Fitzgerald And The Tommy Flanagan Trio With The Basie Orchestra | Jazz At The Santa Monica Civic '72 | Pablo | 2625701-2
Ella Fitzgerald With The Count Basie Orchestra | Ella & Basie-On The Sunny Side Of The Street | Verve | 821576-2
Five + Jazz Comfort | Brazz | Memo Music | MM 6061
Greetje Kauffeld With Jerry Van Rooyen And Jiggs Whigham And The Rias Big Band | Greetje Kauffeld Meets Jerry Van Rooyen And Jiggs Whigham With The Rias Big Band | Mons Records | MR 874786
Jenny Evans And Her Quintet | Shiny Stockings | Enja | ENJ-9317 2
Jesper Thilo Quintet feat. Hank Jones | A Jazz Par 91 Project | Storyville | STCD 4178
Oscar Peterson Trio | The Oscar Peterson Trio Plays | Verve | POCJ 1827 PMS
Sir Charles Thompson | Playing My Way | Jazz Connaisseur | JCCD 9313-2
Super Trio | Brotherhood Of Man | L+R Records | CDLR 45095
The Count Basie Orchestra | Long Live The Chief | Denon Compact Disc | CY-1018
The Three Sounds | Babe's Blues | Blue Note | 784434-2
Earl Hines Quartet | A Night At Johnnie's | Black & Blue | BLE 59.300 2

Shiny Stockings-
Magic Slim Band | The Ralph Bass Sessions Vol.5 | Red Lightnin' | RL 0057

Shipwreck On Te Magnetic Rock-
Chris Barber's Jazz Band | Ottilie Patterson With Chris Barber's Jazzband 1955-1958 | Lake | LACD 30

Shir
Kol Simcha | Contemporary Klezmer | Laika Records | LK 93-048

Shir Hamaalot
Fred Houn & The Afro-Asian Music Ensemble | We Refused To Be Used And Abused | Soul Note | 121167-2

Shirl
Max Roach Quintet | Standard Time | EmArCy | 814190-1 IMS

Shirokko
Benny Goodman's Boys | Big Band Bounce And Boogie:Clarinetitis/The Young BG-Benny Goodman | Affinity | AFS 1018

Shirts Off
Coleman Hawkins And His Rhythm | Coleman Hawkins/Johnny Hodges:Complete 1949-1950 Vogue Master Takes | The Jazz Factory | JFCD 22840

Shi-Sah
Dave Brubeck Quartet | Live | Bandstand | BDCD 1538

Shiva
Percussion Summit | Percussion Summit | Moers Music | 02056 CD

Shiva-Loka
Ingrid Jensen Quintet | Here On Earth | Enja | ENJ-9313 2

Shiva's Dance
Tony Scott | Music For Yoga Meditation And Other Joys | Verve | 2304471 IMS

Shiva-The Third Eye
Noodband | Shiver | Moers Music | 01094

Shoe It Yourself
Benny Goodman Trio | Benny Goodman:The Complete 1947-1949 Small Group Sessions Vol.2(1947-1949) | Blue Moon | BMCD 1043

Shoe Shine Boy
Bill Perkins With The Jan Lundgren Trio | Bill Perkins Recreates The Historic Solos Of Lester Young | Fresh Sound Records | FSR-CD 5010
Count Basie And The Kansas City 7 | Count Basie And The Kansas City 7 | Impulse(MCA) | 951202-2
Dick Wellstood | Live at The Sticky Wicket | Arbors Records | ARCD 19188
The New York Allstars | Count Basie Remembered | Nagel-Heyer | CD 031
Jones-Smith Incorporated | The Lester Young Story Vol.1 | CBS | CBS 88223

Shoe Shiner's Drag
Jelly Roll Morton's Red Hot Peppers | Didn't He Ramble | Black & Blue | BLE 59.228 2

Shoo-Shoo Baby
Nat King Cole Trio | The Early Forties | Fresh Sound Records | FSR-CD 0139

Shoot The Likker To Me,John Boy
Acoustic Alchemy | Against The Grain | GRP | GRP 97832

Shoot The Loop
Jimmy Dorsey And His Orchestra | The Uncollected: Jimmy Dorsey | Hindsight | HSR 101

Shooting Stars
Richard Grossman Trio | Trio Live In Real Time | Nine Winds Records | NWCD 0134

Shop 'Till You Drop
Paul Moer Trio | Live At The Pour House | Fresh Sound Records | FSCD 1025

Shoreway
Graham Haynes & No Image | What Time It Be | Muse | MCD 5402

Short Coat
Cedar Walton Trio | Cedar | Timeless | CD SJP 223

Short Count
Double Drums Project | Double Drums Project | BIT | 11264

Short Cut
Ute Kannenberg Quartet | Kannenberg On Purpose | Jazz Haus Musik | JHM 0109 CD
Gregor Hübner Quintet | Januschke's Time | Satin Doll Productions | SDP 1034-1 CD

Short Cuts
The Huebner Brothers | Memories | Satin Doll Productions | SDP 1025-1 CD
Max Collie And His Rhythm Aces | Max Collie Rhyhtm Aces Vol.3 | GHB Records | BCD-98

Short Film On Diving
Swingle Singers | Swingle Singers Getting Romantic | Philips | 586736-2
Short Fugue from Album For The Young Op.68(Robert Schuman)
Lightnin' Hopkins | The Swartmore Concert | Original Blues Classics | OBCCD 563-2
Short Hare
Arne Domnerus Quartet | Sugar Fingers | Phontastic | NCD 8831
Short Life
Daniel Schnyder With The NDR Radio Philharmonie Hannover | Tanatula | Enja | ENJ-9302 2
Howard McGhee Sextet | Maggie | Savoy | SV 0269
Short Notice
Robert Previt Quintet | Bump The Renaissance | Sound Aspects | sas CD 008
Short People
Steve Klink Trio | Feels Like Home | Minor Music | 801092
Ralph Towner With Strings | In The Light | ECM | 1033/4
Short Piece For Guitar And Strings
Lares | Lares | yvp music | 3017
Short Romantic Schoolgirl Song
Duke Ellington And His Orchestra | Duke Ellington Private Collection/Studio Sessions-Chicago 1956 | Music De Luxe Special | MSCD 22
Short Stop
Michael Session Quintet | Michael Session 'N Session | ITM-Pacific | ITMP 970074
Shorty Rogers And His Orchestra Feat. The Giants | Short Stops | RCA | NL 85917(2)
Short Story
Ralph Lalama & His Manhattan All Stars | Feelin' And Dealin' | Criss Cross | Criss 1046
Short Stuff
Billy Higgins Trio With Harold Land | 3/4 For Peace | Red Records | 123258-2
Short Suite
Al Di Meola-Chick Corea | Land Of The Midnight Sun | CBS | 468214-2
Short Tales Of The Black Forest
Sandor Szabo | Gaia And Aries | Acoustic Music Records | 319.1146.2
Shorter Form
Ron McClure Quartet | Match Point | Steeplechase | SCCD 31517
Shorter Story
New Horizon Ensemble | After The Dawn Has Risen | Open Minds | OM 2414-2
Shorter Voyage
Ken McIntyre Sextet | Introducing The Vibrations | Steeplechase | SCCD 31065
Short'n Stout
Boots Brown(Shorty Rogers) And His Blockbusters | Jimmy Giuffre:Complete 1947-1952 Master Takes | Definitive Records | DRCD 11212
Shortnin' Bread
Jack McDuff Quartet With Orchestra | Prelude:Jack McDuff Big Band | Prestige | PRCD 24283-2
John Mooney And Bluesiana | Travelin' On | Crosscut | CCD 11032
Shorts
Ron McClure Sextet | Sunburst | Steeplechase | SCCD 31306
Shortwave
Julius Hemphill Sextet | Five Chord Stud | Black Saint | 120140-2
Shorty George
Smith Casey | The Greatest In Country Blues Vol.3(1929-1956) | Story Of Blues | CD 3523-2
Shorty's Blues
Bud Freeman All Stars | The Bud Freeman All Stars | Original Jazz Classics | OJC 183(SV 2012)
Shotgun Blues
Cootie Williams And His Orchestra | Typhoon | Swingtime(Contact) | ST 1003
Shotgun Boogie
Dan Burley With Brownie & Sticks McGhee | Circle Blues Session | Southland | SCD 9
Should I
Alvino Rey And His Orchestra | The Uncollected: Alvino Rey And His Orchestra 1946 | Hindsight | HSR 121
Jan Garber And His Orchestra | The Uncollected:Jan Garber, Vol.2 | Hindsight | HSR 155
Oscar Peterson Trio | The Oscar Peterson Trio At The Concertgebouw | Verve | 521649-2
Seger Ellis Group | Prairie Blues-The Music Of Seger Ellis | AZURE Compact Disc | AZ-CD-22
Should I Care
Soul Immigrants Plus Guests | A Healty Vibe | Lipstick Records | LIP 8947-2 HOT
Should I Surrender
Ulrich P. Lask Group | Lask | ECM | 1217
Should We Geanie
David Murray Nonet | Dark Star(The Music Of The Grateful Dead) | Astor Place | TCD 4002
Should've Been
Freddy Cole With Band | To The End Of The Earth | Fantasy | FCD 9675-2
Kendra Shank Group | Wish | Jazz Focus | JFCD 028
Should've Gone Before You Left
Albert Ammons | The Boogie Woogie Boys | Storyville | 6.28469 DP
Shout
Myra Melford Trio | Now & Now | Enemy | EMCD 131(03531)
Shout For Joy
Albert Ammons | The Best Of Boogie Woogie | Zeta | ZET 740
Shoutin'
T.S. Monk,Sextet | Take One | Blue Note | 799614--2
Count Basie And His Orchestra | Count Basie-Basie's Basement | RCA | ???
Shoutin' Blues
The Indispensable Count Basie | RCA | ND 89758
Shouting On A Riff
Dave Brubeck Quintet | Reunion | Original Jazz Classics | OJCCD 150-2
Shouts
Rova Saxophone Quartet | Rova:The Works Vol.1 | Black Saint | 120176-2
Show Eyes
Bianca Ciccu With The Randy Brecker Quintet | The Gusch | ITM Records | ITM 1440
Show Me
Ella Fitzgerald With The Marty Paich Orchestra | Ella Sings Broadway | Verve | 549373-2
Johnny Richards And His Orchestra | My Fair Lady-My Way | Fresh Sound Records | FSR 609(Roulette SR 52114) (835247)
Oscar Peterson Trio | My Fair Lady | Verve | MV 2097 IMS
Shelly Manne And His Friends | My Fair Lady | Mobile Fidelity | MFCD 809
Show Me How(You Milk The Cow)
Carmen Lundy And Her Orchestra | Good Morning Kiss | Black-Hawk | BKH 523
Show Me The Way To Go Out Of This World
Firehouse Five Plus Two | The Firehouse Five Story Vol. 3 | Good Time Jazz | 12012
Show Of Hands
Edmond Hall Quartet With Teddy Wilson | Commodore Classics In Swing | Commodore | 9031-72723-2
Show The Good Side
Benny Goodman And His Orchestra | Camel Caravan Broadcast 1939 Vol.3 | Phontastic | NCD 8819
Show Your Linen,Miss Richardson
Tiny Grimes Quintet | Tiny Grimes:The Complete 1950-1954,Vol.5 | Blue Moon | BMCD 6009
Showboat Shuffle
Duke Ellington And His Famous Orchestra | Reminiscing In Tempo | Naxos Jazz | 8.120589 CD
Showtime Medley:
Tim Berne Group | Tim Berne EmpireThe Five Years Plan/Spectres/Songs And Rituals In Real Time | Screwgun | SC 70009
Show-Type Tune
Bill Evans Trio | The Second Trio | Milestone | M 47046
Bill Evans-Eddie Gomez Duo | The Complete Fantasy Recordings | Fantasy | 9FCD 1012-2
Carlos Denia-Uli Glaszmann | Ten Strings For Bill Evans | Edition Musikat | EDM 069
Larry Schneider-Andy LaVerne Duo | Bill Evans...Person We Know | Steeplechase | SCCD 31307
Show-Type Tune(take 1)
Hugh Davies | Shozyg | FMP | SAJ 36
Shpiel Es
John Handy Group | Musical Dreamland | Boulevard | BLD 515 CD
Shreveport Stomp
Wilbur DeParis And His New New Orleans Band | Atlantic Jazz: New Orleans | Atlantic | 7567-81700-2
Jelly Roll Morton Trio | The Complete Jelly Roll Morton-Vol.3/4 | RCA | NL 89769(2) DP
Shringar
Miles Donahue Quintet | The Good Listener | RAM Records | RMCD 4510
Shrubberies
Perry Robinson Quartet | Call To The Stars | West Wind | WW 2052
Shuckin'
Dinah Washington With The Teddy Stewart Orchestra | John Coltrane:Complete Recordings With Dizzy Gillespie | Definitive Records | DRCD 11249
Shuckin' And Jivin'
Jimmy McGriff Orchestra | Jimmy McGriff-Funkiest Little Band In The Kand | LRC Records | CDC 9046(874379)
Shuffle
Wayne Horvitz Group | Miracle Mile | Nonesuch | 7559-79278-2
Shuffle Boil
Steve Lacy Sextet | We See(Thelonious Monk Songbook) | Hat Art | CD 6127
Shuffle Montgomery
Herbie Nichols Trio | Herbie Nichols:The Complete Blue Note Recordings | Blue Note | 859352-2
Shuffle Montgomery(alt.take)
John King Trio | Electric World | Ear-Rational | ECD 1016
Shufflin'
Frank Wess Meets The Paris-Barcelona Swing Connection | Paris-Barcelona Connection | Fresh Sound Records | FSNT 002 CD
Ed Thigpen Ensemble | Young Men & Old | Timeless | CD SJP 330
Shug
Mahmoud Turkmani | Fayka | Enja | ENJ-9447 2
Shukran Paco De Lucia
Pharoah Sanders Group | Shukuru | Evidence | ECD 22022-2
Shulie A Bop
Sarah Vaughan And Her Trio | Swingin' Easy | EmArCy | 514072-2
Verve Jazz Masters 18:Sarah Vaughan | Verve | 518199-2
Shuma
Dusko Goykovich Quintet With The NDR Radio-Philharmonie,Hannover | Balkan Blues | Enja | ENJ-9320 2
Shumadya
John Lindberg Trio | Give And Take | Black Saint | BSR 0072
Shunyata
Blauer Hirsch | Cyberpunk | FMP | 1240
Shut Up
Samm Bennett And Chunk | Knitting Factory Tours Europe Way 23-June 15,1991 | Enemy | EMCD 121(03521)
Shut Your Big Mouth(Girl)
Joe Sims And Clarence Williams | Big Charlie Thomas 1925-1927 | Timeless | CBC 1-030
Shut Your Mouth
Elmo Hope-Frank Foster Quintet | Hope Meets Foster | Original Jazz Classics | OJCCD 1703-2(P 7021)
Shutterbug
J.J.Johnson Sextet | J.J.Inc. | CBS | CK 65296
Shy Csardas
Hank D'Amico Sextet | Don Byas Complete American Small Group Recordings | Definitive Records | DRCD 11213
Si Ch'io Vorrei Morire
Mike Westbrook Orchestra | Westbrook-Rossini | Hat Art | CD 6002
Si Continua
Paolo Fresu Angel Quartet | Metamorfosi | RCA | 2165202-2
Si Dolce E Il Tormento
Roman Bunka Group | Dein Kopf Ist Ein Schlafendes Auto | ATM Records | ATM 3818-AH
Si Ga Ni Wa Ta
Eliane De Creus & Jean Sablon | Le Jazz En France Vol.5:Django Plus | Pathe | 1727291
Si Llego A Besarte
Gianluigi Trovesi With The Orchestra Da Camera Di Nembro Enea Salmeggia | Around Small Fairy Tales | Soul Note | 121341-2
Si Peu De Temps
Victory Of The Better Man | ...Wegen Brot... | CMP Records | CMP CD 69
Si Se Calla El Cantor
Jerry Bergonzi Quartet | Jerry On Red | Red Records | 123224-2
Si Si
Charlie Parker Quintet | Bird On Verve-Vol.6:South Of The Border | Verve | 817447-1 IMS
Si Tu Savais
Allan Vaché-Jim Galloway Sextet | Raisin' The Roof:Allan Vaché Meets Jim Galloway | Nagel-Heyer | CD 054
Si Tu Vois Ma Mere
Bob Wilber's Bechet Legacy | The Hamburg Concert-Tribute To A Legend | Nagel-Heyer | CD 028
Charlie Byrd Quartet | Moments Like This | Concord | CCD 4627
Sidney Bechet With Claude Luter And His Orchestra | Sidney Bechet | Vogue | 000001 GK
Si Tu Vois Ma Mere-
NuNu! | Ocean | TipToe | TIP-888837 2
Si Verias
Irazu | La Fiesta Del Timbalero | L+R Records | CDLR 45039
Siam
Bobby Hutcherson Sextet | Jazz-Club: Vibraphone | Verve | 840034-2
Siana's Dream
Deborah Henson-Conant | Alter Ego | Laika Records | 35100852
Siana's Dream:The Music Box
Alterd Ego | Laika Records | 35100962
Juhani Aaltonen Group | Springbird | Leo Records | 005
Sibel
Hal Kemp And His Orchestra | Got A Date With An Angel | Pro-Arte | CDD 553
Sibiria(Kosakken Borge)
Dizzy Gillespie-Stan Getz Sextet | Welcome To Jazz: Dizzy Gillespie | Koch Records | 321 972 D1
Siboney(part 1)
Diz And Getz | Verve | 2-2521 IMS
Siboney(part 2)
Ultimate Stan Getz selected by Joe Henderson | Verve | 557532-2
A.D.D.Trio | Sic Bisquitus Disintegrat | Enja | ENJ-9361 2
Sic Et Non
Christoph Schweizer Septet | Normal Garden | Mons Records | MR 874660
Sicherlich
Barbara Thompson's Paraphernalia | Barbara Thompson's Paraphernalia | MCA | 2292-50577-1
Siciliano
Eddie Daniels Quartet With The London Philharmonia Orchestra | Breakthrough | GRP | GRP 95332
Siciliano In G Minor
Jacques Loussier Trio | Focus On Jacques Loussier | Decca | FOS-R 5/6
Sicilienne In G Minor(BWV 1031)
Laurindo Almeida-Bud Shank Duo | Selected Classical Works For Guitar And Flute | Concord | CC 2003
Sickness
JATP All Stars | The Complete Jazz At The Philharmonic On Verve 1944-1949 | Verve | 523893-2
Sid Flips His Lid
Marty Paich Piano Quartet | Take Me Along | Fresh Sound Records | 58111 CD(RCA)
Side By Side
Marty Ehrlich And The Dark Woods Ensemble | Just Before The Dawn | New World Records | 80474-2
Richie Cole Quintet | Side By Side | Muse | MCD 6016
Side By Side-
Miles Davis Quintet | Circle In The Round | CBS | 467898-2
Side Car I
Miles Davis Sextet | Circle In The Round | CBS | 467898-2
Side Car II
Ellery Eskelin Trio | One Great Day... | HatOLOGY | 502
Side Effects
Bruce Ditmas Trio | Aeray Dust | Chiaroscuro | CR 195
Side Mouthin'
Roscoe Mitchell | Sound Songs | Delmark | DE 493(2)
Sideburns
John Abercrombie Quartet | Getting There | ECM | 1321(833494-2)
Sidekicks
Paul Bley | Synth Thesis | Postcards | POST 1001
Sideman
8 Bold Souls | Sideshow | Arabesque Recordings | AJ 0103
Sidewalk
Mike Dietz-Wolfgang Güttler-Henrik Walsdorff | Hart Und Ungerecht | L+R Records | CDLR 45061
Rob Van Den Broeck Trio | Heavy Duty | Timeless | SJP 220
Sidewalk Blues
Alex Welsh And His Band | Best Of British Jazz From The BBC Jazz Club Vol.4 | Upbeat Jazz | URCD 122
Jelly Roll Morton's Red Hot Peppers | Jelly Roll Morton-Doctor Jazz | RCA | CL 89808 SF
Doctor Jazz | Black & Blue | BLE 59.227 2
Birth Of The Hot | Bluebird | 63 66641-2
Sidewalk Stanley
Matthias Petzold Working Band | Elements | Indigo-Records | 1005 CD
Sidewalk Stories
The Sidewalks Of New York | Tin Pan Alley:The Sidewalks Of New York | Winter&Winter | 910038-2
Sidewalk Story:
Astral Project | Astral Project | Astral Project | no No.
Sidewalks Of Cuba
Woody Herman And His Orchestra | Jazz Live & Rare: Woody Herman 1945-1947 | Jazzline | ???
Sidewalks Of New York
Oliver Nelson And His Orchestra | Verve Jazz Masters 48:Oliver Nelson | Verve | 527654-2
Sideway Blues
Anfrew Hill Nonet | Passing Ships | Blue Note | 593871-2
Sideways
Chris Barber's Jazz And Blues Band | Sideways | Black Lion | 147009
Sideways-
Paul Bley Trio | Closer | ESP Disk | ESP 1021-2
Sidewinder
Bill Cosby All Stars | Bill Cosby-Hello,Friend:To Ennis With Love | Verve | 539171-2
Monty Alexander-Sly Dunbar-Robbie Shakespeare Group | Monty Meets Sly And Robbie | Telarc Digital | CD 83494
Sidewinder s In Paradise
Andrew Cyrille And Maono | Junction | IPS Records | 003
Sidney's Soliloquy
Klaus Treuheit Trio | Steinway Afternoon | clearaudio | 42016 CD
Sid's Delight
Clark Terry Sextet | Free And Oozy | Blue Moon | BMCD 3076
Sie Haben Nicht Hingehört(Floyd Westermann)
Das Pferd | Das Pferd | ITM Records | ITM 1416
Sie Schrieen:Lass Ihn Kreuzigen-
Perfcect Trouble | Perfect Trouble | Moers Music | 02070 CD
Sieben Tage, Sieben Nächte
Peter A. Schmid Duos | Duets,Dialogues & Duels | Creative Works Records | CW CD 1034
Sieben Wachteln
Christopher Dell D.R.A. | Future Of The Smallest Form | Jazz 4 Ever Records:Jazz Network | J4E 4754
Siebenunddreissig
Future Of The Smallest Form | Jazz 4 Ever Records:Jazz Network | J4E 4754
Siebenundvierzig
Aera | TÄrkis | Erlkönig | 148409
Siebzehn
Mal Waldron Sextet | Jazzbühne Berlin '79/'83 | Repertoire Records | REPCD 4918-WZ
Sieg Haille
Mal Waldron Trio | Black Glory | Enja | 2004
Siege
Silke Gonska-Frieder W.Bergner Group | Entdeckung Der Langsamkeit | Born&Bellmann | 970909 CD
Siegfried
Michael Cain-Ralph Alessi-Peter Epstein | Circa | ECM | 1622
Siegfried And Roy
Stan Kenton And His Orchestra | Kenton Plays Wagner | Creative World | ST 1024
Sience
Jens Winther And The WDR Big Band | The Escape | dacapo | DCCD 9437
Sience Fiction
John Wolf Brennan | Text, Context, Co-Text & Co-Co-Text | Creative Works Records | CW CD 1025-2
Sience Friction
Tony Purrone Trio | Electric Poetry | B&W Present | BW 028
Sience Friction II(Elephant And Castle)
Dinah Washington With The Rudy Martin Trio | The Complete Dinah Washington On Mercury Vol.1 | Mercury | 832444-2
Sienna
Lyle Mays Trio | Fictionary | Warner | 9362-47906-2
Fictionary | Geffen Records | GED 24521
Sienna: Welcome My Darling
Stanley Cowell | Waiting For The Moment | Galaxy | GXY 5104
Sierra Morena
JMOG | JMOG | Sackville | SKCD2-2031
Sierraflimmern-Föhn Stufe 3
Billy Cobham Group | Life & Times | Atlantic | ATL 50253
Siesta
Roberto Perera Group | Harp And Soul | Inak | 30362
Jimmie Lunceford And His Orchestra | Big Band Bounce & Boogie:Strictly Lunceford | Affinity | AFS 1003
Siesta For The Fiesta
Andrew Hill Quartet | Judgment! | Blue Note | 870079-6
Sig Ep
Niels-Henning Orsted-Pedersen Trio | The Eternal Traveller | Pablo | 2310910
Siga,Siga
Robert Norman In Different Groups | The Best Of Robert Norman(1941-1989) | Hot Club Records | HCRCD 085
Sighin' And Cryin'
Slim Gaillard Trio | Trio-Quartet-Orchestra | Jazz Anthology | 550282
Sight No More
Bud Revels Group | Survivors | Enja | ENJ-6066 2
Sightless Bird

TITELVERZEICHNIS

Radius | Sightseeing | Ear-Rational | ECD 1017

Sigma
Jeff 'Tain' Watts Quartet | Citizen Tain | CBS | CK 69551

Sigmund Stern Groove
Cal Tjader Quintet | Concerts In The Sun | Fantasy | FCD 9688-2
Concerts In The Sun | Fantasy | FCD 9688-2
San Francisco Moods | Original Jazz Classics | OJC 277(F 8017)

Sign Me Up
New York Voices | Hearts Of Fire | GRP | GRP 96532

Signal
Jimmy Raney Quintet | Early Getz | Prestige | P 24088
Stan Getz Quintet | Jazz At Storyville Vol.2 | Fresh Sound Records | FSR 630(Roost RLP 411)

Signal(alt.take)
Stan Getz-The Complete Roost Sessions | The Jazz Factory | JFCD 22839

Signals
Steve Beresford Orchestra | Signals For Tea | Avant | AVAN 039

Signe Lita
Jerry Bergonzi And Joachim Kühn | Signed By | Adda | ZZ 84104

Significant Deciclons
Oscar Peterson-Harry Edison Duo | Oscar Peterson & Harry Edison | Original Jazz Classics | OJCCD 738-2(2310741)

Signify
Count Basie And His Orchestra With Joe Turner & Eddie Cleanhead Vinson | Kansas City Shout | Pablo | 2310859-2

Signifying Monkey
Big Three Trio | Willie Dixon-The Big Three Trio | CBS | 467248-2

Signing Off
Ella Fitzgerald With The Lou Levy Quartet | Clap Hands,Here Comes Charlie! | Verve | 835646-2
Leonard Feather All Stars | Night Blooming | Mainstream | MD CDO 719

Signs On Lines
Michael Hornstein-Robert Di Gioia | Dry Red | Edition Collage | EC 486-2

S'il Vous Plait
Joe Pass-John Pisano | Joe Pass-John Pisano:Duets | Pablo | 2310959-2
Kid Thomas And His Algiers Stompers | Sonnets From Algiers' | American Music | AMCD-53
Miles Davis Nonet | The Real Birth Of The Cool | Bandstand | BDCD 1512

Sila Kale Bal
Bettina Born-Wolfram Born | Schattenspiel | Born&Bellmann | 993004 CD

Silder-
Anthony Braxton Trio | Silence/Time Zones | Black Lion | BLCD 760221

Silence
Charlie Haden Orchestra | The Ballad Of The Fallen | ECM | 1248(811546-2)
Charlie Haden Quartet | Silence | Soul Note | SN 1172
Charlie Haden Trio | The Montreal Tapes | Verve | 537670-2
Charlie Haden-Egberto Gismonti | In Montreal | ECM | 1746(543813-2)
Charlie Haden-Paul Motian Trio Feat.Geri Allen | Etudes | Soul Note | 121162-2
Contact Trio | Musik | Japo | 60036
Franck Avitabile Trio With Louis Petrucciani | In Tradition | Dreyfus Jazz Line | FDM 36594-2
Michael Mantler Group With The Danish Concert Radio Orchestra | Many Have No Speech | Watt | 19(835580-2)
Michael Sagmeister Quintet | Here And Now | Acoustic Music Records | 319.1146.2
Philippe Macé Group | Aventures | AH Records | PAM 969
Geri Allen Sextet | The Nurturer | Blue Note | 795139-2

Silence Comes In Waves
Laszlo Süle Band | Silence Fiction | AH Records | CD 90025

Silence Is The Question
New York Voices | What's Inside | GRP | GRP 97002

Silence So Loud
Nels Cline Trio | Silencer | Enja | ENJ-6098 2

Silenciosa
Joe Lovano-Greg Osby Quintet | Friendly Fire | Blue Note | 499125-2

Silenos
Greg Osby Quintet | Mindgames | JMT Edition | 919021-2

Silent Attitude
Marc Copland-Greg Osby | Round And Round | Nagel-Heyer | CD 2035
Marc Schmolling Trio | Nostalgia Soul Ship | Organic Music | ORGM 9731

Silent Blue
Matt Jazz Quintet | Sharp Blues | SPLASC(H) Records | H 109

Silent Dance-
John Tchicai Trio | Real Tchicai | Steeplechase | SCS 1075

Silent Dream
Christoph Spendel | Thoughts | L+R Records | CDLR 45092

Silent Feet
Thomas Karl Fuchs | Piano Meditation I | Edition Collage | EC 481-2

Silent For A While
Thomas Schiedel | All Alone | AH Records | AH 404001-13

Silent Lake
Dave Grusin Ensemble | Harlequin | GRP | GRP 95222

Silent Night
Christoph Mudrich Trio feat. Sir Henry | Christmas In Blue | Blue Concept | BCCD 93/03
Cleo Brown-Marian McPartland | Living In The Afterglow | Audiophile | ACD-216
Jim Galloway-Jay McShann Quartet | Jim & Jay's Christmas | Sackville | SKCD2-3054
Montreal Jubilation Gospel Choir | Jubilation VI 'Looking Back'-Special 20th Anniversary Compilation | Blues Beacon | BLU-1022 22
The Four Freshmen | Freshmas! | Ranwood | RCD 8239(875344)

Silent Night Holy Night
Erika Rojo & Tim Sund | Das Lied | Nabel Records:Jazz Network | CD 4684

Silent Noon
Billy Bang Quartet | Big Bang Theory | Justin Time | JUST 135-2

Silent Partner
Champion Jack Dupree Group | Jack Dupree-Jimmy Rushing-Muddy Waters | Laserlight | 17062
Meredith d´Ambrosia-Gene Bertoncini | Silent Passion | Sunnyside | SSC 1075 D

Silent Room-
Jan Schaffer Group | Electric Graffiti | VeraBra Records | CDVBR 2027-2

Silent Spring
Gary Burton Quintet With Eberhard Weber | Ring | ECM | 1051
Acoustic Guitars | Acoustic Guitars | Stunt Records | 18703

Silently Invisibly
Arrigo Cappelletti Trio | Reflections | SPLASC(H) Records | H 134

Silhuetten
Elliott Sharp Carbon | Sili/Contemp/Tation | Ear-Rational | ECD 1018

Silk
Nguyen Le Trio | Nguyen Le:3 Trios | ACT | 9245-2
The Rosenberg Trio With Frits Landesbergen | Gypsy Swing | Verve | 527806-2

Silk And Steel
Kenny Drew Trio | Dark Beauty | Steeplechase | SCS 1016

Silk Lake
Sonny Rollins Quintet | Vintage Sessions | Prestige | P 24096

Silk 'N' Soul
Richard Grossman Trio | Trio Live In Real Time | Nine Winds Records | NWCD 0134

Silks And Satins
Vic Lewis West Coast All Stars | Vic Lewis Presenting A Celebration Of Contemporary West Coast Jazz | Candid | CCD 79711/12

Silky
Directors | Directors | Jazz Haus Musik | JHM 0040 CD

Silky Landscape
Franco Ambrosetti Quintet | Light Breeze | Enja | ENJ-9331 2

Silli In The Sky
Light Breeze | Enja | ENJ-9331 2

Silli's Nest
Bengt Hallberg Quartet | Hallberg's Hot Accordion In The Foreground | Phontastic | NCD 7532

Sillsaltarvisan
Bill McHenry Quartet | Rest Stop | Fresh Sound Records | FSNT 033 CD

Silly
Impetus | Down To Earth | Plainisphare | PL 1267-5

Silly Samba
Lee Konitz-Harold Danko Duo | Wild As Springtime | G.F.M. Records | 8002

Silly Shuffle
Tony Scott Quintet Feat. Jan Akkerman | Meditation | Polydor | 2480661

Silver
Modern Jazz Quartet And Laurindo Almeida | Collaboration | Philips | 30JD-10093 PMS
Steve Kuhn | Ecstasy | ECM | 1058
Tom McKinley/Ed Schuller Group | Life Cycle | GM Recordings | GM 3001(807786)

Silver Bells
Jim Galloway-Jay McShann Quartet | Jim & Jay's Christmas | Sackville | SKCD2-3054

Silver Blues
Amstel Octet | Hazy Hugs | Limetree | MLP 198601

Silver City
Bob Scobey's Frisco Band | The Scobey Story Vol.2 | Good Time Jazz | GTCD 12033-2

Silver Fox
Ran Blake | Wende | Owl Records | 05

Silver Hollow
Jack DeJohnette Quartet | New Directions | ECM | 1128
Parallel Realities | Parallel Realities:Live... | Jazz Door | JD 1251/52

Silver Lake
Glen Velez Group | Assyrian Rose | CMP Records | CMP CD 42

Silver Temple
Buddy Rich And His Orchestra | Big Swing Face | Pacific Jazz | 837989-2

Silver Threads Among The Blues
Papa Bue's Viking Jazzband | The Golden Years Of Revival Jazz,Vol.7 | Storyville | STCD 5512

Silver Threads Among The Gold
Sammy Rimington Band | Sammy Rimington Plays The Clarinet Of George Lewis | SAM Records | SAM CD 003

Silver Treads Among My Soul
Jon Burr Quartet | In My Own Words | Cymekob | CYK 804-2

Silver Worth Gold-
Bob Berg Sextet | Back Roads | Denon Compact Disc | CY-79042

Silverbird Is Heading For The Sun
Louis Smith Quintet | Silvering | Steeplechase | SCCD 31336

Silvering
Roland Kirk Quartet | Rip Rig And Panic/Now Please Don't You Cry Beautiful Edith | EmArCy | 832164-2 PMS

Silver's Serenade
Horace Silver Quintet | Horace Silver Retrospective | Blue Note | 495576-2
Michal Urbaniak Quintet | Music For Violin & Jazz Quartet | JAM | 001 IMS

Silverware
Amanda Sedgwick Quintet | Reunion | Touché Music | TMcCD 021

Silvia
Johnny Hodges Orchestra | Johnny Hodges:The Complete 1937-1940 Small Group Sessions(Master Takes),Vol.1 | Blue Moon | BMCD 1019

Sim
Bireli Lagrene Group | A Tribute To Django Reinhardt | Jazzpoint | JP 1061 CD
Bireli Lagrene-Vic Juris | Bireli Lagrene 'Highlights' | Jazzpoint | JP 1027 CD
Vic Juris Quartet | For The Music | Jazzpoint | JP 1034 CD
Vic Juris Quintet | Bleeker Street | Muse | MR 5265
Peter O'Mara Quintet | Back Seat Driver | Enja | 9126-2

Simba
Serge Forté Trio | Vaina | Laika Records | LK 90-021

Simba Samba
Claude Williams With His Twin Pianos And Trio | Claude Williamson Mulls The Mulligan(Plays Gerry Mulligans Compositions) | Fresh Sound Records | FSR-CD 0054

Simbah
Gerry Mulligan Tentette | The Birth Of The Cool Vol.2 | Capitol | 798935-2

Simbora
Denny Christianson Big Band | Doomsday Machine | Justin Time | Just 8

Simona
Andy Middleton Group | Nomad's Notebook | Intuition Records | INT 3264-2

Simone
Bill Saxton Trio | Beneath The Surface | Nilva | NQ 3408 IMS
Jutta Hipp Quintet | Cool Dogs & Two Oranges | L+R Records | LR 41006
Roseanna With Band | Passion Dance | Telarc Digital | CD 83385

Simonpolskan
Bud Shank-Laurindo Almeida Quartet | Braziliance Vol.2 | Pacific Jazz | 796102-2

Simple
Bobo Stenson Trio | Serenity | ECM | 1740/41(543611-2)

Simple & Sweet
Swim Two Birds | No Regrets | Laika Records | 35101342

Simple & True
Artie Shaw And His Orchestra | The Uncollected:Artie Shaw And His Orchestra, Vol.1 | Hindsight | HSR 139

Simple Life
Nils Landgren First Unit And Guests | Nils Landgren-The First Unit | ACT | 9292-2
John Coltrane Quartet | Jazz Gallery:John Coltrane Vol.1 | RCA | 2119540-2

Simple Melody
Gebhard Ullmann Trio | Essencia | Between The Lines | btl 017(Efa 10187-2)
Holger Mantey | Calaufa | L+R Records | CDLR 45058

Simple Pleasures
Matthew Shipp-Joe Morris | Thesis | HatOLOGY | 506

Simple Song
Jaco Pastorius Trio | Live In New York City Volume Four | Big World | BW 1004

Simple Things
Jim Hall Group | Dialogues | Telarc Digital | CD 83369

Simple Thoughts
Mino Cinelu-Kenny Barron | Swamp Sally | Verve | 532268-2

Simple Waltz
George Robert Quartet With Clark Terry | Live At The Q-4 Rheinfelden | TCB Records | TCB 9080

Simplicidad
Shin-Ichi Fukuda | Guitar Legends:Homage To Great Popular Guitarists | Denon Compact Disc | CO-18048

Simplicity-
Bjarne Roupe Group | Passion Play | Stunt Records | 18801

Simply
Peter Brötzmann | Nothing To Say-A Suite Of Breathless Motion Dedicated To Oscar Wild | FMP | CD 73

Sims A-Plenty
Pork Pie | The Door Is Open | MPS | 68038

Simultanuos Images Of Queen Nofretete
Salvatore Tranchini Quintet feat. Jerry Bergonzi And Franco Ambrosetti | Radio Suite | Red Records | 123280-2

Sin Limite
Bajazzo | Caminos | Edition Collage | EC 485-2

Sin Pensar
Gonzalo Rubalcaba Trio | The Blessing | Blue Note | 797197-2

Sin Remedio, El Mar
Victor Mendoza Group | This Is Why | RAM Records | RMCD 4515

Sin Tiempo Y Sin Distancia
Cuarteto Las D'Aida Y Su Grupo | Soy La Mulata | L+R Records | CDLR 45059

Sinatra Speaks
Billy Bang Septet | Live At Carlos 1 | Soul Note | SN 1136

Since Feeling Is First
Uwe Kropinski & John Stowell | Picture In Black And White | Acoustic Music Records | 319.1134.2

Since I Fell For You
Big Joe Turner And His Orchestra | Kansas City Here I Come | Original Jazz Classics | OJCCD 743-2(2310904)
Buddy Johnson And His Orchestra | Buddy And Ella Johnson 1953-1964 | Bear Family Records | BCD 15479 DH
Wails | Official | 6010
Etta Jones With The Houston Person Quartet | My Buddy | HighNote Records | HCD 7026
Houston Person-Ron Carter | Now's The Time | Muse | MCD 5421
Jimmy Smith Trio | On The Sunny Side | Blue Note | LT 1092
Jimmy Witherspoon With Groove Holmes | Cry The Blues | Bulldog | BDL 1012
Kenny Dorham Quintet | But Beautiful | Milestone | M 47036
Mose Allison Trio | Mose Alife!/Wild Man On The Loose | Warner | 8122-75439-2
Nina Simone And Orchestra | Planet Jazz:Nina Simone | Planet Jazz | 2165372-2
Oscar Moore Quartet | Oscar Moore And Friends | Fresh Sound Records | FSR-CD 0202
Stanley Turrentine With The Three Sounds | Blue Hour | Blue Note | 524586-2
The Blue Note Years-The Best Of Stanley Turrentine | Blue Note | 793201-2
Vesna Skorija Band | Niceland | Satin Doll Productions | SDP 1037-1 CD
Vince Guaraldi Trio | Cast Your Fate To The Wind | Original Jazz Classics | OJCCD 437-2(F 8089)
Vince Jones With The Benny Green Quartet | One Day Spent | Intuition Records | INT 3087-2
One Day Spent | Intuition Records | INT 3087-8(CD-Single)
Luciano Federighi & Fabio's Fables | In A Blizzard Of Blue | SPLASC(H) Records | HP 17

Since I Fell For You-(alt.take)
Little Johnny Taylor With Band | The Galaxy Years | Ace Records | CDCHD 967

Since My Baby Gone
Monty Alexander Quartet | Friday Night | Limetree | MCD 0022

Since My Best Gal Turned Me Down
Bix Beiderbecke And His Gang | Riverboat Shuffle | Naxos Jazz | 8.120584 CD

Since We Met
Bill Evans | Eloquence | Fantasy | F 9618
Bill Evans Trio | Since We Met | Original Jazz Classics | OJC 622(F 9501)
The Complete Fantasy Recordings | Fantasy | 9FCD 1012-2
Lonnie Plaxico Orchestra | With All Your Heart | Muse | MCD 5525

Since You Asked
Singers Unlimited | A Capella | MPS | 815671-1
Big Maceo Merriweather | Big Maceo Vol.1 | Blues Classics | BC 28

Since You've Been Gone
Don Byas Quintet | Don Byas Featuring Mary Lou Williams Trio & Beryl Booker Trio | Vogue | 21610212

Sincerely
Art Blakey And The Jazz Messengers | A Night In Tunisia | Blue Note | 784049-2

Sincerely Diana
A Night In Tunisia | Blue Note | 784049-2

Sincerely Diana(alt.take)
Donald Harrison Quartet | Nouveau Swing | Impulse(MCA) | 951209-2

Sincerely Yours
Ari Brown Quartet | Ultimate Frontier | Delmark | DE 486

Sindengo Walzare
Stephan Froleyks | Fine Music With New Instruments | Jazz Haus Musik | JHM 0094 CD

Sine Nomine
Urs Leimgruber/John Wolf Brennan | M.A.P. | L+R Records | CDLR 45021

Sinfonia(BWV 29)
Swingle Singers | Jazz Sebastian Bach | Philips | 542552-2

Sinfonia(BWV 826)
Jacques Loussier Trio | Play Bach No.4 | Decca | 157893-2

Sinfonia, Cantata No.29 'Wir Danken Dir Gott wir Danken Dir'(BWV 29)
Elmore James Group | The Legend Of Elmore James | Anthology of the Blues | AB 5601

Sing
Les Brown And His Band Of Renown | Today | MPS | 68118

Sing A Pure Song
Charles Earland Sextet | Jazzin' With The Soul Brothers | Fantasy | FANCD 6086-2

Sing A Simple Song
Louie Bellson Big Band | The London Gig | Pablo | 2310880

Sing And Swim
Bob Crosby And His Orchestra | The Radio Years | London | HMG 5021 AN

Sing For Your Supper
Benny Goodman Trio | Benny Goodman:The King Of Swing | Musicmasters | 65130-2

Sing Me A Song
George Adams-Don Pullen Quartet | The Best Of Don Pullen:The Blue Note Years | Blue Note | 823513-2

Sing Me Not A Ballad
Jugend Jazzorchester Sachsen-Anhalt | Jugend Jazzorchester Sachsen-Anhalt Spielt Kurt Weill | Born&Bellmann | 972806 CD

Sing Me Softly Of The Blues
Carla Bley Band | Dinner Music | Watt | 6(825815-2)
Carla Bley-Steve Swallow | Go Together | Watt | 24(517673-2)
Gary Burton Quartet | Duster | RCA | 2125730-2
Joe Sachse | Ballade Für Jimi Metag | Born&Bellmann | 991503 CD
Karin Krog With The Archie Shepp Quartet | Karin Krog Jubilee-The Best Of 30 Years | Verve | 523716-2
Tony Purrone Trio | The Tonester | Steeplechase | SCCD 31495

Sing My Heart
Ella Fitzgerald With The Billy May Orchestra | The Harold Arlen Songbook | Verve | 817526-1 IMS

Sing My Heart(alt.take)
Chris Barber's Jazz Band | The Chris Barber Jubilee Album-Vol. 2 | Intercord | 157009

Sing On
Paul Barbarin And His New Orleans Jazz | Paul Barbarin And His New Orleans Jazz | Atlantic | 790977-2

Sing Sing Prison Blues
Anita O'Day With The Russ Garcia Orchestra | Sings The Winners | Verve | 2304255 IMS

Sing Sing Sing
Benny Goodman And His Orchestra | The Benny Goodman Story | Capitol | 833569-2
Planet Jazz:Jazz Greatest Hits | Planet Jazz | 2169648-2
Jazz Collection:Benny Goodman | Laserlight | 24396
Jazz Drumming Vol.2(1937-1938) | Fenn Music | FJD 2702
The Indispensable Benny Goodman Vol.3/4 | RCA | 2115520-2
Chad Rager Modern Big Band | In The Club...Live | Jazz Focus | JFCD 026
Hal Mooney Orchestra & The Gene Lowell Singers | Big Band And Voices | Bainbridge | BT 1008
Seamus Blake Quintet | The Bloomdaddies | Criss Cross | Criss 1110

Sing Sing Sing-
Benny Goodman And His Orchestra | Swing Swing Swing-Rare Recordings From The Yale University Music Library | Limelight | 844312-2

Sing Sing Sing(part 1)
The Harry James Years Vol.1 | Bluebird | 63 66155-2
Sing Sing Sing(part 2)
The Harry James Years Vol.1 | Bluebird | 63 66155-2
Sing Sing Sing(With A Swing)
Bud Shank And Trombones | Cool Fool | Fresh Sound Records | FSR CD 507
Sing Something Simple
June Christy And Her Orchestra | The Misty Miss Christy | Pathe | 1566141(Capitol T 725)
Sing Song
John Abercrombie Trio | Gateway 2 | ECM | 1105(847323-2)
John Abercrombie-John Scofield | Solar | Palo Alto | PA 8031
Sing Song Swing
Ella Fitzgerald And Her Orchestra | Live From The Roseland Ballroom New York | Jazz Anthology | JA 5228
Sing That
René Pretschner & Melo Mafali | The Piano Duo:El Latino | Green House Music | CD 1006
Sing The Song
John Handy Group | Handy Dandy Man | Inak | 8618
Sing With Strings - ...Sing With Strings
Rosemary Clooney With The Buddy Cole Trio | Swing Around Rosie | Coral | 589485-2
Sing You
Anita Boyer & Her Tomboyers | Nat King Cole Trio:The MacGregor Years 1941/45 | Music & Arts | CD 911
Sing You Sinners
Mel Tormé With The Shorty Rogers Orchestra | Comin' Home Baby!/Sings Sunday In New York | Warner | 8122-75438-2
Phillips' Louisville Jug Band | The Jug & Washboard Bands-Vol.2(1928-1930) | Story Of Blues | CD 3514-2
Singende Balalaika-
Greenfish | Perfume Light... | TipToe | TIP-888831 2
SingendesBlau
Oleg Plotnikov Trio | My Little Rolly | Timeless | CD SJP 435
Singin'
Nat King Cole With The Sunset All Stars | Music At Sunset | Jazz Colours | 874738-2
Singin' In The Rain
Al Cohn Quintet | Be Loose | Biograph | BLP 12063
Singin' The Blues
Frankie Trumbauer And His Orchestra | Riverboat Shuffle | Naxos Jazz | 8.120584 CD
Marian McPartland Trio feat. Chris Potter | In My Life | Concord | CCD 4561
Singin' The Blues-
Fletcher Henderson And His Connie's Inn Orchestra | Hocus Pocus | RCA | ND 90413(847143)
Singing In The Rain
Count Basie And His Orchestra | The Greatest | Verve | MV 2650 IMS
Singing Off
| Jazz Classics In Digital Stereo: Henry Red Allen 1929-1936 | CDS Records Ltd. | RPCD 610(CD 685)
Singing Red
Gil Goldstein Quartet | The Sands Of Time | Muse | MCD 5471
Singing Wood
Mikhail Alperin's Moscow Art Trio | Hamburg Concert | JA & RO | JARO 4201-2
Willis Jackson Sextet | Single Action | Muse | MCD 5179
Single Moon
Ella Fitzgerald With The Nelson Riddle Orchestra | Ella Fitzgerald Sings The Johnny Mercer Songbook | Verve | 539057-2
Single 'O
The Johnny Mercer Songbook | Verve | 823247-2 PMS
Single Solo And Group Dance
Bill Mays Trio | An Ellington Affair | Concord | CCD 4651
Sinn Isch D'r Dom... - ...Sinn Isch D'r Dom...
Peter Finger Und Gäste | InnenLeben | Acoustic Music Records | AMC 1019
Sinnen
Nina Simone Groups | Feeling Good-The Very Best Of Nina Simone | Mercury | 522747-2
Sinnerman
Nina Simone Quintet | Nina Simone-The 60s Vol.2:Mood Indigo | Mercury | 838544-2 PMS
Sinpunto Y Contracopa
Dave Liebman Group | Songs For My Daughter | Soul Note | 121295-2
Sinset And The Mocking Birds-
Titi Winterstein Quintet plus Guests | Live! | Boulevard | BLD 508 LP
Sinto Ela Chegar
Titi Winterstein Sextet | Djinee Tu Kowa Ziro | Boulevard | BLD 501 CD
Sinto Sempre Assim
Tete Montoliu | Tete Montoliu Interpreta A Serrat | Fresh Sound Records | FSR 4004(835319)
Sintra
New Art Saxophone Quartet | Songs And Dances | Enja | ENJ-9420 2
Siobeg Siomor-
George Coleman Quartet | Playing Changes | Ronnie Scott's Jazz House | JHCD 002
Sipho
Louisiana Sugar Babes | Planet Jazz:Jazz Trumpet | Planet Jazz | 2169654-2
'Sippi
Jazz Archives Vol.77:Jabbo Smith-The Complete 1929-1938 Sessions | EPM Musique | 158112
Sippin' At Bells
Chet Baker Quintet/NDR Big Band/Radio Orchestra Hannover | The Last Concert Vol.I+II | Enja | ENJ-6074 22
Chet Baker-Stan Getz Quintet | The Stockholm Concerts | Verve | 537555-2
George Russell Sextet | George Russell Sextet At The Five Spot | Verve | 112287-2
Kurt Rosenwinkel Quartet | Intuit | Criss Cross | Criss 1160
Miles Davis All Stars | The Savoy Recordings 2 | Savoy | 650108(881908)
Sonny Clark Quintet | Cool Struttin' | Blue Note | 495327-2
Cool Struttin' | Blue Note | 746513-2
Woody Shaw Quartet | In My Own Sweet Way | IN+OUT Records | 7003-2
Chet Baker-Stan Getz Quintet | The Stockholm Concerts | Verve | 537555-2
Sippin' At Bells(2)
Miles Davis All Stars | The Complete Savoy Studio Sessions | Savoy | 886421
Sipping The Past
Barry Altschul Quartet | Irina | Soul Note | SN 1065
Sir Duke
Les Brown And His Band Of Renown | Les Brown And His Band Of Renown | CDS Records Ltd. | CJCD 834
Sebastian Gramss Underkarl | Jazzscene | TCB Records | TCB 99102
Sir John
Gary Burton Trio | Jazz Special-The Vibe Man | RCA | CL 43237 AF
Johnny Hodges Orchestra | Triple Play | RCA | ND 90208(847147)
Sirabhorn
Dresch Quartet | Live In Cologne | West Wind | WW 0017
Sirba In Caruta
Bik Bent Braam | Howdy | Timeless | CD SJP 388
Siren
Walt Weiskopf Nonet | Siren | Criss Cross | Criss 1187
Siren Song
Bob Cooper With The Mike Wofford Trio | Bob Cooper Plays The Music Of Michel Legrand | Discovery | DS 822 IMS
Siri
The United Women's Orchestra | The Blue One | Jazz Haus Musik | JHM 0099 CD
Siringo Road
Olaf Tarenskeen | Decisions | Acoustic Music Records | 319.1144.2
Sirkle
Chuck Wayne Quartet | The Jazz Guitarist | Savoy | SV 0189(MG 12077)
Sister
Sonny Rollins Quintet | Falling In Love With Jazz | Milestone | M 9179
Sister Andrea
Salvatore Bonafede Trio | Nobody's Perfect | Penta Flowers | CDPIA 022
Sister Caroline
Wild Bill Moore Quintet | Bottom Groove | Milestone | MCD 47098-2
Jacky Terrasson Trio | Alive | Blue Note | 859651-2
Sister Cheryl
Steffen Kamper Trio | Delight | Dr.Jazz Records | 8612-2
Arthur Blythe Quintet & Guests | Elaborations | CBS | FC 38163
Sister Kate -> I Wish I Couls Shimmy Like My Sister Kate
Sister Of Arequipa
Ken McIntyre Quartet | Open Horizon | Steeplechase | SCCD 31049
Sister Sadie
Bill Cosby All Stars | Bill Cosby-Hello,Friend:To Ennis With Love | Verve | 539171-2
Dee Dee Bridgewater With Her Trio | Keeping Tradition | Verve | 519607-2
Eddie Jefferson And His Orchestra | The Jazz Singer | Inner City | IC 1016 IMS
Gil Evans Orchestra | Standards On Impulse! | Impulse(MCA) | IMP 12032
GRP All-Star Big Band | GRP 10th Anniversary | GRP | GRP 96722
Horace Silver Quintet | Blowin' The Blues Away | Blue Note | 495342-2
The Best Of Horace Silver | Blue Note | 791143-2
True Blue | Blue Note | 534032-2
Jan Lundgren Trio | Cooking! At The Jazz Bakery | Fresh Sound Records | FSR-CD 5019
Joe Pass With The NDR Big Band | NDR Big Band-Bravissimo | ACT | 9232-2
Joey DeFrancesco Group | Reboppin' | CBS | CK 48624
Larry Coryell-Michael Urbaniak Duo | The Larry Coryell-Michael Urbaniak Duo | Keytone | KYT 716
Manhattan Jazz Quintet | Funky Strut | Sweet Basil | 660.55.006
Rolf Kühn With The NDR Big Band | Big Band Connection:Rolf Kühn Special | Blue Flame | 40622(2132489-2)
Woody Herman And His Orchestra | Verve Jazz Masters 54:Woody Herman | Verve | 529903-2
Woody Herman-1963 | Philips | 589490-2
Hot Tracks For Cool Cats Vol.2 | Polydor | 816380-2
Sister Sadie-
Larry Coryell | Tributaries | Novus | NL 83072
Sister Salvation
Maceo Parker Group | Southern Exposure | Minor Music | 801033
Sister Sanctified
George Duke Group | I Love The Blues | MPS | 817488-1
Sister Wilson
Nat Adderley Sextet | In The Bag | Original Jazz Classics | OJCCD 648-2(JLP 975)
Irene Schweizer | Piano Solo Vol.2 | Intakt Records | CD 021
Sisyphos
Albert Mangelsdorff | Albert Mangelsdorff-Solo | MPS | 68287
Sit Down, You're Rockin' The Boat
Mel Tormé And His Trio | Night At The Concord Pavillion | Concord | CCD 4433
Sit Sofort
Eduardo M.Kohan Trio | Dies Irae | Hat Art | 3507
Sittin' And Drinkin'
Art Tatum | Art Tatum-The Complete Jazz Chronicle Solo Session | Storyville | STCD 8253
Sittin' And Rockin'
Hoagy Carmichael And His Orchestra | Hoagy Carmichael 1927-1939 | Timeless | CBC 1-011
Sittin' In My Dark Room
Louis Armstrong And His Orchestra | Louis Armstrong:A 100th Birthday Celebration | RCA | 2663694-2
Sittin' In The Dark
Louis Armstrong-The Complete RCA Victor Recordings | RCA | 2668682-2
Sittin' In The Sandtrap
Louis Armstrong And His All Stars With The Jack Pleis Orchestra | Ambassador Louis Armstrong Vol.18:Because Of You(1950-1953) | Ambassador | CLA 1918
Sittin' On The Dock Of The Bay - (Sittin' On) The Dock Of The Bay
Lirico | Sussurro | Jazz Haus Musik | JHM 0129 CD
Ron Ringwood's Crosscut Bluesband | Earth Tones | Organic Music | ORGM 9722
World Saxophone Quartet | Rhythm And Blues | Nonesuch | 7559-60864-2
Sittin' On The Top Of The World
Howlin' Wolf Band | Howlin' Wolf | Chess | 427016
Memphis Slim | Alone With My Friends | Original Blues Classics | OBCCD 581-2(Battle 6118)
Sitting Ducks
Lowell Fulsom Band | Tramp/Soul | Ace Records | CDCHD 339
Sitting In Limbo
Katie Webster | The Many Faces Of Katie Webster | Schubert Records | SCH- 103
Sitting In The Sun
Christian McBride Group | Gettin' To It | Verve | 523989-2
Sitting On A Cloud
Glen Gray And The Casa Loma Orchestra | The Radio Years: Glen Gray And The Casa Loma Orchestra 1943-46 | London | HM-A 5050 AN
Situations
Christine Tobin Band | Aililiu | Babel | BDV 9501
Sivad
Miles Davis Group | Another Bitches Brew | Jazz Door | JD 1284/85
Six Millions Dollars Song
Hank Jones | Maybeck Recital Hall Series Volume Sixteen | Concord | CCD 4502
Six And Eight
Elvin Jones Trio | The Big Beat | Milestone | MCD 47016-2
Six And Four
Oliver Nelson Quintet | Eric Dolphy:The Complete Prestige Recordings | Prestige | 9 PRCD-4418-2
Oscar Peterson Trio | En Concert Avec Europe 1 | Laserlight | 710443/48
Barrett Deems Septet | Deemus | Delmark | DE 492
Six Beauties On A Rooftop
Joe Wilder Quartet | Wilder' N' Wilder | Savoy | SV 0131(MG 12063)
Six Is Nine
Charlie Barnet And His Orchestra | Clap Hands,Here Comes Charlie! | Bluebird | ND 86273
Six Lessons From Madame La Zonga
Clarence Gatemouth Brown Band | The Blues Of Clarence 'Gatemouth Brown | Storyville | 4960563
Six Levels Below Olat Life
Yusef Lateef Orchestra | The Blue Yusef Lateef | Rhino | 8122-73717-2
Six Miles Next Door
Sidsel Endresen-Bugge Wesseltoft | Duplex Ride | ACT | 9000-2
Six Preludes:
Cassiber | The Beauty And The Beast | Riskant | 528-72410
Six To Four
Harry James And His New Jazz Band | Saturday Night Swing | Giants Of Jazz | GOJ 1016
Six Years
Joe Locke Quartet | Wire Walker | Steeplechase | SCCD 31332
Six-Four My Singer
Stan Getz Quartet | The Carnegie Hall Concert | Jazz Door | JD 1221
Sixteen
Thelonious Monk Sextet | More Genius Of Thelonious Monk | Blue Note | 300194(BNJ 61011)
Sixteen(alt.take)
More Genius Of Thelonious Monk | Blue Note | 300194(BNJ 61011)
Sixth (Celebration)-
Cedar Walton | Blues For Myself | Red Records | NS 205
Sixth Avenue Express
Humphrey Lyttelton And His Band | Beano Boogie | Calligraph | CLGCD 021
Sixth Sense
Vital Information | Ray Of Hope | VeraBra Records | CDVBR 2161-2
Dizzy Gillespie With Orchestra | Stonhenge/Carousel Suite | GM Recordings | GM 3014 CD(882949)
Sixty One
Klaus König Orchestra & Guests | The Song Of Songs:Oratorio For Two Solo Voices,Choir And Orchestra | Enja | ENJ-7057 2
Sixty Queens
Christoph Spendel-Michael Sagmeister | So Near So Far | L+R Records | LR 40024
Sixty-Five Faubourg
Earl Hines | Le Jazz En France Vol.15:Earl Hines Paris Session 1965 | Pathe | 1552611
Sixty-One Joys
Eberhard Blum | Sixty-Two Mesostic Re Marce Cunningham | Hat Art | CD 6095(2)
Sizzle
Thilo Wolf Trio With Randy Brecker,Chuck Loeb & New York Strings | A Swinging Hour In New York | Mons Records | MR 874801
Sjerze Djewuschki
Willem Breuker Kollektief With Strings And Choir | Psalm 122 | BVHAAST | CD 9803
Sjöraets Polska-Efter Olof Schyman
Per Gudmundson-Ale Möller-Lene Willemark | Frifot | ECM | 1690(557653-2)
Sjungar Lars-Polska-
Jimmy Witherspoon With The Robben Ford Quartet | Live:Jimmy Witherspoon & Robben Ford | ARG Jazz | 2133292-2
Skal Boyz
Tommy Flanagan Trio | The Complete 'Overseas' | DIW | DIW 305 CD
Skal Brother
Tommy Flanagan Trio In Stockholm 1957 | Dragon | DRLP 87
Skankaroony
Herbert Joos | The Philosophy Of The Fluegelhorn | Japo | 60004 IMS
Skater's Waltz
Roland Kirk-Jack McDuff Quartet | Pre-Rahsan | Prestige | P 24080
Skating
Pete Jolly Trio | Take The 'A' Train | Fresh Sound Records | FSR-CD 0306
Bill Evans-Jim Hall | Undercurrent | Blue Note | 538228-2
Skating In Central Park
Double Image | Open Hand | dmp Digital Music Productions | CD 503
Keith Ingham | Out Of The Past | Sackville | SKCD2-3047
Modern Jazz Quartet | European Concert | Atlantic | SD 2-603
Skating On Thin Ice
Michael Heupel | Stadtgarten Series Vol.2 | Jazz Haus Musik | JHM 1002 SER
Skeleton In The Closet
Bobby Hackett And His Orchestra | Commodore Classics-Bobby Hackett/Miff Mole | Commodore | 6.26171 AG
Skerpla
Ben Waltzer Trio | For Good | Fresh Sound Records | FSNT 013 CD
Sketch
Bill Dixon Sextet | Bill Dixon In Italy - Volume Two | Soul Note | SN 1011
Sketch No.1
Eric Dolphy Quartet | Out There | Original Jazz Classics | OJC20 023-2(NJ 8252)
Sketch Of Melba
Out There | New Jazz | NJSA 8252-6
Eric Dolphy:The Complete Prestige Recordings | Prestige | 9 PRCD-4418-2
Jay Jay Johnson Sextet | Clifford Brown:The Complete Blue Note And Pacific Recordings | Blue Note | 834195-2
Sketch(1)
Nick Brignola With Kenny Barron And Dave Holland | It's Time | Reservoir | RSR CD 123
Sketches
Joshua Redman Quartet | Blues For Pat | Jazz Door | JD 1282
Sketches Of Roses
John Hicks-David Murray | Sketches Of Tokyo | DIW | DIW 812 CD
Sketches(part 1-8)
The New York Composers Orchestra | First Program In Standard Time | New World Records | 80418-2
Ski Jumping Blues
Ellis Larkins Trio With Tony Middleton | Swingin' For Hamp | Concord | CJ 134
Skidoo
Paul Motian Quartet | Bil Evans | JMT Edition | 834445-2
Skies May Be Blue
James Blood Ulmer Group | Music Speaks Louder Than Words:James Blood Ulmer Plays The Music Of Ornette Coleman | DIW | DIW 910 CD
Skies Of Europe:
Teddy Stauffer Und Seine Original Teddies | Das Schönste Von Damals | Vagabond | 6.28039 DP
Skillet
Alan Silva Group | Alan Silva | ESP Disk | ESP 1091-2
Skin Deep
Duke Ellington And His Orchestra | Antibes Concert-Vol.2 | Verve | 2304065 IMS
Ella Fitzgerald And Duke Ellington:Cote D'Azure Concerts on Verve | Verve | 539033-2
Ella Fitzgerald And Duke Ellington:Cote D'Azure Concerts on Verve | Verve | 539033-2
Soul Call | Verve | 539785-2
Friction | Replicant Walk | Enemy | EMCD 109(03509)
Skinnie Minnie
Buddy DeFranco Trio | Do Nothing Till You Hear From Us! | Concord | CCD 4851
Skins
H.P.Salentin Group | It's Up To You | Mons Records | MR 874787
Skip It
Stuff Smith Quartet | Live At The Montmartre | Storyville | STCD 4142
Skip The Gutter
Louis Armstrong And His Hot Five | Jazz:The Essential Collection Vol.2 | IN+OUT Records | 78012-2
Louis Armstrong And His Savoy Ballroom Five | Louis Armstrong-The Hot Fives & Hot Sevens Vol.3 | CBS | 465189-2
Skippin'
James Moody Quartet | Sweet And Lovely | Novus | PD 83063
Skippy
Brad Mehldau Trio | Anything Goes | Warner | 9362-48608-2
Buell Neidlinger's String Jazz | Locomotive | Soul Note | 121161-2
Dave Liebman Trio | Monk's Mood | Double Time Records | DTRCD-154
Steve Lacy-Roswell Rudd Quartet | School Days | Hat Art | CD 6140
Thelonious Monk Sextet | Thelonious Monk:The Complete Blue Note Recordings | Blue Note | 830363-2
Skippy(alt.take)
More Genius Of Thelonious Monk | Blue Note | 300194(BNJ 61011)
Skiss
Cy Laurie's New Orleans Septet | The Golden Years Of Revival Jazz,Vol.6 | Storyville | STCD 5511
Skit Dat De Dat
Jim McNeely Quartet And The WDR Big Band | East Coast Blow Out | Lipstick Records | LIP 890072
Skokiaan
Chris Barber's Jazz Band | Chris Barber's Jazz Band | Ace Of Club | ACL 1163
Skokiaan(edited version without vocal)
Louis Armstrong And His All Stars/Orchestra | The Wonderful World Of Louis Armstrong | MCA | 2292-57202-2

TITELVERZEICHNIS

Skokiaan(part 1&2)
Louis Armstrong With Sy Oliver And His Orchestra | Louis Armstrong-My Greatest Songs | MCA | MCD 18347

Skokiaan(part 1)
Oscar Peterson Quintet | Skol | Original Jazz Classics | OJC20 496-2

Skol Blues
Mikhail Alperin's Moscow Art Trio | Hamburg Concert | JA & RO | JARO 4201-2

Skomorohi
Horace Parlan Quintet | On The Spur Of The Moment | Blue Note | 869178-0

Skookum Spook
Frank Morgan Sextet | Bird Calls 2 | Savoy | 650111(881911)

Skrik & Hyl
Jan Garbarek-Palle Danielsson | Works | ECM | 823266-2

Skrupptie Wupptie
Dave Ballou Quartet | Amongst Ourselves | Steeplechase | SCCD 31436

Skull And Nettlework
Al Haig Sextet | Early Getz | Prestige | P 24088

Skull Buster
Stan Getz:The Complete 1948-1952 Quintet Sessions(Master Takes) | Blue Moon | BMCD 1015

Skull Duggery
Dave Burrell-Beaver Harris Orchestra | In: Sanity | Black Saint | BSR 0006/7

Skur Leja
Jacob Young Quintet | Evening Falls | ECM | 1876(9811780)

Sky
David Jean-Baptiste Group | The Nature Suite | Laika Records | 35101632

Sky & Ocean
Cassandra Wilson Group | Traveling Miles | Blue Note | 854123-2

Sky And Sea(Blue In Green)
Bola Sete Trio | Tour De Force:The Bola Sete Trios | Fantasy | FCD 24766-2

Sky And Sea(Ceu E Mar)
Cassandra Wilson Group | Kind Of Blue:Blue Note Celebrate The Music Of Miles Davis | Blue Note | 534255-2
Nova Bossa Nove | Jazz Influence | Arkadia Jazz | 71241

Sky Blue
Larry Porter Trio | March Blues | Enja | 8092-2

Sky Dive
George Benson Group | George Benson In Concert-Carnegie Hall | CTI | ZK 44167

Sky High
Ramsey Lewis Group | Sky Islands | GRP | GRP 97452

Skycraper
Chris Connor With The Richard Wess Orchestra | Witchcraft | Atlantic | AMCY 1068

Skydance
Taj Mahal Group | Conjure | American Clave | AMCL 1006-2

Skygger
Masqualero | Re-Enter | ECM | 1437(847939-2)

Skykkevis Og Delt
Ahmad Jamal Trio | I Remember Duke,Hoagy & Strayhorn | Telarc Digital | CD 83339

Skylark
Art Blakey And The Jazz Messengers | Caravan | Original Jazz Classics | OJC20 038-2
Ben Waltzer Trio | For Good | Fresh Sound Records | FSNT 013 CD
Bennie Wallace Quartet | The Old Songs | audioquest Music | AQCD 1017
Bill Henderson And His Friends | Live At The Times | Discovery | DS 779 IMS
Cedar Walton Trio | Manhattan Afternoon | Criss Cross | Criss 1082
Christian Elsässer Trio | Venice | Organic Music | ORGM 9727
Clark Terry-Marian McPartland | Clark Terry:One On One | Chesky | JD 198
Dexter Gordon Quartet | American Classic | Discovery | 71009-2
Doug Raney Quartet | Back In New York | Steeplechase | SCCD 31409
Earl Hines | Four Jazz Giants:Earl Hines Plays Tributes To W.C.Handy,Hoagy Carmichael And Louis Armstrong | Solo Art | SACD-111/112
Ella Fitzgerald With The Nelson Riddle Orchestra | The Silver Collection: Ella Fitzgerald-The Songbooks | Verve | 823445-2 PMS
Ella Fitzgerald Sings The Johnny Mercer Songbook | Verve | 539057-2
The Johnny Mercer Songbook | Verve | 823247-2 PMS
Frank Morgan Quartet | Love,Lost & Found | Telarc Digital | CD 83374
Gene Ammons Quartet | The Gene Ammons Story: Gentle Jug | Prestige | P 24079
Glenn Miller And His Orchestra | Glenn Miller Forever | RCA | NL 89214 DP
Gust Williams Tsilis Quartet | Heritage | Ken Music | 660.56.018
Houston Person Quartet | In A Sentimental Mood | HighNote Records | HCD 7060
Jim Hall Group | Dialogues | Telarc Digital | CD 83369
Kenny Barron | Maybeck Recital Hall Series Volume Ten | Concord | CCD 4466
Lionel Hampton And His Orchestra | The Lionel Hampton Big Band | West Wind Orchestra Series | 2404 CD
Manfred Dierkes | It's About Time | Acoustic Music Records | 319.1176.2
Maxine Sullivan With The Doc Cheatham Quintet | We Just Couldn't Say Goodbye | Audiophile | ACD-128
New York Unit | Over The Rainbow | Paddle Wheel | KICJ 136
Paul Motian Quartet With Lee Konitz | Paul Motian On Broadway, Vol.3 | JMT Edition | 849157-2
Rusty Dedrick Quintet | Salute To Bunny | Fresh Sound Records | FSR 534(Counterpoint CPT 552)
Silvia Droste And Her Quartet | Audiophile Voicings | BELL Records | BLR 84004
Singers Unlimited With The Pat Williams Orchestra | Feeling Free | MPS | 68103
Sonny Rollins Quartet | Next Album | Original Jazz Classics | OJC 312 (M 9042)
Steve Houben-Michel Herr Quartet | Steve Houben & Michel Herr Meets Curtis Lundy & Kenny Washington | B.Sharp Records | CDS 094
The European Jazz Guitar Orchestra | The European Jazz Guitar Orchestra | Jardis Records | JRCD 9307
Tommy Smith Quartet | Standards | Blue Note | 796452-2
Walter Davis Trio | Scorpio Rising | Steeplechase | SCCD 31255

Skylark(alt.take)
Art Lande Trio | Skylight | ECM | 1208

Skylight
Bruce Forman Quartet | Pardon Me | Concord | CCD 4368

Skyline
Hans Koller Big Band | New York City | MPS | 68235
Zipflo Reinhardt Quintet | Oceana | Intercord | 160114

Skyliner
June Christy With The Shorty Rogers Orchestra | June Christy Big Band Special | Capitol | 498319-2
Swingle Singers | Back To Swing | Aves | 161530

Skyride
Joachim Kühn | Snow In The Desert | Atlantic | ATL 50718 Digital

Skyscape
Woody Herman And His Orchestra | Chubby Jackson-The Happy Monster:Small Groups 1944-1947 | Cool & Blue | C&B-CD 109

Skyward Bound
Steps Ahead | Steps Ahead | Elektra | 7559-60168-2
Terje Rypdal Group | Skywards | ECM | 1608(533768-2)

Skywards
Stephan Schmolck Quartet | Rites Of Passage | L+R Records | CDLR 45064

Slalom
Philippe Caillat Special Project | Melodic Travel | Laika Records | LK 689-012

Curtis Amy Group | Peace For Love | Fresh Sound Records | FSR CD 5004

Slamboat
Don Byas Quartet | Don Byas Complete American Small Group Recordings | Definitive Records | DRCD 11213

Slang
Maarten Altena Ensemble | Cities & Street | Hat Art | CD 6082

Slängpolskor
Bobby Naughton Unit | The Haunt | Otic | 1005

Slap Happy
Duke Ellington And His Orchestra | Duke Ellington's Masterpieces Vol.1: 1938-1940 | Black & Blue | BLE 59.233 2

Slap Shot
Bruno Tommaso Orchestra | Barga Jazz | SPLASC(H) Records | HP 06

Slapstick
Joshua Redman Quartet | Spirit Of The Moment:Live At The Village Vanguard | Warner | 9362-45923-2
When Granny Sleeps | Welcome | dacapo | DCCD 9447

Slapstick Slope
Count Basie And His Orchestra | Hall Of Fame | Verve | MV 2645 IMS

Slats
Joe Newman Octet | The Complete Joe Newman RCA-Victor Recordings(1955-1956):The Basie Days | RCA | 2122613-2

Slaughter On 10th Avenue
Earl Hines | Live At The New School-Vol. 2 | Chiaroscuro | CR 180

Slava-
Dollar Brand | African Sketch Book | Enja | 2026-2

Slavic Mood
Dorotha Trowbridge | St.Louis Girls(1929-1937) | Story Of Blues | CD 3536-2

Sledge
Jeff Richman Group | The Way In | MGI Records | MGR CD 1016

Sleep
Benny Carter And His Orchestra | The Uncollectet:Banny Carter-Live At The Trianon Ballroom | Hindsight | HSR 218
Milt Buckner Quartet | Green Onions | Black & Blue | BLE 59.087 2
The American Jazz Orchestra | Central City Sketches | Limelight | 820819-2 IMS
Tom Saunders' 'Wild Bill Davison Band' & Guests | Exactly Like You | Nagel-Heyer | CD 023
Tommy Dorsey And His Orchestra | The Indispensable Tommy Dorsey Vol.1/2 | RCA | 2126405-2
Joseph Robechaux And His New Orleans Boys | Joe Robichaux And His New Orleans Boys | Folklyric | 9032

Sleep Loved
Monty Sunshine's Jazz Band | Gotta Travel On | Timeless | CD TTD 570

Sleep Save And Warm(Version 1)
Tomasz Stanko-Terje Rypdal | Litania | ECM | 1636(537551-2)

Sleep Save And Warm(Version 2)
Tomasz Stanko Septet | Litania | ECM | 1636(537551-2)

Sleep Save And Warm(Version 3)
Maynard Ferguson With The Birdland Dreamband | The Birdland Dream Band Vol.2 | Fresh Sound Records | 58057 CD(RCA)

Sleep Tight
Charlie Ventura Quintet | High On An Open Mike | Fresh Sound Records | FSR-CD 314

Sleep Till Noon
The New Charlie Ventura In Hi-Fi | Harlequin | HQ 2009(Baton BL 1202) IMS

Sleep Warm
Sidney Catlett Quartet | Commodore Classics In Swing | Commodore | 9031-72723-2

Sleeper Car
Georgia Kelly/Peter Kent/Anne Pinsker | Winter Classics | Global Pacific Records | 660.52.020

Sleeping Bee
Concord All Stars | Festival Time | Concord | CJ 117
Richard Wyands Trio | The Arrival | DIW | DIW 611 CD
Trumpet Spectacular | The Progressive Records All Star Trumpet Spectacular | Progressive | PRO 7015 IMS

Sleeping In
Guy Barker Sextet | Timeswing | Verve | 533029-2

Sleeping Susan
Gene Ammons-Sonny Stitt Quartet | Soul Summit | Prestige | PCD 24118-2(P 7234/7275)

Sleepwalker
Barry Altschul Quartet | For Stu | Soul Note | SN 1015

Sleepwalker's Serenade
Count Basie And His Orchestra | The Complete Atomic Basie | Roulette | 828635-2

Sleepwalker's Serenade(alt.take)
| Sonic Fiction | Hat Art | CD 6043

Sleepy Boys
Joe Lovano Quintet | Village Rhythm | Soul Note | 121182-2

Sleepy Lagoon
Joe Venuti Quartet | Hooray For Joe | Chiaroscuro | CR 153

Sleepy Time Gal
Eddy Howard And His Orchestra | The Uncollected:Eddy Howard, Vol.2 | Hindsight | HSR 156

Sleepytime Gal
Oscar Peterson Trio | The Complete Young Oscar Peterson(1945-1949) | RCA | 2122612-2
Singers Unlimited With The Robert Farnon Orchestra | Sentimental Journey | MPS | 68102

Sleigh Ride
Mark Shane's X-Mas Allstars | What Would Santa Say? | Nagel-Heyer | CD 055
Mel Tormé And His Trio With The Cincinnati Sinfonietta | Christmas Songs- | Telarc Digital | CD 83315

Sleigh Ride In July
Jackie And Roy | Full Circle | Contemporary | CCD 14046-2
New England Ragtime Ensemble | The Art Of The Rag | GM Recordings | GM 3018 CD(882950)

Slender Thread
Louis Armstrong And His Orchestra | Louis Armstrong Radio Days | Moon Records | MCD 056-2

Slick Chick
Jimmy Rodgers Blues Band | Sloppy Drunk | Black & Blue | BLE 59.544 2

Slick Stud & Sweet Thang
Peter Bolte-Marcio Doctor | Zeitraum | Jazz Haus Musik | JHM 0113 CD

Slick Willie
Barry Altschul Trio | Somewhere Else | Moers Music | 01064

Slickaphonics-In Concert Part 3&4:
Chris Cheek Sextet | A Girl Named Joe | Fresh Sound Records | FSNT 032 CD

Slide
The RH Factor feat. Reuben Hoch | Live In New York | L+R Records | CDLR 45074

Slide By Slide
Miles Davis Quintet | Miles Davis Quintet 1965-1968 | CBS | C6K 67398

Slide Car
Miles Davis Quintet 1965-1968 | CBS | C6K 67398
Miles Davis Quintet 1965-1968 | CBS | C6K 67398

Slide Car(incomplete)
Albion Jazz Band | They're All Nice Tunes | Stomp Off Records | CD 1249

Slide Hamp Slide
Lionel Hampton Orchestra | Vibebrations | Giants Of Jazz | GOJ 1014

Slide's Mambo
Curtis Fuller-Slide Hampton Quintet | Two Bones | Blue Note | GXK 8166

Sliding Horns
Buddy Johnson And His Orchestra | Go Ahead & Rock Rock Rock | Official | 6011

Slieve Russell
Deborah Henson-Conant Group | Deborah Henson-Conant:Best Of Instrumental Music | Laika Records | 35101322

Grant Green With Orchestra | The Final Comedown(Soundtrack) | Blue Note | 581678-2

Slight Fear And Terror
The Final Comedown(Soundtrack) | Blue Note | 581678-2
Chet Baker Quintet | Chet Baker & Crew | Pacific Jazz | 582671-2

Slightly Above Moderate
Shelly Manne Orchestra | Cool California | Savoy | WL 70511(2)(SJL 2254) DP

Slightly Monkish
Jimmy Smith Trio | Groovin' At Smalls' Paradise | Blue Note | 499777-2
Lyle Murphy And His Orchestra | New Orbits In Sound | Fresh Sound Records | FSR 505(GNP 33)

Slightly Oliver
Grant Geissman Quintet | Good Stuff | Concord | CJ 62

Slim Jim
The Prestige All Stars | All Day Long | Prestige | SMJ 6604

Slim Pickings
Slim And Slam | Slim And Slam Vol.3 | Tax | m- 8044

Slim's Cee
Slim Gaillard Trio | Big Band Bounce And Boogie:Rockin' In Rhythm-Piano Portraits Vol.2 | Affinity | AFS 1028

Slin
Zoot Sims Quartet | Zoot Sims:Quartet&Sextet | Vogue | 21511522

Slings And Arrows
Cees Slinger Quartet | Sling Shot! | Timeless | CD SJP 225

Slinky
Guido Manusardi | Contrasti | Penta Flowers | CDPIA 012

Slip Away
American Folk Blues Festival | American Folk Blues Festival 1964 | L+R Records | CDLR 42024

Sliphorn Jive
Glenn Miller And His Orchestra | The Original Sounds Of The Swing Era Vol. 3 | RCA | 26.28131 DP
The Swinging Mr. Miller | RCA | 2115522-2

Slipped Disc
Mel Tormé With The Mike Renzi Trio | An Evening With Mel Tormé | Concord | CCD 4736

Slippery
Monty Alexander 7 | Jamento | Pablo | 2310826
Roy Smeck | Roy Smeck Plays Hawaiian Guitar, Banjo, Ukelele And Guitar | Yazoo | YAZ 1052

Slippery When Wet
Chick Corea Quartet | Three Quartets | Stretch Records | SCD 9002-2

Slippery,Hippery,Flippery
Roland Kirk Quartet | Rip Rig And Panic/Now Please Don't You Cry Beautiful Edith | EmArCy | 832164-2 PMS

Slippin' And Slidin'
Sidney Bechet And His New Orleans Feetwarmers | Sidney Bechet 1932-1943: The Bluebird Sessions | Bluebird | ND 90317
Thomas Brendgens-Mönkemeyer | Beauty | Jardis Records | JRCD 20138
Yusef Lateef Quintet | The Roots Of Acid Jazz | Impulse(MCA) | IMP 12042
Live At Pep's | Impulse(MCA) | GRP 11342

Slippin' Into Darkness
Craig Handy Quartet | Split Second Timing | Arabesque Recordings | AJ 0101

Slippin' On A Star
Paul Bley | Solo Piano | Steeplechase | SCCD 31236

Slipping
The Leaders | Slipping And Sliding | Sound Hills | SSCD 8054

Slipping Away
Niko Schäuble Quintet | On The Other Hand | Naxos Jazz | 86011-2

Slits
Milt Jackson Quintet | In The Beginning | Original Jazz Classics | OJCCD 1771-2(G 204)

Slittin' Sam(The Shaychet Man)
Richard 'Groove' Holmes Sextet | Blues All Day Long | Muse | MCD 5358

Slop
Charles Mingus Orchestra | Nostalgia In Times Square/The Immortal 1959 Sessions | CBS | 88337
Kenny Garrett Trio | Stars And Stripes/Live | Jazz Door | JD 1259

Slop Around
Donald Byrd Orchestra | Black Byrd | Blue Note | 784466-2

Slop Jar Blues
Stefan Bauer-Claudio Puntin-Marcio Doctor | Lingo | Jazz Haus Musik | JHM 0116 CD

Slope Stomp
Eddie Playboy Taylor & The Blueshounds | Ready For Eddie | Big Bear | 146407

Slovakian Folk Song
Nicolas Simion Quartet | Oriental Gates:Live In Vienna | Tutu Records | 888212-2*
Nicolas Simion Group | Balkan Jazz | Intuition Records | INT 3339-2

Slovakian Peasant Song
Liam Noble | Close Your Eyes | FMR | FMR CD 25

Slow Blues
Duke Ellington Trio | The Pianist | Original Jazz Classics | OJCCD 717-2(F 9462)

Slow Blues No.2(take 2)
Big Bill Broonzy | Last Sessions-Vol.3 | Verve | 817779-1 IMS

Slow Boat
Armand Gordon & Son Jazz Clan | Jazz Pure | Jazz Pure Collection | AU 31618 CD

Slow Boat To China
Bing Crosby And Rosemarie Clooney With The Billy May Orchestra | Fancy Meeting You Here | RCA | 2663859-2
Bob Sands Quartet | JumpSTART | Fresh Sound Records | FSNT 042 CD
Bruce Forman Quartet | Coast To Coast | Candid | CRS 1026 IMS
Dee Dee Bridgewater With Her Trio | Dear Ella | Verve | 539102-2
Dutch Swing College Band | Souvenirs From Holland, Vol. 3 | DSC Production | PA 005 (801062)
ITS Jazzband | Welcome To Dr. Jazz | Dr.Jazz Records | 8600-2
Mocambo Jam Session | The Historic Mocambo Sessions '54-Vol.2 | Polydor | MP 2491 IMS
Paramount Jazz Band | The Paramount Jazz Band | Timeless | CD TTD 596
Prowizorka Jazz Band | Prowizorka Jazz Band | Timeless | CD TTD 558
Stan Getz Quartet | Soul Eyes | Concord | CCD 4783
Warne Marsh Quintet With Art Pepper | Jazz Of Two Cities | Fresh Sound Records | FSR-CD 342
Bing Crosby And Rosemarie Clooney With The Billy May Orchestra | Fancy Meeting You Here | RCA | 2663859-2

Slow Boat To China-
Charlie Parker Quintet | Bird Eyes-Last Unissued Vol.14 | Philology | W 844.2

Slow Brook-
Barney Kessel-Herb Ellis Quartet | Great Guitars | Concord | CCD 6004

Slow Burn
Steve Coleman And Metrics | A Tale Of 3 Cities,The EP | Novus | 2124747-2
Count Basie And His Orchestra | King Of Swing | Verve | 837433-2

Slow But Shure
Coun Basie And His Orchestra | Jazz Live & Rare:Count Basie & His Orchestra Live 1954 | Jazzline | ???

Slow But Sure
Jimmy McGriff Orchestra | Swingin' The Blues-Jumpin' The Blues | Laserlight | 24654
Benny Carter Quintet With Nancy Marano | Benny Carter Songbook Vol.2 | Musicmasters | 65155-2

Slow Charleston
Andy Sheppard-Steve Lodder Group | Moving Image | Verve | 533875-2

Slow Dance
John Coltrane Quartet | John Coltrane | Prestige | P 24003
John Coltrane With The Red Garland Trio | John Coltrane-The Prestige Recordings | Prestige | 16 PCD 4405-2

Stanley Clarke Group | Modern Man | CBS | 468220-2
Fred Astaire With The Oscar Peterson Sextet | The Astaire Story | Verve | 835649-2 PMS

Slow Dark
Milt Jackson Quartet | Jazz At The Philharmonic:The Montreux Collection | Pablo | PACD 5306-2

Slow Death
Highlights Of The Montreux Jazz Festival 1975 | Pablo | 2625707
Lucky Thompson Quartet | Lucky Meets Tommy | Fresh Sound Records | FSR-CD 0199

Slow Down
Clarence Gatemouth Brown Quartet | Cold Storage | Black & Blue | BLE 59.096 2
Louis Jordan And His Tympany Five | Louis Jordan-Let The Good Times Roll: The Complete Decca Recordings 1938-1954 | Bear Family Records | BCD 15557 IH
Michael Sagmeister Quintet | Here And Now | Acoustic Music Records | 319.1146.2
Nat King Cole Trio | Hit That Jive Jack | MCA | MCD 42350

Slow Down Baby
You Cindy Lou | Confessin' The Blues | Affinity | AFF 66

Slow Down John
Jimmy Smith Quintet | Root Down | Verve | 559805-2

Slow Down Sagg
Cow Cow Davenport | Boogie Woogie | Laserlight | 24321

Slow Drag
Donald Byrd Quintet | Slow Drag | Blue Note | 535560-2
Essence Of Funk | Essence Of Funk | Hip Bop | HIBD 8007
King Curtis Band | King Curtis-Blow Man Blow | Bear Family Records | BCD 15670 CI
Oscar Peterson All Stars | Oscar Peterson+Harry Edison+Eddie 'Cleanhead' Vinson's | Pablo | 2310927-2

Slow Freight
Glenn Miller And His Orchestra | The Glenn Miller Story Vol.4 | RCA | NL 89223 AG
Ray Bryant | Inimitable | Jazz Connaisseur | JCCD 9430-2
Alone At Montreux | 32 Jazz | 32128

Slow Hot Wind
Steve Eliovson-Collin Walcott | Dawn Dance | ECM | 1198

Slow Jazz
Steve Coleman And Metrics | The Way Of The Cipher | Novus | 2131690-2

Slow Lane
Steve Coleman's Music Live In Paris | Novus | 2131691-2

Slow Mood
Andy Narell Group | Slow Motion | HipPocket | 9971815-2

Slow Motion
Charly Antolini Group | Countdown | BELL Records | BLR 84067
Dudek-Van Den Broek-Haurand | Pulque | Konnex Records | KCD 5055
Family Of Percussion | Message To The Enemies Of Time | Nagara | MIX 1010-N

Slow Motion Blues
Lester Young Quartet | Lester Swings | Verve | 833554-1

Slow Orbit
Michael Mantler Quintet | Live | Watt | 18

Slow Orchestra Piece No.3(Prisonnieres)
Live | Watt | 18

Slow Orchestra Piece No.6
Live | Watt | 18

Slow Orchestra Piece No.8(A L'abattoir)
Arnett Cobb Quartet | Party Time | Original Jazz Classics | OJC 219(P 7165)

Slow River
Jean Goldkette And His Orchestra | The Indispensable Bix Beiderbecke(1924-1930) | RCA | ND 89572
Clarence Williams And His Bottomland Orchestra | Clarence Williams Vol.2(1927) | Village(Jazz Archive) | VILCD 022-2

Slow Scene
Antje Uhle Trio | Majazztic Steps | Mons Records | MR 874824

Slow Storm
David Moss | My Favorite Things | Intakt Records | CD 022

Slow Train Breakdown
Avishai Cohen Group | Devotion | Stretch Records | SCD 9021-2

Slow Waltz
Louis Jordan And His Tympany Five | Rock 'N Roll Call | Bluebird | 63 66145-2

Slowly
Shelly Manne Quartet | Shelly Manne 2-3-4 | Impulse(MCA) | GRP 11492

Slowmotion
Scetches | Different Places | VeraBra Records | CDVBR 2102-2

Slowtrack
John Coltrane Trio | The Last Trane | Original Jazz Classics | OJC 394(P 7378)

Slowtrane
John Coltrane-The Prestige Recordings | Prestige | 16 PCD 4405-2
Donald Harrison Sextet | Free To Be | Impulse(MCA) | 951283-2

Slowvisor
Steve Coleman And Metrics | The Way Of The Cipher | Novus | 2131690-2

S-Ludes
Steve Coleman's Music Live In Paris | Novus | 2131691-2

Slumming On Park Avenue
Ella Fitzgerald With Paul Weston And His Orchestra | The Complete Ella Fitzgerald Song Books of Harold Arlen, Irving Berlin, Duke Ellington, George & Ira Gershwin, Jerome Kern, Johnny Mercer, Cole Porter And Rogers & Hart | Verve | 519832-2

Sly
Jamaaladeen Tacuma Group | Dreamscape | DIW | DIW 904 CD

Smack Dab In The Middle
Count Basie And His Orchestra | Count Basie At Newport | Verve | 9861761
Count On The Coast Vol.2 | Phontastic | NCD 7575
One O'Clock Jump | Verve | 559806-2
Live In Basel 1956 | Jazz Helvet | JH 05

Smack Up
Harold Land Quintet | Groove Yard | Original Jazz Classics | OJCCD 162-2

Small Blue Opus
Kip Hanrahan Group | A Fre Short Notes From The End Run | American Clave | AMCL 1011 EP

Small Drops Of Happiness
Hal Galper-Jeff Johnson | Maybeck Duets | Philology | W 139.2

Small Feet
Die Elefanten | Wasserwüste | Nabel Records:Jazz Network | CD 4634

Small Fish Big Fish
Bruce Gertz Quintet | Third Eye | RAM Records | RMCD 4509

Small Fry
George Melly With John Chilton's Feetwarmers | Melly Sings Hoagy | Ronnie Scott's Jazz House | NSPL 18557
Junior Mance | Jubilation | Sackville | SKCD2-2046

Small Hands
Braff/Barnes Quartet | Salutes Rodgers And Hart | Concord | CCD 6007

Small Picture No.1
Christian Wallumrod Ensemble | Sofienberg Variations | ECM | 1809(017067-2)

Small Picture No.2
Sofienberg Variations | ECM | 1809(017067-2)

Small Picture No.3
Sofienberg Variations | ECM | 1809(017067-2)

Small Picture No.3,5
Mulgrew Miller Trio | With Our Own Eyes | Novus | 4163171-2

Small Talk
Buddy Johnson And His Orchestra | Buddy And Ella Johnson 1953-1964 | Bear Family Records | BCD 15479 DH

Small Taste
Go Ahead & Rock Rock Rock | Official | 6011

Small Town Boy
Louis Jordan And His Tympany Five | Louis Jordan Vol.2-Knock Me Out | Swingtime(Contact) | ST 1012

Small Window Room
John Abercrombie-John Scofield | Solar | Palo Alto | PA 8031

Small World
Mark Murphy And His Septet | I'll Close My Eyes | Muse | MCD 5436
Pearl Bailey With Orchestra | Come On Let's Play With Pearlie Mae | Roulette | CDP 793274-2

Small World-
Michael Feinstein With Jule Styne | Michael Feinstein Sings The Jule Styne Songbook | Nonesuch | 7559-79274-2

Small's Minor
Lars Gullin Quartet | Lars Gullin 1951/52 Vol.5:First Walk | Dragon | DRCD 380

Smart Aleck
Lionel Hampton And His Sextet | Lionel Hampton-Historical Recording Sessions 1939-1941 | RCA | PM 42417

Smashed
Irene Schweizer/Andrew Cyrille | Irene Schweizer-Andrew Cyrille | Intakt Records | CD 008

Smashing Thirds
Fats Waller | Planet Jazz:Fats Waller | Planet Jazz | 2152058-2
Fats Waller-The Joint Is Jumpin' | RCA | ND 86288(874182)
Joe Turner | Another Epoch-Stride Piano | Pablo | 2310763

Smatter
Thierry Péala Group | Inner Traces:A Kenny Wheeler Songbook | Naive | 226102

Smells Like Teen Spirit
The Bad Plus | These Are The Vistas | CBS | 510666-2
The Bad Plus | Fresh Sound Records | FSNT 107 CD
New York Jazz Quartet | Blues For Sarka | Enja | 3025-2

Smile
Benny Carter Quartet | Take The 'A' Train | Fresh Sound Records | FSR-CD 0306
Bireli Lagrene Trio | Live In Marciac | Dreyfus Jazz Line | FDM 36567-2
Buddy Greco Quartet | Route 66-A Personal Tribute To Nat King Cole | Celebrity | CYCD 71901
Dave McKenna Quartet | No More Ouzo For Puzo | Concord | CCD 4365
Jackie McLean Quartet | Live At Montmartre | Steeplechase | SCCD 31001
Jay Leonhart-Joe Beck | There's Gonna Be Trouble | Sunnyside | SSC 1006(952110)
John Swana Quintet | Tug Of War | Criss Cross | Criss 1163
Ken McIntyre-Thierry Bruneau 5tet feat. Richard Davis | Tribute | Serene Records | SER 02
Matt Renzi-Jimmy Weinstein Quartet | Matt Renzi-Jimmy Weinstein Quartet | Fresh Sound Records | FSNT 045 CD
Maximilian Geller Quartet feat. Melanie Bong | Smile | Edition Collage | EC 461-2
Vocal Moments | Take Twelve On CD | TT 008-2
McCoy Tyner Quartet | Prelude And Sonata | Milestone | MCD 9244-2
Michael Karn Quintet | In Focus | Criss Cross | Criss 1191
Peter Herbolzheimer Rhythm Combination & Brass | Smile | Koala Records | CD P 17
Terumasa Hino Quartet | Unforgettable | Blue Note | 781191-2
Toots Thielemans-Kenny Werner Duo | Toots Thielemans & Kenny Werner | EmArCy | 014722-2
Ruby Braff Trio | Bravura Eloquence | Concord | CCD 4423

Smile At Darkness
Billy Cotton And His Band | Sing A New Song | Saville Records | SVL 160 IMS

Smile Of The Beyond
Sunnyland Slim Band | The Ralph Bass Sessions Vol.5 | Red Lightnin' | RL 0057

Smile On You
Freddy Martin And His Orchestra | The Uncollected:Freddy Martin | Hindsight | HSR 151

Smiles
Benny Goodman Quartet | Avalon-The Small Band Vol.2 (1937-1939) | Bluebird | ND 82273
Boyd Senter And His Senterpedes | Boyd Senter:Jazzologist Supreme | Timeless | CBC 1-032
Coleman Hawkins With The Ramblers | The Hawk In Holland | Ace Of Club | ACL 1247
Gambit Jazzmen With Tim Laughlin | King Of The Mardi Gras | Lake | LACD 54
Manfred Schoof/Rainer Brünninghaus | Shadows & Smiles | Wergo | WER 80007-50
Oscar Peterson Trio | The Complete Young Oscar Peterson(1945-1949) | RCA | 2122612-2
Masters Of Jazz Vol.7 | RCA | NL 89721 DP
Papa Bue's Viking Jazzband | A Song Was Born | BELL Records | BLR 84012
Stan Getz Quartet | Stan Getz Highlights | Verve | 847430-2
Stan Getz:East Of The Sun-The West Coast Sessions | Verve | 531935-2
Wrobel-Roberscheuten-Hopkins Jam Session | Jammin' At The IAJRC Convention Hamburg 1999 | Nagel-Heyer | CD 066
The Paragon Ragtime Orchestra | That Demon Rag | Dorian Discovery | DIS 80107

Smiles(alt.take)
Stan Getz Quartet | Award Winner | Verve | 543320-2

Smiles(false start)
Steve Williamson Sextet | Rhyme Time-That Fuss Was Us! | Verve | 511235-2

Smilin'
Don Grusin Group | Native Land | GRP | GRP 97192

Smilin' Jones
Bill Frisell Trio | Bill Frisell With Dave Holnad And Elvin Jones | Nonesuch | 7559-79624-2
Ged Hone's New Orleans Boys | Throwing Stones At The Sun | Lake | LACD 28

Smiling Faces
Incognito | Positivity | Talkin' Loud | 518260-2

Smiling Lingala
Pili-Pili | Pili-Pili | JA & RO | JARO 4141-2
Shinichi Kato-Masahiko Sato | Duet | Nagel-Heyer | CD 2017

Smiling Sunlight
Trevor Richards New Orleans Trio | The Trevor Richards New Orleans Trio | Stomp Off Records | CD 1222

Smith Walk
Louis Smith Quintet | Smithville | Blue Note | BLP 1594

Smithy Street,Stepney(Clavinova)
McCoy Tyner Septet | Expansions | Blue Note | BST 84338

Smog Eyes
Warne Marsh Quintet | Intuition | Capitol | 852771-2

Smoke
Louisiana Red Group | Louisiana Red | The Rising Sun Collection | RSC 0006

Smoke Gets In Your Eyes
Archie Shepp Quartet | Black Ballad | Timeless | CD SJP 386
Art Tatum | Art Tatum-The Complete Pablo Solo Masterpieces | Pablo | 7 PACD 4404-2
The Art Tatum Solo Masterpieces | Pablo | 2625703
Bucky Pizzarelli | Love Songs | Stash Records | ST 213 IMS
Cannonball Adderley And His Orchestra | African Waltz | Original Jazz Classics | OJC 258(RLP 9377)
Clifford Brown With Strings | Brownie-The Complete EmArCy Recordings Of Clifford Brown | EmArCy | 838306-2
Coleman Hawkins Quartet | Good Old Broadway | Prestige | 0902114(Moodsville MV 23)
Danny Moss Quartet | Weaver Of Dreams | Nagel-Heyer | CD 017
David Matthews Trio With Strings | Jazz Ballads With Strings | Sweet Basil | 660.55.012
Don Byas Quartet | New York 1945 | Jazz Anthology | JA 5106
Eartha Kitt With The Joachim Kühn Quartet | Standards/Live | ITM Records | ITM 1484
Freddie Brocksieper Und Seine Solisten | Freddie's Boogie Blues | Bear Family Records | BCD 16388 AH
Freddy Cole With Band | Merry-Go-Round | Telarc Digital | CD 83493
Gene Quill With The Hank Jones Quartet | Rhythm Plus One | Fresh Sound Records | LSP 15597(Epic LN 3297)
Hans Ulrik Sextet | Jazz And Mambo | Stunt Records | STUCD 19818
John Lewis Trio | Improvised Meditations & Excursions | Atlantic | AMCY 1104
Kurt Elling Group With Guests | Live In Chicago | Blue Note | 522211-2
Loren Schoenberg And His Jazz Orchestra | Just A-Settin' And A-Rockin' | Musicmasters | 5039-2
Mark Soskin Quartet | Overjoyed | Jazz City | 660.53.020
Nat King Cole Trio | Vocal Classics & Instrumental Classics | Capitol | 300014(TOCJ 6128)
Red Rodney Quintet | Prestige First Sessions, Vol.3 | Prestige | PCD 24116-2
Stephane Grappelli Quartet | Planet Jazz:Stephane Grappelli | RCA | 2165366-2
Teddy Wilson | Teddy Wilson In Tokyo | Sackville | 2005
The Steve Davis Project | Quality Of Silence | dmp Digital Music Productions | CD 522
Thelonious Monk Quintet | MONK | Original Jazz Classics | OJCCD 016-2
The Jazz Giants Play Jerome Kern:Yesterdays | Prestige | PCD 24202-2
Thelonious Monk:The Complete Prestige Recordings | Prestige | 3 PRCD 4428-2
Thilo Kreitmeier & Group | Soul Call | Organic Music | ORGM 9711
Thomas Clausen Trio | She Touched Me | M.A Music | A 628-2
Tommy Dorsey And His Orchestra | The Indispensable Tommy Dorsey Vol.2/4(1937.1938) | RCA | 2126406-2

Smoke Gets In Your Eyes-
Duke Jordan Trio | When You're Smiling | Steeplechase | SCCD 37023/24
Joe Albany | Live In Paris | Fresh Sound Records | FSCD 1010
Charlie Parker Quintet | Bird's Eyes-Last Unissued Vol.2+3 | Philology | W 12/15.2

Smoke House
Benny Goodman And His Orchestra | Wrappin' It Up-The Harry James Years Part 2 | Bluebird | 63 66549-2
Jaco Pastorius Trio | Heavy'n Jazz | Jazzpoint | JP 1036 CD

Smoke On The Water
Jaco Pastorius Heavy'n Jazz & Stuttgart Aria | Jazzpoint | JP 1058 CD

Smoke On The Water-
Bob Wilber Quartet | A Man And His Music | J&M Records | J&MCD 503

Smoke Stack
Johnny Griffin Septet | A Blowing Session | Blue Note | 0677191
A Blowing Session | Blue Note | 0677191

Smoke Stack(alt.take)
International Commission For The Prevention Of Musical Border Control,The | The International Commission For The Prevention Of Musical Border Control | VeraBra Records | CDVBR 2093-2

Smoke The Carribbean
The Catholics | Simple | Laika Records | 35100802

Smoked Oysters
Jelly Roll Morton's Red Hot Peppers | RCA Victor 80th Anniversary Vol.1:1917-1929 | RCA | 2668777-2

Smokehouse Blues
The Jelly Roll Morton Centennial-His Complete Victor Recordings | Bluebird | ND 82361
Doctor Jazz | Black & Blue | BLE 59.227 2
Lightnin' Hopkins | Smokes Like Lighning | Original Blues Classics | OBCCD 551(BV 1070)

Smokestack Lightnin'
Louisiana Red Group | Louisiana Red | The Rising Sun Collection | RSC 0006
The Rockets | Out Of The Blue | L+R Records | CDLR 42077

Smokestack Shuffle
Billy Usselton Sextet | His First Album | Fresh Sound Records | KL 1051(Kapp)

Smokey Embrace
Ray Brown All Stars(The Be Bop Boys) | The Dizzy Gillespie Story | Savoy | SV 0177(MG 12110)

Smokey Mokes
The Royal Garden Ramblers | Dixieland Jubilee-Vol. 3 | Intercord | 155013

Smokey The Bear
James Rivers Groups | The Best Of New Orleans Rhythm & Blues Vol.3 | Mardi Gras Records | MG 9009

Smokin'
Mal Waldron Sextet | Sweet Love Bitter(Original Soundtrack) | Impulse(MCA) | IMP 12952

Smoky Mokes
Jerry Granelli Sextet | A Song I Thought I Heard Buddy Sing | ITM-Pacific | ITMP 970066

Smooch
Miles Davis Quartet | Welcome To Jazz: Miles Davis Vol.2 | Koch Records | 321 975 D1
Steve Lacy-Mal Waldron | Communiqué | Soul Note | 121298-2

Smooth Attitudes
Lars Gullin Group | Made In Sweden Vol.2: 24.3.1951-12.12.1952 | Magnetic Records | MRCD 113

Smooth Cha Cha
Ray Crawford Sextet | Smooth Groove | Candid | CCD 79028

Smooth Groove
Adonis Rose Quintet | The Unity | Criss Cross | Criss 1173

Smooth One
Mel Tormé With The Mike Renzi Trio | An Evening With Mel Tormé | Concord | CCD 4736

Smooth Sailing
Arnett Cobb-Tiny Grimes Quintet | Live In Paris 1974 | France's Concert | FCD 133
Edmond Hall's All Star Quintet | Edmond Hall Profoundly Blue | Blue Note | 821260-2
Ella Fitzgerald With Bill Doggett's Orchestra | Ella:The Legendary American Decca Recordings | GRP | GRP 46482
JATP All Stars | JATP In Tokyo | Pablo | 2620104-2
Jay McShann Quartet | The Man From Muskogee | Sackville | SKCD2-3005

Snafu
Albert Burbank Jazzband | New Orleans Tarditional Jazz Legends:Albert Burbank/Raymond Burke | Mardi Gras Records | MG 9005

Snag It
Bunk Johnson And His New Orleans Band | Victor Jazz History Vol.1:New Orleans & Dixieland | RCA | 2128555-2
Grand Dominion Jazz Band | Half And Half | Stomp Off Records | CD 3989
Louis Armstrong And His All Stars | Satchmo-A Musical Autobiography Vol.1 | MCA | 2-4173

Snagglepuss
Costa & Cataldo Music Project | Picture Number One | SPLASC(H) Records | H 141

Snake-
Ronald Shannon Jackson And The Decoding Society | Decode Yourself | Island | ILPS 9827(804685)

Snake Crawl
The Sea Ensemble | We Move Together | ESP Disk | ESP 3018-2

Snake Dancing
Jelly Jaw Short | St. Louis Town 1927-1932 | Yazoo | YAZ 1003

Snake Eyes-
The Harlem Footwarmers | The Complete Duke Ellington-Vol. 2 | CBS | CBS 68275

Snake Oil
Joseph Berardi-Kira Vollman | Happy Wretched Family | Victo | CD 033

TITELVERZEICHNIS

Snake Rag
King Oliver's Creole Jazz Band | King Oliver-Louis Armstrong | Milestone | M 47017
King Oliver's Creole Jazzband-The Complete Set | Retrieval | RTR 79007
Snake Soup
Jason Moean Group | Soundtrack To Human Motion | Blue Note | 497431-2
Snakin' The Grass
Peggy Lee With Lou Levy's Orchestra | Pass Me By/Big Spender | Capitol | 535210-2
Snakin' Up On You
Neighbours | Accents | MRC | 066-32854
Snap Crackle
Roy Haynes Quartet | Out Of The Afternoon | Impulse(MCA) | 951180-2
Alvin Queen Trio | Glidin' And Stridin' | Nilva | NQ 3403 IMS
Snapped Cap
Hank Mobley Sextet | The Flip | Blue Note | 593872-2
Snappin' Out
James Morrison Quartet | Tempo Jazz Edition Vol.2-Playin' Now | Polydor | 847903-2
Snapshot
Dusko Goykovich-Gianni Basso Quintet | Live At Birdland Neuburg | Birdland | BN 004
Snare Rattle
Trevor Coleman Group | Kiwi Love | Fiala Music | JFJ 90005
Snaring A Yotte
Gutbucket | Dry Humping The American Dream | Enja | ENJ-9466 2
Snarling Wrath Of Angry Gods
Albert Mangelsdorff Quartet | Live In Berlin | FMP | 0390
Sneakin'
Ron Holloway Group | Slanted | Milestone | MCD 9219-2
Sneakin' Around
Helen Humes And Her All Stars | Sneakin´ Around | Black & Blue | BLE 233083
Sneakin' In The Back
New On The Corner | Left Handed | Jazz 4 Ever Records:Jazz Network | J4E 4758
Sneakin' Out
The Brecker Brothers | The Becker Bros | RCA | 2122103-2
Sneakin' Up Behind You
Derrick James & Wesley 'G' Quintet | Two Sides To Every Story | Jardis Records | JRCD 20137
Sneaking In The Backdoor
Dianne Reeves With Orchestra | For Every Heart | Palo Alto | TB 203
Sneaky Pete
Little Brother Montgomery Trio | Urban Blues | Fantasy | F 24717
Snibor
Duke Ellington And His Orchestra | In The Sixties | RCA | PD 89565
Snide Remarks
Klaus König Orchestra | Reviews | Enja | ENJ-9061 2
Sniffing Attitudes
Christoph Haberer | Mir Was Dir Was | Jazz Haus Musik | JHM 15
Snigglin' The Blues
Theo Jörgensmann Quartet | Snijbloemen | HatOLOGY | 539
Snipp Snapp Snute
Jan Garbarek-Nana Vasconcelos | Works | ECM | 823266-2
Sno' Peas
Jesse Van Ruller Trio | Trio | EmArCy | 017513-2
Phil Markowitz Trio | Sno' Peas | Ken Music | 660.56.010
Claudio Fasoli Quartet | Lido | Soul Note | SN 1071
Snoop
Bud Shank With The Keith Greko Trio | Last Train Outta Flagstaff | Concept | VL 4 IMS
Snoopy's Search
Billy Cobham Group | Spectrum | Atlantic | 7567-81428-2
Bob Enevoldsen Quintet | The Complete Nocturne Recordings:Jazz In Hollywood Series Vol.1 | Fresh Sound Records | NR 3CD-101
Snootie Little Cutie
Jazz In Hollywood:Harry Babasin/Bob Enevoldsen | Original Jazz Classics | OJCCD 1888-2(Nocturne NLP3/NLP-6)
Snooze
Delta Rhythm Boys | Harlem Roots-Jazz On Film:Rhythm In Harmony | Storyville | SLP 6002
Snorkelling Red Sea
Uri Caine | Solitaire | Winter&Winter | 910075-2
Snort
Ronny Cuber Septet | Pin Point | Electric Bird | K 28P 6415
Snow
Eduardo Niebla-Antonio Forcione Group | Poema | Jazzpoint | JP 1035 CD
Joachim Kühn | Wandlungen-Transformations | CMP Records | CMP CD 29
George Winston | December | Windham Hill | 34 11025-2
Snow Blues
Gary Peacock | December Poems | ECM | 1119
Snow Dance
David Benoit Group | Urban Daydreams | GRP | GRP 95872
Snow In March
Joachim Kühn | Snow In The Desert | Atlantic | ATL 50718 Digital
Snow Waltz
Rob McConnell Trio | Trio Sketches | Concord | CCD 4591
Snow...Melting
Carla White And Her Trio | Orient Express | Milestone | M 9147
Snowbound
The Rippingtons | Curves Ahead | GRP | GRP 96512
Snowfall
Singers Unlimited | Four Of Us | MPS | 68106
Snowfall-
Claude Thornhill And His Orchestra | The Uncollected: Claude Thornhill | Hindsight | HSR 108
Snowman
Coryell/Catherine | Splendid | Elektra | ELK K 52086
Snuggled On Your Shoulder
Marlene And Her Quartet | Every Breath I Take | Savoy | SV 0233(MV 12058)
Snygg Olle-
Betty Carter And Her Trio | The Audience With Betty Carter | Bet-Car | MK 1003
So
Henri Chaix Trio | Jumpin' Punkins | Sackville | SKCD2-2020
So Allright
Don 'Sugar Cane' Harris Quartet | Fiddler On The Rock | MPS | 68028
So Alt Wie Nina
Art Farmer With Orchestra | Gentle Eyes | Mainstream | MD CDO 716
So Beats My Heart For You
Art Tatum | The Tatum Solo Masterpieces Vol.7 | Pablo | 2310792
Johnny Richards And His Orchestra | Wide Range | Creative World | ST 1052
So Blue
The Four Brothers | Together Again! | RCA | 2179623-2
Earl Hines | Earl Hines Piano Solos's | Laserlight | 15790
So Danco Samba(I Only Dance The Samba)
Antonio Carlos Jobim With The Claus Ogerman Orchestra | The Composer Of 'Desafinado' Plays | Verve | 521431-2
Baden Powell | Live In Hamburg | Acoustic Music Records | 319.1037.2
Ella Fitzgerald With The Jimmy Jones Trio | Ella Fitzgerald And Duke Ellington:Cote D'Azure Concerts on Verve | Verve | 539033-2
Ella Fitzgerald And Duke Ellington:Cote D'Azure Concerts on Verve | Verve | 539033-2
Getz-Gilberto Quintet | Getz/Gilberto | Polydor | 521414-2
Getz/Gilberto:The Girl From Ipanema | CTI Records | PDCTI 1105-2
Larry Goldings Quartet With Joshua Redman | Caminhos Cruzados | Novus | 4163184-2
Peter Fessler Group | Eastside Moments | Minor Music | 801078
Sadao Watanabe Sextet | Bossa Nova Concert | Denon Compact Disc | DC-8556
Stan Getz Quintet Feat. Astrud Gilberto | Getz/Gilberto | Verve | 589595-2 SACD
Stan Getz-Luiz Bonfa Orchestra | Verve Jazz Masters 13:Antonio Carlos Jobim | Verve | 516409-2
Jazz Samba Encore! | Verve | 823613-2
Jazz Samba Encore! | CTI Records | PDCTI 1125-2
Heiner Goebbels-Alfred Harth Duo | Hommage/Vier F uste FÄr Hans Eisler | FMP | SAJ 08
So Do I
Gogi Grant With The Dennis Farnon Orchestra | Welcome To My Heart | Fresh Sound Records | ND 42126
So Do It
Wes Montgomery Quintet | Wes Montgomery-The Complete Riverside Recordings | Riverside | 12 RCD 4408-2
Wes Montgomery-The Complete Riverside Recordings | Riverside | 12 RCD 4408-2
So Do It(alt.take)
Quincy Jones And His Orchestra | Big Band Bossa Nova | Verve | 557913-2
So E Tarde Me Pardoa(Forgive Me If I'm Late)
Artie Shaw And His Orchestra | Artie Shaw And His Orchestra 1949 | Limelight | 820817-2 IMS
So Easy
Dexter Gordon Quintet | Master Takes-The Savoy Recordings | Savoy | WL 70814 SF
So Far
Michael Mantler Group | Songs And One Symphony | ECM | 1721
So Far-
Benny Bailey Quartet | Islands | Enja | ENJ-2082 2
So Far So Good
Jimmy Rowles Trio | The Complete Nocturne Recordings:Jazz In Hollywood Series Vol.1 | Fresh Sound Records | NR 3CD-101
Jazz Indeed | Under Water | Traumton Records | 2415-2
So Far So Near
Marilyn Crispell Trio | Story Teller | ECM | 1847(0381192)
Piirpauke | The Wild East | JA & RO | JARO 4128-2
So Few OfUs
Astrud Gilberto With Antonio Carlos Jobim And The Marty Paich Orchestra | The Astrud Gilberto Album | Verve | 823009-1
So Good
Bea Booze With The Sammy Price Trio | Sammy Price Vol.1-Singing With Sam | Swingtime(Contact) | BT 2002
Buddy Johnson And His Orchestra | Walkin' | Official | 6008
Clyde Bernhardt And His Kansas City Buddies | Clyde Bernhardt:The Complete Recordings Vol.1 (1945-1948) | Blue Moon | BMCD 6016
So Gracefully
Marc Cary Quintet | Cary On! | Enja | ENJ-9023 2
So Gracefully(radio version)
Gary Peacock Trio | Shift In The Wind | ECM | 1165
So Green
Paul Bley | Solo Piano | Steeplechase | SCCD 31236
So Hard It Hurts
Paul Bley Trio | Ballads | ECM | 1010
So I Better
Etta Jones With The Houston Person Band | Sugar | Muse | MCD 5379
So I Write
Andrew Hill Trio | So In Love | Fresh Sound Records | FSR 653(Warwick W 2002)
So In Love
Bennie Wallace Quartet | Bennie Wallace | audioquest Music | AQCD 1051
Dick Wellstood | Stride Piano | MRC | 066-32859
Ella Fitzgerald With The Buddy Bregman Orchestra | Ella Fitzgerald Sings The Cole Porter Songbook Vol.2 | Verve | 821990-2
Hampton Hawes Trio | Hampton Hawes Trio Vol.1 | Original Jazz Classics | OJC20 316-2(C 3505)
Harold Land Quintet | Eastward Ho! | Original Jazz Classics | OJCCD 493-2
John Tank Quintet | So In Love | TCB Records | TCB 95602
Marc Copland Trio | Softly... | Savoy | CY 18076
Masabumi 'Poo' Kikuchi Trio | Tethered Moon | Paddle Wheel | KICJ 93
Peggy Lee With Jack Marshall's Music | Blue Valentines | Blue Note | 781331-2
Randy Sandke Quintet | The Chase | Concord | CCD 4642
So Ist Es
Brocksi-Quartett | Globetrotter | Bear Family Records | BCD 15912 AH
So Ist Es...(Det Var Det)
Chris Cheek Quintet | Vine | Fresh Sound Records | FSNT 086 CD
So It Seems
Monty Alexander Orchestra | Stir It Up-The Music Of Bob Marley | Telarc Digital | CD 83469
So Little Time
Scott Hamilton Quartet | Apples And Oranges | Concord | CJ 165
So Lonely
Ramblin' Thomas | Country Bottleneck Guitar Classics | Yazoo | YAZ 1026
So Long
Gil Evans Orchestra | Blues In Orbit | Enja | ENJ-3069 2
Joe Beck Quartet | The Journey | dmp Digital Music Productions | CD 481
Zoot Sims Quartet | Suddenly It's Spring | Original Jazz Classics | OJCCD 742-2(2310898)
June Christy With The Johnny Guarnieri Quintet | June Christy And The Johnny Guarnieri Quintet (1949) | Jazz Unlimited | JUCD 2084
So Long-
Marc Cohen Quartet | My Foolish Heart | Jazz City | 660.53.014
So Long Broadway
Louis Armstrong And His All Stars | Jazz Special-Louis Armstrong:Mr.Music | RCA | NL 45333 AG
So Long Eric
Charles Mingus Sextet | Eric Dolphy Birthday Celebration | Fantasy | FANCD 6085-2
Town Hall Concert | America | AM 6140
Jack Walrath And The Masters Of Supense | Out Of The Tradition | Muse | MCD 5403
So Long For Now
Eddy Howard And His Orchestra | The Uncollected: Eddy Howard | Hindsight | HSR 119
So Long Jim
John Lindberg/Marty Ehrlich Duo | Unison | Cecma | 1006
So Long,Big Time
Michael Kneihs Quintet | Quintessence | Mons Records | MR 874313
So Many Stars
Jackie And Roy | Star Sounds | Concord | CJ 115
Norbert Gottschalk-Frank Haunschild | The Art Of The Duo:Favorite Songs | Mons Records | MR 874813
Singers Unlimited With The Pat Williams Orchestra | Feeling Free | MPS | 68103
Eden Atwood Group | A Night In The Life | Concord | CCD 4730
So May It Secretly Begin
Elmore James Group | The Legend Of Elmore James | Anthology of the Blues | AB 5601
So Mild The Wind,So Meek The Water
Phil Haynes Trio | Live Insurgency-Set 1 | Soul Note | 121302-2
So Much 2 Say
Take 6 | So Much To Say | Reprise | 7599-25892-2
Roslyn Burrough And Her Group | Love Is Here | Sunnyside | SSC 1009(952097)
So Near
Ella Fitzgerald With The Nelson Riddle Orchestra | Dream Dancing | Original Jazz Classics | OJCCD 1072-2(2310814)
So Near And Yet So Far
Fred Astaire With The Oscar Peterson Sextet | The Astaire Story | Verve | 835649-2 PMS
So Near So Far
Larry Willis Trio | Serenade | Sound Hills | SSCD 8063
Peter Materna Quartet | Full Moon Party | Village | VILCD 1021-2
Dade | In The Shade | Big World | BW 2001
So Nice
Paul Moer Trio | Paul Moer Trio Plays The Music Of Elmo Hope | Fresh Sound Records | FSR-CD 5008
So Nice(Summer Samba)
Bud Shank And The Sax Section | Bud Shank And The Sax Section | Pacific Jazz | LN 10091
Marcos Valle With Orchestra | Samba '68 | Verve | 559516-2
Ralph Lalama & His Manhattan All Stars | Feelin' And Dealin' | Criss Cross | Criss 1046
So Oder So
Uwe Kropinski | So Oder So | ITM Records | 0025
So Oder So Ist Das Leben-
Ana Caram Group | Blue Bossa | Chesky | JD 219
So Rare
Ella Fitzgerald With Frank De Vol And His Orchestra | Like Someone In Love | Verve | 511524-2
George Shearing Trio | So Rare | Savoy | 650141(882497)
Joe Pass-Jimmy Rowles Duo | Joe Pass:A Man And His Guitar | Original Jazz Classics | OJCCD 8806-2
Mose Allison Trio | High Jinks! The Mose Allison Trilogy | CBS | J3K 64275
So Rühr' Ich Um Mit Meinem Säbel
Alte Leidenschaften | Sketches Of Pain | L+R Records | CDLR 45042
So So
Allan Holdsworth/Gordon Beck | With A Heart In My Song | JMS | 044-1
So Sorry Please
Bud Powell Trio | The Best Of Bud Powell On Verve | Verve | 523392-2
Bud Powell:Complete 1947-1951 Blue Note,Verve & Roost Recordings | The Jazz Factory | JFCD 22837
Red Garland Trio | Bright And Breezy | Original Jazz Classics | OJC 265(JLP 948)
So Sorry To Leave You
Last Of The Hipmen | Last Of The Hipmen | Jazzline | 11126
So Tender
Lynne Arriale Trio | Inspiration | TCB Records | TCB 22102
Vic Juris Quartet | Moonscape | Steeplechase | SCCD 31402
So This Is Love?
Paul Weeden Quintet | Clear Sight | Timeless | JC 11012
So Tired
Art Blakey And The Jazz Messengers | Lee Morgan More Birdland Sessions | Fresh Sound Records | FSCD 1029
A Night In Tunisia | Blue Note | 784049-2
Bobby Timmons Orchestra | Quartet And Orchestra | Milestone | MCD 47091-2
Bobby Timmons Trio | Moanin' | Milestone | M 47031
Chartbusters | Chartbusters! Vol.1 | NYC-Records | NYC 6017-2
Sam Jones Sextet | The Soul Society | Original Jazz Classics | OJCCD 1789-2(RLP 1172)
So Tired,So Lonely Too
Baden Powell Quartet | En Concert Avec Europe 1 | Laserlight | 710703/04
So We'll Go No More A'Roving
Bill Evans Trio | The Jazz Giants Play Miles Davis:Milestones | Prestige | PCD 24225-2
So What
Blue In Green | Milestone | MCD 9185-2
Bill Evans Trio With Jeremy Steig | The Complete Bill Evans On Verve | Verve | 527953-2
What's New | Enoch's Music | 57271053
Cal Collins Trio | Cal Collins In San Francisco | Concord | CJ 71
Centrifugal Funk | Centrifugal Funk | Legato | 652508
Dexter Gordon Quartet | Stable Mable | Steeplechase | SCS 1040
Dwayne Dolphin Quintet | Portrait Of Adrian | Minor Music | 801042
Eddie Jefferson And His Band | Eddie Jefferson:Vocalese | 32 Jazz | 32123
Eddie Louiss-Michel Petrucciani | Conférence De Presse | Dreyfus Jazz Line | FDM 36568-2
Frank Minion With The Bill Evans Trio | The Soft Land Of Make Believe | Fresh Sound Records | FSR 2013(Bethlehem BCP 6052)
Gerry Mulligan With Chubby Jackson's Orchestra | Ezz-Thetic | Original Jazz Classics | OJCCD 1726-2(P 7827)
J.J.Johnson And His Orchestra | J.J.! | RCA | 2125727-2
Joe Diorio/Robben Ford Quartet | Minor Elegance | MGI Records | MGR CD 1012
Johnny Lytle Orchestra | Good Vibes | Muse | MR 5271
Miles Davis Quintet | Miles Davis At Carnegie Hall | CBS | CK 65027
Miles Davis-Heard 'Round The World | CBS | 88626
Miles Davis At Plugged Nickel, Vol. 1/2 | CBS | CBS C 2 38266
The Complete Copenhagen Concert 1964 | Magnetic Records | MRCD 117
Free Trade Hall Vol.2 | Magnetic Records | MRCD 103
Miles Davis In Stockholm Complete | Dragon | DRCD 228
Miles Davis Sextet | The Miles Davis Selection | CBS | 465699-2
Miles Davis With Gil Evans & His Orchestra | Greatest Hits | CBS | CK 65418
Niels Landgren Funk Unit | Live In Stockholm | ACT | 9223-2
Patrick Karlhuber Group | So What | Edition Collage | EC 480-2
Wallace Roney Quintet | Endless Miles:A Tribute To Miles Davis | N2K | 43082
So What-
Jaki Byard And The Apollo Stompers | Phantasies | Soul Note | 121075-2
So What Could Be New
The Herdsmen | The Herdsmen Play Paris | Original Jazz Classics | OJC 116(F 3201)
So Wird's Nie Wieder Sein
Dave Brubeck Quartet | Late Night Brubeck | Telarc Digital | CD 83345
So Would I
Vic Lewis West Coast All Stars | Shake Down The Stars | Candid | CCD 79526
So You Don't
Hal Kemp And His Orchestra | Got A Date With An Angel | Pro-Arte | CDD 553
So(u)loflotz
Andy Sheppard Group | Rhythm Method | Blue Note | 827798-2
Soap Bubbles
Joe Bonner-Johnny Dyani | Suburban Fantasies | Steeplechase | SCCD 31176
Sobbin' Blues
Firehouse Five Plus Two | The Firehouse Five Story Vol. 2 | Good Time Jazz | 12011
Sobbin' Hearted Blues
Cootie Williams And His Orchestra | Big Band Bounce And Boogie:Echoes Of Harlem-Cootie Williams | Affinity | AFS 1031
Sobre Las Olas(Over The Waves)
Hamiet Bluiett Quintet | Endangered Species | India Navigation | IN 1025
Soca Me Nice
Mongo Santamaria Orchestra | Soca Me Nice | Concord | CCD 4362
Soca Symphony
Charlie Byrd Orchestra | Latin Byrd | Milestone | M 47005
Socegadamente(Softly)
George Wallington | Virtuoso | Denon Compact Disc | 35C38-7248
Social Drones
Ravi Coltrane Quintet | From The Round Box | RCA | 2173923-2
Social Intelligence
Greg Osby Quartet With String Quartet | Symbols Of Light(A Solution) | Blue Note | 531395-2
Social Order
Bob Schulz And His Frisco Jazz Band | Thanks Turk! | Stomp Off Records | CD 1288
Social Securities
The Stephen Barry Band | Blues Under A Full Moon | Blues Beacon | BLU-1009 2
Society Red

Dexter Gordon Quintet | Dexter Gordon:The Complete Blue Note Sixties Sessions | Blue Note | 834200-2

Sod House
Red Whale | Queekegg | Maracatu | MAC 940002

Soddy And Bowl
Guido Manusardi Trio | Introduction | Penta Flowers | CDPIA 009

Sofdu Unga Ástin Min
Asian American Jazz Trio,The | Moon Over The World | Paddle Wheel | KICJ 163

Sofi
Carlos Martins Quartet | Passagem | Enja | ENJ-9073 2

Sofienberg Variations:
Christina Nielsen Quintet | From This Time Forward | Stunt Records | STUCD 19503

Sofrito
Mongo Santamaria And His Band | Montreux Heat! | Pablo | PACD 5317-2
Gateway | In The Moment | ECM | 1574(529346-2)

Soft
Scott Hamilton Quintet | Close Up | Concord | CCD 4197

Soft Aberration
Eddie Jefferson And His All Stars | Letter From Home | Original Jazz Classics | OJCCD 307-2

Soft Blue
Joe Bonner | New Beginnings | Evidence | TR 125

Soft Buns
Jörg Kaufmann Trio | Sketches | Blue Concept | BCCD 95/01

Soft Disortions
Count Basie And His Orchestra | Sixteen Men Swinging | Verve | 2-2517 IMS

Soft Drink
Buddy Montgomery Sextet | Ties Of Love | Landmark | LCD 1512-2

Soft Eyes
Rick Laird Quartet | Soft Focus | Timeless | CD SJP 104/112

Soft Landing
Yusef Lateef Ensemble | Nocturnes | Atlantic | 7567-81977-2

Soft Light
Benny Goodman Septet | The Benny Goodman Yale Archives Vol.1 | Limelight | 820802-2

Soft Lights And Sweet Music
John Coltrane With The Red Garland Trio | John Coltrane-The Prestige Recordings | Prestige | 16 PCD 4405-2
Milcho Leviev | Plays The Music Of Irving Berlin-Easter Parade | Trend | TRCD 553(881347)

Soft Movements
Dave Grusin Orchestra | The Fabulous Baker Boys(Soundtrack) | GRP | GRP 20022

Soft Pedal Blues
Stanley Turrentine Quartet | That's Where It's At | Blue Note | 869939-7

Soft Seas
George Adams-Don Pullen Quartet | Life Line | Timeless | CD SJP 154

Soft Shoe
Art Farmer Quintet | Farmer 's Market | Prestige | P 24032
Ernestine Anderson With The Hank Jones Trio | Hello Like Before | Concord | CCD 4031
Gerry Mulligan Quartet | Chet Baker:Complete 1952 Fantasy & Pacific Jazz Sessions | Definitive Records | DRCD 11233
Herb Ellis Quartet | A Taste Of Jazz | Concord | CJ 93
Max Roach-Anthony Braxton | Birth And Rebirth | Black Saint | 120024-2
Eddie Daniels Quartet | Eddie Daniels...This Is Now | GRP | GRP 96352

Soft Song
Fred Wesley Group | Amalgamation | Minor Music | 801045

Soft Soul And All That Jazz
West Coast All Stars | TV Jazz Themes | Fresh Sound Records | FSR 517(Somerset SF 8800)

Soft Strut
Henry Threadgill Septet | When Was That? | About Time | AT 1004

Soft Summer Breeze
Steve Khan Group | Steve Khan-Tightrope | CBS | 82230

Soft Touch
Paul Bley Quartet | In The Evenings Out There | ECM | 1488
Progressive Steps feat. Marty Cook | Hard Core | SPLASC(H) Records | CD H 331-2

Soft Wind
Art Blakey And The Jazz Messengers | The Jazz Messengers At The Cafe Bohemia Vol. 1 | Blue Note | 300087(1507)

Soft Winds
Art Tatum Trio | The Complete Trio Sessions Vol.2 | Official | 3002
Chet Baker Quartet | New Blue Horns | Original Jazz Classics | OJC 256(RLP 294)
Chris Flory Quartet | For All We Know | Concord | CCD 4403
Dinah Washington With The Hal Mooney Orchestra | Compact Jazz:Dinah Washington Sings The Blues | Mercury | 832573-2 PMS
Illinois Jacquet Quintet | The Best Of The Jazz Saxophones Vol.2 | LRC Records | CDC 8529
J.J. Johnson-Al Grey Sextet | Things Are Getting Better All The Time | Original Jazz Classics | OJCCD 745-2(2312141)
Things Are Getting Better All The Time | Pablo | 2312141
Joe Pass With The NDR Big Band | Joe Pass In Hamburg | ACT | 9100-2
Johnny Griffin-Eddie Lockjaw Davis Quintet | Tough Tenors | Original Jazz Classics | OJCCD 1094-2(JLP 931)
Kenny Burrell Trio | Live At The Vanguard | Argo | ARC 500
Lady Bass & The Real Gone Guys | Sneakin'Around | L+R Records | CDLR 40027
Lionel Hampton With The Oscar Peterson Trio | Verve Jazz Masters 26:Lionel Hampton with Oscar Peterson | Verve | 521853-2
Marion Brown Quartet | La Placita-Live In Willisau | Timeless | SJP 108
Oscar Peterson And The Bassists | Montreux '77-The Art Of The Jam Session | Pablo | 2620106
Oscar Peterson Trio | En Concert Avec Europe 1 | Laserlight | 710443/48
Swinging Cooperations:Reunion Blues/Great Connection | MPS | 539085-2
Oscar Peterson Trio: Olympia/Theatre Des Champs-Elysees | Laserlight | 36134
At Zardis' | Pablo | 2CD 2620118
Papa John De Francesco Quintet | Comin' Home | Muse | MCD 5531
Red Garland Quintet | Rediscovered Masters, Vol.2 | Original Jazz Classics | OJCCD 769-2
Ron Eschete Trio | Soft Winds | Concord | CCD 4737
Stephane Grappelli Quintet | Feeling + Finesse = Jazz | Atlantic | 7567-90140-2
Stuff Smith Quartet | Stuff Smith+Dizzy Gillespie+Oscar Peterson | Verve | 521676-2
The Royal Air Force HQ Bomber Command Sextet | RAF HQ Bomber Command Sextet | Celebrity | CYCD 74508
Thomas Siffling Jazz Quartet | Soft Winds | Satin Doll Productions | SDP 1030-1 CD
Vintage Introduction | North Sea Highlights | Timeless | CD SJP 156

Soft Winds(alt.take)
Jazz Indeed | Who The Moon Is | Traumton Records | 4427-2

Softache(My Darling Since)
Aldo Romano Quintet | Dreams & Waters | Owl Records | 063 CD

Softly
George Robert-Tom Harrell Quintet | Cape Verde | Mons Records | CD 1898
André Holst With Chris Dean's European Swing Orchestra | That's Swing | Nagel-Heyer | CD 079

Softly As I Leave You
Patrick Tompert Trio | Moche! | Satin Doll Productions | SDP 1035-1 CD

Softly As In A Morning
| Florian Poser Plays His Favourite Standards | Acoustic Music Records | 319.1067.2

Softly As In A Morning Sunrise
Al Cohn Quintet | Be Loose | Biograph | BLP 12063
Art Pepper Quartet | Gettin' Together | Original Jazz Classics | OJCCD 169-2
Art Pepper Quintet | Gettin' Together | Contemporary | COP 023
Bireli Lagrene Trio | Live In Marciac | Dreyfus Jazz Line | FDM 36567-2
Bobby Timmons Trio | In Person | Original Jazz Classics | OJC20 364-2(RLP 9391)
Bruce Forman Quartet | 20/20 | Muse | MR 5273
David Friesen/Clark Terry/Bud Shank | Three To Get Ready | ITM-Pacific | ITMP 970084
Dianne Reeves With Band | I Remember | Blue Note | 790264-2
Dick Wellstood | This Is The One...Dig! | Solo Art | SACD-119
Donald Harrison Quartet | Free To Be | Impulse(MCA) | 951283-2
Donald Harrison Quintet | For Art's Sake | Candid | CCD 79501
Eric Dolphy-Ron Carter Quartet | Magic | Prestige | P 24053
Freddie Brocksieper Four Stars | Freddie's Boogie Blues | Bear Family Records | BCD 16388 AH
Great Jazz Trio | Standard Collection Vol.2 | Limetree | MCD 0032
J.J. Johnson-Al Grey Sextet | Things Are Getting Better All The Time | Pablo | 2312141
James McMillan plus Original Savoy Recordings | Savoy Remix:Crescente Moon | Savoy | CY 78846
Jenny Evans And Her Quintet | Shiny Stockings | Enja | ENJ-9317 2
Jeri Brown With Band | I've Got Your Number | Justin Time | JUST 122-2
Joe Pass With Red Mitchell | Finally | EmArCy | 512603-2 PMS
John Coltrane Quartet | Live At The Village Vanguard:The Master Takes | Impulse(MCA) | 951251-2
The Best Of John Coltrane-His Greatest Years | MCA | AS 9200-2
John Hicks Trio | Is That So? | Timeless | CD SJP 357
June Christy With The Pete Rugolo Orchestra | Something Cool(The Complete Mono & Stereo Versions) | Capitol | 534069-2
Junior Mance Trio | Softly As In A Morning Sunrise | Enja | 8080-2
Kenny Clarke-Francy Boland And Co. | The Golden 8 | Blue Note | 869935-9
Larry Young Quartet | Unity | Blue Note | GXK 8205 (84221)
Joe Henderson-The Blue Note Years | Blue Note | 789287-2
Martial Solal Trio | Balade Du 10 Mars | Soul Note | 121340-2
Miles Davis Quintet | Miles Davis In Stockholm Complete | Dragon | DRCD 228
Modern Jazz Quartet | The Complete Modern Jazz Quartet Prestige & Pablo Recordings | Prestige | 4PRCD 4438-2
Milt Jackson Birthday Celebration | Fantasy | FANCD 6079-2
The Complete Modern Jazz Quartet Prestige & Pablo Recordings | Prestige | 4PRCD 4438-2
Modern Jazz Quartet | Prestige | P 24005
Ron Carter Quintet | Eric Dolphy:The Complete Prestige Recordings | Prestige | 9 PRCD-4418-2
Roseanna Vitro With Tim Ries And The Fred Hersh Quartet | Softly | Concord | CCD 4587
Shelly Manne Trio | French Concert | Galaxy | GXY 5124
Sonny Clark Trio | Sonny Clark Trio | Blue Note | 533774-2
Sonny Criss Quintet | Sonny Criss Quartet Feat. Wynton Kelly | Fresh Sound Records | FSR-CD 318
At The Crossroad | Fresh Sound Records | 252962-1(Peacock PLP 91)
Sonny Rollins Trio | A Night At The Village Vanguard Vol.1 | Blue Note | 746517-2
Sonny Rollins:The Blue Note Recordings | Blue Note | 821371-2
Ballads | Blue Note | 537562-2
Stafford James Ensemble | Stafford James Ensemble | Red Records | VPA 142
Stanley Cowell | Maybeck Recital Hall Series Volume Five | Concord | CCD 4431
Tete Montoliu | The Music I Like To Play Vol.2 | Soul Note | 121200-2
Wynton Kelly Trio | Kelly Blue | Riverside | RISA 1142-6
Stockholm 1960 | Royal Jazz | RJD 509
Zoot Sims-Bucky Pizzarolli Duo | Elegiac | Storyville | STCD 8238
Lee Morgan-Hank Mobley Quintet | Introducing Lee Morgan | Savoy | SV 0116(MG 12091)

Softly As In A Morning Sunrise(alt.take)
Sonny Rollins Trio | Sonny Rollins:The Blue Note Recordings | Blue Note | 821371-2
Gerald Albright Group | Live At Birdland West | Atlantic | 7567-82334-2

Softly Baby
Bruce Dunlap Quintet | About Home | Chesky | JD 59

Softly With Feeling
Les Hooper Big Band | Look What They've Done | Creative World | CW 3002

Softness
Ronald Shannon Jackson And The Decoding Society | Decode Yourself | Island | ILPS 9827(804685)

Sogno D'Amore
Dresch Quartet | Live In Cologne | West Wind | WW 0017

Soham
Shunzo O'No Orchestra | Manhattan Blue | Electric Bird | K32Y 6168

Soir Bon
Christian Escoude Octet | Gipsy Waltz | EmArCy | 838772-2

Soirée
Bill Evans Quartet | From Left To Right | Verve | 557451-2
Lisa Wahlandt & Mulo Francel And Their Fabulous Bossa Band | Bossa Nova Affair | Edition Collage | EC 534-2

Soiree Mignonne
Bill Evans Quartet | The Complete Bill Evans On Verve | Verve | 527953-2

Soirée(alt.take 1)
From Left To Right | Verve | 557451-2
The Complete Bill Evans On Verve | Verve | 527953-2

Soirée(alt.take 2)
Robert Jeanne Quartet | Quartets | B.Sharp Records | CDS 084

Sojourn
Charlie Elgart Group | Signs Of Life | RCA | PD 83045
Bob Kindler Group | Tiger's Paw | Global Pacific Records | 660.52.019

'Sokay
Jan Jankeje Mlada Muzika | Sokol | Jazzpoint | 1002

Sokrates:Der Skorpion Und Der Alligator
Christina Nielsen-Carsten Dahl Duo | Lys Pa Himlen | dacapo | DCCD 9458

Sol
Bertrand Gallaz | Sweet And Sour | Plainisphare | PL 1267-104 CD

Sol De Nit
International Commission For The Prevention Of Musical Border Control,The | The International Commission For The Prevention Of Musical Border Control | VeraBra Records | CDVBR 2093-2

Sol Di Gioia
Quique Sinesi & Daniel Messina With Guests | Prioridad A la Emoción | art-mode-records | AMR 21061

Sol Naciente
Freddy Studer Orchestra | Seven Songs | VeraBra Records | CDVBR 2056-2

Sol Y Sombra
Trio Asab | Coast To Coast | Aho-Recording | AHO CD 1028(CD 380)

Solacium
Prestige All Stars | The Cats | Original Jazz Classics | OJCCD 079-2(NJ 8217)
John Coltrane-The Prestige Recordings | Prestige | 16 PCD 4405-2
George Robert-Tom Harrell Quintet | Live In Switzerland 1987-89 | Jazz Helvet | JH 04

Solaire
Jon Hassell Group | Power Spot | ECM | 1327
Jeanie Bryson And Her Band | Tonight I Need You So | Telarc Digital | CD 83348

Solamente Una Vez(You Belong To My Heart)
Billy Taylor Trio | Separate Keyboards:Erroll Garner/Billy Taylor | Savoy | SV0223(MG 12008)

Solance
Terry Lightfoot's Jazzmen | Down On Bourbon Street | Timeless | CD TTD 581

Solance-A Mexican Serenade
Lyrik-Performance | Ich Brenne Und Ich Werde Immer Brennen | Born&Bellmann | 973110 CD

Solar
Arnold Klos Trio | Crinkle's Garden | Limetree | MLP 198537
Bill Evans Trio | The Brilliant | West Wind | WW 2058
Billy Pierce Quintet | One For Chuck | Sunnyside | SSC 1053 D
Bud Shank Trio | Crystal Moments | Concord | CJ 126
Chet Baker Quartet | The Jazz Giants Play Miles Davis:Milestones | Prestige | PCD 24225-2
Chet Baker In New York | Original Jazz Classics | OJC20 207-2
Chet Baker Quintet | My Foolish Heart | I.R.D. Records | TDMCD 002
Chuck Mangione Quintet | Jazz Brother | Milestone | M 47042
Dave Holland | Emerald Tears | ECM | 1109(529087-2)
Dave Pike Quartet | It's Time For Dave Pike | Original Jazz Classics | OJCCD 1951-2(RLP 9360)
Dick Katz Trio | 3wayPlay | Reservoir | RSR CD 127(875790)
Doug Raney Trio | Guitar Guitar Guitar | Steeplechase | SCCD 31212
Horace Parlan | Jazzbühne Berlin '79/'83 | Repertoire Records | REPCD 4918-WZ
Keith Jarrett Trio | At The Deer Head Inn | ECM | 1531(517720-2)
Kenny Barron Trio | Live at Bradley's | EmArCy | 549099-2
Kenny Dorham Quintet | Scandia Skies | Steeplechase | SCCD 36011
Larry Willis Trio | Just In Time | Steeplechase | SCS 1251
Mat Maneri Trio | So What? | HatOLOGY | 529
Miles Davis Quintet | The Prestige Legacy Vol.1:The High Priests | Prestige | PCD 24251-2
Oliver Jones | The Many Moods Of Oliver Jones | Justin Time | Just 3
Slide Hampton Quintet | Roots | Criss Cross | Criss 1015
Tete Montoliu Trio | Hot House | Steeplechase | SCCD 37027/28
Peter Weniger Quartet | Tiptap | Mons Records | MR 874768

Solar Winds
Keith Jarrett Trio With Strings | Arbour Zena | ECM | 1070(825592-2)

Solara March
Mat Maneri Trio | So What? | HatOLOGY | 529

Soldier Boy
Phillips' Louisville Jug Band | The Jug & Washboard Bands-Vol.2(1928-1930) | Story Of Blues | CD 3514-2

Soldier In The Rain
Quincy Jones And His Orchestra | Verve Jazz Masters Vol.59:Toots Thielemans | Verve | 535271-2
Eric Reed Trio | Soldier's Hymn-Dedicated To Art Blakey | Candid | CCD 79511

Soldier's Song
Arild Andersen Quartet | Green Shading Into Blue | ECM | 1127

Solea
José Salazar And Trio | Soleá: A Flamenco-Jazz Fantasy | ACT | 9208-2
Miles Davis With Gil Evans & His Orchestra | The Miles Davis Selection | CBS | 465699-2
Naima | Vertigo | Mons Records | MR 874816

Soledad
Pablo Ziegler And His Quintet For New Tango | Asfalto-Street Tango | RCA | 2663266-2

Soleil
Palatino | Palationo Chap.3 | EmArCy | 013610-2

Soleil A Genes
Jean Pierre Mas Trio | Jamais 2 Sans 3 | Owl Records | 06

Soleil Noir
Jean-Louis Matinier Quartet | Confluences | Enja | ENJ-9454 2

Soleil Rouge
Randy Weston Trio | Zulu | Milestone | M 47045

Solemn Meditation
Randy Weston Trio With Cecil Payne | Jazz A La Bohemia | Original Jazz Classics | OJCCD 1747-2

Solfiegietto in C Minor(C.P.E.Bach)
Ingolf Burkhardt-Ludwig Nuß Quintet | Jazzed Friends | Mons Records | MR 874780

Solid
Grant Green Sextet | Solid | Blue Note | 833580-2
Woody Shaw Sextet | Solid | 32 Jazz | 32153

Solid As A Rock
Jack Montrose And All-Stars | The Horn's Full | RCA | NL 45956(RCA LPM 1572)

Solid Citizens
Art Pepper Quintet | Smack Up | Original Jazz Classics | OJC20 176-2

Solid Citizens(alt.take)
Charles Gayle Quartet | Always Born | Silkheart | SHCD 115

Solid Ether
Gunter Hampel-Christian Weider Duo | Solid Fun | Birth | CD 044

Solid Fun
Ronnie Laws With Strings And Voices | Solid Ground | Blue Note | 498544-2

Solid Old Man
Duke Ellington And His Orchestra | Duke Ellington:Complete Prestige Carnegie Hall 1946-1947 Concerts | Definitive Records | DRCD 11211
Keith Ingham Manhattan Swingtet | We're In The Money | Sackville | SKCD2-2055
Rex Stewart And His Feetwarmers | Django Reinhardt:Djangology | EMI Records | 780659-2

Solid Potato Salad
Nat King Cole Trio | Jazz In V.Discs Vol.3 | Collection Hugues Panassié | CTPL 003

Solid Sending Boogie
Nana Simopoulos Group | Still Waters | Enja | 6010-2

Solid State
Dave Stryker Quartet | Guitar On Top | Ken Music | 660.56.019

Solidao
Globe Unity Orchestra | Globe Unity 73 Live in Wuppertal | FMP | 0160

Solidarity
Ed Sarath Quintet | Last Day In May | Konnex Records | KCD 5042
Gary Dial-Dick Oatts Quartet With Brass Ensemble | Brassworks | dmp Digital Music Productions | CD 477

Soliloquy
Lee Konitz-Hal Galper Duo | Windows | Steeplechase | SCCD 31057

Soliloquy (Blues For Dr.John)
Keith Jarrett Quartet | Belonging | ECM | 1050(829115-2)

Solistice
29th Street Saxophone Quartet | Your Move | Antilles | 314512524(875360)

Solitaire
Stan Kenton And His Orchestra | Paris 1953 | Royal Jazz | RJD 504
Chris Barber's Jazz Band | More Of Best Of Dixieland | Philips | 838347-2

Solitary
Steve Adams/Ken Filiano Quartet | Anacrusis | Nine Winds Records | NW 0128

Solitary Woman
(Little)Jimmy Scott With The Lucky Thompson Orchestra | Everybody's Somebody's Fool | Decca | 050669-2

Solitude
Abdullah Ibrahim Trio | African Magic | TipToe | TIP-888845 2
Andy And The Bey Sisters | Andy Bey And The Bey Sisters | Prestige | PCD 24245-2
Billie Holiday And Her All Stars | Billie Holiday:The Great American Songbook | Verve | 523003-2
Clark Terry-Tommy Flanagan | Clark Terry:One On One | Chesky | JD 198
Duke Ellington And His Famous Orchestra | Duke Ellington:The Complete RCA-Victor Mid-Forties Recordings(1944-1946) | RCA | 2663394-2
Duke Ellington And His Orchestra | The Big Bands Vol.1.The Snader Telescriptions | Storyville | 4960043
The Legends Of Swing | Laserlight | 24659
En Concert Avec Europe 1 | Laserlight | 710707/08
Ella Fitzgerald And Barney Kessel | Ella Fitzgerald Day Dream:The Best Of The Duke Ellington Song Book | Verve | 527223-2
Günther Klatt-Tizian Jost | Art Of The Duo:Live In Mexico City | Tutu Records | 888184-2*
Harry Allen With The Bill Charlap Trio | Harry Allen Plays Ellington Songs | RCA | 2170448-2

Henri Crolla Sextet | Jazz In Paris:Henri Crolla-Quand Refleuriront Les Lilas Blancs? | EmArCy | 018418-2
Jack Dieval And The J.A.C.E. All-Stars | Jazz In Paris:Jack Diéval-Jazz Aux Champs Elysées | EmArCy | 018419-2
Jessica Williams Trio | Higher Standards | Candid | CCD 79736
Jill Seifers And Her Quartet | The Waiting | Fresh Sound Records | FSNT 072 CD
Jimmy Scott With Band | Moon Glow | Milestone | MCD 9332-2
Joe Pass Quartet | The Jazz Giants Play Duke Ellington:Caravan | Prestige | PCD 24227-2
Johnny Hodges Orchestra | Johnny Hodges:The Complete 1941-1954 Small Group Sessions(Master Takes),Vol.3 | Blue Moon | BMCD 1030
Louis Armstrong And His All Stars With Duke Ellington | Louis Armstrong-Duke Ellington:The Great Summit-Complete Session | Roulette | 524546-2
Louis Armstrong And His Orchestra | Louis Armstrong:Swings | Memo Music | HDJ 4033
Rebecca Parris With The Gary Burton Group | Gary Burton Collection | GRP | GRP 98512
Sathima Bea Benjamin Group | A Morning In Paris | Enja | ENJ-9309 2
Sonny Rollins Trio | Sonny Rollins-The Freelance Years:The Complete Riverside & Contemporary Recordings | Riverside | 5 RCD 4427-2
Stephen Scott Trio | Renaissance | Verve | 523863-2

Solitude-
Sir Charles Thompson | Playing My Way | Jazz Connaisseur | JCCD 9313-2
$$hide$$ | $$Titelverweise | |

Solitude -> In My Solitude

Solitudes
Tamia/Pierre Favre | Solitudes | ECM | 1446
Mona Larsen And The Danish Radio Big Band Plus Soloists | Michael Mantler:Cerco Un Paese Innocente | ECM | 1556

Solitudine-
Sandro Cerino Action Quartet | Tom Thumb In The Magic Castle | SPLASC(H) Records | HP 03

Solo
Billy Taylor | Ten Fingers-One Voice | Arkadia Jazz | 71602
Bob Keene Septet | Solo For Seven | Fresh Sound Records | FSR 641(Andex A 4001)
Roscoe Mitchell Quartet | Old Quartet | Nessa | N 5

Solo-
Pepe Justicia-Amir Haddad Duo | Internationales Guitarren Festival '99 | ALISO Records | AL 1038

Solo Agua
Clarinet Summit | Clarinet Summit In Concert At The Public Theater | India Navigation | IN 1062 CD

Solo Berlin
Hank Jones | Have You Met Hank Jones ? | Savoy | WL 70544 (809329)

Solo Dancer
Charles Mingus And His Orchestra | Great Moments With Charles Mingus | MCA | MCA 2-4128 (802130)

Solo Dancing
Astrud Gilberto With Orchestra | Astrud Gilberto | Jazz Magazine | 43003

Solo Flight
Benny Goodman And His Orchestra | Benny Goodman Vol.2: Clarinet A La King | CBS | 460829-2

Solo Flute
Eberhard Weber Group | Endless Days | ECM | 1748(013420-2)

Solo For Bass
Stan Kenton And His Orchestra | Kenton Showcase | Creative World | ST 1026

Solo From 'More Travels'
Jon Hiseman With The United Jazz & Rock Ensemble And Babara Thompson's Paraphernalia | About Time Too! | VeraBra Records | CDVBR 2014-2

Solo Hannover
Bunny Berigan | I Can't Get Started | Pro-Arte | CDD 554

Solo One
Gunter Hampel And His Galaxie Dream Band | Vogelfrei | Birth | 0029

Solo Z
Friedrich Gulda | Gegenwart | ERP | E.R.P. 1

Solo(No.1)
Bireli Lagrene Group | Bireli Lagrene & Special Guests | Inak | 8610

Solomon
James Newton | Axum | ECM | 1214

Solomon Chief Of Wise Men
David Murray-James Newton Duo | Solomon's Son's | Circle Records | RK 5-16177/5 IMS

Solopark
Sal Salvador Quartet | A Tribute To The Greats | Fresh Sound Records | FSR 2019(Bethlehem BCP 74)

Solosol
George Wallington Quintet | The New York Scene | Original Jazz Classics | OJCCD 1805-2(NJ 8207)

Solstizie D'Estate(from the movie Il Prezzo)
The Sax Section | The Sax Section | Fresh Sound Records | LSP 15622(Epic LN 3278)

Solution
Jazzartrio | From Time To Time | SPLASC(H) Records | H 148

Solving The Riddle
Baden Powell Solo/Group | Tristeza On Guitar | MPS | 68087

Som Do Carnaval
Milt Jackson Quintet | Opus De Funk | Prestige | P 24048

Soma
The MJQ Box | Prestige | 7711-2

Sombras E Nevoeiro-
Thad Jones Quintet | The Fabulous Thad Jones | Prestige | MPP 2506

Sombre Intrusion
Roy Kawasaki Ensemble | Ring Toss | Chiaroscuro | CR 181

Some Aspects Of Water
Orexis | Orexis | Intercord | 160075

Some Cats Know
Joe Baudisch Quartet | The Meeting Of Two Tenors | Acoustic Music Records | 319.1135.2

Some Changes In Life
Roman Schwaller Jazz Quartet | Live At The Nachtcafé Munich | Bassic-Sound | CD 019
Maria Schneider Jazz Orchestra | Evanescence | Enja | ENJ-8048 2

Some Clark Bars
Bertha 'Chippie' Hill With Georgia Tom | Come On Mama Do That Dance | Yazoo | YAZ 1041

Some Day
Louis Armstrong And His All Stars | Historic Barcelona Concerts At Windsor Palace 1955 | Fresh Sound Records | FSR-CD 3004
Viktoria Tolstoy Group & Strings | Shining On You | ACT | 9701-2
Pete Johnson | Boogie Woggie Classics | Blue Note | BLP 1209

Some Dirge
Cl.W. Jacobi's Bottomland Orchestra | A Tribute To Clarence Williams | Stomp Off Records | CD 1266

Some Echoes
Etta Jones And Her Band | Love Shout | Original Jazz Classics | OJCCD 941-2(P 7272)

Some Enchanted Evening
Joshua Breakstone Quartet | Self-Portrait In Swing | Contemporary | CCD 14050-2

Some Heroes
Tony Williams | Spectrum:The Anthology | Verve | 537075-2

Some Hip Drum Shit
Ernie Watts Quintet | Unity | JVC | JVC 2046-2

Some Kind Of Destruction
Roland Kirk Quartet | Rahsaan/The Complete Mercury Recordings Of Roland Kirk | Mercury | 846630-2

Some Kind Of Love
Jay McShann Quartet | Goin' To Kansas City | Stony Plain | SPCD 1286

Some Kinda Crazy
James Clay/David Fathead Newman Quintet | The Sound Of The Wide Open Spaces | Original Jazz Classics | OJCCD 1075-2(RLP 1178)

Some Kinda Mean
Sam Jones Septet | The Soul Society | Original Jazz Classics | OJCCD 1789-2(RLP 1172)

Some Like It Hot
Mel Tormé With The Mel-Tones | Back In Town | Verve | MV 2675 IMS

Some Like To Love More Than One
Stefano Battaglia Trio | Auryn | SPLASC(H) Records | CD H 162-2

Some Moon
Wild Bill Davis Quartet | Live At Swiss Radio Studio Zürich | Jazz Connaisseur | JCCD 8701-2

Some More
Chuck Israels International Quartet | On Common Ground | Anima Records | DV-CD 002

Some Neck
John Scofield Quartet | Meant To Be | Blue Note | 795479-2

Some Of My Best Friends Are Blues
Jimmy Smith Trio | Talkin' Verve:George Benson | Verve | 553780-2
Jimmy Witherspoon With The Robben Ford Quartet | Live At The Notodden Blues Festival | Crosscut | CCD 11035

Some Of These Days
Art Hodes-Jim Galloway | Live From Toronto's Café Des Copains | Music & Arts | CD 610
Benny Carter And His Orchestra | The Deluxe Recordings | Swingtime(Contact) | ST 1013
Bob Scobey's Frisco Band | The Scobey Story Vol.1 | Good Time Jazz | GTCD 12032-2
Chris Barber-Barry Martin Band | Collaboration | GHB Records | BCD 40
Dutch Swing College Band | Swinging Studio Sessons | Philips | 824256-2 PMS
Earl Hines Sextet | At Club Hangover-Vol.5 | Storyville | SLP 263
Kid Ory-Red Allen Band | We've Got Rhythm | Verve | 2304504 IMS
Nat Pierce/Dick Collins Nonet | Nat Pierce-Dick Collins-Ralph Burns & The Herdsmen Play Paris | Fantasy | FCD 24759-2
Oscar Peterson Quintet With Orchestra | The Personal Touch | Pablo | 2312135-2
Ray Nance Quartet | Jazz-Club: Violin | Verve | 840039-2
Soprano Summit | Chalumeau Blue | Chiaroscuro | CR 148

Some Of These Days(rehersal)
The Sidewalks Of New York | Tin Pan Alley:The Sidewalks Of New York | Winter&Winter | 910038-2

Some Of These Days(the show)
Joe Williams And Friends | Joe Williams At Newport '63 | RCA | NL 70119

Some Of This 'N' Some Of That
Mind Games | Lyrical Life | yvp music | CD 3027

Some Othe Season
Ornette Coleman Quartet | Beauty Is A Rare Thing:Ornette Coleman-The Complete Atlantic Recordings | Atlantic | 8122-71410-2

Some Other
Coe,Oxley & Co. | Nutty On Willisau | Hat Art | CD 6046

Some Other Blues
Jean Toussaint Quartet | Impressions Of Coltrane | September | CD 5104
John Coltrane Quartet | Coltrane Jazz | Atlantic | 7567-81344-2
Junior Mance Quartet | At Town Hall Vol.2 | Enja | 9095-2
Tete Montoliu Trio | Tootie's Tempo | Steeplechase | SCCD 31108

Some Other Spring
Art Tatum Trio | Art Tatum-The Complete Pablo Group Masterpieces | Pablo | 6 PACD 4401-2
The Tatum Group Masterpieces | Pablo | 2310735-2
Benny Carter And His Strings With The Oscar Peterson Quartet | Alone Together | Verve | 2304512 IMS
Billie Holiday And Her All Stars | Verve Jazz Masters 12:Billie Holiday | Verve | 519825-2
Billie Holiday And Her Orchestra | Billie Holiday:The Quintessential Vol.7(1938-1939) | CBS | CK 46180
Charlie Byrd Quartet | Charlie Byrd In Greenwich Village | Milestone | M 47049
Dan Barrett Octet | Strictly Instrumental | Concord | CJ 331
Ella Fitzgerald With Count Basie And His Orchestra | A Perfect Match-Basie And Ella | Pablo | 2312110-2
Jimmy Rowles Septet | Weather In A Jazz Vane | Fresh Sound Records | FSR 502(Andex S-3007)
Scott Hamilton Quartet | After Hours | Concord | CCD 4755

Some Other Spring-
Tommy Flanagan 3 | The Montreux '77 Collection | Pablo | 2620107
David Benoit Group | Waiting For Spring | GRP | GRP 95952

Some Other Time
Bill Evans Trio | Bill Evans:The Complete Live At The Village Vanguard 1961 | Riverside | 3RCD 1961-2
Paris 1965 | Royal Jazz | RJD 503
Bill Evans:The Secret Sessions | Milestone | 8MCD 4421-2
How Deep Is The Ocean | West Wind | WW 2055
Cassandra Wilson Group | Days Aweigh | JMT Edition | 834412-2
Larry Coryell-Miroslav Vitous | Dedicated To Bill Evans And Scott LaFaro | Jazzpoint | JP 1021 CD
LeeAnn Ledgerwood Trio | Paradox | Steeplechase | SCCD 31497
Mark Turner Quintet | Ballad Session | Warner | 9362-47631-2
Marlene And Her Quintet | Every Breath I Take | Savoy | SV 0233(MV 12058)
Monica Zetterlund With The Bill Evans Trio | The Complete Bill Evans On Verve | Verve | 527953-2
Ralph Moore Quartet | Who It Is You Are | Denon Compact Disc | CY-75778
Richie Beirach | Continuum | Eastwind | EWIND 704
Tim Ries Quintet | Universal Spirits | Criss Cross | Criss 1144
Tony Bennett-Bill Evans | The Tony Bennett-Bill Evans Album | Original Jazz Classics | OJC20 439-2(F 9489)
Ian Shaw With The Adrian York Quartet | Ghostsongs | Ronnie Scott's Jazz House | JHCD 025

Some Other Time-
Michael Feinstein With Jule Styne | Michael Feinstein Sings The Jule Styne Songbook | Nonesuch | 7559-79274-2

Some People
Tony Scott Quartet | Tony Scott Plays Gypsy | Fresh Sound Records | FSR 574(Signature SS 6001)

Some Saturday
Rex Stewart And His Orchestra | The Indispensable Duke Ellington And The Small Groups,Vol.9/10 | RCA | NL 89582 (809207)

Some Say You Win
Sam Butler | Guitar Wizards 1926-1935 | Yazoo | YAZ 1016

Some Skunk Funk
The Brecker Brothers | The Becker Bros | RCA | 2122103-2
Heavy Metal Be-Bop | RCA | 2119257-2
The Brecker Brothers Live | Jazz Door | JD 1248

Some Song And Dance:
Bud Powell Trio | Bud Powell:The Complete Blue Note And Roost Recordings | Blue Note | 830083-2

Some Soul
Coleman Hawkins All Stars | Coleman Hawkins All Stars | Original Jazz Classics | OJCCD 225-2(SV 2005)

Some Streching
Duke Ellington And His Orchestra | The Intimate Ellington | Original Jazz Classics | OJCCD 730-2(2310787)

Some Sweet Day
The Black Eagles | Some Sweet Day | Lake | LACD 65

Some Time Ago
Clark Terry-Bob Brookmeyer Quintet | Clark Terry-Bobby Brookmeyer Quintet | Mainstream | MD CDO 728
Joe Pass Sextet | Simplicity | Pacific Jazz | LN 10086
Sal Salvador Sextet | Starfingers | Bee Hive | BH 7002

Some Will Dream
Charlie Rouse And Orrin Keepnews | Epistrophy | Landmark | LCD 1521-2

Somebody Bigger
Mahalia Jackson With Choir/Orchestra/Falls-Jones Ensemble | This Is Mahalia Jackson | CBS | 66241

Somebody Done Changed The Lock On My Door
Louis Jordan And His Tympany Five | Louis Jordan-Let The Good Times Roll: The Complete Decca Recordings 1938-1954 | Bear Family Records | BCD 15557 IH
Louis Jordan Greatest Hits-Vol.2 | MCA | 1337

Somebody Done Hoodooed The Hoodoo Man
Louis Jordan Vol.1-Hoodoo Man | Swingtime(Contact) | ST 1011

Somebody Else Is Taking My Place
Percy Humphrey's Sympathy Five | Percy Humphrey | American Music | AMCD-88

Somebody Gonna Have To Move
Billy Boy Arnold With The Aces | The Devil's Music:Mississippi And Memphis/Chicago Blues | Red Lightnin' | RL 0033

Somebody Loves Me
Anita Boyer & Her Tomboyers | Nat King Cole Trio:The MacGregor Years 1941/45 | Music & Arts | CD 911
Art Tatum | Art Tatum:Over The Rainbow | Dreyfus Jazz Line | FDM 36727-2
Art Tatum:Complete Capitol Recordings | Capitol | 821325-2
Art Tatum:Over The Rainbow | Dreyfus Jazz Line | FDM 36727-2
Pure Genius | Atlantis | ATS 3
Art Tatum Sextet | The Tatum Group Masterpieces | Pablo | 2310731
Benny Goodman Sextet | Verve Jazz Masters 33:Benny Goodman | Verve | 844410-2
Bernard Zacharias Et Ses Solistes | Jazz In Paris:Modern Jazz At Saint-Germain-De-Prés | EmArCy | 013042-2
Bud Powell Trio | Bud Powell:Complete 1947-1951 Blue Note,Verve & Roost Recordings | The Jazz Factory | JFCD 22837
Dan Barrett Octet | Strictly Instrumental | Concord | CJ 331
Dizzy Gillespie Septet | 'S Wonderful | Jazz Society(Vogue) | 670508
Don Byas Quartet | Jazz In Paris:Don Byas-Laura | EmArCy | 013027-2
Earl Hines | Americans Swinging In Paris:Earl Hines | EMI Records | 539661-2
Le Jazz En France Vol.15:Earl Hunes Paris Session 1965 | Pathe | 1552611
Elmo Hope Trio | Last Sessions Vol.2 | Inner City | IC 1037 IMS
Ernie Wilkins And His Orchestra | Here Comes The Swingin' Mr.Wilkins | Fresh Sound Records | FSR 511(Everest LPBR 5077)
George Wettling's New Yorkers | Jazz:The Essential Collection Vol.3 | IN+OUT Records | 78013-2
Hampton Hawes Trio | Everybody Likes Hampton Hawes | Original Jazz Classics | OJCCD 421-2
Nat King Cole Trio | Los Angeles Live Performance | Jazz Anthology | JA 5219
Oscar Peterson Trio | The George Gershwin Songbook | Verve | 823249-1
The Gershwin Songbook(The Instrumentals) | Verve | 525361-2
Paul Gonsalves/Roy Eldridge Quintet | Mexican Bandit Meets Pittsburg Pirate | Original Jazz Classics | OJCCD 751-2(F 9646)
Roy Gerson Quartet | The Gerson Person | The Jazz Alliance | TJA 10012
Stuff Smith Quartet | Cat On A Hot Fiddle | Verve | 9861487
Ted Brown Quartet | Preservation | Steeplechase | SCCD 31539
Ted Heath And His Orchestra | Ted Heath And His Music-It's Swing Time | Magic | DAWE 82
The Jazz Age Quintet And The Kammerorchester Schloß Werneck | Happy Birthday,Mr.Gershwin! | Balthasar Records | Balthasar 001(CD 584)
Woody Herman And His Orchestra | Old Gold Rehearsals 1944 | Jazz Unlimited | JUCD 2079
The Radio Years: Woody Herman And His First Herd 1944 | Hindsight | HSR 134
Zoot Sims Quartet | The Best Of The Jazz Saxophones Vol.2 | LRC Records | CDC 8529

Somebody Loves Me-
Al Cohn-Zoot Sims Quintet | From A To Z | RCA | 2147790-2

Somebody Noboday Loves
Blue Barron And His Orchestra | The Uncollected: Blue Barron, Vol.2 | Hindsight | HSR 137

Somebody Somewhere
Steve Lacy Sextet | Songs | Hat Art | CD 6045

Somebody Stole My Break
Louis Armstrong With The Luis Russell Orchestra | Louis Armstrong Vol.6-Satchmo's Collectors Items | MCA | 1322

Somebody Stole My Gal
Benny Goodman And His Orchestra | Great Swing Classics In Hi-Fi | Capitol | 521223-2
Benny Moten's Kansas City Orchestra | Basie Beginnings | Bluebird | ND 90403
Bix Beiderbecke And His Gang | Riverboat Shuffle | Naxos Jazz | 8.120584 CD
Fats Waller And His Rhythm | The Classic Years In Digital Stereo: Fats Waller And His Rhythm | CDS Records Ltd. | RPCD 315(CD 684)

Somebody Wants Me Down There
Maynard Ferguson With The Birdland Dreamband | The Birdland Dream Band Vol.1 | Fresh Sound Records | 58110 CD(RCA)

Somebody's Been Lying 'Bout Me
Jimmy Rushing And His All Stars | Jack Dupree-Jimmy Rushing-Muddy Waters | Laserlight | 17062

Somebody's On My Mind
Lee Gree With Lafayette Leake | Somebody's Praying,Lord | L+R Records | LR 44013

Someday
Dodo Marmarosa Quartet | The Chicago Sessions | Argo | ARC 502 D
James 'Sing' Miller Quartet | New Orleans Traditional Jazz Legends:Sing Miller | Mardi Gras Records | MG 9006

Someday I'll Find You
Sonny Rollins Trio | Sonny Rollins-The Freelance Years:The Complete Riverside & Contemporary Recordings | Riverside | 5 RCD 4427-2
Irene Kral With Alan Broadbent | Gentle Rain | Candid | CRS 1020 IMS

Someday My Prince Will Come
Bernie Senensky Trio | Rhapsody | Timeless | CD SJP 434
Bill Evans Trio | The Complete Bill Evans On Verve | Verve | 527953-2
Spring Leaves | Milestone | M 47034
Live In Paris 1972 Vol.2 | France's Concert | FCD 114
Bill Evans:The Secret Sessions | Milestone | 8MCD 4421-2
Live In Buenos Aires 1979 | West Wind | WW 2061
You're Gonna Hear From Me | Milestone | M 9164
Bill Evans:The Secret Sessions | Milestone | 8MCD 4421-2
Yesterday I Heard The Rain | Bandstand | BDCD 1535
Portrait In Jazz | Original Jazz Classics | OJC20 088-2
Billy Cobham Trio | The Art Of Three | IN+OUT Records | 77045-2
Billy Higgins Trio With Harold Land | 3/4 For Peace | Red Records | 123258-2
Cassandra Wilson Group | Traveling Miles | Blue Note | 854123-2
Chet Baker Trio | Someday My Prince Will Come | Steeplechase | SCS 1180(Audiophile Pressing)
Chris Anderson Trio | Blues One | DIW | DIW 607 CD
Don Braden Quintet | The Open Road | Double Time Records | DTRCD-114
Frank Castenier Group | For You,For Me For Evermore | EmArCy | 9814976
Frank Morgan Quartet | Love,Lost & Found | Telarc Digital | CD 83374
George Cables Trio | Skylark | Steeplechase | SCCD 31381
Grant Green Quintet | Born To Be Blue | Blue Note | 784432-2
Joe Morello Quartet | Morello Standard Time | dmp Digital Music Productions | CD 506
Kenny Werner | Maybeck Recital Hall Series Volume Thirty-Four | Concord | CCD 4622
Lee Konitz Quartet | Round & Round | Musicmasters | 65140-2
Michel Petrucciani/Niels-Henning Orsted-Pedersen | Michel Petrucciani:Concert Inédits | Dreyfus Jazz Line | FDM 36607-2

Miles Davis Sextet | Hollywood Jazz | CBS | 474373-2
Miles Davis With John Coltrane | CBS | CBS 88029
Niels Lan Doky Quartet | Paris By Night | Soul Note | 121206-2
Olga Konkova | Her Point Of View | Candid | CCD 79757
Oscar Peterson Trio | Paris Jazz Concert:Oscar Peterson | Laserlight | 36155
En Concert Avec Europe 1 | Laserlight | 710443/48
Oscar Peterson Trio With The Nelson Riddle Orchestra | Verve Jazz Masters 16:Oscar Peterson | Verve | 516320-2
Oscar Peterson-Milt Jackson Quartet | Reunion Blues | MPS | 817490-1
Patrick Tompert Trio | Hallelujah Time | Satin Doll Productions | SDP 1020-1 CD
Phil Abraham Quartet | Phil Abraham-At The Sugar Village | Jazz Pure Collection | AU 31604 CD
Rogall & Van Buggenum | Two Piano Jazz: Live | Jazzline | ???
Ron Carter Quartet | The Bass And I | somethin'else | 300258(TOCJ 5585)
Steve Grossman With The Cedar Walton Trio | A Small Hotel | Dreyfus Jazz Line | FDM 36561-2
Tierney Sutton And Her Trio | Blue In Green | Telarc Digital | CD 83522
Tsuyoshi Yamamoto Trio | Live | East Wind | EW 8045 IMS

Someday My Prince Will Come-
Michel Petrucciani | 100 Hearts | Blue Note | 538329-2
Toots Thielemans-Kenny Werner Duo | Toots Thielemans & Kenny Werner | EmArCy | 014722-2
Miles Davis Sextet | Someday My Prince Will Come | CBS | CK 65919

Someday My Prince Will Come(alt.take)
Wynton Kelly Trio | Wynton Kelly! | Vee Jay Recordings | VJ 011

Someday Soon
Dick Sudhalter Band | Melodies Heard,Melodies Sweet... | Challenge | CHR 70055

Someday Sweetheart
Benny Goodman Trio | Benny Goodman:The Complete Small Combinations Vol.1/2(1935-1937) | RCA | ND 89753
Eddie Condon All Stars | That Toodlin' Town-Chicago Jazz Revisited | Atlantic | 90461-1 TIS
Henry Red Allen Sextet | Swing Trumpet Kings:Harry Edison Swings Buck Clayton And Vice Versa/Red Allen Plays King Oliver/Swing Goes Dixie | Verve | 533263-2
Muggsy Spanier And His Band | Memories Of Muggsy | Ember | CJS 845
The Tremble Kids All Stars | Dixieland At Its Best | BELL Records | BLR 89091

Someday We'll All Be Free
Diane Schuur And Her Band | Schuur Thing | GRP | GRP 91022-1(808721)

Someday We'll Be Together
Les McCann Group | Listen Up! | Musicmasters | 65139-2

Someday We'll Meet Again
Willie Mabon & His Combo | Blues Roots Vol. 16: Willie Mabon | Chess | 6.24806 AG

Someday You'll Be Sorry
Benny Carter Sextet | Elegy In Blue | Musicmasters | 65115-2
Carol Sloane With The Art Farmer Sextet | Love You Madly | Contemporary | CCD 14049-2
Louis Armstrong And His All Stars | Planet Jazz:Louis Armstrong | Planet Jazz | 2152052-2
New Orleans Louisiana | Traditional Line | TL 1319
Louis Armstrong:Wintergarden 1947/Blue Note 1948 | Storyville | STCD 8242
Louis Armstrong And His All Stars/Orchestra | Do You Know What It Means To Miss New Orleans? | Verve | 837919-2
Louis Armstrong With The Commanders | Ambassador Louis Armstrong Vol.17:Moments To Remember(1952-1956) | Ambassador | CLA 1917
Louis Armstrong With The Dukes Of Dixieland | Sweetheart Definite Alternatives | Chiaroscuro | CR 2006
The Alex Welsh Legacy Band | The Sound Of Alex Vol.1 | Nagel-Heyer | CD 070
The New York Allstars | Oh,Yeah! The New York Allstars Play More Music Of Louis Armstrong | Nagel-Heyer | CD 046
The Tremble Kids All Stars | The Tremble Kids All Stars Play Chicago Jazz! | Nagel-Heyer | CD 043
Tom Saunders' 'Wild Bill Davison Band' & Guests | Exactly Like You | Nagel-Heyer | CD 023
Woody Herman And The Concord Jam | A Concord Jam-Vol. 1 | Concord | CCD 4142

Someday(alt.take)
Rickey Grundy & The Williams Family | We Shall Walk Through The Valley In Peace | L+R Records | LR 44014

Someday(You'll Want Me To Want You)
Della Reese With The Neal Hefti Orchestra | Della | RCA | 2663912-2
Norrie Cox & His New Orleans Stompers | Dance Hall Days | Delmark | DE 236

Somehow In September
Joe Sample Group | Spellbound | Rhino | 81273726-2

Somehow Our Love Survives
Terje Rypdal Quartet | The Singles Collection | ECM | 1383(837749-2)

Somehow, Somewhere
Duke Ellington And His Famous Orchestra | Duke Ellington:The Blanton-Webster Band | Bluebird | 21 13181-2

Someone
Duke Ellington And His Orchestra | Duke Ellington:Complete Studio Transcriptions | Definitive Records | DRCD 11199
Loren Schoenberg And His Jazz Orchestra | Just A-Settin' And A-Rockin' | Musicmasters | 5039-2

Someone Else's Love
Dizzy Atmosphere | Dizzy Atmosphere | Original Jazz Classics | OJCCD 1762-2

Someone In My Backyard
James Newton-Anthony Davis Duo | Crystal Texts | Moers Music | 01048

Someone To Light Up My Life
Sarah Vaughan With Orchestra | I Love Brazil | Pablo | 2312101-2
Shirley Horn Quintet | Loving You | Verve | 537022-2
Singers Unlimited | The Singers Unlimited:Magic Voices | MPS | 539130-2
A Capella III | MPS | 68245

Someone To Love
Tony Bennett With The Marty Manning Orchestra | I Wanna Be Around | CBS | CK 66504

Someone To Watch Over Me
(Little)Jimmy Scott With The Howard Biggs Sextet | Little Jimmy Scott-All Over Again | Savoy | SV 0263
Art Tatum | Art Tatum:Over The Rainbow | Dreyfus Jazz Line | FDM 36727-2
Art Tatum-The Complete Jazz Chronicle Solo Session | Storyville | STCD 8253
Art Tatum:Over The Rainbow | Dreyfus Jazz Line | FDM 36727-2
Art Tatum-The Complete Pablo Solo Masterpieces | Pablo | 7 PACD 4404-2
Art Tatum:Complete Capitol Recordings | Definitive Records | DRCD 11192
Art Tatum:20th Century Piano Genius | Verve | 531763-2
The Gershwin Songbook(The Instrumentals) | Verve | 525361-2
Benny Carter Quartet | Swingin' The Twenties | Original Jazz Classics | OJCCD 339-2
Benny Goodman And His Orchestra | Live At Carnegie Hall-40th Anniversary Concert | Decca | 6.28451 DP
Betty Roche And Her Quartet | Lightly And Politely | Original Jazz Classics | OJCCD 1802-2(P 7198)
Blossom Dearie Quartet | My Gentleman Friend | Verve | 519905-2
Bob Berg Quintet | Cycles | Denon Compact Disc | CY 72745
Bobby Timmons Trio | From The Bottom | Original Jazz Classics | OJCCD 1032-2(RS 3053)
Buck Hill Quartet | Capitol Hill | Muse | MCD 5384
Buddy DeFranco With The Oscar Peterson Trio And The Russell Garcia Orchestra | Buddy DeFranco And Oscar Peterson Play Gershwin | Verve | 557099-2
Chris Connor With The Herbie Mann Septet | This Is Chris | CTI Records | PDCTI 1127-2
Claire Austin And Her All Stars | When Your Lover Has Gone | Original Jazz Classics | OJCCD 1711-2(C 5002)
Ella Fitzgerald With Ellis Larkins | Ella:The Legendary American Decca Recordings | GRP | GRP 46482
Ella Fitzgerald With Orchestra | Forever Ella | Verve | 529387-2
Ella Fitzgerald With The Nelson Riddle Orchestra | Oh Lady Be Good:The Best Of The Gershwin Songbook | Verve | 529581-2
Ella Sings Gershwin-Vol. 1 | Metro | 2682004 IMS
George Shearing Group | Two Originals:Light,Airy And Swinging/Continental Experience/On Target | MPS | 523522-2
Helen O'Connell With The Page Cavanaugh Trio | The Uncollected:Helen O'Connell | Hindsight | HSR 228
Jim Galloway Trio | Music Is My Life | Sackville | SK2CD-5006
Jimmy Raney Quintet | Jimmy Raney/A | Original Jazz Classics | OJC-1706(P 7089)
Joe Pass | Songs For Ellen | Pablo | 2310955-2
Joe Temperley Quartet | Easy To Remember | Hep | CD 2083
Kai Winding Quartet | Kai Winding-Bop City:Small Groups 1949-1951 | Cool & Blue | C&B-CD 110
Klaus Ignatzek | Gershwin Songs | Nabel Records:Jazz Network | CD 4631
Lee Konitz-Franco D'Andrea | 12 Gershwin In 12 Keys | Philology | W 312.2
Nancy Wilson With Gerald Wilson's Orchestra | Yesterday's Love Songs-Today's Blues | Capitol | 796265-2
Oscar Peterson | My Favorite Instrument | MPS | 821843-2 PMS
Pat Dahl With Orchestra | We Dig Pat Dahl | Fresh Sound Records | Audio Fidelity AF 6157 CD
Paul Motian Quartet | Paul Motian On Broadway Vol.1 | JMT Edition | 919029-2
Pee Wee Ellis-Horace Parlan | Gentle Men Blue | Minor Music | 801073
Pierre Spiers Sextet feat. Stephane Grappelli | Special Stephane Grappelli | Jazztime(EMI) | 251286-2
Roland Kirk Quartet | Rahsaan/The Complete Mercury Recordings Of Roland Kirk | Mercury | 846630-2
Domino | Verve | 543833-2
Roy Eldridge Quartet | Frenchie Roy | Vogue | 655009
Sarah Vaughan With The Hal Mooney Orchestra | Sarah Vaughan Sings Gershwin | Verve | 557567-2
Singers Unlimited With The Roger Kellaway Cello Quartet | The Singers Unlimited:Magic Voices | MPS | 539130-2
Sonny Rollins Quintet | Here's To The People | Milestone | MCD 9194-2
Stan Kenton And His Orchestra | Stan Kenton-Jean Turner | Creative World | ST 1046
Stephane Grappelli Quartet | Stephane Grappelli 1992 Live | Dreyfus Jazz Line | FDM 37006-2
Stephane Grappelli Trio | Live | Justin Time | JTR 8469-2
Teddy Wilson-Peter Schilperoort | Jazz Intimate | DSC Production | PA 2010 (801072)
The Houdini's | The Houdini's Play The Big Five | Challenge | CHR 70027
Toots Thielemans With The Shirley Horn Trio | For My Lady | EmArCy | 510133-2
Zoot Sims Quintet | Zoot Sims And The Gershwin Brothers | Original Jazz Classics | OJC20 444-2(2310744)
Art Blakey And The Jazz Messengers | Originally | CBS | FC 38036

Someone To Watch Over Me-
LaVerne Butler With Band | No Looking Back | Chesky | JD 91
Norman Granz Jam Session | Charlie Parker Jam Session | Verve | 833564-2 PMS
Stephane Grappelli Quartet | Verve Jazz Masters 11:Stéphane Grappelli | Verve | 516758-2
Stephane Grappelli Trio | Live At The Blue Note | Telarc Digital | CD 83397

Someone To Watch Over Me(alt.take)
Stephane Grappelli Quartet | Jazz In Paris:Stephane Grappelli-Improvisations | EmArCy | 549242-2 PMS
Joe Williams With The Robert Farnon Orchestra | Joe Williams:Triple Play | Telarc Digital | CD 83461

Someone's Rocking My Dreamboat
Frank Foster's Living Color | Twelve Shades Of Black-For All Intents And Purposes | Leo Records | 007

Somethin' Else
Cannonball Adderley Quintet | Somethin' Else | Blue Note | 495329-2
Miles Davis:The Blue Note And Capitol Recordings | Blue Note | 827475-2
Miles Davis:The Best Of The Capitol/Blue Note Years | Blue Note | 798287-2
Little Brother Montgomery | Chicago-The Living Legends | Original Blues Classics | OBCCD 525-2(RLP 9410)

Something
Ella Fitzgerald With The Tommy Flanagan Trio | Ella A Nice | Original Jazz Classics | OJC20 442-2
Erroll Garner Quartet | Gemini | RCA | NL 89975(809171)
Junior Mance-Martin Rivera Duo | The Tender Touch Of: | Nilva | NQ 3405 IMS
Pete York Group | String Time In New York | BELL Records | BLR 84015
Sarah Vaughan With Orchestra | Song Of The Beatles | Atlantic | SD 16037

Something-
Duke Ellington And His Orchestra | The Ellington Suites | Original Jazz Classics | OJC20 446-2(2310762)
George Benson With The Don Sebesky Orchestra | Verve Jazz Masters 21:George Benson | Verve | 521861-2
Big Band De Lausanne | Duke Ellington's Sacred Music | TCB Records | TCB 20502

Something About John Coltrane
Matthias Spillmann Septet | Something About Water | JHM Records | JHM 3620

Something About Water
Antoine Hervé Quintet | Invention Is You | Enja | ENJ-9398 2

Something About Wolfgang
Paul Horn Quintet | Something Blue | Original Jazz Classics | OJCCD 1778-2(J 615)

Something Blue
Thelonious Monk | Thelonious Monk Collection | Black Lion | BLCD 7601-2

Something Blues
Tommy Flanagan Trio | Something Borrowed Something Blue | Original Jazz Classics | OJCCD 473-2

Something Close To Love
Carol Sloane And Her Band | When I Look In Your Eyes | Concord | CCD 4619

Something Cool
Dominique Eade With Band | When The Wind Was Cool | RCA | 2668858-2
June Christy With The Pete Rugolo Orchestra | Something Cool(The Complete Mono & Stereo Versions) | Capitol | 534069-2
California Cool | Blue Note | 780707-2

Something ELSE
Rick Hollander Quartet | Out Here | Timeless | CD SJP 309

Something Else
Steve Kuhn Quartet | Trance | ECM | 1052

Something For Liza
Louis Jordan Quartet | I Believe In Music | Black & Blue | BB 876.2

Something For October
Bob Dorough Trio With Joe Lovano | Right On My Way Home | Blue Note | 857729-2

Something For Willie
Larry Coryell | Bolero | String | BLE 233850

Something From A Fool
Giorgio Rosciglione Quartet | Giorgio Rosciglione Quartet | Penta Flowers | CDPIA 013

Something Happens To Me
Das Pferd | Blue Turns To Grey | VeraBra Records | CDVBR 2065-2

Something I Dreamed Last Night
Gene Ammons Quartet | The Gene Ammons Story: Gentle Jug | Prestige | P 24079
John Coltrane Quintet | John Coltrane-The Prestige Recordings | Prestige | 16 PCD 4405-2
Julie London With Pete King And His Orchestra | About The Blues/London By Night | Capitol | 535208-2
Miles Davis New Quintet | Workin',Steamin',Cookin',Relaxin' With The Miles Davis Quintet | Original Jazz Classics | OJCCD 8805-2
Miles Davis Quintet | Steamin' | Original Jazz Classics | OJC20 391-2
Sarah Vaughan With Orchestra | Sweet 'N' Sassy | Roulette | 531793-2
Michael Carvin | Drum Concerto At Dawn | Mapleshade | 03732

Something In You
Dizzy Gillespie Quintet | Swing Low, Sweet Cadillac | Impulse(MCA) | 951178-2

Something In Your Smile
Elmore James Band | One Way Out | Charly | CRB 1008

Something Left Unsaid
Lyle Mays Trio | Fictionary | Geffen Records | GED 24521

Something Like Bags
Wes Montgomery Quintet | So Much Guitar! | Original Jazz Classics | OJC20 233-2
Klaus Ignatzek Trio | The Klaus Ignatzek Trio | yvp music | CD 3020

Something Like This
Lee Morgan Quintet | Live At the Lighthouse '70 | Fresh Sound Records | FSR-CD 0140(2)

Something Lingers
Nat King Cole With The Billy May Orchestra | Let's Face The Music | Capitol | EMS 1112

Something More
Buster Williams Quintet | Jazz Unlimited | IN+OUT Records | 7017-2
Magic Slim Band | Highway Is My Home | Black & Blue | BLE 59.525 2

Something New For You
Don Menza Sextet | Horn Of Plenty | Pausa | PR 7170(952081) Digital

Something On Common
Rolf Von Nordenskjöld-Marc Muellbauer | Sleep Walk | BIT | 11109

Something Restless
Jimmy Witherspoon And His Band | Midnight Lady Called The Blues | Muse | MCD 5327

Something Special
Gary Burton Quintet | Gary Burton & Friends-Six Pack | GRP | GRP 96852
Sonny Clark Memorial Quartet | Voodoo | Black Saint | 120109-2
John McLaughlin | My Goal's Beyond | Vogue | 655907

Something Sweet Something Tender
Eric Dolphy Quintet | Out To Lunch | Blue Note | 498793 2
Joachim Kühn | Dynamics | CMP Records | CMP CD 49
Dave McMurdo Jazz Orchestra | Live at Montreal Bistro | Sackville | SKCD2-2029

Something There
Michael Mantler Quintet With The London Symphony Orchestra | Something There | Watt | 13
Stephen Scott Quintet | Something To Consider | Verve | 849557-2

Something To Live For
Buddy DeFranco Trio | Do Nothing Till You Hear From Us! | Concord | CCD 4851
Chris Connor With The Ralph Burns Orchestra | Chris Connor | Atlantic | 7567-80769-2
Clark Terry With Bob Lark And The DePaul University Big Band | Clark Terry Express | Reference Recordings | RR-73 CD
Dave Ellis Quartet | State Of Mind | Milestone | MCD 9328-2
Duke Ellington And His Orchestra | Unknown Session | CBS | 467180-2
Ella Fitzgerald With The Duke Ellington Orchestra | Ella Fitzgerald-First Lady Of Song | Verve | 517898-2
The Stockholm Concert 1966 | Pablo | 2308242-2
Ella Fitzgerald With The Duke Ellington Orchestra And Jimmy Jones Trio | Ella Fitzgerald And Duke Ellington:Cote D'Azure Concerts on Verve | Verve | 539033-2
Ella Fitzgerald And Duke Ellington:Cote D'Azure Concerts on Verve | Verve | 539033-2
Grant Stewart Quartet | Buen Rollo | Fresh Sound Records | FSNT 053 CD
Howard Alden Trio | A Good Likeness | Concord | CCD 4544

Something To Remember You By
Bud Freeman All Stars | The Bud Freeman All Stars | Original Jazz Classics | OJC 183(SV 2012)
Keith Jarrett | The Melody At Night,With You | ECM | 1675(547949-2)
Lester Young And His Band | Lester Young:The Complete Aladdin Sessions | Blue Note | 832787-2
Lester Young Quintet | Lester Young:The Complete 1936-1951 Small Group Sessions(Studio Recordings-Master Takes),Vol.4 | Blue Moon | BMCD 1004

Something To Remind You
Lee Konitz Quintet | Peacemeal | Milestone | M 9025

Something Within' Me
The Pilgrim Travelers | The Best Of The Pilgrim Travelers | Ace Records | CDCHD 342

Something You've Got
King Curtis Band | King Curtis-Blow Man Blow | Bear Family Records | BCD 15670 CI

Something You've Got(overdub)
Howard Riley | For Four On Two Two | Affinity | AFF 110

Something's Coming
Chris Connor With The Ronnie Ball Quartet | Late Show-At The Village Gate | Fresh Sound Records | FSR 705(FM 3035)(835430)
Oscar Peterson Trio | West Side Story | Verve | 539753-2
Stan Kenton And His Orchestra | West Side Story | Capitol | 829914-2

Something's Coming-
Rhein Brass And Friends | Kant Park | Mons Records | MR 874318

Something's Got A Hold On Me
Etta James With Orchestra | Peaches | Chess | 427014
Lillian Boutté And Her Group | Lipstick Traces(A New Orleans R&B Session) | Blues Beacon | BLU-1011 2

Something's Gotta Give
Ella Fitzgerald With The Nelson Riddle Orchestra | Ella Fitzgerald Sings The Johnny Mercer Songbook | Verve | 539057-2
The Johnny Mercer Songbook | Verve | 823247-2 PMS
Trav'lin' Light:The Johnny Mercer Songbook | Verve | 555402-2
Freddie Green And His All Stars | Mr. Rhythm | RCA | 2130072-2

Somethink
Eddie 'Blues Man' Kirkland Band | It's The Blues Man! | Original Blues Classics | OBCCD 513-2(Tru 15010)

Sometime
Art Pepper Quartet | Art Pepper:The Complete Galaxy Recordings | Galaxy | 16GCD 1016-2
Landscape | Original Jazz Classics | OJCCD 676-2(GXY 5128)

Sometime Ago
John Hicks Trio | Single Petal Of A Rose | Mapleshade | 02532
Marian McPartland-Rene Rosness | Just Friends:Marian McPartland Performs Piano Duets With... | Concord | CCD 4805
Niels-Henning Orsted-Pedersen Trio | Friends Forever | Milestone | MCD 9269-2
Steve Kuhn Trio | Years Later | Concord | CCD 4554
Thomas Stabenow-Lothar Schmitz | Swet Peanuts | Bassic-Sound | CD 007

Sometime Ago-La Fiesta
Sunnyland Slim | Sunnyland Train | Steeplechase | SCB 9002

Sometimes
Jay Clayton And Her Quintet | Circle Dancing | Sunnyside | SSC 1076 D

Sometimes Ago
Lee Konitz Quartet | Satori | Milestone | M 9060
Tierney Sutton And Her Trio | Blue In Green | Telarc Digital | CD 83522

Sometimes I Feel Like A Motherless Child

Artie Shaw And His Orchestra | The Indispensable Artie Shaw Vol.3/4 | RCA | 2126414-2
Bob Stewart First Line Band | First Line | JMT Edition | 919014-2
Bobby Timmons Trio | Moanin' | Milestone | M 47031
Charlie Haden-Hank Jones | Steal Away | Verve | 527249-2
David Murray Quintet | Remembrances | DIW | DIW 849 CD
Golden Gate Quartet | From Spriritual To Swing Vol.2 | EMI Records | 780573-2
Grant Green Quintet | Feelin' The Spirit | Blue Note | 746822-2
Hannibal Marvin Peterson Group | The Angels Of Atlanta | Enja | 3085-2
Jeanne Lee | The Newest Sound Around | RCA | 2122112-2
Louis Armstrong With Sy Oliver's Choir And Orchestra | Louis And The Good Book | Verve | 940130-0
Louis And The Good Book | Verve | 549593-2
Mario Schiano With Archie Savage And Clebert Ford | Meetings | SPLASC(H) Records | CD H 418-2
Ramsey Lewis Trio | Down To Earth | Verve | 538329-2
Ray Brown-Milt Jackson Quintet | Much In Common | Verve | 533259-2
Sadao Watanabe Quintet With Strings | Plays Ballads | Denon Compact Disc | DC-8555
Singers Unlimited | A Capella III | MPS | 68245
Willis Jackson Quartet | At Large | Prestige | PCD 24243-2
James Williams | Live at Maybeck Recital Hall Series Volume Forty-Two:James Williams | Concord | CCD 4694

Sometimes I Feel Like A Motherless Child-
Joe Turner | Walking Through Heaven | Swingtime | 8205
Ramsey Lewis Trio | Down To Earth | Verve | 538329-2

Sometimes I Feel Like A Motherless Child(alt.take)
Max Roach Sextet With The J.C.White Singers | Lift Every Voice And Sing | Atlantic | 7567-80798-2

Sometimes I Feel Like A Motherless Child(for Marcus Garvey)
Michael Brecker Quintet | Nearness Of You-The Ballad Book | Verve | 549705-2

Sometimes I See
Pat Metheny Group | Quartet | Geffen Records | GED 24978
Michael Mantler Group | Silence | Watt | 5 (2313105)

Sometimes I See People
Michael Mantler: No Answer/Silence | Watt | 2/5(543374-2)
Clarence Gatemouth Brown Band | Alright Again! | Edsel | Fiend 2

Sometimes I'm Happy
Arthur Briggs And HisOrchestra | L'Essentiel Django Reinhardt | EMI Records | 780671-2
Benny Goodman And His Orchestra | More Camel Caravans | Phontastic | NCD 8845/6
The Benny Goodman Story | Capitol | 833569-2
The Indispensable Benny Goodman Vol.1/2:Birth Of A Big Band | RCA | NL 89755 (809180)
Billie Holiday With The Ray Ellis Orchestra | Last Recordings | Verve | 835370-2 PMS
Bud Powell Trio | Bud Powell:Complete 1947-1951 Blue Note,Verve & Roost Recordings | The Jazz Factory | JFCD 22837
Cal Collins Trio | Cal Collins In San Francisco | Concord | CJ 71
Dick Hafer Quartet | Prez Impressions-Dedicated To The Memory Of Lester Young | Fresh Sound Records | FSR-CD 5002
Eddie Lockjaw Davis-Shirley Scott Sextet | Bacalao | Original Jazz Classics | OJCCD 1090-2(P 7178)
Fletcher Henderson And His Sextet | New-York December 1950 | Jazz Anthology | JA 5185
Helen Humes And Her All Stars | Sneakin' Around | Black & Blue | BLE 233083
Joe Newman Octet | The Complete Joe Newman RCA-Victor Recordings(1955-1956):The Basie Days | RCA | 2122613-2
John Pizzarelli Trio And Friends | After Hours | Novus | 4163191-2
Johnny Smith-Stan Getz Quintet | Stan Getz-The Complete Roost Sessions | EMI Records | 859622-2
Stan Getz-The Complete Roost Sessions | The Jazz Factory | JFCD 22839
Lester Young Quartet | Lester Young:The Complete 1936-1949 Small Group Alternatives(Studio Recordings),Vol.1 | Blue Moon | BMCD 1505
Lester Young With The Bill Potts Trio | Lester Young In Washington,DC 1956:Vol.3 | Pablo | 2308228
Louis Jordan And His Tympany Five | Five Guys Named Moe | Bandstand | BDCD 1531
Oscar Peterson | Oscar Peterson:Exclusively For My Friends | MPS | 513830-2
Oscar Peterson Trio | The Trio-Live From Chicago | Verve | 823008-2
Roy Eldridge-Dizzy Gillespie With The Oscar Peterson Quartet | Roy And Diz | Verve | 521647-2
Scott Hamilton Quintet | Scott Hamilton Is A Good Wind Who Is Blowing Us No Ill | Concord | CCD 4042
Terry Morel With The Ralph Sharon Quartet | Songs Of A Woman In Love | Fresh Sound Records | FSR 2037(Bethlehem BCP 47)

Sometimes In Winter
Jeannie And Jimmy Cheatham & The Sweet Baby Blues Band | Homeward Bound | Concord | CCD 4321

Sometimes It Snows In April
Peter Bolte Quartet | ...All The April Snow | ITM-Pacific | ITMP 970092

Sometimes Perpetually
Jessica Williams | The Victoria Concert | Jazz Focus | JFCD 015

Somewhere
Arcado | Behind The Myth | JMT Edition | 834441-2
Henry Johnson Group | You're The One | Impulse(MCA) | MCA 5754
Mads Vinding Trio | The Kingdom | Stunt Records | STUCD 19703
Oscar Pettiford Orchestra | Deep Passion | Impulse(MCA) | GRP 11432
Steve Davis Sextet | Vibe Up! | Criss Cross | Criss 1178
Warren Bernhardt Trio | So Real | dmp Digital Music Productions | CD 532
Woody Herman And His Orchestra | The Best Of The Big Dance Bands | LRC Records | CDC9010

Somewhere-
Cal Tjader With The Clare Fischer Orchestra | Cal Tjader Plays Harold Arlen & West Side Story | Fantasy | FCD 24775-2
Cannonball Adderley Quintet | Les Is More | Night Records | VNCD 4(887048)

Somewhere Along The Way
Buster Williams Quintet | Somewhere Along The Way | TCB Records | TCB 97602
Keith Jarrett Trio | Somewhere Before | Atlantic | 7567-81455-2

Somewhere Before
Dave Grusin Group | Night-Lines | GRP | GRP 95042

Somewhere Called Home
Freddy Cole Septet | This Is The Life | Muse | MCD 5503

Somewhere East
Barry Altschul Trio | Somewhere Else | Moers Music | 01064

Somewhere Else
Jay Clayton-Jerry Granelli | Sound Songs | JMT Edition | 919006-2
Mulgrew Miller Trio | With Our Own Eyes | Novus | 4163171-2

Somewhere Else Before
Billy Childs Group | I've Known Rivers | Stretch Records | SCD 9010-2

Somewhere If Not In Heaven
Volker Schlott Quartet | Why Not | Acoustic Music Records | 319.1083.2

Somewhere In My Dreams
Etta Jones With The Houston Person Quintet | The Melody Lingers On | HighNote Records | HCD 7005

Somewhere In The Hills
Cal Tjader's Orchestra | Cal Tjader/Soul Sauce | Verve | 521668-2

Somewhere In The Night
Frant Green Quartet | Street Of Dreams | Blue Note | 821290-2
Gloria Lynne And Her Band/Orchestra | Starry Eyes | Verve | 539777-2

Somewhere In The South
Eddie Kirkland Group | Have Mercy | Evidence | ECD 26018-2

Somewhere My Love
AM 4 | Roots & Fruits | EmArCy | 537495-2

Somewhere Over The Rainbow
Clark Terry-Chris Woods Quintet | Swiss Radio Days Jazz Series Vol.8:Clark Terry-Chris Woods | TCB Records | TCB 02082
Earl Hines | Msters Of Jazz Vol.2:Earl Hines | Storyville | SLP 4102
Harry Allen With The John Pizzarelli Trio | Tenors Anyone? | Novus | 2150684-2
Joe Morello Quartet | Morello Standard Time | dmp Digital Music Productions | CD 506
Paul Motian Quartet | Paul Motian On Broadway Vol.1 | JMT Edition | 919029-2
Phil Minton And Veryan Weston | Ways Past | ITM Records | ITM 1468
Cornelius Claudio Kreusch | Talking To A Goblin | Edition Collage | EC 441-2

Somewhere Over The Rainbow-
Dutch Swing College Band | Digital Date | Philips | 834087-2

Sommerballade
Stötter's Nevertheless | But, Where Is The Exit? | L+R Records | CDLR 45099

Sommernat Ved Fjorden(Summer Night By The Fjord)
Hajo Weber-Ulrich Ingenbold Duo | Winterreise | ECM | 1235

Sommerrest
Gumpert-Sommer Duo plus Manfred Hering | The Old Song | FMP | 0170

Somnamblues
Rob McConnell And The Boss Brass | Brassy & Sassy | Concord | CCD 4508

Somnia
New York Jazz Collective | Everybody Wants To Go To Heaven | Naxos Jazz | 86073-2

Somos Novios(Impossible)
Mario Bauzá And His Afro-Cuban Jazz Orchestra | My Time Is Now | Messidor | 15842 CD

Son De La Loma
Christof Sänger & Cuban Fantasy | Moliendo Café | Mons Records | MR 874302

Son Montuno
Eddie Jefferson And His Band | Come Along With Me | Original Jazz Classics | OJCCD 613-2(P 7698)

Son Of A Preacher Man
Al Cohn And His Orchestra | Drum Suite/Son Of Drum Suite | RCA | 2136409-2

Son Of Alfalfa
Rabih Abou-Khalil Group | Odd Times | Enja | ENJ-9330 2

Son Of Ben Hur
Jaco Pastorius Trio | Live In New York City Volume Two | Big World | BW 1002

Son Of Gaudi
Lonnie Smith Orchestra | Think | Blue Note | 784290-2

Son Ombre
Poncho Sanchez And His Orchestra | El Mejor | Concord | CCD 4519

Son Song-
Fra-Fra Sound | Panja-Gazz +4 | Jazz Pure Collection | AU 31619 CD

Sonanzen
Curtis Counce Group | Landslide | Original Jazz Classics | OJCCD 606-2

Sonar
Victor Feldman Septet | Suite Sixteen | Original Jazz Classics | OJCCD 1768-2C 3541)

Sonata-
Duke Ellington And His Orchestra | Duke Elliongton:Complete Prestige Carnegie Hall 1943-1944 Concerts | Definitive Records | DRCD 11210

Sonata In C Minor(Johann Joachim Quantz):
Eugen Cicero-Decebal Badila | Swinging Piano Classics | IN+OUT Records | 77047-2

Sonata In C-Major
Laurindo Almeida-Bud Shank Duo | Selected Classical Works For Guitar And Flute | Concord | CC 2003

Sonata In D-Dur
Free Flight | Soaring | Palo Alto | PA 8050

Sonate 2. Satz
Eugen Cicero Trio | Eugen Cicero Highlights | MPS | 88028-2

Sonate In E Moll:
Harry James And His Orchestra | James And Haymes | Circle | CCD-5

Sonatesca Gutural(part 1-3)
Josep Maria Balanyà | Sonateskas | Laika Records | 35101102

Sonatesca Prensil Polyphonica(part 1-3)
Joe Bonner Trio | New Life | Steeplechase | SCCD 31239

Sonet For Caesar
Duke Ellington And His Orchestra | Live In Paris 1959 | Affinity | CD AFS 777

Sonet In Search Of Amour
Emborg-Larsen Group | Face The Music | Stunt Records | STUCD 19805

Sonetburger
Heiner Goebbels/Alfred Harth | Berold Brecht:Zeit wird knapp | Riskant | 568-72414

Sonett Till Cornelis
John Tchicai-Pierre Dorge | Ball At Louisiana | Steeplechase | SCCD 31174

Song
Five Voices | Direct Sound | Intakt Records | CD 015
Ketil Bjornstad Group | Grace | EmArCy | 013622-2
Mikhail Alperin/Arkady Shilkloper | Wave Over Sorrow | ECM | 1396
Sibylle Pomorin/Terry Jenoure Group | Auguries Of Speed | ITM Records | ITM 1467

Song-
Joe Lovano Quartet | Live At The Village Vanguard | Blue Note | 829125-2

Song And Dance
Rova Saxophone Quartet | Long On Logic | Sound Aspects | sas CD 037

Song For A Crow
Nancy Harrow With The Gary McFarland Orchestra | You Never Know | Atlantic | AMCY 1070

Song For A Friend
The Atlantic String Trio | First Meeting | Factory Outlet Records | FOR 2501-1 CD
First Meeting | Factory Outlet Records | 2001-1 CD

Song For A Mellow Fellow
Circle | Paris Concert | ECM | 1018/19(843163-2)

Song For A Newborn
Ketil Bjornstad Group | The Sea II | ECM | 1633(537341-2)

Song For A Planet
Houston Person Quintet | The Opening Round | Savant Records | SCD 2005

Song For A Real Friend
Arild Andersen Quartet | Clouds In My Mind | ECM | 1059

Song For A Willow
Thomas Kessler & Group | Thomas Kessler & Group | Laika Records | LK 190-015

Song For A(part 1&2)
Masha Bijlsma Band | Profile | Jazzline | JL 11157-2

Song For Aggerey
Lothar Müller Trio | Müller Q[kju] | JA & RO | JARO 4251-2

Song For Agnes
Marilyn Crispell | Live At Mills College, 1995 | Music & Arts | CD 899

Song For An Unfinished Woman
Andy Fusco Quintet | Out Of The Dark | Criss Cross | Criss 1171

Song For B.
Michel Grailler | In A Spring Way | Red Records | VPA 133

Song For Bam Bam
Wolfgang Haffner Project | Back Home | Jazz 4 Ever Records:Jazz Network | J4E 4730
The Brecker Brothers | Return Of The Brecker Brothers | GRP | GRP 96842

Song For Barry
The Brecker Brothers Live | Jazz Door | JD 1248

Song For Ben
Jimmy Heath Sextet | Peer Pleasure | Landmark | LCD 1514-2

Song For Bilbao
Pat Metheny Group | Travels | ECM | 1252/53
Bunny Brunel Group | Dedication | Accord | 500362

Song For Carlos
Peppino D'Agostino | Close To The Heart | Acoustic Music Records | 319.1039.2

Song For Che
Ellery Eskelin With Andrea Parkins & Jim Black | Five Other Pieces(+2) | HatOLOGY | 533
Christoph Spendel | Dreams & Melodies | Software Music | SOWA 107

Song For Claudia
Russell Malone Quartet | Sweet Georgia Peach | Impulse(MCA) | 951282-2

Song For Darius
Mulgrew Miller Trio | Keys To The City | Landmark | LCD 1507-2

Song For Eda
Enrico Pieranunzi Trio | From Always To Now | EdiPan | NPG 803

Song For Eddie
David Matthews & The Manhattan Jazz Orchestra | Hey Duke! | Milestone | MCD 9320-2

Song For Edward
Phil Moerke Group feat. Victor Mendoza | Multi Colors | Jazz Pure Collection | AU 31625 CD

Song For Ellen
Joe Pass | Joe Pass:Guitar Virtuoso | Pablo | 4 PACD 4423-2
Joe Pass Quintet | My Song | Telarc Digital | CD 83326

Song For Elswhere
Larry Coryell Quintet | The Coryells | Chesky | JD 192

Song For Everyone
Roscoe Mitchell And The Note Factory | This Dance Is For Steve McCall | Black Saint | 120150-2

Song For Hans
Katrina Krimsky-Trevor Watts | Stella Malu | ECM | 1199
Chico Hamilton Trio | Trio! | Soul Note | 121246-2

Song For Helga
Palle Mikkelborg Trio | Heart To Heart | Storyville | STCD 4114

Song For Her
Charles Lloyd Quintet | The Water Is Wide | ECM | 1734(549043-2)
Aki Takase Trio | Song For Hope | Enja | 4012 (807512)

Song For J.&J.
In Spector | Europ' Jazz Contest '92 Belgium | B.Sharp Records | CDS 092

Song For Jobim
Lars Moller Group | Colours | Stunt Records | STUCD 19711

Song For Larry
Joe McPhee Quintet | Black Magic Man | Hat Art | A

Song For Lee Lee
Mal Waldron-Nicolas Simion | Art Of The Duo:The Big Rochade | Tutu Records | 888186-2*

Song For Leo
Nicolas Simion Group | Black Sea | Tutu Records | 888134-2*

Song For Leo(dedicated to Leo Wright)
Ronnie Mathews Trio | So Sorry Please... | Nilva | NQ 3414 IMS

Song For Lila-
Jim McNeely Trio | East Side/West Side | Owl Records | 024

Song For Lynn
Mario Pavone Septet | Song For (Septet) | New World Records | 80452-2

Song For Magali
Hamiet Bluiett Clarinet Family | The Clarinet Family | Black Saint | 120097-2

Song For Maya
Willie Williams Quartet | Spirit Willie | Enja | ENJ-7045 2

Song For Mike
EOS | Mosaico | yvp music | CD 3056

Song For My Father
Don 'Sugar Cane' Harris Quintet | Got The Blues | MPS | 68029
George Benson With Orchestra | The Silver Collection: George Benson | Verve | 823450-2 PMS
Horace Silver Quintet | Blue Note's Three Decade Of Jazz 1959-1969, Vol. 1 | Blue Note | 89904
The Blue Note Years-The Best Of Horace Silver Vol.2 | Blue Note | 793206-2
Horace Silver Retrospective | Blue Note | 495576-2
Jenny Evans And Band | Live At The Allotria | ESM Records | ESM 9301
Girl Talk | ESM Records | ESM 9306
Girl Talk | Enja | ENJ-9363 2
Live At The Allotria | BELL Records | BLR 90003
Larry Coryell-Michael Urbaniak Duo | The Larry Coryell-Michael Urbaniak Duo | Keytone | KYT 716
Manhattan Jazz Quintet | Funky Strut | Sweet Basil | 660.55.006
Twobones | Spiral Stairway | TCB Records | TCB 99752
Larry Coryell | Tributaries | Novus | NL 83072

Song For My Lady
Om | Rautionaha | Japo | 60016 IMS

Song For My Mother
Walt Weiskopf Nonet | Song For My Mother | Criss Cross | Criss 1127

Song For My Parents
Patrick Tompert Trio | Patrick Tompert Trio Live | Satin Doll Productions | SDP 1029-1 CD

Song For My Parents-
Dirk Balthaus-Bert Lochs Quartet | Tales Of The Frog | Acoustic Music Records | 319.1082.2

Song For Patrick
Joey Calderazzo-Branford Marsalis | To Know One | Blue Note | 798165-2

Song For Phyllis
Craig Harris Quintet | Black Bone | Soul Note | 121055-2

Song For René
Robert Jeanne Quartet | Quartets | B.Sharp Records | CDS 084

Song For Sally
Gust Williams Tsilis Quintet | Wood Music | Enja | ENJ-7093 2

Song For Sarah
Thomas Stanko Quartet | Suspended Night | ECM | 1868(9811244)
Phil Woods Quintet | Mile High Jazz:Live In Denver | Concord | CCD 4739

Song For Sathima
Abdullah Ibrahim And Ekaya | Water From An Ancient Well | TipToe | TIP-888812 2

Song For Sathima(Daughter Of Cape Town)
Buster Williams Quintet | Somewhere Along The Way | TCB Records | TCB 97602

Song For Sinners
Joe Henderson Sextet | Multiple | Original Jazz Classics | OJCCD 763-2(M 9050)
Phil Woods & Space Jazz Trio | Live At The Corridonia Jazz Festival 1991 | Philology | W 211.2

Song For Somalia
Chris Kase Sextet | Starting Now | Mons Records | MR 874659

Song For Starsy
Chris Hinze-Sigi Schwab Duo | Backstage | Melos Music | CDGS 801

Song For Stina
Alan Barnes And The David Newton Trio | Below Zero | Concord | CCD 4842

Song For Strayhorn
Gerry Mulligan Quartet | Triple Play:Gerry Mulligan | Telarc Digital | CD 83453

Song For Thad
Buster Williams Quintet | Somewhere Along The Way | TCB Records | TCB 97602

Song For The Boys
Mark Murphy With The Marc Seales Trio & Background Voices | Song For The Geese | RCA | 2144865-2

Song For The Masters
Eric Kloss-Barry Miles Duo | Together | Muse | MR 5112

Song For The Sun
Pierre Dorge's New Jungle Orchestra | Giraf | dacapo | DCCD 9440

Song For The Swan
John Carter-Bobby Bradford's New Art Jazz Ensemble | Seeking | Hat Art | CD 6085

Song For The Whales

Johnny Mbizo Dyani Group | Born Under The Heat | Dragon | DRLP 68

Song For Thomas
Ketil Bjornstad-David Darling | Epigraphs | ECM | 1684(543159-2)

Song For TKJD
Mulgrew Miller Trio | Time And Again | Landmark | LCD 1532-2

Song For Tomas
Boel-Emborg-Vinding-Riel | Shadow Of Love | Stunt Records | 18803

Song For World Forgiveness
Lainie Kazan With Band | In The Groove | Musicmasters | 65168-2

Song For You
Peter O'Mara Quintet | Back Seat Driver | Enja | 9126-2
Tuck And Patti | A Gift Of Love | T&P Records | 9815810
Stefan Pelzl's Juju feat. Idris Muhammad | Juju | L+R Records | CDLR 45026

Song From M.A.S.H.
Bill Evans Trio | Homecoming | Milestone | MCD 9291-2
Cal Tjader Quintet | The Shining Sea | Concord | CCD 4159
Paul Desmond Quartet | Hollywood Jazz | CBS | 474373-2

Song From Moulin Rouge
Duke Ellington And His Orchestra | Duke 56/62 Vol.3 | CBS | 26306

Song From Mountains
David Murray Quartet | Shakill's Warrior | DIW | DIW 850 CD

Song From The Valley
Amina Claudine Myers Group | Amina | RCA | PD 83030

Song Hollandaise
David Friesen | Paths Beyond Tracing | Steeplechase | SCCD 31138

Song Mecanique
Eddie Louiss-Richard Galliano Duo | Face To Face | Dreyfus Jazz Line | FDM 36627-2

Song No.1
Tom Scott Quintet | Born Again | GRP | GRP 96752

Song No.2
Miles Davis With Gil Evans & His Orchestra | Ballads | CBS | 461099-2
Original Phalanx | Original Phalanx | DIW | DIW 801 CD

Song Of A Wayfarer
Jean-Paul Bourelly Group | Blackadelic-Blu | DIW | DIW 883 CD

Song Of India
Tommy Dorsey And His Orchestra | Planet Jazz:Big Bands | Planet Jazz | 2169649-2
Planet Jazz:Tommy Dorsey | Planet Jazz | 2159972-2
This Is Tommy Dorsey | RCA | PL 89536 DP

Song Of Our Country
Art Farmer-Fritz Pauer Duo | Azure | Soul Note | 121126-2

Song Of Praise
John Coltrane Quartet | John Coltrane:The Classic Quartet-Complete Impulse Studio Recordings | Impulse(MCA) | 951280-2
Coltrane Spiritual | Impulse(MCA) | 589099-2
John Coltrane:The Classic Quartet-Complete Impulse Studio Recordings | Impulse(MCA) | 951280-2

Song Of Praise(first version)
Elise Einarsdotter-Olle Steinholz | Sketches Of Roses | Touché Music | TMcCD 008

Song Of Ra
Nils Petter Molvaer Group | Khmer | ECM | 1560(537798-2)

Song Of Sands(I)-
Khmer | ECM | 1560(537798-2)

Song Of Sands(II)
Allan Vaché Big Four | Revisited! | Nagel-Heyer | CD 044

Song Of Songs
Woody Shaw Quintet | Lotus Flower | Enja | 4018-2

Song Of Space
Mike Westbrook Brass Band | Glad Day:Settings Of William Blake | Enja | ENJ-9376 2

Song Of Spring
David Friesen Group | Waterfall Rainbow | Inner City | IC 1027 IMS

Song Of The Countrymen
Guido Manusardi | Concerto | SPLASC(H) Records | CD H 437-2

Song Of The East
Carla Bley Band | Fleur Carnivore | Watt | 21

Song Of The Eternal Waiting Of Canute
Toshiko Mariano Quartet | Live At Birdland | Fresh Sound Records | FSCD 1021

Song Of The Fisherman-
Wadada Leo Smith | Kulture Jazz | ECM | 1507

Song Of The Humanity(Kanto Pri Homaro)
Basie Jam | Basie Jam No. 3 | Original Jazz Classics | OJCCD 687-2(2310840)

Song Of The Islands
Count Basie Quintet | The Swinging Count | Verve | MV 2646 IMS
Sackville All Stars | A Tribute To Louis Armstrong | Sackville | SKCD2-3042

Song Of The Jet -> Samba Do Aviao

Song Of The Jungle Stream
Ted Curson Quartet | Ted Curson & Co | India Navigation | IN 1054

Song Of The Moon(Shadows & Traffic Lights)
Collin Walcott Group | Grazing Dreams | ECM | 1096

Song Of The Morrow
Oregon | Ecotopia | ECM | 1354
Lionel Hampton Orchestra | The Many Sides Of Lionel Hampton | Ember | CJS 805

Song Of The Pharoah Kings
Mike Westbrook Brass Band | The Paris Album | Polydor | 2655008 IMS

Song Of The Soul
Boots Randolph-Richie Cole Sextet | Yakety Madness! | Palo Alto | PA 8041

Song Of The Underground Railroad
John Coltrane Quartet With Brass | The Africa Brass Sessions, Vol. 2 | MCA | 2292-54648-2

Song Of The United Front
Art Tatum | Art Tatum:Memories Of You | Black Lion | BLCD 7608-2

Song Of The Volga Boatmen
Glenn Miller And His Orchestra | The Very Best Of Glenn Miller | RCA | PL 89009 AO

Song Of The Wanderer
Scetches | Different Places | VeraBra Records | CDVBR 2102-2

Song Of The Whales
Chick Corea | Piano Improvisations-Vol.1 | ECM | 1014(811979-2)

Song Of The Wind
Chick Corea Septet | The Complete 'Is' Sessions | Blue Note | 540532-2
John McLaughlin | My Goals Beyond | Elektra | MUS K 52364

Song Of The Wind(alt.take)
Edward Vesala Trio With Orchestra | Bad Luck Good Luck | Leo Records | 015

Song Of The Yearning
Cal Tjader With The Lalo Schifrin Orchestra | Several Shades Of Jade/Breeze From The East | Verve | 537083-2

Song Of Yearning
Paolo Fresu Quartet | Angel | RCA | 2155864-2

Song One
Henry Threadgill Group | Song Out Of My Trees | Black Saint | 120154-2

Song Sung Long
Carla Bley Band | Live! | Watt | 12(815730-2)
Vienna Art Orchestra | European Songbook | Amadeo | 527672-2

Song To Aurore
Oscar Peterson And His Trio | Saturday Night At The Blue Note | Telarc Digital | CD 83306

Song To Gayle
Gary Burton-Chick Corea | Duet | ECM | 1140(829941-2)
Stanley Clarke-Al DiMeola-Jean Luc Ponty | The Rite Of Strings | Gai Saber | 834167-2

Song To The East
Ferenc Snétberger Trio | Obsession | TipToe | TIP-888834 2
Al Di Meola Group | Tiramisu | Manhattan | CDP 7469952

Song With Orange
Charles Mingus Orchestra | Nostalgia In Times Square/The Immortal 1959 Sessions | CBS | 88337
Pepper Adams Quintet | Pepper Adams Plays Charlie Mingus | Fresh Sound Records | FSR-CD 0177

Song With Orange(alt.take)
Lee Konitz-Matt Wilson | Gone With The Wind | Steeplechase | SCCD 31528

Song With Wind
Bill Holman Octet | Group Activity | Affinity | AFF 65

Song Without Words
Stan Getz With The Danish Radio Big Band | Stan Getz In Europe | Laserlight | 24657
Stan Getz | Laserlight | 15761

Song X
Pat Metheny/Ornette Coleman Group | Song X | Geffen Records | GED 24096

Song X Duo
Das Böse Ding | Cleanhappydirty | Acoustic Music Records | 319.1090.2

Song,Tread Lightly
Vic Juris Trio | Songbook | Steeplechase | SCCD 31843

SongFor Helen
Kevin Eubanks Group | Shadow Prophet | GRP | GRP 95652

Songo Baiao
New Generation Cuban All Stars | New Generation Cuban All Stars Vol.2:Nuestro Tiempo | Messidor | 15942

Songs And Moments
Sax Mal Anders | Kontraste | Chaos | CACD 8185

Songs For Tony I
Vienna Art Orchestra | European Songbook | Amadeo | 527672-2

Songs Of Struggle And Songs Of Love
Eric Kloss Quintet | Eric Kloss & The Rhythm Section | Prestige | PCD 24125-2(P 7689/7793)

Song-Song
Ana Caram Group | Amazonia | Chesky | JD 45

Sonia Said
Tomasz Stanko-Manfred Bründl-Michael Riessler | Suite Talk | ITM-Pacific | ITMP 970081

Sonic
Jimmy Giuffre 3 | Flight, Bremen 1961 | Hat Art | CD 6071

Sonic Boom
Joe Farrell Quintet | Sonic Text | Contemporary | C 14002

Sonidos De Aquel Dia
Kenny Barron Group | Spirit Song | Verve | 543180-2

Sonja Braga
Johnny 'Hammond' Smith Quartet | Good 'Nuff | Prestige | PRCD 24282-2

Sonja's Dreamland
Dave Valentine Group | Mind Time | GRP | GRP 91043-1(080738)

Sonnet
Mike Westbrook Trio | Love For Sale | Hat Art | CD 6061

Sonnet For Sister Kate
Horace Tapscott | The Tapscott Sessions Vol.7 | Nimbus | NS 2147

Sonnet To Hank Cinq
Duke Ellington And His Orchestra | En Concert Avec Europe 1 | Laserlight | 710707/08

Sonnifero Per Inamorati
Hans Joachim Roedelius/Alexander Czjzek | Weites Land | Amadeo | 831627-2

Sonny Boy
Cal Tjader's Modern Mambo Quintet(Sextet) | Mambo With Tjader | Original Jazz Classics | OJCCD 271-2(F 3202)
Chet Baker-Art Pepper Sextet | The Route | Pacific Jazz | 792931-2
Oscar Pettiford Quartet | Charles Mingus-The Young Rebel | Swingtime(Contact) | ST 1010
Stephane Grappelli-Marc Fosset Duo | Stephanova | Concord | CJ 225
Toots Thielemans Quartet | Harmonica Jazz | CBS | CBS 21108

Sonny Boy-
Jimmy Rushing And His All Stars | The Bluesway Sessions | Charly | CDX 13

Sonny Sounds
Woody Herman And His Orchestra | Woody Herman:Complete 1948-1950 Capitol Sessions | Definitive Records | DRCD 11195

Sonnymoon For Two
Frank Morgan All Stars | Reflections | Contemporary | CCD 14052-2
Humair-Louiss-Ponty | Volume 2 | Dreyfus Jazz Line | FDM 36510-2
Jimmy Smith Trio | Jimmy Smith: Grazy Baby | Blue Note | 784030-2
Shirley Scott Quartet | Queen Of The Organ-Shirley Scott Memorial Album | Prestige | PRCD 11027-2
Sonny Rollins Quartet | Sonnymoon For Two | Moon Records | MCD 015-2
Sonny Rollins Quintet | The Bop Rebells | Jazz Door | JD 1218
Sonny Rollins Trio | A Night At The Village Vanguard | Blue Note | 499795-2
Sonny Rollins:The Blue Note Recordings | Blue Note | 821371-2
Jazz Gallerie:Sonny Rollins Vol.1 | RCA | 2127283-2
Sonny Rollins With The Kenny Drew Trio | Sonny Rollins In Denmark Vol.2 | Moon Records | MCD 038-2

Sonny's Blues
Sonny Berman Orchestra | Sonny Berman:Woodshopper's Holiday 1946 | Cool & Blue | C&B-CD 111

Sonny's Book
Sonny Stitt Quartet | Soul People | Prestige | PCD 24127-2(P 7372/7852)

Sonny's Crib
Sonny Clark Trio | Blues Mambo | West Wind | WW 2103

Sonny's Mood
Sonny Stitt Sextet | Sonny's Last Recordings | Kingdom Jazz | Gate 7012

Sonny's Tune
Sonny Rollins Quartet | Rollins Meets Cherry Vol.1 | Moon Records | MCD 053-2

Sonnyside
Trombone Scene | Trombone Scene | Fresh Sound Records | NL 45925(RCA LPM 1087)

Sonnysphere
Sonny Rollins Quintet | Sonny Rollins:The Blue Note Recordings | Blue Note | 821371-2
Al Hibbler With Harry Carney's All Stars | Rare Dates Without The Duke 1944/49 | Raretone | 5011 FC

Sono
Duke Ellington And His Orchestra | Carnegie Hall Concert January 1946 | Prestige | 2PCD 24074-2
Duke Ellington:Complete Prestige Carnegie Hall 1946-1947 Concerts | Definitive Records | DRCD 11211

Sonor
Paul Bley Duo | Sonor | Soul Note | SN 1085

Sonrisa
Rade Soric Quartet | Mixturiosities | Edition Collage | EC 502-2

Sons Of The Confidential
Hajo Weber-Ulrich Ingenbold Duo | Winterreise | ECM | 1235

Sony Boy Blues
Miles Davis Group | Doo-Bop | Warner | 7599-26938-2

Sonya
Shelly Berg Trio | The Joy | dmp Digital Music Productions | CD 3002

Soo Yang Kol(The Valley Of Weeping Willows)
Joe Thomas And His Orchestra | Joe Thomas:The Complete Recordings 1945-1950 | Blue Moon | BMCD 1051

Sookie, Sookie
Grant Green Sextet | Grant Green:Blue Breakbeat | Blue Note | 494705-2
Alive! | Blue Note | 525650-2
Ben Waltzer Quintet | In Metropolitan Motion | Fresh Sound Records | FSNT 082 CD

Sooky-Sooky Now
Polo De Haas Quartet | Soolmaan | Timeless | CD SJP 384

Soon
Bob Cooper Quartet | For All We Know | Fresh Sound Records | FSR-CD 5029
Cannonball Adderley Quintet | Them Dirty Blues | Capitol | 495447-2
The Cannonball Adderley Collection Vol.1:Them Dirty Blues | Landmark | CAC 1301-2(882341)
Eddie Duran Quartet | Eddie Duran-Jazz Guitarist | Original Jazz Classics | OJC 120(F 3247)
Ella Fitzgerald With The Nelson Riddle Orchestra | Ella Sings Gershwin-Vol. 2 | Metro | 2682023 IMS
George Masso Allstars | The Wonderful World Of George Gershwin | Nagel-Heyer | CD 001
George Shearing Septet | George Shearing In Dixieland | Concord | CCD 4388
Joe Puma Quartet | Wild Kitten | Dawn | DCD 109
Nicole Metzger With The Christoph Mudrich Trio | Nicole Metzger Sings Gershwin | Blue Concept | BCCD 97/01
Oscar Peterson Trio | En Concert Avec Europe 1 | Laserlight | 710443/48
Paul Kuhn Septet | I Wish You Love:The Philharmonic Concert | Timbre | TRCD 005
Rita Reys With The Nederlands Metropole Orchestra | Once Upon A Summertime | Koch Jazz | 3-6919-2
Shelly Manne Quartet | Essence | Galaxy | GXY 5101
Weslia Whitefield Trio | Live In San Francisco | Landmark | LCD 1531-2

Soon-
Modern Jazz Quartet | The Complete Modern Jazz Quartet Prestige & Pablo Recordings | Prestige | 4PRCD 4438-2
The MJQ Box | Prestige | 7711-2

Soon It's Gonna Rain
Singers Unlimited | Compact Disc:The Singers Unlimited | MPS | 831373-2 PMS

Soothe Me
Stan Kenton And His Orchestra | Artistry In Rhythm | Creative World | ST 1043

Sophie
Jeff Beck Quartet | Wired | Epic | ???
Louis Mazetier | Good Vibrations | Jazz Connaisseur | JCCD 9521-2
Marcus Miller Group | Live & More | Dreyfus Jazz Line | FDM 36585-2
Bill O'Connell Group | Voices | CTI Records | CTI 1011-2

Sophisticated Lady
Allan Botschinsky Quintet | The Night | M.A Music | NU 676-1
Archie Shepp-Horace Parlan Duo | 2nd Set | 52e Rue Est | RECD 016
Art Tatum | The Art Tatum Solo Masterpieces | Pablo | 2625703
Bennie Wallace Quartet | The Free Will | Enja | ENJ-3063 2
Bill Ramsey With The Toots Thielemans Quartet | When I See You | BELL Records | BLR 84022
Blossom Dearie | I'm Hip | CBS | 489123-2
Buddy Childers With The Russ Garcia Strings | Artistry In Jazz | Candid | CCD 79735
Buster Williams Quintet | Something More | IN+OUT Records | 7004-2
Butch Miles With The Bucky Pizzarelli Trio | Lady Be Good | Dreamstreet | DR 102
Carlos Martins Quartet | Passagem | Enja | ENJ-9073 2
Chris Barber's Jazz And Blues Band With Special Guests | Echoes Of Harlem | Black Lion | 187000
Coleman Hawkins Quartet | Jazz At The Philharmonic:The Coleman Hawkins Set | Verve | 815148-1 IMS
Concord Festival All Stars | The 20th Concord Festival All Stars | Concord | CCD 4366
Dexter Gordon Quartet | Dexter Gordon Birthday Celebration | Fantasy | FANCD 6082-2
Nights At The Keystone | Blue Note | BT 85112
Dizzy Gillespie And His Orchestra | A Portrait Of Duke Ellington | Verve | 817107-1 IMS
Duke Ellington And His Orchestra | Greatest Hits | CBS | 462959-2
Live At The 1956 Stratford Festival | Music & Arts | CD 616
The Big Bands Vol.1.The Snader Telescriptions | Storyville | 4960043
Jazz Group 1964 | Jazz Anthology | 550192
Duke Ellington:The Complete RCA-Victor Mid-Forties Recordings(1944-1946) | RCA | 2663394-2
Crystal Ballroom, Fargo Concert | Jazz Anthology | JA 5229/30
Ellington On The Air | Ember | CJS 840
Soul Call | Verve | 539785-2
The Duke At Fargo 1940 | Storyville | STCD 8316/17
Duke Ellington: The Champs-Elysees Theater January 29-30th,1965 | Laserlight | 36131
A True Collectors Item | Jazz Archive | 90.105-2
Duke Ellington At Tanglewood Vol.1 | Queen-Disc | 049
Duke Ellington/Jimmy Blanton | Highlights From The Duke Ellington Centennial Edition | RCA | 2663672-2
The Indispensable Duke Ellington Vol.5/6 | RCA | ND 89750
Ella Fitzgerald And Her All Stars | Ella Fitzgerald Sings The Duke Ellington Songbook | Verve | 559248-2
The Complete Ella Fitzgerald Song Books of Harold Arlen, Irving Berlin, Duke Ellington, George & Ira Gershwin, Jerome Kern, Johnny Mercer, Cole Porter And Rogers & Hart | Verve | 519832-2
Erroll Garner Trio | The Erroll Garner Selection | CBS | 471624-2
George Coleman-Tete Montoliu Duo | Meditation | Timeless | CD SJP 110
Great Jazz Trio With String Quartet | N.Y. Sophisticate-A Tribute To Duke Ellington | Denon Compact Disc | DC-8575
Harry Allen Quintet | A Night At Birdland | Nagel-Heyer | CD 010
Ellington For Lovers | Nagel-Heyer | NH 1009
Love Songs Live! | Nagel-Heyer | NH 1014
Harry Allen With The Bill Charlap Trio | Harry Allen Plays Ellington Songs | RCA | 2170448-2
Hot Mallets | Hot Mallets...Live | Jazzcharge | JC 8302
JazzHorchEster | ...Du Bist Nicht Die Erste! | Elite Special | 73625
Joe Henderson With The Keith Greko Trio | Last Train Outta Flagstaff | Concept | VL 4 IMS
Johnny Hodges-Wild Bill Davis Sextet | Jazz Special-The 40's & 60's | RCA | CL 43236 AF
Kevin Mahogany With The James Williams Trio And Benny Golson | You Got What It Takes | Enja | ENJ-9039 2
Kölner Saxophon Mafia | Mafia Years 1982-86 | Jazz Haus Musik | JHM 0058 CD
Larry Coryell Quartet | Toku Do | Muse | MCD 5350
Max Roach Quartet | Again | Affinity | AFF 32
Orchestra | Duke Ellington's Sophisticated Ladies | RCA | BL 04053 DX
Oscar Peterson Trio | Oscar Peterson Plays The Duke Ellington Song Book | Verve | 559785-2
Oscar Pettiford Quartet | Jazz Legacy Baden Baden Unreleased Radio Tapes | Jazzline | ???
Russell Procope-Wild Bill Davis Quartet | Echoes Of Ellington Vol.2 | Timeless | CD TTD 556
Sarah Vaughan And Her Trio | Sassy At Ronnie's | Ronnie Scott's Jazz House | JHCD 015
Sarah Vaughan With Mundell Lowe And George Duvivier | The Man I Love | Jazz Society(Vogue) | 670504
Shep Fields And His New Music | The Uncollected:Shep Fields | Hindsight | HSR 160
Singers Unlimited With Rob McConnell And The Boss Brass | The Singers Unlimited With Rob McConnell And The Boss Brass | MPS | 817486-1
Thelonious Monk Trio | Thelonious Monk-The Complete Riverside Recordings | Riverside | 15 RCD 022-2
Toots Thielemans And His Orchestra | Harmonica Jazz | CBS | CBS 21108
World Saxophone Quartet | Plays Duke Ellington | Nonesuch | 7559-79137-2
Art Taylor's Wailers | Wailin' At The Vanguard | Verve | 519677-2

Sophisticated Lady-
Boyd Raeburn And His Orchestra | Boyd Raeburn:The Transcription Performances 1946 | Hep | CD 42
Duke Ellington | The Complete Duke Ellington-Vol. 7 | CBS | CBS 88140
Gene Krupa And His Orchestra | The King Of Jazz Big Band | Festival | Album 153
Tana Reid Quintet | Passing Thoughts | Concord | CCD 4505

Sophisticated Lady(Medley part 1)-
Duke Ellington And His Famous Orchestra | The Complete Duke Ellington-Vol. 5 | CBS | CBS 88082

Sophisticated Swing
Count Basie And His Orchestra | The Indispensable Count Basie | RCA | ND 89758

Les Brown And His Orchestra | The Les Brown Story | Capitol | 791226-2

Soppin' The Biscuit
Sidney Bechet With Andre Reweliotty And His Orchestra | Sidney Bechet | Vogue | 000001 GK

Sorcerer Of Antiquity
Ronald Shannon Jackson And The Decoding Society | What Spirit Say | DIW | DIW 895 CD

Sorcery
Jack DeJohnette Group | Sorcery | Prestige | P 10081

Sorcery I
Last Exit | Cassette Recordings 87 | Enemy | EMCD 105(03505)

Sorgmild
Jan Garbarek Trio | Eventyr | ECM | 1200

Soria Maria
The Splendid Master Gnawa Musicians Of Morocco | The Splendid Master Gnawa Musicians Of Morocco | Verve | 521587-2

S'Ornette Margareta
Orchestre National De Jazz | African Dream | Label Bleu | LBLC 6521(882051)

Sorra I Escuma
Conrad Gozzo And His Orchestra | GOZ The Great | Fresh Sound Records | LPM 1124(RCA)

Sorrow Is Not Forever
Urszula Dudziak And Band Walk Away | Magic Lady | IN+OUT Records | 7008-2
Vocal Summit | Sorrow Is Not Forever-Love Is | Moers Music | 02004 CD

Sorrows
Andrew Cyrille Trio | Nuba | Black Saint | 120030-2

Sorry
Bix Beiderbecke And His Gang | Riverboat Shuffle | Naxos Jazz | 8.120584 CD
The New York Allstars | Randy Sandke Meets Bix Beiderbecke | Nagel-Heyer | CD 3002
Lucie Arnaz And Her Orchestra | Just In Time | Concord | CCD 4573

Sort Of
Blue Collar | Diary Of A Working Band | Jazz Haus Musik | JHM 0089 CD

Sort Of A Tap Dance-
Richard Davis Sextet | Dealin' | Muse | MR 5027

Sortie-
Ornette Coleman Trio | Who's Crazy? | Affinity | AFF 102 D

Soso
Ulla Oster-Wollie Kaiser | We Can Do It On Stage Any Time! | Jazz Haus Musik | JHM 0088 CD

Sosolo
Chinese Compass | Chinese Compass | dacapo | DCCD 9443

Sospiro E Gemo
Rüdiger Carl | Rüdiger Carl Solo | FMP | CD 86

Sossity,You're A Woman
Abdullah Ibrahim Group | Ekaya(Home) | Black-Hawk | BKH 50205

Sotto Voce
Gebbia/Kowald/Sommer | Cappuccini Klang | SPLASC(H) Records | CD H 383-2

Sotto Voce(interpunctuated)-
Cappuccini Klang | SPLASC(H) Records | CD H 383-2

Soudfa
BBFC | Souvenir D'Italie | Plainisphare | PL 1267-19

Souga
Glen Velez Group | Pan Eros | CMP Records | CMP CD 63

Soul As A Dance
Cal Tjader Quintet | Soul Bird | Verve | 549111-2

Soul Bird(aka Tin Tin Deo)
Cal Tjader's Orchestra | Verve Jazz Masters 39:Cal Tjader | Verve | 521858-2
Coleman Hawkins Quintet | The Real Thing | Prestige | P 24083

Soul Blues
Jugend-Jazzorchester Des Saarlandes | Chops & Fingers | Blue Concept | BCCD 94/04

Soul Bossa Nova
Quincy Jones And His Orchestra | Big Band Bossa Nova | Verve | 557913-2
Jazz Crusaders | Chile Con Soul | Pacific Jazz | 590957-2

Soul Bourgeoisie
Andrew Cyrille Quintet | My Friend Louis | DIW | DIW 858 CD

Soul Brothers
Cal Tjader's Orchestra | Talkin Verve/Roots Of Acid Jazz:Cal Tjader | Verve | 531562-2

Soul Burst
Poncho Sanchez Band With Tito Puente | Chile Con Soul | Concord | CCD 4406

Soul Burst(Guajera)
Duke Ellington And His Orchestra | Antibes Concert-Vol.2 | Verve | 2304065 IMS

Soul Call
Ella Fitzgerald And Duke Ellington:Cote D'Azure Concerts on Verve | Verve | 539033-2
Soul Call | Verve | 539785-2
Kenny Burrell Quintet | Soul Call | Original Jazz Classics | OJCCD 846-2(P 7315)
Thilo Kreitmeier & Group | Soul Call | Organic Music | ORGM 9711
The Crusaders | The Best Of The Crusaders | MCA | 2292-50536-1

Soul Connection
John Patton Quintet | Soul Connection | Nilva | NQ 3406 IMS

Soul Country
Pat Metheny Trio | Part Metheny Trio Live | Warner | 9362-47907-2

Soul Cowboy
Trio 99-00 | Warner | 9362-47632-2
Art Farmer With The Enrico Pieranunzi Quintet | Isis | Soul Note | SN 1021

Soul Dance
Kai Winding Quintet | Duo Bones | Red Records | VPA 143

Soul Eyes
Bernie Senensky Quartet | Wheel Within A Wheel | Timeless | CD SJP 410
Christoph Spendel Trio | Back To Basics | Blue Flame | 40072(2132485-2)
Eddie Allen Quintet | Another Point Of View | Enja | 8004-2
John Coltrane Quartet | The Best Of John Coltrane-His Greatest Years | MCA | AS 9200-2
John Coltrane:The Classic Quartet-Complete Impulse Studio Recordings | Impulse(MCA) | 951280-2
John Critchinson-Art Themen Quartet | First Moves | Ronnie Scott's Jazz House | JHCD 052
Mal Waldron | One-Upmanship | Enja | 2092 (807490)
Mal Waldron Quartet With Jeanne Lee | Soul Eyes | RCA | 2153887-2
McCoy Tyner-Bobby Hutcherson Duo | Manhattan Moods | Blue Note | 828423-2
Oliver Jones Trio | Speak Low Swing Hard | Justin Time | Just 17
Prestige All Stars | John Coltrane-The Prestige Recordings | Prestige | 16 PCD 4405-2
Interplay | Original Jazz Classics | OJCCD 292-2(P 7112)
Scott Wendholt Quintet | The Scheme Of Things | Criss Cross | Criss 1078
Stan Getz Quartet | The Lost Sessions | Verve | 9801098
Soul Eyes | Concord | CCD 4783
Stan Getz-Kenny Barron | Stan Getz Cafe Montmartre | EmArCy | 586755-2
Steve Grossman Trio | Bouncing With Mr. A.T. | Dreyfus Jazz Line | FDM 36579-2
Tete Montoliu | The Music I Like To Play Vol.4: Let's Call This | Soul Note | 121250-2
Uli Lenz Trio | Echoes Of Mandela | Tutu Records | 888180-2*
Vanessa Rubin With Orchestra | Soul Eyes | Novus | PD 90591(874066)

Soul Eyes-
Ernie Watts-Christof Sänger | Blue Topaz | Laika Records | 35101352

Soul Eyes(I)
Blue Topaz | Laika Records | 35101352

Soul Eyes(II)
Fat Boogie Horns | Fat Boogie Horns(Rhythm And Soul Big Band) | Paul Records | PP 4002

Soul Fingers
Craig Bailey Band | A New Journey | Candid | CCD 79725

Soul Flower
David Phillips & Fredance | David Phillips & Freedance | Naxos Jazz | 86061-2

Soul Food-African Shop
Grant Green With Orchestra | The Final Comedown(Soundtrack) | Blue Note | 581678-2
Jodie Christian Quintet | Soul Fountain | Delmark | DE 498

Soul Fusion
Geri Allen Trio | The Gathering | Verve | 557614-2

Soul Junction
Red Garland Quintet | John Coltrane-The Prestige Recordings | Prestige | 16 PCD 4405-2
Red Garland Quintet feat.John Coltrane | Jazz Junction | Prestige | P 24023

Soul Lament
Anthony Braxton Duo/Quintet | Dances & Orations | Music & Arts | CD 923

Soul Lullaby
Lucky Thompson Quartet | Lucky Thompson | LRC Records | CDC 9029

Soul Makossa
Big John Patton Trio | Blue'n Soul-Do The Jerk | Blue Note | 799105-2

Soul Manifesto
Chick Corea And Origin | A Week At The Blue Note | Stretch Records | SCD 9020-2

Soul Mates
The Rippingtons | Welcome To St. James' Club | GRP | GRP 96182

Soul Meeting
Ray Charles-Milt Jackson Quintet | Soul Meeting | Atlantic | SD 1360
Cassandra Wilson And Her Trio | Live | JMT Edition | 849149-2

Soul Merchant
Richard 'Groove' Holmes Trio | Soul Message | Original Jazz Classics | OJC20 329-2(P 7435)

Soul Message
Ramsey Lewis Trio | Down To Earth | Verve | 538329-2

Soul Mist
Cal Tjader Sextet | Soul Bird | Verve | 549111-2

Soul Motion
Anka Darghel-Klaus Ignatzek Quartet | Soul My Secret Place | Blue Flame | 40152(2132487-2)

Soul Of A Stone - (Soul Of A) Stone
Hans Theessink Group | Call Me | Minor Music | 801022

Soul Of Song
Tomasz Stanko Quartet | Soul Of Things | ECM | 1788(016374-2)

Soul Of Things(part I-XIII)
Ran Blake | The Blue Potato And Other Outrages | Milestone | M 9021

Soul On Soul
Sonny Stitt Quartet | Soul People | Prestige | PCD 24127-2(P 7372/7852)

Soul Pride
Vital Information | Show 'Em Where You Live | Intuition Records | INT 3306-2

Soul Principle
Charles Kynard Quintet | Reelin' With The Feelin' | Original Jazz Classics | OJC 333(P 7688)

Soul Reggae
The Vivino Brothers Band | Chitlins Parmigiana | dmp Digital Music Productions | CD 492

Soul Route
Bola Sete And His New Brazilian Trio | Autentico | Original Jazz Classics | OJC 290(F 8375)

Soul Sauce
Cal Tjader Septet | Talkin Verve/Roots Of Acid Jazz:Cal Tjader | Verve | 531562-2
Cal Tjader's Orchestra | Cal Tjader/Soul Sauce | Verve | 521668-2
Poncho Sanchez Groups | Baila Mi Gente-Salsa | Concord | CCD 4701

Soul Serenade
Sonny Stitt Quartet | The Prestige Collection:Sonny Stitt Soul Classics | Original Jazz Classics | OJCCD 6003-2

Soul Shoutin'
Hampton Hawes Trio | Hampton Hawes At The Piano | Original Jazz Classics | C 7637

Soul Song
Tito Puente And His Ensemble | On Broadway | Concord | CCD 4207

Soul Soothing Beach
Once In A Lifetime | Soul Sound | Acoustic Music Records | 319.1055.2

Soul Special
Andrew Hill Sextet | Grass Roots | Blue Note | 522672-2
Don Braden Octet | The Voice Of The Saxophone | RCA | 2668797-2

Soul Station
Hank Mobley Quartet | Soul Station | Blue Note | 495343-2
James Spaulding Quartet | Blues Nexus | Muse | MCD 5467

Soul Street
Oliver Nelson Sextet | Soul Battle | Original Jazz Classics | OJC 325(P 7223)
Kenny Dorham Sextet | Soul Support | Jazz Colours | 874756-2

Soul Time
Hank Mobley Quintet | Far Away Lands | Blue Note | BST 84425

Soul Time[Chuck]
King Curtis Band | King Curtis-Blow Man Blow | Bear Family Records | BCD 15670 CI

Soul Time[Chuck](alt.take)
David Matthews Trio | Tennessee Waltz | Paddle Wheel | 292 E 6050

Soul Twist
Walter Bishop Jr.Orchestra | Soul Village | Muse | MR 5142

Soul Waltz
George Duke Orchestra | Save The Country | Pacific Jazz | LN 10127

Soul Woman
Fritz Krisse Quartet | Soulcolours | Laika Records | 35100782

Soulcolours
Kenny Burrell Sextet | Up The Street 'Round The Corner, Down The Block | Fantasy | F 9458

Soulful Bill
Jimmy Smith Quartet | Fourmost | Milestone | MCD 9184-2

Soulful Brothers
Kenny Burrell Quartet | Blues-The Common Ground | Verve | 589101-2
Idris Muhammad Trio | Kabsha | Evidence | TR 110

Soulful Drums
Jack McDuff Quartet | Screamin' | Original Jazz Classics | OJCCD 875-2(P 7259)
Vital Information | Live Around The World Where We Come From Tour '98-'99 | Intuition Records | INT 3296-2
Steve Laury Quartet | Stepping Out | Denon Compact Disc | CY-75870

Soulful Kisses
Art Blakey And The Jazz Messengers | Art Blakey | Jazz Classics | AU 36019 CD

Soulful Mr. Timmons
John Swana And The Philadelphians | Pilly Gumbo | Criss Cross | Criss 1203

Soulful Spirit
Horst Jankowski Orchestra With Voices | Jankowskeynotes | MPS | 9814806

Soulful Strut
Monty Alexander-Sly Dunbar-Robbie Shakespeare Group | Monty Meets Sly And Robbie | Telarc Digital | CD 83494

Soulita
Dave Ellis Quintet | State Of Mind | Milestone | MCD 9328-2

Soul-Leo
Mulgrew Miller Sextet | Landmarks-A Compilation(1985-1987) | Landmark | LCD 1311-2

Soulmate
Ben Webster Quintet | Soulmates | Original Jazz Classics | OJC 109(RLP 476)

Soulmates
Mal Waldron/Marion Brown | Much More! | Freelance | FRL-CD 010
Doug Watkins Quintet | Yusef's Bag | Prestige | P 24105

Soulrider
Base Line | Why Really | Challenge | CHR 70002

Soultrane
Chet Baker Quintet | Chet Baker Plays & Sings | West Wind | WW 2108
Larry Vuckovich Sextet | City Sounds,Village Voices | Palo Alto | PA 8012
Joe Henderson And His Orchestra | Black Miracle | Milestone | M 9066

Soulution
Ben Webster Quintet | Soulville | Verve | 521449-2

Soulville
Ben Webster With The Oscar Peterson Quartet | Verve Jazz Masters 43:Ben Webster | Verve | 525431-2
Dee Dee Bridgewater With Her Quintet | Love And Peace-A Tribute To Horace Silver | Verve | 527470-2
Horace Silver Quintet | Stylings Of Silver | Blue Note | 540034-2
Horace Silver Retrospective | Blue Note | 495576-2
The Stylings Of Silver | Blue Note | 300168(1562)
Ran Blake Trio | Horace Is Blue:A Silver Noir | HatOLOGY | 550

Soulville Samba
Céline Rudolph And Her Trio | Book Of Travels | Nabel Records:Jazz Network | CD 4672

Soumolé
James Emery Septet | Spectral Domains | Enja | ENJ-9344 2

Sound Action Seven
David S. Ware Quartet | Great Bliss Vol.1 | Silkheart | SHCD 127

Sound Check
Nils Landgren First Unit And Guests | Nils Landgren-The First Unit | ACT | 9292-2
Vincent Herring Quintet | Dawnbird | Landmark | LCD 1533-2

Sound Lee
World Saxophone Quartet | W.S.Q. | Black Saint | 120046-2

Sound Off
Ekkehard Jost & Chromatic Alarm | Wintertango | Fish Music | FM 008 CD

Sound Piece 1(Yellow)
Wintertango | Fish Music | FM 008 CD

Sound Piece 2(Green)
Wintertango | Fish Music | FM 008 CD

Sound Piece3(Blue)
The Splendid Master Gnawa Musicians Of Morocco | The Splendid Master Gnawa Musicians Of Morocco | Verve | 521587-2

Sound Sketches
Sun Ra And His Solar Arkestra | Other Planes Of There | Evidence | ECD 22037-2

Sound Theatre Of Tukang Pijad
Art Farmer-Fritz Pauer Duo | Azure | Soul Note | 121126-2

Soundings For Solo Violin
Michael Shrieve Trio | Fascination | CMP Records | CMP CD 67

Soundjata
Lee Konitz Quartet | Jazz At Storyville | Black Lion | BLP 60901

Soundlotion
Eric Watson-John Lindberg | Soundpost: Works For Piano And Double Bass | Music & Arts | CD 920

Sounds For Sid
Vienna Art Orchestra | European Songbook | Amadeo | 527672-2

Sounds Of Joy
Joe Lovano-Trio | Sounds Of Joy | Enja | 7013-2

Sounds Of Peru-Submergence-Awakening
Monica Zetterlund With The Thad Jones Quartet | Monica Zetterlund-The Lost Tapes | RCA | 2136332-2

Sounds Of The Way
Bluezeum | Portrait Of A Groove | Telarc Digital | CD 83331

Soundscapes X-XII
Stephan Kurmann Strings | Olan Layé | TCB Records | TCB 03052

Soundtrack
Nazaire | Who's Blues | Ronnie Scott's Jazz House | JHCD 019

Soup Sandwich
Randy Burns-Emery Fletcher | Of Love And War | ESP Disk | ESP 1039-2

Source
Manfred Schoof Quintet | Light Lines | Japo | 60019(2360019)
Pago Libre | Pago Libre | L+R Records | CDLR 45105

Source Of Light And Sound
Duck Baker | The Clear Blue Sky | Acoustic Music Records | 319.1065.2

Sous Le Ciel De Paris
Michel Legrand Trio | Jazz In Paris:Michel Legrand-Paris Jazz Piano | EmArCy | 548148-2 PMS
Tethered Moon | Chansons D'Edith Piaf | Winter&Winter | 910048-2
Michel Legrand Trio | Jazz In Paris:Michel Legrand-Paris Jazz Piano | EmArCy | 548148-2 PMS

Sous Le Ponts De Paris
Pierre Michelot Band | Jazz In Paris:Pierre Michelot-Round About The Bass | EmArCy | 832309-2 PMS

Sous Les Ponts De Paris
Lucky Thompson's Modern Jazz Group Tentet | Jazz In Paris:Lucky Thompson-Modern Jazz Group | EmArCy | 159823-2 PMS

Souscription
Ax Genrich Group | Psychedelic Guitar | ATM Records | ATM 3809-AH

South
Benny Moten's Kansas City Orchestra | RCA Victor 80th Anniversary Vol.1:1917-1929 | RCA | 2668777-2
Chris Barber's Jazz Band | Ice Cream | Storyville | 6.23326 AF
Count Basie And His Orchestra | Count Basie-Basie's Basement | RCA | ???
Dee Dee Pierce And His New Orleans Stompers | In Binghampton,N.Y. Vol.Three | American Music | AMCD-81
Dinah Shore With Orchestra | The Best Of Dinah Shore | Capitol | 792895-2
Karl Berger-James Blood Ulmer Duo | Conversations | IN+OUT Records | 77027-2
Ken Colyer's Jazzmen | The Best Of British Traditional Jazz | Philips | 818651-2
Kid Ory's Creole Jazz Band | The Legendary Crescent Recording Sessions | GHB Records | BCD 10

South African Blues
State Street Ramblers | Chicago South Side Jazz | Village(Jazz Archive) | VILCD 019-2

South Etude
Maurice Magnoni Orchestra | New York Suite | L+R Records | CDLR 45077

South Of Greenwich Village
Ed Hamilton Groups | Planet Jazz | Telarc Digital | CD 83387

South Of The Border
Lou Donaldson Quintet | Gravy Train | Blue Note | 853357-2
Lynn Hope Band | Lynn Hope And His Tenor Sax | Pathe | 1546661(Aladdin)
Norrie Cox & His New Orleans Stompers | Dance Hall Days | Delmark | DE 236
The Ritz | Movin' Up | Denon Compact Disc | CY-72526
Wes Montgomery With The Don Sebesky Orchestra | California Dreaming | Verve | 827842-2
Andrew Cyrille Quintet | My Friend Louis | DIW | DIW 858 CD

South Of The Sun
Festa Group | Strings | Nueva Records | NC 3009

South Print
Allotria Jazz Band | The Best Of Allotria Jazz Band München | Elite Special | 730215

South Rampart Street Parade
Allan Vaché's Florida Jazz Allstars | Allan Vaché's Floridy Jazz Allstars | Nagel-Heyer | CD 032
Billy May And His Orchestra | Sorta Dixie | Creative World | ST 1054
Bob Crosby And His Orchestra | Big Band Boouce And Boogie-Bob Crosby:Mournin' Blues/Accent On The Bobcats | Affinity | AFS 1014

Dixie Kings Meets Sharp & Flats | The World Is Waiting For The Sunrise | Express | CA 38-1027
Flat Foot Stompers & Friends | Flat Foot Stompers & Friends Vol.2 | Timeless | TTD 529
Loverfield Jazzband | Swissmade In Holland | Timeless | CD TTD 601
Papa Bue's Viking Jazzband | Barber-Bue Concerts | Storyville | 671196

South Saturn Delta
Wynton Kelly Quintet | It's All Right! | Verve | 537750-2

South Side
Wardell Gray Quartet | Wardell Gray:Light Gray 1948-1950 | Cool & Blue | C&B-CD 116

South Side People
Benny Carter Quartet | Best Of Benny Carter | Musicmasters | 65133-2

South Side(alt.take 1)
Wardell Gray Quartet | Wardell Gray Memorial Vol.1 | Original Jazz Classics | OJCCD 050-2(P 7008)

South Side(alt.take 2)
Wardell Gray Memorial Vol.1 | Original Jazz Classics | OJCCD 050-2(P 7008)

South Side(alt.take 3)
Wardell Gray Memorial Vol.1 | Original Jazz Classics | OJCCD 050-2(P 7008)

South Side(alt.take 4)
Wardell Gray Memorial Vol.1 | Original Jazz Classics | OJCCD 050-2(P 7008)

South Side(alt.take 5)
Wardell Gray Memorial Vol.1 | Original Jazz Classics | OJCCD 050-2(P 7008)

South Side(alt.take 6)
Wardell Gray:Light Gray 1948-1950 | Cool & Blue | C&B-CD 116

South Stream Road
Beaver Harris | African Drums | Owl Records | 09

South Street Exit
Ed Hamilton Group | Path To The Heartland | Telarc Digital | CD 83404

Southbound Train
Hank Crawford And His Orchestra | South-Central | Milestone | MCD 9201-2

Southern Comfort
James Rivers Groups | The Best Of New Orleans Rhythm & Blues Vol.3 | Mardi Gras Records | MG 9009

Southern Memories
Hans Reichel | Bonobo Beach | FMP | 0830

Southern Pacific
Karl Ratzer Group | Fingerprints | CMP Records | CMP 7

Southern Scandal
Stan Kenton And His Orchestra | Stan Kenton In Hi-Fi | Capitol | EMS 1149

Southern Smiles
King Oliver's Creole Jazz Band | The Blues Heritage | Ember | CJS 846

Southplay
Sonny Thompson | Sonny Thompson:The Complete Recordings Vol.1 (1946-1948) | Blue Moon | BMCD 6024

Southwest Loner
Dave Grusin Group | Migration | GRP | GRP 95922

Southwest Passage
Horace Tapscott | The Tapscott Sessions Vol.7 | Nimbus | NS 2147

Southwick
Keith Ingham & Marty Grosz And Their Hot Cosmopolites | Just Imagine..Songs Of DeSylva, Brown And Henderson | Stomp Off Records | CD 1285

Souvenir
Mel Martin Quartet | Mel Martin Plays Benny Carter | Enja | ENJ-9041 2

Souvenirs
Quintet Du Hot Club De France | Verve Jazz Masters 38:Django Reinhardt | Verve | 516931-2
Django Reinhardt-Stephane Grappelli | Ace Of Club | ACL 1158

Souvenirs De La Nouvelle-Orleans
Sidney Bechet-Teddy Buckner Sextet | Sidney Bechet | Vogue | 000001 GK

Souvenirs De L'Occitanie für A-Klarinette
Lars Gullin Quartet | Lars Gullin 1951/52 Vol.5:First Walk | Dragon | DRCD 380

Sov Du Lilla Vide Ung
Anthony Braxton | 8KN-(B-12)IR10(for string quartet) | Sound Aspects | sas CD 009

Sow Belly Blues
Lou Donaldson Quintet | The Best Of Lou Donaldson Vol.1(1957-1967) | Blue Note | 827298-2

Soweto
Abdullah Ibrahim-Carlos Ward Duo | Live At Sweet Basil Vol.1 | Black-Hawk | BKH 50204

Soweto Messenger-
Tony Williams Quintet | Civilization | Blue Note | BT 85138

Soy Gitano
Gilberto Gil With Band | Gilberto Em Concerto | West Wind Latina | 2200 CD

Sozaboy
The Brecker Brothers | Return Of The Brecker Brothers | GRP | GRP 96842

Sozinho(Alone)
Bass Drum Bone | Bass Drum Bones-Wooferlo | Soul Note | 121187-2

Space
Lost Tribe | Lost Tribe | Windham Hill | 34 10143-2

Space Chants Medley:
John Zorn Group | Spy Vs. Spy-The Music Of Ornette Coleman | Nonesuch | 7559-60844-2

Space Church
Ornette Coleman & Prime Time | In All Languages | Harmolodic | 531915-2

Space Circus(part 1&2)
Chick Corea | Verve Jazz Masters 3:Chick Corea | Verve | 519820-2

Space Circus(part 1)
Chick Corea's Return To Forever | Hymn Of The Seventh Galaxy | Polydor | 2310283

Space Is The Place
Sun Ra And His Intergalactic Solar Arkestra | Space Is The Place(Soundtrack) | Evidence | ECD 22070-2

Space Killer
Billy Cobham-George Duke Band | Live On Tour In Europe | Atlantic | ATL 50316

Space Maker
Sun Ra And His Myth Science Arkestra | Fate In A Pleasant Mood/When Sun Comes Out | Evidence | ECD 22068-2

Space On Earth
booMbooM meets Uli Beckerhoff | Resurection Lounge | Laika Records | 35101512

Space Party
Pete York Group | String Time In New York | BELL Records | BLR 84015

Space Spiritual
Grachan Moncur III Quintet | New Africa | Affinity | AFF 38

Space Walk
Mal Waldron Quartet | Up Popped The Devil | Enja | 2034

Spaced
Jack Wilson Trio | Margo's Theme | Discovery | DS 805 IMS

Spaceman-
Lou Donaldson Quintet | The Natural Soul | Blue Note | 542307-2

Spaceman Twist
Andreas Hansl | Dualism | UAK | UAK 1

Spaces
Joe McPhee-John Snyder Duo | Rotation | Hat Art | D

Spaceship
John Surman-John Warren Group | The Brass Project | ECM | 1478

Spacial Motive
Herb Geller Sextet | That Geller Feller(Fire In The West) | Fresh Sound Records | FSR CD 91(882417)

Spain
Allan Vaché's Florida Jazz Allstars | Allan Vaché's Floridy Jazz Allstars | Nagel-Heyer | CD 032
Andy LaVerne | Buy One, Get One Free | Steeplechase | SCCD 31319
Bireli Lagrene Group | A Tribute To Django Reinhardt | Jazzpoint | JP 1061 CD
Bob Crosby's Bobcats | Big Band Bounce And Boogie-Bob Crosby:Mournin' Blues/Accent On The Bobcats | Affinity | AFS 1014
Bucky Pizzarelli-John Pizzarelli Duo | The Complete Guitar Duos(The Stash Sessions) | Stash Records | ST-CD 536(889114)
Chick Corea And Return To Forever | Compact Jazz: Chick Corea | Polydor | 831365-2
Chick Corea's Return To Forever | Verve Jazz Masters 3:Chick Corea | Verve | 519820-2
Duo Fenix | Karai-Eté | IN+OUT Records | 7009-2
Florian Poser | Winds | Edition Collage | EC 500-2
Frank Marocco Quintet | Road To Marocco | Discovery | DS 854 IMS
Silvan Koopmann Bigband | Silvan Koopmann Big Band | Workshop Records | WR 051
Woody Herman And His Orchestra | Woody Herman:Complete 1948-1950 Capitol Sessions | Definitive Records | DRCD 11195
Bucky Pizzarelli-John Pizzarelli Duo | Live at The Vineyard | Challenge | CHR 70025

Spain(alt.take 1)
Chick Corea And Return To Forever | Light As A Feather | Polydor | 557115-2

Spain(alt.take 2)
Mel Tormé With The Marty Paich Dek-Tette | Reunion | Concord | CCD 4360

Spam-Boo-Limbo
Louis Conte Group | La Cocina Caliente | Denon Compact Disc | CY-30001

Spangled Banner Minor And Other Patriotic Songs
Chris Hinze-Sigi Schwab Duo | Backstage | Melos Music | CDGS 801

Spanish Blue
Ken Colyer's Jazzmen | Best Of British Jazz From The BBC Jazz Club Vol.1 | Upbeat Jazz | URCD 118

Spanish Castle
NDR Big Band feat. Inga Rumpf | The Spirit Of Jimi Hendrix | Extra Records & Tapes | 11542

Spanish Fantasy(part 1-4)
Jimmy Giuffre-Bill Connors | Giuffre/Konitz/Connors/Bley | Improvising Artists Inc. | 123859-2

Spanish Fly
Marc Johnson-Eric Longsworth | If Trees Could Fly | Intuition Records | INT 3228-2
Milt Jackson Quartet | In A New Setting | Verve | 538620-2
Hampton Hawes Trio | High In The Sky | Fresh Sound Records | FSR-CD 0059

Spanish Go-Round
Joe Haider Quintet | Reconciliation | EGO | 4001

Spanish Harlem
Gene McDaniels And His Band | Another Tear Falls | Charly | CRB 1136

Spanish Harlem,125th Esat Street
Loft Line | Nine Steps | Acoustic Music Records | 319.1041.2

Spanish Key
Miles Davis Group | This Is Jazz:Miles Davis Electric | CBS | CK 65449

Spanish Key-
Gene McDaniels And His Band | Another Tear Falls | Charly | CRB 1136

Spanish Melody And Swing
Barbara Thompson's Paraphernalia | Barbara Thompson's Paraphernalia | MCA | 2292-50577-1

Spanish Moss-
Billy Cobham Group | Crosswinds | Atlantic | ATL 50037

Spanish Nights
Super Session | Welcome & Alive | Vagabond | 6.28604 DP

Spanish Phrases For Strings And Bass
Clark Terry & Chico O Farril Orchestra | Spanish Rice | Verve | 9861050

Spanish Rice
Jan Akkerman Group | Puccini's Cafe | Inak | 9027

Spanish Tinge(No.1)
Jaki Byard | Jaki Byard:Solo/Strings | Prestige | PCD 24246-2

Spanish Tinge(No.2)
Empirical | Muse | MCD 6010

Spank-A-Lee
Bruce Williams Quintet | Brotherhood | Savant Records | SCD 2004

Spar Sam!
Michael Hedges | Aerial Boundaries | Windham Hill | 34 11032-2

Spare Change
Michael Hedges Trio | An Evening With Windham Hill:Live | Windham Hill | TA-C- 1026

Sparky
Clint Houston Quintet | Watership Down | Storyville | STCD 4150

Sparta:
Branford Marsalis Quartet | Crazy People Music | CBS | 466870-2

Spartacus
Bill Evans | The Complete Bill Evans On Verve | Verve | 527953-2

Spartacus Love Theme
Conversations With Myself | Verve | 521409-2
Bill Evans Trio With Jeremy Steig | The Complete Bill Evans On Verve | Verve | 527953-2
Dejan Terzic Quartet | Four For One | Naxos Jazz | 86036-2

Spasmodic
Choo Choo Light:Stammberger-Rädler-Schöne | Choo Choo Light | G.N.U. Records | CD A 92.007

Speak Again Brother
Max Roach Quartet | Conversations | Milestone | M 47061

Speak Brother Speak
Clarence Williams And His Orchestra | King Oliver 1928-29 | Village(Jazz Archive) | VILCD 005-2

Speak Easy
John Abercrombie-Jarek Smietana Quartet | Speak Easy | PAO Records | PAO 10610
Shelly Manne Two | The Three & The Two | Original Jazz Classics | OJCCD 172-2(C 3584)

Speak Italian
Torsten Goods Group | Manhattan Walls | Jardis Records | JRCD 20139
Christian McBride/Nicholas Payton/Mark Whitfield | Fingerpainting-The Music Of Herbie Hancock | Verve | 537856-2

Speak Like A Child
Herbie Hancock Sextet | The Best Of Herbie Hancock | Blue Note | 791142-2
Jon Faddis With The Carlos Franzetti Orchestra | Rememberances | Chesky | JD 166
Miles Davis Quintet | Miles Davis Quintet 1965-1968 | CBS | C6K 67398

Speak Like A Child(rehersal)
| Son Song | Fresh Sound Records | FSNT 010 CD

Speak Low
Al Cohn With The Rein De Graaff Trio | Rifftide | Timeless | CD SJP 259
Anirahtak und die Jürgen Sturm Band | Berlin-Paris-New York/Music By Kurt Weil | Nabel Records:Jazz Network | CD 4655
Anita O'Day With The Bill Holman Orchestra | Incomparable! Anita O'Day | Verve | 589516-2
Art Farmer/Benny Golson Jazztet | Back To The City | Original Jazz Classics | C 14020
Betty Miller Trio | A Jazz Piano Heatwave | Fresh Sound Records | Foremost FM 1001 CD
Bill Evans Trio | New Jazz Conceptions | Original Jazz Classics | OJC20 025-2(RLP 223)
The Legendary Bill Evans Trio-The Legendary 1960 Birdland Sessions | Cool & Blue | C&B-CD 106
Bob Howard With The Hank Jones Trio | In A Sentimental Mood | Stash Records | ST 266 IMS
Booker Ervin Quartet | That's It | Candid | CCD 79014
Settin' The Pace | Prestige | PCD 24123-2(P 7455/7462)
Bud Shank And Bob Cooper With The Metropole Orchestra | A Flower Is A Lovesome Thing | Koch Jazz | 3-6912-2
Carmen McRae with the Cal Tjader Orchestra | Heat Wave | Concord | CCD 4189
Christi Black With The Bobby Lyle Trio | With Standard 3 | Paddle Wheel | KICP 54
Danny Moss Quartet | Keeper Of The Flame | Nagel-Heyer | CD 064
Dave Hancock Trio | Out Of Nowhere | Timeless | CD SJP 303
David Linx With The Jack Van Poll Trio | Where Rivers Join | September | CD 5109
Diane Schuur With Orchestra | Love Songs | GRP | GRP 97032
The Best Of Diane Schuur | GRP | GRP 98882
Don Elliott Orchestra | Don Elliott Sings | Fresh Sound Records | FSR 2049(Bethlehem BCP 15)
Eddie Higgins Trio | Those Quiet Days | Sunnyside | SSC 1052 D
Eric Alexander-Lin Halliday Quintet | Stablemates | Delmark | DE 488
Four Freshmen And 5 Trombones | Four Freshmen And 5 Trombones | Capitol | 300004(TOCJ 6117)
Gene DiNovi Trio | Renaissance Of A Jazz Master | Candid | CCD 79708
George Shearing Quintet | Back To Birdland | Telarc Digital | CD 83524
Grant Green Quartet | I Want To Hold Your Hand | Blue Note | 300261(4202)
Hank Jones Quartet | Lazy Afternoon | Concord | CCD 4391
Joe Venuti-Dave McKenna Duo | Alone At The Palace | Chiaroscuro | CR 160
Ken McIntyre Quartet | Ken McIntyre:The Complete United Artists Sessions | Blue Note | 857200-2
Kikuchi-Peacock-Motian | Tethered Moon(Play Kurt Weil) | JMT Edition | 514021-2
Laurindo Almeida Quartet | Brazilliance Vol.1 | Pacific Jazz | 796339-2
Marcus Printup Sextet | The New Boogaloo | Nagel-Heyer | CD 2019
Mark Morganelli And The Jazz Forum All Stars | Speak Low | Candid | CCD 79054
Mark Murphy With The Jack Van Poll Trio & Guests | Another Vision | September | CD 5113
Melvin Sparks Quartet | Sparkling | Muse | MR 5248
Nick Brignola With Kenny Barron And Dave Holland | It's Time | Reservoir | RSR CD 123
Oliver Jones Trio | Speak Low Swing Hard | Justin Time | Just 17
Richard Davis Duo | As One | Muse | MR 5093
Rickey Woodard With The Frank Capp Trio | The Frank Capp Trio Presents Rickey Woodard | Concord | CCD 4469
West Coast Jazz Summit | West Coast Jazz Summit | Mons Records | MR 874773
Earl Hines Trio | The Lengendary Little Theater Concert of 1964 | Savoy | 650139(882495)

Speak No Evil
Wayne Shorter Quintet | The Best Of Wayne Shorter | Blue Note | 791141-2
Billy Stritch With The Benny Carter Band | Benny Carter Songbook | Musicmasters | 65134-2

Speak Out(duet)-
Robert Stewart Quartet | Judgement | Red Records | 123268-2

Speak Yomm
Pata Music Meets Arfi | News Of Roi Ubu | Pata Musik | PATA 10 CD
Roberta Piket Trio | Speak,Memory | Fresh Sound Records | FSNT 088 CD

Speak,Memory
Strata Institute | Transmigration | DIW | DIW 860 CD

Speaking Of Sounds
Count Basie And His Orchestra | Basie On Roulette, Vol. 7: Chairman Of The Board | Vogue | 500007

Specht(1)
KontraSax | KontraSax Plays Getrude Stein | Jazz Haus Musik | JHM 0096 CD

Specht(2)
Joachim Kühn | Cinemascope/Piano | MPS | 88037-2

Special Brew
Martial Solal And His Orchestra | Martial Solal-The Vogue Recordings Vol.3:Trio & Big Band | Vogue | 21131112(875746)

Special Days
Charly Antolini Orchestra | Special Delivery | MPS | 68256

Special Delivery
Sandy Brown's Jazz Band | The Golden Years Of Revival Jazz,Vol.10 | Storyville | STCD 5515
Ugetsu | Cape Town Blues | Naxos Jazz | 86052-2

Special Rider
The Mojo Bluesband | Shake That Boogie | Gold Records | 11048

Special Treatment
David Klein Quintet | My Marilyn | Enja | ENJ-9422 2

Specialisation
Ernie Henry Quartet | Seven Standards And A Blues | Original Jazz Classics | OJCCD 1722-2(RLP 248)

Specific People,Places,Things Or Ideas
David Moss Duos | Time Stories | Intakt Records | CD 054

Spectacular
Chico Hamilton Quintet | Chico Hamilton Quintet | Pacific Jazz | 300002(PJ 1209)

Spectrum
Billy Cobham Group | Spectrum | Atlantic | 7567-81428-2
Bob Mintzer Big Band | Spectrum | dmp Digital Music Productions | CD 461
Sam Rivers' Rivbea All-Star Orchestra | Culmination | RCA | 2168311-2

Speculation
Teddy Wilson Sextet | Teddy Wilson In New York | Jazz Anthology | 550272

Spe-cu-lay-ting
John Schröder-Henrik Walsdorff-Uli Jenneßen | Freedom Of Speech | FMP | OWN-90011

Speech Craft
Matthew Ship 'String' Trio | Expansion,Power,Release | HatOLOGY | 558

Speechless-
Paul Bley Duo | Sonor | Soul Note | SN 1085

Speed Life
Frank Culley Band | Rock 'N Roll | Krazy Kat | KK 784 IMS

Speedball
Bobby Broom Quartet | Waitin' And Waitin' | Criss Cross | Criss 1135
Lee Morgan Quintet | Memorial Album | Blue Note | 84446
Stanley Clarke Group | Time Exposure | Epic | 25486

Speedboats
Illinois Jacquet Quintet | Illinois Jacquet Flying Home-The Best Of The Verve Years | Verve | 521644-2

Speedy Edgar
Enrico Pieranunzi Trio | Moon Pie | yvp music | CD 3011

Speedy's 9 Is 10
Bik Bent Braam | Howdy | Timeless | CD SJP 388

Speil
Paul Smoker Trio | Alone | Sound Aspects | sas CD 018(32018)

Spell
David Torn Group | What Means Solid,Traveler? | CMP Records | CMP CD 1012

Spellbound
Coleman Hawkins Quintet With Strings | Body And Soul Revisited | GRP | GRP 16272
Dave King Group | Wildcat | Off The Wall Records | OTW 9501-CD
Hot Club De Norvege With The Vertavo String Quartet | Vertavo | Hot Club Records | HCRCD 095
Junior Mance Trio & Orchestra | That Lovin' Feelin' | Milestone | MCD 47097-2
Ornette Coleman & Prime Time | Virgin Beauty | CBS | 489433-2

Spelunke
Bobby Scott Quartet | Slowly | Musicmasters | 5053-2

Sphere
Keith Ingham | Out Of The Past | Sackville | SKCD2-3047
Toto Blanke-Rudolf Dasek With The Overtontrio | Meditation | ALISO Records | AL 1026
Steve Slagle Quartet | The Steve Slagle Quartet | Steeplechase | SCCD 31323

Spheres
Urs Leimgruber/John Wolf Brennan | M.A.P. | L+R Records | CDLR 45021
Spheres-1st Movement
Keith Jarrett | Spheres | ECM | 1302(827463-2)
Hymns/Spheres | ECM | 1086/7
Spheres-2nd Movement
Hymns/Spheres | ECM | 1086/7
Spheres-3rd Movement
Spheres | ECM | 1302(827463-2)
Hymns/Spheres | ECM | 1086/7
Spheres-4th Movement
Hymns/Spheres | ECM | 1086/7
Spheres-5th Movement
Hymns/Spheres | ECM | 1086/7
Spheres-6th Movement
Hymns/Spheres | ECM | 1086/7
Spheres-7th Movement
Spheres | ECM | 1302(827463-2)
Hymns/Spheres | ECM | 1086/7
Spheres-8th Movement
Hymns/Spheres | ECM | 1086/7
Spheres-9th Movement
Spheres | ECM | 1302(827463-2)
The Brecker Brothers | Return Of The Brecker Brothers | GRP | GRP 96842
Spherical
The Brecker Brothers Live | Jazz Door | JD 1248
Sphyros
J.R. Monterose Quintet | Jaywalkin' | Fresh Sound Records | FSR-CD 320
Spice
Joe Roland Quartet | Joltin' Joe | Savoy | SV 0215(MG 12039)
Spice Island
Dorothy Ashby Quartet | The Jazz Harpist | Savoy | SV 0194(MG 6039)
Spicy Fried Chicken
Clyde Criner Group | Behind The Sun | RCA | PD 83029
Spider
Tommy Smith Sextet | Beasts Of Scottland | Linn Records | AKD 054
Spider Kelly's Blues
Lozenzo Petrocca Quartet | Stop It | Edition Musikat | EDM 018
Spider Man
Mike Clark-Paul Jackson Quartet | The Funk Stops Here | TipToe | TIP-888811 2
Paul Williams Sextet | Paul Williams:The Complete Recordings Vol.1 (1947-1949) | Blue Moon | BMCD 6020
Spider's Lovesong
Don Lanphere Quartet | First Sessions 1949/50 | Prestige | P 24081
Spiegelmensch
Sven Ake Johansson-Alexander von Schlippenbach Duo | Kalfaktor A.Falke Und Andere Lieder | FMP | 0970
Spielplatz
Gunter Hampel And His Galaxie Dream Band | A Place To Be With Us | Birth | 0032
Gunter Hampel Trio | Companion | Birth | 0036
Theo Jörgensmann Quartet | Next Advanture | CMP Records | CMP 15
Spielraum
Christofer Varner | Christofer Varner-Solo | G.N.U. Records | CD A 96.010
Spiffy Diffy
John Patton Quintet | Along Came John | Blue Note | 831915-2
Marc Ribot | Don't Blame Me | DIW | DIW 902 CD
Spill
John Zorn Group | Spillane | Nonesuch | 7559-79172-2
Spillane
Mats Eden-Jonas Simonson With The Cikada String Quartet | Milvus | ECM | 1660
Spillet
Jeff Beal With The Metropole Orchestra | Concerto For Orchestra | Koch Jazz | 3-6904-2
Spin Cycle
Terry Callier Duo | The New Folk Sound Of Terry Callier | Prestige | PRCD 11026-2
Spin Spin Spin
| In The Beginning...Bebop | Savoy | SV 0169(MG 12119)
Spinky
Christofer Varner | Christofer Varner-Solo | G.N.U. Records | CD A 96.010
Spinning
Cold Sweat | 4 Play | JMT Edition | 834444-2
Spinning Song from Songs Without Words Op.67 No.4(Mendelssohn-Bartholdy)
Lee Konitz-Harold Danko Duo | Wild As Springtime | Candid | CCD 79734
Spinning Waltz
Wild As Springtime | G.F.M. Records | 8002
Spinning Wheel
Catch Up | Catch Up Vol. 1 | Calig | 30613
Ian Shaw With The Adrian York Quartet | Ghostsongs | Ronnie Scott's Jazz House | JHCD 025
Spiral
John Coltrane Quartet | Giant Steps | Atlantic | 8122-75203-2
Kenny Barron | Spiral | Eastwind | EWIND 709
Stan Getz Quartet | Bossas And Ballads:The Lost Sessions | Verve | 9901098
Terri Lyne Carrington Quartet | Structure | ACT | 9427-2
The Crusaders | Those Southern Knights | MCA | ???
Spiral (No.125)
Volker Kriegel & Mild Maniac Orchestra | Octember Variations | MPS | 68147
Spiral Dance
Scarlet Rivera Trio | Behind The Crimson Veil | Erdenklang | 40702
Spiralnebel(I,II)
Stan Kenton And His Innovations Orchestra | The Innovations In Modern Music Orchestra | Laserlight | 15770
Spirals Of Ruby
Ok Nok...Kongo | Moonstone Journey | dacapo | DCCD 9444
Mose Allison Trio | Autumn Song | Original Jazz Classics | OJCCD 894-2(P 7189)
Spiril
Al Jarreau With Band | We Got By | Reprise | 7599-27222-2
Spirit
Brother Virus | Happy Hour | Tutu Records | 888130-2
Spirit Lake
The Paragon Ragtime Orchestra | That Demon Rag | Dorian Discovery | DIS 80107
Spirit Song
Michele Hendricks Trio | Me And My Shadow | Muse | MCD 5404
Spirit War
Marty Cook Quintet | Red, White, Black And Blue | Enja | 5067-2
Spirits And Goddesses
Charles Gayle Trio | Spirits Before | Silkheart | SHCD 117
Spirits In The Night
Jazz Passengers | Live At The Knitting Factory New York City,Vol.1 | Enemy | EMCD 111(03511)
Spirits Of Trane
Gil Scott-Heron Groups | Spirits | Mother Records | 523417-2
Spirits Rejoice
Bob Moses Quartet | Wheels Of Colored Light | Open Minds | OM 2412-2
Spirits Up Above
Keith Jarrett | Spirits | ECM | 1333/34(829467-2)
Spirits(No.1-26)
Julian Priester Sextet | Out Of This World | Milestone | MCD 47087-2
Spiritsville
Art Ensemble Of Chicago | Dreaming Of The Masters Suite | DIW | DIW 854 CD
Spiritual
Charlie Haden-Pat Metheny | Beyond The Missouri Sky | Verve | 537130 2
David Phillips & Fredance | David Phillips & Freedance | Naxos Jazz | 86061-2
John Coltrane Quartet | Afro Blue Impressions | Pablo | 2PACD 2620101
Live In Stockholm 1963 | Charly | CD 33
John Coltrane Quartet With Eric Dolphy | John Coltrane:The Complete 1961 Village Vanguard Recordings | Impulse(MCA) | 954322-2
Jazz Gallery:John Coltrane Vol.2 | RCA | 2127276-2
John Coltrane Quintet | Live At The Village Vanguard | MCA | 2292-54627-2
John Coltrane Quintet With Eric Dolphy | John Coltrane:The Complete 1961 Village Vanguard Recordings | Impulse(MCA) | 954322-2
The Other Village Vanguard Tapes | Impulse(MCA) | MCD 04137
The Other Village Vanguard Tapes | Impulse(MCA) | MCD 04137
Coltrane Spiritual | Impulse(MCA) | 589099-2
Le Jazz Group De Paris | Jazz In Paris | EmArCy | 548793-2
Michal Urbaniak With The Horace Parlan Trio | Take Good Care Of My Heart | Steeplechase | SCCD 31195
Billy Taylor Trio | You Tempt Me | Taylor Made Records | T 1004
Spiritual Medley:
The London Gabrieli Brass Ensemble feat. Chris Barber | Under The Influence Of Jazz | Timeless | CD TTD 569
Spiritual Rebirth
Albert Ayler Septet | The Village Concerts | MCA | IA 9336/2
Spirituals: The Language Of Love
Cecil Payne Sextet | Payne's Window | Delmark | DE 509
Spittlefoelds' Slide
Alex Welsh And His Band | Melody Maker Tribute To Louis Armstrong Vol.2 | Jazz Colours | 874768-2
Splanky
Christian Rover Group feat. Rhoda Scott | Christian Rover Group-Live With Rhoda Scott At The Organ | Organic Music | ORGM 9704
Count Basie And His Orchestra | Breakfast Dance And Barbecue | Roulette | 531791-2
En Concert Avec Europe 1 | Laserlight | 710411/12
Live at The Sands | Reprise | 9362-45946-2
Basie In Sweden | Roulette | CDP 759974-2
Hank Crawford And His Orchestra | South-Central | Milestone | MCD 9201-2
Jimmy McGriff-Hank Crawford Quartet | Blues Groove | Telarc Digital | CD 83381
The Real Group | Jazz:Live | ACT | 9258-2
Splash
Miles Davis Group | Circle In The Round | CBS | 467898-2
Circle In The Round | CBS | 467898-2
Ralph Peterson Trio | Triangular | Blue Note | 792750-2
Splashin'
Centrifugal Funk | Centrifugal Funk | Legato | 652508
Splatch
Richard Galliano Quartet | Gallianissimo! The Best Of Richard Galliano | Dreyfus Jazz Line | FDM 36616-2
Spleen
Spleen | Dreyfus Jazz Line | FDM 36513-9
Richard Galliano Trio | Concert Inedits | Dreyfus Jazz Line | FDM 36606-2
Last Affair | Sound Movie-Suite | Blue Flame | 40312
Splendido
Gerry Mulligan Quartet | Lonesome Boulevard | A&M Records | 397061-2
Splidium-Dow(alt.take)
Sonny Stitt Quartet | Prestige First Sessions, Vol.2 | Prestige | PCD 24115-2
Split
Paul Motian Electric Bebop Band | Reincarnation Of A Love Bird | JMT Edition | 514016-2
Split Feelin's
Mark Helias Quintet | Split Image | Enja | 4086 (807528)
Split Kick
Art Blakey And The Jazz Messengers | Kenny Dorham | Royal Jazz | RJD 515
Paul Bley Trio | Charles Mingus-The Complete Debut Recordings | Debut | 12 DCD 4402-2
Stan Getz Quartet | Stan Getz-The Complete Roost Sessions | EMI Records | 859622-2
Unearthed Masters-Vol.2: Stan Getz | JAM | 5007 IMS
Stan Getz Quintet | Stan Getz:East Of The Sun-The West Coast Sessions | Verve | 531935-2
Split Kick(alt.take)
Stan Getz Quartet | Stan Getz-The Complete Roost Sessions | The Jazz Factory | JFCD 22839
Splittin'
Gigi Gryce-Donald Byrd Quintet | New Formulas From The Lab | RCA | PL 43698
Michel Legrand Sextet | Legrand 'Live' Jazz | Novus | ND 83103(847033)
Spoken Announcement by Perico Sambeat
John Coltrane Quartet | New Thing At Newport | Impulse(MCA) | JAS 22 (AS 94)
Spoken Introduction
Art Pepper Quartet | Art Pepper:The Complete Village Vanguard Sessions | Contemporary | 9CCD-4417-2
Bill Evans Quartet | The Complete Bill Evans On Verve | Verve | 527953-2
Bill Evans Trio | The Complete Bill Evans On Verve | Verve | 527953-2
The Complete Bill Evans On Verve | Verve | 527953-2
The Complete Bill Evans On Verve | Verve | 527953-2
The Complete Bill Evans On Verve | Verve | 527953-2
The Complete Bill Evans On Verve | Verve | 527953-2
At The Montreux Jazz Festival | Verve | 539758-2
Bill Evans:The Complete Live At The Village Vanguard 1961 | Riverside | 3RCD 1961-2
Dave McKenna | Maybeck Recital Hall Series Volume Two | Concord | CCD 4410
Freddie Hubbard Sextet | Keystone Bop Vol.2:Friday/Saturday | Prestige | PCD 24163-2
Keystone Bop | Fantasy | F 9615
Spoken Introduction by Joe Williams
Joe Farrell Quintet | Canned Funk | CTI | 6053
Sponge
The Brecker Brothers | Heavy Metal Be-Bop | RCA | 2119257-2
Barney Bigard And His Jazzopators | The Complete Duke Ellington-Vol. 9 | CBS | CBS 88210
Spontaneity
Christopher Hollyday Quartet | On Course | Novus | PD 83087
Spontaneous Color
Bruce Ditmas & D 3 | Spontaneous Combustion | Tutu Records | 888126-2
Spontaneous Combustion
Cannonball Adderley Quintet | Spontaneous Combustion | Savoy | 650104(881904)
Spontaneous Combustion-The Savoy Sessions | Savoy | ???
Discoveries | Savoy | SV 0251
Spontaneous Energy-
Pamela Fries Group | Alarming States | Nueva Records | NC 1011
Spontaneous Samba
Marion Brown-Gunter Hampel Duo | Gemini | Birth | CD 037
Spontaneous Simplicity
Sun Ra And His Arkestra | Outer Spaceways Incorporated | Freedom | FCD 741085
Spooks
Louis Armstrong With Gordon Jenkins And His Orchestra And Choir | Satchmo In Style | Verve | 549594-2
Marion Brown Quintet | Three For Shepp | Impulse(MCA) | IMP 12692
Spooky
Tok Tok Tok | It Took So Long | Einstein Music | EM 21103
Curley Hamner And His Orchestra | Charles Mingus-The Young Rebel | Swingtime(Contact) | ST 1010
Spooky Takes A Holiday
Jimmy Witherspoon And The Jay McShann Orchestra | Jimmy Witherspoon & Jay McShann | Black Lion | BLCD 760173
Spoonful
Gil Evans Orchestra | The Individualism Of Gil Evans | Verve | 833804-2 PMS
Howlin' Wolf Band | Howlin' Wolf | Chess | CH 9183
Spoonin'
Jack McDuff Quartet | The Concert McDuff | Prestige | PRCD 24270-2
Eric Marienthal Group | Crossroads | GRP | GRP 96102
Spoons
Jimmy Witherspoon And His All Stars | Singin' The Blues | Pacific Jazz | 494108-2
Spor
Jan Garbarek Quartet | Wayfarer | ECM | 1259(811968-2)
Joseph Berardi-Kira Vollman | Happy Wretched Family | Victo | CD 033
Sportin' Crowd
Ken Colyer's Skiffle Group | The Famous Manchester Free Trade Hall Concert | 504 Records | 504CD 50
Spot One
Don Grolnick Septet | Nighttown | Blue Note | 798689-2
Spotlight
Jimmy Knepper Quintet | Cunningbird | Steeplechase | SCCD 31061
Spotlite
Coleman Hawkins' Fifty-Second Street All-Stars | Planet Jazz:Coleman Hawkins | Planet Jazz | 2152055-2
Body And Soul | RCA | 26685152
JATP Jam Session | Return To Happiness-JATP At Yoyogi National Stadium,Tokyo | Pablo | 2620117-2
Spouting Bowl
Marcel Azzola-Itaru Oki Group | Transat Rue Des Orchidées | Zoo Records | J 9001
Spragare
Alex Möller-Lena Willemark Group | Hästen Och Tranan | ACT | 9244-2
Sprang
Ralph Burns And His Orchestra | The Jazz Scene | Verve | 521661-2
Spread Love
Take 6 | Tonight Take 6 | Warner | 9362-47611-2
Spread Love-
Dave King Group | Wildcat | Off The Wall Records | OTW 9501-CD
Sprich Ein Zauberwort-
Dave Liebman Trio | The Seasons | Soul Note | 121245-2
Spring
Taku Sugimoto | Oposite | HatNOIR | 802
Wolfgang Engstfeld Quartet | Songs And Ballads | Nabel Records:Jazz Network | CD 4658
Charlie Mariano Group | Savannah Samurai | Jazzline | JL 11153-2
Spring Ain't Here
Pat Metheny Group | In Concert | Jazz Door | JD 1231
Spring Beautiful Spring
Royce Campbell Quintet | Nighttime Daydreams | Timeless | CD SJP 337
Spring Can Really Hang You Up The Most
Bucky Pizzarelli | Love Songs | Stash Records | ST 213 IMS
Ella Fitzgerald With The Marty Paich Orchestra | Whisper Not | Verve | 589947-2
Ella Fitzgerald With The Tommy Flanagan Trio | Jazz At The Santa Monica Civic '72 | Pablo | 2625701-2
Herb Ellis-Ross Tompkins Duo | A Pair To Draw To | Concord | CJ 17
Jackie And Roy | Jackie And Roy | Black Lion | BLCD 760904
Levitts | We Are The Levitts | ESP Disk | ESP 1095-2
Liz Story/Joel DiBartolo | My Foolish Heart | Windham Hill | 34 11115-2
Marian McPartland Quartet | Portrait Of Marian McPartland | Concord | CCD 4101
Stan Getz-Albert Dailey Duo | Poetry | Blue Note | 960370-1 TIS
Wolfgang Engstfeld Quartet | Songs And Ballads | Nabel Records:Jazz Network | CD 4658
Kenny Dorham Septet | Cannonball Adderley Birthday Celebration | Fantasy | FANCD 6087-2
Spring Cannon
Don Sickler Quintet | The Muisc Of Kenny Dorham | Reservoir | RSR CD 111(882635)
Spring In Versailles(part 1)
Johannes Mössinger | Spring In Versailles | double moon | DMCD 1004-2
Spring In Versailles(part 2)
Ralph Burns And His Orchestra | Lee Konitz Meets Jimmy Giuffre | Verve | 527780-2
Spring Is Here
Bill Evans Trio | Spring Leaves | Milestone | M 47034
Bill Evans Trio:The Last Waltz | Milestone | 8MCD 4430-2
Bill Evans Trio:The Last Waltz | Milestone | 8MCD 4430-2
The Best Of Bill Evans Live | Verve | 533825-2
Bill Evans:The Secret Sessions | Milestone | 8MCD 4421-2
Bill Evans At Town Hall | Verve | 831271-2
Bobby Hackett Quintet | Melody Is A Must-Live At The Roosevelt Grill Vol.1 | Phontastic | PHONT 7571
Cannonball Adderley Quintet | Cannonball Adderley:Sophisticated Swing-The EmArCy Small Group Sessions | Verve | 528408-2
Carl Burnett Quintet | Carl Burnett Plays Music Of Richard Rodgers | Discovery | DS 819 IMS
Charlie Mariano Quartet | Deep In A Dream | Enja | ENJ-9423 2
Chris Connor With The Ellis Larkins Trio | I Hear Music | Affinity | AFF 97
Dave Brubeck Trio | The Dave Brubeck Trio | Fantasy | FCD 24726-2
Don Cherry Quintet | Live At The Montmartre Vol.2 | Magnetic Records | MRCD 112
Ella Fitzgerald With The Buddy Bregman Orchestra | The Rodgers And Hart Song Book, Vol.1 | Verve | 821579-2 PMS
Hal Schaefer And His Orchestra | The RCA Victor Jazz Workshop | Fresh Sound Records | NL 45975(RCA LPM 1199)
Hampton Hawes Trio | I'm All Smiles | Original Jazz Classics | OJCCD 796-2(C 7631)
Helmut Nieberle-Helmut Kagerer | Skyliner | ART BY HEART | ABH 2001 2
Horace Parlan | The Maestro | Steeplechase | SCCD 31167
Joey Calderazzo Quartet | In The Door | Blue Note | 795138-2
John Coltrane Quintet | John Coltrane-The Prestige Recordings | Prestige | 16 PCD 4405-2
John Park Quartet | If Winter Comes | Jazz Mark | 105
Mick Goodrick Quartet | Sunscreams | RAM Records | RMCD 4507
Misako Kano Quartet | Breakthrew | Jazz Focus | JFCD 027
Shirley Scott Trio | Like Cozy | Prestige | PCD 24258-2
Singers Unlimited With The Art Van Damme Quintet | The Singers Unlimited:Magic Voices | MPS | 539130-2
Stan Getz Quartet | Blue Skies | Concord | CCD 4676
The Poll Winners | The Poll Winners Ride Again | Original Jazz Classics | OJC 607(C 7556)
Tierney Sutton Group | Unsung Heroes | Telarc Digital | CD 83477
Warne Marsh Quartet | A Ballad Album | Criss Cross | Criss 1007
Spring Is Here-
Gerry Mulligan Concert Jazz Band | En Concert Avec Europe 1 | Laserlight | 710382/83
Spring Is Sprung
Gerry Mulligan Quartet | Americans In Sweden | Tax | CD 3711-2
Spring Like
Fabio Jegher Trio | Time Zone-Fabio Jegher Boston & L.A.Trios | Red Records | VPA 175
Spring Of Life
JoAnne Brackeen Duo | Trinkets And Things | Timeless | SJP 123
Spring Song
Big Band De Lausanne | Switzerjazz | TCB Records | TCB 96452
Klaus Lenz Jazz & Rock Machine | Fusion | View | VS 005 IMS
Spring Song-
Takuan | Push | dacapo | DCCD 9457
Spring Surprise
Billy Barron Quintet | Jazz Caper | Muse | MR 5235
Spring Will Be A Little Late This Year
Abbey Lincoln And Her Orchestra | Devil's Got Your Tongue | Verve | 513574-2

Dennis Farnon And His Orchestra | Caution! Men Swinging | Fresh Sound Records | LPM 1495(RCA)
Red Garland Trio | All Kinds Of Weather | Original Jazz Classics | OJCCD 193-2
Sathima Bea Benjamin Group | A Morning In Paris | Enja | ENJ-9309 2
Harry James And His Orchestra | James And Haymes | Circle | CCD-5

Spring(part 1)
Nils Wogram Sextet | Odd And Awkward | Enja | ENJ-9416-2

Spring(part 2)
Takashi Yoshimatsu | Tender Toys:Shin-Ichi Fukuda | Denon Compact Disc | CO-18053

Springbirds
Florian Poser-Klaus Ignatzek Duo | Springdale | Acoustic Music Records | 319.1166.2

Springdale
ULG | Spring | Laika Records | 35101382

Springdans-
Cecil Scott And His Bright Boys | Harlem Big Bands | Timeless | CBC 1-010

Springsville
Miles Davis + 19 | Miles Ahead | CBS | CK 65121
The Miles Davis Selection | CBS | 465699-2
Phil Woods Quartet | From New York | West Wind | WW 2101

Springtime In Winter
Wally Rose Trio | Ragtime Classics | Good Time Jazz | GTCD 10034-2

Sprott
Ulli Bögershausen-Reinhold Westerheide | Pictures | Laika Records | LK 35100932

Sprudelde Wasser
Paul Bley/Evan Parker/Barre Phillips | Time Will Tell | ECM | 1537

Sprung
Sam Rivers Quartet | Lazuli | Timeless | CD SJP 291

Spunkwater
Esbjörn Svensson Trio(E.S.T.) | Strange Place For Snow | ACT | 9011-2

Spunky Sprawl
Riccardo Ballerini Group | Blue Mesa | yvp music | CD 3048

Squabble
Rolf Von Nordenskjöld Quartet | First Catalogue | KlangRäume | 30170

Squak
Duke Jordan Quintet | Flight To Jordan | Blue Note | BNJ 71006(BST 84046)

Square Dance
Frank Foster's Living Color | Twelve Shades Of Black-For All Intents And Purposes | Leo Records | 007

Square Roots
James Dapogny's Chicago Jazz Band | Laughing At Life | Discovery | 74006-2

Squares
Duck Baker | Ms.Right | Acoustic Music Records | 319.1130.2

Squatty Roo
Ella Fitzgerald And Her All Stars | The Complete Ella Fitzgerald Song Books of Harold Arlen, Irving Berlin, Duke Ellington, George & Ira Gershwin, Jerome Kern, Johnny Mercer, Cole Porter And Rogers & Hart | Verve | 519832-2
Kenny Barron-Regina Carter | Freefall | Verve | 549706-2
L.A.4 | Montage | Concord | CJ 156

Squatty Roo-
Duke Ellington And His Orchestra | Carnegie Hall Concert December 1947 | Prestige | 2PCD 24075-2
Duke Ellington:Complete Prestige Carnegie Hall 1946-1947 Concerts | Definitive Records | DRCD 11211

Squeaky's Blues
Oscar Peterson Quartet | Paris Jazz Concert:Oscar Peterson | Laserlight | 36155
En Concert Avec Europe 1 | Laserlight | 710443/48
Charles Tyler-John Fischer Duo | 6x1 = 10/Duos For A New Decade | Circle Records | RK 21-7879/21 IMS

Squeb
Lonnie Plaxico Group | Iridescence | Muse | MCD 5427

Squeeze Me
Bobby Henderson | Key One Up | Vanguard | VCD 79612-2
Doc Cheatham And Sammy Price | Doc Cheattam&Sammy Price:Duos And Solos | Sackville | SK2CD-5002
Earl Hines Quartet | Another Monday Date | Prestige | PRCD 24043-2
Harry Strutters Hot Rhythm | Harry Strutters Hot Rhythm Orchestra | Jazz Colours | 874751-2
Louis Armstrong And His All Stars | Satch Plays Fats(Complete) | CBS | CK 64927
Louis Armstrong And His Hot Five | Louis Armstrong:Fireworks | Dreyfus Jazz Line | FDM 36710-2
Satch Plays Fats(Complete) | CBS | CK 64927
Heebie Jeebies | Naxos Jazz | 8.120351 CD
Warren Vaché-Allen Vaché Sextet | Ellington For Lovers | Nagel-Heyer | NH 1009
$$hide$$ | $$Titelverweise | |

Squeeze Me -> Just Squeeze Me

Squids
Barbara Thompson's Paraphernalia | Breathless | VeraBra Records | CDVBR 2057-2

Squiffy
Elliott Sharp Groups | Monster Curve | Ear-Rational | ECD 1031

Squilli Di Morte-
Memphis Convention | Memphis Convention | DIW | DIW 874 CD

St. Mark's Place Among The Sewers
Gary Peacock-Ralph Towner | Oracle | ECM | 1490(521350-2)

St. Helens
Claus Boesser-Ferrari | Welcome | Acoustic Music Records | 319.1117.2

St.Annes's Reel-
Lee Ritenour Group | Stolen Moments | GRP | GRP 96152

St.Bart's
Chad Rager Modern Big Band | In The Club...Live | Jazz Focus | JFCD 026

St.Denis
Elmo Hope Quintet | So Nice | Fresh Sound Records | FSR-CD 0194

St.George's Rag
Chris Barber's Jazz Band | The Best Of British Traditional Jazz | Philips | 818651-2

St.Germain Des Pres
Dusko Goykovich Quartet | In My Dreams | Enja | ENJ-9408 2
Charly Antolini Orchestra | Soul Beat | ATM Records | ATM 3802-AH

St.James Infirmary
Alex Hill And His Orchestra | That's My Stuff | Frog | DGF 7
Artie Shaw And His Orchestra | This Is Artie Shaw Vol. 2 | RCA | NL 89411 DP
Bob Scobey's Frisco Band | Scobey And Clancy | Good Time Jazz | GTCD 12009-2
David Paquette Trio | Mood Swings | ART BY HEART | ABH 2004 2
Dick Wellstood | Stride Piano | MRC | 066-32859
Doc Cheatham Sextet | Hey Doc! | Black & Blue | BLE 59.090 2
Erroll Garner Quartet | The Fascinating Erroll Garner | Fontana | 6430135
Joe Turner | Walking Through Heaven | Swingtime | 8205
King Oliver And His Orchestra | King Oliver And His Orchestra 1929-1930 | RCA | ND 89770
Louis Armstrong And His All Stars | Planet Jazz:Male Jazz Vocalists | Planet Jazz | 2169657-2
Victor Jazz History Vol.20:Jazz & The Blues | RCA | 2135739-2
Louis Armstrong And His Savoy Ballroom Five | Memorial | CBS | 66247
Muggsy Spanier And His Band | Memories Of Muggsy | Ember | CJS 845
Papa Bue's Viking Jazzband | Oldtime Festival | BELL Records | BLR 84005
Sammy Price Septet | Barrelhouse And Blues | Black Lion | BLCD 760159
Slam Stewart Quartet | Fish Scales | Black & Blue | BLE 233109
The Harlem Hot Chocolates | It Don't Mean A Thing(If It Ain't Got That Swing) | Naxos Jazz | 8.120526 CD

St.James Infirmary-
Louis Armstrong And His Orchestra | Louis Armstrong-Satchmo's Greatest Hits | RCA | CL 89799

St.John And The Dragon
Memphis Slim Quartet | Lord Have Mercy On Me | America | AM 6076

St.Louis Blues
Aki Takase Quintet | St.Louis Blues | Enja | 9130-2
Andy Kirk And His Twelve Clouds Of Joy | The Uncollected:Andy Kirk | Hindsight | HSR 227 (835032)
Art Tatum | Art Tatum:Swings | Memo Music | HDJ 4032
Artie Shaw And His Orchestra | In The Blue Room/In The Café Rouge | RCA | 2118527-2
Benny Carter All Stars | Aurex Jazz Festival '80:Gentlemen Of Swing | Eastworld | EWJ 80188
Bessie Smith With Louis Armstrong And Fred Longshaw | Jazz Gallery:Louis Armstrong Vol.1 | RCA | 2114166-2
Bessie Smith With The James P.Johnson Orchestra And The Hal Johnson Choir | The Blues | Storyville | 4960323
Big Bill Broonzy | Big Bill Broonzy-The 1955 London Sessions | Sequel Records | NEX CD 119
Billie & Dee Dee Pierce Trio | New Orleans-The Living Legends:Billie And Dede Pierce | Original Blues Classics | OBCCD 534-2(RLP 370)
Cab Calloway And His Orchestra | Duke Ellington/Cab Calloway | Forlane | UCD 19004
Chris Barber's Jazz And Blues Band | Stardust | Timeless | CD TTD 537
Chris Barber's Jazz Band | Chris Barber-Concert '80 Vol.2 | Jeton | JET 60010
Dave Brubeck Quartet | Dave Brubeck's All-Time Greatest Hits | CBS | 68288
Paper Moon | Concord | CCD 4178
Dizzy Gillespie And His Orchestra | Dizzier And Dizzier | RCA | 26685172
Django Reinhardt And The Quintet Du Hot Club De France | Swingin' With Django | Pro-Arte | CDD 549
Django Reinhardt Trio | Django/Django In Rome 1949-1050 | BGO Records | BGOCD 366
Django Reinhardt:Djangology | EMI Records | 780659-2
Dorothy Donegan Trio | The Explosive Dorothy Donegan | Progressive | PRO 7056 IMS
Duke Ellington And His Orchestra | Duke Ellington:Complete Studio Transcriptions | Definitive Records | DRCD 11199
Duke Ellington-Johnny Hodges All Stars | Back To Back | Verve | 521404-2
Duke Ellington's Spacemen | This Is Jazz:Duke Ellington Play Standards | CBS | CK 65056
Eddie Louiss Trio | Flomela | Dreyfus Jazz Line | FDM 36578-2
Ella Fitzgerald And Her All Stars | These Are The Blues | Verve | 829536-2 PMS
Ella Fitzgerald With The Frank DeVol Orchestra | Get Happy! | Verve | 523321-2
Ella Fitzgerald With The Lou Levy Trio | Ella In Rome-The Birthday Concert | Verve | 835454-2
Ellis Larkins Trio | A Smooth One | Black & Blue | BLE 59.123 2
Fats Waller | The Indispensable Fats Waller Vol.1/2 | RCA | 2122616-2
Frl. Mayer's Hinterhaus Jazzer | Frl. Mayer's Hinterhaus Jazzer | Jazz Classics | AU 11097
Glenn Miller And His Orchestra | Play Selections From The Glenn Miller Story And Other Hits | RCA | NL 89073
Gottfried Böttger-Joe Penzlin Duo | Take Two | L+R Records | CDLR 40030
Harold Nicholas And His Orchestra | Jazz In Paris:Harold Nicholas-June Richmond-Andy Bey | EmArCy | 013036-2
Herman Chittison | JazzIn Paris:Harlem Piano In Montmartre | EmArCy | 018447 2
Ida Cox With The Coleman Hawkins Quintet | Blues For Rampart Street | Original Jazz Classics | OJCCD 1758-2
Jack Teagarden's Big Eight | Planet Jazz | Planet Jazz | 2169652-2
Texas Tea Party | Naxos Jazz | 8.120585 CD
James Moody Quartet | Americans Swinging In Paris:James Moody | EMI Records | 539653-2
Jan Jankeje's Party And Swingband | Mobil | Jazzpoint | JP 1068 CD
Jeanie Lambe And The Danny Moss Quartet | Three Great Concerts:Live In Hamburg 1993-1995 | Nagel-Heyer | CD 019
Jessica Williams Quartet | Jassica's Blues | Jazz Focus | JFCD 018
Jimmy Smith With The Lalo Schifrin Orchestra | The Cat | CTI Records | PDCTI 1110-2
Jimmy Witherspoon And His All Stars | Jimmy Witherspoon | Laserlight | 17069
John Lewis-Hank Jones Duo | An Evening With Two Grand Pianos | Little David | LD 59657
Ken Colyer's Jazzmen | More Of Best Of Dixieland | Philips | 838347-2
Louis Armstrong And His All Stars | Satchmo' 70-Happy Birthday! | CBS | 66242-2
Historic Barcelona Concerts At Windsor Palace 1955 | Fresh Sound Records | FSR-CD 3004
The Louis Armstrong Selection | CBS | 467278-2
The Complete Town Hall Concert 17.May 1947 | RCA | ND 89746
Louis Armstrong And His Orchestra | This Is Jazz:Louis Armstrong Sings | CBS | CK 65039
Louis Armstrong-Satchmo's Greatest Hits | RCA | CL 89799
Victor Jazz History Vol.8:Swing Big Bands | RCA | 2128562-2
RCA Victor 80th Anniversary Vol.2:1930-1939 | RCA | 2668778-2
Lucy Reed With The Eddie Higgins Quartet | This Is Lucy Reed | Original Jazz Classics | OJCCD 1943-2(F 3243)
Machito And His Afro-Cuban Salseros | Mucho Macho | Pablo | 2625712-2
Max Collie And His Rhythm Aces | Sensation | Timeless | CD TTD 530
Mr.Acker Bilk And His Paramount Jazz Band | The Golden Years Of Revival Jazz,Vol.7 | Storyville | STCD 5512
The Golden Years Of Revival Jazz,Vol.9 | Storyville | STCD 5514
New Orleans Days | Lake | LACD 36
Muggsy Spanier And His Dixieland All Stars | At Club Hangover-Vol. 2 | Storyville | SLP 249
Papa Celestin And His New Orleans Band | Marie La Veau | GHB Records | BCD 106
Pete Fountain With Orchestra | The Best Of Pete Fountain | MCA | MCD 4032
Quintet Du Hot Club De France | Jazz Legacy 58: Django Reinhardt-Rythme Futur-Radio Sessions 1947 Vol | Vogue | 500108
Djangology Vol.1 | Naxos Jazz | 8.120515 CD
Ralph Sutton-Jay McShann Quartet | The Last Of The Whorehouse Piano Players | Chaz Jazz | CJ 103
Rod Mason And His Hot Five | Rod Mason's Hot Five feat. Angela Brown | Timeless | CD TTD 563
Seger Ellis | Prairie Blues-The Music Of Seger Ellis | AZURE Compact Disc | AZ-CD-22
Sidney Bechet And The Chamber Music Society Of Lower Basin Street | Sidney Bechet 1932-1943: The Bluebird Sessions | Bluebird | ND 90317
Sidney Bechet's Blue Note Jazzmen | Hot Jazz On Blue Note | Blue Note | 835811-2
South Pacific Jazz | South Pacific Jazz | Savoy | SV 0219(MG 6001)
Stephane Grappelli Quartet | Live In San Francisco | Black-Hawk | BKH 51601
The Sidney Bechet Society | Jam Session Concert | Nagel-Heyer | CD 076
Theo Macero And His Orchestra | Something New, Something Blue | Fresh Sound Records | LSP 15623(CBS CL 1388)
Wild Bill Davis Quartet | The Swinging Organ Of Wild Bill Davis:In The Groove! | Fresh Sound Records | FSR-CD 0308
Wolfgang Sauer With The Glen Buschmann Quintet | Deutsches Jazz Festival 1954/1955 | Bear Family Records | BCD 15430
Wooden Joe's New Orleans Band | Wooden Joe Nicholas | American Music | AMCD-5
Wycliffe Gordon Group | Blues Of Summer | Nagel-Heyer | NH 1011
Chris Barber's Jazz And Blues Band | Live In Munich | Timeless | CD TTD 600

St.Louis Blues-
Louis Armstrong And His Orchestra | Rare Louis Armstrong | Jazz Anthology | 550182

St.Louis Blues March
Glenn Miller And His Orchestra | His Original Recordings | RCA | NL 89026 DP
Glenn Miller And His Orchestra/Army Air Force Band | The Best Of Glenn Miller | RCA | NL 83871 AG

St.Louis Blues(part 2)
Benny Goodman And His Orchestra | The Birth Of Swing | Bluebird | ND 90601(3)

St.Louis Boogie
Count Basie And His Orchestra | Masters Of Jazz Vol.5 | RCA | NL 89530 DP

St.Louis Shuffle
Fletcher Henderson And His Orchestra | The Indispensable Fletcher Henderson(1927-1936) | RCA | 2122618-2
The Dixie Stompers | Fletcher Henderson Vol.2(1927) | Village(Jazz Archive) | VILCD 020-2

St.Louis-Dakar
Idris Muhammad Trio | Kabsha | Evidence | TR 110

St.Pepper
Jimmie Gordon Band | Jimmie Gordon 1934-1941 | Story Of Blues | CD 3510-2

St.Petrian
Chris Barber Trio | The Streets Of New Orleans | Jazz Colours | 874705-2

St.Phillip Street Breakdown
Chris Barber's Jazz Band | 40 Years Jubilee | Timeless | CD TTD 589
Monty Sunshine's Jazz Band | Wonderful Dixieland Vol.2 | Sonia | CD 77269
Mr.Acker Bilk And His Paramount Jazz Band | New Orleans Days | Lake | LACD 36

St.Sticks
Barney Kessel Trio | Jellybeans | Concord | CJ 164

St.Thomas
David Murray Big Band | South Of The Border | DIW | DIW 897 CD
George Young Quartet | Burgundy | Paddle Wheel | K 28P 6449
Jenny Evans And Band | Girl Talk | ESM Records | ESM 9306
Girl Talk | Enja | ENJ-9363 2
Live At The Allotria | BELL Records | BLR 90003
Jiri Stivin & Co. | Reduta Live | clearaudio | LT 0010-2 531
Karl Berger-Ray Anderson Duo | Conversations | IN+OUT Records | 77027-2
Kenny Burrell With Rufus Reid | A La Carte | Muse | MR 5317(952092)
Milt Jackson Quintet | Milt Jackson At The Kosei Nenkin | Pablo | 2620103-2
Monty Alexander | So What | Black & Blue | BLE 59.148 2
Ray Bryant Trio | Through The Years-The 60th Birthday Special Recordings Vol.1 | EmArCy | 512764-2 PMS
Richard 'Groove' Holmes Quintet | Grove Holmes/Jimmy McGriff | LRC Records | CDC 9042
Roots | Salutes The Saxophone: Tributes To John Coltrane, Dexter Gordon, Sonny Rollins, Ben Webster And Lester Young | IN+OUT Records | 7016-1
Sonny Rollins & Co. | Planet Jazz:Sonny Rollins | Planet Jazz | 2152062-2
Planet Jazz Sampler | Planet Jazz | 2152326-2
Now's The Time! | RCA | 2132335-2
Sonny Rollins Quintet | Just Once | Jazz Door | JD 12121
Sonny Rollins Trio | Masters Of Jazz Vol.14 | RCA | CL 42874 AG
The Alternative Rollins | RCA | PL 43268
Soren Lee Quartet | Soren Lee Quartet | L+R Records | CDLR 45073
Dizzy Gillespie Quintet | Angel City | Moon Records | MCD 025-2

St.Vitus Dance
Louis Jordan And His Tympany Five | Louis Jordan Vol.2-Knock Me Out | Swingtime(Contact) | ST 1012

Stabat Mater
Ernst Reijseger & Tenore E Cuncordu De Orosei | Colla Voche | Winter&Winter | 910037-2

Stabismo Di Venere
Allen Farnham Trio | Play-Cation | Concord | CCD 4521

Stablemates
Blue Mitchell Quintet | Last Dance | JAM | 5002 IMS
Dexter Gordon Quartet | Stable Mable | Steeplechase | SCS 1040
Eddie Allen Sextet | Summer Days | Enja | ENJ-9388 2
Eladio Reinon Quintet | Es La Historia De Un Amor | Fresh Sound Records | FSNT 004 CD
Eric Alexander-Lin Halliday Quintet | Stablemates | Delmark | DE 488
Howard Rumsey's Lighthouse All Stars Hosts Charlie Persip's Jazz Statesmen | Double Or Nothin' | Fresh Sound Records | 054 26011491(Liberty LRP 3045)
Milt Jackson-Wes Montgomery Quintet | Wes Montgomery-The Complete Riverside Recordings | Riverside | 12 RCD 4408-2
Paul Chambers Quartet | High Step | Blue Note | 84482
Philly Joe Jones Orchestra | The Big Beat | Milestone | MCD 47016-2
Smiley Winters-Mark Levine Duo | Smiley & Me | Concord | CCD 4352
Super Jazz Trio With Art Farmer | Something Tasty | RCA | PL 45369
Tito Puente Orchestra | Special Delivery | Concord | CCD 4732

Stablemates(alt.take)
Milt Jackson-Wes Montgomery Quintet | Wes Montgomery-The Complete Riverside Recordings | Riverside | 12 RCD 4408-2
Steve Lacy | Stabs | FMP | SAJ 05

Stade Se
Peter Herbert Group | B-A-C-H A Chromatic Universe | Between The Lines | btl 013(Efa 10183)

Stadtpfeifer
Erhard Hirt | Guitar Solo | FMP | OWN-90003

Staffel Shuffle
Frank Gratkowski Trio | Gestalten | Jazz Haus Musik | JHM 0083 CD

Stag Rustler
Anthony Braxton | Saxophone Improvisations Series F | America | AM 011/012

Stages(I,II,III)
Angela Brown | The Voice Of Blues | Schubert Records | SCH- 105

Stagnate
Machiel S. Sextet | For Flora | Limetree | MLP 198506

Staight Life
Buddy Rich And His Orchestra | The Amazing Buddy Rich: Time Being | RCA | ND 86459(847168)

Staight No Chaser
Heinrich Von Kalnein Group | New Directions | Nabel Records:Jazz Network | CD 4670

Stainach Song
Taku Sugimoto | Oposite | HatNOIR | 802

Staircase
Keith Jarrett | Staircase | ECM | 1090/91
Schlosser/Weber/Böhm/Huber/Binder | L 14,16 | Jazz 4 Ever Records:Jazz Network | J4E 4760

Staircase To The Future
Keith Jarrett | Works | ECM | 825425-1

Stairway To Heaven
Motohiko Hino Group | It's Therenyc | Enja | 8030-2
Stanley Jordan Trio | Stolen Moments | Blue Note | 797159-2

Stairway To The Stars
Bill Evans-Jim Hall | Undercurrent | Blue Note | 538228-2
Bud Powell Trio | Masters Of The Modern Piano | Verve | 2-2514 IMS
Cal Collins | By Myself | Concord | CJ 119
Chris Cheek Quartet | I Wish I Knew | Fresh Sound Records | FSNT 022 CD
Dan Faulk Quartet | Focusing In | Criss Cross | Criss 1076
Dee Dee Bridgewater With Orchestra | Dear Ella | Verve | 539102-2
Dexter Gordon Quartet | Our Man In Paris | Blue Note | 591722-2
Dexter Gordon:The Complete Blue Note Sixties Sessions | Blue Note | 834200-2
Glenn Miller And His Orchestra | Glenn Miller Forever | RCA | NL 89214 DP

John Coltrane-Milt Jackson Quintet | John Coltrane-The Heavyweight Champion:The Complete Atlantic Recordings | Atlantic | 8122-71984-2
The Coltrane Legacy | Atlantic | SD 1553
Johnny Hartman And His Quintet | I Just Dropped By To Say Hello | MCA | 951176-2
Kenny Burrell Quintet | Freedom | Blue Note | GXK 8170
Laurindo Almeida Quartet | Brazilliance Vol.1 | Pacific Jazz | 796339-2
Milt Jackson-Wes Montgomery Quintet | Bags Meets Wes! | Original Jazz Classics | OJC20 234-2(RLP 9407)
Wes Montgomery-The Complete Riverside Recordings | Riverside | 12 RCD 4408-2
Morris Lane With Bill Doggett | Tenor Saxation | Official | 6022
Oscar Peterson Trio | Masters Of Jazz Vol.7 | RCA | NL 89721 DP
Peter Leitch Quartet | Mean What You Say | Concord | CCD 4417
Sonny Red (Kyner) Quintet | Out Of The Blue | Blue Note | 852440-2
Teddy Edwards Quartet | Good Gravy | Original Jazz Classics | OJCCD 661-2(S 7592)

Stairway To The Stars(alt.take)
Oscar Peterson Trio | This Is Oscar Peterson | RCA | 2663990-2
Wes Montgomery-Milt Jackson Quintet | The Alternative Wes Montgomery | Milestone | MCD 47065-2

Stalag
Oscar Pettiford Quartet | Artistry In Jazz | Black Lion | BLCD 760100

Stalingrad
Carlo Actis Dato/Laura Culver | Zig Zag | SPLASC(H) Records | H 186

Stamina
Werner Lener Trio | My Own | Satin Doll Productions | SDP 1013-1 CD

Stammba
Marvin Stamm Orchestra | Stampede | Palo Alto | PA 8022

Stampede
Savoy Bearcats | New York Vol.3-Don't You Leave Me Here | Frog | DGF 12

Stand By
Stuff Smith And Poul Olsen With The Kenny Drew Trio | Hot Violins | Storyville | STCD 4170

Stand By Me
Mavis Staples-Lucky Peterson | Spirituals&Gospel:Dedicated To Mahalia Jackson | Verve | 533562-2

Stand In The Sun
Joe Locke Quintet | Wire Walker | Steeplechase | SCCD 31332

Stand Pat
Gerry Mulligan-Paul Desmond Quartet | Blues In Time | Verve | POCJ 1919 PMS

Stand Still
Bob Haggart And His Boys | Jazz In V.Discs Vol.3 | Collection Hugues Panassié | CTPL 003

Standard Imitation(My Funny Valentine)
Franco & Lorenzo Petrocca | Italy | Edition Musikat | EDM 062

Standard Medley
Eckhard Weigt Quartet | Standard Moods | Organic Music | ORGM 9718

Standard Moods
Kenny Garrett Quartet | KG Standard Of Language | Warner | 9362-48404-2

Standard Of Language(I-III)
Derrick James & Wesley 'G' Quintet | Two Sides To Every Story | Jardis Records | JRCD 20137

Standard Procedure
Das Saxophonorchester Frankfurt | Das Saxophonorchester Frankfurt-Live | FMP | SAJ 40

Standin' On The Corner(Whistlin' At The Pretty Girls)
Isaac Scott Blues Band | Big Time Blues Man | Red Lightnin' | RL 0046

Standing At The Crossroads
Luther Allison Blues Band | Love Me Papa | Black & Blue | BLE 233524

Standing In The Dark
WDR Big Band | Harlem Story | Koala Records | CD P 7

Standing On A Whale
James Emery Septet | Spectral Domains | Enja | ENJ-9344 2

Standing On A Whale Fishing For Minnows
First Class Blues Band | First Class Blues | Acoustic Music Records | 319.1031.2

Standing Outside
Johnny Hodges Orchestra | The Rabbit's Work On Verve In Chronological Order Vol. 2: 1951-52 | Verve | 2304448 IMS

Standing Up In A Hammock
Buddy Rich Big Band | The New One! | Pacific Jazz | 494507-2
J.A. Deane | Nomad | Victo | CD 035

Stango
Steve Slagle Quartet | Spread The Words | Steeplechase | SCCD 31354

Stanley The Steamer
Dexter Gordon Sextet | Dexter Gordon Plays-The Bethlehem Years | Fresh Sound Records | FSR-CD 154(882891)

Stan's Blues
Stan Getz Quartet | Anniversary ! | EmArCy | 838769-2
The Carnegie Hall Concert | Jazz Door | JD 1221
Stan Getz With The Bill Evans Trio | But Beautiful | Milestone | MCD 9249-2
Al Casey's Swingin' Blues Band | Al Casey Remembers King Curtis | JSP Records | 1095

Stan's Shuffle
Jimmy McGriff Sextet | Feelin' It | Milestone | MCD 9313-2
Stanley Turrentine Quartet | Ain't No Way | Blue Note | LT 1095

Stan's Tune
Stan Getz With The Kurt Edelhagen Orchestra | Stan Getz | Laserlight | 15761

Star
Sarah Vaughan And Her Trio | Sassy At Ronnie's | Ronnie Scott's Jazz House | JHCD 015

Star Crossed Lovers
Bill Berry's L.A.Big Band | Hello Rev. | Concord | CCD 4027
Günther Klatt-Tizian Jost | Art Of The Duo:Live In Mexico City | Tutu Records | 888184-2*
Guy Barker With The London Metropolitan Orchestra | What Love Is | EmArCy | 558331-2

Star Crossed Lovers-
Gene Harris And The Philip Morris All-Stars | Live | Concord | CCD 4808
Tommy Flanagan 3 | The Montreux '77 Collection | Pablo | 2620107

Star Dance
Abdullah Ibrahim Trio | Yarona | TipToe | TIP-888820 2
David Friesen Quartet/Trio/Duo/Solo | Star Dance | Inner City | IC 1019 IMS

Star Eyes
Barney Kessel Trio | Soaring | Concord | CCD 6033
Bill Evans Trio | Empathy+A Simple Matter Of Conviction | Verve | 837757-2 PMS
Billy Pierce Trio | Equilateral | Sunnyside | SSC 1037 D
Bud Powell Trio | The Genius Of Bud Powell-Vol.2 | Verve | 2-2526 IMS
Buddy Childers Big Band | It's What Happening Now! | Candid | CCD 79749
Cal Tjader Sextet | La Onda Va Bien | Concord | CCD 4113
Cannonball Adderley Sextet | What I Mean | Milestone | M 47053
Charlie Parker And The Swedish All Stars | Complete Bird In Sweden | Definitive Records | DRCD 11216
Charlie Parker Quartet | Charlie Parker:April In Paris | Dreyfus Jazz Line | FDM 36737-2
Summit Meeting At Birdland | CBS | CBS 82291
Charlie Parker | Verve | 539757-2
Charlie Parker Quintet | The Verve Years (1950-51) | Verve | 2-2512 IMS
Swedish Schnapps + | Verve | 849393-2
Chet Baker Sextet | RCA Victor 80th Anniversary Vol.5:1960-1969 | RCA | 2668781-2
Chet Is Back | RCA | NL 70578 AG
Chris Anderson Trio | Blues One | DIW | DIW 607 CD
Conte Candoli Quartet | Portrait Of A Count | Fresh Sound Records | FSR-CD 5015
Dexter Gordon Quartet | The Jumpin' Blues | Original Jazz Classics | OJCCD 899-2(PR 10020)
Donald Byrd Quintet | Long Green | Muse | 650137(882380)
Frank Morgan Quartet | Yardbird Suite | Original Jazz Classics | OJCCD 1060-2(C 14045)
Frits Landesbergen Quartet | Alone Together | Timeless | SJP 268
Joe Pass | Joe Pass:Guitar Virtuoso | Pablo | 4 PACD 4423-2
Joe Pass With The NDR Big Band And Radio Philharmonie Hannover | Joe Pass In Hamburg | ACT | 9100-2
John Bunch Trio | The Best Thing For You | Concord | CJ 328
Larry Schneider Quartet | Jazz | Steeplechase | SCCD 31505
Lover Man | Loose Walk | Palcoscenico | PAL 15009
Mickey Tucker Sextet | Hang In There | Steeplechase | SCCD 31302
Mundell Lowe-Hendrik Meurkens Quartet | When Lights Are Lowe | Acoustic Music Records | 319.1190.2
Sadao Watanabe With The Great Jazz Trio | Bird Of Paradise | Flying Disk | VJJ 6017
Shelly Berg Trio | The Joy | dmp Digital Music Productions | CD 3002
Stan Getz Quartet With Chet Baker | Stan Getz-Chet Baker:Quintessece Vol.1 | Concord | CCD 4807
Stephane Grappelli With The Roland Hanna Trio | Parisian Thoroughfare | Black Lion | BLCD 760132
Xanadu All Stars | Xanadu At Montreux Vol.3 | Vogue | 506616

Star Eyes-
Sonny Rollins Quintet | Sonny Rollins Plays For Bird | Original Jazz Classics | OJCCD 214-2
The Charlie Parker Memorial Band | Bird Still Lives! Vol.1 | Timeless | CD SJP 373

Star Eyes(alt.take)
Joe Beck-David Sanborn Orchestra With Strings | Beck&Sanborn | CTI | ZK 40805

Star Island
David Sills Quintet | Bigs | Naxos Jazz | 86070-2

Star Over Monhegan
Miles Davis Group | Star People | CBS | 25395

Star Song
Jackie And Roy | Star Sounds | Concord | CJ 115

Star Spangled Banner
Duke Ellington And His Orchestra | Duke Ellington -Carnegie Hall Concert | Ember | 800851-370(EMBD 2001)
Jaco Pastorius Trio | Heavy'n Jazz | Jazzpoint | JP 1036 CD
Jean-Paul Bourelly Group | Tribute To Jimi | DIW | DIW 893 CD

Stara Baska
Michel Godard-Miroslav Tadic-Mark Nauseef | Loose Wires | Enja | ENJ-9071 2

Stara Pesma
Duke Jordan Quintet | Flight To Jordan | Blue Note | BNJ 71006(BST 84046)

Starbright
Lee Ritenour Group | On The Line | GRP | GRP 95252

Starburst
Jack DeJohnette's Special Edition | Inflation Blues | ECM | 1244
Red Rodney Sextet | Home Free | Muse | MR 5135

Stardust
Art Pepper-George Cables Duo | Art Pepper:The Complete Galaxy Recordings | Galaxy | 16GCD 1016-2
Art Tatum | Art Tatum-The Standard Transcriptions | Music & Arts | CD 919
Standards | Black Lion | CD 877646-2
Artie Shaw And His Orchestra | Planet Jazz:Big Bands | Planet Jazz | 2169649-2
In The Blue Room/In The Café Rouge | RCA | 2118527-2
Ben Webster With The Kenny Drew Trio | There Is No Greater Love | Black Lion | CD 877626-2
Benny Goodman And His Orchestra | The Birth Of Swing | Bluebird | ND 90601(3)
40th Anniversary Concert-Live At Carnegie Hall | London | 820349-2
The Original Sounds Of The Swing Era Vol. 6 | RCA | NL 85515 DP
Benny Goodman Sextet | Live 1939/1941 | Jazz Anthology | JA 5181
Buddy Childers With The Russ Garcia Strings | Artistry In Jazz | Candid | CCD 79735
Buddy DeFranco Quintet | Cooking The Blues | Verve | MV 2513 IMS
Chris Barber's Jazz And Blues Band | Stardust | Timeless | CD TTD 537
Clifford Brown With Strings | Clifford Brown-Max Roach:Alone Together-The Best Of The Mercury Years | Verve | 526373-2
Compact Jazz: Clifford Brown | EmArCy | 842933-2 PMS
Brownie-The Complete EmArCy Recordings Of Clifford Brown | EmArCy | 838306-2
Coleman Hawkins All Stars | Coleman Hawkins | West Wind | WW 2034
Coleman Hawkins Trio | Coleman Hawkins In Europe | Timeless | CBC 1-006
Coleman Hawkins-Freddy Johnson | Thanks For The Memory | EPM Musique | FDC 5159
Dave Brubeck Quartet | Jazz At Oberlin | Original Jazz Classics | OJCCD 046-2
The Dave Brubeck Quartet feat. Paul Desmond In Concert | Fantasy | FCD 60-013
Once When I Was Very Young | Limelight | 844298-2 IMS
Dave Liebman Quintet | Doin' It Again | Timeless | CD SJP 140
Don Byas Quartet | New York 1945 | Jazz Anthology | JA 5106
Don Byas Sextet | Live At Minton's | Jazz Anthology | JA 5121
Earl Hines | Four Jazz Giants:Earl Hines Plays Tributes To W.C.Handy,Hoagy Carmichael And Louis Armstrong | Solo Art | SACD-111/112
Eiji Kitamura Quintet | Seven Stars | Concord | CJ 217
Ernie Royal Sextet | Accent On Trumpet | Fresh Sound Records | FSR 645(Urania UJLP 1203)
Frank Rosolino Quintet | Free For All | Original Jazz Classics | OJCCD 1763-2
Garnet Clark And His Hot's Club Four | Jazz Piano Vol.1 | Jazztime(EMI) | 251282-2
Glenn Miller And His Orchestra | The Glenn Miller Story | RCA | NL 89005 AG
The Very Best Of Glenn Miller | RCA | PL 89009 AO
Häns'che Weiss Ensemble | Vis-A-Vis | Elite Special | 73229
Harry Allen Quintet | A Night At Birdland Vol. 1 | Nagel-Heyer | CD 5002
Love Songs Live! | Nagel-Heyer | NH 1014
Harry James And His Orchestra | The Uncollected: Harry James | Hindsight | HSR 102
Hoagy Carmichael With Jack Teagarden And His Big Band | Swing Vol.1 | Storyville | 4960343
Hot Mallets | Hot Mallets-Isla Eckinger | BELL Records | BLR 84030
Irving Mills And His Hotsy Totsy Gang | Hoagy Carmichael 1927-1939 | Timeless | CBC 1-011
Jazz At Carnegie Hall All Stars | Ella Fitzgerald:Newport Jazz Festival-Live at Carnegie Hall | CBS | C2K 66809
Joe Pass-Jimmy Rowles Duo | Checkmate | Original Jazz Classics | OJCCD 975-2(2310865)
Joe Pass:A Man And His Guitar | Original Jazz Classics | OJCCD 8806-2
John Colianni | Maybeck Recital Hall Series Volume Thirty-Seven | Concord | CCD 4643
John Coltrane Quintet | John Coltrane-The Prestige Recordings | Prestige | 16 PCD 4405-2
John Lewis And The New Jazz Quartet | Slavic Smiles | Baystate | BVCJ 2005(889371)
Jon Hendricks And Friends | Freddie Freeloader | Denon Compact Disc | CY-76302
Lionel Hampton All Stars | Lionel Hampton:Flying Home | Dreyfus Jazz Line | FDM 36735-2
Just Jazz | MCA | MCA 42329
Lionel Hampton And His Orchestra | Chicago Jazz Concert | CBS | 21107
Lionel Hampton With The Oscar Peterson Trio | Verve Jazz Masters 26:Lionel Hampton with Oscar Peterson | Verve | 521853-2
Lord Nelson And His Boppers | In The Beginning | Original Jazz Classics | OJCCD 1771-2(G 204)
Mel Tormé And His Band | Fujitsu-Concord Jazz Festival In Japan '90 | Concord | CCD 4481
Michel Attenoux And His Dream Band | Great Traditionalists | Jazzpoint | JP 1046 CD
Miles Davis Quintet | Miles Davis In Stockholm Complete | Dragon | DRCD 228
Oscar Pettiford Orchestra | Bohemia After Dark | Affinity | AFF 117
Oscar Pettiford Sextet | Oscar Pettiford Sextet | Vogue | 21409452
Paul Desmond-Gerry Mulligan Quartet | Jazz Special-Two Of A Mind | RCA | CL 42788 AG
Pepper Adams-Donald Byrd Sextet | Pepper Adams&Donald Byrd:Stardust | Bethlehem | BET 6000-2(BCP 6029)
Plas Johnson Band | The Warm Sound Of Plas Johnson Tenor Sax Vol.1:Midnight Blue | Blue Moon | BMCD 3060
Ron Carter-Jim Hall Duo | Telephone | Concord | CCD 4270
Ron Eschete | A Closer Look | Concord | CCD 4607
Sir Charles Thompson | Stardust | Paddle Wheel | KICJ 225
The Newport 'House' Band | That Newport Jazz | CBS | 21139
Tommy Dorsey And His Orchestra | Planet Jazz:Tommy Dorsey | Planet Jazz | 2159972-2
Frank Sinatra And The Tommy Dorsey Orchestra | RCA | 2668701-2
This Is Tommy Dorsey | RCA | PL 89536 DP
Willie Lewis And His Entertainers | Americans Swinging In Paris:Benny Carter | EMI Records | 539647-2
Le Jazz En France Vol.3 | Pathe | 1727271
Wynton Marsalis Sextet | Hot House Flowers | CBS | 468710-2
Al Hirt And His Band | Cherry Pink And Apple Blossom White | Memo Music | HDJ 4085

Stardust-
Joe Henderson With The Wynton Kelly Trio | Four! | Verve | 523657-2
Simon Schott | Bar Piano: Simon Schott Plays Your Favorite Evergreens Vol.1 | Organic Music | ORGM 9733
Stan Kenton And His Orchestra | Stan Kenton 1947 | Queen-Disc | 057
The Lighter Side | Creative World | ST 1050

Stardust(1)
Gene Roland Orchestra feat. Charlie Parker | Bird's Eyes:Last Unissued Vol.15 | Philology | W 845.2

Stardust(2)
Bird's Eyes:Last Unissued Vol.15 | Philology | W 845.2

Stardust(alt.take)
Cal Tjader's Orchestra | Several Shades Of Jade/Breeze From The East | Verve | 537083-2

Starlight
Wes Montgomery Quintet | Wes Montgomery:Complete Live At Jorgies | Definitive Records | DRCD 11247

Starlight Hour
Ella Fitzgerald And Her Famous Orchestra | Ella Fitzgerald Vol.2-Forever Young | Swingtime(Contact) | ST 1007

Starmaker
Circle | Circling In | Blue Note | 84555

Starry Night
Art Farmer Septet | Art Worker | Moon Records | MCD 014-2

Stars Fell On Alabama
Anita O'Day With The Buddy Bregman Orchestra | Pick Yourself Up | Verve | 517329-2
Pick Yourself Up | Official | 3015
Art Tatum | The Tatum Solo Masterpieces Vol.5 | Pablo | 2310790
Benny Goodman And His Orchestra | Breakfast Ball | Saville Records | SVL 172 IMS
Billie Holiday And Her Orchestra | Embraceable You | Verve | 817359-1 IMS
Buddy Tate-Harry Sweets Edison Quintet | After Dark | Progressive | PCD 7028
Cannonball Adderley Quartet | Cannonball & Coltrane | Verve | 559770-2
Radio Nights | Night Records | VNCD 2(887045)
Carol Sloane And Clark Terry With The Bill Charlap Trio | The Songs Ella & Louis Sang | Concord | CCD 4787
Chris Fagan Quartet | Lost Bohemia | Open Minds | OM 2411-2
Dave McKenna | A Handful Of Stars | Concord | CCD 4580
Ella Fitzgerald And Louis Armstrong With The Oscar Peterson Quartet | Ella And Louis | Verve | 543304-2
The Jazz Collector Edition: Ella & Louis | Laserlight | 15706
Ella & Louis | Verve | 825373-2
Eric Alexander Quartet | Man With A Horn | Milestone | MCD 9293-2
Erroll Garner Trio | The Erroll Garner Collection Vol.3: Too Marvelous For Words | EmArCy | 842419-2 PMS
Frankie Laine With Buck Clayton And His Orchestra | Jazz Spectacular | CBS | CK 65507
Helen O'Connell With The Page Cavanaugh Trio | The Uncollected:Helen O'Connell | Hindsight | HSR 228
Jack Teagarden's Chicagoans | The Hollywood Session:The Capitol Jazzmen | Jazz Unlimited | JUCD 2044
Jess Stacy Quartet | Big Band Bounce & Boogie:Stacy 'N' Sutton | Affinity | AFS 1020
Johnny Smith Quintet | Moonlight In Vermont | Roulette | 596593-2
Moonlight In Vermont | Roulette | 300016
Johnny Smith-Stan Getz Quintet | Stan Getz-The Complete Roost Sessions | The Jazz Factory | JFCD 22839
Lee Wiley With The Dean Kincaide Dixieland Band | Bread,Butter And Jam In Hi-Fi | RCA | 2136402-2
Michael Cochrane Quartet | Path Ways | Steeplechase | SCCD 31542
Norman Burns Quintet | Bebop In Britain | Esquire | CD ESQ 100-4
Shelly Manne Trio | Shelly Manne & His Friends | Original Jazz Classics | OJCCD 240-2
Stan Getz Quintet | Ultimate Stan Getz selected by Joe Henderson | Verve | 557532-2
Sun Ra And His Arkestra | Purple Night | A&M Records | 395324-2
The Chicago All Stars | Newport Jazz Festival | RCA | 2121829-2
Boots Randolph-Richie Cole Sextet | Yakety Madness! | Palo Alto | PA 8041

Stars Fell On Alabama-
The Tremble Kids All Stars | Dixieland At Its Best | BELL Records | BLR 89091

Stars Fell On Alabama(alt.take)
Ben Webster With Orchestra And Strings | Music For Loving:Ben Webster With Strings | Verve | 527774-2
Frank Vignola Sextet | Off Broadway | Nagel-Heyer | CD 2006
Creative Arts Ensemble | One Step Out | Nimbus | NS 913

Stars In Your Eyes
Jonas Hellborg With Glen Velez | Ars Moriende | Day Eight Music | DEMCD 034

Start
Paul Bley Trio | Closer | ESP Disk | ESP 1021-2
Volker Kriegel & Mild Maniac Orchestra | Elastic Menu | MPS | 68180

Start Up!
Rob McConnell And The Boss Brass | Present Perfect | MPS | 823543-1

Started
Mingus Big Band | Gunslinging Birds | Dreyfus Jazz Line | FDM 36575-2

Starter
Hank Mobley Quintet | Hank Mobley | Blue Note | 0675622

Startin' From Scratch
Charles Mingus-Eric Dolphy Duo | Mingus In Europe, Vol. 1 | Enja | 3049-2

Starting A Story
Carla Bley Band | Heavy Heart | Watt | 14

Starting Again
Jimmy Patrick Quintet | You Are My Audience | BELL Records | BLR 84036

Starting Over
Frank Morgan All Stars | Reflections | Contemporary | CCD 14052-2
Jay Hoggard Quintet | The Fountain | Muse | MCD 5450

Startle
Jimmy Giuffre-Paul Bley-Steve Swallow | Fly Away Little Bird | Owl Records | 018351-2

Starts
Big Bill Broonzy | The Young Big Bill Broonzy | Yazoo | YAZ 1011

Stata El Sol De Ponenet

Jelly Roll Morton | The Library Of Congress Recordings | Affinity | CD AFS 1010-3

State Of Things
Jimmy Reed | I'm The Man Down There | Charly | CRB 1082

Statements
Klaus König Orchestra | Times Of Devastation/Poco A Poco | Enja | ENJ-6014 22
Page One | Beating Bop Live | Stunt Records | 18808

Station
Bob Smith Band | Radio Face | dmp Digital Music Productions | CD 483

Station Car
Gunter Hampel | Wellen/Waves-Berlin Soloflight | FMP | 0770

Station Monica
Wellen/Waves-Berlin Soloflight | FMP | 0770

Status Quo
The Clifford Jordan Big Band | Down Through The Years | Milestone | MCD 9197-2

Status Seeking
Mal Waldron Quintet | The Git Go-Live At The Village Vanguard | Soul Note | SN 1118
Mal Waldron Sextet | Eric Dolphy Birthday Celebration | Fantasy | FANCD 6085-2
Eric Dolphy:The Complete Prestige Recordings | Prestige | 9 PRCD-4418-2
Peter Herbert Group | B-A-C-H A Chromatic Universe | Between The Lines | btl 013(Efa 10183)

Stauber
Max Neissendorfer Trio | Staubfrei | EGO | 95100

Staubfrei
Dagobert Böhm Quartet | Acoustic Moods | Jazzline | ???

Stay
Sonny Rollins Trio | In Sweden 1959 | Ingo | 9

Stay As Sweet As You Are
Art Tatum | Art Tatum-The Standard Transcriptions | Music & Arts | CD 919
Masters Of Jazz Vol.8:Art Tatum | Storyville | SLP 4108
The Three Sounds | Standards | Blue Note | 821281-2

Stay Close To Me
Paul Moer Trio | Live At The Pour House | Fresh Sound Records | FSCD 1025

Stay Informed
Albert Mangelsdorff Trio | Live In Montreux | MPS | 68261

Stay Off The Carpet
Cannonball Adderley Quintet | Cannonball's Sharpshooters | Mercury | 826986-2 PMS

Stay On It
Dizzy Gillespie And His Big Band | Gene Norman Presents Dizzy Gillespie And His Big Band | GNP Crescendo | GNPD 23
Dizzy Gillespie And His Orchestra | Dizzy Gillespie-Diz Delights | RCA | CL 89804 SF

Stay Out Of Love
Willie Lewis And His Entertainers | Le Jazz En France Vol.3 | Pathe | 1727271

Stay Quite
Barry Harris Trio | Stay Right With It | Milestone | M 47050

Stay With Me
Christian Rover Group feat. Rhoda Scott | Christian Rover Group-Live With Rhoda Scott At The Organ | Organic Music | ORGM 9704

Stay With Me Lord
Christian Rover Group-Live With Rhoda Scott At The Organ | Organic Music | ORGM 9704
Oliver Jones Trio | Cookin' At Sweet Basil | Justin Time | JUST 25

Steady
Ben Sidran Group | Old Songs For New The Depression | Antilles | 846132-2(889648)

Steady Freddy
Mike Clark-Paul Jackson Quartet | The Funk Stops Here | TipToe | TIP-888811 2

Steady Freddy(reprise)
Bill Frisell Band | Before We Were Born | Nonesuch | 7559-60843-2

Steady Girl
Warren Lucky And Combo | Listen To Dr. Jive | Krazy Kat | KK 780 IMS

Steady Roll Boogie
Bumble Bee Slim(Amos Easton) | Bumble Bee Slim(Amos Easton) 1931-1937 | Story Of Blues | CD 3501-2

Steady Rollin' Blues
Robert Lockwood Jr.With The Aces | Steady Rollin' Man | Delmark | 900206 AO

Steal Away
Johnny Mars Band | Life On Mars | Teldec | 6.25959 AP

Steal Away To Jesus
Jimmy Witherspoon With The Randy van Horne Choir | Feelin' The Spirit | Fresh Sound Records | FSR 578(HiFiRecords R422)

Steal Your Licks
Allan Vaché-Harry Allen Quintet | Allan And Allan | Nagel-Heyer | CD 074

Stealin' Apples
André Previn And His Pals | Andre Previn And His Pals | Fresh Sound Records | FSR-CD 0106
Benny Goodman And His Orchestra | The Best Of The Big Bands Vol.2 | LRC Records | CDC 8528
Engelbert Wrobel's Swing Society | A Heartful(!) Of Swing | NCC Jazz | NCC 8502
John Crocker Quartet | All Of Me | Timeless | CD TTD 585
Oscar Klein-Lino Patruno European Jazz Stars | Live at The San Marino Jazz Festival | Jazzpoint | JP 1052 CD
Peanuts Hucko All Stars | Tribute To Benny Goodman | Timeless | CD TTD 513
Van Alexander Orchestra | Home Of Happy Feet/Swing! Staged For Sound! | Capitol | 535211-2
Wild Bill Davison With The Eddie Condon All Stars | Wild Bill Davison | Storyville | SLP 4005

Stealin' Blues
Coleman Hawkins Sextet | Hawk Eyes | Original Jazz Classics | OJCCD 294-2

Stealin' The Bean
Fats Navarro Sextet | Fat Girl | Savoy | 650115(881915)

Stealing Space(I&II)
Eddie Davis And His Beboppers | Nostalgia | Savoy | SV 0123(MG 12133)

Steam
Ulli Bögershausen | Private Stories | Laika Records | 35101542
Charles 'Bobo' Shaw & The Human Arts Ensemble | P'nk J'zz | Muse | MR 5232

Steam Heat
George Gruntz Concert Jazz Band | Global Exellence | TCB Records | TCB 21172

Steamboat Stomp
Jelly Roll Morton's Red Hot Peppers | The Jelly Roll Morton Centennial-His Complete Victor Recordings | Bluebird | ND 82361
Doctor Jazz | Black & Blue | BLE 59.227 2

Steel
Golden Gate Quartet | From Spriritual To Swing Vol.2 | EMI Records | 780573-2

Steel Away
Walter 'Wolfman' Washington And The Roadmasters | Out Of The Dark | Rounder Records | CDRR 2068

Steel Your Heart
The Martin Drew Band | British Jazz Artists Vol. 3 | Lee Lambert | LAM 003

Steeplechase
Charlie Parker All Stars | The Savoy Recordings 2 | Savoy | 650108(881908)
James Zollar Quintet | Soaring With Bird | Naxos Jazz | 86008-2
Martial Solal And The Kentonians | Martial Solal:The Complete Vogue Recordings Vol.3 | Vogue | 21606372

Phil Woods Quartet | Ornithology:Phil Salutes Bird | Philology | W 69.2
Roy Hargrove Trio | Parker's Mood | Verve | 527907-2
Scott Hamilton Quartet | After Hours | Concord | CCD 4755

Stegen Pa Taket-Polska Efter Per Larsson
Luigi Archetti | Das Ohr | ATM Records | ATM 3804-AH

Stein On Vine
Emil Mangelsdorff/Bob Degen | Meditation | L+R Records | CDLR 45088

Steinolphonk
Gabriele Hasler & Foolish Heart | God Is A She | Foolish Music | FM 111186

Steinway And Daughter
Heiner Goebbels/Alfred Harth | Frankfurt-Peking | Riskant | 568-72411

Stella
Erwin Angela Clark & Odie | Live At The Piano Man | Steeplechase | SCB 9003
Yosuke Yamashita | Banslikana | Enja | 2080

Stella Backstage
Cornelius Claudio Kreusch | Piano Moments | Take Twelve On CD | TT 007-2
Dink Johnson | Dink Johnson-Charlie Thompson: The Piano Players | American Music | AMCD-11

Stella By Star Wars
Al Haig Quartet | Al Haig Quartet | Fresh Sound Records | FSR-CD 0012

Stella By Starlight
Attila Zoller-Martial Solal | Zoller-Koller-Solal | MPS | 8431072
Barney Kessel Trio | Jellybeans | Concord | CJ 164
Benny Golson Orchestra | Walkin' | Fresh Sound Records | FSR-CD 0302
Bill Evans | Conversations With Myself | Verve | 521409-2
Bill Evans Trio | The Complete Bill Evans On Verve | Verve | 527953-2
The Complete Bill Evans On Verve | Verve | 527953-2
The Complete Bill Evans On Verve | Verve | 527953-2
The Complete Bill Evans On Verve | Verve | 527953-2
A Simple Matter Of Conviction | Verve | 23MJ 3040 IMS
Live In Buenos Aires 1979 | West Wind | WW 2061
Bill Evans:The Secret Sessions | Milestone | 8MCD 4421-2
Bill Evans/Jazzhouse | Milestone | MCD 9151-2
Bill Goodwin Trio | No Method | Fresh Sound Records | FSR-CD 136(882880)
Billy Eckstine With Bobby Tucker And His Orchestra | Billy Eckstine:Billy's Best! | Verve | 526440-2
Bireli Lagrene Trio | Live In Marciac | Dreyfus Jazz Line | FDM 36567-2
Booker Ervin Quartet | The Freedom And Space Sessions | Prestige | P 24091
Charlie Parker With The Joe Lipman Orchestra | Charlie Parker With Strings:The Master Takes | Verve | 523984-2
Charlie Parker Big Band | Verve | 559835-2
Charlie Shavers With Orchestra | The Most Intimate Charlie Shavers | Bethlehem | BET 6019-2(BCP 27)
Chet Baker Quartet | Stella By Starlight | Bandstand | BDCD 1520
Chet Baker Sextet | Chet Baker/Big Band | Pacific Jazz | 781201-2
Chick Corea | Expressions | GRP | GRP 97732
Chris Connor With The Vinnie Burke Quartet+Art Mardigan | Lullabys Of Birdland | Bethlehem | BTM 6823
Christoph Spendel Trio | Back To Basics | Blue Flame | 40072(2132485-2)
Count Basie And His Orchestra | En Concert Avec Europe 1 | Laserlight | 710411/12
Dave Liebman And The Lluis Vidal Trio | Dave Liebman And The Lluis Vidal Trio | Fresh Sound Records | FSNT 026 CD
Dave Liebman Trio | Classic Ballads | Candid | CCD 79512
Dizzy Gillespie Big Band | Groovin' High | Bandstand | BDCD 1513
Dizzy Gillespie Sextet | The Giant | Accord | 556672
Dorothy Ashby Quartet | The Jazz Harpist | Savoy | SV 0194(MG 6039)
Elvin Jones-Takehisa Tanaka Quartet | Elvin Jones Introduces Takehisa Tanaka | Enja | ENJ-7081 2
Gene Ammons And His All Stars | Juganthology | Prestige | P 24036
Grant Green Quartet | I Want To Hold Your Hand | Blue Note | 300261(4202)
Hampton Hawes Trio | Northern Windows Plus | Prestige | PRCD 24278-2
Bird Song | Original Jazz Classics | OJCCD 1035-2
Live At The Jazz Showcase In Chicago, Vol. 1 | Enja | 3099-2
Hampton Hawes-Martial Solal Quartet | Key For Two | Affinity | AFF 31
Howard Alden-George Van Eps | Seven And Seven | Concord | CCD 4584
Jim Hall Jazzpar Quartet | Jazzpar 98 | Storyville | STCD 4230
Jimmy Knepper Quintet | Special Relationship | Hep | CD 2012
Joe Diorio | Italy | MGI Records | MGR CD 1010
Joe Henderson With The Keith Greko Trio | Last Train Outta Flagstaff | Concept | VL 4 IMS
Joe Pass | Joe Pass:A Man And His Guitar | Original Jazz Classics | OJCCD 8806-2
Joe Pass Duo | Northsea Nights | Pablo | 2308221
John Abercrombie-Marc Johnson-Peter Erskine | John Abercrombie/Marc Johnson/Peter Erskine | ECM | 1390(837756-2)
John Mehegan Quartet | Tasty Pudding | Savoy | SV 0253(SL 1144)
Kenny Dorham Quintet | Ballads For Trumpet | Jazz Colours | 874708-2
Larry Vuckovich Quartet | Blues For Red | Hot House Records | HH 1001 IMS
Lou Blackburn-Freddie Hill Quintet | Perception | Fresh Sound Records | FSR-CD 0307
Lucas Heidepriem Quartet | Voicings | IN+OUT Records | 7011-2
Manfredo Fest Quintet | Jungle Cat | dmp Digital Music Productions | CD 470
Martial Solal Trio | Martial Solal At Newport '63 | RCA | 2174803-2
At Newport '63 | RCA | 2125768-2
Michael Weiss Trio | Milestones | Steeplechase | SCCD 31449
Miles Davis Quintet | Miles Davis At Plugged Nickel, Vol. 1/2 | CBS | CBS C 2 38266
Milt Jackson All Stars | Invitation | Original Jazz Classics | OJCCD 260-2
Milt Jackson Sextet | Opus De Funk | Prestige | P 24048
Nat Adderley Quintet | We Remember Cannon | IN+OUT Records | 7012-2
Nat King Cole With The Nelson Riddle Orchestra | The Piano Style Of Nat King Cole | Capitol | 781203-2
Oscar Peterson Trio | Compact Jazz:Oscar Peterson | Mercury | 830698-2
Oscar Peterson-Joe Pass Duo | Live At Salle Pleyel, Paris | Pablo | 2625705
Pat Thomas With Band | Jazz Patterns | Fresh Sound Records | Strand SLS CD 1015
Red Richards-George Kelly Sextet With Doc Cheatham | Groove Move | Jazzpoint | JP 1045 CD
Red Rodney Quintet | Fiery | Savoy | SV 0148(MG 12148)
Rich Perry Quartet | O Grande Amor | Steeplechase | SCCD 31492
Richie Kamuca Quartet | Jazz Erotica | Fresh Sound Records | FSR-CD 500(881696)
Ron McClure Quartet | McJolt | Steeplechase | SCCD 31262
Stan Getz Quintet | Stan Getz Plays | Verve | 2304387 IMS
Stan Getz Plays | Verve | 833535-2
Stan The Man | Verve | 815239-1 IMS
Stanley Cowell | Maybeck Recital Hall Series Volume Five | Concord | CCD 4431
Steve Davis Quartet | Songs We Know | dmp Digital Music Productions | CD 3005
Tal Farlow Quartet | Poppin' And Burnin' | Verve | 815236-1 IMS
Thomas Hass Group | A Honeymoon Too Soon | Stunt Records | STUCD 19601
Timeless All Stars | It's Timeless | Timeless | CD SJP 178
Tommy Flanagan/Kenny Barron | Together | Denon Compact Disc | DC-8573
Tuck Andress | Reckless Precision | Windham Hill | 34 10124-2

Stella By Starlight(alt.take-1)
Ray Brown-Milt Jackson Quintet | Much In Common | Verve | 533259-2

Stella By Starlight(alt.take-2)
Much In Common | Verve | 533259-2

Stella By Starlight(take 4)
Charles Mingus Workshop | Charles Mingus-The Complete Debut Recordings | Debut | 12 DCD 4402-2

Stella By Starlight(take 5)
John Lee Hooker | The Real Folk Blues | Chess | CHD 9271(872291)

Stella Malu
Katrina Krimsky-Trevor Watts | Stella Malu | ECM | 1199
Estella Mama Yancey With Axel Zwingenberger | Axel Zwingenberger And The Friends Of Boogie Woogie Vol.4: The Blues Of Mama Yancey | Vagabond | VRCD 8.88009

Stella Yancey Blues
Michael Shrieve Group | Two Doors | CMP Records | CMP CD 74

Stellar Regions
John Coltrane Quartet | Stellar Regions | Impulse(MCA) | 951169-2

Stellar Regions(alt.take)
Elmo Hope Trio | Last Sessions Vol.2 | Inner City | IC 1037 IMS

Stella-Wise
Günter Sommer | Hörmusik III:Sächsische Schatulle | Intakt Records | CD 027

Stenskoven
Kenny Garrett Group | Black Hope | Warner | 9362-45017-2

Step
Markovic Gut Sextet | Message From Belgrade | Timeless | SJP 195

Step Aside
Sunny Blair | Arkansas Blues | Anthology of the Blues | AB 5607

Step By Step
John Gordon Sextet | Step By Step | Strata East Records | 660.51.005
Tommy Smith Quintet | Step By Step | Blue Note | 791930-2

Step Lightly
Shelly Manne And His Men | At The Blackhawk Vol.2 | Contemporary | C 7578

Step Lightly(alt.take)
Clifford Brown-Max Roach Quintet | Clifford Brown And Max Roach At Basin Street | Verve | 589826-2

Step Lightly(Junior's Arrival)
More Study In Brown | EmArCy | 814637-2
Steve Wilson Quintet | Step Lively | Criss Cross | Criss 1096

Step One
Young Disciples | Tempo Jazz Edition Vol.1-Talkin' Loud | Talkin' Loud | 848362-2

Step Right Up
Clark Terry-Bob Brookmeyer Quintet | Clark Terry-Bobby Brookmeyer Quintet | Mainstream | MD CDO 728
Jimmy Smith With The Oliver Nelson Orchestra | Bashin' | Verve | 2304481 IMS

Step Tempest
Misha Mengelberg Quintet | Change Of Season | Soul Note | 121104-2

Stephane's Blues
Guy Lafitte Quartet | The Things We Did Last Summer | Black & Blue | BLE 59.192 2

Stephane's Tune
Stochelo Rosenberg | Caravan | Verve | 523030-2

Stephanie
Lee Konitz Quartet | Tranquility | Verve | MV 2508 IMS

Steppenwind
Roger Girod-Peter A.Schmid | Windschief | Creative Works Records | CW CD 1027-2

Steppenwolf
Don Menza Sextet | Hip Pocket | Palo Alto | PA 8010

Steppin' In It
Hilton Ruiz Trio | Steppin' Into Beauty | Steeplechase | SCS 1158

Steppin' Out
Rick Margitza Quartet | Work It | Steeplechase | SCCD 31358

Stepping
Hilton Ruiz Trio | New York Hilton | Steeplechase | SCCD 31094

Stepping On The Blues
Glenn Spearman Double Trio | The Fields | Black Saint | 120197-2

Stepping Stones
Michael Bocian | Premonition:Solo Debut For Nylon String Guitar | Enja | 9118-2

Sterephonic
Cecil Payne With The Joe Palin Trio | Brookfield Andante | Spotlite | SPJ LP 2 (CP 2)

Sternenblume
Ton-Art | Zu | Hat Art | CD 6034

Stess And Trauma
Thomas Clausen Trio | She Touched Me | M.A Music | A 628-2

Steve
Black Eagle Jazz Band | When Your Hair Has Turned To Silver | Stomp Off Records | CD 1303

Stevedore Stomp-
Chris Barber's Jazz And Blues Band | 40 Years Jubilee | Timeless | CD TTD 589

Steveland
Alan Sondheim Quintet | T'Other Little Tune | ESP Disk | ESP 1082-2

Steve's Blues
Steve Allen Sextet | Steve Allen Plays Jazz Tonight | Concord | CCD 4548

Steve's Freedom Principle-
Michel Waisvisz | Crackle | FMP | SAJ 14

Stevie
Tough Young Tenors | Alone Together | Antilles | 848767-2(887317)

Stick Jam
Sharkey Bonano And His Band | Sounds Of New Orleans Vol.4 | Storyville | STCD 6011

Stickin'
Bill Easley Quartet | Wind Inventions | Sunnyside | SSC 1022 D

Sticks
Gene Ammons Septet | Goodbye | Original Jazz Classics | OJCCD 1081-2(P 100939)
Louis Moholo-Evan Parker-Pule Pheto-Gibo Pheto-Barry Guy Quintet | Bush Fire | Ogun | OGCD 009

Sticks Up
Glenn Ferris Trio | Flesh & Stone | Enja | 8088-2

Sticky Wicket
Dexter Gordon Quartet | Swiss Nights Vol.2 | Steeplechase | SCCD 31090
American Classic | Discovery | 71009-2
Kenny Werner's Uncovered Hearts | Ludwigsburger Jazztage | Chaos | CACD 8055-3

Stieselkick & Dat Walzerle
Ekkehard Jost Quintet | Carambolage | View | VS 0028 IMS

Still
John Abercrombie Trio | Current Event | ECM | 1311(827770-2)
Karl Berger-Dave Holland Duo | Conversations | IN+OUT Records | 77027-2
Reiner Winterschladen-Manos Tsangaris | King Kong | Jazz Haus Musik | JHM 0056 CD

Still 99
Muddy Waters Blues Band | Muddy Waters | Chess | 427005

Still A Rose
Heiner Stadler Jazz Alchemy | Jazz Alchemy | Tomato | 2696702

Still Belonging To You
Christian Jacob | Maynard Ferguson Presents Christian Jacob | Concord | CCD 4744

Still Crazy After All These Years
Rosemary Clooney With The John Oddo Big Band | Still On The Road | Concord | CCD 4590

Still Got The Blues
Red Holloway Quintet | Coast To Coast | Milestone | MCD 9335-2

Still Groovin'
David Fathead Newman Septet | Still Hard Times | Muse | MCD 5283

Still In Thalys
Carla Bley Band | Live! | Watt | 12(815730-2)

TITELVERZEICHNIS

Still In The Room
Illinois Jacquet And His Orchestra | The Soul Explosion | Original Jazz Classics | OJCCD 674-2(P 7629)

Still King
Ellery Eskelin Quintet | Vanishing Point | HatOLOGY | 577

Still Life
Paul Bley | Synth Thesis | Postcards | POST 1001

Still Life Still Live
Cafe Du Sport Jazzquartett | Cafe Du Sport Jazzquartett | Minor Music | 801096

Still Missing
Ernie Watts With The RIAS-Bigband | Great European Jazz Orchestras Vol.3:Ticino | ACT | 9229-2

Still She
Jenny Evans And Her Quintet | Gonna Go Fishin' | Enja | ENJ-9403 2

Still Standing
David Benoit Group With Symphony Orchestra | Shadows | GRP | GRP 96542

Still Talkin' To Ya
Cannonball Adderley Quintet | Spontaneous Combustion-The Savoy Sessions | Savoy | ???

Still There
Dexter Gordon Quartet | Round Midnight(Soundtrack) | CBS | 70300

Still Water Stomp
Maynard Ferguson With The Birdland Dreamband | The Birdland Dream Band Vol.1 | Fresh Sound Records | 58110 CD(RCA)

Still Water Stomp(alt.take 1)
Birdland Dream Band | Birdland Dream Band | RCA | 2663873-2

Still Water Stomp(alt.take 2)
The Far East Side Band | Caverns | New World Records | 80458-2

Still We Dream(Ugly Beauty)
Carmen McRae with the Clifford Jordan Quartet | The Collected Carmen McRae | RCA | 2668713-2
Jan Somers Band | Here We Are | Timeless | CD SJP 397

Still Young
Ramsey McLean & The Survivors | New New Orleans Music: Jump Jazz | Line Records | COCD 9.00916 O

Stille
Alfred 23 Harth Group | Sweet Paris | free flow music | ffm 0291

Stille Bars-
Norbert Stein Pata Masters | Blue Slit | Pata Musik | PATA 8 CD

Stille Menschen
Bugge Wesseltoft | It's Snowing On My Piano | ACT | 9260-2

Stille Nacht
David Gazarov Trio | Let's Have A Merry Christmas With The David Gazarov Trio! | Organic Music | ORGM 9712
Deborah Henson-Conant | The Gift:15 Weihnachtslieder der Erde | Laika Records | 35100992
Jan Harrington Sextet | Jan Harrington's Christmas In New Orleans | Nagel-Heyer | NHR SP 4
Joe Kienemann | Liedgut:Amsel,Drossel,Swing & Funk | yvp music | CD 3095
New Orleans Quarter | Christmas Jazz | New Orleans Quarter Records | NOQR-V-DIV-CD 2

Stille Nacht Heilige Nacht
Ulli Bögershausen | Christmas Carols | Laika Records | 35101622
Montreal Jubilation Gospel Choir | Joy To The World | Blues Beacon | BLU-1018 2

Stille Stunden
Raum-Zeit-Klang-Project | Dimensionale X H2O Memory | Born&Bellmann | 970612 CD

Stillness
Furio Di Castri | Solo | SPLASC(H) Records | HP 04

Stima
Hugh Masekela Group | Hope | Triloka Records | 320203-2

Stimmung
Some Other Trio | A Tale Of Three Ducks | L+R Records | CDLR 45109

Stingl & Wadl
David Benoit Group | This Side Up | GRP | GRP 95412

Stinky Pooh!
Titi Winterstein Quintet + Guests | I Raisa(Die Reise) | Intercord | 160134

Stitches
Panama Francis And His Savoy Sultans | Gettin' In The Groove | Black & Blue | BLE 233320

Stitt's It
Paul Kuhn Septet | I Wish You Love:The Philharmonic Concert | Timbre | TRCD 005

Stitt's Tune
Sonny Stitt Orchestra | Sonny Stitt & The Top Brass | Atlantic | 90139-1 TIS

Stjärnan
Vic Lewis West Coast All Stars | Vic Lewis Presenting A Celebration Of Contemporary West Coast Jazz | Candid | CCD 79711/12

Stock And After Shock
Big Joe Williams Duo | Nine String Guitar Blues | Delmark | 900203 AO

Stöckchen In Speiche
Django's Music | Django Reinhardt:Djangology | EMI Records | 780659-2

Stockholm Sweetnin'
Conte Candoli Quartet | Conte-Nuity | Fresh Sound Records | FSR-CD 5028
Gary Smulyan Nonet | Saxophone Mosaic | Criss Cross | Criss 1092
Les Spann Quintet | Gemini | Original Jazz Classics | OJCCD 1948-2(JLP 9355)
Oscar Peterson Trio | En Concert Avec Europe 1 | Laserlight | 710443/48
Paul Thommen Octet | Jazz In Switzerland 1930-1975 | Elite Special | 9544002/1-4

Stockyard Strut
Freddie Keppard's Jazz Cardinals | Johnny Dodds Vol.2 | Village(Jazz Archive) | VILCD 017-2
Joshua Redman Quartet | Beyond | Warner | 9362-47465-2

Stoic Revolutions
Blind Willie McTell | 1927-1935 | Yazoo | YAZ 1037

Stolen From Norway(1)
Mikhail Alperin-Vegar Vardal | Portrait | JA & RO | JARO 4227-2

Stolen From Norway(2)
Portrait | JA & RO | JARO 4227-2

Stolen From Norway(3)
Ahmad Jamal Trio | The Awakening | Impulse(MCA) | IMP 12262

Stolen Moments
Brandon Fields With The Gina Kronstadt Strings | Brandon Fields & Strings | Paras Recordings | PRC 1102
Eddie Lockjaw Davis And His Orchestra | Eric Dolphy:The Complete Prestige Recordings | Prestige | 9 PRCD-4418-2
Emborg-Larsen Quintet | Heart Of The Matter | Stunt Records | STUCD 19102
J.J.Johnson And His Orchestra | J.J.! | RCA | 2125727-2
Jenny Evans And Her Quintet | Gonna Go Fishin' | Enja | ENJ-9403 2
Kenny Burrell Quartet | Moon And Sand | Concord | CCD 4121
Lorne Lofsky Trio | It Could Happen To You | Pablo | 2312122
New York Voices | Hearts Of Fire | GRP | GRP 96532
Oliver Nelson And His Orchestra | The Roots Of Acid Jazz | Impulse(MCA) | IMP 12042
Blues And The Abstract Truth | CTI Records | PDCTI 1122-2
Phil Woods And His European Rhythm Machine | Le Jazz En France-Vol.8 | Pathe | 1727321
Primal Blue | Primal Blue | Hip Bop | HIBD 8006
Roots | Stablemates | IN+OUT Records | 7021-2
Stanley Jordan Trio | Stolen Moments | Blue Note | 797159-2
The Atlantic String Trio | First Meeting | Factory Outlet Records | 2001-1 CD

Stolen Sweets
David Newton | Return Journey | Linn Records | AKD 025

Stolpern
Günter Sommer | Hörmusik III:Sächsische Schatulle | Intakt Records | CD 027

Stolt Oli
Eric Le Lann Group | New York | OMD | VB 053 CD

Stomp
Hubert Nuss Trio | The Shimmering Colours Of The Stained Glass | Green House Music | CD 1008
Lionel Hampton And His Orchestra | Lionel Hampton Story Vol.1 | Black & Blue | BLE 59.237 2

Stomp Blasé
John Lee Hooker | No Friend Around | Charly | CR 30170

Stomp Off-Let's Go
Charleston Chasers | Steaming South | Stomp Off Records | CD 1314

Stomp(Johnny Come Lately)
Duke Ellington And His Orchestra | Duke Elliongton:Complete Prestige Carnegie Hall 1943-1944 Concerts | Definitive Records | DRCD 11210

Stomp(Presto)-
Dick Meldonian And The Jersey Swingers | Some Of These Days | Progressive | PRO 7033 IMS

Stompin' For Mili
Count Basie And His Orchestra | Hall Of Fame | Verve | MV 2645 IMS

Stompin' At Decca
Quintet Du Hot Club De France | Django Reinhardt-Stephane Grappelli | Ace Of Club | ACL 1158

Stompin' At The Philharmonie
Acoustic Jazz Quartet | Acoustic Jazz Quartet | Naxos Jazz | 86033-2

Stompin' At The Savoy
Anita O'Day With The Buddy Bregman Orchestra | Pick Yourself Up | Official | 3015
Art Tatum | The Art Tatum Solo Masterpieces | Pablo | 2625703
Benny Goodman And His Orchestra | Planet Jazz:Benny Goodman | Planet Jazz | 2152054-2
Planet Jazz Sampler | Planet Jazz | 2152326-2
The Hits Of Benny Goodman | Capitol | 791212-2
Jazz Collection:Benny Goodman | Laserlight | 24396
Welcome To Jazz: Benny Goodman | Koch Records | 322 076 D1
Benny Goodman Quartet | 1938 Carnegie Hall Concert | CBS | 450983-2
The Benny Goodman Trio And Quartet Sessions Vol.1-After You've Gone | Bluebird | ND 85631
Benny Goodman Trio | Benny Goodman:The Complete 1947-1949 Small Group Sessions Vol.2(1947-1949) | Blue Moon | BMCD 1043
Bernard Berkhout's Swingmates | Air Mail Special | Timeless | CD SJP 360
Cal Tjader Sextet | A Night At The Blackhawk | Original Jazz Classics | OJC 278(F 8026)
Charlie Christian All Stars | Charlie Christian-Jazz Immortal/Dizzy Gillespie 1944 | Original Jazz Classics | OJCCD 1932-2(ES 548)
Chick Webb And His Little Chicks | Jazz Drumming Vol.3(1938-1939) | Fenn Music | FJD 2703
Clifford Brown-Max Roach Quintet | Brownie-The Complete EmArCy Recordings Of Clifford Brown | EmArCy | 838306-2
Coleman Hawkins All Stars | Timeless Jazz-A Jazztone Society Classic | Fresh Sound Records | FSR-CD 0088
Duke Ellington And His Orchestra | A True Collectors Item | Jazz Archive | 90.105-2
Ella Fitzgerald And Louis Armstrong With The Oscar Peterson Quartet | Ella And Louis Again,Vol.1 | Verve | 2304501 IMS
Ella And Louis Again | Verve | 825374-2
Compact Jazz: Ella Fitzgerald/Louis Armstrong | Verve | 835313-2
Ella Fitzgerald With The JATP All Stars | Compact Jazz: Ella Fitzgerald Live | Verve | 833294-2
Erroll Garner Trio | Penthouse Serenade | Savoy | SV 0162(MG 12002)
Gene Krupa Trio | The Complete Jazz At The Philharmonic On Verve 1944-1949 | Verve | 523893-2
Gene Krupa-Charlie Ventura Trio | Commodore Classics-Town Hall Concert 1945 | Commodore | 6.26169 AG
JATP All Stars | The Complete Jazz At The Philharmonic On Verve 1944-1949 | Verve | 523893-2
Jay Hoggard Quintet | The Fountain | Muse | MCD 5450
Jimmie Grier And His Orchestra | The Uncollected:Jimmie Grier | Hindsight | HSR 177
Joe Pass Trio | Live At Donte's | Pablo | 2620114-2
Intercontinental | MPS | 68121
John Lewis-Hank Jones Duo | An Evening With Two Grand Pianos | Little David | LD 59657
Kenny Burrel Quartet | Jazz-Club: Bass | Verve | 840037-2
Leonard Feather's Esquire All Stars | Metropolitan Opera House Jam Session | Jazz Anthology | 550212
Louis Armstrong And His All Stars | Jazz In Paris:Louis Armstrong-The Best Live Concert Vol.2 | EmArCy | 013031-2
The Legendary Berlin Concert Part 2 | Jazzpoint | JP 1063 CD
Louis Armstrong:The Great Chicago Concert 1956 | CBS | C2K 65119
Mack The Knife | Pablo | 2310941-2
Lucky Thompson Quartet | Kenny Clarke | Swing | SW 8411 IMS
Martial Solal | The Solosolal | MPS | 68221
Minton's Playhouse All Stars | Jazz Legacy 64: Charlie Christian-1941 Live Sessions | Vogue | 500114
Rex Allen's Swing Express | Keep Swingin' | Nagel-Heyer | CD 016
Ronnie Scott Orchestra | Bebop In Britain | Esquire | CD ESQ 100-4
Sebastian Gramss Underkarl | 20th Century Jazz Cover-Live | TCB Records | TCB 96202
Stanley Cowell | Maybeck Recital Hall Series Volume Five | Concord | CCD 4431
Tal Farlow Quartet | The Tal Farlow Album | Verve | MV 2584 IMS
Terry Gibbs-Buddy DeFranco-Herb Ellis Sextet | Kings Of Swing | Contemporary | CCD 14067-2
The New York Allstars | The New York Allstars Play Lionel Hampton,Vol.2: Stompin' At The Savoy | Nagel-Heyer | CD 077
The Super Guitar Fusion | Aranjuez | RCA | PL 40866 AS
Walter Norris Trio | Lush Life | Concord | CCD 4457
Wes Montgomery Quintet | Far Wes | Pacific Jazz | 794475-2
Woody Herman And His Orchestra | The Third Herd, Vol.1 | Discovery | DS 815 IMS
Benny Goodman And His Orchestra | The Yale University Muisc Library Vol.5 | Limelight | 820827-2 IMS

Stompin' At The Savoy-
Big City Swing | Decca | TAB 5

Stompy Jones
Duke Ellington And Johnny Hodges Orchestra | Side By Side | Verve | 521405-2
Duke Ellington-Johnny Hodges All Stars | Verve Jazz Masters 4:Duke Ellington | Verve | 516338-2
Duke Ellington And Johnny Hodges Plus Others | Verve | 2304417 IMS
Loren Schoenberg And His Jazz Orchestra | Just A-Settin' And A-Rockin' | Musicmasters | 5039-2
Paul Gonsalves-Ray Nance Sextet | Just A-Sittin' And A-Rockin' | Black Lion | BLCD 760148
Sidney Bechet And His New Orleans Feetwarmers | Sidney Bechet 1932-1943: The Bluebird Sessions | Bluebird | ND 90317

Stompy Jones-
Barney Bigard And His Jazzopators | The Complete Duke Ellington-Vol. 7 | CBS | CBS 88140

Stone Bone
Steve Coleman And Five Elements | World Expansion | JMT Edition | 834410-2

Stone Cold Dead In The Market
Louis Jordan And His Tympany Five | Louis Jordan-Let The Good Times Roll: The Complete Decca Recordings 1938-1954 | Bear Family Records | BCD 15557 IH
Stephan Schmolck Quartet | Rites Of Passage | L+R Records | CDLR 45064

Stone Crazy
Andy Rinehart Group | Jason's Chord | CMP Records | CMP CD 1003

Stone Flower
Laurindo Almeida-Charlie Byrd Quartet | Brazilian Soul | Concord | CCD 4150

Stone Garden
Eric Kloss Quartet | Eric Kloss & The Rhythm Section | Prestige | PCD 24125-2(P 7689/7793)

Stone Ground Seven
Tom White With Band | Keep It Under Your Hat | Ronnie Scott's Jazz House | JHCD 018

Stone Ridge
Tom Shaka | Hit From The Heart | Crosscut | CCD 11025

Stones In My Passway
John Hammond | The Best Of John Hammond | Vanguard | VCD 11/12
Dick Heckstall-Smith & John Etheridge Group | Obsession Fees | R&M Digital Music | 2-8002

Stonewall
Milt Jackson Quartet | Opus De Funk | Prestige | P 24048

Stooge Blues
Lightnin' Hopkins | Lightnin' Strikes Back | Charly | CRB 1031

Stop
Don Lanphere Quintet | Fats Navarro:The 1946-1949 Small Group Sessions(Studio Recordings-Master Takes),Vol.3 | Blue Moon | BMCD 1018
Sonny Red (Kyner) Quintet | Jazz Is Busting Out All Over | Savoy | SV 0178(12123)

Stop And Go
Klaus Doldinger Group | Back In New York:Blind Date | Atlantic | 3984-26922-2
Artie Shaw Sextet | More Lst Recordings:The Final Sessions | Musicmasters | 65101-2

Stop Breakin' Down Blues
Robert Johnson | Robert Johnson-King Of The Delta Blues | CBS | 493006-2

Stop Breakin' Down Blues(alt.take)
Junior Wells Blues Band | Southside Blues Jam | Delmark | 900204 AO

Stop By
Hans Reichel/Fred Frith | Stop Complaining | FMP | CD 36

Stop It
Lozenzo Petrocca Quartet | Stop It | Edition Musikat | EDM 018
Uli Beckerhoff Group | Stay | Nabel Records:Jazz Network | CD 4636
Rosetta Howard And Her Hep Cats | The 30's Girls | Timeless | CBC 1-026

Stop Look And Listen
Jimmy Dorsey And His Orchestra | The Uncollected:Jimmy Dorsey, Vol.3 | Hindsight | HSR 165

Stop Lying
Big Bill Broonzy Band | Big Bill Broonzy-Midnight Steppers | Swingtime(Contact) | BT 2001

Stop Makin' Music
Benny Carter Quintet With Billy Stritch | Benny Carter Songbook Vol.2 | Musicmasters | 65155-2

Stop 'N' Go
Charlie Ventura Septet | Euphoria | Savoy | SJL 2243 (801889)

Stop Pretending
Buddy Johnson And His Orchestra | Wails | Official | 6010

Stop Pretty Baby
Count Basie And His Orchestra | One O'Clock Jump | Verve | 559806-2
Sonny Boy Williamson Band | More Real Folk Blues | Chess | CHD 9277(872297)

Stop The Red Light's On
Nat King Cole Trio | Hit That Jive Jack | MCA | MCD 42350

Stop The World,I Want To Get Off!
The Couriers Of Jazz | The Couries Of Jazz-England's Greatest Combo | Fresh Sound Records | Carlton STCD 116

Stop This World
Mose Allison Quintet | That's Jazz Vol.19: Mose Allison | Atlantic | ATL 50249
Horace Silver Quintet | Horace Silver | Blue Note | 300097(1518)

Stop! Don't!
Don Lanphere Quintet | Prestige First Sessions, Vol.1 | Prestige | PCD 24114-2

Stopover Bombay
Jazz Africa All Nations Big Band | Jadu(Jazz Africa Down Under) | Enja | ENJ-9339 2

Stopover Sidney
Spark Plug Smith | Country Blues Collector Items Vol.2(1931-1937) | Story Of Blues | CD 3540-2

Stoppin' The Clock
Vince Giordano's Nighthawks | Qualty Shout | Stomp Off Records | CD 1260

Stop-Sound
Duane Eubanks Quintet/Sextet | Second Take | TCB Records | TCB 20602

Stoptime Rag
Morton Gunnar Larsen | Maple Leaf Rag | Herman Records | HJCD 1009

Storby Blues(Big City Blues)
Dixie Rhythm Kings | That's My Stuff | Frog | DGF 7

Stories To Tell
Stanley Clarke Groups | Stanley Clarke Best | Zounds | CD 2700020089
Jeff Gardner-Gary Peacock | Alchemy | fnac Muisc | 662016

Storks Over Rabat
Gary Burton Sextet | Who Is Gary Burton? | RCA | 2136403-2

Storm
Itchy Fingers | Live | Enja | ENJ-6076 2
Ray Warleigh Quartet | Reverie | View | VS 106 IMS

Storm Warning
John Lee Hooker | The Blues Vol. 5 | Big Bear | 156042

Stormy Blues
Albert King Blues Band | Thursday Night In San Francisco | Stax | MPS 8557

Stormy Monday Blues(They Call It Stormy Monday)
Big Joe Turner And His All Stars | Stormy Monday | Pablo | 2310943-2
Diane Schuur With Orchestra | The Best Of Diane Schuur | GRP | GRP 98882
Earl Hines And His Orchestra | The Indispensable Earl Hines Vol.3/4(1939-1945) | RCA | 2126408-2
Victor Jazz History Vol.20:Jazz & The Blues | RCA | 2135739-2
James 'Son' Thomas | James 'Son' Thomas | Blues Classics(L+R) | CDLR 82006
JATP All Stars | J.A.T.P. In London 1969 | Pablo | 2CD 2620119
Jimmy Ponder Sextet | Jump | Muse | MCD 5347
Klaus Doldinger Jubilee | Doldinger's Best | ACT | 9224-2
Bluesy Toosy | ACT | 9200-2
Leslie Drayton Orchestra | Love Is A Four-Letter Word | Optimism | ER 1003
Muddy Waters Blues Band | Live In Switzerland 1976 | Jazz Helvet | JH 02-2
T-Bone Walker And His Band | The Great Blues Vocals And Guitar Of T-Bone Walker | Pathe | 2C 068-86523(Capitol)
WDR Big Band | Harlem Story | Koala Records | CD P 7

Stormy Monday Blues(They Call It Stormy Monday-alt.take)
Chris Barber's Jazz And Blues Band | He's Got The Whole World In His Hand | Timeless | CD TTD 599

Stormy Weather
Art Tatum | Handful Of Keys | ASV | AJA 5073
Billie Holiday And Her All Stars | Recital By Billie Holiday | Verve | 521868-2
Billie Holiday And The Basie Boys | Jazz Live & Rare: Billie Holiday Live 1937/56 | Jazzline | ???
Buddy Tate Trio | Midnight Slows Vol.4 | Black & Blue | BLE 194682
Cab Calloway And His Orchestra | Hi-De-Hi-Di-Ho | RCA | 2118524-2
Charles Mingus Workshop | Abstractions | Bethlehem | BET 6016-2(BCP 65)
Dick Hyman | Dick Hyman Plays The Great American Songbook | Musicmasters | 65120-2
Django Reinhardt And The Quintet Du Hot Club De France | The Indispensable Django Reinhardt | RCA | ND 70929
Don Redman And His Orchestra | Swiss Radio Days Jazz Series Vol.11:Don Redman Orchestra | TCB Records | TCB 02112

Ella Fitzgerald With The Billy May Orchestra | The Complete Ella Fitzgerald Song Books of Harold Arlen, Irving Berlin, Duke Ellington, George & Ira Gershwin, Jerome Kern, Johnny Mercer, Cole Porter And Rogers & Hart | Verve | 519832-2
George Benson Quartet | Grandes Voix Du Jazz | CBS | 467147-2
Houston Person Quintet | Basics | Muse | MCD 5344
Jenny Evans And The Rudi Martini Quartet | At Lloyd's | ESM Records | ESM 9302
At Loyd's | BELL Records | BLR 90004
Joe Sample Group | Invitation | Warner | 9362-45209.2
Joe Turner | I Understand | Black & Blue | BLE 59.153 2
Lena Horne With Orchestra | The Jazz Collector Edition: Cotton Club Days | Laserlight | 15707
Lena Horne With The Lou Bring Orchestra | Planet Jazz:Lena Horne | Planet Jazz | 2165373-2
Lonnie Johnson With Elmer Snowden | Lonnie Johnson With Elmer Snowden Vol.2:Blues Ballads And Jumpin' Jazz | Original Blues Classics | OBCCD 570-2
Madeline Bell With The Metropole Orchestra | Beat Out That Rhythm On A Drum | Koch Jazz | 3-6910-2
Randy Weston Trio | The Modern Art Of Jazz | Dawn | DCD 107
Ruth Brown And Her Band | The Songs Of My Life | Fantasy | FCD 9665-2
The Four Freshmen | Voices In Modern | EMI Records | 1599321

Stormy Weather-
Barbara Dennerlein Duo | Jazzbühne Berlin '88 | Repertoire Records | RR 4903-CC

Stormy Weather(Keeps Rainin' All The Time)
Oscar Peterson Trio | Oscar Peterson Plays The Harold Arlen Song Book | Verve | 589103-2
Oscar Peterson Plays The Harold Arlen Song Book | Verve | 589103-2
Roland Kirk Quartet | Soulful Saxes | Affinity | AFF 758

Stormy Weather(take 1)
Richie Cole Sextet | New York Afternoon | Muse | MCD 5119

Stormz
String Thing | String Thing:Alles Wird Gut | MicNic Records | MN 2

Störungsstelle
Charles Brackeen Quartet | Bannar | Silkheart | SH 105

Story From A Stranger
Bill Evans | The Complete Bill Evans On Verve | Verve | 527953-2

Story Line-
Bill Evans At Town Hall | Verve | 831271-2
Richie Beirach & Andy LaVerne | Universal Mind | Steeplechase | SCCD 31325

Story Of E.
Baron Mingus And His Symphonic Airs | Charles Mingus-The Young Rebel | Swingtime(Contact) | ST 1010

Story Time
Steve LaSpina Quartet | Story Time | Steeplechase | SCCD 31396

Storyteller
Bunk Johnson And His Superior Jazz Band | Authentic New Orleans Jazz | Good Time Jazz | GTCD 12048-2

Storyville Blues
Chris Barber's Jazz Band | The Best Of Dixieland-Live in 1954/55 | London | 820878-2
Chris Barber's Jazz Band | Decca | 6.24024 AL
Louis Armstrong And His All Stars | Louis Armstrong | Forlane | UCD 19002

Storywise
Steve Smith Quintet | Vital Information | CBS | 25682

Stowaway
Michel Waisvisz | Crackle | FMP | SAJ 14

Strahlenspur
Arild Andersen Trio | The Triangle | ECM | 1752(0381212)

Straight
Eliane Elias Group | So Far So Close | Blue Note | B 1-91411

Straight Ahead
Abdul Wadud-Leroy Jenkins Duo | Straight Ahead/Free At Last | Red Records | VPA 147
Harold Danko | After The Rain | Steeplechase | SCCD 31356
Jeanne Lee-Ran Blake | The Newest Sound Around | RCA | 2122112-2
Kenny Dorham Quintet | Last But Not Least 1966 Vol.2 | Raretone | 5022 FC
Oliver Nelson Quintet | Eric Dolphy:The Complete Prestige Recordings | Prestige | 9 PRCD-4418-2
Oscar Pettiford Sextet | Montmartre Blues | Black Lion | BLP 60124

Straight Life
Art Pepper Quartet | Art Pepper:The Complete Galaxy Recordings | Galaxy | 16GCD 1016-2
Art Pepper:The Complete Galaxy Recordings | Galaxy | 16GCD 1016-2
Art Pepper:The Complete Galaxy Recordings | Galaxy | 16GCD 1016-2
Landscape | Original Jazz Classics | OJCCD 676-2(GXY 5128)
Tokyo Encore | Dreyfus Jazz Line | FDM 36551-2
Coun Basie And His Orchestra | Jazz Live & Rare:Count Basie & His Orchestra Live 1954 | Jazzline | ???

Straight Lines
Willem Breuker Kollektief | Deadly Sin/Twice A Woman(Sountracks) | BVHAAST | CD 9708

Straight No Chaser
Art Taylor Quintet | Taylor's Tenors | Prestige | VIJ 5034
Bill Evans Trio With Jeremy Steig | The Complete Bill Evans On Verve | Verve | 527953-2
What's New | Enoch's Music | 57271053
Brad Goode-Von Freeman Quintet | Inside Chicago Vol.1 | Steeplechase | SCCD 31500
Bud Powell Trio | At The Golden Circle, Vol.5 | Steeplechase | SCCD 36017
Buddy DeFranco Group | Blues Bag | Affinity | AFF 55
Cannonball Adderley Quintet | Cannonball's Sharpshooters | Mercury | 826986-2 PMS
Verve Jazz Masters 31:Cannonball Adderley | Verve | 522651-2
Hot Tracks For Cool Cats Vol.3 | Polydor | 816411-2
Chad Rager Modern Big Band | In The Club...Live | Jazz Focus | JFCD 026
Clark Terry-Bob Brookmeyer Quintet | Clark Terry-Bobby Brookmeyer Quintet | Mainstream | MD CDO 728
Dave Burrell/Takashi Mizuhashi | Plays Ellington & Monk | Denon Compact Disc | DC-8550
Dexter Gordon Quintet | After Hours | Steeplechase | SCCD 31224
Eddie Cleanhead Vinson Septet | I Want A Little Girl | Pablo | 2310866-2
Fritz Hartschuh Quartet | Monk Project | L+R Records | CDLR 45081
Giants Of Jazz | Giants Of Jazz | George Wein Collection | AU 36100
Joe Ascione Octet | My Buddy:A Tribute To Buddy Rich | Nagel-Heyer | CD 036
Joe Henderson With The Wynton Kelly Trio | Straight No Chaser | Verve | 531561-2
Keith Jarrett Trio | Bye Bye Blackbird | ECM | 1467(513074-2)
Kenny Barron Trio | Green Chimneys | Criss Cross | Criss 1008
Mal Waldron Quartet | Mal Waldron In Retrospect | Eastwind | EWIND 705
Miles Davis All Stars | Miles Davis All Stars | Jazz Band Records | EB 409(835651)
Miles Davis Sextet | Miles & Monk At Newport | CBS | SRCS 5698
Niels Lan Doky Quartet | An Evening Of Standards | Maracatu | MAC 940005
Peter Herbolzheimer Rhythm Combination & Brass | More Bebop | Koala Records | CD P 6
Quincy Jones And His Orchestra | The Quintessential Charts | MCA | IA 9342/2
Slide Hampton Orchestra | Jazz In Paris:Slide Hampton-Exodus | EmArCy | 013033-2
Tete Montoliu | The Music I Like To Play Vol.3-Let's Call This | Soul Note | 121230-2
Thelonious Monk Quartet | Live In Paris 1964 | France's Concert | FCD 132x2
Live In Switzerland 1966 | Jazz Helvet | JH 06
The Be Bop Legends | Moon Records | MCD 072-2
Thelonious Monk Quintet | Thelonious Monk:Misterioso | Dreyfus Jazz Line | FDM 36743-2
Genius Of Modern Music,Vol.2 | Blue Note | 300404
Jazz Profile:Thelonious Monk | Blue Note | 823518-2
Genius Of Modern Music,Vol.1 | Blue Note | 781510-2
Thelonious Monk-Gerry Mulligan Quartet | 'Round Midnight | Milestone | M 47067
Thelonious Monk-The Complete Riverside Recordings | Riverside | 15 RCD 022-2
Wes Montgomery Quintet | Straight No Chaser | Bandstand | BDCD 1504

Straight No Chaser(alt.take)
Art Pepper Quartet | New York Album | Galaxy | GXY 5154
Thelonious Monk-Gerry Mulligan Quartet | Thelonious Monk-The Complete Riverside Recordings | Riverside | 15 RCD 022-2

Straight No Chaser(I)-
Sebastian Gramss-Lömsch Lehmann | knoM.T | Jazz Haus Musik | JHM 0107 CD

Straight No Chaser(II)
Thelonious Monk-Gerry Mulligan Quartet | 'Round Midnight | Milestone | M 47067

Straight On Red
Charly D'Inverno Trio | Following The Band | Jazz Pure Collection | AU 31622 CD

Straight Street
Archie Shepp Quintet | Down Home New York | Soul Note | 121102-2
Harold Mabern Trio | Straight Street | DIW | DIW 608 CD
John Coltrane Sextet | John Coltrane-The Prestige Recordings | Prestige | 16 PCD 4405-2
The Pilgrim Travelers | The Best Of The Pilgrim Travelers | Ace Records | CDCHD 342

Straight To Love
Earl Hines And His Orchestra | The Indispensable Earl Hines Vol.3/4(1939-1945) | RCA | 2126408-2

Straight Up And Down
Chick Corea Quintet | That's Jazz Vol.25: Tones For Joan's Bones | Atlantic | ATL 50302
Eric Dolphy Quintet | A Blue Conception | Blue Note | 534254-2
Gary Burton Quintet | Like Minds | Concord | CCD 4803

Straighten Up And Fly Right
Buddy Greco Quartet | Route 66-A Personal Tribute To Nat King Cole | Celebrity | CYCD 71901
Four For The Blues | Four For The Blues | Elite Special | 73623
John Hicks | Maybeck Recital Hall Series Volume Seven | Concord | CCD 4442
Jörg Seidel Group | I Feel So Smoochie: A Tribute To Nat King Cole | Edition Collage | EC 532-2
Les Brown And His Orchestra | From The Cafe Rouge | Giants Of Jazz | GOJ 1027
Nat King Cole Trio | The Great Nat King Cole | Laserlight | 15733
Oscar Peterson Trio | With Respect To Nat | Verve | 557486-2
Rosemary Clooney With The John Oddo Big Band | Girl Singer | Concord | CCD 4496
Vince Jones Group | For All Colours | Intuition Records | INT 3071-2
Yusef Lateef Quartet | The Golden Flute | MCA | AS 9125
Freddy Cole Trio | I'm Not My Brother,I'm Me | Sunnyside | SSC 1054 D

Straighten Up Baby
Henry Johnson Group | You're The One | Impulse(MCA) | MCA 5754

Stralsund(Song Of Memories)
Al Grey And The Basie Wing | The Last Of The Big Plungers/The Thinking Man's Trombone | Vogue | 655017

Strange
Elvin Jones Quintet | Youngblood | Enja | ENJ-7051 2
Hilton Ruiz Group | A Moment's Notice | Novus | PD 83123

Strange Arrangement
Adelaide Hall With Band | Art Tatum:Complete Original American Decca Recordings | Definitive Records | DRCD 11200

Strange Behaviour
Bob Scobey's Frisco Band | Bob Scobey's Frisco Band | Good Time Jazz | GTCD 12006-2

Strange Blues
P.U.L.S.E. | Amsterdam Groove | ACT | 9262-2

Strange Feeling-
Duke Ellington And His Orchestra | The Jazz Collector Edition: Duke Ellington | Laserlight | 15710

Strange Fruit
Billie Holiday And Her All Stars | Compact Jazz: Billie Holiday-Live | Verve | 841434-2
4 By 4:Ella Fitzgerald/Sarah Vaughan/Billie Holiday/Dinah Washington | Verve | 559693-2
Billie Holiday And Her Trio | Lady Day-The Storyville Concerts | Jazz Door | JD 1215
Billie Holiday With Frankie Newton And His Orchestra | Jazz Gallery:Billie Holiday Vol.1(1933-49) | RCA | 2119542-2
Billie Holiday With The JATP All Stars | Billie Holiday Story Vol.1:Jazz At The Philharmonic | Verve | 521642-2
Billie Holiday With Tony Scott And His Orchestra | Lady Sings The Blues | Enoch's Music | 57271013
Gene Ammons Quartet | Fine And Mellow | Prestige | PRCD 24281-2
Gil Evans Orchestra With Sting | Strange Fruit | ITM Records | ITM 1499
Lester Bowie's Brass Fantasy | My Way | DIW | DIW 835 CD
Serious Fun | DIW | DIW 834 CD
Marcus Miller Group | Live & More | Dreyfus Jazz Line | FDM 36585-2
Matthias Petzold Septett | Ulysses | Indigo-Records | 1003 CD
Nina Simone | Verve Jazz Masters 17:Nina Simone | Verve | 518198-2
Nina Simone Groups | Feeling Good-The Very Best Of Nina Simone | Mercury | 522747-2
Nina Simone Quintet | Nina Simone-The 60s Vol.2:Mood Indigo | Mercury | 838544-2 PMS

Strange Hours
Lily White Group | Somewhere Between Truth & Fiction | Knitting Factory Works | KFWCD 153

Strange Inspirations
Teddy Wilson | Everytime We Say Goodbye | Musicraft | MSVCD-59

Strange Little Smile-
Georg Ruby | Stadtgarten Series Vol.4 | Jazz Haus Musik | JHM 1004 SER

Strange Loop
London Jazz Composers' Orchestra | Three Pieces For Orchestra | Intakt Records | CD 045

Strange Meadow Lark
Dave Brubeck Quartet | The Dave Brubeck Selection | CBS | 467279-2

Strange Meeting
Bill Frisell Trio | Bill Frisell With Dave Hollnad And Elvin Jones | Nonesuch | 7559-79624-2
Live | Gramavision | GCD 79504

Strange Passion
Dutch Swing College Band | 25th Anniversary Concert | DSC Production | PA 001 (801058)

Strange Place For Snow
Trevor Coleman Group | Kiwi Love | Fiala Music | JFJ 90005

Strange Things Happen
Magic Slim Band | The Ralph Bass Sessions Vol.3:Willie Williams With Carey Bell/Magic Slim | Red Lightnin' | RL 0052

Strange Things Happening Every Day
Sister Rosetta Tharpe With The Sammy Price Trio | Gospel Train | MCA | 1317

Strange Times
Peter Malick Group feat. Norah Jones | New York City | Koch Records | 238678-2

Strange Transmissions
Charles Tyler Ensemble | Charles Tyler Ensemble | ESP Disk | ESP 1029-2

Strange Worlds-
Leni Stern Group | Words | Lipstick Records | LIP 890282

Strangehorn
Günther Klatt Quintet | Strangehorn | Eigen | 01
Rova Saxophone Quartet | Saxophone Diplomacy | Hat Art | CD 6068

Stranger Blues
Jesse Fuller One Man Band | Brother Lowdown | Fantasy | F 24707

Stranger Here
Sonny Terry & Brownie McGhee | Back To New Orleans | Fantasy | FCD 24708-2

Stranger In My Hometown
Andy Goodrich Quintet | Motherless Child | Delmark | DE 495

Stranger In Paradise
George Shearing With The Montgomery Brothers | Wes Montgomery-The Complete Riverside Recordings | Riverside | 12 RCD 4408-2
Ira Sullivan Quintet | Ira Sullivan | Flying Fish | FF 075
Toots Thielemans With Orchestra | Bluesette | Polydor | 2482218 IMS

Stranger In Town
Paul Desmond Quartet | Glad To Be Unhappy | RCA | 2131311-2

Stranger On Earth
Amani A.W.-Murray Quartet | Amani A.W.-Murray | GRP | GRP 96332

Stranger On The Shore
Jimmy Hamilton Quartet | Jimmy Hamilton:As Time Goes By | Memo Music | HDJ 4013
Mr. Acker Bilk With The Leon Young String Chorale | Mr. Acker Bilk Starportrait | Aves | 156503

Stranger Than Jim
First House | Erendira | ECM | 1307

Stranger Than Paradise
Emborg-Larsen Quintet | Ships In The Night | Stunt Records | STUCD 19304

Strangers In The Night-
Fletcher Henderson And His Orchestra | The Indispensable Fletcher Henderson(1927-1936) | RCA | 2122618-2

Strangest Kiss
Sigi.Busch-Alexander Sputh Duo | A New Way Of Living | EGO | 4020

Straßen Plätze-
Peter Bolte-Marcio Doctor | Zeitraum | Jazz Haus Musik | JHM 0113 CD

Strata
Matthew Shipp Horn Quartet | Strata | HatOLOGY | 522

Stratotrumpet Blues
Danny Polo And His Swing Stars | Swingin' Britain-The Thirties | Decca | DDV 5013/14

Stratus
Billy Cobham Group | The Best Of Billy Cobham | Atlantic | 7567-81558-2
Billy Cobham Quintet | Warning | GRP | GRP 95282

Stratusphunk
Gil Evans Orchestra | Out Of The Cool | CTI Records | PDCTI 1114-2
J.J.Johnson And His Orchestra | J.J.! | RCA | 2125727-2

Strauss' Last Waltz
Last Exit | The Noise Of Trouble | Enemy | EMCD 103(03503)

Strawa No Sertao-Maxixe
Egberto Gismonti With The Lithuanian State Symphony Orchestra | Meeting Point | ECM | 1586(533681-2)

Strawa No Sertao-Zabumba
String Trio Of New York | Area Cone 212 | Black Saint | BSR 0048

Strawberries At Midnight
The Real Group | Get Real! | ACT | 9252-2

Strawberry Mango
Tom Creekmore Quintet | She Is It | Discovery | DS 791 IMS

Strawberry Woman
Ray Charles-Cleo Laine With The Frank DeVol Orchestra & Chorus | Porgy And Bess | London | 6.30110 EM

Strawberry Woman-
Gene Harris And The Philip Morris Superband | Live At Town Hall N.Y.C. | Concord | CCD 4397

Stray Geese
John Pizzarelli Collection | One Night With You | Chesky | JD 153

Streak O' Clean
Vocal Summit | Sorrow Is Not Forever-Love Is | Moers Music | 02004 CD

Stream Of Time
Frank Sackenheim Quintet | The Music Of Chance | Jazz 4 Ever Records:Jazz Network | J4E 4753

Stream Walk
Edward Vesala Nordic Gallery | Sound & Fury | ECM | 1541

Streaming Below The Time
Lutz Häfner Quintet | Things & Thoughts | Mons Records | MR 874309

Streams
Friedrich-Herbert-Moreno Trio | Voyage Out | Jazz 4 Ever Records:Jazz Network | J4E 4747
Stefano Battaglia | Baptism | SPLASC(H) Records | CD H 417-2

Streams and Chorus Of Seed(complete performance)
Joshua Redman Quintet | Freedom In The Goove | Warner | 9362-46330-2

Streams Of Conciousness
Matt Penman Quartet | Flipside | Naxos Jazz | 86013-2

Streching Out
Jimmy Giuffre 3 | Flight, Bremen 1961 | Hat Art | CD 6071

Street Bride
Music Revelation Ensemble | Music Revelation Ensemble | DIW | DIW 825 CD

Street Dance
M'Boom | Collage | Soul Note | SN 1059

Street Dancing
Rinde Eckert Group | Story In,Story Out | Intuition Records | INT 3507-2

Street Don't Sleep
Errol Parker Quartet | My Own Bag No.3 | Sahara | 1003

Street Lady
Donald Byrd Orchestra | Street Lady | Blue Note | 84439

Street Of Dreams
Ahmad Jamal Quartet | The Essence Part 1 | Dreyfus Jazz Line | FDM 37007-2
Art Farmer Orchestra | Listen To Art Farmer And The Orchestra | Verve | 537747-2
Cannonball Adderley With Richard Hayman's Orchestra | Julian Cannonball Adderley And Strings/Jump For Joy | Verve | 528699-2
Coleman Hawkins Quartet | Sirius | Original Jazz Classics | OJCCD 861-2(2310707)
Count Basie Quartet | Countin' With Basie | Vogue | 500118
Ernestine Anderson With The Hank Jones Trio | Big City | Concord | CCD 4214
Gene Ammons Orchestra | Red Top-The Savoy Sessions | Savoy | SJL 1103 (801179)
Ray Brown Trio | The Red Hot Ray Brown | Concord | CCD 4315
Stan Kenton And His Orchestra | At The Rendezvous Vol.2 | Status | CD 108(882584)
Tatum-Carter-Bellson Trio | The Tatum Group Masterpieces | Pablo | 2310732

Street Runner With Child
Benny Carter Quintet | Cosmopolite | Verve | 521673-2

Street Scenes
Miles Davis Group | Miles Davis Live From His Last Concert In Avignon | Laserlight | 24327

Street Scenes-
Jackie McLean Sextet | Jackie's Bag | Blue Note | BST 84051

Street Woman
Ornette Coleman Quartet | The Belgrade Concert | Jazz Door | JD 12112

Streets And Rivers
Sonny Stitt Quartet | Sonny's Back | Muse | MR 5204

Strength And Sanity
Dave Douglas Sextet | In Our Lifetime | New World Records | 80471-2

Stressless
Bireli Lagrene Quartet | Acoustic Moments | Blue Note | 795263-2

Stretch The Match
Muhal Richard Abrams Orchestra | Blu Blu Blu | Black Saint | 120117-2

Strictly Confidential
Bud Powell Trio | The Genius Of Bud Powell | Verve | 821690-1

Bud Powell:Complete 1947-1951 Blue Note,Verve & Roost Recordings | The Jazz Factory | JFCD 22837
Sam Most And His Orchestra | Sam Most Plays Bird, Bud, Monk And Miles | Fresh Sound Records | FSR 2039(Bethlehem BCP 75)

Strictly Instrumental
Harry James And His Orchestra | Harry James | Jazz Magazine | 40199

Stride Logic
The Three Sopranos With The HR Big Band | The Three Sopranos | hr music.de | hrmj 001-01 CD

Stride Rite
Chick Corea | Delphi 1 Solo Piano Improvisations | Polydor | 2391402

Striding
Roy Eldridge-Alvin Stoller | The Urban Sessions/New Jazz Sound | Verve | 531637-2

Strike Two
Alfred Lauer Bigband | Just Music | Mons Records | MR 874819

Strike Up The Band
Bob Cooper And His Orchestra | Shifting Winds | Affinity | AFF 59
Clarinet Jazz Quartet | Live At Birdland Neuburg | Birdland | BN 003
Count Basie And His Orchestra With Tony Bennett | Basie-Bennett | Roulette | 7938992
Dick Collins And His Orchestra | King Richard The Swing Hearted | Fresh Sound Records | LJM 1027(RCA)
Greetje Kauffeld With Jerry Van Rooyen And Jiggs Whigham And The Rias Big Band | Greetje Kauffeld Meets Jerry Van Rooyen And Jiggs Whigham With The Rias Big Band | Mons Records | MR 874786
Howard Rumsey's Lighthouse All Stars Plus Ten | Jazz Rolls Royce | Fresh Sound Records | FSR-CD 0310
Lucky Thompson Quartet | Live In Switzerland 1968/69 | Jazz Helvet | JH 03
Oscar Peterson Trio | Verve Jazz Masters 37:Oscar Peterson Plays Broadway | Verve | 516893-2
The George Gershwin Songbook | Verve | 823249-1
The Gershwin Songbook(The Instrumentals) | Verve | 525361-2
Ran Blake | That Certain Feeling(George Gershwin Songbook) | Hat Art | CD 6077
Rob McConnell And The Boss Brass | Brassy & Sassy | Concord | CCD 4508
Sonny Stitt With The Bud Powell Trio | Genesis | Prestige | P 24044
Stan Getz Quartet | Stan Getz-The Complete Roost Sessions | EMI Records | 859622-2
Stan Getz-The Complete Roost Sessions | The Jazz Factory | JFCD 22839
Stu Williamson Quintet | Stu Williamson Plays | Fresh Sound Records | FSR-CD 116(882425)
Tal Farlow Quartet | Autumn In New York | Verve | 2304321 IMS
The Houdini's | The Houdini's Play The Big Five | Challenge | CHR 70027
Vinnie Burke All-Stars | Vinnie Burke All-Stars | Fresh Sound Records | ABC 139(Paramount)
The Tremble Kids | Dixieland Forever Vol.2 | BELL Records | BLR 89046

Strike Zone
Jam Session | Jam Session Vol.2 | Steeplechase | SCCD 31523
Glenn Horiuchi Quartet | Oxnard Beet | Soul Note | 121228-2

String Of Pearls
Glenn Miller And His Orchestra | Play Selections From The Glenn Miller Story And Other Hits | RCA | NL 89073

String Quartet
Mats Eden-Jonas Simonson With The Cikada String Quartet | Milvus | ECM | 1660

String Quartet No.1
Keith Jarrett With String Quartet | Works | ECM | 825425-1

String Theory
Dudek-Van Den Broek-Haurand | Crossing Level | Konnex Records | KCD 5077

String Thing
Howard Alden-Frank Vignola-Jimmy Bruno | Concord Jazz Guitar Collective | Concord | CCD 4672
Horace Tapscott | The Tapscott Sessions Vol.5 | Nimbus | NS 1925

Stringin' The Jug
Count Basie With Strings | Basie On Roulette, Vol. 13: String Along With Basie | Vogue | 500013

Strings
Thilo Kreitmeier Quintet | Mo' Better Blues | Organic Music | ORGM 9706
Dietrich Jeske Groups | Strings And Things | Jazz Classics | AU 11205

Strings Of Thread
James Emery Septet | Spectral Domains | Enja | ENJ-9344 2
Volker Kriegel Quintet | Spectrum | MPS | 9808699

Strings Revisited
Charlie Parker With Strings | Bird's Eyes-Last Unisuued Vol.1+4 | Philology | W 5/18.2

Strip Poker
Bernard Peiffer And His St.Germain Des Pres Orchestra | Jazz In Paris:Modern Jazz At Saint-Germain-De-Prés | EmArCy | 013042-2

Striver's Row
Sonny Rollins Trio | A Night At The Village Vanguard Vol.2 | Blue Note | 746518-2
Sonny Rollins:The Blue Note Recordings | Blue Note | 821371-2
Billy Pierce Quartet | Rolling Monk | Paddle Wheel | KICJ 154

Strode Rode
Bruce Eskovitz Quintet | One For Newk | Koch Jazz | KOC 3-7801-2
Irene Schweizer/Han Bennink | Irene Schweizer & Han Bennink | Intakt Records | CD 010

Stroh-Alm
Luther Allison Blues Band | South Side Safari | Red Lightnin' | RL 0036

Strollin'
Alan Broadbent | Maybeck Recital Hall Series Volume Fourteen | Concord | CCD 4488
Arny Kay Band With Guests | Hang On Jimi | L+R Records | CDLR 42078
Charles Mingus Orchestra | Nostalgia In Times Square/The Immortal 1959 Sessions | CBS | 88337
Charlie Barnet And His Orchestra | Big Band Bounce & Boogie:Skyliner-Charlie Barnet | Affinity | AFS 1012
Chet Baker Trio | Chet Baker-Philip Catherine-Jean Louis Rassinfosse | Igloo | IGL 034
Dave Brubeck Quintet | Reunion | Original Jazz Classics | OJCCD 150-2
Dexter Gordon Quartet | The Apartment | Steeplechase | SCCD 31025
Jack McDuff Quartet | Brother Jack Meets The Boss | Original Jazz Classics | OJCCD 326-2(P 7228)
Kenny Clarke All Stars | Black California Vol.2 | Savoy | SV 0274
Peter Compo Quintet | Hot Jazz Violin-Nostalgia In Times Square | Take Twelve On CD | TT 001-2

Strollin' Down Memory Lane
Jimmy Jones Big Four | Giants Of Small-Band Swing Vol.1 | Original Jazz Classics | OJC- 1723(RLP 143)

Strollin' Home
Pepper Adams Quintet | Pepper Adams Plays Charlie Mingus | Fresh Sound Records | FSR-CD 0177

Strollin' With Pam
T-Bone Walker With Jim Wynn's Band | Classics Of Modern Blues | Blue Note | 84550

Strolling Along-
Jaki Byard Quartet | The Last From Lennie's | Prestige | PRCD 11029-2
Tom Talbert Septet | Things As They Are | Seabreeze | CDSB 2038(881572)

Strolling In Central Park
Norrie Cox & His New Orleans Stompers | Dance Hall Days | Delmark | DE 236

Strömung
Willie Dixon | Lost Blues Tapes, Vol.1 | ACT | 9204-2

Strong Man
Abbey Lincoln With Her Quintet | Sonny Rollins-The Freelance Years:The Complete Riverside & Contemporary Recordings | Riverside | 5 RCD 4427-2
Wynton Kelly Trio | Keep It Moving | Milestone | M 47026
Gary Lucas | Skeleton On The Feast | Enemy | EMCD 126(03526)

Strong Will To Live
Gabor Szabo Quintet | The Sorcerer | Impulse(MCA) | IMP 12112

Stronger Than Us
Louis Sclavis-Hans Koch | Duets,Dithyrambisch | FMP | CD 19/20

Strophe I
Gabriele Hasler-Hans Lüdemann-Andreas Willers plus Jörn Schipper | Familienglück | Foolish Music | FM 211097

Strophe II
Familienglück | Foolish Music | FM 211097

Strophe III
Familienglück | Foolish Music | FM 211097

Strophe IV
Jeff Reynolds Group With Guests | Emotions | BELL Records | BLR 84039

Structured Clay
Jimmy Bertrand's Washboard Wizards | Johnny Dodds 1-Spirit Of New Orleans | MCA | 1328

Strut
The G.B.Horn | The J.B.Horns | Gramavision | GV 79462-2(889094)

Struttin'
Jack DeJohnette's Directions | Untitled | ECM | 1074

Struttin' The Boogie
Darrell Grant Quintet | The New Bop | Criss Cross | Criss 1106

Struttin' With Julie
The Mangione Brothers Sextet | The Jazz Brothers | Original Jazz Classics | OJCCD 997-2(R 9335)

Struttin' With Some Barbecue
Alex Welsh And His Band | Melody Maker Tribute To Louis Armstrong Vol.2 | Jazz Colours | 874768-2
Art Hodes | Someone To Watch Over Me-Live At Hanratty's | Muse | MR 5252
Bobby Jaspar Quartet | Bobby Jaspar/Henri Renaud | Vogue | 21409372
Chubby Jacksons Big Three Plus | Jazz From Then Till Now | Fresh Sound Records | FSR 504(Everest LPBR 5041)
George Wein's Dixie Victors | The Magic Horn | RCA | 2113038-2
George Wettling And His Rhythm Kings | Commodore Classics-Bud Freeman/George Wettling:Commodore Style | Commodore | 6.25894 AG
Henry Red Allen Band | At Newport | Verve | 817792-1 IMS
Johannes Rediske Sextet | Re-Disc Bounce | Bear Family Records | BCD 16119 AH
John Barnes-Roy Williams Group | Like We Do | Lake | LACD 69
Louis Armstrong And His All Stars | New Orleans Louisiana | Traditional Line | TL 1319
Live In Berlin/Friedrichstadtpalast | Jazzpoint | JP 1062 CD
The Great Performer | Traditional Line | TL 1304
Louis Armstrong And His All Stars/Orchestra | St.Louis Blues | Black Lion | 127035
Louis Armstrong And His Orchestra | Jazz:The Essential Collection Vol.2 | IN+OUT Records | 78012-2
Louis Armstrong With Edmond Hall's Orchestra | Jazz Live & Rare: Louis Armstrong & Edmond Hall's Orchestra | Jazzline | ???
Ruby Braff And His Buddies | Controlled Nonchalance At The Regattabar Vol.1 | Arbors Records | ARCD 19134
The Newport Jazz Festival All-Stars | The Newport Jazz Festival All-Stars | Concord | CJ 260
Tom Saunders' 'Wild Bill Davison Band' & Guests | Exactly Like You | Nagel-Heyer | CD 023
Toots Thielemans Quintet | Man Bites Harmonica! | Original Jazz Classics | OJCCD 1738-2(RLP 1125)

Struwelpeter
Lee Konitz Nonet | The Lee Konitz Nonet | Chiaroscuro | CR 186

Stuck In The Dark
Mark Levin Quintet | Social Sketches | Enja | 2058

Studio 1
Pili-Pili | Boogaloo | JA & RO | JARO 4174-2

Studio 150,?
Blue Mitchell Quintet | A Blue Time | Milestone | M 47055

Studio B
Kenny Baker And His Band,| Kenny Baker Presents:The Half Dozen...After Hours | Lake | LACD 88

Studio Rivbea
Andreas Willers | Hie & Als Auch | FMP | 0880

Study Nature
Tom Varner Quartet | Motion/Stillness | Soul Note | SN 1067

Studying Walk A Landscape
Joe Barnikel-Norbert Nagel Group | Zero Gravity | Mons Records | MR 874808

Stufen
Miles Davis Quintet | Miles In The Sky | CBS | CK 65684

Stuff
Miles Davis Quintet 1965-1968 | CBS | C6K 67398
Paul Howard's Quality Serenaders | Early Hamp | Affinity | CD AFS 1011

Stuffed Piano
Willis Jackson Sextet | Nuther'n Like Thuther'n | Prestige | PRCD 24265-2

Stuffin'
Ray Blue Quartet | Always With A Purpose | Ray Blue Music | JN 007(RMB 01)

Stuff'n Such
Larry Coryell-Michael Urbaniak Trio | A Quiet Day In Spring | Steeplechase | SCCD 31187

Stuffy
Coleman Hawkins Quartet | Jazz At The Philharmonic:The Coleman Hawkins Set | Verve | 815148-1 IMS
Coleman Hawkins Quintet | Live Recording At The Birdland | Jazz Anthology | JA 5173
Guy Lafitte Trio feat. Wild Bill Davis | Lotus Blossom | Black & Blue | BLE 59.188 2
Hot Mallets | Hot Mallets-Isla Eckinger | BELL Records | BLR 84030
Joe Pass Quartet | Apassionato | Pablo | 2310946-2
Leo Parker Sextet | Rollin' With Leo | Blue Note | LT 1076
Oscar Peterson All Stars | Oscar Peterson+Harry Edison+Eddie 'Cleanhead' Vinson's | Pablo | 2310927-2
Scott Hamilton And Friends | Blues,Bop & Ballads | Concord | CCD 4866

Stumbling
Dave McKenna | Dave Fingers McKenna | Chiaroscuro | CR 175
The Bobcats | Suddely It's 1939-Bob Crosby | Giants Of Jazz | GOJ 1032

Stumbop
Big Bill Broonzy | Last Session-Vol.1/The Big Bill Broonzy Story | Verve | 2304559 IMS

Stump Blues
Remembering Big Bill Broonzy | BGO Records | BGOCD 91

Stumpy Bossa Nova
Johannes Mössinger-Wolfgang Lackerschmid | Joana's Dance | double moon | CHRDM 71017

Stundenwalzer
Wolfgang Lackerschmid Group | Gently But Deep | Lady Hamilton Productions | BR 39

Stupor Mundi
Stu Williamson Quintet | Stu Williamson Plays | Fresh Sound Records | FSR-CD 116(882425)

Stuttgart 2
Bireli Lagrene & Jaco Pastorius | Stuttgart Aria | Jazzpoint | JP 1019 LP

Stuttgart Aria-1
Stuttgart Aria | Jazzpoint | JP 1019 LP

Stuttgart Aria-2
Jazz Jokers | Jazz-Jokers | Jazzpoint | JP 1024 LP

Style Is Coming Back In Style
Tom Creekmore Quintet | She Is It | Discovery | DS 791 IMS

Su Bolu É S'Astore
Nat Su Quartet | The J.Way | Fresh Sound Records | FSNT 038 CD

Su City
Ernst Reijseger & Tenore E Cuncordu De Orosei | Colla Voche | Winter&Winter | 910037-2

Su Puddhu(Balla Turtumirnu
Django Reinhardt And The Quintet Du Hot Club De France | Django Reinhardt:Djangology | EMI Records | 780659-2

Sual
Andy Martin With The Metropole Orchestra | Andy Martin & Metropole Orchestra | Mons Records | MR 874802

Suave
Madrid Jazz Group | Unreleased Madrid Jazz Sessions 1964-1981 | Fresh Sound Records | FSR-CD 3003

Sub City
Bud Powell Trio | Time Waits | Blue Note | 521227-2
Claude Williamson Trio | Live! At The Jazz Bakery | Fresh Sound Records | FSR-CD 5014

Subconscious-Lee
Boulou Ferre-Elios Ferre Duo | Gypsy Dreams | Steeplechase | SCCD 31140
Lee Konitz Quintet | Live At The Half Note | Verve | 521659-2
Lee Konitz With The Metropole Orchestra | Saxophone Dreams | Koch Jazz | 3-6900-2
Lee Konitz-Martial Solal Duo | Live At The Berlin Jazz Days 1980 | MPS | 68289
Michael Kanan Trio | Convergence | Fresh Sound Records | FSNT 055 CD
Rein de Graaff Quintet | Nostalgia | Timeless | CD SJP 429

Subdued
Martin Koller's Third Movement | Right Now | Traumton Records | 4430-2

Subharmonic Dawn(Liquid Mix)
Bob Stewart First Line Band | Goin' Home | JMT Edition | 834427-1

Sublation
Joshua Redman Quartet | Joshua Redman | Warner | 9362-45242-2

Sublimation
Hank Jones Quartet | Lazy Afternoon | Concord | CCD 4391

Subliminal
Scott Colley Quartet | Subliminal... | Criss Cross | Criss 1157

Submission
Klaus Doldinger Quartet & Attila Zoller | Doldinger Jubilee | Atlantic | ATL 60073

Subsequent Influence
Jim Hall Sextet | Subsequently | Limelight | 844278-2 IMS

Subterranean Blues
Gerry Mulligan Quartet | Jazz At The Philharmonic: The Gerry Mulligan Quartets In Concert | Pablo | PACD 5309-2
Swiss Radio Days Jazz Series:Gerry Mulligan | TCB Records | TCB 02092

Subtle Rebuttal
Buell Neidlinger's String Jazz | Locomotive | Soul Note | 121161-2

Subtle Slough
Rex Stewart And His Orchestra | Victor Jazz History Vol.7:Swing Groups | RCA | 2128561-2

Subtonium No.Three
Bill Connors Trio | Double Up | Line Records | COCD 9.00826 O

Suburban Beauty
Duke Ellington And His Orchestra | Duke 56/62 Vol.1 | CBS | 88653

Suburban Beauty(alt.take)
Thelonious Monk Sextet | Genius Of Modern Music,Vol.2 | Blue Note | 300404

Suburban Eyes
Monk's Mood | Naxos Jazz | 8.120588 CD

Suburban Eyes(alt.take)
More Genius Of Thelonious Monk | Blue Note | 300194(BNJ 61011)

Suburbanite
Duke Ellington And His Orchestra | Duke Ellington:Complete Prestige Carnegie Hall 1946-1947 Concerts | Definitive Records | DRCD 11211

Subversive Resurrektionen
Elefanten | Faust | KlangRäume | 30150

Subway
Esbjörn Svensson Trio(E.S.T.) | Est-From Gagarin's Point Of View | ACT | 9005-2
Jam Session | Jam Session Vol.2 | Steeplechase | SCCD 31523
Ron McClure Quintet | Inner Account | Steeplechase | SCCD 31329

Subway Scenarios-
Tiny Parham And His Musicians | Hot Chicago Jazz From The Late 1920's | Folklyric | 9028

Subwayer
Absolute Ensemble | Absolution | Enja | ENJ-9394 2

Succotash
Meredith d'Ambrosio | Another Time | Sunnyside | SSC 1017 D

Such Sweet Thunder
Duke Ellington And His Orchestra | Ella Fitzgerald And Duke Ellington:Cote D'Azure Concerts on Verve | Verve | 539033-2
Ella Fitzgerald And Duke Ellington:Cote D'Azure Concerts on Verve | Verve | 539033-2
Ella Fitzgerald And Duke Ellington:Cote D'Azure Concerts on Verve | Verve | 539033-2
Soul Call | Verve | 539785-2
Hot Summer Dance | Red Baron | 469285-2
Hot Mallets | Hot Mallets-Isla Eckinger | BELL Records | BLR 84030

Such Sweet Thunder(Cleo)
Sigi Schwab | Meditation | Melos Music | CDGS 701

Sudan Airways Loop-
Art Blakey And The Jazz Messengers | Oh-By The Way | Timeless | CD SJP 165

Suddenly It Jumped
Duke Ellington And His Orchestra | Duke Ellington:The Complete RCA-Victor Mid-Forties Recordings(1944-1946) | RCA | 2663394-2

Suddenly It's Spring
Stan Getz Quintet | Best Of The West Coast Sessions | Verve | 537084-2
Stan Getz:East Of The Sun-The West Coast Sessions | Verve | 531935-2
Vic Lewis West Coast All Stars | Shake Down The Stars | Candid | CCD 79526
Al Cohn Quintet | Broadway | Original Jazz Classics | OJCCD 1812-2(P 7819)

Suddenly(In Walked Bud)
Carmen McRae And Her Quartet | Carmen Sings Monk | RCA | 2663841-2
Duke Pearson Sextet | Sweet Honey Bee | Blue Note | 595974-2

Sudel
Donald Byrd Quintet | Groovin' For Nat | Black Lion | BLP 60134

Südlich Von Hawaii(Flaschenpost)
Südpool Jazz Project V | Marcia Funebre-The Italian Suite | L+R Records | CDLR 45106

Sud-Quest Jump
Ulla Oster-Wollie Kaiser | We Can Do It On Stage Any Time! | Jazz Haus Musik | JHM 0088 CD

Südsee
Kölner Saxophon Mafia | Mafia Years 1982-86 | Jazz Haus Musik | JHM 0058 CD

Südstadt Shuffle
Antonio Carlos Jobim Group | Tide | A&M Records | 393031-2

Sueno Con Mexico
Pat Metheny | Works | ECM | 823270-2

Sueno Vivo
Chuck Loeb-Andy LaVerne Septet | Magic Fingers | dmp Digital Music Productions | CD 472

Suenos
Jorge Strunz-Ardeshir Farah Group | Guitars | Milestone | MCD 9136-2
Poncho Sanchez And His Orchestra | El Mejor | Concord | CCD 4519

Sue's Changes
Mingus Big Band | Live In Time | Dreyfus Jazz Line | FDM 36583-2

Suffering
Alfred 'Blues King' Harris Band | Mumbles Walter Horton:Mouth Harp Maestro | Ace Records | CDCH 252

Sugar
Bobby Hackett Quintet | Melody Is A Must-Live At The Roosevelt Grill Vol.1 | Phontastic | PHONT 7571
Bud Freeman And His Summa Cum Laude Orchestra | Planet Jazz:Bud Freeman | Planet Jazz | 2161240-2
Victor Jazz History Vol.18:Chicago Jazz(1934-64) | RCA | 2135737-2
Count Basie And His Orchestra | 100 Ans De Jazz:Count Basie | RCA | 2177831-2

Count Basie-Basie's Basement | RCA | ???
Dick Wellstood | This Is The One...Dig! | Solo Art | SACD-119
George Wettling Jazz Band | George Wettling Jazz Band | JSP Records | 1103
Humphrey Lyttelton-Acker Bilk Band | More Humph & Acker | Calligraph | CLGCD 030
Louis Armstrong And His Hot Seven | Best Of The Complete RCA Victor Recordings | RCA | 2663636-2
Louis Armstrong:A 100th Birthday Celebration | RCA | 2663694-2
Louis Armstrong-The Complete RCA Victor Recordings | RCA | 2668682-2
Red Nichols' Stompers | Victor Jazz History Vol.4:New York Jazz | RCA | 2128558-2
Ruby Braff-Dick Hyman | Fats Waller's Heavenly Jive | Chiaroscuro | CR 162
Teddy Wilson Trio | Three Little Words | Black & Blue | BLE 233094
The Tremble Kids | The Tremble Kids:The Of 40 Years | BELL Records | BLR 84060

Sugar Babe
Pink Anderson | The Blues Of Pink Anderson:Ballad & Folksinger Vol.3 | Original Blues Classics | OBCCD 577-2(BV 1071)

Sugar Cane Rag-
Don 'Sugar Cane' Harris Quintet | Got The Blues | MPS | 68029

Sugar Daddy
Hank Crawford And His Orchestra | Roadhouse Symphony | Original Jazz Classics | OJCCD 1048-2(M 9140)

Sugar Ditch
Charles Brackeen Quartet | Bannar | Silkheart | SH 105

Sugar Finger
Sonny Boy Williamson Group | Sonny Boy Williamson(1937-1947) | RCA | 2126418-2

Sugar Hill
Jimmy Smith Trio | Home Cookin' | Blue Note | 853360-2
Kenny Burrell With The Johnny Pate Orchestra | Verve Jazz Masters 45:Kenny Burrell | Verve | 527652-2
Will Bradley And His Boogie Woogie Boys | Modern Jazz Played By Wingy Manone And His Cats | Harlequin | HQ 2037 IMS

Sugar Hill Penthouse
Duke Ellington And His Orchestra | Duke Ellington | Bluebird | ND 86641(3)

Sugar In My Bowl
David Chesky Group | Club De Sol | Chesky | JD 33

Sugar Loaf Mountain
Woody Herman And His Orchestra | La Fiesta | West Wind Orchestra Series | 2400 CD

Sugar Mama Blues
John Lee Hooker | It Serve You Right To Suffer | Impulse(MCA) | MCD 18186

Sugar On The Floor
Chick Webb And His Orchestra | Chick Webb Vol.4-Ella Swings The Band | MCA | 1327

Sugar Plum
Bill Evans Trio | The Complete Fantasy Recordings | Fantasy | 9FCD 1012-2
Re: Person I Knew | Original Jazz Classics | OJCCD 749-2(F 9608)
Bill Evans:The Secret Sessions | Milestone | 8MCD 4421-2
Teddy Wilson And His Orchestra | Too Hot For Words | Hep | CD 1012

Sugar Ray
Phineas Newborn Jr. Trio | Back Home | Original Jazz Classics | OJCCD 971-2(C 7648)
Fats Waller And His Rhythm | I'm Going To Sit Right Down...The Early Years-Part 2(1935-1936) | Bluebird | 63 66640-2

Sugarfoot Stomp
Connie's Inn Orchestra | Planet Jazz:Coleman Hawkins | Planet Jazz | 2152055-2
Victor Jazz History Vol.6:Harlem Jazz(1928-33) | RCA | 2128560-2
Fletcher Henderson And His Orchestra | The Indispensable Coleman Hawkins 1927-1956:Body And Soul | RCA | ND 89277
Vince Giordano's Nighthawks | Qualty Shout | Stomp Off Records | CD 1260

Sugarfoot Strut
Oscar Castro-Neves Orchestra | Brazilian Scandals | JVC | ???

Sugarpie
Ray Barretto And His Orchestra | Carnaval | Fantasy | FCD 24713-2

Suger Hips
Manfred Schoof/Rainer Brünninghaus | Shadows & Smiles | Wergo | WER 80007-50

Suggestion
The German Jazz Masters | Old Friends | ACT | 9278-2
Darji With The Hank Jones Quartet | Darji Meets Hank Jones | Timeless | SJP 171

Sugu Mugu Jakakai
Roswell Rudd Quartet | Flexile Flyer | Black Lion | BLCD 760215

Suhka
Pierre Dorge & New Jungle Orchestra | Very Hot Even The Moon Is Dancing | Steeplechase | SCCD 31208

Sui Me
Azymuth feat. Jürgen Seefelder | Volta á Turma | West Wind Latina | 2206 CD

Suicide City
Jack Van Poll Trio | Tree-Oh In One | September | CD 5102

Suitcase Blues
Albert Ammons | Boogie Woggie Classics | Blue Note | BLP 1209
Karrin Allyson And Her Trio | I Didn't Know About You | Concord | CCD 4543
Sippie Wallace With Axel Zwingenberger | Sippie Wallace/Axel Zwingenberger And The Friends Of Boogie Woogie Vol.1 | Vagabond | VRCD 8.84002
Sippie Wallace With Band | American Folk Blues Festival '66 | L+R Records | CDLR 42069

Suitcase Blues(part 1+2)
Lou Stein | Stompin' 'Em Down | Chiaroscuro | CR 173

Suite 3x12
Johannes Mössinger-Wolfgang Lackerschmid | Joana's Dance | double moon | CHRDM 71017

Suite 4-2-5:
Trio Ivoire | Trio Ivoire | Enja | ENJ-9424 2

Suite De Buenos Aires(part 1-5)
Gerardo Nunez Group | Flamencos En Nueva York | VeraBra Records | CDVBR 2028-2

Suite De Nadal:
Steckar Tubapack | Tubakoustik | IDA Record | 024 CD

Suite Domestique
Tom Harrell Septet | Passages | Chesky | JD 64

Suite Eolienne(part 1-3)
Pierre Bensusan Group | Bamboulé | Acoustic Music Records | 319.1040.2

Suite For Five Voices In 6 Parts Without Intermission:
Bud Shank/Bill Mays | Explorations:1980 | Concord | CCD 42002

Suite For Lester
Charles Earland Septet | Charles Earland In Concert | Prestige | PRCD 24267-2

Suite For Martin Luther King:
Charles Earland Sextet | Charles Earland In Concert | Prestige | PRCD 24267-2
Sam Rivers Trio | Sam Rivers Trio Live | Impulse(MCA) | IMP 12682

Suite Fraternidad:
Dave Grusin Band With Orchestra | The Orchestral Album | GRP | GRP 97972

Suite From The Milargo Beanfield War:
Manfred Schulze Bläserquintett | Viertens | FMP | 1230

Suite Für Violincello Nr.1 G-Dur
Christian McBride/Nicholas Payton/Mark Whitfield | Fingerpainting-The Music Of Herbie Hancock | Verve | 537856-2

Suite Noire:
Matthias Spillmann Septet | Something About Water | JHM Records | JHM 3620

Suite Of Gold And Blue(part 1-3)
Brigitte Dietrich-Joe Haider Jazz Orchestra | Consequences | JHM Records | JHM 3624

Suite Of Gold And Blue(part 3)
Charlie Mariano Group | Cascade | Keytone | KYT 707

Suite Portugalia:
Ton-Art | Mal Vu. Mal Dit. | Hat Art | CD 6088

Suite Pour Une Frise
Martial Solal Trio | At Newport '63 | RCA | 2125768-2

Suite Sisters:
Marc Copland Quartet | Second Look | Savoy | CY 18001

Suite Thursday:
Duke Ellington And His Orchestra | Three Suites | CBS | 467913-2

Suite(5 parts)
Circo Del Arca | Dies Irae | Hat Art | 3507

Suite:
John Tchicai & Strange Brothers | Darktown Highlights | Storyville | SLP 1015
Piludu Quattro | Room 626 | Jazz 4 Ever Records:Jazz Network | J4E 4721
Salvatore Bonafede Trio | Plays | Ken Music | 660.56.017

Suite-Golden Dawn:
Curtis Fuller Quintet | Four On The Outside | Timeless | CD SJP 124

Suite-Kontrabaß oder Die Kunst die Reisens
John Tank Quintet | So In Love | TCB Records | TCB 95602

Sukiyaki
Slim Gaillard Group | Slim Gaillard Rides Again | Dot | 589761-2

Sukiyaki Cha Cha
Anders Jormin With Brass Quartet | Xieyi | ECM | 1762(013998-2)

Sul Tasto
Eugen Apostolidis Quartet | Imaginary Directions | Edition Collage | EC 503-2

Sula's Dream
European Jazz Youth Orchestra | Swinging Europe 2 | dacapo | DCCD 9450

Sulkyhoola
Jan Garbarek Trio | Madar | ECM | 1515(519075-2)

Sull Lull
The Two-Bone-Big-Band | The Return Of The Hornplayers | Mons Records | MR 874314

Sultan's Theme-
Joe Pass | Joe Pass:Guitar Virtuoso | Pablo | 4 PACD 4423-2

Sultry
Virtuoso No.3 | Original Jazz Classics | OJC20 684-2(2310805)
Chuck Israels International Quartet | On Common Ground | Anima Records | DV-CD 002

Sultry Serenade
Duke Ellington And His Orchestra | Happy Birthday Duke Vol.2 | Laserlight | 15784
Jim Beebe's Chicago Jazz | A Sultry Serenade | Delmark | DE 230

Sum
Jimmy Smith With Orchestra | Sum Serious Blues | Milestone | MCD 9207-2

Sumatra
Doug Sides Ensemble | Sumblo | Laika Records | 35100882

Sumblo
Toshiko Akiyoshi-Lew Tabackin Big Band | Insights | RCA | PL 43363

Summer
Jens Schliecker & Nils Rohwer | Piano Meets Vibes | Acoustic Music Records | 319.1050.2

Summer 86
Masahiro Sayama Trio | Play Me A Little Music | JVC | ???

Summer Band Camp
Martin Schrack Quintet feat.Tom Harrell | Headin' Home | Storyville | STCD 4253

Summer Bossa
Florian Poser-Klaus Ignatzek Duo | Springdale | Acoustic Music Records | 319.1166.2

Summer Breeze Boogie
The Ritz | The Ritz | Denon Compact Disc | CY-1839

Summer Calling
Eric Watson Trio | Conspiracy | Owl Records | 027

Summer Dance
Pili-Pili | Boogaloo | JA & RO | JARO 4174-2
Ana Caram Group | Rio After Dark | Chesky | JD 28

Summer Days
King Curtis Band | King Curtis-Blow Man Blow | Bear Family Records | BCD 15670 CI

Summer Dream
King Curtis-Blow Man Blow | Bear Family Records | BCD 15670 CI
Roberto Nannetti Quintet | Waiting For You | yvp music | CD 3022

Summer Frost
Victor Feldman Group | Fiesta | TBA Records | TBCD 8066(881839)

Summer In Central Park
Mind Games | Lyrical Life | yvp music | CD 3027

Summer Is Gone
Change Of Mind | Change Of Mind | Aho-Recording | CD 1006

Summer Me Winter Me
Johnny Frigo Quintet | Live From Studio A In New York City | Chesky | JD 1
Morgana King And Her Band | I Just Can't Stop Loving You | Muse | MCD 5408

Summer Night
Andy LaVerne/Dave Samuels | Fountainhead | Steeplechase | SCCD 31261
Bobby Hutcherson Quintet | Stick Up | Blue Note | 84244
Dave Pell Octet | Campus Hop:Jazz Goes Dancing | Fresh Sound Records | LPM 1662(RCA)
Flora Purim And Her Sextet | Joe Henderson:The Milestone Years | Milestone | 8MCD 4413-2
George Masso Quintet | Just For A Thrill | Sackville | SKCD2-2022
Keith Jarrett Trio | Tokyo '96 | ECM | 1666(539955-2)
Bye Bye Blackbird | ECM | 1467(513074-2)
Kenny Drew Trio | Dark Beauty | Steeplechase | SCS 1016
Red Mitchell/Jimmy Rowles | Red'n Me | Dreyfus Jazz Line | FDM 36504-2
Sarah Jane Cion Quartet | Summer Night | Naxos Jazz | 86071-2
Stan Getz Quartet | The Master | CBS | 467138-2
Tony Reedus Quartet | The Far Side | Jazz City | 660.53.016

Summer Nights
Buddy Montgomery Sextet | So Why Not? | Landmark | LCD 1518-2

Summer Of '42(The Summer Knows)
Bill Evans-Eddie Gomez Duo | The Complete Fantasy Recordings | Fantasy | 9FCD 1012-2
Chris Anderson Trio | Blues One | DIW | DIW 607 CD
Monty Sunshine Quartet | Love And Sunshine-Monty Alexander In Concert | MPS | 68043
Meredith d'Ambrosio Quartet | Beware Of Spring! | Sunnyside | SSC 1069 D

Summer Running
$$hide$$ | $$Titelverweise | |

Summer Samba -> So Nice(Summer Samba)

Summer Samba Für Die Dunklen Herrn
Woody Herman And The Herd | Woody Herman (And The Herd) At Carnegie Hall | Verve | 559833-2

Summer Sequence(incomplete)
Woody Herman And His Orchestra | Woody Herman:Four Brother | Dreyfus Jazz Line | FDM 36722-2

Summer Sequence(part 1-3)
Art Farmer Quintet | Blame It On My Youth | Contemporary | CCD 14042-2

Summer Serenade
Herb Geller Trio | Birdland Stomp | Enja | 5019 (807540)
Tanzorchester Der Original Teddies | Teddy Stauffer:Rare And Historical Jazz Recordings | Elite Special | 9522009

Summer Soft
Art Farmer Quartet | A Work Of Art | Concord | CJ 179

Summer Song
Dave Brubeck-Paul Desmond Duo | 1975-The Duets | Verve | 394915-2
Don Rendell With The Joe Palin Trio | Live At The Avgarde Gallery Manchaster | Spotlite | SPJ 501
Martin Classen Quartet | Stop & Go | Acoustic Music Records | 319.1033.2

Summer Wishes,Winter Dreams
John Hart Quartet | Bridges | Concord | CCD 4746
De Novo | L.A. Transit | Denon Compact Disc | CY-1004

Summer(Estate)
Takashi Yoshimatsu | Tender Toys:Shin-Ichi Fukuda | Denon Compact Disc | CO-18053

Summermorning
Joe Locke Quartet | Present Tense | Steeplechase | SCCD 31257

Summers End
Special EFX | Peace Of The World | GRP | GRP 96402
Thom Rotella Band | Thom Rotella Band | dmp Digital Music Productions | CD 460

Summer's Over
Gerry Mulligan Concert Jazz Band | Verve Jazz Masters 36:Gerry Mulligan | Verve | 523342-2
Claude Luter Quintet | Saint Germain Dance | Vogue | 655013

Summerset
Mr.Acker Bilk And His Paramount Jazz Band | Acker's Choice | Vagabond | 6.28490 DP

Summertime
Albert Ayler Quartet | My Name Is Albert Ayler | Black Lion | BLCD 760211
American Jazz Quintet | AJQ-In The Beginning | AFO Records | AFO 91-1028-2
Art Hodes-Kenny Davern | Art Hodes-The Final Sessions | Music & Arts | CD 782
Bill Potts And His Orchestra | The Jazz Soul Of Porgy And Bess | Capitol | 795132-2
Buster Williams Quintet | Somewhere Along The Way | TCB Records | TCB 97602
Charlie Parker With Strings | Charlie Parker: The Verve Years (1948-50) | Verve | 2-2501 IMS
Charlie Parker With Strings:The Master Takes | Verve | 523984-2
Chet Baker Quartet | Verve Jazz Masters Vol.60:The Collection | Verve | 529866-2
Compact Jazz: Chet Baker | Verve | 840632-2 PMS
Chet Baker With The Radio Orchestra Hannover(NDR) | My Favourite Songs: The Last Great Concert Vol.1 | Enja | ENJ-5097 2
The Last Concert Vol.I+II | Enja | ENJ-6074 22
Chet Baket Quartet | Chet Baker In Paris | Frosh Sound Records | FSR Box 1(Barclay)
Dave Ellis Quartet | State Of Mind | Milestone | MCD 9328-2
Dave Liebman Quintet | Return Of The Tenor:Standards | Double Time Records | DTRCD-109
Deborah Henson-Conant Trio | 'Round The Corner | Laika Records | LK 87-203
Derek Smith Trio | Love For Sale | Progressive | PRO 7002 IMS
Don Byas Et Ses Rythmes | Don Byas Complete 1946-1951 European Small Group Master Takes | Definitive Records | DRCD 11214
Duke Ellington And His Orchestra | Duke Ellington And His Orchestra 1943,Vol.1 | Circle | CCD-101
All Star Road Band Vol.2 | Doctor Jazz | ZL 70969(2) (809319)
Ella Fitzgerald And The Paul Smith Quartet | Compact Jazz: Ella Fitzgerald Live | Verve | 833294-2
Ella Fitzgerald With The Paul Smith Quartet | For The Love Of Ella Fitzgerald | Verve | 841765-2
Mack The Knife-Ella In Berlin | Verve | 825670-2
Ella Fitzgerald With The Tommy Flanagan Trio | Ella A Nice | Original Jazz Classics | OJC20 442-2
Ella Fitzgerald In Budapest | Pablo | PACD 5308-2
Elvin Jones-Richard Davis Duo | Heavy Sounds | Impulse(MCA) | 547959-2
Ernestine Anderson And Her Trio | Late At Night | Paddle Wheel | KICJ 113
Erroll Garner Trio | The Greatest Garner | Rhino | SD 1227
George Benson Orchestra | Space | CTI | 63042
George Cables Trio | By George | Original Jazz Classics | OJCCD 1056-2(C 14030)
George Masso Allstars | The Wonderful World Of George Gershwin | Nagel-Heyer | CD 001
George Shearing | Verve Jazz Masters 57:George Shearing | Verve | 529900-2
George Wallington And His Band | George Wallington Showcase | Blue Note | BNJ 71003
Gil Evans Orchestra | Svengali | ACT | 9207-2
Guido Manusardi Quartet With The Laurenziana G. D'Amato Chorus | Velvet Soul | SPLASC(H) Records | HP 14
Heinz Von Hermann Jazz Ahead | A Standard Treatment | Mons Records | MR 874320
Henry Red Allen-Coleman Hawkins All Stars | Stormy Weather | Jazz Groove | JG 002 IMS
Herbie Harper Quintet | The Complete Nocturne Recordings:Jazz In Hollywood Series Vol.1 | Fresh Sound Records | NR 3CD-101
Jazz In Hollywood:Herbie Harper | Original Jazz Classics | OJCCD 1887-2(Nocturne NLP-1/NLP-7)
Holly Hofman-Ron Satterfield | Duo Personality | The Jazz Alliance | TJA 10017
Jack McDuff Group | Bringin' It Home | Concord | CCD 4855
Jay McShann-Major Holley | Havin' Fun | Sackville | SKCD2-2047
Jenny Evans And The Rudi Martini Quartet | At Loyd's | BELL Records | BLR 90004
Joe Newman With The Ove Lind Quintet | Joe Newman At The Atlantic | Phontastic | NCD 8810
Joe Pass Quartet | The Complete 'Catch Me' Sessions | Blue Note | LT 1053
Joe Sullivan | The Commodore Story | Commodore | CMD 24002
Joe Williams With The Count Basie Orchestra | Joe Williams With The Count Basie Orchestra | Telarc Digital | CD 83329
John Coltrane Quartet | John Coltrane-The Heavyweight Champion:The Complete Atlantic Recordings | Atlantic | 8122-71984-2
The Very Best Of John Coltrane | Rhino | 8122-79778-2
My Favorite Things | Atlantic | 8122-75204-2
John Lewis | Afternoon In Paris | Dreyfus Jazz Line | FDM 36507-2
Johnny Hartman With The Mikio Masuda Trio | For Trane | Blue Note | 835346-2
Julie London With The Gerald Wilson Big Band | Julie London Feeling Good | EMI Records | 1599361
Kenny Burrell-Grover Washington Quartet | One Night With Blue Note Vol.3 | Blue Note | BT 85115 Digital
Kenny Davern Trio | Strechin' Out | Jazzology | JCD-187
Klaus Ignatzek | Gershwin Songs | Nabel Records:Jazz Network | CD 4631
Klaus Kreuzeder & Willi Herzinger | Sax As Sax Can | Trick Music | TM 8712 CD
Klaus Treuheit Trio | Sprengwerk | Klaus Treuheit Production | KTMP 9911(CD 164)
Lionel Hampton And His Orchestra | European Tour 1953 | Royal Jazz | RJD 517
Louis Armstrong And Ella Fitzgerald With Russell Garcia's Orchestra | Porgy And Bess | Verve | 2-2507 IMS
The Complete Ella Fitzgerald And Louis Armstrong On Verve | Verve | 537284-2
Louis Armstrong With Orchestra | Satchmo | Verve | 835895-2
Marcus Roberts Trio | Gershwin For Lovers | CBS | 477752-2
Martial Solal Trio | Just Friends | Dreyfus Jazz Line | FDM 36592-2
Maxine Sullivan With The Ellis Larkins Trio | Maxine Sullivan 1944 to 1948 | Legend | CD 6004(875358)

TITELVERZEICHNIS

Michele Hendricks And Her Trio | Me And My Shadow | Muse | MCD 5404
Miles Davis With Gil Evans & His Orchestra | Miles Davis Classics | CBS | CBS 88138
Miltiades Papastamou-Marcos Alexiou | Dialogue Blue | CCn'C Records | 01102
Mongo Santamaria Group With Dizzy Gillespie And Toots Thielemans | Summertime-Digital At Montreux 1980 | Original Jazz Classics | OJCCD 626-2(2308229)
Mundell Lowe And His All Stars | Victor Jazz History Vol.17:Mainstream | RCA | 2135736-2
Mundell Lowe's Jazzmen | Porgy And Bess | RCA | PL 43552
Orquestra De Cambra Teatre Lliure | Porgy And Bess | Fresh Sound Records | FSNT 066 CD
Oscar Peterson | Oscar Peterson:Exclusively For My Friends | MPS | 513830-2
Oscar Peterson Trio | Oscar Peterson In Russia | Pablo | 2CD 2625711
Mellow Mood | MPS | 68077
Oscar Peterson-Joe Pass Duo | Porgy And Bess | Original Jazz Classics | OJCCD 829-2(2310779)
Oscar Peterson-Jon Faddis Duo | Oscar Peterson & Jon Faddis | Original Jazz Classics | OJCCD 1036-2(2310743)
Oscar Peterson-Roy Eldridge Duo | Jousts | Pablo | 2310817
Papa John De Francesco Quintet | Comin' Home | Muse | MCD 5531
Sarah Vaughan With Hal Mooney's Orchestra | Compact Jazz: Sarah Vaughan | Mercury | 830699-2
Schlothauer's Maniacs | Maniakisses | Timescrapper | TSCR 9811
Schnuckenack Reinhardt Quintet | Swing Session | Intercord | 160010
Shelly Manne And His Men | At The Blackhawk Vol.1 | Contemporary | C 7577
Sidney Bechet With Michel Attenoux And His Orchestra | Sidney Bechet | Vogue | 000001 GK
Stan Getz New Quartet | A Life In Jazz:A Musical Biography | Verve | 535119-2
Compact Jazz | Verve | 831368-2
Stan Getz Quintet | Stan Getz:East Of The Sun-The West Coast Sessions | Verve | 531935-2
Stanley Turrentine Quintet | Up At Minton's | Blue Note | 828885-2
Stephane Grappelli Quartet | Les Grand Classiques Du Jazz | Festival | Album 155
Tatsuya Takahashi & Tokyo Union | Plays Miles & Gil | Paddle Wheel | K32Y 6268
The New Stan Getz Quartet | Getz Au Go Go | CTI Records | PDCTI 1124-2
Tim Whitehead Quintet | A Cool Blue | Criss Cross | Criss 1102
Tommy Dorsey And His Orchestra | The Post-War Era | Bluebird | 63 66156-2
Forever | RCA | NL 89859 DP
Zoot Sims Quintet | Zoot Sims And The Gershwin Brothers | Original Jazz Classics | OJC20 444-2(2310744)
All Star Live Jam Session | Brownie-The Complete EmArCy Recordings Of Clifford Brown | EmArCy | 838306-2

Summertime-
Art Blakey And The Jazz Messengers | Originally | CBS | FC 38036
Charlie Parker Quintet | Charlie Parker At Birdland And Cafe Society | Cool & Blue | C&B-CD 108
Deborah Henson-Conant | Alterd Ego | Laika Records | 35100962
Dizzy Gillespie-Roy Eldridge Sextet | The Complete Verve Roy Eldridge Studio Sessions | Verve | 9861278
Eddy Louiss Trio | Eddy Louiss Orgue, Vol. 1 | America | AM 6127
JATP All Stars | Jazz At The Philharmonic:The Trumpet Battle 1952 | Verve | 815152-1 IMS
Stephane Grappelli With The Diz Disley Trio | The Best Of Stephane Grappelli | Black Lion | 147013
The Two-Bone-Big-Band | The Return Of The Hornplayers | Mons Records | MR 874314
Big Bill Broonzy Band | Big Bill Broonzy-Midnight Steppers | Swingtime(Contact) | BT 2001

Summertime Is Over
Lonnie Plaxico Group | Plaxico | Muse | MCD 5389

Summertime(alt.take)
Duke Ellington And His Orchestra | Duke Ellington And His Orchestra 1943,Vol.1 | Circle | CCD-101

Summertime(Samba Version)
Patrick Karlhuber Group | So What | Edition Collage | EC 480-2

Summerwind
Häns'che Weiss Ensemble | Vis-A-Vis | Elite Special | 73229

Summer-Winter(part 2)-
Andrew Cyrille-Vladimir Tarasov Duo | Galaxies | Music & Arts | CD 672

Summit
Gerry Mulligan With Astor Piazzolla And His Orchestra | Tango Nuevo | Atlantic | 2292-42145-2
Gerry Mulligan/Astor Piazolla Group | Gerry Mulligan/Astor Piazolla 1974 | Accord | 556642

Summit Blues
Reggie Workman Quintet | Summit Conference | Postcards | POST 1003

Summit Meeting
Artie Shaw And His Gramercy Five | The Complete Gramercy Five Sessions | Bluebird | ND 87637

Summun,Bukmun,Umyun
| Kenny Wheeler-Norma Winstone-John Taylor With The Maritime Jazz Orchestra | Justin Time | JTR 8465-2

Sun Dance
Eddie Daniels Quartet | Nepenthe | GRP | GRP 96072
The Modern Jazz Society | A Concert Of Contemporary Music | Verve | 559827-2
Ed Mann Group | Have No Fear | CMP Records | CMP CD 72

Sun Day
Bob Degen Quartet | Children Of The Night | Enja | 3027

Sun Dog
Gunter Hampel Next Generation | Köln Concert Part 2 | Birth | CD 048

Sun Down
Bill Evans Quartet | The Gambler-Bill Evans Live At The Blue Note Tokyo | Jazz City | 660.53.025

Sun Flower
Jazz Circle | Sun Games | Timeless | CD SJP 167

Sun Goddness
Tito Puente And His Latin Jazz All Stars | Master Timbalero | Concord | CCD 4594

Sun Gone Down(take 1)
Albert King Blues Band | The Lost Session | Stax | SCD 8534-2

Sun Gone Down(take 2)
MGM Trio | MGM Trio | Ramboy Recordings | No.09

Sun In Aquarius
Soesja Citroen And Her Trio | Song For Ma | Challenge | CHR 70056

Sun King
Mike Westbrook Band | Off Abbey Road | TipToe | TIP-888805 2
Wheeler-O'Mara-Darling-Elgart | Kenny Wheeler-Peter O'Mara-Wayne Darling-Bill Elgart | Koala Records | CD P 22

Sun On My Hands
Gerry Mulligan Quartet | Little Big Horn | GRP | GRP 95032

Sun Prayer
Sergey Strarostin's Vocal Family | Journey | JA & RO | JARO 4226-2

Sun Prayer-
Art Ensemble Of Chicago | Urban Bushmen | ECM | 1211/12

Sun Precondition Two
Sun Ra And His Solar Arkestra | Nothing Is | ESP Disk | ESP 1045-2

Sun Rose
Fairy Tale Trio | Jazz Across The Border | Wergo | SM 1531-2

Sun Sanuvah
Barbara Thompson Group | Shifting Sands | Intuition Records | INT 3174-2

Sun Shapes
John Coltrane Quartet | Sun Ship | Impulse(MCA) | 951166-2

Sun Ship
John Coltrane:The Classic Quartet-Complete Impulse Studio Recordings | Impulse(MCA) | 951280-2
Mat Maneri | Trinity | ECM | 1719
McCoy Tyner Quartet | McCoy Tyner-Reevaluation | MCA | AS 9235-2

Sun Star
John Coltrane Quartet | Stellar Regions | Impulse(MCA) | 951169-2

Sun Star(alt.take)
Albert Mangelsdorff Quintet | Lanaya | Plainisphare | PL 1267-96 CD

Sun Touch
DMP Big Band | Glenn Miller Project | dmp Digital Music Productions | CD 519

Sun Valley Jump
Glenn Miller And His Orchestra | His Original Recordings | RCA | NL 89026 DP
The Swinging Mr. Miller | RCA | 2115522-2
Frank Lowe Quintet | The Flam | Black Saint | 120005-2

Sunda
Ben Webster-Don Byas Quintet | Ben Webster/Don Byas | Jazz Magazine | 48018

Sundance
Errol Parker | Live At St.Peter's Church | Sahara | 1009
Keith Jarrett Group | Expectations | CBS | C2K 65900
Lee Konitz-Karl Berger Duo | Seasons Change | Circle Records | RK 19-291079/19 IMS

Sundance(alt.take)
Digital Masters Feat. Bryan Steele | Sun Dance | Edition Musikat | EDM 038

Sundance(part 1-11)
L.A.4 | The L.A.Four Scores! | Concord | CCD 6008

Sunday
Ben Webster Quartet | Live At The Haarlemse Jazzclub | Limetree | MCD 0040
Gone With The Wind | Black Lion | CD 877644-2
Ben Webster With The Oscar Peterson Trio | Ben Webster Meets Oscar Peterson | Verve | 829167-2
Benny Carter And His Orchestra | Highlights Of The Montreux Jazz Festival 1975 | Pablo | 2625707
Buddy Tate Septet | Jazz Greats | Chiaroscuro | CR 204
Coleman Hawkins-Roy Eldridge Quintet | The Essential Coleman Hawkins | Verve | 2304537 IMS
Gerry Mulligan-Ben Webster Quintet | Gerry Mulligan Meets Ben Webster | Verve | 841661-2 PMS
Ultimate Ben Webster selected by James Carter | Verve | 557537-2
Hank Jones | Handful Of Keys-The Music Of Thomas 'Fats' Waller | EmArCy | 512737-2 PMS
Humphrey Lyttelton And His Band | Movin' And Groovin' | Black Lion | BLCD 760504
JATP Jam Session | Return To Happiness-JATP At Yoyogi National Stadium,Tokyo | Pablo | 2620117-2
John Coltrane-Paul Quinichette Quintet | John Coltrane-The Prestige Recordings | Prestige | 16 PCD 4405-2
Johnny Hartman And The Rudy Traylor Orchestra | And I Thought About You | Blue Note | 857456-2
Kenny Ball And His Jazzmen | Saturday Night At The Mill | Decca | 6.23040 AO
Lester Young And His Band | Lester Young:The Complete 1936-1951 Small Group Sessions(Studio Recordings-Master Takes),Vol.4 | Blue Moon | BMCD 1004
Michael Feinstein With Jule Styne | Michael Feinstein Sings The Jule Styne Songbook | Nonesuch | 7559-79274-2
Oscar Peterson-Roy Eldridge Duo | Oscar Peterson & Roy Eldridge | Original Jazz Classics | OJCCD 727-2(2310739)
Paul Quinichette And His Orchestra | The Vice Pres | Verve | 543750-2
Ralph Sutton Trio | Ralph Sutton Trio-Sunday Session | Sackville | SKCD2-2044
Ruby Braff And His Buddies | Controlled Nonchalance At The Regattabar Vol.1 | Arbors Records | ARCD 19134
Stan Getz With The Oscar Peterson Trio | Compact Jazz: Stan Getz & Friends | Verve | 835317-2
The Dixieland All Stars | The Dixieland All Stars | Jazz Unlimited | JUCD 2037
The Widespread Depression Orchestra | Time To Jump And Shout | Stash Records | ST 212 IMS

Sunday Afternoon
Lajos Dudas Quartet | Urban Blues | Konnex Records | KCD 5050
Bobby Bradford/John Carter Quintet | Comin' On | Hat Art | CD 6016

Sunday At Jack's
Charlie Haden Quartet West | In Angel City | Verve | 837031-2

Sunday At The Hillcrest
Count Basie's Small Band | 88 Basie Street | Original Jazz Classics | OJC 808(2310901)

Sunday At The Savoy
Shannon Jackson & The Decoding Society | Raven Roc | DIW | DIW 862 CD

Sunday Blues
Dry Jack | Dry Jack/Magical Elements | Inner City | IC 1063 IMS

Sunday Child
Big Jay McNeely Group | Roots Of Rock 'N' Roll, Vol. 6: Honkers & Screamers | Savoy | SJL 2234 (801210)

Sunday Girl
The Latin Jazz Quintet | Hot Sauce | Prestige | PCD 24128-2

Sunday Go Meetin'
The Latin Jazz Quintet Plus Guest: Eric Dolphy | Eric Dolphy:The Complete Prestige Recordings | Prestige | 9 PRCD-4418-2
Junior Mance Trio | Softly As In A Morning Sunrise | Enja | 8080-2

Sunday In New York
Ralph Moore Quartet | Who It Is You Are | Denon Compact Disc | CY-75778

Sunday In Savannah
Ellis Larkins Trio With Tony Middleton | Swingin' For Hamp | Concord | CJ 134

Sunday Kind Of Love
Diane Schuur With Orchestra And Strings | The Best Of Diane Schuur | GRP | GRP 98882
Etta James With Orchestra | Peaches | Chess | 427014

Sunday Kind Of Love-
Dollar(Abdullah Ibrahim) Brand | ...Memories | West Wind | WW 2029

Sunday Morning
Art Connection | Stolen Moments | Acoustic Music Records | 319.1035.2
Dick Wellstood | Three Is Company | Sackville | 2007
Kenny Burrell Quintet | Moonglow | Prestige | P 24106

Sunday Morning-
Big Joe Turner And His All Stars | Roots Of Rock And Roll Vol. 2: Big Joe Turner | Savoy | SJL 2223 (801199)

Sunday Morning Blues
Association Urbanetique | Ass Bedient | Jazz 4 Ever Records:Jazz Network | J4E 4723

Sunday Morning Fast Break
Dick de Graaf Septet | Heartbeat | Timeless | CD SJP 420

Sunday Picnic
Pata Horns | New Archaic Music | Pata Musik | PATA 4(JHM 42) CD

Sunday Stroll
Cedar Walton Quartet | Eastern Rebellion 2 | Timeless | CD SJP 106

Sunday Train
Jean-Luc Ponty Quartet | Compact Jazz:Jean-Luc Ponty & Stephane Grappelli | MPS | 835320-2 PMS

Sunday(alt.take)
Tony Parenti And His New Orleanians | Tony Parenti And His New Orleanians | Jazzology | JCD-1

Sunday's On The Way
Keith Jarrett | Staircase | ECM | 1090/91

Sundial
Simon Nabatov, String Gang & Percussion | Inside Lookin' Out | Tutu Records | 888104-2*
Chris Potter Quartet | Sundiata | Criss Cross | Criss 1107

Sundown
Son House | Death Letter | Edsel | CD 167
Wes Montgomery With The Don Sebesky Orchestra | Compact Jazz: Wes Montgomery Plays The Blues | Verve | 835318-2 PMS
Johnny Temple | Chicago Blues(1935-1942) | RCA | 2126404-2

Sundown Express
Frisco Syncopators | Firehouse Stomp | Stomp Off Records | CD 1245

Sundu
Alphonse Mouzon Group | Deep Blue-The United States Of Mind | Blue Note | 521152-2

Sunflower
Freddie Hubbard Sextet feat. Leon Thomas | A Piece Of Cake | Palcoscenico | PAL 15006
Special EFX | Double Feature | GRP | GRP 95592

Sunhat Blues
Thomasz Stanko Freelactronic | The Montreux Performance | ITM Records | ITM 1423

Sunjog
Jamaaladeen Tacuma Group | Dreamscape | DIW | DIW 904 CD

Sunken Boat
Elements | Illumination | RCA | PD 83031(874013)

Sunken Treasure
Gil Evans Orchestra | The Great Arrangers | MCA | IA 9340/2

Sunlight
Pat Metheny Group With Orchestra | Secret Story | Geffen Records | GED 24468
Eddie Higgins Trio | Those Quiet Days | Sunnyside | SSC 1052 D

Sunmaker
Maneri/Phillips/Maneri | Tales Of Rohnlief | ECM | 1678

Sunned
Mat Maneri Trio | So What? | HatOLOGY | 529

Sunny
Count Basie And His Orchestra With The Mills Brothers | The Board Of Directors Annual Report | Dot | DLP 25888
Ernestine Anderson With The Monty Alexander Trio | Sunshine | Concord | CCD 4109
George Benson And His Orchestra | Giblet Gravy | Verve | 543754-2
Talkin' Verve:George Benson | Verve | 553780-2
George Van Eps | Legends | Concord | CCD 4616
Joe Bonner Trio | Parade | Steeplechase | SCCD 31116
Oscar Peterson With Orchestra | Motions & Emotions | MPS | 821289-2 PMS
Thilo Kreitmeier & Group | Changes | Organic Music | ORGM 9725
Toots Thielemans/Jonny Teupen/Paul Kuhn And Friends | Just Friends | Jazzline | ???
Wes Montgomery With The Don Sebesky Orchestra | Compact Jazz: Wes Montgomery | Verve | 831372-2

Sunny Afternoon
Michel Redolfi Ensemble | Sonic Waters No.2 | Hat Art | CD 6026

Sunny Island
Nana Vasconcelos/Antonello Salis | Lester | Soul Note | 121157-2

Sunny Road
Big Joe Williams | Big Joe Williams-The Final Years | Verve | 519943-2

Sunny Sunday
Lisa Ekdahl With The Salvador Poe Quartet, Strings And Guests | Lisa Ekdahl Sings Salvadore Poe | RCA | 2179681-2

Sunny Weather
Ulli Bögershausen-Reinhold Westerheide | Pictures | Laika Records | LK 35100932

Sunny Windo
Wes Montgomery With The Don Sebesky Orchestra | California Dreaming | Verve | 827842-2

Sunny(alt.take)
Les McCann Group | Talkin' Verve:Les McCann | Verve | 557351-2

Sunny(part 1)
Talkin' Verve:Les McCann | Verve | 557351-2

Sunny(part 2)
Elisabeth Kontomanou & Jean-Michel Pilc | Hands & Incantation | Steeplechase | SCCD 31484

Sunnymoon For Two
Sonny Stitt Quartet | Symphony Hall Swing | Savoy | WL 70830 (809327)

Sunnyside Beach
Buddy DeFranco Quartet | Waterbed | Candid | CRS 1017 IMS

Sunrise
Brian Bromberg Group | A New Day | Black-Hawk | BKH 524
Dave Liebman Trio | The Seasons | Soul Note | 121245-2
Jan Fryderyk Trio | tri-o (tri-ou) Trio n. | Jazzline | ???
Steve Tibbetts | Steve Tibbetts | ECM | bzz- 77
The Errol Parker Experience | Graffiti | Sahara | 1011
Toto Blanke-Rudolf Dasek | Meditation | ALISO Records | AL 1026
Ahmed El-Salamouny/Gilson De Assis | Calunga | FSM | FCD 97753

Sunrise Blues
Red Norvo Sextet | Red Play The Blues | RCA | 2113034-2

Sunrise Cajun Style
Clarence Gatemouth Brown Band | One More Mile | Rounder Records | CDRR 2034

Sunrise In Malibu
Clifford Jordan Quintet | Mosaic | Milestone | MCD 47092-2

Sunrise In Mexico
Starting Time | Original Jazz Classics | OJC 147(J 952)
Rabih Abou-Khalil Group | The Sultan's Picnic | Enja | ENJ-8078 2

Sunrise In Montreal
Dusko Goykovich Quintet | Bebop City | Enja | ENJ-9015 2

Sunrise Serenade
Glenn Miller And His Orchestra | The Unforgettable Glenn Miller | RCA | PD 89260
Glenn Miller-The Great Instrumentals 1938-1942 | Retrieval | RTR 79001
A Legendary Performer-Previously Unreleased Live Recordings | RCA | NL 89212 DP

Sunrise Sunset
Tommy Vig Orchestra | Encounter With Time | Discovery | DS 780 IMS

Sunset
Elliot Lawrence And His Orchestra | Big Band Sound | Fresh Sound Records | FSCD 2003
Kenny Barron Quintet | Sunset To Dawn | Muse | MCD 6014
Kenny Drew | Everything I Love | Steeplechase | SCS 1007
Mike DiRubbo Quintet | Keep Steppin' | Criss Cross | Criss 1205
Sonny Stitt With The Bud Powell Trio | Genesis | Prestige | P 24044

Sunset Afternoon
Dee Dee Bridgewater With Band | Victim Of Love | Verve | 841199-2

Sunset And Blue
Duke Ellington And His Orchestra | The Best Of Duke Ellington | Pablo | 2405401-2

Sunset And The Mocking Birds
Ralph Schweizer Big Band | DAY Dream | Chaos | CACD 8177

Sunset And The Mocking Birds-
Sacbe | Sacbe-Street Corner | Discovery | DS 864 IMS

Sunset Boulevard
Beryl Bryden & The Blue Boys | I've Got What It Takes-A BBC Radio Celebration Of The Music Of Bessie Smith | Lake | LACD 71

Sunset Eyes
Jack Sheldon And His Exciting All-Star Big Band | Jack's Groove | Fresh Sound Records | FSR 624(GNP 60)

Sunset II-V
Robin Eubanks Sextet | 4:JJ/Slide/Curtis And Al | TCB Records | TCB 97802

Sunset In Blue
Dollar Brand Trio | Anatomy Of A South African Village | Black Lion | BLCD 760172

Sunset Shuffle
Franco Morone | Melodies Of Memories | Acoustic Music Records | 319.1153.2

Sunset Special
Jimmy Dorsey And His Orchestra | The Uncollected:Jimmy Dorsey, Vol.2 | Hindsight | HSR 153

Sunshine

Joachim Kühn Group | Springfever | Atlantic | 50280
Sunshine Alley
Billy Cotton And His Band | Sing A New Song | Saville Records | SVL 160 IMS
Sunshine Mama
Clifford Gibson | Beat You Doing It | Yazoo | YAZ 1027
Sunshine Of Your Love
Ella Fitzgerald And Her Orchestra | Sunshine Of Your Love | MPS | 533102-2
Gerald Wilson And His Orchestra | Deep Blue-The United States Of Mind | Blue Note | 521152-2
Ginger Baker Group(Cream) | The Album | ITM Records | ITM 1469
Sunshine Sammy
Keith Jarrett Quartet | Nude Ants | ECM | 1171/72(829119-2)
Sunshine Song
Nude Ants | ECM | 1171/72(829119-2)
Blind Lemon Jefferson | Suitcase Full Of Blues | Black Swan Records | HCD-23
Sunshower
Ray Bryant Trio | Ray's Tribute To His Jazz Piano Friends | JVC | JVC 9031-2
Stan Getz Quartet | The Lost Sessions | Verve | 9801098
Havana Flute Summit | Havana Flute Summit | Naxos Jazz | 86005-2
Sunshowers
Seamus Blake-Marc Miralta Trio | Sun Sol | Fresh Sound Records | FSNT 087 CD
Sunsol
Horace Parlan Trio | Blue Parlan | Steeplechase | SCCD 31124
Sunwept Sunday
Terje Gewelt Quartet | Forward Motion:The Berklee Tapes | Hep | 2026
Suomi
Pago Libre | Cinémagique | TCB Records | TCB 01112
Süper
Charles Davis Quartet | Super 80 | Nilva | NQ 3410 IMS
Super Bad
Sun Ra And His Arkestra | Supersonic Jazz | Evidence | ECD 22015-2
Super Funk
Jimmy McGriff Orchestra | Jimmy McGriff-Funkiest Little Band In The Kand | LRC Records | CDC 9046(874379)
Super Jet
Steve Kuhn Trio | The Vanguard Date | Owl Time Line | 3819062
Thilo von Westernhagen Group | Ardent Desire | SHP Records | SHP 202
Super Nova
Hot Club De Norvege With Guests | Swinging With Jimmy | Hot Club Records | HCRCD 082
Super Sex
Ron Carter Quintet With Strings | Pick 'Em/Super Strings | Milestone | MCD 47090-2
Super Strings
Louis Armstrong And His Orchestra | Rare Louis Armstrong | Jazz Anthology | 550182
Super Zortzi
Sonny Red (Kyner) Quintet | Red,Blue & Green | Milestone | MCD 47086-2
Super-20
Amsterdam Jazz Quintet | Portraits | Challenge | CHR 70048
Superfine Love
Kölner Saxophon Mafia With Arno Steffen | Kölner Saxophon Mafia Proudly Presents | Jazz Haus Musik | JHM 0046 CD
Supergut Ne
Kölner Saxophon Mafia | Go Commercial... | Jazz Haus Musik | JHM 0065 CD
Supergutne
Houston Boines Band | Mississippi Blues | Anthology of the Blues | AB 5609
Superlatino
Herbie Mann And His Orchestra | Super Mann | Atlantic | ATL 50569
Superman With A Horn
Ku-umba Frank Lacy & The Poker Bigband | Songs From The Musical 'Poker' | Tutu Records | 888150-2*
Supermarket
Georg Ruby Group | Stange Loops | Jazz Haus Musik | JHM 0057 CD
Supernova
Gonzalo Rubalcaba Trio | Supernova | Blue Note | 531172-2
Supernova(I)
Supernova | Blue Note | 531172-2
Supernova(II)
Peter Giger | Illigitimate Music | Nagara | MIX 1014-N
Supersition
Lennie Tristano Trio | The Story Of Jazz Piano | Laserlight | 24653
Supersonic
The Modern Jazz Piano Album | Savoy | WL 70510(2)(SJL 2247) DP
Superstar
Woody Herman And His Orchestra | Woody Herman Herd At Montreux | Original Jazz Classics | OJCCD 991-2(F 9470)
Eddie Burns Group | Treat Me Like I Treat You | Moonshine | BLP 106
Superstition
Jimmy Ponder Quartet | Down Here On The Ground | Milestone | M 9121
Superwoman(Where Were You When I Needed You)
Leroy Jenkins | Leroy Jenkins Solo Concert | India Navigation | IN 1028
Suppertime
Carol Sloane And Her Trio | The Songs Carmen Sang | Concord | CCD 4663
Ella Fitzgerald With Paul Weston And His Orchestra | The Complete Ella Fitzgerald Song Books of Harold Arlen, Irving Berlin, Duke Ellington, George & Ira Gershwin, Jerome Kern, Johnny Mercer, Cole Porter And Rogers & Hart | Verve | 519832-2
Suppressions
Albert Mangelsdorff | Solo Now | MPS | 68067
Supraconductivity
Duke Ellington And His Orchestra & Choir | Second Sacred Concert | America | AM 006/007
Supreme Loop(to Randy Weston)
Alain Everts | Terra Nueva | Acoustic Music Records | 319.1103.2
Sur L'Antelle
Miles Davis Quintet | Compact Jazz: Miles Davis | Philips | 838254-2
Sur L'Autoroute
Willem Breuker Kollektief | In Holland | BVHAAST | 041/42 (807118)
Sur L'Infini Bleu
Titi Winterstein Sextet | Djinee Tu Kowa Ziro | Boulevard | BLD 501 CD
Sur Un Fil
Astor Piazzolla Group | Piazzolla | American Clave | AMCL 1021-2
Sur:Regresso Al Amor(South:Regression To Love)
Ann Malcom With The Kenny Barron Quartet | Incident'ly | Sound Hills | SSCD 8053
Surabaya Johnny
New On The Corner | Left Handed | Jazz 4 Ever Records:Jazz Network | J4E 4758
Dhafer Youssef Group | Electric Sufi | Enja | ENJ-9412 2
Surbj
L.C. Prigett | Piano Blues Vol.1-The Twenties(1923-1930) | Story Of Blues | CD 3511-2
Sure Thing
Bud Powell Trio | The Legacy | Jazz Door | JD 1204
Inner Fries-The Genius Of Bud Powell | Discovery | 71007-2
The Amazing Bud Powell Vol.2 | Blue Note | 532137-2
Sure Thing(alt.take)
The Fantasy Band | The Fantasy Band | dmp Digital Music Productions | CD 496
Sure, Had A Wonderful Time
Gil Evans Orchestra | Strange Fruit | ITM Records | ITM 1499
Surf Medley
Freddie King Group | Freddie King Gives You A Bonanza Of Instrumentals | Crosscut | CCR 1010
Surf Ride
Art Pepper Quartet | A Night At The Surf Club Vol.1 | EPM Musique | FCD 5153

Black California | Savoy | SJL 2215 (801191)
Surf Walk
The Berlin Workshop Orchestra | The Berlin Jazz Workshop Orchestra -Who Is Who? | FMP | SAJ 24
Surface And Symbol
Ketil Bjornstad Group | Water Stories | ECM | 1503(519076-2)
Surface Movements
David Moss Dense Band | Dense Band | Moers Music | 02040
Surfboard
Yosuke Yamashita New York Trio | Canvas In Vigor | Verve | 537008-2
Surfers' Paradise
Sonny Stitt Quartet | Now! | Impulse(MCA) | JAS 25 (AS 43)
Surfin' Snoopy
| All At Once At Any Time | Victo | CD 029
Surfriding
David Kikoski Trio | Surf's Up | Criss Cross | Criss 1208
Surgin'
Felix Wahnshuffle Trio | Live At The Be-Bop:Blues Against Racism | L+R Records | CDLR 45087
Surinam
The Lizard Brothers | Saxophone Animals | Nine Winds Records | NWCD 0139
Surprise
Gunter Hampel And His Galaxie Dream Band | A Place To Be With Us | Birth | 0032
Surprise Hotel
Flim & The BB's | Tunnel | dmp Digital Music Productions | CD 447
Surprise-Partie Au Bord De L'Eau
Charles Lloyd-Billy Higgins | Which Way Is East | ECM | 1878/79(9811796)
Surrender
Francois Carrier Trio | Compassion | Naxos Jazz | 86062-2
Surrender To The Water
Ahmad Jamal Trio | At The Pershing | Affinity | CD AFS 780
Surrey With The Fringe On Top
Curtis Peagler Quartet | I'll Be Around | Pablo | 2310930
McCoy Tyner Trio | Time For Tyner | Blue Note | 784307-2
Miles Davis Quintet | Steamin' | Original Jazz Classics | OJC20 391-2
The Jazz Giants Play Rodgers & Hammerstein:My Favorite Things | Prestige | PCD 24223-2
Nat King Cole With The Dave Cavanaugh Orchestra | Nat King Cole At The Sands | Capitol | EMS 1110
Oscar Peterson Trio | At Zardis' | Pablo | 2CD 2620118
Paul Smith Trio | Intensive Care | Pausa | PR 7167(952078)
The Mastersounds | The Mastersounds | Prestige | PRCD 24770-2
A Date With The Mastersounds | Original Jazz Classics | OJC 282(F 8062)
Wynton Kelly Trio | Wynton Kelly! | Vee Jay Recordings | VJ 011
Wynton Kelly-George Coleman Quartet | Live at The Left Bank Jazz Society,Baltimore,1968 | Fresh Sound Records | FSCD 1032
Erroll Garner Trio | Dreamstreet & One World Concert | Telarc Digital | CD 83350
Surrey With The Fringe On Top(reconstructed version)
Ray Brown Quintet | Brown's Bag | Concord | CCD 6019
Surucucu-
Hank Crawford Orchestra | Down On The Deuce | Milestone | M 9129
Survival Blues
Eric Person Sextet | More Tales To Tell | Soul Note | 121307-2
Survival Of The Fittest
Herbie Hancock Quintet | Herbie Hancock:The Complete Blue Note Sixties Sessions | Blue Note | 495569-2
Munich Saxophon Family | Survival Song | JHM Records | JHM 3613
Survival Song
Monika Linges Quartet | Songing | Nabel Records:Jazz Network | LP 4615
Survive
Bud Revels Group | Survivors | Enja | ENJ-6066 2
Susanata
George Robert-Dado Moroni | Youngbloods | Mons Records | CD 1897
Susanna
Flip Phillips Quintet | Swing Is The Thing | Verve | 543477-2
Susan's Dream
Rias Big Band Berlin + Strings | Weill | Mons Records | MR 874347
Susan's Song
Piacentini/Bonati/McCandless/Moreno | Circles | Nueva Records | NC 1014
Susenyos And Werzelyna
Joe Newman -Zoot Sims Quintet | Locking Horns | Fresh Sound Records | FSR 657(Rama RLP 1003)
Sushi
Oscar Peterson And His Trio | Live At The Blue Note | Telarc Digital | CD 83304
Sushi My Love
Trio Töykeät | [Sisu] | EmArCy | 536580-2
Susie's Blues
Juan Carlos Quintero Group | Juan Carlos Quintero | Nova | NOVA 9024-2
Suspect Rhythm
Jacques Stotzem | Clear Night | Acoustic Music Records | AMC 1013
Suspended Emanations
Ray Drummond Quintet | Camera In A Bag | Criss Cross | Criss 1040
Suspended View
Tim Brady | Visions | Justin Time | JTR 8413-2
Suspendet Variations(I-X)
Art Blakey And The Jazz Messengers | Des Femmes Disparaissent/Les Tricheurs(Original Soundtracks) | Fontana | 834752-2 PMS
Suspension Blues
Makaya & The Tsotsis | Makaya & The Tsotsis | Enja | 2042
Suspicions
Helen Humes With Leonard Feather's Hip-Tet | E-Baba-Le-Ba The Rhythm And Blues Years | Savoy | WL 70824 (809326)
Suspicious Child,Growing Up
Red Norvo And His Orchestra | Live From The Blue Gardens | Musicmasters | 65090-2
Suspiro Del Moro
Michael Brecker Group | Don't Try This At Home | Impulse(MCA) | 950114-2
Suspone
Naylor's Seven Aces | Oliver Naylor 1924-25 | Retrieval | RTR 79008
Sussurro(1)
Lirico | Sussurro | Jazz Haus Musik | JHM 0129 CD
Sussurro(2)
Ralph Towner Quintet | City Of Eyes | ECM | 1388
Sustained Release
Paquito D'Rivera Orchestra | Tropicana Nights | Chesky | JD 186
Sutartine
Charlie Hunter Quartet | Ready...Set...Shango! | Blue Note | 837101-2
Sutton
Bucky Pizzarelli-John Pizzarelli Duo | The Complete Guitar Duos(The Stash Sessions) | Stash Records | ST-CD 536(889114)
Suyafhu Skin...Snapping The Hollow Reed
Sonny Boy Williamson Group | Sonny Boy Williamson(1937-1947) | RCA | 2126418-2
Suzanne
Dave Pell Octet | A Pell Of A Time | Fresh Sound Records | ND 74408
Suzie Q
Cal Collins | Cross Country | Concord | CJ 166
Enrico Pieranunzi/Enrico Rava | Nausicaa | Quadrivium | SCA 037
Svanegängare-
Alex Möller-Lena Willemark Group | Hästen Och Tranan | ACT | 9244-2
Svantetic
Arild Andersen Sextet | Sagn | ECM | 1435
Svarm
Itchy Fingers | Full English Breakfast | Enja | ENJ-7085 2
Svea Rike
Lena Willemark-Ale Möller Group | Nordan | ECM | 1536(523161-2)
Sven I Rosengard

Martin Schrack Trio | Catplay | yvp music | CD 3037
Sven Svanehvit
Howard Johnson & Gravity | Right Now! | Verve | 537801-2
Svev
Jan Garbarek Quartet | Works | ECM | 823266-2
Svevende
Brew Moore Quartet | Lions Abroad Volume One:Tenor Titans | Black Lion | BLCD 7620-2
Swamp Ballet
Fletcher Henderson And His Orchestra | Fletcher Henderson Vol.2(1927) | Village(Jazz Archive) | VILCD 020-2
Swamp Goo
Duke Ellington And His Orchestra | The Greatest Jazz Concert In The World | Pablo | 2625704-2
Swamp Stomp
Vital Information | Live Around The World Where We Come From Tour '98-'99 | Intuition Records | INT 3296-2
Cecil Brooks III Sextet | Hangin' With Smooth | Muse | MCD 5428
Swamp Thing
Brian Buchanan Quintet | Avenues | Jazz Focus | JFCD 002
Swanee
Woody Herman And His Orchestra | Hommage à George Gershwin | CBS | 471681-2
Swanee River
Art Hodes With Kenny Davern And Jim Galloway | Art Hodes-The Final Sessions | Music & Arts | CD 782
George Williams' Swinging Big Band | Put On Your Dancing Shoes | Fresh Sound Records | 054 2602771(United Artists UAS 6076)
Swanee River Boogie
Bob Hall-George Green Band | Shufflin' The Boogie | Jazz Colours | 874748-2
Swans
Don Friedman Quartet | My Foolish Heart | Steeplechase | SCCD 31534
Double You | Menschbilder | Jazz Haus Musik | JHM 0062 CD
Swansong
Rova Saxophone Quartet | From The Bureau Of Both | Black Saint | 120135-2
Swara Sulina(The Beautiful Sound Of The Flute)
Eddie Daniels Quartet | Brief Encounter | Muse | MCD 5154
Sway
Leni Stern Group | Words | Lipstick Records | LIP 890282
Swedenin'
The Real Group | One For All | ACT | 9003-2
Swedish Hit Medley:
Duke Jordan | Midnight Moonlight | Steeplechase | SCCD 31143
Swedish Pastry
Bud Powell Trio | Planet Jazz:Bud Powell | Planet Jazz | 2152064-2
At The Golden Circle, Vol.3 | Steeplechase | SCCD 36009
Vic Juris Trio | Songbook 2 | Steeplechase | SCCD 31516
Piirpauke | Jazzy World | JA & RO | JARO 4200-2
Swedish Reggae
Piirpauke-Global Servisi | JA & RO | JARO 4150-2
Live In Der Balver Höhle | JA & RO | JARO 4101-2
Charlie Parker Quintet | The Verve Years (1950-51) | Verve | 2-2512 IMS
Swedish Schnapps
Swedish Schnapps + | Verve | 849393-2
Eric Alexander Quintet | New York Calling | Criss Cross | Criss 1077
Swedish Schnapps(take 3)
Charlie Parker And His Orchestra | Bird: The Complete Charlie Parker On Verve | Verve | 837141-2
Swedish Schnapps(take 4)
Dizzy Gillespie And His Orchestra | Dizzy Gillespie-The Complete RCA Victor Recordings | Bluebird | 63 66528-2
Swee Pea
Phil Haynes' 4 Horns & What | 4 Horn Lore | Open Minds | OM 2413-2
Sweep
Count Basie And His Orchestra | The Best Of Count Basie | Pablo | 2405408-2
Swee'pea
Wayne Shorter Orchestra | Super Nova | Blue Note | 784332-2
Sweeping Up
Anderson-Harris-Lewis-Valente | Slideride | Hat Art | CD 6165
Sweet
Antonio Farao Trio | Black Inside | Enja | ENJ-9345 2
Marty Cook Quartet | Red, White, Black And Blue | Enja | 5067-2
Sweet & Bitter Little Death
Count Basie And His Orchestra | Count Basie & His Orchestra:Fresno,California April 24,1959 | Jazz Unlimited | JUCD 2039
Sweet And Lovely
Bill Jennings-Leo Parker Quintet | Billy In The Lion's Den | Swingtime(Contact) | ST 1025
Bill Perkins-Richie Kamuca Quintet | Tenors Head On | Pacific Jazz | 797195-2
Coleman Hawkins Quartet | Jazz Dance | Original Jazz Classics | OJCCD 1002-2(1210890)
Danny Moss Meets Buddha's Gamblers | A Swingin' Affair | Nagel-Heyer | CD 034
Dexter Gordon Quartet | Dexter Gordon:Dexter's Mood 1945-1947 | Cool & Blue | C&B-CD 114
Don Byas Quintet | Savoy Jam Party-The Savoy Sessions | Savoy | WL 70512 (809315)
Eddie Costa-Vinnie Burke Trio | Eddie Costa-Vinnie Burke Trio | Fresh Sound Records | LP 1025(Jubilee)
Ella Fitzgerald With The Frank DeVol Orchestra | Ella Fitzgerald Sings Sweet Songs For Swingers | Verve | 9860417
Elmo Hope Trio | Trio And Quartet | Blue Note | 784438-2
Erroll Garner Trio | Dreamstreet & One World Concert | Telarc Digital | CD 83350
Giants Of Jazz | Giants Of Jazz | George Wein Collection | AU 36100
Herbie Brock Trio | Brock's Top | Savoy | SV 0201(MG 12069)
Jimmy Giuffre-Paul Bley-Steve Swallow | Fly Away Little Bird | Owl Records | 018351-2
Jimmy Raney Quartet | Raney '81! | Criss Cross | Criss 1001
John Marshall Quintet | Theme Of No Repeat | Organic Music | ORGM 9719
Jonny King Quintet | In From The Cold | Criss Cross | Criss 1093
Kenny Davern Quartet | I'll See You In My Dreams | Musicmasters | 5020-2
Lee Konitz-Hal Galper Duo | Windows | Steeplechase | SCCD 31057
Lou Donaldson Orchestra | Lush Life | Blue Note | 784254-2
Ralph Sutton Quartet | Live At Sunnie's Rendezvous Vol.1 | Storyville | STCD 8280
Richie Vitale Quintet | The Richie Vitaleo Quintet feat.Ralph Lalama | TCB Records | TCB 96402
Thelonious Monk | Solo Monk | CBS | 471248-2
Thelonious Monk Quartet | Live In Paris 1964 | France's Concert | FCD 132x2
Thelonious Monk Trio | Thelonious Monk:The Complete Prestige Recordings | Prestige | 3 PRCD 4428-2
Thelonious Monk-Gerry Mulligan Quartet | 'Round Midnight | Milestone | M 47067
Walter Bishop Jr. Trio | Midnight Blue | Red Records | 123251-2
Wild Bill Davison All Stars | Wild Bill Davison All Stars | Timeless | CD TTD 545
Woody Herman And The New Thundering Herd | The 40th Anniversary Carnegie Hall Concert | RCA | 2159151-2
Sweet And Lovely-
Dizzy Gillespie Orchestra And The Operatic String Orchestra | Jazz In Paris:Dizzy Gillespie And His Operatic Strings Orchestra | EmArCy | 018420-2
Sweet And Lovely(alt.take 1)
Jazz In Paris:Dizzy Gillespie And His Operatic Strings Orchestra | EmArCy | 018420-2
Sweet And Lovely(alt.take 2)
Dexter Gordon Quartet | Dexter:The Dial Sessions | Storyville | SLP 814

Sweet And Lovely(alt.take)
Joe Turner | Joe Turner:Sweet And Lovely | Vogue | 2111507-2
Sweet And Slow
Louis Mazetier | Good Vibrations | Jazz Connaisseur | JCCD 9521-2
Pee Wee Russell Sextet | We're In The Money | Black Lion | BLCD 760909
Sweet And Slow(remake)
The G.B.Horn | The J.B.Horns | Gramavision | GV 79462-2(889094)
Sweet As She Can Be
Maynard Ferguson And His Big Bop Nouveau Band | These Cats Can Swing! | Concord | CCD 4669
Sweet Baby Doll
King Oliver's Jazz Band | Louis Armstrong With King Oliver Vol.2 | Village(Jazz Archive) | VILCD 012-2
Sweet Basil
Jim Hall-Bob Brookmeyer | Live At The North Sea Jazz Festival | Challenge | CHR 70063
Sweet Bird
Bowling Green John Cephas & Harmonica Phil Wiggins | Sweet Bitter Blues | L+R Records | CDLR 72004
Sweet Black Night
Bobby Jaspar Quartet | Bobby Jaspar-Tenor And Flute | Original Jazz Classics | SMJ 6156
Sweet Blue
Joe Pass With The NDR Big Band And Radio Philharmonie Hannover | Joe Pass In Hamburg | ACT | 9100-2
Sweet Bossa
Moments Quartet | Original Moments | Fresh Sound Records | FSNT 052 CD
Guido Manusardi | Contrasti | Penta Flowers | CDPIA 012
Sweet Cakes
Count Basie And His Orchestra | Jazz Collection:Count Basie | Laserlight | 24368
Pierre Guyonnet Onzetetes | Joue | Plainisphare | PAV 809
Sweet Chorus
Quintet Du Hot Club De France | Django Reinhardt:Djangology | EMI Records | 780659-2
Stephane Grappelli Quartet | Young Django | MPS | 815672-2 PMS
Stephane Grappelli Quintet | Hommage A Django Reinhardt | Festival | Album 120
Sweet Circle
Dave Brubeck | Dave Brubeck Plays And Plays And Plays... | Original Jazz Classics | OJCCD 716-2(F 3259)
Sweet Cleo Brown
Clifford Brown-Max Roach Quintet | Jazz Gallery:Clifford Brown | RCA | 2114176-2
Sweet Clifford
J.M. Rhythm Four plus One | Lazy Afternoon | TCB Records | TCB 20802
Sweet Clifford(Clifford's Fantasy)
World Saxophone Quartet | Dances And Ballads | Nonesuch | 7559-79164-2
Sweet D
Dicky Wells And His Orchestra | Bones For The King | Affinity | AFF 164
Sweet Devotion
Andy J. Forest Band | Shuffle City | L+R Records | CDLR 42068
Sweet Dulcinea
Bill Evans Quintet | The Complete Fantasy Recordings | Fantasy | 9FCD 1012-2
Gust Williams Tsilis Quartet | Heritage | Ken Music | 660.56.018
Sweet Eloise
Art Tatum | Art Tatum-The Standard Transcriptions | Music & Arts | CD 919
Sweet Emma-
Clarence Williams' Jazz Kings | Clarence Williams-The Columbia Recordings Vol.1:Dreaming The Hours Away | Frog | DGF 14
Sweet Eyes
Pierre Michelot Orchestra | Jazz In Paris:Pierre Michelot-Round About The Bass | EmArCy | 832309-2 PMS
Sweet Fifteen
Rahsaan Roland Kirk & The Vibration Society | Rahsaan Rahsaan | Atlantic | ATL 40127(SD 1575)
Sweet For Evie
Volker Kriegel & Mild Maniac Orchestra | Elastic Menu | MPS | 68180
Sweet Georgia Brown
Anita O'Day With The Buddy Bregman Orchestra | Pick Yourself Up | Official | 3015
Benny Carter And His Chocolate Dandies | Coleman Hawkins & Benny Carter | Swing | SW 8403 IMS
Benny Waters & The Traditional Jazz Studio | Lady Be Good | Vagabond | 6.23364 AO
Billy Taylor Trio | The Billy Taylor Trio At Town Hall | Prestige | VIJ 5020
Bireli Lagrene Ensemble | Bireli Lagrene 15 | Antilles | 802503
Bud Powell Trio | The Best Of Bud Powell On Verve | Verve | 523392-2
Bud Powell:Complete 1947-1951 Blue Note,Verve & Roost Recordings | The Jazz Factory | JFCD 22837
Buddy Tate With The Torsten Swingenberger Swintet | Tate Live | Nagel-Heyer | CD 080
Bunk Johnson With Bertha Gonsoulin | Bunk Johnson In San Francisco | American Music | AMCD-16
Chris Barber's Jazz Band | Chris Barber-Concert '80 Vol.2 | Jeton | JET 60010
Coleman Hawkins And His All Star Jam Band | Django Reinhardt:Djangology | EMI Records | 780659-2
Dave Brubeck Group | In Their Own Sweet Way | Telarc Digital | CD 83355
Dave Brubeck Trio | The Dave Brubeck Trio | Fantasy | FCD 24726-2
Dice Of Dixie Crew | 1st Throw | Inak | 811 Direct Cut
Earl Hines And His Orchestra | Earl Hines Vol.1-South Side Swing | MCA | 1311
Ella Fitzgerald With The Marty Paich Orchestra | For The Love Of Ella Fitzgerald | Verve | 841765-2
Whisper Not | Verve | 589947-2
Compact Jazz: Ella Fitzgerald | Verve | 831367-2
Ellis Marsalis Trio | Heart Of Gold | CBS | CK 47509
H.K.'s Mixie Men | Bavarian Jazz Live | Calig | 30620/21
Harold Danko Quartet | The Harold Danko Quartet feat.Gregory Herbert | Inner City | IC 1029 IMS
Henri Crolla Sextet | Jazz In Paris:Henri Crolla-Quand Refleuriront Les Lilas Blancs? | EmArCy | 018418-2
Herb Ellis Group | Texas Swings | Justice Records | JR 1002-2
JATP All Stars | The Complete Jazz At The Philharmonic On Verve 1944-1949 | Verve | 523893-2
The Complete Jazz At The Philharmonic On Verve 1944-1949 | Verve | 523893-2
Jay McShann And His Orchestra | Early Bird | Spotlite | SPJ 120
Jenny Evans And The Rudi Martini Quartet | At Loyd's | BELL Records | BLR 90004
Joe Pass/Niels-Henning Orsted-Pedersen Duo | Joe Pass:Guitar Virtuoso | Pablo | 4 PACD 4423-2
Joe Turner And Friends | The Giant Of Stride Piano In Switzerland | Jazz Connaisseur | JCCD 9106-2
Joe Venuti Quartet | The Best Of The Jazz Violins | LRC Records | CDC 8532
John Pizzarelli Trio | Dear Mr.Cole | Novus | 4163182-2
Johnnes Rediske Quintet | Deutsches Jazz Fesival 1954/1955 | Bear Family Records | BCD 15430
Johnny Hodges Orchestra | The Rabbit's Work On Verve In Chronological Order Vol. 2: 1951-52 | Verve | 2304448 IMS
Louis Armstrong And His All Stars | Mack The Knife | Pablo | 2310941-2
Louis Armstrong With The Dukes Of Dixieland | Great Alternatives | Chiaroscuro | CR 2003
Max Bennett Quintet | Max Bennett Plays | Fresh Sound Records | FSR 2015(Bethlehem BCP 50)
Nat King Cole Trio | The Legendary 1941-44 Broadcast Transcriptions | Music & Arts | CD 808
The Forgotten Years | Giants Of Jazz | GOJ 1013
Oscar Peterson And His Trio | Live At The Blue Note | Telarc Digital | CD 83304
Oscar Peterson And The Bassists | Montreux '77-The Art Of The Jam Session | Pablo | 2620106
Oscar Peterson Quartet | Fallin' In Love With Oscar | Jazz Door | JD 1276
Oscar Peterson Trio | On The Town | Verve | 543834-2
The London Concert | Pablo | 2CD 2620111
Masters Of Jazz Vol.7 | RCA | NL 89721 DP
Rockin' In Rhythm | RCA | FXM 17327
Oscar Peterson-Joe Pass Duo | Live At Salle Pleyel, Paris | Pablo | 2625705
Quintet Du Hot Club De France | Verve Jazz Masters Vol.60:The Collection | Verve | 529866-2
Welcome To Jazz: Django Reinhardt | Koch Records | 322 074 D1
Roy Eldridge And His Orchestra | At The Arcadia Ballroom New York | Jazz Anthology | JA 5149
Sam Pilafian & Friends | Travelin' Light | Telarc Digital | CD 80281
Singers Unlimited With The Patrick Williams Orchestra | Compact Disc:The Singers Unlimited | MPS | 831373-2 PMS
Slam Stewart Trio | Slam Stewart | Black & Blue | BLE 233027
Stephane Grappelli-David Grisman Group | Live | Warner | BSK 3550
Teddy Buckner And His Dixieland Band | In Concert At The Dixieland Jubilee | Dixieland Jubilee | DJ 503
Terry Lightfoot Sextet | Terry Lightfoot Live In Leipzig | Black Lion | BLCD 760513
The Frank Capp Juggernaut | Play It Again Sam | Concord | CCD 4747
Turk Murphy And His Jazz Band | Victor Jazz History Vol.19:Dixieland Revival | RCA | 2135738-2
Wnew Saturday Night Swing Session | Jazz Off The Air-Vol. 1 | Spotlite | SPJ 144
Bob Stewart First Line Band | Goin' Home | JMT Edition | 834427-1
Sweet Georgia Fame
Tete Montoliu Trio | Catalonian Fire | Steeplechase | SCCD 31017
Sweet Georgia Peach
Blossom Dearie Trio | Sweet Blossom Dearie | Philips | PHCE 1019 PMS
Sweet Henry
Yohichi Murata Solid Brass | Double Edge | JVC | JVC 9005-2
Sweet Home Chicago
Robert Lockwood Jr. | Robert Lockwood Jr. Plays Robert (Johnson) & Robert (Lockwood) | Black & Blue | 33740
Sweet Honey Bee
Lee Morgan Sextet | Charisma | Blue Note | 300260(4312)
Sweet Hour
Cyrus Chestnut Trio | You Are My Sunshine | Warner | 9362-48445-2
Sweet Hour Of Prayer
Billy Bang Quartet | Big Bang Theory | Justin Time | JUST 135-2
Sweet Joan
Lou Donaldson Quintet | Lou Donaldson Quartet/Quintet/Sextet | Blue Note | 300135(1537)
Sweet Lake City Blues
Michal Urbaniak With The Horace Parlan Trio | Take Good Care Of My Heart | Steeplechase | SCCD 31195
Sweet Leilani
Black Eagle Jazz Band | Black Eagle Jazz Band | Stomp Off Records | CD 1224
Sweet Like This
King Oliver And His Orchestra | King Oliver And His Orchestra 1929-1930 | RCA | ND 89770
Max Collie And His Rhythm Aces | World Champions Of Jazz | Black Lion | BLCD 760512
Sweet Little Angel
B.B.King And His Band | Singin' The Blues/The Blues | Ace Records | CDCHD 320
Freddy King Blues Band | Live In Nancy 1975, Vol.1 | France's Concert | FCD 126
Sweet Little Jesus Boy
Take 6 | He Is Christmas | Reprise | 7599-26665-2
Cleve Pozar Quartet | New Music: Second Wave | Savoy | SJL 2235 (801211)
Sweet Little Sixteen
Benny Goodman And His Orchestra | Artie Shaw/Benny Goodman | Forlane | UCD 19006
Sweet Lorraine
Art Tatum | Decca Presents Art Tatum | MCA | MCAD 42327(872084)
Standards | Black Lion | CD 877646-2
Art Tatum:Complete Capitol Recordings | Definitive Records | DRCD 11192
Art Tatum:20th Century Piano Genius | Verve | 531763-2
The Tatum Solo Masterpieces Vol.8 | Pablo | 2310793
Buddy Greco Quartet | Route 66-A Personal Tribute To Nat King Cole | Celebrity | CYCD 71901
Cedar Walton | Maybeck Recital Hall Series Volume Twenty-Five | Concord | CCD 4546
Chet Baker Quartet | The Best Of Chet Baker Plays | Pacific Jazz | 797161-2
Chet Baker-Art Pepper Sextet | The Route | Pacific Jazz | 792931-2
Harry Allen Quintet | Love Songs Live! | Nagel-Heyer | NH 1014
Harry Sweets Edison With The Nat King Cole Quartet | The Complete After Midnight Sessions | Capitol | 748328-2
Henry Red Allen's All Stars | World On A String | RCA | ND 82497847084)
Jeff Hamilton Trio With Frits Landesbergen | Dynavibes | Mons Records | MR 874794
Jo Jones Trio | Key One Up | Vanguard | VCD 79612-2
Joe Newman With The Ove Lind Quintet | Joe Newman At The Atlantic | Phontastic | NCD 8810
Joe Pass | Joe Pass:A Man And His Guitar | Original Jazz Classics | OJCCD 8806-2
Joe Turner And His Band | In The Evening | Pablo | 2310776
Johnny Dodds' Hot Six | Blue Clarinet Stomp | RCA | ND 82293(847121)
Johnny Mercer With Paul Weston's Orchestra | The Uncollected:Johnny Mercer | Hindsight | HSR 152
June Christy And Her Orchestra | Early June | Fresh Sound Records | FSCD 1011
Kirk Lightsey Trio | From Kirk To Nat | Criss Cross | Criss 1050
Louis Armstrong With The Oscar Peterson Quartet | Satchmo/What A Wonderful World | Verve | 837786-2
Louisiana Repertory Jazz Ensemble Of New Orleans | Hot & Sweet Sounds Of Lost New Orleans | Stomp Off Records | CD 1140
Minton's Playhouse All Stars | Thelonious Monk:After Hours At Minton's | Definitive Records | DRCD 11197
Nat King Cole And His Trio | Combo USA | Affinity | CD AFS 1002
Nat King Cole Trio | Nat King Cole:Route 66 | Dreyfus Jazz Line | FDM 36716-2
The Great Nat King Cole | Laserlight | 15733
The Legendary 1941-44 Broadcast Transcriptions | Music & Arts | CD 808
Nat King Cole Trio:The MacGregor Years 1941/45 | Music & Arts | CD 911
Hit That Jive Jack | MCA | MCD 42350
Oscar Moore Trio | Oscar Moore And Friends | Fresh Sound Records | FSR-CD 0202
Oscar Peterson Trio | Masters Of Jazz Vol.7 | RCA | NL 89721 DP
Peck Kelley Jam | Coomodore Classics-Peck Kelley Jam Vol.2 | Commodore | 6.25528 AG
Piccadilly Six + One | The Pearls | Elite Special | 73347
Ralph Sutton-Kenny Davern Trio | Ralph Sutton & Kenny Davern | Chaz Jazz | CJ 105
Roy Eldridge Quintet | Rockin' Chair | Verve | MV 2686 IMS
Singers Unlimited | The Singers Unlimited:Magic Voices | MPS | 539130-2
A Capella III | MPS | 68245
Sonny Criss Quintet | At The Crossroad | Fresh Sound Records | 252962-1(Peacock PLP 91)
This Is Jazz All Stars | The Genius Of Sidney Bechet | Jazzology | JCD-35
Wardell Gray Quartet | Wardell Gray:Light Gray 1948-1950 | Cool & Blue | C&B-CD 116
Woody Herman And His Orchestra | The Radio Years: Woody Herman And His First Herd 1944 | Hindsight | HSR 134
Sweet Lorraine(alt.take)
Oscar Peterson Trio | This Is Oscar Peterson | RCA | 2663990-2
Jimmie Noone-Earl Hines Sextet | Jimmie Noone/Earl Hines Vol.1-At The Apex Club | MCA | 1313
Sweet Lover
Blossom Dearie Trio | Sweet Blossom Dearie | Philips | PHCE 1019 PMS
Sweet Lovin' Man
Chris Barber's Jazz Band | The Chris Barber Jubilee Album-Vol. 1 | Intercord | 157008
George Brunis And His Jazzband | The Davison-Brunis Sessions Vol. 3 | London | HMC 5013 AN
Jacques Gauthé's Creole Rice Yerba Buena Jazz Band | Cassoulet Stomp | Stomp Off Records | CD 1170
King Oliver's Jazz Band | Jazz Classics In Digital Stereo: King Oliver Volume One 1923 To 1929 | CDS Records Ltd. | RPCD 607(CD 787)
Sweet Mercy
Benny Goodman Septet | Benny Goodman:The King Of Swing | Musicmasters | 65130-2
Sweet Mistreater
Orange Kellin Trio | The Orange Kellin Trio | Big Easy Records | BIG CD-004
Sweet 'N' Sour
Dieter Köhnlein-Volker Schlott | Sweet Ballad Sweet | Aho-Recording | AHO CD 1032(CD 660)
Sweet 'N' Sour(alt.take)
Shannon Jackson & The Decoding Society | Nasty | Moers Music | 01086
Sweet Paris:
Jimmy Yancey | Pioneers Of Boogie Woogie | Jazz Anthology | JA 5212
Sweet Patootie(Blues)
Jesse James | Piano Blues Vol.2-The Thirties(1930-1939) | Story Of Blues | CD 3512-2
Sweet Pea
Marty Cook Group feat. Monty Waters | Borderlines | Tutu Records | 888122-2*
Miles Davis Quintet | Water Babies | CBS | CBS PC 34396
Yoron Israel Connection | A Gift For You | Freelance | FRL-CD 024
Sweet Peter Charleston
Jelly Roll Morton's Red Hot Peppers | The Complete Jelly Roll Morton-Vol.3/4 | RCA | NL 89769(2) DP
Sweet Poison
Jay Hoggard Quintet | The Fountain | Muse | MCD 5450
Sweet Potato
Al Jarreau With Band | We Got By | Reprise | 7599-27222-2
Sweet Potato Pie
Glenn Miller And His Orchestra | Glenn Miller | Memo Music | HDJ 4116
Sweet Rain
Klaus Müller-Ekkehard Rössle | Auf Und Davon | Jazz Haus Musik | JHM 0091 CD
Rabih Abou-Khalil Group | Roots & Sprouts | Enja | ENJ-9373 2
Stan Getz Quartet | Stan Getz Highlights | Verve | 847430-2
Sweet Rain | Verve | 815054-2 PMS
Sweet Revival
Jimmy Lunceford And His Chickasaw Syncopators | Victor Jazz History Vol.9:Kansas City(1926-32) | RCA | 2128563-2
Sweet Root Man
Memphis Slim | Steady Rolling Blues | Original Blues Classics | OBCCD 523-2(BV 1075)
Sweet Samba
John Coltrane Quintet | Black Pearls | Original Jazz Classics | OJC 352(P 7316)
Sweet Sapphire Blues
Black Pearls | Prestige | P 24037
Chris Barber's Jazz Band | Echoes Of Harlem | Lake | LACD 87
Sweet Savannah Sue
Louis Armstrong And His Orchestra | Louis Armstrong:Swings | Memo Music | HDJ 4033
Sweet Sixteen
B.B.King With The Philip Morris Super Band | Live At The Apollo | MCA | MCA 09637
Little Milton And His Band | Little Milton | Chess | 427013
Sweet Sixteen Bars
Ray Charles Trio | The Great Ray Charles | Atlantic | SD 1259
Sweet Slumber
Houston Person Quintet | Basics | Muse | MCD 5344
Sweet Smile
Slim And Slam | Slim & Slam:Original 1938-39 Recordings Vol.2 | Tax | S 2-2
Sweet Song
Roy Haynes Quartet | Thank You Thank You | Galaxy | GXY 5103
Sweet Sorrow
Stan Getz Quartet | Nobody Else But Me | Verve | 521660-2
Sweet Soul
St.Louis Kings Of Rhythm | Rhythm And Blues Showtime | Timeless | CD SJP 231/2
Sweet Stuff
Acker Bilk With Ken Colyer's Jazzmen | Together Again | Lake | LACD 53
Sweet Substitute
Turk Murphy And His Jazz Band | Concert In The Park | Merry Makers Record | MMRC-CD-12
Sweet Sucker Dance
Mingus Dynasty | Chair In The Sky | Warner | 99081
Sweet Sue Just You
Benny Goodman And His Orchestra | The Indispensable Benny Goodman(Big Band) Vol.5/6(1938-1939) | RCA | 2122621-2
Benny Goodman Quartet | Benny Goodman:The Complete Small Combinations Vol.1/2(1935-1937) | RCA | ND 89753
Charlie Ventura Quintet | High On An Open Mike | Fresh Sound Records | FSR-CD 314
Chet Baker With Kenny Burrell | Baby Breeze | Verve | 538328-2
Chick Webb And His Little Chicks | Jazz Drumming Vol.2(1937-1938) | Fenn Music | FJD 2702
Dicky Wells And His Orchestra | Django Reinhardt And His American Friends:Paris 1935-1937 | Memo Music | HDJ 4124
Earl Hines | Le Jazz En France Vol.15:Earl Hunes Paris Session 1965 | Pathe | 1552611
Fats Waller And His Rhythm | Fats Waller:The Complete Associated Transcription Sessions 1935-1939 | Jazz Unlimited | JUCD 2076
I'm Gonna Sit Right Down...The Early Years-Part 2(1935-1936) | Bluebird | 63 66640-2
Jack Payne And His BBC Dance Orchestra | Radio Nights | Saville Records | SVL 152 IMS
Louis Armstrong And His Orchestra | Louis Armstrong-Satchmo's Greatest Hits | RCA | CL 89799
Muggsy Spanier And His Ragtimers | Commodore Classics-Muggsy Spanier:Hot Horn 1944 | Commodore | 6.26167 AG
Ralph Sutton | Ralph Sutton At Cafe Des Copains | Sackville | SKCD2-2019
Randy Weston Trio | Zulu | Milestone | M 47045
Ray Noble And His Orchestra | The Radio Years | London | HMG 5019 AN
Retro Quartet | Jazz From The USSR | Mobile Fidelity | MFCD 890
Ruby Braff Quartet | Live At The Regattabar | Arbors Records | ARCD 19131
The Mills Brothers | Four Boys And A Guitar | CBS | CK 57713
Tommy Dorsey And His Orchestra | The Indispensable Tommy Dorsey Vol.2/4(1937.1938) | RCA | 2126406-2
Sweet Sue Just You-
Mel Tormé And Cleo Laine With The John Dankworth Orchestra | Nothing Without You | Concord | CCD 4515

Fats Waller And His Rhythm | I'm Gonna Sit Right Down...The Early Years-Part 2(1935-1936) | Bluebird | 63 66640-2

Sweet Surrender
Horace Silver Quintet | Silver's Serenade | Blue Note | 821288-2

Sweet Sweetie Dee
Jasper Van't Hof | At The Concertgebouw | Challenge | CHR 70010

Sweet Syncopation
Una Mae Carlisle With John Kirby And His Orchestra | TheComplete Una Mae Carlisle(1940-1942) And John Kirby(1941-1942) | RCA | ND 89484

Sweet Thing
Bola Sete Quintet | Bossa Nova | Original Jazz Classics | OJC 286(F 8349)

Sweet Tooth
Tom Beckham Quartet | Suspicions | Fresh Sound Records | FSNT 075 CD
Phil Grenadier Quintet | Sweet Transients | Fresh Sound Records | FSNT 093 CD

Sweet Transients
La Vienta | Forgotten Romance | Telarc Digital | CD 83380

Sweet William
Phil Woods Quartet With Orchestra Strings | Phil Woods/I Remember... | Gryphon | 6.23953 AT

Sweet Woman Blues
| In Pursuite Of The 13th Note | Talkin' Loud | 848493-2

Sweetest Gal In Town
Vince Giordano's Nighthawks | Qualty Shout | Stomp Off Records | CD 1260

Sweethearts On Parade
Cozy Cole's Big Seven | Body And Soul Revisited | GRP | GRP 16272
Down Home Jazz Band | Back To Bodega | Stomp Off Records | CD 1273
Joe Newman And His Orchestra | The Complete Joe Newman RCA-Victor Recordings(1955-1956):The Basie Days | RCA | 2122613-2
Lionel Hampton Sextet | Americans Swinging In Paris:Lionel Hampton | EMI Records | 539649-2
Le Jazz En France-Vol.6 | Pathe | 1727301
Louis Armstrong And His All Stars | Masters Of Jazz Vol.1 | RCA | NL 89723 DP
Louis Armstrong And His Orchestra | Louis Armstrong And His Big Band Vol.1-The Maturity | Black & Blue | BLE 59.225 2
Oscar Peterson Quintet With Orchestra | The Personal Touch | Pablo | 2312135-2
Roy Eldridge Quartet | The Best Of Roy Eldridge | Pablo | 2310857

Sweetie Cakes
Joe Newman Quintet | I Feel Like A New Man | Black Lion | BLCD 760905

Sweetie Dear
Dutch Swing College Band | Digital Date | Philips | 834087-2
Mr.Acker Bilk And His Paramount Jazz Band | New Orleans Days | Lake | LACD 36

Sweetie Pie
Fats Waller And His Rhythm | Breakin' The Ice-The Early Years Part 1(1934-1935) | Bluebird | 63 66618-2
Stan Getz Quartet | Stan Getz-The Complete Roost Sessions | EMI Records | 859622-2
Stan Getz-The Complete Roost Sessions | The Jazz Factory | JFCD 22839

Sweetness
Coleman Hawkins Quintet | Soul | Original Jazz Classics | OJC20 096-2(P 7149)

Sweetnin'
Kenny Burrell Quintet | Moonglow | Prestige | P 24106

Sweet-No Regrets
Marty Cook Group feat. Jim Pepper | Red,White,Black & Blue | Tutu Records | 888174-2*

Sweet-No Regrets Now
Count Basie And His Orchestra | Masters Of Jazz Vol.5 | RCA | NL 89530 DP

Sweets
The Indispensable Count Basie | RCA | ND 89758
Count Basie Octet | Victor Jazz History Vol.10:Kansas City(1935-71) | RCA | 2128564-2
Shelly Manne And His Men | Jimmy Giuffre:The Complete 1947-1953 Small Group Sessions,Vol.2 | Blue Moon | BMCD 1047

Sweety Cakes
Charles Earland Septet | I Ain't Jivin' I'm Jammin' | Muse | MCD 5481

Swimming In The Mist
Jazz Circle | Sun Games | Timeless | CD SJP 167

Swing & Be Funky
James Blood Ulmer Trio | Odyssey | CBS | 25602

Swing '36
| Soprano Summit At Thatchers | J&M Records | J&MCD 501

Swing '39
Charlie Byrd And The Washington Guitar Quartet | Charlie Byrd/The Washington Guitar Quartet | Concord | CCD 42014
Django Reinhardt And The Quintet Du Hot Club De France | Swingin' With Django | Pro-Arte | CDD 549
Quintet Du Hot Club De France | Django Reinhardt-Un Géant Sur Son Image | Melodie | 400052

Swing '41
Bireli Lagrene Group | Gipsy Project | Dreyfus Jazz Line | FDM 36626-2

Swing '42
Quintet Du Hot Club De France | L'Essentiel Django Reinhardt | EMI Records | 780671-2
Stephane Grappelli Quartet | Vintage 1981 | Concord | CCD 4169
Django Reinhardt And The Quintet Du Hot Club De France | Peche À La Mode-The Great Blue Star Sessions 1947/1953 | Verve | 835418-2

Swing '48
Django Reinhardt Portrait | Barclay | DALP 2/1939
Quintet Du Hot Club De France | Verve Jazz Masters 38:Django Reinhardt | Verve | 516931-2
Charlie Byrd Group | Byrd In The Wind | Original Jazz Classics | OJCCD 1086(RS 9449)

Swing '59
Charlie Byrd Quintet | Du Hot Club De Concord | Concord | CCD 4674
Titi Winterstein Sextet | Djinee Tu Kowa Ziro | Boulevard | BLD 501 CD

Swing A Lullaby
Django Reinhardt And The Quintet Du Hot Club De France | Swing De Paris | Arco | 3 ARC 110

Swing Benny Swing
Billie Holiday And Her Orchestra | Billie Holiday:The Quintessential Vol.8/9(1939-1942) | CBS | 477837-2

Swing Cars
Carlo Actis Dato Quartet | Bagdad Boogie | SPLASC(H) Records | CD H 380-2

Swing For Django
Helmut Nieberle-Helmut Kagerer | Flashes | Jardis Records | JRCD 20031
Traubeli Weiß Ensemble | Dreaming Of You | Edition Collage | EC 468-2

Swing For Mangala
Jermaine Landsberger Trio | Gypsy Feeling | Edition Collage | EC 516-2

Swing For Oscar
Henri Crolla Orchestra | Jazz In Paris:Henri Crolla-Notre Ami Django | EmArCy | 014062-2

Swing From Paris
Quintet Du Hot Club De France | Django Reinhardt Vol. 2 | Decca | 180021 AG

Swing Guitars
Bill Coleman Orchestra | Bill Coleman | Swing | SW 8402 IMS
Django Reinhardt And The Quintet Du Hot Club De France | Planet Jazz Sampler | Planet Jazz | 2152326-2
Swing De Paris | Arco | 3 ARC 110
Django Reinhardt Quintet | Masters Of Jazz Vol.4 | RCA | NL 70671 DP
Quintet Du Hot Club De France | Django Reinhardt-Un Géant Sur Son Image | Melodie | 400052

Swing High Swing Low
Ozzie Nelson And His Orchestra | The Uncollected:Ozzie Nelson, Vol.2 | Hindsight | HSR 189

Swing House
Gerry Mulligan Quartet | Gene Norman Presents The Original Gerry Mulligan Tentet And Quartet | GNP Crescendo | GNPD 56
Gerry Mulligan Quartet | Pacific Jazz | 300001(PJ 1)
Stan Kenton And His Orchestra | The Kenton Era | Creative World | ST 1030

Swing Is Here
Dick Hyman Orchestra | Swing Is Here | Reference Recordings | RR-72 CD
Gene Krupa's Swing Band | RCA Victor 80th Anniversary Vol.2:1930-1939 | RCA | 2668778-2

Swing Is The Thing
Ikey Robinson And His Windy City Five | Chicago 1935 | Gannet | CJR 1001

Swing It Easy
Hazy Osterawld And His Orchestra | Jazz In Switzerland 1930-1975 | Elite Special | 9544002/1-4

Swing Jack
Henry Mancini And His Orchestra | Combo! | RCA | 2147794-2

Swing Lightly
Duke Ellington And His Famous Orchestra | The Complete Duke Ellington-vol. 4 | CBS | CBS 88035

Swing Low
Ull Möck Trio | Drilling | Satin Doll Productions | SDP 1023-1 CD
Dizzy Gillespie Quartet | Dizzy Gillespie | LRC Records | CDC 9016(874389)

Swing Low Sweet Cadillac
Dizzy Gillespie Quintet | Dizzy's Diamonds-Best Of The Verve Years | Verve | 513875-2
The Roots Of Acid Jazz | Impulse(MCA) | IMP 12042
Swing Low, Sweet Cadillac | Impulse(MCA) | 951178-2
Dizzy Gillespie:Pleyel 53 | Vogue | 2115466-2
Dizzy Gillespie Sextet | The Champ | Savoy | SV 0170(MG 12047)
Albert Ayler Quartet | Goin' Home | Black Lion | BLCD 760197

Swing Low Sweet Chariot
Archie Shepp-Horace Parlan Duo | Swing Low | Plainisphare | PL 1267-73 CD
David & Roselyn Group | Gospel From The Streets Of New Orleans | Sound Of New Orleans | SONO 1033
Golden Gate Quartet | Best Of Golden Gate Quartet | Sonia | CD 77285
Hannibal Marvin Peterson Quintet | Hanibal In Antibes | Enja | 3011-2
Kid Ory's Creole Jazz Band | Kid Ory '44-'46 | American Music | AMCD-19
Louis Armstrong With Sy Oliver's Choir And Orchestra | Louis And The Good Book | Verve | 549593-2
Jazz Collection:Louis Armstrong | Laserlight | 24300
Mavis Staples-Lucky Peterson | Spirituals&Gospel:Dedicated To Mahalia Jackson | Verve | 533562-2
Mr.Acker Bilk And His Paramount Jazz Band | The Golden Years Of Revival Jazz,Vol.9 | Storyville | STCD 5514
New Orleans Days | Lake | LACD 36
Sonny Rollins Sextet With Rufus Harley | The Cutting Edge | Original Jazz Classics | OJC 468(M 9059)
Ted Heath And His Orchestra | Ted Heath And His Music-It's Swing Time | Magic | DAWE 82

Swing Out To Victory
Cootie Williams And His Orchestra | Duke Ellington's Trumpets | Black & Blue | BLE 59.231 2

Swing Party:
Warren Vaché Quintet | Horn Of Plenty | Muse | MCD 5524

Swing Song
Bill Perkins Quintet | Swing Spring | Candid | CCD 79752

Swing Spr
Art Farmer Quartet Feat Jim Hall | Live At The Half Note | Atlantic | 90666-1 TIS

Swing Spring
J.J.Johnson And His Orchestra | J.J.! | RCA | 2125727-2
Miles Davis All Stars | Miles Davis And The Modern Jazz Giants | Original Jazz Classics | OJC20 347-2(P 7150)
Miles Davis And The Modern Jazz Giants | Miles Davis And The Modern Jazz Giants | Prestige | P 7650
Wallace Roney Quintet | Crunchin' | Muse | MCD 5518

Swing That Music
Bobby Short With The Alden-Barrett Quintet | Swing That Music | Telarc Digital | CD 83317
Louis Armstrong And His All Stars | Louis Armstrong | Forlane | UCD 19002
Louis Armstrong And His Orchestra | Big Band Bounce & Boogie-Louis Armstrong:Struttin' With Some Barbecue | Affinity | AFS 1024
Mostly Blues | Ember | CJS 850
Peanuts Hucko Sextet | Tribute To Louis Armstrong And Benny Goodman | Timeless | TTD 541/42
David Schnitter Quartet | Goliath | Muse | MR 5153

Swing Time
Willie Lewis And His Entertainers | Le Jazz En France Vol.3 | Pathe | 1727271

Swing To Bop
Charlie Christian All Stars | Charlie Christian-Jazz Immortal/Dizzy Gillespie 1944 | Original Jazz Classics | OJCCD 1932-2(ES 548)
Minton's Playhouse All Stars | Charlie Christian:Swing To Bop | Dreyfus Jazz Line | FDM 36715-2
Jazz Legacy 64: Charlie Christian-1941 Live Sessions | Vogue | 500114

Swing Valse
Bireli Lagrene Ensemble | Routes To Django & Bireli Swing '81 | Jazzpoint | JP 1055 CD
Christian Escoude Octet | Gipsy Waltz | EmArCy | 838772-2

Swingin'
Clifford Brown-Max Roach Quintet | Brownie-The Complete EmArCy Recordings Of Clifford Brown | EmArCy | 838306-2
Kenny Burrell Quintet | Swingin' | Blue Note | GXK 8155

Swingin' At Newport
Count Basie And His Orchestra | Count Basie At Newport | Verve | 2304414 IMS

Swingin' At The Daisy Chain
Roy Eldridge And His Orchestra | At The Arcadia Ballroom New York | Jazz Anthology | JA 5149

Swingin' Back
Cootie Williams And His Orchestra | Cootie In Hi-Fi | RCA | NL 89811

Swingin' In November
Benny Carter And His Orchestra | Aspects | Capitol | 852677-2

Swingin' In November(alt.take)
Sammy Price And His Bluesicians | Sammy Price:Blues & Boogie | Vogue | 2111509-2

Swingin' Machine
Mose Allison Quintet | That's Jazz Vol.19: Mose Allison | Atlantic | ATL 50249

Swingin' On Nothin'
Harold Land Septet | Black California | Savoy | SJL 2215 (801191)

Swingin' On The Moon
Louis Armstrong And His Orchestra | Armed Forces Radio Service 1943/1944 | Duke Records | D 1021

Swingin' On The State Line
The Ink Spots | If I Didn't Care | Pro-Arte | CDD 555

Swingin' On The Teagarden Gate
Louis Armstrong And His Orchestra | Louis Armstrong Vol.8:1941-1942 | Ambassador | CLA 1908

Swingin' Parisian Rhythm(Jazz Sur Saine)
Lowell Fulsom Band | Lowell Fulson | Chess | 427007

Swingin' Scotch
Coleman Hawkins Quartet | Today And Now | MCA | AS 34

Swingin' Shepherd Blues
Ella Fitzgerald With The Paul Weston Orchestra | Ella Fitzgerald-First Lady Of Song | Verve | 517898-2
Get Happy! | Verve | 523321-2
Herbie Mann Group With The Tommy McCook Band | Herbie Mann-Reggae | Atlantic | ATL 50053
Moe Koffman Quartet | Moe Koffman 1967 | Just A Memory | JAS 9505-2

Swingin' The Berrys
Sammy Price Quintet | Le Jazz En France Vol.14:Boogie Woogie A La Parisienne | Pathe | 1552601

Swingin' The Blues
Count Basie And His Orchestra | Count Basie-Basie's Basement | RCA | ???
From Spiritual To Swing | Vanguard | VCD 169/71
Jazz Drumming Vol.2(1937-1938) | Fenn Music | FJD 2702
Count Basie,His Instrumentals & Rhyhtm | Victor Jazz History Vol.10:Kansas City(1935-71) | RCA | 2128564-2
Danny Moss Meets Buddha's Gamblers | A Swingin' Affair | Nagel-Heyer | CD 034
Dempsey Wright Quintet | The Wright Approach | Fresh Sound Records | FSR 501(Andex S 3006)
Johnny Otis And His Orchestra | Spirit Of The Black Territory Bands | Arhoolie | CD 384
Shorty Rogers And His Orchestra | Shorty Rogers Courts The Count | RCA | 2132337-2
Zoot Sims Quartet | Zoot Sims:The Complete 1944-1954 Small Group Sessions(Master Takes),Vol.2 | Blue Moon | BMCD 1039

Swingin' The Toreador
Fats Waller And His Rhythm | The Classic Years In Digital Stereo: Fats Waller And His Rhythm | CDS Records Ltd. | RPCD 315(CD 684)

Swingin' Till The Girls Come Home
Eddie Davis Trio + Joe Newman | Countin' With Basie | Vogue | 500118
Lambert, Hendricks And Bavan | At Basin Street East | RCA | 2125756-2
Oscar Peterson Trio | Compact Jazz: Oscar Peterson Plays Jazz Standards | Verve | 833283-2

Swingin' Uptown
Tanzorchester Der Original Teddies | International Schlager & In Mood mit Teddy Stauffer's Original Teddies | Elite Special | 9522003

Swingin' With Daddy-O
Louis Jordan And His Tympany Five | Five Guys Named Moe | Bandstand | BDCD 1531
Sal Salvador All-Star Quartet | Juicy Lucy | Bee Hive | BH 7009

Swingin' With Django
Little Brother Montgomery's Quintet | New Orleans To Chicago:The Forties | Gannet | CJR 1002

Swinging At The Sugar Bowl
The Hot Club Swing Stars | Le Jazz En France Vol.13:Alix Combelle 1937-1940(Tome 1) | Pathe | 1552591

Swinging For Mezz
The Basie Alumni | Swinging For The Count | Candid | CCD 79724

Swinging For The Count
Teddy Charles And His Orchestra | Something New, Something Blue | Fresh Sound Records | LSP 15623(CBS CL 1388)

Swinging In A Cocoanut Tree
Slim Gaillard And His Flat Foot Floogie Boys | Slim And Slam Vol.2 | Tax | m- 8043

Swinging Mood
Hal McIntyre And His Orchestra | The Uncollected:Hal McIntyre | Hindsight | HSR 172

Swinging On A Star
Oscar Peterson Trio | At Zardis' | Pablo | 2CD 2620118
Rosemary Clooney With The Scott Hamilton Quintet | Rosie Sings Bing | Concord | CJ 60

Swinging Shepherd Blues
Oscar Peterson Quintet With Orchestra | The Personal Touch | Pablo | 2312135-2

Swinging St. Fu
Joscho Stephan Group | Swinging Strings | Acoustic Music Records | 319.1195.2

Swinging The Blues
Count Basie And His Orchestra | Big Band Bounce & Boggie:Swingin' The Blues | Affinity | AFS 1010

Swinging The Samba
Horace Silver Quintet | Horace Silver Retrospective | Blue Note | 495576-2
Fats Waller And His Rhythm And His Orchestra | Welcome To Jazz: Fats Waller | Koch Records | 321 984 D1

Swinging Tom Tom(incomplete)
Brocksi-Quintett | Drums Boogie | Bear Family Records | BCD 15988 AH

Swinging Tom Tom(incomplete-2)
Berry Lipman Orchestra | Easy Listening Vol.1 | Sonia | CD 77280

Swinging With Rudolph
Lionel Hampton Quintet | You Better Know It | Impulse(MCA) | IMP 12972

Swingo
Trio Larose | Debut | Jazz 'n' Arts Records | JNA 0802
Jason Rebello Group | Keeping Time | Novus | 2112904-2

Swingtime In Springtime
Django Reinhardt And The Quintet Du Hot Club De France | Django Reinhardt:Djangology | EMI Records | 780659-2

Swingtime In The Rockies
Benny Goodman And His Orchestra | 1938 Carnegie Hall Concert | CBS | 450983-2
The Indispensable Benny Goodman Vol.1/2:Birth Of A Big Band | RCA | NL 89755 (809180)
The Big 18 | More Live Echoes Of The Swinging Bands | RCA | 2113033-2

Swingtime!
Franck Band | Liebeslieder | Jazz Haus Musik | JHM 35 CD

Swirls
Willy Bischof Jazztet | Swiss Air | Jazz Connaisseur | JCCD 9523-2

Swiss Air
Steve Lacy Quintet | The Way | Hat Art | CD 6154(2)

Switch Blade
Yaya 3 | Yaya 3 | Loma | 936248277-2
Ellington/Mingus/Roach Trio | Money Jungle | Blue Note | 538227-2

Switch Blade(alt.take)
Howard Alden-Dan Barrett Quintet | The A.B.Q Salutes Buck Clayton | Concord | CCD 4395

Switch-A-Roo
Warne Marsh Quartet | Star Highs | Criss Cross | Criss 1002

Syanthesia
Dan Gottshall Group | The Golem Shuffle | Timbre | TRCD 002

Syeeda's Song Flute
Art Taylor Quintet | A.T.'s Delight | Blue Note | 868852-0
John Coltrane Quartet | Giant Steps | Atlantic | 8122-75203-2
The Art Of John Coltrane - The Atlantic Years | Atlantic | SD 2-313

Syeeda's Song Flute(alt.take)
Giant Steps | Atlantic | 8122-75203-2
Roosevelt Sykes | The Honeydripper | Queen-Disc | 055

Sykesism
Om | Kirikuki | Japo | 60012 IMS

Sykiyaki
Jonas Knutsson Group | Flower In The Sky | ACT | 9248-2

Sylvan Swizzle
Barbara Dennerlein | Jazz Live Auf Der Böhm | Böhm Records | 65141 IMS

Sylvia
Sonny Criss Quintet | At The Crossroad | Fresh Sound Records | 252962-1(Peacock PLP 91)

Symmetry
Ron McClure Quartet | Pink Cloud | Naxos Jazz | 86002-2

Sympathy
Keith Jarrett Trio | The Mourning Of A Star | Atlantic | 8122-75355-2
Mark Isham-Peter Van Hooke Duo | Vapor Drawings | Windham Hill | TA-C- 1027

Symphonette
Tadd Dameron Sextet | Fats Navarro:The 1946-1949 Small Group Sessions(Studio Recordings-Master Takes),Vol.3 | Blue Moon | BMCD 1018

Symphonette(alt.master)
Tadd Dameron Septet | Fats Navarro/Tadd Dameron:Complete Blue Note & Capitol Sessions | Definitive Records | DRCD 11191
Symphonic Raps
Carroll Dickerson's Savoyagers | Jazz Classics In Digital Stereo: Louis Armstrong | CDS Records Ltd. | REB 597
Symphonie in B-Dur(Schubert)
David Friesen | Paths Beyond Tracing | Steeplechase | SCCD 31138
Symphony In Black:
Clifford Jordan Group | Clifford Jordan...Remembering Me-Me | Muse | MR 5105
Symphony No.1(Titan-3rd Movement)
Uri Caine Group | Urlicht/Primal Light | Winter&Winter | 910004-2
Symphony No.2(Resurrection-Andante Moderato)-
Urlicht/Primal Light | Winter&Winter | 910004-2
Symphony No.2(Resurrection-Primal Light)
NDR Radio Philharmonic Orchestra | Colossus Of Sound | Enja | ENJ-9460 2
Symphony No.4
Uri Caine Group | Urlicht/Primal Light | Winter&Winter | 910004-2
Symphony No.5(Adagietto)
Gunter Hampel Duo | The Music Of Gunter Hampel | Birth | 003
Syn
Cannonball Adderley Sextet | Coast To Coast | Milestone | M 47039
Synapsis-
Manhattan New Music Project | Mood Swing | Soul Note | 121207-2
Synchronicity
Michael Schiefel | I Don't Belong | Traumton Records | 4433-2
Tomato Kiss | Tomato Kiss | Nabel Records:Jazz Network | CD 4624
Walter Norris-Aladar Pege | Synchronicity | Enja | 3035 (807496)
Synchronicity(I)
Christof Lauer-Jens Thomas | Shadows In The Rain | ACT | 9297-2
Synchronicity(II)
David Eyges Quartet | The Captain | Chiaroscuro | CR 191
Syncopate
Milt Buckner Quintet | Organ | Jazz Anthology | JA 5178
Syndrome
Open Circle | Slave To The Sea | SPLASC(H) Records | H 130
Syndrome-
Dave Weckl Band | Synergy | Stretch Records | SCD 9022-2
Synthetic Blues
Engelbert Wrobel-Chris Hopkins-Dan Barrett Sextet | Harlem 2000 | Nagel-Heyer | CD 082
Synthetic Love
Kurt Rosenwinkel Quintet | The Enemies Of Energy | Verve | 543042-2
Synthetics
Lanfranco Malaguti Trio | Synthetismos | SPLASC(H) Records | H 179
Syotanka
Barney Wilen Quartet | French Ballads | IDA Record | 014 CD
Syracuse
The Danish Radio Jazz Orchestra | Nice Work | dacapo | DCCD 9446
Syretha's Gift
Jacques Loussier Trio | Jacques Loussier Trio Plays Debussy | Telarc Digital | CD 83511
Syster Glas
Michael Brecker Group | Michael Brecker | Impulse(MCA) | 950113-2
Syzgy
Chet Baker Quintet | Peace | Enja | ENJ-4016 2
Syzygies
Steve Coleman-Dave Holland | Phase Space | DIW | DIW 865 CD
Szivarvany(for Attila Zoller)
Radu Malfatti-Stephan Wittwer Duo | Thrumblin' Malfatti-Wittwer | FMP | 0350
T & S
Cecil Taylor | Fly! Fly! Fly! | MPS | 68263
'T Was Da Nite
Clare Fischer And His Orchestra | 'T Was Only Yesterday | Discovery | DS 798 IMS
T(h)ree
Bobo Stenson Trio | Serenity | ECM | 1740/41(543611-2)
T.
Ornette Coleman Quartet | Beauty Is A Rare Thing:Ornette Coleman-The Complete Atlantic Recordings | Atlantic | 8122-71410-2
T. & T.
Phil Sunkel's Jazz Band | Every Morning I Listen To..Phil Sunkel's Jazz Band | Fresh Sound Records | 252279-1(ABC-Paramount 136)
T.And S.
Champion Jack Dupree Quintet | Blues Power No.8:Champion Jack Dupree - Blues From The Gutter | Atlantic | 40526
T.B. Blues
Sippie Wallace With Axel Zwingenberger | An Evening With Sippie Wallace | Vagabond | VRCD 8.86006
Sonny Boy Williamson Group | King Of The Blues Harmonica | Black & Blue | BLE 59.251 2
T.B.C.(Terminal Baggage Claim)
Humair-Jeanneau-Texier | Up Date 3.3 | Label Bleu | LBLC 6530(882973)
T.H.-
Intergalactic Maiden Ballet,The | The Intergalactic Maiden Ballet | ITM Records | ITM 1457
T.J.
Tiziana Ghiglioni Trio | Spellbound | yvp music | CD 3058
T.K. On A Mission
Dave Grusin Group | Migration | GRP | GRP 95922
T.K.O.
Sarah Jane Morris Group | Blue Valentine | Ronnie Scott's Jazz House | JHCD 038
T.N.T.
Gene DiNovi Trio | Live At The Montreal Bistro | Candid | CCD 79726
Keith Nichols And The Cotton Club Orchestra | Henderson Stomp | Stomp Off Records | CD 1275
T.N.T.(Twelth Night Tango)
Rob McConnell & The Boss Brass | Live In Digital | Seabreeze | CDSB 106(881884)
T.On A White Horse
Jack Ranger | Piano Blues Vol.1-The Twenties(1923-1930) | Story Of Blues | CD 3511-2
T.T.T.
Bill Evans Trio | The Complete Fantasy Recordings | Fantasy | 9FCD 1012-2
Re: Person I Knew | Original Jazz Classics | OJCCD 749-2(F 9608)
Tome XX | Natura Morte | Jazz Haus Musik | JHM 32
T.T.T.(Twelve Tone Tune)
Bill Evans Trio | The Complete Fantasy Recordings | Fantasy | 9FCD 1012-2
The Tokyo Concert | Original Jazz Classics | OJCCD 345-2
Bill Evans Live In Tokyo | CBS | 481265-2
Enrico Pieranunzi Trio | Deep Down | Soul Note | 121121-2
T.V.
Nueva Manteca | Varadero Blues | Timeless | CD SJP 318
T.V. Special
Big Joe Turner With The Count Basie Orchestra | Flip Flop And Fly | Original Jazz Classics | OJCCD 1053-2(2310937)
T.V.Mama
Big Joe Turner With The Milt Buckner Trio | Texas Style | Black & Blue | BLE 59.547 2
Joe Turner With Band | Great Rhythm & Blues-Vol.4 | Bulldog | BDL 1003
T.V.Time
Count Basie And His Orchestra | Count Down | Jazz Society(Vogue) | 670503
Taabo Taabo
Al Di Meola Group | Orange And Blue | Inak | 700802
Tabarka
Dave Valentine Group | Jungle Garden | GRP | GRP 95232
Tabla Solo
Paul Horn Group | Paul Horn In India | Blue Note | 84551
Table D'Hote
Konstantin Wienstroer-Voit Lange-Felix Elsner | Unfinished Business | Green House Music | CD 1005
Table Talk-
Tristan Honsinger Quintet | Map Of Moods | FMP | CD 76
Taboo
Art Tatum | Art Tatum-The Complete Pablo Solo Masterpieces | Pablo | 7 PACD 4404-2
The Tatum Solo Masterpieces Vol.7 | Pablo | 2310792
Dizzy Gillespie Quintet | Talking Verve:Dizzy Gillespie | Verve | 533846-2
Dorothy Ashby-Frank Wess Quartet | In A Minor Groove | Prestige | PCD 24120-2(P 7140/NJ 8209)
Joe Turner Trio | Joe Turner | Black & Blue | BLE 233031
Stan Kenton And His Orchestra | By Request Vol.4 | Creative World | ST 1064
Frank Newton And His Cafe Society Orchestra | Frankie's Jump | Affinity | CD AFS 1014
Tabu
Johnny Smith Quintet | Moonlight In Vermont | Roulette | 300016
Johnny Smith-Stan Getz Quintet | Stan Getz-The Complete Roost Sessions | The Jazz Factory | JFCD 22839
Tabu Jump
Kusuma Sari(Sading) | Gamelan Batel Wayang Ramayana | CMP Records | CMP CD 3003
Tabular
Trilok Gurtu Group | Living Magic | CMP Records | CMP CD 50
Tacker Herranom-
Charles Earland Quartet | In The Pocket... | Muse | MR 5240
Tacot Blues
Marty Paich Octet | Marty Paich Octet | Fresh Sound Records | FSR 598(GNP 21)
Tact
Bruce Ditmas Trio | Aeray Dust | Chiaroscuro | CR 195
Tadd
Fats Navarro With The Tadd Dameron Band | Fats Navarro Featured With The Tadd Dameron Band | Milestone | M 47041
Taddlin' Awhile
Andy LaVerne | Tadd's Delight-Andy LaVerne Plays Tadd Dameron | Steeplechase | SCCD 31375
Tadd's Delight
Chet Baker Quintet | Chet Baker Plays & Sings | West Wind | WW 2108
Sonny Clark Trio | Sonny Clark Trio | Blue Note | 533774-2
Steve Kuhn Trio | Porgy | Jazz City | 660.53.012
Sonny Clark Trio | The Art Of The Trio | Blue Note | GXK 8157
Tadd's Delight (alt.take)
The Art Of The Trio | Blue Note | 300207(3069)
Taglioni
Charles Lloyd Quartet | Charles Lloyd In Europe | Atlantic | 7567-80788-2
Tagore
Arild Andersen Quartet | A Molde Concert | ECM | 1236
Tahiti
Milt Jackson Quintet | Milt Jackson | Blue Note | 81509
Stan Tracey Trio | Laughin' And Scratchin' | Ronnie Scott's Jazz House | JHAS 608
Tahitian Pearl
Kenny Dorham Quintet | The Bopmasters | MCA | IA 9337/2 (801647)
Tahun Bahu
Boury | Moderne Zeiten-Musik Und Tanz | Jazz Haus Musik | JHM 11
Tai Chi Chai Tea
Mose Allison Quintet | Ever Since The World Ended | Blue Note | 748015-2
Tai-Chi
Robin Eubanks Group | Different Perspectives | JMT Edition | 834424-2
Taiga
Cornelius Claudio Kreusch | Piano Moments | Take Twelve On CD | TT 007-2
Walt Dickerson-Pierre Dorge | Landscape With Open Door | Steeplechase | SCS 1115
Tail Feathers
Glenn Miller And The Army Air Force Band | This Is Glenn Miller And The Army Air Force Band | RCA | NL 89217 DP
Tailgate
George Girard And His Dixieland All Stars | Sounds Of New Orleans Vol.6 | Storyville | STCD 6013
Tailgate Ramble
Teddy Buckner And His Dixieland Band | In Concert At The Dixieland Jubilee | Dixieland Jubilee | DJ 503
Tailor Made
Hal McKusick Quartet | East Coast Jazz Series No.8 | Fresh Sound Records | FSR 2021(Bethlehem BCP 16)
Tailspin Blues
Mound City Blue Blowers | Victor Jazz History Vol.3:White Chicago | RCA | 2128557-2
Tai-Min
Johannes Enders Quartet | Kyoto | Organic Music | ORGM 9726
Tainish
Noble Sissle And His Orchestra | Big Band Bounce And Boogie:The Thirties-Sidney Bechet | Affinity | AFS 1025
Tain't Me
Eddie Heywood Sextet | Commodore Classics-Eddie Heywood:The Biggest Little Band In The Forties | Commodore | 6.25493 AG
Johnny Hartman And His Orchestra | Unforgettable | Impulse(MCA) | IMP 11522
T'Ain't No Need
Chris Barber's Jazz Band | Ottilie Patterson With Chris Barber's Jazzband 1955-1958 | Lake | LACD 30
Tain't No Sin
Benny Goodman And His Orchestra | Planet Jazz:Benny Goodman | Planet Jazz | 2152054-2
Tain't No Use
The Birth Of Swing | Bluebird | ND 90601(3)
Herbie Steward Quintet | Al Haig Meets The Master Saxes Vol.3 | Spotlite | SPJ 143
Maxine Sullivan With The Keith Ingham Sextet | Maxine Sullivan Sings The Music Of Burton Lane | Mobile Fidelity | MFCD 773
Tain't Nobody's Bizness But My Own
Angela Brown | The Voice Of Blues | Schubert Records | SCH- 105
Tain't Nobody's Bizness If I Do
Billie Holiday With The Buster Harding Orchestra | Jazz Gallery:Billie Holiday Vol.1(1933-49) | RCA | 2119542-2
Ella Fitzgerald With The Tommy Flanagan Trio | Ella-At The Montreux Jazz Festival 1975 | Original Jazz Classics | OJC20 789-2(2310751)
Ernestine Anderson With The Hank Jones Trio | Hello Like Before | Concord | CCD 4031
Helen Humes And Her All Stars | 'Tain't Nobody's Biz-ness If I Do | Original Jazz Classics | OJCCD 453-2
Jay McShann Quintet | Roll' Em | Black & Blue | BLE 233022
Jimmy Rushing And His Orchestra | Five Feet Of Soul | Roulette | 581830-2
Jimmy Witherspoon And His Trio | Jimmy Witherspoon & Panama Francis' Savoy Sultans | Black & Blue | BLE 59.177 2
Mary Stallings With The Gene Harris Quartet | I Waited For You | Concord | CCD 4620
Tain't Nobody's Bizness If I Do(take 3)
Bunny Berigan And His Orchestra | Bunny Berigan | Atlantis | ATS 7
Tain't So Honey 'Tain't So
Dick Hyman-Louis Mazetier Duo | Barrel Of Keys | Jazz Connaisseur | JCCD 0140-2
Jack Teagarden And His Orchestra | Think Well Of Me | Verve | 557101-2
Tain't What You Do (It's How You Do It)
Chick Webb And His Orchestra | Big Band Bounce & Boogie:In The Groove | Affinity | AFS 1007
Ella Fitzgerald With The Chick Webb Orchestra | Let's Get Together | Laserlight | 17003
George Wein And The Newport All Stars | Swing That Music | CBS | CK 53317
Taj
Badiane | Flavours | Acoustic Music Records | 319.1071.2
Ta-Ka-Ta-Ki-Ta
Antonio Carlos Jobim Group | Tide | A&M Records | 393031-2
Take A Bebop
Tacuma-Puschnig Duo | Gemini-Gemini | ITM-Pacific | ITMP 970063
Take A Flat Map...
Mighty Joe Young Blues Band | Bluesy Josephine | Black & Blue | BLE 59.521 2
Take A Little Time To Smile
| Boogie Woogie King | Black & Blue | BLE 233520
Take A Little Walk With Me
Robert Lockwood Jr. | 15 Years In The Mississippi Delta 1926-1941 | Yazoo | YAZ 1038
Take A Long Walk
Aretha Franklin With The Bob Mersey Orchestra | Aretha Sings The Blues | CBS | 26676-2
Take A Love Song
Call Boys Inc. | Call Boys Inc. | Moers Music | 02068 CD
Take A Trip With Me
Christoph Spendel-Michael Sagmeister | So Near So Far | L+R Records | LR 40024
Take Care
John Stevens Sextet | Freebop | Affinity | AFF 101
Take Care Of Business
Nina Simone With Orchestra | Nina Simone-The 60s Vol.1: Ne Me Quitte Pas | Mercury | 838543-2 PMS
Take Eight
Vital Information | Live Around The World Where We Come From Tour '98-'99 | Intuition Records | INT 3296-2
Harlan Leonard & His Rockers | Victor Jazz History Vol.10:Kansas City(1935-71) | RCA | 2128564-2
Take Five
Charles Bell Trio | In Concert | Fresh Sound Records | FSR 544(Gateway LP 7012)
Dave Brubeck Quartet | The Dave Brubeck Quartet At Carnegie Hall | CBS | 66234
The Great Concerts | CBS | 462403-2
The Dave Brubeck Selection | CBS | 467279-2
Collection Dave Brubeck | Atlantic | ATL 20269
Dave Brubeck Quartet With Gerry Mulligan | The Last Set At Newport | Atlantic | 7567-81382-2
Dave Brubeck Trio & Gerry Mulligan | Live At The Berlin Philharmonie | CBS | 67261
Deborah Henson-Conant Trio | 'Round The Corner | Laika Records | LK 87-203
George Benson Group | George Benson In Concert-Carnegie Hall | CTI | ZK 44167
Kenny Blake Group | Interior Design | Heads Up Records | 889010
Klaus Kreuzeder & Willi Herzinger | Sax As Sax Can | Trick Music | TM 8712 CD
Manhattan Jazz Orchestra | Moritat | Sweet Basil | 660.55.008
Robert Hohner Persussion Ensemble | The Gamut | dmp Digital Music Productions | CD 505
Take Heart
Dick Charlesworth And His City Gents | The Golden Years Of Revival Jazz,Vol.6 | Storyville | STCD 5511
Take Her To Jamaica
André Previn And His Pals | Pal Joey | Original Jazz Classics | OJCCD 637-2(S 7543)
Take It From Me
Neville Dickie-Louis Mazetier | Dickie-Mazetier:Harlem Strut | Stomp Off Records | CD 1302
Take It From The Top
Humphrey Lyttelton And His Band | Take It From The Top-A Dedication To Duke Ellington | Black Lion | BLCD 760516
Take It On Up
Toots Thielemans-Eugen Cicero Quartet | Nice To Meet You | Intercord | 145034
Take It!
Ernst-Ludwig Petrowsky Quartet | Synopsis/DDR | FMP | 0240
Take Love
Bobby Short With The Alden-Barrett Quintet | Duke Ellington...Swings! | Telarc Digital | CD 83429
Take Love Easy
Ella Fitzgerald-Joe Pass Duo | Take Love Easy | Pablo | 2310702
Joe Pass:A Man And His Guitar | Original Jazz Classics | OJCCD 8806-2
Lena Horne With The Lennie Hayton Orchestra | Lena Goes Latin | DRG | MRS 510 IMS
Take Me Back
Archie Edwards | Blues Live '82-American Folk Blues Festival | L+R Records | LS 42052
Take Me Back Baby
Nancy Harrow And The Buck Clayton All Stars | Wild Women Don't Have The Blues | Candid | CCD 79008
Whispering Smith | The Blues Vol.3 | Big Bear | 156400
Take Me Back To New Orleans
Mike Westbrook Concert Band | Release | Deram | 844851-2
Take Me Girl, I'm Ready
Louie Bellson And His Jazz Orchestra | Air Mail Special-A Salute To The Big Band Masters | Limelight | 820824-2 IMS
Take Me Home
Ray Charles With Orchestra | What Have I Done To Their Songs | London | 6.23173 AF
Take Me In Your Arms
Stan Kenton And His Orchestra | Mellophonium Magic | Status | CD 103(882199)
Take Me Out To The Ballgame
Temperance Seven | Pasadena & The Lost Cylinders-Music From The Archives | Lake | LACD 77
Take Me There
Astrud Gilberto With Joao Donato And His Orchestra | Silver Collection: The Astrud Gilberto Album | Verve | 823451-2 PMS
Take Me To Aruanda
Astrud Gilberto With Orchestra | The Shadow Of Your Smile | Verve | 2304540
Eddie Condon And The Chicagoans | Chicago And All That Jazz! | Verve | MV 2535 IMS
Take Me To The River
Jabbo Smith And His Rhythm Aces | Big Band Bounce & Boogie-Jabbo Smith:Sweet 'N' Low Down | Affinity | AFS 1029
Philadelphia Jerry Ricks | True Blues | Traditional Line | TL 1314
Take Me To The Water
Nina Simone With Hal Mooney's Orchestra | Verve Jazz Masters Vol.58:Nina Simone Sings Nina | Verve | 529867-2
Nina Simone With Orchestra | Nina Simone-The 60s Vol.3:Work Song | Mercury | 838545-2 PMS
Take My Hand Precious Lord
Magnolia Jazzband & Lillian Boutté | New Orleans Gospel In Molde Kirke | Herman Records | HJCD 1004
Take Off
Miles Davis Quartet | Miles Davis Vol.1 | Blue Note | 532610-2
Svend Asmussen Quartet | Fit As A Fiddle | dacapo | DCCD 9429
Take Off Blues
Al Sears Quintet | Swing's The Thing | Original Jazz Classics | OJCCD 838-2(SV 2018)
Take Off Road
Ray Charles And His Orchestra | Love & Peace | London | 6.23662 AO
Take Ten
Paul Desmond Orchestra | Late Night Sax | CBS | 487798-2
Paul Desmond Quartet | Planet Jazz:Paul Desmond | Planet Jazz | 2152061-2
Planet Jazz Sampler | Planet Jazz | 2152326-2
Paul Desmond-Greatest Hits | RCA | CL 89809 SF
Take Ten | RCA | 63661462

Paul Desmond-Gerry Mulligan Quartet | The Ballad Of Paul Desmond | RCA | 21429372
Zoot Sims-Bucky Pizzarelli Duo | Summum | Ahead | 33752

Take The 'A' Train
Billy Strayhorn | The Peaceful Side Of Billy Strayhorn | Capitol | 852563-2
Brocksi-Quintett | Drums Boogie | Bear Family Records | BCD 15988 AH
Buddy Rich And His Orchestra | Buddy Rich Presented by Lionel Hampton | Jazz Classics | CD CA 36014
Caterina Valente With The Count Basie Orchestra | Caterina Valente '86 | Mobile Fidelity | MFCD 889
Clifford Brown-Max Roach Quintet | Study In Brown | EmArCy | 814646-2
Brownie-The Complete EmArCy Recordings Of Clifford Brown | EmArCy | 838306-2
Coleman Hawkins And Friends | Bean Stalkin' | Pablo | 2310933-2
Dave Brubeck Quartet | Jazz Goes To College | CBS | CK 45149
Duke Ellington And His Famous Orchestra | Planet Jazz:Duke Ellington | Planet Jazz | 2152053-2
Planet Jazz Sampler | Planet Jazz | 2152326-2
Duke Ellington:The Blanton-Webster Band | Bluebird | 21 13181-2
Planet Jazz:Big Bands | Planet Jazz | 2169649-2
Victor Jazz History Vol.12:Ellingtonia | RCA | 2135731-2
Duke Ellington And His Orchestra | Ellington At Basin Street:The Complete Concert | Music & Arts | CD 908
Yale Concert | Fantasy | F 9433
Duke Ellington And His Orchestra feat. Paul Gonsalves | Original Jazz Classics | OJCCD 623-2
Live At The 1956 Stratford Festival | Music & Arts | CD 616
Swing | Stereoplay-CD | CD 697042
100 Years Duke | Laserlight | 24906
Highlights From The Duke Ellington Centennial Edition | RCA | 2663672-2
The Story Of Jazz Piano | Laserlight | 24653
Highlights From The Duke Ellington Centennial Edition | RCA | 2663672-2
Big Band Bounce And Boogie:Classic Transcriptions-Duke Ellington | Affinity | AFS 1032
The Greatest Jazz Concert In The World | Pablo | 2625704-2
From The Blue Note, Chicago | Jazz Anthology | JA 5197
Duke Ellington -Carnegie Hall Concert | Ember | 800851-370(EMBD 2001)
Ella Fitzgerald And Duke Ellington:Cote D'Azure Concerts on Verve | Verve | 539033-2
Soul Call | Verve | 539785-2
Duke Ellington: The Champs-Elysees Theater January 29-30th,1965 | Laserlight | 36131
Duke Ellington At The Alhambra | Pablo | PACD 5313-2
Hot Summer Dance | Red Baron | 469285-2
Duke Ellington At Tanglewood Vol.1 | Queen-Disc | 049
Duke Ellington's Jazz Group | Duke Ellington's Jazz Group | Jazz Anthology | JA 5145
Ella Fitzgerald And Her Quintet | Ella In Hollywood-Recorded Live At The Crescendo | Verve | V 6-4052 IMS
Ella Fitzgerald With The Duke Ellington Orchestra | The Complete Ella Fitzgerald Song Books of Harold Arlen, Irving Berlin, Duke Ellington, George & Ira Gershwin, Jerome Kern, Johnny Mercer, Cole Porter And Rogers & Hart | Verve | 519832-2
Gerald 'Gerry' Wiggins | Maybeck Recital Hall Series Volume Eight | Concord | CCD 4450
Harry James And His Orchestra | The Golden Trumpet Of Harry James | London | 820178-2 IMS
Heinz Sauer Quartet With The NDR Big Band | NDR Big Band-Bravissimo | ACT | 9232-2
Heinz Von Hermann Jazz Ahead | A Standard Treatment | Mons Records | MR 874320
Jenny Evans And The Rudi Martini Quartet | At Loyd's | BELL Records | BLR 90004
Jo Jones Quartet | Our Man Papa Jo! | Denon Compact Disc | 38C38-7047
Joe Newman With The Ove Lind Quintet | Joe Newman At The Atlantic | Phontastic | NCD 8810
Jon Hendricks And Friends | Freddie Freeloader | Denon Compact Disc | CY-76302
Kristin Korb With The Ray Brown Trio And Guests | Introducing Kristin Korb | Telarc Digital | CD 83386
Lionel Hampton All Stars | For The Love Of Music | MoJazz | 530554-2
Maynard Ferguson Orchestra | Storm | ARG Jazz | 21374872
Michel Petrucciani | Michel Petrucciani:Concert Inédits | Dreyfus Jazz Line | FDM 36607-2
Oscar Peterson Trio | Oscar Peterson In Russia | Pablo | 2CD 2625711
Oscar Peterson Plays The Duke Ellington Song Book | Verve | 559785-2
Oscar Peterson Plays The Duke Ellington Song Book | Verve | 559785-2
Oscar Peterson With The Duke Ellington Orchestra | Oscar Peterson Plays Duke Ellington | Pablo | 2310966-2
Oscar Peterson-Jon Faddis Duo | Oscar Peterson & Jon Faddis | Original Jazz Classics | OJCCD 1036-2(2310743)
Paul Bley Trio | The Nearness Of You | Steeplechase | SCS 1246
Quadrant | A Celebration Of Duke | Original Jazz Classics | OJC 605(2312119)
Ran Blake | Duke Dreams/The Legacy Of Strayhorn-Ellington | Soul Note | SN 1027
Ray Bryant Trio | Ray Bryant Plays | Fresh Sound Records | FSR .529(Signature SM 6008)
Rex Allen's Swing Express | Keep Swingin' | Nagel-Heyer | CD 016
Rias Big Band | The Music Of Duke Ellington | Mons Records | MR 874306
Russ Freeman-Shelly Manne | One On One | Contemporary | CCD 14090-2
Sarah Vaughan With Orchestra | Compact Jazz: Sarah Vaughan | Mercury | 830699-2
Stuff Smith Quartet | Live At The Montmartre | Storyville | STCD 4142
Sun Ra & His Arkestra | Live At Montreux | Inner City | IC 1039 IMS
The New York Saxophone Quartet | An American Experience | Stash Records | ST 220 IMS
Yusef Lateef Quintet | Blues For The Orient | Prestige | P 24035
Zoot Sims-Bucky Pizzarelli Duo | Elegiac | Storyville | STCD 8238
| Barrelhouse Jazzband Plays Duke Ellington | L+R Records | LR 40026

Take The 'A' Train-
Charles Mingus Quartet | Live In Chateauvallon 1972 | France's Concert | FCD 134
On The Corner With The Philharmonic Orchestra,Würzburg | On The Corner feat. Benny Bailye | Mons Records | MR 874807
Oscar Peterson-Joe Pass Duo | Oscar Pterson Et Joe Pass A La Salle Pleyel | Pablo | 2CD 2625705
Live At Salle Pleyel, Paris | Pablo | 2625705

Take The 'A' Train(alt.take)
World Saxophone Quartet | Plays Duke Ellington | Nonesuch | 7559-79137-2
Duke Ellington And His Orchestra | Duke Ellington In Hamilton | Radiex Music | RDX-1000

Take The 'A' Train(rehersal take)
Ruby Braff-Buddy Tate With The Newport All Stars | Ruby Braff-Buddy Tate With The Newport All Stars | Black Lion | BLCD 760138

Take The 'A' Train(theme)
Duke Ellington And His Orchestra | At The Hurricane:Original 1943 Broadcasts | Storyville | STCD 8359
Live At Carnegie Hall 1964 Vol.2 | Nueva Records | JU 323
Way Low | Duke Records | D 1015

Take The Cake
Buddy Banks Sextet | Buddy Banks:The Complete Recordings 1945-1949 | Blue Moon | BMCD 6015

Take The Coltrane
David Fathead Newman Quintet | Chillin' | HighNote Records | HCD 7036
Don Sebesky Orchestra | Joyful Noise:A Tribute To Duke Ellington | RCA | 2663552-2

John Hicks-Ray Drummond | Two Of A Kind | Evidence | ECD 22017-2
Jon Lloyd Quartet | Four And Five | HatOLOGY | 537
Johnny Griffin-Steve Grossman Quintet | Johnny Griffin & Steve Grossman | Dreyfus Jazz Line | FDM 36615-2

Take The 'D' Train
Woody Herman And His Orchestra | In A Misty Mood | Jazz Society(Vogue) | 670509

Take The Eartrain
Robin Kenyatta Orchestra | Take The Heat Off Me | ITM-Pacific | ITMP 970069

Take The Rest
Louis Jordan Quintet | Jump 'N Jive | JSP Records | 1069

Take The Wess Trane
Helmut Kagerer/Helmut Nieberle | Wes Trane | Edition Collage | EC 453-2
Jeannie And Jimmy Cheatham & The Sweet Baby Blues Band | Back To The Neighborhood | Concord | CCD 4373

Take These Chains From My Heart
King Curtis Band | King Curtis-Blow Man Blow | Bear Family Records | BCD 15670 CI
Ray Charles With Orchestra | Ray Charles | London | 6.24034 AL

Take Three Parts Jazz
Teddy Charles New Directions Quartet With Booker Little And Booker Ervin | Jazz In The Garden At The Museum Of Modern Art | Fresh Sound Records | FSR-CD 0212

Take Twelve
Gottfried Böttger-Joe Penzlin Duo | Take Two | L+R Records | CDLR 40030

Take Your Pick
Mike Durham's West Jesmond Rhythm Kings | Shake 'Em Loose | Lake | LACD 45

Take Your Shoes Off Baby
Artie Shaw And His Orchestra | The Indispensable Artie Shaw Vol.3/4 | RCA | 2126414-2

Take-Off
Frank Gordon Sextet | Clarion Echoes | Soul Note | 121096-2
Zoot Sims-Joe Pass Duo | Blues For Two | Original Jazz Classics | 2310879 Digital

Takes My Breath Away
Louis Armstrong With Sy Oliver And His Orchestra | Ambassador Louis Armstrong Vol.18:Because Of You(1950-1953) | Ambassador | CLA 1918

Takes Two To Tango
Pearl Bailey With Orchestra | Pearl Bailey-The Best Of The Roulette Years | Roulette | CDP 796483-2

Takin' A Chance On Love
Harry Arnold Big Band | Big Band Classics 1957-58 | Dragon | DRLP 139/140
Nat King Cole With The Nelson Riddle Orchestra | The Piano Style Of Nat King Cole | Capitol | 781203-2
Zoot Sims Quintet | Zoot! | Original Jazz Classics | OJCCD 228-2(RLP 228)

Takin' Care O'Business
Lucky Thompson-Emmett Berry Quintet | Lucky Thompson | Swing | SW 8404 IMS

Takin' Care O'Business(alt.take)
Jim Snidero Quartet | Storm Rising | Ken Music | 660.56.006

Takin' It With Me
George Russell And His Sextet | At Beethoven Hall | MPS | 539084-2

Taking A Chance On Love
Charlie Shavers Quartet | Charlie Shavers 1960 | Jazz Anthology | JA 5131
Cy Coleman Trio | Cy Coleman | Fresh Sound Records | FSR 635(Seeco CELP 402)
Davide Petrocca Quartet | Move | Edition Musikat | EDM 026
Ella Fitzgerald And Her Famous Orchestra | Ella Fitzgerald:The Early Years-Part 2 | GRP | GRP 26232
Ella Fitzgerald With The Tommy Flanagan Quartet | Ella Fitzgerald:Newport Jazz Festival-Live at Carnegie Hall | CBS | C2K 66809
George Shearing | Favorite Things | Telarc Digital | CD 83398
Gerry Mulligan Tentette | The Birth Of The Cool Vol.2 | Capitol | 798935-2
Howard Rumsey's Lighthouse All-Stars | Sunday Jazz A La Lighthouse Vol.2 | Original Jazz Classics | OJCCD 972-2(S 2501)
Ian Shaw With Band | The Echo Of A Song | Ronnie Scott's Jazz House | JHCD 048
Lester Young Quartet | Pres And Teddy And Oscar | Verve | 2-2502 IMS
Ray Brown Trio | Bassface | Telarc Digital | CD 83340
Ronny Lang And His All-Stars | Basie Street | Fresh Sound Records | FSR-CD 0501
Sonny Stitt With The Bud Powell Trio | Genesis | Prestige | P 24044
Susannah McCorkle With The Frank Wess Quintet | I'll Take Romance | Concord | CCD 4491
Teddi King With Al Cohn And His Orchestra | Bidin' My Time | Fresh Sound Records | 14465 CD(RCA)

Taking A Chance On Love-
Ella Fitzgerald With The Tommy Flanagan Quartet | Newport Jazz Festival - Live At Carnegie Hall | CBS | CBS 68279

Taking A Chance On Love(alt.take)
Tal Farlow Trio | The Swinging Guitar Of Tal Farlow | Verve | 559515-2
Dizzy Gillespie Quintet | Jazz In Paris:Dizzy Gillespie-Cognac Blues | EmArCy | 014064-2

Taking To Myself
Dirty Butter | Memphis Jug Band Vol.2 | Frog | DGF 16

Takirari
Juxoli | Juxoli | Pannon Jazz/Classic | PJ 1009

Taktik
Charles Lloyd Quartet | Notes From Big Sur | ECM | 1465(511999-2)

Takur
Robin Holcomb Sextet | Larks,They Crazy | Sound Aspects | sas CD 026

Talam Mahalakshimi Tala 9,5 Brats
Ernst-Ludwig Petrowsky Trio | SelbDritt | FMP | 0890

Tale
Shorty Rogers And His Orchestra Feat. The Giants | Short Stops | RCA | NL 85917(2)

Tale Of An African Lobster
Chick Corea Electric Band | Inside Out | GRP | GRP 96012

Tale Of Saverio
John Goldsby Quartet | Tales Of The Fingers | Concord | CCD 4632

Tales
Andre Jaume Trio | Tales And Prophecies | Hat Art | 12 (2R12)

Tales For A Girl,12
Roger Girod-Peter A.Schmid | Windschief | Creative Works Records | CW CD 1027-2

Tales From Blackwood Forest
Chris Hinze Quartet | Wide And Blue | MRC | 066-45420

Tales Of Rumi
Aki Takase-Alexander von Schlippenbach | Piano Duets-Live In Berlin 93/94 | FMP | OWN-90002

Tales Of The Near Future(Clairvoyance)
Benny Carter With The Rutgers University Orchestra | Harlem Renaissance | Limelight | 844299-2 IMS

Tales Retold
Cecil Taylor Unit | Unit Structures | Blue Note | 784237-2

Tales(reprise)
Paul Wertico Trio | Don't Be Scared Anymore | Premonition | 790748-2

Talisman
Mike Nock | Talisman | Enja | 3071

Talk
Toshinori Kondo/Tristan Honsinger Group | This That And The Other | ITM Records | 0021

Talk 1
Jutta Glaser & Bernhard Sperrfechter | Little Girl Blue | Jazz 'n' Arts Records | JNA 0502

Talk 2
Little Girl Blue | Jazz 'n' Arts Records | JNA 0502

Talk 3
Little Girl Blue | Jazz 'n' Arts Records | JNA 0502

Talk 4
Al Haig Quartet | Al Haig Meets The Master Saxes Vol.3 | Spotlite | SPJ 143

Talk For Three
Mikhail Alperin's Moscow Art Trio | Prayer | JA & RO | JARO 4193-2

Talk For Trio
Hamburg Concert | JA & RO | JARO 4201-2
Andy Just Blues Band With Guests | Don't Cry | Crosscut | CCD 11044

Talk Stone
Dave Doran Group | Rhythm Voice | Plainisphare | PL 1267-109 CD

Talk To Me
Dave McKenna Quartet | No More Ouzo For Puzo | Concord | CCD 4365

Talk To Me Baby
Vince Weber | The Boogie Man | Rüssl Räckords | 062-29597

Talk To Me, Talk To Me
Hound Dog Taylor & The House Rockers | Natural Boogie | Sonet | 198044(SNTF 678)

Talk To You
J.B.Lenoir | J.B.Lenoir | Blues Classics(L+R) | CDLR 82001

Talk Together
The New Orleans Spiritualettes | I Believe | Sound Of New Orleans | SONO 6012

Talk With The Band
Mike Longo Septet | Talk With The Spirits | Pablo | 2310769

Talk(An Introduction)
Rahsaan Roland Kirk Sextet | Bright Moments | Rhino | 8122-71409-2

Talkin' About
Dave Stryker Quartet | Blue Degrees | Steeplechase | SCCD 31315

Talkin' About J.C.
Grooveyard Meets Roman Schwaller | Basic Instinct | Organic Music | ORGM 9701
Larry Young Quartet | Groove Street | Original Jazz Classics | OJCCD 1853-2

Talkin' About You, Cannon
Robert Pete Williams | Blues Masters Vol.1-Robert Pete Williams | Storyville | STCD 8001

Talkin' 'Bout You
Incognito | Positivity | Talkin' Loud | 518260-2

Talkin' To Myself
Thomas Faist Sextet | Gentle | Village | VILCD 1020-2

Talkin' To the Mirror
Chico Freeman Quartet | Tradition In Transition | Elektra | MUS K 52412

Talking 'Bout My Woman
Mississippi John Hurt | Today! | Vanguard | VMD 79220

Talking Hands
Brownie McGhee & Sonny Terry | Blues Is My Companion | Aves | 146508

Talking Hearts
Barrelhouse Jazzband | Talking Hot | L+R Records | CDLR 70002

Talking Round
Albert Collins Blues Band | Ice Cold Blues | Charly | CRB 1119

Talking Strings In Silver Grey
Lee Konitz-Karl Berger Duo | Seasons Change | Circle Records | RK 19-291079/19 IMS

Talking With Myself
Greg Tardy Band | Serendipity | Impulse(MCA) | 951258-2

Talking With Tom
Joel Futterman Quartet | Vision In Time | Silkheart | SHCD 125

Tall And Slim
Count Basie And His Orchestra | Basie Big Band | Pablo | 2310756-2

Tally Ho!
Count Basie And The Kansas City 7 | Count Basie And The Kansas City 7 | Impulse(MCA) | 951202-2

Tally-Ho Mr.Basie
Pierre Boussaguet Trio With Guy Lafitte | Charme | EmArCy | 538468-2

Talwin
Jo Jones-Milt Hinton | Percussion And Bass | Fresh Sound Records | FSR-CD 0204

Tamalpais
The New Oscar Pettiford Sextet | The New Oscar Pettiford Sextet | Original Jazz Classics | OJC 112(DLP 8)

Tamanco No Samba
Cal Tjader Sextet | Cuban Fantasy | Fantasy | FCD 24777-2

Tamanco No Samba(Samba Blim)
Alain Monnier Trio | Tribulat | Hat Art | 3505

Tamara
Pension Winnetou | Pension Winnetou | Moers Music | 02028

Tamburitza Boogie
Andy And The Bey Sisters | Andy Bey And The Bey Sisters | Prestige | PCD 24245-2

Tammy
The Three Sounds | Moods | Blue Note | 300420

Tampico
Stan Kenton And His Orchestra | The Early Years | Capitol | 166219-2

Tamzara(turkish folk material)
Chet Baker Quintet | Groovin' With The Chet Baker Quintet | Prestige | PR20 7460-2

Tan Gaugin
Big Al Sears And The Sparrows | Sear-iously | Bear Family Records | BCD 15668 AH

Tan Skin Lad
Loek Dikker Waterland Ensemble | Tan Tango | Waterland | WM 001

Tana
Sfogliare Albi | Tempo Per | yvp music | CD 3029

Tance Dance
Antonio Farao Quartet | Thorn | Enja | ENJ-9399 2

Tandem
Christmann-Schönenberg Duo | Topic | Ring | 01020

Taney County
Charlie Haden | Quartet West | Verve | 831673-2

Tang
Steve Coleman And Five Elements | World Expansion | JMT Edition | 834410-2

Tanga
Mario Bauzá And His Afro-Cuban Jazz Orchestra | Tanga | Messidor | 15819 CD

Tangara
Astor Piazzolla Group | Live at Cine Teatro Gran Rex De Buenos Aires | West Wind Latina | 2212 CD

Tangent A
Heinz Sauer Quintet | Lost Ends:Live at Alte Oper Frankfurt | free flow music | ffm 0594

Tangent B
Ekkehard Jost Quintet | Carambolage | View | VS 0028 IMS

Tangerine
Buddy Tate-Al Grey Quintet | Just Jazz | Reservoir | RSR CD 110(882634)
Dave Brubeck Quartet | The Great Concerts | CBS | 462403-2
The Dave Brubeck Selection | CBS | 467279-2
Dexter Gordon Quartet | Nights At The Keystone | Blue Note | BT 85112
Dexter Gordon Quintet | Dexter Gordon Birthday Celebration | Fantasy | FANCD 6082-2
Earl Hines Trio | Hines '74 | Black & Blue | BLE 233073
Eddie Lockjaw Davis Quartet | Eddie Lockjaw Davis With Shirley Scott | Original Jazz Classics | OJC 218(P 7154)
Harry Babasin Quintet | Jazz In Hollywood:Harry Babasin/Bob Enevoldsen | Original Jazz Classics | OJCCD 1888-2(Nocturne NLP3/NLP-6)
Lennie Tristano | Lennie Tristano:The Copenhagen Concert | Storyville | 4960603
Lou Donaldson Sextet | The Time Is Right | Blue Note | 868498-0
Mark Murphy-Bob Magnusson | Mark Murphy Sings Nat Cing Cole,Volumes 1&2 | Muse | MCD 6001
Singers Unlimited With Rob McConnell And The Boss Brass | The Singers Unlimited With Rob McConnell And The Boss Brass | MPS | 817486-1

Stan Getz Quintet | Stan Getz:The Complete 1952-1954 Small Group Sessions(Master Takes),Vol.2 | Blue Moon | BMCD 1035
Willis Jackson Quintet | Soul Night Live! | Prestige | PRCD 24273-2
Zoot Sims Quartet | The Concert 23.6.1958 | Jazzline | ???
Earl Hines Trio | The Lengendary Little Theater Concert of 1964 | Savoy | 650139(882495)

Tangles Outcome
Gary Burton Quartet | Picture This | ECM | 1226

Tanglewood '63
Stan Getz Quintet With The Boston Pops Orchestra | Stan Getz And Arthur Fiedler At Tanglewood | RCA | 2136406-2

Tango
Doctor Umezu Band | Eight Eyes And Eight Ears | ITM Records | ITM 1412
Gary Campbell Trio | Intersection | Milestone | MCD 9236-2
Jens Schliecker & Nils Rohwer | Duo Fantasie:Piano Meets Vibes | Acoustic Music Records | 319.1094.2
Patrick Bebelaar Quartet | You Never Lose An Island | dml-records | CD 015
Paul Horn Group feat. Egberto Gismonti | The Altitude Of The Sun | Black Sun Music | 15002-2
Peter Fulda Trio With Céline Rudolph | Silent Dances | Jazz 4 Ever Records:Jazz Network | J4E 4731
Roberto Cipelli Quartet | Moona Moore | SPLASC(H) Records | H 173
Zbigniew Namyslowski Quartet | Namyslovski | Inner City | IC 1048 IMS

Tango-
Gato Barbieri Sextet | Gato Barbieri:The Complete Flying Dutchman Recordings 1969-1973 | RCA | 2154555-2

Tango 1
Barbara Thompson's Paraphernalia | Thompson's Tangos | Intuition Records | INT 3290-2

Tango 2
Thompson's Tangos | Intuition Records | INT 3290-2

Tango 3
Thompson's Tangos | Intuition Records | INT 3290-2

Tango 4
Chick Corea-Gary Burton | Native Sense-The New Duets | Stretch Records | SCD 9014-2

Tango A Mi Padre(Nocturno-Elegia)
Ulli Jünemann-Morton Ginnerup European Jazz Project | The Exhibition | Edition Collage | EC 518-2

Tango Al Dente
Laurindo Almeida/Charlie Byrd Quartet | Tango | Concord | CCD 4290

Tango Alemán
Blue Box | Blue Box 10 | TipToe | TIP-888818 2

Tango Corrientes 319
The Tango Kings | The Tango Kings | Big World | BW 2016

Tango Del Mar
Dino Saluzzi Group | Argentina | West Wind Latina | 2201 CD

Tango Du Soleil
Howard Alden Trio | Silver Anniversary Set | Concord | CCD 7002

Tango For Gretchen Rodriguez
Vienna Art Orchestra | Concerto Piccolo | Hat Art | CD 6038

Tango Madrugada
The Tango Kings | The Tango Kings | Big World | BW 2016

Tango No.3
Uwe Werner-Mick Baumeister Duo | Oh Brother | Chaos | CACD 8067-2

Tango Of Oblivion
Bettina Born-Wolfram Born | Schattenspiel | Born&Bellmann | 993004 CD

Tango Op.165 Nr.2
Paul Bley | Tango Palace | Soul Note | 121090-2

Tango Para Lajuana
John Wolf Brennan-Daniele Patumi | Ten Zentences | L+R Records | CDLR 45066

Tango Pour Claude
Richard Galliano Quartet | Gallianissimo! The Best Of Richard Galliano | Dreyfus Jazz Line | FDM 36616-2
Viaggio | Dreyfus Jazz Line | FDM 36562-9
Richard Galliano Trio | Concert Inédits | Dreyfus Jazz Line | FDM 36606-2

Tango Reprise
Fred Van Hove | Verloren Maandag | FMP | SAJ 11

Tango Salsa
Fischbacher Group & Modern String Quartet | Fischbacher Group & Modern String Quartet | Dr.Jazz Records | 8608-2

Tango Subversivo
Al Di Meola World Sinfonia | World Sinfonia | Inak | 700772

Tango 'Til They're Sore
Frank Speer Acoustic Quartet | Dread Nay | Jazz 4 Ever Records:Jazz Network | J4E 4734

Tango Tragico
Othar Turner And The Rising Star Fife And Drum Band | The Introduction To Living Country Blues USA | L+R Records | LS 42030

Tangoa Free
Ferenc Snétberger Quartet | Signature | Enja | ENJ-9017 2
Tom Christensen Quartet | Gualala | Naxos Jazz | 86050-2

Tangorine
Dizzy Gillespie Big Band | Groovin' High | Bandstand | BDCD 1513

Tangos
Roberto Gatto Group feat. John Scofield | Ask | Inak | 8802

Tanguillo
Clemens Maria Peters/Reinhold Bauer | Quadru Mana/Quadru Mania | Edition Collage | EC 464-2

Tanguito
Guitar Moments | Take Twelve On CD | TT 006-2

Tania-
Jukka Tolonen Group | A Passenger To Paramaribo | Sonet | 147120

Tánk
John Tank Quartet | Canadian Sunset | TCB Records | TCB 20902

Tank's Tune
John Zorn Group | Massada Tree | DIW | DIW 890 CD

Tant De Temps
Bobo Stenson Trio | Underwear | ECM | 1012

Tantalizing A Cuban
Earl Hines And His Orchestra | The Indispensable Earl Hines Vol.1/2 | RCA | 2126407-2

Tante Nelly
Slide Hampton-Joe Haider Jazz Orchestra | Give Me A Double | JHM Records | JHM 3627
Barondown | Crackshot | Avant | AVAN 059

Tantrum Clangley
God Is My Co-Pilot | Mir Shlufn Nisht | Avant | AVAN 032

Tantum Ergo(in memoriam Edward Kennedy Ellington)
Lew Tabackin Trio | Black & Tan Fantasy | JAM | 5005 IMS

Tanya
Hank Crawford Quintet | Portrait | Milestone | MCD 9192-2
Robert Lockwood Jr.With The Aces | Steady Rollin' Man | Delmark | 900206 AO

Tanz der Kraniche
Christian Rannenberg & The Pink Piano All Stars | Long Way From Home | Acoustic Music Records | AMC 1006

Tanz Der Tse Tse Fliegen
Sigi Schwab | Meditation Vol.2 | Melos Music | CDGS 705

Taos
Jonas Hellborg Group | Adfa | Demon Records | DEM 020

Tapajack
Ray Anderson Trio | Right Down Your Alley | Soul Note | 121087-2

Tape Worm
Elliot Lawrence Band | Plays Tiny Kahn And Johnny Mandel Arrangements | Fantasy | 0902109(F 3219)

Tapetenwechsel
John Coltrane Sextet | Live In Seatle | Impulse(MCA) | GRP 21462

Tappin' On The Trapps
Benny Goodman And His Orchestra | Benny Goodman's 1934 Dodge All-Star Recordings(Complete) | Circle | CCD-111

Tapping In The Dark
Magnificant Seventh's Brass Band | Authentic New Orleans Jazz Funeral | Mardi Gras Records | MG 1012

Taps Miller
Count Basie And His Orchestra | Jazz In V.Discs Vol.2 | Collection Hugues Panassié | CTPL 002
Disque D'Or | Vogue | 400525

Taqassoum
Jorge Cardoso | Talking Hands:Live | ALISO Records | AL 1021

Taquito Militar-
MOKAVE | MOKAVE Vol.1 | audioquest Music | AQCD 1006

Tar Á Got
Papa Bue's Viking Jazzband | A Tribute To Wingy Manone | Storyville | SLP 210

Taracira
Galliano-Portal | Blow Up | Dreyfus Jazz Line | FDM 36589-2

Taraf
Jon Balke w/Magnetic North Orchestra | Further | ECM | 1517
Michel Portal-Richard Galliano | Concerts | Dreyfus Jazz Line | FDM 36661-2
Richard Galliano | Concert Inédits | Dreyfus Jazz Line | FDM 36606-2

Tarantella
Pino Minafra Quintet | Colori | SPLASC(H) Records | CD H 108-2

Tarantella(3)
Daniel Schnyder Group | Tanatula | Enja | ENJ-9302 2

Tarantula
George Colligan Quintet | Constant Source | Steeplechase | SCCD 31462
Peppino D'Agostino | Close To The Heart | Acoustic Music Records | 319.1039.2

Tara's Theme
Stan Getz With The Claus Ogerman Orchestra | What The World Needs Now-Stan Getz Plays Bacharach And David | Verve | 557450-2
Frankie Laine With Carl Fischer's Orchesrtra | The Uncollected:Frankie Lane Vol.2 | Hindsight | HSR 216 (835570)

Tarde
Joe Pass Quintet | Whitestone | Pablo | 2310912-2

Tarra's Freilach
Paul Brody's Tango Toy | Klezmer Stories | Laika Records | 35101222
Jazz Circle | Sun Games | Timeless | CD SJP 167

Tartaros
Lee Morgan Sextet | Taru | Blue Note | 522670-2

Taru What's Wrong With You
Charly Antolini Quartet | Menue/Finale | BELL Records | BLR 84068

Tasane Maa
Bettina Born-Wolfram Born | Schattenspiel | Born&Bellmann | 993004 CD

Tashunka Witko
Carol Emanuel | Tops Of Trees | Koch Jazz | KOC 3-7802-2

Tastalun
Don Cherry Quartet | Where Is Brooklyn? | Blue Note | 84311

Taste On The Place
Melvin Sparks Group | I'm A 'Gittar' Player | Cannonball Records | CBD 27101

Tastiere
Willie Rodriguez Jazz Quartet | Flatjacks | Milestone | MCD 9331-2

Tasty
Woody Herman And His Orchestra | Woody Herman:Complete 1948-1950 Capitol Sessions | Definitive Records | DRCD 11195

Tasty Pudding
Miles Davis All Stars | Dig | Prestige | P 24054
Stan Getz Quintet | Stan Getz At The Shrine | Verve | POCJ 1904 PMS

Tata's Blues
Tana Reid Sextet | Blue Motion | Paddle Wheel | KICJ 172

Tatort
Klaus Doldinger's Passport | Klaus Doldinger Passport Live | Warner | 8573-84132-2
Der Rote Bereich | Der Rote Bereich | Jazz 4 Ever Records:Jazz Network | J4E 4715

Tattler
Duke Ellington And His Orchestra | Two Great Concerts | Festival | ???

Tattooed Lady
Miles Davis Group | Dark Magus | CBS | C2K 65137

Tatu(part 1)
Dark Magus | CBS | C2K 65137

Tatu(part 2)
Adam Makowicz | Maybeck Recital Hall Series Volume Twenty-Four | Concord | CCD 4541

Tatzelwurm
John Wolf Brennan | Irisations | Creative Works Records | CW CD 1021-2

Tau(2)
Irisations | Creative Works Records | CW CD 1021-2

Tau(3)
Quartett & Brass | More Than Four | Line Records | COCD 9.01068 0

Taugh Enough
Mani Neumeir-Peter Hollinger | Monsters Of Drums-Live | ATM Records | ATM 3821-AH

Taumel
Stan Kenton And His Orchestra | West Side Story | Capitol | 829914-2

Taurian Matador
Billy Cobham Group | Shabazz | Atlantic | ATL 50147

Taurus
Mary Lou Williams Trio | A Keyboard History | Fresh Sound Records | FSR 651(Jazztone J 1206)

Taurus People
Seamus Blake Quartet | Stranger Things Have Happened | Fresh Sound Records | FSNT 063 CD
Steve Grossman Trio | Way Out East Vol.1 | Red Records | 123176-2

Täuschung Der Luft
Uwe Walter | Tauta | Ear-Rational | ECD 1037

Tautology
Lennie Tristano Quintet | First Sessions 1949/50 | Prestige | P 24081
Michael Kanan Trio | The Gentleman Is A Dope | Fresh Sound Records | FSNT 147 CD
Alex Möller-Lena Willemark Group | Hästen Och Tranan | ACT | 9244-2

Tavakkol
Tavil-Nadasvaram-Group | Music From South India/Madras | Moers Music | 01090

Taxi Of The Desert
Ladonna Smith-Davey Williams | Dix Improvisations, Victoriaville 1989 | Victo | CD 009

Taxi Story
Bill Perkins With The Jan Lundgren Trio | Bill Perkins Recreates The Historic Solos Of Lester Young | Fresh Sound Records | FSR-CD 5010

Taxi War Dance
Howard Rumsey's Lighthouse All-Stars | Music For Lighthousekeeping | Original Jazz Classics | OJCCD 636-2(C 7528)

Taxi's Waiting
Ann Dyer & No Good Time Fairies | Revolver:A New Spin | Premonition | 790745-2

Taylor's Test
The Jimmy Giuffre 3 | The Easy Way | Verve | 2304491 IMS

Tbilissi
Lester Bowie-Phillip Wilson | Duet | Improvising Artists Inc. | 123854-2

T-Bone Blues
T-Bone Walker And His Band | The Great Blues Vocals And Guitar Of T-Bone Walker | Pathe | 2C 068-86523(Capitol)

Te Acuerdas
Charles Lloyd Quintet | Lift Every Voice | ECM | 1832/33(018783-2)

Te Amaré
Laurindo Almeida Trio | Artistry In Rhythm | Concord | CCD 4238

Te Tango Entre Suenos
Brodmann-Pausch Percussion Duo | Are You Serious? | Jazz 4 Ever Records:Jazz Network | J4E 4718

TE TIMA TATANGA
Rex Stewart And His Orchestra | Duke Ellington's Trumpets | Black & Blue | BLE 59.231 2

Tea For Three
Richard Galliano Quartet | Spleen | Dreyfus Jazz Line | FDM 36513-9

Tea For Toots
Richard Galliano-Gabriele Mirabassi Duo | Coloriage | Quadrivium | SCA 031

Tea For Two
Anita O'Day With The Tete Montoliu Trio | Tea For Two | Moon Records | MLP 023-1
Art Tatum | Art Tatum-The Standard Transcriptions | Music & Arts | CD 919
The Standard Sessions: Art Tatum 1935-1943 Transcriptions | Music & Arts | CD 673
Pure Genius | Atlantis | ATS 3
The Art Tatum Solo Masterpieces | Pablo | 2625703
Art Tatum Trio | The Complete Trio Sessions Vol.1 | Official | 3001
Benny Carter And His Orchestra | The Uncollecteed:Banny Carter-Live At The Trianon Ballroom | Hindsight | HSR 218
Benny Goodman Quartet | Benny Goodman:The Complete Small Combinations Vol.1/2(1935-1937) | RCA | ND 89753
Bob Gordon Quintet | Bob Gordon Memorial | Fresh Sound Records | FSR-CD 0180
Bud Freeman And His Group | California Session | Jazzology | JCD-277
Bud Powell Trio | From 'Birdland' New York City 1956 | Jazz Anthology | 550202
Charles Mingus Jazz Workshop | Jazz Composers Workshop | Savoy | SV 0171(MG 12059)
Django Reinhardt | Django Reinhardt:Djangology | EMI Records | 780659-2
Duke Ellington And His Orchestra | Duke Ellington -Carnegie Hall Concert | Ember | 800851-370(EMBD 2001)
Earl Hines Trio | Earl Hines:Fine & Dandy | Vogue | 2111508-2
Ella Fitzgerald With The Count Basie Orchestra | Ella & Basie-On The Sunny Side Of The Street | Verve | 821576-2
Ernestine Allen With The King Curtis Group | Let It Roll | Original Blues Classics | OBCCD 539-2(TRU 15004)
Fats Waller | Fats Waller:The Complete Associated Transcription Sessions 1935-1939 | Jazz Unlimited | JUCD 2076
Fats Waller:The Complete Associated Transcription Sessions 1935-1939 | Jazz Unlimited | JUCD 2076
Fats Waller-The Joint Is Jumpin' | RCA | ND 86288(874182)
Hank Jones | Urbanity | Verve | 537749-2
Harry Edison Quartet | The Inventive Mr. Edison | Fresh Sound Records | 054 2402661(Pacific Jazz PJ 11)
Jimmy Hamilton Quintet | Jimmy Hamilton And The New York Jazz Quintet | Fresh Sound Records | FSCD 2002
Joe Venuti Quartet | The Best Of The Jazz Violins | LRC Records | CDC 8532
Junko Onishi Trio | Live At The Village Vanguard | Blue Note | 833418-2
Lester Young And His Band | Tenor Triumvirate:Bean & Prez & Chu | Queen-Disc | 051
Lester Young Quintet | Prez's Hat Vol.4 | Philology | 214 W 9
Lester Young With The Oscar Peterson Quartet | The Pres-ident Plays | Verve | 831670-2 PMS
Lester Young-Nat Cole Trio | Lester Young 'Rarities' | Moon Records | MCD 048-2
Lester Young:The Complete1936-1951 Group Sessions(Studio Recordings-Master Takes),Vol.1 | Blue Moon | BMCD 1001
Louis Armstrong And His All Stars | Satchmo At Symphony Hall | GRP | GRP 16612
Oscar Peterson Trio | The Song Is You-The Best Of The Verve Songbooks | Verve | 531558-2
Oscar Peterson-Austin Roberts | Oscar Peterson 1951 | Just A Memory | JAS 9501-2
Quintet Du Hot Club De France | Django Reinhardt Vol. 5 | Decca | 180024 AG
Ralph Sutton-Len Barnard | Easy Street | Sackville | SKCD2-2040
Sarah Vaughan With Orchestra | !Viva! Vaughan | Mercury | 549374-2
Schnuckenack Reinhardt Quintet | 15.3.1973 | Intercord | 160031
Stephane Grappelli Quartet | I Hear Music | RCA | 2179624-2
Planet Jazz:Stephane Grappelli | RCA | 2165366-2
Stephane Grappelli With The Hot Club Of London | Live In London | Black Lion | BLCD 760139
Sylvia Syms With The Johnny Richards Orchestra | Sylvia Syms Sings | Atlantic | AMCY 1076
Thelonious Monk Trio | Thelonious Monk-The Complete Riverside Recordings | Riverside | 15 RCD 022-2

Tea For Two-
Charlie Parker And His Orchestra | Bird's Eyes Last Unissued Vol.18 | Philology | W 848.2
Helmut Zacharias mit seiner Swing-Besetzung | Ich Habe Rhythmus | Bear Family Records | BCD 15642 AH
Jaki Byard Quartet | The Last From Lennie's | Prestige | PRCD 11029-2
Phineas Newborn Jr. Trio | Tivoli Encounter | Storyville | STCD 8221
Simon Schott | Bar Piano: Simon Schott Plays Your Favorite Evergreens Vol.1 | Organic Music | ORGM 9733
Bud Powell Trio | Bud Powell:Complete 1947-1951 Blue Note,Verve & Roost Recordings | The Jazz Factory | JFCD 22837

Tea For Two(take 1)
Quintet Du Hot Club De France | Django Reinhardt Vol. 4 | Decca | 180023 AG

Tea For Two(take 2)
Django Reinhardt Vol. 4 | Decca | 180023 AG

Tea In The Sahara
Gil Evans Orchestra With Sting | Strange Fruit | ITM Records | ITM 1499
JazzHorchEster | ...Zudem Wird Auch Jazz Komponiert | Elite Special | 73412

Tea Time
Lucky Thompson Quartet | Lucky Thompson | LRC Records | CDC 9029

Tea Time(part 1)
Nils Wogram Sextet | Odd And Awkward | Enja | ENJ-9416-2

Tea Time(part 2)
Charlie Hunter Quartet | Ready...Set...Shango! | Blue Note | 837101-2

Teabaggin'
Melvin Rhyne Trio | Mel's Spell | Criss Cross | Criss 1118

Teach Me Tonight
All That Jazz & Helena Paul | All That Jazz & Helena Paul | Satin Doll Productions | SDP 1031-1 CD
Ann Hampton Callaway And Her Band | After Hours | Denon Compact Disc | CY-18042
Bill Ramsey & The Ron Wilson Trio | Singin' & Swingin' | zyx records | 22001
Count Basie And His Orchestra | Live In Basel 1956 | Jazz Helvet | JH 05
Count Basie And His Orchestra With Sarah Vaughan | Count Basie-Sarah Vaughan | Roulette | 8372412
David Newton Trio | In Good Company | Candid | CCD 79714
Dinah Washington With Orchestra | Mad About The Boy-The Best Of Dinah Washington | Mercury | 512214-2
Dinah Washington With The Quincy Jones Orchestra | Compact Jazz: Dinah Washington | Mercury | 830700-2 PMS
Erroll Garner Trio | Concert By The Sea | CBS | 451042-2
George Shearing-Don Thompson Duo | Live At The Cafe Carlyle | Concord | CCD 4246
Jermaine Landsberger Trio & Gina | Samba In June | Edition Collage | EC 524-2
Jerry Wiggins Trio | Wiggin' Out | Fresh Sound Records | FSR 532(HiFiJazz J 618)
L.A.4 | Montage | Concord | CJ 156
Louis Armstrong And His All Stars | Jazz In Paris:Louis Armstrong-The Best Live Concert Vol.2 | EmArCy | 013031-2
Marshall Royal Quintet | Royal Blue | Concord | CCD 125
Oliver Jones Trio | Requestfully Yours | Justin Time | Just 11
Oscar Peterson And The Bassists | Montreux '77-The Art Of The Jam Session | Pablo | 2620106
Oscar Peterson Trio | Walking The Line | MPS | 68082

Red Holloway With The Matthias Bätzel Trio | A Night Of Blues & Ballads | JHM Records | JHM 3614
Richard Wyands Trio | The Arrival | DIW | DIW 611 CD
Sarah Vaughan With The Oscar Peterson Quartet | How Long Has This Been Going On? | Pablo | 2310821-2
Teresa Brewer With The David Murray Quartet | Softly I Swing | Red Baron | 471575-2

Teach Me Tonight(alt.take)
Nick Woodland And The Magnets | Big Heart | Blues Beacon | BLU-1013 2

Teacher Teacher
Shorty Rogers And His Orchestra | Swings | Bluebird | ND 83012

Teacher(How I Love My Teacher)
The Colson Unity Troup | No Reservation | Black Saint | BSR 0043

Teaching A Rat To Sing
Dan Rose Quartet | The Water's Rising | Enja | 9116-2

Teamwork Song
Cannonball Adderley Quintet | Nancy Wilson/The Cannonball Adderley Quintet | Capitol | 781204-2

Teapot
Paul Bley Trio | Introducing Paul Bley | Original Jazz Classics | OJCCD 201-2(DEB 7)

Teapot Walin' - (Teapot) Walin'
Knut Kiesewetter With Orchestra | Jazz Again | Polydor | 2372016

Tear It Down
Wes Montgomery Quartet | Compact Jazz: Wes Montgomery Plays The Blues | Verve | 835318-2 PMS

Teardrops From My Eyes
Louis Jordan And His Tympany Five | Louis Jordan-Let The Good Times Roll: The Complete Decca Recordings 1938-1954 | Bear Family Records | BCD 15557 IH
Jean-Paul Bourelly Group | Tribute To Jimi | DIW | DIW 893 CD

Tearin' Out
Joe Thomas And His Orchestra | Screaming Saxophones Vol.1 | Swingtime(Contact) | ST 1002

Tears
Charlie Byrd | Solo Flight | Original Jazz Classics | OJCCD 1093-2(RS 9498)
Charlie Byrd And The Washington Guitar Quartet | Charlie Byrd/The Washington Guitar Quartet | Concord | CCD 42014
Django's Music | Django Reinhardt:Djangology | EMI Records | 780659-2
Dutch Swing College Band | Albert Nicholas & The Dutch Swing College Band | Storyville | STCD 5522
Gabriele Hasler-Roger Hanschel Duo | Love Songs | Foolish Music | FM 211003
Graham Stewart And His New Orleans Band | The Golden Years Of Revival Jazz,Vol.10 | Storyville | STCD 5515
Graham Stewart Seven | Best Of British Jazz From The BBC Jazz Club Vol.5 | Upbeat Jazz | URCD 125
King Oliver's Jazz Band | Louis Armstrong With King Oliver Vol.2 | Village(Jazz Archive) | VILCD 012-2
Milt Jackson With Strings | Feelings | Original Jazz Classics | OJC 448(2310774)
Quintet Du Hot Club De France | Django Reinhardt:Djangology | EMI Records | 780659-2
Stephane Grappelli Quartet | Stephane Grappelli 1992 Live | Dreyfus Jazz Line | FDM 37006-2
Stephane Grappelli Quintet | Hommage A Django Reinhardt | Festival | Album 120
Weather Report | Weather Report | CBS | 468212-2

Tears-
Joe Pass And Paulinho Da Costa Sextet | Tudo Bem! | Original Jazz Classics | 2310824

Tears And Joys-
Kamikaze Ground Crew | Madam Marie's Temple Of Knowledge | New World Records | 80438-2

Tears Are Rolling
The Sax Section | The Sax Section | Fresh Sound Records | LSP 15622(Epic LN 3278)

Tears For Johannesburg
Max Roach Group | Live In Europe 1964-Freedom Now Suite | Magnetic Records | MRCD 110

Tears From The Children
John Lewis-Hank Jones Duo | An Evening With Two Grand Pianos | Little David | LD 59657
Modern Jazz Quartet | Blues On Bach | Atlantic | 7567-81393-2
The Complete Last Concert | Atlantic | 81976-2

Tears In Heaven
Niels Lan Doky Trio | Niels Lan Doky | Verve | 559087-2

Tears In The Moonlight
David Linx With The Jack Van Poll Trio | Where Rivers Join | September | CD 5109

Tears Inside
Don Rader Quintet | A Foreign Affair | L+R Records | CDLR 45034
Nick Brignola Quartet | On A Different Level | Reservoir | RSR CD 112(882636)
Pat Metheny Trio | Rejoicing | ECM | 1271(817795-2)
Chris Beier | Roots | Media Arte | CD 587

Tears Of Joy
Charlie Haden-Pat Metheny | Beyond The Missouri Sky | Verve | 537130-2

Tears Of Rain
Gary Burton Quintet | Like Minds | Concord | CCD 4803

Tears Sent By You
Amos Milburn And His Aladdin Chicken-Shackers | Vicious Vicious Vodka | Pathe | 1561401(Aladdin)

Tears To Burn
Larry Willis Sextet | A Tribute To Someone | audioquest Music | AQCD 1022

Technicolor Nightmare
Simon Jeffes | Piano Music | Peregrina Music | PM 50262

Teclado Marfil
Bruce Dunlap Quintet | About Home | Chesky | JD 59

Tecos
Dejan Terzic European Assembly | Coming Up | double moon | DMCHR 71034

Tectonic
Vinny Golia Large Ensemble | Pilgrimage To Obscurity | Nine Winds Records | NWCD 0130

Teddy The Toad
Count Basie And His Orchestra | Atomic Swing | Roulette | 497871-2
The Complete Atomic Basie | Roulette | 828635-2
Jazz Collection:Count Basie | Laserlight | 24368
Count Basie & His Orchestra:Fresno,California April 24,1959 | Jazz Unlimited | JUCD 2039
Ray Bryant Trio | Ray Bryant Plays Basie & Ellington | EmArCy | 832235-2 PMS

Tee Funk
Tiny Grimes Quartet | Some Groovy Fours | Black & Blue | BB 874.2

Teen Age Rock
Aera | TÄrkis | Erlkönig | 148409

Teen Town
Jazz Pistols | 3 On The Floor | Lipstick Records | LIP 8959-2
Normand Guilbeault Ensemble | Basso Continuo | Justin Time | JTR 8452-2
Jaco Pastorius Trio | Live In Italy | Jazzpoint | JP 1031 CD

Teen Town-
Jaco Pastorius Heavy'n Jazz & Stuttgart Aria | Jazzpoint | JP 1058 CD
Heavy'n Jazz | Jazzpoint | JP 1036 CD
T-Bone Walker And His Band | Singing The Blues | Pathe | 1546761(Imperial LP 9116)

Teenager
Smiley Lewis | Ooh La La | Pathe | 1561391(Imperial)

Teenie's Blues
Oliver Nelson And His Orchestra | Blues And The Abstract Truth | CTI Records | PDCTI 1122-2

Teetanz
Cindy Blackman Quintet | Arcane | Muse | MCD 5341

Teeter Totter
Richard Grossman Trio | Trio Live In Real Time | Nine Winds Records | NWCD 0134

Tefka
Jan Garbarek-Kjell Johnsen Duo | Aftenland | ECM | 1169(839304-2)

Tegn
Kim Kristensen | Pulse Of Time | dacapo | DCCD 9435
Duke Ellington And His Orchestra | Togo Brava Swuite | Storyville | STCD 8323

Tego
Steve Reich And Musicians | Tehellim | ECM | 1215(827411-2)

Teilquintet
Daniel Schnyder Group | Words Within Music | Enja | ENJ-9369 2

Teiresias
Daniel Schnyder Quintet | Nucleus | Enja | ENJ-8068 2
John Zorn Group | Masada Seven | DIW | DIW 915 CD

Telares
Herbie Mann Sextet | Let Me Tell You | Milestone | M 47010

Tel-Aviv
Rozie Trio | Afro Algonquin | Moers Music | 01078

Tele-Funky
New Old Way Quintet | Waxing On | SPLASC(H) Records | H 112

Telegram
Eddie Davis Trio + Joe Newman | Countin' With Basie | Vogue | 500118

Telephone Song
Milton Batiste With The Rue Conti Jazz Band | Milton Batiste With The Rue Conti Jazz Band | Lake | LACD 31

Telephones
Slickaphonics | Modern Life | Enja | ENJ-4062 2

Telephony
Chicago Underground Trio | Possible Cube | Delmark | DE 511

Television
Lowell Fulsom Band | San Francisco Blues | Black Lion | BLCD 760176

Telisi Rama
Pork Pie | The Door Is Open | MPS | 68038

Tell Her You Saw Me
Jimmy Witherspoon With Groove Holmes | Cry The Blues | Bulldog | BDL 1012

Tell It All
Art Blakey And The Jazz Messengers | Feedom Rider | Blue Note | 821287-2

Tell It Like It Is
The Freedom Rider | Blue Note | 870076-5
Lennart Ginman-Kirk Lightsey Quartet | 1991 | Stunt Records | STUCD 19003

Tell Me
Brigeen Doran Quartet | Bright Moments | B&W Present | BW 020
Udo Schild Group | Morning | Jazz Haus Musik | ohne Nummer

Tell Me A Secret
Buddy Tate Trio | Midnight Slows Vol.6 | Black & Blue | BLE 190932

Tell Me About It Now
Nat King Cole With The Dave Cavanaugh Orchestra | Tell Me All About Yourself | Capitol | EMS 1109

Tell Me Baby
Sonny Boy Williamson Group | King Of The Blues Harmonica | Black & Blue | BLE 59.251 2

Tell Me 'Bout My Baby
Julia Lee And Her Boy Friends | Julia Lee's Party Time | Pathe | 2C 068-86524(Capitol)

Tell Me I'm Not Too Late
Chris Barber's Jazz And Blues Band With Special Guests | Best Of British Jazz From The BBC Jazz Club Vol.5 | Upbeat Jazz | URCD 125

Tell Me More
Billie Holiday And Her Orchestra | Billie Holiday:The Quintessential Vol.8/9(1939-1942) | CBS | 477837-2

Tell Me More And More And Then Some
Soesja Citroen And Her Trio | Song For Ma | Challenge | CHR 70056

Tell Me Somethin'
Mose Allison Trio | Mose Alife!/Wild Man On The Loose | Warner | 8122-75439-2
Domenic Landolf Quartet | Levitation | JHM Records | JHM 3616

Tell Me The Truth
Jon Hendricks & Company | Love | Muse | MCD 5258

Tell Me This
Mississippi Sheiks | Stop And Listen | Yazoo | YAZ 2006

Tell Me What True Love Is
Nelson Rangell Group | In Every Moment | GRP | GRP 96622

Tell Me When
Gerry Mulligan-Ben Webster Quintet | The Complete Gerry Mulligan Meets Ben Webster Sessions | Verve | 539055-2

Tell Me When(alt.take)
Valery Ponomarev Quintet | Trip To Moscow | Reservoir | RSR CD 107(882631)

Tell Me Wry
Jimmy Reed | I'm The Man Down There | Charly | CRB 1082

Tell Me You Love Me
Sonny Rollins Quintet | Sunny Days Stary Nights | Milestone | M 9122

Tell Me You'll Wait For Me
Dr.John With The John Clayton Big Band | Dr.John-Afterglow | Blue Thumb | GRB 70002

Tell Me Your Dreams
Taragota Hot Seven | Bavarian Jazz Live | Calig | 30620/21

Tell Me(What I Got To Do)
Ray Gaskins | Can't Stp | Lipstick Records | LIP 8946-2

Tell Someone
Big Three Trio | Willie Dixon-The Big Three Trio | CBS | 467248-2

Tell To Mama
Torbjorn Sunde Group | Meridians | ACT | 9263-2

Tell Your Ma,Tell Your Pa
Bill Frisell Trio | Bill Frisell With Dave Hollnad And Elvin Jones | Nonesuch | 7559-79624-2
Claude Bolling And The Show Biz Band | Swing Session | Decca | 6.22649 AO

Tell Your Story
Charles Lloyd Quartet | Fish Out Of Water | ECM | 1398

Tellaro
Jamenco | Conversations | Trick Music | TM 9202 CD
Joe Beard With Ronnie Earl & The Broadcasters | Blues Union | audioquest Music | AQCD 1039

Tema Y Gancho
The Splendid Master Gnawa Musicians Of Morocco | The Splendid Master Gnawa Musicians Of Morocco | Verve | 521587-2

Temoin Dans La Ville
OYEZ | I Mean You | Timeless | CD SJP 282

Temperatur
Charles Musselwhite Band | Charles Musselwhite Memphis,Tennessee | Crosscut | CCR 1008

Tempete A Florence
Ekkehard Jost & Chromatic Alarm | Wintertango | Fish Music | FM 008 CD

Tempi Passati
Maarten Altena Ensemble | Code | Hat Art | CD 6094

Tempo
Lionel Hampton And His Orchestra | Planet Jazz:Lionel Hampton | Planet Jazz | 2152059-2

Tempo And Swing
Lionel Hampton Quartet | Jazz Gallery:Lionel Hampton Vol.1 | RCA | 2114170-2

Tempo Positioned
George Wallington | Virtuoso | Denon Compact Disc | 35C38-7248

Temporarily
Jimmy Giuffre 3 | Jimmy Giuffre 3, 1961 | ECM | 1438/39(849644-2)
Jimmy Giuffre Trio | Live In Europe 1961 Vol.2 | Raretone | 5019 FC

Tempos De Minuano
Ramón Diaz Group | O Si No Que? | Fresh Sound Records | FSNT 044 CD

Temprano
Louis Sclavis-Ernst Reijseger | Et On Ne Parle Pas Du Temps | FMP | CD 66

Temptation
Artie Shaw And His Orchestra | This Is Artie Shaw | RCA | NL 89411 DP
Charlie Parker With The Joe Lipman Orchestra | Charlie Parker With Strings:The Master Takes | Verve | 523984-2
Charlie Parker Big Band | Verve | 559835-2
Diana Krall Group | The Girl In The Other Room | Verve | 9862246
Freddy Cole With Band | A Circle Of Love | Fantasy | FCD 9674-2
Jon Rose Group | Violin Music In The Age Of Shopping | Intakt Records | CD 038
Randy Johnston Quartet | In A-Chord | Muse | MCD 5512

Temptation Flower
Benny Goodman Sextet | Benny Goodman Sextet | CBS | 450411-2

Tempus Fugit
Bud Powell Trio | The Genius Of Bud Powell | Verve | 821690-1
Bud Powell:Complete 1947-1951 Blue Note,Verve & Roost Recordings | The Jazz Factory | JFCD 22837
Charly Antolini-Charly Augschöll Quartet | On The Beat | BELL Records | BLR 84053
Miles Davis Sextet | Kind Of Blue:Blue Note Celebrate The Music Of Miles Davis | Blue Note | 534255-2
Miles Davis:The Blue Note And Capitol Recordings | Blue Note | 827475-2
Miles Davis Vol.1 | Blue Note | 300081(1501)

Tempus Fugit(alt.take)
Miles Davis:The Blue Note And Capitol Recordings | Blue Note | 827475-2

Temurá
Claus Boesser-Ferrari | Ten | Acoustic Music Records | 319.1168.2

Ten Bars Ago
Anita O'Day With The Billy May Orchestra | Verve Jazz Masters 49:Anita O'Day | Verve | 527653-2

Ten Cents A Dance
Chris Connor With The Ronnie Ball Quartet | Chris Connor At The Village Gate:Early Show | Roulette | 300008(TOCJ 6122)
Ella Fitzgerald With The Buddy Bregman Orchestra | The Complete Ella Fitzgerald Song Books of Harold Arlen, Irving Berlin, Duke Ellington, George & Ira Gershwin, Jerome Kern, Johnny Mercer, Cole Porter And Rogers & Hart | Verve | 519832-2
Shorty Rogers And His Giants | Shorty Rogers Plays Richard Rodgers | Fresh Sound Records | NL 45645(RCA LPM 1428)

Ten Dollar High
Hal Russell NRG Ensemble | The Finnish/Swiss Tour | ECM | 1455

Ten Letters Of Love
Ernie Carson And The Castle Jazz Band | Old Bones | Stomp Off Records | CD 1283

Ten Thousand Years Later
Roger Kellaway Quintet | Spirit Feel | Pacific Jazz | LN 10070

Ten Years
Buddy Guy Band | Buddy Guy | Chess | 427006

Ten Years Ago
Buddy Guy-Junior Wells Band | Drinkin' TNT 'N' Smokin' Dynamite | Sequel Records | NEM CD 687
Richard Galliano Quartet | New York Tango | Dreyfus Jazz Line | FDM 36581-2
The Four Brothers | Together Again! | RCA | 2179623-2

Ten Years Later
J.J.Johnson Sextet | Heroes | Verve | 528864-2

Tender As A Rose
Abbey Lincoln And Her Trio | Over The Years | Verve | 549101-2
Carol Stevens With Phil More's Music | That Satin Doll | Atlantic | AMCY 1080

Tender Is The Night
Diederik Wissels Trio | Tender Is The Night | Jazz Pure Collection | AU 31616 CD
Marc Copland Trio | Tracks | L+R Records | CDLR 45050

Tenderly
Art Tatum | Art Tatum:Over The Rainbow | Dreyfus Jazz Line | FDM 36727-2
Art Tatum-The Complete Jazz Chronicle Solo Session | Storyville | STCD 8253
Art Tatum-The Complete Pablo Solo Masterpieces | Pablo | 7 PACD 4404-2
Art Tatum:Complete Capitol Recordings | Definitive Records | DRCD 11192
In Private | Fresh Sound Records | FSR-CD 0127
Artie Shaw And His Gramercy Five | I Can't Get Started | Verve | MV 2559 IMS
Barry Harris-Kenny Barron Quartet | Confirmation | Candid | CCD 79519
Ben Webster With The Oscar Peterson Quartet | King Of The Tenors | Verve | 519806-2
Benny Carter Quartet | 3,4,5 The Verve Small Group Sessions | Verve | 849395-2 PMS
Bill Evans-Don Elliott | Tenderly | Milestone | MCD 9317-2
Bill Perkins Big Band | Our Man Woody | Jazz Mark | 110 CD(889466)
Billie Holiday And Her Orchestra | Billie Holiday: The First Verve Sessions | Verve | 2610027
Billie Holiday With The Buster Harding Orchestra | Billie Holiday Broadcast Performances Vol.1 | ESP Disk | ESP 3002-2
Buddy DeFranco Quartet | Jazz Tones | Verve | MV 2610 IMS
Carmen McRae With The Shirley Horn Trio | Planet Jazz:Female Jazz Vocalists | Planet Jazz | 2169656-2
The Collected Carmen McRae | RCA | 2668713-2
Sarah-Dedicated To You | Novus | PD 90546
Chet Baker Quintet/NDR Big Band/Radio Orchestra Hannover | Straight From The Heart-The Last Concert Vol.2 | Enja | ENJ-6020 2
The Last Concert Vol.I+II | Enja | ENJ-6074 22
Chet Baket Quartet | Chet Baker In Paris | Fresh Sound Records | FSR Box 1(Barclay)
Claude Williams Quintet | Call For The Fiddler | Steeplechase | SCCD 31051
Duke Ellington And His Orchestra | This Is Jazz:Duke Ellington Play Standards | CBS | CK 65056
Hot Summer Dance | Red Baron | 469285-2
Eddie Cleanhead Vinson Septet | The 'Clean' Machine | Muse | MR 5116
Ella Fitzgerald And Louis Armstrong With The Oscar Peterson Quartet | Verve Jazz Masters 24:Ella Fitzgerald & Louis Armstrong | Verve | 521851-2
The Best Of Ella Fitzgerald And Louis Armstrong On Verve | Verve | 537909-2
Ella And Louis | Verve | 543304-2
The Jazz Collector Edition: Ella & Louis | Laserlight | 15706
Welcome To Jazz: Ella Fitzgerald | Koch Records | 322 078 D1
Ella Fitzgerald With Orchestra | Forever Ella | Verve | 529387-2
Elliot Lawrence And His Orchestra | The Elliot Lawrence Big Band Swings Cohn & Kahn | Fantasy | FCD 24761-2
Eric Dolphy | Magic | Prestige | P 24053
Eric Dolphy:The Complete Prestige Recordings | Prestige | 9 PRCD-4418-2
Eric Dolphy Quintet | Far Cry | Original Jazz Classics | OJC20 400-2
Erroll Garner | Way Out Wardell | Ace Records | CDBOP 014
Freddy Martin And His Orchestra | The Uncollected: Freddy Martin, Vol.3 | Hindsight | HSR 190
George Shearing | The Shearing Piano | Capitol | 531574-2
My Ship | MPS | 68096
Häns'che Weiss-Vali Mayer Duo | Just Play | MMM Records | CD 1298
Henri Crolla Sextet | Jazz In Paris:Henri Crolla-Quand Refleuriront Les Lilas Blancs? | EmArCy | 018418-2
Herb Ellis Trio | Herb Mix | Concord | CJ 181
JATP All Stars | Jazz At The Philharmonic 1957 | Tax | CD 3703-2
Jimmy Bruno Trio With The Edgardo Cintron Orchestra | Sleight Of Hand | Concord | CCD 4532

TITELVERZEICHNIS

Jimmy Smith Trio | A New Sound A New Star:Jimmy Smith At The Organ | Blue Note | 857191-2
Jimmy Smith At The Organ | Blue Note | 300154(1512)
Joe Beck-Ali Ryerson | Django | dmp Digital Music Productions | CD 530
Joe Maneri Quartet | Tenderly | HatOLOGY | 525
Joe Pass Quartet | Apassionato | Pablo | 2310946-2
John Pizzarelli Trio | P.S. Mr.Cole | RCA | 2663563-2
John Towner Quartet | The John Towner Touch | Fresh Sound Records | KL 1055(Kapp)
Johnny Smith Quintet | Moonlight In Vermont | Roulette | 300016
Johnny Smith-Stan Getz Quintet | Stan Getz-The Complete Roost Sessions | The Jazz Factory | JFCD 22839
Lionel Hampton And His All Star Jazz Inner Circle | En Concert Avec Europe 1 | Laserlight | 710375/76
Lionel Hampton And His Orchestra | En Concert Avec Europe 1 | Laserlight | 710462
Lionel Hampton Quartet | The Complete Lionel Hampton Quartets And Quintets With Oscar Peterson On Verve | Verve | 559797-2
Lionel Hampton Quintet | Planet Jazz:Lionel Hampton | Planet Jazz | 2152059-2
Jazz Flamenco | RCA | 2136400-2
Louis Hayes Quintet | Quintessential Lou | TCB Records | TCB 99652
Oscar Peterson Trio | JATP In Tokyo | Pablo | 2620104-2
At Zardis' | Pablo | 2CD 2620118
Oscar Peterson-Joe Pass Duo | Oscar Pterson Et Joe Pass A La Salle Pleyel | Pablo | 2CD 2625705
Live At Salle Pleyel, Paris | Pablo | 2625705
Oscar Peterson-Ray Brown Duo | Tenderly | Verve | MV 2662 IMS
Paulo Cardoso | VoceBasso | Organic Music | ORGM 9703
Pete Jolly Duo | Pete Jolly Duo/Trio/Quartet | Fresh Sound Records | ND 42133
Sarah Vaughan And Her Trio | The Complete Sarah Vaughan Live In Japan | Mobile Fidelity | MFCD 844-2
Woody Herman And His Orchestra | Woody Herman Presents Volume 2...Four Others | Concord | CCD 4180

Tenderly-
Louis Armstrong And His All Stars | Louis Armstrong:The Great Chicago Concert 1956 | CBS | C2K 65119
The Best Live Concert | Festival | ???
Sarah Vaughan With The Jimmy Jones Trio | Linger Awhile | Pablo | 2312144-2
Simon Schott | Bar Piano: Simon Schott Plays Your Favorite Evergreens Vol.1 | Organic Music | ORGM 9733
Stan Getz-Lionel Hampton Quintet | Hamp And Getz | Verve | 831672-2
Willie Cook&Paul Gonsalves With The Enrque Villegas Trio | Encuentro | Fresh Sound Records | FSR-CD 0072

Tenderness
Walt Dickerson/Richard Davis | Tenderness | Steeplechase | SCCD 31213

Tendin' To Business
Stephane Grappelli Trio | Unique Piano Session | Jazz Anthology | JA 5216

Teneriffa-Kakerlaken
Geoff Goodman Quintet | Naked Eye | Tutu Records | 888214-2*

Tengelman Girls
Gianluigi Trovesi Octet | Les Hommes Armés | Soul Note | 121311-2

Tengo Tango
Cannonball Adderley Sextet | Nippon Soul | Original Jazz Classics | OJC20 435-2(RLP 9477)
Urs Leimgruber | Ungleich | Hat Art | CD 6049

Tenk
John Lee Hooker Band | Moanin' The Blues | Charly | CRB 1029

Tennessee Waltz
Art Hodes-Jim Galloway | Live From Toronto's Cafe Des Copains | Music & Arts | CD 610
Johnny 'Big Mouse' Walker | Blue Love | Steeplechase | SCB 9005
King Curtis Band | King Curtis-Blow Man Blow | Bear Family Records | BCD 15670 CI
Lillian Boutté And Her Group | The Jazz Book | Blues Beacon | BLU-1020 2

Tenor Conclave
Prestige All Stars | Tenor Conclave | Original Jazz Classics | OJCCD 127-2
Don Rendell Nine | Earth Music | Spotlite | SPJ 515

Tenor Jump
Bruce Eskovitz Sextet | One For Newk | Koch Jazz | KOC 3-7801-2

Tenor Madness
Eddie Harris-Wendell Harrison Quintet | The Battle Of The Tenors-In Memory Of Eddie Harris | Enja | ENJ-9336 2
Sonny Rollins Quintet | The Prestige Legacy Vol.2:Battles Of Saxes | Prestige | PCD 24252-2
John Coltrane-The Prestige Recordings | Prestige | 16 PCD 4405-2
Jazz Gallerie:Sonny Rollins Vol.1 | RCA | 2127283-2
Tenor Tribute | Tenor Tribute Vol.2 | Soul Note | 121194-2
Phil Woods Quintet | Gratitude | Denon Compact Disc | CY-1316

Tenorlee-
Zoot Sims Quartet | Zoot Sims:Quartet&Sextet | Vogue | 21511522

Ten-Sion
Andre Hodeir And His Jazz Group De Paris | Jazz In Paris:Le Jazz Groupe De Paris Joue André Hodeir | EmArCy | 548792-2

Tension Detente
Soul Immigrants Plus Guests | A Healty Vibe | Lipstick Records | LIP 8947-2 HOT

Tensions
Charles Mingus Jazz Workshop | Blues & Roots | Atlantic | 8122-75205-2
Blues & Roots | Atlantic | 7567-81336-2

Tensions(alt.take)
Blues & Roots | Atlantic | 8122-75205-2
Hans Reichel-Rüdiger Carl Duo | Buben...Plus | FMP | CD 78

Tenthousand Only
Bill Carrothers-Bill Stewart | Bill Carrothers Duets With Bill Stewart | Dreyfus Jazz Line | FDM 37002-2

Tenuto
Duke Ellington And His Orchestra | The Intimate Ellington | Original Jazz Classics | OJCCD 730-2(2310787)

Teo
Miles Davis Quintet | Someday My Prince Will Come | CBS | CK 65919
Miles Davis With John Coltrane | CBS | CBS 88029
Michael Blake Group | Drift | Intuition Records | INT 3212-2

Teo Walks
Hector Martignon Group | Portrait In White And Black | Candid | CCD 79727

Teo's Bag
Miles Davis Quintet | Circle In The Round | CBS | 467898-2
Miles Davis Quintet 1965-1968 | CBS | C6K 67398
Miles Davis Quintet 1965-1968 | CBS | C6K 67398

Teo's Bag(alt.take)
Don Cherry/Ed Blackwell | Mu(The Complete Session) | Affinity | AFF 774

Tequila
King Curtis Band | King Curtis-Blow Man Blow | Bear Family Records | BCD 15670 CI
Stan Kenton And His Orchestra | At The Rendezvous Vol.1 | Status | CD 102(882198)
Wes Montgomery Quartet | Tequila | Verve | 547769-2
Wes Montgomery Quintet With The Claus Ogerman Orchestra | Tequila | CTI Records | PDCTI 1118-2

Tequila(alt.take)
Stochelo Rosenberg Group | Gypsy Swing | Verve | 527806-2

Tequilla
Wes Montgomery Quartet | Compact Jazz: Wes Montgomery | Verve | 831372-2
Ramsey Lewis Quintet | Ivory Pyramid | GRP | GRP 96882

Teresa
Jaco Pastorius Groups | Another Side Of Jaco Pastorius | Jazzpoint | JP 1064 CD
Jaco Pastorius Trio | Jaco Pastorius Broadway Blues & Theresa | Jazzpoint | JP 1053 CD
Jaco Pastorius Heavy'n Jazz & Stuttgart Aria | Jazzpoint | JP 1058 CD
Jaco Pastorius Broadway Blues & Theresa | Jazzpoint | JP 1053 CD

Teresa(track 1-3)
Charlie Byrd-Cal Tjader Orchestra | Tambu | Fantasy | FCD 9453-2

Teribee,Three Palm Slammy
Johnny Griffin Quartet | Way Out | Original Jazz Classics | OJCCD 1855-2

Terminal 'B'
Ronald Shannon Jackson And The Decoding Society | What Spirit Say | DIW | DIW 895 CD

Termini's Corner
Roland Kirk Quartet | Talkin' Verve-Roots Of Acid Jazz:Roland Kirk | Verve | 533101-2
Domino | Verve | 543833-2
Domino | Verve | 543833-2

Termini's Corner(6 breakdown takes)
Domino | Verve | 543833-2

Termini's Corner(alt.take)
Louis Moholo Trio | Tern | FMP | SAJ 43/44

Terpsichore
Howard Roberts Quintet | Good Pickins | Verve | MV 2677 IMS

Terra
Joey Baron Trio | Tongue In Groove | JMT Edition | 849158-2

Terra Branca
Batida | Terra Do Sul | Timeless | CD SJP 245

Terra Firma
Joe Gordon Quintet | Lookin' Good | Original Jazz Classics | OJCCD 1934-2(S 7597)

Terra Firma Irma
Adam Rudolph's Moving Pictures | Skyway | Soul Note | 121269-2

Terrace Theme
Kenny Burrell Quintet | Guitar Forms | Verve | 521403-2

Terrace Theme(alt.take 1)
Guitar Forms | Verve | 521403-2

Terrace Theme(alt.take 2)
Guitar Forms | Verve | 521403-2

Terrace Theme(alt.take 3)
Peter Erskine Trio | Time Being | ECM | 1532

Terraces
Shigeharu Mukai Group | Mukai Meets Gilberto | Denon Compact Disc | DC-8569

Terrain
Improvisors Pool | Background For Improvisors | FMP | CD 75

Terrain Turquoise
Rova Saxophone Quartet | The Crowd-For Elias Canetti | Hat Art | CD 6098

Terraplane Blues
Robert Johnson | Robert Johnson-King Of The Delta Blues | CBS | 493006-2
Paul Williams & Friends | In Memory Of Robert Johnson | Black Sun Music | 15017-2

Terre D'Agala
Gilles Torrent Jazztet | Terre Engloutie | Plainisphare | PL 1267-22

Terror Ride
Gus Viseur Quintet | Gus Viseur A Bruxelles | Harmonia Mundi | PJC 222006

Terry Anne
Tito Puente Orchestra | Planet Jazz:Tito Puente | Planet Jazz | 2165369-2

Terry Cloth
Larry Carlton Group | Kid Gloves | GRP | GRP 96832

Terry's Little Tune
Bishop Norman Williams Group | The One Mind Experience-The Bishop | Evidence | TR 101

Terry's Tune
Terry Gibbs Septet | Early Stan | Original Jazz Classics | OJCCD 654-2(P 7255)

Terry's Tune(alt.take 1)
Early Stan | Original Jazz Classics | OJCCD 654-2(P 7255)

Terry's Tune(alt.take 2)
Early Getz | Prestige | P 24088

Terschelling
Dioko | Potosi | Jazz Haus Musik | JHM 20

Teru
Blaufrontal | Stadtgarten Series Vol.5 | Jazz Haus Musik | JHM 1005 SER

Terz
Caoutchouc | Caoutchouc Plays Garcia Lorca | Timeless | CD SJP 399

Teseract
Cal Tjader Septet | A Fuego Vivo | Concord | CCD 4176

Tesoro
John Surman Quartet | Stranger Than Fiction | ECM | 1534

Tess
Michel Benita Quartet | Preferences | Label Bleu | LBLC 6532(882935)
Cootie Williams And His Orchestra | Big Band Bounce And Boogie:Echoes Of Harlem-Cootie Williams | Affinity | AFS 1031

Tessalation Row
Thomas Stabenow Trio | Human Spirit | Bassic-Sound | CD 009

Test
Bucky And John Pizzarelli Duo | The Pizzarellis,Bucky And John:Contrasts | Arbors Records | ARCD 19209

Tete-A-Tete
Art Pepper-George Cables Duo | Art Pepper:The Complete Galaxy Recordings | Galaxy | 16GCD 1016-2
Buddy Tate Band | Rock 'N Roll | Krazy Kat | KK 784 IMS

Tetegramatan-
Trevor Watts Moiré Music Drum Orchestra | A Wider Embrace | ECM | 1449

Tetegramatan(reprise)-
Tete Montoliu/Peter King Quintet | New Year's Morning '89 | Fresh Sound Records | FSR 117(835311)

Tethered Moon
Masabumi 'Poo' Kikuchi Trio | Tethered Moon | Paddle Wheel | KICJ 93

Tetragon
Joe Henderson Quartet | Joe Henderson:The Milestone Years | Milestone | 8MCD 4413-2
Mulgrew Miller Quartet | The Countdown | Landmark | LCD 1519-2

Tetris
I.C.P.Tentet | I.C.P.-Tentet In Berlin | FMP | SAJ 23

Teu(tone)ntanz
Morgenland/Yarinistan | Vielleicht | Riskant | 568-72229

Tex Mex Teevee
Wollie Kaiser Timeghost | Tust Du Fühlen Gut | Jazz Haus Musik | JHM 0060 CD
Mose Allison Quintet | Gimecrats And Gewgaws | Blue Note | 823211-2

Texanna
Allan Holdsworth Group | The Sixteen Man Of Tain | Cream Records | CR 610-2

Texas
Louis Jordan And His Tympany Five | Louis Jordan-Let The Good Times Roll: The Complete Decca Recordings 1938-1954 | Bear Family Records | BCD 15557 IH

Texas And Pacific
Louis Jordan Greatest Hits-Vol.2 | MCA | 1337

Texas Girl At The Funeral Of Her Father
Yakou Tribe | Red & Blue Days | Traumton Records | 4474-2
Dave Bartholomew And His Band | Shrimp And Gumbo | Pathe | 1566311

Texas Koto Blues
Alberta Hunter With The Red Onion Jazz Babies | Louis Armstrong And The Blues Singers 1924-1930 | Affinity | AFS 1018(6)

Texas Moaner Blues
Clarence Williams' Blue Five | Louis Armstrong 1924-25 | Village(Jazz Archive) | VILCD 009-2
Red Onion Jazz Babies,The | King Oliver-Louis Armstrong | Milestone | M 47017

Texas Shuffle
Count Basie And His Orchestra | Disque D'Or | Vogue | 400525

Textures
Herbie Hancock Group | Mr. Hands | CBS | 32362

Thaba Bhosigo
Dollar Brand Quintet | South Africa | Enja | 5007 Digital (807535)

Thag's Dance
Oscar Peterson Trio | Oscar Peterson-The London House Sessions | Verve | 531766-2

Thalia
The Dance Band | Pierides | Line Records | COCD 9.00377 0

Thamar
Chick Corea Trio | A.R.C. | ECM | 1009

Thanatos
Nina Simone Quartet | Fodder On My Wings | CY Records | 733622

Thangs
Bennie Wallace Quartet | The Talk Of The Town | Enja | ENJ-7091 2
Bennie Wallace Quintet | The Art Of The Saxophone | Denon Compact Disc | CY-1648

Thank Heaven For The Little Girls
Shorty Rogers And His Giants | 'Gigi' In Jazz | Fresh Sound Records | 12588 CD(RCA)

Thank You Blues
Enrico Rava Quartet | Opening Night | ECM | 1224

Thank You!!!
Dave Brubeck | Two Generations Of Brubeck | Atlantic | SD 1645

Thank You(For Let Me Be Myself)
Eddie Jefferson And His Band | Eddie Jefferson:Vocalese | 32 Jazz | 32123

Thank You-Fallettinme Be Mice Elf Agin
Ella Fitzgerald And Her Famous Orchestra | The Radio Years 1940 | Jazz Unlimited | JUCD 2065

Thank Your Stars
Louis Armstrong And His Orchestra | Louis Armstrong Vol.2 | Ambassador | CLA 1902

Thanks A Million
Louis Armstrong With Luis Russell And His Orchestra | Ambassador Louis Armstrong Vol.1(1935) | Ambassador | CLA 1901
Randy Sandke Quintet | I Hear Music | Concord | CCD 4566

Thanks A Million-
The New York Allstars | We Love You,Louis! | Nagel-Heyer | CD 029
Louis Armstrong With Luis Russell And His Orchestra | Ambassador Louis Armstrong Vol.1(1935) | Ambassador | CLA 1901

Thanks Again
Vanasse/Vitous | Nouvelle Cuisine | Justin Time | JTR 8406

Thanks For Everything
Count Basie And His Orchestra | Basie On Roulette, Vol. 22: Back With Basie | Vogue | 500022

Thanks For The Beautiful Land On The Delta
Duke Ellington And His Orchestra | That's Jazz Vol.31: New Orleans Suite | Atlantic | ATL 50403

Thanks For The Boogie Ride
Anita O'Day With The Cal Tjader Quartet | Time For 2 | Verve | 559808-2

Thanks For The Memory
Benny Goodman And His Orchestra | Benny Goodman Forever | RCA | NL 89955(2) DP
Erroll Garner | The Erroll Garner Collection Vol.4&5 | EmArCy | 511821-2 PMS
Leonard Feather All Stars | Thanks For The Memory | EPM Musique | FDC 5159
Stacey Kent With The Jim Tomlison Quintet | Dreamsville | Candid | CCD 79775
Stan Getz Quintet | Stan Getz Highlights:The Best Of The Verve Years Vol.2 | Verve | 517330-2
Stan Getz Plays | Verve | 2304387 IMS
Erroll Garner Trio | The Concert Garner | Jazz Groove | 008 IMS

Thanks For The Ride
Gary Smulyan Quartet With Strings | Gary Smulyan With Strings | Criss Cross | Criss 1129

Thanks For You
The Herdsmen | The Herdsmen Play Paris | Original Jazz Classics | OJC 116(F 3201)

Thanks To Isidor
Cassandra | Enten Eller | SPLASC(H) Records | H 176

Thanksgiving
Peter Kater Orchestra | Two Hearts | Optimism | PDK 4001 CD

Thanksgiving Suite:
Vince Guaraldi Group | Charlie Brown's Holiday Hits | Fantasy | FCD 9682-2

Thanksgiving Theme
Dave Grusin | Mountain Dance | GRP | GRP 95072

Thanksong
Dollar Brand | Anthem For The New Nations | Denon Compact Disc | DC-8588

That Ain't Right
Nat King Cole Trio | The Great Nat King Cole | Laserlight | 15733

That Came Down On Me
Gunter Hampel Quartet | Time Is Now-Live At The Eldena Jazz Festival 1992 | Birth | CD 042
Jimmy Smith With The Oliver Nelson Orchestra | Peter & The Wolf | Verve | 547264-2

That Cat-
The Ink Spots | If I Didn't Care | Pro-Arte | CDD 555

That Chicks Too Young To Fry
Ken Hyder's Talisker | The Last Battle | View | VS 107 IMS

That Da-Da Strain
Bud Freeman And His Famous Chicagoans | Bud Freeman(1927-1940) | CDS Records Ltd. | RPCD 604
Muggsy Spanier And His Ragtime Band | Jazz Classics In Digital Stereo: Muggsy Spanier 1931 & 1939 | CDS Records Ltd. | REB 687
Wild Bill Davison And His World Famous Jazz Band | Wild Bill Davison And His Jazz Band 1943 | Jazzology | JCD-103

That Did It,Marie
Margie Evans With Chicago's Young Blues Generation | Blues Live '82-American Folk Blues Festival | L+R Records | LS 42052

That Fat Man
Will Osborne And His Orchestra | The Uncollected:Will Osborne | Hindsight | HSR 197

That Funky Train
Preston Jackson And His New Orleans Band | New Orleans To Chicago:The Forties | Gannet | CJR 1002

That Goldblatt Magic
Ralph Sharon Sextet | Mr.& Mrs. Jazz | Fresh Sound Records | FSR 2028(Bethlehem BCP 13)

That Jones Boy
Maynard Ferguson With The Birdland Dreamband | The Birdland Dream Band Vol.1 | Fresh Sound Records | 58110 CD(RCA)

That Lucky Old Sun(Just Rolls Around Heaven)
Grant Green Quintet | His Majesty King Funk/Up With Donald Byrd | Verve | 527474-2
Louis Armstrong With Gordon Jenkins And His Orchestra And Choir | Louis Armstrong-All Time Greatest Hits | MCA | MCD 11032
Ray Charles With Orchestra | Ray Charles | London | 6.24034 AL

That Man
Rosemary Clooney With The Count Basie Orchestra | At Long Last | Concord | CCD 4795

That Misty Red Beast
Toots Thielemans Quartet With Orchestra | Bluesette | CBS | CDCOL 26604

That Naughty Waltz
Benny Goodman And His Orchestra | The Benny Goodman Caravans Vol.3-One O'Clock Jump | Giants Of Jazz | GOJ 1036

That Old Black Magic
Ashley Alexander Big Band | Power Slide | Pausa | PR 7178(952087)
Billy Eckstine With The Billy May Orchestra | Billy Eckstine | Laserlight | 17070

Ella Fitzgerald And Her Orchestra | Jazz Collection:Ella Fitzgerald | Laserlight | 24397
Ella Fitzgerald With Benny Carter And His Orchestra | Ella:The Legendary American Decca Recordings | GRP | GRP 46482
Ella Fitzgerald With The Billy May Orchestra | The Harold Arlen Songbook | Verve | 817526-1 IMS
Erroll Garner | The Erroll Garner Collection Vol.4&5 | EmArCy | 511821-2 PMS
Glenn Miller And His Orchestra | Original Recordings From 1938 to 1942,Vol.2 | RCA | 2118549-2
Ike Quebec Quartet | Blue And Sentimental | Blue Note | 784098-2
Blue Eyes-Sinatra Songs The Blue Note Way | Blue Note | 789914-2
Lars Gullin Quartet | Lars Gullin 1953,Vol.2:Moden Sounds | Dragon | DRCD 234
Lionel Hampton With The Oscar Peterson Trio | Compact Jazz: Lionel Hampton | Verve | 833287-2
Oscar Peterson Trio | JATP In Tokyo | Pablo | 2620104-2
The Song Is You-The Best Of The Verve Songbooks | Verve | 531558-2
Oscar Peterson Plays The Harold Arlen Song Book | Verve | 589103-2
Peggy Connelly With The Russ Garcia 'Wigville' Band | Peggy Connelly | Fresh Sound Records | FSR 2018(Bethlehem BCP 53)
Shirley Horn With The Quincy Jones Orchestra | Trav'lin' Light:The Johnny Mercer Songbook | Verve | 555402-2

That Old Black Magic(part 1)
Lionel Hampton Quartet | The Complete Lionel Hampton Quartets And Quintets With Oscar Peterson On Verve | Verve | 559797-2

That Old Black Magic(part 2)
André Previn | Previn At Sunset | Black Lion | BLCD 760189

That Old Devil Called Love
Billie Holiday With The Toots Camarata Orchestra | Hot Tracks For Cool Cats Vol.3 | Polydor | 816411-2
Chet Baker And His Orchestra | Compact Jazz: Chet Baker | Verve | 840632-2 PMS
Ella Fitzgerald And Her All Stars | All That Jazz | Pablo | 2310938-2
Gail Wynters With The Gordon Brisker Quintet | My Shining Hour | Naxos Jazz | 86027-2
Miles Davis Quartet | Welcome To Jazz: Miles Davis Vol.2 | Koch Records | 321 975 D1
Zoot Sims Quartet | Warm Tenor | Pablo | 2310831-2

That Old Devil Moon
Clifford Jordan And The Magic Triangle | On Stage Vol. 1 | Steeplechase | SCS 1071

That Old Feeling
Art Tatum | Art Tatum-The Complete Pablo Solo Masterpieces | Pablo | 7 PACD 4404-2
The Tatum Solo Masterpieces Vol.5 | Pablo | 2310790
Chet Baker Quartet | Chet Baker Sings | Pacific Jazz | 300067(PJ 1222)
Ella Fitzgerald With The Frank DeVol Orchestra | Ella Fitzgerald Sings Sweet Songs For Swingers | Verve | 9860417
Ella Fitzgerald-Joe Pass Duo | Fitzgerald & Pass... Again | Original Jazz Classics | OJCCD 1052-2(2310772)
Fats Waller With Adelaide Hall | Fats Waller In London | EMI Records | EG 2604421
George Masso Quintet | Just For A Thrill | Sackville | SKCD2-2022
Joe Temperley Quartet | Easy To Remember | Hep | CD 2083
Julie London With Pete King And His Orchestra | About The Blues/London By Night | Capitol | 535208-2
Karin Krog With Warne Marsh And Red Mitchell | Karin Krog Jubilee-The Best Of 30 Years | Verve | 523716-2
Lee Konitz Trio | Motion | Verve | 557107-2
Louis Armstrong With The Oscar Peterson Quartet | Louis Armstrong Meets Oscar Peterson | Verve | 825713-2
Maxine Sullivan With The Art Hodes Sextet | We Just Couldn't Say Goodbye | Audiophile | ACD-128
Pee Wee Russell And His Orchestra | Portrait Of Pee Wee | Fresh Sound Records | FSR-CD 126(882874)
Warren Vaché Quartet | Warm Evening | Concord | CCD 4392

That Preachin' Man
Billy Cotton And His Band | The Rhythm Man | Saville Records | SVL 149 IMS

That Rhythm Man
Duke Ellington And His Memphis Men | The Complete Duke Ellington-Vol. 2 | CBS | CBS 68275
Louis Armstrong And His Orchestra | Louis Armstrong Vol.4: Hot Fives & Sevens | JSP Records | JSPCD 315

That Slavic Smile
Modern Jazz Quartet | MJQ 40 | Atlantic | 7567-82330-2
Echoes | Pablo | 2312142-2

That Song About The Midway
The Danish Radio Jazz Orchestra | This Train:The Danish Radio Jazz Orchestra Plays The Music Of Ray Pitts | dacapo | DCCD 9428

That Special Feeling
Tommy Dorsey And His Orchestra | The Indispensable Tommy Dorsey Vol.2/4(1937.1938) | RCA | 2126406-2

That Terrific Rainbow
Art Ensemble Of Chicago | The Spiritual | Black Lion | BLCD 760219

That Time
Tommy Flanagan Trio | Jazz Poet | Timeless | CD SJP 301

That Too Do Blues
Benny Moten's Kansas City Orchestra | The Complete Bennie Moten Vol.5/6 | RCA | PM 45688

That Will Never Happen No More
Joe Venuti And His New Yorkers | The Big Bands Of Joe Venuti Vol.1 (1928-30) | JSP Records | 1111

That! Afternoon In Paris
Bob Berg Group | Short Stories | Denon Compact Disc | CY-1768

That´s The Trouble With Us
J.B.Hutto Quartet | Slideslinger | Black & Blue | BLE 59.540 2

That'll Just 'Bout Knock Me Out
Louis Jordan And His Tympany Five | Louis Jordan Vol.2-Knock Me Out | Swingtime(Contact) | ST 1012

That's A Plenty
Alvino Rey And His Orchestra With The King Sisters | The Uncollected:Alvino Rey,Vol.3 | Hindsight | HSR 196
Benny Goodman And His Orchestra | 40th Anniversary Concert-Live At Carnegie Hall | London | 820349-2
Live At Carnegie Hall-40th Anniversary Concert | Decca | 6.28451 DP
Benny Goodman Quartet | The King Of Swing 1958-1967 Era | Festival | ???
George Lewis And His New Orleans Jazzband | George Lewis In Japan | Storyville | SLP 514
Jack Teagarden And His Band | The Club Hangover Broadcast | Arbors Records | ARCD 19150/51
Jimmy McPartland And His Dixielanders | Victor Jazz History Vol.18:Chicago Jazz(1934-64) | RCA | 2135737-2
Muggsy Spanier And His Dixieland All Stars | At Club Hangover-Vol. 2 | Storyville | SLP 249
Muggsy Spanier And His V-Disc All Stars | Muggsy Spanier And Bud Freeman:V-Discs 1944-45 | Jazz Unlimited | JUCD 2049
New Orleans Owls | The Owls' Hoot | Frog | DGF 2
Roy Eldridge And His Central Plaza Dixielanders | The Very Best Of Dixieland Jazz | Verve | 535529-2
Sammy Price Sextet | Sammy Price In Europe | Jazz Anthology | JA 5192
The Steamboat Rats | ...Got That Swing | Elite Special | 73435

That's A Serious Thing
Eddie Condon's Hot Shots | The Indispensable Jack Teagarden(1928-1957) | RCA | ND 89613

That's All
Andrew Hill Trio | So In Love | Fresh Sound Records | FSR 653(Warwick W 2002)
Ben Webster All Stars | Compact Jazz: Coleman Hawkins/Ben Webster | Verve | 833296-2
Ben Webster And His Orchestra | Verve Jazz Masters 43:Ben Webster | Verve | 525431-2
Ben Webster Quartet | Live At The Jazzhus Montmartre,Vol.1 | Jazz Colours | 874710-2
Cal Tjader Sextet | Soul Bird | Verve | 549111-2
CoJazz feat. Gianni Basso | All Those Melodies | TCB Records | TCB 20402
Donald Byrd Quintet | Chant | Blue Note | LT 991 (GXK 8183)
Hank Crawford Quintet | After Dark | Milestone | MCD 9279-2
Haze Greenfield Group | All About You | Black-Hawk | BKH 535 CD
Jimmy Bruno Trio | Burnin' | Concord | CCD 4612
Jimmy McGriff Sextet | McGriff's House Party | Milestone | MCD 9300-2
June Christy And Her Orchestra | The Misty Miss Christy | Capitol | 798452-2
Louis Mazetier | In Concert:What A Treat! | Jazz Connaisseur | JCCD 9522-2
Lucky Millinder And His Orchestra | Big Band Bounce & Boogie:Apollo Jump | Affinity | AFS 1004
Pepper Adams Quartet | Reflectory | Muse | MR 5182
Sarah Vaughan With The Quincy Jones Orchestra | Jazz In Paris:Sarah Vaughan-Vaughan And Violins | EmArCy | 065004-2
Sarah Vaughan With The Roland Hanna Quartet | Sarah Vaughan Birthday Celebration | Fantasy | FANCD 6090-2
Scott Hamilton Quartet | East Of The Sun | Concord | CCD 4583
Sister Rosetta Tharpe With The Original Tuxedo Jazz Band | Live In Paris 1964 | France's Concert | FCD 118
Tete Montoliu | That's All | Steeplechase | SCCD 31199
Wild Bill Davis Super Trio | That's All | Jazz Connaisseur | JCCD 9005-2
All Star Trombone Spectacular | The Progressive Records All Star Trombone Spectacular | Progressive | PRO 7018 IMS

That's All I Want From You
Cadillac George Harris With Band | Mississippi Burnin' Blues | Mardi Gras Records | MG 1017

That's All Right
Eddie Kirkland Duo | Detroit Blues | Anthology of the Blues | AB 5606
Mose Allison Trio | Mose Allison Sings The 7th Son | Prestige | PR20 7279-2
Mose Alife!/Wild Man On The Loose | Warner | 8122-75439-2
Snooks Eaglin | That's All Right | Original Blues Classics | OBCCD 568-2(BV 1046)

That's All She Wrote
Nat King Cole With The Gordon Jenkins Orchestra | Where Did Everyone Go ? | Capitol | EMS 1114

That's All There Is To It
Donald Byrd Quintet | Getting Down To Business | Landmark | LCD 1523-2

That's All There Is To That
Etta Jones With Her Trio | Something Nice | Original Jazz Classics | OJCCD 221-2(P 7194)
Etta Jones With The Houston Person Band | Sugar | Muse | MCD 5379

That's All(single version)
Big Bill Broonzy Group | Big Bill Broonzy 1935-1940 | Black & Blue | BLE 59.253 2

That's Because
Ron Carter Quartet | Stardust | somethin'else | 537813-2

That's Deep
Nicolas Simion Quartet feat. Tomasz Stanko | Transylvanian Dance | Tutu Records | 888164-2*

That's Dope
Alex Smith Quintet | Jazzville Vol.2 | Fresh Sound Records | FSR 601(Dawn DLP 1107)

That's Earl Brother
Dizzy Gillespie Sextet | In The Beginning | Prestige | P 24030
John Marshall Quintet | Theme Of No Repeat | Organic Music | ORGM 9719
Tom Harrell With The Mulgrew Miller Trio | Trumpet Legacy | Milestone | MCD 9286-2
Ann Cole With Band | Got My Mojo Working | Krazy Kat | KK 782 IMS

That's For Me
Louis Armstrong And His All Stars | Louis Armstrong:C'est Si Bon | Dreyfus Jazz Line | FDM 36730-2
Swing Legends:Louis Armstrong | Nimbus Records | NI 2012
Louis Armstrong:Complete 1950-1951 All Stars Decca Recordings | Definitive Records | DRCD 11188

That's For Sure
The Hudson Project | The Hudson Project | Stretch Records | SCD 9024-2

That's For You
Thad Jones-Mel Lewis Orchestra | A Touch Of Class | West Wind Orchestra Series | 2402 CD

That's Grand
Abbey Lincoln With Her Quintet | That's Him! | Original Jazz Classics | OJCCD 085-2

That's Him
Sonny Rollins-The Freelance Years:The Complete Riverside & Contemporary Recordings | Riverside | 5 RCD 4427-2
Nina Simone With The Bob Mercey Orchestra | The Amazing Nina Simone | Official | 6002

That's How I Feel About You
J.J.Johnson-Kai Winding Quintet (Jay&Kai) | Kai Winding And Jay Jay Johnson | Bethlehem | BET 6026-2(BCP 76)

That's In
Buddy Guy Blues Band | Buddy Guy-The Complete Chess Studio Recordings | MCA | MCD 09337

That's It
Buddy Guy Chicago Blues Band | Blues Rarities | Chess | 6.28601 DP
Lars Gullin Quartet | Made In Sweden Vol.1: 1949 to March 1951 | Magnetic Records | MRCD 106

That's Life
Ray Gelato Giants | The Full Flavour | Linn Records | AKD 034

That's Love
Art Pepper Quintet With Strings | Art Pepper:The Complete Galaxy Recordings | Galaxy | 16GCD 1016-2
Lonnie Johnson Trio | He's A Jelly Roll Baker | Bluebird | 63 66064 2

That's Me
Charly Antolini Quartet | Menue/Finale | BELL Records | BLR 84068

That's My Baby
Chris Barber Jazz And Blues Band feat. Wendell Brunious | Panama! | Timeless | CD TTD 568

That's My Desire
Frankie Laine With Carl Fischer And His Orchestra | The Uncollected:Frankie Laine | Hindsight | HSR 198 (835569)
Louis Armstrong And His All Stars | At The Pasadena Civic Auditorium | GNP Crescendo | GNP 11001
The Beautiful American | Jazz Society(Vogue) | 670501
Rockin' Chair | Topline Records | TOP 119
Peanuts Holland Sextet | Jazz In Paris:Peanuts Holland-Buck Clayton-Charlie Singleton | EmArCy | 013032-2

That's My Girl
Nat King Cole And His Trio With Pete Rugolo's Orchestra | Lush Life | Capitol | 780595-2
Nat King Cole Trio With Pete Rugolo's Orchestra | Nat King Cole:For Sentimental Reasons | Dreyfus Jazz Line | FDM 36740-2
Sir Roland Hanna | Plays The Music Of Alec Wilder | EmArCy | 558839-2

That's My Home
Louis Armstrong With Chick Webb's Orchestra | Best Of The Complete RCA Victor Recordings | RCA | 2663636-2
Louis Armstrong With Sy Oliver And His Orchestra | Louis Armstrong:The New And Revisited Musical Autobiography Vol.3 | Jazz Unlimited | JUCD 2005
Punch Miller's New Orleans Band | The Larry Borenstein Collection Vol.11:Punch Miller | 504 Records | 504CD 40

That's My Story
Lloyd Smith's Gut-Bucketeers | That's My Stuff | Frog | DGF 7

That's Nat
Barry Altschul Quintet | That's Nice | Soul Note | SN 1115

That's No Joke
Robert Wilkins | The Greatest In Country Blues Vol.2(1927-1936) | Story Of Blues | CD 3522 2

That's Puente
Howard Rumsey's Lighthouse All-Stars | In The Solo Spotlite | Original Jazz Classics | OJCCD 451-2

That's Right
Nat Adderley And His Orchestra | Work Songs | Milestone | M 47047
The Young Lions | Jazz Gallery:Lee Morgan Vol.1 | RCA | 2127281-2

That's Right I'm Wrong
Jack Teagarden With The Hoagy Carmichael Orchestra | Jack Teagarden | Queen-Disc | 027

That's The Blues Old Man
Johnny Hodges Orchestra | Passion Flower 1940-46 | Bluebird | 63 66616-2

That's The Evening For Santa Claus
Joe Venuti And His New Yorkers | The Big Bands Of Joe Venuti Vol.1 (1928-30) | JSP Records | 1111

That's The Law
Cootie Williams And His Orchestra | Rhythm And Jazz In The Mid Forties | Official | 3014

That's The One
Five Red Caps | Lenox Avenue Jump | Krazy Kat | KK 779 IMS

That's The Stuff You Gotta Watch
Rubberlegs Williams With Herbie Fields' Band | Obscure Blues Shouters Vol.2 | Blue Moon | BMCD 6011

That's The Time
Tampa Red And The Chicago Five | Chicago Blues(1935-1942) | RCA | 2126404-2

That's The Way It Goes
Per Husby Orchestra | Dedications | Affinity | AFF 136

That's The Way It Is
Jimmy Giuffre 3 | The Jimmy Giuffre Three | Atlantic | 7567-90981-2
The Jimmy Giuffre 3-Hollywood & Newport 1957-1958 | Fresh Sound Records | FSCD 1026
Milt Jackson-Ray Brown Jam | Montreux '77-The Art Of The Jam Session | Pablo | 2620106

That's Tough
Jimmy Giuffre 3 | Jimmy Giuffre 3, 1961 | ECM | 1438/39(849644-2)

That's True That's True
Flight, Bremen 1961 | Hat Art | CD 6071

That's What
Nat King Cole Trio | Great Capitol Masters | Pathe | 1566251(Capitol)

That's What Friends Are For
Miles Davis Group | Decoy | CBS | 468702-2

That's What Happened
Osie Johnson And His Orchestra | A Bit Of The Blues | Fresh Sound Records | NL 45989(RCA LPM 1369)

That's What It Takes
Roy Fox & His Band | This Is Romance | Saville Records | SVL 166 IMS

That's What The Man Said
Ben Sidran Group | Heat Wave | VeraBra Records | CDVBR 2096-2

That's What You Gotta Do
Ella Johnson With Orchestra | Swing Me | Official | 6009

That's What You Think
George Williams' Swinging Big Band | Put On Your Dancing Shoes | Fresh Sound Records | 054 2602771(United Artists UAS 6076)
Putney Dandridge Band | Putney Dandridge 1935-1936 | Timeless | CBC 1-023

That's What Zoot Said
Jenny Evans And Her Quintet | Shiny Stockings | Enja | ENJ-9317 2
Dinah Washington With The Tab Smith Orchestra | A Slick Chick(On The Mellow Side)-The Rhythm&Blues Years | EmArCy | 814184-1 IMS

That's When We Thought Of Love
Billy Taylor Trio | Custom Taylored | Fresh Sound Records | FSR-CD 0205

That's Why I Love You Like I Do
Koko Taylor With The Mighty Joe Young Group | I Got What It Takes | Sonet | 198212(SNTF 687)

That's Your Red Wagon
Red Garland Trio | Red In Bluesville | Original Jazz Classics | OJCCD 295-2
Buster Benton Blues Band | Blues At The Top | Black & Blue | BLE 59.001 2

The
Volker Kriegel Group | Inside Missing Link | MPS | 88030-2

The 12,5 % Solution
Bill Dixon Septet | New Music: Second Wave | Savoy | SJL 2235 (801211)

The 37th Chamber
Nexus | Urban Shout | SPLASC(H) Records | H 170

The 490
Archie Shepp Quintet | Down Home New York | Soul Note | 121102-2

The 8th Of July 1969
John Clark Quartet | Faces | ECM | 1176

The Abyss
Triocolor | Colours Of Ghana | ACT | 9285-2

The Accrator I
Colours Of Ghana | ACT | 9285-2

The Accrator II
Renee Rosnes Sextet | Ancestors | Blue Note | 834634-2

The Adventures Of Hasso Sigbjörnsen
John Surman Orchestra | Tales Of The Algonquin | Deram | 844884-2

The Adventures Of Max And Ben
Barbara Thompson's Paraphernalia | Mother Earth | VeraBra Records | CDVBR 2005-2

The Adventures Of Water
Lee Konitz Quintet | Lee Konitz/Rhapsody | Paddle Wheel | KICJ 174

The African As Non-American-
Sangoma Everett Quartet | The Courage To Listen To You Heart | TCB Records | TCB 97202

The African Queen
Yusef Lateef With Eternal Wind And The 'Kölner Rundfunk Orchester' | The African American Epic Suite:Music For Quintet And Orchestra | ACT | 9214-2

The African-American Epic Suite:
Dizzy Gillespie With THE Orchestra | One Night In Washington | Elektra | 96-0300-1 TIS

The After Thought
Ahmad Jamal Trio | Live In Paris 1992 | Dreyfus Jazz Line | FDM 37019-2

The Aftermath
Live In Paris 92 | Birdology | 849408-2
The Tremble Kids All Stars | Dixieland Forever Vol.2 | BELL Records | BLR 89046

The Agent-
Stan Getz With The Eddie Sauter Orchestra | Stan Getz Plays The Music Of Mickey One | Verve | 531232-2
Anthony Braxton With The Rova Saxophone Quartet | The Aggregate | Sound Aspects | sas CD 023

The Alchemist
Wayne Escoffery Quintet | Intuition | Nagel-Heyer | CD 2038
Ornette Coleman Quartet | Beauty Is A Rare Thing:Ornette Coleman-The Complete Atlantic Recordings | Atlantic | 8122-71410-2

The Alchemy Of Scott LaFaro
Marcello Rosa Sextet | The Blue Rose | Penta Flowers | CDPIA 015

The Alien Lounge
Charlie Barnet And His Orchestra | The Indispensable Charlie Barnet Vol.1/2 | RCA | 2135554-2

The Alligatory Abagua
Joe Chambers Sextet | The Almoravid | 32 Jazz | 32099

The Aloe And The Wild Rose-
Gato Barbieri Sextet | Gato Barbieri:The Complete Flying Dutchman Recordings 1969-1973 | RCA | 2154555-2

The Amazon River
Billy Oskay/Michael O'Domhnaill | Nightnoise | Windham Hill | WD 1031

The Ancient Sound

TITELVERZEICHNIS

Cathy Hayes With The Barney Kessel Orchestra | It's All Right With Me | Fresh Sound Records | FSR 531(HiFiJazz R 416)

The Angle
Khan Jamal Sextet | Infinity | Stash Records | ST 278(807425)

The Animal Race
Jelly Roll Morton | The Library Of Congress Recordings | Affinity | CD AFS 1010-3

The Anniversary
Tony Williams Quintet | Tokyo Live | Blue Note | 799031-2

The Answer
Klaus Ignatzek Quintet | The Answer! | Candid | CCD 79534
Grover Washington Jr. Septet | Paradise | Elektra | 7559-60537-2

The Answer In Your Eyes
Sterling Young And His Orchestra | The Uncollected: Sterling Young | Hindsight | HSR 113

The Answer Is The Blues
Jim Hall Quintet | Panorama-Live At The Village Vanguard | Telarc Digital | CD 83408

The Ant & The Elk
Dizzy Gillespie/Max Roach | Max+Dizzy | A&M Records | 396404-2

The Apartment
Stan Getz With The Eddie Sauter Orchestra | Stan Getz Plays The Music Of Mickey One | Verve | 531232-2

The Apartment-
Jimmy Smith With The Claus Ogerman Orchestra | Any Number Can Win | Verve | 557447-2

The Ape Woman
Gerry Mulligan Concert Jazz Band | Swiss Radio Days Jatt Sries Vol.12:Gerry Mulligan And The Concert Jazz Big Band | TCB Records | TCB 02122

The Arch-
World Trio | World Trio | VeraBra Records | CDVBR 2052-2

The Arch Mage
Paul Bley Synthesizer Show | The Paul Bley Synthesizer Show | Milestone | M 9033

The Arrow
Jamie Findlay | Amigos Del Corazon | Acoustic Music Records | 319.1100.2

The Art Of Being
Peter Kowald Group | When The Is Out You Don't See Stars | FMP | CD 38

The Art Of Happiness
Ronald Shannon Jackson And The Decoding Society | Mandance | Antilles | ???

The Art Of Weathering November
Victor Feldman Quartet | The Artful Dodger | Concord | CCD 4038

The Ash Grove
Vienna Art Orchestra | Chapter II | Amadeo | 849066-2

The Awakening
Chico Freeman And Brainstorm | Threshold | IN+OUT Records | 7022-2
Cindy Blackman Quintet | Arcane | Muse | MCD 5341
Woody Shaw Quintet | Song Of Songs | Contemporary | C 7632

The Babel Fish
Hal Galper Quintet | Let's Call This That | Double Time Records | DTRCD-157

The Bach Suite:
Oscar Peterson Quartet | Oscar Peterson:The Composer | Pablo | 2310970-2

The Bach Suite: Allegro
Don Bagley Trio | Basically Bagley | Blue Moon | BMCD 1601

The Back Beat
Horace Silver Quintet | The Stylings Of Silver | Blue Note | 300168(1562)

The Back Sliders
Art Blakey And The Jazz Messengers | Roots And Herbs | Blue Note | 521956-2

The Back Sliders(alt.take)
Dexter Gordon Quartet | A Swingin' Affair | Blue Note | 784133-2

The Bad And The Beautiful
Dominique Eade With Band | When The Wind Was Cool | RCA | 2668858-2
Mark Murphy And His Sextet | Bop For Kerouac | Muse | MCD 5253

The Bad Game
Joe Henderson Quartet | Joe Henderson:The Milestone Years | Milestone | 8MCD 4413-2
Sandy Brown With The Brian Lemon Trio | In The Evening | Hep | CD 2017

The Badger
Horace Silver Quintet | Blowin' The Blues Away | Blue Note | 495342-2

The Bagdad Blues
Chet Baker-Stan Getz Quintet | The Stockholm Concerts | Verve | 537555-2

The Baggage Room Blues
Ketil Bjornstad Group | Grace | EmArCy | 013622-2

The Bait
Susannah McCorkle With The Ken Peplowski Quintet | No More Blues | Concord | CCD 4370

The Balance
Klaus Ignatzek Group Feat.Dave Liebman | Tender Mercies | Nabel Records:Jazz Network | LP 4621

The Balanced Scales-
European Jazz Ensemble | European Jazz Ensemble At The Philharmonic Cologne | M.A Music | A 800-2

The Ballad
Kick | Wolfhound's Kick | BELL Records | BLR 84041

The Ballad Medley:
Johnny Hodges Orchestra | The Rabbit's Work On Verve In Chronological Order, Vol. 6 | Verve | 2304446 IMS

The Ballad Of All The Sad Young Men
Nils Landgren Group | Sentimental Journey | ACT | 9409-2
Georgie Fame & The Danish Radio Big Band | Endangered Species | Music Mecca | CD 1040-2

The Ballad Of Chet Kincaid(Hikky-Burr)
Raphael Fays | Raphael Fays | Decca | 6.24130 AP

The Ballad Of Little Girl Dancer
Taj Mahal | At The New Morning Blues Festival | Spiegelei | 170600

The Ballad Of The Fallen
Irene Schweizer | Piano Solo Vol.1 | Intakt Records | CD 020

The Ballance
Brad Mehldau | Elegiac Cycle | Warner | 9362-47357-2

The Band Returns
Franz Koglmann Pipetet | Orte Der Geometrie | Hat Art | CD 6018

The Banyan Tree Song
New Orleans Klezmer Allstars | Manichalfwitz | Gert Town Records | GT-1117

The Barbara Song
Gil Evans Orchestra | The Individualism Of Gil Evans | Verve | 833804-2 PMS

The Barley
Eric Dolphy Quartet | Out There | Original Jazz Classics | OJC20 023-2(NJ 8252)

The Baron
Out There | New Jazz | NJSA 8252-6
Eric Dolphy:The Complete Prestige Recordings | Prestige | 9 PRCD-4418-2
Red Rodney Quintet | The Red Rodney Quintets | Fantasy | FCD 24758-2
Prestige First Sessions, Vol.3 | Prestige | PCD 24116-2

The Basilisk
John Tchicai-Vitold Rek Duo | Art Of The Duo:Satisfaction | Enja | 7033-2

The Bastard Period
Jerry Bergonzi 4et | On Again | RAM Records | RMCD 4527

The Bat
Pat Metheny Group | Offramp | ECM | 1216(817138-2)

The Bat(part II)
Steve Lacy Trio | Bye-Ya | Freelance | FRL-CD 025

The Bath
Father Tom Vaughn Trio | Joyful Jazz | Concord | CJ 16

The Battle Of Laatzen
Fred Houn & The Afro-Asian Music Ensemble | We Refused To Be Used And Abused | Soul Note | 121167-2

The Beach
Ketil Bjornstad Group | Seafarer's Song | EmArCy | 9865777
Fritz Pauer Trio | Blues Inside Out | MPS | 68218

The Bead Game
Hot Mallets | Hot Mallets...Live | Jazzcharge | JC 8302

The Bean Stalks Again
Günter Lenz Springtime | Roaring Plenties | L+R Records | LR 40005

The Bear Walks
Raymond Scott And His Orchestra | The Uncollected:Raymond Scott Vol.2 | Hindsight | HSR 211

The Beast Inside
Billy Drummond Quartet | Dubai | Criss Cross | Criss 1120

The Beat
Turk Murphy And His Orchestra | Flip Phillips Complete 1947-1951 Verve Master Takes | Definitive Records | DRCD 11201

The Beat Goes On
Gabor Szabo Quintet | The Sorcerer | Impulse(MCA) | IMP 12112
The Roots Of Acid Jazz | Impulse(MCA) | IMP 12042
Sonny Criss Quartet | The Beat Goes On! | Original Jazz Classics | OJCCD 1051-2(P 7558)
Carroll Gibbons And The Savoy Hotel Orpheans | Brighter Than The Sun | Saville Records | SVL 174 IMS

The Beatles
John Scofield Quartet | Who's Who? | Arista Novus | AN 3018 (801317)
Louis Armstrong And His All Stars With Duke Ellington | Louis Armstrong-Duke Ellington:The Great Summit-Complete Session | Roulette | 524546-2

The Beautiful American
The Beautiful American | Jazz Society(Vogue) | 670501

The Beauty Of Meat
Marcus Roberts Trio | In Honor Of Duke | CBS | CK 63630

The Beehive
Steve Cohn Group | The Beggar And The Robot In Diamonds | ITM-Pacific | ITMP 970089

The Beginning
Yusef Lateef Sextet | Morning-The Savoy Sessions | Savoy | SJL 2205 (801181)

The Believer
John Coltrane Quintet | John Coltrane-The Prestige Recordings | Prestige | 16 PCD 4405-2
Winard Harper Sextet | Winard | Savant Records | SCD 2021

The Bell
The Bell Gal & Her Dixieland Boys feat. Jim Robinson | New Orleans-The Living Legends:Sweet Emma | Original Jazz Classics | OJCCD 1832-2

The Bell Piece
Wynton Marsalis Quintet | Think Of One | CBS | 468709-2

The Bells
Jay McShann | Jay McShann At Cafe Des Copains | Sackville | SKCD2-2024

The Bells Of Rhymney
Fats Waller And His Rhythm | The Last Years 1940-1943 | Bluebird | ND 90411(3)

The Belt(Brau)
Allan Botschinsky/Niels-Henning Orsted-Pedersen | Duologue | M.A Music | NU 206-3

The Bench
Winard Harper Sextet | Winard | Savant Records | SCD 2021

The Benevolent One
Phil Minton | The Berlin Station | FMP | SAJ 57

The Best Is
Agneta Baumann And Her Quintet | A Time For Love | Touché Music | TMcCD 006

The Best Is Yet To Come
Carmen McRae With The Shirley Horn Trio | Sarah-Dedicated To You | Novus | PD 90546
Ella Fitzgerald With Orchestra | The Best Is Yet To Come | Original Jazz Classics | OJCCD 889-2(2312138)
Esmeralda Ferrara Group | Day By Day | Philology | W 129.2
Jackie & Roy | We've Got It-The Music Of Cy Coleman | Discovery | DSCD 907(881988)

The Best Man
Nat King Cole Trio | Great Capitol Masters | Pathe | 1566251(Capitol)
Ahmad Jamal Trio | At The Blackhawk | Chess | 515002

The Best Thing For You
Benny Goodman Septet | Benny Goodman:The King Of Swing | Musicmasters | 65130-2
Ernestine Anderson With The George Shearing Trio | A Perfect Match | Concord | CCD 4357
Stan Getz Quartet | Unearthed Masters-Vol.2: Stan Getz | JAM | 5007 IMS

The Best Things Happen While You're Dancing
Bennie Wallace Quartet | The Talk Of The Town | Enja | ENJ-7091 2

The Best Things In Life Are Free
Blue Mitchell With Strings And Brass | Smooth As The Wind | Original Jazz Classics | OJCCD 871-2(R 9367)
Erroll Garner Trio | Closeup In Swing/A New Kind Of Love(Music from The Motion Picture) | Telarc Digital | CD 83383
Harry Sweets Edison With The Ken Peplowski Quintet | Live At Ambassador Auditorium | Concord | CCD 4610
The Three Sounds | Standards | Blue Note | 821281-2

The Best To You
Art Blakey And The Jazz Messengers | New York 1957 | Jazz Anthology | JA 5198

The Big Cat
Terry Gibbs Dream Band | Terry Gibbs Dream Band Vol.5:The Big Cat | Contemporary | CCD 7657-2
Stan Kenton And His Orchestra | Back To Balbao | Creative World | ST 1031

The Big Chase
Meyer-Fleck-Marshall | Unconnon Ritual | CBS | SK 62891

The Big Crash From China
Bob Crosby's Bobcats | Jazz Drumming Vol.2(1937-1938) | Fenn Music | FJD 2702

The Big Dance
8 Bold Souls | Ant Farm | Arabesque Recordings | AJ 0114

The Big Dipper
Thad Jones-Mel Lewis Orchestra | Thad Jones-Mel Lewis | Blue Note | 84498
Tommy Dorsey And His Orchestra | The Indispensable Tommy Dorsey Vol.2/4(1937.1938) | RCA | 2126406-2

The Big Fight-
Stan Getz With The Eddie Sauter Orchestra | Stan Getz Plays The Music Of Mickey One | Verve | 531232-2
Coleman Hawkins All Stars | Verve Jazz Masters 43:Coleman Hawkins | Verve | 521856-2

The Big Head
The Jazz Scene | Verve | 521661-2
Eddie Harris Quartet | A Study In Jazz/Breakfast At Tiffany's | Vee Jay Recordings | VJ 020

The Big Hurt
Wes Montgomery Quintet With The Claus Ogerman Orchestra | Tequila | CTI Records | PDCTI 1118-2

The Big Hurt(alt.take)
Nat Adderley Quintet | Workin'-Live In Subway Vol.1 | Timeless | CD SJP 387

The Big Top
Plas Johnson Band | Rockin' With The Plas | Pathe | 2C 068-86529(Capitol)

The Big Wind
Friedemann Graef Group | Daily New Paradox | FMP | 0450

The Bilbao Song
Jay Migliori Quartet | The Courage | Discovery | DS 859 IMS

The Birch(1)
Christian Wallumrod Trio | No Birch | ECM | 1628(537344-2)

The Birch(2)
No Birch | ECM | 1628(537344-2)

The Birch(3)
No Birch | ECM | 1628(537344-2)

The Birch(4)
Charlie Byrd Septet | Latin Byrd | Milestone | M 47005

The Bird
Charlie Parker Quartet | The Jazz Scene | Verve | 521661-2
Dave Grusin Ensemble | Harlequin | GRP | GRP 95222
Jimmy McGriff Band | Jimmy McGriff featuring Hank Crawford | LRC Records | CDC 9001(874373)

The Bird-
Sheila Jordan-Mark Murphy Group | One For Junior | Muse | MCD 5489

The Birth Of The Blues
Golden Gate Quartet | Spirituals To Swing 1955-69 | EMI Records | 791569-2
Ken Colyer's Jazzmen | Live At The Dancing Slipper 1969 | AZURE Compact Disc | AZ-CD-25
Lionel Hampton With Milt Buckner And The All Stars | Alive & Jumping | MPS | 821283-1

The Birthday Gift
Red Rodney Quintet | No Turn On Red | Denon Compact Disc | CY-73149

The Bisquit Man
Klaus Weiss Sextet | All Night Through | ATM Records | ATM 3816 AH

The Bitches' Circle
Steve Lacy Quartet | Trickles | Black Saint | 120008-2

The Black And Crazy Blues
Roland Kirk Quartet | The Inflated Tear | Atlantic | 7567-90045-2
Rahsaan Roland Kirk Group | The Man Who Cried Fire | Night Records | VNCD 1(887047)

The Black Disciple
Marty Ehrlich Quartet | Can You Hear A Motion? | Enja | ENJ-8052 2

The Black Horse
Marco Tamburini Quartet | Thinking Of You | Penta Flowers | CDPIA 021

The Black Saint And The Sinner Lady
Charles Mingus And His Orchestra | Great Moments With Charles Mingus | MCA | MCA 2-4128 (802130)

The Blackhawk
Memphis Slim | All Kinds Of Blues | Original Blues Classics | OBC-507(BV 1053)

The Blackwiddow Blues
John Zorn Naked City | Naked City-Grand Guignol | Avant | AVAN 002

The Blast Off
Jiri Stivin & Co. | Reduta Live | clearaudio | LT 0010-2 531

The Blessing
Charles Lloyd Quartet | One Night With Blue Note Vol.4 | Blue Note | BT 85116 Digital
Charlie Haden Trio | The Montreal Tapes | Verve | 537670-2
The Montreal Tapes Vol.1 | Verve | 523260-2
Don Cherry Quartet | Art Deco | A&M Records | 395258-2 PMS
Henny Vonk with the Rob van den Broeck Trio | Rerootin' Henny Vonk | Timeless | SJP 164
John Coltrane-Don Cherry Quartet | The Avantgarde | Rhino | 8122-79892-2
That's Jazz Vol.40: The Avant-Garde | Atlantic | ATL 50523
Larry Schneider Quartet | Ornettology | Steeplechase | SCCD 31461
Paul Bley Quintet | The Faboulus Paul Bley Quintet | America | AM 6120
Trombonefire | Sliding Affairs | Laika Records | 35101462

The Blessing Of A Beautiful Bride
Ugetsu | Ugetsu-Live In Athens | Mons Records | MR 874779

The Blonde Bedouin
Duck Baker feat. John Renbourn | A Thousand Words | Acoustic Music Records | AMC 1021

The Blooming Flower
George Handy And His Orchestra | The Jazz Scene | Verve | 521661-2

The Blooz
Klaus Kreuzeder & Henry Sincigno | Sax As Sax Can-Alive | Trick Music | TM 9312 CD

The Blue
Booker Ervin Sextet | The Book Cooks | Fresh Sound Records | FSR 2050(Bethlehem BCP 6048)(835051)

The Blue Danube
Nat King Cole Trio | Nat King Cole Trio Transcriptions Vol.1 | Naxos Jazz | 8.120512 CD

The Blue Room
Benny Moten's Kansas City Orchestra | The Complete Bennie Moten Vol.5/6 | RCA | PM 45688
Ella Fitzgerald With The Buddy Bregman Orchestra | The Rodgers And Hart Song Book, Vol.1 | Verve | 821579-2 PMS
Elliot Lawrence Band | Plays Tiny Kahn And Johnny Mandel Arrangements | Fantasy | 0902109(F 3219)

The Blues
All Star Band | A String Of Swingin' Pearls | RCA | 2113035-2
Coleman Hawkins-Henry Red Allen All Stars | Vol.One: Warhorses | Jass Records | ???
Duke Ellington Quartet | Duke's Big 4 | Pablo | 2310703-2
Henry Mancini And His Orchestra | The Blues And The Beat | Fresh Sound Records | ND 74409
Sarah Vaughan And Her Trio | The Complete Sarah Vaughan Live In Japan | Mobile Fidelity | MFCD 844-2

The Blues-
Duke Ellington And His Orchestra | Carnegie Hall Concert January 1946 | Prestige | 2PCD 24074-2
Duke Ellington | Bluebird | ND 86641(3)

The Blues Are Brewin'
Louis Armstrong And His Orchestra | Louis Armstrong:C'est Si Bon | Dreyfus Jazz Line | FDM 36730-2
Louis Armstrong-The Complete RCA Victor Recordings | RCA | 2668682-2

The Blues Done Come Back
Albert King Blues Band | The Blues Don't Change | Stax | SCD 8570-2(STX 4101)

The Blues From Way Back
Frank Grasso Big Band | Frank Grasso Big Band | Timeless | CD SJP 226

The Blues Is All I Ever Had
Leola Manning | Favorite Country Blues Guitar-Piano Duets | Yazoo | YAZ 1015

The Blues Machine
Frankie Newton And His Orchestra | Frankie's Jump | Affinity | CD AFS 1014

The Blues Never Die
Mary Lou Williams-Cecil Taylor Quartet | Embraced | Pablo | 2620108

The Blues Story
Stan Kenton With The Danish Radio Big Band | Stan Kenton With The Danish Radio Big Band | Storyville | STCD 8340
Hal McKusick Quintet | Jazz Workshop | RCA | PM 43637

The Blues Walk
Brad Goode-Von Freeman Sextet | Inside Chicago Vol.3 | Steeplechase | SCCD 31531
Clifford Brown-Max Roach Quintet | Clifford Brown And Max Roach | Verve | 543306-2
Compact Jazz: Clifford Brown | EmArCy | 842933-2 PMS
Dexter Gordon Quartet | The Panther | Original Jazz Classics | OJCCD 770-2(P 10030)
Donald Byrd Quintet | Byrd In Paris Vol.1 | Polydor | 833394-2
Frank Wess Septet | Live At The 1990 Concord Jazz Festival-Second Set | Concord | CCD 4452

The Blues Walk(alt.take)
Clifford Brown-Max Roach Quintet | Brownie-The Complete EmArCy Recordings Of Clifford Brown | EmArCy | 838306-2
Clifford Roach Quintet | Standard Time | EmArCy | 814190-1 IMS

The Blues Waltz
Darrell Grant Quintet | The New Bop | Criss Cross | Criss 1106
The Blues(from Black Brown And Beige)
Nigel Kennedy And Alec Dankworth | Bartok-Ellington | EMI Records | EL 270538 1
The Blues, That's Me!
Enrico Pieranunzi | What's What | yvp music | CDX 48704
The Bluest Blues
Dizzy Gillespie Quintet | Pleyel Concert 1953 | Vogue | 655608
Dizzy Gillespie Sextet | The Champ | Jazz Anthology | JA 5183
The 'Bone' Zone
Bill Coleman And His Orchestra | From Boogie To Funk | Polydor | 2445035 IMS
The Boogie Hop
Jimmy Gordon With Band | 'The Mississippi Mudder' Jimmie Gordon Vol.2(1934-1941) | Story Of Blues | CD 3518-2
The Boogie Rocks
Christine Chatman And Her Band | Sammy Price Vol.1-Singing With Sam | Swingtime(Contact) | BT 2002
The Booglemeisters
Glenn Miller And His Orchestra | Swing Legends | Nimbus Records | NI 2001
The Booglie Wooglie Piggy
The Glenn Miller Story Vol.4 | RCA | NL 89223 AG
The Boon Companions
Remy Filipovitch Trio | All Day Long | Album | AS 22927
The Booster
The Paragon Ragtime Orchestra | That Demon Rag | Dorian Discovery | DIS 80107
The Bop Be Bops-
Dusko Goykovich Big Band | Balkan Connection | Enja | ENJ-9047 2
The Bopper
Riot | Riot-Black Hill | Nagara | MIX 1017-N
The Bording Hymn
George Benson Quartet | The George Benson Cookbook | CBS | 502470-2
The Borgia Stick
Jimmy Smith Trio | Verve Jazz Masters 21:George Benson | Verve | 521861-2
The Boss
Jimmy Smith:Best Of The Verve Years | Verve | 527950-2
Louie Bellson Trio/Quartet/Quintet | Cool Cool Blue | Pablo | 2310899
The Bossa Scene:
Gus Mancuso Quintet | Gus Mancuso & Special Friends | Fantasy | FCD 24762-2
The Boston Beguine
Gil Scott-Heron/Brian Jackson Group | Winter In America | Strata East Records | 660.51.015
The Boulevard Of Broken Dreams
Richard Carr-Bucky Pizzarelli | String Thing | Savant Records | SCD 2010
The Bowery
Mark Whitfield Quartet | 7th Avenue Stroll | Verve | 529223-2
The Bowery Bunch
John Taylor Trio | Rosslyn | ECM | 1751(159924-2)
The Bowl Song
Jack Bruce-Bernie Worrell | Monkjack | CMP Records | CMP CD 1010
The Boy Friend
Peppino D'Agostino | A Glimpse Of Times Past | Acoustic Music Records | 319.1157.2
The Boy From Ipanema
Shirley Horn Quintet | Antonio Carlos Jobim And Friends | Verve | 531556-2
Vesna Skorija Band | Niceland | Satin Doll Productions | SDP 1037-1 CD
Beryl Bryden And The Piccdilly Six | Beryl Bryden:Queen Of Bues And Washboard | Elite Special | 72430
The Boy From New Orleans
Beryl Bryden With The Rod Mason Band | Dixie From The Island Vol.3 | Jazz Colours | 874704-2
The Boy Next Door
Bill Evans Trio | The Complete Bill Evans On Verve | Verve | 527953-2
Spring Leaves | Milestone | M 47034
At Shelly's Manne-Hole | Original Jazz Classics | OJC20 263-2(RLP 9487)
Blossom Dearie Trio | April In Paris | Fresh Sound Records | FSR 555(Barclay 74017)
Bobby Troup Quartet | The Distinctive Style Of Bobby Troup | Fresh Sound Records | FSR 2024(Bethlehem BCP 35)
Johnny Smith Quartet | The Johnny Smith Foursome | Fresh Sound Records | FSR 581(Roost 2223)
Les Brown And His Orchestra | The Uncollected:Les Brown, Vol.4 | Hindsight | HSR 199
Lorne Lofsky Trio | It Could Happen To You | Pablo | 2312122
The Jimmy Giuffre 4 | Ad Lib | Verve | 2304490 IMS
The Boyish Chest
Barre Phillips-Peter Kowald Duo | Die Jungen: Random Generators | FMP | 0680
The Boys From Brooklyn
Sandole Brothers | The Sandole Brothers | Fantasy | FCD 24763-2
The Boys From Istanbul
Johnny Mbizo Dyani Group | Born Under The Heat | Dragon | DRLP 68
The Brain
Chick Corea Septet | The Complete 'Is' Sessions | Blue Note | 540532-2
The Brain(alt.take)
Dave Douglas Quartet | A Thousand Evenings | RCA | 2663698-2
The Branches(for Dave Tarras-part 1)
A Thousand Evenings | RCA | 2663698-2
The Branches(for Dave Tarras-part 2)
Bennie Wallace With The Blues Ensemble Of Biloxi | Sweeping Through The City | Enja | 4078 (807526)
The Break Strain-King Cotton-
Pili-Pili | Jakko | JA & RO | JARO 4131-2
The Break Tapper
Hank Mobley Quintet | Dippin' | Blue Note | 746511-2
The Breakdown
Michal Urbaniak Group | Urbaniak | Inner City | IC 1036 IMS
The Breakout
Double Drums Project | Double Drums Project | BIT | 11264
The Breath Exchanged-
Ahmad Jamal Trio | Live At The Alhambra | Vogue | 655002
The Breeze And I
Art Pepper Quartet | Art In L.A. | West Wind | WW 2064
Jazz Crusaders | Chile Con Soul | Pacific Jazz | 590957-2
Jimmy Rowles Septet | Weather In A Jazz Vane | Fresh Sound Records | FSR 502(Andex S-3007)
Robin Kenyatta Quartet | Ghost Stories | ITM-Pacific | ITMP 970060
Tad Shull Quintet | Deep Passion | Criss Cross | Criss 1047
Wes Montgomery Trio | Boss Guitar | Original Jazz Classics | OJCCD 261-2
Wes Montgomery-The Complete Riverside Recordings | Riverside | 12 RCD 4408-2
Willis Jackson Quintet | Bar Wars | Muse | MCD 6011
The Breeze From Orlando's Shore
Gerry Hemingway Quintet | The Marmalade King | Hat Art | CD 6164
The Bridge
The Dolphins With Dan Brubeck | Old World New World | dmp Digital Music Productions | CD 487
The Bridge Of Iron Roses
Steve Houben Quartet | Blue Circumstances | Igloo | IGL 102
The Broilers
Eddie Lockjaw Davis Quintet | The Eddie Lockjaw Davis Cookbook Vol.2 | Original Jazz Classics | OJC20 653-2(P 7161)
James Newton Ensemble | Suite For Frida Kahlo | audioquest Music | AQCD 1023
The Brooklyn Bridge
Gene Harris Quartet | Brotherhood | Concord | CCD 4640
The Brown Queen
Great Jazz Trio | Re-Visited:At The Village Vanguard Vol.2 | Eastworld | EWJ 90005
The Buccaneers
Kid Ory's Creole Jazz Band | Kid Ory:Creole Classics 1944-1947 | Naxos Jazz | 8.120587 CD
The Bucket's Got A Hole In It
Ken Colyer's Jazzmen | The Golden Years Of Revival Jazz.Vol.14 | Storyville | STCD 5519
Kid Ory's Creole Jazz Band | Kid Ory:Creole Classics 1944-1947 | Naxos Jazz | 8.120587 CD
The Builder
Beaver Harris | African Drums | Owl Records | 09
The Bullet
Marcus Printup Sextet | The New Boogaloo | Nagel-Heyer | CD 2019
The Bullet Train
Duke Jordan Trio | Flight To Japan | Steeplechase | SCS 1088
The Burgundy Bruise
Adrian Mears And The Australian Composers Ensemble | All For One | Enja | 9124-2
The Bus Blues
Ugetsu | Live In Shanghai | Mons Records | MR 874303
The Business Ain't Nothin' But The Blues
Roland Kirk Quintet | Rahsaan/The Complete Mercury Recordings Of Roland Kirk | Mercury | 846630-2
Frank Butler | Carl's Blues | Original Jazz Classics | OJC 423(C 7574)
The Butler Did It
Jimmy Giuffre Trio | Night Dance | Choice | CHCD 71001
The Butterfly
The Jimmy Giuffre 3 | Music For People,Birds,Butterflies & Mosquitoes | Candid | CRS 1001 IMS
The Buzz
Bud Freeman All Stars | The Bud Freeman All-Star Sessions | Prestige | PRCD 24286-2
The Buzzard
Bud Freeman And His Windy City Five | Bud Freeman(1927-1940) | CDS Records Ltd. | RPCD 604
The Buzzard Song
Don 'Sugar Cane' Harris Quartet | Fiddler On The Rock | MPS | 68028
The Cab Driver
Michael Bocian Quartet | Reverence | Enja | 8096-2
The Caboose
The Ravens | Rarities | Savoy | SV 0261(SJL 1174)
The Cage
Niels Jensen Trio | Nude But Still Stripping | ITM Records | 0038
The Cage Map
Abdullah Ibrahim Trio | Cape Town Flowers | TipToe | TIP-888826 2
The Call
Abdullah Ibrahim Trio And A String Orchestra | African Suite | TipToe | TIP-888832 2
Abdullah Ibrahim Trio With The Munich Radio Symphony Orchestra | African Symphony | Enja | ENJ-9410 2
Anthony Braxton/Mario Pavone | Duets (1993) | Music & Arts | CD 786
Paul Smoker Trio | Come Rain Or Come Shine | Sound Aspects | sas CD 024
Randy Weston | Blues To Africa | Freedom | FCD 741014
Vince Benedetti Quartet | The Dwellers On The High Plateau | EGO | 4005
The Call Of The Blues
Tommy Dorsey And His Orchestra | Tommy Dorsey And His Orchestra With Frank Sinatra | RCA | 2115518-2
The Call(2)
Charles Lloyd Quartet | Montreux 82 | Elektra | 60220-1
The Calling
Ron McClure Quintet | Descendants | Ken Music | 660.56.007
The Canonization
Grant Green Quintet | His Majesty King Funk/Up With Donald Byrd | Verve | 527474-2
The Cape Of Good Hope
Horace Silver Quintet | The Cape Verdean Blues | Blue Note | 576753-2
The Cape Verdean Blues
Horace Silver | Blue Note | 84510
The Blue Note Years-The Best Of Horace Silver Vol.2 | Blue Note | 793206-2
Naked Ear | Acoustik Guitar Duolog | Acoustic Music Records | AMC 1022
The Caravan Moves On
Sandy Brown's Jazz Band | McJazz | Dormouse | DM 6 IMS
The Cascades
Richard Zimmerman | The Complete Works Of Scott Joplin | Laserlight | 15945
The Castaways
Adam Makowicz | The Solo Album | Verve | 517888-2
The Cat
Jimmy Smith With The Lalo Schifrin Orchestra | The Cat | CTI Records | PDCTI 1110-2
Johnny Griffin Sextet | The Cat | Antilles | 848421-2(887313)
Kenny Wheeler Sextet | Uncovered Heart | Sunnyside | SSC 1048 D
Martin Schmitt | Handful Of Blues | AH Records | ESM 9303
Rusty Bryant Quintet | Rusty Bryant Returns | Original Jazz Classics | OJCCD 331-2(P 7626)
Mabel Lee With Orchestra | Harlem Roots-Jazz On Film:Jivin' Time | Storyville | SLP 6003
The Cat From Katmandu
Giko Pavan Quartet | Gino Pavan | SPLASC(H) Records | H 128
The Cat Is Crying
Moscow Art Trio | Once Upon A Time | JA & RO | JARO 4238-2
The Cat Is Crying(continued)
Jimmy Smith With Orchestra | The Big Brawl | Milan | CD CH 128(883460)
The Cat Walk
Gerry Mulligan-Ben Webster Quintet | The Complete Gerry Mulligan Meets Ben Webster Sessions | Verve | 539055-2
The Cat Walk(alt.take 1)
The Complete Gerry Mulligan Meets Ben Webster Sessions | Verve | 539055-2
The Cat Walk(alt.take 2)
The Complete Gerry Mulligan Meets Ben Webster Sessions | Verve | 539055-2
The Cat Walk(alt.take 3)
Lou Donaldson Orchestra | Blue Breaks Beats Vol.2 | Blue Note | 789907-2
The Caterpilar
Sheila Jordan With Te Alan Broadbent Trio And The Hiraga String Quartet | Heart Strings | Muse | MCD 5468
The Cat's Back
Bunk Johnson's Jazz Band | Bunk Johnson 1944/45 | American Music | AMCD-12
The Caverns Of Volere
Max Roach Quintet | Jazz In Paris:Max Roach-Parisian Sketches | EmArCy | 589963-2
The Caves-
Yusef Lateef Orchestra | The Many Faces Of Yusef Lateef | Milestone | M 47009
The Centaur And The Phoenix
Idrees Sulieman Quintet | 'Groovin' | Steeplechase | SCS 1218
The Challenge
JATP All Stars | Jazz At The Philharmonic:One O'Clock Jump 1953 | Verve | 815153-1 IMS
The Champ
Dizzy Gillespie Jam | Montreux '77 | Original Jazz Classics | OJC20 381-2(2308211)
Montreux '77-The Art Of The Jam Session | Pablo | 2620106
Dizzy Gillespie Sextet | The Champ | Jazz Anthology | JA 5183
Jimmy Smith Trio | A New Sound A New Star:Jimmy Smith At The Organ | Blue Note | 857191-2
Jimmy Smith:Best Of The Verve Years | Verve | 527950-2
Groovin' At Smalls' Paradise | Blue Note | 499777-2
The Champ Jimmy Smith At The Organ Vol.2 | Blue Note | 300093(1514)
Ray Brown Trio With Ralph Moore | Moore Makes 4 | Concord | CCD 4477
Sonny Stitt Quintet | The Champ | 32 Jazz | 32084
Michael Blake Group | Kingdom Of Champa | Intuition Records | INT 3189-2
The Champa Theme
Max Roach Quintet | Jazz In Paris:Max Roach-Parisian Sketches | EmArCy | 589963-2
The Champs-
James Newton Trio | Binu | Circle Records | RK 11-21877/11 IMS
The Chant
Cannonball Adderley Quintet | Cannonball Adderley Birthday Celebration | Fantasy | FANCD 6087-2
En Concert Avec Europe 1 | Laserlight | 710466
Julian Cannonball Adderlry: Salle Pleyel/Olympia | Laserlight | 36126
Wes Montgomery-The Complete Riverside Recordings | Riverside | 12 RCD 4408-2
Cannonball Adderley-Nat Adderley Quintet | What Is This Thing Called Soul:In Europe-Live! | Original Jazz Classics | OJCCD 801-2(2308238)
Chuck Loeb Group | My Shing Hour | Jazz City | 660.53.009
Jelly Roll Morton's Red Hot Peppers | Doctor Jazz | Black & Blue | BLE 59.227 2
Patrick Williams' New York Band | 10th Avenue | Soundwings | SWD 2103(881134
The Chanting
The Jimmy Giuffre 3 | Music For People,Birds,Butterflies & Mosquitoes | Candid | CRS 1001 IMS
The Chapel
Alex Welsh And His Band | Great British Jazz Bands Vol.6:Alex Welsh | Lake | LACD 62
The Chase
Andy LaVerne | Tadd's Delight-Andy LaVerne Plays Tadd Dameron | Steeplechase | SCCD 31375
Gene Ammons-Dexter Gordon Quintet | Dexter Gordon Birthday Celebration | Fantasy | FANCD 6082-2
Lionel Hampton And His Orchestra | Chicago Jazz Concert | CBS | 21107
Tadd Dameron-Fats Navarro Sextet | Fats Navarro/Tadd Dameron:Complete Blue Note & Capitol Sessions | Definitive Records | DRCD 11191
The Chase(alt.master)
Fats Navarro/Tadd Dameron:Complete Blue Note & Capitol Sessions | Definitive Records | DRCD 11191
The Chaser
Sadao Watanabe With Lee Ritenour & His Gentle Thought | Autumn Blow | Flying Disk | VIJ 6006
The Chef
Eddie Lockjaw Davis Quintet | Cookbook Vol.1 | Original Jazz Classics | OJC20 652-2(P 7141)
The Eddie Lockjaw Davis Cookbook Vol.1 | Original Jazz Classics | OJCCD 652-2(P 7141)
The Chess Players
Stan Getz Quartet With The Jon Hendricks Ensemble | Grandes Voix Du Jazz | CBS | 467147-2
The Chick From Ipanema
Bireli Lagrene & Jaco Pastorius | Stuttgart Aria | Jazzpoint | JP 1019 LP
The Chicken
Jaco Pastorius' Word Of Mouth Big Band | Invitation | Warner | 92-3876-1
The Chicken And The Hawk Boogie
Louis Jordan And His Tympany Five | Louis Jordan-Let The Good Times Roll: The Complete Decca Recordings 1938-1954 | Bear Family Records | BCD 15557 IH
The Chicks I Pick Are Slender Tender And Tall
Louis Jordan Vol.2-Knock Me Out | Swingtime(Contact) | ST 1012
The Chief
Eddie Lockjaw Davis Quartet | The Best Of Eddie 'Lockjaw' Davis | Pablo | 2405414-2
The Chinese Dog
Red Sun | Samul Nori | Amadeo | 841222-2
The Choice-
Willie Williams Trio | WW3 | Enja | ENJ-8060 2
The Choice Is Yours-
Mitch Farber Group | Starclimber | Muse | MCD 5400
The Christmas Song
Carmen McRae And Her Sextet | Carmen McRae Sings Lover Man | CBS | CK 65115
Dexter Gordon Quartet | The Panther | Original Jazz Classics | OJCCD 770-2(P 10030)
Dexter Gordon Birthday Celebration | Fantasy | FANCD 6082-2
Ella Fitzgerald With The Frank DeVol Orchestra | Ella With You A Swinging Christmas | Verve | 2304445 IMS
Jim Galloway-Jay McShann Quartet | Jim & Jay's Christmas | Sackville | SKCD2-3054
Jimmy Smith With The Billy Byers Orchestra | Jimmy Smith:Best Of The Verve Years | Verve | 527950-2
Christmas Cookin' | Verve | 513711-2
Mel Tormé And His Trio With The Cincinnati Sinfonietta | Christmas Songs- | Telarc Digital | CD 83315
Nat King Cole With Orchestra | Nat King Cole:Route 66 | Dreyfus Jazz Line | FDM 36716-2
Oscar Moore Trio | Oscar Moore And Friends | Fresh Sound Records | FSR-CD 0202
Walter Bishop Jr. Trio | Midnight Blue | Red Records | 123251-2
The Chromatic Persuaders
Dominique Cornil | Scott Joplin Ragtimes | GHA Records | CD 126.004
The Circle With The Hole In The Middle
Paul Bley Trio | New Music: Second Wave | Savoy | SJL 2235 (801211)
The Circular Letter (For J.K.)
Dave Brubeck Quartet | My Favorite Things | CBS | SRCS 9369
The City
Mel Tormé With The Marty Paich Dek-Tette | In Concert Tokyo | Concord | CCD 4382
The City Lights
Steve Kuhn Quartet | Last Year's Waltz | ECM | 1213
The City Sleeps
Lou Blackburn-Freddie Hill Quintet | Perception | Fresh Sound Records | FSR-CD 0307
The Claw
Flip Phillips Quartet | Flipenstein | Progressive | PRO 7063 IMS
Woody Herman Big Band And Special Guests | World Class | Concord | CCD 4240
The Claw And Spur
Eddie Cleanhead Vinson Septet | The 'Clean' Machine | Muse | MR 5116
The Cliffs Of Asturias
Buddy Rich Quintet With The Dave Lambert Singers | At Birdland | Jazz Door | JD 1202
The Closer
JATP All Stars | The Complete Jazz At The Philharmonic On Verve 1944-1949 | Verve | 523893-2
Charlie Parker Jazz At The Philharmonic 1949 | Verve | 519803-2
The Clothed Woman
Duke Ellington And His Orchestra | Duke Ellington:Complete Prestige Carnegie Hall 1946-1947 Concerts | Definitive Records | DRCD 11211
The Cloud Is Crying
Homesick James Quartet | Windy City Blues | Stax | SCD 8612-2
The Cloud Is Crying(alt.take)
Chick Corea And His Orchestra | My Spanish Heart | Polydor | 543303-3
The Clouds
Steve LaSpina Quintet | Distant Dream | Steeplechase | SCCD 31448
The Clown
Charles Mingus Quintet | Charles Mingus-Passion Of A Man:The Complete Atlantic Recordings 1956-1961 | Atlantic | 8122-72871-2
Tome XX | The Red Snapper | Jazz Haus Musik | JHM 0047 CD

Hans Koller-George Mraz Duo | The K & K In New York | L+R Records | LR 40009

The Clownster
Charlie Rouse Quartet | Moment's Notice | Storyville | JC 4

The Coach
Flim & The BB's | The Further Adventures | dmp Digital Music Productions | CD 462

The Coaster
Grachan Moncur III Sextet | Evolution | Blue Note | 870073-4
Roy Fox And His Band | Whispering | Decca | RFL 13

The Collector
Bud Shank-Laurindo Almeida Quartet | Braziliance Vol.2 | Pacific Jazz | 796102-2

The Color Of You
Dave Grusin Band With Orchestra | The Orchestral Album | GRP | GRP 97972

The Colour Of Love
Carola Grey Group | The Age Of Illusions | Jazzline | JL 11139-2

The Colours Of Chloe
Gary Burton Quintet With Eberhard Weber | Ring | ECM | 1051
Count Basie And His Orchestra | Count Basie At Newport | Verve | 9861761

The Comeback
En Concert Avec Europe 1 | Laserlight | 710706/07
Count Basie And The Kansas City 7 | Count Basie: Salle Pleyel, April 17th, 1972 | Laserlight | 36127
Illinois Jacquet Trio | Lions Abroad Volume One:Tenor Titans | Black Lion | BLCD 7620-2
William Hooker Trio | The Firmament Fury | Silkheart | SHCD 123

The Common Ground
Kenny Burrell With The Don Sebesky Orchestra | Blues-The Common Ground | Verve | 589101-2
Billy Drummond Quartet | The Gift | Criss Cross | Criss 1083

The Common Law
Allen Farnham Quartet | The Common Ground | Concord | CCD 4634

The Community
Urs Leimgruber-Fritz Hauser | L'Enigmatique | Hat Art | CD 6091

The Companion
Ray Crawford Sextet | I Know Pres | Candid | SMJ 6196

The Compendium Suite
Tommy Flanagan Trio With Kenny Burrell | Beyond The Bluebird | Timeless | CD SJP 350

The Connection:
Passport | Handmade | Atlantic | 2292-42172-2

The Connexion
Vlado Williams Trio | New Advanced Jazz | Savoy | SV 0238(MG 12188)

The Conquerors
Horace Silver Ensemble | Silver 'N Strings Play The Music Of The Spheres | Blue Note | LWB 1033

The Continental
Blossom Dearie Trio | April In Paris | Fresh Sound Records | FSR 555(Barclay 74017)
Bobby Hackett And His Jazz Band | Gotham Jazz Scene/Big T's Dixieland Band | Dormouse | DMI CDX 03(882985)
Cal Tjader Septet | A Fuego Vivo | Concord | CCD 4176
Nat King Cole With The Dave Cavanaugh Orchestra | Nat King Cole At The Sands | Capitol | EMS 1110
Rene Thomas Quartet | Jazz In Paris:René Thomas-The Real Cat | EmArCy | 549400-2 PMS
Tommy Dorsey And His Orchestra | The Post-War Era | Bluebird | 63 66156-2

The Cooker
Joe Venuti-Zoot Sims Sextet | Joe Venuti And Zoot Sims | Chiaroscuro | CR 142

The Cool Suite:
Art Blakey And The Jazz Messengers | Free For All | Blue Note | 784170-2

The Corner
8 Bold Souls | Ant Farm | Arabesque Recordings | AJ 0114

The Cosmic Lawn
Sun Ra And His Solar Arkestra | Heliocentric World Vol.1 | ESP Disk | ESP 1014-2

The Cost Of Living
Michael Brecker Group | The Cost Of Living | Jazz Door | JD 1260

The Cotton Tail Caper
Sergey Kuryokhin/Boris Grebenshchikov | Subway Culture:The Third Russian Opera | LEO | LR 402/403

The Countdown
Mulgrew Miller Quartet | The Countdown | Landmark | LCD 1519-2

The Country's In The Very Best Hands
Max Roach With Howard Rumsey's Lighthouse All Stars | Drummin' The Blues | Liberty | LPR 3064

The Cow And The Fiddle
Jimmy Giuffre Quartet | In Person | Verve | 2304492 IMS

The Crane's Dance
Tony Scott/Shinichi Yuize | Dedications | Line Records | COCD 9.00803

The Crawl
Mickey Tucker Septet | The Crawl | Muse | MR 5223

The Creator Has A Master Plan
Howard Johnson's Nubia | Arrival | Verve | 523985-2
Pharoah Sanders Orchestra | The Best Of Pharoah Sanders | MCA | AS 9229

The Creator Has A Master Plan(edited version)
Louis Armstrong And His Friends | Louis Armstrong And His Friends | Bluebird | 2663961-2

The Creator Has A Master Plan(Peace alt.take 1)
Louis Armstrong And His Friends | Bluebird | 2663961-2

The Creator Has A Master Plan(Peace alt.take 2)
Leon Thomas With Band | Spirits Known And Unknown | RCA | 2663876-2

The Creator Has A Master Plan(Peace)
Leon Thomas With The Oliver Nelson Quintet | Leon Thomas In Berlin | RCA | 2663877-2
Louis Armstrong And His Friends | Louis Armstrong And His Friends | Bluebird | 2663961-2
Bobby Hutcherson-Harold Land Quintet | Live At The Festival | Enja | 2030-2

The Creek
Michael Blake Group | Drift | Intuition Records | INT 3212-2

The Creep
Sonny Criss Sextet | The Sonny Criss Memorial Album | DIW | DIW 302 CD

The Creeper
Johnny Otis Band | Creepin' With The Cats: The Legendary DIG Masters Vol.1 | Ace Records | CDCHD 325

The Crillon Controller
James Newton Orchestra | Water Mystery | Gramavision | GR 8407-2

The Critic's Choice
Oliver Nelson And His Orchestra | More Blues And The Abstract Truth | MCA | 2292-54643-2

The Crooner(for Johnny Hartman)
Bob Berg Quintet | In The Shadows | Denon Compact Disc | CY-76210

The Crossing Place
Bill Laswell/Jones Hellborg Group | Niels & The New York Street Percussionists | ITM Records | ITM 1453

The Crusade
Mick Goodrick-David Liebman-Wolfgang Muthspiel | In The Same Breath | CMP Records | CMP CD 71

The Crushout-
Stan Getz With The Eddie Sauter Orchestra | Stan Getz Plays The Music Of Mickey One | Verve | 531232-2

The Crushout(Total Death)-
Steve Lacy Quintet | Follies | FMP | SAJ 18

The Cry Of My People
Harold Mabern | Philadelphia Bound | Sackville | SKCD2-3051
Antoine Roney Sextet | The Traveler | Muse | MCD 5469

The Cry(for Booker Little)
Frank Stozier Sextet | Long Night | Milestone | MCD 47095-2

The Crystal Ball
Claude Thornhill And His Orchestra | Snowfall | Fresh Sound Records | NL 46030(RCA)

The Crystal Palace
Steve Lacy Trio | Rushes-10 Songs From Russia | Nueva Records | IN 809

The Cup Bearers
Peter Leitch Trio | On A Misty Night | Criss Cross | Criss 1026

The Cup Bearers-
Duck Baker | The Clear Blue Sky | Acoustic Music Records | 319.1065.2

The Cure
Tippett-Kellers-Tippett | Twilight Etchings | FMP | CD 65

The Curse
Dave McKenna | Dave Fingers McKenna | Chiaroscuro | CR 175

The Cuttin' Edge
Phil Minton And Veryan Weston | Ways Past | ITM Records | ITM 1468

The Cylinder
Modern Jazz Quartet | The Complete Modern Jazz Quartet Prestige & Pablo Recordings | Prestige | 4PRCD 4438-2
The Complete Modern Jazz Quartet Prestige & Pablo Recordings | Prestige | 4PRCD 4438-2
MJQ 40 | Atlantic | 7567-82330-2
The Complete Last Concert | Atlantic | 81976-2
The Modern Jazz Quartet | Reunion At Budokan 1981 | Atlantic | 251210-1 TIS

The Dabtara
Shakti | Natural Elements | CBS | 82329

The Dain Curse
Amsterdam Jazz Quintet | Portraits | Challenge | CHR 70048

The Daly Jump
Count Basie And His Orchestra | Basie On Roulette, Vol. 16: Not Now I'll Tell You When | Vogue | 500016

The Damned Don't Cry
Cool Blue | House In The Country | Foolish Music | FM 211591

The Dance
Jeff Beal Group | Contemplations | Triloka Records | 320204-2
Ellery Eskelin With Andrea Parkins & Jim Black | Five Other Pieces(+2) | HatOLOGY | 533

The Dance Of Maya
Klaus König Orchestra & Guests | The Song Of Songs:Oratorio For Two Solo Voices,Choir And Orchestra | Enja | ENJ-7057 2

The Dance Of The Double Camp
Fischbacher Group feat. Adam Nussbaum | Mysterious Princess | Acoustic Music Records | AMC 1025

The Dance(part 2)-
Billy Cobham Quintet | Warning | GRP | GRP 95282

The Danger Zone
Freddy King Blues Band | Live In Nancy 1975 Vol.2 | France's Concert | FCD 129

The Dark Knight
John McLaughlin With The One Truth Band | Electric Dreams | CBS | CBS 83526

The Dark Side Of Country Music
Vincent Herring Quintet | Dawnbird | Landmark | LCD 1533-2

The Dark Side Of The Moon
Horace Tapscott Quartet | The Dark Tree | Hat Art | CD 6053

The Darker Side
Ella Fitzgerald And Her Savoy Eight | Ella Fitzgerald Vol.1-Forever Young | Swingtime(Contact) | ST 1006

The Daubtful Quest
Joe Newman Octet | The Complete Joe Newman RCA-Victor Recordings(1955-1956):The Basie Days | RCA | 2122613-2

The Dawn
Music Revelation Ensemble | In The Name Of... | DIW | DIW 885 CD

The Dawn Of Time
Gary Thomas And Seventh Quadrant | Code Violations | Enja | 5085

The Day After
Dizzy Gillespie Quintet | Something Old Something New | Verve | 558079-2
Howard McGhee Quartet | Shades Of Blue | Jazz Colours | 874757-2
Ron McClure Quartet | Match Point | Steeplechase | SCCD 31517

The Day After Christmas
Enrico Pieranunzi | The Day After The Silence | EdiPan | NPG 800

The Day It Rained
Deborah Henson-Conant Group | Deborah Henson-Conant:Best Of Instrumental Music | Laika Records | 35101322

The Day It Rained Forever
Thomas Heberer | The Heroic Millepede | ITM Records | ITM 1443

The Day Of Bliss And Joy
Steve Laury-Bob Whitlock | Stepping Out | Denon Compact Disc | CY-75870

The Day Will Come
Swan Silvertones | My Rock/Love Lifted Me | Ace Records | CDCHD 340

The Day You Came Along
Jimmy Rowles Trio | The Complete Nocturne Recordings:Jazz In Hollywood Series Vol.1 | Fresh Sound Records | NR 3CD-101
Lew Stone And His Band | Lew Stone And His Band | Decca | DDV 5005/6 DT

The Day You Came Along(alt.take)
Kenny Drew Jr. | Live At The Montreux Jazz Fesival '99 | TCB Records | TCB 21152

The Deacon
Count Basie And His Orchestra | Breakfast Dance And Barbecue | Roulette | 531791-2
Basie On Roulette, Vol. 7: Chaiman Of The Board | Vogue | 500007

The Dealer
Milt Jackson All Stars | Invitation | Original Jazz Classics | OJCCD 260-2

The Dear Departed Past
Kim Kristensen | Pulse Of Time | dacapo | DCCD 9435

The Death Of A Dreamer
Ran Blake | Realization Of A Dream | Owl Records | 012

The Deccan Queen SKB Express
Third Person | Third Person-The Bends | Enemy | EMCD 124(03524)

The Dedication(part 1)-
Mark White Quartet | Live At Warsaw Jazz Festival 1991 | Jazzmen Records | 660.50.005

The Deep High-
Ellis=Ochs=Robinson | What We Live | DIW | DIW 909 CD

The Depth
Franco Morone | The South Wind | Acoustic Music Records | 319.1115.2

The Desert Story
Dennis Gonzales New Dallasangels | The Desert Wind | Silkheart | SHCD 124

The Deserving Many
Dan Rose Trio | Conversations | Enja | 8006-2

The Devil Is A Busy Man
Ada Moore And Her Quintet | Jazz Workshop Vol.3 | Original Jazz Classics | OJCCD 1701-2(Debut 15)

The Devil's Pulpit
McCoy Tyner Orchestra | Song Of The New World | Original Jazz Classics | OJCCD 618-2

The Dirge
Stan Getz Sextet | Billy Highstreet Samba | EmArCy | 838771-2
Bruce Turner Quartet | The Dirty Bopper | Calligraph | CLG LP 003 IMS

The Dirty Dozen
Budd Johnson Quartet | Mr.Bechet | Black & Blue | BB 882.2

The Disappearance Of Space And Time
Mark Helias/Gerry Hemingway/Ray Anderson | Bassdrumbone(Hence The Reason) | Enja | ENJ-9322 2

The Disappearing Afternoon
Vinny Golia-The Chamber Trio | Worldwide & Portable | Nine Winds Records | NWCD 0143

The Discovery
Stanley Wilson And His Orchestra | The Music From M Squad | Fresh Sound Records | PL 45929(RCA LPM 2062)

The Discovery Of Bhupala
Dave Stryker Quartet | Full Moon | Steeplechase | SCCD 31345

The Disguise
Larry Schneider Quartet | Ornettology | Steeplechase | SCCD 31461
Frederica von Stade With The Chris Brubeck-Bill Croft Ensemble | Across Your Dreams: Frederica von Stade Sings Brubeck | Telarc Digital | CD 80467

The Divide
Benny Goodman And His Orchestra | More Camel Caravans | Phontastic | NCD 8841/2

The Dixieland Band
The Birth Of Swing | Bluebird | ND 90601(3)

The Doctor Is Out
Kim Pensyl | Pensyl Sketches Collection | GRP | GRP 97702

The Dog Who Smokes
Jimmy McGriff Trio | Blues For Mr. Jimmy | EMI Records | SSL 6005

The Dolphin
Ferenc Snétberger | The Budapest Concert | TipToe | TIP-888823 2
George Colligan | Small Room | Steeplechase | SCCD 31470
Luis Bonilla Latin Jazz All Stars | Pasos Gigantes | Candid | CCD 79507
The New Stan Tracy Quartet | For Heaven's Sake | Cadillac | SGCCD 04
Woody Herman Big Band | Live At The Concord Jazz Festival | Concord | CCD 4191

The Dolphin-After
Bill Evans With Orchestra | From Left To Right | Verve | 557451-2
Bill Evans Quartet | The Complete Bill Evans On Verve | Verve | 527953-2

The Dolphin-Before
The Complete Bill Evans On Verve | Verve | 527953-2
From Left To Right | Verve | 557451-2
The Complete Bill Evans On Verve | Verve | 527953-2

The Dolphin-Before(alt.take 1)
The Complete Bill Evans On Verve | Verve | 527953-2

The Dolphin-Before(alt.take 2)
The Complete Bill Evans On Verve | Verve | 527953-2

The Dolphin-Before(alt.take 3)
The Complete Bill Evans On Verve | Verve | 527953-2

The Dolphin-Before(alt.take 4)
The Complete Bill Evans On Verve | Verve | 527953-2

The Dolphin-Before(alt.take 5)
Itchy Fingers | Full English Breakfast | Enja | ENJ-7085 2

The Dome
Ralph Towner-Gary Burton | Slide Show | ECM | 1306

The Donkey Jamboree
Artie Shaw And His Orchestra | The Original Sounds Of The Swing Era Vol.7 | RCA | CL 05517 DP

The Donkey Serenade
Francois Houle 5 | Cryptology | Between The Lines | btl 012(Efa 10182-2)

The Donkey's Tale
Wayne Horvitz Group | This New Generation | Nonesuch | 7559-60759-2

The 'Don't Know Mind'
Miles Davis Group | Doo-Bop | Warner | 7599-26938-2

The Doo Bop Song
Denny Christianson Big Band | Doomsday Machine | Justin Time | Just 8

The Door
Pork Pie | The Door Is Open | MPS | 68038

The Double Rainbow Over Heeper Street
Klaus König Orchestra | Times Of Devastation/Poco A Poco | Enja | ENJ-6014 22
Stefan Karlsson Quintet | The Road Not Taken | Justice Records | JR 0702-2

The Doubtful Guest
Michael Mantler Quintet | Live | Watt | 18
Lynne Arriale Trio | A Long Road Home | TCB Records | TCB 97952

The Dove
Wolfgang Lackerschmid & Lynne Arriale Trio | You Are Here | Bhakti Jazz | BR 43
Lew Stone And His Orchestra | The Bands The Matter | Eclipse | ECM 2047

The Dragon
Marty Paich Octet | Tenors West | GNP Crescendo | GNP 9040
Dave Holland Quintet | Jumpin' In | ECM | 1269

The Dragon And The Samurai
Horace Silver Quintet | Silver's Serenade | Blue Note | 821288-2

The Dragon Lady
Geoff Keezer Sextet | Waiting In The Wings | Sunnyside | SSC 1035 D

The Dreaded Lergy
Buddy DeFranco Quartet | Waterbed | Candid | CRS 1017 IMS

The Dream
Franz Koglmann Tentet | Ich | Hat Art | CD 6033
Tom White With Band | Keep It Under Your Hat | Ronnie Scott's Jazz House | JHCD 018
Hans Reichel | The Death Of The Rare Bird Ymir | FMP | 0640

The Dream Is You
Roscoe Mitchell | Sound Songs | Delmark | DE 493(2)

The Dreamcatcher
Amos Hoffman Quartet | The Dreamer | Fresh Sound Records | FSNT 060 CD

The Dreamer
Charles Fambrough Group | The Proper Angle | CTI Records | CTI 1002-2

The Dreaming
Gust Williams Tsilis Quartet | Possibilities | Ken Music | 660.56.009

The Drink
Axel Zwingenberger With Champion Jack Dupree & Torsten Zwingenberger | Axel Zwingenberger & The Friends Of Boogie Woogie Vol.6 | Vagabond | VRLP 8.90016

The Drinker
Steve Kuhn Quartet | Last Year's Waltz | ECM | 1213

The Drive
Oliver Nelson Sextet | Eric Dolphy Birthday Celebration | Fantasy | FANCD 6085-2
Eric Dolphy:The Complete Prestige Recordings | Prestige | 9 PRCD-4418-2
Memphis Slim And His Band | The Blues Is Everywhere | Vogue | 655503

The Drum Also Waltzes
The Paris All-Stars | Homage To Charlie Parker | A&M Records | 395300-2

The Drum Battle
Guy Cabay Quartet | The Ghost Of McCoy's Castle | B.Sharp Records | CDS 101

The Drum Thing
John Coltrane Trio | John Coltrane:The Classic Quartet-Complete Impulse Studio Recordings | Impulse(MCA) | 951280-2
Art Blakey And The Jazz Messengers | Moanin' | Blue Note | 495324-2

The Drum Thunder (Miniature) Suite:
Moanin' | Blue Note | 300321

The Drummer Boy(from The Boy's Magic Horns)
Allan Holdsworth Group | The Sixteen Man Of Tain | Cream Records | CR 610-2

The Drums Were Yellow
Mercy Dee Walton Trio | Pity And A Shame | Original Blues Classics | OBCCD 552-2(BV 1039)

The Drunkard In Spring(from The Song Of The Earth)
Deborah Henson-Conant | The Celtic Album | Laika Records | 35101022

The Drunken Sailor
Mingus Dynasty | Chair In The Sky | Warner | 99081

The Duck-
$$hide$$ | $$Titelverweise | |

The Duck -> O Pato

The Duck And The Dodo
Dado Moroni Trio | What's New? | SPLASC(H) Records | CD H 378-2

The Duke
Dave Brubeck Quartet | Interchanges '54 | CBS | 467917-2
Dave Brubeck's All-Time Greatest Hits | CBS | 68288
Miles Davis + 19 | The Miles Davis Selection | CBS | 465699-2
Peter Herbolzheimer Rhythm Combination & Brass | Smile | Koala Records | CD P 17

Tony Lakatos Quartet | Live In Budapest | Laika Records | 35100742
Wanja Slavin-Matc Schmolling | Off Minor | Organic Music | ORGM 9732
Dave Brubeck Quartet | Late Night Brubeck | Telarc Digital | CD 83345

The Duke Steps Out
Duke Ellington And His Orchestra | Louis Armstrong & Duke Ellington | Avenue | AVINT 1006

The Duke You Say!
Orquestra De Cambra Teatre Lliure | Tributes To Duke Ellington | Fresh Sound Records | FSNT 084 CD

The Duke(Clare Fischer)
Tributes To Duke Ellington | Fresh Sound Records | FSNT 084 CD

The Duke(Dave Brubeck)
Charlie Barnet And His Orchestra | Charlie Barnet Vol.1 | Zeta | ZET 749

The Duke's King
The Duke Ellington Orchestra | Music Is My Mistress | Limelight | 820801-2 IMS

The Dyin' Crapshooter's Blues
Ella Fitzgerald With The Duke Ellington Orchestra | Ella Fitzgerald Sings The Duke Ellington Song Book Vol.2 | Verve | 2615033 IMS

The E And D Blues(E For Ella D For Duke)
The Complete Ella Fitzgerald Song Books of Harold Arlen, Irving Berlin, Duke Ellington, George & Ira Gershwin, Jerome Kern, Johnny Mercer, Cole Porter And Rogers & Hart | Verve | 519832-2

The Eagle And Me
Huddie Ledbetter | Classics In Jazz-Leadbelly | Pathe | 2C 068-80701(Capitol)

The Earth
Adam Rudolph's Moving Pictures | Skyway | Soul Note | 121269-2

The Easter Islander
Louis Armstrong With Orchestra | Ramblin' Rose | H&L Records | 6.24131 AO

The Edge Of Love
Eric Alexander Quartet | Eric Alexander In Europe | Criss Cross | Criss 1114

The Edge Of The Night
Kip Hanrahan Groups | Desire Develops An Edge | American Clave | AMCL 1008-2

The Eel
Bud Freeman And His Summa Cum Laude Orchestra | Planet Jazz:Bud Freeman | Planet Jazz | 2161240-2
A String Of Swingin' Pearls | RCA | 2113035-2

The Eel's Nephew
Special EFX | Confidential | GRP | GRP 95812

The Egg
Herbie Hancock Quartet | Herbie Hancock:The Complete Blue Note Sixties Sessions | Blue Note | 495569-2
Michele Rosewoman Sextet | Harvest | Enja | ENJ-7069 2

The Egun(Egg-Oon) And The Harvest
Art Blakey And The Jazz Messengers | Indestructible | Blue Note | BST 84193

The Eight Veil
Duke Ellington And His Orchestra | The Uncollected: Duke Ellington, Vol.1 | Hindsight | HSR 125

The Elders
David S.Ware Trio | Passage To Music | Silkheart | SHCD 113

The Eldorado Shuffle
Tad Shull Quintet | Deep Passion | Criss Cross | Criss 1047

The Electric Ballroom
Marilyn Mazur's Future Song | Small Labyrinths | ECM | 1559(533679-2)

The Electric Cave
Peter Herbolzheimer Rhythm Combination & Brass | Bandfire | Koala Records | CD P 1

The Elephant And The Orchid
Khaliq Al-Rouf & Salaam | The Elephant Trop Dance | Nilva | NQ 3404 IMS

The Eleventh Hour(part 1)
Ed Schuller & Band | The Eleventh Hour | Tutu Records | 888124-2*

The Eleventh Hour(part 2)
Hans Reichel-Rüdiger Carl Duo | Buben...Plus | FMP | CD 78

The Embalmers' Waltz
Chick Corea Group | Tap Step | Stretch Records | SCD 9006-2

The Emperor
Teddy Charles Tentet | The Teddy Charles Tentet | Atlantic | 790983-2

The Emporer
Steve Turre Group | Steve Turre | Verve | 537133-2

The Empty Cathedral
Buster Williams-Kenny Barron | Crystal Reflections | 32 Jazz | 32087

The Enchanted Forest
Harry Betts And His Orchestra | The Jazz Soul Of Dr. Kildare | Mobile Fidelity | MFCD 839

The End
Catalogue | Pénétration | Hat Art | CD 6187
Julian Priester Quintet | Keep Swingin' | Original Jazz Classics | SMJ 6081
Stanley Wilson And His Orchestra | The Music From M Squad | Fresh Sound Records | PL 45929(RCA LPM 2062)

The End Of A Book
Ahmad Jamal Quartet | Nature | Dreyfus Jazz Line | FDM 37018-2

The End Of A Love Affair
Nature(The Essence Part III) | Atlantic | 3984-23105-2
Art Blakey And The Jazz Messengers | The Jazz Messengers | CBS | CK 65265
Art Blakey/The Jazz Messengers | CBS | CK 62265
Dan Wall Quartet | Off The Wall | Enja | ENJ-9310 2
Denny Zeitlin | Maybeck Recital Hall Series Volume Twenty-Seven | Concord | CCD 4572
Lou Levy Trio | Baby Grand Jazz | Fresh Sound Records | FSR-CD 94(882168)
Matt Dennis And His Orchestra | Dave Garroway:Some Of My Favorites | Fresh Sound Records | ND 74403
Tom Williams Quintet | Introducing Tom Williams | Criss Cross | Criss 1064
Wes Montgomery Trio | A Dynamic New Jazz Sound | Original Jazz Classics | OJCCD 034-2
Wes Montgomery-The Complete Riverside Recordings | Riverside | 12 RCD 4408-2
Billie Holiday With The Ray Ellis Orchestra | Lady In Satin | CBS | CK 65144

The End Of A Love Affair(Mono)
Lady In Satin | CBS | CK 65144

The End Of A Love Affair(Stereo)
Lady In Satin | CBS | CK 65144

The End Of A Love Affair(The Audio Story)
Allan Botschinsky Quintet | The Night | M.A Music | NU 676-1

The End Of Faith
Dusko Goykovich Quintet | It's About Blues Time | Fresh Sound Records | FSR-CD 0305

The Ending Of The First Side
Return To Forever | Musicmagic | CBS | SRCS 9349

The Enemies Og Enery
Duane Eubanks Quintet/Sextet | Second Take | TCB Records | TCB 20602

The English Man And The Girl
Loek Dikker Waterland Ensemble | Domesticated Doomsday Machine | Waterland | WM 002

The Enlightener
Chicago Underground Trio | Possible Cube | Delmark | DE 511

The Entertainer
Ken Colyers's Jazzmen | Sensation!:The Decca Years 1955-59 | Lake | LACD 1
Peter Bocage With The Love-Jiles Ragtime Orchestra | New Orleans-The Living Legends:Peter Bocage | Original Jazz Classics | OJCCD 1835-2
Singers Unlimited | A Capella III | MPS | 68245

The Escape
George 'Bullet' Williams | Alabama Blues 1927-1931 | Yazoo | YAZ 1006

The Essence
Shorty Rogers-Bud Shank And The Lighthouse All Stars | Eight Brothers | Candid | CCD 79521

The Essence Of You
Hank Jones Trio | Essence | dmp Digital Music Productions | CD 480

The Eternal Present
Gary Thomas Quintet | Seventh Quadrant | Enja | 5047 (807550)

The Eternal Triangle
Eric Alexander-Lin Halliday Quintet | Stablemates | Delmark | DE 488

The Eternal Turn-On
Nat Adderley Group | Soul Of The Bible | Capitol | 358257-2

The Eternal Walk
Jessica Williams | Ain't Misbehavin' | Candid | CCD 79763

The Eulipians
James Newton Septet | Romance And Revolution | Blue Note | BT 85134

The Evergreen Terrace
Peter Brötzmann/Werner Lüdi | Wie Das Leben So Spielt | FMP | CD 22

The Everywhere Calypso
Mark Soskin Trio | Views From Here | Paddle Wheel | KICJ 126

The Exciting Life
Ketil Bjornstad Group | Seafarer's Song | EmArCy | 9865777

The Exile's Line
Tony Scott-Bill Evans Quintet | A Day In New York | Fresh Sound Records | FSR-CD 0160(2)

THe Exquisite Crystal-
Steve Lacy Nine | Futurities Part II | Hat Art | CD 6032

The Eye Of The Hurricane
Herbie Hancock Quintet | Herbie Hancock:The Complete Blue Note Sixties Sessions | Blue Note | 495569-2
Tomasz Stanko-Manfred Bründl-Michael Riessler | Suite Talk | ITM-Pacific | ITMP 970081

The Face I Love
Don Braden Octet | The Voice Of The Saxophone | RCA | 2668797-2
Melissa Walker And Her Band | I Saw The Sky | Enja | ENJ-9409 2
Sarah Vaughan With Orchestra | I Love Brazil | Pablo | 2312101-2
Esbjörn Svensson Trio(E.S.T.) | Good Morning Susie Soho | ACT | 9009-2

The Face Of Love
Uri Caine Trio | Blue Wail | Winter&Winter | 910034-2

The Face Of Space
Ornette Coleman Quartet | Change Of The Century | Atlantic | 7567-81341-2

The Face Of The Bass
Beauty Is A Rare Thing:Ornette Coleman-The Complete Atlantic Recordings | Atlantic | 8122-71410-2
Stephen Scott Sextet | Something To Consider | Verve | 849557-2

The Faithfull Husar
Louis Armstrong And His All Stars | Live In Berlin/Friedrichstadtpalast | Jazzpoint | JP 1062 CD
The Great Performer | Traditional Line | TL 1304
Byron Stripling And Friends | If I Could Be With You | Nagel-Heyer | NH 1010

The Faithfull Husar-
The New York Allstars | We Love You,Louis! | Nagel-Heyer | CD 029
Louis Armstrong And His All Stars | Live In Berlin/Friedrichstadtpalast | Jazzpoint | JP 1062 CD

The Faithfull Husar(radio-version)
The Jazz Passengers | Implement Yourself | New World Records | 80398-2

The Fallen
John Carter Octet | Castles Of Ghana | Gramavision | GR 8603-2

The Falling Rains Of Life
Chris Barber's Jazz Band | The Outstanding Album | BELL Records | BLR 89300

The Family
Wuppertaler Free Jazz Workshop Orchestra | Wuppertaler Free Jazz Workshop 1980 | FMP | 0940

The Famous Alto Break
Charlie Parker Septet | Charlie Parker Story On Dial Vol.1:West Coast Days | Capitol | 300009(TOCJ 6123)

The Far Corners
Roscoe Mitchell And The Note Factory | This Dance Is For Steve McCall | Black Saint | 120150-2

The Farewell
Thad Jones-Mel Lewis Orchestra | Suite For Pops | Horizon | MLJ 701

The Farewell(from The Song Of The Earth)
Avishai Cohen Trio | The Trumpet Player | Fresh Sound Records | FSNT 161 CD

The Fast
Donald & Peggy Knaack | Inside The Plactic Lotus | Hat Art | 3517

The Fat Man
Jackie Cain/Roy Kral Quartet | Bogie | Fantasy | F 9643
Terry Gibbs Dream Band | Terry Gibbs Dream Band Vol.2:The Sundown Sessions | Contemporary | CCD 7652-2
Jack DeJohnette Group | Sorcery | Prestige | P 10081

The Fatha's Getaway
Dave Liebman Ensemble | John Coltrane's Medetation | Arkadia Jazz | 71042

The Father And The Son And The Holy Ghost
Cozy Cole All Stars | Ultimate Coleman Hawkins selected by Sonny Rollins | Verve | 557538-2

The Father Co-Operates
Earl Hines And His Orchestra | The Indispensable Earl Hines Vol.3/4(1939-1945) | RCA | 2126408-2

The Father Jumps
Earl Hines-Piano Man | Bluebird | NK 86750

The Fearless Five
Art Blakey Percussion Ensemble | Afro Blue | Blue Note | 780701-2

The Feeling Of Jazz
Mario Raja Big Band | Ellington | SPLASC(H) Records | CD H 427-2

The Feeling Of You
Jenny Evans And Her Quintet | Nuages | ESM Records | ESM 9308
Steve Kuhn Quartet | Last Year's Waltz | ECM | 1213

The Feeling Within
Hank Mobley Quintet | Straight No Filter | Blue Note | BST 84435

The Festivale
Gerry Mulligan Quartet | Newport Jazz Festival 1958,July 3rd-6th Vol.2:Mulligan The Main Man | Phontastic | NCD 8814

The Festive Minor
Mike Westbrook Concert Band | Release | Deram | 844851-2

The Field
Louis Van Dijk | Aquarelles | Keytone | KYT 715

The Fields
Pat Metheny Group | Travels | ECM | 1252/53

The Fields The Sky
Joe Zawinul Group | The Rise & Fall Of The Third Stream | 32 Jazz | 32133

The Fifth Of Beethoven
Larry Coryell With John Scofield And Joe Beck | Tributaries | Novus | NL 83072

The File
Richard Leo Johnson | Fingertip Ship | EMI Records | 496901-2

The Final Comedown
Grant Green With Orchestra | Blue Break Beats | Blue Note | 799106-2
The Final Comedown(Soundtrack) | Blue Note | 581678-2
The Final Comedown(Soundtrack) | Blue Note | 581678-2
Laszlo Süle Band | Silence Fiction | AH Records | CD 90025

The Fire Still Burns(for Jimi)
Don Braden Quartet | The Fire Within | RCA | 2663297-2

The Fire Within-
Brennan-Cline-Patumi-Voirol-Theissing | Shooting Stars & Traffic Lights | L+R Records | CDLR 45090

The First Circle
Robert Hohner Persussion Ensemble | Lift Off | dmp Digital Music Productions | CD 498

The First Day
United Women's Orchestra | Virgo Supercluster | Jazz Haus Musik | JHM 0123 CD

The First Glimmer Of Dawn-
Das Pferd | Ao Vivo | VeraBra Records | CDVBR 2029-2

The First Milestone
Tender Variations | Tender Variations(Original Sountrack aus dem Film oDer Windhund o) | Decca | 6.23969 AO

The First Night
Al Di Meola Group | Winter Nights | Telarc Digital | CD 83458

The First Noel
Keith Foley | Music For Christmas | dmp Digital Music Productions | CD 452

The First One
Mack Goldsbury And The New York Connection | Songs I Love To Play | Timescraper | TSCR 9615

The First Snow
Bob Rockwell Trio | Born To Be Blue | Steeplechase | SCCD 31333

The First Step
Thilo.Wolf Trio With Randy Brecker,Chuck Loeb & New York Strings | A Swinging Hour In New York | Mons Records | MR 874801

The First Theme
Laura Fygi Meets Michel Legrand | Watch What Happens | Mercury | 534598-2

The First Time
Laura Fygi With Band | Laura Fygi Live At The North Sea Jazz | Spectra | 9811207
Ann Hampton Callaway And Her Band | After Hours | Denon Compact Disc | CY-18042

The First Time Ever I Saw Your Face
Mel Tormé With Band And Symphony Orchestra | A New Album | Paddle Wheel | KICJ 128
Bengt-Arne Wallin Orchestra | The Birth+Rebirth Of Swedish Folk Jazz | ACT | 9254-2

The First Time In The World I Saw Your Eyes
Sabine&Markus Setzer | Between The Words | Lipstick Records | LIP 8970

The First Twinkle
Blues & Boogie Explosion | Blues & Boogie Explosion | BELL Records | BLR 84003

The Fish
Jay McShann Quartet | Goin' To Kansas City | Stony Plain | SPCD 1286

The Fish Fry Boogie
Zoot Sims Quartet | I Wish I Were Twins | Original Jazz Classics | OJCCD 976-2(2310868)

The Fisherman
Kölner Saxophon Mafia | Go Commercial... | Jazz Haus Musik | JHM 0065 CD

The Fisherman's Wife's Friend
Vincent Courtois Trio | The Fitting Room | Enja | ENJ-9411 2

The Fitting Room
Mel Tormé With The George Shearing Trio | Mel & George 'Do' World War II | Concord | CCD 4471

The Five Ways
Bob Hall | Pianissimo-Barpiano | BELL Records | BLR 89063

The Fives
Peggy Stern Trio | Pleiades | Philology | W 82.2

The Flaming Sword
Duke Ellington And His Famous Orchestra | In A Mellow Tone | RCA | 2113029-2
Herbert Joos-Mathias Ruegg Duo | Mel-An-Cho | Pläne | 88261 Digital

The Flat Foot Floogie
Landes Jugend Jazz Orchester Hessen | Touch Of Lips | hr music.de | hrmj 004-01 CD

The Flea
Buddy Bregman And His Orchestra | Swinging Kicks | Verve | 559514-2

The Flight
Jimmy Smith | The Sounds Of Jimmy Smith | Blue Note | 300158(1556)

The Flight Back
Enrico Pieranunzi | The Day After The Silence | EdiPan | NPG 800

The Flip
Hank Mobley Sextet | The Flip | Blue Note | 593872-2
Rova Saxophone Quartet | From The Bureau Of Both | Black Saint | 120135-2

The Flood
Sippie Wallace With Louis Armstrong And Artie Starks | Louis Armstrong And The Blues Singers 1924-1930 | Affinity | AFS 1018(6)

The Flow
Forman/Loeb/Jackson/Haffner | Metro | Lipstick Records | LIP 890232

The Flu
Herb Geller Quartet | Herb Geller Plays The Al Cohn Songbook | Hep | CD 2066

The Fluegelbird
Nathan Davis Quintet | Two Originals:Happy Girl/The Hip Walk | MPS | 539082-2

The Fly
Horace Heidt And His Musical Knights | The Uncollected:Horace Heidt | Hindsight | HSR 194

The Folks Who Live On The Hill
Arthur Prysock And His Orchestra | A Fine Romance | Verve | 523827-2
Carmen McRae And Her Trio | Live | Jazz Door | JD 1280
Derek Smith Trio | Derek Smith Trio Plays Jerome Kern | Progressive | PRO 7055 IMS
Jack Dieval Avec Stephane Grappelli | Special Stephane Grappelli | Jazztime(EMI) | 251286-2
Maxine Sullivan And Her Band | Maxine Sullivan Sings | Fresh Sound Records | FSR-CD 0178
Oscar Peterson-Stephane Grappelli Quartet | Stephane Grappelli & Friends In Paris | Accord | 500762
Randy Sandke Septet | The Chase | Concord | CCD 4642
Stan Getz Quartet | Born To Be Blue | Bandstand | BDCD 1533
Stephane Grappelli With The George Shearing Trio | Verve Jazz Masters 11:Stéphane Grappelli | Verve | 516758-2
Stephane Grappelli-Bucky Pizzarelli Duo | Duet | Ahead | 33755

The Following Morning
Jack Bruce-Bernie Worrell | Monkjack | CMP Records | CMP CD 1010

The Fool On The Hill
Klaus Ignatzek | Plays Beatles Songs | Nabel Records:Jazz Network | CD 4643
Lena Horne And Gabor Szabo | Lena & Gabor | Gryphon | 6.24451 AT
Singers Unlimited | A Capella | MPS | 815671-1

The Force
Francisco Mondragon Rio Group | Natural | DIW | DIW 321 CD

The Four Lovers
Sonny Stitt Orchestra | Sonny Stitt & The Top Brass | Atlantic | 90139-1 TIS

The Four Points Are Thus Beheld
Ray Anderson Alligatory Band | Heads And Tales | Enja | ENJ-9055 2

The Four Reasons:
Don Grolnick Group | Hearts And Numbers | VeraBra Records | CDVBR 2016-2

The Four Sleepers
Bennie Wallace Trio | The Fourteen Bar Blues | Enja | 3029-2

The Fourth Way
David Blamires Group | The David Blamires Group | Nova | NOVA 9144-2

The Fox
Kenny Dorham Quintet | Trompeta Toccata | Blue Note | BST 84181
Lionel Hampton All Stars | Lionel Hampton And His Jazz Giants | Black & Blue | BLE 59.107 2

The Fractar Question
Steve Turre Group | Lotus Flower | Verve | 559787-2

The Free,Chained
Mal Waldron Trio | Breaking New Ground | Eastwind | EWIND 712

The Freedom In There
Art Blakey | Feedom Rider | Blue Note | 821287-2

The Freedom Rider (Drum Solo)
Best Of Blakey 60 | Blue Note | 493072-2
Art Blakey And The Jazz Messengers | The Freedom Rider | Blue Note | 870076-5

TITELVERZEICHNIS

The Freedom Suite
Sonny Rollins Trio | Sonny Rollins-The Freelance Years:The Complete Riverside & Contemporary Recordings | Riverside | 5 RCD 4427-2
Peggy Lee With Benny Goodman And The Paul Weston Orchestra | Peggy Lee & Benny Goodman:The Complete Recordings 1941-1947 | CBS | C2K 65686

The Freedom Train
Ben Selvin And His Orchestra | Cheerful Little Earful | Saville Records | SVL 165 IMS

The Fricticious Motive Of An Imaginary Murder
Buddy Rich And His Orchestra | Live Sessions At The Palladium, Hollywood | Jazz Anthology | JA 5206

The Frim Fram Sauce
Peter Bolte Quartet | ...All The April Snow | ITM-Pacific | ITMP 970092

The Frog And The Snake
Hal Singer Orchestra | Rent Party | Savoy | SV 0258(SJL 1147)

The Front
Wayne Horvitz Group | Miracle Mile | Nonesuch | 7559-79278-2

The Front Door
The Prestige All Stars | Earthy | Original Jazz Classics | OJCCD 1707-2(P 7102)

The Fruit
Roni Ben-Hur Trio | Sofia's Butterfly | TCB Records | TCB 98802

The Full Bronte
James Moody's Modernists | New Sounds | Blue Note | 784436-2

The Funeral
Steve White Quartet | Jazz In Hollywood:Steve White | Original Jazz Classics | OJCCD 1891-2(Nocturne unreleased)

The Funky Fox
Graef-Schippa-Moritz | Orlando Frames | Nabel Records:Jazz Network | CD 4690

The Funky Girl's Broken Heel
The Quartet | Dedications | Konnex Records | ST 5002 IMS

The Fuzz
Al Porcino Big Band | In Oblivion | Jazz Mark | 106 Digital
Bengt-Arne Wallin Orchestra | The Birth+Rebirth Of Swedish Folk Jazz | ACT | 9254-2

The Gaerdeby Tune
The Benny Carter All-Star Sax Ensemble | Over The Rainbow | Limelight | 820810-2 IMS

The Gal From Joe's
Johnny Hodges With Billy Strayhorn And The Duke Ellington Orchestra | Verve Jazz Masters 35:Johnny Hodges | Verve | 521857-2
Nina Simone And Orchestra | Compact Jazz: Nina Simone | Mercury | 838007-2

The Gallery
Huddie Ledbetter | Blues Roots Vol.1 | Storyville | 6.23700 AG

The Galloping Latin
Sam Yahel Trio | Trio | Criss Cross | Criss 1158

The Gambit:
Bill Evans Quartet | The Gambler-Bill Evans Live At The Blue Note Tokyo | Jazz City | 660.53.025

The Gambler
Peter Beets New York Trio | Peter Beets New York Trio | Criss Cross | Criss 1214

The Game Maker
Jack Walrath And The Masters Of Supense | Hip Gnosis | TCB Records | TCB 01062

The Gamut
Jimmy Giuffre Trio | Live In Europe Vol.1 | Raretone | 5018 FC

The Gap Sealer
Harlem Hamfats | Hot Chicago Jazz Blues And Jive 1936-1937 | Folklyric | 9029

The Gardener
Chick Corea And His Orchestra | My Spanish Heart | Polydor | 543303-3

The Gardens
Jean-Luc Ponty Quintet | Imaginary Voyage | Atlantic | SD 19136

The Gate
Peter Apfelbaum & The Hieroglyphics Ensemble | Jodoji Brightness | Antilles | 74321 12050 2(875267)

The Gathering
Lee-Askill-Atherton | Shoalhaven Rise | Black Sun Music | 15019-2

The Generation Gap
Les McCann-Eddie Harris Quintet | Swiss Movements | Atlantic | 7567-81365-2

The Gentle Art Of Love
Mat Mathews Orchestra | The Gentle Art Of Love | Dawn | DCD 111

The Gentle Rain (Chuva Delicada)
Astrud Gilberto With The Don Sebesky Orchestra | Silver Collection: The Astrud Gilberto Album | Verve | 823451-2 PMS
Joe Pass And Paulinho Da Costa Sextet | Tudo Bem! | Original Jazz Classics | 2310824
Kenny Drew Trio | Recollections | Timeless | CDSJP 333
Singers Unlimited + The Oscar Peterson Trio | In Tune | MPS | 68085
Oscar Peterson And His Trio | Encore At The Blue Note | Telarc Digital | CD 83356

The Gentleman & Hizcaine
Will Osborne And His Orchestra | The Uncollected:Will Osborne | Hindsight | HSR 197

The Gentleman Is A Dope
Michael Kanan Trio | The Gentleman Is A Dope | Fresh Sound Records | FSNT 147 CD
Morgana King And Her Quintet | Another Time Another Space | Muse | MCD 5339

The Getaway And The Chase
Gregor Hilden Group | Westcoast Blues | Acoustic Music Records | 319.1162.2

The Giant Guitar And The Black Stick
Horace Tapscott Quintet | West Coast Hot | Novus | ND 83107

The Giddybug Gallop
Duke Ellington And His Famous Orchestra | Passion Flower 1940-46 | Bluebird | 63 66616-2

The Gift
Gordon Brisker Quintet | The Gift | Naxos Jazz | 86001-2
Jon Rose Group | Violin Music In The Age Of Shopping | Intakt Records | CD 038
Mike Nock Quartet | In Out And Around | Timeless | CD SJP 119
Renee Rosnes Quartet | Ancestors | Blue Note | 834634-2

The Gift: One Shot From The Hip
Dave Douglas Trio | Constellations | Hat Art | CD 6173

The Gig
Herbie Nichols Trio | Herbie Nichols Trio | Blue Note | 300098(1519)

The Gig(alt.take)
Harold Mabern-Kieran Overs | Philadelphia Bound | Sackville | SKCD2-3051

The Gipsy
Louis Armstrong And His All Stars | New Orleans Louisiana | Traditional Line | TL 1319

The Girl Friend
Harry Babasin Quintet | Jazz In Hollywood:Harry Babasin/Bob Enevoldsen | Original Jazz Classics | OJCCD 1888-2(Nocturne NLP3/NLP-6)
Shorty Rogers & His Giants | Re-Entry | Eastworld | CP 32-5421

The Girl From East 9th Street
Paul Desmond-Gerry Mulligan Quartet | The Ballad Of Paul Desmond | RCA | 21429372
Randy Burns Quartet | Evening Of The Magician | ESP Disk | ESP 1089-2

The Girl In My Dreams Tries To Look Like You
Roy Fox & His Band | This Is Romance | Saville Records | SVL 166 IMS

The Girl In The Other Room
Benny Green Quintet | Prelude | Criss Cross | Criss 1036

The Girl Next Door
Wes Montgomery With The Jimmy Jones Orchestra | Wes Montgomery-The Complete Riverside Recordings | Riverside | 12 RCD 4408-2

The Girl Next Door(alt.take)
Enver Ismailov | Colours Of A Ferghana Bazar-Live At The International Jazzfestival Münster | Tutu Records | 888142-2*

The Girl Of Meexor
Christian Josi With The Harry Allen Quartet | I Walk With My Feet Off The Ground | Master Mix | CHECD 00111

The Girl Who Cried Champagne
Carla Bley Band | Fleur Carnivore | Watt | 21

The Girl Who Cried Champagne(part 1-3)
Eric Watson Quartet | Your Tonight Is My Tomorrow | Owl Records | 047 CD

The Girl Who Used To Be Me
Four Tenor Brothers | Made In Sweden Vol.2: 24.3.1951-12.12.1952 | Magnetic Records | MRCD 113

The Girl With The Rose Hips
Dave Douglas Quartet | Charms Of The Night Sky | Winter&Winter | 910015-2*

The Girl With The Rose Hips-
Florian Poser Group | Pacific Tales | Acoustic Music Records | 319.1124.2

The Girlfriend Of The Whirling Dervish
Eclipse Ally Five | Original Zenith Brass Band/Eclipse Alley Five/Avery-Tillman Band | American Music | AMCD-75

The Girls Go Crazy About The Way I Walk
Chris Barber's Jazz Band | Barber 's Best | Decca | 6.28128 DP
Kid Ory's Creole Jazz Band | Kid Ory:Creole Classics 1944-1947 | Naxos Jazz | 8.120587 CD

The Girl's In Love With You
Pat Metheny Group | We Live Here | Geffen Records | GED 24729

The Girls Next Door
Klaus Weiss Sextet | All Night Through | ATM Records | ATM 3816 AH

The Git Go
Mal Waldron Quartet | Soul Eyes | RCA | 2153887-2
Mal Waldron Quintet | The Git Go-Live At The Village Vanguard | Soul Note | SN 1118

The Glide
Steve Coleman Group | Motherland Pulse | JMT Edition | 919001-2

The Glide Was In The Ride
Artie Shaw And His Orchestra | Mixed Bag | Musicmasters | 65119-2

The Global Soul
David Binney Group | South | ACT | 9279-2

The Global Soul(reprise)
Brother Virus | Happy Hour | Tutu Records | 888130-2

The Glow Of Temptation
Brian Bromberg Group | It's About Time-The Acoustic Project | Nova | NOVA 9146-2

The Golden Apples Of The Sun
Jay Hoggard Septet | Mystic Winds, Tropic Breezes | India Navigation | IN 1049

The Golden Flute
Benny Golson Orchestra | Tune In,Turn On | Verve | 559793-2

The Golden Horn
Dave Brubeck Quartet | Jazz Impressions Of Eurasia | CBS | SRCS 9360

The Golden Striker
Modern Jazz Quartet | Jazz-Club; Bass | Verve | 840037-2
MJQ 40 | Atlantic | 7567-82330-2
No Sun In Venice | Atlantic | SD 1284
The Modern Jazz Quartet | Reunion At Budokan 1981 | Atlantic | 251210-1 TIS
James Moody And His Band | Wail Moody Wail | Original Jazz Classics | OJCCD 1791-2(P 7036)

The Golden Wedding
Woody Herman And His Orchestra | Compact Jazz: Woody Herman | Verve | 835319-2 PMS

The Good Doctor
Verve Jazz Masters 54:Woody Herman | Verve | 529903-2

The Good Earth
Jazz Live & Rare: Wooody Herman 1945-1947 | Jazzline | ???
Compact Jazz: Woody Herman | Verve | 835319-2 PMS
Woody Herman's 2nd Herd | The Herd Rides Again...In Stereo | Evidence | ECD 22010-2

The Good Life
Ahmad Jamal Trio | Ahmad Jamal:Waltz For Debby | Memo Music | HDJ 4018
Carmen McRae And Her Quintet | Velvet Soul | LRC Records | CDC 7970
Clark Terry Sextet | Free And Oozy | Blue Moon | BMCD 3076
Gary McFarland Orchestra | Soft Samba | Verve | MV 2102 IMS
Kenny Burrell Quintet | Freedom | Blue Note | GXK 8170
Parallel Realities | Parallel Realities:Live... | Jazz Door | JD 1251/52
Sonny Stitt Quartet | In Style | Muse | MR 5228
Willis Jackson Sextet | Gravy | Prestige | PCD 24254-2
Dominik Grimm-Thomas Wallisch Trio | A Brighter Day | Edition Collage | EC 510-2

The Good Life-
Winard Harper Sextet | Winard | Savant Records | SCD 2021

The Good The Bad And The Ugly
Willem Breuker Kollektief | Willem Breuker Kollektief | BVHAAST | CD 9601

The Goof And I
Al Porcino Big Band | In Oblivion | Jazz Mark | 106 Digital
Shorty Rogers & His Giants | Re-Entry | Eastworld | CP 32-5421
Woody Herman And His Orchestra | Hollywood Paladium 1948 | Jazz Anthology | JA 5237

The Gospel Truth
Steve Wilson Quintet | Step Lively | Criss Cross | Criss 1096

The Goutelas Suite:
Ben Webster Quintet | Trav'lin Light | Milestone | M 47056

The Grain Belt Blues
Repercussion Unit | In Need Again | CMP Records | CMP CD 31

The Grandfather-
JoAnne Brackeen Trio | Keyed Up | CBS | 83868

The Gravel And The Bird
Billie & Dee Dee Pierce | De De Pierce With Billie Pierce In Binghampton,NY,Vol.2 | American Music | AMCD-80

The Gravy Waltz
Oscar Peterson Trio | The Jazz Soul Of Oscar Peterson/Affinity | Verve | 533100-2

The Great City
Shirley Horn Trio | The Garden Of The Blues | Steeplechase | SCS 1203
Richard Zimmerman | The Complete Works Of Scott Joplin | Laserlight | 15945

The Great Escape
Larry Coryell Sextet | Barefoot Boy | RCA | CL 13961 DP

The Great Pretender
Lester Bowie's Brass Fantasy | The Fire This Time | IN+OUT Records | 7019-2
George Winston | Linus & Lucy-The Music Of Vince Guaraldi | Windham Hill | 34 11187-2

The Great Pumpkin Waltz
Billy Byers' Jazz Workshop | The Jazz Workshop | Fresh Sound Records | NL 46046(RCA LPM 1269)

The Great Schism
Louis Moholo Trio | Tern | FMP | SAJ 43/44

The Great Unknown
Peter Ponzol Trio | Prism | View | VS 114 IMS

The Greatest Love Of All(single version)
Yusef Lateef Quartet | 1984 | MCA | AS 84

The Green Grass Grows All Around
Louis Jordan And His Tympany Five | Louis Jordan Vol.2-Knock Me Out | Swingtime(Contact) | ST 1012

The Griots
Graham Haynes Group | The Griots Footsteps | Verve | 523262-2

The Griots Song(Djelilou)
Arthur Blythe Sextet | The Grip | India Navigation | IN 1029

The Groom's Sister
Jerry Dodgion Quartet | The Jazz Scene:San Francisco | Fantasy | FCD 24760-2

The Groove
Modern Jazz From San Francisco | Original Jazz Classics | OJC 272(F 3213)

The Groove Merchant
Crystal | Clear | Black-Hawk | BKH 51501

The Group
Dexter Gordon Quintet | Generation | Original Jazz Classics | OJCCD 836-2(P 10069)
Dexter Gordon Birthday Celebration | Fantasy | FANCD 6082-2
John Fedchock New York Big Band | John Fedchock New York Big Band | Reservoir | RSR CD 138

The Guest
The Indica Project | Horn Ok Please | Enja | 9110-2

The Gunks
Thomas Heberer | Kill Yr Darlins | Poise | Poise 05

The Gunslingers Delight
John Marshall Band | Compared To What | DA Records | 73009

The Gypsy
Lou Colombo Quintet | I Remember Bobby | Concord | CCD 4435
Louis Armstrong And His All Stars | At The Pasadena Civic Auditorium | GNP Crescendo | GNP 11001
Louis Armstrong With The Commanders | Ambassador Louis Armstrong Vol.17:Moments To Remember(1952-1956) | Ambassador | CLA 1917
Martin Taylor Quintet With Guests | Spirit Of Django:Years Apart | Linn Records | AKD 058
Snooky Young Quintet | Horn Of Plenty | Concord | CJ 91
The Great British Jazz Band | A British Jazz Odyssey | Candid | CCD 79740
Victor Feldman Orchestra | Latinsville | Contemporary | CCD 9005-2
Werner Pöhlert-Jochen Pöhlert | Impressions,Interlude & 'Only Eyes' | Hohner Records | ohne Nummer(3 Maxi-Single)

The Gypsy's Hip
Michael Musillami Group | GlassArt | Evidence | ECD 22060-2

The Half Of It Deary Blues
Wycliffe Gordon Group | Slidin' Home | Nagel-Heyer | CD 2001

The 'Hallelujah' Shout
Air Mail | Light Blues | Amadeo | 835305-2

The Hapless Child
Michael Mantler Quintet | Live | Watt | 18
Duke Ellington And His Orchestra | The Rare Broadcast Recordings 1951 | Jazz Anthology | JA 5209

The Happy Blues
Herbie Harper Quintet | Jazz In Hollywood:Herbie Harper | Original Jazz Classics | OJCCD 1887-2(Nocturne NLP-1/NLP-7)

The Happy Clown
Herbie Harper Feat.Bud Shank And Bob Gordon | Fresh Sound Records | 054 2600581(Liberty LJH 6003)

The Happy Jazz Singer
Horace Silver Quintet | That Healin' Feelin' | Blue Note | 84352

The Happy Medium
Chubby Jackson Sextet | Chubby Jackson-The Happy Monster:Small Groups 1944-1947 | Cool & Blue | C&B-CD 109

The Happy Sheik
Rabih Abou-Khalil Group | The Sultan's Picnic | Enja | ENJ-8078 2
LaVerne Butler With The Rob Bargad Band | Day Dreamin' | Chesky | JD 117

The Hard One
Gonzalo Rubalcaba Trio With Michael Brecker | Inner Voyage | Blue Note | 499241-2
Otis Spann/Robert Lockwood Jr. | The Blues:A Collection Of Classic Blues Singers | Black Lion | BLCD 7605-2

The Hard Way
Warne Marsh-Sal Mosca | How Deep How High | Discovery | DS 863 IMS

The Hardest Time
Curlew | Live At The Knitting Factory New York City,Vol.1 | Enemy | EMCD 111(03511)

The Harlem Medley:
Stephen Scott Trio | Renaissance | Verve | 523863-2

The Haunted Melody
Steve Wilson Quintet | Blues For Marcus | Criss Cross | Criss 1073

The Hawk Talks
Duke Ellington And His Orchestra | Concert At Carnegie Hall | Atlantis | ATS 2 D

The Haze Of The Frost
Blue Mitchell Sextet | Blue Soul | Original Jazz Classics | OJCCD 765-2(RLP 1155)

The Head
Tiny Parham And His Musicians | Victor Jazz History Vol.2:Black Chicago | RCA | 2128556-2

The Headmasters Daughter
Pili-Pili | Boogaloo | JA & RO | JARO 4174-2

The Headpeeper
Heinz Von Hermann Quintet | Jazz Ahead | Mons Records | MR 874810

The Healer's Voyage On The Sacred River(for Ayl Kwel Armah)
Jan Garbarek Group | Visible World | ECM | 1585(529086-2)

The Healing Smoke
Don Sleet Quintet | All Members | Original Jazz Classics | OJCCD 1949-2(JLP 9455)

The Hearing
Lee Morgan Quintet | Indestructible Lee | Affinity | AFF 762

The Heart Keeps
Jon Hiseman Group | Night In The Sun | Kuckuck | 055

The Heart Of The Matter
Torsten Kamps | Groove Booster | Blackbird Records | BD 40510

The Heat
Roy Eldridge Quintet | Frenchie Roy | Vogue | 655009

The Heat Of Heat
Pat Metheny Group | Imaginary Day | Warner | 9362-46791-2

The Heat Of The Day
Dan Faulk Quartet | Spirit In The Night | Fresh Sound Records | FSNT 024 CD

The Heath Blues
Monty Alexander Orchestra | Stir It Up-The Music Of Bob Marley | Telarc Digital | CD 83469

The Heather On The Hill
Russell Malone Quartet | Look Who's Here | Verve | 543543-2
Jack McDuff Group | The Heatin' System | Concord | CCD 4644

The Heat's On
Dizzy Gillespie All Stars | Dizzy's Diamonds-Best Of The Verve Years | Verve | 513875-2
The Frank Capp Juggernaut | Play It Again Sam | Concord | CCD 4747

The Henhouse
Cannonball Adderley Quartet | Cannonball Adderley Birthday Celebration | Fantasy | FANCD 6087-2

The Henry John Story-
John Benson Brooks Ensemble | Alabama/Africa | Milestone | M 47059

The Hidden Voice
SWR Big Band | Jazz In Concert | Hänssler Classics | CD 93.004

The Hierophant
Billy Eckstine With Bobby Tucker And His Orchestra | Billy Eckstine Now Singing In 12 Great Movies | Verve | 589307-2

The High And The Mighty
Jimmy Smith Trio | A New Sound A New Star:Jimmy Smith At The Organ | Blue Note | 857191-2
Jimmy Smith At The Organ | Blue Note | 300154(1512)
Enrico Rava 4uartet | Animals | Inak | 8801

The High Priest
Art Blakey And The Jazz Messengers | Kyoto | Original Jazz Classics | OJCCD 145-2

The Higher We Jump
Bill Connors | Theme To The Gaurdian | ECM | 1057

The Highest Mountain
Cliffird Jordan Quartet | Half Note | Steeplechase | SCCD 31198

The Hill Of Love

Chuck Mangione Quartet With The Rochester Philharmonic Orchestra | Compact Jazz: Chuck Mangione | Mercury | 830696-2 PMS
The Hiltop
The N.Y. Hardbop Quintet | Rokermotion | TCB Records | TCB 96352
The Hippie
Hank Mobley Quintet | Far Away Lands | Blue Note | BST 84425
The Holey
Jaki Byard | Jaki Byard:Solo/Strings | Prestige | PCD 24246-2
The Hollis Stomp
Charlie Byrd | The Charlie Byrd Christmas Album | Concord | CCD 42004
The Holy Ghost
George Gruntz Concert Jazz Band '83 | Theatre | ECM | 1265
The Holy Grail Of Jazz And Joy
Dave Brubeck Orchestra | Two Generations Of Brubeck | Atlantic | SD 1645
The Home Fire
Dollar Brand Orchestra | Abdullah Ibrahim-African Marketplace | Elektra | ELK K 52217
The Honey-Bird
Cab Calloway And His Orchestra | Soundtracks And Broadcastings | Jazz Anthology | 550232
The Honeydripper
Jack McDuff Quartet | Jack McDuff:The Prestige Years | Prestige | PRCD 24387-2
Honeydripper | Original Jazz Classics | OJC 222(P 7199)
Roosevelt Sykes | The Blues:A Collection Of Classic Blues Singers | Black Lion | BLCD 7605-2
The Honeydripper(alt.take)
Joe Liggins Quintet | Great Rhythm & Blues-Vol.6 | Bulldog | BDL 1005
The Honky-Tonk Cowboy
Axel Zwingenberger With The Mojo Blues Band And Red Holloway | Axel Zwingenberger And The Friends Of Boogie Woogie,Vol.8 | Vagabond | VRCD 8.93019
The Hoochi Coochi Coo
Chick Corea-Herbie Hancock Duo | Corea Hancock | Polydor | 2669049
The Hook
Jukka Tolonen Group | Impressions | Sonet | 147126
The Hop
Glenn Miller And His Orchestra | Glenn Miller In Concert | RCA | NL 89216 DP
The Horn Pipe
Modern Jazz Quartet | Echoes | Pablo | 2312142-2
The Horses Of Nizami
Hans Koller & The International Brass Company | The Horses | L+R Records | LR 40008
The Hotel Lazard Cafe
Sam 'Stretch' Shields | Living Country Blues USA Vol.7: Afro-American Blues Roots | L+R Records | LR 42037
The House Behind The River
Archie Shepp-Lars Gulin Quintet | The House I Live In | Steeplechase | SCCD 36013
The House I Live In
The Ravens | Rarities | Savoy | SV 0261(SJL 1174)
The House Of The Rising Sun
Peter Gullin Trio | Untold Story | Dragon | DRCD 315
The House Of Winchester
Clifford Jordan And The Magic Triangle | The Highest Mountain | Steeplechase | SCS 1047
The Hucklebuck
Lionel Hampton And His Orchestra | Wes Montgomery:Complete Recordings With Lionel Hampton | Definitive Records | DRCD 11242
The Hum Of Its Parts
Wädi Gysi & Hans Reichel | Show-Down | Intakt Records | CD 023
The Human Abstract
Borah Bergman-Andrew Cyrille | The Human Factor | Soul Note | 121212-2
The Hump Bump
Lou Donaldson Quintet | Mr.Shing-A-Ling | Blue Note | 784271-2
The Humpback
Attila Zoller Quartet | The Horizon Beyond | ACT | 9211-2
The Hundred Books(for Idries Shah)
Pete Rugolo And His Orchestra | Thriller/Richard Diamon(Original Jazz Scores From 2 Classics TV Series) | Fresh Sound Records | FSCD 2015
The Hungry Glass
Greetje Kauffeld With Jerry Van Rooyen And Jiggs Whigham And The Rias Big Band | Greetje Kauffeld Meets Jerry Van Rooyen And Jiggs Whigham With The Rias Big Band | Mons Records | MR 874786
The Hunt
Terje Rypdal Quintet | Works | ECM | 825428-1
The Hunter-
Jackie McLean-Michael Carvin Duo | Antiquity | Steeplechase | SCCD 31028
The Hunter Gets Captured By The Game
T-Bone Walker With Jim Wynn's Band | Singing The Blues | Pathe | 1546761(Imperial LP 9116)
The Hustler
The Crusaders | Street Life | MCA | ???
The Hustlers
Anita Boyer & Her Tomboyers | Nat King Cole Trio:The MacGregor Years 1941/45 | Music & Arts | CD 911
The Hymn
Clark Terry-Chris Woods Quintet | Swiss Radio Days Jazz Series Vol.8:Clark Terry-Chris Woods | TCB Records | TCB 02082
The Ice Is Breaking
Dave Bartholomew And His Band | Shrimp And Gumbo | Pathe | 1566311
The Illusion
Bob Neloms | Pretty Music | India Navigation | IN 1050
The Immaculate Conception
Michael Formanek Septet | Low Profile | Enja | ENJ-8050 2
The Impaler
William Ackerman Group | Passage | Windham Hill | TA-C- 1014
The Imperative
Christoph Schweizer Sextet | Normal Garden | Mons Records | MR 874660
The Impossible Rag
Werner Pirchner Quintet | The Loss | Bellaphon | 270-31-003
The Improvizer
Booker Ervin Quintet | The In Between | Blue Note | 859379-2
The 'In' Crowd
Monty Alexander-Sly Dunbar-Robbie Shakespeare Group | Monty Meets Sly And Robbie | Telarc Digital | CD 83494
The Inception
Mal Waldron | Update | Soul Note | 121130-2
The Inch Worm
John Coltrane Quartet | John Coltrane-Live Trane:The European Tours | Pablo | 7PACD 4433-2
The Complete 1962 Stockholm Concert Vol.1 | Magnetic Records | MRCD 108
Live 1962 | Festival | ???
John Coltrane:The Classic Quartet-Complete Impulse Studio Recordings | Impulse(MCA) | 951280-2
John Coltrane:Standards | Impulse(MCA) | 549914-2
Rare John Coltrane Quartet | Duke Records | D 1016
Rachelle Ferrell With The Eddie Green Trio And Alex Foster | First Instrumental | Blue Note | 827820-2
Sheila Jordan And Her Quartet | Confirmation | East Wind | EW 8024 IMS
The Indifferent
Trine-Lise Vaering With The Bobo Stenson Trio And Guests | When I Close My Eyes | Stunt Records | STUCD 19602
The Inevitable Wall
Larry Young Quintet | Heaven On Earth | Blue Note | BNJ 71040(BST 84304)
The Infinite
Muhal Richard Abrams | Afrisong | India Navigation | IN 1058
The Inflated Tear
Roland Kirk Quartet | Atlantic Jazz: The Avant-Garde | Atlantic | 7567-81709-2
The Inflated Tear | Atlantic | 7567-90045-2
Steve Turre Group | Lotus Flower | Verve | 559787-2
The Ingrian Rune Song
Steve Coleman And The Mystic Rhythm Society | Myths, Modes And Means | Novus | 2131692-2
The Injuns
Greg Osby Quintet | Inner Circle | Blue Note | 499871-2
The Inner Circle Principle
Sergey Kuryokhin | The Way Of Freedom | LEO | LR 107
The Inner Look
Kahil El'Zabar Quartet | Sacred Love | Sound Aspects | sas CD 021
The Insect God
Gunter Hampel And His Galaxie Dream Band | Vogelfrei | Birth | 0029
The Inside Lane
Becker/Sclavis/Lindberg | Transition | FMP | 1170
The Interlude(Drinking Music)
Freddie Hubbard Quintet | Red Clay | CTI | 6001
The Intimacy Of My Woman's Beautiful Eyes
Duke Ellington And His Orchestra | Jazz:For Absolute Beginners | RCA | NL 89874 AG
The Intimacy Of The Blues
Duke Ellington Trio | And His Mother Called Him Bill | RCA | 2125762-2
The Introduction
Steve Morse Band | The Introduction | Elektra | 960369-1
The Invisible
John Coltrane-Don Cherry Quartet | The Avantgarde | Rhino | 8122-79892-2
That's Jazz Vol.40: The Avant-Garde | Atlantic | ATL 50523
Terri Lyne Carrington Quartet | Structure | ACT | 9427-2
Sun Ra Group | Janus | Black Lion | CD 877640-2
The Invisible Storm
Phillip Johnston's Big Trouble | Philip Johnston's Big Trouble | Black Saint | 120152-2
The Island
Dave Liebman Quintet | Besame Mucho And Other Latin Jazz Standards | Red Records | 123260-2
Denny Zeitlin-David Friesen Duo | Concord Duo Series Volume Eight | Concord | CCD 4639
Shirley Horn Trio | Loving You | Verve | 537022-2
Stanley Turrentine Sextet | T Time | Musicmasters | 65124-2
Wycliffe Gordon Quintet | The Joyride | Nagel-Heyer | CD 2032
The Island Boy
Prince Lasha-Sonny Simmons Quintet | Firebirds | Original Jazz Classics | OJCCD 1822-2(C 7617)
The Islands
Chris Barber's Jazz Band | The Great Re-Union Concert | Intercord | 157011
The Ivy Walk
Nat Su Quartet | The J.Way | Fresh Sound Records | FSNT 038 CD
The J. Way
Tok Tok Tok | 50 Ways To Leave Your Lover | Einstein Music | EM 91051
The Jack
Geoff Keezer Quartet | Curveball | Sunnyside | SSC 1045 D
The James Bond Theme
Count Basie And His Orchestra | Basie Meets Bond | Capitol | 538225-2
Johnny Griffin Sextet | Bush Dance | Galaxy | GXY 5126
The Jamfs Are Coming
Oscar Peterson Trio | Two Originals:Walking The Line/Another Day | MPS | 533549-2
The Kenny Clarke-Francy Boland Big Band | Two Originals:Sax No End/All Blues | MPS | 523525-2
The Jasmin Tree
Modern Jazz Quartet | The Complete Modern Jazz Quartet Prestige & Pablo Recordings | Prestige | 4PRCD 4438-2
The Jasmine Tree
The Complete Modern Jazz Quartet Prestige & Pablo Recordings | Prestige | 4PRCD 4438-2
MJQ 40 | Atlantic | 7567-82330-2
The Complete Last Concert | Atlantic | 81976-2
The Jeep Is Jumpin'
Dick Hyman Orchestra | Swing Is Here | Reference Recordings | RR-72 CD
Duke Ellington-Coleman Hawkins Orchestra | Duke Ellington Meets Coleman Hawkins | MCA | MCAD 5650
Jay McShann Trio | Swingmatism | Sackville | SKCD2-3046
Johnny Hodges Orchestra | Everybody Knows Johnny Hodges | Impulse(MCA) | JAS 34 (AS 61)
Nat Jaffe And His V-Disc Jumpers | Don Byas Complete American Small Group Recordings | Definitive Records | DRCD 11213
Zoot Sims Quintet | The Swinger | Pablo | 2310861
The Jet Song-
Sal Mosca | For You | Candid | CRS 1022 IMS
The Jive Don't Come From Kokomo
Rosetta Howard And The Harlem Blues Seernaders | Charlie Shavers And The Blues Singers 1938-1939 | Timeless | CBC 1-025
The Jive Samba
Cannonball Adderley Sextet | The Cannonball Adderley Collection Vol.3:Jazz Workshop Revisited | Landmark | CAC 1303-2(882343)
Rene Thomas Quintet | Blue Note,Paris 1964 | Royal Jazz | RJD 512
The Jody Grind
Horace Silver Quintet | Horace Silver | Blue Note | 84510
Vesna Skorija Band | Niceland | Satin Doll Productions | SDP 1037-1 CD
Alphonse Mouzon Group | By All Means | MPS | 817485-1
The Joint Is Jumpin'
Fats Waller And His Rhythm | Fats Waller-The Joint Is Jumpin' | RCA | ND 86288(874182)
The Joker
Lee Morgan Sextet | Search For The New Land | Blue Note | 84169
Matthew Brubeck & David Widelock | Giraffes In A Hurry | B&W Present | BW 042
The Jolly Jumper
The Mills Brothers | The Best Of The Decca Years | MCA | MCD 31348
The Joneses
Cyrus Chestnut Trio With James Carter | Cyrus Chestnut | Atlantic | 7567-83140-2
The Journey
Joe Beck Quartet | The Journey | dmp Digital Music Productions | CD 481
La Vienta | Night Dance | Telarc Digital | CD 83359
Rick Margitza Orchestra | Hope | Blue Note | 794858-2
Threeo | Racing Time | L+R Records | CDLR 45103
Bobby Lyle Group | The Journey | Atlantic | 7567-82138-2
The Journey-
Keith Jarrett Quartet | My Song | ECM | 1115(821406-2)
The Journey Home
Works | ECM | 825425-1
The Journeyers To The East
The Quincy Jones-Sammy Nestico Orchestra | Basie & Beyond | Warner | 9362-47792-2
The Joy Of Cookin'
Willem Breuker Kollektief And Djazzex | Dance Plezier-Joy Of Dance | BVHAAST | CD 9513
The Juggler
Ralph Towner-John Abercrombie | Five Years Later | ECM | 1207
The Juicer Is Wild
Stanley Wilson And His Orchestra | The Music From M Squad | Fresh Sound Records | PL 45929(RCA LPM 2062)
The Jump
Paul Smith Trio | By The Fireside | Savoy | SV 0225(MG 12094)
The Jumpin' Blues
Jay McShann And His Orchestra | Big Band Bounce & Boogie:Hootie's K.C.Blues | Affinity | AFS 1006
Jimmy Smith Quartet | The Best Of Jimmy Smith | Blue Note | 791140-2
Stanley Turrentine-Jimmy Smith Quartet | One Night With Blue Note Vol.3 | Blue Note | BT 85115 Digital
The Jumpin' Blues(alt.take)
Benny Goodman And His Orchestra | More Camel Caravans | Phontastic | NCD 8845/6
The Jumpin' Jive
Cab Calloway And His Orchestra | Cab Calloway: Jumpin' Jive 1938/1946 | Zeta | ZET 732
The Jungle Bit
Mongo Santamaria Orchestra | The Watermelon Man | Milestone | M 47012
The Jungle King
Count Basie And His Orchestra | The Indispensable Count Basie | RCA | ND 89758
The Kakapo
Jonas Knutsson Quartet | Jonas Knutsson Quartet | Touché Music | TMcCD 018
The Kangaroo Woman
Dutch Swing College Band | Digital Dixie | Philips | 800065-2 PMS
The Keep
Wadada Leo Smith | Kulture Jazz | ECM | 1507
The Kemet Omega Reigns(for Billie Holiday)
Claude Williamson Trio | Keys West | Affinity | AFF 62
The Kerry Dancers
Art Ensemble Of Chicago | Fanfare For The Warriors | Atlantic | 90046-1 TIS
The Key To You
David Benoit Group | Every Step Of The Way | GRP | GRP 95582
The Kicker
Horace Silver Quintet | Song For My Father | Blue Note | 499002-2
Joe Henderson-The Blue Note Years | Blue Note | 789287-2
Joe Henderson Sextet | Foresight | Milestone | M 47058
Ray Brown Trio With Nicholas Payton | Some Of My Best Friends Are The Trumpet Players | Telarc Digital | CD 83495
The Kid
Harold Ousley Sextet | The People's Groove | Muse | MR 5107
Lou Donaldson Quintet | So Blue So Funky:Heroes Of The Hammond Vol.2 | Blue Note | 829092-2
The King
Count Basie And His Orchestra | The Legendary Count Basie | CBS | 26033
Harry Allen Quartet | Jazz Im Amerika Haus,Vol.1 | Nagel-Heyer | CD 011
Illinois Jacquet And His Orchestra | How High The Moon | Prestige | P 24057
Nat Pierce/Dick Collins Nonet | Nat Pierce-Dick Collins Nonet/Charlie Mariano Sextet | Original Jazz Classics | OJC 118(F 3224)
Zoot Sims-Bob Brookmeyer Quintet | Morning Fun | Black Lion | BLCD 760914
The King And I(part 1 from Suite Cannon)
Metro | Tree People | Lipstick Records | LIP 090312
The King In The Pallenquin
Eric Felten Group | Gratitude | Soul Note | 121296-2
The King Is Gone(for Miles)
Marcus Miller Group | The Sun Don't Lie | Dreyfus Jazz Line | FDM 36560-2
Steve Davis Sextet | The Jaunt | Criss Cross | Criss 1113
The King Of Kings
Louis Armstrong And His Hot Five | Louis Armstrong-The Hot Fives Vol.1 | CBS | 460821-2
The Kingdom Of Swing
Eric Kloss Quartet | Eric Kloss & The Rhythm Section | Prestige | PCD 24125-2(P 7689/7793)
The Kings
Franklin Kiermyer & Jericho | Break Down The Walls | Konnex Records | KCD 5044
The Kissing Way Home
Takashi Kazamaki & Kalle Laar Group | Floating Frames | Ear-Rational | ECD 1038
The Knowledge Of A Child
Khan Jamal Sextet | Infinity | Stash Records | ST 278(807425)
The Kobayashi Syndrom
Peter Herborn Orchestra | Large One | Jazzline | JL 11174-2
The L.A.Boogie Chase
Duke Ellington And His Orchestra | Duke Ellington And His Orchestra 1929-1943 | Storyville | 4960333
The Laborers-
Toni Harper With The Marty Paich Orchestra | Lady Lonely | Fresh Sound Records | ND 42131
The Lady
Frank Wright Quintet | Your Prayer | ESP Disk | ESP 1053-2
Lee Morgan Quintet | Lee Morgan Indeed | Blue Note | 300136(1538)
The Lady From 300 Central Park West
Horace Silver Septet | Horace Silver-The Hardbop Grandpop | Impulse(MCA) | IMP 11922
The Lady In Blue
Leonard Feather's Blue Six | Clyde Bernhardt:The Complete Recordings Vol.1 (1945-1948) | Blue Moon | BMCD 6016
The Lady In My Life
Mark Murphy With The Ralph Burns Orchestra | Crazy Rhythm:His Debut Recordings | Decca | 050670-2
The Lady In Red
Shorty Rogers And His Giants | Martians Stay Home | Atlantic | 50714
Stan Kenton And His Orchestra | Portraits On Standards | Creative World | ST 1042
Peter Erskine Trio | As It Is | ECM | 1594
The Lady In The Lake
Adam Makowicz Trio | My Favorite Things-The Music Of Richard Rodgers | Concord | CCD 4631
The Lady Is A Tramp
Art Simmons Quartet | Jazz In Paris:Piano Aux Champs Elysées | EmArCy | 014059-2
Bireli Lagrene Quartet | Blue Eyes | Dreyfus Jazz Line | FDM 36591-2
Bobby Troup Quartet | The Distinctive Style Of Bobby Troup | Fresh Sound Records | FSR 2024(Bethlehem BCP 35)
Carl Perkins Trio | Introducing Carl Perkins | Fresh Sound Records | FSR-CD 0010
Chet Baker Quintet | My Foolish Heart | I.R.D. Records | TDMCD 002
Della Reese With The Neal Hefti Orchestra | Della | RCA | 2663912-2
Della | RCA | 2663912-2
Dorothy Donegan Trio | I Just Want To Sing | Audiophile | ACD-281
Ella Fitzgerald With The Buddy Bregman Orchestra | The Rodgers And Hart Songbook | Verve | 821693-1
The Silver Collection: Ella Fitzgerald-The Songbooks | Verve | 823445-2 PMS
Ella Fitzgerald Sings The Rodgers And Hart Song Book | Verve | 537258-2
The Rodgers And Hart Song Book, Vol.1 | Verve | 821579-2 PMS
Ella Fitzgerald With The Tommy Flanagan Trio | Ella Fitzgerald In Budapest | Pablo | PACD 5308-2
Erroll Garner Trio | Dreamstreet & One World Concert | Telarc Digital | CD 83350
Gerald Wiggins Trio | Wig Is Here | Black & Blue | BLE 59.069 2
Gerry Mulligan Quartet | The Jazz Giants Play Rodgers & Hart:Blue Moon | Prestige | PCD 24205-2
Gerry Mulligan Quartet feat.Chet Baker | Original Jazz Classics | OJCCD 711-2(F 8082/P 7641)
Gerry Mulligan:Pleyel Concert Vol.2 | Vogue | 21409432
Gerry Mulligan Sextet | Compact Jazz:Gerry Mulligan | Mercury | 830697-2 PMS
Jenny Evans And The Rudi Martini Quartet | At Loyd's | BELL Records | BLR 90004
Lou Levy Trio | Jazz In Four Colors | Fresh Sound Records | ND 74401
Oscar Peterson Trio | The Song Is You-The Best Of The Verve Songbooks | Verve | 531558-2
Patti Page With Pete Rugolo And HisOrchestra | Patti Page In The Land Of Hi-Fi | Verve | 538320-2
Rosemary Clooney And Her Sextet | Sings Rodgers,Hart & Hammerstein | Concord | CCD 4405

The Lady Is A Tramp
Stephane Grappelli Group | Satin Doll | Accord | 440162
Stephane Grappelli Quartet | Grapelli Story | Verve | 515807-2
Stephane Grappelli Quintet | London Meeting | String | BLE 233852

The Lady Is In Love With You
Maxine Sullivan With The Keith Ingham Sextet | Maxine Sullivan Sings The Music Of Burton Lane | Mobile Fidelity | MFCD 773
Vince Guaraldi Trio | Vince Guaraldi Trio | Original Jazz Classics | OJC20 149-2(F 3225)
Georg Wadenius Group | Cleo | Four Leaf Clover | FLC 5097 CD

The Lady With The Fan
Bob Crosby And His Orchestra | Suddely It's 1939-Bob Crosby | Giants Of Jazz | GOJ 1032

The Lady's In Love With You
Pee Wee Russell Sextet | We're In The Money | Black Lion | BLCD 760909

The Lake
Louis Van Dijk | Aquarelles | Keytone | KYT 715

The Lambeth Walk
Bob Wilber Quintet | Bob Wilbur:Nostalgia | Arbors Records | ARCD 19145

The Lame Dance(Schiopatata)
Oscar Peterson Trio | Paris Jazz Concert:Oscar Peterson | Laserlight | 36155

The Lamp Is
Bill Henderson With The Oscar Peterson Trio | Vocal Classics | Verve | 837937-2

The Lamp Is Low
Buddy DeFranco Quintet | Chip Off The Old Bop | Concord | CCD 4527
George Shearing With The Montgomery Brothers | Wes Montgomery-The Complete Riverside Recordings | Riverside | 12 RCD 4408-2
Glenn Miller And His Orchestra | The Original Sounds Of The Swing Era Vol. 3 | RCA | 26.28131 DP
Johnny Hartman With The Bethlehem Orchestra | All Of Me-The Debonair Mr. Hartman | Fresh Sound Records | FSR 2043(Bethlehem BCP 6014)
Mike Richmond Quartet | Blue In Green | Steeplechase | SCCD 31296
Sarah Vaughan And Her Trio | The Complete Sarah Vaughan Live In Japan | Mobile Fidelity | MFCD 844-2
Vic Dickenson-Buck Clayton All Stars | Atlantic Jazz: Kansas City | Atlantic | 7567-81701-2
Wes Montgomery Sextet | Wes And Friends | Milestone | M 47013

The Lamp Is Low-
Peggy Lee With The Benny Goodman Orchestra | Peggy Lee & Benny Goodman:The Complete Recordings 1941-1947 | CBS | C2K 65686

The Lamp OfMemory(Incertidumbre)
John Surman | Upon Reflection | ECM | 1148(825472-2)

The Lamplighter
Lionel Hampton And His Orchestra | Lionel Hampton Vol.1-Steppin' Out | MCA | 1315

The Lamplighter's Serenade
Rene Toledo Group | The Dreamer | GRP | GRP 96772

The Lark In The Dark
Raymond Scott And His Orchestra | The Uncollected:Raymond Scott Vol.2 | Hindsight | HSR 211

The Last Blues
John Coltrane Trio | John Coltrane:The Classic Quartet-Complete Impulse Studio Recordings | Impulse(MCA) | 951280-2
Thilo Wolf Trio With Randy Brecker,Chuck Loeb & New York Strings | A Swinging Hour In New York | Mons Records | MR 874801

The Last Child
Gary Burton Quintet | Whiz Kids | ECM | 1329

The Last Clown
Jackie Allen With The Bill Cunlife Sextet | Which? | Naxos Jazz | 86042-2

The Last Dance
Louis Van Dijk | Aquarelles | Keytone | KYT 715

The Last Go Pepper Blues
Bill Evans Group | Starfish & The Moon:Radio Edits | Escape | ESC 03695-2

The Last Goodbye
Jack McDuff Quartet | The Last Goodun' | Prestige | PRCD 24274-2

The Last Goodun'
Terje Rypdal Quartet | The Singles Collection | ECM | 1383(837749-2)

The Last Hero
Fernando Tarrés And The Arida Conta Group With Guests | On The Edges Of White | Muse | MCD 5463

The Last One
Henry Johnson Group | Missing You | Inak | 30292

The Last One Out
Phil Woods Quartet | Musique Du Bois | Muse | MCD 5037

The Last Rose Of Summer
Nina Simone With Hal Mooney's Orchestra | Broadway-Blues-Ballads | Verve | 518190-2

The Last Stage Of A Journey
Eberhard Weber Group | Endless Days | ECM | 1748(013420-2)

The Last Stage Of A Long Journey
Dizzy Gillespie With The Lalo Schifrin Orchestra | Free Ride | Pablo | 2310794

The Last Stroke Of Midnight
N.Y. Hardbop Quintet | A Mere Bag Of Shells | TCB Records | TCB 20702

The Last Time
Jimmy Rodgers Blues Band | Sloppy Drunk | Black & Blue | BLE 59.544 2

The Last Time I Saw Paris
Johnny Hodges Orchestra | Not So Dukish | Verve | 2304510 IMS
Sonny Rollins Quartet | The Freedom Suite Plus | Milestone | M 47007
Teddy Stauffer Und Seine Original Teddies | International Schlager & In Mood mit Teddy Stauffer's Original Teddies | Elite Special | 9522003

The Last Time We Saw Paris
The Robert Cray Band | False Accusations | Crosscut | CCD 11012

The Last Waltz(Sergej Kuryokhin)
Howard McGhee Sextet | Howard McGhee & Milt Jackson | Savoy | SV 0167(MG 12026)

The Late Late Blues
John Coltrane-Milt Jackson Quintet | Jazz Gallery:John Coltrane Vol.2 | RCA | 2127276-2
Bill Ramsey With The Paul Kuhn Trio | Caldonia And More... | Bear Family Records | BCD 16151 AH

The Late Late Show
Billy May And His Orchestra | Billy May's Big Fat Brass/Bill's Bag | Capitol | 535206-2
Count Basie And His Orchestra | Atomic Swing | Roulette | 497871-2
The Complete Atomic Basie | Roulette | 828635-2
The Complete Atomic Basie | Roulette | 828635-2
Joe Newman Septet | The Complete Joe Newman RCA-Victor Recordings(1955-1956):The Basie Days | RCA | 2122613-2
Metronome Quintet | Just Friends | Gold Records | 11047

The Latest Thing In HotJazz
Chet Baker-Wolfgang Lackerschmid Quintet | Chet Baker/Wolfgang Lackerschmid | Inak | 857

The Latin Train
Marlena Shaw With Orchestra | From The Depths Of My Soul | Blue Note | 84443

The Law
Bo Carter | Twist It Baby | Yazoo | YAZ 1034

The Law Of Nature
Jon Balke w/Oslo 13 | Nonsentration | ECM | 1445

The Laws Of Freedom
Adam Holzman Group | Overdrive | Lipstick Records | LIP 890252

The Leap
Miles Davis Quartet | Miles Davis:The Blue Note And Capitol Recordings | Blue Note | 827475-2

The Left Bank
Max Roach Quintet | Jazz In Paris:Max Roach-Parisian Sketches | EmArCy | 589963-2

The Left Bank-
Charlie Haden Quartet West With Strings | Now Is The Hour | Verve | 527827-2

The Left Hand Of God
Roy Hargrove Quintet | Of Kindred Souls:Live | Novus | 4163154-2

The Left Side Of The Moon Is Blue
Roland Kirk & His Vibration Society | Paris 1976 | Royal Jazz | RJD 510

The Legend Of A Tartar
Ornette Coleman Quartet | Beauty Is A Rare Thing:Ornette Coleman-The Complete Atlantic Recordings | Atlantic | 8122-71410-2

The Legend Of Bebop
Wynton Marsalis Septet | Live In Swingtown | Jazz Door | JD 1290

The Legendary Profile
Modern Jazz Quartet | The Complete Last Concert | Atlantic | 81976-2

The Lemons's Tree
Bill Barron-Ted Curson Quintet | The Leopard | Fresh Sound Records | CR 2010

The Lewinsky March
David Shea Group | Shock Corridor | Avant | AVAN 013

The Life Of A trio
Alphonse Mouzon Group | In Search Of A Dream | MPS | 68192

The Light
Norbert Stein Pata Masters | Blue Slit | Pata Musik | PATA 8 CD
Rob Brown Trio | Breath Rhyme | Silkheart | SHCD 122

The Light In The Dark
Steven Halpern-Dallas Smith | Natural Light | Gramavision | 18-7834-1

The Lightning Fields(Field 1-5)
Roberto Ottaviano Koiné | Hybrid And Hot | SPLASC(H) Records | CD H 453-2

The Line Forms At The End
Dick Katz Quintet | The Line Forms Here | Reservoir | RSR CD 141

The Lion And The Virgin
Lee Morgan Quintet | Leeway | Blue Note | 84034

The Lion Queen-
Leo Parker Sextet | Rollin' With Leo | Blue Note | LT 1076

The Lion's Roar
Les Brown And His Orchestra | The Uncollected: Les Brown And His Orchestra 1949 | Hindsight | HSR 131

The Listening
Gebhard Ullmann-Andreas Willers | Playful '93 | Nabel Records:Jazz Network | CD 4659

The Listening Room
Ray Anderson With The George Gruntz Concert Jazz Band | Ray Anderson Big Band Record | Gramavision | R2 79497

The Little Bandmaster
New Orleans Quarter | Christmas Jazz | New Orleans Quarter Records | NOQR-V-DIV-CD 2

The Little Boy With The Sad Eyes
Nat Adderley Quintet | On The Move | Evidence | ECD 22064-2

The Little Child
Wolfgang Schlüter-Christoph Spendel Duo | Orange Town | MRC | 066-64599

The Little Girl With The Shells
Jack Montrose And All-Stars | The Horn's Full | RCA | NL 45956(RCA LPM 1572)-

The Little Prince
Duke Ellington And His Orchestra | Yale Concert | Fantasy | F 9433

The Little Purple Flower
Willem Breuker Kollektief | Willem Breuker Kollektief | BVHAAST | CD 9601

The Little Rasti
The Poll Winners | Poll Winners Three | Original Jazz Classics | OJCCD 692-2(C 7576)

The Little Rhumba
Catch Up | Catch Up Vol. 1 | Calig | 30613

The Little Trumpet:
A.C. Reed Trio | I Got Money | Black & Blue | BLE 59.727 2

The LittleThings That Mean So Much
John McLaughlin-Carlos Santana Group | John McLaughlin-Carlos Santana | Jazz Door | JD 1250

The Live People
Alexander von Schlippenbach | The Living Music | FMP | 0100

The Lizard
Dirk Schreurs-Walter Baeken Group | Beyond Ballads | B.Sharp Records | CDS 100

The Lock On My Door
Roman Schwaller Jazz Quartet | Some Changes In Life | JHM Records | JHM 3612

The Loco Motif(Jimmy Cobb And The Locomotive)
Michel Godard-Miroslav Tadic-Mark Nauseef | Loose Wires | Enja | ENJ-9071 2

The Locust Have Returned...And They Are Bigger Than Ever!!!
Peter Bolte-Marcio Doctor | Zeitraum | Jazz Haus Musik | JHM 0113 CD

The Lombardo Method
Barry Harris | Stay Right With It | Milestone | M 47050

The Londonderry Air
Orchestra Jazz Siciliana | Orchestra Jazz Siciliana Plays The Music Of Carla Bley | Watt | XtraWatt/4

The Lone Arranger
The Carla Bley Band | I Hate To Sing | Watt | 12,5
Annette Lowman With Three Of A Kind, Fred Wesley And Rodney Jones | Brown Baby:A Tribute To Oscar Brown Jr. | Minor Music | 801061

The Lone Ranger
Bill Frisell Band | Before We Were Born | Nonesuch | 7559-60843-2
Little Jimmy Scott | Specialty | SPCD 2170-2

The Loneliest House In the Street
OAM Trio | Trilingual | Fresh Sound Records | FSNT 070 CD

The Loneliest Marc
Chris Barber's Jazz Band | The Chris Barber Jubilee Album-Vol. 2 | Intercord | 157009

The Lonely One
Duke Ellington And His Orchestra With Johnnie Ray | Duke 56/62 Vol.3 | CBS | 26306

The Loner
Oscar Peterson Trio | The Trio:Live From Chicago | Verve | 539063-2

The Lonesome One
Oscar Peterson-The London House Sessions | Verve | 531766-2

The Lonesome Road
Louis Armstrong And His Hot Five/All Stars/Orchestra | New Orleans Function | Sonia | CD 77710
Rod Mason And His Hot Five | Rod Mason's Hot Five feat. Angela Brown | Timeless | CD TTD 563

The Long And Winding Road
Lanfranco Malaguti/Enzo Pietropaoli/Fabrizio Sferra | Something | Nueva Records | NC 1010
Sarah Vaughan With Orchestra | Song Of The Beatles | Atlantic | SD 16037

The Long Goodbye
One For All | The Long Haul | Criss Cross | Criss 1193

The Long Narrow Road
Count Basie And His Orchestra | On My Way And Shoutin' Again | Verve | 2304385 IMS

The Long Road
Ernie Watts Trio | The Long Road Home | JVC | JVC 2058-2

The Long Time Ago Suite
George Robert-Tom Harrell Quintet | Live In Switzerland 1987-89 | Jazz Helvet | JH 04

The Long Two-
Marty Ehrlich Group | The Long View | Enja | ENJ-9452 2

The Long View:
Thom Rotella Group | Home Again | dmp Digital Music Productions | CD 469

The Long Winter
Les McCann Quartet | Straight Ahead | Blue Note | 064 240331-1(BT 85105)

The Longest Day
Azimuth With Ralph Towner | Depart | ECM | 1163

The Longest Day(Reprise)
The Crusaders | Standing Tall | MCA | 2292-50436-1

The Longest Summer
Clifford Jordan Orchestra | Inward Fire | Muse | MR 5128

The Look
Barney Kessel Trio | Autumn Leaves | Black Lion | CD 877634-2

The Look Of Love
Carmen McRae With The Johnny Keating Orchestra | For Once In My Life | Atlantic | AMCY 1064
Stan Getz With The Claus Ogerman Orchestra | What The World Needs Now-Stan Getz Plays Bacharach And David | Verve | 557450-2
Joe McPhee & Survival Unit II | At WBAI's Free Music Store | Hat Art | CD 6197

The Lookout
Chick Corea Trio | Trio Music,Live In Europe | ECM | 1310(827769-2)

The Loop
Gary Burton Quintet | Whiz Kids | ECM | 1329
Jens Bunge Group | Meet You In Chicago | Jazz 4 Ever Records:Jazz Network | J4E 4749
Plas Johnson Band | Rockin' With The Plas | Pathe | 2C 068-86529(Capitol)

The Lord Is Listenin' To Ya Hallelujah
Carla Bley/Andy Sheppard/Steve Swallow | Song With Legs | Watt | 26(527069)
Mahalia Jackson | Welcome To Europe | CBS | SPR 32

The Lord's Prayer
Wycliffe Gordon-Eric Reid | The Gospel Truth | Criss Cross | Criss 1192

The Loss Of The Human Soul
Mel Lewis And His Sextet | The Lost Art | Limelight | 820815-2 IMS

The Lost Jewel-
Johannes Enders Quartet | Kyoto | Organic Music | ORGM 9726

The Lost Lenore
Tommy Vig Orchestra | Encounter With Time | Discovery | DS 780 IMS

The Louisiana Two Step
Fats Waller And His Rhythm | The Indispensable Fats Waller Vol.5/6 | RCA | 2126416-2

The Love Nest
Benny Waters Quintet | Benny Waters Plays Songs Of Love | Jazzpoint | JP 1039 CD
Bob Crosby's Bobcats | Big Band Bounce And Boogie-Bob Crosby:Mournin' Blues/Accent On The Bobcats | Affinity | AFS 1014
Nat King Cole Trio | Great Capitol Masters | Pathe | 1566251(Capitol)
Claude Williamson Trio | La Fiesta | Discovery | DS 862 IMS

The Love That Walked By
Fred Wesley Group | New Friends | Minor Music | 801016

The Love We Had
Betty Carter And The John Hicks Quartet | It's Not About The Melody | Verve | 513870-2

The Lovesick Bassplayer's Bassplaying
Albert King With The Willie Dixon Band | Windy City Blues | Stax | SCD 8612-2

The Lovin'est Woman In Town
Arthur Blythe Quintet & Guests | Elaborations | CBS | FC 38163

The Lutemaker
David Binney Group | The Luxury Of Guessing | audioquest Music | AQCD 1030

The Magic Farmer
Count Basie And His Orchestra | I Got Rhythm | Affinity | AFF 48

The Magic Horn
Hein Van De Geyn's Bassline | Bassline Returns | Challenge | CHR 70047

The Magic Smith-
Kenny Barron Trio | Lemuria-Seascape | Candid | CCD 79508

The Magician
Kalifactors | An Introduction To Kalifactors | Fresh Sound Records | FSNT 143 CD
Return To Forever | Romantic Warrior | CBS | SRCS 9348

The Magician In You
Stanley Turrentine Orchestra | The Spoiler | Blue Note | 853359-2

The Magilla
Christof Griese Quartet With Davis Milne | New Friends | Jazz 4 Ever Records:Jazz Network | J4E 4736

The Magnolia Triangle(alt.take)
Woody Herman And His Orchestra | Jazz Legacy 18: Woody Herman-The Fourth Herd | Vogue | 500068

The Maid Is Pretty
Artie Shaw And His Orchestra | The Indispensable Artie Shaw Vol.5/6(1944-1945) | RCA | ND 89914

The Maiden Went To The Spring-
Benny Goodman Sextet | Benny Goodman:The Complete 1947-1949 Small Group Sessions Vol.1(1947) | Blue Moon | BMCD 1042

The Maids Of Cadiz
Miles Davis + 19 | The Miles Davis Selection | CBS | 465699-2

The Major General
Dave McMurdo Jazz Orchestra | Live at Montreal Bistro | Sackville | SKCD2-2029

The Mama Suite:
Eric Alexander Quintet | The Second Milestone | Milestone | MCD 9315-2

The Man From Hydepark
Leszek Zadlo Quartet | Breath | Enja | ENJ-6026 2

The Man From Potters Crossing-
Original Teddies Quartett | Hot Jazz & Swing Mit Teddy Stauffer's Original Teddies | Elite Special | 9522002

The Man From Toledo
Rudy Linka Trio | Always Double Czech! | Enja | ENJ-9301 2

The Man I Love
Anita O'Day & Her Quartet | An Evening With Anita O'Day | Verve | MV 2526 IMS
Art Tatum | Art Tatum-The Standard Transcriptions | Music & Arts | CD 919
Standards | Black Lion | CD 877646-2
Artie Shaw And His Orchestra | The Indispensable Artie Shaw Vol.5/6(1944-1945) | RCA | ND 89914
Benny Goodman Quartet | Avalon-The Small Band Vol.2 (1937-1939) | Bluebird | ND 82273
Benny Goodman Trio | 1938 Carnegie Hall Concert | CBS | 450983-2
Billie Holiday With The JATP All Stars | Billie Holiday Story Vol.1:Jazz At The Philharmonic | Verve | 521642-2
Bob Wilber Octet | Bean:Bob Wilber's Tribute To Coleman Hawkins | Arbors Records | ARCD 19144
Coleman Hawkins Quartet | Classic Tenors | CBS | AK 38445
Coleman Hawkins' Swing Four | Jazz:The Essential Collection Vol.3 | IN+OUT Records | 78013-2
Coleman Hawkins With Leo Mathisen And His Band | Coleman Hawkins Vol.1-Hawk Variation | Swingtime(Contact) | ST 1004
Concord All Stars | Concord All Stars On Cape Cod | Concord | CCD 4530
Dick Hyman | The Gershwin Songbook:Jazz Variations | Musicmasters | 65094-2
Dinah Washington With The Gerald Wilson Orchestra | The Complete Dinah Washington On Mercury Vol.1 | Mercury | 832444-2
Doc Cheatham And Sammy Price | Jazz In Paris:Sammy Price And Doc Cheatham Play Gershwin | EmArCy | 018426-2
Don Byas Et Ses Rythmes | Don Byas Complete 1946-1951 European Small Group Master Takes | Definitive Records | DRCD 11214
Don Byas With Luis Rovira Y Su Orquestra | Don Byas-George Johnson:Those Barcelona Days 1947-1948 | Fresh Sound Records | FSR-CD 3001
Eddie Daniels Quartet | Real Time | Chesky | JD 118
Ella Fitzgerald With The Nelson Riddle Orchestra | Oh Lady Be Good:The Best Of The Gershwin Songbook | Verve | 529581-2
Ella Sings Gershwin-Vol. 1 | Metro | 2682004 IMS
The Complete Ella Fitzgerald Song Books of Harold Arlen, Irving Berlin, Duke Ellington, George & Ira Gershwin, Jerome Kern, Johnny Mercer, Cole Porter And Rogers & Hart | Verve | 519832-2

Ella Fitzgerald With The Tommy Flanagan Quartet | Ella In London | Original Jazz Classics | OJCCD 974-2(2310711)
Ella Fitzgerald With The Tommy Flanagan Trio | Jazz At The Philharmonic:The Montreux Collection | Pablo | PACD 5306-2
Highlights Of The Montreux Jazz Festival 1975 | Pablo | 2625707
Erroll Garner Trio | The King Of Piano Jazz | Festival | Album 166
Freddy Randall's All Stars | A Tribute To Gershwin | Jazz Colours | 874707-2
George Braith Quartet | Soul Stream | Blue Note | 870167-0
Harry Allen Quintet | A Night At Birdland Vol. 1 | Nagel-Heyer | CD 5002
Harry James And His Orchestra | The Uncollected:Harry James, Vol.5 | Hindsight | HSR 142
Howard McGhee Quartet | Howard McGhee & Milt Jackson | Savoy | SV 0167(MG 12026)
JATP All Stars | JATP-1940's | Verve | MV 9070/72 IMS
The Complete Jazz At The Philharmonic On Verve 1944-1949 | Verve | 523893-2
Jenny Evans And Her Quintet | Gonna Go Fishin' | ESM Records | ESM 9307
Gonna Go Fishin' | Enja | ENJ-9403 2
Joe Baudisch And Friends | Joe Baudisch And Friends | Bassic-Sound | CD 013
Kenny Barron/Michael Moore | 1+1+1 | Black-Hawk | BKH 50601
Kenny Davern Trio | Strechin' Out | Jazzology | JCD-187
Lee Konitz-Franco D'Andrea | 12 Gershwin In 12 Keys | Philology | W 312.2
Leny Andrade And Her Quartet | Embraceable You | Timeless | CD SJP 365
Lester Young Trio | Lester Young Trio | Verve | 521650-2
Lucky Thompson's Modern Jazz Group Quartet | Jazz In Paris:Lucky Thompson-Modern Jazz Group | EmArCy | 159823-2 PMS
Mal Waldron | Blues For Lady Day | Black Lion | BLCD 760193
Miriam Klein And Her Allstars | Ladylike-Miriam Klein Sings Billie Holiday | MPS | 523379-2
Nat King Cole Trio | Any Old Time | Giants Of Jazz | GOJ 1031
Oscar Peterson Trio | The George Gershwin Songbook | Verve | 823249-1
Oscar Peterson:The Gershwin Songbooks | Verve | 529698-2
1953 Live | Jazz Band Records | EBCD 2111-2(875389)
Paul Smith Quartet | Softly Baby | Jasmine | JAS 311
Quintet Du Hot Club De France | Django/Django In Rome 1949-1050 | BGO Records | BGOCD 366
Parisian Swing | Ace Of Club | ACL 1189
Red Norvo And His Orchestra | Commodore Classics-Red Norvo:Town Hall Concert 1945 | Commodore | 6.26168 AG
Roy Eldridge Quintet | Roy Eldridge And His Little Jazz Vol.1 | Vogue | 21611412
Sathima Bea Benjamin Group | A Morning In Paris | Enja | ENJ-9309 2
Schnuckenack Reinhardt Quintet | Jak-Swing | RCA | PL 28415 AS
Sue Raney With The Alan Broadbent Sextet | In Good Company | Discovery | DSCD 974(889498)
Teddy Charles' West Coasters | Wardell Gray Memorial Vol.1 | Original Jazz Classics | OJCCD 050-2(P 7008)
Teddy Wilson Quartet | Vintage Hampton | Telarc Digital | CD 83321
Tiny Grimes And His Rockin' Highlanders | Tiny Grimes:The Complete 1950-1954,Vol.4 | Blue Moon | BMCD 6008
Zoot Sims Quintet | Zoot Sims And The Gershwin Brothers | Pablo | PASA 2310-744-6
Zoot Sims And The Gershwin Brothers | Original Jazz Classics | OJC20 444-2(2310744)
Art Blakey And The Jazz Messengers | Originally | CBS | FC 38036

The Man I Love-
JATP All Stars | Jazz At The Philharmonic:The Challenges | Verve | 815154-1 IMS
Norman Granz Jam Session | Charlie Parker Jam Session | Verve | 833564-2 PMS
Sir Roland Hanna | Maybeck Recital Hall Series Volume Thirty-Two | Concord | CCD 4604
Edmond Hall Sextet | Commodore Classics In Swing | Commodore | 9031-72723-2

The Man I Love (take 1)
Miles Davis And The Modern Jazz Giants | Miles Davis And The Modern Jazz Giants | Prestige | P 7650

The Man I Love (take 2)
Miles Davis And The Modern Jazz Giants | Prestige | P 7650

The Man I Love(alt.take)
Johannes Rediske Quintet | Jumpin' At The Badewanne | Bear Family Records | BCD 16172 AH

The Man I Love(dedicated to The Box)
Tiny Grimes And His Rockin' Highlanders | Rock The House | Swingtime(Contact) | ST 1016

The Man In The Middle
Billy Barber | Shades Of Gray | dmp Digital Music Productions | CD 445

The Man In Your Life
Tristan Honsinger Quintet | Map Of Moods | FMP | CD 76

The Man Say Something
Roland Kirk & His Vibration Society | Paris 1976 | Royal Jazz | RJD 510

The Man That Got Away
Cal Tjader Quartet With Strings | Plays Harold Arlen | Original Jazz Classics | OJC 285(F 8072)
Ella Fitzgerald With The Billy May Orchestra | The Complete Ella Fitzgerald Song Books of Harold Arlen, Irving Berlin, Duke Ellington, George & Ira Gershwin, Jerome Kern, Johnny Mercer, Cole Porter And Rogers & Hart | Verve | 519832-2
The Harold Arlen Songbook | Verve | 817526-1 IMS
Lainie Kazan With Band | Body And Soul | Musicmasters | 65126-2
Roberta Piket Trio | Speak,Memory | Fresh Sound Records | FSNT 088 CD
Rosemary Clooney With The Scott Hamilton-Warren Vache Septet | Rosemary Clooney Sings The Lyrics Of Ira Gershwin | Concord | CCD 4112
Joe Bushkin And His Orchestra | Play It Again Joe | Atlantic | 81621-1 TIS

The Man Who Came To Dinner
Charles Mingus Group With Orchestra | Charles Mingus | Denon Compact Disc | DC-8565

The Man With A Horn
Howard McGhee Sextet | Maggie | Savoy | SV 0269

The Man With The Harmonica
Carla White And Her Quartet | Orient Express | Milestone | M 9147

The Man With The Horn
Ray Anthony And His Orchestra | The Hits Of Ray Anthony | Capitol | 791219-2

The Man You Were
Glen Gray And The Casa Loma Orchestra | The Radio Years | London | HMG 5028 AN

The Many Faces Of Cole Porter:
Robin Williamson Group | Skirting The River Road | ECM | 1785(016372-2

The Map With No North
Peter A. Schmid Duos | Duets,Dialogues & Duels | Creative Works Records | CW CD 1034

The Marabou
Carlo Mombelli'a Abstractions | Dancing In A Museum | ITM-Pacific | ITMP 970078

The March Of The Swing Parade
Curlew | Bee | Open Minds | OM 2408-2

The Mark Of Zoro(intro)
Flip Phillips Septet | Swing Is The Thing | Verve | 543477-2

The Mark Of Zoro(outro)
Dado Moroni Trio | What's New? | SPLASC(H) Records | CD H 378-2

The Marksman
Benny Carter And His Band | The Urban Sessions/New Jazz Sound | Verve | 531637-2

The Martinique
Chris Barber's Jazz Band | Ice Cream | Storyville | 6.23326 AF

The Martyr
Modern Jazz Quartet | Milt Jackson Birthday Celebration | Fantasy | FANCD 6079-2
The Legendary Profile | Atlantic | AMCY 1103
Herb Robertson Group | The Little Trumpet | JMT Edition | 919007-2

The Marvelous Event
Rickey Kelly Group | My Kind Of Music | New Note Records | NNR 001

The Masher
Jimmy McGriff-Hank Crawford Quartet | Right Turn On Blue | Telarc Digital | CD 83366

The Masher(alt.take)
Bernie Worrell 'The Other Side' | Pieces Of Woo | CMP Records | CMP CD 65

The Mask
Miles Davis Group | Live At The Fillmore East | CBS | C2K 65139
Live At The Fillmore East | CBS | C2K 65139
George Winston | Linus & Lucy-The Music Of Vince Guaraldi | Windham Hill | 34 11187-2

The Masked Marvel
Tippett-Kellers-Tippett | Twilight Etchings | FMP | CD 65

The Mason's Apron
$$hide$$ | $$Titelverweise | |

The Masquerade Is Over -> I'm Affraid The Masquerade Is Over

The Matador
Room | Room | Sound Aspects | sas CD 028

The Maze
Herbie Hancock Quintet | Herbie Hancock:The Complete Blue Note Sixties Sessions | Blue Note | 495569-2
Roscoe Mitchell Percussion Ensemble | Roscoe Mitchell | Nessa | N 14/15

The Meaning Of The Blues
Gil Evans Orchestra | Little Wing | West Wind | WW 2042
Miles Davis + 19 | The Miles Davis Selection | CBS | 465699-2
Stan Kenton And His Orchestra | Standards In Silhouette | Capitol | ST 1049
Tatsuya Takahashi & Tokyo Union | Plays Miles & Gil | Paddle Wheel | K32Y 6268
Toni Harper With The Marty Paich Orchestra | Night Mood | Fresh Sound Records | NL 46049(RCA LSP 2253)

The Meaning Of The Blues-
Miles Davis With Gil Evans & His Orchestra | Miles Davis At Carnegie Hall | CBS | CK 65027
Cleve Pozar Quartet | New Music: Second Wave | Savoy | SJL 2235 (801211)

The Mechanical Bird
Les Baxter And His Orchestra | Baxter's Best | Capitol | 791218-2

The Meetin'
Oliver Nelson Sextet | Images | Prestige | P 24060
Eric Dolphy Quintet | Berlin Concerts | Enja | 3007/9-2

The Melancholy Of Departure
Kenneth Knudsen-Christian Skeel | Music For Eyes | dacapo | DCCD 9433

The Melancholy Speed Skater's Dream
Jimmy Yancey | The Best Of Boogie Woogie | Zeta | ZET 740

The Meltdown
Freddie Hubbard Quintet | Life Flight | Blue Note | BT 85139

The Mercenary
David Torn Quartet | Cloud About Mercury | ECM | 1322(831108-2)

The Mercury Grid
Bruce Dunlap Trio | The Rhythm Of Wings | Chesky | JD 92

The Merry-Go-Round Broke Down
Bill Coleman Quintet | Dicky Wells & Bill Coleman In Paris | Affinity | CD AFS 1004
Thomas Morris And His Seven Hot Babies | When A Gator Hollers | Frog | DGF 1

The Mess Is Here
Lionel Hampton And His Orchestra | The Mess Is Here | Magic | AWE 18(807364)

The Message
Hugh Fraser Quintet | In The Mean Time | Jazz Focus | JFCD 020
Tommy Chase Quartet | Hard! | Contemporary | BOP 5

The Middle Of Love
Matthew Shipp-Joe Morris | Thesis | HatOLOGY | 506

The Midgets
Art Blakey And The Jazz Messengers | Live In Copenhagen 1959 | Royal Jazz | RJD 516
Joe Newman Septet | The Complete Joe Newman RCA-Victor Recordings(1955-1956):The Basie Days | RCA | 2122613-2

The Midnight Blues
Firehouse Five Plus Two | Goes To A Fire | Good Time Jazz | GTCD 10052-2

The Midnight Fire Alarm
Big Bill Broonzy | Trouble In Mind | Spotlite | SPJ 900

The Midnight Sun Will Never Set
Count Basie And His Orchestra | One More Time-Muisc From The Pen Of Quincy Jones | Roulette | CDP 797271-2
The Great Concert Of Count Basie | Festival | 402311
Harry Allen-Tommy Flanagan | Day Dream | RCA | 2167152-2
William Galison-Mulo Franzl Group | Midnight Sun | Edition Collage | EC 508-2
Charles Earland Sextet | Black Talk! | Original Jazz Classics | OJCCD 335-2(P 7758)

The Mighty Burner
Hamiet Bluiett | Birthright-A Solo Blues Concert | India Navigation | IN 1030

The Mill
Robben Ford & The Blue Line | Handful Of Blues | Blue Thumb | BTR 70042

The Miller's Son
Chris Potter Quartet | Gratitude | Verve | 549433-2

The Mind's Eye
Gratitude | Verve | 549433-2

The Mind's Eye(Intro)
Ingrid Jensen Sextet | Vernal Fields | Enja | ENJ-9013 2

The Mingus That I Knew
Duke Ellington With Tommy Dorsey And His Orchestra | Duke Ellington:The Complete RCA-Victor Mid-Forties Recordings(1944-1946) | RCA | 2663394-2

The Minor Goes Muggin'
Dan Barrett Octet | Strictly Instrumental | Concord | CJ 331

The Minor Passions
John Gill's Novelty Orchestra Of New Orleans | Smile, Darn Ya, Smile | Stomp Off Records | CD 1227

The Mirror(Oglinda)
Jelly Roll Morton | The Library Of Congress Recordings | Affinity | CD AFS 1010-3

The Mistake
Bobby Watson Quartet | Love Remains | Red Records | 123212-2

The Modal Thing
Sonny Red (Kyner) Quintet | Red,Blue & Green | Milestone | MCD 47086-2

The Mode
JATP All Stars | Jazz At The Philharmonic:Blues In Chicago 1955 | Verve | 815155-1 IMS

The Mohawk Special
Don Byas-Tyree Glenn Orchestra | Don Byas Complete 1946-1951
European Small Group Master Takes | Definitive Records | DRCD 11214

The Mole
Jack Teagarden And His Orchestra | A Standard Library Of Jazz Vol. 2 | Storyville | SLP 704

The Monk And The Mermaid
Dave Bartholomew And His Orchestra | The Monkey | Pathe | 1561331(Imperial)

The Monkey Thing
Fats Waller And His Buddies | The Indispensable Fats Waller Vol.1/2 | RCA | 2122616-2

The Monster
Leipziger Saxophon Quartet + Rolf Von Nordenskjöld | Passages: Leipziger Saxophon Quartet Plays Rolf Von Nordenskjöld | BIT | 11158

The Monster And The Flower
Hendrik Meurkens Band | A View From Manhattan | Concord | CCD 4585

The Montrane
| Soprano Summit At Thatchers | J&M Records | J&MCD 501

The Mooche
DMP Big Band | DMP Big Band Salutes Duke Ellington | dmp Digital Music Productions | CD 520
Duke Ellington And His Orchestra | The Complete Duke Ellington-Vol. 1 | CBS | CBS 67264
Highlights From The Duke Ellington Centennial Edition | RCA | 2663672-2
Big Band Bounce And Boogie:Classic Transcriptions-Duke Ellington | Affinity | AFS 1032
Duke Ellington:Complete Studio Transcriptions | Definitive Records | DRCD 11199
Jazz Special-The Popular Duke Ellington | RCA | NL 89095 AG
The Rare Broadcast Recordings 1953 | Jazz Anthology | JA 5220
In The Sixties | RCA | PD 89565
Jay McShann Trio | Swingmatism | Sackville | SKCD2-3046
Louis Armstrong-Duke Ellington Group | The Complete Louis Armstrong & Duke Ellington Sessions | Roulette | 793844-2
Ray Barretto Orchestra | Portraits In Jazz And Clave | RCA | 2168452-2
Sidney Bechet And His New Orleans Feetwarmers | Sidney Bechet 1932-1943: The Bluebird Sessions | Bluebird | ND 90317
Swing And Blues Band | Talk To Me | Plainisphare | PAV 808
Toots Thielemans Quintet | Toots Thielemans Live-Vol. 2 | Polydor | 2441063 IMS
Toots Thielemans With The Shirley Horn Trio | For My Lady | EmArCy | 510133-2

The Mooche-
Duke Ellington And His Orchestra | Ella Fitzgerald And Duke Ellington:Cote D'Azure Concerts on Verve | Verve | 539033-2
Duke Ellington At The Alhambra | Pablo | PACD 5313-2
Hot Summer Dance | Red Baron | 469285-2

The Mood To Be Wooed
Jazz Live & Rare: The First And Second Esquire Concert | Jazzline | ???

The Mood To Be Wooed-
Holly Slater Quartet | The Mood Was There | Ronnie Scott's Jazz House | JHCD 053

The Moon
Frank Wright Trio | Frank Wright Trio | ESP Disk | ESP 1023-2

The Moon Is A Harsh Mistress
Rigmor Gustafsson With The Nils Landgren Quartet And The Fleshquartet | I Will Wait For You | ACT | 9418-2
Ruth Cameron With The Chris Dawson Trio | First Songs | EmArCy | 559031-2

The Moon Is Full Tonight
Julia Hülsman Trio With Rebekka Bakken | Scattering Poems | ACT | 9405-2

The Moon Is Hiding
Franz Koglmann Pipetet | Schlaf Schlemmer, Schlaf Magritte | Hat Art | CD 6108

The Moon Is Low
Art Tatum | The Art Tatum Solo Masterpieces | Pablo | 2625703
Art Tatum Quartet | The Tatum Group Masterpieces | Pablo | 2310734
Fats Waller And His Rhythm | The Middle Years Part 2(1938-40) | RCA | 6366552-2
Roy Eldridge-Benny Carter Quintet | The Urban Sessions/New Jazz Sound | Verve | 531637-2
Urbie Green And His Orchestra | Let's Face The Music And Dance | Fresh Sound Records | NL 45906(RCA LPM 1667)

The Moon Is Low(78rpm-take)
Fats Waller And His Rhythm | Fats Waller:The Complete Associated Transcription Sessions 1935-1939 | Jazz Unlimited | JUCD 2076

The Moon Is Low(alt.take)
The Middle Years Part 2(1938-40) | RCA | 6366552-2
Rob Wasserman Duet | Duets | GRP | GRP 97122

The Moon Is Made Of Gold
Jimmy Witherspoon With Orchestra | Spoonful | Blue Note | 84545

The Moon Of Manakoora
Sonny Rollins Quartet | This Is What I Do | Milestone | MCD 9310-2
Jan Garbarek Group | Rites | ECM | 1685/86(559006-2)

The Moon Over Mtatsminda
Charlie Haden-Pat Metheny | Beyond The Missouri Sky | Verve | 537130-2

The Moon Song
Lee Konitz-Gil Evans | Anti Heroes | Verve | 511622-2 PMS

The Moon Was Yellow
Al Haig Trio | The Piano Collection Vol.2 | Vogue | 21610222
Count Basie And His Orchestra | The Great 1959 Band In Concert | Jazz Groove | 003 IMS

The Moontrane
Dexter Gordon And His Orchestra | Sophisticated Giant | CBS | 450316-1
Larry Young Quartet | Unity | Blue Note | GXK 8205 (84221)

The Moor Man
Return To Forever | Return To Forever Live | CBS | 82808

The Moors-
Charlie Barnet And His Orchestra | Big Band Bounce & Boogie:Skyliner-Charlie Barnet | Affinity | AFS 1012

The More I See You
Brad Mehldau Trio | Art Of The Trio Vol.5:Progression | Warner | 9362-48005-2
Carol Sloane And Her Band | Out Of The Blue | Fresh Sound Records | LSP 15823(CBS CS 8566)
Count Basie And His Orchestra | The Jazz Giants Play Harry Warren:Lullaby Of Broadway | Prestige | PCD 24204-2
Basie In Europe | LRC Records | CDC 7481
Diane Schuur With Orchestra | Love Songs | GRP | GRP 97032
Ella Fitzgerald With The Jimmy Jones Trio | Ella & Duke At The Cote D'Azur | Verve | 539030-2
Compact Jazz: Ella Fitzgerald Live | Verve | 833294-2
Etta Jones With The Oliver Nelson Quintet | Hollar! | Original Jazz Classics | OJCCD 1061(PR 7284)
Frankie Randall With The Marty Paich Orchestra | A Swingin' Touch | Fresh Sound Records | NL 45978(RCA)
Herb Ellis-Ross Tompkins Duo | A Pair To Draw To | Concord | CJ 17
Johnny Hartman With The Hank Jones Quartet | The Voice That Is! | Impulse(MCA) | IMP 12982
Mark Murphy With The Jack Van Poll Trio & Guests | Another Vision | September | CD 5113
Rosemary Clooney And Her Band With Strings | For The Duration | Concord | CCD 4444
Sarah Vaughan With The Jimmy Jones Orchestra | Dreamy | Fresh Sound Records | SR 52046(Roulette)
Singers Unlimited With The Robert Farnon Orchestra | Sentimental Journey | MPS | 68102
Spike Robinson Quartet | Music Of Harry Warren | Discovery | DS 870 IMS
Tiziana Ghiglioni With Paul Bley | Lyrics | SPLASC(H) Records | CD H 348-2
Warren Vaché Quartet | Iridescece | Concord | CJ 153

The More You Get
Aki Takase-Alexander von Schlippenbach | Piano Duets-Live In Berlin 93/94 | FMP | OWN-90002

The Morning After
Mongo Santamaria Orchestra | The Watermelon Man | Milestone | M 47012

The Morning Of This Night
Jack McDuff Quintet | The Last Goodun' | Prestige | PRCD 24274-2

The Morning Song

TITELVERZEICHNIS

Les McCann Group | Another Beginning | Atlantic | 7567-80790-2
Robin Williamson Group | Skirting The River Road | ECM | 1785(016372-2

The Morning Watch-
Kim Pensyl | Pensyl Sketches Collection | GRP | GRP 97702

The Most Beautiful Girl In The World
Dave Brubeck Quartet | Brubeck Plays Music From West Side Story And... | CBS | 450410-2
Caterina Valente-Catherine Michel | Girltalk | Nagel-Heyer | NH 1015

The Most Beautiful Sea-
John LaPorta Quartet | The Most Minor | Fresh Sound Records | FSR-CD 0208

The Moth And The Flame:
Ketil Bjornstad Group | The Sea II | ECM | 1633(537341-2)

The Mother
Salvatore Bonafede Trio | Nobody's Perfect | Penta Flowers | CDPIA 022

The Mountain
Abdullah Ibrahim Trio | Cape Town Revisited | TipToe | TIP-888836 2
African Magic | TipToe | TIP-888845 2
Tom Harrell Quintet | Stories | Contemporary | CCD 14043-2

The Mountain Of Night
Dollar(Abdullah Ibrahim) Brand Group | African River | Enja | ENJ-6018 2
Roy Hargrove's Crisol | Habana | Verve | 537563-2

The Mountaincs
Keith Jarrett Trio | The Mourning Of A Star | Atlantic | 8122-75355-2

The Mourning Of A Star
Fabien Degryse Group | Quadruplex | B.Sharp Records | CDS 077

The Mousing Minuets:
Alphonse Mouzon Quartet | Virtue | MPS | 821281-1

The Move
John Tchicai-Pierre Favre Quartet(Naked Hamlet Ensemble) | Jazz In Switzerland 1930-1975 | Elite Special | 9544002/1-4

The Mozdok's Train
Ella Fitzgerald And Her Famous Orchestra | A-Tisket, A-Tasket | Naxos Jazz | 8.120540 CD

The Mule Walk
Dick Wellstood | This Is The One...Dig! | Solo Art | SACD-119
Louis Mazetier | In Concert:What A Treat! | Jazz Connaisseur | JCCD 9522-2
Matthew Shipp Trio | The Multiplication Table | HatOLOGY | 516

The Mummy Club
Lionel Hampton | The Best Of Boogie Woogie | Zeta | ZET 740

The Munson Street Breakdown
Lionel Hampton Orchestra | Lionel Hampton Story Vol.2 | Black & Blue | BLE 59.238 2

The Murmuring Sound Of The Mountain Stream
Lee Morgan Sextet | Charisma | Blue Note | 300260(4312)

The Music Goes 'Round And 'Round
Louis Armstrong And His Orchestra | Louis Armstrong Vol.2 | Ambassador | CLA 1902
Mound City Blue Blowers | Mound City Blue Blowers(1935-1936) | Timeless | CBC 1-018
Tommy Dorsey And His Clambake Seven | Planet Jazz:Tommy Dorsey | Planet Jazz | 2159972-2
Having Wonderful Time | RCA | 2121824-2
Andreas Willers Octet | The Ground Music | Enja | ENJ-9368 2

The Music Grinder(A German Sax Waltz)
Andrew Cyrille Quartet | The Navigator | Soul Note | SN 1062

The Music Of Chance
Jeff Gardner Trio | The Music Must Change:Jazz Compositions Inspired By The Works Of Paul Auster | Naive | 225079

The Music Of The People
Stephan Micus | The Muisc Of Stones | ECM | 1384(837750-2)

The Music Of The Stones(part 1)
The Muisc Of Stones | ECM | 1384(837750-2)

The Music Of The Stones(part 2)
The Muisc Of Stones | ECM | 1384(837750-2)

The Music Of The Stones(part 3)
The Muisc Of Stones | ECM | 1384(837750-2)

The Music Of The Stones(part 4)
The Muisc Of Stones | ECM | 1384(837750-2)

The Music Of The Stones(part 5)
The Muisc Of Stones | ECM | 1384(837750-2)

The Music Of The Stones(part 6)
Joe Reichman And His Orchestra | The Uncollected:Joe Reichman | Hindsight | HSR 166

The Music That Makes Me Dance
Steve Kuhn Trio | Oceans In The Sky | Owl Records | 013428-2
Ann Hampton Callaway And Her Band | After Hours | Denon Compact Disc | CY-18042

The Musical Clock
Return To Forever | Return To Forever Live | CBS | 82808

The Mystery Song
Kamikaze Ground Crew | The Scenic Route | New World Records | 80400-2

The Mystical Dreamer
Don Cherry/Ed Blackwell | Mu(The Complete Session) | Affinity | AFF 774

The Mystified Churchgoer
Randy Weston Orchestra | Volcano Blues | Verve | 519269-2

The Nango
Stan Kenton And His Orchestra | The Formative Years(1941-1942) | Creative World | ST 1061

The Narrator
29th Street Saxophone Quartet | Underground | Antilles | 848415-2(889151)

The Natives Are Restless Tonight
Jazz City Workshop | Jazz City Workshop | Fresh Sound Records | FSR 2025(Bethlehem BCP 44)

The Natural Piano
Robin Holcomb Sextet | Larks,They Crazy | Sound Aspects | sas CD 026

The Nature Line
Bill Evans Duo | Intuition | Original Jazz Classics | OJCCD 470-2

The Nature Of Things
Bill Evans-Eddie Gomez Duo | The Complete Fantasy Recordings | Fantasy | 9FCD 1012-2
Bill Evans Trio | Bill Evans:From The 70's | Original Jazz Classics | OJCCD 1069-2(F 9630)

The Nature Of Things(take 9)
Herbert Joos | Still Life | Extraplatte | 316139

The Navigator
Kevin Eubanks Group | Opening Night | GRP | GRP 91013-1(808716)

The Nearness Of You
Bill Charlap Trio | Stardust | Blue Note | 535985-2
Blue Mitchell And His Orchestra | A Blue Time | Milestone | M 47055
Bruce Forman Quartet With Bobby Hutcherson | There Are Times | Concord | CCD 4332
Cécile Verny Quartet | Kekeli | double moon | CHRDM 71028
Charlie Parker With The Woody Herman Orchestra | Bird's Eyees Last Unissued Vol.23 | Philology | W 853.2
Clark Terry Quintet | Having Fun | Delos | DE 4021(882677)
Coleman Hawkins-Roy Eldridge Quintet | Coleman Hawkins And Roy Eldridge At The Opera House | Verve | 2304432 IMS
Dave McKenna | A Celebration Of Hoagy Carmichael | Concord | CCD 4227
Duke Pearson Sextet | Dedication! | Original Jazz Classics | OJCCD 1939-2(P 7729)
Earl Hines | Four Jazz Giants:Earl Hines Plays Tributes To W.C.Handy,Hoagy Carmichael And Louis Armstrong | Solo Art | SACD-111/112
Eden Atwood Group | There Again | Concord | CCD 4645
Ella Fitzgerald And Louis Armstrong With The Oscar Peterson Quartet | The Best Of Ella Fitzgerald And Louis Armstrong On Verve | Verve | 537909-2
Ella And Louis | Verve | 543304-2
The Jazz Collector Edition: Ella & Louis | Laserlight | 15706
Ella & Louis | Verve | 825373-2
Erroll Garner Trio | The Concert Garner | Jazz Groove | 008 IMS
Gerry Mulligan Quartet | Gerry Mulligan Quartet | Pacific Jazz | 300001(PJ 1)
Gerry Mulligan:Pleyel Concert Vol.2 | Vogue | 21409432
Glenn Miller And His Orchestra | Candelight Miller | RCA | 2668716-2
Glenn Miller Forever | RCA | NL 89214 DP
James Moody And His Band | Wail Moody Wail | Original Jazz Classics | OJCCD 1791-2(P 7036)
Johnny Hodges Orchestra | Triple Play | RCA | ND 90208(847147)
Johnny Richards And His Orchestra | Wide Range | Creative World | ST 1052
Lee Konitz Quartet | Tranquility | Verve | MV 2508 IMS
Les Haricots Rouges + Sam Lee | En Concert | Black & Blue | BLE 59215 2
Lou Donaldson Sextet | The Time Is Right | Blue Note | 868498-0
Mel Tormé With Orchestra | That's All Mel Tormé | CBS | CK 65165
Mike Mainieri | Man Behaind Bars | NYC-Records | NYC 6019-2
Milt Jackson Quartet | Opus De Funk | Prestige | P 24048
Oscar Peterson-Ray Brown Duo | An Evening With Oscar Peterson | Verve | MV 2691 IMS
Peter Beets New York Trio | Peter Beets New York Trio | Criss Cross | Criss 1214
Rick Hollander Quartet | Once Upon A Time-The Music Of Hoagy Carmichael | Concord | CCD 4666
Sarah Vaughan And Her Trio | The Complete Sarah Vaughan Live In Japan | Mobile Fidelity | MFCD 844-2
Stephane Grappelli With The Diz Disley Trio | Violinspiration | MPS | 68058
The Four Freshmen | Voices In Modern | EMI Records | 1599321

The Nearness Of You-
Dizzy Gillespie-Roy Eldridge Sextet | The Complete Verve Roy Eldridge Studio Sessions | Verve | 9861278
Gillespie-Eldridge-Edison Septet | Tour De Force | Verve | MV 2524 IMS
Jane Ira Bloom Quintet | The Nearness | Arabesque Recordings | AJ 0120
Mel Tormé And Cleo Laine With The John Dankworth Orchestra | Nothing Without You | Concord | CCD 4515
Norman Granz Jam Session | Charlie Parker Jam Session | Verve | 833564-2 PMS
Saxophone Connection | Saxophone Connection | L+R Records | CDLR 45046

The Nearness Of You(harm-solo)
Freddie Hubbard Sextet | Minor Mishap | Black Lion | BLP 60122

The Need For Love
Dardanelle Quintet | The Colors Of My Life | Stash Records | ST 217 IMS

The Needless Kiss
Marvin 'Smitty' Smith Group | The Road Less Traveled | Concord | CCD 4379

The Neser
Till Brönner Quartet & Deutsches Symphonieorchester Berlin | German Songs | Minor Music | 801057

The Never Ending Process
Wolfhound-Anne Haigis | The Never Ending Story | BELL Records | BLR 84025

The New Ark
Brian Lynch Sextet | In Process | Ken Music | 660.56.011

The New Boogaloo
Darrell Grant Quintet | The New Bop | Criss Cross | Criss 1106

The New Funeral March
Oscar Klein's Jazz Show | Oscar Klein's Jazz Show | Jazzpoint | JP 1043 CD

The New Harmonica Shuffle
Sonny Terry-Bull City Red | From Spiritual To Swing | Vanguard | VCD 169/71

The New John Henry
Duke Ellington And His Orchestra | Carnegie Hall Concert December 1947 | Prestige | 2PCD 24075-2

The New Look(Snibor)
Duke Ellington:Complete Prestige Carnegie Hall 1946-1947 Concerts | Definitive Records | DRCD 11211

The New National Anthem-
John Surman-John Warren Group | The Brass Project | ECM | 1478

The New One Two(part 1)
The Brass Project | ECM | 1478

The New One Two(part 2)
Muhal Richard Abrams | Afrisong | India Navigation | IN 1058

The New York City Ghost
Herbie Harper Quintet | Jazz In Hollywood:Herbie Harper | Original Jazz Classics | OJCCD 1887-2(Nocturne NLP-1/NLP-7)

The Newcomer
Cedar Walton Trio | Manhattan Afternoon | Criss Cross | Criss 1082

The Next Level
Humphrey Lyttelton And His Band | Jazz At The Royal Festival Hall/Jazz At The Conway Hall | Dormouse | DM 22 CD

The Next Stop
Fred Wesley Group | Amalgamation | Minor Music | 801045

The Next Thing I Knew
Betty Bennett And Her Orchestra | Nobody Else But Me-Betty Bennett Sings The Arrangements Of Shorty Rogers & André Previn | Atlantic | AMCY 1065

The Niger Oar(Niger Lalaba)
Allan Botschinsky Quintet | The Night | M.A Music | NU 676-1

The Night
Joachim Kühn Group | Universal Time | EmArCy | 016671-2
Ketil Bjornstad | New Life | EmArCy | 017265-2
Roscoe Mitchell | Sound Songs | Delmark | DE 493(2)
Bob Mover Trio Feat. Paul Bley And John Abercrombie | The Night Bathers | Justin Time | Just 14

The Night Before
Sir Roland Hanna Quartet | Double Exposure | LRC Records | CDC 9040

The Night Comes Down
Anthony Kerr Quartet | Now Hear This | Ronnie Scott's Jazz House | JHCD 055

The Night Has A Thousand Eyes
Buddy Montgomery | Maybeck Recital Hall Series Volume Fifteen | Concord | CCD 4494
Dan Faulk Trio | Spirit In The Night | Fresh Sound Records | FSNT 024 CD
Dave Liebman Trio | Spirit Renewed | Owl Time Line | 3819112
Gary Burton-Stephane Grappelli Quartet | Paris Encounter | Atlantic | 7567-80763-2
George Duke Quartet | Presented By The Jazz Workshop 1966 In San Francisco | MPS | 68233
Joe Zawinul And The Austrian All Stars | His Majesty Swinging Nephews 1954-1957 | RST-Records | 91549-2
John Coltrane Quartet | Coltrane's Sound | Atlantic | 7567-81358-2
John Handy Quintet | Live At Yoshi's Nightspot | Boulevard | BLD 531 CD
McCoy Tyner Trio | McCoy Tyner With Stanley Clarke And Al Foster | Telarc Digital | CD 83488
Paul Desmond With Different Groups | 100 Ans De Jazz:Paul Desmond | RCA | 2177830-2
Paul Desmond-Gerry Mulligan Quartet | The Ballad Of Paul Desmond | RCA | 21429372
Pete Minger Quartet | Look To The Sky | Concord | CCD 4555
Shelly Manne Double Piano Jazz Quartet | In Concert At Carmelo's | Trend | TR 526 Digital
Sonny Rollins Septet | The Complete Sonny Rollins RCA Victor Recordings | RCA | 2668675-2

The Night Has A Thousand Eyes(alt.take)
Red Norvo And His Swing Septet | Knock On Wood | Affinity | CD AFS 1017

The Night Is Blue
Red Norvo Sextet | Red Play The Blues | RCA | 2113034-2

The Night Is Darking Round Me
Dick Hyman | Dick Hyman Plays The Great American Songbook | Musicmasters | 65120-2

The Night Of A Champion
Bireli Lagrene Group | A Tribute To Django Reinhardt | Jazzpoint | JP 1061 CD
Dusko Goykovich Sextet | Swinging Macedonia | Enja | 4048-2

The Night Shepherd
Achim Kaufmann Trio | Weave | Jazz 4 Ever Records:Jazz Network | J4E 4737

The Night Sky Is A Rock
David Matthews Trio With Strings | Jazz Ballads With Strings | Sweet Basil | 660.55.012

The Night We Called It A Day
Bob James Trio | Bold Conceptions | Verve | 557454-2
Carol Kidd With The David Newton Trio | The Night We Called It A Day | Linn Records | AKD 007
Chet Baker Trio | Embraceable You | Pacific Jazz | 831676-2
Chris Connor And Her Quinet | Chris Craft | Atlantic | AMCY 1062
John Coltrane-Milt Jackson Quintet | Bags & Trane | Rhino | 8122-73685-2
June Christy With The Pete Rugolo Orchestra | Something Cool(The Complete Mono & Stereo Versions) | Capitol | 534069-2
Something Cool(The Complete Mono & Stereo Versions) | Capitol | 534069-2
Matt Dennis With Orchestra | The Original Matt Dennis | Glendale | GLS 6006 IMS
Oscar Peterson Trio | The Sound Of The Trio | Verve | 543321-2
The Trio-Live From Chicago | Verve | 823008-2
Ron Crotty Trio | Modern Jazz From San Francisco | Original Jazz Classics | OJC 272(F 3213)
Mark Murphy With The Bill Mays Trio | Kerouac, Then And Now | Muse | MCD 5359

The Night You Looked Two Ways
Deborah Henson-Conant | Alterd Ego | Laika Records | 35100962

The Nightingale
Piacentini/Bonati/McCandless/Moreno | Circles | Nueva Records | NC 1014

The Nightwalker
Eliane Elias Group | A Long Story | Manhattan | CDP 795476-2

The Noodle Song
Mahavishnu Orchestra | The Inner Mounting Flame | CBS | CK 65523

The Noonward Race
John Zorn Naked City | Naked City-Grand Guignol | Avant | AVAN 002

The Norm
Emborg-Larsen Quintet | Ships In The Night | Stunt Records | STUCD 19304

The Note
Larry Porter/Allan Praskin Quartet | Acoustic Music | Popular Records | PR 140

The Nymph
Charlie Mariano Sextet | Nat Pierce-Dick Collins Nonet/Charlie Mariano Sextet | Original Jazz Classics | OJC 118(F 3224)

The Object Lesson
Joe Morris Quartet | You Be Me | Soul Note | 121304-2

The Old Circus Train Turn-Around Blues
Duke Ellington And His Orchestra | Perdido | Moon Records | MCD 070-2
Ella Fitzgerald And Duke Ellington:Cote D'Azure Concerts on Verve | Verve | 539033-2
Scott Hamilton Quartet | Organic Duke | Concord | CCD 4623

The Old Circus Train Turn-Around Blues(rehersal)
Jens Sondergaard Quartet | No Coast | Storyville | SLP 4126

The Old Country
Melissa Walker And Her Band | May I Feel | Enja | ENJ-9335 2
Nat Adderley Quintet | The Old Country | Enja | ENJ-7027 2
Philip Harper Sextet | Soulful Sin | Muse | MCD 5505

The Old Couple
Galardini-Lessmann-Morena Trio | Insolitudine | SPLASC(H) Records | H 155

The Old Rugged Cross
Chris Barber's Jazz And Blues Band | 30 Years Chris Barber:Can't We Get Together | Timeless | CD TTD 517/8
New York Jazz Ensemble | The Bunk Project | Limelight | 514937-2
Rahsaan Roland Kirk And His Orchestra | Blacknuss | Rhino | 8122-71408-2
The Heavenly Stars | Old Time Religion | Sound Of New Orleans | SONO 6009

The One And Lonely Bass Clarinet Blues
Jimmy Smith All Stars | Damn! | Verve | 527631-2

The One For Me
Buddy Tate With The Humphrey Lyttelton Band | Buddy Tate With Humphrey Lyttelton And Ruby Braff | Jazz Colours | 874713-2

The One I Love
Ike Lloyd And His Orchestra | Clyde Bernhardt:The Complete Recordings Vol.2 (1949-1953) | Blue Moon | BMCD 6017
Paul Desmond Quartet | Take Ten | RCA | 63661462
Tommy Dorsey And His Orchestra | Tommy Dorsey And His Orchestra With Frank Sinatra | RCA | 2115518-2

The One I Love Belongs To Somebody Else
Count Basie Kansas City 3 | For The Second Time | Original Jazz Classics | OJC 600(2310878)
Count Basie Quartet With Joe Williams | Basie On Roulette, Vol. 4: Memories Ad-Lib | Vogue | 500004
Ella Fitzgerald-Joe Pass Duo | Fitzgerald & Pass... Again | Original Jazz Classics | OJCCD 1052-2(2310772)
Etta Jones With The Houston Person Quintet | Ain't She Sweet(Save Your Love For Me/I'll Be Seeing You) | 32 Jazz | 32120
Ken Peplowski Quintet | The Natural Touch | Concord | CCD 4517
Red Norvo-Ross Tompkins Quartet | Red & Ross | Concord | CJ 90
Tommy Dorsey And His Orchestra | Frank Sinatra Sings The Standards | RCA | NL 89102 AP

The Oneness Of Two(In Three)
Humphrey Lyttelton And His Band | A Tribute To Humph-Vol.4 | Dormouse | DM 4 IMS

The Open Trio
Paolo Fresu Sextet | Ossi Di Seppia | SPLASC(H) Records | CD H 350-2

The Opener
Art Blakey And The Jazz Messengers | Meet You At The Jazz Corner Of The World Vol. 1 | Blue Note | 84054
Bill Evans | The Complete Fantasy Recordings | Fantasy | 9FCD 1012-2
Bill Evans Trio | The Complete Fantasy Recordings | Fantasy | 9FCD 1012-2
I Will Say Goodbye | Original Jazz Classics | OJCCD 761-2(F 9593)
Cecil Payne With The Joe Palin Trio | Brookfield Andante | Spotlite | SPJ LP 2 (CP 2)
Duke Ellington And His Orchestra | Harlem | Pablo | 2308245-2
Ella Fitzgerald And Duke Ellington:Cote D'Azure Concerts on Verve | Verve | 539033-2
Soul Call | Verve | 539785-2
Duke Ellington: The Champs-Elysees Theater January 29-30th,1965 | Laserlight | 36131
Eje Thelin Quintet | At The German Jazz Festival 1964 | Dragon | DRCD 374
JATP All Stars | Jazz At The Philharmonic:Bird & Pres-Carnegie Hall 1949 | Verve | 815150-1 IMS
The Complete Jazz At The Philharmonic On Verve 1944-1949 | Verve | 523893-2
Charlie Parker Jazz At The Philharmonic 1949 | Verve | 519803-2
Tim Berne Bloodcount | Discretion | Screwgun | SC 70003

The Opener-
Vienna Art Orchestra | Inside Out | Moers Music | 02062/3 CD

The Opening-
Nexus | Urban Shout | SPLASC(H) Records | H 170

The Oracle
Hank Jones Trio | The Oracle | EmArCy | 846376-2 PMS

The Ordinary Fortune
Have You Met This Jones? | MPS | 68195

The Oregon Grinder

Steve Turre Group | Lotus Flower | Verve | 559787-2

The Orient
Badal Roy & Amit Chatterjee | Art Of The Duo: Endless Radiance | Tutu Records | 888178-2*

The Origin
Isham Jones And His Orchestra | Jazz Museum-Hot Dance Bands Of The Twenties,Vol.2 | MCA | 52057 (801842)

The Orinoco Paddle Stick
Great Jazz Trio | Re-Visited:At The Village Vanguard Vol.1 | Eastworld | EWJ 90002

The Other Half Of Me
Adam Rudolph's Moving Pictures | Skyway | Soul Note | 121269-2

The Other Side Of Five
Bill Evans-Toots Thielemans Quintet | Affinity | Warner | 7599-27387-2

The Other Side Of Midnight(Noelle's Theme)
Joe Henderson Sextet | Joe Henderson:The Milestone Years | Milestone | 8MCD 4413-2

The Other Side Of Right
Joe Van Enkhuizen Quartet | Back On The Scene | Criss Cross | Criss 1013 (835601)

The Other Side Of Time
Gil Scott-Heron Groups | Spirits | Mother Records | 523417-2

The Other Woman
Nina Simone Groups | You Can Have Him | Memo Music | HDJ 4087
Nina Simone Trio | At Town Hall | Official | 6012

The Other World
Bruce Gertz Quintet | Blueprint | Freelance | FRL-CD 017

The Outer View
George Russell Sextet | The Outer View | Original Jazz Classics | OJCCD 616-2(RLP 9440)

The Outer View(alt.take)
Art Blakey Big Band | Ain't Life Grand | Affinity | AFF 106

The Outlaw
Horace Silver Quintet | Further Explorations By The Horace Silver Quintet | Blue Note | 300044(1589)

The Pain After
Marty Ehrlich And The Dark Woods Ensemble | Emergency Peace | New World Records | 80409-2

The Pakistani Fruit Box
Henry Kaiser-Jim O'Rourke | Tomorrow Knows Where You Live | Victo | CD 014

The Palantir
George Russell And The Living Time Orchestra | The African Game | Blue Note | 746335-2

The Pan Galactic Gargle Blaster(or Beeblebrox' Blues)
Miles Davis With Gil Evans & His Orchestra | Sketches Of Spain | CBS | CK 65142

The Pan Piper
The Miles Davis Selection | CBS | 465699-2
Bukka White | Country Bottleneck Guitar Classics | Yazoo | YAZ 1026

The Panderer
Dick Wellstood And The Friends Of Fats | Ain't Misbehavin' | Chiaroscuro | CR 183

The Panic Is On
Soprano Summit | Soprano Summit Live At Concord '77 | Concord | CCD 4052

The Panther
Dexter Gordon With The Junior Mance Trio | At Montreux | Prestige | P 7861
Buddy Bolden's Blues | Buddy Bolden's Blues | ITM Records | ITM 14101

The Parry Game
Doug Raney Quintet | The Doug Raney Quintet | Steeplechase | SCCD 31249

The Party's Over
Agneta Baumann And Her Quintet | A Time For Love | Touché Music | TMcCD 006
Ahmad Jamal Trio | Live At The Alhambra | Vogue | 655002
Anita O'Day With The Cal Tjader Quartet | Time For 2 | Verve | 559808-2
Blossom Dearie Quartet | Verve Jazz Masters 51:Blossom Dearie | Verve | 529906-2
Blossom Dearie Sings Comden And Green | Verve | 589102-2
Bobby Timmons Trio | This Here Is Bobby Timmons | Original Jazz Classics | OJC20 104-2(RLP 1164)
Christian Josi With The Harry Allen Quartet | I Walk With My Feet Off The Ground | Master Mix | CHECD 00111
Jimmy McGriff Trio | Blues For Mr. Jimmy | EMI Records | SSL 6005
Ray Anthony And His Orchestra | Dancing Alone Together | Capitol | EMS 1156
Stan Kenton And His Orchestra | The Stage Door Swings | Capitol | EMS 1159

The Party's Over-
Jan Gunnar Hoff Trio | Moving | Curling Legs Prod. | C.L.P. CD 016

The Passage Of Life
Phil Haynes Quartet | Continuum:The Passing | Owl Time Line | 3819072

The Path
Eddie Daniels Quartet | Brief Encounter | Muse | MCD 5154
Norbert Stein Pata Orchester | The Secret Act Of Painting | Pata Musik | PATA 7 CD
Bill Evans Group | The Alternative Man | Blue Note | BT 85111

The Patriot
Lucille Bogan | Lucille Bogan(Bessie Jackson) | Story Of Blues | CD 3535-2

The Peacocks
Bill Evans Trio | The Brilliant | West Wind | WW 2058
Bill Holman Band | A View From The Side | JVC | JVC 2050-2
Gary Foster Quartet | Make Your Own Fun | Concord | CCD 4459
Lynne Arriale Trio | With Words Unspoken | dmp Digital Music Productions | CD 518
Stan Getz With The Bill Evans Trio | But Beautiful | Jazz Door | JD 1208
Tim Sund Trio | Trialogue | Nabel Records:Jazz Network | CD 4692
Toots Thielemans Quintet | Verve Jazz Masters Vol.59:Toots Thielemans | Verve | 535271-2
Werner Lener Quartet | Personal Moments | Satin Doll Productions | SDP 1026-1 CD
Winck-Büning-Schoenefeld | Truth And The Abstract Blues | Acoustic Music Records | 319.1061.2

The Peacock's Tail
John McLaughlin Group | The Promise | Verve | 529828-2

The Peacocks(with verse of Garcia Lorca)
Steve Lacy-Mal Waldron | Live at Dreher Paris 1981 Vol.2 | Hat Art | CD 6186(2)

The Peanut Vendor
Herbie Mann Sextet | Verve Jazz Masters 56:Herbie Mann | Verve | 529901-2
Jimmy Dorsey And His Orchestra | The Radio Years | London | HMG 5022 AN
Raymond Scott And His Orchestra | The Uncollected:Raymond Scott | Hindsight | HSR 201
Stan Kenton And His Orchestra | Return To Biloxi | Magic | DAWE 35(881848)
Stan Kenton Orchestra | Rhapsody In Blue | Moon Records | MCD 012-2

The Pearls
Jelly Roll Morton's Red Hot Peppers | Jelly Roll Morton-Doctor Jazz | RCA | CL 89808 SF
Doctor Jazz | Black & Blue | BLE 59.227 2
Wally Rose Trio | Ragtime Classics | Good Time Jazz | GTCD 10034-2
Jelly Roll Morton's Red Hot Peppers | The Complete Jelly Roll Morton-Vol.1/2 | RCA | ND 89768

The Pelican
Bubber Miley And His Mileage Makers | New York Vol.3-Don't You Leave Me Here | Frog | DGF 12

The Pendulum At Falcon's Lair
The New Oscar Pettiford Sextet | The New Oscar Pettiford Sextet | Original Jazz Classics | OJC 112(DLP 8)

The People Don't Do Like They Used To Do
Norbert Stein Pata Orchester | The Secret Act Of Painting | Pata Musik | PATA 7 CD

The People Of Yomm
Claire Martin With The Jim Mullen Quartet | The Waiting Game | Linn Records | AKD 018

The People United Will Never Be Defeated
Frederic Rzewski | The People United Will Never Be Defeated! | Hat Art | CD 6066

The Perfect Date
Vital Information | Live Around The World Where We Come From Tour '98-'99 | Intuition Records | INT 3296-2
Steve White Quartet | Jazz In Hollywood:Steve White | Original Jazz Classics | OJCCD 1891-2(Nocturne unreleased)

The Perfumed Forest Wet With Rain
Dollar Brand Quintet | Montreux '80 | Enja | 3079-2

The Pesky Serpent
Shorty Rogers And His Giants | Short Stops | RCA | NL 85917(2)

The Pharoah
Maynard Ferguson And His Orchestra | Maynard '61 | Fresh Sound Records | R 52064(Roulette)

The Philanthropist
Mike Nock Quintet | Ozboppin' | Naxos Jazz | 86019-2

The Phineas Train
Pat Martino Quintet | Think Tank | Blue Note | 592009-2
Deborah Henson-Conant Group | Deborah Henson-Conant:Best Of Instrumental Music | Laika Records | 35101322

The Phoenix
Deborah Henson-Conant Trio | Just For You | Laika Records | LK 95-063
George Lewis-Douglas Ewart | George Lewis-Douglas Ewart | Black Saint | BSR 0026

The Piano Lesson
Duke Ellington And His Orchestra | Eastbourne Performance | RCA | 2122106-2

The Picayune
Mel Tormé With The Marty Paich Dek-Tette | Mel Torme Sings Fred Astaire | Charly | CD 96

The Picture
Jan Garbarek Group | Photo With Blue Skie, White Clouds, Wires, Windows And A Red Roof | ECM | 1135 (843168-2)
Pekka Pylkkännen's Tube Factory | Opaque | Naxos Jazz | 86068-2

The Pilgrim And The Stars
John Surman-Jack DeJohnette | The Amazing Adventures Of Simon Simon | ECM | 1193(829160-2)

The Pilgrim's Way (To The Seventeen Walls)
Albert King Blues Band | The Blues Don't Change | Stax | SCD 8570-2(STX 4101)

The Pineapple Rag
Centrifuge | Big T's Sunglasses | Jazz Pure Collection | AU 31606 CD

The Pink Panther
Rodney Jones Quintet | Right Now | Minor Music | 801054

The Pivot
Peter Bernstein Trio | Earth Tones | Criss Cross | Criss 1151

The Place
Benny Green Trio | The Place To Be | Blue Note | 829268-2

The Plains
Duo Due | Tre | Amadeo | 837950-2

The Planet
Roberto Ottaviano Koiné | Hybrid And Hot | SPLASC(H) Records | CD H 453-2

The Pleasant Pheasant
Herbie Hancock Septet | My Point Of View | Blue Note | 521226-2

The Pleasure Is Mine
Herbie Hancock Sextet | Herbie Hancock:The Complete Blue Note Sixties Sessions | Blue Note | 495569-2
Laurent De Wilde Trio | Odd And Blue | IDA Record | 023 CD

The Pleasure Is Mine,I'm Sure
Flemming Agerskov Quintet | Face To Face | dacapo | DCCD 9445

The Pleasure Of Everyday Activity
Enrico Rava Quartet | The Plot | ECM | 1078

The Plot
Jim McNeely Quartet | The Plot Thickens | Muse | MCD 5378

The Plum Blossom
Robben Ford & The Blue Line | Mystic Line | Stretch Records | GRS 00082

The Poet
Ornette Coleman Trio | Who's Crazy? | Affinity | AFF 102 D

The Point
Klaus Doldinger | Constellation | Warner | 2292-40132-2
Gene McDaniels And His Band | Another Tear Falls | Charly | CRB 1136

The Pointsman's Contract
Mitchel Forman | Only A Memory | Soul Note | 121070-2

The Polish Landlady-
Kurt Rosenwinkel Quintet | The Enemies Of Energy | Verve | 543042-2

The Polish Song
The Tango Kings | The Tango Kings | Big World | BW 2016

The Polka Of Doom
Odean Pope Trio | Out For A Walkf Happiness | Moers Music | 02072 CD

The Popeye
Karl Berger Quartet | We Are You | Enja | 6060-2

The Postman
Albion Jazz Band | They're All Nice Tunes | Stomp Off Records | CD 1249

The Potato That Became Tomato
Dave Liebman | One Of A Kind | Line Records | COCD 9.00887 0

The Praise Song
King Curtis Band | King Curtis-Blow Man Blow | Bear Family Records | BCD 15670 CI

The Prance
Gene Ammons Quartet | Preachin' | Original Jazz Classics | OJCCD 792-2(P 7270)

The Prayer
John Tchicai-Vitold Rek Duo | Art Of The Duo:Satisfaction | Enja | 7033-2
Alex Welsh And His Band | Melody Maker Tribute To Louis Armstrong Vol.1 | Jazz Colours | 874767-2

The Preacher
Art Hodes | Keepin' Out Of Mischief Now | Candid | CCD 79717
Art Hodes-Jim Galloway | Live From Toronto's Cafe Des Copains | Music & Arts | CD 610
Babs Gonzales Group | Properly Presenting Babs Gonzales | Fresh Sound Records | FSR 702(835422)
Buddy Morrow And His Orchestra | The Uncollected:Buddy Morrow | Hindsight | HSR 154
Charly Antolini Orchestra | Charly Antolini | Jazz Magazine | 48017
Eddie Jefferson And His Band | Come Along With Me | Original Jazz Classics | OJCCD 613-2(P 7698)
Gottfried Böttger-Joe Penzlin Duo | Take Two | L+R Records | CDLR 40030
Jimmy Smith Trio | Jimmy Smith At The Organ | Blue Note | 300154(1512)
Kenny Ball And His Jazzmen | The Very Best Of Kenny Ball | Timeless | CD TTD 598
Larry Carlton Group | Kid Gloves | GRP | GRP 96832

The Preacher And The Voodoo Woman
Charlie Haden-Pat Metheny | Beyond The Missouri Sky | Verve | 537130-2

The Precious Jewel
Terence Blanchard Quintet | Romantic Defiance | CBS | 480489-2

The Present
Peter Ponzol Trio | Prism | View | VS 114 IMS

The Pretty One
Jacques Schwarz-Bart/James Hurt Quartet | Immersion | Fresh Sound Records | FSNT 057 CD

The Price I Thought I'd Pay
Richie Cole Septet | Alto Madness | Muse | MCD 5155

The Price Of Experience-
Marty Ehrlich Quartet | Song | Enja | ENJ-9396 2

The Price Of The Ticket(after James Baldwin)
Jacques Schwarz-Bart/James Hurt Quartet | Immersion | Fresh Sound Records | FSNT 057 CD

The Price To Pay
Ian Bargh | Only Trust Your Heart | Sackville | SKCD2-2053

The Prince And The Sage
Ralph Towner | Works | ECM | 823268-1

The Princess
Rick Margitza Orchestra | Hope | Blue Note | 794858-2
Ronnie Taheny Group | Briefcase | Laika Records | 35101152

The Princess And The Frog
Sputnik 27 | But Where's The Moon? | dml-records | CD 011

The Princess Coming Home
Shelly Manne Orchestra | Cool California | Savoy | WL 70511(2)(SJL 2254) DP

The Prisoner
Art Pepper Quintet With Strings | Art Pepper:The Complete Galaxy Recordings | Galaxy | 16GCD 1016-2
Gil Scott-Heron Sextet | The Revolution Will Not Be Televised | RCA | ND 86994(874175)
Herbie Hancock Orchestra | Herbie Hancock:The Complete Blue Note Sixties Sessions | Blue Note | 495569-2
Joe Henderson-The Blue Note Years | Blue Note | 789287-2

The Prisoner(alt.take)
Art Pepper Quintet With Strings | Art Pepper:The Complete Galaxy Recordings | Galaxy | 16GCD 1016-2
Herbie Hancock Orchestra | Herbie Hancock:The Complete Blue Note Sixties Sessions | Blue Note | 495569-2
Fred Frith Maybe Monday | Digital Wildlife | Winter&Winter | 910071-2

The Prisoner's Dilemma
Bunny Berigan | I Can't Get Started | Pro-Arte | CDD 554

The Prisoner's Song
Louis Armstrong With Sy Oliver's Choir And Orchestra | Louis Armstrong-Heavenly Music | Ambassador | CLA 1916

The Process Of Creation Suite Part 3:Assimilation
Kenny Barron Sextet | Peruvian Blue | 32 Jazz | 32083

The Profit
Max Roach Quartet | To The Max! | Enja | ENJ-7021 22
Max Roach Sextet With Choir | It's Time | Impulse(MCA) | 951185-2
Gerry Niewood Group | Share My Dream | dmp Digital Music Productions | CD 450

The Promise
John Coltrane Quartet | The Promise | Moon Records | MCD 058-2
The Best Of John Coltrane | Pablo | 2405417-2
The Best Of John Coltrane-His Greatest Years, Vol. 2 | MCA | AS 9223

The Proof
Charles Fambrough Group | The Proper Angle | CTI Records | CTI 1002-2

The Prophet
Cal Tjader's Orchestra | Verve Jazz Masters 39:Cal Tjader | Verve | 521858-2
Donald Harrison-Terence Blanchard Quintet | Eric Dolphy & Booker Little Remembered Live At Sweet Basil | Paddle Wheel | K32Y 6145
Eric Dolphy-Booker Little Quintet | At The Five Spot,Vol.1 | Original Jazz Classics | OJC20 133-2
Eric Dophy Quintet | Eric Dolphy:The Complete Prestige Recordings | Prestige | 9 PRCD-4418-2
Harold Danko Quintet | Prestigious-A Tribute To Eric Dolphy | Steeplechase | SCCD 31508
Kühn/Nauseef/Newton/Tadic | Let's Be Generous | CMP Records | CMP CD 53
Milt Jackson Quintet | Milt Jackson At The Kosei Nenkin | Pablo | 2620103-2

The Prophet Speaks
The Al Di Meola Project | Kiss My Axe | Inak | 700782

The Proverbs
Ralph Towner | Anthem | ECM | 1743(543814-2)

The Prowler
Duke Ellington And His Orchestra | Harlem | Pablo | 2308245-2

The Purple Room
John Surman Orchestra | Tales Of The Algonquin | Deram | 844884-2

The Pursuit Of The Woman With The Feathered Hat
Dizzy Gillespie Quintet | The Cool World/Dizzy Goes Hollywood | Verve | 531230-2

The Pusher
Nina Simone | RCA Victor 80th Anniversary Vol.6:1970-1979 | RCA | 2668782-2
Niels-Henning Orsted-Pedersen And The Danish Radio Big Band | Ambiance | dacapo | DCCD 9417

The Puzzle
Niels-Henning Orsted-Pedersen/Philip Catherine Duo | The Viking | Pablo | 2310894-2

The Python
Erroll Garner Trio | Relaxin' | Vogue | 500117

The Quay Of Meditative Future
Dick Griffin Orchestra | A Dream For Rahsaan & More | Konnex Records | KCD 5062

The Queen's Fancy
Modern Jazz Quartet | The Complete Modern Jazz Quartet Prestige & Pablo Recordings | Prestige | 4PRCD 4438-2
Modern Jazz Quartet | Prestige | P 24005
The Modern Jazz Society | A Concert Of Contemporary Music | Verve | 559827-2

The Queen's Fancy(rehersal take)
Randy Johnson Quintet | Walk On WalkOn Walk ON | Muse | MCD 5432

The Queen's Suite:
Duke Ellington And His Orchestra | The Best Of Duke Ellington | Pablo | 2405401-2

The Quest
Jan Garbarek Group | Visible World | ECM | 1585(529086-2)
Lutz Häfner Quartet | Lutz Häfner | Mons Records | MR 874804

The Question Is
Tom Varner Quintet | Martian Heartache | Soul Note | 121286-2

The Quiet American
Jasper Van't Hof Trio | Tomorrowland | Challenge | CHR 70040

The Quiet Man
James McMillan Group | Up All Day All Night | Savoy | CY 78899

The Rabbit-
Peter Erskine Group | Transition | Denon Compact Disc | CY-1484

The Race Is On
Ronnie Foster Group | The Racer | Electric Bird | K 28P 6441

The Rain Forest
Billy Taylor With The Quincy Jones Orchestra | My Fair Lady Loves Jazz | MCA | AS 72

The Rain King
Motohiko Hino Group | It's Therenyc | Enja | 8030-2

The Rainbow People
Dexter Gordon-Benny Bailey Quintet | The Rainbow People | Steeplechase | SCCD 31521
Blues & Boogie Explosion | Blues & Boogie Explosion | BELL Records | BLR 84003

The Rains From A Cloud Do Not Wet The Sky
Frank Vignola Trio | Appel Direct | Concord | CCD 4576

The Rat Race
Gigi Gryce Quintet | The Rat Race Blues | Original Jazz Classics | OJCCD 081-2(NJ 8262)

The Raven Speaks
Woody Herman And His Orchestra | The Raven Speaks | Original Jazz Classics | OJCCD 663-2(F 9416)
James Weiman Trio | People Music | TCB Records | TCB 96302

The Razor's Edge
Dave Holland Quintet | The Razor's Edge | ECM | 1353
Philipp Wachsmann-Paul Lytton | Some Other Season | ECM | 1662

The Re(de)fining Of Methods And Means
Dave Brubeck Quartet | The Great Concerts | CBS | 462403-2

The Real Ambassador

TITELVERZEICHNIS

The Dave Brubeck Selection | CBS | 467279-2
The Real Cat
James 'Son' Thomas | James 'Son' Thomas | Blues Classics(L+R) | CDLR 82006
The Real McCoy
Gene Ammons And His All Stars | The Big Sound | Original Jazz Classics | OJCCD 651-2(P 7132)
Niels Lan Doky Quartet | Friendship | Milestone | MCD 9183-2
The Real Softshoe
Carol Sloane With The Phil Woods Quartet | The Real Thing | Contemporary | CCD 14060-2
The Rebel
Sibylle Pomorin/Terry Jenoure Group | Auguries Of Speed | ITM Records | ITM 1467
The Recitic
Duke Ellington-Coleman Hawkins Orchestra | Duke Ellington Meets Coleman Hawkins | MCA | MCAD 5650
The Red Baron
Eddie Higgins Quartet | Zoot's Hyms | Sunnyside | SSC 1064 D
The Red Blues
Red Rodney Sextet | The Red Tornado | Muse | MR 5088
The Red Broom
Red Norvo Sextet | Muisc To Listen To Red Norvo By | Original Jazz Classics | OJC 155(C 7534)
The Red Door
Gerry Mulligan Sextet | California Concerts Vol.2 | Pacific Jazz | 746864-2
Stuff Smith Trio | The Stuff Smith Trio 1943 | Progressive | PCD 7053
The Red One
Howlin' Wolf | Heavy Heads | Chess | 6.24835 AS
The Red Rooster
Willie Dixon Blues Band | Blues Roots Vol. 12: Willie Dixon | Chess | 6.24802 AG
The Red Rooster(Rehearsal)
The Fringe | The Fringe Live In Israel | Soul Note | 121305-2
The Red Sea
Dave Samuels Group | Natural Selections | GRP | GRP 96562
The Red Snapper
Red Rodney Sextet | The Red Tornado | Muse | MR 5088
The Red Wing
Rusty Bryant Group | For The Good Times | Prestige | PRCD 24269-2
The Red-Eye Special
Fats Waller | Louis Armstrong In The Thirties/Fats Waller Last Testament | Forlane | UCD 19005
The Regenerative Landscape(for AMM)
Bazillus | The Regulator | ACT | 9206-2
The Reluctant Bride
Ron McClure Quartet | Pink Cloud | Naxos Jazz | 86002-2
The Remembered Visit
Michael Mantler Quintet | Live | Watt | 18
Steve Lacy Group | Anthem | Novus | PD 83079
The Rent
Kurt Elling Group With Guests | Live In Chicago | Blue Note | 522211-2
The Rent Party
Live In Chicago | Blue Note | 522211-2
The Rent Party(Intro)
Ahmad Jamal Quartet | Nature | Dreyfus Jazz Line | FDM 37018-2
The Reprise-
Nature(The Essence Part III) | Atlantic | 3984-23105-2
Sonic Fiction | Changing With The Times | Naxos Jazz | 86034-2
The Restaurant At The End Of The Universe(including Trillian's Dance)
Lan Xang | Hidden Gardens | Naxos Jazz | 86046-2
The Return
Paquito D'Rivera Group | Havana Cafe | Chesky | JD 60
The Return Of Mohammed
Terje Rypdal Group | If Mountains Could Sing | ECM | 1554(523987-2)
The Return Of Per Ulv
Cornelius Claudio Kreusch | The Vision | Enja | 8082-2
The Return Of The Pleasures
Ganelin Trio | Con Fuoco | LEO | LR 106
The Return Of The Undead Mescalworm
Rabih Abou-Khalil Group | Nafas | ECM | 1359(835781-2)
The Return(I)
Nafas | ECM | 1359(835781-2)
The Return(II)
John Surman-John Warren Group | The Brass Project | ECM | 1478
The Returning Exile
Bob Mintzer Big Band | Spectrum | dmp Digital Music Productions | CD 461
The Rev
Jasper Van't Hof Quintet | Eyeball | Limetree | FCD 0002
Ray Brown Trio Plus | Bye Bye Blackbird | Paddle Wheel | K 28P 6303
The Revelation(Ritual)
Joey DeFrancesco-Jimmy Smith Quartet | Incredible! | Concord | CCD 4890
The Rhumba
Jim Brent-Bruce Kaminsky Duo | Greensleeves | Steeplechase | SCS 4003
The Rhumba Jumps
Glenn Miller And His Orchestra | Glenn Miller Live-15 Rare Broadcast Performances From 1940-1942 | RCA | NL 89485 AG
Swim Two Birds | Sweet Relief | Laika Records | 35101182
The Rhyme
Loope | Prinz Henry | ITM Records | ITM 1447
The Rhythm Of Our Hearts
Dick Robertson And His Orchestra | The New York Session Man | Timeless | CBC 1-008
The Rhythm Thing
Sonny Red (Kyner) Sextet | Images:Sonny Red | Original Jazz Classics | OJC 148(J 974)
The Right Of Love
Rufus 'Speckled Red' Perryman | Big Band Bounce & Boogie-The Boogie Woogie Masters | Affinity | AFS 1005
The Right Time
Carmen McRae And Her Quintet | Velvet Soul | LRC Records | CDC 7970
The Right To Love
Gail Wynters With The Gordon Brisker Quintet | My Shining Hour | Naxos Jazz | 86027-2
The River
Abbey Lincoln With Her Band | Talking To The Sun | Enja | ENJ-4060 2
Monty Alexander Trio | The River | Concord | CCD 4422
The River Is So Blue
Ryuichi Sakamoto-Kazumi Watanabe Groups | Tokyo Joe | Denon Compact Disc | DC-8586
The River(I-XII)
The Crossover Ensemble | The River:Image Of Time And Life | dacapo | DCCD 9434
The River:Image Of Time And Life:
Blossom Dearie Quartet | Give Him The Ooh-La-La | Verve | 517067-2
The Riviera
Jackie & Roy | We've Got It-The Music Of Cy Coleman | Discovery | DSCD 907(881988)
The Road Less Traveled
Marvin 'Smitty' Smith Group | The Road Less Traveled | Concord | CCD 4379
The Road To Woy Woy
Pat Metheny Group | The Road To You | Geffen Records | GED 24601
The Road To You
Wayne Horvitz Trio | Todos Santos | Sound Aspects | sas CD 019
The Rock 'N' Roll Waltz
Frans Bak & Jazz Group 90 | Hymn To The Rainbow | L+R Records | CDLR 45055
The Rocks Of The Cliffs
Trevor Watts Moiré Music Drum Orchestra | A Wider Embrace | ECM | 1449
The Rocky Road To Dublin
World Quintet With The London Mozart Players | World Quintet | TipToe | TIP-888843 2
The Rod
Roscoe Mitchell And The Note Factory | This Dance Is For Steve McCall | Black Saint | 120150-2
The Roman Swing Of Mrs. Stone
Oscar Klein's Jazz Show | A' Portrait Of Jan Jankeje | Jazzpoint | JP 1054 CD
Return To Forever | Romantic Warrior | CBS | SRCS 9348
The Rook
Jack McDuff Orchestra | Write On, Capt'n | Concord | CCD 4568
The Roots Of Coincidence
Pauline Oliveros | The Roots Of The Moment | Hat Art | CD 6009
The Rotten Kid
Thilo Berg Big Band And Barbara Morrison | Blues For Ella | Mons Records | CD 1902
The Rotten Kid(alt.take)
Michel Petrucciani | Note'n Notes | Owl Records | 037 CD
The Rubber Man
Esbjörn Svensson Trio(E.S.T.) | E.S.T. Live | ACT | 9295-2
The Rube Thing
Gus Mancuso Quartet | Introducing Gus Mancuso | Fresh Sound Records | 3233(Fantasy)
The Ruble And The Yen
Guido Manusardi | Concerto | SPLASC(H) Records | CD H 437-2
The Rumproller
Lee Morgan Quintet | The Best Of Lee Morgan | Blue Note | 791138-2
Nelson Rangell Groups | Yes, Then Yes | GRP | GRP 97552
The Sad Sergeant
Jimmy Giuffre-Lee Konitz | Giuffre/Konitz/Connors/Bley | Improvising Artists Inc. | 123859-2
The Sadness After
AM 4 | ...And She Answered | ECM | 1394
The Sadness Of Yuki
Wolfgang Puschnig-Uli Scherer | Puschnig-Scherer | EmArCy | 014103-2
Sarah Jane Cion Trio | Summer Night | Naxos Jazz | 86071-2
The Saga Of Jenny
Dee Dee Bridgewater With Band | Dee Dee Bridgewater Sings Kurt Weil | EmArCy | 9809601
Rias Big Band Berlin + Strings | Weill | Mons Records | MR 874347
The Scat Song
Dutch Swing College Band | Souvenirs From Holland, Vol. 3 | DSC Production | PA 005 (801062)
The Scavenger
Cannonball Adderley Quintet | Country Preacher | Capitol | 830452-2
The Scene Is Clean
Clifford Brown-Max Roach Quintet | Brownie-The Complete EmArCy Recordings Of Clifford Brown | EmArCy | 838306-2
Continuum | Mad About Tadd | Palo Alto | PA 8029
Red Rodney Quintet | Then And Now | Chesky | JD 79
Nat Adderley Quintet | On The Move | Evidence | ECD 22064-2
The Scent Of The Healer
Paul Brody's Tango Toy | Klezmer Stories | Laika Records | 35101222
The Schlemiel As A Modern Hero
John Swana And The Philadelphians | Pilly Gumbo | Criss Cross | Criss 1203
The Scorpion(alt.take)
Jack McDuff Group | Bringin' It Home | Concord | CCD 4855
The Scribe
Yaya 3 | Yaya 3 | Loma | 936248277-2
Lynn Hope Band | Lynn Hope And His Tenor Sax | Pathe | 1546661(Aladdin)
The Scythe
Ketil Bjornstad Group | The Sea | ECM | 1545(521718-2)
The Sea(part 1-12)
Mal Waldron Quintet | Live At The Village Vanguard | Soul Note | 121148-2
The Search
David Friedman Quartet | Shades Of Change | Enja | ENJ-5017 2
Peter Herbolzheimer Rhythm Combination & Brass | Friends And Sihouettes | Koala Records | CD P 25
The Search For Direction-
Carola Grey & Noisy Mama | Girls Can't Hit! | Lipstick Records | LIP 8945-2
The Search(part 1)
Wycliffe Gordon Group | The Search | Nagel-Heyer | CD 2007
The Search(part 1)-
Nils Wogram Octet | Odd And Awkward | Enja | ENJ-9416-2
The Search(part 2)
Wycliffe Gordon Group | The Search | Nagel-Heyer | CD 2007
The Search(part 2)-
Tubby Hayes Quartet | Mexican Green | Mole Jazz | MOLE 2
The Second Day
String Trio Of New York | Time Never Lies | Stash Records | ST-CD 544(889796)
The Second Milestone
One For All | Live At Smoke Vol.1 | Criss Cross | Criss 1211
The Second Night
Booker Ervin Quartet | The Freedom And Space Sessions | Prestige | P 24091
The Second Page
Monday Night Big Band | Thanks To Thad:Monday Night Big Band Plays The Music Of Thad Jones | TCB Records | TCB 97902
The Second Race
Thad Jones-Mel Lewis Orchestra | Body And Soul | West Wind Orchestra Series | 2407 CD
The Second Time Around
Count Basie And His Orchestra | Frankly Basie-Count Basie Plays The Hits Of Frank Sinatra | Verve | 519849-2
Mel Tormé With Orchestra | That's All Mel Tormé | CBS | CK 65165
Teddy Wilson Quintet | Air Mail Special | Black Lion | BLCD 760115
The Secret
John Tchicai Group | Put Up The Flight | Storyville | SLP 4141
Passport | Ataraxia | Atlantic | 2292-42148-2
Steve Tibbetts/Tim Weinhold Duo | Steve Tibbetts | ECM | bzz- 77
The Seduction
Wynton Marsalis Quartet | Tempo Jazz Edition Vol.2-Playin' Now | Polydor | 847903-2
The Seed And All
Robin Williamson | The Seed-At-Zero | ECM | 1732(543819-2)
The Seed-At-Zero
Elements | Illumination | RCA | PD 83031(874013)
The Senate-
Bobby Vega Group | Down The Road | Lipstick Records | LIP 8955-2
The Sentimental Blues
Shirley Horn With Band | The Santimental Touch Of Albert Van Dam | RCA | PL 70465 TIS
The Sermon
Jimmy McGriff Orchestra | Jimmy McGriff-Funkiest Little Band In The Kand | LRC Records | CDC 9046(874379)
Jimmy Smith Quartet | Any Number Can Win | Verve | 557447-2
Jimmy Smith Sextet | Jimmy Smith: The Sermon | Blue Note | 746097-2
Jimmy Smith With Orchestra | Sum Serious Blues | Milestone | MCD 9207-2
Phineas Newborn Jr. Trio | The Newborn Touch | Original Jazz Classics | OJCCD 270-2
The Serpent's Tooth(I)
Miles Davis Sextet | The Jazz Giants Play Miles Davis:Milestones | Prestige | PCD 24225-2
Miles Davis And His Orchestra | Collector's Items | Original Jazz Classics | OJC20 071-2(P 7044)
The Serpent's Tooth(II)
Landes Jugend Jazz Orchester Hessen | Touch Of Lips | hr music.de | hrmj 004-01 CD
The Session
Gil Melle Quintet | Patterns In Jazz | Blue Note | 300096(1517)
The Seventh Son
Mose Allison Trio | Mose Allison Sings The 7th Son | Prestige | PR20 7279-2
Mose In Your Ear | Atlantic | SD 1627
The Shade Of The Cedar Tree
Joris Teepe Quintet | Bottom Line | Mons Records | MR 874770
The Shadow Of Lo
Return To Forever | Where Have I Known You Before | Polydor | 825206-2
Dieter Ilg Sextet | Summerhill | Lipstick Records | LIP 890062
The Shadow Of Your Smile
Astrud Gilberto With Orchestra | The Shadow Of Your Smile | Verve | 2304540
Astrud Gilberto With The Don Sebesky Orchestra | Verve Jazz Masters 9:Astrud Gilberto | Verve | 519824-2
Silver Collection: The Astrud Gilberto Album | Verve | 823451-2 PMS
Bill Evans | Further Conversations With Myself | Verve | 559832-2
Bill Evans Trio | Bill Evans:The Secret Sessions | Milestone | 8MCD 4421-2
Bill Perkins Quintet | Quietly There | Original Jazz Classics | OJCCD 1776-2
Blossom Dearie Trio | At Ronnie Scott's:Blossom Time | EmArCy | 558683-2
Bobby Lyle Trio | Night Breeze | Electric Bird | K 28P 6457
Carmen McRae And Her Sextet | Woman Talk | Mainstream | MD CDO 706
Eddie Harris Quartet | The Best Of Eddie Harris | Atlantic | 7567-81370-2
Eddie Lockjaw Davis Quartet | Jazz Legends:Eddie Lockjaw Davis Quartet Vol.1&2 | Storyville | 4960263
The Best Of The Jazz Saxophones Vol.3 | LRC Records | CDC 9009
Erroll Garner Quintet | That's My Kick | RCA | NL 89433
Jack Sheldon Quartet | Stand By For The Jack Sheldon Quartet | Concord | CJ 229
Jenny Evans And The Rudi Martini Quartet | At Loyd's | BELL Records | BLR 90004
Joe Pass With Red Mitchell | Finally | EmArCy | 512603-2 PMS
Leny Andrade And Her Trio | Embraceable You | Timeless | CD SJP 365
Lou Donaldson Quintet | Mr.Shing-A-Ling | Blue Note | 784271-2
Lous Dassen With Holger Clausen/Atlanta Jazzband | Let's Do It... | Dr.Jazz Records | 8606-2
Oliver Nelson Quartet | Three Dimensions | MCA | IA 9335/2
Richard 'Groove' Holmes Trio | Misty | Original Jazz Classics | OJCCD 724-2(P 7485)
Singers Unlimited + The Oscar Peterson Trio | In Tune | MPS | 68085
The Rosenberg Trio | Suenos Gitanos | Polydor | 549581-2
Thilo Kreitmeier Quintet | Mo' Better Blues | Organic Music | ORGM 9706
Toots Thielemans Quartet With Orchestra | Bluesette | CBS | CDCOL 26604
Wes Montgomery With The Don Sebesky Orchestra | Verve Jazz Masters 14:Wes Montgomery | Verve | 519826-2
Herbert Joos Trio | Ballade Noire | free flow music | ffm 0392
The Shadow Of Your Smile-
Jiri Stivin & Co. | Reduta Live | clearaudio | LT 0010-2 531
Yutaka Yokokura Group | Yutaka | GRP | GRP 95572
The Shake
Stanley Turrentine Orchestra | Rough 'N' Tumble | Blue Note | 524552-2
Jump'n Jive | We The Cats Shall Hep Ya | Timeless | CD SJP 378
The Shang
Charlie Hunter Quartet | Ready...Set...Shango! | Blue Note | 837101-2
The Shango Pt.III
Joe Roccisano Orchestra | The Shape I'm In | Landmark | LCD 1535-2
The Shape Of Things
John Stubblefield Quartet | Morning Song | Enja | ENJ-8036 2
The Shaw Of Newark
Victor Lewis Trio | Three Way Conversations | Red Records | 123276-2
The Sheik Of Araby
Art Tatum | Art Tatum:Complete Original American Decca Recordings | Definitive Records | DRCD 11200
Benny Goodman Quartet | Welcome To Jazz: Benny Goodman | Koch Records | 321 973 D1
Bernie Privin Orchestra | Brothers And Other Mothers, Vol. 2 | Savoy | SJL 2236 (801212)
Coleman Hakins And His Orchestra | Body And Soul | RCA | 26685152
Dave McKenna & Gray Sargent | Concord Duo Series Volume Two | Concord | CCD 4552
Eddie Condon All Stars | Eddie Condon Town Hall Concerts Vol.1 | Jazzology | JCECD-1001
Emile Barnes' Louisiana Joymakers | Opening Night At Preservation Hall | American Music | AMCD-86
Fats Waller And His Rhythm | Live Vol.3 | Giants Of Jazz | GOJ 1041
Ken Colyer's Jazzmen | Best Of British Jazz From The BBC Jazz Club Vol.1 | Upbeat Jazz | URCD 118
Lester Young Quintet | Lester Young:The Complete 1936-1951 Small Group Sessions(Studio Recordings-Master Takes),Vol.4 | Blue Moon | BMCD 1004
Oscar Peterson Trio | The Complete Young Oscar Peterson(1945-1949) | RCA | 2122612-2
Masters Of Jazz Vol.7 | RCA | NL 89721 DP
Red Nichols And His Five Pennies | Big Band Bounce And Boogie:Clarinetitis/The Young BG-Benny Goodman | Affinity | AFS 1018
Schnuckenack Reinhardt Quintet | Live | Intercord | 160035
Teddy Wilson Trio | Revisited The Goodman Years | Storyville | STCD 4046
The Tremble Kids | 25 Jahre The Tremble Kids | Intercord | 180036
Wild Bill Davison All Stars | Wild Bill Davison | Storyville | SLP 4005
The Sheik Of Araby Boogie
Art Hodes Trio | Apex Blues 1944 | Jazzology | JCD-104
The Sheikh
Elvin Jones Jazz Machine | Going Home | Enja | ENJ-7095 2
The Shell Game
Big Band De Lausanne | Duke Ellington's Sacred Music | TCB Records | TCB 20502
The Shepherd Of Breton
Duke Ellington Trio | In The Uncommon Market | Pablo | 2308247-2
The Shepherd(rehersal)
In The Uncommon Market | Pablo | 2308247-2
The Shimmering Colours Of The Stained Glass(I)
Hubert Nuss Trio | The Shimmering Colours Of The Stained Glass | Green House Music | CD 1008
The Shimmering Colours Of The Stained Glass(II)
Bill Perkins Quintet | Quietly There | Original Jazz Classics | OJCCD 1776-2
The Shining Sea
Scott Hamilton With Strings | Scott Hamilton With Strings | Concord | CCD 4538
The Shout
Art Tatum | Art Tatum:Complete Original American Decca Recordings | Definitive Records | DRCD 11200
Les McCann Trio | Plays The Shout | Pacific Jazz | LN 10083
The Show Has Begun
Bert Ambrose And His Orchestra | The Bands That Matter | Eclipse | ECM 2044
The Show Must Go On
Swim Two Birds | No Regrets | Laika Records | 35101342
The Showliness Of Beeing Sane
Randy Weston African Rhythm | Khepera | Verve | 557821-2
The Shrine
Rob McConnell And The Boss Brass | Even Canadians Get The Blues | Concord | CCD 4722
The Shuttle
Stanley Cowell Trio | Travellin' Man | Black Lion | BLCD 760178
The Shy One
Batman | Naked City | Nonesuch | 7559-79238-2
The Sicilian Clan

Shelly Manne Trio | Shelly Manne 2-3-4 | Impulse(MCA) | GRP 11492

The Sidewalks Of New York

Cannonball Adderley Quintet | Cannonball And Eight Giants | Milestone | M 47001
Duke Ellington And His Famous Orchestra | Duke Ellington:The Blanton-Webster Band | Bluebird | 21 13181-2
Duke Ellington And His Orchestra | The Duke At Fargo 1940 | Storyville | STCD 8316/17
The Indispensable Duke Ellington Vol.5/6 | RCA | ND 89750

The Sidewalks Of New York-

The Sidewalks Of New York | Tin Pan Alley:The Sidewalks Of New York | Winter&Winter | 910038-2

The Sidewalks Of New York(coda)

Tin Pan Alley:The Sidewalks Of New York | Winter&Winter | 910038-2

The Sidewalks Of New York(finale)

Tin Pan Alley:The Sidewalks Of New York | Winter&Winter | 910038-2

The Sidewalks Of New York(interlude)

Bud Shank And The Sax Section | Bud Shank And The Sax Section | Pacific Jazz | LN 10091

The Sidewinder

Lee Morgan Quintet | The Best Of Lee Morgan | Blue Note | 791138-2
We Remember You | Fresh Sound Records | FSCD 1024
Lee Morgan:Blue Breakbeats | Blue Note | 494704-2
Manhattan Jazz Quintet | The Sidewinder | Paddle Wheel | K32Y 6170
Ralph Towner-Peter Erskine | Open Letter | ECM | 1462(511980-2)

The Sigh

Ginger Baker/Jens Johansson/Jonas Hellborg | Unseen Rain | Day Eight Music | DEMCD 028

The Sign-

Dusko Goykovich-Gianni Basso Quintet | Live At Birdland Neuburg | Birdland | BN 004

The Sign Says 'West'

Big Band De Lausanne & Charles Papasoff | Astor | TCB Records | TCB 95502

The Silence Of A Candle

Carlo Mombelli'a Abstractions | Dancing In A Museum | ITM-Pacific | ITMP 970078

The Silver Meter

Big John Patton Quintet | The Organization! The Best Of Big John Patton | Blue Note | 830728-2
John Patton Quintet | Along Came John | Blue Note | 0675614
Scott Joplin | Piano Rags-Vol. 2 | Jazz Anthology | JA 5137

The Singing Song

The New Stan Getz Quartet | Getz Au Go Go | CTI Records | PDCTI 1124-2

The Single Petal Of A Rose-

Ralph Schweizer Big Band | DAY Dream | Chaos | CACD 8177
Johnny 'Hammond' Smith Sextet | The Soulful Blues | Prestige | PCD 24244-2

The Sin-In

Michael Mantler Group | The Hapless Child | Watt | 4

The Sinking Spell

Michael Mantler Sextet | More Movies | Watt | 10 (2313110)
Bruce Turner Quartet | The Dirty Bopper | Calligraph | CLG LP 003 IMS

The Sinner

Tim Ries Septet | Alternate Side | Criss Cross | Criss 1199

The Sinner's March

John Bergamo | On The Edge | CMP Records | CMP CD 27

The Sit-In

Allan Holdsworth Group | The Sixteen Man Of Tain | Cream Records | CR 610-2

The Sixteen Men Of Tain

David Murray Quartet | Shakill's II | DIW | DIW 884 CD

The Sixth Sense

Trine-Lise Vaering With The Bobo Stenson Trio And Guests | When I Close My Eyes | Stunt Records | STUCD 19602
Joey DeFrancesco-Jimmy Smith Quartet | Incredible! | Concord | CCD 4890

The Skunk(alt.master)

Chick Corea And His Orchestra | My Spanish Heart | Polydor | 543303-3

The Sky

Blueprint Stage | Puzzle | Mons Records | MR 874817

The Sky Bird That Flies Away

Glenn Miller And His Orchestra | Glenn Miller:The Complete Studio Recordings Vol.2:In The Mood | Memo Music | HDJ 4115

The Sky Fell Down

Vienna Art Orchestra | Vienna Art Orchestra Plays For Jean Cocteau | Amadeo | 529290-2

The Sleeper

Duke Ellington And His Orchestra | Latin America Suite | Original Jazz Classics | OJC20 469-2

The Sleeping Lady And The Giant Who Watches Over Her

Nicholas Payton Quintet | From This Moment... | Verve | 527073-2

The Sleeve Job

Chick Corea Group | Tap Step | Stretch Records | SCD 9006-2

The Slider

Count Basie And His Orchestra | Masters Of Jazz Vol.5 | RCA | NL 89530 DP

The Slur

Planet Blow | Alien Lunatic | Jazz Haus Musik | JHM 0071 CD
Yusef Lateef Quartet | The Golden Flute | MCA | AS 9125

The Smart Set

Das Pferd | The World Of 'Das Pferd' | ITM Records | ITM 1488

The Smile Of Menja

Kenny Drew | It Might As Well Be Spring | Soul Note | SN 1040

The Smiling Hour

Sarah Vaughan With Band | Copacabana | Pablo | 2312125

The Snake

George Young Orchestra | Chant | Electric Bird | K32Y 6033
Rob Bargad Sextet | Better Times | Criss Cross | Criss 1086

The Snake's Dance

Clark Terry Quintet | Having Fun | Delos | DE 4021(882677)

The Snapper

Chico Hamilton | Dancing To A Different Drummer | Soul Note | 121291-2

The Snooper

Kölner Saxophon Mafia | Licence To Thrill | Jazz Haus Musik | JHM 0100 CD
Yusef Lateef Quartet | Yusef's Bag | Prestige | P 24105

The Soccerball

Frank Minion With The Tommy Flanagan Quartet | The Soft Land Of Make Believe | Fresh Sound Records | FSR 2013(Bethlehem BCP 6052)

The Song I Used To Play

Al Cohn And His Orchestra | The Jazz Workshop:Four Brass One Tenor | RCA | PM 45164

The Song Is Ended

Ella Fitzgerald With Paul Weston And His Orchestra | The Complete Ella Fitzgerald Song Books of Harold Arlen, Irving Berlin, Duke Ellington, George & Ira Gershwin, Jerome Kern, Johnny Mercer, Cole Porter And Rogers & Hart | Verve | 519832-2
Oscar Peterson Trio | The Song Is You-The Best Of The Verve Songbooks | Verve | 531558-2
Papa Bue's Viking Jazzband | In The Mood | Timeless | TTD 539
Roy Eldridge Quintet | Roy Eldridge 'Little Jazz'-The Best Of The Verve Years | Verve | 523338-2

The Song Is Love

John Purcell Orchestra | Naturally | Novus | 4163151-2

The Song Is You

Anthony Braxton Duo | Trio And Duet | Sackville | 3007
Art Van Damme Group | State Of Art | MPS | 841413-2
Art Van Damme Quintet | Keep Going/Blue World | MPS | 529093-2
Attila Zoller-Lee Konitz | When It's Time | Enja | ENJ-9031 2
Barrett Deems Big Band | Groovin' Hard | Delmark | DE 505
Cannonball Adderley And His Orchestra | Verve Jazz Masters 31:Cannonball Adderley | Verve | 522651-2
Cannonball Adderley Group | Julian 'Cannonball' Adderley | EmArCy | 830381-2
Charlie Mariano With The Don Sebesky Orchestra | A Jazz Portrait Of Charlie Mariano | Fresh Sound Records | FSR-CD 0176
Charlie Parker Quartet | Charlie Parker:The Best Of The Verve Years | Verve | 527815-2
Charlie Parker | Verve | 539757-2
Charlie Parker:Bird's Best Bop On Verve | Verve | 527452-2
Birdland All Stars At Carnegie Hall | Roulette | CDP 798660-2
Chet Baker Quintet | Peace | Enja | ENJ-4016 2
Chet Baker With String-Orchestra And Voices | Chet Baker With Fifty Italian Strings | Original Jazz Classics | OJC20 492-2(JLP 921)
Chuck Wayne Trio | Morning Mist | Original Jazz Classics | OJCCD 1097-2(P-7367)
Claude Williamson Trio | Live! At The Jazz Bakery | Fresh Sound Records | FSR-CD 5014
Count Basie And His Orchestra | En Concert Avec Europe 1 | Laserlight | 710411/12
Eddie Miller And His Orchestra | The Uncollected:Eddie Miller | Hindsight | HSR 225 (835033)
Fred Hersch | Maybeck Recital Hall Series Volume Thirty-One | Concord | CCD 4596
Gene Harris Quartet | Black And Blue | Concord | CCD 4482
Helmut Nieberle & Cordes Sauvages | Salut To Django | Jardis Records | JRCD 9926
Herb Steward Quintet | One Brother | Mobile Fidelity | MFCD 884
Howard Rumsey's Lighthouse All-Stars | Howard Rumsey's Lighthouse All Stars Vol.3 | Original Jazz Classics | OJCCD 266-2(C 3508)
Jimmy Giuffre 3 | Atlantic Jazz: West Coast | Atlantic | 7567-81703-2
Joe Pass | Joe Pass:A Man And His Guitar | Original Jazz Classics | OJCCD 8806-2
Joe Pass Quartet | Live At Yoshi's | Pablo | 2310951-2
Jutta Hipp Quintet | Deutsches Jazz Fesival 1954/1955 | Bear Family Records | BCD 15430
Keith Jarrett Trio | Still Live | ECM | 1360/61(835008-2
LaVerne Butler With Band | No Looking Back | Chesky | JD 91
Lee Konitz-Jimmy Giuffre Octet | Lee Konitz Meets Jimmy Giuffre | Verve | 2304381 IMS
Mark Nightingale With The RIAS Big Band | Destiny | Mons Records | MR 874793
Paul Bollenback Quintet | Original Visions | Challenge | CHR 70022
Rob Mullins Quartet | Jazz Jazz | Nova | NOVA 8918-2
Sonny Rollins And The Contemporary Leaders | Contemporary Sonny Rollins-Alternate Takes | Contemporary | C 7651
Stan Getz Quartet | Stan Getz/Zoot Sims | LRC Records | CDC 9041
Stan Getz Quintet | Stan Getz-The Complete Roost Sessions | EMI Records | 859622-2
Jazz At Storyville Vol.1 | Fresh Sound Records | FSR 629(Roost RLP 407)
Terry Gibbs Dream Band | Terry Gibbs Dream Band Vol.2:The Sundown Sessions | Contemporary | CCD 7652-2
The Tenor Triangle & The Melvin Rhyne Trio | Aztec Blues | Criss Cross | Criss 1143
Tommy Dorsey And His Orchestra | The Post-War Era | Bluebird | 63 66156-2
Frank Sinatra And The Tommy Dorsey Orchestra | RCA | 2668701-2
Tommy Dorsey In Concert | RCA | NL 89780 DP

The Song Is You(alt.take)

Lee Konitz | Lee Konitz 'Self Portrait'(In Celebration Of Lee Konitz' 70th Birthday) | Philology | W 121.2

The Song My Lady Sings

Freddie Hubbard All Stars | MMTC(Monk,Miles,Trane And Cannon) | Musicmasters | 65132-2

The Song Of Autmn

Jenny Evans And Her Quintet | Shiny Stockings | ESM Records | ESM 9305

The Song Of Autumn

Stephan Micus | Behind Eleven Deserts | Intuition Records | INT 2042-2

The Song Of Danijar

Sadao Watanabe Sextet | Bossa Nova Concert | Denon Compact Disc | DC-8556

The Song Of Rosebuds

Ernie Krivda Quintet | Satanic | Inner City | IC 1031 IMS

The Song You Sing

The Robert Hohner Percussion Ensemble | Different Strokes | dmp Digital Music Productions | CD 485

The Sons

Eckinger/Manning Quintet | L.A. Calling | TCB Records | TCB 9090

The Soon-A Baby

Louis Jordan And His Tympany Five | Louis Jordan-Let The Good Times Roll: The Complete Decca Recordings 1938-1954 | Bear Family Records | BCD 15557 IH
Andy LaVerne | Jazz Piano Lineage | dmp Digital Music Productions | CD 463

The Sorcerer

Eye Of The Hurricane | Eye Of The Hurricane | Aho-Recording | AHO CD 1007(CD 662)
Herbie Hancock Sextet | Herbie Hancock:The Complete Blue Note Sixties Sessions | Blue Note | 495569-2
Larry Coryell Quartet | Shining Hour | 32 Jazz | 32112
Miles Davis Quintet | Miles Davis Quintet 1965-1968 | CBS | C6K 67398
Wallace Roney Quintet | Endless Miles:A Tribute To Miles Davis | N2K | 43082

The Soul And Its Expression:

Horace Silver Ensemble | Silver 'N Strings Play The Music Of The Spheres | Blue Note | LWB 1033

The Soul And The Atma

Charles Kynard Sextet | The Soul Brotherhood | Prestige | PCD 24257-2

The Soul Brotherhood

Illinois Jacquet And His Orchestra | The Soul Explosion | Original Jazz Classics | OJCCD 674-2(P 7629)

The Soulful Blues

The Houdini's | Headlines-The Houdini's In New York | Timeless | CD SJP 382

The Soulful One

Friedemann Graef Group | Orlando Fragments | Nabel Records:Jazz Network | CD 4681

The Soulful Turnaround Of Giovanni Sebastiano B.

Horace Silver Ensemble | Silver 'N Strings Play The Music Of The Spheres | Blue Note | LWB 1033

The Soundville Syndrome(part 1-3)

Chris Potter Quartet | Gratitude | Verve | 549433-2

The Source

Michele Rosewoman And Quintessence | Contrast High | Enja | ENJ-5091 2

The Southern Stomps

King Oliver's Jazz Band | Louis Armstrong With King Oliver Vol.1 | Village(Jazz Archive) | VILCD 003-2

The Space Of The Bass

Bobby Timmons Trio | Quartet And Orchestra | Milestone | MCD 47091-2

The Spanish Count

Jasper Van't Hof Quintet | Eyeball | CMP Records | CMP 11

The Spell

Vassilis Tsabropoulos Trio | Achirana | ECM | 1728(157462-2)
Vincent Chancey Quartet | Welcome Mr. Chancey | IN+OUT Records | 7020-1
The Dorsey Brothers Orchestra | The Dorsey Brothers' Orchestra Vol.2 | Jazz Oracle | BDW 8005

The Sphinx

Dave Stryker Quartet | Full Moon | Steeplechase | SCCD 31345
Rabih Abou-Khalil Group | Odd Times | Enja | ENJ-9330 2

The Sphinx And I

Bob Hall | No.29 | BELL Records | BLR 84038

The Spider

Fats Waller And His Rhythm | The Indispensable Fats Waller Vol.7/8(1938-1940) | RCA | 2126417-2

The Spider And The Fly

The Middle Years Part 2(1938-40) | RCA | 6366552-2

The Spin

Charlie Hunter-Leon Parker | Duo | Blue Note | 499187-2

The Spin Seekers

Chick Corea & Origin | Change | Stretch Records | SCD 9023-2

The Spinning Song

Herbie Nichols Trio | Herbie Nichols Trio Vol.2 | Blue Note | 300198

The Spinning Song(alt.take)

Enrico Rava-Ran Blake | Duo En Noir | Between The Lines | btl 004(Efa 10174-2)

The Spiral Staircase

Chico Freeman Group | The Emissary | Clarity Recordings | CCD-1015

The Spirit Is Willing

Glenn Miller And His Orchestra | Glenn Miller And His Orchestra-Swinging Instrumentals | Bluebird | 63 66529-2

The Spirit Lives On

Wollie Kaiser Timeghost | Post Art Core | Jazz Haus Musik | JHM 0077 CD

The Spirit Of Life

Horace Silver Ensemble | Silver 'N Percussion | Blue Note | 300216

The Spirit Wheel

Plas Johnson Band | The Warm Sound Of Plas Johnson Tenor Sax Vol.2:The Madison Avenue Strut | Blue Moon | BMCD 3061

The Sports Page

Last Exit | Live At Knitting Factory Vol.4 | Enemy | EMCD 118(03518)

The Squirrel

Dizzy Gillespie And His Orchestra | Good Bait | Spotlite | SPJ 122
Kenny Clarke Quartet | Americans Swinging In Paris:Kenny Clarke | EMI Records | 539652-2
Jazz In Paris:Kenny Clarke Sextet Plays André Hodair | EmArCy | 834542-2 PMS
Lars Gullin With The Wade Legge Trio | Lars Gullin 1953,Vol.2:Moden Sounds | Dragon | DRCD 234
Lou Donaldson Quintet | Midnight Sun | Blue Note | LT 1028 (GXK 8173)
Tadd Dameron-Fats Navarro Quintet | Live At The Birdland | Jazz Anthology | JA 5176
Tadd Dameron-Fats Navarro Sextet | Fats Navarro/Tadd Dameron:Complete Blue Note & Capitol Sessions | Definitive Records | DRCD 11191

The Squirrel(alt.master)

Fats Navarro/Tadd Dameron:Complete Blue Note & Capitol Sessions | Definitive Records | DRCD 11191

The St.Vitus Dance

Ran Blake Trio | Horace Is Blue:A Silver Noir | HatOLOGY | 550

The Star Spangled Banner

Duke Ellington And His Orchestra | Duke Ellingotn:Complete Prestige Carnegie Hall 1943-1944 Concerts | Definitive Records | DRCD 11210
Sir Roland Hanna | Plays The Music Of Alec Wilder | EmArCy | 558839-2

The Star-Crossed Lovers

Duke Ellington And His Orchestra | Such Sweet Thunder | CBS | CK 65568
Ella Fitzgerald And Duke Ellington:Cote D'Azure Concerts on Verve | Verve | 539033-2
Ella Fitzgerald And Duke Ellington:Cote D'Azure Concerts on Verve | Verve | 539033-2
Ella Fitzgerald And Duke Ellington:Cote D'Azure Concerts on Verve | Verve | 539033-2
Ella Fitzgerald And Duke Ellington:Cote D'Azure Concerts on Verve | Verve | 539033-2
Ed Bickert-Lorne Lofsky Quartet | This Is New | Concord | CCD 4414
Fred Hersch Trio | Horizons | Concord | CJ 267
Lorne Lofsky Trio | The Concord Jazz Guitar Collection Volume 3 | Concord | CCD 4507

The Star-Crossed Lovers-

Duke Ellington And His Orchestra | Such Sweet Thunder | CBS | CK 65568

The Star-Crossed Lovers(stereo-LP-master)

Sorgen/Rust/Windbiel Trio | Outlet | ESP Disk | ESP 3029-2

The Stevedor's Serenade

Duke Ellington And His Famous Orchestra | The Complete Duke Ellington-Vol.11 | CBS | CBS 88242

The Stinger

Stanley Cowell Ensemble | Talkin' 'Bout Love | Galaxy | GXY 5111

The Stopper

Sonny Rollins With The Modern Jazz Quartet | Milt Jackson Birthday Celebration | Fantasy | FANCD 6079-2
Welcome To Jazz: Sonny Rollins | Koch Records | 322 079 D1
Sonny Rollins With The Modern Jazz Quintet | Vintage Sessions | Prestige | P 24096

The Story

The Jimmy Giuffre 3 | 7 Pieces | Verve | 2304438 IMS

The Storyteller

Christian Elsässer Trio | Future Days | Organic Music | ORGM 9721

The Story-Teller

J.M. Rhythm Four plus One | Lazy Afternoon | TCB Records | TCB 20802

The Stream Is Stony

Westbrook & Company | Platterback | PAO Records | PAO 10530

The Streets

Steve Coleman And Five Elements | Steve Coleman's Music Live In Paris | Novus | 2131691-2

The Stride

Abdullah Ibrahim Trio | African Magic | TipToe | TIP-888845 2
Abdullah Ibrahim-Carlos Ward Duo | Live At Sweet Basil Vol.1 | Black-Hawk | BKH 50204

The String

Stan Getz With The Eddie Sauter Orchestra | Stan Getz Plays The Music Of Mickey One | Verve | 531232-2

The Stripper-

Al Casey's Swingin' Blues Band | Al Casey Remembers King Curtis | JSP Records | 1095

The Strollers

Stan Kenton And His Orchestra | Plays Bob Graettinger:City Of Glass | Capitol | 832084-2

The Struggle Of The Turtle To The Sea(part 1-3)

John Tchicai Quartet | Timo's Message | Black Saint | 120094-2

The Stuffed Monk

Ronnie Earl & The Broadcasters | Blues And Forgiveness | Crosscut | CCD 11042

The Subtle Sermon

Duke Ellington And His Orchestra | Duke Ellington:Complete Studio Transcriptions | Definitive Records | DRCD 11199

The Succuba

Michael Cain-Ralph Alessi-Peter Epstein | Circa | ECM | 1622

The Suchness Of Dory Philpott

Giancarlo Nicolai Trio | The Giancarlo Nicolai Trio | LEO | LR 134

The Summer '95

Ali Ryerson Quartet | Portrait In Silver | Concord | CCD 4638

The Summer Knows

Joe Diorio/Ira Sullivan | The Breeze And I | RAM Records | RMCD 4508

The Summer Knows-

Sue Raney-Dick Shreve | Autumn In The Air | Fresh Sound Records | FSR-CD 5017

The Summit

Art Blakey And The Jazz Messengers | Art Blakey & The Jazz Messengers: Olympia, May 13th, 1961 | Laserlight | 36128
Live In Stockholm 1959 | DIW | DIW 313 CD

The Sun

Alice Coltrane Trio | Cosmic Music | MCA | AS 9148

The Sun Died

Marcus Miller Group | The Sun Don't Lie | Dreyfus Jazz Line | FDM 36560-2

The Sun Don't Lie

Georgia Carr With The Nelson Riddle Orchestra | Softly Baby | Pathe | 1566241(Capitol)

The Sun Goes Down

Sid Lipton And His Orchestra | The Classic Years In Digital Stereo: Dance Bands U.K. | CDS Records Ltd. | RPCD 303(CD 681)

The Sun In Montreal
Eye Of The Hurricane | Eye Of The Hurricane | Aho-Recording | AHO CD 1007(CD 662)

The Sunflower
Paul Motian Trio | Le Voyage | ECM | 1138
You Took The Words Right Out Of My Heart | JMT Edition | 514028-2
The Mahavishnu Orchestra | Between Nothingness & Eternity | CBS | CK 32766

The Sunlit Path-
Friedemann Graef Group | Orlando Fragments | Nabel Records:Jazz Network | CD 4681

The Sunny Jingle Of The Camino De Cadaques
Dennis Gonzales And The Dallas-London Quartet | Catechism(The Name We Are Knows By) | Music & Arts | CD 913

The Sunset Bell
Lilian Terry With The Dizzy Gillespie Quartet | Oo-Shoo-Be-Doo-Be...Oo,Oo ...Oo,Oo | Soul Note | SN 1147

The Sunshine Of Love
Bud Freeman Trio | The Joy Of Sax | Chiaroscuro | CR 135

The Surrey With The Fringe On Top
Beverly Kenney With The Johnny Smith Quartet | Sings For Johnny Smith | Fresh Sound Records | FSR-CD 79(882164)
Blossom Dearie Trio | April In Paris | Fresh Sound Records | FSR 555(Barclay 74017)
Cannonball Adderley With Richard Hayman's Orchestra | Julian Cannonball Adderley And Strings/Jump For Joy | Verve | 528699-2
Sphere | Sphere | Verve | 557796-2
The Jay And Kai Trombone Octet | Jay & Kai + 6 | CBS | 480990-2
Wynton Kelly-George Coleman Quartet | Live In Baltimore | Affinity | AFF 108

The Survivor
Gary Burton Quartet With Orchestra | A Genuine Tong Funeral(Dark Opera Without Words) | RCA | 2119255-2

The Survivors-
A Genuine Tong Funeral(Dark Opera Without Words) | RCA | 2119255-2
Billy Pierce Quartet | Rio-Ballads & Bossa Novas | Sunnyside | SSC 1065 D

The Survivors' Suite: Beginning
Keith Jarrett Quartet | The Survivor's Suite | ECM | 1085(827131-2)

The Survivors' Suite: Conclusion
Jerry Granelli UFB | News From The Street | VeraBra Records | CDVBR 2146-2

The Swamp
Willie 'The Lion' Smith And His Cubs | Willie The Lion Smith And His Cubs | Timeless | CBC 1-012

The Swarm
George Benson With The Jack McDuff Quartet | The New Boss Guitar | Original Jazz Classics | OJCCD 461-2

The Sweet Alice Blues
Kim Pensyl | Pensyl Sketches Collection | GRP | GRP 97702

The Sweet Smell Of Success
European Music Orchestra | Guest | Soul Note | 121299-2

The Sweetest Girl I've Ever Known
Art Pepper-George Cables Duo | Art Pepper:The Complete Galaxy Recordings | Galaxy | 16GCD 1016-2

The Sweetest Sounds
Goin' Home | Original Jazz Classics | GXY 5143
J.J.Johnson's All Stars | J.J.'s Broadway | Verve | 9860308
Lester Lanin And His Orchestra | The Uncollected:Lester Lanin | Hindsight | HSR 210

The Sweetheart Of Sigma Chi
Shorty Rogers And His Giants | The Big Shorty Rogers Express | RCA | 2118519-2

The Sweetheart Of Sigmund Freud
Celestin's Original Tuxedo Jazz Orchestra | New Orleans Classics:Papa Celestin And Sam Morgan | AZURE Compact Disc | AZ-CD-12

The Swinger
Duke Ellington And His Orchestra | Duke 56/62 Vol.2 | CBS | 88654

The Swinging Door
Jon Hendricks & Company | Love | Muse | MCD 5258

The Swinging Preacher
Kenny Burrell Quintet | Kenny Burrell-Bluesin' Around | CBS | FC 38507

The Sword-Swallower
Richard Zimmerman | The Complete Works Of Scott Joplin | Laserlight | 15945

The Syndicate-
John Lee Hooker | Half A Stranger | Mainstream | MD CDO 903

The Tadd Walk
Thomas Hass Group | A Honeymoon Too Soon | Stunt Records | STUCD 19601

The Tag In Bb
The New Roman Schwaller Jazzquartet | Welcome Back From Outer Space | JHM Records | JHM 3605

The Tag In F
Chris Potter Quintet | Presenting Chriss Potter | Criss Cross | Criss 1067

The Tall Tears Trees
Sandole Brothers | The Sandole Brothers | Fantasy | FCD 24763-2

The Tamaret
Del Ferro/Overwater/Paeffgen | Evening Train | Acoustic Music Records | 319.1063.2

The Teaser
Count Basie And His Orchestra | Birdland All Stars At Carnegie Hall | Roulette | CDP 798660-2

The Telecasters
Ana Caram Group | Blue Bossa | Chesky | JD 219

The Telephone Song
The New Stan Getz Quintet Feat. Astrud Gilberto | Getz Au Go Go | CTI Records | PDCTI 1124-2

The Temple Of Isfahan
Kenny Burrell Quartet | The Tender Gender | Chess | 515001

The Tender Trap
Stacey Kent And Her Quintet | The Tender Trap | Candid | CCD 79751
Mose Allison Sextet | Middle Class White Boy | Discovery | 71011-2

The Terrible Doubt-
Marty Ehrlich/Anthony Cox | Falling Man | Muse | MCD 5398

The Thang
Roy Hargrove Quintet | The Vibe | Novus | PD 90668

The Theme
Art Blakey And The Jazz Messengers | Straight Ahead | Concord | CCD 4168
At The Jazz Corner Of The World | Blue Note | 828888-2
Meet You At The Jazz Corner Of The World | Blue Note | 535565-2
Meet You At The Jazz Corner Of The World | Blue Note | 535565-2
Ben Webster Quartet | Stormy Weather | Black Lion | BLP 60108
Horace Silver Quintet | Doin' The Thing - The Horace Silver Quintet At The Village Gate | Blue Note | 300414
Joe Gordon Quintet | Blakey | Verve | 538634-2
Miles Davis New Quintet | Workin' With The Miles Davis Qoartet | Original Jazz Classics | OJC 296(P 7166)
Miles Davis Quintet | Live In Stockholm | Dragon | DRCD 228
En Concert Avec Europe 1 | Laserlight | 710455/58
Miles Davis In Stockholm Complete | Dragon | DRCD 228
Paul Bley Trio | Introducing Paul Bley | Original Jazz Classics | OJCCD 201-2(DEB 7)
My Standard | Steeplechase | SCCD 31214

The Theme-
Miles Davis Group | Live At The Fillmore East | CBS | C2K 65139
Live At The Fillmore East | CBS | C2K 65139
Miles Davis Quintet | The Complete Copenhagen Concert 1964 | Magnetic Records | MRCD 117
Lee Morgan-Clifford Jordan Quintet | Live In Baltimore 1968 | Fresh Sound Records | FSCD 1037

The Theme Of The Defeat
Miles Davis New Quintet | Workin',Steamin',Cookin',Relaxin' With The Miles Davis Quintet | Original Jazz Classics | OJCCD 8805-2

The Theme(alt.take)
Workin' With The Miles Davis Quartet | Original Jazz Classics | OJC 296(P 7166)
Three Of A Kind | Drip Some Grease | Minor Music | 801056

The Theory Of Monkness
The Waltzer-McHenry Quartet | Jazz Is Where You Find It | Fresh Sound Records | FSNT 021 CD

The Thick Plottens
Mike Westbrook Orchestra | Westbrook-Rossini | Hat Art | CD 6002

The Thing That Came Out Of The Swamp
Blue Mitchell Quintet | The Thing To Do | Blue Note | 784178-2

The Things I Leave Behind-
Blue Barron And His Orchestra | The Uncollected: Blue Barron | Hindsight | HSR 110

The Things I Love
Memphis Slim | So Long | America | AM 6130

The Things I Want I Can't Get At Home
Junior Wells Blues Band | Mesing With The Kid | Charly | CRB 1133

The Things We Did Last Summer
Bennie Green And His Band | Walkin' Down | Original Jazz Classics | OJCCD 1752-2
Buddy DeFranco Quartet | Jazz Tones | Verve | MV 2610 IMS
Lucie Arnaz And Her Orchestra | Just In Time | Concord | CCD 4573
Oscar Peterson Trio | Romance-The Vocal Style Of Oscar Peterson | Verve | POCJ 1911 PMS
Richie Kamuca Octet | Jazz Erotica | Fresh Sound Records | FSR-CD 500(881696)
Gene DiNovi Trio | Live At The Montreal Bistro | Candid | CCD 79726

The Things We Did Last Summer-
Michael Feinstein With Jule Styne | Michael Feinstein Sings The Jule Styne Songbook | Nonesuch | 7559-79274-2

The Things We Love
Tex Allen Quintet | Late Night | Muse | MCD 5492

The Third Day
Don Menza Sextet | Hip Pocket | Palo Alto | PA 8010

The Third Night
Johnny King Septet | The Meltdown | Enja | ENJ-9329 2

The Third Rail
Spies & Guests | By The Way Of The World | Telarc Digital | CD 83305

The Third Stone From The Sun-
Jaco Pastorius Trio | Heavy'n Jazz | Jazzpoint | JP 1036 CD
Jiggs Whigham With The WDR Big Band | The Third Stone | Koala Records | CD P 4

The Third Time Is A Charm
D-Code | D-Code And Introducing Ben Herman | Timeless | CD SJP 359

The Third World
Herbie Nichols Trio | Herbie Nichols:The Complete Blue Note Recordings | Blue Note | 859352-2

The Third World(alt.take)
Leo Smith Group | Procession Of The Great Ancestry | Chief Records | CD 6

The Three Day Thang
Yusef Lateef Quartet | Blues For The Orient | Prestige | P 24035

The Three Faces Of Balal
Julian Argüelles-Steve Argüelles | Scapes | Babel | BDV 9614

The Three Madonnas
Andy Summers Trio | The Last Dance Of Mr.X | RCA | 2668937-2

The Three Minors
Jam Session | Jam Session Vol.10 | Steeplechase | SCCD 31555

The Three Muscateers
Randy Weston Septet | Saga | Verve | 529237-2

The Three Trumpeters
Cindy Blackman-Carlton Holmes | Works On Canvas | HighNote Records | HCD 7038

The Thrill Is Gone
Atli Bjorn Trio | Cry Me A River | Steeplechase | SCCD 36004
B.B.King With The Philip Morris Super Band | Live At The Apollo | MCA | MCA 09637
Charlie Mariano Sextet | Nat Pierce-Dick Collins Nonet/Charlie Mariano Sextet | Original Jazz Classics | OJC 118(F 3224)
Chet Baker Quartet | Chet Baker Sings | Pacific Jazz | 300067(PJ 1222)
Jazz Fresh | Jazz Fresh | GGG-Verlag:GGG Verlag und Mailorder | CD 01.03
Jeanie Lambe And The Danny Moss Quartet | The Blue Noise Session | Nagel-Heyer | CD 052
Jimmy Rowles-Red Mitchell Quartet | The Jimmy Rowles/Red Mitchell Trio | Contemporary | C 14016
Patti Page With Pete Rugolo And HisOrchestra | Patti Page In The Land Of Hi-Fi | Verve | 538320-2
Ron Ringwood's Crosscut Bluesband | Earth Tones | Organic Music | ORGM 9722
Roni Ben-Hur With The Barry Harris Trio | Backyard | TCB Records | TCB 95902
Sheila Jordan/Harvie Swartz | Old Time Feeling | Muse | MCD 5366

The Thrill Is Gone(Medley)
Steve Rochinski Quartet | Otherwise | Jardis Records | JRCD 20133

The Thrill Of It All
Lee Konitz-Hein Van De Geyn | Hein Van De Geyn Meets Lee Konitz | September | CD 5110

The Thumb
Joshua Breakstone Quintet | Evening Star | Contemporary | CCD 14040-2
Wes Montgomery Quartet | Tequila | Verve | 547769-2
Compact Jazz: Wes Montgomery Plays The Blues | Verve | 835318-2 PMS
Wes Montgomery Quintet With The Claus Ogerman Orchestra | Tequila | CTI Records | PDCTI 1118-2

The Tide Is In
Phil Upchurch Group | Whatever Happened To The Blues | VeraBra Records | CDVBR 2066-2

The Tiger And The Lamb
Clarinet Jazz Trio | Live At Birdland Neuburg | Birdland | BN 003

The Tiger Trap
Brad Dutz | Brad Dutz | Nine Winds Records | NWCD 0141

The Time Of The Barracudas
Miles Davis With Gil Evans & His Orchestra | Quiet Nights | CBS | CK 65293
Billy Gault Quintet | When Destiny Calls | Steeplechase | SCCD 31027

The Timeless Space
Joshua Redman Quartet | Timeless Tales | Warner | 9362-47052-2

The Times They Are A-Changin'
Lirico | Sussurro | Jazz Haus Musik | JHM 0129 CD
Tim Berne Quartet | Mutant Variations | Soul Note | 121091-2

The Token
Dee Dee Bridgewater With Her Quintet | Love And Peace-A Tribute To Horace Silver | Verve | 527470-2

The Tokyo Blues
Horace Silver Quintet | Paris Blues | Pablo | PACD 5316-2
Horace Silver Retrospective | Blue Note | 495576-2
The Tokyo Blues | Blue Note | 853355-2
Rickey Woodard Quartet | The Tokyo Express | Candid | CCD 79527

The Tonica
Rod Piazza & The Mighty Flyers | Blues In The Dark | Black Top | BT 1062 CD

The Touch
Trio Ivoire | Trio Ivoire | Enja | ENJ-9424 2

The Touch Of Your Hand
Sarah Vaughan With Hal Mooney's Orchestra | Sarah Vaughan Sings Broadway:Grat Songs From Hit Shows | Verve | 526464-2

The Touch Of Your Hands
Ack Van Rooyen And The Metropole Orchestra | Colores | Koala Records | CD P 21

The Touch Of Your Lips
Ben Webster With The Oscar Peterson Trio | Compact Jazz: Oscar Peterson & Friends | Verve | 835315-2
Bill Evans | The Complete Fantasy Recordings | Fantasy | 9FCD 1012-2
The Complete Fantasy Recordings | Fantasy | 9FCD 1012-2
Bill Evans Trio | The Complete Bill Evans On Verve | Verve | 527953-2
The Complete Bill Evans On Verve | Verve | 527953-2
At The Montreux Jazz Festival | Verve | 539758-2
Bill Evans Trio:The Last Waltz | Milestone | 8MCD 4430-2
The Best Of Bill Evans Live | Verve | 533825-2
Cal Collins Trio | Cincinnati To L.A. | Concord | CJ 59
Chet Baker Quartet | Chet Baker-The Legacy Vol.4:Oh You Crazy Moon | Enja | ENJ-9453 2
Conception | Circle Records | RK 32-27680/32 IMS
Compact Jazz: Chet Baker | Verve | 840632-2 PMS
Clare Fischer And The Brunner-Schwer Steinway | Alone Together | MPS | 68178
Doug Raney Quartet | Back In New York | Steeplechase | SCCD 31409
George Masso Quintet | Just For A Thrill | Sackville | SKCD2-2022
Howard Alden-George Van Eps Quartet | 13 Strings | Concord | CCD 4464
Knud Jorgensen-Bengt Hanson-Gustavo Bergalli | Day Dream | Touché Music | TMcCD 003
Lee Konitz-Harold Danko Duo | Once Upon A Live | Accord | 500162
Ray Walker-John Pisano | Affinity | Jardis Records | JRCD 20032
Rob McConnell And The Boss Brass | Overtime | Concord | CCD 4618
Tom Harrell Quintet | Open Air | Steeplechase | SCCD 31220
Tony Bennett-Bill Evans | The Tony Bennett-Bill Evans Album | Original Jazz Classics | OJC20 439-2(F 9489)
Warren Vaché Trio | Live at The Vineyard | Challenge | CHR 70028

The Tower-
Eric Alexander Quintet | The First Milestone | Milestone | MCD 9302-2

The Towering Inferno
Cool Blue | House In The Country | Foolish Music | FM 211591

The Town And Country Suite:
Richie Beirach & Andy LaVerne | Universal Mind | Steeplechase | SCCD 31325

The Tractor
Karl Denson Group | Herbal Turkey Breast | Minor Music | 801032

The Train And The River
Jimmy Giuffre 3 | The Jimmy Giuffre 3-Hollywood & Newport 1957-1958 | Fresh Sound Records | FSCD 1026
Jimmy Giuffre Trio | Jimmy Giuffre Trios Live | Raretone | 5013 FC

The Train Blues
Chicago's Young Blues Generation | American Folk Blues Festival '82 | L+R Records | LR 50001

The Train I Ride
Fred McDowell | Mississippi Blues | Black Lion | BLCD 760179

The Traitor
Booker Ervin Quartet | Settin' The Pace | Prestige | PCD 24123-2(P 7455/7462)

The Tranquilizer Suite Part 2:Slow Down
A Band Of Friends | Roots & Fruits | EmArCy | 537495-2

The Trans-Love Express
Kölner Saxophon Mafia | Licence To Thrill | Jazz Haus Musik | JHM 0100 CD

The Trap
Winard Harper Group | Trap Dancer | Savant Records | SCD 2013

The Traveller
Rene Toledo Group | The Dreamer | GRP | GRP 96772

The Travelling Suite:
Bob Belden Ensemble | Treasure Island | Sunnyside | SSC 1041 D

The Treasure Untold
James Hurt Group | Dark Grooves-Mystcal Rhythms | Blue Note | 495104-2

The Tree Of Live
Cecil Taylor | The Tree Of Life | FMP | CD 98

The Trial
We Three | East Coasting | Organic Music | ORGM 9702

The Triangle
Philly Joe Jones Septet | The Big Beat | Milestone | MCD 47016-2

The Tribe
Ornette Coleman Quartet | Beauty Is A Rare Thing:Ornette Coleman-The Complete Atlantic Recordings | Atlantic | 8122-71410-2

The Tribes Of New York
Guy Barker With The London Metropolitan Orchestra | What Love Is | EmArCy | 558331-2

The Trick Bag
Wes Montgomery Trio | Wes Montgomery-The Complete Riverside Recordings | Riverside | 12 RCD 4408-2
Wes Montgomery-The Complete Riverside Recordings | Riverside | 12 RCD 4408-2

The Trick Bag(alt.take)
Encores | Milestone | M 9110

The Trill Of Real Love
Art Pepper Quartet | The Trip | Original Jazz Classics | OJC 410(C 7638)

The Trip
In San Francisco | Fresh Sound Records | FSCD 1005
Art Pepper:The Complete Village Vanguard Sessions | Contemporary | 9CCD-4417-2
Duke Ellington And His Orchestra | Ella & Duke At The Cote D'Azur | Verve | 539030-2
Ella Fitzgerald And Duke Ellington:Cote D'Azure Concerts on Verve | Verve | 539033-2
Modern Jazz Quartet | MJQ 40 | Atlantic | 7567-82330-2
Plastic Dreams | Atlantic | AMCY 1099

The Trolley Song
Lou Levy Trio | My Old Flame | Fresh Sound Records | FSR-CD 312

The Trolley Song-
Mel Tormé With The Marty Paich Dek-Tette | Reunion | Concord | CCD 4360

The Trouble With Hello Is Good-Bye
Sue Raney With The Bob Florence Trio | Flight Of Fancy-A Journey Of Allan & Marilyn Bergman | Discovery | DSCD 931

The Trouble With Me Is You
Nat King Cole And His Trio | Nat King Cole:The Snader Telescriptions | Storyville | 4960103
Combo USA | Affinity | CD AFS 1002

The Trumpet Player
Louis Armstrong And His Orchestra | Louis Armstrong:Swing That Music | Laserlight | 36056

The Trumpet Player's Lament
Louis Armstrong With Luis Russell And His Orchestra | Louis Armstrong Vol.7-Satchmo's Discoveries | MCA | 1326

The Trumpeter In The Forest-
King Oliver And His Orchestra | Luis Russell And His Orchestra 1927-29 | Village(Jazz Archive) | VILCD 018-2

The Truth Is Unavailable
Louis Jordan And His Tympany Five | Louis Jordan-Let The Good Times Roll: The Complete Decca Recordings 1938-1954 | Bear Family Records | BCD 15557 IH

The Truth Of The Matter
Pat Metheny Group With Orchestra | Secret Story | Geffen Records | GED 24468

The Truth Will Always Be
Pili-Pili | Ballads Of Timbuktu | JA & RO | JARO 4240-2

The Tuareg's Desert(Tseng Tseng Can)
Ahmad Jamal Trio | Live In Paris 1992 | Dreyfus Jazz Line | FDM 37019-2

The Tube
Live In Paris 92 | Birdology | 849408-2

The Tunnel
Bob Mintzer Big Band | Urban Contours | dmp Digital Music Productions | CD 467

The Turnaround
John Patton Quartet | Let 'Em Roll | Blue Note | 789795-2

The Twelve Powers
Elmore James Band | One Way Out | Charly | CRB 1008

The Twiligth Clone
Eric Watson-John Lindberg | Soundpost: Works For Piano And Double Bass | Music & Arts | CD 920

The Twister
Gene Ammons And His All Stars | Jammin' In Hi Fi With Gene Ammons | Original Jazz Classics | OJCCD 129-2(P 7110)
The Twister(1)
Paul Williams Sextet | Paul Williams:The Complete Recordings Vol.1 (1947-1949) | Blue Moon | BMCD 6020
The Twitch
Quincy Jones And His Orchestra | The Quintessence | Impulse(MCA) | 951222-2
The Quintessential Charts | MCA | IA 9342/2
The Two Little Squirrels(Nuts To You)
Louis Jordan And His Tympany Five | Louis Jordan Vol.2: Knock Me Out | Swingtime(Contact) | ST 1012
The Two Lonely People
Bill Evans Trio | Bill Evans Trio In Buenos Aires Vol.1 | Jazz Lab | JLCD 1(889053)
Emilio Solla Y Afines | Folcolores | Fresh Sound Records | FSWJ 001
Kenny Drew Jr. | This One's For Bill | TCB Records | TCB 99352
Stefano Battaglia Trio | Bill Evans Compositions Vol.2 | SPLASC(H) Records | CD H 410-2
The Two Lonely People(aka The Man And The Woman)
Charles Maxfield Group | R&B Guitars 1950-1954 | Blue Moon | BMCD 6018
The Unbearable Lightness Of Beeing
Mahavishnu | Mahavishnu | Warner | 251351-1
The Underdog
Irene Kral With Alan Broadbent | Gentle Rain | Candid | CRS 1020 IMS
The Underdog Has Arisen
Dizzy Gillespie/Max Roach | Max+Dizzy | A&M Records | 396404-2
The Undertow
Rodney Jones Group | The Undiscoverd Few | Blue Note | 496902-2
The Unknown Warrior(Song For My Forefathers)
The Enja Band | The Enja Band-Live At Sweet Basil | Enja | ENJ-8034 2
The Unwelcome Morbidy Of Replicant Pris
Albert Mangelsdorff Trio | The Wild Point | MPS | 68071
The Up And Down Man
Jazz Gala Big Band With Guest Soloists | Jazz Special-Gala Concert | RCA | CL 30069 DP
The Urghins Of Shermese
Tony Williams Lifetime | Spectrum:The Anthology | Verve | 537075-2
The Uwis Suite:
Peggy Lee With Orchestra | The Basin Street Proudly Presents Peggy Lee | Capitol | 832744-2
The Vampire(Soubacha)
Shelly Manne And His Men | West Coast Jazz In England | Jazz Groove | JG 006 IMS
The Vamp's Blues
At The Blackhawk Vol.2 | Contemporary | C 7578
The Veil
Paul Plimley-Lisle Ellis | Both Sides Of The Same Mirror | Nine Winds Records | NWCD 0135
The Venture Of Living
James Newton Ensemble | Suite For Frida Kahlo | audioquest Music | AQCD 1023
The Verticale Circle
White Orange | White Orange | Caprice | CAP 1215
The Very Last Waltz
Jimmy Rowles Quartet | Fiorello-Uptown/Mary Sunshine-Downtown | Fresh Sound Records | FSR 587(Signature SM 6011)
The Very Thought
Al Bowlly With Monia Liter | On The Sentimental Side | Decca | DDV 5009/10
The Very Thought Of You
Art Farmer Quartet | Portrait Of Art Farmer | Contemporary | C 7554
Art Tatum | The Tatum Solo Masterpieces Vol.10 | Pablo | 2310862
Carl Ravazza And His Orchestra | The Uncollected: Carl Ravazza | Hindsight | HSR 117
Charlie Mariano Quartet | Swingin' With Mariano | Affinity | AFF 767
Dunstan Coulber Quartet | Standards For A New Century | Nagel-Heyer | CD 081
Earl Bostic And His Orchestra | For You | Sing | 503
Ella Fitzgerald With The Tommy Flanagan Quartet | Ella In London | Original Jazz Classics | OJCCD 974-2(2310711)
Everett Greene With The Houston Person Quartet | My Foolish Heart | Savant Records | SCD 2014
Helen Humes And Her All Stars | Swingin' With Helen | Original Jazz Classics | OJCCD 608-2
Jesse Belvin With Marty Paich And His Orchestra | Mr. Easy | Fresh Sound Records | ND 74402
Joe Pass | Joe Pass At The Montreux Jazz Festival 1975 | Original Jazz Classics | OJC20 934-2(2310752)
Joe Temperley Quartet With Strings | Easy To Remember | Hep | CD 2083
Johnny Hartman And His Orchestra | Unforgettable | Impulse(MCA) | IMP 11522
Johnny Hodges Orchestra | RCA Victor 80th Anniversary Vol.5:1960-1969 | RCA | 2668781-2
Lezlie Anders And Her Band | With Love,Lezlie | Celebrity | CYCD 74801
Maximilian Geller Quartet feat. Melanie Bong | Smile | Edition Collage | EC 461-2
Vocal Moments | Take Twelve On CD | TT 008-2
Nancy Wilson With Gerald Wilson's Orchestra | Yesterday's Love Songs-Today's Blues | Capitol | 796265-2
Red Nichols And His Five Pennies | Red Nichols And His Five Pennies | Laserlight | 15743
Terrie Richard With The Harry Allen Quartet | I Cried For You | Master Mix | CHECD 00107
Tommy Flanagan | Alone Too Long | Denon Compact Disc | DC-8572
André Previn Trio | Jazz At The Musikverein | Verve | 537704-2
The Very Thought Of You-
Ray Brown | The Very Tall Band | Telarc Digital | CD 83443
The View(From The House)
Ketil Bjornstad Group | Water Stories | ECM | 1503(519076-2)
The View(I)
Water Stories | ECM | 1503(519076-2)
The View(II)
Jack DeJohnette's Directions | Untitled | ECM | 1074
The Villa
Kenny Dorham Octet | Afro-Cuban | Blue Note | 746815-2
The Village Caller
Johnny Lytle Sextet | Everything Must Change | Muse | MR 5158
The Villain
Charles McPherson Quintet | The Quintet/Live! | Original Jazz Classics | OJCCD 1804-2(P 7480)
The Viper's Drag
United Women's Orchestra | Virgo Supercluster | Jazz Haus Musik | JHM 0123 CD
The Virgo Supercluster Suite:
Trio Ivoire | Trio Ivoire | Enja | ENJ-9424 2
The Vision
Gary Lucas/Walter Horn | Skeleton On The Feast | Enemy | EMCD 126(03526)
The Visit
Chris Potter Quartet | Gratitude | Verve | 549433-2
The Visitor
Arild Andersen Quartet | If You Look Far Enough | ECM | 1493(513902-2)
The Voice
Joanne Grauer Quintet With Lorraine Feather | Joanne Grauer Indtroducing Lorraine Feather | MPS | 68198
Triocolor | Colours Of Ghana | ACT | 9285-2
Dennis Gonzales And The Dallas-London Quartet | Catechism(The Name We Are Knows By) | Music & Arts | CD 913
The Voice Of Old Man River
Irene Scruggs | The Voice Of The Blues-Bottleneck Guitar Masterpieces | Yazoo | YAZ 1046
The Voodoo Music
Annabelle Wilson With The Jerry Granelli-Jane Ira Bloom Group | On Music | ITM-Pacific | ITMP 970071
The Voyager Returns
Chico Hamilton Quintet | That's Jazz Vol.20: Chico Hamilton | Warner | WB 56239
The Wailing Boat
Birdland Dream Band | Birdland Dream Band | RCA | 2663873-2
Maynard Ferguson With The Birdland Dreamband | The Birdland Dream Band Vol.1 | Fresh Sound Records | 58110 CD(RCA)
The Waiting
Jimmy Giuffre Trio | Night Dance | Choice | CHCD 71001
The Jimmy Giuffre 3 | Music For People,Birds,Butterflies & Mosquitoes | Candid | CRS 1001 IMS
The Waiting Game
Jo Swan And Her Quartet | Primal Schmaltz | Timbre | TRCD 004
The Walkin' Blues
Snooks Eaglin | That's All Right | Original Blues Classics | OBCCD 568-2(BV 1046)
The Waltz
Maynard Ferguson And His Orchestra | A Message From Newport | Roulette | CDP 793272-2
The Waltz I Blew For You
Rob McConnell And The Boss Brass | Present Perfect | MPS | 823543-1
The Wanderer
McCoy Tyner Sextet | Extensions | Blue Note | 837646-2
Ahmad Mansour Quartet | Episode | Timeless | CD SJP 341
The Washington Twist
Bill Evans Trio | Empathy+A Simple Matter Of Conviction | Verve | 837757-2 PMS
The Watcher & The Moon
Clifford Jordan Quintet | Two Tenor Winner | Criss Cross | Criss 1011
The Water Is Wide
Christoph Oeding Trio | Taking A Chance | Mons Records | MR 874784
The Water Of Life-
Tim Berne Group | Tim Berne EmpireThe Five Years Plan/Spectres/Songs And Rituals In Real Time | Screwgun | SC 70009
The Watergate Blues
Modern Jazz Quartet | The Best Of The Modern Jazz Quartet | Pablo | 2405423-2
The Waters Of March(Aguas De Marco)
Zona Sul | Pure Love | Nagel-Heyer | CD 3039
The Waters Of March(Aguas De Marco-alt.take)
Dan Rose Quartet | The Water's Rising | Enja | 9116-2
The Wave Police
Steve Lacy | Remains | Hat Art | CD 6102
The Way He Makes Me Feel
Vanessa Rubin With Band | Language Of Love | Telarc Digital | CD 83465
The Way Home
Bob Mintzer Big Band | Urban Contours | dmp Digital Music Productions | CD 467
The Way I Feel
Jimmy Rushing And His All Stars | Jack Dupree-Jimmy Rushing-Muddy Waters | Laserlight | 17062
The Way Of...
Witzel's Venue | Perceptions | Lipstick Records | LIP 8963-2
The Way To The Vestibule
Michael Gregory | The Way We Used To Do | TipToe | TIP-888806 2
The Way We Used To Do
The Crusaders | Free As The Wind | MCA | 2292-50776-1
The Way We Were
Charlie Byrd Trio | Byrd By The Sea | Fantasy | F 9466
Rosemary Clooney & The All Stars | With Love | Concord | CCD 4144
Singers Unlimited | A Capella III | MPS | 68245
The Way You Are
Denise Lawrence & Storeyville Tickle | Let It Shine | Lake | LACD 37
The Way You Look Tonight
Art Blakey And The Jazz Messengers | A Night At Birdland Vol. 3 | Blue Note | 300192(BNJ 61002)
Art Pepper Quartet | A Night At The Surf Club Vol.2 | EPM Musique | FDC 5154
Art Pepper-George Cables Duo | Art Pepper:The Complete Galaxy Recordings | Galaxy | 16GCD 1016-2
Art Tatum | Art Tatum-The Complete Pablo Solo Masterpieces | Pablo | 7 PACD 4404-2
The Tatum Solo Masterpieces Vol.6 | Pablo | 2310791
Cal Tjader Quintet | Breathe Easy | Galaxy | GXY 5107
Cannonball Adderley Quintet | Verve Jazz Masters 31:Cannonball Adderley | Verve | 522651-2
Cannonball Adderley:Sophisticated Swing-The EmArCy Small Group Sessions | Verve | 528408-2
Charlie Parker All Stars | Bird On 52nd Street | Original Jazz Classics | OJC 114(F 6011/JWS 501)
Clare Teal And Her Band | Orsino's Songs | Candid | CCD 79783
Coleman Hawkins Quartet | Blowin' Up A Breeze | Spotlite | SPJ 137
Dave Brubeck Quartet | Jazz At The College Of The Pacific Vol.2 | Original Jazz Classics | OJCCD 1076-2
Jazz At Oberlin | Original Jazz Classics | OJCCD 046-2
The Dave Brubeck Quartet feat. Paul Desmond In Concert | Fantasy | FCD 60-013
The Art Of Dave Brubeck - The Fantasy Years:Jazz At Oberlin/College OPacific | Atlantic | SD 2-317
Dizzy Gillespie Sextet | Jazz In Paris:Dizzy Gillespie-Cognac Blues | EmArCy | 014064-2
Eric Dolphy With Erik Moseholm's Trio | Eric Dolphy:The Complete Prestige Recordings | Prestige | 9 PRCD-4418-2
Erroll Garner Trio | Gems | CBS | 21062
The Greatest Garner | Rhino | SD 1227
Fred Astaire With The Oscar Peterson Quartet | A Fine Romance | Verve | 523827-2
Hugh Fraser-Jean Toussaint Quartet | Back To Back | Jazz Focus | JFCD 025
Jimmy Raney Trio | But Beautiful | Criss Cross | Criss 1065
Jimmy Smith Trio | Jimmy Smith At The Organ | Blue Note | 300154(1512)
Johnny Pace With The Chet Baker Quintet | Chet Baker Introduces Johnny Pace | Original Jazz Classics | OJCCD 433-2(RLP 12-292)
Jonathan Schwartz & Quintet | Anyone Would Love You | Muse | MCD 5325
Kenny Hagood With John Lewis' Orchestra | The Bebop Boys | Savoy | WL 70547 (809278)
Lionel Hampton Quintet | Air Mail Special | Verve | MV 2547 IMS
The Lional Hampton Quintet | Verve | 589100-2
Louis Smith Quintet | The Bopsmith | Steeplechase | SCCD 31489
Mal Waldron Sextet | Mal-2 | Original Jazz Classics | OJCCD 671-2(P 7111)
John Coltrane-The Prestige Recordings | Prestige | 16 PCD 4405-2
Mal Waldron Trio | You And The Night And The Muisc | Paddle Wheel | K 28P 6272
Martial Solal And The Kentonians | Martial Solal:The Complete Vogue Recordings Vol.3 | Vogue | 21606372
Mel Tormé With The George Shearing Trio | A Vintage Year | Concord | CJ 341
Oscar Peterson-Ray Brown Duo | An Evening With Oscar Peterson | Verve | MV 2691 IMS
Paul Desmond-Gerry Mulligan Quartet | Two Of A Mind | RCA | 2179620-2
Jazz Special-Two Of A Mind | RCA | CL 42788 AG
Peter Beets New York Trio | Peter Beets New York Trio | Criss Cross | Criss 1214
Scott Kreitzer Group | New York State Of Mind | Jazz City | 660.53.022
Sonny Rollins Quartet | Thelonious Monk:The Complete Prestige Recordings | Prestige | 3 PRCD 4428-2
Jazz Gallerie:Sonny Rollins Vol.1 | RCA | 2127283-2
Sonny Stitt-Red Holloway Quintet | Just Friends | Affinity | AFF 51
Stan Getz Quintet | Stan Getz Plays | Verve | 2304387 IMS
Ultimate Stan Getz selected by Joe Henderson | Verve | 557532-2
Stan Kenton And His Orchestra | Stan Kenton At Ukiah 1959 | Status | CD 109(882969)
Tete Montoliu | The Music I Like To Play Vol.4: Let's Call This | Soul Note | 121250-2
Wes Montgomery Trio | Guitar On The Go | Original Jazz Classics | OJCCD 489-2(RLP 9494)
Guitar On The Go | Original Jazz Classics | OJCCD 489-2(RLP 9494)
Wes Montgomery-The Complete Riverside Recordings | Riverside | 12 RCD 4408-2
Zoot Sims And His Three Brothers | Zoot Sims:The Complete 1944-1954 Small Group Sessions(Master Takes),Vol.1 | Blue Moon | BMCD 1038
The Way You Look Tonight-
Billy Bauer Quartet | Billy Bauer Plectrist | Verve | MV 2678 IMS
The Way You Look Tonight(alt.take)
Lee Konitz | Lee Konitz 'Self Portrait'(In Celebration Of Lee Konitz' 70th Birthday) | Philology | W 121.2
The Weaver
Yusef Lateef Quintet | Live At Pep's | Impulse(MCA) | GRP 11342
The Web
Peter Madsen Group | Snuggling Snakes | Minor Music | 801030
The Wedding
Abdullah Ibrahim Quartet | Duke's Memories | String | BLE 233853
Abdullah Ibrahim Trio And A String Orchestra | African Suite | TipToe | TIP-888832 2
Abdullah Ibrahim Trio With The Munich Radio Symphony Orchestra | African Symphony | Enja | ENJ-9410 2
Archie Shepp Quintet | Live In San Francisco | Impulse(MCA) | JAS 68(AS 9162)
Henning Berg-Andreas Genschel Duo | Beim 5.Kölner Jazz Haus Festival 1982 | Jazz Haus Musik | JHM 13
Darius Brubeck And The Nu Jazz Connection | African Tributes | B&W Present | BW 023
The Wedding Of All Essential Parts
Keith Ingham & Marty Grosz And Their Hot Cosmopolites | Going Hollywood | Stomp Off Records | CD 1323
The Weeping Prince(for Malcolm)
Chris Barber's Jazz And Blues Band | Who's Blues | BELL Records | BLR 84009
The Weight
Leroy Jenkins-Muhal Richard Abrams Duo | Lifelong Ambitions | Black Saint | 120033-2
The Well
Pauline Oliveros With Relache,The Ensemble For Contemporary Music | The Well & The Gentle | Hat Art | 2020 Digital
The Wellcoming
Johnny King Septet | The Meltdown | Enja | ENJ-9329 2
The Wellspring
Pauline Oliveros With Relache,The Ensemble For Contemporary Music | The Well & The Gentle | Hat Art | 2020 Digital
The Whale(A Green Piece For Blue People)
Steve Lacy Group | Two,Five & Six/Blinks | Hat Art | CD 6189(2)
The Wheel Of Misfortune
Claire Martin With Band | Old Boyfriends | Linn Records | AKD 028
The Whirling Dervish
Steve Lacy Trio | Rushes-10 Songs From Russia | Nueva Records | IN 809
The Whisper In The Shell
The Goofus Five | The Goofus Five feat. Adrian Rollini | Timeless | CBC 1-017
The White Clown
Melo Mafali | Ten Piano Players,Vol.1 | Green House Music | CD 1002
The White Lady And The Black Tarot
Dave Samuels Group | Natural Selections | GRP | GRP 96562
The Whopper
Chris Barber's Jazz And Blues Band With Dr.John | On A Mardy Gras Day | Great Southern Records | GS 11024
The Widow In The Window
Norma Winstone With Group | Live At Roccella Jonica | SPLASC(H) Records | CD H 508-2
The Wiffenproof Song
Bill Carrothers-Bill Stewart | Bill Carrothers Duets With Bill Stewart | Dreyfus Jazz Line | FDM 37002-2
Louis Armstrong With Gordon Jenkins And His Orchestra And Choir | Ambassador Louis Armstrong Vol.17:Moments To Remember(1952-1956) | Ambassador | CLA 1917
Satchmo In Style | Verve | 549594-2
Red Garland Quartet | Red Alert | Original Jazz Classics | OJCCD 647-2(GXY 5109)
The Wild East
Geoff Keezer Trio | World Music | CBS | 472811-2
The Wild Point
Clarion Fracture Zone | Blue Shift | VeraBra Records | CDVBR 2075-2
The Wild Uproar
Mitch Watkins Group | Strings With Wings | TipToe | TIP-888814 2
The Willie Walk
Charlie Mariano With The Don Sebesky Orchestra | A Jazz Portrait Of Charlie Mariano | Fresh Sound Records | FSR-CD 0176
The Wind
Chet Baker Quintet And Strings | Chet Baker And Strings | CBS | 21142
Edward Vesala Group | Lumi | ECM | 1339
Gabe Baltazar Quartet | Birdology | Fresh Sound Records | FSR-CD 5001
Lennie Niehaus Quintet | Seems Like Old Times | Fresh Sound Records | FSR-CD 5016
Misha Alperin | At Home | ECM | 1768(549610-2)
Ran Blake-Jeanne Lee | You Stepped Out Of A Cloud | Owl Records | 055 CD
Stan Getz Quartet | The Lost Sessions | Verve | 9801098
Bossas And Ballads:The Lost Sessions | Verve | 9901098
Stan Kenton And His Orchestra | At The Rendezvous Vol.2 | Status | CD 108(882584)
The Wind Beneath Your Wings
Nguyen Le Group | Tales From Viet-Nam | ACT | 9225-2
The Wind Blew It Away
Mark Nauseef/Miroslav Tadic Group | The Snake Music | CMP Records | CMP CD 60
The Wind Is A Lady
The Guest Stars | Out At Night | Eigelstein | 568-72228
The Wind Whales If Ishmael
Dave Holland Qartet | Dream Of The Elders | ECM | 1572(529084-2)
The Winding Way
Scolohofo | Oh! | Blue Note | 542081-2
Grant Green Orchestra | Green Is Beautiful | Blue Note | 300275(4342)
The Windjammer
Allen Harris With The Metropole Orchestra | Here Comes Allen Harris... | Mons Records | MR 874771
The Windmills Of You Mind
George Benson Quartet | Talkin' Verve:George Benson | Verve | 553780-2
Michel Legrand Big Band | Michel Legrand Big Band | Verve | 538937-2
The Windmills Of Your Mind
Oscar Peterson Trio | Two Originals:Walking The Line/Another Day | MPS | 533549-2
Walking The Line | MPS | 68082
The Windup
Meredith d'Ambrosia Group | Little Jazz Bird | Sunnyside | SSC 1040 D
The Wing Key
Blaufrontal With Hank Roberts & Mark Feldman | Bad Times Roll | Jazz Haus Musik | JHM 0061 CD
The Winner's Tears
Peter Leitch Quintet | Portraits And Dedications | Criss Cross | Criss 1039
The Winters Tale[Epilugue](Lars-Erik Larsen)

TITELVERZEICHNIS

Jay Hoggard Quintet | Love Is The Answer | Muse | MCD 5527

The Wise One
Eric Kloss-Barry Miles Duo | Together | Muse | MR 5112

The Wish
John McLaughlin Group | Remember Shakti | Verve | 559945-2
Duke Ellington And His Orchestra | Indiana Live Session | Jazz Anthology | JA 5135

The Witch
Art Blakey And The Jazz Messengers | The Witch Doctor | Blue Note | 521957-2

The Witch Doctor
The Witch Doctor | Blue Note | 521957-2

The Witch Doctor(alt.take)
Le Petit Chien | Woof | Enja | 9122-2

The Witching Hour
Al Di Meola Group | Land Of The Midnight Sun | CBS | 468214-2

The Wizard
Al Di Meola Groups | Guitar Heroes Vol.1:Al Di Meola | Zounds | CD 2700044001
Albert Ayler Trio | Spiritual Unity | ESP Disk | ESP 1002-2
Christian McBide Quartet | Vertcal Vision | Warner | 9362-48278-2

The Wizard Of Montara
Charlie Mariano Group | Boston All Stars/New Sound From Boston | Original Jazz Classics | OJCCD 1745-2

The Wizzard
John Surman | Private City | ECM | 1366

The Wizzard Song
Eddie Harris-Wendell Harrison Quintet | The Battle Of The Tenors-In Memory Of Eddie Harris | Enja | ENJ-9336 2

The Wolf-
Tal Farlow Trio | Trilogy | Inner City | IC 1099 IMS

The Woman
Blind John Davis | Blind John Davis | L+R Records | CDLR 72002

The Woman I'm Lovin'
Henry Johnson Group | You're The One | Impulse(MCA) | MCA 5754

The Wonderful World Of Sports
Georgie Fame Group | The Blues And Me | VeraBra Records | CDVBR 2104-2

The Words Don't Fit In My Mouth
Bennie Maupin-Dr. Patrick Gleeson | Driving While Black... | Intuition Records | INT 3242-2

The Work
Annette Lowman With Three Of A Kind And Maceo Parker | Anette Lowman | Minor Music | 801050

The Work Song
Cannonball Adderley Quintet | Cannonball In Japan | Capitol | 793560-2
Cannonball Adderley-Nat Adderley Sextet | The Best Of Cannonball Adderley:The Capitol Years | Capitol | 795482-2
Charles Bell Trio | In Concert | Fresh Sound Records | FSR 544(Gateway LP 7012)
Charles Mingus Quintet | Charles Mingus-The Complete Debut Recordings | Debut | 12 DCD 4402-2
Claude Bolling And His Orchestra With Joe Williams | Jazz Gala 79 | America | AM 015/16
Nat Adderley Quintet | Workin'-Live In Subway Vol.1 | Timeless | CD SJP 387
We Remember Cannon | IN+OUT Records | 7012-2
Nat Adderley Sextet | Work Songs | Milestone | M 47047
Work Song | Sweet Basil | 660.55.007
Nina Simone With Hal Mooney's Orchestra | Verve Jazz Masters 17:Nina Simone | Verve | 518198-2
Nina Simone With Orchestra | Nina Simone-The 60s Vol.3:Work Song | Mercury | 838545-2 PMS
Oscar Peterson Trio With Milt Jackson | Very Tall | Verve | 827821-2
Paul Horn Group | 500 Miles High | West Wind | WW 2043
Duke Ellington And His Orchestra | Carnegie Hall Concert January 1946 | Prestige | 2PCD 24074-2

The Work Song-
Carnegie Hall Concert December 1944 | Prestige | 2PCD 24073-2
Duke Ellington | Bluebird | ND 86641(3)
The Indispensable Duke Ellington Vol.11/12 | RCA | 2115524-2

The World
Lucky Thompson Trio | Lucky Thompson:The Complete Vogue Recordings Vol.2 | Vogue | 21559502

The World Is Falling Down
Mississippi Sheiks | Stop And Listen | Yazoo | YAZ 2006

The World Is Waiting For The Sunrise
Benny Goodman Quartet | The King Of Swing 1958-1967 Era | Festival | ???
Benny Goodman Trio | Jazz Live & Rare: Benny Goodman & His Group/Orchestra | Jazzline | ???
Chris Barber's Jazz Band | Chris Barber's Jazz Band | Ace Of Club | ACL 1163
Coleman Hawkins With The Oscar Peterson Quartet | The Genius Of Coleman Hawkins | Verve | 825673-2 PMS
Dick Hyman-Ralph Sutton Duo | Concord Duo Series Volume Six | Concord | CCD 4603
Oscar Peterson Quartet | Jazz Dance | Original Jazz Classics | OJCCD 1002-2(1210890)
Oscar Peterson Quintet With Orchestra | The Personal Touch | Pablo | 2312135-2
Rainer Sander Swing Wing | Shine | Elite Special | 73611
The Original Tuxedo 'Jass' Band | The Original Tuxedo oJass o Band | MPS | 68229

The World Of Light
Golden Gate Quartet With The Martial Solal Orchestra | From Spiritual To Swing Vol.2 | EMI Records | 780573-2

The World Outside(Warsow Concerto)
Cora Fuker & Ola Mae Bell | Living Country Blues USA Vol.11:Country Gospel Rock | L+R Records | LR 42041

The World Was Young
Myra Melford Trio | Jump | Enemy | EMCD 115(03515)

The World Within
Kid Ory's Creole Jazz Band | New Orleans | CBS | 21061

The Worm
Jimmy McGriff Organ Blues Band | The Worm | Blue Note | 538699-2
Pullin' Out The Stops! The Best Of Jimmy McGriff | Blue Note | 830724-2
Neighbours | Accents | MRC | 066-32854

The Worm Turns
Jimmy McGriff Orchestra | Jimmy McGriff-Funkiest Little Band In The Kand | LRC Records | CDC 9046(874379)

The Wraith
Jay Collins Quintet | Reality Tonic | Reservoir | RSR CD 142

The Wrong Blues
Charlie Bamet And His Orchestra | The Indispensable Charlie Barnet Vol.1/2 | RCA | 2135554-2

The X Festival
Rodney Jones Quintet | Rodney Jones-The 'X' Field | Musicmasters | 65147-2

The XX Meter Decoder
Barry Guy-Howard Riley-John Stevens-Trevor Watts | Endgame | Japo | 60028

The Yam
Benny Goodman And His Orchestra | More Camel Caravans | Phontastic | NCD 8843/4
All Of Me | Black Lion | 127034

The Years
Benny Goodman Forever | RCA | NL 89955(2) DP

The Yellow Rose Of Brooklyn
George Gruntz Concert Jazz Band | 25 Years George Gruntz Concert Jazz Band:The World's Greatest Unknown Hits | TCB Records | TCB 96602

The Yodel
George Hall And His Orchestra | The Uncollected:George Hall | Hindsight | HSR 144

The You And Me That Used To Be
Michel Petrucciani Quintet | Michel Petrucciani Live | Blue Note | 780589-2

The You Note
Bill Evans Quintet | Living In The Crest Of A Wave | Elektra | MUS 96.0349-1

The Zennuugh People
Dave Weckl Band | Rhythm In My Soul | Stretch Records | SCD 9016-2

Thelonica(1)
Tommy Flanagan | Thelonica | Enja | ENJ-4052 2

Thelonica(2)
Anthony Davis Septet | Interpertations Of Monk | DIW | DIW 395/8 CD

Thelonious
Ran Blake | Epistrophy | Soul Note | 121177-2
Thelonious Monk And His Orchestra | Thelonious Monk-The Complete Riverside Recordings | Riverside | 15 RCD 022-2
Thelonious Monk Quartet | Live At The Jazz Workshop-Complete | CBS | C2K 65189
Thelonious Monk Quintet | The Blue Note Years-The Best Of Thelonious Monk | Blue Note | 796636-2
Thelonious Monk Sextet | Thelonious Monk:Misterioso | Dreyfus Jazz Line | FDM 36743-2
Genius Of Modern Music,Vol.1 | Blue Note | 300403
Thelonious Monk:The Complete Blue Note Recordings | Blue Note | 830363-2
Wynton Marsalis Group | Standard Time Vol.4:Marsalis Plays Monk | CBS | CK 67503
Geri Allen Trio | Twenty One | Blue Note | 830028-2

Thelonious Monk Medley:
Frank Collett | Perfectly Frank | Fresh Sound Records | FSR-CD 5024

Thelonious Theonlyus
J.J.Johnson Sextet | Heroes | Verve | 528864-2

Theloniously Speaking
John McLaughlin Group | The Promise | Verve | 529828-2

Thelonius Melodius
Bobby McFerrin | Simple Pleasures | Manhattan | 748059-2

Them Changes
Linda Sharrock With The Wolfgang Puschnig Trio | Linda Sharrock & The Three Man Band | Moers Music | 02078 CD

Them Dirty Blues
Cannonball Adderley Quintet | Them Dirty Blues | Capitol | 495447-2
The Cannonball Adderley Collection Vol.1:Them Dirty Blues | Landmark | CAC 1301-2(882341)

Them Jive New Yorkers
Babs Gonzales Group | Properly Presenting Babs Gonzales | Fresh Sound Records | FSR 702(835422)

Them Old Blues
The Little Ramblers | Adrian Rollini Groups 1924-27 | Village(Jazz Archive) | VILCD 023-2

Them That Got
Roseanna Vitro With The Ken Werner Group | Catchin' Some Rays-The Music Of Ray Charles | Telarc Digital | CD 83419

Them That's Got
Al Cohn Quintet | Cohn On The Saxophone | Dawn | DCD 102

Them There Eyes
Benny Carter And His Orchestra | Benny Carter-Live And Well In Japan! | Pablo | 2308216
Benny Goodman And His Orchestra | Swing Swing Swing-Rare Recordings From The Yale University Music Library | Limelight | 844312-2
Billie Holiday | My Greatest Songs | MCA | MCD 18767
Billie Holiday And Her Orchestra | Billie Holiday:The Quintessential Vol.8/9(1939-1942) | CBS | 477837-2
Billie Holiday With The Carl Drinkard Trio | Billie Holiday At Storyville | Black Lion | 147015
Billie Holiday At Storyville | Black Lion | CD 877625-2
Buck Clayton Quintet | Jazz Legacy 56: Buck Clayton-A La Buck | Vogue | 500106
Carmen McRae And Her Sextet | Carmen McRae Sings Lover Man | CBS | CK 65115
Diane Schuur With Orchestra | The Best Of Diane Schuur | GRP | GRP 98882
Earl Hines Trio | Earl Hines In Paris | America | AM 6107
Ella Fitzgerald With The Count Basie Orchestra | Ella & Basie-On The Sunny Side Of The Street | Verve | 821576-2
Ella Fitzgerald With The Oscar Peterson Quartet | Ella Fitzgerald At The Opera House | Verve | 831269-2 PMS
Marie Bergman With Band | Fruit | Stunt Records | STUCD 19603
Peggy Lee With Orchestra | The Basin Street Proudly Presents Peggy Lee | Capitol | 832744-2
Quintet Du Hot Club De France | Swing '35 -'39 | Eclipse | ECM 2051
Red Richards Quintet | Echoes Of Spring | Sackville | SKCD2-2049
Sarah Vaughan With The Billy May Orchestra | Jazz Profile | Blue Note | 823517-2
Schnuckenack Reinhardt Quintet | Swing Session | Intercord | 160010
Stephane Grappelli Quartet | Stephane Grappelli | Jazz Colours | 874717-2
The Tremble Kids All Stars | The Tremble Kids All Stars Play Chicago Jazz! | Nagel-Heyer | CD 043
The Whoopee Makers | The Complete Duke Ellington-Vol. 3 | CBS | CBS 88000

Thema For Monk
Wolfgang Lauth Quartet | Deutsches Jazz Festival 1954/1955 | Bear Family Records | BCD 15430

Thema In B
David S.Ware Trio | Birth Of A Being | Hat Art | W

Thembi
Pharoah Sanders Sextet | The Best Of Pharoah Sanders | MCA | AS 9229

Theme
Art Ensemble Of Chicago | Urban Bushmen | ECM | 1211/12
Benny Carter Big Band | On The Air | Nueva Records | JU 327
Dizzy Gillespie Group | Bird Songs | Telarc Digital | CD 83421
Ella Fitzgerald And Her Orchestra | Live From The Roseland Ballroom New York | Jazz Anthology | JA 5228
Ken McIntyre Sextet | Introducing The Vibrations | Steeplechase | SCCD 31065
Lester Young Quartet | Live At The Royal Roost | Jazz Anthology | JA 5214
Wynton Kelly-George Coleman Quartet | In Concert | Affinity | AFF 54

Theme-
Miles Davis Group | In Concert | CBS | C2K 65140
Roland Kirk Quintet | Petite Fleur | Moon Records | MCD 027-2
Les Brown And His Band Of Renown | Today | MPS | 68118

Theme D'Amour
Art Ensemble Of Chicago | Americans Swinging In Paris:Art Ensemble Of Chicago | EMI Records | 539667-2

Theme De Celine
Les Stances A Sophie | Nessa | N 4

Theme De L'Amour Universel
1969-1970 People In Sorrow/Les Stances A Sophie(Soundtrack) | Jazztime(EMI) | 795818-2

Theme De Liz
Americans Swinging In Paris:Art Ensemble Of Chicago | EMI Records | 539667-2

Theme De Yoyo
Les Stances A Sophie | Nessa | N 4

Theme For Augustine
Stan Kenton And His Orchestra | Live At Butler University | Creative World | ST 1058

Theme For Bond
Oscar Peterson Quintet With Orchestra | The Personal Touch | Pablo | 2312135-2

Theme For Charlie
Tina Brooks Quintet | True Blue | Blue Note | 868846-9

Theme For Duke
Cal Tjader Quintet | Concert On The Campus | Original Jazz Classics | OJC 279(F 8044)

Theme For Ernie
Archie Shepp Quartet | Ballads For Trane | Denon Compact Disc | DC-8570
Frank Foster Quintet | Chiquito Loco | Arco | 3 ARC 120
John Coltrane Quartet | Soultrane | Original Jazz Classics | OJC20 021-2
John Coltrane-The Prestige Recordings | Prestige | 16 PCD 4405-2
John Coltrane | Prestige | P 24003
Steve Kuhn Trio | Oceans In The Sky | Owl Records | 013428-2
Tete Montoliu Trio | Tete! | Steeplechase | SCCD 31029
Hot House | Steeplechase | SCCD 37027/28

Theme For Lester Young
Dannie Richmond Quintet | Three Or Four Shades Of Dannie Richmond Quintet | Tutu Records | 888120-2*

Theme For Lester Young: Goodbye Pork Pie Hat
Hamiet Bluiett Group | ...You Don't Need To Know...If You Have To Ask | Tutu Records | 888128-2*
Jessica Williams | The Next Step | Hep | CD 2054

Theme For Malcolm
Donald Brown Group | Cause And Effect | Muse | MCD 5447

Theme For Manuel
Stan Getz Quartet | The Best Of The Jazz Saxophones Vol.3 | LRC Records | CDC 9009

Theme For Martha
Billy Bang | Distinction Without A Difference | Hat Art | 4 (1Ro4)

Theme For Nana
Geir Lysne Listening Ensemble | Korall | ACT | 9236-2

Theme For O.J.
Art Blakey And The Jazz Messengers | One For All | A&M Records | 395329-2

Theme For Sco:
Daniel Humair Soultet | Jazz In Paris | EmArCy | 548793-2

Theme For Sister Salvation
Freddie Redd Quartet | The Music From The Connection | Blue Note | 84027

Theme For Trambean
Duke Ellington And His Orchestra | Duke Ellington At Tanglewood Vol.1 | Queen-Disc | 049

Theme From 'Asphalt Jungle'
Harry Betts And His Orchestra | The Jazz Soul Of Dr. Kildare | Mobile Fidelity | MFCD 839

Theme From 'I Want To Live'
Gerry Mulligan Concert Jazz Band | Compact Jazz: Gerry Mulligan Concert Jazz Band | Verve | 838933-2

Theme From 'Picnic'
Esther Phillips With The Ray Ellis Orchestra | And I Love Him! | Atlantic | AMCY 1061

Theme From 'Summer Of 42' (The Summer Knows)
Gene Bertoncici Trio | Acoustic Romance | Paddle Wheel | KICJ 155

Theme From Any Number Can Win
Jimmy Rowles-Eric Von Essen | Lilac Time | Kokopelli Records | KOKO 1297

Theme From Black Orpheus
Paul Desmond Quartet | Paul Desmond-Greatest Hits | RCA | CL 89809 SF
Take Ten | RCA | 63661462
Paul Desmond-Gerry Mulligan Quartet | The Ballad Of Paul Desmond | RCA | 21429372
Bobby Hutcherson Quartet | Herbie Hancock:The Complete Blue Note Sixties Sessions | Blue Note | 495569-2

Theme From Blow Up
Cal Tjader's Orchestra | Several Shades Of Jade/Breeze From The East | Verve | 537083-2

Theme From Cleopatra
Dizzy Gillespie Quintet | Talking Verve:Dizzy Gillespie | Verve | 533846-2

Theme From 'Cool World'
Rusty Bryant Sextet | For The Good Times | Prestige | PRCD 24269-2

Theme From Deep Throat
Betty Carter With Orchestra | 'Round Midnight | Atlantic | AMCY 1060

Theme From Elvira Madigan
Joe McPhee | Rotation | Hat Art | D

Theme From Jack Johnson
Miles Davis Group | In Concert | CBS | C2K 65140

Theme From Jack Johnson-
Hank Jones Trio | I Remember You | Black & Blue | BLE 233122

Theme From 'Lillies Of The Field[Amen]'(part 1)
King Curtis Band | King Curtis-Blow Man Blow | Bear Family Records | BCD 15670 CI

Theme From 'Lillies Of The Field[Amen]'(part 2)
Cedar Walton Trio | Left Bank Encores | Prestige | PRCD 11022-2

Theme From Love Story
Cedar Walton-Hank Mobley Quintet | Breakthrough | Muse | MR 5132
Stan Kenton And His Orchestra | Live At Brigham Young University | Creative World | STD 1039

Theme From M Suad
Ahmad Jamal Orchestra | Night Song | MoJazz | 530303-2

Theme From M.A.S.H.
Jimmy Smith Quartet | Off The Top | Elektra | MUS K 52418

Theme From Mahogany
Nina Simone With The Bob Mercey Orchestra | The Amazing Nina Simone | Official | 6002

Theme From Mr.Broadway
Oliver Nelson And His Orchestra | More Blues And The Abstract Truth | MCA | 2292-54643-2

Theme From Our Fairytale
Swim Two Birds | No Regrets | Laika Records | 35101342

Theme From Perry Mason
Quincy Jones And His Orchestra | Talkin' Verve-Roots Of Acid Jazz:Roland Kirk | Verve | 533101-2

Theme From Peter Gunn
Marian McPartland | Maybeck Recital Hall Series Volume Nine | Concord | CCD 4460

Theme From 'Rhapsody In Blue'(take 1)
Spaulding Givens Trio | Debut Rarities Vol.2 | Original Jazz Classics | OJCCD 1808-2

Theme From 'Rhapsody In Blue'(take 2)
Bernard Purdie's Soul To Jazz | Bernard Purdie's Soul To Jazz II | ACT | 9253-2

Theme From 'Shaft'
Uli Beckerhoff Quartet | New York Meeting | L+R Records | CDLR 45082

Theme From Tchaikovsky's Symphony Pathetic
Sonny Rollins Quintet | The Bop Rebells | Jazz Door | JD 1218

Theme From The Bad And The Beautiful
Graham Stewart Seven | Best Of British Jazz From The BBC Jazz Club Vol.5 | Upbeat Jazz | URCD 125

Theme From The Carpetbaggers
Stan Getz With The Bill Evans Trio | The Complete Bill Evans On Verve | Verve | 527953-2
The Complete Bill Evans On Verve | Verve | 527953-2

Theme From The Carpetbaggers(alt.take 1)
The Complete Bill Evans On Verve | Verve | 527953-2

Theme From The Carpetbaggers(alt.take 2)
The Complete Bill Evans On Verve | Verve | 527953-2

Theme From The Carpetbaggers(alt.take 3)
The Complete Bill Evans On Verve | Verve | 527953-2

Theme From The Carpetbaggers(alt.take 4)
The Complete Bill Evans On Verve | Verve | 527953-2

Theme From The Carpetbaggers(incomplete take)
Dave Grusin And The N.Y./L.A. Dream Band | Dave Grusin And The NY-LA Dream Band | GRP | GRP 91001-1(808561)

Theme From The Motion Picture Rosemary's Baby
Joey Baron Trio | RAIsedpleasuredot | New World Records | 80449-2

Theme From The Pink Panther
Sergio Salvatore Trio | Always A Beginning | Concord | CCD 4704

Theme From Thriller
Herbie Mann Group | Astral Island | Atlantic | 78-0077-1

Theme From Trambean
Duke Ellington And His Orchestra | Sophisticated Lady | Jazz Society(Vogue) | 670502

Theme From'Joy House'
Eddie Harris Group | The Best Of Eddie Harris | Atlantic | 7567-81370-2

Theme In Search Of A Movie
Woody Herman Big Band | Live At The Concord Jazz Festival | Concord | CCD 4191

Theme Medley:
Duke Ellington And His Orchestra | Duke Ellington:Complete Prestige Carnegie Hall 1946-1947 Concerts | Definitive Records | DRCD 11211

Theme Of No Repeat
Tadd Dameron And His Orchestra | Clifford Brown Memorial | Original Jazz Classics | OJC20 017-2(P 7055)
Jazz Gallery:Clifford Brown | RCA | 2114176-2

Theme Of The Stargazers
Neal Hefti Sextet | The Changing Face Of Harlem, Vol. 2 | Savoy | SJL 2224 (801200)

Theme There Eyes
Don Byas All Star Quintet | Don Byas Complete American Small Group Recordings | Definitive Records | DRCD 11213

Theme To Grace-
Bill Connors | Theme To The Gaurdian | ECM | 1057

Theme To The Gaurdian
Chick Corea's Return To Forever | Hymn Of The Seventh Galaxy | Polydor | 2310283

Theme To The Mothership
Return To Forever | Return To The 7th Galaxy-Return To Forever:The Anthology | Verve | 533108-2
Stan Kenton | Solo:Stan Kenton | Creative World | ST 1071

Theme(I)
Sidsel Endresen Sextet | Exile | ECM | 1524(521721-2)

Theme(II)
Duke Ellington And His Orchestra | A True Collectors Item | Jazz Archive | 90.105-2

Theme:Blues Chorale
Willie 'The Lion' Smith | The Memoirs Of Willie 'The Lion' Smith | RCA | 2126415-2

Them's Graveyard Words
Chris Cheek Sextet | A Girl Named Joe | Fresh Sound Records | FSNT 032 CD

Then
Dave Liebman | Time Immemorial | Enja | ENJ-9389 2
Eddie Prevost Band | Now Here This Then | Spotlite | SPJ 505

Then From Now
Rich Perry Quartet | Hearsay | Steeplechase | SCCD 31515

Then I'll Be Tired Of You
Cal Tjader Quintet | Concert On The Campus | Original Jazz Classics | OJC 279(F 8044)
Danny Moss Quartet | Weaver Of Dreams | Nagel-Heyer | CD 017
Ella Fitzgerald With Frank De Vol And His Orchestra | Like Someone In Love | Verve | 511524-2
Ellis Larkins | Duologue | Black Lion | BLP 60911
John Coltrane Quintet | John Coltrane-The Prestige Recordings | Prestige | 16 PCD 4405-2
John Pizzarelli Trio With Harry Allen | P.S. Mr.Cole | RCA | 2663563-2
Jonathan Schwartz & Quintet | Alone Together | Muse | MR 5143
Paul Desmond With Strings | Desmond Blue | RCA | 2663898-2
Sally Blair And The Bethlehem Strings | Squeeze Me | Fresh Sound Records | FSR 2023(Bethlehem BCP 6009)

Then Or Now
McKinney's Cotton Pickers | The Complete McKinney's Cotton Pickers Vol.3/4 | RCA | NL 89738(2) DP

Then Steal
Jimmy Witherspoon And His All Stars | Singin' The Blues | Pacific Jazz | 494108-2

Then The Lights Go Out
Levitts | We Are The Levitts | ESP Disk | ESP 1095-2

Then You've Never Been Blue
Janet Blair With The Lou Busch Orchestra | Janet Blair Flame Out! | Fresh Sound Records | DICO D 1301 CD

Theo
Old Merrytale Jazz Band | Dixieland Jubilee-Vol. 3 | Intercord | 155013

Theodora
Richard 'Groove' Holmes Quartet | Swedish Lullaby | Sison | Sis 0003 IMS
Sergey Kuryokhin | The Way Of Freedom | LEO | LR 107

Theory Of Art
Art Blakey And The Jazz Messengers | Theory Of Art | RCA | ND 86286(886235)
A Night In Tunisia | RCA | 2663896-2

Theory Of Art(alt.take)
Peter Brötzmann/Alfred 23 Harth | Go-No-Go | FMP | 1150

There Ain't No Sweet Man Worth The Salt Of My Tears
Dick Morrissey Quartet | There And Back | Ronnie Scott's Jazz House | JHAS 607

There And Back Again
Joachim Raffel Sextet | ...In Motion | Jazz 4 Ever Records:Jazz Network | J4E 4746

There And Now
Brötzmann-Mengelberg-Bennink Trio | 3 Points And A Mountain...Plus | FMP | CD 107

There Are No Doors
Woody Herman And His Orchestra | The V-Disc Years 1944-45 Vol.1 | Hep | 34

There Are So Many
Billy Eckstine And His Orchestra | Billy Eckstine Sings | Savoy | SJL 1127 (801176)

There Are Such Things
Matthias Nadolny-Gunnar Plümer | You'll Never Walk Alone | Nabel Records:Jazz Network | CD 4667
Sonny Rollins Quartet | Worktime | Original Jazz Classics | OJC20 007-2(P 7020)
Taking Care Of Business | Prestige | P 24082
Tommy Dorsey And His Orchestra | This Is Tommy Dorsey | RCA | PL 89536 DP

There But For The Grace Of...
Geoff Keezer Quartet | Here And Now | Blue Note | 796691-2

There Comes A Time
Gil Evans Orchestra With Sting | Strange Fruit | ITM Records | ITM 1499
Tony Williams Lifetime | Spectrum:The Anthology | Verve | 537075-2

There Goes My Heart
Louis Smith Quintet | There Goes My Heart | Steeplechase | SCCD 31415

There Goes My Heart-
Henry Busse And His Shuffle Rhythm Orchestra | The Uncollected:Henry Busse,Vol.2 | Hindsight | HSR 193 (835574)

There He Goes
Jamaaladeen Takuma Group | Renaissance Man | Gramavision | GR 8308-2

There I Go There I Go Again
Andy Kirk And His Twelve Clouds Of Joy | Live Sessions 1937 | Jazz Anthology | JA 5133

There In A Dream
Archie Shepp Group | Blase | Charly | CD 77

There Is A Balm In Gilead
Mahalia Jackson | In Memoriam Mahalia Jackson | CBS | 66501

There Is A Hot Lady In My Bedroom And I Need A Drink
Rolf Kühn And Friends | Affairs:Rolf Kühn & Friends | Intuition Records | INT 3211-2

There Is A Mingus Amonk Us
Orrin Evans Sextet | Listen To The Band | Criss Cross | Criss 1195

There Is A Sun Chase
Leonard Feather And Ye Olde English Swynge Band | Swingin' Britain-The Thirties | Decca | DDV 5013/14

There Is More
Horace Silver Quintet | That Healin' Feelin' | Blue Note | 84352

There Is No Greater Love
Ahmad Jamal Trio | At The Pershing | Affinity | CD AFS 780
Allan Vaché Swingtet | The First Sampler | Nagel-Heyer | NHR SP 5
Jazz Im Amerikahaus,Vol.3 | Nagel-Heyer | CD 013
Anthony Braxton-Chick Corea Quintet | Woodstock Jazz Festival Vol.2 | Douglas Music | DM 10009
Ben Webster With Orchestra And Strings | Ultimate Ben Webster selected by James Carter | Verve | 557537-2
Ben Webster With The Kenny Drew Trio | There Is No Greater Love | Black Lion | CD 877626-2
Billie Holiday With Bobby Tucker | Billie Holiday Story Vol.1:Jazz At The Philharmonic | Verve | 521642-2
Bobby Watson & Open Form Trio | Round Trip | Red Records | VPA 187
Bucky Pizzarelli-John Pizzarelli Duo | The Complete Guitar Duos(The Stash Sessions) | Stash Records | ST-CD 536(889114)
Cedar Walton Trio | Manhattan Afternoon | Criss Cross | Criss 1082
Claude Williams Quintet | Call For The Fiddler | Steeplechase | SCCD 31051
Conte Candoli Quartet | Candoli Live | Nagel-Heyer | CD 2024
Danny Moss-Roy Williams Quintet | Steamers! | Nagel-Heyer | CD 049
Dave Bargeron Quartet | Barge Burns...Slide Flies | Mapleshade | 02832
Dexter Gordon Quartet | Swiss Nights Vol.2 | Steeplechase | SCCD 31090
Dick Katz Trio | 3wayPlay | Reservoir | RSR CD 127(875790)
Frank Rosolino Quintet | Free For All | Original Jazz Classics | OJCCD 1763-2
Greg Clayton Trio | Live At Boomers | String Jazz | SJRCD 1013
Guido Manusardi | Concerto | SPLASC(H) Records | CD H 437-2
Horace Parlan Trio | Pannonica | Enja | ENJ-4076 2
Joe Albany Trio | Portrair Of A Legend | Fresh Sound Records | FSR-CD 317
Live In Paris | Fresh Sound Records | FSCD 1010
John Abercrombie Trio | Straight Flight | JAM | 5001 IMS
Kahil El'Zabar Quartet | Sacred Love | Sound Aspects | sas CD 021
Kenny Barron Trio | Green Chimneys | Criss Cross | Criss 1008
Klaus Ignatzek Group | Jacaranda | Timeless | CD SJP 292
Knud Jorgensen-Bengt Hanson | Bojangles | Touché Music | TMcCD 002
Lennie Niehaus Quintet + One | Seems Like Old Times | Fresh Sound Records | FSR-CD 5016
Lex Jasper Trio With Orchestra | Lexpression | Limetree | MCD 0016
Matthias Nadolny-Gunnar Plümer | You'll Never Walk Alone | Nabel Records:Jazz Network | CD 4667
McCoy Tyner Trio | Just Feelin' | Palo Alto | PA 8083
Michael Sagmeister-Christoph Spendel | Binary | Acoustic Music Records | 319.1192.2
Mikio Masuda Trio | Black Daffodils | JVC | JVC 9030-2
Miles Davis Quintet | Four & More | CBS | SRCS 5145
Oscar Peterson And The Bassists | Montreux '77 | Original Jazz Classics | OJC 383(2308213)
Montreux '77-The Art Of The Jam Session | Pablo | 2620106
Peter Weniger Trio | I Mean You | Mons Records | MR 874300
Sonny Rollins Trio | Sonny Rollins-The Freelance Years:The Complete Riverside & Contemporary Recordings | Riverside | 5 RCD 4427-2
Stacy Rowles With The Jimmy Rowles Quartet | Tell It Like It Is | Concord | CJ 249
Stan Kenton And His Orchestra | By Request Vol.3 | Creative World | ST 1062
Stefon Harris Group | Black Action Figure | Blue Note | 499546-2
Steve Kuhn Trio | Seasons Of Romance | Postcards | POST 1009
The Mastersounds | Swinging With The Mastersounds | Original Jazz Classics | OJC 280(F 8050)
The Trumpet Kings | The Trumpet Kings At The Montreux Jazz Festival 1975 | Original Jazz Classics | OJCCD 445-2
Tommy Flanagan Trio | Communication-Live At Fat Tuesday's New York | Paddle Wheel | KICJ 73
Toots Thielemans Quartet | When I See You | BELL Records | BLR 84022
Vic Juris-John Etheridge Quartet | Bohemia | Jazzpoint | JP 1023 CD
Victor Feldman Trio | The Arrival Of Victor Feldman | Original Jazz Classics | OJC 268(C 7549)
Woody Shaw Quartet | Setting Standards | Muse | MR 5318(952093)

There Is No Greater Love-
Dizzy Gillespie Quintet | Have Trumpet Will Exite | Verve | MV 2696 IMS

There Is No Greater Love(alt.take)
Masqualero | Re-Enter | ECM | 1437(847939-2)

There Is No Jungle In Baltimore
Peter Brötzmann | Nothing To Say-A Suite Of.Breathless Motion Dedicated To Oscar Wild | FMP | CD 73

There Is No You
Miles Davis Quintet | Charles Mingus-The Complete Debut Recordings | Debut | 12 DCD 4402-2
Oscar Peterson Quartet | Live At The Northsea Jazz Festival | Pablo | 2620115-2

There Is Nobody Looking
Phillip Johnston's Big Trouble | The Unknown | Avant | AVAN 037

There Must Be A Way
Louis Jordan And His Tympany Five | Louis Jordan-Let The Good Times Roll: The Complete Decca Recordings 1938-1954 | Bear Family Records | BCD 15557 IH
Benny Goodman And His Orchestra | Rare Broadcasting Transcription-Vol. 2 | Jazz Anthology | JA 5152

There Never Was A Baby Like My Baby
Rebecka Gordon Quartet | Yiddish'n Jazz | Touché Music | TMcCD 014

There Once Was A Jew
Blossom Dearie | I'm Hip | CBS | 489123-2

There Shall Be No Night
Duke Ellington And His Orchestra | The Duke At Fargo 1940 | Storyville | STCD 8316/17
Cassandra Wilson Group | After The Beginning Again | JMT Edition | 514001-2

There She Goes
Ben Sidran Group | A Good Travel Agent | VeraBra Records | CDVBR 2095-2

There Was A Time
Once In A Lifetime | Soul Sound | Acoustic Music Records | 319.1055.2

There Was A Time-
Reverend Blind Gary Davis | Gospel, Blues And Street Songs | Original Blues Classics | OBCCD 524-2(RLP 148)

There Was A Time-Echo Of Harlem
Thilo Kreitmeier Quintet | Mo' Better Blues | Organic Music | ORGM 9706
Oregon | Oregon | ECM | 1258(811711-2)

There Was No Moon That Night
Dado Moroni | With Duke In Mind | Jazz Connaisseur | JCCD 9415-2

There Was Nobody Looking
Kip Hanrahan Groups | Tenderness | American Clave | AMCL 1016-2

There Were Swallows...
Luther Kent & Trick Bag | It's In The Bag | Enja | 4066

There Won't Be A Shortage Of Love
Bobby McFerrin Groups | Spontaneous Inventions | Blue Note | 746298-2

There Ya Go
De 8 Baan | Europ' Jazz Contest Belgium '93 | B.Sharp Records | CDS 097

There'll Be A Hot Time In The Old Town Tonight
Ottilie Patterson With Chris Barber Jazz Band | Ottilie Patterson With Chris Barber | Jazz Colours | 874742-2

There'll Be A Jubilee
Tiny Hill And His Orchestra | The Uncollected:Tiny Hill | Hindsight | HSR 159

There'll Be No Days Like That
Dutch Swing College Band & Teddy Wilson | Jazz Intimate | DSC Production | PA 2010 (801072)

There'll Be Other Spring
George Shearing-Marion McPartland Duo | Alone Together | Concord | CCD 4171

There'll Be Some Changes Made
Billie Holiday With The Ray Ellis Orchestra | Last Recordings | Verve | 835370-2 PMS
Bud Freeman And His Summa Cum Laude Orchestra | Victor Jazz History Vol.18:Chicago Jazz(1934-64) | RCA | 2135737-2
Ken Peplowski Quintet | Mr.Gentle And Mr.Cool | Concord | CCD 4419
Una Mae Carlisle Septet | Lester Young:The Complete 1936-1951 Small Group Sessions(Studio Recordings-Master Takes),Vol.6 Rare Items | Blue Moon | BMCD 1006

There'll Never Be Another You
Al Caiola Quintet | Deep In A Dream | Savoy | SV 0205(MG 12033)
Art Pepper Quartet | Art Pepper:The Complete Galaxy Recordings | Galaxy | 16GCD 1016-2
One September Afternoon | Original Jazz Classics | OJCCD 678-2(GXY 5141)
Art Tatum | Art Tatum:20th Century Piano Genius | Verve | 531763-2
The Art Tatum Solo Masterpieces | Pablo | 2625703
Billy Usselton Sextet | Modern Jazz Gallery | Fresh Sound Records | KXL 5001(252282-1 Kapp)
Bob Keene Septet | Solo For Seven | Fresh Sound Records | FSR 641(Andex A 4001)
Bobby Jaspar/Jymie Merritt Trio | Bobby Jaspar | Fresh Sound Records | 84063(Barclay)
Bud Powell Trio | Blues For Bouffemont | Black Lion | BLCD 760135
California Jam Sessions | Chet Baker:California Jam Sessions | Definitive Records | DRCD 11232
Chet Baker Quartet | Live In Chateauvallon 1978 | France's Concert | FCD 128
Chet Baker-Lee Konitz Quartet | In Concert | India Navigation | IN 1052 CD
Coleman Hawkins With Billy Byers And His Orchestra | The Hawk In Hi-Fi | RCA | 2663842-2
Conte Candoli-Carl Fontana Quintet | The Complete Phoenix Recordings Vol.6 | Woofy Productions | WPCD 126
Count Basie And His Orchestra | The Greatest | Verve | MV 2650 IMS
Dick Hyman | There Will Never Be Another You | Jazz Connaisseur | JCCD 9831-2
14 Jazz Piano Favorites | Music & Arts | CD 622
Gerry Mulligan Octet | The Best Of Gerry Mulligan | CTI | 63047
Hank Mobley Quintet | Complete 'The Jazz Message Sessions With Kenny Clarke' | The Jazz Factory | JFCD 22858
J.J.Johnson Quintet | Vivian | Concord | CCD 4523
Jenny Evans And Band | Girl Talk | ESM Records | ESM 9306
Girl Talk | Enja | ENJ-9363 2
Live At The Allotria | BELL Records | BLR 90003
Jimmy Raney-Doug Raney | Nardis | Steeplechase | SCCD 31184
Joe Williams With The Count Basie Orchestra | Joe Williams:Triple Play | Telarc Digital | CD 83461
Lee Konitz-Warne Marsh Sextet | That's Jazz Vol.21: Lee Konitz & Warne Marsh | Atlantic | ATL 50298
Lester Young Quintet | Pres And Teddy And Oscar | Verve | 2-2502 IMS
Lionel Hampton And His Orchestra | Wes Montgomery:Complete Recordings With Lionel Hampton | Definitive Records | DRCD 11242
Major Holley Trio | Mule | Black & Blue | BLE 233074
Michel Petrucciani/Ron McClure | Cold Blues | Owl Records | 042 CD
Norvo-Farlow-Stewart Trio | Swingin' The Forties With The Great Eight | Timeless | SJP 185/6
Red Richards Quintet | Echoes Of Spring | Sackville | SKCD2-2049
Richard 'Groove' Holmes Trio | Misty | Original Jazz Classics | OJCCD 724-2(P 7485)
Sonny Rollins & Co. | The Complete Sonny Rollins RCA Victor Recordings | RCA | 2668675-2
Sonny Stitt Quartet | Back To My Home Town | Black & Blue | BB 877.2
Stan Getz Quartet | Stan Getz:East Of The Sun-The West Coast Sessions | Verve | 531935-2
Steve Grossman Quartet | Hold The Line | DIW | DIW 912 CD
Tal Farlow Quartet | Poppin' And Burnin' | Verve | 815236-1 IMS
Warren Vaché Quintet With Special Guest Allan Vaché | Jazz Im Amerikahaus,Vol.2 | Nagel-Heyer | CD 012
Werner Pöhlert Combo | Something Cool:Werner Pöhlert Combo Recordings 1985-1009 | Hohner Records | ohne Nummer(2)

There'll Never Be Another You-
Stan Getz Quartet | The Steamer | Verve | 547771-2

There'll Never Be Another You(2 incomplete takes)
Coleman Hawkins With Billy Byers And His Orchestra | The Hawk In Hi-Fi | RCA | 2663842-2

There'll Never Be Another You(alt.take 1)
The Hawk In Hi-Fi | RCA | 2663842-2

There'll Never Be Another You(alt.take 2)
Art Pepper Quartet | Art Pepper:The Complete Galaxy Recordings | Galaxy | 16GCD 1016-2

There'll Never Be Another You(alt.take)
One September Afternoon | Originál Jazz Classics | OJCCD 678-2(GXY 5141)
Billie Holiday With Teddy Wilson And His Orchestra | Rare And Unissued Recordings From The Golden Years Vol.4 | Queen-Disc | 068

There's A Boat
Andy Martin With The Metropole Orchestra | Andy Martin & Metropole Orchestra | Mons Records | MR 874802

There's A Boat Dat's Leavin' Soon For New York
Karin Krog With The Egil Kapstad Quartet | Gershwin With Karin Krog | Polydor | 2382045 IMS
Louis Armstrong And Ella Fitzgerald With Russell Garcia's Orchestra | The Complete Ella Fitzgerald And Louis Armstrong On Verve | Verve | 537284-2
Louis Armstrong With The Russell Garcia Orchestra | Compact Jazz: Louis Armstrong | Verve | 833293-2
Lucy Reed With The Bill Evans Quartet | The Singing Reed | Original Jazz Classics | OJCCD 1777-2(F 3212)
Miles Davis With Gil Evans & His Orchestra | The Miles Davis Selection | CBS | 465699-2
Oscar Peterson Trio | Porgy And Bess | Verve | 519807-2
Oscar Peterson-Joe Pass Duo | Porgy And Bess | Original Jazz Classics | OJCCD 829-2(2310779)
Ray Charles Quartet | Porgy And Bess | London | 6.30110 EM
Slide Hampton Octet | Two Sides Of Slide | Fresh Sound Records | FSR-CD 0206

There's A Broken Heart For Every Light In Broadway
Cab Calloway And His Cotton Club Orchestra | Cab Calloway & Co | RCA | ND 89560

There's A Cabin In The Cotton
Louis Armstrong And His Orchestra | Laughin' Louie | RCA | ND 90404

There's A Cabin In The Pines
Louis Armstrong-The Complete RCA Victor Recordings | RCA | 2668682-2

There's A Lull In My Life
Ahmad Jamal Trio | Big Byrd | Dreyfus Jazz Line | FDM 37008-2
Anita O'Day With The Buddy Bregman Orchestra | Pick Yourself Up | Verve | 517329-2
Pick Yourself Up | Official | 3015
Daryl Sherman With Orchestra | Look What I Found | Arbors Records | ARCD 19154
Ella Fitzgerald With The Frank DeVol Orchestra feat. Stan Getz | Compact Jazz: Stan Getz & Friends | Verve | 835317-2
Hank Mobley And His Orchestra | A Slic Of The Top | Blue Note | 833588-2
Kay Starr With Orchestra | The Uncollected:Kay Starr Vol.2 | Hindsight | HSR 229
Duke Ellington And His Famous Orchestra | The Complete Duke Ellington-Vol. 8 | CBS | CBS 88185

There's A Paddle

Duke Ellington And His Orchestra | Togo Brava Swuite | Storyville | STCD 8323

There's A Place

Al Jolson With Orchestra | Al Jolson-Great Original Performances(1926-1932) | CDS Records Ltd. | RPCD 300

There's A Road (God's River)

Juez | There's A Room | Stunt Records | 18806

There's A Small Hotel

Art Tatum | The Art Tatum Solo Masterpieces | Pablo | 2625703
Chamber Jazz Sextet | Plays Pal Joey | Candid | CCD 79030
Charlie Byrd Trio | Au Courant | Concord | CCD 4779
Chet Baker Quintet/NDR Big Band/Radio Orchestra Hannover | Straight From The Heart-The Last Concert Vol.2 | Enja | ENJ-6020 2
The Last Concert Vol.I+II | Enja | ENJ-6074 22
Claude Thornhill And His Orchestra | Snowfall | Fresh Sound Records | NL 46030(RCA)
Ella Fitzgerald With The Buddy Bregman Orchestra | The Rodgers And Hart Songbook | Verve | 821693-1
The Best Of The Song Books:The Ballads | Verve | 521867-2
The Complete Ella Fitzgerald Song Books of Harold Arlen, Irving Berlin, Duke Ellington, George & Ira Gershwin, Jerome Kern, Johnny Mercer, Cole Porter And Rogers & Hart | Verve | 519832-2
Ella Fitzgerald With The Hank Jones Trio | Ella Fitzgerald:The Royal Roost Sessions | Cool & Blue | C&B-CD 112
Erroll Garner Quartet | Plays Misty | Fresh Sound Records | FSR-CD 0158
Hank Jones Trio | The Jazz Trio Of Hank Jones | Savoy | SV 0184(MG 12023)
Jaye P. Morgan With Marion Evens And His Orchestra | Just You Just Me | Fresh Sound Records | ND 38627
Joe Turner | I Understand | Black & Blue | BLE 59.153 2
Joe Zawinul And The Austrian All Stars | His Majesty Swinging Nephews 1954-1957 | RST-Records | 91549-2
Martial Solal | Martial Solal:The Complete Vogue Recordings Vol.2 | Vogue | 21409332
Oscar Peterson Trio | At Zardis' | Pablo | 2CD 2620118
Ralph Flanagan And His Orchestra | Dance Again Part 2 | Magic | DAWE 75
Stan Getz Quartet | The Jazz Giants Play Rodgers & Hart:Blue Moon | Prestige | PCD 24205-2
Stan Getz:The Complete 1946-1951 Quartet Sessions(Master Takes),Vol.1 | Blue Moon | BMCD 1013
Stan Kenton And His Orchestra | Sketches On Standards | Creative World |

There's A Small Hotel-

Bobby Jaspar Quartet | Bobby Jaspar & His Modern Jazz | Vogue | 21559512

There's Danger In Your Eyes Cherie

Thelonious Monk | Thelonious Monk-The Complete Riverside Recordings | Riverside | 15 RCD 022-2

There's Danger In Your Eyes Cherie(alt.take)

Thelonious Monk-The Complete Riverside Recordings | Riverside | 15 RCD 022-2

There's No Business Like Show Business

Sonny Rollins Quartet | Taking Care Of Business | Prestige | P 24082

There's No Disappointment In Heaven

Benny Goodman And His Orchestra | Live At The International World Exhibition,Brussels 1958: The Unissued Recordings | Magic | DAWE 36(881849)

There's No Forgetting You

Full Moon Trio | Live At Birdland Neuburg | double moon | CHRDM 71024

There's No Greater Lunch

Lonnie Johnson Quintet | Blues By Lonnie Johnson | Original Blues Classics | OBCCD 502-2(BV 1007)

There's No One But You

Buddy Johnson And His Orchestra | Buddy And Ella Johnson 1953-1964 | Bear Family Records | BCD 15479 DH

There's No One Like You

Walkin' | Official | 6008

There's No You

Ben Webster With Strings | The Warm Mood | Discovery | DS 818 IMS
Benny Bailey Quartet With Strings | I Remember Love | Laika Records | 35101752
Charlie Ventura Quartet | Charlie Ventura Complete 1951-1952 Verve Studio Recordings | Definitive Records | DRCD 11202
Danny Moss Quartet | Weaver Of Dreams | Nagel-Heyer | CD 017
Eddie Henderson With The Mulgrew Miller Trio | Trumpet Legacy | Milestone | MCD 9286-2
Ella Fitzgerald With Joe Pass | Speak Love | Pablo | 2310888
Enrico Rava-Ran Blake | Duo En Noir | Between The Lines | btl 004(Efa 10174-2)
Frank Rosolino Quintet | Frankly Speaking | Affinity | AFF 69
Louis Armstrong With The Oscar Peterson Quartet | Louis Armstrong Meets Oscar Peterson | Verve | 539060-2
Louis Armstrong Meets Oscar Peterson | Verve | 825713-2
Marty Elkins And Her Sextet | Fuse Blues | Nagel-Heyer | CD 062
Marty Paich Octet | Tenors West | GNP Crescendo | GNP 9040
Ray Charles And His Orchestra | The Great Ray Charles | Atlantic | SD 1259
Stacey Kent And Her Quintet | Close Your Eyes | Candid | CCD 79737
The Birdlanders | The Birdlanders | Fresh Sound Records | FSR-CD 0170

There's No You(alt.take)

The Minstrel Stars | The Minstrel Stars | Upbeat Jazz | URCD 105

There's Nothing Else That I Can Do

Louis Jordan And His Tympany Five | Louis Jordan-Let The Good Times Roll: The Complete Decca Recordings 1938-1954 | Bear Family Records | BCD 15557 IH
Montreal Jubilation Gospel Choir | Jubilation II | Blues Beacon | BLU-1006 2

There's Nowhere To Go But Up

Steve Laury Quintet | Keepin' The Faith | Denon Compact Disc | CY-75283

Thermidor

Art Blakey And The Jazz Messengers | Caravan | Original Jazz Classics | OJC20 038-2

Thermo

Don Braden Trio | The Fire Within | RCA | 2663297-2
Freddie Hubbard-Oscar Peterson Quintet | Face To Face | Original Jazz Classics | OJCCD 937-2(2310876)
George Cables Quartet | Beyond Forever | Steeplechase | SCCD 31305
Art Blakey And The Jazz Messengers | Caravan | Original Jazz Classics | OJC20 038-2

Thermo(alt.take)

Howard McGhee Quartet | Trumpet At Tempo | Spotlite | SPJ 131

These Are My Dreams

Benny Green Trio | These Are Soulful Days | Blue Note | 499527-2

These Are Soulful Days

Cal Massey Sextet | Blues To Coltrane | Candid | CCD 79029
Grooveyard featuring Red Holloway | Grooveyard Featuring Red Holloway | JHM Records | JHM 3607

These Are The Things I Love

Warne Marsh Quintet | Jazz Of Two Cities | Fresh Sound Records | FSR-CD 342
Dorothy Love Coates And The Original Gospel Harmonettes | The Best Of Dorothy Love Coates And The Original Gospel Harmonettes | Ace Records | CDCHD 343

These Blues

The Hawks | Dave Bartholomew Presents The Hawks | Pathe | 1561371(Imperial)

These Foolish Strings

Abbey Lincoln With The Harold Vick Quartet | A Tribute To Billie Holiday | Enja | 6012-2

These Foolish Things Remind Me On You

Anthony Ortega With The Nat Pierce Orchestra | Earth Dance | Fresh Sound Records | FSR-CD 325
Art Pepper Quartet | Complete Discovery-Savoy Master Takes | Definitive Records | DRCD 11218
Art Pepper:The Complete Village Vanguard Sessions | Contemporary | 9CCD-4417-2
Black California | Savoy | SJL 2215 (801191)
Art Tatum | The Art Tatum Solo Masterpieces | Pablo | 2625703
Barry Ulanov's All Star Modern Jazz Musicians | Bird's Eyes Last Unissued Vol.17 | Philology | W 847.2
Bobby Watson | This Little Light Of Mine-The Bobby Watson Solo Album | Red Records | 123250-2
Chet Baker Sextet | Chet Baker-The Italian Sessions | Bluebird | ND 82001
Victor Jazz History Vol.13:Modern Jazz-Cool & West Coast | RCA | 2135732-2
Coleman Hawkins Quartet | Late Night Sax | CBS | 487798-2
Count Basie All Stars | Ain't It The Truth | Black Lion | 147014
Count Basie Jam | Montreux '77-The Art Of The Jam Session | Pablo | 2620106
Dave Brubeck Quartet | Jazz At Oberlin | Original Jazz Classics | OJCCD 046-2
The Dave Brubeck Quartet feat. Paul Desmond In Concert | Fantasy | FCD 60-013
The Art Of Dave Brubeck - The Fantasy Years:Jazz At Oberlin/College OPacific | Atlantic | SD 2-317
David Fathead Newman Quintet | Chillin' | HighNote Records | HCD 7036
Don Byas And His Orchestra | Don Byas Complete 1946-1951 European Small Group Master Takes | Definitive Records | DRCD 11214
Don Friedman | My Romance | Steeplechase | SCCD 31403
Ella Fitzgerald With Joe Pass | Ella Fitzgerald:Newport Jazz Festival-Live at Carnegie Hall | CBS | C2K 66809
Ella Fitzgerald With The Lou Levy Trio | Ella In Rome-The Birthday Concert | Verve | 835454-2
Ella Fitzgerald With The Oscar Peterson Quartet | Ella And Louis Again, Vol.2 | Verve | 711122 IMS
Verve Jazz Masters 6:Ella Fitzgerald | Verve | 519822-2
Compact Jazz: Ella Fitzgerald Live | Verve | 833294-2
George Wallington Trio | The Piano Collection Vol.2 | Vogue | 21610222
Hampton Hawes Trio | Hampton Hawes Trio Vol.1 | Original Jazz Classics | OJC20 316-2(C 3505)
Harold Ashby Quartet | On The Sunny Side Of The Street | Timeless | CD SJP 385
Harry Edison Quartet | The Inventive Mr. Edison | Fresh Sound Records | 054 2402661(Pacific Jazz PJ 11)
Herman Chittison Trio | Piano Genius | Musicraft | MVS 506
Hot Lips Page And His Orchestra | Commodore Classics-Swing Street Showcase | Commodore | 6.25524 AG
Jackie McLean Quartet | A Long Drink Of The Blues | Original Jazz Classics | OJCCD 253-2(NJ 8253)
James Moody And His Swedish Crowns | Made In Sweden Vol.1: 1949 to March 1951 | Magnetic Records | MRCD 106
Jimmy McGriff Orchestra | Jimmy McGriff-Funkiest Little Band In The Kand | LRC Records | CDC 9046(874379)
Johnny Guarnieri Swing Men | Lester Young:The Complete 1936-1951 Small Group Sessions(Studio Recordings-Master Takes),Vol.2 | Blue Moon | BMCD 1002
Jutta Hipp Quintet | Jutta Hipp With Zoot Sims | Blue Note | 852439-2
Lee Konitz Quartet | Jazz At Storyville | Black Lion | BLP 60901
Lee Konitz-Harold Danko Duo | Once Upon A Live | Accord | 500162
Lennie Tristano Quartet | That's Jazz Vol.15: Lennie Tristano | Atlantic | ATL 50245
Lester Young And His Band | Lester Young:The Complete Aladdin Sessions | Blue Note | 832787-2
Lester Young:The Complete 1936-1951 Small Group Sessions(Studio Recordings-Master Takes),Vol.3 | Blue Moon | BMCD 1003
Lester Young And His Orchestra | Pres/The Complete Savoy Recordings | Savoy | WL 70505 (809309)
Lew Stone And His Band | Lew Stone And His Band | Decca | DDV 5005/6 DT
Lionel Hampton Quintet | The Lional Hampton Quintet | Verve | 589100-2
Marc Ribot | Don't Blame Me | DIW | DIW 902 CD
Max Roach-Clifford Brown Quintet | Daahoud | Mobile Fidelity | MFCD 826
Nat King Cole Trio | The Instrumental Classics | Capitol | 798288-2
The Legendary 1941-44 Broadcast Transcriptions | Music & Arts | CD 808
Paul Bley Trio | The Nearness Of You | Steeplechase | SCS 1246
Sir Charles Thompson Quartet | Key One Up | Vanguard | VCD 79612-2
Sonny Criss Quintet | Jazz-U.S.A. | Blue Note | 300013(TOCJ 6127)
Stan Getz Quintet | Unearthed Masters-Vol.2: Stan Getz | JAM | 5007 IMS
Stan Kenton And His Orchestra | By Request Vol.6 | Creative World | ST 1069
Sue Raney With The Alan Broadbent Sextet | In Good Company | Discovery | DSCD 974(889498)
Thelonious Monk | Solo Monk | CBS | 471248-2
Thelonious Monk Trio | Thelonious Monk:85th Birthday Celebration | zyx records | FANCD 6076-2
Thelonious Monk:The Complete Prestige Recordings | Prestige | 3 PRCD 4428-2
Tommy Flanagan Trio | Communication-Live At Fat Tuesday's New York | Paddle Wheel | KICJ 73
Woody Herman And His Orchestra | Woody Herman 1954 And 1959 | Status | DSTS 1021

These Foolish Things Remind Me On You-

Roy Eldridge-Coleman Hawkins Quintet | Just You Just Me-Live In 1959! | Stash Records | ST-CD 531(882689)
Art Pepper Quartet | Art Pepper:The Complete Galaxy Recordings | Galaxy | 16GCD 1016-2

These Foolish Things Remind Me On You(alt.take)

Count Basie All Stars | Ain't It The Truth | Black Lion | 147014

These Foolish Things Remind Me On You(Medley part 2)-

Hot Lips Page And His Orchestra | Classics In Swing:Buck Clayton-Jonah Jones-Hot Lips Page | Commodore | 9031-72735-2

These Instrumental Pieces Were

Eddie Harris Quartet | Is It In | Atlantic | 780240-1

These Things Called Changes

Bill Evans Trio | A Simple Matter Of Conviction | Verve | 23MJ 3040 IMS

Theseus And Minotauros

Jim Hall With The Zapolski Quartet | Jazzpar 98 | Storyville | STCD 4230

Thesis

Matthew Shipp-Joe Morris | Thesis | HatOLOGY | 506

Theta

New Orleans All Stars | At The Dixieland Jubilee | Dixieland Jubilee | DJ 502

That's It

Ronnie Mathews Quartet | Roots Branches & Dances | Bee Hive | BH 7008

They All Fall In Love

Stan Getz Quartet | Stan Getz With European Friends | LRC Records | CDC 7679(874365)

They All Laughed

Ella Fitzgerald And Louis Armstrong With The Oscar Peterson Quartet | Ella And Louis Again,Vol.1 | Verve | 2304501 IMS
Ella And Louis Again | Verve | 825374-2
Ella Fitzgerald With The Nelson Riddle Orchestra | Ella Sings Gershwin-Vol. 1 | Metro | 2682004 IMS
Fred Astaire With The Oscar Peterson Sextet | Fred Astaire Steppin' Out:Astaire Sings | Verve | 523006-2
Manny Albam And His Orchestra | Jazz Horizons | Fresh Sound Records | DLP 9004(Dot)
Rosemary Clooney With The Scott Hamilton-Warren Vache Septet | Rosemary Clooney Sings The Lyrics Of Ira Gershwin | Concord | CCD 4112
Soesja Citroen With The Metropole Orchestra | Yesterdays | Challenge | CHR 70049
Stacey Kent And Her Quintet | The Tender Trap | Candid | CCD 79751
Trudy Desmond Band | My One And Only Love | Justin Time | JTR 8468-2

They All Laughed-

Joe Pass | Blues For Fred | Pablo | 2310931-2

They All Say I'm The Biggest Fool

Buddy Johnson And His Orchestra | Wails | Official | 6010

They Call It Stormy Monday -> Stormy Monday Blues

They Can't Take That Away From Me

Anita Boyer & Her Tomboyers | Nat King Cole Trio:The MacGregor Years 1941/45 | Music & Arts | CD 911
Art Tatum | The Art Tatum Solo Masterpieces | Pablo | 2625703
Billie Holiday And Her All Stars | Billie Holiday:The Great American Songbook | Verve | 523003-2
Billie Holiday And Her Orchestra | Billie Holiday:The Quintessential Vol.4(1937) | CBS | 463333-2
Bob Howard With The Hank Jones Trio | In A Sentimental Mood | Stash Records | ST 266 IMS
Charlie Parker With Strings | Bird With Strings-Live At The Apollo, Carnegie Hall & Birdland | CBS | CBS 82292
Charlie Parker With The Joe Lipman Orchestra | Charlie Parker With Strings:The Master Takes | Verve | 523984-2
Charlie Ventura Quintet | Bop For The People | Affinity | AFF 104
Cy Coleman Trio | Cy Coleman | Fresh Sound Records | FSR 635(Seeco CELP 402)
Dick Collins And His Orchestra | King Richard The Swing Hearted | Fresh Sound Records | LJM 1027(RCA)
Dizzy Gillespie Sextet | The Champ | Jazz Anthology | JA 5183
Ella Fitzgerald And Louis Armstrong With The Oscar Peterson Quartet | The Best Of Ella Fitzgerald And Louis Armstrong On Verve | Verve | 537909-2
Ella And Louis | Verve | 543304-2
The Jazz Collector Edition: Ella & Louis | Laserlight | 15706
Compact Jazz: Ella Fitzgerald/Louis Armstrong | Verve | 835313-2
Ella Fitzgerald With Andre Previn | Nice Work If You Can Get It-Ella Fitzgerald And Andre Previn Do Gershwin | Pablo | 2312140-2
Ella Fitzgerald With The Nelson Riddle Orchestra | Ella Sings Gershwin-Vol. 1 | Metro | 2682004 IMS
Sings The Ira And George Gershwin Songbook | Verve | 825024-2
Ella Fitzgerald With The Tommy Flanagan Trio | Ella A Nice | Original Jazz Classics | OJC20 442-2
Elliot Lawrence Band | Plays Tiny Kahn And Johnny Mandel Arrangements | Fantasy | 0902109(F 3219)
Fran Warren With The Marty Paich Orchestra | Hey There! Here's Fran Warren | Fresh Sound Records | Tops T 1585 CD
Gene Harris | Maybeck Recital Hall Series Volume Twenty-Three | Concord | CCD 4536
James Clay/David Fathead Newman Quintet | The Sound Of The Wide Open Spaces | Original Jazz Classics | OJCCD 1075-2(RLP 1178)
Janet Blair With The Lou Busch Orchestra | Janet Blair Flame Out! | Fresh Sound Records | DICO D 1301 CD
Joe Pass | I Remember Charlie Parker | Original Jazz Classics | OJC 602(2312109)
Blues For Fred | Pablo | 2310931-2
John Pizzarelli Trio And Friends | After Hours | Novus | 4163191-2
Lester Young-Roy Eldridge-Harry Edison Band | Jazz Gallery:Lester Young Vol.2(1946-59) | RCA | 2119541-2
Marcus Roberts Trio | Gershwin For Lovers | CBS | 477752-2
Peter Herbolzheimer Orchestra | Music For Swinging Dancers,Vol.3:Cheek To Cheek | Koala Records | CD P 10
Red Garland Quintet | John Coltrane-The Prestige Recordings | Prestige | 16 PCD 4405-2
Red Garland Quintet feat.John Coltrane | Jazz Junction | Prestige | P 24023
Ruby Braff-George Barnes Quartet | Plays Gershwin | Concord | CCD 6005
Sir Roland Hanna | Maybeck Recital Hall Series Volume Thirty-Two | Concord | CCD 4604
Stan Getz And The Swedish All Stars | Stockholm Sessions '58 | Dragon | DRLP 157/158
Stanley Turrentine Quartet | Never Let Me Go | Blue Note | 576750-2
Stuff Smith Quartet | Cat On A Hot Fiddle | Verve | 9861487
Sue Raney With Dick Shreve And Bob Magnusson | Autumn In The Air | Fresh Sound Records | FSR-CD 5017
Tommy Dorsey And His Orchestra | The Indispensable Tommy Dorsey Vol.1/2 | RCA | 2126405-2
Wolfgang Schlüter's Swing Revival | Swing der 30er-40er Jahre | Koala Records | Panda 11(941331)
Zoot Sims Quintet | Zoot Sims And The Gershwin Brothers | Original Jazz Classics | OJC20 444-2(2310744)
Anita O'Day With The Oscar Peterson Quartet | Jazz-Club: Vocal | Verve | 840029-2

They Can't Take That Away From Me-

Simon Schott | Bar Piano: Simon Schott Plays Your Favorite Evergreens Vol.1 | Organic Music | ORGM 9733
Sonny Rollins Quintet | Sonny Rollins Plays For Bird | Original Jazz Classics | OJCCD 214-2
Uli Wewelsiep-Thomas Brill | Live At The Forum | Aho-Recording | CD 1010

They Didn't Believe Me

Bobby Timmons Trio | In Person | Original Jazz Classics | OJC20 364-2(RLP 9391)
Bud Powell Trio | Strictly Powell | RCA | 6351423-2
Dinah Washington With The Quincy Jones Orchestra | Verve Jazz Masters 40:Dinah Washington | Verve | 522055-2
A Fine Romance | Verve | 523827-2
Ernestine Anderson With Orchestra | My Kinda Swing | Mercury | 842409-2
Frank Sinatra With Orchestra | Frank Sinatra | Koch Records | 321 942 D1
Georgie Auld And His Orchestra | Cool California | Savoy | WL 70511(2)(SJL 2254) DP
Lars Gullin Quartet | Lars Gullin 1953,Vol.2:Moden Sounds | Dragon | DRCD 234
Oscar Peterson-Ray Brown Duo | Oscar Peterson:Get Happy | Dreyfus Jazz Line | FDM 36738-2
Tenderly | Verve | MV 2662 IMS
Pete Jolly Trio | Pete Jolly Duo/Trio/Quartet | Fresh Sound Records | ND 42133
The Paragon Ragtime Orchestra | That Demon Rag | Dorian Discovery | DIS 80107
Tommy Flanagan Quintet | Jazz...It's Magic | Savoy | SV 0153(MG 12209)

They Don't Want Me To Rock No More

Buddy Johnson And His Orchestra | Walkin' | Official | 6008

They Heard It Twice

Horace Henderson And His Orchestra | Fletcher Henderson Vol.1-The End Of An Era | Swingtime(Contact) | ST 1008

They Pass By Singin'

Ray Charles-Cleo Laine With The Frank DeVol Orchestra & Chorus | Porgy And Bess | London | 6.30110 EM

They Pass By Singin'-

Billy Bang Quartet | Bang On! | Justin Time | JUST 105-2

They Raided The House

Jump'n Jive | We The Cats Shall Hep Ya | Timeless | CD SJP 378

They Say It's Spring

Blossom Dearie Quartet | Tempo Jazz Edition Vol.3-Stayin' Cool | Verve | 847902-2
Bobby Short With The Alden-Barrett Quintet | Swing That Music | Telarc Digital | CD 83317

They Say It's Wonderful

Bob Brookmeyer Quartet | The Duale Roll Of Bob Brookmeyer | Original Jazz Classics | OJCCD 1729-2
Clusone 3 | Soft Lights And Sweet Music | Hat Art | CD 6153

Dave Pell Octet | The Dave Pell Octet Plays Irving Berlin | Fresh Sound Records | 252963-1(Kapp KL 1036) (835207)
Johnny Hartman With The John Coltrane Quartet | John Coltrane And Johnny Hartman | MCA | AS 40 (254617-2)
Johnny O'Neal Trio | Coming Out | Concord | CJ 228
Quincy Jones And His Orchestra | The Birth Of A Band | EmArCy | 818177-1 IMS
Sonny Stitt Trio | The Boss Men | Prestige | PCD 24253-2
Stacey Kent And Her Quintet | The Tender Trap | Candid | CCD 79751
Modern Jazz Quartet | The Modern Jazz Quartet | Atlantic | 7567-81331-2

They Say That Falling In Love Is Wonderful
Martial Solal And The Kentonians | Martial Solal:The Complete Vogue Recordings Vol.3 | Vogue | 21606372

They Say You Cry
Gene Ammons Quartet | A Stranger In Town | Prestige | PRCD 24266-2

They Say You're Laughing At Me
Pili-Pili | Ballads Of Timbuktu | JA & RO | JARO 4240-2

They Speak Their Heart Freely(Kanajoro Ka Kouma)
Sun Ra And His Myth Arkestra | The Solar Myth Approach | Affinity | AFF 760

They're Red Hot
Chris Barber's Jazz Band With Alex Bradford | Hot Gospel | Lake | LACD 39

Thibodeaux Twister
Lenny White Group | Present Tense | Hip Bop | HIBD 8004

Thick
Gary Campbell Quartet | Thick & Thin | Double Time Records | DTRCD-115

Thierno De Conakry
Gene Shaw Sextet | Debut In Blues | Argo | ARC 501

Thieves In The Temple
Ronald Shannon Jackson And The Decoding Society | Decode Yourself | Island | ILPS 9827(804685)

Thin Ice
Lucky Thompson Trio | Lucky Thompson | Swing | SW 8404 IMS

Thin Ice(alt.take)
Rinde Eckert Group | Story In,Story Out | Intuition Records | INT 3507-2

Thin Walls
George Shearing Group | Two Originals:Light,Airy And Swinging/Continental Experience/On Target | MPS | 523522-2

Thingin
Lee Konitz With Don Friedman & Attila Zoller | Thingin | HatOLOGY | 547
Lee Konitz With The Oliver Strauch Group & Peter Decker | Lee Konitz With Oliver Strauch Group & Peter Decker | Edition Collage | EC 497-2

Thing'In
Lee Konitz Quintet | Sound Of Surprise | RCA | 2169309-2

Thingin'
Lee Konitz Trio | It's You | Steeplechase | SCCD 31398

Things
Tampa Red | Don't Tampa With The Blues | Original Blues Classics | OBCCD 516-2

Things Ain't What They Used To Be
Booker Little And His Orchestra | Booker Little 4 & Max Roach | Blue Note | 784457-2
Charles Mingus Group | Mingus Dynasty | CBS | CK 65513
Charles Mingus Orchestra | Nostalgia In Times Square/The Immortal 1959 Sessions | CBS | 88337
Charlie Barnet And His Orchestra | Big Band Bounce & Boogie:Skyliner-Charlie Barnet | Affinity | AFS 1012
Clark Terry Five | The Jazz Giants Play Duke Ellington:Caravan | Prestige | PCD 24227-2
Memories Of Duke | Original Jazz Classics | OJCCD 604-2
Count Basie Big Band | The Montreux '77 Collection | Pablo | 2620107
Duke Ellington And His Orchestra | At The Hurricane:Original 1943 Broadcasts | Storyville | STCD 8359
Afro-Bossa | Reprise | 9362-47876-2
Concert In The Virgin Islands | Discovery | DS 841 (807431)
Ella & Duke At The Cote D'Azur | Verve | 539030-2
The Best Of Duke Ellington | Capitol | 831501-2
Duke Ellington Live ! | EmArCy | 842071-2
Two Great Concerts | Festival | ???
Duke Ellington -Carnegie Hall Concert | Ember | 800851-370(EMBD 2001)
Ella Fitzgerald And Duke Ellington:Cote D'Azure Concerts on Verve | Verve | 539033-2
Ella Fitzgerald And Duke Ellington:Cote D'Azure Concerts on Verve | Verve | 539033-2
Ella Fitzgerald And Duke Ellington:Cote D'Azure Concerts on Verve | Verve | 539033-2
Duke Ellington At The Alhambra | Pablo | PACD 5313-2
Duke Ellington: The Champs-Elysees Theater January 29-30th,1965 | Laserlight | 36131
Happy Birthday Duke Vol.3 | Laserlight | 15785
Live At Click Restaurant Philadelphia 1949-Vol.4 | Raretone | 5005 FC
Ellis Larkins | Maybeck Recital Hall Series Volume Twenty-Two | Concord | CCD 4533
J.J. Johnson-Al Grey Sextet | Things Are Getting Better All The Time | Pablo | 2312141
James Clay Quartet | I Let A Song Go Out Of My Heart | Antilles | 848279-2(889265)
Joe Venuti-George Barnes Quintet | Live At The Concord Summer Festival | Concord | CJ 30
Johnny Hodges Orchestra | Highlights From The Duke Ellington Centennial Edition | RCA | 2663672-2
Passion Flower 1940-46 | Bluebird | 63 66616-2
Johnny Hodges:The Complete 1941-1954 Small Group Sessions(Master Takes),Vol.1 | Blue Moon | BMCD 1028
Jazz Special-The 40's & 60's | RCA | CL 43236 AF
Keith Jarrett Trio | Keith Jarrett At The Blue Note-The Complete Recordings | ECM | 1575/80(527638-2)
The Cure | ECM | 1440(849650-2)
Klaus Spencker Trio | Invisible | Jardis Records | JRCD 9409
Mal Waldron-John Coltrane Sextet | Wheelin' | Prestige | P 24069
Mighty Sam McClain Group | Sledgehammer Soul & Down Home Blues | audioquest Music | AQCD 1042
Oscar Peterson Jam | Montreux '77 | Original Jazz Classics | OJC20 378-2(2308208)
Montreux '77-The Art Of The Jam Session | Pablo | 2620106
Oscar Peterson Trio | Night Train | Verve | 821724-2
Oscar Peterson Plays The Duke Ellington Song Book | Verve | 559785-2
Oscar Peterson-Jon Faddis Duo | Oscar Peterson & Jon Faddis | Original Jazz Classics | OJCCD 1036-2(2310743)
Paul Desmond Quartet | Live | Verve | 543501-2
Like Someone In Love | Telarc Digital | CD 83319
Prestige All Stars | John Coltrane-The Prestige Recordings | Prestige | 16 PCD 4405-2
Prestige Blues Swingers | Jam Session In Swingville | Prestige | P 24051
Ray Brown Trio | Black Orpheus | Paddle Wheel | KICJ 109
Return To The Wide Open Spaces | Live At The Caravan Of Dreams | Amazing Records | AMCD 1021
The Atlantic String Trio | First Meeting | Factory Outlet Records | FOR 2501-1 CD
First Meeting | Factory Outlet Records | 2001-1 CD
Tiny Grimes And His Rockin' Highlanders | Tiny Grimes:The Complete 1950-1954,Vol.3 | Blue Moon | BMCD 6007

Things Ain't What They Used To Be-
Duke Ellington And His Orchestra | All Star Road Band Vol.2 | Doctor Jazz | ZL 70969(2) (809319)
Oscar Peterson-Joe Pass Duo | Live At Salle Pleyel, Paris | Pablo | 2625705

Things Ain't What They Used To Be(2)
Duke Ellington And His Orchestra | Ella Fitzgerald And Duke Ellington:Cote D'Azure Concerts on Verve | Verve | 539033-2
Buell Neidlinger All Stars | Cecil Taylor Jumpin' Punkins | Candid | CS 9013

Things Are Getting Better
Cannonball Adderley-Milt Jackson Quintet | Milt Jackson Birthday Celebration | Fantasy | FANCD 6079-2
To Bags...With Love:Memorial Album | Pablo | 2310967-2
David Benoit Group | Letter To Evan | GRP | GRP 96872
J.J. Johnson-Al Grey Sextet | Things Are Getting Better All The Time | Pablo | 2312141
Piet Noordijk Quartet | Live In Sesjun Vol.2:The Song Is You | Timeless | CD SJP 393
Dizzy Gillespie With Gil Fuller & The Monterey Jazz Festival Orchestra | Gil Fuller And The Monterey Jazz Festival Orchestra | Pacific Jazz | 780370-2

Things Are Looking Up
Trudy Desmond Band | My One And Only Love | Justin Time | JTR 8468-2

Things Are Looking Up(rehersal)
J.B.& His Hawks | Combination Blues | Charly | CRB 1042

Things Are Swingin'
Tom Talbert Septet | Things As They Are | Seabreeze | CDSB 2038(881572)

Things That Happen
Big Joe Turner And His All Stars | The Best Of Joe Turner | Pablo | 2405404-2

Things To Come
Dizzy Gillespie Big Band | In The Beginning | Prestige | P 24030
Peter Herbolzheimer Rhythm Combination & Brass | Colors Of A Band | Mons Records | MR 874799
Tito Puente And His Ensemble | Mambo Of The Times | Concord | CCD 4499

Things To Do
Kenny Barron Group | Things Unsee | Verve | 537315-2

Things We Did Last Summer
John McNeil Quintet | Things We Did Last Summer | Steeplechase | SCCD 31231

Things We Said Today
Larry Carlton Group | The Gift | GRP | GRP 98542
Bill Frisell Band | Blues Dream | Nonesuch | 7559-79615-2

Things Will Never Be The Same
Hamiet Bluiett Quartet | EBU | Soul Note | 121088-2

Things You Don't Have To Do
Doug MacLeod Group | You Can't Take My Blues | audioquest Music | AQCD 1041

Think
Joe Beard With Ronnie Earl & The Broadcasters | Blues Union | audioquest Music | AQCD 1039
Lonnie Smith Orchestra | Blue'n Soul-Do The Jerk | Blue Note | 799105-2
The '5' Royales | Dedicated To You | Sing | 580

Think Beautiful
Chet Baker Quartet | Baby Breeze | Verve | 538328-2

Think Beautiful(alt.take)
Bill Stewart Qaurtet | Think Before You Think | Jazz City | 660.53.024

Think It Over
Guitar Slim And His Band | The Things That I Used To Do | Ace Records | CDCHD 318

Think Low
Phil Nimmons 'N' Nine Plus Six | The Atlantic Suite/Suite P.E.I./Tributes | Sackville | SK2CD-5003

Think Of Me
Lola Albright With The Dean Elliott Orchestra | Lola Wants You | Fresh Sound Records | FSR-CD 0007
Earl Hines | Four Jazz Giants:Earl Hines Plays Tributes To W.C.Handy,Hoagy Carmichael And Louis Armstrong | Solo Art | SACD-111/112

Think Of Mingus
Andy Summers Group | Green Chimneys:The Music Of Thelonious Monk | RCA | 2663472-2

Think Of One
Christian Scheuber Quartet | Clara's Smile | double moon | DMCHR 71025
Danilo Perez Quartet | Panamonk | Impulse(MCA) | 951190-2
Fred Hersch Trio | The Fred Hersch Trio Plays | Chesky | JD 116
Lynne Arriale Trio | With Words Unspoken | dmp Digital Music Productions | CD 518
Orage Then Blue Orchestra | Orange Then Blue | GM Recordings | GM 3006(807787)
Wynton Marsalis Quintet | Think Of One | CBS | 468709-2

Think Of One(alt.take)
Thelonious Monk Quintet | MONK | Original Jazz Classics | OJCCD 016-2

Think Of One(take 1+2)
Eddie Henderson Quintet | Think On Me | Steeplechase | SCCD 31264

Think Tank
Reunion | Flight Charts And Plans | Blue Flame | 40242(2132481-2)

Think Twice
Lowell Fulsom Blues Band | Think Twice Before You Speak | JSP Records | 1082

Think,Think,Think
Al Jarreau With Band | All Fly Home | Warner | 7599-27362-2

Thinkin' About It Too
Incognito | Positivity | Talkin' Loud | 518260-2

Thinkin' About Your Body
Lightnin' Hopkins | Lightnin' Hopkins Sings The Blues | Pathe | 2C 068-83075(Imperial)

Thinkin' 'Bout An Old Friend
Jean-Paul Bourelly Group | Blackadelic-Blu | DIW | DIW 883 CD

Thinkin' Of You
George Shearing | Piano | Concord | CCD 4400
Jukka Tolonen Group | Impressions | Sonet | 147126

Thinkin' One Thing And Doin' Another
Mulgrew Miller Septet | Hand In Hand | Novus | 4163153-2

Thinkin' Out Loud
Marty Paich Piano Quartet | Take Me Along | Fresh Sound Records | 58111 CD(RCA)

Thinking About The Future And The Past
Loope | Prinz Henry | ITM Records | ITM 1447

Thinking Blues
Down Town Jazz Band | Hear Us Talkin' To Ya | Timeless | TTD 514

Thinking Good,Thinking Bad
Greg Osby Quintet | Mindgames | JMT Edition | 919021-2

Thinking Inside
Buddy Johnson And His Orchestra | Buddy And Ella Johnson 1953-1964 | Bear Family Records | BCD 15479 DH

Thinking It Over
Ella Johnson With Orchestra | Swing Me | Official | 6009

Thinking Of Wayne
Chick Corea | Standards | Stretch Records | SCD 9028-2

Thinking Of You-
Amos Milburn With Johnny Mandell And His Orchestra | Vicious Vicious Vodka | Pathe | 1561401(Aladdin)

Thinking Of You, MJQ
Jean-Paul Bourelly Group | Vibe Music | PAO Records | PAO 10500

Thinx
Urs Leimgruber-Joelle Léandre-Fritz Hauser | No Try No Fail | HatOLOGY | 509

Third (Power, Resolve)-
Art Farmer Quintet | Blame It On My Youth | Contemporary | CCD 14042-2

Third Decade
Big John Wrencher With Eddie Playboy Taylor & The Blueshounds | Big John's Boogie | Big Bear | 146402

Third Dynasty
Rez Abbasi Group | Modern Memory | String Jazz | SJRCD 102

Third Ear
David S. Ware Quartet | Third Ear Recitation | DIW | DIW 870 CD

Third Hand
Tomasz Stanko Trio | Bluish | Power Bros | 00113

Third Impression
Teddy Charles Quartet | Live At The Verona Jazz Festival 1988 | Soul Note | 121183-2

Third Line Samba
James Emery | Exo Eso | FMP | SAJ 59

Third Man Theme
Edward Vesala Group | Lumi | ECM | 1339

Third Moon
Tony Scott-Bill Evans Sextet | A Day In New York | Fresh Sound Records | FSR-CD 0160(2)

Third Movement
Steve Cohn Trio | Ittekemasu | ITM-Pacific | ITMP 970059

Third Movement-Beige-
Duke Ellington And His Orchestra | Duke Elliongton:Complete Prestige Carnegie Hall 1943-1944 Concerts | Definitive Records | DRCD 11210

Third Plane
V.S.O.P. | The Quintet | CBS | 88273

Third Rail
Ensemble Modern | Ensemble Modern-Fred Frith:Traffic Continues | Winter&Winter | 910044-2

Third Riddle
Gerry Hemingway Quintet | Special Detail | Hat Art | CD 6084

Third Stone From The Sun
Paul Plimley-Lisle Ellis | Both Sides Of The Same Mirror | Nine Winds Records | NWCD 0135

Third Stream Samba
Marty Cook Conspiracy | Phases Of The Moon | Tutu Records | 888160-2*

Third Street
Spyro Gyra & Guests | Love & Other Obsessions | GRP | GRP 98112
Cedar Walton Trio | Cedar | Timeless | CD SJP 223

Third Street Blues
Frank Morgan Quartet | Easy Living | Original Jazz Classics | OJCCD 833-2(C 14013)
Blind Willie Reynolds | The Greatest In Country Blues Vol.1(1927-1930) | Story Of Blues | CD 3521-2

Third Time Around
Hank Mobley Quintet | Straight No Filter | Blue Note | BST 84435

Third Wind
Freddie Hubbard Sextet | Bolivia | Limelight | 820837-2

Third World Anthem
Alvin Queen-Bill Saxton Sextet | Ashanti | Divox | CDX 48703

Thirteen
Mal Waldron Sextet | Eric Dolphy:The Complete Prestige Recordings | Prestige | 9 PRCD-4418-2
Spanish Fly | Rags To Britches | Knitting Factory Works | KFWCD 114

Thirteen Eagles
Thomas Schiedel | All Alone | AH Records | AH 404001-13

Thirteenth Floor
Philip Harper Sextet | The Thirteenth Moon | Muse | MCD 5520

Thirty Five
Vincent Herring Quintet | Change The World | Musicmasters | 65163-2

Thirty-Three, Ninety-Six
Chick Corea Quartet | Chick Corea | America | AM 6144

This
Eddie Prevost Band | Now Here This Then | Spotlite | SPJ 505

This Bitter Earth
Irene Redfield With The Charles Earland Quintet | Million Dollar Secret | Savant Records | SCD 2007
Louis Armstrong And His Friends | Jazz Special-His Last Recordings | RCA | ND 89527

This Black Cat Has Nine Lives
Glenn Miller And His Orchestra | Live At Meadowbrook Ballroom 1939 | Magic | DAWE 34(881864)

This Can't Be Love
Art Tatum | The Tatum Solo Masterpieces Vol. 2 | Pablo | 2310729
Art Tatum Quartet | The Tatum Group Masterpieces | Pablo | 2310734
Art Tatum-Buddy DeFranco Quartet | The Tatum Group Masterpieces | Pablo | 2625706
Ben Webster With The Oscar Peterson Trio | Ben Webster Meets Oscar Peterson | Verve | 829167-2
Charlie Byrd Trio | Au Courant | Concord | CCD 4779
Charlie Rouse/Paul Quinichette Quintet | The Chase Is On | Affinity | AFF 154
Dinah Washington And Her Orchestra | Verve Jazz Masters 19:Dinah Washington | Verve | 518200-2
Ella Fitzgerald With The Buddy Bregman Orchestra | The Rodgers And Hart Song Book, Vol.1 | Verve | 821579-2 PMS
Erroll Garner Trio | The King Of Piano Jazz | Festival | Album 166
Johnny Smith Quartet | The Sound Of Johnny Smith Guitar | Fresh Sound Records | FSR 583(Roost 2246)
Michel Legrand Orchestra | Compact Jazz: Michel Legrand | Philips | 840944-2
Red Holloway With The Jack McDuff Quartet | Cookin' Together | Original Jazz Classics | OJC 327(P 7325)
Ruby Braff And His New England Songhounds | Volume One | Concord | CCD 4478
Shannon Gibbons With The Cecil Bridgewater Quartet | Shannon Gibbons | Soul Note | 121163-2
Sonny Stitt Quartet | Kaleidoscope | Original Jazz Classics | OJCCD 060-2(P 7077)
Genesis | Prestige | P 24044
Stan Getz Quartet | Award Winner | Verve | 543320-2
Stan Getz:East Of The Sun-The West Coast Sessions | Verve | 531935-2
Thad Jones-Mel Lewis Quartet | The Thad Jones-Mel Lewis Quartet | Artists House | AH 3 IMS
Weslia Whitefield With The Mike Greensill Trio | Nice Work... | Landmark | LCD 1544-2

This Can't Be Love(alt.take)
Art Tatum-Lionel Hampton-Buddy Rich | The Tatum Group Masterpieces Vol.4 | Pablo | 2405427-2
Tatum-Hampton-Rich Trio | Art Tatum-The Complete Pablo Group Masterpieces | Pablo | 6 PACD 4401-2
Ella Fitzgerald And Her Famous Orchestra | The Radio Years 1940 | Jazz Unlimited | JUCD 2065

This Changing World
Glenn Miller And His Orchestra | Glenn Miller:The Complete Studio Recordings Vol.2:In The Mood | Memo Music | HDJ 4115

This Could Be The Start Of Something
Lambert, Hendricks And Bavan | At Basin Street East | RCA | 2125756-2
Oscar Peterson Trio | The Jazz Soul Of Oscar Peterson/Affinity | Verve | 533100-2

This Could Be The Start Of Something Big
Ella Fitzgerald And Her Quintet | Ella In Hollywood-Recorded Live At The Crescendo | Verve | V 6-4052 IMS
Peter Bernstein Quartet | Somethin's Burnin' | Criss Cross | Criss 1079

This Fol-Ish Thing
Erroll Garner Trio | Relaxin' | Vogue | 500117

This Girl's In Love With You
Etta Jones With Orchestra | My Mother's Eyes | Muse | MR 5145

This Guy's In Love With You
Hampton Hawes Trio | Live At The Montmartre | Black Lion | BLCD 760202
Oscar Peterson With Orchestra | Motions & Emotions | MPS | 821289-2 PMS
Ella Fitzgerald With The Tommy Flanagan Trio | Ella Fitzgerald In Budapest | Pablo | PACD 5308-2

This Guy's In Love With You-
Dexter Gordon With Orchestra | Strings & Things | Steeplechase | SCCD 31145

This Has To Be The One
Boyd Raeburn And His Orchestra | Experiments In Big Band Jazz-1945 | Musicraft | MVS 505 IMS

This Heart Of Mine
Dave McKenna Trio | Plays The Music Of Harry Warren | Concord | CJ 174

Art Blakey And The Jazz Messengers | Live At Birdland | Fresh Sound Records | FSCD 1020

This Here

Cannonball Adderley And His Orchestra | African Waltz | Original Jazz Classics | OJC 258(RLP 9377)
Cannonball Adderley Quintet | Coast To Coast | Milestone | M 47039
Cannonball Adderley Birthday Celebration | Fantasy | FANCD.6087-2
Live In San Francisco | Riverside | RISA 1157-6
Cannonball In Japan | Capitol | 793560-2
Cannonball Adderley Sextet | THE Sextet | Milestone | M 9106
Jimmy Smith All Stars | Damn! | Verve | 527631-2
Richard 'Groove' Holmes Trio | On Basie's Bandstand | Prestige | PRCD 11028-2
After Hours | Blue Note | 837986-2
Tony Williams Trio | Young At Heart | CBS | 487313-2

This I Dig Of You

Holly Slater Quartet | The Mood Was There | Ronnie Scott's Jazz House | JHCD 053

This Is

Chuck Foster And His Orchestra | The Uncollected: Chuck Foster | Hindsight | HSR 115

This Is A Hard Hat Area

Thomas Heberer | Kill Yr Darlins | Poise | Poise 05

This Is A Hard Hat Area(reprise remix)

Sweet Honey In The Rock | In This Land | FMS-Records | 2054 CD

This Is All I Ask

Bill Evans-Toots Thielemans Quintet | Affinity | Warner | 7599-27387-2
Buddy DeFranco Meets The Oscar Peterson Quartet | Hark | Original Jazz Classics | OJCCD 867-2(2310915)
Buddy Greco Group | MacArthur Park | Celebrity | CYCD 71911
Flip Phillips Quartet | Spanish Eyes | Choice | CRS 1013 IMS
Frank Foster-Frank Wess Quintet | Frankly Speaking | Concord | CCD 4276
John Abercrombie Quartet | The Toronto Concert | Maracatu | MAC 940003
Ralph Sutton | Ralph Sutton At Cafe Des Copains | Sackville | SKCD2-2019
Ruby Braff-Dick Hyman | A Pipe Organ Recital Plus One | Concord | CCD 43003
Sue Raney With Dick Shreve And Bob Magnusson | Autumn In The Air | Fresh Sound Records | FSR-CD 5017
Annie Ross With The Gerry Mulligan Quartet | Annie Ross Sings A Song With Mulligan | Fresh Sound Records | 054 2602321(World Pacific WP 1253)

This Is Always

Chet Baker-Lee Konitz Quartet | In Concert | India Navigation | IN 1052 CD
King Pleasure With The John Lewis Trio And The Dave Lambert Singers | Annie Ross & King Pleasure Sings | Original Jazz Classics | OJC 217(P 7128)
Morgana King And Her Sextet | This Is Always | Muse | MCD 5493
Shelly Manne And His Men | At The Black Hawk Vol.5 | Original Jazz Classics | OJCCD 660-2
Sonny Stitt Quartet | The Last Stitt Sessions Vol. One And Two | 32 Jazz | 32127

This Is Always-

Lester Young's JAPT Quartet | Prez's Hat Vol.1 | Philology | 214 W 6

This Is An Empty Bottle Of Wine

Greg Osby Quartet With String Quartet | Symbols Of Light(A Solution) | Blue Note | 531395-2

This Is Bliss

Hampton Hawes-Charlie Haden Duo | As Long As There's Music | Artists House | AH 4 IMS

This Is For Albert

LeeAnn Ledgerwood Trio | Walkin' Up | Steeplechase | SCCD 31541
Rob Schneiderman Trio | Keepin' In The Groove | Reservoir | RSR CD 144

This Is For David

Trio Da Paz With Special Guests | Brazil From The Inside | Concord | CCD 4524

This Is For Us To Share

Phillip Wilson Quartet | Live At Moers Festival | Moers Music | 01062

This Is My First Affair So Please Be Kind -> Please Be Kind - (This Is My First Affair So) Please Be Kind -> Please Be Kind

This Is My Night To Dream

Nat King Cole Trio | Nat King Cole:For Sentimental Reasons | Dreyfus Jazz Line | FDM 36740-2
Love Songs | Nimbus Records | NI 2010
Vocal Classics & Instrumental Classics | Capitol | 300014(TOCJ 6128)

This Is My Story,This Is My Song

Stan Kenton And His Orchestra | A Concert In Progressive Jazz | Creative World | ST 1037

This Is New

Chick Corea Quintet | Chick Corea-Herbie Hancock-Keith Jarrett-McCoy Tyner | Atlantic | 7567-81402-2
Chick Corea-Herbie Hancock-Keith Jarrett-McCoy Tyner | Atlantic | ATL 50326
Dee Dee Bridgewater With Band | Dee Dee Bridgewater Sings Kurt Weil | EmArCy | 9809601
Ed Bickert-Lorne Lofsky Quartet | This Is New | Concord | CCD 4414
HR Big Band | The American Songs Of Kurt Weill | hr music.de | hrmj 006-01 CD
Jimmy Raney Quartet | Raney '81! | Criss Cross | Criss 1001
Magni Wentzel Trio | Turn Out The Stars | Hot Club Records | HCRCD 092
Peter Leitch Quartet | Mean What You Say | Concord | CCD 4417

This Is Not A Test

Silje Nergard Group with Strings | Nightwatch | EmArCy | 9865648

This Is Not America

Denny Christianson Big Band | Doomsday Machine | Justin Time | Just 8

This Is The Blues

Otis Spann | Otis Spann And His Piano | Crosscut | CCR 1003(Candid)

This Is The End Of... A Beautiful Friendship - (This Is The End Of...) A Beautiful Friendship

Great British Jazz Band | The Great British Jazz Band:Jubilee | Candid | CCD 79720
Howard Alden-George Van Eps Quartet | 13 Strings | Concord | CCD 4464
Milt Jackson-Ray Brown Jam | Montreux '77-The Art Of The Jam Session | Pablo | 2620106
Nat King Cole With The George Shearing Quintet Plus String Choir | Nat King Cole Sings/George Shearing Plays | Capitol | EMS 1113
Singers Unlimited With Rob McConnell And The Boss Brass | The Singers Unlimited With Rob McConnell And The Boss Brass | MPS | 817486-1
Woody Herman Band | Woody Herman Presents A Great American Evening | Concord | CJ 220

This Is The Life

Guy Barker Quintet | Into The Blue | Verve | 527656-2

This Is The Movie

Junior Cook Quartet | The Place To Be | Steeplechase | SCCD 31240

This Is The Thing

Chet Baker Sextet | Compact Jazz: Chet Baker | Verve | 840632-2 PMS

This Is The Way

Dizzy Gillespie Big Band | Carnegie Hall Concert | Verve | 2304429 IMS

This Life A Road

Nancy Harrow Group | Lost Lady | Soul Note | 121263-2

This Little Girl Of Mine

Bobby Watson | This Little Light Of Mine-The Bobby Watson Solo Album | Red Records | 123250-2

This Love Of Mine

Stan Kenton And His Orchestra | Stan Kenton-The Formative Years | Decca | 589489-2
The Formative Years(1941-1942) | Creative World | ST 1061
Tommy Dorsey And His Orchestra | Frank Sinatra And The Tommy Dorsey Orchestra | RCA | 2668701-2
This Js Tommy Dorsey Vol. 2 | RCA | 26.28041 DP

This Love That I've Found

Dizzy Gillespie Quintet | Something Old Something New | Verve | 558079-2

This Lovely Feling

Dizzy Gillespie Sextet | Dizzy's Diamonds-Best Of The Verve Years | Verve | 513875-2

This Man's Dream

Barbara Dennerlein Quartet | Orgelspiele | Böhm Records | 65145 IMS

This Masquerade

George Benson Group/Orchestra | George Benson Anthology | Warner | 8122-79934-2
Jack McDuff Group | Bringin' It Home | Concord | CCD 4855
Milt Jackson And His Orchestra | Reverence And Compassion | Reprise | 9362-45204-2
Morgana King And Her Quintet | Everything Must Change | Muse | MCD 5190
Richard Davis Quintet | Harvest | Muse | MR 5115

This Masquerade(single-edit)

The Original Five Blind Boys Of Mississippi | Oh Lord-Stand By Me/Marching Up To Zion | Ace Records | CDCHD 341

This Means So Much

Jimmy Patrick Quintet | You Are My Audience | BELL Records | BLR 84036

This Moment

Jim Jackson | Memphis Blues 1928-1930 | RCA | 2126409-2

This Morning

Bucky Pizzarelli-John Pizzarelli Duo | The Complete Guitar Duos(The Stash Sessions) | Stash Records | ST-CD 536(889114)

This Nearly Was Mine

Chick Corea | Expressions | GRP | GRP 97732
Ethan Iverson Trio | Decontruction Zone(Originals) | Fresh Sound Records | FSNT 047 CD
Les Brown And His Orchestra | South Pacific | Capitol | ED 2604131

This Old Fairy-Tale

Buddy Guy Band | Blues Power No.9: Buddy Guy & Junior Wells Play The Blues | Atlantic | 40240

This One

Mark Soskin Quartet | Calypso & Jazz-Around The Corner | Paddle Wheel | KICJ 175

This One Is For Trunk(In Memoriam Peter Trunk)

Fritz Krisse Quartet | Soulcolours | Laika Records | 35100782
Fred Wesley Group | Comme Ca | Minor Music | 801020

This Over That

Mitch Seidman-Fred Fried | Jazz Guitar Highlights 1 | Jardis Records | JRCD 20141
Scott Colley Trio | This Place | Steeplechase | SCCD 31443

This Quietness

Sister Rosetta Tharpe With The Otis Spann Trio | Live In Paris 1964 | France's Concert | FCD 118

This Rhythm On My Mind

Paulus Potters Trio With Guests | The Argonauts | Timeless | CD SJP 423

This Time

Pete Malinverni Trio | This Time | Reservoir | RSR CD 147

This Time The Dream's On Me

Christian Josi With The Harry Allen Quartet | I Walk With My Feet Off The Ground | Master Mix | CHECD 00111
Ella Fitzgerald With The Billy May Orchestra | The Complete Ella Fitzgerald Song Books of Harold Arlen, Irving Berlin, Duke Ellington, George & Ira Gershwin, Jerome Kern, Johnny Mercer, Cole Porter And Rogers & Hart | Verve | 519832-2
The Harold Arlen Songbook | Verve | 817526-1 IMS
Ella Fitzgerald With The Nelson Riddle Orchestra | Ella Fitzgerald Sings The Johnny Mercer Songbook | Verve | 539057-2
The Johnny Mercer Songbook | Verve | 823247-2 PMS
Harry Allen Quartet | Love Songs Live! | Nagel-Heyer | NH 1014
Jeri Southern With The Lennie Hayton Orchestra | Coffee Cigarettes And Memories | Fresh Sound Records | FSR-CD 29(882157)
June Christy With The Pete Rugolo Orchestra | Something Cool(The Complete Mono & Stereo Versions) | Capitol | 534069-2
Something Cool(The Complete Mono & Stereo Versions) | Capitol | 534069-2
Kenny Burrell Quintet | Introducing Kenny Burrell | Blue Note | 300104(1523)
Paul Bley Trio | Charles Mingus-The Complete Debut Recordings | Debut | 12 DCD 4402-2
Red Garland Quintet | Red's Good Groove | Original Jazz Classics | OJCCD 1064-2(987)
Red Norvo And His Orchestra | Live From The Blue Gardens | Musicmasters | 65090-2
Red Rodney Quintet | Prestige First Sessions, Vol.3 | Prestige | PCD 24116-2

This Time's Hard

Big Bill Broonzy | Last Session, Vol.2 | Verve | 813367-1 IMS

This Train

Louis Armstrong With Sy Oliver's Choir And Orchestra | Louis And The Good Book | Verve | 549593-2
Sister Rosetta Tharpe With The Sammy Price Trio | Gospel Train | MCA | 1317

This Way

Al Di Meola Group | Orange And Blue | Inak | 700802

This Way Out

Nat King Cole Trio | The Instrumental Classics | Capitol | 798288-2
Vocal Classics & Instrumental Classics | Capitol | 300014(TOCJ 6128)

This Will Be

Chris Potter Quintet | Vertigo | Concord | CCD 4843

This Will Make You Laugh

Nat King Cole Trio | The Early Forties | Fresh Sound Records | FSR-CD 0139

This Yeah

Rhoda Scott | Rhoda Scott:Alone | Verve | 537635-2

This Year's Kisses

Billie Holiday With Teddy Wilson And His Orchestra | Billie Holiday:The Quintessential Vol.3(1936-1937) | CBS | 460820-2
Hal Kemp And His Orchestra | Got A Date With An Angel | Pro-Arte | CDD 553
Soesja Citroen And Her Quartet | Song For Ma | Challenge | CHR 70056

This Younger Generation

Chick Corea Septet | The Complete 'Is' Sessions | Blue Note | 540532-2

This(alt.take)

Stan Kenton And His Orchestra | Kenton Showcase | Creative World | ST 1026

This'll Get To Ya

Miles Davis Quintet | Miles Davis Quintet 1965-1968 | CBS | C6K 67398

Thisness(rehersal)

Annette Peacock With The Cikada String Quartet | An Acrobat's Heart | ECM | 1733(159496-2)

Tho

Alex De Santis Jazz Quartet | Le Canzoni Italiana | Edition Collage | EC 514-2

T'Ho Volute Bene

Aldo Romano Quartet | Canzoni | Enja | 9102-2

Thomas Wartet

Rene Thomas Quintet | The 1954 Paris Sessions | Vogue | 21622912

Thomey

Eric St.Laurent & Osmose | Eric St-Laurent & Osmose | BIT | 11190

Thorn

Alexander von Schlippenbach And Tony Oxley | Digger's Harvest | FMP | CD 103

Thoroughbred

Gil Evans Orchestra | Svengali | ACT | 9207-2
Temperance Seven | Pasadena & The Lost Cylinders-Music From The Archives | Lake | LACD 77

Thorstadlin'

Gebhard Ullmann Quartet | Kreuzberg Park East | Soul Note | 121371-2

Those Dirty Blues

Ma Rainey With Lovie Austin And Her Blues Serenaders | Ma Rainey-Complete Recordings Vol.1 | VJM | VLP 81 IMS

Those Little White Lies

John Mehegan | Johnny Mehegan's Reflections | Savoy | SV 0204(MG 12028)

Those Things Money Can't Buy

Frank Catalano Quartet | Cut It Out!?! | Delmark | DE 501

Those Were The

Dexter Gordon Quartet | Power! | Prestige | P 24087

Those Were The Days

Joey & 'Papa' John DeFrancesco Group | All In The Family | HighNote Records | HCD 7021

Those Who Sit And Wait

Jimmy Scott With Band | Moon Glow | Milestone | MCD 9332-2

Those Who Were

Niels-Henning Orsted-Pedersen/Ulf Wakenius Duo With Lisa Nilsson | Those Who Were | Verve | 533232-2
Two-Bone Big Band | Two-Bone Big Band | MKW-Records | ???

Thou Swell

Benny Carter Quartet | The Jazz Giants Play Rodgers & Hart:Blue Moon | Prestige | PCD 24205-2
Swingin' The Twenties | Original Jazz Classics | OJCCD 339-2
Billy Byers' Jazz Workshop | The Jazz Workshop | Fresh Sound Records | NL 46046(RCA LPM 1269)
Bix Beiderbecke And His Gang | Riverboat Shuffle | Naxos Jazz | 8.120584 CD
Bud Powell | Strictly Confidental | Black Lion | BLCD 760196
Della Reese With The Neal Hefti Orchestra | Della | RCA | 2663912-2
Della | RCA | 2663912-2
Dorothy Ashby Quartet | The Jazz Harpist | Savoy | SV 0194(MG 6039)
Ella Fitzgerald With The Buddy Bregman Orchestra | The Complete Ella Fitzgerald Song Books of Harold Arlen, Irving Berlin, Duke Ellington, George & Ira Gershwin, Jerome Kern, Johnny Mercer, Cole Porter And Rogers & Hart | Verve | 519832-2
Ella Fitzgerald With The Hank Jones Trio | Ella Fitzgerald:Mr.Paganini | Dreyfus Jazz Line | FDM 36741-2
Ella Fitzgerald:The Royal Roost Sessions | Cool & Blue | C&B-CD 112
J.J.Johnson-Kai Winding Quintet (Jay&Kai) | Kai Winding And Jay Jay Johnson | Bethlehem | BET 6026-2(BCP 76)
Lester Lanin And His Orchestra | The Uncollected:Lester Lanin | Hindsight | HSR 210
Paul Kuhn Quintet | Deutsches Jazz Fesival 1954/1955 | Bear Family Records | BCD 15430
Pete Jolly Trio | Take The 'A' Train | Fresh Sound Records | FSR-CD 0306
Sarah Vaughan And Her Trio | Sarah Vaughan At Mister Kelly's | EmArCy | 832791-2 PMS
Stan Getz Quintet | Stan Getz-The Complete Roost Sessions | EMI Records | 859622-2
Jazz At Storyville Vol.1 | Fresh Sound Records | FSR 629(Roost RLP 407)

Thou Swell(incomplete)

Louisiana Sugar Babes | Jazz Archives Vol.77:Jabbo Smith-The Complete 1929-1938 Sessions | EPM Musique | 158112

Though Sledding

Mahalia Jackson With Orchestra | In Memoriam Mahalia Jackson | CBS | 66501

Thought Of Happines

Joachim Kühn | The Diminished Augmented System | EmArCy | 542320-2

Thought Of JF

Dave Liebman Quintet | The Last Call | EGO | 4016

Thoughtful

Mal Waldron | One-Upmanship | Enja | 2092 (807490)

Thoughts

Christoph Spendel | Thoughts | L+R Records | CDLR 45092
Great Friends | Great Friends | Black & Blue | BLE 233222

Thoughts About Duke

Pipe Trio | We Thought About Duke | Hat Art | CD 6163

Thoughts About My Mother

Richie Hart Quartet With Strings | Remembering Wes | Blue Flame | 40222

Thoughts And Dreams

Randy Burns-Emery Fletcher | Of Love And War | ESP Disk | ESP 1039-2

Thoughts Of Loss

Lars Danielsson Group | Fresh Enough | L+R Records | CDLR 45051

Thre For The Festival

J.A. Deane | Nomad | Victo | CD 035

Three

Bill Dixon Sextet | Bill Dixon In Italy - Volume Two | Soul Note | SN 1011
Gary Burton Quartet With Chamber Orchestra | Seven Songs For Quartet And Chamber Orchestra | ECM | 1040
Khan Jamal Trio | Three | Steeplechase | SCCD 31201
Errol Parker Trio | My Own Bag No.1 | Sahara | 1001

Three Acts Of Recognition

Machito And His Orchestra | Afro-Cuban Jazz Moods | Original Jazz Classics | OJC20 447-2

Three Afro-Cuban Jazz Moods:

Stan Tracey-John Surman | Stan Tracey Duets(Sonatinas/TNT) | Blue Note | 789450-2

Three And One

Ed Neumeister Trio | The Mohican And The Great Spirit | TCB Records | TCB 01072

Three Angels

Walt Weiskopf Nonet | Song For My Mother | Criss Cross | Criss 1127

Three Aspects

The Heath Brothers Orchestra | Jazz Family | Concord | CCD 4846

Three Bags Full

Herbie Hancock Quintet | Herbie Hancock:The Complete Blue Note Sixties Sessions | Blue Note | 495569-2
Takin' Off | Blue Note | 837643-2

Three Bags Full(alt.take)

Herbie Hancock:The Complete Blue Note Sixties Sessions | Blue Note | 495569-2
Stan Getz Quintet With The Boston Pops Orchestra | Stan Getz And Arthur Fiedler At Tanglewood | RCA | 2136406-2

Three Blind Mice

Duke Ellington And His Orchestra | Live Recording At The Cotton Club-Vol. 2 | Jazz Anthology | JA 5169

Three Bopeteers

Guitar Madness | Guitar Madness | Nueva Records | HM 705

Three Cheers For Paul Chambers

Fabien Degryse Quintet | Medor Sadness | Edition Collage | EC 454-2

Three Children In The Garden

Mickey Tucker | Gettin' There | Steeplechase | SCCD 31365

Three Clowns

Susan Weinert Band | Mysterious Stories | VeraBra Records | CDVBR 2111-2

Three Coices

Billy Eckstine With Bobby Tucker And His Orchestra | Billy Eckstine Now Singing In 12 Great Movies | Verve | 589307-2

Three Coins In The Fountain

Hank Mobley Quartet | Workout | Blue Note | 784080-2
Hank Mobley Quintet | Blue Eyes-Sinatra Songs The Blue Note Way | Blue Note | 789914-2
Ralph Towner | Anthem | ECM | 1743(543814-2)

Three Comments

Bruno Castellucci Groups | Bim Bam | Koala Records | CD P 19

Three Dances

Duke Ellington And His Orchestra | The Indispensable Duke Ellington Vol.11/12 | RCA | 2115524-2

Three Dances(West Indian Dance-Creamy Brown-Emancipation Celebration)-

Duke Ellingtonton:Complete Prestige Carnegie Hall 1943-1944 Concerts | Definitive Records | DRCD 11210

Three Day Sucker
Dave Grusin And The N.Y./L.A. Dream Band | Dave Grusin And The NY-LA Dream Band | GRP | GRP 91001-1(808561)

Three Deuces
Eddie Lockjaw Davis Quintet | The Eddie Lockjaw Davis Cookbook Vol.1 | Original Jazz Classics | OJCCD 652-2(P 7141)

Three Faces Of Intimate Game
Billy Sheehan-John Novello-Dennis Chambers | Niacin | Stretch Records | SCD 9011-2

Three Flowers
Frank Morgan Quartet | Easy Living | Original Jazz Classics | OJCCD 833-2(C 14013)
McCoy Tyner | Soliloquy | Blue Note | 796429-2

Three For Dizzy
Roland Kirk-Jack McDuff Quartet | Pre-Rahsan | Prestige | P 24080

Three For D'reen-
Jimmy Smith Trio | Bucket! | Blue Note | 524550-2

Three For Four
Jim Pepper Quartet | West End Avenue | Nabel Records:Jazz Network | CD 4633

Three For Gemini
Matthias Schubert Quartet | Blue And Grey Suite | Enja | ENJ-9045 2

Three For The Festival
Rahsaan Roland Kirk With The George Gruntz Trio | Rahsaan Rolnd Kirk:Dog Years In The Fourth Ring | 32 Jazz | 32032
Roland Kirk Quintet | Live In Paris 1970 Vol.1 | France's Concert | FCD 109

Three Forgotten Magic Words
Michel Petrucciani Trio | Live At The Village Vanguard | Blue Note | 540382-2
Soviet Jazz Ensemble | Boomerang | Mobile Fidelity | MFCD 908

Three Handed Woman
Louis Jordan Quintet | I Believe In Music | Black & Blue | BB 876.2

Three Hearts
Steve Erquiaga Group | Erkiology | Windham Hill | 34 10127-2

Three Hots And A Cot-
Johnny 'Guitar' Watson | California Blues | Anthology of the Blues | AB 5603

Three In Four Or More
Humphrey Lyttelton-Acker Bilk Band | More Humph & Acker | Calligraph | CLGCD 030

Three In One
Geoff Keezer Trio | Waiting In The Wings | Sunnyside | SSC 1035 D

Three Little Initials
Don Redman And His Orchestra | The Complete McKinney's Cotton Pickers Vol.5 Plus Don Redman & His Orchestra | RCA | NL 89161 (809233)

Three Little Words
Benny Carter 4 | The Montreux '77 Collection | Pablo | 2620107
Bucky And John Pizzarelli Duo | The Pizzarellis,Bucky And John:Contrasts | Arbors Records | ARCD 19209
David Janeway Quartet | Inside Out | Timeless | CD SJP 402
Gerald Wiggins Trio | Mary Lou Williams/Gerry Wiggins:On Vogue | Vogue | 2111505-2
John Coltrane-Milt Jackson Quintet | Bags & Trane | Rhino | 8122-73685-2
John Swana Quintet | Introducing John Swana | Criss Cross | Criss 1045
Lester Young Quintet | Prez's Hat Vol.4 | Philology | 214 W 9
Lester Young With The Bill Potts Trio | Lester Young In Washington,DC 1956:Vol.2 | Pablo | 2308225-2
Milt Jackson Quartet | Mostly Duke | Pablo | 2310944-2
Quintet Du Hot Club De France | Django Reinhardt Vol. 2 | Decca | 180021 AG
Richie Kamuca Quartet | Drop Me Off In Harlem | Concord | CJ 39
Sonny Rollins Quartet | Sonny Rollins On Impulse | MCA | 2292-54613-2
Sonny Rollins With The Kenny Drew Trio | Sonny Rollins In Denmark Vol.2 | Moon Records | MCD 038-2
Stan Getz Quartet | Award Winner | Verve | 543320-2
Stan Getz:East Of The Sun-The West Coast Sessions | Verve | 531935-2
Teddy Wilson Trio | Three Little Words | Black & Blue | BLE 233094
Mel Tormé With The Mike Renzi Trio | An Evening With Mel Tormé | Concord | CCD 4736

Three Men In A Boat
Joe Maneri-Joe Morris-Mat Maneri | Three Men Walking | ECM | 1597

Three Men Walking
David Moss Dense Band | Dense Band | Moers Music | 02040

Three Mountains
Elisabeth Kontomanou & Jean-Michel Pilc | Hands & Incantation | Steeplechase | SCCD 31484

Three Note Samba
Huub Janssen's Amazing Jazzband | Huub Janssen's Amazing Jazzband | Timeless | CD TTD 536

Three O'Clock Blues
Cootie Williams Quintet | Jazz In Paris:Joe Newman-Jazz At Midnight-Cootie Williams | EmArCy | 018446-2

Three O'Clock In The Morning
Dexter Gordon Quartet | It's You Or No One | Steeplechase | SCC 6022
The Best Of Dexter Gordon | Blue Note | 791139-2
Dexter Gordon:The Complete Blue Note Sixties Sessions | Blue Note | 834200-2
Oscar Peterson-Ray Brown Duo | Oscar Peterson:Get Happy | Dreyfus Jazz Line | FDM 36738-2
Tenderly | Verve | MV 2662 IMS

Three O'Clock Jump
Diederik Wissels Trio With Larry Schneider | Crystals | Timeless | CD SJP 218/254

Three Of A Kind
Lew Davis Trombone Trio | Swingin' Britain-The Thirties | Decca | DDV 5013/14

Three On A Match
Daniel Flors Group | When Least Expected | Fresh Sound Records | FSNT 080 CD

Three On A Row
Shelly Manne Three | The Three & The Two | Original Jazz Classics | OJCCD 172-2(C 3584)

Three Or Four Shades Of Blues
Danny Richmond Quintet | Dionysius | Red Records | VPA 161

Three Poems:
David Blamires Group | The David Blamires Group | Nova | NOVA 9144-2

Three Points-
Mike Nock-Marty Ehrlich | The Waiting Game | Naxos Jazz | 86048-2

Three Preludes:
Steve Tibbetts Group | Yr | ECM | 1355(835245-2)

Three Primates
Heiner Stadler Jazz Alchemy | Jazz Alchemy | Tomato | 2696702

Three Seconds
Oliver Nelson Sextet | Images | Prestige | P 24060
Ran Blake | The Blue Potato And Other Outrages | Milestone | M 9021

Three Silver Quarters
Mat Maneri Trio | So What? | HatOLOGY | 529

Three Stories,One End
Wayne Horvitz-Butch Morris-Robert Previte | Nine Below Zero | Sound Aspects | sas CD 014

Three Thimbles
John Rapson Octet | bing | Sound Aspects | sas CD 036

Three Thousand Miles Back Home
Dave Bartholomew And His Orchestra | The Monkey | Pathe | 1561331(Imperial)

Three To Get Ready And Four To Go
Dave Brubeck Quartet | The Dave Brubeck Selection | CBS | 467279-2

Three To Got Ready
Gerard Pansanel Quintet | Voices | Owl Time Line | 3819102

Three Views Of A Secret
George Cables Trio | Night And Day | DIW | DIW 606 CD
Jaco Pastorius Trio | Live In New York City Volume Two | Big World | BW 1002
Toots Thielemans Quartet | Toots Thielemans:The Live Takes Vol.1 | IN+OUT Records | 77041-2
Weather Report | Night Passage | CBS | 468211-2
Darrell Grant Quintet | The New Bop | Criss Cross | Criss 1106

Three Way Split
Zoom | Three Ways | Bhakti Jazz | BR 101

Three Ways In One
Ornette Coleman-Joachim Kühn Duo | Colors | Harmolodic | 537789-2

Three Wishes
Klaus Ignatzek Group | Day For Night | Nabel Records:Jazz Network | CD 4639
Makoto Ozone Group | Treasure | Verve | 021906-2
Ornette Coleman & Prime Time | Virgin Beauty | CBS | 489433-2
Spyro Gyra | Three Wishes | GRP | GRP 96742

Three Worlds(based on Akazehe Greeting from Burundi)
Abdullah Ibrahim | Knysna Blue | TipToe | TIP-888816 2

Three-Fourth Blues
Rex Stewart And His Orchestra | That's Earl Brother | Spotlite | SPJ 152

Three-Quarter Gemini
Jim Pepper & Eagle Wing | Remembrance-Live At The International Jazzfestival Münster | Tutu Records | 888152-2*
Jim Pepper Flying Eagle | Live At New Morning,Paris | Tutu Records | 888194-2*
William Ackerman Groups | Past Light-Visiting | Windham Hill | 34 11028-2

Threewe
Pete York-Wolfgang Schmid-Lenny MacDowell | Once Upon A Time | BELL Records | BLR 84028

Thren
Marian McPartland Trio With Strings | Marian McPartland With Strings | Concord | CCD 4745

Thrill Seekers
Chris Barber's Jazz Band | Elite Syncopations-Great British Traditional Jazzbands Vol.2 | Lake | LACD 43

Thriller Rag
Steve Swallow Group | Swallow | Watt | XtraWatt/6

Thrills And Spills
Al Haig Trio | Al Haig Today! | Fresh Sound Records | FSR-CD 0006

Thriving On A Riff
Charlie Parker's Reboppers | The Complete Savoy Studio Sessions | Savoy | 886421

Through
Joe Maneri-Joe Morris-Mat Maneri | Three Men Walking | ECM | 1597

Through A Glas Darkly
Erroll Garner Trio | Relaxin' | Vogue | 500117

Through For The Night
Johnny Hodges Orchestra | The Rabbit's Work On Verve In Chronological Order Vol. 3: 1952-54 | Verve | 2304449 IMS

Through The Clouds
Charles Brown Band | Boss Of The Blues | Mainstream | MD CDO 908

Through The Orchard
Marty Fogel Quartet | Many Bobbing Heads, At Last... | CMP Records | CMP CD 37

Through The Test Of Time
Patti Austin And Her Band | Patti Austin Live | GRP | GRP 96822

Through The Window
Bheki Mseleku Group | Timelessness | Verve | 521306-2

Through The Years
Sibongile Khumalo Group | Live At The Market Theatre | CBS | 491322-2

Throughout
Bill Frisell Trio | Live | Gramavision | GCD 79504

Throw It Away
Gilbert Paeffgen Trio | Pedestrian Tales | Edition Musikat | EDM 061
Norbert Gottschalk-Frank Haunschild | The Art Of The Duo:Favorite Songs | Mons Records | MR 874813

Thrrillr
Cozy Cole All Stars | Ultimate Coleman Hawkins selected by Sonny Rollins | Verve | 557538-2

Thru For The Night
Gustl Mayer's Jazz Stampede | Yellow Cab | L+R Records | LR 40004

Thruway
Manny Albam And His Orchestra | Jazz Horizons | Fresh Sound Records | DLP 9004(Dot)

Thruway(alt.take)
Lowell Fulsom Band | Man Of Motion | Charly | CRB 1018

Thumbs Up
Mark Helias Group | Loopin' The Cool | Enja | ENJ-9049 2
Walter Norris-George Mraz Duo | Drifting | Enja | ENJ-2044 2
Ray Brown With The Allstar Big Band | Much In Common | Verve | 533259-2

Thunder Walk
George Benson Quintet | Blue Benson | Polydor | 2391242 IMS
George Benson Sextet | Talkin' Verve:George Benson | Verve | 553780-2
Herbie Hancock Quintet | Jazz-Club: Piano | Verve | 840032-2

Thunderball
Al Caiola Quintet | Deep In A Dream | Savoy | SV 0205(MG 12033)

Thunderbird
Tito Puente's Golden Latin Jazz All Stars | In Session | RMM Records | 660.58.037

Thundering Noise
Bireli Lagrene Ensemble | Routes To Django & Bireli Swing '81 | Jazzpoint | JP 1055 CD
Maggie Jones With Louis Armstrong And Fletcher Henderson | Louis Armstrong And The Blues Singers 1924-1930 | Affinity | AFS 1018(6)

Thursday 2:55 p.m.
Victoria Spivey With Lonnie Johnson | Woman Blues! | Original Blues Classics | OBCCD 566-2(BV 1054)

Thursday The 12th
Tom Williams Quintet | Introducing Tom Williams | Criss Cross | Criss 1064

Thursday's Child
Arne Domnerus Quartet | Sugar Fingers | Phontastic | NCD 8831
Barbara Lea With The Johnny Windhurst Quartet | Barbara Lea | Original Jazz Classics | OJCCD 1713-2(PR 7065)

Thursday's Theme
Larry Coryell Group | Fallen Angel | CTI Records | CTI 1014-2

Thy Way Home
Mahalia Jackson | In Memoriam Mahalia Jackson | CBS | 66501

Thyme Time
Art Pepper Quintet | Rediscoveries | Savoy | WL 70828 (809328)

Tia Juana
Barrelhouse Jazzband | Barrelhouse Jazzband Plays Jelly Roll Morton | Intercord | 145038
The Wolverines | Bix Beiderbecke | Milestone | MCD 47019-2

Tibet
Lounge Lizards | Berlin 1991 Part 1 | Intuition Records | INT 2044-2
Radius | Sightseeing | Ear-Rational | ECD 1017

Tibetan Sun
Barbara Thompson Group | Heavenly Bodies | VeraBra Records | CDVBR 2015-2

Tibetan Sunrise
New Orchestra Workshop | The Future Is N.O.W. | Nine Winds Records | NWCD 0131

Tic Toc
Chris Walden Orchestra | Great European Jazz Orchestras Vol.3:Ticino | ACT | 9229-2

Tick Tock
The Dynatones feat.Charlie Musselwhite | Live | Red Lightnin' | RL 0044

Ticker
Lightnin' Hopkins | Lightnin Hopkins-A Legend In His Own Time | Anthology of the Blues | AB 5608

Ticket To Tokyo
Mal Waldron & Jim Pepper | Art Of The Duo | Tutu Records | 888106-2*
Mal Waldron Quartet feat.Jim Pepper | Quadrologue At Utopia Vol.1 | Tutu Records | 888118-2*

Ticket To Utopia
Mark Murphy-Jose Roberto Bertrami | Night Mood | Milestone | MCD 9145-2

Tickle Toe
Anders Lindskog Quartet | Cry Me A River | Touché Music | TMcCD 005
Anders Lindskog Trio | Fine Together | Touché Music | TMcCD 010
Art Pepper Quartet | Complete Discovery-Savoy Master Takes | Definitive Records | DRCD 11218
Benny Carter And His Orchestra | Tickle Toe | Vee Jay Recordings | VJ 024
Butch Miles-Howard Alden Sextet | Cookin' | Nagel-Heyer | CD 5003
Charly Antolini Jazz Power | Cookin' | L+R Records | CDLR 45024
Chico Hamilton And Euphoria | Arroyo | Soul Note | 121241-2
Count Basie And His Orchestra | Disque D'Or | Vogue | 400525
Harald Rüschenbaum Orchestra | Rondo | Swingtime | 8208
Hot Mallets | Hot Mallets...Live! | JHM Records | JHM 3610
Jan Lundgren Trio With Herb Geller | Stockholm Get-Together | Fresh Sound Records | FSR CD 5007
Johnny Smith Quartet | The Johnny Smith Foursome | Fresh Sound Records | FSR 581(Roost 2223)
Lester Young And His Band | Jazz Gallery:Lester Young Vol.1(1936-46) | RCA | 2114171-2

Ticklin' The Blues
Jesse Fuller | Jesse Fuller's Favorites | Original Blues Classics | OBCCD 528-2(P 7368)

Tickling The Strings
Jesse Fuller One Man Band | Brother Lowdown | Fantasy | F 24707

Tico Tico
Carlo Actis Dato/Laura Culver | Zig Zag | SPLASC(H) Records | H 186
Charlie Parker Sextet | Charlie Parker:The Best Of The Verve Years | Verve | 527815-2
The Latin Bird | Memo Music | HDJ 4076
Christoph Sänger | Live At The Montreal Jazz Festival | Laika Records | 35100822
Frank Vignola Trio With Davis Grisman | Let It Happen | Concord | CCD 4625
The Rosenberg Trio | The Rosenberg Trio:The Collection | Verve | 537152-2
Urszula Dudziak And Band Walk Away | Magic Lady | IN+OUT Records | 7008-2
Clusone 3 | Rare Avis | HatOLOGY | 523

Tidal Breeze
Harold Danko Quartet | Tidal Breeze | Steeplechase | SCCD 31411

Tidal Waves
Lloyd Glenn Trio | After Hours | Pathe | 1546641(Aladdin)

Tide
Hartschuh-Reiter-Sauer | Eternal Verities | L+R Records | CDLR 45096

Tidevann(Tide)
Tango Orkestret | Tango Orkestret | Stunt Records | STUCD 19303

Tie Me To Your Apron String Again
The United Women's Orchestra | The Blue One | Jazz Haus Musik | JHM 0099 CD

Tiebreak
Christoph Spendel Group | Out Of Town | TCB Records | TCB 01032

Tiefseejahrmarkt
Cafe Du Sport Jazzquartett | Cafe Du Sport Jazzquartett | Minor Music | 801096

Tiefseetaucher
Enrico Rava-Dino Saluzzi Quintet | Volver | ECM | 1343

Tiempos De Ausencias
Gary Burton Quintet | Reunion | GRP | GRP 95982

Tiempos Viejos
Nils Petter Molvaer Group | Khmer | ECM | 1560(537798-2)

Tien
Henrichs-Kuchenbuch-Rilling | Ohpsst | FMP | SAJ 22

Tierra Baja
Gary Burton Quartet | Picture This | ECM | 1226

Tierra Espanola
Alain Everts | Terra Nueva | Acoustic Music Records | 319.1103.2

Tierra Tibia
Buddy Montgomery Quartet | Ties Of Love | Landmark | LCD 1512-2

Tiffany
Bill Evans Trio | Consecration 2 | Timeless | CD SJP 332

Tiffany's Waltz
Jukka Tolonen Group | Crossection | Sonet | 147119

Tiger Dreams
Philip Catherine Quartet | Summer Night | Dreyfus Jazz Line | FDM 36637-2

Tiger Groove
Eric Person Quartet | Arrival | Soul Note | 121237-2

Tiger Man
Joe Hill Louis Band | Joe Hill Louis: The Be-Bop Boy | Bear Family Records | BCD 15524 AH
State Street Ramblers | Chicago South Side Jazz | Village(Jazz Archive) | VILCD 019-2

Tiger No.33
Hans Koller & The International Brass Company | Live At The Jazz Festival Frankfurt | L+R Records | LR 40014

Tiger Rag
Albert Nicholas Quartet | A Tribute To Jelly Roll Morton | Storyville | SLP 4050
Art Tatum | Art Tatum:Complete Original American Decca Recordings | Definitive Records | DRCD 11200
Benny Goodman Quartet | The Benny Goodman Trio And Quartet Sessions Vol.1-After You've Gone | Bluebird | ND 85631
Castle Jazz Band | The Famous Castle Jazz Band In Stereo | Good Time Jazz | GTCD 10030-2
Chris Barber's Jazz Band | In The Beginning... | Black Lion | BLCD 760520
Dutch Swing College Band Meets Billy Butterfield | Swing That Music | DSC Production | PA 1009 (801066)
Gregor Et Son Gregoriens | Le Jazz En France Vol.9:Pionniers Du Jazz Francais 1906-1931 | Pathe | 1552551
Helmut Zacharias | Ich Habe Rhythmus | Bear Family Records | BCD 15642 AH
Heritage Hall Jazz Band | New Orleans | Dixieland Jubilee | DJ 512
Ken Colyer's Jazzmen | Up Jumped The Devil | Upbeat Jazz | URCD 114
Kid Ory's Creole Jazz Band | New Orleans | CBS | 21061
Louis Armstrong And His All Stars | Masters Of Jazz Vol.1:Louis Armstrong | Storyville | STCD 4101
En Concert Avec Europe 1 | Laserlight | 710415
Louis Armstrong:Wintergarden 1947/Blue Note 1948 | Storyville | STCD 8242
The Complete Town Hall Concert 17.May 1947 | RCA | ND 89746
Punch Miller's Bunch & George Lewis | Jazz At Preservation Hall, Vol.3 | Atlantic | SD 1410
Stephane Grappelli And His Musicians | Grapelli Story | Verve | 515807-2
Stephane Grappelli-David Grisman Group | Live | Warner | BSK 3550
The Thames River Jazz Band | Riverboat Shuffle | Black Lion | 157003
Wolverine Orchestra | Bix Beiderbecke & The Wolverines | Village(Jazz Archive) | VILCD 008-2

Tiger Rag-
Piccadilly Six | Fans' Favourites | Elite Special | 73319

Tiger Twist
Robben Ford Band | Tiger Walk | Blue Thumb | BTR 70122

Tiger Walk
Carla Bley Band | Fancy Chamber Music | Watt | 28(539937-2)

Tigers In Training
Bob Kindler Group | Tiger's Paw | Global Pacific Records | 660.52.019

Tight Like That
Louis Armstrong And His Savoy Ballroom Five | Louis Armstrong:Fireworks | Dreyfus Jazz Line | FDM 36710-2

Tight Like This
Pili-Pili | Boogaloo | JA & RO | JARO 4174-2

Tight Lips
Marc Ducret-Bobby Previt | In The Grass | Enja | ENJ-9343 2
Tight Lipstick
Yosuke Yamashita & Adelhard Roidinger | Inner Space | Enja | 3001
Tight Squeeze
Leroy Carr | Leroy Carr-Singin' The Blues | Biograph | BLP C 9
Tightrope
Franco Morone | Guitarea | Acoustic Music Records | 319.1046.2
Tight-Rope-Walker
Duke Ellington And His Orchestra | Afro-Bossa | Reprise | 9362-47876-2
Tigress
Sorry.It's Jazz | Sorry,It's Jazz! | Satin Doll Productions | SDP 1040-1 CD
Tigri-Bing
Rinus Groeneveld Trio | Dare To Be Different | Timeless | CD SJP 321
Tijuana Gift Shop
Charles Mingus Septet | Jazz:For Absolute Beginners | RCA | NL 89874 AG
Tijuana Gift Shop(alt.take)
Charles Mingus Orchestra | Tijuana Moods(The Complete Edition) | RCA | 2663840-2
Tijuana Gift Shop(alt.take-2)
Tijuana Moods(The Complete Edition) | RCA | 2663840-2
Tijuana Gift Shop(short-take)
Jimmy McGriff Orchestra | Swingin' The Blues-Jumpin' The Blues | Laserlight | 24654
Tiki
The Best Of The Jazz Organs | LRC Records | CDC 9006
Til Bakeblikk
Emborg-Larsen Group | Face The Music | Stunt Records | STUCD 19805
'Til I Can Gain Control Again
Arild Andersen Quintet | Masqualero | Odin | LP 08
Til Sjaellands Morke Skove(To The Dark Forest Of Zealand)
Bobby Hutcherson Orchestra | Knucklebean | Blue Note | LA 789
Till The Clouds Roll By
Mel Tormé With The Al Pellegrini Orchestra | It's A Blue World | Bethlehem | BET 6023-2(BCP 6041)
Till The End Of Times
Herb Ellis Quintet | Roll Call | Justice Records | JR 1001-2
Till Then
The Mills Brothers | Harlem Roots-Jazz On Film:Rhythm In Harmony | Storyville | SLP 6002
Till There Was You
Gene Ammons Quartet | The Gene Ammons Story: Gentle Jug | Prestige | P 24079
Steve Grossman Quintet | Time To Smile | Dreyfus Jazz Line | FDM 36566-2
Sonny Rollins Trio | Sonny Rollins-The Freelance Years:The Complete Riverside & Contemporary Recordings | Riverside | 5 RCD 4427-2
Till There Was You(alt.take)
Freedom Suite | Original Jazz Classics | OJCCD 067-2
Till There Was You(take 1)
Freedom Suite | Original Jazz Classics | OJCCD 067-2
Till There Was You(take 2)
The Freedom Suite Plus | Milestone | M 47007
Till Vennene
Monika Linges Quartet | Floating | Nabel Records:Jazz Network | CD 4607
Till We Get There
Albert Burbank Jazzband | New Orleans Tarditional Jazz Legends:Albert Burbank/Raymond Burke | Mardi Gras Records | MG 9005
Tillie
Jaki Byard Trio | Giant Steps | Prestige | P 24086
Tillie's Downtown Now
Bud Freeman And His Windy City Five | Bud Freeman(1927-1940) | CDS Records Ltd. | RPCD 604
Tilly's Two Step
Darrell Grant Quartet | Black Art | Criss Cross | Criss 1087
Tim Booked Two
| Playing To The Moon | Ronnie Scott's Jazz House | JHCD 047
Timbale Groove
Mongo Santamaria And His Rhythm Afro-Cubanos | Afro Roots | Prestige | PCD 24018-2(F 8012/8032)
Timba-Tumba
Odetta | The Tin Angel | Original Blues Classics | OBCCD 565-2(F 3252)
Timbiktu
Lauren Newton Quartet | Timbre | Hat Art | 3511
Timbuktu
Cindy Blackman Quartet | Trio + Two | Freelance | FRL-CD 015
Time
Clifford Brown-Max Roach Quintet | Brownie-The Complete EmArCy Recordings Of Clifford Brown | EmArCy | 838306-2
D.D.Jackson-Don Byron | Paired Down,Vol.2 | Justin Time | JUST 104-2
Joe Newman And His Orchestra | Joe Newman With Woodwinds | Fresh Sound Records | FSR 663(Roulette R 52014)
Marcus Klossek Imagination | As We Are | Jardis Records | JRCD 20134
Michael Sagmeister Quartet | Motions And Emotions | BELL Records | BLR 84054
Roland Kirk Quartet | Rahsaan/The Complete Mercury Recordings Of Roland Kirk | Mercury | 846630-2
Domino | Verve | 543833-2
Sarah Vaughan With The Jimmy Jones Trio | Birdland All Stars At Carnegie Hall | Roulette | CDP 798660-2
Time-
Sarah Vaughan Birthday Celebration | Fantasy | FANCD 6090-2
Linger Awhile | Pablo | 2312144-2
John Goldsby Quartet | Tales Of The Fingers | Concord | CCD 4632
Time After Time
Abbey Lincoln With Hank Jones | When There Is Love | Verve | 519697-2
Ann Hampton Callaway And Her Band | After Hours | Denon Compact Disc | CY-18042
Ben Webster And His Associates | Ultimate Ben Webster selected by James Carter | Verve | 557537-2
Ben Webster With Strings | The Warm Mood | Discovery | DS 818 IMS
Benny Green Trio | Greens | Blue Note | 796485-2
Cecil Payne Quartet | Casbah | Empathy Records | E 1005
Chet Baker Quartet | Chet Baker Sings | Pacific Jazz | 300067(PJ 1222)
Dodo Greene With The Ike Quebec Sextet | My Hour Of Need | Blue Note | 852442-2
Eddie Lockjaw Davis Sextet feat. Paul Gonsalves | Love Calls | RCA | 2125729-2
Ella Fitzgerald With The Marty Paich Orchestra | Whisper Not | Verve | 589947-2
Ernestine Anderson With The Monty Alexander Trio | Sunshine | Concord | CCD 4109
Jack DeJohnette Trio | The Jack DeJohnette Piano Album | Landmark | LCD 1504-2
JATP All Stars | Jazz At The Philharmonic 1983 | Pablo | 2310882
John Coltrane Quartet | The Jazz Giants Play Sammy Cahn:It's Magic | Prestige | PCD 24226-2
John Coltrane-The Prestige Recordings | Prestige | 16 PCD 4405-2
Keith Jarrett Trio | Keith Jarrett At The Blue Note-The Complete Recordings | ECM | 1575/80(527638-2)
Lawrence Brown With The Ralph Burns Orchestra | Slide Trombone | Verve | 559930-2
Lionel Hampton All Stars | For The Love Of Music | MoJazz | 530554-2
Miles Davis Group | This Is Jazz:Miles Davis Plays Ballads | CBS | CK 65038
Miles In Montreux | Jazz Door | JD 1287/88
Milt Jackson Quintet | At The Village Gate | Original Jazz Classics | OJCCD 309-2
Morgana King With Orchestra | Looking Through The Eyes Of Love | Muse | MR 5257
Plas Johnson Sextet | The Blues | Concord | CCD 4015
Sonny Stitt-Jack McDuff Quintet | Stitt Meets Brother Jack | Original Jazz Classics | OJCCD 703-2(P 7244)
Stan Getz Quartet | Stan Getz:The Golden Years Vol.1(1952-1958) | Moon Records | MCD 039-2
Stan Getz:East Of The Sun-The West Coast Sessions | Verve | 531935-2
Stephane Grappelli Quartet | Grapelli Story | Verve | 515807-2
Afternoon In Paris | MPS | 68156
Stephane Grappelli With The George Shearing Trio | Compact Jazz:George Shearing | MPS | 833284-2 PMS
Teddy Wilson Quartet | I Want To Be Happy | Naxos Jazz | 8.120538 CD
Tuck And Patti | Everything Is Gonna Be Alright | Jazz Door | JD 1297
Vince Jones With The Benny Green Quartet | One Day Spent | Intuition Records | INT 3087-2
Vito Price Quintet | Swingin' The Loop | Fresh Sound Records | FSR-CD 110(882418)
Time After Time-
Stephane Grappelli | 7.Zelt-Musik-Festival:Jazz Events | Zounds | CD 2730001
Stephane Grappelli Trio With Marcel Azzola | Stephane Grappelli In Toky | Denon Compact Disc | CY-77130
Time After Time(2 false start)
Stan Getz Quartet | Award Winner | Verve | 543320-2
Time After Time(alt.take)
Stan Getz:East Of The Sun-The West Coast Sessions | Verve | 531935-2
Time After Time(first version)
Freddie Hubbard Sextet | Minor Mishap | Black Lion | BLP 60122
Time After Time(The Savior Is Waiting)
Art Kassel And His 'Kassels-In-The-Air' Orchestra | The Uncollected:Art Kassel | Hindsight | HSR 162
Time And Again
Stuff Smith Quartet | Stuff Smith+Dizzy Gillespie+Oscar Peterson | Verve | 521676-2
Time And More
Nelson Riddle And His Orchestra | Communication | MPS | 9814795
Time And Space
Marty Ehrlich Quintet | New York Child | Enja | ENJ-9025 2
Time And The Wild Words
John Scofield Quartet | Time On My Hands | Blue Note | 792894-2
Time And Us
Antonio Farao Trio | Thorn | Enja | ENJ-9399 2
Time Back
Jazz Indeed | Under Water | Traumton Records | 2415-2
Time Bandits
Buddy Rich And His Orchestra | The Amazing Buddy Rich: Time Being | RCA | ND 86459(847168)
Time Check
Louis Bellson And His Big Band | 150 MPH | Concord | CCD 4036
Time Dust Gathered
Roland Hanna | Perugia | Freedom | FLP 41010
Time For A Rainy Day
Laurent De Wilde Sextet | Time Change | Warner | 8573-84315-2
Time For Change
Stan Kenton And His Orchestra | Kenton '76 | Creative World | STD 1076
Time For Duke
Borah Bergman | A New Frontier | Soul Note | 121030-2
Time For Joy,Time Of Song
Ahmad Jamal Quartet | Digital Works | Atlantic | 781258-2
Time For Love
Slide Hampton-Joe Haider Jazz Orchestra | Give Me A Double | JHM Records | JHM 3627
Lionel Hampton And His All Stars | Lionel Hampton And His All Stars 1956 | Jazz Anthology | 550152
Time For The Tupan
Mike Melillo | Live And Well | Red Records | VPA 188
Time Game
Claudio Fasoli | Egotrip | SPLASC(H) Records | H 161
Time Into Space Into Time
Ingrid Sertso/Karl Berger Group | Jazz Dance | ITM Records | ITM 1427
Time Is Now
Wollie Kaiser Timeghost | Post Art Core | Jazz Haus Musik | JHM 0077 CD
Santi Debriano Quintet | Obeah | Freelance | FRL-CD 008
Time Is On Our Side
Byron Allen Trio | The Byron Allen Trio | ESP Disk | ESP 1005-2
Time Lapse Photos
Dave Matthews' Big Band | Night Flight | Muse | MR 5098
Time Line
Mitch Farber Group | Starclimber | Muse | MCD 5400
Time Marches On
Dave McKenna & Gray Sargent | Concord Duo Series Volume Two | Concord | CCD 4552
Time Of Change
Andreas Heuser | Continuum | Acoustic Music Records | 319.1086.2
Time Of The Baracudas
Gil Evans Orchestra | The Individualism Of Gil Evans | Verve | 833804-2 PMS
Art Blakey And The Jazz Messengers | Ugetsu | Original Jazz Classics | OJC20 090-2(RLP 9464)
Time Off
John Gordon's Trombones Unlimited | Live In Concert | Mons Records | CD 1890
Time On Monday
(Little)Jimmy Scott With The Howard Biggs Sextet | Little Jimmy Scott-All Over Again | Savoy | SV 0263
Time On My Hands
Art Tatum | Art Tatum:Complete Capitol Recordings | Definitive Records | DRCD 11192
Benny Goodman Quartet | Welcome To Jazz: Benny Goodman | Koch Records | 321 973 D1
Charlie Shavers With The Al Waslon Trio | A Man And His Music | Storyville | SLP 4073
Coleman Hawkins Quartet | Sirius | Original Jazz Classics | OJCCD 861-2(2310707)
Body And Soul Revisited | GRP | GRP 16272
Coleman Hawkins Quintet | Jazz At The Philharmonic:The Coleman Hawkins Set | Verve | 815148-1 IMS
Dan Barrett And His Extra-Celestials | Moon Song | Arbors Records | ARCD 19158
Duke Ellington And His Orchestra | The Rare Broadcast Recordings 1953 | Jazz Anthology | JA 5220
Joe Daniels And His Hot Shots | Steppin' Out To Swing | Saville Records | SVL 167 IMS
Lee Konitz Quartet | Lee Konitz In Harvard Square | Black Lion | BLCD 760928
Oscar Peterson Trio | Masters Of Jazz Vol.7 | RCA | NL 89721 DP
Richie Vitale Quintet | The Richie Vitaleo Quintet feat.Ralph Lalama | TCB Records | TCB 96402
Stan Getz Quintet | Stan Getz Plays | Verve | 2304387 IMS
Stan Kenton And His Orchestra | At The Rendezvous Vol.1 | Status | CD 102(882198)
Stephane Grappelli-Django Reinhard | A Swinging Affair | Decca | 6.24725 AO
Tommy Dorsey And His Orchestra | Tommy Dorsey In Concert | RCA | NL 89780 DP
Time On My Hands(alt.take)
Fourth World | Fourth World | Ronnie Scott's Jazz House | JHCD 026
Time Out
Count Basie And His Orchestra | Basie On Roulette, Vol. 15: The Best Of Basie-Vol. 2 | Vogue | 500015
Time Out For Chris
Bill Evans Trio With Jeremy Steig | What's New | Enoch's Music | 57271053
Time Out(part 1)
Miroslav Vitous/Jan Garbarek | Atmos | ECM | 1475(513373-2)
Time Out(part 2)
Enrico Pieranunzi Quintet | Don't Forget The Poet | Challenge | CHR 70065
Time Races With Emit
Akio Sasajima Trio | Time Remembered | Muse | MCD 5417
Time Remembered
Bill Evans Trio | The Complete Bill Evans On Verve | Verve | 527953-2
Since We Met | Original Jazz Classics | OJC 622(F 9501)
In His Own Way | West Wind | WW 2028
How Deep Is The Ocean | West Wind | WW 2055
The Complete Fantasy Recordings | Fantasy | 9FCD 1012-2
The Best Of The Jazz Pianos | LRC Records | CDC 8519
Bill Evans:The Secret Sessions | Milestone | 8MCD 4421-2
Bill Evans:The Secret Sessions | Milestone | 8MCD 4421-2
Bill Evans Trio With Symphony Orchestra | Bach-Chopin-Scriabin-Granados-Faure-Evans | Verve | 2304525 IMS
Bill Evans Trio With The Claus Ogerman Orchestra | The Complete Bill Evans On Verve | Verve | 527953-2
Carlos Denia-Uli Glaszmann | Ten Strings For Bill Evans | Edition Musikat | EDM 069
Chris Cheek Quartet | I Wish I Knew | Fresh Sound Records | FSNT 022 CD
Dylan Fowler | Portrait | Acoustic Music Records | 319.1185.2
Fred Hersch Trio | Evanessence: A Tribute To Bill Evans | Jazz City | 660.53.027
Howard Alden Trio | Your Story-The Music Of Bill Evans | Concord | CCD 4621
John McLaughlin With The Aighette Quartet And Yan Marez | Time Remembered:John McLaughlin Plays Bill Evans | Verve | 519861-2
Kenny Werner Trio | Introducing The Trio | Sunnyside | SSC 1038 D
Time Remembered-
Denny Zeitlin-Charlie Haden Duo | Time Remembers One Time Once | ECM | 1239
Time Remembers One Time Once
Jack Bruce-Bernie Worrell | Monkjack | CMP Records | CMP CD 1010
Time Signal
Benny Golson Quintet | Domingo | Dreyfus Jazz Line | FDM 36557-2
Time Stream
Takashi Ohi With The Junior Mance Trio | Time Stream | Denon Compact Disc | CY-78898
Time Sublime Stone
Jasper Van't Hof | Solo Piano | Timeless | CD SJP 286
Time To Change
Joey Baron Quartet | We'll Soon Find Out | Intuition Records | INT 3515-2
Time To Cry
Jon Burr Quartet | In My Own Words | Cymekob | CYK 804-2
Time To Go Now...Really by Cannonball Adderley
Kenny Davers/Humphrey Lyttelton Sextet | This Old Gang Of Ours | Calligraph | CLG LP 012 IMS
Time To Remember
Louie Bellson Septet | Louie Bellson Jam | Original Jazz Classics | OJCCD 802-2(2310838)
Time To Ride A Moonbeam-
Michele Hendricks And Her Band | Keepin' Me Satisfied | Muse | MCD 5363
Time To Tell The Truth
Edward Vesala Ensemble | Ode Of The Death Of Jazz | ECM | 1413(843196-2)
Time To Think
Chick Corea Electric Band | GRP Super Live In Concert | GRP | GRP 16502
Time Track
Roberto Perera Group | Seduction | Inak | 30302
Time Traveling
The Tough Tenors With The Antonio Farao European Trio | Tough Tenors | Jazz 4 Ever Records:Jazz Network | J4E 4761
Time Tunel
Time Unit | Time Unit | Dragon | DRLP 69
Time Waits
Franck Avitabile Trio With Louis Petrucciani | In Tradition | Dreyfus Jazz Line | FDM 36594-2
Time Warps
Bud Powell Trio | The Genius Of Bud Powell-Vol.2 | Verve | 2-2526 IMS
Time Was
John Coltrane Quartet | John Coltrane-The Prestige Recordings | Prestige | 16 PCD 4405-2
Kenny Barron Trio | Green Chimneys | Criss Cross | Criss 1008
Time Was(Duerme)
Morgana King And Her Sextet | Portraits | Muse | MR 5301(952107)
Time Will Tell
Nelson Rangell Groups | Yes, Then Yes | GRP | GRP 97552
Till Brönner Group | Love | Verve | 559058-2
Wynton Marsalis With Art Blakey And His Jazz Messengers | An American Hero | Kingdom Jazz | ???
Time Will Tell-
Chris Potter Quartet | Unspoken | Concord | CCD 4775
Timekeeper
Count Basie's Kansas City Five | Count Basie: Kansas City 5 | Pablo | 2312126
Timeless
John Abercrombie Trio | Timeless | ECM | 1047(829114-2)
Marc Copland Quartet | Second Look | Savoy | CY 18001
Steven Halpern | Timeless | Gramavision | 18-7833-1
Time's A Rhythm
dAs prOjekT | dAs prOjekT | Foolish Music | FM 211288
Papa Charlie McCoy | Country Blues Collector Items Vol.2(1931-1937) | Story Of Blues | CD 3540-2
Times Change
Marty Ehrlich Quintet | Side By Side | Enja | ENJ-6092 2
Time's Mirror
Klaus König Orchestra | Times Of Devastation/Poco A Poco | Enja | ENJ-6014 22
Times Of Devestation
Quintet Du Hot Club De France | The Very Best Of Django Reinhardt | Decca | 6.28441 DP
Times Past
Scott Wendholt Sextet | From Now On | Criss Cross | Criss 1123
Times Slimes
David Chesky-Romero Lubambo Duo | The New York Chorinhos | Chesky | JD 39
Time's Up
Warne Marsh Quintet | Modern Jazz Gallery | Fresh Sound Records | KXL 5001(252282-1 Kapp)
Timesignature
Guy Barker Sextet | Timeswing | Verve | 533029-2
Timezone Earth
Zollsounds 4 feat. Lee Konitz | Open Hearts | Enja | 9123-2
Timothy
Vincent Herring Quintet | Change The World | Musicmasters | 65163-2
Tin Drum Stories Part 1:Shelter
Andreas Willers Group | Tin Drum Stories(inspired by the novel 'Die Blechtrommel' by Günter Grass) | Between The Lines | btl 009(Efa 10179-2)
Tin Drum Stories Part 2:Glass
Tin Drum Stories(inspired by the novel 'Die Blechtrommel' by Günter Grass) | Between The Lines | btl 009(Efa 10179-2)
Tin Drum Stories Part 3:Ahead,Apart
Tin Drum Stories(inspired by the novel 'Die Blechtrommel' by Günter Grass) | Between The Lines | btl 009(Efa 10179-2)
Tin Drum Stories Part 4:Fortuna X
Richie Cole Quartet | Pure Imagination | Concord | CCD 4314
Tin Pan Alley
Christian Willisohn Group | Blues On The World | Blues Beacon | BLU-1025 2
Homesick James Quartet | Got To Move | Trix Records | TRIX 3320
Tin Roof Blues
Dutch Swing College Band | Albert Nicholas & The Dutch Swing College Band | Storyville | STCD 5522
Earl Hines | Basin Street Blues | Milan | CD CH 560(883626)
George Brunis And His Jazzband | The Commodore Story | Commodore | CMD 24002
George Lewis And His Original New Orleans Jazzmen | George Lewis In Stockholm,1959 | Dragon | DRCD 221

George Lewis And His Ragtime Band | The Second Bakersfield Concert,1954 | Storyville | SLP 4022
Herb Morand And His New Orleans Jazz Band | Herb Morand 1949 | American Music | AMCD-9
Louis Armstrong And His All Stars | Rare Performances Of The 50's And The 60's | CBS | CBS 88669
Satchmo In Stockholm | Queen-Disc | 053
Muggsy Spanier And His V-Disc All Stars | Muggsy Spanier And Bud Freeman:V-Discs 1944-45 | Jazz Unlimited | JUCD 2049
New Orleans Rhythm Kings | New Orleans Rhythm Kings | Village(Jazz Archive) | VILCD 004-2
Raymond Burke With Vincent Cass' Band | Raymond Burke 1937-1949 | American Music | AMCD-47
Sharkey Bonano And His Band | Sounds Of New Orleans Vol.8 | Storyville | STCD 6015
Silver Leaf Jazz Band | Streets And Scenes Of New Orleans | Good Time Jazz | GTCD 15001-2

Tin Roof Blues(alt.take 1)
New Orleans Rhythm Kings | New Orleans Rhythm Kings | Village(Jazz Archive) | VILCD 004-2

Tin Roof Blues(alt.take 2)
New Orleans Rhythm Kings | Village(Jazz Archive) | VILCD 004-2

Tin Roof Blues(false start 1)
Muggsy Spanier And His V-Disc All Stars | Muggsy Spanier And Bud Freeman:V-Discs 1944-45 | Jazz Unlimited | JUCD 2049

Tin Roof Blues(false start 2)
Johnny Wiggs' New Orleans Boys | Sounds Of New Orleans Vol.2 | Storyville | STCD 6009

Tin Shack Out Back
Dave Brubeck Orchestra | Two Generations Of Brubeck | Atlantic | SD 1645

Tin Soldier
Anachronic Jazz Band | Anachronic Jazz Band | Calig | 30622

Tin Tin Deo
Art Pepper Quartet | Art Pepper:The Complete Galaxy Recordings | Galaxy | 16GCD 1016-2
Art Pepper-Shorty Rogers Quintet | Art Pepper & Shorty Rogers:Complete Lighthouse Sessions | The Jazz Factory | JFCD 22836
Conte Candoli With The Joe Haider Trio | Conte Candoli Meets The Joe Haider Trio | JHM Records | JHM 3602
David Fathead Newman Sextet | Fathead:Ray Charles Presents David Newman | Atlantic | 8122-73708-2
Dizzy Gillespie And His Orchestra | Dizzy In Greece | Verve | MV 2630 IMS
Dizzy Gillespie And The United Nation Orchestra | Live At The Royal Festival Hall | Enja | ENJ-6044 2
Dizzy Gillespie Quintet | Dizzy Gillespie:Pleyel 53 | Vogue | 2115466-2
Dizzy Gillespie Sextet | The Champ | Jazz Anthology | JA 5183
Eddie Lockjaw Davis-Johnny Griffin Quintet | The Toughest Tenors | Milestone | M 47035
Giants Of Jazz | Giants Of Jazz In Berlin '71 | EmArCy | 834567-2
Jesper Thilo Quintet feat. Hank Jones | A Jazz Par 91 Project | Storyville | STCD 4178
Machito And His Afro Cuban Jazz Ensemble | Machito And His Afro Cuban Jazz Ensemble | Caliente | Hot 120
Oscar Peterson Quintet | Oscar Peterson Meets Roy Hargrove And Ralph Moore | Telarc Digital | CD 83399
Pee Wee Russell-Coleman Hawkins Septet | Jazz Reunion | Candid | CS 9020
Poncho Sanchez Band | El Conguero | Concord | CJ 286
Vladimir Shafranov Trio | White Nights | The Jazz Alliance | TJA 10018
Your Neighborhood Saxophone Quartet | Boogie Stop Shuffle | Coppens | CCD 3004(882623)

Tina
Franco D'Andrea Trio | Franco D'Andrea Trio | yvp music | 3021
Phil Guy Blues Band | I Once Was A Gambler | JSP Records | 1114

Tina's Canteen
Ron Carter Orchestra | Parade | Original Jazz Classics | OJCCD 1047-2(M 9088)

Tinderbox
Nguyen Le Group | Tales From Viet-Nam | ACT | 9225-2

Ting Ning
Duke Ellington And His Orchestra | The Rare Broadcast Recordings 1952 | Jazz Anthology | JA 5213

Tinka's Dreams
Dogs Don't Sing In The Rain | Vocal Moments | Take Twelve On CD | TT 008-2
Irene Schweizer-Rüdiger Carl Duo | The Very Centre Of Middle Europe | Hat Art | X

Tintagel
Franco Ambrosetti Orchestra | Grazie Italia | Enja | ENJ-9379 2

Tintenfisch Inki
Michel Godard Ensemble | Castel Del Monte II | Enja | ENJ-9431 2

Tintinnabullum
Abdullah Ibrahim Quartet | Cape Town Revisited | TipToe | TIP-888836 2

Tintinyana
Abdullah Ibrahim Trio | Yarona | TipToe | TIP-888820 2
Abdullah Ibrahim Trio And A String Orchestra | African Suite | TipToe | TIP-888832 2
Abdullah Ibrahim Trio With The Munich Radio Symphony Orchestra | African Symphony | Enja | ENJ-9410 2
Dollar Brand | African Piano | Japo | 60002(835020-2)
Ancient Africa | Japo | 60005(2360005)

Tintiyana
Bill Coleman Quintet | Really I Do | Black & Blue | BLE 59.162 2

Tiny Tune
Tito Puente Orchestra | Planet Jazz:Tito Puente | Planet Jazz | 2165369-2

Tiny-Not Ghengis
Al Porcino Big Band | Al Cohn Meets Al Porcino | Organic Music | ORGM 9730

Tiny's Blues
Bud Powell Trio With The Joe Timer Orchestra | More Unissued Vol.1 | Royal Jazz | RJD 507
Tadd Dameron Band | Fats Navarro Featured With The Tadd Dameron Band | Milestone | M 47041

Tiny's Boogie Woogie
Tiny Grimes Swingtet | Tiny Grimes:The Complete 1944-1950 Vol.1 | Blue Moon | BMCD 6005

Tiny's Exercise
Lou Levy Trio | Jazz In Hollywood Series | Fresh Sound Records | FSR-CD 58(882430)

Tiny's Other Blues
Jazz In Hollywood:Bud Shank/Lou Levy | Original Jazz Classics | OJCCD 1890-2(Nocturne NLP-2/NLP-10)

Tioga
Jones And Collins Astoria Hot Eight | Sizzling The Blues | Frog | DGF 5

Tipatina's
Jim McNeely Quintet | Rain's Dance | Steeplechase | SCS 4001

Ti-Pi-Tin
Percy Humphrey-Louis Nelson Jazz Band | New Orleans To Scandinavia | Storyville | SLP 232

Tippin'
Horace Silver Quintet | Newport Jazz Festival 1958,July 3rd-6th,Vol.1:Mostly Miles | Phontastic | NCD 8813
Oliver Jones Trio | A Class Act | Enja | ENJ-7059 2

Tippin' In
Shirley Scott Trio | Roll 'Em | Impulse(MCA) | GRP 11472

Tippy-Toeing Through The Jungle Garden
Steve Lacy-Steve Potts | Tips | Hat Art | 20 (1R20)

Tipsy
Jesse Davis Quintet | Young At Art | Concord | CCD 4565

Tiptap
Excelsior New Orleans Brass Band | Excelsior New Orleans Brass Band | Bartrax | BARX 051 CD

Tiptoe
The Mel Lewis Jazz Orchestra | The Definitive Thad Jones-Live From The Village Vanguard Vol.2 | Musicmasters | 5046-2

Tira Tira
Peter Schärli Quintet With Glenn Ferris | Willisau And More Live | Creative Works Records | CW CD 1020-2
Al Di Meola Group | Tiramisu | Manhattan | CDP 7469952

Tiramisu
Sieverts-Enders-Salfellner Trio | Brooklyn Blue | Jazz 4 Ever Records:Jazz Network | J4E 4732

Tirate
Bernard Peiffer Trio | Jazz In Paris:Bernard Peiffer-La Vie En Rose | EmArCy | 013980-2

Tired But Not Sleepy
Willie William Group With Carey Bell | The Ralph Bass Sessions Vol.3:Willie Williams With Carey Bell/Magic Slim | Red Lightnin' | RL 0052

Tired Of Pretty Women
Whistlin' Rufus(Rufus Bridey) | Piano Blues Rarities 1933-1937 | Story Of Blues | CD 3507-2

Tired Of Talkin'
Alice Moore | St.Louis Girls(1929-1937) | Story Of Blues | CD 3536-2

Tired Of You Clowning
Johnny Hodges Orchestra | Johnny Hodges:The Complete 1937-1940 Small Group Sessions(Master Takes),Vol.2 | Blue Moon | BMCD 1020

'Tis Autumn
Eddie Higgins Quartet | Zoot's Hyms | Sunnyside | SSC 1064 D
Esther Phillips With The Ray Ellis Orchestra | And I Love Him! | Atlantic | AMCY 1061
Joe Pass-Jimmy Rowles Duo | Joe Pass:A Man And His Guitar | Original Jazz Classics | OJCCD 8806-2
Lee Konitz Trio | Tenorlee | Choice | CHCD 71019
Mark Murphy-Joe Lo Duca | Mark Murphy Sings Nat Cing Cole,Volumes 1&2 | Muse | MCD 6001
Ranee Lee And Her Quartet With David Murray | Seasons Of Love | Justin Time | JUST 103-2
Stan Getz Quintet | Stan Getz Plays | Verve | 2304387 IMS
Steve White Quintet | Jazz In Hollywood:Virgil Gonsalves/Steve White | Original Jazz Classics | OJCCD 1889-2(Nocturne NLP-8/NLP-9)

'Tis(Theme)
A Band Of Friends | Teatime Vol.2 | Poise | Poise 06/2

Tisch Und Bett
Art Hodes Quartet | Art Hodes Trios & Quartete | Jazzology | JCD-113

Tishomingo Blues
George Lewis And His Band | George Lewis At Manny's Tavern 1949 | American Music | AMCD-85
George Lewis And The Barry Martyn Band | For Dancers Only | GHB Records | BCD 37
John Eaton | It Seems Like Old Times | Chiaroscuro | CR 174

Tishomingo Blues(alt.take)
Ken Colyer And His Jazz Band | Ken Colyer-The Unknown New Orleans Sessions With Raymond Burke 1952-1953 | 504 Records | 504CD 23

Tit Er Jeg Glad
Bob Crosby And His Orchestra | So Far So Good | Halcyon | DHDL 132

Titi Boom
Tim Whitehead Quintet | A Cool Blue | Criss Cross | Criss 1102

Titmouse
Henri Chaix Trio | Jumpin' Punkins | Sackville | SKCD2-2020

Tito'in
Yusef Lateef Orchestra | The Centaur And The Phoenix | Original Jazz Classics | OJCCD 721-2(RLP 9337)

Titora
Yusef Lateef Sextet With Voices | The Many Faces Of Yusef Lateef | Milestone | M 47009

Tituber-
Dexter Gordon And Orchestra | More Than You Know | Steeplechase | SCS 1030

Tivoli Gardens Swing
Kenny Drew Trio | Afternoon In Europe | RCA | PL 45373

Tizzy
Khan Jamal Trio | Three | Steeplechase | SCCD 31201

Tjelvar
Arild Andersen Sextet | Sagn | ECM | 1435

Tjovane
Per Gudmundson-Ale Möller-Lene Willemark | Frifot | ECM | 1690(557653-2)

Tjugmyren
NuNu! | Ocean | TipToe | TIP-888837 2

Tkanje
Roscoe Mitchell | Congliptions | Nessa | N 2

TNT
Alguimia | Alguimia Dos | Fresh Sound Records | FSNT 050 CD
Cy Touff Octet | Cy Touff His Octet & Quintet | Fresh Sound Records | 054 2402651(Pacific Jazz PJ 1211)
Shorty Rogers-Bud Shank Quintet | Yesterday Today And Forever | Concord | CCD 4223

To A Broadway Rose
Shelly Berg Trio | The Joy | dmp Digital Music Productions | CD 3002

To A Moment Of Truth
Eje Thelin Quartet | Ejs Thelin 1966 With Barney Wilen | Dragon | DRCD 366
Lucky Thompson Quintet | Americans Swinging In Paris:Lucky Thompson | EMI Records | 539651-2

To A Mornin' Sunrise
Lucky Thompson | Swing | SW 8404 IMS

To A Wild Rose
Stuff Smith Trio | The Stuff Smith Trio 1943 | Progressive | PCD 7053

To Anne's Eyes
George Shearing-Jim Hall Duo | First Edition | Concord | CCD 4177

To B.E. (t '80)
Clark Terry-Max Roach Quartet | Friednship | CBS | 510886-2

To Basie With Love
John Abercrombie Quartet | M | ECM | 1191

To Be
John Coltrane Quintet | Expression | MCA | 2292-54646-2

To Be Agog
Agog | Eat Time | Jazz Haus Musik | JHM 0072 CD

To Be Agog(II)
Henry Threadgill Sextet | You Know The Number | RCA | PL 83013

To Be Continued
Jack DeJohnette Trio | Works | ECM | 825427-2
Tome XX | The Red Snapper | Jazz Haus Musik | JHM 0047 CD
Stadtgarten Series Vol.4 | Jazz Haus Musik | JHM 1004 SER

To Be Exposed
Seger Ellis With Louis Armstrong And His Orchestra | Louis Armstrong-Louis In New York Vol.5 | CBS | 466965-2

To Be Or Not To Bop
The Atlantic Jazz Trio | Some Other Time | Factory Outlet Records | FOR 2002-1 CD

To Be Or To U.B.
Seamus Blake Quintet | The Bloomdaddies | Criss Cross | Criss 1110

To Benny Golson
George Shearing-Marion McPartland Duo | Alone Together | Concord | CCD 4171

To Carry Beans
Scarlet Rivera Trio | Behind The Crimson Veil | Erdenklang | 40702

To Change Nature
Kazumi Watanabe-Mike Mainieri | To Chi Ka | Denon Compact Disc | DC-8568

To Dance Ot Not To Dance
Joelle Leandre's Canvas Trio | L'Histoire De Mme.Tasco | Hat Art | CD 6122

To Django
Stephane Grappelli Quartet | To Django | Arco | 3 ARC 106

To Dorette
Tony Scott Trio | Music For Zen Meditation | Verve | 521444-2

To Drift Like Clouds
Ginger Baker/Jens Johansson/Jonas Hellborg | Unseen Rain | Day Eight Music | DEMCD 028

To Each His Own
Gato Barbieri-Dollar Brand | Hamba Khale | Charly | CD 79

To Elvin And Cleve
Joe Maneri Quartet | Coming Down The Mountain | HatOLOGY | 501

To Erlinda
Michel Petrucciani Trio | Live At The Village Vanguard | Blue Note | 540382-2
Salvatore Bonafede Trio | Plays | Ken Music | 660.56.017

To Gil(to Gil Evans)
Hilaria Kramer 6 | Trigon | SPLASC(H) Records | H 191

To God In God's Absence
John Wolf Brennan | The Well-Prepared Clavier/Das Wohlpräparierte Klavier | Creative Works Records | CW CD 1032-2

To Györgi K.(Ur Tag)
George Shearing/Hank Jones | The Spirit Of 176 | Concord | CCD 4371

To Hank Mobley
Fred Astaire With The Oscar Peterson Sextet | Fred Astaire Steppin' Out:Astaire Sings | Verve | 523006-2

To Hear A Teardrop In The Rain
Eric Kloss Quartet | Eric Kloss & The Rhythm Section | Prestige | PCD 24125-2(P 7689/7793)

To Henry C.(O Well)
Joe Lovano Sextet | Tenor Legacy | Blue Note | 827014-2

To Her Ladyship
John Coltrane Group | Olé Coltrane | Rhino | 8122-73699-2
Olé Coltrane | Atlantic | 7567-81349-2
John Coltrane Sextet | The Coltrane Legacy | Atlantic | SD 1553

To Hip For Your Own Good
Sibylle Pomorin/Terry Jenoure Group | Auguries Of Speed | ITM Records | ITM 1467

To Jackie And Roy
Macrino-Rovagna Ensemble | New Age Jazz | Penta Flowers | CDPIA 003

To John C.(Age)
Blossom Dearie With The Russ Garcia Orchestra | My Funny Valentine-The Rogers & Hart Songbook | Verve | 526448-2

To Keep My Love Alive
John Balke Group | Saturation | EmArCy | 538160-2

To Let You Know
Ron Eschete Quintet | To Let You Know I Care | Muse | MR 5186

To Live & Let Die
Defunkt | Live At The Knitting Factory | Enemy | EMCD 122(03522)

To Love Is To Love You
Bill Ware And The Club Bird All-Stars | Long And Skinny | Knitting Factory Works | KFWCD 131

To M.
Paolo Fresu Sextet | Ossi Di Seppia | SPLASC(H) Records | CD H 350-2

To Me,Fair Friend
Axel Donner | To Michèle | KlangRäume | 30020

To Mickey's Memory
Chet Baker Sextet | Chet Baker & Crew | Pacific Jazz | 582671-2
Chet Baker & Crew | Pacific Jazz | 582671-2

To Mickey's Memory(alt.take)
Joshua Breakstone Quintet | Echoes | Contemporary | C 14025

To My Friends
Papo Vazquez Group | Breakout | Timeless | CD SJP 311

To My Mother
Walt Dickerson Quartet | To My Queen Revisited | Steeplechase | SCCD 31112

To My Sister
Jaki Byard Trio | Giant Steps | Prestige | P 24086

To Rigmor
Hans Kumpf Duo | On A Baltic Trip | LEO | LR 122

To Say Goodbye
Sarah Vaughan With Band | Copacabana | Pablo | 2312125

To Stay In Good With You
Charlie Mariano Quintet | A Jazz Portrait Of Charlie Mariano | Fresh Sound Records | FSR-CD 0176

To The East
Trine-Lise Vaering With The Bobo Stenson Trio And Guests | When I Close My Eyes | Stunt Records | STUCD 19602

To The End Of The Of The World
Freddy Cole With Band | To The End Of The Earth | Fantasy | FCD 9675-2

To The Ends Of The Earth
Monty Alexander's Ivory & Steel | To The Ends Of The Earth | Concord | CCD 4721

To The Evening Child
Montreal Jubilation Gospel Choir | Jubilatio III-Glory Train | Blues Beacon | BLU-1008 2

To The Point
John Tchicai-Hartmut Geerken | Continent | Praxis | CM 102

To The Women In My Life
Herb Pomeroy Ensemble | Lenox School Of Jazz Concert | Royal Jazz | RJD 513

To Treat Love Lightly
Albrecht Maurer Trio Works | Movietalks | Jazz Haus Musik | JHM 0119 CD

To Unknown Movies
Ornette Coleman Quartet | Beauty Is A Rare Thing:Ornette Coleman-The Complete Atlantic Recordings | Atlantic | 8122-71410-2

To Us
Kjell Jansson Quartet | Back From Where We Came | Touché Music | TMcCD 009

To Vana
Andy Lumpp | Dreamin' Man | Nabel Records:Jazz Network | CD 4662

To Walk Back Home
Armen Donelian Sextet | The Wayfarer | Sunnyside | SSC 1049 D

To You
Gene Harris Quartet | Listen Here! | Concord | CCD 4385

To You S.A.
Louis Armstrong With The Polynesians | Early Hamp | Affinity | CD AFS 1011

To Your Perfection
Rolf Kühn And His Orchestra | Rolf Kühn-Picture CD | Blue Flame | 40162(2132489-2)

Toaca De Paste
Bud Freeman Trio | The Joy Of Sax | Chiaroscuro | CR 135

Toast My Bread
Cootie Williams And His Orchestra | Duke Ellington's Trumpets | Black & Blue | BLE 59.231 2

Tobago
Art Studio & Tiziana Ghiglioni | Onde | SPLASC(H) Records | CD H 133-2

Tobi Ilu
Benny Moten's Kansas City Orchestra | Basie Beginnings | Bluebird | ND 90403

Tocata-
The Rosenberg Trio | Suenos Gitanos | Polydor | 549581-2

Tocata Para Billy Blanco
Astor Piazzolla Y Su Orquesta | Pulsacion | West Wind Latina | 2220 CD

Toccata
Bernard Peiffer | Jazz In Paris:Bernard Peiffer-La Vie En Rose | EmArCy | 013980-2
Ernst Reijseger | Colla Parta | Winter&Winter | 910012-2
Klaus Treuheit-Rudi Mahall | 2 Duos | Klaus Treuheit Production | GR 9412(CD 160)
Ulli Bögershausen-Reinhold Westerheide | Pictures | Laika Records | LK 35100932
Dizzy Gillespie And His Orchestra | Talking Verve:Dizzy Gillespie | Verve | 533846-2

Toccata-
Gillespiana And Carnegie Hall Concert | Verve | 519809-2
Dizzy Gillespie Quintet | En Concert Avec Europe 1 | Laserlight | 710705

Free Flight | Beyond The Clouds | Palo Alto | PA 8075

Toccata And Fugue
Eugen Cicero Trio | Rococo Jazz 2 | Timeless | CD SJP 255

Toccata And Fugue In D Minor(BWV 565)
Jacques Loussier Trio | Jacques Loussier Plays Bach | Telarc Digital | CD 83411
Play Bach | Decca | 6.30006 DX
René Marino Rivero | Che Bandoneon | ALISO Records | AL 1020
Jacques Loussier Trio | Play Bach No.5 | Decca | 159194-2

Toccata In C Major(BWV 564):
Play Bach | Accord | 500372

Tod Auf Deutsch
Ulrich Gumpert Quintet | Markowitz' Blues(Soundtrack) | Basic | 50002

Todas Las Cosas Se Van
Andrew Hill Quartet | Spiral | Freedom | FCD 741007

Today I Love Ev'rybody
Annette Lowman With Three Of A Kind, Maceo Parker And Rodney Jones | Anette Lowman | Minor Music | 801050

Today Is Tomorrow
Stanley Cowell | Waiting For The Moment | Galaxy | GXY 5104

Tödlicher Irrtum-
Jeff Hamilton Trio With Frits Landesbergen | Dynavibes | Mons Records | MR 874794

Todo Lo Que Queda Por Decir
Herbie Mann Group | Flautista! Herbie Mann Plays Afro Cuban Jazz | Verve | 557448-2

Todos Locos
Daniel Messina Band | Imagenes | art-mode-records | 990014

Todos Los Reencuentros
Quique Sinesi & Daniel Messina | Prioridad A la Emoción | art-mode-records | AMR 21061
John Blake Sextet | Maiden Dance | Gramavision | GR 8309-2

Toe Jam
Uri Caine Trio | Bedrock | Winter&Winter | 910068-2
Johannes Enders Group | Reflections Of South Africa | Jazz 4 Ever Records:Jazz Network | J4E 4729

Toenails
Hans Reichel | Bonobo | FMP | 0280

Together
Edward Vesala Quartet With Strings | Satu | ECM | 1088
Keith Ingham & Marty Grosz And Their Hot Cosmopolites | Just Imagine..Songs Of DeSylva, Brown And Henderson | Stomp Off Records | CD 1285

Together-
Count Basie And His Orchestra | On My Way And Shoutin' Again | Verve | 2304385 IMS

Together Again
The Timeless Art Orchestra | Without Words | Satin Doll Productions | SDP 1005-1 CD

Togetherness
Don Cherry Trio | Orient | Affinity | CD AFS 769
Walt Dickerson Quartet | A Sense Of Direction | Original Jazz Classics | OJCCD 1794-2(NJ 8268)

Togi
Chucho Valdes Quartet | Chucho Veldes Solo Piano | Blue Note | 780597-2

Togo
Luis Agudo & Friends | Dona Fia | Red Records | 123244-2
Duke Ellington And His Orchestra | Togo Brava Swuite | Storyville | STCD 8323

Togo Brava Suite:
Togo Brava Swuite | Storyville | STCD 8323

Togo Or Yoyo(Naturellement)
John Scofield Trio | En Route | Verve | 9861357

Togs
Fabien Degryse Quintet | Medor Sadness | Edition Collage | EC 454-2

Tohama
Q4 Orchester Project | Yavapai | Creative Works Records | CW CD 1028-2

Tohono O'Otam
Elvin Jones Quintet | Live At The Village Vanguard Vol.1 | Landmark | LCD 1534-2

Toi Qui Sait
United Women's Orchestra | Virgo Supercluster | Jazz Haus Musik | JHM 0123 CD

Toil And Truble-
Dollar(Abdullah Ibrahim) Brand Group | African River | Enja | ENJ-6018 2

Toi-Toi
Joe McPhee | As Serious As Your Life | HatOLOGY | 514

Token Cello
Dave Brubeck Quartet | Jazz Impressions Of Japan | CBS | SRCS 9367

Toku-Do
Larry Coryell Quartet | Toku Do | Muse | MCD 5350
Roots | Saying Something | IN+OUT Records | 77031-2
Sphere | Live At Umbria Jazz | Red Records | NS 207

Tokyo Blue
Cal Tjader With The Lalo Schifrin Orchestra | Several Shades Of Jade/Breeze From The East | Verve | 537083-2

Tokyo Blues
Chartbusters | Chartbusters! Vol.1 | NYC-Records | NYC 6017-2
John McLaughlin Group | The Promise | Verve | 529828-2

Tokyo Decadence
Red Holloway Quartet | Red Holloway & Company | Concord | CJ 322

Tokyo Girl
Ryuichi Sakamoto-Kazumi Watanabe Groups | Tokyo Joe | Denon Compact Disc | DC-8586

Tokyo(part 1&2)
Joseph Berardi-Kira Vollman | Happy Wretched Family | Victo | CD 033

Told My Story
Count Basie And His Orchestra | I Told You So | Original Jazz Classics | OJCCD 824-2(2310767)

Told You So
JoAnne Brackeen | Mythical Magic | MPS | 68211

Toledo
Paulinho Da Costa Orchestra | Agora | Original Jazz Classics | OJCCD 630-2(2310785)

Toledo Bagel
Lionel Hampton Quintet | Planet Jazz:Lionel Hampton | Planet Jazz | 2152059-2

Toledo Blade
Jazz Flamenco | RCA | 2136400-2

Toleranz-
Arild Andersen Sextet | Sagn | ECM | 1435

Toll
Cecil Taylor Quartet | Looking Ahead | Original Jazz Classics | OJC 452(C 7562)

Toll Bridge
Wilbur DeParis And His New New Orleans Band | Wilbur DeParis At Symphony Hall | Atlantic | 7567-82268-2

Toll Road
Golden Gate Quartet | Golden Gate Quartet | CBS | 471559-2

Tom
Jens Schliecker & Nils Rohwer | Piano Meets Vibes | Acoustic Music Records | 319.1050.2

Tom Brown's Buddy
King Oliver-Jelly Roll Morton Duo | King Oliver's Creole Jazzband-The Complete Set | Retrieval | RTR 79007

Tom Cat Blues
Chris Barber's Jazz Band | Folk Barber Style | Decca | 6.22314 AG

Tom Thumb
Wayne Shorter Sextet | Blue N' Groovy | Blue Note | 780679-2
Sandro Cerino Action Quartet | Tom Thumb In The Magic Castle | SPLASC(H) Records | HP 03

Tom, Dick 'N' Harry
Billy Taylor Trio | You Tempt Me | Taylor Made Records | T 1004

Tomaas
Egberto Gismonti/Nana Vasconcelos | Duas Vozes | ECM | 1279

Tomarapeba
Dave Weckl Group | Heads Up | GRP | GRP 96732

Tomatillo
Dave Liebman Group | Songs For My Daughter | Soul Note | 121295-2

Tomato Kiss
Moscow Rachmaninov Trio | Groupe Lacroix:The Composer Group | Creative Works Records | CW CD 1030-2

Tombal(Marianne Schroeder)
Michel Camilo Trio | In Trio | Electric Bird | K32Y 6118

Tom-Cat Mambo
Lucky Thompson Quintet | Tricotism | Impulse(MCA) | GRP 11352

Tomma Suki
Jesse Davis Quartet | Second Nature | Concord | CCD 4883

Tommin'
Salvatore Bonafede Trio | Plays | Ken Music | 660.56.017

Tommy Hawk
Hal McKusick Octet | Jazz Workshop | RCA | PM 43637
Oscar Klein-Philadelphia Jerry Ricks | Blues Panorama | Koch Records | 121 705

Tommy Medley:
Charles Bell Trio | In Concert | Fresh Sound Records | FSR 544(Gateway LP 7012)

Tommy's Blues
Christian Rannenberg & The Pink Piano All Stars | Long Way From Home | Acoustic Music Records | AMC 1006

Tommy's Time
Prestige All Stars | John Coltrane-The Prestige Recordings | Prestige | 16 PCD 4405-2
Marty Paich Big Band | What's New | Discovery | DS 857 IMS

Tomoki
Jonathan Schwartz & Quintet | Anyone Would Love You | Muse | MCD 5325

Tomorrow
Milt Jackson With The Quincy Jones Orchestra | The Ballad Artistry Of Milt Jackson | Atlantic | 7567-82269-2
John Gill's Novelty Orchestra Of New Orleans | Smile, Darn Ya, Smile | Stomp Off Records | CD 1227

Tomorrow Afternoon
Sarah Vaughan With The Ernie Wilkins Orchestra | A Time In My Life | Mobile Fidelity | MFCD 855

Tomorrow Is Another Day
Nina Simone With Horace Ott's Orchestra | In Concert/I Put A Spell On You | Mercury | 846543-2

Tomorrow Is My Turn
Nina Simone With Orchestra | Nina Simone-The 60s Vol.1: Ne Me Quitte Pas | Mercury | 838543-2 PMS

Tomorrow Is The Question
Jasper Van't Hof Trio | Tomorrowland | Challenge | CHR 70040

Tomorrow Mountain
Ian Shaw With Band | Soho Stories | Milestone | MCD 9316-2

Tomorrow Never Came
Nicki Leighton-Thomas Group | Forbidden Games | Candid | CCD 79778
Ann Dyer & No Good Time Fairies | Revolver:A New Spin | Premonition | 790745-2

Tomorrow Today
Nelson Rangell Group | Nelson Rangell | GRP | GRP 96242

Tomorrow's Story Not The Same-
Gary Lucas | Skeleton On The Feast | Enemy | EMCD 126(03526)

Tom's Diner
Larry Schneider Quintet | So Easy | Label Bleu | LBLC 6516(881241)

Tom's Idea
Thomas Shaw | Do Lord Remember Me | Blues Beacon | BLU-1001 2

Tom-Song
Loope | Prinz Henry | ITM Records | ITM 1447

Ton Sur Ton
Marc Johnson-Eric Longsworth | If Trees Could Fly | Intuition Records | INT 3228-2

Ton Sur Ton(reprise)
Soledad Bravo With Band | Volando Voy | Messidor | 15966 CD

Tonal Weights & Blue Fire(No.Two)
Carlos Patato Valdes Group | Master Pieces | Messidor | 15827 CD

Tone
Ornette Coleman & Prime Time | Tone Dialing | Verve | 527483-2

Tone Field
Dodo Marmarosa | Dodo's Bounce | Fresh Sound Records | FSCD 1019

Tone Paralell To Harlem
Andy Sheppard-Steve Lodder Group | Moving Image | Verve | 533875-2

Tones For Elvin Jones
Jürgen Seefelder Quartet | Naide | West Wind | WW 2096

Tones For Joan's Bones
Chick Corea Trio | Chick Corea-Herbie Hancock-Keith Jarrett-McCoy Tyner | Atlantic | ATL 50326
Duke Pearson Big Band | Introducing Duke Pearson's Big Band | Blue Note | 494508-2

Tongsi
Jan Garbarek Group | Legend Of The Seven Dreams | ECM | 1381(837344-2)

Tongue Of Secrets
Kenny Barron Group | Things Unsee | Verve | 537315-2

Toni
Jaki Byard | Empirical | Muse | MCD 6010

Toni,Du Dodl
Kenny Dorham Quintet | Kenny Dorham | Bainbridge | BT 1048

Tonight
Cal Tjader With The Clare Fischer Orchestra | Cal Tjader Plays Harold Arlen & West Side Story | Fantasy | FCD 24775-2
CMMC Bigband | Modern Times | Blue Concept | BCCD 93/02
Earl Hines Trio | Boogie Woogie On St.Louis Blues | Prestige | MPP 2515
Ramsey Lewis Group | Sky Islands | GRP | GRP 97452

Tonight At Noon
Charles Mingus Orchestra | Tonight At Noon...Three Or Four Shades Of Love | Dreyfus Jazz Line | FDM 36633-2
Charles Mingus Quintet | Charles Mingus-Passion Of A Man:The Complete Atlantic Recordings 1956-1961 | Atlantic | 8122-72871-2
The Very Best Of Charles Mingus | Rhino | 8122-79988-2
Charles Mingus -Passions Of A Man | Atlantic | ATL 60143
Jeanie Bryson And Her Band | Tonight I Need You So | Telarc Digital | CD 83348

Tonight I Shall Sleep With A Smile On My Face
Duke Ellington And His Orchestra | Unknown Session | CBS | 467180-2
Scott Hamilton Quartet | Radio City | Concord | CCD 4428
The Danish-German Slide Combination | Fugue For Tinhorns | L+R Records | LR 45011

Tonight's The Night
Julia Lee And Her Boy Friends | Julia Lee's Party Time | Pathe | 2C 068-86524(Capitol)

Toni's Carnival II
Blueslady Toni Spearman + Wetsox | Rock With Mama ! | Star Club | SWX 186

Tonk
Duke Ellington-Billy Strayhorn Duo | Duke Ellington:The Complete RCA-Victor Mid-Forties Recordings(1944-1946) | RCA | 2663394-2
Dutch Jazz Orchestra | Portrait Of A Silk Thread | Kokopelli Records | KOKO 1310

Tonus
John McLaughlin Group | Live In Paris | Verve | 543536-2

Tony
Tony Williams Quartet | The Joy Of Flying | CBS | SRCS 5825

Too Bad
Max Collie And His Rhythm Aces | World Champions Of Jazz | Black Lion | BLCD 760512
Eddie Boyd And His Blues Band | Eddie Boyd And His Blues Band Featuring Peter Green | Crosscut | CCR 1002

Too Close For Comfort
Art Pepper Quartet | Intensity | Original Jazz Classics | OJCCD 387-2
Art Van Damme Quintet | Keep Going/Blue World | MPS | 529093-2
Benny Goodman And His All Star Sextet | On Stage | Decca | 6.28101 DP
Bob Keene Quintet | The Bob Keene Quintet | Fresh Sound Records | FSR 586(Del-Fi DFLP 1202)
Count Basie And His Orchestra | One O'Clock Jump | Verve | 559806-2
One O'Clock Jump | Verve | 559806-2
I Told You So | Original Jazz Classics | OJCCD 824-2(2310767)
Compact Jazz: Count Basie & Joe Williams | Verve | 835329-2 PMS
Curtis Counce Group | You Get More Bounce With Curtis Counce | Original Jazz Classics | OJCCD 159-2
Eddie Lockjaw Davis Quartet | Eddie Lockjaw Davis With Shirley Scott | Original Jazz Classics | OJC 218(P 7154)
George Shearing Trio | Compact Jazz:George Shearing | MPS | 833284-2 PMS
Jenny Evans And Band | Live At The Allotria | ESM Records | ESM 9301
Girl Talk | ESM Records | ESM 9306
Girl Talk | Enja | ENJ-9363 2
Live At The Allotria | BELL Records | BLR 90003
Peggy Lee With Billy May And His Orchestra | Pretty Eyes | Capitol | EMS 1153
Sarah Jane Morris Group | Blue Valentine | Ronnie Scott's Jazz House | JHCD 038
Stan Getz Quartet | Stan Getz:East Of The Sun-The West Coast Sessions | Verve | 531935-2
Thilo Berg Big Band | Footing | Mons Records | CD 1877

Too Darn Hot
Ella Fitzgerald With The Buddy Bregman Orchestra | The Complete Ella Fitzgerald Song Books of Harold Arlen, Irving Berlin, Duke Ellington, George & Ira Gershwin, Jerome Kern, Johnny Mercer, Cole Porter And Rogers & Hart | Verve | 519832-2
Ella Fitzgerald With The Paul Smith Quartet | Mack The Knife-Ella In Berlin | Verve | 825670-2
Mel Tormé And His Trio | Night At The Concord Pavillion | Concord | CCD 4433
Teddy Wilson | Cole Porter Classics | Black Lion | CD 877648-2

Too Early To Leave
Eddie Kirkland Group | Have Mercy | Evidence | ECD 26018-2

Too Fat To Boogie
Martin Schmitt | Handful Of Blues | AH Records | ESM 9303

Too Fond Samba
Benny Goodman Trio | The Original Sounds Of The Swing Era Vol. 6 | RCA | NL 85515 DP

Too Hot
Tom Scott Group | Them Changes | GRP | GRP 96132

Too Kee(Amour.Amour)
Barrelhouse Jazzband | 25 Jahre Barrelhouse Jazzband Frankfurt | Intercord | 155030

Too Late
Duane Eubanks Quintet/Sextet | Second Take | TCB Records | TCB 20602
King Oliver And His Orchestra | King Oliver And His Orchestra 1929-1930 | RCA | ND 89770
Clarence Gatemouth Brown Band | Gate Swings | Verve | 537617-2

Too Late For A Picture
Hubert Sumlin Group | Blues Anytime | L+R Records | CDLR 72010

Too Late Now
Eden Atwood Group | No One Ever Tells You | Concord | CCD 4560
Maxine Sullivan With The Keith Ingham Trio | Maxine Sullivan Sings The Music Of Burton Lane | Mobile Fidelity | MFCD 773
Roland Kirk-Jack McDuff Quartet | Pre-Rahsan | Prestige | P 24080
Terry Morel With The Ralph Sharon Quartet | Songs Of A Woman In Love | Fresh Sound Records | FSR 2037(Bethlehem BCP 47)
Wes Montgomery Trio | Wes Montgomery-The Complete Riverside Recordings | Riverside | 12 RCD 4408-2
Johnny Frigo Sextet | Debut Of A Legend | Chesky | JD 119

Too Late Too Late
T-Bone Walker With Marl Young's Band | Hot Leftovers | Pathe | 1561451(Imperial)

Too Little Tenderness
Herb Geller Quartet | You're Looking At Me | Fresh Sound Records | FSR-CD 5018

Too Little Time
Nat King Cole With The Billy May Orchestra | Let's Face The Music | Capitol | EMS 1112

Too Little Too Late
Mississippi Sheiks | Stop And Listen | Yazoo | YAZ 2006

Too Many Fish In The Sea
Jeannie And Jimmy Cheatham & The Sweet Baby Blues Band | Blues And The Boogie Masters | Concord | CCD 4579

Too Many Old Flames
Monty Alexander Sextet | Three Originals:Love And Sunshine/Estade/Cobilimbo | MPS | 523526-2

Too Many Rivers To Cross
Benny Goodman And His Orchestra | Benny Goodman:The King Of Swing | Musicmasters | 65130-2

Too Many Ways
Buddy Guy Blues Band | Buddy Guy-The Complete Chess Studio Recordings | MCA | MCD 09337

Too Many Ways(alt.take)
Bill Gaither | Bill Gaither(Leroy's Buddy) 1935-1941 | Story Of Blues | CD 3503-2

Too Marvelous For Words
Art Tatum | Art Tatum:20th Century Piano Genius | Verve | 531763-2
The Tatum Solo Masterpieces Vol.9 | Pablo | 2310835
Ella Fitzgerald With The Nelson Riddle Orchestra | Ella Fitzgerald Sings The Johnny Mercer Songbook | Verve | 539057-2
The Johnny Mercer Songbook | Verve | 823247-2 PMS
Helen O'Connell With The Page Cavanaugh Trio | The Uncollected:Helen O'Connell | Hindsight | HSR 228
Jackie And Roy | High Standards | Concord | CJ 186
Jerry Wiggins Trio | The Piano Collection Vol.1 | Vogue | 21610242
Jimmy Raney Quintet | Too Marvelous For Words | Biograph | BLP 12060
June Christy With The Johnny Guarnieri Quintet | June Christy And The Johnny Guarnieri Quintet (1949) | Jazz Unlimited | JUCD 2084
Lee Konitz & The Gerry Mulligan Quartet | Konitz Meets Mulligan | Pacific Jazz | 746847-2
Lee Konitz-Gerry Mulligan Quintet | Blue Eyes-Sinatra Songs The Blue Note Way | Blue Note | 789914-2
Lester Young Quartet | Lester Young:Blue Lester | Dreyfus Jazz Line | FDM 36729-2
Lester Swings | Verve | 833554-1
Lester Young Quintet | Prez's Hat Vol.3 | Philology | 214 W 8
Monty Alexander Sextet | To Nat, With Love From Monty Alexander | Master Mix | CHECD 12
Nat King Cole Trio | Nat King Cole:Route 66 | Dreyfus Jazz Line | FDM 36716-2
Nat King Cole Trio 1943-49-The Vocal Sides | Laserlight | 15718
Ronnie Scott Quartet | Bebop In Britain | Esquire | CD ESQ 100-4
Stan Getz Quartet | Stan Getz:The Complete 1946-1951 Quartet Sessions(Master Takes),Vol.1 | Blue Moon | BMCD 1013
Stan Kenton And His Orchestra | Stan Kenton On The Air | Status | DSTS 1022
Virgil Gonsalves Sextet | Jazz In Hollywood:Virgil Gonsalves/Steve White | Original Jazz Classics | OJCCD 1889-2(Nocturne NLP-8/NLP-9)

Too Much
Jack Millman And His All-Stars | Jack Millman And His All-Stars | Fresh Sound Records | FSR-CD 0502

Too Much - Not Enough
Christof Thewes Little Big Band | Greyhound | Jazz Haus Musik | JHM 0133 CD

Too Much At Once
James Booker | The Piano Prince From New Orleans | Aves | 146509

Too Much Grey
Jack Hylton And His Orchestra | The Talk Of The Town | Saville Records | SVL 164 IMS

Too Much Mama-
The Sidewalks Of New York | Tin Pan Alley:The Sidewalks Of New York | Winter&Winter | 910038-2
Too Much Mustard
Ellery Eskelin Trio | One Great Day... | HatOLOGY | 502
Too Much Sake
Joseph Warner Quartet | Mood Pieces | Jardis Records | JRCD 9921
Kamikaze Ground Crew | Madam Marie's Temple Of Knowledge | New World Records | 80438-2
Too Much Too Soon
T-Bone Walker Band | T-Bone Jumps Again | Charly | CRB 1019
Too Phat Blues
Warren Vaché With Joe Puma | Blues Of Summer | Nagel-Heyer | NH 1011
Louisiana Red | The Blues Purity Of Louisiana Red | Blue Labor | BL 104
Too Rich For My Blood
Glenn Miller And His Orchestra | Glenn Miller | Memo Music | HDJ 4116
Too Sensible
Martin Schrack Trio | Catplay | yvp music | CD 3037
Too Soon
Lowell Fulsom Band | Man Of Motion | Charly | CRB 1018
Esther Phillips And The Mort Garson Orchestra | And I Love Him! | Atlantic | AMCY 1061
Too Soon Tomorrow
Florian Poser-Klaus Ignatzek Duo | Reunion | Acoustic Music Records | 319.1084.2
Too Soon Too Late
Peter Guidi Meets Michael Herr And Riccardo Del Fra | A Weaver Of Dreams | Timeless | CD SJP 401
Too Soon-Exit
Sylvie Courvoisier Group | Y2K | Enja | ENJ-9383 2
Too Suite
Lovie Austin Serenaders | Chicago South Side Jazz | Village(Jazz Archive) | VILCD 019-2
Too Trite
Jim McNeely Trio | Winds Of Change | Steeplechase | SCCD 31256
Too Young
Nat King Cole Trio | Penthouse Serenade | Capitol | 494504-2
Ella Fitzgerald With The Buddy Bregman Orchestra | Ella Fitzgerald-First Lady Of Song | Verve | 517898-2
Too Young For The Blues
Sonny Boy Williamson Band | The Real Folk Blues | Chess | CHD 9272(872292)
Too Young To Go Steady
John Coltrane Quartet | Ballads | Impulse(MCA) | MCD 05885
John Coltrane:The Classic Quartet-Complete Impulse Studio Recordings | Impulse(MCA) | 951280-2
Keith Jarrett Trio | Standards Live | ECM | 1317(827827-2)
Kurt Elling Group | This Time Its Love | Blue Note | 493543-2
Pharoah Sanders Group | Shukuru | Evidence | ECD 22022-2
Toodle-Loo On Down
Roger Sturgis With Lovie Jordan's Elks Rendez-Vous Band | Louis Jordan-Let The Good Times Roll: The Complete Decca Recordings 1938-1954 | Bear Family Records | BCD 15557 IH
Ed Neumeister Trio | The Mohican And The Great Spirit | TCB Records | TCB 01072
Toodlin' Blues
Bix And His Rhythm Jugglers | Bix Beiderbecke & The Wolverines | Village(Jazz Archive) | VILCD 008-2
Toodlin' Home
Alex Hill And His Orchestra | That's My Stuff | Frog | DGF 7
Too-Kah
Elmore James And His Broomdusters | Whose Muddy Shoes | Chess | CH 9114
Toot Sweet
The Buck Clayton Legacy | Encore Live | Nagel-Heyer | CD 018
Henry Busse And His Shuffle Rhythm Orchestra | The Uncollected:Henry Busse,Vol.2 | Hindsight | HSR 193 (835574)
Toot Toot Tootsie
Sonny Rollins Quartet | Sonny Rollins-The Freelance Years:The Complete Riverside & Contemporary Recordings | Riverside | 5 RCD 4427-2
Sonny Rollins:Brown Skin Girl | Memo Music | HDJ 4041
Toot Your Roots
Woody Herman And His Orchestra | King Cobra | Original Jazz Classics | OJCCD 1068-2(F 9499)
Toothless
Barondown | Crackshot | Avant | AVAN 059
Tootsie Roll
Stan Getz Quartet | Stan Getz:Imagination | Dreyfus Jazz Line | FDM 36733-2
Stan Getz-The Complete Roost Sessions | The Jazz Factory | JFCD 22839
Toot-Toot's
Albert Mangelsdorff | Albert Mangelsdorff-Solo | MPS | 68287
Top Brass
Michel Grailler | Dream Drops | Owl Records | 013434-2
Top Dance
Alexander von Schlippenbach And Sunny Murray | Smoke | FMP | CD 23
Top Forty
Andy McKee And NEXT with Hamiet Bluiett | Sound Root | Mapleshade | 04432
Top Hat
Roy Gerson Quartet | The Gerson Person | The Jazz Alliance | TJA 10012
Top Hat White Tie And Tails
Ella Fitzgerald With Paul Weston And His Orchestra | The Complete Ella Fitzgerald Song Books of Harold Arlen, Irving Berlin, Duke Ellington, George & Ira Gershwin, Jerome Kern, Johnny Mercer, Cole Porter And Rogers & Hart | Verve | 519832-2
Mel Tormé With The Marty Paich Dek-Tette | Mel Torme Sings Fred Astaire | Charly | CD 96
Top Of The Gate Rag
Robben Ford & The Blue Line | Handful Of Blues | Blue Thumb | BTR 70042
Top Of The Hill
Jesper Lundgaard & MadsVinding | Two Basses | Touché Music | TMcCD 020
Top Of The Mountain
George Benson Orchestra | Body Talk | CTI | 6033
Top O'The Dunes
Barbara Dennerlein Quartet | Hot Stuff | Enja | ENJ-6050 2
Top Secret
New York Voices | New York Voices | GRP | GRP 95892
Top Shelf
Stanley Clarke-Al DiMeola-Jean Luc Ponty | The Rite Of Strings | Gai Saber | 834167-2
Topplue Votter & Skjerf
Terje Rypdal Trio | Works | ECM | 825428-1
Topspin
ULG | Spring | Laika Records | 35101382
Topspring
Allan Vaché Sextette | Swing And Other Things | Arbors Records | ARCD 19171
Topsy
Art Tatum Trio | The Complete Trio Sessions Vol.2 | Official | 3002
Buck Clayton All Stars feat.Ben Webster | Ben And Buck | Sackville | SKCD2-2037
Django Reinhardt And The Quintet Du Hot Club De France | Django Reinhardt Portrait | Barclay | DALP 2/1939
Frank Collett Trio | Perfectly Frank | Fresh Sound Records | FSR-CD 5024
Geoff Goodman Quintet | Naked Eye | Tutu Records | 888214-2*
Hot Lips Page Band | After Hours In Harlem | HighNote Records | HCD 7031
Jack Van Poll Trio | Cats Groove | September | CD 5107
Jimmy Giuffre 3 | Atlantic Jazz: West Coast | Atlantic | 7567-81703-2
Joe Morello Quartet | Going Places | dmp Digital Music Productions | CD 497
Lee Konitz-Warne Marsh Quintet | Lee Konitz With Warne Marsh | Atlantic | 8122-75356-2
That's Jazz Vol.21: Lee Konitz & Warne Marsh | Atlantic | ATL 50298
Modern Jazz Quartet | The Complete Modern Jazz Quartet Prestige & Pablo Recordings | Prestige | 4PRCD 4438-2
Topsy-This One's For Basie | Original Jazz Classics | OJCCD 1073-2(2310917)
Oliver Jackson Quintet | Billie's Bounce | Black & Blue | BLE 59.183 2
Ray Brown Trio With Ulf Wakenius | Summertime | Telarc Digital | CD 83430
Topsy Turvy
Bud Powell Trio | Strictly Powell | RCA | 6351423-2
Toque
Gus Viseur Sextet | Gus Viseur A Bruxelles | Harmonia Mundi | PJC 222006
Torch Song
Jackie McLean Quintet | Bluesnik | Blue Note | 784067-2
Toreador(Carmen)
Craig Handy Quartet | Split Second Timing | Arabesque Recordings | AJ 0101
Toro Y Miguel
Sammy Price | Doc Cheattam&Sammy Price:Duos And Solos | Sackville | SK2CD-5002
Toronto Experience
Joe Temperley Quartet | Easy To Remember | Hep | CD 2083
Torpedo
Axel Zwingenberger | Powerhouse Boogie | Vagabond | 6.24210 AS-Digital
Torrent
A Band Of Friends | Teatime Vol.2 | Poise | Poise 06/2
Torrid Zone
Eddie Condon And His Band | Commodore Classics In Swing | Commodore | 9031-72723-2
Toru
Sam Newsome Quartet | This Masquerade | Steeplechase | SCCD 31503
Toscanian Sunset
Barbara Dennerlein Quintet | Bebab | Bebab Records | 250964(880159)
Toshiko's Elegy
Four Or More Flutes | Influtenza | L+R Records | CDLR 45079
Tot Just
John Swana And The Philadelphians | Pilly Gumbo | Criss Cross | Criss 1203
Total Eclipse
Billy Cobham Group | Total Eclipse | Atlantic | ATL 50098
Total Jazz(Final Movement Of 'Portrait Of Ella Fitzgerald'
Lincoln Center Jazz Orchestra | Portraits By Ellington | CBS | 472814-2
Total Jazz(Fourth Movement)
Ella Fitzgerald With The Duke Ellington Orchestra | The Complete Ella Fitzgerald Song Books of Harold Arlen, Irving Berlin, Duke Ellington, George & Ira Gershwin, Jerome Kern, Johnny Mercer, Cole Porter And Rogers & Hart | Verve | 519832-2
Total Praise
Rolf Kühn Group | Internal Eyes | Intuition Records | INT 3328-2
Total Refections
Internal Eyes | Intuition Records | INT 3328-2
Total Reflections
Horace Silver Quintet/Sextet With Vocals | Total Response | Blue Note | 300212
Totem
Don Grusin Group | Native Land | GRP | GRP 97192
Totem Pole
Lee Morgan Quintet | The Sidewinder | Blue Note | 495332-2
Totem Pole(alt.take)
Morgenland/Yarinistan | Vielleicht | Riskant | 568-72229
Toto(Afrique)
Dick Oatts Quintet | South Paw | Steeplechase | SCCD 31511
Touch
Eberhard Weber Quartet | Works | ECM | 825429-2
Touch-
Hank Mobley Sextet | Hank Mobley With Donald Byrd And Lee Morgan | Blue Note | 300138(1540)
Touch Down At Falconara
Ingrid Jensen Quintet | Higher Grounds | Enja | ENJ-9353 2
Touch Her Soft Lips And Part
Jam Session | Jam Session Vol.4 | Steeplechase | SCCD 31527
Lynne Arriale Trio | Melody | TCB Records | TCB 99552
Wycliffe Gordon Group | The Search | Nagel-Heyer | CD 2007
Touch It Lightly
Larry Porter/Allan Praskin Quartet With Sal Nistico | Sonnet For Sal | Enja | 8026-2
Touch Of Strange
Sonny Stitt Septet | Prestige First Sessions, Vol.2 | Prestige | PCD 24115-2
Touch Of Trash
Abdullah Ibrahim | South African Sunshine | Pläne | CD 88778
Touch Of Your Lips
Leo Smith Trio | Touch The Earth | FMP | 0730
Touch[e]!(Michael Schneider)
Rebop | To Duke | Blue Concept | BCCD 93/01
Touche
Gunter Hampel And His Galaxie Dream Band | Enfant Terrible | Birth | 0025
Touches
World Saxophone Quartet | Live In Zurich | Black Saint | 120077-2
Touching
Paul Bley Trio | Ramblin' | Affinity | AFF 37
Touching In Love
Stan Getz With The Eddie Sauter Orchestra | Stan Getz Plays The Music Of Mickey One | Verve | 531232-2
Touching In Love-
Paul Bley-Hans Lüdemann | Moving Hearts | West Wind | WW 2085
Touching Points:
Krzyaztof Scieranski Trio | No Radio | ITM Records | ITM 001 JP
Tough 'Duff
Jack McDuff Quartet | Tough 'Duff | Original Jazz Classics | OJCCD 324-2(P 7185)
Joe Houston Band | Earthquake | Pathe | 1561381(Imperial)
Tough Guy
Tom Varner Quintet | Martian Heartache | Soul Note | 121286-2
Tough Talk
John C. Marshall Group | Same Old Story | Traditional Line | TL 1317
Toujours
Stefano Maltese Quintet | Amor Fati | SPLASC(H) Records | H 184
Toulouse
Bireli Lagrene Group | A Tribute To Django Reinhardt | Jazzpoint | JP 1061 CD
Toulouse Blues
Bireli Lagrene Trio | Live At The Carnegie Hall: A Tribute To Django Reinhardt | Jazzpoint | JP 1040 CD
Hank Jones Meets Cheik-Tidiana Seck | Sarala | Verve | 528783-2
Tounia Kanibala
Milt Jackson And His Colleagues | Bag's Bag | Original Jazz Classics | OJCCD 935-2(2310842)
Tour Angel
Alex Riel Quartet | D.S.B. Kino | Stunt Records | STUCD 19811
Tour De Force
Dizzy Gillespie All Stars | Village Vanguard Live Sessions No.1 | LRC Records | CDC 9011
Dizzy Gillespie And His Orchestra | Dizzy Gillespie:Birks Works-The Verve Big Band Sessions | Verve | 527900-2
Dizzy Gillespie Orchestra | Verve Jazz Masters 10:Dizzy Gillespie | Verve | 516319-2
Dizzy Gillespie Quintet | No More Blues | Moon Records | MCD 065-2
Roy Eldridge-Dizzy Gillespie-Harry Edison With The Oscar Peterson Quartet | The Complete Verve Roy Eldridge Studio Sessions | Verve | 9861278
Slide Hampton & The Jazz Masters | Dedicated To Diz | Telarc Digital | CD 83323
Tourist In Paradise
Duke Ellington And His Orchestra | Duke Ellington's Far East Suite | RCA | 2174797-2
Tourist Point Of View
Duke Ellington's Far East Suite | RCA | 2174797-2
Tourist Point Of View(alt.take)
Doctor Umezu Band | Eight Eyes And Eight Ears | ITM Records | ITM 1412
Tournaround
Michel Godard Ensemble | Castel Del Monte II | Enja | ENJ-9431 2
Tourne Ton Esprit
Ugly White Belly | South Of No North | Timeless | CD SJP 415
Tour's End
Gary Meek Groups | Gary Meek | Lipstick Records | LIP 890032
Tous Demandaient Pour Toi
Clifton Chenier And His Band | Frenchin' The Boogie | Verve | 519724-2
Tout Ca(Count Every Star)
Miles Davis Quintet | Filles De Kilimanjaro | CBS | 86555-2
Tout De Suite
Miles Davis Quintet 1965-1968 | CBS | C6K 67398
Miles Davis Quintet 1965-1968 | CBS | C6K 67398
Tout De Suite(alt.take)
Miles Davis Quintet 1965-1968 | CBS | C6K 67398
Tout De Suite(incomplete)
Eddie Barclay Et Son Grand Orchestre | Et Voila! | Fresh Sound Records | FSR 515(Barclay 82138)
Tout Passe
BBFC | Live | Plainisphare | PL 1267-14
Tout Va Lew
Les Blue Stars | Jazz In Paris:Blossom Dearie-The Pianist/Les Blue Stars | EmArCy | 064784-2
Toute Ma Joie(That's My Girl)
Denis Badault Trio | Et Voila! | AH Records | PAM 968
Tow Zone Away
Louis Dumaine's Jazzola Eight | The Classic Years In Digital Stereo: Hot Town | CDS Records Ltd. | RPCD 616(CD 647)
Toward The Margins
Horace Tapscott | The Tapscott Sessions-Vol.4 | Nimbus | NS 1814
Towards The Precipice
Stephan Micus | Towards The Wind | ECM | 1804(159453-2)
Towards The Wind:
Neil Ardley And His Harmony Of The Spheres | Harmony Of The Spheres | Decca | 6.23985 AS
Tower Of Inspiration
James Blood Ulmer Quartet | Black And Blues | DIW | DIW 845 CD
Tower Of Time
Oscar Brown Jr. With The Floyd Morris Quartet | Mr.Oscar Brown Jr. Goes To Washington | Verve | 557452-2
Towers Of Faith
Albert Mangelsdorff Quintet | Lanaya | Plainisphare | PL 1267-96 CD
Town
Les Jazz Modes | Les Jazz Modes | Dawn | DCD 104
Toy
Cannonball Adderley Quartet | Cannonball Adderley Birthday Celebration | Fantasy | FANCD 6087-2
Clifford Jordan Orchestra | Inward Fire | Muse | MR 5128
Twice A Week & Steve Elson | Play Of Colours | Edition Collage | EC 511-2
Flim & The BB's | Neon | dmp Digital Music Productions | CD 458
Toy Parade-
Festa Group | Strings | Nueva Records | NC 3009
Toy Room
Kenneth Knudsen-Christian Skeel | Music For Eyes | dacapo | DCCD 9433
Toy Shop At Night
Al Hirt And His Band | Cherry Pink And Apple Blossom White | Memo Music | HDJ 4085
Toyland
Herbie Hancock Sextet | V.S.O.P. Herbie Hancock-Live At The City Center N.Y. | CBS | 486569-2
Toys
Speak Like A Child | Blue Note | 746136-2
Herbie Hancock Trio | Herbie Hancock:The Complete Blue Note Sixties Sessions | Blue Note | 495569-2
Ted Pilzecker Group | Destinations | Mons Records | CD 1885
Tra La Folla,Mora,Mormora
Billy Jenkins And Fun Horns | East/West Now Wear The Same Vest | Babel | BDV 9601
Trabucco
Jim Black Quartet | Alasnoaxis | Winter&Winter | 910061-2
Trace
Jacques Stotzem | Straight On | Acoustic Music Records | 319.1030.2
Traces
Rolf Schimmermann Group | Suru | B&W Present | BW 009
Sebastian Whittaker Septet | First Outing | Justice Records | JR 0202-2
Traces Of Darkness
John Wolf Brennan | Text, Context, Co-Text & Co-Co-Text | Creative Works Records | CW CD 1025-2
Traces Of Origin
Wolfgang Puschnig-Uli Scherer | Puschnig-Scherer | EmArCy | 014103-2
Traces Of Taegum
Puschnig-Scherer | EmArCy | 014103-2
Traces Of The East
Keith Jarrett Trio | The Mourning Of A Star | Atlantic | 8122-75355-2
Traces Of You
Al Di Meola Group | Soaring Through A Dream | Manhattan | CDP 7463372
Traci
Nils Landgren Funk Unit | Live In Montreux | ACT | 9265-2
Grant Green Quartet | Sunday Mornin' | Blue Note | 852434-2
Track 360(Trains That Pass In The Night)
Duke Ellington And His Orchestra | Duke 56/62 Vol.1 | CBS | 88653
Track Meet
Francesco Branciamore Quartet | Flash In Four | SPLASC(H) Records | HP 11
Tracy
Dodo Marmarosa Trio | The Chicago Sessions | Argo | ARC 502 D
Trädet(The Tree)
Rodney Jones Group | The Undiscoverd Few | Blue Note | 496902-2
Tradition
Stanley Clarke Group | If This Bass Could Only Talk | CBS | 460883-2
Helmut Kagerer 4 & Roman Schwaller | Gamblin' | Jardis Records | JRCD 9714
Tradition Trap
Rahsaan Roland Kirk Group | The Man Who Cried Fire | Night Records | VNCD 1(887047)
Traditional New Orleans Piece-
Hamiet Bluiett | Walkin' & Talkin' | Tutu Records | 888172-2*
Traditional New Orleans Tune-
Jon Rose Group | Violin Music In The Age Of Shopping | Intakt Records | CD 038
Traditional Song-
Charlie Mariano-Chris Hinze Quintet | Blue Stone | Black Lion | BLCD 760203
Traffic
Bobby Previte Septet | Weather Clear, Track Fast | Enja | ENJ-6082 2
Traffic Continues II:Gusto(for Tom Cora)
Ensemble Modern | Ensemble Modern-Fred Frith:Traffic Continues | Winter&Winter | 910044-2
Traffic Continues:

Ensemble Modern-Fred Frith:Traffic Continues | Winter&Winter | 910044-2

Traffic I-
Ensemble Modern-Fred Frith:Traffic Continues | Winter&Winter | 910044-2

Traffic II
Ensemble Modern-Fred Frith:Traffic Continues | Winter&Winter | 910044-2

Traffic III-
Artie Shaw And His Orchestra | The Uncollected:Artie Shaw, Vol.4 | Hindsight | HSR 149

Traffic Jam
Nat Adderley Orchestra | Double Expusure | Prestige | P 10090

Tragamar
Don Ellis Quintet | New Ideas | Original Jazz Classics | OJCCD 431-2(NJ 8257)

Tragick Magick
E.M.T. | Canadian Cup Of Coffee | FMP | SAJ 02

Trahütten
Brad Mehldau | Elegiac Cycle | Warner | 9362-47357-2

Trailer Park Ghost
Philly Joe Jones Septet | Mo' Joe | Black Lion | BLCD 760154

Train
Mose Allison Trio | Back Country Suite | Original Jazz Classics | OJC 075(P 7091)

Train-
Charles Tyler Quartet | Definite Vol.2 | Storyville | SLP 4099

Train Of Thought
The Quartet | Loaded | Leo Records | 010

Train Shuffle
Tom Harrell Sextet | Upswing | Chesky | JD 103

Train Song
Frank Wright Quintet | Your Prayer | ESP Disk | ESP 1053-2

Train To St.Gallen
Duke Robillard-Herb Ellis Quintet | More Conversations In Swing Guitar | Stony Plain | SPCD 1292

Train To Texas
Massimo Urbani Quintet | The Blessing | Red Records | 123257-2

Train(23 Stops)
Philippe Caillat Group | French Connection,Dirty Rats | JA & RO | 003(08-4103)

Trainer
Michel Petrucciani Sextet | Both Worlds | Dreyfus Jazz Line | FDM 36590-2

Training
Michel Petrucciani Trio | Trio In Tokyo | Dreyfus Jazz Line | FDM 36605-2
Roosevelt Sykes | The Honeydripper | Queen-Disc | 055

Trains And Boats And Planes
Willie 'The Lion' Smith Duo | Willie 'The Lion ' Smith:The Lion's In Town | Vogue | 2111506-2

Trakeando
Cal Tjader Quintet | Solar Heat | Memo Music | HDJ 4078

Tram
Albert Mangelsdorff Quartet | Live In Berlin | FMP | 0390

Tramline
Trio Concepts | Trio Concepts | yvp music | CD 3010

Tramonto
John Stowell-Bebo Ferra | Elle | Jardis Records | JRCD 20028
John Taylor Trio | Rosslyn | ECM | 1751(159924-2)
Lowell Fulsom Band | Tramp/Soul | Ace Records | CDCHD 339

Tramp Blues
John Benson Brooks Ensemble | Alabama/Africa | Milestone | M 47059

Tramps
Pino Distaso/Roberto Gotta/Beto Cutillo | Tell Her It's All Right | Edition Collage | EC 463-2

Tramps Road
Billy Barber | Lighthouse | dmp Digital Music Productions | CD 455

Trance
Steve Kuhn Trio | Life's Magic | Black-Hawk | BKH 522
Marty Cook & The New York Sound Explosion | Trance | Circle Records | RK 20-31279/20 IMS

Trance Angle
Jean-Paul Bourelly Trance Atlantic | Boom Bop II | double moon | CHRDM 71023

Trance Atlantic
Robin Eubanks/Steve Turre Group | Dedication | JMT Edition | 834433-2

'Trane
Louis Sclavis-Evan Parker | Duets,Dithyrambisch | FMP | CD 19/20

Trane Up
Eddie Lockjaw Davis And His Orchestra | Eric Dolphy:The Complete Prestige Recordings | Prestige | 9 PRCD-4418-2

Trane Whistle
Oliver Nelson Quintet | Taking Care Of Business | Original Jazz Classics | OJCCD 1784-2(NJ 8233)

Traneing In
John Coltrane Quartet | John Coltrane-Live Trane:The European Tours | Pablo | 7PACD 4433-2
The Complete 1962 Stockholm Concert Vol.2 | Magnetic Records | MRCD 109
Live In Stockholm 1963 | Charly | CD 33
John Coltrane With The Red Garland Trio | John Coltrane-The Prestige Recordings | Prestige | 16 PCD 4405-2
McCoy Tyner Trio | McCoy Tyner With Stanley Clarke And Al Foster | Telarc Digital | CD 83488

Trane's Blues
Miles Davis New Quintet | Workin',Steamin',Cookin',Relaxin' With The Miles Davis Quintet | Original Jazz Classics | OJCCD 8805-2
Workin' With The Miles Davis Qoartet | Original Jazz Classics | OJC 296(P 7166)

Trane's Slow Blues
John Coltrane Trio | Lush Life | Original Jazz Classics | OJC20 131-2
Steve Grossman Trio | Way Out East Vol.2 | Red Records | 123183-2

Tranesonic
John Coltrane Quartet | Stellar Regions | Impulse(MCA) | 951169-2

Tranesonic(alt.take)
Bobby Hutcherson Sextet | Components | Blue Note | 829027-2

Tranquil
Hamiet Bluiett Septet | New York City Jazz-4 | Polydor | 815109-1 IMS

Tranquility
Mike LeDonne Quintet | Waltz For An Urbanite | Criss Cross | Criss 1111
Tania Maria Sextet | Taurus | Concord | CCD 4175
Los Angeles Neophonic Orchestra | Stan Kenton Conducts The Los Angeles Neophonic Orchestra | Capitol | 494502-2

Tranquilizer
Trigger Alpert's All Stars | Trigger Happy! | Fresh Sound Records | RLP 12-225(Riverside)

Tranquilo
Albert Mangelsdorff-Wolfgang Dauner & Family Of Percussion | Moon At Noon | Musikant | 066 1472811

Trans Tanz
Lester Bowie Group | All The Magic! | ECM | 1246/47

Transblucency-
Duke Ellington And His Orchestra | Duke Ellington:Complete Prestige Carnegie Hall 1946-1947 Concerts | Definitive Records | DRCD 11211

Transformate Transcend Tones And Images
Gunter Hampel And His Galaxie Dream Band | Transformation | Birth | 0026

Transformation
Miroslav Vitous | Emergence | ECM | 1312
Reinhard Flatischler | Transformation | VeraBra Records | CDVBR 2033-2

Transition
Graham Haynes Group | Transition | Verve | 529039-2
LeeAnn Ledgerwood Trio | Transition | Steeplechase | SCCD 31468
Trilok Gurtu Group | Living Magic | CMP Records | CMP CD 50

Transition Inzwischen
Dave Weckl Band | Rhythm In My Soul | Stretch Records | SCD 9016-2

Transition Theme For Minor Blues Or Little Malcolm Loves His Dad
Chris Jarrett | Fire | Edition Collage | EC 443-2

Transitions
Emily Remler Quartet | Transitions | Concord | CCD 4236

Translucide
Joe Morris Quartet | You Be Me | Soul Note | 121304-2

Transmitter
Dino Saluzzi | Andina | ECM | 1375(837186-2)

Transmutation
Stefano Battaglia | Baptism | SPLASC(H) Records | CD H 417-2

Transmutation-
Benjamin Koppel Double Quartet | Europ' Jazz Contest '94 | B.Sharp Records | CDS 104

Transparency
Herb Robertson Quintet | Transparency | JMT Edition | 834402-1

Transylvanian Dance
Nicolas Simion Quartet feat. Tomasz Stanko | Transylvanian Dance | Tutu Records | 888164-2*
Nicolas Simion Trio | Back To The Roots | Tutu Records | 888176-2
Harry Tavitian/Corneliu Stroe | Transilvanian Suite | LEO | LR 132

Trapeze
Marty Cook Group feat. Jim Pepper | Red,White,Black & Blue | Tutu Records | 888174-2*
Marty Cook Quintet | Red, White, Black And Blue | Enja | 5067-2

Trapping The Foot, Trapping The Brain
Barry Altschul | Another Time Another Place | Muse | MR 5176

Traps(Song Of The Hidden Path)
Raum-Zeit-Klang-Project | Dimensionale X H2O Memory | Born&Bellmann | 970612 CD

Trash Dance
Michel Wintsch & Road Movie | Michel Wintsch & Road Movie featuring Gerry Hemingway | Between The Lines | btl 002(Efa 10172-2)

Trash Road
Albert Collins Blues Band | Ice Cold Blues | Charly | CRB 1119

Trau Schau Wem
Ulla Oster Group | Beyond Janis | Jazz Haus Musik | JHM 0052 CD
World Quintet With The London Mozart Players And Herbert Grönemeyer | World Quintet | TipToe | TIP-888843 2

Trauer
Willem Breuker Kollektief | Live at The Donaueschingen Music Festival | MPS | 529089-2

Traum
Martin Theurer & Paul Lovens | Der Traum Der Roten Palme | FMP | 0950

Traumbilder
Teddy Stauffer Und Seine Original Teddies | Das Schönste Von Damals | Vagabond | 6.28039 DP

Travel Alone
Oregon | Crossing | ECM | 1291(825323-2)

Travel By Day
Don Cherry/Nana Vasconcelos/Collin Walcott | Codona 3 | ECM | 1243

Travel By Night
Evan Parker Electro-Acoustic Ensemble | Drawn Inward | ECM | 1693

Travel In The Homeland
John Scofield Trio | En Route | Verve | 9861357

Travel John
Allotria Jazz Band | All That Jazz | Elite Special | 730217

Traveler
Perry Robinson Quartet | The Traveler | Chiaroscuro | CR 190

Traveler There Is No Road
Chuck Wayne Quartet | Traveling | Progressive | PRO 7008 IMS

Travelin'
McCoy Tyner Quartet | It's About Time | Blue Note | BT 85102

Travelin' Blues
Barrelhouse Jazzband | 40 Jahre Barrelhouse Jazzband | L+R Records | CDLR 8001
Mr.Acker Bilk And His Paramount Jazz Band | The Golden Years Of Revival Jazz,Vol.7 | Storyville | STCD 5512
1+2=3:The Best Of Barber And Bilk | Lake | LACD 73

Travelin' Light
Billie Holiday With The JATP All Stars | Billie Holiday Story Vol.1:Jazz At The Philharmonic | Verve | 521642-2
Billie Holiday With The Paul Whiteman Orchestra | Billie's Blues | Blue Note | 748786-2
Billie Holiday With Tony Scott And His Orchestra | Lady Sings The Blues | Enoch's Music | 57271013
Carmen McRae And Her Sextet | Carmen McRae Sings Lover Man | CBS | CK 65115
Ella Fitzgerald With The Nelson Riddle Orchestra | The Best Of The Song Books:The Ballads | Verve | 521867-2
Enrico Rava Quintet | Andanada | Soul Note | SN 1064
Shirley Scott Quintet | Workin' | Prestige | PCD 24126-2(P 7424/7456)
Zoot Sims Quartet | For Lady Day | Pablo | 2310942-2

Travelin' Man
Stan Kenton And His Orchestra | Some Women I've Known | Creative World | ST 1029

Travelin' On
John Mooney And Bluesiana | Travelin' On | Crosscut | CCD 11032

Travelin'(alt.take)
Joachim Kühn & The String Orchestra | Cinemascope/Piano | MPS | 88037-2

Travelin'(uncomplete take)
Robert Balzar Trio | Travelling | Jazzpoint | JP 1050 CD

Traveling
Draft | Traveling Birds | Jazz Haus Musik | JHM 68 CD

Traveling By Flying Carpet
Lazy Lester Band | Rides Again | Line Records | STLP 400396 J

Traveling Miles
Enrico Rava Quintet | Easy Living | ECM | 1760(9812050)

Traveling Night
John Hammond Band | The Best Of John Hammond | Vanguard | VCD 11/12

Traveling Riverside Blues
Woody Mann-Jo Ann Kelly | Been Here And Gone | Acoustic Music Records | 319.1174.2

Traveling Tatars-
Grant Green With Orchestra | The Final Comedown(Soundtrack) | Blue Note | 581678-2

Traveling To Get To Doc
The Final Comedown(Soundtrack) | Blue Note | 581678-2
Christian Wallumrod Trio | No Birch | ECM | 1628(537344-2)

Traveling:
European Jazz Ensemble | European Jazz Ensemble 25th Anniversary | Konnex Records | KCD 5100

Traveller
Gene Shaw Sextet | Debut In Blues | Argo | ARC 501

Travels
Loope | Red & Yellow | Aho-Recording | CD 1003
Pat Metheny Group | Works | ECM | 823270-2
Glen Moore | Dragonetti's Dream | VeraBra Records | CDVBR 2154-2

Travels With My Foot
Mosalini/Beytelmann/Caratini | Imagenes | Riskant | ???

Trav'lin'
Modern Jazz Quartet | The Complete Last Concert | Atlantic | 81976-2

Trav'lin' Light
Billie Holiday With The JATP All Stars | The Complete Jazz At The Philharmonic On Verve 1944-1949 | Verve | 523893-2
Billie Holiday With The Mal Waldron Trio+Guests | At Monterey 1958 | Black-Hawk | BKH 50701
Ella Fitzgerald With The Nelson Riddle Orchestra | Ella Fitzgerald Sings The Johnny Mercer Songbook | Verve | 539057-2
The Johnny Mercer Songbook | Verve | 823247-2 PMS
Peggy Connelly With The Russ Garcia 'Wigville' Band | Peggy Connelly | Fresh Sound Records | FSR 2018(Bethlehem BCP 53)
Sonny Rollins Sextet | The Standard Sonny Rollins | RCA | 2174801-2

Trav'lin' Light(alt take)
Dado Moroni Trio | What's New? | SPLASC(H) Records | CD H 378-2

Trayra Boia
Nana Vasconcelos/Antonello Salis | Lester | Soul Note | 121157-2

Tré
Marco Piludu International Quartet | New York Travels | Jazz 4 Ever Records:Jazz Network | J4E 4733

Tre Abandonati
Gianluigi Trovesi-Gianni Coscia | In Cerca Di Cibo | ECM | 1703(543034-2)

Tre Bimbi Di Campagna
Flemming Agerskov Quintet | Face To Face | dacapo | DCCD 9445

Tre Fortaellinger
Riccardo Fassi Trio | Riccardo Fassi New York Trio | yvp music | CD 3036

Tre Sma Soldater
Clark Terry Orchestra | Free And Oozy | Blue Moon | BMCD 3076

Treason
Roy Ayers Group | Nasté | RCA | 6366613-2

Treat Me Rough
Trigger Alpert's All Stars | Trigger Happy! | Fresh Sound Records | RLP 12-225(Riverside)

Treat Street
Arnie Lawrence Quartet | Reneval | Palo Alto | PA 8033

Treck 'N' Dorough
Trio Clastrier-Riessler-Rizzo | Palude | Wergo | WER 8010-2

Tredue
Swim Two Birds | Apsion | VeraBra Records | CDVBR 2101-2

Tree Frog
Count Basie And His Orchestra | The Best Of Count Basie | Pablo | 2405408-2

Tree Patterns
Jimmy Giuffre Trio | The Train And The River | Choice | CHCD 71011

Tree People
Metro | Tree People | Lipstick Records | LIP 890312

Tree Top Tall Papa
Sunny Murray Quartet | Live At Moers Festival | Moers Music | 01054 CD

Trees
Louis Armstrong With Gordon Jenkins And His Orchestra And Choir | Satchmo In Style | Verve | 549594-2
Mahalia Jackson With Choir/Orchestra/Falls-Jones Ensemble | This Is Mahalia Jackson | CBS | 66241
Riot | Green And Blue | Nagara | MIX 1012-N
Roland Kirk Quintet | Rahsaan/The Complete Mercury Recordings Of Roland Kirk | Mercury | 846630-2
Sarah Vaughan With The Jimmy Jones Orchestra | Dreamy | Fresh Sound Records | SR 52046(Roulette)

Trees-
George Adams-Don Pullen Quartet | Decisions | Timeless | CD SJP 205

Trellis
The Tremble Kids | The Tremble Kids:The Of 40 Years | BELL Records | BLR 84060

Treme Terra
Chris Jarrett | Short Stories For Piano | Edition Musikat | EDM 056

Tremolo
Bob Sands Quintet | JumpSTART | Fresh Sound Records | FSNT 042 CD

Tren A Palencia
Anthony Coleman Quartet | Disco By Night | Avant | AVAN 011

Trendsition Zildjian
Matthias Petzold Septett | Ulysses | Indigo-Records | 1003 CD

Trentadue Panini
Gary Smulyan Quartet | Homage | Criss Cross | Criss 1068

Trenzinho Do Caipira
Egberto Gismonti | Danca Dos Escravos | ECM | 1387(837753-2)

Trenzinho Do Caipira(Verde)
Pata Music Meets Arfi | News Of Roi Ubu | Pata Musik | PATA 10 CD

Treomphe
Herman Chittison | JazzIn Paris:Harlem Piano In Montmartre | EmArCy | 018447-2

Tres
No Square Trio | Empreintes | Elite Special | 73612

Tres Chouette
Jimmy Raney Quintet | Too Marvelous For Words | Biograph | BLP 12060

Tres De Azucar
Samba Trio | Tristeza | Timeless | CD SJP 169

Tres Minutos Con La Realidad
Merseysippi Jazz Band 1954-1957 | Mersey Tunnel Jazz | Lake | LACD 85

Tres Palabras
Brad Mehldau Trio | Anything Goes | Warner | 9362-48608-2
Christoph Sänger Trio | Imagination | Laika Records | 35100752
Gonzalo Rubalcaba Group | Suite 4 y 20 | Blue Note | 780054-2
Kenny Burrell Sextet | Moonglow | Prestige | P 24106

Tres Palabras(Without You)
Lou Levy Trio | Jazz In Hollywood:Bud Shank/Lou Levy | Original Jazz Classics | OJCCD 1890-2(Nocturne NLP-2/NLP-10)

Tres Para S.
Toto Blanke-Rudolf Dasek | Talking Hands:Live | ALISO Records | AL 1021

Tres Pinas
Pau Brasil | Babel | ACT | 5009-2

Tres Tangos For Bandoneon And Orchestra
René Marino Rivero | Che Bandoneon | ALISO Records | AL 1020

Tres Tangos Nostalgicos Para Marianne Von Allmen:
Sören Fischer Quartet | Don't Change Your Hair For Me | Edition Collage | EC 513-2

Tres Tequilas
Baden Powell Quartet | Canto On Guitar | MPS | 68157

Tres-Cun-Deo-La
Joe Henderson Sextet | Multiple | Original Jazz Classics | OJCCD 763-2(M 9050)
Willem Breuker Kollektief And Djazzex | Dance Plezier-Joy Of Dance | BVHAAST | CD 9513

Trespass
Chico Freeman And Brainstorm | Threshold | IN+OUT Records | 7022-2

Trespasser
John Surman | Road To Saint Ives | ECM | 1418(843849-2)

Trethevy Quoit
Gene Ammons And His All Stars | Dexter Gordon Birthday Celebration | Fantasy | FANCD 6082-2

'Treux Bleu
Peter Giger Group | Illigitimate Music | Nagara | MIX 1014-N

Trey Of Hearts
Matthew Fries Quintet | Song For Today | TCB Records | TCB 20752

Triads
Larry Karush-Glen Moore Duo | May 24, 1976 | Japo | 60014(2360014)

Trial
Triple Helix | Triple Helix | Enja | ENJ-8056 2

Trial By Error
Chuck Loeb Group | Simple Things | dmp Digital Music Productions | CD 504

Trialogue
Tim Sund Trio | Trialogue | Nabel Records:Jazz Network | CD 4692

Trialogue No.1:
Trialogue | Nabel Records:Jazz Network | CD 4692

Trialogue No.2:
Trialogue | Nabel Records:Jazz Network | CD 4692

Trialogue No.3:
Trialogue | Nabel Records:Jazz Network | CD 4692

Trialogue No.4:
Ronald Shannon Jackson And The Decoding Society | Barbeque Dog | Antilles | AN 1015(802757)

Triangle
Ray Barretto And His Orchestra | Handprints | Concord | CCD 4473

Tribalism
Enrico Rava Quartet | The Plot | ECM | 1078

Tribe

Soul Immigrants Plus Guests | A Healty Vibe | Lipstick Records | LIP 8947-2 HOT

Tribilin Cantore
Johnny Dankworth Quintet | Cleo At Carnegie Hall-The 10th Anniversary Concert | DRG | DARC 2-2101 IMS

Tribu
Alain Monnier Trio | Tribulat | Hat Art | 3505

Tributaries
Alex Riel Trio | Emergence | Red Records | 123263-2

Tribute
Hendrik Meurkens Quintet | Slidin' | Concord | CCD 4628
Slide Hampton-Joe Haider Jazz Orchestra | Give Me A Double | JHM Records | JHM 3627
Stan Kenton And His Orchestra | The Complete MacGregor Transcriptions Vol.1 | Naxos Jazz | 8.120517 CD

Tribute To Brownie
Louis Smith Quintet | Here Comes Louis Smith | Blue Note | 852438-2

Tribute To E.W.
John Hicks Trio | Nightwind:An Erroll Garner Songbook | HighNote Records | HCD 7035

Tribute To Fitzcaraldo
Alex Gunia-Philipp Van Endert Group | Beauty Of Silence | Laika Records | 35101052

Tribute To Glenn Miller
Ray Anthony Orchestra | 1988 & All THat Jazz | Aero Space | RACD 1030(881833)

Tribute To Hodges & Ellington-
Nat Adderley Sextet | Autumn Leaves-Live At Sweet Basil | Sweet Basil | 660.55.013

Tribute To S.M.
Bowling Green John Cephas & Harmonica Phil Wiggins | Sweet Bitter Blues | L+R Records | CDLR 72004

Tribute To The Elders
Peter Materna Quartet | Aquarius | Jazzline | JL 11142-2

Tribute To The Ticklers
Jaki Byard | Maybeck Recital Hall Series Volume Seventeen | Concord | CCD 4511

Tribute To Valente(I Love Paris)
Melvin Taylor Quartet | Plays The Blues For You | Isabel | BLE 59.920 2

Tribute To Wild Bill
Mark Soskin Trio | Views From Here | Paddle Wheel | KICJ 126

Trick Bag
Jesse Van Ruller Trio | Trio | EmArCy | 017513-2

Trick Of The Light
Everyman Band | Without Warning | ECM | 1290

Trick Of The Wool
Count Basie And His Orchestra | Hall Of Fame | Verve | MV 2645 IMS

Tricks Ain't Walkin' No More
Jimmy Rushing | The Jazz Odyssey Of James Rushing Esq. | Fresh Sound Records | FSR 591(CBS CL 963)

Tri-Colour Blues
Andreas Willers Group | Andreas Willers & Friends Play Jimi Hendrix:Experience | Nabel Records:Jazz Network | CD 4665

Tricons
Carl Leukaufe Quintet | Warrior | Delmark | DE 491

Tricotism
Eddie Daniels Quartet | Real Time | Chesky | JD 118
Joe Pass/Niels-Henning Orsted-Pedersen Duo | Chops | Original Jazz Classics | OJCCD 786-2(2310830)
Joe Temperley Quintet | Double Duke | Naxos Jazz | 86032-2
Kenny Clarke Meets The Detroit Jazzmen | Kenny Clarke Meets The Detroit Jazz Men | Savoy | SV 0243(SJL 1111)
Michael Lutzeier Quartet | Music 4 Food | Jazz 4 Ever Records:Jazz Network | J4E 4739
Monty Alexander | Solo | Jeton | JET 60002
Oscar Peterson Trio | Oscar Peterson-The London House Sessions | Verve | 531766-2

Tricotism-
Oscar Pettiford Quintet | Oscar Rides Again | Affinity | AFF 160

Trieste
Gene Harris-The Three Sounds | Yesterday Today And Tomorrow | Blue Note | 84441
Keith Jarrett Quartet | Byablue | Impulse(MCA) | MCD 10648
Modern Jazz Quartet | Lonely Woman | Atlantic | 7567-90665-2
Modern Jazz Quartet And Laurindo Almeida | Collaboration | Philips | 30JD-10093 PMS

Triftig O Du Triftig
Benny Goodman And His Orchestra | Benny Goodman:Bangkok 1956/Basel 1959/Santiago De Chile 1961/Berlin 1980 | TCB Records | TCB 43012

Trigger Fantasy
Trigger Alpert's All Stars | Trigger Happy! | Fresh Sound Records | RLP 12-225(Riverside)

Trigger Happy
Trigger Alpert's Absolutely All Star Seven | East Coast Sound | Original Jazz Classics | OJCCD 1012-2(JLP 11)
Trigger Alpert's All Stars | Trigger Happy! | Fresh Sound Records | RLP 12-225(Riverside)

Triggerfinger Suite:
John Zorn Naked City | Naked City:Radio | Avant | AVAN 003

Triggerfingers-
Konstantin Wienstroer-Veit Lange-Felix Elsner | Unfinished Business | Green House Music | CD 1005

Triggerfingers(2)-
Hilaria Kramer 6 | Trigon | SPLASC(H) Records | H 191

Trigonomerty
Roy Haynes Quintet | Te-Vou! | Dreyfus Jazz Line | FDM 36569-2

Trill Ride
Trio De Clarinettes | Trio De Clarinettes | FMP | CD 39

Trilo
Sorgen/Rust/Windbiel Trio | Outlet | ESP Disk | ESP 3029-2

Trilogie Über Gewisse Situationen Im Leben Eines Menschen:
dAs prOjekT | dAs prOjekT | Foolish Music | FM 211288

Trilogie:
Mangelsdorff-Pastorius-Mouzon | Trilogue-Live At The Berliner Jazztage | MPS | 821282-1

Trilogue
Bob James Trio | Bold Conceptions | Verve | 557454-2

Trilogy
Nguyen Le Trio | Million Waves | ACT | 9221-2
Odean Pope Trio | Ninety-Six | Enja | 9091-2

Trilogy In Blois(Morning Sun,Noon Sun And Night Sun In Blois)
Gary Peacock Trio | Tales Of Another | ECM | 1101(827418-2)

Trilogy(1)
Klaus Ignatzek Group Feat.Dave Liebman | The Spell | Nabel Records:Jazz Network | CD 4614
Gary Peacock Trio | Tales Of Another | ECM | 1101(827418-2)

Trilogy(2)
Klaus Ignatzek Group Feat.Dave Liebman | The Spell | Nabel Records:Jazz Network | CD 4614
Gary Peacock Trio | Tales Of Another | ECM | 1101(827418-2)

Trilogy(3)
Klaus Ignatzek Group Feat.Dave Liebman | The Spell | Nabel Records:Jazz Network | CD 4614
Dixie-O-Naires | Strike Up The Band | Timeless | CD TTD 576

Trilogy:
Seamus Blake Quintet | The Bloomdaddies | Criss Cross | Criss 1110
Mark Nauseef Group | Dark | CMP Records | CMP CD 36

Trinidad
Joe Pass | Virtuoso No.3 | Original Jazz Classics | OJC20 684-2(2310805)
Les McCann Group | Listen Up! | Musicmasters | 65139-2
Dizzy Gillespie Sextet | Jambo Caribe | Verve | 557492-2

Trinidad,Goodbye
Jambo Caribe | Verve | 557492-2

Trinidad,Hello
Masahiko Sato Trio | Trinity | Enja | 2008

Trinity
Tomasz Stanko Quartet | Leosia | ECM | 1603(531693-2)
Lan Xang | Hidden Gardens | Naxos Jazz | 86046-2

Trinkets
JoAnne Brackeen Duo | Trinkets And Things | Timeless | SJP 123

Trinkle Tinkle
Alexander von Schlippenbach And Sunny Murray | Smoke | FMP | CD 23
Chick Corea Quartet | Live In Montreux | Stretch Records | SCD 9009-2
Don Pullen | Plays Monk | Paddle Wheel | K 28P 6368
John Coltrane-Thelonious Monk Quartet | Monk & Trane | Milestone | M 47011
Keith Copeland Trio | Postcard From Vancouver | Jazz Focus | JFCD 023
Kirk Lightsey | Lightsey Live | Sunnyside | SSC 1014 D
Peter Leitch Quintet | Exhilaration | Reservoir | RSR CD 118(889465)
Roy Haynes Quintet | Te-Vou! | Dreyfus Jazz Line | FDM 36569-2
Thelonious Monk | Nice Work In London | Freedom | 147307
Thelonious Monk Quartet | Thelonious Monk:85th Birthday Celebration | zyx records | FANCD 6076-2
Thelonious Monk-The Complete Riverside Recordings | Riverside | 15 RCD 022-2
Thelonious Monk Trio | Thelonious Monk | Original Jazz Classics | OJC20 010-2(P 7027)
Thelonious Monk:The Complete Prestige Recordings | Prestige | 3 PRCD 4428-2
Chick Corea | Ludwigsburger Jazztage | Chaos | CACD 8055-3

Trio
Erroll Garner Trio | Erroll Garner:Trio | Dreyfus Jazz Line | FDM 36719-2
Relaxin' With Erroll | Vogue | 655008
Joelle Leandre's Canvas Trio | L'Histoire De Mme.Tasco | Hat Art | CD 6122
Mark Nauseef/Miroslav Tadic Group | The Snake Music | CMP Records | CMP CD 60

Trio 2
Noodband | Shiver | Moers Music | 01094

Trio And Group Dancers
Charles Mingus And His Orchestra | Great Moments With Charles Mingus | MCA | MCA 2-4128 (802130)

Trio Blues
Art Tatum Trio | The Tatum Group Masterpieces | Pablo | 2625706
Count Basie Jam | Montreux '77-The Art Of The Jam Session | Pablo | 2620106

Trio Con Arco
Paolo Fresu Sextet | Ensalada Mistica | SPLASC(H) Records | CD H 415-2

Trio For Flute Bassoon And Piano
Uwe Kropinski | So Oder So | ITM Records | 0025

Trio For Soprano Saxophone,Bass Trombone And Piano
Joe Sachse | Ballade Für Jimi Metag | Born&Bellmann | 991503 CD

Trio Imitation
Chick Corea Trio | Trio Music | ECM | 1232/33(159454-2)

Trio Improvisations(1-5)
Toto Blanke-Rudolf Dasek | Two Much Guitar! | ALISO Records | AL 1022

Trio Infernal
Trio Ivoire | Trio Ivoire | Enja | ENJ-9424 2

Trio No.1
Lyle Mays Trio | Fictionary | Geffen Records | GED 24521

Trio No.2
Fictionary | Warner | 9362-47906-2
Fictionary | Geffen Records | GED 24521

Trio Sonata (part 1-4)
Paul Plimley Trio | Density Of The Lovestruck Demons | Music & Arts | CD 906

Trio Walk
Herbie Nichols Trio | Herbie Nichols:The Complete Blue Note Recordings | Blue Note | 859352-2

Trio(alt.take)
Steps Ahead | Steps Ahead | Elektra | 7559-60168-2

Trio(An Improvisation)
Thomas Chapin Trio Plus Brass | Insomnia | Knitting Factory Works | KFWCD 132

Trip
Woody Schabata Quintet | May-Rimba | Amadeo | 829324-2

Trip To Ghana
Valery Ponomarev Quintet | Trip To Moscow | Reservoir | RSR CD 107(882631)

Trip To The Bar
Mind Games With Claudio Roditi | Vocal Moments | Take Twelve On CD | TT 008-2

Trip To Your Town
Mind Games With Philip Catherine | Pretty Fonky | Edition Collage | EC 482-2
The Clarke/Duke Project | The Clarke/Duke Project 2 | Epic | EK 38934

Triple Dance
Dave Holland Trio | Triplicate | ECM | 1373
Daniel Humair Trio | Triple Hip Trip | Owl Records | 014 CD

Triple Play
Franco Ambrosetti Quintet | Heart Bop | Enja | 3087 (807508)

Triple X
Albert Mangelsdorff-John Surman Quintet | Room 1220 | Konnex Records | KCD 5037

Triplets,You Say
Daniel Schnyder Quintet | Nucleus | Enja | ENJ-8068 2

Triplex
Urs Leimgruber/John Wolf Brennan | M.A.P. | L+R Records | CDLR 45021

Triplicate
Jam Session | Jam Session Vol.1 | Steeplechase | SCCD 31522
Red Mitchell-Harold Land Quintet | Atlantic Jazz: West Coast | Atlantic | 7567-81703-2

Trippin'
Eric Alexander Quartet | Eric Alexander In Europe | Criss Cross | Criss 1114
Steve Davis Sextet | Dig Deep | Criss Cross | Criss 1136

Tripti
David Friedman Quartet | Other Worlds | Intuition Records | INT 3210-2

Triptych
Denny Zeitlin-David Friesen | Live At The Jazz Bakery | Intuition Records | INT 3257-2
Archie Shepp-Max Roach Duo | The Long March Part 2 | Hat Art | CD 6042

Triptych:
Maarten Altena Ensemble | Cities & Street | Hat Art | CD 6082
Jan Garbarek Trio | Triptychon | ECM | 1029(847321-2)

Triptykon
Peter Kuhn Quintet | Ghost Of A Trance | Hat Art | 9 (1R09)

Triste
Baden Powell Trio | L'Ame De Baden Powell | Festival | 114811
Cal Tjader Sextet | Talkin Verve/Roots Of Acid Jazz:Cal Tjader | Verve | 531562-2
Carlo Domeniconi | Nil | MRC | 066-32856
Elis Regina Group | Compact Jazz: Antonio Carlos Jobim | Verve | 843273-2
Franco D'Andrea New Quartet | Jobim | Philology | W 125.2
Joe Kienemann Trio | All That Jazz Special | Blue Flame | 40742(2132446-2)
Lee Konitz Quartet | Pride | Steeplechase | SCCD 31479
Oscar Peterson Trio | Paris Jazz Concert:Oscar Peterson | Laserlight | 36155
En Concert Avec Europe 1 | Laserlight | 710443/48
Three Originals:Motion&Emotions/Tristeza On Piano/Hello Herbie | MPS | 521059-2
Paul Bley Quartet | The Paul Bley Quartet | ECM | 1365(835250-2)
Sarah Vaughan With Orchestra | Sarah Vaughan Birthday Celebration | Fantasy | FANCD 6090-2
I Love Brazil | Pablo | 2312101-2
Shirley Scott Trio | Blues Everywhere | Candid | CCD 79525
Herbie Hancock | Antonio Carlos Jobim And Friends | Verve | 531556-2

Triste-
Barney Wilen Quintet | La Note Bleue | IDA Record | 010 CD

Tristeza
Baden Powell Ensemble | Samba Triste | Accord | 102772
Baden Powell Trio | Compact Jazz: Best Of Bossa Nova | Verve | 833269-2
Oscar Peterson Trio | En Concert Avec Europe 1 | Laserlight | 710443/48
Three Originals:Motion&Emotions/Tristeza On Piano/Hello Herbie | MPS | 521059-2
Sadao Watanabe And His Brazilian Friends | Sadao Meets Brazilian Friends | Denon Compact Disc | DC-8557

Tristeza e Solidao
Susannah McCorkle And Her Sextet | Sabia | Concord | CCD 4418

Triton Et Demi
Henry Butler | Blues & More Vol.1 | Windham Hill | 34 10138-2

Tritone Samba
Andy LaVerne Trio | Between Mars & Earth | Steeplechase | SCCD 31478

Tritt Mir Bloß Nicht Auf Die Schuh
Astor Piazzolla Y Su Orquesta | Pulsacion | West Wind Latina | 2220 CD

Tri-Van Drumming
Tony Scott | Music For Yoga Meditation And Other Joys | Verve | 2304471 IMS

Triveni-Sacred Knot
Muhal Richard Abrams Ensemble | Spihumonesty | Black Saint | 120032-2

Tri-X
Hermann Breuer-Carolyn Breuer Quintet | Family Affair | Enja | 8002-2

Trixie
Sidney Bechet Sextet With Trixie Smith | Blackstick | MCA | 1330

TRM'PT FLY FLY
Koch-Schütz-Käppeli | The Art Of The Staccato | Sound Aspects | sas CD 033

Trogener Chibliläbe
Grand Dominion Jazz Band | Half And Half | Stomp Off Records | CD 3989

Troika
Viktoria Tabatchnikowa-Eugenij Belov | Troika | ALISO Records | AL 1036

Troika-
Dave Liebman | One Of A Kind | Line Records | COCD 9.00887 0

Trois Images
Gianluigi Trovesi Octet | Les Hommes Armés | Soul Note | 121311-2

Trolley Song
Dave Brubeck Quartet | Dave Brubeck-Paul Desmond | Fantasy | FCD 24727-2

Trombone Butter(aka Trombone Chilly)
Dinah Washington With The Eddie Chamblee Orchestra | Dinah Sings Bessie Smith | Verve | 538635-2

Trombone Butter(aka Trombone Chilly-alt.take)
Beryl Bryden & The Blue Boys | I've Got What It Takes-A BBC Radio Celebration Of The Music Of Bessie Smith | Lake | LACD 71

Trombone Cholly
Chris Barber's Jazz Band | Ottilie Patterson With Chris Barber's Jazzband 1955-1958 | Lake | LACD 30

Trombonia-Bustoso-Issimo
Duke Ellington And His Orchestra | Ella Fitzgerald And Duke Ellington:Cote D'Azure Concerts on Verve | Verve | 539033-2
Eddie Johnson Quartet | Love You Madly | Delmark | DE 515

Trombosphere
Luigi Archetti | Das Ohr | ATM Records | ATM 3804-AH

Trommelgeflüster(part 1&2)
Drümmele Maa | Stadtgarten Series Vol.5 | Jazz Haus Musik | JHM 1005 SER

Trompe L'Oreille
Kenny Dorham Quintet | Trompeta Toccata | Blue Note | BST 84181

Trong Com(The Rice Drum)
Hubert Rostaing Et Son Orchestre | Jazz In Paris:Clarinettes À Saint-Germain Des Prés | EmArCy | 013543-2

Tropea
Jon Hiseman Group | Night In The Sun | Kuckuck | 055

Tropical Breeze
Oscar Castro-Neves Orchestra | Brazilian Scandals | JVC | ???

Tropical Storm
Stanley Jordan Group | Flying Home | Blue Note | 748682-2

Tropican Sunday
Gil Fuller And His Orchestra | The Bebop Boys | Savoy | WL 70547 (809278)

Tropicville
Poncho Sanchez Group | Soul Sauce-Memories Of Cal Tjader | Concord | CCD 4662

Tröste Dich
Joe Baudisch Quartet | The Meeting Of Two Tenors | Acoustic Music Records | 319.1135.2

Trotting
Zoot Sims Quartet | Zoot Sims:The Complete 1944-1954 Small Group Sessions(Master Takes),Vol.2 | Blue Moon | BMCD 1039

Trotting(alt.take 1)
Zoot Sims Quartets | Original Jazz Classics | OJCCD 242-2(P 7026)

Trotting(alt.take 2)
New Art Saxophone Quartet | Songs And Dances | Enja | ENJ-9420 2

Troubador Tale
Don Friedman Quartet | Metamorphosis | Original Jazz Classics | OJCCD 1914-2(P 7488)

Troublant Bolero
Christian Escoude Quartet With Strings | Plays Django Reinhardt | EmArCy | 510132-2
Organ Jazztrio & Martin Weiss | Hommage | Edition Collage | EC 492-2
Stochelo Rosenberg Trio | Seresta | Hot Club Records | HCRCD 059
The Rosenberg Trio | The Rosenberg Trio:The Collection | Verve | 537152-2
Leni Stern Group | Ten Songs | Lipstick Records | LIP 890092

Trouble
Sarah Vaughan With The Ernie Wilkins Orchestra | A Time In My Life | Mobile Fidelity | MFCD 855
Stanley Turrentine Quintet | Never Let Me Go | Blue Note | 576750-2
Wayne Horvitz Group | 4+1 Ensemble | Intuition Records | INT 3224-2
Thomas Stabenow Trio | Human Spirit | Bassic-Sound | CD 009

Trouble At The South Bend
Charles Brown | Great Rhythm & Blues-Vol.1 | Bulldog | BDL 1001

Trouble If I Don't Use My Head
Jesse Fuller One Man Band | Brother Lowdown | Fantasy | F 24707

Trouble In Mind
Archie Shepp-Horace Parlan Duo | 2nd Set | 52e Rue Est | RECD 016
Dinah Washington With Orchestra | Compact Jazz:Dinah Washington Sings The Blues | Mercury | 832573-2 PMS
Dinah Washington With The Jimmy Cobb Orchestra | The Complete Dinah Washington Vol.7 | Official | 3018
Dodo Greene With The Ike Quebec Quintet | My Hour Of Need | Blue Note | 852442-2
Jay McShann Quartet | Goin' To Kansas City | Stony Plain | SPCD 1286
Jeannie And Jimmy Cheatham & The Sweet Baby Blues Band | Homeward Bound | Concord | CCD 4321
Jimmy Rushing And The Buck Clayton All Stars | Jimmy Rushing And The Smith Girls | Fresh Sound Records | FSR 594(CBS CS 8405)
Jimmy Witherspoon And His All Stars | Blues For Easy Livers | Original Blues Classics | OBCCD 585-2(PR 7475)
Jimmy Witherspoon | Laserlight | 17069
Memphis Slim | Tribute To Big Bill Broonzy etc. | Candid | CS 9023
Mose Allison Trio | Mose Allison:Greatest Hits | Original Jazz Classics | OJCCD 6004-2
Local Color | Original Jazz Classics | OJCCD 457-2
Mr.Acker Bilk And His Paramount Jazz Band | New Orleans Days | Lake | LACD 36

TITELVERZEICHNIS

Ruth Brown With The Thad Jones-Mel Lewis Orchestra | Fine Brown Frame | Capitol | 781200-2

Trouble In Paradise
Noma Kosazana & Uli Lenz | Art Of The Duo: Trouble In Paradise | Tutu Records | 888144-2*
Dinah Washington And Her Quartet | Compact Jazz:Dinah Washington Sings The Blues | Mercury | 832573-2 PMS

Trouble Is A Man
Charlie Mariano Sextet | Nat Pierce-Dick Collins Nonet/Charlie Mariano Sextet | Original Jazz Classics | OJC 118(F 3224)
Ella Fitzgerald With The Tommy Flanagan Trio | Sunshine Of Your Love | MPS | 533102-2
Ernestine Anderson With Orchestra | My Kinda Swing | Mercury | 842409-2
Larry Sonn And His Orchestra | Jazz Band Having A Ball | Fresh Sound Records | DLP 9005(Dot)
Lottie Murrell | The Introduction To Living Country Blues USA | L+R Records | LS 42030

Trouble Man
Pucho & His Latin Soul Brothers | Jazzin' With The Soul Brothers | Fantasy | FANCD 6086-2
Lloyd Jones Blues Band | Trouble Monkey | audioquest Music | AQCD 1037

Trouble Then Satisfaction
Earl Hines Sextet | The Dukeless Gang | Queen-Disc | 041

Trouble With Joe
Monty Alexander Sextet | To Nat, With Love From Monty Alexander | Master Mix | CHECD 12

Trouble With Mutation
Lowell Fulsom Band | Lowell Fulson | Chess | 427007

Troubled Skies
John Swana Sextet | In The Moment | Criss Cross | Criss 1119

Troubled Times
Duke Ellington And His Orchestra | The Indispensable Duke Ellington Vol.3/4(1930-1934) | RCA | 2122620-2

Troubled Waters(for Paul Robeson)
Al Rapone & The Zydeco Express | Troubled Woman | Traditional Line | TL 1306

Troubles
Steve Lacy Quintet | The Way | Hat Art | CD 6154(2)

Trough A Long And Sleepless Night
Josh Roseman Unit | Cherry | Enja | ENJ-9392 2

Trousertrout
Marcio Tubino Group | Festa Do Olho | Organic Music | ORGM 9723

Trovas
Louie Bellson's 7 | Live At The Concord Summer Festival | Concord | CCD 4026

Trubadur
Ken Peplowski Quintet | Illumination | Concord | CCD 4449

Trubbel (Trouble)
Ralph R.Hübner-Christoph Lauer Quartet | Mondspinner | free flow music | ffm 0796

Trüblich?
Double Image | Double Image | Enja | ENJ-2096 2

Truce
Joe Locke Quintet | Inner Space | Steeplechase | SCCD 31380

Truckin'
Fats Waller And His Rhythm | I'm Gonna Sit Right Down...The Early Years-Part 2(1935-1936) | Bluebird | 63 66640-2
Mel Tormé With The Marty Paich Orchestra | Compact Jazz: Mel Torme | Verve | 833282-2 PMS

Truddelutter
Jimmy Giuffre 3 | Jimmy Giuffre 3, 1961 | ECM | 1438/39(849644-2)

Trudgin'
Jimmy Giuffre Trio | Live In Europe Vol.1 | Raretone | 5018 FC

True
Louis Gallaud With Emanuel Sayles | Punch Miller/Louis Gallaud | American Music | AMCD-68

True Blue
Booker Ervin Quintet | The Blues Book | Original Jazz Classics | OJCCD 780-2(P 7340)
Cees Smal Quintet | Just Friends | Limetree | MLP 198607
Barbara Lea And The Legendary Lawson-Haggart Jazz Band | You're The Cats! | Audiophile | ACD-252

True Blues
Art Pepper Quartet | Landscape | Original Jazz Classics | OJCCD 676-2(GXY 5128)

True Colors
Klaus Suonsaari Quintet | True Colours | L+R Records | CDLR 45080

True Friends
Marcus Miller Group | Tales | Dreyfus Jazz Line | FDM 36571-2

True Geminis
Bob Cooper Quartet | Tenor Sax Jazz Impressions | Trend | TR 518 Direct-to-Disc

True Love
Little Johnny Taylor With Band | The Galaxy Years | Ace Records | CDCHD 967

True Love-
Simon Schott | Bar Piano: Simon Schott Plays Your Favorite Evergreens Vol.2 | Organic Music | ORGM 9735
Sandy Brown With The Brian Lemon Trio | In The Evening | Hep | CD 2017

True Or False
Roy Haynes Quartet | True Or False | Freelance | FRL-CD 007

True Romance
Tommy Smith Sextet | Paris | Blue Note | 780612-2

True Stories(part 1-3)
Darol Anger-Barbara Higbie Duo | Tideline | Windham Hill | WD 1021

Trumba
Bix Beiderbecke Orchestra/Gang | The Golden Age Of Bix Beiderbecke | EMI Records | CD MFP 6046

Trumpet
Heinrich Köbberling-Matt Renzi Quartet | Pisces | Nabel Records:Jazz Network | CD 4677
Joe McPhee | Graphics | Hat Art | I/J

Trumpet Blues
Dizzy Gillespie-Roy Eldridge Sextet | Diz And Roy | Verve | 2-2524 IMS
Roy Eldridge-Dizzy Gillespie With The Oscar Peterson Quartet | The Complete Verve Roy Eldridge Studio Sessions | Verve | 9861278
Harry James And His Orchestra | The Hits Of Harry James | Capitol | 791220-2

Trumpet Concerto(3 movements)
Duke Ellington And His Orchestra | The Complete Duke Ellington-Vol. 7 | CBS | CBS 88140

Trumpet March-
Stan Kenton And His Orchestra | The Complete MacGregor Transcriptions Vol.2 | Naxos Jazz | 8.120518 CD

Trumpets No End(Blue Skies)
Duke Ellington And His Orchestra | Duke Ellington:Complete Prestige Carnegie Hall 1946-1947 Concerts | Definitive Records | DRCD 11211

Trust
Monty Alexander 7 | Goin' Yard | Telarc Digital | CD 83527

Trust In Me
Coleman Hawkins All Star Octet | Bean And The Boys | Prestige | PCD 24124-2
Houston Person Quintet | Trust In Me | Prestige | PCD 24264-2
James 'Sing' Miller Quartet | New Orleans Traditional Jazz Legends:Sing Miller | Mardi Gras Records | MG 9006
Louis Jordan And His Tympany Five | Louis Jordan-Let The Good Times Roll: The Complete Decca Recordings 1938-1954 | Bear Family Records | BCD 15557 IH
Mildred Bailey And Her Orchestra | Squeeze Me | Affinity | CD AFS 1013

Trust In Me-
Herbie Hancock Group | Feet's Don't Fail Me Now | CBS | SRCS 9504

Trust Me
Kip Hanrahan Groups | Desire Develops An Edge | American Clave | AMCL 1008-2

Truth
Duke Jordan | Duke Jordan-Solo Masterpieces Vol.2 | Steeplechase | SCCD 31300
Gunter Hampel Jazz Sextet | Gunter Hampel: The 8th Of Sept.1999 | Birth | CD 049
Music Inc | Live In Tokyo | Strata East Records | 660.51.016
Shannon Jackson & The Decoding Society | Raven Roc | DIW | DIW 862 CD

Truth Be Told
Victor Lewis Trio | Three Way Conversations | Red Records | 123276-2

Truth Is Fallen
Albert Ayler Quintet | In Memory Of Albert Ayler | Jazz Door | JD 1203

Truth Is Marching In
Marcus Roberts Quintet | The Truth Is Spoken Here | Novus | PD 83051

Truth(II)
Dave Brubeck With The Erich Kunzel Orchestra | Truth Is Fallen | Atlantic | 7567-80761-2

Truth(Planets Are Spinning)
Wolfhound-Anne Haigis | The Never Ending Story | BELL Records | BLR 84025

Try A Little Tenderness
Buddy Childers Big Band | Just Buddy's | Candid | CCD 79761
Chris Connor With The Ellis Larkins Trio | I Hear Music | Affinity | AFF 97
Don Lanphere/Marc Seales | Don Loves Midge | Hep | 2027
World Saxophone Quartet | Rhythm And Blues | Nonesuch | 7559-60864-2

Try A Little Tenderness-
George Howard Group | Do I Ever Cross Your Mind | GRP | GRP 96692

Try It
Matthias Petzold Working Band | Elements | Indigo-Records | 1005 CD

Try It Again
Matthias Frey Group | Liquid Crystal | Inak | 9026

Try Me
The Clarke/Duke Project | The Clarke/Duke Project 2 | Epic | EK 38934

Try Some Of That
Macon Ed[Eddie Anthony] And Tampa Joe[prob.Jim Hill] | Georgia String Bands(1928-1930) | Story Of Blues | CD 3516-2

Try To Fly
Doctor Feelgood-The Original Piano Red | Music Is Medicine | L+R Records | LR 42019

Try To Remember
Morgana King With Orchestra | A Taste Of Honey | Mainstream | MD CDO 707
Singers Unlimited | A Capella | MPS | 815671-1

Try Your Wings
Ben Sidran Quartet feat. Johnny Griffin | Have You Met...Barcelona? | Orange Blue | OB 002 CD

Tryin' To Get Over
Reverend Blind Gary Davis | Say No To The Devil | Original Blues Classics | OBC 519

Tryst
Rod Williams Quintet | Hanging In The Ballance | Muse | MCD 5380

Tryst Revisited
Larry Willis Trio | Just In Time | Steeplechase | SCS 1251

Tsakve
Abdullah Ibrahim Trio And A String Orchestra | African Suite | TipToe | TIP-888832 2

Tsakwe
Abdullah Ibrahim Trio | African Magic | TipToe | TIP-888845 2

Tsakwe-
Sibongile Khumalo Group | Live At The Market Theatre | CBS | 491322-2

Tsakwe-Royal Blue
Rabih Abou-Khalil Group | Blue Camel | Enja | ENJ-7053 2

Tsarka
Jürgen Sturm's Ballstars | Tango Subversivo | Nabel Records:Jazz Network | CD 4613

Tscha Tscha Para Abeja
Steve Coleman And Five Elements | RCA Victor 80th Anniversary Vol.7:1980-1989 | RCA | 2668783-2

Tschastuschka
Günther Klatt & New York Razzmatazz | Fa Mozzo | Tutu Records | 888138-2

Tschirglo Waltz
Bireli Lagrene Ensemble | Routes To Django & Bireli Swing '81 | Jazzpoint | JP 1055 CD
Bireli Lagrene Quartet | A' Portrait Of Jan Jankeje | Jazzpoint | JP 1054 CD
Titi Winterstein Quintet plus Guests | Live! | Boulevard | BLD 508 LP

Tsidi
Michael Moore Group | Tunes For Horn Guys | Ramboy Recordings | No.08

Tsunami
Richard Beirach-Masahiko Togashi | Richie Beirach-Masahiko Togashi-Terumasa Hino | Konnex Records | KCD 5043

TT (A Tete Montoliu)
Steve Gibbons Band | Birmingham To Memphis | Linn Records | AKD 019

T-Time
Stefano Di Battista Quintet | A Prima Vista | Blue Note | 497945-2

T-T-Tim
Roscoe Mitchell | The Roscoe Mitchell Solo Saxophone Concerts | Sackville | 2006

Tu Crees Que
Cal Tjader Sextet | Monterey Concerts | Prestige | PCD 24026-2
Here | Galaxy | GXY 5121

Tu Es A Flor
Clifton Chenier Group | Live At Montreux | Charly | CDX 2

Tu' Gether
Eddie Barclay Et Son Grand Orchestre | Et Voila! | Fresh Sound Records | FSR 515(Barclay 82138)

Tu Madre
Guillermo Marchena Y El Grupo Irazu | Boleros | L+R Records | CDLR 45068

Tu Mi Delirio
Cuarteto Las D'Aida Y Su Grupo | Soy La Mulata | L+R Records | CDLR 45059

Tu Olvido
Clifton Chenier And His Band | Frenchin' The Boogie | Verve | 519724-2

Tu Rostro Oculto
Louis Conte Group | La Cocina Caliente | Denon Compact Disc | CY-30001

Tu Scendi Dalle Stelle
La Vienta | Jazzmenco | Telarc Digital | CD 83353

Tuang Guru
Abdullah Ibrahim Trio | Cape Town Revisited | TipToe | TIP-888836 2
Yarona | TipToe | TIP-888820 2
African Magic | TipToe | TIP-888845 2
Gerry Hemingway | Tubworks:Solo-Percussion | Sound Aspects | sas 022

Tuba
James Newton Quintet | The Mystery School | India Navigation | IN 1046

Tuba Boons
Max Roach New Quintet | Max Roach | Bainbridge | BT 1042

Tuba Tune
Steckar Tubapack | Tubakoustik | IDA Record | 024 CD

Tubs
The Music Improvisation Company | The Music Improvisation Company | ECM | 1005

Tuck Me To Sleep
Frisco Syncopators | Firehouse Stomp | Stomp Off Records | CD 1245

Tudo Bem
Greg Marvin Quartet | I'll Get By | Timeless | CD SJP 347

Tuesday
Tome XX | Third Degree | Jazz Haus Musik | JHM 0063 CD

Tuesday 3:35 p.m.
Third Degree | Jazz Haus Musik | JHM 0063 CD

Tuesday 8:12 p.m.
Ran Blake-Christine Correa | Round About | Music & Arts | CD 807

Tuesday Afternoon
Count Basie And His Orchestra | Prez's Hat Vol.4 | Philology | 214 W 9

Tuesday Ends Saturday
Teddy Wilson | The Keystone Transcriptions 1939-1940 | Storyville | STCD 8258

Tuesday Jump
Allotria Jazz Band | The Best Of Allotria Jazz Band München | Elite Special | 730215

Tuesday Next
Joel Weiskopf Quintet | New Beginning | Criss Cross | Criss 1204

Tuesday's Death
Andy Bey Group | Tuesdays In Chinatown | Minor Music | 801099

Tuesdays In Chinatown
Gordon Brisker Quintet | The Gift | Naxos Jazz | 86001-2

Tuition Blues
Buddy Johnson And His Orchestra | Buddy And Ella Johnson 1953-1964 | Bear Family Records | BCD 15479 DH

Tuke Number One
Buck Hill Quartet | This Is Buck Hill | Steeplechase | SCCD 31095

Tuku Tuku
Piirpauke | Tuku Tuku | JA & RO | JARO 4158-2

Tuku Tuku(II)
Abdullah Ibrahim | South African Sunshine | Pläne | CD 88778

Tula Hula
Sibongile Khumalo Group | Live At The Market Theatre | CBS | 491322-2

Tu-Le
Mongo Santamaria And His Band | Sabroso | Original Jazz Classics | OJCCD 281-2

Tuli Bamba
Bill Berry's L.A.Big Band | Hello Rev. | Concord | CCD 4027

Tulip Or Turnip
Duke Ellington And His Orchestra | Duke Ellington:Complete Musicraft Recordings | Definitive Records | DRCD 11215
Happy Birthday Duke Vol.4 | Laserlight | 15786

Tulips Are Better Than One
Oliver Strauch Group With Lee Konitz | City Lights | Blue Concept | BCCD 94/03

Tulle
Koch-Schütz-Studer & El Nil Troop | Heavy Cairo Trafic | Intuition Records | INT 3175-2

Tulli Men Al Maschkabeia
Clark Terry Septet | Clark Terry | Verve | 537754-2

Tumbao
Cal Tjader Quintet | Concerts In The Sun | Fantasy | FCD 9688-2
Concerts In The Sun | Fantasy | FCD 9688-2
Cal Tjader Sextet | Monterey Concerts | Prestige | PCD 24026-2

Tumbleweed
The Berlin Workshop Orchestra | Sib Langis | FMP | SAJ 30

Tumbling Derwish
Cal Collins Quartet | Ohio Style | Concord | CCD 4447

Tumbling Tumbleweeds
Alain Trudel Quartet | Jericho's Legacy | Naxos Jazz | 86021-2

Tundra
Sainkho Namtchylak | Lost Rivers | FMP | CD 42

Tune Axle Grease
Lee Konitz Quintet | Stereokonitz | RCA | 2159146-2

Tune For Duke
Anthony Ortega With The Nat Pierce Orchestra | Earth Dance | Fresh Sound Records | FSR-CD 325

Tune For Mona
Tony Ortega Octet | Jazz For Young Moderns | Fresh Sound Records | FSR 2006(Bethlehem BCP 79)

Tune For The Moon
Sal Salvador All-Star Quartet | Juicy Lucy | Bee Hive | BH 7009

Tune In
Florian Ross Quartet With The Event String Ensemble | Suite For Soprano Sax And String Orchestra | Naxos Jazz | 86037-2

Tune In 5-
James 'Son' Thomas | James 'Son' Thomas | Blues Classics(L+R) | CDLR 82006

Tune In Three
Mark Turner Quintet | Yam Yam | Criss Cross | Criss 1094

Tune Up
Chet Baker Trio | Chet Baker In Bologna | Dreyfus Jazz Line | FDM 36558-9
Cindy Blackman Quartet | Cindy Blackman Telepathy | Muse | MCD 5437
Max Roach Quartet | Standard Time | EmArCy | 814190-1 IMS
Miles Davis Quartet | Blue Haze | Original Jazz Classics | OJC20 093-2(P 7054)
Tune Up | Prestige | P 24077
Monty Alexander Trio | Facets | Concord | CJ 108
Sonny Rollins Quartet | Sonny Rollins:The Blue Note Recordings | Blue Note | 821371-2
True Blue | Blue Note | 534032-2
Newk's Time | Blue Note | 576752-2
Sonny Stitt Quartet | The Jazz Giants Play Miles Davis:Milestones | Prestige | PCD 24225-2
Brothers 4 | Prestige | PCD 24261-2
Tune Up | Muse | MCD 5334
Wes Montgomery Quintet | Wes Montgomery-The Complete Riverside Recordings | Riverside | 12 RCD 4408-2
Wes Montgomery With Strings | Fusion! | Original Jazz Classics | OJC 368(RLP 9472)
Wes Montgomery Quintet | Movin' Along | Original Jazz Classics | OJC20 089-2

Tune Up(alt.take)
Wes Montgomery-The Complete Riverside Recordings | Riverside | 12 RCD 4408-2
Wes Montgomery With The Jimmy Jones Orchestra | Wes Montgomery-The Complete Riverside Recordings | Riverside | 12 RCD 4408-2
Wes Montgomery With Orchestra | Pretty Blue | Milestone | M 47030

Tune Up(take 5)
Wes Montgomery Quintet | The Alternative Wes Montgomery | Milestone | MCD 47065-2

Tune With A View
Tom Harrell Sextet | Upswing | Chesky | JD 103

Tune-Up(take 4)
Gianluigi Trovesi Octet | Les Hommes Armés | Soul Note | 121311-2

Tunin' In
Duke Ellington And His Orchestra | Ellington At Newport 1956(Complete) | CBS | CK 64932

Tuning Up-
Dizzy Gillespie And His Orchestra | Gillespiana And Carnegie Hall Concert | Verve | 519809-2

Tunisian Fantasy
Dizzy Gillespie Big Band | Carnegie Hall Concert | Verve | 2304429 IMS

Tunisian Journey
Arturo Sandoval And His Cuban Jazz Masters | Tumbaito | Inak | 2003

Tunji
John Coltrane Quartet | Coltrane | Impulse(MCA) | 589567-2
John Coltrane:The Classic Quartet-Complete Impulse Studio Recordings | Impulse(MCA) | 951280-2
Coltrane Spiritual | Impulse(MCA) | 589099-2
Coltrane | Impulse(MCA) | 589567-2

Tunji(alt.take 1)
Coltrane | Impulse(MCA) | 589567-2

Tunji(alt.take 2)
Coltrane | Impulse(MCA) | 589567-2

Tunji(alt.take 3)
Chris McGregor's Brotherhood Of Breath | Liv At Willisau | Ogun | OGCD 001

Tunnel

Rob Van Den Broeck Quintet | Free Fair | Timeless | SJP 122

Tunnel For Love
Gary Burton Sextet | Works | ECM | 823267-2

Tunnelflug Mit Klimawechsel
Gato Barbieri Group | Masters Of Jazz Vol.9 | RCA | NL 89722

Tupac Amaru
Gato Barbieri Septet | Fenix | RCA | FD 10144

Tupelo Blues
Cassandra Wilson Group | Misty Blue:Sweet Sisters Swing Songs Of Sorrow And Sadness | Blue Note | 521151-2

Tupelo Honey
Blue Light 'Til Dawn | Blue Note | 781357-2
God Is My Co-Pilot | Mir Shlufn Nisht | Avant | AVAN 032

Turbulence
Marion Brown-Gunter Hampel Duo | Gemini | Birth | CD 037
Rickey Woodard Quintet | Yazoo | Concord | CCD 4629

Turbulent Mirror
Zbigniew Seifert Quartet | Man Of The Light | MPS | 68163

Turiya And Ramakrishna
Axel Zwingenberger With Teddy Ibing | Boogie Woogie Breakdown | Vagabond | VRCD 8.78013

Turk Street Boogie
Stefan Isaksson Quartet | Stefan Isaksson Live! | Dragon | DRLP 54

Turkish Bath
Don Ellis Orchestra | Electric Bath | CBS | CK 65522

Turkish Bath(single-version)
Orexis | Inspiration | Intercord | 160108

Turkish Mambo
Lennie Tristano Trio | That's Jazz Vol.15: Lennie Tristano | Atlantic | ATL 50245

Turkish March
Nexus | Urban Shout | SPLASC(H) Records | H 170

Turklaten-
Turk Murphy And His Jazz Band | Turk Murphy's San Francisco Jazz-Vol.1 | Good Time Jazz | 12026

Turn
Jimmy Ponder With Orchestra | Jimmy Ponder | LRC Records | CDC 9031

Turn Again
Count Basie And Friends | Basie And Friends | Pablo | 2310925

Turn Around
Ornette Coleman Quartet | Tomorrow Is The Question | Original Jazz Classics | OJC20 342-2(S 7569)
Pat Metheny Quintet | 80/81 | ECM | 1180/81 (843169-2)
Guido Manusardi | Contrasti | Penta Flowers | CDPIA 012

Turn 'Em On(Mono)
King Curtis Band | King Curtis-Blow Man Blow | Bear Family Records | BCD 15670 CI

Turn 'Em On(Stereo)
Karl Ratzer Group | Gumbo Dive | RST-Records | 91540-2

Turn It Over Baby
Charlie Hunter & Pound For Pound | Return Of The Candyman | Blue Note | 823108-2

Turn Me Loose
Lionel Hampton Big Band | Newport Uproar! | RCA | NL 89590

Turn Me On
Charlie Love Trio | Charlie Love With George Lewis And Louis Nelson | American Music | AMCD-60

Turn Out Of The Stars
Eric Marienthal Group | Oasis | GRP | GRP 96552

Turn Out The Stars
Bill Evans Trio | Since We Met | Original Jazz Classics | OJC 622(F 9501)
Getting Sentimental | Milestone | MCD 9346-2
In His Own Way | West Wind | WW 2028
Bill Evans Trio:The Last Waltz | Milestone | 8MCD 4430-2
Bill Evans Trio:The Last Waltz | Milestone | 8MCD 4430-2
The Best Of Bill Evans Live | Verve | 533825-2
Bill Evans:The Secret Sessions | Milestone | 8MCD 4421-2
Live In Buenos Aires 1979 | West Wind | WW 2061
The Complete Fantasy Recordings | Fantasy | 9FCD 1012-2
Live In Paris 1972 Vol.1 | France's Concert | FCD 107
Bill Evans:The Secret Sessions | Milestone | 8MCD 4421-2
Homecoming | Milestone | MCD 9291-2
Bill Evans-Jim Hall | The Complete Bill Evans On Verve | Verve | 527953-2
Trio (Motian Peacock)-Duo(Hall) | Verve | 2-2509 IMS
Carlos Denia-Uli Glaszmann | Ten Strings For Bill Evans | Edition Musikat | EDM 069
David Benoit Group | Waiting For Spring | GRP | GRP 95952
John Abercrombie-Andy LaVerne | Where We Were | Double Time Records | DTRCD-110
Judy Niemack With The Kenny Werner Quartet | ...Night And The Music | Freelance | FRL-CD 026
Kronos Quartet With Jim Hall | Music Of Bill Evans | Landmark | LCD 1510-2
Liz Story/Joel DiBartolo | My Foolish Heart | Windham Hill | 34 11115-2
Meredith d'Ambrosia Group | The Cove | Sunnyside | SSC 1028 D
Thomas Clausen-Pyysalo Severi | Turn Out The Stars | Storyville | STCD 4215

Turn Out The Stars-
Bill Evans | Bill Evans At Town Hall | Verve | 831271-2
Marilyn Crispell | Contrasts: Live At Yoshi's | Music & Arts | CD 930

Turn Over The Musket
Johnny Lytle Orchestra | Good Vibes | Muse | MR 5271

Turn The Tables
Things | Mother Nature | Jazzpoint | JP 1028 CD

Turn To East
Hannes Beckmann Quartet | Violin Tales | Tutu Records | 888202-2*

Turn To G
Steve Kuhn Quartet | Last Year's Waltz | ECM | 1213

Turn Your Love Around
Art Van Damme Quintet | Keep Going/Blue World | MPS | 529093-2

Turnabout
Count Basie And His Orchestra | Count Basie-The Best Of The Roulette Years | Roulette | CDP 797969-2

Turnaround
Paul Bley Trio | Notes On Ornette | Steeplechase | SCCD 31437
Steve Khan Quartet | Headline | Polydor | 517690-2
Charlie Haden Trio | The Montreal Tapes | Verve | 523295-2

Turnaroundphrase-
Walt Weiskopf Nonet | Song For My Mother | Criss Cross | Criss 1127

Turned Around
Takashi Kazamaki & Kalle Laar Group | Floating Frames | Ear-Rational | ECD 1038

Turned Me Around
Luther Thomas & Dizzazz | Yo' Momma | Moers Music | 01088

Turner Brown Blues
Bruce Turner Quartet | The Dirty Bopper | Calligraph | CLG LP 003 IMS

Turning Around
Sadao Watanabe Orchestra & Strings | California Shower | Flying Disk | VIJ 6012

Turning Point
Kevin Eubanks Group | Turning Point | Blue Note | 798170-2

Turnpike
J.J.Johnson Sextet | J.J.Inc. | CBS | CK 65296

Turnpike(alt.take)
Jay Jay Johnson Sextet | Clifford Brown:The Complete Blue Note And Pacific Recordings | Blue Note | 834195-2

Turnpike(rehersal take)
J.J.Johnson Sextet | The Eminent J.J.Johnson Vol.1 | Blue Note | BLP 1505 (CDP 7815052)

Turns
Paul Bley Trio | Footoose | Savoy | SV 0140(MG 12182)
Paul Bley-Paul Motian Duo | Notes | Soul Note | 121190-2

Turnstile
Gerry Mulligan Quartet | Gerry Mulligan Quartet feat.Chet Baker | Original Jazz Classics | OJCCD 711-2(F 8082/P 7641)
Gerry Mulligan:Pleyel Concert Vol.1 | Vogue | 21409422
Harry Allen And Randy Sandke Meets The RIAS Big Band Berlin | The Music Of The Trumpet Kings | Nagel-Heyer | CD 037
Gerry Mulligan Quartet | My Funny Valentine | Jazz Society(Vogue) | 670511

Turquesa
Charlie Mariano Quartet | Crystal Balls | CMP Records | CMP 10

Turquoise
Jimmy Smith Trio | The Champ-Jimmy Smith At The Organ Vol.2 | Blue Note | 300093(1514)

Turribo
John Benson Brooks' Orchestra | Folk Jazz U.S.A. | RCA | PM 43767

Turtle Shoes
Didier Lockwood Group | Live In Montreux | MPS | 821284-1

Turtle Talk
Winner's Circle | Turning Point(John Coltrane | Bethlehem | BET 6003-2(BCP 6024)

Turtle Twist
Jelly Roll Morton Trio | The Jelly Roll Morton Centennial-His Complete Victor Recordings | Bluebird | ND 82361

Turtle Walk
Lou Donaldson Quintet | Hot Dog | Blue Note | 828267-2

Tuskegee Experiment
Don Byron Quartet | Tuskegee Experiments | Nonesuch | 7559-79280-2

Tuskegee Strutter's Ball
Kosh | Groovy Strings | Elite Special | 73325

Tutankhamun(Tutanchamon)
Art Ensemble Of Chicago | Tutankhamun | Black Lion | BLCD 760199

Tutta Comprendo,O Misera
Masqualero | Bande A Part | ECM | 1319

Tutte
Chinese Compass | Chinese Compass | dacapo | DCCD 9443

Tutte Le Bocche Belle
Ornette Coleman Quartet | Languages | Moon Records | MCD 044-2

Tutti Flutti
Duke Ellington And His Orchestra | All Star Road Band Vol.2 | Doctor Jazz | ZL 70969(2) (809319)

Tutti For Cootie
Carnegie Hall '64 Vol.2 | Moon Records | MCD 068-2
Duke Ellington: The Champs-Elysees Theater January 29-30th,1965 | Laserlight | 36131
The Tremble Kids All Stars | The Tremble Kids All Stars Play Chicago Jazz! | Nagel-Heyer | CD 043

Tutti For Eddie
Trygve Seim-Oyvind Braekke-Per Oddvar Johansen Orchestra | The Source And Different Cikadas | ECM | 1764(014432-2)

Tutti Free
Jan Klare/Tom Lorenz Quartett | Das Böse Ding | Acoustic Music Records | 319.1060.2

Tutto E Il Contrario Di Tutto
Mike Westbrook Orchestra | Westbrook-Rossini | Hat Art | CD 6002

Tutto Ho Perduto-
Dreyfus All Stars | Dreyfus Night In Paris | Dreyfus Jazz Line | FDM 36652-2

Tutu
Marcus Miller Group | Live & More | Dreyfus Jazz Line | FDM 36585-2
Michel Petrucciani Trio | Michel Petrucciani:Concert Inédits | Dreyfus Jazz Line | FDM 36607-2
Miles Davis Group | Tutu | Warner | 7599-25490-2
Time After Time | Jazz Door | JD 1256/57

Tuuna
Georg Ruby-Wollie Kaiser | Ruby Domesticus Vugaris | Jazz Haus Musik | JHM 26

Tu-Way-Pock-E-Way
Albert Ammons Rhythm Kings | The King Of Boogie Woogie | Blues Classics | BC 27

Tuxedo Junction
Erskine Hawkins And His Orchestra | The Original Tuxedo Junction | RCA | ND 90363(874142)
Victor Jazz History Vol.8:Swing Big Bands | RCA | 2128562-2
Glenn Miller And His Orchestra | In The Mood | Intercord | 125403
The Unforgettable Glenn Miller | RCA | PD 89260
Glenn Miller-The Great Instrumentals 1938-1942 | Retrieval | RTR 79001
His Original Recordings | RCA | NL 89026 DP
The Ultimate Glenn Miller-22 Original Hits From The King Of Swing | RCA | 2113137-2
Play Selections From The Glenn Miller Story And Other Hits | RCA | NL 89073
Jimmy Smith Trio | Compact Jazz: George Benson | Verve | 833292-2 PMS

Tva Solröda Segel
Harald Rüschenbaum Orchestra | Rondo | Swingtime | 8208

Twas But Piety
Chick Corea-Gary Burton | In Concert, Zürich, October 28, 1979 | ECM | 1182/83

Tweak
Fred Van Hove | Verloren Maandag | FMP | SAJ 11

Tweed And Tropical
John Kirby And His Orchestra | TheComplete Una Mae Carlisle(1940-1942) And John Kirby(1941-1942) | RCA | ND 89484

Tweedle Dee
Chick Corea With String Quartet | Verve Jazz Masters 3:Chick Corea | Verve | 519820-2
Red Garland Trio | The P.C. Blues | Original Jazz Classics | OJCCD 898-2(PR 7752)

'Tween Dusk And Dawn In Via Urbana-
Fred Elizalde And His Orchestra | An Evening At The Savoy | Decca | DDV 5011/12

Twelfth Of The Twelfth
Django Reinhardt And The Quintet Du Hot Club De France | Swingin' With Django | Pro-Arte | CDD 549

Twelfth Year(take 1)
Quintet Du Hot Club De France | Django Reinhardt Vol. 4 | Decca | 180023 AG

Twelfth Year(take 2)
Django Reinhardt Vol. 4 | Decca | 180023 AG

Twelve
Peter Erskine Trio | Juni | ECM | 1657(539726-2)
Uri Caine | Solitaire | Winter&Winter | 910075-2
Pee Wee Ellis Trio | Twelve And More Blues | Minor Music | 801034

Twelve And More Blues
Larry Coryell Quartet | Comin' Home | Muse | MCD 5303

Twelve Bars But Not Blues
Bunny Brunel Group | Dedication | Accord | 500362

Twelve By Two For Squatty Boo
Stafford James Ensemble | Stafford James Ensemble | Red Records | VPA 142

Twelve Inches Wide
String Thing | String Thing:Turtifix | MicNic Records | MN 4

Twelve Months
Jan Garbarek Group | Twelve Moons | ECM | 1500(519500-2)

Twelve Moons:
Tony Purrone Trio | Rascality | Steeplechase | SCCD 31514

Twelve More Bars To Go
Wayne Shorter Quartet | Juju | Blue Note | 499005-2
Juju | Blue Note | 837644-2

Twelve O'Clock Blues
Sammy Price | Le Jazz En France Vol.14:Boogie Woogie A La Parisienne | Pathe | 1552601

Twelve Tone Stomp-
Bill Evans Trio | Live In Paris 1972 Vol.2 | France's Concert | FCD 114

Twelve(alt.take)
Curtis Fuller Quintet | Blues-ette | Savoy | SV 0127(ST 13006)

Twenty
Philip Catherine Trio | Moods Vol.II | Criss Cross | Criss 1061

Twenty One
Steve Lacy-Fred Van Hove | Five Facings | FMP | CD 85

Twenty Years
Bill Frisell Trio | Bill Frisell With Dave Hollnad And Elvin Jones | Nonesuch | 7559-79624-2
Das Pferd | Blue Turns To Grey | VeraBra Records | CDVBR 2065-2

Twenty-Five
Marc Copland & Vic Juris | Double Play | Steeplechase | SCCD 31509

Twenty-Four Hours A Day
Eddie Boyd Blues Band | Five Long Years | L+R Records | CDLR 72009

Twenty-Four Robbers
Glenn Miller And His Orchestra | Glenn Miller In Concert | RCA | NL 89216 DP

Twenty-Seven-91
Bob Rockwell Quartet | No Rush | Steeplechase | SCCD 31219

Twice Around The Sun
Lutz Wichert Trio | Ambiguous | Edition Musikat | EDM 068

Twice Is Nice
John Surman Quartet | Adventure Playground | ECM | 1463(511981-2)

Twice Said Once
Bill Dixon Quartet | Vade Mecum | Soul Note | 121208-2

Twilight
Frank Rosolino Quintet | Free For All | Original Jazz Classics | OJCCD 1763-2
Jörg Kaufmann Trio | Sketches | Blue Concept | BCCD 95/01
Mary Lou Williams Quartet | Mary Lou Williams:The London Sessions | Vogue | 21409312
Sphere | Sphere | Verve | 557796-2
Wynton Marsalis Quintet | Wynton Marsalis | CBS | 468708-2
Milan Swoboda Quartet | Dedication | P&J Music | P&J 001 CD

Twilight Blue
Steve Turre Group | Rhythm Within | Verve | 527159-2

Twilight Fields(part 1-5)
Misha Alperin Group With John Surman | First Impression | ECM | 1664(557650-2)

Twilight Hour
Buck Ram All-Stars | The Black Swing Tradition | Savoy | SJL 2246 (801854)

Twilight Rain
Naylor's Seven Aces | Oliver Naylor 1924-25 | Retrieval | RTR 79008

Twilight Song
Melissa Walker And Her Band | I Saw The Sky | Enja | ENJ-9409 2
Triple Helix | Triple Helix | Enja | ENJ-8056 2

Twilight...And Beyond
Don Friedman Trio | Almost Everything | Steeplechase | SCCD 31368

Twins
Thomas Heberer | Stella | Poise | Poise 08
Christmann-Schönenberg Duo | Topic | Ring | 01020

Twist Time
Annie Ross & PonyPoindexter With The Berlin All Stars | Annie Ross & Pony Poindexter with The Berlin All Stars | MPS | 9811257

Twisted
Annie Ross And Her Quartet | Annie Ross & King Pleasure Sings | Original Jazz Classics | OJC 217(P 7128)
Mar Murphy With The Ernie Wilkins Orchestra | RAH | Original Jazz Classics | OJCCD 141-2(R 9395)
Urs Leimgruber-Adelhard Roidinger-Fritz Hauser | Lines | Hat Art | CD 6149
Wardell Gray Quartet | Wardell Gray:Light Gray 1948-1950 | Cool & Blue | C&B-CD 116

Twisted Blues
Wes Montgomery Quintet | So Much Guitar! | Original Jazz Classics | OJC20 233-2
Wes Montgomery With The Johnny Pate Orchestra | Verve Jazz Masters 14:Wes Montgomery | Verve | 519826-2
Wes Montgomery With The Oliver Nelson Orchestra | Wes Montgomery:The Verve Jazz Sides | Verve | 521690-2
Compact Jazz: Wes Montgomery Plays The Blues | Verve | 835318-2 PMS

Twisted Image
Bengt Berger & Bitter Funeral Beer Band | Praise Drumming | Dragon | DRLP 142

Twisted Roots
Copenhagen Art Ensemble | Angels' Share | dacapo | DCCD 9452

Twisted Song
Wardell Gray Quartet | Wardell Gray Memorial Vol.1 | Original Jazz Classics | OJCCD 050-2(P 7008)

Twisted(alt.take 1)
Wardell Gray Memorial Vol.1 | Original Jazz Classics | OJCCD 050-2(P 7008)

Twisted(alt.take 2)
Wardell Gray Memorial Vol.1 | Original Jazz Classics | OJCCD 050-2(P 7008)

Twisted(alt.take 3)
Wardell Gray:Light Gray 1948-1950 | Cool & Blue | C&B-CD 116

Twistedology
Marc Johnson's Bass Desires | Second Sight | ECM | 1351(833038-2)

Twister
Stanko-Finkel-Schuller-Elgart | Caoma | Konnex Records | KCD 5053

Twistin' The Night Away
Barbecue Bob | Chocolate To The Bone | Yazoo | YAZ 2005

Twitter Pat
Steve Lacy-Evan Parker | Chirps | FMP | CD 29

Twixt The Sheets
Bill Dixon Sextet | Bill Dixon In Italy - Volume Two | Soul Note | SN 1011

Two
Paul Millns | Finally Falls The Rain | BELL Records | BLR 84707

Two Arms
George Gruntz Concert Jazz Band | Global Exellence | TCB Records | TCB 21172

Two Bass Hit
Dizzy Gillespie And His Orchestra | Dizzy Gillespie-Diz Delights | RCA | CL 89804 SF
The Greatest Of Dizzy Gillespie | RCA | 2113164-2
Dizzy Gillespie (1946-1949) | RCA | ND 89763
Miles Davis Quintet | Circle In The Round | CBS | 467898-2
Circle In The Round | CBS | 467898-2
Miles Davis In Person-Friday Night At The Blackhawk,San Francisco,Vol.1 | CBS | C4K 87106
En Concert Avec Europe 1 | Laserlight | 710455/58
Miles Davis Sextet | Miles & Monk At Newport | CBS | SRCS 5698
Red Garland Quintet feat.John Coltrane | High Pressure | Original Jazz Classics | OJCCD 349-2(P 7209)
Sonny Clark Trio | Sonny Clark | Blue Note | 533774-2
Sonny Clark Trio | Blue Note | 533774-2
Buddy Rich And His Orchestra With Dizzy Gillespie | Jazz Monterey 1958-1980 | Palo Alto | PA 8080-2

Two Bass Hit (alt.take)
Sonny Clark Trio | The Art Of The Trio | Blue Note | 300207(3069)

Two Become One
Peter Brötzmann | Brötzmann/Solo | FMP | 0360

Two Blocks From The Edge
Return To The Wide Open Spaces | Live At The Caravan Of Dreams | Amazing Records | AMCD 1021

Two Brothers
Nat Adderley Quintet | Compact Jazz: Cannonball Adderley | EmArCy | 842930-2 PMS

Two Brothers(for Gilbert + George)
Brian Barley Trio | Brian Barley Trio 1970 | Just A Memory | JAS 9502-2

Two Catalan Songs
The Poll Winners | Straight Ahead | Original Jazz Classics | OJCCD 409-2

Two Degrees East Three Degrees West
John Lewis And Members Of The Stuttgart Symphony Orchestra | Victor Jazz History Vol.15:Progressive Jazz | RCA | 2135734-2
Alan Elsdon Band | Jazz Journeymen | Black Lion | BLCD 760519

Two Deuces

TITELVERZEICHNIS

Louis Armstrong And His Hot Five | Jazz:The Essential Collection Vol.2 | IN+OUT Records | 78012-2
Louis Armstrong With Bob Haggart's Orchestra | Louis Armstrong:The New And Revisited Musical Autobiography Vol.2 | Jazz Unlimited | JUCD 2004

Two Different Worlds
Walter Davis Trio | Scorpio Rising | Steeplechase | SCCD 31255

Two Drinks Of Wine
Jon Faddis-Billy Harper Sextet | Jon & Billy | Black-Hawk | BKH 532

Two Eels Waltzing On An Icecake
Scott Hamilton Quintet | Plays Ballads | Concord | CCD 4386

Two Faces
Martin Schrack Quintet | Reflection | yvp music | CD 3024

Two Fishes In A Foreign City
Jiri Stivin & Jiri Stivin | Two Generations In Jazz | P&J Music | P&J 005 CD

Two Five Jive
Wolfgang Muthspiel Group | In & Out | Amadeo | 521385-2

Two Flutes
Pat Metheny Quartet | 80/81 | ECM | 1180/81 (843169-2)

Two Folk Songs
John Tchicai Group | Put Up The Flight | Storyville | SLP 4141

Two For Blues Suite
Grant Green Quartet | Gooden's Corner | Blue Note | GXK 8168

Two For The Blues
Count Basie And His Orchestra | The Basie Band 1952-1957 | Jazz Magazine | 40200
Lambert, Hendricks And Ross | Lambert,Hendricks & Ross:Sing A Song Of Basie | CTI Records | PDCTI 1115-2

Two For The Road
Dave Grusin Orchestra | Two For The Road:The Music Of Henry Mancini | GRP | GRP 98652
Earl Klugh Group With Strings | Late Night Guitar | Blue Note | 498573-2
Eddie Daniels/Bucky Pizzarelli Duo | Blue Bossa | Choice | CHCD 71002

Two For The Road-
Rob McConnell-Ed Bickert-Don Thompson | Three For The Road | Concord | CCD 4765

Two For Timbuctu
Enrico Pieranunzi-Bert Van Den Brink | Daedalus' Wings | Challenge | CHR 70069

Two For Two
Hendrik Meurkens Octet | Sambahia | Concord | CCD 4474

Two Franks
Count Basie And His Orchestra | Sixteen Men Swinging | Verve | 2-2517 IMS

Two Friends
Leszek Zadlo Quartet | Thoughts | EGO | 4003

Two Funky People
Bucky And John Pizzarelli Duo | The Pizzarellis,Bucky And John:Contrasts | Arbors Records | ARCD 19209

Two Getting Together
Klaus Doldinger-Peter Trunk | Bluesy Toosy | ACT | 9200-2

Two Kinds Of Blues
Jimmy Giuffre 3 | The Jimmy Giuffre 3-Hollywood & Newport 1957-1958 | Fresh Sound Records | FSCD 1026

Two Kings
Chris Connor With The Maynard Ferguson Orchestra | Double Exposure | Atlantic | AMCY 1074

Two Little Fishes Five Loaves Of Bread
Sister Rosetta Tharpe With The Otis Spann Trio | Live In Paris 1964 | France's Concert | FCD 118

Two Little Pearls
Stan Getz With The Danish Radio Big Band | Stan Getz | Laserlight | 15761

Two Loves Have I
Stuff Smith With The Nat King Cole Quartet | The Complete After Midnight Sessions | Capitol | 748328-2

Two Magpies
Stephan Froleyks | Fine Music With New Instruments | Jazz Haus Musik | JHM 0094 CD

Two Men,Two Boats
Duke Pearson Trio | Profile | Blue Note | 868495-9

Two Not One
Lee Konitz-Warne Marsh Sextet | That's Jazz Vol.21: Lee Konitz & Warne Marsh | Atlantic | ATL 50298

Two O'Clock Jump
Harry James And His Orchestra | Trumpet Blues:The Best Of Harry James | Capitol | 521224-2
Welcome To Jazz: Harry James | Koch Records | 321 983 D1

Two O'Clock Mood
Art Blakey And The Jazz Messengers | The Art Of Jazz | IN+OUT Records | 77028-2

Two Of A Kind
Blue Night | Timeless | CD SJP 217

Two Of A Mind
Paul Desmond-Gerry Mulligan Quartet | Jazz Special-Two Of A Mind | RCA | CL 42788 AG

Two Old Ships
David Darling | Cello | ECM | 1464(511982-2)

Two Or Three Things
Jutta Hipp Quintet | Cool Dogs & Two Oranges | L+R Records | LR 41006

Two Part Invention No.1 In C Major(BWV 772)
Swingle Singers | Jazz Sebastian Bach | Philips | 542552-2
Warne Marsh-Lee Konitz Quintet | Live At The Club Montmartre,Vol.2 | Storyville | STCD 8202

Two Part Invention No.13 In A Minor(BWV 784)
Live At The Club Montmartre,Vol.2 | Storyville | STCD 8202

Two Part Invention No.14 In B Flat Major(BWV 785)
Jacques Loussier Trio | Play Bach No.3 | Decca | 157892-2

Two Part Invention No.15 In B Minor(BWV 796)
Play Bach Aux Champs-Élysées | Decca | 159203-2

Two Part Invention No.8 In F Major(BWV 779)
Play Bach No.3 | Decca | 157892-2
Mehmet Ergin Group | Beyond The Seven Hills | MCA | MCD 70020

Two People
Javier Feierstein Quartet | Wysiwyg | Fresh Sound Records | FSNT 040 CD

Two People In Boston
Charles Davis & Captured Moments | Strange Goodbyes | L+R Records | CDLR 45101

Two Preludes For Tales
Bill Evans Quintet | Petite Blonde | Lipstick Records | LIP 890122

Two Remember, One Forgets
Herbie Mann Group | Opalescence | Kokopelli Records | KOKO 1298

Two Sides
Frank Vaganee 5 | Picture A View | B.Sharp Records | CDS 080

Two Sides To Every Story
The Meeting | Update | Hip Bop | HIBD 8008

Two Singers
Jakob Magnusson Group | Time Zone | Optimism | GBJ 2002

Two Sleepy People
Benny Goodman And His Orchestra | Birth Of A Band | Giants Of Jazz | GOJ 1038
Dave McKenna | A Celebration Of Hoagy Carmichael | Concord | CCD 4227
Hoagy Carmichael With Perrry Botkin And His Orchestra | Hoagy Carmichael 1927-1939 | Timeless | CBC 1-011
Johannes Rediske Quintet | Jumpin' At The Badewanne | Bear Family Records | BCD 16172 AH
Keith Ingham Trio | A Star Dust Melody | Sackville | SKCD2-2051
Oscar Peterson-Major Holley Duo | Tenderly | Verve | MV 2662 IMS
Earl Hines | Live At The New School | Chiaroscuro | CR 157

Two Sleepy People-
Jack Teagarden With The Hoagy Carmichael Orchestra | Jack Teagarden | Queen-Disc | 027
Stephane Grappelli | 7.Zelt-Musik-Festival:Jazz Events | Zounds | CD 2730001
Stephane Grappelli Trio | Stephane Grappelli | Hot Club Records | HCRCD 101

Two Sons
Black Note | Nothin' But Swing | Impulse(MCA) | IMP 11772

Two Spanish Flies
Dollar(Abdullah Ibrahim) Brand | Ode To Duke Ellington | West Wind | WW 0020

Two Stories
Clifford Jordan Quintet | Two Tenor Winner | Criss Cross | Criss 1011

Two To Tango
Lester Young With The Oscar Peterson Quartet | Lester Young With The Oscar Peterson Trio | Verve | 521451-2
Polo De Haas Quartet | Soolmaan | Timeless | CD SJP 384

Two Trains
James Cotton Group | Deep In The Blues | Verve | 529849-2

Two Trains Runnin'
Bob Mintzer With The Peter Erskine Trio | The Saxophone Featuring Two T's | Novus | 2114068-2

Two Waltzing,One Square And Then
Eliane Elias Group | So Far So Close | Blue Note | B 1-91411

Two Weeks In Another Town
Johnny Parker With Pete Rugolo And His Orchestra | Way To The West | Fresh Sound Records | 054 2602131(Capitol)

Two Women From Padua
Blasnost | Blasnost | Acoustic Music Records | AMC 1023

Two Worlds
Tony Williams Lifetime | Ego | Verve | 559512-2
Spectrum:The Anthology | Verve | 537075-2

Two-Face Flash
Tony Pastor And His Orchestra | Let's Dance With Tony Pastor | Fresh Sound Records | R 25024(Roulette)

Two-Lane Highway:
David Friedman-Jasper Van't Hof | Birds Of A Feather | Traumton Records | 2428-2

Twomblish
Dave Brubeck | Brubeck Plays Brubeck | CBS | CK 65722

Twos And Fews
Albert Ammons-Meade Lux Lewis | Boogie Woggie Classics | Blue Note | BLP 1209

Txatxatxell
David Xirgu Quartet | Idolents | Fresh Sound Records | FSNT 077 CD

Txi-Khan
Idolents | Fresh Sound Records | FSNT 077 CD

Txitxiriko
Jeanie Bryson With The Ronnie Mathews Trio | Live at Warsaw Jazz Festival 1991 | Jazzmen Records | 660.50.002

Tyawo
Robert Dick Group With The Soldier String Quartet | Third Stone From The Sun | New World Records | 80435-2

Tying Up Loose Ends
Chet Baker-Art Pepper Sextet | The Route | Pacific Jazz | 792931-2

Tynan Tyme
Luca Flores Matt Jazz Quintet & Guests | Where Extremes Meet | SPLASC(H) Records | H 123

Tytte
Bill Marx And His Trio | My Son The Folk Swinger/Jazz Kaleidoscope | Vee Jay Recordings | VJ 021

Ü 7
Dogs Don't Sing In The Rain | Bones For Breakfast | Edition Collage | EC 472-2

U Always Know
Vocal Moments | Take Twelve On CD | TT 008-2
Bones For Breakfast | Edition Collage | EC 472-2

U Always Know(blue remix)
Keith Jarrett Trio | Tribute | ECM | 1420/21

U Dance
Miroslav Vitous Group | Journey's End | ECM | 1242(843171-2)

U Dunaje U Prespurka
Reunion | Flight Charts And Plans | Blue Flame | 40242(2132481-2)

U Slide
Andre Jaume 3 | Musique Pour 3 & 8:Errance | Hat Art | 2003 Digital

U Turn
Jasper Van't Hof Group | Blue Corner | ACT | 9228-2

'U'(for Francis Picabia)
Horace Parlan Quintet | Frank-ly Speaking | Steeplechase | SCS 1076

U.M.M.G.(Upper Manhattan Medical Group)
Chick Corea Akoustic Band | Alive | GRP | GRP 96272
Joe Romano Quartet | And Finally Romano | Fresh Sound Records | FSR 108
Tommy Flanagan Trio | The Best Of Tommy Flanagan | Pablo | 2405410-2
Herb Geller Quartet | Birdland Stomp | Fresh Sound Records | FSR-CD 0174

U.'N.I.
U.P. Wilson Band | On My Way | Red Lightnin' | RL 0078

UB 40
Dudu Pukwana Group | Ubagile | Jazz Colours | 874744-2

Über Die Wahrheit Des Schönen Scheins
Ekkehard Jost & Chromatic Alarm | Von Zeit Zu Zeit | Fish Music | FM 005 CD

Über Meiner Mütze Nur Die Sterne
Giessen-Köln-Nonett | Some Other Tapes | Fish Music | FM 009/10 CD

Über Meiner Mütze Nur Die Sterne & The End
Stefan Bauer-Claudio Puntin-Marcio Doctor | Lingo | Jazz Haus Musik | JHM 0116 CD

Überall Und Nirgands
Peter Koch | Die Farbe Blau | Born&Bellmann | 972306 CD

Überleitung
Franz Koglmann Group | Venus In Transit | Between The Lines | btl 017(Efa 10186)

Überstöhrung
Percfect Trouble | Perfect Trouble | Moers Music | 02070 CD

Überverbot Am Richard-Strauss-Konservatorium
Pino Distaso/Roberto Gotta/Beto Cutillo | Tell Her It's All Right | Edition Collage | EC 463-2

Ubik
Fritz Krisse Quartet | Soulcolours | Laika Records | 35100782

Ubique
Rebecca Coupe Franks Group | Suit Of Amor | Justice Records | JR 0901-2

Ubu's Logbook
Pata Music Meets Arfi | News Of Roi Ubu | Pata Musik | PATA 10 CD

Ubu's Love
News Of Roi Ubu | Pata Musik | PATA 10 CD

Ubu's Talking
Archie Shepp-Dollar Brand Duo | Duet | Denon Compact Disc | DC-8561

Uckermark
Georg Hofmann-Lucas Niggli Duo | Mute Songs & Drumscapes | Creative Works Records | CW CD 1022-2

Udu Udu
Hugh Masekela Group | GRRR | Verve | 9860309

U-DWI(Smallpox)
Baden Powell Quartet | Le Genie De Baden Powell | Accord | 114852

Uffe's Solo
Claudio Fasoli/Kenny Wheeler/J.F. Jenny-Clark | Land | Nueva Records | IN 802

Ufo
Amanda Sedgwick Quintet | Reunion | Touché Music | TMcCD 021

Ugetsu
Art Blakey And The Jazz Messengers | Ugetsu | Original Jazz Classics | OJC20 090-2(RLP 9464)
Cedar Walton Quintet | Cedar's Blues-Live | Red Records | VPA 179
Ed Bickert-Lorne Lofsky Quartet | This Is New | Concord | CCD 4414

Ugly Beauty
Andy Summers Group | Green Chimneys:The Music Of Thelonious Monk | RCA | 2663472-2
Bennie Wallace Trio | Live At The Public Theater | Enja | 9127-2
Johannes Mössinger-Wolfgang Lackerschmid | Joana's Dance | double moon | CHRDM 71017
John Swana-Joe Magnarelli Sextet | Philly-New York Junction | Criss Cross | Criss 1150
Monk By Five | Monk By Five | Touché Music | TMcCD 012
Paul Motian Trio | Monk In Motian | JMT Edition | 919020-2
Scott Colley Trio | This Place | Steeplechase | SCCD 31443
Wynton Marsalis Group | Standard Time Vol.4:Marsalis Plays Monk | CBS | CK 67503
Alvin Alcorn New Orleans Jazz Babies | Sounds Of New Orleans Vol.5 | Storyville | STCD 6012

Ugly Music
Mark Murphy And His Septet | I'll Close My Eyes | Muse | MCD 5436

Ugo In Love
Joan Monné Trio | Mireia | Fresh Sound Records | FSNT 100 CD

Ugrix
Don Ellis Quintet | New Ideas | Original Jazz Classics | OJCCD 431-2(NJ 8257)

Uh Huh
Universal Congress Of | The Sad And Tragic Demise Of Big Fine Hot Salty Black Wind | Enemy | EMCD 117(03517)

Uh! Oh!
Billy May And His Orchestra | Billy May's Big Fat Brass/Bill's Bag | Capitol | 535206-2

Uh! Oh!(Nutty Squirrels)
Chico Freeman Quartet | No Time Left | Black Saint | 120036-2

Uhren
Doug Hammond Group | Spaces | DIW | DIW 359 CD

Ujaku
Archie Shepp Quartet | Archie Shepp | The Rising Sun Collection | RSC 0005

Ujama
Archie Shepp Quintet | Montreux One | Freedom | FCD 741027

Uki-Ah
Holger Mantey | Calaufa | L+R Records | CDLR 45058

Uli's Delight
Stefania Tallini Trio | New Life | yvp music | CD 3114

Ulisse E L'Arco
Steve Kuhn | Ecstasy | ECM | 1058

Ulla
Ulli Bögershausen | Private Stories | Laika Records | 35101542
Best Of Ulli Bögershausen | Laika Records | LK 93-045
Sax Mal Anders | Kontraste | Chaos | CACD 8185

Ulla In Africa
Hans Koller Groups And Orchestra | Hans Koller Masterpieces | MPS | 529078-2

Ulla M. & 22-8
Last Exit | Cassette Recordings 87 | Enemy | EMCD 105(03505)

Ulls Verds
Giochi Proibiti Quartet | Stoparding | SPLASC(H) Records | H 120

Ulrikas Dans
Catalogue | Pénétration | Hat Art | CD 6187

Ultima Hora
Phil Woods And His European Rhythm Machine | Phil Woods And His European Rhythm Machine | Inner City | IC 1002 IMS

Ultimo Fandango
Sfogliare Albi | Tempo Per | yvp music | CD 3029

Ultra
Hank Mobley All Stars | Hank Mobley & All Stars | Blue Note | 300144(1544)

Ultra Violet
Django Reinhardt And The Quintet Du Hot Club De France | Swingin' With Django | Pro-Arte | CDD 549

Ulysses 95
Carlos Barbosa-Lima | Music Of The Americas | Concord | CCD 4461

Um Abraco No Getz(A Tribute To Getz)
Stan Getz-Luiz Bonfa Orchestra | Jazz Samba Encore! | CTI Records | PDCTI 1125-2

Um Anjo
Don Grusin Group | Raven | GRP | GRP 96022

Um Beijo(A Kiss)
Joao Gilberto Trio | Getz/Gilberto-Recorded Live At Carnegie Hall | CTI Records | PDCTI 1129-2

Um Braco No Bronfa
Stephan Diez-Mirrors | Lost In A Dream | BELL Records | BLR 84048

Um Dia Mama
Berlin Jazz Composers Orchestra(JayJayBeCe) | How Rook | BIT | 11185

Um Mitternacht
Leon Thomas With Band | Spirits Known And Unknown | RCA | 2663876-2

Um,Um,Um
Luis Agudo | Afrorera | Red Records | VPA 185

Uma Fita De Tres Cores-
Folklore E Bossa Nova Do Brasil | Folklore E Bossa Nova Do Brasil | MPS | 68098

Uma Nuvam No Céu(Prelude To The Rains)
Luiz Bonfa/Cafe | Non Stop To Brazil | Chesky | JD 29

Umamoya Jabula
Bill Laswell/Jones Hellborg Group | Niels & The New York Street Percussionists | ITM Records | ITM 1453

Umaningi Bona(Long River)
Agog | Eat Time | Jazz Haus Musik | JHM 0072 CD

Umanqoba
Tome XX | Natura Morte | Jazz Haus Musik | JHM 32

Umbo Weti
Sibongile Khumalo Group | Live At The Market Theatre | CBS | 491322-2

Umbrella Bob
Benny Goodman Quartet | Camel Caravan Broadcast 1939 Vol.1 | Phontastic | NCD 8817

Umbrella Man
Benny Goodman Quartet With Guests | The Benny Goodman Caravans-The Small Groups Vol.1 | Giants Of Jazz | GOJ 1034
Dizzy Gillespie Quintet | School Days | Savoy | SV 0157(MG 6043)
Chazz! | Passing The Bar | Timeless | CD SJP 381

Umbrellas-
Bermuda Viereck | Noblesse Galvanisee | Plainisphare | PL 1267-20/21

Umh, Umh
Hugh Masekela Quintet | The African Connection | MCA | IA 9343/2

Ummh
Bobby Hutcherson-Harold Land Quintet | San Francisco | Blue Note | 828268-2

Umpachene Falls
Jazz Indeed | Under Water | Traumton Records | 2415-2

Umsonst Und Draußen
Steve Barta Quintet | Blue River | Kokopelli Records | KOKO 1303

Un
Florian Poser-Klaus Ignatzek Duo | Springdale | Acoustic Music Records | 319.1166.2

Un Abraco No Bonfa
Joao Gilberto Trio | The Carnegie Hall Concert | Jazz Door | JD 1221

Un Basso Nel Buio
Eddie Henderson Quartet | Flight On Mind | Steeplechase | SCCD 31284

Un Claire De Lune A Maubeuge
Papa Bue's Viking Jazzband | Greatest Hits | Storyville | 6.23336 AF

Un Claire De Lune(Moonlight Tango)
Charlie Rouse Orchestra | Bossa Nova Bacchanal | Blue Note | 593875-2

Un Dia
Mongo Santamaria And His Orchestra | Soy Yo | Concord | CCD 4327

Un Flambeau,Jeannette Isabella
Joan Abril Quintet | Eric | Fresh Sound Records | FSNT 092 CD

Un Gato Deprimido
Tiziana Ghiglioni And Her Band | Tiziana Ghiglioni Canta Luigi Tenco | Philology | W 60.2

Un Grao De Areia-
Barney Wilen With The Mal Waldron Trio | Movie Themes From France | Timeless | CD SJP 335

Un Home Et Une Femme
Quatuor De Saxophones Gabriel Pierné | Musiques De Films | Nocturne Productions | NPCD 507
Un Instand
Nitta Rette Et Son Trio Hot | Jazz In Paris:Django Reinhardt-Django Et Compagnie | EmArCy | 549241-2 PMS
Un Instand D'Infini
Babik Reinhardt Group | Babik Reinhardt-Live | Melodie | 400032
Un Machito
Eddy Palermo Trio | The Way I See | EdiPan | NPG 806
Un Mercredi En Juillet
John Zorn Naked City | Absinthe | Avant | AVAN 004
Un Negre Amb Un Saxo
Max Roach Quintet | Jazz In Paris:Max Roach-Parisian Sketches | EmArCy | 589963-2
Un Nouveau Complet
Seis Del Solar | Decision | Messidor | 15821 CD
Un Perfil A L'Horitzó
Michel Pilz Trio | Carpathes | FMP | 0250
Un Placer
Salsaya Big Band | Live | Timeless | CD SJP 209
Un Poco Loco
Bud Powell Trio | The Amazing Bud Powell Vol.1 | Blue Note | 300366
Bud Powell:The Complete Blue Note And Roost Recordings | Blue Note | 830083-2
Jim McNeely | Maybeck Recital Hall Series Volume Twenty | Concord | CCD 4522
Mark Soskin Sextet | 17(Seventeen) | TCB Records | TCB 20652
Un Poco Loco(alt.take 1)
Bud Powell Trio | Bud Powell:The Complete Blue Note And Roost Recordings | Blue Note | 830083-2
Un Poco Loco(alt.take 2)
Bud Powell:The Complete Blue Note And Roost Recordings | Blue Note | 830083-2
Un Point Bleu
Charlie Parker Sextet | The Verve Years (1950-51) | Verve | 2-2512 IMS
Un Poquito De Tu Amor
Machito And His Afro-Cuban Salseros | Mucho Macho | Pablo | 2625712-2
Un Setier D'Alliance
Andre Jaume | Saxanimalier | Hat Art | R
Un Temois Dans La Ville
Moments Quartet | Original Moments | Fresh Sound Records | FSNT 052 CD
Un Toc De Groc
Pekka Pylkkännen's Tube Factory | Opaque | Naxos Jazz | 86068-2
Un Ultimo Esfuerzo
Arrigo Cappelletti Trio | Singulari Equilibri | SPLASC(H) Records | CD H 390-2
Una Lotta Machinosa(And A New Delaying Tactic)
Charles Davis Quartet | Super 80 | Nilva | NQ 3410 IMS
Una Mas
Larry Goldings Quartet | Caminhos Cruzados | Novus | 4163184-2
T.S. Monk Sextet | Changing Of The Guard | Blue Note | 789050-2
Una Mas(One More Time)
Ran Blake Quartet | Short Life Of Barbara Monk | Soul Note | SN 1127
Una Muy Bonita
Ornette Coleman Quartet | Change Of The Century | Atlantic | 7567-81341-2
Tiziana Ghiglioni And Her Band | SONB-Something Old Something New Something Borrowed Something Blue | SPLASC(H) Records | CD H 370-2
Una Noche Con Francis
Dexter Gordon Sextet | Round Midnight(Soundtrack) | CBS | 70300
Una Notte Sul Divano
Jazz Detroit & Lee Harper | Jazz Detroit | Die Mühle Records | 850101
Una Serenata
Willem Breuker Kollektief | La Banda/Banda And Jazz | Enja | ENJ-9326 2
Seis Del Solar | Decision | Messidor | 15821 CD
Una Volta, Danny
Bebo Valdés Trio | El Arte Del Sabor | Blue Note | 535193-2
Una, Dos Y Tres-
Asgard | Songs Of G. | Acoustic Music Records | 319.1042.2
Un'Altra Notte-
Art Ensemble Of Chicago | Bap-Tizum | Atlantic | 7567-80757-2
Unanka
Christian Willisohn New Band | Heart Broken Man | Blues Beacon | BLU-1026 2
Un-Autentic Blues
Christian Willisohn-Manuel Lopez | Boogie Woogie And Some Blues | Blues Beacon | BLU-1007 2
Unbelieveable
Alfred 23 Harth Group | Sweet Paris | free flow music | ffm 0291
Unberührbarkeit & Vergewaltigung
Marius Ungureanu-Sergiu Nastase-Räto Harder | Musikversuche | Experimente 93 | MU/EX 93
Unbreakable Heart
The Dolphins With Dan Brubeck | Old World New World | dmp Digital Music Productions | CD 487
Unchain My Heart
(Little)Jimmy Scott And His Quintet With Horns And Strings | Lost And Found | Sequel Records | RSA CD 804
Unchained Melody
Les Baxter And His Orchestra | Baxter's Best | Capitol | 791218-2
Lee Konitz-Jimmy Giuffre Octet | Lee Konitz Meets Jimmy Giuffre | Verve | 2304381 IMS
Uncle
Freddie Hubbard Orchestra | First Light | CTI | EPC 450562-2
Uncle Bob's Your Uncle
Gary Bartz Quartet | Monsoon | Steeplechase | SCCD 31234
Uncle Horsley Writhes Again
Buddy DeFranco Quartet | Waterbed | Candid | CRS 1017 IMS
Uncle Rough
Eddie Condon All Stars | Eddie Condon Town Hall Concerts Vol.1 | Jazzology | JCECD-1001
Uncomposed Appendix
Pete Jolly Trio | When Lights Are Low | Fresh Sound Records | 58109 CD(RCA)
Und
Michael Riessler Group | Heloise | Wergo | WER 8008-2
Werner Müller Mit Dem Rias-Tanzorchester | Swing Tanzen Gestattet | Vagabond | 6.28415 DP
Und Ewig Dröhnt Der Orient
Nickendes Perlgras | Die Hintere Vase | Jazz Haus Musik | JHM 0105 CD
Und Plasikschweine
Volker Kriegel & Mild Maniac Orchestra | Octember Variations | MPS | 68147
Und So Weiter,And So On
Georg Ruby Village Zone | Mackeben Revisited:The Ufa Years | Jazz Haus Musik | JHM 0121 CD
Und Über Uns Der Himmel
Anirahtak und die Jürgen Sturm Band | Das Kurt Weill Programm | Nabel Records:Jazz Network | CD 4638
Und Was Bekam Des Soldaten Weib
Uri Caine Ensemble | Love Fugue-Robert Schumann | Winter&Winter | 910049-2
Und Wüsten's Die Blumen
Malfatti-Wittwer Duo | Und? | FMP | 0470
Unde Atoluwe Naiowe
Al Haig Quartet | Al Haig Quartet | Fresh Sound Records | FSR-CD 0012
Undecided
Benny Carter 4 | The Montreux '77 Collection | Pablo | 2620107
Benny Goodman And His Orchestra | Benny Goodman Forever | RCA | NL 89955(2) DP
Bob Florence And His Orchestra | Name Band:1959 | Fresh Sound Records | FSCD 2008
Dee Dee Bridgewater With Her Trio | Live At Yoshi's | Verve | 543354-2
Dexter Gordon Sextet | Midnight Dream | West Wind | WW 2040
Dizzy Gillespie Sextet | Jazz In Paris:Dizzy Gillespie-Cognac Blues | EmArCy | 014064-2
Ella Fitzgerald With Louis Armstrong And The All Stars | Ella Fitzgerald-First Lady Of Song | Verve | 517898-2
Ella Fitzgerald With The Chick Webb Orchestra | Ella Fitzgerald 75th Birthday Celebration:The Original Decca Recordings | GRP | GRP 26192
Erroll Garner Trio | Body & Soul | CBS | 467916-2
The Complete Savoy Sessions Vol.2 | Savoy | WL 70542 (809296)
Gerry Hayes-Charlie Antolini Quintet | Swing Explosion | BELL Records | BLR 84061
JATP Jam Session | Return To Happiness-JATP At Yoyogi National Stadium,Tokyo | Pablo | 2620117-2
John Kirby And His Onyx Club Boys | The Swinging Small Bands Vol. 1/1937-39 | MCA | 1324
Kenny Davers/Humphrey Lyttelton Sextet | This Old Gang Of Ours | Calligraph | CLG LP 012 IMS
Louis Armstrong And His All Stars | At The Pasadena Civic Auditorium | GNP Crescendo | GNP 11001
Lucky Thompson With Gerard Pochonet And His Orchestra | Lullaby In Rhythm | Biograph | BLP 12061
Red Garland Quintet feat.John Coltrane | High Pressure | Original Jazz Classics | OJCCD 349-2(P 7209)
Rob McConnell Septet With Harry 'Sweets' Edison | Live At The 1990 Concord Jazz Festival-First Set | Concord | CCD 4451
Roy Eldridge Quintet | Roy Eldridge And His Little Jazz Vol.1 | Vogue | 21511412
Sultans Of Swing | This Joint Is Jumping | Mons Records | MR 874319
Tatum-Carter-Bellson Trio | The Tatum Group Masterpieces | Pablo | 2625706
Teddy Wilson With The Dutch Swing College Band | The Dutch Swing College Band Meets Teddy Wilson | Timeless | TTD 525
The Tremble Kids All Stars | Dixieland At Its Best | BELL Records | BLR 89091
Vic Dickenson-Buck Clayton All Stars | Atlantic Jazz: Kansas City | Atlantic | 7567-81701-2
Willy Bischof Jazztet | Swiss Air | Jazz Connaisseur | JCCD 9523-2
Jimmy Rushing With Oliver Nelson And His Orchestra | The Bluesway Sessions | Affinity | CDX 13
Undecided Blues
Duke Jordan | Duke Jordan Solo Masterpieces Vol.1 | Steeplechase | SCCD 31299
Undecided Lady
Duke Jordan Trio | Wait And See | Steeplechase | SCCD 31211
Undecided(alt.take)
Roy Eldridge Quintet | Roy Eldridge And His Little Jazz Vol.1 | Vogue | 21511412
Under A Blanket Of Blue
Ben Webster With Orchestra And Strings | Music For Loving:Ben Webster With Strings | Verve | 527774-2
Benny Goodman Sextet | The Benny Goodman Selection | CBS | 467280-2
Coleman Hawkins Quintet | Ultimate Coleman Hawkins selected by Sonny Rollins | Verve | 557538-2
Ella Fitzgerald And Louis Armstrong With The Oscar Peterson Quartet | Verve Jazz Masters 24:Ella Fitzgerald & Louis Armstrong | Verve | 521851-2
The Best Of Ella Fitzgerald And Louis Armstrong On Verve | Verve | 537909-2
Ella And Louis | Verve | 543304-2
The Complete Ella Fitzgerald And Louis Armstrong On Verve | Verve | 537284-2
Ella & Louis | Verve | 825373-2
Gene Ammons Quartet | The Gene Ammons Story: Gentle Jug | Prestige | P 24079
Glenn Miller And His Orchestra | Glenn Miller In Concert | RCA | NL 89216 DP
Stan Kenton And His Orchestra | Portraits On Standards | Creative World | ST 1042
Tatum-Carter-Bellson Trio | Art Tatum-The Complete Pablo Group Masterpieces | Pablo | 6 PACD 4401-2
The Tatum Group Masterpieces | Pablo | 2310732
Under A Blanket Of Blue(alt.take 1)
Ben Webster With Orchestra And Strings | Music For Loving:Ben Webster With Strings | Verve | 527774-2
Under A Blanket Of Blue(alt.take 2)
Luciano Federighi & Fabio's Fables | In A Blizzard Of Blue | SPLASC(H) Records | HP 17
Under A Dorian Sky
Bill Frisell | Ghost Town | Nonesuch | 7559-79583-2
Under A Golden Sky
Gerry Mulligan Quartet | Little Big Horn | GRP | GRP 95032
Under My Thumb
Cassiber | The Beauty And The Beast | Riskant | 528-72410
Under Paris Skies
Coleman Hawkins With Many Albam And His Orchestra | The Hawk In Paris | Bluebird | 63 51059-2
Travelin' Light | Cookin' With Frank And Sam | Concord | CCD 4647
Under Redwoods
Greg Marvin Sextet | Taking Off! | Timeless | CD SJP 348
Under The Bamboo Tree
Ken Colyer's Jazzmen | Dixieland Forever | BELL Records | BLR 89025
Under The Bed
Joe Bonner Quartet | Suite For Chocolate | Steeplechase | SCCD 31215
Under The Mountain
Francesco Branciamore Quartet | Flash In Four | SPLASC(H) Records | HP 11
Under The Spell Of The Blues
Ella Fitzgerald With The Chick Webb Orchestra | Let's Get Together | Laserlight | 17003
Under The Surface
Julian Priester Quintet | Keep Swingin' | Original Jazz Classics | SMJ 6081
Under Water
Perception With Bill Molenhof | Another Perception Of Jazz | Aho-Recording | AHO CD 1012(CD 663)
Undercover Girl Blues
Lester Young Quartet | Lester Young:The Complete 1936-1951 Small Group Session(Studio Recordings-Master Takes),Vol.5 | Blue Moon | BMCD 1005
Underfelt
29th Street Saxophone Quartet | Underground | Antilles | 848415-2(889151)
Underground Dream
George Colligan | Return To Copenhagen | Steeplechase | SCCD 31519
Underground Emotions(Way Way Down)
Kerry Campbell Quintet | Phoenix Rising | Contemporary | CCD 14041-2
Underground Movement
Marty Ehrlich And The Dark Woods Ensemble | Just Before The Dawn | New World Records | 80474-2
Underneath It All
Mitch Watkins Group | Underneath It All | Enja | ENJ-5099 2
Underneath The Mango Tree
Ralph Flanagan And His Orchestra | Dance Again Part 2 | Magic | DAWE 75
Undernote
Mike Cuozzo Quintet | Mighty Mike Cuozzo | Savoy | SV 0207(MG 12051)
Understanding
McCoy Tyner Quintet | Dimensions | Elektra | 960350-1
Thomas Franck Quartet | Bewitched | Stunt Records | STUCD 18905
Understatement
The Mitchell-Marsh Big Two | Hot House | Storyville | SLP 4092
Underworld Blues
Gerd Baumann-Alessandro Ricciarelli Quartet | Say No More | Edition Collage | EC 489-2
Undicesima Strada(The Crossing Of Water)
Peter Rühmkorf Mit Dem Michael Naura Trio | Kein Apolloprogramm Für Lyrik | ECM | 801 SP
Undisonus Op.23 for Violin And Orchestra
Koch-Schütz-Studer & Musicos Cubanos | Fidel | Intakt Records | CD 056
Une Casa Leccera
Fischbacher Group & Modern String Quartet | Fischbacher Group & Modern String Quartet | Dr.Jazz Records | 8608-2
Une Nuit Au Violon
Albert Louis Jazzband | Live Im Neumeyer Dr. Flotte | Jazz Classics | AU 11089
Uneac(Suite)
Chris Potter Quintet | Presenting Chriss Potter | Criss Cross | Criss 1067
Unending
Horst Grabosch Quartet | Alltage | Jazz Haus Musik | JHM 80 CD
Unerwünscht
Stefano Battaglia-Tony Oxley Duo | Explore | SPLASC(H) Records | CD H 304-2
Uneven Image
Edward Vesala Nordic Gallery | Sound & Fury | ECM | 1541
Unexpected Guests
Zahara | Flight Of The Spirit | Antilles | AN 1011(802688)
Unfinished Column
Shorty Rogers-Bud Shank And The Lighthouse All Stars | Eight Brothers | Candid | CCD 79521
Unfinished Self-Portrait
Gary Burton Quintet With Eberhard Weber | Ring | ECM | 1051
Unfinished Sympathy
Dave Brubeck Quartet With Gerry Mulligan | We're All Together Again For The First Time | Atlantic | 7567-81390-2
Unfinished Woman
Trio Töykeät | [Sisu] | EmArCy | 536580-2
Unfold Twice
Benny Carter Quartet | 3,4,5 The Verve Small Group Sessions | Verve | 849395-2 PMS
Unforgettable
Dinah Washington With The Belford Hendricks Orchestra | Verve Jazz Masters 19:Dinah Washington | Verve | 518200-2
Hal Galper Trio With Jerry Bergonzi | Just Us | Enja | ENJ-8058 2
John Pizzarelli Trio | Dear Mr.Cole | Novus | 4163182-2
Johnny Hartman And His Orchestra | Standards On Impulse! | Impulse(MCA) | IMP 12032
Larry Willis | Unforgettable | Steeplechase | SCCD 31318
Oscar Peterson With Orchestra | With Respect To Nat | Verve | 557486-2
Pepper Adams Quintet | My One And Only Love | West Wind | WW 2053
Ung Forelsket Kvinne
Bobby Hutcherson Quintet | Medina | Blue Note | LT 1086
Ungarische Lieder
Eugen Cicero Trio | Swings Tschaikowsky & Liszt | MPS | 88039-2
Ungarisches Potpourri
Dizzy Gillespie Sextet | Dizzy's Diamonds-Best Of The Verve Years | Verve | 513875-2
Unhappy Happy Soul
Dave Douglas Trio | Constellations | Hat Art | CD 6173
Unicorn
Kazumi Watanabe Group | To Chi Ka | Denon Compact Disc | DC-8568
Unidentified Objects
Wes Montgomery | Guitar On The Go | Original Jazz Classics | OJCCD 489-2(RLP 9494)
Unidentified Solo Guitar
Thelonious Monk | Blues Five Spot | Milestone | M 9124
Unidentified Title
Duke Ellington And His Orchestra | The Duke At Fargo 1940 | Storyville | STCD 8316/17
Lionel Hampton And His Orchestra | En Concert Avec Europe 1 | Laserlight | 710462
Miles Davis Group | En Concert Avec Europe 1 | Laserlight | 710460
Unidentified Title-
Paris Jazz Concert:Miles Davis | Laserlight | 17445
Roland Kirk Quintet | Petite Fleur | Moon Records | MCD 027-2
Unilateral
Franz Koglmann Tentet | Ich | Hat Art | CD 6033
Union Pacific
Lincoln Center Jazz Orchestra | Big Train | CBS | CK 69860
Union Pacific Big Boy
Chris McGregor's Brotherhood Of Breath | Liv At Willisau | Ogun | OGCD 001
Union Station Blues
Christopher Dell Quartet | Other Voices, Other Rooms | L+R Records | CDLR 45093
Unison
J.F. Jenny Clark/Christof Lauer | Unison | CMP Records | CMP CD 32
Unisons
Dave Brubeck Quartet | Adventures In Time | CBS | CBS 66291
Unit 7
Cannonball Adderley Quintet | Nancy Wilson/The Cannonball Adderley Quintet | Capitol | 781204-2
Sam Jones & Co | The Riverside Collection: Sam Jones-Right Down Front | Original Jazz Classics | OJC- 6008
The Riverside Reunion Band | Hi-Fly | Milestone | MCD 9228-2
Wynton Kelly Trio With Wes Montgomery | Smokin' At The Half Note | CTI Records | PDCTI 1117-2
Wynton Kelly-George Coleman Quartet | Live In Baltimore | Affinity | AFF 108
United
Art Blakey And The Jazz Messengers | Roots And Herbs | Blue Note | 521956-2
Pisces | Blue Note | GXK 8151
George Colligan Trio | Activism | Steeplechase | SCCD 31382
Chris Barber's Jazz And Blues Band | Who's Blues | BELL Records | BLR 84009
United Blues
Trio Karel Boehlee | Switch | Timeless | CD SJP 206
United Dish
Joachim Kühn | United Nations | Atlantic | ATL 50719
United States
Kenny Garrett Sextet | Garrett 5 | Paddle Wheel | K32Y 6280
Unité-Multiple
Amalgam | Samanna | View | VS 104 IMS
Unity
Ernie Watts Quintet | Unity | JVC | JVC 2046-2
Unity Village
Pat Metheny Trio | Part Metheny Trio Live | Warner | 9362-47907-2
Muhal Richard Abrams Feat.Malachi Favors | Sightsong | Black Saint | BSR 0003
Universal
Phil Minton | A Doughnut In One Hand | FMP | CD 91
Universal Thoughts
Marty Cook Conspiracy | Phases Of The Moon | Tutu Records | 888160-2*
Universal Trains
Essence | Last Flight | DIW | DIW 831 CD
Univisible
Michele Rosewoman Quintet | Quintessence | Enja | 5039 (807547)
Univoyage
Hot Club The Zigan | Witchcraft | Jazz Pure Collection | AU 31605 CD
Unknown Realms(Shirli Sees)
Weather Report | I Sing The Body Electric | CBS | 468207-2
Unknown Title
Dizzy Gillespie Big Band | The Legendary Dizzy Gillespie Big Band-Live 1946 | Bandstand | BDCD 1534
Unleemited(take 1)
Louis Armstrong And His All Stars | Louis Armstrong:Complete 1950-1951 All Stars Decca Recordings | Definitive Records | DRCD 11188

Unlisted Blues
Kowalt-Smith-Sommer Trio | If You Want The Kernels, You Have To Break The Shells | FMP | 0920

Unmade Films
Allen Eager Quintet | Brothers And Other Mothers, Vol. 2 | Savoy | SJL 2236 (801212)

Unnecessary Town
Laurent De Wilde Sextet | Time Change | Warner | 8573-84315-2

Uno
Primal Blue | Primal Blue | Hip Bop | HIBD 8006

Unquity Road
Henry Threadgill Very Very Circus | Spirit Of Nuff...Nuff | Black Saint | 120134-2

Unrequited
Toshiko Akiyoshi Jazz Orchestra | Wishing Peace | Ken Music | 660.56.001

Unresolved
Jack DeJohnette Group | Sorcery | Prestige | P 10081

Uns
Max Neissendorfer Trio | Staubfrei | EGO | 95100

Unsa Oide Kath Mecht A No
David Moss Dense Band | Dense Band | Moers Music | 02040

Unsaid(1)
Michael Mantler Orchestra | Hide And Seek | ECM | 1738(549612-2)

Unsaid(2)
Hide And Seek | ECM | 1738(549612-2)

Unsaid(3)
Hide And Seek | ECM | 1738(549612-2)

Unsaid(4)
Hide And Seek | ECM | 1738(549612-2)

Unsaid(5)
Hide And Seek | ECM | 1738(549612-2)

Unsaid(6)
Sonny Boy Williamson Group | Blues Rarities | Chess | 6.28601 DP

Unseen Sea Scene
Conrad Herwig Sextet | Unseen Universe | Criss Cross | Criss 1194

Unshielded Desire
Ray Anderson Alligatory Band | Heads And Tales | Enja | ENJ-9055 2

Unsong Songs
Jimmie Lunceford And His Orchestra | Jimmie Lunceford Vol.5-Jimmie's Legacy | MCA | 1320

Unspoken
Chris Potter Quartet | Unspoken | Concord | CCD 4775

Unspoken Words
Dave Brubeck Orchestra | Two Generations Of Brubeck | Atlantic | SD 1645

Unsquare Dance
Dave Brubeck Quartet | Time Out/Time Further Out | CBS | CBS 22013

Unstable Symetry
Michael Riessler Group | Tentations D'Abélard | Wergo | WER 8009-2

Unstern
Ella Fitzgerald With The Tommy Flanagan Trio | Sunshine Of Your Love | MPS | 533102-2

Unsuless Landscape
Eric Alexander Quartet | Man With A Horn | Milestone | MCD 9293-2

Unsung Hero
Jay Collins Quintet | Reality Tonic | Reservoir | RSR CD 142

Unsung Heros
Khan Jamal Trio | The Traveller | Steeplechase | SCCD 31217

Unter Den Linden
Klaus Kreuzeder & Henry Sincigno | Saxappeal | Trick Music | TM 9013 MC
Günter Sommer | Hörmusik III:Sächsische Schatulle | Intakt Records | CD 027

Unterste Zeit
The Contemporary Alphorn Orchestra | Mytha | Hat Art | CD 6110

Unterwegs:
Kenny Wheeler/Lee Konitz/Dave Holland/Bill Frisell | Angel Song | ECM | 1607(533098-2)

Unti
Ahmad Mansour Quintet | Penumbra | Timeless | CD SJP 404

Until
Victor Lewis Sextet | Eeeyyess! | Enja | ENJ-9311 2

Un-Til
Billy Barron Quintet | Jazz Caper | Muse | MR 5235

Until I Met You
Tee Carson & The Basie Bandsmen | Basically Count | Palo Alto | PA 8005

Until It's Time For Me To Go
Carmen McRae With The Johnny Keating Orchestra | For Once In My Life | Atlantic | AMCY 1064

Until It's Time For You To Go
Ray Bryant | Alone At Montreux | 32 Jazz | 32128
Turk Mauro Quintet | The Underdog | Storyville | SLP 4076

Until The Rain Comes
Andy Kirk And His Twelve Clouds Of Joy | Big Band Bounce & Boogie-Andy Kirk And His Clouds Of Joy:Walkin' & Swingin' | Affinity | AFS 1011

Until The Real Thing Comes Along
Cal Collins Quartet | Ohio Style | Concord | CCD 4447
Carmen McRae With The Red Holloway Quintet | Fine And Mellow | Concord | CCD 4342
Coleman Hawkins Quintet | The Real Thing | Prestige | P 24083
Dexter Gordon Quartet | A Swingin' Affair | Blue Note | 784133-2
Dexter Gordon:The Complete Blue Note Sixties Sessions | Blue Note | 834200-2
Ella Fitzgerald With Ellis Larkins | Ella Fitzgerald 75th Birthday Celebration:The Original Decca Recordings | GRP | GRP 26192
Gene Harris Quartet | Like A Lover | Concord | CCD 4526
June Christy And Her Orchestra | The Misty Miss Christy | Pathe | 1566141(Capitol T 725)
Mel Tormé With Band/Orchestra | Mel Torme | Musicraft | MVS 508 IMS
Ruth Price With The Johnny Smith Quartet | Ruth Price Sings With The Johnny Smith Quartet | Fresh Sound Records | FSR 596(Roost 2217)
The Ravens | Rarities | Savoy | SV 0261(SJL 1174)
Weslia Whitefield With The Mike Greensill Quartet | Teach Me Tonight | HighNote Records | HCD 7009

Until Then
Kenny Barron Quintet | Quickstep | Enja | ENJ-6084 2
Fletcher Henderson And His Orchestra | The Indispensable Fletcher Henderson(1927-1936) | RCA | 2122618-2

Until Tonight
Duke Ellington And His Famous Orchestra | Duke Ellington & His Famous Orchestra | Forlane | UCD 19003

Until We Sleep(Lullaby)
Hugh Masekela Group | Hope | Triloka Records | 320203-2

Until(The Mole)
Amina Claudine Myers Sextet | Country Girl | Minor Music | 1012

Untitled
Keith Jarrett | Concerts(Bregenz) | ECM | 1227(827286-2)
Larry Karush-Glen Moore Duo | May 24, 1976 | Japo | 60014(2360014)
Monty Alexander | Pianissimo-Barpiano | BELL Records | BLR 89063

Untitled 90314
John Coltrane Quartet | Living Space | Impulse(MCA) | 951246-2
The Mastery Of John Coltrane/Vol. 1: Feelin' Good | MCA | 2292-54641-2

Untitled 90320
John Coltrane:The Classic Quartet-Complete Impulse Studio Recordings | Impulse(MCA) | 951280-2
Albert Ammons | The First Day | Blue Note | 798450-2

Untitled Blues
Billy Taylor Trio | Jazz At Massey Hall,Vol.2 | Original Jazz Classics | OJCCD 111-2(DLP 9)
Roland Kirk Quintet | Rahsaan/The Complete Mercury Recordings Of Roland Kirk | Mercury | 846630-2
Sonny Criss With The George Arvanitas Trio | Live In Italy | Fresh Sound Records | FSR-CD 67(881947)

Untitled Blues(Original)
Lee Morgan Sextet | Sonic Boom | Blue Note | 590414-2

Untitled Boogaloo
Sonic Boom | Blue Note | 590414-2
Deep Blue-The United States Of Mind | Blue Note | 521152-2
Sammy Price-J.C.Heard | Boogie And Jazz Classics | Black & Blue | BLE 59.111 2

Untitled In Ab Minor
Buddy Guy Blues Band | Buddy Guy-The Complete Chess Studio Recordings | MCA | MCD 09337

Untitled Instrumental
Buddy Guy Chicago Blues Band | Blues Rarities | Chess | 6.28601 DP
Buddy Johnson And His Orchestra | Buddy And Ella Johnson 1953-1964 | Bear Family Records | BCD 15479 DH
Miles Davis Quintet | Live In Europe | Nueva Records | JU 320

Untitled Original
Dave Liebman With Gunnar Mossblad And The James Madison University Jazz Esemble | The Music Of John Coltrane | Candid | CCD 79531
Charles Mingus Workshop | Charles Mingus-The Complete Debut Recordings | Debut | 12 DCD 4402-2

Untitled Original Blues(take 1)
Charles Mingus-The Complete Debut Recordings | Debut | 12 DCD 4402-2

Untitled Original Blues(take 2)
Charles Mingus-The Complete Debut Recordings | Debut | 12 DCD 4402-2

Untitled Original Composition(take 3)
Charles Mingus-The Complete Debut Recordings | Debut | 12 DCD 4402-2

Untitled Original Composition(take 5)
John Coltrane Quartet | John Coltrane-The Heavyweight Champion:The Complete Atlantic Recordings | Atlantic | 8122-71984-2

Untitled Original(Exotica)
Coltrane Plays The Blues | Rhino | 8122-79966-2
Charles Mingus Workshop | Charles Mingus-The Complete Debut Recordings | Debut | 12 DCD 4402-2

Untitled Percussion Composition
Count Basie And His Orchestra | The Uncollected:Count Basie | Hindsight | HSR 224 (835571)

Untitled Train-
Sun Ra & His Omniverse Arkestra | Destination Unknown | Enja | 7071-2

Untitled(per Carletto)
Matthias Müller Quartet | Bhavam | Jazz Haus Musik | JHM 0126 CD

Untitled-Undefined
Wolfgang Puschnig-Jamaladeen Tacuma Group With Guests | Journey Into The Gemini Territory | ITM-Pacific | ITMP 970091

Unwritten Letter
The Berlin Workshop Orchestra | Sib Langis | FMP | SAJ 30

Up A Lazy River
Allotria Jazz Band | All That Jazz | Elite Special | 730217
Ben Sidran Group | Heat Wave | VeraBra Records | CDVBR 2096-2
Benny Goodman-Jimmy Rowles | Benny Goodman:The Complete 1947-1949 Small Group Sessions Vol.1(1947) | Blue Moon | BMCD 1042
Chris Barber Quartet | Ballads For Trombone | Jazz Colours | 874718-2
Papa Bue's Viking Jazzband | The Golden Years Of Revival Jazz,Vol.11 | Storyville | STCD 5516
Live At Slukefter,Tivoli | Music Mecca | CD 1028-2
The Alex Welsh Legacy Band | The Sound Of Alex Vol.1 | Nagel-Heyer | CD 070
The Mills Brothers | The Best Of The Decca Years | MCA | MCD 31348

Up A Step
Ricky Ford Quintet | Tenor Madness Too! | Muse | MCD 5478

Up Abow My Head There's Music In The Air
Wayne Horvitz Group | 4+1 Ensemble | Intuition Records | INT 3224-2

Up All Night
Cannonball Adderley Quintet With Brass Reeds And Voices | Accent On Africa | Affinity | AFF 148

Up And Ad It
Lester Young Quintet | Pres Lives-The Savoy Sessions | Savoy | WL 70528 (SJL 1109) SF

Up And At 'Em
Lester Young Quartet | Lester Young:The Complete 1936-1951 Small Group Session(Studio Recordings-Master Takes),Vol.5 | Blue Moon | BMCD 1005

Up And At It
Live Recordings In New York City | Jazz Anthology | JA 5174

Up And Down
Mike Richmond Quartet | Blue In Green | Steeplechase | SCCD 31296
Steve Wilson Quartet | Four For Time | Criss Cross | Criss 1115

Up And Down East Street(For Ulysse Hardy)
Paul Dunmall Trio | Ghostly Thoughts | HatOLOGY | 503

Up And Down,Up And Down(Puck)
Mark Ford With The Robben Ford Band | Mark Ford With The Robben Ford Band | Crosscut | CCD 11031

Up And Push
Masabumi Kikuchi Trio | Feel You | Paddle Wheel | KICJ 141

Up Blues
Marlow Morris Quintet | Organ Boogie Woogie | CBS | 21079

Up From Limbo-
Stan Getz With The Eddie Sauter Orchestra | Stan Getz Plays The Music Of Mickey One | Verve | 531232-2
Gil Evans And The Monday Night Orchestra | Live At Sweet Basil | Electric Bird | K32Y 6017/8

Up From The Skies
Gil Evans Orchestra | Live At The Public Theater Vol.1(New York 1980) | Black-Hawk | BKH 525 CD
Lucky Peterson Group | Beyond Cool | Verve | 521147-2
Sarah Jane Morris Group | Blue Valentine | Ronnie Scott's Jazz House | JHCD 038

Up From The Skies(alt.take)
Gil Evans Orchestra | Plays The Muisc Of Jimmy Hendrix | RCA | 2125755-2

Up 'Gainst The Wall
John Coltrane Quartet | John Coltrane-His Greatest Years, Vol. 3 | MCA | AS 9278
John Coltrane Trio | Coltrane | Impulse(MCA) | 589567-2
McCoy Tyner Trio | Remembering John | Enja | ENJ-6080 2
Jiri Stivin-Ali Haurand | Just The Two Of Us | Konnex Records | KCD 5095

Up Hahn The Swing
Paul Bley | Blues For Red | Red Records | 123238 2

Up In A Fir Tree
Barney Wilen Quintet | Barney Wilen Quintet | Fresh Sound Records | FSR-CD 0048

Up In Cynthia's Room
Howard McGhee Sextet | Teddy Edwards:Steady With Teddy 1946-1948 | Cool & Blue | C&B-CD 115

Up In Quincy's Room
Doug Raney Sextet | Meeting The Tenors | Criss Cross | Criss 1006

Up In Sidney's Flat
Bunk Johnson-Sidney Bechet Sextet | Jazz Classics Vol.2 | Blue Note | 789385-2

Up Jump
Duke Ellington And His Orchestra | The Greatest Jazz Concert In The World | Pablo | 2625704-2

Up Jumped Spring
Art Blakey And The Jazz Messengers | The History Of Art Blakey And The Jazz Messengers | Blue Note | 797190-2
Frank Morgan Quartet | Mood Indigo | Antilles | 791320-2(881863)
Freddie Hubbard Quintet | Backlash | Atlantic | 7567-90466-2
Kirk Lightsey Quartet | First Affairs | Limetree | MCD 0015
Oliver Jones Trio | Just In Time | Justin Time | JUST 120/1-2
Trio Transition | Trio Transition | DIW | DIW 808 CD

Up Jumped The Devil
Earl Hines And His Orchestra | The Indispensable Earl Hines Vol.3/4(1939-1945) | RCA | 2126408-2
Earl Hines-Piano Man | Bluebird | NK 86750

Up Jumped You With Love
Fats Waller And His Rhythm | The Last Years 1940-1943 | Bluebird | ND 90411(3)

Up 'N Adam
Lester Young Quartet | Lester Swings | Verve | 833554-1
Live At Birdland Vol.2 | Bandstand | BDCD 1526

Up On Teddy's Hill
Minton's Playhouse All Stars | Charlie Christian:Swing To Bop | Dreyfus Jazz Line | FDM 36715-2
Jazz Legacy 64: Charlie Christian-1941 Live Sessions | Vogue | 500114

Up On the Roof
Hank Mobley Sextet | Reach Out! | Blue Note | 300259(4288)

Up Side Down-
Anita O'Day With The Gary McFarland Orchestra | All The Sad Youn Men | Verve | 517065-2

Up State
Red Richards-George Kelly Sextet With Doc Cheatham | Groove Move | Jazzpoint | JP 1045 CD

Up Stream
Jeremy Steig Quartet Feat. Jan Hammer | Something Else | LRC Records | CDC 8512

Up The Creek
Bola Sete Quintet | Bossa Nova | Original Jazz Classics | OJC 286(F 8349)

Up There
Buddy Rich And His Orchestra | Swingin' New Big Band | Pacific Jazz | 835232-2

Up Tight(Everything's Alright)
Swingin' New Big Band | Pacific Jazz | 835232-2
Ramsey Lewis Trio With Orchestra | Ramsey Lewis | Chess | 6.24473 AL

Up Town
Bobby Timmons Orchestra | Quartet And Orchestra | Milestone | MCD 47091-2

Up Up And Away
Jim Hall Trio | Jazz-Club: Guitar | Verve | 840035-2
Chick Corea Quartet | Live In Montreux | Stretch Records | SCD 9009-2

Up With The Lark
Bill Evans Trio | Bill Evans Trio:The Last Waltz | Milestone | 8MCD 4430-2
Bill Evans Trio:The Last Waltz | Milestone | 8MCD 4430-2
Live In Buenos Aires 1979 | West Wind | WW 2061
The Complete Fantasy Recordings | Fantasy | 9FCD 1012-2
The Tokyo Concert | Original Jazz Classics | OJCCD 345-2
Homecoming | Milestone | MCD 9291-2
Bill Evans Live In Tokyo | CBS | 481265-2
The Paris Concert-Edition One | Blue Note | MUS 96.0164-1
Thomas Fink Trio | Big Brown Eyes | clearaudio | WOR 161 CD

Up, Sometimes Down
Baden Powell Quartet | L'Art De Baden Powell | Accord | 114842

Upa Nequinho
Tom Scott Groups | Reed My Lips | GRP | GRP 97592

Upepidde
Sonny Sharrock Band | Highlife | Enemy | EMCD 119(03519)

Upland
Paul Nash Ensemble | Second Impression | Soul Note | SN 1107

Upline
New York Jazz Collective | Everybody Wants To Go To Heaven | Naxos Jazz | 86073-2

Upon A Time
Third Kind Of Blue | Third Kind Of Blue | Minor Music | 006

Upon The Swing
Hal Galper Quintet | Let's Call This That | Double Time Records | DTRCD-157

Upper And Outest
Georg Hofmann-Lucas Niggli Duo | Mute Songs & Drumscapes | Creative Works Records | CW CD 1022-2

Upper Bakossi
Rod Levitt Orchestra | The Dynamic Sound Patterns Of The Rod Levitt Orchestra | Original Jazz Classics | OJCCD 1955-2(RS 9471)

Upper Bay
Tommy Flanagan Quintet | Jazz...It's Magic | Savoy | SV 0153(MG 12209)

Upper Manhattan Medical Group 'U.M.M.G.'
George Colligan Trio | Stomping Ground | Steeplechase | SCCD 31441

Upper Wess Side
Anke Helfrich Trio With Mark Turner | You'll See | double moon | CHRDM 71013

Upper Westside
Burkhard Beins-Martin Pfleiderer-Peter Niklas Wilson | Yarbles | HatOLOGY | 510

Uprising
Ken Schaphorst Big Band | Purple | Naxos Jazz | 86030-2

Uprising(for Jessie And Yvonne)
Craig Taborn Trio | Craig Taborn Trio | DIW | DIW 618 CD

Ups And Downs
Carla Bley-Steve Swallow | Duets | Watt | 20(837345-2)
Gino Lattuca Quartet | My Impression | B.Sharp Records | CDS 085

Upside Out
String Trio Of New York | Octagon | Black Saint | 120131-2

Upswing
Lynne Arriale Trio | Arise | IN+OUT Records | 77059-2
Tom Harrell Sextet | Upswing | Chesky | JD 103

Uptight
Art Blakey And The Jazz Messengers | Pisces | Blue Note | GXK 8151

Uptime Down
Don Byas Group | Don Byas:Midnight At Mintons | HighNote Records | HCD 7044

Uptown
Lee Ritenour Sextet | Alive In L.A. | GRP | GRP 98822
Lee Ritenour With Special Guests | Festival International De Jazz De Montreal | Spectra | 9811661
McCoy Tyner Big Band | Uptown/Downtown-Recorded Live At The Blue Note | Milestone | MCD 9167-2
Peter O'Mara Quintet | Avenue 'U' | Enja | 6046-2

Uptown Conversation
Nelson Riddle And His Orchestra | Communication | MPS | 9814795

Uptown Dance
Pat Martino Quintet | Stone Blue | Blue Note | 830822-2

Uptown Downunder
Rein De Graaff-Dick Vennik Quartet | Jubilee | Timeless | CD SJP 294

Uptown Rendezvous
Van Alexander Orchestra | Home Of Happy Feet/Swing! Staged For Sound! | Capitol | 535211-2

Uptown Rhapsody
Donald Harrison With The Guardians Of The Flame And The Mardi Gras Indians | Indian Blues | Candid | CCD 79514

Ur
Piirpauke | Zerenade | JA & RO | JARO 4142-2

Ural-Caravana(Bajot Soi 1)
Franz Koglmann Group | Venus In Transit | Between The Lines | btl 017(Efa 10186)

Urania,Wien
The Dance Band | Pierides | Line Records | COCD 9.00377 0

Uranus
Jorgen Emborg Group | Keyword | Stunt Records | 18904
Walter Davis | 400 Years Ago Tomorrow | Owl Records | 020

Uranus-
The Guest Stars | Out At Night | Eigelstein | 568-72228

Urbal Tea
World Saxophone Quartet | Moving Right Along | Black Saint | 120127-2

Urban Blues
Bob Mintzer Big Band | Urban Contours | dmp Digital Music Productions | CD 467

Urban Daydreams
Tony Dagradi Trio | Live At The Columns | Turnipseed | TMCD 07
Urban Magic:
Glen Velez Group | Pan Eros | CMP Records | CMP CD 63
Urban Music
Thomas Kessler Group | On Earth | Laika Records | 8695069
Urban Music(Vol.2)
Ralph Peterson Quartet | Ralph Peterson Presents The Fo'tet | Blue Note | 795475-2
Urbanate The Area 2
Association Urbanetique | Ass Bedient | Jazz 4 Ever Records:Jazz Network | J4E 4723
Urbanetique
Manny Albam And His Orchestra | The Jazz Workshop | RCA | 2159157-2
Uromkvaed(Primal Chorus)
Marilyn Mazur's Future Song | Marilyn Mazure's Future Song | VeraBra Records | CDVBR 2105-2
Urstrom
Harold Land Sextet | Westcoast Blues | Original Jazz Classics | OJCCD 146-2(J 920)
Ursula
Miles Davis Group | The Man With The Horn | CBS | 468701-2
Peter Leitch Quartet | Colors & Dimensions | Reservoir | RSR CD 140
Ursus Maior
Salamander | Spirit Of Fire | amf records | amf 1017
Urumchi
Jimmy McGriff Quartet | Feelin' It | Milestone | MCD 9313-2
Us
Swingle Singers | Back To Swing | Aves | 161530
Usage De Faux
Louis Moholo's Viva-La-Black | Freedom Tour-Live In South Afrika 1993 | Ogun | OGCD 006
Use Of Light
Steve Wolfe Quintet Feat.Nancy King | First Date | Inner City | IC 1049 IMS
Used To Be Jackson
Hank Crawford Orchestra | Down On The Deuce | Milestone | M 9129
Used To Have A Yellow Jacket
Ella Fitzgerald With Orchestra | Ella Abraca Jobim | Pablo | 2630201-2
Useless Landscape
Dave Frishberg Trio | Classics | Concord | CCD 4462
Usis Blues
Sammy Price Trio | Le Jazz En France Vol.14:Boogie Woogie A La Parisienne | Pathe | 1552601
Utaforr Skapet(In Front Of The Cupboard)
Andy LaVerne Trio | Another World | Steeplechase | SCCD 31086
Uten Forbindelse
Agnes Buen Garnas-Jan Garbarek | Rosensfole-Medieval Songs From Norway | ECM | 1402(839293 2)
Utfred
String Trio Of New York | Rebirth Of A Feeling | Black Saint | BSR 0068
Utopia Ballad
Mike Westbrook Orchestra | Bar Utopia-A Big Band Cabaret | Enja | ENJ-9333 2
Utopia Blues
John Klemmer Quintet | Waterfalls | MCA | AS 9220
Utter Chaos
Gerry Mulligan Quartet | Jazz At The Philharmonic: The Gerry Mulligan Quartets In Concert | Pablo | PACD 5309-2
Gerry Mulligan Quartet | Pacific Jazz | 300001(PJ 1)
Utter Chaos-
Gerry Mulligan:Pleyel Concert Vol.2 | Vogue | 21409432
Gerry Mulligan Quartet | Pacific Jazz | 300001(PJ 1)
Utviklingssang
Carla Bley-Steve Swallow | Duets | Watt | 20(837345-2)
The Carla Bley Band | Social Studies | Watt | 11(831831-2)
Astral Project | Astral Project | Astral Project | no No.
Uwis-
Ray Foxley | Professor Foxley's Sporting House Music | BELL Records | BLR 84021
Uxorious
Swiss Jazz Quintet feat. Franco Ambrosetti | Imagination | Jazz Publications | JPV 8201
V.I.P.'s Boogie
Duke Ellington And His Orchestra | Duke Ellington Live ! | EmArCy | 842071-2
From The Blue Note, Chicago | Jazz Anthology | JA 5197
Jazz Festival Vol.2 | Storyville | 4960743
V.I.P.'s Boogie-
Leszek Zadlo Quartet | Breath | Enja | ENJ-6026 2
Va En Serio
BLU | Rhythm & Blu. | Gramavision | 18-8606-1
Va,Crudele!
Madrid Jazz Group | Unreleased Madrid Jazz Sessions 1964-1981 | Fresh Sound Records | FSR-CD 3003
Vacation
T-Bone Walker And His Band | Good Feelin' | Verve | 519723-2
Vaccio
Warren Vaché Trio | Live at The Vineyard | Challenge | CHR 70028
Vadana
Collin Walcott Quartet | Cloud Dance | ECM | 1062(825469-2)
Richie Beirach | Common Heart | Owl Records | 048 CD
Vagabond Dreams
Glenn Miller And His Orchestra | Glenn Miller:The Complete Studio Recordings Vol.2:In The Mood | Memo Music | HDJ 4115
Vagabundo
Alex Möller-Lena Willemark Group | Hästen Och Tranan | ACT | 9244-2
Vaggvisa
Arild Andersen Quartet | Shimri | ECM | 1082
Vague
Ivan Paduart Trio | Europ' Jazz Contest '92 Belgium | B.Sharp Records | CDS 092
Vagus
Mario Piacentini Trio | Canto Atavico | SPLASC(H) Records | H 146
Vai Passar
Serge Forté Trio | Vaina | Laika Records | LK 90-021
Vaina
Christine Wodrascka | Vertical | FMP | CD 79
Vai-Te Embora,O Papao-
Loope | Prinz Henry | ITM Records | ITM 1447
Valdivia
Jon Gordon Quartet/Quintet | Along The Way | Criss Cross | Criss 1138
Vale Do Eco
Elisabet Raspall Grup | Lila | Fresh Sound Records | FSNT 058 CD
Vale La Pena
George Gruntz Concert Jazz Band | Global Exellence | TCB Records | TCB 21172
Valentine
Ron McClure Trio | Never Always | Steeplechase | SCCD 31355
Valeria
Modern Jazz Quartet | Topsy-This One's For Basie | Original Jazz Classics | OJCCD 1073-2(2310917)
The Best Of The Modern Jazz Quartet | Pablo | 2405423-2
Valetta
Gianluigi Trovesi Octet | Les Hommes Armés | Soul Note | 121311-2
Valinor
Les McCann Group | Music Lets Me Be | MCA | 28916 XOT
Vallat
Ekkehard Jost Quartet | Deep | Fish Music | FM 007 CD
Vallat For Four
Nils Landgren-Esbjörn Svensson | Swedish Folk Modern | ACT | 9428-2
Vallat Fran Härjedalen
Swedish Folk Modern | ACT | 9428-2
Vallat Fran Jämtland
Bengt-Arne Wallin Orchestra | The Birth+Rebirth Of Swedish Folk Jazz | ACT | 9254-2
Vallat(2)-
Mark Egan-Danny Gottlieb Quartet | Elements | Antilles | AN 1017(802738)
Valley
Walter Bishop Jr. Trio | Valley Land | Muse | MR 5060
Valley Of Fragments
Sergio Salvatore Quartet | Sergio Salvatore | GRP | GRP 97202
Valley Of Life
Jamie Findlay | Wings Of Light | Acoustic Music Records | 319.1076.2
Vallsvit
Lucky Four | Lucky Four | Tutu Records | 888108-2
Valmontana
Art Blakey And The Jazz Messengers | Les Liaisons Dangereuses(Original Soundtrack) | Fontana | 812017-2
Valmontana(take 2)
Larry Willis Trio | Steal Away | audioquest Music | AQCD 1009
Vals 7
John Blake Septet | Quest | Sunnyside | SSC 1058 D
Vals Criollo-
Ferenc Snétberger | For My People | Enja | ENJ-9387 2
Vals Gitano-
Susanne Lundeng Quartet | Waltz For The Red Fiddle | Laika Records | 35101402
Vals Til Den Rode Fela(Waltz For The Red Fiddle)
Paquito D'Rivera Group With The Absolute Ensemble | Habanera | Enja | ENJ-9395 2
Vals Venezolano
Pau Brasil | La Vem A Tribo | GHA Records | CD 126.005
Valsa Tupi
Bill Evans Trio With Symphony Orchestra | Bach-Chopin-Scriabin-Granados-Faure-Evans | Verve | 2304525 IMS
Valse
Billy Taylor And The Jazzmobile Allstars | The Jazzmobile Allstars | Taylor Made Records | T 1003
Valse À Clignancourt
Helmut Kagerer/Helmut Nieberle | Guitar Moments | Take Twelve On CD | TT 006-2
Valse Á Häns'che
Salut! | Green & Orange | Edition Collage | EC 488-2
Valse Á Hojok
Rainer Pusch-Horace Parlan | In Between Those Changes | yvp music | CD 3046
Valse A Nieb
Stochelo Rosenberg Trio | Seresta | Hot Club Records | HCRCD 059
Valse A Rosental
Titi Winterstein Quintet plus Guests | Live! | Boulevard | BLD 508 LP
Valse De Weiß
Traubeli Weiß Ensemble | Dreaming Of You | Edition Collage | EC 468-2
Valse De Weiß(II)
Titi Winterstein Quintet | Saitenstra en | Intercord | 160117
Valse Du Passe
Simon Cato Spang-Hansen Quartet | Identified | dacapo | DCCD 9448
Valse Du Vendredi
Yes Yes Yes Trio | 12th Jazz Hoeilaart International Europ' Jazz Contest 90 | B.Sharp Records | CDS 081
Valse Hot
Larry Goldings Trio | Light Blue | Minor Music | 801026
Max Roach Quintet | Hot Tracks For Cool Cats Vol.3 | Polydor | 816411-2
Sonny Rollins Plus Four | Sonny Rollins Plus 4 | Original Jazz Classics | OJC20 243-2(P 7038)
Jazz Gallery:Clifford Brown | RCA | 2114176-2
Vienna Art Orchestra | Nightride Of A Lonely Saxophoneplayer | Moers Music | 02054/5 CD
Valse Lento
Lindemann Sextet | En Public Aux Faux-nez | Plainisphare | PL 1267-13
Valse Manouche
Matelo Ferret Ensemble | Tribute To Django | France's Concert | FCD 124
Valse Oubliée
Lajos Dudas | Music For Clarinet | Pannon Jazz/Classic | PCL 8007
Valse Robin
The Carla Bley Band | Social Studies | Watt | 11(831831-2)
Valse Sinistre
Häns'che Weiss Ensemble | Vis-A-Vis | Elite Special | 73229
Valse Triste
Art Pepper Quartet | Art Pepper:The Complete Galaxy Recordings | Galaxy | 16GCD 1016-2
Art Pepper:The Complete Village Vanguard Sessions | Contemporary | 9CCD-4417-2
Art Pepper:The Complete Village Vanguard Sessions | Contemporary | 9CCD-4417-2
APQ-The Maiden Voyage Sessions,Vol.3 | Galaxy | GXY 5151
The Caribbean Jazz Project | The Caribbean Jazz Project | Inak | 9038
Randy Weston | Marrakech In The Cool Of The Evening | Verve | 521588-2
Valse Tzigane
Charlie Byrd | Latin Byrd | Milestone | MCD 47005-2
Valse(Opus 8 No.4)
Bill Evans Trio With The Claus Ogerman Orchestra | The Complete Bill Evans On Verve | Verve | 527953-2
Valse(Siciliano in G Minor[Bach])
Badi Assad | Solo | Chesky | JD 99
Valsitude
Evan Parker/Barry Guy/Paul Lytton | Imaginary Values | MAYA Recordings | MCD 9401
Valve Head
Lionel Hampton Allstar Big Band feat.Woody Herman | Aurex Jazz Festival '81:Live Special | Eastworld | EWJ 80254
Vamonos
Omar Belmonte's Latin Lover | Vamos A Ver | EGO | 96170
Vamos A Ver
Mmotia-The Little People | Dwight Andrews | Otic | 1007
Vamp
Chick Corea Group | Early Days | LRC Records | CDC 7969(874370)
Django Reinhardt And His Quintet | Django Reinhardt Vol. 6 | Decca | 180025 AG
Frank Newton And His Cafe Society Orchestra | Frankie's Jump | Affinity | CD AFS 1014
Vamp For Ochum
Michele Rosewoman Quintet | Quintessence | Enja | 5039 (807547)
Van Gogh Admist The Flowers
Kenny Garrett Group | Black Hope | Warner | 9362-45017-2
Vancouver Lights
Sotto In Su | Südamerika Sept. 90 | Jazz Haus Musik | JHM 0051 CD
Vandalis Electrica
Charlie Mariano & The Karnataka College Of Percussion | Jyothi | ECM | 1256
Vandanam
Hans Reichel-Rüdiger Carl Duo | Buben...Plus | FMP | CD 78
Vandrere
Gregorio-Gustafsson-Nordeson | Background Music | HatOLOGY | 526
Vänge
Clifford Jordan-Ran Blake Groups | Masters From Different Worlds | Mapleshade | 01732
Vanguard Max
Art Pepper Quartet | Art Pepper:The Complete Village Vanguard Sessions | Contemporary | 9CCD-4417-2
David Milne Group | Berlin Connection | BIT | 11254
Vanilje
Eddie Palmieri Group | Vortex | RMM Records | 660.58.116
Vanishing Time
Arild Andersen Quintet With The Cikada String Quartet | Hyperborean | ECM | 1631(537342-2)
Vanishing Waltz
Mona Larsen And The Danish Radio Big Band Plus Soloists | Michael Mantler:Cerco Un Paese Innocente | ECM | 1556
Vanità-
Dave Douglas Trio | Constellations | Hat Art | CD 6173
Vanity
Elise Einarsdotter-Olle Steinholz | Sketches Of Roses | Touché Music | TMcCD 008
Vanja
Simon Phillips-Jeff Babko Group | Vantage Point | Jazzline | JL 11159-2
Vapallia
Keith Jarrett Quintet | Back Hand | MCA | 62746 (801436)
Varadero
Nueva Manteca | Varadero Blues | Timeless | CD SJP 318
Vardag
Astor Piazzolla Group | Onda Nueve | West Wind Latina | 2213 CD
Variant I-
Gunther Schuller Ensemble | Beauty Is A Rare Thing:Ornette Coleman-The Complete Atlantic Recordings | Atlantic | 8122-71410-2
Variant II-
Beauty Is A Rare Thing:Ornette Coleman-The Complete Atlantic Recordings | Atlantic | 8122-71410-2
Variant III-
Beauty Is A Rare Thing:Ornette Coleman-The Complete Atlantic Recordings | Atlantic | 8122-71410-2
Variant VI-
Oliver Lake/Donal Leonellis Fox | Boston Duets | Music & Arts | CD 732
Variants On A Theme Of Thelonious Monk(Criss Cross):
Marcus Sukiennik Big Band | A Night In Tunisia Suite(7 Variationen über Dizzy Gillespie's 'A Night In Tunisia') | Jazz Haus Musik | ohne Nummer
Variation 1:Verschleierung
Ketil Bjornstad | The Bach Variations | EmArCy | 017267-2
Variation 1-23
Uri Caine With The Concerto Köln | Concerto Köln | Winter&Winter | 910086-2
Variation 1-33
Joachim Kühn-Walter Quintus | Get Up Early | Ambiance(CMP) | AMB-CD 2
Variation 2:Erstarrung und Befreiung
Marcus Sukiennik Big Band | A Night In Tunisia Suite(7 Variationen über Dizzy Gillespie's 'A Night In Tunisia') | Jazz Haus Musik | ohne Nummer
Variation 3:Atem
A Night In Tunisia Suite(7 Variationen über Dizzy Gillespie's 'A Night In Tunisia') | Jazz Haus Musik | ohne Nummer
Variation 4:Geselligkeit
A Night In Tunisia Suite(7 Variationen über Dizzy Gillespie's 'A Night In Tunisia') | Jazz Haus Musik | ohne Nummer
Variation 5:Der Kern
A Night In Tunisia Suite(7 Variationen über Dizzy Gillespie's 'A Night In Tunisia') | Jazz Haus Musik | ohne Nummer
Variation 6:Das Fest
A Night In Tunisia Suite(7 Variationen über Dizzy Gillespie's 'A Night In Tunisia') | Jazz Haus Musik | ohne Nummer
Variation 7:Ausklang
Michael Naura-Wolfgang Schlüter Duo | Country Children | ECM | 803 SP
Variation I
Charles Gayle 3 | Abiding Variations | FMP | CD 100
Variation II
Abiding Variations | FMP | CD 100
Variation On A Theme(Tales From The Farside)
Moscow Rachmaninov Trio | Groupe Lacroix:The Composer Group | Creative Works Records | CW CD 1030-2
Variation On A Thme By Schubert(Edison Denissov)
Günther Klatt Trio | Live At Leverkusen | Enja | 5069-2
Variation(dedicated to Django Reinhardt)
Friedrich Gulda | The Long Road To Freedom | MPS | 88021-2
Variationen Über BWV 38
Jürg Sommer Trio | Jazz In Switzerland 1930-1975 | Elite Special | 9544002/1-4
Variationen Über 'Rauch Und Moder'
Art Ensemble Of Chicago And Lester Bowie's Brass Fantasy | Live at The 6th Tokyo Muisc Joy '90 | DIW | DIW 842 CD
Variations On A Theme (Trinkle Tinkle)
Mal Waldron | Update | Soul Note | 121130-2
Variations On A Theme Of Hindemith
Meade Lux Lewis | Boogie Woogie, Stride & The Piano Blues | Blue Note | 799099-2
Variations on Ah! Vous Dirais-Je Maman(KV 265)
Eddie Daniels/Bucky Pizzarelli Duo | Blue Bossa | Choice | CHCD 71002
Variations On I Got Rhythm And Cuban Overture
Ferenc Snétberger Quartet | Signature | Enja | ENJ-9017 2
Variations On Nuages
Don Pullen's African-Brazilian Connection | Ode To Live-A Tribute To George Adams | Blue Note | 789233-2
Variations On Spanish Themes
Joe Bonner Quintet | Angel Eyes | Muse | MR 5114
Variations On The Misery
Gil Evans Orchestra | Live At The Public Theater Vol.1(New York 1980) | Black-Hawk | BKH 525 CD
Variations Sur Un Theme De Monteverdi(part 1-3)
Art Ensemble Of Chicago | Les Stances A Sophie | Nessa | N 4
Variations(III)
Paolo Fresu Quartet | Angel | RCA | 2155864-2
Variazione Cinque
Lee Konitz Quartet | Lee Konitz:Move | Moon Records | MCD 057-2
Variazione Otto
Paolo Fresu Quintet | Melos | RCA | 2178289-2
Variazione Sei
Paolo Fresu Sextet | Ensalada Mistica | SPLASC(H) Records | CD H 415-2
Variety(for Guy Klucevsek)
Alex Möller-Lena Willemark Group | Hästen Och Tranan | ACT | 9244-2
Varshini
Charlie Mariano & The Karnataka College Of Percussion | Live | VeraBra Records | CDVBR 2034-2
Anita O'Day And Her Trio | Tea For Two | Moon Records | MLP 023-1
Varsity Drag
Jimmie Grier And His Orchestra | The Uncollected:Jimmie Grier | Hindsight | HSR 177
Vashkar
Jaco Pastorius Quartet | Jaco | DIW | DIW 312 CD
Paul Bley Trio | Footoose | Savoy | SV 0140(MG 12182)
Tony Williams Lifetime | Emergency! | Verve | 539117-2
Vassarlean
Charles Mingus Group | The Jazz Life! | Candid | CCD 79019
Jan Garbarek Group | Rites | ECM | 1685/86(559006-2)
Vast Plain,Clouds
Kamafra | Kamafra Live | Edition Musikat | EDM 072
Vatapá
Dicke Luft | Halb So Wild-Wie Schlimm | Riskant | 568-722416
Vater Und Mutter Erde
Karl Scharnweber Trio | Coral Concert II/Another View | Nabel Records:Jazz Network | CD 4650
Vater Unser Im Himmelreich
Willie 'The Lion' Smith | The Memoirs Of Willie 'The Lion' Smith | RCA | 2126415-2
Vauva(Baby)
Achim Knipsel-Willi Kellers Duo | Eickendorfballade | FMP | 0910
Vaya Con Dios
Machito And His Afro-Cuban Salseros | Mucho Macho | Pablo | 2625712-2
Vector
Oliver Augst-Rüdiger Carl-Christoph Korn | Blank | FMP | OWN-90013
Ved Sorevatn
Dave Holland Quintet | The Razor's Edge | ECM | 1353
Vedana
Dave Liebman Quartet | 1st Visit | West Wind | WW 2067
Vegas Drag
Christine Wodrascka | Vertical | FMP | CD 79

TITELVERZEICHNIS

Veien
Mat Maneri | Trinity | ECM | 1719
Veiled
Terry Gibbs Octet | Jewis Melodies In Jazztime | Mercury | 589673-2
Veiloch
Gary Campbell Quartet | Thick & Thin | Double Time Records | DTRCD-115
Vein Melter
Bebo Valdés Group | Bebo Rides Again | Messidor | 15834 CD
Veldt(Seven Pieces For Twelve Strings)
Alberto Nacci Alma Quartet | Isola Lontana | SPLASC(H) Records | CD H 310-2
Velejar
Roy Hargrove Quintet | Family | Verve | 527630-2
Velera
Ahmed El-Salamouny/Gilson De Assis | Tango Brasileiro | FSM | FCD 97725
Velhos Tempos
Oriental Wind | Life Road | JA & RO | JARO 4113-2
Veli Aga
Jazzy World | JA & RO | JARO 4200-2
Pep O'Callaghan Grup | Port O'Clock | Fresh Sound Records | FSNT 069 CD
Vell Pelegri
Louis Armstrong And His All Stars | Historic Barcelona Concerts At Windsor Palace 1955 | Fresh Sound Records | FSR-CD 3004
Velma's Blues
Bird's Eyes-Last Unissued Vol.16 | Philology | W 846.2
Véloce(Bolling)
John Wolf Brennan | The Well-Prepared Clavier/Das Wohlpräparierte Klavier | Creative Works Records | CW CD 1032-2
Veloce(very fast)-
Hermeto Pascoal Orchestra With Strings | Brazilian Adventure | Muse | MCD 6006
Velvet
Bill Dixon Quartet | November 1981 | Soul Note | 121038-2
Velvet Rain
Lucky Thompson Quartet | Lucky Thompson | Swing | SW 8404 IMS
Velvet Scene
Prestige All Stars | John Coltrane-The Prestige Recordings | Prestige | 16 PCD 4405-2
Gene Ammons Quintet | The Gene Ammons Story: Organ Combos | Prestige | P 24071
Vem Kan Segla Förutan Vind
Jorge Degas-Wolfgang Loos | Cantar A Vida | Traumton Records | 4446-2
Vem Morena
Tania Maria Quintet | Piquant | Concord | CCD 4151
Vemond
Antonio Hart Group | Here I Stand | Impulse(MCA) | 951208-2
Ven Devorame Otra Vez
Latin On Impulse! Various Artists | Impulse(MCA) | IMP 12762
Vendaval
Conrad Herwig Quartet | New York Hardball | Ken Music | 660.56.002
Vendome
Modern Jazz Quartet | MJQ 40 | Atlantic | 7567-82330-2
Modern Jazz Quartet | Prestige | P 24005
European Concert | Atlantic | SD 2-603
The MJQ Box | Prestige | 7711-2
Venecia
A Band Of Friends | Teatime Vol.2 | Poise | Poise 06/2
Venedig
Agnes Buen Garnas-Jan Garbarek | Rosensfole-Medieval Songs From Norway | ECM | 1402(839293-2)
Venelite
Dick Heckstall-Smith & John Etheridge Group | Live 1990 | L+R Records | CDLR 45028
Venez Punir Son Injustice
Südpool Jazz Project V | Marcia Funebre-The Italian Suite | L+R Records | CDLR 45106
Veni Creator Spiritus
Benny Goodman And His Orchestra | The King Of Jazz Big Band | Festival | Album 153
Venice
Christian Elsässer Trio | Venice | Organic Music | ORGM 9727
Enrico Rava Quartet | Opening Night | ECM | 1224
Modern Jazz Quartet | No Sun In Venice | Atlantic | SD 1284
John Zorn-George Lewis-Bill Frisell | News For Lulu | Hat Art | CD 6005
Venita's Dance
Kenny Dorham Octet | Afro-Cuban | Blue Note | 746815-2
Ventarron
Paolo Fresu Quintet | Ostinato | SPLASC(H) Records | H 106
Ventidue
Flavio Boltro Quartet | Flabula | Penta Flowers | CDPIA 020
Ventura
Howard McGhee Sextet | Sunset Swing | Black Lion | BLCD 760171
Venture
Jimmy Giuffre 3 | Emphasis,Stuttgart 1961 | Hat Art | CD 6072
Venture Inward
Andrew Hill Sextet | Grass Roots | Blue Note | 522672-2
Wolfgang Puschnig-Jamaladeen Tacuma Group With Guests | Journey Into The Gemini Territory | ITM-Pacific | ITMP 970091
Venus
John Coltrane-Rashied Ali Duo | Interstellar Space | Impulse(MCA) | 543415-2
LeeAnn Ledgerwood | Compassion | Steeplechase | SCCD 31477
Venus-
Viktoria Tolstoy With The Esbjörn Svensson Trio | Viktoria Tolstoy:White Russian | Blue Note | 821220-2
Venus And Mars
Johnny Griffin Sextet | The Little Giant | Original Jazz Classics | OJCCD 136-2(R 1149)
Venus As A Boy
Dave Valentine Group | Musical Portraits | GRP | GRP 96642
Venus De Mildrew
Gerry Mulligan And The Sax Section | The Gerry Mulligan Songbook | Pacific Jazz | 833575-2
Venus De Milo
Gerry Mulligan Orchestra | Re-Birth Of The Cool | GRP | GRP 96792
Miles Davis And His Orchestra | The Complete Birth Of The Cool | Capitol | 494550-2
Birth Of The Cool | Capitol | 530117-2
Miles Davis:The Blue Note And Capitol Recordings | Blue Note | 827475-2
Venus In Transit:
Steve Lampert Group | Venus Perplexed | Steeplechase | SCCD 31557
Venus Perplexed
Venus Perplexed | Steeplechase | SCCD 31557
Venus Perplexed Suite:
Tom Varner Quintet | Martian Heartache | Soul Note | 121286-2
Venutian Rhythm Dance
Bill Evans-Eddie Gomez Duo | The Complete Fantasy Recordings | Fantasy | 9FCD 1012-2
Guido Manusardi Quintet | Bridge Into The New Generation | SPLASC(H) Records | H 102
Vera Cruz
Dan Papaila Quartet | Positively! | Timeless | CD SJP 403
Helen Merrill With Orchestra | Casa Forte | EmArCy | 558848-2
Jim Hall Quartet | Where Would I Be? | Original Jazz Classics | M 9037
Verano Porteno
Toto Blanke-Rudolf Dasek | Mona Lisa | ALISO Records | AL 1037
Verano Sin Velo
Kevin Eubanks Group | Opening Night | GRP | GRP 91013-1(808716)
Vera's Song
Jones Hellborg | The Silent Life | Demon Records | DEM 026
Verd Mari
Lluis Vidal Trio | Milikituli | Fresh Sound Records | FSNT 009 CD
Jerry Gonzalez & Fort Apache Band | Moliendo Cafe-To Wisdom The Price | Sunnyside | SSC 1061 D
Verdammter Atlantic
Tommy Flanagan Trio | The Complete 'Overseas' | DIW | DIW 305 CD
Verdandi
The Complete 'Overseas' | DIW | DIW 305 CD
Verdandi(alt.take)
Tommy Flanagan Trio In Stockholm 1957 | Dragon | DRLP 87
Verdulac
Adam Noidlt-Intermission | Eine Permanent Helle Fläche | Jazz Haus Musik | JHM 53 CD
Vergebung
Bettina Born-Wolfram Born | Irgenwo Zwischen Tango,Musette Und Jazz | Born&Bellmann | 972708 CD
Verhallt-
Alfred 23 Harth-Bob Degen Duo | Melchior | Biber Records | BI 6240
Veris Leta Facies
Jenny Evans And Her Quintet | Nuages | ESM Records | ESM 9308
Steve Coleman And Five Elements | Def Trance Beat(Modalities Of Rhythm) | Novus | 4163181-2
Verlangen
Karl Scharnweber Trio | Coral Concert II/Another View | Nabel Records:Jazz Network | CD 4650
Verleih Uns Frieden Gnädiglich
Alfred 23 Harth-Bob Degen Duo | Melchior | Biber Records | BI 6240
Verlorene Liebesmüh:
Ingrid Jensen Sextet | Vernal Fields | Enja | ENJ-9013 2
Vernal Fields
Christoph Lauer Quintet | Fragile Network | ACT | 9266-2
Vernasio
Jackie McLean Quintet | Consequence | Blue Note | LT 994 (GXK 8172)
Verrückte Beine
Franco Ambrosetti Quintet | Light Breeze | Enja | ENJ-9331 2
Versace
Hugh Marsh Duo/Quartet/Orchestra | The Bear Walks | VeraBra Records | CDVBR 2011-2
Joachim Kühn Trio And The WDR Big Band | Carambolage | CMP Records | CMP CD 58(EFA 03058)
Versailles
Ronnie Taheny Group | Briefcase | Laika Records | 35101152
Lalo Schifrin Sextet | Marquis De Sade | Verve | 537751-2
Verses At Balwearie Tower
Matt Jazz Quintet | Sharp Blues | SPLASC(H) Records | H 109
Versprechen Und Neid
Hans-Günther Wauer/Günter Baby Sommer | Dedication | FMP | 0900
Versus
Glen Moore | Dragonetti's Dream | VeraBra Records | CDVBR 2154-2
Vertebra
Christine Wodrascka | Vertical | FMP | CD 79
Vertical Invader-
Marianne Schroeder | Piano (Morton Feldman 1926-1987) | Hat Art | CD 6035
Verticalement-
Thierry Lang-Daniel Perrin | Tusitala | Plainisphare | PL 1267-105 CD
Vertigo
Jackie McLean Quintet | Vertigo | Blue Note | 522669-2
Jim Snidero Quintet | Vertigo | Criss Cross | Criss 1112
Vertigo-
Roland Kirk Quartet | Rahsaan/The Complete Mercury Recordings Of Roland Kirk | Mercury | 846630-2
Vertigo Ro
Alfred 23 Harth-Bob Degen Duo | Melchior | Biber Records | BI 6240
Verve Blues
Art Tatum Sextet | The Tatum Group Masterpieces | Pablo | 2310731
Verve Y Agua
Bill Evans Trio | Quiet Now | Affinity | AFF 73
Very Early
Allen Farnham Trio | The Common Ground | Concord | CCD 4634
Bill Evans Trio | The Second Trio | Milestone | M 47046
The Brilliant | West Wind | WW 2058
Moonbeams | Original Jazz Classics | OJC20 434-2(RLP 9428)
Bill Evans:The Secret Sessions | Milestone | 8MCD 4421-2
Homecoming | Milestone | MCD 9291-2
Bill Evans:The Secret Sessions | Milestone | 8MCD 4421-2
Bill Evans:The Secret Sessions | Milestone | 8MCD 4421-2
Bill Evans-Montreux II | CBS | 481264-2
Carlos Denia-Uli Glaszmann | Ten Strings For Bill Evans | Edition Musikat | EDM 069
Charles Lloyd Quartet | Montreux 82 | Elektra | 60220-1
Dezsö Lakatos With The Super Trio | Elliptic Dance | Timeless | CD SJP 298
John Hicks-Ray Drummond | Two Of A Kind | Evidence | ECD 22017-2
Kronos Quartet With Eddie Gomez | Music Of Bill Evans | Landmark | LCD 1510-2
Very Early-
Toots Thielemans-Kenny Werner Duo | Toots Thielemans & Kenny Werner | EmArCy | 014722-2
John McLaughlin Group | Belo Horizonte | Warner | 99185
Very Early-(Excerpts)
Bill Evans Trio | Re: Person I Knew | Original Jazz Classics | OJCCD 749-2(F 9608)
Martial Solal Trio | Le Jazz En France-Vol.7 | Pathe | 1727311
Very Handy
Marc Ducret-Bobby Previt | In The Grass | Enja | ENJ-9343 2
Very Handy Indeed
Felix Wahnshuffle Trio | Live At The Be-Bop:Blues Against Racism | L+R Records | CDLR 45087
Very Late
Ernie Wilkins And His Orchestra | The Big New Band Of The '60s | Fresh Sound Records | FSCD 2006
Very Near Blues
Thelonious Monk Quartet | Thelonious Monk-The Complete Riverside Recordings | Riverside | 15 RCD 022-2
Very Saxy
Dick Collins And The Runaway Heard | Horn Of Plenty | Fresh Sound Records | NL 45632(RCA LJM 1019)
Very Slow
Ellington/Mingus/Roach Trio | Money Jungle | Blue Note | 538227-2
Very Special
Vienna Art Orchestra | Duke Ellington's Sound Of Love | TCB Records | TCB 99802
Very Tenor
Duke Ellington And His Orchestra | The Greatest Jazz Concert In The World | Pablo | 2625704-2
Very Very Simple
Andreas Hansl | Dualism | UAK | UAK 1
Vessel
Vaughn Monroe And His Orchestra | Vaughn Monroe And His Orchestra 1943 | Circle | CCD-45
Vette
Django Reinhardt And The Quintet Du Hot Club De France | Django Reinhardt Portrait | Barclay | DALP 2/1939
Alex Möller-Lena Willemark Group | Hästen Och Tranan | ACT | 9244-2
Via Appia
Bourbon Street | Jazzpuzzle | GIC | GD 4.1411
Via Ronco
Guido Manusardi Sextet | Acqua Fragia | SPLASC(H) Records | H 178
Viable
Phil Woods' The Little Big Band | Real Life | Chesky | JD 47
Viaggio
Michel Portal-Richard Galliano | Concerts | Dreyfus Jazz Line | FDM 36661-2
Richard Galliano Quartet | Gallianissimo! The Best Of Richard Galliano | Dreyfus Jazz Line | FDM 36616-2
Viaggio | Dreyfus Jazz Line | FDM 36562-9
Richard Galliano Trio | Concert Inédits | Dreyfus Jazz Line | FDM 36606-2
Viaggio Imaginario
The Enriquillo Winds | Melodia Para Congas | Mapleshade | 04632
Vibe Boogie
Steve Davis Sextet | Vibe Up! | Criss Cross | Criss 1178
Vibes-
Leonard Feather's Esquire All Stars | Metropolitan Opera House Jam Session | Jazz Anthology | 550212
Vibraphone Blues
Benny Goodman Quartet | Jazz Gallery:Lionel Hampton Vol.1 | RCA | 2114170-2
Victor Jazz History Vol.20:Jazz & The Blues | RCA | 2135739-2
Lionel Hampton Sextet | You Better Know It | Impulse(MCA) | IMP 12972
Vibraphonissina
Connie Crothers Trio | Perception | Steeplechase | SCCD 31022
Vibration
Keith Tippett Group | Warm Spirits-Cool Spirits | View | VS 101 IMS
Vibrations
Dewey Redman Trio | Tarik | Affinity | AFF 42
Teddy Charles Tentet | The Teddy Charles Tentet | Atlantic | 790983-2
Vice Versa
Rick Hollander Quartet | Out Here | Timeless | CD SJP 309
Vicksburg Is My Home
Harold Vick Orchestra Quintet | Steppin' Out | Blue Note | 852433-2
Vicky's Dream
Dan Barrett Septet | Dan Barrett's International Swing Party | Nagel-Heyer | CD 067
Vic's Spot
Prestige Blues Swingers | Jam Session In Swingville | Prestige | P 24051
Victim
Claire Martin With The Jim Mullen Quartet And Special Guests | Devil May Care | Linn Records | AKD 021
Victor
Uli Beckerhoff Septet | Private Life | Nabel Records:Jazz Network | CD 4657
Dave Stryker And The Bill Warfield Big Band | Nomad | Steeplechase | SCCD 31371
Victoria
Lonnie Plaxico Group | Plaxico | Muse | MCD 5389
Ran Blake-Jaki Byard Duo | Improvisations | Soul Note | 121022-2
Victory Ball
The Metronome All Stars | Dizzy Gillspie-The Complete RCA Victor Recordings | Bluebird | 63 66528-2
Jazz Gallery:Charlie Parker Vol.1 | RCA | 2114174-2
Victory Blues
John Handy's Louisiana Shakers | John Handy-The Very First Recordings | American Music | AMCD-51
Victory Stride
Swing And Blues Band | Talk To Me | Plainisphare | PAV 808
Victory Stride(alt.take)
Barry Martyn's Band | Kid Thomas And Emanuel Paul With Bary Martyn's Band' | GHB Records | BCD 257
Vidala
Gato Barbieri Group | Bolivia | RCA | FD 10158
Viddene
Eddy Palermo Quartet | Ganimede | EdiPan | NPG 808
Video Games
Gordon Brisker Quintet | The Gift | Naxos Jazz | 86001-2
Vidit Suum Dulcem
Vido Musso's All Stars | Loaded:Vido Musso/Stan Getz | Savoy | SV 0227(MG 12074)
Vieil Aller
Véronique Gillet And Fernando Freitez With Carlos Franco | Terracota | Acoustic Music Records | 319.1056.2
Viejos Tiempos
Dirk Raulf Group | Theater I (Bühnenmusik) | Poise | Poise 07
Viel Lärm Um Nichts(Schauspielhaus Graz)
Günter Sommer | Hörmusik III:Sächsische Schatulle | Intakt Records | CD 027
Viele Haben Keine Sprache
Morgenland/Yarinistan | Vielleicht | Riskant | 568-72229
Vienen Del Sur Los Recuerdos
Carl Ravazza And His Orchestra | The Uncollected: Carl Ravazza | Hindsight | HSR 117
Vienna
Greenfish | Perfume Light... | TipToe | TIP-888831 2
The Rippingtons | Weekend In Monaco | GRP | GRP 96812
Vienna Discussion(Theme Song)
Joachim Palden | Boogie Woogie And Ragtime Piano Contest | Gold Records | 11046
Vienna(part 1)
Keith Jarrett | Vienna Concert | ECM | 1481(513437-2)
Vienna(part 2)
Thomas Reimer Trio | Vienna's Heardt | Edition Collage | EC 506-2
Vienna's Heardt
Jim Tomlinson Quintet | Only Trust Your Heart | Candid | CCD 79758
Vienne Blues
Mike Westbrook Orchestra | The Orchestra Of Smith's Academy | Enja | ENJ-9358 2
Viennese Waltz
Stephane Grappelli Trio | Unique Piano Session | Jazz Anthology | JA 5216
Vierd Blues
Dave Pike Quartet | Bill Evans:Piano Player | CBS | CK 65361
Hampton Hawes Trio | The Green Leaves Of Summer | Original Jazz Classics | OJCCD 476-2
Oscar Peterson Quartet | The Jazz Giants Play Miles Davis:Milestones | Prestige | PCD 24225-2
Phineas Newborn Jr. Quartet | Stockholm Jam Session, Vol.2 | Steeplechase | SCCD 36026
Viernes Santo(Introduccion-Part a-Part b)
Manfred Schulze Bläserquintett | Viertens | FMP | 1230
Vierundfünfzig
Christopher Dell D.R.A. | Future Of The Smallest Form | Jazz 4 Ever Records:Jazz Network | J4E 4754
Vierundvierzig A
Wolfgang Fuchs-Hans Schneider-Klaus Huber | Momente | FMP | 0610
View From The Outside
Muhal Richard Abrams Octet | View From Within | Black Saint | 120081-2
Viewpoint
Frank Vaganee 5 | Picture A View | B.Sharp Records | CDS 080
Vigil
John Coltrane-Elvin Jones | John Coltrane:The Classic Quartet-Complete Impulse Studio Recordings | Impulse(MCA) | 951280-2
Liz Story Group | Speechless | RCA | PL 83037
Vignette
Coleman Hawkins Quintet | The High And Mighty Hawk | Affinity | AFF 163
Owen Howard Quintet | Sojourn | Koch Jazz | KOC 3-7807-2
Vignette I
Andrew Rathbun Group | True Stories | Fresh Sound Records | FSNT 099 CD
Vignette II
True Stories | Fresh Sound Records | FSNT 099 CD
Vignette III
Joe Maneri Quartet | Tenderly | HatOLOGY | 525
Vilderness 1
Nils Petter Molvaer Group | Solid Ether | ECM | 1722(543365-2)
Vilderness 2
Artie Shaw And His Orchestra | The Original Sounds Of The Swing Era Vol.7 | RCA | CL 05517 DP
Vilia
Johnny Smith Quintet | Moonlight In Vermont | Roulette | 596593-2
Zoot Sims:The Complete 1944-1954 Small Group Sessions(Master Takes),Vol.3 | Blue Moon | BMCD 1040

Villa
Tome XX | The Red Snapper | Jazz Haus Musik | JHM 0047 CD
Villa Air Bell
Katrina Krimsky-Trevor Watts | Stella Malu | ECM | 1199
Villa In Brazil
Stella Malu | ECM | 1199
Tony Scott-Bill Evans Quintet | A Day In New York | Fresh Sound Records | FSR-CD 0160(2)
Villa Paradiso
Kenny Clarke-Francy Boland Big Band | Three Latin Adventures | MPS | 529095-2
Villa Radieuse-
Drümmele Maa | Villa Rhododendron | Jazz Haus Musik | JHM 25
Villa Tiamo
Bobby Hackett All Stars | Giants Of Traditional Jazz | Savoy | SV 0277
Village Blues
John Coltrane Quartet | Coltrane Jazz | Atlantic | 7567-81344-2
John Coltrane-The Heavyweight Champion:The Complete Atlantic Recordings | Atlantic | 8122-71984-2
Village Blues(alt.take)
Tom Beckham Quartet | Suspicions | Fresh Sound Records | FSNT 075 CD
Village Children
Bill Watrous Big Band | Space Available | Double Time Records | DTRCD-124
Village Dance-
Badal Roy & Amit Chatterjee | Art Of The Duo: Endless Radiance | Tutu Records | 888178-2*
Village Dance No.1
Karl Ratzer Group | Moon Dancer | Enja | ENJ-9357 2
Village Lee
John Patton Quartet | The Lost Grooves | Blue Note | 831883-2
Village Lee(alt.take)
Jack Walrath Sextet | Neohippus | Blue Note | B 1-91101
Village Voice
Larry Vuckovich Septet | City Sounds,Village Voices | Palo Alto | PA 8012
Villanella
Gianluigi Trovesi-Gianni Coscia | In Cerca Di Cibo | ECM | 1703(543034-2)
Ran Blake-David 'Knife' Fabris | Something To Live For | HatOLOGY | 527
Vilshofen
Joe Farrell/Louis Hayes Quartet | Vim 'N' Vigor | Timeless | CD SJP 197
Vindarna Sucka(Sorrow Wind)
Paul Giger Trio | Vindonissa | ECM | 1836(066069-2)
Vindonissa
Vindonissa | ECM | 1836(066069-2)
Vindonissa(intro)
Chris Cheek Quintet | Vine | Fresh Sound Records | FSNT 086 CD
Vine
George Adams & Blue Brass Connection | Cool Affairs | PAO Records | PAO 10010
Vine Laces
The Ritz | Movin' Up | Denon Compact Disc | CY-72526
Vineyard Blues
Susan Weinert Band | The Bottom Line | VeraBra Records | CDVBR 2177-2
Vinnie
Dick Berk Sextet | One By One | Reservoir | RSR CD 143
Vinsonology
Dick de Graaf-Tony Lakatos Quintet | New York Straight Ahead | Challenge | CHR 70033
Vinyl Junkie
Tom Bennecke & Space Gurilla | Wind Moments | Take Twelve On CD | TT 009-2
Vinz
Toots Thielemans-Eugen Cicero Quartet | Nice To Meet You | Intercord | 145034
Violet
Miles Davis With The Danish Radio Big Band | Aura | CBS | CK 63962
Sax Appeal Saxophone Quartet plus Claudio Fasoli | Giotto | Soul Note | 121309-2
Violet Into The Blue
Blind John Davis | You Better Cut That Out | Steeplechase | SCB 9008
Violet Song
Marilyn Crispell-Barry Guy-Gerry Hemingway | Cascades | Music & Arts | CD 853
Violeta
Roberto Ottaviano Koiné | Hybrid And Hot | SPLASC(H) Records | CD H 453-2
Violets For Your Furs
Billie Holiday With The Ray Ellis Orchestra | Grandes Voix Du Jazz | CBS | 467147-2
Dave Brubeck Quartet | Angel Eyes | CBS | SRCS 9368
J.R. Monterose Quartet | The Message | Fresh Sound Records | FSR-CD 0201
John Coltrane Quartet | John Coltrane-The Prestige Recordings | Prestige | 16 PCD 4405-2
Johnny Hartman With The Masahiko Kikuchi Trio | For Trane | Blue Note | 835346-2
Nat Adderley Trio | Wes Montgomery-The Complete Riverside Recordings | Riverside | 12 RCD 4408-2
Ray Brown Trio With Nicholas Payton | Some Of My Best Friends Are The Trumpet Players | Telarc Digital | CD 83495
Singers Unlimited With The Art Van Damme Quintet | The Singers Unlimited:Magic Voices | MPS | 539130-2
Stacey Kent With The Jim Tomlison Quintet | Dreamsville | Candid | CCD 79775
Tommy Dorsey And His Orchestra | Frank Sinatra And The Tommy Dorsey Orchestra | RCA | 2668701-2
Forever | RCA | NL 89859 DP
Violin Concerto(3 movements)
Shem Guibbory | Steve Reich | ECM | 1168(827287-2)
Violoncello Bastardo
Duke Ellington And His Orchestra | Live In Paris 1959 | Affinity | CD AFS 777
Viper's Drag
Dick Wellstood | This Is The One...Dig! | Solo Art | SACD-119
Neville Dickie-Louis Mazetier | Dickie-Mazetier:Harlem Strut | Stomp Off Records | CD 1302
Viper's Dream
Quintet Du Hot Club De France | Django Reinhardt:Echoes Of France | Dreyfus Jazz Line | FDM 36726-2
Django/Django In Rome 1949-1050 | BGO Records | BGOCD 366
Django Reinhardt:Djangology | EMI Records | 780659-2
George Russell Sextet | Trip to Prillarguri | Soul Note | 121029-2
Virgen De Regla-
Ornette Coleman & Prime Time | Virgin Beauty | CBS | 489433-2
Virgin De La Nieve
Abdullah Ibrahim Quartet | Duke's Memories | String | BLE 233853
Virgin Jungle
James Newton Ensemble | The African Flower | Blue Note | 746292-2
Pili-Pili | Pili-Pili | JA & RO | JARO 4141-2
Steve Lacy Septet | The Door | RCA | PL 83049
Virginia
Ken Colyers's Jazzmen | Colyer's Pleasure | Lake | LACD 34
Virginia's Song
Willem Breuker Kollektief | Willem Breuker Kollektief | BVHAAST | 031
Virgo
Dejan Terzic European Assembly | Coming Up | double moon | DMCHR 71034
Frank Morgan-George Cables Duo | Double Image | Contemporary | CCD 14035-2
Jazz Detroit & Lee Harper | Jazz Detroit | Die Mühle Records | 850101
The Tough Tenors With The Antonio Farao European Trio | Tough Tenors | Jazz 4 Ever Records:Jazz Network | J4E 4761

Tito Puente Orchestra | Royal T | Concord | CCD 4553
Mary Lou Williams Orchestra | Masters Of The Modern Piano | Verve | 2-2514 IMS
Virtue
Franco Ambrosetti Quintet | Light Breeze | Enja | ENJ-9331 2
Virtuosismo
George Wallington | Virtuoso | Denon Compact Disc | 35C38-7248
Visa
Charlie Parker Quintet | Bird At St. Nick's | Original Jazz Classics | OJC20 041-2(JWS 500)
Charlie Parker Septet | Charlie Parker: The Verve Years (1948-50) | Verve | 2-2501 IMS
Charlie Parker Sextet | Charlie Parker 1950-1951:The Complete Bird At Birdland Vol.1 | Fat Boy Jazz | FBB 901
The Charlie Parker Memorial Band | Bird Still Lives! Vol.1 | Timeless | CD SJP 373
Visa Fran Leksand
Art Farmer Quartet Feat Jim Hall | To Sweden With Love | Atlantic | AMCY 1016
Vis-A-Vis
Joe Henderson Quartet | Joe Henderson:The Milestone Years | Milestone | 8MCD 4413-2
Anne Morre | Anne Morre | Bellaphon | BCH 33008
Viscosity
J.J.Johnson Quintet | The Eminent J.J.Johnson Vol.2 | Blue Note | 532144-2
Viscosity(alt.take)
Johnny Hodges And The Ellington Men | The Big Sound | Verve | MV 2525 IMS
Viscous Consistency
Tabla & Strings | Islands Everywhere | Tutu Records | 888208-2*
Vishnu Blues
Yusef Lateef Ensemble | Nocturnes | Atlantic | 7567-81977-2
Visible Particles
Eberhard Weber Group | Fluid Rustle | ECM | 1137
Visible Thoughts
Jan Garbarek Group | Visible World | ECM | 1585(529086-2)
Visible World(chiaro)
Visible World | ECM | 1585(529086-2)
Visible World(scuro)
Frank Marocco Quintet | Road To Marocco | Discovery | DS 854 IMS
Vision
Lee Konitz-Frank Wunsch | Into It(Solos & Duos) | West Wind | WW 2090
Steve Tibbetts Group | Bye Bye Safe Journey | ECM | 1270
The Timeless Art Orchestra | Without Words | Satin Doll Productions | SDP 1005-1 CD
Vision Is A Naked Sword
Oregon | Out Of The Woods | Elektra | ELK K 52101
Vision Quest
Mike Nock Trio | Ondas | ECM | 1220
Visionary
Thomas Faist Jazzquartet | Visionary | JHM Records | JHM 3609
Ellery Eskelin Trio | Kulak, 29 & 30 | HatOLOGY | 521
Visions
Bobby Hutcherson Quintet | Spiral | Blue Note | LT 996 (GXK 8178)
Jimmy Ponder Group | The Best Of The Jazz Guitars | LRC Records | CDC 8531(874372)
Larry Young Quartet | Mother Ship | Blue Note | LT 1038
Marcus Miller Group | Tales | Dreyfus Jazz Line | FDM 36571-2
Mark Turner Quintet | Ballad Session | Warner | 9362-47631-2
Michael Cochrane Quartet | Path Ways | Steeplechase | SCCD 31542
Mick Goodrick-David Liebman-Wolfgang Muthspiel | In The Same Breath | CMP Records | CMP CD 71
Visions-
Kenny Wheeler With L'Orchestre Chambre de Montréal | Visions | Justin Time | JTR 8413-2
Visions In The Wood
Phil Woods Quartet | Here´s To My Lady | Chesky | JD 3
Visions Of Gaudi
Tom Harrell Sextet | Sail Away | Original Jazz Classics | OJCCD 1095-2(C- 14054-2)
Dave Pike Sextet | On A Gentle Note | Muse | MR 5168
Visitation
Sam Jones Quintet | Visitation | Steeplechase | SCS 1097
Visite Du Vigile
Nazaire | Who's Blues | Ronnie Scott's Jazz House | JHCD 019
Visitor From Nowhere
Wayne Shorter-Herbie Hancock | 1+1:Herbie Hancock-Wayne Shorter | Verve | 537564-2
Visitor From Somewhere
Modern Jazz Quartet | Space | EMI Records | 8538162
Visitors
Loft Line | Visitors | Acoustic Music Records | 319.1085.2
Vista
Al Di Meola World Sinfonia | Heart Of The Immigrants | Inak | 700792
Visur Vatnsenda-Rósu
John Wolf Brennan-Daniele Patumi | Ten Zentences | L+R Records | CDLR 45066
Vital Transformation
Big Joe Williams | Blues Masters Vol.2 | Storyville | STCD 8002
Vite Ayi
Bill Carrothers-Bill Stewart | Bill Carrothers Duets With Bill Stewart | Dreyfus Jazz Line | FDM 37002-2
Vitrines
Eric Le Lann Group | New York | OMD | VB 053 CD
Viva Brazilia
Cal Tjader Quintet | Cal Tjader's Latin Concert | Original Jazz Classics | OJCCD 643-2(F 8014)
Viva Cepeda
San Francisco Moods | Original Jazz Classics | OJC 277(F 8017)
Viva Coltrane
Toto Blanke-Rudolf Dasek | Meditation | ALISO Records | AL 1026
Viva Dell' Amore
Barney Kessel And His Orchestra | Barney Kessel Plays Carmen | Original Jazz Classics | OJC 269(C 7563)
Viva El Toro
Gato Barbieri Orchestra | Chapter Three:Viva Emiliano Zapata | Impulse(MCA) | 2292-52001-1
Viva La Danzarina-
Allen Toussaint Group | Motion | Warner | WPCP 4416
Viva La Quince Brigada(Long Live The Fifteenth Brigade)
Gabriel Pérez Group | La Chipaca | Green House Music | CD 1011
Viva Los Novios
Bobby Lyle Group | The Journey | Atlantic | 7567-82138-2
Viva Mandela-
Stan Kenton And His Orchestra | One Night Stand | Choice | CHCD 71051
Viva Prado
Innovations-Live 1951 | Bandstand | BDCD 1519
Viva Tirado
Gerald Wilson Big Band | Moment Of The Truth | Pacific Jazz | 792928-2
Vivace-
Swingle Singers | Jazz Sebastian Bach Vol.2 | Philips | 542553-2
Vivace-Concerto for two Violins In D Minor(BWV 1043)
Jacques Loussier Trio | Reflections Of Bach | Teldec | 2292-44431-2
Vivien
Herb Geller-Brian Kellock | Hollywood Portraits | Hep | CD 2078
Vivien Leigh
Astrud Gilberto With The Marty Paich Orchestra | Verve Jazz Masters 9:Astrud Gilberto | Verve | 519824-2
Vivo Sohando
Getz-Gilberto Quintet | Getz/Gilberto | Polydor | 521414-2
Getz/Gilberto:The Girl From Ipanema | CTI Records | PDCTI 1105-2
Stan Getz Quintet Feat. Astrud Gilberto | Getz/Gilberto | Verve | 589595-2 SACD
Antonio Carlos Jobim With The Claus Ogerman Orchestra | Verve Jazz Masters 13:Antonio Carlos Jobim | Verve | 516409-2

Vivo Sohando(Dreamer)
Compact Jazz: Antonio Carlos Jobim | Verve | 843273-2
Zona Sul | Pure Love | Nagel-Heyer | CD 3039
Pure Love | Nagel-Heyer | CD 3039
Vivo Sohando(Dreamer-alt.take)
Susannah McCorkle And Her Sextet | Sabia | Concord | CCD 4418
Vivre Avec Toi
Andre Pasdoc With The Orchestra Vola | Jazz In Paris:Django Reinhardt-Django Et Compagnie | EmArCy | 549241-2 PMS
Vivre Pour Toi
Jazz Pistols | Special Treatment | Lipstick Records | LIP 8971-2
Vix 9
Jimmy Cleveland And His All Stars | Introducing Jimmy Cleveland | Verve | 543752-2
Vocal Tracked
Wolfgang Fuchs | Solos & Duets | FMP | OWN-90004
Voce E Eu(You And I)
Stan Getz Quintet Feat. Astrud Gilberto | Verve Jazz Masters 53:Stan Getz-Bossa Nova | Verve | 529904-2
Lisa Wahlandt & Mulo Francel And Their Fabulous Bossa Band | Bossa Nova Affair | Edition Collage | EC 534-2
Voce E Linda
Astrud Gilberto With The Walter Wanderley Quartet | A Certain Smile A Certain Sadness | Verve | 557449-2
Voce Ja Foi Bahia
Ana Caram Group | Bossa Nova | Chesky | JD 129
Voce Vai Ver(You'll See)
Art Studio & Tiziana Ghiglioni | Onde | SPLASC(H) Records | CD H 133-2
Vodka
George Gruntz Trio With Franco Ambrosetti | Mock-Lo-Motion | TCB Records | TCB 95552
Vodoun Amon
Pili-Pili | Pili-Pili Live 88 | JA & RO | JARO 4139-2
David Fiuczynski-John Medeski Group | Lunar Crush | Gramavision | R2 79498
Vogel Jakob
Duo Due | Tre | Amadeo | 837950-2
Vogelpredigt
Thilo von Westernhagen Group | Forgotten Gardens | Acoustic Music Records | AMC 1011
Voi Che Amate
Chinese Compass | Chinese Compass | dacapo | DCCD 9443
Voi,Che Sapete
Gary Peacock Quartet | Voice From The Past-Paradigm | ECM | 1210(517768-2)
Voice From The Past
Marilyn Crispell-Gary Peacock-Paul Motian | Amaryllis | ECM | 1742(013400-2)
Charles Lloyd Quartet | Voice In The Night | ECM | 1674(559445-2)
Voice In The Night
Johannes Mössinger | Spring In Versailles | double moon | DMCD 1004-2
Voice Of A Lion
Last Exit | Last Exit | Enemy | EMCD 101(03501)
Voice Of The North
Bill Carrothers Quartet | The Electric Bill | Dreyfus Jazz Line | FDM 36631-2
Voice Of The People
Don Cherry/Ed Blackwell | El Corazon | ECM | 1230
Voice Of The Silence
Ed Sarath Quintet | Voice Of The Wind | Owl Time Line | 3819012
Voice Solo
Walter 'Buddy Boy' Hawkins | The Greatest In Country Blues Vol.1(1927-1930) | Story Of Blues | CD 3521-2
Voices
Spies & Guests | By The Way Of The World | Telarc Digital | CD 83305
Voices Behind Locked Doors
Barbara Thompson's Paraphernalia | A Cry From The Heart | VeraBra Records | CDVBR 2021-2
Cedar Walton Quintet | As Long As There's Music | Muse | MCD 5405
Voices Deep Within Me
Jimmy Rowles-Red Mitchell Trio | I'm Glad There Is You | Contemporary | CCD 14032-2
Voicings
George Colligan Quintet | Constant Source | Steeplechase | SCCD 31462
Voila
Wiener Art Orchester | Tango From Obango | Art Record | 1002(ES 7819)
Vol D'Elephant(part 1)
Vincent Courtois Quartet | Translucide | Enja | ENJ-9380 2
Vol D'Elephant(part 2)
Jacky Terrasson-Emmanuel Pahud Quartet | Into The Blue | Blue Note | 557257-2
Vol Du Bourdon(Rimsky-Korsakov)
Slim And Slam | Slim & Slam:Original 1938 Recordings Vol.1 | Tax | S 1-2
Volando
Steve Lacy Sextet | The Condor | Soul Note | 121135-2
Volare
Francesca Simone Trio | Guardia Li | Minor Music | 801093
Lionel Hampton Sextet | Seven Come Eleven | Memo Music | HDJ 4054
Louis Armstrong And His All Stars | Live At The Cote D'Azur | Bandstand | BDCD 1521
Ran Blake | Third Stream Recompositions | Owl Records | 017
Volare (Nel Blu Dipinto Di Blu)
Joelle Leandre | Palimpseste | Hat Art | CD 6103
Volcano
Randy Weston Orchestra | Volcano Blues | Verve | 519269-2
Volcano For Hire
Weather Report | In Performance At The Playboy Jazz Festival | Elektra | MUS 96.0298-1
Volcano's Daughter
Massimo De Mattia Group | The Silent Drama | SPLASC(H) Records | CD H 442-2
Volière(Saint-Saens)
Dave Ballou Trio | Volition | Steeplechase | SCCD 31460
Volition
Orrin Evans Trio | Grown Folk Bizness | Criss Cross | Criss 1175
Volkslieder:
Volker Schlott Quartet | Akribik | Acoustic Music Records | 319.1165.2
Volta Trais
Franco D'Andrea Trio | Volte | Owl Records | 052 CD
Volunteered Slavery
Roland Kirk Quintet | Live In Paris 1970 Vol.2 | France's Concert | FCD 115
Volupte
Ernie Krivda-Bill Dobbins | The Art Of The Ballad | Koch Jazz | KOC 3-7806-2
Volver
Horacio Molina With Band | Tango Cancion | Messidor | 15910
Volvio Una Noche
Michael Kersting Quintet | Michael Kersting 'Five' | Bassic-Sound | CD 004
Vom Himmel Hoch
Wolf Mayer Trio | I Do Believe In Spring | Triptychon | 400403
Heinz Sauer Quintet | Lost Ends:Live at Alte Oper Frankfurt | free flow music | ffm 0594
Vom Himmel Hoch...
Heinz Sauer-Bob Degen Duo | Plaza Lost And Found | L+R Records | CDLR 45044
Chris Hinze-Sigi Schwab Duo | Backstage | Melos Music | CDGS 801
Vom Wind
Andreas Willers | Can I Go Like This? | Jazz Haus Musik | JHM 0070 CD
Von Allen Guten Geistern
Norbert Stein Pata Orchester | Die Wilden Pferde Der Armen Leute | Pata Musik | JHM 39
Von Der Gewöhnlichen Traurigkeit

Attila Zoller Trio | The K & K In New York | L+R Records | LR 40009
Von Der Tönenden Insel(Carnet De La Vie)
Sigi Schwab | Meditation Vol.2 | Melos Music | CDGS 705
Von Gott Will Ich Nicht Lassen
Ulli Bögershausen | Best Of Ulli Bögershausen | Laika Records | LK 93-045
Von Irgendwo Nach Nirgendwo
Ulli Bögershausen-Reinhold Westerheide | Pictures | Laika Records | LK 35100932
David Binney Group | South | ACT | 9279-2
Von Joshua
Ekkehard Jost & Chromatic Alarm | Von Zeit Zu Zeit | Fish Music | FM 005 CD
Von Teit Zu Zeit
Rüdiger Carl | Vorn:Lieder Und Improvisationen Für Akkordeon, Bandoneon Und Ziehharmonika | FMP | 1110
Vonetta
Miles Davis Quintet | Miles Davis Quintet 1965-1968 | CBS | C6K 67398
Dirty Dozen Brass Band | Voodoo | CBS | CK 45042
Voodoo
Sonny Clark Memorial Quartet | Voodoo | Black Saint | 120109-2
Voodoo Child(Slight Return)
Robert Dick Group With The Soldier String Quartet | Third Stone From The Sun | New World Records | 80435-2
Voodoo Child(Slight Return)-
Gil Evans And The Monday Night Orchestra | Live At Sweet Basil | Electric Bird | K32Y 6017/8
Voodoo Chile
NDR Big Band | NDR Big Band-Bravissimo | ACT | 9232-2
NDR Big Band feat. Inga Rumpf | The Spirit Of Jimi Hendrix | Extra Records & Tapes | 11542
Voodoo Chile-
Pinguin Moschner-Joe Sachse | If 69 Was 96/The Music Of Jimi Hendrix | Aho-Recording | CD 1016
Voodoo Man
J.B.Lenoir | J.B.Lenoir | Blues Classics(L+R) | CDLR 82001
VooDoo Reprise
Tiziano Tononi Group | Going For The Magic | SPLASC(H) Records | HP 13
Vor Elise
Franz Koglmann Group | Venus In Transit | Between The Lines | btl 017(Efa 10186)
Voralberger Schuhgroßhändler(Some Like It Hot)
Claudio Puntin/Gerdur Gunnarsdóttir | Ýlir | ECM | 1749(158570-2)
Vorbankar
Emil Mangelsdorff Quartet | 10 Jahre Interaction Jazz | L+R Records | LR 40021
Vorgestern
Tabasco | Live Music | Jazz Classics | AU 11160
Vor-Nach I
Uwe Oberg | Dedicated | Jazz 'n' Arts Records | JNA 1603
Vor-Nach II
| Box:Billy Tipton Memorial Saxophone Quartet | New World Records | 80495-2
Vorspiel
David Friedman Trio | Other Worlds | Intuition Records | INT 3210-2
Vorstellung
Dave Holland Quintet | The Razor's Edge | ECM | 1353
Vortex
Flip Phillips Quartet | Flip Phillips Complete 1947-1951 Verve Master Takes | Definitive Records | DRCD 11201
The Blue Notes Legacy | Live In South Afrika 1964 | Ogun | OGCD 007
Vo-Sa
God Is My Co-Pilot | Mir Shlufn Nisht | Avant | AVAN 032
Vote For Miles
Chick Webb And His Orchestra | Jazz Drumming Vol.1(1927-1937) | Fenn Music | FJD 2701
Vous Et Moi
Victory Of The Better Man | ...Wegen Brot... | CMP Records | CMP CD 69
Vouz Et Moi
Vladimir Shafranov Trio | White Nights | The Jazz Alliance | TJA 10018
Vox Humana
Gary Burton Quintet | Dreams So Real | ECM | 1072
Works | ECM | 823267-2
Voy Cantando
Alain Trudel Quartet | Jericho's Legacy | Naxos Jazz | 86021-2
Voyage
B&H | Groovin' Jazz Regensburg | I-Records | IR 319101
George Colligan | Small Room | Steeplechase | SCCD 31470
Lito Voyatzoglou Quintet | Tili-Tili-Tili | Praxis | GM 1003
Stan Getz Quartet | Soul Eyes | Concord | CCD 4783
Vincent Herring Quintet | Evidence | Landmark | LCD 1527-2
Voyage Noir
Jeremy Steig-Eddie Gomez | Music For Flute & Double-Bass | CMP Records | CMP 6
Voyage Out
Sunday Night Orchestra | Voyage Out | Mons Records | MR874305
Vozes(Saudades)
Ran Blake | The Blue Potato And Other Outrages | Milestone | M 9021
Vrancea
Badi Assad | Solo | Chesky | JD 99
Vuelvo Al Sur
John McLaughlin's Free Spirits | Tokyo Live | Verve | 521870-2
Vulcan Princess
Chick Corea Quartet | Compact Jazz: Chick Corea | Polydor | 831365-2
Vulcan Worlds
Art Erios | Thebe Stofar Terios | Nueva Records | NC 3010
Vulnerability
Christine Wodrascka | Vertical | FMP | CD 79
Vutu
Jonas Knutsson Group | Flower In The Sky | ACT | 9248-2
W(Souvenirs D'Enfance)
Kieler Saxophon Quartett | JazzNord | KlangRäume | 30100
W.R.U.
Ornette Coleman Quartet | Beauty Is A Rare Thing:Ornette Coleman-The Complete Atlantic Recordings | Atlantic | 8122-71410-2
Paul Plimley Trio | Density Of The Lovestruck Demons | Music & Arts | CD 906
W.W.
Thomas Heidepriem Quartet | Brooklyn Shuffle | L+R Records | CDLR 45084
Wabash
Mike Turk With The Alkaline Jazz Trio | A Little Taste Of Cannonball | Organic Music | ORGM 9708
Scott Hamilton And Friends | Blues,Bop & Ballads | Concord | CCD 4866
Wabash Blues
A Salute To Eddie Condon | A Salute To Eddie Condon | Nagel-Heyer | CD 004
Alex Welsh And His Jazz Band | Doggin' Around | Black Lion | BLCD 760510
Duke Ellington-Johnny Hodges All Stars | Back To Back | Verve | 521404-2
Dutch Swing College Band | Digital Anniversary | Philips | 824585-2 PMS
Echoes Of New Orleans | Live At Sweet Basil | Big Easy Records | BIG CD-005
Ken Colyer's Jazzmen | When I Leave The World Behind | GHB Records | BCD-152
Wabash Cannonball
Boots Randolph-Richie Cole Orchestra | Yakety Madness! | Palo Alto | PA 8041
Wabun
Köln Connection | Stadtgarten Series Vol.1 | Jazz Haus Musik | JHM 1001 SER
Wach,Nachtigal,Wach Auf
Keith Foley | Music For Christmas | dmp Digital Music Productions | CD 452
Wachet Auf Ruft Uns Die Stimme
Cal Tjader's Modern Mambo Sextet | Tjader Plays Mambo | Original Jazz Classics | OJC 274(F 3221)
Wack Wack
Stephan Schmolck Quartet | Rites Of Passage | L+R Records | CDLR 45064
Wacked Cat 'Lisa'
Chick Webb And His Orchestra | Chick Webb Vol.4-Ella Swings The Band | MCA | 1327
Wa-Da-Da
Marty Grosz And His Honoris Causa Jazz Band | Hooray For Bix! | Good Time Jazz | GTCD 10065-2
Willem Breuker Kollektief | Willem Breuker Kollektief | BVHAAST | 031
Wade
Bernard Purdie's Soul To Jazz | Bernard Purdie's Soul To Jazz | ACT | 9242-2
Wade In The Water
Charlie Haden-Hank Jones | Steal Away | Verve | 527249-2
David & Roselyn Group | Gospel From The Streets Of New Orleans | Sound Of New Orleans | SONO 1033
First Revolution Singers | A Cappella Gospel Anthology | Tight Harmony Records | TH 199404
Golden Gate Quartet | Golden Gate Quartet | CBS | 471559-2
Russell Gunn Quartet | Young Gunn | Muse | MCD 5539
Joe Williams And Friends | Feel The Spirit | Telarc Digital | CD 83362
Wadi Rum
Renaud Garcia-Fons Group | Navigatore | Enja | ENJ-9418 2
Wadi Rum(introducing)
Horace Parlan Quintet | The Best Of Blue Note Vol.2 | Blue Note | 797960-2
Wadin'
Speakin' My Piece | Blue Note | 868848-3
Wagging Along
Bola Sete Quintet | Bossa Nova | Original Jazz Classics | OJC 286(F 8349)
Wagon Wheels
Ray Anthony And His Orchestra | Ray Anthony's Houseparty Hop | Capitol | 1565471
Sonny Rollins Trio | Sonny Rollins-The Freelance Years:The Complete Riverside & Contemporary Recordings | Riverside | 5 RCD 4427-2
Michael Riessler Group | Orange | ACT | 9274-2
Wagon(1)
Orange | ACT | 9274-2
Wagon(2)-
Orange | ACT | 9274-2
Wagon(3)
Orange | ACT | 9274-2
Wagon(4)
Orange | ACT | 9274-2
Wagon(5)-
Dave Spencer & The Bluebirds | Live In Europe | Crosscut | CCD 11047
Wahaila
Perry Robinson 4 | Funk Dumpling | Savoy | SV 0255(MG 12177)
Waheera
Miles Davis/Tadd Dameron Quintet | All the Things You Are | Jazz Door | JD 12110
Wahlverwandtschaften:
Adam Noidlt-Intermission | Eine Permanent Helle Fläche | Jazz Haus Musik | JHM 53 CD
Waikikian
Andy LaVerne | In The Mood For A Classic-Andy LaVerne Plays Bud Powell | Steeplechase | SCCD 31342
Wail
Bud Powell Quintet | The Amazing Bud Powell Vol.1 | Blue Note | 300366
Fats Navarro/Tadd Dameron:Complete Blue Note & Capitol Sessions | Definitive Records | DRCD 11191
Rein de Graaff Quintet | New York Jazz | Timeless | CD SJP 130
Stanley Cowell Quartet | Back To The Beautiful | Concord | CCD 4398
Wail Bait
Clifford Brown Sextet | More Memorable Tracks | Blue Note | 300195(BNJ 61001)
Wail Bait(alt.take)
Clifford Brown-Gigi Gryce Sextet | Alternate Takes | Blue Note | BST 84428
Wail March
Sonny Rollins Quintet | Sonny Rollins:The Blue Note Recordings | Blue Note | 821371-2
James Moody And His Band | James Moody | Prestige | P 24015
Wail(alt.master)
Bud Powell Quintet | Fats Navarro/Tadd Dameron:Complete Blue Note & Capitol Sessions | Definitive Records | DRCD 11191
Wail(alt.take)
Fats Navarro And Tadd Dameron:The Complete Blues Note And Capitol Recordings | Blue Note | 833373-2
Wailea
David Benoit Group | Shaken Not Stirred | GRP | GRP 97872
Wailin' With Saury
Carlo Mombelli Quartet | Abstractions | West Wind | WW 2024
Wailing
Roy Eldridge-Alvin Stoller | The Urban Sessions/New Jazz Sound | Verve | 531637-2
Wailing Vessel
Bud Shank And Trombones | Cool Fool | Fresh Sound Records | FSR CD 507
Wailing Vessel(alt.take)
Don Lanphere Quintet | Fats Navarro:Nostalgia | Dreyfus Jazz Line | FDM 36736-2
Wailing Wall
Fats Navarro:The 1946-1949 Small Group Sessions(Studio Recordings-Master Takes),Vol.3 | Blue Moon | BMCD 1018
Waillie-Waillie
Woody Herman And His Orchestra | Live In Antibes 1965 | France's Concert | FCD 117
Wait A Little While
Patti Austin And Her Band | Live At The Bottom Line | CBS | 467922-2
Wait And Smile
Vanessa Rubin With Orchestra | Soul Eyes | Novus | PD 90591(874066)
Wait For The Magic
Steve Lacy Octet | Vespers | Soul Note | 121260-2
Wait No Longer
Sam Morrison Group | Natural Layers | Chiaroscuro | CR 184
Wait 'Till You See Her
Cy Coleman Trio | Cy Coleman | Fresh Sound Records | FSR 635(Seeco CELP 402)
Ella Fitzgerald With The Buddy Bregman Orchestra | The Rodgers And Hart Songbook | Verve | 821693-1
George Shearing Trio | Windows | MPS | 68200
Joe Venuti-Zoot Sims Quintet | Joe Venuti And Zoot Sims | Chiaroscuro | CR 142
Ross Tompkins Trio | Lost In The Stars | Concord | CJ 46
Wait 'Till You See My Cherie
Ben Pollack And His Park Central Orchestra | Ben Pollack Vol.3 | Jazz Oracle | BDW 8017
Wait!
Eb Davis Bluesband | Good Time Blues | Acoustic Music Records | AMC 1016
Waiter The Check
Niko Schäuble Quintet | On The Other Hand | Naxos Jazz | 86011-2
Waiter, Make Mine Blues
Giacomo Gates With The Harold Danko Quartet | Blue Skies | dmp Digital Music Productions | CD 3001
Waitin' For Robert E.Lee -> Waiting For The Robert E.Lee
Waiting
Gunter Hampel All Stars | Jubilation | Birth | 0038
Gunter Hampel And His Galaxie Dream Band | Ruomi | Birth | 0023
Hans Reichel | The Dawn Of Dachsman | FMP | 1140
Karen Mantler Group | Karen Mantler And Her Cat Arnold Get The Flu | Watt | XtraWatt/5
Lina Nyberg-Esbjörn Svensson | Close | Touché Music | TMcCD 004
Manfred Zepf Meets Andrew Cyrille | Paintings | West Wind | 003
Peter O'Mara Quintet | Avenue 'U' | Enja | 6046-2
Special EFX | Special Delivery | Limetree | FCD 0004
Gunter Hampel And His Galaxie Dream Band | Journey To The Song Within | Birth | 0017
Waiting (No.161)
Calvin Boze With Maxwell Davis & His Orchestra | Calvin Boze:The Complete Recordings 1945-1952 | Blue Moon | BMCD 6014
Waiting At The End Of The Road
Orange Kellin Trio | The Orange Kellin Trio | Big Easy Records | BIG CD-004
Waiting For An Answer
Henning Wolter Trio | Two Faces | double moon | DMCD 1003-2
Waiting For Angel Eyes
Rhythmstick(various groups) | Rhythmstick | CTI Records | CTI 1006-2
Waiting For Daylight
David Kikoski Trio | Almost Twilight | Criss Cross | Criss 1190
Waiting For Irene
Louis Mazetier-Peter Ecklund | A Friendly Chat | Jazz Connaisseur | JCCD 9932-2
Waiting For Katy
David Benoit Group | Letter To Evan | GRP | GRP 96872
Waiting For Maria
Munoz And His Group | Rendezvous With Now | India Navigation | IN 1034
Waiting For Siro
Anna Lauvergnac-Andy Bey | Anna Lauvergnac | TCB Records | TCB 21132
Waiting For Summer
Donald & Peggy Knaack | Inside The Plactic Lotus | Hat Art | 3517
Waiting For The Rain
| Pete Fountain And His Basin Street Six | 504 Records | 504CD 16
Waiting For The Robert E.Lee
Louis Jordan And His Tympany Five | Louis Jordan Vol.1-Hoodoo Man | Swingtime(Contact) | ST 1011
Turk Murphy And His Jazz Band | Turk Murphy's San Francisco Jazz-Vol.1 | Good Time Jazz | 12026
Waiting For Tom
Branford Marsalis Quartet | Scenes In The City | CBS | 468458-2
Waiting On A Sign From You
Bryan Lee And The Jump Street Five | The Blues Is... | Blues Beacon | BLU-1012 2
Waiting On You-
Harold Danko Quartet | Next Age | Steeplechase | SCCD 31350
Waiting Train
Hans Reichel | The Dawn Of Dachsman...Plus | FMP | CD 60
Wakaria(What's Up?)
The Guest Stars | The Guest Stars | Eigelstein | 568-72227
Wake Nicodemus
Magnificant Seventh's Brass Band | Authentic New Orleans Jazz Funeral | Mardi Gras Records | MG 1012
Wake Up
Patrick Karlhuber Group | So What | Edition Collage | EC 480-2
Wake Up Call
Urszula Dudziak And Band Walk Away | Magic Lady | IN+OUT Records | 7008-2
Rodney Jones Group | Soul Manifesto | Blue Note | 530499-2
Wake Up Call(interlude)
Soprano Summit | Chalumeau Blue | Chiaroscuro | CR 148
Wake Up Jacob
James Rivers Groups | The Best Of New Orleans Rhythm & Blues Vol.3 | Mardi Gras Records | MG 9009
Wake Up Old Lady
Russell Jacquet And His Yellow Jackets | Black California Vol.2 | Savoy | SV 0274
Wake Up Song
Billy Cobham Group | Life & Times | Atlantic | ATL 50253
Wakening
Ahmed Abdul-Malik Orchestra | Jazz Sounds Of Africa | Prestige | PRCD 24279-2
Wakida Hena
Jean-Luc Ponty Quintet | Aurora | Atlantic | 7567-81543-2
Waking Dream
Jon Gordon Sextet | Witness | Criss Cross | Criss 1121
Waking Up
Page One | Page One | Storyville | STCD 4171
Waktz Op.64 No.2 In C Sharp Minor(Chopin)
Jonas Hellborg | Elegant Punk | Day Eight Music | DEMCD 004
Walcott's Pendulum
Sven Ake Johansson-Alexander von Schlippenbach Duo | Kalfaktor A.Falke Und Andere Lieder | FMP | 0970
Waldsterben(Dying Of The Forest)
Bud Shank Quartet | At Jazz Alley | Contemporary | C 14027
Walidi Ya
Graham Haynes Group | Transition | Verve | 529039-2
Walk
Rolf Kühn-Joachim Kühn | Brothers | VeraBra Records | CDVBR 2184-2
Tom McKinley/Ed Schuller Group | Life Cycle | GM Recordings | GM 3001(807786)
Walk Away
Oscar Brown Jr. And His Group | Movin' On | Rhino | 8122-73678-2
Memphis Slim | So Long | America | AM 6130
Walk In The Night
Joe Lutcher's Jump Band | Joe Joe Jump | Charly | CRB 1038
Walk On
Leroy Vinnegar Sextet | Leroy Walks! | Contemporary | COP 011
Randy Johnson Quintet | Walk On WalkOn Walk ON | Muse | MCD 5432
Walk On Air
Anita O'Day And Her Trio | Anita And The Rhythm Section | Glendale | GLS 6001 IMS
Walk On By
George Benson With Orchestra | The Silver Collection: George Benson | Verve | 823450-2 PMS
Lenny White Group | Renderers Of Spirit | Hip Bop | HIBD 8014
Roland Kirk And His Orchestra | Rahsaan/The Complete Mercury Recordings Of Roland Kirk | Mercury | 846630-2
Sonny Stitt Quartet | Brothers 4 | Prestige | PCD 24261-2
The Prestige Collection:Sonny Stitt Soul Classics | Original Jazz Classics | OJCCD 6003-2
Stanley Turrentine Orchestra | Rough 'N' Tumble | Blue Note | 524552-2
Blue'n Soul-Do The Jerk | Blue Note | 799105-2
Franco Morone | Melodies Of Memories | Acoustic Music Records | 319.1153.2
Walk On The Wild Side
Herbie Mann Orchestra | Yellow Fever | Atlantic | SD 19252
Jimmy Smith With The Oliver Nelson Orchestra | Verve Jazz Masters 29:Jimmy Smith | Verve | 521855-2
Bashin' | Verve | 2304481 IMS
Walk On The Wild Side | CTI Records | PDCTI 1109-2
Tok Tok Tok | Love Again | Einstein Music | EM 01081
Gunter Hampel And His Galaxie Dream Band | Out From Under | Birth | 0016
Walk Right In
Willis Jackson Sextet | Gravy | Prestige | PCD 24254-2
The Dynatones feat.Charlie Musselwhite | Live | Red Lightnin' | RL 0044
Walk Tall
Cannonball Adderley Quintet | Julian Cannonball Adderlry: Salle Pleyel/Olympia | Laserlight | 36126
Nils Landgren Funk Unit | Paint It Blue:A Tribute To Cannonball Adderley | ACT | 9243-2
Live In Montreux | ACT | 9265-2
Cannonball Adderley Group | Phenix | Fantasy | FCD 79004-2
Walk Tall-

Cannonball Adderley Sextet | Cannonball Adderley Birthday Celebration | Fantasy | FANCD 6087-2
Clarence Williams' Jazz Kings | Clarence Williams-The Columbia Recordings Vol.1:Dreaming The Hours Away | Frog | DGF 14

Walk The Walk
Bill Matthews And His New Orleans Dixieland Band | Recorded In New Orleans Vol. 1 | Good Time Jazz | GTCD 12019-2

Walk With My Father
Five Blind Boys Of Mississippi | My Desire/There's A God Somewhere | Mobile Fidelity | MFCD 769

Walkabout
Paolo Fresu Sextet | Ensalada Mistica | SPLASC(H) Records | CD H 415-2

Walk-A-Way
Buddy Johnson And His Orchestra | Buddy And Ella Johnson 1953-1964 | Bear Family Records | BCD 15479 DH

Walk'Em
Go Ahead & Rock Rock Rock | Official | 6011

Walkie Talkie
Arnett Cobb Quintet | Movin' Right Along | Original Jazz Classics | OJCCD 1074-2(P 7216)

Walkin'
Art Pepper Plus Eleven | Art Pepper + Eleven | Contemporary | CSA 7568-6
Modern Jazz Classics | Original Jazz Classics | OJC20 341-2
A Treasury Of Modern Jazz Classics | Mobile Fidelity | MFCD 805
Candid Jazz Masters | The Candid Jazz Masters:For Miles | Candid | CCD 79710
Chet Baker Quintet | Chet Baker:The Most Important Jazz Album Of 1964/65 | Roulette | 581829-2
Chet Baker Plays & Sings | West Wind | WW 2108
Cornell Dupree Group | Bop 'N' Blues | Kokopelli Records | KOKO 1302
Elements | Illumination | RCA | PD 83031(874013)
Gene Ammons-Sonny Stitt Quintet | Verve Jazz Masters 50:Sonny Stitt | Verve | 527651-2
George Shearing Quintet | Jazz Concert | Capitol | EMS 1157
Jam Session | The Concert 23.6.1958 | Jazzline | ???
Joe Lovano With The Junko Onishi Trio | Tenor Time | somethin'else | 300230(TOCJ 5584)
Leroy Vinnegar Sextet | Leroy Walks! | Contemporary | COP 011
Marc Cohen Quartet | My Foolish Heart | Jazz City | 660.53.014
Michel Portal-Martial Solal | Fast Mood | RCA | 2169310-2
Miles Davis All Star Sextet | Walkin' | Original Jazz Classics | OJC20 213-2
Miles Davis All Stars | Miles Davis All Stars | Jazz Band Records | EB 409(835651)
Miles Davis Quintet | Greatest Hits | CBS | CK 65418
Stockholm 1960 | Royal Jazz | RJD 509
Paris,France | Moon Records | MCD 021-1
Seven Steps To Heaven | Jazz Door | JD 1225
Miles Davis In Stockholm Complete | Dragon | DRCD 228
Miles Davis With Gil Evans & His Orchestra | Live Miles-More From The Legendary Carnegie Hall Concert | CBS | 460064-2
Paul Gonsalves Quintet | Gettin' Together | Original Jazz Classics | OJCCD 203-2
Phineas Newborn Jr. Quartet | Stockholm Jam Session, Vol.2 | Steeplechase | SCCD 36026
Robin Eubanks Group | Different Perspectives | JMT Edition | 834424-2
Sonny Stitt And His West Coast Friends | Groovin' High | Eastworld | CP 32-5423
Sonny Stitt Quintet | The Champ | 32 Jazz | 32084

Walkin'-
Andy Kirk And His Twelve Clouds Of Joy | Big Band Bounce & Boogie-Andy Kirk And His Clouds Of Joy:Walkin' & Swingin' | Affinity | AFS 1011

Walkin' And Cookin' Blues
B.B.King And His Band | B. B. King, 1949-1950 | Anthology of the Blues | AB 5611

Walkin' Blues
Muddy Waters Blues Band | Muddy Waters-The Collection | MCA | MCD 18961
Oscar Klein | Oscar Klein Pickin' The Blues-Vol. 1 | Intercord | 150005

Walkin' By The River
Stan Kenton And His Orchestra | Rendezvous With Kenton | Creative World | ST 1057

Walkin' Down The Highway In A Raw Red Egg
Donald Harrison With The Guardians Of The Flame And The Mardi Gras Indians & Dr. John | Indian Blues | Candid | CCD 79514

Walkin' In Brussels
Bill Coleman And His Seven | Eartha Kitt-Doc Cheatham-Bill Coleman | Swing | SW 8410 IMS

Walkin' My Baby Back Home
Ed Bickert-Don Thompson Duo | Ed Bickert/Don Thompson | Sackville | 4005
Joe Pass | Unforgettable | Pablo | 2310964-2
John Pizzarelli Trio | P.S. Mr.Cole | RCA | 2663563-2
Jörg Seidel Group | I Feel So Smoochie: A Tribute To Nat King Cole | Edition Collage | EC 532-2
Leroy Vinnegar Sextet | Leroy Walks! | Contemporary | COP 011
Oscar Peterson-Stephane Grappelli Quartet | Jazz In Paris:Oscar Peterson-Stephane Grappelli Quartet Vol.1 | EmArCy | 013028-2
Papa Bue's Viking Jazzband Feat.Wild Bill Davison & Gustav Winckler | All That Meat And No Potatoes | Storyville | SLP 280

Walkin' On The Air
Clifton Chenier Group | On Tour | EPM Musique | FDC 5505

Walkin' On The Moon...
Amy Kay Band With Guests | Walking On Thin Ice | L+R Records | CDLR 42072

Walkin' Shoes
Art Pepper Plus Eleven | Art Pepper + Eleven | Contemporary | CSA 7568-6
Modern Jazz Classics | Original Jazz Classics | OJC20 341-2
A Treasury Of Modern Jazz Classics | Mobile Fidelity | MFCD 805
Gerry Mulligan Quartet | Chet Baker:Complete 1952 Fantasy & Pacific Jazz Sessions | Definitive Records | DRCD 11233
Gerry Mulligan Quartet | Pacific Jazz | 300001(PJ 1)

Walkin' Stomp
Modern Jazz Quartet | Plastic Dreams | Atlantic | AMCY 1099

Walkin' The Blues
Otis Spann | Otis Spann And His Piano | Crosscut | CCR 1003(Candid)

Walkin' The Boogie
John Lee Hooker | Heavy Heads | Chess | 6.24835 AS

Walkin' The Dog
Down Home Jazz Band | Back To Bodega | Stomp Off Records | CD 1273
Big Mama Thornton Group | Big Mama Thornton | The Rising Sun Collection | RSC 0002

Walkin' The Dog(alt.take)
Johnny Hodges Sextet | Masters Of Jazz Vol.9:Johnny Hodges | Storyville | STCD 4109

Walkin' The Line
Champion Jack Dupree Group | Chamion Jack Dupree | EPM Musique | FDC 5504

Walkin' Tiptoe
Barrelhouse Jazzband & Angi Domdey | Barrelhouse Jazzband & Angi Domdey | L+R Records | CDLR 70003

Walkin' Up
Bill Evans Trio | At The Montreux Jazz Festival | Verve | 539758-2
The Best Of Bill Evans Live | Verve | 533825-2
Bill Evans:The Secret Sessions | Milestone | 8MCD 4421-2
Don Friedman Quartet | Metamorphosis | Original Jazz Classics | OJCCD 1914-2(P 7488)
Paul Motian Quartet | Bil Evans | JMT Edition | 834445-2

Walkin' Wadin' Sittin' Ridin'
Buddy Collette Quintet | Buddy's Best | Fresh Sound Records | FSR 652(Dooto DTL 245)

Walkin' With Wally
Cal Tjader Quintet | Concerts In The Sun | Fantasy | FCD 9688-2
Concerts In The Sun | Fantasy | FCD 9688-2
Cal Tjader Sextet | Monterey Concerts | Prestige | PCD 24026-2

Walkin'(alt.take 1)
Art Pepper Plus Eleven | Modern Jazz Classics | Original Jazz Classics | OJC20 341-2
Art Pepper + Eleven | Contemporary | CSA 7568-6

Walkin'(alt.take 2)
Modern Jazz Classics | Original Jazz Classics | OJC20 341-2
Leon Thomas With Orchestra | Spirits Known And Unknown | RCA | 2663876-2

Walkin'(alt.take)
Miles Davis Quintet | Miles Davis In Person-Friday Night At The Blackhawk,San Francisco,Vol.1 | CBS | C4K 87106
Free Trade Hall Vol.1 | Magnetic Records | MRCD 102

Walking
Steve Tibbetts Duo | Northern Song | ECM | 1218
Tarheel Slim | No Time At All | Trix Records | TRIX 3310
Blind Blake | Blind Blake-No Dough Blues | Biograph | BLP 12031

Walking Around
Don Byas Ree-Boppers | Don Byas Complete 1946-1951 European Small Group Master Takes | Definitive Records | DRCD 11214
Lionel Hampton And His Orchestra | Lionel Hampton's Paris All Stars | Vogue | 21511502

Walking At The Trocadero
Lionel Hampton:Real Crazy | Vogue | 2113409-2

Walking Batteriewoman
The Carla Bley Band | Social Studies | Watt | 11(831831-2)
Big Joe Williams | Classic Delta Blues | Original Blues Classics | OBCCD 545-2

Walking Blues
Chris Jones-Steve Baker | Everybody's Cryin' Mercy | Acoustic Music Records | 319.1147.2
Sammy Womacka | Ragtime,Blues & Jazz Guitar | Wonderland Records | 319.9022.2

Walking Death
Big Bill Broonzy | Black Brown And White | Mercury | 842743-2

Walking Down The Keys
The Real Group | One For All | ACT | 9003-2

Walking Down The Street
Jean-Luc Ponty Quintet | Aurora | Atlantic | SD 19158

Walking Foreward,Not Back
Carmen McRae With The Oliver Nelson Orchestra | Portrait Of Carmen | Atlantic | AMCY 1053

Walking Home Together
L.Subramaniam/Stephane Grappelli Group | Conversations | Milestone | M 9130

Walking In A Maze
Ed Mann Group | Perfect World | CMP Records | CMP MC 45

Walking In The Afternoon
Hans Kumpf Duo | On A Baltic Trip | LEO | LR 122

Walking In The Dust
Billy Taylor Trio | You Tempt Me | Taylor Made Records | T 1004

Walking In The Moonlight
Teddy Edwards Quintet | Midnight Creeper | HighNote Records | HCD 7011

Walking My Baby Back Home
Nat King Cole With The Billy May Orchestra | Nat King Cole:For Sentimental Reasons | Dreyfus Jazz Line | FDM 36740-2
Rex Stewart-Cootie Williams Orchestra | Hawk Variation | Swingtime(Contact) | ST 1004

Walking On Air
Friedemann Graef-Albrecht Riermeier Duo | Exit | FMP | 0820

Walking On Eggs
Michael Hornstein-Robert Di Gioia | Dry Red | Edition Collage | EC 486-2

Walking On The Moon
Sarah Jane Cion Trio | Summer Night | Naxos Jazz | 86071-2

Walking Poem No.2
Lightnin' Hopkins | Lightnin' Strikes Back | Charly | CRB 1031

Walking Shoes
Gerry Mulligan Septet | Gerry Mulligan:Gerry Meets Hamp | Memo Music | HDJ 4009
Gerry Mulligan Tentette | The Birth Of The Cool Vol.2 | Capitol | 798935-2

Walking Slow Behind You
Count Basie And His Orchestra | The Indispensable Count Basie | RCA | ND 89758

Walking The Basses
Champion Jack Dupree Group | Jack Dupree-Jimmy Rushing-Muddy Waters | Laserlight | 17062

Walking The Blues
Salut! | Green & Orange | Edition Collage | EC 488-2
Hound Dog Taylor & The House Rockers | Hound Dog Taylor And The House Rockers | Sonet | 198045(SNTF 676)

Walking The Dog
Jack McDuff Sextet | The Reentry | Muse | MCD 5361

Walking The Fish
King Curtis Band | King Curtis-Blow Man Blow | Bear Family Records | BCD 15670 CI

Walking The Floor Over You
The Three Sounds | Babe's Blues | Blue Note | 784434-2

Walking Through The Park
Paul Barbarin And His New Orleans Jazz | Paul Barbarin And His New Orleans Jazz | Atlantic | 790977-2

Walking Together
Walt Barr Quintet | Artful Dancer | Muse | MR 5238

Walking Up
Bill Evans Trio | How My Heart Sings! | Original Jazz Classics | OJCCD 369-2
Ultimate Bill Evans selected by Herbie Hancock | Verve | 557536-2
Joe Pass Quartet | The Complete 'Catch Me' Sessions | Blue Note | LT 1053

Walking With The King
George Lewis Ragtime Jazz Band Of New Orleans | The Oxford Series Vol.14 | American Music | AMCD-34
Papa Bue's Viking Jazzband | Church Concert | Timeless | CD TTD 571

Wall Of Love
Steve Baker-Chris Jones | Slow Roll | Acoustic Music Records | 319.1070.2

Wals De Fantasia
Olaf Tarenskeen | Decisions | Acoustic Music Records | 319.1144.2

Walter Davis
Michael Weiss Trio | Milestones | Steeplechase | SCCD 31449

Walter's Altar
Walter Horton | Memphis Blues | Anthology of the Blues | AB 5602

Walter's Instrumental
Vinny Golia-The Chamber Trio | Worldwide & Portable | Nine Winds Records | NWCD 0143

Waltswing
Art Ensemble Of Chicago | Complete Live In Japan-April 22, 1984 Tokyo | DIW | DIW 815/16 CD

Waltz
Jimmy Giuffre 3 | The Jimmy Giuffre 3-Hollywood & Newport 1957-1958 | Fresh Sound Records | FSCD 1026
Matthew Ship 'String' Trio | Expansion,Power,Release | HatOLOGY | 558

Waltz-
Jazz Indeed | Who The Moon Is | Traumton Records | 4427-2

Waltz 4
Clarinet Summit | Clarinet Summit In Concert At The Public Theater | India Navigation | IN 1062 CD

Waltz Beautiful
Dave Douglas Group | Soul On Soul | RCA | 2663603-2

Waltz Boogie
Gunter Hampel And His Galaxie Dream Band | Journey To The Song Within | Birth | 0017

Waltz For 11 Universes In A Corridor (No.57)
Gunter Hampel Trio | Waltz For 3 Universes In A Corridor | Birth | 0010

Waltz For A
Bill Easley Quartet | Wind Inventions | Sunnyside | SSC 1022 D

Waltz For A Princess
Richie Cole Sextet | New York Afternoon | Muse | MCD 5119

Waltz For AZ
Thomas Stabenow-Lothar Schmitz | Swet Peanuts | Bassic-Sound | CD 007

Waltz For Berlin
Wolfgang Lackerschmid-Günter Lenz Duo | Live Conversation | Inak | 852

Waltz For Bette
Chick Corea Group | Early Days | LRC Records | CDC 7969(874370)

Waltz For Carmen
Lee Ritenour Sextet | Alive In L.A. | GRP | GRP 98822
George Shearing | Piano | Concord | CCD 4400

Waltz For Coop
Imre Köszegi Trio | Drummer's Dream | yvp music | CD 3044

Waltz For Debby
Bill Evans | The Complete Fantasy Recordings | Fantasy | 9FCD 1012-2
Bill Evans Trio | The Village Vanguard Sessions | Milestone | M 47002
His Last Concert In Germany | West Wind | WW 2022
Bill Evans Trio:The Last Waltz | Milestone | 8MCD 4430-2
Bill Evans:The Secret Sessions | Milestone | 8MCD 4421-2
Live In Paris 1972 Vol.3 | France's Concert | FCD 125
Live In Paris 1972 Vol.1 | France's Concert | FCD 107
Bill Evans:The Secret Sessions | Milestone | 8MCD 4421-2
Bill Evans:The Secret Sessions | Milestone | 8MCD 4421-2
Half Moon Bay | Milestone | MCD 9282-2
More From The Vanguard | Milestone | M 9125
Bobby Jaspar Quartet | Bobby Jaspar With Friends | Fresh Sound Records | FSR-CD 0166
Bud Shank Quartet | Bud Shank Plays The Music Of Bill Evans | Fresh Sound Records | FSR-CD 5012
Cannonball Adderley Quartet | Cannonball Adderley Birthday Celebration | Fantasy | FANCD 6087-2
Carol Kidd With The Sandy Taylor Trio | Carol Kidd | Linn Records | AKD 003
Johnny Hartman With The Hank Jones Quartet | The Voice That Is! | Impulse(MCA) | IMP 12982
Oscar Peterson Trio | Compact Jazz: Oscar Peterson Plays Jazz Standards | Verve | 833283-2
The Moscow Sax Quintet | The Jazznost Tour | Arkadia Jazz | 71161
Tony Bennett-Bill Evans | The Tony Bennett-Bill Evans Album | Original Jazz Classics | OJC20 439-2(F 9489)
Oscar Peterson Trio | Nigerian Marketplace | Pablo | 2308231-2

Waltz For Debby-
Tierney Sutton And Her Trio | Blue In Green | Telarc Digital | CD 83522

Waltz For Debby(alt.take)
Bill Evans Trio | Waltz For Debby | Original Jazz Classics | OJC20 210-2
Frank Rosolino Quartet | Frank Talks! | Storyville | STCD 8284

Waltz For Diana
Joe Pass With The NDR Big Band | Joe Pass In Hamburg | ACT | 9100-2

Waltz For Django
Lenny Carlson | Search For The Floor | Flying High | FH 9501

Waltz For Ellen
CoJazz Plus | CoJazz Plus Vol.2 | TCB Records | TCB 97302

Waltz For Geri
Carola Grey Group | The Age Of Illusions | Jazzline | JL 11139-2

Waltz For Jim
Joe Baudisch And Friends | Joe Baudisch And Friends | Bassic-Sound | CD 013

Waltz For John
Rudy Linka Quartet | News From Home | ARTA Records | F 1 0026-2511

Waltz For Katharina
John McLaughlin Group | Belo Horizonte | Warner | 99185

Waltz For My Lady
Slide Hampton-Joe Haider Jazz Orchestra | Give Me A Double | JHM Records | JHM 3627
Mal Waldron Trio | You And The Night And The Muisc | Paddle Wheel | K 28P 6272

Waltz For Nicky
Richard Galliano Quartet | Viaggio | Dreyfus Jazz Line | FDM 36562-9
Richard Galliano Trio | Concert Inédits | Dreyfus Jazz Line | FDM 36606-2

Waltz For Pee Wee
Michael Sagmeister Quartet | A Certain Gift | MGI Records | MGR CD 1014
Geoff Keezer Quartet | Curveball | Sunnyside | SSC 1045 D

Waltz For Ruth
Charlie Haden-Pat Metheny | Beyond The Missouri Sky | Verve | 537130-2
Florian Poser-Klaus Ignatzek Duo | Springdale | Acoustic Music Records | 319.1166.2

Waltz For S.
Nino De Rose & Friends | Jazz Voices: It's Always Jazz | SPLASC(H) Records | H 124

Waltz For Snoopy
Jim Hall Sextet | Subsequently | Limelight | 844278-2 IMS

Waltz For Stan
Rudy Linka Quartet | Live It Up | Timeless | CD SJP 407

Waltz For Susann
Roy Brooks-Randy Weston | Duet In Detroit | Enja | ENJ-7067 2

Waltz For Sweetie
Johnny Griffin-Sal Nistico-Roman Schwaller Sextet | Three Generations Of Tenorsaxophone | JHM Records | JHM 3611
Frank Strozier-Booker Little Quintet | The Fantastic Frank Strozier | Vee Jay Recordings | VJ 012

Waltz For The Lonely Ones
Viktoria Tolstoy Group & Strings | Shining On You | ACT | 9701-2
Buddy Rich Big Band | Backwoods Siseman/Pieces Of Dream | Laserlight | 24655

Waltz For The Mushroom Hunters
Tim Sund Quartet | About Time | Laika Records | LK 93-043

Waltz For The Night
Tim Whitehead Quintet | A Cool Blue | Criss Cross | Criss 1102

Waltz For Universes In A Corridor
Paolo Fresu Sextet | Ensalada Mistica | SPLASC(H) Records | CD H 415-2

Waltz For Verena
Walter Norris | Maybeck Recital Hall Series Volume Four | Concord | CCD 4425

Waltz For Wasili
John Abercrombie With The Ansgar Striepens Quintet | Dreams And Realities | Laika Records | 35101642

Waltz For Wheeler
Ben van den Dungen/Jarmo Hoogendijk Quintet | Speak Up | Timeless | CD SJP 342

Waltz For Zweetie
Bud Shank-Laurindo Almeida Quartet | Braziliance Vol.2 | Pacific Jazz | 796102-2

Waltz Hollandaise
Max Roach-Clifford Brown Quintet | Brownie Lives! | Fresh Sound Records | FSCD 1012

Waltz Me Blues
Louis Mazetier | Good Vibrations | Jazz Connaisseur | JCCD 9521-2

Waltz Medley:
Dick Griffin Septet | The Eighth Wonder & More | Konnex Records | KCD 5059

Waltz My Son
Bill Charlap Trio | Souvenir | Criss Cross | Criss 1108

Waltz New
Klaus Ignatzek Trio | The Klaus Ignatzek Trio | yvp music | CD 3020
Tommy Flanagan Trio | Communication-Live At Fat Tuesday's New York | Paddle Wheel | KICJ 73

Waltz No.5

Larry Coryell-Brian Keane-Diego Cortez | Bolero | String | BLE 233850

Waltz Of The Friends
NDR-Workshop | Doldinger's Best | ACT | 9224-2

Waltz Of The Jive Cats
Bluesy Toosy | ACT | 9200-2

Waltz Of The Prophets
Stan Kenton And His Orchestra | Adventures In Jazz | Capitol | 521222-2

Waltz Of The Prophets(alt.take)
Phillip Johnston's Big Trouble | Philip Johnston's Big Trouble | Black Saint | 120152-2

Waltz Three
David Murray Quartet | A Sanctuary Within | Black Saint | 120145-2

Waltzin' Over T'Yours
Baden Powell Ensemble | Apaixonado | MPS | 68090

Waltzing
Dave Brubeck Quartet | Double Live From The USA & UK | Telarc Digital | CD 83400(2)

Waltzing Is Hip
Oscar Peterson Trio | En Concert Avec Europe 1 | Laserlight | 710443/48

Waltzing Mathilda
Chad Wackerman Quartet | Forty Reasons | CMP Records | CMP CD 48

Walz'er
Joe Sachse/David Moss/George Lewis | Berlin Tango | ITM Records | ITM 1448

Walzer Für Sabinchen
Kelm 3 | Per Anno | dml-records | CD 013

Walzer Nr.4
Charles Mingus Quintet With Roland Kirk | Oh Yeah | Atlantic | 90667-1 TIS

Wami
Denise Jannah And Her Band | A Heart Full Of Music | Timeless | CD SJP 414

Wanderer
Jimmy Witherspoon And His Band | Jumping On The West Coast-Buddy Tate & Friends | Black Lion | BLCD 760175

Wandering
Oscar Peterson With Orchestra | Motions & Emotions | MPS | 821289-2 PMS

Wandering Souls
Chris Jarrett | Live In Tübingen | Edition Collage | EC 490-2

Wanderings
Jukka Tolonen Group | Tolonen! | Sonet | 147117

Wanderlust
Duke Ellington-Coleman Hawkins Orchestra | Duke Ellington Meets Coleman Hawkins | MCA | MCAD 5650

Wanderlust-
Duke Ellington And His Orchestra | Carnegie Hall Concert December 1947 | Prestige | 2PCD 24075-2
Duke Ellington:Complete Prestige Carnegie Hall 1946-1947 Concerts | Definitive Records | DRCD 11211

Wandlungen
Paul Smith Quartet | By The Fireside | Savoy | SV 0225(MG 12094)

Wandring Eyes
Joe Marsala And His Delta Four | Hickory House Jazz | Affinity | CD AFS 1012

Wang Dang Doodle
Koko Taylor With The Jimmy Rogers Blues Band | South Side Lady | Black & Blue | BLE 59.542 2

Wang Tang
Ben's Bad Boys | Ben Pollack Vol.2 | Jazz Oracle | BDW 8016

Wang Wang Blues
Fletcher Henderson And His Orchestra | Jazz Classics In Digital Stereo: Fletcher Henderson Swing | CDS Records Ltd. | RPCD 628(CD 682)

Wang Wang Doodle
Willie Dixon Blues Band | Blues Roots Vol. 12: Willie Dixon | Chess | 6.24802 AG

Wanna See Me Down
Blue Box | Blue Box 10 | TipToe | TIP-888818 2

Wanton Spirit
Kenny Barron Trio | Wanton Spirit | Verve | 522364-2

Wapango
Gary Peacock-Bill Frisell | Just So Happens | Postcards | POST 1005

Waqt
Michael Mantler Group With The Danish Radio Concert Orchestra Strings | The School Of Understanding(Sort-Of-An-Opera) | ECM | 1648/49(537963-2)

War
Jim Black Alasnoaxis | Splay | Winter&Winter | 910076-2

War Again Error
Louie Bellson Drum Explosion | Matterhorn | Original Jazz Classics | 2310834

War Horse
Lightnin' Hopkins | Lightnin' Strikes Back | Charly | CRB 1031

War On Drugs
Anders Jormin | Xieyi | ECM | 1762(013998-2)

War Orphans
Bobo Stenson Trio | War Orphans | ECM | 1604(539723-2)
Charlie Haden's Liberation Music Orchestra | Liberation Music Orchestra | Impulse(MCA) | 951188-2
Paul Motian Quintet | Tribute | ECM | 1048
Sonny Boy Williamson Group | King Of The Blues Harmonica | Black & Blue | BLE 59.251 2

War Was?
Nat Adderley Quintet | Good Company | Challenge | CHR 70009

Wared
Frank Tannehill | Frank Tannehill(1932-1941) | Story Of Blues | CD 3526-2

Warm All Over
Herlin Riley Quintet | Watch What You're Doing | Criss Cross | Criss 1179

Warm Blue
Gunther Klatt And Elephantrombones | Live At Leverkusen | Enja | 5069-2

Warm Blue Stream
Stan Kenton And His Orchestra | Some Women I've Known | Creative World | ST 1029

Warm Canto
Ensemble Indigo | Reflection | Enja | ENJ-9417 2
Mal Waldron Sextet | The Quest | Original Jazz Classics | OJCCD 082-2(NJ 8269)
Fire Waltz | Prestige | P 24085
Eric Dolphy:The Complete Prestige Recordings | Prestige | 9 PRCD-4418-2
Richard Davis Trio | Way Out West | Muse | MR 5180

Warm Color
Yusef Lateef Quartet | 1984 | MCA | AS 84

Warm Intensity
Blind Willie McTell | Blind Willie McTell-Death Cell Blues | Biograph | BLP C 14

Warm Night-
Art Ensemble Of Chicago | Urban Bushmen | ECM | 1211/12

Warm Night Blues Stroll-
Blues Comany And Guests | Invitation To The Blues | Inak | 9064

Warm Puppies
Mal Waldron Quartet feat. Jim Pepper | The Git-Go At Utopia,Volume Two | Tutu Records | 888148-2*
Keith Tippett Group | Warm Spirits-Cool Spirits | View | VS 101 IMS

Warm Valley
Allan Vaché Swingtet | Jazz Im Amerikahaus,Vol.3 | Nagel-Heyer | CD 013
Art Farmer Quartet | Warm Valley | Concord | CCD 4212
Don Sebesky Orchestra | Joyful Noise:A Tribute To Duke Ellington | RCA | 2663552-2
Duke Ellington And His Famous Orchestra | Passion Flower 1940-46 | Bluebird | 63 66616-2
Duke Ellington And His Orchestra | Duke Ellington In Hamilton | Radiex Music | RDX-1000
The Duke At Fargo 1940 | Storyville | STCD 8316/17
Happy Birthday Duke Vol.2 | Laserlight | 15784
Earl Hines | Earl Hine Plays Duke Ellington | New World Records | 80361/362-2
Gary Bartz-Sonny Fortune Quintet | Alto Memories | Verve | 523268-2
Günther Klatt-Tizian Jost | Art Of The Duo:Live In Mexico City | Tutu Records | 888184-2*
Herb Geller Quartet | To Benny & Johnny | Hep | CD 2084
Howard Alden Trio | Take Your Pick | Concord | CCD 4743
Joe Van Enkhuizen Quartet | Ellington My Way | Timeless | CD SJP 419
Marty Paich Band | I Get A Boot Out Of You | Discovery | DS 829 IMS
Mulgrew Miller | Keys To The City | Landmark | LCD 1507-2
Duke Ellington And His Orchestra | Yale Concert | Fantasy | F 9433

Warm Valley-
Phil Woods/Jim McNeely | Flowers For Hodges | Concord | CCD 4485

Warm Winds
Macon Ed[Eddie Anthony] And Tampa Joe[prob.Jim Hill] | Georgia String Bands(1928-1930) | Story Of Blues | CD 3516-2

Warme Melk Met Chokolade
John Lewis-Barry Galbraith | The John Lewis Piano | Atlantic | AMCY 1035

Warming Up
Soul Immigrants Plus Guests | A Healty Vibe | Lipstick Records | LIP 8947-2 HOT

Warming Up(These Things Called Changes)
Miriam Alter Quintet | Alter Ego | Intuition Records | INT 3258-2

Warmness
Art Blakey And The Jazz Messengers | Moanin' | Blue Note | 495324-2

Warm-Up And Dialogue Between Lee And Rudy
Hans Koller Groups | Out Of The Rim | IN+OUT Records | 7014-2

Warne Marsh(In Memoriam)
Warne Marsh/Hans Koller | Jazz Unlimited | IN+OUT Records | 7017-2
Warne Marsh Quintet | Jazz Of Two Cities | Fresh Sound Records | FSR-CD 342

Warne Marsh(talking with Bobby Troupe)
Warne Marsh Trio | Warne Out | Interplay | IP 7709

Warp And Woof
Mal Waldron Sextet | Fire Waltz | Prestige | P 24085
Steve Adams/Ken Filiano Quartet | Anacrusis | Nine Winds Records | NW 0128

Warrior
Tony Williams Quintet | Civilization | Blue Note | BT 85138

Warriors(Guerreros)
Claude Thornhill And His Orchestra | Tapestries | Affinity | ???

Warten Auf Die Pinguine
Brodmann-Pausch Percussion Duo | Are You Serious? | Jazz 4 Ever Records:Jazz Network | J4E 4718

Warten Auf Thomas
Glenn Horiuchi Quartet | Oxnard Beet | Soul Note | 121228-2

Warum Bist Du Fortgegangen
Wolfgang Lauth Quartet | Lauther | Bear Family Records | BCD 15717 AH
Charlie Mariano Quartet | Warum Bist Du Traurig(Why Are You So Sad) | B&W Present | BW 019

Was A Sunny Day
Peter Kowald | Was Da Ist | FMP | CD 62

Washboard Blues
Hoagy Carmichael With Jack Teagarden And His Big Band | Swing Vol.1 | Storyville | 4960343
John Barnes Dixieland Band | Dixieland Forever Vol.2 | BELL Records | BLR 89046

Washday
Chris Potter Group | Traveling Mercies | Verve | 018243-2

Washed Ashore
Urs Blöchlinger | Cinema Invisible | Plainisphare | PL 1267-24/25

Washington And Lee Swing
Ken Colyer Trust Band | The Ken Colyer Trust Band Pay New Orleans Jazz | Upbeat Jazz | URCD 112

Washington Post March
Claude Hopkins And His Orchestra | Harlem 1935 | Jazz Anthology | JA 5156

Wassail Song
Singers Unlimited | Christmas | MPS | 821859-2

Wasser, Brot, Schuhe
Martin Auer Quintet | Martin Auer Quintett | Jazz 4 Ever Records:Jazz Network | J4E 4762

Wasserzeichen
Stochelo Rosenberg Trio | Seresta | Hot Club Records | HCRCD 059

Wastelands
Joe Venuti And His Orchestra | The Big Bands Of Joe Venuti Vol.2 (1930-1933) | JSP Records | 1112

Watanabe
Trilok Gurtu Group | Bad Habits Die Hard | CMP Records | CMP CD 80

Watch Out
Jeremy Davenport Quartet | Jeremy Davenport | Telarc Digital | CD 83376
Rene McLean Sextet | Watch Out | Steeplechase | SCCD 31037

Watch The Birdie
Hatchett's Swingtette | In The Mood | Decca | RFL 11

Watch The Boogie
Uli Beckerhoff Quintet | Dedication | Fusion | 8009

Watch What Happens
Erroll Garner Sextet | Magician & Gershwin And Kern | Telarc Digital | CD 83337
Joe Pass Trio | Intercontinental | MPS | 68121
Lena Horne And Gabor Szabo | Lena & Gabor | Gryphon | 6.24451 AT
Phil Woods Quartet | The Birth Of The ERM | Philology | 214 W 16/17
Stanley Turrentine Quartet | Ain't No Way | Blue Note | LT 1095
Vince Jones Group | Watch What Happens | Intuition Records | INT 3070-2
Zoot Sims-Bucky Pizzarelli Duo | Summum | Ahead | 33752

Watch You Sleepin'
Wolfgang Lackerschmid Group | Gently But Deep | Lady Hamilton Productions | BR 39
Billy Strayhorn's Septet | Cue For Saxophone | Affinity | AFF 166

Watch Yourself
Lonnie Brooks Blues Band | Bayou Lightning | Sonet | 147108

Watching For The Signal
Eric Essix Sextet | First Impressions | Nova | NOVA 8920-2

Watching Shadows
Hans Reichel | The Dawn Of Dachsman | FMP | 1140

Watching You
Freddy Cole With Band | Merry-Go-Round | Telarc Digital | CD 83493

Watching You Watching Me
Saheb Sarbib Quintet | It Couldn't Happen Without You | Soul Note | 121098-2

Water
Cecil Taylor | Erzulie Maketh Scent | FMP | CD 18
David Kikoski Trio | Almost Twilight | Criss Cross | Criss 1190
Jens Winther And The IASJ Big Band | The Four Elements | Stunt Records | STUCD 19802

Water Babies
Robert Dick Group With The Soldier String Quartet | Jazz Standard On Mars | Enja | ENJ-9327 2
Steve Khan Trio | Headline | Polydor | 517690-2

Water Ballet
Don Cherry Group | Don Cherry-The Sonet Recordings:Eternal Now/Live Ankara | Verve | 533049-2

Water Boy
Earl Hines And His Orchestra | The Indispensable Earl Hines Vol.3/4(1939-1945) | RCA | 2126408-2
Odetta | The Tin Angel | Original Blues Classics | OBCCD 565-2(F 3252)

Water Dream
Darrell Grant Quintet | The New Bop | Criss Cross | Criss 1106

Water From An Ancient Well
Abdullah Ibrahim Trio | Cape Town Revisited | TipToe | TIP-888836 2
Dave Grusin Quintet | GRP Super Live In Concert | GRP | GRP 16502

Water Girl
Gene Ammons Quintet | The Gene Ammons Story: Organ Combos | Prestige | P 24071

Water Jug
Rickey Woodard Quartet | California Cooking No.2 | Candid | CCD 79762
Enrico Rava Group | Quotation Marks | Japo | 60010 IMS (2360010)

Water Mile
Doug Hammond Group | Spaces | DIW | DIW 359 CD

Water Music
The Jeff Lorber Fusion | Fusion | Inner City | IC 1026 IMS

Water On The Pond
Miles Davis Sextet | This Is Jazz:Miles Davis Electric | CBS | CK 65449

Water Pistol
Yusef Lateef Trio | Yusef's Bag | Prestige | P 24105
Fritz Pauer Trio | Water Plants | EGO | 4007

Water Shed
Michael Gibbs Orchestra | Great European Jazz Orchestras Vol.1:Big Music | ACT | 9231-2

Water Stone
Mark Turner-Chris Cheek Quintet | The Music Of Mercedes Rossy | Fresh Sound Records | FSNT 043 CD

Water Stones
Steve Lampert Group | Venus Perplexed | Steeplechase | SCCD 31557

Water Test With Question
Dave Liebman Quartet | The Elements:Water | Arkadia Jazz | 71043

Water To Drink -> Agua De Beber

Waterbed
Buddy DeFranco Quartet | Waterbed | Candid | CRS 1017 IMS

Watercolor Dream
Pat Metheny Group | Blue Asphalt | Jazz Door | JD 1223

Watercolors
Ralph Peterson Trio | Triangular | Blue Note | 792750-2

Waterfall
Ketil Bjornstad Group | Water Stories | ECM | 1503(519076-2)
Lester Bowie's Brass Fantasy | When The Spitit Returns | Dreyfus Jazz Line | FDM 37016-2
Marlena Shaw With Orchestra | From The Depths Of My Soul | Blue Note | 84443

Watering
Boyd Senter And His Senterpedes | Boyd Senter:Jazzologist Supreme | Timeless | CBC 1-032

Waterloop
Frank Minion With The Jimmy Jones Quartet | The Soft Land Of Make Believe | Fresh Sound Records | FSR 2013(Bethlehem BCP 6052)

Watermelon
Deborah Henson-Conant Trio | Just For You | Laika Records | LK 95-063

Watermelon Boogie
Jo Ambros Group | Wanderlust | dml-records | CD 016

Watermelon In Easterhay
Albert King Blues Band | Wednesday Night In San Francisco | Stax | SCD 8556-2

Watermelon Man
Blues At Sunset(Live at Wattstax And Montreux) | Stax | SCD 8581-2
Herbie Hancock Quintet | Takin' Off | Blue Note | 837643-2
The Best Of Herbie Hancock | Blue Note | 89907
The Best Of Herbie Hancock | Blue Note | 791142-2
Cantaloupe Island | Blue Note | 829331-2
Herbie Mann Group | Sunbelt | Atlantic | ATL 50536
Jazz Jokers | Jazz-Jokers | Jazzpoint | JP 1024 LP
Lambert, Hendricks And Bavan | At Newport '63 | RCA | 2125757-2
Moe Koffman Quartet | Moe Koffman 1967 | Just A Memory | JAS 9505-2
Mongo Santamaria Group With Dizzy Gillespie And Toots Thielemans | Montreux Heat! | Pablo | PACD 5317-2
Mongo Santamaria Orchestra | The Watermelon Man | Milestone | M 47012
Woody Herman And His Orchestra | Live In Antibes 1965 | France's Concert | FCD 117

Watermelon Man(alt.take)
Herbie Hancock Quintet | Herbie Hancock:The Complete Blue Note Sixties Sessions | Blue Note | 495569-2
Xu Feng Xia | Difference And Similarity | FMP | CD 96

Waters Of March
Mark Murphy With Richie Cole And His Orchestra | Stolen Moments | Muse | MCD 5102
Eliane Elias Quartet | Eliane Elias Plays Jobim | Blue Note | 793089-2

Waterwheel
Kai Winding Septet | Early Bones | Prestige | P 24067

Watsoning
Bobby Watson & Open Form Trio | Appointment In Milano | Red Records | VPA 184

Watusa
Sun Ra And His Intergalactic Solar Arkestra | Space Is The Place(Soundtrack) | Evidence | ECD 22070-2

Wave
Alexander von Schlippenbach | The Living Music | FMP | 0100
Alvin Queen & Junior Mance With Martin Rivera | Watch What Happens | Divox | CDX 48702
Art Van Damme & The Singers Unlimited | Invitation | MPS | 68107
Benny Carter 4 | Montreux '77 | Original Jazz Classics | OJC20 374-2(2308204)
The Montreux '77 Collection | Pablo | 2620107
Bireli Lagrene Ensemble | Routes To Django & Bireli Swing '81 | Jazzpoint | JP 1055 CD
Cecil Payne Quartet | Casbah | Empathy Records | E 1005
De Novo | L.A. Transit | Denon Compact Disc | CY-1004
Dorothy Donegan Trio | I Just Want To Sing | Audiophile | ACD-281
Eddie Lockjaw Davis Quartet | Swingin' Till The Girls Come Home | Steeplechase | SCCD 31058
Ella Fitzgerald With The Tommy Flanagan Trio | Ella-At The Montreux Jazz Festival 1975 | Original Jazz Classics | OJC20 789-2(2310751)
Gerry Mulligan Group With Jane Duboc | Triple Play:Gerry Mulligan | Telarc Digital | CD 83453
Herb Ellis Quartet | Soft & Mellow | Concord | CCD 4077
Joe Pass | Joe Pass:A Man And His Guitar | Original Jazz Classics | OJCCD 8806-2
Live At Long Beach City College | Pablo | 2308239-2
Manfredo Fest Quartet | Just Jobim | dmp Digital Music Productions | CD 524
Oscar Peterson Trio | The Good Life | Original Jazz Classics | OJC 627(2308241)
Oscar Peterson Trio With The Claus Ogermann Orchestra | The Antonio Carlos Jobim Songbook | Verve | 525472-2
Three Originals:Motion&Emotions/Tristeza On Piano/Hello Herbie | MPS | 521059-2
Oscar Peterson With Orchestra | Motions & Emotions | MPS | 821289-2 PMS
Richard 'Groove' Holmes Orchestra | Comin' On Home | Blue Note | 538701-2
Rosemary Clooney With The John Oddo Big Band | Girl Singer | Concord | CCD 4496
Stanley Turrentine Quartet | Ain't No Way | Blue Note | LT 1095
Tony Bennett With Orchestra | Tony Bennet's Something | CBS | CK 64601

Wave Cut
Paul Moer Trio | Live At The Pour House | Fresh Sound Records | FSCD 1025

Wave Forms No. One
Ed Schuller & The Eleventh Hour Band | Snake Dancing | Tutu Records | 888188-2*

Wave Forms No. Two
The Sea Ensemble | We Move Together | ESP Disk | ESP 3018-2

Wave Over Sorrow
Raum-Zeit-Klang-Project | Dimensionale X H2O Memory | Born&Bellmann | 970612 CD

Wave(Intro)
Jeff Lorber Group | Worth Waiting For | Verve | 517998-2
Waverly
Glenda Powrie Group | Asha | Muse | MCD 5392
Waverly Street
Aparis | Despite The Fire Fighters' Efforts... | ECM | 1496(517717-2)
Waverterms
Andy Lumpp | Andy Lump Piano Solo | Nabel Records:Jazz Network | LP 4608(Audiophile)
Waves
Christoph Sänger Trio | Caprice | Laika Records | LK 94-057
Joerg Reiter | Caprice | BELL Records | BLR 84040
Martin Kolbe-Ralf Illenberger With Wolfgang Dauner | Waves/Colouring The Leaves | BELL Records | BLR 83751
Terje Rypdal Quartet | Waves | ECM | 1110(827419-2)
Works | ECM | 825428-1
The Contemporary Alphorn Orchestra | Mytha | Hat Art | CD 6110
Waves Of Beeing
Juhani Aaltonen Trio | Prana-Live At Groovy | Leo Records | 013
Wavy Gravy
Johnny Otis Band | Creepin' With The Cats: The Legendary DIG Masters Vol.1 | Ace Records | CDCHD 325
Wa-Wa-Wa
Marilyn Middleton Pollock & Steve Mellor's Chicago Hoods | Red Hot And Blue | Lake | LACD 42
Wawina Era Wo
Maria Schneider Jazz Orchestra | Coming About | Enja | ENJ-9062 2
Way Back Home
Junior Parker With Orchestra feat.Jimmy McGriff | Little Junior Parker | LRC Records | CDC 9002
The Boswell Sisters With The Dorsey Brothers' Orchestra | Everybody Loves My Baby | Pro-Arte | CDD 550
Gray Gordon And His Tic-Toc Rhythm Orchestra | The Uncollected Gray Gordon | Hindsight | HSR 206
Way Beyond Cave
Howard Johnson & Gravity | Gravity!!! | Verve | 531021-2
Way Down
Casey Bill Weldon | Masters Of Jazz Vol. 15-Blues Giants | RCA | NL 89728 DP
Way Down Yonder In New Orleans
Bill Coleman Quintet | Dicky Wells & Bill Coleman In Paris | Affinity | CD AFS 1004
Dutch Swing College Band | Dutch Swing College Band Live In 1960 | Philips | 838765-2
Digital Dixie | Philips | 800065-2 PMS
Howard Alden-Dan Barrett Quintet | The A.B.Q Salutes Buck Clayton | Concord | CCD 4395
Kansas City Six | Lester Young:The Complete1936-1951 Group Sessions(Studio Recordings-Master Takes),Vol.1 | Blue Moon | BMCD 1001
Lester Young And The Kansas City Six | The Commodore Story | Commodore | CMD 24002
Louis Armstrong And His Orchestra | Mostly Blues | Ember | CJS 850
Oscar Klein Quartet | Early Oscar Klein(1954-1964) | RST-Records | 91564-2
Thomas Jefferson's International New Orleans Jazz Band | Thomas Jefferson's International New Orleans Jazz Band | Storyville | SLP 254
Willy Bischof Jazztet | Swiss Air | Jazz Connaisseur | JCCD 9523-2
Bill Perkins With The Jan Lundgren Trio | Bill Perkins Recreates The Historic Solos Of Lester Young | Fresh Sound Records | FSR-CD 5010
Way Down Yonder In New Orleans(Theme)
This Is Jazz All Stars | Jazz Live & Rare: This Is Jazz Radio Series-Live 1947 | Jazzline | ???
Way Early Subtone
Lutz Häfner Quartet | Way In Way Out | Jazz 4 Ever Records:Jazz Network | J4E 4757
Way In
Mal Waldron Trio | Plays The Blues | Enja | 5021
Way Out
Lutz Häfner Quartet | Way In Way Out | Jazz 4 Ever Records:Jazz Network | J4E 4757
Phil Minton/Veryan Weston | Ways | ITM Records | ITM 1420
Way Out Basie
Chris Connor With Band | Chris Connor | Atlantic | 7567-80769-2
Way Out There
Gerald Wiggins Trio | Around The World In 80 Days | Original Jazz Classics | OJCCD 1761-2(SP 2101)
Way Out West
Sonny Rollins Trio | Contemporary Sonny Rollins-Alternate Takes | Contemporary | C 7651
Bobby Short Sextet | Songs Of New York | Telarc Digital | CD 83346
Way Out West(alt.take)
Sonny Rollins Trio | Sonny Rollins-The Freelance Years:The Complete Riverside & Contemporary Recordings | Riverside | 5 RCD 4427-2
Harold Danko | This Isn't Maybe... | Steeplechase | SCCD 31471
Way To Your Heart
Eugene Chadbourne Group | The Hellingtunes | Intakt Records | CD 052
Wayfarer
John Surman | A Biography Of The Rev. Absolom Dawe | ECM | 1528(523749-2)
Phil Minton/Veryan Weston | Ways | ITM Records | ITM 1420
Wayfaring Stranger
Charles Lloyd Quintet | Lift Every Voice | ECM | 1832/33(018783-2)
Charlie Haden With String Quartet | The Art Of The Song | Verve | 547403-2
Joe Williams And Friends | Joe Williams At Newport '63 | RCA | NL 70119
John Benson Brooks' Orchestra | Folk Jazz U.S.A. | RCA | PM 43767
Larry Willis Sextet | A Tribute To Someone | audioquest Music | AQCD 1022
Wayne
Jim McNeely Trio | East Side/West Side | Owl Records | 024
Wayne War Schneller
Antonio Hart Group | Ama Tu Sonrisa | Enja | ENJ-9404 2
Wayne's Lament
Miles Davis Group | Miles Davis Live From His Last Concert In Avignon | Laserlight | 24327
Wayne's Tune
Billy Pierce Quintet | One For Chuck | Sunnyside | SSC 1053 D
Wayne's World
Frank Sackenheim Quartet | The Music Of Chance | Jazz 4 Ever Records:Jazz Network | J4E 4753
James Emery | Exo Eso | FMP | SAJ 59
Ways It Isnt
Arild Andersen Quartet | Shimri | ECM | 1082
Ways To Leave Your Lover
Phil Minton/Veryan Weston | Ways | ITM Records | ITM 1420
Wazemmes
Oregon | Ecotopia | ECM | 1354
WBAI
Phil Moerke Group | Multi Colors | Jazz Pure Collection | AU 31625 CD
We Agree
Count Basie's Kansas City Five | Count Basie: Kansas City 5 | Pablo | 2312126
We All Got To Go
Joe Hill Louis Band | Joe Hill Louis: The Be-Bop Boy | Bear Family Records | BCD 15524 AH
We All Gotta Go Sometime(take 2)
Joe Hill Louis: The Be-Bop Boy | Bear Family Records | BCD 15524 AH
We All Gotta Go Sometime(take 3)
Horace Silver Ensemble | Silver 'N Strings Play The Music Of The Spheres | Blue Note | LWB 1033
We All Remember Wes
Al Jones Blues Band | Sharper Than A Tack | Blues Beacon | BLU-1034 2
We All Wanna Boogie
Billy Jenkins And Fun Horns | East/West Now Wear The Same Vest | Babel | BDV 9601
We Always Cried
Arnold Ross Trio | Just You & He & Me | Fresh Sound Records | FSR-CD 313
We Always Knew
Ingrid Sertso/Karl Berger Group | Jazz Dance | ITM Records | ITM 1427
We Are
Yosuke Yamashita-Hozan Yamamoto Duo | Yosuke Yamashita-Hozan Yamamoto | Enja | 5003/4
We Are All Alone
Five Blind Boys Of Mississippi | My Desire/There's A God Somewhere | Mobile Fidelity | MFCD 769
We Are In Love
Peter Brötzmann/Werner Lüdi | Wie Das Leben So Spielt | FMP | CD 22
We Are The Blues
Dino Saluzzi Quartet | Once Upon A Time-Far Away In The South | ECM | 1309(827768-2)
We Are The Children
Cleo Laine With The Johnny Dankworth Quintet | Cleo At Carnegie Hall-The 10th Anniversary Concert | DRG | DARC 2-2101 IMS
We Are The Stars
Fisherman's Break | Fisherman's Break | Edition Collage | EC 450-2
We Are The Two Only Ones
Esther Phillips And The Dave Matthews Orchestra | A Way To Say Goodbye | Muse | MCD 5302
We Begin
Heikki Sarmanto Ensemble And Gregg Smith Vocal Quartet | New Hope Jazz Mass | Finlandia | FA 201
We Blue It
Ramsey Lewis Trio | Down To Earth | Verve | 538329-2
We Blue It(alt.take)
Art Ensemble Of Chicago | Naked | DIW | DIW 818 CD
We Can't Agree
Louis Jordan And His Tympany Five | Look Out Sisters-Unissued Film Soundtracks 1944-1948 | Krazy Kat | KK 7415 IMS
We Can't Go On This Way
Ella Fitzgerald With Orchestra | The Jazz Collector Edition: Ella Fitzgerald | Laserlight | 15705
We Could Be Flying
Hank Jones Trio | The Jazz Trio Of Hank Jones | Savoy | SV 0184(MG 12023)
We Could Make Such Beautiful Music Together
Marlene And Her Quartet | Every Breath I Take | Savoy | SV 0233(MV 12058)
We Diddit
Mal Waldron Sextet | Fire Waltz | Prestige | P 24085
Steve Lacy Three | N.Y.Capers & Quirks | HatOLOGY | 532
We Fell In Love Anyway
Rosemary Clooney With The John Oddo Big Band | Girl Singer | Concord | CCD 4496
We Fell Out Of Love
Till Brönner Group | Love | Verve | 559058-2
We Fly Around The World
Johnny Hodges And Shorty Baker And Their Orchestra | Ellingtonians In Paris | Jazztime(EMI) | 251275-2
We Free Kings
Michael Hornstein-Robert Di Gioia | Dry Red | Edition Collage | EC 486-2
We Got By
Al Jarreau With Band | L Is For Lover | i.e. Music | 557850-2
We Got Telepathy - (We Got) Telepathy
The Vivino Brothers Band | Chitlins Parmigiana | dmp Digital Music Productions | CD 492
We Had A Sister
Pat Metheny Trio | Trio 99-00 | Warner | 9362-47632-2
Ray Charles And His Orchestra | Love & Peace | London | 6.23662 AO
We Just Want To Dance Our Steps
Ahmad Jamal Trio | Live At The Alhambra | Vogue | 655002
We Kiss In The Shadow
Red Garland Trio | The Jazz Giants Play Rodgers & Hammerstein:My Favorite Things | Prestige | PCD 24223-2
Roger Kellaway Quartet | In Japan | All Art Jazz | AAJ 11002
Stan Kenton-June Christy | Duet | Capitol | 789285-2
We Laughed At Love
Stan Kenton And His Orchestra | At The Rendezvous Vol.1 | Status | CD 102(882198)
We Like It
Günther Klatt & New York Razzmatazz | Fa Mozzo | Tutu Records | 888138-2
We Live Here
Roy Ayers Quintet | Hot | Ronnie Scott's Jazz House | JHCD 021
We Might As Well Call It Thrtough(I Didn't Get Married To Your Two-Timing Mother)
Jeanne Lee-Gunter Hampel Duo | Freedom Of The Universe | Birth | 0030
We Move(take 1)
Gunter Hampel Group | The 8th Of July 1969 | Birth | CD 001
We Move(take 2)
The 8th Of July 1969 | Birth | CD 001
We Move(take 3)
Peter Brötzmann Quartet | Dare Devil | DIW | DIW 857 CD
We Remember Pres
Jimmy Rushing All Stars | The Bluesway Sessions | Charly | CDX 13
We See
Ellery Eskelin With Andrea Parkins & Jim Black | The Secret Museum | HatOLOGY | 552
Sphere | Sphere | Verve | 557796-2
Thelonious Monk Quintet | MONK | Original Jazz Classics | OJCCD 016-2
On Tour In Europe | Charly | CD 122
Trio Impossible | Trio Impossible | Jazz 4 Ever Records:Jazz Network | J4E 4738
Phil Mason's New Orleans All-Stars With Christine Tyrrell | Spirituals & Gospels | Lake | LACD 64
We Shall Overcome
Charlie Haden-Hank Jones | Steal Away | Verve | 527249-2
Charlie Haden's Liberation Music Orchestra | Liberation Music Orchestra | Impulse(MCA) | 951188-2
Louis Armstrong And His Friends | Jazz Special-His Last Recordings | RCA | ND 89527
Mahalia Jackson And Her Trio With The Drayton Singers | Live In Antibes 1968 | France's Concert | FCD 122
We Shall Walk Through The Streets Of The City
Chris Barber's Jazz Band | Copulatin' Jazz | Great Southern Records | GS 11025
George Lewis Band | The George Lewis Band At Herbert Otto's Party | American Music | AMCD-74
Percy Humphrey's Crescent City Joy Makers | New Orleans-The Living Legends:Percy Humphey's Crescent City Joy Makers | Original Jazz Classics | OJCCD 1834-2
We Speak
Rick Margitza Septet | Color | Blue Note | 792279-2
We Supply
Chris Barber's Jazz Band | 40 Years Jubilee At The Opera House Nürnberg | Timeless | CD TTD 590
We Sure Do Need Him
Chris Barber Original Jazzband Of 1954 | Chris Barber:40 Years Jubilee Concert | Storyville | 4990013
We Sure Do Need Him Now
Chris Barber's Jazz And Blues Band | Class Of '78 | Black Lion | 187001
We Three
Michael Carvin | Drum Concerto At Dawn | Mapleshade | 03732
We Three Kings Of Orient Are
Donald Brown Quartet | Jazz City Christmas,Vol.1 | Jazz City | 660.53.006
We Travel The Spaceways
Sun Ra And His Intergalactic Solar Arkestra | Space Is The Place(Soundtrack) | Evidence | ECD 22070-2
We Were In Love
Benny Carter Quintet | All That Jazz-Live At Princeton | Limelight | 820841-2 IMS
We Will Meet Again
Fred Hersch Trio With Toots Thielemans | Evanessence: A Tribute To Bill Evans | Jazz City | 660.53.027
We Will Met Again
Kenny Drew Jr. Trio | Remembrance | TCB Records | TCB 20202
We Will Met Again (For Harry)
Roosevelt Sykes | Roosevelt Sykes(1929-1941) | Story Of Blues | CD 3542-2
We Wish You A Merry Christmas
Keith Foley | Music For Christmas | dmp Digital Music Productions | CD 452
Weak-Minded Blues
Willie Baker | The Georgia Blues 1927-1933 | Yazoo | YAZ 1012
Wealthy Clients
Jack Hylton And His Orchestra | The Bands That Matter | Eclipse | ECM 2046
Wear And Tear
Philip Aaberg | High Plains | Windham Hill | WD 1037
Weary Blues
Alvin Alcorn Band With George Lewis | George Lewis With Red Allen-The Circle Records | American Music | AMCD-71
Bunk Johnson's Jazz Band | Commodore Classics-Old New Orleans Jazz 1942 | Commodore | 6.24547 AG
Dutch Swing College Band | Dutch Swing College Band Live In 1960 | Philips | 838765-2
Erskine Hawkins And His Orchestra | The Original Tuxedo Junction | RCA | ND 90363(874142)
New Orleans Rhythm Kings | New Orleans Rhythm Kings | Milestone | MCD 47020-2
The Metro Stompers | The Metro Stompers | Sackville | 4002
Tommy Dorsey And His Orchestra | The Original Sounds Of The Swing Era Vol. 8 | RCA | CL 05521 DP
Tommy Ladnier And His Orchestra | Victor Jazz History Vol.19:Dixieland Revival | RCA | 2135738-2
Weary Way Blues
Conrad Janis And His Tailgate Band | Conrad Janis And His Tailgate Band Vol.2 | GHB Records | BCD-81
Weaselocity
Miniature | I Can't Put My Finger On It | JMT Edition | 849147-2
Weasil
Donald Byrd Orchestra | Fancy Free | Blue Note | 789796-2
Weather Bird
Harry James And His Orchestra With The Dixieland Five | Compact Jazz | Verve | 833285-2 PMS
Louis Armstrong With Earl Hines | Heebie Jeebies | Naxos Jazz | 8.120351 CD
Steve Lane's Famour Red Hot Peppers | Easy Come-Easy Go:A Jazz Cocktail | AZURE Compact Disc | AZ-CD-14
Barrelhouse Jazzband | The King Oliver Heritage Jazz Band | L+R Records | CDLR 40033
Weather Bird Rag
King Oliver's Creole Jazz Band | King Oliver's Creole Jazzband-The Complete Set | Retrieval | RTR 79007
Louisiana Repertory Jazz Ensemble Of New Orleans | Hot & Sweet Sounds Of Lost New Orleans | Stomp Off Records | CD 1140
Weathercock's Call
Gary Dial-Dick Oatts Quartet With Brass Ensemble | Brassworks | dmp Digital Music Productions | CD 477
Weaver Of Dreams
Eddie Daniels Quartet | Under The Influence | GRP | GRP 97172
John Hicks Quartet | In The Mix | Landmark | LCD 1542-2
Tete Montoliu/Peter King Quintet | New Year's Morning '89 | Fresh Sound Records | FSR 117(835311)
Weaving A Garland
Hampton Hawes Orchestra | Northern Windows | Prestige | P 10088
Web
Hayden Chisholm | Circe | Jazz Haus Musik | JHM 0081 CD
Joe Lovano Sextet | Tenor Legacy | Blue Note | 827014-2
Web Of Fire
Art Blakey And The Jazz Messengers | Straight Ahead | Concord | CCD 4168
Wedding In The Wild Forest(part 1&2)
Mikhail Alperin's Moscow Art Trio | Hamburg Concert | JA & RO | JARO 4201-2
Wedding In The Wild Forest(part 2)
Stanley Cowell Trio | Travellin' Man | Black Lion | BLCD 760178
Wedding Music
Ralph Towner | Blue Sun | ECM | 1250(829162-2)
Wedding Of The Streams
Liz Story | Solid Colors | Windham Hill | TA-C- 1023
Wedding Song
Jukka Tolonen Group | Crossection | Sonet | 147119
Wedding Suite
Jaco Pastorius/Brian Melvin Group | Jazz Street | Timeless | CD SJP 258
Wednesday Evening Blues
Heartbop | Wednesday Night | yvp music | CD 3033
Wednesday Night Prayer Meeting
Charles Mingus Jazz Workshop | Blues & Roots | Atlantic | 8122-75205-2
Rhino Presents The Atlantic Jazz Gallery | Atlantic | 8122-71257-2
Blues & Roots | Atlantic | 7567-81336-2
Charles Mingus Orchestra | Me Myself An Eye | Atlantic | 50571
Charles Mingus Quintet | Charles Minus-Live | Affinity | CD AFS 778
Mingus Big Band | Live In Time | Dreyfus Jazz Line | FDM 36583-2
Wednesday Night Prayer Meeting-
Charles Mingus And His Orchestra | Charles Mingus-Passion Of A Man:The Complete Atlantic Recordings 1956-1961 | Atlantic | 8122-72871-2
Wednesday Night Prayer Meeting(alt.take)
Charles Mingus Jazz Workshop | Blues & Roots | Atlantic | 8122-75205-2
Joe Newman Quintet | Jive At Five | Prestige | 61159
Wee
Gillespie-Stitt-Getz Septet | Diz And Getz | Verve | 2-2521 IMS
James Spaulding Quartet | Songs Of Courage | Muse | MCD 5382
Johnny Griffin Quartet | Live At The Jazzhus Montmartre,Copenhagen Vol.2 | Jazz Colours | 874724-2
Quintet Of The Year | Charlie Parker The Immortal Sessions Vol.2:1949-1953 | SAGA Jazz Classics | EC 3319-2
Red Holloway Quartet | Nica's Dream | Steeplechase | SCCD 31192
Roy Hargrove Quintet | The Collected Roy Hargrove | RCA | 2668710-2
Charlie Parker Sextet | Charlie Parker Live Feb.14, 1950 | EPM Musique | FCD 5710
Wee Baby Blues
Big Joe Turner With The Count Basie Band | The Bosses | Original Jazz Classics | OJCCD 821-2(2310709)
Shakey Horton Band | The Soul Of Blues Harmonica | Chess | CH 9268
Wee Dot
Art Blakey And The Jazz Messengers | A Night At Birdland Vol. 2 | Blue Note | 532147-2
The History Of Art Blakey And The Jazz Messengers | Blue Note | 797190-2
Dexter Gordon Quartet | The Apartment | Steeplechase | SCCD 31025
Jutta Hipp Quintet | Jutta Hipp With Zoot Sims | Blue Note | 852439-2
Art Blakey And The Jazz Messengers | A Night At Birdland Vol. 3 | Blue Note | 300192(BNJ 61002)
Wee Dot(Blues For Some Bones)
Earl Bostic Quintet | Alto Magic In Hi Fi | Sing | 597
Wee See
Scalesenders | This And More | Edition Collage | EC 498-2
Wee(Allen's Alley)

Dizzy Gillespie Septet | Stan Getz Highlights | Verve | 847430-2
For Musicians Only | For Musicians Only | Verve | 837435-2
Ultimate Stan Getz selected by Joe Henderson | Verve | 557532-2
Quintet Of The Year | The Quintet-Jazz At Massey Hall | Debut | DSA 124-6
Charlie Parker Quintet | Bird Eyes-Last Unissued Vol.14 | Philology | W 844.2

Wee,Too
Bazillus | The Regulator | ACT | 9206-2

Weed
Harlem Mamfats | I'm So Glad | Queen-Disc | 062

Weehawken Mad Pad
Elmo Hope Sextet | The All Star Sessions | Milestone | M 47037

Weeja
L'Orchestre De Contrebasses | Les Cargos | Label Bleu | LBLC 6536(889138)

Weekly Blues
Mama Estella Yancey With Erwin Helfer | Maybe I'll Cry | Steeplechase | SCB 9001

Weep
Gerry Mulligan Concert Jazz Band | Verve Jazz Masters 36:Gerry Mulligan | Verve | 523342-2
Manfred Schoof Quintet | Scales | Japo | 60013

Weep No More,My Lady
The Guest Stars | The Guest Stars | Eigelstein | 568-72227

Weeping Willow
John Lee Hooker | The Blues | America | AM 6078
Pete Christlieb Quartet | Conversations With Warne Vol.1 | Criss Cross | Criss 1043

Weeping Willow Blues
Pink Anderson | Pink Anderson Vol.1:Carolina Blues Man | Original Blues Classics | OBC- 504(BV 1038)

Weightless
Inge Brandenburg mit Kurt Edelhaben und seinem Orchester | Why Don't You Take All Of Me | Bear Family Records | BCD 15614 AH

Weil Ich Angst Hab' Vor Dir
Vienna Art Orchestra | All That Strauss | TCB Records | TCB 20052

Weinsberg Dance With Me
Oscar Klein Band | Pick-A-Blues Live | Jazzpoint | JP 1071
Jack Walrath And The Masters Of Supense | Serious Hang | Muse | MCD 5475

Weird Beard
Bob Mintzer Big Band | Art Of The Big Band | dmp Digital Music Productions | CD 479

Weird Nightmare
Michele Rosewoman And Quintessence | Guardians Of The Light | Enja | ENJ-9378 2
Michele Rosewoman Trio | Occasion To Rise | Evidence | ECD 22042-2
Jack Bruce-Bernie Worrell | Monkjack | CMP Records | CMP CD 1010

Weird Poetry
Chase | Pure Music | Epic | EPC 80017

Weird Walsje No.1
Miles Davis Quartet | Miles Davis Vol.1 | Blue Note | 532610-2

Weirdo
Peter Weniger Quartet | Weirdoes | Mons Records | MR 874826

Weird-O
Art Blakey And The Jazz Messengers | Art Blakey/The Jazz Messengers | CBS | CK 62265
Miles Davis Quartet | Miles Davis:The Blue Note And Capitol Recordings | Blue Note | 827475-2
Miles Davis:The Best Of The Capitol/Blue Note Years | Blue Note | 798287-2
Miles Davis Vol.2 | Blue Note | 300082(1502)

Weißt Du Noch?
Ulli Bögershausen | Best Of Ulli Bögershausen | Laika Records | LK 93-045
Motus Quartett | Grimson Flames | Creative Works Records | CW CD 1023-2

Weit Zurück, Auf Einer Enlosen Landstraße...-
Hans Joachim Roedelius/Alexander Czjzek | Weites Land | Amadeo | 831627-2

Welcome
Big Band De Lausanne & Charles Papasoff | Astor | TCB Records | TCB 95502
Good Fellas | Good Fellas 2 | Paddle Wheel | KICJ 115
John Coltrane Quartet | The Gentle Side Of John Coltrane | Impulse(MCA) | 951107-2
John Coltrane-His Greatest Years, Vol. 3 | MCA | AS 9278
Coltrane Spiritual | Impulse(MCA) | 589099-2
Kenny Wheeler Quartet | Welcome | Soul Note | 121171-2
Larry Ochs Quartet | John Coltrane's Ascension | Black Saint | 120180-2
Wiregrass Sacred Harp Singers | The Colored Sacred Harp | New World Records | 80433-2

Welcome Back
Jack DeJohnette Quartet | Oneness | ECM | 1637(537343-2)

Welcome Blessing
The Ethnic Heritage Ensemble | Ethnic Heritage Ensemble | Leo Records | 014

Welcome Herr Lazaro
Errol Dixon with Mickey Baker & The Alex Sanders Funk Time Band | Fighting The Boogie | Bellaphon | BCH 33021

Welcome Home
Liz Story Group | Speechless | RCA | PL 83037

Welcome To A Prayer
Axel Zwingenberger-Vince Weber | The Boogiemeisters | Vagabond | VRCD 8.99026

Welcome To Boogie City
Lous Dassen With Holger Clausen/Atlanta Jazzband | Let's Do It... | Dr.Jazz Records | 8606-2

Welcome To New York
Oliver Nelson And His Orchestra | Black Brown And Beautiful | RCA | ND 86993

Welcome To Our World
The Rippingtons | Welcome To St. James' Club | GRP | GRP 96182

Welcome To The Club
Mel Tormé With The Wally Stott Orchestra | Compact Jazz: Mel Torme | Verve | 833282-2 PMS
Patricia Covair-Greg Troyer | New Orleans After Dark | Challenger Productions | AE 1000-2

Welcome To What You Think You Hear
Hans Reichel | Shamghaied On Tor Road | FMP | CD 46

We'll Always Be Together
Robin Kenyatta Quartet | Girl From Martinique | ECM | 1008 (2301008)

We'll Be Together Again
Benny Carter With The Oscar Peterson Quartet | 3,4,5 The Verve Small Group Sessions | Verve | 849395-2 PMS
Billy Pierce Quartet | The Complete William The Conqueror Sessions | Sunnyside | SSC 9013 D
Christian Rover Group feat. Rhoda Scott | Christian Rover Group-Live With Rhoda Scott At The Organ | Organic Music | ORGM 9704
Cologne Concert Big Band | Live | Mons Records | MR 874811
David Sills Quintet | Journey Together | Naxos Jazz | 86023-2
Ella Fitzgerald With Frank De Vol And His Orchestra | Like Someone In Love | Verve | 511524-2
Elvin Jones Trio | The Ultimate Elvin Jones | Blue Note | 84305
Gene Ammons-Sonny Stitt Quintet | Gentle Jug Vol.3 | Prestige | PCD 24249-2
We'll Be Together Again | Original Jazz Classics | OJCCD 708-2(P 7606)
J.J.Johnson-Joe Pass | We'll Be Together Again | Pablo | 2310911-2
Joe Newman Octet | The Complete Joe Newman RCA-Victor Recordings(1955-1956):The Basie Days | RCA | 2122613-2
Joe Pass-Jimmy Rowles Duo | Checkmate | Original Jazz Classics | OJCCD 975-2(2310865)
Joe Pass:A Man And His Guitar | Original Jazz Classics | OJCCD 8806-2
John Hicks Trio | Gentle Rain | Sound Hills | SSCD 8062
Leroy Vinnegar Quartet | Integrity-The Walker Live At Lairmont | Jazz Focus | JFCD 009
Lurlean Hunter And Her All Stars | Blue & Sentimantel | Atlantic | AMCY 1081
Marty Elkins And Her Sextet | Fuse Blues | Nagel-Heyer | CD 062
Mary Fettig Quintet | In Good Company | Concord | CJ 273
Melvin Rhyne Quintet | To Cannonball With Love | Paddle Wheel | KICJ 147
Pat Martino-Gil Goldstein Duo | We'll Be Together Again | Muse | MR 5090
Ray Sherman | Ray Sherman At The Keyboard | Arbors Records | ARCD 19133
Ron McClure Sextet | Double Triangle | Naxos Jazz | 86044-2
Sonny Criss Quintet | Blues Pour Flirter | Polydor | 2445034 IMS
Tony Bennett-Bill Evans | The Tony Bennett-Bill Evans Album | Original Jazz Classics | OJC20 439-2(F 9489)
Toots Thielemans Quartet | Jazz In Paris:Toots Thielemans-Blues Pour Flirter | EmArCy | 549403-2 PMS
Toots Thielemans Trio | Only Trust Your Heart | Concord | MC CJ 355C
Viktoria Tolstoy With The Jacob Karlzon Trio | Blame It On My Youth | Kaza(EMI) | 536620-2

We'll Be Together Again-
Roland Kirk Quintet | Rahsaan/The Complete Mercury Recordings Of Roland Kirk | Mercury | 846630-2
Sheila Jordan With The Kenny Barron Trio | Lost And Found | Muse | MCD 5390

We'll Be Together Again(2)
Tal Farlow Quartet | This Is Tal Farlow | Verve | 537746-2

We'll Do It
Ella Johnson With Orchestra | Swing Me | Official | 6009

We'll Go No More A-Roving
Zbigniew Namyslowski Sextet | Air Condition | Affinity | AFF 83

Well Hello There
Tom Mega + Band | Backyards Of Pleasure | ITM Records | ITM 1432

Well In That Case
Unternehmen Kobra | Central Europe Suite | G.N.U. Records | CD A 94.007

Well Make It
John Surman Orchestra | Tales Of The Algonquin | Deram | 844884-2

We'll Meet Again
Preservation Hall Jazz Band | Because Of You | CBS | SK 60327

Well Of Clouds
Jack Teagarden And His Orchestra | Jack Teagarden | Queen-Disc | 027

We'll See
Les McCann Trio | In San Francisco | Pacific Jazz | LN 10077

We'll See Yaw'll After While Ya Heah
Stanley Turrentine Quartet | That's Where It's At | Blue Note | 869939-7

Well Sir
Gerald Wilson Orchestra | Feelin' Kinda Blues | Pacific Jazz | CDP 79-2

We'll Wait For You
Sun Ra And His Intergalactic Solar Arkestra | Space Is The Place(Soundtrack) | Evidence | ECD 22070-2

Well You Needn't
Cannonball Adderley Sextet | What I Mean | Milestone | M 47053
Chet Baker Sextet | Chet Is Back | RCA | NL 70578 AG
Chet Baker With The NDR-Bigband | The Last Concert Vol.I+II | Enja | ENJ-6074 22
Cindy Blackman Quartet | Cindy Blackman Telepathy | Muse | MCD 5437
Dave Bailey Sextet | One Foot In The Gutter | Epic | ESCA 7759
Jeff Hamilton Trio | Jeff Hamilton Trio Live | Mons Records | MR 874777
Jimmy Smith Trio | Incredible Jimmy Smith Vol.3 | Blue Note | 300106(1525)
John Coltrane-Thelonious Monk Septet | Monk & Trane | Milestone | M 47011
Miles Davis Quartet | Kind Of Blue:Blue Note Celebrate The Music Of Miles Davis | Blue Note | 534255-2
Miles Davis Vol.1 | Blue Note | 532610-2
Miles Davis:The Blue Note And Capitol Recordings | Blue Note | 827475-2
Miles Davis:The Best Of The Capitol/Blue Note Years | Blue Note | 798287-2
Miles Davis Vol.2 | Blue Note | 300082(1502)
Miles Davis Quintet | Miles Davis In Person-Friday Night At The Blackhawk,San Francisco,Vol.1 | CBS | C4K 87106
Free Trade Hall Vol.2 | Magnetic Records | MRCD 103
Oliver Jones Trio | Just In Time | Justin Time | JUST 120/1-2
Thelonious Monk Quartet | Monk-Misterioso | CBS | 468406-2
Paris Jazz Concert:Thelonious Monk And His Quartet | Laserlight | 17250
Thelonious Monk:85th Birthday Celebration | zyx records | FANCD 6076-2
Live In Paris 1964 | France's Concert | FCD 132x2
En Concert Avec Europe 1 | Laserlight | 710377/78
Thelonious Monk-The Complete Riverside Recordings | Riverside | 15 RCD 022-2
Thelonious Monk In Copenhagen | Storyville | STCD 8283
Live At Monterey Jazz Festival,1963 | Jazz Unlimited | JUCD 2045/2046
Thelonious Monk Septet | Thelonious Monk-The Complete Riverside Recordings | Riverside | 15 RCD 022-2
Thelonious Monk Trio | Genius Of Modern Music,Vol.1 | Blue Note | 300403
Monk's Mood | Naxos Jazz | 8.120588 CD
Thelonious Monk:Complete 1947-1952 Blue Note Recordings | The Jazz Factory | JFCD 22838
Wolfgang Puschnig-Jamaladeen Tacuma Trio | Gemini Gemini-The Flavors Of Thelonious Monk | ITM-Pacific | ITMP 970082
Donald Byrd Quartet With Bobby Jaspar | Au Chat Qui Peche 1958 | Fresh Sound Records | FSCD 1028

Well You Needn't-
Steve Kuhn Quartet | Last Year's Waltz | ECM | 1213

Well You Needn't(alt.take)
Thelonious Monk Trio | Genius Of Modern Music,Vol.1 | Blue Note | 532138-2
More Genius Of Thelonious Monk | Blue Note | 300194(BNJ 61011)

Well,Add Black
Buck Clayton's Big Four | The Classic Swing Of Buck Clayton | Original Jazz Classics | OJCCD 1709-2(RLP 142)

Wellen Und Wolken
Art Blakey And The Jazz Messengers | Kyoto | Original Jazz Classics | OJCCD 145-2

Wells Fargo
Wilbur Harden Quintet | Countdown | Savoy | 650102(881902)

Welt Ohne Morgen(Floyd Westermann)
Peter Kowald | Open Secrets | FMP | 1190

Wendekreis Des Steinbocks
George Shearing | Piano | Concord | CCD 4400

Wendy
Rob McConnell And The Boss Brass | Tribute | MPS | 68276

Wenn Der Sommer Wieder Einzieht
Lisa Wahland And Her Trio | Marlene | Fine Music | FM 108-2

Wenn Der Sommer Wieder Einzieht(intro)
No Nett | Wenn Der Weiße Flieder Wieder Blüht | Jazz Haus Musik | JHM 14

Wenn Ein Junger Mann Kommt
Max Greger Und Sein Orchester | Swing Tanzen Gestattet | Vagabond | 6.28415 DP

Wenn Ich In Deine Augen Seh'
Lisa Wahland And Her Trio | Marlene | Fine Music | FM 108-2

Wenn Ich Mir Was
Georg Ruby Village Zone | Mackeben Revisited:The Ufa Years | Jazz Haus Musik | JHM 0121 CD

Wenn Ich Mir Was Wünschen Dürfte
Peter Brötzmann/Werner Lüdi | Wie Das Leben So Spielt | FMP | CD 22

Wenn Nix Höre,Muß Spille
Georg Ruby Village Zone | Mackeben Revisited:The Ufa Years | Jazz Haus Musik | JHM 0121 CD

Wenn Verliebte Bummeln Gehen
Peter Kowald Quintett | Peter Kowald Quintett | FMP | 0070

Wenn's Im Sommer Ins Kino Schneit
Matthias Bätzel Trio | Green Dumplings | JHM Records | JHM 3618

Wenn's Mailüfterl Weht
Don Rendell Five | Just Music | Spotlite | SPJ 502

Weps
Aki Takase Quintet | St.Louis Blues | Enja | 9130-2

Wer Kommt Mehr Vom Sozialamt?
Tilman Jäger Tape 4 | Abendlieder | Satin Doll Productions | SDP 1043-1 CD

Wer Nur Den Lieben Gott Lässt Walten
Der Rote Bereich | Risky Business | ACT | 9407-2

Wer Wird Wird Wirt
Barbara Dennerlein Quartet | Orgelspiele | Böhm Records | 65145 IMS

We're Five
WDR Big Band | Harlem Story | Koala Records | CD P 7

We're In Love Again
Dave Pell Octet | Campus Hop:Jazz Goes Dancing | Fresh Sound Records | LPM 1662(RCA)

We're In The Money-
Connie Francis With Orchestra | The Swinging Connie Francis | Audiophile | ACD-286

We're In This Love Together
Alexis Korner & Memphis Slim | The Blues Vol. 5 | Big Bear | 156042

We're Still Friends
Dick Hyman | Cole Porter:All Through The Night | Musicmasters | 5060-2

Were You There
Mahalia Jackson | In Memoriam Mahalia Jackson | CBS | 66501

Werther
Göbels-Harth Group | Es Herrscht Uhu Im Land | Japo | 60037 (2360037)

Wes
Lee Ritenour Sextet | Alive In L.A. | GRP | GRP 98822

Wes Bound
Wes Montgomery Quintet | Straight No Chaser | Bandstand | BDCD 1504

West
Paul Bley-Paul Motian Duo | Notes | Soul Note | 121190-2

West 42nd Street
Kenny Dorham Quintet | Soul Support | Jazz Colours | 874756-2

West Africa Blue
World Saxophone Quartet | Dances And Ballads | Nonesuch | 7559-79164-2

West African Snap
Arcado-String Trio | Arcado-String Trio | JMT Edition | 919028-2

West Bank City
Craig Handy Trio | Three For All + One | Arabesque Recordings | AJ 0109

West Coast
Blind Blake | Blind Blake-Rope Stretchin' Blues | Biograph | BLP 12037

West Coast Blues
Blue Mitchell Orchestra | A Blue Time | Milestone | M 47055
Horace Parlan Trio | Hi-Fly | Steeplechase | SCCD 31417
Klaus Weiss Quintet | A Taste Of Jazz | ATM Records | ATM 3810-AH
Lightnin' Hopkins | Lightnin' Hopkins Sings The Blues | Pathe | 2C 068-83075(Imperial)
Project G-5 | Tribute To Wes Montgomery | Paddle Wheel | KICJ 146
Rene Thomas Quintet | Meeting Mister Thomas | Fresh Sound Records | FSR 554(Barclay 84091)
The Mastersounds | Swinging With The Mastersounds | Original Jazz Classics | OJC 280(F 8050)
Wes Montgomery Quartet | The Incredible Guitar Of Wes Montgomery | Original Jazz Classics | OJC20 036-2
Live In Paris 1965 | France's Concert | FCD 108
Wes Montgomery With Orchestra | Compact Jazz: Wes Montgomery Plays The Blues | Verve | 835318-2 PMS
Project G-7 | Tribute To Wes Montgomery, Vol.2 | Paddle Wheel | KICJ 131

West End Avenue
Ralph Sutton Quartet | Partners In Crime | Sackville | SKCD2-2023

West End Blues
Beryl Bryden With The Rod Mason Band | Dixie From The Island Vol.3 | Jazz Colours | 874704-2
Charlie Barnet And His Orchestra | Big Band Bounce & Boogie:Skyliner-Charlie Barnet | Affinity | AFS 1012
King Oliver And His Orchestra | Luis Russell And His Orchestra 1927-29 | Village(Jazz Archive) | VILCD 018-2
Louis Armstrong And His All Stars | Ambassador Satch | CBS | CK 64926
Louis Armstrong And His All Stars/Orchestra | The Wonderful World Of Louis Armstrong | MCA | 2292-57202-2
Louis Armstrong And His Hot Five | Jazz Gallery:Louis Armstrong Vol.1 | RCA | 2114166-2
Heebie Jeebies | Naxos Jazz | 8.120351 CD
Louis Armstrong And His Orchestra | Louis Armstrong:Swing That Music | Laserlight | 36056
Louis Armstrong And His Big Band Vol.1-The Maturity | Black & Blue | BLE 59.225 2
Thomas Heberer-Dieter Manderscheid | What A Wonderful World | Jazz Haus Musik | JHM 0118 CD

West End Blues-
Sammy Price | Dixieland Jubilee-Vol. 1 | Intercord | 155002

West From California's Shores
Brad Mehldau Trio | Places | Warner | 9362-47693-2

West Hartford
Honeyboy Edwards | White Windows | Evidence | ECD 26039-2

West Indian Pancake
Duke Ellington And His Orchestra | Ella Fitzgerald And Duke Ellington:Cote D'Azure Concerts on Verve | Verve | 539033-2
Ella Fitzgerald And Duke Ellington:Cote D'Azure Concerts on Verve | Verve | 539033-2
Soul Call | Verve | 539785-2
Duke Ellington And His Famous Orchestra | Duke Ellington & His Famous Orchestra | Forlane | UCD 19003

West Of Pecos
Donald Byrd Sextet | Blackjack | Blue Note | 784466-2

West Print
Dinah Washington With The Rudy Martin Trio | The Complete Dinah Washington On Mercury Vol.1 | Mercury | 832444-2

West Side Blues
T-Bone Walker And His Band | The Great Blues Vocals And Guitar Of T-Bone Walker | Pathe | 2C 068-86523(Capitol)

West Side Story Medley:
Earl Hines Trio | Boogie Woogie On St.Louis Blues | Prestige | MPP 2515

West Side Story(Medley)
Dave Burrell Trio | High Won-High Two | Black Lion | BLCD 760206

West Side Stroll
Memphis Slim | Boogie Woogie Piano | CBS | CBS 21106

West Winds Are Blowing(take 1)
Andrew Hill Quintet | But Not Farewell | Blue Note | 794971-2

Western Suite:
Gerry Mulligan Sextet | California Concerts Vol.2 | Pacific Jazz | 746864-2

Western Woman
Oliver Augst-Rüdiger Carl-Christoph Korn | Blank | FMP | OWN-90013

West-Östlicher Divan
Louisiana Red | New York Blues | L+R Records | LR 42002

Westwind
Joe Venuti-Zoot Sims Sextet | Joe Venuti And Zoot Sims | Chiaroscuro | CR 142

Westwood Walk
Gerry Mulligan Tentette | The Birth Of The Cool Vol.2 | Capitol | 798935-2
The Mike Hennessey Chastet | Shades Of Chas Burchell | IN+OUT Records | 7025-2
David Becker Tribune | In Motion | Bluemoon | R 27-7916-2

Wet Back In The Left Bank
The Herdsmen | The Herdsmen Play Paris | Original Jazz Classics | OJC 116(F 3201)

Wet In Paris
Erik Truffaz Quartet Quintet | Out Of A Dream | Blue Note | 855855-2
Straight Talk | Pure | Jazz 4 Ever Records:Jazz Network | J4E 4719
Wet Point
Dave Weckl Band | Synergy | Stretch Records | SCD 9022-2
We've Made Some Good Money, Man
Art Farmer With Orchestra | Gentle Eyes | Mainstream | MD CDO 716
We've Only Just Begun
Charlie Byrd Trio With Strings & Brass | Crystal Silence | Fantasy | F 9429
Singers Unlimited | Four Of Us | MPS | 68106
WGZFM
The Boswell Sisters | It's The Girls | ASV | AJA 5014
Wham
Duke Ellington And His Orchestra | The Duke At Fargo 1940 | Storyville | STCD 8316/17
Jack Teagarden And His Orchestra | Varsity Sides | Savoy | WL 70827 (809324)) SF
Wham And They're Off
Charles Mingus Quintet With Roland Kirk | Charles Mingus-Passion Of A Man:The Complete Atlantic Recordings 1956-1961 | Atlantic | 8122-72871-2
Wham Bam Thank You Ma'Am
The Very Best Of Charles Mingus | Rhino | 8122-79988-2
Charles Mingus -Passions Of A Man | Atlantic | ATL 60143
Whap!
Jack McDuff Quartet | Honeydripper | Original Jazz Classics | OJC 222(P 7199)
What
Subwave | Subwave | G.N.U. Records | CD A 96.X22
What A B.T.
Klaus Ignatzek Quintet | Son Of Gaudi | Nabel Records:Jazz Network | CD 4660
Sonny Terry & Brownie McGhee | Just A Closer Walk With Thee | Original Blues Classics | OBCCD 541-2(F 3296)
What A Beautiful City
Oliver Jones Trio | Northern Summit | Enja | ENJ-6086 2
What A Beautiful Yesteryear
The Pilgrim Travelers | The Best Of The Pilgrim Travelers | Ace Records | CDCHD 342
What A Day
Ella Johnson With Orchestra | Swing Me | Official | 6009
What A Difference A Day Made
Coleman Hawkins With Michel Warlop And His Orchestra | Django Reinhardt And His American Friends:Paris 1935-1937 | Memo Music | HDJ 4124
Dinah Washington With Orchestra | Mad About The Boy-The Best Of Dinah Washington | Mercury | 512214-2
Dinah Washington With The Belford Hendricks Orchestra | Verve Jazz Masters 20:Introducing | Verve | 510853-2
Verve Jazz Masters 19:Dinah Washington | Verve | 518200-2
4 By 4:Ella Fitzgerald/Sarah Vaughan/Billie Holiday/Dinah Washington | Verve | 559693-2
Donna Drake With The Wynton Kelly Trio | Donna Sings Dinah | Fresh Sound Records | FSR-CD 0060
Jens Bunge Group | Meet You In Chicago | Jazz 4 Ever Records:Jazz Network | J4E 4749
Jimmie Lunceford And His Orchestra | The King Of Big Band Jazz | Festival | Album 146
Kay Starr With Orchestra | The Uncollected:Kay Starr Vol.2 | Hindsight | HSR 229
Lonnie Johnson | Losing Game | Original Blues Classics | OBCCD 543-2(BV 1924)
Sarah Vaughan With The Jimmy Jones Quartet | Tenderly | Bulldog | BDL 1009
Stephane Grappelli Quartet | Stephane Grappelli | LRC Records | CDC 9014
Hank Crawford And His Orchestra | Cajun Sunrise | Kudu | 63048
What A Fellowship
Niels Lan Doky Trio | Niels Lan Doky | Verve | 559087-2
What A Friend We Have In Jesus
George Lewis And His New Orleans All Stars | King Of New Orleans | Vagabond | 6.28053 DP
What A Friend We Have In Jesus-
Ornette Coleman Quartet | Sound Museum | Verve | 531914-2
What A Little Moonlight Can Do
Billie Holiday And Her All Stars | The Billie Holiday Song Book | Verve | 823246-2
4 By 4:Ella Fitzgerald/Sarah Vaughan/Billie Holiday/Dinah Washington | Verve | 559693-2
Billie Holiday And Her Orchestra | Billie Holiday: The First Verve Sessions | Verve | 2610027
Billie Holiday With The Mal Waldron Trio | Compact Jazz: Billie Holiday-Live | Verve | 841434-2
Ella Fitzgerald, Billie Holiday And Carmen McRae At Newport | Verve | 559809-2
Carmen McRae And Her Sextet | Carmen McRae Sings Lover Man | CBS | CK 65115
Dee Dee Bridgewater With Her Trio | Keeping Tradition | Verve | 519607-2
Dick Collins And The Runaway Heard | Horn Of Plenty | Fresh Sound Records | NL 45632(RCA LJM 1019)
Melissa Walker And Her Band | May I Feel | Enja | ENJ-9335 2
Ralph Sutton Quartet | Live At Sunnie's Rendezvous Vol.1 | Storyville | STCD 8280
The Ralph Sutton Quartet With Ruby Braff,Vol.2 | Storyville | STCD 8246
Rex Allen's Swing Express | Keep Swingin' | Nagel-Heyer | CD 016
Teddy Wilson And His Orchestra | Jazz Gallery:Billie Holiday Vol.1(1933-49) | RCA | 2119542-2
Gloria Lynne With The Ernie Wilkins Orchestra | Go!Go!Go! | Fresh Sound Records | FSR 536(Evererst SDBR 1237)
What A Shame
Chick Webb And His Orchestra | Big Band Bounce & Boogie:In The Groove | Affinity | AFS 1007
What A Woman
Sonny Clay And His Band | Sonny Clay 1922-1960 | Harlequin | HQ 2007 IMS
What A Wonderful World
Jay McShann Quintet | What A Wonderful World | Groove Note | GN 1005(180gr-Pressung)
What A Wonderful World | Groove Note | GRV 1005-2
Jimmy Smith Sextet | Angel Eyes-Ballads & Slow Jams | Verve | 527632-2
Joe Williams With The Robert Farnon Orchestra | Joe Williams:Triple Play | Telarc Digital | CD 83461
Lionel Hampton All Stars | For The Love Of Music | MoJazz | 530554-2
Louis Armstrong And His Friends | Planet Jazz:Louis Armstrong | Planet Jazz | 2152052-2
Louis Armstrong-All Time Greatest Hits | MCA | MCD 11032
Louis Armstrong And His Orchestra | What A Wonderful World | MCA | MCD 01876
Louis Armstrong With Orchestra | RCA Victor 80th Anniversary Vol.6:1970-1979 | RCA | 2668782-2
Louis Moholo's Viva-La-Black | Freedom Tour-Live In South Afrika 1993 | Ogun | OGCD 006
Prowizorka Jazz Band | Prowizorka Jazz Band | Timeless | CD TTD 558
Teresa Brewer & Friends | Memories Of Louis | Red Baron | 469283-2
Vinny Valentino & Here No Evil | Now And Again | dmp Digital Music Productions | CD 3003
What A Wonderful World-
Bill Frisell | Ghost Town | Nonesuch | 7559-79583-2
What A World
Andrew Cyrille | What About? | Affinity | AFF 75
What Am I Here For
Ben Webster With Orchestra And Strings | Music For Loving:Ben Webster With Strings | Verve | 527774-2
Clifford Brown-Max Roach Quintet | Clifford Brown-Max Roach:Alone Together-The Best Of The Mercury Years | Verve | 526373-2
Clifford Brown And Max Roach | Verve | 543306-2
Brownie-The Complete EmArCy Recordings Of Clifford Brown | EmArCy | 838306-2
Count Basie And His Orchestra | April In Paris | Verve | 521402-2
Cy Touff Octet | Cy Touff His Octet & Quintet | Fresh Sound Records | 054 2402651(Pacific Jazz PJ 1211)
David Fathead Newman Sextet | Mr.Gentle, Mr.Cool:A Tribute To Duke Ellington | Kokopelli Records | KOKO 1300
Duke Ellington And His Famous Orchestra | Ben Webster-Cotton Tail | RCA | 63667902
Duke Ellington And His Orchestra | The Feeling Of Jazz | Black Lion | BLCD 760123
Duke Ellington-Count Basie | CBS | 473753-2
George Wein And The Newport All Stars | Swing That Music | CBS | CK 53317
Nat Pierce Quintet | Crosby-Bennett-Clooney-Herman:A Tribute To Duke | Concord | CCD 4050
Sarah Vaughan And Her Band | Duke Ellington Song Book Two | Pablo | CD 2312116
Shelly Manne Quartet | Essence | Galaxy | GXY 5101
The Jazz Age Sextet And The Kammerorchester Schloß Werneck | Happy Birthday,Duke! | Balthasar Records | Balthasar 004(CD 589-1)
Marty Paich Band | I Get A Boot Out Of You | Discovery | DS 829 IMS
What Am I Here For(alt.take)
Dado Moroni | With Duke In Mind | Jazz Connaisseur | JCCD 9415-2
What Am I Here For(spoken closing by Dado Moroni)
With Duke In Mind | Jazz Connaisseur | JCCD 9415-2
What Am I Here For(spoken introduction by Dado Moroni)
Kid Thomas Valentine's Creaole Jazz Band | Kid Thomas Valentine's Creole Jazz Band | American Music | AMCD-49
What Are Days For
John Abercrombie Quartet | M | ECM | 1191
What Are You Doin' Honey
Ella Fitzgerald With The Frank DeVol Orchestra | Ella With You A Swinging Christmas | Verve | 2304445 IMS
What Are You Doing New Year's Eve?
Nancy Wilson With Gerald Wilson's Orchestra | Yesterday's Love Songs-Today's Blues | Capitol | 796265-2
What Are You Doing The Rest Of Your Life
Art Farmer With The Great Jazz Trio And String | Ambrosia | Denon Compact Disc | DC-8574
Bill Evans Quartet With Orchestra | The Complete Bill Evans On Verve | Verve | 527953-2
From Left To Right | Verve | 557451-2
Bill Evans Trio | My Romance | Zeta | ZET 702
Live In Paris 1972 Vol.1 | France's Concert | FCD 107
Yesterday I Heard The Rain | Bandstand | BDCD 1535
Bill Evans With Orchestra | The Complete Bill Evans On Verve | Verve | 527953-2
Bob Cooper With The Mike Wofford Trio | Bob Cooper Plays The Music Of Michel Legrand | Discovery | DS 822 IMS
Gene Ammons And His Orchestra | Free Again | Prestige | P 10040
Joe Venuti-George Barnes Quintet | Live At The Concord Summer Festival | Concord | CJ 30
Lorez Alexandria With The Houston Person Sextet | May I Come In | Muse | MCD 5420
Milt Jackson And His Orchestra | The Best Of Milt Jackson | CTI | 63045
Ray Bryant | Solo Flight | Pablo | 2310798
Roswell Rudd Quartet | Flexile Flyer | Black Lion | BLCD 760215
Tsuyoshi Yamamoto Trio | Live | East Wind | EW 8045 IMS
Woody Herman And The Young Thundering Herd With Friends | Woody And Friends At Monterey Jazz Festival 1979 | Concord | CCD 4170
What Are You Doing The Rest Of Your Life-
Oscar Peterson-Joe Pass Duo | Live At Salle Pleyel, Paris | Pablo | 2625705
What Are You Doing The Rest Of Your Life(alt.take 1)
Bill Evans With Orchestra | The Complete Bill Evans On Verve | Verve | 527953-2
What Are You Doing The Rest Of Your Life(alt.take 2)
Paquito D'Rivera Group | Havana Cafe | Chesky | JD 60
What Cames Out Of A Dog
Jeanie Bryson And Her Band | Tonight I Need You So | Telarc Digital | CD 83348
What Can I Give
Dave Doran Group | Rhythm Voice | Plainisphare | PL 1267-109 CD
What Can I Say
Kenny Blake Group | Interior Design | Heads Up Records | 889010
What Can I Say After I Say I'm Sorry
Allan Vaché-Harry Allen Quintet | Allan And Allan | Nagel-Heyer | CD 074
Ann Gilbert With The Elliot Lawrence Orchestra | In A Swingin' Mood | Fresh Sound Records | NL 45997(RCA LX 1090)
Bud Freeman Trio | The Joy Of Sax | Chiaroscuro | CR 135
Kay Starr With Orchestra | The Uncollected:Kay Starr Vol.2 | Hindsight | HSR 229
Nat King Cole Trio | Nat King Cole Trio 1943-49-The Vocal Sides | Laserlight | 15718
Nat King Cole With The Nelson Riddle Orchestra | The Piano Style Of Nat King Cole | Capitol | 781203-2
Ray Anthony And His Orchestra | Swingin' On Campus! | Pathe | 1566131(Capitol T 645)
Sammy Price Sextet | Rockin' Boogie | Black & Blue | BB 921.2
What Can I Say After I Say I'm Sorry-
Red Rodney-Ira Sullivan Quintet | Live At The Village Vanguard | Muse | MR 5209
What Can We Do?
Linda Hopkins And Her All Stars | How Blue Can You Get | Palo Alto | PA 8034
What 'cha Gonna Do With That
Charly Antolini Orchestra | Soul Beat | ATM Records | ATM 3802-AH
What 'cha Talkin'
Bugge Wesseltoft | It's Snowing On My Piano | ACT | 9260-2
What Child Is This(Greensleeves)
Charlie Byrd | The Charlie Byrd Christmas Album | Concord | CCD 42004
John Colianni Trio With The Cincinnati Sinfonietta | Christmas Songs-Telarc Digital | CD 83315
Vince Guaraldi Trio | A Charlie Brown Christmas | Fantasy | FSA 8431-6
Keith Foley | Music For Christmas | dmp Digital Music Productions | CD 452
What Cild Is This -> Greensleeves
What Could I Do Without You
$$hide$$ | $$Titelverweise | |
What Did I Do To Be So Black And Blue -> Black And Blue
What Did You Buy Today
Low Flying Aircraft | Low Flying Aircraft | Line Records | COCD 9.00426 O
What Did You Say?
Mitchel Forman | Only A Memory | Soul Note | 121070-2
What Do I Owe Here
Jeannie And Jimmy Cheatham & The Sweet Baby Blues Band | Blues And The Boogie Masters | Concord | CCD 4579
What Do We Do?
James Moody Quartet | Moving Forward | Novus | PD 83026
What Do You Do After You Ruin Your Life
Mose Allison Trio | Your Mind Is In Vacation | Atlantic | SD 1691
What Do You See In Her
Sarah Vaughan And Her Band | The Devine One | Fresh Sound Records | FSR 659(Roulette R 52060)
What Do You See?
Michael Mantler Orchestra | Hide And Seek | ECM | 1738(549612-2)
The New Orleans Spiritualettes | I Believe | Sound Of New Orleans | SONO 6012
What Do You Want?
Roland Hanna-George Mraz | Sir Elf Plus 1 | Candid | CRS 1018 IMS
What Does It Take
Art Tatum | The Tatum Solo Masterpieces Vol.7 | Pablo | 2310792
What Does The Snail Say?
Duke Ellington And His Orchestra | En Concert Avec Europe 1 | Laserlight | 710707/08
What Else Is In There
Bobby McFerrin Group | The Young Lions | Elektra | MUS 96.0196-1
What Game Shall We Play Today
Chick Corea Quartet | Return To Forever | ECM | 1022(811978-2)
Chick Corea/Gary Burton | Crystal Silence | ECM | 1024(831331-2)
Chick Corea And Return To Forever | Light As A Feather | Polydor | 557115-2
What Game Shall We Play Today(alt.take 1)
Light As A Feather | Polydor | 557115-2
What Game Shall We Play Today(alt.take 2)
Light As A Feather | Polydor | 557115-2
What Game Shall We Play Today(alt.take 3)
Dave Holland Big Band | What Goes Around | ECM | 1777(014002-2)
What Goes Around Comes Around
Dave Holland Quintet | Not For Nothin' | ECM | 1758(014004-2)
Jeannie And Jimmy Cheatham & The Sweet Baby Blues Band | Back To The Neighborhood | Concord | CCD 4373
What Good Would It Do?
29th Street Saxophone Quartet | Underground | Antilles | 848415-2(889151)
What Have They Done To My Song Ma
Ray Charles With Orchestra | Ray Charles | London | 6.24034 AL
What Have You Done To Me
The International Jazz Group | The International Jazz Group | Swing | SW 8407 IMS
What I Can Do You Can Do Too
Irene Redfield With The Charles Earland Quintet | Million Dollar Secret | Savant Records | SCD 2007
What I Say
Miles Davis Group | Another Bitches Brew | Jazz Door | JD 1284/85
What If
Kenny Barron Quintet | What If | Enja | ENJ-5013 2
Kenny Barron-Regina Carter | Freefall | Verve | 549706-2
Leslie Drayton Orchestra | Love Is A Four-Letter Word | Optimism | ER 1003
What Is Happening
Slide Hampton-Joe Haider Jazz Orchestra | Give Me A Double | JHM Records | JHM 3627
Bernie Senensky Quartet | Wheel Within A Wheel | Timeless | CD SJP 410
What Is Left
Huey Connell Group | Songs For Joy And Sadness | Minor Music | 801095
What Is Love?
Charles Lloyd-Billy Higgins | Which Way Is East | ECM | 1878/79(9811796)
What Is Man
Paul Nero Sound | Doldinger Jubilee | Atlantic | ATL 60073
What Is The Meaning Of This
Ornette Coleman & Prime Time Band | Of Human Feelings | Antilles | AN 2001(802385)
What Is The Word
Michael Mantler Group With The Danish Radio Concert Orchestra Strings | The School Of Understanding(Sort-Of-An-Opera) | ECM | 1648/49(537963-2)
What Is The Word(by Samuel Beckett)
André Previn | Plays Vernon Duke | Contemporary | C 7558
What Is There To Say
Benny Green Trio | In This Direction | Criss Cross | Criss 1038
Billy Butterfield And His Orchestra | The Uncollected:Billy Butterfield | Hindsight | HSR 173
Carmen McRae-George Shearing Duo | Two For The Road | Concord | CCD 4128
Chris Connor With The Ellis Larkins Trio | I Hear Music | Affinity | AFF 97
Dizzy Gillespie With Johnny Richard And His Orchestra | Cool California | Savoy | WL 70511(2)(SJL 2254) DP
Ernie Royal Sextet | Accent On Trumpet | Fresh Sound Records | FSR 645(Urania UJLP 1203)
John Pizzarelli Group | Let There Be Love | Telarc Digital | CD 83518
Maxine Sullivan With The Doc Cheatham Quintet | We Just Couldn't Say Goodbye | Audiophile | ACD-128
Peggy Connelly With The Russ Garcia 'Wigville' Band | Peggy Connelly | Fresh Sound Records | FSR 2018(Bethlehem BCP 53)
Red Garland Quintet feat.John Coltrane | High Pressure | Original Jazz Classics | OJCCD 349-2(P 7209)
Red Garland Trio | Bright And Breezy | Original Jazz Classics | OJC 265(JLP 948)
Sonny Rollins Quartet | The Freedom Suite Plus | Milestone | M 47007
Sonny Rollins-The Freelance Years:The Complete Riverside & Contemporary Recordings | Riverside | 5 RCD 4427-2
Sylvia Syms With The Barbara Carroll Trio | Sylvia Syms Sings | Atlantic | AMCY 1076
Willie 'The Lion' Smith | Commodore Classics-Willie 'The Lion' Smith:Composer-Entertainer | Commodore | 6.25491 AG
What Is This Thing
Thad Jones-Mel Lewis Quartet | The Thad Jones-Mel Lewis Quartet | Artists House | AH 3 IMS
What Is This Thing Called Jazz
Larry Schneider Trio | Freedom Jazz Dance | Steeplechase | SCCD 31390
Tim Ries Septet | Alternate Side | Criss Cross | Criss 1199
What Is This Thing Called Love
Alvin Queen Quartet | Introducing:RTB Big Band | Plainisphare | PL 1267-23
Antonio Farao Trio | Next Stories | Enja | ENJ-9430 2
Art Blakey-Paul Chambers | Drums Around The Corner | Blue Note | 521455-2
Art Pepper Quartet | Among Friends | Discovery | DSCD 837
Art Simmons Quartet | Jazz In Paris:Piano Aux Champs Elysées | EmArCy | 014059-2
Artie Shaw And His Orchestra | The Indispensable Artie Shaw Vol.1/2(1938-1939) | RCA | 2126413-2
Benny Carter Quintet | New York Nights | Musicmasters | 65154-2
Bill Coleman Quintet | Americans Swinging In Paris:Don Byas | EMI Records | 539655-2
Bill Evans Quartet | Modern Days & Night:Music Of Cole Porter | Double Time Records | DTRCD-120
Bill Evans Trio | The Complete Bill Evans On Verve | Verve | 527953-2
The Complete Bill Evans On Verve | Verve | 527953-2
Spring Leaves | Milestone | M 47034
Portrait In Jazz | Original Jazz Classics | OJC20 088-2
Bireli Lagrene Group | Gipsy Project | Dreyfus Jazz Line | FDM 36626-2
Budd Johnson Quartet | In Memory Of A Very Dear Friend | Dragon | DRLP 94
Cannonball Adderley Quintet | The Cannonball Adderley Collection Vol.5:At The Lighthouse | Landmark | CAC 1305-2(882344)
Carmel Jones Quintet | Jay Hawk Talk | Original Jazz Classics | OJCCD 1938-2(P7401)
Charles Mingus Jazz Workshop | Jazzical Moods | Fresh Sound Records | FSR-CD 0062
Charles Mingus Workshop | Abstractions | Bethlehem | BET 6016-2(BCP 65)
Charlie Parker And His Orchestra | Bird: The Complete Charlie Parker On Verve | Verve | 837141-2
Charlie Parker Big Band | Bird On Verve-Vol.7:Charlie Parker Big Band | Verve | 817448-1 IMS
Charlie Parker With Strings | Bird With Strings-Live At The Apollo, Carnegie Hall & Birdland | CBS | CBS 82292

TITELVERZEICHNIS

Charlie Parker With Strings:The Master Takes | Verve | 523984-2
Charlie Parker With The Joe Lipman Orchestra | Verve Jazz Masters 28:Charlie Parker Plays Standards | Verve | 521854-2
Charlie Parker Big Band | Verve | 559835-2
Charlie Shavers With The Al Waslon Trio | A Man And His Music | Storyville | SLP 4073
Clifford Brown-Max Roach Quintet | Brownie-The Complete EmArCy Recordings Of Clifford Brown | EmArCy | 838306-2
Cologne Concert Big Band | Live | Mons Records | MR 874811
Darrell Grant Quartet | Black Art | Criss Cross | Criss 1087
Dave Brubeck Quartet | Brubeck Plays Music From West Side Story And... | CBS | 450410-2
Dick Hafer Quartet | Prez Impressions-Dedicated To The Memory Of Lester Young | Fresh Sound Records | FSR-CD 5002
Ella Fitzgerald With Orchestra | Essential Ella | Verve | 523990-2
Ella Fitzgerald With The Buddy Bregman Orchestra | The Cole Porter Song Book | Verve | 2683044 IMS
Ella Fitzgerald Sings The Cole Porter Songbook Vol.2 | Verve | 821990-2
Firehouse Five Plus Two | Plays For Lovers | Good Time Jazz | GTCD 12014-2
George Garzone Group | Alone | NYC-Records | NYC 6018-2
George Shearing Trio | Jazz Moments | Capitol | 832085-2
Gerry Mulligan-Ben Webster Quintet | Gerry Mulligan Meets Ben Webster | Verve | 841661-2 PMS
Grant Green Quartet | Gooden's Corner | Blue Note | GXK 8168
Hampton Hawes Trio | Hampton Hawes Trio Vol.1 | Original Jazz Classics | OJC20 316-2(C 3505)
Hank Jones | Maybeck Recital Hall Series Volume Sixteen | Concord | CCD 4502
Harry James And His Orchestra | The Uncollected:Harry James, Vol.5 | Hindsight | HSR 142
Helen Merrill With The George Gruntz Trio | Jazz In Switzerland 1930-1975 | Elite Special | 9544002/1-4
Herb Ellis Trio With Hendrik Meurkens | Burnin' | Acoustic Music Records | 319.1164.2
JATP All Stars | J.A.T.P. In London 1969 | Pablo | 2CD 2620119
Jessica William-Leroy Williams Trio | Encounters II | Jazz Focus | JFCD 021
Jochen Voss/Thomas Brendgens-Mönkemeyer | Alterations | Acoustic Music Records | 319.1029.2
Joey Calderazzo Trio | The Traveler | Blue Note | 780902-2
Johnny Griffin-Art Taylor Quartet | Johnny Griffin/Art Taylor In Copenhagen | Storyville | STCD 8300
Jon Gordon Quintet | Ask Me Now | Criss Cross | Criss 1099
Kenny Werner | Copenhagen Calypso | Steeplechase | SCCD 31346
Larry Schneider Quartet | Just Cole Porter | Steeplechase | SCCD 31291
Les Brown And His Band Of Renown | Digital Swing | Fantasy | FCD 9650-2
Louis Armstrong And His Orchestra | Jazz Drumming Vol.3(1938-1939) | Fenn Music | FJD 2703
Louis Smith Quintet | Silvering | Steeplechase | SCCD 31336
Marcus Roberts | If I Could Be With You | Novus | 4163149-2
Martial Solal Trio | Martial Solal NY-1 | Blue Note | 584232-2
Martial Solal At Newport '63 | RCA | 2174803-2
At Newport '63 | RCA | 2125768-2
Nat King Cole Trio | Vocal Classics & Instrumental Classics | Capitol | 300014(TOCJ 6128)
Norman Granz Jam Session | Jam Session No. 2 | Verve | MV 2654 IMS
Charlie Parker Jam Session | Verve | 833564-2 PMS
Paul Motian Quartet | Paul Motian On Broadway Vol.1 | JMT Edition | 919029-2
Paula Haliday With Orchestra | Haliday Sings Holiday | Fresh Sound Records | FSR 709(835321)
Ralph Flanagan And His Orchestra | Dance Again Part 2 | Magic | DAWE 75
Red Garland Trio | A Garland Of Red | Original Jazz Classics | OJC 126(P 7064)
Rein De Graaff Trio | Chasin' The Bird | Timeless | SJP 159
Sally Blair And The Bethlehem Orchestra | Squeeze Me | Fresh Sound Records | FSR 2023(Bethlehem BCP 6009)
Sergio Salvatore Trio | Always A Beginning | Concord | CCD 4704
Sidney Bechet And His New Orleans Feetwarmers | Sidney Bechet 1932-1943: The Bluebird Sessions | Bluebird | ND 90317
Sonny Rollins Trio | Sonny Rollins:The Blue Note Recordings | Blue Note | 821371-2
Spaulding Givens/Charles Mingus | Debut Rarities Vol.2 | Original Jazz Classics | OJCCD 1808-2
Stan Getz Quartet | Yours And Mine | Concord | CCD 4740
Nobody Else But Me | Verve | 521660-2
Steve Hobbs Quartet | On The Lower East Side | Candid | CCD 79704
Tatum-Hampton-Rich Trio | The Tatum Group Masterpieces | Pablo | 2625706
Thilo Wagner Trio | Wagner,Mörike.Beck,Finally. | Nagel-Heyer | CD 078
Thomas Clausen | Pianomusic | M.A Music | A 801-2
Thomas Stabenow Quartet | What's New | Bassic-Sound | CD 014
Tommy Dorsey And His Orchestra | This Is Tommy Dorsey Vol. 2 | RCA | 26.28041 DP
Wycliffe Gordon Group | The Search | Nagel-Heyer | CD 2007
Zoot Sims-Bucky Pizzarelli Duo | Summum | Ahead | 33752

What Is This Thing Called Love(alt.take)
Clifford Brown-Max Roach Quintet | Clifford Brown And Max Roach At Basin Street | Verve | 589826-2
Brownie-The Complete EmArCy Recordings Of Clifford Brown | EmArCy | 838306-2
Jimmy Raney Quartet | Raney '81! | Criss Cross | Criss 1001

What Is This Thing Called Swing
Louis Armstrong And His Orchestra | Big Band Bounce & Boogie-Louis Armstrong:Struttin' With Some Barbecue | Affinity | AFS 1024

What Is This?
Percfect Trouble | Perfect Trouble | Moers Music | 02070 CD

What It Was
The Afro-Asian Music Ensemble | Tomorrow Is Now | Soul Note | 121117-2

What It's All About
Jenny Evans And Her Quintet | Nuages | ESM Records | ESM 9308

What Joy
Nuages | Enja | ENJ-9467 2
Baby Mack With Louis Armstrong And Richard M. Jones | Louis Armstrong And The Blues Singers 1924-1930 | Affinity | AFS 1018(6)

What Kind Of Fool Am I
Bill Evans | The Solo Sessions Vol.1 | Milestone | MCD 9170-2
Bill Evans Trio | The Complete Bill Evans On Verve | Verve | 527953-2
The Complete Bill Evans On Verve | Verve | 527953-2
Billy May And His Orchestra Plus Guests | The Capitol Years | EMI Records | EMS 1275
Ray Brown-Milt Jackson Quintet | Much In Common | Verve | 533259-2
Bill Evans Trio | The Complete Bill Evans On Verve | Verve | 527953-2

What Kind Of Fool Am I(2)
Lightnin' Hopkins | Sittin' In With Lightnin' Hopkins | Mainstream | MD CDO 905

What Know
Wynton Kelly Quintet | Wrinkles-Wynton Kelly & Friends | Affinity | AFF 151

What Laurie Likes
Art Pepper Quartet | Renascene | Galaxy | GCD 4202-2
Dave Ballou Quintet | On This Day | Steeplechase | SCCD 31504

What Lies Beyond - (What Lies) Beyond
Charles Mingus Quartet | Charles Mingus Presents Charles Mingus | Candid | CCD 79005

What Love
Charles Minus-Live | Affinity | CD AFS 778
Charles Mingus Quintet | Charles Mingus-Passion Of A Man:The Complete Atlantic Recordings 1956-1961 | Atlantic | 8122-72871-2
Ed Schuller & Mack Goldbury | Art Of The Duo: Savignyplatz | Tutu Records | 888206-2*

Inez Andrews And The Andrewettes | The Famous Spiritual + Gospel Festival Of 1965 | L+R Records | LR 44005
The ARC Choir | Walk With Me | Mapleshade | 04132

What Love Is This
Shirley Scott Quintet | A Wakin' Thing | Candid | CCD 79719

What Makes Harold Sing?
Louie Bellson And His Jazz Orchestra | East Side Suite | Musicmasters | 5009-2

What Me Worry
The Guest Stars | Out At Night | Eigelstein | 568-72228

What More Can A Woman Do
Mildred Anderson With The Al Sears Quintet | No More In Life | Original Blues Classics | OBCCD 579-2(BV 1017)
Al Bowlly With Lew Stone And His Band | On The Sentimental Side | Decca | DDV 5009/10

What More Can Jesus Do
American Folk Blues Festival | American Folk Blues Festival '80 | L+R Records | CDLS 42013

What Need Have I For This...
Dave McMurdo Jazz Orchestra | Different Paths | Sackville | SKCD2-2034

What Now My Love
Richard 'Groove' Holmes Trio | Misty | Original Jazz Classics | OJCCD 724-2(P 7485)

What Price Love
Giacomo Gates With The Harold Danko Quartet | Blue Skies | dmp Digital Music Productions | CD 3001

What Reason Could I Give
Ingrid Sertso And Her Sextet | Dance With Me | Enja | 8024-2

What Stays
George Duke Group | Liberated Fantasies | MPS | 68026

What The Hell
Ethan Iverson Trio | Contruction Zone(Originals) | Fresh Sound Records | FSNT 046 CD

What The Kraken Knows
Phil Mason's New Orleans All-Stars | West Indies Blues | Lake | LACD 93

What The World Needs Now Is Love
Stan Getz With The Richard Evans Orchestra | What The World Needs Now-Stan Getz Plays Bacharach And David | Verve | 557450-2
The Capp/Pierce Juggernaut | Live At The Century Plaza | Concord | CCD 4072
Wes Montgomery Quartet | Verve Jazz Masters 14:Wes Montgomery | Verve | 519826-2
Wes Montgomery Quintet With The Claus Ogerman Orchestra | Tequila | CTI Records | PDCTI 1118-2

What They Were Written About
John Scofield Quartet | What We Do | Blue Note | 799586-2

What Thy Did
Barbara Carroll | Barbara Carroll At The Piano | Discovery | DS 847 IMS

What Was
The Magic Triangle | The Magic Triangle | Black Saint | BSR 0038

What We Know We Think About
Kip Hanrahan Groups | Exotica | American Clave | AMCL 1027-2

What We Think We Know - ...What We Think We Know
Jukka Tolonen Group | A Passenger To Paramaribo | Sonet | 147120

What Will Be Left Between Us And The Moon Tonight
Rebecka Gordon Quartet | Yiddish'n Jazz | Touché Music | TMcCD 014

What Will Happen When The Messiah Comes?
Freddie Brocksieper Und Seine Solisten | Freddie's Boogie Blues | Bear Family Records | BCD 16388 AH

What Will I Do
Hal Galper Trio | Naturally | Black-Hawk | BKH 529

What Will I Tell My Heart
Ella Fitzgerald With Jackie Davis And Louis Bellson | Lady Time | Original Jazz Classics | OJCCD 864-2(2310825)
Jim Tomlinson Sextet | Only Trust Your Heart | Candid | CCD 79758
Joe Williams With The Jimmy Mundy Orchestra | A Man Ain't Supposed To Cry | Roulette | CDP 793269-2

What Will It Be
Mark Shane's X-Mas Allstars | What Would Santa Say? | Nagel-Heyer | CD 055

What Will Santa Claus Say
Thom Rotella Group | Home Again | dmp Digital Music Productions | CD 469

What Will Tomorrow Bring
Bertha Hope Trio | Between Two Kings | Minor Music | 801025

What Without The Beauty Within?
Matthias Daneck's N.O.W. | Seven Portraits Of Obviously Unpredictable Mood Swings And Subsequent Behaviour | Satin Doll Productions | SDP 1012-1 CD

What Would I Do Without You
Joe Beck-Ali Ryerson-Steve Davis | Alto | dmp Digital Music Productions | CD 521
Herbie Mann Group | Sunbelt | Atlantic | ATL 50536

What You Do To Me
Clarence Williams And His Novelty Four | Jazz Classics In Digital Stereo: King Oliver Volume Two 1927 To 1930 | CDS Records Ltd. | ZCF 788

What You Like
Little Johnny Taylor With Band | The Galaxy Years | Ace Records | CDCHD 967

What You Want Wid Bess
Louis Armstrong And Ella Fitzgerald With Russell Garcia's Orchestra | The Complete Ella Fitzgerald And Louis Armstrong On Verve | Verve | 537284-2
Paolo Fresu Quartet | Kind Of Porgy & Bess | RCA | 21951952
Ray Charles-Cleo Laine With The Frank DeVol Orchestra & Chorus | Porgy And Bess | London | 6.30110 EM

What? Where? Hum Hum
Melanie Bong With Band | Fantasia | Jazz 4 Ever Records:Jazz Network | J4E 4755

What? Where? Why?
Wycliffe Gordon Group | Slidin' Home | Nagel-Heyer | CD 2001

What?!
Oscar Peterson Trio | Tristeza On Piano | MPS | 817489-2 PMS

Whatch What Happens
Three Originals:Motion&Emotions/Tristeza On Piano/Hello Herbie | MPS | 521059-2
Keith Nichols And The Cotton Club Orchestra | Henderson Stomp | Stomp Off Records | CD 1275

What'd I Say
Freddie King Orchestra | My Feeling For The Blues | Repertoire Records | REPCD 4170-WZ
Maynard Ferguson And His Orchestra | The Blues Roar | Mainstream | MD CDO 717

Whatever
The Page Cavanaugh Trio | The Digital Page | Star Line Productions | SLCD 9001(875581)

Whatever It Is
Baby Face Willette Quartet | Face To Face | Blue Note | 859382-2

Whatever Lola Wants
Louis Jordan And His Tympany Five | Rock 'N Roll Call | Bluebird | 63 66145-2

Whatever Possessed Me
Chet Baker Quintet | Chet Baker Plays & Sings | West Wind | WW 2108
Lew Soloff Group | My Romance | Paddle Wheel | K32Y 6278

Whatever The Moon
Rinde Eckert Group | Story In,Story Out | Intuition Records | INT 3507-2

Whatever The Reason
Roswell Rudd Quartet | Flexile Flyer | Black Lion | BLCD 760215

What'll I Do
Clusone 3 | Soft Lights And Sweet Music | Hat Art | CD 6153
Maynard Ferguson And His Orchestra | Si Si M.F. | Fresh Sound Records | R 52084(Roulette)
West Coast Jazz Summit | West Coast Jazz Summit | Mons Records | MR 874773

What's Going On
Charles Lloyd Quintet | Lift Every Voice | ECM | 1832/33(018783-2)
Dieter Ilg-Marc Copeland-Jeff Hirshfield | What's Goin' On | Jazzline | JL 11138-2
Herbie Mann Group | Push Push | Embryo | SD 532
Tom Mega + Band | A Moon Of Roses | ITM Records | ITM 1487

What's Going On-
John Stubblefield Sextet | Prelude | Storyville | SLP 1018

What's Happening
Paul Williams Orchestra | Paul Williams:The Complete Recordings Vol.2 (1949-1952) | Blue Moon | BMCD 6021

What's Left
Pierre Boussaguet Trio With Guy Lafitte | Charme | EmArCy | 538468-2

What's Left To Say
Gene Quill All Stars | 3 Bones And A Quill | Fresh Sound Records | FSR-CD 105(882183)

What's My Name?
Sonny Rollins Trio | Jazz-Club: Tenor Sax | Verve | 840031-2
Marty Cook Group | Theory Of Strange | Enja | 9107-2

What's New?
Ahmad Jamal Trio | At The Pershing-But Not For Me | Chess | 940910-2
At The Pershing | Affinity | CD AFS 780
Annie Ross With The Johnny Spence Orchestra | Annie Ross Sings A Handful Of Songs | Fresh Sound Records | FSR-CD 0061
Art Blakey And The Jazz Messengers | At The Cafe Bohemia Vol.3 | Blue Note | 300193(BNJ 61007)
Art Pepper Quartet | Among Friends | Interplay | IP 7718
Art Tatum | Art Tatum-The Complete Pablo Solo Masterpieces | Pablo | 7 PACD 4404-2
The Art Tatum Solo Masterpieces | Pablo | 2625703
Bill Evans Trio With Jeremy Steig | What's New | Enoch's Music | 57271053
Billie Holiday And Her Orchestra | Velvet Mood Songs By Billie Holliday | Verve | MV 2596 IMS
Cannonball Adderley Quintet | Cannonball Adderley:Sophisticated Swing-The EmArCy Small Group Sessions | Verve | 528408-2
Carl Allen And Manhattan Projects | Piccadilly Square | Timeless | CD SJP 406
Charlie Parker Quintet | Bird At St. Nick's | Original Jazz Classics | OJC20 041-2(JWS 500)
Charlie Parker 1950-1951:The Complete Bird At Birdland Vol.1 | Fat Boy Jazz | FBB 901
Christof Lauer Trio | Evidence | CMP Records | CMP CD 70
Clifford Brown With Strings | Clifford Brown-Max Roach:Alone Together-The Best Of The Mercury Years | Verve | 526373-2
Verve Jazz Masters 44:Clifford Brown and Max Roach | Verve | 528109-2
Clifford Brown-Max Roach Quintet | Pure Genius | Elektra | MUS K 52388
David Gibson Sextet | Maya | Nagel-Heyer | CD 2018
Denny Christianson Big Band | Doomsday Machine | Justin Time | Just 8
Dinah Washington With The Don Costa Orchestra | In Love | Roulette | CDP 797273-2
Don Menza & Frank Strazzeri | Ballads | Fresh Sound Records | FSR 103 (807728)
Ed Kröger Quartet | What's New | Laika Records | 35101172
Eddie Condon All Stars | Eddie Condon Town Hall Concerts Vol.1 | Jazzology | JCECD-1001
Edmond Hall-Bobby Hackett Band | Edmond Hall's Last Concert | Jazzology | JCD-223
Frank Morgan-Bud Shank Quintet | Quiet Fire | Contemporary | CCD 14064-2
George Benson Quintet | Verve Jazz Masters 21:George Benson | Verve | 521861-2
Blue Benson | Polydor | 2391242 IMS
George Shearing Trio | Jazz Moments | Capitol | 832085-2
Hank Jones Trio | The Jazz Skyline | Savoy | SV 0173(MG 12070)
Helen Merrill With The Quincy Jones Orchestra | Brownie-The Complete EmArCy Recordings Of Clifford Brown | EmArCy | 838306-2
Henri Crolla Sextet | Jazz In Paris:Henri Crolla-Notre Ami Django | EmArCy | 014062-2
Jack Wilkins Sextet | You Can't Live Without It | Chiaroscuro | CR 185
Jane Jarvis Quartet | Jane Jarvis Jams | Arbors Records | ARCD 19152
JATP Jam Session | Return To Happiness-JATP At Yoyogi National Stadium,Tokyo | Pablo | 2620117-2
Jimmy Raney Quintet | Too Marvelous For Words | Biograph | BLP 12060
Jimmy Smith Trio | Jimmy Smith: Grazy Baby | Blue Note | 784030-2
Joe Williams With The Jimmy Mundy Orchestra | A Man Ain't Supposed To Cry | Roulette | CDP 793269-2
John Coltrane Quartet | Ballads | Impulse(MCA) | 589548-2
John Coltrane:The Classic Quartet-Complete Impulse Studio Recordings | Impulse(MCA) | 951280-2
John Coltrane:Standards | Impulse(MCA) | 549914-2
Johnny Griffin Quartet | Little Giant | Milestone | M 47054
June Christy And Her Orchestra | Early June | Fresh Sound Records | FSCD 1011
Klaus Weiss Quintet | A Taste Of Jazz | ATM Records | ATM 3810-AH
Knud Jorgensen-Bengt Hanson-Gustavo Bergalli | Day Dream | Touché Music | TMcCD 003
Lee Konitz Quartet | Satori | Milestone | M 9060
Lee Konitz Trio With Bill Evans | Lee Konitz:Move | Moon Records | MCD 057-2
Lionel Hampton Trio | Paris Session 1956 | Jazztime(EMI) | 251274-2
Louis Armstrong With The Oscar Peterson Quartet | Louis Armstrong Meets Oscar Peterson | Verve | 825713-2
Marian McPartland Trio feat. Chris Potter | In My Life | Concord | CCD 4561
Milt Jackson Quintet | The Jazz Skyline | Savoy | WL 70821 (809325)
Oliver Jackson Orchestra | The Last Great Concert | Nagel-Heyer | CD 063
Oliver Nelson Quintet | Oliver Nelson Feat. Kenny Dorham | Original Jazz Classics | OJCCD 227-2(NJ 8224)
Olivier Peters Quartet | What Is New | NCC Jazz | NCC 8503
Randy Sandke Quintet | Cliffhanger | Nagel-Heyer | CD 2037
Ray Anthony And His Orchestra | Dancing Alone Together | Capitol | EMS 1156
Shelly Manne And His Men | At The Black Hawk Vol.2 | Original Jazz Classics | OJCCD 657-2(S 7578)
At The Blackhawk Vol.2 | Contemporary | C 7578
Stan Getz Quartet | Stan Getz:Imagination | Dreyfus Jazz Line | FDM 36733-2
Early Getz | Prestige | P 24088
Stan Kenton And His Orchestra | Stan Kenton On The Air | Status | DSTS 1022
Thomas Stabenow Quartet | What's New | Bassic-Sound | CD 014
Wynton Kelly Trio With Wes Montgomery | Smokin' At The Half Note | CTI Records | PDCTI 1117-2

What's New?-
Klaus Ignatzek Quintet | All Systems Go | Candid | CCD 79738
Norman Granz Jam Session | Bird: The Complete Charlie Parker On Verve | Verve | 837141-2
Charlie Parker Jam Session | Verve | 833564-2 PMS

What's New?(alt.take 1)
George Benson Quintet | Giblet Gravy | Verve | 543754-2

What's New?(alt.take 2)
Anthony Ortega Trio | Scattered Clouds | HatOLOGY | 555

What's New?(alt.take)
Lionel Hampton Trio | Paris Session 1956 | Jazztime(EMI) | 251274-2
Art Pepper Quintet | Rediscoveries | Savoy | WL 70828 (809328)

What's Next?
Nat Adderley Sextet | Much Brass | Original Jazz Classics | OJCCD 848-2(R 1143)
Teo Macero With The Prestige Jazz Quartet | Teo Macero With The Prestige Jazz Quartet | Original Jazz Classics | OJCCD 1715-2(P 7104)

What's Shakin'
Fra-Fra Sound | Panja-Gazz +4 | Jazz Pure Collection | AU 31619 CD

What's The Matter With Me

Ella Fitzgerald And Her Famous Orchestra | Ella Fitzgerald Vol.2-Forever Young | Swingtime(Contact) | ST 1007

What's The News
Mick Goodrick Trio | Biorhythms | CMP Records | CMP CD 46

What's The Reason(I'm Not Pleasing You)
Fats Waller And His Rhythm | The Classic Years In Digital Stereo: Fats Waller And His Rhythm | CDS Records Ltd. | RPCD 315(CD 684)

What's The Resolution
Gerry Mulligan-Johnny Hodges Quintet | Gerry Mulligan Meets Johnny Hodges | Verve | MV 2682 IMS

What's The Rush
Main Stream Power Band | Memories In Swing | MWM Records | MWM 002

What's The Use
Eddie Condon And His Band With Johnny Windhurst | The Doctor Jazz Series,Vol.1:Eddie Condon | Storyville | STCD 6041

What's The Use Of Getting Sober
Louis Jordan And His Tympany Five | Louis Jordan Greatest Hits-Vol.2 | MCA | 1337

What's The Word
Charlie Parker All Stars | Bird At The Roost Vol.4 | Savoy | 650127(882237)

What's Up
Henry Butler Quintet | The Village | Impulse(MCA) | ???

What's Up,Dogs?
Nils Landgren Funk Unit | Fonk Da World | ACT | 9299-2

What's Up,What's Up
Enrico Pieranunzi | Top Jazz From Italy-The Winners Of Musica Jazz Critics Poll '88 | yvp music | CD 3018

What's With You
Mose Allison Trio | Mose Alife!/Wild Man On The Loose | Warner | 8122-75439-2
Cal Massey Sextet | Blues To Coltrane | Candid | CCD 79029

What's Wrong
James 'Sugarboy' Crawford Band | Sugarboy Crawford | Chess | 427017

What's Wrong With You
Donald & Peggy Knaack | Inside The Plactic Lotus | Hat Art | 3517

What's Your Movie?
Big John Patton Septet | Blue Planet Man | Paddle Wheel | KICJ 168

What's Your Story(Morning Glory)
Glenn Miller And His Orchestra | The Glenn Miller Collection | RCA | ???
Joe Pass-Jimmy Rowles Duo | Joe Pass:A Man And His Guitar | Original Jazz Classics | OJCCD 8806-2
John Colianni | Maybeck Recital Hall Series Volume Thirty-Seven | Concord | CCD 4643
Milt Jackson And Big Brass | For Someone I Love | Original Jazz Classics | OJCCD404-2(RLP 9478)

Whatta Ya Gonna Do
Louis Armstrong And His Orchestra | Louis Armstrong-The Complete RCA Victor Recordings | RCA | 2668682-2

Whe I Run
Michael Mantler Group | Michael Mantler: No Answer/Silence | Watt | 2/5(543374-2)
The Poll Winners | The Poll Winners Ride Again | Original Jazz Classics | OJC 607(C 7556)

Whe The Red Red Robin Come Bob Bob Bobbin' Along
Christoph Stiefel Group | Ancient Longing | Jazzline | JL 11141-2

Wheatland
Oscar Peterson Trio | Oscar Peterson Trio: Olympia/Theatre Des Champs-Elysees | Laserlight | 36134
The Good Life | Original Jazz Classics | OJC 627(2308241)
Curtis Fuller Sextet | The Curtis Fuller Jazztet feat. Benny Golson | Savoy | SV 0134(MG 12143)

Whee Baby
Peggy Lee With Orchestra | All Aglow Again | Capitol | 1565541

Wheel Of Fortune
Steve Coleman And Five Elements | Genesis & The Opening Of The Way | RCA | 2152934-2

Wheel Of Nature
29th Street Saxophone Quartet | The Real Deal | New Note Records | ???

Wheelin'(take 1)
Prestige All Stars | John Coltrane-The Prestige Recordings | Prestige | 16 PCD 4405-2
Mal Waldron-John Coltrane Sextet | Wheelin' | Prestige | P 24069

Wheelin'(take 2)
Prestige All Stars | John Coltrane-The Prestige Recordings | Prestige | 16 PCD 4405-2
Ari Ambrose Quartet | Chainsaw | Steeplechase | SCCD 31481

Wheels Of Fortune(When Face Gets Pale)
Wheelz With Ingrid Jensen | Around The World I | ACT | 9247-2

When
Elvin Jones-Takehisa Tanaka Quartet | Elvin Jones Introduces Takehisa Tanaka | Enja | ENJ-7081 2

When A Man Loves A Woman
Dan Papaila Trio | Positively! | Timeless | CD SJP 403
Hank Crawford Orchestra | Down On The Deuce | Milestone | M 9129
Shirley Scott Quintet | A Wakin' Thing | Candid | CCD 79719
Jörg Krückel-Brad Leali Quartet | Cookin' Good | Edition Collage | EC 507-2

When A Sinner Kissed An Angel
Carey Bell's Blues Harp Band | Carey Bell | Blues Classics(L+R) | CDLR 82013

When A Woman Loves A Man
Abbey Lincoln With Her Quintet | Sonny Rollins-The Freelance Years:The Complete Riverside & Contemporary Recordings | Riverside | 5 RCD 4427-2
Art Tatum | Art Tatum-The Complete Pablo Solo Masterpieces | Pablo | 7 PACD 4404-2
The Tatum Solo Masterpieces Vol.13 | Pablo | 2310875
Dinah Washington With The Gus Chappell Orchestra | The Complete Dinah Washington On Mercury Vol.1 | Mercury | 832444-2
Ella Fitzgerald With The Nelson Riddle Orchestra | The Johnny Mercer Songbook | Verve | 823247-2 PMS
Ruby Braff-Scott Hamilton Sextet | A First | Concord | CJ 274

When All Was Chet
Ian Bargh | Only Trust Your Heart | Sackville | SKCD2-2053

When April Comes Again
Chubby Newsom With The David Clowney Orchestra | The Original Hip Shakin' Mama | Official | 6020

When Autumn Comes
Bill Evans Trio | The Tokyo Concert | Original Jazz Classics | OJCCD 345-2
Bill Evans Live In Tokyo | CBS | 481265-2

When Autumn Sings
Slim Gaillard And His Band | Cement Mixer Put-Ti Put-Ti | Folklyric | 9038

When Buddah Smiles
Benny Goodman And His Orchestra | The Birth Of Swing | Bluebird | ND 90601(3)

When Can I See You
Ronald Shannon Jackson And The Decoding Society | Barbeque Dog | Antilles | AN 1015(802757)

When Day Is Done
Coleman Hawkins With Different Bands | 100 Ans De Jazz:Coleman Hawkins | RCA | 2177832-2
Cozy Cole All Stars | Thanks For The Memory | EPM Musique | FDC 5159
Django Reinhardt And The Quintet Du Hot Club De France | Swingin' With Django | Pro-Arte | CDD 549
Quintet Du Hot Club De France | Django Reinhardt:Djangology | EMI Records | 780659-2

When Did You Leave Heaven
Ernie Andrews With The Houston Person Quintet | No Regrets | Muse | MCD 5484
Lisa Ekdahl With The Peter Nordahl Trio | When Did You Leave Heaven | RCA | 2143175-2

Louis Armstrong With Sy Oliver And His Orchestra | Louis And The Angels | Verve | 549592-2
Louis Armstrong With Sy Oliver's Choir And Orchestra | Louis Armstrong-Heavenly Music | Ambassador | CLA 1916

When Did You Stop Loving Me,When Did I Stop Loving You
Big Bill Broonzy | Big Bill Broonzy-The 1955 London Sessions | Sequel Records | NEX CD 119

When Elephants Fall In Love
Jacques Gauthé-Alain Marquet Clarinet Serenaders | Paris Blues | Stomp Off Records | CD 1216

When God Created The Coffebreak
Stephen Scott Septet | Aminah's Dream | Verve | 517996-2

When I Dream Of You
Gene Ammons Quartet | The Gene Ammons Story: The 78 Era | Prestige | P 24058

When I Fall In Love
Arrigo Cappelletti Trio | Reflections | SPLASC(H) Records | H 134
Betty Carter With Orchestra | 'Round Midnight | Atlantic | AMCY 1060
Bill Evans Trio | Spring Leaves | Milestone | M 47034
Bill Evans:The Secret Sessions | Milestone | 8MCD 4421-2
Portrait In Jazz | Original Jazz Classics | OJC20 088-2
Bill Evans Trio With Lee Konitz & Warne Marsh | Crosscurrents | Original Jazz Classics | OJCCD 718-2(F 9568)
Blue Mitchell Quartet | Blue's Moods | Original Jazz Classics | OJC 138(R 9336)
Buddy Greco Quartet | Route 66-A Personal Tribute To Nat King Cole | Celebrity | CYCD 71901
Chucho Valdes Trio | Chucho Veldes Solo Piano | Blue Note | 780597-2
Deborah Brown With The Horace Parlan Trio | Jazz 4 Jazz | Reckless Records | RR 9901 CD
George Shearing | Compact Jazz:George Shearing | MPS | 833284-2 PMS
Jackie McLean Quartet | Contour | Prestige | P 24076
Jerry Gonzalez & Fort Apache Band | Earth Dance | Sunnyside | SSC 1050 D
Keith Jarrett Trio | Inside Out | ECM | 1780(014005-2)
Still Live | ECM | 1360/61(835008-2
Whisper Not | ECM | 1724/25(543813-2)
Kevin Mahogany With Orchestra | Songs And Moments | Enja | ENJ-8072 2
Lainie Kazan With Band | Body And Soul | Musicmasters | 65126-2
McCoy Tyner | Revelations | Blue Note | 791651-2
Miles Davis New Quintet | Workin',Steamin',Cookin',Relaxin' With The Miles Davis Quintet | Original Jazz Classics | OJCCD 8805-2
Miles Davis Quintet | Steamin' | Original Jazz Classics | OJC20 391-2
Miles Donahue Quartet | Double Dribble | Timeless | CD SJP 392
Monty Alexander's Ivory & Steel | To The Ends Of The Earth | Concord | CCD 4721
Oscar Peterson-Milt Jackson Quartet | Reunion Blues | MPS | 817490-1
Ray Brown Trio | Live At Starbucks | Telarc Digital | CD 83502
Rickey Woodard Quartet | California Cooking | Candid | CCD 79509
Stan Kenton And His Orchestra | Stan Kenton At Ukiah 1959 | Status | CD 109(882969)
Tiziana Ghiglioni-Giancarlo Schiaffini Duo | Well Actually | SPLASC(H) Records | H 117
Clark Terry With The Summit Jazz Orchestra | Clark | Edition Collage | EC 530-2

When I Fall In Love-
Enrico Pieranunzi Trio | Trilogues Vol.3 | yvp music | CD 3026
Morgana King And Her Quintet | Higher Ground | Muse | MR 5224

When I Get Low I Get High
Ella Fitzgerald With The Chick Webb Orchestra | Let's Get Together | Laserlight | 17003

When I Get To The Mountain
Bill Frisell Quintet | Rambler | ECM | 1287

When I Go
Artie Shaw And His Orchestra | The Uncollected:Artie Shaw And His Orchestra, Vol.1 | Hindsight | HSR 139

When I Go A-Dreamin'
Champion Jack Dupree | Champion Jack Dupree | Storyville | 4960383

When I Got Married
Allan Vaché-Jim Galloway Sextet | Raisin' The Roof:Allan Vaché Meets Jim Galloway | Nagel-Heyer | CD 054

When I Grow Too Old To Dream
Benny Goodman And His Orchestra | B.G. In Hi-Fi | Capitol | 792864-2
Emile Barnes-Peter Bocage Big Five | Barnes-Bocage Big Five 1954 | American Music | AMCD-84
Jay McShann Quartet | Just A Lucky So And So | Sackville | SKCD2-3035
Jimmy Smith Quartet | Back At The Chicken Shack | Blue Note | 746402-2
John Purcell Orchestra | Naturally | Novus | 4163151-2
Louis Armstrong And His All Stars | The Legendary Berlin Concert Part 2 | Jazzpoint | JP 1063 CD
En Concert Avec Europe 1 | Laserlight | 710415
Phil Mason's New Orleans All-Stars | You Do Something To Me! | Lake | LACD 33
Roger Kellaway | The Art Of Interconnectedness | Challenge | CHR 70042
Sidney Bechet With Andre Reweliotty And His Orchestra | Sidney Bechet | Vogue | 000001 GK
Wrobel-Roberscheuten-Hopkins Jam Session | Jammin' At The IAJRC Convention Hamburg 1999 | Nagel-Heyer | CD 066
Arnett Cobb & His Orchestra | The Complete Apollo Sessions | Vogue | 500116

When I Leave Here
Bunk Johnson's Jazz Band | Commodore Classica-Old New Orleans Jazz 1942 | Commodore | 6.24547 AG

When I Leave This World Behind
The Sidewalks Of New York | Tin Pan Alley:The Sidewalks Of New York | Winter&Winter | 910038-2
Buddy Guy Blues Band | The Blues Giant | Black & Blue | BLE 59.900 2

When I Look At You
Carol Sloane And Her Band | When I Look In Your Eyes | Concord | CCD 4619

When I Look In Your Eyes
Helen Merrill-Gordon Beck | No Tears No Goodbyes | Owl Records | 013435-2
Irene Kral With Alan Broadbent | Where Is Love? | Choice | CHCD 71012
Ray Bryant | Inimitable | Jazz Connaisseur | JCCD 9430-2
Tony Bennett With Orchestra | Tony Bennet's Something | CBS | CK 64601

When I Met You
Satoko Fuji Trio | Toward,To West | Enja | ENJ-9382 2

When I Move To The Sky
Chris Barber's Jazz Band | Chris Barber-40 Years Jubilee(1954-1956) | Timeless | CD TTD 586

When I Run
L.C. Prigett | Piano Blues Vol.1-The Twenties(1923-1930) | Story Of Blues | CD 3511-2

When I Take My Sugar To Tea
Nat King Cole Trio | Nat King Cole Trio 1943-49-The Vocal Sides | Laserlight | 15718

When I Think Of One
Jack Linx And His Birmingham Society Serenaders | Jack Linx And Maurice Sigler | Jazz Oracle | BDW 8018

When I Was One Year Old
Champion Jack Dupree Group | Champ's Housewarming | Vagabond | VRCD 8.88014
Big Joe Turner And His All Stars | Big Joe Rides Again | Atlantic | 790668-2

When I'm 64
Benny Moten's Kansas City Orchestra | Basie Beginnings | Bluebird | ND 90403

When I'm Alone
Steve LaSpina Quintet | When I'm Alone | Steeplechase | SCCD 31376

When I'm Called Home
Rodney Kendrick Trio | We Don't Die We Multiply | Verve | 537447-2

When I'm Drinking
J.B.Lenoir Blues Band | J. B. Lenoir | Chess | 427003

When I'm With My Baby
Charlie Elgart Group | Signs Of Life | RCA | PD 83045

When In Rome
Bill Evans | Eloquence | Fantasy | F 9618
Blossom Dearie Trio | At Ronnie Scott's:Blossom Time | EmArCy | 558683-2
Blossom Dearie Sings & Plays Songs Of Chelsea | Master Mix | CHECD 2
Tony Bennett-Bill Evans | The Tony Bennett-Bill Evans Album | Original Jazz Classics | OJC20 439-2(F 9489)
Andy Lutter Trio | Nichtendende Geschichten | Extra Records & Tapes | 57230463

When Irish Eyes Are Smiling
Red Norvo And His Orchestra | Jivin The Jeep | Hep | CD 1019

When It Was
Bill Evans Quintet | Living In The Crest Of A Wave | Elektra | MUS 96.0349-1

When It's Over
Allotria Jazz Band | 69-89 Good Times | Elite Special | 30224

When It's Sleepy Time Down South
Anson Weeks And His Orchestra | The Radio Years: Anson Weeks And His Hotel Mark Hopkins Orchestra 193 | Hindsight | HSR 146
Billie Holiday With The Ray Ellis Orchestra | Last Recordings | Verve | 835370-2 PMS
Carol Sloane And Clark Terry With The Bill Charlap Trio | The Songs Ella & Louis Sang | Concord | CCD 4787
Earl Hines | Four Jazz Giants:Earl Hines Plays Tributes To W.C.Handy,Hoagy Carmichael And Louis Armstrong | Solo Art | SACD-111/112
Lillian Bouté And Her Group | You've Gotta Love Pops:Lillian Bouté Sings Louis Armstrong | ART BY HEART | ABH 2005 2
Louis Armstrong And His All Stars | This Is Jazz:Louis Armstrong Sings | CBS | CK 65039
Louis Armstrong & The All Stars 1965 | EPM Musique | FDC 5100
Masters Of Jazz Vol.1:Louis Armstrong | Storyville | STCD 4101
En Concert Avec Europe 1 | Laserlight | 710415
Live In Berlin/Friedrichstadtpalast | Jazzpoint | JP 1062 CD
The Great Performer | Traditional Line | TL 1304
Louis Armstrong And His Orchestra | Jazz Gallery:Louis Armstrong Vol.1 | RCA | 2114166-2
Fist Recorded Concerts 1932/1933 | Jazz Anthology | JA 5238
Louis Armstrong Plays And Sings The Great Standards, Vol.1 | Black & Blue | BLE 59.226 2
Louis Armstrong With Orchestra | High Society | Intercord | 125400
Roy Eldridge-Dizzy Gillespie With The Oscar Peterson Quartet | Jazz Maturity... Where It's Coming From | Original Jazz Classics | OJCCD 807-2(2310816)
Ruby Braff All Stars | Being With You:Ruby Braff Remembers Louis Armstrong | Arbors Records | ARCD 19163
The New York Allstars | The Second Sampler | Nagel-Heyer | NHR SP 6
Broadway | Nagel-Heyer | CD 003
Oh,Yeah! The New York Allstars Play More Music Of Louis Armstrong | Nagel-Heyer | CD 046
The Tremble Kids | 25 Jahre The Tremble Kids | Intercord | 180036

When It's Sleepy Time Down South-
Louis Armstrong And His Orchestra | Louis Armstrong Vol.8:1941-1942 | Ambassador | CLA 1908
Laughin' Louie | RCA | ND 90404
Louis Armstrong-Satchmo's Greatest Hits | RCA | CL 89799
Ray Gelato Giants | The Full Flavour | Linn Records | AKD 034
Louis Armstrong With Gordon Jenkins And His Orchestra And Choir | Satchmo In Style | Verve | 549594-2

When It's Sleepy Time Down South(alt.take)
Roy Eldridge Quintet | The Complete Verve Roy Eldridge Studio Sessions | Verve | 9861278
Alex Welsh And His Band | Melody Maker Tribute To Louis Armstrong Vol.2 | Jazz Colours | 874768-2

When It's Sleepy Time Down South(Finale)
Louis Armstrong And His All Stars | Historic Barcelona Concerts At Windsor Palace 1955 | Fresh Sound Records | FSR-CD 3004
Historic Barcelona Concerts At Windsor Palace 1955 | Fresh Sound Records | FSR-CD 3004

When It's Sleepy Time Down South(Opening Theme)
Historic Barcelona Concerts At Windsor Palace 1955 | Fresh Sound Records | FSR-CD 3004
Earl Hines | Four Jazz Giants:Earl Hines Plays Tributes To W.C.Handy,Hoagy Carmichael And Louis Armstrong | Solo Art | SACD-111/112

When It's Sleepy Time Down South(Theme)
Louis Armstrong And His All Stars | Satchmo In Stockholm | Queen-Disc | 053
Attila Zoller | Lasting Love | Acoustic Music Records | 319.1131.2

When It's Time
Attila Zoller-Wolfgang Lackerschmid | Live Highlights '92 | Bhakti Jazz | BR 28
Wolfgang Lackerschmid-Donald Johnston Group | New Singers-New Songs | Bhakti Jazz | BR 31
Steve LaSpina Quintet | Distant Dream | Steeplechase | SCCD 31448

When It's Twilight On The Trail
Blind John Davis | Blind John Davis | L+R Records | CDLR 72002

When Joanna Loved Me
Paul Desmond Quartet | Masters Of Jazz Vol.13 | RCA | CL 42790 AG

When Johnny Comes Marching Home
Eddie Brunner Und Die Original Teddies | Teddy Stauffer:Rare And Historical Jazz Recordings | Elite Special | 9522009
Glenn Miller And His Orchestra | Glenn Miller Forever | RCA | NL 89214 DP
Jimmy Smith Trio | The Master | Blue Note | 830451-2
John Swana Quintet | The Feeling's Mutual | Criss Cross | Criss 1090

When Joy Hits Town
Stanley Jordan Group | Flying Home | Blue Note | 748682-2

When Lights Are Low
Anders Lindskog Trio | Fine Together | Touché Music | TMcCD 010
Archie Shepp-Chet Baker Quintet | In Memory Of: First And Last Meeting In Frankfurt And Paris 1988 | L+R Records | CDLR 45006
Cal Tjader Quintet | Breathe Easy | Galaxy | GXY 5107
Chuck Wayne Quartet | Traveling | Progressive | PRO 7008 IMS
Eric Dolphy With Erik Moseholm's Trio | Eric Dolphy:The Complete Prestige Recordings | Prestige | 9 PRCD-4418-2
Gary Bartz-Sonny Fortune Quintet | Alto Memories | Verve | 523268-2
J.J.Johnson-Joe Pass | We'll Be Together Again | Pablo | 2310911-2
JATP Jam Session | Return To Happiness-JATP At Yoyogi National Stadium,Tokyo | Pablo | 2620117-2
Lionel Hampton And His Orchestra | The Complete Lionel Hampton Vol.3/4(1939) | RCA | 2122614-2
Hot Mallets Vol.1 | Bluebird | ND 86458
Benny Carter(1928-1952) | RCA | ND 89761
Miles Davis Quartet | Blue Haze | Original Jazz Classics | OJC20 093-2(P 7054)
Tune Up | Prestige | P 24077
Welcome To Jazz: Miles Davis Vol.2 | Koch Records | 321 975 D1
Monty Alexander Trio | Triple Treat | Concord | CCD 4193
Oscar Peterson Trio | Compact Jazz: Oscar Peterson Plays Jazz Standards | Verve | 833283-2
Pete Jolly Trio | When Lights Are Low | Fresh Sound Records | 58109 CD(RCA)

When Love Begins
David Allyn With The Johnny Richards Orchestra | Jewells | Savoy | SV 0273

When Love Is Far Away

John McLaughlin's Free Spirits | Tokyo Live | Verve | 521870-2

When Love Was You And Me
Babs Gonzales And His Orchestra | Sonny Rollins | Definitive Records | DRCD 11243

When Malindy Sings
Freddie Roach Quintet | Good Move | Blue Note | 524551-2
So Blue So Funky:Heroes Of The Hammond Vol.2 | Blue Note | 829092-2

When Miss Jessye Sings
David Linx With The Jack Van Poll Trio | Where Rivers Join | September | CD 5109

When My Baby Smiles At Me
Benny Goodman Quintet | 1938 Carnegie Hall Concert | CBS | 450983-2

When My Dreamboat Comes Home
Johnny Lytle Quintet | Got That Feeling/Moon Child | Milestone | MCD 47093-2
Kid Howard's La Vida Band | Kid Howard's La Vida Band | American Music | AMCD-54

When My Left Eye Jumps
Washboard Sam & His Washboard Band | Chicago Blues(1935-1942) | RCA | 2126404-2

When My Sugar Walks Down The Street
Miyuki Koga With The Dick Hyman Quintet | Dreamin' | Concord | CCD 4588
Red Nichols And His Five Pennies | Red Nichols And His Five Pennies | Laserlight | 15743
Wolverine Orchestra | Chicago Jazz 1924-28 | Village(Jazz Archive) | VILCD 007-2

When Police Came They Also Hit Me
Ben Bernie And His Hotel Roosevelt Orchestra | Jazz Museum-Hot Dance Bands Of The Twenties,Vol.1 | MCA | 52056 (801841)

When Ruben Swings The Cuban
Ian Shaw With The Adrian York Quartet | Ghostsongs | Ronnie Scott's Jazz House | JHCD 025

When Sleep Brings Us Apart
Fats Waller And His Rhythm | I'm Gonna Sit Right Down...The Early Years-Part 2(1935-1936) | Bluebird | 63 66640-2

When Something Is Wrong With My Baby
Herbie Mann Group | Deep Pocket | Kokopelli Records | KOKO 1296

When Summer Comes
Hal Kemp And His Orchestra | The Radio Years: Hal Kemp And His Orchestra 1934 | Hindsight | HSR 143

When Sunny Gets Blue
Keith McDonald | This Is Keith McDonald | Landmark | LLP 503
Sonny Stitt Quintet | The Prestige Collection:Sonny Stitt Soul Classics | Original Jazz Classics | OJCCD 6003-2
Stan Kenton And His Orchestra | Standards In Silhouette | Capitol | ST 1049

When The Doom (Moon) Comes Over The Mountain
Giko Pavan Quartet | Gino Pavan | SPLASC(H) Records | H 128

When The Fire Burns Low
Shin-Ichi Fukuda | Guitar Legends:Homage To Great Popular Guitarists | Denon Compact Disc | CO-18048

When The Lights Go On Again
Acoustic Alchemy | Back On The Case | GRP | GRP 96482

When The Lights Go Out
Richard Elliot Sextet | City Speak | Blue Note | 832620-2
Sonny Boy Williamson | Blues Roots Vol.10 | Storyville | 6.23709 AG

When The Quail Come Back To San Quentin
Johnny Copeland Group | Texas Twister | Edsel | 66.23401 AS

When The Red Red Robin Comes Bob Bob Bobbin' Along
Clusone 3 | Rare Avis | HatOLOGY | 523
Joshua Breakstone Quartet | 4/4=1 | Mobile Fidelity | MFCD 774

When The Roll Is Called Up Yonder
Peggy Lee With The Benny Goodman Orchestra | Peggy Lee & Benny Goodman:The Complete Recordings 1941-1947 | CBS | C2K 65686

When The Roses Bloom Again
Sammy Price Sextet | Sammy Price In Europe | Jazz Anthology | JA 5192

When The Saints Go Marching In
Benny Waters Sextet | A' Portrait Of Jan Jankeje | Jazzpoint | JP 1054 CD
Bill Ramsey With Eric Krans Dixieland Pipers And Guests | Caldonia And More... | Bear Family Records | BCD 16151 AH
Billie Pierce With The Raymond Burke Quintet | Billie Pierce(With Raymond Burke) | American Music | AMCD-76
Bo Diddley And Chuck Berry | Two Great Guitars | Chess | CH 9170
Buck Clayton And His Band | Jammin' At Condon's Vol.2 | Nueva Records | JU 312
Chris Barber's Brass Band | Take Me Back To New Orleans | Black Lion | 157007
Chris Barber's Jazz Band | Copulatin' Jazz | Great Southern Records | GS 11025
Coleman Hawkins-Henry Red Allen All Stars | Vol.One: Warhorses | Jass Records | ???
Erich Kunzel Cincinnati Pops Big Band Orchestra | Big Band Hit Parade | Telarc Digital | CD 80177
Firehouse Five Plus Two | Crashes A Party | Good Time Jazz | GTCD 10038-2
Frank Edwards | Done Some Travelin' | Trix Records | TRIX 3303
George Lewis And His Ragtime Band | Jazz At Vesper | Original Jazz Classics | OJCCD 1721-2(RLP 230)
Golden Gate Quartet | Best Of Golden Gate Quartet | Sonia | CD 77285
Jimmy McPartland And His Dixielanders | Planet Jazz | Planet Jazz | 2169652-2
The Happy Dixieland Jazz | RCA | 2118518-2
Joe Newman And His Orchestra | The Complete Joe Newman RCA-Victor Recordings(1955-1956):The Basie Days | RCA | 2122613-2
Louis Armstrong | Satchmo-When The Saints Go Marching In | Verve | 711051 IMS
Louis Armstrong And His All Stars | Jazz In Paris:Louis Armstrong-The Best Live Concert Vol.2 | EmArCy | 013031-2
Historic Barcelona Concerts At Windsor Palace 1955 | Fresh Sound Records | FSR-CD 3004
Masters Of Jazz Vol.1:Louis Armstrong | Storyville | STCD 4101
En Concert Avec Europe 1 | Laserlight | 710415
The Great Performer | Traditional Line | TL 1304
What A Wonderful World | Moon Records | MCD 066-2
Louis Armstrong And His Orchestra | Louis Armstrong-My Greatest Songs | MCA | MCD 18347
Jazz:The Essential Collection Vol.2 | IN+OUT Records | 78012-2
Louis Armstrong:Swing That Music | Laserlight | 36056
Louis Armstrong | London | 6.24023 AL
Magnificant Seventh's Brass Band | Authentic New Orleans Jazz Funeral | Mardi Gras Records | MG 1012
Olympia Brass Band | Best Of Jazz Fest-Live From New Orleans | Mardi Gras Records | MG 1011
Oscar Klein Band | Pick-A-Blues Live | Jazzpoint | JP 1071
Oscar Klein Jazzshow | Koch Records | 321 704
Oscar Papa Celestin's Jazzband | Hello Friends... | Storyville | SLP 103
Papa Bue's Viking Jazzband | A Song Was Born | BELL Records | BLR 84012
Ray Brown-Milt Jackson Quintet | Much In Common | Verve | 533259-2
Sidney Bechet With Claude Luter And His Orchestra | In Concert | Vogue | 655625
Sinleton Palmer And His Dixieland Band | Dixie By Gaslight | Dixieland Jubilee | DJ 511
The Heavenly Stars | Old Time Religion | Sound Of New Orleans | SONO 6009

When The Saints Go Marching In-
Lionel Hampton And His Orchestra | En Concert Avec Europe 1 | Laserlight | 710462
Treme Brass Band | I Got A Big Fat Woman | Sound Of New Orleans | SONO 1029

When The Saints Go Marching In(instrumental version)
Nicolas Simion Quartet feat. Tomasz Stanko | Transylvanian Dance | Tutu Records | 888164-2*

When The Shepherd Lost His Sheep
Maneri/Phillips/Maneri | Tales Of Rohnlief | ECM | 1678

When The Ship Went Down
Plimley/Ellis/Cyrille | When Silence Pulls | Music & Arts | CD 692

When The Spirit Hits
Lester Bowie's Brass Fantasy | When The Spitit Returns | Dreyfus Jazz Line | FDM 37016-2

When The Spirit Returns
I Only Have Eyes For You | ECM | 1296(825902-2)
Lester Bowie's New York Organ Ensemble | Funky T. Cool T. | DIW | DIW 853 CD

When The Sun Comes Down
Al Hibbler With Gerald Wilson's Orchestra | Monday Every Day | Discovery | DS 842 IMS

When The Sun Comes Out
Art Pepper Quintet With Strings | Art Pepper:The Complete Galaxy Recordings | Galaxy | 16GCD 1016-2
Benny Goodman And His Orchestra | The Benny Goodman Selection | CBS | 467280-2
Cal Tjader Quartet | Jazz At The Blackhawk | Original Jazz Classics | OJCCD 436-2(F 8096)
Plays Harold Arlen | Original Jazz Classics | OJC 285(F 8072)
Ella Fitzgerald With The Billy May Orchestra | The Harold Arlen Songbook | Verve | 817526-1 IMS
Marian McPartland Trio | Personal Choice | Concord | CCD 4202
Mel Tormé And His Trio | Mel Tormé In New York | Jazz Door | JD 12103
Roland Kirk Quartet | Rahsaan/The Complete Mercury Recordings Of Roland Kirk | Mercury | 846630-2
Talkin' Verve-Roots Of Acid Jazz:Roland Kirk | Verve | 533101-2
Domino | Verve | 543833-2
Singers Unlimited With Orchestra | Friends | MPS | 821286-1
Soesja Citroen With The Metropole Orchestra | Yesterdays | Challenge | CHR 70049
Sun Ra And His Myth Science Arkestra | Fate In A Pleasant Mood/When Sun Comes Out | Evidence | ECD 22068-2

When The Sun Comes Out(alt.take 1)
Roland Kirk Quartet | Domino | Verve | 543833-2

When The Sun Comes Out(alt.take 2)
Art Pepper Quintet With Strings | Art Pepper:The Complete Galaxy Recordings | Galaxy | 16GCD 1016-2

When The Sun Comes Out(alt.take)
Big Bill Broonzy | Last Session, Vol.2 | Verve | 813367-1 IMS

When The Sun Goes Down
Count Basie Quartet | Big Band Bounce & Boogie-Count Basie:Swingin' At The Daisy Chain | Affinity | AFS 1019

When The Sun Sets Down South(Southern Sunset)
Sidney Bechet With Noble Sissle's Swingsters | Blackstick | MCA | 1330

When The Swallows Come Back To Capistrano
Doc Houlind & His Copenhagen Ragtime Band | What A Wonderful World | Timeless | CD TTD 591

When The Time Comes
Flora Molton And The Truth Band | Living Country Blues USA Vol.11:Country Gospel Rock | L+R Records | LR 42041

When The Work Is Done
Boyd Rivers | Living Country Blues USA Vol.11:Country Gospel Rock | L+R Records | LR 42041

When The World Was Young
Anita O'Day And Her Orchestra | Mello'day | GNP Crescendo | GNP 2126
Anita O'Day With The Three Sounds | Trav'lin' Light:The Johnny Mercer Songbook | Verve | 555402-2
Dick Johnson Quartet | Dick Johnson Plays | Concord | CCD 4107
Nat King Cole With The Gordon Jenkins Orchestra | Where Did Everyone Go ? | Capitol | EMS 1114
Sheila Jordan And Her Trio | Portrait Of Sheila | Blue Note | 789002-2
Stan Getz Quartet | The Stan Getz Quartet In Paris | Enoch's Music | 57271043

When There's Nothing Left To Do Or Say
Ernie Andrews With The Houston Person Quintet | No Regrets | Muse | MCD 5484

When They Ring The Golden Bell
Mark Isham-Peter Van Hooke Duo | Vapor Drawings | Windham Hill | TA-C- 1027

When Tomorrow Comes
Vienna Art Orchestra | Artistry In Rhythm-A European Suite | TCB Records | TCB 01102

When We Two Walked
Secret Agent Men | Secret Agent Men | Paddle Wheel | KICJ 135

When We Were Free
Deborah Brown With The Horace Parlan Trio | Jazz 4 Jazz | Timeless | CD SJP 409

When We Were One
Vanessa Rubin With Orchestra | Soul Eyes | Novus | PD 90591(874066)

When Were You Born?
Hank Jones Trio | A Jazz Par 91 Project | Storyville | STCD 4180

When Will I Loose My Memory
Ornette Coleman & Prime Time | Tone Dialing | Verve | 527483-2

When Will I See You Again
David Newton Trio | In Good Company | Candid | CCD 79714

When Will The Blues Leave
Chet Baker Quintet | Stella By Starlight | West Wind | WW 0033
Ornette Coleman Quintet | Something Else | Contemporary | C 7551
Paul Bley Group | The Paul Bley Group | Soul Note | SN 1140
Paul Bley Trio | Footoose | Savoy | SV 0140(MG 12182)
Notes On Ornette | Steeplechase | SCCD 31437
Charlie Haden Trio | The Montreal Tapes | Verve | 523295-2

When You And I Were Young Maggie
Eddie Edwards Original Dixieland Jazz Band | Commodore Classics-Eddie Edwards Original Dixieland Jazz Band | Commodore | 6.26170 AG

When You Come...
Bruce Forman Quartet | 20/20 | Muse | MR 5273

When You Got A Good Friend
Robert Johnson | Robert Johnson-King Of The Delta Blues | CBS | 493006-2

When You Got A Good Friend(alt.take)
Moose Vinson Group | The Devil's Music:Mississippi And Memphis/Chicago Blues | Red Lightnin' | RL 0033

When You Leave Me Alone To Pine
Jimmy Reed | I'm The Man Down There | Charly | CRB 1082

When You Love A Woman But She Don't Love You Back Blues
Al Cohn Quartet | Standards Of Excellence | Concord | CJ 241

When You Lover Has Gone
Art Tatum | Art Tatum-The Complete Pablo Solo Masterpieces | Pablo | 7 PACD 4404-2
Benny Carter Trio | 3,4,5 The Verve Small Group Sessions | Verve | 849395-2 PMS
George Colligan | Small Room | Steeplechase | SCCD 31470
Lee Konitz-Jimmy Giuffre Octet | Lee Konitz Meets Jimmy Giuffre | Verve | 527780-2

When You Meet Her
Toshiko Mariano Quartet | Live At Birdland | Fresh Sound Records | FSCD 1021

When You Said Goodbye
Buddy Guy-Junior Wells Band | Drinkin' TNT 'N' Smokin' Dynamite | Sequel Records | NEM CD 687

When You Surrender
Nat King Cole With The Dave Cavanaugh Orchestra | Tell Me All About Yourself | Capitol | EMS 1109

When You Wish Upon A Star
Christian Minh Doky Quartet | Appreciation | Storyville | STCD 4169
Glenn Miller And His Orchestra | Candlelight Miller | RCA | 2668716-2
The Glenn Miller Collection | RCA | ???
Harry Babasin Quintet | Jazz In Hollywood:Harry Babasin/Bob Enevoldsen | Original Jazz Classics | OJCCD 1888-2(Nocturne NLP3/NLP-6)
Joe Morello Quartet | Morello Standard Time | dmp Digital Music Productions | CD 506
Malta And His Orchestra | Obsession | JVC | ???
Sonny Rollins Quartet | The Alternative Rollins | RCA | PL 43268
Weslia Whitefield With The Mike Greensill Quartet | Teach Me Tonight | HighNote Records | HCD 7009
Zigmund-Richmond-Berkman | Dark Street | Freelance | FRL-CD 022

When You Wish Upon A Star-
Mel Tormé With The Marty Paich Dek-Tette | Reunion | Concord | CCD 4360
Alex Welsh | Dixieland Jubilee | Intercord | 155032

When You Wore A Tulip
George Lewis And His New Orleans Stompers | George Lewis And His New Orleans Stompers | Blue Note | 821261-2
George Lewis Ragtime Jazz Band Of New Orleans | The Oxford Series Vol.12:George Lewis Ragtime Jazz Band | American Music | AMCD-32

When Your Lover Has Gone
Archie Shepp-Mal Waldron | Left Alone Revisited | Enja | 9141-2
Art Blakey And The Jazz Messengers | A Night In Tunisia | Blue Note | 784049-2
Art Farmer Quartet | Plays The Arrangements And Compositions Of Gigi Gryce And Quincy Jones | Original Jazz Classics | OJCCD 054-2
House Of Byrd | Prestige | P 24066
Art Van Damme Quintet | Keep Going/Blue World | MPS | 529093-2
Ben Webster With Orchestra And Strings | Music For Loving:Ben Webster With Strings | Verve | 527774-2
Ben Webster With The Oscar Peterson Trio | Ben Webster Meets Oscar Peterson | Verve | 521448-2
Ben Webster Meets Oscar Peterson | Verve | 829167-2
Bill Watrous Quartet | Bill Watrous In London | Mole Jazz | MOLE 7
Billie Holiday And Her Orchestra | Velvet Mood Songs By Billie Holliday | Verve | MV 2596 IMS
Buddy DeFranco Quartet | Jazz Tones | Verve | MV 2610 IMS
Earl Hines | Tour De Force | Black Lion | BLCD 760140
Eddie Lockjaw Davis-Shirley Scott Sextet | Bacalao | Original Jazz Classics | OJCCD 1090-2(P 7178)
Ella Fitzgerald-Oscar Peterson Duo | Ella And Oscar | Pablo | 2310759-2
George Shearing Group | Two Originals:Light,Airy And Swinging/Continental Experience/On Target | MPS | 523522-2
Harold Harris Trio | At The Playboy Club | Vee Jay Recordings | VJR 502
Herb Ellis-Jimmy Giuffre Orchestra | Herb Ellis Meets Jimmy Giuffre | Verve | 559826-2
Jo Jones Trio | Jo Jones Trio | EmArCy | 512534-2
John Colianni | Maybeck Recital Hall Series Volume Thirty-Seven | Concord | CCD 4643
LaVerne Butler With The Rob Bargad Band | Day Dreamin' | Chesky | JD 117
Louis Armstrong With The Russell Garcia Orchestra | Verve Jazz Masters 1:Louis Armstrong | Verve | 519818-2
Louis Armstrong With Zilmer Randolph's Orchestra | Louis Armstrong V.S.O.P. Vol. 7/8 | CBS | CBS 88004
Mary Osborne Quintet | Now And Then | Stash Records | ST 215 IMS
Ruby Braff All Stars | Being With You:Ruby Braff Remembers Louis Armstrong | Arbors Records | ARCD 19163
Sarah Vaughan With The Oscar Peterson Quartet | Sarah Vaughan Birthday Celebration | Fantasy | FANCD 6090-2
How Long Has This Been Going On? | Pablo | 2310821-2
Shirley Horn Trio | All Night Long | Steeplechase | SCCD 31157
Sonny Rollins Quartet | Tenor Madness | Original Jazz Classics | OJC20 124-2
Stacey Kent With The Jim Tomlison Quintet | Dreamsville | Candid | CCD 79775
Stan Getz All Stars | Stan The Man | Verve | 815239-1 IMS
The Newport All Stars | That Newport Jazz | CBS | 21139

When You're Far Away
Chet Baker Quintet | Comin' On With The Chet Baker Quintet | Prestige | PR20 7478-2

When You're Gone
Johnny Griffin-Martial Solal | Griffin-Solal In&Out | Dreyfus Jazz Line | FDM 36610-2

When You're Smiling
Art Pepper Quartet | Roadgame | Galaxy | GXY 5142
Roadgame | Original Jazz Classics | OJCCD 774-2(GXY 5142)
Barbara Long With The Billy Howell Quintet | Soul-The Voice Of Babara Long | Savoy | SV 0216(MG 12161)
Benny Waters Quartet | When You're Smiling | Hep | CD 2010
Jimmy Rushing And His Orchestra | Jimmy Rushing And The Big Brass/Rushing Lullabies | CBS | CK 65118
Lester Young With The Bill Potts Trio | Lester Young In Washington,DC 1956:Vol.1 | Original Jazz Classics | OJCCD 782-2(2308219)
Louis Armstrong And His All Stars | Satchmo-A Musical Autobiography Vol.2 | MCA | 2-4174
Michel Silva Trio With Jimmy Slyde | Explosive Drums | Black & Blue | BLE 59.080 2
Papa Bue's Viking Jazzband With Wingy Manone | A Tribute To Wingy Manone | Storyville | SLP 210
Ruby Braff And His Orchestra | The Mighty Braff | Affinity | AFF 757
The European Jazz Ginats | Jazz Party | Nagel-Heyer | CD 009
The Feetwarmers | Doldinger Jubilee | Atlantic | ATL 60073
Thomas Jefferson/Kid Thomas Jazz Band | New Orleans Traditional Jazz Legends:Kid Thomas/Thomas Jefferson/Percy Humphrey | Mardi Gras Records | MG 9003
Warren Vaché And The New York City All-Star Big Band | Swingtime! | Nagel-Heyer | CD 059
Wild Bill Davison All Stars | Wild Bill Davison All Stars | Timeless | CD TTD 545
Benny Carter And His Orchestra | Benny Carter-Live And Well In Japan! | Pablo | 2308216

When You're Smiling-
Louis Armstrong And His Orchestra | Louis Armstrong-Satchmo's Greatest Hits | RCA | CL 89799

When Zweeble Walked By
Al Jarreau With Band | Heaven And Earth | i.e. Music | 557852-2

Whenever I Hear Your Name
Terje Rypdal With Strings | When Ever I Seem To Be Far Away | ECM | 1045

Whenever I Seem To Be Far Away
Horace Silver Quintet | A Prescription For The Blues | Impulse(MCA) | 951238-2

Whenever Lester Plays The Blues
Christian Josi With The Harry Allen Quartet | I Walk With My Feet Off The Ground | Master Mix | CHECD 00111

Whenever,Whenever,Whenever
Kalifactors | An Introduction To Kalifactors | Fresh Sound Records | FSNT 143 CD

Wher Am I
Mezzrow-Bechet Quintet | The King Jazz Story Vol. 6 | Storyville | STCD 4115

Where
Tony Williams Lifetime | Emergency! | Verve | 539117-2

Where Am I Going
Tubby Hayes Quartet | Live 1969 | Harlequin | HQ 3006 IMS

Where Are The Hebrew Children
Carmen McRae And Her Quintet | Velvet Soul | LRC Records | CDC 7970

Where Are You
Ahmad Jamal Trio | Chicago Revisited | Telarc Digital | CD 83327
Archie Shepp Quartet | Ballads For Trane | Denon Compact Disc | DC-8570
Bill Harris And Friends | Bill Harris And Friends | Original Jazz Classics | OJC 083(F 3263)
David Hazeltine Quintet | How It Is | Criss Cross | 1142
Dexter Gordon Quartet | Dexter Gordon:The Complete Blue Note Sixties Sessions | Blue Note | 834200-2

Tete Montoliu | Yellow Dolphin Street/Catalonian Folk Songs | Timeless | CD SJP 107/116

Where Are You-
Patti Page With Lou Stein's Music | The Uncollected:Patti Page | Hindsight | HSR 223

Where Are You From Today
Lyle Mays Trio | Fictionary | Geffen Records | GED 24521

Where Are You Going
Django Reinhardt And The Quintet Du Hot Club De France | The Indispensable Django Reinhardt | RCA | ND 70929

Where Are You Now?
Chick Corea | Piano Improvisations-Vol.1 | ECM | 1014(811979-2)
Mal Waldron Quintet | Where Are You? | Soul Note | 121248-2

Where Breathing Starts
Wingy Mannone Septet | Trumpet Jive! | Prestige | PCD 24119-2(P 7812/SV 2006)

Where Did The Gentleman Go
Bob Enevoldsen Quintet | Jazz In Hollywood:Harry Babasin/Bob Enevoldsen | Original Jazz Classics | OJCCD 1888-2(Nocturne NLP3/NLP-6)

Where Do I Go From Here
Jimmy Rowles Quartet | Fiorello-Uptown/Mary Sunshine-Downtown | Fresh Sound Records | FSR 587(Signature SM 6011)
Peggy Lee With Orchestra | All Aglow Again | Capitol | 1565541

Where Do The Children Play?
Andre Ceccarelli 4tet | 61:32 00 | RCA | 2165773-2

Where Do We Go From Here
Makoto Ozone Group | Treasure | Verve | 021906-2
Oscar Peterson Trio | Swinging Cooperations:Reunion Blues/Great Connection | MPS | 539085-2
Bill Frisell Band | Blues Dream | Nonesuch | 7559-79615-2

Where Do We Go?
Helen Merrill With The Dick Katz Group | A Shade Of Difference | EmArCy | 558851-2

Where Do You Go
Maynard Ferguson Orchestra With Chris Connor | Two's Company | Roulette | 837201-2
Stan Getz Quartet | Stan Getz:The Golden Years Vol.2(1958-1961) | Moon Records | MCD 040-2

Where Do You Start
Grady Tate Quintet | TNT/Grady Tate Sings | Milestone | MCD 9193-2
Susannah McCorkle With The Frank Wess Quintet | I'll Take Romance | Concord | CCD 4491
Kahil El'Zabar's The Ritual Trio | Alika Rising | Sound Aspects | sas CD 040

Where Does Love Come From(for My Father)
Roland Kirk Quartet | Rahsaan/The Complete Mercury Recordings Of Roland Kirk | Mercury | 846630-2

Where Does The Blame Lie
The Goofus Five | The Goofus Five feat. Adrian Rollini | Timeless | CBC 1-017

Where Eagles Fly-
Bruce Barth Quintet | Morning Call | Enja | 8084-2

Where Flamingos Fly
Gil Evans Orchestra | Out Of The Cool | CTI Records | PDCTI 1114-2

Where Have I Danced With You Before
Gijs Hendriks Quartet | Close To The Edge | Timeless | SJP 113

Where Have I Known You Before
Return To Forever | Where Have I Known You Before | Polydor | 825206-2

Where Have I Loved You Before
Maxine Sullivan-Keith Ingham | Maxine Sullivan Sings The Music Of Burton Lane | Mobile Fidelity | MFCD 773

Where Have You Been?
Joe Lovano Quintet | Landmarks | Blue Note | 796108-2

Where Home Is
Kurt Elling Group | This Time Its Love | Blue Note | 493543-2

Where I Belong
Michael Gregory | The Way We Used To Do,| TipToe | TIP-888806 2

Where I Come From
Chico Hamilton Quintet | Gongs East | Discovery | DS 831 IMS

Where I Live
Stan Getz With The Eddie Sauter Orchestra | Stan Getz Plays The Music Of Mickey One | Verve | 531232-2

Where I Live-
Elisabeth Kontomanou Group | Embrace | Steeplechase | SCCD 31467

Where In The World
Duke Ellington And His Orchestra | Duke 56/62 Vol.3 | CBS | 26306

Where Is Love
Jack Wilson Trio | Margo's Theme | Discovery | DS 805 IMS
Singers Unlimited | Four Of Us | MPS | 68106
Vincent Herring And Sandy Lomax With The Thomas Fink Trio | Big Brown Eyes | clearaudio | WOR 161 CD

Where Is My Yellow Lighter?
Krzyaztof Scieranski Trio | No Radio | ITM Records | ITM 001 JP

Where Is The Love
Singers Unlimited With The Pat Williams Orchestra | The Singers Unlimited:Magic Voices | MPS | 539130-2
Feeling Free | MPS | 68103
Zachary Breaux Group | Groovin' | Ronnie Scott's Jazz House | JHCD 023

Where Is The One
Vic Juris Quintet | Music Of Alec Wilder | Double Time Records | DTRCD-118

Where It Comes From
Michele Rosewoman Quintet | Quintessence | Enja | 5039 (807547)

Where Monk And Mingus Live
Roland Kirk Quartet | Verve Jazz Masters 27:Roland Kirk | Verve | 522062-2

Where Monk And Mingus Live-
Phil Haynes' 4 Horns & What | 4 Horn Lore | Open Minds | OM 2413-2

Where Or Wayne
Jack DeJohnette Quartet | New Directions | ECM | 1128
Jack DeJohnette Special Edition | Earth Walk | Blue Note | 796690-2

Where Or When
Antonio Hart Quartet | For The First Time | Novus | PD 83120
Art Tatum | The V-Discs | Black Lion | BLP 60114
Art Tatum-Ben Webster Quartet | Art Tatum-The Complete Pablo Group Masterpieces | Pablo | 6 PACD 4401-2
The Tatum Group Masterpieces | Pablo | 2310737-2
Benny Golson Quartet | Three Little Words | Ronnie Scott's Jazz House | JHAS 609
Benny Goodman Trio | Benny Goodman:The Complete Small Combinations Vol.3/4 | RCA | ND 89754
Candy Johnson Quartet | Midnight Slow Vol.2 | Black & Blue | BLE 233055
Clarence Gatemouth Brown Trio | Midnight Slows Vol.2 | Black & Blue | 190552
Clifford Brown With Strings | Brownie-The Complete EmArCy Recordings Of Clifford Brown | EmArCy | 838306-2
Danny Moss Quartet | Keeper Of The Flame | Nagel-Heyer | CD 064
Dardanelle Quintet | The Colors Of My Life | Stash Records | ST 217 IMS
Don Wilkerson Quartet | The Texas Twister | Original Jazz Classics | OJCCD 1950-2(RLP 1186)
Edmond Hall Quartet With Teddy Wilson | Commodore Classics In Swing | Commodore | 9031-72723-2
Erroll Garner Trio | Concert By The Sea | CBS | 451042-2
Etta Jones And Her Quintet | Don't Go To Strangers | Original Jazz Classics | OJCCD 298-2(P 7186)
Frank Newton And His Uptown Serenaders | Frankie's Jump | Affinity | CD AFS 1014
Hal Kemp And His Orchestra | The Uncollected:Hal Kemp,Vol.3 | Hindsight | HSR 222
Johnny Smith Quintet | Moonlight In Vermont | Roulette | 300016
Johnny Smith-Stan Getz Quintet | Stan Getz-The Complete Roost Sessions | The Jazz Factory | JFCD 22839
Lena Horne With The Lou Bring Orchestra | Planet Jazz:Lena Horne | Planet Jazz | 2165373-2
Lionel Hampton And His Orchestra | Wes Montgomery:Complete Recordings With Lionel Hampton | Definitive Records | DRCD 11242
Oscar Peterson-Ray Brown Duo | Tenderly | Verve | MV 2662 IMS
Ralph Flanagan And His Orchestra | Dance Again Part 2 | Magic | DAWE 75
Red Mitchell Quintet | Red Mitchell | Bethlehem | BTM 6825
Singers Unlimited | Easy To Love | MPS | 68281
Sonny Rollins Quintet | Old Flames | Milestone | MCD 9215-2
Stan Getz Quartet | Stan Getz Highlights:The Best Of The Verve Years Vol.2 | Verve | 517330-2
Award Winner | Verve | 543320-2
Stan Getz:East Of The Sun-The West Coast Sessions | Verve | 531935-2
Stefan Scaggiari Trio | Stefanitely | Concord | CCD 4570
Woody Herman Herd | Road Band:The Woody Herman Herd | Capitol | 1565511

Where The Blues Were Born In New Orleans
Louis Armstrong And His Dixieland Seven | Louis Armstrong:A 100th Birthday Celebration | RCA | 2663694-2
Swing Legends:Louis Armstrong | Nimbus Records | NI 2012
Victor Jazz History Vol.1:New Orleans & Dixieland | RCA | 2128555-2

Where The Mulchair River Flows
Tom Harrell Quintet | Live At The Village Vanguard | RCA | 2663910-2

Where The Rain Begins
Jan Garbarek Group | Rites | ECM | 1685/86(559006-2)

Where The Rivers Meet
The Rippingtons | Weekend In Monaco | GRP | GRP 96812

Where The Southern Crosses The Dog
Woody Mann-Bob Brozman | Get Together | Acoustic Music Records | 319.1187.2

Where Were We?
Fats Waller | Fats Waller:The Complete Associated Transcription Sessions 1935-1939 | Jazz Unlimited | JUCD 2076

Where Were You On The Night Of June The Third?
Diederik Wissels Trio | Tender Is The Night | Jazz Pure Collection | AU 31616 CD

Where You At?
Horace Silver Quintet | Horace-Scope | Blue Note | 784042-2

Where You Belong
Eddie Boyd Blues Band | Five Long Years | L+R Records | CDLR 72009

Where You There
Lillian Boutté And Her Music Friends | I Sing Because I'm Happy | Timeless | CD JC 11003

Where You There When They Crucified My Lord(for Malcolm,Martin,Medgar And Many More)
Tom Harrell Sextet | Play Of Light | Black-Hawk | BKH 50901

Where?
Red Mitchell | Simple Isn´t Easy | Sunnyside | SSC 1016 D

Where's Art?
Roy Eldridge-Alvin Stoller | The Urban Sessions/New Jazz Sound | Verve | 531637-2

Where's That Rainbow
Trigger Alpert's All Stars | Trigger Happy! | Fresh Sound Records | RLP 12-225(Riverside)

Where's That Summer
Meredith d'Ambrosio | Another Time | Sunnyside | SSC 1017 D

Where's The Exit
Bob Cooper With The Mike Wofford Trio | Bob Cooper Plays The Music Of Michel Legrand | Discovery | DS 822 IMS

Where's The Love
Chubby Newsom With Orchestra | The Original Hip Shakin' Mama | Official | 6020

Where's Tom
Johnny Griffin Quartet | Little Giant | Milestone | M 47054

Wherever There's A Will There's A Way(My Baby)
McKinney's Cotton Pickers | The Indispensable Coleman Hawkins 1927-1956:Body And Soul | RCA | ND 89277

Wherever There's Love
Dutch Swing College Band Meets Billy Butterfield | Swing That Music | DSC Production | PA 1009 (801066)
Billie Holiday With Teddy Wilson And His Orchestra | Billie Holiday:The Quintessential Vol.8/9(1939-1942) | CBS | 477837-2

Whew! What A Dream
Benny Green Trio | The Place To Be | Blue Note | 829268-2

Which Way Is It Going
Myra Melford-Han Bennink | Eleven Ghosts | HatOLOGY | 507

Which Way?
Dollar Brand | Pre Abdullah Ibrahim | Jazz Colours | 874711-2

Whiffenproof Song
Clark Terry Trio | Intimate Stories | Challenge | CHR 70050

While My Guitar Gently Weeps
Chet Baker Quartet | Sings/It Could Happen To You | Original Jazz Classics | OJC20 303-2

While My Lady Sleeps
Chet Baker Trio | Embraceable You | Pacific Jazz | 831676-2
Chuck Wayne Quintet | Zoot Sims:The Complete 1944-1954 Small Group Sessions(Master Takes),Vol.3 | Blue Moon | BMCD 1040
John Coltrane Quintet | The Mal Waldron Memorial Album:Soul Eyes | Prestige | PRCD 11024-2
Jazz Gallery:John Coltrane Vol.1 | RCA | 2119540-2
John Coltrane Sextet | The Prestige Legacy Vol.1:The High Priests | Prestige | PCD 24251-2
Phineas Newborn Jr. With Dennis Farnon And His Orchestra | While My Lady Sleeps | RCA | 2185157-2
Ray Barretto + New World Spirit | My Summertime | Owl Records | 835830-2

While On Earth
Oliver Lake Quintet | Heavy Spirits | Black Lion | BLCD 760209

While The City Sleeps
Saxophon And Organ | Above The Clouds | Naxos Jazz | 86041-2

While We're Young
Bob Rockwell Trio | Born To Be Blue | Steeplechase | SCCD 31333
Dinah Washington With The Belford Hendricks Orchestra | Brook Benton-Dinah Washington:The Two Of Us | Verve | 526467-2
Jimmy Rowles Trio | Grandpaws | Candid | CRS 1014 IMS
John Towner Quartet | The John Towner Touch | Fresh Sound Records | KL 1055(Kapp)
Lorez Alexandria And Her Quintet | How Will I Remember You | Discovery | DS 782 IMS
Joshua Breakstone Quartet | 4/4=1 | Mobile Fidelity | MFCD 774

While You Are Mine
Gunter Hampel And His Galaxie Dream Band | All Is Real | Birth | 0028

While You Think Keep An Eye On Your Thoughts
All The Things You Could Be If Charles Mingus Was Your Daddy | Birth | CD 031
Bruce Gertz Quintet | Blueprint | Freelance | FRL-CD 017

Whims Of Chambers
Engstfeld-Plümer-Weiss | Drivin' | Nabel Records:Jazz Network | CD 4618
Lee Konitz & His West Coast Friends | High Jingo | Eastworld | CP 32-5422
Maurice Vander Trio | Maurice Vander | Dreyfus Jazz Line | FDM 36502-2
Wallace Roney Quartet | Munchin' | Muse | MCD 5533

Whims Of Chambers(alt.take)
Charles Earland Septet | Whip Appeal | Muse | MCD 5409

Whip The Mule
Nat Adderley Quintet | A Little New York Midtown Music | Original Jazz Classics | OJCCD 1008-2(GXY 5120)

Whipitup
John Zorn Naked City | Naked City-Grand Guignol | Avant | AVAN 002

Whippersnapper
Frank Morgan Septet | Frank Morgan | Vogue | 655018

Whirl
Tony Dagradi Quintet | Lunar Eclipse | Gramavision | GR 8103-2

Whirling
Christian McBride Group | Number Two Express | Verve | 529585-2

Whirlpool
Eric Vloeiman Quartet | Bestiarium | Challenge | CHR 70038

Whirly Bird
Count Basie And His Orchestra | The Atomic Band Live In Europe | Bandstand | BDLP 1506
The Best Of The Big Bands | LRC Records | CDC 8518
I Got Rhythm | Affinity | AFF 48
Live at The Sands | Reprise | 9362-45946-2
Count Basie: Salle Pleyel, April 17th, 1972 | Laserlight | 36127
Count Basie & His Orchestra:Fresno,California April 24,1959 | Jazz Unlimited | JUCD 2039

Whirrrr
Jimmy Giuffre 3 | Flight, Bremen 1961 | Hat Art | CD 6071

Whiser Not
Memphis Slim | Boogie Woogie Hits-Various Artists | RCA | CL 89803 SF

Whiskey Blues
The Harlem Ramblers | Dixieland Jubilee-Vol. 1 | Intercord | 155002

Whiskey Headed Woman
Harmonica Slim Blues Group | Black Bottom Blues | Trix Records | TRIX 3323

Whisper Not
Art Blakey And The Jazz Messengers | At The Club St.Germain | RCA | ND 74897(2)
Live In Holland 1958 | Bandstand | BDCD 1532
Art Farmer/Benny Golson Jazztet | Here And Now | Verve | 558052-2
Bobby Hutcherson Quartet | Bobby Hutcherson:Landmarks(A Compilation 1984-1986) | Landmark | LCD 1310-2
Dizzy Gillespie Big Band | Groovin' High | Bandstand | BDCD 1513
Erwin Müller Trio | Jazz In Switzerland 1930-1975 | Elite Special | 9544002/1-4
Great Jazz Trio & Friends | Aurex Jazz Festival '81 | Eastworld | EWJ 80209
Kenny Drew | Kenny Drew/Solo-Duo | Storyville | STCD 8274
Knut Kiesewetter Train | Knut Kiesewetter | Jazz Magazine | 48020
Milt Jackson Sextet | Bag's Opus | Blue Note | 784458-2
Oscar Peterson Trio | The Trio:Live From Chicago | Verve | 539063-2
The Trio-Live From Chicago | Verve | 823008-2
Shelly Manne And His Men | At The Blackhawk Vol.3 | Contemporary | C 7579
The Mastersounds | A Date With The Mastersounds | Original Jazz Classics | OJC 282(F 8062)
Wes Montgomery Trio | Wes Montgomery-The Complete Riverside Recordings | Riverside | 12 RCD 4408-2
Wynton Kelly Quartet | Keep It Moving | Milestone | M 47026
Mel Tormé With The George Shearing Trio | A Vintage Year | Concord | CJ 341

Whisper Not(alt.take 1)
Dizzy Gillespie And His Orchestra | Dizzy Gillespie:Birks Works-The Verve Big Band Sessions | Verve | 527900-2

Whisper Not(alt.take 2)
Dizzy Atmosphere | Dizzy Atmosphere | Original Jazz Classics | OJCCD 1762-2

Whisper Not(alt.take)
Takashi Ohi With The Junior Mance Trio | Time Stream | Denon Compact Disc | CY-78898

Whispering
Miles Davis Sextet | Sonny Rollins:Complete 1949-1951 Prestige Studio Recordings | Definitive Records | DRCD 11240
Welcome To Jazz: Miles Davis | Koch Records | 321 944 D1

Whispering-
Roy Fox And His Band | Hello Ladies And Gentleman. This Is Roy Fox Speaking | Ace Of Club | ACL 1172

Whispering Chambers
Duke Ellington And His Orchestra | Crystal Ballroom, Fargo Concert | Jazz Anthology | JA 5229/30

Whispering Grass
Hank Crawford Orchestra | Rhino Presents The Atlantic Jazz Gallery | Atlantic | 8122-71257-2
The Ink Spots | If I Didn't Care | Pro-Arte | CDD 555

Whisperings
Doug Hammond Trio | Perspicuity | L+R Records | CDLR 45031

Whispers In The Dark
Dick Jurgens And His Orchestra | The Radio Years: Dick Jurgens And His Orchestra 1937-39 | London | HMP 5046 AN

Whistful Thinking
Billy Cotton And His Band | Sing A New Song | Saville Records | SVL 160 IMS

Whistle Stop
Big Joe Turner And His All Stars | Roots Of Rock And Roll Vol. 2: Big Joe Turner | Savoy | SJL 2223 (801199)

Whistling Away The Dark
Freddie Hubbard & The Festival All Stars | Sweet Return | Atlantic | 780108-1

White
Miles Davis With The Danish Radio Big Band | Aura | CBS | CK 63962
Hans Koller & The International Brass Company | The Horses | L+R Records | LR 40008

White Birds On Bare Trees
Bob Brookmeyer Group With The WDR Big Band | Electricity | ACT | 9219-2

White Blues
Chet Baker Trio | Mr.B | Timeless | CD SJP 192

White Buffalo
Dave Liebman Quartet | The Elements:Water | Arkadia Jazz | 71043

White Christmas
Ella Fitzgerald With The Frank DeVol Orchestra | Ella With You A Swinging Christmas | Verve | 2304445 IMS
Golden Gate Quartet | Spirituals To Swing 1955-69 | EMI Records | 791569-2
HR Big Band With Marjorie Barnes And Frits Landesbergen And Strings | Swinging Christmas | hr music.de | hrmj 012-02 CD
Jim Galloway-Jay McShann Quartet | Jim & Jay's Christmas | Sackville | SKCD2-3054
Marcus Roberts | Prayer For Peace | Novus | ND 90585(847064)

White City Kids
Mr.Acker Bilk And His Paramount Jazz Band | White Cliffs Of Dover | Intercord | 125408

White Cliffs Of Dover
The Storyville Jassband | Trad Tavern | Timeless | CD TTD 577

White Cloud
Intergalactic Maiden Ballet,The | The Intergalactic Maiden Ballet | ITM Records | ITM 1457

White Line
Uli Trepte Group | Guru Guru/Uli Trepte | ATM Records | ATM 3815-AH

White Line Fever
John Zorn Group | Spillane | Nonesuch | 7559-79172-2

White Line Fever-
John Taylor Group | Pause, And Think Again | FMR | FMR CD 24

White Magic
Enver Ismailov & Geoff Warren | Art Of The Duo:Dancing Over The Moon | Tutu Records | 888168-2*

White Minarets
Vladimir Shafranov Trio | White Nights | The Jazz Alliance | TJA 10018

White Nights-
Chris Jarrett | Piano Moments | Take Twelve On CD | TT 007-2
Rössler/Kühn/Heidepriem/Stefanski Quartet | Coloured | Fusion | 8015

White Noise Of Forgetfulness
Henry Mancini And His Orchestra | Experiment In Terror(Sountrack) | Fresh Sound Records | NL 45964(RCA LSP 2442)

White Paint On Silver Wood
Jimmy Giuffre-Paul Bley-Steve Swallow | Conversations With A Goose | Soul Note | 121258-2

White Rabbit
George Benson Orchestra | Star Edition-George Benson | CTI | 83002

White Song
Jimmy Yancey | The Yancey-Lofton Sessions Vol. 2 | Storyville | SLP 239

White With Eyes
Jonas Hellborg | Elegant Punk | Day Eight Music | DEMCD 004

Whitewash
Neville Dickie-Louis Mazetier | Dickie-Mazetier:Harlem Strut | Stomp Off Records | CD 1302

Whittlin'
Charlie Mariano Quartet | Tea For Four | Leo Records | 012

Who
Benny Goodman Trio | Jazz Collection:Benny Goodman | Laserlight | 24396
Jazz Drumming Vol.1(1927-1937) | Fenn Music | FJD 2701

Who Am I
Mark Nauseef/Miroslav Tadic Group | The Snake Music | CMP Records | CMP CD 60

Who Are You
Ramsey Lewis Group | Sky Islands | GRP | GRP 97452
Friedemann Graef Group | Daily New Paradox | FMP | 0450

Who Bought The Car?
Louie Bellson's Big Band Explosion | The Art Of The Chart | Concord | CCD 4800

Who But Mariah
Ada Montellanico With The Jimmy Cobb Trio | The Encounter | Philology | W 66.2

Who Can I Turn To
Bill Evans Trio | The Complete Bill Evans On Verve | Verve | 527953-2
Trio '65 | Verve | 2304517 IMS
Bill Evans Trio:The Last Waltz | Milestone | 8MCD 4430-2
Bill Evans:The Secret Sessions | Milestone | 8MCD 4421-2
Bill Evans:The Secret Sessions | Milestone | 8MCD 4421-2
The Brilliant | West Wind | WW 2058
Bill Evans:The Secret Sessions | Milestone | 8MCD 4421-2
Yesterday I Heard The Rain | Bandstand | BDCD 1535
Half Moon Bay | Milestone | MCD 9282-2
Bob Neloms | Pretty Music | India Navigation | IN 1050
Larry Willis Trio | Let's Play | Steeplechase | SCCD 31283
Oscar Peterson Trio | The Paris Concert | Pablo | 2PACD 2620112
Mellow Mood | MPS | 68077
The Concord All Stars | Take 8-Jazz Festival Japan '87 | Concord | CJ 347
Alan Clare With Lenny Bush | Alan Clare's Holland Park:Love Music To Unwind | Master Mix | CHECD 00108

Who Can I Turn To-
Oscar Peterson Quartet | Time After Time | Pablo | 2310947-2
Gerry Brown-John Lee Group | Infinite Jones | Keytone | KYT 710

Who Cares
Andreas Lonardoni Group | Snooze | Lipstick Records | LIP 8956-2
Bert Ambrose And His Orchestra | Happy Days | Saville Records | SVL 147 IMS
Bob Brookmeyer Quintet | Sony Jazz Collection:Stan Getz | CBS | 488623-2
Buddy Montgomery | Maybeck Recital Hall Series Volume Fifteen | Concord | CCD 4494
Carol Sloane And Her Band | Out Of The Blue | Fresh Sound Records | LSP 15823(CBS CS 8566)
Dick Hyman | The Gershwin Songbook:Jazz Variations | Musicmasters | 65094-2
Ella Fitzgerald With Andre Previn | Nice Work If You Can Get It-Ella Fitzgerald And Andre Previn Do Gershwin | Pablo | 2312140-2
Henri Renaud Trio With Jimmy Gourley | Henri Reanaud Trio,Sextet & All Stars | Vogue | 21606382
Karin Krog Quintet | Karin Krog Jubilee-The Best Of 30 Years | Verve | 523716-2
Klaus Weiss Quintet | A Taste Of Jazz | ATM Records | ATM 3810-AH
Lionel Hampton Orchestra | The Big Bands Vol.1.The Snader Telescriptions | Storyville | 4960043
Michael Moore Trio | Michael Moore Trio Plays Gershwin | Master Mix | CHECD 00110
Susannah McCorkle With The Ken Peplowski Quintet | No More Blues | Concord | CCD 4370

Who Cares-
June Christy With The Pete Rugolo Orchestra | The Song Is June | Capitol | 855455-2

Who Cares About April
Niacin | High Bias | Stretch Records | SCD 9017-2

Who Cares(alt.take)
Horace Parlan Trio | Hi-Fly | Steeplechase | SCCD 31417
Bob Brookmeyer Quartet | Oslo | Concord | CCD 4312

Who Could Care
Stan Getz-Bob Brookmeyer Quintet | A Life In Jazz:A Musical Biography | Verve | 535119-2
Stan Getz-Bob Brookmeyer Recorded Fall 1961 | Verve | 813359-1 IMS

Who Do You Love
John Hammond Band | The Best Of John Hammond | Vanguard | VCD 11/12
Lenny White Group | Hot Jazz Bisquits | Hip Bop | HIBD 8801
Lee Morgan Quartet | Jazz Gallery:Lee Morgan Vol.1 | RCA | 2127281-2

Who Ever Thinks Or Hope Of Love
Elliot Lawrence And His Orchestra | The Elliot Lawrence Big Band Swings Cohn & Kahn | Fantasy | FCD 24761-2

Who Fard That Shot
Elliot Lawrence Band | Plays Tiny Kahn And Johnny Mandel Arrangements | Fantasy | 0902109(F 3219)

Who Is Heinz?
Bill Holman And His Orchestra | Satin Nights | Black-Hawk | BKH 536

Who Knows
Ari Ambrose Quartet | Jazmin | Steeplechase | SCCD 31535
Art Farmer Sextet | The Company I Keep-Art Farmer Meets Tom Harrell | Arabesque Recordings | AJ 0112
New York Voices | New York Voices | GRP | GRP 95892
Thelonious Monk Quintet | Thelonious Monk:The Complete Blue Note Recordings | Blue Note | 830363-2

Who Knows Them?
Dianne Reeves With Orchestra | For Every Heart | Palo Alto | TB 203

Who Knows(alt.take)
Thelonious Monk Quintet | More Genius Of Thelonious Monk | Blue Note | 300194(BNJ 61011)

Who Loves You
Nick LaRocca And His Original Dixieland Band | Original Dixieland Jazz Band | RCA | ND 90026

Who Me
Count Basie And His Orchestra | Count On The Coast Vol.2 | Phontastic | NCD 7575
Breakfast Dance And Barbecue | Roulette | 531791-2
En Concert Avec Europe 1 | Laserlight | 710411/12
Basie In Sweden | Roulette | CDP 759974-2

Who Needs Forever?
Jimmy Heath Sextet | The Riverside Collection: Jimmy Heath-Nice People | Original Jazz Classics | OJCCD 6006-2

Who She Do
Joe Williams With The Norman Simmons Quartet | Ballad And Blues Master | Verve | 511354-2 PMS

Who' Sit
Lars Gullin Sextet | Lars Gullin 1951/52 Vol.5:First Walk | Dragon | DRCD 380

Who Sleeps
The Rythmakers | The Hottest Jazz Ever Recorded | VJM | VLP 53 IMS

Who T.F. Is Calling
James 'Sing' Miller Quartet | New Orleans Traditional Jazz Legends:Sing Miller | Mardi Gras Records | MG 9006

Who Throught Up This Song(from The Boy's Magic Horn)
Roy Eldridge And His Orchestra | The Varsity Sessions Vol.1 | Storyville | SLP 701

Who Used To Dance
Ella Fitzgerald And Louis Armstrong With Dave Barbour And His Orchestra | Ella Fitzgerald:Mr.Paganini | Dreyfus Jazz Line | FDM 36741-2

Who Walks In When I Walk Out
Ella Fitzgerald With Dave Barbour And His Orchestra | Ella:The Legendary American Decca Recordings | GRP | GRP 46482

Who Will Buy
J.J.Johnson's All Stars | J.J.'s Broadway | Verve | 9860308
Max Roach Group | Live In Europe 1964-Freedom Now Suite | Magnetic Records | MRCD 110

Who Will Rescue You?
Carla Bley Big Band | The Carla Bley Big Band Goes To Church | Watt | 27(533682-2)
Dave Brubeck Quartet | Late Night Brubeck | Telarc Digital | CD 83345

Who Will The Next Fool Be
Klaus König Orchestra | Reviews | Enja | ENJ-9061 2

Who Would Have Thought That
Lennie Niehaus Quintet | Patterns | Fresh Sound Records | FSR-CD 5013

Who?
Benny Goodman Quintet | Benny Goodman:The King Of Swing | Musicmasters | 65130-2

Whole Lotta Loving
Katie Webster | The Many Faces Of Katie Webster | Schubert Records | SCH- 103

Whole Nelson
Lares | Lares | yvp music | 3017

Whole Tone Stomp
Andy Jaffe Sextet | Manhattan Projections | Stash Records | ST-CD 549(875045)

Who'll Buy My Bublitckki?
Benny Goodman And His Orchestra | Benny Goodman Forever | RCA | NL 89955(2) DP

Who'll Buy My Dreams
Ruby Braff Trio | Bravura Eloquence | Concord | CCD 4423

Wholly Cats
Kenny Burrell Sextet | Verve Jazz Masters 45:Kenny Burrell | Verve | 527652-2
The European Jazz Guitar Orchestra | The European Jazz Guitar Orchestra | Jardis Records | JRCD 9307
Abbey Lincoln With Her Band | Wholly Earth | Verve | 559538-2

Wholly Earth
Bill Crosby All Stars | Bill Crosby-My Appreciation | Verve | 847892-2 PMS

Whoopi
Algiers Brass Band | Lord Lord Lord | Sound Of New Orleans | SONO 1030

Whoopin' Blues
Sarah Spencer's Rue Conti Jazz Band | Laisses Les Bons Temps Rouler! | Lake | LACD 22

Who's Afraid Of Virginia Woolf
Jimmy Smith With Orchestra | Who's Afraid Of Virginia Woolf? | Verve | 823309-2 PMS

Who's Been Eatin' My Porridge
Johnny 'Big Mouse' Walker | Blue Love | Steeplechase | SCB 9005

Who's Been Here
Larry Johnson & Nat Riddles | Johnson! Where Did You Get That Sound? New York Really Has The Blues | L+R Records | LR 42046

Who's Been Talkin'?
Howlin' Wolf Band | Howlin' Wolf | Chess | 427016
Marty Hall Band | Who's Been Talkin'?s | Blues Beacon | BLU-1033 2
Robert Cray Band | The Robert Cray Band | Charly | ???

Who's Controlling Whom?
Joe Newman-Bill Byers Sextet | Byers' Guide | Fresh Sound Records | FSCD 2004

Who's Got Rhythm
Hal McIntyre And His Orchestra | The Uncollected:Hal McIntyre | Hindsight | HSR 172

Who's Got You?
The Rippingtons | Welcome To St. James' Club | GRP | GRP 96182

Who's In Control?
Bob Barnard Quintet | New York Notes | Sackville | SKCD2-3061

Who's Making Love
Lou Donaldson Quintet | Hot Dog | Blue Note | 828267-2

Who's Sam?
Howard Rumsey's Lighthouse All-Stars | Howard Rumsey's Lighthouse All-Stars Vol.6 | Original Jazz Classics | OJCCD 386-2(C 3504)

Who's Sleepy
J.P.Torres Band | Trombone Man | RMM Records | 660.58.085

Who's Smoking?
Paquito D'Rivera Group feat. James Moody | Who's Smooking?! | Candid | CCD 79523

Who's Sorry Now
Alvin Alcorn Band With George Lewis | George Lewis With Red Allen-The Circle Records | American Music | AMCD-71
Bob Crosby's Bobcats | Big Band Bounce And Boogie-Bob Crosby:Mournin' Blues/Accent On The Bobcats | Affinity | AFS 1014
Earl Hines | Tour De Force Encore | Black Lion | BLCD 760157
Frank 'Big Boy' Goudie Trio | Frank 'Big Boy' Goudie With Amos White | American Music | AMCD-50
Ken Colyer's Jazzmen | When I Leave The World Behind | GHB Records | BCD-152
Sweet Emma Barrett And Herr Bell Boys | Mardi Grax Day 1960-Live | 504 Records | 504CD 67

Who's Sorry Now(alt.take)
Klaus König Orchestra | Reviews | Enja | ENJ-9061 2

Who's That Guy?
Peg Leg Sam | Medicine Show Man | Trix Records | TRIX 3302

Who's Who Is It?
Anson Weeks And His Orchestra | The Radio Years: Anson Weeks And His Hotel Mark Hopkins Orchestra 193 | Hindsight | HSR 146

Whose Blues
Jimmy Jewell Sextet | From The First Time I Met You | Affinity | AFF 5
Jimmy Witherspoon And His Quartet | Blues Around The Clock | Original Blues Classics | OBCCD 576-2(P 7314)

Whoza Mtwana
Abdullah Ibrahim With The NDR Big Band | Ekapa Lodumo | TipToe | TIP-888840 2
Dollar Brand Quintet | Montreux '80 | Enja | 3079-2

Why
Kol Simcha | Contemporary Klezmer | Laika Records | LK 93-048
Mary Lou Williams Quartet | Mary Lou Williams:The London Sessions | Vogue | 21409312
Mitch Watkins Group | Underneath It All | Enja | ENJ-5099 2
Tad Shull Quintet | Deep Passion | Criss Cross | Criss 1047

Why Am I
Barbara Sutton Curtis | Solos & Duets | Sackville | SKCD2-2027

Why Am I Treated So Bad
Nils Landgren Funk Unit | Paint It Blue:A Tribute To Cannonball Adderley | ACT | 9243-2
Art Pepper Quintet | Gettin' Together | Contemporary | COP 023

Why Are You Blue
Nancy Harrow With The Gary McFarland Orchestra | You Never Know | Atlantic | AMCY 1070

Why Begin Again
The Brecker Brothers | Straphagin' | RCA | 2131312-2

Why Can't You Behave
Ella Fitzgerald With The Buddy Bregman Orchestra | The Cole Porter Song Book | Verve | 2683044 IMS

Why Can't You Behave?
Till Brönner-Gregoire Peters Quintet | Generations Of Jazz | Minor Music | 801037

Why Change
Connie Jones & Dick Sudhalter Group | Live at The Vineyard | Challenge | CHR 70054

Why Did I Choose You
Bill Evans Quartet | From Left To Right | Verve | 557451-2
Bill Evans Quartet With Orchestra | The Complete Bill Evans On Verve | Verve | 527953-2
From Left To Right | Verve | 557451-2
Bucky Pizzarelli-John Pizzarelli Duo | The Complete Guitar Duos(The Stash Sessions) | Stash Records | ST-CD 536(889114)
Eden Atwood Group | A Night In The Life | Concord | CCD 4730
Martin Taylor | Portraits | Linn Records | AKD 048
Sue Raney-Dick Shreve | Autumn In The Air | Fresh Sound Records | FSR-CD 5017

Why Did I Choose You(alt.take 1)
Bill Evans Quartet | The Complete Bill Evans On Verve | Verve | 527953-2

Why Did I Choose You(alt.take 2)
The Complete Bill Evans On Verve | Verve | 527953-2

Why Did I Choose You(alt.take 3)
The Complete Bill Evans On Verve | Verve | 527953-2

Why Did I Choose You(alt.take 4)
The Complete Bill Evans On Verve | Verve | 527953-2

Why Did I Choose You(alt.take 5)
The Complete Bill Evans On Verve | Verve | 527953-2

Why Did I Choose You(alt.take 6)
Huey 'Piano' Smith & His Clowns | The Imperial Sides 1960-61 | Pathe | 1546731(Imperial)

Why Do I Love You
Charlie Parker Sextet | The Verve Years (1950-51) | Verve | 2-2512 IMS
Dodo Marmarosa Trio | The Chicago Sessions | Argo | ARC 502 D
Kenny Dorham Quintet | Showboat | Bainbridge | BT 1043
Margaret Whiting With Russel Garcia And His Orchestra | A Fine Romance | Verve | 523827-2
Miles Davis Nonet | The Real Birth Of The Cool | Bandstand | BDCD 1512

Why Do I Love You(take 2)
Sonny Stitt Quartet | Symphony Hall Swing | Savoy | WL 70830 (809327)

Why Do I Love You(take 6)
Charlie Parker's Jazzers | Bird: The Complete Charlie Parker On Verve | Verve | 837141-2

Why Do I Love You(take 7)
Niko Schäuble Quintet | On The Other Hand | Naxos Jazz | 86011-2

Why Do You Have To Go Home
Harry James And His Orchestra | Sounds Familiar | Saville Records | SVL 151 IMS

Why Does It Happen To Me Every Time?
Jonas Hellborg Group | Adfa | Demon Records | DEM 020

Why Don't
Buddy Johnson And His Orchestra | Buddy And Ella Johnson 1953-1964 | Bear Family Records | BCD 15479 DH

Why Don't Cha Stop It
Joe Lovano With The Junko Onishi Trio | Tenor Time | somethin'else | 300230(TOCJ 5584)

Why Don't I
Sonny Rollins Quintet | Sonny Rollins | Blue Note | 84508
Sonny Rollins:The Blue Note Recordings | Blue Note | 821371-2
Steve Grossman Quartet | Steve Grossman Quartet | Dreyfus Jazz Line | FDM 36602-2
Steve Grossman Trio | Bouncing With Mr. A.T. | Dreyfus Jazz Line | FDM 36579-2

Why Don't You Do Right
Ernst Höllerhagen And His Band | Ernst Höllerhagen 1942-1948 | Elite Special | 9522001
Herbie Mann Group | The Evolution Of Mann | Atlantic | SD 2-300
Jeanie Bryson And Her Band | Som Cats Know-Jeannie Bryson Sings Songs Of Peggy Lee | Telarc Digital | CD 83391
Peggy Lee With The Benny Goodman Orchestra | Peggy Lee & Benny Goodman:The Complete Recordings 1941-1947 | CBS | C2K 65686
Ruth Brown With The Richard Wess Orchestra | Late Date With Ruth Brown | Atlantic | AMCY 1055
Singers Unlimited With The Clare Fischer Orchestra | Compact Disc:The Singers Unlimited | MPS | 831373-2 PMS

Why Don't You Do Right-
Benny Goodman And His Orchestra | Big City Swing | Decca | TAB 5

Why D'You Do It
Jonathan Schwartz & Quintet | Anyone Would Love You | Muse | MCD 5325

Why Go To The Moon-
Mike Mainieri Group | An American Diary:The Dreaming | NYC-Records | NYC 6026-2

Why I Was Born
Albert Ammons Rhythm Kings | The King Of Boogie Woogie | Blues Classics | BC 27

Why Is It That It's Not
Patty Waters With The Burton Greene Trio | Patty Waters Sings | ESP Disk | ESP 1025-2

Why Nogales?
Jim Hall | Dedications & Inspirations | Telarc Digital | CD 83365

Why Not You
Bill Watrous And His Orchestra | Reflections | Soundwings | SW 2104(807408)

Why Not?
Count Basie And His Orchestra | The Count | Verve | MV 2644 IMS
Live At Birdland | Jazz Anthology | JA 5225
Diederik Wissels Trio | Tender Is The Night | Jazz Pure Collection | AU 31616 CD
Peppino D'Agostino | Close To The Heart | Acoustic Music Records | 319.1039.2
Volker Schlott Quartet | Why Not | Acoustic Music Records | 319.1083.2

Why She Couldn't Come
Kerry Campbell Quintet | Phoenix Rising | Contemporary | CCD 14041-2

Why Shouldn't I
Betty Roche And Her Quartet | Lightly And Politely | Original Jazz Classics | OJCCD 1802-2(P 7198)
Jaye P. Morgan With Marion Evens And His Orchestra | Just You Just Me | Fresh Sound Records | ND 38627
Tony Perkins With The Marty Paich Orchestra | Tony Perkins | Fresh Sound Records | LN 3394(Epic)

Why Shouldn't You Cry
Stefanie Schlesinger And Her Group | What Love Is | Enja | ENJ-9434 2
Wolfgang Lackerschmid & Lynne Arriale Trio | You Are Here | Bhakti Jazz | BR 43
The Andrew Sisters | The Andrew Sisters | ASV | AJA 5096

Why Try To Change Me Now
Elvin Jones Quartet | Familiar Ground | West Wind | WW 2104

Why Was I Born
Art Tatum | Art Tatum-The Standard Transcriptions | Music & Arts | CD 919
Dick Collins And The Runaway Heard | Horn Of Plenty | Fresh Sound Records | NL 45632(RCA LJM 1019)
Ella Fitzgerald With The Nelson Riddle Orchestra | The Complete Ella Fitzgerald Song Books of Harold Arlen, Irving Berlin, Duke Ellington, George & Ira Gershwin, Jerome Kern, Johnny Mercer, Cole Porter And Rogers & Hart | Verve | 519832-2
George Barnes Quartet | Blues Going Up | Concord | CJ 43
Jackie McLean Quartet | Contour | Prestige | P 24076
Jerry Wiggins Trio | The Piano Collection Vol.1 | Vogue | 21610242
Kenny Burrell Quintet | John Coltrane-The Prestige Recordings | Prestige | 16 PCD 4405-2
Kenny Burrell-John Coltrane Duo | Kenny Burrell & John Coltrane | Original Jazz Classics | OJC20 300-2
Kenny Burrell & John Coltrane | New Jazz | NJSA 8276-2
Jazz Gallery:John Coltrane Vol.1 | RCA | 2119540-2
Mick Pyne | Alone Together | Spotlite | SPJ 506
Sun Ra Arkestra | Cosmo Omnibus Imaginable Illusion/Live At Pit-Inn,Tokyo | DIW | DIW 824 CD
Tony Perkins With Orchestra | On A Rainy Afternoon | Fresh Sound Records | ND 42123

Why Was I Born-
James Williams | Live at Maybeck Recital Hall Series Volume Forty-Two:James Williams | Concord | CCD 4694

Why Weep
Lucky Thompson Quintet | Lucky Thompson | Swing | SW 8404 IMS

Why You So Mean To Me
Albert King Blues Band | Crosscut Saw:Albert King In San Francisco | Stax | SCD 8571-2(F 9627)

Why?
Jelly Roll Morton's Hot Six | Jelly Roll Morton:Last Sessions-The Complete General Recordings | Commodore | CMD 14032

Wichita Lineman
Ray Charles With Orchestra | What Have I Done To Their Songs | London | 6.23173 AF

Wichi-Tai-To
Jim Pepper Group | Comin' And Goin' | Bellaphon | 290.31.029

Wide Open
Jenny Evans And Her Quintet | Whisper Not | ESM Records | Panda 16(941336)

Wide Open Spaces
Michael Formanek Quintet | Wide Open Space | Enja | ENJ-6032 2

Widele Wedele,Hinterm Städele Hält Der Bettelmann Hochzeit
John Surman-John Warren Group | The Brass Project | ECM | 1478

Wider Vision
Wanja Slavin-Matc Schmolling | Off Minor | Organic Music | ORGM 9732

Widmung
Thierry Péala Group | Inner Traces:A Kenny Wheeler Songbook | Naive | 226102

Wie Du
Brötzmann-Mangelsdorff-Sommer Trio | Pica | FMP | 1050

Wie Du(Like You)
Grosses Tanzorchester Vom Palace-Hotel St.Moritz | International Schlager & In Mood mit Teddy Stauffer's Original Teddies | Elite Special | 9522003

Wie Lange Noch?
Klaus Spencker Trio | Invisible | Jardis Records | JRCD 9409

Wie Leif Erikson Amerika Entdeckte
Christoph Thewes-Rudi Mahall Quartet | Quartetto Pazzo | Jazz Haus Musik | JHM 0122 CD

Wie Man's Macht,Man Macht's Verkehrt
Joe Kienemann Trio | Liedgut:Amsel,Drossel,Swing & Funk | yvp music | CD 3095

Wie Schön Blüht Uns Der Maien
Fun Horns | Choral Concert(Weihnachtsoratorium/Choräle) | KlangRäume | 30090

Wiegenlied
Joachim Kühn | Cinemascope/Piano | MPS | 88037-2

Wien Wien Nur Du Allein
Charly Antolini Orchestra | Soul Beat | ATM Records | ATM 3802-AH

Wiener Dog
Andy Lumpp | Piano Solo | Nabel Records:Jazz Network | CD 4646

Wiener Gerd
Piano Solo | Nabel Records:Jazz Network | CD 4646

Wiener Peter
Björn Alke Quartet | Jazz Sverige 1974 | Caprice | CAP 1072

Wig Wise
Major Holley Trio | Mule | Black & Blue | BLE 233074

Wiggle Wobble
Count Basie And His Orchestra | Count Basie And His Orchestra-1944 | Circle | CCD-60

Wigglin'
Freddie Redd Quartet | The Music From The Connection | Blue Note | 84027

Wights Waits For Weights
Mark Alban Lotz/Tjitze Anne Vogel | Mostly Harmless... | Edition Collage | EC 470-2
Steve Coleman Group | Motherland Pulse | JMT Edition | 919001-2
Steve Coleman Quintet | Jump On It | Enja | 4094

Wild And Free-
Friedemann Graef-Albrecht Riermeier Duo | Exit | FMP | 0820

Wild Bill Blues At The Huchette
Wild Bill Moore Quintet | Bottom Groove | Milestone | MCD 47098-2

Wild Bill's Beat
Count Basie And His Orchestra | Basie Boogie | CBS | 21063

Wild Bird
Dave Douglas Group | Dave Douglas Freak In | Bluebird | 2664008-2

Wild Blue
Duke Ellington And His Orchestra | Duke 56/62 Vol.2 | CBS | 88654

Wild Cat
Bob Wilber-Dick Wellstood | The Duet | Progressive | PCD 7080

Wild Cat Blues
Clarence Williams' Blue Five | The Complete 1923-1926 Clarence Williams Sessions Vol.1 | EPM Musique | FDC 5107
Dick Wellstood And The Friends Of Fats | Ain't Misbehavin' | Chiaroscuro | CR 183
John Crocker Quartet | Tribute To Fats Waller | Jazz Colours | 874730-2
Monty Sunshine Trio | Dixieland Collection | Aves | 146535
The Very Best Of Dixieland Jazz | Verve | 535529-2
Hot Jazz Meeting | Polydor | 834745-2

Wild Coffee-
Big Joe Williams | Baby Please Don't Go | Swingtime(Contact) | BT 2007

Wild Disputes
Joe Venuti Quartet | Happy Joe | Vagabond | 6.23757 AO

Wild Dog
Stanley Clarke-George Duke Band | Live In Montreux | Jazz Door | JD 1234

Wild Flower
Herbie Nichols Trio | Herbie Nichols Trio | Blue Note | 300098(1519)
Frank Kimbrough Quintet | The Herbie Nichols Project | Soul Note | 121313-2

Wild Honey
Bob Hall | No.29 | BELL Records | BLR 84038

Wild Is Love
Shirley Horn With Orchestra | Loads Of Love + Shirley Horn With Horns | Mercury | 843454-2
Chuck Brown And The Second Chapter Band | Timeless | Minor Music | 801068

Wild Is The Wind
Dave Pike Quartet | Pike's Peak | Epic | 489772-2
Fred Hersch Trio | Dancing In The Dark | Chesky | JD 90
J.J.Johnson With The Brass Orchestra | The Brass Orchestra | Verve | 537321-2
Nina Simone Quartet | Nina Simone-The 60s Vol.3:Work Song | Mercury | 838545-2 PMS
Nina Simone Trio | At Town Hall | Official | 6012
Roseanna Vitro With Tim Ries And The Fred Hersh Quartet | Softly | Concord | CCD 4587

Wild Is The Wind-
Ahmad Jamal Trio | Live In Paris 92 | Birdology | 849408-2
Patty Waters With The Burton Greene Trio | College Tour | ESP Disk | ESP 1055-2

Wild Man
Alex Welsh & His Band With Guests | Salute To Satchmo | Black Lion | 157005

Wild Man Blues
Don Byas/Claude Bolling | Frenchie Roy | Vogue | 655009
Jacques Gauthé's Creole Rice Yerba Buena Jazz Band | Cassoulet Stomp | Stomp Off Records | CD 1170
Jelly Roll Morton's Red Hot Peppers | Jelly Roll Morton-Doctor Jazz | RCA | CL 89808 SF
Doctor Jazz | Black & Blue | BLE 59.227 2
Louis Armstrong And His Hot Seven | The Louis Armstrong Selection Vol.1 | CBS | 474764-2
Nicholas Payton Quartet | Gumbo Nouveau | Verve | 531199-2
Rod Mason's Hot Five | Tribute To Jelly Roll Morton | Jazz Colours | 874728-2
Theis/Nyegaard Jazzband | The Golden Years Of Revival Jazz,Vol.5 | Storyville | STCD 5510
Trumpets TRPTS. | Transforming Traditions | Black-Hawk | BKH 51701
Sidney Bechet And His New Orleans Feetwarmers | Sidney Bechet 1932-1943: The Bluebird Sessions | Bluebird | ND 90317

Wild Man On The Loose
Mose Allison Trio | Mose Alife!/Wild Man On The Loose | Warner | 8122-75439-2
Chicago Stompers | Washboard Story | Zeta | ZET 741

Wild Man(aka Wild Man Moore)
Duke Ellington And Count Basie With Their Orchestras | First Time! | CBS | CK 65571

Wild Man(aka Wild Man Moore-alt.take)
Deborah Henson-Conant | Alter Ego | Laika Records | 35100852

Wild Mountain Thyme-
Alterd Ego | Laika Records | 35100962
Miff Mole's Molers | That's A Plenty | Memo Music | HDJ 4112

Wild Party
Fletcher Henderson And His Orchestra | Jazz Classics In Digital Stereo: Fletcher Henderson Swing | CDS Records Ltd. | RPCD 628(CD 682)

Wild Rice
Nelson Rangell Group | In Every Moment | GRP | GRP 96622

Wild Rose
Babik Reinhardt Group | All Love | Melodie | 400012

Wild Village Dance
Kokomo Arnold | King Of The Bottelneck Guitar | Black & Blue | BLE 59.250 2

Wild Woman
Albert King Blues Band | Door To Door | Chess | 515021

Wild Women Don't Have The Blues
Jasper Van't Hof Trio | Tomorrowland | Challenge | CHR 70040

Wildcat
Tommy Smith Sextet | Beasts Of Scottland | Linn Records | AKD 054

Wildes Denken
Pata Masters | Pata-Bahia | Pata Musik | PATA 11 CD
Randy Sandke Quintet | I Hear Music | Concord | CCD 4566

Wildlife
Carla Bley Band | Night-Glo | Watt | 16

Wildlife:
Maynard Ferguson And His Orchestra | Verve Jazz Masters 52:Maynard Ferguson | Verve | 529905-2

Wildman
Jack Bruce Group | Somethinelse | CMP Records | CMP CD 1001

Wildroot
Woody Herman And The Herd | Woody Herman (And The Herd) At Carnegie Hall | Verve | 559833-2
Woody Herman's 2nd Herd | The Herd Rides Again...In Stereo | Evidence | ECD 22010-2

Wildwood
Art Farmer Septet | Farmer's Market | Prestige | P 24032
Stan Getz Quintet | Stan Getz-The Complete Roost Sessions | EMI Records | 859622-2
Chamber Music | Fresh Sound Records | FSR-CD 78(882177)

Wildwood Flower
Michael Riessler Group | Heloise | Wergo | WER 8008-2

Wilhelm Von Champeaux
Cecil Payne Septet | Scotch And Milk | Delmark | DE 494

Wili(part 1)
Miles Davis Group | Dark Magus | CBS | C2K 65137

Wili(part 2)
Willie 'The Lion' Smith | The Memoirs Of Willie 'The Lion' Smith | RCA | 2126415-2

Will
Weather Report | Sweetnighter | CBS | 485102-2
Ensemble Modern | Ensemble Modern-Fred Frith:Traffic Continues | Winter&Winter | 910044-2

Will Cast Some Light On
Bobby Shew-Chuck Findley Quintet | Trumpets No End | Delos | DE 4003(882204)

Will I Forget?
Paul Desmond Quartet With The Bill Bates Singers | Desmond | Original Jazz Classics | OJCCD 712-2(F 3235/8082)

Will I Know
John Klemmer Quartet | Involvement | Chess | 076139-2

Will 'N' Jug
Harry Verbeke Quartet | Short Speech | Timeless | SJP 136

Will O'The Wisp
Miles Davis With Gil Evans & His Orchestra | Soleá: A Flamenco-Jazz Fantasy | ACT | 9208-2
World Trio | World Trio | VeraBra Records | CDVBR 2052-2
John Graas Nonet | Jazzmantics | Fresh Sound Records | 252283-1(Decca DL 8677)

Will The Circle Be Unbroken
John Lee Hooker Group | Everybody Rockin' | Charly | CRB 1004

Will We Meet Again
Michael Mantler Sextet | More Movies | Watt | 10 (2313110)

Will We Meet Tonight
Danny 'Run Joe' Taylor And His Band | Listen To Dr. Jive | Krazy Kat | KK 780 IMS

Will You Make My Soup Hot And Silver
Billy Wright Band | Goin' Down Slow | Savoy | SV 0257

Will You Still Be Mine
Benny Bailey-Quartet With Strings | I Remember Love | Laika Records | 35101752
Benny Bailey With On The Corner And The Philharmonic Orchestra,Würzburg | On The Corner feat. Benny Bailye | Mons Records | MR 874807
Carol Sloane And Her Band | Out Of The Blue | Fresh Sound Records | LSP 15823(CBS CS 8566)
Hampton Hawes Quartet | All Night Session Vol.2 | Original Jazz Classics | OJCCD 639-2(C 7546)
Joshua Breakstone Quartet | Self-Portrait In Swing | Contemporary | CCD 14050-2
Lem Winchester Quintet | Winchester Special | Original Jazz Classics | OJCCD 1719-2(NJ 8223)
Max Greger Quintet | Night Train | Polydor | 543393-2
McCoy Tyner Trio | Live At Sweet Basil Vol.2 | Paddle Wheel | KICJ 1
Miles Davis Quartet | Green Haze | Prestige | P 24064
Oscar Peterson Trio | The Oscar Peterson Trio,Roy Eldridge,Sonny Stitt And Jo Jones At Newp | Verve | MV 2618 IMS
Pete Jolly Trio | Jolly Jumps In | Fresh Sound Records | 12582 CD(RCA)
Red Garland Trio | I Left My Heart... | Muse | MR 5311(952091)
Rosemary Clooney & The All Stars | With Love | Concord | CCD 4144
Sonny Rollins Trio | Sonnymoon For Two | Moon Records | MCD 015-2
Steve Kuhn Trio | Looking Back | Concord | CCD 4446
Tommy Dorsey And His Orchestra | Forever | RCA | NL 89859 DP

William And Mary
Billy Pierce Quartet | The Complete William The Conqueror Sessions | Sunnyside | SSC 9013 D

William Turner-
Gary McFarland Orchestra | The Great Arrangers | MCA | IA 9340/2

Willie & Muddy
Willie Jackson With Steve Lewis | Piron's New Orleans Orchestra | AZURE Compact Disc | AZ-CD-13

Willie Nelson-
Miles Davis Quintet | Black Beauty-Miles Davis At Filmore West | CBS | C2K 65138
Maynard Ferguson Band | Verve Jazz Masters 52:Maynard Ferguson | Verve | 529905-2

Willie Nillie
Michael Brecker Group | Tales From The Hudson | Impulse(MCA) | 951191-2

Willie T.
John Eaton | It Seems Like Old Times | Chiaroscuro | CR 174

Willie The Wailer
| The Nixa 'Jazz Today' Collection | Lake | LACD 48

Willie The Weeper
Bob Wilber And His Wildcats | The Commodore Story | Commodore | CMD 24002
Louis Armstrong And His Hot Seven | Heebie Jeebies | Naxos Jazz | 8.120351 CD
Mr.Acker Bilk And His Paramount Jazz Band | Golden Hour Of Acker Bilk And His Paramount Jazz Band | Golden Hour | 88 368 XAT

Willow
Dianne Reeves With Orchestra | For Every Heart | Palo Alto | TB 203
Marian McPartland | Willow Creek And Other Ballads | Concord | CCD 4272

Willow Groove
Chick Corea & Friends | Remembering Bud Powell | Stretch Records | SCD 9012-2

Willow Tree
Joe Turner | Stride By Stride | Solo Art | SACD-106
Sonny Boy Williamson Blues Band | Masters Of Jazz Vol. 15-Blues Giants | RCA | NL 89728 DP

Willow Weep For Me
Angelo Di Pippo Quartet | Arthur Street | Stash Records | ST-CD 557(875135)
Art Tatum | Art Tatum:Over The Rainbow | Dreyfus Jazz Line | FDM 36727-2
Art Tatum-The Complete Pablo Solo Masterpieces | Pablo | 7 PACD 4404-2
Art Tatum-The Complete Pablo Solo Masterpieces | Pablo | 7 PACD 4404-2
Art Tatum:Complete Capitol Recordings | Definitive Records | DRCD 11192
The Art Tatum Solo Masterpieces | Pablo | 2625703
Ben Webster Quartet | Ben Webster Plays Ballads | Storyville | SLP 4118
Benny Goodman And His Orchestra | Benny Goodman:The King Of Swing | Musicmasters | 65130-2
Bill Perkins & Frank Strazzeri | Warm Moods | Fresh Sound Records | FSR-CD 0191
Billie Holiday And Her Band | Lady Sings The Blues | Enoch's Music | 57271013
Billie Holiday With The Mal Waldron Trio | Billie Holiday Radio & TV Broadcast(1953-56) | ESP Disk | ESP 3003-2
Charles Musselwhite Band | Charles Musselwhite Memphis,Tennessee | Crosscut | CCR 1008
Clark Terry With Orchestra & Strings | Clark After Dark | MPS | 529088-2
Clifford Brown With Strings | Brownie-The Complete EmArCy Recordings Of Clifford Brown | EmArCy | 838306-2
Coleman Hawkins Quintet | Lover Man | France's Concert | FCD 104
David Fathead Newman Sextet | Fathead:Ray Charles Presents David Newman | Atlantic | 8122-73708 2
Atlantic Saxophones | Rhino | 8122-71256-2
Dexter Gordon Quartet | Our Man In Paris | Blue Note | 591722-2
Live At The Amsterdam Paradiso | Affinity | AFF 751
Dizzy Gillespie Quintet | The Great Modern Jazz Trumpet | Festival | 402151
Duke Ellington And His Orchestra | This Is Jazz:Duke Ellington Play Standards | CBS | CK 65056
Eden Atwood Group | A Night In The Life | Concord | CCD 4730
Ella Fitzgerald With Orchestra | Ella/Things Ain't What They Used To Be | Warner | 9362-47875-2
Ella Fitzgerald With The Paul Smith Trio | Return To Happiness-JATP At Yoyogi National Stadium,Tokyo | Pablo | 2620117-2
Frank Tate Quintet | Live In Belfast | Nagel-Heyer | CD 069
Fred Hunt Trio | Yesterdays | BELL Records | BLR 84037
Gottfried Böttger-Reiner Regel Duo | Reedin' Piano | L+R Records | CDLR 40034
Harry James And His Orchestra | Harry's Choice | Pathe | 2C 068-54575(Capitol T 1093)
Helen Merrill With The Roger Kellaway Trio And Wayne Shorter | Clear Oot Of This World | EmArCy | 510691-2 PMS
Herbie Mann-Bill Evans Quartet | That's Jazz Vol.8: Nirvana | Atlantic | ATL 50238
JATP All Stars | OW! All Star Jam Session | Moon Records | MCD 075-2
Jenny Evans And Her Quintet | Shiny Stockings | Enja | ENJ-9317 2
Jesper Thilo Quintet | Strike Up The Band | Sackville | SKCD2-2050
Jimmy Smith Trio | Incredible Jimmy Smith Vol.3 | Blue Note | 300106(1525)
Joe Turner | Another Epoch-Stride Piano | Pablo | 2310763
John Lewis | Evolution | Atlantic | 7567-83211-2
John Lewis And Hank Jones | An Evening With Two Grand Pianos | Atlantic | 7567-80787-2
John Lewis-Hank Jones Duo | An Evening With Two Grand Pianos | Little David | LD 59657
June Christy With Orchestra | This Is June Christy/June Christy Recalls Those Kenton Days | Capitol | 535209-2
June Christy Recalls Those Kenton Days | EMI Records | 1599311
King Curtis Quartet | The New Scene Of King Curtis | Original Jazz Classics | OJC 198(NJ 8237)
King Curtis Quintet | I Remember King Curtis | Prestige | P 24033
Laura Fygi With Band | Bewitched | Verve | 514724-2
Lawrence Marable Quartet | Tenorman | Fresh Sound Records | 054 2608851(Jazz West JWLP 8)
Lester Young Quintet | Lester Swings | Verve | 2683066 IMS
Lou Rawls With Les McCann Ltd. | Stormy Monday | Blue Note | 791441-2
Louis Armstrong With The Oscar Peterson Quartet | Louis Armstrong Meets Oscar Peterson | Verve | 539060-2
Ella And Louis Again, Vol.2 | Verve | 711122 IMS
Marian McPartland | Maybeck Recital Hall Series Volume Nine | Concord | CCD 4460
Muriel Zoe Group | Red And Blue | ACT | 9416-2
Nannie Porres Quintet | Music In Sweden 3: Jazz | Caprice | CAP 1131
Oliver Jones | Just 88 | Enja | ENJ-8062 2
Oscar Peterson Trio With Roy Eldridge & Jo Jones | The Oscar Peterson Trio,Roy Eldridge,Sonny Stitt And Jo Jones At Newp | Verve | MV 2618 IMS
Oscar Pettiford Sextet | Montmartre Blues | Black Lion | BLP 60124
Ray Charles With Orchestra | 20 Superhits | London | 6.22554 AP
Richard Carr-Bucky Pizzarelli | String Thing | Savant Records | SCD 2010
Roy Eldridge Quintet | Happy Time | Original Jazz Classics | OJCCD 628-2(2310746)
Sammy Price Sextet | Rockin' Boogie | Black & Blue | BB 921.2
Slam Stewart Quartet | Fish Scales | Black & Blue | BLE 233109
Stanley Jordan Group | Cornucopia | Blue Note | 792356-2
Stanley Turrentine With The Three Sounds | Blue Hour | Blue Note | 524586-2
Midnight Blue(The [Be]witching Hour) | Blue Note | 854365-2
Stanley Turrentine:Ballads | Blue Note | 795581-2
Stephane Grappelli Quartet | At The Winery | Concord | CCD 4139
Terry Smith With The Tony Lee Trio | British Jazz Artists Vol. 2 | Lee Lambert | LAM 002
Thelonious Monk Quartet | Thelonious Monk:Misterioso | Dreyfus Jazz Line | FDM 36743-2
Thelonious Monk:Complete 1947-1952 Blue Note Recordings | The Jazz Factory | JFCD 22838
Thilo Kreitmeier Quintet | Mo' Better Blues | Organic Music | ORGM 9706
Thomas Clausen-Pyysalo Severi | Turn Out The Stars | Storyville | STCD 4215
Toots Thielemans Quartet | Jazz In Paris:Toots Thielemans-Blues Pour Flirter | EmArCy | 549403-2 PMS
Toots Thielemans With The Shirley Horn Trio | For My Lady | EmArCy | 510133-2
Vince Guaraldi Trio | A Flower Is A Lovesome Thing | Original Jazz Classics | OJC 235(F 3257)
Wes Montgomery Quartet | The Small Group Recordings | Verve | 2-2513 IMS

Wild Bill Davison Quartet | Midnight Slows No.1 | Black & Blue | BLE 233026
Wynton Kelly Trio | Keep It Moving | Milestone | M 47026
Kelly Blue | Riverside | RISA 1142-6
Wynton Kelly Trio With Wes Montgomery | Wes Montgomery:The Verve Jazz Sides | Verve | 521690-2
Zoot Sims Quartet | Soprano Sax | Pablo | 2310770-2
Zoot Sims-Bucky Pizzarelli Duo | Summum | Ahead | 33752

Willow Weep For Me-
JATP All Stars | Jam Session 1955 | Moon Records | MCD 029-2
Ray Bryant | Alone At Montreux | 32 Jazz | 32128

Willow Weep For Me(alt.take)
Tommy Flanagan Trio | The Complete 'Overseas' | DIW | DIW 305 CD
Harold Danko | Ink And Water | Sunnyside | SSC 1008(952101)

Willowcrest
Cannonball Adderley Group | Julian 'Cannonball' Adderley | EmArCy | 830381-2

Willows
Mike Santiago/Entity | White Trees | Chiaroscuro | CR 193

Willy Nilly
Mal Waldron & Jim Pepper | Art Of The Duo | Tutu Records | 888106-2*

Willy's Blues
Eddie Bert Sextet | The Human Factor | Fresh Sound Records | FSR-CD 5005

Wilpan's Walk
Blind Blake | Blind Blake-That Lovin' I Crave | Biograph | BLP 12050

Winchester Cathedral
Hank Jones With Oliver Nelson's Orchestra | Happenings | Impulse(MCA) | JAS 61(AS 9132)

Wind
Naima | Vertigo | Mons Records | MR 874816

Wind Chant
Carter Jefferson Sextet | The Rise Of Atlantis | Timeless | CD SJP 126

Wind Danse
Chick Corea Group | Verve Jazz Masters 3:Chick Corea | Verve | 519820-2
Julian Priester And Marine Intrusion | Polarization | ECM | 1098

Wind Parade
Donald Byrd Orchestra | Donald Byrd:Blue Breakbeats | Blue Note | 494708-2

Wind Sons
John Patitucci Group | John Patitucci | GRP | GRP 95602

Wind,Sand And Stars-
Franco Morone | Guitarea | Acoustic Music Records | 319.1046.2

Windchime
Barbara Thompson | Songs From The Center Of The Earth | Black Sun Music | 15014-2

Windfall
Peter Erskine Trio | Juni | ECM | 1657(539726-2)
Sadao Watanabe Group | Earth Step | Verve | 521287-2

Windfall-
John Surman With String Quartet | Coruscating | ECM | 1702(543033-2)

Winding Passages
Rinde Eckert Group | Story In,Story Out | Intuition Records | INT 3507-2

Winding The World
Lee Konitz-Matt Wilson | Gone With The Wind | Steeplechase | SCCD 31528

Winding Town
Gone With The Wind | Steeplechase | SCCD 31528

Winding Up
Alvin Batiste Ensemble | Musique D'Afrique Nouvelle Orleans | India Navigation | IN 1064

Windjammer
Howard McGhee Sextet | Sunset Swing | Black Lion | BLCD 760171

Windmill
Clifford Jordan Quintet | Starting Time | Original Jazz Classics | OJC 147(J 952)
Kirk Lightsey Quintet feat. Marcus Belgrave | Kirk 'N Marcus | Criss Cross | Criss 1030

Windmills Of Your Mind
George Benson Quartet | The Silver Collection: George Benson | Verve | 823450-2 PMS

Windmills Of Your Mind-
Charly Antolini Jazz Power | Bop Dance | BELL Records | BLR 84043

Window
Stan Getz Quartet | Verve Jazz Masters 8:Stan Getz | Verve | 519823-2
David Digs Orchestra | Realworld | Palo Alto | PA 8037

Windows
Chick Corea Trio | Circling In | Blue Note | 84555
Frank Marocco-Ray Pizzi Duo | Jazz Accordeon | Discovery | DS 797 IMS
Jerry Bergonzi Quartet | Vertical Reality | Accord | 500642
Marian McPartland Trio | Marion McPartland At The Festival | Concord | CCD 4118
Rogall & Van Buggenum | Two Piano Jazz: Live | Jazzline | ???
Hubert Laws And His Orchestra | Carnegie Hall | CTI | 6025

Windows Of The World
Lutz Potthoff Quartet With Uli Beckerhoff | Windrush | Acoustic Music Records | 319.1111.2

Winds
Axel Fischbacher Quartet | Coast To Coast | L+R Records | CDLR 45025
Wes Montgomery With The Don Sebesky Orchestra | California Dreaming | Verve | 827842-2

Winds Of Barcelona
Jerry Moore Quintet | Ballad Of Birmingham | ESP Disk | ESP 1061-2

Winds Of Sahara
Juhani Aaltonen Group | Springbird | Leo Records | 005

Windschief
Dave McKenna | Giant Strides | Concord | CCD 4099

Windsor Quartet
Jean-Pierre Pasquier Group | Firegold | Plainisphare | PAV 810

Windy
Super Session | Welcome & Alive | Vagabond | 6.28604 DP

Windy City
Anita Boyer & Her Tomboyers | Nat King Cole Trio:The MacGregor Years 1941/45 | Music & Arts | CD 911

Windy City Jive
Earl Hines And His Orchestra | Earl Hines-Piano Man | Bluebird | NK 86750

Windy Wendy
Ray Anderson Quartet | Old Bottles-New Wine | Enja | ENJ-4098 2

Wine Wine Wine
George Mraz Quartet | Morava | Milestone | MCD 9309-2

Wine,Oh Wine
Bryan Lee Group | Crawfish Lady | Blues Beacon | BLU-1035 2

Winestone
Cannonball Adderley Sextet | What I Mean | Milestone | M 47053

Winetou
Hayden Chisholm | Circe | Jazz Haus Musik | JHM 0081 CD

Wing
Jane Ira Bloom Quintet | The Nearness | Arabesque Recordings | AJ 0120

Wing Melodies
Jon Hassell Group | Power Spot | ECM | 1327
Cecil Taylor Orchestra Of Two Continents | Segments II | Soul Note | 121089-2

Wingin'
Inga Lühning With Trio | Lühning | Jazz Haus Musik | JHM 0111 CD

Wingman
011 Jazz Quintet | Rising | SPLASC(H) Records | H 168

Wings
James Blood Ulmer Quartet | America-Do You Remember The Love? | Blue Note | BT 85136

Wings And Things
Duke Ellington And His Orchestra | Passion Flower | Moon Records | MCD 074-2
Ella Fitzgerald And Duke Ellington:Cote D'Azure Concerts on Verve | Verve | 539033-2
Ella Fitzgerald And Duke Ellington:Cote D'Azure Concerts on Verve | Verve | 539033-2
Soul Call | Verve | 539785-2
Johnny Hodges-Wild Bill Davis Orchestra | Compact Jazz: Johnny Hodges-Wild Bill Davis | Verve | 839288-2

Wings Og Karma
Sandole Brothers | The Sandole Brothers | Fantasy | FCD 24763-2

Wings Over Persia
Stephan Micus | Wings Over Water | Japo | 60038(831058-2)

Wings Over Water
Carol Welsman With Band | Inclined | Justin Time | JTR 8478-2

Winin' Boy Blues
Albert Nicholas With The Henri Chaix Trio | Kornhaus Theater Baden 1969 | Sackville | SKCD2-2045
Jelly Roll Morton's New Orleans Jazzmen | Sidney Bechet 1932-1943: The Bluebird Sessions | Bluebird | ND 90317

Winky(Gigi)
Die Elefanten | Wasserwüste | Nabel Records:Jazz Network | CD 4634

Winner? Loser?
The Clarke/Duke Project | The Clarke/Duke Project | Epic | 468223-2

Winners Circle
Travis Haddix Band With The Kala Horns | Winners Never Quit | Elite Special | 73432

Winning The West
Frederic Rzewski | North American Ballads & Squares | Hat Art | CD 6089

Winter
Daniel Schnyder Group | Words Within Music | Enja | ENJ-9369 2
Dave Liebman Trio | The Seasons | Soul Note | 121245-2
Dino Saluzzi Trio | Cité De La Musique | ECM | 1616(533316-2)
Howard Riley Trio | The Day Will Come | CBS | 494434-2
Jasper Van't Hof | My World Of Music | Keytone | KYT 3-100 Digital
Jimmy Gourley-Richard Galliano 4 | Flyin' The Coop | 52e Rue Est | RECD 020
Uli Beckerhoff Quintet | Original Motion Picture Soundtrack:Das Geheimnis(Secret Of Love) | Nabel Records:Jazz Network | CD 4666
Charlie Mariano Group | Savannah Samurai | Jazzline | JL 11153-2

Winter Always Turns To Spring
Dave Brubeck Quartet | Jazz Impressions Of New York | CBS | CK 46189

Winter In Madrid
Esbjörn Svensson Trio(E.S.T.) | Winter In Venice | ACT | 9007-2

Winter In Venice
Rob McConnell And The Boss Brass | The Brass Is Back | Concord | CCD 4458

Winter Light
Nexus | Urban Shout | SPLASC(H) Records | H 170

Winter Moon
Art Pepper Quintet With Strings | Art Pepper:The Complete Galaxy Recordings | Galaxy | 16GCD 1016-2
Hoagy Carmichael Quintet | Blue Moon-Blue Note The Night And The Music | Blue Note | 789910-2
Stan Getz-Laurindo Almeida Orchestra | Verve Jazz Masters 53:Stan Getz-Bossa Nova | Verve | 529904-2
Art Pepper Quintet With Strings | Art Pepper:The Complete Galaxy Recordings | Galaxy | 16GCD 1016-2

Winter Moon(alt.take)
Don Menza Sextet | Hip Pocket | Palo Alto | PA 8010

Winter Of My Discontent
Vic Juris Quintet | Music Of Alec Wilder | Double Time Records | DTRCD-118

Winter Solstice
Enrico Pieranunzi Trio | Trioscape | yvp music | CD 3050

Winter Song
Jens Schliecker & Nils Rohwer | Piano Meets Vibes | Acoustic Music Records | 319.1050.2
Bill Dixon Septet | New Music: Second Wave | Savoy | SJL 2235 (801211)

Winter Song(alt.take)
Akio Sasajima Trio | Time Remembered | Muse | MCD 5417

Winter Sun
Dave Valentine Group | Musical Portraits | GRP | GRP 96642

Winter Tale
Modern Jazz Quartet | A Quartet Is A Quartet Is A Quartet | Atlantic | AMCY 1098

Winter Weather
Jimmy Rowles Septet | Weather In A Jazz Vane | Fresh Sound Records | FSR 502(Andex S-3007)
Peggy Lee With The Benny Goodman Orchestra | Peggy Lee & Benny Goodman:The Complete Recordings 1941-1947 | CBS | C2K 65686
Ralph Sutton | More At Cafe Des Copains | Sackville | SKCD2-2036

Winter Wonderful
Sonny Rollins Quartet | The Complete Sonny Rollins RCA Victor Recordings | RCA | 2668675-2

Winter Wonderland
Ken Colyer And His Jazz Band | Ken Colyer In New Orleans:The Complete 1953 Recordings | 504 Records | 504CD 53
Maryland Jazzband Of Cologne feat. Papa Don Vappie And Erny Elly | Christmas In New Orleans | Maryland Records | MJCD 0895
Sackville All Stars | The Sackville All Star Christmas Records | Sackville | SKCD2-3038
Thilo Wolf Big Band | Sternstunden Des Swing | MDL-Jazz | CD 27768

Winterballade
Joerg Reiter | Caprice | BELL Records | BLR 84040

Winterlude
Al Di Meola Group | Winter Nights | Telarc Digital | CD 83458

Winter-Summer(part 1)-
Azimuth | How It Was Then...Never Again | ECM | 1538

Wintersweet
Don Thompson's Banff Jazz All Stars | Celebration | Jazz Focus | JFCD 024

Wintertango
Amsterdam String Trio | Winter Theme | Winter&Winter | 910060-2

Wintertheme(1)
Winter Theme | Winter&Winter | 910060-2

Wintertheme(2)
Winter Theme | Winter&Winter | 910060-2

Wintertheme(3)
Robert Balzar Trio | Travelling | Jazzpoint | JP 1050 CD

Wintertime
Tok Tok Tok | Love Again | Einstein Music | EM 01081

Winterwonderland
Larry Willis Quintet | Heavy Blue | Steeplechase | SCCD 31269

Wipe It Off
Jaco Pastorius Trio | Live In New York City Volume Two | Big World | BW 1002

Wir Machen Musik
Daniel Schnyder Group | Words Within Music | Enja | ENJ-9369 2

Wir Setzen Uns In Tränen Nieder-
Dicke Luft | Halb So Wild-Wie Schlimm | Riskant | 568-722416

Wir Sind Die Sieger
Franck Band | Dufte | Jazz Haus Musik | JHM 0054 CD

Wir Sind Dufte
Lask | Sucht + Ordnung | ECM | 1268

Wires
Rinus Groeneveld Trio | Dare To Be Different | Timeless | CD SJP 321

Wisdom
Yellowjackets | Run For Your Life | GRP | GRP 97542
Mitch Seidman-Fred Fried-Harvie Swartz | This Over That | Jardis Records | JRCD 9816

Wisdom Of Notes
Thomas Brendgens-Mönkemeyer | Beauty | Jardis Records | JRCD 20138
David S. Ware Quartet | Davis S.Ware Quartet | DIW | DIW 916 CD

Wise One
John Coltrane Quartet | The Gentle Side Of John Coltrane | Impulse(MCA) | 951107-2
John Coltrane:The Classic Quartet-Complete Impulse Studio Recordings | Impulse(MCA) | 951280-2
Coltrane Spiritual | Impulse(MCA) | 589099-2
LeeAnn Ledgerwood | Compassion | Steeplechase | SCCD 31477
Klaus Doldinger & Passport | Down To Earth | Warner | 4509-93207-2

Wise Up
Sylvester Mike And His Orchestra | Clyde Bernhardt:The Complete Recordings Vol.2 (1949-1953) | Blue Moon | BMCD 6017

Wisely
Joshua Redman Quartet | Joshua Redman | Warner | 9362-45242-2

Wish
Wish | Warner | 9362-45365-2
Kendra Shank Group | Wish | Jazz Focus | JFCD 028
Ray Anderson Sextet | Wishbone | Gramavision | GV 79454-2(882568)

Wish I Were There
Don Braden Sextet | Wish List | Criss Cross | Criss 1069

Wish You Were Here
NColor | NColor | clearaudio | 220391 LP

Wishing And Hoping
Johnny Hodges Orchestra | Jazz Legacy 9: Johnny Hodges-The Rabbit In Paris | Vogue | 500059

Wishing And Waiting
Toshiko Akiyoshi Jazz Orchestra | Wishing Peace | Ken Music | 660.56.001

Wishing Well
Gil Goldstein Quartet | The Sands Of Time | Muse | MCD 5471
Sandy Graham And Her Quintet | Sandy Graham | Muse | MCD 5425
Wycliffe Gordon Quintet | The Joyride | Nagel-Heyer | CD 2032
Dave Ballou Trio | Volition | Steeplechase | SCCD 31460

Wisteria
Bob Wilber-Dick Hyman Sextet | A Perfect Match:A Tribute To Johnny Hodges & Wild Bill Davis | Arbors Records | ARCD 19193

Witch Hunt
Henning Berg-Andreas Genschel Duo | Beim 5.Kölner Jazz Haus Festival 1982 | Jazz Haus Musik | JHM 13
Kirk Lightsey Trio | Isotope | Criss Cross | Criss 1003 (835592)
Wayne Shorter Quintet | Speak No Evil | Blue Note | 499001-2
Wayne Shorter:The Classic Blue Note Recordings | Blue Note | 540856-2
Scapes | Changes In Time | Timeless | CD SJP 361

Witchcraft
Bireli Lagrene Quartet | Blue Eyes | Dreyfus Jazz Line | FDM 36591-2
Bo Thorpe And His Orchestra | Live At The Omni | Hindsight | HSR 231
Donald Byrd Sextet | Byrd In Hand | Blue Note | 542305-2
Duke Pearson Trio | Profile | Blue Note | GXK 8212 (84022)
Lucie Arnaz And Her Orchestra | Just In Time | Concord | CCD 4573
Mark Murphy Band | Mark Murphy's Hip Parade | Fresh Sound Records | 054 2613281(Capitol ST 1299)
Ross Tompkins-Joe Venuti Quintet | Live At Concord '77 | Concord | CJ 51

Witchdoctor
Chet Baker And The Lighthouse All Stars | Witch Doctor | Original Jazz Classics | OJCCD 609-2
Howard Rumsey's Lighthouse All-Stars | Howard Rumsey's Lighthouse All Stars Vol.3 | Original Jazz Classics | OJCCD 266-2(C 3508)

Witches Pit
Prestige All Stars | John Coltrane-The Prestige Recordings | Prestige | 16 PCD 4405-2
Walt Dickerson-Pierre Dorge | Landscape With Open Door | Steeplechase | SCS 1115

Witchi-Tai-To
Jan Garbarek-Bobo Stenson Quartet | Witchi-Tai-To | ECM | 1041(833330-2)
Jim Pepper Sextet | The Path | Enja | 5087-2

Witchi-Tai-To-
Shelly Manne All Stars | Mannekind | Mainstream | MD CDO 727

With (Exit)
Cecil Taylor Sextet | Conquistador | Blue Note | 576749-2

With (Exit-alt.take)
Allan Holdsworth/Gordon Beck | With A Heart In My Song | JMS | 044-1

With A Heart In My Song
Billy Taylor With The Quincy Jones Orchestra | My Fair Lady Loves Jazz | MCA | AS 72

With A Little Bit Of Luck
Shelly Manne And His Friends | My Fair Lady | Mobile Fidelity | MFCD 809

With A Little Help From My Friends
Renee Rosnes Trio | Art & Soul | Blue Note | 499997-2
Uwe Kropinski | Faces | ITM Records | ITM 14100

With A Song In My Heart
Bill Evans Trio | Empathy+A Simple Matter Of Conviction | Verve | 837757-2 PMS
Chet Baker With The Don Sebesky Orchestra | She Was Too Good To Me | Epic | 450954-2
Ella Fitzgerald With The Buddy Bregman Orchestra | The Rodgers And Hart Songbook | Verve | 821693-1
George Robert Quintet | Tribute | Jazz Focus | JFCD 004
Ian Shaw With Band | Taking It To Hart | Ronnie Scott's Jazz House | JHCD 036
José Luis Gámez Quintet | Rumbo Dorte | Fresh Sound Records | FSNT 089 CD
Kenny Werner Group | Beauty Secrets | RCA | 2169904-2
Los Angeles Jazz Quartet | Conversation Piece | Naxos Jazz | 86045-2
Mal Waldron Trio | Impressions | Original Jazz Classics | OJCCD 132-2(NJ 8242)
Paul Kuhn Septet | I Wish You Love:The Philharmonic Concert | Timbre | TRCD 005
Ralph Flanagan And His Orchestra | Dance Again Part 2 | Magic | DAWE 75
Tana Reid Quintet | Blue Motion | Paddle Wheel | KICJ 172

With A Song In My Heart-
Abe Lyman And His Californians | The Uncollected:Abe Lyman | Hindsight | HSR 184

With Every Breath I Take
Billy Eckstine With The Billy May Orchestra | Once More With Feeling | Roulette | 581862-2
Marlene And Her Quartet | Every Breath I Take | Savoy | SV 0233(MV 12058)
Lee Konitz | Lee Konitz 'Self Portrait'(In Celebration Of Lee Konitz' 70th Birthday) | Philology | W 121.2

With Malice Towards None
Tommy Flanagan/George Mraz | Ballads & Blues | Enja | 3031-2

With My Boots On
Lew Stone And His Orchestra | The Bands The Matter | Eclipse | ECM 2047

With Respect
Karl Berger Company | With Silence | Enja | 2022

With Someone New
David Azarian Trio | Stairway To Seventh Heaven | Mobile Fidelity | MFCD 902

With Strings Attached
John Surman Orchestra | Tales Of The Algonquin | Deram | 844884-2

With The Devil In The Backseat
The New York Composers Orchestra | Music By Marty Ehrlich, Robin Holcomb, Wayne Horvitz, Doug Wieselman | New World Records | 80397-2

With The Wind And The Rain In Your Hair
Don Elliott Octet | Don Elliott:Mellophone | Fresh Sound Records | FSR 2009(Bethlehem BCP 12)
Stan Getz Quartet | Stan Getz Plays | Verve | 833535-2
Stan Kenton And His Orchestra | Rendezvous With Kenton | Creative World | ST 1057
Tal Farlow Trio | Tal Farlow '78 | Concord | CJ 57

With Thee I Swing
Bernhard Arndt | Insight Insight | FMP | OWN-90005

With You I'm Born Again-

Allen Toussaint Group | Motion | Warner | WPCP 4416

Within' The Hall Of Neptune
Jenny Evans And Her Quintet | Nuages | Enja | ENJ-9467 2

Within' You,Without You
Nuages | ESM Records | ESM 9308
John Surman Orchestra | Tales Of The Algonquin | Deram | 844884-2

Without A Song
Art Blakey And The Jazz Messengers | Anthenagin | Prestige | P 10076
Art Tatum | Art Tatum:20th Century Piano Genius | Verve | 531763-2
The Tatum Solo Masterpieces Vol.11 | Pablo | 2310864
Billy Eckstine And His Orchestra | Mister B. And The Band/Billy Eckstine | Savoy | SV 0264(SJL 2214)
Houston Person Quartet | In A Sentimental Mood | HighNote Records | HCD 7060
Jessica Williams | Intuition | Jazz Focus | JFCD 010
Joe Henderson Sextet | Joe Henderson:The Milestone Years | Milestone | 8MCD 4413-2
Joe Lee Wilson With Orchestra | Without A Song | Inner City | IC 1064 IMS
John Hicks | Steadfast | Strata East Records | 660.51.010
Mack Goldsbury And The New York Connection | Songs I Love To Play | Timescrapper | TSCR 9615
Mary Lou Williams Trio | May Lou Williams Trio At Rick's Cafe Americain,Chicago,Ill. | Storyville | STCD 8285
Mulgrew Miller Trio | Work! | Landmark | LCD 1511-2
Nat Su Quartet | The J.Way | Fresh Sound Records | FSNT 038 CD
Oscar Peterson Trio | The Song Is You-The Best Of The Verve Songbooks | Verve | 531558-2
Ralph Flanagan And His Orchestra | Dance Again Part 2 | Magic | DAWE 75
Stan Getz Quartet | Stan Getz:The Golden Years Vol.2(1958-1961) | Moon Records | MCD 040-2
Tex Beneke And His Orchestra | Dancer's Delight | Magic | DAWE 79
Tommy Dorsey And His Orchestra | Frank Sinatra Sings The Standards | RCA | NL 89102 AP
Willis Jackson Quintet | Together Again: Willis Jackson With Jack McDuff | Prestige | PRCD 24284-2
Dorothy Donegan Trio | I Just Want To Sing | Audiophile | ACD-281

Without Him
Johnny Thompson & The Pennsylvania District Choir | Live At Lausanne | Bellaphon | BCH 33007

Without Love
Little Milton And His Band | Little Milton | Chess | 427013

Without Words(New Ballad)
The Timeless Art Orchestra | Without Words | Satin Doll Productions | SDP 1005-1 CD

Without You
Bola Sete Quintet | Bossa Nova | Original Jazz Classics | OJC 286(F 8349)
Pat Peterson Quintet | Introducing Pat Peterson | Enja | 4020
Wild Bill Davis Trio | Impulsions | Black & Blue | BLE 233037

Witness
Gordon Brisker Quintet | My Son John | Naxos Jazz | 86064-2

Witte Bloemen-
Martin Theurer | Moon Mood | FMP | 0700

Wittgenstein Blues
Clifford Jordan-Ran Blake Groups | Masters From Different Worlds | Mapleshade | 01732

Wives And Lovers
Ella Fitzgerald With The Duke Ellington Orchestra | The Stockholm Concert 1966 | Pablo | 2308242-2
Ella Fitzgerald With The Duke Ellington Orchestra And Jimmy Jones Trio | Ella Fitzgerald And Duke Ellington:Cote D'Azure Concerts on Verve | Verve | 539033-2
Ella Fitzgerald And Duke Ellington:Cote D'Azure Concerts on Verve | Verve | 539033-2
Ella Fitzgerald With The Marty Paich Orchestra | Whisper Not | Verve | 589947-2
Eric Alexander Quintet | New York Calling | Criss Cross | Criss 1077
Jimmy Smith With Orchestra | Who's Afraid Of Virginia Woolf? | Verve | 823309-2 PMS
Thad Jones-Pepper Adams Quintet | Mean What You Say | Original Jazz Classics | OJCCD 464-2
Wes Montgomery Trio | Tequila | Verve | 547769-2
Bill Frisell Quintet | Rambler | ECM | 1287

Wizard Of Odds
The Moscow Chambers Jazz Ensemble | Kadans | Mobile Fidelity | MFCD 916

Wizzin' The Wizz
Lionel Hampton And His Orchestra | Chu Berry: Berry Story | Zeta | ZET 738

WNEW
Stan Getz-Bill Evans Quartet | Stan Getz & Bill Evans | Verve | 833802-2

WNEW(Theme Song)
Gumpert-Sommer Duo plus Manfred Hering | The Old Song | FMP | 0170

Wo Die Vasen Grasen
Sven Ake Johansson-Alexander von Schlippenbach Duo | Kalfaktor A.Falke Und Andere Lieder | FMP | 0970

Wo Ist Die 1
Irene Schweizer | Piano Solo Vol.1 | Intakt Records | CD 020

Wobblin' Baby
Tok | Paradox | Japo | 60029

Wocai
Old Merrytale Jazz Band | 25 Jahre Old Merrytale Jazzband Hamburg | Intercord | 155043

Woe
Fats Waller And His Rhythm | I'm Gonna Sit Right Down...The Early Years-Part 2(1935-1936) | Bluebird | 63 66640-2

Wogen
Klaus Ignatzek-Florian Poser Duo | Music For Grandpiano And Vibraphone | Fusion | 8021 Digital

Wohin?
Montreal Jubilation Gospel Choir | Joy To The World | Blues Beacon | BLU-1018 2

Woke Up This Morning
Freddie King Orchestra | My Feeling For The Blues | Repertoire Records | REPCD 4170-WZ

Wolf 424
Wolfhound | Wolfhound Live | BELL Records | BLR 84047

Wolf Stump
Andrew Cyrille-Peter Brötzman Duo | Andrew Cyrille Meets Peter Brötzmann In Berlin | FMP | 1000

Wolfbane
Tony Purrone Trio | Set 'Em Up | Steeplechase | SCCD 31389

Wolfgang Tango
The Music Improvisation Company | The Music Improvisation Company | ECM | 1005

Wolkenbilder(1)
Harry Pepl/Herbert Joos/Jon Christensen | Cracked Mirrors | ECM | 1356

Wolkenbilder(2)
Sigi Schwab | Meditation Vol.2 | Melos Music | CDGS 705

Wolverine
Albert Burbank With Kid Ory And His Creole Jazzband | Sounds Of New Orleans Vol.3 | Storyville | STCD 6010

Wolverine Blues
Bob Scobey's Frisco Band | The Scobey Story Vol.1 | Good Time Jazz | GTCD 12032-2
Dejan's Young Olympia Brass Band | New Orleans Louisiana | Traditional Line | TL 1319
Earl Hines And His Orchestra | The Earl | Naxos Jazz | 8.120581 CD
Jelly Roll Morton Trio | Doctor Jazz | Black & Blue | BLE 59.227 2
Louis Armstrong And His Orchestra | Louis Armstrong And His Big Band Vol.1-The Maturity | Black & Blue | BLE 59.225 2

Wolynka
Bobby Bradford With The Frank Sullivan Trio | Bobby Bradford Live:One Night Stand | Soul Note | 121168-2

Woman
James Newton | Flutes! | Circle Records | RK 7-7677/7 IMS

Woman At Point Zero
Angela Brown | The Voice Of Blues | Schubert Records | SCH- 105

Woman Be Wise
Sippie Wallace With Little Brother Montgomery | Blues Roots Vol.6 | Storyville | 6.23705 AG

Woman Of Heart And Mind
Donald Byrd Orchestra | Street Lady | Blue Note | 84439

Woman On A Train
Cassandra Wilson Group | Jumpworld | JMT Edition | 834434-2

Woman You Must Be Crazy
Joe Turner And His Band | Have No Fear Joe Turner Is Here | Pablo | 2310863

Women And Money
John Lee Hooker | Blues Roots Vol. 13: John Lee Hooker | Chess | 6.24803 AG

Womisch Kloi Tomisch
Roger Hanschel/Gabriele Hasler | Go In Green | Jazz Haus Musik | JHM 0073 CD

Won
Sam Morrison Group | Natural Layers | Chiaroscuro | CR 184

Wonder Why
Bill Evans Trio | Bill Evans:The Secret Sessions | Milestone | 8MCD 4421-2
Bob Rockwell Quartet | Shades Of Blue | Steeplechase | SCCD 31378
Etta Jones With The Houston Person Sextet | At Last | Muse | MCD 5511
George Shearing Trio | Jazz Moments | Capitol | 832085-2
Kenny Burrell With The Don Sebesky Orchestra | Blues-The Common Ground | Verve | 589101-2
Koko Taylor With The Jimmy Rogers Blues Band | South Side Lady | Black & Blue | BLE 59.542 2
Milt Jackson Quartet | Opus De Funk | Prestige | P 24048
The Jazz Giants Play Sammy Cahn:It's Magic | Prestige | PCD 24226-2
Randy Johnston Quartet | In A-Chord | Muse | MCD 5512
Sarah Vaughan With Mundell Lowe And George Duvivier | After Hours | Roulette | 855468-2
Shelly Manne Trio | At The Black Hawk Vol.5 | Original Jazz Classics | OJCCD 660-2
Tal Farlow Quartet | This Is Tal Farlow | Verve | 537746-2
Brad Mehldau With The Rossy Trio | New York-Barcelona Crossing Vol.1 | Fresh Sound Records | FSNT 031 CD

Wonderful
John Campbell Trio | Workin' Out | Criss Cross | Criss 1198

Wonderful Copenhagen
Dave Brubeck Quartet | The Dave Brubeck Selection | CBS | 467279-2

Wonderful Life
Walt Weiskopf Sextet | Simplicity | Criss Cross | Criss 1075

Wonderful Thing
Count Basie And His Orchestra | The Indispensable Count Basie | RCA | ND 89758

Wonderful Wonderful
Perico Sambeat Quartet | Dual Force | Ronnie Scott's Jazz House | JHCD 031
Rene Thomas Quintet | Meeting Mister Thomas | Fresh Sound Records | FSR 554(Barclay 84091)
Sonny Rollins Quartet | Newk's Time | Blue Note | 576752-2
Teddy Edwards Quintet | Teddy Edwards:Steady With Teddy 1946-1948 | Cool & Blue | C&B-CD 115

Wonderful You
Roy Haynes Group | Vistalita | Galaxy | GXY 5116

Wondering
Lil' Son Jackson With Band | Rockin' And Rollin' | Pathe | 1546671(Imperial)

Wonders Never Cease
Cassandra Wilson Group | Dance To The Drums Again | CBS | CK 53451(DIW 863)

Wood
Markus Stockhausen Quartet | Karta | ECM | 1704(543035-2)

Wood And Naphta
Travis 'Moonchild' Haddix And The Travis Haddix Band | Shootum Up | Elite Special | 73613

Wood Chips-
Alex Welsh And His Jazz Band | At Home With... | Dormouse | DM 16 IMS

Wood Is A Pleasant Thing To Think About
Koch-Schütz-Studer & Musicos Cubanos | Fidel | Intakt Records | CD 056

Woodcarvings
Papa Celestin And His New Orleans Band | The Radio Broadcast: 1950-1951 | Folklyric | 9030

Woodcocks
European Jazz Youth Orchestra | Swinging Europe 1 | dacapo | DCCD 9449

Wooden Fantasy
Eddie Chamblee And His Orchestra | Eddie Chamblee:The Complete Recordings 1947-1952 | Blue Moon | BMCD 1049

Wooden Voices
Brigeen Doran Quartet | Bright Moments | B&W Present | BW 020

Woodlore
John Carter Quintet | Variations On Selected Themes For Jazz Quintet | Moers Music | 01056

Woodpecker Song
Duke Ellington And His Orchestra | Eastbourne Performance | RCA | 2122106-2

Woodshed
Woody Herman And His Orchestra | Big Band Bounce & Boogie:The Bad That Plays The Blues | Affinity | AFS 1008

Woodshopper's Ball
Herman's Heat & Puente's Beat | Palladium Records | PDC 156(889168)
The Band That Plays The Blues | Naxos Jazz | 8.120527 CD
Woody Herman 1954 And 1959 | Status | DSTS 1021

Woody & Wu
Woody Shaw And His Orchestra | Woody 3 | CBS | 83778

Woody 1:On The New Ark
Woody 3 | CBS | 83778

Woody'n You
Ahmad Jamal Trio | At The Pershing | Affinity | CD AFS 780
Billy Pierce Trio | Equilateral | Sunnyside | SSC 1037 D
Carl Perkins Trio | Introducing Carl Perkins | Fresh Sound Records | FSR-CD 0010
Curtis Counce Group | Sonority | Contemporary | CCD 7655-2
Eric Dolphy With Erik Moseholm's Trio | Eric Dolphy In Europe, Vol.3 | Original Jazz Classics | OJCCD 416-2
Eric Dolphy:The Complete Prestige Recordings | Prestige | 9 PRCD-4418-2
Freddie Hubbard All Stars | Aurex Jazz Festival '81:Live Special | Eastworld | EWJ 80254
Gonzalo Rubalcaba Trio | Diz... | Blue Note | 830490-2
Hampton Hawes Quartet | All Night Session Vol.2 | Original Jazz Classics | OJCCD 639-2(C 7546)
Johnny Griffin Quartet | Little Giant | Milestone | M 47054
Kenny Burrell Trio | Live At The Village Vanguard | Muse | 600623(882378)
Lou Levy Trio | Jazz In Hollywood:Bud Shank/Lou Levy | Original Jazz Classics | OJCCD 1890-2(Nocturne NLP-2/NLP-10)
Miles Davis All Stars | Miles Davis Vol.1 | Blue Note | 532610-2
Miles Davis New Quintet | Miles Davis | Prestige | P 24001
Miles Davis Quintet | Relaxin' | Original Jazz Classics | OJC20 190-2
Relaxin' | Prestige | PRSA 7129-6
Miles Davis Sextet | Miles Davis:Milestones | Dreyfus Jazz Line | FDM 36731-2
Miles Davis:The Blue Note And Capitol Recordings | Blue Note | 827475-2
Milt Jackson Septet | Bebop | East-West | ???

Modern Jazz Quartet | Fontessa | Rhino | 8122-73687-2
Together Again | Pablo | PACD20 244-2(2308244)
OAM Trio | Trilingual | Fresh Sound Records | FSNT 070 CD
Oscar Peterson All Stars | Jazz At The Philharmonic:The Montreux Collection | Pablo | PACD 5306-2
Highlights Of The Montreux Jazz Festival 1975 | Pablo | 2625707
Oscar Peterson Trio | The Trio:Live From Chicago | Verve | 539063-2
The Jazz Soul Of Oscar Peterson | Verve | MV 2098 IMS
The Jazz Soul Of Oscar Peterson/Affinity | Verve | 533100-2
Phineas Newborn Jr. Quartet | Stockholm Jam Session Vol.1 | Steeplechase | SCCD 36025
Red Garland Quintet | John Coltrane-The Prestige Recordings | Prestige | 16 PCD 4405-2
Red Garland Quintet feat.John Coltrane | Jazz Junction | Prestige | P 24023
Sonny Rollins Trio | Sonny Rollins:The Blue Note Recordings | Blue Note | 821371-2
Stan Getz Quartet | Award Winner | Verve | 543320-2
Stan Getz:East Of The Sun-The West Coast Sessions | Verve | 531935-2
Tommy Flanagan Trio | The Best Of Tommy Flanagan | Pablo | 2405410-2
Wallace Roney Quintet | Crunchin' | Muse | MCD 5518

Woody'n You(alt.take)
Miles Davis All Stars | Miles Davis Vol.1 | Blue Note | 532610-2
Miles Davis Sextet | Miles Davis:The Blue Note And Capitol Recordings | Blue Note | 827475-2
Stan Getz Quartet | Award Winner | Verve | 543320-2

Woody'n You(false start)
Award Winner | Verve | 543320-2

Woody'n You(inserts)
Bill Evans Trio | Peace Piece And Other Pieces | Milestone | M 47024

Woody's Lament
Woody Herman And His Orchestra | Woody Herman Presents Volume 2...Four Others | Concord | CCD 4180

Woof
Bass Drum Bone | Bass Drum Bones-Wooferlo | Soul Note | 121187-2

Woolaphant
Philip DeGruy | Innuendo Out The Other | NYC-Records | NYC 6013-2

Word For Bird
Ornette Coleman Quartet | In All Languages | Harmolodic | 531915-2

Word Of Mouth
Ravi Coltrane Quintet | From The Round Box | RCA | 2173923-2

Wordless
Kudsi Erguner/Süleyman Erguner | Sufi Music Of Turkey | CMP Records | CMP CD 3005

Wordless(I)
Gabriele Hasler-Georg Ruby | Spider's Lovesong | Foolish Music | FM 211893

Wordless(II)
Bob Berg Group | Short Stories | Denon Compact Disc | CY-1768

Words
Temperance Seven | Pasadena & The Lost Cylinders-Music From The Archives | Lake | LACD 77

Words Can't Describe
Sarah Vaughan And Her Trio | Swingin' Easy | EmArCy | 514072-2
Verve Jazz Masters Vol.60:The Collection | Verve | 529866-2
McKinney's Cotton Pickers | The Complete McKinney's Cotton Pickers Vol.3/4 | RCA | NL 89738(2) DP

Words For A Loss
Eddy Howard And His Orchestra | The Uncollected:Eddy Howard, Vol.2 | Hindsight | HSR 156

Words Of Truth
Alvin Batiste Ensemble | Musique D'Afrique Nouvelle Orleans | India Navigation | IN 1064

Words Of Wisdom
Art De Fakt | Art De Fakt-Ray Federman:Surfiction Jazz No.2 | double moon | CHRDM 71007

Words Out Of A Bad Dream
Steve Williamson Quintet | A Waltz For Grace | Verve | 843088-2 PMS

Work
Matt Renzi-Jimmy Weinstein Quartet | Matt Renzi-Jimmy Weinstein Quartet | Fresh Sound Records | FSNT 045 CD
Matthias Bätzel Trio | Monk's Mood | JHM Records | JHM 3628
Mulgrew Miller Trio | Work! | Landmark | LCD 1511-2
Steve Lacy | Only Monk | Soul Note | SN 1160
Thelonious Monk Trio | Thelonious Monk/Sonny Rollins | Original Jazz Classics | OJCCD 059-2
Thelonious Monk:The Complete Prestige Recordings | Prestige | 3 PRCD 4428-2
Gil Scott-Heron Groups | Spirits | Mother Records | 523417-2

Work Of Art
Bernard Purdie's Soul To Jazz | Bernard Purdie's Soul To Jazz | ACT | 9242-2

Work Song
Cannonball Adderley Quintet | Them Dirty Blues | Blue Note | 495447-2
Cannonball Adderley Birthday Celebration | Fantasy | FANCD 6087-2
Them Dirty Blues | Capitol | 495447-2
The Cannonball Adderley Quintet:Paris 1960 | Pablo | PACD 5303-2
Julian Cannonball Adderlry: Salle Pleyel/Olympia | Laserlight | 36126
Julian Cannonball Adderlry: Salle Pleyel/Olympia | Laserlight | 36126
Duke Ellington And His Famous Orchestra | Victor Jazz History Vol.12:Ellingtonia | RCA | 2135731-2
Duke Ellington And His Orchestra | Duke Ellington:The Complete RCA-Victor Mid-Forties Recordings(1944-1946) | RCA | 2663394-2
Elek Bacsik Trio | Jazz In Paris:Elek Baczik | EmArCy | 542231-2
Florian Bührich Quintet | endlich Jazz...? | Jazz 4 Ever Records:Jazz Network | J4E 4764
Gene Ammons-James Moody Quintet | Chicago Concert | Original Jazz Classics | OJCCD 1091-2(PR 10065)
Junior Mance Trio | Milestones | Sackville | SKCD2-3065
Masha Bijlsma Band With Bob Malach | Lebo | Jazzline | JL 11145-2
Nina Simone Groups | You Can Have Him | Memo Music | HDJ 4087

Work Song-
Cannonball Adderley Quintet | Them Dirty Blues | Blue Note | 495447-2

Work Song(alt take)
Them Dirty Blues | Capitol | 495447-2
Ray Brown With The Allstar Big Band | Much In Common | Verve | 533259-2

Work, Baby, Work
Lonnie Brooks | The Blues, Vol. 6 | Sonet | 157102

Workin' Man
Joe Williams With The Jimmy Jones Orchestra | Me And The Blues | RCA | 2121823-2

Working
The Berlin Workshop Orchestra | Sib Langis | FMP | SAJ 30

Working Eyes
Ed Mann Group | Perfect World | CMP Records | CMP MC 45

Working Inside
Otis Rush And His Band | Blues Power No.3:Otis Rush - Mourning In The Morning | Atlantic | 40495

Working Man Blues
Graham Stewart And His New Orleans Band | The Golden Years Of Revival Jazz,Vol.10 | Storyville | STCD 5515
Humphrey Lyttelton And His Band | Delving Back With Humph:Humphrey Lyttelton 1948-1949 | Lake | LACD 72
King Oliver's Jazz Band | Louis Armstrong With King Oliver Vol.2 | Village(Jazz Archive) | VILCD 012-2

Working Week
Homesick James Quartet | Blues On The Southside | Original Blues Classics | OBCCD 529-2(P 7388)

Working With Homesick
Calvin Boze With Maxwell Davis & His Orchestra | Calvin Boze:The Complete Recordings 1945-1952 | Blue Moon | BMCD 6014

Workinoot
Jutta Gruber & The Martin Schrack Trio | Keep Hanging On | yvp music | CD 3043

Workout
Joe Lovano Septet | Universal Language | Blue Note | 799830-2

Workshop
Eddie Jefferson And His Orchestra | The Jazz Singer | Inner City | IC 1016 IMS

Worksong
Johnny Lytle Quintet | Got That Feeling/Moon Child | Milestone | MCD 47093-2
Lyambiko And Her Trio | Out Of This Mood | Nagel-Heyer | CD 2021
Willem Breuker Kollektief And Djazzex | Dance Plezier-Joy Of Dance | BVHAAST | CD 9513

World Class-
Oscar Brown Jr. with The NDR Big Band | Live Every Minute | Minor Music | 801071

World Full Of Gray
The Colson Unity Troup | No Reservation | Black Saint | BSR 0043

World Of Ideas
David Murray Big Band | South Of The Border | DIW | DIW 897 CD

World Protection Blues
Herbie Mann Sextet | The Jazz We Heard Last Summer | Savoy | SV 0228(MG 12112)

World Wide Web
Reinhard Flatischler | Transformation | VeraBra Records | CDVBR 2033-2

Worms
Medeski Martin & Wood With Guests | It's A Jungle In Here | Gramavision | R2 79495

Worried About My Baby
Sunnyland Slim | Sunnyland Train | Steeplechase | SCB 9002

Worried Life Blues
Jeannie And Jimmy Cheatham & The Sweet Baby Blues Band | Midnight Mama | Concord | CJ 297
Lightnin' Hopkins | The Blues Vol.2 | Intercord | 158601
Otis Spann | Blues Roots Vol.9 | Storyville | 6.23708 AG
Robben Ford & The Blue Line | Mystic Line | Stretch Records | GRS 00082

Worried Man Blues
Chris Barber's Jazz Band | 40 Years Jubilee At The Opera House Nürnberg | Timeless | CD TTD 590

Worried Mind(aka Stick Around)
Don Byas And His Orchestra | Don Byas Complete American Small Group Recordings | Definitive Records | DRCD 11213

Worry
Walter 'Wolfman' Washington Group | Best Of New Orleans Rhyhtm & Blues Vol.2 | Mardi Gras Records | MG 9008

Worry Doll
Joe Baudisch Quartet | The Meeting Of Two Tenors | Acoustic Music Records | 319.1135.2

Worry Later
Steve Slagle Quartet | Steve Slaggle Plays Monk | Steeplechase | SCCD 31446
Walter Blanding Quintet | The Olive Tree | Criss Cross | Criss 1186
Katie Webster | Pounds Of Blues | Charly | CRB 1087

Worry You Off My Mind
Sonny Terry & Brownie McGhee | Sonny Terry And Brownie McGhee At Suger Hill | Original Blues Classics | OBCCD 536-2(F 8091)

Worry, Worry, Worry
Luke Jones With Joe Alexander's Highlanders | Luke Jones:The Complete Recordings 1946-1949 | Blue Moon | BMCD 6012

Worryin' The Life Out Of Me
Ralph Sutton | More At Cafe Des Copains | Sackville | SKCD2-2036

Worship
Charles Brackeen Quartet | Worshippers Come Nigh | Silkheart | SHCD 111

Worte
Bob Degen Trio | Catability | Enja | ENJ-9332 2

Worth A Week's Anguish
Terence Blanchard/Donald Harrison Quintet | Discernment | Concord | CCD 43008

Wortlaut - (Wort)laut
Michael Sell Brass Ensemble | 5 Stücke für 11 Instrumentalisten oder Instrumentalistinnen | Misp Records | MISP 505

Would You Like To Take A Walk
Art Tatum | The Tatum Solo Masterpieces Vol.10 | Pablo | 2310862
Art Tatum Trio | Art Tatum:Complete Capitol Recordings | Definitive Records | DRCD 11192
Ella Fitzgerald With Dave Barbour And His Orchestra | Ella:The Legendary American Decca Recordings | GRP | GRP 46482
Leroy Vinnegar Sextet | Leroy Walks! | Original Jazz Classics | OJCCD 160-2
Art Tatum | Art Tatum:20th Century Piano Genius | Verve | 531763-2

Would You Like To Take A Walk-
Dave McKenna Trio | Plays The Music Of Harry Warren | Concord | CJ 174

Wouldn't It Be Loverly
Johnny Richards And His Orchestra | My Fair Lady-My Way | Fresh Sound Records | FSR 609(Roulette SR 52114) (835247)
Oscar Peterson Trio | Oscar Peterson Plays My Fair Lady And The Music From Fiorello! | Verve | 521677-2
Shelly Manne And His Friends | My Fair Lady | Mobile Fidelity | MFCD 809
Toshiko Akiyoshi Trio | Finesse | Concord | CCD 4069

Wounded Knee(Buddy Red Bow)
Dutch Jazz Orchestra | Portrait Of A Silk Thread | Kokopelli Records | KOKO 1310

Wow!
Bill Doggett And His Orchestra | Wow! | Verve | 549372-2

Wrap It Up
Zoot Sims Quartet | The Best Of Zoot Sims | Pablo | 2405406-2

Wrap Your Troubles In Dreams
Art Tatum | Art Tatum-The Complete Jazz Chronicle Solo Session | Storyville | STCD 8253
Art Tatum-The Complete Pablo Solo Masterpieces | Pablo | 7 PACD 4404-2
Art Tatum:20th Century Piano Genius | Verve | 531763-2
In Private | Fresh Sound Records | FSR-CD 0127
Bill Evans Trio | The Complete Bill Evans On Verve | Verve | 527953-2
The Complete Bill Evans On Verve | Verve | 527953-2
The Best Of Bill Evans Live | Verve | 533825-2
Billy Taylor | Ten Fingers-One Voice | Arkadia Jazz | 71602
Cozy Cole All Stars | Concerto For Cozy | Jazz Anthology | JA 5161
Daryl Sherman-John Cocuzzi Orchestra | Daryl Sherman And John Cocuzzi Celebrating Mildred Bailey And Red Norvo | Audiophile | ACD-295
Don Byas Quartet | New York 1945 | Jazz Anthology | JA 5106
Jessica William-Leroy Williams Trio | Encounters | Jazz Focus | JFCD 005
Joe Williams,With The Oliver Nelson Orchestra | Jump For Joy | Bluebird | 63 52713-2
Jonah Jones Sextet | Harlem Jump And Swing | Affinity | AFF 96
Ken Colyer Jazz Quartet | Wrap Your Troubles In Dreams | AZURE Compact Disc | AZ-CD-34
Papa Benny's Jazzband | The Golden Years Of Revival Jazz,Vol.12 | Storyville | STCD 5517
Red Norvo Quintet | Swing That Music | Affinity | AFF 776
Roy Eldridge Quintet | Roy Eldridge And His Little Jazz Vol.1 | Vogue | 21511412
Sidney Bechet With The Martial Solal Trio | Sidney Bechet | Vogue | 000001 GK
Sue Raney With The Billy May Orchestra | Songs For A Raney Day | Capitol | 300015(TOCJ 6129)

Wrap Your Troubles In Dreams(2)
Bill Evans Trio | The Complete Bill Evans On Verve | Verve | 527953-2
The Complete Bill Evans On Verve | Verve | 527953-2

Wrap Your Troubles In Dreams(3)
Dizzy Gillespie Septet | Dizzy Gillespie Plays In Paris | Vogue | 21409402

Wrappin' It Up
Benny Goodman And His Orchestra | Wrappin' It Up-The Harry James Years Part 2 | Bluebird | 63 66549-2
Harry Arnold Big Band | Big Band Classics 1957-58 | Dragon | DRLP 139/140

Write Me A Few Lines
Mississippi Fred McDowell | Standing At The Burying Ground | Red Lightnin' | RL 0053

Writing On Ice
Blind Willie McTell | The Early Years | Yazoo | YAZ 1005

Written In Your Face
Ornette Coleman Quartet | The Belgrade Concert | Jazz Door | JD 12112

Wrong Key Donkey
Carla Bley/Andy Sheppard/Steve Swallow | Song With Legs | Watt | 26(527069)
Cootie Williams And His Orchestra | Rhythm And Jazz In The Mid Forties | Official | 3014

Wrong Neighborhood
Dizzy Gillespie With The Lalo Schifrin Orchestra | Free Ride | Pablo | 2310794

Wrong Number
Susan Weinert Band | Mysterious Stories | VeraBra Records | CDVBR 2111-2

Wrong Time, Wrong Place
Steve Swallow Group | Real Book | Watt | XtraWatt/7(521637-2)

Wrong Together
Sonny Terry & Brownie McGhee | Back To New Orleans | Fantasy | FCD 24708-2

Wrong Wrong Wrong
Gabriele Hasler-Roger Hanschel Duo | Love Songs | Foolish Music | FM 211003

Wrongs
The Harlem Ramblers | Dixieland Jubilee-Vol. 2 | Intercord | 155005

Wu Chou
Cadavre Exquis | Cadavre Exquis | Creative Works Records | CW CD 1014-1

Wucherung II
Norbert Stein Pata Masters meets Djaduk Ferianto Kua Etnika | Pata Java | Pata Musik | PATA 16 CD

Wulang Sunu
European Jazz Youth Orchestra | Swinging Europe 1 | dacapo | DCCD 9449

Wulongcha
Peter Kowald/Irene Schweizer | Duos: Europa | FMP | 1260

Wünsch Dir Was
Per Henrik Wallin Trio | Per Henrik Wallin Trio | Caprice | CAP 1185

Wurundjeri The Majestic
Acoustic Art | Interlude | Acoustic Music Records | AMC 1024

WW3:
Hans-Günther Wauer/Günter Baby Sommer | Dedication | FMP | 0900

Wy Are We Afraid
June Christy With The Johnny Guarnieri Quintet | June Christy And The Johnny Guarnieri Quintet (1949) | Jazz Unlimited | JUCD 2084

Wy Oh Why?
Albert Brunies And His Halfway House Orchestra | The Halfway House Orchestra-The Complete Recordings In Chronological Order | Jazz Oracle | BDW 8001

Wynola
Sonny Rollins Quintet | Sunny Days,Starry Nights | Milestone | MCD 9122-2

Wynton
Sunny Days Stary Nights | Milestone | M 9122

Wyoming Bill Kelso
Maria Schneider Jazz Orchestra | Evanescence | Enja | ENJ-8048 2

Wysiwyg
Mike Longo Septet | Talk With The Spirits | Pablo | 2310769

X
Kelm 3 | Per Anno | dml-records | CD 013
Malachi Thompson Quintet | 47th Street | Delmark | DE 497

X Y Z
Earl Hines And His Orchestra | The Indispensable Earl Hines Vol.1/2 | RCA | 2126407-2
Matthew Ship 'String' Trio | By The Law Of Music | Hat Art | CD 6200

Xaba
Dollar Brand | Ancient Africa | Japo | 60005(2360005)

Xanas
Arcado String Trio | Live In Europe | Avant | AVAN 058

X-Dream
John Wolf Brennan | Willisau And More Live | Creative Works Records | CW CD 1020-2

Xednindex
Irisations | Creative Works Records | CW CD 1021-2
Spencer Barefield-Anthony Holland-Tani Tabbal | Live At Nickelsdorf Konfrontation | Sound Aspects | sas CD 007

Xi
Cal Tjader Group | Amazonas | Original Jazz Classics | OJCCD 840-2(F 9502)

Xibaba
Donald Byrd & His Orchestra | Electric Byrd | Blue Note | 836195-2

Xieyi
Jon Lloyd Quartet | Four And Five | HatOLOGY | 537

Xiste
Galardini-Lessmann-Morena Trio | Insolitudine | SPLASC(H) Records | H 155

X-Mas
New Orleans Quarter | Christmas Jazz | New Orleans Quarter Records | NOQR-V-DIV-CD 2

X-Ray Blues
Ray Charles-Milt Jackson Quintet | Soul Meeting | Atlantic | SD 1360

X-Rism
Mitch Watkins Group | Underneath It All | Enja | ENJ-5099 2

Y A Du Soleil Dans La Boutique
Josep Maria Balanyà | Sonateskas | Laika Records | 35101102

Y Cuando Oigas El Agua Caer...
Tomasz Stanko Sextet | From The Green Hill | ECM | 1680(547336-2)

Y Despues De Todo - ...Y Despues De Todo
Barre Phillips Group | For All It Is | Japo | 60003 IMS

Y II
8 1/2 Souvenirs | Happy Feet | RCA | 2663226-2

Y La Negra Ballada
Charly Antolini Orchestra | In The Groove | Inak | 806

Y Todavia La Quiero
Joe Henderson Trio | The State Of The Tenor-Live At The Village Vanguard Vol.2 | Blue Note | 746426-2

Y Ya La Quiero
Joe Henderson-The Blue Note Years | Blue Note | 789287-2

Y.I.Blues
Pete Jolly And His West Coast Friends | Art Pepper:The Hollywood All-Star Sessions | Galaxy | 5GCD 4431-2

Y.I.Blues(alt.take)
Barre Phillips Group | For All It Is | Japo | 60003 IMS

Y2K
Sylvie Courvoisier Group | Y2K | Enja | ENJ-9383 2
Ahmed Abdul-Malik's Middle-Eastern Music | Jazz Sahara | Original Jazz Classics | OJCCD 1820-2(R 12-287)

Ya Annas(Oh, People)
Gertrude 'Ma' Rainey With Lovie Austin And Her Blues Serenaders | Gertrude 'Ma' Rainey-Queen Of The Blues | Biograph | BLP 12032

Ya Na Ho
Jim Pepper Flying Eagle | Live At New Morning,Paris | Tutu Records | 888194-2*

Ya Na Ho-
Karim Ziad Groups | Ifrikya | ACT | 9282-2

Ya Rijal
Art Blakey Percussion Ensemble | Orgy In Rhythm Vol.1 | Blue Note | 300156(1554)

Yaaba
Irene Schweizer Trio & Dewan Motihar Trio With Barney Wilen & Manfred Schoof | Jazz Meets Asia:Sakura Sakura-Jazz Meets India-Djanger Bali | MPS | 533132-2

Yaaka Hula Hickey Dula
Alexander von Schlippenbach And Sven-Ake Johansson | Live 1976/77 | FMP | CD 111

Yabay
Moye-Tchicai-Geerken | The African Tapes Vol.1 | Praxis | CM 114

Yacht Club Swing
Dick Wellstood's Wallerites | Uptown And Lowdown | Prestige | PCD 24262-2
Fats Waller And His Rhythm | The Indispensable Fats Waller Vol.7/8(1938-1940) | RCA | 2126417-2
Vic Dickenson-Red Richards All Stars | Yacht Club Swing | Harlequin | HQ 2045 IMS

Yagapriya
Mariano-Humair-Haurand | Frontier Traffic | Konnex Records | KCD 5110
Slim Gaillard Trio | Trio-Quartet-Orchestra | Jazz Anthology | 550282

Yahllah
Paul Motian Band | Psalm | ECM | 1222
Paul Motian Trio | You Took The Words Right Out Of My Heart | JMT Edition | 514028-2

Yakety Yak
Darius Brubeck And The Nu Jazz Connection | African Tributes | B&W Present | BW 023

Yakhbeir John
Teddy Charles Septet | On Campus! Ivy League Jazz Concert | Fresh Sound Records | FSR 2026(Bethlehem BCP 6044)

Y'all
Jin Hi Kim Group | Sargeng | Ear-Rational | ECD 1014

Yama
Art Blakey And The Jazz Messengers | A Night In Tunisia | Blue Note | 784049-2
Joe Sachse | European House | FMP | CD 41

Yama Yama Blues
Black Bottom Stompers | Ace In The Hole | Elite Special | 73357

Yams
Jackie McLean Quintet | Herbie Hancock:The Complete Blue Note Sixties Sessions | Blue Note | 495569-2
George Duke Group | George Duke & Feel | MPS | 68023

Yancey Special
Bob Crosby And His Orchestra | Big Band Bounce And Boogie-Bob Crosby:Mournin' Blues/Accent On The Bobcats | Affinity | AFS 1014
Lloyd Glenn Quartet | Old Time Shuffle | Black & Blue | BLE 59.077 2
Meade Lux Lewis | Big Band Bounce & Boogie-The Boogie Woogie Masters | Affinity | AFS 1005
Sugar Chile Robinson Trio | Go Boy Go | Oldie Blues | OL 2828

Yang
Bheki Mseleku Group | Timelessness | Verve | 521306-2

Yankee No-How
Bob Crosby And His Orchestra | The Uncollected:Bob Crosby | Hindsight | HSR 192

Yano
Milt Jackson With The Monty Alexander Trio | Soul Fusion | Original Jazz Classics | OJCCD 731-2(2310804)
Tome XX | Natura Morte | Jazz Haus Musik | JHM 32

Yao And Mama's Dance
Rainer Pusch-Horace Parlan | In Between Those Changes | yvp music | CD 3046

Yara
Alexander von Schlippenbach Trio | Elf Bagatellen | FMP | CD 27

Yard Dog
Roy Eldridge Quintet | Rockin' Chair | Verve | MV 2686 IMS

Yardbird Suite
Al Haig Trio | The Piano Collection Vol.2 | Vogue | 21610222
Art Pepper Quartet | Bird Lives! | Milestone | MCD 9166-2
Five Birds And A Monk | Galaxy | GXY 5134
Blossom Dearie | I'm Hip | CBS | 489123-2
Earl Coleman And His All Stars | Dexter Gordon: Move! | Spotlite | SPJ 133 (835055)
Gene Ammons-James Moody Quintet | Chicago Concert | Original Jazz Classics | OJCCD 1091-2(PR 10065)
Gene Krupa And His Orchestra | Gene Krupa Plays Gerry Mulligan Arrangements | Verve | 2304430 IMS
Hank Jones Trio | 'Bop Redux | Muse | MCD 5444
Herbie Mann Sextet | Yardbird Suite | Jazz Anthology | JA 5162
Joe Pass/Niels-Henning Orsted-Pedersen Duo | Chops | Original Jazz Classics | OJCCD 786-2(2310830)
Junior Cook Quartet | Pressure Cooker | Affinity | AFF 53
Martial Solal | Bluesine | Soul Note | 121060-2
Modern Jazz Quartet | The Modern Jazz Quartet At Music Inn With Sonny Rollins,Vol.2 | Atlantic | 7567-80794-2
Mose Allison Trio | Creek Bank | Prestige | PCD 24055-2
Richie Cole Quintet | Alive! | Muse | MR 5270
Roy Hargrove-Stephen Scott | Parker's Mood | Verve | 527907-2
Roy Haynes Quintet | Birds Of A Feather:A Tribute To Charlie Parker | Dreyfus Jazz Line | FDM 36625-2
Sadao Watanabe With The Great Jazz Trio | Bird Of Paradise | Flying Disk | VJJ 6017
Ted Brown Trio | Free Spirit | Criss Cross | Criss 1031

Yardbird Suite(alt.take)
Jay McShann | Vine Street Boogie | Black Lion | BLCD 760187

Yarum
Archie Shepp And His Orchestra | Yasmina/Poem For Malcolm | Affinity | AFF 771

Yasmina
Trio Concepts | Trio Concepts | yvp music | CDX 48801

Yavapai
John Scofield Trio | Shinola | Enja | ENJ-4004 2

Yaz Geldi(turkish folk material)
Benny Moten's Kansas City Orchestra | The Complete Bennie Moten Vol.1/2 | RCA | NL 89881(2) DP

Yazoo Moon
Night Ark | Moments | RCA | PD 83028(874049)

Ye Banks & Braes-
George Russell Smalltet | The RCA Victor Jazz Workshop | RCA | 2159144-2

Ye Hypocrite,Ye Beelzebub
Dizzy Reece Quintet | Comin' On | Blue Note | 522019-2

Ye Olde Curiosity Shape
Gene Ammons Quintet | Blue Groove | Prestige | MPP 2514

Yea Truth Faileth
Pete York & His All Star Group | It's You Or No One | Mons Records | MR 874772

Yeah
Mal Waldron Trio | Set Me Free | Affinity | AFF 116

Yeah Baby
Jack McDuff Quartet | Tough 'Duff | Original Jazz Classics | OJCCD 324-2(P 7185)
Charly Antolini Orchestra | Drum Beat | MPS | 9808191

Yeah Man
Charly Antolini | Jazz Magazine | 48017
Dink Johnson | Dink Johnson-Charlie Thompson: The Piano Players | American Music | AMCD-11
Original Motion Picture Soundtrack | Kansas City | Verve | 529554-2

Yeah Yeah Yeah
Ralph Moore Quartet | Who It Is You Are | Denon Compact Disc | CY-75778

Yeah,Man(Amen)
Vinny Golia-The Chamber Trio | Worldwide & Portable | Nine Winds Records | NWCD 0143

Year Of The Pig
Oliver Nelson & His Sextet | Three Dimensions | MCA | IA 9335/2

Yearnin'
Oliver Nelson And His Orchestra | Blues And The Abstract Truth | CTI Records | PDCTI 1122-2

Yearning
Tommy Dorsey And His Orchestra | Tommy Dorsey In Concert | RCA | NL 89780 DP
Year's End
Steve Kuhn Trio | Years Later | Concord | CCD 4554
Years Of Solitude
Gerry Mulligan/Astor Piazolla Group | Gerry Mulligan/Astor Piazolla 1974 | Accord | 556642
Years Of Yearning
Bobby Watson | This Little Light Of Mine-The Bobby Watson Solo Album | Red Records | 123250-2
Yeehaw Junction
Jeanne Lee Ensemble | Conspiracy | Earthform | 1
Yellow
Mark Helias Quintet | Split Image | Enja | 4086 (807528)
Yellow Bird
Gene Ammons Septet | Gene Ammons Bossa Nova | Original Jazz Classics | OJCCD 351-2(PR 7257)
The Mills Brothers With Orchestra | The Golden Years Of The Mills Brothers | Ember | NR 5090
Yellow Cab
Die Dozenten | Take It Easy | L+R Records | CDLR 45054
Yellow Car III
Albert Louis Jazzband | Live Im Neumeyer Dr. Flotte | Jazz Classics | AU 11089
Yellow Days
Freddy Cole With Band | Rio De Janeiro Blue | Telarc Digital | CD 83525
Yellow Dog Blues
Art Hodes' Chicagoans | Hot Jazz On Blue Note | Blue Note | 835811-2
Franz Jackson's Original Jass All-Stars feat. Bob Shoffner | Chicago-The Living Legends:Franz Jackson | Original Jazz Classics | OJCCD 1824-2(RLP 9406)
Henry Red Allen Sextet | Swing Trumpet Kings:Harry Edison Swings Buck Clayton And Vice Versa/Red Allen Plays King Oliver/Swing Goes Dixie | Verve | 533263-2
Louis Armstrong And His All Stars | The Louis Armstrong Selection | CBS | 467278-2
Ben's Bad Boys | Ben Pollack Vol.2 | Jazz Oracle | BDW 8016
Yellow Dream
Zoot Sims And His Five Brothers | Made In Sweden Vol.1: 1949 to March 1951 | Magnetic Records | MRCD 106
Yellow Earth
Rössler/Kühn/Heidepriem/Stefanski Quartet | Coloured | Fusion | 8015
Yellow Fever
Herbie Mann Orchestra | Yellow Fever | Atlantic | SD 19252
Yellow Fields
Gary Burton Quartet With Eberhard Weber | Passengers | ECM | 1092(835016-2)
Peter Wölpl Group | Mr. Wölps & Dr. Fudge | Blue Flame | 40422(3984042-2)
Yellow Flag
Mind Games | Lyrical Life | yvp music | CD 3027
Yellow Hill
Lew Tabackin Quartet | Nature | Inner City | IC 1028 IMS
Yellow Man
Sachi Hayasaka & Stir Up! | 2.26 | Enja | 8014-2
Yellow Shadow
Thierry Lang-Daniel Perrin | Tusitala | Plainisphare | PL 1267-105 CD
Yellow Umbrella
Andrew Hill Quintet | Dance With Death | Blue Note | LT 1030 (GXK 8184)
Yemaya
Lazaro Ros Ensemble | Ori Batá (Cuban Yoruba Music) | Enja | ENJ-9381 2
Leni Stern Group | Words | Lipstick Records | LIP 890282
Yemaye
John Hicks Quartet | In The Mix | Landmark | LCD 1542-2
Yes And No
Uptown Express | Uptown Express | Palo Alto | PA 8048
Yes Baby
Tim Berne-Marc Ducret-Tom Rainey | Big Satan | Winter&Winter | 910005-2
Yes Dear
Gunter Hampel And His Galaxie Dream Band | Enfant Terrible | Birth | 0025
Yes Earth
Montreal Jubilation Gospel Choir | Highway To Heaven | Blues Beacon | BLU-1005 2
Yes I'm In The Barrel
Chubby Jackson And His All Star Big Band | Chubby Takes Over | Fresh Sound Records | FSR-CD 324
Yes Indeed
Eric Dolphy-Ron Carter Quintet | Magic | Prestige | P 24053
Ron Carter Quintet | Where | Original Jazz Classics | OJCCD 432-2
Eric Dolphy:The Complete Prestige Recordings | Prestige | 9 PRCD-4418-2
Slam Stewart Quartet | Slam Stewart | Black & Blue | BLE 233027
Yes Is A Pleasant Country
James Spaulding Quartet | The Smile Of The Snake | HighNote Records | HCD 7006
Yes It Is
Amina Claudine Myers Group | Amina | RCA | PD 83030
Yes Love
Benny Goodman And His Orchestra | Benny Goodman Vol.2: Clarinet A La King | CBS | 460829-2
Yes My Darling Daughter
Joe Henderson Quartet | Relaxin' At Camarillo | Original Jazz Classics | OJCCD 776-2(C 14006)
Yes My Dear
Bill Barron Quartet | The Next Plateau | Muse | MCD 5368
Yes Or No
Brian Bromberg Group | It's About Time-The Acoustic Project | Nova | NOVA 9146-2
Wayne Shorter Quartet | Juju | Blue Note | 837644-2
1239A | Artistry | Verve | 847956-2
Yes Sir That's My Baby
J.J.Johnson-Kai Winding Quintet (Jay&Kai) | Kai Winding And Jay Jay Johnson | Bethlehem | BET 6026-2(BCP 76)
Kai Winding-J.J.Johnson Quintet | Kai & Jay! | Affinity | AFF 161
Milt Jackson All Stars | The Best Of Milt Jackson | Pablo | 2405405-2
Nat King Cole Trio | Jazz In Paris:nat king cole | Dreyfus Jazz Line | fdm 36000
Ruth Brown With The Thad Jones-Mel Lewis Orchestra | Fine Brown Frame | Capitol | 781200-2
Yes Suh
Lew Stone And His Band | Lew Stone And His Band | Decca | DDV 5005/6 DT
Yes To Be
Benny Goodman And His Orchestra | Rare Broadcasting Transcriptions-Vol. 1 | Jazz Anthology | JA 5151
Yes We Have No Bananas
Hazy Osterawld And His Orchestra | Rare And Historical Jazz Recordings | Elite Special | 73414
Yes Yes
Lennie Niehaus Octet | Lennie Niehaus Vol.3:The Octet No.2 | Contemporary | COP 017
Yes, Lord I'm Crippled
Excelsior New Orleans Brass Band | Excelsior New Orleans Brass Band | Bartrax | BARX 051 CD
Yesterday
Benny Goodman And His Orchestra | Live At Carnegie Hall-40th Anniversary Concert | Decca | 6.28451 DP
Count Basie And His Orchestra | Basie's Beatle Bag | Verve | 557455-2
Dorothy Donegan | Makin' Whoopee | Black & Blue | BLE 59.146 2
Lanfranco Malaguti/Enzo Pietropaoli/Fabrizio Sferra | Something | Nueva Records | NC 1010
Oscar Peterson With Orchestra | Motions & Emotions | MPS | 821289-2 PMS
Sarah Vaughan With Orchestra | Song Of The Beatles | Atlantic | SD 16037
Singers Unlimited | A Capella 2 | MPS | 821860-2
Fred Hunt Trio | Yesterdays | BELL Records | BLR 84037
Yesterday And Long Ago
Blue Barron And His Orchestra | The Uncollected: Blue Barron | Hindsight | HSR 110
Yesterday I Heard The Rain
Bill Evans Trio | The Tokyo Concert | Original Jazz Classics | OJCCD 345-2
Bill Evans:The Secret Sessions | Milestone | 8MCD 4421-2
Bill Evans Live In Tokyo | CBS | 481265-2
Yesterday, Today And Tomorrow
Joe Williams With The Cannonball Adderley Septet | Joe Williams Live | Original Jazz Classics | OJCCD 438-2(F 9441)
Yesterdays
Art Pepper Quartet | Art Pepper:The Complete Galaxy Recordings | Galaxy | 16GCD 1016-2
Art Tatum | Art Tatum:Memories Of You | Black Lion | BLCD 7608-2
Art Tatum:20th Century Piano Genius | Verve | 531763-2
Art Tatum:20th Century Piano Genius | Verve | 531763-2
The Tatum Solo Masterpieces Vol. 3 | Pablo | 2310730
Bernard Berkhout '5' | Royal Flush | Timeless | CD SJP 425
Bill Evans | Further Conversations With Myself | Verve | 559832-2
Bill Evans/Hank Jones/Red Mitchell | Moods Unlimited | Paddle Wheel | KICJ 65
Billie Holiday And Her Orchestra | Billie Holiday: The First Verve Sessions | Verve | 2610027
Billie Holiday And Her Quintet | Billie Holiday:The Complete Commodore Recordings | GRP | AFS 1019-8
Boulou & Elios Ferre Quintet | New York,N.Y. | Steeplechase | SCCD 31404
Bud Powell | Bud Powell:Complete 1947-1951 Blue Note,Verve & Roost Recordings | The Jazz Factory | JFCD 22837
Bud Powell Trio | More Unissued Vol.1 | Royal Jazz | RJD 507
Cal Tjader Quintet | Tjader Plays Mambo | Original Jazz Classics | OJCCD 274-2(F 3221)
Cal Tjader's Modern Mambo Sextet | Tjader Plays Mambo | Original Jazz Classics | OJC 274(F 3221)
Carmen McRae And Her Sextet | Carmen McRae Sings Lover Man | CBS | CK 65115
Charlie Byrd Trio With Bud Shank | Brazilville | Concord | CCD 4173
Clifford Brown With Strings | Brownie-The Complete EmArCy Recordings Of Clifford Brown | EmArCy | 838306-2
Coleman Hakins And His Orchestra | Rainbow Mist | Delmark | DE 459
Daniel Küffer Quartet | Daniel Küffer Quartet | Satin Doll Productions | SDP 1010-1 CD
Dizzy Gillespie And His Orchestra | Dizzy In Greece | Verve | MV 2630 IMS
Dizzy Gillespie Big Band | Groovin' High | Bandstand | BDCD 1513
Don Byas Quartet | Americans Swinging In Paris:Don Byas | EMI Records | 539655-2
A Night In Tunisia | Black Lion | BLCD 760136
Ella Fitzgerald With The Nelson Riddle Orchestra | The Complete Ella Fitzgerald Song Books of Harold Arlen, Irving Berlin, Duke Ellington, George & Ira Gershwin, Jerome Kern, Johnny Mercer, Cole Porter And Rogers & Hart | Verve | 519832-2
Erroll Garner Sextet | Magician & Gershwin And Kern | Telarc Digital | CD 83337
Frank Ku-Umba Lacy Group | Tonal Weights & Blue Fire | Tutu Records | 888112-2*
Franz Koglmann Quintet | About Yesterdays Ezzthetics | Hat Art | CD 6003
Gato Barbieri Group | The Third World Revisited | Bluebird | ND 86995
Gato Barbieri Septet | Yesterdays | RCA | 2147797-2
Gato Barbieri:The Complete Flying Dutchman Recordings 1969-1973 | RCA | 2154555-2
Greg Marvin Quartet | I'll Get By | Timeless | CD SJP 347
Hampton Hawes Trio | Bird Song | Original Jazz Classics | OJCCD 1035-2
The Trio Vol.2 | Original Jazz Classics | OJCCD 318-2
Hank Jones | Urbanity | Verve | 537749-2
Helen Merrill With The Stan Getz Quartet | Just Friends | EmArCy | 842007-2 PMS
J.J.Johnson Quintet | J.J. Johnson's Jazz Quintets | Savoy | SV 0151(MG 12106)
Jeff Hamilton Trio | Jeff Hamilton Trio Live | Mons Records | MR 874777
Jimmy Rowles-Red Mitchell Trio | The Jimmy Rowles/Red Mitchell Trio | Contemporary | C 14016
Johnny Smith | Johnny Smith | Verve | 537752-2
Johnny Smith Quintet | Moonlight In Vermont | Roulette | 300016
June Christy With The Johnny Guarnieri Quintet | June Christy And The Johnny Guarnieri Quintet (1949) | Jazz Unlimited | JUCD 2084
Kenny Drew | It Might As Well Be Spring | Soul Note | SN 1040
Kenny Drew Quintet | Lite Flite | Steeplechase | SCCD 31077
Klaus Weiss Quintet | A Taste Of Jazz | ATM Records | ATM 3810-AH
Knud Jorgensen-Bengt Hanson-Gustavo Bergalli | Day Dream | Touché Music | TMcCD 003
Kühn/Humair/Jenny-Clark | Live-Théatre de la Ville, Paris 1989 | CMP Records | CMP CD 43
Louis Mazetier | In Concert:What A Treat! | Jazz Connaisseur | JCCD 9522-2
Louis Scherr-Tommy Cecil Duo | The Song Is You | Limetree | MLP 0026
Marion McPartland Trio | Great Britain's | Savoy | SV 0160(MG 12016)
McCoy Tyner | Revelations | Blue Note | 791651-2
Miles Davis Quartet | Ballads & Blues | Blue Note | 836633-2
Miles Davis Quintet | Miles Davis At Plugged Nickel, Vol. 1/2 | CBS | CBS C 2 38266
Miles Davis Sextet | Miles Davis:The Blue Note And Capitol Recordings | Blue Note | 827475-2
Miles Davis Vol.1 | Blue Note | 300081(1501)
Nueva Manteca | Varadero Blues | Timeless | CD SJP 318
Oscar Peterson Trio | En Concert Avec Europe 1 | Laserlight | 710443/48
Oscar Peterson-Austin Roberts | Oscar Peterson 1951 | Just A Memory | JAS 9501-2
Paul Smith Trio | Intensive Care | Pausa | PR 7167(952078)
Phil Markowitz Trio | Sno' Peas | Ken Music | 660.56.010
Rickey Kelly Quintet | Limited Stops Only | Nimbus | NS 3146
Sal Salvador Quartet | Boo Boo Be Doop | Affinity | AFF 68
Shelly Manne Quartet | Essence | Galaxy | GXY 5101
Soesja Citroen With The Metropole Orchestra | Yesterdays | Challenge | CHR 70049
Sonny Rollins & Co. | Sonny Rollins-All The Things You Are (1963-1964) | Bluebird | ND 82179
Sonny Stitt Quartet | In Style | Muse | MR 5228
Stan Getz And J.J. Johnson With The Oscar Peterson Quartet | Stan Getz And J.J. Johnson At The Opera House | Verve | 831272-2 PMS
Stan Getz Quartet | Stan Getz:Imagination | Dreyfus Jazz Line | FDM 36733-2
Scandinavian Days | Fresh Sound Records | FSCD 1009
Stan Getz Quintet | Jazz At Storyville Vol.2 | Fresh Sound Records | FSR 630(Roost RLP 411)
Stan Getz With The Danish Radio Big Band | Stan Getz | Laserlight | 15761
Stan Kenton And His Orchestra | Live In Biloxi | Magic | DAWE 32(881539)
Stan Kenton With The Danish Radio Big Band | Stan Kenton With The Danish Radio Big Band | Storyville | STCD 8340
Stan Levey's Sextet | Grand Stan | Fresh Sound Records | FSR 2000(Bethlehem BCP 71)
Tal Farlow Trio | Tal Farlow Complete 1956 Private Recordings | Definitive Records | DRCD 11263
Teddy Charles Septet | On Campus! Ivy League Jazz Concert | Fresh Sound Records | FSR 2026(Bethlehem BCP 6044)
Tiziana Ghiglioni With Paul Bley | Lyrics | SPLASC(H) Records | CD H 348-2
Wes Montgomery Trio | A Dynamic New Jazz Sound | Original Jazz Classics | OJCCD 034-2
Wes Montgomery-The Complete Riverside Recordings | Riverside | 12 RCD 4408-2
Wild Bill Davison And The Jazz Giants | The Jazz Giants | Sackville | SKCD2-3002
Yesterdays-
Joey DeFrancesco-Jimmy Smith Quartet | Incredlble! | Concord | CCD 4890
Yesterday's Child
Wes Montgomery Trio | Wes Montgomery-The Complete Riverside Recordings | Riverside | 12 RCD 4408-2
Horace Tapscott | The Tapscott Sessions Vol.7 | Nimbus | NS 2147
Yesterday's Tomorrow
Marion Montgomery And Her Quartet | I Gotta Right To Sing... | Ronnie Scott's Jazz House | JHCD 003
Yesterdays(alt.take)
Kenny Drew Trio | New Faces New Sounds:Introducing The Kenny Drew Trio | Blue Note | 871245-4
Yester-Me, Yester-You, Yesterday
Steve Slagle Quartet | Reincarnation | Steeplechase | SCCD 31367
Yesternow
Stan Getz With The Eddie Sauter Orchestra | Stan Getz Plays The Music Of Mickey One | Verve | 531232-2
Yes-The Creature Machine-
Toshiko Akiyoshi-Lew Tabackin Big Band | Tanuki's Night Out | JAM | 006 IMS
Yet Never Broken
Bill Evans Trio | Bill Evans Trio:The Last Waltz | Milestone | 8MCD 4430-2
Bill Evans Trio:The Last Waltz | Milestone | 8MCD 4430-2
Christoph Schweizer Sextet | Normal Garden | Mons Records | MR 874660
Yeti
Mongo Santamaria And His Rhythm Afro-Cubanos | Afro Roots | Prestige | PCD 24018-2(F 8012/8032)
Yggdrasill
Maurizio Rolli-Diana Torto Group | Norwegian Mood | Philology | W 124.2
Yhadik Allah
Winston Mankunku Band | Crossroads | ITM Records | ITM 1441
Yidl With The Fiddle
Nat Adderley Group | Soul Of The Bible | Capitol | 358257-2
Yield
Gene Ammons Quartet | Preachin' | Original Jazz Classics | OJCCD 792-2(P 7270)
Yield Not
Bobby Bland And His Band | Bobby Bland The Voice: Duke Recordings 1959-1969 | Ace Records | CDCHD 323
Yin
Ornette Coleman & Prime Time | Tone Dialing | Verve | 527483-2
Ÿlir
Jasper Van't Hof | My World Of Music | Keytone | KYT 3-100 Digital
Yntest
Modern String Quartet | Elephants & Strings | Upsolute Music Records | UMR 102 ST
Yo Ho
Steve Coleman And Five Elements | World Expansion | JMT Edition | 834410-2
Yo' Jeans
Piirpauke | Piirpauke-Global Servisi | JA & RO | JARO 4150-2
Yö Kyöpelinvuorella
Gato Barbieri Group | Masters Of Jazz Vol.9 | RCA | NL 89722
Yo Le Canto A La Luna
Gato Barbieri:The Complete Flying Dutchman Recordings 1969-1973 | RCA | 2154555-2
Yo M'enamori D'un Aire
Luther Thomas & Dizzazz | Yo' Momma | Moers Music | 01088
Yo No Quiero Bailar
Conexion Latina | La Conexión | Enja | ENJ-9065 2
Yo Quiero También
Soledad Bravo With Band | Volando Voy | Messidor | 15966 CD
Yodel Lady Blues
The Andrew Sisters With The Glenn Miller Orchestra | The Chesterfield Broadcasts Vol.1 | RCA | 2663113-2
Yodelin' Jive
Bessie Smith With Fletcher Henderson | Bessie Smith-The Complete Recordings Vol.1 | CBS | 467895-2
Yolanda Anas
Pat Metheny Group | First Circle | ECM | 1278(823342-2)
Yolanda You Learn
Alain Everts | Terra Nueva | Acoustic Music Records | 319.1103.2
Yomm L'Amour Absolu
| All At Once At Any Time | Victo | CD 029
Yonder Came The Blues
Cora Fluker | Living Country Blues USA Vol.11:Country Gospel Rock | L+R Records | LR 42041
Yor Ladab
Pili-Pili | Hotel Babo | JA & RO | JARO 4147-2
Yoraba Gospel
John Zorn Group | Masada Five | DIW | DIW 899 CD
Yorke
Eje Thelin Group | Eje Thelin Group | Caprice | CAP 1091
You
Christof Lauer Trio | Evidence | CMP Records | CMP CD 70
Joe Haider Trio | Grandfather's Garden | JHM Records | JHM 3619
Joe Haider-Bert Joris Anniversary Big Band | Joe Haider-Bert Joris Anniversary Big Band '92 | JHM Records | JHM 3603
Sonny Rollins And The Contemporary Leaders | Contemporary Sonny Rollins-Alternate Takes | Contemporary | C 7651
Tommy Dorsey And His Orchestra | Planet Jazz:Tommy Dorsey | Planet Jazz | 2159972-2
2nd Nature | What Comes Natural | Inak | 41232
You Ain't Nowhere
Louis Jordan And His Tympany Five | Louis Jordan Vol.1-Hoodoo Man | Swingtime(Contact) | ST 1011
You Alway
Bohana Jazzband | The Golden Years Of Revival Jazz,Vol.6 | Storyville | STCD 5511
You Always Hurt The One You Love
Christie Brothers Stompers | Christie Brothers Stompers | Cadillac | SGC/MEL CD 20/1
Ken Colyer's All Stars | The Sunny Side Of Ken Colyer | Upbeat Jazz | URCD 113
The Mills Brothers | The Best Of The Decca Years | MCA | MCD 31348
You And I
Sadao Watanabe Sextet | Bossa Nova Concert | Denon Compact Disc | DC-8556
You And It
Barre Phillips | Carmouflage | Victo | CD 008
You And Me
Joe Pass Sextet | Simplicity | Pacific Jazz | LN 10086
Monty Waters Quartet | Monty Waters New York Calling Vol.2 | Tutu Records | 888182-2*
Phil Moerke Group feat. Victor Mendoza | Multi Colors | Jazz Pure Collection | AU 31625 CD
Zakir Hussain Group | Making Music | ECM | 1349
Abbey Lincoln & Dave Liebman | People In Me | Verve | 514626-2
You And Music
Donald Byrd Orchestra | Donald Byrd:Blue Breakbeats | Blue Note | 494708-2
You And The Night And The Music

Bill Evans Quintet | The 'Interplay' Sessions | Milestone | M 47066
Bill Evans Trio | Peace Piece And Other Pieces | Milestone | M 47024
Consecration 1 | Timeless | CD SJP 331
Billy May And His Orchestra | Bacchanalia | Capitol | ED 2604201
Brad Goode-Von Freeman Sextet | Inside Chicago Vol.4 | Steeplechase | SCCD 31532
Buddy DeFranco Trio | Do Nothing Till You Hear From Us! | Concord | CCD 4851
Conte Candoli Quartet | Candoli Live | Nagel-Heyer | CD 2024
Dave McKenna | Dancing In The Dark And Other Music Of Arthur Schwartz | Concord | CCD 4292
Hampton Hawes Trio | The Trio Vol.2 | Original Jazz Classics | OJCCD 318-2
Hector Martignon Group | Portrait In White And Black | Candid | CCD 79727
Jeff 'Tain' Watts Trio | MegaWatts | Sunnyside | SSC 1055 D
Joe Bonner Quartet | The Lost Melody | Steeplechase | SCCD 31227
John Abercrombie Trio | Tactics | ECM | 1623(533680-2)
John Campbell | Maybeck Recital Hall Series Volume Twenty-Nine | Concord | CCD 4581
Keith Jarrett Trio | At The Deer Head Inn | ECM | 1531(517720-2)
Kendra Shank Group | Wish | Jazz Focus | JFCD 028
Klaus Spencker Trio | Invisible | Jardis Records | JRCD 9409
Lennie Niehaus Octet | Lennie Niehaus Vol.3:The Octet No.2 | Contemporary | COP 017
Melvin Rhyne Quartet | To Cannonball With Love | Paddle Wheel | KICJ 147
On The Corner With The Philharmonic Orchestra,Würzburg | On The Corner feat. Benny Bailye | Mons Records | MR 874807
Paul Motian Quartet | Paul Motian On Broadway Vol.2 | JMT Edition | 834440-2
Renee Rosnes Trio With String Orchestra | Without Words | Blue Note | 798168-2
Stan Getz With The Bill Evans Trio | But Beautiful | Jazz Door | JD 1208
Tal Farlow Quartet | The Tal Farlow Album | Verve | MV 2584 IMS
Tierney Sutton And Her Trio | Blue In Green | Telarc Digital | CD 83522
Warren Vaché And Bill Charlap | 2Gether | Nagel-Heyer | CD 2011
Woody Shaw Quintet | Time Is Right-Woody Shaw Quintet Live In Europe | Red Records | 123168-2

You And Your Love
Benny Goodman And His Orchestra | Wrappin' It Up-The Harry James Years Part 2 | Bluebird | 63 66549-2

You Are In My Thoughts
Clint Houston Quartet | Inside The Plain Of The Elliptic | Timeless | SJP 132

You Are My Dream
Dave Pike With The Cedar Walton Trio | Pike's Groove | Criss Cross | Criss 1021

You Are My Everything
Charles Brown Band | Boss Of The Blues | Mainstream | MD CDO 908

You Are My Heart's Delight
Shirley Scott Trio | Skylark | Candid | CCD 79705

You Are My Heart's Delight-
Joe McBride | Keys To Your Heart | Inak | 30352

You Are My Lucky Star-
Bernard Peiffer Trio | Jazz In Paris:The Bernard Peiffer Trio Plays Standards | EmArCy | 018425-2

You Are My Seetheart
Natty Dominique's Creole Dance Band | Natty Dominique's Creole Dance Band | American Music | AMCD-18

You Are My Sunshine
Dave Liebman Group | Songs For My Daughter | Soul Note | 121295-2
Firehouse Five Plus Two | Crashes A Party | Good Time Jazz | GTCD 10038-2
Gene Harris-Scott Hamilton Quintet | At Last | Concord | CCD 4434
James Morrison Quartet | Snappy Doo | Warner | 9031-71211-2
Magnificant Seventh's with Milton Batiste And Alton Carson | Best Of New Orleans:Bourbon Street Jazz After Dark | Mardi Gras Records | MG 1022
Milt Jackson-Ray Brown Jam | Montreux '77-The Art Of The Jam Session | Pablo | 2620106
Mose Allison Trio | Mose In Your Ear | Atlantic | SD 1627
Oscar Peterson-Ray Brown Duo | Jazz At The Santa Monica Civic '72 | Pablo | 2625701-2
Singers Unlimited With Rob McConnell And The Boss Brass | The Singers Unlimited With Rob McConnell And The Boss Brass | MPS | 817486-1

You Are My Tree
Michel Petrucciani With The Graffiti String Quartet | Marvellous | Dreyfus Jazz Line | FDM 36564-2

You Are My Waltz
Lightnin' Hopkins | Lightnin' Hopkins(1946-1960) | Story Of Blues | CD 3524-2

You Are So Beautiful
Dorothy Donegan | Piano Giants Vol.1 | Swingtime | 8201

You Are So Strong
Earl Hines-Kenny Clarke Duo | Hine's Tune | France's Concert | FCD 101

You Are The Sunshine Of My Life
Berry Lipman Orchestra | Easy Listening Vol.1 | Sonia | CD 77280
Ella Fitzgerald With The Tommy Flanagan Trio | Jazzin' Vol.2: The Music Of Stevie Wonder | Fantasy | FANCD 6088-2
Montreux '77 | Original Jazz Classics | OJC20 376-2(2308206)
Father Tom Vaughn Trio | Joyful Jazz | Concord | CJ 16
Joe Pass Trio | Live At Donte's | Pablo | 2620114-2
Kenny Ball And His Jazzmen | The Very Best Of Kenny Ball | Timeless | CD TTD 598
Monty Sunshine Quartet | Love And Sunshine-Monty Alexander In Concert | MPS | 68043
Singers Unlimited With The Pat Williams Orchestra | Feeling Free | MPS | 68103
Stephane Grappelli Quartet | At The Winery | Concord | CCD 4139
Vintage Introiduction | North Sea Highlights | Timeless | CD SJP 156

You Are There
Irene Kral With Alan Broadbent | Gentle Rain | Candid | CRS 1020 IMS
Joe Pass Trio | Eximious | Original Jazz Classics | OJCCD 1037-2(2310877)

You Are To Me Everything
Al Caiola Quintet | Deep In A Dream | Savoy | SV 0205(MG 12033)

You Are Too Beautiful
Buddy Childers With The Russ Garcia Strings | Artistry In Jazz | Candid | CCD 79735
Cannonball Adderley With Richard Hayman's Orchestra | Julian Cannonball Adderley And Strings/Jump For Joy | Verve | 528699-2
Eddie Lockjaw Davis Trio | Eddie's Function | Affinity | AFF 153
Jesse Davis Sextet | As We Speak | Concord | CCD 4512
Junior Mance Trio | At The Village Vanguard | Original Jazz Classics | OJC 204(JLP 941)
Les Brown And His Orchestra | Les Brown And His Orchestra 1944 & 1946 | Circle | CCD-90
Pete Rugolo And His Orchestra | Adventures In Rhythm | Fresh Sound Records | LSP 15560(CBS CL 604) (835208)
Sarah Vaughan With Her Quartet | Crazy And Mixed Up | Pablo | 2312137-2
Sonny Rollins Quartet | Sonny Rollins And The Big Brass | Verve | 557545-2
Stephen Scott Trio | Aminah's Dream | Verve | 517996-2
Thelonious Monk Trio | Thelonious Monk-The Complete Riverside Recordings | Riverside | 15 RCD 022-2

You Are Too Beautiful-
Perry Robinson Quartet | The Traveler | Chiaroscuro | CR 190

You Be You
John Lee Hooker | Boogie Chillun | Fantasy | FCD 24706-2

You Bet
Herbie Hancock Group | Feet's Don't Fail Me Now | CBS | SRCS 9504

You Better Change Your Way
Buddy Johnson And His Orchestra | Go Ahead & Rock Rock Rock | Official | 6011

You Better Go Now
Billie Holiday With The Percy Faith Orchestra | Masters Of Jazz Vol.3:Billie Holiday | Storyville | STCD 4103
Chet Baker Quartet And Strings | Chet Baker And Strings | CBS | 21142
Gene DiNovi Trio | Live At The Montreal Bistro | Candid | CCD 79726
Jerri Southern And The Toots Camarata Orchestra | The Very Thought Of You:The Decca Years 1951-1957 | Decca | 050671-2
Jimmy Smith Sextet | Angel Eyes-Ballads & Slow Jams | Verve | 527632-2
Mark Murphy And His Sextet | Bop For Kerouac | Muse | MCD 5253
Stephane Grappelli Quintet | Feeling + Finesse = Jazz | Atlantic | 7567-90140-2
Stephane Grappelli-Hank Jones Quartet | London Meeting | String | BLE 233852

You Better Love Me
Big Bill Broonzy | An Evening With Big Bill Broonzy,Vol.2 | Storyville | STCD 8017

You Better Stop Here
Michael Sagmeister | Still With Me | MGI Records | MGR CD 1004

You Better Watch Yourself
Little Walter Blues Band | Little Walter | Chess | 427001

You Blew Out The Flame
Coleman Hawkins All Stars | In A Mellow Tone | Original Jazz Classics | OJCCD 6001-2

You Bossa Nova Me
Bobby Short With The Benny Carter Band | Benny Carter Songbook | Musicmasters | 65134-2

You Broke Your Promise
Sammy Rimington Band | Sammy Rimington Plays The Clarinet Of George Lewis | SAM Records | SAM CD 003

You Brought A New Kind Of Love To Me
Erroll Garner With The Leith Stevens Orchestra | Closeup In Swing/A New Kind Of Love(Music from The Motion Picture) | Telarc Digital | CD 83383
Jonah Jones And His Orchestra | Commodore Classics In Swing | Commodore | 9031-72723-2
Ruby Braff Quintet | Mr. Braff To You | Phontastic | PHONT 7568
Wrobel-Roberscheuten-Hopkins Jam Session | Jammin' At The IAJRC Convention Hamburg 1999 | Nagel-Heyer | CD 066
Bumble Bee Slim(Amos Easton) | Bumble Bee Slim(Amos Easton) 1931-1937 | Story Of Blues | CD 3501-2

You Call It Jogging
Billy Cotton And His Band | The Rhythm Man | Saville Records | SVL 149 IMS

You Call It Madness But I Call It Love
Dodo Marmarosa Trio | The Chicago Sessions | Argo | ARC 502 D
Nat King Cole Trio | Nat King Cole Trio 1943-49-The Vocal Sides | Laserlight | 15718
Nat King Cole Vol.1 | Laserlight | 15746
Sidsel Endresen-Bugge Wesseltoft | Duplex Ride | ACT | 9000-2

You Call-We Fly
Abbey Lincoln With Hank Jones | When There Is Love | Verve | 519697-2

You Came A Long Way From St. Louis
Bing Crosby And Rosemarie Clooney With The Billy May Orchestra | Fancy Meeting You Here | RCA | 2663859-2
Charlie Byrd Group | Byrd In The Wind | Original Jazz Classics | OJCCD 1086(RS 9449)
Chris Connor With The Ronnie Ball Quartet | Late Show-At The Village Gate | Fresh Sound Records | FSR 705(FM 3035)(835430)
Jeanie Lambe And The Danny Moss Quartet | The Second Sampler | Nagel-Heyer | NHR SP 6
Jimmy Smith With The Claus Ogerman Orchestra | Any Number Can Win | Verve | 557447-2
June Christy With The Shorty Rogers Orchestra | June Christy Big Band Special | Capitol | 498319-2
Marion Montgomery And Her Quartet | I Gotta Right To Sing... | Ronnie Scott's Jazz House | JHCD 003
Chad Wackerman Quartet | Forty Reasons | CMP Records | CMP CD 48

You Can Be Anything
Little Ester With Band | Roots Of Rock 'N' Roll, Vol. 5: Ladies Sing The Blues | Savoy | SJL 2233

You Can Count On Me
Duke Ellington And His Orchestra | Duke Ellington/Cab Calloway | Forlane | UCD 19004
The Soul Stirrers | Negro Spirituals,Gospel & Jubilee Songs | Vogue | 655015

You Can Count On Me To Do My Part
Billie & Dee Dee Pierce | De De Pierce With Billie Pierce In Binghampton,NY,Vol.2 | American Music | AMCD-80

You Can Depend On Me
David Paquette Trio | Mood Swings | ART BY HEART | ABH 2004 2
Dexter Gordon Quartet | Dexter Gordon Plays-The Bethlehem Years | Fresh Sound Records | FSR-CD 154(882891)
Earl Hines And His Orchestra | Once Upon A Time | MCA | 2292-50608-1
Fletcher Henderson And His Orchestra | The Indispensable Fletcher Henderson(1927-1936) | RCA | 2122618-2
Frankie Laine With Carl Fischer's Orchestra | The Uncollected:Frankie Lane Vol.2 | Hindsight | HSR 216 (835570)
Harry Sweets Edison With The Nat King Cole Quartet | The Complete After Midnight Sessions | Capitol | 748328-2
Joe Newman And His Orchestra | The Complete Joe Newman RCA-Victor Recordings(1955-1956):The Basie Days | RCA | 2122613-2
Oscar Peterson Trio | The History Of An Artist | Pablo | 2625702-2
Tommy Dorsey And His Orchestra | Tommy Dorsey In Concert | RCA | NL 89780 DP

You Can Depend On Me-
Punch Miller's New Orleans Band | The Larry Borenstein Collection Vol.11:Punch Miller | 504 Records | 504CD 40

You Can Have Him
Ella Fitzgerald With Paul Weston And His Orchestra | The Complete Ella Fitzgerald Song Books of Harold Arlen, Irving Berlin, Duke Ellington, George & Ira Gershwin, Jerome Kern, Johnny Mercer, Cole Porter And Rogers & Hart | Verve | 519832-2
Nina Simone Groups | You Can Have Him | Memo Music | HDJ 4087

You Can It If You Try
John Lee Hooker | Solid Sender | Charly | CRB 1081

You Can Leave Your Hat On
Julia Hülsmann Trio With Anna Lauvergnac | Come Closer | ACT | 9702-2
David Linx With The Jack Van Poll Trio | Where Rivers Join | September | CD 5109

You Can Make It
Joe McPhee Po Music | Oleo & A Future Retrospective | Hat Art | 3514

You Can See
Jimmy Heath Sextet | Peer Pleasure | Landmark | LCD 1514-2

You Can Stay But The Noise Must Go
Walter 'Wolfman' Washington And The Roadmasters | Out Of The Dark | Rounder Records | CDRR 2068

You Cannot Take My Dignity(Jinga Horonja)
Howlin' Wolf Band | More Real Folk Blues | Chess | CHD 9279(872299)

You Can't Be Sirius!
Barry Martyn's Band | Kid Thomas And Emanuel Paul With Bary Martyn's Band' | GHB Records | BCD 257

You Can't Get Away
Louis Armstrong And His Orchestra | Louis Armstrong Radio Days | Moon Records | MCD 056-2

You Can't Get That No More
Kenny Ball And His Jazzmen | Saturday Night At The Mill | Decca | 6.23040 AO

You Can't Hide
Morgana King And Her Quintet | Higher Ground | Muse | MR 5224

You Can't Keep A Good Man Down
Jesse Fuller One Man Band | Brother Lowdown | Fantasy | F 24707

You Can't Lose A Broken Heart
Paris Washboard | Waiting For The Sunrise | Stomp Off Records | CD 1261

You Can't Run Around
Duke Ellington And His Famous Orchestra | The Complete Duke Ellington-Vol. 8 | CBS | CBS 88185

You Can't Take That Away From Me
Alberta Hunter Trio | The 30's Girls | Timeless | CBC 1-026

You Cought Me Smilin' - (You Cought Me) Smilin'
Anita O'Day And Her Orchestra | Mello'day | GNP Crescendo | GNP 2126

You Couldn't Be Cuter
Peggy Lee With Orchestra | All Aglow Again | Capitol | 1565541

You Did It You Did It
Roland Kirk Quartet | Talkin' Verve-Roots Of Acid Jazz:Roland Kirk | Verve | 533101-2
Roland Kirk Quintet | France's Concert Anthology Vol.1 | France's Concert | FCD 130

You Didn't Think
Louis Jordan And His Tympany Five | Louis Jordan-Let The Good Times Roll: The Complete Decca Recordings 1938-1954 | Bear Family Records | BCD 15557 IH

You Didn't Want Me Baby
Dinah Washington With The Gerald Wilson Orchestra | The Complete Dinah Washington On Mercury Vol.1 | Mercury | 832444-2

You Dig
Nils Landgren Funk Unit | Live In Montreux | ACT | 9265-2
The Three Sounds | Black Orchid | Blue Note | 821289-2

You Dig It
Duke Ellington-Coleman Hawkins Orchestra | Duke Ellington Meets Coleman Hawkins | Impulse(MCA) | 951162-2

You Dirty Dog
Duke Ellington Meets Coleman Hawkins | MCA | MCAD 5650

You Do Something To Me
Ella Fitzgerald With Orchestra | Forever Ella | Verve | 529387-2
Ella Fitzgerald With The Buddy Bregman Orchestra | The Cole Porter Song Book | Verve | 2683044 IMS
Ella Fitzgerald Sings The Cole Porter Songbook Vol.2 | Verve | 821990-2
Ingrid Jensen Quintet | Here On Earth | Enja | ENJ-9313 2
Jessica Williams Trio | Momentum | Jazz Focus | JFCD 003
Phil Mason's New Orleans All-Stars | You Do Something To Me! | Lake | LACD 33
Shorty Rogers And His Giants | Collaboration-Shorty Rogers And Andre Previn | Fresh Sound Records | ND 74398
Sonny Rollins Quartet | The Complete Sonny Rollins RCA Victor Recordings | RCA | 2668675-2
Wrobel-Roberscheuten-Hopkins Jam Session | Jammin' At The IAJRC Convention Hamburg 1999 | Nagel-Heyer | CD 066
Anson Weeks And His Orchestra | The Radio Years: Anson Weeks And His Hotel Mark Hopkins Orchestra 193 | Hindsight | HSR 146

You Do Something To Me-
Ella Fitzgerald With The Tommy Flanagan Trio | Ella A Nice | Original Jazz Classics | OJC20 442-2
John Colianni Trio | Blues-O-Matic | Concord | CCD 4367

You Don't Have To Say You're Sorry
Peggy Lee With Orchestra | All Aglow Again | Capitol | 1565541

You Don't Know
Sonny Criss Quintet | At The Crossroad | Fresh Sound Records | 252962-1(Peacock PLP 91)

You Don't Know Me
Thomas Chapin Quintet | You Don't Know Me | Arabesque Recordings | AJ 0115
Louie Bellson Sextet | Side Track | Concord | CJ 141

You Don't Know What It Means To Miss New Orleans-
Al Haig Trio | Al Haig Today! | Fresh Sound Records | FSR-CD 0006

You Don't Know What Love Is
Allen Harris With The Metropole Orchestra | Here Comes Allen Harris... | Mons Records | MR 874771
Barbara Long With The Billy Howell Quintet | Soul-The Voice Of Babara Long | Savoy | SV 0216(MG 12161)
Billie Holiday With The Ray Ellis Orchestra | This Is Jazz:Billie Holiday Sings Standards | CBS | CK 65048
Bob Stewart Groups | Then & Now | Postcards | POST 1014
Booker Ervin Quintet | Down In The Dumps | Savoy | SV 0245(SJL 1119)
Buddy Arnold Septet | Wailing | Fresh Sound Records | ABC 114(Paramount)
Cassandra Wilson Group | Midnight Blue(The [Be]witching Hour) | Blue Note | 854365-2
Blue Light 'Til Dawn | Blue Note | 781357-2
Cathy Hayes With The Barney Kessel Orchestra | It's All Right With Me | Fresh Sound Records | FSR 531(HiFiJazz R 416)
Charlie Hunter-Leon Parker | Duo | Blue Note | 499187-2
Chet Baker Quartet | Let's Get Lost: The Best Of Chet Baker Sings | Pacific Jazz | 792932-2
Chet Baker Quintet | Live In Europe 1956 | Accord | 556622
Chris Connor With The Richard Wess Orchestra | Witchcraft | Atlantic | AMCY 1068
Dinah Washington And Her Orchestra | Verve Jazz Masters 19:Dinah Washington | Verve | 518200-2
Dusko Goykovich Big Band | Balkan Connection | Enja | ENJ-9047 2
Earl Hines And His Orchestra | The Indispensable Earl Hines Vol.3/4(1939-1945) | RCA | 2126408-2
Eddie Condon All Stars | Eddie Condon Town Hall Concerts Vol.1 | Jazzology | JCECD-1001
Eric Dolphy Quartet | Last Date | EmArCy | 510124-2 PMS
Fred Hersch-Jay Clayton | Beautiful Love | Sunnyside | SSC 1066 D
Gray Sargent Quartet | Shades Of Gray | Concord | CCD 4571
Gust Williams Tsilis Quartet | Heritage | Ken Music | 660.56.018
Herbert Joos Quartet | Herbert Joos Plays Billie Holiday Songs | EmArCy | 522634-2
Jo Albany | Proto-Bopper | Spotlite | SPJ LP 3 (JA 3)
John Coltrane Quartet | John Coltrane:The Classic Quartet-Complete Impulse Studio Recordings | Impulse(MCA) | 951280-2
John Klemmer Quartet | Involvement | Chess | 076139-2
John Swana Sextet | John Swana And Friends | Criss Cross | Criss 1055
Johnny Lytle Quintet | The Village Caller | Original Jazz Classics | OJCCD 110-2(R 9480)
Jon Eardley/Mick Pyne | Two Of A Kind | Spotlite | SPJ LP 16
Kenn Drew Trio | Kenny Drew Trio At The Brewhouse | Storyville | 4960633
Kenny Barron Quartet | Invitation | Criss Cross | Criss 1044
Klaus Treuheit | Solo | Klaus Treuheit Production | A+P 9304(CD 161)
Larry Coryell Duo | Lady Coryell | Vanguard | 662125
Lennie Tristano | Lennie Tristano:The Copenhagen Concert | Storyville | 4960603
The New Tristano | Atlantic | 7567-80475-2
Lew Del Gatto Septet | Katewalk | Naxos Jazz | 86058-2
Mal Waldron | Blues For Lady Day | Black Lion | BLCD 760193
Martin Fredebeul Quartet | Search | Nabel Records:Jazz Network | CD 4652
Marty Ehrlich/Anthony Cox | Falling Man | Muse | MCD 5398
McCoy Tyner Trio | Just Feelin' | Palo Alto | PA 8083
Milt Jackson With Strings | Feelings | Original Jazz Classics | OJC 448(2310774)
Nat Adderley Quintet | Good Company | Challenge | CHR 70009
Overtone | All The Things We Are | Workshop Records | WR 071
Peter Weniger Trio | I Mean You | Mons Records | MR 874300
Ran Blake-Christine Correa | Round About | Music & Arts | CD 807
Rich Perry Quartet | What Is This? | Steeplechase | SCCD 31374
Richie Beirach | Maybeck Recital Hall Series Volume Nineteen | Concord | CCD 4518
Roots | Salutes The Saxophone | IN+OUT Records | 7016-2
Roy Hargrove Quintet | Public Eye | Novus | PD 83113
Sir Charles Thompson Trio | Robbin's Nest | Paddle Wheel | KICJ 181
Sonny Criss Quintet | The Bopmasters | MCA | IA 9337/2 (801647)

Sonny Stitt-Red Holloway Quintet | Just Friends | Affinity | AFF 51
Stephan Noel Lang Trio | Echoes | Nagel-Heyer | CD 2033
Steve Davis Quartet | Songs We Know | dmp Digital Music Productions | CD 3005
Tete Montoliu | Words Of Love | Steeplechase | SCCD 31084
The Baltimore Syndicate | The Baltimore Syndicate | Paddle Wheel | KICJ 72
Thomas Brendgens-Mönkemeyer | Beauty | Jardis Records | JRCD 20138
Thomas Hass Group | A Honeymoon Too Soon | Stunt Records | STUCD 19601
Toni Harper With The Oscar Peterson Quartet | Toni | Verve | MV 2684 IMS
Vince Jones Group | It All Ends Up In Tears | Intuition Records | INT 3069-2
Vinnie Burke All-Stars | Vinnie Burke All-Stars | Fresh Sound Records | ABC 139(Paramount)
Warne Marsh-Lee Konitz Quintet | Warne Marsh-Lee Konitz,Vol.3 | Storyville | SLP 4096

You Don't Know What Love Is-
Larry Vuckovich Quintet | Blues For Red | Hot House Records | HH 1001 IMS

You Don't Know What Love Is(No.1)
Monty Waters' Hot Rhythm Junction | Jazzoerty | Tutu Records | 888196-2*

You Don't Know What Love Is(No.2)
Lee Konitz Trio | Motion | Verve | 557107-2

You Don't Learn That In School
Louis Armstrong And His Orchestra | Swing Legends:Louis Armstrong | Nimbus Records | NI 2012
Louis Armstrong-The Complete RCA Victor Recordings | RCA | 2668682-2

You Don't Love Me Anymore
Albert C. Humphrey With Christian Christl | Breath Taking Boogie Shaking | Acoustic Music Records | AMC 1004

You Don't See Me
Al Jarreau With Band | Tenderness | i.e. Music | 557853-2
Grand Dominion Jazz Band | Half And Half | Stomp Off Records | CD 3989

You Don't Want To Live?
Harlem Mamfats | I'm So Glad | Queen-Disc | 062

You Drove Me From Your Door
Louis Jordan And His Tympany Five | Louis Jordan-Let The Good Times Roll: The Complete Decca Recordings 1938-1954 | Bear Family Records | BCD 15557 IH

You Dyed Your Hair Chartreuse - (You Dyed Your Hair) Chartreuse
Gunter Hampel Next Generation | Köln Concert Part 1 | Birth | CD 047

You Ever Saw Birds Gather And Lift Off?
Blossom Dearie | I'm Hip | CBS | 489123-2

You Fascinate Me So
Blossom Dearie Trio | Blossom Dearie Sings & Plays Songs Of Chelsea | Master Mix | CHECD 2

You For Me
Count Basie And His Orchestra | Live In Basel 1956 | Jazz Helvet | JH 05

You Forgot To Remember
Ella Fitzgerald With Paul Weston And His Orchestra | The Complete Ella Fitzgerald Song Books of Harold Arlen, Irving Berlin, Duke Ellington, George & Ira Gershwin, Jerome Kern, Johnny Mercer, Cole Porter And Rogers & Hart | Verve | 519832-2

You Get 'Cha
Jimmy Smith Trio | Jimmy Smith At The Organ | Blue Note | 300154(1512)

You Go To My Head
Alex Norris Quintet | A New Beginning | Fresh Sound Records | FSNT 081 CD
All Star Live Jam Session | Brownie-The Complete EmArCy Recordings Of Clifford Brown | EmArCy | 838306-2
Allan Vaché-Harry Allen Quintet | Allan And Allan | Nagel-Heyer | CD 074
Ann Malcom With The Robi Szakcsi Jr. Trio | R.S.V.P. | Mons Records | MR 874301
Art Pepper | Artworks | Galaxy | GXY 5148
Art Pepper Quartet | Art Pepper:The Complete Village Vanguard Sessions | Contemporary | 9CCD-4417-2
Art Pepper Quintet | The Return Of Art Pepper -The Complete Art Pepper Aladdin Recordings Vol.1 | Blue Note | 870601-9
Art Pepper-George Cables Duo | Tete-A-Tete | Original Jazz Classics | OJCCD 843-2(GXY 5147)
Art Pepper:The Complete Galaxy Recordings | Galaxy | 16GCD 1016-2
Art Tatum | Art Tatum-The Complete Pablo Solo Masterpieces | Pablo | 7 PACD 4404-2
Art Tatum Trio | The Art Tatum Trip | Jazz Anthology | JA 5138
Betty Carter And The Cyrus Chetsnut Trio | It's Not About The Melody | Verve | 513870-2
Billie Holiday And Her Orchestra | Billie Holiday:The Quintessential Vol.6(1938) | CBS | 466313-2
Billie Holiday And Her Trio | Lady Day-The Storyville Concerts | Jazz Door | JD 1215
Bud Powell Trio | Bud Powell:Bouncing With Bud | Dreyfus Jazz Line | FDM 36725-2
Bud Powell:Complete 1947-1951 Blue Note,Verve & Roost Recordings | The Jazz Factory | JFCD 22837
Chet Baker Quartet | Jazz In Paris:Chet Baker Quartet Plays Standards | EmArCy | 014378-2 PMS
Chet Baker-Paul Bley | Diane | Steeplechase | SCM 51207
Clifford Brown All Stars | Brownie-The Complete EmArCy Recordings Of Clifford Brown | EmArCy | 838306-2
Clifford Brown All Stars With Dinah Washington | Verve Jazz Masters 40:Dinah Washington | Verve | 522055-2
Coleman Hawkins All Star Octet | Bean And The Boys | Prestige | PCD 24124-2
Dave Brubeck Quartet | Buried Treasures | CBS | CK 65777
Dave Brubeck Sextet | Nightshift | Telarc Digital | CD 83351
Dizzy Gillespie And His Orchestra | Dizzier And Dizzier | RCA | 26685172
Ella Fitzgerald-Joe Pass Duo | Take Love Easy | Pablo | 2310702
Joe Pass:A Man And His Guitar | Original Jazz Classics | OJCCD 8806-2
Gary Smulyan Quintet | The Lure Of Beauty | Criss Cross | Criss 1049
Gordon Brisker Quintet | My Son John | Naxos Jazz | 86064-2
Ian McDougall Quartet | The Warmth Of The Horn | Concord | CCD 4652
James Moody And His Band | Moody's Blues | Vogue | 655016
Jeanne Lee-Mal Waldron | After Hours | Owl Records | 013426-2
Jeff Jerolamon Quintet | Jeff Jerolamon's Swing Thing! | Candid | CCD 79538
Jenny Evans And Her Quintet | Shiny Stockings | Enja | ENJ-9317 2
Jimmy Raney Quartet | Jimmy Raney Visits Paris Vol.1 | Vogue | 21409352
John Abercrombie-Andy LaVerne | Timeline | Steeplechase | SCCD 31538
John Basile Quartet | The Desmond Project | Chesky | JD 156
Lainie Kazan With Band | In The Groove | Musicmasters | 65168-2
Lars Gullin Quartet | Lars Gullin 1953,Vol.2:Moden Sounds | Dragon | DRCD 234
Lee Konitz Quartet | Subconcious-Lee | Original Jazz Classics | OJCCD 186-2(P 7004)
Lee Morgan Quintet | The Gigolo | Blue Note | 784212-2
Lennie Tristano Quartet | That's Jazz Vol.15: Lennie Tristano | Atlantic | ATL 50245
Louis Armstrong With The Oscar Peterson Quartet | Louis Armstrong Meets Oscar Peterson | Verve | 539060-2
Jazz-Club: Trumpet | Verve | 840038-2
Nick Brignola Quintet | Like Old Times | Reservoir | RSR CD 133
Oscar Peterson-Harry Edison Duo | Oscar Peterson & Harry Edison | Original Jazz Classics | OJCCD 738-2(2310741)
Paul Bley | Solo Piano | Steeplechase | SCCD 31236
Paul Desmond And The Modern Jazz Quartet | Paul Demond With The Modern Jazz Quartet | CBS | JK 57337
Paul Desmond Quartet | That's Jazz Vol.29: Paul Desmond | Warner | WB 56294
Peter Fessler Quartet | Foot Prints | Minor Music | 801058
Primal Blue | Primal Blue | Hip Bop | HIBD 8006
Sal Salvador Quartet | Stop Smoking Or Else Blues | Fresh Sound Records | FSR 556(Roulette SR 25262)
Sarah Vaughan With John Kirby And His Orchestra | Sarah Vaughan:Lover Man | Dreyfus Jazz Line | FDM 36739-2
Sarah Vaughan Birthday Celebration | Fantasy | FANCD 6090-2
Shirley Horn Quartet | The Main Ingredient | Verve | 529555-2
Sir Charles Thompson | Portrait Of A Piano | Sackville | 3037
Stan Getz Quartet | Stan Getz-The Complete Roost Sessions | EMI Records | 859622-2
Stan Getz:Imagination | Dreyfus Jazz Line | FDM 36733-2
Unearthed Masters-Vol.2: Stan Getz | JAM | 5007 IMS
Susannah McCorkle With The Allen Farnham Orchestra | From Bessie To Brazil | Concord | CCD 4547
Teddy Wilson Trio | Teddy Wilson | LRC Records | CDC 9003
Walt Dickerson Quartet | A Sense Of Direction | Original Jazz Classics | OJCCD 1794-2(NJ 8268)

You Go To My Head-
Ella Fitzgerald With The Tommy Flanagan Trio | Ella Fitzgerald In Budapest | Pablo | PACD 5308-2
Hank Jones Trio | Charles Mingus-The Complete Debut Recordings | Debut | 12 DCD 4402-2
Quincy Jones All Stars | Go West Man | Fresh Sound Records | ABC 186 (Paramount)
Art Pepper-George Cables Duo | Art Pepper:The Complete Galaxy Recordings | Galaxy | 16GCD 1016-2

You Go To My Head(alt.take)
Goin' Home | Original Jazz Classics | GXY 5143

You Got It
Cannonball Adderley Quintet | Live In San Francisco | Riverside | RISA 1157-6
Dizzy Gillespie-Count Basie Quartet | The Gifted Ones | Original Jazz Classics | OJCCD 886-2(2310833)
Etta James With Orchestra | Peaches | Chess | 427014

You Got It Bad Girl
Ran Blake | Third Stream Recompositions | Owl Records | 017

You Got It In Your Soulness
Les McCann-Eddie Harris Quintet | Swiss Movements | Atlantic | 7567-81365-2

You Got It Made
John Brim & His Stompers | Whose Muddy Shoes | Chess | CH 9114

You Got My Nose Open
Charlie Shavers Quartet | Swing Along With Charlie Shavers | Fresh Sound Records | FSR-CD 327

You Got To Go When The Wagon Comes
Louis Jordan And His Tympany Five | Louis Jordan Vol.1: Hoodoo Man | Swingtime(Contact) | ST 1011

You Got To Know How
Sippie Wallace With Jim Dapogny's Chicago Jazz Band | Sippie | Atlantic | SD 19350

You Got To My Head
Larry Clinton And His Orchestra | Larry Clinton And His Orchestra 1937-38 | Decca | 6.23557 AG

You Got To Pay
Little Sam & Orchestra | Don Byas Complete American Small Group Recordings | Definitive Records | DRCD 11213

You Gotta Go
Howard Johnson's Nubia | Arrival | Verve | 523985-2

You Gotta Pay The Band
Alberta Hunter With Buster Bailey's Blues Blasters | Songs We Taught Your Mother | Original Blues Classics | OBCCD 520-2

You Gotta Reap What You Sow
Albert King Blues Band | I'm In A Phone Booth,Baby | Fantasy | F 9633

You Gotta Shake That Thing
Jerry Coker Orchestra | Modern Music From Indiana University | Fantasy | 0902116(F 3214)

You Gotta Try...Harder!
Dieter Antritter And His Traveling Jazz Band | Great Traditionalists | Jazzpoint | JP 1046 CD

You GotTo See Your Mama
Laura Fygi Meets Michel Legrand | Watch What Happens | Mercury | 534598-2

You Had To Be There
Dee Dee Bridgewater With Her Quintet | Love And Peace-A Tribute To Horace Silver | Verve | 527470-2

You Happened My Way
Horace Silver Quintet | Finger Poppin' | Blue Note | 542304-2
Chet Baker Quartet | As Time Goes By | Timeless | CD SJP 251/252

You Have Everything You Need
Blossom Dearie | I'm Hip | CBS | 489123-2

You Hit The Spot
Ella Fitzgerald With The Marty Paich Dek-tette | Verve Jazz Masters 46:Ella Fitzgerald-The Jazz Sides | Verve | 527655-2
Marty Grosz & The Collectors Items Cats | Thanks | J&M Records | J&MCD 502
Dave Holland Quintet | Jumpin' In | ECM | 1269

You I Love
Frank Minion With The Jimmy Jones Quartet | The Soft Land Of Make Believe | Fresh Sound Records | FSR 2013(Bethlehem BCP 6052)

You Keep Coming Back Like A Song
Ella Fitzgerald With Paul Weston And His Orchestra | The Complete Ella Fitzgerald Song Books of Harold Arlen, Irving Berlin, Duke Ellington, George & Ira Gershwin, Jerome Kern, Johnny Mercer, Cole Porter And Rogers & Hart | Verve | 519832-2
Joseph Robechaux And His New Orleans Boys | Joe Robichaux And His New Orleans Boys | Folklyric | 9032

You Knew
Gerald Wilson Orchestra Of The 80's | Lomelin | Discovery | DS 833 IMS

You Know
Paul Millns Groups | Unsong Heroes | Acoustic Music Records | 319.1143.2

You Know It Too
Martin Taylor-David Newton | Don't Fret | Linn Records | AKD 014

You Know Who(I Mean You)
Big Joe Williams | Baby Please Don't Go | Swingtime(Contact) | BT 2007

You Know You Know
Mahavishnu Orchestra | The Inner Mounting Flame | CBS | CK 65523
Lutz Wichert Trio | Ambiguous | Edition Musikat | EDM 068

You Know You Never Know
Bobby Bradford Quintet | Lost In L.A. | Soul Note | 121068-2

You Leave Me Breathless
Eddie Higgins Quintet | The Swingin'est | Vee Jay Recordings | VJ 015
Howard Alden Trio With Monty Alexander | Snowy Morning Blues | Concord | CCD 4424
John Coltrane With The Red Garland Trio | John Coltrane-The Prestige Recordings | Prestige | 16 PCD 4405-2
Johnny Griffin Quartet | Ballads For Tenor | Jazz Colours | 874709-2
Nat Adderley And The Big Sax Section | That's Right | Original Jazz Classics | OJCCD 791-2(RLP 9330)
Nat King Cole With The Dave Cavanaugh Orchestra | Nat King Cole At The Sands | Capitol | EMS 1110

You Leave Me Breathless-
Illinois Jacquet And His Orchestra | Illinois Jacquet:All Stars Studio Recordings 1945-1947(Master Takes) | Blue Moon | BMCD 1011

You Let My Love Grow Cold
Dinah Washington With The Quincy Jones Orchestra | The Swingin' Miss 'D' | Verve | 558074-2

You Let My Love Grow Old
Jeanie Bryson And Her Band | Som Cats Know-Jeannie Bryson Sings Songs Of Peggy Lee | Telarc Digital | CD 83391

You Live Your Life And I'll Live Mine
Fats Waller And His Rhythm | The Indispensable Fats Waller Vol.7/8(1938-1940) | RCA | 2126417-2

You Look Good To Me
Oscar Peterson And The Bassists | Montreux '77-The Art Of The Jam Session | Pablo | 2620106
Oscar Peterson Trio | En Concert Avec Europe 1 | Laserlight | 710443/48
Ron Eschete Quintet | To Let You Know I Care | Muse | MR 5186

You Made Me Funny
Benny Moten's Kansas City Orchestra | The Complete Bennie Moten Vol.5/6 | RCA | PM 45688

You Made Me Love You
Dutch Swing College Band | Souvenirs From Holland, Vol. 2 | DSC Production | PA 004 (801061)
Harry James And His Orchestra | Trumpet Blues:The Best Of Harry James | Capitol | 521224-2
Hatchett's Swingtette | Stephane's Tune | Naxos Jazz | 8.120570 CD
Jimmy Witherspoon And His Quartet | Blues Around The Clock | Original Blues Classics | OBCCD 576-2(P 7314)

You Make Me Feel Like A Natural Woman - (You Make Me Feel) Like A Natural Woman
Hans Theessink | Hans Theessink:Solo | Minor Music | 801047

You Make Me Feel So Good
Benny Green | Green's Blues | Telarc Digital | CD 83539

You Make Me Feel So Young
Carol Simpson With Orchestra | All About Carole | Jasmine | JAS 309
Chris Connor With Band | Chris Connor | Atlantic | 7567-80769-2
Clare Teal And Her Band | Orsino's Songs | Candid | CCD 79783
Claude Williamson Trio | The Fabulous Claude Williamson Trio | Fresh Sound Records | FSR-CD 0051
Donna Brooks With The Alex Smith Trio | I'll Take Romance | Dawn | DCD 113
Four Freshmen With The Billy May Orchestra | Voices In Fun | Pathe | 1566151(Capitol ST 1543)
Paul Kuhn Trio With Greetje Kauffeld And Jean 'Toots' Thielemans | Play It Again Paul | IN+OUT Records | 77040-2
Peggy Connelly With The Marty Paich Orchestra | Peggy Connelly Sings | Fresh Sound Records | FSR 607(835386)

You Make Me So Happy
Matchbox Bluesband | Live Recordings Extravaganza! | L+R Records | CDLR 42074

You May Be Asked For
The Georgians | The Georgians 1922-23 | Retrieval | RTR 79003

You Move You Lose
Lucky Thompson Quartet | Lucky Thompson | Swing | SW 8404 IMS

You Must Be Blind
Nat King Cole Trio | The Early Forties | Fresh Sound Records | FSR-CD 0139

You Must Be Jokin'
Fats Waller And His Rhythm And His Orchestra | The Last Years 1940-1943 | Bluebird | ND 90411(3)

You Must Believe In Spring
Bill Perkins Quartet | Journey To The East | Contemporary | C 14011
Esmeralda Ferrara Group | Day By Day | Philology | W 129.2
George Colligan & Jesper Bodilsen | A Wish | Steeplechase | SCCD 31507
Sheila Jordan With Her Quartet | The Crossing | Black-Hawk | BKH 50501 CD

You Must Believe In Spring-
Abbey Lincoln And Her All Stars | The World Is Falling Down | Verve | 843476-2

You Must Believe In Spring And Love
Allotria Jazz Band | The Best Of Allotria Jazz Band München | Elite Special | 730215

You Must Have Been A Beautiful Baby
Russ Morgan And His Orchestra | The Uncollected:Russ Morgan | Hindsight | HSR 145

You Must Met My Wife
Benny Goodman Trio | Berlin 1980 | TCB Records | TCB 43022

You Mustn't Kick It Around
Charlie Haden Quartet West With Strings | The Art Of The Song | Verve | 547403-2

You My Love
Al Cohn-Zoot Sims Quintet | You 'N' Me | Verve | 589318-2

You 'N' Me
Herb Geller Quartet | Herb Geller Plays The Al Cohn Songbook | Hep | CD 2066
Shelly Manne Quintet | Atlantic Jazz: West Coast | Atlantic | 7567-81703-2

You Need To Rock
Oscar Peterson Quintet With Orchestra | The Personal Touch | Pablo | 2312135-2

You Never Be Anything
Albert Sarko Quintet | Blues And Views(Bagdad Christmas) | Enja | 8018-2

You Never Give Me Your Money
Sarah Vaughan And Her Band | Songs Of The Beatles | Atlantic | 16037-2
Sarah Vaughan With Orchestra | Song Of The Beatles | Atlantic | SD 16037

You Never Lose An Island:
(Little)Jimmy Scott With The Lucky Thompson Orchestra | Everybody's Somebody's Fool | Decca | 050669-2

You Never Miss The Water Till The Well Runs Dry
Count Basie And His Orchestra With The Mills Brothers | The Board Of Directors Annual Report | Dot | DLP 25888

You Never Told Me That You Care
Golden Gate Quartet | From Spriritual To Swing Vol.2 | EMI Records | 780573-2

You Never Walk Alone
Louis Armstrong And His All Stars | The Best Live Concert | Festival | ???

You Open My Eyes
Jimmy Heath Quartet | You Or Me | Steeplechase | SCCD 31370

You Owe Me
Joe Williams,With The Oliver Nelson Orchestra | Jump For Joy | Bluebird | 63 52713-2

You Rascal You -> I'll Be Glad When You're Dead You Rascal You

You Really Don't Know
Sippie Wallace With Axel Zwingenberger | Sippie Wallace/Axel Zwingenberger And The Friends Of Boogie Woogie Vol.1 | Vagabond | VRCD 8.84002
An Evening With Sippie Wallace | Vagabond | VRCD 8.86006
Simon Phillips Group | Symbiosis | Lipstick Records | LIP 890362

You Run Your Mouth,I'll Run My Business
Coleman Hawkins And His Orchestra | Coleman Hawkins Vol.1-Hawk Variation | Swingtime(Contact) | ST 1004

You Saved Me
Eddie Allen Quintet | Summer Days | Enja | ENJ-9388 2

You Say
Nelson Rangell Group | Playing For Keeps | GRP | GRP 95932

You Say You Care
John Coltrane Quartet | The Prestige Legacy Vol.1:The High Priests | Prestige | PCD 24251-2
John Coltrane-The Prestige Recordings | Prestige | 16 PCD 4405-2
John Coltrane | Prestige | P 24003
Kendra Shank Group | Wish | Jazz Focus | JFCD 028
Scott Hamilton Quartet | Race Point | Concord | CCD 4492
Junior Wells Blues Band | Southside Blues Jam | Delmark | 900204 AO

You Send Me
Patricia Covair With The Willie Metcalf Jr. Jazz Quartet | New Orleans After Dark | Challenger Productions | AE 1000-2
Roy Ayers Quintet | Searchin' | Ronnie Scott's Jazz House | JHCD 013

You Send Me Flowers
Frank Stokes | Creator Of The Memphis Blues | Yazoo | YAZ 1056

You Shook Me
Julie Wilson With The Phil Moore Orchestra | Love | Fresh Sound Records | Dolphin 6

TITELVERZEICHNIS

You Should Stay
Robert Jeanne Quartet | Quartets | B.Sharp Records | CDS 084
You Speak My Language
Cleo Laine With The Johnny Dankworth Quintet | Cleo At Carnegie Hall-The 10th Anniversary Concert | DRG | DARC 2-2101 IMS
You Stepped Out Of A Dream
Al Haig Quartet | Al Haig Quartet | Fresh Sound Records | FSR-CD 0012
Bobby Lyle Group | Pianomagic | Atlantic | 7567-82346-2
Boots Mussuli Quartet | Little Man | Affinity | AFF 67
Brew Moore Quintet | Svinget 14 | Black Lion | BLCD 760164
Carlo Atti With The Hal Galper Trio | Sweet Beat Blues | Red Records | 123277-2
Charlie Mariano With The Tete Montoliu Trio | It's Standard Time Vol.2 | Fresh Sound Records | FSR-CD 5022
Double Image | Open Hand | dmp Digital Music Productions | CD 503
Eddie Lockjaw Davis Quartet | Eddie Lockjaw Davis With Shirley Scott | Original Jazz Classics | OJC 218(P 7154)
Glenn Miller And His Orchestra | Candelight Miller | RCA | 2668716-2
Glenn Miller Forever | RCA | NL 89214 DP
Hal Schaefer Trio | The Extraordinary Jazz Pianist | Discovery | DS 781 IMS
Ian Shaw With Band | The Echo Of A Song | Ronnie Scott's Jazz House | JHCD 048
Joe Pass Quartet | The Complete 'Catch Me' Sessions | Blue Note | LT 1053
Joe Williams With The Frank Hunter Orchestra | Planet Jazz:Joe Williams | Planet Jazz | 2165370-2
John Campbell Trio | Turning Point | Contemporary | CCD 14061-2
Johnny Griffin-Martial Solal | Griffin-Solal In&Out | Dreyfus Jazz Line | FDM 36610-2
Kenny Clarke-Francy Boland Big Band | En Concert Avec Europe 1 | Laserlight | 710413/14
Lee Konitz Quintet | Live At The Half Note | Verve | 521659-2
Lennie Niehaus Quintet | Vol.1:The Quintets | Original Jazz Classics | OJC 319(C 3518)
McCoy Tyner Trio With Woodwinds And Strings | Fly With The Wind | Original Jazz Classics | OJCCD 699-2(M 9067)
Oscar Peterson Quartet | Live At The Northsea Jazz Festival | Pablo | 2620115-2
Oscar Peterson Trio | Three Originals:Motion&Emotions/Tristeza On Piano/Hello Herbie | MPS | 521059-2
Pete Rugolo And His Orchestra | Introducing | Fresh Sound Records | LSP 15824(CBS CL 635)
Shorty Rogers And His Giants | Collaboration-Shorty Rogers And Andre Previn | Fresh Sound Records | ND 74398
Sonny Rollins Quintet | Sonny Rollins | Blue Note | 84508
Jazz Profile:Sonny Rollins | Blue Note | 823516-2
Stan Getz Quartet | Stan Getz:Imagination | Dreyfus Jazz Line | FDM 36733-2
Early Getz | Prestige | P 24088
Stan Kenton And His Orchestra | Mellophonium Magic | Status | CD 103(882199)
Steve Wolfe Quintet Feat.Nancy King | First Date | Inner City | IC 1049 IMS
Teddy Edwards-Howard McGhee Quintet | Together Again! | Original Jazz Classics | OJCCD 424-2
Terry Morel With The Ralph Sharon Quartet | Songs Of A Woman In Love | Fresh Sound Records | FSR 2037(Bethlehem BCP 47)
Toon Van Vliet Quartet | Toon Van Vliet | BVHAAST | 059
You Stepped Out Of A Dream-
Peter Sprague Quartet | Musica Del Mar | Concord | CJ 237
You Stole My Heart
Eddie Harris Group With The WDR Big Band | Eddie Harris-The Last Concert | ACT | 9249-2
You Stole My Heart(The Last Encore)
Dizzy Gillespie And His Orchestra | John Coltrane:Complete Recordings With Dizzy Gillespie | Definitive Records | DRCD 11249
You Sweet And Fancy Lady
Grant Stewart Quartet | More Urban Tones | Criss Cross | Criss 1124
You Tell Me
Brubeck/LaVerne Trio | See How It Feels | Black-Hawk | BKH 51401
You The Night And The Music
Jasper Van't Hof | At The Concertgebouw | Challenge | CHR 70010
You Took Advantage Of Me
Art Tatum | Art Tatum:Over The Rainbow | Dreyfus Jazz Line | FDM 36727-2
Art Tatum:Complete Capitol Recordings | Capitol | 821325-2
The Standard Sessions: Art Tatum 1935-1943 Transcriptions | Music & Arts | CD 673
Art Tatum At The Piano Vol.1 | GNP Crescendo | GNPD 9025
Solos 1937 & Classic Piano Solos | Forlane | UCD 19010
Art Tatum Quartet | The Tatum Group Masterpieces | Pablo | 2310734
Betty Bennett And Her Orchestra | Nobody Else But Me-Betty Bennett Sings The Arrangements Of Shorty Rogers & André Previn | Atlantic | AMCY 1065
Bud Freeman And His Summa Cum Laude Orchestra | Bread,Butter And Jam In Hi-Fi | RCA | 2136402-2
Chris Barber's Jazz Band | The Chris Barber Concerts | Lake | LACD 55/56
Dutch Swing College Band | Souvenirs From Holland, Vol. 3 | DSC Production | PA 005 (801062)
Ella Fitzgerald With The Buddy Bregman Orchestra | The Rodgers And Hart Songbook | Verve | 821693-1
The Complete Ella Fitzgerald Song Books of Harold Arlen, Irving Berlin, Duke Ellington, George & Ira Gershwin, Jerome Kern, Johnny Mercer, Cole Porter And Rodgers & Hart | Verve | 519832-2
Elliot Lawrence Band | Plays Tiny Kahn And Johnny Mandel Arrangements | Fantasy | 0902109(F 3219)
Gerry Mulligan Concert Jazz Band | Verve Jazz Masters 36:Gerry Mulligan | Verve | 523342-2
En Concert Avec Europe 1 | Laserlight | 710382/83
Harry Allen Quintet | A Night At Birdland Vol. 1 | Nagel-Heyer | CD 5002
Jack Dieval Avec Stephane Grappelli | Special Stephane Grappelli | Jazztime(EMI) | 251286-2
June Christy With Maynard Ferguson And His Orchestra | The Misty Miss Christy | Capitol | 798452-2
Lawrence Brown With The Ralph Burns Orchestra | Slide Trombone | Verve | 559930-2
Lee Wiley With The Ruby Braff Quartet | Duologue | Black Lion | BLP 60911
Paul Whiteman And His Orchestra | The Indispensable Bix Beiderbecke(1924-1930) | RCA | ND 89572
Ruby Braff-Ellis Larkins | Duets Vol.2 | Vanguard | VCD 79611-2
Scott Hamilton Sextet | In New York City | Concord | CCD 4070
You Took Advantage Of Me(alt.take 1)
Muggsy Spanier And His V-Disc All Stars | Muggsy Spanier And Bud Freeman:V-Discs 1944-45 | Jazz Unlimited | JUCD 2049
You Took Advantage Of Me(alt.take 2)
Muggsy Spanier And Bud Freeman:V-Discs 1944-45 | Jazz Unlimited | JUCD 2049
You Took Advantage Of Me(false start)
Ake Stan Hasselgard Quintet | Young Clarinet | Dragon | DRLP 163
You Took The Words Right Out Of My Heart
Paul Motian Trio | You Took The Words Right Out Of My Heart | JMT Edition | 514028-2
Thelonious Monk | Thelonious Monk-The Complete Riverside Recordings | Riverside | 15 RCD 022-2
You Tought My Heart To Sing
Eden Atwood Group | A Night In The Life | Concord | CCD 4730
You Turn Me On I'm A Radio
Howlin' Wolf | Blues Roots Vol. 14: Howlin' Wolf | Chess | 6.24804 AG
You Turned The Tables On Me
Benny Goodman And His Orchestra | Roll 'Em, Vol.1 | CBS | 460062-2
Billie Holiday And Her Orchestra | Billie Holiday: The First Verve Sessions | Verve | 2610027
Billy Mitchell Sextet | This Is Billy Mitchell | Smash | 065507-2
Bobby Scott Quartet | Slowly | Musicmasters | 5053-2
Harry James And His Orchestra | The Radio Years: Harry James And His Orchestra 1948-49 | Hindsight | HSR 135
Mose Allison Trio | High Jinks! The Mose Allison Trilogy | CBS | J3K 64275
Putney Dandridge Band | Putney Dandridge 1935-1936 | Timeless | CBC 1-023
Stan Kenton And His Orchestra | At The Rendezvous Vol.1 | Status | CD 102(882198)
Woody Herman's 2nd Herd | Woody Herman's 2nd Herd Live 1948-Vol.1 | Raretone | 5001 FC
You Understand
Albert King Blues Band | Thursday Night In San Francisco | Stax | MPS 8557
You Want Me To Stop Loving You
Roscoe Mitchell And The Sound And Space Ensembles | Roscoe Mitchell | Black Saint | BSR 0070
You Wear Love So Well
Tommy Smith Sextet | Misty Morning And No Time | Linn Records | AKD 040
You Were Meant For Me
Dutch Swing College Band | Souvenirs From Holland, Vol. 3 | DSC Production | PA 005 (801062)
Leslie Scott With The Coleman Hawkins Orchestra | The Indispensable Coleman Hawkins 1927-1956:Body And Soul | RCA | ND 89277
You Were Never Lovelier
Stephane Grappelli Quartet | Afternoon In Paris | MPS | 68156
You Were Out
Ben Selvin And His Orchestra | Cheerful Little Earful | Saville Records | SVL 165 IMS
You Who Brought Me Love
Walt Dickerson Trio | To My Son | Steeplechase | SCS 1130
You Will Always Have A Friend
Flip Phillips With The Woody Herman Orchestra | Together Flip & Woody | CDS Records Ltd. | CJCD 828
You Will Be Shot
Russell Malone Quartet | Look Who's Here | Verve | 543543-2
You Will Know
Lonnie Johnson Quintet | Blues By Lonnie Johnson | Original Blues Classics | OBCCD 502-2(BV 1007)
You Will,Oscar,You Will
Little Johnny Taylor With Band | The Galaxy Years | Ace Records | CDCHD 967
You Won't Be Satisfied Until You Break My Heart
Ella Fitzgerald With Louis Armstrong And The All Stars | The Complete Ella Fitzgerald And Louis Armstrong On Verve | Verve | 537284-2
Gary Crosby And His All Stars | The Happy Bachelor | Verve | MV 2664 IMS
Abbey Lincoln With Hank Jones | When There Is Love | Verve | 519697-2
You Won't Forget Me
On The Corner With The Philharmonic Orchestra,Würzburg | On The Corner feat. Benny Bailye | Mons Records | MR 874807
Vic Juris Trio | Songbook 2 | Steeplechase | SCCD 31516
Walt Weiskopf Nonet | Song For My Mother | Criss Cross | Criss 1127
You Won't Let Me Go
Ray Charles With Ralph Burns' Orchestra | The Genius Of Ray Charles | Atlantic | 1312-2
You Would Rather Have The Blues
Billy Cotton And His Band | The Rhythm Man | Saville Records | SVL 149 IMS
You You Darlin'
Jimmy Dorsey And His Orchestra | The Uncollected: Jimmy Dorsey | Hindsight | HSR 101
You(alt.take)
Inno | Insonnie | SPLASC(H) Records | CD H 321-2
You'd Be So Nice
Adam Makowicz | Maybeck Recital Hall Series Volume Twenty-Four | Concord | CCD 4541
You'd Be So Nice To Come Home To
André Previn's Jazz Trio | King Size! | Original Jazz Classics | OJCCD 691-2(S 7570)
Art Pepper Quartet | Art Pepper Meets The Rhythm Section | Original Jazz Classics | OJC20 338-2
The Jazz Giants Play Cole Porter:Night And Day | Prestige | PCD 24203-2
Axel Beineke Jazz Trio | Let's Be True | Edition Collage | EC 469-2
Bobby Timmons Trio | Moanin' | Milestone | M 47031
Cannonball Adderley And His Orchestra | Compact Jazz: Cannonball Adderley | EmArCy | 842930-2 PMS
Carla White And Her Trio | Orient Express | Milestone | M 9147
Chet Baker Quartet | When Sunny Gets Blue | Steeplechase | SCS 1221
Chuck Brown And The Second Chapter Band | Timeless | Minor Music | 801068
Claude Tissendier Saxomania | Saxomania | OMD | CD 1522
Coleman Hawkins And Ben Webster With The Oscar Peterson Quartet | Compact Jazz: Coleman Hawkins/Ben Webster | Verve | 833296-2
Dave Brubeck | Dave Brubeck Plays And Plays And Plays... | Original Jazz Classics | OJCCD 716-2(F 3259)
David Friesen Quartet | Four To Go | ITM-Pacific | ITMP 970088
Dick Hyman | Cole Porter:All Through The Night | Musicmasters | 5060-2
Frankie Laine With Buck Clayton And His Orchestra | Jazz Spectacular | CBS | CK 65507
Fraser MacPherson Quintet | Jazz Prose | Concord | CJ 269
Great Jazz Trio | Standard Collection Vol.1 | Limefree | MCD 0031
Henri Renaud All Stars | Henri Reanaud Trio,Sextet & All Stars | Vogue | 21606382
James Williams Trio | The Arioso Touch | Concord | CJ 192
Kenny Clarke-Francy Boland And Co. | The Golden 8 | Blue Note | 869935-9
Lee Konitz Trio | Motion | Verve | 557107-2
Manfred Junker Quartet | Cole Porter-Live! | Edition Collage | EC 531-2
Manhattan Jazz Quintet | My Favorite Things | Paddle Wheel | K32Y 6210
Matt Dennis Trio With Sy Oliver And His Orchestra | Welcome Matt Dennnis! | Fresh Sound Records | FSR-CD 87(882167)
Paolo Radoni Trio | A Day Or Two | B.Sharp Records | CDS 095
Warren Vaché Sextet | Easy Going | Concord | CCD 4323
You'd Be So Nice To Come Home To(alt.take)
David Klein Quintet | My Marilyn | Enja | ENJ-9422 2
You'd Be Surprised
Kid Thomas-Louis Nelson Jazz Band | Kid Thomas & Louis Nelson In Denmark Vol. 2 | Storyville | SLP 246
You'd Better Believe Me
Buddy Johnson And His Orchestra | Walkin' | Official | 6008
You'd Better Go Now
Buddy Collette Quintet | Everybody's Buddy | Fresh Sound Records | FSR 506(Challenge CHL 603)
You'd Better Love Me
Mel Tormé With Orchestra | That's All Mel Tormé | CBS | CK 65165
Youkali
Dee Dee Bridgewater With Band | This Is New | Verve | 016884-2
Dee Dee Bridgewater Sings Kurt Weil | EmArCy | 9801601
Jugend Jazzorchester Sachsen-Anhalt | Jugend Jazzorchester Sachsen-Anhalt Spielt Kurt Weill | Born&Bellmann | 972806 CD
You'll Aways Be Mine
Carmen Lundy With Band | Moment To Moment | Arabesque Recordings | AJ 0102
You'll Be My Lover
Jimmy Patrick Quintet | You Are My Audience | BELL Records | BLR 84036
You'll Be Sorry
Teddy Wilson | The Keystone Transcriptions 1939-1940 | Storyville | STCD 8258
Tarika Blue | Tarika Blue | Chiaroscuro | CR 164
You'll Get Them Blues
Chick Webb And His Orchestra | Big Band Bounce & Boogie:In The Groove | Affinity | AFS 1007
You'll Have To Swing It(If You Can't Sing It) -> Mr.Paganini
You'll Have To Swing It(Mr.Paganini part 1+2)
Chico Freeman Group | You'll Know When You Get There | Black Saint | 120128-2
You'll Know When You Get There
Clarence Williams' Jazz Kings | Clarence Williams-The Columbia Recordings Vol.1:Dreaming The Hours Away | Frog | DGF 14
You'll Never Get Away From Me
Tony Scott Quartet | Tony Scott Plays Gypsy | Fresh Sound Records | FSR 574(Signature SS 6001)
You'll Never Know
Earl Hines | Earl Hines At Home | Delmark | 900240 AO
John Pizzarelli Group | Let There Be Love | Telarc Digital | CD 83518
Rosemary Clooney With Les Brown & His Band Of Renown | Aurex Jazz Festival '83 | Eastworld | EWJ 80268
You'll Never Know(dedicated to my Father)
Vanessa Rubin With Band | Girl Talk | Telarc Digital | CD 83480
You'll Never Walk Alone
Gene Ammons Quartet | Preachin' | Original Jazz Classics | OJCCD 792-2(P 7270)
The Jazz Giants Play Rodgers & Hammerstein:My Favorite Things | Prestige | PCD 24223-2
Grady Tate And His Quartet | Body & Soul | Milestone | MCD 9208-2
You'll Never Walk Alone-
Louis Armstrong And His All Stars | Louis Armstrong:The Great Chicago Concert 1956 | CBS | C2K 65119
Old Favorites | MCA | 1335
You'll See
Jimmy Smith-Eddie Harris Trio | All The Way | Milestone | MCD 9251-2
$$hide$$ | $$Titelverweise | |
You'll See -> Voce Vai Ver
You'll Want My Love
Louis Armstrong And His Orchestra | Young Louis Armstrong | RCA | 2115517-2
Young And Fine
Once In A Lifetime | Soul Sound | Acoustic Music Records | 319.1055.2
Young And Foolish
Bill Evans Trio | Peace Piece And Other Pieces | Milestone | M 47024
Bill Henderson With The Oscar Peterson Trio | Vocal Classics | Verve | 837937-2
Cedar Walton Quintet | As Long As There's Music | Muse | MCD 5405
Charlie Shoemake Quartet | Away From The Crowd | Discovery | DS 856 IMS
Oscar Peterson Trio With The All Star Big Band | Bursting Out/Swinging Brass | Verve | 529699-2
Tony Bennett-Bill Evans | The Tony Bennett-Bill Evans Album | Original Jazz Classics | OJC20 439-2(F 9489)
Von Freeman Quartet | Young And Foolish | Affinity | AFF 184
Young At Heart
Claude Williamson Trio | The Fabulous Claude Williamson Trio | Fresh Sound Records | FSR-CD 0051
Young Bean
Ben Webster And His Associates | Ultimate Ben Webster selected by James Carter | Verve | 557537-2
Elvin Jones Quintet | Youngblood | Enja | ENJ-7051 2
Young Blood
Gerry Mulligan Concert Jazz Band | The Complete Verve Gerry Mulligan Concert Band | Verve | 9860613
Stan Kenton And His Orchestra | Paris 1953 | Royal Jazz | RJD 504
The Young Blues Thrillers | American Folk Blues Festival Live '85 | L+R Records | CDLR 42065
Young Man
Oscar Brown Jr. And His Group | Movin' On | Rhino | 8122-73678-2
Paul Williams Orchestra | Paul Williams:The Complete Recordings Vol.2 (1949-1952) | Blue Moon | BMCD 6021
Young Man's Blues
George Winston | Linus & Lucy-The Music Of Vince Guaraldi | Windham Hill | 34 11187-2
Young Man's Fancy
Stephan Micus | To The Evening Child | ECM | 1486(513780-2)
Young Moon
Don Weller Spring Quartet | Commit No Nuisance | Affinity | AFF 44
Young Prince And Princess-
Sonny Rollins Quintet | Here's To The People | Milestone | MCD 9194-2
Young Roy
Brad Mehldau Trio | Introducing Brad Mehldau | Warner | 9362-45997-2
Young Werther
Beryl Bryden & The Blue Boys | I've Got What It Takes-A BBC Radio Celebration Of The Music Of Bessie Smith | Lake | LACD 71
Younger Than Springtime
Oscar Peterson Trio | Jazz-Club: Bass | Verve | 840037-2
Verve Jazz Masters 16:Oscar Peterson | Verve | 516320-2
Ruby Braff-Dick Hyman | Younger Than Swingtime-Music From South Pacific | Concord | CCD 4445
Your Ballad
Jeanne Lee Ensemble | Conspiracy | Earthform | 1
Your Cat
King Curtis Band | King Curtis-Blow Man Blow | Bear Family Records | BCD 15670 CI
Your Cheatin' Heart
Louis Armstrong And His All Stars With The Sy Oliver Orchestra | Ambassador Louis Armstrong Vol.18:Because Of You(1950-1953) | Ambassador | CLA 1918
Ray Charles With Orchestra | Portrait In Music | London | 6.28338 DP
Your Eyes
Eric Marienthal Group | Voices Of The Heart | GRP | GRP 95632
Dave McKenna Quartet | Piano Mover | Concord | CJ 146
Your Father's Moustache
Woody Herman And His Orchestra | The V-Disc Years 1944-45 Vol.1 | Hep | 34
Jazz Live & Rare: Wooody Herman 1945-1947 | Jazzline | ???
Your Feet's Too Big
Fats Waller And His Rhythm | The Middle Years Part 2(1938-40) | RCA | 6366552-2
Your Good Teath(II)
Etta James & The Roots Band | Burnin' Down he House | RCA | 3411633-2
Your Good Thing Is About To End
Lucky Peterson Group | Beyond Cool | Verve | 521147-2
Your Host
Dakota Staton With Her Quartet | Darling Please Save Your Love For Me | Muse | MCD 5462
Your Lady
John Coltrane Quartet | Coltrane Live At Birdland | MCA | 2292-54654-2
Rich Perry Trio | Doxy | Steeplechase | SCCD 31473
Your Little Voice
Jan Hammer Group | Melodies | Epic | 82405
Your Love Has Faded
Duke Ellington And His Orchestra | Duke 56/62 Vol.3 | CBS | 26306
Terrie Richard With The Harry Allen Quartet | I Cried For You | Master Mix | CHECD 00107
Lucky Peterson Group | Beyond Cool | Verve | 521147-2
Your Love Is So Doggone Good - (Your Love Is) So Doggone Good
Sonny Stitt Quartet | Goin' Down Slow | Prestige | PRCD 24276-2
The Three Sounds | Blue Break Beats | Blue Note | 799106-2
Your Love Is Too Much
Eubie Blake | Tricky Fingers | Traditional Line | TL 1362
Your Mind Is On Vacation
Mose Allison Trio | I Don't Worry About A Thing | Rhino | 8122-71417-2
That's Jazz Vol.19: Mose Allison | Atlantic | ATL 50249
You'r Mind's On Vacation
Mose Allison Sextet | Your Mind Is In Vacation | Atlantic | SD 1691
Your Mother's Son-In-Law

29th Street Saxophone Quartet | Your Move | Antilles | 314512524(875360)

Your Name Is Snake Anthony
Jack McDuff Quartet | The Last Goodun' | Prestige | PRCD 24274-2

Your Nose Is Open
Thierry Lang Trio | Between Smile And Tears | Plainisphare | PL 1267-108 CD

Your Picture Hanging Crooked On The Wall
Frank Wright Quintet | Your Prayer | ESP Disk | ESP 1053-2

Your Red Wagon
Count Basie And His Orchestra | Planet Jazz:Jimmy Rushing | RCA | 2165371-2
RCA Victor 80th Anniversary Vol.3:1940-1949 | RCA | 2668779-2
Jimmy Witherspoon With The Ben Webster Quintet | That's Jazz Vol.30: Jimmy Witherspoon & Ben Webster | Warner | WB 56295
Carol Grimes And Her Quintet | Alive At Ronnie Scott's | Ronnie Scott's Jazz House | JHCD 034

Your Socks Don't Match
Louis Jordan And His Tympany Five | Louis Jordan-Let The Good Times Roll: The Complete Decca Recordings 1938-1954 | Bear Family Records | BCD 15557 IH
Louis Jordan-Let The Good Times Roll: The Complete Decca Recordings 1938-1954 | Bear Family Records | BCD 15557 IH
Kenny Drew Trio | Your Soft Eyes | Soul Note | 121031-2

Your Song
Dominik Grimm-Thomas Wallisch Trio | A Brighter Day | Edition Collage | EC 510-2
Harry Happel Trio | North Sea High Lights | Timeless | SJP 156/7

Your Story
Bill Evans Trio | Bill Evans Trio:The Last Waltz | Milestone | 8MCD 4430-2
Consecration 2 | Timeless | CD SJP 332
Howard Alden Trio | Your Story-The Music Of Bill Evans | Concord | CCD 4621

Your Wonderful Love
Carol Sloane With The Benny Aronov Quartet | Cottontail | Candid | CRS 1025 IMS

You're A Bad Influence On Me
David Lahm Group | Real Jazz For The Folks Who Feel Jazz | Palo Alto | PA 8027

You're A Grand Old Flag
Benny Goodman And His Orchestra | The Original Sounds Of The Swing Era Vol. 1 | RCA | NL 89861 DP

You're A Heavenly Thing
Louis Armstrong With Sy Oliver's Choir And Orchestra | Louis Armstrong-Heavenly Music | Ambassador | CLA 1916

You're A Lucky Guy
Artie Shaw And His Orchestra | The Indispensable Artie Shaw Vol.1/2(1938-1939) | RCA | 2126413-2

You're A Memory
Lillie Delk Christian With The Louis Armstrong Quartet | Louis Armstrong And The Blues Singers 1924-1930 | Affinity | AFS 1018(6)

You're A Sweetheart
Benny Goodman Quintet | B.G. In Hi-Fi | Capitol | 792864-2
Dick Robertson And His Orchestra | The New York Session Man | Timeless | CBC 1-008

You're A Weaver Of Dreams
John Coltrane Quartet | Jazz-Club: Tenor Sax | Verve | 840031-2

You're All I Need To Get By
Stan Hope | Christmas With Houston Person And Friends | Muse | MCD 5530

You're An Old Smoothie
Ella Fitzgerald With The Marty Paich Dek-tette | Ella Fitzgerald-First Lady Of Song | Verve | 517898-2
Jack Hylton And His Orchestra | The Bands That Matter | Eclipse | ECM 2046

You're Blasé
Ahmad Jamal Trio | Live At The Alhambra | Vogue | 655002
Art Tatum | The Art Tatum Solo Masterpieces | Pablo | 2625703
Benny Goodman Trio | More Camel Caravans | Phontastic | NCD 8845/6
Buddy DeFranco Quintet | Chip Off The Old Bop | Concord | CCD 4527
Craig Handy Quartet | Split Second Timing | Arabesque Recordings | AJ 0101
Ella Fitzgerald With The Frank DeVol Orchestra | A Life In Jazz:A Musical Biography | Verve | 535119-2
Stan Getz Highlights | Verve | 847430-2
Ella Fitzgerald-Joe Pass Duo | Take Love Easy | Pablo | 2310702
Joe Pass:A Man And His Guitar | Original Jazz Classics | OJCCD 8806-2
Erroll Garner Trio | Body & Soul | CBS | 467916-2
The Erroll Garner Selection | CBS | 471624-2
Mark Murphy With The Marc Seales Trio & Background Voices | Song For The Geese | RCA | 2144865-2
Roy Eldridge With The Russell Garcia Orchestra | The Complete Verve Roy Eldridge Studio Sessions | Verve | 9861278
Sarah Vaughan With Orchestra | The Best Of Sarah Vaughan | Pablo | 2405416-2
Shirley Horn With Band | Travelin' Light | Impulse(MCA) | GRP 11382
Stan Getz Quartet | Best Of The West Coast Sessions | Verve | 537084-2
Stan Getz:East Of The Sun-The West Coast Sessions | Verve | 531935-2

You're Blasé-
Hal Russell NRG Ensemble | The Hal Russell Story | ECM | 1498
Stan Getz Quartet | The Steamer | Verve | 547771-2

You're Blasé(false start)
Otis Rush Quartet | Live In Europe | Isabel | BLE 59.921 2

You're Driving Me Crazy
Art Tatum | Art Tatum-The Complete Pablo Solo Masterpieces | Pablo | 7 PACD 4404-2
In Private | Fresh Sound Records | FSR-CD 0127
Benny Goodman And His Orchestra | Live At The International World Exhibition Brussels, 1958 | Jazz Anthology | 550172
Billie Holiday With Bobby Tucker | Compact Jazz: Billie Holiday-Live | Verve | 841434-2
Billie Holiday Story Vol.1:Jazz At The Philharmonic | Verve | 521642-2
Billie Holiday With Her Trio And Stan Getz | Lady Day-The Storyville Concerts | Jazz Door | JD 1215
Bourbon St.Jazzband Luzern | I Must Have It | Elite Special | 76347
Claude Hopkins | Soliloquy | Sackville | 3004
Concord Super Band | Concord Super Band | Concord | CJ 80
Della Reese With The Neal Hefti Orchestra | Della | RCA | 2663912-2
Don Elliott Orchestra | Don Elliott Sings | Fresh Sound Records | FSR 2049(Bethlehem BCP 15)
Ella Fitzgerald With The Lou Levy Quartet | Ella Returns To Berlin | Verve | 837758-2
Erroll Garner Trio | The Erroll Garner Selection | CBS | 471624-2
Jack Payne And His BBC Dance Orchestra | Radio Nights | Saville Records | SVL 152 IMS
Joe Turner And His Band | That's Jazz Vol.14: The Boss Of The Blues | Atlantic | ATL 50244
Joe Turner With Orchestra | The Boss Of The Blues | Atlantic | SD 8812
Lester Young And His Band | Lester Young:The Complete 1936-1951 Small Group Sessions(Studio Recordings-Master Takes),Vol.4 | Blue Moon | BMCD 1004
Louis Armstrong And His Orchestra | Lionel Hampton Story Vol.1 | Black & Blue | BLE 59.237 2
Quintet Du Hot Club De France | Django Reinhardt:Djangology | EMI Records | 780659-2
Stan Getz Quintet | Stan Getz-The Complete Roost Sessions | The Jazz Factory | JFCD 22839

You're Easy To Dance With
Carmen McRae And Her Orchestra | Can't Hide Love | Blue Note | 789540-2

You're Everything
Chick Corea's Return To Forever | Verve Jazz Masters 3:Chick Corea | Verve | 519820-2
Buddy Johnson And His Orchestra | Buddy And Ella Johnson 1953-1964 | Bear Family Records | BCD 15479 DH

You're Everything My Heart Desires
Walkin' | Official | 6008

You're Financially Disturbed
Sir Roland Hanna | Plays The Music Of Alec Wilder | EmArCy | 558839-2

You're Getting To Be A Habit With Me
Carol Sloane And Her Trio | Sweet And Slow | Concord | CCD 4564
Earl Hines Trio | Jazz In Paris:Earl Hines-Paris One Night Stand | EmArCy | 548207-2 PMS
Eddy Howard And His Orchestra | The Uncollected:Eddy Howard, Vol.2 | Hindsight | HSR 156
Henri Chaix Trio | Jive At Five | Sackville | SKCD2-2035
Scott Hamilton Sextet | In New York City | Concord | CCD 4070
Shelly Manne And His Men | Vol.1:The West Coast Sound | Original Jazz Classics | OJCCD 152-2
Steve Lane's Famour Red Hot Peppers And Pam | Easy Come-Easy Go:A Jazz Cocktail | AZURE Compact Disc | AZ-CD-14
Dave McKenna Trio | Plays The Music Of Harry Warren | Concord | CJ 174

You're Getting To Be A Habit With Me(vocal)
Cecil Gant | Cecil Gant:The Complete Recordings Vol.1 (1944) | Blue Moon | BMCD 6022

You're Gonna Hear From Me
Bill Evans Trio | The Complete Bill Evans On Verve | Verve | 527953-2
Bill Evans:The Secret Sessions | Milestone | 8MCD 4421-2
You're Gonna Hear From Me | Milestone | M 9164
Rosemary Clooney With The Woody Herman Big Band | My Buddy | Concord | CCD 4226
Terry Smith With The Tony Lee Trio | British Jazz Artists Vol. 2 | Lee Lambert | LAM 002
Bill Evans Trio | The Complete Bill Evans On Verve | Verve | 527953-2

You're Gonna Hear From Me(2)
The Complete Bill Evans On Verve | Verve | 527953-2

You're Gonna Hear From Me(3)
Freddie Hubbard Orchestra | Splash | Fantasy | F 9610

You're Gonna See A Lot Of Me
Teddy Wilson And His Orchestra | Rare And Unissued Recordings From The Golden Years,Vol.2 | Queen-Disc | 065

You're In Charge
Ed Bickert Quartet | Bye Bye Baby | Concord | CJ 232

You're In Love,Charlie Brown
Randy Brecker Quintet | In The Idiom | Denon Compact Disc | CY-1483

You're Just In Love
Sarah Vaughan And Billy Eckstine With Hal Mooney And His Orchestra | The Irving Berlin Songbook | EmArCy | 822526-1 IMS

You're Laughing At Me
Ella Fitzgerald With Paul Weston And His Orchestra | The Complete Ella Fitzgerald Song Books of Harold Arlen, Irving Berlin, Duke Ellington, George & Ira Gershwin, Jerome Kern, Johnny Mercer, Cole Porter And Rogers & Hart | Verve | 519832-2
Fats Waller And His Rhythm | The Indispensable Fats Waller Vol.5/6 | RCA | 2126416-2

You're Laughing At Me(alt.take)
Jazz Gillum Group | Harmonica And Washboard Blues | Black & Blue | BLE 59.252 2

You're Leavin' Me, Baby
Fats Waller And His Rhythm | The Indispensable Fats Waller Vol.7/8(1938-1940) | RCA | 2126417-2

You're Living Yours
Stacey Kent With The Jim Tomlison Quintet | Dreamsville | Candid | CCD 79775

You're Looking
Carmen McRae With The John Collins Quartet | You're Lookin' At Me-A Collection Of Nat King Cole Songs | Concord | CJ 235

You're Looking At Me
Herb Geller Quartet | You're Looking At Me | Fresh Sound Records | FSR-CD 5018
Wilie Smith With The Nat King Cole Quartet | The Complete After Midnight Sessions | Capitol | 748328-2

You're Lucky To Me
Charleston Chasers | The Charleston Chasers 1929-1931 | VJM | VLP 44 IMS
Ruby Braff-Dick Hyman | Ruby Braff And Dick Hyman Play Nice Tunes | Arbors Records | ARCD 19141

You're Mine You
Art Tatum | The Tatum Solo Masterpieces Vol.11 | Pablo | 2310864
Art Tatum-Buddy DeFranco Quartet | The Tatum Group Masterpieces | Pablo | 2625706
Ben Webster With The Teddy Wilson Trio | Music For Loving:Ben Webster With Strings | Verve | 527774-2
Bennie Green Quintet | Back On The Scene | Blue Note | BLP 1587
Gerald 'Gerry' Wiggins | Maybeck Recital Hall Series Volume Eight | Concord | CCD 4450
Lee Morgan Sextet | City Lights | Blue Note | 300183(1575)
Sarah Vaughan With The Quincy Jones Orchestra | You're Mine You | Fresh Sound Records | 857157-2
Stan Kenton And His Orchestra | The Romantic Approach | Creative World | ST 1017
Tatum-Carter-Bellson Trio | The Tatum Group Masterpieces | Pablo | 2625706

You're Much Too Fat(And That's That)
Sonny Boy Williamson Group | The Blues | Storyville | 4960323

You're My Baby
Count Basie And His Orchestra | Duke Ellington-Count Basie | CBS | 473753-2

You're My Blues Machine
Toots Thielemans Group | Live | Polydor | 831694-2 PMS
Teddy Wilson And His Orchestra | The Rarest 1937-42 | Everybody's | 1003

You're My Everything
Al Bowlly With Roy Fox And His Band | On The Sentimental Side | Decca | DDV 5009/10
Dave Pell Octet | Campus Hop:Jazz Goes Dancing | Fresh Sound Records | LPM 1662(RCA)
Ernestine Anderson With The Metropole Orchestra | Isn't It Romantic | Koch Jazz | 3-6906-2
Gene Harris And The Philip Morris Superband | Live At Town Hall N.Y.C. | Concord | CCD 4397
Miles Davis Quintet | Relaxin' | Prestige | PRSA 7129-6
Monty Alexander Quartet | Three Originals:Love And Sunshine/Estade/Cobilimbo | MPS | 523526-2
Peter Madsen Trio With Stanley Turrentine | Three Of A Kind Meets Mister T. | Minor Music | 801043
Urbie Green And His Orchestra | Let's Face The Music And Dance | Fresh Sound Records | NL 45906(RCA LPM 1667)
Freddie Hubbard Quintet | Hub-Tones | Blue Note | 499008-2

You're My Everything(alt.take)
Teddy Wilson | The Keystone Transcriptions 1939-1940 | Storyville | STCD 8258

You're My Favorite Memory
Teddy Wilson Sextet | The Complete Associated Transcriptions,1944 | Storyville | STCD 8236
Cleo Brown Quartet | Boogie Woogie | Official | 3010

You're My Meat
Joe Venuti And His New Yorkers | The Big Bands Of Joe Venuti Vol.2 (1930-1933) | JSP Records | 1112

You're My Thrill
Big Nick Nicholas Quintet | Big And Warm | India Navigation | IN 1061
Billie Holiday With Gordon Jenkins And His Orchestra | Billie's Love Songs | Nimbus Records | NI 2000
Lover Man | MCA | 2292-52317-1
Hal McKusick Sextet | Now's The Time(1957-58) | GRP | GRP 16512
Howard Alden-Renee Rosnes | Take Your Pick | Concord | CCD 4743
Ray Draper Sextet | Tuba Sounds | Original Jazz Classics | OJCCD 1936-2(P 7096)
Scott Hamilton Quintet | Race Point | Concord | CCD 4492
Zoot Sims Quartet | Warm Tenor | Pablo | 2310831-2

You're Nearer
Shirley Horn With Strings | Here's To Life | Verve | 511879-2
Tony Bennett-Bill Evans | Together Again | DRG | MRS 901 IMS

You're Nice To Be Around
Mal Waldron & Jim Pepper | Art Of The Duo | Tutu Records | 888106-2*

You're No Bunny Unless Some Bunny Loves You
Jesse Fuller One Man Band | Brother Lowdown | Fantasy | F 24707

You're No.1 In My Book
Cab Calloway And His Orchestra | The Cab Calloway Show | Zounds | CD 697110

You're Nobody 'Til Somebody Loves You
Les Brown & His Band Of Renown | Aurex Jazz Festival '83 | Eastworld | EWJ 80267
Pete Fountain With Orchestra | The Best Of Pete Fountain | MCA | MCD 4032
The Mills Brothers With Orchestra | The Golden Years Of The Mills Brothers | Ember | NR 5090

You're Not The Kind
Count Basie And His Orchestra | Class Of '54 | Black Lion | BLCD 760924
Sarah Vaughan With The Clifford Brown All Stars | Sarah Vaughan | Verve | 543305-2
Brownie-The Complete EmArCy Recordings Of Clifford Brown | EmArCy | 838306-2
Scott Hamilton Quartet | After Hours | Concord | CCD 4755

You're On The Right Track, Baby
Red McKenzie And His Orchestra | Red McKenzie(1935-1937) | Timeless | CBC 1-019

You're Sensational-
Keith Ingham & Marty Grosz And Their Hot Cosmopolites | Going Hollywood | Stomp Off Records | CD 1323

You're So Cute
Fats Waller And His Rhythm | I'm Gonna Sit Right Down...The Early Years-Part 2(1935-1936) | Bluebird | 63 66640-2

You're So Desirable
Teddy Wilson And His Orchestra | Rare And Unissued Recordings From The Golden Years,Vol.2 | Queen-Disc | 065

You're Sweetheart-
Howard McGhee Quintet | The Bop Master | Affinity | AFF 765

You're The Cream In My Coffee
Cat Anderson And His Orchestra | Ellingtonians In Paris | Jazztime(EMI) | 251275-2
Nat King Cole Trio | Great Capitol Masters | Pathe | 1566251(Capitol)
Stephane Grappelli And His Quintet | Stephane's Tune | Naxos Jazz | 8.120570 CD

You're The One For Me
Lucky Peterson Group | Move | Verve | 537897-2

You're The Only Girl In The Next World For Me
Annie Laurie And Her Orchestra | It Hurts To Be In Love | Sing | 1155

You're The Reason
Bola Sete Quintet | Bossa Nova | Original Jazz Classics | OJC 286(F 8349)

You're The Top
Ella Fitzgerald With The Buddy Bregman Orchestra | The Complete Ella Fitzgerald Song Books of Harold Arlen, Irving Berlin, Duke Ellington, George & Ira Gershwin, Jerome Kern, Johnny Mercer, Cole Porter And Rogers & Hart | Verve | 519832-2
Louis Armstrong With The Russell Garcia Orchestra | I've Got The World On A String/Louis Under The Stars | Verve | 2304428 IMS
Verve Jazz Masters 1:Louis Armstrong | Verve | 519818-2
Rosemary Clooney And Her Band | Rosemary Clooney Sings The Music Of Cole Porter | Concord | CCD 4185
Stan Kenton And His Orchestra | Stan Kenton-Jean Turner | Creative World | ST 1046

You're The Top(alt.take)
Dixieland Jug Blowers | The Dixieland Jug Blowers | Yazoo | YAZ 1054

Yourna
Tim Sund Quartet | About Time | Laika Records | LK 93-043

Yours
Akira Tana-Rufus Reid Quintet | Yours And Mine | Concord | CCD 4440

Yours And Mine
Stan Getz Quartet | Bossas And Ballads:The Lost Sessions | Verve | 9901098
Sumi Tonooka Quartet | Taking Time | Candid | CCD 79502

Yours Is My Heart Alone
Cannonball Adderley Quintet | Wes Montgomery-The Complete Riverside Recordings | Riverside | 12 RCD 4408-2
Charlie Mariano Quartet | Deep In A Dream | Enja | ENJ-9423 2
Dave McKenna | The Key Man | Concord | CJ 261
The Rosenberg Trio | Gypsy Swing | Verve | 527806-2
Tommy Dorsey And His Orchestra | Frank Sinatra Sings The Standards | RCA | NL 89102 AP

Yours Truly
Ron Carter Quartet | Patrao | Milestone | M 9099

Yours Truly Rosa
Jose Lopretti Group | Candombe | Challenge | CHR 70013

You've Been A Good Old Wagon(Daddy But You Done Broke Down)
Dinah Washington With The Eddie Chamblee Orchestra | Dinah Sings Bessie Smith | Verve | 538635-2
Dinah Washington With The Fred Norman Orchestra | Back To The Blues | Roulette | 8543342
Marilyn Middleton Pollock With The Lake Records All-Star Jazzband |
Marilyn Middleton Pollock With The Lake Records All-Star Jazzband | Lake | LACD 35
Sippie Wallace With Jim Dapogny's Chicago Jazz Band | Sippie | Atlantic | SD 19350

You've Changed
Barney Kessel Quintet | Red Hot And Blues | Contemporary | CCD 14044-2
Billie Holiday With The Ray Ellis Orchestra | Ella,Billie,Sarah,Aretha,Mahalia | CBS | 473733-2
Buddy Montgomery | Maybeck Recital Hall Series Volume Fifteen | Concord | CCD 4494
Dexter Gordon Quintet | Dexter Gordon | Blue Note | 84502
Dexter Gordon:The Complete Blue Note Sixties Sessions | Blue Note | 834200-2
Don Lanphere Quintet Feat. Jon Pugh | From Out Of Nowhere | Hep | 2019
Eddie Harris Group | Live In Berlin | Timeless | CD SJP 289
Ella Fitzgerald With The Marty Paich Orchestra | Ella Fitzgerald-First Lady Of Song | Verve | 517898-2
Elvin Jones Jazz Machine | Going Home | Enja | ENJ-7095 2
Francine Griffin With Band | Francine Griffin:The Song Bird | Delmark | DE 512
Grooveyard Meets Houston Person | Basic Instinct | Organic Music | ORGM 9701
Hamiet Bluiett Quartet | Ballads & Blues:Live At The Village Vanguard | Soul Note | 121288-2
Larry Vuckovich Sextet | City Sounds,Village Voices | Palo Alto | PA 8012
Lew Tabackin Trio | Black & Tan Fantasy | JAM | 5005 IMS
Meredith d'Ambrosia Group | Shadowland | Sunnyside | SSC 1060 D
Nathan Davis Quintet | London By Night | DIW | DIW 813 CD
The Riverside Reunion Band | Hi-Fly | Milestone | MCD 9228-2
Willis Jackson Sextet | The Gator Horn | Muse | MR 5146
Orange Kellin Trio | The Orange Kellin Trio | Big Easy Records | BIG CD-004

You've Got A Friend
Ella Fitzgerald And The Tommy Flanagan Trio With The Basie Orchestra | Jazz At The Santa Monica Civic '72 | Pablo | 2625701-2
Night Ark | Moments | RCA | PD 83028(874049)
Singers Unlimited | Four Of Us | MPS | 68106
The Fabulous New Jimmy Dorsey Orchestra | Dorsey Then And Now | Atlantic | 81801-1 TIS

You've Got A Friend In Me
Stephane Grappelli Quartet | Jazz In Paris:Stephane Grappelli Plays Cole Porter | EmArCy | 014061-2
You've Got It Bad Girl
Toots Thielemans With Orchestra | Old Friend | Polydor | 2925029 IMS
Bert Ambrose And His Orchestra | The Bands That Matter | Eclipse | ECM 2044
You've Got Possibilities
Blossom Dearie Quartet | My Gentleman Friend | Verve | 519905-2
You've Got Something I Want
Bobby Short And His Orchestra | Celebrating 30 Years At The Cafe Carlyle | Telarc Digital | CD 83428
You've Got To Be Modernistic
Jimmy Johnson And His Orchestra | Thumpin' & Bumpin'-New York Vol.2 | Frog | DGF 11
You've Got To Hurt Before You Heal
Nina Simone With Horace Ott's Orchestra | In Concert/I Put A Spell On You | Mercury | 846543-2
You've Got To Learn
Nina Simone With Orchestra | Nina Simone-The 60s Vol.1: Ne Me Quitte Pas | Mercury | 838543-2 PMS
You've Left Me
Junior Mance Quartet | That Lovin' Feelin' | Milestone | MCD 47097-2
You've Lost That Lovin' Feelin'
Ben Pollack And His Park Central Orchestra | Ben Pollack Vol.3 | Jazz Oracle | BDW 8017
You've Never Been There
Mark Murphy And His Sextet | Bop For Kerouac | Muse | MCD 5253
You've Really Got A Hold On Me
John Lee Hooker Group | Everybody Rockin' | Charly | CRB 1014
Yo-Yo
Das Dritte Ohr | Black & White Blues-The Little Red Rooster | Chess | 2292-44598-1
Ypsilon
Larry Ridley & The Jazz Legacy Ensemble | Live At Rutgers University | Strata East Records | 660.51.020
Yr
Nick Brignola Quintet | Like Old Times | Reservoir | RSR CD 133
Ysabel's Table Dance
Charles Mingus Orchestra | New Tijuana Moods | Bluebird | ND 85644
Ysabel's Table Dance(alt.take)
New Tijuana Moods | Bluebird | ND 85644
Ysabel's Table Dance(alt.take-2)
The Fraterman | Spielerlaubnis | Aho-Recording | CD 1014
YTNOP Blues
Bill Frisell Band | Is That You? | Nonesuch | 7559-60956-2
Yuba City
Wayne Horvitz Group | Miracle Mile | Nonesuch | 7559-79278-2
Yucan 2
Sun Ra And His Astro-Infinity Arkestra | Atlantis | Evidence | ECD 22067-2
Yukio-Khalifa
Stephan Micus | To The Evening Child | ECM | 1486(513780-2)
Yuko's Eyes
Andreas Heuser | Unknown Places | Acoustic Music Records | 319.1191.2
Yum
George Young Quartet | Burgundy | Paddle Wheel | K 28P 6449
Yunjanna
Thilo Wolf Big Band | I Got Rhythm | MDL-Jazz | CD 1911(CD 050)
Yuppieville Rodeo
Erik Truffaz Quartet | The Dawn | Blue Note | 493916-2
Yuri's Choice
Donald Byrd Sextet | First Flight | Delmark | DE 407
Yusef
Yusef Lateef Quintet | Live at Pep's Vol.2 | Impulse(MCA) | 547961-2
Yusef's Mood
Yusef Lateef Sextet | Morning-The Savoy Sessions | Savoy | SJL 2205 (801181)
Yussufs Traum
Paul Dresher-Ned Rothenberg Group | Opposites Attract | New World Records | 80411-2
Yuyo
Michel Philip Mossman Sextet | Mama Soho | TCB Records | TCB 98102
Yvette
Cecil Brooks III And The CB3 Band | For Those Who Love To Groove | Savant Records | SCD 2023
Stan Getz Quintet | Stan Getz-The Complete Roost Sessions | EMI Records | 859622-2
Chamber Music | Fresh Sound Records | FSR-CD 78(882177)
Zacinto
Eric St-Laurent-Thomy Jordi-Thomas Alkier feat. Helge Schneider | Rock,Jazz & Music:Laut! | BIT | 11212
Zagreb
Frank Rehak Sextet | Jazzville Vol.2 | Fresh Sound Records | FSR 601(Dawn DLP 1107)
Zag-Zig
Michel Portal-Martial Solal | Fast Mood | RCA | 2169310-2
Ekkehard Jost Quintet | Some Other Tapes | Fish Music | FM 009/10 CD
Zahara De Los Atunes
Ryuichi Sakamoto-Kazumi Watanabe Groups | Tokyo Joe | Denon Compact Disc | DC-8586
Zakatak
Joseph Bowie-Oliver Lake | Joseph Bowie-Oliver Lake | Sackville | 2010
Zakir
Zakir Hussain Group | Making Music | ECM | 1349
Dudu Pukwana & Spear | In The Townships | Caroline | C 1504
Zal
Conrad Herwig Quartet | New York Hardball | Ken Music | 660.56.002
Zambujeira Do Mar
John McLaughlin Group | Belo Horizonte | Warner | 99185
Zampona
Buddy Collette Quintet | Man Of Many Parts | Original Jazz Classics | OJCCD 239-2(C 3522)
Zana
Pork Pie | The Door Is Open | MPS | 68038
Zanshin
David Murray-Dave Burrell | Windward Passages | Black Saint | 120165-2
Zanza
Ronaldo Folegatti Groups | Sound Of Watercolors | AH Records | AH 403001-11
Zanzibar
Joe Beck Quartet | The Journey | dmp Digital Music Productions | CD 481
Zap Zap Zap(für Mutter)
Eddie Jefferson And His Band | Godfather Of Vocalese | Muse | MCD 6013
Zapata
Larry Coryell | Solo's Duo's And Trio's | Keytone | KYT 718
Zapevala Sojka Ptica
Tabasco | Live Music | Jazz Classics | AU 11160
Zapp
Frank Paul Schubert Quartet | Der Verkauf Geht Weiter | Jazz Haus Musik | JHM 0114 CD
Zappenduster
Elliott Sharp + Guitarists | 'Dyners Club | Intakt Records | CD 036
Zapzarap
Eddie Higgins Quintet | The Swingin'est | Vee Jay Recordings | VJ 015
Zara's Song
Elmo Hope-Frank Foster Quintet | Hope Meets Foster | Original Jazz Classics | OJCCD 1703-2(P 7021)
'Zat You,Zanta Claus?
Mark Shane's X-Mas Allstars | What Would Santa Say? | Nagel-Heyer | CD 055
Bert Saeger Jazz Quintet | Live At The Yardbird Suite | L+R Records | CDLR 45023
Zatopek
Nana | Schwarze Nana | Jazz Haus Musik | JHM 23
Zaubertrick
Paul Giger Trio | Alpstein | ECM | 1426(847940-2)
Zäuerli
Alpstein | ECM | 1426(847940-2)
Zäuerli(II)
Alpstein | ECM | 1426(847940-2)
Zäuerli(III)
Peter Giger's Family Of Percussion & Friends And Gripo Timbila Eduardo Durao | Mozambique Meets Europe | B&W Present | BW 031
Zawose
Cab Calloway And His Cotton Club Orchestra | Cab Calloway & Co | RCA | ND 89560
Zaz Zuh Zaz
Eddie Condon All Stars | Eddie Condon Town Hall Concerts Vol.1 | Jazzology | JCECD-1001
Za-Zen(Meditation)
Andre Jaume Music Pour 8 | L'Oc | Hat Art | CD 6058
Ze Kol Ma Sheyesh
Jasper Van't Hof | Axioma | JA & RO | JARO 4250-2
Zeal
John Zorn Group | Masada One | DIW | DIW 888 CD
Zebu
Pucho & His Latin Soul Brothers | Rip A Dip | Milestone | MCD 9247-2
Zebula
Didier Lockwood Group | Live In Montreux | MPS | 821284-1
Zee Zee
Gil Evans Orchestra | Svengali | ACT | 9207-2
Zeilen Der Zärtlichkeit
Clemens Maria Peters/Reinhold Bauer | Guitar Moments | Take Twelve On CD | TT 006-2
Zeitlupenländler
John Zorn Group | Masada One | DIW | DIW 888 CD
Zelao
Gato Barbieri Sextet | Gato Barbieri:The Complete Flying Dutchman Recordings 1969-1973 | RCA | 2154555-2
Zelim
John Zorn Group | Masada Seven | DIW | DIW 915 CD
Zendances 4 Too(I,II,III,IV,VI,VII)
Peter A. Schmid Duos | Duets,Dialogues & Duels | Creative Works Records | CW CD 1034
Zendances:
Doug Sides Ensemble | Sumblo | Laika Records | 35100882
Zenith
Stephane Metraux/Bernard Ogay | Oxymore | Plainisphare | PAV 803
Zeno's Dream
Lee-Askill-Atherton | Shoalhaven Rise | Black Sun Music | 15019-2
Zep Di
Diederik Wissels Trio | Tender Is The Night | Jazz Pure Collection | AU 31616 CD
Zephyr
Mitch Watkins Group | Strings With Wings | TipToe | TIP-888814 2
John McNeil Quintet | Clean Sweep | Steeplechase | SCS 1154
Zerenade
J.F. Jenny Clark/Joachim Kühn | Unison | CMP Records | CMP CD 32
Zerkall Bleu
Art Ensemble Of Chicago | Complete Live In Japan-April 22, 1984 Tokyo | DIW | DIW 815/16 CD
Zero
Brunies Brothers Dixieland Jazz Band | Brunies Brothers | American Music | AMCD-77
Zero Tolerance
Pat Metheny | Zero Tolerance For Silence | Geffen Records | GED 24626
Zero Tolerance For Silence(part 1-5)
Art Ensemble Of Chicago | Tribute To Lester | ECM | 1808(017066-2)
Zero-Alternate Line
Horst Jankowski Quartet | Jankowskinetik | MPS | 9808189
Zerocasion
Alfred 23 Harth-Bob Degen Duo | Melchior | Biber Records | BI 6240
Zhivago
Hans Koller Trio | Relax With My Horns | MPS | 9813445
Ziag Hin
La Vienta | Forgotten Romance | Telarc Digital | CD 83380
Zig Billion
George Russell Sextet | The Outer View | Original Jazz Classics | OJCCD 616-2(RLP 9440)
Zig Zag
John Zorn Group | Spy Vs. Spy-The Music Of Ornette Coleman | Nonesuch | 7559-60844-2
Julian Dash And His Orchestra | Eddie Chamblee/Julian Dash/Joe Thomas:The Complete Recordings 1951-1955 | Blue Moon | BMCD 1052
Tab Smith Sextet | Top 'N' Bottom | Delmark | DE 499
Zigaboogaloo
Friedeman Graef-Achim Goettert | Saxoridoo | FMP | OWN-90010
Zigeuner
John Towner Quartet | The John Towner Touch | Fresh Sound Records | KL 1055(Kapp)
Zigeuner Romanze (e-moll)
Karol Adam Ensemble | Gipsy Fascination | G&J Records | GJ 2001
Zigeuner Tanz
Meyer-Fleck-Marshall | Unconnon Ritual | CBS | SK 62891
Zikr(Remembrance Of Allah)
Mahmoud Turkmani | Fayka | Enja | ENJ-9447 2
Zikra
Jon Lloyd Quartet | Four And Five | HatOLOGY | 537
Zimbabwe
Larry Coryell Quintet | The Coryells | Chesky | JD 192
Zimbabwe(part 1&2)
Jacques Stotzem | Connections | Acoustic Music Records | 319.1194.2
Zing! Went The Strings Of My Heart
Chet Baker Quartet | Chet Baker Quartet Live Vol.3: May Old Flame | Pacific Jazz | 531573-2
Donald Byrd Quintet | Young Byrd | Milestone | M 47044
Red Norvo Trio | Move! | Savoy | SV 0168(MG 12088)
Susannah McCorkle With The Frank Wess Quintet | I'll Take Romance | Concord | CCD 4491
Zip
Greg Marvin Quintet | Workout! | Criss Cross | Criss 1037 (835629)
Zip-A-Dee-Doo-Dah
Singers Unlimited With The Roger Kellaway Cello Quartet | Compact Disc:The Singers Unlimited | MPS | 831373-2 PMS
John Zorn Group | Massada Tree | DIW | DIW 890 CD
Zipor
Sweetman With His South Side Groove Kings | Austin Backalley Blue | Mapleshade | 02752
Ziriab
Peter Rühmkorf Mit Dem Michael Naura Trio | Kein Apolloprogramm Für Lyrik | ECM | 801 SP
Znefu For Y'All
Mary Lou Williams Orchestra | Masters Of The Modern Piano | Verve | 2-2514 IMS
Zoe
Lee Konitz With The Ed Partyka Jazz Orchestra | Dreams And Realities | Laika Records | 35101642
Ralph Towner | Solo Concert | ECM | 1173(827268-2)
Zoetrope
Vienna Art Choir | Five Old Songs | Moers Music | 02036 CD
Zoltan
Tone Jansa Quartet feat. Woody Shaw | Dr. Chi | Timeless | CD SJP 241
Zone
Walt Weiskopf Nonet | Siren | Criss Cross | Criss 1187
Zone I
Allan Holdsworth Group | The Name Of A Woman | Cream Records | JMS 18733-2
Zone II
The Name Of A Woman | Cream Records | JMS 18733-2
Zone III
Sal Salvador Sextet | Starfingers | Bee Hive | BH 7002
Zonish
Tony Scott-Bill Evans Quintet | A Day In New York | Fresh Sound Records | FSR-CD 0160(2)
Zonky
Fats Waller | Piano Solos | RCA | ND 89741
Mary Lou Williams Orchestra | The Black Swing Tradition | Savoy | SJL 2246 (801854)
Zoo 23:28
Rusty Bryant Quintet | Rusty Bryant Returns | Original Jazz Classics | OJCCD 331-2(P 7626)
Zoo Boogaloo
Synopsis | UDU | Chaos | CACD 8030-3
Zoology
Tom McKinley/Ed Schuller Group | Life Cycle | GM Recordings | GM 3001(807786)
Zoom
Jean-Pierre Catoul Quintet | Modern Gardens | B.Sharp Records | CDS 076
Zooming On A Corner On The Mandelbrot Set
Count Basie And Friends | Basie And Friends | Pablo | 2310925
Zoot
Javon Jackson Sextet | A Look Within | Blue Note | 836490-2
Zoot Suite
Jack DeJohnette's Special Edition | Album Album | ECM | 1280
Joe Zawinul And The Austrian All Stars | His Majesty Swinging Nephews 1954-1957 | RST-Records | 91549-2
Zoot Swings The Blues(take 1)
Zoot Sims Quartet | Zootcase | Prestige | P 24061
Zoot Swings The Blues(take 2)
John Pizzarelli Sextet | My Blue Heaven | Chesky | JD 38
Zootcase
Paul Bley Trio | Charles Mingus-The Complete Debut Recordings | Debut | 12 DCD 4402-2
Zoot Sims Quintet | Zoot Sims:The Complete 1944-1954 Small Group Sessions(Master Takes),Vol.3 | Blue Moon | BMCD 1040
Lutz Wichert Trio | Ambiguous | Edition Musikat | EDM 068
Zootphone Dance
Eddie Higgins Quartet | Zoot's Hyms | Sunnyside | SSC 1064 D
Zores Mores
Flor De Tango | Armenonville | Minor Music | 801097
Zorro Gris
Christian Bleiming & His Boogie Boys | Jivin' Time | Acoustic Music Records | AMC 1010
Zortzico(Albinez)
Duke Robillard Group | Swing | Demon Records | Fiend CD 191
Zovirax
Claude Hopkins And His Orchestra | Big Bands Uptown 1931-40 | MCA | 1323
Zu Allein
Ulli Bögershausen-Reinhold Westerheide | Pictures | Laika Records | LK 35100932
Thilo Wolf Big Band | Sternstunden Des Swing | MDL-Jazz | CD 27768
Zu Doof
Claus Stötter's Nevertheless | Die Entdeckung Der Banane | Jazz 'n' Arts Records | JNA 1403
Zu Guter Letzt
JazzHorchEster | ...Zudem Wird Auch Jazz Komponiert | Elite Special | 73412
Zug & Druck:
Theo Jörgensmann | Laterna Magica | CMP Records | CMP 19
Zugabe
Ernst-Ludwig Petrowsky Quartet | Just For Fun | FMP | 0140
Trio Friedrich-Hebert-Moreno | Surfacing | Naxos Jazz | 86060-2
Zul
Gene Harris Orchestra | In A Special Way | Blue Note | 300215(TOCJ 1625)
Zulu
Roy Brooks-Randy Weston | Duet In Detroit | Enja | ENJ-7067 2
Zulu And The Mexican
Last Exit | Last Exit | Enemy | EMCD 101(03501)
Zum
Tango Orkestret | Tango Orkestret | Stunt Records | STUCD 19303
Zum Trotz
Jan Jankeje Trio | A' Portrait Of Jan Jankeje | Jazzpoint | JP 1054 CD
Heiner Goebbels-Alfred Harth Duo | Hommage/Vier F uste FÄr Hans Eisler | FMP | SAJ 08
Zumbi
The Voodoo Gang | Return Of The Turtle-Old And New Songs From Africa | Enja | 9112-2
Zurdo
Sylvain Luc-Biréli Lagrène | Duet | Dreyfus Jazz Line | FDM 36604-2
Zurezat
Mark Turner Quartet | Dharma Days | Warner | 9362-47998-2
Zürich
Mark Turner Septet | Yam Yam | Criss Cross | Criss 1094
Zürich-Berlin
Vinko Globokar | 5, Die Sich Nicht Ertragen Können! | FMP | 1180
Zvoncekova Koleda
Fun Horns | Choral Concert(Weihnachtsoratorium/Choräle) | KlangRäume | 30090
Zweet Zurzday-
Georg Ruby Village Zone | Mackeben Revisited:The Ufa Years | Jazz Haus Musik | JHM 0121 CD
Zwei In Einer Großen Stadt
Joe Kienemann Trio | Integration | yvp music | CD 3023
Zwei Schwestern
Schmid-Hübner-Krill | Time Makes The Tune | Mons Records | MR 874825
Zweifünfeins
Ernst-Ludwig Petrowsky Quartet | Synopsis/DDR | FMP | 0240
Zweiundvierzig
Stefan Bauer Quintet | Best Of Two Worlds | Jazzline | JL 11147-2
Zwischenspiel
Peter Finger Und Gäste | InnenLeben | Acoustic Music Records | AMC 1019
Zwoncekova Koleda-
Seamus Blake Quintet | The Call | Criss Cross | Criss 1088
Zyghanigili & Zimto Cardas
Olaf Tarenskeen | Decisions | Acoustic Music Records | 319.1144.2
Zygotos
Michael Jülich | Das Befreite Schlagzeug | Moers Music | 01068
| |

Teil 2
Interpretenverzeichnis

Legende: Zeile 1: Interpret • Zeile 2: Gruppe • Zeile 3: Lied-Titel | Label | Bestellnummer

(Leon Chandler),Ndugu(dr,perc,toms) |
Jean-Luc Ponty Quintet
The Very Best Of Jean-Luc Ponty | Rhino | 8122-79862-2

(unkn. 3 tb,fl, b-cl) |
Eje Thelin Group
Ejs Thelin 1966 With Barney Wilen | Dragon | DRCD 366

100 Voices on the streets of Boston |
Heiner Goebbels Group
Shadow/Landscape With Argonauts | ECM | 1480

10-voice-choir |
Louis Armstrong With Sy Oliver's Choir And Orchestra
Jazz Collection:Louis Armstrong | Laserlight | 24366
Louis And The Good Book | Verve | 549593-2
Louis And The Good Book | Verve | 940130-0

3-Ology |
Debriano-Hart-Blythe
3-Ology | Konnex Records | KCD 5047

52nd Street All Stars |
52nd Street All Stars
Planet Jazz:Bebop | RCA | 2169650-2

A Jam Session At Victor |
A Jam Session At Victor
Planet Jazz:Fats Waller | Planet Jazz | 2152058-2
Planet Jazz:Jazz Greatest Hits | Planet Jazz | 2169648-2

A Salute To Eddie Condon |
A Salute To Eddie Condon
A Salute To Eddie Condon | Nagel-Heyer | CD 004
One Two Three | Nagel-Heyer | CD 008
The First Sampler | Nagel-Heyer | NHR SP 5

A Watts Prophet | (voice)
Don Cherry Group
Multi Kulti | A&M Records | 395323-2

A&M Symphony Orchestra |
Roger Kellaway Cello Quartet With The A&M Symphony Orchestra
Roger Kellaway Cello Quartet | A&M Records | 9861062

Aalefjaer,Knut | (drperc)
Geir Lysne Listening Ensemble
Korall | ACT | 9236-2
Aurora Borealis-Nordic Lights | ACT | 9406-2

Aaltonen,Juhani | (alto-fl,as,ts,fl,bells,voice,b-fl)
Edward Vesala Group
Nan Madol | ECM | 1077

Aaron,Lorin | (tb)
Stan Kenton And His Orchestra
Stan Kenton-The Formative Years | Decca | 589489-2

Aarons,Albert 'Al' | (tpfl-h)
Count Basie And His Orchestra
Atomic Swing | Roulette | 497871-2
Verve Jazz Masters 2:Count Basie | Verve | 519819-2
Basie Meets Bond | Capitol | 538225-2
Basie's Beatle Bag | Verve | 557455-2
Live at The Sands | Reprise | 9362-45946-2
Ella Fitzgerald With Orchestra
The Best Is Yet To Come | Original Jazz Classics | OJCCD 889-2(2312138)
Ella Fitzgerald With The Nelson Riddle Orchestra
Dream Dancing | Original Jazz Classics | OJCCD 1072-2(2310814)
Frank Sinatra With The Count Basie Orchestra
Sinatra-Basie:An Historic Musical First | Reprise | 7599-27023-2
It Might As Well Be Spring | Reprise | 7599-27027-2
Frank Wess And His Orchestra
The Long Road | Prestige | PCD 24247-2
Zoot Sims With Orchestra
Passion Flower | Original Jazz Classics | OJCCD 939-2(2312120)

Aarset,Eivind | (g,electronics,talk-boxtreatments)
Ketil Bjornstad Group
Grace | EmArCy | 013622-2
Seafarer's Song | EmArCy | 9865777
Marilyn Mazur With Ars Nova And The Copenhagen Art Ensemble
Jordsange | dacapo | DCCD 9454
Marilyn Mazur's Future Song
Small Labyrinths | ECM | 1559(533679-2)
Nils Petter Molvaer Group
Khmer | ECM | 1560(537798-2)
Solid Ether | ECM | 1722(543365-2)

Aarset,Vidar | (fr-h)
Terje Rypdal With The Borealis Ensemble
Q.E.D. | ECM | 1474

Abate,Greg | (as,ts,fl,ssbs)
Greg Abate Quintet
Dr. Jeckyll & Mr. Hyde | Candid | CCD 79715

Abato,Jimmy | (as,bs,ts,clsax)
Glenn Miller And His Orchestra
Planet Jazz:Glenn Miller | Planet Jazz | 2152056-2
The Chesterfield Broadcasts Vol.1 | RCA | 2663113-2
Swing Legends | Nimbus Records | NI 2001
Sarah Vaughan With The Norman Leyden Orchestra
Sarah Vaughan:Lover Man | Dreyfus Jazz Line | FDM 36739-2
The Andrew Sisters With The Glenn Miller Orchestra
The Chesterfield Broadcasts Vol.1 | RCA | 2663113-2

Abbas,Ihab | (re)
Koch-Schütz-Studer & El Nil Troop
Heavy Cairo Trafic | Intuition Records | INT 3175-2

Abbasi,Rez | (g,el-g,tablasperc)
Rez Abbasi Group
Modern Memory | String Jazz | SJRCD 102
Out Of Body | String Jazz | SJRCD 1021

Abbuehl,Susanne | (voice)
Susanne Abbuehl Group
April | ECM | 1766(013999-2)

Abbühl,Martin | (v)
Asita Hamidi & Arcobaleno
Mosaic | Laika Records | 8695067

Abdenour,Djemai | (algerian-bjmandola)
Nguyen Le Group
Maghreb And Friends | ACT | 9261-2

Abderson,Vance | (bongo)
Pat Martino Sextet
El Hombre | Original Jazz Classics | OJCCD 195-2(P 7513)

Abdul-Khaliq,Fuasi | (asts)
Dook Joint
Who's Been Talkin'... | Organic Music | ORGM 9728

Abdul-Malik,Ahmed | (boud)
Ahmed Abdullah Sextet
Jazz Sounds Of Africa | Prestige | PRCD 24279-2
Ahmed Abdul-Malik Orchestra
Planet Jazz:Lee Morgan | Planet Jazz | 2161238-2
Jazz Sounds Of Africa | Prestige | PRCD 24279-2
Ahmed Abdul-Malik's Middle-Eastern Music
Jazz Sahara | Original Jazz Classics | OJCCD 1820-2(R 12-287)
Anthony Ortega With The Robert Zieff Orchestra
Earth Dance | Fresh Sound Records | FSR-CD 325
Art Blakey And The Afro Drum Ensemble
The African Beat | Blue Note | 522666-2
Dave Pike Quintet
Carnavals | Prestige | PCD 24248-2
Herbie Mann Group
The Best Of Herbie Mann | Atlantic | 7567-81369-2
Rhino Presents The Atlantic Jazz Gallery | Atlantic | 8122-71257-2
Herbie Mann Septet
Herbie Mann At The Village Gate | Atlantic | 7567-81350-2
Herbie Mann Sextet
Herbie Mann At The Village Gate | Atlantic | 7567-81350-2
John Coltrane Septet With Eric Dolphy
John Coltrane:The Complete 1961 Village Vanguard Recordings | Impulse(MCA) | 954322-2
The Other Village Vanguard Tapes | Impulse(MCA) | MCD 04137
John Coltrane Sextet
John Coltrane:The Complete 1961 Village Vanguard Recordings | Impulse(MCA) | 954322-2
Odetta With The Buck Clayton Sextet
Odetta And The Blues | Original Blues Classics | OBCCD 509-2(RLP 9417)
Thelonious Monk Quartet
Jazz Profile:Thelonious Monk | Blue Note | 823518-2
Thelonious Monk:85th Birthday Celebration | zyx records | FANCD 6076-2
Misterioso | Original Jazz Classics | OJC20 206-2
Thelonious In Action | Original Jazz Classics | OJCCD 103-2

Abdurrahman,Bilal | (cl,darabeka,perc,duftambourine)
Ahmed Abdullah Sextet
Jazz Sounds Of Africa | Prestige | PRCD 24279-2
Ahmed Abdul-Malik Orchestra
Planet Jazz:Lee Morgan | Planet Jazz | 2161238-2
Jazz Sounds Of Africa | Prestige | PRCD 24279-2
Ahmed Abdul-Malik's Middle-Eastern Music
Jazz Sahara | Original Jazz Classics | OJCCD 1820-2(R 12-287)

Abdur-Rahman,Kenyatte | (clave,perc,xyl,bass-drcabasa)
Cold Sweat
Cold Sweat Plays J.B. | JMT Edition | 919025-2

Abe,Chiharu | (v)
Uri Caine With The Concerto Köln
Concerto Köln | Winter&Winter | 910086-2

Abelein,Ralph | (p,el-p,orgvoc)
Ralph Abelein Group
Mr. B's Time Machine | Satin Doll Productions | SDP 1042-1 CD

Abercrombie,John | (el-g,el-mand,g-synth,g,mand)
Barre Phillips Quintet
Mountainscapes | ECM | 1076
Billy Cobham Group
The Best Of Billy Cobham | Atlantic | 7567-81558-2
Bob Brookmeyer Group With The WDR Big Band
Electricity | ACT | 9219-2
Charles Lloyd Quartet
Voice In The Night | ECM | 1674(559445-2)
Charles Lloyd Quintet
The Water Is Wide | ECM | 1734(549043-2)
Hyperion With Higgins | ECM | 1784(014000-2)
Lift Every Voice | ECM | 1832/33(018783-2)
Charles Lloyd Sextet
Lift Every Voice | ECM | 1832/33(018783-2)
Collin Walcott Group
Grazing Dreams | ECM | 1096
Collin Walcott Quartet
Cloud Dance | ECM | 1062(825469-2)
Enrico Rava Quartet
The Pilgrim And The Stars | ECM | 1063(847322-2)
The Plot | ECM | 1078
Franco Ambrosetti Quintet
Light Breeze | Enja | ENJ-9331 2
Gateway
In The Moment | ECM | 1574(529346-2)
Gato Barbieri Group
Planet Jazz:Gato Barbieri | RCA | 2165364-2
Gato Barbieri:The Best Of The Early Years | RCA | 2663523-2
Gil Evans Orchestra
PLay The Music Of Jimi Hendrix | RCA | 2663872-2
Jack DeJohnette New Directions
In Europe | ECM | 1157
Jack DeJohnette Quartet
New Directions | ECM | 1128
Jack DeJohnette-John Abercrombie Duo
Pictures | ECM | 1079
Jan Garbarek Trio
Eventyr | ECM | 1200
John Abercrombie
Characters | ECM | 1117
John Abercrombie Quartet
Night | ECM | 1272(823212-2)
Getting There | ECM | 1321(833494-2)
November | ECM | 1502(519073-2)
Cat 'N' Mouse | ECM | 1770(014001-2)
Class Trip | ECM | 1846(0381182)
John Abercrombie Sextet
Open Land | ECM | 1683(557652-2)
John Abercrombie Trio
Timeless | ECM | 1047(829114-2)
Gateway | ECM | 1061(829192-2)
Gateway 2 | ECM | 1105(847323-2)
Current Event | ECM | 1311(827770-2)
Animato | ECM | 1411
While We're Young | ECM | 1489
Speak To The Devil | ECM | 1511
Gateway | ECM | 1562(527637-2)
Tactics | ECM | 1623(533680-2)
John Abercrombie With The Ansgar Striepens Quintet
Dreams And Realities | Laika Records | 35101642
John Abercrombie-Andy LaVerne
Timeline | Steeplechase | SCCD 31538
John Abercrombie-Marc Johnson-Peter Erskine
John Abercrombie/Marc Johnson/Peter Erskine | ECM | 1390(837756-2)
John Abercrombie-Ralph Towner Duo
Sargasso Sea | ECM | 1080
Johnny 'Hammond' Smith Quartet
The Soulful Blues | Prestige | PCD 24244-2
Kenny Wheeler Ensemble
Muisc For Large & Small Ensembles | ECM | 1415/16
Kenny Wheeler Quintet
The Widow In The Window | ECM | 1417(843198-2)
Lee Konitz Quintet
Sound Of Surprise | RCA | 2169309-2
Michel Petrucciani Quartet
Michel Plays Petrucciani | Blue Note | 748679-2
Tom Harrell Quintet
Sail Away | Original Jazz Classics | OJCCD 1095-2(C- 14054-2)
Tom Harrell Sextet
Visions | Contemporary | CCD 14063-2
Sail Away | Original Jazz Classics | OJCCD 1095-2(C- 14054-2)
Uli Beckerhoff Quartet
Secret Obsession | Nabel Records:Jazz Network | CD 4647
Uli Beckerhoff Septet
Private Life | Nabel Records:Jazz Network | CD 4657

Aberg,Lennart | (alto-fl,ss,ts,as,fl,sopraninoperc)
Don Cherry Group
Dona Nostra | ECM | 1448(521727-2)
Oriental Wind
Life Road | JA & RO | JARO 4113-2
Jazzy World | JA & RO | JARO 4200-2

Abernathy,Bob | (fr-h)
Stan Getz With The Eddie Sauter Orchestra
Stan Getz Plays The Music Of Mickey One | Verve | 531232-2

Able,Milt | (b)
Jay McShann Quartet
Goin' To Kansas City | Stony Plain | SPCD 1286

Ables,Charles | (b,el-bg)
Carmen McRae With The Shirley Horn Trio
Planet Jazz:Female Jazz Vocalists | Planet Jazz | 2169656-2
The Collected Carmen McRae | RCA | 2668713-2
Shirley Horn Quartet
Light Out Of Darkness(A Tribute To Ray Charles) | Verve | 519703-2
The Main Ingredient | Verve | 529555-2
You Won't Forget Me | Verve | 847482-2
Shirley Horn Quintet
Light Out Of Darkness(A Tribute To Ray Charles) | Verve | 519703-2
The Main Ingredient | Verve | 529555-2
Shirley Horn Trio
Light Out Of Darkness(A Tribute To Ray Charles) | Verve | 519703-2
The Antonio Carlos Jobim Songbook | Verve | 525472-2
The Main Ingredient | Verve | 529555-2
You Won't Forget Me | Verve | 847482-2
Violets For Your Furs | Steeplechase | SCCD 31164
Shirley Horn Trio with Branford Marsalis
You Won't Forget Me | Verve | 847482-2
Shirley Horn Trio with Miles Davis
You Won't Forget Me | Verve | 847482-2
Shirley Horn Trio with Toots Thielemans
You Won't Forget Me | Verve | 847482-2
Shirley Horn Trio with Wynton Marsalis
You Won't Forget Me | Verve | 847482-2
Shirley Horn With Strings
Here's To Life | Verve | 511879-2
Toots Thielemans With The Shirley Horn Trio
Verve Jazz Masters Vol.59:Toots Thielemans | Verve | 535271-2

Abney,Don | (p)
Al Sears Quintet
Swing's The Thing | Original Jazz Classics | OJCCD 838-2(SV 2018)
Benny Carter And His Orchestra
Further Definitions/Additions To Further Definotions | Impulse(MCA) | 951229-2
Carmen McRae With Orchestra
Birds Of A Feather | Decca | 589515-2
Carmen McRae With The Ralph Burns Orchestra
Birds Of A Feather | Decca | 589515-2
Ella Fitzgerald With The Don Abney Trio
Ella Fitzgerald-First Lady Of Song | Verve | 517898-2
Louis Armstrong With Sy Oliver And His Orchestra
Satchmo Serenaders | Verve | 543792-2
Lucy Reed With Orchestra
This Is Lucy Reed | Original Jazz Classics | OJCCD 1943-2(F 3243)

Abou Higazi,Khaled | (doff)
Mahmoud Turkmani Group
Zakira | Enja | ENJ-9475 2

Abou-Khalil,Rabih | (bass-oud,oud,fl,glockenspiel,voice)
Glen Moore -Rabih Abou-Khalil
Nude Bass Ascending... | Intuition Records | INT 3192-2
Michael Riessler Group
Heloise | Wergo | WER 8008-2
Rabih Abou-Khalil
Il Sospiro | Enja | ENJ-9440 2
Rabih Abou-Khalil Group
Nafas | ECM | 1359(835781-2)
Al-Jadida | Enja | ENJ-6090 2
Blue Camel | Enja | ENJ-7053 2
Tarab | Enja | ENJ-7083 2
The Sultan's Picnic | Enja | ENJ-8078 2
Arabian Waltz | Enja | ENJ-9059 2
Odd Times | Enja | ENJ-9330 2
Yara | Enja | ENJ-9360 2
Bukra | Enja | ENJ-9372 2
Roots & Sprouts | Enja | ENJ-9373 2
The Cactus Of Knowledge | Enja | ENJ-9401 2
Rabih Abou-Khalil Quintet
Between Dusk And Dawn | Enja | ENJ-9771 2
Rabih Abou-Khalil Septet
Between Dusk And Dawn | Enja | ENJ-9771 2

Abraham,Phil | (tb)
Dee Dee Bridgewater With Band
Dee Dee Bridgewater Sings Kurt Weil | EmArCy | 9809601

Abramowitz,Jonathan | (cellostrings)
Earl Klugh Group With Strings
Late Night Guitar | Blue Note | 498573-2
Grover Washington Jr. Orchestra
Inside Moves | Elektra | 7559-60318-2
Nina Simone And Orchestra
Baltimore | Epic | 476906-2
Ron Carter Group
Songs For You | Milestone | MCD 47099-2

Abrams,Lee | (drcongas)
Al Haig Trio
Al Haig Trio And Sextets | Original Jazz Classics | OJCCD 1929-2(SPL 1118)
Duke Jordan Trio
The Birdlanders Vol.1 | Original Jazz Classics | OJCCD 1930-2

Abrams,Marc | (b)
Christian Elsässer Trio
Venice | Organic Music | ORGM 9727
Christian Wegscheider Trio
Live | Village | VILCD 1015-2
Claus Raible Sextet
Loopin' With Lea | Organic Music | ORGM 9724
Gerd Baumann-Alessandro Ricciarelli Quartet
Say No More | Edition Collage | EC 489-2
Johannes Enders Quintet
Quiet Fire | Enja | ENJ-9390 2

Abrams,Muhal Richard | (alto-cl,p,cello,arr,cl,el-p,gongs)
Eddie Harris Group
The Best Of Eddie Harris | Atlantic | 7567-81370-2

Abrams,Ray | (ts)
Little Jimmy Scott | Specialty | SPCD 2170-2
Coleman Hawkins And His Orchestra
Jazz:The Essential Collection Vol.3 | IN+OUT Records | 78013-2
Kenny Clarke And His 52nd Street Boys
Planet Jazz:Bebop | RCA | 2169650-2
Fats Navarro:Nostalgia | Dreyfus Jazz Line | FDM 36736-2

Abreu,Juan Carlos | (drperc)
Lazaro Ros Con Mezcla
Cantos | Intuition Records | INT 3080-2

Abril,Joan | (g)
Joan Abril Quartet
Insomnio | Fresh Sound Records | FSNT 034 CD
Joan Abril Quintet
Insomnio | Fresh Sound Records | FSNT 034 CD
Eric | Fresh Sound Records | FSNT 092 CD
Joan Abril Sextet
Eric | Fresh Sound Records | FSNT 092 CD

Absolute Ensemble |
Absolute Ensemble
African Symphony | Enja | ENJ-9410 2
Paquito D'Rivera Group With The Absolute Ensemble
Habanera | Enja | ENJ-9395 2

Academic Jazz Band |
Academic Jazz Band
7.Zelt-Musik-Festival:Jazz Events | Zounds | CD 2730001

Acea,Adrian | (p)
Coleman Hawkins With The Adrian Acea Trio
Coleman Hawkins At The Golden Circle | Dragon | DRCD 265
Acea,Johnny | (p)
Big Al Sears Band
Sear-iously | Bear Family Records | BCD 15668 AH
Grant Green Sextet
Blue Bossa | Blue Note | 795590-2
Leo Parker Sextet
True Blue | Blue Note | 534032-2
Acey,Sinclair | (tp)
Sam Rivers Orchestra
Crystals | Impulse(MCA) | 589760-2
Achhammer,Siegfried | (tp)
Helmut Zacharias mit dem Orchester Frank Folken
Ich Habe Rhythmus | Bear Family Records | BCD 15642 AH
Kurt Edelhagen All Stars
Deutsches Jazz Fesival 1954/1955 | Bear Family Records | BCD 15430
Kurt Edelhagen All Stars Und Solisten
Deutsches Jazz Fesival 1954/1955 | Bear Family Records | BCD 15430
Quartet Der Kurt Edelhagen All Stars
Deutsches Jazz Fesival 1954/1955 | Bear Family Records | BCD 15430
Acker,Werner | (el-gg)
All That Jazz & Helena Paul
All That Jazz & Helena Paul | Satin Doll Productions | SDP 1031-1 CD
Uli Gutscher Quintet
Wind Moments | Take Twelve On CD | TT 009-2
Ackermann,Gottfried | (v)
Bernd Konrad Jazz Group With Symphonie Orchestra
Wen Die Götter Lieben | Creative Works Records | CW CD 1010-1
Acosta,Jose Antonio | (keyboards,b,arrvoc)
Lazaro Ros Con Mezcla
Cantos | Intuition Records | INT 3080-2
Acoustic Alchemy |
Acoustic Alchemy
Against The Grain | GRP | GRP 97832
Acuna,Alejandro Neciosup | (bj,dr,perc,congas,cajon,cymbal)
Antonio Carlos Jobim Group
Antonio Carlos Jobim And Friends | Verve | 531556-2
Antonio Carlos Jobim With The Herbie Hancock Sextet
Antonio Carlos Jobim And Friends | Verve | 531556-2
Antonio Carlos Jobim-Gal Costa Septet
Antonio Carlos Jobim And Friends | Verve | 531556-2
Ella Fitzgerald With Orchestra
Ella Abraca Jobim | Pablo | 2630201-2
Gal Costa With The Herbie Hancock Sextet
Antonio Carlos Jobim And Friends | Verve | 531556-2
Gonzalo Rubalcaba-Herbie Hancock Quintet
Antonio Carlos Jobim And Friends | Verve | 531556-2
Herbie Hancock Quartet
Antonio Carlos Jobim And Friends | Verve | 531556-2
Joe Henderson Septet
Antonio Carlos Jobim And Friends | Verve | 531556-2
John Patitucci Group
Sketchbook | GRP | GRP 96172
Mistura Fina | GRP | GRP 98022
Jon Hendricks With The Herbie Hancock Quintet
Antonio Carlos Jobim And Friends | Verve | 531556-2
Lee Ritenour Group
Rio | GRP | GRP 95242
Shirley Horn Quintet
Antonio Carlos Jobim And Friends | Verve | 531556-2
Loving You | Verve | 537022-2
Shirley Horn Sextet
Antonio Carlos Jobim And Friends | Verve | 531556-2
Shirley Horn Trio
Loving You | Verve | 537022-2
Weather Report
Black Market | CBS | 468210-2
Heavy Weather | CBS | CK 65108
Acuna,Claudia | (voc)
Alex Norris Quintet
A New Beginning | Fresh Sound Records | FSNT 081 CD
Antonio Hart Group
Ama Tu Sonrisa | Enja | ENJ-9404 2
Adair,Andrew | (pvoc)
Andrew Adair Group
States | Fresh Sound Records | FSNT 061 CD
Donald Harrison Quartet
Free To Be | Impulse(MCA) | 951283-2
Donald Harrison Sextet
Free To Be | Impulse(MCA) | 951283-2
Adaker,Ulf | (tpfl-h)
Mingus By Five
Mingus By Five | Touché Music | TMcCD 019
Monk By Five
Monk By Five | Touché Music | TMcCD 012
Ulf Adaker Quartet
Reflections | Touché Music | TMcCD 016
Adam,Karol | (v)
Karol Adam Ensemble
Gipsy Fascination | G&J Records | GJ 2001
Adamietz,Peter | (p)
Florian Bührich Quintet
endlich Jazz...? | Jazz 4 Ever Records:Jazz Network | J4E 4764
Adamopoulos,Dahlia | (viola)
Abdullah Ibrahim Trio And A String Orchestra
African Suite | TipToe | TIP-888832 2
String Orchestra
African Suite | TipToe | TIP-888832 2
Adams,Alec | (dr)
Chas Burchell Trio/Quartet
Unsong Hero:The Undiscovered Genius Of Chas Burchell | IN+OUT Records | 7026-2
Adams,Arnold | (g)
Willie Bryant And His Orchestra
Planet Jazz:Ben Webster | RCA | 2165368-2
Adams,Arthur | (b,el-g,gvoc)
Al Jarreau With Band
We Got By | Reprise | 7599-27222-2
Bobby Hutcherson Orchestra
Deep Blue-The United States Of Mind | Blue Note | 521152-2
Jimmy Smith Quintet
Root Down | Verve | 559805-2
Jimmy Smith Sextet
Jimmy Smith:Best Of The Verve Years | Verve | 527950-2
Root Down | Verve | 559805-2
Nina Simone Trio
Verve Jazz Masters 17:Nina Simone | Verve | 518198-2
Verve Jazz Masters Vol.58:Nina Simone Sings Nina | Verve | 529867-2
Adams,Brian | (dr)
Dollar(Abdullah Ibrahim) Brand Group
African River | Enja | ENJ-6018 2
Adams,Christoph | (pkeyboards)
Joachim Ullrich Orchestra
Faces Of The Duke | Jazz Haus Musik | JHM 0045 CD
Reiner Witzel Group
Passage To The Ear | Nabel Records:Jazz Network | CD 4668
Adams,Clifford | (tbvoc)
Charles Earland Septet
Charles Earland In Concert | Prestige | PRCD 24267-2
Charles Earland Sextet
Charles Earland In Concert | Prestige | PRCD 24267-2
Adams,Dave | (dr,vibchimes)
Michael Mantler Quintet With The Balanescu Quartet
Folly Seeing All This | ECM | 1485
Adams,Dwight | (tpfl-h)
Muneer B.Fennell & The Rhythm String Band
An Encounter With Higher Forces | double moon | CHRDM 71019

Adams,George | (alto-fl,ts,b-cl,fl,ss,perc,vocsax)
Charles Mingus Orchestra
Cumbia & Jazz Fusion | Atlantic | 8122-71785-2
Charles Mingus Quintet
Changes One | Rhino | 8122-71403-2
Changes Two | Rhino | 8122-71404-2
Charles Mingus Sextet
Changes Two | Rhino | 8122-71404-2
George Adams Sextet
Soung Suggestions | ECM | 1141
Gil Evans Orchestra
There Comes A Time | RCA | 2131392-2
James Blood Ulmer Quartet
Revealing | IN+OUT Records | 7007-2
Jazz Unlimited | IN+OUT Records | 7017-2
Miles Davis With Gil Evans Orchestra, The George Gruntz Concert Jazz Band And Guests
Miles & Quincy Live At Montreux | Warner | 9362-45221-2
Adams,Greg | (tp)
Diane Schuur With Orchestra
Blues For Schuur | GRP | GRP 98632
The Best Of Diane Schuur | GRP | GRP 98882
Adams,Pepper | (bs,cameo,clsax)
Barry Harris Sextet
Bull's Eye! | Original Jazz Classics | OJCCD 1082-2(P 7600)
Blue Mitchell And His Orchestra
Blue Breaks Beats Vol.2 | Blue Note | 789907-2
A Sure Thing | Original Jazz Classics | OJCCD 837-2
Charles Mingus And His Orchestra
Charles Mingus-Passion Of A Man:The Complete Atlantic Recordings 1956-1961 | Atlantic | 8122-72871-2
The Complete Town Hall Concert | Blue Note | 828353-2
Charles Mingus Jazz Workshop
Rhino Presents The Atlantic Jazz Gallery | Atlantic | 8122-71257-2
Blues & Roots | Atlantic | 8122-75205-2
Charles Mingus Orchestra
The Very Best Of Charles Mingus | Rhino | 8122-79988-2
Charles Mingus Workshop
Charles Mingus-The Complete Debut Recordings | Debut | 12 DCD 4402-2
Chet Baker Quintet
Chet Baker Plays The Best Of Lerner And Loewe | Original Jazz Classics | OJC20 137-2
Chet Baker Septet
Chet | Original Jazz Classics | OJC20 087-2
Chet Baker Plays The Best Of Lerner And Loewe | Original Jazz Classics | OJC20 137-2
Chet Baker Sextet
Chet | Original Jazz Classics | OJC20 087-2
Donald Byrd Quintet
Free Form | Blue Note | 595961-2
Blue N' Groovy | Blue Note | 780679-2
Donald Byrd Sextet
Byrd In Hand | Blue Note | 542305-2
Duke Pearson Sextet
Dedication! | Original Jazz Classics | OJCCD 1939-2(P 7729)
Gene Ammons And His All Stars
John Coltrane-The Prestige Recordings | Prestige | 16 PCD 4405-2
Blue Gene | Original Jazz Classics | OJC20 192-2(P 7146)
The Big Sound | Original Jazz Classics | OJCCD 651-2(P 7132)
Groove Blues | Original Jazz Classics | OJCCD 723-2(PR 7201)
The Prestige Legacy Vol.2:Battles Of Saxes | Prestige | PCD 24252-2
George Benson And His Orchestra
Giblet Gravy | Verve | 543754-2
Talkin' Verve:George Benson | Verve | 553780-2
George Benson Orchestra
Verve Jazz Masters 21:George Benson | Verve | 521861-2
Talkin' Verve:George Benson | Verve | 553780-2
Grover Washington Jr. Orchestra
Jazzrock-Anthology Vol.3:Fusion | Zounds | CD 27100555
Helen Merrill With The Pepper Adams Quintet
Chasin' The Bird(Gershwin) | EmArCy | 558850-2
Herbie Mann And His Orchestra
The Best Of Herbie Mann | Atlantic | 7567-81369-2
Houston Person Sextet
Blue Odyssey | Original Jazz Classics | OJCCD 1045-2(P 7566)
Jimmy Witherspoon And His All Stars
Blues For Easy Livers | Original Blues Classics | OBCCD 585-2(PR 7475)
John Coltrane All Stars
Dakar | Original Jazz Classics | OJC20 393-2(P 7280)
John Coltrane Sextet
The Mal Waldron Memorial Album:Soul Eyes | Prestige | PRCD 11024-2
Lee Morgan Orchestra
Standards | Blue Note | 823213-2
Lee Morgan Quintet
True Blue | Blue Note | 534032-2
Oliver Nelson And His Orchestra
More Blues And The Abstract Truth | Impulse(MCA) | 951212-2
Pepper Adams Quartet
10 To 4 At The 5-Spot | Original Jazz Classics | OJCCD 031-2(RLP 265)
Pepper Adams Quintet
10 To 4 At The 5-Spot | Original Jazz Classics | OJCCD 031-2(RLP 265)
Prestige All Stars
John Coltrane-The Prestige Recordings | Prestige | 16 PCD 4405-2
Prestige Blues-Swingers
Soul Street | Original Jazz Classics | OJCCD 987-2(NJ 8293)
Quincy Jones And His Orchestra
Verve Jazz Masters Vol.59:Toots Thielemans | Verve | 535271-2
Quincy Jones Big Band
Rahsaan/The Complete Mercury Recordings Of Roland Kirk | Mercury | 846630-2
Red Garland Quintet
Red's Good Groove | Original Jazz Classics | OJCCD 1064-2(987)
Stanley Turrentine Orchestra
Rough 'N' Tumble | Blue Note | 524552-2
The Spoiler | Blue Note | 853359-2
Thad Jones-Mel Lewis Orchestra
The Groove Merchant/The Second Race | Laserlight | 24656
Thelonious Monk And His Orchestra
Thelonious Monk:85th Birthday Celebration | zyx records | FANCD 6076-2
At Town Hall | Original Jazz Classics | OJCCD 135-2
Adams,Terry | (cello,porg)
Art Pepper Quintet With Strings
Art Pepper:The Complete Galaxy Recordings | Galaxy | 16GCD 1016-2
Winter Moon | Original Jazz Classics | OJC20 677-2(GXY 5140)
Carla Bley Band
European Tour 1977 | Watt | 8
Musique Mecanique | Watt | 9
Herbie Hancock Group
Sunlight | CBS | 486570-2
Adderley Jr.,Nat | (el-p,keyboards,psynth)
Nat Adderley Group
Soul Of The Bible | Capitol | 358257-2
Adderley,Julian \'Cannonball\' | (asss)
Cannonball Adderley And His Orchestra
Verve Jazz Masters 31:Cannonball Adderley | Verve | 522651-2
Ballads | Blue Note | 537563-2
Cannonball Adderley Birthday Celebration | Fantasy | FANCD 6087-2
Cannonball Adderley And The Poll Winners
Cannonball Adderley And The Poll Winners | Capitol | 520086-2
Cannonball Adderley Duo
Cannonball Adderley Birthday Celebration | Fantasy | FANCD 6087-2
Cannonball Adderley Group
Julian 'Cannonball' Adderley | EmArCy | 830381-2

Phenix | Fantasy | FCD 79004-2
Cannonball Adderley Quartet
Takes Charge | Blue Note | 534071-2
Ballads | Blue Note | 537563-2
Cannonball & Coltrane | Verve | 559770-2
Cannonball Adderley Birthday Celebration | Fantasy | FANCD 6087-2
Know What I Mean? | Original Jazz Classics | OJC 105(R 12-433)
Cannonball Adderley Quintet
Wes Montgomery-The Complete Riverside Recordings | Riverside | 12 RCD 4408-2
The Art Of Saxophone | Laserlight | 24652
Julian Cannonball Adderlry: Salle Pleyel/Olympia | Laserlight | 36126
Somethin' Else | Blue Note | 495329-2
Them Dirty Blues | Capitol | 495447-2
Them Dirty Blues | Blue Note | 495447-2
Them Dirty Blues | Capitol | 495447-2
Them Dirty Blues | Blue Note | 495447-2
Them Dirty Blues | Capitol | 495447-2
Them Dirty Blues | Blue Note | 495447-2
Them Dirty Blues | Capitol | 495447-2
Verve Jazz Masters 31:Cannonball Adderley | Verve | 522651-2
Cannonball Adderley:Sophisticated Swing-The EmArCy Small Group Sessions | Verve | 528408-2
Jazz Workshop Revisited | Capitol | 529441-2
At The Lighthouse | Capitol | 531572-2
Kind Of Blue:Blue Note Celebrate The Music Of Miles Davis | Blue Note | 534255-2
Ballads | Blue Note | 537563-2
The Best Of Cannonball Adderley:The Capitol Years | Capitol | 795482-2
The Best Of Blue Note Vol.2 | Blue Note | 797960-2
Miles Davis:The Best Of The Capitol/Blue Note Years | Blue Note | 798287-2
Jazz Profile:Miles Davis | Blue Note | 823515-2
Mercy Mercy Mercy | Capitol | 829915-2
Ballads & Blues | Blue Note | 836633-2
Cannonball Adderley Birthday Celebration | Fantasy | FANCD 6087-2
Live In San Francisco | Original Jazz Classics | OJC20 035-2
Cannonball Adderley Quintet Plus | Original Jazz Classics | OJC20 306-2
Portrait Of Cannonball | Original Jazz Classics | OJCCD 361-2(RLP 269)
The Cannonball Adderley Quintet:Paris 1960 | Pablo | PACD 5303-2
At Newport | Pablo | PACD 5315-2
The Jazz Giants Play Rodgers & Hammerstein:My Favorite Things | Prestige | PCD 24223-2
Live In San Francisco | Riverside | RISA 1157-6
Cannonball Adderley Quintet In Chicago
Cannonball & Coltrane | Verve | 559770-2
Cannonball Adderley Quintet Plus
Cannonball Adderley Birthday Celebration | Fantasy | FANCD 6087-2
Cannonball Adderley Quintet Plus | Original Jazz Classics | OJC20 306-2
Cannonball Adderley Septet
Inside Straight | Original Jazz Classics | OJCCD 750-2(F 9435)
Cannonball Adderley Sextet
Julian Cannonball Adderlry: Salle Pleyel/Olympia | Laserlight | 36126
Jazz Workshop Revisited | Capitol | 529441-2
Ballads | Blue Note | 537563-2
Cannonball Adderley Birthday Celebration | Fantasy | FANCD 6087-2
Dizzy's Business-Live In Concert | Milestone | MCD 47069-2
Cannonball Adderley In New York | Original Jazz Classics | OJC20 142-2(RLP 9404)
Nippon Soul | Original Jazz Classics | OJC20 435-2(RLP 9477)
Cannonball Adderley With Sergio Mendes And The Bossa Rio Quartet
Cannonball's Bossa Nova | Blue Note | 522667-2
Cannonball Adderley With Sergio Mendes And The Bossa Rio Sextet
Cannonball's Bossa Nova | Blue Note | 522667-2
Ballads | Blue Note | 537563-2
Blue Bossa | Blue Note | 795590-2
Cannonball Adderley-Milt Jackson Quintet
To Bags...With Love:Memorial Album | Pablo | 2310967-2
Milt Jackson Birthday Celebration | Fantasy | FANCD 6079-2
Cannonball Adderley Birthday Celebration | Fantasy | FANCD 6087-2
Things Are Getting Better | Original Jazz Classics | OJC20 032-2
Cannonball Adderley-Nat Adderley Quintet
What Is This Thing Called Soul:In Europe-Live! | Original Jazz Classics | OJCCD 801-2(2308238)
Cannonball Adderley-Nat Adderley Sextet
The Best Of Cannonball Adderley:The Capitol Years | Capitol | 795482-2
Eddie Cleanhead Vinson With The Cannonball Adderley Quintet
Cannonball Adderley Birthday Celebration | Fantasy | FANCD 6087-2
Eddie 'Cleanhead' Vinson With The Cannonball Adderley Quintet | Milestone | MCD 9324-2
Gene Ammons And His All Stars
Dexter Gordon Birthday Celebration | Fantasy | FANCD 6082-2
George Shearing Quintet With Cannonball And Nat Adderley
At Newport | Pablo | PACD 5315-2
Horace Silver Sextet
The Story Of Jazz Piano | Laserlight | 24653
Jimmy Heath Orchestra
Cannonball Adderley Birthday Celebration | Fantasy | FANCD 6087-2
Joe Williams With The Cannonball Adderley Sextet
Cannonball Adderley Birthday Celebration | Fantasy | FANCD 6087-2
Kenny Dorham Septet
Cannonball Adderley Birthday Celebration | Fantasy | FANCD 6087-2
Miles Davis Quintet
Newport Jazz Festival 1958,July 3rd-6th,Vol.1:Mostly Miles | Phontastic | NCD 8813
Miles Davis Sextet
Circle In The Round | CBS | 467898-2
Kind Of Blue | CBS | 480410-2
Kind Of Blue | CBS | CK 64935
This Is Jazz:Miles Davis Plays Ballads | CBS | CK 65038
Miles Davis With Gil Evans & His Orchestra
This Is Jazz:Miles Davis Plays Ballads | CBS | CK 65038
Porgy And Bess | CBS | CK 65141
Nat Adderley And The Big Sax Section
Cannonball Adderley Birthday Celebration | Fantasy | FANCD 6087-2
That's Right | Original Jazz Classics | OJCCD 791-2(RLP 9330)
Nat Adderley Group
Soul Of The Bible | Capitol | 358257-2
Nat Adderley Quintet
Introducing Nat Adderley | Verve | 543828-2
Nat Adderley Sextet
Cannonball Adderley Birthday Celebration | Fantasy | FANCD 6087-2
In The Bag | Original Jazz Classics | OJCCD 648-2(JLP 975)
Philly Joe Jones Big Band
Cannonball Adderley Birthday Celebration | Fantasy | FANCD 6087-2
Raul De Souza Orchestra
Cannonball Adderley Birthday Celebration | Fantasy | FANCD 6087-2
Sam Jones Plus 10
Cannonball Adderley Birthday Celebration | Fantasy | FANCD 6087-2
Adderley,Julian 'Cannonball' | (narration,ss,asel-as)
Cannonball Adderley Group
Phenix | Fantasy | FCD 79004-2
Adderley,Julian 'Cannonball'[as 'Jud Brotherly'] | (as)
Oscar Peterson With The Ernie Wilkins Orchestra
Verve Jazz Masters 16:Oscar Peterson | Verve | 516320-2
Adderley,Nat | (co,voctp)
Cannonball Adderley And His Orchestra
Verve Jazz Masters 31:Cannonball Adderley | Verve | 522651-2
Cannonball Adderley Birthday Celebration | Fantasy | FANCD 6087-2
Cannonball Adderley Group
Julian 'Cannonball' Adderley | EmArCy | 830381-2
Phenix | Fantasy | FCD 79004-2

Cannonball Adderley Quintet
The Art Of Saxophone | Laserlight | 24652
Julian Cannonball Adderlry: Salle Pleyel/Olympia | Laserlight | 36126
Them Dirty Blues | Blue Note | 495447-2
Them Dirty Blues | Capitol | 495447-2
Them Dirty Blues | Blue Note | 495447-2
Them Dirty Blues | Capitol | 495447-2
Verve Jazz Masters 31:Cannonball Adderley | Verve | 522651-2
Cannonball Adderley:Sophisticated Swing-The EmArCy Small Group Sessions | Verve | 528408-2
Jazz Workshop Revisited | Capitol | 529441-2
At The Lighthouse | Capitol | 531572-2
Ballads | Blue Note | 537563-2
The Best Of Cannonball Adderley:The Capitol Years | Capitol | 795482-2
Mercy Mercy Mercy | Capitol | 829915-2
Cannonball Adderley Birthday Celebration | Fantasy | FANCD 6087-2
Live In San Francisco | Original Jazz Classics | OJC20 035-2
Cannonball Adderley Quintet Plus | Original Jazz Classics | OJC20 306-2
The Cannonball Adderley Quintet:Paris 1960 | Pablo | PACD 5303-2
At Newport | Pablo | PACD 5315-2
Live In San Francisco | Riverside | RISA 1157-6
Cannonball Adderley Quintet Plus
Cannonball Adderley Birthday Celebration | Fantasy | FANCD 6087-2
Cannonball Adderley Quintet Plus | Original Jazz Classics | OJC20 306-2
Cannonball Adderley Septet
Inside Straight | Original Jazz Classics | OJCCD 750-2(F 9435)
Cannonball Adderley Sextet
Julian Cannonball Adderlry: Salle Pleyel/Olympia | Laserlight | 36126
Jazz Workshop Revisited | Capitol | 529441-2
Ballads | Blue Note | 537563-2
Cannonball Adderley Birthday Celebration | Fantasy | FANCD 6087-2
Dizzy's Business-Live In Concert | Milestone | MCD 47069-2
Cannonball Adderley In New York | Original Jazz Classics | OJC20 142-2(RLP 9404)
Nippon Soul | Original Jazz Classics | OJC20 435-2(RLP 9477)
Cannonball Adderley-Nat Adderley Quintet
What Is This Thing Called Soul:In Europe-Live! | Original Jazz Classics | OJCCD 801-2(2308238)
Cannonball Adderley-Nat Adderley Sextet
The Best Of Cannonball Adderley:The Capitol Years | Capitol | 795482-2
Don Wilkerson Quintet
The Texas Twister | Original Jazz Classics | OJCCD 1950-2(RLP 1186)
Eddie Cleanhead Vinson With The Cannonball Adderley Quintet
Cannonball Adderley Birthday Celebration | Fantasy | FANCD 6087-2
Eddie 'Cleanhead' Vinson With The Cannonball Adderley Quintet | Milestone | MCD 9324-2
Gene Ammons And His All Stars
Dexter Gordon Birthday Celebration | Fantasy | FANCD 6082-2
Gene Ammons Septet
Goodbye | Original Jazz Classics | OJCCD 1081-2(P 100939)
George Shearing Quintet With Cannonball And Nat Adderley
At Newport | Pablo | PACD 5315-2
Horace Silver Sextet
The Story Of Jazz Piano | Laserlight | 24653
J.J.Johnson-Nat Adderley Quintet
Yokohama Concert Vol.2:Chain Reaction | Pablo | PACD 2620121-2
The J.J.Johnson Memorial Album | Prestige | PRCD 11025-2
Jan Harrington With The Nat Adderley Quintet
Remembering Dinah-A Salute To Dinah Washington | Hot Shot Records | HSR 8313-2
Jimmy Heath Orchestra
Cannonball Adderley Birthday Celebration | Fantasy | FANCD 6087-2
Lionel Hampton All Stars
Jazz In Paris:Lionel Hampton And His French New Sound Vol.1 | EmArCy | 549405-2 PMS
Jazz In Paris:Lionel Hampton And His French New Sound Vol.2 | EmArCy | 549406-2 PMS
Milt Jackson Orchestra
Big Bags | Original Jazz Classics | OJCCD 366-2(RLP 9429)
Nat Adderley And The Big Sax Section
Cannonball Adderley Birthday Celebration | Fantasy | FANCD 6087-2
That's Right | Original Jazz Classics | OJCCD 791-2(RLP 9330)
Nat Adderley Group
Soul Of The Bible | Capitol | 358257-2
Nat Adderley Quartet
Wes Montgomery-The Complete Riverside Recordings | Riverside | 12 RCD 4408-2
Cannonball Adderley:Sophisticated Swing-The EmArCy Small Group Sessions | Verve | 528408-2
Work Song | Original Jazz Classics | OJC20 363-2
Naturally! | Original Jazz Classics | OJCCD 1088-2(JLP 947)
Nat Adderley Quintet
Wes Montgomery-The Complete Riverside Recordings | Riverside | 12 RCD 4408-2
Introducing Nat Adderley | Verve | 543828-2
We Remember Cannon | IN+OUT Records | 7012-2
Jazz Unlimited | IN+OUT Records | 7017-2
Joe Henderson:The Milestone Years | Milestone | 8MCD 4413-2
The Old Country | Enja | ENJ-7027 2
Remembering Dinah-A Salute To Dinah Washington | Hot Shot Records | HSR 8313-2
Work Song | Original Jazz Classics | OJC20 363-2
A Little New York Midtown Music | Original Jazz Classics | OJCCD 1008-2(GXY 5120)
Much Brass | Original Jazz Classics | OJCCD 848-2(R 1143)
Nat Adderley Quintet(incl.The Three Sounds)
Branching Out | Original Jazz Classics | OJCCD 255-2(R 285)
Nat Adderley Septet
Don't Look Back | Steeplechase | SCCD 31059
Nat Adderley Sextet
Wes Montgomery-The Complete Riverside Recordings | Riverside | 12 RCD 4408-2
Joe Henderson:The Milestone Years | Milestone | 8MCD 4413-2
Cannonball Adderley Birthday Celebration | Fantasy | FANCD 6087-2
Work Song | Original Jazz Classics | OJC20 363-2
In The Bag | Original Jazz Classics | OJCCD 648-2(JLP 975)
Much Brass | Original Jazz Classics | OJCCD 848-2(R 1143)
Nat Adderley Trio
Wes Montgomery-The Complete Riverside Recordings | Riverside | 12 RCD 4408-2
Work Song | Original Jazz Classics | OJC20 363-2
Nat Adderley With Jim Hall And The Junior Mance Trio
Little Big Horn! | Original Jazz Classics | OJCCD 1001-2(R 9474)
Nat Adderley With Kenny Burrell And The Junior Mance Trio
Little Big Horn! | Original Jazz Classics | OJCCD 1001-2(R 9474)
Nat Adderley With The Three Sounds
Branching Out | Original Jazz Classics | OJCCD 255-2(R 285)
Paul Gonsalves Quintet
Gettin' Together | Original Jazz Classics | OJCCD 203-2
Quincy Jones Big Band
Rahsaan/The Complete Mercury Recordings Of Roland Kirk | Mercury | 846630-2
Sal Nistico Quintet
Heavyweights | Milestone | MCD 47096-2
Sam Jones Plus 10
Cannonball Adderley Birthday Celebration | Fantasy | FANCD 6087-2
Sonny Rollins Orchestra
Sonny Rollins And The Big Brass | Verve | 557545-2
Wynton Kelly Sextet
Kelly Blue | Original Jazz Classics | OJC20 033-2(RLP 1142)
Kelly Blue | Riverside | RISA 1142-6

Adderley,Nat[as 'Little Brother'] | (tp)
King Curtis Quintet
The New Scene Of King Curtis | Original Jazz Classics | OJC 198(NJ 8237)

Adderley,Nat[as 'Pat Brotherly'] | (tp)
Oscar Peterson With The Ernie Wilkins Orchestra
Verve Jazz Masters 16:Oscar Peterson | Verve | 516320-2

Addison,Bernard | (g)
Coleman Hawkins And His Orchestra
Jazz:The Essential Collection Vol.3 | IN+OUT Records | 78013-2
Coleman Hawkins And His Rhythm
Jazz:The Essential Collection Vol.3 | IN+OUT Records | 78013-2
Fletcher Henderson And His Orchestra
Jazz:The Essential Collection Vol.1 | IN+OUT Records | 78011-2
Jazz:The Essential Collection Vol.3 | IN+OUT Records | 78013-2
Louis Armstrong And His Orchestra
Jazz:The Essential Collection Vol.2 | IN+OUT Records | 78012-2
Louis Armstrong:C'est Si Bon | Dreyfus Jazz Line | FDM 36730-2
Swing Legends:Louis Armstrong | Nimbus Records | NI 2012
New Orleans Feetwarmers
Jazz:The Essential Collection Vol.1 | IN+OUT Records | 78011-2
Sidney Bechet And His New Orleans Feetwarmers
Sidney Bechet:Summertime | Dreyfus Jazz Line | FDM 36712-2

Addison,Bernard prob. | (g)
Bessie Smith With The James P.Johnson Orchestra And The Hal Johnson Choir
The Blues | Storyville | 4960323

Addy,Mustapha Tettey | (african-perc)
Chico Freeman & Franco Ambrosetti Meet Reto Weber Percussion Orchestra
Face To Face | double moon | CHRDM 71018

Aderhold,Bubi | (bs,reedsts)
Helmut Zacharias mit dem Orchester Frank Folken
Ich Habe Rhythmus | Bear Family Records | BCD 15642 AH
Kurt Edelhagen All Stars
Deutsches Jazz Fesival 1954/1955 | Bear Family Records | BCD 15430
Kurt Edelhagen All Stars Und Solisten
Deutsches Jazz Fesival 1954/1955 | Bear Family Records | BCD 15430
Quartet Der Kurt Edelhagen All Stars
Deutsches Jazz Fesival 1954/1955 | Bear Family Records | BCD 15430
Stan Getz With The Kurt Edelhagen Orchestra
Stan Getz In Europe | Laserlight | 24657

Adilifu,Kamau | (tpfl-h)
McCoy Tyner Big Band
The Best Of McCoy Tyner Big Band | Dreyfus Jazz Line | FDM 37012-2

Adkins,Bill | (assax)
Count Basie And His Orchestra
Afrique | RCA | 2179618-2

Adler,Murray | (concertmasterv)
Charlie Haden Quartet West
Always Say Goodbye | Verve | 521501-2
Charlie Haden Quartet West With Strings
The Art Of The Song | Verve | 547403-2
Charlie Haden With String Quartet
The Art Of The Song | Verve | 547403-2

Adler,Rudolph | (ts)
Dr. Henry Levine's Barefoot Dixieland Philharmonic feat.Prof. Sidney Bechet
Planet Jazz | Planet Jazz | 2169652-2
Sidney Bechet And The Chamber Music Society Of Lower Basin Street
Sidney Bechet:Summertime | Dreyfus Jazz Line | FDM 36712-2

Adler,Stanley | (cellovoice)
Mike Westbrook Orchestra
Bar Utopia-A Big Band Cabaret | Enja | ENJ-9333 2

Adnet,Maucha | (voc)
Antonio Carlos Jobim With Orchestra
Verve Jazz Masters 13:Antonio Carlos Jobim | Verve | 516409-2
Kenny Barron Group With Trio De Paz
Canta Brazil | EmArCy | 017993-2

Adolfsson,Jürgen | (ss,assopranino)
Beng Berger Band
Bitter Funeral Beer | ECM | 1179

Adolfsson,Tommy | (sogo,tpperc)

Adriaansen,Charice | (b)
Abdullah Ibrahim Trio And A String Orchestra
African Suite | TipToe | TIP-888832 2
String Orchestra
African Suite | TipToe | TIP-888832 2

Aebi,Daniel | (dr)
Brigitte Dietrich-Joe Haider Jazz Orchestra
Consequences | JHM Records | JHM 3624
Horn Knox
The Song Is You | JHM Records | JHM 3625
Joe Haider Trio
Grandfather's Garden | JHM Records | JHM 3619
A Magyar-The Hungarian-Die Ungarische | JHM Records | JHM 3626

Aebi,Irene | (cello,v,bellsvoice)
Steve Lacy-Roswell Rudd Quartet
Monk's Dream | Verve | 543090-2

Aerts,Jos | (ddr)
Django Reinhardt With Stan Brenders Et Son Grand Orchestre
Verve Jazz Masters 38:Django Reinhardt | Verve | 516931-2

Aerts,Philippe | (b)
Philip Catherine Quartet
Summer Night | Dreyfus Jazz Line | FDM 36637-2
Philip Catherine Trio
Summer Night | Dreyfus Jazz Line | FDM 36637-2

Affif,Ron | (el-gg)
Ron Affif Quartet
The Jazz Giants Play Miles Davis:Milestones | Prestige | PCD 24225-2

Africa,Mervyn | (psynth)
Gail Thompson Orchestra
Gail Thompson's Jazz Africa | Enja | ENJ-9053 2
Jazz Africa All Nations Big Band
Jadu(Jazz Africa Down Under) | Enja | ENJ-9339 2

Agee,Jack | (reeds)
Jimmy Smith With The Oliver Nelson Orchestra
Verve Jazz Masters 29:Jimmy Smith | Verve | 521855-2
Jimmy Smith:Best Of The Verve Years | Verve | 527950-2
Jimmy Smith-Talkin' Verve | Verve | 531563-2

Agee,Stafford | (tb)
Maceo Parker With The Rebirth Brass Band
Southern Exposure | Minor Music | 801033

Agergaard,Thomas | (fl,alto-fl,ts,ssfl-h)
Copenhagen Art Ensemble
Shape To Twelve | dacapo | DCCD 9430
Angels' Share | dacapo | DCCD 9452
Marilyn Mazur With Ars Nova And The Copenhagen Art Ensemble
Jordsange | dacapo | DCCD 9454
Ok Nok...Kongo
Moonstone Journey | dacapo | DCCD 9444

Agerholm,Kenneth | (tb,african-hvoc)
Pierre Dorge's New Jungle Orchestra
Giraf | dacapo | DCCD 9440

Agerskov,Flemming | (tp,fl-hvoc-effects)
Flemming Agerskov Quintet
Face To Face | dacapo | DCCD 9445
Marilyn Mazur With Ars Nova And The Copenhagen Art Ensemble
Jordsange | dacapo | DCCD 9454
Takuan
Push | dacapo | DCCD 9457
The Crossover Ensemble
The River:Image Of Time And Life | dacapo | DCCD 9434
The Crossover Ensemble With The Zapolski Quartet
Helios Suite | dacapo | DCCD 9459

Agog |
Agog
Eat Time | Jazz Haus Musik | JHM 0072 CD

Agostini,Gloria | (harp)
Bob James And His Orchestra
Jazzrock-Anthology Vol.3:Fusion | Zounds | CD 27100555
Earl Klugh Group With Strings
Late Night Guitar | Blue Note | 498573-2
Earl Klugh-Gloria Agostine
Late Night Guitar | Blue Note | 498573-2
Helen Merrill With Orchestra
Casa Forte | EmArCy | 558848-2
Paul Desmond With Strings
Planet Jazz:Paul Desmond | Planet Jazz | 2152061-2
Desmond Blue | RCA | 2663898-2
Quincy Jones And His Orchestra
The Quintessence | Impulse(MCA) | 951222-2
Stan Getz With The Eddie Sauter Orchestra
Stan Getz Plays The Music Of Mickey One | Verve | 531232-2
Stan Getz With The Richard Evans Orchestra
What The World Needs Now-Stan Getz Plays Bacharach And David | Verve | 557450-2
Wes Montgomery With The Jimmy Jones Orchestra
Wes Montgomery-The Complete Riverside Recordings | Riverside | 12 RCD 4408-2
The Jazz Giants Play Rodgers & Hart:Blue Moon | Prestige | PCD 24205-2

Aguabella,Francisco | (congas,percconga)
Joe Henderson And His Orchestra
Joe Henderson:The Milestone Years | Milestone | 8MCD 4413-2

Agüeros,Salvador 'Rabito' | (congasbongos)
Dave Brubeck Sextet
Bravo! Brubeck! | CBS | CK 65723

Agyapon,Kweyao | (perc)
Cold Sweat
Cold Sweat Plays J.B. | JMT Edition | 919025-2

Ahern,Bob | (bg)
Stan Kenton And His Orchestra
Swing Vol.1 | Storyville | 4960343

Ahlers,Jens | (dr)
Uli Beckerhoff Group
Stay | Nabel Records:Jazz Network | CD 4636

Ahlers,Wolfgang | (tbtp)
Albert Mangelsdorff With The NDR Big Band
NDR Big Band-Bravissimo | ACT | 9232-2
Chet Baker With The NDR-Bigband
NDR Big Band-Bravissimo | ACT | 9232-2
My Favourite Songs: The Last Great Concert Vol.1 | Enja | ENJ-5097 2
The Last Concert Vol.I+II | Enja | ENJ-6074 22
Chet Baker-The Legacy Vol.1 | Enja | ENJ-9021 2
Heinz Sauer Quartet With The NDR Big Band
NDR Big Band-Bravissimo | ACT | 9232-2
Joe Pass With The NDR Big Band
Joe Pass In Hamburg | ACT | 9100-2
NDR Big Band-Bravissimo | ACT | 9232-2
NDR Big Band
NDR Big Band-Bravissimo | ACT | 9232-2
Pee Wee Ellis & NDR Bigband
What You Like | Minor Music | 801064

Ahrens,Kai | (cl)
Bernd Konrad Jazz Group With Symphonie Orchestra
Wen Die Götter Lieben | Creative Works Records | CW CD 1010-1

Ahrens,Rolf | (dr)
Helmut Zacharias Sextet
Ich Habe Rhythmus | Bear Family Records | BCD 15642 AH

Aichinger,Oskar | (p)
Oskar Aichinger Trio
Elelents Of Poetry | Between The Lines | btl 005(Efa 10175-2)

Aighetta Quartet,The |
John McLaughlin With The Aighette Quartet And Yan Marez
Time Remembered:John McLaughlin Plays Bill Evans | Verve | 519861-2

Aiken,Gus | (tp)
Louis Armstrong And His Orchestra
Louis Armstrong:Swing That Music | Laserlight | 36056
Swing Legends:Louis Armstrong | Nimbus Records | NI 2012

Ainsworth,William 'Billy' | (assax)
Tommy Dorsey And His Orchestra
Planet Jazz:Tommy Dorsey | Planet Jazz | 2159972-2

Akahoshi,Akira | (b)
Till Brönner Quartet & Deutsches Symphonieorchester Berlin
German Songs | Minor Music | 801057

Akchoté,Noel | (el-gg)
Noel Akchoté Trio
Rien | Winter&Winter | 910057-2
Noel Akchoté-Marc Ribot-Eugene Chadbourne
Lust Corner | Winter&Winter | 910019-2
Vincent Courtois Quartet
Translucide | Enja | ENJ-9380 2

Akerberg,Sture | (b)
Arne Domnerus Quartet
Sugar Fingers | Phontastic | NCD 8831
Arne Domnerus Quintet
Sugar Fingers | Phontastic | NCD 8831
Jan Lundgren Trio
Sugar Fingers | Phontastic | NCD 8831

Akerberg,Yngve | (b)
Lars Gullin Quartet
Lars Gullin 1953,Vol.2:Moden Sounds | Dragon | DRCD 234
Lars Gullin 1951/52 Vol.5:First Walk | Dragon | DRCD 380
Lars Gullin Quintet
Lars Gullin 1951/52 Vol.5:First Walk | Dragon | DRCD 380
Lars Gullin Septet
Lars Gullin 1951/52 Vol.5:First Walk | Dragon | DRCD 380
Lars Gullin Sextet
Lars Gullin 1951/52 Vol.5:First Walk | Dragon | DRCD 380

Akihary,Monica | (voc)
Boi Akih
Uwa I | Enja | ENJ-9472 2

Akili |
Akili
Maasai Mara | M.A Music | A 802-2
Akili | M.A Music | NU 730-2

Akinro,Tokunbo | (voc)
Tok Tok Tok
Love Again | Einstein Music | EM 01081
It Took So Long | Einstein Music | EM 21103
50 Ways To Leave Your Lover | Einstein Music | EM 91051

Akiyoshi,Toshiko | (p,arrp-solo)
Charles Mingus And His Orchestra
The Complete Town Hall Concert | Blue Note | 828353-2
Toshiko Akiyoshi-Lew Tabackin Big Band
Monterey Jazz Festival 1975 | Storyville | 4960213
Toshiko Mariano Quartet
Toshiko Mariano Quartet | Candid | CCD 79012

AkLaff,Pheeroan | (dr,perc,gong,voice,voc,recitation)
Craig Harris And Tailgater's Tales
Shelter | JMT Edition | 919008-2
Don Byron Quartet
Tuskegee Experiments | Nonesuch | 7559-79280-2
Don Byron Quintet
Tuskegee Experiments | Nonesuch | 7559-79280-2
Marty Ehrlich Group
The Long View | Enja | ENJ-9452 2

Al Aarons | (tp)
Ella Fitzgerald With The Count Basie Orchestra
Ella Fitzgerald-First Lady Of Song | Verve | 517898-2
Ella And Basie | Verve | 539059-2

Alaadeen,Ahmad | (ts)
Jay McShann Quintet
What A Wonderful World | Groove Note | GN 1005(180gr-Pressung)
What A Wonderful World | Groove Note | GRV 1005-2

Al-Assi,Ali | (oud)

Ute Kannenberg Quartet With Guests
Kannenberg On Purpose | Jazz Haus Musik | JHM 0109 CD

Albam,Manny | (arr,bell-tree,bs,condts)
Charlie Parker With The Neal Hefti Orchestra
Charlie Parker:The Best Of The Verve Years | Verve | 527815-2
Bird: The Complete Charlie Parker On Verve | Verve | 837141-2
Coleman Hawkins With Many Albam And His Orchestra
Planet Jazz:Coleman Hawkins | Planet Jazz | 2152055-2
Ella Fitzgerald With Sy Oliver And His Orchestra
Ella Fitzgerald:The Decca Years 1949-1954 | Decca | 050668-2
Joe Lovano Orchestra
Blue Note Plays Gershwin | Blue Note | 520808-2
Oscar Peterson With Orchestra
With Respect To Nat | Verve | 557486-2
Terry Gibbs Dream Band
Terry Gibbs Dream Band Vol.2:The Sundown Sessions | Contemporary | CCD 7652-2
The Four Brothers
Planet Jazz:Jazz Saxophone | Planet Jazz | 2169653-2
Together Again! | RCA | 2179623-2

Albany,Joe | (p,vocp-solo)
Joe Albany Trio
Portrair Of A Legend | Fresh Sound Records | FSR-CD 317
Lester Young And His Band
Jazz:The Essential Collection Vol.3 | IN+OUT Records | 78013-2
Lester Young:The Complete Aladdin Sessions | Blue Note | 832787-2
Lester Young:Blue Lester | Dreyfus Jazz Line | FDM 36729-2

Albers,Eef | (g)
Akili
Maasai Mara | M.A Music | A 802-2
Akili | M.A Music | NU 730-2
Pili-Pili
Be In Two Minds | JA & RO | JARO 4134-2
Toots Thielemans And His Orchestra
Verve Jazz Masters Vol.59:Toots Thielemans | Verve | 535271-2

Albert,Chris | (tpco)
Count Basie Big Band
Farmers Market Barbecue | Original Jazz Classics | OJCCD 732-2(2310874)

Albert,Ingrid | (viola)
HR Big Band With Marjorie Barnes And Frits Landesbergen And Strings
Swinging Christmas | hr music.de | hrmj 012-02 CD

Albert,Miss C.J. | (voc)
Roland Kirk Group
I Talk With The Spirits | Verve | 558076-2
Roland Kirk Quintet
Rahsaan/The Complete Mercury Recordings Of Roland Kirk | Mercury | 846630-2

Albert,Sam | (v)
Ella Fitzgerald With The Frank DeVol Orchestra
Get Happy! | Verve | 523321-2

Albin,Helge | (cond,fl,asld)
European Jazz Youth Orchestra
Swinging Europe 3 | dacapo | DCCD 9461

Albrecht,Marcello | (bsequencer)
booMbooM meets Uli Beckerhoff
Resurection Lounge | Laika Records | 35101512

Albrechtsen,Claus | (dr)
Chris Barber & The Ramblers
The Golden Years Of Revival Jazz,Vol.12 | Storyville | STCD 5517

Albright,Gerald | (as,synth,ts,b,arr,reedssax)
Bobby Lyle Group
The Journey | Atlantic | 7567-82138-2
Michael 'Patches' Stewart Group
Blue Patches | Hip Bop | HIBD 8016
The Quincy Jones-Sammy Nestico Orchestra
Basie & Beyond | Warner | 9362-47792-2

Albright,Tim | (tb)
Steve Coleman And Five Elements
The Sonic Language Of Myth | RCA | 2164123-2
Steve Coleman And The Council Of Balance
Genesis & The Opening Of The Way | RCA | 2152934-2

Alcántara,Victor | (p)
Victor Alcántara Trio
Stabat Mater Inspirations | Organic Music | ORGM 9716

Alcaraz,Angie | (fl)
Jack Costanzo Group
Latin Fever:The Wild Rhythms Of Jack Costanza | Capitol | 590955-2

Alcorn,Alvin | (tpvoc)
Kid Ory And His Band
The Very Best Of Dixieland Jazz | Verve | 535529-2
Kid Ory's Creole Jazz Band
This Kid's The Greatest! | Good Time Jazz | GTCD 12045-2

Alcroft,Randy | (tb)
Buddy Childers Big Band
It's What Happening Now! | Candid | CCD 79749

Aldama,Carlos | (perc)
Gonzalo Rubalcaba & Cuban Quartet
Antiguo | Blue Note | 837717-2

Aldama,Michael | (perc)

Aldazabar,Barbaro Ramos | (claves)
Steve Coleman And The Council Of Balance
Genesis & The Opening Of The Way | RCA | 2152934-2

Aldebert,Louis | (voc)
Les Double Six
Les Double Six | RCA | 2164314-2

Aldebert,Monique | (voc)

Aldegon,Jean | (as,b-cl,flsax)
Kenny Clarke 8
Americans Swinging In Paris:Kenny Clarke | EMI Records | 539652-2

Alden,Howard | (bj,el-g,gg-solo)
Allan Vaché-Jim Galloway Sextet
Raisin' The Roof:Allan Vaché Meets Jim Galloway | Nagel-Heyer | CD 054
Butch Miles And Friends
Blues Of Summer | Nagel-Heyer | NH 1011
The Second Sampler | Nagel-Heyer | NHR SP 6
Butch Miles-Howard Alden Sextet
Cookin' | Nagel-Heyer | CD 5003
David Ostwald's Gully Low Jazz Band
Blues In Your Heart | Nagel-Heyer | CD 051
Flip Phillips Quintet
Swing Is The Thing | Verve | 543477-2
Flip Phillips Septet
Swing Is The Thing | Verve | 543477-2
Flip Phillips Sextet
Swing Is The Thing | Verve | 543477-2
Flip Phillips Trio
Swing Is The Thing | Verve | 543477-2
Flip Phillips-Howard Alden
Swing Is The Thing | Verve | 543477-2
Frank Tate Quintet
Live In Belfast | Nagel-Heyer | CD 069
Harry Allen Quintet
Love Songs Live! | Nagel-Heyer | NH 1014
International Allstars
The International Allstars Play Benny Goodman:Vol.1 | Nagel-Heyer | CD 025
The Second Sampler | Nagel-Heyer | NHR SP 6
John Lewis Quartet
Evolution II | Atlantic | 7567-83313-2
Randy Sandke And The New York Allstars
The Re-Discovered Louis And Bix | Nagel-Heyer | CD 058
Randy Sandke-Howard Alden
Ellington For Lovers | Nagel-Heyer | NH 1009
Ruby Braff Trio
Ruby Braff Trio:In Concert | Storyville | 4960543
As Time Goes By... | Candid | CCD 79741
Terrie Richard Alden And The Warren Vaché Quartet
Voice With Heart | Nagel-Heyer | CD 048
Terrie Richard Alden-Howard Alden
Love | Nagel-Heyer | CD 071
The International Allstars
The International Allstars Play Benny Goodman Vol.1 | Nagel-Heyer | CD 045
The Nagel-Heyer Allstars
Uptown Lowdown:A Jazz Salute To The Big Apple | Nagel-Heyer | CD 2004
Warren Vaché-Allen Vaché Sextet
Mrs.Vaché's Boys | Nagel-Heyer | CD 050
Ellington For Lovers | Nagel-Heyer | NH 1009

Aleman,Oscar | (g)
Eddie Brunner And His Orchestra
Americans Swinging In Paris:Bill Coleman-The Elegance | EMI Records | 539662-2

Aleong,Aki | (perc)
Les McCann Orchestra
Talkin' Verve:Les McCann | Verve | 557351-2

Aless,Tony | (parr)
Charlie Parker And His Orchestra
Charlie Parker:The Best Of The Verve Years | Verve | 527815-2
The Cole Porter Songbook | Verve | 823250-2
Bird: The Complete Charlie Parker On Verve | Verve | 837141-2
Charlie Parker With Orchestra
Charlie Parker Big Band | Verve | 559835-2
Charlie Parker With Orchestra & The Dave Lambert Singers
Verve Jazz Masters 28:Charlie Parker Plays Standards | Verve | 521854-2
Charlie Parker With Strings
Charlie Parker With Strings:The Master Takes | Verve | 523984-2
Charlie Parker With The Neal Hefti Orchestra
Charlie Parker:The Best Of The Verve Years | Verve | 527815-2
Bird: The Complete Charlie Parker On Verve | Verve | 837141-2
Chubby Jackson Big Band
Gerry Mulligan Quartet feat.Chet Baker | Original Jazz Classics | OJCCD 711-2(F 8082/P 7641)
Stan Getz Quartet
Stan Getz:Imagination | Dreyfus Jazz Line | FDM 36733-2
Stan Getz Quartets | Original Jazz Classics | OJC20 121-2(P 7002)
Woody Herman And His Orchestra
The Legends Of Swing | Laserlight | 24659
Woody Herman:Four Brother | Dreyfus Jazz Line | FDM 36722-2
Woody Herman And His Woodshoppers
Woody Herman (And The Herd) At Carnegie Hall | Verve | 559833-2
Woody Herman And The Herd
Woody Herman (And The Herd) At Carnegie Hall | Verve | 559833-2

Alessi,Ralph | (tpfl-h)
Michael Cain-Ralph Alessi-Peter Epstein
Circa | ECM | 1622
Steve Coleman And Five Elements
The Sonic Language Of Myth | RCA | 2164123-2
Steve Coleman And Metrics
A Tale Of 3 Cities,The EP | Novus | 2124747-2
The Way Of The Cipher | Novus | 2131690-2
Steve Coleman And The Council Of Balance
Genesis & The Opening Of The Way | RCA | 2152934-2
The Sidewalks Of New York
Tin Pan Alley:The Sidewalks Of New York | Winter&Winter | 910038-2

Aleuda | (percvoc)
Azymuth
Jazzrock-Anthology Vol.3:Fusion | Zounds | CD 27100555

Alexander,Bob | (tb)
Benny Goodman And His Orchestra
The Legends Of Swing | Laserlight | 24659
Lena Horne With The Lennie Hayton Orchestra
Planet Jazz:Lena Horne | Planet Jazz | 2165373-2

Alexander,Charlie | (p)
Louis Armstrong And His Orchestra
Satch Plays Fats(Complete) | CBS | CK 64927

Alexander,Dan | (g)
John Lee Hooker Group
Endless Boogie | MCA | MCD 10413

Alexander,Eric | (ssts)
Eric Alexander Quartet
Solid! | Milestone | MCD 9283-2
Man With A Horn | Milestone | MCD 9293-2
The First Milestone | Milestone | MCD 9302-2
The Second Milestone | Milestone | MCD 9315-2
Summit Meeting | Milestone | MCD 9322-2
Nightlife In Tokyo | Milestone | MCD 9330-2
Eric Alexander Quintet
Solid! | Milestone | MCD 9283-2
The First Milestone | Milestone | MCD 9302-2
The Second Milestone | Milestone | MCD 9315-2
Summit Meeting | Milestone | MCD 9322-2
Eric Alexander Sextet
Man With A Horn | Milestone | MCD 9293-2
Freddy Cole With The Eric Alexander Band
Love Makes The Changes | Fantasy | FCD 9681-2
Ian Shaw With Band
Soho Stories | Milestone | MCD 9316-2
Jimmy Cobb's Mob
Cobb's Groove | Milestone | MCD 9334-2
Jimmy McGriff Quintet
McGriff's House Party | Milestone | MCD 9300-2
Jimmy McGriff Sextet
McGriff's House Party | Milestone | MCD 9300-2
Jimmy Scott With Band
But Beautiful | Milestone | MCD 9321-2
Moon Glow | Milestone | MCD 9332-2

Alexander,Honey | (flp)
Leon Thomas With Band
Leon Thomas In Berlin | RCA | 2663877-2

Alexander,Jerome | (voc)
First Revolution Singers
First Revolution Gospel Singers:A Capella | Laserlight | 24338

Alexander,Joe | (tsvoc)
Tadd Dameron And His Orchestra
Fontainebleau | Original Jazz Classics | OJCCD 055-2

Alexander,Kirkby | (as)
(Little)Jimmy Scott With The Lucky Thompson Orchestra
Everybody's Somebody's Fool | Decca | 050669-2

Alexander,Monty | (p,melodica,talk,whistle,voc,p-solo)
Dizzy Gillespie Jam
Montreux '77 | Original Jazz Classics | OJC20 381-2(2308211)
Dizzy Gillespie Sextet
The Jazz Giants Play Harold Arlen:Blues In The Night | Prestige | PCD 24201-2
Kristian Jorgensen Quartet With Monty Alexander
Meeting Monty | Stunt Records | STUCD 01212
Milt Jackson Quartet
Milt Jackson Birthday Celebration | Fantasy | FANCD 6079-2
Milt Jackson With The Monty Alexander Trio
To Bags...With Love:Memorial Album | Pablo | 2310967-2
Soul Fusion | Original Jazz Classics | OJCCD 731-2(2310804)
Milt Jackson-Ray Brown Jam
Milt Jackson Birthday Celebration | Fantasy | FANCD 6079-2
Montreux '77 | Original Jazz Classics | OJC 385(2620105)
Montreux '77 | Original Jazz Classics | OJC20 375-2(2308205)
Monty Alexander Quartet
Three Originals:Love And Sunshine/Estade/Cobilimbo | MPS | 523526-2
Monty Alexander Sextet
Three Originals:Love And Sunshine/Estade/Cobilimbo | MPS | 523526-2
Monty Alexander Trio
Montreux Alexander-Live! At The Montreux Festival | MPS | 817487-2
Quincy Jones And His Orchestra
Verve Jazz Masters Vol.59:Toots Thielemans | Verve | 535271-2
Red Rodney All Stars
A Tribute To Charlie Parker Vol.1 | Storyville | 4960483

Alexander,Mousie | (dr)
Benny Goodman And His All Star Sextet
Verve Jazz Masters 33:Benny Goodman | Verve | 844410-2
Benny Goodman Quintet
Verve Jazz Masters 33:Benny Goodman | Verve | 844410-2
Buck Clayton-Buddy Tate Quintet
Buck & Buddy | Original Jazz Classics | OJCCD 757-2(SV 2017)
Charlie Ventura Quintet
High On An Open Mike | Fresh Sound Records | FSR-CD 314
Jimmy Witherspoon With Jay McShann And His Band
Planet Jazz:Male Jazz Vocalists | Planet Jazz | 2169657-2
Johnny Smith Quartet
The Sound Of The Johnny Smith Guitar | Roulette | 531792-2
Mike Bryan Sextet
Jazz Festival Vol.2 | Storyville | 4960743
Ralph Sutton Quartet
The Ralph Sutton Quartet With Ruby Braff,Vol.2 | Storyville | STCD 8246
Zoot Sims-Jimmy Rowles Quartet
If I'm Lucky | Original Jazz Classics | OJCCD 683-2(2310803)
The Jazz Giants Play Harry Warren:Lullaby Of Broadway | Prestige | PCD 24204-2

Alexander,Roland | (fl,ss,ts,pharm)
Roland Alexander Quintet
Ronnie Mathews-Roland Alexander-Freddie Hubbard | Prestige | PRCD 24271-2
Sam Rivers Orchestra
Crystals | Impulse(MCA) | 589760-2

Alexander,Taru | (dr)
Abbey Lincoln With Her Band
Who Used To Dance | Verve | 533559-2

Alexander,Van | (ld)
Van Alexander Orchestra
Home Of Happy Feet/Swing! Staged For Sound! | Capitol | 535211-2

Alexandria,Lorez | (voc)
Lorez Alexandria With Orchestra
Misty Blue:Sweet Sisters Swing Songs Of Sorrow And Sadness | Blue Note | 521151-2
Deep Blue-The United States Of Mind | Blue Note | 521152-2

Algedon,Jean | (as)
Andre Hodeir And His Jazz Groupe De Paris
Jazz In Paris:Le Jazz Groupe De Paris Joue André Hodeir | EmArCy | 548792-2

Algoed,Karel | (b)
The Swingcats
Face To Face:The Swingcats Live | Nagel-Heyer | CD 072

Alguimia |
Alguimia
Alguimia 'U' | Fresh Sound Records | FSNT 023 CD
Alguimia:Standards | Fresh Sound Records | FSNT 049 CD
Alguimia Dos | Fresh Sound Records | FSNT 050 CD

Alguire,Danny | (cotp)
Firehouse Five Plus Two
Dixieland Favorites | Good Time Jazz | FCD 60-008
Crashes A Party | Good Time Jazz | GTCD 10038-2
Goes To A Fire | Good Time Jazz | GTCD 10052-2
Goes South | Good Time Jazz | GTCD 12018-2

Ali Khan,Ustad Fateh | (voice)
Jan Garbarek With Ustad Fateh Ali Khan & Musicians From Pakistan
Ragas And Sagas | ECM | 1442(511263-2)

Ali Khan,Ustad Nazim | (sarangi)

Ali,Amin | (el-bvoc)
James Blood Ulmer Blues Experience
Live at The Bayerischer Hof | IN+OUT Records | 7018-2

Ali,Mohammed Neseehu | (talking-drdjimbe)
Ben Waltzer Quintet
In Metropolitan Motion | Fresh Sound Records | FSNT 082 CD

Ali,Rashied | (drperc)
Alice Coltrane Quintet
Journey In Satchidananda | Impulse(MCA) | 951228-2
Alice Coltrane Sextet
Journey In Satchidananda | Impulse(MCA) | 951228-2
Alice Coltrane Trio
A Monastic Trio | Impulse(MCA) | 951267-2
John Coltrane And His Orchestra
Meditations | Impulse(MCA) | 951199-2
John Coltrane Group
The Olatunji Concert:The Last Live Recording | Impulse(MCA) | 589120-2
John Coltrane Quartet
Coltrane Spiritual | Impulse(MCA) | 589099-2
Stellar Regions | Impulse(MCA) | 951169-2
John Coltrane Quintet
Live At The Village Vanguard Again | Impulse(MCA) | 951213-2
John Coltrane-Rashied Ali Duo
Interstellar Space | Impulse(MCA) | 543415-2

Ali,Roshan | (cholek)
Remember Shakti
Saturday Night In Bombay | Verve | 014184-2

Alias,Charles | (dr)
Miles Davis Group
Bitches Brew | CBS | C2K 65774

Alias,Don | (bongos,congas,dr,conga,perc,clap-dr)
Al Jarreau With Band
Tenderness | i.e. Music | 557853-2
Barbara Dennerlein Group
Take Off | Verve | 527664-2
Junkanoo | Verve | 537122-2
Outhipped | Verve | 547503-2
Carla Bley Band
Fleur Carnivore | Watt | 21
The Very Big Carla Bley Band | Watt | 23
Carla Bley Sextet
Sextet | Watt | 17
Chick Corea And His Orchestra
My Spanish Heart | Polydor | 543303-3
Chick Corea Group
Verve Jazz Masters 3:Chick Corea | Verve | 519820-2
Herbie Hancock Group
Herbie Hancock The New Standards | Verve | 527715-2
Herbie Hancock Group With String Quartet
Herbie Hancock The New Standards | Verve | 527715-2
Herbie Hancock Group With String Quartet,Woodwinds And Brass
Herbie Hancock The New Standards | Verve | 527715-2
Herbie Hancock Group With Woodwinds And Brass
Herbie Hancock The New Standards | Verve | 527715-2
Jack DeJohnette Quartet
Oneness | ECM | 1637(537343-2)
Joe Lovano Sextet
Tenor Legacy | Blue Note | 827014-2
John McLaughlin Group
The Promise | Verve | 529828-2
John Scofield Groups
Groove Elation | Blue Note | 832801-2
John Scofield Sextet
Hand Jive | Blue Note | 827327-2
Leni Stern Group
Secrets | Enja | ENJ-5093 2
Closer To The Light | Enja | ENJ-6034 2
Marcus Miller Group
The Sun Don't Lie | Dreyfus Jazz Line | FDM 36560-2
Michael Brecker Group
Tales From The Hudson | Impulse(MCA) | 951191-2
Now You See It...(Now You Don't) | GRP | GRP 96222
Michael Brecker Quintet

Two Blocks From The Edge | Impulse(MCA) | 951261-2
Mike Stern Group
Odds Or Evens | Atlantic | 7567-82297-2
Give And Take | Atlantic | 7567-83036-2
Miles Davis Group
Amandla | Warner | 7599-25873-2
On The Corner | CBS | CK 63980
Nils Landgren Funk Unit With Guests
5000 Miles | ACT | 9271-2
Pat Metheny Group
Imaginary Day | Warner | 9362-46791-2
Peter Erskine Orchestra
Peter Erskine | Original Jazz Classics | OJC 610(C 14010)
Steve Swallow Group
Carla | Watt | XtraWatt/2
Swallow | Watt | XtraWatt/6
The Brecker Brothers
Return Of The Brecker Brothers | GRP | GRP 96842
Tony Williams Lifetime
Ego | Verve | 559512-2
Victor Lewis Sextet
Eeeyyess! | Enja | ENJ-9311 2
Wayne Krantz Duo
Signals | Enja | ENJ-6048 2
Weather Report
Black Market | CBS | 468210-2

Alibo,Michel | (bel-b)
Karim Ziad Groups
Ifrikya | ACT | 9282-2
Nguyen Le Group
Maghreb And Friends | ACT | 9261-2
Nguyen Le Trio With Guests
Purple:Celebrating Jimi Hendrix | ACT | 9410-2

Aliva,José | (p)
Conexion Latina
Mambo 2000 | Enja | ENJ-7055 2

Alkaline Jazz Trio |
Mike Turk With The Alkaline Jazz Trio
A Little Taste Of Cannonball | Organic Music | ORGM 9708

Alkier,Thomas | (dr)
Klaus König Orchestra
The Heart Project | Enja | ENJ-9338 2
Markus Stockhausen Orchestra
Sol Mestizo:Markus Stockhausen Plays The Music Of Enrique Diaz | ACT | 9222-2
NDR Big Band
NDR Big Band-Bravissimo | ACT | 9232-2
NDR Big Band With Guests
50 Years Of NDR Big Band:Bravissimo II | ACT | 9259-2

All Star Live Jam Session |
All Star Live Jam Session
Brownie-The Complete EmArCy Recordings Of Clifford Brown | EmArCy | 838306-2

All That Jazz |
All That Jazz & Helena Paul
All That Jazz & Helena Paul | Satin Doll Productions | SDP 1031-1 CD

Allaert,Philippe | (dr)
Jasper Van't Hof Group
Blue Corner | ACT | 9228-2
Philippe Caillat Group
Stream Of Time | Laika Records | LK 92-030
Pili-Pili
Pili-Pili Live 88 | JA & RO | JARO 4139-2

Allalah,Laurence | (cello)
Stephane Grappelli With The Michel Legrand Orchestra
Grapelli Story | Verve | 515807-2

Allayialis,Toni | (voc)
Vince Jones Group
Here's To The Miracles | Intuition Records | INT 3198-2

Allen,Carl | (bass-dr,dr,tambourinevoc)
Benny Green Trio
Blue Note Plays Gershwin | Blue Note | 520808-2
Dave Ellis Quartet
State Of Mind | Milestone | MCD 9328-2
Dave Ellis Quintet
State Of Mind | Milestone | MCD 9328-2
Donald Harrison Quartet
Nouveau Swing | Impulse(MCA) | 951209-2
Free To Be | Impulse(MCA) | 951283-2
Donald Harrison Quintet
Free To Be | Impulse(MCA) | 951283-2
Donald Harrison Sextet
Free To Be | Impulse(MCA) | 951283-2
Kind Of New | Candid | CCD 79768
Eddie Henderson With The Mulgrew Miller Trio
Trumpet Legacy | Milestone | MCD 9286-2
Eric Reed Trio
Pure Imagination | Impulse(MCA) | 951259-2
Freddie Hubbard Quartet
Topsy | Enja | ENJ-7025 2
Freddie Hubbard Quintet
Topsy | Enja | ENJ-7025 2
Lew Soloff With The Mulgrew Miller Trio
Trumpet Legacy | Milestone | MCD 9286-2
Nicholas Payton With The Mulgrew Miller Trio
Trumpet Legacy | Milestone | MCD 9286-2
Tom Harrell Orchestra
Time's Mirror | RCA | 2663524-2
Tom Harrell With The Mulgrew Miller Trio
Trumpet Legacy | Milestone | MCD 9286-2
Vince Jones With The Benny Green Quartet
One Day Spent | Intuition Records | INT 3087-2
Wayne Escoffery Quartet
Time Changes | Nagel-Heyer | CD 2015

Allen,Charlie | (tp)
Earl Hines And His Orchestra
Jazz:The Essential Collection Vol.2 | IN+OUT Records | 78012-2

Allen,Doug | (perc)
Jimmy Smith With The Claus Ogerman Orchestra
Any Number Can Win | Verve | 557447-2

Allen,Ed | (cotp)
Cliff Jackson's Washboard Wanderers
Uptown And Lowdown | Prestige | PCD 24262-2

Allen,Eddie E.J. | (tp,fl-h,arr,perc,voicepiccolo-tp)
Cold Sweat
Cold Sweat Plays J.B. | JMT Edition | 919025-2
Craig Harris And Tailgater's Tales
Shelter | JMT Edition | 919008-2
Blackout In The Square Root Of Soul | JMT Edition | 919015-2
Cyrus Chestnut Sextet
Earth Stories | Atlantic | 7567-82876-2
Eddie Allen Quintet
R 'N' B | Enja | ENJ-9033 2
Summer Days | Enja | ENJ-9388 2
Eddie Allen Sextet
Summer Days | Enja | ENJ-9388 2
Lester Bowie's Brass Fantasy
The Fire This Time | IN+OUT Records | 7019-2
Marty Ehrlich Group
The Long View | Enja | ENJ-9452 2
Mongo Santamaria And His Band
Brazilian Sunset | Candid | CCD 79703
Mongo Santamaria And His Orchestra
Jazzin' Vol.2: The Music Of Stevie Wonder | Fantasy | FANCD 6088-2
Rabih Abou-Khalil Group
The Cactus Of Knowledge | Enja | ENJ-9401 2

Allen,Fletcher | (as,clts)
Benny Carter And His Orchestra
Django Reinhardt All Star Sessions | Capitol | 531577-2

Americans Swinging In Paris:Benny Carter | EMI Records | 539647-2

Allen,Gene | (bar-h,b-cl,bs,cl,oboe,reedssax)
Benny Goodman And His Orchestra
The Legends Of Swing | Laserlight | 24659
George Russell And His Orchestra
George Russell New York N.Y. | Impulse(MCA) | 951278-2
Gerry Mulligan And His Orchestra
Mullenium | CBS | CK 65678
Gerry Mulligan Concert Jazz Band
Verve Jazz Masters 36:Gerry Mulligan | Verve | 523342-2
Verve Jazz Masters Vol.60:The Collection | Verve | 529866-2
Gerry Mulligan And The Concert Band At The Village Vanguard | Verve | 589488-2
The Complete Verve Gerry Mulligan Concert Band | Verve | 9860613
Rod Levitt Orchestra
The Dynamic Sound Patterns Of The Rod Levitt Orchestra | Original Jazz Classics | OJCCD 1955-2(RS 9471)
Thelonious Monk And His Orchestra
Greatest Hits | CBS | CK 65422
Woody Herman And His Orchestra
Verve Jazz Masters 54:Woody Herman | Verve | 529903-2
Woody Herman-1963 | Philips | 589490-2

Allen,Geri | (keyboards,p,el-p,synth,orgp-solo)
Bobby Hutcherson Group
Skyline | Verve | 559616-2
Charles Lloyd Quintet
Lift Every Voice | ECM | 1832/33(018783-2)
Charles Lloyd Sextet
Lift Every Voice | ECM | 1832/33(018783-2)
Charlie Haden And The Liberation Music Orchestra
The Montreal Tapes:Liberation Music Orchestra | Verve | 527469-2
Charlie Haden Trio
The Montreal Tapes | Verve | 537483-2
Courtney Pine Group
Modern Day Jazz Stories | Verve | 529028-2
Fred Wesley Group
New Friends | Minor Music | 801016
Geri Allen And The Jazzpar 1996 Nonet
Some Aspects Of Water | Storyville | STCD 4212
Geri Allen Trio
Some Aspects Of Water | Storyville | STCD 4212
Geri Allen Trio With Johny Coles
Some Aspects Of Water | Storyville | STCD 4212
Geri Allen/Charlie Haden/Paul Motian
In The Year Of The Dragon | JMT Edition | 919027-2
Geri Allen/Charlie Haden/Paul Motian & Guest
In The Year Of The Dragon | JMT Edition | 919027-2
Greg Osby Quintet
Mindgames | JMT Edition | 919021-2
Lenny White Group
Renderers Of Spirit | Hip Bop | HIBD 8014
Paul Motian Quartet
Monk In Motian | JMT Edition | 919020-2
Steve Coleman And Five Elements
On The Edge Of Tomorrow | JMT Edition | 919005-2
Steve Coleman Group
Motherland Pulse | JMT Edition | 919001-2
Woody Shaw Quartet
Bemsha Swing | Blue Note | 829029-2

Allen,Harry | (ts)
Allan Vaché-Harry Allen Quintet
Allan And Allan | Nagel-Heyer | CD 074
Butch Miles And Friends
The Second Sampler | Nagel-Heyer | NHR SP 6
Butch Miles-Howard Alden Sextet
Cookin' | Nagel-Heyer | CD 5003
Eddie Metz And His Gang
Tough Assignment:A Tribute To Dave Tough | Nagel-Heyer | CD 053
Frank Tate Quintet
Live In Belfast | Nagel-Heyer | CD 069
George Masso Sextet
C'Est Magnifique! | Nagel-Heyer | CD 060
Harry Allen And Randy Sandke Meets The RIAS Big Band Berlin
The Music Of The Trumpet Kings | Nagel-Heyer | CD 037
Harry Allen Quartet
Jazz Im Amerika Haus,Vol.1 | Nagel-Heyer | CD 011
Blues Of Summer | Nagel-Heyer | NH 1011
Love Songs Live! | Nagel-Heyer | NH 1014
The First Sampler | Nagel-Heyer | NHR SP 5
Harry Allen Quintet
A Night At Birdland | Nagel-Heyer | CD 010
A Night At Birdland Vol. 1 | Nagel-Heyer | CD 5002
Ellington For Lovers | Nagel-Heyer | NH 1009
Love Songs Live! | Nagel-Heyer | NH 1014
The First Sampler | Nagel-Heyer | NHR SP 5
John Pizzarelli Trio With Harry Allen
P.S. Mr.Cole | RCA | 2663563-2
Karl Schloz Quartet
A Mooth One | Nagel-Heyer | CD 2012
Mark Shane's X-Mas Allstars
What Would Santa Say? | Nagel-Heyer | CD 055
Christmas Jazz! | Nagel-Heyer | NH 1008
Oliver Jackson Orchestra
The Last Great Concert | Nagel-Heyer | CD 063
Randy Sandke Quintet
Cliffhanger | Nagel-Heyer | CD 2037
Randy Sandke Sextet
Cliffhanger | Nagel-Heyer | CD 2037
Rex Allen's Swing Express
Keep Swingin' | Nagel-Heyer | CD 016
Ellington For Lovers | Nagel-Heyer | NH 1009
The Second Sampler | Nagel-Heyer | NHR SP 6
The Buck Clayton Legacy
All The Cats Join In(Buck Clayton Remembered) | Nagel-Heyer | CD 006
Encore Live | Nagel-Heyer | CD 018
The First Sampler | Nagel-Heyer | NHR SP 5
The Second Sampler | Nagel-Heyer | NHR SP 6
The Yamaha International Allstar Band
Hapy Birthday Jazzwelle Plus | Nagel-Heyer | CD 005
The First Sampler | Nagel-Heyer | NHR SP 5
Warren Vaché And The New York City All-Star Big Band
Swingtime! | Nagel-Heyer | CD 059

Allen,Henry Red | (tpvoc)
Coleman Hawkins And His Orchestra
Jazz:The Essential Collection Vol.3 | IN+OUT Records | 78013-2
Fats Waller And His Buddies
Planet Jazz:Jack Teagarden | Planet Jazz | 2161236-2
Jazz:The Essential Collection Vol.3 | IN+OUT Records | 78013-2
Fletcher Henderson And His Orchestra
Jazz:The Essential Collection Vol.1 | IN+OUT Records | 78011-2
Jazz:The Essential Collection Vol.3 | IN+OUT Records | 78013-2
Henry Allen Jr. And His New York Orchestra
Planet Jazz:Jazz Saxophone | Planet Jazz | 2169653-2
Planet Jazz:Jazz Trumpet | Planet Jazz | 2169654-2
Henry Red Allen Band
The Very Best Of Dixieland Jazz | Verve | 535529-2
Henry Red Allen's All Stars
Planet Jazz:Coleman Hawkins | Planet Jazz | 2152055-2
Jack Teagarden With The Red Allen Band
The Very Best Of Dixieland Jazz | Verve | 535529-2
Louis Armstrong And His Orchestra
Louis Armstrong:Swing That Music | Laserlight | 36056
Jazz:The Essential Collection Vol.2 | IN+OUT Records | 78012-2
Satch Plays Fats(Complete) | CBS | CK 64927
Louis Armstrong-My Greatest Songs | MCA | MCD 18347
Swing Legends:Louis Armstrong | Nimbus Records | NI 2012
New Orleans Feetwarmers
Jazz:The Essential Collection Vol.1 | IN+OUT Records | 78011-2
Spike Hughes And His Negro Orchestra

Jazz:The Essential Collection Vol.3 | IN+OUT Records | 78013-2

Allen,Jackie | (voc)
Jens Bunge Group
Meet You In Chicago | Jazz 4 Ever Records:Jazz Network | J4E 4749

Allen,Jimmy | (bts)
Jimmy Witherspoon And His Band
Baby, Baby, Baby | Original Blues Classics | OBCCD 527-2(P 7290)

Allen,Marshall | (as,bells,cymbal,piccolo,spiral)
Sun Ra And His Astro-Infinity Arkestra
Space Is The Place | Impulse(MCA) | 951249-2
Sun Ra And His Intergalactic Research Arkestra
Black Myth/Out In Space | MPS | 557656-2

Allen,Moses | (b,tubapreaching)
Jimmy Lunceford And His Orchestra
Planet Jazz:Swing | Planet Jazz | 2169651-2

Allen,Napoleon | (g)
Ike Quebec Quintet
The Blue Note Swingtets | Blue Note | 495697-2

Allen,Nat | (tb)
Louis Armstrong And His Orchestra
Louis Armstrong:C'est Si Bon | Dreyfus Jazz Line | FDM 36730-2

Allen,Red | (as)
James Moody Boptet
Americans Swinging In Paris:James Moody | EMI Records | 539653-2

Allen,Rex | (tbvib)
Rex Allen's Swing Express
Keep Swingin' | Nagel-Heyer | CD 016
Ellington For Lovers | Nagel-Heyer | NH 1009
The Second Sampler | Nagel-Heyer | NHR SP 6

Allen,Sam | (gp)
Dicky Wells And His Orchestra
Americans Swinging In Paris:Dicky Wells | EMI Records | 539664-2

Allen,Sanford | (strings,vconcertmaster)
Andrew Hill Orchestra
Deep Blue-The United States Of Mind | Blue Note | 521152-2
Earl Klugh Group With Strings
Late Night Guitar | Blue Note | 498573-2
Freddy Cole With Band
Le Grand Freddy:Freddy Cole Sings The Music Of Michel Legrand | Fantasy | FCD 9683-2
Grover Washington Jr. Orchestra
Inside Moves | Elektra | 7559-60318-2
Les McCann Group
Another Beginning | Atlantic | 7567-80790-2
Ron Carter Quintet With Strings
Pick 'Em/Super Strings | Milestone | MCD 47090-2
Ron Carter With Strings
Pastels | Original Jazz Classics | OJCCD 665-2(M 9073)

Allen,Sue | (voc)
Paul Desmond Quartet With The Bill Bates Singers
Desmond | Original Jazz Classics | OJCCD 712-2(F 3235/8082)

Allen,Tex | (tpvoc)
Gil Evans Orchestra
Svengali | Rhino | 8122-73720-2

Allen,Woody | (cl)
Woody Allen And His New Orleans Jazz Band
Wild Man Blues | RCA | 2663353-2
Woody Allen Trio
Wild Man Blues | RCA | 2663353-2

Allende,Angel | (perc)
Idris Muhammad Group
Jazzin' With The Soul Brothers | Fantasy | FANCD 6086-2

Allende,Victor | (perc)
Lalo Schifrin And His Orchestra
Tin Tin Deo | Fresh Sound Records | FSR-CD 319

Alley Scatz: |
Landes Jugend Jazz Orchester Hessen
Touch Of Lips | hr music.de | hrmj 004-01 CD

Alley,Vernon | (b)
Charlie Mariano Quartet
The Jazz Scene:San Francisco | Fantasy | FCD 24760-2
Charlie Mariano Sextet
The Jazz Scene:San Francisco | Fantasy | FCD 24760-2
Count Basie And His Orchestra
Jazz Collection:Count Basie | Laserlight | 24368
Lionel Hampton And His Orchestra
Lionel Hampton:Flying Home | Dreyfus Jazz Line | FDM 36735-2

Alleyne,Archie | (dr)
Jim Galloway-Jay McShann Quartet
Christmas Jazz! | Nagel-Heyer | NH 1008

Alleyne,Cheryl | (dr)
Gail Thompson Orchestra
Gail Thompson's Jazz Africa | Enja | ENJ-9053 2

Alleyne,Rupert | (fl)
Ahmed Abdul-Malik Orchestra
Jazz Sounds Of Africa | Prestige | PRCD 24279-2

Allier,Pierre | (tp)
Coleman Hawkins With Michel Warlop And His Orchestra
Django Reinhardt All Star Sessions | Capitol | 531577-2
Wal-Berg Et Son Jazz Francais
Jazz In Paris:Django Reinhardt-Django Et Compagnie | EmArCy | 549241-2 PMS

Allier,Roger | (b)

Allison,Ben | (b)
Michael Blake Group
Drift | Intuition Records | INT 3212-2
Tim Sund & Tom Christensen Quartet
Americana | Nabel Records:Jazz Network | CD 4697

Allison,Mose | (p,el-p,voc,orgtp)
Al Cohn Quintet feat. Zoot Sims
Al And Zoot | GRP | 951827-2
Al Cohn-Zoot Sims Quintet
You 'N' Me | Verve | 589318-2
Mose Allison Quartet
The Mose Chronicles-Live In London,Vol.2 | Blue Note | 529748-2
Mose Allison Quintet
Gimeracs And Gewgaws | Blue Note | 823211-2
Mose Allison Trio
Blue Velvet: Crooners, Swooners And Velvet Vocals | Blue Note | 521153-2
The Mose Chronicles-Live In London,Vol.1 | Blue Note | 529747-2
Rhino Presents The Atlantic Jazz Gallery | Atlantic | 8122-71257-2
I Don't Worry About A Thing | Rhino | 8122-71417-2
The Word From Mose | Atlantic | 8122-72394-2
Mose Alife!/Wild Man On The Loose | Warner | 8122-75439-2
Back Country Suite | Original Jazz Classics | OJC 075(P 7091)
Local Color | Original Jazz Classics | OJCCD 457-2
Mose Allison:Greatest Hits | Original Jazz Classics | OJCCD 6004-2
Mose Allison Sings The 7th Son | Prestige | PR20 7279-2
Zoot Sims-Al Cohn Quintet
Jazz Alive:A Night At The Half Note | Blue Note | 494105-2
Zoot Sims-Al Cohn-Phil Woods Sextet
Jazz Alive:A Night At The Half Note | Blue Note | 494105-2

Allmond,Peck | (bs,tp,peck-horn,tsss)
Don Cherry Group
Multi Kulti | A&M Records | 395323-2
Michael Blake Group
Drift | Intuition Records | INT 3212-2

Allouche,Joel | (dr,cymbals,perctablas)
Nguyen Le Group
Tales From Viet-Nam | ACT | 9225-2
Philippe Caillat Special Project
Melodic Travel | Laika Records | LK 689-012
Soriba Kouyaté Quartet
Live In Montreux | ACT | 9414-2

Allred,Bill | (tb)
Bill Allred-Roy Williams Quintet
Absolutely | Nagel-Heyer | CD 024

INTERPRETENVERZEICHNIS

Ellington For Lovers | Nagel-Heyer | NH 1009
Blues Of Summer | Nagel-Heyer | NH 1011
The Second Sampler | Nagel-Heyer | NHR SP 6
International Chicago-Jazz Orchestra
That's A Plenty | JHM Records | JHM 3621
Jeanie Lambe And The Danny Moss Septet
Three Great Concerts:Live In Hamburg 1993-1995 | Nagel-Heyer | CD 019
Ralph Sutton And His Allstars
Echoes Of Spring:The Complete Hamburg Concert | Nagel-Heyer | CD 038
The Vaché-Allred-Metz Family Jazz Band
Side By Side | Nagel-Heyer | CD 042
Tom Saunders' 'Wild Bill Davison Band' & Guests
Exactly Like You | Nagel-Heyer | CD 023
The Second Sampler | Nagel-Heyer | NHR SP 6

Allred,John | (tb)
Allan Vaché's Florida Jazz Allstars
Allan Vaché's Floridy Jazz Allstars | Nagel-Heyer | CD 032
Eddie Metz And His Gang
Tough Assignment:A Tribute To Dave Tough | Nagel-Heyer | CD 053
The Vaché-Allred-Metz Family Jazz Band
Side By Side | Nagel-Heyer | CD 042
Warren Vaché And The New York City All-Star Big Band
Swingtime! | Nagel-Heyer | CD 059

Almario,Justo | (as,fl,ts,sssax)
Dianne Reeves With Band
I Remember | Blue Note | 790264-2

Almeida,Laurindo | (cabassa,g,arr,perctambourine)
Herbie Mann Sextet
Verve Jazz Masters Vol.60:The Collection | Verve | 529866-2
Verve Jazz Masters 56:Herbie Mann | Verve | 529901-2
June Christy With The Pete Rugolo Orchestra
Something Cool(The Complete Mono & Stereo Versions) | Capitol | 534069-2
Modern Jazz Quartet And Laurindo Almeida
MJQ 40 | Atlantic | 7567-82330-2
Stan Getz Group Feat.Laurindo Almeida
Stan Getz With Guest Artist Laurindo Almeida | Verve | 823149-2
Stan Getz-Laurindo Almeida Orchestra
Stan Getz Highlights:The Best Of The Verve Years Vol.2 | Verve | 517330-2
Verve Jazz Masters 53:Stan Getz-Bossa Nova | Verve | 529904-2
Stan Getz Highlights | Verve | 847430-2
Stan Kenton And His Orchestra
Stan Kenton Portraits On Standards | Capitol | 531571-2

Almendra,John Andreu | (dr,perc,timbalesvoc)
Mongo Santamaria And His Band
Brazilian Sunset | Candid | CCD 79703
Mongo Santamaria And His Orchestra
Jazzin' Vol.2: The Music Of Stevie Wonder | Fantasy | FANCD 6088-2

Almond,Frank | (v)
Absolute Ensemble
African Symphony | Enja | ENJ-9410 2

Almond,Peck | (brass)
David Binney Group
Balance | ACT | 9411-2

Almsted,Gunnar | (b)
Lars Gullin Quartet
Lars Gullin 1951/52 Vol.5:First Walk | Dragon | DRCD 380

Alnaes,Frode | (g)
Arild Andersen Sextet
Sagn | ECM | 1435
Dee Dee Bridgewater With Band
Victim Of Love | Verve | 841199-2
Masqualero
Aero | ECM | 1367

Alois,Louis | (as)
Louis Armstrong With Sy Oliver And His Orchestra
Satchmo Serenaders | Verve | 543792-2

Alonge,Ray | (fr-h)
Bill Evans Quartet With Orchestra
The Complete Bill Evans On Verve | Verve | 527953-2
From Left To Right | Verve | 557451-2
Dizzy Gillespie And His Orchestra
Ultimate Dizzy Gillespie | Verve | 557535-2
Freddie Hubbard With Orchestra
This Is Jazz:Freddie Hubbard | CBS | CK 65041
Gato Barbieri Orchestra
The Roots Of Acid Jazz | Impulse(MCA) | IMP 12042
Gil Evans Orchestra
Verve Jazz Masters 23:Gil Evans | Verve | 521860-2
The Individualism Of Gil Evans | Verve | 833804-2
Blues In Orbit | Enja | ENJ-3069 2
Grover Washington Jr. Orchestra
Jazzrock-Anthology Vol.3:Fusion | Zounds | CD 27100555
Jimmy Smith With The Lalo Schifrin Orchestra
Jimmy Smith:Best Of The Verve Years | Verve | 527950-2
Jimmy Smith-Talkin' Verve | Verve | 531563-2
The Cat | Verve | 539756-2
Joe Williams With The Frank Hunter Orchestra
Planet Jazz:Joe Williams | Planet Jazz | 2165370-2
Kenny Burrell With The Gil Evans Orchestra
Guitar Forms | Verve | 521403-2
Verve Jazz Masters 23:Gil Evans | Verve | 521860-2
Verve Jazz Masters 45:Kenny Burrell | Verve | 527652-2
Verve Jazz Masters Vol.60:The Collection | Verve | 529866-2
Milt Jackson Orchestra
Milt Jackson Birthday Celebration | Fantasy | FANCD 6079-2
Oscar Peterson With The Ernie Wilkins Orchestra
Verve Jazz Masters 16:Oscar Peterson | Verve | 516320-2
Phil Woods Quartet With Orchestra & Strings
Round Trip | Verve | 559804-2
Quincy Jones And His Orchestra
Rahsaan/The Complete Mercury Recordings Of Roland Kirk | Mercury | 846630-2
The Quintessence | Impulse(MCA) | 951222-2
Stan Getz With The Eddie Sauter Orchestra
Stan Getz Plays The Music Of Mickey One | Verve | 531232-2
Stan Getz With The Gary McFarland Orchestra
Stan Getz Highlights:The Best Of The Verve Years Vol.2 | Verve | 517330-2
Verve Jazz Masters 53:Stan Getz-Bossa Nova | Verve | 529904-2
Big Band Bossa Nova | Verve | 825771-2 PMS
Stan Getz Highlights | Verve | 847430-2

Alonso,Armando | (gvoice)
Dino Saluzzi Group
Mojotoro | ECM | 1447

Alonso,Robert | (tp)
Horst Faigle's Jazzkrement
Gans Normal | Jazz 4 Ever Records:Jazz Network | J4E 4748

Alperin,Mikhail 'Misha' | (claviola,p,melodica,plastic-tubes)
Mikhail Alperin/Arkady Shilkloper
Wave Over Sorrow | ECM | 1396
Mikhail Alperin's Moscow Art Trio
Folk Dreams | JA & RO | JARO 4187-2
Prayer | JA & RO | JARO 4193-2
Hamburg Concert | JA & RO | JARO 4201-2
Mikhail Alperin's Moscow Art Trio With The Russkaja Pesnja Folk Choir
Folk Dreams | JA & RO | JARO 4187-2
Mikhail Alperin's Moscow Art Trio With The Tuva Folk & Russian Folk Ensemble
Prayer | JA & RO | JARO 4193-2
Mikhail Alperin-Vegar Vardal
Portrait | JA & RO | JARO 4227-2
Misha Alperin
At Home | ECM | 1768(549610-2)
Portrait | JA & RO | JARO 4227-2
Misha Alperin Group With John Surman
First Impression | ECM | 1664(557650-2)
Misha Alperin Group With The Brazz Brothers
Portrait | JA & RO | JARO 4227-2
Misha Alperin Quintet
North Story | ECM | 1596
Misha Alperin Trio
Night After Night | ECM | 1769(014431-2)
Moscow Art Trio
Jazzy World | JA & RO | JARO 4200-2
Music | JA & RO | JARO 4214-2
Portrait | JA & RO | JARO 4227-2
Once Upon A Time | JA & RO | JARO 4238-2
Moscow Art Trio And The Bulgarian Voices Angelite
Portrait | JA & RO | JARO 4227-2
Trigon
Oglinda | JA & RO | JARO 4215-2

Alpert,Lorenzo | (bassoon)
Uri Caine With The Concerto Köln
Concerto Köln | Winter&Winter | 910086-2

Alpert,Trigger | (b)
Bud Freeman And His Stars
Muggsy Spanier And Bud Freeman:V-Discs 1944-45 | Jazz Unlimited | JUCD 2049
Bud Freeman And The V-Disc Jumpers
Muggsy Spanier And Bud Freeman:V-Discs 1944-45 | Jazz Unlimited | JUCD 2049
Coleman Hawkins Quintet
Body And Soul Revisited | GRP | GRP 16272
Coleman Hawkins Quintet With Strings
Body And Soul Revisited | GRP | GRP 16272
Coleman Hawkins Sextet
Body And Soul Revisited | GRP | GRP 16272
Eight Squares And A Critic
Muggsy Spanier And Bud Freeman:V-Discs 1944-45 | Jazz Unlimited | JUCD 2049
Frank Trumbauer And His Orchestra
The Hollywood Session:The Capitol Jazzmen | Jazz Unlimited | JUCD 2044
Glenn Miller And His Orchestra
Planet Jazz:Glenn Miller | Planet Jazz | 2152056-2
Planet Jazz:Jazz Greatest Hits | Planet Jazz | 2169648-2
Planet Jazz:Big Bands | Planet Jazz | 2169649-2
Louis Armstrong And Ella Fitzgerald With Bob Hagger's Orchestra
Louis Armstrong:C'est Si Bon | Dreyfus Jazz Line | FDM 36730-2
Muggsy Spanier And His V-Disc All Stars
Muggsy Spanier And Bud Freeman:V-Discs 1944-45 | Jazz Unlimited | JUCD 2049
The V-Disc Jumpers
Muggsy Spanier And Bud Freeman:V-Discs 1944-45 | Jazz Unlimited | JUCD 2049
Trigger Alpert's Absolutely All Star Seven
East Coast Sound | Original Jazz Classics | OJCCD 1012-2(JLP 11)

Alsberg,Mats | (el-b)
Oriental Wind
Life Road | JA & RO | JARO 4113-2
Jazzy World | JA & RO | JARO 4200-2

Alsop,LaMar | (stringsviola)
A Band Of Friends
Wynton Marsalis Quartet With Strings | CBS | CK 68921
Earl Klugh Group With Strings
Late Night Guitar | Blue Note | 498573-2
Helen Merrill With Orchestra
Casa Forte | EmArCy | 558848-2
Nina Simone And Orchestra
Baltimore | Epic | 476906-2
Ron Carter Quintet With Strings
Pick 'Em/Super Strings | Milestone | MCD 47090-2

Al-Sous,Mohammad | (darabuka)
Rabih Abou-Khalil Group
Roots & Sprouts | Enja | ENJ-9373 2

Alspach,Scott | (tpfl-h)
Dave Weckl Group
Master Plan | GRP | GRP 96192
Hard-Wired | GRP | GRP 97602

Altbart,Heini | (dr)
Oscar Klein & Katie Kern Group
Pick-A-Blues | Jazzpoint | JP 1065 CD
Oscar Klein Band
Pick-A-Blues Live | Jazzpoint | JP 1071

Alter,Myriam | (comp)
Dino Saluzzi Group
If | Enja | ENJ-9451 2
Miriam Alter Quintet
Alter Ego | Intuition Records | INT 3258-2

Alterhaug,Bjorn | (b)
Ketil Bjornstad Group
Early Years | EmArCy | 013271-2

Altmann,Thomas | (bongos,timbalesperc)
Joe Gallardo's Latino Blue
A Latin Shade Of Blue | Enja | ENJ-9421 2

Altschul,Barry | (dr,perc,bells,cymbals,gongs,quica)
Chick Corea Trio
A.R.C. | ECM | 1009
The Story Of Jazz Piano | Laserlight | 24653
Circle
Paris Concert | ECM | 1018/19(843163-2)
David Holland Quartet
Conference Of The Birds | ECM | 1027(829373-2)

Alvares,Enrico | (v)
Abdullah Ibrahim Trio And A String Orchestra
African Suite | TipToe | TIP-888832 2
String Orchestra
African Suite | TipToe | TIP-888832 2

Alvarez,Chico | (tp)
Nat King Cole Quartet With The Stan Kenton Orchestra
Nat King Cole:For Sentimental Reasons | Dreyfus Jazz Line | FDM 36740-2
Stan Kenton And His Orchestra
Swing Vol.1 | Storyville | 4960343
Stan Kenton-The Formative Years | Decca | 589489-2
One Night Stand | Choice | CHCD 71051

Alves,Luiz | (b)
Cal Tjader Group
Amazonas | Original Jazz Classics | OJCCD 840-2(F 9502)

Alvim,Cesarius | (b)
Dee Dee Bridgewater With Band
Victim Of Love | Verve | 841199-2

Alvin,Danny | (dr)
Bud Freeman And His Summa Cum Laude Orchestra
Planet Jazz:Bud Freeman | Planet Jazz | 2161240-2
Planet Jazz:Jazz Saxophone | Planet Jazz | 2169653-2

Alvis,Hayes | (b,tubavoc)
Duke Ellington And His Famous Orchestra
Greatest Hits | CBS | 462959-2
Jazz:The Essential Collection Vol.2 | IN+OUT Records | 78012-2
Duke Ellington And His Orchestra
Jazz:The Essential Collection Vol.2 | IN+OUT Records | 78012-2
Jazz:The Essential Collection Vol.3 | IN+OUT Records | 78013-2
Earl Hines And His Orchestra
Jazz:The Essential Collection Vol.2 | IN+OUT Records | 78012-2
Louis Armstrong And His Orchestra
Louis Armstrong:Swing That Music | Laserlight | 36056
Jazz:The Essential Collection Vol.2 | IN+OUT Records | 78012-2
Louis Armstrong:C'est Si Bon | Dreyfus Jazz Line | FDM 36730-2

AM 4 |
AM 4
...And She Answered | ECM | 1394

Amalbert,Juan | (conga,ldtimbales)
The Latin Jazz Quintet Plus Guest: Eric Dolphy
Eric Dolphy:The Complete Prestige Recordings | Prestige | 9 PRCD-4418-2
Eric Dolphy Birthday Celebration | Fantasy | FANCD 6085-2
Willis Jackson Group
At Large | Prestige | PCD 24243-2
Willis Jackson Quintet
At Large | Prestige | PCD 24243-2

Amar,Illya | (marimbatuned-gongs)
Nguyen Le Trio With Guests
Bakida | ACT | 9275-2

Amargós,Joan Albert | (p,keyboardscond)
Orquestra De Cambra Teatre Lliure
Porgy And Bess | Fresh Sound Records | FSNT 066 CD

Amaro,David | (el-gg)
Cal Tjader Group
Amazonas | Original Jazz Classics | OJCCD 840-2(F 9502)
Flora Purim And Her Quintet
Joe Henderson:The Milestone Years | Milestone | 8MCD 4413-2
Flora Purim And Her Sextet
Joe Henderson:The Milestone Years | Milestone | 8MCD 4413-2
Butterfly Dreams | Original Jazz Classics | OJCCD 315-2

Amarosa,John | (tp)
Tommy Dorsey And His Orchestra
Planet Jazz:Tommy Dorsey | Planet Jazz | 2159972-2

Amberson,Norman | (dr)
Chris Barber's Jazzband & das Große Rundfunkorchester Berlin,DDR
Jazz Zounds: Chris Barber | Zounds | CD 2720007

Ambros,Jo | (gel-g)
Jo Ambros Group
Wanderlust | dml-records | CD 016

Ambrose,Ari | (ts)
Ari Ambrose Quartet
Jazmin | Steeplechase | SCCD 31535
Ari Ambrose Trio
United | Steeplechase | SCCD 31518
Jam Session
Jam Session Vol.6 | Steeplechase | SCCD 31537

Ambrosetti,Franco | (fl-htp)
Chico Freeman & Franco Ambrosetti Meet Reto Weber Percussion Orchestra
Face To Face | double moon | CHRDM 71018
Franco Ambrosetti Quintet
Live At The Blue Note | Enja | ENJ-7065 2
Light Breeze | Enja | ENJ-9331 2
George Gruntz Concert Jazz Band
Blues 'N Dues Et Cetera | Enja | ENJ-6072 2

Ambrosini,Marco | (dudelsack,schlüsselfidelnickelarpa)
Michael Riessler Group
Tentations D'Abélard | Wergo | WER 8009-2

Ambush,Scott | (b)
Spyro Gyra & Guests
Love & Other Obsessions | GRP | GRP 98112

Ameen,Robert 'Robbie' | (dr,guiro,perc,timbalestrap-dr)
Michael Riessler And The Ensemble 13
Momentum Mobile | Enja | ENJ-9003 2
Michael Riessler Group
Tentations D'Abélard | Wergo | WER 8009-2
Mongo Santamaria And His Orchestra
Jazzin' Vol.2: The Music Of Stevie Wonder | Fantasy | FANCD 6088-2
Steve Swallow Group
Swallow | Watt | XtraWatt/6

Amendola,Scott | (dr)
Charlie Hunter Quartet
Ready...Set...Shango! | Blue Note | 837101-2

America,Yma | (voccoro)
Conexion Latina
Mambo Nights | Enja | ENJ-9402 2

American Brass Quintet |
Keith Jarrett With The American Brass Quintet
In The Light | ECM | 1033/4

Amero,Eugene | (fl,clts)
Singers Unlimited With Rob McConnell And The Boss Brass
The Singers Unlimited:Magic Voices | MPS | 539130-2

Ames,Morgan | (voc)
Les McCann Group
Another Beginning | Atlantic | 7567-80790-2

Amico,Sal | (tp)
Sal Nistico Quintet
Heavyweights | Milestone | MCD 47096-2

Amlotte,Jim | (b-tb,tbtp)
Stan Kenton And His Orchestra
Adventures In Blues | Capitol | 520089-2
Adventures In Jazz | Capitol | 521222-2
Stan Kenton Orchestra
Stompin' At Newport | Pablo | PACD 5312-2

AMM III |
AMM III
It Had Been An Ordinary Enough Day In Pueblo, Colorado | Japo | 60031

Amman Boutz |
Amman Boutz
Some Other Tapes | Fish Music | FM 009/10 CD

Ammerlaan,Gerard | (b,percel-b)
Greetje Bijma Kwintet
Tales Of A Voice | TipToe | TIP-888808 2

Ammon,Jacques | (p)
Eckart Runge-Jacques Ammon
Cello Tango | Edition Musikat | EDM 053

Ammons,Albert | (pp-solo)
Albert Ammons
Boogie Woogie | Laserlight | 24321
From Spiritual To Swing | Vanguard | VCD 169/71
Albert Ammons-Meade Lux Lewis
Boogie Woogie | Laserlight | 24321
Albert Ammons-Pete Johnson-Meade Lux Lewis
From Spiritual To Swing | Vanguard | VCD 169/71
Big Bill Broonzy With Albert Ammons
From Spiritual To Swing | Vanguard | VCD 169/71
Boogie Woogie Trio
Boogie Woogie | Laserlight | 24321
Count Basie And His Orchestra
From Spiritual To Swing | Vanguard | VCD 169/71
Sister Rosetta Tharpe With Albert Ammons
From Spiritual To Swing | Vanguard | VCD 169/71

Ammons,Gene | (bs,tsvoc)
Count Basie Octet
Planet Jazz:Count Basie | Planet Jazz | 2152068-2
Gene Ammons And His All Stars
John Coltrane-The Prestige Recordings | Prestige | 16 PCD 4405-2
Dexter Gordon Birthday Celebration | Fantasy | FANCD 6082-2
Blue Gene | Original Jazz Classics | OJC20 192-2(P 7146)
Jammin' With Gene | Original Jazz Classics | OJCCD 211-2(P 7060)
The Big Sound | Original Jazz Classics | OJCCD 651-2(P 7132)
Groove Blues | Original Jazz Classics | OJCCD 723-2(PR 7201)
The Prestige Legacy Vol.2:Battles Of Saxes | Prestige | PCD 24252-2
Gene Ammons And His Orchestra
A Stranger In Town | Prestige | PRCD 24266-2
Gene Ammons Quartet
Preachin' | Original Jazz Classics | OJCCD 792-2(P 7270)
God Bless Jug And Sonny | Prestige | PCD 11019-2
The Jazz Giants Play Rodgers & Hart:Blue Moon | Prestige | PCD 24205-2
The Jazz Giants Play Rodgers & Hammerstein:My Favorite Things | Prestige | PCD 24223-2
Gentle Jug Vol.3 | Prestige | PCD 24249-2
Brother Jug! | Prestige | PR20 7792-2

The Mal Waldron Memorial Album:Soul Eyes | Prestige | PRCD 11024-2
A Stranger In Town | Prestige | PRCD 24266-2
Fine And Mellow | Prestige | PRCD 24281-2
Gene Ammons Quintet
Boss Tenor | Original Jazz Classics | OJC20 297-2(P-7180)
The Jazz Giants Play Jerome Kern:Yesterdays | Prestige | PCD 24202-2
The Jazz Giants Play Cole Porter:Night And Day | Prestige | PCD 24203-2
Gentle Jug Vol.3 | Prestige | PCD 24249-2
Brother Jug! | Prestige | PR20 7792-2
A Stranger In Town | Prestige | PRCD 24266-2
Fine And Mellow | Prestige | PRCD 24281-2
Gene Ammons Septet
Bad! Bossa Nova | Original Jazz Classics | OJC20 351-2(P 7257)
Goodbye | Original Jazz Classics | OJCCD 1081-2(P 100939)
A Stranger In Town | Prestige | PRCD 24266-2
Gene Ammons Sextet
Gentle Jug Vol.3 | Prestige | PCD 24249-2
Fine And Mellow | Prestige | PRCD 24281-2
Gene Ammons Sextet With Strings
Fine And Mellow | Prestige | PRCD 24281-2
Gene Ammons-Dexter Gordon Quintet
Dexter Gordon Birthday Celebration | Fantasy | FANCD 6082-2
Gene Ammons-James Moody Quintet
Chicago Concert | Original Jazz Classics | OJCCD 1091-2(PR 10065)
Gene Ammons-Sonny Stitt Quartet
Gentle Jug Vol.3 | Prestige | PCD 24249-2
Gene Ammons-Sonny Stitt Quintet
Verve Jazz Masters 50:Sonny Sitt | Verve | 527651-2
Boss Tenors In Orbit!!! | Verve | 549371-2
God Bless Jug And Sonny | Prestige | PCD 11019-2
Gentle Jug Vol.3 | Prestige | PCD 24249-2
The Prestige Legacy Vol.2:Battles Of Saxes | Prestige | PCD 24252-2
Left Bank Encores | Prestige | PRCD 11022-2
Jack McDuff Quartet
The Last Goodun' | Prestige | PRCD 24274-2
Jack McDuff Quartet With Gene Ammons
Brother Jack Meets The Boss | Original Jazz Classics | OJCCD 326-2(P 7228)
Jack McDuff Quintet
Jack McDuff:The Prestige Years | Prestige | PRCD 24387-2
Woody Herman And His Orchestra
Woody Herman:Four Brother | Dreyfus Jazz Line | FDM 36722-2

Amorin,Jorge | (perc)
Hank Jones Meets Cheik-Tidiana Seck
Sarala | Verve | 528783-2

Amouroux,Jean-Paul | (o,orgceleste)
Memphis Slim Trio
Americans Swinging In Paris:Memphis Slim | EMI Records | 539666-2

Amram,David | (fr-h,fl,g,arr,claves,ocarina)
Curtis Fuller And Hampton Hawes With French Horns
Curtis Fuller And Hampton Hawes With French Horns | Original Jazz Classics | OJCCD 1942-2(NJ 8305)
Curtis Fuller And Teddy Charles With French Horns
Curtis Fuller And Hampton Hawes With French Horns | Original Jazz Classics | OJCCD 1942-2(NJ 8305)
Kenny Dorham Septet
Cannonball Adderley Birthday Celebration | Fantasy | FANCD 6087-2
Lionel Hampton All Stars
Jazz In Paris:Lionel Hampton And His French New Sound Vol.1 | EmArCy | 549405-2 PMS
Jazz In Paris:Lionel Hampton And His French New Sound Vol.2 | EmArCy | 549406-2 PMS

Amros,Jo | (g)
Sputnik 27
But Where's The Moon? | dml-records | CD 011

Amstad,Bruno | (djembevoc)
Christy Doran's New Bag With Muthuswamy Balasubramoniam
Black Box | double moon | CHRDM 71022

Amster,Rob | (b)
Kurt Elling Group
This Time Its Love | Blue Note | 493543-2
Blue Velvet: Crooners, Swooners And Velvet Vocals | Blue Note | 521153-2
Kurt Elling Group With Guests
Live In Chicago | Blue Note | 522211-2

Amsterdam String Trio |
Amsterdam String Trio
Winter Theme | Winter&Winter | 910060-2

Amsterdam,Chet | (b)
Ben Webster With Orchestra And Strings
Music For Loving:Ben Webster With Strings | Verve | 527774-2
Ultimate Ben Webster selected by James Carter | Verve | 557537-2
Jimmy McGriff Orchestra
Swingin' The Blues-Jumpin' The Blues | Laserlight | 24654

Amuedo,Leonardo | (g,el-bg-synth)
The Rosenberg Trio
Suenos Gitanos | Polydor | 549581-2
The Rosenberg Trio With Orchestra
Noches Calientes | Verve | 557022-2

Amy,Curtis | (ss,tsvoc)
Johnny Hartman And His Orchestra
Unforgettable | Impulse(MCA) | IMP 11522

An,Thai | (moon-fl)
Nguyen Le Group
Tales From Viet-Nam | ACT | 9225-2

Anastas,Tom | (bsts)
Woody Herman And His Orchestra
Verve Jazz Masters 54:Woody Herman | Verve | 529903-2
The Raven Speaks | Original Jazz Classics | OJCCD 663-2(F 9416)

Ande,Akira | (b)
Takabanda
La Leggenda Del Pescatore | Jazz 4 Ever Records:Jazz Network | J4E 4752

Anders,Christoph | (el-g,org,synth,perc,sounds,voice)
Alfred 23 Harth Group
Sweet Paris | free flow music | ffm 0291

Anders,Jörn | (tp)
Florian Poser Group
Say Yes! | Edition Collage | EC 452-2

Andersen,Arild | (b,el-b,xylthumb-p)
Arild Andersen Quartet
If You Look Far Enough | ECM | 1493(513902-2)
Arild Andersen Quintet With The Cikada String Quartet
Hyperborean | ECM | 1631(537342-2)
Arild Andersen Sextet
Sagn | ECM | 1435
Arild Andersen Trio
The Triangle | ECM | 1752(0381212)
Bill Frisell-Arild Andersen
In Line | ECM | 1241(837019-2)
David Darling Group
Cycles | ECM | 1219
Jan Garbarek Quintet
Sart | ECM | 1015(839305-2)
Jan Garbarek Trio
Triptychon | ECM | 1029(847321-2)
Ketil Bjornstad Group
Early Years | EmArCy | 013271-2
Grace | EmArCy | 013622-2
Markus Stockhausen Quartet
Karta | ECM | 1704(543035-2)
Joyosa | Enja | ENJ-9468 2
Masqualero
Bande A Part | ECM | 1319
Aero | ECM | 1367
Re-Enter | ECM | 1437(847939-2)
Roy Powell Quartet
North By Northwest | Nagel-Heyer | CD 2013
Terje Rypdal Sextet
Terje Rypdal | ECM | 1016(527645-2)
Uli Beckerhoff Quartet
Secret Obsession | Nabel Records:Jazz Network | CD 4647
Vassilis Tsabropoulos Trio
Achirana | ECM | 1728(157462-2)

Andersen,Erik 'Krolle' | (cl)
Adrian Bentzon's Jazzband
The Golden Years Of Revival Jazz,Sampler | Storyville | 109 1001
The Golden Years Of Revival Jazz,Vol.1 | Storyville | STCD 5506
The Golden Years Of Revival Jazz,Vol.2 | Storyville | STCD 5507
The Golden Years Of Revival Jazz,Vol.3 | Storyville | STCD 5508
The Golden Years Of Revival Jazz,Vol.4 | Storyville | STCD 5509
The Golden Years Of Revival Jazz,Vol.7 | Storyville | STCD 5512
The Golden Years Of Revival Jazz,Vol.13 | Storyville | STCD 5518
The Golden Years Of Revival Jazz,Vol.14 | Storyville | STCD 5519
Theis/Nyegaard Jazzband
The Golden Years Of Revival Jazz,Sampler | Storyville | 109 1001
The Golden Years Of Revival Jazz,Vol.3 | Storyville | STCD 5508
The Golden Years Of Revival Jazz,Vol.5 | Storyville | STCD 5510
The Golden Years Of Revival Jazz,Vol.12 | Storyville | STCD 5517
The Golden Years Of Revibal Jazz,Vol.15 | Storyville | STCD 5520

Andersen,Jacob | (perc)
Caecilie Norby With Band
My Corner Of The Sky | Blue Note | 853422-2
Simon Spang-Hanssen & Maneklar
Wondering | dacapo | DCCD 9436

Andersen,Jay | (b)
Jam Session
Jam Session Vol.1 | Steeplechase | SCCD 31522
Woody Herman And His Orchestra
Verve Jazz Masters 54:Woody Herman | Verve | 529903-2

Andersen,Jorn | (dr)
Hugh Marsh Duo/Quartet/Orchestra
The Bear Walks | VeraBra Records | CDVBR 2011-2

Andersen,Martin | (dr)
Ok Nok...Kongo
Moonstone Journey | dacapo | DCCD 9444

Anderson,Adrienne | (voc)
McCoy Tyner Group With Horns And Voices
Inner Voices | Original Jazz Classics | OJCCD 1039-2(M 9079)
McCoy Tyner Group With Voices
Inner Voices | Original Jazz Classics | OJCCD 1039-2(M 9079)

Anderson,Bill | (p)
Conte Candoli-Carl Fontana Quintet
The Complete Phoenix Recordings Vol.1 | Woofy Productions | WPCD 121
The Complete Phoenix Recordings Vol.2 | Woofy Productions | WPCD 122
The Complete Phoenix Recordings Vol.3 | Woofy Productions | WPCD 123
The Complete Phoenix Recordings Vol.4 | Woofy Productions | WPCD 124
The Complete Phoenix Recordings Vol.5 | Woofy Productions | WPCD 125
The Complete Phoenix Recordings Vol.6 | Woofy Productions | WPCD 126

Anderson,Carl | (voc)
The Rippingtons
Tourist In Paradise | GRP | GRP 95882

Anderson,Cat | (tp,fl-hperc)
Billy Strayhorn Orchestra
Johnny Hodges With Billy Strayhorn And The Orchestra | Verve | 557543-2
Cat Anderson And His All Stars
Americans Swinging In Paris:Cat Anderson | EMI Records | 539658-2
Cat Anderson And His Orchestra
Americans Swinging In Paris:Cat Anderson | EMI Records | 539658-2
Django Reinhardt With Duke Ellington And His Orchestra
Django Reinhardt:Souveniers | Dreyfus Jazz Line | FDM 36744-2
Duke Ellington And Count Basie With Their Orchestras
First Time! | CBS | CK 65571
Duke Ellington And His Famous Orchestra
Planet Jazz:Johnny Hodges | Planet Jazz | 2152065-2
Duke Ellington And His Orchestra
Planet Jazz:Duke Ellington | Planet Jazz | 2152053-2
Planet Jazz:Johnny Hodges | Planet Jazz | 2152065-2
Planet Jazz:Jazz Greatest Hits | Planet Jazz | 2169648-2
Duke Ellington's Far East Suite | RCA | 2174797-2
Jazz Collection:Duke Ellington | Laserlight | 24369
The Art Of Saxophone | Laserlight | 24652
The Legends Of Swing | Laserlight | 24659
100 Years Duke | Laserlight | 24906
Highlights From The Duke Ellington Centennial Edition | RCA | 2663672-2
The Popular Duke Ellington | RCA | 2663880-2
Carnegie Hall Concert December 1944 | Prestige | 2PCD 24073-2
Carnegie Hall Concert January 1946 | Prestige | 2PCD 24074-2
Duke Ellington: The Champs-Elysees Theater January 29-30th,1965 | Laserlight | 36131
Greatest Hits | CBS | 462959-2
The Big Bands Vol.1.The Snader Telescriptions | Storyville | 4960043
Jazz Festival Vol.2 | Storyville | 4960743
Verve Jazz Masters 4:Duke Ellington | Verve | 516338-2
Verve Jazz Masters 20:Introducing | Verve | 519853-2
Ellington '55 | Capitol | 520135-2
Great Swing Classics In Hi-Fi | Capitol | 521223-2
Ella & Duke At The Cote D'Azur | Verve | 539030-2
Ella Fitzgerald And Duke Ellington:Cote D'Azure Concerts on Verve | Verve | 539033-2
Soul Call | Verve | 539785-2
The Great Paris Concert | Atlantic | 7567-81303-2
Jazz:The Essential Collection Vol.2 | IN+OUT Records | 78012-2
New Orleans Suite | Rhino | 812273670-2
Afro-Bossa | Reprise | 9362-47876-2
Ellington At Newport 1956(Complete) | CBS | CK 64932
Black Brown And Beige | CBS | CK 65566
Such Sweet Thunder | CBS | CK 65568
Anatomy Of A Murder | CBS | CK 65569
Welcome To Jazz At The Philharmonic | Fantasy | FANCD 6081-2
The Ellington Suites | Original Jazz Classics | OJC20 446-2(2310762)
Latin America Suite | Original Jazz Classics | OJC20 469-2
Duke Ellington And His Orchestra feat. Paul Gonsalves | Original Jazz Classics | OJCCD 623-2
Yale Concert | Original Jazz Classics | OJCCD 664-2
Jazz At The Philharmonis Berlin '65/Paris '67 | Pablo | PACD 5304-2
Duke Ellington At The Alhambra | Pablo | PACD 5313-2
The Jazz Giants Play Duke Ellington:Caravan | Prestige | PCD 24227-2
Duke Ellington Small Band
The Intimacy Of The Blues | Original Jazz Classics | OJCCD 624-2
Ella Fitzgerald With The Duke Ellington Orchestra
The Stockholm Concert 1966 | Pablo | 2308242-2
Ella Fitzgerald-First Lady Of Song | Verve | 517898-2
The Best Of The Song Books | Verve | 519804-2
Verve Jazz Masters 6:Ella Fitzgerald | Verve | 519822-2
The Best Of The Song Books:The Ballads | Verve | 521867-2
Verve Jazz Masters 46:Ella Fitzgerald-The Jazz Sides | Verve | 527655-2
Ella At Duke's Place | Verve | 529700-2
Love Songs:The Best Of The Song Books | Verve | 531762-2
Ella & Duke At The Cote D'Azur | Verve | 539030-2
Ella Fitzgerald And Duke Ellington:Cote D'Azure Concerts on Verve | Verve | 539033-2
Ella Fitzgerald Sings The Duke Ellington Songbook | Verve | 559248-2
For The Love Of Ella Fitzgerald | Verve | 841765-2
Ella Fitzgerald With The Duke Ellington Orchestra And Jimmy Jones Trio
Ella & Duke At The Cote D'Azur | Verve | 539030-2
Ella Fitzgerald And Duke Ellington:Cote D'Azure Concerts on Verve | Verve | 539033-2
Johnny Hodges And The Ellington Men
Verve Jazz Masters 35:Johnny Hodges | Verve | 521857-2
Johnny Hodges With Billy Strayhorn And The Duke Ellington Orchestra
Verve Jazz Masters 35:Johnny Hodges | Verve | 521857-2
Lionel Hampton And His Orchestra
Lionel Hampton:Flying Home | Dreyfus Jazz Line | FDM 36735-2
Oscar Peterson With The Duke Ellington Orchestra
Oscar Peterson Plays Duke Ellington | Pablo | 2310966-2
Rosemary Clooney With The Duke Ellington Orchestra
Blue Rose | CBS | CK 65506

Anderson,Chris | (pel-p)
Frank Stozier Sextet
Long Night | Milestone | MCD 47095-2
Frank Strozier Quartet
Long Night | Milestone | MCD 47095-2

Anderson,Clarence 'Sleepy' | (orgp)
Billy Mitchell Quintet
This Is Billy Mitchell | Smash | 065507-2
Dinah Washington And Her Band
After Hours With Miss D | Verve | 0760562
Dinah Washington With The Quincy Jones Orchestra
Verve Jazz Masters 40:Dinah Washington | Verve | 522055-2
The Swingin' Miss 'D' | Verve | 558074-2
Gene Ammons Quartet
Preachin' | Original Jazz Classics | OJCCD 792-2(P 7270)
The Jazz Giants Play Rodgers & Hammerstein:My Favorite Things | Prestige | PCD 24223-2
Gene Ammons Quintet
Gentle Jug Vol.3 | Prestige | PCD 24249-2

Anderson,Clifton | (tb)
Sonny Rollins Quintet
Sunny Days,Starry Nights | Milestone | MCD 9122-2
Old Flames | Milestone | MCD 9215-2
This Is What I Do | Milestone | MCD 9310-2
The Jazz Giants Play Harry Warren:Lullaby Of Broadway | Prestige | PCD 24204-2
Sonny Rollins Quintet With Brass
Old Flames | Milestone | MCD 9215-2
Sonny Rollins Sextet
Sunny Days,Starry Nights | Milestone | MCD 9122-2
Here's To The People | Milestone | MCD 9194-2
Global Warming | Milestone | MCD 9280-2

Anderson,Dave | (b,el-bfretless-b)
Tony Purrone Trio
Rascality | Steeplechase | SCCD 31514

Anderson,Dorral | (dr)
Gene Ammons Quartet
Preachin' | Original Jazz Classics | OJCCD 792-2(P 7270)
The Jazz Giants Play Rodgers & Hammerstein:My Favorite Things | Prestige | PCD 24223-2

Anderson,Edward | (cotp)
Jelly Roll Morton And His Orchestra
Planet Jazz:Jelly Roll Morton | Planet Jazz | 2152060-2
Jazz:The Essential Collection Vol.1 | IN+OUT Records | 78011-2

Anderson,Eric | (b)
Steve Tibbetts Group
The Fall Of Us All | ECM | 1527(521144-2)

Anderson,Ernestine | (voc)
Ernestine Anderson With Orchestra
My Kinda Swing | Mercury | 842409-2

Anderson,Frank | (orgp)
Willie Bobo Group
Bobo's Beat | Roulette | 590954-2

Anderson,Gary | (alto-fl,cl,ts,b-cl,contra-b-cl,fl)
Charles Mingus Orchestra
Cumbia & Jazz Fusion | Atlantic | 8122-71785-2
Woody Herman And His Orchestra
Jazzin' Vol.2: The Music Of Stevie Wonder | Fantasy | FANCD 6088-2
King Cobra | Original Jazz Classics | OJCCD 1068-2(F 9499)
Woody Herman Herd At Montreux | Original Jazz Classics | OJCCD 991-2(F 9470)
Woody Herman And The New Thundering Herd
Woody Herman:Thundering Herd | Original Jazz Classics | OJCCD 841-2
Woody Herman's Thundering Herd
Planet Jazz:Jazz Saxophone | Planet Jazz | 2169653-2

Anderson,Gene | (pceleste)
Louis Armstrong And His Orchestra
Satch Plays Fats(Complete) | CBS | CK 64927

Anderson,Ivie | (voc)
Duke Ellington And His Famous Orchestra
Duke Ellington:The Blanton-Webster Band | Bluebird | 21 13181-2
Planet Jazz:Duke Ellington | Planet Jazz | 2152053-2
Planet Jazz:Female Jazz Vocalists | Planet Jazz | 2169656-2
Duke Ellington And His Orchestra
Highlights From The Duke Ellington Centennial Edition | RCA | 2663672-2
Jazz:The Essential Collection Vol.3 | IN+OUT Records | 78013-2
The Duke At Fargo 1940 | Storyville | STCD 8316/17

Anderson,J. | (tuba)
Dee Dee Bridgewater With Orchestra
Dear Ella | Verve | 539102-2

Anderson,Jay | (b,el-b,keyboardscomputer)
Ari Ambrose Trio
United | Steeplechase | SCCD 31518
Dave Stryker Octet
Blue To The Bone III | Steeplechase | SCCD 31524
Jam Session
Jam Session Vol.3 | Steeplechase | SCCD 31526
Jam Session Vol.5 | Steeplechase | SCCD 31536
Lynne Arriale Trio
Arise | IN+OUT Records | 77059-2
Michael Brecker Group
Now You See It...(Now You Don't) | GRP | GRP 96222
Mike Stern Group
Standards(And Other Songs) | Atlantic | 7567-82419-2
Toots Thielemans Quartet
Toots Thielemans:The Live Takes Vol.1 | IN+OUT Records | 77041-2
Vic Juris Quartet
For The Music | Jazzpoint | JP 1034 CD

Anderson,Jim | (rainmaker)
Gonzalo Rubalcaba Quartet
Supernova | Blue Note | 531172-2

Anderson,John | (ptp)
Stan Kenton And His Orchestra
Swing Vol.1 | Storyville | 4960343

Anderson,Kenny | (sax)
Arturo Sandoval And The Latin Train Band
Arturo Sandoval & The Latin Train | GRP | GRP 98202

Anderson,Marc | (congas,cymbal,rattles,triangle)
Steve Tibbetts Duo
Northern Song | ECM | 1218
Steve Tibbetts Group
Bye Bye Safe Journey | ECM | 1270
Exploded View | ECM | 1335
Yr | ECM | 1355(835245-2)
Big Map Idea | ECM | 1380
The Fall Of Us All | ECM | 1527(521144-2)
Steve Tibbetts | ECM | 1814(017068-2)

Anderson,Maxine | (voc)
Bobby Lyle Group
The Journey | Atlantic | 7567-82138-2

Anderson,Michael | (tp)
Eric Schaefer & Demontage
Eric Schaefer & Demontage | Jazz Haus Musik | JHM 0117 CD

Franz Bauer Quintet
Plüschtier | Jazz Haus Musik | JHM 0097 CD
Nickendes Perlgras
Die Hintere Vase | Jazz Haus Musik | JHM 0105 CD

Anderson,Mildred | (voc)
Mildred Anderson With The Eddie Lockjaw Davis Quartet
Queen Of The Organ-Shirley Scott Memorial Album | Prestige | PRCD 11027-2

Anderson,Nancy | (voc)
The Sidewalks Of New York
Tin Pan Alley:The Sidewalks Of New York | Winter&Winter | 910038-2

Anderson,Patrice | (v)
Art Pepper Quintet With Strings
Art Pepper:The Complete Galaxy Recordings | Galaxy | 16GCD 1016-2
Winter Moon | Original Jazz Classics | OJC20 677-2(GXY 5140)

Anderson,Pink | (gvoc)
Pink Anderson
Bawdy Blues | Original Blues Classics | OBCCD 544-2(BV 1055)

Anderson,Ray | (tb,alto-tb,co,little instruments)
Barbara Dennerlein Group
Take Off | Verve | 527664-2
Outhipped | Verve | 547503-2
Barbara Dennerlein Quintet
That's Me | Enja | ENJ-7043 2
Carlos Bica Group
Azul | Traumton Records | 4425-2
Charlie Haden And The Liberation Music Orchestra
The Montreal Tapes:Liberation Music Orchestra | Verve | 527469-2
George Gruntz Concert Jazz Band
Blues 'N Dues Et Cetera | Enja | ENJ-6072 2
Hank Roberts Group
Black Pastels | JMT Edition | 919016-2
Karl Berger-Ray Anderson Duo
Conversations | IN+OUT Records | 77027-2
Klaus König Orchestra
Times Of Devastation/Poco A Poco | Enja | ENJ-6014 22
Reviews | Enja | ENJ-9061 2
Mark Helias/Gerry Hemingway/Ray Anderson
Bassdrumbone(Hence The Reason) | Enja | ENJ-9322 2
Marty Ehrlich Group
The Long View | Enja | ENJ-9452 2
Marty Ehrlich Quintet
Song | Enja | ENJ-9396 2
Ray Anderson Alligatory Band
Don't Mow Your Lawn | Enja | ENJ-8070 2
Heads And Tales | Enja | ENJ-9055 2
Ray Anderson Lapis Lazuli Band
Funkorific | Enja | ENJ-9340 2
Ray Anderson Pocket Brass Band
Where Home Is | Enja | ENJ-9366 2
Ray Anderson Quintet
Blues Bred In The Bone | Enja | ENJ-5081 2
Ray Anderson Sextet
It Just So Happens | Enja | ENJ-5037 2

Anderson,Reid | (bel-b)
Ben Waltzer Trio
For Good | Fresh Sound Records | FSNT 013 CD
Bill Carrothers Quartet
The Electric Bill | Dreyfus Jazz Line | FDM 36631-2
Bill McHenry Quartet
Graphic | Fresh Sound Records | FSNT 056 CD
Ethan Iverson Trio
Contruction Zone(Originals) | Fresh Sound Records | FSNT 046 CD
Decontruction Zone(Originals) | Fresh Sound Records | FSNT 047 CD
The Minor Passions | Fresh Sound Records | FSNT 064 CD
Mark Turner Quartet
Dharma Days | Warner | 9362-47998-2
Reid Anderson Quartet
Dirty Show Tunes | Fresh Sound Records | FSNT 030 CD
Abolish Bad Architecture | Fresh Sound Records | FSNT 062 CD
The Bad Plus
These Are The Vistas | CBS | 510666-2
The Bad Plus | Fresh Sound Records | FSNT 107 CD
Till Brönner Quartet & Deutsches Symphonieorchester Berlin
German Songs | Minor Music | 801057
Tom Beckham Quartet
Suspicions | Fresh Sound Records | FSNT 075 CD

Anderson,Wessell 'Wes' | (as,sopraninocl)
Eric Reed Orchestra
Happiness | Nagel-Heyer | CD 2010
Eric Reed Quartet
Musicale | Impulse(MCA) | 951196-2
Eric Reed Quintet
Musicale | Impulse(MCA) | 951196-2
Lincoln Center Jazz Orchestra
Big Train | CBS | CK 69860
Wynton Marsalis Group
Standard Time Vol.4:Marsalis Plays Monk | CBS | CK 67503
Standard Time Vol.6:Mr.Jelly Lord | CBS | CK 69872

Andersson,Hansd | (b)
Flemming Agerskov Quintet
Face To Face | dacapo | DCCD 9445
The Crossover Ensemble With The Zapolski Quartet
Helios Suite | dacapo | DCCD 9459

Andersson,Ulf | (cl,ss,ts,fl,aspiccolo)
Eje Thelin Quintet
At The German Jazz Festival 1964 | Dragon | DRCD 374

Ando,Naoki | (synth-programming)
Toshinori Kondo & Ima
Red City Smoke | JA & RO | JARO 4173-2

Andos,Randy | (bar-horn,tuba,b-tb,euphoniumtb)
Spyro Gyra & Guests
Love & Other Obsessions | GRP | GRP 98112

Andre,Vaughn | (g)
Milt Jackson And His Colleagues
Bag's Bag | Original Jazz Classics | OJCCD 935-2(2310842)

Andre,Wayne | (tb,bar-h,bar-hornbass-tb)
Benny Goodman And His Orchestra
40th Anniversary Concert-Live At Carnegie Hall | London | 820349-2
Verve Jazz Masters 33:Benny Goodman | Verve | 844410-2
Bill Evans Quartet With Orchestra
The Complete Bill Evans On Verve | Verve | 527953-2
From Left To Right | Verve | 557451-2
Bob James And His Orchestra
Jazzrock-Anthology Vol.3:Fusion | Zounds | CD 27100555
Freddie Hubbard With Orchestra
This Is Jazz:Freddie Hubbard | CBS | CK 65041
George Benson With The Don Sebesky Orchestra
Verve Jazz Masters 21:George Benson | Verve | 521861-2
Gerry Mulligan Concert Jazz Band
Verve Jazz Masters 36:Gerry Mulligan | Verve | 523342-2
The Complete Verve Gerry Mulligan Concert Band | Verve | 9860613
Glenn Miller And His Orchestra
The Glenn Miller Orchestra In Digital Mood | GRP | GRP 95022
Grover Washington Jr. Orchestra
Jazzrock-Anthology Vol.3:Fusion | Zounds | CD 27100555
Jimmy McGriff Orchestra
Swingin' The Blues-Jumpin' The Blues | Laserlight | 24654
Jimmy Smith With Orchestra
Jimmy Smith-Talkin' Verve | Verve | 531563-2
Jimmy Smith With The Johnny Pate Orchestra
Jimmy Smith-Talkin' Verve | Verve | 531563-2
Kenny Burrell With The Don Sebesky Orchestra
Verve Jazz Masters 45:Kenny Burrell | Verve | 527652-2
Blues-The Common Ground | Verve | 589101-2
Oscar Peterson With Orchestra
With Respect To Nat | Verve | 557486-2
Quincy Jones And His Orchestra
Verve Jazz Masters Vol.59:Toots Thielemans | Verve | 535271-2
Sarah Vaughan With Orchestra
!Viva! Vaughan | Mercury | 549374-2
Sarah Vaughan Sings The Mancini Songbook | Verve | 558401-2
Sarah Vaughan With The Frank Foster Orchestra
The Antonio Carlos Jobim Songbook | Verve | 525472-2
Wes Montgomery With The Don Sebesky Orchestra
Verve Jazz Masters 14:Wes Montgomery | Verve | 519826-2
Wes Montgomery:The Verve Jazz Sides | Verve | 521690-2
Talkin' Jazz:Roots Of Acid Jazz | Verve | 529580-2
California Dreaming | Verve | 827842-2
Wes Montgomery With The Oliver Nelson Orchestra
Verve Jazz Masters 14:Wes Montgomery | Verve | 519826-2
Wes Montgomery:The Verve Jazz Sides | Verve | 521690-2
Talkin' Jazz:Roots Of Acid Jazz | Verve | 529580-2

Andrees,Juwe | (pkeyboards)
Bajazzo
Caminos | Edition Collage | EC 485-2

Andresen,Bjornar | (bel-b)
Terje Rypdal Sextet
Terje Rypdal | ECM | 1016(527645-2)

Andress,Tuck | (el-g,el-g-solog)
Tuck And Patti
Tears Of Joy | Windham Hill | 34 10111-2
Love Warriors | Windham Hill | 34 10116-2
Dream | Windham Hill | 34 10130-2
A Gift Of Love | T&P Records | 9815810

Andreu,Jose | (v)
Herbie Mann And His Orchestra
The Best Of Herbie Mann | Atlantic | 7567-81369-2

Andrew Sisters,The | (voc-group)
The Andrew Sisters With The Glenn Miller Orchestra
The Chesterfield Broadcasts Vol.1 | RCA | 2663113-2

Andrews,Dwight | (alto-fl,bass-fl,piccolo,b-cl,as,ts)
Leo Smith Group
Devine Love | ECM | 1143

Andrews,Jeff | (bel-b)
Michael Brecker Group
Don't Try This At Home | Impulse(MCA) | 950114-2
Mike Stern Group
Jigsaw | Atlantic | 7567-82027-2
Vital Information
Ray Of Hope | VeraBra Records | CDVBR 2161-2
Where We Come From | Intuition Records | INT 3218-2

Andrews,Laverne | (voc)
The Andrew Sisters With The Glenn Miller Orchestra
The Chesterfield Broadcasts Vol.1 | RCA | 2663113-2

Andrews,Maxine | (voc)

Andrews,Patti | (voc)
Glenn Miller And His Orchestra
The Chesterfield Broadcasts Vol.1 | RCA | 2663113-2
The Andrew Sisters With The Glenn Miller Orchestra
The Chesterfield Broadcasts Vol.1 | RCA | 2663113-2

Andrews,Reggie | (keyboards)
Bobby Hutcherson Orchestra
Deep Blue-The United States Of Mind | Blue Note | 521152-2

Andrews,Russ | (ts)
Duke Ellington And His Orchestra
The Ellington Suites | Original Jazz Classics | OJC20 446-2(2310762)
Super Black Blues Band
Super Black Blues Vol.II | RCA | 2663874-2

Andrews,Stanley | (as,v,tpcl)
Arthur Young And Hatchett's Swingtette
Grapelli Story | Verve | 515807-2
Stephane Grappelli And His Musicians
Grapelli Story | Verve | 515807-2

Andrus,Chuck | (b)
Woody Herman And His Orchestra
Verve Jazz Masters 54:Woody Herman | Verve | 529903-2
Woody Herman-1963 | Philips | 589490-2

Andueza,Mikel | (asss)
Big Band Bellaterra
Don't Git Sassy | Fresh Sound Records | FSNT 048 CD
Mikel Andueza Quintet
BCN | Fresh Sound Records | FSNT 036 CD
Pep O'Callaghan Grup
Tot Just | Fresh Sound Records | FSNT 017 CD
Ramón Diaz Group
O Si No Que? | Fresh Sound Records | FSNT 044 CD

Anelli,Tony | (tp)
Gene Krupa And His Orchestra
Mullenium | CBS | CK 65678

Angeli,Primo | (pcembalo)
Brocksieper-Jazz-Ensemble
Drums Boogie | Bear Family Records | BCD 15988 AH
Brocksieper-Solisten-Orchester
Globetrotter | Bear Family Records | BCD 15912 AH
Brocksieper-Solisten-Orchester(Brocksi-Quartet)
Drums Boogie | Bear Family Records | BCD 15988 AH
Brocksieper-Special-Ensemble
Globetrotter | Bear Family Records | BCD 15912 AH
Brocksi-Quartett
Globetrotter | Bear Family Records | BCD 15912 AH
Freddie Brocksieper Und Seine Solisten
Globetrotter | Bear Family Records | BCD 15912 AH

Angelica,Maria | (castanets)
Lionel Hampton And His Orchestra
Planet Jazz:Lionel Hampton | Planet Jazz | 2152059-2
Lionel Hampton And His Quintet
Planet Jazz:Jazz Greatest Hits | Planet Jazz | 2169648-2
Lionel Hampton Quintet
Planet Jazz:Lionel Hampton | Planet Jazz | 2152059-2

Angelo,Nelson | (el-g,g,parr)
Ithamara Koorax With Band
Love Dance:The Ballad Album | Milestone | MCD 9327-2
Sarah Vaughan With Orchestra
I Love Brazil | Pablo | 2312101-2
Sarah Vaughan Birthday Celebration | Fantasy | FANCD 6090-2

Anger,Darol | (mand,v,cello,octave-mand,octave-v)
Stephane Grappelli-David Grisman Group
Stephane Grappelli:Live In San Francisco | Storyville | 4960723

Angione,Gianluigi | (cl)
Banda Cittá Ruvo Di Puglia
La Banda/Banda And Jazz | Enja | ENJ-9326 2

Angster,Armand | (b-cl,ss,mand,clcontra-b-cl)
Double Trio(Trio De Clarinettes&Arcado)
Green Dolphy Suite | Enja | ENJ-9011 2

Anirahtak | (voc)
Anirahtak und die Jürgen Sturm Band
Das Kurt Weill Programm | Nabel Records:Jazz Network | CD 4638
Berlin-Paris-New York/Music By Kurt Weil | Nabel Records:Jazz Network | CD 4655

Anker,Lotte | (ss,asts)
Copenhagen Art Ensemble
Shape To Twelve | dacapo | DCCD 9430
Angels' Share | dacapo | DCCD 9452
Lotte Anker-Marilyn Crispell-Marilyn Mazur
Poetic Justice | dacapo | DCCD 9460
Marilyn Mazur With Ars Nova And The Copenhagen Art Ensemble
Jordsange | dacapo | DCCD 9454

Anliker,Hans | (tb)
Anliker-Parker-Schmid-Senn-Solothurnmann
September Winds | Creative Works Records | CW CD 1038/39
Q4 Orchester Project
Lyon's Brood | Creative Works Records | CW CD 1018-3
Yavapai | Creative Works Records | CW CD 1028-2

Annabi,Amina | (voc)
Hank Jones Meets Cheik-Tidiana Seck
Sarala | Verve | 528783-2

Anot,César | (perc,b-gvoc)

Ansah,Thomas Ebow | (gvoc)
Hamiet Bluiett Group
...You Don't Need To Know...If You Have To Ask | Tutu Records | 888128-2*

Anthony,Bill | (b)
Stan Getz Quintet
Stan Getz Highlights:The Best Of The Verve Years Vol.2 | Verve | 517330-2
Stan Getz And The 'Cool' Sounds | Verve | 547317-2
Stan Getz Highlights | Verve | 847430-2

Anthony,Mike | (g)
Bobby Bryant Orchestra
Deep Blue-The United States Of Mind | Blue Note | 521152-2
Gerald Wilson And His Orchestra
Deep Blue-The United States Of Mind | Blue Note | 521152-2

Anthony,Ray | (arr,ldtp)
Glenn Miller And His Orchestra
Planet Jazz:Glenn Miller | Planet Jazz | 2152056-2
Planet Jazz:Jazz Greatest Hits | Planet Jazz | 2169648-2
Planet Jazz:Big Bands | Planet Jazz | 2169649-2

Antolini,Charly | (drperc)
Art Van Damme Group
State Of Art | MPS | 841413-2
Baden Powell Quartet
Three Originals:Tristeza On Guitar/Poema On Guitar/Apaixonado | MPS | 519216-2
Baden Powell Trio
Three Originals:Tristeza On Guitar/Poema On Guitar/Apaixonado | MPS | 519216-2
Charly Antolini Orchestra
Drum Beat | MPS | 9808191
Danny Moss Quartet
Keeper Of The Flame | Nagel-Heyer | CD 064
Danny Moss-Roy Williams Quintet
Steamers! | Nagel-Heyer | CD 049
Ellington For Lovers | Nagel-Heyer | NH 1009
Dieter Reith Group
Reith On! | MPS | 557423-2
Dieter Reith Quintet
Reith On! | MPS | 557423-2
Dieter Reith Trio
Reith On! | MPS | 557423-2
Jeanie Lambe And The Danny Moss Quartet
The Blue Noise Session | Nagel-Heyer | CD 052
Joe Turner-Albert Nicholas Quartet
The Giant Of Stride Piano In Switzerland | Jazz Connaisseur | JCCD 9106-2
Max Greger Quintet
Night Train | Polydor | 543393-2
Oscar Klein's Anniversary Band
Moonglow | Nagel-Heyer | CD 021
Ellington For Lovers | Nagel-Heyer | NH 1009
The Second Sampler | Nagel-Heyer | NHR SP 6
Schlüter-Nabatov-Antolini
Swing Kings | ACT | 9298-2
Singers Unlimited With The Art Van Damme Quintet
The Singers Unlimited:Magic Voices | MPS | 539130-2
The European Jazz Ginats
Jazz Party | Nagel-Heyer | CD 009
The First Sampler | Nagel-Heyer | NHR SP 5
The Tremble Kids All Stars
The Tremble Kids All Stars Play Chicago Jazz! | Nagel-Heyer | CD 043

Anton,Artie | (congas,drperc)
Stan Kenton And His Orchestra
Adventures In Blues | Capitol | 520089-2

Anton,Jim | (bel-b)
Steve Tibbetts Group
The Fall Of Us All | ECM | 1527(521144-2)
Steve Tibbetts | ECM | 1814(017068-2)

Antonelli,Tony | (as,reeds,saxts)
Jack Teagarden And His Orchestra
Jazz:The Essential Collection Vol.3 | IN+OUT Records | 78013-2

Antonini,Claire | (lute,cistre,tambur,saz,tartheorbe)
Renaud Garcia-Fons
Navigatore | Enja | ENJ-9418 2
Renaud Garcia-Fons Group
Oriental Bass | Enja | ENJ-9334 2
Navigatore | Enja | ENJ-9418 2
Entremundo | Enja | ENJ-9464 2

Antoniou,Giorgos | (b)
Brigitte Dietrich-Joe Haider Jazz Orchestra
Consequences | JHM Records | JHM 3624
Horn Knox
The Song Is You | JHM Records | JHM 3625
Joe Haider Trio
Grandfather's Garden | JHM Records | JHM 3619
A Magyar-The Hungarian-Die Ungarische | JHM Records | JHM 3626

Antonsen,Jens Petter | (tp)
Jon Balke w/Magnetic North Orchestra
Further | ECM | 1517

Antritter,Dieter | (clsax)
Dieter Antritter And His Traveling Jazz Band
Great Traditionalists | Jazzpoint | JP 1046 CD

Anzar,Pedro | (ts,vib,marimba,g,perc,charango)
Pat Metheny Group
Letter From Home | Geffen Records | GED 24245
The Road To You | Geffen Records | GED 24601

Anzenhofer,Thomas | (recitation)
Dirk Raulf Group
Die Welt Ist Immer Wieder Schön | Poise | Poise 03

Aoki,Tatsuyuki | (dr)
United Future Organizatio
United Future Organization | Talkin' Loud | 518166-2

Apap,Jean Marc | (viola)
Richard Galliano Septet
Piazzolla Forever | Dreyfus Jazz Line | FDM 36642-2

Aparicio,Eddie | (dr)
Jack Costanzo Group
Latin Fever:The Wild Rhythms Of Jack Costanza | Capitol | 590955-2

Aparis |
Aparis
Aparis | ECM | 1404
Despite The Fire Fighters' Efforts... | ECM | 1496(517717-2)

Aperdannier,Bene | (p,el-porg)
Jazz Indeed
Under Water | Traumton Records | 2415-2
Who The Moon Is | Traumton Records | 4427-2

Apfelbaum,Peter | (bs,dr,perc,ts,marimba,cowbell,p)
Don Cherry Group
Multi Kulti | A&M Records | 395323-2

Aplanalp,Richard | (bs)
Ella Fitzgerald With Orchestra
Ella/Things Ain't What They Used To Be | Warner | 9362-47875-2

Apostolidis,Eugen | (b)
Eugen Apostolidis Quartet
Imaginary Directions | Edition Collage | EC 503-2
Helmut Kagerer 4 & Roman Schwaller
Jazz Guitar Highlights 1 | Jardis Records | JRCD 20141
Gamblin' | Jardis Records | JRCD 9714
Jermaine Landsberger Trio
Gypsy Feeling | Edition Collage | EC 516-2
Jermaine Landsberger Trio With Bireli Lagrene
Gypsy Feeling | Edition Collage | EC 516-2
Piludu Quattro
Room 626 | Jazz 4 Ever Records:Jazz Network | J4E 4721

Appel,Dirk | (voc)
Jazzensemble Des Hessischen Rundfunks
Jazz Messe-Messe Für Unsere Zeit | hr music.de | hrmj 003-01 CD

Appiah,Nana | (brekete-dr,cabasa,cowbell)
Trevor Watts Moiré Music Drum Orchestra
A Wider Embrace | ECM | 1449
Applebaum,Stan | (cond,arrceleste)
Cal Tjader's Orchestra
Talkin Verve/Roots Of Acid Jazz:Cal Tjader | Verve | 531562-2
Appleman,Abe | (v)
A Band Of Friends
Wynton Marsalis Quartet With Strings | CBS | CK 68921
Appleton,Pat | (vocvoice)
Ax Genrich Group
Psychedelic Guitar | ATM Records | ATM 3809-AH
Appleton,Ray | (dr,percshakes)
Pat Martino Septet
Strings! | Original Jazz Classics | OJCCD 223-2(P 7547)
Appleyard,Peter | (vib)
Benny Goodman And His All Star Sextet
Verve Jazz Masters 33:Benny Goodman | Verve | 844410-2
Bill Mays Quartet
The Story Of Jazz Piano | Laserlight | 24653
Aquabella,Francisco | (bata-dr,claves,conga,quinto,congas)
Dizzy Gillespie And His Orchestra
Talking Verve:Dizzy Gillespie | Verve | 533846-2
Peggy Lee With Lou Levy's Orchestra
Pass Me By/Big Spender | Capitol | 535210-2
Arap,Jean-Marc | (viola)
Stephane Grappelli With The Michel Legrand Orchestra
Grapelli Story | Verve | 515807-2
Araujo,Juarez | (cl)
Ithamara Koorax With Band
Love Dance:The Ballad Album | Milestone | MCD 9327-2
Araujo,Lourival | (berimbauvoice)
Pata Masters
Pata-Bahia | Pata Musik | PATA 11 CD
Arbello,Fernando | (tb)
Fletcher Henderson And His Orchestra
Jazz:The Essential Collection Vol.1 | IN+OUT Records | 78011-2
Arcadio,Bernard | (keyboardsvoc)
Dee Dee Bridgewater With Band
Victim Of Love | Verve | 841199-2
Arcado String Trio |
Arcado-String Trio
Arcado-String Trio | JMT Edition | 919028-2
Archer,Jim | (v)
Dee Dee Bridgewater With Orchestra
Dear Ella | Verve | 539102-2
Archer,Vincente | (b)
Donald Harrison Quartet
Free To Be | Impulse(MCA) | 951283-2
Donald Harrison Sextet
Kind Of New | Candid | CCD 79768
Marcus Printup Sextet
The New Boogaloo | Nagel-Heyer | CD 2019
Archey,Jimmy | (tb)
Earl Hines-Muggsy Spanier All Stars
Earl Hines/Muggsy Spanier All Stars:The Chicago Dates | Storyville | STCD 6037
King Oliver And His Orchestra
Jazz:The Essential Collection Vol.1 | IN+OUT Records | 78011-2
Louis Armstrong And His Orchestra
Louis Armstrong:Swing That Music | Laserlight | 36056
Swing Legends:Louis Armstrong | Nimbus Records | NI 2012
Sidney Bechet's Blue Note Jazzmen
Runnin' Wild | Blue Note | 821259-2
Archibald,Paul | (tp)
John Surman-Jack DeJohnette With The London Brass
Printed In Germany | ECM | 1802(017065-2)
Archibald,Tim | (b)
Deborah Henson-Conant
Alterd Ego | Laika Records | 35100962
Arens,Lars | (tb)
Clark Terry With The Summit Jazz Orchestra
Clark | Edition Collage | EC 530-2
Arfi |
Pata Music Meets Arfi
News Of Roi Ubu | Pata Musik | PATA 10 CD
Argent,Rod | (el-p,synth,voc,keyboards,pvocoder)
Barbara Thompson's Paraphernalia
Barbara Thompson's Special Edition | VeraBra Records | CDVBR 2017-2
Argüelles,Julian | (as,bs,fl,b-cl,sax,keyboards)
Carla Bley Band
Big Band Theory | Watt | 25(519966-2)
Carla Bley Big Band
The Carla Bley Big Band Goes To Church | Watt | 27(533682-2)
Flemming Agerskov Quintet
Face To Face | dacapo | DCCD 9445
Kenny Wheeler Ensemble
Muisc For Large & Small Ensembles | ECM | 1415/16
NDR Big Band
The Theatre Of Kurt Weil | ACT | 9234-2
Argüelles,Steve | (dr,electronicsperc)
Creative Works Orchestra
Willisau And More Live | Creative Works Records | CW CD 1020-2
Heinz Sauer Quintet
Lost Ends:Live at Alte Oper Frankfurt | free flow music | ffm 0594
Nguyen Le Group
Tales From Viet-Nam | ACT | 9225-2
Robert Dick Group With The Soldier String Quartet
Jazz Standard On Mars | Enja | ENJ-9327 2
Ariovaldo | (perc)
Sarah Vaughan With Orchestra
I Love Brazil | Pablo | 2312101-2
Sarah Vaughan Birthday Celebration | Fantasy | FANCD 6090-2
Arkatov,James | (cello)
Ella Fitzgerald With The Nelson Riddle Orchestra
The Best Of The Song Books:The Ballads | Verve | 521867-2
Arkin,Eddie | (g)
Charles Earland Septet
Charlie's Greatest Hits | Prestige | PCD 24250-2
Arkin,Edward | (synth)
Stanley Clarke Group
If This Bass Could Only Talk | CBS | 460883-2
Arlt,Michael | (g)
Grooveyard Meets Houston Person
Basic Instinct | Organic Music | ORGM 9701
Grooveyard Meets Red Holloway
Basic Instinct | Organic Music | ORGM 9701
Grooveyard Meets Roman Schwaller
Basic Instinct | Organic Music | ORGM 9701
We Three
East Coasting | Organic Music | ORGM 9702
The Drivin' Beat | Organic Music | ORGM 9707
We Three With Roman Schwaller
East Coasting | Organic Music | ORGM 9702
Arm,Theodore | (v)
Chick Corea With String Quartet,Flute And French Horn
Septet | ECM | 1297
Armando,Ray | (congas,percbongos)
Buddy Rich Big Band
Backwoods Siseman/Pieces Of Dream | Laserlight | 24655
Gato Barbieri Orchestra
The Roots Of Acid Jazz | Impulse(MCA) | IMP 12042
Grant Green Sextet
Grant Green:Blue Breakbeat | Blue Note | 494705-2
Lee Konitz Orchestra
The Art Of Saxophone | Laserlight | 24652
Lou Donaldson Orchestra
Blue Breaks Beats Vol.2 | Blue Note | 789907-2

Richard 'Groove' Holmes Orchestra
Comin' On Home | Blue Note | 538701-2
Richard 'Groove' Holmes Sextet
Blue Break Beats | Blue Note | 799106-2
Stan Getz-Joao Gilberto Orchestra
Sony Jazz Collection:Stan Getz | CBS | 488623-2
Armann,Michael | (pvoice)
Rabih Abou-Khalil Septet
Between Dusk And Dawn | Enja | ENJ-9771 2
Armitage,Dennis | (ts)
Joe Turner And Friends
The Giant Of Stride Piano In Switzerland | Jazz Connaisseur | JCCD 9106-2
Armour,Ed | (fl-htp)
Charles Mingus And His Orchestra
The Complete Town Hall Concert | Blue Note | 828353-2
Freddie Hubbard Orchestra
The Body And The Soul | Impulse(MCA) | 951183-2
Armstead,Joshie | (voc)
Nina Simone And Orchestra
Baltimore | Epic | 476906-2
Armstrong [Hardin],Lil | (p,vocp-solo)
Jimmy Rodgers With Louis And Lil Armstrong
Best Of The Complete RCA Victor Recordings | RCA | 2663636-2
King Oliver's Creole Jazz Band
Jazz:The Essential Collection Vol.1 | IN+OUT Records | 78011-2
King Oliver's Jazz Band
Jazz:The Essential Collection Vol.1 | IN+OUT Records | 78011-2
Lil's Hot Shots
Jazz:The Essential Collection Vol.2 | IN+OUT Records | 78012-2
Louis Armstrong And His Hot Five
Jazz:The Essential Collection Vol.2 | IN+OUT Records | 78012-2
Louis Armstrong And His Hot Seven
Jazz:The Essential Collection Vol.2 | IN+OUT Records | 78012-2
Sidney Bechet Trio
Planet Jazz:Sidney Bechet | Planet Jazz | 2152063-2
Armstrong,Adam | (bel-b)
Wanderlust
Border Crossing | Laika Records | 35100812
Wanderlust + Guests
Full Bronte | Laika Records | 35101412
Armstrong,Jim | (tbvoc)
Dieter Antritter And His Traveling Jazz Band
Great Traditionalists | Jazzpoint | JP 1046 CD
Armstrong,Joseph | (congas)
Grant Green Sextet
Grant Green:Blue Breakbeat | Blue Note | 494705-2
Alive! | Blue Note | 525650-2
Blue Break Beats | Blue Note | 799106-2
The Lost Grooves | Blue Note | 831883-2
Armstrong,Louis | (co,slide-whistle,voc,p,talking,tp)
Bessie Smith And Her Band
Jazz:The Essential Collection Vol.1 | IN+OUT Records | 78011-2
Bessie Smith With Louis Armstrong And Fred Longshaw
Jazz:The Essential Collection Vol.1 | IN+OUT Records | 78011-2
Carroll Dickerson's Savoyagers
Louis Armstrong:Fireworks | Dreyfus Jazz Line | FDM 36710-2
Clarence Williams' Blue Five
Jazz:The Essential Collection Vol.1 | IN+OUT Records | 78011-2
Ella Fitzgerald And Louis Armstrong With Dave Barbour And His Orchestra
Ella Fitzgerald:Mr.Paganini | Dreyfus Jazz Line | FDM 36741-2
Ella Fitzgerald And Louis Armstrong With Sy Oliver And His Orchestra
Ella Fitzgerald:Mr.Paganini | Dreyfus Jazz Line | FDM 36741-2
Ella Fitzgerald And Louis Armstrong With The Oscar Peterson Quartet
Ella Fitzgerald-First Lady Of Song | Verve | 517898-2
Verve Jazz Masters 1:Louis Armstrong | Verve | 519818-2
Verve Jazz Masters 6:Ella Fitzgerald | Verve | 519822-2
Verve Jazz Masters 24:Ella Fitzgerald & Louis Armstrong | Verve | 521851-2
Verve Jazz Masters 46:Ella Fitzgerald-The Jazz Sides | Verve | 527655-2
Verve Jazz Masters Vol.60:The Collection | Verve | 529866-2
The Complete Ella Fitzgerald And Louis Armstrong On Verve | Verve | 537284-2
The Best Of Ella Fitzgerald And Louis Armstrong On Verve | Verve | 537909-2
Ella And Louis | Verve | 543304-2
Ella & Louis | Verve | 825373-2
Ella And Louis Again | Verve | 825374-2
For The Love Of Ella Fitzgerald | Verve | 841765-2
Ella Fitzgerald And Louis Armstrong With The Russell Garcia Orchestra
Ella Fitzgerald-First Lady Of Song | Verve | 517898-2
Verve Jazz Masters 24:Ella Fitzgerald & Louis Armstrong | Verve | 521851-2
Ella Fitzgerald With Louis Armstrong And The All Stars
Ella Fitzgerald-First Lady Of Song | Verve | 517898-2
The Complete Ella Fitzgerald And Louis Armstrong On Verve | Verve | 537284-2
The Best Of Ella Fitzgerald And Louis Armstrong On Verve | Verve | 537909-2
Ella Fitzgerald With Sy Oliver And His Orchestra
Ella Fitzgerald:The Decca Years 1949-1954 | Decca | 050668-2
Esquire All-American Award Winners
Best Of The Complete RCA Victor Recordings | RCA | 2663636-2
Highlights From The Duke Ellington Centennial Edition | RCA | 2663672-2
Fletcher Henderson And His Orchestra
Jazz:The Essential Collection Vol.1 | IN+OUT Records | 78011-2
Jimmy Rodgers With Louis And Lil Armstrong
Best Of The Complete RCA Victor Recordings | RCA | 2663636-2
King Oliver's Creole Jazz Band
Jazz:The Essential Collection Vol.1 | IN+OUT Records | 78011-2
King Oliver's Jazz Band
Jazz:The Essential Collection Vol.1 | IN+OUT Records | 78011-2
Leonard Feather's Esquire All-Americans
Louis Armstrong:C'est Si Bon | Dreyfus Jazz Line | FDM 36730-2
Lil's Hot Shots
Jazz:The Essential Collection Vol.2 | IN+OUT Records | 78012-2
Louis Armstrong And Billie Holiday With Sy Oliver's Orchestra
Louis Armstrong:C'est Si Bon | Dreyfus Jazz Line | FDM 36730-2
Louis Armstrong And Bing Crosby With Orchestra
The Very Best Of Dixieland Jazz | Verve | 535529-2
Louis Armstrong And Ella Fitzgerald With Bob Haggers's Orchestra
Louis Armstrong:C'est Si Bon | Dreyfus Jazz Line | FDM 36730-2
Louis Armstrong And Ella Fitzgerald With Russell Garcia's Orchestra
The Complete Ella Fitzgerald And Louis Armstrong On Verve | Verve | 537284-2
The Best Of Ella Fitzgerald And Louis Armstrong On Verve | Verve | 537909-2
Porgy And Bess | Verve | 827475-2
Louis Armstrong And Ella Fitzgerald With Sy Oliver's Orchestra
Louis Armstrong:C'est Si Bon | Dreyfus Jazz Line | FDM 36730-2
Louis Armstrong And Gary Crosby With Sonny Burke's Orchestra
Louis Armstrong-My Greatest Songs | MCA | MCD 18347
Louis Armstrong And His All Stars
Jazz In Paris:Louis Armstrong:The Best Live Concer Vol.1 | EmArCy | 013030-2
Jazz In Paris:Louis Armstrong-The Best Live Concert Vol.2 | EmArCy | 013031-2
Planet Jazz:Louis Armstrong | Planet Jazz | 2152052-2
Planet Jazz:Jack Teagarden | Planet Jazz | 2161236-2
Planet Jazz:Male Jazz Vocalists | Planet Jazz | 2169657-2
Jazz Collection:Louis Armstrong | Laserlight | 24366
Best Of The Complete RCA Victor Recordings | RCA | 2663636-2
Louis Armstrong:A 100th Birthday Celebration | RCA | 2663694-2
Jazz Festival Vol.1 | Storyville | 4960733

Verve Jazz Masters 1:Louis Armstrong | Verve | 519818-2
I Love Jazz | Verve | 543747-2
Satchmo Serenaders | Verve | 543792-2
Louis Armstrong:The Great Chicago Concert 1956 | CBS | C2K 65119
Louis Armstrong Plays W.C.Handy | CBS | CK 64925
Ambassador Satch | CBS | CK 64926
Satch Plays Fats(Complete) | CBS | CK 64927
Louis Armstrong:C'est Si Bon | Dreyfus Jazz Line | FDM 36730-2
Historic Barcelona Concerts At Windsor Palace 1955 | Fresh Sound Records | FSR-CD 3004
Live In Berlin/Friedrichstadtpalast | Jazzpoint | JP 1062 CD
The Legendary Berlin Concert Part 2 | Jazzpoint | JP 1063 CD
What A Wonderful World | MCA | MCD 01876
Louis Armstrong-My Greatest Songs | MCA | MCD 18347
Swing Legends:Louis Armstrong | Nimbus Records | NI 2012
Louis Armstrong:Wintergarden 1947/Blue Note 1948 | Storyville | STCD 8242
Louis Armstrong And His All Stars With A Studio Orchestra
What A Wonderful World | MCA | MCD 01876
Louis Armstrong And His All Stars With Benny Carter's Orchestra
Ambassador Louis Armstrong Vol.17:Moments To Remember(1952-1956) | Ambassador | CLA 1917
Louis Armstrong And His All Stars With Duke Ellington
Louis Armstrong-Duke Ellington:The Great Summit-Complete Session | Roulette | 524546-2
Louis Armstrong And His All Stars With Sonny Burke's Orchestra
Ambassador Louis Armstrong Vol.17:Moments To Remember(1952-1956) | Ambassador | CLA 1917
Louis Armstrong And His All Stars With The Sy Oliver Orchestra
Ambassador Louis Armstrong Vol.17:Moments To Remember(1952-1956) | Ambassador | CLA 1917
Louis Armstrong And His Dixieland Seven
Planet Jazz:Louis Armstrong | Planet Jazz | 2152052-2
Planet Jazz:Jazz Greatest Hits | Planet Jazz | 2169648-2
Planet Jazz:Jazz Trumpet | Planet Jazz | 2169654-2
Planet Jazz:Male Jazz Vocalists | Planet Jazz | 2169657-2
Best Of The Complete RCA Victor Recordings | RCA | 2663636-2
Louis Armstrong:A 100th Birthday Celebration | RCA | 2663694-2
Louis Armstrong:C'est Si Bon | Dreyfus Jazz Line | FDM 36730-2
Swing Legends:Louis Armstrong | Nimbus Records | NI 2012
Louis Armstrong And His Friends
Planet Jazz:Louis Armstrong | Planet Jazz | 2152052-2
Planet Jazz Sampler | Planet Jazz | 2152326-2
Louis Armstrong And His Friends | Bluebird | 2663961-2
Louis Armstrong And His Hot Five
Jazz:The Essential Collection Vol.2 | IN+OUT Records | 78012-2
Satch Plays Fats(Complete) | CBS | CK 64927
Louis Armstrong:Fireworks | Dreyfus Jazz Line | FDM 36710-2
Louis Armstrong And His Hot Seven
Planet Jazz:Louis Armstrong | Planet Jazz | 2152052-2
Best Of The Complete RCA Victor Recordings | RCA | 2663636-2
Louis Armstrong:A 100th Birthday Celebration | RCA | 2663694-2
Jazz:The Essential Collection Vol.2 | IN+OUT Records | 78012-2
Louis Armstrong:C'est Si Bon | Dreyfus Jazz Line | FDM 36730-2
Louis Armstrong And His Orchestra
Planet Jazz:Louis Armstrong | Planet Jazz | 2152052-2
Best Of The Complete RCA Victor Recordings | RCA | 2663636-2
Louis Armstrong:A 100th Birthday Celebration | RCA | 2663694-2
Louis Armstrong:Swing That Music | Laserlight | 36056
I Love Jazz | Verve | 543747-2
Satchmo Serenaders | Verve | 543792-2
Jazz:The Essential Collection Vol.2 | IN+OUT Records | 78012-2
Jazz:The Essential Collection Vol.3 | IN+OUT Records | 78013-2
Satch Plays Fats(Complete) | CBS | CK 64927
Louis Armstrong:Fireworks | Dreyfus Jazz Line | FDM 36710-2
Louis Armstrong:C'est Si Bon | Dreyfus Jazz Line | FDM 36730-2
What A Wonderful World | MCA | MCD 01876
Louis Armstrong-My Greatest Songs | MCA | MCD 18347
Swing Legends:Louis Armstrong | Nimbus Records | NI 2012
Louis Armstrong And His Savoy Ballroom Five
Jazz:The Essential Collection Vol.2 | IN+OUT Records | 78012-2
Louis Armstrong:Fireworks | Dreyfus Jazz Line | FDM 36710-2
Louis Armstrong And Omer Simeon With The Sy Oliver Orchestra
Ambassador Louis Armstrong Vol.17:Moments To Remember(1952-1956) | Ambassador | CLA 1917
Louis Armstrong And The Commanders under the Direction of Camarata
Satchmo Serenaders | Verve | 543792-2
Louis Armstrong And The Mills Brothers
Louis Armstrong:Swing That Music | Laserlight | 36056
Louis Armstrong With Benny Carter's Orchestra
Louis Armstrong-My Greatest Songs | MCA | MCD 18347
Louis Armstrong With Chick Webb's Orchestra
Best Of The Complete RCA Victor Recordings | RCA | 2663636-2
Louis Armstrong:A 100th Birthday Celebration | RCA | 2663694-2
Louis Armstrong With Earl Hines
Jazz:The Essential Collection Vol.2 | IN+OUT Records | 78012-2
Louis Armstrong With Gordon Jenkins And His Orchestra
Satchmo In Style | Verve | 549594-2
Louis Armstrong With Gordon Jenkins And His Orchestra And Choir
Satchmo In Style | Verve | 549594-2
Ambassador Louis Armstrong Vol.17:Moments To Remember(1952-1956) | Ambassador | CLA 1917
Louis Armstrong-My Greatest Songs | MCA | MCD 18347
Swing Legends:Louis Armstrong | Nimbus Records | NI 2012
Louis Armstrong With Harry Mills And Choir
Louis And The Good Book | Verve | 549593-2
Louis Armstrong With Jimmy Dorsey And His Orchestra
Louis Armstrong:Swing That Music | Laserlight | 36056
Swing Legends:Louis Armstrong | Nimbus Records | NI 2012
Louis Armstrong With Louis Jordan And His Tympany Five
Louis Armstrong:C'est Si Bon | Dreyfus Jazz Line | FDM 36730-2
Louis Armstrong With Orchestra
Jazz Collection:Louis Armstrong | Laserlight | 24366
Louis Armstrong With Sy Oliver And His Orchestra
Satchmo Serenaders | Verve | 543792-2
Louis And The Angels | Verve | 549592-2
Louis Armstrong:C'est Si Bon | Dreyfus Jazz Line | FDM 36730-2
Louis Armstrong-My Greatest Songs | MCA | MCD 18347
Louis Armstrong With Sy Oliver's Choir And Orchestra
Jazz Collection:Louis Armstrong | Laserlight | 24366
Louis And The Good Book | Verve | 549593-2
Louis And The Good Book | Verve | 940130-0
Louis Armstrong With The Casa Loma Orchestra
Louis Armstrong:Swing That Music | Laserlight | 36056
Louis Armstrong With The Commanders
Ambassador Louis Armstrong Vol.17:Moments To Remember(1952-1956) | Ambassador | CLA 1917
Louis Armstrong With The Gordon Jenkins Orchestra
Ambassador Louis Armstrong Vol.17:Moments To Remember(1952-1956) | Ambassador | CLA 1917
Louis Armstrong With The Hal Mooney Orchestra
Ambassador Louis Armstrong Vol.17:Moments To Remember(1952-1956) | Ambassador | CLA 1917
Louis Armstrong With The Lyn Murray Chorus
Louis And The Good Book | Verve | 549593-2
Louis Armstrong With The Oscar Peterson Quartet
Verve Jazz Masters 1:Louis Armstrong | Verve | 519818-2
Verve Jazz Masters 20:Introducing | Verve | 519853-2
Louis Armstrong Meets Oscar Peterson | Verve | 539060-2
Louis Armstrong With The Russell Garcia Orchestra
Verve Jazz Masters 1:Louis Armstrong | Verve | 519818-2
The Silver Collection: Louis Armstrong | Verve | 823446-2
Louis Armstrong-Duke Ellington Group
Blue Velvet: Crooners, Swooners And Velvet Vocals | Blue Note | 521153-2
Louis Armstrong-Earl Hines
Louis Armstrong:Fireworks | Dreyfus Jazz Line | FDM 36710-2
Louis Jordan And His Tympany Five

INTERPRETENVERZEICHNIS

Louis Jordan-Let The Good Times Roll: The Complete Decca Recordings 1938-1954 | Bear Family Records | BCD 15557 IH
V-Disc All Star Jam Session
Louis Armstrong-Jack Teagarden-Woody Herman:Midnights At V-Disc | Jazz Unlimited | JUCD 2048
V-Disc All Stars
Jazz:The Essential Collection Vol.3 | IN+OUT Records | 78013-2

Armstrong,Ralphe | (b,b-g,vocel-b)
Earl Klugh Trio
The Earl Klugh Trio Volume One | Warner | 7599-26750-2
Jean-Luc Ponty Group
Atlantic Jazz: Fusion | Atlantic | 7567-81711-2
Jean-Luc Ponty Quartet
Cosmic Messenger | Atlantic | 7567-81550-2
The Very Best Of Jean-Luc Ponty | Rhino | 8122-79862-2
Jean-Luc Ponty Quintet
Cosmic Messenger | Atlantic | 7567-81550-2
The Very Best Of Jean-Luc Ponty | Rhino | 8122-79862-2
Jean-Luc Ponty Sextet
Enigmatic Ocean | Atlantic | 19110-2
Cosmic Messenger | Atlantic | 7567-81550-2
The Very Best Of Jean-Luc Ponty | Rhino | 8122-79862-2
Mahavishnu Orchestra
Apocalypse | CBS | 467092-2

Armstrong,Tippy | (g)
Albert King Blues Band
Lovejoy | Stax | SCD 8517-2(STS 2040)

Arnaud,Francois | (v)
Stephane Grappelli With The Michel Legrand Orchestra
Grapelli Story | Verve | 515807-2

Arnberg,Elisabeth | (strings)
Esbjörn Svensson Trio(E.S.T) With Strings
EST Plays Monk | ACT | 9010-2

Arndt,Andreas | (cello)
Kölner Saxophon Mafia With The Auryn Quartet
Kölner Saxophon Mafia Proudly Presents | Jazz Haus Musik | JHM 0046 CD

Arnesen,Rune | (drbongos)
Nils Petter Molvaer Group
Khmer | ECM | 1560(537798-2)
Solid Ether | ECM | 1722(543365-2)

Arnheim,Yossi | (fl)
SheshBesh
SheshBesh | TipToe | TIP-888830 2

Arno,Victor | (v)
Ella Fitzgerald With The Nelson Riddle Orchestra
The Best Of The Song Books:The Ballads | Verve | 521867-2
Love Songs:The Best Of The Song Books | Verve | 531762-2
Phineas Newborn Jr. With Dennis Farnon And His Orchestra
While My Lady Sleeps | RCA | 2185157-2

Arnold,Billy Boy | (harmvoc)
Billy Boy Arnold Group
Eldorado Cadillac | Alligator Records | ALCD 4836
Windy City Blues | Stax | SCD 8612-2

Arnold,Buddy | (reedsts)
Stan Kenton And His Orchestra
Adventures In Blues | Capitol | 520089-2
Adventures In Jazz | Capitol | 521222-2

Arnold,Harry | (arr,ld,talkingts)
Coleman Hawkins With The Thore Ehrlings Orchestra
Coleman Hawkins At The Golden Circle | Dragon | DRCD 265

Arnold,Horacee | (drperc)
Chick Corea Septet
The Complete 'Is' Sessions | Blue Note | 540532-2

Arnold,Jay | (ts)
Jack McDuff Group
So Blue So Funky-Heroes Of The Hammond | Blue Note | 796563-2

Arnold,Jerome | (el-b)
Billy Boy Arnold Group
Windy City Blues | Stax | SCD 8612-2

Arnold,John | (dr)
Gary Thomas Quartet
Pariah's Pariah | Winter&Winter | 910033-2

Arnold,Marcina | (voc)
David Jean-Baptiste Group
The Nature Suite | Laika Records | 35101632

Arnold,Ronald | (ts)
Jimmy McGriff Quintet
Swingin' The Blues-Jumpin' The Blues | Laserlight | 24654

Arnopol,Michael | (b)
Jens Bunge Group
Meet You In Chicago | Jazz 4 Ever Records:Jazz Network | J4E 4749
Patricia Barber Group
Modern Cool | Blue Note | 521811-2
Patricia Barber Quartet
Café Blue | Blue Note | 521810-2

Arnström,Agneta | (dousso kynia)
Don Cherry Group
Don Cherry-The Sonet Recordings:Eternal Now/Live Ankara | Verve | 533049-2

Aronov,Ben | (keyboards,p,celesteel-p)
Carol Sloane With The Norris Turney Quartet
Something Cool | Choice | CHCD 71025
Ken Peplowski Quartet
Lost In The Stars | Nagel-Heyer | CD 2020
Terry Gibbs Dream Band
Terry Gibbs Dream Band Vol.3:Flying Home | Contemporary | CCD 7654-2
Terry Gibbs Dream Band Vol.6:One More Time | Contemporary | CCD 7658-2

Aronson,Stanley | (as,bsts)
Glenn Miller And His Orchestra
Planet Jazz:Glenn Miller | Planet Jazz | 2152056-2
Planet Jazz:Swing | Planet Jazz | 2169651-2
Candelight Miller | RCA | 2668716-2

Arpino,André | (dr)
Swingle Singers
Jazz Sebastian Bach | Philips | 542552-2

Arpino,Thierry | (dr)
Tony Purrone Trio
Rascality | Steeplechase | SCCD 31514

Arriaga Quartet |
Chick Corea And His Orchestra
My Spanish Heart | Polydor | 543303-3

Arriale,Lynne | (p)
Lynne Arriale Trio
Arise | IN+OUT Records | 77059-2
Wolfgang Lackerschmid & Lynne Arriale Trio
You Are Here | Bhakti Jazz | BR 43

Arrom,Juanjo | (tb)
Big Band Bellaterra
Don't Git Sassy | Fresh Sound Records | FSNT 048 CD

Arron,Robert | (reeds)
Al Jarreau With Band
L Is For Lover | i.e. Music | 557850-2

Ars Nova |
Marilyn Mazur With Ars Nova And The Copenhagen Art Ensemble
Jordsange | dacapo | DCCD 9454

Ars Vitale | (band)
Kölner Saxophon Mafia With Guests
Kölner Saxophon Mafia: 20 Jahre Saxuelle Befreiung | Jazz Haus Musik | JHM 0115 CD

Arslan,Vern | (tp)
Tommy Dorsey And His Orchestra
Planet Jazz:Tommy Dorsey | Planet Jazz | 2159972-2

Art De Fakt |
Art De Fakt
Art De Fakt-Ray Federman:Surfiction Jazz No.2 | double moon | CHRDM 71007

Art Ensemble Of Chicago |
Art Ensemble Of Chicago
Nice Guys | ECM | 1126
Full Force | ECM | 1167(829197-2)
Urban Bushmen | ECM | 1211/12
The Third Decade | ECM | 1273
Tribute To Lester | ECM | 1808(017066-2)
Americans Swinging In Paris:Art Ensemble Of Chicago | EMI Records | 539667-2
Bap-Tizum | Atlantic | 7567-80757-2
Coming Home Jamaica | Dreyfus Jazz Line | FDM 37003-2

Art Of Brass Vienna: |
Hans Theessink Group
Crazy Moon | Minor Music | 801052

Arte String Quartet |
Gabriel Pérez Group
Alfonsina | Jazz 4 Ever Records:Jazz Network | J4E 4751

Artero,Patrick | (dr,tpfl-h)
Frank Wess Meets The Paris-Barcelona Swing Connection
Paris-Barcelona Connection | Fresh Sound Records | FSNT 002 CD

Artin,Tom | (tb)
Mark Shane-Terry Blaine Group
With Thee I Swing! | Nagel-Heyer | CD 040

Arus,George | (tb)
Artie Shaw And His Orchestra
Planet JazzArtie Shaw | Planet Jazz | 2152057-2
Planet Jazz Sampler | Planet Jazz | 2152326-2
Planet Jazz:Swing | Planet Jazz | 2169651-2
Planet Jazz:Female Jazz Vocalists | Planet Jazz | 2169656-2
The Legends Of Swing | Laserlight | 24659
Tommy Dorsey And His Orchestra
Planet Jazz:Frank Sinatra & Tommy Dorsey | Planet Jazz | 2152067-2
Planet Jazz Sampler | Planet Jazz | 2152326-2
Planet Jazz:Tommy Dorsey | Planet Jazz | 2159972-2
Planet Jazz:Big Bands | Planet Jazz | 2169649-2
Planet Jazz:Male Jazz Vocalists | Planet Jazz | 2169657-2
Frank Sinatra And The Tommy Dorsey Orchestra | RCA | 2668701-2

Arvanitas,Georges | (porg)
Cat Anderson And His Orchestra
Americans Swinging In Paris:Cat Anderson | EMI Records | 539658-2
Les Double Six
Les Double Six | RCA | 2164314-2
Phil Woods-Benny Carter Quintet
The Art Of Saxophone | Laserlight | 24652
Sonny Criss Quintet
Jazz In Paris:Saxophones Á Saint-Germain Des Prés | EmArCy | 014060-2
Jazz In Paris:Sonny Criss-Mr.Blues Pour Flirter | EmArCy | 549231-2 PMS
Toots Thielemans Quartet
Jazz In Paris:Toots Thielemans-Blues Pour Flirter | EmArCy | 549403-2 PMS

Asaf,Ofer | (sax)
Kamafra
Kamafra Live | Edition Musikat | EDM 072

Asante | (voice)
Pharoah Sanders Group
Save Our Children | Verve | 557297-2

Asante,Okeryema | (african-dr,perc,kalimbavoc)
Hamiet Bluiett Group
...You Don't Need To Know...If You Have To Ask | Tutu Records | 888128-2*

Asatrian,Karen | (keyboards,synth,programmingvoice)
Couch Ensemble
Winnetou | Jazz 'n' Arts Records | JNA 1503

Asbjornsen,Kristin | (voc)
Ketil Bjornstad Group
Seafarer's Song | EmArCy | 9865777

Ascher,Kenny | (el-pkeyboards)
Earl Klugh Group
Late Night Guitar | Blue Note | 498573-2

Ascione,Joseph 'Joe' | (dr,percbongos)
Allan Vaché-Antti Sarpila & 1 Sextet
Summit Meeting | Nagel-Heyer | CD 027
Allan Vaché-Antti Sarpila Quintet
Swing Is Here | Nagel-Heyer | CD 026
Blues Of Summer | Nagel-Heyer | NH 1011
The Second Sampler | Nagel-Heyer | NHR SP 6
Bob Wilber And Friends
What Swing Is All About | Nagel-Heyer | CD 035
Blues Of Summer | Nagel-Heyer | NH 1011
Byron Stripling And Friends
If I Could Be With You | Nagel-Heyer | NH 1010
Frank Vignola Sextet
Off Broadway | Nagel-Heyer | CD 2006
International Allstars
The International Allstars Play Benny Goodman:Vol.1 | Nagel-Heyer | CD 025
The Second Sampler | Nagel-Heyer | NHR SP 6
Joe Ascione Octet
My Buddy:A Tribute To Buddy Rich | Nagel-Heyer | CD 036
Randy Sandke And The New York Allstars
The Re-Discovered Louis And Bix | Nagel-Heyer | CD 058
Randy Sandke-Dick Hyman
The Re-Discovered Louis And Bix | Nagel-Heyer | CD 058
The International Allstars
The International Allstars Play Benny Goodman Vol.1 | Nagel-Heyer | CD 045
The Nagel-Heyer Allstars
Uptown Lowdown:A Jazz Salute To The Big Apple | Nagel-Heyer | CD 2004
The New York Allstars
We Love You,Louis! | Nagel-Heyer | CD 029
Count Basie Remembered | Nagel-Heyer | CD 031
Count Basie Remembered Vol.2 | Nagel-Heyer | CD 041
Oh,Yeah! The New York Allstars Play More Music Of Louis Armstrong | Nagel-Heyer | CD 046
The Second Sampler | Nagel-Heyer | NHR SP 6

Ash,Steve | (p)
Warren Vaché And The New York City All-Star Big Band
Swingtime! | Nagel-Heyer | CD 059

Ashby,Harold | (cl,tsfl)
Ben Webster Septet
The Soul Of Ben Webster | Verve | 527475-2
Duke Ellington And His Orchestra
Highlights From The Duke Ellington Centennial Edition | RCA | 2663672-2
New Orleans Suite | Rhino | 812273670-2
The Ellington Suites | Original Jazz Classics | OJC20 446-2(2310762)
The Afro-Eurasian Eclipse-A Suite In Eight Parts | Original Jazz Classics | OJCCD 645-2(F 9498)
Togo Brava Swuite | Storyville | STCD 8323
Duke Ellington Orchestra
Continuum | Fantasy | FCD 24765-2
Duke Ellington Small Band
The Intimacy Of The Blues | Original Jazz Classics | OJCCD 624-2
Willie Dixon-Memphis Slim Quintet
Windy City Blues | Stax | SCD 8612-2

Ashby,Irving | (g)
Erroll Garner Quartet
Erroll Garner:Trio | Dreyfus Jazz Line | FDM 36719-2
Fats Waller And His Rhythm
Planet Jazz:Fats Waller | Planet Jazz | 2152058-2
JATP All Stars
Verve Jazz Masters 28:Charlie Parker Plays Standards | Verve | 521854-2
The Complete Jazz At The Philharmonic On Verve 1944-1949 | Verve | 523893-2
Bird: The Complete Charlie Parker On Verve | Verve | 837141-2
Jubilee All Stars
Jazz Gallery:Lester Young Vol.2(1946-59) | RCA | 2119541-2
Lester Young And His Band
Jazz:The Essential Collection Vol.3 | IN+OUT Records | 78013-2
Lester Young:The Complete Aladdin Sessions | Blue Note | 832787-2
Lester Young:Blue Lester | Dreyfus Jazz Line | FDM 36729-2
Lionel Hampton And His Orchestra
Lionel Hampton:Flying Home | Dreyfus Jazz Line | FDM 36735-2
Nat King Cole And His Trio
Nat King Cole:The Snader Telescriptions | Storyville | 4960103
Nat King Cole:Route 66 | Dreyfus Jazz Line | FDM 36716-2
Nat King Cole And His Trio With Strings
Nat King Cole:The Snader Telescriptions | Storyville | 4960103
Nat King Cole Quartet
The Instrumental Classics | Capitol | 798288-2
Nat King Cole:For Sentimental Reasons | Dreyfus Jazz Line | FDM 36740-2
Nat King Cole Quartet With The Pete Rugolo Orchestra
The Instrumental Classics | Capitol | 798288-2
Nat King Cole Quartet With The Stan Kenton Orchestra
Nat King Cole:For Sentimental Reasons | Dreyfus Jazz Line | FDM 36740-2
Nat King Cole Trio
Nat King Cole:The Snader Telescriptions | Storyville | 4960103
Nat King Cole:Route 66 | Dreyfus Jazz Line | FDM 36716-2
Nat King Cole:For Sentimental Reasons | Dreyfus Jazz Line | FDM 36740-2
Love Songs | Nimbus Records | NI 2010
Nat King Cole Trio With Pete Rugolo's Orchestra
Nat King Cole:For Sentimental Reasons | Dreyfus Jazz Line | FDM 36740-2
Nat King Cole Trio With Strings
Nat King Cole:For Sentimental Reasons | Dreyfus Jazz Line | FDM 36740-2
Oscar Peterson Trio
Gitanes Jazz 'Round Midnight: Oscar Peterson | Verve | 511036-2 PMS
Verve Jazz Masters 37:Oscar Peterson Plays Broadway | Verve | 516893-2
The Hollywood Hucksters
The Hollywood Session:The Capitol Jazzmen | Jazz Unlimited | JUCD 2044

Ashby,Irving prob. | (g)
JATP All Stars
The Complete Jazz At The Philharmonic On Verve 1944-1949 | Verve | 523893-2

Ashley,Ernest | (g)
Lionel Hampton And His Orchestra
Planet Jazz:Lionel Hampton | Planet Jazz | 2152059-2

Ashton,Bob | (bs,cl,ts,fl,b-cl,reedssax)
Cannonball Adderley And His Orchestra
Ballads | Blue Note | 537563-2
Cannonball Adderley Quintet
Ballads | Blue Note | 537563-2
Cannonball Adderley With Sergio Mendes And The Bossa Rio Sextet
Ballads | Blue Note | 537563-2
Count Basie And His Orchestra
Afrique | RCA | 2179618-2
Eddie Lockjaw Davis And His Orchestra
Eric Dolphy:The Complete Prestige Recordings | Prestige | 9 PRCD-4418-2
Gene Ammons And His Orchestra
A Stranger In Town | Prestige | PRCD 24266-2
Hank Jones With Oliver Nelson's Orchestra
The Roots Of Acid Jazz | Impulse(MCA) | IMP 12042
Jimmy McGriff Organ Blues Band
The Worm | Blue Note | 538699-2
Jimmy Rushing With Oliver Nelson And His Orchestra
Every Day I Have The Blues | Impulse(MCA) | 547967-2
Jimmy Smith And Wes Montgomery With Orchestra
Jimmy & Wes-The Dynamic Duo | Verve | 521445-2
Jimmy Smith And Wes Montgomery With The Oliver Nelson Orchestra
Wes Montgomery:The Verve Jazz Sides | Verve | 521690-2
Jimmy Smith:Best Of The Verve Years | Verve | 527950-2
Talkin' Jazz:Roots Of Acid Jazz | Verve | 529580-2
Jimmy Smith With The Oliver Nelson Orchestra
Verve Jazz Masters 29:Jimmy Smith | Verve | 521855-2
Jimmy Smith:Best Of The Verve Years | Verve | 527950-2
Jimmy Smith-Talkin' Verve | Verve | 531563-2
Peter & The Wolf | Verve | 547264-2
King Curtis Band
King Curtis-Blow Man Blow | Bear Family Records | BCD 15670 CI
Louis Armstrong And His Friends
Louis Armstrong And His Friends | Bluebird | 2663961-2
Sonny Rollins Orchestra
Alfie | Impulse(MCA) | 951224-2
Wes Montgomery With The Oliver Nelson Orchestra
Verve Jazz Masters 14:Wes Montgomery | Verve | 519826-2
Wes Montgomery:The Verve Jazz Sides | Verve | 521690-2
Talkin' Jazz:Roots Of Acid Jazz | Verve | 529580-2

Ashworth,Don | (bs,fl,b-cl,oboe,fr-h,ocarina)
Bill Evans Quartet With Orchestra
The Complete Bill Evans On Verve | Verve | 527953-2
From Left To Right | Verve | 557451-2
Bill Evans With Orchestra
The Complete Bill Evans On Verve | Verve | 527953-2
From Left To Right | Verve | 557451-2
George Benson With The Don Sebesky Orchestra
Verve Jazz Masters 21:George Benson | Verve | 521861-2
Jack McDuff Quartet With Orchestra
Prelude:Jack McDuff Big Band | Prestige | PRCD 24283-2
Stan Getz With The Eddie Sauter Orchestra
Stan Getz Plays The Music Of Mickey One | Verve | 531232-2

Ashworth.Nigel | (reeds)
André Holst With Chris Dean's European Swing Orchestra
That's Swing | Nagel-Heyer | CD 079

Askari,Mohamed | (nay)
Ute Kannenberg Quartet With Guests
Kannenberg On Purpose | Jazz Haus Musik | JHM 0109 CD

Askeur,Mahdi | (voc)
Nguyen Le Group
Maghreb And Friends | ACT | 9261-2

Askew,Greg | (chekere)
Mongo Santamaria And His Orchestra
Jazzin' Vol.2: The Music Of Stevie Wonder | Fantasy | FANCD 6088-2

Askey,Gil | (arr,keyboards,tpvoc)
(Little)Jimmy Scott With The Lucky Thompson Orchestra
Everybody's Somebody's Fool | Decca | 050669-2
Buddy Johnson And His Orchestra
Buddy And Ella Johnson 1953-1964 | Bear Family Records | BCD 15479 DH

Aslop,LaMar | (viola)
Nina Simone And Orchestra
Baltimore | Epic | 476906-2

Asmussen,Svend | (v,vocviola)
John Lewis Sextet
Monterey Jazz Festival 1975 | Storyville | 4960213
Sathima Bea Benjamin Group
A Morning In Paris | Enja | ENJ-9309 2
Svend Asmussen Quartet
Fit As A Fiddle | dacapo | DCCD 9429
Still Fiddling | Storyville | STCD 4252
Svend Asmussen Sextet
Svend Asmussen At Slukafter | Phontastic | NCD 8804

Aspar,Henri | (bs)
Ernie Royal And The Duke Knights
Americans Swinging In Paris:James Moody | EMI Records | 539653-2

Aspery,Ron | (as)

Heinz Sauer Quartet With The NDR Big Band
NDR Big Band-Bravissimo | ACT | 9232-2
Asplund,Peter | (tpfl-h)
Silje Nergard Group with Strings
Nightwatch | EmArCy | 9865648
Viktoria Tolstoy With The Esbjörn Svensson Trio
Viktoria Tolstoy:White Russian | Blue Note | 821220-2
Assael,Deborah | (cello)
Hank Jones Trio With The Meridian String Quartet
The Story Of Jazz Piano | Laserlight | 24653
Association Urbanetique |
Association Urbanetique
Ass Bedient | Jazz 4 Ever Records:Jazz Network | J4E 4723
Assumpacao,Zeca | (brainwood)
Egberto Gismonti & Academia De Dancas
Sanfona | ECM | 1203/04(829391-2)
Egberto Gismonti Group
Infancia | ECM | 1428
Musica De Sobrevivencia | ECM | 1509(519706-2)
Egberto Gismonti Trio
ZigZag | ECM | 1582
Assumpcao,Nico | (bel-b)
Duo Fenix
Karai-Eté | IN+OUT Records | 7009-2
Joe Henderson Group
Double Rainbow | Verve | 527222-2
Astor,Felix | (drperc)
Christopher Dell D.R.A.
Future Of The Smallest Form | Jazz 4 Ever Records:Jazz Network | J4E 4754
Jazzensemble Des Hessischen Rundfunks
Jazz Messe-Messe Für Unsere Zeit | hr music.de | hrmj 003-01 CD
Matthias Bröde Quartet
European Faces | Edition Collage | EC 517-2
Matthias Bröde Quintet
European Faces | Edition Collage | EC 517-2
Reiner Witzel Group
Passage To The Ear | Nabel Records:Jazz Network | CD 4668
Aszodi,Ference | (tp)
Hans Koller Big Band
New York City | MPS | 9813437
Atef,Cyril | (dr,perc,berimbao,voc,cuica,kakabobe)
Cornelius Claudio Kreusch Group
Scoop | ACT | 9255-2
Yves Robert Trio
In Touch | ECM | 1787(016375-2)
Atkins,André | (tb)
Steve Coleman And The Council Of Balance
Genesis & The Opening Of The Way | RCA | 2152934-2
Atkins,Ed | (tb)
King Oliver's Jazz Band
Jazz:The Essential Collection Vol.1 | IN+OUT Records | 78011-2
Atkins,Leonard | (ts,vviola)
Phineas Newborn Jr. With Dennis Farnon And His Orchestra
While My Lady Sleeps | RCA | 2185157-2
Tommy Dorsey And His Orchestra
Planet Jazz:Frank Sinatra & Tommy Dorsey | Planet Jazz | 2152067-2
Atkins,Nat | (tb)
Earl Hines And His Orchestra
Planet Jazz:Earl Hines | Planet Jazz | 2159973-2
Atkinson,Karen | (fl)
Lisle Atkinson Quintet
Bass Contra Bass | Storyville | STCD 8270
Atkinson,Lisle | (b)
Jeanne Lee Group
Natural Affinities | Owl Records | 018352-2
Lisle Atkinson Quartet
Bass Contra Bass | Storyville | STCD 8270
Lisle Atkinson Quintet
Bass Contra Bass | Storyville | STCD 8270
Nina Simone Quartet
Verve Jazz Masters 17:Nina Simone | Verve | 518198-2
Verve Jazz Masters 20:Introducing | Verve | 519853-2
Nina Simone After Hours | Verve | 526702-2
In Concert/I Put A Spell On You | Mercury | 846543-2
Nina Simone Quintet
Nina Simone After Hours | Verve | 526702-2
Nina Simone Trio
Nina Simone After Hours | Verve | 526702-2
Verve Jazz Masters Vol.58:Nina Simone Sings Nina | Verve | 529867-2
Nina Simone With Horace Ott's Orchestra
Nina Simone After Hours | Verve | 526702-2
Nina Simone-Lisle Atkinson
Verve Jazz Masters Vol.58:Nina Simone Sings Nina | Verve | 529867-2
Richard Wyands Trio
Then Here And Now | Storyville | STCD 8269
Atkinson,Sweet Pea | (voc)
Jimmy Smith All Stars
Jimmy Smith:Dot Com Blues | Blue Thumb | 543978-2
Atlantic Jazz Trio |
The Atlantic Jazz Trio
Some Other Time | Factory Outlet Records | FOR 2002-1 CD
Atlantic String Trio,The |
The Atlantic String Trio
First Meeting | Factory Outlet Records | FOR 2501-1 CD
Atlas,Jim | (bel-b)
Singers Unlimited
The Singers Unlimited:Magic Voices | MPS | 539130-2
ATonALL |
ATonALL
ATonALL | Creative Works Records | CW CD 1024-2
Attenbourough,Terbour | (b)
Terry Callier Duo
The New Folk Sound Of Terry Callier | Prestige | PRCD 11026-2
Attenoux,Michel | (asss)
Lionel Hampton All Stars
Jazz In Paris:Lionel Hampton-Ring Dem Bells | EmArCy | 159825-2 PMS
Michel Attenoux And His Dream Band
Great Traditionalists | Jazzpoint | JP 1046 CD
Quartier Latin Jazz Band
Great Traditionalists | Jazzpoint | JP 1046 CD
Sidney Bechet With Michel Attenoux And His Orchestra
Planet Jazz:Sidney Bechet | Planet Jazz | 2152063-2
Atterburry Thomas,Rosa | (voc)
Mike Westbrook Brass Band
Glad Day:Settings Of William Blake | Enja | ENJ-9376 2
Attig,Jürgen | (b,el-bfretless-b)
Gunter Hampel Quartet
Time Is Now-Live At The Eldena Jazz Festival 1992 | Birth | CD 042
Atwood,Fred | (b)
Lou Levy Trio
My Old Flame | Fresh Sound Records | FSR-CD 312
Atzmon,Gilad | (cl,ss,sol,ts,keyboardszorna)
Gilad Atzmon & The Orient House Ensemble
Gilad Atzmon & The Orient House Ensemble | TipToe | TIP-888839 2
Aubel,David | (fl)
Karim Ziad Groups
Ifrikya | ACT | 9282-2
Aubert,Henri | (v)
Phil Woods Quartet With Orchestra & Strings
Round Trip | Verve | 559804-2
Aubry,Philippe | (ts)
Louis Sclavis & The Bernard Struber Jazztet
La Phare | Enja | ENJ-9359 2
Auchtor,Carmen | (voc)
Christian Willisohn New Band
Heart Broken Man | Blues Beacon | BLU-1026 2
Auders,Josef | (sax)
Hans Koller Big Band
New York City | MPS | 9813437
Audi,Cesar | (dr,effects,surdovoice)
Raiz De Pedra
Diario De Bordo | TipToe | TIP-888822 2
Raiz De Pedra feat. Egberto Gismonti
Diario De Bordo | TipToe | TIP-888822 2
Audin,Jean-Philippe | (cello)
Charlie Haden Quartet West With Strings
Now Is The Hour | Verve | 527827-2
Audino,Johnny | (tp)
Ella Fitzgerald With The Nelson Riddle Orchestra
Ella Fitzgerald Sings The Johnny Mercer Songbook | Verve | 539057-2
Gerald Wilson And His Orchestra
Blue Breaks Beats Vol.2 | Blue Note | 789907-2
Terry Gibbs Dream Band
Terry Gibbs Dream Band Vol.2:The Sundown Sessions | Contemporary | CCD 7652-2
Terry Gibbs Dream Band Vol.3:Flying Home | Contemporary | CCD 7654-2
Terry Gibbs Dream Band Vol.6:One More Time | Contemporary | CCD 7658-2
The Jazz Giants Play Jerome Kern:Yesterdays | Prestige | PCD 24202-2
Auer,Martin | (tpfl-h)
Clark Terry With The Summit Jazz Orchestra
Clark | Edition Collage | EC 530-2
HR Big Band
The American Songs Of Kurt Weill | hr music.de | hrmj 006-01 CD
Libertango:Homage An Astor Piazolla | hr music.de | hrmj 014-02 CD
HR Big Band With Marjorie Barnes And Frits Landesbergen
Swinging Christmas | hr music.de | hrmj 012-02 CD
HR Big Band With Marjorie Barnes And Frits Landesbergen And Strings
Swinging Christmas | hr music.de | hrmj 012-02 CD
Martin Auer Quintet
Martin Auer Quintett | Jazz 4 Ever Records:Jazz Network | J4E 4762
Rainer Tempel Big Band
Album 03 | Jazz 'n' Arts Records | JNA 1102
The Three Sopranos With The HR Big Band
The Three Sopranos | hr music.de | hrmj 001-01 CD
Auer,Pepsi | (p)
Freddy Christman Quartet
Deutsches Jazz Fesival 1954/1955 | Bear Family Records | BCD 15430
Auger,Brian | (keyboards,synth,orgp)
Passport And Guests
Doldinger Jubilee Concert | Atlantic | 2292-44175-2
Augsburg String Quartet |
Stefanie Schlesiger And Her Group plus String Quartet
What Love Is | Enja | ENJ-9434 2
Augusto,Luiz | (drper)
Richard Galliano Quartet
Spleen | Dreyfus Jazz Line | FDM 36513-9
Gallianissimo! The Best Of Richard Galliano | Dreyfus Jazz Line | FDM 36616-2
Richard Galliano Quintet
Spleen | Dreyfus Jazz Line | FDM 36513-9
Augustsson,Filip | (b)
Rebecka Gordon Quartet
Yiddish'n Jazz | Touché Music | TMcCD 014
Auld,Georgie | (as,ts,sax,ss,vocwoodwinds)
Anita O'Day With The Buddy Bregman Orchestra
Pick Yourself Up | Verve | 517329-2
Artie Shaw And His Orchestra
Planet JazzArtie Shaw | Planet Jazz | 2152057-2
Planet Jazz:Male Jazz Vocalists | Planet Jazz | 2169657-2
The Legends Of Swing | Laserlight | 24659
Swing Vol.1 | Storyville | 4960343
Barney Kessel And His Septet
To Swing Or Not To Swing | Original Jazz Classics | OJCCD 317-2
Benny Goodman And His All Star Sextet
Charlie Christian:Swing To Bop | Dreyfus Jazz Line | FDM 36715-2
Benny Goodman And His Orchestra
Charlie Christian:Swing To Bop | Dreyfus Jazz Line | FDM 36715-2
Benny Goodman Septet feat.Count Basie
Charlie Christian:Swing To Bop | Dreyfus Jazz Line | FDM 36715-2
Big Joe Turner And Pete Johnson With The Blues Band
Newport Jazz Festival 1958,July 3rd-6th Vol.3:Blues In The Night No.1 | Phontastic | NCD 8815
Big Maybelle With The Blues Band
Newport Jazz Festival 1958,July 3rd-6th Vol.3:Blues In The Night No.1 | Phontastic | NCD 8815
Billie Holiday With The JATP All Stars
Billie Holiday Story Vol.1:Jazz At The Philharmonic | Verve | 521642-2
The Complete Jazz At The Philharmonic On Verve 1944-1949 | Verve | 523893-2
Verve Jazz Masters 47:Billie Holiday Sings Standards | Verve | 527650-2
Jazz At The Philharmonic:Best Of The 1940's Concerts | Verve | 557534-2
Buddy Bregman And His Orchestra
Swinging Kicks | Verve | 559514-2
Chubby Jackson Big Band
Gerry Mulligan Quartet feat.Chet Baker | Original Jazz Classics | OJCCD 711-2(F 8082/P 7641)
Chuck Berry With The Blues Band
Newport Jazz Festival 1958,July 3rd-6th Vol.3:Blues In The Night No.1 | Phontastic | NCD 8815
Count Basie Octet
Planet Jazz:Count Basie | Planet Jazz | 2152068-2
Ella Fitzgerald With Benny Carter's Magnificent Seven
30 By Ella | Capitol | 520090-2
Maynard Ferguson And His Orchestra
Verve Jazz Masters 52:Maynard Ferguson | Verve | 529905-2
Mike Bryan Sextet
Jazz Festival Vol.2 | Storyville | 4960743
Sarah Vaughan With The Allstars
Sarah Vaughan:Lover Man | Dreyfus Jazz Line | FDM 36739-2
Woody Herman And The Vanderbilt All Stars
Louis Armstrong-Jack Teagarden-Woody Herman:Midnights At V-Disc | Jazz Unlimited | JUCD 2048
Auryn String Quartet |
Kölner Saxophon Mafia With The Auryn Quartet
Kölner Saxophon Mafia Proudly Presents | Jazz Haus Musik | JHM 0046 CD
Aussem,Peter | (bassoon)
Harald Banter Ensemble
Deutsches Jazz Fesival 1954/1955 | Bear Family Records | BCD 15430
Austin,Henry | (voc)
Lillian Boutté And Her Group & The Soulful Heavenly Stars
The Gospel Book | Blues Beacon | BLU-1017 2
Austin,Johnny | (tp)
Glenn Miller And His Orchestra
Planet Jazz:Glenn Miller | Planet Jazz | 2152056-2
Austin,Patti | (voc)
Patti Austin And Her Band
Patti Austin:The Ultimate Collection | GRP | GRP 98212
Austin,Sil | (ts)
Buddy Johnson And His Orchestra
Buddy And Ella Johnson 1953-1964 | Bear Family Records | BCD 15479 DH
Austin,William | (p)
Louis Jordan And His Tympany Five
Louis Jordan-Let The Good Times Roll: The Complete Decca Recordings 1938-1954 | Bear Family Records | BCD 15557 IH
Austria Drei |
Austria Drei
Jazz Portraits | EGO | 95080
Authier,Patrice | (p)
Bill Coleman Sextet
Americans Swinging In Paris:Bill Coleman | EMI Records | 539663-2
Autin,Jean-Paul | (assopranino)
Pata Music Meets Arfi
News Of Roi Ubu | Pata Musik | PATA 10 CD
Autrey,Herman | (tpvoc)
Bud Freeman All Stars
The Bud Freeman All-Star Sessions | Prestige | PRCD 24286-2
Dick Wellstood's Wallerites
Uptown And Lowdown | Prestige | PCD 24262-2
Fats Waller And His Rhythm
Planet Jazz:Fats Waller | Planet Jazz | 2152058-2
Planet Jazz Sampler | Planet Jazz | 2152326-2
Planet Jazz:Male Jazz Vocalists | Planet Jazz | 2169657-2
Auvray,Lydie | (accordeon)
Kölner Saxophon Mafia With Lydie Auvray
Kölner Saxophon Mafia Proudly Presents | Jazz Haus Musik | JHM 0046 CD
Avakian,George | (interviewer)
Louis Armstrong And His All Stars
Louis Armstrong Plays W.C.Handy | CBS | CK 64925
Avellar,Luiz | (keyboards)
Toots Thieleman And Sivuca
Verve Jazz Masters Vol.59:Toots Thielemans | Verve | 535271-2
Avenel,Jean-Jacques | (bcora)
Nguyen Le Group
Maghreb And Friends | ACT | 9261-2
Steve Lacy-Roswell Rudd Quartet
Monk's Dream | Verve | 543090-2
Avery,Charles | (dr,pp-solo)
Charles Avery
Boogie Woogie | Laserlight | 24321
Avery,Teodross | (ssts)
Dee Dee Bridgewater With Big Band
Dear Ella | Verve | 539102-2
Donald Harrison Quintet
Free To Be | Impulse(MCA) | 951283-2
Teodross Avery Quartet
My Generation | Impulse(MCA) | 951181-2
Teodross Avery Quintet
My Generation | Impulse(MCA) | 951181-2
Avila,José | (p)
Conexion Latina
La Conexión | Enja | ENJ-9065 2
Avila,Miguel | (perc)
Lalo Schifrin And His Orchestra
Tin Tin Deo | Fresh Sound Records | FSR-CD 319
Avison,Keith | (tb)
Mr.Acker Bilk And His Paramount Jazz Band
The Golden Years Of Revival Jazz,Vol.2 | Storyville | STCD 5507
The Golden Years Of Revival Jazz,Vol.6 | Storyville | STCD 5511
The Golden Years Of Revival Jazz,Vol.12 | Storyville | STCD 5517
The Golden Years Of Revival Jazz.Vol.14 | Storyville | STCD 5519
The Golden Years Of Revibal Jazz,Vol.15 | Storyville | STCD 5520
Avital,Omer | (b)
Charles Owens Quartet
Eternal Balance | Fresh Sound Records | FSNT 067 CD
OAM Trio
Trilingual | Fresh Sound Records | FSNT 070 CD
Avola,Al | (garr)
Artie Shaw And His Orchestra
Planet JazzArtie Shaw | Planet Jazz | 2152057-2
Planet Jazz Sampler | Planet Jazz | 2152326-2
Planet Jazz:Swing | Planet Jazz | 2169651-2
Planet Jazz:Female Jazz Vocalists | Planet Jazz | 2169656-2
The Legends Of Swing | Laserlight | 24659
Tommy Dorsey And His Orchestra
Planet Jazz:Frank Sinatra & Tommy Dorsey | Planet Jazz | 2152067-2
Axelsson,Lennart | (tpfl-h)
Abdullah Ibrahim With The NDR Big Band
Ekapa Lodumo | TipToe | TIP-888840 2
Albert Mangelsdorff With The NDR Big Band
NDR Big Band-Bravissimo | ACT | 9232-2
Chet Baker With The NDR-Bigband
NDR Big Band-Bravissimo | ACT | 9232-2
My Favourite Songs: The Last Great Concert Vol.1 | Enja | ENJ-5097 2
The Last Concert Vol.I+II | Enja | ENJ-6074 22
Chet Baker-The Legacy Vol.1 | Enja | ENJ-9021 2
Heinz Sauer Quartet With The NDR Big Band
NDR Big Band-Bravissimo | ACT | 9232-2
Joe Pass With The NDR Big Band
Joe Pass In Hamburg | ACT | 9100-2
NDR Big Band-Bravissimo | ACT | 9232-2
Joe Pass With The NDR Big Band And Radio Philharmonie Hannover
Joe Pass In Hamburg | ACT | 9100-2
Johnny Griffin With The NDR Big Band
NDR Big Band-Bravissimo | ACT | 9232-2
NDR Big Band
NDR Big Band-Bravissimo | ACT | 9232-2
The Theatre Of Kurt Weil | ACT | 9234-2
Oscar Brown Jr. with The NDR Big Band
Live Every Minute | Minor Music | 801071
Pee Wee Ellis & NDR Bigband
What You Like | Minor Music | 801064
Axen,Bent | (p)
Don Byas Quartet
The Art Of Saxophone | Laserlight | 24652
Eric Dolphy Quartet
Eric Dolphy Birthday Celebration | Fantasy | FANCD 6085-2
Eric Dolphy With Erik Moseholm's Trio
Eric Dolphy:The Complete Prestige Recordings | Prestige | 9 PRCD-4418-2
Eric Dolphy in Europe, Vol.1 | Original Jazz Classics | OJC 413(P 7304)
Eric Dolphy In Europe, Vol.2 | Original Jazz Classics | OJCCD 414-2
Eric Dolphy In Europe, Vol.3 | Original Jazz Classics | OJCCD 416-2
Stan Getz With Ib Glindemann And His Orchestra
Stan Getz In Europe | Laserlight | 24657
Axenkopf,Klaus | (b)
Marcus Klossek Imagination
As We Are | Jardis Records | JRCD 20134
Jazz Guitar Highlights 1 | Jardis Records | JRCD 20141
Axis |
Axis
Axis | Jazz 4 Ever Records:Jazz Network | J4E 4735
Ayers,Roy | (KAT,voc,marimba,vib)
Herbie Mann Group
Memphis Underground | Atlantic | 7567-81364-2
The Best Of Herbie Mann | Atlantic | 7567-81369-2
Ayler,Albert | (as,ss,ts,bagpipevoc)
Albert Ayler Duo
Albert Ayler Live In Greenwich Village:The Complete Impulse Recordings | Impulse(MCA) | IMP 22732
Albert Ayler Group
Albert Ayler Live In Greenwich Village:The Complete Impulse Recordings | Impulse(MCA) | IMP 22732
Albert Ayler Quintet
Albert Ayler Live In Greenwich Village:The Complete Impulse Recordings | Impulse(MCA) | IMP 22732
Albert Ayler Sextet
Albert Ayler Live In Greenwich Village:The Complete Impulse Recordings | Impulse(MCA) | IMP 22732
Ayler,Donald | (tp)
Albert Ayler Group
Albert Ayler Live In Greenwich Village:The Complete Impulse Recordings | Impulse(MCA) | IMP 22732
Albert Ayler Quintet
Albert Ayler Live In Greenwich Village:The Complete Impulse Recordings | Impulse(MCA) | IMP 22732

Albert Ayler Sextet
Albert Ayler Live In Greenwich Village:The Complete Impulse Recordings | Impulse(MCA) | IMP 22732

Azevedo,Mike | (congasperc)
Caldera
Jazzrock-Anthology Vol.3:Fusion | Zounds | CD 27100555

Azimuth |
Azimuth
Azimuth '85 | ECM | 1298
How It Was Then...Never Again | ECM | 1538
Azimuth | ECM | 1546/48(523010-2)
Azimuth With Ralph Towner
Azimuth | ECM | 1546/48(523010-2)

Aziz | (cholak)
Remember Shakti
Saturday Night In Bombay | Verve | 014184-2

Aziz,Moustapha Abdel | (arghoul)
Koch-Schütz-Studer & El Nil Troop
Heavy Cairo Trafic | Intuition Records | INT 3175-2

Aznar,Pedro | (g,perc,glockenspiel,voice,whistle)
Pat Metheny Group
First Circle | ECM | 1278(823342-2)

Azuma,Christina | (g)
Christina Azuma
Internationales Guitarren Festival '94 | ALISO Records | AL 1030

Azymuth |
Azymuth
Jazzrock-Anthology Vol.3:Fusion | Zounds | CD 27100555

Azzi,Christian | (p)
Claude Luter Et Ses L'Orientais
Jazz In Paris:Sidney Bechet Et Claude Luther | EmArCy | 159821-2 PMS
Sidney Bechet With Claude Luter And His Orchestra
Planet Jazz:Sidney Bechet | Planet Jazz | 2152063-2
Sidney Bechet:Summertime | Dreyfus Jazz Line | FDM 36712-2

Azzola,Marcel | (accordeon)
Florin Niculescu Quartet
Four Friends | Jardis Records | JRCD 9923

Baan,Frans | (bassoon)
Toots Thielemans And His Orchestra
Verve Jazz Masters Vol.59:Toots Thielemans | Verve | 535271-2

Baba,Chili | (voc)
Roman Bunka Group
Dein Kopf Ist Ein Schlafendes Auto | ATM Records | ATM 3818-AH

Babafemi | (congasperc)
Gato Barbieri Group
Planet Jazz:Gato Barbieri | RCA | 2165364-2
Gato Barbieri Septet
Yesterdays | RCA | 2147797-2

Babasin,Harry | (b,ldcello)
Arnold Ross Trio
Just You & He & Me | Fresh Sound Records | FSR-CD 313
Barney Kessel Quintet
Easy Like | Original Jazz Classics | OJCCD 153-2
Bob Enevoldsen Quintet
The Complete Nocturne Recordings:Jazz In Hollywood Series Vol.1 | Fresh Sound Records | NR 3CD-101
Bob Enevoldsen Sextet
The Complete Nocturne Recordings:Jazz In Hollywood Series Vol.1 | Fresh Sound Records | NR 3CD-101
Bud Shank Quintet
The Complete Nocturne Recordings:Jazz In Hollywood Series Vol.1 | Fresh Sound Records | NR 3CD-101
Harry Babasin Quintet
The Complete Nocturne Recordings:Jazz In Hollywood Series Vol.1 | Fresh Sound Records | NR 3CD-101
Herbie Harper Quartet
The Complete Nocturne Recordings:Jazz In Hollywood Series Vol.1 | Fresh Sound Records | NR 3CD-101
Herbie Harper Quintet
The Complete Nocturne Recordings:Jazz In Hollywood Series Vol.1 | Fresh Sound Records | NR 3CD-101
Lou Levy Trio
The Complete Nocturne Recordings:Jazz In Hollywood Series Vol.1 | Fresh Sound Records | NR 3CD-101
Virgil Gonsalves Sextet
The Complete Nocturne Recordings:Jazz In Hollywood Series Vol.1 | Fresh Sound Records | NR 3CD-101

Babbington,Roy | (bb-g)
Mose Allison Quartet
The Mose Chronicles-Live In London,Vol.2 | Blue Note | 529748-2
Mose Allison Trio
The Mose Chronicles-Live In London,Vol.1 | Blue Note | 529747-2

Babel,Zoro | (dr)
Markus Stockhausen Quartet
Cosi Lontano...Quasi Dentro | ECM | 1371

Babkina,Nadezhda | (ld)
Mikhail Alperin's Moscow Art Trio With The Russkaja Pesnja Folk Choir
Folk Dreams | JA & RO | JARO 4187-2

Babualt,Michel | (dr)
Phil Woods-Benny Carter Quintet
The Art Of Saxophone | Laserlight | 24652

Baccus,Eddie | (org)
Eddie Baccus Quartet
Rahsaan/The Complete Mercury Recordings Of Roland Kirk | Mercury | 846630-2

Bachelder,Ken | (b)
The Jimmy And Marion McPartland Sessions
Vic Lewis:The Golden Years | Candid | CCD 79754

Bachmann,Thomas | (ts)
HR Big Band
The American Songs Of Kurt Weill | hr music.de | hrmj 006-01 CD

Bachträgl,Erich | (drperc)
Art Farmer Quintet
From Vienna With Art | MPS | 9811443

Baciu,Ion | (p)
Tim Hagans With Norrbotten Big Band
Future Miles | ACT | 9235-2

Backenroth,Hans | (b)
Agneta Baumann And Her Quartet
Comes Love... | Touché Music | TMcCD 011

Background Vocals |
Al Jarreau With Band
High Crime | i.e. Music | 557848-2
L Is For Lover | i.e. Music | 557850-2
Heart's Horizon | i.e. Music | 557851-2
Heaven And Earth | i.e. Music | 557852-2
We Got By | Reprise | 7599-27222-2
Bobby McFerrin Group
Bobby McFerrin | Elektra | 7559-60023-2
Joe Williams With The Frank Hunter Orchestra
Planet Jazz:Joe Williams | Planet Jazz | 2165370-2

Backhouse,Tony | (voc)
Vince Jones Group
Here's To The Miracles | Intuition Records | INT 3198-2

Backlund,Kaj | (tp)
Edward Vesala Group
Nan Madol | ECM | 1077

Bäckman,Rolf | (as)
Bengt-Arne Wallin Orchestra
The Birth+Rebirth Of Swedish Folk Jazz | ACT | 9254-2

Backus,Earl | (g)
Anita O'Day And Her Combo
Verve Jazz Masters 49:Anita O'Day | Verve | 527653-2

Bacon,Louis | (tpvoc)
Duke Ellington And His Orchestra
Highlights From The Duke Ellington Centennial Edition | RCA | 2663672-2
Louis Armstrong And His Orchestra
Louis Armstrong:Swing That Music | Laserlight | 36056
Louis Armstrong-My Greatest Songs | MCA | MCD 18347
Swing Legends:Louis Armstrong | Nimbus Records | NI 2012
Louis Armstrong With Chick Webb's Orchestra
Best Of The Complete RCA Victor Recordings | RCA | 2663636-2
Louis Armstrong:A 100th Birthday Celebration | RCA | 2663694-2

Bacsik,Elek | (g)
Dizzy Gillespie Septet
The Antonio Carlos Jobim Songbook | Verve | 525472-2
Elek Bacsik Quartet
Jazz In Paris:Elek Baczik | EmArCy | 542231-2
Elek Bacsik Trio
Jazz In Paris:Elek Baczik | EmArCy | 542231-2
Les Double Six
Les Double Six | RCA | 2164314-2

Baden Powell | (g,agogo,surdo,arr,vocg-solo)
Baden Powell
Three Originals:Tristeza On Guitar/Poema On Guitar/Apaixonado | MPS | 519216-2
Baden Powell Ensemble
Three Originals:Tristeza On Guitar/Poema On Guitar/Apaixonado | MPS | 519216-2
Baden Powell Quartet
Three Originals:Tristeza On Guitar/Poema On Guitar/Apaixonado | MPS | 519216-2
Baden Powell Solo/Group
Three Originals:Tristeza On Guitar/Poema On Guitar/Apaixonado | MPS | 519216-2
Baden Powell Trio
Three Originals:Tristeza On Guitar/Poema On Guitar/Apaixonado | MPS | 519216-2

Bader,Klaus | (sax)
Great Traditionalists In Europe
Great Traditionalists | Jazzpoint | JP 1046 CD

Badgley,Ed | (tp)
Gene Krupa And His Orchestra
Mullenium | CBS | CK 65678

Badie,Peter | (b)
Lionel Hampton And His Orchestra
Planet Jazz:Lionel Hampton | Planet Jazz | 2152059-2
Lionel Hampton And His Quintet
Planet Jazz:Jazz Greatest Hits | Planet Jazz | 2169648-2
Lionel Hampton Quintet
Planet Jazz:Lionel Hampton | Planet Jazz | 2152059-2

Badila,Decebal | (b)
Eugen Cicero-Decebal Badila
Swinging Piano Classics | IN+OUT Records | 77047-2

Badini,Gerard | (cl,tsld)
Gérard Badini Quartet
Jazz In Paris:Gérard Badini-The Swing Machine | EmArCy | 018417-2
Lionel Hampton All Stars
Jazz In Paris:Lionel Hampton-Ring Dem Bells | EmArCy | 159825-2 PMS
Sidney Bechet With Michel Attenoux And His Orchestra
Planet Jazz:Sidney Bechet | Planet Jazz | 2152063-2

Badrena,Manolo | (african bells,chekere,cowbell)
Ahmad Jamal Quartet
The Essence Part 1 | Dreyfus Jazz Line | FDM 37007-2
Big Byrd | Dreyfus Jazz Line | FDM 37008-2
Ahmad Jamal Quintet
The Essence Part 1 | Dreyfus Jazz Line | FDM 37007-2
Big Byrd | Dreyfus Jazz Line | FDM 37008-2
Ahmad Jamal Septet
Live In Paris 1996 | Dreyfus Jazz Line | FDM 37020-2
Carla Bley Band
Heavy Heart | Watt | 14
Night-Glo | Watt | 16
Ivo Perlman Group
Children Of Ibeji | Enja | ENJ-7005 2
Mark Whitfield Group
Patrice | Warner | 7599-26659-2
Mike Stern Group
Jigsaw | Atlantic | 7567-82027-2
Randy Brecker Group
Jazzrock-Anthology Vol.3:Fusion | Zounds | CD 27100555
Weather Report
Mr. Gone | CBS | 468208-2
Heavy Weather | CBS | CK 65108

Bae,Ikwhan | (vviola)
Steve Swallow Group
Carla | Watt | XtraWatt/2

Baez,Aquiles | (cuatro)
Danilo Perez Group
Central Avenue | Impulse(MCA) | 951281-2

Bagby,Doc | (orgp)
Sister Rosetta Tharpe And Her Group
Gospel Train | Mercury | 841134-2
Sister Rosetta Tharpe And Her Group With The Harmonizing Four
Gospel Train | Mercury | 841134-2

Bagge,Lasse | (condarr)
Toots Thielemans With Gals And Pals
Verve Jazz Masters Vol.59:Toots Thielemans | Verve | 535271-2

Bagley,Don | (b)
Ben Webster With Strings
The Warm Moods-With Strings | Rhino | 8122-73721-2
Lars Gullin American All Stars
Lars Gullin 1953,Vol.2:Moden Sounds | Dragon | DRCD 234
Stan Kenton And His Orchestra
Great Swing Classics In Hi-Fi | Capitol | 521223-2
Stan Kenton Portraits On Standards | Capitol | 531571-2
One Night Stand | Choice | CHCD 71051

Bah,Hassan | (congas)
Piirpauke
Piirpauke-Global Servisi | JA & RO | JARO 4150-2

Bahler,Tom | (vocvoc-arr)
Quincy Jones And His Orchestra
Verve Jazz Masters Vol.59:Toots Thielemans | Verve | 535271-2

Bahner,Michael | (b)
Jürgen Knieper Quintet
State Of Things | Jazz Haus Musik | JHM 0104 CD

Baierl,Ferry | (g)
Helmut Nieberle & Cordes Sauvages
Jazz Guitar Highlights 1 | Jardis Records | JRCD 20141
Salut To Django | Jardis Records | JRCD 9926

Baika,Imre | (b)
Terra Brazil
Café Com Leite | art-mode-records | AMR 2101

Bailey,Benny | (tp,fl-hvoc)
(Little)Jimmy Scott With The Lionel Hampton Orchestra
Everybody's Somebody's Fool | Decca | 050669-2
Abbey Lincoln And Her All Stars(Newport Rebels)
Candid Dolphy | Candid | CCD 79033
Benny Bailey Quartet
I Thought About You | Laika Records | 35100762
Angel Eyes | Laika Records | 8695068
Benny Bailey Quartet With Strings
I Remember Love | Laika Records | 35101752
Benny Bailey Quartet With Wayne Bartlett
I Thought About You | Laika Records | 35100762
Benny Bailey Quintet
Jazz Portraits | EGO | 95080
The Satchmo Legacy | Enja | ENJ-9407 2
Benny Bailey Septet
Big Brass | Candid | CCD 79011
Benny Bailey With The Bernhard Pichl Trio
On The Corner | Jazz 4 Ever Records:Jazz Network | J4E 4726
Berlin Contemporary Jazz Orchestra
Berlin Contemporary Jazz Orchestra | ECM | 1409
Conexion Latina
Calorcito | Enja | ENJ-4072 2
Mambo 2000 | Enja | ENJ-7055 2
Dexter Gordon-Benny Bailey Quintet
Revelation | Steeplechase | SCCD 31373
The Rainbow People | Steeplechase | SCCD 31521
Dizzy Gillespie And His Orchestra
Dizzy Gillespie:Pleyel Jazz Concert 1948 + Max Roach Quintet 1949 | Vogue | 21409412
Planet Jazz:Dizzy Gillespie | Planet Jazz | 2152069-2
Planet Jazz:Bebop | RCA | 2169650-2
Four For Jazz & Benny Bailey
The Best Of Four For Jazz & Benny Bailey | JHM Records | JHM 3615
Freddie Redd Sextet
Redd's Blues | Blue Note | 540537-2
Hans Koller Big Band
New York City | MPS | 9813437
Jazz Artists Guild
Newport Rebels-Jazz Artists Guild | Candid | CCD 79022
Kenny Clarke-Francy Boland Big Band
Clark-Boland Big Band: TNP, October 29th, 1969 | Laserlight | 36129
Three Latin Adventures | MPS | 529095-2
More Smiles | MPS | 9814789
All Smiles | MPS | 9814790
Francy Boland-Fellini 712 | MPS | 9814805
Les McCann-Eddie Harris Quintet
Rhino Presents The Atlantic Jazz Gallery | Atlantic | 8122-71257-2
Swiss Movement | Atlantic | 8122-72452-2
Lionel Hampton All Stars
Jazz In Paris:Lionel Hampton And His French New Sound Vol.1 | EmArCy | 549405-2 PMS
Jazz In Paris:Lionel Hampton And His French New Sound Vol.2 | EmArCy | 549406-2 PMS
Lionel Hampton And His Orchestra
Lionel Hampton:Flying Home | Dreyfus Jazz Line | FDM 36735-2
Lionel Hampton Orchestra
The Big Bands Vol.1.The Snader Telescriptions | Storyville | 4960043
Max Greger Quintet
Night Train | Polydor | 543393-2
Max Roach Septet
The Jazz Life! | Candid | CCD 79019
Miles Davis With Gil Evans Orchestra, The George Gruntz Concert Jazz Band And Guests
Miles & Quincy Live At Montreux | Warner | 9362-45221-2
NDR Big Band With Guests
50 Years Of NDR Big Band:Bravissimo II | ACT | 9259-2
NDR-Workshop
Doldinger's Best | ACT | 9224-2
Slide Hampton-Joe Haider Jazz Orchestra
Give Me A Double | JHM Records | JHM 3627
Stan Getz And The Swedish All Stars
Stan Getz Highlights:The Best Of The Verve Years Vol.2 | Verve | 517330-2
Stan Getz Highlights | Verve | 847430-2
The Upper Manhattan Jazz Society
The Upper Manhattan Jazz Society | Enja | ENJ-4090 2

Bailey,Buster | (as,cl,ss,tsvoc)
Alberta Hunter With Buster Bailey's Blues Blasters
Songs We Taught Your Mother | Original Blues Classics | OBCCD 520-2
Bessie Smith And Her Band
Jazz:The Essential Collection Vol.1 | IN+OUT Records | 78011-2
Bessie Smith With The James P.Johnson Orchestra And The Hal Johnson Choir
The Blues | Storyville | 4960323
Billie Holiday And Her Band
Billie's Love Songs | Nimbus Records | NI 2000
Billie Holiday With Teddy Wilson And His Orchestra
Billie's Love Songs | Nimbus Records | NI 2000
Fletcher Henderson And His Orchestra
Jazz:The Essential Collection Vol.1 | IN+OUT Records | 78011-2
Jazz:The Essential Collection Vol.3 | IN+OUT Records | 78013-2
Henry Red Allen's All Stars
Planet Jazz:Coleman Hawkins | Planet Jazz | 2152055-2
Jack Teagarden With The Red Allen Band
The Very Best Of Dixieland Jazz | Verve | 535529-2
John Kirby Band
The Small Black Groups | Storyville | 4960523
Juanita Hall With The Claude Hopkins All Stars
Juanita Hall Sings The Blues | Original Jazz Classics | OJCCD 1928-2(CPST 556)
King Oliver's Jazz Band
Jazz:The Essential Collection Vol.1 | IN+OUT Records | 78011-2
Lionel Hampton And His Orchestra
Planet Jazz:Male Jazz Vocalists | Planet Jazz | 2169657-2
Sarah Vaughan With John Kirby And His Orchestra
Sarah Vaughan Birthday Celebration | Fantasy | FANCD 6090-2
Sarah Vaughan:Lover Man | Dreyfus Jazz Line | FDM 36739-2
The Lousiana Stompers
Jazz:The Essential Collection Vol.1 | IN+OUT Records | 78011-2
Victoria Spivey With Buster Bailey's Blues Blasters
Songs We Taught Your Mother | Original Blues Classics | OBCCD 520-2
Wingy Mannone And His Orchestra
Planet Jazz:Jazz Trumpet | Planet Jazz | 2169654-2

Bailey,Colin | (dr)
Joe Pass Quartet
Apassionato | Pablo | 2310946-2
Nuages | Pablo | 2310961-2
Joe Pass:Guitar Virtuoso | Pablo | 4 PACD 4423-2
Joy Spring | Blue Note | 835222-2
The Jazz Giants Play Duke Ellington:Caravan | Prestige | PCD 24227-2
Ron Affif Quartet
The Jazz Giants Play Miles Davis:Milestones | Prestige | PCD 24225-2
Vince Guaraldi Group
Charlie Brown's Holiday Hits | Fantasy | FCD 9682-2
Vince Guaraldi Trio
Cast Your Fate To The Wind | Original Jazz Classics | OJCCD 437-2(F 8089)

Bailey,Colin or Jerry Grannelly | (dr)
A Charlie Brown Christmas | Fantasy | FSA 8431-6

Bailey,Craig | (asfl)
Craig Bailey Band
A New Journey | Candid | CCD 79725
Tom Harrell Orchestra
Time's Mirror | RCA | 2663524-2

Bailey,Dave | (cldr)
A Band Of Friends
The Best Of The Gerry Mulligan Quartet With Chet Baker | Pacific Jazz | 795481-2
Al Sears & His Rock 'N' Rollers
Sear-iously | Bear Family Records | BCD 15668 AH
Ben Webster Septet
The Soul Of Ben Webster | Verve | 527475-2
Bola Sete Quintet
Tour De Force:The Bola Sete Trios | Fantasy | FCD 24766-2
Gerry Mulligan And His Orchestra
Mullenium | CBS | CK 65678
Gerry Mulligan And The Sax Section
The Gerry Mulligan Songbook | Pacific Jazz | 833575-2
Gerry Mulligan Concert Jazz Band
The Complete Verve Gerry Mulligan Concert Band | Verve | 9860613
Gerry Mulligan Quartet
Newport Jazz Festival 1958,July 3rd-6th Vol.2:Mulligan The Main Man | Phontastic | NCD 8814
Gerry Mulligan Quintet
Late Night Sax | CBS | 487798-2

Gerry Mulligan Sextet
The Gerry Mulligan Songbook | Pacific Jazz | 833575-2
Gerry Mulligan-Paul Desmond Quartet
Gerry Mulligan-Paul Desmond Quartet | Verve | 519850-2
Grant Green Trio
Ballads | Blue Note | 537560-2
Green Street | Blue Note | 540032-2
Lou Donaldson Quintet
Blue Bossa | Blue Note | 795590-2
The Best Of Blue Note | Blue Note | 796110-2
Gravy Train | Blue Note | 853357-2
Stan Getz Group Feat.Laurindo Almeida
Stan Getz With Guest Artist Laurindo Almeida | Verve | 823149-2
Stan Getz-Laurindo Almeida Orchestra
Stan Getz Highlights:The Best Of The Verve Years Vol.2 | Verve | 517330-2
Verve Jazz Masters 53:Stan Getz-Bossa Nova | Verve | 529904-2
Stan Getz Highlights | Verve | 847430-2
Stan Getz-Luiz Bonfa Quintet
Jazz Samba Encore! | Verve | 823613-2

Bailey,Derek | (el-gg)
Tony Oxley Quintet
The Baptist Traveller | CBS | 494438-2
Tony Oxley Sextet
4 Compositions For Sextet | CBS | 494437-2

Bailey,Don | (bharm)
Bobby Bryant Orchestra
Deep Blue-The United States Of Mind | Blue Note | 521152-2
Sonny Rollins Trio
A Night At The Village Vanguard | Blue Note | 499795-2
Sonny Rollins:The Blue Note Recordings | Blue Note | 821371-2

Bailey,Donald | (drperc)
Babs Gonzales With The Jimmy Smith Trio
Blue Velvet: Crooners, Swooners And Velvet Vocals | Blue Note | 521153-2
Carmen McRae And Her Trio
The Collected Carmen McRae | RCA | 2668713-2
Carmen McRae And Her Trio With Zoot Sims
The Collected Carmen McRae | RCA | 2668713-2
Gerry Mulligan Quartet
Jazz At The Philharmonic: The Gerry Mulligan Quartets In Concert | Pablo | PACD 5309-2
Hampton Hawes Trio
The Jazz Giants Play Rodgers & Hart:Blue Moon | Prestige | PCD 24205-2
Jimmy Rowles Trio
Jimmy Rowles/Subtle Legend Vol.1 | Storyville | STCD 8287
Jimmy Smith All Stars
House Party | Blue Note | 524542-2
Jimmy Smith Quartet
Blue Note Plays Gershwin | Blue Note | 520808-2
Six Views Of The Blues | Blue Note | 521435-2
Cool Blues | Blue Note | 535587-2
Prayer Meetin' | Blue Note | 576754-2
Back At The Chicken Shack | Blue Note | 746402-2
The Best Of Blue Note | Blue Note | 796110-2
Home Cookin' | Blue Note | 853360-2
Midnight Blue(The [Be]witching Hour) | Blue Note | 854365-2
Jimmy Smith Quintet
Prayer Meetin' | Blue Note | 576754-2
Rockin' the Boat | Blue Note | 576755-2
Jimmy Smith Trio
Paris Jazz Concert:Jimmy Smith And The Trio | Laserlight | 36159
Groovin' At Smalls' Paradise | Blue Note | 499777-2
Verve Jazz Masters 29:Jimmy Smith | Verve | 521855-2
Verve Jazz Masters 21:George Benson | Verve | 521861-2
Bucket! | Blue Note | 524550-2
Jimmy Smith:Best Of The Verve Years | Verve | 527950-2
Cool Blues | Blue Note | 535587-2
Talkin' Verve:George Benson | Verve | 553780-2
So Blue So Funky-Heroes Of The Hammond | Blue Note | 796563-2
Standards | Blue Note | 821282-2
I'm Movin' On | Blue Note | 832750-2
Home Cookin' | Blue Note | 853360-2
A New Sound A New Star:Jimmy Smith At The Organ | Blue Note | 857191-2

Bailey,Elden | (perc)
Stan Getz With The Eddie Sauter Orchestra
Stan Getz Plays The Music Of Mickey One | Verve | 531232-2

Bailey,Joe | (b,tubavoc)
Babs Gonzales And His Band
Voilà | Fresh Sound Records | FSR CD 340

Bailey,John | (tp)
Ray Barretto Orchestra
Portraits In Jazz And Clave | RCA | 2168452-2

Bailey,Mildred | (voc)
Mildred Bailey With The Ellis Larkins Trio
Planet Jazz:Female Jazz Vocalists | Planet Jazz | 2169656-2

Bailey,Philip | (arr,vocperc)
Paulinho Da Costa Orchestra
Happy People | Original Jazz Classics | OJCCD 783-2(2312102)

Bailey,Steve | (b,el-b,b-gfretless-b)
The Rippingtons
Tourist In Paradise | GRP | GRP 95882

Bailey,Victor | (b,el-bfretless-b)
Deborah Henson-Conant Group
Budapest | Laika Records | LK 93-039
Lenny White Group
Present Tense | Hip Bop | HIBD 8004
Renderers Of Spirit | Hip Bop | HIBD 8014
Michael Brecker Group
Now You See It...(Now You Don't) | GRP | GRP 96222

Bailly,Octavio | (b,vocb-g)
Cannonball Adderley With Sergio Mendes And The Bossa Rio Quartet
Cannonball's Bossa Nova | Blue Note | 522667-2
Cannonball Adderley With Sergio Mendes And The Bossa Rio Sextet
Cannonball's Bossa Nova | Blue Note | 522667-2
Ballads | Blue Note | 537563-2
Joe Pass Sextet
Joe Pass:Guitar Virtuoso | Pablo | 4 PACD 4423-2
Paulinho Da Costa Orchestra
Agora | Original Jazz Classics | OJCCD 630-2(2310785)

Bain,Bob | (gb-g)
Duke Ellington With Tommy Dorsey And His Orchestra
Highlights From The Duke Ellington Centennial Edition | RCA | 2663672-2
Ella Fitzgerald With The Nelson Riddle Orchestra
Ella Fitzgerald Sings The Johnny Mercer Songbook | Verve | 539057-2
Henry Mancini And His Orchestra
Combo! | RCA | 2147794-2
Peggy Lee With Lou Levy's Orchestra
Pass Me By/Big Spender | Capitol | 535210-2
Peggy Lee With The Quincy Jones Orchestra
Blues Cross Country | Capitol | 520088-2
Pete Rugolo And His Orchestra
Thriller/Richard Diamon(Original Jazz Scores From 2 Classics TV Series) | Fresh Sound Records | FSCD 2015
Tommy Dorsey And His Orchestra
Planet Jazz:Tommy Dorsey | Planet Jazz | 2159972-2
Planet Jazz:Jazz Greatest Hits | Planet Jazz | 2169648-2

Bain,Robert 'Bob' | (gel-g)
Ella Fitzgerald With The Nelson Riddle Orchestra
The Best Of The Song Books:The Ballads | Verve | 521867-2
Oh Lady Be Good:The Best Of The Gershwin Songbook | Verve | 529581-2
Love Songs:The Best Of The Song Books | Verve | 531762-2
Louie Bellson Septet
Louie Bellson Jam | Original Jazz Classics | OJCCD 802-2(2310838)

Baird,Taswell | (tb)
Dizzy Gillespie And His Orchestra
Planet Jazz:Dizzy Gillespie | Planet Jazz | 2152069-2
Planet Jazz:Bebop | RCA | 2169650-2
Ella Fitzgerald With The Dizzy Gillespie Orchestra
Ella Fitzgerald:Mr.Paganini | Dreyfus Jazz Line | FDM 36741-2

Bajazzo |
Bajazzo
Caminos | Edition Collage | EC 485-2
Harlequin Galaxy | Edition Collage | EC 519-2

Baker,Abe | (b)
Leon Thomas With Orchestra
Spirits Known And Unknown | RCA | 2663876-2

Baker,Anita | (voc)
Cyrus Chestnut Trio With Anita Baker
Cyrus Chestnut | Atlantic | 7567-83140-2

Baker,Art | (asb)
Ella Fitzgerald With Sy Oliver And His Orchestra
Ella Fitzgerald:The Decca Years 1949-1954 | Decca | 050668-2

Baker,Artie | (asbs)
Louis Armstrong With Sy Oliver And His Orchestra
Satchmo Serenaders | Verve | 543792-2

Baker,Chet | (fl-h,voc,tp,boo-bamp)
A Band Of Friends
The Best Of The Gerry Mulligan Quartet With Chet Baker | Pacific Jazz | 795481-2
Chet Baker & The Boto Brasilian Quartet
Chet Baker & The Boto Brasilian Quartet | Dreyfus Jazz Line | FDM 36511-9
Chet Baker And The Lighthouse All Stars
Witch Doctor | Original Jazz Classics | OJCCD 609-2
The Jazz Giants Play Harry Warren:Lullaby Of Broadway | Prestige | PCD 24204-2
Chet Baker Big Band
The Best Of Chet Baker Plays | Pacific Jazz | 797161-2
Chet Baker Group
Blue Velvet: Crooners, Swooners And Velvet Vocals | Blue Note | 521153-2
Chet Baker Quartet
Jazz In Paris:Chet Baker-Broken Wing | EmArCy | 013043-2
Jazz In Paris:Chet Baker Quartet Plays Standards | EmArCy | 014378-2 PMS
Chet Baker Quartet Live Vol.1:This Time The Dreams's On Me | Pacific Jazz | 525248-2
Verve Jazz Masters Vol.60:The Collection | Verve | 529866-2
Chet Baker Quartet Live Vol.3: May Old Flame | Pacific Jazz | 531573-2
Baby Breeze | Verve | 538328-2
Let's Get Lost: The Best Of Chet Baker Sings | Pacific Jazz | 792932-2
The Best Of Chet Baker Plays | Pacific Jazz | 797161-2
Chet Baker-The Legacy Vol.2:I Remember You | Enja | ENJ-9077 2
Chet Baker-The Legacy Vol.4:Oh You Crazy Moon | Enja | ENJ-9453 2
Chet | Original Jazz Classics | OJC20 087-2
Chet Baker In New York | Original Jazz Classics | OJC20 207-2
Sings/It Could Happen To You | Original Jazz Classics | OJC20 303-2
Chet Baker In Milan | Original Jazz Classics | OJC20 370-2(JLP 18)
At Last! | Original Jazz Classics | OJCCD 480-2
The Jazz Giants Play Miles Davis:Milestones | Prestige | PCD 24225-2
Chet Baker Quintet
Chet Baker:The Most Important Jazz Album Of 1964/65 | Roulette | 581829-2
Chet Baker & Crew | Pacific Jazz | 582671-2
Peace | Enja | ENJ-4016 2
My Favourite Songs: The Last Great Concert Vol.1 | Enja | ENJ-5097 2
The Last Concert Vol.I+II | Enja | ENJ-6074 22
Chet Baker Plays The Best Of Lerner And Loewe | Original Jazz Classics | OJC20 137-2
Chet Baker In New York | Original Jazz Classics | OJC20 207-2
Once Upon A Summertime | Original Jazz Classics | OJCCD 405-2
The Jazz Giants Play Rodgers & Hart:Blue Moon | Prestige | PCD 24205-2
Groovin' With The Chet Baker Quintet | Prestige | PR20 7460-2
Comin' On With The Chet Baker Quintet | Prestige | PR20 7478-2
Cool Burnin' With The Chet Baker Quintet | Prestige | PR20 7496-2
Boppin' With The Chet Baker Quintet | Prestige | PR20 7512-2
Smokin' With The Chet Baker Quintet | Prestige | PR20 7749-2
Chet Baker Quintet/NDR Big Band/Radio Orchestra Hannover
Straight From The Heart-The Last Concert Vol.2 | Enja | ENJ-6020 2
The Last Concert Vol.I+II | Enja | ENJ-6074 22
Chet Baker Septet
The Best Of Chet Baker Plays | Pacific Jazz | 797161-2
Chet | Original Jazz Classics | OJC20 087-2
Chet Baker Plays The Best Of Lerner And Loewe | Original Jazz Classics | OJC20 137-2
Chet Baker Sextet
Baby Breeze | Verve | 538328-2
Chet Baker & Crew | Pacific Jazz | 582671-2
The Best Of Chet Baker Plays | Pacific Jazz | 797161-2
Chet Baker-The Italian Sessions | Bluebird | ND 82001
Chet | Original Jazz Classics | OJC20 087-2
Chet Baker In Milan | Original Jazz Classics | OJC20 370-2(JLP 18)
Chet Baker Trio
Embraceable You | Pacific Jazz | 831676-2
Strollin' | Enja | ENJ-5005 2
Chet Baker In Bologna | Dreyfus Jazz Line | FDM 36558-9
The Touch Of Your Lips | Steeplechase | SCCD 31122
This Is Always | Steeplechase | SCCD 31168
Daybreak | Steeplechase | SCS 1142(Audiophile Pressing)
Chet Baker With Bobby Scott
Baby Breeze | Verve | 538328-2
Chet Baker With Bobby Scott And Kenny Burrell
Baby Breeze | Verve | 538328-2
Chet Baker With Kenny Burrell
Baby Breeze | Verve | 538328-2
Chet Baker With String-Orchestra And Voices
Chet Baker With Fifty Italian Strings | Original Jazz Classics | OJC20 492-2(JLP 921)
Chet Baker With The NDR-Bigband
NDR Big Band-Bravissimo | ACT | 9232-2
My Favourite Songs: The Last Great Concert Vol.1 | Enja | ENJ-5097 2
The Last Concert Vol.I+II | Enja | ENJ-6074 22
Chet Baker-The Legacy Vol.1 | Enja | ENJ-9021 2
Chet Baker With The Radio Orchestra Hannover(NDR)
My Favourite Songs: The Last Great Concert Vol.1 | Enja | ENJ-5097 2
The Last Concert Vol.I+II | Enja | ENJ-6074 22
Chet Baker-Art Pepper-Phil Urso Sextet
Picture Of Heath | Pacific Jazz | 494106-2
Chet Baker-Gerry Mulligan Group
Carnegie Hall Concert Vol. 1/2 | CTI | EPC 450554-2
Chet Baker-Stan Getz Quintet
The Stockholm Concerts | Verve | 537555-2
Stan Meets Chet | Verve | 837436-2
Chet Baker-Wolfgang Lackerschmid Duo
Chet Baker:The Legacy Vol.3:Why Shouldn't You Cry | Enja | ENJ-9337 2
Chet Baker-Wolfgang Lackerschmid Quintet
Chet Baker:The Legacy Vol.3:Why Shouldn't You Cry | Enja | ENJ-9337 2
Chet Baker-Wolfgang Lackerschmid Trio
Chet Baker:The Legacy Vol.3:Why Shouldn't You Cry | Enja | ENJ-9337 2
Gerry Mulligan Quartet
Gene Norman Presents The Original Gerry Mulligan Tentet And Quartet | GNP Crescendo | GNPD 56
Gerry Mulligan Quartet feat.Chet Baker | Original Jazz Classics | OJCCD 711-2(F 8082/P 7641)
The Jazz Giants Play Rodgers & Hart:Blue Moon | Prestige | PCD 24205-2
Gerry Mulligan Tentette
Gene Norman Presents The Original Gerry Mulligan Tentet And Quartet | GNP Crescendo | GNPD 56
Howard Rumsey's Lighthouse All-Stars
Sunday Jazz A La Lighthouse Vol.2 | Original Jazz Classics | OJCCD 972-2(S 2501)
Johnny Pace With The Chet Baker Quintet
Chet Baker Introduces Johnny Pace | Original Jazz Classics | OJCCD 433-2(RLP 12-292)
Lars Gullin And The Chet Baker Quartet
Lars Gullin 1955/56 Vol.1 | Dragon | DRCD 224
Lee Konitz & The Gerry Mulligan Quartet
Konitz Meets Mulligan | Pacific Jazz | 746847-2
Michel Grailler-Chet Baker
Dream Drops | Owl Records | 013434-2

Baker,Cy | (tp)
Benny Goodman And His Orchestra
Camel Caravan Broadcast 1939 Vol.1 | Phontastic | NCD 8817
Camel Caravan Broadcast 1939 Vol.2 | Phontastic | NCD 8818
Camel Caravan Broadcast 1939 Vol.3 | Phontastic | NCD 8819

Baker,Dave | (b-tb,condtb)
George Russell Sextet
Eric Dolphy Birthday Celebration | Fantasy | FANCD 6085-2
Ezz-thetics | Original Jazz Classics | OJCCD 070-2(RLP 9375)
The Jazz Giants Play Miles Davis:Milestones | Prestige | PCD 24225-2

Baker,Ginger | (dr)
Bob Wallis Storyville Jazzmen
The Golden Years Of Revival Jazz,Vol.7 | Storyville | STCD 5512

Baker,Harold 'Shorty' | (tp)
(Little)Jimmy Scott With The Billy Taylor Orchestra
Everybody's Somebody's Fool | Decca | 050669-2
Big Al Sears Band
Sear-iously | Bear Family Records | BCD 15668 AH
Billy Strayhorn Orchestra
Johnny Hodges With Billy Strayhorn And The Orchestra | Verve | 557543-2
Bud Freeman All Stars
The Bud Freeman All-Star Sessions | Prestige | PRCD 24286-2
Count Basie And His Orchestra
April In Paris | Verve | 521402-2
Della Reese With The Sy Oliver Orchestra
Misty Blue:Sweet Sisters Swing Songs Of Sorrow And Sadness | Blue Note | 521151-2
Django Reinhardt With Duke Ellington And His Orchestra
Django Reinhardt:Souveniers | Dreyfus Jazz Line | FDM 36744-2
Duke Ellington And His Orchestra
Planet Jazz:Duke Ellington | Planet Jazz | 2152053-2
Jazz Collection:Duke Ellington | Laserlight | 24369
The Legends Of Swing | Laserlight | 24659
Highlights From The Duke Ellington Centennial Edition | RCA | 2663672-2
Carnegie Hall Concert December 1947 | Prestige | 2PCD 24075-2
Carnegie Hall Concert January 1943 | Prestige | 2PCD 34004-2
Greatest Hits | CBS | 462959-2
Jazz Festival Vol.2 | Storyville | 4960743
Verve Jazz Masters 4:Duke Ellington | Verve | 516338-2
Jazz:The Essential Collection Vol.2 | IN+OUT Records | 78012-2
Jazz:The Essential Collection Vol.3 | IN+OUT Records | 78013-2
Black Brown And Beige | CBS | CK 65566
Anatomy Of A Murder | CBS | CK 65569
The Ellington Suites | Original Jazz Classics | OJC20 446-2(2310762)
Duke Ellington At The Alhambra | Pablo | PACD 5313-2
At The Hurricane:Original 1943 Broadcasts | Storyville | STCD 8359
Ella Fitzgerald With The Duke Ellington Orchestra
The Best Of The Song Books:The Ballads | Verve | 521867-2
Johnny Hodges And The Ellington Men
Verve Jazz Masters 35:Johnny Hodges | Verve | 521857-2
Johnny Hodges Orchestra
Coleman Hawkins/Johnny Hodges:The Vogue Recordings | Vogue | 21559712
Verve Jazz Masters 43:Ben Webster | Verve | 525431-2
Johnny Hodges With Billy Strayhorn And The Duke Ellington Orchestra
Verve Jazz Masters 35:Johnny Hodges | Verve | 521857-2
Lena Horne With The Lennie Hayton Orchestra
Planet Jazz:Lena Horne | Planet Jazz | 2165373-2
Shorty Baker-Doc Cheatham Quintet
Shorty & Doc | Original Jazz Classics | OJCCD 839-2(SV 2021)

Baker,Israel | (tpv)
Charlie Haden Quartet West With Strings
The Art Of The Song | Verve | 547403-2
Ella Fitzgerald With The Billy May Orchestra
The Best Of The Song Books:The Ballads | Verve | 521867-2
Ella Fitzgerald Sings The Harold Arlen Song Book | Verve | 589108-2
Ella Fitzgerald With The Frank DeVol Orchestra
Get Happy! | Verve | 523321-2
Ella Fitzgerald With The Nelson Riddle Orchestra
The Best Of The Song Books:The Ballads | Verve | 521867-2
Love Songs:The Best Of The Song Books | Verve | 531762-2
Frank Sinatra With The Count Basie Orchestra
It Might As Well Be Spring | Reprise | 7599-27027-2
Herbie Mann With The Frank DeVol Orchestra
Verve Jazz Masters 56:Herbie Mann | Verve | 529901-2

Baker,Julius | (fl,reedswoodwinds)
Coleman Hawkins With Billy Byers And His Orchestra
Planet Jazz:Coleman Hawkins | Planet Jazz | 2152055-2
The Hawk In Hi-Fi | RCA | 2663842-2
Don Senay With Orchestra And Strings
Charles Mingus-The Complete Debut Recordings | Debut | 12 DCD 4402-2
Thad Jones And His Orchestra
Charles Mingus-The Complete Debut Recordings | Debut | 12 DCD 4402-2

Baker,Kenny | (tpfl-h)
Vic Lewis Jam Session
Vic Lewis:The Golden Years | Candid | CCD 79754

Baker,Marilyn | (viola)
Milt Jackson And His Orchestra
Reverence And Compassion | Reprise | 9362-45204-2

Baker,Michael | (dr,vocdr-machine-programming)
Bobby Lyle Group
The Journey | Atlantic | 7567-82138-2

Baker,Mickey | (arr,gvoc)
Al Sears And His Orchestra
Sear-iously | Bear Family Records | BCD 15668 AH
Buddy Johnson And His Orchestra
Buddy And Ella Johnson 1953-1964 | Bear Family Records | BCD 15479 DH

Baker,Newman | (dr,percspoons)
Erica Lindsay Quintet
Dreamers | Candid | CCD 79040
Erica Lindsay Sextet
Dreamers | Candid | CCD 79040
Jeanne Lee Group
Natural Affinities | Owl Records | 018352-2
Monnette Sudler Sextet
Brighter Days For You | Steeplechase | SCCD 31087

Baker,Tom | (co,tb,as,tp,ts,vib,percconga)
Dan Barrett Septet
Dan Barrett's International Swing Party | Nagel-Heyer | CD 067
The Swingcats
Face To Face:The Swingcats Live | Nagel-Heyer | CD 072

Baker,Virginia | (v)
Ron Carter With Strings
Pastels | Original Jazz Classics | OJCCD 665-2(M 9073)

Baker,Ysrael | (v)
Phineas Newborn Jr. With Dennis Farnon And His Orchestra
While My Lady Sleeps | RCA | 2185157-2

Bakken,Rebekka | (voc)

Christoph Lauer & Norwegian Brass
Heaven | ACT | 9420-2
Julia Hülsman Trio With Rebekka Bakken
Scattering Poems | ACT | 9405-2

Bala,Carlos | (dr)
Duo Fenix
Karai-Eté | IN+OUT Records | 7009-2

Balakrishna,Khalil | (el-sitar,tambourasitar)
Miles Davis Group
Circle In The Round | CBS | 467898-2
Live-Evil | CBS | C2K 65135
In Concert | CBS | C2K 65140
On The Corner | CBS | CK 63980

Balance |
Balance
Elements | double moon | DMCHR 71033
Some Other Tapes | Fish Music | FM 009/10 CD

Balanescu Quartet: |
Michael Mantler Quintet With The Balanescu Quartet
Folly Seeing All This | ECM | 1485
Rabih Abou-Khalil Group
Arabian Waltz | Enja | ENJ-9059 2

Balanescu,Alexander | (v)
Michael Mantler Quintet With The Balanescu Quartet
Folly Seeing All This | ECM | 1485
Rabih Abou-Khalil Group
Arabian Waltz | Enja | ENJ-9059 2

Balanyà,Josep Maria | (p-solo)
Josep Maria Balanyà
Sonateskas | Laika Records | 35101102
Elements Of Development | Laika Records | 8695070

Balasubramoniam,Musthwamy | (mridangam)
Chico Freeman & Franco Ambrosetti Meet Reto Weber Percussion Orchestra
Face To Face | double moon | CHRDM 71018
Christy Doran's New Bag With Muthuswamy Balasubramoniam
Black Box | double moon | CHRDM 71022

Balazs,Elemer | (dr)
Ferenc Snétberger Trio
Obsession | TipToe | TIP-888834 2

Balboa,Buddy | (reeds)
Billy Eckstine And His Orchestra
Blue Velvet: Crooners, Swooners And Velvet Vocals | Blue Note | 521153-2

Baldan,Alberto | (marimba)
Gerry Mulligan With Astor Piazzolla And His Orchestra
Tango Nuevo | Atlantic | 2292-42145-2

Baldauf,Rüdiger | (tpfl-h)
Eddie Harris Group With The WDR Big Band
Eddie Harris-The Last Concert | ACT | 9249-2
HR Big Band
Libertango:Homage An Astor Piazolla | hr music.de | hrmj 014-02 CD
SWR Big Band
Jazz In Concert | Hänssler Classics | CD 93.004

Baldin,Dileno | (fr-h)
Uri Caine With The Concerto Köln
Concerto Köln | Winter&Winter | 910086-2

Baldwin,Bob | (b)
Tommy Dorsey And His Orchestra
Planet Jazz:Tommy Dorsey | Planet Jazz | 2159972-2

Baldwin,Lennie | (tbvoc)
Lennie Baldwin's Dauphin Street Six
The Golden Years Of Revival Jazz,Sampler | Storyville | 109 1001
The Golden Years Of Revival Jazz,Vol 1 | Storyville | STCD 5506
The Golden Years Of Revival Jazz,Vol.3 | Storyville | STCD 5508
The Golden Years Of Revival Jazz,Vol.6 | Storyville | STCD 5511
The Golden Years Of Revival Jazz,Vol.9 | Storyville | STCD 5514
The Golden Years Of Revival Jazz,Vol.10 | Storyville | STCD 5515
The Golden Years Of Revival Jazz,Vol.13 | Storyville | STCD 5518

Baldwin,Peggy | (cello)
Jacintha With Band And Strings
Lush Life | Groove Note | GRV 1011-2(Gold CD 2011)

Bales,Burt | (p,vocp-solo)
Bunk Johnson With The Yerba Buena Jazz Band
Bunk & Lu | Good Time Jazz | GTCD 12024-2

Balfour,Robbin L. | (voc)
Max Roach Chorus & Orchestra
To The Max! | Enja | ENJ-7021 22

Balint,Eszter | (voc)
Marc Ribot Y Los Cubanos Postizos
Nuy Divertido(Very Entertaining) | Atlantic | 7567-83293-2

Balke,Jon | (el-p,keyboards,perc,psynth)
Jon Balke w/Magnetic North Orchestra
Further | ECM | 1517
Kyanos | ECM | 1822(017278-2)
Jon Balke w/Oslo 13
Nonsentration | ECM | 1445
Masqualero
Bande A Part | ECM | 1319
Nguyen Le Trio With Guests
Bakida | ACT | 9275-2

Ball,Dave | (b-g)
Barbara Thompson Group
Heavenly Bodies | VeraBra Records | CDVBR 2015-2
Barbara Thompson's Paraphernalia
Barbara Thompson's Special Edition | VeraBra Records | CDVBR 2017-2

Ball,Leo | (tp)
Herbie Mann's Cuban Band
Verve Jazz Masters 56:Herbie Mann | Verve | 529901-2

Ball,Marcia | (pvoc)
Hans Theessink Group
Crazy Moon | Minor Music | 801052

Ball,Roger | (as,synth,el-pkeyboards)
Klaus Doldinger With Orchestra
Lifelike | Warner | 2292-46478-2

Ball,Ronnie | (parr)
Art Pepper-Warne Marsh Quintet
The Way It Is | Original Jazz Classics | OJCCD 389-2
Lee Konitz-Warne Marsh Sextet
Lee Konitz With Warne Marsh | Atlantic | 8122-75356-2
Roy 'Little Jazz' Eldridge Quartet
The Complete Verve Roy Eldridge Studio Sessions | Verve | 9861278
Warne Marsh Quintet
Jazz Of Two Cities | Fresh Sound Records | FSR-CD 342
Warne Marsh Quintet With Art Pepper
Jazz Of Two Cities | Fresh Sound Records | FSR-CD 342

Ballamy,Iain | (sax,ssts)
Ian Shaw With The Cedar Walton Trio
In A New York Minute | Milestone | MCD 9297-2

Ballanti,Paolo | (cello)
Gianluigi Trovesi Nonet
Round About A Midsummer's Dream | Enja | ENJ-9384 2

Ballard,Butch | (dr)
Duke Ellington And His Orchestra
The Legends Of Swing | Laserlight | 24659
Johnny Hodges Orchestra
Coleman Hawkins/Johnny Hodges:The Vogue Recordings | Vogue | 21559712
Louis Armstrong And His Orchestra
Best Of The Complete RCA Victor Recordings | RCA | 2663636-2
Louis Armstrong:A 100th Birthday Celebration | RCA | 2663694-2
Louis Armstrong:C'est Si Bon | Dreyfus Jazz Line | FDM 36730-2

Ballard,Fred | (tp)
Lou Donaldson Quintet
The Lost Grooves | Blue Note | 831883-2

Ballard,George | (dr)
Count Basie And His Orchestra
Planet Jazz:Count Basie | Planet Jazz | 2152068-2

Ballard,Jeff | (dr,hand-clapsperc)
Avishai Cohen Quartet
The Trumpet Player | Fresh Sound Records | FSNT 161 CD
Avishai Cohen Trio
The Trumpet Player | Fresh Sound Records | FSNT 161 CD
Danilo Perez Trio
Central Avenue | Impulse(MCA) | 951281-2
Kurt Rosenwinkel Quartet
The Next Stop | Verve | 549162-2
Kurt Rosenwinkel Quintet
The Enemies Of Energy | Verve | 543042-2
Perico Sambeat Quartet
Friendship | ACT | 9421-2
Perico Sambeat Quintet
Friendship | ACT | 9421-2
Reid Anderson Quartet
Abolish Bad Architecture | Fresh Sound Records | FSNT 062 CD

Ballard,Red | (tb)
Benny Goodman And His Orchestra
Planet Jazz:Benny Goodman | Planet Jazz | 2152054-2
Planet Jazz Sampler | Planet Jazz | 2152326-2
Planet Jazz:Jazz Greatest Hits | Planet Jazz | 2169648-2
Planet Jazz:Big Bands | Planet Jazz | 2169649-2
Planet Jazz:Swing | Planet Jazz | 2169651-2
Planet Jazz:Jazz Trumpet | Planet Jazz | 2169654-2
Planet Jazz:Female Jazz Vocalists | Planet Jazz | 2169656-2
Benny Goodman At Carnegie Hall 1938(Complete) | CBS | C2K 65143
Charlie Christian:Swing To Bop | Dreyfus Jazz Line | FDM 36715-2
Camel Caravan Broadcast 1939 Vol.1 | Phontastic | NCD 8817
Camel Caravan Broadcast 1939 Vol.2 | Phontastic | NCD 8818
Camel Caravan Broadcast 1939 Vol.3 | Phontastic | NCD 8819
More Camel Caravans | Phontastic | NCD 8841/2
More Camel Caravans | Phontastic | NCD 8843/4
More Camel Caravans | Phontastic | NCD 8845/6
Benny Goodman Band
Benny Goodman At Carnegie Hall 1938(Complete) | CBS | C2K 65143
Jam Session
Benny Goodman At Carnegie Hall 1938(Complete) | CBS | C2K 65143
Louis Armstrong With Gordon Jenkins And His Orchestra
Satchmo In Style | Verve | 549594-2

Ballin,Peter | (sax)
Buddy Childers Big Band
Just Buddy's | Candid | CCD 79761

Ballou,Dave | (tpfl-h)
Dave Ballou Quartet
Rothko | Steeplechase | SCCD 31525
Dancing Foot | Steeplechase | SCCD 31556
Jam Session
Jam Session Vol.5 | Steeplechase | SCCD 31536
Paquito D'Rivera Group With The Absolute Ensemble
Habanera | Enja | ENJ-9395 2
Rabih Abou-Khalil Group
The Cactus Of Knowledge | Enja | ENJ-9401 2
Steve LaSpina Quintet
Remember When | Steeplechase | SCCD 31540

Ballou,Marty | (b)
Duke Robillard-Herb Ellis Quintet
Conversation In Swing Guitar | Stony Plain | SPCD 1260
More Conversations In Swing Guitar | Stony Plain | SPCD 1292

Ballou,Monte | (bjvoc)
Lu Watters' Jazz Band
Blues Over Bodega | Good Time Jazz | GTCD 12066-2

Bally,Alex | (dr,percfl)
Hans Koller Free Sound
Phoenix | MPS | 9813438

Balogh,Elemar | (cymbal)
Wedeli Köhler Group
Swing & Folk | Jazzpoint | JP 1067 CD

Balrak,Patricia | (voc)
Pili-Pili
Stolen Moments | JA & RO | JARO 4159-2
Boogaloo | JA & RO | JARO 4174-2
Jazzy World | JA & RO | JARO 4200-2

Baltaga,Oleg | (dr)
Trigon
Oglinda | JA & RO | JARO 4215-2

Baltazar,Gabe | (as,clreeds)
Johnny Hartman And His Orchestra
Unforgettable | Impulse(MCA) | IMP 11522
Stan Kenton And His Orchestra
Adventures In Blues | Capitol | 520089-2
Adventures In Jazz | Capitol | 521222-2

Baltazar,Norman | (tp)
Adventures In Blues | Capitol | 520089-2
Adventures In Jazz | Capitol | 521222-2

Balzar,Robert | (b)
Benny Bailey Quartet With Strings
I Remember Love | Laika Records | 35101752
Robert Balzar Trio
Travelling | Jazzpoint | JP 1050 CD

Bamert,Bernhard | (tb)
Brigitte Dietrich-Joe Haider Jazz Orchestra
Consequences | JHM Records | JHM 3624
European Jazz Youth Orchestra
Swinging Europe 3 | dacapo | DCCD 9461
Horn Knox
The Song Is You | JHM Records | JHM 3625
Matthias Spillmann Septet
Something About Water | JHM Records | JHM 3620

Bamont,Johnnie | (sax)
Diane Schuur With Orchestra
Blues For Schuur | GRP | GRP 98632
The Best Of Diane Schuur | GRP | GRP 98882

Banana,Milton | (dr)
Baden Powell Solo/Group
Three Originals:Tristeza On Guitar/Poema On Guitar/Apaixonado | MPS | 519216-2
Getz-Gilberto Quintet
Verve Jazz Masters 13:Antonio Carlos Jobim | Verve | 516409-2
Stan Getz Highlights:The Best Of The Verve Years Vol.2 | Verve | 517330-2
Verve Jazz Masters 20:Introducing | Verve | 519853-2
Getz/Gilberto | Polydor | 521414-2
A Life In Jazz:A Musical Biography | Verve | 535119-2
Stan Getz Quintet
Verve Jazz Masters 53:Stan Getz-Bossa Nova | Verve | 529904-2
Stan Getz Quintet Feat. Astrud Gilberto
Verve Jazz Masters 8:Stan Getz | Verve | 519823-2
Getz/Gilberto | Verve | 589595-2 SACD
Stan Getz-Joao Gilberto Quintet
The Antonio Carlos Jobim Songbook | Verve | 525472-2
Stan Getz Highlights | Verve | 847430-2

Banchi | (v)
United Future Organizatio
United Future Organization | Talkin' Loud | 518166-2

Band |
Al Jarreau With Band
Heart's Horizon | i.e. Music | 557851-2
Clarence Gatemouth Brown Band
The Blues Of Clarence 'Gatemouth Brown | Storyville | 4960563
Laura Fygi With Band
Laura Fygi Live At The North Sea Jazz | Spectra | 9811207
Rockin' Dopsie And The Zydeco Twisters
Rockin' Dopsie And The Zydeco Twister | Storyville | 4960423

Banda Cittá Ruvo Di Puglia |
Banda Cittá Ruvo Di Puglia
La Banda/Banda And Jazz | Enja | ENJ-9326 2
Willem Breuker Kollektief
La Banda/Banda And Jazz | Enja | ENJ-9326 2

Bandy,Riley T. | (as)
Abbey Lincoln With Her Band
Who Used To Dance | Verve | 533559-2

Bang,Jan | (live-samplingvoc-resampling)
Ketil Bjornstad Group
Grace | EmArCy | 013622-2

Bangoura,Epizo | (percdjembe)
Mark Helias Group
Loopin' The Cool | Enja | ENJ-9049 2

Bani,Zahra | (percvoc)
Nguyen Le Group
Maghreb And Friends | ACT | 9261-2

Bank,Bob | (reeds)
Miles Davis With Gil Evans & His Orchestra
Quiet Nights | CBS | CK 65293

Bank,Danny | (alto-fl,b-cl,bs,b-fl,cl,fl,bassoon)
(Little)Jimmy Scott With The Billy Taylor Orchestra
Everybody's Somebody's Fool | Decca | 050669-2
Art Farmer Septet
Plays The Arrangements And Compositions Of Gigi Gryce And Quincy Jones | Original Jazz Classics | OJCCD 054-2
Ben Webster With Orchestra And Strings
Verve Jazz Masters 43:Ben Webster | Verve | 525431-2
Music For Loving:Ben Webster With Strings | Verve | 527774-2
Ultimate Ben Webster selected by James Carter | Verve | 557537-2
Cannonball Adderley And His Orchestra
Verve Jazz Masters 31:Cannonball Adderley | Verve | 522651-2
Charles Mingus And His Orchestra
The Complete Town Hall Concert | Blue Note | 828353-2
Charles Mingus Orchestra
Charles Mingus:Pre-Bird(Mingus Revisited) | Verve | 538636-2
Charlie Parker And His Orchestra
The Cole Porter Songbook | Verve | 823250-2
Bird: The Complete Charlie Parker On Verve | Verve | 837141-2
Charlie Parker With Orchestra
Charlie Parker:The Best Of The Verve Years | Verve | 527815-2
Charlie Parker With The Joe Lipman Orchestra
Verve Jazz Masters 28:Charlie Parker Plays Standards | Verve | 521854-2
Charlie Parker Big Band | Verve | 559835-2
Chris Connor With Band
Chris Connor | Atlantic | 7567-80769-2
Chubby Jackson And His All Star Big Band
Chubby Takes Over | Fresh Sound Records | FSR-CD 324
Dinah Washington With The Quincy Jones Orchestra
Verve Jazz Masters 40:Dinah Washington | Verve | 522055-2
The Swingin' Miss 'D' | Verve | 558074-2
Dizzy Gillespie And His Orchestra
Afro | Verve | 517052-2
Gato Barbieri Group
Planet Jazz:Gato Barbieri | RCA | 2165364-2
Gato Barbieri:The Best Of The Early Years | RCA | 2663523-2
Hank Jones With Oliver Nelson's Orchestra
The Roots Of Acid Jazz | Impulse(MCA) | IMP 12042
Helen Merrill With The Quincy Jones Orchestra
Clifford Brown-Max Roach:Alone Together-The Best Of The Mercury Years | Verve | 526373-2
Verve Jazz Masters 44:Clifford Brown and Max Roach | Verve | 528109-2
Brownie-The Complete EmArCy Recordings Of Clifford Brown | EmArCy | 838306-2
Jimmy Smith And Wes Montgomery With Orchestra
Jimmy & Wes-The Dynamic Duo | Verve | 521445-2
Jimmy Smith And Wes Montgomery With The Oliver Nelson Orchestra
Wes Montgomery:The Verve Jazz Sides | Verve | 521690-2
Jimmy Smith:Best Of The Verve Years | Verve | 527950-2
Talkin' Jazz:Roots Of Acid Jazz | Verve | 529580-2
Jimmy Smith With The Oliver Nelson Orchestra
Jimmy Smith:Best Of The Verve Years | Verve | 527950-2
Peter & The Wolf | Verve | 547264-2
Joe Williams With The Frank Hunter Orchestra
Planet Jazz:Joe Williams | Planet Jazz | 2165370-2
Joe Williams With The Jimmy Jones Orchestra
Planet Jazz:Joe Williams | Planet Jazz | 2165370-2
Johnny Hodges Orchestra
Verve Jazz Masters 35:Johnny Hodges | Verve | 521857-2
Junior Mance Trio & Orchestra
That Lovin' Feelin' | Milestone | MCD 47097-2
Lawrence Brown With The Ralph Burns Orchestra
Slide Trombone | Verve | 559930-2
Louis Armstrong And His Friends
Louis Armstrong And His Friends | Bluebird | 2663961-2
Miles Davis + 19
Miles Ahead | CBS | CK 65121
Miles Davis With Gil Evans & His Orchestra
Miles Davis At Carnegie Hall | CBS | CK 65027
This Is Jazz:Miles Davis Plays Ballads | CBS | CK 65038
Porgy And Bess | CBS | CK 65141
Sketches Of Spain | CBS | CK 65142
Quiet Nights | CBS | CK 65293
Nancy Harrow And The Buck Clayton All Stars
Wild Women Don't Have The Blues | Candid | CCD 79008
Oliver Nelson And His Orchestra
Verve Jazz Masters Vol.60:The Collection | Verve | 529866-2
Quincy Jones And His Orchestra
Verve Jazz Masters Vol.59:Toots Thielemans | Verve | 535271-2
Ralph Burns And His Orchestra
The Complete Verve Roy Eldridge Studio Sessions | Verve | 9861278
Sonny Rollins Orchestra
Alfie | Impulse(MCA) | 951224-2
Tommy Dorsey And His Orchestra
Planet Jazz:Tommy Dorsey | Planet Jazz | 2159972-2
Wes Montgomery With The Oliver Nelson Orchestra
Verve Jazz Masters 14:Wes Montgomery | Verve | 519826-2
Wes Montgomery:The Verve Jazz Sides | Verve | 521690-2
Talkin' Jazz:Roots Of Acid Jazz | Verve | 529580-2
Woody Herman And His Orchestra
The Legends Of Swing | Laserlight | 24659

Bank,Danny prob | (bs)
Charles Mingus And His Orchestra
Charles Mingus-The Complete Debut Recordings | Debut | 12 DCD 4402-2
Joe Williams With The Frank Hunter Orchestra
Planet Jazz:Joe Williams | Planet Jazz | 2165370-2

Banks,Alvin 'Buddy' | (b)
James Moody Boptet
Americans Swinging In Paris:James Moody | EMI Records | 539653-2
Sidney Bechet With Michel Attenoux And His Orchestra
Planet Jazz:Sidney Bechet | Planet Jazz | 2152063-2

Banks,Billy | (voc)
Cy Laurie's New Orleans Septet
The Golden Years Of Revival Jazz,Vol 1 | Storyville | STCD 5506

Banks,Cheryl | (dancervoc)
Sun Ra And His Astro-Infinity Arkestra
Space Is The Place | Impulse(MCA) | 951249-2

Banks,Clarence | (tb)
Dee Dee Bridgewater With Big Band
Dear Ella | Verve | 539102-2
Diane Schuur With The Count Basie Orchestra
The Best Of Diane Schuur | GRP | GRP 98882

Banks,Danny | (bs,fl,b-clsax)
Cannonball Adderley And His Orchestra
Ballads | Blue Note | 537563-2
Cannonball Adderley Quintet
Ballads | Blue Note | 537563-2
Cannonball Adderley With Sergio Mendes And The Bossa Rio Sextet
Ballads | Blue Note | 537563-2

Lena Horne With The Lennie Hayton Orchestra
Planet Jazz:Lena Horne | Planet Jazz | 2165373-2

Banks,Kenneth | (b)
Mose Vinson Band
Joe Hill Louis: The Be-Bop Boy | Bear Family Records | BCD 15524 AH

Banks,Martin | (fl-htp)
Roland Kirk And His Orchestra
Rahsaan/The Complete Mercury Recordings Of Roland Kirk | Mercury | 846630-2

Banks,Robert | (orgp)
Al Smith With The King Curtis Quintet
Midnight Special | Original Blues Classics | OBCCD 583-2(BV 1013)
St.Louis Jimmy Oden Group
Goin' Down Slow | Original Blues Classics | OBCCD 584-2(BV 1028)
Sunnyland Slim Band
Windy City Blues | Stax | SCD 8612-2

Banks,Stanley | (bel-b)
Bernard Purdie's Soul To Jazz
Bernard Purdie's Soul To Jazz II | ACT | 9253-2
George Benson Group
Breezin' | Warner | 8122-76713-2
Hank Crawford Quartet
The World Of Hank Crawford | Milestone | MCD 9304-2
Hank Crawford Quintet
After Dark | Milestone | MCD 9279-2
The World Of Hank Crawford | Milestone | MCD 9304-2
The Jazz Giants Play Sammy Cahn:It's Magic | Prestige | PCD 24226-2
Hank Crawford Septet
The World Of Hank Crawford | Milestone | MCD 9304-2

Bannet,John | (tp)
Toots Thielemans And His Orchestra
Verve Jazz Masters Vol.59:Toots Thielemans | Verve | 535271-2

Banse,Hans | (bassoon)
Bernd Konrad Jazz Group With Symphonie Orchestra
Wen Die Götter Lieben | Creative Works Records | CW CD 1010-1

Banter,Harald | (ld)
Harald Banter Ensemble
Deutsches Jazz Fesival 1954/1955 | Bear Family Records | BCD 15430

Bantzer,Claus | (org)
Nils Landgren-Tomasz Stanko With Anders Eljas And Claus Bantzer
Gotland | ACT | 9226-2

Banzer,Russ | (sax)
Sarah Vaughan With The Norman Leyden Orchestra
Sarah Vaughan:Lover Man | Dreyfus Jazz Line | FDM 36739-2

Baptist,Rick | (tpfl-h)
Stan Getz With Orchestra
Apasionado | A&M Records | 395297-2
The Quincy Jones-Sammy Nestico Orchestra
Basie & Beyond | Warner | 9362-47792-2

Baptista,Cyro | (bass-dr,triangle,percshaker)
Bill Frisell Band
Before We Were Born | Nonesuch | 7559-60843-2
Cassandra Wilson Group
Blue Light 'Til Dawn | Blue Note | 781357-2

Baquet,George | (cl)
Jelly Roll Morton And His Orchestra
Planet Jazz:Jelly Roll Morton | Planet Jazz | 2152060-2

Barab,Seymour | (cello)
Bill Evans Quartet With Orchestra
The Complete Bill Evans On Verve | Verve | 527953-2
From Left To Right | Verve | 557451-2
Bill Evans With Orchestra
The Complete Bill Evans On Verve | Verve | 527953-2
From Left To Right | Verve | 557451-2
Charles Mingus Group
Mingus Dynasty | CBS | CK 65513
Charles Mingus Orchestra
Charles Mingus:The Complete 1959 Columbia Recordings | CBS | C3K 65145
Grant Green With Orchestra
The Final Comedown(Soundtrack) | Blue Note | 581678-2
Phil Woods Quartet With Orchestra & Strings
Round Trip | Verve | 559804-2

Baraka,Amiri | (recitation)
Roswell Rudd-Archie Shepp Group
Live In New York | EmArCy | 013482-2

Barakaat,Nasir | (g)
Lester Young And His Band
Lester Young:The Complete Aladdin Sessions | Blue Note | 832787-2
Lester Young:Blue Lester | Dreyfus Jazz Line | FDM 36729-2

Barbarin,Lucien | (tb)
Lucien Barbarin With The Henri Chaix Trio
Trombone Tradition | Jazz Connaisseur | JCCD 8803-2
Lucien Barbarin-Henri Chaix Duo
Trombone Tradition | Jazz Connaisseur | JCCD 8803-2
Wynton Marsalis Group
Standard Time Vol.6:Mr.Jelly Lord | CBS | CK 69872

Barbarin,Paul | (dr,voc,snare-drvib)
Henry Allen Jr. And His New York Orchestra
Planet Jazz:Jazz Saxophone | Planet Jazz | 2169653-2
Planet Jazz:Jazz Trumpet | Planet Jazz | 2169654-2
King Oliver And His Dixie Syncopators
Jazz:The Essential Collection Vol.1 | IN+OUT Records | 78011-2
King Oliver And His Orchestra
Planet Jazz:Jazz Trumpet | Planet Jazz | 2169654-2
King Oliver's Jazz Band
Jazz:The Essential Collection Vol.1 | IN+OUT Records | 78011-2
Louis Armstrong And His Orchestra
Louis Armstrong:Swing That Music | Laserlight | 36056
Jazz:The Essential Collection Vol.2 | IN+OUT Records | 78012-2
Satch Plays Fats(Complete) | CBS | CK 64927
Louis Armstrong-My Greatest Songs | MCA | MCD 18347
Swing Legends:Louis Armstrong | Nimbus Records | NI 2012
Louis Armstrong And His Savoy Ballroom Five
Jazz:The Essential Collection Vol.2 | IN+OUT Records | 78012-2
Paul Barbarin And His Band
Atlantic Jazz: New Orleans | Atlantic | 7567-81700-2

Barber,Bill | (tuba)
Gil Evans Orchestra
Verve Jazz Masters 23:Gil Evans | Verve | 521860-2
The Individualism Of Gil Evans | Verve | 833804-2
Out Of The Cool | Impulse(MCA) | 951186-2
John Coltrane And His Orchestra
John Coltrane:Standards | Impulse(MCA) | 549914-2
John Coltrane Quartet With Brass
The Complete Africa/Brass Sessions | Impulse(MCA) | 952168-2
Kenny Burrell With The Gil Evans Orchestra
Guitar Forms | Verve | 521403-2
Verve Jazz Masters 23:Gil Evans | Verve | 521860-2
Verve Jazz Masters 45:Kenny Burrell | Verve | 527652-2
Verve Jazz Masters Vol.60:The Collection | Verve | 529866-2
Miles Davis + 19
Miles Ahead | CBS | CK 65121
Miles Davis And His Orchestra
The Complete Birth Of The Cool | Capitol | 494550-2
Birth Of The Cool | Capitol | 530117-2
Miles Davis:The Best Of The Capitol/Blue Note Years | Blue Note | 798287-2
Jazz Profile:Miles Davis | Blue Note | 823515-2
Ballads & Blues | Blue Note | 836633-2
Miles Davis:Milestones | Dreyfus Jazz Line | FDM 36731-2
Miles Davis With Gil Evans & His Orchestra
Miles Davis At Carnegie Hall | CBS | CK 65027
This Is Jazz:Miles Davis Plays Ballads | CBS | CK 65038
Porgy And Bess | CBS | CK 65141
Quiet Nights | CBS | CK 65293

Barber,Chris | (3-tb-multitrack,4-tb-multitrack,b)
Chris Barber & The Ramblers
The Golden Years Of Revival Jazz,Vol.12 | Storyville | STCD 5517
Chris Barber Original Jazzband Of 1954
Chris Barber:40 Years Jubilee Concert | Storyville | 4990013
Chris Barber's Jazz And Blues Band
Chris Barber On The Road:A Jazz Documentary | Storyville | 4960683
Chris Barber:40 Years Jubilee Concert | Storyville | 4990013
Chris Barber's Jazz Band
The Very Best Of Dixieland Jazz | Verve | 535529-2
The Best Of Dixieland-Live in 1954/55 | London | 820878-2
The Golden Years Of Revival Jazz,Vol 1 | Storyville | STCD 5506
The Golden Years Of Revival Jazz,Vol.2 | Storyville | STCD 5507
The Golden Years Of Revival Jazz,Vol.3 | Storyville | STCD 5508
The Golden Years Of Revival Jazz,Vol.4 | Storyville | STCD 5509
The Golden Years Of Revival Jazz,Vol.7 | Storyville | STCD 5512
The Golden Years Of Revival Jazz,Vol.9 | Storyville | STCD 5514
The Golden Years Of Revival Jazz,Vol.11 | Storyville | STCD 5516
The Golden Years Of Revival Jazz,Vol.13 | Storyville | STCD 5518
The Golden Years Of Revival Jazz,Vol.14 | Storyville | STCD 5519
The Golden Years Of Revibal Jazz,Vol.15 | Storyville | STCD 5520
Chris Barber's Jazzband & das Große Rundfunkorchester Berlin,DDR
Jazz Zounds: Chris Barber | Zounds | CD 2720007
Ken Colyer Trio
The Golden Years Of Revival Jazz.Vol.3 | Storyville | STCD 5508
Ken Colyer's Jazzmen
The Very Best Of Dixieland Jazz | Verve | 535529-2
The Golden Years Of Revival Jazz,Vol 1 | Storyville | STCD 5506
The Golden Years Of Revival Jazz,Vol.7 | Storyville | STCD 5512
The Golden Years Of Revival Jazz,Vol.11 | Storyville | STCD 5516
The Golden Years Of Revival Jazz,Vol.13 | Storyville | STCD 5518
The Golden Years Of Revival Jazz,Vol.14 | Storyville | STCD 5519
The Golden Years Of Revibal Jazz,Vol.15 | Storyville | STCD 5520
Lonnie Donegan Skiffle Group
The Best Of Dixieland-Live in 1954/55 | London | 820878-2
Monty Sunshine Trio
The Very Best Of Dixieland Jazz | Verve | 535529-2
The Golden Years Of Revival Jazz.Vol.3 | Storyville | STCD 5508
The Golden Years Of Revival Jazz,Vol.11 | Storyville | STCD 5516
The Golden Years Of Revival Jazz,Vol.13 | Storyville | STCD 5518
The Golden Years Of Revibal Jazz,Vol.15 | Storyville | STCD 5520

Barber,Danny | (tp)
Buddy Childers Big Band
Just Buddy's | Candid | CCD 79761

Barber,John | (tuba)
Miles Davis With Gil Evans & His Orchestra
Sketches Of Spain | CBS | CK 65142

Barber,Julian | (strings,vviola)
Gary McFarland And His Orchestra
The Complete Bill Evans On Verve | Verve | 527953-2
Grant Green With Orchestra
The Final Comedown(Soundtrack) | Blue Note | 581678-2
Grover Washington Jr. Orchestra
Inside Moves | Elektra | 7559-60318-2
Les McCann Group
Another Beginning | Atlantic | 7567-80790-2
Louis Armstrong And His Friends
Planet Jazz:Louis Armstrong | Planet Jazz | 2152052-2
Planet Jazz Sampler | Planet Jazz | 2152326-2
Louis Armstrong And His Friends | Bluebird | 2663961-2
Phil Woods Quartet With Orchestra & Strings
Round Trip | Verve | 559804-2
Stan Getz With The Eddie Sauter Orchestra
Stan Getz Plays The Music Of Mickey One | Verve | 531232-2

Barber,Patricia | (p,table-knifes on stringsvoc)
Patricia Barber Group
Modern Cool | Blue Note | 521811-2
Patricia Barber Quartet
Café Blue | Blue Note | 521810-2

Barber,Stephen | (string-orchestration)
Steps Ahead
N.Y.C. | Intuition Records | INT 3007-2

Barbieri,Gato | (as,ts,cl,fl,hands,voc,handclaps)
Carla Bley Group
Tropic Appetites | Watt | 1
Charlie Haden's Liberation Music Orchestra
Liberation Music Orchestra | Impulse(MCA) | 951188-2
Don Cherry Quartet
Complete Communion | Blue Note | 522673-2
Essence All Stars
Afro Cubano Chant | Hip Bop | HIBD 8009
Hot Jazz Bisquits | Hip Bop | HIBD 8801
Gary Burton Quartet With Orchestra
A Genuine Tong Funeral(Dark Opera Without Words) | RCA | 2119255-2
Gato Barbieri Group
Planet Jazz:Gato Barbieri | RCA | 2165364-2
Gato Barbieri:The Best Of The Early Years | RCA | 2663523-2
Gato Barbieri Orchestra
Latino America | Impulse(MCA) | 952236-2
The Roots Of Acid Jazz | Impulse(MCA) | IMP 12042
Gato Barbieri Quintet
The Art Of Saxophone | Laserlight | 24652
Gato Barbieri Septet
Yesterdays | RCA | 2147797-2
Gato Barbieri Sextet
The Third World | RCA | 2179617-2
The Jazz Composer's Orchestra
Comminications | JCOA | 1001/2

Barbour,Dave | (g,arr,ldtb)
Artie Shaw And His Orchestra
Planet JazzArtie Shaw | Planet Jazz | 2152057-2
Billie Holiday With The JATP All Stars
The Complete Jazz At The Philharmonic On Verve 1944-1949 | Verve | 523893-2
Ella Fitzgerald And Louis Armstrong With Dave Barbour And His Orchestra
Ella Fitzgerald:Mr.Paganini | Dreyfus Jazz Line | FDM 36741-2
Helen Humes And Her All Stars
Lester Young:The Complete Aladdin Sessions | Blue Note | 832787-2
Jack Teagarden's Chicagoans
Jazz:The Essential Collection Vol.3 | IN+OUT Records | 78013-2
The Hollywood Session:The Capitol Jazzmen | Jazz Unlimited | JUCD 2044
JATP All Stars
The Complete Jazz At The Philharmonic On Verve 1944-1949 | Verve | 523893-2
Jerri Southern And The Dave Barbour Trio
The Very Thought Of You:The Decca Years 1951-1957 | Decca | 050671-2
Lena Horne With The Horace Henderson Orchestra
Planet Jazz:Lena Horne | Planet Jazz | 2165373-2
Louis Armstrong And His Orchestra
Louis Armstrong:Swing That Music | Laserlight | 36056
Peggy Lee With The Benny Goodman Orchestra
Peggy Lee & Benny Goodman:The Complete Recordings 1941-1947 | CBS | C2K 65686
Ten Cats And A Mouse
The Hollywood Session:The Capitol Jazzmen | Jazz Unlimited | JUCD 2044
The Capitol Jazzmen
Jazz:The Essential Collection Vol.3 | IN+OUT Records | 78013-2
The Hollywood Session:The Capitol Jazzmen | Jazz Unlimited | JUCD 2044

Barbour,Dave prob. | (g)
Billie Holiday With The JATP All Stars
Billie Holiday Story Vol.1:Jazz At The Philharmonic | Verve | 521642-2
The Complete Jazz At The Philharmonic On Verve 1944-1949 | Verve | 523893-2
Verve Jazz Masters 47:Billie Holiday Sings Standards | Verve | 527650-2

Barcelona,Danny | (dr)
Louis Armstrong And His All Stars
Jazz In Paris:Louis Armstrong:The Best Live Concer Vol.1 | EmArCy | 013030-2
Jazz In Paris:Louis Armstrong-The Best Live Concert Vol.2 | EmArCy | 013031-2
Jazz Collection:Louis Armstrong | Laserlight | 24366
Jazz Festival Vol.1 | Storyville | 4960733
Live In Berlin/Friedrichstadtpalast | Jazzpoint | JP 1062 CD
The Legendary Berlin Concert Part 2 | Jazzpoint | JP 1063 CD
What A Wonderful World | MCA | MCD 01876
Louis Armstrong And His All Stars With A Studio Orchestra
What A Wonderful World | MCA | MCD 01876
Louis Armstrong And His All Stars With Duke Ellington
Louis Armstrong-Duke Ellington:The Great Summit-Complete Session | Roulette | 524546-2
Louis Armstrong And His Orchestra
I Love Jazz | Verve | 543747-2
Louis Armstrong-Duke Ellington Group
Blue Velvet: Crooners, Swooners And Velvet Vocals | Blue Note | 521153-2

Barclay,John | (tp)
John Surman-Jack DeJohnette With The London Brass
Printed In Germany | ECM | 1802(017065-2)
Kenny Wheeler Brass Ensemble
A Long Time Ago | ECM | 1691

Bardagi,Pere | (v)
Orquestra De Cambra Teatre Lliure
Tributes To Duke Ellington | Fresh Sound Records | FSNT 084 CD

Bardaro,Pasquale | (vib)
European Jazz Youth Orchestra
Swinging Europe 3 | dacapo | DCCD 9461

Barefield,Eddie | (as,cl,bs,reeds,sax,ldts)
Benny Moten's Kansas City Orchestra
Planet Jazz:Ben Webster | RCA | 2165368-2
Planet Jazz:Jimmy Rushing | RCA | 2165371-2
Planet Jazz:Swing | Planet Jazz | 2169651-2
Jazz:The Essential Collection Vol.3 | IN+OUT Records | 78013-2
Big Al Sears Band
Sear-iously | Bear Family Records | BCD 15668 AH
Billie Holiday With Eddie Heywood And His Orchestra
Billie's Love Songs | Nimbus Records | NI 2000
Cab Calloway And His Orchestra
Planet Jazz:Cab Calloway | Planet Jazz | 2161237-2
Ella Fitzgerald And Her Famous Orchestra
The Radio Years 1940 | Jazz Unlimited | JUCD 2065
Roy Eldridge And His Central Plaza Dixielanders
The Very Best Of Dixieland Jazz | Verve | 535529-2
The Complete Verve Roy Eldridge Studio Sessions | Verve | 9861278

Barene,Robert | (v)
Artie Shaw And His Orchestra
Planet JazzArtie Shaw | Planet Jazz | 2152057-2
Planet Jazz:Jazz Greatest Hits | Planet Jazz | 2169648-2
Cal Tjader With The Clare Fischer Orchestra
Cal Tjader Plays Harold Arlen & West Side Story | Fantasy | FCD 24775-2
Ella Fitzgerald With The Frank DeVol Orchestra
Get Happy! | Verve | 523321-2

Bargad,Rob | (p,arrld)
Nat Adderley Quintet
The Old Country | Enja | ENJ-7027 2

Barge,Claudine | (voc)
Les Double Six
Les Double Six | RCA | 2164314-2

Barge,Gene | (ts)
Albert King With The Willie Dixon Band
Windy City Blues | Stax | SCD 8612-2
Buddy Guy Blues Band
Buddy Guy-The Complete Chess Studio Recordings | MCA | MCD 09337

Bargeron,Dave | (b-tb,tuba,euphoniumtb)
Bob James And His Orchestra
Jazzrock-Anthology Vol.3:Fusion | Zounds | CD 27100555
George Gruntz Concert Jazz Band
Blues 'N Dues Et Cetera | Enja | ENJ-6072 2
George Gruntz Concert Jazz Band '83
Theatre | ECM | 1265
Miles Davis With Gil Evans Orchestra, The George Gruntz Concert Jazz Band And Guests
Miles & Quincy Live At Montreux | Warner | 9362-45221-2
Rabih Abou-Khalil Group
The Cactus Of Knowledge | Enja | ENJ-9401 2

Barguiarena,Ed | (perc)
Terri Lyne Carrington Group
Jazz Is A Spirit | ACT | 9408-2

Bargy,Roy | (parr)
Bix Beiderbecke And His Gang
Jazz:The Essential Collection Vol.2 | IN+OUT Records | 78012-2
Paul Whiteman And His Orchestra
Planet Jazz:Jack Teagarden | Planet Jazz | 2161236-2
Jazz:The Essential Collection Vol.3 | IN+OUT Records | 78013-2
The Three T's
Jazz:The Essential Collection Vol.3 | IN+OUT Records | 78013-2

Barile,Salvatore | (fl-h)
Banda Città Ruvo Di Puglia
La Banda/Banda And Jazz | Enja | ENJ-9326 2

Barkan,Todd | (percsynth)
Rahsaan Roland Kirk Sextet
Atlantic Saxophones | Rhino | 8122-71256-2

Barker,Danny | (bj,vocg)
Billie Holiday With Teddy Wilson And His Orchestra
Billie's Love Songs | Nimbus Records | NI 2000
George Wein's Dixie Victors
The Magic Horn | RCA | 2113038-2
Planet Jazz | Planet Jazz | 2169652-2
Louis Armstrong And His Orchestra
I Love Jazz | Verve | 543747-2
Louis Armstrong And Omer Simeon With The Sy Oliver Orchestra
Ambassador Louis Armstrong Vol.17:Moments To Remember(1952-1956) | Ambassador | CLA 1917
Louis Armstrong With Sy Oliver And His Orchestra
Louis Armstrong-My Greatest Songs | MCA | MCD 18347
Paul Barbarin And His Band
Atlantic Jazz: New Orleans | Atlantic | 7567-81700-2
This Is Jazz All Stars
Sidney Bechet:Summertime | Dreyfus Jazz Line | FDM 36712-2
Vic Dickenson-Buck Clayton All Stars
Atlantic Jazz: Kansas City | Atlantic | 7567-81701-2

Barker,Guy | (tp,fl-hflumpet)
Barbara Thompson Group
Heavenly Bodies | VeraBra Records | CDVBR 2015-2
Billy Cobham Group
Art Of Five | IN+OUT Records | 77063-2
Carla Bley Band
The Very Big Carla Bley Band | Watt | 23
Big Band Theory | Watt | 25(519966-2)
Carla Bley Big Band
The Carla Bley Big Band Goes To Church | Watt | 27(533682-2)
Jim Tomlinson Sextet
Only Trust Your Heart | Candid | CCD 79758

Barksdale,Everett | (el-b,el-g,gbj)
Art Tatum Trio
Art Tatum:Complete Capitol Recordings | Capitol | 821325-2
Billie Holiday With Sy Oliver And His Orchestra
Billie's Love Songs | Nimbus Records | NI 2000
Cab Calloway And His Orchestra
Planet Jazz:Cab Calloway | Planet Jazz | 2161237-2
Planet Jazz:Male Jazz Vocalists | Planet Jazz | 2169657-2

INTERPRETENVERZEICHNIS

Clark Terry & Chico O Farril Orchestra
Spanish Rice | Verve | 9861050
Eddie Lockjaw Davis Sextet feat. Paul Gonsalves
Planet Jazz:Jazz Saxophone | Planet Jazz | 2169653-2
Ella Fitzgerald With Sy Oliver And His Orchestra
Ella Fitzgerald:Mr.Paganini | Dreyfus Jazz Line | FDM 36741-2
Ella Fitzgerald And Louis Armstrong With Sy Oliver And His Orchestra
Ella Fitzgerald:Mr.Paganini | Dreyfus Jazz Line | FDM 36741-2
Ella Fitzgerald With Bill Doggett's Orchestra
Ella Fitzgerald:Mr.Paganini | Dreyfus Jazz Line | FDM 36741-2
Ella Fitzgerald With Sy Oliver And His Orchestra
Ella Fitzgerald:The Decca Years 1949-1954 | Decca | 050668-2
Ella Fitzgerald With The Hank Jones Quartet
Ella Fitzgerald:Mr.Paganini | Dreyfus Jazz Line | FDM 36741-2
Henry Red Allen's All Stars
Planet Jazz:Coleman Hawkins | Planet Jazz | 2152055-2
Jerome Richardson Sextet
Night Life | Prestige | PCD 24260-2
Johnny Hodges Orchestra
Verve Jazz Masters 35:Johnny Hodges | Verve | 521857-2
Louis Armstrong And Billie Holiday With Sy Oliver's Orchestra
Louis Armstrong:C'est Si Bon | Dreyfus Jazz Line | FDM 36730-2
Louis Armstrong And Ella Fitzgerald With Sy Oliver's Orchestra
Louis Armstrong:C'est Si Bon | Dreyfus Jazz Line | FDM 36730-2
Louis Armstrong And His All Stars With The Sy Oliver Orchestra
Ambassador Louis Armstrong Vol.17:Moments To Remember(1952-1956) | Ambassador | CLA 1917
Louis Armstrong And His Orchestra
Satchmo Serenaders | Verve | 543792-2
Louis Armstrong With Sy Oliver And His Orchestra
Satchmo Serenaders | Verve | 543792-2
Louis And The Angels | Verve | 549592-2
Louis Armstrong:C'est Si Bon | Dreyfus Jazz Line | FDM 36730-2
Louis Armstrong-My Greatest Songs | MCA | MCD 18347
Louis Armstrong With Sy Oliver's Choir And Orchestra
Jazz Collection:Louis Armstrong | Laserlight | 24366
Louis And The Good Book | Verve | 549593-2
Louis And The Good Book | Verve | 940130-0
Sidney Bechet And His New Orleans Feetwarmers
Planet Jazz | Planet Jazz | 2169652-2
Sidney Bechet:Summertime | Dreyfus Jazz Line | FDM 36712-2
Stanley Turrentine And His Orchestra
The Lost Grooves | Blue Note | 831883-2

Barlow,Clarence | (computer-programming)
Kölner Saxophon Mafia With Clarence Barlow
Kölner Saxophon Mafia Proudly Presents | Jazz Haus Musik | JHM 0046 CD

Barlow,Dale | (ts)
Vince Jones Group
Future Girl | Intuition Records | INT 3109-2
Vince Jones With The Benny Green Quartet
One Day Spent | Intuition Records | INT 3087-2

Barnardi,Noni | (as)
Benny Goodman And His Orchestra
Camel Caravan Broadcast 1939 Vol.1 | Phontastic | NCD 8817
Camel Caravan Broadcast 1939 Vol.2 | Phontastic | NCD 8818
Camel Caravan Broadcast 1939 Vol.3 | Phontastic | NCD 8819

Barnes,Alan | (as,ts,bs,cl,sssax)
Clare Teal And Her Band
Orsino's Songs | Candid | CCD 79783
Mike Westbrook Orchestra
The Orchestra Of Smith's Academy | Enja | ENJ-9358 2
Warren Vaché And The New York City All-Star Big Band
Swingtime! | Nagel-Heyer | CD 059

Barnes,George | (el-gg)
Coleman Hawkins Sextet
Body And Soul Revisited | GRP | GRP 16272
Della Reese With The Sy Oliver Orchestra
Misty Blue:Sweet Sisters Swing Songs Of Sorrow And Sadness | Blue Note | 521151-2
Jimmy McPartland And His Dixielanders
Planet Jazz | Planet Jazz | 2169652-2
Louis Armstrong And His Orchestra
I Love Jazz | Verve | 543747-2
Louis Armstrong With Gordon Jenkins And His Orchestra And Choir
Satchmo In Style | Verve | 549594-2
Ambassador Louis Armstrong Vol.17:Moments To Remember(1952-1956) | Ambassador | CLA 1917
Louis Armstrong With Sy Oliver And His Orchestra
Louis And The Angels | Verve | 549592-2
Louis Armstrong With Sy Oliver's Choir And Orchestra
Jazz Collection:Louis Armstrong | Laserlight | 24366
Louis And The Good Book | Verve | 549593-2
Louis And The Good Book | Verve | 940130-0

Barnes,John | (as,bs,voc,cl,ts,fl,b-cl,sax)
A Salute To Eddie Condon
A Salute To Eddie Condon | Nagel-Heyer | CD 004
One Two Three | Nagel-Heyer | CD 008
The First Sampler | Nagel-Heyer | NHR SP 5
Great British Jazz Band
The Great British Jazz Band:Jubilee | Candid | CCD 79720
Marty Grosz Quartet
Just For Fun! | Nagel-Heyer | CD 039
Paulinho Da Costa Orchestra
Happy People | Original Jazz Classics | OJCCD 783-2(2312102)
The Alex Welsh Legacy Band
The Sound Of Alex Vol.1 | Nagel-Heyer | CD 070
The Great British Jazz Band
A British Jazz Odyssey | Candid | CCD 79740
Tom Saunders' 'Wild Bill Davison Band' & Guests
Exactly Like You | Nagel-Heyer | CD 023
The Second Sampler | Nagel-Heyer | NHR SP 6

Barnes,Marjorie | (voc)
HR Big Band With Marjorie Barnes And Frits Landesbergen
Swinging Christmas | hr music.de | hrmj 012-02 CD
HR Big Band With Marjorie Barnes And Frits Landesbergen And Strings
Swinging Christmas | hr music.de | hrmj 012-02 CD

Barnes,Paul | (as,cl,vocs)
Jelly Roll Morton And His Orchestra
Planet Jazz:Jelly Roll Morton | Planet Jazz | 2152060-2
Jazz:The Essential Collection Vol.1 | IN+OUT Records | 78011-2

Barnes,Peter | (fl)
Deborah Henson-Conant
The Celtic Album | Laika Records | 35101022

Barneschi,Stefano | (v)
La Gaia Scienza
Love Fugue-Robert Schumann | Winter&Winter | 910049-2

Barnet,Charlie | (as,ts,bells,chimes,maracas,ss,bsld)
Charlie Bamet And His Orchestra
Planet Jazz:Big Bands | Planet Jazz | 2169649-2
Planet Jazz:Swing | Planet Jazz | 2169651-2

Barney ? | (bj)
Jelly Roll Morton And His Orchestra
Planet Jazz:Jelly Roll Morton | Planet Jazz | 2152060-2

Barnikel,Johannes 'Jo' | (keyboards,synthp)
Gerwin Eisenhauer's The Gaff Gang feat. Lisa Wahland
Favorite Tunes | Edition Collage | EC 527-2

Baro,Evaristo | (b)
Sabu L. Martinez Group
Palo Congo | Blue Note | 522665-2

Baro,Sarah | (voc)

Baron,Art | (tb,bass-recorder,conch-chell,b-tb)
Duke Ellington And His Orchestra
Highlights From The Duke Ellington Centennial Edition | RCA | 2663672-2
Duke Ellington Orchestra
Continuum | Fantasy | FCD 24765-2
George Gruntz Concert Jazz Band
Blues 'N Dues Et Cetera | Enja | ENJ-6072 2
Mingus Big Band 93
Nostalgia In Times Square | Dreyfus Jazz Line | FDM 36559-2

Baron,Frank | (p)
Arthur Young And Hatchett's Swingtette
Grapelli Story | Verve | 515807-2

Baron,Joey | (dr,electronics,membranophone)
Batman
Naked City | Nonesuch | 7559-79238-2
Bill Frisell Band
Before We Were Born | Nonesuch | 7559-60843-2
Is That You? | Nonesuch | 7559-60956-2
Where In The World | Nonesuch | 7559-61181-2
Carmen McRae With The Dizzy Gillespie Quartet
Misty Blue:Sweet Sisters Swing Songs Of Sorrow And Sadness | Blue Note | 521151-2
Dave Douglas Group
Soul On Soul | RCA | 2663603-2
Dave Douglas Freak In | Bluebird | 2664008-2
Dino Saluzzi Group
If | Enja | ENJ-9451 2
Hank Roberts Group
Black Pastels | JMT Edition | 919016-2
Herb Robertson Brass Ensemble
Shades Of Bud Powell | JMT Edition | 919019-2
Herb Robertson Quintet
'X'-cerpts:Live At Willisau | JMT Edition | 919013-2
James Carter Group
Chasin' The Gypsy | Atlantic | 7567-83304-2
Joey Baron Quartet
We'll Soon Find Out | Intuition Records | INT 3515-2
John Abercrombie Quartet
Cat 'N' Mouse | ECM | 1770(014001-2)
Class Trip | ECM | 1846(0381182)
John Taylor Trio
Rosslyn | ECM | 1751(159924-2)
John Zorn Group
Spy Vs. Spy-The Music Of Ornette Coleman | Nonesuch | 7559-60844-2
Josh Roseman Unit
Cherry | Enja | ENJ-9392 2
Lee Konitz Quintet
Sound Of Surprise | RCA | 2169309-2
Marc Johnson Group
The Sound Of Summer Running | Verve | 539299-2
Miriam Alter Quintet
Alter Ego | Intuition Records | INT 3258-2
Richard Galliano Group
Laurita | Dreyfus Jazz Line | FDM 36572-9
Richard Galliano Quartet
Gallianissimo! The Best Of Richard Galliano | Dreyfus Jazz Line | FDM 36616-2
Richard Galliano Trio
Gallianissimo! The Best Of Richard Galliano | Dreyfus Jazz Line | FDM 36616-2
Steve Kuhn Trio
Remembering Tomorrow | ECM | 1573(529035-2)
The Bill Frisell Band
Lookout For Hope | ECM | 1350(833495-2)
Uri Caine Group
Urlicht/Primal Light | Winter&Winter | 910004-2

Baron,Moran | (tb)
European Jazz Youth Orchestra
Swinging Europe 1 | dacapo | DCCD 9449
Swinging Europe 2 | dacapo | DCCD 9450

Barone,Gary | (fl-htp)
Matthias Stich Sevensenses
...mehrschichtig | Satin Doll Productions | SDP 1038-1 CD
Shelly Manne Sextet
Alive In London | Original Jazz Classics | OJCCD 773-2(S 7629)

Barone,Mike | (tb)
Dizzy Gillespie And His Orchestra
Talking Verve:Dizzy Gillespie | Verve | 533846-2
Johnny Hartman And His Orchestra
Unforgettable | Impulse(MCA) | IMP 11522

Baronian,Souren | (dumbek)
Tony Scott Group
Tony Scott | Verve | 9861063

Baroudi,Nadja | (dr)
Sören Fischer Quartet
Don't Change Your Hair For Me | Edition Collage | EC 513-2

Barr,Gene | (ts)
Funk Inc.
Jazzin' With The Soul Brothers | Fantasy | FANCD 6086-2

Barrajanos,Danny | (congas)
Arnett Cobb Quintet
Movin' Right Along | Original Jazz Classics | OJCCD 1074-2(P 7216)
More Party Time | Original Jazz Classics | OJCCD 979-2(P 7175)

Barrero,Tony | (tp)
Lester Bowie's Brass Fantasy
The Fire This Time | IN+OUT Records | 7019-2

Barreto,Julio | (drtimbales)
Gonzalo Rubalcaba & Cuban Quartet
Antiguo | Blue Note | 837717-2
Gonzalo Rubalcaba Quartet
Imagine | Blue Note | 830491-2

Barrett,Dan | (co,tb,arr,voc,v-tbtp)
Allan Vaché Swingtet
Ellington For Lovers | Nagel-Heyer | NH 1009
Barbara Dennerlein Group
Outhipped | Verve | 547503-2
Dan Barrett Septet
Dan Barrett's International Swing Party | Nagel-Heyer | CD 067
Engelbert Wrobel-Chris Hopkins-Dan Barrett Sextet
Harlem 2000 | Nagel-Heyer | CD 082
Joe Ascione Octet
My Buddy:A Tribute To Buddy Rich | Nagel-Heyer | CD 036
Randy Sandke And The New York Allstars
The Re-Discovered Louis And Bix | Nagel-Heyer | CD 058
Rex Allen's Swing Express
Keep Swingin' | Nagel-Heyer | CD 016
Ellington For Lovers | Nagel-Heyer | NH 1009
The Second Sampler | Nagel-Heyer | NHR SP 6
The New York Allstars
Broadway | Nagel-Heyer | CD 003
One Two Three | Nagel-Heyer | CD 008
Count Basie Remembered | Nagel-Heyer | CD 031
Count Basie Remembered Vol.2 | Nagel-Heyer | CD 041
Randy Sandke Meets Bix Beiderbecke | Nagel-Heyer | CD 3002
The First Sampler | Nagel-Heyer | NHR SP 5

Barrett,Dave | (as,ts,saxellotp)
Lennie Baldwin's Dauphin Street Six
The Golden Years Of Revival Jazz,Sampler | Storyville | 109 1001
The Golden Years Of Revival Jazz,Vol 1 | Storyville | STCD 5506
The Golden Years Of Revival Jazz,Vol.3 | Storyville | STCD 5508
The Golden Years Of Revival Jazz,Vol.6 | Storyville | STCD 5511
The Golden Years Of Revival Jazz,Vol.9 | Storyville | STCD 5514
The Golden Years Of Revival Jazz,Vol.10 | Storyville | STCD 5515
The Golden Years Of Revival Jazz,Vol.13 | Storyville | STCD 5518

Barretto,Carlos | (b)
Bob Sands Quartet
JumpSTART | Fresh Sound Records | FSNT 042 CD
Bob Sands Quintet
JumpSTART | Fresh Sound Records | FSNT 042 CD

Barretto,Ray | (bongos,congas,quinto,tambourine)
Art Blakey Percussion Ensemble
Drums Around The Corner | Blue Note | 521455-2
Billy Cobham Group
Spectrum | Atlantic | 7567-81428-2
Buddy Tate With The Marlow Morris Quintet
Late Night Sax | CBS | 487798-2
Cal Tjader Quintet
Talkin Verve/Roots Of Acid Jazz:Cal Tjader | Verve | 531562-2
Cal Tjader's Orchestra
Verve Jazz Masters 39:Cal Tjader | Verve | 521858-2
Dave Pike Quintet
Carnavals | Prestige | PCD 24248-2
Dave Pike Sextet
Carnavals | Prestige | PCD 24248-2
Dizzy Gillespie And His Orchestra
Gillespiana And Carnegie Hall Concert | Verve | 519809-2
Talking Verve:Dizzy Gillespie | Verve | 533846-2
Ultimate Dizzy Gillespie | Verve | 557535-2
Eddie Harris Group
The Best Of Eddie Harris | Atlantic | 7567-81370-2
Eddie Lockjaw Davis Orchestra
Afro-Jaws | Original Jazz Classics | OJCCD 403-2(RLP 9373)
Eddie Lockjaw Davis-Shirley Scott Sextet
Bacalao | Original Jazz Classics | OJCCD 1090-2(P 7178)
Frank Wess And His Orchestra
The Long Road | Prestige | PCD 24247-2
Freddie Hubbard With Orchestra
This Is Jazz:Freddie Hubbard | CBS | CK 65041
Gene Ammons And His All Stars
Blue Gene | Original Jazz Classics | OJC20 192-2(P 7146)
Gene Ammons And His Orchestra
A Stranger In Town | Prestige | PRCD 24266-2
Gene Ammons Quintet
Boss Tenor | Original Jazz Classics | OJC20 297-2(P-7180)
The Jazz Giants Play Jerome Kern:Yesterdays | Prestige | PCD 24202-2
The Jazz Giants Play Cole Porter:Night And Day | Prestige | PCD 24203-2
Gentle Jug Vol.3 | Prestige | PCD 24249-2
Gene Ammons Septet
Goodbye | Original Jazz Classics | OJCCD 1081-2(P 100939)
Gene Ammons Sextet
Gentle Jug Vol.3 | Prestige | PCD 24249-2
George Benson With Orchestra
Verve Jazz Masters 21:George Benson | Verve | 521861-2
George Benson With The Don Sebesky Orchestra
Verve Jazz Masters 21:George Benson | Verve | 521861-2
Herbie Mann And His Orchestra
The Best Of Herbie Mann | Atlantic | 7567-81369-2
Herbie Mann's Cuban Band
Verve Jazz Masters 56:Herbie Mann | Verve | 529901-2
Horace Parlan Quartet
Blue Bossa | Blue Note | 795590-2
Jimmy Forrest Quintet
Soul Street | Original Jazz Classics | OJCCD 987-2(NJ 8293)
Jimmy Smith And Wes Montgomery With Orchestra
Jimmy & Wes-The Dynamic Duo | Verve | 521445-2
Jimmy Smith And Wes Montgomery With The Oliver Nelson Orchestra
Jimmy Smith:Best Of The Verve Years | Verve | 527950-2
Talkin' Jazz:Roots Of Acid Jazz | Verve | 529580-2
Jimmy Smith-Wes Montgomery Quartet
Jimmy & Wes-The Dynamic Duo | Verve | 521445-2
Wes Montgomery:The Verve Jazz Sides | Verve | 521690-2
Verve Jazz Masters 29:Jimmy Smith | Verve | 521855-2
Jimmy Smith:Best Of The Verve Years | Verve | 527950-2
Talkin' Jazz:Roots Of Acid Jazz | Verve | 529580-2
Jimmy Smith-Talkin' Verve | Verve | 531563-2
Joe Zawinul Quartet
To You With Love | Fresh Sound Records | Strand SLS CD 1007
Johnny 'Hammond' Smith Septet
Open House | Milestone | MCD 47089-2
Johnny Lytle Quartet
Got That Feeling/Moon Child | Milestone | MCD 47093-2
Johnny Lytle Quintet
Got That Feeling/Moon Child | Milestone | MCD 47093-2
Kenny Burrell Quintet
Midnight Blue | Blue Note | 495335-2
The Best Of Blue Note | Blue Note | 796110-2
Soul Call | Original Jazz Classics | OJCCD 846-2(P 7315)
Lou Donaldson Quintet
The Best Of Blue Note | Blue Note | 796110-2
Ray Barretto Orchestra
Portraits In Jazz And Clave | RCA | 2168452-2
Red Garland Quartet
The Jazz Giants Play Rodgers & Hart:Blue Moon | Prestige | PCD 24205-2
Red Garland Trio With Ray Barretto
Manteca | Original Jazz Classics | OJCCD 428-2(PR 7139)
Sonny Stitt-Jack McDuff Quintet
Stitt Meets Brother Jack | Original Jazz Classics | OJCCD 703-2(P 7244)
Stanley Turrentine Quintet
Never Let Me Go | Blue Note | 576750-2
Wes Montgomery Quartet
Verve Jazz Masters 14:Wes Montgomery | Verve | 519826-2
Talkin' Jazz:Roots Of Acid Jazz | Verve | 529580-2
Tequila | Verve | 547769-2
Wes Montgomery Quartet With The Claus Ogerman Orchestra
Tequila | Verve | 547769-2
Wes Montgomery Quintet
Wes Montgomery-The Complete Riverside Recordings | Riverside | 12 RCD 4408-2
So Much Guitar! | Original Jazz Classics | OJC20 233-2
The Jazz Giants Play Duke Ellington:Caravan | Prestige | PCD 24227-2
Wes Montgomery Quintet With The Claus Ogerman Orchestra
The Antonio Carlos Jobim Songbook | Verve | 525472-2
Talkin' Jazz:Roots Of Acid Jazz | Verve | 529580-2
Wes Montgomery Sextet
Tequila | Verve | 547769-2
Wes Montgomery With The Claus Ogerman Orchestra
Verve Jazz Masters 14:Wes Montgomery | Verve | 519826-2
Wes Montgomery With The Don Sebesky Orchestra
Verve Jazz Masters 14:Wes Montgomery | Verve | 519826-2
Wes Montgomery:The Verve Jazz Sides | Verve | 521690-2
Talkin' Jazz:Roots Of Acid Jazz | Verve | 529580-2
California Dreaming | Verve | 827842-2
Wild Bill Moore Quintet
Bottom Groove | Milestone | MCD 47098-2
Yusef Lateef Ensemble
Atlantic Saxophones | Rhino | 8122-71256-2

Barron,Bill | (cl,tsss)
Cecil Taylor Quintet
Love For Sale | Blue Note | 494107-2
Charles Mingus Orchestra
Charles Mingus:Pre-Bird(Mingus Revisited) | Verve | 538636-2

Barron,Farid | (p)
Lincoln Center Jazz Orchestra
Big Train | CBS | CK 69860
Wycliffe Gordon Quintet
The Joyride | Nagel-Heyer | CD 2032

Barron,George | (ssts)
Lonnie Liston Smith & His Cosmic Echoes
Astral Travelling | RCA | 2663878-2

Barron,Kenny | (el-p,keyboards,p,el-keyboards,synth)
(Little)Jimmy Scott And His Quintet
All The Way | Warner | 7599-26955-2
Abbey Lincoln With The Rodney Kendrick Trio And Guests
A Turtle's Dream | Verve | 527382-2
Billy Cobham Trio
The Art Of Three | IN+OUT Records | 77045-2
Buddy Rich Septet
Swingin' The Blues-Jumpin' The Blues | Laserlight | 24654
Candid Jazz Masters

The Candid Jazz Masters:For Miles | Candid | CCD 79710
Charlie Haden-Kenny Barron
Night And The City | Verve | 539961-2
Dizzy Gillespie And His Orchestra
Talking Verve:Dizzy Gillespie | Verve | 533846-2
Dizzy Gillespie Quintet
Dizzie Gillespie: Salle Pleyel/Olympia | Laserlight | 36132
Verve Jazz Masters 10:Dizzy Gillespie | Verve | 516319-2
Talking Verve:Dizzy Gillespie | Verve | 533846-2
Ultimate Dizzy Gillespie | Verve | 557535-2
Something Old Something New | Verve | 558079-2
Dizzy Gillespie Sextet
Talking Verve:Dizzy Gillespie | Verve | 533846-2
Jambo Caribe | Verve | 557492-2
Ultimate Dizzy Gillespie | Verve | 557535-2
Donald Harrison Sextet
Kind Of New | Candid | CCD 79768
Eddie Harris Quartet
There Was A Time-Echo Of Harlem | Enja | ENJ-6068 2
Ella Fitzgerald And Her All Stars
All That Jazz | Pablo | 2310938-2
Franco Ambrosetti Quintet
Live At The Blue Note | Enja | ENJ-7065 2
J.J. Johnson-Al Grey Sextet
Things Are Getting Better All The Time | Original Jazz Classics | OJCCD 745-2(2312141)
The J.J.Johnson Memorial Album | Prestige | PRCD 11025-2
James Moody Orchestra
The Blues And Other Colors | Original Jazz Classics | OJCCD 954-2(M 9023)
Joe Henderson Quartet
Joe Henderson:The Milestone Years | Milestone | 8MCD 4413-2
The Kicker | Original Jazz Classics | OJCCD 465-2
Tetragon | Original Jazz Classics | OJCCD 844-2(M 9017)
The Jazz Giants Play Cole Porter:Night And Day | Prestige | PCD 24203-2
Joe Henderson Sextet
Joe Henderson:The Milestone Years | Milestone | 8MCD 4413-2
The Kicker | Original Jazz Classics | OJCCD 465-2
Kenny Barron
What If | Enja | ENJ-5013 2
Kenny Barron Group
Spirit Song | Verve | 543180-2
Kenny Barron Group With Trio De Paz
Canta Brazil | EmArCy | 017993-2
Kenny Barron Quintet
What If | Enja | ENJ-5013 2
Live At Fat Tuesdays | Enja | ENJ-5071 2
Quickstep | Enja | ENJ-6084 2
Kenny Barron Trio
Live at Bradley's | EmArCy | 549099-2
What If | Enja | ENJ-5013 2
Kenny Barron-John Hicks Quartet
Rhythm-A-Ning | Candid | CCD 79044
Kenny Barron-Regina Carter
Freefall | Verve | 549706-2
Kenny Barron-Victor Lewis
What If | Enja | ENJ-5013 2
Mark Morganelli And The Jazz Forum All Stars
Speak Low | Candid | CCD 79054
Mark Whitfield Group
Patrice | Warner | 7599-26659-2
Melissa Walker And Her Band
I Saw The Sky | Enja | ENJ-9409 2
Ron Carter Group
Songs For You | Milestone | MCD 47099-2
Peg Leg | Original Jazz Classics | OJCCD 621-2
Ron Carter Octet
New York Slick | Original Jazz Classics | OJCCD 916-2(M 9096)
Ron Carter Quartet
Pick 'Em/Super Strings | Milestone | MCD 47090-2
Ron Carter Quintet With Strings
Pick 'Em/Super Strings | Milestone | MCD 47090-2
Ron Carter Sextet
New York Slick | Original Jazz Classics | OJCCD 916-2(M 9096)
Ron Carter With Strings
Pastels | Original Jazz Classics | OJCCD 665-2(M 9073)
Russell Malone Quartet
Sweet Georgia Peach | Impulse(MCA) | 951282-2
Russell Malone Quintet
Sweet Georgia Peach | Impulse(MCA) | 951282-2
Stan Getz Quartet
A Life In Jazz:A Musical Biography | Verve | 535119-2
Stan Getz Cafe Montmartre | EmArCy | 586755-2
Anniversary ! | EmArCy | 838769-2
Serenity | EmArCy | 838770-2
The Lost Sessions | Verve | 9801098
Bossas And Ballads:The Lost Sessions | Verve | 9901098
Stan Getz With Orchestra
Apasionado | A&M Records | 395297-2
Stan Getz-Kenny Barron
People Time | EmArCy | 510134-2
A Life In Jazz:A Musical Biography | Verve | 535119-2
Stan Getz Cafe Montmartre | EmArCy | 586755-2
Tommy Flanagan/Kenny Barron
The Story Of Jazz Piano | Laserlight | 24653
Yusef Lateef Orchestra
Rhino Presents The Atlantic Jazz Gallery | Atlantic | 8122-71257-2

Barrosa,Sergio | (b)
Ithamara Koorax With Band
Love Dance:The Ballad Album | Milestone | MCD 9327-2

Barroso,Juan M. | (dr)
Joaquin Chacon Group
San | Fresh Sound Records | FSNT 015 CD

Barroso,Sergio | (b)
Sarah Vaughan With Orchestra
I Love Brazil | Pablo | 2312101-2
Sarah Vaughan Birthday Celebration | Fantasy | FANCD 6090-2

Barrow,George | (bs,reeds,saxts)
Bobby Timmons Orchestra
Quartet And Orchestra | Milestone | MCD 47091-2
Charles Mingus Quintet
Charles Mingus-The Complete Debut Recordings | Debut | 12 DCD 4402-2
Mingus At The Bohemia | Original Jazz Classics | OJC20 045-2
The Charles Mingus Quintet+Max Roach | Original Jazz Classics | OJC20 440-2(F 6009)
Eddie Lockjaw Davis And His Orchestra
Eric Dolphy:The Complete Prestige Recordings | Prestige | 9 PRCD-4418-2
Frank Wess And His Orchestra
The Long Road | Prestige | PCD 24247-2
Gene Ammons And His Orchestra
A Stranger In Town | Prestige | PRCD 24266-2
Jimmy Forrest With The Oliver Nelson Orchestra
Soul Street | Original Jazz Classics | OJCCD 987-2(NJ 8293)
Jimmy Smith With The Oliver Nelson Orchestra
Verve Jazz Masters 29:Jimmy Smith | Verve | 521855-2
Jimmy Smith:Best Of The Verve Years | Verve | 527950-2
John LaPorta Octet
Theme And Variations | Fantasy | FCD 24776-2
King Curtis Band
King Curtis-Blow Man Blow | Bear Family Records | BCD 15670 CI
Oliver Nelson And His Orchestra
Blues And The Abstract Truth | Impulse(MCA) | 951154-2
The Roots Of Acid Jazz | Impulse(MCA) | IMP 12042
Sandole Brothers
The Sandole Brothers | Fantasy | FCD 24763-2

The Jazz Composer's Orchestra
Comminications | JCOA | 1001/2

Barrows,John | (fr-h)
Dizzy Gillespie And His Orchestra
Gillespiana And Carnegie Hall Concert | Verve | 519809-2
Talking Verve:Dizzy Gillespie | Verve | 533846-2
Ultimate Dizzy Gillespie | Verve | 557535-2
Miles Davis With Gil Evans & His Orchestra
Ballads | CBS | 461099-2
Sketches Of Spain | CBS | CK 65142
Quiet Nights | CBS | CK 65293
Woody Herman And The Herd
Woody Herman (And The Herd) At Carnegie Hall | Verve | 559833-2

Barry,Dave | (drperc)
Mike Westbrook Brass Band
Glad Day:Settings Of William Blake | Enja | ENJ-9376 2

Barsby,Helen | (tp)
The United Women's Orchestra
The Blue One | Jazz Haus Musik | JHM 0099 CD
United Women's Orchestra
Virgo Supercluster | Jazz Haus Musik | JHM 0123 CD

Barsimento,Mike | (dr)
Dave Liebman Quintet
Jazz Portraits | EGO | 95080

Bartee,Claude | (ssts)
Grant Green Orchestra
Grant Green:Blue Breakbeat | Blue Note | 494705-2
Blue Breaks Beats Vol.2 | Blue Note | 789907-2
So Blue So Funky-Heroes Of The Hammond | Blue Note | 796563-2
Grant Green Septet
Live At The Lighthouse | Blue Note | 493381-2
Grant Green Sextet
Grant Green:Blue Breakbeat | Blue Note | 494705-2
Alive! | Blue Note | 525650-2
Blue Break Beats | Blue Note | 799106-2
The Lost Grooves | Blue Note | 831883-2

Bartee,Ellis | (dr)
(Little)Jimmy Scott With The Lionel Hampton Orchestra
Everybody's Somebody's Fool | Decca | 050669-2
Lionel Hampton And His Orchestra
Lionel Hampton:Flying Home | Dreyfus Jazz Line | FDM 36735-2
Lionel Hampton Orchestra
The Big Bands Vol.1.The Snader Telescriptions | Storyville | 4960043

Bartek,Mosmir | (tb)
Hans Koller Big Band
New York City | MPS | 9813437

Bartels,Gerald | (b)
Jan Harrington And Friends
I Feel The Spirit | Nagel-Heyer | NHR SP 7
Jan Harrington Band
Christmas Jazz! | Nagel-Heyer | NH 1008
Jan Harrington Sextet
Jan Harrington's Christmas In New Orleans | Nagel-Heyer | NHR SP 4

Bartelt,Marcus | (bs,fl,b-cl,reedssax)
HR Big Band
The American Songs Of Kurt Weill | hr music.de | hrmj 006-01 CD
Nana Mouskouri With The Berlin Radio Big Band
Nana Swings | Mercury | 074394-2

Barth,Benny | (dr)
The Mastersounds
The Mastersounds | Prestige | PRCD 24770-2

Barth,Bruce | (keyboards,p,orgsynth)
Bruce Barth Quartet
Where Eagles Fly | Fresh Sound Records | FSNT 090 CD
Ingrid Jensen Sextet
Vernal Fields | Enja | ENJ-9013 2

Barthelmy,Claude | (el-b,el-g,bg)
Aldo Romano Duo
Il Piacere | Owl Records | 013575-2
Aldo Romano Trio
Il Piacere | Owl Records | 013575-2
Claude Barthelmy Group
Moderne | Owl Records | 014739-2

Barthelmy,Paul | (tb)
Eric Dolphy Quartet With The University Of Illinois Big Band
The Illinois Concert | Blue Note | 499826-2

Bartlett,Wayne | (arrvoc)
Benny Bailey Quartet With Wayne Bartlett
I Thought About You | Laika Records | 35100762
Wayne Bartlett With The Thomas Hufschmidt Group
Tokyo Blues | Laika Records | 35101212
Wayne Bartlett With The Thomas Hufschmidt Trio And Wolfgang Engstfeld
Senor Blues | Laika Records | LK 95-066

Bartley,Dallas | (b)
Louis Jordan And His Tympany Five
The Small Black Groups | Storyville | 4960523
Louis Jordan-Let The Good Times Roll: The Complete Decca Recordings 1938-1954 | Bear Family Records | BCD 15557 IH

Bartney,Kathy | (voc)
Passport
Garden Of Eden | Atlantic | 2292-44147-2

Bartoccini,Gerardo | (b)
Nicola Puglielli Group
In The Middle | Jardis Records | JRCD 9924

Barton,Bob | (pvoc)
Oscar Klein-Lino Patruno European Jazz Stars
Live at The San Marino Jazz Festival | Jazzpoint | JP 1052 CD

Barton,Dee | (dr,comptb)
Stan Kenton And His Orchestra
Adventures In Blues | Capitol | 520089-2
Adventures In Jazz | Capitol | 521222-2

Barton,Johnny | (bj,vocg)
Graham Stewart And His New Orleans Band
The Golden Years Of Revival Jazz,Sampler | Storyville | 109 1001
The Golden Years Of Revival Jazz,Vol.4 | Storyville | STCD 5509
The Golden Years Of Revival Jazz,Vol.10 | Storyville | STCD 5515
Graham Stewart Seven
The Golden Years Of Revival Jazz,Vol.8 | Storyville | STCD 5513

Barton,Mary Jane | (harp)
Ella Fitzgerald With The Marty Paich Orchestra
Get Happy! | Verve | 523321-2

Bartz,Gary | (as,bells,perc,shakers,cl,ss)
Gary Bartz Ntu Troop
Jazzin' Vol.2: The Music Of Stevie Wonder | Fantasy | FANCD 6088-2
Gary Bartz Quartet
Libra/Another Earth | Milestone | MCD 47077-2
Gary Bartz Quintet
West 42nd Street | Candid | CCD 79049
Libra/Another Earth | Milestone | MCD 47077-2
Gary Bartz Sextet
Libra/Another Earth | Milestone | MCD 47077-2
Gene Ammons Septet
Goodbye | Original Jazz Classics | OJCCD 1081-2(P 100939)
Helen Merrill With Richard Davis & Gary Bartz
A Shade Of Difference | EmArCy | 558851-2
Ingrid Jensen Quintet
Here On Earth | Enja | ENJ-9313 2
Louis Hayes Sextet
The Crawl | Candid | CCD 79045
McCoy Tyner Orchestra
Sama Layuca | Original Jazz Classics | OJCCD 1071-2(M 9056)
McCoy Tyner Septet
Focal Point | Original Jazz Classics | OJCCD 1009-2(M 9072)
McCoy Tyner Sextet
Asante | Blue Note | 493384-2
Extensions | Blue Note | 837646-2
Focal Point | Original Jazz Classics | OJCCD 1009-2(M 9072)
Miles Davis Group
Live-Evil | CBS | C2K 65135
Pharoah Sanders Orchestra
Deaf Dumb Blind | Impulse(MCA) | 951265-2
Roy Hargrove's Crisol
Habana | Verve | 537563-2
Shirley Horn Quartet
Light Out Of Darkness(A Tribute To Ray Charles) | Verve | 519703-2
Shirley Horn Quintet
Light Out Of Darkness(A Tribute To Ray Charles) | Verve | 519703-2

Bartz,Hartwig | (dr)
Fritz Münzer Quintet
Jazz für junge Leute:Live im HR 1962 | Jazz 'n' Arts Records | C 01

Bascomb,Dud | (tp)
Duke Ellington And His Orchestra
Ella & Duke At The Cote D'Azur | Verve | 539030-2
Ella Fitzgerald And Duke Ellington:Cote D'Azure Concerts on Verve | Verve | 539033-2

Bascomb,Wilbur | (b,el-btp)
David Fathead Newman Septet
Jazzin' Vol.2: The Music Of Stevie Wonder | Fantasy | FANCD 6088-2
Erskine Hawkins And His Orchestra
Planet Jazz:Big Bands | Planet Jazz | 2169649-2
Hank Crawford And His Orchestra
Roadhouse Symphony | Original Jazz Classics | OJCCD 1048-2(M 9140)
Hank Crawford Quintet
After Dark | Milestone | MCD 9279-2
Jimmy McGriff Septet
McGriff Avenue | Milestone | MCD 9325-2
Rusty Bryant Group
For The Good Times | Prestige | PRCD 24269-2

Basie Alumni,The |
The Basie Alumni
Swinging For The Count | Candid | CCD 79724

Basie,Count | (arr,ld,org,p,celeste,el-p,voc)
Benny Goodman Septet
Jazz:The Essential Collection Vol.3 | IN+OUT Records | 78013-2
Charlie Christian:Swing To Bop | Dreyfus Jazz Line | FDM 36715-2
Benny Goodman Septet feat.Count Basie
Charlie Christian:Swing To Bop | Dreyfus Jazz Line | FDM 36715-2
Benny Moten's Kansas City Orchestra
Planet Jazz:Ben Webster | RCA | 2165368-2
Planet Jazz:Jimmy Rushing | RCA | 2165371-2
Planet Jazz:Swing | Planet Jazz | 2169651-2
Jazz:The Essential Collection Vol.3 | IN+OUT Records | 78013-2
Big Joe Turner With The Count Basie Orchestra
Flip Flop And Fly | Original Jazz Classics | OJCCD 1053-2(2310937)
Count Basie All Stars
The Legends Of Swing | Laserlight | 24659
Count Basie And His Orchestra
Jazz Gallery:Lester Young Vol.2(1946-59) | RCA | 2119541-2
Planet Jazz:Count Basie | Planet Jazz | 2152068-2
Planet Jazz Sampler | Planet Jazz | 2152326-2
Planet Jazz:Jimmy Rushing | RCA | 2165371-2
Planet Jazz:Jazz Greatest Hits | Planet Jazz | 2169648-2
Planet Jazz:Big Bands | Planet Jazz | 2169649-2
100 Ans De Jazz:Count Basie | RCA | 2177831-2
Afrique | RCA | 2179618-2
Fun Time | Pablo | 2310945-2
Jazz Collection:Count Basie | Laserlight | 24368
The Legends Of Swing | Laserlight | 24659
Count Basie: Salle Pleyel, April 17th, 1972 | Laserlight | 36127
Atomic Swing | Roulette | 497871-2
Verve Jazz Masters 2:Count Basie | Verve | 519819-2
Count Basie Swings-Joe Williams Sings | Verve | 519852-2
Verve Jazz Masters 20:Introducing | Verve | 519853-2
April In Paris | Verve | 521402-2
Breakfast Dance And Barbecue | Roulette | 531791-2
Basie Meets Bond | Capitol | 538225-2
Basie's Beatle Bag | Verve | 557455-2
One O'Clock Jump | Verve | 559806-2
Chairman Of The Board | Roulette | 581664-2
Jazz:The Essential Collection Vol.3 | IN+OUT Records | 78013-2
The Complete Atomic Basie | Roulette | 828635-2
King Of Swing | Verve | 837433-2
Live at The Sands | Reprise | 9362-45946-2
Count Basie At Newport | Verve | 9861761
Count On The Coast Vol.1 | Phontastic | NCD 7555
Count On The Coast Vol.2 | Phontastic | NCD 7575
88 Basie Street | Original Jazz Classics | OJC 808(2310901)
Jazz Dance | Original Jazz Classics | OJCCD 1002-2(1210890)
Fancy Pants | Original Jazz Classics | OJCCD 1038-2(2310920)
I Told You So | Original Jazz Classics | OJCCD 824-2(2310767)
Digital III At Montreux | Original Jazz Classics | OJCCD 996-2(2308223)
The Jazz Giants Play Harry Warren:Lullaby Of Broadway | Prestige | PCD 24204-2
From Spiritual To Swing | Vanguard | VCD 169/71
Count Basie And The Kansas City 7
Count Basie: Salle Pleyel, April 17th, 1972 | Laserlight | 36127
Count Basie And The Kansas City 7 | Impulse(MCA) | 951202-2
Count Basie Band
Basie Jam No. 2 | Original Jazz Classics | OJCCD 631-2(2310786)
Count Basie Big Band
Montreux '77 | Original Jazz Classics | OJCCD 377-2
Farmers Market Barbecue | Original Jazz Classics | OJCCD 732-2(2310874)
Count Basie Jam
Montreux '77 | Original Jazz Classics | OJC 379(2308209)
Montreux '77 | Original Jazz Classics | OJC 385(2620105)
Count Basie Jam Session
Count Basie Jam Session At The Montreux Jazz Festival 1975 | Original Jazz Classics | OJC20 933-2(2310750)
Count Basie Kansas City 3
For The Second Time | Original Jazz Classics | OJC 600(2310878)
Count Basie Kansas City 5
Milt Jackson Birthday Celebration | Fantasy | FANCD 6079-2
Count Basie Kansas City 7
Count Basie Kansas City 7 | Original Jazz Classics | OJCCD 690-2(2310908)
Count Basie Octet
Planet Jazz:Count Basie | Planet Jazz | 2152068-2
Count Basie Quartet
Planet Jazz:Jazz Piano | RCA | 2169655-2
Jazz:The Essential Collection Vol.3 | IN+OUT Records | 78013-2
Count Basie Sextet
Verve Jazz Masters 2:Count Basie | Verve | 519819-2
Jazz:The Essential Collection Vol.3 | IN+OUT Records | 78013-2
Jazz At The Philharmonic:The Montreux Collection | Pablo | PACD 5306-2
Count Basie Trio
The Story Of Jazz Piano | Laserlight | 24653
The Jazz Giants Play Harold Arlen:Blues In The Night | Prestige | PCD 24201-2
From Spiritual To Swing | Vanguard | VCD 169/71
Count Basie,His Instrumentals & Rhythm
Planet Jazz:Count Basie | Planet Jazz | 2152068-2
Jazz:The Essential Collection Vol.3 | IN+OUT Records | 78013-2
Count Basie-Oscar Peterson
The Jazz Giants Play Sammy Cahn:It's Magic | Prestige | PCD 24226-2
Count Basie-Oscar Peterson Quartet
The Timekeepers-Count Basie Meets Oscar Peterson | Original Jazz Classics | OJC20 790-2(2310896)
Count Basie-Oscar Peterson Quintet
Satch And Josh | Pablo | 2310722-2
Jazz Dance | Original Jazz Classics | OJCCD 1002-2(1210890)
Count Basie's Kansas City Seven
Jazz:The Essential Collection Vol.3 | IN+OUT Records | 78013-2
Count Basie's Small Band

88 Basie Street | Original Jazz Classics | OJC 808(2310901)
Count Basie-Zoot Sims Quartet
Basie & Zoot | Original Jazz Classics | OJCCD 822-2(2310745)
Dizzy Gillespie-Count Basie Quartet
The Gifted Ones | Original Jazz Classics | OJCCD 886-2(2310833)
Duke Ellington And Count Basie With Their Orchestras
First Time! | CBS | CK 65571
Ella Fitzgerald And Count Basie With The JATP All Stars
Bluella:Ella Fitzgerald Sings The Blues | Pablo | 2310960-2
Ella Fitzgerald And Joe Williams With The Count Basie Octet
For The Love Of Ella Fitzgerald | Verve | 841765-2
Ella Fitzgerald With The Count Basie Orchestra
Bluella:Ella Fitzgerald Sings The Blues | Pablo | 2310960-2
Ella Fitzgerald-First Lady Of Song | Verve | 517898-2
Verve Jazz Masters 46:Ella Fitzgerald-The Jazz Sides | Verve | 527655-2
Ella And Basie | Verve | 539059-2
For The Love Of Ella Fitzgerald | Verve | 841765-2
Ella Fitzgerald With The Count Basie Septet
Ella And Basie | Verve | 539059-2
Frank Sinatra With The Count Basie Orchestra
Sinatra-Basie:An Historic Musical First | Reprise | 7599-27023-2
It Might As Well Be Spring | Reprise | 7599-27027-2
Harry Edison Quintet
Edison's Light | Original Jazz Classics | OJCCD 804-2(2310780)
Helen Humes With James P. Johnson And The Count Basie Orchestra
From Spiritual To Swing | Vanguard | VCD 169/71
Helen Humes With The Kansas City Five
From Spiritual To Swing | Vanguard | VCD 169/71
JATP All Stars
Welcome To Jazz At The Philharmonic | Fantasy | FANCD 6081-2
Jimmy Rushing With Count Basie And His Orchestra
From Spiritual To Swing | Vanguard | VCD 169/71
Jones-Smith Incorporated
Jazz:The Essential Collection Vol.3 | IN+OUT Records | 78013-2
Kansas City 6
Count Basie:Kansas City 6 | Original Jazz Classics | OJC20 449-2(2310871)
Kansas City Five
Lester Young:Blue Lester | Dreyfus Jazz Line | FDM 36729-2
From Spiritual To Swing | Vanguard | VCD 169/71
Kansas City Seven
Jazz:The Essential Collection Vol.3 | IN+OUT Records | 78013-2
The J.J.Johnson Memorial Album | Prestige | PRCD 11025-2
Lester Young Quintet
The Art Of Saxophone | Laserlight | 24652
Jazz:The Essential Collection Vol.3 | IN+OUT Records | 78013-2
Lester Young:Blue Lester | Dreyfus Jazz Line | FDM 36729-2
Milt Jackson Orchestra
Sarah Vaughan Birthday Celebration | Fantasy | FANCD 6090-2
Milt Jackson With The Count Basie Orchestra
To Bags...With Love:Memorial Album | Pablo | 2310967-2
Milt Jackson Birthday Celebration | Fantasy | FANCD 6079-2
Milt Jackson + Count Basie + Big Band Vol.1 | Original Jazz Classics | OJCCD 740-2(2310822)
Milt Jackson + Count Basie + Big Band Vol.2 | Original Jazz Classics | OJCCD 741-2(2310823)
Sarah Vaughan And Joe Williams With The Count Basie Orchestra
Jazz Profile | Blue Note | 823517-2
Sarah Vaughan And The Count Basie Orchestra
Ballads | Roulette | 537561-2
Sarah Vaughan Birthday Celebration | Fantasy | FANCD 6090-2
Sarah Vaughan With The Count Basie Band
Jazz Profile | Blue Note | 823517-2
Zoot Sims Quartet feat.Count Basie
Jazz Dance | Original Jazz Classics | OJCCD 1002-2(1210890)

Basie,Count[as 'Prince Charming'] | (p)
Kansas City Five
Lester Young:Blue Lester | Dreyfus Jazz Line | FDM 36729-2
Kansas City Seven
Jazz:The Essential Collection Vol.3 | IN+OUT Records | 78013-2

Baskerville,Priscilla | (voc)
Max Roach Chorus & Orchestra
To The Max! | Enja | ENJ-7021 22

Basmann,Günther | (dr,perc,vibraphonettemarimba)
Radtke/Bauer/Basmann
A Contrast Music | Edition Collage | EC 491-2

Bass,Fontella | (p,orgvoc)
Art Ensemble Of Chicago
Americans Swinging In Paris:Art Ensemble Of Chicago | EMI Records | 539667-2
Lester Bowie Group
The Great Pretender | ECM | 1209(829369-2)

Bass,Lester | (b-tptb)
Lionel Hampton And His Orchestra
Lionel Hampton:Flying Home | Dreyfus Jazz Line | FDM 36735-2

Bass,Mickey | (b)
Lee Morgan Quintet
The Sixth Sense | Blue Note | 522467-2

Bassenge,Lisa | (voc)
Lisa Bassenge Trio
Going Home | Minor Music | 801091
A Sight, A Song | Minor Music | 801100
Lisa Bassenge Trio With Guests
A Sight, A Song | Minor Music | 801100

Bassey,Bus | (asts)
Artie Shaw And His Orchestra
Planet JazzArtie Shaw | Planet Jazz | 2152057-2
Planet Jazz:Big Bands | Planet Jazz | 2169649-2
Benny Goodman And His Orchestra
Charlie Christian:Swing To Bop | Dreyfus Jazz Line | FDM 36715-2
More Camel Caravans | Phontastic | NCD 8845/6

Bassey,Mark | (tb)
Mike Westbrook Orchestra
Bar Utopia-A Big Band Cabaret | Enja | ENJ-9333 2

Bassi,Aldo | (tpfl-h)
Stefania Tallini Trio With Guests
New Life | yvp music | CD 3114

Bassini,Rubens | (atabaques,pandeiro,paus,congasperc)
Dave Grusin Group
Mountain Dance | GRP | GRP 95072
Helen Merrill With Orchestra
Casa Forte | EmArCy | 558848-2
Lee Ritenour Group
Rio | GRP | GRP 95242
Stan Getz-Joao Gilberto Orchestra
Sony Jazz Collection:Stan Getz | CBS | 488623-2

Basso,Gianni | (ts)
Chet Baker Sextet
Chet Baker In Milan | Original Jazz Classics | OJC20 370-2(JLP 18)
Chet Baker With String-Orchestra And Voices
Chet Baker With Fifty Italian Strings | Original Jazz Classics | OJC20 492-2(JLP 921)
Dusko Goykovich Big Band
Balkan Connection | Enja | ENJ-9047 2
Dusko Goykovich Quintet
Balkan Blues | Enja | ENJ-9320 2
Jenny Evans And Her Quintet
Shiny Stockings | Enja | ENJ-9317 2
Shiny Stockings | ESM Records | ESM 9305

Basso,Guido | (tp,fl-hharm)
Singers Unlimited With Rob McConnell And The Boss Brass
The Singers Unlimited:Magic Voices | MPS | 539130-2

Bastien,Biddy | (b)
Anita O'Day With Gene Krupa And His Orchestra
Let Me Off Uptown:Anita O'Day With Gene Krupa | CBS | CK 65625

Bastos,Ivan | (b)
Pata Masters
Pata-Bahia | Pata Musik | PATA 11 CD

Batagello,Walter | (tp)
Buddy Rich And His Orchestra
Swingin' New Big Band | Pacific Jazz | 835232-2

Bateman,Charles | (p)
Sonny Stitt Quartet
Kaleidoscope | Original Jazz Classics | OJCCD 060-2(P 7077)

Batera,Chico | (dr,agogo,tambourineperc)
Lee Ritenour Group
Rio | GRP | GRP 95242
Sarah Vaughan With Orchestra
I Love Brazil | Pablo | 2312101-2
Sarah Vaughan Birthday Celebration | Fantasy | FANCD 6090-2

Bates,Bob | (b)
Dave Brubeck Quartet
Jazz:Ted Hot And Cool | CBS | CK 61468
Brubeck Time | CBS | CK 65724
Paul Desmond Quartet With The Bill Bates Singers
Desmond | Original Jazz Classics | OJCCD 712-2(F 3235/8082)
Paul Desmond Quintet
Desmond | Original Jazz Classics | OJCCD 712-2(F 3235/8082)

Bates,Django | (e-flat-peckhorn,keyboards,ptenor-h)
First House
Erendira | ECM | 1307
Cantilena | ECM | 1393
Joachim Kühn And The Radio Philharmonie Hannover NDR With Jazz Soloists
Europeana | ACT | 9220-2
Sidsel Endresen Quartet
So I Write | ECM | 1408(841776-2)
Sidsel Endresen Sextet
Exile | ECM | 1524(521721-2)

Bates,Lefty | (gb-g)
Buddy Guy Blues Band
Buddy Guy-The Complete Chess Studio Recordings | MCA | MCD 09337

Bates,Norman | (b)
Dave Brubeck Quintet
Reunion | Original Jazz Classics | OJCCD 150-2
Paul Desmond Quartet
Desmond | Original Jazz Classics | OJCCD 712-2(F 3235/8082)
The Jazz Giants Play Jerome Kern:Yesterdays | Prestige | PCD 24202-2

Bates,Walter | (ts)
Anita O'Day With Gene Krupa And His Orchestra
Let Me Off Uptown:Anita O'Day With Gene Krupa | CBS | CK 65625

Bateson,Chris | (blueblowing,jug,tptp-mouthpiece)
Henrik Johansen With The City Ramblers
The Golden Years Of Revival Jazz,Sampler | Storyville | 109 1001
Hylda Sims And The Citty Ramblers Skiffle Group With Henrik Johansen
The Golden Years Of Revival Jazz,Vol.9 | Storyville | STCD 5514

Batista,Ciro | (perc)
James Carter Group
Chasin' The Gypsy | Atlantic | 7567-83304-2

Batiste,Alvin | (cl,voc,el-cl,flts)
Mark Whitfield Group
Patrice | Warner | 7599-26659-2

Batnes,Elise | (vld)
Terje Rypdal Quartet With The Bergen Chamber Ensemble
Lux Aeterna | ECM | 1818(017070-2)

Batoru |
Batoru
Tree Of Sounds | Nabel Records:Jazz Network | CD 4685

Batta,Amancio | (african-perc,voc,doundoumbaperc)
Pili-Pili
Jakko | JA & RO | JARO 4131-2
Pili-Pili | JA & RO | JARO 4141-2
Hoomba-Hoomba | JA & RO | JARO 4192-2

Battistessa,Gustavo | (bandoneon)
Quique Sinesi & Daniel Messina With Guests
Prioridad A la Emoción | art-mode-records | AMR 21061

Battle,Bobby | (drtambourine)
Arthur Blythe Quartet
Retroflection | Enja | ENJ-8046 2
Calling Card | Enja | ENJ-9051 2

Battle,Edgar | (arr,tpv-tb)
Willie Bryant And His Orchestra
Planet Jazz:Ben Webster | RCA | 2165368-2

Battle,Kathleen | (voc)
Al Jarreau With Band
Tenderness | i.e. Music | 557853-2

Battle,Turner | (keyboards)
Tom Browne Groups
Mo' Jamaica Funk | Hip Bop | HIBD 8002

Bätzel,Alexander | (dr)
Alberto Marsico Quintet
Them That's Got | Organic Music | ORGM 9705
Christian Rover Group feat. Rhoda Scott
Christian Rover Group-Live With Rhoda Scott At The Organ | Organic Music | ORGM 9704
Organ Jazztrio & Martin Weiss
Hommage | Edition Collage | EC 492-2
Stanley Blume Quartet
Movin' Up | Organic Music | ORGM 9709
Stanley Blume Quintet
Movin' Up | Organic Music | ORGM 9709

Bätzel,Matthias | (orgp)
Ed Kröger Quartet
What's New | Laika Records | 35101172
Ed Kröger Quartet plus Guests
Movin' On | Laika Records | 35101332
Grooveyard Meets Houston Person
Basic Instinct | Organic Music | ORGM 9701
Grooveyard Meets Red Holloway
Basic Instinct | Organic Music | ORGM 9701
Grooveyard Meets Roman Schwaller
Basic Instinct | Organic Music | ORGM 9701
Matthias Bätzel Trio
Green Dumplings | JHM Records | JHM 3618
Monk's Mood | JHM Records | JHM 3628
Matthias Bätzel-Michael Keul
Green Dumplings | JHM Records | JHM 3618
Organ Jazztrio & Martin Weiss
Hommage | Edition Collage | EC 492-2
Red Holloway With The Matthias Bätzel Trio
A Night Of Blues & Ballads | JHM Records | JHM 3614
Stanley Blume Quartet
Movin' Up | Organic Music | ORGM 9709
Stanley Blume Quintet
Movin' Up | Organic Music | ORGM 9709

Bauch,Arthur | (viola)
Ron Carter With Strings
Pastels | Original Jazz Classics | OJCCD 665-2(M 9073)

Baucomont,Jeanette | (voc)
Modern Jazz Quartet And The Swingle Singers
MJQ 40 | Atlantic | 7567-82330-2
Swingle Singers
Jazz Sebastian Bach | Philips | 542552-2
Jazz Sebastian Bach Vol.2 | Philips | 542553-2
Swingle Singers Going Baroque | Philips | 546746-2
Swingle Singers Singing Mozart | Philips | 548538-2
Swingling Telemann | Philips | 586735-2
Swingle Singers Getting Romantic | Philips | 586736-2

Baudisch,Joe | (dr)
Joseph Warner Quartet
Mood Pieces | Jardis Records | JRCD 9921

Bauduc,Ray | (dr)
All Star Band
Planet Jazz:Jack Teagarden | Planet Jazz | 2161236-2
Ben Pollack And His Park Central Orchestra
Planet Jazz:Jack Teagarden | Planet Jazz | 2161236-2
Jazz:The Essential Collection Vol.3 | IN+OUT Records | 78013-2
Bob Crosby And His Orchestra
Swing Legens:Bob Crosby | Nimbus Records | NI 2011
Bob Crosby's Bobcats
Swing Legens:Bob Crosby | Nimbus Records | NI 2011
Bob Haggart/Ray Bauduc
Swing Legens:Bob Crosby | Nimbus Records | NI 2011
Gene Gifford And His Orchestra
Planet Jazz:Bud Freeman | Planet Jazz | 2161240-2
Jack Teagarden And His Band
Meet Me Where They Play The Blues | Good Time Jazz | GTCD 12063-2

Bauer,Andreas | (bmarimba)
Radtke/Bauer/Basmann
A Contrast Music | Edition Collage | EC 491-2

Bauer,Billy | (gg-solo)
Billie Holiday And Her All Stars
Billie Holiday Story Vol.4:Lady Sings The Blues | Verve | 521429-2
Charlie Parker Quintet
Verve Jazz Masters 28:Charlie Parker Plays Standards | Verve | 521854-2
The Cole Porter Songbook | Verve | 823250-2
Bird: The Complete Charlie Parker On Verve | Verve | 837141-2
Cozy Cole's Big Seven
Body And Soul Revisited | GRP | GRP 16272
Harry Carney And His Orchestra With Strings
Music For Loving:Ben Webster With Strings | Verve | 527774-2
Jimmy Smith With The Johnny Pate Orchestra
Jimmy Smith-Talkin' Verve | Verve | 531563-2
Lee Konitz Quartet
Subconcious-Lee | Original Jazz Classics | OJCCD 186-2(P 7004)
Lee Konitz Quintet
Subconcious-Lee | Original Jazz Classics | OJCCD 186-2(P 7004)
Lee Konitz-Billy Bauer Duo
Subconcious-Lee | Original Jazz Classics | OJCCD 186-2(P 7004)
Lee Konitz-Warne Marsh Quintet
Lee Konitz With Warne Marsh | Atlantic | 8122-75356-2
Lee Konitz-Warne Marsh Sextet
Lee Konitz With Warne Marsh | Atlantic | 8122-75356-2
Lennie Tristano Trio
The Story Of Jazz Piano | Laserlight | 24653
Lenny Tristano Quartet
Subconcious-Lee | Original Jazz Classics | OJCCD 186-2(P 7004)
Lenny Tristano Quintet
Subconcious-Lee | Original Jazz Classics | OJCCD 186-2(P 7004)
The Metronome All Stars
Jazz Gallery:Lester Young Vol.2(1946-59) | RCA | 2119541-2
Planet Jazz:Dizzy Gillespie | Planet Jazz | 2152069-2
Woody Herman And His Orchestra
The Legends Of Swing | Laserlight | 24659
Songs For Hip Lovers | Verve | 559872-2
Woody Herman:Four Brother | Dreyfus Jazz Line | FDM 36722-2
Louis Armstrong-Jack Teagarden-Woody Herman:Midnights At V-Disc | Jazz Unlimited | JUCD 2048
Old Gold Rehearsals 1944 | Jazz Unlimited | JUCD 2079
Woody Herman And The Herd
Woody Herman (And The Herd) At Carnegie Hall | Verve | 559833-2
Woody Herman And The Vanderbilt All Stars
Louis Armstrong-Jack Teagarden-Woody Herman:Midnights At V-Disc | Jazz Unlimited | JUCD 2048

Bauer,Conrad | (tbtb-solo)
Conrad Bauer
European Jazz Ensemble 25th Anniversary | Konnex Records | KCD 5100
European Jazz Ensemble
20th Anniversary Tour | Konnex Records | KCD 5078
European Jazz Ensemble 25th Anniversary | Konnex Records | KCD 5100
Klaus König Orchestra
Hommage A Douglas Adams | Enja | ENJ-6078 2

Bauer,Franz | (marimbavib)
Batoru
Tree Of Sounds | Nabel Records:Jazz Network | CD 4685
Dirk Strakhof & Batoru
Arabesque | Nabel Records:Jazz Network | CD 4696
Frank Paul Schubert Quartet
Der Verkauf Geht Weiter | Jazz Haus Musik | JHM 0114 CD
Franz Bauer Quintet
Plüschtier | Jazz Haus Musik | JHM 0097 CD
Nils Petter Molvaer Group
Elegy For Africa | Nabel Records:Jazz Network | CD 4678

Bauer,Joe | (tp)
Tommy Dorsey And His Orchestra
Planet Jazz:Tommy Dorsey | Planet Jazz | 2159972-2
Planet Jazz:Big Bands | Planet Jazz | 2169649-2
Planet Jazz:Swing | Planet Jazz | 2169651-2

Bauer,Peter | (dr-programming)
Alfred 23 Harth Group
Sweet Paris | free flow music | ffm 0291

Bauer,Reinhold | (percvoc)
Clemens Maria Peters/Reinhold Bauer
Quadru Mana/Quadru Mania | Edition Collage | EC 464-2

Bauer,Stefan | (marimba,vib,synthvoc)
Christoph Haberer Group
Pulsation | Jazz Haus Musik | JHM 0066 CD
Jürgen Sturm's Ballstars
Tango Subversivo | Nabel Records:Jazz Network | CD 4613
Klaus König Orchestra
Time Fragments:Seven Studies In Time And Motion | Enja | ENJ-8076 2
Stefan Bauer-Claudio Puntin-Marcio Doctor
Lingo | Jazz Haus Musik | JHM 0116 CD
Wayne Bartlett With The Thomas Hufschmidt Group
Tokyo Blues | Laika Records | 35101212

Baulch,Sarah | (voc)
Mike Westbrook Brass Band
Glad Day:Settings Of William Blake | Enja | ENJ-9376 2

Baumann,Agneta | (voc)
Agneta Baumann And Her Quartet
Comes Love... | Touché Music | TMcCD 011
Agneta Baumann And Her Quintet
A Time For Love | Touché Music | TMcCD 006
Agneta Baumann Group
Sentimental Lady | Touché Music | TMcCD 017

Baumann,Christoph | (p)
Cadavre Exquis
Cadavre Exquis | Creative Works Records | CW CD 1014-1

Baumann,Franz D. | (fl-h)
Litschie Hrdlicka Group
Falling Lovers | EGO | 93020

Baumann,Franziska | (flvoc)
Michel Wintsch & Road Movie
Michel Wintsch & Road Movie featuring Gerry Hemingway | Between The Lines | btl 002(Efa 10172-2)

Baumann,Gerd | (g,el-g,mand,balalaikafretless-g)
Gerd Baumann-Alessandro Ricciarelli Quartet
Say No More | Edition Collage | EC 489-2

Baumeister,Peter | (drperc)
Dave Pike Set
Dave Pike Set:Masterpieces | MPS | 531848-2
Volker Kriegel Quintet
Spectrum | MPS | 9808699

Baumel,Herbert | (stringsv)
Sonny Stitt With Orchestra
Goin' Down Slow | Prestige | PRCD 24276-2
Stan Getz With The Eddie Sauter Orchestra
Stan Getz Plays The Music Of Mickey One | Verve | 531232-2

Baumgart,Werner | (as,arr,cl,tsoboe)
Erwin Lehn Und Sein Südfunk-Tanzorchester
Deutsches Jazz Fesival 1954/1955 | Bear Family Records | BCD 15430
Baumgartner,Ariane | (voc)
Matthias Petzold Working Band
Elements | Indigo-Records | 1005 CD
Baumgartner,Heiri | (asbs)
Q4 Orchester Project
Lyon's Brood | Creative Works Records | CW CD 1018-3
Baur,Eckhard | (tp,fl-hf-horn)
Geir Lysne Listening Ensemble
Korall | ACT | 9236-2
Aurora Borealis-Nordic Lights | ACT | 9406-2
Bauschulte,Meinolf | (drelectronic-perc)
Ulrich P. Lask Group
Lask | ECM | 1217
Bautista,Roland | (gperc)
Ella Fitzgerald With Orchestra
Ella Abraca Jobim | Pablo | 2630201-2
George Duke Group
Jazzrock-Anthology Vol.3:Fusion | Zounds | CD 27100555
Willie Bobo Group
Jazzrock-Anthology Vol.3:Fusion | Zounds | CD 27100555
Bauza,Mario | (cl,as,ldtp)
Charlie Parker With Machito And His Orchestra
Charlie Parker:The Best Of The Verve Years | Verve | 527815-2
Talkin' Bird | Verve | 559859-2
Bird: The Complete Charlie Parker On Verve | Verve | 837141-2
Charlie Parker:April In Paris | Dreyfus Jazz Line | FDM 36737-2
Ella Fitzgerald With The Chick Webb Orchestra
Jazz Collection:Ella Fitzgerald | Laserlight | 24397
Machito And His Orchestra
Afro-Cuban Jazz Moods | Original Jazz Classics | OJC20 447-2
Bauzo,Louis | (congasperc)
Mongo Santamaria And His Orchestra
Jazzin' Vol.2: The Music Of Stevie Wonder | Fantasy | FANCD 6088-2
Bavan,Yolanda | (voc)
Lambert, Hendricks And Bavan
Planet Jazz:Male Jazz Vocalists | Planet Jazz | 2169657-2
Bawelino,Joe | (g)
Joe Bawelino Quartet
Happy Birthday Stéphane | Edition Collage | EC 458-2
Joe Bawelino Quartet & Martin Stegner
Happy Birthday Stéphane | Edition Collage | EC 458-2
Traubeli Weiß Ensemble
Dreaming Of You | Edition Collage | EC 468-2
Bay,Victor | (v)
Ella Fitzgerald With The Nelson Riddle Orchestra
The Best Of The Song Books:The Ballads | Verve | 521867-2
Oh Lady Be Good:The Best Of The Gershwin Songbook | Verve | 529581-2
Love Songs:The Best Of The Song Books | Verve | 531762-2
Bayer,Franz | (violavoc)
Motus Quartett
Grimson Flames | Creative Works Records | CW CD 1023-2
Baylor,Marcus | (drperc)
Cassandra Wilson Group
Traveling Miles | Blue Note | 854123-2
Bayol,Gerard | (tp)
Sidney Bechet And His Orchestra
Jazz In Paris:Sidney Bechet Et Claude Luther | EmArCy | 159821-2 PMS
Bazley,Tony | (dr)
Leroy Vinnegar Sextet
The Jazz Giants Play Harry Warren:Lullaby Of Broadway | Prestige | PCD 24204-2
Beach,Frank | (tp)
Billy May And His Orchestra
Billy May's Big Fat Brass/Bill's Bag | Capitol | 535206-2
Ella Fitzgerald With Frank De Vol And His Orchestra
Get Happy! | Verve | 523321-2
Ella Fitzgerald With The Billy May Orchestra
Ella Fitzgerald Sings The Harold Arlen Song Book | Verve | 589108-2
June Christy With The Pete Rugolo Orchestra
Something Cool(The Complete Mono & Stereo Versions) | Capitol | 534069-2
Louis Armstrong With The Hal Mooney Orchestra
Ambassador Louis Armstrong Vol.17:Moments To Remember(1952-1956) | Ambassador | CLA 1917
Mel Tormé With The Billy May Orchestra
Mel Tormé Goes South Of The Border With Billy May | Verve | 589517-2
Pete Rugolo And His Orchestra
Thriller/Richard Diamon(Original Jazz Scores From 2 Classics TV Series) | Fresh Sound Records | FSCD 2015
Stan Kenton And His Orchestra
Stan Kenton-The Formative Years | Decca | 589489-2
Beach,Thelma | (v)
Frank Sinatra With The Count Basie Orchestra
It Might As Well Be Spring | Reprise | 7599-27027-2
Beachill,Pete | (tbv-tb)
Carla Bley Big Band
The Carla Bley Big Band Goes To Church | Watt | 27(533682-2)
Kenny Wheeler Brass Ensemble
A Long Time Ago | ECM | 1691
Beadle,Gordon | (ts)
Jimmy McGriff Septet
McGriff Avenue | Milestone | MCD 9325-2
Beal,Charlie | (p)
Louis Armstrong And His Dixieland Seven
Planet Jazz:Louis Armstrong | Planet Jazz | 2152052-2
Planet Jazz:Jazz Greatest Hits | Planet Jazz | 2169648-2
Planet Jazz:Jazz Trumpet | Planet Jazz | 2169654-2
Planet Jazz:Male Jazz Vocalists | Planet Jazz | 2169657-2
Best Of The Complete RCA Victor Recordings | RCA | 2663636-2
Louis Armstrong:A 100th Birthday Celebration | RCA | 2663694-2
Louis Armstrong:C'est Si Bon | Dreyfus Jazz Line | FDM 36730-2
Swing Legends:Louis Armstrong | Nimbus Records | NI 2012
Louis Armstrong And His Hot Seven
Planet Jazz:Louis Armstrong | Planet Jazz | 2152052-2
Best Of The Complete RCA Victor Recordings | RCA | 2663636-2
Louis Armstrong:A 100th Birthday Celebration | RCA | 2663694-2
Louis Armstrong And His Orchestra
Planet Jazz:Louis Armstrong | Planet Jazz | 2152052-2
Best Of The Complete RCA Victor Recordings | RCA | 2663636-2
Louis Armstrong:A 100th Birthday Celebration | RCA | 2663694-2
Beal,Jeff | (cond,arr,comp,fl-h,p,electronics,tp)
Dave Weckl Group
Heads Up | GRP | GRP 96732
Beal,John | (bel-b)
A Band Of Friends
Wynton Marsalis Quartet With Strings | CBS | CK 68921
Bill Evans Quartet
The Complete Bill Evans On Verve | Verve | 527953-2
From Left To Right | Verve | 557451-2
Nina Simone And Orchestra
Baltimore | Epic | 476906-2
Paul Desmond-Gerry Mulligan Quartet
The Ballad Of Paul Desmond | RCA | 21429372
Two Of A Mind | RCA | 2179620-2
Rod Levitt Orchestra
The Dynamic Sound Patterns Of The Rod Levitt Orchestra | Original Jazz Classics | OJCCD 1955-2(RS 9471)
Bean,Billy | (g)
Billy Bean-Dennis Budimir
West Coast Sessions | String Jazz | SJRCD 1006
Charlie Ventura Quintet
High On An Open Mike | Fresh Sound Records | FSR-CD 314
John Pisano-Billy Bean-Dennis Budimir
West Coast Sessions | String Jazz | SJRCD 1006
The Trio
The Trio:Rediscovered | String Jazz | SJRCD 1007
Bean,Clarence 'Tootsie' | (dr)
Red Richards Quartet
Swingtime | Jazzpoint | JP 1041 CD
Beard,Jim | (el-p,synth,clavinet,keyboards,org,p)
Bob Berg Quintet
The Art Of Saxophone | Laserlight | 24652
Dave Liebman Quintet
Homage To John Coltrane | Owl Records | 018357-2
John McLaughlin Group
The Promise | Verve | 529828-2
The Heart Of Things | Verve | 539153-2
Michael Brecker Group
Don't Try This At Home | Impulse(MCA) | 950114-2
Now You See It...(Now You Don't) | GRP | GRP 96222
Michael 'Patches' Stewart Group
Penetration | Hip Bop | HIBD 8018
Mike Stern Group
Jigsaw | Atlantic | 7567-82027-2
Odds Or Evens | Atlantic | 7567-82297-2
Play | Atlantic | 7567-83219-2
Philip Catherine Quartet
Guitar Groove | Dreyfus Jazz Line | FDM 36599-2
Wayne Krantz Quartet
Signals | Enja | ENJ-6048 2
Beasley,John | (keyboards,p,keyboard-programming)
John Patitucci Group
Sketchbook | GRP | GRP 96172
Mistura Fina | GRP | GRP 98022
Beason,Bill | (dr)
Dicky Wells And His Orchestra
Americans Swinging In Paris:Dicky Wells | EMI Records | 539664-2
Ella Fitzgerald And Her Famous Orchestra
The Radio Years 1940 | Jazz Unlimited | JUCD 2065
Ella Fitzgerald And Her Orchestra
Jazz Collection:Ella Fitzgerald | Laserlight | 24397
Sarah Vaughan With John Kirby And His Orchestra
Sarah Vaughan Birthday Celebration | Fantasy | FANCD 6090-2
Sarah Vaughan:Lover Man | Dreyfus Jazz Line | FDM 36739-2
Beatrix,Ssana | (recitation)
John McLaughlin Group
The Promise | Verve | 529828-2
Beats,Bob | (b)
Al Jarreau With Band
High Crime | i.e. Music | 557848-2
Beau,Heinie | (arr,as,cl,tsreeds)
Ella Fitzgerald And Louis Armstrong With Dave Barbour And His Orchestra
Ella Fitzgerald:Mr.Paganini | Dreyfus Jazz Line | FDM 36741-2
Ella Fitzgerald With The Billy May Orchestra
Love Songs:The Best Of The Song Books | Verve | 531762-2
Frank Sinatra With Orchestra
Planet Jazz:Frank Sinatra & Tommy Dorsey | Planet Jazz | 2152067-2
Jack Teagarden's Chicagoans
Jazz:The Essential Collection Vol.3 | IN+OUT Records | 78013-2
The Hollywood Session:The Capitol Jazzmen | Jazz Unlimited | JUCD 2044
Tommy Dorsey And His Orchestra
Planet Jazz:Frank Sinatra & Tommy Dorsey | Planet Jazz | 2152067-2
Planet Jazz:Tommy Dorsey | Planet Jazz | 2159972-2
Frank Sinatra And The Tommy Dorsey Orchestra | RCA | 2668701-2
Beau,Henry | (reeds)
Ella Fitzgerald With The Billy May Orchestra
Ella Fitzgerald Sings The Harold Arlen Song Book | Verve | 589108-2
Beaussier,Daniel | (floboe)
Carla Bley Band
Fleur Carnivore | Watt | 21
Beaux-Arts String Quartet,The |
Stan Getz With The Eddie Sauter Orchestra
Verve Jazz Masters 8:Stan Getz | Verve | 519823-2
Beaver,Paul | (synthtape-recorder)
Quincy Jones And His Orchestra
Verve Jazz Masters Vol.59:Toots Thielemans | Verve | 535271-2
Beazley,Graham | (b)
Dick Charlesworth And His City Gents
The Golden Years Of Revival Jazz,Vol.4 | Storyville | STCD 5509
The Golden Years Of Revival Jazz,Vol.6 | Storyville | STCD 5511
The Golden Years Of Revival Jazz,Vol.11 | Storyville | STCD 5516
Bebelaar,Patrick | (psynth)
Frank Kroll Quintet
Landscape | dml-records | CD 014
Jazz Orchester Rheinland-Pfalz
Like Life | Jazz Haus Musik | LJBB 9405
Patrick Bebelaar Group
Point Of View | dml-records | CD 017
Patrick Bebelaar Quartet
Never Thought It Could Happen | dml-records | CD 007
You Never Lose An Island | dml-records | CD 015
Beccham,Chloe | (voc)
Mike Westbrook Brass Band
Glad Day:Settings Of William Blake | Enja | ENJ-9376 2
Becher,Rudi | (tb)
Erwin Lehn Und Sein Südfunk-Tanzorchester
Deutsches Jazz Fesival 1954/1955 | Bear Family Records | BCD 15430
Bechet,Sidney | (cl,as,ss,comp,ts,p,b,dr,voc)
Bechet-Spanier Big Four
Jazz:The Essential Collection Vol.1 | IN+OUT Records | 78011-2
Bunk Johnson-Sidney Bechet Sextet
Jazz:The Essential Collection Vol.1 | IN+OUT Records | 78011-2
Clarence Williams' Blue Five
Jazz:The Essential Collection Vol.1 | IN+OUT Records | 78011-2
Dr. Henry Levine's Barefoot Dixieland Philharmonic feat.Prof. Sidney Bechet
Planet Jazz | Planet Jazz | 2169652-2
Jelly Roll Morton's New Orleans Jazzmen
Planet Jazz | Planet Jazz | 2169652-2
Planet Jazz:Male Jazz Vocalists | Planet Jazz | 2169657-2
Louis Armstrong And His Orchestra
Jazz:The Essential Collection Vol.2 | IN+OUT Records | 78012-2
Louis Armstrong:C'est Si Bon | Dreyfus Jazz Line | FDM 36730-2
Swing Legends:Louis Armstrong | Nimbus Records | NI 2012
New Orleans Feetwarmers
Planet Jazz | Planet Jazz | 2169652-2
Jazz:The Essential Collection Vol.1 | IN+OUT Records | 78011-2
From Spiritual To Swing | Vanguard | VCD 169/71
Sidney Bechet All Stars
Planet Jazz:Sidney Bechet | Planet Jazz | 2152063-2
Planet Jazz Sampler | Planet Jazz | 2152326-2
Sidney Bechet And His All Stars
Sidney Bechet:Summertime | Dreyfus Jazz Line | FDM 36712-2
Sidney Bechet And His Feetwarmers
Jazz In Paris:Sidney Bechet Et Claude Luther | EmArCy | 159821-2 PMS
Sidney Bechet:Summertime | Dreyfus Jazz Line | FDM 36712-2
Sidney Bechet And His New Orleans Feetwarmers
Planet Jazz | Planet Jazz | 2169652-2
Sidney Bechet:Summertime | Dreyfus Jazz Line | FDM 36712-2
Sidney Bechet And His Orchestra
Jazz In Paris:Sidney Bechet Et Claude Luther | EmArCy | 159821-2 PMS
Sidney Bechet:Summertime | Dreyfus Jazz Line | FDM 36712-2
Sidney Bechet And The Chamber Music Society Of Lower Basin Street
Sidney Bechet:Summertime | Dreyfus Jazz Line | FDM 36712-2
Sidney Bechet Quartet
Planet Jazz:Sidney Bechet | Planet Jazz | 2152063-2
Sidney Bechet Trio
Planet Jazz:Sidney Bechet | Planet Jazz | 2152063-2
Jazz:The Essential Collection Vol.1 | IN+OUT Records | 78011-2
Sidney Bechet With Bob Wilber's Wildcats
Sidney Bechet:Summertime | Dreyfus Jazz Line | FDM 36712-2
Sidney Bechet With Claude Luter And His Orchestra
Planet Jazz:Sidney Bechet | Planet Jazz | 2152063-2
Sidney Bechet:Summertime | Dreyfus Jazz Line | FDM 36712-2
Sidney Bechet With Michel Attenoux And His Orchestra
Planet Jazz:Sidney Bechet | Planet Jazz | 2152063-2
Sidney Bechet With Noble Sissle's Swingsters
Sidney Bechet:Summertime | Dreyfus Jazz Line | FDM 36712-2
Sidney Bechet With Sammy Price's Bluesicians
Planet Jazz:Sidney Bechet | Planet Jazz | 2152063-2
Sidney Bechet's Blue Note Jazzmen
Jazz:The Essential Collection Vol.1 | IN+OUT Records | 78011-2
Runnin' Wild | Blue Note | 821259-2
Sidney Bechet:Summertime | Dreyfus Jazz Line | FDM 36712-2
Sidney Bechet-Teddy Buckner Sextet
Planet Jazz:Sidney Bechet | Planet Jazz | 2152063-2
This Is Jazz All Stars
Sidney Bechet:Summertime | Dreyfus Jazz Line | FDM 36712-2
Tommy Ladnier And His Orchestra
Planet Jazz | Planet Jazz | 2169652-2
Jazz:The Essential Collection Vol.1 | IN+OUT Records | 78011-2
Becht,Erich | (p)
Erhard Wenig Quartet
Deutsches Jazz Fesival 1954/1955 | Bear Family Records | BCD 15430
Heinz Schönberger Quintet
Deutsches Jazz Fesival 1954/1955 | Bear Family Records | BCD 15430
Bechtel,Dirk | (tpfl-h)
Jazz Orchester Rheinland-Pfalz
Kazzou | Jazz Haus Musik | LJBB 9104
Bechtold,Lynn | (v)
Absolute Ensemble
African Symphony | Enja | ENJ-9410 2
Beck,Al | (tp)
Anita O'Day With Gene Krupa And His Orchestra
Let Me Off Uptown:Anita O'Day With Gene Krupa | CBS | CK 65625
Beck,Art | (cl,as,reeds,saxts)
Jack Teagarden And His Orchestra
Jazz:The Essential Collection Vol.3 | IN+OUT Records | 78013-2
Beck,Donny | (b)
Willie Bobo Group
Jazzrock-Anthology Vol.3:Fusion | Zounds | CD 27100555
Beck,Fred | (ts)
Jan Jankeje Septet
A' Portrait Of Jan Jankeje | Jazzpoint | JP 1054 CD
Beck,Gordon | (digital-p,keyboards,p,el-p,org)
Allan Holdsworth Group
None Too Soon | Cream Records | CR 400-2
Helen Merrill-Gordon Beck
No Tears No Goodbyes | Owl Records | 013435-2
Ronnie Scott And The Band
Live At Ronnie Scott's | CBS | 494439-2
Beck,Gregor | (dr)
Benny Waters Quartet
Swinging Again | Jazzpoint | JP 1037 CD
A' Portrait Of Jan Jankeje | Jazzpoint | JP 1054 CD
Heiner Franz' Swing Connection
Heiner Franz' Swing Connection | Jardis Records | JRCD 9817
Oscar Klein-Lino Patruno European Jazz Stars
Live at The San Marino Jazz Festival | Jazzpoint | JP 1052 CD
Oscar Klein's Jazz Show
Oscar Klein's Jazz Show | Jazzpoint | JP 1043 CD
Oscar Klein's Jazz Show Vol.2 | Jazzpoint | JP 1048 CD
A' Portrait Of Jan Jankeje | Jazzpoint | JP 1054 CD
Ralph Sutton And His Allstars
Echoes Of Spring:The Complete Hamburg Concert | Nagel-Heyer | CD 038
Rex Allen's Swing Express
Keep Swingin' | Nagel-Heyer | CD 016
Ellington For Lovers | Nagel-Heyer | NH 1009
The Second Sampler | Nagel-Heyer | NHR SP 6
Thilo Wagner Trio
Wagner,Mörike.Beck,Finally. | Nagel-Heyer | CD 078
Beck,Horst | (b)
Ralph Schweizer Big Band
DAY Dream | Chaos | CACD 8177
Beck,Jeff | (el-g,g,talk-boxg-synth)
John McLaughlin Group
The Promise | Verve | 529828-2
Beck,Joe | (alto-g,as,gel-g)
(Little)Jimmy Scott And His Band
Mood Indigo | Milestone | MCD 9305-2
Bobby Timmons Quartet
Quartet And Orchestra | Milestone | MCD 47091-2
Buddy Rich Big Band
Backwoods Siseman/Pieces Of Dream | Laserlight | 24655
Gato Barbieri Group
Planet Jazz:Gato Barbieri | RCA | 2165364-2
Gato Barbieri:The Best Of The Early Years | RCA | 2663523-2
Gene Ammons Sextet
Fine And Mellow | Prestige | PRCD 24281-2
Gene Ammons Sextet With Strings
Fine And Mellow | Prestige | PRCD 24281-2
Gil Evans Orchestra
Blues In Orbit | Enja | ENJ-3069 2
Helen Merrill With Orchestra
Casa Forte | EmArCy | 558848-2
Ian Shaw With Band
Soho Stories | Milestone | MCD 9316-2
Jimmy Scott With Band
Over The Rainbow | Milestone | MCD 9314-2
But Beautiful | Milestone | MCD 9321-2
Moon Glow | Milestone | MCD 9332-2
Lew Soloff Group
Rainbow Mountain | TipToe | TIP-888838 2
Lonnie Liston Smith & His Cosmic Echoes
Astral Travelling | RCA | 2663878-2
Miles Davis Quintet
Miles Davis Quintet 1965-1968 | CBS | C6K 67398
Miles Davis Sextet
Circle In The Round | CBS | 467898-2
Rusty Bryant Sextet
For The Good Times | Prestige | PRCD 24269-2
Beck,Michael | (pel-p)
Horn Knox
The Song Is You | JHM Records | JHM 3625
Michael Beck Trio
Michael Beck Trio | JHM Records | JHM 3623
Beck,Roscoe | (b,background-voc,el-bvoc)
Robben Ford & The Blue Line
Handful Of Blues | Blue Thumb | BTR 70042
Beckenbridge,Dardanelle | (p)
Lionel Hampton And His Orchestra
Lionel Hampton:Flying Home | Dreyfus Jazz Line | FDM 36735-2
Beckenstein,Jay | (as,p,sax,el-p,perc,whistle,ss)
King Curtis Band
King Curtis-Blow Man Blow | Bear Family Records | BCD 15670 CI
Spyro Gyra & Guests
Love & Other Obsessions | GRP | GRP 98112
Beckenstein,Ray | (as,piccolo,cl,fl,bs,b-cl,reeds,sax)
Chris Connor With Band
Chris Connor | Atlantic | 7567-80769-2
Coleman Hawkins With Many Albam And His Orchestra
Planet Jazz:Coleman Hawkins | Planet Jazz | 2152055-2
Gil Evans Orchestra
Out Of The Cool | Impulse(MCA) | 951186-2
J.J.Johnson And His Orchestra

INTERPRETENVERZEICHNIS

Planet Jazz:J.J.Johnson | Planet Jazz | 2159974-2
Jimmy Smith With The Oliver Nelson Orchestra
Jimmy Smith:Best Of The Verve Years | Verve | 527950-2
Kenny Burrell With The Gil Evans Orchestra
Guitar Forms | Verve | 521403-2
Verve Jazz Masters 23:Gil Evans | Verve | 521860-2
Verve Jazz Masters 45:Kenny Burrell | Verve | 527652-2
Verve Jazz Masters Vol.60:The Collection | Verve | 529866-2
Louis Armstrong And His Friends
Louis Armstrong And His Friends | Bluebird | 2663961-2
Oscar Brown Jr. And His Group
Movin' On | Rhino | 8122-73678-2
Stan Getz With The Gary McFarland Orchestra
Stan Getz Highlights:The Best Of The Verve Years Vol.2 | Verve | 517330-2
Verve Jazz Masters 53:Stan Getz-Bossa Nova | Verve | 529904-2
Big Band Bossa Nova | Verve | 825771-2 PMS
Stan Getz Highlights | Verve | 847430-2
Wes Montgomery With The Don Sebesky Orchestra
Verve Jazz Masters 14:Wes Montgomery | Verve | 519826-2
Wes Montgomery:The Verve Jazz Sides | Verve | 521690-2
Talkin' Jazz:Roots Of Acid Jazz | Verve | 529580-2
California Dreaming | Verve | 827842-2

Becker,Adi | (tb)
Jazz Orchester Rheinland-Pfalz
Kazzou | Jazz Haus Musik | LJBB 9104
Like Life | Jazz Haus Musik | LJBB 9405
Marcus Sukiennik Big Band
A Night In Tunisia Suite(7 Variationen über Dizzy Gillespie's 'A Night In Tunisia') | Jazz Haus Musik | ohne Nummer

Becker,Freddie | (accordeonp)
Giessen-Köln-Nonett
Some Other Tapes | Fish Music | FM 009/10 CD
Transalpin Express Orchestra
Some Other Tapes | Fish Music | FM 009/10 CD

Becker,Irene | (keyboards,caxixi,voc,p,orgvoice)
Pierre Dorge's New Jungle Orchestra
Giraf | dacapo | DCCD 9440

Becker,Kurt | (flvib)
Harald Banter Ensemble
Deutsches Jazz Fesival 1954/1955 | Bear Family Records | BCD 15430
Paul Kuhn Quintet
Deutsches Jazz Fesival 1954/1955 | Bear Family Records | BCD 15430
Rolf Kühn And His Quintet
Deutsches Jazz Fesival 1954/1955 | Bear Family Records | BCD 15430

Becker,Manfred | (accordeonp)
Ekkehard Jost Ensemble
Weimarer Balladen | Fish Music | FM 004 CD
Ekkehard Jost Nonet
Out Of Jost's Songbook | Fish Music | FM 006 CD

Becker,Markus | (keyboards,psynth)
Heinz Sauer Quintet
Lost Ends:Live at Alte Oper Frankfurt | free flow music | ffm 0594
Jazzensemble Des Hessischen Rundfunks
Atmosphering Conditions Permitting | ECM | 1549/50
Radio Jazzgroup Frankfurt
Jubilee Edition | double moon | CHRDM 71020

Becker,Meret | (voc)
Kölner Saxophon Mafia With Guests
Kölner Saxophon Mafia: 20 Jahre Saxuelle Befreiung | Jazz Haus Musik | JHM 0115 CD

Becker,Rüdiger | (tb)
Marcus Sukiennik Big Band
A Night In Tunisia Suite(7 Variationen über Dizzy Gillespie's 'A Night In Tunisia') | Jazz Haus Musik | ohne Nummer

Beckerhoff,Uli | (tp,fl-h,keyboardspiccolo-tp)
La Voce-Music For Voices,Trumpet And Bass | JA & RO | JARO 4208-2
Ansgar Striepens Quintet
Dreams And Realities | Laika Records | 35101642
booMbooM meets Uli Beckerhoff
Resurection Lounge | Laika Records | 35101512
Changes
Jazz Portraits | EGO | 95080
Jazzensemble Des Hessischen Rundfunks
Atmosphering Conditions Permitting | ECM | 1549/50
John Abercrombie With The Ansgar Striepens Quintet
Dreams And Realities | Laika Records | 35101642
Peter Weiss Orchestra
Personal Choice | Nabel Records:Jazz Network | CD 4669
Tomato Kiss
Tomato Kiss | Nabel Records:Jazz Network | CD 4624
Uli Beckerhoff Group
Stay | Nabel Records:Jazz Network | CD 4636
Uli Beckerhoff Quartet
Secret Obsession | Nabel Records:Jazz Network | CD 4647
Uli Beckerhoff Quintet
Original Motion Picture Soundtrack:Das Geheimnis(Secret Of Love) | Nabel Records:Jazz Network | CD 4666
Uli Beckerhoff Septet
Private Life | Nabel Records:Jazz Network | CD 4657
Uli Beckerhoff Trio
Camporondo | Nabel Records:Jazz Network | CD 4629
Wayne Bartlett With The Thomas Hufschmidt Group
Tokyo Blues | Laika Records | 35101212

Beckett,Barry | (keyboards)
Albert King Blues Band
Lovejoy | Stax | SCD 8517-2(STS 2040)
Dee Dee Bridgewater With Band
Dee Dee Bridgewater | Atlantic | 7567-80760-2

Beckett,Darren | (dr)
Stéphane Mercier Group
Flor De Luna | Fresh Sound Records | FSNT 097 CD

Beckett,Fred | (tb)
Lionel Hampton And His Orchestra
Lionel Hampton:Flying Home | Dreyfus Jazz Line | FDM 36735-2

Beckett,Harry | (fl-htp)
Gail Thompson Orchestra
Gail Thompson's Jazz Africa | Enja | ENJ-9053 2
John Surman Orchestra
How Many Clouds Can You See? | Deram | 844882-2

Beckett,Paul C. | (computer-programming)
Toshinori Kondo & Ima
Red City Smoke | JA & RO | JARO 4173-2

Beckett,Samuel | (words)
Michael Mantler Quintet With The Balanescu Quartet
Folly Seeing All This | ECM | 1485

Beckham,Tom | (vib)
Tom Beckham Quartet
Suspicions | Fresh Sound Records | FSNT 075 CD

Beckmann,Hannes | (v)
Hannes Beckmann Group
Jazzy World | JA & RO | JARO 4200-2
Hannes Beckmann Quartet
Violin Tales | Tutu Records | 888202-2*

Becton,Clarence | (dr)
Benny Bailey Quartet
I Thought About You | Laika Records | 35100762
Benny Bailey Quartet With Wayne Bartlett
I Thought About You | Laika Records | 35100762
Mal Waldron Trio
Free At Last | ECM | 1001

Bedford,Ronnie | (dr,percwhistle)
Chuck Wayne Trio
Morning Mist | Original Jazz Classics | OJCCD 1097-2(P-7367)
Pee Wee Russell Quartet
Ask Me Now! | Impulse(MCA) | 755742-2
Rod Levitt Orchestra
The Dynamic Sound Patterns Of The Rod Levitt Orchestra | Original Jazz Classics | OJCCD 1955-2(RS 9471)

Bee Jays,The | (voc-group)
Buddy Johnson And His Orchestra
Buddy And Ella Johnson 1953-1964 | Bear Family Records | BCD 15479 DH

Beebe,Jim | (tb)
Bob Scobey's Frisco Band
Planet Jazz | Planet Jazz | 2169652-2

Beenen,Martin | (drtp)
Dutch Swing College Band
Swinging Studio Sessons | Philips | 824256-2 PMS
Dutch Swing College Band Live In 1960 | Philips | 838765-2

Beets,Marius | (b)
Lotz Of Music
Puasong Daffriek | Laika Records | LK 94-054

Beets,Peter | (p)
The Rosenberg Trio
Suenos Gitanos | Polydor | 549581-2

Behrendt,Bob | (tp)
Stan Kenton And His Orchestra
Adventures In Blues | Capitol | 520089-2
Adventures In Jazz | Capitol | 521222-2

Behrendt,Manfred | (b)
Johannes Rediske Quintet
Deutsches Jazz Fesival 1954/1955 | Bear Family Records | BCD 15430
Re-Disc Bounce | Bear Family Records | BCD 16119 AH
Jumpin' At The Badewanne | Bear Family Records | BCD 16172 AH
Johannes Rediske Sextet
Re-Disc Bounce | Bear Family Records | BCD 16119 AH
Johnnes Rediske Quintet
Deutsches Jazz Fesival 1954/1955 | Bear Family Records | BCD 15430

Behrens,Stanley | (flsax)
Jimmy Smith With Orchestra
Verve Jazz Masters 29:Jimmy Smith | Verve | 521855-2

Beiderbecke,Bix | (co,p,co-solo)
Bix And His Rhythm Jugglers
Jazz:The Essential Collection Vol.2 | IN+OUT Records | 78012-2
Bix Beiderbecke
Jazz:The Essential Collection Vol.2 | IN+OUT Records | 78012-2
Bix Beiderbecke And His Gang
Jazz:The Essential Collection Vol.2 | IN+OUT Records | 78012-2
Frankie Trumbauer And His Orchestra
Jazz:The Essential Collection Vol.2 | IN+OUT Records | 78012-2
Hoagy Carmichael And His Orchestra
Planet Jazz:Bud Freeman | Planet Jazz | 2161240-2
Irving Mills And His Hotsy Totsy Gang
Jazz:The Essential Collection Vol.3 | IN+OUT Records | 78013-2
Paul Whiteman And His Orchestra
Planet Jazz:Jazz Trumpet | Planet Jazz | 2169654-2
The Wolverines
Jazz:The Essential Collection Vol.2 | IN+OUT Records | 78012-2

Beier,Detlev | (bel-b)
Changes
Jazz Portraits | EGO | 95080
Pee Wee Ellis & NDR Bigband
What You Like | Minor Music | 801064
Peter Weiss Quartet
Personal Choice | Nabel Records:Jazz Network | CD 4669
Rolf Kühn Group
Inside Out | Intuition Records | INT 3276-2
Internal Eyes | Intuition Records | INT 3328-2
The Three Sopranos With The HR Big Band
The Three Sopranos | hr music.de | hrmj 001-01 CD
Tomato Kiss
Tomato Kiss | Nabel Records:Jazz Network | CD 4624
Uli Beckerhoff Group
Stay | Nabel Records:Jazz Network | CD 4636

Beigang,Klaus Martell | (dr,percvoc)
Wollie Kaiser Timeghost
New Traces For Old Aces | Jazz Haus Musik | JHM 0102 CD

Beirach,Richard | (el-p,p,clavinet,percp-solo)
Beirach-Hübner-Mraz
Round About Bartok | ACT | 9276-2
George Adams Sextet
Soung Suggestions | ECM | 1141
Richard Beirach Trio
Round About Federico Mompou | ACT | 9296-2
The Huebner Brothers
Memories | Satin Doll Productions | SDP 1025-1 CD

Bejar,Quino | (pailas)
Eladio Reinon Quintet
Es La Historia De Un Amor | Fresh Sound Records | FSNT 004 CD

Bejerano,Martin | (p)
Roy Haynes Quartet
Fountain Of Youth | Dreyfus Jazz Line | FDM 36663-2

Beldeanu,Michael | (v)
Bernd Konrad Jazz Group With Symphonie Orchestra
Wen Die Götter Lieben | Creative Works Records | CW CD 1010-1

Belden,Bob | (arr,ldts)
McCoy Tyner Big Band
The Best Of McCoy Tyner Big Band | Dreyfus Jazz Line | FDM 37012-2

Beldini,Al | (dr)
Bill Evans Quartet
The Complete Bill Evans On Verve | Verve | 527953-2
Bill Evans Trio
The Complete Bill Evans On Verve | Verve | 527953-2

Belenguer,Toni | (tb)
Daniel Flors Group
When Least Expected | Fresh Sound Records | FSNT 080 CD

Belew,Adrian | (el-g)
Herbie Hancock Group
Magic Window | CBS | 486572-2

Belgrave,Marcus | (tpfl-h)
Charles Mingus Orchestra
Charles Mingus:Pre-Bird(Mingus Revisited) | Verve | 538636-2
Charles Mingus Sextet
Changes Two | Rhino | 8122-71404-2
David Fathead Newman Sextet
Atlantic Saxophones | Rhino | 8122-71256-2
Rhino Presents The Atlantic Jazz Gallery | Atlantic | 8122-71257-2
Fathead:Ray Charles Presents David Newman | Atlantic | 8122-73708-2
George Gruntz Concert Jazz Band '83
Theatre | ECM | 1265
Hank Crawford Septet
The World Of Hank Crawford | Milestone | MCD 9304-2
Ray Charles And His Orchestra
Ray Charles At Newport | Atlantic | 7567-80765-2
Ray Charles Sextet With The Raylets
Newport Jazz Festival 1958,July 3rd-6th Vol.4:Blues In The Night No.2 | Phontastic | NCD 8816
Roland Alexander Quintet
Ronnie Mathews-Roland Alexander-Freddie Hubbard | Prestige | PRCD 24271-2

Bell,Aaron | (b)
Billie Holiday And Her All Stars
Verve Jazz Masters 12:Billie Holiday | Verve | 519825-2
Billie Holiday Story Vol.4:Lady Sings The Blues | Verve | 521429-2
4 By 4:Ella Fitzgerald/Sarah Vaughan/Billie Holiday/Dinah Washington | Verve | 559693-2
The Billie Holiday Song Book | Verve | 823246-2
Billy Strayhorn Orchestra
Johnny Hodges With Billy Strayhorn And The Orchestra | Verve | 557543-2
Carmen McRae With Orchestra
Birds Of A Feather | Decca | 589515-2
Carmen McRae With The Ralph Burns Orchestra
Birds Of A Feather | Decca | 589515-2
Duke Ellington And Count Basie With Their Orchestras
First Time! | CBS | CK 65571
Duke Ellington And His Orchestra
Planet Jazz:Johnny Hodges | Planet Jazz | 2152065-2
Jazz Festival Vol.2 | Storyville | 4960743
Duke Ellington And His Orchestra feat. Paul Gonsalves | Original Jazz Classics | OJCCD 623-2
The Jazz Giants Play Duke Ellington:Caravan | Prestige | PCD 24227-2
Duke Ellington-Coleman Hawkins Orchestra
Duke Ellington Meets Coleman Hawkins | Impulse(MCA) | 951162-2
Friedrich Gulda Septet
Friedrich Gulda At Birdland | RCA | 2112587-2
Friedrich Gulda Trio
Friedrich Gulda At Birdland | RCA | 2112587-2
John Coltrane-Duke Ellington Quartet
The Gentle Side Of John Coltrane | Impulse(MCA) | 951107-2
Duke Ellington & John Coltrane | Impulse(MCA) | 951166-2
Johnny Hodges Orchestra
Johnny Hodges At The Sportpalast, Berlin | Pablo | 2CD 2620102
The Jazz Giants Play Harry Warren:Lullaby Of Broadway | Prestige | PCD 24204-2
Johnny Hodges With Billy Strayhorn And The Duke Ellington Orchestra
Verve Jazz Masters 35:Johnny Hodges | Verve | 521857-2

Bell,Aaron or Bob Cunningham | (b)
Junior Mance Trio
That Lovin' Feelin' | Milestone | MCD 47097-2

Bell,Clive | (shakuhachi)
Nicki Leighton-Thomas Group
Forbidden Games | Candid | CCD 79778

Bell,Dave | (b-g)
Jon Hiseman With The United Jazz & Rock Ensemble And Babara Thompson's Paraphernalia
About Time Too! | VeraBra Records | CDVBR 2014-2

Bell,Janice | (voc)
Louis Armstrong And His Friends
Louis Armstrong And His Friends | Bluebird | 2663961-2

Bell,Kelvyn | (el-g,vocg)
Arthur Blythe Group
Hipmotism | Enja | ENJ-6088 2
Bob Stewart First Line Band
First Line | JMT Edition | 919014-2
Jean-Paul Bourelly Group
Jungle Cowboy | JMT Edition | 919009-2
Steve Coleman And Five Elements
On The Edge Of Tomorrow | JMT Edition | 919005-2

Bell,Khalil Kwame | (perc)
Russel Gunn Group
Ethnomusicology Vol.1 | Atlantic | 7567-83165-2

Bell,Larry | (drvoc)
First Revolution Singers
First Revolution Gospel Singers:A Capella | Laserlight | 24338

Bell,Leard | (dr)
Johnny Otis And His Orchestra
Verve Jazz Masters 43:Ben Webster | Verve | 525431-2

Bell,Madeleine | (voc)
Landes Jugend Jazz Orchester Hessen
Touch Of Lips | hr music.de | hrmj 004-01 CD

Bell,Poogie | (drdr-programming)
Marcus Miller Group
The Sun Don't Lie | Dreyfus Jazz Line | FDM 36560-2
Tales | Dreyfus Jazz Line | FDM 36571-2
Live & More | Dreyfus Jazz Line | FDM 36585-2

Bell,Richard | (accordeon,org,wurlitzer-p,p)
Hans Theessink Group
Call Me | Minor Music | 801022
Crazy Moon | Minor Music | 801052
Journey On | Minor Music | 801062

Bell,Rick | (ts)
Zoot Sims Quintet
Zoot Sims | Storyville | STCD 8367

Bell,Vincent | (g)
Quincy Jones And His Orchestra
Talkin' Verve-Roots Of Acid Jazz:Roland Kirk | Verve | 533101-2
Rahsaan/The Complete Mercury Recordings Of Roland Kirk | Mercury | 846630-2

Bell,Vincent or Carl Lynch | (g)
Les McCann Group
Talkin' Verve:Les McCann | Verve | 557351-2

Bellantese,Regina | (v)
Taylor Hawkins Group
Wake Up Call | Fresh Sound Records | FSCD 145 CD

Beller,Alex 'Al' | (v)
Artie Shaw And His Orchestra
Planet JazzArtie Shaw | Planet Jazz | 2152057-2
Planet Jazz:Big Bands | Planet Jazz | 2169649-2
Ben Pollack And His Park Central Orchestra
Planet Jazz:Jack Teagarden | Planet Jazz | 2161236-2
Jazz:The Essential Collection Vol.3 | IN+OUT Records | 78013-2
Ella Fitzgerald With The Nelson Riddle Orchestra
The Best Of The Song Books:The Ballads | Verve | 521867-2
Oh Lady Be Good:The Best Of The Gershwin Songbook | Verve | 529581-2
Love Songs:The Best Of The Song Books | Verve | 531762-2
Tommy Dorsey And His Orchestra
Planet Jazz:Frank Sinatra & Tommy Dorsey | Planet Jazz | 2152067-2

Bellincampi,Giordano | (b-tb,condtb)
Michael Mantler Group With The Danish Radio Concert Orchestra Strings
The School Of Understanding(Sort-Of-An-Opera) | ECM | 1648/49(537963-2)
Mona Larsen And The Danish Radio Big Band Plus Soloists
Michael Mantler:Cerco Un Paese Innocente | ECM | 1556

Bellingieri,Osvaldo | (p)
Gato Barbieri Orchestra
Latino America | Impulse(MCA) | 952236-2

Bello,John | (tpfl-h)
Eddie Lockjaw Davis Orchestra
Afro-Jaws | Original Jazz Classics | OJCCD 403-2(RLP 9373)
Maynard Ferguson And His Orchestra
Verve Jazz Masters 52:Maynard Ferguson | Verve | 529905-2
Quincy Jones And His Orchestra
Talkin' Verve-Roots Of Acid Jazz:Roland Kirk | Verve | 533101-2
Rahsaan/The Complete Mercury Recordings Of Roland Kirk | Mercury | 846630-2

Bellonzi,Charles | (dr)
Golden Gate Quartet With The Martial Solal Orchestra
From Spriritual To Swing Vol.2 | EMI Records | 780573-2
Rene Thomas Quartet
Jazz In Paris:René Thomas-Meeting Mister Thomas | EmArCy | 549812-2
Rene Thomas Quintet
Jazz In Paris:René Thomas-Meeting Mister Thomas | EmArCy | 549812-2
Richard Galliano Quartet
Viaggio | Dreyfus Jazz Line | FDM 36562-9
Gallianissimo! The Best Of Richard Galliano | Dreyfus Jazz Line | FDM 36616-2

Bellson,Louie | (dr,arr,moog-dr,percvoc)
Ben Webster With Orchestra And Strings
Verve Jazz Masters 43:Ben Webster | Verve | 525431-2
Music For Loving:Ben Webster With Strings | Verve | 527774-2
Ultimate Ben Webster selected by James Carter | Verve | 557537-2
Ben Webster With The Billy Strayhorn Trio
Music For Loving:Ben Webster With Strings | Verve | 527774-2
Coleman Hawkins Quartet
The Art Of Saxophone | Laserlight | 24652
Count Basie Band
Basie Jam No. 2 | Original Jazz Classics | OJCCD 631-2(2310786)
Count Basie Jam Session
Count Basie Jam Session At The Montreux Jazz Festival 1975 | Original Jazz Classics | OJC20 933-2(2310750)

Count Basie Kansas City 3
For The Second Time | Original Jazz Classics | OJC 600(2310878)
Count Basie Kansas City 5
Milt Jackson Birthday Celebration | Fantasy | FANCD 6079-2
Count Basie Sextet
Jazz At The Philharmonic:The Montreux Collection | Pablo | PACD 5306-2
Count Basie Trio
The Jazz Giants Play Harold Arlen:Blues In The Night | Prestige | PCD 24201-2
Count Basie-Oscar Peterson Quartet
The Timekeepers-Count Basie Meets Oscar Peterson | Original Jazz Classics | OJC20 790-2(2310896)
Count Basie-Oscar Peterson Quintet
Satch And Josh | Pablo | 2310722-2
Jazz Dance | Original Jazz Classics | OJCCD 1002-2(1210890)
Count Basie-Zoot Sims Quartet
Basie & Zoot | Original Jazz Classics | OJCCD 822-2(2310745)
Dizzy Gillespie Sextet
Verve Jazz Masters 10:Dizzy Gillespie | Verve | 516319-2
Dizzy Gillespie-Roy Eldridge Sextet
Ultimate Dizzy Gillespie | Verve | 557535-2
Duke Ellington And His Orchestra
Highlights From The Duke Ellington Centennial Edition | RCA | 2663672-2
Greatest Hits | CBS | 462959-2
The Big Bands Vol.1.The Snader Telescriptions | Storyville | 4960043
Duke Ellington Quartet
Joe Pass:Guitar Virtuoso | Pablo | 4 PACD 4423-2
The Jazz Giants Play Duke Ellington:Caravan | Prestige | PCD 24227-2
Duke Ellington Trio With The Boston Pops Orchestra
Highlights From The Duke Ellington Centennial Edition | RCA | 2663672-2
Ella Fitzgerald And Louis Armstrong With The Oscar Peterson Quartet
Ella Fitzgerald-First Lady Of Song | Verve | 517898-2
Verve Jazz Masters 1:Louis Armstrong | Verve | 519818-2
Verve Jazz Masters 6:Ella Fitzgerald | Verve | 519822-2
Verve Jazz Masters 24:Ella Fitzgerald & Louis Armstrong | Verve | 521851-2
Verve Jazz Masters Vol.60:The Collection | Verve | 529866-2
The Complete Ella Fitzgerald And Louis Armstrong On Verve | Verve | 537284-2
The Best Of Ella Fitzgerald And Louis Armstrong On Verve | Verve | 537909-2
Ella And Louis Again | Verve | 825374-2
For The Love Of Ella Fitzgerald | Verve | 841765-2
Ella Fitzgerald Jam
Bluella:Ella Fitzgerald Sings The Blues | Pablo | 2310960-2
Ella Fitzgerald With Benny Carter's Magnificent Seven
30 By Ella | Capitol | 520090-2
Ella Fitzgerald With Jackie Davis And Louis Bellson
Bluella:Ella Fitzgerald Sings The Blues | Pablo | 2310960-2
Lady Time | Original Jazz Classics | OJCCD 864-2(2310825)
Ella Fitzgerald With Orchestra
Ella/Things Ain't What They Used To Be | Warner | 9362-47875-2
Ella Fitzgerald With The Duke Ellington Orchestra
Ella Fitzgerald-First Lady Of Song | Verve | 517898-2
Verve Jazz Masters 46:Ella Fitzgerald-The Jazz Sides | Verve | 527655-2
Ella Fitzgerald With The Marty Paich Orchestra
Whisper Not | Verve | 589947-2
Ella Fitzgerald With The Nelson Riddle Orchestra
Dream Dancing | Original Jazz Classics | OJCCD 1072-2(2310814)
Ella Fitzgerald With The Oscar Peterson Quartet
Verve Jazz Masters 6:Ella Fitzgerald | Verve | 519822-2
Verve Jazz Masters 24:Ella Fitzgerald & Louis Armstrong | Verve | 521851-2
For The Love Of Ella Fitzgerald | Verve | 841765-2
Harry Carney And His Orchestra With Strings
Music For Loving:Ben Webster With Strings | Verve | 527774-2
JATP All Stars
J.A.T.P. In London 1969 | Pablo | 2CD 2620119
Welcome To Jazz At The Philharmonic | Fantasy | FANCD 6081-2
Kansas City 6
Count Basie:Kansas City 6 | Original Jazz Classics | OJC20 449-2(2310871)
Lawrence Brown Quintet
Slide Trombone | Verve | 559930-2
Louie Bellson Septet
Louie Bellson Jam | Original Jazz Classics | OJCCD 802-2(2310838)
Louis Armstrong With The Oscar Peterson Quartet
Verve Jazz Masters 1:Louis Armstrong | Verve | 519818-2
Verve Jazz Masters 20:Introducing | Verve | 519853-2
Louis Armstrong Meets Oscar Peterson | Verve | 539060-2
Oscar Peterson All Stars
Jazz At The Philharmonic:The Montreux Collection | Pablo | PACD 5306-2
Oscar Peterson Quartet
Oscar Peterson:The Composer | Pablo | 2310970-2
Night Child | Original Jazz Classics | OJCCD 1030-2(2312108)
Oscar Peterson Trio
The London Concert | Pablo | 2CD 2620111
The Jazz Giants Play Rodgers & Hart:Blue Moon | Prestige | PCD 24205-2
Ralph Burns And His Orchestra
The Complete Verve Roy Eldridge Studio Sessions | Verve | 9861278
Roy Eldridge Quintet
Decidedly | Pablo | PACD 5314-2
Roy Eldridge Sextet
Decidedly | Pablo | PACD 5314-2
Roy Eldridge-Dizzy Gillespie With The Oscar Peterson Quartet
The Complete Verve Roy Eldridge Studio Sessions | Verve | 9861278
Sarah Vaughan With The Oscar Peterson Quartet
How Long Has This Been Going On? | Pablo | 2310821-2
Joe Pass:Guitar Virtuoso | Pablo | 4 PACD 4423-2
Sarah Vaughan Birthday Celebration | Fantasy | FANCD 6090-2
Tatum-Carter-Bellson Trio
Art Tatum-The Complete Pablo Group Masterpieces | Pablo | 6 PACD 4401-2
Teddy Wilson Trio
J.A.T.P. In London 1969 | Pablo | 2CD 2620119
Tommy Dorsey And His Orchestra
Planet Jazz:Tommy Dorsey | Planet Jazz | 2159972-2
Zoot Sims Quartet feat.Count Basie
Jazz Dance | Original Jazz Classics | OJCCD 1002-2(1210890)

Belmondo,Lionel | (saxts)
Dee Dee Bridgewater With Her Quartet With Horace Silver
Love And Peace-A Tribute To Horace Silver | Verve | 527470-2
Dee Dee Bridgewater With Her Quintet
Love And Peace-A Tribute To Horace Silver | Verve | 527470-2
Dee Dee Bridgewater With Her Quintet With Jimmy Smith
Love And Peace-A Tribute To Horace Silver | Verve | 527470-2

Belmondo,Stephane | (tp)
Dee Dee Bridgewater With Her Quartet With Horace Silver
Love And Peace-A Tribute To Horace Silver | Verve | 527470-2
Dee Dee Bridgewater With Her Quintet
Love And Peace-A Tribute To Horace Silver | Verve | 527470-2
Dee Dee Bridgewater With Her Quintet With Jimmy Smith
Love And Peace-A Tribute To Horace Silver | Verve | 527470-2

Belmonte,Omar | (perc)
Litschie Hrdlicka Group
Falling Lovers | EGO | 93020

Belmote,Omar | (dr,percvoc)
Omar Belmonte's Latin Lover
Vamos A Ver | EGO | 96170

Belnick,Arnold | (v)
Hank Crawford Orchestra
Rhino Presents The Atlantic Jazz Gallery | Atlantic | 8122-71257-2
Milt Jackson With Strings
To Bags...With Love:Memorial Album | Pablo | 2310967-2

Belov,Eugenji | (balalaika)
Belov Duo
Internationales Guitarren Festival '99 | ALISO Records | AL 1038
Viktoria Tabatchnikowa-Eugenij Belov
Troika | ALISO Records | AL 1036

Below,Freddie | (drtambourine)
Buddy Guy Blues Band
Buddy Guy-The Complete Chess Studio Recordings | MCA | MCD 09337

Beltraminelli,Daniela | (v)
Michel Wintsch & Road Movie
Michel Wintsch & Road Movie featuring Gerry Hemingway | Between The Lines | btl 002(Efa 10172-2)

Bemiss,Albert | (org,psynth)
Lillian Boutté And Her Group
The Gospel Book | Blues Beacon | BLU-1017 2
Lillian Boutté And Her Group & The Soulful Heavenly Stars
The Gospel Book | Blues Beacon | BLU-1017 2

Bemko,Harold | (cello)
Tommy Dorsey And His Orchestra
Planet Jazz:Frank Sinatra & Tommy Dorsey | Planet Jazz | 2152067-2

Benavent,Carlos | (b,el-b,oud,b-g,mandola)
Los Jovenes Flamencos
Jazzpana | ACT | 9212-2
Los Jovenes Flamencos With The WDR Big Band And Guests
Jazzpana | ACT | 9212-2
Miles Davis With Gil Evans Orchestra, The George Gruntz Concert Jazz Band And Guests
Miles & Quincy Live At Montreux | Warner | 9362-45221-2
Nguyen Le Trio With Guests
Bakida | ACT | 9275-2

Benaventi,Joe | (cello)
Charlie Parker With Strings
Charlie Parker With Strings:The Master Takes | Verve | 523984-2
Charlie Parker With The Neal Hefti Orchestra
Charlie Parker:The Best Of The Verve Years | Verve | 527815-2
Bird: The Complete Charlie Parker On Verve | Verve | 837141-2

Bender,Helmut | (voc)
Jazzensemble Des Hessischen Rundfunks
Jazz Messe-Messe Für Unsere Zeit | hr music.de | hrmj 003-01 CD

Bender,Pete 'Wyoming' | (voc)
Gunther Schuller With The WDR Radio Orchestra & Rememberance Band
Witchi Tia To, The Music Of Jim Pepper | Tutu Records | 888204-2*

Bender,Walter | (dr,samples,special-effectsvoice)
Ax Genrich Group
Psychedelic Guitar | ATM Records | ATM 3809-AH
Wave Cut | ATM Records | ATM 3813-AH

Benders,Mart | (fl)
The Rosenberg Trio With Orchestra
Noches Calientes | Verve | 557022-2

Bendik | (saxkeyboards)
Steps Ahead
N.Y.C. | Intuition Records | INT 3007-2

Bendiksen,Havar | (g,mandaccordeon)
Susanne Lundeng Quartet
Waltz For The Red Fiddle | Laika Records | 35101402

Bendzko,Thomas | (tp)
Conexion Latina
Mambo Nights | Enja | ENJ-9402 2
Dusko Goykovich Big Band
Balkan Connection | Enja | ENJ-9047 2

Benedetti,Vince | (arrp)
Hank Mobley Sextet
The Flip | Blue Note | 593872-2

Beneke,Gordon 'Tex' | (as,cl,ts,vocsax)
Glenn Miller And His Orchestra
The Ultimate Glenn Miller-22 Original Hits From The King Of Swing | RCA | 2113137-2
Planet Jazz:Glenn Miller | Planet Jazz | 2152056-2
Planet Jazz Sampler | Planet Jazz | 2152326-2
Planet Jazz:Jazz Greatest Hits | Planet Jazz | 2169648-2
Planet Jazz:Big Bands | Planet Jazz | 2169649-2
Planet Jazz:Swing | Planet Jazz | 2169651-2
The Chesterfield Broadcasts Vol.1 | RCA | 2663113-2
Candlelight Miller | RCA | 2668716-2
The Glenn Miller Story Vol. 2 | RCA | ND 89221
The Glenn Miller Story Vol. 3 | RCA | ND 89222
Swing Legends | Nimbus Records | NI 2001
The Andrew Sisters With The Glenn Miller Orchestra
The Chesterfield Broadcasts Vol.1 | RCA | 2663113-2

Benesch,Rolf | (tsbs)
Swim Two Birds
Sweet Relief | Laika Records | 35101182
No Regrets | Laika Records | 35101342

Beneventano,Andrea | (p)
Nicola Puglielli Group
In The Middle | Jardis Records | JRCD 9924

Benford,Bill | (tuba)
Jelly Roll Morton's Red Hot Peppers
Planet Jazz:Jelly Roll Morton | Planet Jazz | 2152060-2
Jazz:The Essential Collection Vol.1 | IN+OUT Records | 78011-2

Benford,Tommy | (dr)
Benny Carter And His Orchestra
Americans Swinging In Paris:Benny Carter | EMI Records | 539647-2
Bill Coleman Quintet
Americans Swinging In Paris:Bill Coleman-The Elegance | EMI Records | 539662-2
Coleman Hawkins And His All Star Jam Band
Django Reinhardt All Star Sessions | Capitol | 531577-2
Americans Swinging In Paris:Benny Carter | EMI Records | 539647-2
Jazz:The Essential Collection Vol.3 | IN+OUT Records | 78013-2
Dick Wellstood-Tommy Benford
Uptown And Lowdown | Prestige | PCD 24262-2
Eddie Brunner And His Orchestra
Americans Swinging In Paris:Bill Coleman-The Elegance | EMI Records | 539662-2
Jelly Roll Morton's Red Hot Peppers
Planet Jazz:Jelly Roll Morton | Planet Jazz | 2152060-2
Jazz:The Essential Collection Vol.1 | IN+OUT Records | 78011-2

Benge,Alfreda | (voice)
Michael Mantler Group
The Hapless Child | Watt | 4

Bengtsson,Tord | (el-g,vperc)
Beng Berger Band
Bitter Funeral Beer | ECM | 1179

Benita,Michel | (bel-b)
Erik Truffaz Quartet
Mantis | Blue Note | 535101-2
Erik Truffaz Quartet Quintet
Mantis | Blue Note | 535101-2
Nguyen Le Group
Tales From Viet-Nam | ACT | 9225-2
Palatino
Palationo Chap.3 | EmArCy | 013610-2
Peter Erskine Trio
ELB | ACT | 9289-2

Benitez,Gorka | (fl,ssts)
Alguimia
Alguimia 'U' | Fresh Sound Records | FSNT 023 CD
David Xirgu Quartet
Idolents | Fresh Sound Records | FSNT 077 CD
Gorka Benitez Quartet
Gorka Benitez Trio | Fresh Sound Records | FSNT 073 CD
Gorka Benitez Quintet
Gorka Benitez Trio | Fresh Sound Records | FSNT 073 CD
Gorka Benitez Trio
Gorka Benitez Trio | Fresh Sound Records | FSNT 073 CD
Orquestra De Cambra Teatre Lliure
Porgy And Bess | Fresh Sound Records | FSNT 066 CD

Benitez,John | (b,el-bvoc)
Antonio Hart Group
Here I Stand | Impulse(MCA) | 951208-2
Danilo Perez Group
Central Avenue | Impulse(MCA) | 951281-2
Danilo Perez Trio
Central Avenue | Impulse(MCA) | 951281-2
Mongo Santamaria And His Orchestra
Jazzin' Vol.2: The Music Of Stevie Wonder | Fantasy | FANCD 6088-2
Roy Hargrove's Crisol
Habana | Verve | 537563-2

Benjamin,Joe | (b)
Big Al Sears Band
Sear-iously | Bear Family Records | BCD 15668 AH
Billie Holiday With The Mal Waldron Trio
Billie Holiday Story Vol.1:Jazz At The Philharmonic | Verve | 521642-2
Clark Terry Orchestra
Color Changes | Candid | CCD 79009
Della Reese With The Sy Oliver Orchestra
Misty Blue:Sweet Sisters Swing Songs Of Sorrow And Sadness | Blue Note | 521151-2
Dizzy Gillespie Orchestra And The Operatic String Orchestra
Jazz In Paris:Dizzy Gillespie And His Operatic Strings Orchestra | EmArCy | 018420-2
Don Byas Quartet
Jazz In Paris:Don Byas-Laura | EmArCy | 013027-2
Duke Ellington And His Orchestra
Highlights From The Duke Ellington Centennial Edition | RCA | 2663672-2
New Orleans Suite | Rhino | 812273670-2
The Ellington Suites | Original Jazz Classics | OJC20 446-2(2310762)
The Afro-Eurasian Eclipse-A Suite In Eight Parts | Original Jazz Classics | OJCCD 645-2(F 9498)
Togo Brava Swuite | Storyville | STCD 8323
Duke Ellington Quartet
Togo Brava Swuite | Storyville | STCD 8323
Duke Ellington Small Band
The Intimacy Of The Blues | Original Jazz Classics | OJCCD 624-2
Duke Ellington Trio
Duke Ellington Live At The Whitney | Impulse(MCA) | 951173-2
George Russell And His Orchestra
Bill Evans:Piano Player | CBS | CK 65361
Gerry Mulligan And His Orchestra
Mullenium | CBS | CK 65678
Gerry Mulligan Quartet
Jazz At The Philharmonic: The Gerry Mulligan Quartets In Concert | Pablo | PACD 5309-2
Gerry Mulligan-Paul Desmond Quartet
Gerry Mulligan-Paul Desmond Quartet | Verve | 519850-2
Harry Sweets Edison Sextet
Mr.Swing Harry Edison | Verve | 559868-2
Joe Williams And His Band
Blue Velvet: Crooners, Swooners And Velvet Vocals | Blue Note | 521153-2
Joe Williams With The Harry 'Sweets' Edison Band
Together/Have A Good Time | Roulette | 531790-2
Johnny Hodges Orchestra
Planet Jazz:Johnny Hodges | Planet Jazz | 2152065-2
Kenny Burrell Quintet
Guitar Forms | Verve | 521403-2
Verve Jazz Masters 45:Kenny Burrell | Verve | 527652-2
Kenny Clarke Quintet
Verve Jazz Masters 45:Kenny Burrell | Verve | 527652-2
Louis Armstrong And Billie Holiday With Sy Oliver's Orchestra
Louis Armstrong:C'est Si Bon | Dreyfus Jazz Line | FDM 36730-2
Louis Armstrong With Sy Oliver And His Orchestra
Satchmo Serenaders | Verve | 543792-2
Louis And The Angels | Verve | 549592-2
Louis Armstrong With Sy Oliver's Choir And Orchestra
Louis And The Good Book | Verve | 549593-2
Mal Waldron Sextet
Eric Dolphy:The Complete Prestige Recordings | Prestige | 9 PRCD-4418-2
Eric Dolphy Birthday Celebration | Fantasy | FANCD 6085-2
The Quest | Original Jazz Classics | OJCCD 082-2(NJ 8269)
The Mal Waldron Memorial Album:Soul Eyes | Prestige | PRCD 11024-2
Paul Desmond-Gerry Mulligan Quartet
Two Of A Mind | RCA | 2179620-2
Roland Kirk With The Jack McDuff Trio
Kirk's Work | Original Jazz Classics | OJC20 459-2(P 7210)
Sarah Vaughan And Her Trio
Swingin' Easy | EmArCy | 514072-2
Verve Jazz Masters 42:Sarah Vaughan-The Jazz Sides | Verve | 526817-2
4 By 4:Ella Fitzgerald/Sarah Vaughan/Billie Holiday/Dinah Washington | Verve | 559693-2
Sarah Vaughan With The Clifford Brown All Stars
Verve Jazz Masters 20:Introducing | Verve | 519853-2
Clifford Brown-Max Roach:Alone Together-The Best Of The Mercury Years | Verve | 526373-2
Sarah Vaughan | Verve | 543305-2
4 By 4:Ella Fitzgerald/Sarah Vaughan/Billie Holiday/Dinah Washington | Verve | 559693-2
Brownie-The Complete EmArCy Recordings Of Clifford Brown | EmArCy | 838306-2
Sarah Vaughan | EmArCy | 9860779
Sarah Vaughan With The Jimmy Jones Trio
Sarah Vaughan | Verve | 543305-2
Wild Bill Moore Quintet
Bottom Groove | Milestone | MCD 47098-2

Benjamin,Sathima Bea | (voc)
Sathima Bea Benjamin Group
A Morning In Paris | Enja | ENJ-9309 2

Benkenstein,Thorsten | (tpfl-h)
Lee Konitz With The Ed Partyka Jazz Orchestra
Dreams And Realities | Laika Records | 35101642

Bennett,Benny | (dr)
Clifford Brown Quartet
Planet Jazz:Clifford Brown | Planet Jazz | 2161239-2
Don Byas Quartet
Planet Jazz:Jazz Saxophone | Planet Jazz | 2169653-2
Don Byas Quintet
Jazz In Paris:Don Byas-Laura | EmArCy | 013027-2
James Moody Boptet
Americans Swinging In Paris:James Moody | EMI Records | 539653-2

Bennett,Chuck | (tb)
Vince Guaraldi Group
Charlie Brown's Holiday Hits | Fantasy | FCD 9682-2

Bennett,Ed | (btb)
Carmen McRae With The Dizzy Gillespie Quartet
Misty Blue:Sweet Sisters Swing Songs Of Sorrow And Sadness | Blue Note | 521151-2

Bennett,Errol 'Crusher' | (perccongas)
Steve Khan Group
Jazzrock-Anthology Vol.3:Fusion | Zounds | CD 27100555

Bennett,H.B. | (dr)
Bobby McFerrin Group
Bobby McFerrin | Elektra | 7559-60023-2

Bennett,Joe | (tbvoc)
Miles Davis + 19
Miles Ahead | CBS | CK 65121
Miles Davis With Gil Evans & His Orchestra

INTERPRETENVERZEICHNIS

This Is Jazz:Miles Davis Plays Ballads | CBS | CK 65038
Porgy And Bess | CBS | CK 65141

Bennett,Lou | (org)
Lou Bennett Trio
Jazz In Paris | EmArCy | 548790-2
Lou Bennett Trio With The Paris Jazz All Stars
Jazz In Paris | EmArCy | 548790-2
Rene Thomas Quartet
Jazz In Paris:René Thomas-Meeting Mister Thomas | EmArCy | 549812-2
Rene Thomas Quintet
Jazz In Paris:René Thomas-Meeting Mister Thomas | EmArCy | 549812-2

Bennett,Mark | (tbtp)
Benny Goodman And His Orchestra
The Legends Of Swing | Laserlight | 24659
Bob Crosby And His Orchestra
Swing Legens:Bob Crosby | Nimbus Records | NI 2011
Jack Teagarden And His Orchestra
Jazz:The Essential Collection Vol.3 | IN+OUT Records | 78013-2

Bennett,Max | (bel-b)
Ella Fitzgerald With The Lou Levy Trio
Ella Fitzgerald-First Lady Of Song | Verve | 517898-2
For The Love Of Ella Fitzgerald | Verve | 841765-2
Peggy Lee With The Quincy Jones Orchestra
Blues Cross Country | Capitol | 520088-2
Terry Gibbs Dream Band
Terry Gibbs Dream Band Vol.3:Flying Home | Contemporary | CCD 7654-2
Terry Gibbs Dream Band Vol.6:One More Time | Contemporary | CCD 7658-2

Bennett,Russ | (bj)
Yerba Buena Jazz Band
Bunk & Lu | Good Time Jazz | GTCD 12024-2

Bennett,Tony | (voc)
Tony Bennett With The Bill Charlap Trio
Stardust | Blue Note | 535985-2
Tony Bennett-Bill Evans
The Complete Fantasy Recordings | Fantasy | 9FCD 1012-2
The Tony Bennett-Bill Evans Album | Original Jazz Classics | OJC20 439-2(F 9489)

Bennion Feeney ,Krista | (v)
A Band Of Friends
Wynton Marsalis Quartet With Strings | CBS | CK 68921
Steve Kuhn With Strings
Promises Kept | ECM | 1815(0675222)

Benno,Norman | (oboe)
Ella Fitzgerald With The Nelson Riddle Orchestra
The Best Of The Song Books:The Ballads | Verve | 521867-2
Love Songs:The Best Of The Song Books | Verve | 531762-2
Ella Fitzgerald Sings The Johnny Mercer Songbook | Verve | 539057-2
Dream Dancing | Original Jazz Classics | OJCCD 1072-2(2310814)

Benny Diggs Singers |
Bernard Purdie's Soul To Jazz
Bernard Purdie's Soul To Jazz II | ACT | 9253-2

Benoit,David | (keyboards,p,el-p,synth,electronics)
David Benoit Group
The Best Of David Benoit 1987-1995 | GRP | GRP 98312
Lee Ritenour With Special Guests
Festival International De Jazz De Montreal | Spectra | 9811661

Benoit,Olivier | (g)
Orchestre National De Jazz
Charmediterranéen | ECM | 1828(018493-2)

Benskin,Sammy | (p)
Benny Morton's All Stars
The Blue Note Swingtets | Blue Note | 495697-2
Jazz:The Essential Collection Vol.3 | IN+OUT Records | 78013-2
John Hardee Sextet
The Blue Note Swingtets | Blue Note | 495697-2
John Hardee Swingtet
The Blue Note Swingtets | Blue Note | 495697-2

Benson,George | (el-g,vocg)
Freddie Hubbard Trio
This Is Jazz:Freddie Hubbard | CBS | CK 65041
Freddie Hubbard With Orchestra
This Is Jazz:Freddie Hubbard | CBS | CK 65041
George Benson And His Orchestra
Giblet Gravy | Verve | 543754-2
Talkin' Verve:George Benson | Verve | 553780-2
George Benson Group
Verve Jazz Masters 21:George Benson | Verve | 521861-2
Breezin' | Warner | 8122-76713-2
George Benson Group/Orchestra
George Benson Anthology | Warner | 8122-79934-2
George Benson Orchestra
Verve Jazz Masters 21:George Benson | Verve | 521861-2
Talkin' Verve:George Benson | Verve | 553780-2
George Benson Quartet
It's Uptown | CBS | 502469-2
The George Benson Cookbook | CBS | 502470-2
Talkin' Verve:George Benson | Verve | 553780-2
George Benson Quartet + Guests
The George Benson Cookbook | CBS | 502470-2
George Benson Quartet With The Sweet Inspirations
Talkin' Verve:George Benson | Verve | 553780-2
George Benson Quintet
It's Uptown | CBS | 502469-2
Verve Jazz Masters 21:George Benson | Verve | 521861-2
Giblet Gravy | Verve | 543754-2
George Benson Sextet
Talkin' Verve:George Benson | Verve | 553780-2
George Benson With Orchestra
Verve Jazz Masters 21:George Benson | Verve | 521861-2
George Benson With The Don Sebesky Orchestra
Verve Jazz Masters 21:George Benson | Verve | 521861-2
George Benson With The Jack McDuff Quartet
The New Boss Guitar | Original Jazz Classics | OJCCD 461-2
Jack McDuff Quartet
The Soulful Drums | Prestige | PCD 24256-2
The Concert McDuff | Prestige | PRCD 24270-2
The Last Goodun' | Prestige | PRCD 24274-2
Jack McDuff:The Prestige Years | Prestige | PRCD 24387-2
Jack McDuff Quartet With Orchestra
Prelude:Jack McDuff Big Band | Prestige | PRCD 24283-2
Jack McDuff Quintet
The Last Goodun' | Prestige | PRCD 24274-2
Jack McDuff Sextet
Silken Soul | Prestige | PCD 24242-2
The Soulful Drums | Prestige | PCD 24256-2
Jaki Byard Sextet
Jaki Byard:Solo/Strings | Prestige | PCD 24246-2
Jimmy Smith Trio
Verve Jazz Masters 21:George Benson | Verve | 521861-2
Jimmy Smith:Best Of The Verve Years | Verve | 527950-2
Talkin' Verve:George Benson | Verve | 553780-2
Lee Morgan Sextet
Taru | Blue Note | 522670-2
Lena Horne With The George Benson Quintet
Misty Blue:Sweet Sisters Swing Songs Of Sorrow And Sadness | Blue Note | 521151-2
Lou Donaldson Quintet
Midnight Creeper | Blue Note | 524546-2
Miles Davis Quintet
Miles Davis Quintet 1965-1968 | CBS | C6K 67398
Miles Davis Sextet
Circle In The Round | CBS | 467898-2
Miles In The Sky | CBS | CK 65684
Patti Austin And Her Band
Patti Austin:The Ultimate Collection | GRP | GRP 98212

Benson,George or Joe Beck | (g)
Miles Davis Quintet
Miles Davis Quintet 1965-1968 | CBS | C6K 67398

Benson,Peter | (v)
Dee Dee Bridgewater With Orchestra
Dear Ella | Verve | 539102-2

Benson,Walt | (tb)
Tommy Dorsey And His Orchestra
Planet Jazz:Tommy Dorsey | Planet Jazz | 2159972-2
Planet Jazz:Jazz Greatest Hits | Planet Jazz | 2169648-2

Bensoussan,Aaron | (cantorhand-dr)
Uri Caine Group
Urlicht/Primal Light | Winter&Winter | 910004-2

Bent,Phillip | (fl)
GRP All-Star Big Band
GRP All-Star Big Band:Live! | GRP | GRP 97402

Bentall,Dave | (tb)
Buddy Childers Big Band
Just Buddy's | Candid | CCD 79761

Benton,Bob | (voc)
Bob Benton With The Charles Mingus Quintet
Charles Mingus-The Complete Debut Recordings | Debut | 12 DCD 4402-2

Benton,Franz | (gvoc)
Klaus Kreuzeder & Franz Benton
Big little Gigs: First Takes Live | Trick Music | TM 0112 CD

Benton,Walter | (ts)
Abbey Lincoln And Her Orchestra
Straight Ahead | Candid | CCD 79015
Clifford Brown All Stars
Verve Jazz Masters 44:Clifford Brown and Max Roach | Verve | 528109-2
Brownie-The Complete EmArCy Recordings Of Clifford Brown | EmArCy | 838306-2
Jazz Artists Guild
Newport Rebels-Jazz Artists Guild | Candid | CCD 79022
Julian Priester Sextet
Out Of This World | Milestone | MCD 47087-2
Max Roach All Stars
Candid Dolphy | Candid | CCD 79033
Max Roach Group
We Insist: Freedom Now Suite | Candid | CCD 79002
Max Roach Septet
The Jazz Life! | Candid | CCD 79019
Victor Feldman Orchestra
Latinsville | Contemporary | CCD 9005-2
Walter Benton Quintet
Out Of This World | Milestone | MCD 47087-2

Bentyne,Cheryl | (voc)
Rob Wasserman Duet
Duets | GRP | GRP 97122

Bentzon,Adrian | (celestep)
Adrian Bentzon's Jazzband
The Golden Years Of Revival Jazz,Sampler | Storyville | 109 1001
The Golden Years Of Revival Jazz,Vol 1 | Storyville | STCD 5506
The Golden Years Of Revival Jazz,Vol.2 | Storyville | STCD 5507
The Golden Years Of Revival Jazz,Vol.3 | Storyville | STCD 5508
The Golden Years Of Revival Jazz,Vol.4 | Storyville | STCD 5509
The Golden Years Of Revival Jazz,Vol.7 | Storyville | STCD 5512
The Golden Years Of Revival Jazz,Vol.13 | Storyville | STCD 5518
The Golden Years Of Revival Jazz,Vol.14 | Storyville | STCD 5519
Albert Nicholas With Adrian Bentzon's Jazzband
The Golden Years Of Revival Jazz,Sampler | Storyville | 109 1001
Albert Nicholas & The Dutch Swing College Band | Storyville | STCD 5522

Bentzon,Fridolin | (b)
Adrian Bentzon's Jazzband
The Golden Years Of Revival Jazz,Sampler | Storyville | 109 1001
Albert Nicholas With Adrian Bentzon's Jazzband
The Golden Years Of Revival Jazz,Sampler | Storyville | 109 1001
Albert Nicholas & The Dutch Swing College Band | Storyville | STCD 5522

Bentzon,Nikolaj | (p,keyboardssynth)
Jens Winther And The Danish Radio Jazz Orchestra
Angels | dacapo | DCCD 9442
Mona Larsen And The Danish Radio Big Band Plus Soloists
Michael Mantler:Cerco Un Paese Innocente | ECM | 1556
The Danish Radio Jazz Orchestra
This Train:The Danish Radio Jazz Orchestra Plays The Music Of Ray Pitts | dacapo | DCCD 9428
Nice Work | dacapo | DCCD 9446

Beracz,Gerti | (voc)
Wollie Kaiser Timeghost
Tust Du Fühlen Gut | Jazz Haus Musik | JHM 0060 CD

Berbé,Thierry | (cello)
Charlie Haden Quartet West With Strings
Now Is The Hour | Verve | 527827-2

Berberian,John | (oud)
Tony Scott Group
Tony Scott | Verve | 9861063

Beresford,Steve | (p,voc,tb,el-g,beat-box,farfisa)
Alfred 23 Harth Group
Sweet Paris | free flow music | ffm 0291

Berg,Bill | (dr,perctimpani)
Bill Perkins Quintet
Swing Spring | Candid | CCD 79752

Berg,Bob | (sax,ss,tsrecorder)
Barbara Dennerlein Quintet
That's Me | Enja | ENJ-7043 2
Bob Berg Quintet
The Art Of Saxophone | Laserlight | 24652
Cedar Walton Quartet
First Set | Steeplechase | SCCD 31085
Third Set | Steeplechase | SCCD 31179
Horace Silver Quintet With Brass
Horace Silver Retrospective | Blue Note | 495576-2
Horace Silver Quintet With Vocals
Horace Silver Retrospective | Blue Note | 495576-2
Leni Stern Group
Secrets | Enja | ENJ-5093 2
Mike Stern Group
Jigsaw | Atlantic | 7567-82027-2
Odds Or Evens | Atlantic | 7567-82297-2
Standards(And Other Songs) | Atlantic | 7567-82419-2
Tom Harrell Quintet
Visions | Contemporary | CCD 14063-2

Berg,Dick | (fr-h)
Carmen McRae With The Ralph Burns Orchetra
Birds Of A Feather | Decca | 589515-2
Jimmy Heath Orchestra
Cannonball Adderley Birthday Celebration | Fantasy | FANCD 6087-2
Thad Jones-Mel Lewis Orchestra
The Groove Merchant/The Second Race | Laserlight | 24656

Berg,George | (as,b-cl,bassoon,bs,cl,ts,fl,reeds)
(Little)Jimmy Scott With The Billy Taylor Orchestra
Everybody's Somebody's Fool | Decca | 050669-2
Cal Tjader With The Lalo Schifrin Orchestra
Talkin Verve/Roots Of Acid Jazz:Cal Tjader | Verve | 531562-2
Charles Mingus And His Orchestra
The Complete Town Hall Concert | Blue Note | 828353-2
Lalo Schifrin And His Orchestra
Verve Jazz Masters 39:Cal Tjader | Verve | 521858-2
Louis Armstrong With Gordon Jenkins And His Orchestra And Choir
Satchmo In Style | Verve | 549594-2
Ambassador Louis Armstrong Vol.17:Moments To Remember(1952-1956) | Ambassador | CLA 1917
Louis Armstrong With The Gordon Jenkins Orchestra
Ambassador Louis Armstrong Vol.17:Moments To Remember(1952-1956) | Ambassador | CLA 1917
Peggy Lee With The Benny Goodman Orchestra
Peggy Lee & Benny Goodman:The Complete Recordings 1941-1947 | CBS | C2K 65686
Quincy Jones And His Orchestra
Talkin' Verve-Roots Of Acid Jazz:Roland Kirk | Verve | 533101-2

Berg,Henning | (tb)
Berlin Contemporary Jazz Orchestra
Berlin Contemporary Jazz Orchestra | ECM | 1409
Eddie Harris Group With The WDR Big Band
Eddie Harris-The Last Concert | ACT | 9249-2
Henning Berg & John Taylor With 'Tango'
Tango & Company | Jazz Haus Musik | JHM 0085 CD
Henning Berg Quartet
Minnola | Jazz Haus Musik | JHM 0127 CD
Jens Winther And The WDR Big Band
The Escape | dacapo | DCCD 9437
Joachim Ullrich Orchestra
Faces Of The Duke | Jazz Haus Musik | JHM 0045 CD
Vince Mendoza With The WDR Big Band And Guests
Sketches | ACT | 9215-2

Berg,Kirsten Braten | (voc)
Arild Andersen Sextet
Sagn | ECM | 1435

Berg,Richard | (fr-h)
Dizzy Gillespie And His Orchestra
Gillespiana And Carnegie Hall Concert | Verve | 519809-2
Talking Verve:Dizzy Gillespie | Verve | 533846-2
Ultimate Dizzy Gillespie | Verve | 557535-2
Stan Getz With The Eddie Sauter Orchestra
Stan Getz Plays The Music Of Mickey One | Verve | 531232-2

Berg,Rolf | (g)
Lars Gullin Quartet
Lars Gullin 1955/56 Vol.1 | Dragon | DRCD 224
Lars Gullin Quintet
Lars Gullin 1955/56 Vol.1 | Dragon | DRCD 224

Berg,Thilo | (dr)
Louis Stewart-Heiner Franz Quartet
Jazz Guitar Highlights 1 | Jardis Records | JRCD 20141
Winter Song | Jardis Records | JRCD 9005

Bergalli,Facundo | (g)
Gustavo Bergalli Group
Tango In Jazz | Touché Music | TMcCD 007

Bergalli,Gustavo | (tpfl-h)
Irene Sjögren Group
Song For A Willow | Touché Music | TMcCD 015
Klaus Ignatzek Quintet
Today Is Tomorrow/Live In Leverkusen | Nabel Records:Jazz Network | CD 4654
Son Of Gaudi | Nabel Records:Jazz Network | CD 4660
Klaus Ignatzek-Claudio Roditi Quintet
Live at Bird's Eye | Village | VILCD 1023-2
Knud Jorgensen-Bengt Hanson-Gustavo Bergalli
Skiss | Touché Music | TMcCD 001
Day Dream | Touché Music | TMcCD 003

Bergen Chamber Ensemble |
Terje Rypdal Quartet With The Bergen Chamber Ensemble
Lux Aeterna | ECM | 1818(017070-2)

Bergendy,Istvan | (as)
Mihaly Tabany Orchestra
Jubilee Edition | double moon | CHRDM 71020

Bergendy,Peter | (ts)

Berger,Bengt | (african-finger-p,tibetan-bell)
Beng Berger Band
Bitter Funeral Beer | ECM | 1179
Don Cherry Group
Don Cherry-The Sonet Recordings:Eternal Now/Live Ankara | Verve | 533049-2

Berger,Dave | (harm)
John Lee Hooker Group
Endless Boogie | MCA | MCD 10413

Berger,Dirk | (g)
Dirk Berger Quartet
Garagenjazz | Jazz Haus Musik | JHM 0090 CD

Berger,Eugene | (v)
Billie Holiday With The Ray Ellis Orchestra
Lady In Satin | CBS | CK 65144

Berger,Karl | (marimba,p,vib,keyboards,balafon)
Albert Mangelsdorff-Karl Berger
Albert Mangelsdorff And His Friends | MPS | 067375-2
Don Cherry Group
Multi Kulti | A&M Records | 395323-2
Gato Barbieri Quintet
The Art Of Saxophone | Laserlight | 24652
Karl Berger-Carlos Ward Duo
Conversations | IN+OUT Records | 77027-2
Karl Berger-Dave Holland Duo
Conversations | IN+OUT Records | 77027-2
Karl Berger-Ingrid Sertso Duo
Conversations | IN+OUT Records | 77027-2
Karl Berger-James Blood Ulmer Duo
Conversations | IN+OUT Records | 77027-2
Karl Berger-Marc Feldman Duo
Conversations | IN+OUT Records | 77027-2
Karl Berger-Ray Anderson Duo
Conversations | IN+OUT Records | 77027-2
Lajos Dudas Quintet
Talk Of The Town | double moon | CHRDM 71012
Lajos Dudas Sextet
Talk Of The Town | double moon | CHRDM 71012

Berger,Michael | (keyboards,samples,vocp)
booMbooM meets Uli Beckerhoff
Resurection Lounge | Laika Records | 35101512
Uli Beckerhoff Group
Stay | Nabel Records:Jazz Network | CD 4636
Uli Beckerhoff Quintet
Original Motion Picture Soundtrack:Das Geheimnis(Secret Of Love) | Nabel Records:Jazz Network | CD 4666
Uli Beckerhoff Septet
Private Life | Nabel Records:Jazz Network | CD 4657

Berger,Sy | (tb)
Elliot Lawrence And His Orchestra
Mullenium | CBS | CK 65678

Bergeron,Deborah | (tpfl-h)
Buddy Childers Big Band
It's What Happening Now! | Candid | CCD 79749

Bergeron,Wayne | (tpfl-h)
Diane Schuur With Orchestra And Strings
The Best Of Diane Schuur | GRP | GRP 98882
The Quincy Jones-Sammy Nestico Orchestra
Basie & Beyond | Warner | 9362-47792-2

Berghofer,Chuck | (b,vocel-b)
Diane Schuur And Her Band
Music Is My Life | Atlantic | 7567-83150-2
Diane Schuur Quintet With B.B.King
The Best Of Diane Schuur | GRP | GRP 98882
Diane Schuur With Orchestra
Love Songs | GRP | GRP 97032
The Best Of Diane Schuur | GRP | GRP 98882
Ella Fitzgerald With The Marty Paich Orchestra
Whisper Not | Verve | 589947-2
Herb Geller Quartet
To Benny & Johnny | Hep | CD 2084
Herb Geller-Chuck Berghofer
To Benny & Johnny | Hep | CD 2084
Ray Walker-John Pisano Trio
Affinity | Jardis Records | JRCD 20032

Jazz Guitar Highlights 1 | Jardis Records | JRCD 20141
Shelly Manne And His Men
Live! At The Manne Hole Vol.1 | Original Jazz Classics | OJCCD 714-2(S 7593)
Live! At The Manne Hole Vol.2 | Original Jazz Classics | OJCCD 715-2(S 7594)
Singers Unlimited With The Patrick Williams Orchestra
The Singers Unlimited:Magic Voices | MPS | 539130-2
The Quincy Jones-Sammy Nestico Orchestra
Basie & Beyond | Warner | 9362-47792-2
Zoot Sims Quintet
Quietly There-Zoot Sims Plays Johnny Mandel | Original Jazz Classics | OJCCD 787-2(2310903)

Berglund,Dan | (b,percstring-arr)
Esbjörn Svensson Trio(E.S.T) With Strings
EST Plays Monk | ACT | 9010-2
Esbjörn Svensson Trio(E.S.T.)
Est-From Gagarin's Point Of View | ACT | 9005-2
Winter In Venice | ACT | 9007-2
Good Morning Susie Soho | ACT | 9009-2
EST Plays Monk | ACT | 9010-2
Strange Place For Snow | ACT | 9011-2
Seven Days Of Falling | ACT | 9012-2
E.S.T. Live | ACT | 9295-2
Nils Landgren Funk Unit With Guests
5000 Miles | ACT | 9271-2
Nils Landgren With The Esbjörn Svensson Trio
Ballads | ACT | 9268-2
Viktoria Tolstoy Group & Strings
Shining On You | ACT | 9701-2
Viktoria Tolstoy With The Esbjörn Svensson Trio
Viktoria Tolstoy:White Russian | Blue Note | 821220-2

Bergman,Eddie | (v)
Ben Pollack And His Park Central Orchestra
Planet Jazz:Jack Teagarden | Planet Jazz | 2161236-2
Jazz:The Essential Collection Vol.3 | IN+OUT Records | 78013-2

Bergman,Matthias | (fl-htp)
Andreas Schnerman Quartet
Welcome To My Backyard | Edition Collage | EC 535-2
Andreas Schnerman Quintet
Welcome To My Backyard | Edition Collage | EC 535-2
Andreas Schnerman Sextet
Welcome To My Backyard | Edition Collage | EC 535-2
Frank Sackenheim Quintet
The Music Of Chance | Jazz 4 Ever Records:Jazz Network | J4E 4753

Bergmann,Matthias | (tpfl-h)
Andreas Schnerman Quartet
4 In One | Edition Collage | EC 526-2

Bergmann,Thomas | (tb)
Brass Attack
Brecht Songs | Tutu Records | 888190-2*

Bergonzi,Jerry | (ss,ts,bel-b)
George Gruntz Concert Jazz Band
Blues 'N Dues Et Cetera | Enja | ENJ-6072 2
Miles Davis With Gil Evans Orchestra, The George Gruntz Concert Jazz Band And Guests
Miles & Quincy Live At Montreux | Warner | 9362-45221-2

Bergström,Jonas | (as)
Lars Gullin Octet
Lars Gullin 1951/52 Vol.5:First Walk | Dragon | DRCD 380

Beridot,Marie-Hélène | (v)
Stephane Grappelli With The Michel Legrand Orchestra
Grapelli Story | Verve | 515807-2

Berigan,Bunny | (tp,arrvoc)
A Jam Session At Victor
Planet Jazz:Fats Waller | Planet Jazz | 2152058-2
Planet Jazz:Jazz Greatest Hits | Planet Jazz | 2169648-2
All Star Band
Planet Jazz:Jack Teagarden | Planet Jazz | 2161236-2
Benny Goodman And His Orchestra
Planet Jazz:Benny Goodman | Planet Jazz | 2152054-2
Planet Jazz:Swing | Planet Jazz | 2169651-2
Bud Freeman All Stars
The Bud Freeman All-Star Sessions | Prestige | PRCD 24286-2
Gene Gifford And His Orchestra
Planet Jazz:Bud Freeman | Planet Jazz | 2161240-2
Louis Armstrong And His Orchestra
Louis Armstrong:Swing That Music | Laserlight | 36056
Tommy Dorsey And His Orchestra
Planet Jazz:Frank Sinatra & Tommy Dorsey | Planet Jazz | 2152067-2
Planet Jazz:Tommy Dorsey | Planet Jazz | 2159972-2
Planet Jazz:Big Bands | Planet Jazz | 2169649-2
Planet Jazz:Swing | Planet Jazz | 2169651-2
Planet Jazz:Male Jazz Vocalists | Planet Jazz | 2169657-2
Frank Sinatra And The Tommy Dorsey Orchestra | RCA | 2668701-2

Berk,Ata | (dr)
Bill Ramsey & His Trio
Caldonia And More... | Bear Family Records | BCD 16151 AH

Berkovitz,Joe | (p)
Don Byron Quintet
Tuskegee Experiments | Nonesuch | 7559-79280-2
Don Byron-Joe Berkovitz
Tuskegee Experiments | Nonesuch | 7559-79280-2

Berle,Joe | (p)
Johnny Pace With The Chet Baker Quintet
Chet Baker Introduces Johnny Pace | Original Jazz Classics | OJCCD 433-2(RLP 12-292)

Berlin Contemporary Jazz Orchestra |
Berlin Contemporary Jazz Orchestra
Berlin Contemporary Jazz Orchestra | ECM | 1409

Berlin Radio Big Band,The |
Nana Mouskouri With The Berlin Radio Big Band
Nana Swings | Mercury | 074394-2

Berlin,Frieder | (p)
Frieder Berlin Trio
Soul Fingers | Satin Doll Productions | SDP 1039-1 CD
Regina Büchner's Jazz 4 Fun
Jazz 4 Fun | Satin Doll Productions | SDP 1017-1 CD

Berlin,Jeff | (b,distortion-b,el-b,voc,el-b-solo)
Klaus Doldinger Jubilee
Doldinger's Best | ACT | 9224-2
Klaus Doldinger With Orchestra
Lifelike | Warner | 2292-46478-2
Klaus Doldinger With Orchestra And Etta James
Lifelike | Warner | 2292-46478-2

Berliner,Jay | (el-gg)
Charles Mingus Orchestra
Mingus Mingus Mingus | Impulse(MCA) | 951170-2
The Black Saint And The Sinner Lady | Impulse(MCA) | 951174-2
James Carter Group
Chasin' The Gypsy | Atlantic | 7567-83304-2
Milt Jackson And His Orchestra
Sunflower | CTI | ZK 65131
Ron Carter Group
Songs For You | Milestone | MCD 47099-2
Peg Leg | Original Jazz Classics | OJCCD 621-2
Ron Carter Octet
New York Slick | Original Jazz Classics | OJCCD 916-2(M 9096)

Berlipp,Friedel | (bongos)
Harald Banter Ensemble
Deutsches Jazz Festival 1954/1955 | Bear Family Records | BCD 15430

Berman,Marty | (as,b-cl,bscl)
Tommy Dorsey And His Orchestra
Planet Jazz:Tommy Dorsey | Planet Jazz | 2159972-2

Berman,Sonny | (tp)
Woody Herman And His Orchestra
The Legends Of Swing | Laserlight | 24659
Woody Herman:Four Brother | Dreyfus Jazz Line | FDM 36722-2

Louis Armstrong-Jack Teagarden-Woody Herman:Midnights At V-Disc | Jazz Unlimited | JUCD 2048
Woody Herman And His Woodshoppers
Woody Herman (And The Herd) At Carnegie Hall | Verve | 559833-2
Woody Herman And The Herd
Woody Herman (And The Herd) At Carnegie Hall | Verve | 559833-2

Bern,Alan | (accordeon)
Guy Klucevsek-Alan Bern
Accordance | Winter&Winter | 910058-2

Bernal,Gil | (ts)
Lionel Hampton Orchestra
The Big Bands Vol.1.The Snader Telescriptions | Storyville | 4960043

Bernard Wright | (synth)
Miles Davis Group
Tutu | Warner | 7599-25490-2

Bernard,Cy | (cello)
Frank Sinatra With Orchestra
Planet Jazz:Frank Sinatra & Tommy Dorsey | Planet Jazz | 2152067-2
Harry James And His Orchestra
Trumpet Blues:The Best Of Harry James | Capitol | 521224-2

Bernard,Eddie | (p)
Django Reinhardt And His Quintet
Peche À La Mode-The Great Blue Star Sessions 1947/1953 | Verve | 835418-2
Django Reinhardt And The Quintet Du Hot Club De France
Planet Jazz:Django Reinhardt | Planet Jazz | 2152071-2
Planet Jazz Sampler | Planet Jazz | 2152326-2
Django's Music
Peche À La Mode-The Great Blue Star Sessions 1947/1953 | Verve | 835418-2
Sidney Bechet And His Feetwarmers
Jazz In Paris:Sidney Bechet Et Claude Luther | EmArCy | 159821-2 PMS
Sidney Bechet:Summertime | Dreyfus Jazz Line | FDM 36712-2
Sidney Bechet And His Orchestra
Jazz In Paris:Sidney Bechet Et Claude Luther | EmArCy | 159821-2 PMS
Sidney Bechet-Teddy Buckner Sextet
Planet Jazz:Sidney Bechet | Planet Jazz | 2152063-2

Bernard,Will | (el-gg)
Don Cherry Group
Multi Kulti | A&M Records | 395323-2
Rinde Eckert Group
Story In,Story Out | Intuition Records | INT 3507-2

Bernardi,Noni | (as,arrsax)
Benny Goodman And His Orchestra
More Camel Caravans | Phontastic | NCD 8843/4
More Camel Caravans | Phontastic | NCD 8845/6
Bob Crosby And His Orchestra
Swing Legens:Bob Crosby | Nimbus Records | NI 2011
Tommy Dorsey And His Orchestra
Planet Jazz:Tommy Dorsey | Planet Jazz | 2159972-2

Bernardo,Noni | (as)
Bob Crosby And His Orchestra
Swing Legens:Bob Crosby | Nimbus Records | NI 2011

Berne,Tim | (as,bs,reverse-voodoo-vib,tsvoice)
Hank Roberts Group
Black Pastels | JMT Edition | 919016-2
Herb Robertson Group
The Little Trumpet | JMT Edition | 919007-2
Herb Robertson Quintet
'X'-cerpts:Live At Willisau | JMT Edition | 919013-2
John Zorn Group
Spy Vs. Spy-The Music Of Ornette Coleman | Nonesuch | 7559-60844-2
Tim Berne-Marc Ducret-Tom Rainey
Big Satan | Winter&Winter | 910005-2

Bernhardt,Jens | (p)
Landes Jugend Jazz Orchester Hessen
Touch Of Lips | hr music.de | hrmj 004-01 CD

Bernhardt,Warren | (el-p,keyboards,synth,p,clavinet)
Kenny Burrell With The Don Sebesky Orchestra
Verve Jazz Masters 45:Kenny Burrell | Verve | 527652-2
Mike Mainieri Group
Jazz Life Vol.2:From Seventh At Avenue South | Storyville | 4960763
Steps Ahead
Modern Times | Elektra | 7559-60351-2

Bernhart,Milton 'Milt' | (tbv-tb)
Anita O'Day With The Buddy Bregman Orchestra
Pick Yourself Up | Verve | 517329-2
Astrud Gilberto With Antonio Carlos Jobim And The Marty Paich Orchestra
The Antonio Carlos Jobim Songbook | Verve | 525472-2
Astrud Gilberto With The Marty Paich Orchestra
Verve Jazz Masters 9:Astrud Gilberto | Verve | 519824-2
Buddy Bregman And His Orchestra
Swinging Kicks | Verve | 559514-2
Ella Fitzgerald With The Billy May Orchestra
Ella Fitzgerald-First Lady Of Song | Verve | 517898-2
The Best Of The Song Books | Verve | 519804-2
Verve Jazz Masters 6:Ella Fitzgerald | Verve | 519822-2
The Best Of The Song Books:The Ballads | Verve | 521867-2
Verve Jazz Masters 46:Ella Fitzgerald-The Jazz Sides | Verve | 527655-2
Love Songs:The Best Of The Song Books | Verve | 531762-2
Ella Fitzgerald Sings The Harold Arlen Song Book | Verve | 589108-2
For The Love Of Ella Fitzgerald | Verve | 841765-2
Ella Fitzgerald With The Buddy Bregman Orchestra
Ella Fitzgerald-First Lady Of Song | Verve | 517898-2
Love Songs:The Best Of The Song Books | Verve | 531762-2
Ella Fitzgerald Sings The Cole Porter Songbook | Verve | 537257-2
Ella Fitzgerald Sings The Rodgers And Hart Song Book | Verve | 537258-2
Ella Fitzgerald With The Frank DeVol Orchestra
Get Happy! | Verve | 523321-2
Ella Fitzgerald With The Nelson Riddle Orchestra
The Best Of The Song Books:The Ballads | Verve | 521867-2
Oh Lady Be Good:The Best Of The Gershwin Songbook | Verve | 529581-2
Love Songs:The Best Of The Song Books | Verve | 531762-2
Ella Fitzgerald Sings The Johnny Mercer Songbook | Verve | 539057-2
Howard Rumsey's Lighthouse All-Stars
Sunday Jazz A La Lighthouse Vol.2 | Original Jazz Classics | OJCCD 972-2(S 2501)
June Christy With The Pete Rugolo Orchestra
Something Cool(The Complete Mono & Stereo Versions) | Capitol | 534069-2
Maynard Ferguson And His Orchestra
Verve Jazz Masters 52:Maynard Ferguson | Verve | 529905-2
Maynard Ferguson Band
Verve Jazz Masters 52:Maynard Ferguson | Verve | 529905-2
Nat King Cole Quartet With The Stan Kenton Orchestra
Nat King Cole:For Sentimental Reasons | Dreyfus Jazz Line | FDM 36740-2
Pete Rugolo And His Orchestra
Thriller/Richard Diamon(Original Jazz Scores From 2 Classics TV Series) | Fresh Sound Records | FSCD 2015
Shorty Rogers And His Giants
PLanet Jazz:Shorty Rogers | Planet Jazz | 2159976-2
Shorty Rogers And His Orchestra Feat. The Giants
PLanet Jazz:Shorty Rogers | Planet Jazz | 2159976-2
Stan Kenton And His Orchestra
Swing Vol.1 | Storyville | 4960343
Great Swing Classics In Hi-Fi | Capitol | 521223-2
Stan Kenton Portraits On Standards | Capitol | 531571-2
One Night Stand | Choice | CHCD 71051
Van Alexander Orchestra
Home Of Happy Feet/Swing! Staged For Sound! | Capitol | 535211-2

Berns,Pepe | (b)
Andreas Schnerman Quartet
4 In One | Edition Collage | EC 526-2
Welcome To My Backyard | Edition Collage | EC 535-2
Andreas Schnerman Quintet
Welcome To My Backyard | Edition Collage | EC 535-2
Andreas Schnerman Sextet
Welcome To My Backyard | Edition Collage | EC 535-2
Jan Von Klewitz Quintet
Bonehenge Suite | Jazz Haus Musik | JHM 0078 CD
Joachim Ullrich Orchestra
Faces Of The Duke | Jazz Haus Musik | JHM 0045 CD
Rolf Zielke Trio Feat. Mustafa Boztüy
Rolf Zielke Trio Feat. Mustafa Boztüy | Jazz 'n' Arts Records | JNA 0602

Bernstein,Artie | (b)
Adrian Rollini And His Orchestra
Jazz:The Essential Collection Vol.3 | IN+OUT Records | 78013-2
Benny Goodman And His All Star Sextet
Charlie Christian:Swing To Bop | Dreyfus Jazz Line | FDM 36715-2
Benny Goodman And His Orchestra
Jazz:The Essential Collection Vol.3 | IN+OUT Records | 78013-2
Charlie Christian:Swing To Bop | Dreyfus Jazz Line | FDM 36715-2
More Camel Caravans | Phontastic | NCD 8845/6
Benny Goodman Septet feat.Count Basie
Charlie Christian:Swing To Bop | Dreyfus Jazz Line | FDM 36715-2
Benny Goodman Sextet
Charlie Christian:Swing To Bop | Dreyfus Jazz Line | FDM 36715-2
More Camel Caravans | Phontastic | NCD 8845/6
From Spiritual To Swing | Vanguard | VCD 169/71
Billie Holiday With Teddy Wilson And His Orchestra
Billie's Love Songs | Nimbus Records | NI 2000
Count Basie And His Orchestra
From Spiritual To Swing | Vanguard | VCD 169/71
Jack Teagarden And His Orchestra
Jazz:The Essential Collection Vol.3 | IN+OUT Records | 78013-2
Jack Teagarden With Orchestra
Jazz:The Essential Collection Vol.3 | IN+OUT Records | 78013-2
Lena Horne With The Lou Bring Orchestra
Planet Jazz:Lena Horne | Planet Jazz | 2165373-2
Planet Jazz:Female Jazz Vocalists | Planet Jazz | 2169656-2
Lionel Hampton And His Orchestra
Planet Jazz:Coleman Hawkins | Planet Jazz | 2152055-2
Planet Jazz:Lionel Hampton | Planet Jazz | 2152059-2
Planet Jazz Sampler | Planet Jazz | 2152326-2
Planet Jazz:Jazz Saxophone | Planet Jazz | 2169653-2
Jazz:The Essential Collection Vol.3 | IN+OUT Records | 78013-2

Bernstein,Peter | (g)
Helmut Kagerer-Peter Bernstein Quartet
Jazz Guitar Highlights 1 | Jardis Records | JRCD 20141
April In New York | Jardis Records | JRCD 9818
Jason Seizer With The Larry Goldings Trio
Sketches | Organic Music | ORGM 9710
Jimmy Cobb's Mob
Cobb's Groove | Milestone | MCD 9334-2
Joshua Redman Quintet
Freedom In The Goove | Warner | 9362-46330-2
Klaus Doldinger Group
Back In New York:Blind Date | Atlantic | 3984-26922-2
Teodross Avery Quartet
My Generation | Impulse(MCA) | 951181-2

Bernstein,Steven | (slide-tp,tp,co,fl-h,crooning)
Carla Bley Band
The Very Big Carla Bley Band | Watt | 23
Karen Mantler Group
My Cat Arnold | Watt | XtraWatt/3
Karen Mantler And Her Cat Arnold Get The Flu | Watt | XtraWatt/5
Lounge Lizards
Live In Berlin 1991-Vol.2 | Intuition Records | INT 2055-2
Michael Blake Group
Kingdom Of Champa | Intuition Records | INT 3189-2
Drift | Intuition Records | INT 3212-2

Berriel,Almeida Pedro F. | (percvoc)
Conjunto Clave Y Guaguanco
Dejala En La Puntica | TipToe | TIP-888829 2

Berrios,Steve | (bata,bells,clave,cabasa,checkere)
Essence All Stars
Afro Cubano Chant | Hip Bop | HIBD 8009
Hot Jazz Bisquits | Hip Bop | HIBD 8801
Freddy Cole With Band
A Circle Of Love | Fantasy | FCD 9674-2
To The End Of The Earth | Fantasy | FCD 9675-2
Jerry Gonzalez & Fort Apache Band
The River Is Deep | Enja | ENJ-4040 2
Michael Brecker Group
Now You See It...(Now You Don't) | GRP | GRP 96222
Mongo Santamaria And His Band
Montreux Heat! | Pablo | PACD 5317-2
Mongo Santamaria And His Orchestra
Jazzin' Vol.2: The Music Of Stevie Wonder | Fantasy | FANCD 6088-2
Mongo Santamaria Group With Dizzy Gillespie And Toots Thielemans
Summertime-Digital At Montreux 1980 | Original Jazz Classics | OJCCD 626-2(2308229)
Montreux Heat! | Pablo | PACD 5317-2
Pucho & His Latin Soul Brothers
Jazzin' With The Soul Brothers | Fantasy | FANCD 6086-2
Rip A Dip | Milestone | MCD 9247-2

Berroa,Ignacio | (dr,rainmaker,timbalestrap-dr)
Dizzy Gillespie And The United Nation Orchestra
7.Zelt-Musik-Festival:Jazz Events | Zounds | CD 2730001
Gonzalo Rubalcaba Quartet
Supernova | Blue Note | 531172-2
Gonzalo Rubalcaba Trio
Inner Voyage | Blue Note | 499241-2
Supernova | Blue Note | 531172-2
Gonzalo Rubalcaba Trio With Michael Brecker
Inner Voyage | Blue Note | 499241-2

Berry,Bill | (co,tpvib)
Billy Strayhorn Orchestra
Johnny Hodges With Billy Strayhorn And The Orchestra | Verve | 557543-2
Duke Ellington And His Orchestra
Jazz Festival Vol.2 | Storyville | 4960743
Duke Ellington And His Orchestra feat. Paul Gonsalves | Original Jazz Classics | OJCCD 623-2
The Jazz Giants Play Duke Ellington:Caravan | Prestige | PCD 24227-2
Jimmy Smith With Orchestra
Jimmy Smith-Talkin' Verve | Verve | 531563-2
Johnny Hodges Orchestra
Verve Jazz Masters 35:Johnny Hodges | Verve | 521857-2
Johnny Hodges With Billy Strayhorn And The Duke Ellington Orchestra
Verve Jazz Masters 35:Johnny Hodges | Verve | 521857-2
Maynard Ferguson Orchestra With Chris Connor
Two's Company | Roulette | 837201-2
Ruth Brown With Orchestra
Fine And Mellow | Fantasy | FCD 9663-2
Thad Jones-Mel Lewis Orchestra
The Groove Merchant/The Second Race | Laserlight | 24656

Berry,Chuck | (gvoc)
Bessie Smith And Her Band
Jazz:The Essential Collection Vol.3 | IN+OUT Records | 78013-2
Chuck Berry With The Blues Band
Newport Jazz Festival 1958,July 3rd-6th Vol.3:Blues In The Night No.1 | Phontastic | NCD 8815

Berry,Emmett | (tp)
Billie Holiday With Teddy Wilson And His Orchestra
Billie's Love Songs | Nimbus Records | NI 2000
Cannonball Adderley And His Orchestra
Verve Jazz Masters 31:Cannonball Adderley | Verve | 522651-2

Count Basie And His Orchestra
Planet Jazz:Count Basie | Planet Jazz | 2152068-2
Planet Jazz Sampler | Planet Jazz | 2152326-2
Planet Jazz:Jimmy Rushing | RCA | 2165371-2
Planet Jazz:Jazz Greatest Hits | Planet Jazz | 2169648-2
Planet Jazz:Big Bands | Planet Jazz | 2169649-2
Jazz:The Essential Collection Vol.3 | IN+OUT Records | 78013-2
Count Basie,His Instrumentals & Rhyhtm
Planet Jazz:Count Basie | Planet Jazz | 2152068-2
Jazz:The Essential Collection Vol.3 | IN+OUT Records | 78013-2
Della Reese With The Sy Oliver Orchestra
Misty Blue:Sweet Sisters Swing Songs Of Sorrow And Sadness | Blue Note | 521151-2
Emmett Berry-Sammy Price Orchestra
Americans Swinging In Paris:Sammy Price | EMI Records | 539650-2
Fletcher Henderson And His Orchestra
Jazz:The Essential Collection Vol.3 | IN+OUT Records | 78013-2
Johnny Hodges And His Band
Verve Jazz Masters 35:Johnny Hodges | Verve | 521857-2
Johnny Hodges Orchestra
Highlights From The Duke Ellington Centennial Edition | RCA | 2663672-2
Lucky Thompson Quintet
Americans Swinging In Paris:Lucky Thompson | EMI Records | 539651-2
Sammy Price Quintet
Americans Swinging In Paris:Sammy Price | EMI Records | 539650-2
Sidney Bechet With Sammy Price's Bluesicians
Planet Jazz:Sidney Bechet | Planet Jazz | 2152063-2
Teddy Wilson Sextet
The Complete Associated Transcriptions,1944 | Storyville | STCD 8236

Berry,Leon 'Chu' | (tsbs)
Billie Holiday With Teddy Wilson And His Orchestra
Billie's Love Songs | Nimbus Records | NI 2000
Fletcher Henderson And His Orchestra
Jazz:The Essential Collection Vol.1 | IN+OUT Records | 78011-2
Gene Krupa's Swing Band
Planet Jazz:Swing | Planet Jazz | 2169651-2
Lionel Hampton And His Orchestra
Planet Jazz:Coleman Hawkins | Planet Jazz | 2152055-2
Planet Jazz:Ben Webster | RCA | 2165368-2
Planet Jazz:Jazz Saxophone | Planet Jazz | 2169653-2
Jazz:The Essential Collection Vol.3 | IN+OUT Records | 78013-2
Spike Hughes And His Negro Orchestra
Jazz:The Essential Collection Vol.3 | IN+OUT Records | 78013-2
Wingy Mannone And His Orchestra
Planet Jazz:Jazz Trumpet | Planet Jazz | 2169654-2
Planet Jazz:Male Jazz Vocalists | Planet Jazz | 2169657-2

Berry,Leroy | (bjg)
Benny Moten's Kansas City Orchestra
Planet Jazz:Ben Webster | RCA | 2165368-2
Planet Jazz:Jimmy Rushing | RCA | 2165371-2
Planet Jazz:Swing | Planet Jazz | 2169651-2
Jazz:The Essential Collection Vol.3 | IN+OUT Records | 78013-2

Berry,Steve | (b,el-btb)
Mike Westbrook Brass Band
Glad Day:Settings Of William Blake | Enja | ENJ-9376 2
Mike Westbrook Orchestra
Bar Utopia-A Big Band Cabaret | Enja | ENJ-9333 2
The Orchestra Of Smith's Academy | Enja | ENJ-9358 2

Berson,Ingrid | (voc)
Freddie Brocksieper Orchester
Shot Gun Boogie | Bear Family Records | BCD 16277 AH

Berstein,Steven | (tpco)
Lounge Lizards
Berlin 1991 Part 1 | Intuition Records | INT 2044-2

Bert,Eddie | (tbvoc)
Birdland Dream Band
Birdland Dream Band | RCA | 2663873-2
Charles Mingus And His Orchestra
The Complete Town Hall Concert | Blue Note | 828353-2
Charles Mingus Orchestra
Charles Mingus:Pre-Bird(Mingus Revisited) | Verve | 538636-2
Charles Mingus Quintet
Charles Mingus-The Complete Debut Recordings | Debut | 12 DCD 4402-2
Mingus At The Bohemia | Original Jazz Classics | OJC20 045-2
The Charles Mingus Quintet+Max Roach | Original Jazz Classics | OJC20 440-2(F 6009)
Elliot Lawrence And His Orchestra
The Elliot Lawrence Big Band Swings Cohn & Kahn | Fantasy | FCD 24761-2
Jimmy McGriff Orchestra
Swingin' The Blues-Jumpin' The Blues | Laserlight | 24654
Lena Horne With The Lennie Hayton Orchestra
Planet Jazz:Lena Horne | Planet Jazz | 2165373-2
Stan Getz With The Eddie Sauter Orchestra
Stan Getz Plays The Music Of Mickey One | Verve | 531232-2
Thad Jones-Mel Lewis Orchestra
The Groove Merchant/The Second Race | Laserlight | 24656
Thelonious Monk And His Orchestra
Greatest Hits | CBS | CK 65422
Thelonious Monk:85th Birthday Celebration | zyx records | FANCD 6076-2
At Town Hall | Original Jazz Classics | OJCCD 135-2

Berthenet,Gilles | (tp)
Frank Wess Meets The Paris-Barcelona Swing Connection
Paris-Barcelona Connection | Fresh Sound Records | FSNT 002 CD

Berton,Vic | (b,dr,celesteharpophone)
Red And Miff's Stompers
Planet Jazz:Jazz Trumpet | Planet Jazz | 2169654-2
Roger Wolfe Kahn And His Orchestra
Planet Jazz:Jack Teagarden | Planet Jazz | 2161236-2

Bertoncini,Gene | (el-gg)
Grover Washington Jr. Orchestra
Jazzrock-Anthology Vol.3:Fusion | Zounds | CD 27100555
Paul Desmond Orchestra
Late Night Sax | CBS | 487798-2
Skylark | CTI | ZK 65133
Wayne Shorter Orchestra
Wayne Shorter:The Classic Blue Note Recordings | Blue Note | 540856-2

Bertram,Walter | (p)
Elke Reiff Quartett
There Is More | Laika Records | 35101112

Bertrami,Jose Roberto | (el-p,org,keyboards,perc,voc,vocoder)
Azymuth
Jazzrock-Anthology Vol.3:Fusion | Zounds | CD 27100555
Ithamara Koorax With Band
Love Dance:The Ballad Album | Milestone | MCD 9327-2
Sarah Vaughan With Orchestra
I Love Brazil | Pablo | 2312101-2
Sarah Vaughan Birthday Celebration | Fantasy | FANCD 6090-2

Bertrand,Pierre | (ts)
Susan Weinert Band
Point Of View | Intuition Records | INT 3272-2

Bertz,Simone | (v)
Abdullah Ibrahim Trio And A String Orchestra
African Suite | TipToe | TIP-888832 2
String Orchestra
African Suite | TipToe | TIP-888832 2

Bery,Shelly | (p)
Michael 'Patches' Stewart Group
Blue Patches | Hip Bop | HIBD 8016

Beschi,Paolo | (cello)
La Gaia Scienza
Love Fugue-Robert Schumann | Winter&Winter | 910049-2

Besiakov,Ben | (p,celesteorg)
Joaquin Chacón-Uffe Markussen European Quintet
Time | Fresh Sound Records | FSNT 051 CD

Bessa,Alfredo | (atabaque,berimbau,guicaperc)
Baden Powell Solo/Group
Three Originals:Tristeza On Guitar/Poema On Guitar/Apaixonado | MPS | 519216-2

Besson,Airelle | (tp)
European Jazz Youth Orchestra
Swinging Europe 3 | dacapo | DCCD 9461

Best,Cliff | (g)
Frankie Laine With Buck Clayton And His Orchestra
Jazz Spectacular | CBS | CK 65507

Best,Denzil | (dr)
Ben Webster Quintet
Jazz:The Essential Collection Vol.3 | IN+OUT Records | 78013-2
Billie Holiday With The Bobby Tucker Quartet
Billie's Love Songs | Nimbus Records | NI 2000
Coleman Hawkins And His Orchestra
Jazz:The Essential Collection Vol.3 | IN+OUT Records | 78013-2
Coleman Hawkins Quartet
Thelonious Monk:The Complete Prestige Recordings | Prestige | 3 PRCD 4428-2
Jazz:The Essential Collection Vol.3 | IN+OUT Records | 78013-2
Thelonious Monk:85th Birthday Celebration | zyx records | FANCD 6076-2
Coleman Hawkins Quintet
Ultimate Coleman Hawkins selected by Sonny Rollins | Verve | 557538-2
Don Byas All Star Quintet
Don Byas:Laura | Dreyfus Jazz Line | FDM 36714-2
Fats Navarro Quintet
Fats Navarro:Nostalgia | Dreyfus Jazz Line | FDM 36736-2
George Shearing Quintet
Verve Jazz Masters 57:George Shearing | Verve | 529900-2
George Shearing Trio
The Story Of Jazz Piano | Laserlight | 24653
Lee Konitz Quintet
Subconcious-Lee | Original Jazz Classics | OJCCD 186-2(P 7004)
Phineas Newborn Jr. Quartet
Fabulous Phineas | RCA | 2179622-2

Best,Donald | (vib)
Donald Byrd Orchestra With Voices
True Blue | Blue Note | 534032-2
The Best Of Blue Note | Blue Note | 796110-2
Donald Byrd Septet + Voices
A New Perspective | Blue Note | 499006-2

Best,John | (tp)
Artie Shaw And His Orchestra
Planet JazzArtie Shaw | Planet Jazz | 2152057-2
Planet Jazz Sampler | Planet Jazz | 2152326-2
Planet Jazz:Swing | Planet Jazz | 2169651-2
Planet Jazz:Female Jazz Vocalists | Planet Jazz | 2169656-2
The Legends Of Swing | Laserlight | 24659
Billy May And His Orchestra
Billy May's Big Fat Brass/Bill's Bag | Capitol | 535206-2
Ella Fitzgerald With Paul Weston And His Orchestra
Ella Fitzgerald Sings The Irving Berlin Song Book | Verve | 543830-2
Ella Fitzgerald With The Paul Weston Orchestra
Get Happy! | Verve | 523321-2
Glenn Miller And His Orchestra
Planet Jazz:Glenn Miller | Planet Jazz | 2152056-2
Planet Jazz:Jazz Greatest Hits | Planet Jazz | 2169648-2
Planet Jazz:Big Bands | Planet Jazz | 2169649-2
The Chesterfield Broadcasts Vol.1 | RCA | 2663113-2
Swing Legends | Nimbus Records | NI 2001
Nat King Cole With The Billy May Orchestra
Nat King Cole:For Sentimental Reasons | Dreyfus Jazz Line | FDM 36740-2
Peggy Lee With The Benny Goodman Orchestra
Peggy Lee & Benny Goodman:The Complete Recordings 1941-1947 | CBS | C2K 65686
The Andrew Sisters With The Glenn Miller Orchestra
The Chesterfield Broadcasts Vol.1 | RCA | 2663113-2
Vic Lewis Jam Session
Vic Lewis:The Golden Years | Candid | CCD 79754

Best,Ravi | (tp)
Lester Bowie's Brass Fantasy
The Odyssee Of Funk & Popular Music | Dreyfus Jazz Line | FDM 37004-2
When The Spitit Returns | Dreyfus Jazz Line | FDM 37016-2

Best,Skeeter | (el-gg)
Earl Hines And His Orchestra
Planet Jazz:Earl Hines | Planet Jazz | 2159973-2
Modern Jazz Sextet
Verve Jazz Masters 50:Sonny Sitt | Verve | 527651-2
The Modern Jazz Sextet | Verve | 559834-2
Ray Charles-Milt Jackson Sextet
Soul Brothers/Soul Meeting | Atlantic | 7567-81951-2

Beths,Gijsbert | (v)
Toots Thielemans And His Orchestra
Verve Jazz Masters Vol.59:Toots Thielemans | Verve | 535271-2

Betrami,Claudio | (b)
Sarah Vaughan With Orchestra
I Love Brazil | Pablo | 2312101-2
Sarah Vaughan Birthday Celebration | Fantasy | FANCD 6090-2

Betsch,John | (dr,cowbellperc)
Dollar Brand Quartet
Africa Tears And Laugher | Enja | ENJ-3039 2
Elvira Plenar Trio
I Was Just... | free flow music | ffm 0191
Jim Pepper & Eagle Wing
Remembrance-Live At The International Jazzfestival Münster | Tutu Records | 888152-2*
Jim Pepper Flying Eagle
Live At New Morning,Paris | Tutu Records | 888194-2*
Klaus König Orchestra
Times Of Devastation/Poco A Poco | Enja | ENJ-6014 22
Hommage A Douglas Adams | Enja | ENJ-6078 2
Mal Waldron Quartet feat. Jim Pepper
The Git-Go At Utopia,Volume Two | Tutu Records | 888148-2*
Mal Waldron Quartet feat.Jim Pepper
Mal, Dance And Soul | Tutu Records | 888102-2*
Quadrologue At Utopia Vol.1 | Tutu Records | 888118-2*
Mal Waldron Trio
Mal, Dance And Soul | Tutu Records | 888102-2*
Marty Cook Group feat. Jim Pepper
Internationales Jazzfestival Münster | Tutu Records | 888110-2*
Red,White,Black & Blue | Tutu Records | 888174-2*
Muneer B.Fennell & The Rhythm String Band
An Encounter With Higher Forces | double moon | CHRDM 71019
Simon Nabatov, String Gang & Percussion
Inside Lookin' Out | Tutu Records | 888104-2*
Steve Lacy-Roswell Rudd Quartet
Monk's Dream | Verve | 543090-2

Bettis,Nat | (perc,xylyodeling)
Donald Byrd Orchestra
Blue Break Beats | Blue Note | 799106-2
Pharoah Sanders Orchestra
Karma | Impulse(MCA) | 951153-2
Thembi | Impulse(MCA) | 951253-2
Deaf Dumb Blind | Impulse(MCA) | 951265-2
The Roots Of Acid Jazz | Impulse(MCA) | IMP 12042

Betts,Harry | (arr,ld,slide-whistle,b-tbtb)
Anita O'Day With The Russ Garcia Orchestra
Verve Jazz Masters 49:Anita O'Day | Verve | 527653-2
Barney Kessel And His Orchestra
Barney Kessel Plays Carmen | Original Jazz Classics | OJC 269(C 7563)
Ella Fitzgerald With Frank De Vol And His Orchestra
Get Happy! | Verve | 523321-2
June Christy With The Pete Rugolo Orchestra
Something Cool(The Complete Mono & Stereo Versions) | Capitol | 534069-2
Nat King Cole Quartet With The Stan Kenton Orchestra
Nat King Cole:For Sentimental Reasons | Dreyfus Jazz Line | FDM 36740-2
Shorty Rogers And His Orchestra Feat. The Giants
PLanet Jazz:Shorty Rogers | Planet Jazz | 2159976-2
Stan Kenton And His Orchestra
Stan Kenton Portraits On Standards | Capitol | 531571-2
One Night Stand | Choice | CHCD 71051

Betts,Keter | (b,b-solocello)
All Star Live Jam Session
Brownie-The Complete EmArCy Recordings Of Clifford Brown | EmArCy | 838306-2
Benny Carter And His Orchestra
Jazz At The Philharmonic:The Montreux Collection | Pablo | PACD 5306-2
Bobby Timmons Trio
Bobby Timmons:The Prestige Trio Sessions | Prestige | PRCD 24277-2
Cannonball Adderley And His Orchestra
Verve Jazz Masters 31:Cannonball Adderley | Verve | 522651-2
Charlie Byrd Group
Byrd In The Wind | Original Jazz Classics | OJCCD 1086(RS 9449)
Charlie Byrd Orchestra
Latin Byrd | Milestone | MCD 47005-2
Charlie Byrd Quartet
Latin Byrd | Milestone | MCD 47005-2
Blues Sonata | Original Jazz Classics | OJC20 1063(RS 9453)
Byrd's Word! | Original Jazz Classics | OJCCD 1054-2(R 9448)
Charlie Byrd Quintet
Latin Byrd | Milestone | MCD 47005-2
Charlie Byrd Septet
Latin Byrd | Milestone | MCD 47005-2
Charlie Byrd Sextet
Byrd's Word! | Original Jazz Classics | OJCCD 1054-2(R 9448)
Charlie Byrd Trio
Blues Sonata | Original Jazz Classics | OJC20 1063(RS 9453)
Byrd At The Gate | Original Jazz Classics | OJC20 262-2
Byrd's Word! | Original Jazz Classics | OJCCD 1054-2(R 9448)
At The Village Vanguard | Original Jazz Classics | OJCCD 669-2(RLP 9452)
Mr. Guitar Charlie Byrd | Original Jazz Classics | OJCCD 998-2(R 9450)
Charlie Byrd Trio And Guests
Byrd At The Gate | Original Jazz Classics | OJC20 262-2
Charlie Byrd Trio With Voices
Byrd Song | Original Jazz Classics | OJCCD 1092-2(RS 9481)
Charlie Byrd-Keter Betts
Byrd's Word! | Original Jazz Classics | OJCCD 1054-2(R 9448)
Chuck Brown And The Second Chapter Band
Timeless | Minor Music | 801068
Dinah Washington And Her Band
After Hours With Miss D | Verve | 0760562
Verve Jazz Masters 40:Dinah Washington | Verve | 522055-2
Dinah Washington And Her Orchestra
For Those In Love | EmArCy | 514073-2
Ella Fitzgerald With Count Basie And His Orchestra
Digital III At Montreux | Original Jazz Classics | OJCCD 996-2(2308223)
Ella Fitzgerald With The Count Basie Orchestra
Bluella:Ella Fitzgerald Sings The Blues | Pablo | 2310960-2
Ella Fitzgerald With The Tommy Flanagan Quartet
Bluella:Ella Fitzgerald Sings The Blues | Pablo | 2310960-2
Ella In London | Original Jazz Classics | OJCCD 974-2(2310711)
Ella Fitzgerald With The Tommy Flanagan Trio
Bluella:Ella Fitzgerald Sings The Blues | Pablo | 2310960-2
Jazz Collection:Ella Fitzgerald | Laserlight | 24397
Ella Fitzgerald-First Lady Of Song | Verve | 517898-2
Jazzin' Vol.2: The Music Of Stevie Wonder | Fantasy | FANCD 6088-2
Montreux '77 | Original Jazz Classics | OJC20 376-2(2308206)
Ella-At The Montreux Jazz Festival 1975 | Original Jazz Classics | OJC20 789-2(2310751)
Jazz At The Philharmonic:The Montreux Collection | Pablo | PACD 5306-2
Jan Harrington With The Mike Hennesey Trio
Remembering Dinah-A Salute To Dinah Washington | Hot Shot Records | HSR 8313-2
Jan Harrington With The Nat Adderley Quintet
Remembering Dinah-A Salute To Dinah Washington | Hot Shot Records | HSR 8313-2
Joao Gilberto Trio
Getz/Gilberto No.2 | Verve | 519800-2
The Antonio Carlos Jobim Songbook | Verve | 525472-2
Keter Betts
Remembering Dinah-A Salute To Dinah Washington | Hot Shot Records | HSR 8313-2
Nat Adderley Quartet
Wes Montgomery-The Complete Riverside Recordings | Riverside | 12 RCD 4408-2
Work Song | Original Jazz Classics | OJC20 363-2
Nat Adderley Quintet
Wes Montgomery-The Complete Riverside Recordings | Riverside | 12 RCD 4408-2
Remembering Dinah-A Salute To Dinah Washington | Hot Shot Records | HSR 8313-2
Work Song | Original Jazz Classics | OJC20 363-2
Nat Adderley Sextet
Wes Montgomery-The Complete Riverside Recordings | Riverside | 12 RCD 4408-2
Work Song | Original Jazz Classics | OJC20 363-2
Stan Getz Sextet
Verve Jazz Masters 8:Stan Getz | Verve | 519823-2
Stan Getz-Charlie Byrd Sextet
Jazz Samba | Verve | 521413-2
The Antonio Carlos Jobim Songbook | Verve | 525472-2
Verve Jazz Masters 53:Stan Getz-Bossa Nova | Verve | 529904-2
Ultimate Stan Getz selected by Joe Henderson | Verve | 557532-2
Stan Getz Highlights | Verve | 847430-2
Tommy Flanagan 3
Montreux '77 | Original Jazz Classics | OJC 372(2308202)

Betz,Werner | (tb)
Helmut Zacharias mit dem Orchester Frank Folken
Ich Habe Rhythmus | Bear Family Records | BCD 15642 AH
Kurt Edelhagen All Stars
Deutsches Jazz Fesival 1954/1955 | Bear Family Records | BCD 15430
Kurt Edelhagen All Stars Und Solisten
Deutsches Jazz Fesival 1954/1955 | Bear Family Records | BCD 15430
Quartet Der Kurt Edelhagen All Stars
Deutsches Jazz Fesival 1954/1955 | Bear Family Records | BCD 15430

Beutler,Allan | (bs,bass-saxreeds)
Stan Kenton And His Orchestra
Adventures In Blues | Capitol | 520089-2
Adventures In Jazz | Capitol | 521222-2

Bey,Andy | (el-p,vocp)
Andy And The Bey Sisters
Andy Bey And The Bey Sisters | Prestige | PCD 24245-2
Andy Bey
Tuesdays In Chinatown | Minor Music | 801099
Andy Bey Group
Tuesdays In Chinatown | Minor Music | 801099
Duke Pearson Orchestra
Deep Blue-The United States Of Mind | Blue Note | 521152-2
Blue Bossa | Blue Note | 795590-2
Gary Bartz Ntu Troop
Jazzin' Vol.2: The Music Of Stevie Wonder | Fantasy | FANCD 6088-2
Horace Silver Quintet

Horace Silver Retrospective | Blue Note | 495576-2
Blue Velvet: Crooners, Swooners And Velvet Vocals | Blue Note | 521153-2
Horace Silver Sextet
Horace Silver Retrospective | Blue Note | 495576-2
Deep Blue-The United States Of Mind | Blue Note | 521152-2
Horace Silver Sextet With Vocals
Horace Silver Retrospective | Blue Note | 495576-2

Bey,Chief | (african-dr,voc,ashiko-dr,balafon)
Ahmed Abdul-Malik Orchestra
Jazz Sounds Of Africa | Prestige | PRCD 24279-2
Art Blakey And The Afro Drum Ensemble
The African Beat | Blue Note | 522666-2
Herbie Mann Group
The Best Of Herbie Mann | Atlantic | 7567-81369-2
Rhino Presents The Atlantic Jazz Gallery | Atlantic | 8122-71257-2
Herbie Mann Septet
Herbie Mann At The Village Gate | Atlantic | 7567-81350-2
Herbie Mann Sextet
Herbie Mann At The Village Gate | Atlantic | 7567-81350-2
Pharoah Sanders Orchestra
Thembi | Impulse(MCA) | 951253-2
Randy Weston African Rhythm
Khepera | Verve | 557821-2

Bey,Geraldine | (voc)
Andy And The Bey Sisters
Andy Bey And The Bey Sisters | Prestige | PCD 24245-2

Bey,Ronnell | (voc)
Max Roach Chorus & Orchestra
To The Max! | Enja | ENJ-7021 22
Wolfgang Lackerschmid-Donald Johnston Group
New Singers-New Songs | Bhakti Jazz | BR 31

Bey,Sadiq | (voc)
The Sidewalks Of New York
Tin Pan Alley:The Sidewalks Of New York | Winter&Winter | 910038-2

Bey,Salome | (voc)
Andy And The Bey Sisters
Andy Bey And The Bey Sisters | Prestige | PCD 24245-2

Beyer,Raymund | (synth)
Ax Genrich Group
Psychedelic Guitar | ATM Records | ATM 3809-AH

Bhattacharya,Debashish | (hindustani-slide-g)
Remember Shakti
Saturday Night In Bombay | Verve | 014184-2

Bhattacharya,Sandip | (tablas,balafonframe-dr)
Boi Akih
Uwa I | Enja | ENJ-9472 2

Biancaniello,Louis | (keyboards,synthprogramming)
Al Jarreau With Band
Heaven And Earth | i.e. Music | 557852-2

Bianchi Chiols,Janaina | (voc)
Toshinori Kondo & Ima plus Guests
Human Market | JA & RO | JARO 4146-2

Bianchi,Marcel | (g)
Quintet Du Hot Club De France
Django/Django In Rome 1949-1050 | BGO Records | BGOCD 366
Django Reinhardt:Echoes Of France | Dreyfus Jazz Line | FDM 36726-2
Django Reinhardt:Souveniers | Dreyfus Jazz Line | FDM 36744-2

Bianchi,Marco | (viola)
La Gaia Scienza
Love Fugue-Robert Schumann | Winter&Winter | 910049-2

Bianchini,Roland | (b)
Claude Luter Et Ses L'Orientais
Jazz In Paris:Sidney Bechet Et Claude Luther | EmArCy | 159821-2 PMS
Sidney Bechet With Claude Luter And His Orchestra
Planet Jazz:Sidney Bechet | Planet Jazz | 2152063-2
Sidney Bechet:Summertime | Dreyfus Jazz Line | FDM 36712-2
Sidney Bechet-Teddy Buckner Sextet
Planet Jazz:Sidney Bechet | Planet Jazz | 2152063-2

Bianco,Francisco | (bs)
Daniel Flors Group
When Least Expected | Fresh Sound Records | FSNT 080 CD

Bianco,Gene | (harp)
Gil Evans Orchestra
Blues In Orbit | Enja | ENJ-3069 2
Grant Green With Orchestra
The Final Comedown(Soundtrack) | Blue Note | 581678-2
Paul Desmond Orchestra
Planet Jazz:Jazz Saxophone | Planet Jazz | 2169653-2
Paul Desmond With Strings
Desmond Blue | RCA | 2663898-2

Bica,Carlos | (b)
Carlos Bica & Azul
Look What They've Done To My Song | Enja | ENJ-9458 2
Carlos Bica Group
Azul | Traumton Records | 4425-2
Gebhard Ullmann Trio
Essencia | Between The Lines | btl 017(Efa 10187-2)
Joel Frahm Quintet
The Rains From A Cloud Do Not Wet The Sky | Nabel Records:Jazz Network | CD 4686
Kölner Saxophon Mafia With Guests
Kölner Saxophon Mafia: 20 Jahre Saxuelle Befreiung | Jazz Haus Musik | JHM 0115 CD
Maria Joao Quintet
Conversa | Nabel Records:Jazz Network | CD 4628
Paul Brody's Tango Toy
Klezmer Stories | Laika Records | 35101222

Bickel,Doug | (pkeyboards)
Maynard Ferguson And His Big Bop Nouveau Band
Maynard Ferguson '93-Footpath Café | Hot Shot Records | HSR 8312-2

Bickert,Ed | (gel-g)
Paul Desmond Quartet
Live | Verve | 543501-2
Singers Unlimited With Rob McConnell And The Boss Brass
The Singers Unlimited:Magic Voices | MPS | 539130-2

Bickford,Bill | (el-g,12-string-g,gvoc)
Ed Schuller & Band
The Eleventh Hour | Tutu Records | 888124-2*
Ed Schuller & The Eleventh Hour Band
Snake Dancing | Tutu Records | 888188-2*
Ed Schuller Quartet feat. Dewey Redman
Mu-Point | Tutu Records | 888154-2*
Gunther Schuller With The WDR Radio Orchestra & Rememberance Band
Witchi Tia To, The Music Of Jim Pepper | Tutu Records | 888204-2*
Jim Pepper & Eagle Wing
Rerembrance-Live At The International Jazzfestival Münster | Tutu Records | 888152-2*
Ku-umba Frank Lacy & The Poker Bigband
Songs From The Musical 'Poker' | Tutu Records | 888150-2*
Marty Cook Conspiracy
Phases Of The Moon | Tutu Records | 888160-2*
Paradox
The First Second | TipToe | TIP-888833 2

Bickl,Gerhard 'Zwei' | (keyboards,grand-pp)
Jenny Evans And Band
Girl Talk | Enja | ENJ-9363 2
Live At The Allotria | ESM Records | ESM 9301
Girl Talk | ESM Records | ESM 9306
Litschie Hrdlicka Group
Falling Lovers | EGO | 93020
Jazz Portraits | EGO | 95080

Bieber,Thomas | (fr-h)
Hans Theessink Group
Crazy Moon | Minor Music | 801052

Biel,Ernst | (dr)
Ernst Bier-Mack Goldsbury Quartet
At Night When You Go To Sleep | Timescrapper | TSCR 9611
Ernst Bier-Mack Goldsbury Quintet
At Night When You Go To Sleep | Timescrapper | TSCR 9611

Bieler,Barbara | (voc)
Jazzensemble Des Hessischen Rundfunks
Jazz Messe-Messe Für Unsere Zeit | hr music.de | hrmj 003-01 CD

Bielly Jr.,Octavio | (b)
Cannonball Adderley With Sergio Mendes And The Bossa Rio Sextet
Blue Bossa | Blue Note | 795590-2

Bier,Ernst | (dr)
Perry Robinson Quartet
Perry Robinson Quartet | Timescrapper | TSCR 9613

Big Allanbik |
Big Allanbik
Batuque Y Blues | Blues Beacon | BLU-1031 2

Big Band |
Louis Armstrong And His All Stars With A Studio Orchestra
What A Wonderful World | MCA | MCD 01876
Peggy Lee With Orchestra
Pass Me By/Big Spender | Capitol | 535210-2

Big Band Bellaterra |
Big Band Bellaterra
Don't Git Sassy | Fresh Sound Records | FSNT 048 CD

Big Bill | (gp)
Bill Ramsey & His Trio
Caldonia And More... | Bear Family Records | BCD 16151 AH

Big Maybelle[Mabel Smith] | (voc)
Big Maybelle With The Blues Band
Newport Jazz Festival 1958,July 3rd-6th Vol.3:Blues In The Night No.1 | Phontastic | NCD 8815

Big Three,The |
The Big Three
Milt Jackson Birthday Celebration | Fantasy | FANCD 6079-2
The Big Three | Original Jazz Classics | OJCCD 805-2(2310757)

Bigard,Barney | (cl,dr,ts,vocss)
Barney Bigard And His Orchestra
Highlights From The Duke Ellington Centennial Edition | RCA | 2663672-2
Jazz:The Essential Collection Vol.3 | IN+OUT Records | 78013-2
Benny Morton's All Stars
The Blue Note Swingtets | Blue Note | 495697-2
Jazz:The Essential Collection Vol.3 | IN+OUT Records | 78013-2
Duke Ellington And His Cotton Club Orchestra
Planet Jazz:Duke Ellington | Planet Jazz | 2152053-2
Jazz:The Essential Collection Vol.2 | IN+OUT Records | 78012-2
Duke Ellington And His Famous Orchestra
Duke Ellington:The Blanton-Webster Band | Bluebird | 21 13181-2
Planet Jazz:Duke Ellington | Planet Jazz | 2152053-2
Planet Jazz:Johnny Hodges | Planet Jazz | 2152065-2
Planet Jazz Sampler | Planet Jazz | 2152326-2
Planet Jazz:Ben Webster | RCA | 2165368-2
Planet Jazz:Big Bands | Planet Jazz | 2169649-2
Planet Jazz:Jazz Trumpet | Planet Jazz | 2169654-2
Planet Jazz:Female Jazz Vocalists | Planet Jazz | 2169656-2
Highlights From The Duke Ellington Centennial Edition | RCA | 2663672-2
Greatest Hits | CBS | 462959-2
Jazz:The Essential Collection Vol.2 | IN+OUT Records | 78012-2
Jazz:The Essential Collection Vol.3 | IN+OUT Records | 78013-2
Duke Ellington:Ko-Ko | Dreyfus Jazz Line | FDM 36717-2
Duke Ellington And His Orchestra
Highlights From The Duke Ellington Centennial Edition | RCA | 2663672-2
Jazz:The Essential Collection Vol.2 | IN+OUT Records | 78012-2
Jazz:The Essential Collection Vol.3 | IN+OUT Records | 78013-2
The Duke At Fargo 1940 | Storyville | STCD 8316/17
Esquire Metropolitan Opera House Jam Session
Jazz:The Essential Collection Vol.3 | IN+OUT Records | 78013-2
Jack Teagarden's Big Eight
Jazz:The Essential Collection Vol.3 | IN+OUT Records | 78013-2
Jelly Roll Morton Trio
Planet Jazz:Jelly Roll Morton | Planet Jazz | 2152060-2
Jelly Roll Morton's Red Hot Peppers
Planet Jazz:Jelly Roll Morton | Planet Jazz | 2152060-2
Jazz:The Essential Collection Vol.1 | IN+OUT Records | 78011-2
King Oliver And His Dixie Syncopators
Jazz:The Essential Collection Vol.1 | IN+OUT Records | 78011-2
King Oliver's Jazz Band
Jazz:The Essential Collection Vol.1 | IN+OUT Records | 78011-2
Louis Armstrong And Gary Crosby With Sonny Burke's Orchestra
Louis Armstrong-My Greatest Songs | MCA | MCD 18347
Louis Armstrong And His All Stars
Jazz Collection:Louis Armstrong | Laserlight | 24366
I Love Jazz | Verve | 543747-2
Satchmo Serenaders | Verve | 543792-2
Louis Armstrong Plays W.C.Handy | CBS | CK 64925
Satch Plays Fats(Complete) | CBS | CK 64927
Louis Armstrong:C'est Si Bon | Dreyfus Jazz Line | FDM 36730-2
Louis Armstrong-My Greatest Songs | MCA | MCD 18347
Swing Legends:Louis Armstrong | Nimbus Records | NI 2012
Louis Armstrong:Wintergarden 1947/Blue Note 1948 | Storyville | STCD 8242
Louis Armstrong And His All Stars With Benny Carter's Orchestra
Ambassador Louis Armstrong Vol.17:Moments To Remember(1952-1956) | Ambassador | CLA 1917
Louis Armstrong And His All Stars With Duke Ellington
Louis Armstrong-Duke Ellington:The Great Summit-Complete Session | Roulette | 524546-2
Louis Armstrong And His All Stars With Sonny Burke's Orchestra
Ambassador Louis Armstrong Vol.17:Moments To Remember(1952-1956) | Ambassador | CLA 1917
Louis Armstrong And His Dixieland Seven
Planet Jazz:Louis Armstrong | Planet Jazz | 2152052-2
Planet Jazz:Jazz Greatest Hits | Planet Jazz | 2169648-2
Planet Jazz:Jazz Trumpet | Planet Jazz | 2169654-2
Planet Jazz:Male Jazz Vocalists | Planet Jazz | 2169657-2
Best Of The Complete RCA Victor Recordings | RCA | 2663636-2
Louis Armstrong:A 100th Birthday Celebration | RCA | 2663694-2
Louis Armstrong:C'est Si Bon | Dreyfus Jazz Line | FDM 36730-2
Swing Legends:Louis Armstrong | Nimbus Records | NI 2012
Louis Armstrong And His Hot Seven
Planet Jazz:Louis Armstrong | Planet Jazz | 2152052-2
Best Of The Complete RCA Victor Recordings | RCA | 2663636-2
Louis Armstrong:A 100th Birthday Celebration | RCA | 2663694-2
Louis Armstrong:C'est Si Bon | Dreyfus Jazz Line | FDM 36730-2
Louis Armstrong And His Orchestra
I Love Jazz | Verve | 543747-2
Satchmo Serenaders | Verve | 543792-2
Louis Armstrong And Omer Simeon With The Sy Oliver Orchestra
Ambassador Louis Armstrong Vol.17:Moments To Remember(1952-1956) | Ambassador | CLA 1917
Louis Armstrong With Benny Carter's Orchestra
Louis Armstrong-My Greatest Songs | MCA | MCD 18347
Louis Armstrong With Sy Oliver And His Orchestra
Satchmo Serenaders | Verve | 543792-2
Louis Armstrong-My Greatest Songs | MCA | MCD 18347
Rex Stewart And His Feetwarmers
Django Reinhardt All Star Sessions | Capitol | 531577-2
The Capitol Jazzmen
The Hollywood Session:The Capitol Jazzmen | Jazz Unlimited | JUCD 2044

Bigband Der Musikschule Der Stadt Brühl |
Bigband Der Musikschule Der Stadt Brühl Mit Gastsolisten
Pangäa | Indigo-Records | 1004 CD

Bigerille,Rene | (fl)
Dizzy Gillespie Orchestra And The Operatic String Orchestra
Jazz In Paris:Dizzy Gillespie And His Operatic Strings Orchestra | EmArCy | 018420-2

Bigge,Carolina | (dr)
The United Women's Orchestra
The Blue One | Jazz Haus Musik | JHM 0099 CD
United Women's Orchestra
Virgo Supercluster | Jazz Haus Musik | JHM 0123 CD

Biggs,Caroline | (voc)
Mike Westbrook Brass Band
Glad Day:Settings Of William Blake | Enja | ENJ-9376 2

Bigham,John | (g,keyboardsdr-programming)
Miles Davis Group
Amandla | Warner | 7599-25873-2

Bigler,Heinz | (ascl)
Four For Jazz
The Best Of Four For Jazz & Benny Bailey | JHM Records | JHM 3615
Four For Jazz & Benny Bailey
The Best Of Four For Jazz & Benny Bailey | JHM Records | JHM 3615
International Chicago-Jazz Orchestra
That's A Plenty | JHM Records | JHM 3621

Bigorna | (fl)
Ithamara Koorax With Band
Love Dance:The Ballad Album | Milestone | MCD 9327-2

Bihlmaier,Dieter | (fl)
Dieter Bihlmaier Selection
Mallet Connection | Bhakti Jazz | BR 33

Bijma,Greetje | (voice)
Greetje Bijma Kwintet
Tales Of A Voice | TipToe | TIP-888808 2
Greetje Bijma Trio
Barefoot | Enja | ENJ-8038 2

Bildhauer,Shekilua | (perc)
Jamenco
Conversations | Trick Music | TM 9202 CD

Bildo,Tom | (tbtuba)
Edward Vesala Group
Lumi | ECM | 1339

Bilhorn,Brad | (dr)
Art Pepper Quartet
Renascene | Galaxy | GCD 4202-2

Bilk,Bernhard 'Mr.Acker' | (clvoc)
Mr.Acker Bilk And His Paramount Jazz Band
The Very Best Of Dixieland Jazz | Verve | 535529-2
The Golden Years Of Revival Jazz,Vol.2 | Storyville | STCD 5507
The Golden Years Of Revival Jazz,Vol.5 | Storyville | STCD 5510
The Golden Years Of Revival Jazz,Vol.6 | Storyville | STCD 5511
The Golden Years Of Revival Jazz,Vol.7 | Storyville | STCD 5512
The Golden Years Of Revival Jazz,Vol.8 | Storyville | STCD 5513
The Golden Years Of Revival Jazz,Vol.9 | Storyville | STCD 5514
The Golden Years Of Revival Jazz,Vol.10 | Storyville | STCD 5515
The Golden Years Of Revival Jazz,Vol.12 | Storyville | STCD 5517
The Golden Years Of Revival Jazz,Vol.13 | Storyville | STCD 5518
The Golden Years Of Revival Jazz,Vol.14 | Storyville | STCD 5519
The Golden Years Of Revibal Jazz,Vol.15 | Storyville | STCD 5520

Bilker,Kurt | (dr)
Lajos Dudas Quartet
Jubilee Edition | double moon | CHRDM 71020
Lajos Dudas Trio
Jubilee Edition | double moon | CHRDM 71020
Olaf Kübler Quartet
When I'm 64 | Village | VILCD 1016-2

Bill Bates Singers: |
Paul Desmond Quartet With The Bill Bates Singers
Desmond | Original Jazz Classics | OJCCD 712-2(F 3235/8082)

Billberg,Rolf | (asts)
Lars Gullin Quintet
Lars Gullin 1955/56 Vol.1 | Dragon | DRCD 224
Stan Kenton With The Danish Radio Big Band
Stan Kenton With The Danish Radio Big Band | Storyville | STCD 8340

Billen,Louis | (cl,asts)
Django Reinhardt With Stan Brenders Et Son Grand Orchestre
Verve Jazz Masters 38:Django Reinhardt | Verve | 516931-2

Biller,Thomas | (b)
Florian Poser Group
Say Yes! | Edition Collage | EC 452-2

Billert-Kucharski,Renate | (viola)
Bernd Konrad Jazz Group With Symphonie Orchestra
Wen Die Götter Lieben | Creative Works Records | CW CD 1010-1

Billings,Bernie | (ts)
Muggsy Spanier And His Ragtime Band
Planet Jazz | Planet Jazz | 2169652-2

Billings,Frank 'Josh' | (drsuitcase)
Mound City Blue Blowers
Planet Jazz:Jack Teagarden | Planet Jazz | 2161236-2

Billingslea,Sandra 'Sandy' | (v)
Abbey Lincoln With The Rodney Kendrick Trio And Guests
A Turtle's Dream | Verve | 527382-2
Ron Carter Quintet With Strings
Pick 'Em/Super Strings | Milestone | MCD 47090-2

Billker,Kurt | (dr)
Frank Kirchner Group
Frank Kirchner | Laika Records | LK 93-036
Lajos Dudas Quartet
Nightlight | double moon | DMCHR 71030
Lajos Dudas Quintet
Talk Of The Town | double moon | CHRDM 71012
Some Great Songs | double moon | DMCD 1005-2
Nightlight | double moon | DMCHR 71030
Lajos Dudas Sextet
Talk Of The Town | double moon | CHRDM 71012

Bilsheim,Dieter | (tp,fl-hpiccolo-tp)
Harry Allen And Randy Sandke Meets The RIAS Big Band Berlin
The Music Of The Trumpet Kings | Nagel-Heyer | CD 037

Bilyk,Matt | (tb)
Warren Vaché And The New York City All-Star Big Band
Swingtime! | Nagel-Heyer | CD 059

Bimbi,Stephania | (recitation)
John McLaughlin Group
The Promise | Verve | 529828-2

Binder,Andreas 'Andi' | (fr-h)
Mind Games
Pretty Fonky | Edition Collage | EC 482-2
Wind Moments | Take Twelve On CD | TT 009-2
Mind Games With Claudio Roditi
Live | Edition Collage | EC 501-2
Vocal Moments | Take Twelve On CD | TT 008-2
Mind Games With Philip Catherine
Pretty Fonky | Edition Collage | EC 482-2
Tom Bennecke & Space Gurilla
Wind Moments | Take Twelve On CD | TT 009-2
William Galison-Mulo Franzl Group
Midnight Sun | Edition Collage | EC 508-2

Binder,Lars | (dr)
Changes
Jazz Changes? | Jazz 'n' Arts Records | 0100
Fritz Münzer Tentet
Blue Ideas | Jazz 'n' Arts Records | 0200
Schlosser/Weber/Böhm/Huber/Binder
L 14,16 | Jazz 4 Ever Records:Jazz Network | J4E 4760

Binetsch,Uli | (tbshell)
Uli Binetsch's Own Bone
Boone Up Blues | Rockwerk Records | CD 011001

Bings,Herbert | (dr)
HR Big Band
The American Songs Of Kurt Weill | hr music.de | hrmj 006-01 CD
Libertango:Homage An Astor Piazolla | hr music.de | hrmj 014-02 CD
HR Big Band With Marjorie Barnes And Frits Landesbergen
Swinging Christmas | hr music.de | hrmj 012-02 CD
HR Big Band With Marjorie Barnes And Frits Landesbergen And Strings
Swinging Christmas | hr music.de | hrmj 012-02 CD
The European Jazz Guitar Orchestra

INTERPRETENVERZEICHNIS

The European Jazz Guitar Orchestra | Jardis Records | JRCD 9307

Binney,David 'Dave' | (as,sampler,cl,live-samples,ss)
Chris Potter Group
Traveling Mercies | Verve | 018243-2
David Binney Group
South | ACT | 9279-2
Balance | ACT | 9411-2
Uri Caine Group
Urlicht/Primal Light | Winter&Winter | 910004-2

Binyon,Larry | (cl,ts,flss)
Ben Pollack And His Park Central Orchestra
Planet Jazz:Jack Teagarden | Planet Jazz | 2161236-2
Jazz:The Essential Collection Vol.3 | IN+OUT Records | 78013-2
Billie Holiday With Toots Camarata And His Orchestra
Billie's Love Songs | Nimbus Records | NI 2000
Fats Waller And His Buddies
Planet Jazz:Jack Teagarden | Planet Jazz | 2161236-2
Jazz:The Essential Collection Vol.3 | IN+OUT Records | 78013-2
Jess Stacy And His Orchestra
Planet Jazz:Jazz Piano | RCA | 2169655-2

Biondi,Gino | (b)
Earl Klugh Group With Strings
Late Night Guitar | Blue Note | 498573-2

Biondi,Ray | (gv)
Anita O'Day With Gene Krupa And His Orchestra
Let Me Off Uptown:Anita O'Day With Gene Krupa | CBS | CK 65625

Biondini,Luciano | (acc)
Gabriele Mirabassi Trio
Latakia Blend | Enja | ENJ-9441 2

Biondo,Chris | (b)
Chuck Brown And The Second Chapter Band
Timeless | Minor Music | 801068

Bird,Jerry | (g)
Jack McDuff Quartet With Orchestra
Moon Rappin' | Blue Note | 538697-2

Bird,Rudy | (perc)
Miles Davis Group
Miles Davis Live From His Last Concert In Avignon | Laserlight | 24327

Birdland Dreamband,The |
Birdland Dream Band
Birdland Dream Band | RCA | 2663873-2

Birdsall,Butch | (voc)
Charlie Parker And His Orchestra
Bird: The Complete Charlie Parker On Verve | Verve | 837141-2
Charlie Parker With Orchestra & The Dave Lambert Singers
Verve Jazz Masters 28:Charlie Parker Plays Standards | Verve | 521854-2

Birdsong,Blanche | (harp)
Stan Getz With Orchestra
Stan Getz Highlights | Verve | 847430-2

Birger,Arne | (b)
Ricardo's Jazzmen
The Golden Years Of Revival Jazz,Vol.4 | Storyville | STCD 5509
The Golden Years Of Revival Jazz,Vol.5 | Storyville | STCD 5510

Birkeland,Oystein | (cello)
Terje Rypdal Group
If Mountains Could Sing | ECM | 1554(523987-2)

Birkle,Markus | (g)
Ralph Abelein Group
Mr. B's Time Machine | Satin Doll Productions | SDP 1042-1 CD

Bisceglie,Nino | (tuba)
Banda Città Ruvo Di Puglia
La Banda/Banda And Jazz | Enja | ENJ-9326 2

Bischof,Willy | (keyboardsp)
Willy Bischof Jazztet
Swiss Air | Jazz Connaisseur | JCCD 9523-2
Willy Bischof Trio
Swiss Air | Jazz Connaisseur | JCCD 9523-2

Biscoe,Chris | (alto-cl,sax,ss,as,bspiccolo)
Mike Westbrook Brass Band
Glad Day:Settings Of William Blake | Enja | ENJ-9376 2
Mike Westbrook Orchestra
Bar Utopia-A Big Band Cabaret | Enja | ENJ-9333 2
The Orchestra Of Smith's Academy | Enja | ENJ-9358 2

Bisharat,Charles | (v)
Charlie Haden Quartet West With Strings
The Art Of The Song | Verve | 547403-2

Bishop Jr.,Walter | (el-p,keyboardsp)
Charlie Parker And His Orchestra
Bird: The Complete Charlie Parker On Verve | Verve | 837141-2
Charlie Parker Quintet
Verve Jazz Masters 28:Charlie Parker Plays Standards | Verve | 521854-2
Charlie Parker:Bird's Best Bop On Verve | Verve | 527452-2
Charlie Parker:The Best Of The Verve Years | Verve | 527815-2
Talkin' Bird | Verve | 559859-2
The Cole Porter Songbook | Verve | 823250-2
Bird: The Complete Charlie Parker On Verve | Verve | 837141-2
Charlie Parker Septet
Talkin' Bird | Verve | 559859-2
Charlie Parker Sextet
Verve Jazz Masters 28:Charlie Parker Plays Standards | Verve | 521854-2
Charlie Parker:The Best Of The Verve Years | Verve | 527815-2
Talkin' Bird | Verve | 559859-2
The Cole Porter Songbook | Verve | 823250-2
Charlie Parker's Jazzers
Bird: The Complete Charlie Parker On Verve | Verve | 837141-2
Jackie McLean Quintet
Capuchin Swing | Blue Note | 540033-2
Ken McIntyre Quintet feat.Eric Dolphy
Eric Dolphy:The Complete Prestige Recordings | Prestige | 9 PRCD-4418-2
Eric Dolphy Birthday Celebration | Fantasy | FANCD 6085-2
Kenny Dorham Quintet
The Jazz Giants Play Sammy Cahn:It's Magic | Prestige | PCD 24226-2
Miles Davis And His Orchestra
Collector's Items | Original Jazz Classics | OJC20 071-2(P 7044)
Miles Davis Sextet
Dig | Original Jazz Classics | OJC20 005-2
The Jazz Giants Play Harold Arlen:Blues In The Night | Prestige | PCD 24201-2
The Jazz Giants Play Miles Davis:Milestones | Prestige | PCD 24225-2
The Prestige Legacy Vol.1:The High Priests | Prestige | PCD 24251-2
Oscar Pettiford Sextet
Charles Mingus-The Complete Debut Recordings | Debut | 12 DCD 4402-2
Shorty Baker-Doc Cheatham Quintet
Shorty & Doc | Original Jazz Classics | OJCCD 839-2(SV 2021)
Stan Getz And His Four Brothers
The Brothers | Original Jazz Classics | OJCCD 008-2
The Prestige Legacy Vol.2:Battles Of Saxes | Prestige | PCD 24252-2
Stan Getz Five Brothers Bop Tenor Sax Stars
Stan Getz:Imagination | Dreyfus Jazz Line | FDM 36733-2
Tubby Hayes And The All Stars
Rahsaan/The Complete Mercury Recordings Of Roland Kirk | Mercury | 846630-2

Bishop,Wallace | (dr)
Earl Hines And His Orchestra
Jazz:The Essential Collection Vol.2 | IN+OUT Records | 78012-2
Great Traditionalists In Europe
Great Traditionalists | Jazzpoint | JP 1046 CD
Lena Horne With The Phil Moore Four
Planet Jazz:Lena Horne | Planet Jazz | 2165373-2
Louis Armstrong With Sy Oliver And His Orchestra
Satchmo Serenaders | Verve | 543792-2
Stuff Smith With The Henri Chaix Trio
Late Woman Blues | Storyville | STCD 8328

Bisquay,Anne-Gaelle | (cello)
Abbey Lincoln With The Rodney Kendrick Trio And Guests
A Turtle's Dream | Verve | 527382-2

Bisquay,Yann | (v)
Stephane Grappelli With The Michel Legrand Orchestra
Grapelli Story | Verve | 515807-2

Biss,Harry | (p)
Zoot Sims Quartet
Zoot Sims Quartets | Original Jazz Classics | OJCCD 242-2(P 7026)

Bissill,Richard | (fr-h)
Dee Dee Bridgewater With Orchestra
Dear Ella | Verve | 539102-2
John Surman-Jack DeJohnette With The London Brass
Printed In Germany | ECM | 1802(017065-2)

Bissonette,Gregg | (drperc)
Larry Carlton Group
The Gift | GRP | GRP 98542

Biste,Paul | (as)
Helmut Zacharias mit dem Orchester Frank Folken
Ich Habe Rhythmus | Bear Family Records | BCD 15642 AH

Bitelli,Dave | (cl,as,tssax)
Mike Westbrook Orchestra
Bar Utopia-A Big Band Cabaret | Enja | ENJ-9333 2
The Orchestra Of Smith's Academy | Enja | ENJ-9358 2

Bitkicks |
Bitkicks
Kickbit Information | ATM Records | ATM 3823-AH

Bitran,Mariane | (flalto-fl)
Simon Spang-Hanssen & Maneklar
Wondering | dacapo | DCCD 9436

Bitto,Stefan | (v)
Till Brönner Quartet & Deutsches Symphonieorchester Berlin
German Songs | Minor Music | 801057

Bivens,William 'Yam' | (vib)
Grant Green Sextet
Grant Green:Blue Breakbeat | Blue Note | 494705-2
Alive! | Blue Note | 525650-2
Blue Break Beats | Blue Note | 799106-2
The Lost Grooves | Blue Note | 831883-2
John Hardee Sextet
The Blue Note Swingtets | Blue Note | 495697-2
Pucho & His Latin Soul Brothers
Rip A Dip | Milestone | MCD 9247-2

Biviano,Lyn | (tp)
Count Basie And His Orchestra
Jazz Dance | Original Jazz Classics | OJCCD 1002-2(1210890)
The Jazz Giants Play Harry Warren:Lullaby Of Broadway | Prestige | PCD 24204-2
Count Basie Big Band
Montreux '77 | Original Jazz Classics | OJCCD 377-2
Milt Jackson Orchestra
Sarah Vaughan Birthday Celebration | Fantasy | FANCD 6090-2
Milt Jackson With The Count Basie Orchestra
To Bags...With Love:Memorial Album | Pablo | 2310967-2
Milt Jackson Birthday Celebration | Fantasy | FANCD 6079-2
Milt Jackson + Count Basie + Big Band Vol.1 | Original Jazz Classics | OJCCD 740-2(2310822)
Milt Jackson + Count Basie + Big Band Vol.2 | Original Jazz Classics | OJCCD 741-2(2310823)

Bivins,Willie | (congasvib)
Pucho & His Latin Soul Brothers
Jazzin' With The Soul Brothers | Fantasy | FANCD 6086-2

Bivona,Gus | (ascl)
Benny Goodman And His Orchestra
Charlie Christian:Swing To Bop | Dreyfus Jazz Line | FDM 36715-2
Duke Ellington With Tommy Dorsey And His Orchestra
Highlights From The Duke Ellington Centennial Edition | RCA | 2663672-2
June Christy With The Pete Rugolo Orchestra
Something Cool(The Complete Mono & Stereo Versions) | Capitol | 534069-2

Bjerkestrand,Kjetil | (keyboards)
Dee Dee Bridgewater With Band
Victim Of Love | Verve | 841199-2

Björkenheim,Raoul | (g,bass-recorder,gongshekere)
Edward Vesala Group
Lumi | ECM | 1339
Krakatau
Volition | ECM | 1466
Matinale | ECM | 1529

Björklund,Mats | (g)
Klaus Doldinger's Passport
Earthborn | Atlantic | 2292-46477-2
Passport
Iguacu | Atlantic | 2292-46031-2

Björkman,Ake | (fl-hfr-h)
Lars Gullin Septet
Lars Gullin 1951/52 Vol.5:First Walk | Dragon | DRCD 380
Lars Gullin Sextet
Lars Gullin 1951/52 Vol.5:First Walk | Dragon | DRCD 380

Bjorn,Atli | (p)
Brew Moore Quartet
No More Brew | Storyville | STCD 8275

Björninen,Juha | (g)
Piirpauke
Piirpauke-Global Servisi | JA & RO | JARO 4150-2

Bjornstad,Ketil | (p,keyboardsp-solo)
Ketil Bjornstad
New Life | EmArCy | 017265-2
The Bach Variations | EmArCy | 017267-2
Ketil Bjornstad Group
Early Years | EmArCy | 013271-2
Grace | EmArCy | 013622-2
Water Stories | ECM | 1503(519076-2)
The Sea | ECM | 1545(521718-2)
The Sea II | ECM | 1633(537341-2)
Seafarer's Song | EmArCy | 9865777
Ketil Bjornstad-David Darling
The River | ECM | 1593(531170-2)
Epigraphs | ECM | 1684(543159-2)

Black Indian | (lyricist)
Steve Coleman And Five Elements
Curves Of Life | Novus | 2131693-2

Black Thought of 'The Roots' | (rap)
Teodross Avery Quartet
My Generation | Impulse(MCA) | 951181-2

Black,Arnold | (v)
Louis Armstrong And His Friends
Planet Jazz:Louis Armstrong | Planet Jazz | 2152052-2
Planet Jazz Sampler | Planet Jazz | 2152326-2
Louis Armstrong And His Friends | Bluebird | 2663961-2

Black,Dave | (dr)
Bob Scobey's Frisco Band
Planet Jazz | Planet Jazz | 2169652-2
Duke Ellington And His Orchestra
The Legends Of Swing | Laserlight | 24659
100 Years Duke | Laserlight | 24906
Ellington '55 | Capitol | 520135-2
Great Swing Classics In Hi-Fi | Capitol | 521223-2

Black,Emma | (cello)
Carla Bley Band
Fancy Chamber Music | Watt | 28(539937-2)

Black,James | (dr)
Nat Adderley Sextet
Cannonball Adderley Birthday Celebration | Fantasy | FANCD 6087-2
In The Bag | Original Jazz Classics | OJCCD 648-2(JLP 975)
Yusef Lateef Quartet
Live at Pep's Vol.2 | Impulse(MCA) | 547961-2
Yusef Lateef Quintet
Live at Pep's Vol.2 | Impulse(MCA) | 547961-2
The Roots Of Acid Jazz | Impulse(MCA) | IMP 12042

Black,Jim | (drperc)
Andreas Willers Group
Andreas Willers & Friends Play Jimi Hendrix:Experience | Nabel Records:Jazz Network | CD 4665
Carlos Bica & Azul
Look What They've Done To My Song | Enja | ENJ-9458 2
Carlos Bica Group
Azul | Traumton Records | 4425-2
Dave Douglas Tiny Bell Trio
Wandering Souls | Winter&Winter | 910042-2
David Binney Group
South | ACT | 9279-2
Balance | ACT | 9411-2
Ed Schuller Group feat. Dewey Redman
The Force | Tutu Records | 888166-2*
Franz Bauer Quintet
Plüschtier | Jazz Haus Musik | JHM 0097 CD
Jim Black Alasnoaxis
Splay | Winter&Winter | 910076-2
Jim Black Quartet
Alasnoaxis | Winter&Winter | 910061-2
Marty Cook Conspiracy
Phases Of The Moon | Tutu Records | 888160-2*

Black,Seneca | (tp)
Lincoln Center Jazz Orchestra
Big Train | CBS | CK 69860

Blackburn,Lou | (tb,african-shawn,percshenai)
Duke Ellington And Count Basie With Their Orchestras
First Time! | CBS | CK 65571
Gerald Wilson And His Orchestra
Blue Breaks Beats Vol.2 | Blue Note | 789907-2

Blackman,Cindy | (drdr-solo)
Eddie Allen Quintet
Summer Days | Enja | ENJ-9388 2
Eddie Allen Sextet
Summer Days | Enja | ENJ-9388 2

Blackman,Donald | (el-p,org,keyboards,psynth)
Lenny White Group
Renderers Of Spirit | Hip Bop | HIBD 8014

Blackmon,Junior | (dr)
Billy Boy Arnold Group
Windy City Blues | Stax | SCD 8612-2

Blackwell,Ed | (dr,cowbell,wood-dr,gong,perc)
Charlie Haden Trio
The Montreal Tapes Vol.1 | Verve | 523260-2
Dewey Redman Quartet
The Struggle Continues | ECM | 1225
Don Cherry Group
Multi Kulti | A&M Records | 395323-2
Don Cherry Quartet
Complete Communion | Blue Note | 522673-2
Don Cherry/Ed Blackwell
El Corazon | ECM | 1230
Ed Blackwell Project
Vol.1:What It Is? | Enja | ENJ-7089 2
Vol.2:What It Be Like? | Enja | ENJ-8054 2
Eric Dolphy Quintet
Eric Dolphy At The Five Spot Vol.2 | Original Jazz Classics | OJC20 247-2(P 7294)
Eric Dolphy-Booker Little Quintet
Eric Dolphy Birthday Celebration | Fantasy | FANCD 6085-2
At The Five Spot,Vol.1 | Original Jazz Classics | OJC20 133-2
Eric Dolphy Memorial Album | Original Jazz Classics | OJCCD 353-2
Eric Dophy Quintet
Eric Dolphy:The Complete Prestige Recordings | Prestige | 9 PRCD-4418-2
Joe Lovano Quartet
From The Soul | Blue Note | 798636-2
John Coltrane-Don Cherry Quartet
The Avant-Garde | Atlantic | 7567-90041-2
The Avantgarde | Rhino | 8122-79892-2
Old And New Dreams
Old And New Dreams | ECM | 1154
Playing | ECM | 1205
Ornette Coleman Double Quartet
Beauty Is A Rare Thing:Ornette Coleman-The Complete Atlantic Recordings | Atlantic | 8122-71410-2
Free Jazz | Atlantic | 8122-75208-2
Ornette Coleman Quartet
This Is Our Music | Atlantic | 7567-80767-2
Beauty Is A Rare Thing:Ornette Coleman-The Complete Atlantic Recordings | Atlantic | 8122-71410-2
Ornette On Tenor | Atlantic | 8122-71455-2

Blade,Brian | (cymbalsdr)
Brad Mehldau Trio
Introducing Brad Mehldau | Warner | 9362-45997-2
Brian Blade Group
Fellowship | Blue Note | 859417-2
Charlie Haden Quartet With Orchestra
American Dreams | Verve | 064096-2
Chris Potter Quartet
Gratitude | Verve | 549433-2
David Binney Group
South | ACT | 9279-2
Directions In Music
Live at Massey Hall:Celebrating Miles Davis & John Coltrane | Verve | 589654-2
Joshua Redman Quartet
MoodSwing | Warner | 9362-45643-2
Spirit Of The Moment:Live At The Village Vanguard | Warner | 9362-45923-2
Timeless Tales | Warner | 9362-47052-2
Joshua Redman Quintet
Freedom In The Goove | Warner | 9362-46330-2
Mark Turner Quartet
Ballad Session | Warner | 9362-47631-2
Mark Turner Quintet
Ballad Session | Warner | 9362-47631-2
Mark Turner Trio
Ballad Session | Warner | 9362-47631-2
Wayne Shorter Quartet
Footprints Live! | Verve | 589679-2
Yaya 3
Yaya 3 | Loma | 936248277-2

Blaha,Josef | (poboe)
Hans Koller Big Band
New York City | MPS | 9813437

Blaine,Terry | (voc)
Mark Shane-Terry Blaine Group
With Thee I Swing! | Nagel-Heyer | CD 040

Blair,Lee | (bjg)
Jelly Roll Morton And His Orchestra
Planet Jazz:Jelly Roll Morton | Planet Jazz | 2152060-2
Jazz:The Essential Collection Vol.1 | IN+OUT Records | 78011-2
Jelly Roll Morton's Red Hot Peppers
Planet Jazz:Jelly Roll Morton | Planet Jazz | 2152060-2
Jazz:The Essential Collection Vol.1 | IN+OUT Records | 78011-2
Louis Armstrong And His Orchestra
Louis Armstrong:Swing That Music | Laserlight | 36056
Jazz:The Essential Collection Vol.2 | IN+OUT Records | 78012-2
Louis Armstrong-My Greatest Songs | MCA | MCD 18347
Swing Legends:Louis Armstrong | Nimbus Records | NI 2012
Wilbur DeParis And His New New Orleans Band
Atlantic Jazz: New Orleans | Atlantic | 7567-81700-2

Blairman,Allen | (drperc)

Bireli Lagrene Ensemble
Bireli Swing '81 | Jazzpoint | JP 1009 CD
Routes To Django & Bireli Swing '81 | Jazzpoint | JP 1055 CD
Blaise,Catherine | (cello)
Till Brönner Quartet & Deutsches Symphonieorchester Berlin
German Songs | Minor Music | 801057
Blake Jr.,John E. | (v)
Grover Washington Jr. Septet
Paradise | Elektra | 7559-60537-2
Blake,Alex | (bel-b)
Billy Cobham Group
The Best Of Billy Cobham | Atlantic | 7567-81558-2
Chico Freeman And Brainstorm
Sweet Explosion | IN+OUT Records | 7010-2
Jazz Unlimited | IN+OUT Records | 7017-2
Pharoah Sanders Group
Save Our Children | Verve | 557297-2
Randy Weston African Rhythm
Khepera | Verve | 557821-2
Randy Weston African Rhythm Quintet and The Gnawa Master Musicians of Marocco
Spirit! The Power Of Music | Verve | 543256-2
Sun Ra And His Intergalactic Research Arkestra
Black Myth/Out In Space | MPS | 557656-2
Blake,Ellsworth | (ts)
Louis Armstrong And His Orchestra
Planet Jazz:Louis Armstrong | Planet Jazz | 2152052-2
Louis Armstrong:A 100th Birthday Celebration | RCA | 2663694-2
Blake,Jerry | (cl,as,arr,voc,bsts)
Fletcher Henderson And His Orchestra
Jazz:The Essential Collection Vol.3 | IN+OUT Records | 78013-2
Blake,Jimmy | (tp)
Tommy Dorsey And His Orchestra
Planet Jazz:Frank Sinatra & Tommy Dorsey | Planet Jazz | 2152067-2
Planet Jazz Sampler | Planet Jazz | 2152326-2
Planet Jazz:Tommy Dorsey | Planet Jazz | 2159972-2
Planet Jazz:Big Bands | Planet Jazz | 2169649-2
Planet Jazz:Male Jazz Vocalists | Planet Jazz | 2169657-2
Frank Sinatra And The Tommy Dorsey Orchestra | RCA | 2668701-2
Blake,Joanna | (voc)
Mike Westbrook Brass Band
Glad Day:Settings Of William Blake | Enja | ENJ-9376 2
Blake,John | (org,strings,synthv)
Archie Shepp Orchestra
The Cry Of My People | Impulse(MCA) | 9861488
Muneer B.Fennell & The Rhythm String Band
An Encounter With Higher Forces | double moon | CHRDM 71019
Blake,Johnathan | (drtambourine)
Mingus Big Band
Tonight At Noon...Three Or Four Shades Of Love | Dreyfus Jazz Line | FDM 36633-2
Blake,Meredith | (voc)
Hoagy Carmichael With Jack Teagarden And His Big Band
Swing Vol.1 | Storyville | 4960343
Blake,Michael | (b-cl,ss,ts,fingersnaps,handclaps)
Lounge Lizards
Berlin 1991 Part 1 | Intuition Records | INT 2044-2
Live In Berlin 1991-Vol.2 | Intuition Records | INT 2055-2
Michael Blake Group
Kingdom Of Champa | Intuition Records | INT 3189-2
Drift | Intuition Records | INT 3212-2
Slow Poke
Redemption | Intuition Records | INT 3260-2
Blake,Ran | (pp-solo)
Enrico Rava-Ran Blake
Duo En Noir | Between The Lines | btl 004(Efa 10174-2)
Blake,Ron | (fl,ssts)
Christian McBride Quartet
Vertcal Vision | Warner | 9362-48278-2
Cornelius Claudio Kreusch Group
Scoop | ACT | 9255-2
Roy Hargrove Quintet
Roy Hargrove Quintet With The Tenors Of Our Time | Verve | 523019-2
Family | Verve | 527630-2
Roy Hargrove Quintet With Branford Marsalis
Roy Hargrove Quintet With The Tenors Of Our Time | Verve | 523019-2
Roy Hargrove Quintet With Joe Henderson
Roy Hargrove Quintet With The Tenors Of Our Time | Verve | 523019-2
Roy Hargrove Quintet With Johnny Griffin
Roy Hargrove Quintet With The Tenors Of Our Time | Verve | 523019-2
Roy Hargrove Quintet With Joshua Redman
Roy Hargrove Quintet With The Tenors Of Our Time | Verve | 523019-2
Roy Hargrove Quintet With Stanley Turrentine
Roy Hargrove Quintet With The Tenors Of Our Time | Verve | 523019-2
Roy Hargrove Sextet
Family | Verve | 527630-2
Blake,Russell | (el-b)
Sonny Rollins Quintet
Sunny Days,Starry Nights | Milestone | MCD 9122-2
Sonny Rollins Sextet
Sunny Days,Starry Nights | Milestone | MCD 9122-2
Blake,Seamus | (sax,ss,tswindchimes)
Charles Mingus Orchestra
Tonight At Noon...Three Or Four Shades Of Love | Dreyfus Jazz Line | FDM 36633-2
Dave Douglas Group
Dave Douglas Freak In | Bluebird | 2664008-2
Franco Ambrosetti Quintet
Live At The Blue Note | Enja | ENJ-7065 2
Mark Zubeck Quintet
Horse With A Broken Leg | Fresh Sound Records | FSNT 078 CD
Mingus Big Band
Tonight At Noon...Three Or Four Shades Of Love | Dreyfus Jazz Line | FDM 36633-2
Phil Grenadier Quintet
Sweet Transients | Fresh Sound Records | FSNT 093 CD
Seamus Blake Quartet
Stranger Things Have Happened | Fresh Sound Records | FSNT 063 CD
Seamus Blake Quintet
Stranger Things Have Happened | Fresh Sound Records | FSNT 063 CD
Seamus Blake-Marc Miralta Trio
Sun Sol | Fresh Sound Records | FSNT 087 CD
Victor Lewis Sextet
Eeeyyess! | Enja | ENJ-9311 2
Blake,Stewart | (bs)
Ella Fitzgerald With Sy Oliver And His Orchestra
Ella Fitzgerald:The Decca Years 1949-1954 | Decca | 050668-2
Blakey,Art | (dr,voc,dr-solotalking)
Art Blakey
Best Of Blakey 60 | Blue Note | 493072-2
The Art Of Jazz | IN+OUT Records | 77028-2
Feedom Rider | Blue Note | 821287-2
Art Blakey And The Afro Drum Ensemble
The African Beat | Blue Note | 522666-2
Art Blakey And The Afrocuban Boys
Les Liaisons Dangereuses(Original Soundtrack) | Fontana | 812017-2
Art Blakey And The Jazz Messengers
Planet Jazz:Art Blakey | Planet Jazz | 2152066-2
Planet Jazz Sampler | Planet Jazz | 2152326-2
Planet Jazz:Lee Morgan | Planet Jazz | 2161238-2
A Night In Tunisia | RCA | 2663896-2
Art Blakey & The Jazz Messengers: Olympia, May 13th, 1961 | Laserlight | 36128
Paris Jazz Concert:Art Blakey & The Jazz Messengers | Laserlight | 36158
Best Of Blakey 60 | Blue Note | 493072-2
Moanin' | Blue Note | 495324-2
Horace Silver Retrospective | Blue Note | 495576-2
Jazz Life Vol.2:From Seventh At Avenue South | Storyville | 4960763
Roots And Herbs | Blue Note | 521956-2
The Witch Doctor | Blue Note | 521957-2
A Night At Birdland Vol. 1 | Blue Note | 532146-2
A Night At Birdland Vol. 2 | Blue Note | 532147-2
At The Cafe Bohemia Vol.1 | Blue Note | 532148-2
At The Cafe Bohemia Vol.2 | Blue Note | 532149-2
True Blue | Blue Note | 534032-2
Meet You At The Jazz Corner Of The World | Blue Note | 535565-2
Wayne Shorter:The Classic Blue Note Recordings | Blue Note | 540856-2
The Art Of Jazz | IN+OUT Records | 77028-2
Blue N' Groovy | Blue Note | 780679-2
A Night In Tunisia | Blue Note | 784049-2
The Best Of Blue Note | Blue Note | 796110-2
The Best Of Blue Note Vol.2 | Blue Note | 797960-2
Night In Tunisia | Philips | 800064-2
Les Liaisons Dangereuses(Original Soundtrack) | Fontana | 812017-2
Feedom Rider | Blue Note | 821287-2
Jazz In Paris:Art Blakey-1958-Paris Olympia | EmArCy | 832659-2 PMS
Jazz In Paris:Paris Jam Session | EmArCy | 832692-2 PMS
Impulse!Art Blakey!Jazz Messengers! | Impulse(MCA) | 951175-2
The Jazz Messengers | CBS | CK 65265
At The Club St.Germain | RCA | ND 74897(2)
Caravan | Original Jazz Classics | OJC20 038-2
Ugetsu | Original Jazz Classics | OJC20 090-2(RLP 9464)
Art Blakey And The Jazz Messengers With Barney Wilen And Bud Powell
Jazz In Paris:Paris Jam Session | EmArCy | 832692-2 PMS
Art Blakey And The Jazz Messengers With Thelonious Monk
Art Blakey's Jazz Messengers With Thelonious Monk | Atlantic | 7567-81332-2
Art Blakey Percussion Ensemble
Drums Around The Corner | Blue Note | 521455-2
Art Blakey Quartet
A Jazz Message | Impulse(MCA) | 547964-2
Art Blakey-Barney Wilen Quartet
Les Liaisons Dangereuses(Original Soundtrack) | Fontana | 812017-2
Art Blakey-Paul Chambers
Drums Around The Corner | Blue Note | 521455-2
Art Blakey-Sabu
Horace Silver Trio And Spotlight On Drums:Art Blakey-Sabu | Blue Note | 591725-2
Benny Golson Quintet
Groovin' | Original Jazz Classics | OJCCD 226-2(NJ 8220)
Blue Mitchell Quintet
Out Of The Blue | Original Jazz Classics | OJCCD 667-2(RLP 1131)
Bud Powell Trio
The Best Of Bud Powell On Verve | Verve | 523392-2
Buddy DeFranco Quartet
Mr. Clarinet | Verve | 847408-2
Cannonball Adderley Quartet
Ballads | Blue Note | 537563-2
Cannonball Adderley Quintet
Somethin' Else | Blue Note | 495329-2
Kind Of Blue:Blue Note Celebrate The Music Of Miles Davis | Blue Note | 534255-2
The Best Of Blue Note Vol.2 | Blue Note | 797960-2
Miles Davis:The Best Of The Capitol/Blue Note Years | Blue Note | 798287-2
Jazz Profile:Miles Davis | Blue Note | 823515-2
Ballads & Blues | Blue Note | 836633-2
Cannonball Adderley-Milt Jackson Quintet
To Bags...With Love:Memorial Album | Pablo | 2310967-2
Milt Jackson Birthday Celebration | Fantasy | FANCD 6079-2
Cannonball Adderley Birthday Celebration | Fantasy | FANCD 6087-2
Things Are Getting Better | Original Jazz Classics | OJC20 032-2
Cliff Jordan-John Gilmore Quintet
Blowing In From Chicago | Blue Note | 542306-2
Clifford Brown Sextet
Clifford Brown Memorial Album | Blue Note | 532141-2
Coleman Hawkins Quintet
Monk's Music | Original Jazz Classics | OJC20 084-2
Dexter Gordon Quintet
The Art Of Saxophone | Laserlight | 24652
Donald Brown Quintet
Donald Byrd & Doug Watkins:The Tradition Sessions | Blue Note | 540528-2
Donald Byrd Sextet
Donald Byrd & Doug Watkins:The Tradition Sessions | Blue Note | 540528-2
Fats Navarro Quintet
Fats Navarro:Nostalgia | Dreyfus Jazz Line | FDM 36736-2
Grant Green Quartet
Ballads | Blue Note | 537560-2
Midnight Blue(The [Be]witching Hour) | Blue Note | 854365-2
Hank Mobley Quartet
Soul Station | Blue Note | 495343-2
Hank Mobley Quintet
Hank Mobley | Blue Note | 0675622
Roll Call | Blue Note | 540030-2)
Herbie Nichols Trio
Herbie Nichols:The Complete Blue Note Recordings | Blue Note | 859352-2
Horace Silver Trio
Horace Silver Retrospective | Blue Note | 495576-2
Horace Silver Trio And Spotlight On Drums:Art Blakey-Sabu | Blue Note | 591725-2
Ike Quebec Quartet
Blue Note Plays Gershwin | Blue Note | 520808-2
Jimmy Smith All Stars
House Party | Blue Note | 524542-2
Jimmy Smith Quartet
Six Views Of The Blues | Blue Note | 521435-2
Jimmy Smith Quintet
Cool Blues | Blue Note | 535587-2
Johnny Griffin Septet
A Blowing Session | Blue Note | 0677191
Trane's Blues | Blue Note | 498240-2
Kenny Burrell Quartet
Blue Lights Vol.1&2 | Blue Note | 857184-2
Kenny Burrell Septet
Blue Lights Vol.1&2 | Blue Note | 857184-2
Kenny Dorham Octet
Afro-Cuban | Blue Note | 0675619
Kenny Dorham Orchestra
Blue Bossa | Blue Note | 795590-2
Miles Davis All Stars
Miles Davis Vol.2 | Blue Note | 532611-2
Miles Davis Quartet
Miles Davis Vol.1 | Blue Note | 532610-2
Kind Of Blue:Blue Note Celebrate The Music Of Miles Davis | Blue Note | 534255-2
Miles Davis:The Best Of The Capitol/Blue Note Years | Blue Note | 798287-2
Jazz Profile:Miles Davis | Blue Note | 823515-2
Ballads & Blues | Blue Note | 836633-2
Blue Haze | Original Jazz Classics | OJC20 093-2(P 7054)
Miles Davis Quintet
The Prestige Legacy Vol.1:The High Priests | Prestige | PCD 24251-2
Miles Davis Sextet
Kind Of Blue:Blue Note Celebrate The Music Of Miles Davis | Blue Note | 534255-2
Miles Davis:The Best Of The Capitol/Blue Note Years | Blue Note | 798287-2
Jazz Profile:Miles Davis | Blue Note | 823515-2
Ballads & Blues | Blue Note | 836633-2
Miles Davis:Milestones | Dreyfus Jazz Line | FDM 36731-2
Dig | Original Jazz Classics | OJC20 005-2
The Jazz Giants Play Harold Arlen:Blues In The Night | Prestige | PCD 24201-2
Paul Bley Trio
Charles Mingus-The Complete Debut Recordings | Debut | 12 DCD 4402-2
Introducing Paul Bley | Original Jazz Classics | OJCCD 201-2(DEB 7)
Quincy Jones Big Band
Rahsaan/The Complete Mercury Recordings Of Roland Kirk | Mercury | 846630-2
Randy Weston Trio
Randy Weston:Solo,Duo,Trio | Milestone | MCD 47085-2
Sonny Clark Quintet
My Conception | Blue Note | 522674-2
Sonny Rollins Quartet
Sonny Rollins Vol.2 | Blue Note | 497809-2
Sonny Rollins:The Blue Note Recordings | Blue Note | 821371-2
Jazz Profile:Sonny Rollins | Blue Note | 823516-2
Sonny Rollins With The Modern Jazz Quartet | Original Jazz Classics | OJCCD 011-2
The Prestige Legacy Vol.1:The High Priests | Prestige | PCD 24251-2
Sonny Rollins Quartet feat.Thelonious Monk
Ballads | Blue Note | 537562-2
Sonny Rollins Quintet
Sonny Rollins Vol.2 | Blue Note | 497809-2
Ballads | Blue Note | 537562-2
The Blue Note Years-The Best Of Sonny Rollins | Blue Note | 793203-2
Sonny Rollins:The Blue Note Recordings | Blue Note | 821371-2
Jazz Profile:Sonny Rollins | Blue Note | 823516-2
Sonny Rollins Sextet
Sonny Rollins Vol.2 | Blue Note | 497809-2
Sonny Rollins:The Blue Note Recordings | Blue Note | 821371-2
Sonny Stitt Quartet
Kaleidoscope | Original Jazz Classics | OJCCD 060-2(P 7077)
Thelonious Monk Quartet
Thelonious Monk:85th Birthday Celebration | zyx records | FANCD 6076-2
Thelonious Monk:Misterioso | Dreyfus Jazz Line | FDM 36743-2
Thelonious Monk Quintet
Thelonious Monk:The Complete Prestige Recordings | Prestige | 3 PRCD 4428-2
Genius Of Modern Music,Vol.1 | Blue Note | 532138-2
Genius Of Modern Music,Vol.2 | Blue Note | 532139-2
The Best Of Thelonious Monk:The Blue Note Years | Blue Note | 795636-2
Jazz Profile:Thelonious Monk | Blue Note | 823518-2
Thelonious Monk:85th Birthday Celebration | zyx records | FANCD 6076-2
Thelonious Monk:Misterioso | Dreyfus Jazz Line | FDM 36743-2
MONK | Original Jazz Classics | OJCCD 016-2
The Jazz Giants Play Jerome Kern:Yesterdays | Prestige | PCD 24202-2
The Prestige Legacy Vol.1:The High Priests | Prestige | PCD 24251-2
Thelonious Monk Septet
Thelonious Monk:85th Birthday Celebration | zyx records | FANCD 6076-2
Thelonious Monk With John Coltrane | Jazzland | JZSA 946-6
Thelonious Monk With John Coltrane | Original Jazz Classics | OJC20 039-2
Monk's Music | Original Jazz Classics | OJC20 084-2
Thelonious Monk Sextet
Genius Of Modern Music,Vol.1 | Blue Note | 532138-2
Jazz Profile:Thelonious Monk | Blue Note | 823518-2
Thelonious Monk:Misterioso | Dreyfus Jazz Line | FDM 36743-2
Thelonious Monk Trio
Thelonious Monk:The Complete Prestige Recordings | Prestige | 3 PRCD 4428-2
Genius Of Modern Music,Vol.1 | Blue Note | 532138-2
The Best Of Thelonious Monk:The Blue Note Years | Blue Note | 795636-2
Jazz Profile:Thelonious Monk | Blue Note | 823518-2
Thelonious Monk:85th Birthday Celebration | zyx records | FANCD 6076-2
Thelonious Monk:Misterioso | Dreyfus Jazz Line | FDM 36743-2
Thelonious Monk | Original Jazz Classics | OJC20 010-2(P 7027)
Thelonious Monk/Sonny Rollins | Original Jazz Classics | OJCCD 059-2
The Unique Thelonious Monk | Original Jazz Classics | OJCCD 064-2
The Prestige Legacy Vol.1:The High Priests | Prestige | PCD 24251-2
Tina Brooks Quintet
True Blue | Blue Note | 534032-2
Zoot Sims Quartet
Zoot Sims Quartets | Original Jazz Classics | OJCCD 242-2(P 7026)
Zoot Sims-Al Cohn Sextet
The Brothers | Original Jazz Classics | OJCCD 008-2
Blam,Michael 'Mischa' | (b)
Hannes Beckmann Quartet
Violin Tales | Tutu Records | 888202-2*
Blamires,David | (g,el-g,voc,mellophone,melodica,tp)
Pat Metheny Group
Imaginary Day | Warner | 9362-46791-2
We Live Here | Geffen Records | GED 24729
Blanc,Daniel 'Dani' | (flas)
Brigitte Dietrich-Joe Haider Jazz Orchestra
Consequences | JHM Records | JHM 3624
Blanchard,Pierre | (v)
Abbey Lincoln With The Rodney Kendrick Trio And Guests
A Turtle's Dream | Verve | 527382-2
Toots Thielemans Quintet
Verve Jazz Masters Vol.59:Toots Thielemans | Verve | 535271-2
Blanchard,Terence | (tp)
Art Blakey And The Jazz Messengers
The Art Of Jazz | IN+OUT Records | 77028-2
Rachelle Ferrell With The Terrence Blanchard Quartet
First Instrumental | Blue Note | 827820-2
Terri Lyne Carrington Group
Jazz Is A Spirit | ACT | 9408-2
Blanchet,Alain 'T-Blanc' | (perc)
Marty Hall Band
Tried & True | Blues Beacon | BLU-1030 2
Blanchette,Jack | (g)
Louis Armstrong With The Casa Loma Orchestra
Louis Armstrong:Swing That Music | Laserlight | 36056
Bland,Bobby | (gvoc)
Bobby Bland And His Band
Monterey Jazz Festival 1975 | Storyville | 4960213
Bland,Jack | (bj,gvoc)
Mound City Blue Blowers
Planet Jazz:Jack Teagarden | Planet Jazz | 2161236-2
Jazz:The Essential Collection Vol.3 | IN+OUT Records | 78013-2
Bland,Milton | (ts)
Buddy Guy Blues Band
Buddy Guy-The Complete Chess Studio Recordings | MCA | MCD 09337
Blandings Jr.,Walter | (cl,ss,asts)
Eric Reed Orchestra
Happiness | Nagel-Heyer | CD 2010
Lincoln Center Jazz Orchestra
Big Train | CBS | CK 69860
Marcus Printup Sextet
The New Boogaloo | Nagel-Heyer | CD 2019
Wycliffe Gordon Group
The Search | Nagel-Heyer | CD 2007
Wynton Marsalis Group
Standard Time Vol.4:Marsalis Plays Monk | CBS | CK 67503
Blane,John | (tb)
Buddy Childers Big Band

Just Buddy's | Candid | CCD 79761

Blanke,Toto | (el-g,g,bj,midi-g,vocwhistling)

Das Obertontrio Und Toto Blanke
Energy Fields | ALISO Records | AL 1029
Lajos Dudas Quartet
Jubilee Edition | double moon | CHRDM 71020
Lajos Dudas Quintet
Jubilee Edition | double moon | CHRDM 71020
Toto Blanke Group
Fools Paradise | ALISO Records | AL 1019
Electric Circus' Best | ALISO Records | AL 1034
Toto Blanke-Diego Jasca
Sur | ALISO Records | AL 1035
Toto Blanke-Rudolf Dasek
Talking Hands:Live | ALISO Records | AL 1021
Two Much Guitar! | ALISO Records | AL 1022
Meditation | ALISO Records | AL 1026
Mona Lisa | ALISO Records | AL 1037
Toto Blanke-Rudolf Dasek With The Overtontrio
Meditation | ALISO Records | AL 1026

Blanket,F. | (v)

Toots Thielemans And His Orchestra
Verve Jazz Masters Vol.59:Toots Thielemans | Verve | 535271-2

Blanton,Jimmy | (b)

Barney Bigard And His Orchestra
Highlights From The Duke Ellington Centennial Edition | RCA | 2663672-2
Jazz:The Essential Collection Vol.3 | IN+OUT Records | 78013-2
Duke Ellington And His Famous Orchestra
Duke Ellington:The Blanton-Webster Band | Bluebird | 21 13181-2
Planet Jazz:Duke Ellington | Planet Jazz | 2152053-2
Planet Jazz:Johnny Hodges | Planet Jazz | 2152065-2
Planet Jazz Sampler | Planet Jazz | 2152326-2
Planet Jazz:Ben Webster | RCA | 2165368-2
Planet Jazz:Big Bands | Planet Jazz | 2169649-2
Planet Jazz:Jazz Trumpet | Planet Jazz | 2169654-2
Planet Jazz:Female Jazz Vocalists | Planet Jazz | 2169656-2
Highlights From The Duke Ellington Centennial Edition | RCA | 2663672-2
Jazz:The Essential Collection Vol.2 | IN+OUT Records | 78012-2
Jazz:The Essential Collection Vol.3 | IN+OUT Records | 78013-2
Duke Ellington:Ko-Ko | Dreyfus Jazz Line | FDM 36717-2
Duke Ellington And His Orchestra
Highlights From The Duke Ellington Centennial Edition | RCA | 2663672-2
The Duke At Fargo 1940 | Storyville | STCD 8316/17
Duke Ellington/Jimmy Blanton
Highlights From The Duke Ellington Centennial Edition | RCA | 2663672-2
Duke Ellington:Ko-Ko | Dreyfus Jazz Line | FDM 36717-2
Johnny Hodges Orchestra
Planet Jazz:Johnny Hodges | Planet Jazz | 2152065-2
Planet Jazz Sampler | Planet Jazz | 2152326-2
Planet Jazz:Jazz Saxophone | Planet Jazz | 2169653-2
Highlights From The Duke Ellington Centennial Edition | RCA | 2663672-2
Rex Stewart And His Orchestra
Planet Jazz:Ben Webster | RCA | 2165368-2
Planet Jazz:Jazz Trumpet | Planet Jazz | 2169654-2
Jazz:The Essential Collection Vol.3 | IN+OUT Records | 78013-2

Blareau,Charlie | (b)

Guy Lafitte-Peanuts Holland And Their Orchestra
Jazz In Paris:Guy Lafitte-Blue And Sentimental | EmArCy | 159852-2 PMS

Blaschke,Ralf | (g)

Acoustic Affaire
Mira | Jazz 'n' Arts Records | JNA 1303

Blaser,Beat | (bs)

Q4 Orchester Project
Yavapai | Creative Works Records | CW CD 1028-2

Blasorchester Dicke Luft |

Kölner Saxophon Mafia With Blasorchester Dicke Luft
Kölner Saxophon Mafia Proudly Presents | Jazz Haus Musik | JHM 0046 CD

Blaszczyk,Marek | (bel-b)

Walkaway With Urszula Dudziak
Saturation | IN+OUT Records | 77024-2

Blaufrontal |

Blaufrontal
Blaufrontal | Jazz Haus Musik | JHM 0037 CD
Blaufrontal With Hank Roberts & Mark Feldman
Bad Times Roll | Jazz Haus Musik | JHM 0061 CD

Blaut,Bill | (as)

Buddy Rich Big Band
Backwoods Siseman/Pieces Of Dream | Laserlight | 24655

Blauth,Johnny | (tb)

Freddie Brocksieper Orchester
Drums Boogie | Bear Family Records | BCD 15988 AH

Blaze,Ralph | (gmaracas)

Stan Kenton And His Orchestra
Great Swing Classics In Hi-Fi | Capitol | 521223-2
Stan Kenton Portraits On Standards | Capitol | 531571-2

Blazer,Harry | (dr)

Gary Burton Quartet
The New Quartet | ECM | 1030

Bleckmann,Theo | (vocvoice)

Theo Bleckman & Kirk Nurock
Looking-Glass River | Traumton Records | 2412-2
Theo Bleckman & Kirk Nurock Quartet
Looking-Glass River | Traumton Records | 2412-2

Bleibel,Wolfgang | (as)

Joe Pass With The NDR Big Band
Joe Pass In Hamburg | ACT | 9100-2

Bleige,Scott | (tb)

Buddy Childers Big Band
Just Buddy's | Candid | CCD 79761

Blenzig,Charles | (keyboards,perc,voc,psynth)

Steve Lampert Group
Venus Perplexed | Steeplechase | SCCD 31557

Bless,Noah | (tb)

Andy Middleton Group
Nomad's Notebook | Intuition Records | INT 3264-2

Blessing,Lyon | (vib,org,keyboardssynth)

Al Jarreau With Band
All Fly Home | Warner | 7599-27362-2
Les McCann Group
Talkin' Verve:Les McCann | Verve | 557351-2
Les McCann Orchestra
Talkin' Verve:Les McCann | Verve | 557351-2

Bley,Carla | (c-mel-sax,ld,marimba,p,el-p,org)

Carla Bley - Michael Mantler & Orchestra
13-3/4 | Watt | 3 (2313103)
Carla Bley Band
Live! | Watt | 12(815730-2)
Heavy Heart | Watt | 14
Night-Glo | Watt | 16
Fleur Carnivore | Watt | 21
The Very Big Carla Bley Band | Watt | 23
Big Band Theory | Watt | 25(519966-2)
Fancy Chamber Music | Watt | 28(539937-2)
4X4 | Watt | 30(159547-2)
Dinner Music | Watt | 6(825815-2)
European Tour 1977 | Watt | 8
Musique Mecanique | Watt | 9
Carla Bley Big Band
The Carla Bley Big Band Goes To Church | Watt | 27(533682-2)
Carla Bley Group
Tropic Appetites | Watt | 1
Carla Bley Sextet
Sextet | Watt | 17
Carla Bley/Andy Sheppard/Steve Swallow
Song With Legs | Watt | 26(527069)
Carla Bley-Steve Swallow
Duets | Watt | 20(837345-2)
Go Together | Watt | 24(517673-2)
Are We There Yet? | Watt | 29(547297)
Charlie Haden Orchestra
The Ballad Of The Fallen | ECM | 1248(811546-2)
Charlie Haden's Liberation Music Orchestra
Liberation Music Orchestra | Impulse(MCA) | 951188-2
Gary Burton Quartet With Orchestra
A Genuine Tong Funeral(Dark Opera Without Words) | RCA | 2119255-2
Glen Moore Group
Nude Bass Ascending... | Intuition Records | INT 3192-2
Karen Mantler Group
Karen Mantler And Her Cat Arnold Get The Flu | Watt | XtraWatt/5
Farewell | Watt | XtraWatt/8
Michael Mantler Group
Michael Mantler: No Answer/Silence | Watt | 2/5(543374-2)
The Hapless Child | Watt | 4
Silence | Watt | 5 (2313105)
Movies | Watt | 7 (2313107)
Movies/More Movies | Watt | 7/10(543377-2)
Michael Mantler Quintet With The London Symphony Orchestra
Something There | Watt | 13
Michael Mantler Sextet
Movies/More Movies | Watt | 7/10(543377-2)
Steve Swallow Group
Carla | Watt | XtraWatt/2
Swallow | Watt | XtraWatt/6
The Carla Bley Band
Social Studies | Watt | 11(831831-2)
I Hate To Sing | Watt | 12,5
The Jazz Composer's Orchestra
Comminications | JCOA | 1001/2

Bley,Paul | (el-p,p,synthp-solo)

Alfred Harth Quintet
This Earth! | ECM | 1264
Charles Mingus Orchestra
Charles Mingus:Pre-Bird(Mingus Revisited) | Verve | 538636-2
Mingus | Candid | CCD 79021
Don Ellis Trio
Out Of Nowhere | Candid | CCD 79032
Ivo Perlman Group
Children Of Ibeji | Enja | ENJ-7005 2
Jimmy Giuffre 3
Jimmy Giuffre 3, 1961 | ECM | 1438/39(849644-2)
Jimmy Giuffre Three
Free Fall | CBS | CK 65446
Jimmy Giuffre-Paul Bley-Steve Swallow
Fly Away Little Bird | Owl Records | 018351-2
John Surman Quartet
Adventure Playground | ECM | 1463(511981-2)
Paul Bley
Homage To Carla | Owl Records | 013427-2
Partners | Owl Records | 014730-2
The Life Of A Trio:Saturday | Owl Records | 014731-2
The Life Of A Trio:Sunday | Owl Records | 014735-2
Open, To Love | ECM | 1023
Solo Piano | Steeplechase | SCCD 31236
Paul Bley Quartet
Fragments | ECM | 1320
The Paul Bley Quartet | ECM | 1365(835250-2)
In The Evenings Out There | ECM | 1488
Paul Bley Trio
Paul Bley With Gary Peacock | ECM | 1003
Charles Mingus-The Complete Debut Recordings | Debut | 12 DCD 4402-2
Not Two, Not One | ECM | 1670(559447-2)
The Story Of Jazz Piano | Laserlight | 24653
Introducing Paul Bley | Original Jazz Classics | OJCCD 201-2(DEB 7)
Paul Bley/Barre Phillips
Time Will Tell | ECM | 1537
Paul Bley/Evan Parker
Time Will Tell | ECM | 1537
Paul Bley/Evan Parker/Barre Phillips
Time Will Tell | ECM | 1537
St.Gerold | ECM | 1609(157899-2)
Paul Bley/Jimmy Giuffre
The Life Of A Trio:Saturday | Owl Records | 014731-2
The Life Of A Trio:Sunday | Owl Records | 014735-2
Paul Bley/Jimmy Giuffre/Steve Swallow
The Life Of A Trio:Saturday | Owl Records | 014731-2
The Life Of A Trio:Sunday | Owl Records | 014735-2
Paul Bley/Steve Swallow
The Life Of A Trio:Saturday | Owl Records | 014731-2
The Life Of A Trio:Sunday | Owl Records | 014735-2
Paul Bley-Gary Peacock Duet
Partners | Owl Records | 014730-2
Sonny Rollins-Coleman Hawkins Quintet
Planet Jazz:Sonny Rollins | Planet Jazz | 2152062-2
Sonny Meets Hawk! | RCA | 2174800-2

Blind Willie Dunn's Gin Bottle Four |

Blind Willie Dunn's Gin Bottle Four
Jazz:The Essential Collection Vol.1 | IN+OUT Records | 78011-2

Blix,Brynjulf | (fender-borg)

Terje Rypdal Group
Odyssey | ECM | 1067/8

Blo,Harald | (v)

Terje Rypdal Quartet With The Bergen Chamber Ensemble
Lux Aeterna | ECM | 1818(017070-2)

Blöchlinger,Urs | (as,sopranino,bass-sax,fl,anklung)

Cadavre Exquis
Cadavre Exquis | Creative Works Records | CW CD 1014-1

Block,Al | (as,fl,cl,ts,piccoloreeds)

Charlie Parker And His Orchestra
Charlie Parker:The Best Of The Verve Years | Verve | 527815-2
The Cole Porter Songbook | Verve | 823250-2
Charlie Parker With Orchestra
Charlie Parker Big Band | Verve | 559835-2
Gil Evans Orchestra
Verve Jazz Masters 23:Gil Evans | Verve | 521860-2
The Individualism Of Gil Evans | Verve | 833804-2
Miles Davis With Gil Evans & His Orchestra
Sketches Of Spain | CBS | CK 65142
Stan Getz With The Eddie Sauter Orchestra
Stan Getz Plays The Music Of Mickey One | Verve | 531232-2

Block,Sandy | (b)

Ella Fitzgerald With Sy Oliver And His Orchestra
Ella Fitzgerald:The Decca Years 1949-1954 | Decca | 050668-2
Ella Fitzgerald With The Hank Jones Quartet
Ella Fitzgerald:Mr.Paganini | Dreyfus Jazz Line | FDM 36741-2
Joe Williams With The Frank Hunter Orchestra
Planet Jazz:Joe Williams | Planet Jazz | 2165370-2
Louis Armstrong And The Commanders under the Direction of Camarata
Satchmo Serenaders | Verve | 543792-2
Louis Armstrong With Sy Oliver And His Orchestra
Satchmo Serenaders | Verve | 543792-2
Louis Armstrong-My Greatest Songs | MCA | MCD 18347
Louis Armstrong With The Commanders
Ambassador Louis Armstrong Vol.17:Moments To Remember(1952-1956) | Ambassador | CLA 1917

Block,Sid | (bts)

Duke Ellington With Tommy Dorsey And His Orchestra
Highlights From The Duke Ellington Centennial Edition | RCA | 2663672-2
Louis Armstrong With Sy Oliver And His Orchestra
Louis And The Angels | Verve | 549592-2
Tommy Dorsey And His Orchestra
Planet Jazz:Tommy Dorsey | Planet Jazz | 2159972-2
Planet Jazz:Jazz Greatest Hits | Planet Jazz | 2169648-2

Blocker,Joe | (dr-synth)

Bobby Lyle Quintet
Jazzrock-Anthology Vol.3:Fusion | Zounds | CD 27100555

Bloedow,Oren | (bvoc)

Lounge Lizards
Berlin 1991 Part 1 | Intuition Records | INT 2044-2
Live In Berlin 1991-Vol.2 | Intuition Records | INT 2055-2

Blomquist,Curt | (bs)

Coleman Hawkins With The Thore Ehrlings Orchestra
Coleman Hawkins At The Golden Circle | Dragon | DRCD 265

Blomquist,Rolf | (fl,clts)

Bengt-Arne Wallin Orchestra
The Birth+Rebirth Of Swedish Folk Jazz | ACT | 9254-2
Lars Gullin Sextet
Lars Gullin 1951/52 Vol.5:First Walk | Dragon | DRCD 380

Blonk,Jaap | (vocvoice)

Kölner Saxophon Mafia With Guests
Kölner Saxophon Mafia: 20 Jahre Saxuelle Befreiung | Jazz Haus Musik | JHM 0115 CD

Blood,Sweat And Tears |

Blood,Sweat And Tears
Monterey Jazz Festival 1975 | Storyville | 4960213

Bloom,Jane Ira | (sslive-electronics)

Jane Ira Bloom-Fred Hersch Duo
As One | JMT Edition | 919003-2
Klaus König Orchestra
Hommage A Douglas Adams | Enja | ENJ-6078 2

Bloom,Kurt | (ts)

Charlie Barnet And His Orchestra
Planet Jazz:Big Bands | Planet Jazz | 2169649-2
Planet Jazz:Swing | Planet Jazz | 2169651-2

Bloom,Marty | (effectsvoc)

Jelly Roll Morton's Red Hot Peppers
Planet Jazz:Jelly Roll Morton | Planet Jazz | 2152060-2
Jazz:The Essential Collection Vol.1 | IN+OUT Records | 78011-2

Bloom,Ted | (v)

Charlie Parker With Strings
Charlie Parker With Strings:The Master Takes | Verve | 523984-2

Bloomfield,Mike | (el-g,gp)

Woody Herman And His Orchestra
Brand New | Original Jazz Classics | OJCCD 1044-2(F 8414)

Blowers,Johnny | (dr)

Billie Holiday With Toots Camarata And His Orchestra
Billie's Love Songs | Nimbus Records | NI 2000
Ella Fitzgerald With Bill Doggett's Orchestra
Ella Fitzgerald:Mr.Paganini | Dreyfus Jazz Line | FDM 36741-2
Ella Fitzgerald With Sy Oliver And His Orchestra
Ella Fitzgerald:The Decca Years 1949-1954 | Decca | 050668-2
Frank Trumbauer And His Orchestra
The Hollywood Session:The Capitol Jazzmen | Jazz Unlimited | JUCD 2044
Louis Armstrong And Ella Fitzgerald With Sy Oliver's Orchestra
Louis Armstrong:C'est Si Bon | Dreyfus Jazz Line | FDM 36730-2
Louis Armstrong And His Orchestra
Louis Armstrong:Swing That Music | Laserlight | 36056
Louis Armstrong:C'est Si Bon | Dreyfus Jazz Line | FDM 36730-2
Louis Armstrong With Gordon Jenkins And His Orchestra And Choir
Satchmo In Style | Verve | 549594-2
Louis Armstrong-My Greatest Songs | MCA | MCD 18347
Swing Legends:Louis Armstrong | Nimbus Records | NI 2012
Louis Armstrong With Sy Oliver And His Orchestra
Satchmo Serenaders | Verve | 543792-2
Louis Armstrong:C'est Si Bon | Dreyfus Jazz Line | FDM 36730-2
Louis Armstrong-My Greatest Songs | MCA | MCD 18347
Louis Armstrong With Sy Oliver's Choir And Orchestra
Louis And The Good Book | Verve | 549593-2
Woody Herman And The Vanderbilt All Stars
Louis Armstrong-Jack Teagarden-Woody Herman:Midnights At V-Disc | Jazz Unlimited | JUCD 2048

Blue Collar |

Blue Collar
Diary Of A Working Band | Jazz Haus Musik | JHM 0089 CD

Blue Note All Stars |

Blue Note All Stars
Town Hall Concert | Blue Note | 497811-2

Blue Room Ensemble |

Blue Room Ensemble
Solitude | Foolish Music | FM 211993

Blue,Peggie | (voc)

Archie Shepp Orchestra
The Cry Of My People | Impulse(MCA) | 9861488

Blue,Ray | (ts)

Ray Blue Quartet
Always With A Purpose | Ray Blue Music | JN 007(RMB 01)

Blue,William Thornton | (clas)

Louis Armstrong And His Orchestra
Satch Plays Fats(Complete) | CBS | CK 64927

Bluesharp Slim | (harmvoc)

Thilo Kreitmeier & Group
Changes | Organic Music | ORGM 9725

Bluestone,Harry | (tp,vconcert-master)

Artie Shaw And His Orchestra
Planet JazzArtie Shaw | Planet Jazz | 2152057-2
Planet Jazz:Jazz Greatest Hits | Planet Jazz | 2169648-2
Frank Sinatra With Orchestra
Planet Jazz:Frank Sinatra & Tommy Dorsey | Planet Jazz | 2152067-2

Bluiett,Hamiet | (alto-cl,bs,alto-fl,b-cl)

Arthur Blythe Group
Hipmotism | Enja | ENJ-6088 2
Hamiet Bluiett
Walkin' & Talkin' | Tutu Records | 888172-2*
Hamiet Bluiett Group
...You Don't Need To Know...If You Have To Ask | Tutu Records | 888128-2*
James Carter Group
Conversin' With The Elders | Atlantic | 7567-82988-2
Lester Bowie Group
The Great Pretender | ECM | 1209(829369-2)
World Saxophone Quartet
Plays Duke Ellington | Nonesuch | 7559-79137-2
Dances And Ballads | Nonesuch | 7559-79164-2

Blumberg,Stuart | (tp)

Chick Corea And His Orchestra
My Spanish Heart | Polydor | 543303-3
Chick Corea Group
Verve Jazz Masters 3:Chick Corea | Verve | 519820-2

Blume,Dave | (gelectronics)

Uri Caine Group
Urlicht/Primal Light | Winter&Winter | 910004-2

Blume,Stanley | (asss)

Alberto Marsico Quintet
Them That's Got | Organic Music | ORGM 9705
Christian Rover Group feat. Rhoda Scott
Christian Rover Group-Live With Rhoda Scott At The Organ | Organic Music | ORGM 9704
Stanley Blume Quartet
Movin' Up | Organic Music | ORGM 9709
Stanley Blume Quintet
Movin' Up | Organic Music | ORGM 9709

Blume,Steffen | (tb)

European Jazz Youth Orchestra
Swinging Europe 3 | dacapo | DCCD 9461

Blume,Teddy | (v)

Charlie Parker With Strings
Bird: The Complete Charlie Parker On Verve | Verve | 837141-2
Blümlein,Dirk | (bvoc)
Ralph Abelein Group
Mr. B's Time Machine | Satin Doll Productions | SDP 1042-1 CD
Blythe,Arthur | (as,saxss)
Arthur Blythe Group
Hipmotism | Enja | ENJ-6088 2
Arthur Blythe Quartet
Retroflection | Enja | ENJ-8046 2
Calling Card | Enja | ENJ-9051 2
Cold Sweat
Cold Sweat Plays J.B. | JMT Edition | 919025-2
Debriano-Hart-Blythe
3-Ology | Konnex Records | KCD 5047
Jack DeJohnette Quartet
Special Edition | ECM | 1152
Jan Harrington With The Arthur Blythe Quartet
Remembering Dinah-A Salute To Dinah Washington | Hot Shot Records | HSR 8313-2
Joey Baron Quartet
We'll Soon Find Out | Intuition Records | INT 3515-2
Kevin Mahogany With Orchestra
Songs And Moments | Enja | ENJ-8072 2
Rodney Jones Group
Soul Manifesto | Blue Note | 530499-2
Roots
Salutes The Saxophone | IN+OUT Records | 7016-2
Salutes The Saxophones: Tributes To Gene Ammons, Eric Dolphy, Coleman Hawkins And Charlie Parker | IN+OUT Records | 7016-3
Jazz Unlimited | IN+OUT Records | 7017-2
Stablemates | IN+OUT Records | 7021-2
Saying Something | IN+OUT Records | 77031-2
For Diz & Bird | IN+OUT Records | 77039-2
Board,Johnny | (as,fl,bsts)
(Little)Jimmy Scott With The Lionel Hampton Orchestra
Everybody's Somebody's Fool | Decca | 050669-2
Albert King With The Willie Dixon Band
Windy City Blues | Stax | SCD 8612-2
Lionel Hampton And His Orchestra
Lionel Hampton:Flying Home | Dreyfus Jazz Line | FDM 36735-2
Lionel Hampton Orchestra
The Big Bands Vol.1.The Snader Telescriptions | Storyville | 4960043
Bobadillis,Isidro | (tambara)
Paquito D'Rivera Orchestra
Jazzrock-Anthology Vol.3:Fusion | Zounds | CD 27100555
Bobè,Eddie | (bongos,cowbell,congas,cajon,palitos)
Marty Ehrlich Group
The Long View | Enja | ENJ-9452 2
Michele Rosewoman Sextet
Harvest | Enja | ENJ-7069 2
Bobo,Willie | (congas,bongos,cowbell,dr,timbales)
Bobby Hutcherson Orchestra
Montara | Blue Note | 590956-2
Cal Tjader Group
Verve Jazz Masters Vol.60:The Collection | Verve | 529866-2
Cal Tjader Quartet
Black Hawk Nights | Fantasy | FCD 24755-2
Our Blues | Fantasy | FCD 24771-2
Cal Tjader Plays Harold Arlen & West Side Story | Fantasy | FCD 24775-2
Cal Tjader Quintet
Our Blues | Fantasy | FCD 24771-2
Concerts In The Sun | Fantasy | FCD 9688-2
Cal Tjader's Latin Concert | Original Jazz Classics | OJCCD 643-2(F 8014)
Cal Tjader Septet
Talkin Verve/Roots Of Acid Jazz:Cal Tjader | Verve | 531562-2
Cal Tjader Sextet
Black Hawk Nights | Fantasy | FCD 24755-2
The Jazz Giants Play Cole Porter:Night And Day | Prestige | PCD 24203-2
Charlie Rouse Orchestra
Bossa Nova Bacchanal | Blue Note | 593875-2
Blue Bossa | Blue Note | 795590-2
Chico Hamilton
The Dealer | Impulse(MCA) | 547958-2
Chico Hamilton Sextet
The Dealer | Impulse(MCA) | 547958-2
Grant Green Sextet
Blue Bossa | Blue Note | 795590-2
Herbie Hancock Quartet
Herbie Hancock:The Complete Blue Note Sixties Sessions | Blue Note | 495569-2
Ike Quebec Quintet
Blue Bossa | Blue Note | 795590-2
Miles Davis Sextet
Sorcerer | CBS | CK 65680
Mongo Santamaria And His Band
Sabroso | Original Jazz Classics | OJCCD 281-2
Sarah Vaughan With Orchestra
!Viva! Vaughan | Mercury | 549374-2
Victor Feldman Orchestra
Latinsville | Contemporary | CCD 9005-2
Wes Montgomery Orchestra
Muvin' Wes | Verve | 521433-2
Wes Montgomery With The Johnny Pate Orchestra
Verve Jazz Masters 14:Wes Montgomery | Verve | 519826-2
Wes Montgomery:The Verve Jazz Sides | Verve | 521690-2
Talkin' Jazz:Roots Of Acid Jazz | Verve | 529580-2
Willie Bobo Group
Juicy | Verve | 519857-2
Bobo's Beat | Roulette | 590954-2
Jazzrock-Anthology Vol.3:Fusion | Zounds | CD 27100555
Bobs,The: |
Klaus König Orchestra
Reviews | Enja | ENJ-9061 2
Bocage,Peter | (tpv)
Eureka Brass Band
Atlantic Jazz: New Orleans | Atlantic | 7567-81700-2
Böck,Charly | (perc)
Gerwin Eisenhauer's The Gäff Gang feat. Lisa Wahland
Favorite Tunes | Edition Collage | EC 527-2
Bock,Deborah | (v)
Melissa Walker And Her Band
I Saw The Sky | Enja | ENJ-9409 2
Bock,Hans-Jürgen | (pel-p)
Old Merrytale Jazz Band
The Very Best Of Dixieland Jazz | Verve | 535529-2
Bockholt,Johannes | (dr)
Céline Rudolph And Her Trio
Paintings | Nabel Records:Jazz Network | CD 4661
Book Of Travels | Nabel Records:Jazz Network | CD 4672
Volker Kottenhahn Trio
Out Of Print | Nabel Records:Jazz Network | CD 4680
Bockius,Frank | (dr,tambourinevoc)
Jan Harrington With The Arthur Blythe Quartet
Remembering Dinah-A Salute To Dinah Washington | Hot Shot Records | HSR 8313-2
Matthias Stich & Whisper Not
Bach Lives!! | Satin Doll Productions | SDP 1018-1 CD
Bockius,Peter | (b)
Jan Harrington With The Arthur Blythe Quartet
Remembering Dinah-A Salute To Dinah Washington | Hot Shot Records | HSR 8313-2
Thomas Reimer Trio
Vienna's Heardt | Edition Collage | EC 506-2
Boddicker,Michael | (synth,lyricon,vocoder)
Paulinho Da Costa Orchestra
Happy People | Original Jazz Classics | OJCCD 783-2(2312102)
Bodenseh,Markus | (bel-b)
Frank Eberle Septet
Scarlet Sunrise | Satin Doll Productions | SDP 1041-1 CD
Polyphonix
Alarm | Jazz 'n' Arts Records | 0300
Rainer Tempel Big Band
Melodies Of '98 | Jazz 4 Ever Records:Jazz Network | J4E 4744
Album 03 | Jazz 'n' Arts Records | JNA 1102
Rainer Tempel Quintet
Blick In Die Welt | Edition Musikat | EDM 038
Bodker,Niels | (drwbd)
Henrik Johansen's Jazzband
The Golden Years Of Revival Jazz,Vol 1 | Storyville | STCD 5506
The Golden Years Of Revival Jazz,Vol.2 | Storyville | STCD 5507
Theis/Nyegaard Jazzband
The Golden Years Of Revival Jazz,Sampler | Storyville | 109 1001
The Golden Years Of Revival Jazz,Vol.3 | Storyville | STCD 5508
The Golden Years Of Revival Jazz,Vol.5 | Storyville | STCD 5510
The Golden Years Of Revival Jazz,Vol.6 | Storyville | STCD 5511
The Golden Years Of Revival Jazz,Vol.12 | Storyville | STCD 5517
The Golden Years Of Revibal Jazz,Vol.15 | Storyville | STCD 5520
Bodner,Phil | (alto-fl,cl,contra-b-cl,ss,ts,bs)
Billie Holiday With The Ray Ellis Orchestra
Lady In Satin | CBS | CK 65144
Cal Tjader With The Lalo Schifrin Orchestra
Talkin Verve/Roots Of Acid Jazz:Cal Tjader | Verve | 531562-2
Coleman Hawkins With Billy Byers And His Orchestra
Planet Jazz:Coleman Hawkins | Planet Jazz | 2152055-2
The Hawk In Hi-Fi | RCA | 2663842-2
Earl Klugh Group With Strings
Late Night Guitar | Blue Note | 498573-2
Freddie Hubbard With Orchestra
This Is Jazz:Freddie Hubbard | CBS | CK 65041
Gato Barbieri Group
Planet Jazz:Gato Barbieri | RCA | 2165364-2
Gato Barbieri:The Best Of The Early Years | RCA | 2663523-2
George Benson With The Don Sebesky Orchestra
Verve Jazz Masters 21:George Benson | Verve | 521861-2
Glenn Miller And His Orchestra
The Glenn Miller Orchestra In Digital Mood | GRP | GRP 95022
Grant Green Orchestra
Grant Green:Blue Breakbeat | Blue Note | 494705-2
Grant Green With Orchestra
The Final Comedown(Soundtrack) | Blue Note | 581678-2
J.J.Johnson And His Orchestra
Planet Jazz:J.J.Johnson | Planet Jazz | 2159974-2
Joe Williams With The Frank Hunter Orchestra
Planet Jazz:Joe Williams | Planet Jazz | 2165370-2
Joe Williams With The Jimmy Jones Orchestra
Planet Jazz:Joe Williams | Planet Jazz | 2165370-2
Joe Williams,With The Oliver Nelson Orchestra
Planet Jazz:Joe Williams | Planet Jazz | 2165370-2
Lalo Schifrin And His Orchestra
Verve Jazz Masters 39:Cal Tjader | Verve | 521858-2
Miles Davis With Gil Evans & His Orchestra
Porgy And Bess | CBS | CK 65141
Milt Jackson And His Orchestra
Sunflower | CTI | ZK 65131
Oliver Nelson And His Orchestra
More Blues And The Abstract Truth | Impulse(MCA) | 951212-2
Paul Desmond Quartet With The Don Sebesby Orchestra
From The Hot Afternoon | Verve | 543487-2
Paul Desmond With Strings
Desmond Blue | RCA | 2663898-2
Wes Montgomery With The Jimmy Jones Orchestra
Wes Montgomery-The Complete Riverside Recordings | Riverside | 12 RCD 4408-2
The Jazz Giants Play Rodgers & Hart:Blue Moon | Prestige | PCD 24205-2
Boelens,Miguel | (as)
René Pretschner Quartet
Floating Pictures | Green House Music | CD 1001
Boeren,Bert | (co,tbfl)
Dutch Swing College Band
Digital Anniversary | Philips | 824585-2 PMS
Bogaart,Robert | (tp)
Landes Jugend Jazz Orchester Hessen
Touch Of Lips | hr music.de | hrmj 004-01 CD
Bogas,Ed | (condarr)
Gene Ammons Sextet With Strings
Fine And Mellow | Prestige | PRCD 24281-2
Bögershausen,Ulli | (g,g-solo12-string-g)
Ulli Bögershausen
Sologuitar | Laika Records | 35101132
Private Stories | Laika Records | 35101542
Christmas Carols | Laika Records | 35101622
Ageless Guitar Solos | Laika Records | 8695071
Best Of Ulli Bögershausen | Laika Records | LK 93-045
Ulli Bögershausen-Reinhold Westerheide
Pictures | Laika Records | LK 35100932
Boggs,Peter | (dr)
Marty Grosz And His Honoris Causa Jazz Band
Hooray For Bix! | Good Time Jazz | GTCD 10065-2
Boghossian,Sam | (viola)
Johnny Hartman And His Orchestra
Unforgettable | Impulse(MCA) | IMP 11522
Milt Jackson And His Orchestra
Reverence And Compassion | Reprise | 9362-45204-2
Bohana Jazzband |
Bohana Jazzband
The Golden Years Of Revival Jazz,Vol.6 | Storyville | STCD 5511
The Golden Years Of Revival Jazz,Vol.10 | Storyville | STCD 5515
Bohannon,Hoyt | (tb)
Harry James And His Orchestra
Trumpet Blues:The Best Of Harry James | Capitol | 521224-2
Bohanon,George | (tb,bar-h,percmaracas)
Bobby Bryant Orchestra
Deep Blue-The United States Of Mind | Blue Note | 521152-2
Chico Hamilton Quintet
The Dealer | Impulse(MCA) | 547958-2
Donald Byrd Orchestra
Places And Spaces | Blue Note | 854326-2
Flora Purim With Orchestra
Joe Henderson:The Milestone Years | Milestone | 8MCD 4413-2
GRP All-Star Big Band
GRP All-Star Big Band:Live! | GRP | GRP 97402
All Blues | GRP | GRP 98002
Hampton Hawes Orchestra
Northern Windows Plus | Prestige | PRCD 24278-2
Jimmy Smith All Stars
Jimmy Smith:Dot Com Blues | Blue Thumb | 543978-2
Joe Henderson And His Orchestra
Joe Henderson:The Milestone Years | Milestone | 8MCD 4413-2
Joe Henderson Group
Jazzin' Vol.2: The Music Of Stevie Wonder | Fantasy | FANCD 6088-2
Milt Jackson And His Orchestra
Reverence And Compassion | Reprise | 9362-45204-2
Raul De Souza Orchestra
Cannonball Adderley Birthday Celebration | Fantasy | FANCD 6087-2
Stan Getz With Orchestra
Apasionado | A&M Records | 395297-2
The Quincy Jones-Sammy Nestico Orchestra
Basie & Beyond | Warner | 9362-47792-2
Bohanon,Hoyt | (tb)
Peggy Lee With The Quincy Jones Orchestra
Blues Cross Country | Capitol | 520088-2
Bohanon,Steve | (dr)
Don Ellis Orchestra
Electric Bath | CBS | CK 65522
Bohländer,Carlo | (tp)
Kurt Edelhagen All Stars Und Solisten
Deutsches Jazz Fesival 1954/1955 | Bear Family Records | BCD 15430
Böhlke,Andreas | (flas)
Wayne Bartlett With The Thomas Hufschmidt Group
Tokyo Blues | Laika Records | 35101212
Böhlke,Edgar M. | (narration)
Okschila Tatanka
Wounded Knee-Lyrik Und Jazz | Wergo | SM 1088-2
Böhm,Rainer | (p)
Changes
Jazz Changes? | Jazz 'n' Arts Records | 0100
Fritz Münzer Tentet
Blue Ideas | Jazz 'n' Arts Records | 0200
Schlosser/Weber/Böhm/Huber/Binder
L 14,16 | Jazz 4 Ever Records:Jazz Network | J4E 4760
Thomas Siffling Jazz Quartet
Soft Winds | Satin Doll Productions | SDP 1030-1 CD
Thomas Stiffling Group
Stories | Jazz 4 Ever Records:Jazz Network | J4E 4756
Bohn,Carsten | (dr,percvoice)
Bitkicks
Kickbit Information | ATM Records | ATM 3823-AH
Uli Trepte Group
Guru Guru/Uli Trepte | ATM Records | ATM 3815-AH
Bohn,Rudi | (p,harpsichordorg)
Helmut Zacharias mit Kleiner Tanz-Besetzung
Ich Habe Rhythmus | Bear Family Records | BCD 15642 AH
Helmut Zacharias mit seinem Orchester
Ich Habe Rhythmus | Bear Family Records | BCD 15642 AH
Helmut Zacharias Quintet
Ich Habe Rhythmus | Bear Family Records | BCD 15642 AH
Helmut Zacharias Sextet
Ich Habe Rhythmus | Bear Family Records | BCD 15642 AH
Böhringer,Peter | (tpmellophone)
Peter A. Schmid Trio With Guests
Profound Sounds In An Empty Reservoir | Creative Works Records | CW CD 1033
Q4 Orchester Project
Lyon's Brood | Creative Works Records | CW CD 1018-3
Yavapai | Creative Works Records | CW CD 1028-2
Boi Akih |
Boi Akih
Uwa I | Enja | ENJ-9472 2
Boiadjiev String-Ensemble |
Bill Ramsey With Orchestra
Gettin' Back To Swing | Bear Family Records | BCD 15813 AH
Boiadjiev,Nedeltcho | (cond)
Boice,Johnny | (tb)
Buddy Rich And His Orchestra
Swingin' New Big Band | Pacific Jazz | 835232-2
Buddy Rich Big Band
The New One! | Pacific Jazz | 494507-2
Boine,Mari | (voc)
Jan Garbarek Group
Twelve Moons | ECM | 1500(519500-2)
Visible World | ECM | 1585(529086-2)
Boissenin,Anne-Sophie | (cello)
Stephane Grappelli With The Michel Legrand Orchestra
Grapelli Story | Verve | 515807-2
Bojorquez,Ray | (ts)
Ella Fitzgerald With Orchestra
Ella/Things Ain't What They Used To Be | Warner | 9362-47875-2
Bolado,Vidal | (congas)
Tadd Dameron Tentet
Jazz Profile:Dexter Gordon | Blue Note | 823514-2
Boland,Francy | (arr,pel-p)
Kenny Clarke-Francy Boland Big Band
Clark-Boland Big Band: TNP, October 29th, 1969 | Laserlight | 36129
Three Latin Adventures | MPS | 529095-2
More Smiles | MPS | 9814789
All Smiles | MPS | 9814790
Francy Boland-Fellini 712 | MPS | 9814805
NDR Big Band With Guests
50 Years Of NDR Big Band:Bravissimo II | ACT | 9259-2
Bolanos,Angel Pedro | (iya)
Lazaro Ros Ensemble
Ori Batá (Cuban Yoruba Music) | Enja | ENJ-9381 2
Bolar,Abe | (b)
Cliff Jackson's Washboard Wanderers
Uptown And Lowdown | Prestige | PCD 24262-2
Hot Lips Page Band
Planet Jazz:Jazz Trumpet | Planet Jazz | 2169654-2
Bolato,Jean | (bvoice)
Pata Music Meets Arfi
News Of Roi Ubu | Pata Musik | PATA 10 CD
Bolberg Pedersen,Herik | (tpfl-h)
Geri Allen And The Jazzpar 1996 Nonet
Some Aspects Of Water | Storyville | STCD 4212
Jens Winther And The Danish Radio Jazz Orchestra
Angels | dacapo | DCCD 9442
The Danish Radio Jazz Orchestra
This Train:The Danish Radio Jazz Orchestra Plays The Music Of Ray Pitts | dacapo | DCCD 9428
Bolden,Arnold | (dr)
Fats Waller And His Rhythm
Planet Jazz Sampler | Planet Jazz | 2152326-2
Bolden,James 'Buddy' | (tp)
B.B.King And His Band
Live At San Quentin | MCA | MCD 06103
Duke Ellington Orchestra
Continuum | Fantasy | FCD 24765-2
Bolden,Walter | (dr)
Stan Getz Quartet
Stan Getz-The Complete Roost Sessions | EMI Records | 859622-2
Stan Getz:Imagination | Dreyfus Jazz Line | FDM 36733-2
Tony Scott And The All Stars
Body And Soul Revisited | GRP | GRP 16272
Bolds,Kenny | (dr)
Lionel Hampton And His All Star Jazz Inner Circle
Lionel Hampton: Salle Pleyel, March 9th, 1971 | Laserlight | 36133
Bolin,Tommy | (el-gg)
Billy Cobham Group
Spectrum | Atlantic | 7567-81428-2
The Best Of Billy Cobham | Atlantic | 7567-81558-2
Billy Cobham Quartet
Atlantic Jazz: Fusion | Atlantic | 7567-81711-2
Bollani,Stefano | (pperc)
Enrico Rava Quintet
Easy Living | ECM | 1760(9812050)
Richard Galliano Group I Solisti Dell'Orchestra Della Toscana
Gallianissimo! The Best Of Richard Galliano | Dreyfus Jazz Line | FDM 36616-2
Richard Galliano With Orchestra
Passatori | Dreyfus Jazz Line | FDM 36601-2
Bollenback,Paul | (el-g,g,g-synth,kalimbasynth)
Christian Scheuber Quartet
Clara's Smile | double moon | DMCHR 71025
Christian Scheuber Quintet
Clara's Smile | double moon | DMCHR 71025
Gary Thomas Group
Found On Sordid Street | Winter&Winter | 910002-2
Ron Holloway-Paul Bollenback
Jazzin' Vol.2: The Music Of Stevie Wonder | Fantasy | FANCD 6088-2
Terri Lyne Carrington Group
Jazz Is A Spirit | ACT | 9408-2

INTERPRETENVERZEICHNIS

Bolling,Claude | (p,arr,compp-solo)
Cat Anderson And His All Stars
Americans Swinging In Paris:Cat Anderson | EMI Records | 539658-2
Claude Bolling
Jazz In Paris:Claude Bolling Plays Original Piano Greats | EmArCy | 548151-2 PMS
Lionel Hampton And His Orchestra
Lionel Hampton's Paris All Stars | Vogue | 21511502
Lionel Hampton Quintet
Americans Swinging In Paris:Lionel Hampton | EMI Records | 539649-2
Lionel Hampton Sextet
Americans Swinging In Paris:Lionel Hampton | EMI Records | 539649-2

Bollman,Günter | (tb)
The Three Sopranos With The HR Big Band
The Three Sopranos | hr music.de | hrmj 001-01 CD

Bollmann,Günter | (tb,euphoniumtb.euphonium)
HR Big Band
The American Songs Of Kurt Weill | hr music.de | hrmj 006-01 CD
Libertango:Homage An Astor Piazolla | hr music.de | hrmj 014-02 CD
HR Big Band With Marjorie Barnes And Frits Landesbergen
Swinging Christmas | hr music.de | hrmj 012-02 CD
HR Big Band With Marjorie Barnes And Frits Landesbergen And Strings
Swinging Christmas | hr music.de | hrmj 012-02 CD

Bolte,Peter | (as,woodwinds,fl,cl,ss,p,el-p,dr)
Abdullah Ibrahim With The NDR Big Band
Ekapa Lodumo | TipToe | TIP-888840 2
Matthias Petzold Esperanto-Music
Lifelines | Indigo-Records | 1001 CD
NDR Big Band
The Theatre Of Kurt Weil | ACT | 9234-2
Oscar Brown Jr. with The NDR Big Band
Live Every Minute | Minor Music | 801071
Pee Wee Ellis & NDR Bigband
What You Like | Minor Music | 801064
Peter Bolte
Trio | Jazz Haus Musik | JHM 0095 CD
Peter Bolte Quartet
Evocation | Jazz Haus Musik | JHM 0079 CD
Peter Bolte Trio
Trio | Jazz Haus Musik | JHM 0095 CD
Peter Bolte-Imgmar Heller
Trio | Jazz Haus Musik | JHM 0095 CD
Peter Bolte-Marcio Doctor
Zeitraum | Jazz Haus Musik | JHM 0113 CD

Bolton,Dupree | (tp)
Harold Land Quintet
The Fox | Original Jazz Classics | OJCCD 343-2

Boltro,Flavio | (tpfl-h)
Laurent De Wilde Sextet
Time Change | Warner | 8573-84315-2
Michel Petrucciani Sextet
Both Worlds | Dreyfus Jazz Line | FDM 36590-2

Bolvig,Palle | (tpfl-h)
Miles Davis With The Danish Radio Big Band
Aura | CBS | CK 63962
Mona Larsen And The Danish Radio Big Band Plus Soloists
Michael Mantler:Cerco Un Paese Innocente | ECM | 1556
Stan Getz With Ib Glindemann And His Orchestra
Stan Getz In Europe | Laserlight | 24657
Stan Getz With The Danish Radio Big Band
Stan Getz In Europe | Laserlight | 24657
Stan Kenton With The Danish Radio Big Band
Stan Kenton With The Danish Radio Big Band | Storyville | STCD 8340
The Danish Radio Big Band
Aura | CBS | CK 63962
The Danish Radio Jazz Orchestra
This Train:The Danish Radio Jazz Orchestra Plays The Music Of Ray Pitts | dacapo | DCCD 9428

Boman,Patrik | (b)
Lisa Ekdahl With The Peter Nordahl Trio
When Did You Leave Heaven | RCA | 2143175-2
Back To Earth | RCA | 2161463-2

Bombardo,Pau | (dr)
Mitchell-Terraza Group
Shell Blues | Fresh Sound Records | FSNT 005 CD

Bona,Richard | (djembe,shaker,udu,el-b,voc,kalimba)
Cornelius Claudio Kreusch Group
Scoop | ACT | 9255-2
Jacky Terrasson Group
What It Is | Blue Note | 498756-2
Renee Rosnes Quartet
Art & Soul | Blue Note | 499997-2
Robert Dick Group With The Soldier String Quartet
Jazz Standard On Mars | Enja | ENJ-9327 2

Bonaccio,Benny | (cl,as,b-cl,bsreeds)
Paul Whiteman And His Orchestra
Planet Jazz:Jack Teagarden | Planet Jazz | 2161236-2
Jazz:The Essential Collection Vol.3 | IN+OUT Records | 78013-2

Bonaccorso,Rosario | (b)
Enrico Rava Quintet
Easy Living | ECM | 1760(9812050)

Bonal,Jean | (g)
Guy Lafitte Sextet
Jazz In Paris:Guy Lafitte-Blue And Sentimental | EmArCy | 159852-2 PMS

Bond,Jimmy | (arrb)
Art Pepper Quartet
Intensity | Original Jazz Classics | OJCCD 387-2
The Way It Is | Original Jazz Classics | OJCCD 389-2
The Jazz Giants Play Jerome Kern:Yesterdays | Prestige | PCD 24202-2
Art Pepper Quintet
Smack Up | Original Jazz Classics | OJC20 176-2
Art Pepper Quintet With Strings
Art Pepper:The Complete Galaxy Recordings | Galaxy | 16GCD 1016-2
Chet Baker Big Band
The Best Of Chet Baker Plays | Pacific Jazz | 797161-2
Chet Baker Quartet
Jazz In Paris:Chet Baker Quartet Plays Standards | EmArCy | 014378-2 PMS
Verve Jazz Masters Vol.60:The Collection | Verve | 529866-2
Let's Get Lost: The Best Of Chet Baker Sings | Pacific Jazz | 792932-2
Chet Baker Quintet
Chet Baker & Crew | Pacific Jazz | 582671-2
Chet Baker Sextet
Chet Baker & Crew | Pacific Jazz | 582671-2
The Best Of Chet Baker Plays | Pacific Jazz | 797161-2
Gerald Wilson And His Orchestra
Blue Breaks Beats Vol.2 | Blue Note | 789907-2
Jimmy Witherspoon And His Band
Baby, Baby, Baby | Original Blues Classics | OBCCD 527-2(P 7290)
Joe Gordon Quintet
Lookin' Good | Original Jazz Classics | OJCCD 1934-2(S 7597)
Johnny Griffin Quintet
Grab This! | Original Jazz Classics | OJCCD 1941-2(RLP 9437)
Johnny Hartman And His Orchestra
Unforgettable | Impulse(MCA) | IMP 11522
Lars Gullin And The Chet Baker Quartet
Lars Gullin 1955/56 Vol.1 | Dragon | DRCD 224
Lawrence Marable Quartet feat. James Clay
Midnight Blue(The [Be]witching Hour) | Blue Note | 854365-2

Bondell,Jordi | (g)
Joan Abril Quintet
Insomnio | Fresh Sound Records | FSNT 034 CD
Victor De Diego Group
Amaia | Fresh Sound Records | FSNT 012 CD

Bone,E.W. 'Red' | (tb)
Tommy Dorsey And His Orchestra
Planet Jazz:Tommy Dorsey | Planet Jazz | 2159972-2
Planet Jazz:Big Bands | Planet Jazz | 2169649-2
Planet Jazz:Swing | Planet Jazz | 2169651-2

Bone,Ponty | (accordeon)
Hans Theessink Group
Crazy Moon | Minor Music | 801052

Bonfa,Luiz | (gvoc)
Ithamara Koorax With Band
Love Dance:The Ballad Album | Milestone | MCD 9327-2
Stan Getz Group
Verve Jazz Masters 53:Stan Getz-Bossa Nova | Verve | 529904-2
Stan Getz Quartet
Verve Jazz Masters 53:Stan Getz-Bossa Nova | Verve | 529904-2
Stan Getz-Luiz Bonfa Group
The Antonio Carlos Jobim Songbook | Verve | 525472-2
Stan Getz-Luiz Bonfa Orchestra
Verve Jazz Masters 13:Antonio Carlos Jobim | Verve | 516409-2
Jazz Samba Encore! | Verve | 823613-2
Stan Getz-Luiz Bonfa Quartet
Jazz Samba Encore! | Verve | 823613-2
Stan Getz-Luiz Bonfa Quintet
Jazz Samba Encore! | Verve | 823613-2

Bonfils,Tony | (bb-g)
Dee Dee Bridgewater With Band
Victim Of Love | Verve | 841199-2
Dee Dee Bridgewater With Her Trio
Live In Paris | Verve | 014317-2

Bong,Kurt | (bongosdr)
Dieter Reith Quintet
Reith On! | MPS | 557423-2

Bong,Melanie | (voc)
Maximilian Geller Group
Maximilian Geller Goes Bossa | Edition Collage | EC 496-2
Maximilian Geller Quartet feat. Melanie Bong
Smile | Edition Collage | EC 461-2
Maimilian Geller Goes Bossa Encore | Edition Collage | EC 505-2
Vocal Moments | Take Twelve On CD | TT 008-2
Melanie Bong With Band
Fantasia | Jazz 4 Ever Records:Jazz Network | J4E 4755

Bonica,Joe | (dr,percrain-stick)
Amman Boutz
Some Other Tapes | Fish Music | FM 009/10 CD
Chromatic Alarm
Some Other Tapes | Fish Music | FM 009/10 CD
Ekkehard Jost & Chromatic Alarm
Von Zeit Zu Zeit | Fish Music | FM 005 CD
Wintertango | Fish Music | FM 008 CD
Ekkehard Jost Ensemble
Weimarer Balladen | Fish Music | FM 004 CD
Ekkehard Jost Nonet
Out Of Jost's Songbook | Fish Music | FM 006 CD
Ekkehard Jost Quartet
Some Other Tapes | Fish Music | FM 009/10 CD
Ekkehard Jost Quintet
Some Other Tapes | Fish Music | FM 009/10 CD
Ekkehard Jost Trio
Some Other Tapes | Fish Music | FM 009/10 CD
Giessen-Köln-Nonett
Some Other Tapes | Fish Music | FM 009/10 CD
Olaf Kübler Quartet
Midnight Soul | Village | VILCD 1024-2
Transalpin Express Orchestra
Some Other Tapes | Fish Music | FM 009/10 CD

Bonilla,Edwin | (cowbell,maracas,timbalesperc)
Arturo Sandoval And The Latin Train Band
Arturo Sandoval & The Latin Train | GRP | GRP 98202

Bonilla,Luis | (tbb-tb)
Lester Bowie's Brass Fantasy
The Fire This Time | IN+OUT Records | 7019-2
The Odysse Of Funk & Popular Music | Dreyfus Jazz Line | FDM 37004-2
When The Spitit Returns | Dreyfus Jazz Line | FDM 37016-2

Bonisteel,Peter | (perc)
Dave Brubeck With The Erich Kunzel Orchestra
Truth Is Fallen | Atlantic | 7567-80761-2

Bonnen,Dietmar | (phardpaper-box)
Kölner Saxophon Mafia With Fleisch
Kölner Saxophon Mafia Proudly Presents | Jazz Haus Musik | JHM 0046 CD

Bonner,Joe | (keyboards,p,arr,chimes,bamboo-fl)
Pharoah Sanders Group
Black Unity | Impulse(MCA) | 951219-2

Bonsel,Hans | (cello)
Stochelo Rosenberg Group With Strings
Gypsy Swing | Verve | 527806-2

Booker Jr.,Marion | (dr)
Jimmy McGriff Quintet
Swingin' The Blues-Jumpin' The Blues | Laserlight | 24654

Booker,Beryl | (p)
Billie Holiday And Her All Stars
Billie's Blues | Blue Note | 748786-2
Slam Stewart Trio
The Small Black Groups | Storyville | 4960523

Booker,Marion | (dr)
George Benson Quartet + Guests
The George Benson Cookbook | CBS | 502470-2

Booker,Walter | (b,el-bg)
Archie Shepp Septet
The Way Ahead | Impulse(MCA) | 951272-2
Cannonball Adderley Group
Phenix | Fantasy | FCD 79004-2
Cannonball Adderley Quintet
The Best Of Cannonball Adderley:The Capitol Years | Capitol | 795482-2
Cannonball Adderley Septet
Inside Straight | Original Jazz Classics | OJCCD 750-2(F 9435)
Cannonball Adderley Sextet
Cannonball Adderley Birthday Celebration | Fantasy | FANCD 6087-2
Donald Byrd Quintet
Slow Drag | Blue Note | 535560-2
Donald Byrd Sextet
Blue Breaks Beats Vol.2 | Blue Note | 789907-2
Blue Break Beats | Blue Note | 799106-2
Blackjack | Blue Note | 821286-2
Joe Williams With The Cannonball Adderley Sextet
Cannonball Adderley Birthday Celebration | Fantasy | FANCD 6087-2
Joe Zawinul Group
Zawinul | Atlantic | 7567-81375-2
Kenny Barron-John Hicks Quartet
Rhythm-A-Ning | Candid | CCD 79044
Lee Morgan Sextet
Deep Blue-The United States Of Mind | Blue Note | 521152-2
Sonic Boom | Blue Note | 590414-2
Nat Adderley Group
Soul Of The Bible | Capitol | 358257-2
Nat Adderley Quintet
We Remember Cannon | IN+OUT Records | 7012-2
Jazz Unlimited | IN+OUT Records | 7017-2
Roy Hargrove Quartet
Family | Verve | 527630-2
Roy Hargrove Quintet
Family | Verve | 527630-2
Roy Hargrove-Walter Booker
Family | Verve | 527630-2
Sonny Rollins Orchestra
Alfie | Impulse(MCA) | 951224-2
Sonny Rollins Quartet
Sonny Rollins On Impulse | Impulse(MCA) | 951223-2
The Roots Of Acid Jazz | Impulse(MCA) | IMP 12042
Stan Getz With The Richard Evans Orchestra
What The World Needs Now-Stan Getz Plays Bacharach And David | Verve | 557450-2

Boom,Ricky | (voc)
Johannes Rediske Quintet
Jumpin' At The Badewanne | Bear Family Records | BCD 16172 AH

booMbooM |
booMbooM meets Uli Beckerhoff
Resurection Lounge | Laika Records | 35101512

Boone,Harvey | (as,bscl)
Connie's Inn Orchestra
Planet Jazz:Coleman Hawkins | Planet Jazz | 2152055-2
Fletcher Henderson And His Orchestra
Jazz:The Essential Collection Vol.1 | IN+OUT Records | 78011-2

Boone,Lester | (as,cl,bsreeds)
Earl Hines And His Orchestra
Jazz:The Essential Collection Vol.2 | IN+OUT Records | 78012-2
Louis Armstrong And His Orchestra
Satch Plays Fats(Complete) | CBS | CK 64927

Boone,Richard | (tbvoc)
Stan Getz With The Danish Radio Big Band
Stan Getz In Europe | Laserlight | 24657

Booth,David | (dr)
Ben Webster Quartet
Jazz:The Essential Collection Vol.3 | IN+OUT Records | 78013-2

Boozier,Henry | (tp)
Milt Jackson Quintet
Milt Jackson Birthday Celebration | Fantasy | FANCD 6079-2
MJQ | Original Jazz Classics | OJCCD 125-2

Bop City |
Bop City
Hot Jazz Bisquits | Hip Bop | HIBD 8801

Börcsök,Aliosa | (dr)
Jaco Pastorius Trio
Live In Italy & Honestly | Jazzpoint | JP 1059 CD

Bordas,Oriol | (as,vibld)
Frank Wess Meets The Paris-Barcelona Swing Connection
Paris-Barcelona Connection | Fresh Sound Records | FSNT 002 CD

Borealis Ensemble |
Terje Rypdal With The Borealis Ensemble
Q.E.D. | ECM | 1474

Borel,Felix | (v)
Rainer Tempel Band
Suite Ellington | Jazz 'n' Arts Records | JNA 0401

Borg,George | (reeds)
Quincy Jones And His Orchestra
Rahsaan/The Complete Mercury Recordings Of Roland Kirk | Mercury | 846630-2

Born,Michael | (percvib)
Jazzensemble Des Hessischen Rundfunks
Jazz Messe-Messe Für Unsere Zeit | hr music.de | hrmj 003-01 CD
Landes Jugend Jazz Orchester Hessen
Touch Of Lips | hr music.de | hrmj 004-01 CD

Börner,Till | (tp)
Till Brönner-Gregoire Peters Quintet
Generations Of Jazz | Minor Music | 801037

Böröcz,Thomas | (dr)
Jaco Pastorius Groups
Another Side Of Jaco Pastorius | Jazzpoint | JP 1064 CD
Jaco Pastorius Trio
Live In Italy | Jazzpoint | JP 1031 CD

Borodkin,Abram | (cello)
Ben Webster With Orchestra And Strings
Music For Loving:Ben Webster With Strings | Verve | 527774-2
Ultimate Ben Webster selected by James Carter | Verve | 557537-2

Borsarello,Jacques | (viola)
Charlie Haden Quartet West With Strings
Now Is The Hour | Verve | 527827-2

Bos,Ruud | (cond,arrp)
Toots Thielemans And His Orchestra
Verve Jazz Masters Vol.59:Toots Thielemans | Verve | 535271-2
Toots Thielemans With The Ruud Bos Orchestra
The Silver Collection: Toots Thielemans | Polydor | 825086-2 PMS

Bosch,Ilse | (b)
The United Women's Orchestra
The Blue One | Jazz Haus Musik | JHM 0099 CD

Bosch,Miguel Angel | (tpfl-h)
Daniel Flors Group
When Least Expected | Fresh Sound Records | FSNT 080 CD
Orquestra De Cambra Teatre Lliure
Porgy And Bess | Fresh Sound Records | FSNT 066 CD

Bosco,Joao | (gvoc)
John Patitucci Group
Mistura Fina | GRP | GRP 98022

Bose,Sterling | (tpvoc)
Benny Goodman And His Orchestra
Planet Jazz:Benny Goodman | Planet Jazz | 2152054-2
Bob Crosby And His Orchestra
Swing Legens:Bob Crosby | Nimbus Records | NI 2011
Jack Teagarden And His Orchestra
Jazz:The Essential Collection Vol.3 | IN+OUT Records | 78013-2
Jack Teagarden With Orchestra
Jazz:The Essential Collection Vol.3 | IN+OUT Records | 78013-2
Tommy Dorsey And His Clambake Seven
Planet Jazz:Tommy Dorsey | Planet Jazz | 2159972-2
Planet Jazz:Swing | Planet Jazz | 2169651-2
Tommy Dorsey And His Orchestra
Planet Jazz:Tommy Dorsey | Planet Jazz | 2159972-2

Bossche,Henk | (tb)
Brocksieper-Jazz-Ensemble
Drums Boogie | Bear Family Records | BCD 15988 AH
Brocksieper-Solisten-Orchester
Globetrotter | Bear Family Records | BCD 15912 AH
Brocksieper-Special-Ensemble
Globetrotter | Bear Family Records | BCD 15912 AH

Bosse,Stoor | (dr)
Lars Gullin Quartet
Lars Gullin 1955/56 Vol.1 | Dragon | DRCD 224
Lars Gullin Quintet
Lars Gullin 1955/56 Vol.1 | Dragon | DRCD 224

Bostic,Earl | (asb)
Hot Lips Page And His Orchestra
Don Byas:Laura | Dreyfus Jazz Line | FDM 36714-2
Lionel Hampton And His Orchestra
Lionel Hampton:Flying Home | Dreyfus Jazz Line | FDM 36735-2

Boston Percussion Ensemble,The |
Max Roach With The Boston Percussion Ensemble
Clifford Brown-Max Roach:Alone Together-The Best Of The Mercury Years | Verve | 526373-2

Boston Pops Orchestra |
Duke Ellington Trio With The Boston Pops Orchestra
Highlights From The Duke Ellington Centennial Edition | RCA | 2663672-2

Boswell,Bobby | (b)
Abbey Lincoln With The Max Roach Quintet
Abbey Is Blue | Original Jazz Classics | OJC20 069-2(RLP 1153)
Abbey Lincoln With The Max Roach Sextet
Abbey Is Blue | Original Jazz Classics | OJC20 069-2(RLP 1153)
Max Roach Quintet
Clifford Brown-Max Roach:Alone Together-The Best Of The Mercury Years | Verve | 526373-2
Jazz In Paris:Max Roach-Parisian Sketches | EmArCy | 589963-2
Max Roach Sextet
Clifford Brown-Max Roach:Alone Together-The Best Of The Mercury Years | Verve | 526373-2

Botelho,Cesarius Alvim | (b)
Franz Koglmann Quintet
Opium | Between The Lines | btl 011(Efa 10181-2)

Both,Wim | (fl-htp)
Stochelo Rosenberg Group
Gypsy Swing | Verve | 527806-2
Bothen,Christer | (b-cl,ts,bells,dousso n'koni,p)
Beng Berger Band
Bitter Funeral Beer | ECM | 1179
Don Cherry Group
Don Cherry-The Sonet Recordings:Eternal Now/Live Ankara | Verve | 533049-2
Böther,Andreas | (as,fl,tssax)
Chet Baker With The NDR-Bigband
NDR Big Band-Bravissimo | ACT | 9232-2
My Favourite Songs: The Last Great Concert Vol.1 | Enja | ENJ-5097 2
The Last Concert Vol.I+II | Enja | ENJ-6074 22
Heinz Sauer Quartet With The NDR Big Band
NDR Big Band-Bravissimo | ACT | 9232-2
Joe Pass With The NDR Big Band And Radio Philharmonie Hannover
Joe Pass In Hamburg | ACT | 9100-2
NDR Big Band
NDR Big Band-Bravissimo | ACT | 9232-2
Bothner,Jürgen | (ts)
Frank Eberle Septet
Scarlet Sunrise | Satin Doll Productions | SDP 1041-1 CD
Fritz Münzer Tentet
Blue Ideas | Jazz 'n' Arts Records | 0200
Bothwell,Johnny | (as)
Anita O'Day With Gene Krupa And His Orchestra
Let Me Off Uptown:Anita O'Day With Gene Krupa | CBS | CK 65625
Botkin,Perry | (gld)
Jack Teagarden With Orchestra
Jazz:The Essential Collection Vol.3 | IN+OUT Records | 78013-2
Lena Horne With The Lou Bring Orchestra
Planet Jazz:Lena Horne | Planet Jazz | 2165373-2
Planet Jazz:Female Jazz Vocalists | Planet Jazz | 2169656-2
Boto,José | (drperc)
Chet Baker & The Boto Brasilian Quartet
Chet Baker & The Boto Brasilian Quartet | Dreyfus Jazz Line | FDM 36511-9
Botschinsky,Allan | (fl-htp)
Allan Botschinsky Quartet
Last Summer | M.A Music | A 804-2
I've Got Another Rhythm | M.A Music | A 916-2
Allan Botschinsky/Niels-Henning Orsted-Pedersen
Duologue | M.A Music | NU 206-3
European Jazz Ensemble
European Jazz Ensemble At The Philharmonic Cologne | M.A Music | A 800-2
20th Anniversary Tour | Konnex Records | KCD 5078
European Jazz Ensemble 25th Anniversary | Konnex Records | KCD 5100
European Trumpet Summit
European Trumpet Summit | Konnex Records | KCD 5064
First Brass
First Brass | M.A Music | NU 158-3
Stan Getz With Ib Glindemann And His Orchestra
Stan Getz In Europe | Laserlight | 24657
Stan Getz With The Danish Radio Big Band
Stan Getz In Europe | Laserlight | 24657
Stan Kenton With The Danish Radio Big Band
Stan Kenton With The Danish Radio Big Band | Storyville | STCD 8340
Wilton Gaynair Quintet
Alpharian | Konnex Records | KCD 5032
Böttcher,Andreas | (org)
Andreas Böttcher-Günter Heinz
Ghost Busters | Organic Music | ORGM 9715
Böttcher,Martin | (g)
Helmut Zacharias & His Sax-Team
Ich Habe Rhythmus | Bear Family Records | BCD 15642 AH
Helmut Zacharias mit seinem Orchester
Ich Habe Rhythmus | Bear Family Records | BCD 15642 AH
Botti,Chris | (keyboard-b-dr-programming,tpfl-h)
The Brecker Brothers
Out Of The Loop | GRP | GRP 97842
Bottom,Davis | (voc)
Herbie Hancock Group
Magic Window | CBS | 486572-2
Boucaya,William | (bssax)
Alain Goraguer Orchestra
Jazz In Paris | EmArCy | 548793-2
Golden Gate Quartet With The Martial Solal Orchestra
Americans Swinging In Paris:Golden Gate Quartet | EMI Records | 539659-2
From Spiritual To Swing Vol.2 | EMI Records | 780573-2
Lionel Hampton All Stars
Jazz In Paris:Lionel Hampton And His French New Sound Vol.1 | EmArCy | 549405-2 PMS
Jazz In Paris:Lionel Hampton And His French New Sound Vol.2 | EmArCy | 549406-2 PMS
Lucky Thompson With The Gerard Pochonet All-Stars
Planet Jazz:Jazz Saxophone | Planet Jazz | 2169653-2
Lucky Thompson's Modern Jazz Group Tentet
Jazz In Paris:Lucky Thompson-Modern Jazz Group | EmArCy | 159823-2 PMS
Sarah Vaughan With The Quincy Jones Orchestra
Jazz In Paris:Sarah Vaughan-Vaughan And Violins | EmArCy | 065004-2
4 By 4:Ella Fitzgerald/Sarah Vaughan/Billie Holiday/Dinah Washington | Verve | 559693-2
Bouchety,Jean | (b)
Bill Coleman And His Orchestra
Don Byas:Laura | Dreyfus Jazz Line | FDM 36714-2
Bill Coleman Quintet
Americans Swinging In Paris:Don Byas | EMI Records | 539655-2
Django Reinhardt And The Quintet Du Hot Club De France
Planet Jazz:Django Reinhardt | Planet Jazz | 2152071-2
Don Byas Quartet
Americans Swinging In Paris:Don Byas | EMI Records | 539655-2
Don Byas:Laura | Dreyfus Jazz Line | FDM 36714-2
Don Byas Ree-Boppers
Don Byas:Laura | Dreyfus Jazz Line | FDM 36714-2
Tyree Glenn
Don Byas:Laura | Dreyfus Jazz Line | FDM 36714-2
Bouck,Aubrey | (fr-h)
Peggy Lee With The Quincy Jones Orchestra
Blues Cross Country | Capitol | 520088-2
Boudreaux,Jeff | (dr)
Caecilie Norby With Band
My Corner Of The Sky | Blue Note | 853422-2
Boukouya,Marc | (tb)
Association Urbanetique
Ass Bedient | Jazz 4 Ever Records:Jazz Network | J4E 4723
Boulware,Will | (keyboards,orgp)
Maceo Parker Group
Southern Exposure | Minor Music | 801033
Maceo(Soundtrack) | Minor Music | 801046
Maceo Parker With The Rebirth Brass Band
Maceo(Soundtrack) | Minor Music | 801046
Pee Wee Ellis Quartet
Sepia Tonality | Minor Music | 801040
Pee Wee Ellis Quintet
Sepia Tonality | Minor Music | 801040
Remy Filipovitch-Will Boulware
Alone Together | Album | AS 55417 CD
Bourelly,Carl | (synth,programmingvoc)
Jean-Paul Bourelly Group
Jungle Cowboy | JMT Edition | 919009-2
Jean-Paul Bourelly Trance Atlantic
Boom Bop II | double moon | CHRDM 71023
Bourelly,Jean-Paul | (el-g,g,b-g,effects,voc,g-synth)
Cassandra Wilson And Her Quintet
Point Of View | JMT Edition | 919004-2
Craig Harris And Tailgater's Tales
Blackout In The Square Root Of Soul | JMT Edition | 919015-2
Jean-Paul Bourelly Group
Jungle Cowboy | JMT Edition | 919009-2
Jean-Paul Bourelly Trance Atlantic
Boom Bop II | double moon | CHRDM 71023
Miles Davis Group
Amandla | Warner | 7599-25873-2
Muneer B.Fennell & The Rhythm String Band
An Encounter With Higher Forces | double moon | CHRDM 71019
Bourgeyx,Vincent | (p,el-porg)
Stéphane Mercier Group
Flor De Luna | Fresh Sound Records | FSNT 097 CD
Bourguignon,José | (dr)
Rene Thomas Quintet
Jazz In Paris:René Thomas-The Real Cat | EmArCy | 549400-2 PMS
Bourne[Notorious] | (rap)
Tom Browne Groups
Mo' Jamaica Funk | Hip Bop | HIBD 8002
Bourree,Francis | (ts)
Dee Dee Bridgewater With Band
Victim Of Love | Verve | 841199-2
Bouterwerk,Thomas | (as)
Dusko Goykovich Big Band
Balkan Connection | Enja | ENJ-9047 2
Boutté,Lillian | (voc)
Christian Willisohn Group
Blues On The World | Blues Beacon | BLU-1025 2
Christian Willisohn-Lillian Boutté
Come Together | ART BY HEART | ABH 2002 2
Lillian Boutté And Her Group
You've Gotta Love Pops:Lillian Bouté Sings Louis Armstrong | ART BY HEART | ABH 2005 2
The Gospel Book | Blues Beacon | BLU-1017 2
Lillian Boutté And Her Group & The Soulful Heavenly Stars
The Gospel Book | Blues Beacon | BLU-1017 2
Bova,Jeff | (electronic-keyboards,programming)
Pharoah Sanders Group
Save Our Children | Verve | 557297-2
Pharoah Sanders Orchestra
Message From Home | Verve | 529578-2
Bover,Albert | (p)
Albert Bover-Horacio Fumero
Duo | Fresh Sound Records | FSNT 025 CD
Eladio Reinon Quintet
Es La Historia De Un Amor | Fresh Sound Records | FSNT 004 CD
José Luis Gámez Quartet
Dr.Jeckyl | Fresh Sound Records | FSNT 006 CD
José Luis Gámez Quintet
Dr.Jeckyl | Fresh Sound Records | FSNT 006 CD
Victor De Diego Group
Amaia | Fresh Sound Records | FSNT 012 CD
Bowden,Colin | (dr,snare-drwbd)
Doug Richford's London Jazzmen
The Golden Years Of Revival Jazz,Sampler | Storyville | 109 1001
Lonnie Donegan Skiffle Group
The Best Of Dixieland-Live in 1954/55 | London | 820878-2
Bowden,Ron | (drwbd)
Chris Barber Original Jazzband Of 1954
Chris Barber:40 Years Jubilee Concert | Storyville | 4990013
Chris Barber's Jazz Band
The Very Best Of Dixieland Jazz | Verve | 535529-2
The Best Of Dixieland-Live in 1954/55 | London | 820878-2
The Golden Years Of Revival Jazz,Vol 1 | Storyville | STCD 5506
The Golden Years Of Revival Jazz,Vol.2 | Storyville | STCD 5507
The Golden Years Of Revival Jazz.Vol.3 | Storyville | STCD 5508
The Golden Years Of Revival Jazz,Vol.4 | Storyville | STCD 5509
The Golden Years Of Revival Jazz,Vol.7 | Storyville | STCD 5512
The Golden Years Of Revival Jazz,Vol.9 | Storyville | STCD 5514
The Golden Years Of Revival Jazz,Vol.11 | Storyville | STCD 5516
The Golden Years Of Revival Jazz,Vol.13 | Storyville | STCD 5518
The Golden Years Of Revival Jazz,Vol.14 | Storyville | STCD 5519
The Golden Years Of Revibal Jazz,Vol.15 | Storyville | STCD 5520
Ken Colyer's Jazzmen
The Very Best Of Dixieland Jazz | Verve | 535529-2
The Golden Years Of Revival Jazz,Vol 1 | Storyville | STCD 5506
The Golden Years Of Revival Jazz,Vol.7 | Storyville | STCD 5512
The Golden Years Of Revival Jazz,Vol.11 | Storyville | STCD 5516
The Golden Years Of Revival Jazz,Vol.13 | Storyville | STCD 5518
The Golden Years Of Revival Jazz,Vol.14 | Storyville | STCD 5519
The Golden Years Of Revibal Jazz,Vol.15 | Storyville | STCD 5520
Bowen III,Bob | (b)
Sebastian Weiss Trio
Polaroid Memory | Fresh Sound Records | FSNT 085 CD
Bowen,Claude | (tp)
Artie Shaw And His Orchestra
Planet JazzArtie Shaw | Planet Jazz | 2152057-2
Planet Jazz Sampler | Planet Jazz | 2152326-2
Planet Jazz:Swing | Planet Jazz | 2169651-2
Planet Jazz:Female Jazz Vocalists | Planet Jazz | 2169656-2
The Legends Of Swing | Laserlight | 24659
Harry James And His Orchestra
The Legends Of Swing | Laserlight | 24659
Bowen,Gregg | (tp)
Benny Goodman And His Orchestra
Verve Jazz Masters 33:Benny Goodman | Verve | 844410-2
Harry Allen And Randy Sandke Meets The RIAS Big Band Berlin
The Music Of The Trumpet Kings | Nagel-Heyer | CD 037
Nana Mouskouri With The Berlin Radio Big Band
Nana Swings | Mercury | 074394-2
Bowens,Harry | (voc)
Jimmy Smith All Stars
Jimmy Smith:Dot Com Blues | Blue Thumb | 543978-2
Bower,B. | (v)
Artie Shaw And His Orchestra
Planet JazzArtie Shaw | Planet Jazz | 2152057-2
Planet Jazz:Big Bands | Planet Jazz | 2169649-2
Bowers,Gil | (p)
Bob Crosby And His Orchestra
Swing Legens:Bob Crosby | Nimbus Records | NI 2011
Bowie,Bahnamous Lee | (keyboardssynth)
Art Ensemble Of Chicago
Coming Home Jamaica | Dreyfus Jazz Line | FDM 37003-2
Bowie,Dougie | (drperc)
Holly Cole And Her Quartet
It Happened One Night | Metro Blue | 852699-0
Bowie,Joseph | (perc,tb,congas,vocmarimba)
Jean-Paul Bourelly Trance Atlantic
Boom Bop II | double moon | CHRDM 71023
Lester Bowie's Brass Fantasy
The Odysse Of Funk & Popular Music | Dreyfus Jazz Line | FDM 37004-2
Bowie,Lester | (tp,bass-dr,celeste,long-horn,voice)
Art Ensemble Of Chicago
Nice Guys | ECM | 1126
Full Force | ECM | 1167(829197-2)
Urban Bushmen | ECM | 1211/12
The Third Decade | ECM | 1273
Americans Swinging In Paris:Art Ensemble Of Chicago | EMI Records | 539667-2
Bap-Tizum | Atlantic | 7567-80757-2
Coming Home Jamaica | Dreyfus Jazz Line | FDM 37003-2
Jack DeJohnette New Directions
In Europe | ECM | 1157
Jack DeJohnette Quartet
New Directions | ECM | 1128
James Carter Group
Conversin' With The Elders | Atlantic | 7567-82988-2
Josh Roseman Unit
Cherry | Enja | ENJ-9392 2
Leo Smith Group
Devine Love | ECM | 1143
Lester Bowie Group
The Great Pretender | ECM | 1209(829369-2)
Lester Bowie Quartet
The Great Pretender | ECM | 1209(829369-2)
Lester Bowie's Brass Fantasy
I Only Have Eyes For You | ECM | 1296(825902-2)
Avant Pop | ECM | 1326
The Fire This Time | IN+OUT Records | 7019-2
The Odysse Of Funk & Popular Music | Dreyfus Jazz Line | FDM 37004-2
When The Spitit Returns | Dreyfus Jazz Line | FDM 37016-2
Bowie,Michael | (bvoc)
Abbey Lincoln With Her Band
Who Used To Dance | Verve | 533559-2
Wholly Earth | Verve | 559538-2
Abbey Lincoln With The Rodney Kendrick Trio And Guests
A Turtle's Dream | Verve | 527382-2
Bowler,David | (dr)
Ahmad Jamal Trio
Live In Paris 1992 | Dreyfus Jazz Line | FDM 37019-2
Ahmad Jamal Trio with Orchestra
Pittsburgh | Atlantic | 7567-8209-2
Bowles,Paul | (narration)
Ute Kannenberg Quartet With Guests
Kannenberg On Purpose | Jazz Haus Musik | JHM 0109 CD
Bowles,Russell | (tb)
Jimmy Lunceford And His Orchestra
Planet Jazz:Swing | Planet Jazz | 2169651-2
The Legends Of Swing | Laserlight | 24659
Bowman,Babe | (tb)
Artie Shaw And His Orchestra
Planet JazzArtie Shaw | Planet Jazz | 2152057-2
Planet Jazz:Jazz Greatest Hits | Planet Jazz | 2169648-2
Bowman,Carl | (euphonium)
John Coltrane Quartet With Brass
The Complete Africa/Brass Sessions | Impulse(MCA) | 952168-2
Bowman,Dave | (p)
Billie Holiday With Toots Camarata And His Orchestra
Billie's Love Songs | Nimbus Records | NI 2000
Bud Freeman And His Famous Chicagoans
Jazz:The Essential Collection Vol.3 | IN+OUT Records | 78013-2
Bud Freeman And His Summa Cum Laude Orchestra
Planet Jazz:Bud Freeman | Planet Jazz | 2161240-2
Planet Jazz:Jazz Saxophone | Planet Jazz | 2169653-2
Frank Trumbauer And His Orchestra
The Hollywood Session:The Capitol Jazzmen | Jazz Unlimited | JUCD 2044
Louis Armstrong And His Orchestra
Louis Armstrong:Swing That Music | Laserlight | 36056
Louis Armstrong:C'est Si Bon | Dreyfus Jazz Line | FDM 36730-2
Muggsy Spanier And His V-Disc All Stars
Muggsy Spanier And Bud Freeman:V-Discs 1944-45 | Jazz Unlimited | JUCD 2049
Sidney Bechet And His Orchestra
Sidney Bechet:Summertime | Dreyfus Jazz Line | FDM 36712-2
Bowman,Dean | (vocvoice)
Lester Bowie's Brass Fantasy
The Odysse Of Funk & Popular Music | Dreyfus Jazz Line | FDM 37004-2
When The Spitit Returns | Dreyfus Jazz Line | FDM 37016-2
Uri Caine Group
Urlicht/Primal Light | Winter&Winter | 910004-2
Bown,Patti | (p)
Bill Coleman Septet
Jazz In Paris:Bill Coleman-From Boogie To Funk | EmArCy | 549401-2 PMS
Cal Massey Sextet
The Jazz Life! | Candid | CCD 79019
Blues To Coltrane | Candid | CCD 79029
Cal Tjader's Orchestra
Verve Jazz Masters 39:Cal Tjader | Verve | 521858-2
Gene Ammons Quartet
A Stranger In Town | Prestige | PRCD 24266-2
Jimmy Rushing And His Orchestra
Five Feet Of Soul | Roulette | 581830-2
Quincy Jones And His Orchestra
The Quintessence | Impulse(MCA) | 951222-2
The Roots Of Acid Jazz | Impulse(MCA) | IMP 12042
Bown,Russ | (tb)
Benny Carter And His Orchestra
Aspects | Capitol | 852677-2
Boyd,Curtis | (dr)
The Dave Glasser/Clark Terry/Barry Harris Project
Uh! Oh! | Nagel-Heyer | CD 2003
Blues Of Summer | Nagel-Heyer | NH 1011
Boyd,Douglas | (oboe)
Joachim Kühn And The Radio Philharmonie Hannover NDR With Jazz Soloists
Europeana | ACT | 9220-2
Boyd,Nelson | (b)
Bud Powell Orchestra
Bebop | Pablo | PACD 2310978-2
Charles McPherson Quintet
The Jazz Giants Play Rodgers & Hammerstein:My Favorite Things | Prestige | PCD 24223-2
Coleman Hawkins All Stars
Verve Jazz Masters 43:Coleman Hawkins | Verve | 521856-2
Dexter Gordon Quintet
The Art Of Saxophone | Laserlight | 24652
Fats Navarro:Nostalgia | Dreyfus Jazz Line | FDM 36736-2
Dizzy Gillespie And His Orchestra
Verve Jazz Masters 20:Introducing | Verve | 519853-2
Dizzy Gillespie:Birks Works-The Verve Big Band Sessions | Verve | 527900-2
Dizzy Gillespie Orchestra
Verve Jazz Masters 10:Dizzy Gillespie | Verve | 516319-2
Fats Navarro Quintet
Fats Navarro:Nostalgia | Dreyfus Jazz Line | FDM 36736-2
J.J.Johnson Quintet
The J.J.Johnson Memorial Album | Prestige | PRCD 11025-2
J.J.Johnson Sextet
The J.J.Johnson Memorial Album | Prestige | PRCD 11025-2
Max Roach Quartet
Clifford Brown-Max Roach:Alone Together-The Best Of The Mercury Years | Verve | 526373-2
Miles Davis All Stars
Miles Davis:Milestones | Dreyfus Jazz Line | FDM 36731-2
Miles Davis And His Orchestra
The Complete Birth Of The Cool | Capitol | 494550-2
Birth Of The Cool | Capitol | 530117-2
Jazz Profile:Miles Davis | Blue Note | 823515-2
Miles Davis:Milestones | Dreyfus Jazz Line | FDM 36731-2
Sonny Stitt Quintet
Sonny Stitt | Original Jazz Classics | OJCCD 009-2
Tadd Dameron Sextet
The Fabulous Fats Navarro Vol.1 | Blue Note | 0677207
Tadd Dameron-Fats Navarro Sextet
Fats Navarro:Nostalgia | Dreyfus Jazz Line | FDM 36736-2
Thelonious Monk Sextet
Genius Of Modern Music,Vol.2 | Blue Note | 532139-2
Jazz Profile:Thelonious Monk | Blue Note | 823518-2

Boyd,Reggie | (b-gg)
Buddy Guy Blues Band
Buddy Guy-The Complete Chess Studio Recordings | MCA | MCD 09337
Boyd,Wayne | (el-gg)
Jimmy McGriff Quartet
Feelin' It | Milestone | MCD 9313-2
Boyden,Phil | (v)
Steve Martland Band
The Orchestra Of Smith's Academy | Enja | ENJ-9358 2
Boyer,Jo | (tp)
Django's Music
Peche À La Mode-The Great Blue Star Sessions 1947/1953 | Verve | 835418-2
Boyer,Joe | (arr)
Dizzy Gillespie Orchestra And The Operatic String Orchestra
Jazz In Paris:Dizzy Gillespie And His Operatic Strings Orchestra | EmArCy | 018420-2
Boykins,Ronnie | (b,bells,sousaphone,space-gong,tuba)
Elmo Hope Ensemble
Sounds From Rikers Island | Fresh Sound Records | FSR CD 338
George Benson With The Jack McDuff Quartet
The New Boss Guitar | Original Jazz Classics | OJCCD 461-2
Roland Kirk Quartet
Talkin' Verve-Roots Of Acid Jazz:Roland Kirk | Verve | 533101-2
Boyle,Barbara | (voc)
Steve Klink-Barbara Boyle
Places To Come From,Places To Go | Minor Music | 801098
Boys From The Choir Solvguttene |
Jan Garbarek Group
Rites | ECM | 1685/86(559006-2)
Bozem,Günter | (drperc)
Colin Dunwoodie Quartet
Glad To See You | Edition Collage | EC 460-2
Wind Moments | Take Twelve On CD | TT 009-2
Boztüy,Mustafa | (bendir,darbouka,sazudu)
Rolf Zielke Trio Feat. Mustafa Boztüy
Rolf Zielke Trio Feat. Mustafa Boztüy | Jazz 'n' Arts Records | JNA 0602
Bozzio,Terry | (dr,voc,p,dumbek,perc.bodhran)
The Brecker Brothers
Heavy Metal Be-Bop | RCA | 2119257-2
Bracey,Marty | (perc)
Dizzy Gillespie And His Orchestra
Closer To The Source | Atlantic | 7567-80776-2
Brackeen,Charles | (ss,ts,vocvoice)
Paul Motian Trio
Le Voyage | ECM | 1138
Brackeen,JoAnne | (p,el-pp-solo)
Stan Getz Quartet
Live At Montmartre(CD=Stan's Party) | Steeplechase | SCCD 37021/22
Tony Lakatos Quartet
Live In Budapest | Laika Records | 35100742
Toots Thielemans Quartet
Images | Choice | CHCD 71007
Bradburry,J. | (v)
Dee Dee Bridgewater With Orchestra
Dear Ella | Verve | 539102-2
Braden,Don | (fl,ts,sstalking)
Freddy Cole With Band
A Circle Of Love | Fantasy | FCD 9674-2
Jam Session
Jam Session Vol.3 | Steeplechase | SCCD 31526
Jam Session Vol.9 | Steeplechase | SCCD 31554
Tom Harrell Orchestra
Time's Mirror | RCA | 2663524-2
Bradfield,Geoff | (ssts)
Tucy Connell Group
Songs For Joy And Sadness | Minor Music | 801096
Bradford,Kirkland | (ascl)
Jimmy Lunceford And His Orchestra
The Legends Of Swing | Laserlight | 24659
Bradley,Bill | (dr)
J.R. Monterose Quintet
Jaywalkin' | Fresh Sound Records | FSR-CD 320
Bradley,Julius | (bs)
Jess Stacy And His Orchestra
Planet Jazz:Jazz Piano | RCA | 2169655-2
Bradley,Will | (tbtp)
Benny Goodman And His Orchestra
Great Swing Classics In Hi-Fi | Capitol | 521223-2
More Camel Caravans | Phontastic | NCD 8843/4
Charlie Parker With Strings
Bird: The Complete Charlie Parker On Verve | Verve | 837141-2
Charlie Parker With The Joe Lipman Orchestra
Charlie Parker With Strings:The Master Takes | Verve | 523984-2
Charlie Parker Big Band | Verve | 559835-2
Jess Stacy And His Orchestra
Planet Jazz:Jazz Piano | RCA | 2169655-2
Louis Armstrong With Gordon Jenkins And His Orchestra And Choir
Satchmo In Style | Verve | 549594-2
Louis Armstrong-My Greatest Songs | MCA | MCD 18347
Swing Legends:Louis Armstrong | Nimbus Records | NI 2012
Sarah Vaughan The The Joe Lippman Orchestra
Sarah Vaughan:Lover Man | Dreyfus Jazz Line | FDM 36739-2
Sarah Vaughan With The Hugo Winterhalter Orchestra
Sarah Vaughan:Lover Man | Dreyfus Jazz Line | FDM 36739-2
Tommy Dorsey And His Orchestra
Planet Jazz:Tommy Dorsey | Planet Jazz | 2159972-2
Brady,Francesca | (voc)
Mike Westbrook Brass Band
Glad Day:Settings Of William Blake | Enja | ENJ-9376 2
Braekke,Oyvind | (tb)
Christoph Lauer & Norwegian Brass
Heaven | ACT | 9420-2
Trygve Seim Group
Different Rivers | ECM | 1744(159521-2)
Trygve Seim-Oyvind Braekke-Per Oddvar Johansen Orchestra
The Source And Different Cikadas | ECM | 1764(014432-2)
Braff,Ruby | (co,voc,ptp)
Benny Goodman And His Orchestra
Great Swing Classics In Hi-Fi | Capitol | 521223-2
George Wein's Dixie Victors
The Magic Horn | RCA | 2113038-2
Planet Jazz | Planet Jazz | 2169652-2
Ralph Sutton Quartet
The Ralph Sutton Quartet With Ruby Braff,Vol.2 | Storyville | STCD 8246
Ruby Braff Trio
Ruby Braff Trio:In Concert | Storyville | 4960543
As Time Goes By... | Candid | CCD 79741
Ruby Braff-Ellis Larkins
Duets Vol.1 | Vanguard | VCD 79609-2
Duets Vol.2 | Vanguard | VCD 79611-2
Vic Dickenson Septet
Nice Work | Vanguard | VCD 79610-2
Vic Dickenson Septet With Ruby Braff
Nice Work | Vanguard | VCD 79610-2
Braga,Ohana | (perc)
Antonio Carlos Jobim With Orchestra
Verve Jazz Masters 13:Antonio Carlos Jobim | Verve | 516409-2
Braga,Paulinho | (dr)
Lee Ritenour Group
Rio | GRP | GRP 95242
Braga,Paulo | (drperc)
Antonio Carlos Jobim Group
Verve Jazz Masters 13:Antonio Carlos Jobim | Verve | 516409-2
Antonio Carlos Jobim With Orchestra
Verve Jazz Masters 13:Antonio Carlos Jobim | Verve | 516409-2
Antonio Carlos Jobim-Elis Regina Group
The Antonio Carlos Jobim Songbook | Verve | 525472-2
Joe Henderson Group
Double Rainbow | Verve | 527222-2
Toots Thieleman And Sivuca
Verve Jazz Masters Vol.59:Toots Thielemans | Verve | 535271-2
Brahem,Anouar | (oud)
Anouar Brahem Group
Khomsa | ECM | 1561(527093-2)
Anouar Brahem Quartet
Conte De L'Incroyable Amour | ECM | 1457(511959-2)
Anouar Brahem Trio
Barzakh | ECM | 1432(847540-2)
Thimar | ECM | 1641(539888-2)
Astrakan Café | ECM | 1718(159494-2)
Le Pas Du Chat Noir | ECM | 1792(016373-2)
Erik Truffaz Quartet Quintet
Mantis | Blue Note | 535101-2
Jan Garbarek Trio
Madar | ECM | 1515(519075-2)
Orchestre National De Jazz
Charmediterranéen | ECM | 1828(018493-2)
Brainstorm |
Brainstorm feat. Chico Freeman
The Mystical Dreamer | IN+OUT Records | 7006-2
Chico Freeman And Brainstorm
Sweet Explosion | IN+OUT Records | 7010-2
Jazz Unlimited | IN+OUT Records | 7017-2
Threshold | IN+OUT Records | 7022-2
Braith,George | (ss,strich,tsbraith-horn)
George Braith Quartet
So Blue So Funky-Heroes Of The Hammond | Blue Note | 796563-2
Bralower,Jimmy | (dr,percdr-programming)
Al Jarreau With Band
L Is For Lover | i.e. Music | 557850-2
Michael Brecker Group
Now You See It...(Now You Don't) | GRP | GRP 96222
Bramerie,Thomas | (b)
Dee Dee Bridgewater With Her Trio
Live At Yoshi's | Verve | 543354-2
Branch,Russell 'Odun' | (perc)
Sun Ra And His Astro-Infinity Arkestra
Space Is The Place | Impulse(MCA) | 951249-2
Brand,Dirk | (chicken shakedr)
Philippe Caillat Group
Stream Of Time | Laika Records | LK 92-030
Philippe Caillat Special Project
Melodic Travel | Laika Records | LK 689-012
Brand,Dollar[Abdullah Ibrahim] | (fl,p,voc,p-solo,fl-solo,cello)
Abdullah Ibrahim
Desert Flowers | Enja | ENJ-7011 2
Abdullah Ibrahim And Ekaya
Water From An Ancient Well | TipToe | TIP-888812 2
Abdullah Ibrahim Quartet
Cape Town Revisited | TipToe | TIP-888836 2
Abdullah Ibrahim Septet
No Fear, No Die(S'en Fout La Mort):Original Soundtrack | TipToe | TIP-888815 2
Abdullah Ibrahim Sextet
Mindif | Enja | ENJ-5073 2
Abdullah Ibrahim Trio
Yarona | TipToe | TIP-888820 2
Cape Town Flowers | TipToe | TIP-888826 2
Cape Town Revisited | TipToe | TIP-888836 2
African Magic | TipToe | TIP-888845 2
Abdullah Ibrahim Trio And A String Orchestra
African Suite | TipToe | TIP-888832 2
Abdullah Ibrahim Trio With The Munich Radio Symphony Orchestra
African Symphony | Enja | ENJ-9410 2
Abdullah Ibrahim With The NDR Big Band
Ekapa Lodumo | TipToe | TIP-888840 2
Archie Shepp-Dollar Brand Duo
The Art Of Saxophone | Laserlight | 24652
Dollar Brand
African Piano | Japo | 60002(835020-2)
African Dawn | Enja | ENJ-4030 2
Dollar Brand Quartet
Africa Tears And Laugher | Enja | ENJ-3039 2
Dollar Brand Trio
The Children Of Africa | Enja | ENJ-2070 2
Dollar Brand-Johnny Dyani Duo
Echoes From Africa | Enja | ENJ-3047 2
Dollar(Abdullah Ibrahim) Brand
African Suite | TipToe | TIP-888832 2
Dollar(Abdullah Ibrahim) Brand Group
African River | Enja | ENJ-6018 2
Sathima Bea Benjamin Group
A Morning In Paris | Enja | ENJ-9309 2
Brand,Helmut | (arrbs)
Helmut Brandt Combo
Deutsches Jazz Fesival 1954/1955 | Bear Family Records | BCD 15430
Inge Brandenburg And Her All-Stars
Why Don't You Take All Of Me | Bear Family Records | BCD 15614 AH
Till Brönner Quartet & Deutsches Symphonieorchester Berlin
German Songs | Minor Music | 801057
Brand,Julius | (stringsv)
Phil Woods Quartet With Orchestra & Strings
Round Trip | Verve | 559804-2
Sonny Stitt With Orchestra
Goin' Down Slow | Prestige | PRCD 24276-2
Brandao,Sergio | (bel-b)
Paquito D'Rivera Orchestra
Jazzrock-Anthology Vol.3:Fusion | Zounds | CD 27100555
Brandenburg,Helmut | (ts)
Freddie Brocksieper And His Boys
Freddie's Boogie Blues | Bear Family Records | BCD 16388 AH
Brandenburg,Inge | (voc)
Inge Brandenburg
Why Don't You Take All Of Me | Bear Family Records | BCD 15614 AH
Inge Brandenburg & Otto 'Fats' Ortwein und die King Beats
Why Don't You Take All Of Me | Bear Family Records | BCD 15614 AH
Inge Brandenburg And Her All-Stars
Why Don't You Take All Of Me | Bear Family Records | BCD 15614 AH
Inge Brandenburg mit Hans Martin Majewski und seinem Orchester
Why Don't You Take All Of Me | Bear Family Records | BCD 15614 AH
Inge Brandenburg mit Kurt Edelhaben und seinem Orchester
Why Don't You Take All Of Me | Bear Family Records | BCD 15614 AH
Inge Brandenburg mit Werner Müller und seinem Orchester
Why Don't You Take All Of Me | Bear Family Records | BCD 15614 AH
Brandolino,Cathy | (voc)
John Patitucci Group
Mistura Fina | GRP | GRP 98022
Brandom,Dave | (sax)
Buddy Childers Big Band
Just Buddy's | Candid | CCD 79761
Brandon,Kevin | (b)
Jimmy Smith With Orchestra
Verve Jazz Masters 29:Jimmy Smith | Verve | 521855-2
Brandt,Mette | (v)
Michael Mantler Group With The Danish Radio Concert Orchestra Strings
The School Of Understanding(Sort-Of-An-Opera) | ECM | 1648/49(537963-2)
Branford,Jay | (bscl)
Antonio Hart Group
Here I Stand | Impulse(MCA) | 951208-2
Brannon,Teddy | (pceleste)
Little Jimmy Scott | Specialty | SPCD 2170-2
Don Byas Quartet
Don Byas:Laura | Dreyfus Jazz Line | FDM 36714-2
Roy Eldridge And His Orchestra
The Complete Verve Roy Eldridge Studio Sessions | Verve | 9861278
Branson,Bruce | (asbs)
Duke Ellington With Tommy Dorsey And His Orchestra
Highlights From The Duke Ellington Centennial Edition | RCA | 2663672-2
Tommy Dorsey And His Orchestra
Planet Jazz:Tommy Dorsey | Planet Jazz | 2159972-2
Planet Jazz:Jazz Greatest Hits | Planet Jazz | 2169648-2
Brashear,Oscar | (fl-htp)
Bobby Hutcherson Orchestra
Montara | Blue Note | 590956-2
Diane Schuur And Her Band
The Best Of Diane Schuur | GRP | GRP 98882
Dizzy Gillespie With The Lalo Schifrin Orchestra
Free Ride | Original Jazz Classics | OJCCD 784-2(2310794)
Flora Purim With Orchestra
Joe Henderson:The Milestone Years | Milestone | 8MCD 4413-2
Herbie Hancock Group With String Quartet,Woodwinds And Brass
Herbie Hancock The New Standards | Verve | 527715-2
Herbie Hancock Group With Woodwinds And Brass
Herbie Hancock The New Standards | Verve | 527715-2
Horace Silver Quintet With Brass
Horace Silver Retrospective | Blue Note | 495576-2
Jimmy Smith All Stars
Jimmy Smith:Dot Com Blues | Blue Thumb | 543978-2
Joe Henderson And His Orchestra
Joe Henderson:The Milestone Years | Milestone | 8MCD 4413-2
Joe Henderson Group
Jazzin' Vol.2: The Music Of Stevie Wonder | Fantasy | FANCD 6088-2
McCoy Tyner Orchestra
13th House | Original Jazz Classics | OJCCD 1089-2(M 9102)
Milt Jackson And His Orchestra
Reverence And Compassion | Reprise | 9362-45204-2
Raul De Souza Orchestra
Cannonball Adderley Birthday Celebration | Fantasy | FANCD 6087-2
The Quincy Jones-Sammy Nestico Orchestra
Basie & Beyond | Warner | 9362-47792-2
Willie Bobo Group
Jazzrock-Anthology Vol.3:Fusion | Zounds | CD 27100555
Zoot Sims And His Orchestra
The Jazz Giants Play Duke Ellington:Caravan | Prestige | PCD 24227-2
Zoot Sims With Orchestra
Passion Flower | Original Jazz Classics | OJCCD 939-2(2312120)
Brass |
Diane Schuur Trio With Orchestra And Strings
In Tribute | GRP | GRP 20062
Diane Schuur With Orchestra
In Tribute | GRP | GRP 20062
Love Songs | GRP | GRP 97032
The Best Of Diane Schuur | GRP | GRP 98882
Stan Getz With The Michel Legrand Orchestra
Stan Getz Highlights | Verve | 847430-2
Brass & Strings |
Johnny Hartman And The Rudy Traylor Orchestra
And I Thought About You | Blue Note | 857456-2
Brass Attack |
Brass Attack
Brecht Songs | Tutu Records | 888190-2*
Brass Section |
Keith Jarrett Group With Brass
Expectations | CBS | C2K 65900
brass,Strings and woodwinds,details unkn. |
Carla Bley - Michael Mantler & Orchestra
13-3/4 | Watt | 3 (2313103)
Brassfield,Don | (sax)
Anita O'Day With Gene Krupa And His Orchestra
Let Me Off Uptown:Anita O'Day With Gene Krupa | CBS | CK 65625
Bratberg,Hallgrim | (g)
Geir Lysne Listening Ensemble
Korall | ACT | 9236-2
Aurora Borealis-Nordic Lights | ACT | 9406-2
Silje Nergard Group with Strings
Nightwatch | EmArCy | 9865648
Bratland,Sondre | (voc)
Christoph Lauer & Norwegian Brass
Heaven | ACT | 9420-2
Geir Lysne Listening Ensemble
Korall | ACT | 9236-2
Bratt,Andrew | (dr)
John Mayer's Indio-Jazz Fusions
Ragatal | Nimbus Records | NI 5569
Braud,Wellman | (btuba)
Bechet-Spanier Big Four
Jazz:The Essential Collection Vol.1 | IN+OUT Records | 78011-2
Duke Ellington And His Cotton Club Orchestra
Planet Jazz:Duke Ellington | Planet Jazz | 2152053-2
Jazz:The Essential Collection Vol.2 | IN+OUT Records | 78012-2
Duke Ellington And His Orchestra
Highlights From The Duke Ellington Centennial Edition | RCA | 2663672-2
Jazz:The Essential Collection Vol.2 | IN+OUT Records | 78012-2
Jelly Roll Morton's New Orleans Jazzmen
Planet Jazz | Planet Jazz | 2169652-2
Planet Jazz:Male Jazz Vocalists | Planet Jazz | 2169657-2
Kid Ory And His Band
The Very Best Of Dixieland Jazz | Verve | 535529-2
Kid Ory's Creole Jazz Band
This Kid's The Greatest! | Good Time Jazz | GTCD 12045-2
Louis Armstrong And His Orchestra
Jazz:The Essential Collection Vol.2 | IN+OUT Records | 78012-2
Louis Armstrong:C'est Si Bon | Dreyfus Jazz Line | FDM 36730-2
Swing Legends:Louis Armstrong | Nimbus Records | NI 2012
Mezz Mezzrow And His Swing Band
Planet Jazz:Bud Freeman | Planet Jazz | 2161240-2
New Orleans Feetwarmers
Jazz:The Essential Collection Vol.1 | IN+OUT Records | 78011-2
Sidney Bechet And His New Orleans Feetwarmers
Planet Jazz | Planet Jazz | 2169652-2
Sidney Bechet:Summertime | Dreyfus Jazz Line | FDM 36712-2
Braufman,Alan | (as,fl,pipe-horn,clss)
Carla Bley Band
Musique Mecanique | Watt | 9
Braun,Thomas | (fr-h)
Litschie Hrdlicka Group
Falling Lovers | EGO | 93020
Braun,Werner | (dr)
Jan Jankeje Quintet
Zum Trotz | Jazzpoint | JP 1016 CD
Jan Jankeje Septet
A' Portrait Of Jan Jankeje | Jazzpoint | JP 1054 CD
Jan Jankeje Trio
A' Portrait Of Jan Jankeje | Jazzpoint | JP 1054 CD
Patrick Tompert Trio
Hallelujah Time | Satin Doll Productions | SDP 1020-1 CD
Patrick Tompert Trio Live | Satin Doll Productions | SDP 1029-1 CD
Moche! | Satin Doll Productions | SDP 1035-1 CD
Stuttgarter Dixieland All Stars
It's The Talk Of The Town | Jazzpoint | JP 1069 CD
Braune,Buggy | (p)
Florian Poser Group
Say Yes! | Edition Collage | EC 452-2
Brause Horns,The |
International Commission For The Prevention Of Musical Border Control,The
The International Commission For The Prevention Of Musical Border Control | VeraBra Records | CDVBR 2093-2
Brawn,Robert | (b-tbtb)

Buddy Rich Big Band
The New One! | Pacific Jazz | 494507-2
Braxhoofden,Dick | (bj)
Albert Nicholas With The Dutch Swing College Band
Albert Nicholas & The Dutch Swing College Band | Storyville | STCD 5522
Dutch Swing College Band
Albert Nicholas & The Dutch Swing College Band | Storyville | STCD 5522
Braxton,Anthony | (as,sopranino,as-solo,cl)
Circle
Paris Concert | ECM | 1018/19(843163-2)
Dave Brubeck Quartet
All The Things We Are | Atlantic | 7567-81399-2
Dave Brubeck Quintet
All The Things We Are | Atlantic | 7567-81399-2
David Holland Quartet
Conference Of The Birds | ECM | 1027(829373-2)
Gunter Hampel And His Galaxie Dream Band
Enfant Terrible | Birth | 0025
Gunter Hampel Group
Familie | Birth | 008
The 8th Of July 1969 | Birth | CD 001
Marion Brown Orchestra
Afternoon Of A Georgia Faun | ECM | 1004
Bray,Jim | (b,sousaphone,tubabj)
Chris Barber Original Jazzband Of 1954
Chris Barber:40 Years Jubilee Concert | Storyville | 4990013
Chris Barber's Jazz Band
The Very Best Of Dixieland Jazz | Verve | 535529-2
The Best Of Dixieland-Live in 1954/55 | London | 820878-2
The Golden Years Of Revival Jazz,Vol 1 | Storyville | STCD 5506
The Golden Years Of Revival Jazz,Vol.2 | Storyville | STCD 5507
The Golden Years Of Revival Jazz,Vol.3 | Storyville | STCD 5508
The Golden Years Of Revival Jazz,Vol.4 | Storyville | STCD 5509
The Golden Years Of Revival Jazz,Vol.7 | Storyville | STCD 5512
The Golden Years Of Revival Jazz,Vol.9 | Storyville | STCD 5514
The Golden Years Of Revival Jazz,Vol.11 | Storyville | STCD 5516
The Golden Years Of Revival Jazz,Vol.13 | Storyville | STCD 5518
The Golden Years Of Revival Jazz,Vol.14 | Storyville | STCD 5519
The Golden Years Of Revibal Jazz,Vol.15 | Storyville | STCD 5520
Graham Stewart And His New Orleans Band
The Golden Years Of Revival Jazz,Vol.4 | Storyville | STCD 5509
Johnny Parker Trio
The Golden Years Of Revival Jazz,Vol.5 | Storyville | STCD 5510
Ken Colyer's Jazzmen
The Very Best Of Dixieland Jazz | Verve | 535529-2
The Golden Years Of Revival Jazz,Vol 1 | Storyville | STCD 5506
The Golden Years Of Revival Jazz,Vol.7 | Storyville | STCD 5512
The Golden Years Of Revival Jazz,Vol.11 | Storyville | STCD 5516
The Golden Years Of Revival Jazz,Vol.13 | Storyville | STCD 5518
The Golden Years Of Revival Jazz,Vol.14 | Storyville | STCD 5519
The Golden Years Of Revibal Jazz,Vol.15 | Storyville | STCD 5520
Lonnie Donegan Skiffle Group
The Best Of Dixieland-Live in 1954/55 | London | 820878-2
Brazel,Gerald | (tp)
Lester Bowie's Brass Fantasy
The Fire This Time | IN+OUT Records | 7019-2
The Odysse Of Funk & Popular Music | Dreyfus Jazz Line | FDM 37004-2
When The Spitit Returns | Dreyfus Jazz Line | FDM 37016-2
Brazz Brothers,The |
The Brazz Brothers
Ngoma | Laika Records | 35101562
Brecher,Sid | (viola)
Billie Holiday With The Ray Ellis Orchestra
Lady In Satin | CBS | CK 65144
Brechtlein,Tommy | (dr,background-vocperc)
Robben Ford & The Blue Line
Handful Of Blues | Blue Thumb | BTR 70042
Brecker Brothers,The |
The Brecker Brothers
Heavy Metal Be-Bop | RCA | 2119257-2
The Becker Bros | RCA | 2122103-2
Brecker,Michael | (alto-fl,voc,el-ts,handclaps,EWI,fl)
Al Jarreau With Band
Tenderness | i.e. Music | 557853-2
Bernard Purdie's Soul To Jazz
Bernard Purdie's Soul To Jazz | ACT | 9242-2
Billy Cobham Group
The Best Of Billy Cobham | Atlantic | 7567-81558-2
Caecilie Norby With Band
My Corner Of The Sky | Blue Note | 853422-2
Charlie Haden Quartet With Orchestra
American Dreams | Verve | 064096-2
Dave Weckl Group
Master Plan | GRP | GRP 96192
Directions In Music
Live at Massey Hall:Celebrating Miles Davis & John Coltrane | Verve | 589654-2
Don Grolnick Group
Hearts And Numbers | VeraBra Records | CDVBR 2016-2
Gonzalo Rubalcaba Trio With Michael Brecker
Inner Voyage | Blue Note | 499241-2
Herbie Hancock Group
Magic Window | CBS | 486572-2
Herbie Hancock The New Standards | Verve | 527715-2
Herbie Hancock Group With String Quartet
Herbie Hancock The New Standards | Verve | 527715-2
Herbie Hancock Group With String Quartet,Woodwinds And Brass
Herbie Hancock The New Standards | Verve | 527715-2
Herbie Hancock Group With Woodwinds And Brass
Herbie Hancock The New Standards | Verve | 527715-2
Horace Silver Quintet
Horace Silver Retrospective | Blue Note | 495576-2
A Prescription For The Blues | Impulse(MCA) | 951238-2
Hugh Marsh Duo/Quartet/Orchestra
The Bear Walks | VeraBra Records | CDVBR 2011-2
Jacky Terrasson Group
What It Is | Blue Note | 498756-2
Jaco Pastorius With Orchestra
Word Of Mouth | Warner | 7599-23525-2
John Abercrombie Quartet
Night | ECM | 1272(823212-2)
Getting There | ECM | 1321(833494-2)
John McLaughlin Group
The Promise | Verve | 529828-2
John Patitucci Group
Sketchbook | GRP | GRP 96172
Kenny Wheeler Quintet
Double, Double You | ECM | 1262(815675-2)
Kevin Mahogany With The Bob James Trio And Michael Brecker
My Romance | Warner | 9362-47025-2
Lenny White Group
Present Tense | Hip Bop | HIBD 8004
Renderers Of Spirit | Hip Bop | HIBD 8014
Los Jovenes Flamencos With The WDR Big Band And Guests
Jazzpana | ACT | 9212-2
Makoto Ozone Group
Treasure | Verve | 021906-2
Michael Brecker Group
Time Is Of The Essence | Verve | 547844-2
Michael Brecker | Impulse(MCA) | 950113-2
Don't Try This At Home | Impulse(MCA) | 950114-2
Tales From The Hudson | Impulse(MCA) | 951191-2
Now You See It...(Now You Don't) | GRP | GRP 96222
Michael Brecker Quindectet
Wide Angles | Verve | 076142-2
Michael Brecker Quintet
Nearness Of You-The Ballad Book | Verve | 549705-2
Two Blocks From The Edge | Impulse(MCA) | 951261-2
Mike Stern Group
Jigsaw | Atlantic | 7567-82027-2
Give And Take | Atlantic | 7567-83036-2
Nils Landgren Funk Unit
Paint It Blue:A Tribute To Cannonball Adderley | ACT | 9243-2
Pat Metheny Quartet
80/81 | ECM | 1180/81 (843169-2)
Pat Metheny Quintet
80/81 | ECM | 1180/81 (843169-2)
Peter Erskine Orchestra
Peter Erskine | Original Jazz Classics | OJC 610(C 14010)
Randy Brecker Group
Jazzrock-Anthology Vol.3:Fusion | Zounds | CD 27100555
Rolf Kühn Group
Inside Out | Intuition Records | INT 3276-2
Steps Ahead
Steps Ahead:Copenhagen Live | Storyville | 4960363
Steps Ahead | Elektra | 7559-60168-2
Modern Times | Elektra | 7559-60351-2
Steve Khan Group
Jazzrock-Anthology Vol.3:Fusion | Zounds | CD 27100555
The Brecker Brothers
Heavy Metal Be-Bop | RCA | 2119257-2
The Becker Bros | RCA | 2122103-2
Retum Of The Brecker Brothers | GRP | GRP 96842
Out Of The Loop | GRP | GRP 97842
Brecker,Randy | (fl-h,tp,el-tp,handclaps,keyboards)
Barbara Dennerlein Group
Junkanoo | Verve | 537122-2
Bernard Purdie's Soul To Jazz
Bernard Purdie's Soul To Jazz | ACT | 9242-2
Billy Cobham Group
The Best Of Billy Cobham | Atlantic | 7567-81558-2
Brecker-Engstfeld-Plümer-Weiss
ToGether | Nabel Records:Jazz Network | CD 4648
Caecilie Norby With Band
My Corner Of The Sky | Blue Note | 853422-2
Carla Bley Band
Night-Glo | Watt | 16
Dave Weckl Group
Heads Up | GRP | GRP 96732
George Gruntz Concert Jazz Band
Blues 'N Dues Et Cetera | Enja | ENJ-6072 2
GRP All-Star Big Band
GRP All-Star Big Band:Live! | GRP | GRP 97402
All Blues | GRP | GRP 98002
Hank Crawford And His Orchestra
Roadhouse Symphony | Original Jazz Classics | OJCCD 1048-2(M 9140)
Horace Silver Quintet
Horace Silver Retrospective | Blue Note | 495576-2
Blue Velvet: Crooners, Swooners And Velvet Vocals | Blue Note | 521153-2
A Prescription For The Blues | Impulse(MCA) | 951238-2
John Scofield Groups
Quiet | Verve | 533185-2
Groove Elation | Blue Note | 832801-2
Lenny White Group
Renderers Of Spirit | Hip Bop | HIBD 8014
Mike Stern Group
Standards(And Other Songs) | Atlantic | 7567-82419-2
Mingus Big Band
Tonight At Noon...Three Or Four Shades Of Love | Dreyfus Jazz Line | FDM 36633-2
Mingus Big Band 93
Nostalgia In Times Square | Dreyfus Jazz Line | FDM 36559-2
Nils Landgren Funk Unit
Paint It Blue:A Tribute To Cannonball Adderley | ACT | 9243-2
Peter Erskine Orchestra
Peter Erskine | Original Jazz Classics | OJC 610(C 14010)
Randy Brecker Group
Jazzrock-Anthology Vol.3:Fusion | Zounds | CD 27100555
Randy Brecker-Wolfgang Engstfeld Quartet
Mr. Max! | Nabel Records:Jazz Network | CD 4637
Rolf Kühn And Friends
Affairs:Rolf Kühn & Friends | Intuition Records | INT 3211-2
Steve Khan Group
Jazzrock-Anthology Vol.3:Fusion | Zounds | CD 27100555
The Brecker Brothers
Heavy Metal Be-Bop | RCA | 2119257-2
The Becker Bros | RCA | 2122103-2
Retum Of The Brecker Brothers | GRP | GRP 96842
Out Of The Loop | GRP | GRP 97842
The Jazz Composer's Orchestra
Comminications | JCOA | 1001/2
Bredberg,Arne | (tb)
Leonardo Pedersen's Jazzkapel
The Golden Years Of Revival Jazz,Sampler | Storyville | 109 1001
The Golden Years Of Revival Jazz,Vol.11 | Storyville | STCD 5516
Brederode,Wolfert | (p,harmoniummelodia)
Arnulf Ochs Group
In The Mean Time | Jazz 'n' Arts Records | JNA 1202
Susanne Abbuehl Group
April | ECM | 1766(013999-2)
Bredesen-Vestby,Ellen | (perc)
Terje Rypdal Quartet With The Bergen Chamber Ensemble
Lux Aeterna | ECM | 1818(017070-2)
Bredl,Otto | (tb)
Helmut Zacharias mit dem Orchester Frank Folken
Ich Habe Rhythmus | Bear Family Records | BCD 15642 AH
Kurt Edelhagen All Stars
Deutsches Jazz Fesival 1954/1955 | Bear Family Records | BCD 15430
Kurt Edelhagen All Stars Und Solisten
Deutsches Jazz Fesival 1954/1955 | Bear Family Records | BCD 15430
Quartet Der Kurt Edelhagen All Stars
Deutsches Jazz Fesival 1954/1955 | Bear Family Records | BCD 15430
Bredwell,Merle | (bs)
Elliot Lawrence And His Orchestra
Mullenium | CBS | CK 65678
Bregman,Buddy | (arr,voccond)
Anita O'Day With The Buddy Bregman Orchestra
Pick Yourself Up | Verve | 517329-2
Verve Jazz Masters 49:Anita O'Day | Verve | 527653-2
Buddy Bregman And His Orchestra
Swinging Kicks | Verve | 559514-2
Ella Fitzgerald With The Buddy Bregman Orchestra
Ella Fitzgerald-First Lady Of Song | Verve | 517898-2
The Best Of The Song Books | Verve | 519804-2
The Best Of The Song Books:The Ballads | Verve | 521867-2
Love Songs:The Best Of The Song Books | Verve | 531762-2
Ella Fitzgerald Sings The Cole Porter Songbook | Verve | 537257-2
Ella Fitzgerald Sings The Rodgers And Hart Song Book | Verve | 537258-2
The Silver Collection: Ella Fitzgerald-The Songbooks | Verve | 823445-2 PMS
For The Love Of Ella Fitzgerald | Verve | 841765-2
Brehm,Alvin | (b)
Gunther Schuller Ensemble
Beauty Is A Rare Thing:Ornette Coleman-The Complete Atlantic Recordings | Atlantic | 8122-71410-2
Brehm,Simon | (b)
Lars Gullin With The Bob Laine Trio
Lars Gullin 1953,Vol.2:Moden Sounds | Dragon | DRCD 234
Rita Reys With The Lars Gullin Quartet
Lars Gullin 1953,Vol.2:Moden Sounds | Dragon | DRCD 234
Breidis,Vic | (pceleste)
Ben Pollack And His Park Central Orchestra
Planet Jazz:Jack Teagarden | Planet Jazz | 2161236-2
Jazz:The Essential Collection Vol.3 | IN+OUT Records | 78013-2
Breit,Kevin | (el-g,bozouki,el-mand,g,mand)
Cassandra Wilson Group
Traveling Miles | Blue Note | 854123-2
Holly Cole And Her Quartet
It Happened One Night | Metro Blue | 852699-0
Breitkreuz,Falk | (fl,saxts)
Bajazzo
Caminos | Edition Collage | EC 485-2
Harlequin Galaxy | Edition Collage | EC 519-2
Rudi Neuwirth Group
Sand | Traumton Records | 2413-2
Brenders,Stan | (condarr)
Django Reinhardt With Stan Brenders Et Son Grand Orchestre
Verve Jazz Masters 38:Django Reinhardt | Verve | 516931-2
Brendgens-Mönkemeyer,Thomas | (gg-solo & overdubbing)
Thomas Brendgens-Mönkemeyer
Beauty | Jardis Records | JRCD 20138
Thomas Brendgens-Mönkemeyer & Jochen Voss
Jazz Guitar Highlights 1 | Jardis Records | JRCD 20141
Textures | Jardis Records | JRCD 9920
Brennan,John Wolf | (church-org,p,arco-p,pizzicato-p)
Corina Curschellas-John Wolf Brennan
Entupadas | Creative Works Records | CW CD 1013-1
Willisau And More Live | Creative Works Records | CW CD 1020-2
Creative Works Orchestra
Willisau And More Live | Creative Works Records | CW CD 1020-2
John Wolf Brennan
The Beauty Of Fractals | Creative Works Records | CW CD 1017-1
Willisau And More Live | Creative Works Records | CW CD 1020-2
Irisations | Creative Works Records | CW CD 1021-2
Text, Context, Co-Text & Co-Co-Text | Creative Works Records | CW CD 1025-2
The Well-Prepared Clavier/Das Wohlpräparierte Klavier | Creative Works Records | CW CD 1032-2
Flügel | Creative Works Records | CW CD 1037-2
John Wolf Brennan-Marianne Schroeder
The Well-Prepared Clavier/Das Wohlpräparierte Klavier | Creative Works Records | CW CD 1032-2
Brennecke,Rainer | (tpfl-h)
Association Urbanetique
Ass Bedient | Jazz 4 Ever Records:Jazz Network | J4E 4723
Brenner,Phil | (alto-flss)
Kevin Mahogany With Orchestra
Songs And Moments | Enja | ENJ-8072 2
Brenner,Udo | (b)
Colin Dunwoodie Quartet
Glad To See You | Edition Collage | EC 460-2
Wind Moments | Take Twelve On CD | TT 009-2
Brereton,Clarence | (tp)
Sarah Vaughan With John Kirby And His Orchestra
Sarah Vaughan Birthday Celebration | Fantasy | FANCD 6090-2
Sarah Vaughan:Lover Man | Dreyfus Jazz Line | FDM 36739-2
Sidney Bechet With Noble Sissle's Swingsters
Sidney Bechet:Summertime | Dreyfus Jazz Line | FDM 36712-2
Bret,Alix | (b)
Guy Lafitte Sextet
Jazz In Paris:Guy Lafitte-Blue And Sentimental | EmArCy | 159852-2 PMS
Michel De Villers Octet
Jazz In Paris:Saxophones À Saint-Germain Des Prés | EmArCy | 014060-2
Breuer,Cordula | (fl)
Uri Caine With The Concerto Köln
Concerto Köln | Winter&Winter | 910086-2
Breuer,Gerd | (drroto-tom)
Elke Reiff Quartett
There Is More | Laika Records | 35101112
Monika Linges Quartet
Floating | Nabel Records:Jazz Network | CD 4607
Breuer,Harry | (drperc)
Jimmy Smith With The Oliver Nelson Orchestra
Peter & The Wolf | Verve | 547264-2
Breuer,Hermann | (tbp)
Berlin Contemporary Jazz Orchestra
Berlin Contemporary Jazz Orchestra | ECM | 1409
Christian Willisohn New Band
Heart Broken Man | Blues Beacon | BLU-1026 2
Mal Waldron
Moods | Enja | ENJ-3021 2
Mal Waldron Sextet
Moods | Enja | ENJ-3021 2
NDR Big Band
NDR Big Band-Bravissimo | ACT | 9232-2
Trombonefire
Sliding Affairs | Laika Records | 35101462
Breuer,Reinhold | (drperc)
Sotto In Su
Südamerika Sept. 90 | Jazz Haus Musik | JHM 0051 CD
Vanitas | Poise | Poise 04
Breuker,Willem | (b-cl,as,ts,bs,sax,ss,cl,perc)
Berlin Contemporary Jazz Orchestra
Berlin Contemporary Jazz Orchestra | ECM | 1409
Gunter Hampel Group
The 8th Of July 1969 | Birth | CD 001
Willem Breuker Kollektief
La Banda/Banda And Jazz | Enja | ENJ-9326 2
Brewer,Dave | (gguira)
The Catholics
Simple | Laika Records | 35100802
Breyere,Josse | (tb)
Brocksieper-Jazz-Ensemble
Drums Boogie | Bear Family Records | BCD 15988 AH
Brocksieper-Solisten-Orchester
Globetrotter | Bear Family Records | BCD 15912 AH
Brocksieper-Special-Ensemble
Globetrotter | Bear Family Records | BCD 15912 AH
Brocksi-Quartett
Globetrotter | Bear Family Records | BCD 15912 AH
Brice,Percy | (dr)
Billy Taylor Trio
Billy Taylor Trio | Prestige | PRCD 24285-2
Dexter Gordon Quartet
Dexter Gordon Birthday Celebration | Fantasy | FANCD 6082-2
L.T.D. | Prestige | PCD 11018-2
XXL | Prestige | PCD 11033-2
George Shearing And His Quintet
Beauty And The Beat | Capitol | 542308-2
George Shearing Quintet
At Newport | Pablo | PACD 5315-2
George Shearing Quintet With Cannonball And Nat Adderley
At Newport | Pablo | PACD 5315-2
George Shearing Sextet
At Newport | Pablo | PACD 5315-2
Oscar Pettiford Sextet
Charles Mingus-The Complete Debut Recordings | Debut | 12 DCD 4402-2
Peggy Lee With George Shearing
Beauty And The Beat | Capitol | 542308-2
Peggy Lee With The George Shearing Trio
Beauty And The Beat | Capitol | 542308-2
Sarah Vaughan With The Jimmy Jones Orchestra
Ballads | Roulette | 537561-2
Jazz Profile | Blue Note | 823517-2
Bridgewater Kowalski,Tulani | (voc)

Dee Dee Bridgewater With Band
This Is New | Verve | 016884-2
Bridgewater,Cecil | (fr-h,kalimba,tp,fl-harr)
Dee Dee Bridgewater With Her Septet
Dear Ella | Verve | 539102-2
Eric Dolphy Quartet With The University Of Illinois Big Band
The Illinois Concert | Blue Note | 499826-2
Eric Dolphy Quartet With The University Of Illinois Brass Ensemble
The Illinois Concert | Blue Note | 499826-2
Horace Silver Sextet
Horace Silver Retrospective | Blue Note | 495576-2
Deep Blue-The United States Of Mind | Blue Note | 521152-2
Horace Silver Sextet With Vocals
Horace Silver Retrospective | Blue Note | 495576-2
Klaus Weiss Septet
All Night Through | ATM Records | ATM 3816 AH
Klaus Weiss Sextet
All Night Through | ATM Records | ATM 3816 AH
Max Roach Double Quartet
To The Max! | Enja | ENJ-7021 22
Max Roach Quartet
To The Max! | Enja | ENJ-7021 22
Max Roach Sextet With The J.C.White Singers
Lift Every Voice And Sing | Atlantic | 7567-80798-2
McCoy Tyner Group With Horns
Inner Voices | Original Jazz Classics | OJCCD 1039-2(M 9079)
McCoy Tyner Group With Horns And Voices
Inner Voices | Original Jazz Classics | OJCCD 1039-2(M 9079)
Bridgewater,Dee Dee | (narrationvoc)
Dee Dee Bridgewater With Band
This Is New | Verve | 016884-2
Dee Dee Bridgewater | Atlantic | 7567-80760-2
Victim Of Love | Verve | 841199-2
Dee Dee Bridgewater Sings Kurt Weil | EmArCy | 9809601
7.Zelt-Musik-Festival:Jazz Events | Zounds | CD 2730001
Dee Dee Bridgewater With Big Band
Dear Ella | Verve | 539102-2
Dee Dee Bridgewater With Her Quartet With Horace Silver
Love And Peace-A Tribute To Horace Silver | Verve | 527470-2
Dee Dee Bridgewater With Her Quintet
Love And Peace-A Tribute To Horace Silver | Verve | 527470-2
Dee Dee Bridgewater With Her Quintet With Jimmy Smith
Love And Peace-A Tribute To Horace Silver | Verve | 527470-2
Dee Dee Bridgewater With Her Septet
Dear Ella | Verve | 539102-2
Dee Dee Bridgewater With Her Trio
Live In Paris | Verve | 014317-2
Keeping Tradition | Verve | 519607-2
Dear Ella | Verve | 539102-2
Live At Yoshi's | Verve | 543354-2
Dee Dee Bridgewater In Montreux | Polydor | 847913-2
Dee Dee Bridgewater With Orchestra
Dear Ella | Verve | 539102-2
Dee Dee Bridgewater-Kenny Burrell
Dear Ella | Verve | 539102-2
Bridgewater,Ron | (as,ts,fl,clss)
McCoy Tyner Septet
Focal Point | Original Jazz Classics | OJCCD 1009-2(M 9072)
McCoy Tyner Sextet
Focal Point | Original Jazz Classics | OJCCD 1009-2(M 9072)
Bridwell,Hollis | (cl,tssax)
Stan Kenton And His Orchestra
Stan Kenton-The Formative Years | Decca | 589489-2
Brieff,Frank | (viola)
Charlie Parker With Strings
Verve Jazz Masters 28:Charlie Parker Plays Standards | Verve | 521854-2
Charlie Parker With Strings:The Master Takes | Verve | 523984-2
Charlie Parker:The Best Of The Verve Years | Verve | 527815-2
Bird: The Complete Charlie Parker On Verve | Verve | 837141-2
Charlie Parker:April In Paris | Dreyfus Jazz Line | FDM 36737-2
Briegleb,Christian | (sax)
Marcus Sukiennik Big Band
A Night In Tunisia Suite(7 Variationen über Dizzy Gillespie's 'A Night In Tunisia') | Jazz Haus Musik | ohne Nummer
Briggs,Arthur | (tp)
Coleman Hawkins With Michel Warlop And His Orchestra
Django Reinhardt All Star Sessions | Capitol | 531577-2
Briggs,Jimmy | (saxvoc-arr)
Lou Donaldson Orchestra
Blue Breaks Beats Vol.2 | Blue Note | 789907-2
Briggs,Pete | (tuba)
Carroll Dickerson's Savoyagers
Louis Armstrong:Fireworks | Dreyfus Jazz Line | FDM 36710-2
Louis Armstrong And His Hot Seven
Jazz:The Essential Collection Vol.2 | IN+OUT Records | 78012-2
Louis Armstrong And His Orchestra
Satch Plays Fats(Complete) | CBS | CK 64927
Bright,Ernest | (reeds)
Dizzy Gillespie And His Orchestra
Ultimate Dizzy Gillespie | Verve | 557535-2
Bright,Ronnell | (p)
Coleman Hawkins Quintet
The Hawk Relaxes | Original Jazz Classics | OJCCD 709-2(MV 15)
Sarah Vaughan And The Thad Jones Orchestra
Verve Jazz Masters 42:Sarah Vaughan-The Jazz Sides | Verve | 526817-2
Sarah Vaughan With Her Quartet
Verve Jazz Masters 42:Sarah Vaughan-The Jazz Sides | Verve | 526817-2
Sarah Vaughan With The Jimmy Jones Orchestra
Ballads | Roulette | 537561-2
Jazz Profile | Blue Note | 823517-2
Sarah Vaughan With The Quincy Jones Orchestra
Jazz In Paris:Sarah Vaughan-Vaughan And Violins | EmArCy | 065004-2
4 By 4:Ella Fitzgerald/Sarah Vaughan/Billie Holiday/Dinah Washington | Verve | 559693-2
Shirley Scott Quintet
Queen Of The Organ-Shirley Scott Memorial Album | Prestige | PRCD 11027-2
Briglia,Tony | (dr)
Louis Armstrong With The Casa Loma Orchestra
Louis Armstrong:Swing That Music | Laserlight | 36056
Brilhart,Arnold | (as,cl,floboe)
Hoagy Carmichael And His Orchestra
Planet Jazz:Bud Freeman | Planet Jazz | 2161240-2
Brilhart,Verlye | (harp)
Ella Fitzgerald With The Billy May Orchestra
The Best Of The Song Books:The Ballads | Verve | 521867-2
Ella Fitzgerald Sings The Harold Arlen Song Book | Verve | 589108-2
Brillhart,Arnold | (fl,clas)
Roger Wolfe Kahn And His Orchestra
Planet Jazz:Jack Teagarden | Planet Jazz | 2161236-2
Brillinger,Jeff | (dr)
Chet Baker Quartet
Jazz In Paris:Chet Baker-Broken Wing | EmArCy | 013043-2
Chet Baker-The Legacy Vol.4:Oh You Crazy Moon | Enja | ENJ-9453 2
Jed Levy Quartet
Round And Round | Steeplechase | SCCD 31529
Ron McClure Quartet
Match Point | Steeplechase | SCCD 31517
Woody Herman And His Orchestra
Jazzin' Vol.2: The Music Of Stevie Wonder | Fantasy | FANCD 6088-2
King Cobra | Original Jazz Classics | OJCCD 1068-2(F 9499)
Woody Herman Herd At Montreux | Original Jazz Classics | OJCCD 991-2(F 9470)
Bring,Lou | (cond)
Lena Horne With The Lou Bring Orchestra
Planet Jazz:Lena Horne | Planet Jazz | 2165373-2
Planet Jazz:Female Jazz Vocalists | Planet Jazz | 2169656-2
Bringolf,Serge | (dr,percvoc)
Bireli Lagrene Group
Bireli Lagrene 'Highlights' | Jazzpoint | JP 1027 CD
Jaco Pastorius Groups
Another Side Of Jaco Pastorius | Jazzpoint | JP 1064 CD
Jaco Pastorius Trio
Heavy'n Jazz | Jazzpoint | JP 1036 CD
Jaco Pastorius Heavy'n Jazz & Stuttgart Aria | Jazzpoint | JP 1058 CD
Brink Christensen,Ellen Marie | (voc)
Marilyn Mazur With Ars Nova And The Copenhagen Art Ensemble
Jordsange | dacapo | DCCD 9454
Brinkmann,Georg | (cl-aditiv)
Horst Faigle's Jazzkrement
Gans Normal | Jazz 4 Ever Records:Jazz Network | J4E 4748
Briodin,Jean-Claude | (voc)
Les Double Six
Les Double Six | RCA | 2164314-2
Swingle Singers
Jazz Sebastian Bach | Philips | 542552-2
Swingle Singers Going Baroque | Philips | 546746-2
Briquet,Christoph | (viola)
Stephane Grappelli With The Michel Legrand Orchestra
Grapelli Story | Verve | 515807-2
Brisbois,Wilbur 'Bud' | (tp)
Duke Ellington And His Orchestra
Planet Jazz:Johnny Hodges | Planet Jazz | 2152065-2
The Popular Duke Ellington | RCA | 2663880-2
Herbie Hancock Group
Man-Child | CBS | 471235-2
Johnny Hartman And His Orchestra
Unforgettable | Impulse(MCA) | IMP 11522
Stan Kenton And His Orchestra
Adventures In Blues | Capitol | 520089-2
Adventures In Jazz | Capitol | 521222-2
Briscoe,Ted | (b)
Jubilee All Stars
Jazz Gallery:Lester Young Vol.2(1946-59) | RCA | 2119541-2
Lester Young And His Band
Lester Young:The Complete Aladdin Sessions | Blue Note | 832787-2
Briseno,Modesto | (bs,clts)
Chamber Jazz Sextet
Plays Pal Joey | Candid | CCD 79030
Brisker,Gordon | (flts)
Woody Herman And His Orchestra
Verve Jazz Masters 54:Woody Herman | Verve | 529903-2
Woody Herman-1963 | Philips | 589490-2
Brister,William | (drcongas)
Sun Ra And His Intergalactic Research Arkestra
Black Myth/Out In Space | MPS | 557656-2
Broadbent,Alan | (arr,cond,keyboards,p,el-p,synth)
Bill Perkins-Bud Shank Quintet
The Jazz Giants Play Harold Arlen:Blues In The Night | Prestige | PCD 24201-2
Charlie Haden Quartet West
Haunted Heart | Verve | 513078-2
Always Say Goodbye | Verve | 521501-2
Now Is The Hour | Verve | 527827-2
Quartet West | Verve | 831673-2
In Angel City | Verve | 837031-2
Charlie Haden Quartet West With Strings
Now Is The Hour | Verve | 527827-2
The Art Of The Song | Verve | 547403-2
Diane Schuur And Her Band
Music Is My Life | Atlantic | 7567-83150-2
Diane Schuur Trio With Orchestra And Strings
In Tribute | GRP | GRP 20062
Diane Schuur With Orchestra
In Tribute | GRP | GRP 20062
The Best Of Diane Schuur | GRP | GRP 98882
Irene Kral With Alan Broadbent
Where Is Love? | Choice | CHCD 71012
Lee Konitz With Alan Broadbent
Live-Lee | Milestone | MCD 9329-2
Lee Ritenour Group
Stolen Moments | GRP | GRP 96152
Woody Herman And His Orchestra
Brand New | Original Jazz Classics | OJCCD 1044-2(F 8414)
Broadnax,Dwayne 'Cook' | (dr)
Jimmy Scott With Band
But Beautiful | Milestone | MCD 9321-2
Broadnax,Paul | (pvoc)
Jeanne Lee Group
Natural Affinities | Owl Records | 018352-2
Broberg,Bosse | (tp)
Agneta Baumann And Her Quartet
Comes Love... | Touché Music | TMcCD 011
Agneta Baumann Group
Sentimental Lady | Touché Music | TMcCD 017
Brock,Werner | (dr)
Harald Banter Ensemble
Deutsches Jazz Fesival 1954/1955 | Bear Family Records | BCD 15430
Brocksieper,Freddie | (drbongos)
Brocksieper-Jazz-Ensemble
Drums Boogie | Bear Family Records | BCD 15988 AH
Brocksieper-Solisten-Orchester
Globetrotter | Bear Family Records | BCD 15912 AH
Brocksieper-Solisten-Orchester(Brocksi-Quartet)
Drums Boogie | Bear Family Records | BCD 15988 AH
Brocksieper-Special-Ensemble
Globetrotter | Bear Family Records | BCD 15912 AH
Brocksi-Quartett
Globetrotter | Bear Family Records | BCD 15912 AH
Drums Boogie | Bear Family Records | BCD 15988 AH
Brocksi-Quintett
Drums Boogie | Bear Family Records | BCD 15988 AH
Brocksi-Sextett
Drums Boogie | Bear Family Records | BCD 15988 AH
Shot Gun Boogie | Bear Family Records | BCD 16277 AH
Freddie Brocksieper And His Boys
Freddie's Boogie Blues | Bear Family Records | BCD 16388 AH
Freddie Brocksieper Four Stars
Freddie's Boogie Blues | Bear Family Records | BCD 16388 AH
Freddie Brocksieper Orchester
Drums Boogie | Bear Family Records | BCD 15988 AH
Shot Gun Boogie | Bear Family Records | BCD 16277 AH
Freddie Brocksieper Quartett
Shot Gun Boogie | Bear Family Records | BCD 16277 AH
Freddie Brocksieper Quintett
Shot Gun Boogie | Bear Family Records | BCD 16277 AH
Freddie Brocksieper Star-Quintett
Shot Gun Boogie | Bear Family Records | BCD 16277 AH
Freddie Brocksieper Trio
Shot Gun Boogie | Bear Family Records | BCD 16277 AH
Freddie Brocksieper Und Seine Solisten
Globetrotter | Bear Family Records | BCD 15912 AH
Shot Gun Boogie | Bear Family Records | BCD 16277 AH
Freddie's Boogie Blues | Bear Family Records | BCD 16388 AH
Brodahl,Frank | (tpfl-h)
Christoph Lauer & Norwegian Brass
Heaven | ACT | 9420-2
Geir Lysne Listening Ensemble
Aurora Borealis-Nordic Lights | ACT | 9406-2
Brodbeck,Jean-Paul | (p)
Domenic Landolf Quartet
Levitation | JHM Records | JHM 3616
Bröde,Matthias | (keyboards,harmp)
Matthias Bröde Quartet
European Faces | Edition Collage | EC 517-2
Matthias Bröde Quintet
European Faces | Edition Collage | EC 517-2
Brodie,Hugh | (ts)
Cal Massey Sextet
The Jazz Life! | Candid | CCD 79019
Blues To Coltrane | Candid | CCD 79029
Brodmann,Hans-Günter | (drperc)
Brodmann-Pausch Percussion Duo
Are You Serious? | Jazz 4 Ever Records:Jazz Network | J4E 4718
Brodsky,Irving | (p,arr,celestevoc)
Hoagy Carmichael And His Orchestra
Planet Jazz:Bud Freeman | Planet Jazz | 2161240-2
Brody,Paul | (tp)
Paul Brody's Tango Toy
Klezmer Stories | Laika Records | 35101222
Brofsky,Alex | (fr-h)
Miles Davis With Gil Evans Orchestra, The George Gruntz Concert Jazz Band And Guests
Miles & Quincy Live At Montreux | Warner | 9362-45221-2
Sonny Rollins Quintet With Brass
Old Flames | Milestone | MCD 9215-2
Broger,Werner | (b)
Q4 Orchester Project
Lyon's Brood | Creative Works Records | CW CD 1018-3
Brohdal,Frank | (tpfl-h)
Geir Lysne Listening Ensemble
Korall | ACT | 9236-2
Brohdal,Rune | (fr-h)
Christoph Lauer & Norwegian Brass
Heaven | ACT | 9420-2
Brohm,Jörg | (tp)
Nana Mouskouri With The Berlin Radio Big Band
Nana Swings | Mercury | 074394-2
Brokaw,Sid | (v)
Artie Shaw And His Orchestra
Planet JazzArtie Shaw | Planet Jazz | 2152057-2
Planet Jazz:Jazz Greatest Hits | Planet Jazz | 2169648-2
Brom Jr.,Gustav | (tb)
Hans Koller Big Band
New York City | MPS | 9813437
Bromberg,Brian | (b,fretless-b,keyboards,synth)
Gonzalo Rubalcaba Trio
The Trio | somethin'else | 494442-2
Bromley,Tom | (b)
Vic Lewis Jam Session
Vic Lewis:The Golden Years | Candid | CCD 79754
Brönner,Till | (fl-h,voc,tp,keyboards,programming)
Frank Castenier Group
For You,For Me For Evermore | EmArCy | 9814976
Harry Allen And Randy Sandke Meets The RIAS Big Band Berlin
The Music Of The Trumpet Kings | Nagel-Heyer | CD 037
Nils Landgren Funk Unit
Paint It Blue:A Tribute To Cannonball Adderley | ACT | 9243-2
Nils Landgren Funk Unit With Guests
5000 Miles | ACT | 9271-2
Pee Wee Ellis Quintet With Guests
A New Shift | Minor Music | 801060
Rolf Kühn Group
Inside Out | Intuition Records | INT 3276-2
Three Of A Kind
Drip Some Grease | Minor Music | 801056
Till Brönner Group
Chattin' With Chet | Verve | 157534-2
Love | Verve | 559058-2
Till Brönner Quartet & Deutsches Symphonieorchester Berlin
German Songs | Minor Music | 801057
Till Brönner Quintet
My Secret Love | Minor Music | 801051
Till Brönner Quintet With Annette Lowman
My Secret Love | Minor Music | 801051
Brook,Michael | (gelectonics)
Jon Hassell Group
Power Spot | ECM | 1327
Brook,Paige | (flas)
Jackie Paris With The Charles Mingus Quintet
Charles Mingus-The Complete Debut Recordings | Debut | 12 DCD 4402-2
Brooke,Paul | (dr-computer)
Jasper Van't Hof
Pili-Pili | Warner | 2292-40458-2
Brookmeyer,Bob | (arr,comp,p,tbv-tb)
Anita O'Day With The Gary McFarland Orchestra
All The Sad Youn Men | Verve | 517065-2
Verve Jazz Masters 49:Anita O'Day | Verve | 527653-2
Astrud Gilberto With The Al Cohn Orchestra
Verve Jazz Masters 9:Astrud Gilberto | Verve | 519824-2
Astrud Gilberto With The Gil Evans Orchestra
Verve Jazz Masters 9:Astrud Gilberto | Verve | 519824-2
Verve Jazz Masters 23:Gil Evans | Verve | 521860-2
Bob Brookmeyer Group With The WDR Big Band
Electricity | ACT | 9219-2
Bob Brookmeyer Quartet
Old Friends | Storyville | STCD 8292
Bob Brookmeyer Quintet
Sony Jazz Collection:Stan Getz | CBS | 488623-2
Bob Brookmeyer Sextet
Late Night Sax | CBS | 487798-2
Bud Shank And Trombones
Cool Fool | Fresh Sound Records | FSR CD 507
Chet Baker Sextet
The Best Of Chet Baker Plays | Pacific Jazz | 797161-2
Chubby Jackson And His All Star Big Band
Chubby Takes Over | Fresh Sound Records | FSR-CD 324
George Russell And His Orchestra
Geogre Russell New York N.Y. | Impulse(MCA) | 951278-2
Gerry Mulligan And His Orchestra
Mullenium | CBS | CK 65678
Gerry Mulligan Concert Jazz Band
Verve Jazz Masters 36:Gerry Mulligan | Verve | 523342-2
Verve Jazz Masters Vol.60:The Collection | Verve | 529866-2
Gerry Mulligan And The Concert Band At The Village Vanguard | Verve | 589488-2
The Complete Verve Gerry Mulligan Concert Band | Verve | 9860613
Gerry Mulligan Quartet
Paris Jazz Concert:Gerry Mulligan And His Quartet | Laserlight | 17433
Gerry Mulligan:Pleyel Concert Vol.1 | Vogue | 21409422
Gerry Mulligan:Pleyel Concert Vol.2 | Vogue | 21409432
Planet Jazz:Gerry Mulligan | Planet Jazz | 2152070-2
Planet Jazz Sampler | Planet Jazz | 2152326-2
Planet Jazz:Jazz Saxophone | Planet Jazz | 2169653-2
Jazz At The Philharmonic: The Gerry Mulligan Quartets In Concert | Pablo | PACD 5309-2
Jimmy Giuffre 3
Western Suite | Atlantic | 7567-80777-2
Michel Petrucciani Sextet
Both Worlds | Dreyfus Jazz Line | FDM 36590-2
Oliver Nelson And His Orchestra
Verve Jazz Masters Vol.60:The Collection | Verve | 529866-2
Stan Getz Quintet
Stan Getz Highlights:The Best Of The Verve Years Vol.2 | Verve | 517330-2
Stan Getz And The 'Cool' Sounds | Verve | 547317-2
Stan Getz Highlights | Verve | 847430-2
Stan Getz With The Gary McFarland Orchestra
Stan Getz Highlights:The Best Of The Verve Years Vol.2 | Verve | 517330-2

Verve Jazz Masters 53:Stan Getz-Bossa Nova | Verve | 529904-2
Big Band Bossa Nova | Verve | 825771-2 PMS
Stan Getz-Bob Brookmeyer Quintet
Stan Getz Highlights:The Best Of The Verve Years Vol.2 | Verve | 517330-2
A Life In Jazz:A Musical Biography | Verve | 535119-2
Thad Jones-Mel Lewis Orchestra
The Groove Merchant/The Second Race | Laserlight | 24656
Woody Herman And His Orchestra
The Legends Of Swing | Laserlight | 24659

Brooks,Anna | (sax)
John Mayer's Indio-Jazz Fusions
Ragatal | Nimbus Records | NI 5569

Brooks,Billy | (dr,bamboo-fl,b-fl,dun-dun,voctp)
Eddie Harris Group
Here Comes The Judge | CBS | 492533-2
Fritz Pauer Trio
Jazz Portraits | EGO | 95080
Live At The Berlin Jazz Galerie | MPS | 9811263
Horace Parlan Quartet
Jazz Portraits | EGO | 95080
Slide Hampton-Joe Haider Jazz Orchestra
Give Me A Double | JHM Records | JHM 3627
Woody Shaw Quartet
Bemsha Swing | Blue Note | 829029-2

Brooks,Gene | (dr)
Lucille Hegamin With Willie The Lion And His Cubs
Songs We Taught Your Mother | Original Blues Classics | OBCCD 520-2

Brooks,Harry | (p)
Sidney Bechet With Noble Sissle's Swingsters
Sidney Bechet:Summertime | Dreyfus Jazz Line | FDM 36712-2

Brooks,Harvey | (el-bp)
Miles Davis Group
Circle In The Round | CBS | 467898-2
Bitches Brew | CBS | C2K 65774

Brooks,Jerry | (b)
Lenny White Group
Renderers Of Spirit | Hip Bop | HIBD 8014

Brooks,Ron | (b)
Bob James Trio
Bold Conceptions | Verve | 557454-2

Brooks,Roy | (concert-tom-toms,dr,perc)
Charles McPherson Quartet
Jazzin' Vol.2: The Music Of Stevie Wonder | Fantasy | FANCD 6088-2
McPherson's Mood | Original Jazz Classics | OJCCD 1947-2(PR 7743)
Chet Baker Quintet
The Jazz Giants Play Rodgers & Hart:Blue Moon | Prestige | PCD 24205-2
Groovin' With The Chet Baker Quintet | Prestige | PR20 7460-2
Comin' On With The Chet Baker Quintet | Prestige | PR20 7478-2
Cool Burnin' With The Chet Baker Quintet | Prestige | PR20 7496-2
Boppin' With The Chet Baker Quintet | Prestige | PR20 7512-2
Smokin' With The Chet Baker Quintet | Prestige | PR20 7749-2
Dexter Gordon Quartet
Dexter Gordon Birthday Celebration | Fantasy | FANCD 6082-2
The Jumpin' Blues | Original Jazz Classics | OJCCD 899-2(PR 10020)
Dollar Brand Trio
The Children Of Africa | Enja | ENJ-2070 2
Horace Silver Quintet
Horace Silver Retrospective | Blue Note | 495576-2
Song For My Father | Blue Note | 499002-2
Silver's Serenade | Blue Note | 821288-2
Paris Blues | Pablo | PACD 5316-2
Horace Silver Trio
Song For My Father | Blue Note | 499002-2
M'Boom
To The Max! | Enja | ENJ-7021 22
Shirley Scott Quintet
Blue Seven | Original Jazz Classics | OJCCD 1050-2(P 7376)
Queen Of The Organ-Shirley Scott Memorial Album | Prestige | PRCD 11027-2
Yusef Lateef Orchestra
The Blue Yusef Lateef | Rhino | 8122-73717-2
Yusef Lateef Quartet
The Golden Flute | Impulse(MCA) | 9681049

Brooks,Stuart | (tpfl-h)
Barbara Thompson Group
Heavenly Bodies | VeraBra Records | CDVBR 2015-2
John Surman-John Warren Group
The Brass Project | ECM | 1478
Mike Westbrook Orchestra
The Orchestra Of Smith's Academy | Enja | ENJ-9358 2

Brooks,Tina | (ts)
Freddie Hubbard Quintet
Open Sesame | Blue Note | 495341-2
Freddie Redd Sextet
Redd's Blues | Blue Note | 540537-2
Jimmy Smith All Stars
House Party | Blue Note | 524542-2
Jimmy Smith Quintet
Cool Blues | Blue Note | 535587-2
Kenny Burrell Septet
Blue Lights Vol.1&2 | Blue Note | 857184-2
Tina Brooks Quintet
True Blue | Blue Note | 534032-2
The Waiting Game | Blue Note | 540536-2
Blue N' Groovy | Blue Note | 780679-2

Brookshire,Nell | (voc)
Duke Ellington And His Orchestra
Togo Brava Swuite | Storyville | STCD 8323

Broom,Bobby | (el-gg)
Sonny Rollins Quintet
No Problem | Original Jazz Classics | OJCCD 1014-2(M 9104)

Broonzy,Big Bill | (g,vocv)
Big Bill Broonzy
The Blues | Storyville | 4960323
Classic Blues | Zounds | CD 2700048
Big Bill Broonzy With Albert Ammons
From Spiritual To Swing | Vanguard | VCD 169/71

Brosseau,Robert | (v)
Charlie Haden Quartet West With Strings
The Art Of The Song | Verve | 547403-2

Broström,Hakan | (fl,ssas)
Tim Hagans With Norrbotten Big Band
Future Miles | ACT | 9235-2

Brötzmann,Peter | (as,ts,bass-s,bass-sax,tarogata,bs)
Achim Jaroschek-Peter Brötzmann
Neurotransmitter | double moon | DMCD 1006-2
Ekkehard Jost Quartet
Some Other Tapes | Fish Music | FM 009/10 CD

Brouwer,Niels | (g)
Boi Akih
Uwa ! | Enja | ENJ-9472 2

Browden,Marlon | (drperc)
Greg Osby Quartet With String Quartet
Symbols Of Light(A Solution) | Blue Note | 531395-2

Brown Jr.,Oscar | (voc)
Oscar Brown Jr. And His Group
Live Every Minute | Minor Music | 801071
Movin' On | Rhino | 8122-73678-2
Oscar Brown Jr. with The NDR Big Band
Live Every Minute | Minor Music | 801071

Brown,Alan | (dr)
Vince Jones Group
For All Colours | Intuition Records | INT 3071-2

Brown,Alfred | (as,strings,tp,v,condviola)
Andrew Hill Orchestra
Deep Blue-The United States Of Mind | Blue Note | 521152-2
Bill Evans Quartet With Orchestra
The Complete Bill Evans On Verve | Verve | 527953-2
From Left To Right | Verve | 557451-2
Bob James And His Orchestra
Jazzrock-Anthology Vol.3:Fusion | Zounds | CD 27100555
Freddy Cole With Band
Le Grand Freddy:Freddy Cole Sings The Music Of Michel Legrand | Fantasy | FCD 9683-2
Grover Washington Jr. Orchestra
Inside Moves | Elektra | 7559-60318-2
James Moody Orchestra
The Blues And Other Colors | Original Jazz Classics | OJCCD 954-2(M 9023)
Les McCann Group
Another Beginning | Atlantic | 7567-80790-2
Louis Armstrong And His Friends
Planet Jazz:Louis Armstrong | Planet Jazz | 2152052-2
Planet Jazz Sampler | Planet Jazz | 2152326-2
Louis Armstrong And His Friends | Bluebird | 2663961-2
Nina Simone And Orchestra
Baltimore | Epic | 476906-2
Phil Woods Quartet With Orchestra & Strings
Round Trip | Verve | 559804-2
Stan Getz With The Eddie Sauter Orchestra
Stan Getz Plays The Music Of Mickey One | Verve | 531232-2
Wes Montgomery With The Jimmy Jones Orchestra
Wes Montgomery-The Complete Riverside Recordings | Riverside | 12 RCD 4408-2
The Jazz Giants Play Rodgers & Hart:Blue Moon | Prestige | PCD 24205-2
Yusef Lateef Orchestra
The Blue Yusef Lateef | Rhino | 8122-73717-2

Brown,Andrew | (as,bs,b-cl,bass-sax,tscl)
Cab Calloway And His Orchestra
Planet Jazz:Cab Calloway | Planet Jazz | 2161237-2

Brown,Benjamin 'Ben' | (bel-b)
Buddy Rich Big Band
Backwoods Siseman/Pieces Of Dream | Laserlight | 24655
Lena Horne With The George Benson Quintet
Misty Blue:Sweet Sisters Swing Songs Of Sorrow And Sadness | Blue Note | 521151-2

Brown,Bert | (b)
Oscar Peterson Quartet
Planet Music:Oscar Peterson | RCA | 2165365-2
This Is Oscar Peterson | RCA | 2663990-2
Oscar Peterson Trio
This Is Oscar Peterson | RCA | 2663990-2

Brown,Bill | (voc)
Paul Desmond Quartet With The Bill Bates Singers
Desmond | Original Jazz Classics | OJCCD 712-2(F 3235/8082)

Brown,Bob 'Bobby' | (as,tsfl)
Johnny Hodges-Wild Bill Davis Sextet
Planet Jazz:Johnny Hodges | Planet Jazz | 2152065-2
Willie Bobo Group
Juicy | Verve | 519857-2

Brown,Cameron | (b)
Dannie Richmond Quintet
Three Or Four Shades Of Dannie Richmond Quintet | Tutu Records | 888120-2*
Dave Ballou Quartet
Rothko | Steeplechase | SCCD 31525
Joe Lovano-Greg Osby Quintet
Friendly Fire | Blue Note | 499125-2
Mal Waldron
Moods | Enja | ENJ-3021 2
Mal Waldron Sextet
Moods | Enja | ENJ-3021 2

Brown,Carlinhos | (perc)
Lee Ritenour Group
Festival | GRP | GRP 95702

Brown,Charlie | (b,gts)
Bernard Purdie Group
Jazzin' With The Soul Brothers | Fantasy | FANCD 6086-2

Brown,Chris | (b,el-b,voc,dr,gazamba,wing,p)
Dave Brubeck With The Erich Kunzel Orchestra
Truth Is Fallen | Atlantic | 7567-80761-2

Brown,Chuck | (gvoc)
Chuck Brown And The Second Chapter Band
Timeless | Minor Music | 801068

Brown,Clarence Gatemouth | (g,harm,vocv)
Clarence Gatemouth Brown Band
The Blues Of Clarence 'Gatemouth Brown | Storyville | 4960563

Brown,Clifford | (tp)
All Star Live Jam Session
Brownie-The Complete EmArCy Recordings Of Clifford Brown | EmArCy | 838306-2
Art Blakey And The Jazz Messengers
A Night At Birdland Vol. 1 | Blue Note | 532146-2
A Night At Birdland Vol. 2 | Blue Note | 532147-2
Clifford Brown & The Neal Hefti Orchestra
Clifford Brown With Strings | Verve | 558078-2
Clifford Brown All Stars
Verve Jazz Masters 44:Clifford Brown and Max Roach | Verve | 528109-2
Brownie-The Complete EmArCy Recordings Of Clifford Brown | EmArCy | 838306-2
Clifford Brown All Stars With Dinah Washington
Verve Jazz Masters 40:Dinah Washington | Verve | 522055-2
Clifford Brown And Art Farmer With The Swedish All Stars
Clifford Brown Memorial | Original Jazz Classics | OJC20 017-2(P 7055)
Clifford Brown Quartet
Planet Jazz:Clifford Brown | Planet Jazz | 2161239-2
Clifford Brown Sextet
Clifford Brown Memorial Album | Blue Note | 532141-2*
Clifford Brown With Strings
Clifford Brown-Max Roach:Alone Together-The Best Of The Mercury Years | Verve | 526373-2
Verve Jazz Masters 44:Clifford Brown and Max Roach | Verve | 528109-2
Brownie-The Complete EmArCy Recordings Of Clifford Brown | EmArCy | 838306-2
Clifford Brown-Max Roach Quartet
Verve Jazz Masters 44:Clifford Brown and Max Roach | Verve | 528109-2
Clifford Brown-Max Roach Quintet
Clifford Brown-Max Roach:Alone Together-The Best Of The Mercury Years | Verve | 526373-2
Verve Jazz Masters 44:Clifford Brown and Max Roach | Verve | 528109-2
Verve Jazz Masters Vol.60:The Collection | Verve | 529866-2
Clifford Brown And Max Roach | Verve | 543306-2
Clifford Brown And Max Roach At Basin Street | Verve | 589826-2
Study In Brown | EmArCy | 814646-2
Brownie-The Complete EmArCy Recordings Of Clifford Brown | EmArCy | 838306-2
Gigi Gryce-Clifford Brown Octet
Planet Jazz:Clifford Brown | Planet Jazz | 2161239-2
Gigi Gryce-Clifford Brown Sextet
Planet Jazz:Clifford Brown | Planet Jazz | 2161239-2
Helen Merrill With The Quincy Jones Orchestra
Clifford Brown-Max Roach:Alone Together-The Best Of The Mercury Years | Verve | 526373-2
Verve Jazz Masters 44:Clifford Brown and Max Roach | Verve | 528109-2
Brownie-The Complete EmArCy Recordings Of Clifford Brown | EmArCy | 838306-2
J.J.Johnson Sextet
The Eminent J.J.Johnson Vol.1 | Blue Note | 532143-2
Lou Donaldson Quintet
Clifford Brown Memorial Album | Blue Note | 532141-2
Sarah Vaughan With The Clifford Brown All Stars
Verve Jazz Masters 20:Introducing | Verve | 519853-2
Clifford Brown-Max Roach:Alone Together-The Best Of The Mercury Years | Verve | 526373-2
Sarah Vaughan | Verve | 543305-2
4 By 4:Ella Fitzgerald/Sarah Vaughan/Billie Holiday/Dinah Washington | Verve | 559693-2
Brownie-The Complete EmArCy Recordings Of Clifford Brown | EmArCy | 838306-2
Sarah Vaughan | EmArCy | 9860779
Sonny Rollins Plus Four
Sonny Rollins Plus 4 | Original Jazz Classics | OJC20 243-2(P 7038)
The Prestige Legacy Vol.1:The High Priests | Prestige | PCD 24251-2
Tadd Dameron And His Orchestra
Clifford Brown Memorial | Original Jazz Classics | OJC20 017-2(P 7055)

Brown,Dean | (g)
Bernard Purdie's Soul To Jazz
Bernard Purdie's Soul To Jazz | ACT | 9242-2
Eddie Harris Group With The WDR Big Band
Eddie Harris-The Last Concert | ACT | 9249-2
Lenny White Group
Present Tense | Hip Bop | HIBD 8004
Renderers Of Spirit | Hip Bop | HIBD 8014
Hot Jazz Bisquits | Hip Bop | HIBD 8801
Marcus Miller Group
The Sun Don't Lie | Dreyfus Jazz Line | FDM 36560-2
Tales | Dreyfus Jazz Line | FDM 36571-2
Live & More | Dreyfus Jazz Line | FDM 36585-2
The Brecker Brothers
Return Of The Brecker Brothers | GRP | GRP 96842
Out Of The Loop | GRP | GRP 97842
Till Brönner Group
Chattin' With Chet | Verve | 157534-2

Brown,Delmar | (keyboards,voc,psynth)
Brainstorm feat. Chico Freeman
The Mystical Dreamer | IN+OUT Records | 7006-2
Chico Freeman And Brainstorm
Sweet Explosion | IN+OUT Records | 7010-2
Jazz Unlimited | IN+OUT Records | 7017-2
Lew Soloff Group
Rainbow Mountain | TipToe | TIP-888838 2
Miles Davis With Gil Evans Orchestra, The George Gruntz Concert Jazz Band And Guests
Miles & Quincy Live At Montreux | Warner | 9362-45221-2

Brown,Donald | (p,voc,p-solosynth)
Art Blakey And The Jazz Messengers
Jazz Life Vol.2:From Seventh At Avenue South | Storyville | 4960763
Dianne Reeves With Band
Misty Blue:Sweet Sisters Swing Songs Of Sorrow And Sadness | Blue Note | 521151-2
I Remember | Blue Note | 790264-2

Brown,Eddie | (as,bsoboe)
Charlie Parker With Strings
Charlie Parker:The Best Of The Verve Years | Verve | 527815-2
Bird: The Complete Charlie Parker On Verve | Verve | 837141-2
Charlie Parker:April In Paris | Dreyfus Jazz Line | FDM 36737-2
Charlie Parker With The Joe Lipman Orchestra
Verve Jazz Masters 28:Charlie Parker Plays Standards | Verve | 521854-2
Charlie Parker With Strings:The Master Takes | Verve | 523984-2
Charlie Parker Big Band | Verve | 559835-2

Brown,Edwin C. | (oboe)
Charlie Parker Quartet With Strings
The Cole Porter Songbook | Verve | 823250-2

Brown,Garnett | (tbbass-tb)
Billy Cobham Group
The Best Of Billy Cobham | Atlantic | 7567-81558-2
Booker Ervin Sextet
Heavy!!! | Original Jazz Classics | OJCCD 981-2(P 7499)
Diane Schuur And Her Band
The Best Of Diane Schuur | GRP | GRP 98882
Duke Pearson Orchestra
Blue N' Groovy | Blue Note | 780679-2
Freddie Hubbard With Orchestra
This Is Jazz:Freddie Hubbard | CBS | CK 65041
George Benson Orchestra
Talkin' Verve:George Benson | Verve | 553780-2
George Benson With Orchestra
Verve Jazz Masters 21:George Benson | Verve | 521861-2
George Russell Sextet
The Outer View | Original Jazz Classics | OJCCD 616-2(RLP 9440)
Gil Evans Orchestra
Blues In Orbit | Enja | ENJ-3069 2
Herbie Hancock Group
Man-Child | CBS | 471235-2
Sunlight | CBS | 486570-2
Herbie Hancock Orchestra
Herbie Hancock:The Complete Blue Note Sixties Sessions | Blue Note | 495569-2
The Prisoner | Blue Note | 525649-2
Horace Silver Quintet With Brass
Horace Silver Retrospective | Blue Note | 495576-2
Jack Wilson Sextet
Blue N' Groovy | Blue Note | 780679-2
Les McCann Group
Another Beginning | Atlantic | 7567-80790-2
Lionel Hampton And His Orchestra
Planet Jazz:Big Bands | Planet Jazz | 2169649-2
Louis Armstrong And His Friends
Louis Armstrong And His Friends | Bluebird | 2663961-2
Modern Jazz Quartet & Guests
MJQ 40 | Atlantic | 7567-82330-2
Roland Kirk And His Orchestra
Rahsaan/The Complete Mercury Recordings Of Roland Kirk | Mercury | 846630-2
Stanley Turrentine And His Orchestra
The Lost Grooves | Blue Note | 831883-2
Thad Jones-Mel Lewis Orchestra
The Groove Merchant/The Second Race | Laserlight | 24656

Brown,George | (congas,drperc)
Gene Ammons Septet
A Stranger In Town | Prestige | PRCD 24266-2
Gene Ammons-Sonny Stitt Quintet
Gentle Jug Vol.3 | Prestige | PCD 24249-2
Wes Montgomery Trio
Wes Montgomery-The Complete Riverside Recordings | Riverside | 12 RCD 4408-2
Portrait Of Wes | Original Jazz Classics | OJCCD 144-2
Guitar On The Go | Original Jazz Classics | OJCCD 489-2(RLP 9494)
The Jazz Giants Play Miles Davis:Milestones | Prestige | PCD 24225-2

Brown,Gerry | (drperc)
NDR Big Band With Guests
50 Years Of NDR Big Band:Bravissimo II | ACT | 9259-2
Oscar Brown Jr. And His Group
Live Every Minute | Minor Music | 801071
Oscar Brown Jr. with The NDR Big Band
Live Every Minute | Minor Music | 801071
Stanley Clarke Group
If This Bass Could Only Talk | CBS | 460883-2

Brown,Greg | (b)
Dollar Brand Quartet
Africa Tears And Laughter | Enja | ENJ-3039 2

Brown,Henry | (p,vocp-solo)
Henry Brown

INTERPRETENVERZEICHNIS

Boogie Woogie | Laserlight | 24321

Brown,Henry 'Pucho' | (congastimbales)

Gene Ammons Quintet

A Stranger In Town | Prestige | PRCD 24266-2

Brown,Hillard | (dr)

Duke Ellington And His Orchestra

Carnegie Hall Concert December 1944 | Prestige | 2PCD 24073-2

Brown,Irving 'Skinny' | (asts)

Louis Jordan And His Tympany Five

Louis Jordan-Let The Good Times Roll: The Complete Decca Recordings 1938-1954 | Bear Family Records | BCD 15557 IH

Brown,Jeremy | (bel-b)

Gerard Presencer Group

Chasing Reality | ACT | 9422-2

Brown,Jewel | (voc)

Louis Armstrong And His All Stars

Jazz In Paris:Louis Armstrong:The Best Live Concer Vol.1 | EmArCy | 013030-2

Jazz In Paris:Louis Armstrong-The Best Live Concert Vol.2 | EmArCy | 013031-2

Jazz Festival Vol.1 | Storyville | 4960733

The Legendary Berlin Concert Part 2 | Jazzpoint | JP 1063 CD

Brown,John | (as,voc,btp)

Dizzy Gillespie And His Orchestra

Dizzy Gillespie:Pleyel Jazz Concert 1948 + Max Roach Quintet 1949 | Vogue | 21409412

Planet Jazz:Dizzy Gillespie | Planet Jazz | 2152069-2

Planet Jazz:Bebop | RCA | 2169650-2

Planet Jazz:Male Jazz Vocalists | Planet Jazz | 2169657-2

Ella Fitzgerald With The Dizzy Gillespie Orchestra

Ella Fitzgerald:Mr.Paganini | Dreyfus Jazz Line | FDM 36741-2

Ella Fitzgerald With The Hank Jones Trio

Ella Fitzgerald:Mr.Paganini | Dreyfus Jazz Line | FDM 36741-2

Brown,John V. | (b)

Tom Browne Groups

Mo' Jamaica Funk | Hip Bop | HIBD 8002

Brown,Lawrence | (tbarr)

Al Sears And His Orchestra

Sear-iously | Bear Family Records | BCD 15668 AH

Billy Strayhorn Orchestra

Johnny Hodges With Billy Strayhorn And The Orchestra | Verve | 557543-2

Django Reinhardt With Duke Ellington And His Orchestra

Django Reinhardt:Souveniers | Dreyfus Jazz Line | FDM 36744-2

Duke Ellington And Count Basie With Their Orchestras

First Time! | CBS | CK 65571

Duke Ellington And His Famous Orchestra

Duke Ellington:The Blanton-Webster Band | Bluebird | 21 13181-2

Planet Jazz:Duke Ellington | Planet Jazz | 2152053-2

Planet Jazz:Johnny Hodges | Planet Jazz | 2152065-2

Planet Jazz Sampler | Planet Jazz | 2152326-2

Planet Jazz:Ben Webster | RCA | 2165368-2

Planet Jazz:Big Bands | Planet Jazz | 2169649-2

Planet Jazz:Jazz Trumpet | Planet Jazz | 2169654-2

Planet Jazz:Female Jazz Vocalists | Planet Jazz | 2169656-2

Highlights From The Duke Ellington Centennial Edition | RCA | 2663672-2

Greatest Hits | CBS | 462959-2

Jazz:The Essential Collection Vol.2 | IN+OUT Records | 78012-2

Jazz:The Essential Collection Vol.3 | IN+OUT Records | 78013-2

Duke Ellington:Ko-Ko | Dreyfus Jazz Line | FDM 36717-2

Duke Ellington And His Orchestra

Planet Jazz:Duke Ellington | Planet Jazz | 2152053-2

Planet Jazz:Johnny Hodges | Planet Jazz | 2152065-2

Planet Jazz:Jazz Greatest Hits | Planet Jazz | 2169648-2

Duke Ellington's Far East Suite | RCA | 2174797-2

The Art Of Saxophone | Laserlight | 24652

The Legends Of Swing | Laserlight | 24659

Highlights From The Duke Ellington Centennial Edition | RCA | 2663672-2

The Popular Duke Ellington | RCA | 2663880-2

Carnegie Hall Concert December 1944 | Prestige | 2PCD 24073-2

Carnegie Hall Concert January 1946 | Prestige | 2PCD 24074-2

Carnegie Hall Concert December 1947 | Prestige | 2PCD 24075-2

Carnegie Hall Concert January 1943 | Prestige | 2PCD 34004-2

Duke Ellington: The Champs-Elysees Theater January 29-30th,1965 | Laserlight | 36131

Jazz Festival Vol.2 | Storyville | 4960743

Ella & Duke At The Cote D'Azur | Verve | 539030-2

Ella Fitzgerald And Duke Ellington:Cote D'Azure Concerts on Verve | Verve | 539033-2

Soul Call | Verve | 539785-2

The Great Paris Concert | Atlantic | 7567-81303-2

Jazz:The Essential Collection Vol.2 | IN+OUT Records | 78012-2

Jazz:The Essential Collection Vol.3 | IN+OUT Records | 78013-2

Afro-Bossa | Reprise | 9362-47876-2

Latin America Suite | Original Jazz Classics | OJC20 469-2

Duke Ellington And His Orchestra feat. Paul Gonsalves | Original Jazz Classics | OJCCD 623-2

Yale Concert | Original Jazz Classics | OJCCD 664-2

Jazz At The Philharmonis Berlin '65/Paris '67 | Pablo | PACD 5304-2

The Jazz Giants Play Duke Ellington:Caravan | Prestige | PCD 24227-2

The Duke At Fargo 1940 | Storyville | STCD 8316/17

At The Hurricane:Original 1943 Broadcasts | Storyville | STCD 8359

Duke Ellington Small Band

The Intimacy Of The Blues | Original Jazz Classics | OJCCD 624-2

Duke Ellington-Coleman Hawkins Orchestra

Duke Ellington Meets Coleman Hawkins | Impulse(MCA) | 951162-2

Ella Fitzgerald With The Duke Ellington Orchestra

The Stockholm Concert 1966 | Pablo | 2308242-2

Ella Fitzgerald-First Lady Of Song | Verve | 517898-2

Verve Jazz Masters 46:Ella Fitzgerald-The Jazz Sides | Verve | 527655-2

Ella At Duke's Place | Verve | 529700-2

Ella & Duke At The Cote D'Azur | Verve | 539030-2

Ella Fitzgerald And Duke Ellington:Cote D'Azure Concerts on Verve | Verve | 539033-2

Ella Fitzgerald With The Duke Ellington Orchestra And Jimmy Jones Trio

Ella & Duke At The Cote D'Azur | Verve | 539030-2

Ella Fitzgerald And Duke Ellington:Cote D'Azure Concerts on Verve | Verve | 539033-2

Frankie Laine With Buck Clayton And His Orchestra

Jazz Spectacular | CBS | CK 65507

Joe Turner With Orchestra

Atlantic Jazz: Kansas City | Atlantic | 7567-81701-2

Johnny Hodges And His Band

Verve Jazz Masters 35:Johnny Hodges | Verve | 521857-2

Johnny Hodges Orchestra

Planet Jazz:Johnny Hodges | Planet Jazz | 2152065-2

Planet Jazz Sampler | Planet Jazz | 2152326-2

Planet Jazz:Jazz Saxophone | Planet Jazz | 2169653-2

Highlights From The Duke Ellington Centennial Edition | RCA | 2663672-2

Johnny Hodges At The Sportpalast, Berlin | Pablo | 2CD 2620102

Side By Side | Verve | 521405-2

The Jazz Giants Play Harry Warren:Lullaby Of Broadway | Prestige | PCD 24204-2

Johnny Hodges With Billy Strayhorn And The Duke Ellington Orchestra

Verve Jazz Masters 35:Johnny Hodges | Verve | 521857-2

Johnny Hodges-Wild Bill Davis Sextet

Planet Jazz:Johnny Hodges | Planet Jazz | 2152065-2

Lawrence Brown Quintet

Slide Trombone | Verve | 559930-2

Lawrence Brown With The Ralph Burns Orchestra

Slide Trombone | Verve | 559930-2

Oscar Peterson With The Duke Ellington Orchestra

Oscar Peterson Plays Duke Ellington | Pablo | 2310966-2

Rex Stewart And His Orchestra

Planet Jazz:Ben Webster | RCA | 2165368-2

Planet Jazz:Jazz Trumpet | Planet Jazz | 2169654-2

Jazz:The Essential Collection Vol.3 | IN+OUT Records | 78013-2

Brown,Les | (arr,ld,cl,asg)

Les Brown And His Orchestra

Great Swing Classics In Hi-Fi | Capitol | 521223-2

Brown,Maggie | (voc)

Abbey Lincoln With Her Band

Wholly Earth | Verve | 559538-2

Brown,Marion | (as,perc,wood-fl,zomari,as-solo,fl)

Archie Shepp Sextet

Fire Music | Impulse(MCA) | 951158-2

Gunter Hampel All Stars

Jubilation | Birth | 0038

John Coltrane And His Orchestra

Ascension | Impulse(MCA) | 543413-2

Marion Brown & Jazz Cussion

Echoes Of Blue | double moon | CHRDM 71015

Marion Brown Orchestra

Afternoon Of A Georgia Faun | ECM | 1004

Marion Brown-Gunter Hampel Duo

Gemini | Birth | CD 037

Brown,Mark P. | (b)

Tim Sund Quintet

In The Midst Of Change | Nabel Records:Jazz Network | CD 4679

Brown,Marshall | (cond,tb,bar-h,v-tb,bass-tp)

Pee Wee Russell Quartet

Ask Me Now! | Impulse(MCA) | 755742-2

Brown,Maurice | (celloviola)

Billie Holiday With The Ray Ellis Orchestra

Lady In Satin | CBS | CK 65144

Charles Mingus Group

Mingus Dynasty | CBS | CK 65513

Charles Mingus Orchestra

Charles Mingus:The Complete 1959 Columbia Recordings | CBS | C3K 65145

Charlie Parker Quartet With Strings

The Cole Porter Songbook | Verve | 823250-2

Charlie Parker With Strings

Charlie Parker:The Best Of The Verve Years | Verve | 527815-2

Bird: The Complete Charlie Parker On Verve | Verve | 837141-2

Charlie Parker:April In Paris | Dreyfus Jazz Line | FDM 36737-2

Charlie Parker With The Joe Lipman Orchestra

Verve Jazz Masters 28:Charlie Parker Plays Standards | Verve | 521854-2

Charlie Parker With Strings:The Master Takes | Verve | 523984-2

Charlie Parker Big Band | Verve | 559835-2

Brown,Mel | (dr,bellsg)

Jessica Williams Trio

Higher Standards | Candid | CCD 79736

Jazz In The Afternoon | Candid | CCD 79750

John Lee Hooker Group

Endless Boogie | MCA | MCD 10413

Mel Brown Quartet

Chicken Fat | Impulse(MCA) | 9861047

Mel Brown Quintet

Chicken Fat | Impulse(MCA) | 9861047

Brown,Mildred | (voc)

Lou Donaldson Orchestra

Blue Breaks Beats Vol.2 | Blue Note | 789907-2

Brown,Norman | (g)

Louis Armstrong And The Mills Brothers

Louis Armstrong:Swing That Music | Laserlight | 36056

Brown,Pete | (as,voctp)

52nd Street All Stars

Planet Jazz:Bebop | RCA | 2169650-2

Coleman Hawkins And His 52nd Street All Stars

Jazz:The Essential Collection Vol.3 | IN+OUT Records | 78013-2

Coleman Hawkins' Fifty-Second Street All-Stars

Planet Jazz:Coleman Hawkins | Planet Jazz | 2152055-2

JATP All Stars

The Complete Jazz At The Philharmonic On Verve 1944-1949 | Verve | 523893-2

Joe Turner With Orchestra

Atlantic Jazz: Kansas City | Atlantic | 7567-81701-2

Brown,Phil | (dr)

Red Rodney Quintet

The Red Rodney Quintets | Fantasy | FCD 24758-2

Brown,Pud | (as,clss)

Kid Ory's Creole Jazz Band

This Kid's The Greatest! | Good Time Jazz | GTCD 12045-2

Brown,Ray | (b,dr,b-solo,cello,ptp)

All Stars

Alternate Blues | Original Jazz Classics | OJCCD 744-2

Anita O'Day With The Oscar Peterson Quartet

Verve Jazz Masters 49:Anita O'Day | Verve | 527653-2

Art Pepper-Zoot Sims Quintet

Art 'N' Zoot | Pablo | 2310957-2

Ben Webster All Stars

King Of The Tenors | Verve | 519806-2

Ben Webster And His Associates

Verve Jazz Masters 43:Ben Webster | Verve | 525431-2

Ultimate Ben Webster selected by James Carter | Verve | 557537-2

Ben Webster And Associates | Verve | 835254-2

Ben Webster And His Orchestra

Verve Jazz Masters 43:Ben Webster | Verve | 525431-2

Ben Webster Quartet

Soulville | Verve | 521449-2

Ultimate Ben Webster selected by James Carter | Verve | 557537-2

Ben Webster Quintet

Soulville | Verve | 521449-2

Ben Webster With The Oscar Peterson Quartet

King Of The Tenors | Verve | 519806-2

Verve Jazz Masters 43:Ben Webster | Verve | 525431-2

Ultimate Ben Webster selected by James Carter | Verve | 557537-2

Ben Webster With The Oscar Peterson Trio

Ben Webster Meets Oscar Peterson | Verve | 521448-2

Verve Jazz Masters 43:Ben Webster | Verve | 525431-2

Ben Webster With The Teddy Wilson Trio

Verve Jazz Masters 43:Ben Webster | Verve | 525431-2

Music For Loving:Ben Webster With Strings | Verve | 527774-2

Benny Carter And His Orchestra

Further Definitions/Additions To Further Definotions | Impulse(MCA) | 951229-2

Bill Evans Quintet

The Complete Fantasy Recordings | Fantasy | 9FCD 1012-2

Quintessence | Original Jazz Classics | OJCCD 698-2(F 9529)

The Jazz Giants Play Jerome Kern:Yesterdays | Prestige | PCD 24202-2

The Jazz Giants Play Sammy Cahn:It's Magic | Prestige | PCD 24226-2

Billie Holiday And Her All Stars

Verve Jazz Masters 12:Billie Holiday | Verve | 519825-2

Verve Jazz Masters 47:Billie Holiday Sings Standards | Verve | 527650-2

Verve Jazz Masters Vol.60:The Collection | Verve | 529866-2

4 By 4:Ella Fitzgerald/Sarah Vaughan/Billie Holiday/Dinah Washington | Verve | 559693-2

The Billie Holiday Song Book | Verve | 823246-2

Billie Holiday And Her Orchestra

Solitude | Verve | 519810-2

Billie Holiday And Her Quintet

Verve Jazz Masters 47:Billie Holiday Sings Standards | Verve | 527650-2

Blossom Dearie Quartet

Give Him The Ooh-La-La | Verve | 517067-2

My Gentleman Friend | Verve | 519905-2

Verve Jazz Masters 51:Blossom Dearie | Verve | 529906-2

Blossom Dearie Sings Comden And Green | Verve | 589102-2

Blossom Dearie Quintet

My Gentleman Friend | Verve | 519905-2

Verve Jazz Masters 51:Blossom Dearie | Verve | 529906-2

Blossom Dearie Trio

Verve Jazz Masters 51:Blossom Dearie | Verve | 529906-2

Blossom Dearie Sings Comden And Green | Verve | 589102-2

Bud Powell Trio

The Best Of Bud Powell On Verve | Verve | 523392-2

Jazz Giant | Verve | 543832-2

Bud Powell:Bouncing With Bud | Dreyfus Jazz Line | FDM 36725-2

Buddy DeFranco With The Oscar Peterson Trio

The Complete Lionel Hampton Quartets And Quintets With Oscar Peterson On Verve | Verve | 559797-2

Buddy Rich Orchestra

Krupa And Rich | Verve | 521643-2

Buddy Rich-Gene Krupa Orchestra

Krupa And Rich | Verve | 521643-2

Cannonball Adderley And The Poll Winners

Cannonball Adderley And The Poll Winners | Capitol | 520086-2

Cannonball Adderley Quintet

Wes Montgomery-The Complete Riverside Recordings | Riverside | 12 RCD 4408-2

Charlie Parker All Stars

Charlie Parker:The Best Of The Verve Years | Verve | 527815-2

Charlie Parker And His Orchestra

The Cole Porter Songbook | Verve | 823250-2

Bird: The Complete Charlie Parker On Verve | Verve | 837141-2

Charlie Parker Quartet

Verve Jazz Masters 20:Introducing | Verve | 519853-2

Charlie Parker | Verve | 539757-2

Bird: The Complete Charlie Parker On Verve | Verve | 837141-2

Charlie Parker:April In Paris | Dreyfus Jazz Line | FDM 36737-2

Charlie Parker Quartet With Strings

The Cole Porter Songbook | Verve | 823250-2

Charlie Parker Quintet

Charlie Parker:Bird's Best Bop On Verve | Verve | 527452-2

Charlie Parker:The Best Of The Verve Years | Verve | 527815-2

Charlie Parker | Verve | 539757-2

Charlie Parker With Orchestra

Charlie Parker:The Best Of The Verve Years | Verve | 527815-2

Charlie Parker With Strings

Verve Jazz Masters 28:Charlie Parker Plays Standards | Verve | 521854-2

Charlie Parker With Strings:The Master Takes | Verve | 523984-2

Charlie Parker:The Best Of The Verve Years | Verve | 527815-2

Bird: The Complete Charlie Parker On Verve | Verve | 837141-2

Charlie Parker:April In Paris | Dreyfus Jazz Line | FDM 36737-2

Charlie Parker With The Joe Lipman Orchestra

Verve Jazz Masters 28:Charlie Parker Plays Standards | Verve | 521854-2

Charlie Parker With Strings:The Master Takes | Verve | 523984-2

Charlie Parker Big Band | Verve | 559835-2

Christian McBride/Ray Brown/Milt Hinton

Gettin' To It | Verve | 523989-2

Clark Terry Five

The Jazz Giants Play Duke Ellington:Caravan | Prestige | PCD 24227-2

Clark Terry With The Oscar Peterson Trio

Verve Jazz Masters 37:Oscar Peterson Plays Broadway | Verve | 516893-2

Oscar Peterson Trio + One | Verve | 558075-2

Coleman Hawkins And Ben Webster With The Oscar Peterson Quartet

Coleman Hawkins Encounters Ben Webster | Verve | 521427-2

Verve Jazz Masters 43:Coleman Hawkins | Verve | 521856-2

Verve Jazz Masters 43:Ben Webster | Verve | 525431-2

Verve Jazz Masters Vol.60:The Collection | Verve | 529866-2

Ultimate Coleman Hawkins selected by Sonny Rollins | Verve | 557538-2

Coleman Hawkins And Confreres

Coleman Hawkins And Confreres | Verve | 835255-2 PMS

Coleman Hawkins Quartet

Verve Jazz Masters 43:Coleman Hawkins | Verve | 521856-2

The Complete Jazz At The Philharmonic On Verve 1944-1949 | Verve | 523893-2

Coleman Hawkins With The Oscar Peterson Quartet

Verve Jazz Masters 43:Coleman Hawkins | Verve | 521856-2

The Genius Of Coleman Hawkins | Verve | 539065-2

Ultimate Coleman Hawkins selected by Sonny Rollins | Verve | 557538-2

Count Basie Jam

Montreux '77 | Original Jazz Classics | OJC 379(2308209)

Montreux '77 | Original Jazz Classics | OJC 385(2620105)

Count Basie Kansas City 3

For The Second Time | Original Jazz Classics | OJC 600(2310878)

Count Basie Trio

The Jazz Giants Play Harold Arlen:Blues In The Night | Prestige | PCD 24201-2

Count Basie-Oscar Peterson Quintet

Satch And Josh | Pablo | 2310722-2

Jazz Dance | Original Jazz Classics | OJCCD 1002-2(1210890)

Dee Dee Bridgewater With Big Band

Dear Ella | Verve | 539102-2

Dee Dee Bridgewater With Her Septet

Dear Ella | Verve | 539102-2

Dee Dee Bridgewater With Her Trio

Dear Ella | Verve | 539102-2

Dee Dee Bridgewater With Orchestra

Dear Ella | Verve | 539102-2

Dizzy Gillespie And His Orchestra

Planet Jazz:Dizzy Gillespie | Planet Jazz | 2152069-2

Planet Jazz Sampler | Planet Jazz | 2152326-2

Planet Jazz:Jazz Greatest Hits | Planet Jazz | 2169648-2

Planet Jazz:Bebop | RCA | 2169650-2

Dizzy Gillespie:Night In Tunisia | Dreyfus Jazz Line | FDM 36734-2

Dizzy Gillespie Jam

Montreux '77 | Original Jazz Classics | OJC 385(2620105)

Montreux '77 | Original Jazz Classics | OJC20 381-2(2308211)

Dizzy Gillespie Septet

Stan Getz Highlights:The Best Of The Verve Years Vol.2 | Verve | 517330-2

Verve Jazz Masters 25:Stan Getz & Dizzy Gillespie | Verve | 521852-2

Stan Getz Highlights | Verve | 847430-2

Dizzy Gillespie Sextet

Verve Jazz Masters 10:Dizzy Gillespie | Verve | 516319-2

Dizzy Gillespie:Night In Tunisia | Dreyfus Jazz Line | FDM 36734-2

The Jazz Giants Play Harold Arlen:Blues In The Night | Prestige | PCD 24201-2

Dizzy Gillespie-Count Basie Quartet

The Gifted Ones | Original Jazz Classics | OJCCD 886-2(2310833)

Dizzy Gillespie-Roy Eldridge Sextet

Ultimate Dizzy Gillespie | Verve | 557535-2

The Complete Verve Roy Eldridge Studio Sessions | Verve | 9861278

Dizzy Gillespie-Stan Getz Sextet

Verve Jazz Masters 25:Stan Getz & Dizzy Gillespie | Verve | 521852-2

Diz And Getz | Verve | 549749-2

Ultimate Stan Getz selected by Joe Henderson | Verve | 557532-2

Stan Getz Highlights | Verve | 847430-2

Duke Ellington Quartet

Joe Pass:Guitar Virtuoso | Pablo | 4 PACD 4423-2

The Jazz Giants Play Duke Ellington:Caravan | Prestige | PCD 24227-2

Ella Fitzgerald With Sy Oliver And His Orchestra

Ella Fitzgerald:Mr.Paganini | Dreyfus Jazz Line | FDM 36741-2

Ella Fitzgerald And Count Basie With The JATP All Stars

Bluella:Ella Fitzgerald Sings The Blues | Pablo | 2310960-2

Ella Fitzgerald And Her All Stars

All That Jazz | Pablo | 2310938-2

Ella Fitzgerald-First Lady Of Song | Verve | 517898-2

Verve Jazz Masters 6:Ella Fitzgerald | Verve | 519822-2

Love Songs:The Best Of The Song Books | Verve | 531762-2

Ella Fitzgerald Sings The Duke Ellington Songbook | Verve | 559248-2
For The Love Of Ella Fitzgerald | Verve | 841765-2
Ella Fitzgerald:Mr.Paganini | Dreyfus Jazz Line | FDM 36741-2
Ella Fitzgerald And Her Quintet
Verve Jazz Masters 46:Ella Fitzgerald-The Jazz Sides | Verve | 527655-2
Ella Fitzgerald And Louis Armstrong With Dave Barbour And His Orchestra
Ella Fitzgerald:Mr.Paganini | Dreyfus Jazz Line | FDM 36741-2
Ella Fitzgerald And Louis Armstrong With Sy Oliver And His Orchestra
Ella Fitzgerald:Mr.Paganini | Dreyfus Jazz Line | FDM 36741-2
Ella Fitzgerald And Louis Armstrong With The Oscar Peterson Quartet
Ella Fitzgerald-First Lady Of Song | Verve | 517898-2
Verve Jazz Masters 1:Louis Armstrong | Verve | 519818-2
Verve Jazz Masters 6:Ella Fitzgerald | Verve | 519822-2
Verve Jazz Masters 24:Ella Fitzgerald & Louis Armstrong | Verve | 521851-2
Verve Jazz Masters 46:Ella Fitzgerald-The Jazz Sides | Verve | 527655-2
Verve Jazz Masters Vol.60:The Collection | Verve | 529866-2
The Complete Ella Fitzgerald And Louis Armstrong On Verve | Verve | 537284-2
The Best Of Ella Fitzgerald And Louis Armstrong On Verve | Verve | 537909-2
Ella And Louis | Verve | 543304-2
Ella & Louis | Verve | 825373-2
Ella And Louis Again | Verve | 825374-2
For The Love Of Ella Fitzgerald | Verve | 841765-2
Ella Fitzgerald Jam
Bluella:Ella Fitzgerald Sings The Blues | Pablo | 2310960-2
Ella Fitzgerald With Orchestra
Ella/Things Ain't What They Used To Be | Warner | 9362-47875-2
Ella Fitzgerald With Sy Oliver And His Orchestra
Ella Fitzgerald:The Decca Years 1949-1954 | Decca | 050668-2
Ella Fitzgerald With The Count Basie Orchestra
Bluella:Ella Fitzgerald Sings The Blues | Pablo | 2310960-2
For The Love Of Ella Fitzgerald | Verve | 841765-2
Ella Fitzgerald With The Hank Jones Trio
The Complete Jazz At The Philharmonic On Verve 1944-1949 | Verve | 523893-2
Ella Fitzgerald:Mr.Paganini | Dreyfus Jazz Line | FDM 36741-2
Ella Fitzgerald With The JATP All Stars
Ella Fitzgerald-First Lady Of Song | Verve | 517898-2
For The Love Of Ella Fitzgerald | Verve | 841765-2
Ella Fitzgerald With The Oscar Peterson Quartet
Verve Jazz Masters 6:Ella Fitzgerald | Verve | 519822-2
Verve Jazz Masters 24:Ella Fitzgerald & Louis Armstrong | Verve | 521851-2
For The Love Of Ella Fitzgerald | Verve | 841765-2
Ella Fitzgerald With The Oscar Peterson Quartet And Ben Webster
Verve Jazz Masters 43:Ben Webster | Verve | 525431-2
Ella Fitzgerald-Oscar Peterson Trio
Ella And Oscar | Pablo | 2310759-2
For Musicians Only
Ultimate Stan Getz selected by Joe Henderson | Verve | 557532-2
Ultimate Dizzy Gillespie | Verve | 557535-2
For Musicians Only | Verve | 837435-2
Gene Krupa Orchestra
Krupa And Rich | Verve | 521643-2
Hampton Hawes Trio
The Jazz Giants Play Miles Davis:Milestones | Prestige | PCD 24225-2
Hank Jones Trio
The Complete Jazz At The Philharmonic On Verve 1944-1949 | Verve | 523893-2
Harry Sweets Edison Sextet
The Soul Of Ben Webster | Verve | 527475-2
Herb Ellis Quintet
Stan Getz Highlights:The Best Of The Verve Years Vol.2 | Verve | 517330-2
Nothing But The Blues | Verve | 521674-2
J.J. Johnson-Al Grey Sextet
Things Are Getting Better All The Time | Original Jazz Classics | OJCCD 745-2(2312141)
The J.J.Johnson Memorial Album | Prestige | PRCD 11025-2
J.J.Johnson & Stan Getz With The Oscar Peterson Quartet
Stan Getz Highlights:The Best Of The Verve Years Vol.2 | Verve | 517330-2
A Life In Jazz:A Musical Biography | Verve | 535119-2
Stan Getz Highlights | Verve | 847430-2
J.J.Johnson Sextet
The J.J.Johnson Memorial Album | Prestige | PRCD 11025-2
Jam Session
Jazz Gallery:Lester Young Vol.2(1946-59) | RCA | 2119541-2
James Morrison-Ray Brown Quartet
Two The Max | East-West | 9031-77125-2
JATP All Stars
JATP In Tokyo | Pablo | 2620104-2
Nothing But The Blues | Verve | 521674-2
Verve Jazz Masters 28:Charlie Parker Plays Standards | Verve | 521854-2
The Complete Jazz At The Philharmonic On Verve 1944-1949 | Verve | 523893-2
Charlie Parker:The Best Of The Verve Years | Verve | 527815-2
Jazz At The Philharmonic:Best Of The 1940's Concerts | Verve | 557534-2
The Drum Battle:Gene Krupa And Buddy Rich At JATP | Verve | 559810-2
Talkin' Bird | Verve | 559859-2
The Cole Porter Songbook | Verve | 823250-2
Bird: The Complete Charlie Parker On Verve | Verve | 837141-2
Welcome To Jazz At The Philharmonic | Fantasy | FANCD 6081-2
Jazz At The Philharmonic-Frankfurt 1952 | Pablo | PACD 5305-2
Norman Granz' JATP: Carnegie Hall 1949 | Pablo | PACD 5311-2
Joe Pass Trio
Joe Pass:Guitar Virtuoso | Pablo | 4 PACD 4423-2
Johnny Frigo Quartet
I Love John Frigo...He Swings | Mercury | 9861061
Johnny Frigo Sextet
I Love John Frigo...He Swings | Mercury | 9861061
Johnny Hartman And His Orchestra
Unforgettable | Impulse(MCA) | IMP 11522
Johnny Hodges Orchestra
Verve Jazz Masters 43:Ben Webster | Verve | 525431-2
Lalo Schifrin Trio With The London Philharmonic
Jazz Meets The Symphony | East-West | 4509-92004-2
Lester Young Quartet
Jazz Gallery:Lester Young Vol.2(1946-59) | RCA | 2119541-2
Verve Jazz Masters 30:Lester Young | Verve | 521859-2
Verve Jazz Masters Vol.60:The Collection | Verve | 529866-2
Lester Young:Blue Lester | Dreyfus Jazz Line | FDM 36729-2
Lester Young With The Oscar Peterson Quartet
Jazz Gallery:Lester Young Vol.2(1946-59) | RCA | 2119541-2
Lester Young With The Oscar Peterson Trio | Verve | 521451-2
Verve Jazz Masters 30:Lester Young | Verve | 521859-2
Lester Young-Harry Edison With The Oscar Peterson Quartet
Jazz Gallery:Lester Young Vol.2(1946-59) | RCA | 2119541-2
Lionel Hampton Quartet
The Complete Lionel Hampton Quartets And Quintets With Oscar Peterson On Verve | Verve | 559797-2
The Lional Hampton Quintet | Verve | 589100-2
Lionel Hampton Quintet
The Complete Lionel Hampton Quartets And Quintets With Oscar Peterson On Verve | Verve | 559797-2
The Lional Hampton Quintet | Verve | 589100-2
Lionel Hampton With Buddy DeFranco And The Oscar Peterson Trio
Verve Jazz Masters 26:Lionel Hampton with Oscar Peterson | Verve | 521853-2
Lionel Hampton With The Oscar Peterson Quartet
Verve Jazz Masters 26:Lionel Hampton with Oscar Peterson | Verve | 521853-2
Lionel Hampton With The Oscar Peterson Trio
Verve Jazz Masters 26:Lionel Hampton with Oscar Peterson | Verve | 521853-2
Louis Armstrong And Ella Fitzgerald With Sy Oliver's Orchestra
Louis Armstrong:C'est Si Bon | Dreyfus Jazz Line | FDM 36730-2
Louis Armstrong With The Oscar Peterson Quartet
Verve Jazz Masters 1:Louis Armstrong | Verve | 519818-2
Verve Jazz Masters 20:Introducing | Verve | 519853-2
Louis Armstrong Meets Oscar Peterson | Verve | 539060-2
Louis Jordan And His Tympany Five
Louis Jordan-Let The Good Times Roll: The Complete Decca Recordings 1938-1954 | Bear Family Records | BCD 15557 IH
Maynard Ferguson And His Orchestra
Verve Jazz Masters 52:Maynard Ferguson | Verve | 529905-2
Milt Jackson And His Colleagues
Bag's Bag | Original Jazz Classics | OJCCD 935-2(2310842)
Milt Jackson Quartet
Milt Jackson Birthday Celebration | Fantasy | FANCD 6079-2
Soul Route | Original Jazz Classics | OJCCD 1059-2(2310900)
Ain't But A Few Of Us Left | Original Jazz Classics | OJCCD 785-2(2310873)
Milt Jackson Quintet
Milt Jackson At The Kosei Nenkin | Pablo | 2620103-2
Milt Jackson Septet
Milt Jackson Birthday Celebration | Fantasy | FANCD 6079-2
Milt Jackson With Strings
To Bags...With Love:Memorial Album | Pablo | 2310967-2
Milt Jackson With The Oscar Peterson Trio
Gitanes Jazz 'Round Midnight: Oscar Peterson | Verve | 511036-2 PMS
Milt Jackson-Ray Brown Jam
Milt Jackson Birthday Celebration | Fantasy | FANCD 6079-2
Montreux '77 | Original Jazz Classics | OJC 385(2620105)
Montreux '77 | Original Jazz Classics | OJC20 375-2(2308205)
Milt Jackson-Ray Brown Quartet
It Don't Mean A Thing If You Can't Tap Your Foot To It | Original Jazz Classics | OJCCD 601-2
Norman Granz Jam Session
Verve Jazz Masters 26:Lionel Hampton with Oscar Peterson | Verve | 521853-2
Verve Jazz Masters 35:Johnny Hodges | Verve | 521857-2
Charlie Parker:The Best Of The Verve Years | Verve | 527815-2
Verve Jazz Masters Vol.60:The Collection | Verve | 529866-2
Talkin' Bird | Verve | 559859-2
Bird: The Complete Charlie Parker On Verve | Verve | 837141-2
Oscar Peterson And The Bassists
Montreux '77 | Original Jazz Classics | OJC 383(2308213)
Oscar Peterson Quartet
Verve Jazz Masters 37:Oscar Peterson Plays Broadway | Verve | 516893-2
Oscar Peterson Sextet
Oscar Peterson Trio: Olympia/Theatre Des Champs-Elysees | Laserlight | 36134
Oscar Peterson Trio
JATP In Tokyo | Pablo | 2620104-2
At Zardis' | Pablo | 2CD 2620118
Oscar Peterson Trio: Olympia/Theatre Des Champs-Elysees | Laserlight | 36134
Gitanes Jazz 'Round Midnight: Oscar Peterson | Verve | 511036-2 PMS
At The Stratford Shakespearean Festival | Verve | 513752-2
Verve Jazz Masters 16:Oscar Peterson | Verve | 516320-2
Verve Jazz Masters 37:Oscar Peterson Plays Broadway | Verve | 516893-2
Porgy And Bess | Verve | 519807-2
Verve Jazz Masters 20:Introducing | Verve | 519853-2
Night Train | Verve | 521440-2
We Get Request | Verve | 521442-2
The Oscar Peterson Trio At The Concertgebouw | Verve | 521649-2
Exclusively For My Friends-The Lost Tapes | MPS | 529096-2
Oscar Peterson:The Gershwin Songbooks | Verve | 529698-2
The Song Is You-The Best Of The Verve Songbooks | Verve | 531558-2
The Trio:Live From Chicago | Verve | 539063-2
West Side Story | Verve | 539753-2
The Sound Of The Trio | Verve | 543321-2
On The Town | Verve | 543834-2
With Respect To Nat | Verve | 557486-2
Oscar Peterson Plays The Duke Ellington Song Book | Verve | 559785-2
Oscar Peterson Plays The Harold Arlen Song Book | Verve | 589103-2
Oscar Peterson Plays The Cole Porter Song Book | Verve | 821987-2
The Silver Collection: Oscar Peterson | Verve | 823447-2 PMS
A Jazz Portrait Of Frank Sinatra | Verve | 825769-2
Oscar Peterson Trio With Milt Jackson
Very Tall | Verve | 559830-2
Very Tall | Verve | 827821-2
Oscar Peterson Trio With Roy Eldridge
Oscar Peterson Trio: Olympia/Theatre Des Champs-Elysees | Laserlight | 36134
Oscar Peterson Trio With The Nelson Riddle Orchestra
Verve Jazz Masters 16:Oscar Peterson | Verve | 516320-2
The Silver Collection: Oscar Peterson | Verve | 823447-2 PMS
Oscar Peterson Trio With The Russell Garcia Orchestra
Verve Jazz Masters 16:Oscar Peterson | Verve | 516320-2
Oscar Peterson With The Ernie Wilkins Orchestra
Verve Jazz Masters 16:Oscar Peterson | Verve | 516320-2
Oscar Peterson-Milt Jackson Quartet
Swinging Cooperations:Reunion Blues/Great Connection | MPS | 539085-2
Oscar Peterson-Ray Brown Duo
Gitanes Jazz 'Round Midnight: Oscar Peterson | Verve | 511036-2 PMS
Verve Jazz Masters 37:Oscar Peterson Plays Broadway | Verve | 516893-2
The Complete Jazz At The Philharmonic On Verve 1944-1949 | Verve | 523893-2
Oscar Peterson:Get Happy | Dreyfus Jazz Line | FDM 36738-2
Quadrant
Milt Jackson Birthday Celebration | Fantasy | FANCD 6079-2
Quincy Jones And His Orchestra
Verve Jazz Masters Vol.59:Toots Thielemans | Verve | 535271-2
Ralph Burns And His Orchestra
The Complete Verve Roy Eldridge Studio Sessions | Verve | 9861278
Ray Brown Trio
Something For Lester | Original Jazz Classics | OJCCD 412-2
Roy Eldridge And His Orchestra
The Complete Verve Roy Eldridge Studio Sessions | Verve | 9861278
Roy Eldridge Quintet
The Complete Verve Roy Eldridge Studio Sessions | Verve | 9861278
Roy Eldridge Sextet
The Complete Verve Roy Eldridge Studio Sessions | Verve | 9861278
Roy Eldridge-Dizzy Gillespie With The Oscar Peterson Quartet
The Complete Verve Roy Eldridge Studio Sessions | Verve | 9861278
Jazz Maturity... Where It's Coming From | Original Jazz Classics | OJCCD 807-2(2310816)
Roy Eldridge-Dizzy Gillespie-Harry Edison With The Oscar Peterson Quartet
The Complete Verve Roy Eldridge Studio Sessions | Verve | 9861278
Sarah Vaughan With The Oscar Peterson Quartet
How Long Has This Been Going On? | Pablo | 2310821-2
Joe Pass:Guitar Virtuoso | Pablo | 4 PACD 4423-2
Sarah Vaughan Birthday Celebration | Fantasy | FANCD 6090-2
Sarah Vaughan-Ray Brown
Sarah Vaughan Birthday Celebration | Fantasy | FANCD 6090-2
Sonny Rollins Trio
Sonny Rollins-The Freelance Years:The Complete Riverside & Contemporary Recordings | Riverside | 5 RCD 4427-2
Way Out West | Original Jazz Classics | OJC20 337-2(S 7530)
Sonny Stitt Quartet
Verve Jazz Masters 50:Sonny Sitt | Verve | 527651-2
Sonny Stitt Sextet
Verve Jazz Masters 50:Sonny Sitt | Verve | 527651-2
Sonny Stitt With The Oscar Peterson Trio
Verve Jazz Masters 50:Sonny Sitt | Verve | 527651-2
Stan Getz And J.J. Johnson With The Oscar Peterson Quartet
Ultimate Stan Getz selected by Joe Henderson | Verve | 557532-2
Stan Getz And The Oscar Peterson Trio
The Silver Collection: Stan Getz And The Oscar Peterson Trio | Verve | 827826-2
Stan Getz With The Oscar Peterson Quartet
Verve Jazz Masters 8:Stan Getz | Verve | 519823-2
Ultimate Stan Getz selected by Joe Henderson | Verve | 557532-2
Stan Getz With The Oscar Peterson Trio
Stan Getz Highlights | Verve | 847430-2
Stan Getz-Gerry Mulligan Quintet
Stan Getz Highlights | Verve | 847430-2
Getz Meets Mulligan In Hi-Fi | Verve | 849392-2
Tal Farlow Quartet
Verve Jazz Masters 41:Tal Farlow | Verve | 527365-2
Teddy Edwards-Howard McGhee Quintet
Together Again! | Original Jazz Classics | OJCCD 424-2
Tempo Jazzmen
Dizzy Gillespie:Night In Tunisia | Dreyfus Jazz Line | FDM 36734-2
The Big Three
Milt Jackson Birthday Celebration | Fantasy | FANCD 6079-2
The Big Three | Original Jazz Classics | OJCCD 805-2(2310757)
The Poll Winners
The Poll Winners Ride Again | Original Jazz Classics | OJC 607(C 7556)
Poll Winners Three | Original Jazz Classics | OJCCD 692-2(C 7576)
Exploring The Scene | Original Jazz Classics | OJCCD 969-2(C 7581)
The Jazz Giants Play Harry Warren:Lullaby Of Broadway | Prestige | PCD 24204-2
The Trumpet Summit With The Oscar Peterson Big 4
The Trumpet Summit Meets The Oscar Peterson Big 4 | Original Jazz Classics | OJCCD 603-2
Till Brönner-Gregoire Peters Quintet
Generations Of Jazz | Minor Music | 801037
Zoot Sims Quartet
Art 'N' Zoot | Pablo | 2310957-2
Zoot Sims Quintet
Art 'N' Zoot | Pablo | 2310957-2

Brown,Ray or Carol Kaye | (b)
Jimmy Smith With The Oliver Nelson Orchestra
Jimmy Smith:Best Of The Verve Years | Verve | 527950-2

Brown,Raymond | (fl-h,condtp)
Count Basie And His Orchestra
Digital III At Montreux | Original Jazz Classics | OJCCD 996-2(2308223)
Donald Byrd Orchestra
Places And Spaces | Blue Note | 854326-2
Ella Fitzgerald With Count Basie And His Orchestra
Digital III At Montreux | Original Jazz Classics | OJCCD 996-2(2308223)
Ella Fitzgerald With The Count Basie Orchestra
Bluella:Ella Fitzgerald Sings The Blues | Pablo | 2310960-2
For The Love Of Ella Fitzgerald | Verve | 841765-2

Brown,Rod | (drperc)
Clare Teal And Her Band
Orsino's Songs | Candid | CCD 79783

Brown,Ron | (b,el-btb)
Bobbi Humphrey
Blue Break Beats | Blue Note | 799106-2
Mel Brown Quartet
Chicken Fat | Impulse(MCA) | 9861047
Mel Brown Quintet
Chicken Fat | Impulse(MCA) | 9861047
Stanley Turrentine And His Orchestra
Pieces Of Dream | Original Jazz Classics | OJCCD 831-2(F 9465)

Brown,Ronald | (ts)
Milt Jackson And His Orchestra
Reverence And Compassion | Reprise | 9362-45204-2

Brown,Rosalyn | (voc)
Lou Donaldson Orchestra
Blue Breaks Beats Vol.2 | Blue Note | 789907-2

Brown,Roy | (el-b)
Bobbi Humphrey Group
Blue Breaks Beats Vol.2 | Blue Note | 789907-2

Brown,Russell | (tb)
Harry James And His Orchestra
The Legends Of Swing | Laserlight | 24659

Brown,Ruth | (voc)
Ruth Brown With Orchestra
Fine And Mellow | Fantasy | FCD 9663-2

Brown,Sam | (el-g,g,tanganyikan-gthumb-p)
Bill Evans Quartet
The Complete Bill Evans On Verve | Verve | 527953-2
From Left To Right | Verve | 557451-2
Bill Evans Quartet With Orchestra
The Complete Bill Evans On Verve | Verve | 527953-2
From Left To Right | Verve | 557451-2
Bill Evans Trio
The Complete Bill Evans On Verve | Verve | 527953-2
Bill Evans With Orchestra
The Complete Bill Evans On Verve | Verve | 527953-2
From Left To Right | Verve | 557451-2
Charlie Haden's Liberation Music Orchestra
Liberation Music Orchestra | Impulse(MCA) | 951188-2
Gary Burton-Keith Jarrett Quintet
Gary Burton & Keith Jarrett | Atlantic | 7567-81374-2
Gene Harris And The Three Sounds
Deep Blue-The United States Of Mind | Blue Note | 521152-2
James Moody Orchestra
The Blues And Other Colors | Original Jazz Classics | OJCCD 954-2(M 9023)
Keith Jarrett Group
Expectations | CBS | C2K 65900
Keith Jarrett Group With Brass
Expectations | CBS | C2K 65900
Keith Jarrett Group With Strings
Expectations | CBS | C2K 65900
Louis Armstrong And His Friends
Planet Jazz:Louis Armstrong | Planet Jazz | 2152052-2
Planet Jazz Sampler | Planet Jazz | 2152326-2
Louis Armstrong And His Friends | Bluebird | 2663961-2
Paul Motian Quintet
Tribute | ECM | 1048
Paul Motian Trio
Conception Vessel | ECM | 1028(519279-2)
Thad Jones-Mel Lewis Orchestra
The Groove Merchant/The Second Race | Laserlight | 24656

Brown,Sam Leigh | (voc)
Tomatic 7
Haupstrom | Jazz Haus Musik | JHM 0101 CD

Brown,Sandy | (clvoc)
Sandy Brown's Jazz Band
The Golden Years Of Revival Jazz,Sampler | Storyville | 109 1001
The Golden Years Of Revival Jazz,Vol.5 | Storyville | STCD 5510
The Golden Years Of Revival Jazz,Vol.6 | Storyville | STCD 5511
The Golden Years Of Revival Jazz,Vol.8 | Storyville | STCD 5513
The Golden Years Of Revival Jazz,Vol.10 | Storyville | STCD 5515

Brown,Scoville | (as,clsax)
Lionel Hampton And His Orchestra
Planet Jazz:Lionel Hampton | Planet Jazz | 2152059-2
Louis Armstrong And His Orchestra
Planet Jazz:Louis Armstrong | Planet Jazz | 2152052-2
Best Of The Complete RCA Victor Recordings | RCA | 2663636-2

INTERPRETENVERZEICHNIS

Louis Armstrong:A 100th Birthday Celebration | RCA | 2663694-2
Jazz:The Essential Collection Vol.2 | IN+OUT Records | 78012-2

Brown,Sonny | (drnagoya-harp)
Roland Kirk And His Orchestra
Rahsaan/The Complete Mercury Recordings Of Roland Kirk | Mercury | 846630-2
Roland Kirk Quartet
Talkin' Verve-Roots Of Acid Jazz:Roland Kirk | Verve | 533101-2
Rahsaan/The Complete Mercury Recordings Of Roland Kirk | Mercury | 846630-2

Brown,Sonny or Crosby,Charles | (dr)
Rahsaan Roland Kirk Sextet
Volunteered Slavery | Rhino | 8122-71407-2

Brown,Steve | (b,congas,drg)
David Newton Quartet
DNA | Candid | CCD 79742
Dunstan Coulber Quartet
Standards For A New Century | Nagel-Heyer | CD 081
Jim Tomlinson Quintet
Only Trust Your Heart | Candid | CCD 79758
Jim Tomlinson Sextet
Only Trust Your Heart | Candid | CCD 79758
Joe Temperley Quartet
Easy To Remember | Hep | CD 2083
Joe Temperley Quartet With Strings
Easy To Remember | Hep | CD 2083
Joe Temperley Quintet
Easy To Remember | Hep | CD 2083
Joe Temperley Quintet With Strings
Easy To Remember | Hep | CD 2083
Paul Whiteman And His Orchestra
Planet Jazz:Jazz Trumpet | Planet Jazz | 2169654-2
Stacey Kent And Her Quintet
Close Your Eyes | Candid | CCD 79737
Let Yourself Go-Celebrating Fred Astaire | Candid | CCD 79764

Brown,Ted | (ts)
Lee Konitz Quintet
Sound Of Surprise | RCA | 2169309-2
Ted Brown Quartet
Preservation | Steeplechase | SCCD 31539
Warne Marsh Quintet
Jazz Of Two Cities | Fresh Sound Records | FSR-CD 342
Warne Marsh Quintet With Art Pepper
Jazz Of Two Cities | Fresh Sound Records | FSR-CD 342

Brown,Tiny Bam | (b,drvoc)
Slim Gaillard Trio
The Small Black Groups | Storyville | 4960523
Slim Gaillard-Bam Brown
The Complete Jazz At The Philharmonic On Verve 1944-1949 | Verve | 523893-2

Brown,Trevor | (p)
André Holst With Chris Dean's European Swing Orchestra
That's Swing | Nagel-Heyer | CD 079

Brown,Tyrone | (bel-b)
Grover Washington Jr. Septet
Paradise | Elektra | 7559-60537-2
Max Roach Double Quartet
To The Max! | Enja | ENJ-7021 22
Max Roach Quartet
To The Max! | Enja | ENJ-7021 22
Monnette Sudler Sextet
Brighter Days For You | Steeplechase | SCCD 31087
Pat Martino Quartet
Desperado | Original Jazz Classics | OJCCD 397-2(P 7795)
Pat Martino Quintet
Desperado | Original Jazz Classics | OJCCD 397-2(P 7795)
Rachelle Ferrell With The Eddie Green Trio
First Instrumental | Blue Note | 827820-2
Rachelle Ferrell With The Eddie Green Trio And Alex Foster
First Instrumental | Blue Note | 827820-2

Brown,Vernell | (p)
Kenny Garrett Quartet
KG Standard Of Language | Warner | 9362-48404-2

Brown,Vernon | (tb)
Artie Shaw And His Orchestra
Planet JazzArtie Shaw | Planet Jazz | 2152057-2
Planet Jazz:Big Bands | Planet Jazz | 2169649-2
Benny Goodman And His Orchestra
Planet Jazz:Big Bands | Planet Jazz | 2169649-2
Great Swing Classics In Hi-Fi | Capitol | 521223-2
Benny Goodman At Carnegie Hall 1938(Complete) | CBS | C2K 65143
Charlie Christian:Swing To Bop | Dreyfus Jazz Line | FDM 36715-2
Camel Caravan Broadcast 1939 Vol.1 | Phontastic | NCD 8817
Camel Caravan Broadcast 1939 Vol.2 | Phontastic | NCD 8818
Camel Caravan Broadcast 1939 Vol.3 | Phontastic | NCD 8819
More Camel Caravans | Phontastic | NCD 8843/4
More Camel Caravans | Phontastic | NCD 8845/6
Benny Goodman And His V-Disc All Star Band
The Legends Of Swing | Laserlight | 24659
Benny Goodman Band
Benny Goodman At Carnegie Hall 1938(Complete) | CBS | C2K 65143
Benny Goodman Combo
Benny Goodman At Carnegie Hall 1938(Complete) | CBS | C2K 65143
Benny Goodman Dixieland Quintet
Benny Goodman At Carnegie Hall 1938(Complete) | CBS | C2K 65143
Jam Session
Benny Goodman At Carnegie Hall 1938(Complete) | CBS | C2K 65143
Leon Thomas With Orchestra
Spirits Known And Unknown | RCA | 2663876-2

Brown,Vernon prob | (tb)
Benny Goodman Combo
Benny Goodman At Carnegie Hall 1938(Complete) | CBS | C2K 65143

Brown,William | (suosaphonvoc)
Mitchell's Christian Singers
From Spiritual To Swing | Vanguard | VCD 169/71

Brown,William 'Billy' | (p)
The Modern Jazz Disciples
Disciples Blues | Prestige | PCD 24263-2

Browne,Allan | (dr)
Vince Jones Group
Tell Me A Secret | Intuition Records | INT 3072-2
Vince Jones Septet
On The Brink Of It | Intuition Records | INT 3068-2

Browne,Baron | (bel-b)
Jean-Luc Ponty Quartet
The Very Best Of Jean-Luc Ponty | Rhino | 8122-79862-2
Vital Information
Live Around The World Where We Come From Tour '98-'99 | Intuition Records | INT 3296-2
Show 'Em Where You Live | Intuition Records | INT 3306-2

Browne,Scoville | (as,clts)
Louis Armstrong And His Orchestra
Best Of The Complete RCA Victor Recordings | RCA | 2663636-2
Louis Armstrong:A 100th Birthday Celebration | RCA | 2663694-2

Browne,Tom | (tp,fl-h,keyboards,dr-programming)
Essence All Stars
Hot Jazz Bisquits | Hip Bop | HIBD 8801
Tom Browne Group
Hot Jazz Bisquits | Hip Bop | HIBD 8801
Tom Browne Groups
Mo' Jamaica Funk | Hip Bop | HIBD 8002
Tom Browne Quintet
Another Shade Of Browne | Hip Bop | HIBD 8011
Hot Jazz Bisquits | Hip Bop | HIBD 8801
Urbanator
Urbanator II | Hip Bop | HIBD 8012
Hot Jazz Bisquits | Hip Bop | HIBD 8801

Brubeck,Chris | (b-tb,b,el-b,tb,keyboards,vocp)
Dave Brubeck With The Erich Kunzel Orchestra
Truth Is Fallen | Atlantic | 7567-80761-2

Brubeck,Darius | (el-drones,el-p,org,clavinet)
Dave Brubeck Sextet
Bravo! Brubeck! | CBS | CK 65723

Brubeck,Dave | (el-p,p,oscillatorp-solo)
Dave Brubeck
We're All Together Again For The First Time | Atlantic | 7567-81390-2
Dave Brubeck Plays And Plays And Plays... | Original Jazz Classics | OJCCD 716-2(F 3259)
Dave Brubeck Octet
The Dave Brubeck Octet | Original Jazz Classics | OJCCD 101-2(F 3239)
Dave Brubeck Quartet
The Great Concerts | CBS | 462403-2
Dave Brubeck's Greatest Hits | CBS | 465703-2
We're All Together Again For The First Time | Atlantic | 7567-81390-2
All The Things We Are | Atlantic | 7567-81399-2
Jazz:Ted Hot And Cool | CBS | CK 61468
Time Out | CBS | CK 65122
Brubeck Time | CBS | CK 65724
Buried Treasures | CBS | CK 65777
The Dave Brubeck Quartet feat. Paul Desmond In Concert | Fantasy | FCD 60-013
Jazz At The College Of The Pacific | Original Jazz Classics | OJC20 047-2(F 3223)
Jazz At Oberlin | Original Jazz Classics | OJCCD 046-2
Jazz At The College Of The Pacific Vol.2 | Original Jazz Classics | OJCCD 1076-2
Dave Brubeck Quartet With Gerry Mulligan
The Last Set At Newport | Atlantic | 7567-81382-2
We're All Together Again For The First Time | Atlantic | 7567-81390-2
Dave Brubeck Quartet With Orchestra
Brandenburg Gate:Revisited | CBS | CK 65725
Dave Brubeck Quintet
All The Things We Are | Atlantic | 7567-81399-2
Reunion | Original Jazz Classics | OJCCD 150-2
Dave Brubeck Trio
All The Things We Are | Atlantic | 7567-81399-2
Dave Brubeck With The Erich Kunzel Orchestra
Truth Is Fallen | Atlantic | 7567-80761-2
Dave Brubeck-Lee Konitz Duo
All The Things We Are | Atlantic | 7567-81399-2
Dave Brubeck-Paul Desmond Duo
1975-The Duets | Verve | 394915-2
Jimmy Rushing With The Dave Brubeck Quartet
Brubeck & Rushing | CBS | CK 65727

Brubeck,Howard | (ldtubular-chimes)
Dave Brubeck Quartet With Orchestra
Brandenburg Gate:Revisited | CBS | CK 65725

Brubeck,Matthew | (cello)
Matthew Brubeck & David Widelock
Really! | Jazzpoint | JP 1030 CD

Bruce,Bobby | (v)
Charlie Haden Quartet West With Strings
The Art Of The Song | Verve | 547403-2

Bruce,Jack | (b,el-b,voice,b-g,harm,keyboards,voc)
Michael Mantler Group
Michael Mantler: No Answer/Silence | Watt | 2/5(543374-2)
Michael Mantler Group With The Danish Concert Radio Orchestra
Many Have No Speech | Watt | 19(835580-2)
Michael Mantler Group With The Danish Radio Concert Orchestra Strings
The School Of Understanding(Sort-Of-An-Opera) | ECM | 1648/49(537963-2)
Michael Mantler Quintet
Live | Watt | 18
Michael Mantler Quintet With The Balanescu Quartet
Folly Seeing All This | ECM | 1485
Tony Williams Lifetime
Ego | Verve | 559512-2

Bruce-Mitford,Myrtle | (cello)
Joe Temperley Quartet With Strings
Easy To Remember | Hep | CD 2083
Joe Temperley Quintet With Strings
Easy To Remember | Hep | CD 2083

Brücker,Kai | (gel-g)
Jerry Granelli UFB
News From The Street | VeraBra Records | CDVBR 2146-2
Rinde Eckert Group
Story In,Story Out | Intuition Records | INT 3507-2

Bruckner,Heinrich | (tp)
Hans Theessink Group
Crazy Moon | Minor Music | 801052

Brückner,Kai | (gdobro)
Andreas Schnerman Quintet
Welcome To My Backyard | Edition Collage | EC 535-2
Andreas Schnerman Sextet
Welcome To My Backyard | Edition Collage | EC 535-2
Thärichens Tentett
Lady Moon | Minor Music | 801094
Yakou Tribe
Red & Blue Days | Traumton Records | 4474-2

Bruetsch,Florian | (vib,marimbaperc)
Jo Ambros Group
Wanderlust | dml-records | CD 016

Bruford,Bill | (dr,el-dr,perc,simmons-drsynth-dr)
David Torn Quartet
Cloud About Mercury | ECM | 1322(831108-2)

Bruil,Michelle | (viola)
Abdullah Ibrahim Trio And A String Orchestra
African Suite | TipToe | TIP-888832 2
String Orchestra
African Suite | TipToe | TIP-888832 2

Bruinsma,Ray | (tp)
European Jazz Youth Orchestra
Swinging Europe 1 | dacapo | DCCD 9449
Swinging Europe 2 | dacapo | DCCD 9450

Brunborg,Tore | (sax,ssts)
Arild Andersen Quintet With The Cikada String Quartet
Hyperborean | ECM | 1631(537342-2)
Jon Balke w/Magnetic North Orchestra
Further | ECM | 1517
Jon Balke w/Oslo 13
Nonsentration | ECM | 1445
Masqualero
Bande A Part | ECM | 1319
Aero | ECM | 1367
Re-Enter | ECM | 1437(847939-2)
Misha Alperin Quintet
North Story | ECM | 1596
Silje Nergard Group with Strings
Nightwatch | EmArCy | 9865648

Bründl,Manfred | (b)
Gabriele Hasler & Foolish Heart
God Is A She | Foolish Music | FM 111186
Gabriele Hasler Group
Listening To Löbering | Foolish Music | FM 211389

Brunies,George | (tb,kazoovoc)
Muggsy Spanier And His Ragtime Band
Planet Jazz | Planet Jazz | 2169652-2
Planet Jazz:Jazz Trumpet | Planet Jazz | 2169654-2

Brüning,Uschi | (voc)
European Jazz Ensemble
European Jazz Ensemble At The Philharmonic Cologne | M.A Music | A 800-2

Brüninghaus,Rainer | (el-p,synth,keyboardsp)
Acoustic Alchemy
Against The Grain | GRP | GRP 97832
Bob Brookmeyer Group With The WDR Big Band
Electricity | ACT | 9219-2
Eberhard Weber Colours
Little Movements | ECM | 1186
Eberhard Weber Group
The Colours Of Chloe | ECM | 1042
Endless Days | ECM | 1748(013420-2)
Eberhard Weber Quartet
Yellow Fields | ECM | 1066(843205-2)
Eberhard Weber With Orchestra
The Following Morning | ECM | 1084(829116-2)
Eberhard Weber/Colours
Silent Feet | ECM | 1107(835017-2)
Freddy Studer Orchestra
Seven Songs | VeraBra Records | CDVBR 2056-2
Jan Garbarek Group
Legend Of The Seven Dreams | ECM | 1381(837344-2)
I Took Up The Runes | ECM | 1419(843850-2)
Twelve Moons | ECM | 1500(519500-2)
Visible World | ECM | 1585(529086-2)
Rites | ECM | 1685/86(559006-2)
Jazzensemble Des Hessischen Rundfunks
Atmosphering Conditions Permitting | ECM | 1549/50
Manfred Schoof/Rainer Brüninghaus
Shadows & Smiles | Wergo | WER 80007-50
Rainer Brüninghaus Quartet
Freigeweht | ECM | 1187(847329-2)
Rainer Brüninghaus Trio
Continuum | ECM | 1266(815679-2)

Brunious,John | (tp)
Paul Barbarin And His Band
Atlantic Jazz: New Orleans | Atlantic | 7567-81700-2

Brunn,Andreas | (7-string-g,el-ge-bow)
For Free Hands
Eastern Moods | Laika Records | 35101502

Brunner,Eddie | (cl,tsld)
Eddie Brunner And His Orchestra
Americans Swinging In Paris:Bill Coleman-The Elegance | EMI Records | 539662-2

Brunner,Giga | (dr)
Thilo Wagner Quintet
Just In Time | Satin Doll Productions | SDP 1011-1 CD
Thilo Wagner Trio
Just In Time | Satin Doll Productions | SDP 1011-1 CD

Bruno,Alessandro | (el-g)
Europa String Choir
Internationales Guitarren Festival '99 | ALISO Records | AL 1038

Bruno,Sam | (b)
Etta Jones And Her Band
Love Shout | Original Jazz Classics | OJCCD 941-2(P 7272)
Etta Jones With The Jerome Richardson Sextet
Hollar! | Original Jazz Classics | OJCCD 1061(PR 7284)

Brunon,Karen | (v)
Stephane Grappelli With The Michel Legrand Orchestra
Grapelli Story | Verve | 515807-2

Bruns,George | (b,tubatb)
Firehouse Five Plus Two
Dixieland Favorites | Good Time Jazz | FCD 60-008

Brunton,John 'Lee' | (g)
Thilo Kreitmeier & Group
Changes | Organic Music | ORGM 9725

Brüssau,Brigitte | (voc)
Jazzensemble Des Hessischen Rundfunks
Jazz Messe-Messe Für Unsere Zeit | hr music.de | hrmj 003-01 CD

Brüssau,Reinhard | (voc)

Brutsch,Alex | (viola)
Rainer Tempel Band
Suite Ellington | Jazz 'n' Arts Records | JNA 0401

Bruun,Buster | (clvoc)
Bohana Jazzband
The Golden Years Of Revival Jazz,Vol.6 | Storyville | STCD 5511
The Golden Years Of Revival Jazz,Vol.10 | Storyville | STCD 5515
Chris Barber & The Ramblers
The Golden Years Of Revival Jazz,Vol.12 | Storyville | STCD 5517

Bruynen,Rob | (tpfl-h)
Eddie Harris Group With The WDR Big Band
Eddie Harris-The Last Concert | ACT | 9249-2
Gianlugi Trovesi Quartet With The WDR Big Band
Dedalo | Enja | ENJ-9419 2
Jens Winther And The WDR Big Band
The Escape | dacapo | DCCD 9437
Kevin Mahogany With The WDR Big Band And Guests
Pussy Cat Dues:The Music Of Charles Mingus | Enja | ENJ-9316 2
Los Jovenes Flamencos With The WDR Big Band And Guests
Jazzpana | ACT | 9212-2
Vince Mendoza With The WDR Big Band And Guests
Sketches | ACT | 9215-2

Bryan,Mike | (el-gg)
Artie Shaw And His Orchestra
Planet Jazz:Male Jazz Vocalists | Planet Jazz | 2169657-2

Bryan,Mike prob. | (g)
Woody Herman And The Vanderbilt All Stars
Louis Armstrong-Jack Teagarden-Woody Herman:Midnights At V-Disc | Jazz Unlimited | JUCD 2048

Bryant Sr.,Robert O. | (tp)
Herbie Hancock Group
Sunlight | CBS | 486570-2

Bryant,Bobby | (arr,tp,fl-hfr-h)
Bobby Bryant Orchestra
Deep Blue-The United States Of Mind | Blue Note | 521152-2
Cal Tjader's Orchestra
Verve Jazz Masters 39:Cal Tjader | Verve | 521858-2
Eddie Lockjaw Davis And His Orchestra
Eric Dolphy:The Complete Prestige Recordings | Prestige | 9 PRCD-4418-2
Ella Fitzgerald With Orchestra
Ella/Things Ain't What They Used To Be | Warner | 9362-47875-2
Horace Silver Quintet With Brass
Horace Silver Retrospective | Blue Note | 495576-2
Jimmy Witherspoon And His Band
Baby, Baby, Baby | Original Blues Classics | OBCCD 527-2(P 7290)
Roland Kirk And His Orchestra
Talkin' Verve-Roots Of Acid Jazz:Roland Kirk | Verve | 533101-2
Zoot Sims With Orchestra
Passion Flower | Original Jazz Classics | OJCCD 939-2(2312120)

Bryant,Carmen | (voc)
Les McCann Group
Another Beginning | Atlantic | 7567-80790-2

Bryant,Dana | (voc)
Laurent De Wilde Sextet
Time Change | Warner | 8573-84315-2

Bryant,Freddie | (el-gg)
Freddie Bryant Group
Brazilian Rosewood | Fresh Sound Records | FSNT 035 CD
Jam Session
Jam Session Vol.10 | Steeplechase | SCCD 31555
Tom Harrell Group
Paradise | RCA | 2663738-2

Bryant,Lance | (fl,tss)
Lance Bryant With The Christoph Spendel Trio
West End Avenue II | Nabel Records:Jazz Network | CD 4644

Bryant,Mike | (el-g)
Artie Shaw And His Orchestra
Planet JazzArtie Shaw | Planet Jazz | 2152057-2

Bryant,Paul | (org)
Johnny Griffin Quintet
Grab This! | Original Jazz Classics | OJCCD 1941-2(RLP 9437)

Bryant,Ray | (pp-solo)

Benny Carter 4
Montreux '77 | Original Jazz Classics | OJC20 374-2(2308204)
Benny Golson Quintet
Nemmy Golson And The Philadelphians | Blue Note | 494104-2
Groovin' | Original Jazz Classics | OJCCD 226-2(NJ 8220)
Big Joe Turner And Pete Johnson With The Blues Band
Newport Jazz Festival 1958,July 3rd-6th Vol.3:Blues In The Night No.1 | Phontastic | NCD 8815
Big Maybelle With The Blues Band
Newport Jazz Festival 1958,July 3rd-6th Vol.3:Blues In The Night No.1 | Phontastic | NCD 8815
Carmen McRae With The Tadd Dameron Orchestra
Blue Moon | Verve | 543829-2
Chuck Berry With The Blues Band
Newport Jazz Festival 1958,July 3rd-6th Vol.3:Blues In The Night No.1 | Phontastic | NCD 8815
Coleman Hawkins Quintet
Soul | Original Jazz Classics | OJC20 096-2(P 7149)
The Jazz Giants Play Sammy Cahn:It's Magic | Prestige | PCD 24226-2
Coleman Hawkins Sextet
Hawk Eyes | Original Jazz Classics | OJCCD 294-2
Dizzy Gillespie Sextet
Verve Jazz Masters 50:Sonny Sitt | Verve | 527651-2
Dizzy Gillespie-Sonny Rollins-Sonny Stitt Sextet
Sonny Side Up | Verve | 521426-2
Dizzy Gillespie-Sonny Stitt Quintet
Verve Jazz Masters 10:Dizzy Gillespie | Verve | 516319-2
Hal Singer-Charlie Shavers Quintet
Blue Stompin' | Original Jazz Classics | OJCCD 834-2(P 7153)
Jo Jones Trio
Key One Up | Vanguard | VCD 79612-2
Max Roach Plus Four
Clifford Brown-Max Roach:Alone Together-The Best Of The Mercury Years | Verve | 526373-2
Max Roach Sextet
Clifford Brown-Max Roach:Alone Together-The Best Of The Mercury Years | Verve | 526373-2
Miles Davis-Milt Jackson Quintet
Milt Jackson Birthday Celebration | Fantasy | FANCD 6079-2
Miles Davis And Milt Jackson | Original Jazz Classics | OJC20 012-2(P 7034)
Miles Davis-Milt Jackson Sextet
Miles Davis And Milt Jackson | Original Jazz Classics | OJC20 012-2(P 7034)
Oliver Nelson Quintet
Oliver Nelson Feat. Kenny Dorham | Original Jazz Classics | OJCCD 227-2(NJ 8224)
Prestige Blues-Swingers
Soul Street | Original Jazz Classics | OJCCD 987-2(NJ 8293)
Ray Bryant
Ray Bryant Plays Blues And Ballads | Jazz Connaisseur | JCCD 9107-2
Inimitable | Jazz Connaisseur | JCCD 9430-2
Jazz Dance | Original Jazz Classics | OJCCD 1002-2(1210890)
Ray Bryant Trio
Ray Bryant Trio | Original Jazz Classics | OJCCD 793-2(P 7098)
The Jazz Giants Play Miles Davis:Milestones | Prestige | PCD 24225-2
Roy Eldridge Quintet
Decidedly | Pablo | PACD 5314-2
Roy Eldridge Sextet
Decidedly | Pablo | PACD 5314-2
Sonny Rollins Quartet
Sonny Rollins On Impulse | Impulse(MCA) | 951223-2
The Roots Of Acid Jazz | Impulse(MCA) | IMP 12042
Worktime | Original Jazz Classics | OJC20 007-2(P 7020)
Yusef Lateef Orchestra
Rhino Presents The Atlantic Jazz Gallery | Atlantic | 8122-71257-2

Bryant,Rusty | (as,tsvaritone-as)
Boogaloo Joe Jones Quintet
Charlie's Greatest Hits | Prestige | PCD 24250-2
Rusty Bryant Group
For The Good Times | Prestige | PRCD 24269-2
Rusty Bryant Quintet
Jazzin' With The Soul Brothers | Fantasy | FANCD 6086-2
Rusty Bryant Returns | Original Jazz Classics | OJCCD 331-2(P 7626)
Rusty Bryant Sextet
For The Good Times | Prestige | PRCD 24269-2

Bryant,Sam | (voc)
Mitchell's Christian Singers
From Spiritual To Swing | Vanguard | VCD 169/71

Bryant,Tommy | (b)
Big Joe Turner And Pete Johnson With The Blues Band
Newport Jazz Festival 1958,July 3rd-6th Vol.3:Blues In The Night No.1 | Phontastic | NCD 8815
Big Maybelle With The Blues Band
Newport Jazz Festival 1958,July 3rd-6th Vol.3:Blues In The Night No.1 | Phontastic | NCD 8815
Chuck Berry With The Blues Band
Newport Jazz Festival 1958,July 3rd-6th Vol.3:Blues In The Night No.1 | Phontastic | NCD 8815
Dizzy Gillespie Sextet
Verve Jazz Masters 50:Sonny Sitt | Verve | 527651-2
Dizzy Gillespie-Sonny Rollins-Sonny Stitt Sextet
Sonny Side Up | Verve | 521426-2
Dizzy Gillespie-Sonny Stitt Quintet
Verve Jazz Masters 10:Dizzy Gillespie | Verve | 516319-2
Jo Jones Trio
Key One Up | Vanguard | VCD 79612-2

Bryant,Willie | (ld,vocv)
Willie Bryant And His Orchestra
Planet Jazz:Ben Webster | RCA | 2165368-2

Bryden,Beryl | (vocwbd)
Bill Ramsey With Eric Krans Dixieland Pipers And Guests
Caldonia And More... | Bear Family Records | BCD 16151 AH

Bsiri,Linda | (voc)
Michel Godard Ensemble
Castel Del Monte | Enja | ENJ-9362 2
Castel Del Monte II | Enja | ENJ-9431 2

Bucci,Vincenzo | (fl-h)
Banda Cittá Ruvo Di Puglia
La Banda/Banda And Jazz | Enja | ENJ-9326 2

Buchacher,Willy | (dr)
Peter Möltgen Quartet
Mellow Acid | Edition Collage | EC 495-2

Buchanan,Robbie | (synth,bsynth-programming)
Al Jarreau With Band
High Crime | i.e. Music | 557848-2
Al Jarreau In London | i.e. Music | 557849-2
Joe Sample Group
Spellbound | Rhino | 81273726-2

Buchanon,Tony | (clbs)
Grace Knight With Orchestra
Come In Spinner | Intuition Records | INT 3052-2
Vince Jones With Orchestra
Come In Spinner | Intuition Records | INT 3052-2

Büchel,Richard | (tpfl-h)
Conexion Latina
La Conexión | Enja | ENJ-9065 2

Büchner,Lutz | (as,cl,ts,fl,ss,reedssax)
Abdullah Ibrahim With The NDR Big Band
Ekapa Lodumo | TipToe | TIP-888840 2
Albert Mangelsdorff With The NDR Big Band
NDR Big Band-Bravissimo | ACT | 9232-2
Heinz Sauer Quartet With The NDR Big Band
NDR Big Band-Bravissimo | ACT | 9232-2
Joe Gallardo's Latino Blue
A Latin Shade Of Blue | Enja | ENJ-9421 2
NDR Big Band
NDR Big Band-Bravissimo | ACT | 9232-2
The Theatre Of Kurt Weil | ACT | 9234-2
Oscar Brown Jr. with The NDR Big Band
Live Every Minute | Minor Music | 801071
Pee Wee Ellis & NDR Bigband
What You Like | Minor Music | 801064

Büchner,Regina | (ts)
Regina Büchner's Jazz 4 Fun
Jazz 4 Fun | Satin Doll Productions | SDP 1017-1 CD

Buchtel,Forrest | (tp)
Woody Herman And His Orchestra
Brand New | Original Jazz Classics | OJCCD 1044-2(F 8414)

Buck Clayton Legacy,The |
The Buck Clayton Legacy
All The Cats Join In(Buck Clayton Remembered) | Nagel-Heyer | CD 006
Encore Live | Nagel-Heyer | CD 018
The First Sampler | Nagel-Heyer | NHR SP 5
The Second Sampler | Nagel-Heyer | NHR SP 6

Buck,Greta | (v)
Don Byron Quartet
Tuskegee Experiments | Nonesuch | 7559-79280-2

Buck,Matthias | (vviola)
Jan Jankeje Quintet
Zum Trotz | Jazzpoint | JP 1016 CD

Buckholz,Dawn | (cello)
Robert Dick Group With The Soldier String Quartet
Jazz Standard On Mars | Enja | ENJ-9327 2

Buckingham,Katisse | (ss)
Terri Lyne Carrington Group
Jazz Is A Spirit | ACT | 9408-2

Buckner,Milt | (org,p,arr,vibvoc)
Eddie Lockjaw Davis Quartet
The Art Of Saxophone | Laserlight | 24652
Lionel Hampton And His All Star Jazz Inner Circle
Lionel Hampton: Salle Pleyel, March 9th, 1971 | Laserlight | 36133
Lionel Hampton And His Orchestra
Planet Jazz:Big Bands | Planet Jazz | 2169649-2
Lionel Hampton:Flying Home | Dreyfus Jazz Line | FDM 36735-2
Lionel Hampton Orchestra
The Big Bands Vol.1.The Snader Telescriptions | Storyville | 4960043

Buckner,Ted | (as,bs,cl,flts)
Billie Holiday With Teddy Wilson And His Orchestra
Billie's Love Songs | Nimbus Records | NI 2000

Buckner,Teddy | (tpvoc)
Kid Ory And His Band
The Very Best Of Dixieland Jazz | Verve | 535529-2
Kid Ory's Creole Jazz Band
This Kid's The Greatest! | Good Time Jazz | GTCD 12045-2
Lionel Hampton And His Orchestra
Lionel Hampton:Flying Home | Dreyfus Jazz Line | FDM 36735-2
Sidney Bechet-Teddy Buckner Sextet
Planet Jazz:Sidney Bechet | Planet Jazz | 2152063-2

Bucky,Myra | (v)
Ron Carter With Strings
Pastels | Original Jazz Classics | OJCCD 665-2(M 9073)

Budd,Harry | (th)
Marty Grosz And His Honoris Causa Jazz Band
Hooray For Bix! | Good Time Jazz | GTCD 10065-2

Buddha's Gamblers |
Danny Moss Meets Buddha's Gamblers
A Swingin' Affair | Nagel-Heyer | CD 034
Blues Of Summer | Nagel-Heyer | NH 1011

Budimir,Dennis | (g)
Billy Bean-Dennis Budimir
West Coast Sessions | String Jazz | SJRCD 1006
Bobby Hutcherson Orchestra
Montara | Blue Note | 590956-2
Chico Hamilton Orchestra
With Strings Attached/The Three Faces Of Chico | Warner | 9362-47874-2
Chico Hamilton Quintet
With Strings Attached/The Three Faces Of Chico | Warner | 9362-47874-2
Chico Hamilton Quintet With Strings
With Strings Attached/The Three Faces Of Chico | Warner | 9362-47874-2
Diane Schuur Trio With Orchestra And Strings
In Tribute | GRP | GRP 20062
Diane Schuur With Orchestra
In Tribute | GRP | GRP 20062
The Best Of Diane Schuur | GRP | GRP 98882
Ella Fitzgerald With Orchestra
Ella/Things Ain't What They Used To Be | Warner | 9362-47875-2
Harry James And His Orchestra
Trumpet Blues:The Best Of Harry James | Capitol | 521224-2
John Pisano-Billy Bean-Dennis Budimir
West Coast Sessions | String Jazz | SJRCD 1006
Milt Jackson With Strings
To Bags...With Love:Memorial Album | Pablo | 2310967-2
Peggy Lee With Lou Levy's Orchestra
Pass Me By/Big Spender | Capitol | 535210-2
Peggy Lee With The Quincy Jones Orchestra
Blues Cross Country | Capitol | 520088-2
Singers Unlimited With The Clare Fischer Orchestra
The Singers Unlimited:Magic Voices | MPS | 539130-2
Singers Unlimited With The Pat Williams Orchestra
The Singers Unlimited:Magic Voices | MPS | 539130-2

Budson,Buddy | (p)
Buddy Rich Big Band
Backwoods Siseman/Pieces Of Dream | Laserlight | 24655

Budwig, Monty or Fred Marshall | (b)
Vince Guaraldi Trio
A Charlie Brown Christmas | Fantasy | FSA 8431-6

Budwig,Monty | (bdr)
Annie Ross With Her Quintet
Misty Blue:Sweet Sisters Swing Songs Of Sorrow And Sadness | Blue Note | 521151-2
Barney Kessel Quintet
Barney Kessel Plays Standards | Original Jazz Classics | OJCCD 238-2
Bill Evans Trio
Verve Jazz Masters 5:Bill Evans | Verve | 519821-2
The Complete Bill Evans On Verve | Verve | 527953-2
Ultimate Bill Evans selected by Herbie Hancock | Verve | 557536-2
Bill Holman Octet
The Jazz Giants Play Sammy Cahn:It's Magic | Prestige | PCD 24226-2
Bill Smith Quartet
Folk Jazz U.S.A. | Original Jazz Classics | OJCCD 1956-2(S 7591)
Gary Burton Quartet
Planet Jazz:Gary Burton | RCA | 2165367-2
Jackie Cain-Roy Kral Group
Full Circle | Fantasy | FCD 24768-2
Jimmy Rowles Trio
Jimmy Rowles/Subtle Legend Vol.1 | Storyville | STCD 8287
Joe Pass Quartet
Nuages | Pablo | 2310961-2
Lennie Niehaus Quintet
Lennie Niehaus Vol.1:The Quintets | Original Jazz Classics | OJCCD 1933-2(C 3518)
Shelly Manne And His Hollywood All Stars
Art Pepper:The Hollywood All-Star Sessions | Galaxy | 5GCD 4431-2
Shelly Manne And His Men
At The Black Hawk Vol.1 | Original Jazz Classics | OJCCD 656-2(S 7577)
At The Black Hawk Vol.2 | Original Jazz Classics | OJCCD 657-2(S 7578)
At The Black Hawk Vol.3 | Original Jazz Classics | OJCCD 658-2(S 7579)
At The Black Hawk Vol.4 | Original Jazz Classics | OJCCD 659-2(S 7580)
At The Black Hawk Vol.5 | Original Jazz Classics | OJCCD 660-2
Jazz At The Philharmonic-Yesterdays | Pablo | PACD 5318-2
Shelly Manne Trio
At The Black Hawk Vol.5 | Original Jazz Classics | OJCCD 660-2
Tal Farlow Sextet
Verve Jazz Masters 41:Tal Farlow | Verve | 527365-2
Vince Guaraldi Group
Charlie Brown's Holiday Hits | Fantasy | FCD 9682-2
Vince Guaraldi Trio
Cast Your Fate To The Wind | Original Jazz Classics | OJCCD 437-2(F 8089)
Zoot Sims And His Orchestra
The Jazz Giants Play Duke Ellington:Caravan | Prestige | PCD 24227-2

Budziat,Eberhard | (b-tb,tubatb)
Dusko Goykovich Big Band
Balkan Connection | Enja | ENJ-9047 2
Rainer Tempel Big Band
Melodies Of '98 | Jazz 4 Ever Records:Jazz Network | J4E 4744
Album 03 | Jazz 'n' Arts Records | JNA 1102
SWR Big Band
Jazz In Concert | Hänssler Classics | CD 93.004
Trombonefire
Sliding Affairs | Laika Records | 35101462

Bues,Martin | (drperc)
Gunter Hampel And His Galaxie Dream Band
Enfant Terrible | Birth | 0025
Live At The Berlin Jazzfestival 1978 | Birth | 0027
All Is Real | Birth | 0028
All The Things You Could Be If Charles Mingus Was Your Daddy | Birth | CD 031

Buffington,Jimmy | (fr-h)
Anthony Ortega With The Robert Zieff Orchestra
Earth Dance | Fresh Sound Records | FSR-CD 325
Coleman Hawkins With Billy Byers And His Orchestra
The Hawk In Hi-Fi | RCA | 2663842-2
Dizzy Gillespie And His Orchestra
Verve Jazz Masters 10:Dizzy Gillespie | Verve | 516319-2
Gillespiana And Carnegie Hall Concert | Verve | 519809-2
Talking Verve:Dizzy Gillespie | Verve | 533846-2
Ultimate Dizzy Gillespie | Verve | 557535-2
Freddie Hubbard With Orchestra
This Is Jazz:Freddie Hubbard | CBS | CK 65041
Gato Barbieri Orchestra
The Roots Of Acid Jazz | Impulse(MCA) | IMP 12042
George Russell And His Orchestra
Bill Evans:Piano Player | CBS | CK 65361
Gil Evans Orchestra
The Individualism Of Gil Evans | Verve | 833804-2
Helen Merrill With Orchestra
Casa Forte | EmArCy | 558848-2
J.J.Johnson And His Orchestra
Planet Jazz:J.J.Johnson | Planet Jazz | 2159974-2
James Moody Orchestra
The Blues And Other Colors | Original Jazz Classics | OJCCD 954-2(M 9023)
Jimmy Smith With The Billy Byers Orchestra
Jimmy Smith:Best Of The Verve Years | Verve | 527950-2
Jimmy Smith With The Lalo Schifrin Orchestra
Jimmy Smith:Best Of The Verve Years | Verve | 527950-2
Jimmy Smith-Talkin' Verve | Verve | 531563-2
The Cat | Verve | 539756-2
Jimmy Smith With The Oliver Nelson Orchestra
Peter & The Wolf | Verve | 547264-2
John Coltrane And His Orchestra
John Coltrane:Standards | Impulse(MCA) | 549914-2
John Coltrane Quartet With Brass
The Complete Africa/Brass Sessions | Impulse(MCA) | 952168-2
Miles Davis + 19
Miles Ahead | CBS | CK 65121
Miles Davis With Gil Evans & His Orchestra
Ballads | CBS | 461099-2
Sketches Of Spain | CBS | CK 65142
Quiet Nights | CBS | CK 65293
Modern Jazz Quartet & Guests
MJQ 40 | Atlantic | 7567-82330-2
Oscar Peterson With The Ernie Wilkins Orchestra
Verve Jazz Masters 16:Oscar Peterson | Verve | 516320-2
Paul Desmond Quartet With The Don Sebesby Orchestra
From The Hot Afternoon | Verve | 543487-2
Phil Woods Quartet With Orchestra & Strings
Round Trip | Verve | 559804-2
Quincy Jones And His Orchestra
Rahsaan/The Complete Mercury Recordings Of Roland Kirk | Mercury | 846630-2
The Quintessence | Impulse(MCA) | 951222-2
Stan Getz With The Eddie Sauter Orchestra
Stan Getz Plays The Music Of Mickey One | Verve | 531232-2
Stan Getz With The Richard Evans Orchestra
What The World Needs Now-Stan Getz Plays Bacharach And David | Verve | 557450-2
Thad Jones-Mel Lewis Orchestra
The Groove Merchant/The Second Race | Laserlight | 24656
Wes Montgomery With The Don Sebesky Orchestra
Verve Jazz Masters 14:Wes Montgomery | Verve | 519826-2
Wes Montgomery:The Verve Jazz Sides | Verve | 521690-2
Talkin' Jazz:Roots Of Acid Jazz | Verve | 529580-2
California Dreaming | Verve | 827842-2

Bufford,George 'Mojo' | (harm)
Muddy Waters Band
Muddy Waters:Paris 1972 | Pablo | PACD 5302-2

Buffum,Denyse | (viola)
Chick Corea With String Quartet
Verve Jazz Masters 3:Chick Corea | Verve | 519820-2

Bugnon,Cyrille | (ts)
Erik Truffaz Quartet Quintet
Out Of A Dream | Blue Note | 855855-2

Bühler,Heinz | (tp)
Danny Moss Meets Buddha's Gamblers
A Swingin' Affair | Nagel-Heyer | CD 034
Blues Of Summer | Nagel-Heyer | NH 1011

Buhrer,Rolf | (tb)
Bill Coleman Sextet
Americans Swinging In Paris:Bill Coleman | EMI Records | 539663-2

Bührich,Florian | (vib)
Florian Bührich Quintet
endlich Jazz...? | Jazz 4 Ever Records:Jazz Network | J4E 4764

Buhrs,Han | (voice)
Norbert Stein Pata Masters
Pata Maroc | Pata Musik | PATA 12(AMF 1063)

Buhs,Han | (voc)
Pata Music Meets Arfi
News Of Roi Ubu | Pata Musik | PATA 10 CD

Bukovsky,Miroslav | (tp,fl-hperc)
Wanderlust
Border Crossing | Laika Records | 35100812
Wanderlust + Guests
Full Bronte | Laika Records | 35101412

Buldrini,Frederick | (stringsv)
Bob James And His Orchestra
Jazzrock-Anthology Vol.3:Fusion | Zounds | CD 27100555
Phil Woods Quartet With Orchestra & Strings
Round Trip | Verve | 559804-2

Bulgarian Voices Angelie | (voc)
Moscow Art Trio And The Bulgarian Voices Angelite
Portrait | JA & RO | JARO 4227-2

Bulkin,Sid | (dr)
Stuff Smith Quartet
Cat On A Hot Fiddle | Verve | 9861487

Bull City Red[George Washington] | (g,vocwbd)
Sonny Terry-Bull City Red
From Spiritual To Swing | Vanguard | VCD 169/71

Bulling,Erich | (arrcond)
Ella Fitzgerald With Orchestra
Ella Abraca Jobim | Pablo | 2630201-2
Paulinho Da Costa Orchestra
Happy People | Original Jazz Classics | OJCCD 783-2(2312102)

Bullman,Morton | (tb)
Billie Holiday With Sy Oliver And His Orchestra
Billie's Love Songs | Nimbus Records | NI 2000
Ella Fitzgerald With Sy Oliver And His Orchestra
Ella Fitzgerald:The Decca Years 1949-1954 | Decca | 050668-2
Leon Thomas With Orchestra
Spirits Known And Unknown | RCA | 2663876-2
Louis Armstrong With Sy Oliver And His Orchestra
Satchmo Serenaders | Verve | 543792-2
Louis Armstrong:C'est Si Bon | Dreyfus Jazz Line | FDM 36730-2
Louis Armstrong-My Greatest Songs | MCA | MCD 18347

Bullock,Belden | (b)
Abdullah Ibrahim Trio
African Magic | TipToe | TIP-888845 2
Abdullah Ibrahim Trio And A String Orchestra
African Suite | TipToe | TIP-888832 2

Bullock,Hiram | (b,dr-program,el-g,keyboardsg)
Al Jarreau With Band
L Is For Lover | i.e. Music | 557850-2
Carla Bley Band
Heavy Heart | Watt | 14
Night-Glo | Watt | 16
Carla Bley Sextet
Sextet | Watt | 17
Dizzy Gillespie And His Orchestra
Closer To The Source | Atlantic | 7567-80776-2
Don Grolnick Group
Hearts And Numbers | VeraBra Records | CDVBR 2016-2
Freddy Cole With The Eric Alexander Band
Love Makes The Changes | Fantasy | FCD 9681-2
Lew Soloff Group
Rainbow Mountain | TipToe | TIP-888838 2
Marcus Miller Group
The Sun Don't Lie | Dreyfus Jazz Line | FDM 36560-2
Tales | Dreyfus Jazz Line | FDM 36571-2
Live & More | Dreyfus Jazz Line | FDM 36585-2
Michael 'Patches' Stewart Group
Penetration | Hip Bop | HIBD 8018
Steve Swallow Group
Carla | Watt | XtraWatt/2
Swallow | Watt | XtraWatt/6
Wayne Krantz Duo
Signals | Enja | ENJ-6048 2

Bulterman,Jack | (tp)
Coleman Hawkins Trio
Jazz:The Essential Collection Vol.3 | IN+OUT Records | 78013-2

Buma,Wybe | (tp)
Albert Nicholas With The Dutch Swing College Band
Albert Nicholas & The Dutch Swing College Band | Storyville | STCD 5522
Dutch Swing College Band
Albert Nicholas & The Dutch Swing College Band | Storyville | STCD 5522

Bummerl,Franz | (tp)
Erwin Lehn Und Sein Südfunk-Tanzorchester
Deutsches Jazz Fesival 1954/1955 | Bear Family Records | BCD 15430

Bunch,John | (porg)
Allan Vaché-Jim Galloway Sextet
Raisin' The Roof:Allan Vaché Meets Jim Galloway | Nagel-Heyer | CD 054
Benny Bailey Quintet
The Satchmo Legacy | Enja | ENJ-9407 2
Benny Goodman And His Orchestra
The Legends Of Swing | Laserlight | 24659
40th Anniversary Concert-Live At Carnegie Hall | London | 820349-2
Verve Jazz Masters 33:Benny Goodman | Verve | 844410-2
Benny Goodman Septet
Verve Jazz Masters 33:Benny Goodman | Verve | 844410-2
Benny Goodman Sextet
Verve Jazz Masters 33:Benny Goodman | Verve | 844410-2
Buddy Rich And His Orchestra
Swingin' New Big Band | Pacific Jazz | 835232-2
Harry Allen Quartet
Jazz Im Amerika Haus,Vol.1 | Nagel-Heyer | CD 011
Blues Of Summer | Nagel-Heyer | NH 1011
Love Songs Live! | Nagel-Heyer | NH 1014
The First Sampler | Nagel-Heyer | NHR SP 5
Rolf Kühn Quartet
Rolf Kühn And His Sound Of Jazz | Fresh Sound Records | FSR-CD 326
Rolf Kühn Quintet
Rolf Kühn And His Sound Of Jazz | Fresh Sound Records | FSR-CD 326
Rolf Kühn Sextet
Rolf Kühn And His Sound Of Jazz | Fresh Sound Records | FSR-CD 326

Bunch,Kenji | (viola)
Jim Snidero Quartet With Strings
Strings | Milestone | MCD 9326-2

Bunda,Vojtech | (b)
Karol Adam Ensemble
Gipsy Fascination | G&J Records | GJ 2001

Bundock,Rowland 'Rolly' | (b)
Glenn Miller And His Orchestra
Planet Jazz:Glenn Miller | Planet Jazz | 2152056-2
Planet Jazz Sampler | Planet Jazz | 2152326-2
Planet Jazz:Big Bands | Planet Jazz | 2169649-2
Planet Jazz:Swing | Planet Jazz | 2169651-2
The Chesterfield Broadcasts Vol.1 | RCA | 2663113-2
Candlelight Miller | RCA | 2668716-2
Swing Legends | Nimbus Records | NI 2001
Henry Mancini And His Orchestra
Combo! | RCA | 2147794-2
Pete Rugolo And His Orchestra
Thriller/Richard Diamon(Original Jazz Scores From 2 Classics TV Series) | Fresh Sound Records | FSCD 2015
The Andrew Sisters With The Glenn Miller Orchestra
The Chesterfield Broadcasts Vol.1 | RCA | 2663113-2

Bundy,Bill | (celloharp)
Charlie Parker With Strings
Verve Jazz Masters 28:Charlie Parker Plays Standards | Verve | 521854-2
Charlie Parker With Strings:The Master Takes | Verve | 523984-2

Bunge,Fred | (tp)
Die Deutsche All Star Band 1953
1.Deutsches Jazz Festival 1953 Frankfurt/Main | Bear Family Records | BCD 15611 AH
Fred Bunge Star Band
Deutsches Jazz Fesival 1954/1955 | Bear Family Records | BCD 15430

Bunge,Jens | (harm)
Jens Bunge Group
Meet You In Chicago | Jazz 4 Ever Records:Jazz Network | J4E 4749

Bunick,Floris Nico | (p)
Charles Mingus Group
The Jazz Life! | Candid | CCD 79019
Candid Dolphy | Candid | CCD 79033
Mysterious Blues | Candid | CCD 79042
Mingus Dynasty | CBS | CK 65513
Charles Mingus Orchestra
Charles Mingus:The Complete 1959 Columbia Recordings | CBS | C3K 65145
Mingus | Candid | CCD 79021

Bunka,Roman | (g,keyboard,oudvoc)
Roman Bunka Group
Dein Kopf Ist Ein Schlafendes Auto | ATM Records | ATM 3818-AH
Uli Trepte Group
Guru Guru/Uli Trepte | ATM Records | ATM 3815-AH

Bunker,Larry | (dr,perc,vib,b,bongos,congas,marimba)
A Band Of Friends
The Best Of The Gerry Mulligan Quartet With Chet Baker | Pacific Jazz | 795481-2
Al Jarreau With Band
We Got By | Reprise | 7599-27222-2
Anita O'Day And Her Combo
Pick Yourself Up | Verve | 517329-2
Benny Carter And His Orchestra
Aspects | Capitol | 852677-2
Bill Evans Trio
Verve Jazz Masters 5:Bill Evans | Verve | 519821-2
The Complete Bill Evans On Verve | Verve | 527953-2
The Best Of Bill Evans Live | Verve | 533825-2
Ultimate Bill Evans selected by Herbie Hancock | Verve | 557536-2
At Shelly's Manne-Hole | Original Jazz Classics | OJC20 263-2(RLP 9487)
Billie Holiday And Her All Stars
Verve Jazz Masters 12:Billie Holiday | Verve | 519825-2
Verve Jazz Masters 20:Introducing | Verve | 519853-2
Songs For Distingué Lovers | Verve | 539056-2
Billie Holiday And Her Band
Verve Jazz Masters 47:Billie Holiday Sings Standards | Verve | 527650-2
Bud Shank And Trombones
Cool Fool | Fresh Sound Records | FSR CD 507
Chet Baker Quartet
Chet Baker Quartet Live Vol.1:This Time The Dreams's On Me | Pacific Jazz | 525248-2
The Best Of Chet Baker Plays | Pacific Jazz | 797161-2
Diana Krall Group With Orchestra
When I Look In Your Eyes | Verve | 9513304
Diane Schuur With Orchestra
The Best Of Diane Schuur | GRP | GRP 98882
Dizzy Gillespie And His Orchestra
Talking Verve:Dizzy Gillespie | Verve | 533846-2
Ella Fitzgerald With The Billy May Orchestra
Ella Fitzgerald-First Lady Of Song | Verve | 517898-2
The Best Of The Song Books | Verve | 519804-2
Verve Jazz Masters 6:Ella Fitzgerald | Verve | 519822-2
Verve Jazz Masters 46:Ella Fitzgerald-The Jazz Sides | Verve | 527655-2
Ella Fitzgerald Sings The Harold Arlen Song Book | Verve | 589108-2
For The Love Of Ella Fitzgerald | Verve | 841765-2
Gerry Mulligan Quartet
Gene Norman Presents The Original Gerry Mulligan Tentet And Quartet | GNP Crescendo | GNPD 56
Gerry Mulligan Tentette
Gene Norman Presents The Original Gerry Mulligan Tentet And Quartet | GNP Crescendo | GNPD 56
Harry Babasin Quintet
The Complete Nocturne Recordings:Jazz In Hollywood Series Vol.1 | Fresh Sound Records | NR 3CD-101
Henry Mancini And His Orchestra
Combo! | RCA | 2147794-2
Jimmy Smith With The Oliver Nelson Orchestra
Jimmy Smith:Best Of The Verve Years | Verve | 527950-2
Jimmy Smith-Talkin' Verve | Verve | 531563-2
June Christy With The Pete Rugolo Orchestra
Something Cool(The Complete Mono & Stereo Versions) | Capitol | 534069-2
Lee Konitz & The Gerry Mulligan Quartet
Konitz Meets Mulligan | Pacific Jazz | 746847-2
Lou Levy Trio
The Complete Nocturne Recordings:Jazz In Hollywood Series Vol.1 | Fresh Sound Records | NR 3CD-101
Mark Murphy And His Septet
Blue Velvet: Crooners, Swooners And Velvet Vocals | Blue Note | 521153-2
Maynard Ferguson And His Orchestra
Verve Jazz Masters 52:Maynard Ferguson | Verve | 529905-2
Mel Tormé With The Billy May Orchestra
Mel Tormé Goes South Of The Border With Billy May | Verve | 589517-2
Monica Zetterlund With The Bill Evans Trio
The Complete Bill Evans On Verve | Verve | 527953-2
Peggy Lee With The Quincy Jones Orchestra
Blues Cross Country | Capitol | 520088-2
Pete Rugolo And His Orchestra
Thriller/Richard Diamon(Original Jazz Scores From 2 Classics TV Series) | Fresh Sound Records | FSCD 2015
Singers Unlimited With The Pat Williams Orchestra
The Singers Unlimited:Magic Voices | MPS | 539130-2
Singers Unlimited With The Patrick Williams Orchestra
The Singers Unlimited:Magic Voices | MPS | 539130-2
Virgil Gonsalves Sextet
The Complete Nocturne Recordings:Jazz In Hollywood Series Vol.1 | Fresh Sound Records | NR 3CD-101
Woody Herman And His Sextet
Songs For Hip Lovers | Verve | 559872-2

Bunker,Larry or Grady Tate | (dr)
Bill Evans Trio With The Claus Ogerman Orchestra
Bill Evans Trio With Symphony Orchestra | Verve | 821983-2

Bunn,Jimmy | (p)
Helen Humes And Her All Stars
Lester Young:The Complete Aladdin Sessions | Blue Note | 832787-2
Wardell Gray Sextet
The Prestige Legacy Vol.2:Battles Of Saxes | Prestige | PCD 24252-2
Wardell Gray's Los Angeles All Stars
Dexter Gordon Birthday Celebration | Fantasy | FANCD 6082-2
Wardell Gray Memorial Vol.2 | Original Jazz Classics | OJCCD 051-2(P 7009)

Bunn,Teddy | (bj,gvoc)
Mezzrow-Ladnier Quintet
Planet Jazz:Jazz Trumpet | Planet Jazz | 2169654-2
Tommy Ladnier And His Orchestra
Planet Jazz | Planet Jazz | 2169652-2

Bunt,Belinda | (v)
Dee Dee Bridgewater With Orchestra
Dear Ella | Verve | 539102-2

Bünting,Erhard | (g)
Lajos Dudas Quintet
Jubilee Edition | double moon | CHRDM 71020

Buono,Nick | (tp)
Harry James And His Orchestra
Trumpet Blues:The Best Of Harry James | Capitol | 521224-2

Buquet,Anthomy Bo Bo | (b,tubatb)
Claude Barthelmy Group
Moderne | Owl Records | 014739-2
Henrik Johansen With The City Ramblers
The Golden Years Of Revival Jazz,Sampler | Storyville | 109 1001
Hylda Sims And The Citty Ramblers Skiffle Group With Henrik Johansen
The Golden Years Of Revival Jazz,Vol.9 | Storyville | STCD 5514

Burbidge,Graham | (bdr)
Henrik Johansen's Jazzband
The Golden Years Of Revival Jazz,Vol.6 | Storyville | STCD 5511
The Golden Years Of Revival Jazz,Vol.7 | Storyville | STCD 5512
The Golden Years Of Revibal Jazz,Vol.15 | Storyville | STCD 5520
Sandy Brown's Jazz Band
The Golden Years Of Revival Jazz,Sampler | Storyville | 109 1001
The Golden Years Of Revival Jazz,Vol.5 | Storyville | STCD 5510
The Golden Years Of Revival Jazz,Vol.6 | Storyville | STCD 5511
The Golden Years Of Revival Jazz,Vol.8 | Storyville | STCD 5513
The Golden Years Of Revival Jazz,Vol.10 | Storyville | STCD 5515

Burchard,Christian | (marimba,p,drperc)
Rabih Abou-Khalil Septet
Between Dusk And Dawn | Enja | ENJ-9771 2
Uli Trepte Group
Guru Guru/Uli Trepte | ATM Records | ATM 3815-AH

Burchell,Chas | (ts)
Chas Burchell Quartet
Unsong Hero:The Undiscovered Genius Of Chas Burchell | IN+OUT Records | 7026-2
Chas Burchell Quintet
Unsong Hero:The Undiscovered Genius Of Chas Burchell | IN+OUT Records | 7026-2
Chas Burchell Sextet
Unsong Hero:The Undiscovered Genius Of Chas Burchell | IN+OUT Records | 7026-2
Chas Burchell Trio/Quartet
Unsong Hero:The Undiscovered Genius Of Chas Burchell | IN+OUT Records | 7026-2
Clark Terry Quintet
Unsong Hero:The Undiscovered Genius Of Chas Burchell | IN+OUT Records | 7026-2
Ronnie Scott With The Chas Burchell Quintet
Unsong Hero:The Undiscovered Genius Of Chas Burchell | IN+OUT Records | 7026-2

Burdine,Johnny | (ts)
Buddy Johnson And His Orchestra
Buddy And Ella Johnson 1953-1964 | Bear Family Records | BCD 15479 DH

Burger,Dominik | (drvib)
Peter A. Schmid Duos
Duets,Dialogues & Duels | Creative Works Records | CW CD 1034
Schmilz
Schmilz | Creative Works Records | CW CD 1041

Burger,Markus | (pkeyboards)
Jazz Orchester Rheinland-Pfalz
Kazzou | Jazz Haus Musik | LJBB 9104

Bürger,Michael 'Barny' | (dr)
Balance
Elements | double moon | DMCHR 71033

Burgess,Bob 'Bobby' | (tb)
Bernd Konrad With Erwin Lehn und sein Südfunk Orchester Stuttgart
Wen Die Götter Lieben | Creative Works Records | CW CD 1010-1
Louis Jordan And His Tympany Five
Louis Jordan-Let The Good Times Roll: The Complete Decca Recordings 1938-1954 | Bear Family Records | BCD 15557 IH
Maynard Ferguson And His Orchestra
Verve Jazz Masters 52:Maynard Ferguson | Verve | 529905-2
Slide Hampton-Joe Haider Jazz Orchestra
Give Me A Double | JHM Records | JHM 3627
Stan Kenton And His Orchestra
Stan Kenton Portraits On Standards | Capitol | 531571-2
Terry Gibbs Dream Band
Terry Gibbs Dream Band Vol.2:The Sundown Sessions | Contemporary | CCD 7652-2
Terry Gibbs Dream Band Vol.3:Flying Home | Contemporary | CCD 7654-2
Terry Gibbs Dream Band Vol.6:One More Time | Contemporary | CCD 7658-2
The Jazz Giants Play Jerome Kern:Yesterdays | Prestige | PCD 24202-2
Woody Herman And His Orchestra
Brand New | Original Jazz Classics | OJCCD 1044-2(F 8414)
The Raven Speaks | Original Jazz Classics | OJCCD 663-2(F 9416)

Burgess,Glenn | (org,pceleste)
Golden Gate Quartet
Americans Swinging In Parïs:Golden Gate Quartet | EMI Records | 539659-2
From Spiritual To Swing Vol.2 | EMI Records | 780573-2
Spirituals To Swing 1955-69 | EMI Records | 791569-2
Golden Gate Quartet With The Martial Solal Orchestra
From Spiritual To Swing Vol.2 | EMI Records | 780573-2

Burghardt,Victor | (arr,ascl)
NDR Big Band With Guests
50 Years Of NDR Big Band:Bravissimo II | ACT | 9259-2

Burkard,Thilo | (b)
Takabanda
La Leggenda Del Pescatore | Jazz 4 Ever Records:Jazz Network | J4E 4752

Burkart,Ingolf | (tp)
Brigitte Dietrich-Joe Haider Jazz Orchestra
Consequences | JHM Records | JHM 3624

Burke,Edward | (tb)
Buddy Johnson And His Orchestra
Buddy And Ella Johnson 1953-1964 | Bear Family Records | BCD 15479 DH
Earl Hines And His Orchestra
Planet Jazz:Earl Hines | Planet Jazz | 2159973-2
The Legends Of Swing | Laserlight | 24659
Jazz:The Essential Collection Vol.2 | IN+OUT Records | 78012-2

Burke,Jimmie | (b)
Johnny Pace With The Chet Baker Quintet
Chet Baker Introduces Johnny Pace | Original Jazz Classics | OJCCD 433-2(RLP 12-292)

Burke,Kevin Fitzgerald | (voc)
Jon Hendricks Group
A Tribute To Charlie Parker Vol.2 | Storyville | 4960493

Burke,Sonny | (arr,cond,keyboards,synth,pel-p)
Dizzy Gillespie With The Lalo Schifrin Orchestra
Free Ride | Original Jazz Classics | OJCCD 784-2(2310794)
Jerri Southern And The Sonny Burke Orchestra
The Very Thought Of You:The Decca Years 1951-1957 | Decca | 050671-2
Lionel Hampton And His Orchestra
Lionel Hampton:Flying Home | Dreyfus Jazz Line | FDM 36735-2
Louis Armstrong And His All Stars With Sonny Burke's Orchestra
Ambassador Louis Armstrong Vol.17:Moments To Remember(1952-1956) | Ambassador | CLA 1917
Stanley Turrentine And His Orchestra
Pieces Of Dream | Original Jazz Classics | OJCCD 831-2(F 9465)

Burke,Tim | (tpfl-h)
Woody Herman And His Orchestra
Verve Jazz Masters 54:Woody Herman | Verve | 529903-2

Burke,Vinnie | (b)
Gerry Mulligan Sextet
The Gerry Mulligan Songbook | Pacific Jazz | 833575-2
Tal Farlow Trio
Verve Jazz Masters 41:Tal Farlow | Verve | 527365-2
The Swinging Guitar Of Tal Farlow | Verve | 559515-2

Burkhardt,Ingolf | (fl-htp)
Abdullah Ibrahim With The NDR Big Band
Ekapa Lodumo | TipToe | TIP-888840 2
Albert Mangelsdorff With The NDR Big Band
NDR Big Band-Bravissimo | ACT | 9232-2
Heinz Sauer Quartet With The NDR Big Band
NDR Big Band-Bravissimo | ACT | 9232-2
Joe Gallardo's Latino Blue
A Latin Shade Of Blue | Enja | ENJ-9421 2
Joe Pass With The NDR Big Band
Joe Pass In Hamburg | ACT | 9100-2
NDR Big Band-Bravissimo | ACT | 9232-2
Joe Pass With The NDR Big Band And Radio Philharmonie Hannover
Joe Pass In Hamburg | ACT | 9100-2
Johnny Griffin With The NDR Big Band
NDR Big Band-Bravissimo | ACT | 9232-2
Nana Mouskouri With The Berlin Radio Big Band
Nana Swings | Mercury | 074394-2

NDR Big Band
NDR Big Band-Bravissimo | ACT | 9232-2
The Theatre Of Kurt Weil | ACT | 9234-2
Oscar Brown Jr. And His Group
Live Every Minute | Minor Music | 801071
Oscar Brown Jr. with The NDR Big Band
Live Every Minute | Minor Music | 801071
Pee Wee Ellis & NDR Bigband
What You Like | Minor Music | 801064
Ralph Schweizer Big Band
DAY Dream | Chaos | CACD 8177
Stanley Blume Quintet
Movin' Up | Organic Music | ORGM 9709

Burman,Anders 'Andrew' | (drmaracas)
Lars Gullin Quartet
Lars Gullin 1951/52 Vol.5:First Walk | Dragon | DRCD 380
Stan Getz Quartet
Stan Getz Highlights | Verve | 847430-2

Burness,Lester | (p)
Artie Shaw And His Orchestra
Planet JazzArtie Shaw | Planet Jazz | 2152057-2
Planet Jazz Sampler | Planet Jazz | 2152326-2
Planet Jazz:Swing | Planet Jazz | 2169651-2
Planet Jazz:Female Jazz Vocalists | Planet Jazz | 2169656-2
The Legends Of Swing | Laserlight | 24659

Burnet,Bobby | (tp)
Charlie Barnet And His Orchestra
Planet Jazz:Big Bands | Planet Jazz | 2169649-2
Planet Jazz:Swing | Planet Jazz | 2169651-2

Burnett,Carl | (drperc)
Art Pepper Quartet
Art Pepper:The Complete Galaxy Recordings | Galaxy | 16GCD 1016-2
The Art Of Saxophone | Laserlight | 24652
No Limit | Original Jazz Classics | OJCCD 411-2
Arthur's Blues | Original Jazz Classics | OJCCD 680-2
Roadgame | Original Jazz Classics | OJCCD 774-2(GXY 5142)
The Jazz Giants Play Harry Warren:Lullaby Of Broadway | Prestige | PCD 24204-2
Art Pepper Quintet
Art Pepper:The Complete Galaxy Recordings | Galaxy | 16GCD 1016-2
Art Pepper Quintet With Strings
Art Pepper:The Complete Galaxy Recordings | Galaxy | 16GCD 1016-2
Winter Moon | Original Jazz Classics | OJC20 677-2(GXY 5140)
Art Pepper With The Duke Jordan Trio
Art Pepper With Duke Jordan In Copenhagen 1981 | Galaxy | 2GCD 8201-2
Bill Watrous And His West Coast Friends
Art Pepper:The Hollywood All-Star Sessions | Galaxy | 5GCD 4431-2
Cal Tjader Quintet
Talkin Verve/Roots Of Acid Jazz:Cal Tjader | Verve | 531562-2
Gene Harris And The Three Sounds
Deep Blue-The United States Of Mind | Blue Note | 521152-2
Jack Sheldon And His West Coast Friends
Art Pepper:The Hollywood All-Star Sessions | Galaxy | 5GCD 4431-2
Sonny Stitt And His West Coast Friends
Art Pepper:The Hollywood All-Star Sessions | Galaxy | 5GCD 4431-2
The Three Sounds
Blue Break Beats | Blue Note | 799106-2

Burnett,Joe | (mellophone,tpfl-h)
Maynard Ferguson And His Orchestra
Verve Jazz Masters 52:Maynard Ferguson | Verve | 529905-2
Stan Kenton And His Orchestra
Adventures In Blues | Capitol | 520089-2

Burney,Mike | (reeds)
André Holst With Chris Dean's European Swing Orchestra
That's Swing | Nagel-Heyer | CD 079

Burnham,Charles | (perc,voc,vmandocello)
Cassandra Wilson Group
Misty Blue:Sweet Sisters Swing Songs Of Sorrow And Sadness | Blue Note | 521151-2
Blue Light 'Til Dawn | Blue Note | 781357-2
Midnight Blue(The [Be]witching Hour) | Blue Note | 854365-2

Burno,Dwayne | (bel-b)
Alex Norris Quintet
A New Beginning | Fresh Sound Records | FSNT 081 CD
Bop City
Hot Jazz Bisquits | Hip Bop | HIBD 8801
David Gibson Sextet
Maya | Nagel-Heyer | CD 2018
Eric Alexander Quartet
Man With A Horn | Milestone | MCD 9293-2
Eric Alexander Sextet
Man With A Horn | Milestone | MCD 9293-2
Helmut Kagerer-Peter Bernstein Quartet
Jazz Guitar Highlights 1 | Jardis Records | JRCD 20141
April In New York | Jardis Records | JRCD 9818
Ingrid Jensen Quintet
Here On Earth | Enja | ENJ-9313 2
Johannes Enders Quintet
Bright Nights | Enja | ENJ-9352 2
New Jazz Composers Octet
Walkin' the Line | Fresh Sound Records | FSNT 151 CD
The New Jazz Composers Octet
First Step Into Reality | Fresh Sound Records | FSNT 059 CD

Burns,Bob | (as,saxtp)
Benny Goodman And His Orchestra
Verve Jazz Masters 33:Benny Goodman | Verve | 844410-2

Burns,Dave | (tp)
Al Grey And His Allstars
Snap Your Fingers | Verve | 9860307
Billy Mitchell Sextet
This Is Billy Mitchell | Smash | 065507-2
Dizzy Gillespie And His Orchestra
Dizzy Gillespie:Pleyel Jazz Concert 1948 + Max Roach Quintet 1949 | Vogue | 21409412
Planet Jazz:Dizzy Gillespie | Planet Jazz | 2152069-2
Planet Jazz:Bebop | RCA | 2169650-2
Eddie Jefferson With The James Moody Quintet
Body And Soul | Original Jazz Classics | OJCCD 396-2(P 7619)
Ella Fitzgerald With The Dizzy Gillespie Orchestra
Ella Fitzgerald:Mr.Paganini | Dreyfus Jazz Line | FDM 36741-2
Leo Parker Sextet
True Blue | Blue Note | 534032-2
Milt Jackson Orchestra
To Bags...With Love:Memorial Album | Pablo | 2310967-2
Milt Jackson Birthday Celebration | Fantasy | FANCD 6079-2
Big Bags | Original Jazz Classics | OJCCD 366-2(RLP 9429)

Burns,Ralph | (arr,cond,pcomp)
Ben Webster With Orchestra And Strings
Verve Jazz Masters 43:Ben Webster | Verve | 525431-2
Music For Loving:Ben Webster With Strings | Verve | 527774-2
Ultimate Ben Webster selected by James Carter | Verve | 557537-2
Carmen McRae With The Ralph Burns Orchestra
Birds Of A Feather | Decca | 589515-2
Chris Connor With The Ralph Burns Orchestra
Chris Connor | Atlantic | 7567-80769-2
JATP All Stars
The Complete Jazz At The Philharmonic On Verve 1944-1949 | Verve | 523893-2
Jerri Southern And The Ralph Burns Orchestra
The Very Thought Of You:The Decca Years 1951-1957 | Decca | 050671-2
Lawrence Brown With The Ralph Burns Orchestra
Slide Trombone | Verve | 559930-2
Lena Horne With The Lennie Hayton Orchestra
Planet Jazz:Lena Horne | Planet Jazz | 2165373-2
Mark Murphy With The Ralph Burns Orchestra
Crazy Rhythm:His Debut Recordings | Decca | 050670-2

Ralph Burns And His Orchestra
The Complete Verve Roy Eldridge Studio Sessions | Verve | 9861278
Sonny Stitt With The Ralph Burns Orchestra
Verve Jazz Masters 50:Sonny Sitt | Verve | 527651-2
The Herdsmen
Nat Pierce-Dick Collins-Ralph Burns & The Herdsmen Play Paris | Fantasy | FCD 24759-2
Woody Herman And His Orchestra
Woody Herman:Four Brother | Dreyfus Jazz Line | FDM 36722-2
Louis Armstrong-Jack Teagarden-Woody Herman:Midnights At V-Disc | Jazz Unlimited | JUCD 2048
Old Gold Rehearsals 1944 | Jazz Unlimited | JUCD 2079
Woody Herman And The Herd
Woody Herman (And The Herd) At Carnegie Hall | Verve | 559833-2
Woody Herman And The Vanderbilt All Stars
Louis Armstrong-Jack Teagarden-Woody Herman:Midnights At V-Disc | Jazz Unlimited | JUCD 2048
Woody Herman's Thundering Herd
Planet Jazz:Jazz Saxophone | Planet Jazz | 2169653-2

Burr,Jon | (b)
Roland Hanna Quartet
The Story Of Jazz Piano | Laserlight | 24653

Burrage,Ronnie | (dr,perc,voc,keyboards,synthtrap-dr)
Chico Freeman Quartet
Destiny's Dance | Original Jazz Classics | OJCCD 799-2(C 14008)
Chico Freeman Quintet
Destiny's Dance | Original Jazz Classics | OJCCD 799-2(C 14008)
Chico Freeman Septet
Destiny's Dance | Original Jazz Classics | OJCCD 799-2(C 14008)
Chico Freeman Sextet
Destiny's Dance | Original Jazz Classics | OJCCD 799-2(C 14008)
Courtney Pine Group
Modern Day Jazz Stories | Verve | 529028-2
Ed Schuller & The Eleventh Hour Band
Snake Dancing | Tutu Records | 888188-2*
Gunther Klatt & New York Razzmatazz
Volume One:Fa Mozzo | Tutu Records | 888158-2*
Monty Waters Quartet
Monty Waters New York Calling Vol.2 | Tutu Records | 888182-2*
Nicolas Simion Group
Black Sea | Tutu Records | 888134-2*
Ray Anderson Sextet
It Just So Happens | Enja | ENJ-5037 2
Roland Hanna Quartet
The Story Of Jazz Piano | Laserlight | 24653
Vincent Chancey Quartet
Welcome Mr. Chancey | IN+OUT Records | 7020-1

Burrell,Dave | (el-p,p,arr,cond,org,celeste,perc)
Archie Shepp Orchestra
The Cry Of My People | Impulse(MCA) | 9861488
Archie Shepp Septet
The Way Ahead | Impulse(MCA) | 951272-2

Burrell,Kenny | (g,arr,el-g,6-string-bj,ld,whistling)
Andy And The Bey Sisters
Andy Bey And The Bey Sisters | Prestige | PCD 24245-2
Astrud Gilberto With The Al Cohn Orchestra
Verve Jazz Masters 9:Astrud Gilberto | Verve | 519824-2
Astrud Gilberto With The Gil Evans Orchestra
Verve Jazz Masters 9:Astrud Gilberto | Verve | 519824-2
Verve Jazz Masters 23:Gil Evans | Verve | 521860-2
Big Joe Turner And Pete Johnson With The Blues Band
Newport Jazz Festival 1958,July 3rd-6th Vol.3:Blues In The Night No.1 | Phontastic | NCD 8815
Big Maybelle With The Blues Band
Newport Jazz Festival 1958,July 3rd-6th Vol.3:Blues In The Night No.1 | Phontastic | NCD 8815
Bill Evans Quintet
The Complete Fantasy Recordings | Fantasy | 9FCD 1012-2
Quintessence | Original Jazz Classics | OJCCD 698-2(F 9529)
The Jazz Giants Play Jerome Kern:Yesterdays | Prestige | PCD 24202-2
The Jazz Giants Play Sammy Cahn:It's Magic | Prestige | PCD 24226-2
Billie Holiday And Her All Stars
Verve Jazz Masters 12:Billie Holiday | Verve | 519825-2
Billie Holiday Story Vol.4:Lady Sings The Blues | Verve | 521429-2
4 By 4:Ella Fitzgerald/Sarah Vaughan/Billie Holiday/Dinah Washington | Verve | 559693-2
The Billie Holiday Song Book | Verve | 823246-2
Blossom Dearie Quartet
My Gentleman Friend | Verve | 519905-2
Verve Jazz Masters 51:Blossom Dearie | Verve | 529906-2
Blossom Dearie Sings Comden And Green | Verve | 589102-2
Blossom Dearie Quintet
My Gentleman Friend | Verve | 519905-2
Verve Jazz Masters 51:Blossom Dearie | Verve | 529906-2
Cal Tjader's Orchestra
Talkin Verve/Roots Of Acid Jazz:Cal Tjader | Verve | 531562-2
Charlie Rouse Orchestra
Bossa Nova Bacchanal | Blue Note | 593875-2
Blue Bossa | Blue Note | 795590-2
Chet Baker Quartet
Chet | Original Jazz Classics | OJC20 087-2
Chet Baker Septet
Chet | Original Jazz Classics | OJC20 087-2
Chet Baker Sextet
Chet | Original Jazz Classics | OJC20 087-2
Chet Baker With Bobby Scott And Kenny Burrell
Baby Breeze | Verve | 538328-2
Chet Baker With Kenny Burrell
Baby Breeze | Verve | 538328-2
Chuck Berry With The Blues Band
Newport Jazz Festival 1958,July 3rd-6th Vol.3:Blues In The Night No.1 | Phontastic | NCD 8815
Coleman Hawkins Quintet
Soul | Original Jazz Classics | OJC20 096-2(P 7149)
The Hawk Relaxes | Original Jazz Classics | OJCCD 709-2(MV 15)
The Jazz Giants Play Sammy Cahn:It's Magic | Prestige | PCD 24226-2
Dave Pike Quintet
Carnavals | Prestige | PCD 24248-2
Dave Pike Sextet
Carnavals | Prestige | PCD 24248-2
Dee Dee Bridgewater-Kenny Burrell
Dear Ella | Verve | 539102-2
Dinah Washington With The Belford Hendricks Orchestra
What A Diff'rence A Day Makes! | Verve | 543300-2
Donald Byrd Orchestra With Voices
True Blue | Blue Note | 534032-2
The Best Of Blue Note | Blue Note | 796110-2
Donald Byrd Septet + Voices
A New Perspective | Blue Note | 499006-2
Doug Watkins Sextet
Donald Byrd & Doug Watkins:The Tradition Sessions | Blue Note | 540528-2
Eddie Harris Group
Here Comes The Judge | CBS | 492533-2
Ernestine Anderson With Orchestra
My Kinda Swing | Mercury | 842409-2
Essence All Stars
Hot Jazz Bisquits | Hip Bop | HIBD 8801
Etta Jones And Her Band
Love Shout | Original Jazz Classics | OJCCD 941-2(P 7272)
Etta Jones With The Jerome Richardson Sextet
Hollar! | Original Jazz Classics | OJCCD 1061(PR 7284)
Gene Ammons Septet
Bad! Bossa Nova | Original Jazz Classics | OJC20 351-2(P 7257)
Gil Evans Orchestra
Verve Jazz Masters 23:Gil Evans | Verve | 521860-2
The Individualism Of Gil Evans | Verve | 833804-2
Herbie Mann Sextet

Just Wailin' | Original Jazz Classics | OJCCD 900-2(NJ 8211)
Ike Quebec Quintet
Blue Bossa | Blue Note | 795590-2
Jack McDuff Quartet
Screamin' | Original Jazz Classics | OJCCD 875-2(P 7259)
Jack McDuff:The Prestige Years | Prestige | PRCD 24387-2
Jimmy McGriff Orchestra
Swingin' The Blues-Jumpin' The Blues | Laserlight | 24654
Jimmy Rushing With Oliver Nelson And His Orchestra
Every Day I Have The Blues | Impulse(MCA) | 547967-2
Jimmy Smith All Stars
House Party | Blue Note | 524542-2
Jimmy Smith Quartet
Six Views Of The Blues | Blue Note | 521435-2
Verve Jazz Masters 45:Kenny Burrell | Verve | 527652-2
Jimmy Smith:Best Of The Verve Years | Verve | 527950-2
Jimmy Smith-Talkin' Verve | Verve | 531563-2
Any Number Can Win | Verve | 557447-2
Back At The Chicken Shack | Blue Note | 746402-2
The Best Of Blue Note | Blue Note | 796110-2
Home Cookin' | Blue Note | 853360-2
Fourmost Return | Milestone | MCD 9311-2
Jimmy Smith Trio
Verve Jazz Masters 29:Jimmy Smith | Verve | 521855-2
Jimmy Smith:Best Of The Verve Years | Verve | 527950-2
Verve Jazz Masters Vol.60:The Collection | Verve | 529866-2
Jimmy Smith-Talkin' Verve | Verve | 531563-2
Organ Grinder Swing | Verve | 543831-2
Standards | Blue Note | 821282-2
Home Cookin' | Blue Note | 853360-2
Jimmy Smith With Orchestra
Jimmy Smith-Talkin' Verve | Verve | 531563-2
Jimmy Smith With The Billy Byers Orchestra
Jimmy Smith:Best Of The Verve Years | Verve | 527950-2
Jimmy Smith With The Claus Ogerman Orchestra
Verve Jazz Masters 29:Jimmy Smith | Verve | 521855-2
Any Number Can Win | Verve | 557447-2
Jimmy Smith With The Lalo Schifrin Orchestra
Jimmy Smith:Best Of The Verve Years | Verve | 527950-2
Jimmy Smith-Talkin' Verve | Verve | 531563-2
The Cat | Verve | 539756-2
Jimmy Smith With The Oliver Nelson Orchestra
Verve Jazz Masters 29:Jimmy Smith | Verve | 521855-2
Jimmy Smith:Best Of The Verve Years | Verve | 527950-2
Jimmy Smith-Talkin' Verve | Verve | 531563-2
Jimmy Witherspoon And His Band
Baby, Baby, Baby | Original Blues Classics | OBCCD 527-2(P 7290)
Jimmy Witherspoon With Jay McShann And His Band
Planet Jazz:Male Jazz Vocalists | Planet Jazz | 2169657-2
Joe Williams With The Jimmy Jones Orchestra
Planet Jazz:Joe Williams | Planet Jazz | 2165370-2
Joe Williams,With The Oliver Nelson Orchestra
Planet Jazz:Joe Williams | Planet Jazz | 2165370-2
Johnny Hodges-Earl Hines Quintet
Verve Jazz Masters 35:Johnny Hodges | Verve | 521857-2
Kenny Burrel Quartet
'Round Midnight | Original Jazz Classics | OJCCD 990-2(F 9417)
Kenny Burrell
Verve Jazz Masters 45:Kenny Burrell | Verve | 527652-2
Blues-The Common Ground | Verve | 589101-2
Stormy Monday Blues | Fantasy | FCD 24767-2
Kenny Burrell Quartet
Verve Jazz Masters 45:Kenny Burrell | Verve | 527652-2
Blues-The Common Ground | Verve | 589101-2
Blue Lights Vol.1&2 | Blue Note | 857184-2
Stormy Monday Blues | Fantasy | FCD 24767-2
Kenny Burrell Quintet
John Coltrane-The Prestige Recordings | Prestige | 16 PCD 4405-2
Midnight Blue | Blue Note | 495335-2
Guitar Forms | Verve | 521403-2
Verve Jazz Masters 45:Kenny Burrell | Verve | 527652-2
The Best Of Blue Note | Blue Note | 796110-2
Stormy Monday Blues | Fantasy | FCD 24767-2
Kenny Burrell | Original Jazz Classics | OJCCD 019-2(P 7088)
Soul Call | Original Jazz Classics | OJCCD 846-2(P 7315)
Kenny Burrell Septet
Blue Lights Vol.1&2 | Blue Note | 857184-2
Kenny Burrell Sextet
Verve Jazz Masters 45:Kenny Burrell | Verve | 527652-2
Kenny Burrell With The Don Sebesky Orchestra
Verve Jazz Masters 45:Kenny Burrell | Verve | 527652-2
Blues-The Common Ground | Verve | 589101-2
Kenny Burrell With The Gil Evans Orchestra
Guitar Forms | Verve | 521403-2
Verve Jazz Masters 23:Gil Evans | Verve | 521860-2
Verve Jazz Masters 45:Kenny Burrell | Verve | 527652-2
Verve Jazz Masters Vol.60:The Collection | Verve | 529866-2
Kenny Burrell With The Johnny Pate Orchestra
Verve Jazz Masters 45:Kenny Burrell | Verve | 527652-2
Kenny Burrell-Grover Washington Quartet
Blue Note Plays Gershwin | Blue Note | 520808-2
Kenny Burrell-Jimmy Smith Quartet
Blue Bash | Verve | 557453-2
Kenny Burrell-Jimmy Smith Trio
Blue Bash | Verve | 557453-2
Kenny Burrell-John Coltrane Duo
Kenny Burrell & John Coltrane | New Jazz | NJSA 8276-2
Kenny Burrell & John Coltrane | Original Jazz Classics | OJC20 300-2
Kenny Burrell-John Coltrane Quintet
Kenny Burrell & John Coltrane | New Jazz | NJSA 8276-2
Kenny Burrell & John Coltrane | Original Jazz Classics | OJC20 300-2
Kenny Clarke Quintet
Verve Jazz Masters 45:Kenny Burrell | Verve | 527652-2
Kenny Dorham Sextet
The Complete Round About Midnight At The Cafe Bohemia | Blue Note | 533775-2
Louis Armstrong And His Friends
Planet Jazz:Louis Armstrong | Planet Jazz | 2152052-2
Planet Jazz Sampler | Planet Jazz | 2152326-2
Louis Armstrong And His Friends | Bluebird | 2663961-2
Nancy Harrow And The Buck Clayton All Stars
Wild Women Don't Have The Blues | Candid | CCD 79008
Nat Adderley With Kenny Burrell And The Junior Mance Trio
Little Big Horn! | Original Jazz Classics | OJCCD 1001-2(R 9474)
Paul Chambers Sextet
Trane's Blues | Blue Note | 498240-2
Prestige All Stars
John Coltrane-The Prestige Recordings | Prestige | 16 PCD 4405-2
All Day Long | Original Jazz Classics | OJC20 456-2(P 7081)
The Cats | Original Jazz Classics | OJCCD 079-2(NJ 8217)
The Mal Waldron Memorial Album:Soul Eyes | Prestige | PRCD 11024-2
Ray Barretto Orchestra
Portraits In Jazz And Clave | RCA | 2168452-2
Ray Charles-Milt Jackson Quintet
Soul Brothers/Soul Meeting | Atlantic | 7567-81951-2
Red Garland Quartet
Red Garland Revisited! | Original Jazz Classics | OJCCD 985-2(P 7658)
Shirley Horn With Band
The Roots Of Acid Jazz | Impulse(MCA) | IMP 12042
Shirley Horn With Orchestra
Loads Of Love + Shirley Horn With Horns | Mercury | 843454-2
Shirley Scott Quartet
Queen Of The Organ-Shirley Scott Memorial Album | Prestige | PRCD 11027-2
Sonny Clark Quintet
My Conception | Blue Note | 522674-2
Sonny Rollins Orchestra
Alfie | Impulse(MCA) | 951224-2
Stan Getz Quintet Feat. Astrud Gilberto

Verve Jazz Masters 53:Stan Getz-Bossa Nova | Verve | 529904-2
Stan Getz With Strings And Voices
Reflections | Verve | 523322-2
Stan Getz With The Richard Evans Orchestra
What The World Needs Now-Stan Getz Plays Bacharach And David | Verve | 557450-2
Stanley Turrentine Quintet
Hustlin' | Blue Note | 540036-2
The New Stan Getz Quintet Feat. Astrud Gilberto
Getz Au Go Go | Verve | 821725-2
Wes Montgomery With The Jimmy Jones Orchestra
Wes Montgomery-The Complete Riverside Recordings | Riverside | 12 RCD 4408-2
The Jazz Giants Play Rodgers & Hart:Blue Moon | Prestige | PCD 24205-2
Willis Jackson Group
At Large | Prestige | PCD 24243-2
Wynton Kelly Quartet
Wynton Kelly-Piano | Original Jazz Classics | OJCCD 401-2(RLP 12-254)
Wynton Kelly Trio
Wynton Kelly-Piano | Original Jazz Classics | OJCCD 401-2(RLP 12-254)
Yusef Lateef Orchestra
The Blue Yusef Lateef | Rhino | 8122-73717-2

Burrell,Kenny or Jim Hall | (g)
Johnny Hartman And His Quintet
I Just Dropped By To Say Hello | MCA | 951176-2

Burrell,Kenny or Jimmy Raney | (g)
Cal Tjader's Orchestra
Verve Jazz Masters 39:Cal Tjader | Verve | 521858-2

Burri,Bobby | (b)
Doran/Studer/Burri/Magnenat
Musik Für Zwei Kontrabässe, Elektrische Gitarre & Schlagzeug | ECM | 1436

Burriesce,Joe | (b)
Jimmy McPartland And His Dixielanders
Planet Jazz | Planet Jazz | 2169652-2

Burroughs,Alvin | (dr)
Earl Hines And His Orchestra
Planet Jazz:Earl Hines | Planet Jazz | 2159973-2
The Legends Of Swing | Laserlight | 24659
Jazz:The Essential Collection Vol.2 | IN+OUT Records | 78012-2

Burrowes,Roy | (tp,fl-hperc)
Duke Ellington And His Orchestra
The Great Paris Concert | Atlantic | 7567-81303-2
Afro-Bossa | Reprise | 9362-47876-2
Duke Ellington And His Orchestra feat. Paul Gonsalves | Original Jazz Classics | OJCCD 623-2
The Jazz Giants Play Duke Ellington:Caravan | Prestige | PCD 24227-2

Burtis,Sam | (b-tb,tubatb)
Buddy Rich Big Band
The New One! | Pacific Jazz | 494507-2
Earl Klugh Group
Late Night Guitar | Blue Note | 498573-2
Mingus Big Band 93
Nostalgia In Times Square | Dreyfus Jazz Line | FDM 36559-2

Burton,Abraham | (asts)
Abraham Burton Quartet
Closest To The Sun | Enja | ENJ-8074 2
The Magician | Enja | ENJ-9037 2
James Hurt Group
Dark Grooves-Mystcal Rhythms | Blue Note | 495104-2
Taylor's Wailers
Mr. A.T. | Enja | ENJ-7017 2

Burton,Gary | (vib,marimba,org,p,el-p,perc)
Astor Piazzolla-Gary Burton Sextet
The New Tango | Warner | 2292-55069-2
Astrud Gilberto With The New Stan Getz Quartet
Verve Jazz Masters 9:Astrud Gilberto | Verve | 519824-2
Bob Brookmeyer Quintet
Sony Jazz Collection:Stan Getz | CBS | 488623-2
Bob Brookmeyer Sextet
Late Night Sax | CBS | 487798-2
Chick Corea/Gary Burton
Crystal Silence | ECM | 1024(831331-2)
Chick Corea-Gary Burton
In Concert, Zürich, October 28, 1979 | ECM | 1182/83
Eberhard Weber Group
Fluid Rustle | ECM | 1137
Gary Burton
Alone At Last | Atlantic | 7567-80762-2
Gary Burton Quartet
The New Quartet | ECM | 1030
Times Square | ECM | 1111
Real Life Hits | ECM | 1293
Planet Jazz:Gary Burton | RCA | 2165367-2
Gary Burton Quartet With Eberhard Weber
Passengers | ECM | 1092(835016-2)
Gary Burton Quartet With Orchestra
A Genuine Tong Funeral(Dark Opera Without Words) | RCA | 2119255-2
Gary Burton Quintet
Dreams So Real | ECM | 1072
Whiz Kids | ECM | 1329
Gary Burton Quintet With Eberhard Weber
Ring | ECM | 1051
Gary Burton Sextet
Planet Jazz:Gary Burton | RCA | 2165367-2
Gary Burton Trio
Planet Jazz:Gary Burton | RCA | 2165367-2
Gary Burton-Chick Corea
Duet | ECM | 1140(829941-2)
Gary Burton-Keith Jarrett Quintet
Gary Burton & Keith Jarrett | Atlantic | 7567-81374-2
Gary Burton-Stephane Grappelli Quartet
Paris Encounter | Atlantic | 7567-80763-2
Gary Burton-Steve Swallow
Hotel Hello | ECM | 1055(835586-2)
Getz-Gilberto Quintet
Getz/Gilberto No.2 | Verve | 519800-2
GRP All-Star Big Band
GRP All-Star Big Band:Live! | GRP | GRP 97402
Makoto Ozone Group
Treasure | Verve | 021906-2
NDR Big Band With Guests
50 Years Of NDR Big Band:Bravissimo II | ACT | 9259-2
Quincy Jones And His Orchestra
Talkin' Verve-Roots Of Acid Jazz:Roland Kirk | Verve | 533101-2
Verve Jazz Masters Vol.59:Toots Thielemans | Verve | 535271-2
Rahsaan/The Complete Mercury Recordings Of Roland Kirk | Mercury | 846630-2
Ralph Towner-Gary Burton
Matchbook | ECM | 1056(835014-2)
Slide Show | ECM | 1306
Stan Getz New Quartet
Stan Getz Highlights:The Best Of The Verve Years Vol.2 | Verve | 517330-2
A Life In Jazz:A Musical Biography | Verve | 535119-2
Stan Getz Quartet
Getz/Gilberto No.2 | Verve | 519800-2
Stan Getz Quintet Feat. Astrud Gilberto
Verve Jazz Masters 53:Stan Getz-Bossa Nova | Verve | 529904-2
Stan Getz With Strings And Voices
Reflections | Verve | 523322-2
Steve Swallow Group
Swallow | Watt | XtraWatt/6
The New Stan Getz Quartet
Getz Au Go Go | Verve | 821725-2
The New Stan Getz Quartet Feat. Astrud Gilberto
Getz Au Go Go | Verve | 821725-2
The New Stan Getz Quintet Feat. Astrud Gilberto
Getz Au Go Go | Verve | 821725-2
Thomas Clausen Trio With Gary Burton
Flowers And Trees | M.A Music | A 805-2
Café Noir | M.A Music | INTCD 004

Burton,M. | (voc)
Sonny Rollins Group
What's New? | RCA | 2179626-2

Burton,Princess Patience | (voc)
Rahsaan Roland Kirk And His Orchestra
Blacknuss | Rhino | 8122-71408-2

Burton,Ron | (porg)
Dick Griffin Septet
The Eighth Wonder & More | Konnex Records | KCD 5059
Nicolas Simion Group
Black Sea | Tutu Records | 888134-2*
Rahsaan Roland Kirk Quartet
Rhino Presents The Atlantic Jazz Gallery | Atlantic | 8122-71257-2
Rahsaan Roland Kirk Sextet
Atlantic Saxophones | Rhino | 8122-71256-2
Volunteered Slavery | Rhino | 8122-71407-2
Roland Kirk Quartet
The Inflated Tear | Atlantic | 7567-90045-2
The Inflated Tear | Atlantic | 8122-75207-2
Roland Kirk Quintet
The Inflated Tear | Atlantic | 7567-90045-2
The Inflated Tear | Atlantic | 8122-75207-2

Busby,Laddie | (tb)
Vic Lewis Jam Session
Vic Lewis:The Golden Years | Candid | CCD 79754

Busch,Andreas | (tp)
Jazz Fresh
Jazz Fresh | GGG-Verlag:GGG Verlag und Mailorder | CD 01.03

Busch,Gregor | (sax)

Busch,Hanno | (g)
Clark Terry With The Summit Jazz Orchestra
Clark | Edition Collage | EC 530-2
Matthias Petzold Working Band
Elements | Indigo-Records | 1005 CD
Nana Mouskouri With The Berlin Radio Big Band
Nana Swings | Mercury | 074394-2

Busch,Heiko | (dr)
Jazz Orchester Rheinland-Pfalz
Kazzou | Jazz Haus Musik | LJBB 9104
Like Life | Jazz Haus Musik | LJBB 9405
Last Season | Jazz Haus Musik | LJBB 9706

Busch,Johannes | (voc)
Jazzensemble Des Hessischen Rundfunks
Jazz Messe-Messe Für Unsere Zeit | hr music.de | hrmj 003-01 CD

Busch,Oliver | (fl,b-cl,bs,piccolocl)
Jazz Orchester Rheinland-Pfalz
Kazzou | Jazz Haus Musik | LJBB 9104
Like Life | Jazz Haus Musik | LJBB 9405
Last Season | Jazz Haus Musik | LJBB 9706

Busch,Sigi | (b)
Sigi Busch-Alexander Sputh Duo
Jazz Portraits | EGO | 95080

Busch,Thomas | (b-tb)
Jazz Orchester Rheinland-Pfalz
Kazzou | Jazz Haus Musik | LJBB 9104

Buschhaus,Jörg | (v)
Uri Caine With The Concerto Köln
Concerto Köln | Winter&Winter | 910086-2

Buschmann,Pit | (g)
Glen Buschmann Quintet
Deutsches Jazz Fesival 1954/1955 | Bear Family Records | BCD 15430
Wolfgang Sauer With The Glen Buschmann Quintet
Deutsches Jazz Fesival 1954/1955 | Bear Family Records | BCD 15430

Buschmann,Rainer Glen | (cl)
Glen Buschmann Quintet
Deutsches Jazz Fesival 1954/1955 | Bear Family Records | BCD 15430
Wolfgang Sauer With The Glen Buschmann Quintet
Deutsches Jazz Fesival 1954/1955 | Bear Family Records | BCD 15430

Bush,Andy | (tp)
Mike Westbrook Orchestra
Bar Utopia-A Big Band Cabaret | Enja | ENJ-9333 2

Bush,Lennie | (b)
Benny Goodman And His Orchestra
Verve Jazz Masters 33:Benny Goodman | Verve | 844410-2
Benny Goodman Sextet
Verve Jazz Masters 33:Benny Goodman | Verve | 844410-2
Stephane Grappelli And Friends
Grapelli Story | Verve | 515807-2

Bushell,Garvin | (as,bassoon,cl,bs,sax,ss)
Ella Fitzgerald And Her Orchestra
Jazz Collection:Ella Fitzgerald | Laserlight | 24397
Gil Evans Orchestra
Verve Jazz Masters 23:Gil Evans | Verve | 521860-2
The Individualism Of Gil Evans | Verve | 833804-2
John Coltrane And His Orchestra
John Coltrane:Standards | Impulse(MCA) | 549914-2
John Coltrane Quartet With Brass
The Complete Africa/Brass Sessions | Impulse(MCA) | 952168-2
John Coltrane Quintet With Eric Dolphy
John Coltrane:The Complete 1961 Village Vanguard Recordings | Impulse(MCA) | 954322-2
The Other Village Vanguard Tapes | Impulse(MCA) | MCD 04137
John Coltrane Septet With Eric Dolphy
John Coltrane:The Complete 1961 Village Vanguard Recordings | Impulse(MCA) | 954322-2
The Other Village Vanguard Tapes | Impulse(MCA) | MCD 04137
Louisiana Sugar Babes
Planet Jazz:Jazz Trumpet | Planet Jazz | 2169654-2

Bushkin,Joe | (celeste,p,voctp)
Kansas City Six
Lester Young:Blue Lester | Dreyfus Jazz Line | FDM 36729-2
Louis Armstrong And Ella Fitzgerald With Bob Haggert's Orchestra
Louis Armstrong:C'est Si Bon | Dreyfus Jazz Line | FDM 36730-2
Louis Armstrong And His Orchestra
Satchmo Serenaders | Verve | 543792-2
Muggsy Spanier And His Ragtime Band
Planet Jazz | Planet Jazz | 2169652-2
Planet Jazz:Jazz Trumpet | Planet Jazz | 2169654-2
Tommy Dorsey And His Orchestra
Planet Jazz:Frank Sinatra & Tommy Dorsey | Planet Jazz | 2152067-2
Planet Jazz Sampler | Planet Jazz | 2152326-2
Planet Jazz:Tommy Dorsey | Planet Jazz | 2159972-2
Planet Jazz:Big Bands | Planet Jazz | 2169649-2
Planet Jazz:Male Jazz Vocalists | Planet Jazz | 2169657-2
Frank Sinatra And The Tommy Dorsey Orchestra | RCA | 2668701-2

Bushler,Herb | (bel-b)
Dee Dee Bridgewater With Band
Dee Dee Bridgewater | Atlantic | 7567-80760-2
Gil Evans Orchestra
There Comes A Time | RCA | 2131392-2
Svengali | Rhino | 8122-73720-2
Blues In Orbit | Enja | ENJ-3069 2
Les McCann Group
Another Beginning | Atlantic | 7567-80790-2

Bushnell,Bob | (bel-b)
Billy Butler Quintet
Night Life | Prestige | PCD 24260-2
Cal Tjader's Orchestra
Talkin Verve/Roots Of Acid Jazz:Cal Tjader | Verve | 531562-2
Dickie Wells-Buddy Tate Quintet
Every Day I Have The Blues | Impulse(MCA) | 547967-2
Ella Fitzgerald With Louis Jordan And His Tympany Five
Ella Fitzgerald:Mr.Paganini | Dreyfus Jazz Line | FDM 36741-2
Freddie Hubbard Septet
This Is Jazz:Freddie Hubbard | CBS | CK 65041
Gene Ammons Quartet
Gentle Jug Vol.3 | Prestige | PCD 24249-2
Brother Jug! | Prestige | PR20 7792-2
Gene Ammons Quintet
Brother Jug! | Prestige | PR20 7792-2
Houston Person Sextet
Goodness! | Original Jazz Classics | OJC20 332-2(P 7678)
Jimmy McGriff Organ Blues Band
The Worm | Blue Note | 538699-2
Jimmy Rushing And His Orchestra
Every Day I Have The Blues | Impulse(MCA) | 547967-2
Jimmy Smith Quartet
Jimmy Smith-Talkin' Verve | Verve | 531563-2
Jimmy Smith With Orchestra
Jimmy Smith-Talkin' Verve | Verve | 531563-2
Jimmy Smith With The Claus Ogerman Orchestra
Any Number Can Win | Verve | 557447-2
King Curtis Band
King Curtis-Blow Man Blow | Bear Family Records | BCD 15670 Cl
Louis Armstrong With Louis Jordan And His Tympany Five
Louis Armstrong:C'est Si Bon | Dreyfus Jazz Line | FDM 36730-2
Louis Jordan And His Tympany Five
Louis Jordan-Let The Good Times Roll: The Complete Decca Recordings 1938-1954 | Bear Family Records | BCD 15557 IH
Nina Simone And Orchestra
Planet Jazz:Nina Simone | Planet Jazz | 2165372-2
Nina Simone-Bob Bushnell
Planet Jazz:Nina Simone | Planet Jazz | 2165372-2
Planet Jazz:Female Jazz Vocalists | Planet Jazz | 2169656-2
Rusty Bryant Quintet
Rusty Bryant Returns | Original Jazz Classics | OJCCD 331-2(P 7626)

Busnello,Eddie | (asbs)
Stan Getz With The Kurt Edelhagen Orchestra
Stan Getz In Europe | Laserlight | 24657

Busse,Christoph | (keyboards)
Gunter Hampel Next Generation
Next Generation | Birth | CD 043

Busse,Henry | (co,ldtp)
Paul Whiteman And His Orchestra
Planet Jazz:Jazz Trumpet | Planet Jazz | 2169654-2

Butcher,George prob. | (tp)
Della Reese With The Neal Hefti Orchestra
Della | RCA | 2663912-2

Butera,Sam | (ts)
Little Jimmy Scott | Specialty | SPCD 2170-2

Butler,Art | (cond)
Louis Armstrong And His All Stars With A Studio Orchestra
What A Wonderful World | MCA | MCD 01876

Butler,Artie | (org,pperc)
Big Joe Turner And His Orchestra
Planet Jazz:Male Jazz Vocalists | Planet Jazz | 2169657-2
Stan Getz With Orchestra And Voices
Stan Getz Highlights | Verve | 847430-2
Stan Getz With The Claus Ogerman Orchestra
What The World Needs Now-Stan Getz Plays Bacharach And David | Verve | 557450-2

Butler,Billy | (el-g,g,b-gvoc)
Billy Butler Quintet
Night Life | Prestige | PCD 24260-2
Dinah Washington And Her Orchestra
Misty Blue:Sweet Sisters Swing Songs Of Sorrow And Sadness | Blue Note | 521151-2
Dizzy Gillespie And His Orchestra
Talking Verve:Dizzy Gillespie | Verve | 533846-2
Frank Foster Sextet
Soul Outing! | Original Jazz Classics | OJCCD 984-2(7479)
Gene Ammons Quintet
Brother Jug! | Prestige | PR20 7792-2
Herbie Hancock Septet
Herbie Hancock:The Complete Blue Note Sixties Sessions | Blue Note | 495569-2
Houston Person Sextet
Goodness! | Original Jazz Classics | OJC20 332-2(P 7678)
Jimmy Smith With The Oliver Nelson Orchestra
Verve Jazz Masters 29:Jimmy Smith | Verve | 521855-2
Jimmy Smith:Best Of The Verve Years | Verve | 527950-2
Jimmy Smith-Talkin' Verve | Verve | 531563-2
Peter & The Wolf | Verve | 547264-2
Johnny Hodges Orchestra
Planet Jazz:Johnny Hodges | Planet Jazz | 2152065-2
King Curtis Band
King Curtis-Blow Man Blow | Bear Family Records | BCD 15670 Cl
Rahsaan Roland Kirk Sextet
Blacknuss | Rhino | 8122-71408-2
Sonny Stitt With Orchestra
Goin' Down Slow | Prestige | PRCD 24276-2

Butler,Frank | (dr,percdr-solo)
Art Pepper Quartet
Intensity | Original Jazz Classics | OJCCD 387-2
The Way It Is | Original Jazz Classics | OJCCD 389-2
The Jazz Giants Play Jerome Kern:Yesterdays | Prestige | PCD 24202-2
Art Pepper Quintet
Smack Up | Original Jazz Classics | OJC20 176-2
Ben Webster Quintet
At The Renaissance | Original Jazz Classics | OJC 390(C 7646)
Hampton Hawes Trio
Bird Song | Original Jazz Classics | OJCCD 1035-2
Harold Land Quintet
The Fox | Original Jazz Classics | OJCCD 343-2
John Coltrane And His Orchestra
Kulu Se Mama | Impulse(MCA) | 543412-2
Miles Davis Quartet
This Is Jazz:Miles Davis Plays Ballads | CBS | CK 65038
Miles Davis Quintet
Ballads | CBS | 461099-2
Seven Steps To Heaven | CBS | CK 48827

Butler,Henry | (p,synthvoc)
Robben Ford & The Blue Line
Handful Of Blues | Blue Thumb | BTR 70042

Butler,Jonathan | (g)
Marcus Miller Group
The Sun Don't Lie | Dreyfus Jazz Line | FDM 36560-2

Butler,Lee | (tp)
Steve Martland Band
The Orchestra Of Smith's Academy | Enja | ENJ-9358 2

Butler,Melvin | (ssts)
Brian Blade Group
Fellowship | Blue Note | 859417-2
Stéphane Mercier Group
Flor De Luna | Fresh Sound Records | FSNT 097 CD

Butler,Robert | (tp)
Louis Armstrong And His Orchestra
Louis Armstrong:C'est Si Bon | Dreyfus Jazz Line | FDM 36730-2
Swing Legends:Louis Armstrong | Nimbus Records | NI 2012

Butman,Igor | (sax,ld,ss,asts)
Grover Washington Jr. Orchestra
Late Night Sax | CBS | 487798-2

Buttacavoli,Ronnie | (fl-htp)
Etta James & The Roots Band
Burnin' Down he House | RCA | 3411633-2

Butterfield,Billy | (tp,fl-h,ldvoc)
Artie Shaw And His Orchestra
Planet JazzArtie Shaw | Planet Jazz | 2152057-2
Planet Jazz:Big Bands | Planet Jazz | 2169649-2

Swing Vol.1 | Storyville | 4960343
Billy Butterfield And His Modern Dixie Stompers
Soft Strut | Fresh Sound Records | FSR-CD 318
Bob Crosby And His Orchestra
Swing Legens:Bob Crosby | Nimbus Records | NI 2011
Bob Crosby's Bobcats
Swing Legens:Bob Crosby | Nimbus Records | NI 2011
Bud Freeman And His Summa Cum Laude Orchestra
Planet Jazz:Jack Teagarden | Planet Jazz | 2161236-2
Planet Jazz:Bud Freeman | Planet Jazz | 2161240-2
Eddie Condon And His Boys
The Very Best Of Dixieland Jazz | Verve | 535529-2
Eddie Condon And His Orchestra
Jazz:The Essential Collection Vol.3 | IN+OUT Records | 78013-2
Jess Stacy And His Orchestra
Planet Jazz:Jazz Piano | RCA | 2169655-2
Jimmy Smith With The Lalo Schifrin Orchestra
The Cat | Verve | 539756-2
Lee Wiley With The Dean Kincaide Dixieland Band
Planet Jazz:Female Jazz Vocalists | Planet Jazz | 2169656-2
Louis Armstrong And Ella Fitzgerald With Bob Hagger's Orchestra
Louis Armstrong:C'est Si Bon | Dreyfus Jazz Line | FDM 36730-2
Louis Armstrong And His Orchestra
Louis Armstrong:Swing That Music | Laserlight | 36056
Louis Armstrong:C'est Si Bon | Dreyfus Jazz Line | FDM 36730-2
Louis Armstrong And The Commanders under the Direction of Camarata
Satchmo Serenaders | Verve | 543792-2
Louis Armstrong With Gordon Jenkins And His Orchestra And Choir
Satchmo In Style | Verve | 549594-2
Ambassador Louis Armstrong Vol.17:Moments To Remember(1952-1956) | Ambassador | CLA 1917
Louis Armstrong-My Greatest Songs | MCA | MCD 18347
Swing Legends:Louis Armstrong | Nimbus Records | NI 2012
Louis Armstrong With The Commanders
Ambassador Louis Armstrong Vol.17:Moments To Remember(1952-1956) | Ambassador | CLA 1917
Peggy Lee With The Benny Goodman Orchestra
Peggy Lee & Benny Goodman:The Complete Recordings 1941-1947 | CBS | C2K 65686
Sarah Vaughan The The Joe Lippman Orchestra
Sarah Vaughan:Lover Man | Dreyfus Jazz Line | FDM 36739-2
Sarah Vaughan With The Hugo Winterhalter Orchestra
Sarah Vaughan:Lover Man | Dreyfus Jazz Line | FDM 36739-2
V-Disc All Star Jam Session
Louis Armstrong-Jack Teagarden-Woody Herman:Midnights At V-Disc | Jazz Unlimited | JUCD 2048
V-Disc All Stars
Jazz:The Essential Collection Vol.3 | IN+OUT Records | 78013-2

Butterfield,Don | (tuba)

Cal Tjader With The Lalo Schifrin Orchestra
Talkin Verve/Roots Of Acid Jazz:Cal Tjader | Verve | 531562-2
Cannonball Adderley And His Orchestra
Ballads | Blue Note | 537563-2
Cannonball Adderley Birthday Celebration | Fantasy | FANCD 6087-2
Cannonball Adderley Quintet
Ballads | Blue Note | 537563-2
Cannonball Adderley With Sergio Mendes And The Bossa Rio Sextet
Ballads | Blue Note | 537563-2
Charles Mingus Orchestra
Charles Mingus:Pre-Bird(Mingus Revisited) | Verve | 538636-2
Mingus Mingus Mingus | Impulse(MCA) | 951170-2
The Black Saint And The Sinner Lady | Impulse(MCA) | 951174-2
Dizzy Gillespie And His Orchestra
Verve Jazz Masters 10:Dizzy Gillespie | Verve | 516319-2
Gillespiana And Carnegie Hall Concert | Verve | 519809-2
Talking Verve:Dizzy Gillespie | Verve | 533846-2
Ultimate Dizzy Gillespie | Verve | 557535-2
Jimmy Smith With The Lalo Schifrin Orchestra
Jimmy Smith:Best Of The Verve Years | Verve | 527950-2
Jimmy Smith-Talkin' Verve | Verve | 531563-2
Jimmy Smith With The Oliver Nelson Orchestra
Verve Jazz Masters 29:Jimmy Smith | Verve | 521855-2
Jimmy Smith:Best Of The Verve Years | Verve | 527950-2
Jimmy Smith-Talkin' Verve | Verve | 531563-2
Kenny Burrell With The Don Sebesky Orchestra
Verve Jazz Masters 45:Kenny Burrell | Verve | 527652-2
Blues-The Common Ground | Verve | 589101-2
Lalo Schifrin And His Orchestra
Verve Jazz Masters 39:Cal Tjader | Verve | 521858-2
Modern Jazz Quartet & Guests
MJQ 40 | Atlantic | 7567-82330-2
Oscar Peterson With The Ernie Wilkins Orchestra
Verve Jazz Masters 16:Oscar Peterson | Verve | 516320-2
Roland Kirk With The Benny Golson Orchestra
Rahsaan/The Complete Mercury Recordings Of Roland Kirk | Mercury | 846630-2
Sonny Rollins Orchestra
Sonny Rollins And The Big Brass | Verve | 557545-2
Wes Montgomery With The Don Sebesky Orchestra
Verve Jazz Masters 14:Wes Montgomery | Verve | 519826-2
Wes Montgomery:The Verve Jazz Sides | Verve | 521690-2
Talkin' Jazz:Roots Of Acid Jazz | Verve | 529580-2
California Dreaming | Verve | 827842-2
Wes Montgomery With The Johnny Pate Orchestra
Verve Jazz Masters 14:Wes Montgomery | Verve | 519826-2
Wes Montgomery:The Verve Jazz Sides | Verve | 521690-2
Talkin' Jazz:Roots Of Acid Jazz | Verve | 529580-2

Butterfield,Don or Harvey Phillips | (tuba)

Wes Montgomery Orchestra
Movin' Wes | Verve | 521433-2

Büttermann,Max | (btb)

Freddie Brocksieper And His Boys
Freddie's Boogie Blues | Bear Family Records | BCD 16388 AH

Büttner,Jochen | (perc)

Lajos Dudas Quintet
Talk Of The Town | double moon | CHRDM 71012
Some Great Songs | double moon | DMCD 1005-2
Lajos Dudas Sextet
Talk Of The Town | double moon | CHRDM 71012
Lajos Dudas Trio
Talk Of The Town | double moon | CHRDM 71012

Butts,Jimmy | (bvoc)

Tiny Grimes Swingtet
The Blue Note Swingtets | Blue Note | 495697-2

Butts,Johnny | (dr)

Blossom Dearie Trio
At Ronnie Scott's:Blossom Time | EmArCy | 558683-2

Buyukas,Patty | (voc)

Al Di Meola Group
Land Of The Midnight Sun | CBS | 468214-2

Byam,Roger Gordon | (sax,ss,asts)

Mongo Santamaria And His Orchestra
Jazzin' Vol.2: The Music Of Stevie Wonder | Fantasy | FANCD 6088-2

Byard,Jaki | (arr,as,p,ts,el-p,g,orgp-solo)

Booker Ervin Quartet
The Freedom Book | Original Jazz Classics | OJCCD 845-2(P 7295)
The Space Book | Original Jazz Classics | OJCCD 896-2(PR 7386)
Heavy!!! | Original Jazz Classics | OJCCD 981-2(P 7499)
Booker Ervin Sextet
Heavy!!! | Original Jazz Classics | OJCCD 981-2(P 7499)
Booker Ervin-Dexter Gordon Quintet
Dexter Gordon Birthday Celebration | Fantasy | FANCD 6082-2
Booker Little Quintet
Eric Dolphy Birthday Celebration | Fantasy | FANCD 6085-2
Charles Mingus And His Orchestra
The Complete Town Hall Concert | Blue Note | 828353-2
Charles Mingus Orchestra
Mingus Mingus Mingus | Impulse(MCA) | 951170-2
The Black Saint And The Sinner Lady | Impulse(MCA) | 951174-2
Charles Mingus Sextet
Eric Dolphy Birthday Celebration | Fantasy | FANCD 6085-2
Town Hall Concert 1964, Vol.1 | Original Jazz Classics | OJCCD 042-2
Eric Dolphy Quartet
Eric Dolphy Birthday Celebration | Fantasy | FANCD 6085-2
Eric Dolphy Quintet
Eric Dolphy:The Complete Prestige Recordings | Prestige | 9 PRCD-4418-2
Eric Dolphy Birthday Celebration | Fantasy | FANCD 6085-2
Far Cry | Original Jazz Classics | OJC20 400-2
Eric Dolphy-Booker Little Quintet
Eric Dolphy:The Complete Prestige Recordings | Prestige | 9 PRCD-4418-2
Jaki Byard
Blues For Smoke | Candid | CCD 79018
Jaki Byard:Solo/Strings | Prestige | PCD 24246-2
Jaki Byard Quartet
The Last From Lennie's | Prestige | PRCD 11029-2
Jaki Byard Sextet
Jaki Byard:Solo/Strings | Prestige | PCD 24246-2
Jaki Byard Trio
Sunshine Of My Soul | Original Jazz Classics | OJCCD 1946-2(PR 7550)
Maynard Ferguson Orchestra With Chris Connor
Two's Company | Roulette | 837201-2
Ricky Ford Quartet
Manhattan Blues | Candid | CCD 79036
Ebony Rhapsody | Candid | CCD 79053
Roland Kirk Quartet
Talkin' Verve-Roots Of Acid Jazz:Roland Kirk | Verve | 533101-2
Rahsaan/The Complete Mercury Recordings Of Roland Kirk | Mercury | 846630-2
Sam Rivers Quartet
A Blue Conception | Blue Note | 534254-2
Fuchsia Swing Song | Blue Note | 593874-2

Byas,Don | (ts)

Bill Coleman And His Orchestra
Don Byas:Laura | Dreyfus Jazz Line | FDM 36714-2
Bill Coleman Quintet
Americans Swinging In Paris:Don Byas | EMI Records | 539655-2
Charlie Christian All Stars
Charlie Christian-Jazz Immortal/Dizzy Gillespie 1944 | Original Jazz Classics | OJCCD 1932-2(ES 548)
Coleman Hawkins And His Orchestra
Jazz:The Essential Collection Vol.3 | IN+OUT Records | 78013-2
Count Basie And His Orchestra
Jazz Collection:Count Basie | Laserlight | 24368
Jazz:The Essential Collection Vol.3 | IN+OUT Records | 78013-2
Dizzy Gillespie All Stars
Dizzy Gillespie:Night In Tunisia | Dreyfus Jazz Line | FDM 36734-2
Dizzy Gillespie And His Orchestra
Planet Jazz:Dizzy Gillespie | Planet Jazz | 2152069-2
Planet Jazz Sampler | Planet Jazz | 2152326-2
Planet Jazz:Jazz Greatest Hits | Planet Jazz | 2169648-2
Planet Jazz:Bebop | RCA | 2169650-2
Dizzy Gillespie:Night In Tunisia | Dreyfus Jazz Line | FDM 36734-2
Don Byas All Star Quintet
Don Byas:Laura | Dreyfus Jazz Line | FDM 36714-2
Don Byas All Stars
Don Byas:Laura | Dreyfus Jazz Line | FDM 36714-2
Don Byas And His Orchestra
Americans Swinging In Paris:Don Byas | EMI Records | 539655-2
Don Byas:Laura | Dreyfus Jazz Line | FDM 36714-2
Don Byas Quartet
Jazz In Paris:Don Byas-Laura | EmArCy | 013027-2
Planet Jazz:Jazz Saxophone | Planet Jazz | 2169653-2
The Art Of Saxophone | Laserlight | 24652
Americans Swinging In Paris:Don Byas | EMI Records | 539655-2
Don Byas:Laura | Dreyfus Jazz Line | FDM 36714-2
Don Byas Quintet
Jazz In Paris:Don Byas-Laura | EmArCy | 013027-2
Don Byas Ree-Boppers
Don Byas:Laura | Dreyfus Jazz Line | FDM 36714-2
Don Byas/Slam Stewart
Don Byas:Laura | Dreyfus Jazz Line | FDM 36714-2
Don Byas-Bud Powell Quartet
A Tribute To Cannonball | CBS | CK 65186
Don Byas-Bud Powell Quintet
A Tribute To Cannonball | CBS | CK 65186
Esquire All-American Award Winners
Best Of The Complete RCA Victor Recordings | RCA | 2663636-2
Highlights From The Duke Ellington Centennial Edition | RCA | 2663672-2
Hot Lips Page And His Orchestra
Don Byas:Laura | Dreyfus Jazz Line | FDM 36714-2
JATP All Stars
Stan Getz Highlights:The Best Of The Verve Years Vol.2 | Verve | 517330-2
Johnny Hodges Orchestra
Coleman Hawkins/Johnny Hodges:The Vogue Recordings | Vogue | 21559712
Leonard Feather's Esquire All-Americans
Louis Armstrong:C'est Si Bon | Dreyfus Jazz Line | FDM 36730-2
Minton's Playhouse All Stars
Charlie Christian:Swing To Bop | Dreyfus Jazz Line | FDM 36715-2
Peanuts Holland And His Orchestra
Americans Swinging In Paris:Don Byas | EMI Records | 539655-2
Tyree Glenn
Don Byas:Laura | Dreyfus Jazz Line | FDM 36714-2
Tyree Glenn And His Orchestra
Americans Swinging In Paris:Don Byas | EMI Records | 539655-2
V-Disc All Star Jam Session
Louis Armstrong-Jack Teagarden-Woody Herman:Midnights At V-Disc | Jazz Unlimited | JUCD 2048
Woody Herman And The Vanderbilt All Stars
Louis Armstrong-Jack Teagarden-Woody Herman:Midnights At V-Disc | Jazz Unlimited | JUCD 2048

Byas,Don prob. | (ts)

Charlie Christian All Stars
Charlie Christian-Jazz Immortal/Dizzy Gillespie 1944 | Original Jazz Classics | OJCCD 1932-2(ES 548)

Byers,Billy | (arr,ld,supervisiontb)

Anita O'Day With The Gary McFarland Orchestra
All The Sad Youn Men | Verve | 517065-2
Billy Eckstine With Bobby Tucker And His Orchestra
The Antonio Carlos Jobim Songbook | Verve | 525472-2
Billy Eckstine Now Singing In 12 Great Movies | Verve | 589307-2
Coleman Hawkins With Billy Byers And His Orchestra
Planet Jazz:Coleman Hawkins | Planet Jazz | 2152055-2
The Hawk In Hi-Fi | RCA | 2663842-2
Dizzy Gillespie Quintet
Talking Verve:Dizzy Gillespie | Verve | 533846-2
Elliot Lawrence And His Orchestra
The Elliot Lawrence Big Band Swings Cohn & Kahn | Fantasy | FCD 24761-2
Jack McDuff Quartet With Orchestra
Prelude:Jack McDuff Big Band | Prestige | PRCD 24283-2
Jimmy Rushing And His Orchestra
Five Feet Of Soul | Roulette | 581830-2
Jimmy Smith With The Billy Byers Orchestra
Jimmy Smith:Best Of The Verve Years | Verve | 527950-2
Jimmy Smith With The Claus Ogerman Orchestra
Any Number Can Win | Verve | 557447-2
Jimmy Smith With The Lalo Schifrin Orchestra
Jimmy Smith-Talkin' Verve | Verve | 531563-2
Jimmy Smith With The Oliver Nelson Orchestra
Jimmy Smith:Best Of The Verve Years | Verve | 527950-2
Jimmy Smith-Talkin' Verve | Verve | 531563-2
Johnny Hartman And His Orchestra
Unforgettable | Impulse(MCA) | IMP 11522
Kenny Clarke 8
Americans Swinging In Paris:Kenny Clarke | EMI Records | 539652-2
Kenny Clarke Quartet
Jazz In Paris:Kenny Clarke Sextet Plays André Hodair | EmArCy | 834542-2 PMS
Kenny Clarke Quintet
Jazz In Paris:Kenny Clarke Sextet Plays André Hodair | EmArCy | 834542-2 PMS
Kenny Clarke Sextet
Jazz In Paris:Kenny Clarke Sextet Plays André Hodair | EmArCy | 834542-2 PMS
Lena Horne With The Lennie Hayton Orchestra
Planet Jazz:Lena Horne | Planet Jazz | 2165373-2
Quincy Jones And His Orchestra
Talkin' Verve-Roots Of Acid Jazz:Roland Kirk | Verve | 533101-2
Verve Jazz Masters Vol.59:Toots Thielemans | Verve | 535271-2
Rahsaan/The Complete Mercury Recordings Of Roland Kirk | Mercury | 846630-2
The Quintessence | Impulse(MCA) | 951222-2
The Roots Of Acid Jazz | Impulse(MCA) | IMP 12042
Quincy Jones Big Band
Rahsaan/The Complete Mercury Recordings Of Roland Kirk | Mercury | 846630-2
Sarah Vaughan With Band
Linger Awhile | Pablo | 2312144-2
Sarah Vaughan With Orchestra
!Viva! Vaughan | Mercury | 549374-2
Sarah Vaughan Sings The Mancini Songbook | Verve | 558401-2
Sarah Vaughan Birthday Celebration | Fantasy | FANCD 6090-2
Sarah Vaughan With Small Group & Orchestra
Duke Ellington Song Book One | Pablo | CD 2312111
Sarah Vaughan With The Frank Foster Orchestra
The Antonio Carlos Jobim Songbook | Verve | 525472-2
Sonny Rollins Orchestra
Sonny Rollins And The Big Brass | Verve | 557545-2
Woody Herman And His Orchestra
The Legends Of Swing | Laserlight | 24659

Byers,Bryant | (b-tb)

Buddy Childers Big Band
It's What Happening Now! | Candid | CCD 79749

Byrd,Charlie | (g,arr,el-g,el-q,vocg-solo)

Charlie Byrd
Latin Byrd | Milestone | MCD 47005-2
Solo Flight | Original Jazz Classics | OJCCD 1093-2(RS 9498)
Charlie Byrd Group
Byrd In The Wind | Original Jazz Classics | OJCCD 1086(RS 9449)
Charlie Byrd Orchestra
Latin Byrd | Milestone | MCD 47005-2
Charlie Byrd Quartet
Latin Byrd | Milestone | MCD 47005-2
Blues Sonata | Original Jazz Classics | OJC20 1063(RS 9453)
Byrd's Word! | Original Jazz Classics | OJCCD 1054-2(R 9448)
Charlie Byrd Quintet
Latin Byrd | Milestone | MCD 47005-2
Charlie Byrd Septet
Latin Byrd | Milestone | MCD 47005-2
Charlie Byrd Sextet
Byrd's Word! | Original Jazz Classics | OJCCD 1054 2(R 9448)
Charlie Byrd Trio
Blues Sonata | Original Jazz Classics | OJC20 1063(RS 9453)
Byrd At The Gate | Original Jazz Classics | OJC20 262-2
Byrd's Word! | Original Jazz Classics | OJCCD 1054-2(R 9448)
At The Village Vanguard | Original Jazz Classics | OJCCD 669-2(RLP 9452)
Mr. Guitar Charlie Byrd | Original Jazz Classics | OJCCD 998-2(R 9450)
Charlie Byrd Trio And Guests
Byrd At The Gate | Original Jazz Classics | OJC20 262-2
Charlie Byrd Trio With Voices
Byrd Song | Original Jazz Classics | OJCCD 1092-2(RS 9481)
Charlie Byrd-Ginny Byrd
Byrd's Word! | Original Jazz Classics | OJCCD 1054-2(R 9448)
Charlie Byrd-Keter Betts
Byrd's Word! | Original Jazz Classics | OJCCD 1054-2(R 9448)
Stan Getz Sextet
Verve Jazz Masters 8:Stan Getz | Verve | 519823-2
Stan Getz-Charlie Byrd Sextet
Jazz Samba | Verve | 521413-2
The Antonio Carlos Jobim Songbook | Verve | 525472-2
Verve Jazz Masters 53:Stan Getz-Bossa Nova | Verve | 529904-2
Ultimate Stan Getz selected by Joe Henderson | Verve | 557532-2
Stan Getz Highlights | Verve | 847430-2

Byrd,Donald | (fl-h,co,p,tp,arr,el-tpvoc)

Ahmad Jamal Quintet
Big Byrd | Dreyfus Jazz Line | FDM 37008-2
Al Grey And His Allstars
Snap Your Fingers | Verve | 9860307
Art Blakey And The Jazz Messengers
The Jazz Messengers | CBS | CK 65265
Bill Henderson With The Horace Silver Quintet
Horace Silver Retrospective | Blue Note | 495576-2
Cal Tjader's Orchestra
Talkin Verve/Roots Of Acid Jazz:Cal Tjader | Verve | 531562-2
Dexter Gordon Quintet
Dexter Gordon:Ballads | Blue Note | 796579-2
Donald Brown Quintet
Donald Byrd & Doug Watkins:The Tradition Sessions | Blue Note | 540528-2
Donald Byrd & His Orchestra
Blue Breaks Beats Vol.2 | Blue Note | 789907-2
Donald Byrd Orchestra
Black Byrd | Blue Note | 784466-2
Blue Break Beats | Blue Note | 799106-2
Places And Spaces | Blue Note | 854326-2
Ethiopian Knights | Blue Note | 854328-2
Donald Byrd Orchestra With Voices
True Blue | Blue Note | 534032-2
The Best Of Blue Note | Blue Note | 796110-2
Donald Byrd Quartet
Donald Byrd & Doug Watkins:The Tradition Sessions | Blue Note | 540528-2
Donald Byrd Quintet
Herbie Hancock:The Complete Blue Note Sixties Sessions | Blue Note | 495569-2
Slow Drag | Blue Note | 535560-2
Free Form | Blue Note | 595961-2
Blue N' Groovy | Blue Note | 780679-2
Blue Bossa | Blue Note | 795590-2
Byrd In Paris Vol.1 | Polydor | 833394-2
Donald Byrd Septet + Voices
A New Perspective | Blue Note | 499006-2
Donald Byrd Sextet
Donald Byrd & Doug Watkins:The Tradition Sessions | Blue Note | 540528-2
Byrd In Hand | Blue Note | 542305-2
Blue Breaks Beats Vol.2 | Blue Note | 789907-2
Blue Break Beats | Blue Note | 799106-2
Blackjack | Blue Note | 821286-2
Doug Watkins Sextet
Donald Byrd & Doug Watkins:The Tradition Sessions | Blue Note | 540528-2
Duke Pearson Sextet
Deep Blue-The United States Of Mind | Blue Note | 521152-2
Elmo Hope Sextet
John Coltrane-The Prestige Recordings | Prestige | 16 PCD 4405-2
Gene Ammons And His All Stars

Jammin' With Gene | Original Jazz Classics | OJCCD 211-2(P 7060)
Gigi Gryce-Donald Byrd Jazz Laboratory
At Newport | Verve | 589764-2
Hank Mobley Quintet
The Art Of Saxophone | Laserlight | 24652
No Room For Squares | Blue Note | 524539-2
Herbie Hancock Quintet
Herbie Hancock:The Complete Blue Note Sixties Sessions | Blue Note | 495569-2
Herbie Hancock Septet
Herbie Hancock:The Complete Blue Note Sixties Sessions | Blue Note | 495569-2
My Point Of View | Blue Note | 521226-2
Cantaloupe Island | Blue Note | 829331-2
Herbie Hancock Sextet
Herbie Hancock:The Complete Blue Note Sixties Sessions | Blue Note | 495569-2
Horace Silver Quintet
Horace Silver Retrospective | Blue Note | 495576-2
Blue Velvet: Crooners, Swooners And Velvet Vocals | Blue Note | 521153-2
Six Pieces Of Silver | Blue Note | 525648-2
The Best Of Blue Note Vol.2 | Blue Note | 797960-2
Horace Silver Sextet
The Story Of Jazz Piano | Laserlight | 24653
Jackie McLean Quintet
Herbie Hancock:The Complete Blue Note Sixties Sessions | Blue Note | 495569-2
Vertigo | Blue Note | 522669-2
4, 5 And 6 | Original Jazz Classics | OJC 056(P 7048)
Jackie McLean Sextet
4, 5 And 6 | Original Jazz Classics | OJC 056(P 7048)
John Coltrane Quintet
John Coltrane-The Prestige Recordings | Prestige | 16 PCD 4405-2
Black Pearls | Original Jazz Classics | OJC 352(P 7316)
The Last Trane | Original Jazz Classics | OJC 394(P 7378)
Lush Life | Original Jazz Classics | OJC20 131-2
The Believer | Original Jazz Classics | OJCCD 876-2(P 7292)
The Jazz Giants Play Harold Arlen:Blues In The Night | Prestige | PCD 24201-2
Lou Bennett Trio With The Paris Jazz All Stars
Jazz In Paris | EmArCy | 548790-2
NDR-Workshop
Doldinger's Best | ACT | 9224-2
Paul Chambers Sextet
Trane's Blues | Blue Note | 498240-2
Pepper Adams Quintet
10 To 4 At The 5-Spot | Original Jazz Classics | OJCCD 031-2(RLP 265)
Prestige All Stars
All Day Long | Original Jazz Classics | OJC20 456-2(P 7081)
Red Garland Quintet
John Coltrane-The Prestige Recordings | Prestige | 16 PCD 4405-2
All Mornin' Long | Original Jazz Classics | OJC20 293-2(P-7130)
Dig It | Original Jazz Classics | OJC20 392-2(PR 7229)
Soul Junction | Original Jazz Classics | OJCCD 481-2
The Jazz Giants Play Duke Ellington:Caravan | Prestige | PCD 24227-2
Red Garland Quintet feat.John Coltrane
High Pressure | Original Jazz Classics | OJCCD 349-2(P 7209)
Sonny Clark Quintet
My Conception | Blue Note | 522674-2
Sonny Clark Sextet
Trane's Blues | Blue Note | 498240-2
Sonny Rollins Quintet
Ballads | Blue Note | 537562-2
Sonny Rollins:Vol.1 | Blue Note | 591724-2
The Blue Note Years-The Best Of Sonny Rollins | Blue Note | 793203-2
The Best Of Blue Note Vol.2 | Blue Note | 797960-2
Sonny Rollins:The Blue Note Recordings | Blue Note | 821371-2
Jazz Profile:Sonny Rollins | Blue Note | 823516-2
Sonny Rollins Sextet
Don't Stop The Carnival | Milestone | MCD 55005-2
Thelonious Monk And His Orchestra
Thelonious Monk:85th Birthday Celebration | zyx records | FANCD 6076-2
At Town Hall | Original Jazz Classics | OJCCD 135-2
Walter Davis Quintet
Davis Cup | Blue Note | 0675597
Wes Montgomery With The Oliver Nelson Orchestra
Verve Jazz Masters 14:Wes Montgomery | Verve | 519826-2
Wes Montgomery:The Verve Jazz Sides | Verve | 521690-2
Talkin' Jazz:Roots Of Acid Jazz | Verve | 529580-2
Yusef Lateef Sextet
The Art Of Saxophone | Laserlight | 24652
Byrd,Eddie | (dr)
Louis Jordan And His Tympany Five
Louis Jordan-Let The Good Times Roll: The Complete Decca Recordings 1938-1954 | Bear Family Records | BCD 15557 IH
Byrd,Freddie | (tp)
John Coltrane Quintet
The Jazz Giants Play Rodgers & Hammerstein:My Favorite Things | Prestige | PCD 24223-2
Byrd,Gene | (bg)
Charlie Byrd Orchestra
Latin Byrd | Milestone | MCD 47005-2
Charlie Byrd Quartet
Latin Byrd | Milestone | MCD 47005-2
Charlie Byrd Quintet
Latin Byrd | Milestone | MCD 47005-2
Charlie Byrd Septet
Latin Byrd | Milestone | MCD 47005-2
Stan Getz Sextet
Verve Jazz Masters 8:Stan Getz | Verve | 519823-2
Stan Getz-Charlie Byrd Sextet
Jazz Samba | Verve | 521413-2
The Antonio Carlos Jobim Songbook | Verve | 525472-2
Verve Jazz Masters 53:Stan Getz-Bossa Nova | Verve | 529904-2
Ultimate Stan Getz selected by Joe Henderson | Verve | 557532-2
Stan Getz Highlights | Verve | 847430-2
Byrd,Ginny | (voc)
Charlie Byrd Group
Byrd In The Wind | Original Jazz Classics | OJCCD 1086(RS 9449)
Charlie Byrd-Ginny Byrd
Byrd's Word! | Original Jazz Classics | OJCCD 1054-2(R 9448)
Byrd,Jerry | (g)
Freddy Cole With Band
A Circle Of Love | Fantasy | FCD 9674-2
Byrne,Billy | (tpfl-h)
Woody Herman And His Orchestra
Verve Jazz Masters 54:Woody Herman | Verve | 529903-2
Jazzin' Vol.2: The Music Of Stevie Wonder | Fantasy | FANCD 6088-2
Brand New | Original Jazz Classics | OJCCD 1044-2(F 8414)
King Cobra | Original Jazz Classics | OJCCD 1068-2(F 9499)
The Raven Speaks | Original Jazz Classics | OJCCD 663-2(F 9416)
Woody Herman Herd At Montreux | Original Jazz Classics | OJCCD 991-2(F 9470)
Woody Herman And The New Thundering Herd
Planet Jazz:Big Bands | Planet Jazz | 2169649-2
Woody Herman:Thundering Herd | Original Jazz Classics | OJCCD 841-2
Woody Herman's Thundering Herd
Planet Jazz:Jazz Saxophone | Planet Jazz | 2169653-2
Byrne,Bobby | (tbv-tb)
Cannonball Adderley And His Orchestra
Verve Jazz Masters 31:Cannonball Adderley | Verve | 522651-2
Della Reese With The Sy Oliver Orchestra
Misty Blue:Sweet Sisters Swing Songs Of Sorrow And Sadness | Blue Note | 521151-2
Ella Fitzgerald With Sy Oliver And His Orchestra
Ella Fitzgerald:The Decca Years 1949-1954 | Decca | 050668-2
Lena Horne With The Lennie Hayton Orchestra
Planet Jazz:Lena Horne | Planet Jazz | 2165373-2
Louis Armstrong With Jimmy Dorsey And His Orchestra
Louis Armstrong:Swing That Music | Laserlight | 36056
Swing Legends:Louis Armstrong | Nimbus Records | NI 2012
Byrne,Ed | (tb)
Chet Baker-Gerry Mulligan Group
Carnegie Hall Concert Vol. 1/2 | CTI | EPC 450554-2
Byron,Don | (b-cl,soprano-cl,bs,cl,saxcl-solo)
Cassandra Wilson Group
Blue Light 'Til Dawn | Blue Note | 781357-2
Craig Harris And Tailgater's Tales
Shelter | JMT Edition | 919008-2
Blackout In The Square Root Of Soul | JMT Edition | 919015-2
Don Byron
Tuskegee Experiments | Nonesuch | 7559-79280-2
Don Byron Quartet
Romance With The Unseen | Blue Note | 499545-2
Tuskegee Experiments | Nonesuch | 7559-79280-2
Don Byron Quintet
Tuskegee Experiments | Nonesuch | 7559-79280-2
Don Byron-Joe Berkovitz
Tuskegee Experiments | Nonesuch | 7559-79280-2
Don Byron-Reggie Workman
Tuskegee Experiments | Nonesuch | 7559-79280-2
The Sidewalks Of New York
Tin Pan Alley:The Sidewalks Of New York | Winter&Winter | 910038-2
Uri Caine Group
Urlicht/Primal Light | Winter&Winter | 910004-2
Byrt,Andrew | (viola)
Carla Bley Band
Fancy Chamber Music | Watt | 28(539937-2)
Cabell,Marvin | (fl,saxello,tsss)
John Patton Quartet
The Lost Grooves | Blue Note | 831883-2
Accent On The Blues | Blue Note | 853924-2
Cabera,Yosvany Terry | (ts)
Steve Coleman And The Council Of Balance
Genesis & The Opening Of The Way | RCA | 2152934-2
Cables,George | (el-p,clavinet,pp-solo)
Art Pepper Quartet
Art Pepper:The Complete Galaxy Recordings | Galaxy | 16GCD 1016-2
Art Pepper:The Complete Village Vanguard Sessions | Contemporary | 9CCD-4417-2
San Francisco Samba | Contemporary | CCD 14086-2
No Limit | Original Jazz Classics | OJCCD 411-2
Arthur's Blues | Original Jazz Classics | OJCCD 680-2
Thursday Night At The Village Vanguard | Original Jazz Classics | OJCCD 694-2(7642)
Friday Night At The Village Vanguard | Original Jazz Classics | OJCCD 695-2(C 7643)
Saturday Night At The Village Vanguard | Original Jazz Classics | OJCCD 696-2(C 7644)
Roadgame | Original Jazz Classics | OJCCD 774-2(GXY 5142)
The Jazz Giants Play Harold Arlen:Blues In The Night | Prestige | PCD 24201-2
Art Pepper-George Cables Duo
Art Pepper:The Complete Galaxy Recordings | Galaxy | 16GCD 1016-2
Jazzin' Vol.2: The Music Of Stevie Wonder | Fantasy | FANCD 6088-2
Tete-A-Tete | Original Jazz Classics | OJCCD 843-2(GXY 5147)
Bennie Wallace Quartet
Bennie Wallace In Berlin | Enja | ENJ-9425 2
David Fathead Newman Septet
Jazzin' Vol.2: The Music Of Stevie Wonder | Fantasy | FANCD 6088-2
Dexter Gordon Quartet
Dexter Gordon:Ballads | Blue Note | 796579-2
Dexter Gordon Birthday Celebration | Fantasy | FANCD 6082-2
Freddie Hubbard Quintet
This Is Jazz:Freddie Hubbard | CBS | CK 65041
George Cables
By George | Original Jazz Classics | OJCCD 1056-2(C 14030)
George Cables Trio
By George | Original Jazz Classics | OJCCD 1056-2(C 14030)
Joe Henderson And His Orchestra
Joe Henderson:The Milestone Years | Milestone | 8MCD 4413-2
Joe Henderson Quartet
Joe Henderson:The Milestone Years | Milestone | 8MCD 4413-2
Joe Henderson Quintet
Joe Henderson:The Milestone Years | Milestone | 8MCD 4413-2
Joe Henderson Sextet
Joe Henderson:The Milestone Years | Milestone | 8MCD 4413-2
John Stubblefield Quartet
Morning Song | Enja | ENJ-8036 2
Max Roach Chorus & Orchestra
To The Max! | Enja | ENJ-7021 22
Max Roach Sextet With The J.C.White Singers
Lift Every Voice And Sing | Atlantic | 7567-80798-2
Sonny Rollins Quartet
Next Album | Original Jazz Classics | OJC 312 (M 9042)
Sonny Rollins Quintet
Next Album | Original Jazz Classics | OJC 312 (M 9042)
Cabral,Artie | (dr)
Greg Abate Quintet
Dr. Jeckyll & Mr. Hyde | Candid | CCD 79715
Cabrera,Arturo Martinez | (vocperc)
Conjunto Clave Y Guaguanco
Dejala En La Puntica | TipToe | TIP-888829 2
Cabrera,Felipe | (b,bassoonel-b)
Gonzalo Rubalcaba & Cuban Quartet
Antiguo | Blue Note | 837717-2
Gonzalo Rubalcaba Quartet
Imagine | Blue Note | 830491-2
Cabrera,Julian | (perc)
Mongo Santamaria And His Band
Mongo At The Village Gate | Original Jazz Classics | OJCCD 490-2(RLP 9529)
Cabuto,Marcus | (tp)
Sabroso | Original Jazz Classics | OJCCD 281-2
Caceres,Ernie | (as,bs,bass-s,cl,sax,tsvoc)
Benny Goodman And His Orchestra
The Legends Of Swing | Laserlight | 24659
Benny Goodman And His V-Disc All Star Band
The Legends Of Swing | Laserlight | 24659
Eddie Condon And His Orchestra
Jazz:The Essential Collection Vol.3 | IN+OUT Records | 78013-2
George Wein's Dixie Victors
The Magic Horn | RCA | 2113038-2
Planet Jazz | Planet Jazz | 2169652-2
Glenn Miller And His Orchestra
Planet Jazz:Glenn Miller | Planet Jazz | 2152056-2
Planet Jazz:Jazz Greatest Hits | Planet Jazz | 2169648-2
Planet Jazz:Big Bands | Planet Jazz | 2169649-2
The Chesterfield Broadcasts Vol.1 | RCA | 2663113-2
Candelight Miller | RCA | 2668716-2
Swing Legends | Nimbus Records | NI 2001
Jack Teagarden And His Orchestra
Jazz:The Essential Collection Vol.3 | IN+OUT Records | 78013-2
Jimmy McPartland And His Dixielanders
Planet Jazz | Planet Jazz | 2169652-2
Louis Armstrong And His All Stars
Planet Jazz:Louis Armstrong | Planet Jazz | 2152052-2
Planet Jazz:Jack Teagarden | Planet Jazz | 2161236-2
Planet Jazz:Male Jazz Vocalists | Planet Jazz | 2169657-2
Best Of The Complete RCA Victor Recordings | RCA | 2663636-2
Louis Armstrong:A 100th Birthday Celebration | RCA | 2663694-2
Louis Armstrong:Wintergarden 1947/Blue Note 1948 | Storyville | STCD 8242
Louis Armstrong And His Orchestra
Louis Armstrong:C'est Si Bon | Dreyfus Jazz Line | FDM 36730-2
Swing Legends:Louis Armstrong | Nimbus Records | NI 2012
Muggsy Spanier And His Dixieland Band
Muggsy Spanier-Manhattan Masters,1945 | Storyville | STCD 6051
Sidney Bechet And His Orchestra
Sidney Bechet:Summertime | Dreyfus Jazz Line | FDM 36712-2
The Andrew Sisters With The Glenn Miller Orchestra
The Chesterfield Broadcasts Vol.1 | RCA | 2663113-2
The Metronome All Stars
Planet Jazz:Dizzy Gillespie | Planet Jazz | 2152069-2
V-Disc All Star Jam Session
Louis Armstrong-Jack Teagarden-Woody Herman:Midnights At V-Disc | Jazz Unlimited | JUCD 2048
V-Disc All Stars
Jazz:The Essential Collection Vol.3 | IN+OUT Records | 78013-2
Cadavieco,Juan | (perc)
Sarah Vaughan With Orchestra
!Viva! Vaughan | Mercury | 549374-2
Sarah Vaughan With The Frank Foster Orchestra
The Antonio Carlos Jobim Songbook | Verve | 525472-2
Cadavre Exquis |
Cadavre Exquis
Cadavre Exquis | Creative Works Records | CW CD 1014-1
Cadé,Thierry | (v)
Charlie Haden Quartet West With Strings
Now Is The Hour | Verve | 527827-2
Cadell,Eddie | (ts)
Buster Smith Orchestra
Atlantic Jazz: Kansas City | Atlantic | 7567-81701-2
Cadena,Joe | (tbtp)
Terry Gibbs Dream Band
Terry Gibbs Dream Band Vol.3:Flying Home | Contemporary | CCD 7654-2
Terry Gibbs Dream Band Vol.6:One More Time | Contemporary | CCD 7658-2
Cafe Du Sport Jazzquartett |
Cafe Du Sport Jazzquartett
Cafe Du Sport Jazzquartett | Minor Music | 801096
Café[Edson Café Adasilva] | (percshaker)
Peter Fessler Group
Eastside Moments | Minor Music | 801078
Tom Harrell Group
Paradise | RCA | 2663738-2
Caffey,Bill | (voc)
Count Basie And His Orchestra
Fun Time | Pablo | 2310945-2
Cagnolatti,Ernie | (tpvoc)
Jim Robinson's New Orleans Band
Atlantic Jazz: New Orleans | Atlantic | 7567-81700-2
Cagwin,Jarrod | (dr)
Charlie Mariano Quartet
Deep In A Dream | Enja | ENJ-9423 2
Dusko Goykovich Quartet
In My Dreams | Enja | ENJ-9408 2
Samba Do Mar | Enja | ENJ-9473 2
Rabih Abou-Khalil Group
The Cactus Of Knowledge | Enja | ENJ-9401 2
Stefanie Schlesiger And Her Group plus String Quartet
What Love Is | Enja | ENJ-9434 2
Stefanie Schlesinger And Her Group
What Love Is | Enja | ENJ-9434 2
Cahill,Seamus | (bouzouki,gvoc)
ULG
Spring | Laika Records | 35101382
Cahn,Max | (v)
Billie Holiday With The Ray Ellis Orchestra
Lady In Satin | CBS | CK 65144
Coleman Hawkins With Billy Byers And His Orchestra
The Hawk In Hi-Fi | RCA | 2663842-2
Phil Woods Quartet With Orchestra & Strings
Round Trip | Verve | 559804-2
Caiati,Fernando | (spoken lyrics in Italian)
Helen Merrill With The Piero Umilliani Group
Parole E Musica | RCA | 2174798-2
Caiazza,Nick | (saxts)
Muggsy Spanier And His Ragtime Band
Planet Jazz | Planet Jazz | 2169652-2
Planet Jazz:Jazz Trumpet | Planet Jazz | 2169654-2
V-Disc All Star Jam Session
Louis Armstrong-Jack Teagarden-Woody Herman:Midnights At V-Disc | Jazz Unlimited | JUCD 2048
V-Disc All Stars
Jazz:The Essential Collection Vol.3 | IN+OUT Records | 78013-2
Caillat,Bruno | (tablas,dafkanjeera)
Renaud Garcia-Fons
Navigatore | Enja | ENJ-9418 2
Renaud Garcia-Fons Group
Navigatore | Enja | ENJ-9418 2
Entremundo | Enja | ENJ-9464 2
Caillat,Philippe | (el-gg)
Philippe Caillat Group
Stream Of Time | Laika Records | LK 92-030
Philippe Caillat Special Project
Melodic Travel | Laika Records | LK 689-012
Cain,Jackie | (voc)
Jackie Cain/Roy Kral Quartet
Full Circle | Fantasy | FCD 24768-2
Jackie Cain-Roy Kral Group
Full Circle | Fantasy | FCD 24768-2
Cain,Michael 'Mike' | (keyboards,p,synthgrand-p)
Jack DeJohnette Quartet
Oneness | ECM | 1637(537343-2)
Jack DeJohnette Trio
Dancing With Nature Spirits | ECM | 1558(531024-2)
Marty Ehrlich Quintet
New York Child | Enja | ENJ-9025 2
Michael Cain-Ralph Alessi-Peter Epstein
Circa | ECM | 1622
Caine,Eddie | (alto-fl,as,cl,fl,piccolo,reeds,sax)
Charles Mingus And His Orchestra
Charles Mingus-The Complete Debut Recordings | Debut | 12 DCD 4402-2
Gerry Mulligan Concert Jazz Band
Verve Jazz Masters 36:Gerry Mulligan | Verve | 523342-2
Verve Jazz Masters Vol.60:The Collection | Verve | 529866-2
The Complete Verve Gerry Mulligan Concert Band | Verve | 9860613
Gil Evans Orchestra
Out Of The Cool | Impulse(MCA) | 951186-2
Lena Horne With The Lennie Hayton Orchestra
Planet Jazz:Lena Horne | Planet Jazz | 2165373-2
Miles Davis + 19
Miles Ahead | CBS | CK 65121
Miles Davis With Gil Evans & His Orchestra
Miles Davis At Carnegie Hall | CBS | CK 65027
This Is Jazz:Miles Davis Plays Ballads | CBS | CK 65038
Sketches Of Spain | CBS | CK 65142
Quiet Nights | CBS | CK 65293
Stan Getz With The Gary McFarland Orchestra
Stan Getz Highlights:The Best Of The Verve Years Vol.2 | Verve | 517330-2
Verve Jazz Masters 53:Stan Getz-Bossa Nova | Verve | 529904-2
Big Band Bossa Nova | Verve | 825771-2 PMS
Stan Getz Highlights | Verve | 847430-2
Caine,Shulamith Wechter | (narration)
Uri Caine Ensemble
Love Fugue-Robert Schumann | Winter&Winter | 910049-2
Caine,Uri | (el-p,keyboards,p,arr,synth,voice)

Dave Douglas Group
Soul On Soul | RCA | 2663603-2
The Infinite | RCA | 2663918-2
David Binney Group
South | ACT | 9279-2
Balance | ACT | 9411-2
Marty Ehrlich Quartet
Song | Enja | ENJ-9396 2
Marty Ehrlich Quintet
Song | Enja | ENJ-9396 2
The Sidewalks Of New York
Tin Pan Alley:The Sidewalks Of New York | Winter&Winter | 910038-2
Uri Caine
Solitaire | Winter&Winter | 910075-2
Uri Caine Ensemble
Wagner E Venezia | Winter&Winter | 910013-2
Love Fugue-Robert Schumann | Winter&Winter | 910049-2
Uri Caine Group
Urlicht/Primal Light | Winter&Winter | 910004-2
Uri Caine Trio
Blue Wail | Winter&Winter | 910034-2
Bedrock | Winter&Winter | 910068-2
Uri Caine With The Concerto Köln
Concerto Köln | Winter&Winter | 910086-2

Caiola,Al | (g)
Joe Williams With The Frank Hunter Orchestra
Planet Jazz:Joe Williams | Planet Jazz | 2165370-2
Sarah Vaughan The The Joe Lippman Orchestra
Sarah Vaughan:Lover Man | Dreyfus Jazz Line | FDM 36739-2

Caldarell,Bart | (bs,saxts)
Stan Kenton And His Orchestra
Stan Kenton Portraits On Standards | Capitol | 531571-2

Caldera |
Caldera
Jazzrock-Anthology Vol.3:Fusion | Zounds | CD 27100555

Calderal,Bert | (ts)
Nat King Cole Quartet With The Stan Kenton Orchestra
Nat King Cole:For Sentimental Reasons | Dreyfus Jazz Line | FDM 36740-2

Calderazzo,Gene | (dr)
Eugen Apostolidis Quartet
Imaginary Directions | Edition Collage | EC 503-2

Calderazzo,Joey | (p,synthp-solo)
Caecilie Norby With Band
My Corner Of The Sky | Blue Note | 853422-2
Michael Brecker Group
Don't Try This At Home | Impulse(MCA) | 950114-2
Tales From The Hudson | Impulse(MCA) | 951191-2
Now You See It...(Now You Don't) | GRP | GRP 96222
Michael Brecker Quintet
Two Blocks From The Edge | Impulse(MCA) | 951261-2

Calderell,Bart | (tsbassoon)
Stan Kenton And His Orchestra
One Night Stand | Choice | CHCD 71051

Caldwell,Buddy | (congasperc)
Boogaloo Joe Jones Sextet
Jazzin' With The Soul Brothers | Fantasy | FANCD 6086-2
Discovery:Grover Washington Jr.-The First Recordings | Prestige | PCD 11020-2
Charles Earland Sextet
Black Talk! | Original Jazz Classics | OJCCD 335-2(P 7758)
Charlie's Greatest Hits | Prestige | PCD 24250-2
Houston Person Sextet
Jazzin' With The Soul Brothers | Fantasy | FANCD 6086-2
Goodness! | Original Jazz Classics | OJC20 332-2(P 7678)
Idris Muhammad Group
Jazzin' With The Soul Brothers | Fantasy | FANCD 6086-2
Leon Spencer Sextet
Jazzin' With The Soul Brothers | Fantasy | FANCD 6086-2
Discovery:Grover Washington Jr.-The First Recordings | Prestige | PCD 11020-2
Rusty Bryant Quintet
Jazzin' With The Soul Brothers | Fantasy | FANCD 6086-2
Sonny Stitt With Orchestra
Goin' Down Slow | Prestige | PRCD 24276-2

Caldwell,Chris | (bssax)
Mike Westbrook Orchestra
Bar Utopia-A Big Band Cabaret | Enja | ENJ-9333 2
The Orchestra Of Smith's Academy | Enja | ENJ-9358 2
Steve Martland Band
The Orchestra Of Smith's Academy | Enja | ENJ-9358 2

Caldwell,George | (congas,psynth)
Craig Bailey Band
A New Journey | Candid | CCD 79725

Caldwell,Happy | (clts)
Bessie Smith With The James P.Johnson Orchestra And The Hal Johnson Choir
The Blues | Storyville | 4960323
Eddie Condon's Hot Shots
Jazz:The Essential Collection Vol.3 | IN+OUT Records | 78013-2
Eddie's Hot Shots
Planet Jazz:Jack Teagarden | Planet Jazz | 2161236-2
Jelly Roll Morton's New Orleans Jazzmen
Planet Jazz | Planet Jazz | 2169652-2
Planet Jazz:Male Jazz Vocalists | Planet Jazz | 2169657-2
Louis Armstrong And His Orchestra
Jazz:The Essential Collection Vol.3 | IN+OUT Records | 78013-2

Calhoun,Charles 'Jesse Stone' | (voc)
Al Sears And His Orchestra
Sear-iously | Bear Family Records | BCD 15668 AH

Calhoun,Eddie | (b)
Willis Jackson Group
At Large | Prestige | PCD 24243-2

Calhoun,Will | (clay-dr,dr,korg-wave-dr,loops,perc)
Cornelius Claudio Kreusch Group
Scoop | ACT | 9255-2
Dhafer Youssef Group
Electric Sufi | Enja | ENJ-9412 2
Jean-Paul Bourelly Trance Atlantic
Boom Bop II | double moon | CHRDM 71023
Marcus Miller Group
The Sun Don't Lie | Dreyfus Jazz Line | FDM 36560-2

Caliman,Hadley | (fl,b-cl,ssts)
Eddie Henderson Orchestra
Blue Break Beats | Blue Note | 799106-2
Joe Henderson And His Orchestra
Joe Henderson:The Milestone Years | Milestone | 8MCD 4413-2
Joe Henderson Group
Jazzin' Vol.2: The Music Of Stevie Wonder | Fantasy | FANCD 6088-2

Calister,Isaline | (voc)
Pili-Pili
Dance Jazz Live 1995 | JA & RO | JARO 4189-2

Call,Marjorie | (harp)
Miles Davis With Gil Evans & His Orchestra
Quiet Nights | CBS | CK 65293

Calle,Ed | (as,bs,fl,alto-fl,ts,sax,synth,voice)
Arturo Sandoval And The Latin Train Band
Arturo Sandoval & The Latin Train | GRP | GRP 98202
Arturo Sandoval Quintet
I Remember Clifford | GRP | GRP 96682

Callender,Red | (b,tuba,vocbs)
Art Tatum Sextet
Art Tatum-The Complete Pablo Group Masterpieces | Pablo | 6 PACD 4401-2
Art Tatum Trio
Art Tatum-The Complete Pablo Group Masterpieces | Pablo | 6 PACD 4401-2
The Jazz Giants Play Rodgers & Hart:Blue Moon | Prestige | PCD 24205-2
Art Tatum-Ben Webster Quartet
The Art Tatum Group Masterpieces Vol.8 | Pablo | 2405431-2
Art Tatum-The Complete Pablo Group Masterpieces | Pablo | 6 PACD 4401-2
The Tatum Group Masterpieces Vol.8 | Pablo | PACD20 431-2
The Jazz Giants Play Jerome Kern:Yesterdays | Prestige | PCD 24202-2
Art Tatum-Buddy DeFranco Quartet
Art Tatum-The Complete Pablo Group Masterpieces | Pablo | 6 PACD 4401-2
Billie Holiday And Her All Stars
Verve Jazz Masters 12:Billie Holiday | Verve | 519825-2
The Billie Holiday Song Book | Verve | 823246-2
Billy Eckstine With The Billy May Orchestra
Once More With Feeling | Roulette | 581862-2
Billy May And His Orchestra
Billy May's Big Fat Brass/Bill's Bag | Capitol | 535206-2
Cal Tjader With The Clare Fischer Orchestra
Cal Tjader Plays Harold Arlen & West Side Story | Fantasy | FCD 24775-2
Charlie Parker's New Stars
Charlie Parker:Now's The Time | Dreyfus Jazz Line | FDM 36724-2
Dizzy Gillespie And His Orchestra
Talking Verve:Dizzy Gillespie | Verve | 533846-2
Erroll Garner Quartet
Erroll Garner:Trio | Dreyfus Jazz Line | FDM 36719-2
Erroll Garner Trio
Erroll Garner:Trio | Dreyfus Jazz Line | FDM 36719-2
JATP All Stars
The Complete Jazz At The Philharmonic On Verve 1944-1949 | Verve | 523893-2
Jazz At The Philharmonic:Best Of The 1940's Concerts | Verve | 557534-2
Jesse Price And His Blues Band
Jazz Profile:Dexter Gordon | Blue Note | 823514-2
Lester Young And His Band
Jazz:The Essential Collection Vol.3 | IN+OUT Records | 78013-2
Lester Young:The Complete Aladdin Sessions | Blue Note | 832787-2
Lester Young:Blue Lester | Dreyfus Jazz Line | FDM 36729-2
Lester Young-Nat Cole Trio
Lester Young:The Complete Aladdin Sessions | Blue Note | 832787-2
Midnight Blue(The [Be]witching Hour) | Blue Note | 854365-2
Lester Young:Blue Lester | Dreyfus Jazz Line | FDM 36729-2
Louis Armstrong And His Dixieland Seven
Planet Jazz:Louis Armstrong | Planet Jazz | 2152052-2
Planet Jazz:Jazz Greatest Hits | Planet Jazz | 2169648-2
Planet Jazz:Jazz Trumpet | Planet Jazz | 2169654-2
Planet Jazz:Male Jazz Vocalists | Planet Jazz | 2169657-2
Best Of The Complete RCA Victor Recordings | RCA | 2663636-2
Louis Armstrong:A 100th Birthday Celebration | RCA | 2663694-2
Louis Armstrong:C'est Si Bon | Dreyfus Jazz Line | FDM 36730-2
Swing Legends:Louis Armstrong | Nimbus Records | NI 2012
Louis Armstrong And His Hot Seven
Planet Jazz:Louis Armstrong | Planet Jazz | 2152052-2
Best Of The Complete RCA Victor Recordings | RCA | 2663636-2
Louis Armstrong:A 100th Birthday Celebration | RCA | 2663694-2
Louis Armstrong:C'est Si Bon | Dreyfus Jazz Line | FDM 36730-2
Louis Armstrong And His Orchestra
Louis Armstrong:Swing That Music | Laserlight | 36056
Swing Legends:Louis Armstrong | Nimbus Records | NI 2012
Lucky Thompson And His Lucky Seven
Planet Jazz:Bebop | RCA | 2169650-2
Mel Tormé With The Billy May Orchestra
Mel Tormé Goes South Of The Border With Billy May | Verve | 589517-2
Mel Tormé With The Russell Garcia Orchestra
Swingin' On The Moon | Verve | 511385-2
Pete Rugolo And His Orchestra
Thriller/Richard Diamon(Original Jazz Scores From 2 Classics TV Series) | Fresh Sound Records | FSCD 2015
Red Norvo Septet
Jazz Profile:Dexter Gordon | Blue Note | 823514-2
Roland Kirk And His Orchestra
Talkin' Verve-Roots Of Acid Jazz:Roland Kirk | Verve | 533101-2
The Hollywood Hucksters
The Hollywood Session:The Capitol Jazzmen | Jazz Unlimited | JUCD 2044

Callier,Terry | (gvoc)
Terry Callier Duo
The New Folk Sound Of Terry Callier | Prestige | PRCD 11026-2

Calloway,Cab | (ldvoc)
Cab Calloway And His Cab Jivers
Planet Jazz:Cab Calloway | Planet Jazz | 2161237-2
Cab Calloway And His Hi De Ho Orchestra
7.Zelt-Musik-Festival:Jazz Events | Zounds | CD 2730001
Cab Calloway And His Orchestra
Planet Jazz:Cab Calloway | Planet Jazz | 2161237-2
Planet Jazz:Male Jazz Vocalists | Planet Jazz | 2169657-2

Calloway,Joe | (b)
Stan Getz Quartet
Stan Getz-The Complete Roost Sessions | EMI Records | 859622-2
Stan Getz:Imagination | Dreyfus Jazz Line | FDM 36733-2

Calogero,Pablo | (b-cl,bsfl)
Carla Bley Band
The Very Big Carla Bley Band | Watt | 23
Karen Mantler Group
My Cat Arnold | Watt | XtraWatt/3
Karen Mantler And Her Cat Arnold Get The Flu | Watt | XtraWatt/5

Calquin,Mauricio | (bongos,congasperc)
Joe Gallardo's Latino Blue
A Latin Shade Of Blue | Enja | ENJ-9421 2

Calvo,Omar Rodriguez | (bel-b)
Ramon Valle Trio
No Escape | ACT | 9424-2

Calypso Boys,The | (clavesmaracas)
Louis Jordan And His Tympany Five
Louis Jordan-Let The Good Times Roll: The Complete Decca Recordings 1938-1954 | Bear Family Records | BCD 15557 IH

Calzado,Rudi | (percvoc)
Bobby Hutcherson Orchestra
Montara | Blue Note | 590956-2
Mongo Santamaria And His Band
Sabroso | Original Jazz Classics | OJCCD 281-2

Camara,Alpha | (percvoc)
Pili-Pili
Be In Two Minds | JA & RO | JARO 4134-2

Camara,Damoyé Titti | (voc)
Stolen Moments | JA & RO | JARO 4159-2
Jazzy World | JA & RO | JARO 4200-2

Camara,Gilbert | (percvoc)
Be In Two Minds | JA & RO | JARO 4134-2

Camara,Manfrain | (voc)
Nomans Land | JA & RO | JARO 4209-2

Camarata,Toots | (arr,ldtp)
Billie Holiday With Toots Camarata And His Orchestra
Billie's Love Songs | Nimbus Records | NI 2000
Jerri Southern And The Toots Camarata Orchestra
The Very Thought Of You:The Decca Years 1951-1957 | Decca | 050671-2
Louis Armstrong And The Commanders under the Direction of Camarata
Satchmo Serenaders | Verve | 543792-2
Louis Armstrong With Jimmy Dorsey And His Orchestra
Louis Armstrong:Swing That Music | Laserlight | 36056
Swing Legends:Louis Armstrong | Nimbus Records | NI 2012
Louis Armstrong With The Commanders
Ambassador Louis Armstrong Vol.17:Moments To Remember(1952-1956) | Ambassador | CLA 1917

Camel,William | (b)
Lenny White Group
Renderers Of Spirit | Hip Bop | HIBD 8014

Cameron,Jay | (b-cl,bssax)
Anthony Ortega With The Nat Pierce Orchestra
Earth Dance | Fresh Sound Records | FSR-CD 325

Cameron,John | (arrts)
Albert King With The Willie Dixon Band
Windy City Blues | Stax | SCD 8612-2
Ella Fitzgerald With Orchestra
Ella/Things Ain't What They Used To Be | Warner | 9362-47875-2

Camerun,Romy | (voc)
Ed Kröger Quartet
What's New | Laika Records | 35101172
Ed Kröger Quartet plus Guests
Movin' On | Laika Records | 35101332

Camilleri,Charles | (tp)
Buddy Rich Big Band
Backwoods Siseman/Pieces Of Dream | Laserlight | 24655

Camilo,Michel | (p,el-p,synthp-solo)
Katia Labeque-Michel Camilo
Little Girl Blue | Dreyfus Jazz Line | FDM 36186-2
Paquito D'Rivera Orchestra
Jazzrock-Anthology Vol.3:Fusion | Zounds | CD 27100555

Cammack,James | (bb-g)
Ahmad Jamal Quartet
Nature(The Essence Part III) | Atlantic | 3984-23105-2
Ahmad Jamal A L'Olympia | Dreyfus Jazz Line | FDM 36629-2
The Essence Part 1 | Dreyfus Jazz Line | FDM 37007-2
Big Byrd | Dreyfus Jazz Line | FDM 37008-2
Nature | Dreyfus Jazz Line | FDM 37018-2
Ahmad Jamal Quartet With Stanley Turrentine
Nature(The Essence Part III) | Atlantic | 3984-23105-2
Nature | Dreyfus Jazz Line | FDM 37018-2
Ahmad Jamal Trio
Picture Perfect-70th Anniversary | Warner | 8573-85268-2
In Search Of Momentum (1-10) | Dreyfus Jazz Line | FDM 36644-2
Big Byrd | Dreyfus Jazz Line | FDM 37008-2
Live In Paris 1992 | Dreyfus Jazz Line | FDM 37019-2
Ahmad Jamal Trio with Orchestra
Pittsburgh | Atlantic | 7567-8209-2

Cammalleria,Sergio | (perc)
Orchestra Jazz Siciliana
Orchestra Jazz Siciliana Plays The Music Of Carla Bley | Watt | XtraWatt/4

Cammara,Ladzi | (perc)
Yusef Lateef Orchestra
Rhino Presents The Atlantic Jazz Gallery | Atlantic | 8122-71257-2

Camp,Manel | (p)
Manel Camp & Matthew Simon Acustic Jazz Quintet
Rosebud | Fresh Sound Records | FSNT 011 CD

Campagnol,Niclas | (dr)
Martin Schrack Quartet
Headin' Home | Storyville | STCD 4253
Martin Schrack Quintet feat.Tom Harrell
Headin' Home | Storyville | STCD 4253

Campbell,Arthur | (ptuba)
Roger Wolfe Kahn And His Orchestra
Planet Jazz:Jack Teagarden | Planet Jazz | 2161236-2

Campbell,Charles | (congasvoc)
Monty Alexander Quartet
Three Originals:Love And Sunshine/Estade/Cobilimbo | MPS | 523526-2
Monty Alexander Sextet
Three Originals:Love And Sunshine/Estade/Cobilimbo | MPS | 523526-2

Campbell,Jeff | (b)
Rich Perry Quintet
At Eastman | Steeplechase | SCCD 31533

Campbell,Jimmy | (as,drtp)
Birdland Dream Band
Birdland Dream Band | RCA | 2663873-2
Tal Farlow Quartet
Verve Jazz Masters 41:Tal Farlow | Verve | 527365-2

Campbell,Paul | (tp)
Count Basie And His Orchestra
Jazz Gallery:Lester Young Vol.2(1946-59) | RCA | 2119541-2
Verve Jazz Masters 2:Count Basie | Verve | 519819-2
King Of Swing | Verve | 837433-2

Campbell,Royce | (g)
Royce Campbell-Adrian Ingram Group
Hands Across The Water | String Jazz | SJRCD 1002

Campbell,Stacy | (voc)
Al Jarreau With Band
Tenderness | i.e. Music | 557853-2

Campbell,Tommy | (dr)
Chico Freeman And Brainstorm
Sweet Explosion | IN+OUT Records | 7010-2
Jazz Unlimited | IN+OUT Records | 7017-2
Ray Anderson Alligatory Band
Don't Mow Your Lawn | Enja | ENJ-8070 2
Ray Anderson Lapis Lazuli Band
Funkorific | Enja | ENJ-9340 2
Roots
Salutes The Saxophone | IN+OUT Records | 7016-2
Salutes The Saxophones: Tributes To Gene Ammons, Eric Dolphy, Coleman Hawkins And Charlie Parker | IN+OUT Records | 7016-3
Jazz Unlimited | IN+OUT Records | 7017-2
Sonny Rollins Quintet
Sunny Days,Starry Nights | Milestone | MCD 9122-2
Sonny Rollins Sextet
Sunny Days,Starry Nights | Milestone | MCD 9122-2
Stanley Jordan Trio
Festival International De Jazz De Montreal | Spectra | 9811660

Campbell,Wilbur | (dr)
Gene Ammons-Dexter Gordon Quintet
Dexter Gordon Birthday Celebration | Fantasy | FANCD 6082-2
John Klemmer Quartet
Involvement | Chess | 076139-2

Campbell,William | (tb)
Louis Armstrong And His Friends
Louis Armstrong And His Friends | Bluebird | 2663961-2

Canada,Enric | (perc)
Perico Sambeat Group
Ademuz | Fresh Sound Records | FSNT 041 CD

Canadian Brass |
Canadian Brass
Take The A Train | RCA | 2663455-2

Candid Jazz Masters,The |
Candid Jazz Masters
The Candid Jazz Masters:For Miles | Candid | CCD 79710

Candido[Camero] | (bongos,congas,vocperc)
Charles Mingus Orchestra
Cumbia & Jazz Fusion | Atlantic | 8122-71785-2
Dinah Washington And Her Band
After Hours With Miss D | Verve | 0760562
Dizzy Gillespie And His Orchestra
Verve Jazz Masters 10:Dizzy Gillespie | Verve | 516319-2
Afro | Verve | 517052-2
Gillespiana And Carnegie Hall Concert | Verve | 519809-2
Talking Verve:Dizzy Gillespie | Verve | 533846-2
Dizzy Gillespie Group
Verve Jazz Masters 10:Dizzy Gillespie | Verve | 516319-2
Dizzy Gillespie Sextet
Dizzie Gillespie: Salle Pleyel/Olympia | Laserlight | 36132
Dizzy Gillspie And His Latin American Rhythm
Afro | Verve | 517052-2
Erroll Garner Quartet
Verve Jazz Masters 7:Erroll Garner | Verve | 518197-2
Verve Jazz Masters 20:Introducing | Verve | 519853-2
Contrasts | Verve | 558077-2
Grant Green Orchestra
Grant Green:Blue Breakbeat | Blue Note | 494705-2
Blue Breaks Beats Vol.2 | Blue Note | 789907-2

So Blue So Funky-Heroes Of The Hammond | Blue Note | 796563-2
JATP All Stars
Verve Jazz Masters 25:Stan Getz & Dizzy Gillespie | Verve | 521852-2
Sonny Rollins Quartet
What's New? | RCA | 2179626-2
Wes Montgomery With The Don Sebesky Orchestra
Verve Jazz Masters 14:Wes Montgomery | Verve | 519826-2
Talkin' Jazz:Roots Of Acid Jazz | Verve | 529580-2
Bumpin' | Verve | 539062-2
Wes Montgomery With The Oliver Nelson Orchestra
Verve Jazz Masters 14:Wes Montgomery | Verve | 519826-2

Candoli,Conte | (dr,perc,tp,fl-hvoc)
Anita O'Day With The Buddy Bregman Orchestra
Pick Yourself Up | Verve | 517329-2
Art Pepper Quintet
Gettin' Together | Original Jazz Classics | OJCCD 169-2
Bill Holman Octet
The Jazz Giants Play Sammy Cahn:It's Magic | Prestige | PCD 24226-2
Bud Shank Sextet
New Gold! | Candid | CCD 79707
Buddy Bregman And His Orchestra
Swinging Kicks | Verve | 559514-2
Chet Baker Big Band
The Best Of Chet Baker Plays | Pacific Jazz | 797161-2
Conte Candoli Quartet
Candoli Live | Nagel-Heyer | CD 2024
Conte Candoli With The Joe Haider Trio
Conte Candoli Meets The Joe Haider Trio | JHM Records | JHM 3602
Conte Candoli-Carl Fontana Quintet
The Complete Phoenix Recordings Vol.1 | Woofy Productions | WPCD 121
The Complete Phoenix Recordings Vol.2 | Woofy Productions | WPCD 122
The Complete Phoenix Recordings Vol.3 | Woofy Productions | WPCD 123
The Complete Phoenix Recordings Vol.4 | Woofy Productions | WPCD 124
The Complete Phoenix Recordings Vol.5 | Woofy Productions | WPCD 125
The Complete Phoenix Recordings Vol.6 | Woofy Productions | WPCD 126
Dizzy Gillespie And His Orchestra
Talking Verve:Dizzy Gillespie | Verve | 533846-2
Gerry Mulligan Concert Jazz Band
Verve Jazz Masters 36:Gerry Mulligan | Verve | 523342-2
The Complete Verve Gerry Mulligan Concert Band | Verve | 9860613
Howard Rumsey's Lighthouse All-Stars
Howard Rumsey's Lighthouse All-Stars Vol.6 | Original Jazz Classics | OJCCD 386-2(C 3504)
Jackie Cain-Roy Kral Group
Full Circle | Fantasy | FCD 24768-2
Jimmy Smith With The Oliver Nelson Orchestra
Jimmy Smith:Best Of The Verve Years | Verve | 527950-2
Jimmy Smith-Talkin' Verve | Verve | 531563-2
Johnny Hartman And His Orchestra
Unforgettable | Impulse(MCA) | IMP 11522
June Christy With The Pete Rugolo Orchestra
Something Cool(The Complete Mono & Stereo Versions) | Capitol | 534069-2
June Christy With The Shorty Rogers Orchestra
June Christy Big Band Special | Capitol | 498319-2
Lars Gullin American All Stars
Lars Gullin 1953,Vol.2:Moden Sounds | Dragon | DRCD 234
Mark Murphy And His Septet
Blue Velvet: Crooners, Swooners And Velvet Vocals | Blue Note | 521153-2
Maynard Ferguson Band
Verve Jazz Masters 52:Maynard Ferguson | Verve | 529905-2
Shelly Manne And His Men
Live! At The Manne Hole Vol.1 | Original Jazz Classics | OJCCD 714-2(S 7593)
Live! At The Manne Hole Vol.2 | Original Jazz Classics | OJCCD 715-2(S 7594)
Stan Getz Quintet
Stan Getz Highlights:The Best Of The Verve Years Vol.2 | Verve | 517330-2
Verve Jazz Masters 8:Stan Getz | Verve | 519823-2
Best Of The West Coast Sessions | Verve | 537084-2
Ultimate Stan Getz selected by Joe Henderson | Verve | 557532-2
West Coast Jazz | Verve | 557549-2
Stan Getz Highlights | Verve | 847430-2
Stan Kenton And His Orchestra
Stan Kenton Portraits On Standards | Capitol | 531571-2
Terry Gibbs Big Band
Terry Gibbs Dream Band Vol.4:Main Stem | Contemporary | CCD 7656-2
Terry Gibbs Dream Band
Terry Gibbs Dream Band Vol.2:The Sundown Sessions | Contemporary | CCD 7652-2
Terry Gibbs Dream Band Vol.3:Flying Home | Contemporary | CCD 7654-2
Terry Gibbs Dream Band Vol.5:The Big Cat | Contemporary | CCD 7657-2
Terry Gibbs Dream Band Vol.6:One More Time | Contemporary | CCD 7658-2
The Jazz Giants Play Jerome Kern:Yesterdays | Prestige | PCD 24202-2
Victor Feldman Orchestra
Latinsville | Contemporary | CCD 9005-2
Woody Herman And His Orchestra
The Legends Of Swing | Laserlight | 24659
Woody Herman:Four Brother | Dreyfus Jazz Line | FDM 36722-2
Old Gold Rehearsals 1944 | Jazz Unlimited | JUCD 2079

Candoli,Pete | (perc,tpfl-h)
Anita O'Day With The Billy May Orchestra
Verve Jazz Masters 49:Anita O'Day | Verve | 527653-2
Anita O'Day With The Buddy Bregman Orchestra
Pick Yourself Up | Verve | 517329-2
Art Pepper Plus Eleven
Art Pepper + Eleven | Contemporary | CSA 7568-6
Modern Jazz Classics | Original Jazz Classics | OJC20 341-2
Benny Carter And His Orchestra
Aspects | Capitol | 852677-2
Billy Eckstine With The Billy May Orchestra
Once More With Feeling | Roulette | 581862-2
Billy May And His Orchestra
Billy May's Big Fat Brass/Bill's Bag | Capitol | 535206-2
Ella Fitzgerald With Frank De Vol And His Orchestra
Get Happy! | Verve | 523321-2
Ella Fitzgerald With Paul Weston And His Orchestra
Ella Fitzgerald Sings The Irving Berlin Song Book | Verve | 543830-2
Ella Fitzgerald With The Buddy Bregman Orchestra
Ella Fitzgerald-First Lady Of Song | Verve | 517898-2
Love Songs:The Best Of The Song Books | Verve | 531762-2
Ella Fitzgerald Sings The Cole Porter Songbook | Verve | 537257-2
Ella Fitzgerald Sings The Rodgers And Hart Song Book | Verve | 537258-2
Ella Fitzgerald With The Frank DeVol Orchestra
Get Happy! | Verve | 523321-2
Ella Fitzgerald With The Marty Paich Orchestra
Get Happy! | Verve | 523321-2
Ella Fitzgerald With The Paul Weston Orchestra
Get Happy! | Verve | 523321-2
Gerry Mulligan Tentette
Gene Norman Presents The Original Gerry Mulligan Tentet And Quartet | GNP Crescendo | GNPD 56
Henry Mancini And His Orchestra
Combo! | RCA | 2147794-2
Louis Armstrong And Gary Crosby With Sonny Burke's Orchestra
Louis Armstrong-My Greatest Songs | MCA | MCD 18347
Louis Armstrong And His All Stars With Benny Carter's Orchestra
Ambassador Louis Armstrong Vol.17:Moments To Remember(1952-1956) | Ambassador | CLA 1917
Louis Armstrong And His All Stars With Sonny Burke's Orchestra
Ambassador Louis Armstrong Vol.17:Moments To Remember(1952-1956) | Ambassador | CLA 1917
Louis Armstrong With Benny Carter's Orchestra
Louis Armstrong-My Greatest Songs | MCA | MCD 18347
Mark Murphy And His Septet
Blue Velvet: Crooners, Swooners And Velvet Vocals | Blue Note | 521153-2
Mel Tormé With The Billy May Orchestra
Mel Tormé Goes South Of The Border With Billy May | Verve | 589517-2
Peggy Lee With The Quincy Jones Orchestra
Blues Cross Country | Capitol | 520088-2
Pete Rugolo And His Orchestra
Verve Jazz Masters 52:Maynard Ferguson | Verve | 529905-2
Thriller/Richard Diamon(Original Jazz Scores From 2 Classics TV Series) | Fresh Sound Records | FSCD 2015
Shorty Rogers And His Orchestra Feat. The Giants
Planet Jazz:Shorty Rogers | Planet Jazz | 2159976-2
Stan Kenton And His Orchestra
Great Swing Classics In Hi-Fi | Capitol | 521223-2
Stan Kenton Portraits On Standards | Capitol | 531571-2
Woody Herman And His Orchestra
The Legends Of Swing | Laserlight | 24659
Woody Herman:Four Brother | Dreyfus Jazz Line | FDM 36722-2
Louis Armstrong-Jack Teagarden-Woody Herman:Midnights At V-Disc | Jazz Unlimited | JUCD 2048
Old Gold Rehearsals 1944 | Jazz Unlimited | JUCD 2079
Woody Herman And The Herd
Woody Herman (And The Herd) At Carnegie Hall | Verve | 559833-2

Candreva,Philip | (tp)
Ella Fitzgerald With The Marty Paich Orchestra
Get Happy! | Verve | 523321-2

Canedy,Todd | (dr,synth,percbackground-voc)
Austria Drei
Jazz Portraits | EGO | 95080
Stephan Dietz Quartet
Jazz Portraits | EGO | 95080

Canela,Carme | (voc)
Carme Canela With The Joan Monné Trio
Introducing Carme Canela | Fresh Sound Records | FSNT 014 CD
Orquestra De Cambra Teatre Lliure
Porgy And Bess | Fresh Sound Records | FSNT 066 CD
Perico Sambeat Quartet
Friendship | ACT | 9421-2

Canier,Charles | (v)
Charlie Haden Quartet West With Strings
Now Is The Hour | Verve | 527827-2

Canizares,Juan Manuel | (flamenco-g)
Los Jovenes Flamencos
Jazzpana | ACT | 9212-2
Los Jovenes Flamencos With The WDR Big Band And Guests
Jazzpana | ACT | 9212-2

Cannarozzi,Pete | (synth)
Al Di Meola Group
Jazzrock-Anthology Vol.3:Fusion | Zounds | CD 27100555

Canning,Tom | (keyboards,p,el-psynth)
Al Jarreau With Band
Jarreau | i.e. Music | 557847-2
We Got By | Reprise | 7599-27222-2
All Fly Home | Warner | 7599-27362-2

Cannon,Gerald | (b)
Wayne Escoffery Quintet
Intuition | Nagel-Heyer | CD 2038

Cannon,Sean | (voc)
Hans Theessink Group
Crazy Moon | Minor Music | 801052

Cano,Eddie | (arrp)
Bobby Hutcherson Orchestra
Montara | Blue Note | 590956-2
Jack Costanzo Group
Latin Fever:The Wild Rhythms Of Jack Costanza | Capitol | 590955-2

Cantarano,Stefano | (b)
Stefania Tallini Trio
New Life | yvp music | CD 3114
Stefania Tallini Trio With Guests
New Life | yvp music | CD 3114

Canto,Humberto | (conga,perctumbas)
Dizzy Gillespie Quintet
Jazz In Paris:Dizzy Gillespie-The Giant | EmArCy | 159734-2 PMS

Canto,Umberto | (perc)
Bobby Jaspar Quintet
Jazz In Paris:Bobby Jaspar-Jeux De Quartes | EmArCy | 018423-2

Cantor,Russ | (v)
Charlie Haden Quartet West With Strings
The Art Of The Song | Verve | 547403-2

Cantos,Bill | (voc)
John Patitucci Group
Mistura Fina | GRP | GRP 98022

Capellas,Xavier 'Xavi' | (org,keyboardsp)
Big Band Bellaterra
Don't Git Sassy | Fresh Sound Records | FSNT 048 CD
José Luis Gámez Quartet
Colores | Fresh Sound Records | FSNT 028 CD
José Luis Gámez Quintet
Colores | Fresh Sound Records | FSNT 028 CD

Capello,Carlo | (dr)
Danny Moss Meets Buddha's Gamblers
A Swingin' Affair | Nagel-Heyer | CD 034
Blues Of Summer | Nagel-Heyer | NH 1011

Capers,Bob | (as,bs,fl,reedsts)
Mongo Santamaria And His Band
Mongo At The Village Gate | Original Jazz Classics | OJCCD 490-2(RLP 9529)

Capi,Frank | (b-clbs)
Buddy Rich Big Band
The New One! | Pacific Jazz | 494507-2

Capitol Jazzmen,The |
The Capitol Jazzmen
Jazz:The Essential Collection Vol.3 | IN+OUT Records | 78013-2
The Hollywood Session:The Capitol Jazzmen | Jazz Unlimited | JUCD 2044

Caplan,Sam | (v)
Charlie Parker Quartet With Strings
The Cole Porter Songbook | Verve | 823250-2
Charlie Parker With Strings
Verve Jazz Masters 28:Charlie Parker Plays Standards | Verve | 521854-2
Charlie Parker With Strings:The Master Takes | Verve | 523984-2
Charlie Parker:The Best Of The Verve Years | Verve | 527815-2
Bird: The Complete Charlie Parker On Verve | Verve | 837141-2
Charlie Parker:April In Paris | Dreyfus Jazz Line | FDM 36737-2
Charlie Parker With The Joe Lipman Orchestra
Verve Jazz Masters 28:Charlie Parker Plays Standards | Verve | 521854-2
Charlie Parker With Strings:The Master Takes | Verve | 523984-2
Charlie Parker Big Band | Verve | 559835-2
Charlie Parker With The Neal Hefti Orchestra
Charlie Parker:The Best Of The Verve Years | Verve | 527815-2
Bird: The Complete Charlie Parker On Verve | Verve | 837141-2

Caplan,Sam prob. | (v)
Charlie Parker With Strings
Bird: The Complete Charlie Parker On Verve | Verve | 837141-2
Charlie Parker With The Joe Lipman Orchestra
Charlie Parker With Strings:The Master Takes | Verve | 523984-2
Charlie Parker Big Band | Verve | 559835-2

Capo,Willie | (voc)
Sabu L. Martinez Group
Palo Congo | Blue Note | 522665-2

Capozzo,Jean-Luc | (tpfl-h)
Louis Sclavis & The Bernard Struber Jazztet
La Phare | Enja | ENJ-9359 2

Capp,Frank | (drperc)
André Previn' s Jazz Trio
King Size! | Original Jazz Classics | OJCCD 691-2(S 7570)
Ben Webster With Strings
The Warm Moods-With Strings | Rhino | 8122-73721-2
Jerri Southern And The Dick Hazard Quartet
Misty Blue:Sweet Sisters Swing Songs Of Sorrow And Sadness | Blue Note | 521151-2
Joe Albany Trio
Portrair Of A Legend | Fresh Sound Records | FSR-CD 317
Ralph Sutton And Friends
Sweet Sue-The Music Of Fats Waller Vol.1 | Nagel-Heyer | CD 057
Turk Murphy And His Jazz Band
Planet Jazz | Planet Jazz | 2169652-2

Cappadocia,Rufus | (cello)
Michael Blake Group
Kingdom Of Champa | Intuition Records | INT 3189-2

Cappola,John | (tp)
Louis Sclavis Quartet
L'Affrontement Des Prétendants | ECM | 1705(159927-2)

Captein,Dave | (b)
Jessica Williams Trio
Higher Standards | Candid | CCD 79736
Jazz In The Afternoon | Candid | CCD 79750

Cara,Mancy | (bj,vocg)
Louis Armstrong And His Hot Five
Jazz:The Essential Collection Vol.2 | IN+OUT Records | 78012-2
Louis Armstrong:Fireworks | Dreyfus Jazz Line | FDM 36710-2
Louis Armstrong And His Orchestra
Jazz:The Essential Collection Vol.2 | IN+OUT Records | 78012-2
Louis Armstrong And His Savoy Ballroom Five
Jazz:The Essential Collection Vol.2 | IN+OUT Records | 78012-2

Carabellese,Nunzio | (cl)
Banda Cittá Ruvo Di Puglia
La Banda/Banda And Jazz | Enja | ENJ-9326 2

Caramouche,Greg | (percvoc)
Jean-Paul Bourelly Group
Jungle Cowboy | JMT Edition | 919009-2

Carco,Zito | (p)
Mary Lou Williams Quartet
The Story Of Jazz Piano | Laserlight | 24653

Cardas,Emery | (cello)
Christof Lauer-Jens Thomas With The Cikada String Quartet
Shadows In The Rain | ACT | 9297-2

Cardenas,Steve | (el-gg)
Paul Motian And The E.B.B.B.
Holiday For Strings | Winter&Winter | 910069-2
Paul Motian Electric Bebop Band
Monk And Powell | Winter&Winter | 910045-2
Europe | Winter&Winter | 910063-2
Steve Cárdenas Trio
Shebang | Fresh Sound Records | FSNT 079 CD

Cardinali,Peter | (b)
Hugh Marsh Duo/Quartet/Orchestra
The Bear Walks | VeraBra Records | CDVBR 2011-2

Cardo,Ramon | (asss)
Daniel Flors Group
When Least Expected | Fresh Sound Records | FSNT 080 CD
Dave Liebman And The Lluis Vidal Trio With The Orquestra De Cambra Theatre Lliure
Dave Liebman And The Lluis Vidal Trio | Fresh Sound Records | FSNT 026 CD
Orquestra De Cambra Teatre Lliure
Orquestra De Cambra Teatre Lliure and Lluis Vidal Trio feat.Dave Liebman | Fresh Sound Records | FSNT 027 CD
Porgy And Bess | Fresh Sound Records | FSNT 066 CD
Orquestra De Cambra Teatre Lliure feat. Dave Liebman
Orquestra De Cambra Teatre Lliure and Lluis Vidal Trio feat.Dave Liebman | Fresh Sound Records | FSNT 027 CD

Cardona,Milton | (atchere,checkere,lya,voc,bata-dr)
Johnny King Septet
The Meltdown | Enja | ENJ-9329 2
Michael Brecker Group
Now You See It...(Now You Don't) | GRP | GRP 96222
Rabih Abou-Khalil Group
Blue Camel | Enja | ENJ-7053 2
The Sultan's Picnic | Enja | ENJ-8078 2

Cardoso,Jorge | (g)
Jorge Cardoso
Talking Hands:Live | ALISO Records | AL 1021

Cardoso,Paulo | (b,vocb-solo)
Al Porcino Big Band
Al Cohn Meets Al Porcino | Organic Music | ORGM 9730
Claus Raible Trio
Introducing The Exciting Claus Raible Trio | Organic Music | ORGM 9714
David Gazarov Trio
Let's Have A Merry Christmas With The David Gazarov Trio! | Organic Music | ORGM 9712
Marcio Tubino Group
Festa Do Olho | Organic Music | ORGM 9723
Monty Waters' Hot Rhythm Junction
Jazzoerty | Tutu Records | 888196-2*
Paulo Cardoso
VoceBasso | Organic Music | ORGM 9703
Sabina Sciubba-Paulo Cardoso
VoceBasso | Organic Music | ORGM 9703

Carey David | (vib)
Stan Getz With The Richard Evans Orchestra
What The World Needs Now-Stan Getz Plays Bacharach And David | Verve | 557450-2

Carey,Dave | (dr,percwbd)
J.J. Johnson-Al Grey Sextet
Things Are Getting Better All The Time | Original Jazz Classics | OJCCD 745-2(2312141)
The J.J.Johnson Memorial Album | Prestige | PRCD 11025-2

Carey,Scoops | (as)
Fletcher Henderson And His Orchestra
Jazz:The Essential Collection Vol.1 | IN+OUT Records | 78011-2

Cargill,Mark | (v)
Ahmad Jamal Trio
Picture Perfect-70th Anniversary | Warner | 8573-85268-2

Carisi,Johnny | (arrtp)
Gil Evans And Ten
Gil Evans And Ten | Original Jazz Classics | OJC 346(P 7120)
Gil Evans And Ten | Prestige | PRSA 7120-6
James Chirillo-Johnny Carisi
Sultry Serenade | Nagel-Heyer | CD 061
Miles Davis + 19
Miles Ahead | CBS | CK 65121
Miles Davis And His Orchestra
The Complete Birth Of The Cool | Capitol | 494550-2
Birth Of The Cool | Capitol | 530117-2
Jazz Profile:Miles Davis | Blue Note | 823515-2
Miles Davis With Gil Evans & His Orchestra
This Is Jazz:Miles Davis Plays Ballads | CBS | CK 65038

Carl,Rüdiger | (accordeon,bandoneon,voc)
Jazzensemble Des Hessischen Rundfunks
Atmosphering Conditions Permitting | ECM | 1549/50

Carlberg,Frank | (p)

Frank Carlberg Group
Variations On A Summer Day | Fresh Sound Records | FSNT 083 CD
Carley,Dale | (tpfl-h)
Count Basie And His Orchestra
88 Basie Street | Original Jazz Classics | OJC 808(2310901)
Fancy Pants | Original Jazz Classics | OJCCD 1038-2(2310920)
Count Basie Big Band
Farmers Market Barbecue | Original Jazz Classics | OJCCD 732-2(2310874)
Sarah Vaughan And The Count Basie Orchestra
Sarah Vaughan Birthday Celebration | Fantasy | FANCD 6090-2
Carlisle,Una Mae | (pvoc)
Una Mae Carlisle Quintet
Jazz:The Essential Collection Vol.3 | IN+OUT Records | 78013-2
Una Mae Carlisle Septet
Planet Jazz:Female Jazz Vocalists | Planet Jazz | 2169656-2
Carlos,Jose | (drperc)
Stan Getz Group
Verve Jazz Masters 53:Stan Getz-Bossa Nova | Verve | 529904-2
Stan Getz-Luiz Bonfa Group
The Antonio Carlos Jobim Songbook | Verve | 525472-2
Stan Getz-Luiz Bonfa Orchestra
Verve Jazz Masters 13:Antonio Carlos Jobim | Verve | 516409-2
Jazz Samba Encore! | Verve | 823613-2
Carlos,Ze | (fl)
Ithamara Koorax With Band
Love Dance:The Ballad Album | Milestone | MCD 9327-2
Carlsen,Morten | (cl,ts,bass-s,ney,taragot,bass-sax)
Pierre Dorge's New Jungle Orchestra
Giraf | dacapo | DCCD 9440
Carlson,Frank | (bongo,dr,p,perctympani)
Glenn Miller And His Orchestra
Planet Jazz:Glenn Miller | Planet Jazz | 2152056-2
Candelight Miller | RCA | 2668716-2
June Christy With The Pete Rugolo Orchestra
Something Cool(The Complete Mono & Stereo Versions) | Capitol | 534069-2
Carlsson,Bengt | (b)
Lars Gullin Quartet
Lars Gullin 1955/56 Vol.1 | Dragon | DRCD 224
Carlsson,Lars-Göran | (tb)
Anders Jormin With Brass Quartet
Xieyi | ECM | 1762(013998-2)
Carlsson,Rune | (dr)
Coleman Hawkins With The Göran Lindberg Trio
Coleman Hawkins At The Golden Circle | Dragon | DRCD 265
Eje Thelin Group
Ejs Thelin 1966 With Barney Wilen | Dragon | DRCD 366
Eje Thelin Quartet
Ejs Thelin 1966 With Barney Wilen | Dragon | DRCD 366
Eje Thelin Quintet
At The German Jazz Festival 1964 | Dragon | DRCD 374
Carlton,Bud | (as)
Artie Shaw And His Orchestra
Planet JazzArtie Shaw | Planet Jazz | 2152057-2
Planet Jazz:Jazz Greatest Hits | Planet Jazz | 2169648-2
Carlton,Larry | (as,el-g,gvoc)
Fourplay
Heartfelt | RCA | 2663916-2
Fourplay...Yes,Please! | Warner | 9362-47694-2
Larry Carlton Group
The Gift | GRP | GRP 98542
Paulinho Da Costa Orchestra
Happy People | Original Jazz Classics | OJCCD 783-2(2312102)
Carlton,Michele Pillar | (voc)
Larry Carlton Group
The Gift | GRP | GRP 98542
Carlucci,Nathalie | (v)
Charlie Haden Quartet West With Strings
Now Is The Hour | Verve | 527827-2
Stephane Grappelli With The Michel Legrand Orchestra
Grapelli Story | Verve | 515807-2
Carmadell,Onias | (atabaques,berimbaupandeiro)
The New Dave Pike Set & Grupo Baiafra De Bahia
Dave Pike Set:Masterpieces | MPS | 531848-2
Carmello,Carolee | (voc)
Wolfgang Lackerschmid-Donald Johnston Group
New Singers-New Songs | Bhakti Jazz | BR 31
Carmen,Eli | (bassoon)
Stan Getz With The Eddie Sauter Orchestra
Stan Getz Plays The Music Of Mickey One | Verve | 531232-2
Carmichael,Greg | (g)
Acoustic Alchemy
Against The Grain | GRP | GRP 97832
Carmichael,Hoagy | (p,celeste,voc,coperc)
Blind Willie Dunn's Gin Bottle Four
Jazz:The Essential Collection Vol.1 | IN+OUT Records | 78011-2
Hoagy Carmichael And His Orchestra
Planet Jazz:Bud Freeman | Planet Jazz | 2161240-2
Blue Velvet: Crooners, Swooners And Velvet Vocals | Blue Note | 521153-2
Hoagy Carmichael With Jack Teagarden And His Big Band
Swing Vol.1 | Storyville | 4960343
Carneiro,Edmundo | (perc)
Kamafra
Kamafra Live | Edition Musikat | EDM 072
Carneiro,Nando | (g,synth,caxixig-synth)
Egberto Gismonti Group
Musica De Sobrevivencia | ECM | 1509(519706-2)
Egberto Gismonti Trio
ZigZag | ECM | 1582
Carneiro,Zeca | (gsynth)
Egberto Gismonti Group
Infancia | ECM | 1428
Carney,Harry | (as,bs,b-cl,voc,clss)
Benny Goodman Band
Benny Goodman At Carnegie Hall 1938(Complete) | CBS | C2K 65143
Billy Strayhorn Orchestra
Johnny Hodges With Billy Strayhorn And The Orchestra | Verve | 557543-2
Django Reinhardt With Duke Ellington And His Orchestra
Django Reinhardt:Souveniers | Dreyfus Jazz Line | FDM 36744-2
Duke Ellington And Count Basie With Their Orchestras
First Time! | CBS | CK 65571
Duke Ellington And His Award Winners
Greatest Hits | CBS | 462959-2
Duke Ellington And His Cotton Club Orchestra
Planet Jazz:Duke Ellington | Planet Jazz | 2152053-2
Jazz:The Essential Collection Vol.2 | IN+OUT Records | 78012-2
Duke Ellington And His Famous Orchestra
Duke Ellington:The Blanton-Webster Band | Bluebird | 21 13181-2
Planet Jazz:Duke Ellington | Planet Jazz | 2152053-2
Planet Jazz:Johnny Hodges | Planet Jazz | 2152065-2
Planet Jazz Sampler | Planet Jazz | 2152326-2
Planet Jazz:Ben Webster | RCA | 2165368-2
Planet Jazz:Big Bands | Planet Jazz | 2169649-2
Planet Jazz:Jazz Trumpet | Planet Jazz | 2169654-2
Planet Jazz:Female Jazz Vocalists | Planet Jazz | 2169656-2
Highlights From The Duke Ellington Centennial Edition | RCA | 2663672-2
Greatest Hits | CBS | 462959-2
Jazz:The Essential Collection Vol.2 | IN+OUT Records | 78012-2
Jazz:The Essential Collection Vol.3 | IN+OUT Records | 78013-2
Duke Ellington:Ko-Ko | Dreyfus Jazz Line | FDM 36717-2
Duke Ellington And His Orchestra
Planet Jazz:Duke Ellington | Planet Jazz | 2152053-2
Planet Jazz:Johnny Hodges | Planet Jazz | 2152065-2
Planet Jazz:Jazz Greatest Hits | Planet Jazz | 2169648-2
Duke Ellington's Far East Suite | RCA | 2174797-2
Jazz Collection:Duke Ellington | Laserlight | 24369
The Art Of Saxophone | Laserlight | 24652
The Legends Of Swing | Laserlight | 24659
100 Years Duke | Laserlight | 24906
Highlights From The Duke Ellington Centennial Edition | RCA | 2663672-2
The Popular Duke Ellington | RCA | 2663880-2
Carnegie Hall Concert December 1944 | Prestige | 2PCD 24073-2
Carnegie Hall Concert January 1946 | Prestige | 2PCD 24074-2
Carnegie Hall Concert December 1947 | Prestige | 2PCD 24075-2
Carnegie Hall Concert January 1943 | Prestige | 2PCD 34004-2
Duke Ellington: The Champs-Elysees Theater January 29-30th,1965 | Laserlight | 36131
Greatest Hits | CBS | 462959-2
The Big Bands Vol.1.The Snader Telescriptions | Storyville | 4960043
Jazz Festival Vol.2 | Storyville | 4960743
Verve Jazz Masters 4:Duke Ellington | Verve | 516338-2
Verve Jazz Masters 20:Introducing | Verve | 519853-2
Ellington '55 | Capitol | 520135-2
Great Swing Classics In Hi-Fi | Capitol | 521223-2
Ella & Duke At The Cote D'Azur | Verve | 539030-2
Ella Fitzgerald And Duke Ellington:Cote D'Azure Concerts on Verve | Verve | 539033-2
Soul Call | Verve | 539785-2
The Great Paris Concert | Atlantic | 7567-81303-2
Jazz:The Essential Collection Vol.2 | IN+OUT Records | 78012-2
Jazz:The Essential Collection Vol.3 | IN+OUT Records | 78013-2
New Orleans Suite | Rhino | 812273670-2
Afro-Bossa | Reprise | 9362-47876-2
Ellington At Newport 1956(Complete) | CBS | CK 64932
Black Brown And Beige | CBS | CK 65566
Such Sweet Thunder | CBS | CK 65568
Anatomy Of A Murder | CBS | CK 65569
Welcome To Jazz At The Philharmonic | Fantasy | FANCD 6081-2
The Ellington Suites | Original Jazz Classics | OJC20 446-2(2310762)
Latin America Suite | Original Jazz Classics | OJC20 469-2
Duke Ellington And His Orchestra feat. Paul Gonsalves | Original Jazz Classics | OJCCD 623-2
The Afro-Eurasian Eclipse-A Suite In Eight Parts | Original Jazz Classics | OJCCD 645-2(F 9498)
Yale Concert | Original Jazz Classics | OJCCD 664-2
Jazz At The Philharmonis Berlin '65/Paris '67 | Pablo | PACD 5304-2
Duke Ellington At The Alhambra | Pablo | PACD 5313-2
The Jazz Giants Play Duke Ellington:Caravan | Prestige | PCD 24227-2
The Duke At Fargo 1940 | Storyville | STCD 8316/17
Togo Brava Swuite | Storyville | STCD 8323
At The Hurricane:Original 1943 Broadcasts | Storyville | STCD 8359
Duke Ellington Orchestra
Continuum | Fantasy | FCD 24765-2
Duke Ellington Small Band
The Intimacy Of The Blues | Original Jazz Classics | OJCCD 624-2
Duke Ellington-Coleman Hawkins Orchestra
Duke Ellington Meets Coleman Hawkins | Impulse(MCA) | 951162-2
Ella Fitzgerald With The Duke Ellington Orchestra
The Stockholm Concert 1966 | Pablo | 2308242-2
Ella Fitzgerald-First Lady Of Song | Verve | 517898-2
The Best Of The Song Books | Verve | 519804-2
Verve Jazz Masters 6:Ella Fitzgerald | Verve | 519822-2
The Best Of The Song Books:The Ballads | Verve | 521867-2
Verve Jazz Masters 46:Ella Fitzgerald-The Jazz Sides | Verve | 527655-2
Ella At Duke's Place | Verve | 529700-2
Love Songs:The Best Of The Song Books | Verve | 531762-2
Ella & Duke At The Cote D'Azur | Verve | 539030-2
Ella Fitzgerald And Duke Ellington:Cote D'Azure Concerts on Verve | Verve | 539033-2
Ella Fitzgerald Sings The Duke Ellington Songbook | Verve | 559248-2
For The Love Of Ella Fitzgerald | Verve | 841765-2
Ella Fitzgerald With The Duke Ellington Orchestra And Jimmy Jones Trio
Ella & Duke At The Cote D'Azur | Verve | 539030-2
Ella Fitzgerald And Duke Ellington:Cote D'Azure Concerts on Verve | Verve | 539033-2
Esquire All-American Award Winners
Planet Jazz:Jazz Trumpet | Planet Jazz | 2169654-2
Harry Carney And His Orchestra With Strings
Music For Loving:Ben Webster With Strings | Verve | 527774-2
Jam Session
Benny Goodman At Carnegie Hall 1938(Complete) | CBS | C2K 65143
Jimmy Hamilton And The Duke's Men
The Blue Note Swingtets | Blue Note | 495697-2
Johnny Hodges And His Band
Verve Jazz Masters 35:Johnny Hodges | Verve | 521857-2
Johnny Hodges And The Ellington All-Stars Without Duke
Verve Jazz Masters 35:Johnny Hodges | Verve | 521857-2
Johnny Hodges And The Ellington Men
Verve Jazz Masters 35:Johnny Hodges | Verve | 521857-2
Johnny Hodges Orchestra
Planet Jazz:Johnny Hodges | Planet Jazz | 2152065-2
Planet Jazz Sampler | Planet Jazz | 2152326-2
Planet Jazz:Jazz Saxophone | Planet Jazz | 2169653-2
Highlights From The Duke Ellington Centennial Edition | RCA | 2663672-2
Johnny Hodges At The Sportpalast, Berlin | Pablo | 2CD 2620102
The Jazz Giants Play Harry Warren:Lullaby Of Broadway | Prestige | PCD 24204-2
Johnny Hodges With Billy Strayhorn And The Duke Ellington Orchestra
Verve Jazz Masters 35:Johnny Hodges | Verve | 521857-2
Oscar Peterson With The Duke Ellington Orchestra
Oscar Peterson Plays Duke Ellington | Pablo | 2310966-2
Rex Stewart And His Orchestra
Planet Jazz:Ben Webster | RCA | 2165368-2
Planet Jazz:Jazz Trumpet | Planet Jazz | 2169654-2
Jazz:The Essential Collection Vol.3 | IN+OUT Records | 78013-2
Rosemary Clooney With The Duke Ellington Orchestra
Blue Rose | CBS | CK 65506
Caro,Joe | (g)
Bobby McFerrin Group
Bobby McFerrin | Elektra | 7559-60023-2
Caroline | (sruthi,talam,synth,tambouravoc)
Shankar Group
Nobody Told Me | ECM | 1397
Shankar Quartet
Pancha Nadai Pallavi | ECM | 1407(841641-2)
Shankar/Caroline
The Epidemics | ECM | 1308
Caron,Elise | (voc)
Michael Riessler Group
Orange | ACT | 9274-2
Caron,Natalie | (cello)
Abdullah Ibrahim Trio And A String Orchestra
African Suite | TipToe | TIP-888832 2
Stephane Grappelli With The Michel Legrand Orchestra
Grapelli Story | Verve | 515807-2
String Orchestra
African Suite | TipToe | TIP-888832 2
Carone,Don | (as)
Stan Kenton And His Orchestra
Stan Kenton Portraits On Standards | Capitol | 531571-2
Carp,Jeffrey M. | (harm)
Howlin' Wolf London Session
Howlin' Wolf:The London Sessions | Chess | MCD 09297
Carpenter,Dave | (6-string-b,bel-b)
Allan Holdsworth Group
The Sixteen Man Of Tain | Cream Records | CR 610-2
Carpenter,Thelma | (voc)
Coleman Hawkins And His Orchestra
Planet Jazz:Coleman Hawkins | Planet Jazz | 2152055-2
Carr,Bruno | (dr)
Hank Crawford And His Orchestra
Atlantic Saxophones | Rhino | 8122-71256-2
Herbie Mann Group
The Best Of Herbie Mann | Atlantic | 7567-81369-2
Carr,Ian | (tp,fl-h,el-pfl-h.grand-p)
Jon Hiseman With The United Jazz & Rock Ensemble And Babara Thompson's Paraphernalia
About Time Too! | VeraBra Records | CDVBR 2014-2
Carr,Mancy | (bjvoc)
Carroll Dickerson's Savoyagers
Louis Armstrong:Fireworks | Dreyfus Jazz Line | FDM 36710-2
Louis Armstrong And His Hot Five
Jazz:The Essential Collection Vol.2 | IN+OUT Records | 78012-2
Satch Plays Fats(Complete) | CBS | CK 64927
Louis Armstrong:Fireworks | Dreyfus Jazz Line | FDM 36710-2
Louis Armstrong And His Orchestra
Jazz:The Essential Collection Vol.2 | IN+OUT Records | 78012-2
Satch Plays Fats(Complete) | CBS | CK 64927
Louis Armstrong:Fireworks | Dreyfus Jazz Line | FDM 36710-2
Louis Armstrong And His Savoy Ballroom Five
Jazz:The Essential Collection Vol.2 | IN+OUT Records | 78012-2
Louis Armstrong:Fireworks | Dreyfus Jazz Line | FDM 36710-2
Carr,Norman | (v)
Stan Getz With The Eddie Sauter Orchestra
Stan Getz Plays The Music Of Mickey One | Verve | 531232-2
Ultimate Stan Getz selected by Joe Henderson | Verve | 557532-2
Carr,Pete | (g)
Dee Dee Bridgewater With Band
Dee Dee Bridgewater | Atlantic | 7567-80760-2
Carr,Richard | (v)
Richard Carr Trio
Coast To Coast | Nabel Records:Jazz Network | CD 4675
Along The Edge | Nabel Records:Jazz Network | CD 4683
Carr,Sonny | (perc)
Stan Getz-Joao Gilberto Orchestra
Sony Jazz Collection:Stan Getz | CBS | 488623-2
Carrascosa,Alfons | (as)
Moments Quartet
Original Moments | Fresh Sound Records | FSNT 052 CD
Carrier,Eugene | (keyboards,porg)
B.B.King And His Band
Live At San Quentin | MCA | MCD 06103
Carrière,Pokey | (tp)
Jack Teagarden And His Orchestra
Jazz:The Essential Collection Vol.3 | IN+OUT Records | 78013-2
Carrington,Steven | (ts)
Cyrus Chestnut Sextet
Earth Stories | Atlantic | 7567-82876-2
Carrington,Terri Lyne | (dr,perc,voc,programming,dr-solo)
Caecilie Norby With Band
My Corner Of The Sky | Blue Note | 853422-2
Cassandra Wilson With The Mulgrew Miller Trio
Blue Skies | JMT Edition | 919018-2
Cornelius Claudio Kreusch Group
Scoop | ACT | 9255-2
Danilo Perez Quartet
Panamonk | Impulse(MCA) | 951190-2
Diana Krall Group
The Girl In The Other Room | Verve | 9862246
Dianne Reeves With Band
I Remember | Blue Note | 790264-2
John Patitucci Group
Sketchbook | GRP | GRP 96172
Nguyen Le Trio With Guests
Purple:Celebrating Jimi Hendrix | ACT | 9410-2
Terri Lyne Carrington Group
Jazz Is A Spirit | ACT | 9408-2
Terri Lyne Carrington Quartet
Structure | ACT | 9427-2
Carroll,Baikida | (fl-h,tp,live-electronics,prep-tp)
Jack DeJohnette's Special Edition
Inflation Blues | ECM | 1244
Carroll,Charles | (dr)
Miff Mole And His Dixieland Band
Muggsy Spanier-Manhattan Masters,1945 | Storyville | STCD 6051
Muggsy Spanier And His Dixieland Band
Muggsy Spanier-Manhattan Masters,1945 | Storyville | STCD 6051
Carroll,Diahann | (voc)
Modern Jazz Quartet
MJQ 40 | Atlantic | 7567-82330-2
Carroll,Frank | (b)
Sarah Vaughan With The Norman Leyden Orchestra
Sarah Vaughan:Lover Man | Dreyfus Jazz Line | FDM 36739-2
Carroll,Jimmy | (arr,dir,condld)
Charlie Parker With Strings
Verve Jazz Masters 28:Charlie Parker Plays Standards | Verve | 521854-2
Charlie Parker With Strings:The Master Takes | Verve | 523984-2
Charlie Parker:The Best Of The Verve Years | Verve | 527815-2
Bird: The Complete Charlie Parker On Verve | Verve | 837141-2
Charlie Parker:April In Paris | Dreyfus Jazz Line | FDM 36737-2
Carroll,Joe | (voc)
Dizzy Gillespie And His Orchestra
Planet Jazz:Dizzy Gillespie | Planet Jazz | 2152069-2
Gillespiana And Carnegie Hall Concert | Verve | 519809-2
Ultimate Dizzy Gillespie | Verve | 557535-2
Dizzy Gillespie Sextet
Pleyel Jazz Concert 1953 | Vogue | 21409392
Carrothers,Bill | (el-pp)
Bill Carrothers Quartet
The Electric Bill | Dreyfus Jazz Line | FDM 36631-2
Carrott,Bryan | (vib,marimba,glockenspiel,tympany)
Dave Douglas Group
Witness | RCA | 2663763-2
Lounge Lizards
Berlin 1991 Part 1 | Intuition Records | INT 2044-2
Live In Berlin 1991-Vol.2 | Intuition Records | INT 2055-2
Michael Blake Group
Kingdom Of Champa | Intuition Records | INT 3189-2
Carruthers,Earl | (bs,cl,as,reedssax)
Jimmy Lunceford And His Orchestra
Planet Jazz:Swing | Planet Jazz | 2169651-2
Carry,George | (ascl)
Earl Hines And His Orchestra
Planet Jazz:Earl Hines | Planet Jazz | 2159973-2
Carson,Donald T. | (p)
Diane Schuur With The Count Basie Orchestra
The Best Of Diane Schuur | GRP | GRP 98882
Carson,Everett Ernest | (tpco)
Turk Murphy And His Jazz Band
Planet Jazz | Planet Jazz | 2169652-2
Carson,Tee | (maracasp)
Charlie Byrd Sextet
Byrd's Word! | Original Jazz Classics | OJCCD 1054-2(R 9448)
Carsten,Per | (flas)
Miles Davis With The Danish Radio Big Band
Aura | CBS | CK 63962
Per Carsten Quintet
Via | dacapo | DCCD 9462
The Danish Radio Big Band
Aura | CBS | CK 63962
Carstensen,Stian | (accordeon)
Trygve Seim Group
Different Rivers | ECM | 1744(159521-2)
Carter,Benjamin | (voc)
McCoy Tyner Group With Horns And Voices
Inner Voices | Original Jazz Classics | OJCCD 1039-2(M 9079)
McCoy Tyner Group With Voices

Inner Voices | Original Jazz Classics | OJCCD 1039-2(M 9079)

Carter,Benny | (arr,comp,ld,as,as ld,p,ts,voc,cl,ss)

Ben Webster All Stars
King Of The Tenors | Verve | 519806-2
Ben Webster And His Orchestra
Verve Jazz Masters 43:Ben Webster | Verve | 525431-2
Ben Webster Sextet
Verve Jazz Masters 43:Ben Webster | Verve | 525431-2
Verve Jazz Masters 52:Maynard Ferguson | Verve | 529905-2
Benny Carter 4
Montreux '77 | Original Jazz Classics | OJC20 374-2(2308204)
Benny Carter And His Chocolate Dandies
Planet Jazz:Ben Webster | RCA | 2165368-2
Jazz:The Essential Collection Vol.3 | IN+OUT Records | 78013-2
Benny Carter And His Orchestra
The Art Of Saxophone | Laserlight | 24652
Django Reinhardt All Star Sessions | Capitol | 531577-2
Americans Swinging In Paris:Benny Carter | EMI Records | 539647-2
Aspects | Capitol | 852677-2
Further Definitions/Additions To Further Definotions | Impulse(MCA) | 951229-2
Jazz At The Philharmonic:The Montreux Collection | Pablo | PACD 5306-2
Benny Carter Quartet
The Jazz Giants Play Rodgers & Hart:Blue Moon | Prestige | PCD 24205-2
Benny Carter Quintet
Jazz Giant | Original Jazz Classics | OJC20 167-2(C 7555)
Benny Carter Sextet
To Bags...With Love:Memorial Album | Pablo | 2310967-2
Milt Jackson Birthday Celebration | Fantasy | FANCD 6079-2
Jazz Giant | Original Jazz Classics | OJC20 167-2(C 7555)
Benny Carter-Coleman Hawkins-Johnny Hodges With The Oscar Peterson Trio
The Jazz Giants Play Duke Ellington:Caravan | Prestige | PCD 24227-2
Billie Holiday And Her All Stars
Verve Jazz Masters 12:Billie Holiday | Verve | 519825-2
Verve Jazz Masters 20:Introducing | Verve | 519853-2
Billie Holiday And Her Band
Verve Jazz Masters 47:Billie Holiday Sings Standards | Verve | 527650-2
Billie Holiday With Teddy Wilson And His Orchestra
Billie's Love Songs | Nimbus Records | NI 2000
Billy Eckstine With The Billy May Orchestra
Once More With Feeling | Roulette | 581862-2
Chocolate Dandies
Jazz:The Essential Collection Vol.3 | IN+OUT Records | 78013-2
Coleman Hawkins All Star Octet
Planet Jazz:Coleman Hawkins | Planet Jazz | 2152055-2
Coleman Hawkins And His All Star Jam Band
Django Reinhardt All Star Sessions | Capitol | 531577-2
Americans Swinging In Paris:Benny Carter | EMI Records | 539647-2
Jazz:The Essential Collection Vol.3 | IN+OUT Records | 78013-2
Coleman Hawkins Quartet
The Art Of Saxophone | Laserlight | 24652
Count Basie Band
Basie Jam No. 2 | Original Jazz Classics | OJCCD 631-2(2310786)
Count Basie Jam
Montreux '77 | Original Jazz Classics | OJC 379(2308209)
Montreux '77 | Original Jazz Classics | OJC 385(2620105)
Dizzy Gillespie And His Orchestra
Talking Verve:Dizzy Gillespie | Verve | 533846-2
Duke Ellington And His Orchestra
The Jazz Giants Play Duke Ellington:Caravan | Prestige | PCD 24227-2
Ella Fitzgerald And Her All Stars
All That Jazz | Pablo | 2310938-2
Ella Fitzgerald With Benny Carter's Magnificent Seven
30 By Ella | Capitol | 520090-2
Ella Fitzgerald With The Billy May Orchestra
Ella Fitzgerald-First Lady Of Song | Verve | 517898-2
The Best Of The Song Books | Verve | 519804-2
Verve Jazz Masters 6:Ella Fitzgerald | Verve | 519822-2
The Best Of The Song Books:The Ballads | Verve | 521867-2
Verve Jazz Masters 46:Ella Fitzgerald-The Jazz Sides | Verve | 527655-2
Love Songs:The Best Of The Song Books | Verve | 531762-2
Ella Fitzgerald Sings The Harold Arlen Song Book | Verve | 589108-2
For The Love Of Ella Fitzgerald | Verve | 841765-2
Ella Fitzgerald With The Nelson Riddle Orchestra
Get Happy! | Verve | 523321-2
Fats Waller And His Rhythm
Planet Jazz:Fats Waller | Planet Jazz | 2152058-2
Fletcher Henderson And His Orchestra
Jazz:The Essential Collection Vol.1 | IN+OUT Records | 78011-2
JATP All Stars
JATP In Tokyo | Pablo | 2620104-2
J.A.T.P. In London 1969 | Pablo | 2CD 2620119
The Drum Battle:Gene Krupa And Buddy Rich At JATP | Verve | 559810-2
The Cole Porter Songbook | Verve | 823250-2
Welcome To Jazz At The Philharmonic | Fantasy | FANCD 6081-2
Lionel Hampton And His Orchestra
Planet Jazz:Coleman Hawkins | Planet Jazz | 2152055-2
Planet Jazz:Lionel Hampton | Planet Jazz | 2152059-2
Planet Jazz:Ben Webster | RCA | 2165368-2
Planet Jazz:Swing | Planet Jazz | 2169651-2
Planet Jazz:Jazz Saxophone | Planet Jazz | 2169653-2
Jazz:The Essential Collection Vol.3 | IN+OUT Records | 78013-2
Louis Armstrong And His All Stars With Benny Carter's Orchestra
Ambassador Louis Armstrong Vol.17:Moments To Remember(1952-1956) | Ambassador | CLA 1917
Louis Armstrong With Benny Carter's Orchestra
Louis Armstrong-My Greatest Songs | MCA | MCD 18347
Lucky Thompson And His Lucky Seven
Planet Jazz:Bebop | RCA | 2169650-2
McKinney's Cotton Pickers
Jazz:The Essential Collection Vol.3 | IN+OUT Records | 78013-2
Mezz Mezzrow And His Orchestra
Planet Jazz:Bud Freeman | Planet Jazz | 2161240-2
Norman Granz Jam Session
Verve Jazz Masters 35:Johnny Hodges | Verve | 521857-2
Charlie Parker:The Best Of The Verve Years | Verve | 527815-2
Talkin' Bird | Verve | 559859-2
Bird: The Complete Charlie Parker On Verve | Verve | 837141-2
Peggy Lee With The Quincy Jones Orchestra
Blues Cross Country | Capitol | 520088-2
Phil Woods-Benny Carter Quintet
The Art Of Saxophone | Laserlight | 24652
Roy Eldridge-Benny Carter Quintet
The Complete Verve Roy Eldridge Studio Sessions | Verve | 9861278
Sarah Vaughan With The Benny Carter Orchestra
Ballads | Roulette | 537561-2
Jazz Profile | Blue Note | 823517-2
Spike Hughes And His Negro Orchestra
Jazz:The Essential Collection Vol.3 | IN+OUT Records | 78013-2
Tatum-Carter-Bellson Trio
Art Tatum-The Complete Pablo Group Masterpieces | Pablo | 6 PACD 4401-2
Ten Cats And A Mouse
The Hollywood Session:The Capitol Jazzmen | Jazz Unlimited | JUCD 2044
The Capitol Jazzmen
The Hollywood Session:The Capitol Jazzmen | Jazz Unlimited | JUCD 2044
The Hollywood Hucksters
The Hollywood Session:The Capitol Jazzmen | Jazz Unlimited | JUCD 2044
The Metronome All-Star Nine
Jazz:The Essential Collection Vol.3 | IN+OUT Records | 78013-2
Willie Lewis And His Entertainers
Americans Swinging In Paris:Benny Carter | EMI Records | 539647-2
Zoot Sims With Orchestra
Passion Flower | Original Jazz Classics | OJCCD 939-2(2312120)

Carter,Betty | (vocwbd)

Betty Carter And The Harold Mabern Trio
Misty Blue:Sweet Sisters Swing Songs Of Sorrow And Sadness | Blue Note | 521151-2
Lionel Hampton And His Orchestra
Lionel Hampton:Flying Home | Dreyfus Jazz Line | FDM 36735-2

Carter,Bob | (b,ptp)

Red Norvo Sextet
Planet Jazz:Ben Webster | RCA | 2165368-2

Carter,Clifford | (el-p,keyboards,dr-loops,tambourine)

Don Grolnick Group
Hearts And Numbers | VeraBra Records | CDVBR 2016-2

Carter,Don | (dr)

Muggsy Spanier And His Ragtime Band
Planet Jazz | Planet Jazz | 2169652-2

Carter,Doretta | (voc)

Hans Theessink Group
Crazy Moon | Minor Music | 801052
Journey On | Minor Music | 801062

Carter,Geoff | (clts)

Geoff Carter Quintet
Unsong Hero:The Undiscovered Genius Of Chas Burchell | IN+OUT Records | 7026-2
Lilly Thornton With The Benny Golson Sextet
Remembering Dinah-A Salute To Dinah Washington | Hot Shot Records | HSR 8313-2
The Mike Hennessey Chastet
Shades Of Chas Burchell | IN+OUT Records | 7025-2

Carter,James | (as,ts,bs,b-cl,bass-fl,dr,ss)

Cyrus Chestnut Trio With James Carter
Cyrus Chestnut | Atlantic | 7567-83140-2
Cyrus Chestnut Trio With James Carter And Joe Lovano
Cyrus Chestnut | Atlantic | 7567-83140-2
Donald Byrd Orchestra
Places And Spaces | Blue Note | 854326-2
Flip Phillips Septet
Swing Is The Thing | Verve | 543477-2
Flip Phillips Sextet
Swing Is The Thing | Verve | 543477-2
James Carter Group
Conversin' With The Elders | Atlantic | 7567-82988-2
Chasin' The Gypsy | Atlantic | 7567-83304-2
Layin' In The Cut | Atlantic | 7567-83305-2
James Carter Quartet
The Real Quietstorm | Atlantic | 7567-82742-2
James Carter-Craig Tahorn
The Real Quietstorm | Atlantic | 7567-82742-2
James Carter-Shahid Jaribu
The Real Quietstorm | Atlantic | 7567-82742-2

Carter,Kent | (bcello)

The Jazz Composer's Orchestra
Comminications | JCOA | 1001/2

Carter,Lance | (dr,percsnare-dr)

Cassandra Wilson Group
Misty Blue:Sweet Sisters Swing Songs Of Sorrow And Sadness | Blue Note | 521151-2
Blue Light 'Til Dawn | Blue Note | 781357-2

Carter,Lou | (parr)

The Dixieland All Stars
The Dixieland All Stars | Jazz Unlimited | JUCD 2037

Carter,Neil | (bodhran)

Thomas Kessler Group
On Earth | Laika Records | 8695069

Carter,Regina | (v)

Cassandra Wilson Group
Traveling Miles | Blue Note | 854123-2
James Carter Group
Chasin' The Gypsy | Atlantic | 7567-83304-2
Kenny Barron Group
Spirit Song | Verve | 543180-2
Kenny Barron-Regina Carter
Freefall | Verve | 549706-2
Mark Helias Group
Loopin' The Cool | Enja | ENJ-9049 2
Robert Dick Group With The Soldier String Quartet
Jazz Standard On Mars | Enja | ENJ-9327 2

Carter,Ron | (b,dr,el-b,perc,piccolo-bcello)

(Little)Jimmy Scott And His Quintet
All The Way | Warner | 7599-26955-2
Alice Coltrane Quintet
Ptah The El Daoud | Impulse(MCA) | 951201-2
Andrew Hill Orchestra
Deep Blue-The United States Of Mind | Blue Note | 521152-2
Andrew Hill Quintet
Grass Roots | Blue Note | 522672-2
Blue Bossa | Blue Note | 795590-2
Andy Bey Group
Tuesdays In Chinatown | Minor Music | 801099
Anfrew Hill Nonet
Passing Ships | Blue Note | 593871-2
Antonio Carlos Jobim Group
Antonio Carlos Jobim And Friends | Verve | 531556-2
Antonio Carlos Jobim With The Herbie Hancock Sextet
Antonio Carlos Jobim And Friends | Verve | 531556-2
Antonio Carlos Jobim-Gal Costa Septet
Antonio Carlos Jobim And Friends | Verve | 531556-2
Archie Shepp Orchestra
The Cry Of My People | Impulse(MCA) | 9861488
Archie Shepp Sextet
The Way Ahead | Impulse(MCA) | 951272-2
Art Pepper Quartet
Art Pepper:The Complete Galaxy Recordings | Galaxy | 16GCD 1016-2
Art Pepper-Ron Carter Duo
Art Pepper:The Complete Galaxy Recordings | Galaxy | 16GCD 1016-2
Barry Harris Trio
Magnificent! | Original Jazz Classics | OJCCD 1026-2(P 7733)
Billy Cobham Group
Spectrum | Atlantic | 7567-81428-2
Billy Cobham Trio
The Art Of Three | IN+OUT Records | 77045-2
Blue Note All Stars
Town Hall Concert | Blue Note | 497811-2
Bob Brookmeyer Quintet
Sony Jazz Collection:Stan Getz | CBS | 488623-2
Bob Brookmeyer Sextet
Late Night Sax | CBS | 487798-2
Bobby Timmons Orchestra
Quartet And Orchestra | Milestone | MCD 47091-2
Bobby Timmons Quartet
Quartet And Orchestra | Milestone | MCD 47091-2
Bobby Timmons Trio
In Person | Original Jazz Classics | OJC20 364-2(RLP 9391)
Born To Be Blue! | Original Jazz Classics | OJC20 873-2(R 9468)
Booker Little Quintet
Eric Dolphy Birthday Celebration | Fantasy | FANCD 6085-2
Booker Little Sextet
Out Front | Candid | CCD 79027
Candid Dolphy | Candid | CCD 79033
Cal Tjader's Orchestra
Verve Jazz Masters 39:Cal Tjader | Verve | 521858-2
Cannonball Adderley Sextet
Julian Cannonball Adderlry: Salle Pleyel/Olympia | Laserlight | 36126
Charles Earland Septet
Charles Earland In Concert | Prestige | PRCD 24267-2
Charles Mingus Orchestra
Three Or Four Shades Of Blues | Atlantic | 7567-81403-2
Chet Baker Quintet
Once Upon A Summertime | Original Jazz Classics | OJCCD 405-2
Chet Baker-Gerry Mulligan Group
Carnegie Hall Concert Vol. 1/2 | CTI | EPC 450554-2
Chick Corea Quartet
Inner Space | Atlantic | 7567-81304-2
Coleman Hawkins Quintet
The Hawk Relaxes | Original Jazz Classics | OJCCD 709-2(MV 15)
Coleman Hawkins With Eddie Lockjaw Davis And The Tommy Flanagan Trio
Night Hawk | Original Jazz Classics | OJC20 420-2(SV 2016)
Cyrus Chestnut Trio
Cyrus Chestnut | Atlantic | 7567-83140-2
Cyrus Chestnut Trio With Anita Baker
Cyrus Chestnut | Atlantic | 7567-83140-2
Cyrus Chestnut Trio With James Carter
Cyrus Chestnut | Atlantic | 7567-83140-2
Cyrus Chestnut Trio With James Carter And Joe Lovano
Cyrus Chestnut | Atlantic | 7567-83140-2
Cyrus Chestnut Trio With Joe Lovano
Cyrus Chestnut | Atlantic | 7567-83140-2
Dexter Gordon Quartet
Dexter Gordon Birthday Celebration | Fantasy | FANCD 6082-2
Don Sickler Orchestra
Tribute To Charlie Parker Vol.2 | Dreyfus Jazz Line | FDM 37015-2
Don Sleet Quintet
All Members | Original Jazz Classics | OJCCD 1949-2(JLP 9455)
Donald Harrison Trio
Heroes | Nagel-Heyer | CD 2041
Duke Pearson Quartet
Sweet Honey Bee | Blue Note | 595974-2
Duke Pearson Quintet
Sweet Honey Bee | Blue Note | 595974-2
Duke Pearson Sextet
Sweet Honey Bee | Blue Note | 595974-2
Midnight Blue(The [Be]witching Hour) | Blue Note | 854365-2
Eddie Harris Quartet
The Best Of Eddie Harris | Atlantic | 7567-81370-2
Eddie Harris Quintet
The Best Of Eddie Harris | Atlantic | 7567-81370-2
Atlantic Saxophones | Rhino | 8122-71256-2
Eric Alexander Quartet
Nightlife In Tokyo | Milestone | MCD 9330-2
Eric Dolphy Quartet
Eric Dolphy:The Complete Prestige Recordings | Prestige | 9 PRCD-4418-2
Eric Dolphy Birthday Celebration | Fantasy | FANCD 6085-2
Out There | New Jazz | NJSA 8252-6
Out There | Original Jazz Classics | OJC20 023-2(NJ 8252)
Eric Dolphy Quintet
Far Cry | Original Jazz Classics | OJC20 400-2
Eric Dolphy-Booker Little Quintet
Eric Dolphy:The Complete Prestige Recordings | Prestige | 9 PRCD-4418-2
Eric Reed Quartet
Musicale | Impulse(MCA) | 951196-2
Eric Reed Quintet
Musicale | Impulse(MCA) | 951196-2
Essence All Stars
Hot Jazz Bisquits | Hip Bop | HIBD 8801
Frank Morgan All Stars
Reflections | Original Jazz Classics | OJCCD 1046-2(C 14052)
Frank Morgan Quartet
Yardbird Suite | Original Jazz Classics | OJCCD 1060-2(C 14045)
Freddie Hubbard Quintet
This Is Jazz:Freddie Hubbard | CBS | CK 65041
Freddie Hubbard Septet
This Is Jazz:Freddie Hubbard | CBS | CK 65041
Freddie Hubbard Trio
This Is Jazz:Freddie Hubbard | CBS | CK 65041
Freddie Hubbard With Orchestra
This Is Jazz:Freddie Hubbard | CBS | CK 65041
Gal Costa With The Herbie Hancock Sextet
Antonio Carlos Jobim And Friends | Verve | 531556-2
Gato Barbieri Group
Planet Jazz:Gato Barbieri | RCA | 2165364-2
Gato Barbieri:The Best Of The Early Years | RCA | 2663523-2
Gato Barbieri Orchestra
The Roots Of Acid Jazz | Impulse(MCA) | IMP 12042
Gato Barbieri Septet
Yesterdays | RCA | 2147797-2
Gene Ammons Quartet
Fine And Mellow | Prestige | PRCD 24281-2
Gene Ammons Quintet
Fine And Mellow | Prestige | PRCD 24281-2
Gene Ammons Sextet
Fine And Mellow | Prestige | PRCD 24281-2
Gene Ammons Sextet With Strings
Fine And Mellow | Prestige | PRCD 24281-2
Gene Harris And The Three Sounds
Deep Blue-The United States Of Mind | Blue Note | 521152-2
George Benson And His Orchestra
Giblet Gravy | Verve | 543754-2
George Benson Orchestra
Verve Jazz Masters 21:George Benson | Verve | 521861-2
Talkin' Verve:George Benson | Verve | 553780-2
George Benson Quintet
Verve Jazz Masters 21:George Benson | Verve | 521861-2
Giblet Gravy | Verve | 543754-2
George Benson Sextet
Talkin' Verve:George Benson | Verve | 553780-2
George Benson With The Don Sebesky Orchestra
Verve Jazz Masters 21:George Benson | Verve | 521861-2
Gil Evans Orchestra
Verve Jazz Masters 23:Gil Evans | Verve | 521860-2
The Individualism Of Gil Evans | Verve | 833804-2
Out Of The Cool | Impulse(MCA) | 951186-2
Gonzalo Rubalcaba-Herbie Hancock Quintet
Antonio Carlos Jobim And Friends | Verve | 531556-2
Grover Washington Jr. Orchestra
Jazzrock-Anthology Vol.3:Fusion | Zounds | CD 27100555
Harbie Hancock/Ron Carter
Lifetime | Blue Note | 499004-2
Helen Merrill With The Dick Katz Group
The Feeling Is Mutual | EmArCy | 558849-2
A Shade Of Difference | EmArCy | 558851-2
Helen Merrill-Don Carter Duo
A Shade Of Difference | EmArCy | 558851-2
Herbie Hancock Quartet
Herbie Hancock:The Complete Blue Note Sixties Sessions | Blue Note | 495569-2
Empyrean Isles | Blue Note | 498796-2
Antonio Carlos Jobim And Friends | Verve | 531556-2
Blue N' Groovy | Blue Note | 780679-2
Blue Break Beats | Blue Note | 799106-2
Cantaloupe Island | Blue Note | 829331-2
Herbie Hancock Quintet
V.S.O.P. Herbie Hancock-Live At The City Center N.Y. | CBS | 486569-2
Maiden Voyage | Blue Note | 495331-2
Herbie Hancock:The Complete Blue Note Sixties Sessions | Blue Note | 495569-2
The Best Of Blue Note | Blue Note | 796110-2
Cantaloupe Island | Blue Note | 829331-2
Herbie Hancock Sextet

Herbie Hancock:The Complete Blue Note Sixties Sessions | Blue Note | 495569-2
Speak Like A Child | Blue Note | 746136-2
Herbie Hancock Trio
Herbie Hancock:The Complete Blue Note Sixties Sessions | Blue Note | 495569-2
Chick Corea-Herbie Hancock-Keith Jarrett-McCoy Tyner | Atlantic | 7567-81402-2
Horace Silver Quintet
Horace Silver Retrospective | Blue Note | 495576-2
A Prescription For The Blues | Impulse(MCA) | 951238-2
Horace Silver Quintet With Brass
Horace Silver Retrospective | Blue Note | 495576-2
Horace Silver Quintet With Vocals
Horace Silver Retrospective | Blue Note | 495576-2
J.J.Johnson And His Orchestra
Planet Jazz:J.J.Johnson | Planet Jazz | 2159974-2
J.J.Johnson Quintet
The J.J.Johnson Memorial Album | Prestige | PRCD 11025-2
Jaki Byard Sextet
Jaki Byard:Solo/Strings | Prestige | PCD 24246-2
James Moody Orchestra
The Blues And Other Colors | Original Jazz Classics | OJCCD 954-2(M 9023)
Jim Hall-Ron Carter Duo
Alone Together | Original Jazz Classics | OJC 467(M 9045)
Jimmy Smith Quartet
Jimmy Smith:Best Of The Verve Years | Verve | 527950-2
Jimmy Smith With Orchestra
Jimmy Smith-Talkin' Verve | Verve | 531563-2
Jimmy Smith With The Johnny Pate Orchestra
Jimmy Smith-Talkin' Verve | Verve | 531563-2
Joe Henderson And His Orchestra
Joe Henderson:The Milestone Years | Milestone | 8MCD 4413-2
Joe Henderson Group
Jazzin' Vol.2: The Music Of Stevie Wonder | Fantasy | FANCD 6088-2
Joe Henderson Quartet
Joe Henderson:The Milestone Years | Milestone | 8MCD 4413-2
The Kicker | Original Jazz Classics | OJCCD 465-2
Tetragon | Original Jazz Classics | OJCCD 844-2(M 9017)
The Jazz Giants Play Cole Porter:Night And Day | Prestige | PCD 24203-2
Joe Henderson Quintet
Joe Henderson:The Milestone Years | Milestone | 8MCD 4413-2
Joe Henderson Septet
Antonio Carlos Jobim And Friends | Verve | 531556-2
Mode For Joe | Blue Note | 591894-2
The Blue Note Years-The Best Of Joe Henderson | Blue Note | 795627-2
Joe Henderson Sextet
Joe Henderson:The Milestone Years | Milestone | 8MCD 4413-2
The Kicker | Original Jazz Classics | OJCCD 465-2
Joe Henderson Trio
The Blue Note Years-The Best Of Joe Henderson | Blue Note | 795627-2
The State Of The Tenor Vol.1&2 | Blue Note | 828879-2
Joe Henderson:The Milestone Years | Milestone | 8MCD 4413-2
Joey Baron Quartet
We'll Soon Find Out | Intuition Records | INT 3515-2
Johnny Griffin Quartet
The Kerry Dancers | Original Jazz Classics | OJCCD 1952-2(RLP 9420)
Johnny Smith Quintet
Moonlight In Vermont | Roulette | 596593-2
Jon Hendricks With The Herbie Hancock Quintet
Antonio Carlos Jobim And Friends | Verve | 531556-2
Kenny Burrell Quartet
Verve Jazz Masters 45:Kenny Burrell | Verve | 527652-2
Blues-The Common Ground | Verve | 589101-2
Kenny Burrell Sextet
Verve Jazz Masters 45:Kenny Burrell | Verve | 527652-2
Kenny Burrell With The Don Sebesky Orchestra
Verve Jazz Masters 45:Kenny Burrell | Verve | 527652-2
Blues-The Common Ground | Verve | 589101-2
Kenny Burrell With The Gil Evans Orchestra
Guitar Forms | Verve | 521403-2
Verve Jazz Masters 23:Gil Evans | Verve | 521860-2
Verve Jazz Masters 45:Kenny Burrell | Verve | 527652-2
Verve Jazz Masters Vol.60:The Collection | Verve | 529866-2
Lee Morgan Orchestra
Standards | Blue Note | 823213-2
Lee Morgan Quintet
Sonic Boom | Blue Note | 590414-2
Lee Morgan Sextet
Wayne Shorter:The Classic Blue Note Recordings | Blue Note | 540856-2
Mal Waldron Sextet
Eric Dolphy:The Complete Prestige Recordings | Prestige | 9 PRCD-4418-2
Eric Dolphy Birthday Celebration | Fantasy | FANCD 6085-2
The Quest | Original Jazz Classics | OJCCD 082-2(NJ 8269)
The Mal Waldron Memorial Album:Soul Eyes | Prestige | PRCD 11024-2
Mark Morganelli And The Jazz Forum All Stars
Speak Low | Candid | CCD 79054
Mark Whitfield Group
Patrice | Warner | 7599-26659-2
McCoy Tyner Group With Horns
Inner Voices | Original Jazz Classics | OJCCD 1039-2(M 9079)
McCoy Tyner Group With Horns And Voices
Inner Voices | Original Jazz Classics | OJCCD 1039-2(M 9079)
McCoy Tyner Group With Voices
Inner Voices | Original Jazz Classics | OJCCD 1039-2(M 9079)
McCoy Tyner Orchestra
13th House | Original Jazz Classics | OJCCD 1089-2(M 9102)
McCoy Tyner Quartet
The Real McCoy | Blue Note | 497807-2
McCoy Tyner Sextet
Extensions | Blue Note | 837646-2
McCoy Tyner Trio
Trident | Original Jazz Classics | OJC20 720-2(M 9063)
Miles Davis Group
Live-Evil | CBS | C2K 65135
Miles Davis Quartet
This Is Jazz:Miles Davis Plays Ballads | CBS | CK 65038
Miles Davis Quintet
Ballads | CBS | 461099-2
Circle In The Round | CBS | 467898-2
The Complete Concert 1964:My Funny Valentine+Four & More | CBS | 471246-2
Highlights From The Plugged Nickel | CBS | 481434-2
Filles De Kilimanjaro | CBS | 86555-2
Miles Davis Quintet 1965-1968 | CBS | C6K 67398
Seven Steps To Heaven | CBS | CK 48827
This Is Jazz:Miles Davis Plays Ballads | CBS | CK 65038
Sorcerer | CBS | CK 65680
Nefertiti | CBS | CK 65681
Miles Smiles | CBS | CK 65682
Miles In The Sky | CBS | CK 65684
E.S.P. | CBS | CK65683
Miles Davis Sextet
Circle In The Round | CBS | 467898-2
Miles In The Sky | CBS | CK 65684
Miles Davis With Gil Evans & His Orchestra
Quiet Nights | CBS | CK 65293
Milt Jackson And His Orchestra
Sunflower | CTI | ZK 65131
Milt Jackson Orchestra
To Bags...With Love:Memorial Album | Pablo | 2310967-2
Milt Jackson Birthday Celebration | Fantasy | FANCD 6079-2
Big Bags | Original Jazz Classics | OJCCD 366-2(RLP 9429)
Milt Jackson Sextet
Milt Jackson Birthday Celebration | Fantasy | FANCD 6079-2
Nat Adderley Quintet
A Little New York Midtown Music | Original Jazz Classics | OJCCD 1008-2(GXY 5120)
Oliver Nelson And His Orchestra
Verve Jazz Masters Vol.60:The Collection | Verve | 529866-2
Paul Desmond Orchestra
Late Night Sax | CBS | 487798-2
Skylark | CTI | ZK 65133
Paul Desmond Quartet With The Don Sebesby Orchestra
From The Hot Afternoon | Verve | 543487-2
Pharoah Sanders Orchestra
Karma | Impulse(MCA) | 951153-2
Ron Carter Group
Songs For You | Milestone | MCD 47099-2
Peg Leg | Original Jazz Classics | OJCCD 621-2
Ron Carter Octet
New York Slick | Original Jazz Classics | OJCCD 916-2(M 9096)
Ron Carter Orchestra
Parade | Original Jazz Classics | OJCCD 1047-2(M 9088)
Ron Carter Quartet
Stardust | somethin'else | 537813-2
Pick 'Em/Super Strings | Milestone | MCD 47090-2
Songs For You | Milestone | MCD 47099-2
Parade | Original Jazz Classics | OJCCD 1047-2(M 9088)
Carnaval | Original Jazz Classics | OJCCD 1070-2(GXY 5144)
Ron Carter Quintet
Stardust | somethin'else | 537813-2
Eric Dolphy:The Complete Prestige Recordings | Prestige | 9 PRCD-4418-2
Eric Dolphy Birthday Celebration | Fantasy | FANCD 6085-2
Where | Original Jazz Classics | OJCCD 432-2
Ron Carter Quintet With Strings
Pick 'Em/Super Strings | Milestone | MCD 47090-2
Ron Carter Sextet
New York Slick | Original Jazz Classics | OJCCD 916-2(M 9096)
Ron Carter Trio
Stardust | somethin'else | 537813-2
The Golden Striker | Blue Note | 590831-2
Third Plane | Original Jazz Classics | OJCC20 754-2(M 9105)
Ron Carter With Strings
Pastels | Original Jazz Classics | OJCCD 665-2(M 9073)
Ron Carter-Richard Galliano Duo
Panamanhattan | Dreyfus Jazz Line | FDM 36514-2
Ron Carter-Roland Hanna
Stardust | somethin'else | 537813-2
Russell Malone Quartet
Sweet Georgia Peach | Impulse(MCA) | 951282-2
Russell Malone Quintet
Sweet Georgia Peach | Impulse(MCA) | 951282-2
Sam Rivers Quartet
A Blue Conception | Blue Note | 534254-2
Fuchsia Swing Song | Blue Note | 593874-2
Shirley Horn Quintet
Antonio Carlos Jobim And Friends | Verve | 531556-2
Shirley Horn Sextet
Antonio Carlos Jobim And Friends | Verve | 531556-2
Sonny Rollins & Co.
Planet Jazz:Sonny Rollins | Planet Jazz | 2152062-2
Planet Jazz Sampler | Planet Jazz | 2152326-2
Sonny Rollins Quartet
Planet Jazz:Sonny Rollins | Planet Jazz | 2152062-2
Stan Getz Quartet
Stan Getz Highlights:The Best Of The Verve Years Vol.2 | Verve | 517330-2
Verve Jazz Masters 8:Stan Getz | Verve | 519823-2
Verve Jazz Masters 53:Stan Getz-Bossa Nova | Verve | 529904-2
A Life In Jazz:A Musical Biography | Verve | 535119-2
Ultimate Stan Getz selected by Joe Henderson | Verve | 557532-2
Stan Getz Highlights | Verve | 847430-2
Stan Getz With Orchestra And Voices
Stan Getz Highlights | Verve | 847430-2
Stan Getz With The Bill Evans Trio
Verve Jazz Masters 5:Bill Evans | Verve | 519821-2
The Complete Bill Evans On Verve | Verve | 527953-2
Ultimate Bill Evans selected by Herbie Hancock | Verve | 557536-2
Stan Getz With The Claus Ogerman Orchestra
What The World Needs Now-Stan Getz Plays Bacharach And David | Verve | 557450-2
Stan Getz With The Richard Evans Orchestra
What The World Needs Now-Stan Getz Plays Bacharach And David | Verve | 557450-2
Stan Getz-Bill Evans Quartet
Stan Getz & Bill Evans | Verve | 833802-2
Stanley Turrentine Quartet
The Roots Of Acid Jazz | Impulse(MCA) | IMP 12042
Stephen Scott Quartet
Vision Quest | Enja | ENJ-9347 2
Stephen Scott Trio
Vision Quest | Enja | ENJ-9347 2
The Jazz Composer's Orchestra
Comminications | JCOA | 1001/2
Tom Browne Quintet
Another Shade Of Browne | Hip Bop | HIBD 8011
Hot Jazz Bisquits | Hip Bop | HIBD 8801
Tony Williams Lifetime
Ego | Verve | 559512-2
Wayne Shorter Orchestra
Wayne Shorter:The Classic Blue Note Recordings | Blue Note | 540856-2
Wayne Shorter Quartet
Sorcerer | CBS | CK 65680
Wayne Shorter Quintet
Speak No Evil | Blue Note | 499001-2
Wayne Shorter:The Classic Blue Note Recordings | Blue Note | 540856-2
Wayne Shorter Sextet
Wayne Shorter:The Classic Blue Note Recordings | Blue Note | 540856-2
Blue N' Groovy | Blue Note | 780679-2
Wes Montgomery Quartet
Wes Montgomery-The Complete Riverside Recordings | Riverside | 12 RCD 4408-2
Verve Jazz Masters 14:Wes Montgomery | Verve | 519826-2
Talkin' Jazz:Roots Of Acid Jazz | Verve | 529580-2
Tequila | Verve | 547769-2
The Jazz Giants Play Harold Arlen:Blues In The Night | Prestige | PCD 24201-2
Wes Montgomery Quartet With The Claus Ogerman Orchestra
Tequila | Verve | 547769-2
Wes Montgomery Quintet
Wes Montgomery-The Complete Riverside Recordings | Riverside | 12 RCD 4408-2
So Much Guitar! | Original Jazz Classics | OJC20 233-2
The Jazz Giants Play Duke Ellington:Caravan | Prestige | PCD 24227-2
Wes Montgomery Quintet With The Claus Ogerman Orchestra
The Antonio Carlos Jobim Songbook | Verve | 525472-2
Talkin' Jazz:Roots Of Acid Jazz | Verve | 529580-2
Tequila | Verve | 547769-2
Wes Montgomery Sextet
Tequila | Verve | 547769-2
Wes Montgomery Trio
Wes Montgomery:The Verve Jazz Sides | Verve | 521690-2
Tequila | Verve | 547769-2
Wes Montgomery Trio With The Claus Ogerman Orchestra
Tequila | Verve | 547769-2
Wes Montgomery With The Claus Ogerman Orchestra
Verve Jazz Masters 14:Wes Montgomery | Verve | 519826-2
Wynton Marsalis Quartet
Wynton Marsalis | CBS | 468708-2
Wynton Marsalis Quintet
Wynton Marsalis | CBS | 468708-2
Wynton Marsalis Sextet
Hot House Flowers | CBS | 468710-2

Carter,Viv Clambake | (drwbd)
Mr.Acker Bilk And His Paramount Jazz Band
The Golden Years Of Revival Jazz,Vol.2 | Storyville | STCD 5507
The Golden Years Of Revival Jazz,Vol.6 | Storyville | STCD 5511
The Golden Years Of Revival Jazz,Vol.7 | Storyville | STCD 5512
The Golden Years Of Revival Jazz,Vol.8 | Storyville | STCD 5513
The Golden Years Of Revival Jazz,Vol.9 | Storyville | STCD 5514
The Golden Years Of Revival Jazz,Vol.10 | Storyville | STCD 5515
The Golden Years Of Revival Jazz,Vol.12 | Storyville | STCD 5517
The Golden Years Of Revival Jazz,Vol.13 | Storyville | STCD 5518
The Golden Years Of Revival Jazz,Vol.14 | Storyville | STCD 5519
The Golden Years Of Revibal Jazz,Vol.15 | Storyville | STCD 5520

Caruthers,Earl | (as,bscl)
Jimmy Lunceford And His Orchestra
The Legends Of Swing | Laserlight | 24659

Carvalho,Alexandro | (v)
Duo Fenix
Karai-Eté | IN+OUT Records | 7009-2

Carvalho,Jorjao | (el-b)
Ithamara Koorax With Band
Love Dance:The Ballad Album | Milestone | MCD 9327-2

Carver,Dwight | (mellophone)
Stan Kenton And His Orchestra
Adventures In Blues | Capitol | 520089-2
Adventures In Jazz | Capitol | 521222-2

Carver,Wayman | (bs,cl,as,fl,ts,arrsax)
Ella Fitzgerald And Her Famous Orchestra
The Radio Years 1940 | Jazz Unlimited | JUCD 2065
Ella Fitzgerald And Her Orchestra
Jazz Collection:Ella Fitzgerald | Laserlight | 24397
Ella Fitzgerald With The Chick Webb Orchestra
Jazz Collection:Ella Fitzgerald | Laserlight | 24397
Spike Hughes And His Negro Orchestra
Jazz:The Essential Collection Vol.3 | IN+OUT Records | 78013-2

Carvin,Michael | (dr,perc,tympani,voc,whistle,voice)
Frank Ku-Umba Lacy Group
Tonal Weights & Blue Fire | Tutu Records | 888112-2*
Hamiet Bluiett Group
...You Don't Need To Know...If You Have To Ask | Tutu Records | 888128-2*

Carwell,Carl | (arrvoc)
Paulinho Da Costa Orchestra
Happy People | Original Jazz Classics | OJCCD 783-2(2312102)

Cary,Dick | (alto-h,p,arr,orgtp)
Bud Freeman And His Summa Cum Laude Orchestra
Planet Jazz:Bud Freeman | Planet Jazz | 2161240-2
Eddie Condon And His Boys
The Very Best Of Dixieland Jazz | Verve | 535529-2
Jack Teagarden And His Band
Meet Me Where They Play The Blues | Good Time Jazz | GTCD 12063-2
Jimmy McPartland And His Dixielanders
Planet Jazz | Planet Jazz | 2169652-2
Louis Armstrong And His All Stars
Planet Jazz:Louis Armstrong | Planet Jazz | 2152052-2
Planet Jazz:Jack Teagarden | Planet Jazz | 2161236-2
Planet Jazz:Male Jazz Vocalists | Planet Jazz | 2169657-2
Jazz Collection:Louis Armstrong | Laserlight | 24366
Best Of The Complete RCA Victor Recordings | RCA | 2663636-2
Louis Armstrong:A 100th Birthday Celebration | RCA | 2663694-2
Louis Armstrong:C'est Si Bon | Dreyfus Jazz Line | FDM 36730-2
Louis Armstrong:Wintergarden 1947/Blue Note 1948 | Storyville | STCD 8242
Max Kaminsky And His Dixieland Bashers
Planet Jazz | Planet Jazz | 2169652-2

Cary,Marc Anthony | (p)
Abbey Lincoln With Her Band
Who Used To Dance | Verve | 533559-2
Wholly Earth | Verve | 559538-2
Abraham Burton Quartet
Closest To The Sun | Enja | ENJ-8074 2
The Magician | Enja | ENJ-9037 2
Taylor's Wailers
Mr. A.T. | Enja | ENJ-7017 2

Casamenti,Al | (g)
Bud Freeman And His Summa Cum Laude Orchestra
Planet Jazz:Bud Freeman | Planet Jazz | 2161240-2
Wes Montgomery With The Don Sebesky Orchestra
Verve Jazz Masters 14:Wes Montgomery | Verve | 519826-2
Talkin' Jazz:Roots Of Acid Jazz | Verve | 529580-2
California Dreaming | Verve | 827842-2

Casany,David M. | (fl)
Daniel Flors Group
When Least Expected | Fresh Sound Records | FSNT 080 CD

Cascaro,Jeff | (voc)
HR Big Band
The American Songs Of Kurt Weill | hr music.de | hrmj 006-01 CD

Casero,Ricardo | (tb)
Dave Liebman And The Lluis Vidal Trio With The Orquestra De Cambra Theatre Lliure
Dave Liebman And The Lluis Vidal Trio | Fresh Sound Records | FSNT 026 CD
Orquestra De Cambra Teatre Lliure
Orquestra De Cambra Teatre Lliure and Lluis Vidal Trio feat.Dave Liebman | Fresh Sound Records | FSNT 027 CD
Orquestra De Cambra Teatre Lliure feat. Dave Liebman
Orquestra De Cambra Teatre Lliure and Lluis Vidal Trio feat.Dave Liebman | Fresh Sound Records | FSNT 027 CD

Casey,Al | (gvoc)
Al Casey Quartet
A Tribute To Fats | Jazzpoint | JP 1044 CD
A' Portrait Of Jan Jankeje | Jazzpoint | JP 1054 CD
Billie Holiday With Teddy Wilson And His Orchestra
Billie's Love Songs | Nimbus Records | NI 2000
Coleman Hawkins And His Orchestra
Jazz:The Essential Collection Vol.3 | IN+OUT Records | 78013-2
Doc Cheatham Sextet
A' Portrait Of Jan Jankeje | Jazzpoint | JP 1054 CD
Esquire Metropolitan Opera House Jam Session
Jazz:The Essential Collection Vol.3 | IN+OUT Records | 78013-2
Fats Waller And His Rhythm
Planet Jazz:Fats Waller | Planet Jazz | 2152058-2
Planet Jazz Sampler | Planet Jazz | 2152326-2
Planet Jazz:Male Jazz Vocalists | Planet Jazz | 2169657-2
George Kelly Quintet
A' Portrait Of Jan Jankeje | Jazzpoint | JP 1054 CD
Leonard Feather's Esquire All Stars
Jazz:The Essential Collection Vol.2 | IN+OUT Records | 78012-2
Lionel Hampton And His Orchestra
Planet Jazz:Lionel Hampton | Planet Jazz | 2152059-2
Planet Jazz Sampler | Planet Jazz | 2152326-2
Louis Armstrong And His All Stars
Planet Jazz:Louis Armstrong | Planet Jazz | 2152052-2
Planet Jazz:Jack Teagarden | Planet Jazz | 2161236-2
Planet Jazz:Male Jazz Vocalists | Planet Jazz | 2169657-2
Best Of The Complete RCA Victor Recordings | RCA | 2663636-2
Louis Armstrong:A 100th Birthday Celebration | RCA | 2663694-2
Louis Armstrong And His Orchestra
Louis Armstrong:C'est Si Bon | Dreyfus Jazz Line | FDM 36730-2
Swing Legends:Louis Armstrong | Nimbus Records | NI 2012

Mezz Mezzrow And His Swing Band
Planet Jazz:Bud Freeman | Planet Jazz | 2161240-2
Red Richards-George Kelly Sextet With Doc Cheatham
Groove Move | Jazzpoint | JP 1045 CD

Casey,Bob | (bg)
Muggsy Spanier And His Dixieland Band
Muggsy Spanier-Manhattan Masters,1945 | Storyville | STCD 6051
Muggsy Spanier And His Ragtime Band
Planet Jazz | Planet Jazz | 2169652-2
Planet Jazz:Jazz Trumpet | Planet Jazz | 2169654-2
Pee Wee Russell And His Dixieland Band
Muggsy Spanier-Manhattan Masters,1945 | Storyville | STCD 6051

Casey,Floyd | (dr,wbdkazoo)
Cliff Jackson's Washboard Wanderers
Uptown And Lowdown | Prestige | PCD 24262-2

Casey,Gene | (p)
Oliver Nelson Sextet
Soul Street | Original Jazz Classics | OJCCD 987-2(NJ 8293)
The Latin Jazz Quintet Plus Guest: Eric Dolphy
Eric Dolphy:The Complete Prestige Recordings | Prestige | 9 PRCD-4418-2
Eric Dolphy Birthday Celebration | Fantasy | FANCD 6085-2

Cash | (jazz-rock-group)
Cash
Jazzy World | JA & RO | JARO 4200-2

Cash,Freddie | (bvoc)
Jean-Paul Bourelly Group
Jungle Cowboy | JMT Edition | 919009-2

Cashdollar,Cindy | (dobro)
Hans Theessink Group
Crazy Moon | Minor Music | 801052
Journey On | Minor Music | 801062

Casimenti,Al | (g)
Coleman Hawkins Quintet
Body And Soul Revisited | GRP | GRP 16272
Coleman Hawkins Quintet With Strings
Body And Soul Revisited | GRP | GRP 16272

Casimir,Olaf | (b)
Klaus Spencker Trio
Invisible | Jardis Records | JRCD 9409
Tok Tok Tok
Love Again | Einstein Music | EM 01081
50 Ways To Leave Your Lover | Einstein Music | EM 91051

Casino,Vincent | (tp)
Django's Music
Peche Á La Mode-The Great Blue Star Sessions 1947/1953 | Verve | 835418-2

Caspar,Peter | (tbtuba)
Jazz Orchester Rheinland-Pfalz
Like Life | Jazz Haus Musik | LJBB 9405
Last Season | Jazz Haus Musik | LJBB 9706

Casper,Peter | (tb)
Kazzou | Jazz Haus Musik | LJBB 9104

Cassard,Jules | (btuba)
Wingy Mannone And His Orchestra
Planet Jazz:Jazz Trumpet | Planet Jazz | 2169654-2

Casserley,Lawrence | (electronics,sound-processing)
Evan Parker Electro-Acoustic Ensemble
Drawn Inward | ECM | 1693
Memory/Vision | ECM | 1852(0381172)

Cassidy,Bruce | (tpfl-h)
Singers Unlimited With Rob McConnell And The Boss Brass
The Singers Unlimited:Magic Voices | MPS | 539130-2

Castaldo,Charlie | (tb)
Peggy Lee With The Benny Goodman Orchestra
Peggy Lee & Benny Goodman:The Complete Recordings 1941-1947 | CBS | C2K 65686

Castaldo,Lee | (tp)
Benny Goodman And His Orchestra
The Legends Of Swing | Laserlight | 24659

Castellucci,Bruno | (dr,percsampling)
Dusko Goykovich Quintet With The NDR Radio-Philharmonie,Hannover
Balkan Blues | Enja | ENJ-9320 2
Klaus Ignatzek-Claudio Roditi Quintet
Live at Bird's Eye | Village | VILCD 1023-2
NDR Big Band With Guests
50 Years Of NDR Big Band:Bravissimo II | ACT | 9259-2
Toots Thielemans And His Orchestra
Verve Jazz Masters Vol.59:Toots Thielemans | Verve | 535271-2
Toots Thielemans Quartet
Toots Thielemans:The Live Takes Vol.1 | IN+OUT Records | 77041-2
Toots Thielemans Quintet
Verve Jazz Masters Vol.59:Toots Thielemans | Verve | 535271-2
The Silver Collection: Toots Thielemans | Polydor | 825086-2 PMS

Castillo,Carlos | (el-b)
Machito And His Orchestra
Afro-Cuban Jazz Moods | Original Jazz Classics | OJC20 447-2

Castle,Ben | (ts)
Jamie Cullum Group
Pointless Nostalgic | Candid | CCD 79782

Castle,Lee | (tpvoc)
Artie Shaw And His Orchestra
Planet JazzArtie Shaw | Planet Jazz | 2152057-2
Planet Jazz:Male Jazz Vocalists | Planet Jazz | 2169657-2
Jack Teagarden And His Orchestra
Jazz:The Essential Collection Vol.3 | IN+OUT Records | 78013-2
Tommy Dorsey And His Orchestra
Planet Jazz:Frank Sinatra & Tommy Dorsey | Planet Jazz | 2152067-2
Planet Jazz:Tommy Dorsey | Planet Jazz | 2159972-2

Castleman,Jeff | (b)
Duke Ellington And His Orchestra
Latin America Suite | Original Jazz Classics | OJC20 469-2
Yale Concert | Original Jazz Classics | OJCCD 664-2

Caston,Leonard | (g,org,pvoc)
Buddy Guy Blues Band
Buddy Guy-The Complete Chess Studio Recordings | MCA | MCD 09337

Castrillo,Manuel 'Egui' | (congas,bongos,guiro,timbalesperc)
Arturo Sandoval And The Latin Train Band
Arturo Sandoval & The Latin Train | GRP | GRP 98202

Castro,George | (flperc)
Cal Tjader's Orchestra
Talkin Verve/Roots Of Acid Jazz:Cal Tjader | Verve | 531562-2

Castro,Joe | (p)
Anita O'Day With The Billy May Orchestra
Verve Jazz Masters 49:Anita O'Day | Verve | 527653-2
June Christy With The Pete Rugolo Orchestra
Something Cool(The Complete Mono & Stereo Versions) | Capitol | 534069-2
Zoot Sims With The Joe Castro Trio
Live At Falcon Lair | Pablo | PACD 2310977-2

Castro,Lenny | (perc)
Jimmy Smith All Stars
Jimmy Smith:Dot Com Blues | Blue Thumb | 543978-2
Joe Sample Group
Ashes To Ashes | Warner | 7599-26318-2
Spellbound | Rhino | 81273726-2
Invitation | Warner | 9362-45209.2

Castronari,Mario | (bel-b)
Gail Thompson Orchestra
Gail Thompson's Jazz Africa | Enja | ENJ-9053 2
Jazz Africa All Nations Big Band
Jadu(Jazz Africa Down Under) | Enja | ENJ-9339 2

Castro-Neves,Mario | (pkeyboards)
Ithamara Koorax With Band
Love Dance:The Ballad Album | Milestone | MCD 9327-2

Castro-Neves,Oscar | (g,cavaquinho,synth,percvoc)
Antonio Carlos Jobim Group
Antonio Carlos Jobim And Friends | Verve | 531556-2
Antonio Carlos Jobim With The Herbie Hancock Sextet
Antonio Carlos Jobim And Friends | Verve | 531556-2
Antonio Carlos Jobim-Elis Regina Group
The Antonio Carlos Jobim Songbook | Verve | 525472-2
Antonio Carlos Jobim-Gal Costa Septet
Antonio Carlos Jobim And Friends | Verve | 531556-2
David Darling Group
Cycles | ECM | 1219
Ella Fitzgerald With Orchestra
Ella Abraça Jobim | Pablo | 2630201-2
Gal Costa With The Herbie Hancock Sextet
Antonio Carlos Jobim And Friends | Verve | 531556-2
Joe Henderson Group
Double Rainbow | Verve | 527222-2
Joe Henderson Septet
Antonio Carlos Jobim And Friends | Verve | 531556-2
Joe Pass Sextet
Joe Pass:Guitar Virtuoso | Pablo | 4 PACD 4423-2
Jon Hendricks With The Herbie Hancock Quintet
Antonio Carlos Jobim And Friends | Verve | 531556-2
Shirley Horn Quintet
Antonio Carlos Jobim And Friends | Verve | 531556-2
Shirley Horn Sextet
Antonio Carlos Jobim And Friends | Verve | 531556-2

Catalano,Billy | (tp)
Stan Kenton Orchestra
Stompin' At Newport | Pablo | PACD 5312-2

Catalyne,Joe | (cl,asts)
Jack Teagarden And His Orchestra
Jazz:The Essential Collection Vol.3 | IN+OUT Records | 78013-2

Cathcart,Jack | (tp)
Artie Shaw And His Orchestra
Planet JazzArtie Shaw | Planet Jazz | 2152057-2
Planet Jazz:Big Bands | Planet Jazz | 2169649-2

Cathcart,Jim | (el-p,tp,orgvoc)
Dave Brubeck With The Erich Kunzel Orchestra
Truth Is Fallen | Atlantic | 7567-80761-2

Cathcart,Patti | (voc)
Tuck And Patti
Tears Of Joy | Windham Hill | 34 10111-2
Love Warriors | Windham Hill | 34 10116-2
Dream | Windham Hill | 34 10130-2
A Gift Of Love | T&P Records | 9815810

Catherine,Philip | (12-string-g,el-g,g,tarang,bj,p,el-b)
Aldo Romano Group
AlmaLatina | Owl Records | 018364-2
Bireli Lagrene-Philip Catherine
Bireli Lagrene 'Highlights' | Jazzpoint | JP 1027 CD
Charles Mingus Orchestra
Three Or Four Shades Of Blues | Atlantic | 7567-81403-2
Chet Baker Trio
Strollin' | Enja | ENJ-5005 2
Chet Baker In Bologna | Dreyfus Jazz Line | FDM 36558-9
European Jazz Ensemble
European Jazz Ensemble At The Philharmonic Cologne | M.A Music | A 800-2
European Jazz Ensemble & The Khan Family feat. Joachim Kühn
European Jazz Ensemble Meets The Khan Family | M.A Music | A 807-2
Klaus Weiss Orchestra
Live At The Domicile | ATM Records | ATM 3805-AH
Larry Coryell-Alphonse Mouzon Quartet
Atlantic Jazz: Fusion | Atlantic | 7567-81711-2
Laura Fygi With Band
Bewitched | Verve | 514724-2
Markus Stockhausen Orchestra
Sol Mestizo:Markus Stockhausen Plays The Music Of Enrique Diaz | ACT | 9222-2
Michael Mantler Sextet
Movies/More Movies | Watt | 7/10(543377-2)
Mind Games With Philip Catherine
Pretty Fonky | Edition Collage | EC 482-2
NDR Big Band With Guests
50 Years Of NDR Big Band:Bravissimo II | ACT | 9259-2
Niels-Henning Orsted-Pedersen/Sam Jones Quartet
Double Bass | Steeplechase | SCS 1055(Audiophile Pressing)
Niels-Henning Orsted-Pedersen/Sam Jones Quintet
Double Bass | Steeplechase | SCS 1055(Audiophile Pressing)
Passport And Guests
Doldinger's Best | ACT | 9224-2
Philip Catherine Quartet
Guitar Groove | Dreyfus Jazz Line | FDM 36599-2
Blue Prince | Dreyfus Jazz Line | FDM 36614-2
Summer Night | Dreyfus Jazz Line | FDM 36637-2
Philip Catherine Trio
Summer Night | Dreyfus Jazz Line | FDM 36637-2
Philip Catherine/Niels-Henning Orsted-Pedersen With The Royal Copenhagen Chamber Orchestra
Spanish Nights | Enja | ENJ-7023 2
Stephane Grappelli Quartet
Grapelli Story | Verve | 515807-2
Verve Jazz Masters 11:Stéphane Grappelli | Verve | 516758-2
Stephane Grappelli 1992 Live | Dreyfus Jazz Line | FDM 37006-2

Catholics,The |
The Catholics
Simple | Laika Records | 35100802

Catlett,Big Sid | (dr)
Benny Carter And His Chocolate Dandies
Planet Jazz:Ben Webster | RCA | 2165368-2
Jazz:The Essential Collection Vol.3 | IN+OUT Records | 78013-2
Big Sid Catlett And His Orchestra
The Small Black Groups | Storyville | 4960523
Billie Holiday With Eddie Heywood And His Orchestra
Billie Holiday:The Complete Commodore Recordings | GRP | 543272-2
Coleman Hawkins' All-American Four
Verve Jazz Masters 43:Coleman Hawkins | Verve | 521856-2
Coleman Hawkins And His Rhythm
Jazz:The Essential Collection Vol.3 | IN+OUT Records | 78013-2
Coleman Hawkins Quartet
Ultimate Coleman Hawkins selected by Sonny Rollins | Verve | 557538-2
Dizzy Gillespie All Stars
Dizzy Gillespie:Night In Tunisia | Dreyfus Jazz Line | FDM 36734-2
Edmond Hall's Blue Note Jazzmen
The Blue Note Jazzmen | Blue Note | 821262-2
Esquire Metropolitan Opera House Jam Session
Jazz:The Essential Collection Vol.3 | IN+OUT Records | 78013-2
Fletcher Henderson And His Orchestra
Jazz:The Essential Collection Vol.1 | IN+OUT Records | 78011-2
James P.Johnson's Blue Note Jazzmen
Jazz:The Essential Collection Vol.3 | IN+OUT Records | 78013-2
The Blue Note Jazzmen | Blue Note | 821262-2
JATP All Stars
The Complete Jazz At The Philharmonic On Verve 1944-1949 | Verve | 523893-2
Jimmy Hamilton And The Duke's Men
The Blue Note Swingtets | Blue Note | 495697-2
John Hardee Sextet
The Blue Note Swingtets | Blue Note | 495697-2
John Hardee Swingtet
The Blue Note Swingtets | Blue Note | 495697-2
John Kirby Band
The Small Black Groups | Storyville | 4960523
Lena Horne With The Horace Henderson Orchestra
Planet Jazz:Lena Horne | Planet Jazz | 2165373-2
Leonard Feather's Esquire All Stars
Jazz:The Essential Collection Vol.2 | IN+OUT Records | 78012-2
Lester Young Quartet
Verve Jazz Masters 30:Lester Young | Verve | 521859-2
Jazz:The Essential Collection Vol.3 | IN+OUT Records | 78013-2
Lester Young:Blue Lester | Dreyfus Jazz Line | FDM 36729-2
Louis Armstrong And His All Stars
Planet Jazz:Louis Armstrong | Planet Jazz | 2152052-2
Planet Jazz:Jack Teagarden | Planet Jazz | 2161236-2
Planet Jazz:Male Jazz Vocalists | Planet Jazz | 2169657-2
Jazz Collection:Louis Armstrong | Laserlight | 24366
Best Of The Complete RCA Victor Recordings | RCA | 2663636-2
Louis Armstrong:A 100th Birthday Celebration | RCA | 2663694-2
Louis Armstrong:C'est Si Bon | Dreyfus Jazz Line | FDM 36730-2
Louis Armstrong:Wintergarden 1947/Blue Note 1948 | Storyville | STCD 8242
Louis Armstrong And His Orchestra
Louis Armstrong:A 100th Birthday Celebration | RCA | 2663694-2
Louis Armstrong:Swing That Music | Laserlight | 36056
Jazz:The Essential Collection Vol.2 | IN+OUT Records | 78012-2
Louis Armstrong:C'est Si Bon | Dreyfus Jazz Line | FDM 36730-2
Swing Legends:Louis Armstrong | Nimbus Records | NI 2012
New Orleans Feetwarmers
Jazz:The Essential Collection Vol.1 | IN+OUT Records | 78011-2
Peggy Lee With The Benny Goodman Orchestra
Peggy Lee & Benny Goodman:The Complete Recordings 1941-1947 | CBS | C2K 65686
Sarah Vaughan With Dizzy Gillespie And His All Star Quintet
Sarah Vaughan:Lover Man | Dreyfus Jazz Line | FDM 36739-2
Sidney Bechet And His New Orleans Feetwarmers
Planet Jazz | Planet Jazz | 2169652-2
Sidney Bechet:Summertime | Dreyfus Jazz Line | FDM 36712-2
Sidney Catlett Quartet
Jazz:The Essential Collection Vol.3 | IN+OUT Records | 78013-2
Sidney DeParis' Blue Note Jazzmen
The Blue Note Jazzmen | Blue Note | 821262-2
Spike Hughes And His Negro Orchestra
Jazz:The Essential Collection Vol.3 | IN+OUT Records | 78013-2
Teddy Wilson Sextet
The Complete Associated Transcriptions,1944 | Storyville | STCD 8236

Catlett,Buddy | (b)
Babs Gonzales And His Band
Voilà | Fresh Sound Records | FSR CD 340
Benny Bailey Septet
Big Brass | Candid | CCD 79011
Bill Coleman Septet
Jazz In Paris:Bill Coleman-From Boogie To Funk | EmArCy | 549401-2 PMS
Count Basie And His Orchestra
Verve Jazz Masters 2:Count Basie | Verve | 519819-2
Eddie Lockjaw Davis-Johnny Griffin Quintet
The Jazz Giants Play Cole Porter:Night And Day | Prestige | PCD 24203-2
Ella Fitzgerald With The Count Basie Orchestra
Ella Fitzgerald-First Lady Of Song | Verve | 517898-2
Verve Jazz Masters 46:Ella Fitzgerald-The Jazz Sides | Verve | 527655-2
Ella And Basie | Verve | 539059-2
Ella Fitzgerald With The Count Basie Septet
Ella And Basie | Verve | 539059-2
Frank Sinatra With The Count Basie Orchestra
Sinatra-Basie:An Historic Musical First | Reprise | 7599-27023-2
It Might As Well Be Spring | Reprise | 7599-27027-2
Frank Wess Quintet
The Long Road | Prestige | PCD 24247-2
Louis Armstrong And His All Stars
Jazz In Paris:Louis Armstrong:The Best Live Concer Vol.1 | EmArCy | 013030-2
Jazz In Paris:Louis Armstrong-The Best Live Concert Vol.2 | EmArCy | 013031-2
Jazz Collection:Louis Armstrong | Laserlight | 24366
What A Wonderful World | MCA | MCD 01876
Louis Armstrong And His All Stars With A Studio Orchestra
What A Wonderful World | MCA | MCD 01876

Catlett,George | (b)
Quincy Jones And His Orchestra
The Quintessence | Impulse(MCA) | 951222-2

Caton,Lauderic | (g)
Vic Lewis Jam Session
Vic Lewis:The Golden Years | Candid | CCD 79754

Cattedra,Leonardo | (cl)
Banda Città Ruvo Di Puglia
La Banda/Banda And Jazz | Enja | ENJ-9326 2

Caulder,Albert | (voice)
Michael Mantler Group
The Hapless Child | Watt | 4

Cavaion,Cesare | (b)
Brocksi-Quartett
Globetrotter | Bear Family Records | BCD 15912 AH

Cavallanti,Daniele | (ts,bsclaps)
Italian Instabile Orchestra
Skies Of Europe | ECM | 1543

Cavallaro,Armand | (drperc)
Raymond Fol Big Band
Jazz In Paris:Raymond Fol-Les 4 Saisons | EmArCy | 548791-2

Cavalli,Pierre | (el-gg)
NDR-Workshop
Doldinger's Best | ACT | 9224-2
Stephane Grappelli Quartet
Jazz In Paris:Stephane Grappelli-Django | EmArCy | 018421-1
Stephane Grappelli Quintet
Grapelli Story | Verve | 515807-2
Feeling + Finesse = Jazz | Atlantic | 7567-90140-2

Cavanaugh,Dave | (arr,bs,condts)
Ten Cats And A Mouse
The Hollywood Session:The Capitol Jazzmen | Jazz Unlimited | JUCD 2044
The Hollywood Hucksters
The Hollywood Session:The Capitol Jazzmen | Jazz Unlimited | JUCD 2044

Cave,Jack | (fr-h)
Artie Shaw And His Orchestra
Planet JazzArtie Shaw | Planet Jazz | 2152057-2
Planet Jazz:Jazz Greatest Hits | Planet Jazz | 2169648-2
Billy Eckstine With The Billy May Orchestra
Once More With Feeling | Roulette | 581862-2
Billy May And His Orchestra
Billy May's Big Fat Brass/Bill's Bag | Capitol | 535206-2
Ella Fitzgerald With The Nelson Riddle Orchestra
Ella Fitzgerald Sings The Johnny Mercer Songbook | Verve | 539057-2

Cave,John | (fr-h)
The Best Of The Song Books:The Ballads | Verve | 521867-2
Love Songs:The Best Of The Song Books | Verve | 531762-2
Hank Crawford Orchestra
Rhino Presents The Atlantic Jazz Gallery | Atlantic | 8122-71257-2

Cavelier,Hervé | (concertmaster)
Charlie Haden Quartet West With Strings
Now Is The Hour | Verve | 527827-2

Cavicchiolo,Romano | (dr)
Benny Carter And His Orchestra
The Art Of Saxophone | Laserlight | 24652
Lucien Barbarin With The Henri Chaix Trio
Trombone Tradition | Jazz Connaisseur | JCCD 8803-2

Caviglia,Aldo | (dr)
Victor De Diego Group
Amaia | Fresh Sound Records | FSNT 012 CD

Cavill,Chris | (voc)
Big Allanbik
Batuque Y Blues | Blues Beacon | BLU-1031 2

Caymmi,Danilo | (flvoc)
Antonio Carlos Jobim With Orchestra

Verve Jazz Masters 13:Antonio Carlos Jobim | Verve | 516409-2
Sarah Vaughan With Orchestra
I Love Brazil | Pablo | 2312101-2
Sarah Vaughan Birthday Celebration | Fantasy | FANCD 6090-2

Caymmi,Dori | (g,arrvoc)
Diane Schuur With Orchestra
Love Songs | GRP | GRP 97032
The Best Of Diane Schuur | GRP | GRP 98882
John Patitucci Group
Sketchbook | GRP | GRP 96172
Mistura Fina | GRP | GRP 98022
Sarah Vaughan With Dori Caymmi
Sarah Vaughan Birthday Celebration | Fantasy | FANCD 6090-2

Caymmi,Simone | (voc)
Antonio Carlos Jobim With Orchestra
Verve Jazz Masters 13:Antonio Carlos Jobim | Verve | 516409-2

Ceccarelli,André | (drperc)
Bireli Lagrene Quartet
Standards | Blue Note | 780251-2
Blue Eyes | Dreyfus Jazz Line | FDM 36591-2
Bireli Lagrene Trio
Standards | Blue Note | 780251-2
Dee Dee Bridgewater With Band
This Is New | Verve | 016884-2
Victim Of Love | Verve | 841199-2
Dee Dee Bridgewater Sings Kurt Weil | EmArCy | 9809601
Dee Dee Bridgewater With Her Quartet With Horace Silver
Love And Peace-A Tribute To Horace Silver | Verve | 527470-2
Dee Dee Bridgewater With Her Quintet
Love And Peace-A Tribute To Horace Silver | Verve | 527470-2
Dee Dee Bridgewater With Her Quintet With Jimmy Smith
Love And Peace-A Tribute To Horace Silver | Verve | 527470-2
Dee Dee Bridgewater With Her Trio
Live In Paris | Verve | 014317-2
Keeping Tradition | Verve | 519607-2
Dear Ella | Verve | 539102-2
Dee Dee Bridgewater In Montreux | Polydor | 847913-2
Dee Dee Bridgewater With Orchestra
Dear Ella | Verve | 539102-2
Richard Galliano Group
French Touch | Dreyfus Jazz Line | FDM 36596-2
Stephane Grappelli With The Michel Legrand Orchestra
Grapelli Story | Verve | 515807-2
Verve Jazz Masters 11:Stéphane Grappelli | Verve | 516758-2
Sylvain Luc-André Ceccarelli-Jean Marc Jafet
SUD | Dreyfus Jazz Line | FDM 36612-2

Cedras,Tony | (accordeon,perc,voiceharmonium)
Cassandra Wilson Group
Blue Light 'Til Dawn | Blue Note | 781357-2
Pharoah Sanders Group
Save Our Children | Verve | 557297-2

Celea,Jean-Paul | (b,drp)
John McLaughlin Group
The Heart Of Things | Verve | 539153-2

Centalonza,Richard | (bs,floboe)
Jacky Terrasson Group
What It Is | Blue Note | 498756-2

Centeno,Francisco | (b,jokesel-b)
Helen Merrill With Orchestra
Casa Forte | EmArCy | 558848-2

Ceppos,Mac | (v)
Ben Webster With Orchestra And Strings
Music For Loving:Ben Webster With Strings | Verve | 527774-2
Ultimate Ben Webster selected by James Carter | Verve | 557537-2
Ernestine Anderson With Orchestra
My Kinda Swing | Mercury | 842409-2
Harry Carney And His Orchestra With Strings
Music For Loving:Ben Webster With Strings | Verve | 527774-2
Wes Montgomery With The Jimmy Jones Orchestra
Wes Montgomery-The Complete Riverside Recordings | Riverside | 12 RCD 4408-2
The Jazz Giants Play Rodgers & Hart:Blue Moon | Prestige | PCD 24205-2

Cerletti,Marco | (synth,el-b,sticksvoc)
Marco Cerletti Group
Random And Providence | VeraBra Records | CDVBR 2039-2

Cernota,Johannes | (p-solo)
Johannes Cernota
Sparta | JA & RO | JARO 4136-2
Jazzy World | JA & RO | JARO 4200-2

Ceroli,Nick | (dr)
Zoot Sims And His Orchestra
The Jazz Giants Play Duke Ellington:Caravan | Prestige | PCD 24227-2
Zoot Sims Quintet
Quietly There-Zoot Sims Plays Johnny Mandel | Original Jazz Classics | OJCCD 787-2(2310903)

Cerri,Franco | (bg)
Chet Baker With String-Orchestra And Voices
Chet Baker With Fifty Italian Strings | Original Jazz Classics | OJC20 492-2(JLP 921)

Cervera,Bertrand | (vconcertmaster)
Stephane Grappelli With The Michel Legrand Orchestra
Grapelli Story | Verve | 515807-2

Cevasco,Adalberto | (el-b)
Gato Barbieri Orchestra
Latino America | Impulse(MCA) | 952236-2

Cevero,Maurice | (contractor)
Stephane Grappelli With The Michel Legrand Orchestra
Grapelli Story | Verve | 515807-2

Chaarani,Abdellatif | (bendir,chimes,darbuka,tarperc)
Louis Sclavis & The Bernard Struber Jazztet
La Phare | Enja | ENJ-9359 2

Chabrier,Mlle.E. | (?)
Stephan-Max Wirth Quartet
Jazzchanson 20th Century Suite | double moon | DMCD 1008-2

Chace,Frank | (clbs)
Marty Grosz And His Honoris Causa Jazz Band
Hooray For Bix! | Good Time Jazz | GTCD 10065-2

Chacón,Joaquin | (g,12-string-gel-g)
Joaquin Chacón Group
San | Fresh Sound Records | FSNT 015 CD
Joaquin Chacón-Uffe Markussen European Quintet
Time | Fresh Sound Records | FSNT 051 CD

Chadbourne,Eugene | (el-g,bj,voc,g,birdcage,noise)
Carla Bley Band
Musique Mecanique | Watt | 9
Noel Akchoté-Marc Ribot-Eugene Chadbourne
Lust Corner | Winter&Winter | 910019-2

Chagne,Philippe | (as,ts,bssax)
Frank Wess Meets The Paris-Barcelona Swing Connection
Paris-Barcelona Connection | Fresh Sound Records | FSNT 002 CD

Chaikin,Jules | (string-contractortp)
Gerald Wilson And His Orchestra
Blue Breaks Beats Vol.2 | Blue Note | 789907-2
Johnny Hartman And His Orchestra
Unforgettable | Impulse(MCA) | IMP 11522

Chaillou,Maurice | (drvoc)
Coleman Hawkins With Michel Warlop And His Orchestra
Django Reinhardt All Star Sessions | Capitol | 531577-2
Wal-Berg Et Son Jazz Francais
Jazz In Paris:Django Reinhardt-Django Et Compagnie | EmArCy | 549241-2 PMS

Chaisson,Warren | (vib)
George Shearing And His Quintet
The Swingin's Mutual | Capitol | 799190-2
Nancy Wilson With George Shearing And His Quintet
The Swingin's Mutual | Capitol | 799190-2

Chaix,Henri | (pp-solo)
Benny Carter And His Orchestra
The Art Of Saxophone | Laserlight | 24652
Great Traditionalists In Europe
Great Traditionalists | Jazzpoint | JP 1046 CD
Henri Chaix
Trombone Tradition | Jazz Connaisseur | JCCD 8803-2
Hot Mallets
Hot Mallets...Live! | JHM Records | JHM 3610
Lucien Barbarin With The Henri Chaix Trio
Trombone Tradition | Jazz Connaisseur | JCCD 8803-2
Lucien Barbarin-Henri Chaix Duo
Trombone Tradition | Jazz Connaisseur | JCCD 8803-2
Stuff Smith With The Henri Chaix Trio
Late Woman Blues | Storyville | STCD 8328
The European Jazz Ginats
Jazz Party | Nagel-Heyer | CD 009
The First Sampler | Nagel-Heyer | NHR SP 5
The Tremble Kids All Stars
The Tremble Kids All Stars Play Chicago Jazz! | Nagel-Heyer | CD 043

Challis,William 'Bill' | (arr)
Paul Whiteman And His Orchestra
Planet Jazz:Jazz Trumpet | Planet Jazz | 2169654-2

Chaloff,Serge | (bs)
Serge Chaloff Quartet
Blue Serge | Capitol | 494505-2
The Four Brothers
Planet Jazz:Jazz Saxophone | Planet Jazz | 2169653-2
Together Again! | RCA | 2179623-2
Woody Herman And His Orchestra
The Legends Of Swing | Laserlight | 24659
Woody Herman:Four Brother | Dreyfus Jazz Line | FDM 36722-2

Chamber Jazz Sextet |
Chamber Jazz Sextet
Plays Pal Joey | Candid | CCD 79030

Chamberlain,Dave | (b)
Stacy Kent With The Jim Tomlinson Quintet
The Boy Next Door | Candid | CCD 79797

Chamberlain,Gerald | (tb)
Buddy Rich Big Band
Backwoods Siseman/Pieces Of Dream | Laserlight | 24655
Machito And His Orchestra
Afro-Cuban Jazz Moods | Original Jazz Classics | OJC20 447-2

Chamberlain,Ronnie | (fl,asss)
The Jimmy And Marion McPartland Sessions
Vic Lewis:The Golden Years | Candid | CCD 79754
Vic Lewis Jam Session
Vic Lewis:The Golden Years | Candid | CCD 79754

Chambers,Dan | (voc)
Clare Teal And Her Band
Orsino's Songs | Candid | CCD 79783

Chambers,Dennis | (dr)
Barbara Dennerlein Group
Take Off | Verve | 527664-2
Junkanoo | Verve | 537122-2
Barbara Dennerlein Quintet
That's Me | Enja | ENJ-7043 2
Bireli Lagrene Quartet
My Favorite Django | Dreyfus Jazz Line | FDM 36574-2
Bob Berg Quintet
The Art Of Saxophone | Laserlight | 24652
Gonzalo Rubalcaba Trio
The Trio | somethin'else | 494442-2
Jean-Paul Bourelly Trance Atlantic
Boom Bop II | double moon | CHRDM 71023
John McLaughlin Group
The Promise | Verve | 529828-2
The Heart Of Things | Verve | 539153-2
Live In Paris | Verve | 543536-2
Leni Stern Group
Secrets | Enja | ENJ-5093 2
Closer To The Light | Enja | ENJ-6034 2
Mike Stern Group
Jigsaw | Atlantic | 7567-82027-2
Odds Or Evens | Atlantic | 7567-82297-2
Play | Atlantic | 7567-83219-2
The Brecker Brothers
Return Of The Brecker Brothers | GRP | GRP 96842
Wayne Krantz Quartet
Signals | Enja | ENJ-6048 2

Chambers,Elmer | (cotp)
Fletcher Henderson And His Orchestra
Jazz:The Essential Collection Vol.1 | IN+OUT Records | 78011-2

Chambers,Henderson | (tb)
Al Sears And His Orchestra
Sear-iously | Bear Family Records | BCD 15668 AH
Billie Holiday With Sy Oliver And His Orchestra
Billie's Love Songs | Nimbus Records | NI 2000
Count Basie And His Orchestra
Basie Meets Bond | Capitol | 538225-2
Basie's Beatle Bag | Verve | 557455-2
King Of Swing | Verve | 837433-2
Live at The Sands | Reprise | 9362-45946-2
Ella Fitzgerald With Sy Oliver And His Orchestra
Ella Fitzgerald:Mr.Paganini | Dreyfus Jazz Line | FDM 36741-2
Ella Fitzgerald With Sy Oliver And His Orchestra
Ella Fitzgerald:The Decca Years 1949-1954 | Decca | 050668-2
Frank Sinatra With The Count Basie Orchestra
It Might As Well Be Spring | Reprise | 7599-27027-2
Gene Ammons Septet
A Stranger In Town | Prestige | PRCD 24266-2
Jimmy Hamilton And The Duke's Men
The Blue Note Swingtets | Blue Note | 495697-2
Louis Armstrong And His Orchestra
Louis Armstrong:Swing That Music | Laserlight | 36056
Jazz:The Essential Collection Vol.2 | IN+OUT Records | 78012-2
Louis Armstrong:C'est Si Bon | Dreyfus Jazz Line | FDM 36730-2
Louis Armstrong With Sy Oliver And His Orchestra
Satchmo Serenaders | Verve | 543792-2

Chambers,Jeff | (b)
Ahmad Jamal Septet
Live In Paris 1996 | Dreyfus Jazz Line | FDM 37020-2
Gonzalo Rubalcaba Trio
Inner Voyage | Blue Note | 499241-2
Gonzalo Rubalcaba Trio With Michael Brecker
Inner Voyage | Blue Note | 499241-2

Chambers,Joe | (bass-marimba,dr,perc,marimba,p,el-p)
Andrew Hill Quartet
A Blue Conception | Blue Note | 534254-2
Archie Shepp Sextet
Fire Music | Impulse(MCA) | 951158-2
Bobby Hutcherson Quartet
Herbie Hancock:The Complete Blue Note Sixties Sessions | Blue Note | 495569-2
Bobby Hutcherson Sextet
A Blue Conception | Blue Note | 534254-2
Dialogue | Blue Note | 535586-2
Candid Jazz Masters
The Candid Jazz Masters:For Miles | Candid | CCD 79710
Chet Baker Quintet
Peace | Enja | ENJ-4016 2
Chick Corea Quintet
Inner Space | Atlantic | 7567-81304-2
Chick Corea-Herbie Hancock-Keith Jarrett-McCoy Tyner | Atlantic | 7567-81402-2
Chick Corea Trio
Chick Corea-Herbie Hancock-Keith Jarrett-McCoy Tyner | Atlantic | 7567-81402-2
Donald Byrd Orchestra
Blue Break Beats | Blue Note | 799106-2
Joe Chambers
Mirrors | Blue Note | 496685-2
Joe Chambers Quartet
Mirrors | Blue Note | 496685-2
Joe Chambers Quintet
Mirrors | Blue Note | 496685-2
Joe Chambers Trio
Mirrors | Blue Note | 496685-2
Joe Henderson Septet
Mode For Joe | Blue Note | 591894-2
The Blue Note Years-The Best Of Joe Henderson | Blue Note | 795627-2
Joe Zawinul Group
Zawinul | Atlantic | 7567-81375-2
M'Boom
To The Max! | Enja | ENJ-7021 22
Sonny Fortune Quartet
Monk's Mood | Konnex Records | KCD 5048
Wayne Shorter Quartet
Herbie Hancock:The Complete Blue Note Sixties Sessions | Blue Note | 495569-2
Kind Of Blue:Blue Note Celebrate The Music Of Miles Davis | Blue Note | 534255-2
Wayne Shorter:The Classic Blue Note Recordings | Blue Note | 540856-2
Adams Apple | Blue Note | 591901-2
Wayne Shorter Sextet
Wayne Shorter:The Classic Blue Note Recordings | Blue Note | 540856-2
Blue N' Groovy | Blue Note | 780679-2

Chambers,Paul | (b)
Abbey Lincoln With Her Quintet
Sonny Rollins-The Freelance Years:The Complete Riverside & Contemporary Recordings | Riverside | 5 RCD 4427-2
That's Him! | Original Jazz Classics | OJCCD 085-2
Abbey Lincoln With The Benny Golson Quintet
It's Magic | Original Jazz Classics | OJCCD 205-2
Abbey Lincoln With The Benny Golson Septet
It's Magic | Original Jazz Classics | OJCCD 205-2
Art Blakey-Paul Chambers
Drums Around The Corner | Blue Note | 521455-2
Art Pepper Quartet
Art Pepper Meets The Rhythm Section | Original Jazz Classics | OJC20 338-2
Gettin' Together | Original Jazz Classics | OJCCD 169-2
The Way It Is | Original Jazz Classics | OJCCD 389-2
The Jazz Giants Play Cole Porter:Night And Day | Prestige | PCD 24203-2
Art Pepper Quintet
Gettin' Together | Original Jazz Classics | OJCCD 169-2
Barry Harris Sextet
Bull's Eye! | Original Jazz Classics | OJCCD 1082-2(P 7600)
Barry Harris Trio
Bull's Eye! | Original Jazz Classics | OJCCD 1082-2(P 7600)
Benny Golson Quintet
Groovin' | Original Jazz Classics | OJCCD 226-2(NJ 8220)
Benny Golson Sextet
The J.J.Johnson Memorial Album | Prestige | PRCD 11025-2
Bill Evans Trio
On Green Dolphin Street | Milestone | MCD 9235-2
The Jazz Giants Play Rodgers & Hart:Blue Moon | Prestige | PCD 24205-2
Blue Mitchell Quintet
Out Of The Blue | Original Jazz Classics | OJCCD 667-2(RLP 1131)
Bud Powell Quartet
The Amazing Bud Powell Vol.3:Bud! | Blue Note | 535585-2
Bud Powell Trio
The Amazing Bud Powell Vol.3:Bud! | Blue Note | 535585-2
Cannonball Adderley And His Orchestra
Verve Jazz Masters 31:Cannonball Adderley | Verve | 522651-2
Cannonball Adderley Group
Julian 'Cannonball' Adderley | EmArCy | 830381-2
Cannonball Adderley Quartet
Takes Charge | Blue Note | 534071-2
Ballads | Blue Note | 537563-2
Cannonball & Coltrane | Verve | 559770-2
Cannonball Adderley Quintet
The Art Of Saxophone | Laserlight | 24652
Verve Jazz Masters 31:Cannonball Adderley | Verve | 522651-2
Cannonball Adderley Quintet In Chicago
Cannonball & Coltrane | Verve | 559770-2
Chet Baker Quartet
Chet | Original Jazz Classics | OJC20 087-2
Chet Baker In New York | Original Jazz Classics | OJC20 207-2
The Jazz Giants Play Miles Davis:Milestones | Prestige | PCD 24225-2
Chet Baker Quintet
Chet Baker In New York | Original Jazz Classics | OJC20 207-2
Chet Baker Septet
Chet | Original Jazz Classics | OJC20 087-2
Chet Baker Sextet
Chet | Original Jazz Classics | OJC20 087-2
Dexter Gordon Quartet
Dexter Gordon:Ballads | Blue Note | 796579-2
Jazz Profile:Dexter Gordon | Blue Note | 823514-2
Elmo Hope Sextet
John Coltrane-The Prestige Recordings | Prestige | 16 PCD 4405-2
Freddie Redd Sextet
Redd's Blues | Blue Note | 540537-2
Gil Evans And Ten
Gil Evans And Ten | Original Jazz Classics | OJC 346(P 7120)
The Jazz Giants Play Cole Porter:Night And Day | Prestige | PCD 24203-2
Gil Evans And Ten | Prestige | PRSA 7120-6
Gil Evans Orchestra
Verve Jazz Masters 23:Gil Evans | Verve | 521860-2
The Individualism Of Gil Evans | Verve | 833804-2
Hampton Hawes Trio
Bird Song | Original Jazz Classics | OJCCD 1035-2
Hank Mobley Quartet
Soul Station | Blue Note | 495343-2
Workout | Blue Note | 784080-2
Hank Mobley Quintet
The Turnaround | Blue Note | 524540-2
Roll Call | Blue Note | 540030-2)
Workout | Blue Note | 784080-2
Herbie Hancock Quartet
Herbie Hancock:The Complete Blue Note Sixties Sessions | Blue Note | 495569-2
Horace Silver Sextet
The Story Of Jazz Piano | Laserlight | 24653
Ike Quebec Quartet
Blue And Sentimental | Blue Note | 784098-2
Ike Quebec Quintet
Blue And Sentimental | Blue Note | 784098-2
J.J.Johnson Quintet
The Eminent J.J.Johnson Vol.2 | Blue Note | 532144-2
Jackie McLean Quintet
Capuchin Swing | Blue Note | 540033-2
Jackie McLean Sextet
A Long Drink Of The Blues | Original Jazz Classics | OJCCD 253-2(NJ 8253)
John Coltrane All Stars
The Believer | Original Jazz Classics | OJCCD 876-2(P 7292)
Stardust | Original Jazz Classics | OJCCD 920-2(P 7268)
John Coltrane Quartet
John Coltrane-The Prestige Recordings | Prestige | 16 PCD 4405-2
Trane's Blues | Blue Note | 498240-2

INTERPRETENVERZEICHNIS

Cannonball & Coltrane | Verve | 559770-2
Coltrane Jazz | Atlantic | 7567-81344-2
The Best Of John Coltrane | Atlantic | 7567-81366-2
Atlantic Saxophones | Rhino | 8122-71256-2
John Coltrane-The Heavyweight Champion:The Complete Atlantic Recordings | Atlantic | 8122-71984-2
Giant Steps | Atlantic | 8122-75203-2
The Very Best Of John Coltrane | Rhino | 8122-79778-2
Coltrane | Original Jazz Classics | OJC20 020-2
Soultrane | Original Jazz Classics | OJC20 021-2
Lush Life | Original Jazz Classics | OJC20 131-2
Bahia | Original Jazz Classics | OJCCD 415-2
Stardust | Original Jazz Classics | OJCCD 920-2(P 7268)
The Jazz Giants Play Sammy Cahn:It's Magic | Prestige | PCD 24226-2
The Prestige Legacy Vol.1:The High Priests | Prestige | PCD 24251-2
John Coltrane Quartet With Brass
The Complete Africa/Brass Sessions | Impulse(MCA) | 952168-2
John Coltrane Quintet
John Coltrane-The Prestige Recordings | Prestige | 16 PCD 4405-2
Black Pearls | Original Jazz Classics | OJC 352(P 7316)
The Last Trane | Original Jazz Classics | OJC 394(P 7378)
Coltrane | Original Jazz Classics | OJC20 020-2
Lush Life | Original Jazz Classics | OJC20 131-2
Standard Coltrane | Original Jazz Classics | OJCCD 246-2
Bahia | Original Jazz Classics | OJCCD 415-2
The Believer | Original Jazz Classics | OJCCD 876-2(P 7292)
Stardust | Original Jazz Classics | OJCCD 920-2(P 7268)
The Jazz Giants Play Harold Arlen:Blues In The Night | Prestige | PCD 24201-2
The Jazz Giants Play Rodgers & Hammerstein:My Favorite Things | Prestige | PCD 24223-2
The Mal Waldron Memorial Album:Soul Eyes | Prestige | PRCD 11024-2
John Coltrane Sextet
John Coltrane-The Prestige Recordings | Prestige | 16 PCD 4405-2
Trane's Blues | Blue Note | 498240-2
Blue Train | Blue Note | 591721-2
The Best Of Blue Note | Blue Note | 796110-2
Blue Train(The Ultimate Blue Train) | Blue Note | 853428-0
Coltrane | Original Jazz Classics | OJC20 020-2
The Prestige Legacy Vol.1:The High Priests | Prestige | PCD 24251-2
John Coltrane Trio
John Coltrane-The Prestige Recordings | Prestige | 16 PCD 4405-2
Bahia | Original Jazz Classics | OJCCD 415-2
John Coltrane With The Red Garland Trio
John Coltrane-The Prestige Recordings | Prestige | 16 PCD 4405-2
The Last Trane | Original Jazz Classics | OJC 394(P 7378)
Settin' The Pace | Original Jazz Classics | OJC20 078-2
Traning In | Original Jazz Classics | OJCCD 189-2
John Coltrane-Milt Jackson Quintet
John Coltrane-The Heavyweight Champion:The Complete Atlantic Recordings | Atlantic | 8122-71984-2
Bags & Trane | Rhino | 8122-73685-2
Johnny Griffin Septet
A Blowing Session | Blue Note | 0677191
Trane's Blues | Blue Note | 498240-2
Kai Winding-J.J.Johnson Quintet
The Great Kai & J.J. | Impulse(MCA) | 951225-2
Kenny Burrell Quintet
John Coltrane-The Prestige Recordings | Prestige | 16 PCD 4405-2
Kenny Burrell-John Coltrane Quintet
Kenny Burrell & John Coltrane | New Jazz | NJSA 8276-2
Kenny Burrell & John Coltrane | Original Jazz Classics | OJC20 300-2
Kenny Dorham Quartet
The Jazz Giants Play Harry Warren:Lullaby Of Broadway | Prestige | PCD 24204-2
Kenny Dorham Quintet
Whistle Stop | Blue Note | 525646-2
Kenny Dorham Septet
Cannonball Adderley Birthday Celebration | Fantasy | FANCD 6087-2
Kenny Drew Trio
The Kenny Drew Trio | Original Jazz Classics | OJC20 065-2(RLP 224)
King Curtis Quartet
The New Scene Of King Curtis | Original Jazz Classics | OJC 198(NJ 8237)
King Curtis Quintet
The New Scene Of King Curtis | Original Jazz Classics | OJC 198(NJ 8237)
Lee Morgan Quintet
True Blue | Blue Note | 534032-2
Miles Davis + 19
Miles Ahead | CBS | CK 65121
Miles Davis New Quintet
Workin',Steamin',Cookin',Relaxin' With The Miles Davis Quintet | Original Jazz Classics | OJCCD 8805-2
Miles Davis Quartet
Bill Evans:Piano Player | CBS | CK 65361
Someday My Prince Will Come | CBS | CK 65919
Miles Davis Quintet
Miles Davis: Olympia, March 29th,1960 | Laserlight | 36130
Ballads | CBS | 461099-2
Circle In The Round | CBS | 467898-2
Kind Of Blue | CBS | 480410-2
Miles Davis In Person-Friday Night At The Blackhawk,San Francisco,Vol.1 | CBS | C4K 87106
Kind Of Blue | CBS | CK 64935
Miles Davis At Carnegie Hall | CBS | CK 65027
This Is Jazz:Miles Davis Plays Ballads | CBS | CK 65038
Someday My Prince Will Come | CBS | CK 65919
Live In Stockholm | Dragon | DRCD 228
Newport Jazz Festival 1958,July 3rd-6th,Vol.1:Mostly Miles | Phontastic | NCD 8813
Collector's Items | Original Jazz Classics | OJC20 071-2(P 7044)
Cookin' With The Miles Davis Quintet | Original Jazz Classics | OJC20 128-2
Relaxin' | Original Jazz Classics | OJC20 190-2
Miles Davis And The Modern Jazz Giants | Original Jazz Classics | OJC20 347-2(P 7150)
Steamin' | Original Jazz Classics | OJC20 391-2
The Jazz Giants Play Rodgers & Hammerstein:My Favorite Things | Prestige | PCD 24223-2
The Jazz Giants Play Duke Ellington:Caravan | Prestige | PCD 24227-2
Relaxin' | Prestige | PRSA 7129-6
Miles Davis Sextet
Circle In The Round | CBS | 467898-2
Kind Of Blue | CBS | 480410-2
Kind Of Blue | CBS | CK 64935
This Is Jazz:Miles Davis Plays Ballads | CBS | CK 65038
Sorcerer | CBS | CK 65680
Someday My Prince Will Come | CBS | CK 65919
Miles Davis With Gil Evans & His Orchestra
Miles Davis At Carnegie Hall | CBS | CK 65027
This Is Jazz:Miles Davis Plays Ballads | CBS | CK 65038
Porgy And Bess | CBS | CK 65141
Sketches Of Spain | CBS | CK 65142
Quiet Nights | CBS | CK 65293
Nat Adderley Quartet
Naturally! | Original Jazz Classics | OJCCD 1088-2(JLP 947)
Nat Adderley Quintet
Introducing Nat Adderley | Verve | 543828-2
Oliver Nelson And His Orchestra
Blues And The Abstract Truth | Impulse(MCA) | 951154-2
The Roots Of Acid Jazz | Impulse(MCA) | IMP 12042
Paul Chambers Sextet
Trane's Blues | Blue Note | 498240-2
Prestige All Stars
John Coltrane-The Prestige Recordings | Prestige | 16 PCD 4405-2
Tenor Conclave | Original Jazz Classics | OJCCD 127-2
The Mal Waldron Memorial Album:Soul Eyes | Prestige | PRCD 11024-2
Red Garland Quartet
Red Garland Revisited! | Original Jazz Classics | OJCCD 985-2(P 7658)
The Jazz Giants Play Rodgers & Hart:Blue Moon | Prestige | PCD 24205-2
Red Garland Trio
A Garland Of Red | Original Jazz Classics | OJC 126(P 7064)
Red Garland's Piano | Original Jazz Classics | OJC20 073-2(P 7086)
Dig It | Original Jazz Classics | OJC20 392-2(PR 7229)
Groovy | Original Jazz Classics | OJCCD 061-2
It's A Blue World | Original Jazz Classics | OJCCD 1028-2(P 7838)
Can't See For Lookin' | Original Jazz Classics | OJCCD 918-2(PR 7276)
Red Garland Revisited! | Original Jazz Classics | OJCCD 985-2(P 7658)
Red Garland Trio With Ray Barretto
Manteca | Original Jazz Classics | OJCCD 428-2(PR 7139)
Roy Haynes Trio
We Three | Original Jazz Classics | OJCCD 196-2(NJ 8210)
Sonny Clark Quintet
Cool Struttin' | Blue Note | 495327-2
My Conception | Blue Note | 522674-2
Sonny Clark Sextet
Trane's Blues | Blue Note | 498240-2
Sonny Clark Trio
Sonny Clark | Blue Note | 533774-2
Sonny Clark Trio | Blue Note | 533774-2
Standards | Blue Note | 821283-2
Sonny Criss Quartet
This Is Criss | Original Jazz Classics | OJCCD 430-2(P 7511)
Sonny Rollins Quartet
Sonny Rollins Vol.2 | Blue Note | 497809-2
Sonny Rollins-The Freelance Years:The Complete Riverside & Contemporary Recordings | Riverside | 5 RCD 4427-2
Sonny Rollins:The Blue Note Recordings | Blue Note | 821371-2
Jazz Profile:Sonny Rollins | Blue Note | 823516-2
Tenor Madness | Original Jazz Classics | OJC20 124-2
Tenor Madness | Prestige | PRSA 7047-6
Sonny Rollins Quartet feat.Thelonious Monk
Ballads | Blue Note | 537562-2
Sonny Rollins Quintet
John Coltrane-The Prestige Recordings | Prestige | 16 PCD 4405-2
Sonny Rollins Vol.2 | Blue Note | 497809-2
Ballads | Blue Note | 537562-2
The Blue Note Years-The Best Of Sonny Rollins | Blue Note | 793203-2
Sonny Rollins:The Blue Note Recordings | Blue Note | 821371-2
Jazz Profile:Sonny Rollins | Blue Note | 823516-2
Tenor Madness | Original Jazz Classics | OJC20 124-2
The Prestige Legacy Vol.2:Battles Of Saxes | Prestige | PCD 24252-2
Tenor Madness | Prestige | PRSA 7047-6
Sonny Rollins Sextet
Sonny Rollins Vol.2 | Blue Note | 497809-2
Sonny Rollins:The Blue Note Recordings | Blue Note | 821371-2
Sonny Rollins Trio
The Sound Of Sonny | Original Jazz Classics | OJC20 029-2
Sonny Stitt Quartet
Verve Jazz Masters 50:Sonny Sitt | Verve | 527651-2
Taylor's Wailers
John Coltrane-The Prestige Recordings | Prestige | 16 PCD 4405-2
The New Miles Davis Quintet
Miles | Original Jazz Classics | OJC20 006-2(P 7014)
Thelonious Monk Quintet
Sonny Rollins-The Freelance Years:The Complete Riverside & Contemporary Recordings | Riverside | 5 RCD 4427-2
Brilliant Corners | Original Jazz Classics | OJC20 026-2
Walter Benton Quintet
Out Of This World | Milestone | MCD 47087-2
Wes Montgomery Quartet
Wes Montgomery-The Complete Riverside Recordings | Riverside | 12 RCD 4408-2
Verve Jazz Masters 14:Wes Montgomery | Verve | 519826-2
Verve Jazz Masters 20:Introducing | Verve | 519853-2
Talkin' Jazz:Roots Of Acid Jazz | Verve | 529580-2
Wes Montgomery Quartet With The Claus Ogerman Orchestra
Willow Weep For Me | Verve | 589486-2
Wes Montgomery Quintet
Wes Montgomery-The Complete Riverside Recordings | Riverside | 12 RCD 4408-2
Full House | Original Jazz Classics | OJC20 106-2
Wes Montgomery Trio
Wes Montgomery-The Complete Riverside Recordings | Riverside | 12 RCD 4408-2
Wynton Kelly Quartet
Wynton Kelly-Piano | Original Jazz Classics | OJCCD 401-2(RLP 12-254)
Wynton Kelly Sextet
Kelly Blue | Original Jazz Classics | OJC20 033-2(RLP 1142)
Kelly Blue | Riverside | RISA 1142-6
Wynton Kelly Trio
The Story Of Jazz Piano | Laserlight | 24653
Kelly Blue | Original Jazz Classics | OJC20 033-2(RLP 1142)
Wynton Kelly-Piano | Original Jazz Classics | OJCCD 401-2(RLP 12-254)
Kelly Blue | Riverside | RISA 1142-6
Wynton Kelly Trio With Wes Montgomery
Wes Montgomery:The Verve Jazz Sides | Verve | 521690-2

Chamblee,Eddie | (as,ts,cl,vocg)
Dinah Washington And Her Band
After Hours With Miss D | Verve | 0760562
Verve Jazz Masters 40:Dinah Washington | Verve | 522055-2
Dinah Washington And Her Orchestra
Misty Blue:Sweet Sisters Swing Songs Of Sorrow And Sadness | Blue Note | 521151-2
Dinah Washington With The Eddie Chamblee Orchestra
Verve Jazz Masters 40:Dinah Washington | Verve | 522055-2
Dinah Sings Bessie Smith | Verve | 538635-2
Lionel Hampton And His Orchestra
Planet Jazz:Lionel Hampton | Planet Jazz | 2152059-2

Chamorro,Joan | (bs)
Big Band Bellaterra
Don't Git Sassy | Fresh Sound Records | FSNT 048 CD

Champbell,Charles | (perc)
Paul Nero Sound
Doldinger's Best | ACT | 9224-2

Champlin,Bill | (arrvoc)
Herbie Hancock Group
Monster | CBS | 486571-2
Paulinho Da Costa Orchestra
Happy People | Original Jazz Classics | OJCCD 783-2(2312102)

Chancey,Vincent | (fr-h)
Carla Bley Band
Live! | Watt | 12(815730-2)
Herb Robertson Brass Ensemble
Shades Of Bud Powell | JMT Edition | 919019-2
Lester Bowie's Brass Fantasy
I Only Have Eyes For You | ECM | 1296(825902-2)
Avant Pop | ECM | 1326
The Fire This Time | IN+OUT Records | 7019-2
The Odyssey Of Funk & Popular Music | Dreyfus Jazz Line | FDM 37004-2
When The Spitit Returns | Dreyfus Jazz Line | FDM 37016-2
The Carla Bley Band
I Hate To Sing | Watt | 12,5
Vincent Chancey Quartet
Welcome Mr. Chancey | IN+OUT Records | 7020-1

Chandler,Gary | (tp)
Charles Earland Sextet
Charlie's Greatest Hits | Prestige | PCD 24250-2

Chandler,Jesse | (org)
Vic Juris Trio
While My Guitar Gently Weeps | Steeplechase | SCCD 31553

Chandler,Taft | (ts)
Ahmed Abdul-Malik Orchestra
Jazz Sounds Of Africa | Prestige | PRCD 24279-2

Chaney,Marvin | (voc)
Lillian Boutté And Her Group & The Soulful Heavenly Stars
The Gospel Book | Blues Beacon | BLU-1017 2

Changes |
Changes
Jazz Changes? | Jazz 'n' Arts Records | 0100
Jazz Portraits | EGO | 95080

Chanson,Dominique | (saxts)
Raymond Fol Big Band
Jazz In Paris:Raymond Fol-Les 4 Saisons | EmArCy | 548791-2

Chantrain,Raymond | (tp)
Django Reinhardt With Stan Brenders Et Son Grand Orchestre
Verve Jazz Masters 38:Django Reinhardt | Verve | 516931-2

Chapin,Earl | (fr-h)
Jimmy Smith With The Billy Byers Orchestra
Jimmy Smith:Best Of The Verve Years | Verve | 527950-2
Jimmy Smith With The Lalo Schifrin Orchestra
Jimmy Smith:Best Of The Verve Years | Verve | 527950-2
Jimmy Smith-Talkin' Verve | Verve | 531563-2
The Cat | Verve | 539756-2
Miles Davis With Gil Evans & His Orchestra
Sketches Of Spain | CBS | CK 65142
Quincy Jones And His Orchestra
The Quintessence | Impulse(MCA) | 951222-2
Stan Getz With The Eddie Sauter Orchestra
Stan Getz Plays The Music Of Mickey One | Verve | 531232-2
Thad Jones-Mel Lewis Orchestra
The Groove Merchant/The Second Race | Laserlight | 24656

Chapin,Thomas[Tom] | (as,fl,alto-fl,perc,voice,b-fl)
Axel Zwingenberger With The Lionel Hampton Big Band
The Boogie Woogie Album | Vagabond | VRCD 8.88008
Barbara Dennerlein Group
Junkanoo | Verve | 537122-2
Daniel Schnyder Group
Tanatula | Enja | ENJ-9302 2
Michael Blake Group
Kingdom Of Champa | Intuition Records | INT 3189-2

Chaplin,Ian | (asss)
Vince Jones Group
It All Ends Up In Tears | Intuition Records | INT 3069-2

Chapman,Christine | (fr-h)
Lee Konitz With The Ed Partyka Jazz Orchestra
Dreams And Realities | Laika Records | 35101642

Chapman,Harry | (harp)
Stephane Grappelli And His Musicians
Grapelli Story | Verve | 515807-2

Chappell,Gus | (tb)
Dinah Washington And Her Band
After Hours With Miss D | Verve | 0760562
Verve Jazz Masters 40:Dinah Washington | Verve | 522055-2

Chaput,Roger | (g)
Alix Combelle Et Son Orchestre
Americans Swinging In Paris:Bill Coleman-The Elegance | EMI Records | 539662-2
Dicky Wells And His Orchestra
Americans Swinging In Paris:Dicky Wells | EMI Records | 539664-2
Eddie South/Stephane Grappelli Quintet
Django Reinhardt:Echoes Of France | Dreyfus Jazz Line | FDM 36726-2
Quintet Du Hot Club De France
Grapelli Story | Verve | 515807-2
Verve Jazz Masters 38:Django Reinhardt | Verve | 516931-2
Verve Jazz Masters Vol.60:The Collection | Verve | 529866-2
Django Reinhardt:Souveniers | Dreyfus Jazz Line | FDM 36744-2
Wal-Berg Et Son Jazz Francais
Jazz In Paris:Django Reinhardt-Django Et Compagnie | EmArCy | 549241-2 PMS

Charbonnier,Patrick | (tb)
Pata Music Meets Arfi
News Of Roi Ubu | Pata Musik | PATA 10 CD

Charial,Pierre | (barrel-org)
Michael Riessler And The Ensemble 13
Momentum Mobile | Enja | ENJ-9003 2
Michael Riessler Group
Orange | ACT | 9274-2
Sylvie Courvoisier Group
Ocre | Enja | ENJ-9323 2
Y2K | Enja | ENJ-9383 2

Charlap,Bill | (p)
Bill Charlap Trio
Stardust | Blue Note | 535985-2
Byron Stripling Quartet
Byron,Get On Free | Nagel-Heyer | CD 2016
Byron Stripling Quintet
Byron,Get On Free | Nagel-Heyer | CD 2016
Byron Stripling Sextet
Striplingnow! | Nagel-Heyer | CD 2002
Byron,Get On Free | Nagel-Heyer | CD 2016
Byron Stripling Trio
Byron,Get On Free | Nagel-Heyer | CD 2016
Frank Wess With The Bill Charlap Trio
Stardust | Blue Note | 535985-2
Jim Hall With The Bill Charlap Trio
Stardust | Blue Note | 535985-2
Shirley Horn With The Bill Charlap Trio
Stardust | Blue Note | 535985-2
Tony Bennett With The Bill Charlap Trio
Stardust | Blue Note | 535985-2
Warren Vaché And Bill Charlap
2Gether | Nagel-Heyer | CD 2011

Charlap,Emile | (contractor)
A Band Of Friends
Wynton Marsalis Quartet With Strings | CBS | CK 68921

Charles |
Charles
Jazzy World | JA & RO | JARO 4200-2

Charles Mingus Orchestra |
Charles Mingus Orchestra
Tonight At Noon...Three Or Four Shades Of Love | Dreyfus Jazz Line | FDM 36633-2

Charles,David | (keyboards,synth,percsnare-dr)
Till Brönner Group
Chattin' With Chet | Verve | 157534-2
Love | Verve | 559058-2

Charles,Dennis | (congas,dr,voiceperc)
Cecil Taylor Quartet
At Newport | Verve | 589764-2
The World Of Cecil Taylor | Candid | CCD 79006
Cecil Taylor: Air | Candid | CCD 79046
Cecil Taylor Quintet
Love For Sale | Blue Note | 494107-2
Cecil Taylor Trio
Love For Sale | Blue Note | 494107-2
The World Of Cecil Taylor | Candid | CCD 79006
Cecil Taylor/Buell Neidlinger Quintet
New York City R&B | Candid | CCD 79017
Sonny Rollins Group
What's New? | RCA | 2179626-2
Sonny Rollins Quartet
Planet Jazz:Sonny Rollins | Planet Jazz | 2152062-2
Steve Lacy Quartet
Soprano Sax | Original Jazz Classics | OJCCD 130-2(P 7125)

Charles,Frank | (bongosperc)
Sonny Rollins Group
What's New? | RCA | 2179626-2

Sonny Rollins Quartet
Planet Jazz:Sonny Rollins | Planet Jazz | 2152062-2

Charles,Ray | (as,el-p,p,voc,orgceleste)

Carmen McRae With Orchestra
Birds Of A Feather | Decca | 589515-2
David Fathead Newman Sextet
Atlantic Saxophones | Rhino | 8122-71256-2
Rhino Presents The Atlantic Jazz Gallery | Atlantic | 8122-71257-2
Fathead:Ray Charles Presents David Newman | Atlantic | 8122-73708-2
Dee Dee Bridgewater With Band
Victim Of Love | Verve | 841199-2
Ray Charles And His Orchestra
Ray Charles At Newport | Atlantic | 7567-80765-2
Ray Charles Sextet With The Raylets
Newport Jazz Festival 1958,July 3rd-6th Vol.4:Blues In The Night No.2 | Phontastic | NCD 8816
Ray Charles Trio
Rhino Presents The Atlantic Jazz Gallery | Atlantic | 8122-71257-2
Ray Charles-Milt Jackson Quartet
Soul Brothers/Soul Meeting | Atlantic | 7567-81951-2
Ray Charles-Milt Jackson Quintet
Soul Brothers/Soul Meeting | Atlantic | 7567-81951-2
Ray Charles-Milt Jackson Sextet
Soul Brothers/Soul Meeting | Atlantic | 7567-81951-2

Charles,Teddy | (pvib)

Charles Mingus Group
Mingus Dynasty | CBS | CK 65513
Charles Mingus Orchestra
Charles Mingus:The Complete 1959 Columbia Recordings | CBS | C3K 65145
Curtis Fuller And Teddy Charles With French Horns
Curtis Fuller And Hampton Hawes With French Horns | Original Jazz Classics | OJCCD 1942-2(NJ 8305)
George Russell And His Orchestra
Bill Evans:Piano Player | CBS | CK 65361
J.R. Monterose Sextet
Jaywalkin' | Fresh Sound Records | FSR-CD 320
Miles Davis Quintet
Charles Mingus-The Complete Debut Recordings | Debut | 12 DCD 4402-2
Blue Moods | Original Jazz Classics | OJC20 043-2(DEB 120)
Prestige Jazz Quartet
The Mal Waldron Memorial Album:Soul Eyes | Prestige | PRCD 11024-2
Teddy Charles Quartet
Charles Mingus-Passion Of A Man:The Complete Atlantic Recordings 1956-1961 | Atlantic | 8122-72871-2
Teddy Charles' West Coasters
Wardell Gray Memorial Vol.1 | Original Jazz Classics | OJCCD 050-2(P 7008)
The Prestige All Stars
Olio | Original Jazz Classics | OJCCD 1004-2(P 7084)
The Prestige Jazz Quartet
The Prestige Jazz Quartet | Original Jazz Classics | OJCCD 1937-2(P 7108)

Charleston,Erik | (voc)

Steve Coleman And Five Elements
The Sonic Language Of Myth | RCA | 2164123-2

Charlesworth,Dick | (cl,ss,tsvoc)

Dick Charlesworth And His City Gents
The Golden Years Of Revival Jazz,Vol.4 | Storyville | STCD 5509
The Golden Years Of Revival Jazz,Vol.6 | Storyville | STCD 5511
The Golden Years Of Revival Jazz,Vol.11 | Storyville | STCD 5516

Charlton,Lee | (dr)

Vince Guaraldi Group
Charlie Brown's Holiday Hits | Fantasy | FCD 9682-2

Charma,Arthur | (voc)

Nat Adderley Group
Soul Of The Bible | Capitol | 358257-2

Chartrand,Pat | (assax)

Harry James And His Orchestra
Trumpet Blues:The Best Of Harry James | Capitol | 521224-2

Charvoni | (voc)

Lenny White Group
Present Tense | Hip Bop | HIBD 8004

Chase,Bill | (tp,arr,fl-hel-tp)

Woody Herman And His Orchestra
Verve Jazz Masters 54:Woody Herman | Verve | 529903-2
Woody Herman-1963 | Philips | 589490-2

Chase,Russ | (tp)

Billie Holiday With Toots Camarata And His Orchestra
Billie's Love Songs | Nimbus Records | NI 2000

Chassau,Robert | (v)

A Band Of Friends
Wynton Marsalis Quartet With Strings | CBS | CK 68921

Chasson,Barbara | (viola)

Toots Thielemans And His Orchestra
Verve Jazz Masters Vol.59:Toots Thielemans | Verve | 535271-2

Chastca,Heinrich | (b)

Andy Lumpp Trio
Ostara | Nabel Records:Jazz Network | CD 4682
Andy Lumpp Trio Feat. Andy Przybielski
Musica Ex Spiritu Sancto | Nabel Records:Jazz Network | CD 4694
Andy Lumpp Trio With Andy Przybielski
Music From Planet Earth | Nabel Records:Jazz Network | CD 4687

Chastenier,Frank | (el-p,keyboards,orgp)

Bernard Purdie's Soul To Jazz
Bernard Purdie's Soul To Jazz | ACT | 9242-2
Bob Brookmeyer Group With The WDR Big Band
Electricity | ACT | 9219-2
Eddie Harris Group With The WDR Big Band
Eddie Harris-The Last Concert | ACT | 9249-2
Frank Castenier Group
For You,For Me For Evermore | EmArCy | 9814976
Gianlugi Trovesi Quartet With The WDR Big Band
Dedalo | Enja | ENJ-9419 2
Jens Winther And The WDR Big Band
The Escape | dacapo | DCCD 9437
John Goldsby Sextet
Viewpoint | Nagel-Heyer | CD 2014
Kevin Mahogany With The WDR Big Band And Guests
Pussy Cat Dues:The Music Of Charles Mingus | Enja | ENJ-9316 2
Rolf Kühn Group
Inside Out | Intuition Records | INT 3276-2
Internal Eyes | Intuition Records | INT 3328-2
Till Brönner Group
Chattin' With Chet | Verve | 157534-2
Love | Verve | 559058-2
Till Brönner-Gregoire Peters Quintet
Generations Of Jazz | Minor Music | 801037
Vince Mendoza With The WDR Big Band And Guests
Sketches | ACT | 9215-2

Chatel,Corinne | (voc)

Corinne Chatel Quintet
Ma Vie En Rose | Edition Collage | EC 525-2

Chatman,Susan | (v)

Jacintha With Band And Strings
Lush Life | Groove Note | GRV 1011-2(Gold CD 2011)

Chatterjee,Amit | (el-g)

Badal Roy & Amit Chatterjee
Art Of The Duo: Endless Radiance | Tutu Records | 888178-2*

Chatterjee,Samir | (perc,dumbektable)

Ned Rothenberg Trio
Port Of Entry | Intuition Records | INT 3249-2

Chatz,Milton | (bsreeds)

Louis Armstrong And Ella Fitzgerald With Bob Hagger's Orchestra
Louis Armstrong:C'est Si Bon | Dreyfus Jazz Line | FDM 36730-2

Chaudagne,Remy | (bel-b)

Philippe Caillat Group
Stream Of Time | Laika Records | LK 92-030

Chaurasia,Hariprasad | (bansurifl)

John McLaughlin Group
Remember Shakti | Verve | 559945-2
Zakir Hussain Group
Making Music | ECM | 1349

Chautemps,Jean-Louis | (bs,cl,fl,saxts)

Daniel Humair Soultet
Jazz In Paris | EmArCy | 548793-2
Golden Gate Quartet With The Martial Solal Orchestra
Americans Swinging In Paris:Golden Gate Quartet | EMI Records | 539659-2
From Spriritual To Swing Vol.2 | EMI Records | 780573-2
Lucky Thompson With The Gerard Pochonet All-Stars
Planet Jazz:Jazz Saxophone | Planet Jazz | 2169653-2
Lucky Thompson's Modern Jazz Group Tentet
Jazz In Paris:Lucky Thompson-Modern Jazz Group | EmArCy | 159823-2 PMS
Raymond Fol Big Band
Jazz In Paris:Raymond Fol-Les 4 Saisons | EmArCy | 548791-2
Stan Getz With The Kurt Edelhagen Orchestra
Stan Getz In Europe | Laserlight | 24657

Chavanat,Joan-Claude | (g)

Dee Dee Bridgewater With Band
Victim Of Love | Verve | 841199-2

Chavauché,Corinne | (v)

Stephane Grappelli With The Michel Legrand Orchestra
Grapelli Story | Verve | 515807-2

Chawes,Benni | (voice)

Benni Chaves-Laszlo Gardony
Human Bass | Laika Records | 35101042

Chayeb,Philippe | (el-b)

Serge Forté Trio
Vaina | Laika Records | LK 90-021

Chea,Alvin | (voc)

Take 6
Goldmine | Reprise | 7599-25670-2
So Much To Say | Reprise | 7599-25892-2
He Is Christmas | Reprise | 7599-26665-2
Take 6 With The Yellow Jackets
He Is Christmas | Reprise | 7599-26665-2

Cheatham,Doc | (tpvoc)

Billie Holiday With Eddie Heywood And His Orchestra
Billie Holiday:The Complete Commodore Recordings | GRP | 543272-2
Cab Calloway And His Orchestra
Planet Jazz:Cab Calloway | Planet Jazz | 2161237-2
Doc Cheatham And Sammy Price
Jazz In Paris:Sammy Price And Doc Cheatham Play Gershwin | EmArCy | 018426-2
Doc Cheatham Sextet
A' Portrait Of Jan Jankeje | Jazzpoint | JP 1054 CD
Juanita Hall With The Claude Hopkins All Stars
Juanita Hall Sings The Blues | Original Jazz Classics | OJCCD 1928-2(CPST 556)
Red Richards-George Kelly Sextet With Doc Cheatham
Groove Move | Jazzpoint | JP 1045 CD
Shorty Baker-Doc Cheatham Quintet
Shorty & Doc | Original Jazz Classics | OJCCD 839-2(SV 2021)

Cheek,Chris | (ssts)

Chris Cheek Quartet
I Wish I Knew | Fresh Sound Records | FSNT 022 CD
Chris Cheek Quintet
Vine | Fresh Sound Records | FSNT 086 CD
Chris Cheek Sextet
A Girl Named Joe | Fresh Sound Records | FSNT 032 CD
Elisabet Raspall Quintet
Triangles | Fresh Sound Records | FSNT 018 CD
Frank Carlberg Group
Variations On A Summer Day | Fresh Sound Records | FSNT 083 CD
Freddie Bryant Group
Brazilian Rosewood | Fresh Sound Records | FSNT 035 CD
Georgina Weinstein With Her Quartet
Come Rain Or Come Shine | Fresh Sound Records | FSNT 020 CD
Mark Turner-Chris Cheek Quintet
The Music Of Mercedes Rossy | Fresh Sound Records | FSNT 043 CD
Mark Zubeck Quintet
Horse With A Broken Leg | Fresh Sound Records | FSNT 078 CD
Paul Motian And The E.B.B.B.
Holiday For Strings | Winter&Winter | 910069-2
Paul Motian Electric Bebop Band
Flight Of The Blue Jay | Winter&Winter | 910009-2
Monk And Powell | Winter&Winter | 910045-2
Europe | Winter&Winter | 910063-2
Tom Beckham Quartet
Suspicions | Fresh Sound Records | FSNT 075 CD

Cheikes,Mac | (g)

Tommy Dorsey And His Orchestra
Planet Jazz:Tommy Dorsey | Planet Jazz | 2159972-2

Chemirani,Djamchid | (zarb)

Chico Freeman & Franco Ambrosetti Meet Reto Weber Percussion Orchestra
Face To Face | double moon | CHRDM 71018

Chemirani,Keyvan | (perczarb)

Albert Mangelsdorff-Reto Weber Percussion Orchestra
Live At Montreux | double moon | CHRDM 71009
Mahmoud Turkmani
Fayka | Enja | ENJ-9447 2

Cherico,Gene | (b)

Astrud Gilberto With The New Stan Getz Quartet
Verve Jazz Masters 9:Astrud Gilberto | Verve | 519824-2
Gary Burton Trio
Planet Jazz:Gary Burton | RCA | 2165367-2
Getz-Gilberto Quintet
Getz/Gilberto No.2 | Verve | 519800-2
Paul Desmond Orchestra
Planet Jazz:Jazz Saxophone | Planet Jazz | 2169653-2
Paul Desmond Quartet
Planet Jazz:Paul Desmond | Planet Jazz | 2152061-2
Bossa Antigua | RCA | 2174795-2
Easy Living | RCA | 2174796-2
Take Ten | RCA | 2179621-2
Paul Desmond With Strings
Desmond Blue | RCA | 2663898-2
Paul Desmond-Gerry Mulligan Quartet
The Ballad Of Paul Desmond | RCA | 21429372
Stan Getz Quartet
Getz/Gilberto No.2 | Verve | 519800-2
Stan Getz Quintet Feat. Astrud Gilberto
Verve Jazz Masters 53:Stan Getz-Bossa Nova | Verve | 529904-2
The New Stan Getz Quartet
Getz Au Go Go | Verve | 821725-2
The New Stan Getz Quartet Feat. Astrud Gilberto
Getz Au Go Go | Verve | 821725-2
Toshiko Mariano Quartet
Toshiko Mariano Quartet | Candid | CCD 79012

Cherico,Vince | (dr)

Ray Barretto Orchestra
Portraits In Jazz And Clave | RCA | 2168452-2

Chermiset,Valerie | (flpiccolo)

Paquito D'Rivera Group With The Absolute Ensemble
Habanera | Enja | ENJ-9395 2

Chéroned,Philippe | (cello)

Charlie Haden Quartet West With Strings
Now Is The Hour | Verve | 527827-2

Cherry,David | (synth)

Don Cherry Group
Multi Kulti | A&M Records | 395323-2

Cherry,Don | (bamboo-fl,bangali-fl,bfl,co,gamelan)

Albert Mangelsdorff-Don Cherry
Albert Mangelsdorff And His Friends | MPS | 067375-2
Beng Berger Band
Bitter Funeral Beer | ECM | 1179
Charlie Haden Orchestra
The Ballad Of The Fallen | ECM | 1248(811546-2)
Charlie Haden Trio
The Montreal Tapes Vol.1 | Verve | 523260-2
Charlie Haden's Liberation Music Orchestra
Liberation Music Orchestra | Impulse(MCA) | 951188-2
Collin Walcott Group
Grazing Dreams | ECM | 1096
Don Cherry
Multi Kulti | A&M Records | 395323-2
Don Cherry Group
Dona Nostra | ECM | 1448(521727-2)
Multi Kulti | A&M Records | 395323-2
Don Cherry-The Sonet Recordings:Eternal Now/Live Ankara | Verve | 533049-2
Don Cherry Quartet
Complete Communion | Blue Note | 522673-2
Don Cherry/Ed Blackwell
El Corazon | ECM | 1230
Don Cherry/Nana Vasconcelos/Collin Walcott
Codona | ECM | 1132(829371-2)
Codona 2 | ECM | 1177(833332-2)
Codona 3 | ECM | 1243
Ed Blackwell Project
Vol.2:What It Be Like? | Enja | ENJ-8054 2
Gato Barbieri Quintet
The Art Of Saxophone | Laserlight | 24652
Heiner Goebbels/Heiner Müller
Der Mann Im Fahrstuhl | ECM | 1369(837110-2)
John Coltrane-Don Cherry Quartet
The Avant-Garde | Atlantic | 7567-90041-2
John Coltrane-The Heavyweight Champion:The Complete Atlantic Recordings | Atlantic | 8122-71984-2
The Avantgarde | Rhino | 8122-79892-2
Michael Mantler Group
Michael Mantler: No Answer/Silence | Watt | 2/5(543374-2)
Old And New Dreams
Old And New Dreams | ECM | 1154
Playing | ECM | 1205
Ornette Coleman Double Quartet
Beauty Is A Rare Thing:Ornette Coleman-The Complete Atlantic Recordings | Atlantic | 8122-71410-2
Free Jazz | Atlantic | 8122-75208-2
Ornette Coleman Quartet
This Is Our Music | Atlantic | 7567-80767-2
Change Of The Century | Atlantic | 7567-81341-2
Atlantic Saxophones | Rhino | 8122-71256-2
Rhino Presents The Atlantic Jazz Gallery | Atlantic | 8122-71257-2
Beauty Is A Rare Thing:Ornette Coleman-The Complete Atlantic Recordings | Atlantic | 8122-71410-2
Ornette On Tenor | Atlantic | 8122-71455-2
Tomorrow Is The Question | Original Jazz Classics | OJC20 342-2(S 7569)
Ornette Coleman Quintet
The Music Of Ornette Coleman:Something Else!! | Original Jazz Classics | OJC20 163-2
Sonny Rollins & Co.
Planet Jazz:Sonny Rollins | Planet Jazz | 2152062-2
The Jazz Composer's Orchestra
Comminications | JCOA | 1001/2

Cherry,Ed | (el-gg)

Dizzy Gillespie And The United Nation Orchestra
7.Zelt-Musik-Festival:Jazz Events | Zounds | CD 2730001

Cherry,Vivian | (voc)

Dee Dee Bridgewater With Band
Dee Dee Bridgewater | Atlantic | 7567-80760-2

Chester,Gary | (drperc)

Bill Evans Quartet With Orchestra
The Complete Bill Evans On Verve | Verve | 527953-2
From Left To Right | Verve | 557451-2
Bill Evans With Orchestra
The Complete Bill Evans On Verve | Verve | 527953-2
From Left To Right | Verve | 557451-2
King Curtis Band
King Curtis-Blow Man Blow | Bear Family Records | BCD 15670 CI

Chestnut,Cyrus | (p,el-p,percp-solo)

(Little)Jimmy Scott And His Band
Mood Indigo | Milestone | MCD 9305-2
Christian McBride Group
Gettin' To It | Verve | 523989-2
Cyrus Chestnut
Cyrus Chestnut | Atlantic | 7567-83140-2
Cyrus Chestnut Sextet
Earth Stories | Atlantic | 7567-82876-2
Cyrus Chestnut Trio
Earth Stories | Atlantic | 7567-82876-2
Cyrus Chestnut | Atlantic | 7567-83140-2
You Are My Sunshine | Warner | 9362-48445-2
Cyrus Chestnut Trio With Anita Baker
Cyrus Chestnut | Atlantic | 7567-83140-2
Cyrus Chestnut Trio With James Carter
Cyrus Chestnut | Atlantic | 7567-83140-2
Cyrus Chestnut Trio With James Carter And Joe Lovano
Cyrus Chestnut | Atlantic | 7567-83140-2
Cyrus Chestnut Trio With Joe Lovano
Cyrus Chestnut | Atlantic | 7567-83140-2
Freddie Cole
Jazzin' Vol.2: The Music Of Stevie Wonder | Fantasy | FANCD 6088-2
Freddy Cole With Band
A Circle Of Love | Fantasy | FCD 9674-2
To The End Of The Earth | Fantasy | FCD 9675-2
Le Grand Freddy:Freddy Cole Sings The Music Of Michel Legrand | Fantasy | FCD 9683-2
George Mraz Quartet
Bottom Line | Milestone | MCD 9272-2
Duke's Place | Milestone | MCD 9292-2
George Mraz Trio
Duke's Place | Milestone | MCD 9292-2
Jimmy Scott With Band
Moon Glow | Milestone | MCD 9332-2
Roy Hargrove Quintet
Roy Hargrove Quintet With The Tenors Of Our Time | Verve | 523019-2
Roy Hargrove Quintet With Branford Marsalis
Roy Hargrove Quintet With The Tenors Of Our Time | Verve | 523019-2
Roy Hargrove Quintet With Joe Henderson
Roy Hargrove Quintet With The Tenors Of Our Time | Verve | 523019-2
Roy Hargrove Quintet With Johnny Griffin
Roy Hargrove Quintet With The Tenors Of Our Time | Verve | 523019-2
Roy Hargrove Quintet With Joshua Redman
Roy Hargrove Quintet With The Tenors Of Our Time | Verve | 523019-2
Roy Hargrove Quintet With Stanley Turrentine
Roy Hargrove Quintet With The Tenors Of Our Time | Verve | 523019-2

Chevallier,Christian | (arr,p,vibvoc)

Kenny Clarke 8
Americans Swinging In Paris:Kenny Clarke | EMI Records | 539652-2
Les Blue Stars
Jazz In Paris:Blossom Dearie-The Pianist/Les Blue Stars | EmArCy | 064784-2
Lionel Hampton All Stars
Jazz In Paris:Lionel Hampton And His French New Sound Vol.1 | EmArCy | 549405-2 PMS
Jazz In Paris:Lionel Hampton And His French New Sound Vol.2 | EmArCy | 549406-2 PMS

Chevillon,Bruno | (b)

Louis Sclavis Quartet
Acoustic Quartet | ECM | 1526
L'Affrontement Des Prétendants | ECM | 1705(159927-2)
Louis Sclavis Quintet
Rouge | ECM | 1458
Louis Sclavis Sextet
Les Violences De Rameau | ECM | 1588(533128-2)
Stephan Oliva Trio
Fantasm | RCA | 2173925-2

Chiasson,Warren | (vib)
Les McCann Group
Talkin' Verve:Les McCann | Verve | 557351-2

Chiboust,Noel | (tpts)
Coleman Hawkins With Michel Warlop And His Orchestra
Django Reinhardt All Star Sessions | Capitol | 531577-2
Eddie Brunner And His Orchestra
Americans Swinging In Paris:Bill Coleman-The Elegance | EMI Records | 539662-2

Chicago All Stars,The |
The Chicago All Stars
Planet Jazz:Bud Freeman | Planet Jazz | 2161240-2

Childers,Buddy | (fl-htp)
Bobby Bryant Orchestra
Deep Blue-The United States Of Mind | Blue Note | 521152-2
Buddy Childers Big Band
It's What Happening Now! | Candid | CCD 79749
Just Buddy's | Candid | CCD 79761
Buddy Childers With The Russ Garcia Strings
Artistry In Jazz | Candid | CCD 79735
Ella Fitzgerald With The Marty Paich Orchestra
Get Happy! | Verve | 523321-2
Jimmy Smith With The Oliver Nelson Orchestra
Jimmy Smith:Best Of The Verve Years | Verve | 527950-2
Jimmy Smith-Talkin' Verve | Verve | 531563-2
June Christy With The Pete Rugolo Orchestra
Something Cool(The Complete Mono & Stereo Versions) | Capitol | 534069-2
Maynard Ferguson And His Orchestra
Verve Jazz Masters 52:Maynard Ferguson | Verve | 529905-2
Nat King Cole Quartet With The Stan Kenton Orchestra
Nat King Cole:For Sentimental Reasons | Dreyfus Jazz Line | FDM 36740-2
Pete Rugolo And His Orchestra
Thriller/Richard Diamon(Original Jazz Scores From 2 Classics TV Series) | Fresh Sound Records | FSCD 2015
Singers Unlimited With The Patrick Williams Orchestra
The Singers Unlimited:Magic Voices | MPS | 539130-2
Stan Kenton And His Orchestra
Swing Vol.1 | Storyville | 4960343
Stan Kenton Portraits On Standards | Capitol | 531571-2

Children's Chorus |
Vince Guaraldi Group
Charlie Brown's Holiday Hits | Fantasy | FCD 9682-2

Childs,Billy | (keyboards,p,el-psynth)
Craig Bailey Band
A New Journey | Candid | CCD 79725
Dianne Reeves With Band
I Remember | Blue Note | 790264-2
Essence All Stars
Hot Jazz Bisquits | Hip Bop | HIBD 8801
Freddie Hubbard And His Orchestra
Born To Be Blue | Original Jazz Classics | OJCCD 734-2(2312134)
Freddie Hubbard Quintet
Live At The Northsea Jazz Festival | Pablo | 2620113-2
Freddie Hubbard Sextet
Keystone Bop Vol.2:Friday/Saturday | Prestige | PCD 24163-2
J.J.Johnson Sextet
The J.J.Johnson Memorial Album | Prestige | PRCD 11025-2
J.J.Johnson-Nat Adderley Quintet
Yokohama Concert Vol.2:Chain Reaction | Pablo | PACD 2620121-2
The J.J.Johnson Memorial Album | Prestige | PRCD 11025-2
Joe Henderson Quartet
Keystone Bop Vol.2:Friday/Saturday | Prestige | PCD 24163-2

Childs,Oliver | (voc)
Fats Waller And His Buddies
Planet Jazz:Jack Teagarden | Planet Jazz | 2161236-2

Chimelis,Richard | (bongoes,conga,timbalesperc)
George Shearing With The Montgomery Brothers
Wes Montgomery-The Complete Riverside Recordings | Riverside | 12 RCD 4408-2
George Shearing And The Montgomery Brothers | Original Jazz Classics | OJCCD 040-2

Chindamo,Joe | (keyboards,paccordeon)
Vince Jones Group
Tell Me A Secret | Intuition Records | INT 3072-2
Vince Jones Septet
On The Brink Of It | Intuition Records | INT 3068-2

Chinese Compass |
Chinese Compass
Chinese Compass | dacapo | DCCD 9443

Ching,Fei-Pang | (v)
Ron Carter With Strings
Pastels | Original Jazz Classics | OJCCD 665-2(M 9073)

Chirillo,James | (bj,el-g,gld)
Buck Clayton Swing Band
Swing's The Village | Nagel-Heyer | CD 5004
Blues Of Summer | Nagel-Heyer | NH 1011
James Chirillo Quartet with Vera Mara
Sultry Serenade | Nagel-Heyer | CD 061
James Chirillo Sextet
Sultry Serenade | Nagel-Heyer | CD 061
James Chirillo-Johnny Carisi
Sultry Serenade | Nagel-Heyer | CD 061
Joe Ascione Octet
My Buddy:A Tribute To Buddy Rich | Nagel-Heyer | CD 036
Mark Shane's X-Mas Allstars
What Would Santa Say? | Nagel-Heyer | CD 055
Christmas Jazz! | Nagel-Heyer | NH 1008
Randy Sandke And The New York Allstars
The Re-Discovered Louis And Bix | Nagel-Heyer | CD 058
Randy Sandke-Dick Hyman
The Re-Discovered Louis And Bix | Nagel-Heyer | CD 058
The New York Allstars
Count Basie Remembered | Nagel-Heyer | CD 031
Count Basie Remembered Vol.2 | Nagel-Heyer | CD 041
Hey Ba-Ba-Re-Bop!! The New York Allstars Play Lionel Hampton Vol.1 | Nagel-Heyer | CD 047
The New York Allstars Play Lionel Hampton,Vol.2: Stompin' At The Savoy | Nagel-Heyer | CD 077

Chisholm,George | (tb)
Vic Lewis And His Band
Vic Lewis:The Golden Years | Candid | CCD 79754

Chisholm,Hayden | (as,cl,ss,bs,voicedidgeridoo)
Hans Lüdemann Rism 7
FutuRISM | Jazz Haus Musik | JHM 0092/93 CD
Hayden Chisholm
Circe | Jazz Haus Musik | JHM 0081 CD
John Goldsby Sextet
Viewpoint | Nagel-Heyer | CD 2014
Nils Wogram Octet
Odd And Awkward | Enja | ENJ-9416-2
Nils Wogram Sextet
Odd And Awkward | Enja | ENJ-9416-2

Chittinson,Herman | (pp-solo)
Herman Chittison
JazzIn Paris:Harlem Piano In Montmartre | EmArCy | 018447-2

Chittison,Herman | (p,arr,celestep-solo)
Eddie Brunner And His Orchestra
Americans Swinging In Paris:Bill Coleman-The Elegance | EMI Records | 539662-2
George Wettling's New Yorkers
Jazz:The Essential Collection Vol.3 | IN+OUT Records | 78013-2
Willie Lewis And His Entertainers
Americans Swinging In Paris:Benny Carter | EMI Records | 539647-2

Chivily,Pete | (b)
Stan Kenton And His Orchestra
Adventures In Blues | Capitol | 520089-2

Chocolate Dandies,The |
Chocolate Dandies
Jazz:The Essential Collection Vol.3 | IN+OUT Records | 78013-2

Choir |
Donald Byrd Orchestra With Voices
True Blue | Blue Note | 534032-2
Louis Armstrong And His Orchestra
Swing Legends:Louis Armstrong | Nimbus Records | NI 2012
Louis Armstrong With Gordon Jenkins And His Orchestra And Choir
Louis Armstrong-My Greatest Songs | MCA | MCD 18347
Swing Legends:Louis Armstrong | Nimbus Records | NI 2012
Louis Armstrong With Harry Mills And Choir
Louis And The Good Book | Verve | 549593-2
Louis Armstrong With Sy Oliver's Choir And Orchestra
Louis And The Good Book | Verve | 549593-2
Louis Armstrong With The Lyn Murray Chorus
Louis And The Good Book | Verve | 549593-2
Max Roach Sextet With Choir
It's Time | Impulse(MCA) | 951185-2
Roland Kirk And His Orchestra
Rahsaan/The Complete Mercury Recordings Of Roland Kirk | Mercury | 846630-2

Cholewa,Martin | (fr-h)
Michael Mantler Orchestra
Hide And Seek | ECM | 1738(549612-2)

Choral Thunder Vocal Choir |
Patricia Barber Group
Modern Cool | Blue Note | 521811-2

Chorberg,Israel | (v)
A Band Of Friends
Wynton Marsalis Quartet With Strings | CBS | CK 68921

Chorus |
Eberhard Weber Group
The Colours Of Chloe | ECM | 1042
Louis Armstrong And His Orchestra
What A Wonderful World | MCA | MCD 01876
Louis Armstrong With Gordon Jenkins And His Orchestra And Choir
Satchmo In Style | Verve | 549594-2
Ambassador Louis Armstrong Vol.17:Moments To Remember(1952-1956) | Ambassador | CLA 1917
Louis Armstrong With The Gordon Jenkins Orchestra
Ambassador Louis Armstrong Vol.17:Moments To Remember(1952-1956) | Ambassador | CLA 1917
Sonny Rollins Quartet
Planet Jazz:Sonny Rollins | Planet Jazz | 2152062-2
Stan Getz With Orchestra And Voices
Stan Getz Highlights | Verve | 847430-2

Chouraqui,Ahmed | (el-g)
Schlothauer's Maniacs
Maniakisses | Timescrapper | TSCR 9811

Chowdhury,Subroto Roy | (sitar)
Subroto Roy Chowdhury Group
Serenity | Jazzpoint | JP 1017 CD
Explorations | Jazzpoint | JP 1020 CD
Subroto Roy Chowdhury-Steve Lacy Group
Explorations | Jazzpoint | JP 1020 CD

Christ,Peter | (org)
Peter Möltgen Quartet
Mellow Acid | Edition Collage | EC 495-2

Christensen,Anders | (bel-b)
Paul Motian And The E.B.B.B.
Holiday For Strings | Winter&Winter | 910069-2
Paul Motian Electric Bebop Band
Europe | Winter&Winter | 910063-2

Christensen,Erling | (as,cello,reedssax)
Stan Kenton With The Danish Radio Big Band
Stan Kenton With The Danish Radio Big Band | Storyville | STCD 8340

Christensen,Jon | (dr,percorg)
Anouar Brahem Group
Khomsa | ECM | 1561(527093-2)
Bobo Stenson Trio
Reflections | ECM | 1516(523160-2)
War Orphans | ECM | 1604(539723-2)
Serenity | ECM | 1740/41(543611-2)
Charles Lloyd Quartet
Fish Out Of Water | ECM | 1398
Eberhard Weber Quartet
Yellow Fields | ECM | 1066(843205-2)
Enrico Rava Quartet
The Pilgrim And The Stars | ECM | 1063(847322-2)
The Plot | ECM | 1078
Harry Pepl/Herbert Joos/Jon Christensen
Cracked Mirrors | ECM | 1356
Jacob Young Quintet
Evening Falls | ECM | 1876(9811780)
Jan Garbarek Group
Photo With Blue Skie, White Clouds, Wires, Windows And A Red Roof | ECM | 1135 (843168-2)
Jan Garbarek Quartet
Paths, Prints | ECM | 1223(829377-2)
Jan Garbarek Quintet
Sart | ECM | 1015(839305-2)
Jan Garbarek-Bobo Stenson Quartet
Witchi-Tai-To | ECM | 1041(833330-2)
Dansere | ECM | 1075(829193-2)
Joachim Kühn And The Radio Philharmonie Hannover NDR With Jazz Soloists
Europeana | ACT | 9220-2
John Abercrombie Trio
Animato | ECM | 1411
Jon Balke w/Oslo 13
Nonsentration | ECM | 1445
Keith Jarrett Quartet
Belonging | ECM | 1050(829115-2)
My Song | ECM | 1115(821406-2)
Nude Ants | ECM | 1171/72(829119-2)
Personal Mountains | ECM | 1382(837361-2)
Ketil Bjornstad Group
Early Years | EmArCy | 013271-2
Water Stories | ECM | 1503(519076-2)
The Sea | ECM | 1545(521718-2)
The Sea II | ECM | 1633(537341-2)
Masqualero
Bande A Part | ECM | 1319
Aero | ECM | 1367
Re-Enter | ECM | 1437(847939-2)
Mike Nock Trio
Ondas | ECM | 1220
Miroslav Vitous Group
Journey's End | ECM | 1242(843171-2)
Miroslav Vitous Quartet
First Meeting | ECM | 1145
Misha Alperin Group With John Surman
First Impression | ECM | 1664(557650-2)
Misha Alperin Quintet
North Story | ECM | 1596
Rainer Brünninghaus Quartet
Freigeweht | ECM | 1187(847329-2)
Ralph Towner Quartet
Solstice | ECM | 1060(825458-2)
Lost And Found | ECM | 1563(529347-2)
Shankar Quartet
M.R.C.S. | ECM | 1403
Sidsel Endresen Quartet
So I Write | ECM | 1408(841776-2)
Sidsel Endresen Sextet
Exile | ECM | 1524(521721-2)
Terje Rypdal Group
Skywards | ECM | 1608(533768-2)
Terje Rypdal Quartet
Waves | ECM | 1110(827419-2)
Terje Rypdal Quintet
What Comes After | ECM | 1031
When Ever I Seem To Be Far Away | ECM | 1045
Terje Rypdal Sextet
Terje Rypdal | ECM | 1016(527645-2)
Terje Rypdal Trio
Descendre | ECM | 1144
Tomasz Stanko Septet
Litania | ECM | 1636(537551-2)
Tomasz Stanko Sextet
Litania | ECM | 1636(537551-2)
From The Green Hill | ECM | 1680(547336-2)

Christensen,Thomas 'Tom' | (alto-fl,engl-h,b-cl,ss,ts,cl,oboe)
Joe Lovano Orchestra
Blue Note Plays Gershwin | Blue Note | 520808-2
Tim Sund & Tom Christensen Quartet
Americana | Nabel Records:Jazz Network | CD 4697

Christian,Buddy | (bjg)
Clarence Williams' Blue Five
Jazz:The Essential Collection Vol.1 | IN+OUT Records | 78011-2

Christian,Charlie | (g)
Benny Goodman And His All Star Sextet
Charlie Christian:Swing To Bop | Dreyfus Jazz Line | FDM 36715-2
Benny Goodman And His Orchestra
Charlie Christian:Swing To Bop | Dreyfus Jazz Line | FDM 36715-2
Benny Goodman Septet
Jazz:The Essential Collection Vol.3 | IN+OUT Records | 78013-2
Charlie Christian:Swing To Bop | Dreyfus Jazz Line | FDM 36715-2
Benny Goodman Septet feat.Count Basie
Charlie Christian:Swing To Bop | Dreyfus Jazz Line | FDM 36715-2
Benny Goodman Sextet
Charlie Christian:Swing To Bop | Dreyfus Jazz Line | FDM 36715-2
More Camel Caravans | Phontastic | NCD 8845/6
From Spiritual To Swing | Vanguard | VCD 169/71
Charlie Christian All Stars
Thelonious Monk:85th Birthday Celebration | zyx records | FANCD 6076-2
Charlie Christian-Jazz Immortal/Dizzy Gillespie 1944 | Original Jazz Classics | OJCCD 1932-2(ES 548)
Count Basie And His Orchestra
From Spiritual To Swing | Vanguard | VCD 169/71
Kansas City Six
Charlie Christian:Swing To Bop | Dreyfus Jazz Line | FDM 36715-2
From Spiritual To Swing | Vanguard | VCD 169/71
Lionel Hampton And His Orchestra
Planet Jazz:Coleman Hawkins | Planet Jazz | 2152055-2
Planet Jazz:Ben Webster | RCA | 2165368-2
Planet Jazz:Jazz Saxophone | Planet Jazz | 2169653-2
Jazz:The Essential Collection Vol.3 | IN+OUT Records | 78013-2
Minton's Playhouse All Stars
Charlie Christian:Swing To Bop | Dreyfus Jazz Line | FDM 36715-2
The Metronome All-Star Nine
Jazz:The Essential Collection Vol.3 | IN+OUT Records | 78013-2

Christian,Harry | (v)
Stefanie Schlesiger And Her Group plus String Quartet
What Love Is | Enja | ENJ-9434 2

Christian,Jodie | (el-p,p,bellsp-solo)
Chet Baker-Stan Getz Quintet
Stan Meets Chet | Verve | 837436-2
Eddie Harris Group
The Best Of Eddie Harris | Atlantic | 7567-81370-2
Eddie Harris Quartet
The Best Of Eddie Harris | Atlantic | 7567-81370-2
Eddie Harris Quintet
The Best Of Eddie Harris | Atlantic | 7567-81370-2
Gene Ammons-Dexter Gordon Quintet
Dexter Gordon Birthday Celebration | Fantasy | FANCD 6082-2
Gene Ammons-James Moody Quintet
Chicago Concert | Original Jazz Classics | OJCCD 1091-2(PR 10065)
John Klemmer Quartet
Involvement | Chess | 076139-2
Les McCann Group
Atlantic Jazz: Fusion | Atlantic | 7567-81711-2
Stan Getz Quartet
Verve Jazz Masters 8:Stan Getz | Verve | 519823-2

Christiansen,Ole | (b)
Bohana Jazzband
The Golden Years Of Revival Jazz,Vol.6 | Storyville | STCD 5511
The Golden Years Of Revival Jazz,Vol.10 | Storyville | STCD 5515
Cy Laurie's New Orleans Septet
The Golden Years Of Revival Jazz,Vol.1 | Storyville | STCD 5506
The Golden Years Of Revival Jazz,Vol.5 | Storyville | STCD 5510
The Golden Years Of Revival Jazz,Vol.8 | Storyville | STCD 5513
The Golden Years Of Revival Jazz,Vol.9 | Storyville | STCD 5514
The Golden Years Of Revival Jazz,Vol.11 | Storyville | STCD 5516
Henrik Johansen's Jazzband
The Golden Years Of Revival Jazz.Vol.14 | Storyville | STCD 5519

Christiansen,Svein | (dr)
Terje Rypdal Group
Odyssey | ECM | 1067/8

Christie,Keith | (tb)
Benny Goodman And His Orchestra
Verve Jazz Masters 33:Benny Goodman | Verve | 844410-2

Christlieb,Don | (bassoon)
Ella Fitzgerald With The Nelson Riddle Orchestra
Dream Dancing | Original Jazz Classics | OJCCD 1072-2(2310814)

Christlieb,Pete | (as,ts,cl,sax,fl,reeds,piccolo)
Bobby Bryant Orchestra
Deep Blue-The United States Of Mind | Blue Note | 521152-2
Diane Schuur With Orchestra
Love Songs | GRP | GRP 97032
The Best Of Diane Schuur | GRP | GRP 98882
Diane Schuur With Orchestra And Strings
The Best Of Diane Schuur | GRP | GRP 98882
Louie Bellson Septet
Louie Bellson Jam | Original Jazz Classics | OJCCD 802-2(2310838)
Singers Unlimited With Orchestra
The Singers Unlimited:Magic Voices | MPS | 539130-2
Singers Unlimited With The Clare Fischer Orchestra
The Singers Unlimited:Magic Voices | MPS | 539130-2
Singers Unlimited With The Pat Williams Orchestra
The Singers Unlimited:Magic Voices | MPS | 539130-2
The Quincy Jones-Sammy Nestico Orchestra
Basie & Beyond | Warner | 9362-47792-2

Christman,Gene | (dr)
Herbie Mann Group
Memphis Underground | Atlantic | 7567-81364-2
The Best Of Herbie Mann | Atlantic | 7567-81369-2

Christmann,Egon | (b-tbtb)
Albert Mangelsdorff With The NDR Big Band
NDR Big Band-Bravissimo | ACT | 9232-2
Chet Baker With The NDR-Bigband
NDR Big Band-Bravissimo | ACT | 9232-2
My Favourite Songs: The Last Great Concert Vol.1 | Enja | ENJ-5097 2
The Last Concert Vol.I+II | Enja | ENJ-6074 22
Chet Baker-The Legacy Vol.1 | Enja | ENJ-9021 2
Fred Bunge Star Band

Deutsches Jazz Fesival 1954/1955 | Bear Family Records | BCD 15430
Heinz Sauer Quartet With The NDR Big Band
NDR Big Band-Bravissimo | ACT | 9232-2
Horst Jankowski Orchestra With Voices
Jankowskeynotes | MPS | 9814806
Joe Pass With The NDR Big Band
Joe Pass In Hamburg | ACT | 9100-2
NDR Big Band-Bravissimo | ACT | 9232-2
Joe Pass With The NDR Big Band And Radio Philharmonie Hannover
Joe Pass In Hamburg | ACT | 9100-2
Johnny Griffin With The NDR Big Band
NDR Big Band-Bravissimo | ACT | 9232-2
NDR Big Band
NDR Big Band-Bravissimo | ACT | 9232-2
Pee Wee Ellis & NDR Bigband
What You Like | Minor Music | 801064

Christmann,Freddy | (tp)
Freddy Christman Quartet
Deutsches Jazz Fesival 1954/1955 | Bear Family Records | BCD 15430

Christmann,Günter | (b,kamm,cello,tb,mandoline,sounds)
Jazzensemble Des Hessischen Rundfunks
Atmosphering Conditions Permitting | ECM | 1549/50

Christopher,Evan | (cl)
The Sidney Bechet Society
Jam Session Concert | Nagel-Heyer | CD 076

Christopher,Gavin | (brass-arrvoc)
Herbie Hancock Group
Monster | CBS | 486571-2
Magic Window | CBS | 486572-2

Christy,June | (voc)
June Christy With Orchestra
This Is June Christy/June Christy Recalls Those Kenton Days | Capitol | 535209-2
June Christy With The Johnny Guarnieri Quintet
June Christy And The Johnny Guarnieri Quintet (1949) | Jazz Unlimited | JUCD 2084
June Christy With The Pete Rugolo Orchestra
Something Cool(The Complete Mono & Stereo Versions) | Capitol | 534069-2
The Song Is June | Capitol | 855455-2
June Christy With The Shorty Rogers Orchestra
June Christy Big Band Special | Capitol | 498319-2

Chromatic Alarm |
Chromatic Alarm
Some Other Tapes | Fish Music | FM 009/10 CD

Chromatic Persuaders,The |
The Chromatic Persuaders
The Chromatic Persuaders | Timescrapper | TSCR 9617

Chuffo,Paul | (dr)
Gutbucket
Dry Humping The American Dream | Enja | ENJ-9466 2

Chulo | (b)
Lew Soloff Group
Rainbow Mountain | TipToe | TIP-888838 2

Chycoski,Arnie | (tpfl-h)
Singers Unlimited With Rob McConnell And The Boss Brass
The Singers Unlimited:Magic Voices | MPS | 539130-2

Ciardina,Phil | (tb)
Louis Armstrong And The Commanders under the Direction of Camarata
Satchmo Serenaders | Verve | 543792-2

Cicada String Quartet |
Christof Lauer-Jens Thomas With The Cikada String Quartet
Shadows In The Rain | ACT | 9297-2

Cicero,Eugen | (p)
Eugen Cicero-Decebal Badila
Swinging Piano Classics | IN+OUT Records | 77047-2

Cikada String Quartet |
Annette Peacock With The Cikada String Quartet
An Acrobat's Heart | ECM | 1733(159496-2)
Arild Andersen Quintet With The Cikada String Quartet
Hyperborean | ECM | 1631(537342-2)
Mats Eden-Jonas Simonson With The Cikada String Quartet
Milvus | ECM | 1660

Ciliberti,Giambattista | (cl)
Banda Città Ruvo Di Puglia
La Banda/Banda And Jazz | Enja | ENJ-9326 2

Cimiotti.André | (ass)
Frank Eberle Septet
Scarlet Sunrise | Satin Doll Productions | SDP 1041-1 CD

Cincinnati Symphony Orchestra,The |
Dave Brubeck With The Erich Kunzel Orchestra
Truth Is Fallen | Atlantic | 7567-80761-2

Cinelu,Mino | (bj,synth,mand,dr,perc,sound effects)
Andy Bey Group
Tuesdays In Chinatown | Minor Music | 801099
Cassandra Wilson Group
Traveling Miles | Blue Note | 854123-2
Dhafer Youssef Group
Electric Sufi | Enja | ENJ-9412 2
Dizzy Gillespie And His Orchestra
Closer To The Source | Atlantic | 7567-80776-2
Jacky Terrasson Group
What It Is | Blue Note | 498756-2
Miles Davis Group
Decoy | CBS | 468702-2
We Want Miles | CBS | 469402-2
Amandla | Warner | 7599-25873-2
Nguyen Le Trio
Nguyen Le:3 Trios | ACT | 9245-2
Paquito D'Rivera Group With The Absolute Ensemble
Habanera | Enja | ENJ-9395 2
Pat Metheny Group
Imaginary Day | Warner | 9362-46791-2
World Trio
World Trio | VeraBra Records | CDVBR 2052-2

Cintron,Tony | (dr)
Dizzy Gillespie And His Orchestra
Closer To The Source | Atlantic | 7567-80776-2

Cipelli,Roberto | (p,keyboardssynth)
Paolo Fresu Quintet
Night On The City | Owl Records | 013425-2
Melos | RCA | 2178289-2

Cipriano,Gene | (alto-fl,ts,oboe,bs,engl-h,fl,cl)
Ella Fitzgerald With Frank De Vol And His Orchestra
Get Happy! | Verve | 523321-2
Ella Fitzgerald With Paul Weston And His Orchestra
Love Songs:The Best Of The Song Books | Verve | 531762-2
Ella Fitzgerald Sings The Irving Berlin Song Book | Verve | 543830-2
Ella Fitzgerald With The Nelson Riddle Orchestra
Ella Fitzgerald Sings The Johnny Mercer Songbook | Verve | 539057-2
Herbie Hancock Group With String Quartet,Woodwinds And Brass
Herbie Hancock The New Standards | Verve | 527715-2
Herbie Hancock Group With Woodwinds And Brass
Herbie Hancock The New Standards | Verve | 527715-2
Mel Tormé With The Billy May Orchestra
Mel Tormé Goes South Of The Border With Billy May | Verve | 589517-2
Miles Davis With Gil Evans & His Orchestra
Quiet Nights | CBS | CK 65293
Pete Rugolo And His Orchestra
Thriller/Richard Diamon(Original Jazz Scores From 2 Classics TV Series) | Fresh Sound Records | FSCD 2015

Circle |
Circle
Paris Concert | ECM | 1018/19(843163-2)

Cirillo,Wally | (p)
John LaPorta Octet
Theme And Variations | Fantasy | FCD 24776-2
John LaPorta Septet
Theme And Variations | Fantasy | FCD 24776-2

Cissokho,Malang | (b,koravoc)
Piirpauke
Tuku Tuku | JA & RO | JARO 4158-2

Citerman,Ty | (g)
Gutbucket
Dry Humping The American Dream | Enja | ENJ-9466 2

City Ramblers |
Henrik Johansen With The City Ramblers
The Golden Years Of Revival Jazz,Sampler | Storyville | 109 1001

Civilotti,Anibal | (perc)
Francis Coletta Trio + One
Cris De Balaines | IN+OUT Records | 77030-2

Cizeron,Maurice | (flas)
Michel Warlop Et Son Orchestre
Jazz In Paris:Django Reinhardt-Django Et Compagnie | EmArCy | 549241-2 PMS

Cizmek,Rolf | (b)
Joe Turner-Albert Nicholas Quartet
The Giant Of Stride Piano In Switzerland | Jazz Connaisseur | JCCD 9106-2

Clairborne,Deszon X. | (dr)
Don Cherry Group
Multi Kulti | A&M Records | 395323-2

Claire,Dorothy | (voc)
Glenn Miller And His Orchestra
The Ultimate Glenn Miller-22 Original Hits From The King Of Swing | RCA | 2113137-2

Clais,George | (tp)
Django Reinhardt With Stan Brenders Et Son Grand Orchestre
Verve Jazz Masters 38:Django Reinhardt | Verve | 516931-2

Clapton,Eric | (g,bottleneck-gvoc)
Howlin' Wolf London Session
Howlin' Wolf:The London Sessions | Chess | MCD 09297

Clare,Kenny | (dr)
Art Van Damme Group
State Of Art | MPS | 841413-2
Art Van Damme Quintet
Keep Going/Blue World | MPS | 529093-2
Kenny Clarke-Francy Boland Big Band
Clark-Boland Big Band: TNP, October 29th, 1969 | Laserlight | 36129
Three Latin Adventures | MPS | 529095-2
More Smiles | MPS | 9814789
All Smiles | MPS | 9814790
Francy Boland-Fellini 712 | MPS | 9814805
Knut Kiesewetter With The Dieter Reith Orchestra
Reith On! | MPS | 557423-2
Monty Alexander Quartet
Three Originals:Love And Sunshine/Estade/Cobilimbo | MPS | 523526-2
Ronnie Scott And The Band
Live At Ronnie Scott's | CBS | 494439-2
Stephane Grappelli Quartet
Grapelli Story | Verve | 515807-2
Verve Jazz Masters 11:Stéphane Grappelli | Verve | 516758-2

Clarion Fracture Zone |
Clarion Fracture Zone
Blue Shift | VeraBra Records | CDVBR 2075-2

Clark,Arthur | (bs,cl,flts)
Cannonball Adderley And His Orchestra
Cannonball Adderley Birthday Celebration | Fantasy | FANCD 6087-2
George Benson Orchestra
Talkin' Verve:George Benson | Verve | 553780-2
George Benson With Orchestra
Verve Jazz Masters 21:George Benson | Verve | 521861-2

Clark,Babe | (bs,cl,saxts)
Stan Getz With The Gary McFarland Orchestra
Stan Getz Highlights:The Best Of The Verve Years Vol.2 | Verve | 517330-2
Verve Jazz Masters 53:Stan Getz-Bossa Nova | Verve | 529904-2
Big Band Bossa Nova | Verve | 825771-2 PMS
Stan Getz Highlights | Verve | 847430-2

Clark,Bill | (dr,tpts)
Dizzy Gillespie Orchestra And The Operatic String Orchestra
Jazz In Paris:Dizzy Gillespie And His Operatic Strings Orchestra | EmArCy | 018420-2
Don Byas Quartet
Jazz In Paris:Don Byas-Laura | EmArCy | 013027-2
George Shearing And His Quintet
Verve Jazz Masters 57:George Shearing | Verve | 529900-2
George Shearing Quintet
Verve Jazz Masters 57:George Shearing | Verve | 529900-2
Verve Jazz Masters Vol.59:Toots Thielemans | Verve | 535271-2
Lester Young Quartet
Jazz Gallery:Lester Young Vol.2(1946-59) | RCA | 2119541-2

Clark,Buck | (congasperc)
Arnett Cobb Quintet
Movin' Right Along | Original Jazz Classics | OJCCD 1074-2(P 7216)
Jimmy Smith Quintet
Root Down | Verve | 559805-2
Jimmy Smith Sextet
Root Down | Verve | 559805-2

Clark,Buddy | (b,vvoc)
Bud Shank And Trombones
Cool Fool | Fresh Sound Records | FSR CD 507
Dizzy Gillespie And His Orchestra
Talking Verve:Dizzy Gillespie | Verve | 533846-2
Gerry Mulligan Concert Jazz Band
Verve Jazz Masters 36:Gerry Mulligan | Verve | 523342-2
The Complete Verve Gerry Mulligan Concert Band | Verve | 9860613
Gerry Mulligan-Johnny Hodges Quintet
Gerry Mulligan Meets Johnny Hodges | Verve | 065513-2
Verve Jazz Masters 35:Johnny Hodges | Verve | 521857-2
Herbie Mann Quartet
Verve Jazz Masters 56:Herbie Mann | Verve | 529901-2
Herbie Mann With The Frank DeVol Orchestra
Verve Jazz Masters 56:Herbie Mann | Verve | 529901-2
Herbie Mann's Californians
Great Ideas Of Western Man | Original Jazz Classics | OJCCD 1065-2(RLP 245)
Lennie Niehaus Sextet
Lennie Niehaus Vol.5:The Sextet | Original Jazz Classics | OJCCD 1944-2(C 3524)
Maynard Ferguson And His Orchestra
Verve Jazz Masters 52:Maynard Ferguson | Verve | 529905-2
Mel Tormé With The Billy May Orchestra
Mel Tormé Goes South Of The Border With Billy May | Verve | 589517-2
Sonny Stitt Orchestra
Verve Jazz Masters 50:Sonny Sitt | Verve | 527651-2
Terry Gibbs Big Band
Terry Gibbs Dream Band Vol.4:Main Stem | Contemporary | CCD 7656-2
Terry Gibbs Dream Band
Terry Gibbs Dream Band Vol.2:The Sundown Sessions | Contemporary | CCD 7652-2
Terry Gibbs Dream Band Vol.3:Flying Home | Contemporary | CCD 7654-2
Terry Gibbs Dream Band Vol.5:The Big Cat | Contemporary | CCD 7657-2
Terry Gibbs Dream Band Vol.6:One More Time | Contemporary | CCD 7658-2
The Jazz Giants Play Jerome Kern:Yesterdays | Prestige | PCD 24202-2

Clark,Dave | (b,b-clbs)
Kölner Saxophon Mafia
Mafia Years 1982-86 | Jazz Haus Musik | JHM 0058 CD

Clark,Dick | (bs,tpts)
Artie Shaw And His Orchestra
Planet JazzArtie Shaw | Planet Jazz | 2152057-2
Planet Jazz:Jazz Greatest Hits | Planet Jazz | 2169648-2
Benny Goodman And His Orchestra
Planet Jazz:Benny Goodman | Planet Jazz | 2152054-2
Planet Jazz Sampler | Planet Jazz | 2152326-2
Planet Jazz:Swing | Planet Jazz | 2169651-2

Clark,George | (ts)
Cootie Williams Quintet
Jazz In Paris:Joe Newman-Jazz At Midnight-Cootie Williams | EmArCy | 018446-2

Clark,Harold | (ts)
Louis Armstrong With Sy Oliver And His Orchestra
Satchmo Serenaders | Verve | 543792-2

Clark,James | (g)
Johnny 'Hammond' Smith Quintet
Discovery:Grover Washington Jr.-The First Recordings | Prestige | PCD 11020-2

Clark,John | (brass,el-fr-h,fr-h,el-g,g,hornette)
Carla Bley Band
Night-Glo | Watt | 16
European Tour 1977 | Watt | 8
Musique Mecanique | Watt | 9
Daniel Schnyder Group
Tanatula | Enja | ENJ-9302 2
David Matthews & The Manhattan Jazz Orchestra
Back To Bach | Milestone | MCD 9312-2
Hey Duke! | Milestone | MCD 9320-2
George Gruntz Concert Jazz Band
Blues 'N Dues Et Cetera | Enja | ENJ-6072 2
Gil Evans Orchestra
There Comes A Time | RCA | 2131392-2
Helen Merrill With Orchestra
Casa Forte | EmArCy | 558848-2
Jaco Pastorius With Orchestra
Word Of Mouth | Warner | 7599-23525-2
John Scofield Groups
Quiet | Verve | 533185-2
Marty Ehrlich Group
The Long View | Enja | ENJ-9452 2
McCoy Tyner Big Band
The Best Of McCoy Tyner Big Band | Dreyfus Jazz Line | FDM 37012-2
Miles Davis With Gil Evans Orchestra, The George Gruntz Concert Jazz Band And Guests
Miles & Quincy Live At Montreux | Warner | 9362-45221-2

Clark,Lillian | (voc)
Louis Armstrong With Sy Oliver And His Orchestra
Louis And The Angels | Verve | 549592-2

Clark,Mahlon | (clreeds)
Ella Fitzgerald With The Nelson Riddle Orchestra
Dream Dancing | Original Jazz Classics | OJCCD 1072-2(2310814)
Van Alexander Orchestra
Home Of Happy Feet/Swing! Staged For Sound! | Capitol | 535211-2

Clark,Mike | (dr,dr-solotrap-dr)
Ed Neumeister Quartet
Ed Neumeister Quartet/Quintet | Timescrapper | TSCR 9614
Herbie Hancock Group
Man-Child | CBS | 471235-2
Thrust | CBS | CK 64984
Mike Clark-Paul Jackson Quartet
The Funk Stops Here | TipToe | TIP-888811 2
Vince Guaraldi Group
Charlie Brown's Holiday Hits | Fantasy | FCD 9682-2

Clark,Neil | (congas,african-perc,djimbe,gong)
Randy Weston African Rhythm
Khepera | Verve | 557821-2

Clark,Pete | (as,cl,bsreeds)
Louis Armstrong And His Orchestra
Louis Armstrong:Swing That Music | Laserlight | 36056
Louis Armstrong-My Greatest Songs | MCA | MCD 18347
Swing Legends:Louis Armstrong | Nimbus Records | NI 2012
Louis Armstrong With Chick Webb's Orchestra
Best Of The Complete RCA Victor Recordings | RCA | 2663636-2
Louis Armstrong:A 100th Birthday Celebration | RCA | 2663694-2

Clark,Sonny | (p,orgp-solo)
Billie Holiday And Her All Stars
Billie's Blues | Blue Note | 748786-2
Cal Tjader Quintet
Cal Tjader Plays Jazz | Original Jazz Classics | OJCCD 986-2(F 3-211)
Dexter Gordon Quartet
Go! | Blue Note | 498794-2
Dexter Gordon:Ballads | Blue Note | 796579-2
The Best Of Blue Note Vol.2 | Blue Note | 797960-2
Jazz Profile:Dexter Gordon | Blue Note | 823514-2
Midnight Blue(The [Be]witching Hour) | Blue Note | 854365-2
Don Wilkerson Quintet
Preach Brother! | Blue Note | 0677212
Blue N' Groovy | Blue Note | 780679-2
Grant Green Quartet
Ballads | Blue Note | 537560-2
Midnight Blue(The [Be]witching Hour) | Blue Note | 854365-2
Grant Green Quintet
Kind Of Blue:Blue Note Celebrate The Music Of Miles Davis | Blue Note | 534255-2
Ballads | Blue Note | 537560-2
Howard Rumsey's Lighthouse All-Stars
Oboe/Flute | Original Jazz Classics | OJCCD 154-2(C 3520)
Ike Quebec Quartet
Blue Note Plays Gershwin | Blue Note | 520808-2
Ike Quebec Quintet
Blue And Sentimental | Blue Note | 784098-2
Jackie McLean Quartet
A Fickle Sonance | Blue Note | 524544-2
Jackie McLean Quintet
Vertigo | Blue Note | 522669-2
A Fickle Sonance | Blue Note | 524544-2
Jerry Dodgion Quartet
The Jazz Scene:San Francisco | Fantasy | FCD 24760-2
Jimmy Raney Quartet
Jimmy Raney Visits Paris Vol.1 | Vogue | 21409352
Lawrence Marable Quartet feat. James Clay
Midnight Blue(The [Be]witching Hour) | Blue Note | 854365-2
Serge Chaloff Quartet
Blue Serge | Capitol | 494505-2
Sonny Clark All Stars
Dial S For Sonny | Blue Note | 0675621
Sonny Clark Quintet
Cool Struttin' | Blue Note | 495327-2
My Conception | Blue Note | 522674-2
Sonny Clark Sextet
Trane's Blues | Blue Note | 498240-2
Sonny Clark Trio
Dial S For Sonny | Blue Note | 0675621
Blue Note Plays Gershwin | Blue Note | 520808-2
Sonny Clark | Blue Note | 533774-2
Sonny Clark Trio | Blue Note | 533774-2
Standards | Blue Note | 821283-2
Sonny Rollins Quartet
Sonny Rollins-The Freelance Years:The Complete Riverside & Contemporary Recordings | Riverside | 5 RCD 4427-2
The Sound Of Sonny | Original Jazz Classics | OJC20 029-2
The Jazz Giants Play Jerome Kern:Yesterdays | Prestige | PCD 24202-2
The Jazz Giants Play Cole Porter:Night And Day | Prestige | PCD 24203-2
Teddy Charles' West Coasters
Wardell Gray Memorial Vol.1 | Original Jazz Classics | OJCCD 050-2(P 7008)
Tina Brooks Quintet
True Blue | Blue Note | 534032-2

Clark,Terry | (dr)
Oscar Peterson Trio

Nigerian Marketplace | Pablo | 2308231-2

Clark,William 'Buck' | (percafrican-dr)

Les McCann Group
Atlantic Jazz: Fusion | Atlantic | 7567-81711-2

Clarke,Arthur | (b-cl,bs,fl,ts,reedssax)

Grover Washington Jr. Orchestra
Jazzrock-Anthology Vol.3:Fusion | Zounds | CD 27100555
Lawrence Brown With The Ralph Burns Orchestra
Slide Trombone | Verve | 559930-2
Milt Jackson Orchestra
Big Bags | Original Jazz Classics | OJCCD 366-2(RLP 9429)
Oscar Brown Jr. And His Group
Movin' On | Rhino | 8122-73678-2

Clarke,Babe | (bs,clts)

Jimmy Smith With The Oliver Nelson Orchestra
Verve Jazz Masters 29:Jimmy Smith | Verve | 521855-2
Jimmy Smith:Best Of The Verve Years | Verve | 527950-2

Clarke,Buck | (congasperc)

Arnett Cobb Quintet
More Party Time | Original Jazz Classics | OJCCD 979-2(P 7175)
Jimmy Smith Sextet
Jimmy Smith:Best Of The Verve Years | Verve | 527950-2
Jimmy Smith With Orchestra
Verve Jazz Masters 29:Jimmy Smith | Verve | 521855-2
Les McCann Group
Another Beginning | Atlantic | 7567-80790-2
Willis Jackson Sextet
Together Again: Willis Jackson With Jack McDuff | Prestige | PRCD 24284-2

Clarke,Buddy | (b)

Gerry Mulligan Quartet
The Art Of Saxophone | Laserlight | 24652

Clarke,Dick | (tp)

Willie Bryant And His Orchestra
Planet Jazz:Ben Webster | RCA | 2165368-2

Clarke,Kenny | (brushes on phone book,dr,arr,percp)

Art Blakey And The Jazz Messengers
At The Club St.Germain | RCA | ND 74897(2)
Art Farmer Quintet
Early Art | Original Jazz Classics | OJCCD 880-2(NJ 8258)
Barney Wilen Quartet
Jazz In Paris:Barney Wilen-Jazz Sur Saine | EmArCy | 548317-2 PMS
Barney Wilen Quintet
Jazz In Paris:Barney Wilen-Jazz Sur Saine | EmArCy | 548317-2 PMS
Jazz In Paris:Jazz & Cinéma Vol.1 | EmArCy | 548318-2 PMS
Benny Bailey Quintet
Jazz Portraits | EGO | 95080
Billie Holiday With Eddie Heywood And His Orchestra
Billie's Love Songs | Nimbus Records | NI 2000
Bobby Jaspar Quintet
Jazz In Paris:Bobby Jaspar-Jeux De Quartes | EmArCy | 018423-2
Bud Powell Quartet
Parisian Thoroughfare | Pablo | CD 2310976-2
Bud Powell Quintet
The Story Of Jazz Piano | Laserlight | 24653
Parisian Thoroughfare | Pablo | CD 2310976-2
Bud Powell Paris Sessions | Pablo | PACD 2310972-2
Bud Powell Trio
The Best Of Bud Powell On Verve | Verve | 523392-2
Parisian Thoroughfare | Pablo | CD 2310976-2
Bud Powell Paris Sessions | Pablo | PACD 2310972-2
Bebop | Pablo | PACD 2310978-2
Cannonball Adderley And His Orchestra
Verve Jazz Masters 31:Cannonball Adderley | Verve | 522651-2
Cannonball Adderley Group
Julian 'Cannonball' Adderley | EmArCy | 830381-2
Cannonball Adderley Quintet
The Art Of Saxophone | Laserlight | 24652
Charles Mingus And His Orchestra
Charles Mingus-The Complete Debut Recordings | Debut | 12 DCD 4402-2
Charlie Christian All Stars
Thelonious Monk:85th Birthday Celebration | zyx records | FANCD 6076-2
Charlie Christian-Jazz Immortal/Dizzy Gillespie 1944 | Original Jazz Classics | OJCCD 1932-2(ES 548)
Charlie Parker And His Orchestra
Bird: The Complete Charlie Parker On Verve | Verve | 837141-2
Charlie Parker Quintet
Charlie Parker:Bird's Best Bop On Verve | Verve | 527452-2
Charlie Parker:The Best Of The Verve Years | Verve | 527815-2
Charlie Parker At Storyville | Blue Note | 785108-2
Coleman Hawkins And His Rhythm
Coleman Hawkins/Johnny Hodges:The Vogue Recordings | Vogue | 21559712
Dexter Gordon Quartet
Blue Note Plays Gershwin | Blue Note | 520808-2
True Blue | Blue Note | 534032-2
Our Man In Paris | Blue Note | 591722-2
Dexter Gordon:Ballads | Blue Note | 796579-2
Jazz Profile:Dexter Gordon | Blue Note | 823514-2
Dexter Gordon Birthday Celebration | Fantasy | FANCD 6082-2
Dizzy Gillespie And His Orchestra
Dizzy Gillespie:Pleyel Jazz Concert 1948 + Max Roach Quintet 1949 | Vogue | 21409412
Planet Jazz:Dizzy Gillespie | Planet Jazz | 2152069-2
Planet Jazz:Bebop | RCA | 2169650-2
Dizzy Gillespie Quintet
Jazz In Paris:Dizzy Gillespie-The Giant | EmArCy | 159734-2 PMS
Dizzy Gillespie Sextet
Dizzy Gillespie:Night In Tunisia | Dreyfus Jazz Line | FDM 36734-2
Don Byas-Bud Powell Quartet
A Tribute To Cannonball | CBS | CK 65186
Don Byas-Bud Powell Quintet
A Tribute To Cannonball | CBS | CK 65186
Ella Fitzgerald With The Dizzy Gillespie Orchestra
Ella Fitzgerald:Mr.Paganini | Dreyfus Jazz Line | FDM 36741-2
Ella Fitzgerald With The Hank Jones Trio
Ella Fitzgerald:Mr.Paganini | Dreyfus Jazz Line | FDM 36741-2
Ernie Royal And The Duke Knights
Americans Swinging In Paris:James Moody | EMI Records | 539653-2
Gene Ammons And His All Stars
Dexter Gordon Birthday Celebration | Fantasy | FANCD 6082-2
Hampton Hawes Trio
Northern Windows Plus | Prestige | PRCD 24278-2
Hank Mobley Quintet
The Art Of Saxophone | Laserlight | 24652
Horace Silver Sextet
The Story Of Jazz Piano | Laserlight | 24653
Hubert Fol And His Be-Bop Minstrels
Americans Swinging In Paris:Kenny Clarke | EMI Records | 539652-2
J.J.Johnson Quintet
The Eminent J.J.Johnson Vol.2 | Blue Note | 532144-2
J.J.Johnson Sextet
The Eminent J.J.Johnson Vol.1 | Blue Note | 532143-2
J.R. Monterose Sextet
Jaywalkin' | Fresh Sound Records | FSR-CD 320
Jack Dieval And His Quartet
Americans Swinging In Paris:James Moody | EMI Records | 539653-2
James Moody Quartet
Americans Swinging In Paris:James Moody | EMI Records | 539653-2
Kenny Clarke 8
Americans Swinging In Paris:Kenny Clarke | EMI Records | 539652-2
Kenny Clarke And His 52nd Street Boys
Planet Jazz:Bebop | RCA | 2169650-2
Fats Navarro:Nostalgia | Dreyfus Jazz Line | FDM 36736-2
Kenny Clarke And His Orchestra
Americans Swinging In Paris:James Moody | EMI Records | 539653-2
Kenny Clarke Quartet
Americans Swinging In Paris:Kenny Clarke | EMI Records | 539652-2
Jazz In Paris:Kenny Clarke Sextet Plays André Hodair | EmArCy | 834542-2 PMS
Kenny Clarke Quintet
Jazz In Paris:Kenny Clarke Sextet Plays André Hodair | EmArCy | 834542-2 PMS
Kenny Clarke Sextet
Jazz In Paris:Kenny Clarke Sextet Plays André Hodair | EmArCy | 834542-2 PMS
Kenny Clarke-Francy Boland Big Band
Clark-Boland Big Band: TNP, October 29th, 1969 | Laserlight | 36129
Three Latin Adventures | MPS | 529095-2
More Smiles | MPS | 9814789
All Smiles | MPS | 9814790
Francy Boland-Fellini 712 | MPS | 9814805
Kenny Dorham Quintet
The Jazz Giants Play Sammy Cahn:It's Magic | Prestige | PCD 24226-2
Lee Konitz-Warne Marsh Quintet
Lee Konitz With Warne Marsh | Atlantic | 8122-75356-2
Lee Konitz-Warne Marsh Sextet
Lee Konitz With Warne Marsh | Atlantic | 8122-75356-2
Les Double Six
Les Double Six | RCA | 2164314-2
Lester Young Quartet
Jazz Gallery:Lester Young Vol.2(1946-59) | RCA | 2119541-2
Lou Bennett Trio
Jazz In Paris | EmArCy | 548790-2
Lou Bennett Trio With The Paris Jazz All Stars
Jazz In Paris | EmArCy | 548790-2
Lucky Thompson Quartet
The Jazz Life! | Candid | CCD 79019
Miles Davis All Star Sextet
Walkin' | Original Jazz Classics | OJC20 213-2
Miles Davis All Stars
Miles Davis Vol.1 | Blue Note | 532610-2
Milt Jackson Birthday Celebration | Fantasy | FANCD 6079-2
Bags' Groove | Original Jazz Classics | OJC20 245-2
Miles Davis And The Modern Jazz Giants | Original Jazz Classics | OJC20 347-2(P 7150)
The J.J.Johnson Memorial Album | Prestige | PRCD 11025-2
Miles Davis And His Orchestra
The Complete Birth Of The Cool | Capitol | 494550-2
Birth Of The Cool | Capitol | 530117-2
Jazz Profile:Miles Davis | Blue Note | 823515-2
Miles Davis:Milestones | Dreyfus Jazz Line | FDM 36731-2
Miles Davis And The Modern Jazz Giants
Thelonious Monk:85th Birthday Celebration | zyx records | FANCD 6076-2
Miles Davis Quartet
Ballads & Blues | Blue Note | 836633-2
Miles Davis Quintet
To Bags...With Love:Memorial Album | Pablo | 2310967-2
Thelonious Monk:The Complete Prestige Recordings | Prestige | 3 PRCD 4428-2
Ascenseur Pour LÉchafaud | Fontana | 836305-2
Blue Haze | Original Jazz Classics | OJC20 093-2(P 7054)
Walkin' | Original Jazz Classics | OJC20 213-2
Miles Davis Septet
Miles Davis And Horns | Original Jazz Classics | OJC20 053-2(P 7025)
Miles Davis Sextet
Miles Davis:The Best Of The Capitol/Blue Note Years | Blue Note | 798287-2
Jazz Profile:Miles Davis | Blue Note | 823515-2
Miles Davis/Tadd Dameron Quintet
Miles Davis:Milestones | Dreyfus Jazz Line | FDM 36731-2
Milt Jackson Quintet
Wizard Of The Vibes | Blue Note | 532140-2
Milt Jackson Birthday Celebration | Fantasy | FANCD 6079-2
MJQ | Original Jazz Classics | OJCCD 125-2
Minton's Playhouse All Stars
Charlie Christian:Swing To Bop | Dreyfus Jazz Line | FDM 36715-2
Modern Jazz Quartet
The Complete Modern Jazz Quartet Prestige & Pablo Recordings | Prestige | 4PRCD 4438-2
MJQ 40 | Atlantic | 7567-82330-2
Milt Jackson Birthday Celebration | Fantasy | FANCD 6079-2
Django | Original Jazz Classics | OJC20 057-2
MJQ | Original Jazz Classics | OJCCD 125-2
Oscar Peterson-Stephane Grappelli Quartet
Jazz In Paris:Oscar Peterson-Stephane Grappelli Quartet Vol.1 | EmArCy | 013028-2
Jazz In Paris:Oscar Peterson-Stephane Grappelli Quartet Vol.2 | EmArCy | 013029-2
Rhoda Scott-Kenny Clarke
Jazz In Paris:Rhoda Scott + Kenny Clarke | EmArCy | 549287-2 PMS
Sarah Vaughan With The Jimmy Jones Quartet
Sarah Vaughan:Lover Man | Dreyfus Jazz Line | FDM 36739-2
Sarah Vaughan With The Quincy Jones Orchestra
Jazz In Paris:Sarah Vaughan-Vaughan And Violins | EmArCy | 065004-2
4 By 4:Ella Fitzgerald/Sarah Vaughan/Billie Holiday/Dinah Washington | Verve | 559693-2
Sidney Bechet And His All Stars
Sidney Bechet:Summertime | Dreyfus Jazz Line | FDM 36712-2
Sidney Bechet And His Feetwarmers
Jazz In Paris:Sidney Bechet Et Claude Luther | EmArCy | 159821-2 PMS
Sidney Bechet:Summertime | Dreyfus Jazz Line | FDM 36712-2
Sidney Bechet And His New Orleans Feetwarmers
Planet Jazz | Planet Jazz | 2169652-2
Sidney Bechet:Summertime | Dreyfus Jazz Line | FDM 36712-2
Sidney Bechet Quartet
Planet Jazz:Sidney Bechet | Planet Jazz | 2152063-2
Sonny Rollins With The Modern Jazz Quartet
The Complete Modern Jazz Quartet Prestige & Pablo Recordings | Prestige | 4PRCD 4438-2
Milt Jackson Birthday Celebration | Fantasy | FANCD 6079-2
Sonny Rollins With The Modern Jazz Quartet | Original Jazz Classics | OJCCD 011-2
The Jazz Giants Play Duke Ellington:Caravan | Prestige | PCD 24227-2
Stan Getz Quartet
Stan Getz In Europe | Laserlight | 24657
Stan Getz Quintet
Stan Getz In Europe | Laserlight | 24657
Stephane Grappelli Quartet
Planet Jazz:Stephane Grappelli | RCA | 2165366-2
I Hear Music | RCA | 2179624-2
Stephane Grappelli Trio
I Hear Music | RCA | 2179624-2
Stephane Grappelli-Kenny Clarke
Planet Jazz:Stephane Grappelli | RCA | 2165366-2
Tadd Dameron Septet
The Fabulous Fats Navarro Vol.2 | Blue Note | 0677208
Fats Navarro:Nostalgia | Dreyfus Jazz Line | FDM 36736-2
Tadd Dameron Tentet
Jazz Profile:Dexter Gordon | Blue Note | 823514-2
Tadd Dameron-Fats Navarro Quintet
Fats Navarro:Nostalgia | Dreyfus Jazz Line | FDM 36736-2
Thad Jones Quintet
Charles Mingus-The Complete Debut Recordings | Debut | 12 DCD 4402-2
The McGhee-Navarro Boptet
The Fabulous Fats Navarro Vol.1 | Blue Note | 0677207
The Fabulous Fats Navarro Vol.2 | Blue Note | 0677208
Thelonious Monk Trio
Thelonious Monk:85th Birthday Celebration | zyx records | FANCD 6076-2
Plays The Music Of Duke Ellington | Original Jazz Classics | OJC20 024-2
Wild Bill Davis Group
Americans Swinging In Paris:Wild Bill Davis | EMI Records | 539665-2

Clarke,Kim | (b,vocel-b)

Ku-umba Frank Lacy & The Poker Bigband
Songs From The Musical 'Poker' | Tutu Records | 888150-2*

Clarke,Mike | (perc)

Eddie Henderson Orchestra
Blue Break Beats | Blue Note | 799106-2

Clarke,Neil | (congas,percvoc)

Randy Weston African Rhythm Quintet and The Gnawa Master Musicians of Marocco
Spirit! The Power Of Music | Verve | 543256-2

Clarke,Selwart | (v,concertmasterviola)

Andrew Hill Orchestra
Deep Blue-The United States Of Mind | Blue Note | 521152-2
Les McCann Group
Another Beginning | Atlantic | 7567-80790-2
Louis Armstrong And His Friends
Planet Jazz:Louis Armstrong | Planet Jazz | 2152052-2
Planet Jazz Sampler | Planet Jazz | 2152326-2
Louis Armstrong And His Friends | Bluebird | 2663961-2
Yusef Lateef Orchestra
The Blue Yusef Lateef | Rhino | 8122-73717-2

Clarke,Stanley | (b,bells,el-b,piccolo-b,voc,keyboard)

Al Di Meola Group
Land Of The Midnight Sun | CBS | 468214-2
Chick Corea And His Orchestra
My Spanish Heart | Polydor | 543303-3
Chick Corea And Return To Forever
Light As A Feather | Polydor | 557115-2
Chick Corea Group
Verve Jazz Masters 3:Chick Corea | Verve | 519820-2
Chick Corea Quartet
Return To Forever | ECM | 1022(811978-2)
Verve Jazz Masters 20:Introducing | Verve | 519853-2
My Spanish Heart | Polydor | 543303-3
Chick Corea's Return To Forever
Verve Jazz Masters 3:Chick Corea | Verve | 519820-2
Chick Corea-Stanley Clarke
Verve Jazz Masters 3:Chick Corea | Verve | 519820-2
Dexter Gordon Quintet
Dexter Gordon Birthday Celebration | Fantasy | FANCD 6082-2
Tangerine | Original Jazz Classics | OJCCD 1041-2(P 10091)
Flora Purim And Her Quartet
Joe Henderson:The Milestone Years | Milestone | 8MCD 4413-2
Flora Purim And Her Quintet
Joe Henderson:The Milestone Years | Milestone | 8MCD 4413-2
Flora Purim And Her Sextet
Joe Henderson:The Milestone Years | Milestone | 8MCD 4413-2
Butterfly Dreams | Original Jazz Classics | OJCCD 315-2
Gato Barbieri Group
Planet Jazz:Gato Barbieri | RCA | 2165364-2
Gato Barbieri:The Best Of The Early Years | RCA | 2663523-2
Joe Henderson Sextet
Joe Henderson:The Milestone Years | Milestone | 8MCD 4413-2
Lenny White Group
Present Tense | Hip Bop | HIBD 8004
Renderers Of Spirit | Hip Bop | HIBD 8014
Manhattan Project,The
Kind Of Blue:Blue Note Celebrate The Music Of Miles Davis | Blue Note | 534255-2
Wayne Shorter:The Classic Blue Note Recordings | Blue Note | 540856-2
Pharoah Sanders Group
Black Unity | Impulse(MCA) | 951219-2
Rachelle Ferrell With The Wayne Shorter Sextet
First Instrumental | Blue Note | 827820-2
Return To Forever
Return To The 7th Galaxy-Return To Forever:The Anthology | Verve | 533108-2
Where Have I Known You Before | Polydor | 825206-2
Hymn Of The Seventh Galaxy | Polydor | 825336-2
Stan Getz Quartet
Sony Jazz Collection:Stan Getz | CBS | 488623-2
Stanley Clarke Group
If This Bass Could Only Talk | CBS | 460883-2
Stanley Clarke Groups
Stanley Clarke Best | Zounds | CD 2700020089
Stanley Clarke-Gregory Himes
If This Bass Could Only Talk | CBS | 460883-2
Stanley Clarke-John Robinson
If This Bass Could Only Talk | CBS | 460883-2

Clarke,Terry | (dr,percshakers)

Gene DiNovi Trio
Renaissance Of A Jazz Master | Candid | CCD 79708
Live At The Montreal Bistro | Candid | CCD 79726
Jim Hall Jazzpar Quartet
Jazzpar 98 | Storyville | STCD 4230
Jim Hall Jazzpar Quartet +4
Jazzpar 98 | Storyville | STCD 4230
Singers Unlimited With Rob McConnell And The Boss Brass
The Singers Unlimited:Magic Voices | MPS | 539130-2

Clarke,William 'Buck' | (congas,percafrican-dr)

Freddie Hubbard And His Orchestra
Born To Be Blue | Original Jazz Classics | OJCCD 734-2(2312134)

Clarkson,Geoff | (p)

Anita O'Day With The Russ Garcia Orchestra
Verve Jazz Masters 49:Anita O'Day | Verve | 527653-2
June Christy With The Pete Rugolo Orchestra
Something Cool(The Complete Mono & Stereo Versions) | Capitol | 534069-2
Van Alexander Orchestra
Home Of Happy Feet/Swing! Staged For Sound! | Capitol | 535211-2

Classen,Martin | (ld,ssts)

Marcus Sukiennik Big Band
A Night In Tunisia Suite(7 Variationen über Dizzy Gillespie's 'A Night In Tunisia') | Jazz Haus Musik | ohne Nummer

Clastrier,Valentin | (drehleiervielle a roue)

Michael Riessler Group
Heloise | Wergo | WER 8008-2
Tentations D'Abélard | Wergo | WER 8009-2
Trio Clastrier-Riessler-Rizzo
Palude | Wergo | WER 8010-2

Claumir | (tambourine)

Duo Fenix
Karai-Eté | IN+OUT Records | 7009-2

Clausen,Bent | (vib,dr,perc,balafon,sirenesynth)

Pierre Dørge's New Jungle Orchestra
Giraf | dacapo | DCCD 9440

Clausen,Thomas | (keyboards,p,el-p,mini-moogp-solo)

Bob Brookmeyer Quartet
Old Friends | Storyville | STCD 8292
Copenhagen Art Ensemble
Shape To Twelve | dacapo | DCCD 9430
Angels' Share | dacapo | DCCD 9452
Frank Rosolino Quartet
Frank Talks! | Storyville | STCD 8284
Marilyn Mazur With Ars Nova And The Copenhagen Art Ensemble
Jordsange | dacapo | DCCD 9454
Miles Davis With The Danish Radio Big Band
Aura | CBS | CK 63962
Simon Cato Spang-Hansen Quartet
Identified | dacapo | DCCD 9448
The Danish Radio Big Band
Aura | CBS | CK 63962
Thomas Clausen

Pianomusic | M.A Music | A 801-2
Thomas Clausen Trio
She Touched Me | M.A Music | A 628-2
Thomas Clausen Trio With Gary Burton
Flowers And Trees | M.A Music | A 805-2
Café Noir | M.A Music | INTCD 004

Claussell,Jose | (perctimbales)
Donald Harrison Sextet
Free To Be | Impulse(MCA) | 951283-2

Clavies,Paul | (perc)
Eduardo Niebla-Antonio Forcione Group
Poema | Jazzpoint | JP 1035 CD

Clay,Francis | (dr)
Muddy Waters Blues Band
Muddy Waters-The Collection | MCA | MCD 18961

Clay,James | (flts)
James Clay/David Fathead Newman Quintet
The Sound Of The Wide Open Spaces | Original Jazz Classics | OJCCD 1075-2(RLP 1178)
Lawrence Marable Quartet feat. James Clay
Midnight Blue(The [Be]witching Hour) | Blue Note | 854365-2
Wes Montgomery Quintet
Wes Montgomery-The Complete Riverside Recordings | Riverside | 12 RCD 4408-2
Movin' Along | Original Jazz Classics | OJC20 089-2

Clay,John | (dr)
Zoot Sims With Orchestra
Passion Flower | Original Jazz Classics | OJCCD 939-2(2312120)

Clay,Omar | (american-indian-perc,dr,perc)
Gene Harris And The Three Sounds
Deep Blue-The United States Of Mind | Blue Note | 521152-2
M'Boom
To The Max! | Enja | ENJ-7021 22

Clay,Shirley | (cotp)
Benny Goodman And His Orchestra
Jazz:The Essential Collection Vol.3 | IN+OUT Records | 78013-2
Earl Hines And His Orchestra
Planet Jazz:Earl Hines | Planet Jazz | 2159973-2
Jazz:The Essential Collection Vol.2 | IN+OUT Records | 78012-2

Clayton Jr.,John | (b)
Count Basie And His Orchestra
Digital III At Montreux | Original Jazz Classics | OJCCD 996-2(2308223)
Ella Fitzgerald With The Count Basie Orchestra
For The Love Of Ella Fitzgerald | Verve | 841765-2
Milt Jackson Orchestra
Sarah Vaughan Birthday Celebration | Fantasy | FANCD 6090-2
Milt Jackson With The Count Basie Orchestra
To Bags...With Love:Memorial Album | Pablo | 2310967-2
Milt Jackson Birthday Celebration | Fantasy | FANCD 6079-2
Milt Jackson + Count Basie + Big Band Vol.1 | Original Jazz Classics | OJCCD 740-2(2310822)
Milt Jackson + Count Basie + Big Band Vol.2 | Original Jazz Classics | OJCCD 741-2(2310823)
Milt Jackson With The Monty Alexander Trio
To Bags...With Love:Memorial Album | Pablo | 2310967-2
Soul Fusion | Original Jazz Classics | OJCCD 731-2(2310804)
Monty Alexander Trio
Montreux Alexander-Live! At The Montreux Festival | MPS | 817487-2

Clayton Thomas,David | (voc)
Blood,Sweat And Tears
Monterey Jazz Festival 1975 | Storyville | 4960213

Clayton,Buck | (arr,ldtp)
Benny Carter And His Chocolate Dandies
Planet Jazz:Ben Webster | RCA | 2165368-2
Jazz:The Essential Collection Vol.3 | IN+OUT Records | 78013-2
Benny Goodman Septet
Jazz:The Essential Collection Vol.3 | IN+OUT Records | 78013-2
Charlie Christian:Swing To Bop | Dreyfus Jazz Line | FDM 36715-2
Big Joe Turner And Pete Johnson With The Blues Band
Newport Jazz Festival 1958,July 3rd-6th Vol.3:Blues In The Night No.1 | Phontastic | NCD 8815
Big Maybelle With The Blues Band
Newport Jazz Festival 1958,July 3rd-6th Vol.3:Blues In The Night No.1 | Phontastic | NCD 8815
Billie Holiday And Her All Stars
The Billie Holiday Song Book | Verve | 823246-2
Billie Holiday And Her Band
Billie's Love Songs | Nimbus Records | NI 2000
Billie Holiday And Her Orchestra
Jazz:The Essential Collection Vol.3 | IN+OUT Records | 78013-2
Billie's Love Songs | Nimbus Records | NI 2000
Billie Holiday With Buck Clayton And The Mal Waldron Trio
Billie Holiday Story Vol.1:Jazz At The Philharmonic | Verve | 521642-2
Billie Holiday With Teddy Wilson And His Orchestra
Billie's Love Songs | Nimbus Records | NI 2000
Billie Holiday With The JATP All Stars
Billie Holiday Story Vol.1:Jazz At The Philharmonic | Verve | 521642-2
The Complete Jazz At The Philharmonic On Verve 1944-1949 | Verve | 523893-2
Buck Clayton Quartet
The Complete Jazz At The Philharmonic On Verve 1944-1949 | Verve | 523893-2
Buck Clayton Swing Band
Swing's The Village | Nagel-Heyer | CD 5004
Blues Of Summer | Nagel-Heyer | NH 1011
Buck Clayton-Buddy Tate Quintet
Buck & Buddy | Original Jazz Classics | OJCCD 757-2(SV 2017)
Buck & Buddy Blow The Blues | Original Jazz Classics | OJCCD 850-2(SV 2030)
Buddy Tate With The Marlow Morris Quintet
Late Night Sax | CBS | 487798-2
Chuck Berry With The Blues Band
Newport Jazz Festival 1958,July 3rd-6th Vol.3:Blues In The Night No.1 | Phontastic | NCD 8815
Coleman Hawkins Quintet
Ultimate Coleman Hawkins selected by Sonny Rollins | Verve | 557538-2
Count Basie And His Orchestra
Jazz Collection:Count Basie | Laserlight | 24368
Jazz:The Essential Collection Vol.3 | IN+OUT Records | 78013-2
From Spiritual To Swing | Vanguard | VCD 169/71
Count Basie's Kansas City Seven
Jazz:The Essential Collection Vol.3 | IN+OUT Records | 78013-2
Don Byas All Star Quintet
Don Byas:Laura | Dreyfus Jazz Line | FDM 36714-2
Esquire All-American Award Winners
Planet Jazz:Jazz Trumpet | Planet Jazz | 2169654-2
Frankie Laine With Buck Clayton And His Orchestra
Jazz Spectacular | CBS | CK 65507
Harry James And His Orchestra
The Legends Of Swing | Laserlight | 24659
Helen Humes With James P. Johnson And The Count Basie Orchestra
From Spiritual To Swing | Vanguard | VCD 169/71
Helen Humes With The Kansas City Five
From Spiritual To Swing | Vanguard | VCD 169/71
Ike Quebec Swing Seven
The Blue Note Swingtets | Blue Note | 495697-2
Jam Session
Benny Goodman At Carnegie Hall 1938(Complete) | CBS | C2K 65143
JATP All Stars
The Complete Jazz At The Philharmonic On Verve 1944-1949 | Verve | 523893-2
Jazz At The Philharmonic:Best Of The 1940's Concerts | Verve | 557534-2
Bird: The Complete Charlie Parker On Verve | Verve | 837141-2
Jimmy Rushing With Count Basie And His Orchestra
From Spiritual To Swing | Vanguard | VCD 169/71
Jubilee All Stars
Jazz Gallery:Lester Young Vol.2(1946-59) | RCA | 2119541-2
Kansas City Five
From Spiritual To Swing | Vanguard | VCD 169/71
Kansas City Seven
Jazz:The Essential Collection Vol.3 | IN+OUT Records | 78013-2
Kansas City Six
Jazz:The Essential Collection Vol.3 | IN+OUT Records | 78013-2
Charlie Christian:Swing To Bop | Dreyfus Jazz Line | FDM 36715-2
From Spiritual To Swing | Vanguard | VCD 169/71
Louis Armstrong With Sy Oliver And His Orchestra
Satchmo Serenaders | Verve | 543792-2
Nancy Harrow And The Buck Clayton All Stars
Wild Women Don't Have The Blues | Candid | CCD 79008
Odetta With The Buck Clayton Sextet
Odetta And The Blues | Original Blues Classics | OBCCD 509-2(RLP 9417)
Teddy Wilson And His Orchestra
Jazz:The Essential Collection Vol.3 | IN+OUT Records | 78013-2
The Dixieland All Stars
The Dixieland All Stars | Jazz Unlimited | JUCD 2037
Vic Dickenson-Buck Clayton All Stars
Atlantic Jazz: Kansas City | Atlantic | 7567-81701-2

Clayton,Greg | (g)
Greg Clayton Trio
Live At Boomers | String Jazz | SJRCD 1013

Clayton,Jay | (p,voicevoc)
Jay Clayton-Jerry Granelli
Sound Songs | JMT Edition | 919006-2
Klaus König Orchestra & Guests
The Song Of Songs:Oratorio For Two Solo Voices,Choir And Orchestra | Enja | ENJ-7057 2

Clayton,Jeff | (as,ts,oboe,bs,fl,clsax)
Dee Dee Bridgewater With Big Band
Dear Ella | Verve | 539102-2
Kurt Elling Group
Flirting With Twilight | Blue Note | 531113-2
Milt Jackson And His Orchestra
Reverence And Compassion | Reprise | 9362-45204-2
Ruth Brown With Orchestra
Fine And Mellow | Fantasy | FCD 9663-2
The Clayton Brothers Quintet
Siblingity | Warner | 9362-47813-2

Clayton,Joe | (congas)
Stanley Turrentine And His Orchestra
Pieces Of Dream | Original Jazz Classics | OJCCD 831-2(F 9465)

Clayton,John | (arr,ld,b,voccond)
Bud Shank Sextet
New Gold! | Candid | CCD 79707
Diana Krall Group
When I Look In Your Eyes | Verve | 9513304
The Girl In The Other Room | Verve | 9862246
Diana Krall Group With Orchestra
When I Look In Your Eyes | Verve | 9513304
Diane Schuur Trio With Orchestra And Strings
In Tribute | GRP | GRP 20062
Diane Schuur With Orchestra
In Tribute | GRP | GRP 20062
The Best Of Diane Schuur | GRP | GRP 98882
Jimmy Smith All Stars
Jimmy Smith:Dot Com Blues | Blue Thumb | 543978-2
Milt Jackson And His Orchestra
Reverence And Compassion | Reprise | 9362-45204-2
The Clayton Brothers Quintet
Siblingity | Warner | 9362-47813-2
Vic Lewis West Coast All Stars
Me And You! | Candid | CCD 79739

Clayton,Merry | (voc)
Dee Dee Bridgewater With Band
Dee Dee Bridgewater | Atlantic | 7567-80760-2

Clearmountain,Bob | (handclaps)
The Brecker Brothers
Heavy Metal Be-Bop | RCA | 2119257-2

Cleary,Jon | (el-p,psynth)
Jimmy Smith All Stars
Jimmy Smith:Dot Com Blues | Blue Thumb | 543978-2

Cleaver,Gerald | (dr)
Ben Waltzer Quintet
In Metropolitan Motion | Fresh Sound Records | FSNT 082 CD
Bill McHenry Quartet
Graphic | Fresh Sound Records | FSNT 056 CD
Chris Lightcap Quartet
Lay-Up | Fresh Sound Records | FSNT 074 CD
Roscoe Mitchell And The Note Factory
Nine To Get Ready | ECM | 1651(539725-2)

Clebanoff,Herman | (v)
Cal Tjader With The Clare Fischer Orchestra
Cal Tjader Plays Harold Arlen & West Side Story | Fantasy | FCD 24775-2
Milt Jackson With Strings
To Bags...With Love:Memorial Album | Pablo | 2310967-2
Pete Rugolo And His Orchestra
Thriller/Richard Diamon(Original Jazz Scores From 2 Classics TV Series) | Fresh Sound Records | FSCD 2015

Clemens,Gabriele | (voc)
Jazzensemble Des Hessischen Rundfunks
Jazz Messe-Messe Für Unsere Zeit | hr music.de | hrmj 003-01 CD

Clempson,Clem | (el-g,b-g,gkeyboards)
Barbara Thompson's Paraphernalia
Barbara Thompson's Special Edition | VeraBra Records | CDVBR 2017-2

Cless,Rod | (ascl)
Muggsy Spanier And His Ragtime Band
Planet Jazz | Planet Jazz | 2169652-2
Planet Jazz:Jazz Trumpet | Planet Jazz | 2169654-2

Cleveland,Jimmy | (tb)
Anthony Ortega With The Nat Pierce Orchestra
Earth Dance | Fresh Sound Records | FSR-CD 325
Antonio Carlos Jobim With The Claus Ogerman Orchestra
Verve Jazz Masters 13:Antonio Carlos Jobim | Verve | 516409-2
The Composer Of 'Desafinado' Plays | Verve | 521431-2
Art Farmer Septet
Plays The Arrangements And Compositions Of Gigi Gryce And Quincy Jones | Original Jazz Classics | OJCCD 054-2
Billie Holiday With The Ray Ellis Orchestra
Verve Jazz Masters 47:Billie Holiday Sings Standards | Verve | 527650-2
Birdland Dream Band
Birdland Dream Band | RCA | 2663873-2
Cannonball Adderley And His Orchestra
Verve Jazz Masters 31:Cannonball Adderley | Verve | 522651-2
Ballads | Blue Note | 537563-2
Cannonball Adderley Birthday Celebration | Fantasy | FANCD 6087-2
Cannonball Adderley Group
Julian 'Cannonball' Adderley | EmArCy | 830381-2
Charles Mingus And His Orchestra
The Complete Town Hall Concert | Blue Note | 828353-2
Dinah Washington And Her Orchestra
For Those In Love | EmArCy | 514073-2
Dinah Washington With The Quincy Jones Orchestra
Verve Jazz Masters 40:Dinah Washington | Verve | 522055-2
The Swingin' Miss 'D' | Verve | 558074-2
Eddie Lockjaw Davis And His Orchestra
Eric Dolphy:The Complete Prestige Recordings | Prestige | 9 PRCD-4418-2
Ella Fitzgerald With Orchestra
Ella/Things Ain't What They Used To Be | Warner | 9362-47875-2
Friedrich Gulda Septet
Friedrich Gulda At Birdland | RCA | 2112587-2
George Russell And His Orchestra
George Russell New York N.Y. | Impulse(MCA) | 951278-2
Gigi Gryce-Clifford Brown Octet
Planet Jazz:Clifford Brown | Planet Jazz | 2161239-2
Gil Evans And Ten
Gil Evans And Ten | Original Jazz Classics | OJC 346(P 7120)
The Jazz Giants Play Cole Porter:Night And Day | Prestige | PCD 24203-2
Gil Evans And Ten | Prestige | PRSA 7120-6
Gil Evans Orchestra
Verve Jazz Masters 23:Gil Evans | Verve | 521860-2
The Individualism Of Gil Evans | Verve | 833804-2
Blues In Orbit | Enja | ENJ-3069 2
Hank Jones With Oliver Nelson's Orchestra
The Roots Of Acid Jazz | Impulse(MCA) | IMP 12042
J.J.Johnson And His Orchestra
Planet Jazz:J.J.Johnson | Planet Jazz | 2159974-2
Jimmy Forrest With The Oliver Nelson Orchestra
Soul Street | Original Jazz Classics | OJCCD 987-2(NJ 8293)
Jimmy Rushing And His Orchestra
Five Feet Of Soul | Roulette | 581830-2
Jimmy Smith And Wes Montgomery With Orchestra
Jimmy & Wes-The Dynamic Duo | Verve | 521445-2
Jimmy Smith And Wes Montgomery With The Oliver Nelson Orchestra
Wes Montgomery:The Verve Jazz Sides | Verve | 521690-2
Jimmy Smith:Best Of The Verve Years | Verve | 527950-2
Talkin' Jazz:Roots Of Acid Jazz | Verve | 529580-2
Jimmy Smith With Orchestra
Jimmy Smith-Talkin' Verve | Verve | 531563-2
Jimmy Smith With The Billy Byers Orchestra
Jimmy Smith:Best Of The Verve Years | Verve | 527950-2
Jimmy Smith With The Claus Ogerman Orchestra
Verve Jazz Masters 29:Jimmy Smith | Verve | 521855-2
Any Number Can Win | Verve | 557447-2
Jimmy Smith With The Lalo Schifrin Orchestra
Jimmy Smith:Best Of The Verve Years | Verve | 527950-2
Jimmy Smith-Talkin' Verve | Verve | 531563-2
The Cat | Verve | 539756-2
Jimmy Smith With The Oliver Nelson Orchestra
Verve Jazz Masters 29:Jimmy Smith | Verve | 521855-2
Jimmy Smith:Best Of The Verve Years | Verve | 527950-2
Jimmy Smith-Talkin' Verve | Verve | 531563-2
Junior Mance Trio & Orchestra
That Lovin' Feelin' | Milestone | MCD 47097-2
Kenny Burrell With The Don Sebesky Orchestra
Verve Jazz Masters 45:Kenny Burrell | Verve | 527652-2
Blues-The Common Ground | Verve | 589101-2
Kenny Burrell With The Gil Evans Orchestra
Guitar Forms | Verve | 521403-2
Verve Jazz Masters 23:Gil Evans | Verve | 521860-2
Verve Jazz Masters 45:Kenny Burrell | Verve | 527652-2
Verve Jazz Masters Vol.60:The Collection | Verve | 529866-2
King Curtis Band
King Curtis-Blow Man Blow | Bear Family Records | BCD 15670 CI
Lionel Hampton And His Orchestra
Lionel Hampton's Paris All Stars | Vogue | 21511502
Lionel Hampton Orchestra
The Big Bands Vol.1:The Snader Telescriptions | Storyville | 4960043
Lucy Reed With Orchestra
This Is Lucy Reed | Original Jazz Classics | OJCCD 1943-2(F 3243)
Mar Murphy With The Ernie Wilkins Orchestra
RAH | Original Jazz Classics | OJCCD 141-2(R 9395)
Maynard Ferguson And His Orchestra
Verve Jazz Masters 52:Maynard Ferguson | Verve | 529905-2
Miles Davis + 19
Miles Ahead | CBS | CK 65121
Miles Davis With Gil Evans & His Orchestra
This Is Jazz:Miles Davis Plays Ballads | CBS | CK 65038
Porgy And Bess | CBS | CK 65141
Milt Jackson Orchestra
To Bags...With Love:Memorial Album | Pablo | 2310967-2
Milt Jackson Birthday Celebration | Fantasy | FANCD 6079-2
Big Bags | Original Jazz Classics | OJCCD 366-2(RLP 9429)
Modern Jazz Quartet And Orchestra
MJQ 40 | Atlantic | 7567-82330-2
Oliver Nelson And His Orchestra
Verve Jazz Masters Vol.60:The Collection | Verve | 529866-2
Oscar Peterson With Orchestra
With Respect To Nat | Verve | 557486-2
Oscar Peterson With The Ernie Wilkins Orchestra
Verve Jazz Masters 16:Oscar Peterson | Verve | 516320-2
Phil Woods Quartet With Orchestra & Strings
Round Trip | Verve | 559804-2
Sarah Vaughan With Orchestra
!Viva! Vaughan | Mercury | 549374-2
Sarah Vaughan With The Frank Foster Orchestra
The Antonio Carlos Jobim Songbook | Verve | 525472-2
Shirley Horn With The Quincy Jones Orchestra
Loads Of Love + Shirley Horn With Horns | Mercury | 843454-2
Sonny Rollins Orchestra
Sonny Rollins And The Big Brass | Verve | 557545-2
Alfie | Impulse(MCA) | 951224-2
Sonny Rollins Quintet
Sonny Rollins-The Freelance Years:The Complete Riverside & Contemporary Recordings | Riverside | 5 RCD 4427-2
Wes Montgomery Orchestra
Movin' Wes | Verve | 521433-2
Wes Montgomery With The Johnny Pate Orchestra
Verve Jazz Masters 14:Wes Montgomery | Verve | 519826-2
Wes Montgomery:The Verve Jazz Sides | Verve | 521690-2
Talkin' Jazz:Roots Of Acid Jazz | Verve | 529580-2
Wes Montgomery With The Oliver Nelson Orchestra
Verve Jazz Masters 14:Wes Montgomery | Verve | 519826-2
Wes Montgomery:The Verve Jazz Sides | Verve | 521690-2
Talkin' Jazz:Roots Of Acid Jazz | Verve | 529580-2

Clevelanders,The |
Lalo Schifrin And His Orchestra
Tin Tin Deo | Fresh Sound Records | FSR-CD 319

Cleyndert,Andrew | (b)
Joe Temperley Quartet
Easy To Remember | Hep | CD 2083
Joe Temperley Quartet With Strings
Easy To Remember | Hep | CD 2083
Joe Temperley Quintet
Easy To Remember | Hep | CD 2083
Joe Temperley Quintet With Strings
Easy To Remember | Hep | CD 2083

Cliff,Billy | (voc)
Spyro Gyra & Guests
Love & Other Obsessions | GRP | GRP 98112

Cliff,Dave | (gel-g)
Bob Wilber's Bechet Legacy
The Hamburg Concert-Tribute To A Legend | Nagel-Heyer | CD 028
The Second Sampler | Nagel-Heyer | NHR SP 6
Summit Reunion
Jazz Im Amerikahaus,Vol.5 | Nagel-Heyer | CD 015
The First Sampler | Nagel-Heyer | NHR SP 5
Warren Vaché Quintet
The First Sampler | Nagel-Heyer | NHR SP 5
Warren Vaché Quintet With Special Guest Allan Vaché
Jazz Im Amerikahaus,Vol.2 | Nagel-Heyer | CD 012

Clifton,Bill | (p)
V-Disc All Star Jam Session
Louis Armstrong-Jack Teagarden-Woody Herman:Midnights At V-Disc | Jazz Unlimited | JUCD 2048

Cline,Alex | (dr,cymbals,perc,overtone-singing)
Alex Cline Group

The Lamp And The Star | ECM | 1372
Charlie Haden Quartet West
In Angel City | Verve | 837031-2
Vinny Golia Quintet
Regards From Norma Desmond | Fresh Sound Records | FSNT 008 CD

Cline,Nels | (el-g,steel-g,gvoice)
Alex Cline Group
The Lamp And The Star | ECM | 1372

Clinkscales,Charles | (voc)
Fats Waller And His Buddies
Planet Jazz:Jack Teagarden | Planet Jazz | 2161236-2

Clinton,George | (voc)
Maceo Parker Group
Maceo(Soundtrack) | Minor Music | 801046

Clooney,Rosemary | (talkingvoc)
Bing Crosby And Rosemarie Clooney With The Billy May Orchestra
Fancy Meeting You Here | RCA | 2663859-2
Rosemary Clooney With The Buddy Cole Trio
Swing Around Rosie | Coral | 589485-2
Rosemary Clooney With The Duke Ellington Orchestra
Blue Rose | CBS | CK 65506

Cloud,Vennette | (voc)
Paulinho Da Costa Orchestra
Happy People | Original Jazz Classics | OJCCD 783-2(2312102)

Clute,Pete | (p)
Turk Murphy And His Jazz Band
Planet Jazz | Planet Jazz | 2169652-2
The Very Best Of Dixieland Jazz | Verve | 535529-2
Atlantic Jazz: New Orleans | Atlantic | 7567-81700-2

Clyde,'The Slide' | (tpel-p)
Dogslyde
Hair Of The Dog | Intuition Records | INT 3223-2

Clyne,Jeff | (b)
Blossom Dearie Trio
At Ronnie Scott's:Blossom Time | EmArCy | 558683-2
Tony Oxley Quintet
The Baptist Traveller | CBS | 494438-2
Tony Oxley Sextet
4 Compositions For Sextet | CBS | 494437-2

Coassin,Bob | (tp)
Conexion Latina
Calorcito | Enja | ENJ-4072 2

Coates,Michael | (flts)
Jazz Africa All Nations Big Band
Jadu(Jazz Africa Down Under) | Enja | ENJ-9339 2

Cobb,Arnett | (ts)
Arnett Cobb Quintet
Movin' Right Along | Original Jazz Classics | OJCCD 1074-2(P 7216)
Smooth Sailing | Original Jazz Classics | OJCCD 323-2
More Party Time | Original Jazz Classics | OJCCD 979-2(P 7175)
Axel Zwingenberger With The Lionel Hampton Big Band
The Boogie Woogie Album | Vagabond | VRCD 8.88008
Lionel Hampton And His Orchestra
Lionel Hampton:Flying Home | Dreyfus Jazz Line | FDM 36735-2
Lionel Hampton And His Septet
Lionel Hampton:Flying Home | Dreyfus Jazz Line | FDM 36735-2
Shirley Scott All Stars
Queen Of The Organ-Shirley Scott Memorial Album | Prestige | PRCD 11027-2
Very Saxy
Very Saxy | Original Jazz Classics | OJCCD 458-2
The Prestige Legacy Vol.2:Battles Of Saxes | Prestige | PCD 24252-2

Cobb,Bert | (tuba)
King Oliver And His Dixie Syncopators
Jazz:The Essential Collection Vol.1 | IN+OUT Records | 78011-2
King Oliver's Jazz Band
Jazz:The Essential Collection Vol.1 | IN+OUT Records | 78011-2

Cobb,Jimmy | (co,dr,bells,perc,p-solotp)
Art Pepper Quartet
Gettin' Together | Original Jazz Classics | OJCCD 169-2
The Way It Is | Original Jazz Classics | OJCCD 389-2
Art Pepper Quintet
Gettin' Together | Original Jazz Classics | OJCCD 169-2
Bobby Timmons Orchestra
Quartet And Orchestra | Milestone | MCD 47091-2
Bobby Timmons Quartet
Quartet And Orchestra | Milestone | MCD 47091-2
Bobby Timmons Trio
This Here Is Bobby Timmons | Original Jazz Classics | OJC20 104-2(RLP 1164)
From The Bottom | Original Jazz Classics | OJCCD 1032-2(RS 3053)
Cannonball Adderley And His Orchestra
Verve Jazz Masters 31:Cannonball Adderley | Verve | 522651-2
Cannonball Adderley Quartet
Takes Charge | Blue Note | 534071-2
Ballads | Blue Note | 537563-2
Cannonball & Coltrane | Verve | 559770-2
Cannonball Adderley Quintet
Verve Jazz Masters 31:Cannonball Adderley | Verve | 522651-2
Cannonball Adderley:Sophisticated Swing-The EmArCy Small Group Sessions | Verve | 528408-2
Cannonball Adderley Birthday Celebration | Fantasy | FANCD 6087-2
At Newport | Pablo | PACD 5315-2
Cannonball Adderley Quintet In Chicago
Cannonball & Coltrane | Verve | 559770-2
Dinah Washington And Her Orchestra
For Those In Love | EmArCy | 514073-2
Dinah Washington With The Jimmy Cobb Orchestra
Verve Jazz Masters 40:Dinah Washington | Verve | 522055-2
Ultimate Ben Webster selected by James Carter | Verve | 557537-2
Don Sleet Quintet
All Members | Original Jazz Classics | OJCCD 1949-2(JLP 9455)
Hubert Laws Quartet
The Laws Of Jazz | Atlantic | 8122-71636-2
Jan Harrington With The Mike Hennesey Trio
Remembering Dinah-A Salute To Dinah Washington | Hot Shot Records | HSR 8313-2
Jan Harrington With The Nat Adderley Quintet
Remembering Dinah-A Salute To Dinah Washington | Hot Shot Records | HSR 8313-2
Jimmy Cobb's Mob
Cobb's Groove | Milestone | MCD 9334-2
John Coltrane Quartet
Cannonball & Coltrane | Verve | 559770-2
Coltrane Jazz | Atlantic | 7567-81344-2
The Best Of John Coltrane | Atlantic | 7567-81366-2
John Coltrane-The Heavyweight Champion:The Complete Atlantic Recordings | Atlantic | 8122-71984-2
Giant Steps | Atlantic | 8122-75203-2
The Very Best Of John Coltrane | Rhino | 8122-79778-2
John Coltrane Quintet
John Coltrane-The Prestige Recordings | Prestige | 16 PCD 4405-2
Black Pearls | Original Jazz Classics | OJC 352(P 7316)
Standard Coltrane | Original Jazz Classics | OJCCD 246-2
Bahia | Original Jazz Classics | OJCCD 415-2
Stardust | Original Jazz Classics | OJCCD 920-2(P 7268)
Jon Hendricks Group
A Tribute To Charlie Parker Vol.2 | Storyville | 4960493
Kenny Barron-John Hicks Quartet
Rhythm-A-Ning | Candid | CCD 79044
Kenny Burrell Quintet
John Coltrane-The Prestige Recordings | Prestige | 16 PCD 4405-2
Kenny Burrell-John Coltrane Quintet
Kenny Burrell & John Coltrane | New Jazz | NJSA 8276-2
Kenny Burrell & John Coltrane | Original Jazz Classics | OJC20 300-2
Mar Murphy With The Ernie Wilkins Orchestra
RAH | Original Jazz Classics | OJCCD 141-2(R 9395)
Mark Morganelli And The Jazz Forum All Stars
Speak Low | Candid | CCD 79054
Miles Davis Quartet
Someday My Prince Will Come | CBS | CK 65919
Miles Davis Quintet
Miles Davis: Olympia, March 29th,1960 | Laserlight | 36130
Ballads | CBS | 461099-2
Kind Of Blue | CBS | 480410-2
Miles Davis In Person-Friday Night At The Blackhawk,San Francisco,Vol.1 | CBS | C4K 87106
Kind Of Blue | CBS | CK 64935
Miles Davis At Carnegie Hall | CBS | CK 65027
This Is Jazz:Miles Davis Plays Ballads | CBS | CK 65038
Someday My Prince Will Come | CBS | CK 65919
Live In Stockholm | Dragon | DRCD 228
Newport Jazz Festival 1958,July 3rd-6th,Vol.1:Mostly Miles | Phontastic | NCD 8813
Miles Davis Sextet
Circle In The Round | CBS | 467898-2
Kind Of Blue | CBS | 480410-2
Kind Of Blue | CBS | CK 64935
This Is Jazz:Miles Davis Plays Ballads | CBS | CK 65038
Sorcerer | CBS | CK 65680
Someday My Prince Will Come | CBS | CK 65919
Miles Davis With Gil Evans & His Orchestra
Ballads | CBS | 461099-2
Miles Davis At Carnegie Hall | CBS | CK 65027
This Is Jazz:Miles Davis Plays Ballads | CBS | CK 65038
Porgy And Bess | CBS | CK 65141
Sketches Of Spain | CBS | CK 65142
Quiet Nights | CBS | CK 65293
Nat Adderley And The Big Sax Section
Cannonball Adderley Birthday Celebration | Fantasy | FANCD 6087-2
That's Right | Original Jazz Classics | OJCCD 791-2(RLP 9330)
Nat Adderley Quintet
We Remember Cannon | IN+OUT Records | 7012-2
Jazz Unlimited | IN+OUT Records | 7017-2
Remembering Dinah-A Salute To Dinah Washington | Hot Shot Records | HSR 8313-2
Paul Gonsalves Quintet
Gettin' Together | Original Jazz Classics | OJCCD 203-2
Roman Schwaller Jazz Quartet
Some Changes In Life | JHM Records | JHM 3612
Roy Hargrove Quartet
Family | Verve | 527630-2
Roy Hargrove Quintet
Family | Verve | 527630-2
Roy Hargrove Sextet
Family | Verve | 527630-2
Sonny Red (Kyner) Quartet
Red,Blue & Green | Milestone | MCD 47086-2
Sonny Red (Kyner) Quintet
Red,Blue & Green | Milestone | MCD 47086-2
Walter Benton Quintet
Out Of This World | Milestone | MCD 47087-2
Warren Vaché Quintet
Warren Plays Warrey | Nagel-Heyer | CD 033
Blues Of Summer | Nagel-Heyer | NH 1011
Wes Montgomery Quartet
Wes Montgomery-The Complete Riverside Recordings | Riverside | 12 RCD 4408-2
Verve Jazz Masters 14:Wes Montgomery | Verve | 519826-2
Verve Jazz Masters 20:Introducing | Verve | 519853-2
Talkin' Jazz:Roots Of Acid Jazz | Verve | 529580-2
Wes Montgomery Quartet With The Claus Ogerman Orchestra
Willow Weep For Me | Verve | 589486-2
Wes Montgomery Quintet
Wes Montgomery-The Complete Riverside Recordings | Riverside | 12 RCD 4408-2
Full House | Original Jazz Classics | OJC20 106-2
Wes Montgomery Trio
Wes Montgomery-The Complete Riverside Recordings | Riverside | 12 RCD 4408-2
Boss Guitar | Original Jazz Classics | OJCCD 261-2
Guitar On The Go | Original Jazz Classics | OJCCD 489-2(RLP 9494)
Wynton Kelly Sextet
Kelly Blue | Original Jazz Classics | OJC20 033-2(RLP 1142)
Kelly Blue | Riverside | RISA 1142-6
Wynton Kelly Trio
The Story Of Jazz Piano | Laserlight | 24653
Kelly Blue | Original Jazz Classics | OJC20 033-2(RLP 1142)
Full View | Original Jazz Classics | OJCCD 912-2(M 9004)
Kelly Blue | Riverside | RISA 1142-6
Wynton Kelly Trio With Hank Mobley
Live at The Left Bank Jazz Society,Baltimore,1967 | Fresh Sound Records | FSCD 1031
Wynton Kelly Trio With Wes Montgomery
Wes Montgomery:The Verve Jazz Sides | Verve | 521690-2
Wynton Kelly-George Coleman Quartet
Live at The Left Bank Jazz Society,Baltimore,1968 | Fresh Sound Records | FSCD 1032

Cobbs,Al | (ts)
Jimmy Lunceford And His Orchestra
The Legends Of Swing | Laserlight | 24659

Cobbs,Alfred | (tb)
Duke Ellington And His Orchestra
Ellington '55 | Capitol | 520135-2
Louis Armstrong And His Orchestra
Best Of The Complete RCA Victor Recordings | RCA | 2663636-2
Louis Armstrong:A 100th Birthday Celebration | RCA | 2663694-2
I Love Jazz | Verve | 543747-2
Louis Armstrong:C'est Si Bon | Dreyfus Jazz Line | FDM 36730-2
Louis Armstrong And Omer Simeon With The Sy Oliver Orchestra
Ambassador Louis Armstrong Vol.17:Moments To Remember(1952-1956) | Ambassador | CLA 1917
Louis Armstrong With Sy Oliver And His Orchestra
Louis Armstrong-My Greatest Songs | MCA | MCD 18347
Louis Jordan And His Tympany Five
Louis Jordan-Let The Good Times Roll: The Complete Decca Recordings 1938-1954 | Bear Family Records | BCD 15557 IH

Cobbs,Call prob. | (p)
Albert Ayler Duo
Albert Ayler Live In Greenwich Village:The Complete Impulse Recordings | Impulse(MCA) | IMP 22732

Cobbs,Robert | (dr)
Buster Smith Orchestra
Atlantic Jazz: Kansas City | Atlantic | 7567-81701-2

Cobham,Billy | (dr,field-dr,perc,dr-synth,voc)
Billy Cobham Group
Spectrum | Atlantic | 7567-81428-2
The Best Of Billy Cobham | Atlantic | 7567-81558-2
Art Of Five | IN+OUT Records | 77063-2
Billy Cobham Quartet
Atlantic Jazz: Fusion | Atlantic | 7567-81711-2
Billy Cobham Trio
The Art Of Three | IN+OUT Records | 77045-2
Charles Earland Orchestra
Charlie's Greatest Hits | Prestige | PCD 24250-2
Donald Harrison Trio
Heroes | Nagel-Heyer | CD 2041
Freddie Hubbard With Orchestra
This Is Jazz:Freddie Hubbard | CBS | CK 65041
Gene Ammons Quintet
Fine And Mellow | Prestige | PRCD 24281-2
George Benson And His Orchestra
Giblet Gravy | Verve | 543754-2
Talkin' Verve:George Benson | Verve | 553780-2
George Benson Orchestra
Verve Jazz Masters 21:George Benson | Verve | 521861-2
Talkin' Verve:George Benson | Verve | 553780-2
George Benson Quintet
Verve Jazz Masters 21:George Benson | Verve | 521861-2
Giblet Gravy | Verve | 543754-2
George Benson Sextet
Talkin' Verve:George Benson | Verve | 553780-2
Grover Washington Jr. Orchestra
Jazzrock-Anthology Vol.3:Fusion | Zounds | CD 27100555
Herbie Hancock Trio
Chick Corea-Herbie Hancock-Keith Jarrett-McCoy Tyner | Atlantic | 7567-81402-2
Horace Silver Quintet
Horace Silver Retrospective | Blue Note | 495576-2
Mahavishnu Orchestra
The Inner Mounting Flame | CBS | CK 65523
Miles Davis Group
Circle In The Round | CBS | 467898-2
Live-Evil | CBS | C2K 65135
Bitches Brew | CBS | C2K 65774
Milt Jackson And His Orchestra
Sunflower | CTI | ZK 65131
Paradox
The First Second | TipToe | TIP-888833 2
Ron Carter Octet
New York Slick | Original Jazz Classics | OJCCD 916-2(M 9096)
Ron Carter Sextet
New York Slick | Original Jazz Classics | OJCCD 916-2(M 9096)
The Mahavishnu Orchestra
Between Nothingness & Eternity | CBS | CK 32766
Wolfgang Schmid's Kick
No Filters | TipToe | TIP-888809 2

Coburger,Gabriel | (ts)
Albert Mangelsdorff With The NDR Big Band
NDR Big Band-Bravissimo | ACT | 9232-2
Johnny Griffin With The NDR Big Band
NDR Big Band-Bravissimo | ACT | 9232-2

Cochrane,Michael | (porg)
Louis Smith Quintet
Louisville | Steeplechase | SCCD 31552
Michael Cochrane Quartet
Path Ways | Steeplechase | SCCD 31542

Cochrane,Steve | (tablas)
Steve Tibbetts Group
Bye Bye Safe Journey | ECM | 1270
Yr | ECM | 1355(835245-2)

Cockburn,Bruce | (g)
Hugh Marsh Duo/Quartet/Orchestra
The Bear Walks | VeraBra Records | CDVBR 2011-2

Cocker,Henry | (tb)
Joe Newman And His Band
Jazz In Paris:Joe Newman-Jazz At Midnight-Cootie Williams | EmArCy | 018446-2

Cockerly,Jack | (org)
Pete Rugolo And His Orchestra
Thriller/Richard Diamon(Original Jazz Scores From 2 Classics TV Series) | Fresh Sound Records | FSCD 2015

Codjia,Manu | (g)
Erik Truffaz Quartet
Mantis | Blue Note | 535101-2
Erik Truffaz Quartet Quintet
Mantis | Blue Note | 535101-2

Codona |
Don Cherry/Nana Vasconcelos/Collin Walcott
Codona 2 | ECM | 1177(833332-2)
Codona 3 | ECM | 1243

Codrington,Ray | (tp)
Eddie Harris Quintet
The Best Of Eddie Harris | Atlantic | 7567-81370-2
Atlantic Saxophones | Rhino | 8122-71256-2

Coe,Jimmy | (bsts)
Roy Eldridge-Alvin Stoller
The Complete Verve Roy Eldridge Studio Sessions | Verve | 9861278

Coe,Tony | (as,cl,b-cl,ts,sax,ss,vocfl)
Franz Koglmann Quintet
Make Believe | Between The Lines | btl 001(Efa 10171-2)
Joe Temperley Quintet
Easy To Remember | Hep | CD 2083
Kenny Clarke-Francy Boland Big Band
Clark-Boland Big Band: TNP, October 29th, 1969 | Laserlight | 36129
Three Latin Adventures | MPS | 529095-2
More Smiles | MPS | 9814789
All Smiles | MPS | 9814790
Francy Boland-Fellini 712 | MPS | 9814805
Monoblue Quartet
An Affair With Strauss | Between The Lines | btl 006(Efa 10176-2)
Norma Winstone Trio
Somewhere Called Home | ECM | 1337
Tony Coe-Roger Kellaway
British-American Blue | Between The Lines | btl 007(Efa 10177-2)

Coelho,Amauri | (atabaquepandeiro)
Baden Powell Solo/Group
Three Originals:Tristeza On Guitar/Poema On Guitar/Apaixonado | MPS | 519216-2

Cogbill,Tommy | (el-b)
Herbie Mann Group
Memphis Underground | Atlantic | 7567-81364-2
The Best Of Herbie Mann | Atlantic | 7567-81369-2

Coggins,Gil | (p)
Jackie McLean Sextet
A Long Drink Of The Blues | Original Jazz Classics | OJCCD 253-2(NJ 8253)
Miles Davis All Stars
Miles Davis Vol.1 | Blue Note | 532610-2
Miles Davis Vol.2 | Blue Note | 532611-2
Miles Davis Quartet
Ballads & Blues | Blue Note | 836633-2
Miles Davis Sextet
Kind Of Blue:Blue Note Celebrate The Music Of Miles Davis | Blue Note | 534255-2
Miles Davis:The Best Of The Capitol/Blue Note Years | Blue Note | 798287-2
Jazz Profile:Miles Davis | Blue Note | 823515-2
Ballads & Blues | Blue Note | 836633-2
Ray Draper Quintet
John Coltrane-The Prestige Recordings | Prestige | 16 PCD 4405-2
Sonny Rollins Quintet
Sonny Rollins-The Freelance Years:The Complete Riverside & Contemporary Recordings | Riverside | 5 RCD 4427-2

Cohen,Avishai | (b,p,synth,perc,el-btp)
Amos Hoffman Quartet
The Dreamer | Fresh Sound Records | FSNT 060 CD
Avishai Cohen Quartet
The Trumpet Player | Fresh Sound Records | FSNT 161 CD
Avishai Cohen Trio
The Trumpet Player | Fresh Sound Records | FSNT 161 CD
Danilo Perez Quartet
Panamonk | Impulse(MCA) | 951190-2
Freddie Bryant Group
Brazilian Rosewood | Fresh Sound Records | FSNT 035 CD
Kurt Rosenwinkel Trio
East Coast Love Affair | Fresh Sound Records | FSNT 016 CD
Seamus Blake-Marc Miralta Trio
Sun Sol | Fresh Sound Records | FSNT 087 CD

Cohen,Gil | (tb)
Gil Evans And His Orchestra
The Individualism Of Gil Evans | Verve | 833804-2

Cohen,Greg | (bvoc)
Byron Stripling And Friends

If I Could Be With You | Nagel-Heyer | NH 1010
Dave Douglas Quartet
A Thousand Evenings | RCA | 2663698-2
Charms Of The Night Sky | Winter&Winter | 910015-2
Dino Saluzzi Group
If | Enja | ENJ-9451 2
James Chirillo Quartet with Vera Mara
Sultry Serenade | Nagel-Heyer | CD 061
James Chirillo Sextet
Sultry Serenade | Nagel-Heyer | CD 061
Ken Peplowski Quartet
Lost In The Stars | Nagel-Heyer | CD 2020
Marty Grosz And His Swinging Fools
Ring Dem Bells | Nagel-Heyer | CD 022
The Second Sampler | Nagel-Heyer | NHR SP 6
Randy Sandke And The New York Allstars
The Re-Discovered Louis And Bix | Nagel-Heyer | CD 058
The New York Allstars
We Love You,Louis! | Nagel-Heyer | CD 029
The Second Sampler | Nagel-Heyer | NHR SP 6
Woody Allen And His New Orleans Jazz Band
Wild Man Blues | RCA | 2663353-2
Woody Allen Trio
Wild Man Blues | RCA | 2663353-2

Cohen,Jeffrey | (voc)
Herbie Hancock Group
Magic Window | CBS | 486572-2

Cohen,Leon | (fl,alto-fl,cl,as,ts,oboe,piccolo)
Cal Tjader With The Lalo Schifrin Orchestra
Talkin Verve/Roots Of Acid Jazz:Cal Tjader | Verve | 531562-2
Joe Williams With The Frank Hunter Orchestra
Planet Jazz:Joe Williams | Planet Jazz | 2165370-2
Lalo Schifrin And His Orchestra
Verve Jazz Masters 39:Cal Tjader | Verve | 521858-2

Cohen,Paul | (drtp)
Artie Shaw And His Orchestra
Planet Jazz:Jazz Trumpet | Planet Jazz | 2169654-2
Big Joe Turner With The Count Basie Orchestra
Flip Flop And Fly | Original Jazz Classics | OJCCD 1053-2(2310937)
Count Basie And His Orchestra
Afrique | RCA | 2179618-2
Count Basie: Salle Pleyel, April 17th, 1972 | Laserlight | 36127
Digital III At Montreux | Original Jazz Classics | OJCCD 996-2(2308223)
Ella Fitzgerald With Count Basie And His Orchestra
Digital III At Montreux | Original Jazz Classics | OJCCD 996-2(2308223)
Ella Fitzgerald With The Count Basie Orchestra
Bluella:Ella Fitzgerald Sings The Blues | Pablo | 2310960-2

Cohen,Porky | (tb)
The Six
The Very Best Of Dixieland Jazz | Verve | 535529-2

Cohn,Al | (arr,ld,b-cl,ts,bs,cl,as,reedssax)
Al Cohn Quartet
The Birdlanders Vol.2 | Original Jazz Classics | OJCCD 1931-2
Al Cohn Quintet feat. Zoot Sims
Al And Zoot | GRP | 951827-2
Al Cohn-Zoot Sims Duo
You 'N' Me | Verve | 589318-2
Al Cohn-Zoot Sims Quintet
Planet Jazz:Jazz Saxophone | Planet Jazz | 2169653-2
You 'N' Me | Verve | 589318-2
Al Porcino Big Band
Al Cohn Meets Al Porcino | Organic Music | ORGM 9730
Astrud Gilberto With The Al Cohn Orchestra
Verve Jazz Masters 9:Astrud Gilberto | Verve | 519824-2
Billie Holiday And Her All Stars
The Billie Holiday Song Book | Verve | 823246-2
Birdland Dream Band
Birdland Dream Band | RCA | 2663873-2
Carmen McRae With Orchestra
Birds Of A Feather | Decca | 589515-2
Chubby Jackson And His All Star Big Band
Chubby Takes Over | Fresh Sound Records | FSR-CD 324
Coleman Hawkins With Billy Byers And His Orchestra
The Hawk In Hi-Fi | RCA | 2663842-2
Elliot Lawrence And His Orchestra
The Elliot Lawrence Big Band Swings Cohn & Kahn | Fantasy | FCD 24761-2
George Russell And His Orchestra
George Russell New York N.Y. | Impulse(MCA) | 951278-2
Gerry Mulligan And The Sax Section
The Gerry Mulligan Songbook | Pacific Jazz | 833575-2
Gerry Mulligan Concert Jazz Band
Verve Jazz Masters 36:Gerry Mulligan | Verve | 523342-2
Jimmy Rushing And His Band
Planet Jazz:Jimmy Rushing | RCA | 2165371-2
Jimmy Smith With The Oliver Nelson Orchestra
Verve Jazz Masters 29:Jimmy Smith | Verve | 521855-2
Jimmy Smith:Best Of The Verve Years | Verve | 527950-2
Jimmy Smith-Talkin' Verve | Verve | 531563-2
Lawrence Brown With The Ralph Burns Orchestra
Slide Trombone | Verve | 559930-2
Lena Horne With The Lennie Hayton Orchestra
Planet Jazz:Lena Horne | Planet Jazz | 2165373-2
Maynard Ferguson And His Orchestra
Verve Jazz Masters 52:Maynard Ferguson | Verve | 529905-2
Miles Davis Septet
Miles Davis And Horns | Original Jazz Classics | OJC20 053-2(P 7025)
Milt Jackson Septet
The Birdlanders Vol.1 | Original Jazz Classics | OJCCD 1930-2
Oscar Pettiford Sextet
The Birdlanders Vol.2 | Original Jazz Classics | OJCCD 1931-2
Prestige All Stars
John Coltrane-The Prestige Recordings | Prestige | 16 PCD 4405-2
Tenor Conclave | Original Jazz Classics | OJCCD 127-2
Ralph Burns And His Orchestra
The Complete Verve Roy Eldridge Studio Sessions | Verve | 9861278
Shirley Horn With Orchestra
Loads Of Love + Shirley Horn With Horns | Mercury | 843454-2
Stan Getz Five Brothers Bop Tenor Sax Stars
Stan Getz:Imagination | Dreyfus Jazz Line | FDM 36733-2
Terry Gibbs Dream Band
Terry Gibbs Dream Band Vol.2:The Sundown Sessions | Contemporary | CCD 7652-2
The Four Brothers
Planet Jazz:Jazz Saxophone | Planet Jazz | 2169653-2
Together Again! | RCA | 2179623-2
Trigger Alpert's Absolutely All Star Seven
East Coast Sound | Original Jazz Classics | OJCCD 1012-2(JLP 11)
Woody Herman And His Orchestra
The Legends Of Swing | Laserlight | 24659
Woody Herman:Four Brother | Dreyfus Jazz Line | FDM 36722-2
Woody Herman And The New Thundering Herd
Planet Jazz:Big Bands | Planet Jazz | 2169649-2
Zoot Sims-Al Cohn Quintet
Jazz Alive:A Night At The Half Note | Blue Note | 494105-2
Zoot Sims-Al Cohn Sextet
The Brothers | Original Jazz Classics | OJCCD 008-2
Zoot Sims-Al Cohn-Phil Woods Sextet
Jazz Alive:A Night At The Half Note | Blue Note | 494105-2

Cohn,George | (tp)
Count Basie And His Orchestra
Afrique | RCA | 2179618-2

Cohn[Cohen],Sonny | (tpfl-h)
Big Joe Turner With The Count Basie Orchestra
Flip Flop And Fly | Original Jazz Classics | OJCCD 1053-2(2310937)
Count Basie And His Orchestra
Fun Time | Pablo | 2310945-2
Jazz Collection:Count Basie | Laserlight | 24368
The Legends Of Swing | Laserlight | 24659
Count Basie: Salle Pleyel, April 17th, 1972 | Laserlight | 36127
Atomic Swing | Roulette | 497871-2
Verve Jazz Masters 2:Count Basie | Verve | 519819-2
Basie Meets Bond | Capitol | 538225-2
Basie's Beatle Bag | Verve | 557455-2
Live at The Sands | Reprise | 9362-45946-2
88 Basie Street | Original Jazz Classics | OJC 808(2310901)
Jazz Dance | Original Jazz Classics | OJCCD 1002-2(1210890)
Fancy Pants | Original Jazz Classics | OJCCD 1038-2(2310920)
I Told You So | Original Jazz Classics | OJCCD 824-2(2310767)
Digital III At Montreux | Original Jazz Classics | OJCCD 996-2(2308223)
The Jazz Giants Play Harry Warren:Lullaby Of Broadway | Prestige | PCD 24204-2
Count Basie Big Band
Montreux '77 | Original Jazz Classics | OJCCD 377-2
Farmers Market Barbecue | Original Jazz Classics | OJCCD 732-2(2310874)
Diane Schuur With The Count Basie Orchestra
The Best Of Diane Schuur | GRP | GRP 98882
Duke Ellington And Count Basie With Their Orchestras
First Time! | CBS | CK 65571
Ella Fitzgerald With Count Basie And His Orchestra
Digital III At Montreux | Original Jazz Classics | OJCCD 996-2(2308223)
Ella Fitzgerald With The Count Basie Orchestra
Bluella:Ella Fitzgerald Sings The Blues | Pablo | 2310960-2
Ella Fitzgerald-First Lady Of Song | Verve | 517898-2
Ella And Basie | Verve | 539059-2
For The Love Of Ella Fitzgerald | Verve | 841765-2
Frank Sinatra With The Count Basie Orchestra
Sinatra-Basie:An Historic Musical First | Reprise | 7599-27023-2
It Might As Well Be Spring | Reprise | 7599-27027-2
Milt Jackson Orchestra
Sarah Vaughan Birthday Celebration | Fantasy | FANCD 6090-2
Milt Jackson With The Count Basie Orchestra
To Bags...With Love:Memorial Album | Pablo | 2310967-2
Milt Jackson Birthday Celebration | Fantasy | FANCD 6079-2
Milt Jackson + Count Basie + Big Band Vol.1 | Original Jazz Classics | OJCCD 740-2(2310822)
Milt Jackson + Count Basie + Big Band Vol.2 | Original Jazz Classics | OJCCD 741-2(2310823)
Sarah Vaughan And Joe Williams With The Count Basie Orchestra
Jazz Profile | Blue Note | 823517-2
Sarah Vaughan And The Count Basie Orchestra
Ballads | Roulette | 537561-2
Sarah Vaughan Birthday Celebration | Fantasy | FANCD 6090-2
Sarah Vaughan With The Count Basie Band
Jazz Profile | Blue Note | 823517-2

Coil,Pat | (keyboards,p,el-psynth)
Woody Herman And The New Thundering Herd
Planet Jazz:Big Bands | Planet Jazz | 2169649-2

Coker,Dolo | (p)
Art Pepper Quartet
Intensity | Original Jazz Classics | OJCCD 387-2
The Way It Is | Original Jazz Classics | OJCCD 389-2
The Jazz Giants Play Jerome Kern:Yesterdays | Prestige | PCD 24202-2
Dexter Gordon Quartet
Dexter Gordon Birthday Celebration | Fantasy | FANCD 6082-2
Harry Edison Quintet
Edison's Light | Original Jazz Classics | OJCCD 804-2(2310780)

Coker,Henry | (tbtp)
Count Basie And His Orchestra
Jazz Gallery:Lester Young Vol.2(1946-59) | RCA | 2119541-2
Jazz Collection:Count Basie | Laserlight | 24368
The Legends Of Swing | Laserlight | 24659
Atomic Swing | Roulette | 497871-2
Verve Jazz Masters 2:Count Basie | Verve | 519819-2
Count Basie Swings-Joe Williams Sings | Verve | 519852-2
Verve Jazz Masters 20:Introducing | Verve | 519853-2
April In Paris | Verve | 521402-2
Breakfast Dance And Barbecue | Roulette | 531791-2
One O'Clock Jump | Verve | 559806-2
Chairman Of The Board | Roulette | 581664-2
The Complete Atomic Basie | Roulette | 828635-2
King Of Swing | Verve | 837433-2
Count Basie At Newport | Verve | 9861761
Count On The Coast Vol.1 | Phontastic | NCD 7555
Count On The Coast Vol.2 | Phontastic | NCD 7575
Duke Ellington And Count Basie With Their Orchestras
First Time! | CBS | CK 65571
Ella Fitzgerald And Joe Williams With The Count Basie Octet
For The Love Of Ella Fitzgerald | Verve | 841765-2
Ella Fitzgerald With The Count Basie Orchestra
Ella Fitzgerald-First Lady Of Song | Verve | 517898-2
Ella And Basie | Verve | 539059-2
Frank Sinatra With The Count Basie Orchestra
Sinatra-Basie:An Historic Musical First | Reprise | 7599-27023-2
It Might As Well Be Spring | Reprise | 7599-27027-2
Sarah Vaughan And Joe Williams With The Count Basie Orchestra
Jazz Profile | Blue Note | 823517-2
Sarah Vaughan And The Count Basie Orchestra
Ballads | Roulette | 537561-2
Sarah Vaughan And The Thad Jones Orchestra
Verve Jazz Masters 42:Sarah Vaughan-The Jazz Sides | Verve | 526817-2
Sarah Vaughan With The Count Basie Band
Jazz Profile | Blue Note | 823517-2
Tadd Dameron And His Orchestra
Fontainebleau | Original Jazz Classics | OJCCD 055-2

Coker,Jerry | (cl,tsarr)
Nat Pierce/Dick Collins Nonet
Nat Pierce-Dick Collins-Ralph Burns & The Herdsmen Play Paris | Fantasy | FCD 24759-2
The Herdsmen
Nat Pierce-Dick Collins-Ralph Burns & The Herdsmen Play Paris | Fantasy | FCD 24759-2

Cola,George 'Kid Sheik' | (tpvoc)
Eureka Brass Band
Atlantic Jazz: New Orleans | Atlantic | 7567-81700-2

Colaiuta,Vinnie | (dr,perc,keyboards,synth,b,sampling)
Diane Schuur Quintet With B.B.King
The Best Of Diane Schuur | GRP | GRP 98882
John McLaughlin Group
The Promise | Verve | 529828-2
John Patitucci Group
Sketchbook | GRP | GRP 96172
The Quincy Jones-Sammy Nestico Orchestra
Basie & Beyond | Warner | 9362-47792-2

Colazo,Julio | (perc)
Dizzy Gillespie And His Orchestra
Gillespiana And Carnegie Hall Concert | Verve | 519809-2
Talking Verve:Dizzy Gillespie | Verve | 533846-2
Ultimate Dizzy Gillespie | Verve | 557535-2

Cold Sweat |
Cold Sweat
Cold Sweat Plays J.B. | JMT Edition | 919025-2

Cole,Buddy | (orgp)
JATP All Stars
The Complete Jazz At The Philharmonic On Verve 1944-1949 | Verve | 523893-2
Rosemary Clooney With The Buddy Cole Trio
Swing Around Rosie | Coral | 589485-2

Cole,Buddy prob. | (celeste)
Nat King Cole Trio
Nat King Cole:Route 66 | Dreyfus Jazz Line | FDM 36716-2

Cole,Dick | (tb)
Stan Kenton And His Orchestra
Stan Kenton-The Formative Years | Decca | 589489-2

Cole,Freddy | (pvoc)
Freddie Cole
Jazzin' Vol.2: The Music Of Stevie Wonder | Fantasy | FANCD 6088-2
Freddy Cole With Band
A Circle Of Love | Fantasy | FCD 9674-2
To The End Of The Earth | Fantasy | FCD 9675-2
Le Grand Freddy:Freddy Cole Sings The Music Of Michel Legrand | Fantasy | FCD 9683-2
Freddy Cole With The Cedar Walton Trio
Love Makes The Changes | Fantasy | FCD 9681-2
Freddy Cole With The Cedar Walton Trio And Grover Washington Jr.
Love Makes The Changes | Fantasy | FCD 9681-2
Freddy Cole With The Eric Alexander Band
Love Makes The Changes | Fantasy | FCD 9681-2
Jimmy Scott With Band
But Beautiful | Milestone | MCD 9321-2

Cole,Holly | (voc)
Holly Cole And Her Quartet
It Happened One Night | Metro Blue | 852699-0
Holly Cole Trio
Misty Blue:Sweet Sisters Swing Songs Of Sorrow And Sadness | Blue Note | 521151-2

Cole,June | (b,voctuba)
Bessie Smith And Her Band
Jazz:The Essential Collection Vol.1 | IN+OUT Records | 78011-2
Willie Lewis And His Entertainers
Americans Swinging In Paris:Benny Carter | EMI Records | 539647-2

Cole,Nat King | (p,orgvoc)
JATP All Stars
The Complete Jazz At The Philharmonic On Verve 1944-1949 | Verve | 523893-2
Jazz At The Philharmonic:Best Of The 1940's Concerts | Verve | 557534-2
Lester Young Trio
Verve Jazz Masters 30:Lester Young | Verve | 521859-2
Lester Young:Blue Lester | Dreyfus Jazz Line | FDM 36729-2
Lester Young-Nat Cole Trio
Lester Young:The Complete Aladdin Sessions | Blue Note | 832787-2
Midnight Blue(The [Be]witching Hour) | Blue Note | 854365-2
Lester Young:Blue Lester | Dreyfus Jazz Line | FDM 36729-2
Lester Young-Nat King Cole
Jazz:The Essential Collection Vol.3 | IN+OUT Records | 78013-2
Lester Young:Blue Lester | Dreyfus Jazz Line | FDM 36729-2
Lionel Hampton And His Orchestra
Planet Jazz:Lionel Hampton | Planet Jazz | 2152059-2
Lionel Hampton:Flying Home | Dreyfus Jazz Line | FDM 36735-2
Nat King Cole And George Shearing With Orchestra
Midnight Blue(The [Be]witching Hour) | Blue Note | 854365-2
Nat King Cole And His Trio
Nat King Cole:The Snader Telescriptions | Storyville | 4960103
Nat King Cole:Route 66 | Dreyfus Jazz Line | FDM 36716-2
Nat King Cole And His Trio With Strings
Nat King Cole:The Snader Telescriptions | Storyville | 4960103
Nat King Cole Duo
Nat King Cole:The Snader Telescriptions | Storyville | 4960103
Nat King Cole Quartet
Penthouse Serenade | Capitol | 494504-2
The Instrumental Classics | Capitol | 798288-2
Nat King Cole:For Sentimental Reasons | Dreyfus Jazz Line | FDM 36740-2
Nat King Cole Quartet With The Pete Rugolo Orchestra
The Instrumental Classics | Capitol | 798288-2
Nat King Cole Quartet With The Stan Kenton Orchestra
Nat King Cole:For Sentimental Reasons | Dreyfus Jazz Line | FDM 36740-2
Nat King Cole Quintet
Penthouse Serenade | Capitol | 494504-2
After Midnight | Capitol | 520087-2
Nat King Cole Sextet
After Midnight | Capitol | 520087-2
Nat King Cole Trio
The Legends Of Swing | Laserlight | 24659
Penthouse Serenade | Capitol | 494504-2
Nat King Cole:The Snader Telescriptions | Storyville | 4960103
The Small Black Groups | Storyville | 4960523
Live At The Circle Room | Capitol | 521859-2
The Instrumental Classics | Capitol | 798288-2
The Best Of The Nat King Cole Trio:The Vocal Classics(1942-1946) | Blue Note | 833571-2
Nat King Cole:Route 66 | Dreyfus Jazz Line | FDM 36716-2
Nat King Cole:For Sentimental Reasons | Dreyfus Jazz Line | FDM 36740-2
Love Songs | Nimbus Records | NI 2010
Nat King Cole Trio With Frank DeVol's Orchestra
Nat King Cole:Route 66 | Dreyfus Jazz Line | FDM 36716-2
Nat King Cole Trio With Pete Rugolo's Orchestra
Nat King Cole:For Sentimental Reasons | Dreyfus Jazz Line | FDM 36740-2
Nat King Cole Trio With Strings
Nat King Cole:For Sentimental Reasons | Dreyfus Jazz Line | FDM 36740-2
Nat King Cole With Orchestra
Nat King Cole:Route 66 | Dreyfus Jazz Line | FDM 36716-2
Nat King Cole With The Billy May Orchestra
Nat King Cole:For Sentimental Reasons | Dreyfus Jazz Line | FDM 36740-2
The Capitol Jazzmen
The Hollywood Session:The Capitol Jazzmen | Jazz Unlimited | JUCD 2044

Cole,Richie | (as,mega-universal-sax-orchestra,ts)
Buddy Rich Big Band
Keep The Customer Satisfied | EMI Records | 523999-2
Greg Abate Quintet
Dr. Jeckyll & Mr. Hyde | Candid | CCD 79715
Richie Cole Group
Jazz Life Vol.1:From Village Vanguard | Storyville | 4960753

Cole,Rupert | (as,clreeds)
Louis Armstrong And His Orchestra
Louis Armstrong:Swing That Music | Laserlight | 36056
Jazz:The Essential Collection Vol.2 | IN+OUT Records | 78012-2
Louis Armstrong:C'est Si Bon | Dreyfus Jazz Line | FDM 36730-2
Louis Armstrong-My Greatest Songs | MCA | MCD 18347
Swing Legends:Louis Armstrong | Nimbus Records | NI 2012

Cole,William 'Cozy' | (dr,speechtimales)
Billie Holiday And Her All Stars
Billie Holiday Story Vol.4:Lady Sings The Blues | Verve | 521429-2
Billie Holiday With Sy Oliver And His Orchestra
Billie's Love Songs | Nimbus Records | NI 2000
Billie Holiday With Teddy Wilson And His Orchestra
Billie's Love Songs | Nimbus Records | NI 2000
Bud Freeman All Stars
The Bud Freeman All-Star Sessions | Prestige | PRCD 24286-2
Coleman Hawkins Quartet
Verve Jazz Masters 43:Coleman Hawkins | Verve | 521856-2
Ultimate Coleman Hawkins selected by Sonny Rollins | Verve | 557538-2
Coleman Hawkins Quintet
Verve Jazz Masters 43:Coleman Hawkins | Verve | 521856-2
Ultimate Coleman Hawkins selected by Sonny Rollins | Verve | 557538-2
Jazz:The Essential Collection Vol.3 | IN+OUT Records | 78013-2
Cozy Cole All Stars
Ultimate Coleman Hawkins selected by Sonny Rollins | Verve | 557538-2
Jazz:The Essential Collection Vol.3 | IN+OUT Records | 78013-2
Cozy Cole's Big Seven
Body And Soul Revisited | GRP | GRP 16272
Dizzy Gillespie Sextet

Dizzy Gillespie:Night In Tunisia | Dreyfus Jazz Line | FDM 36734-2
Henry Red Allen's All Stars
Planet Jazz:Coleman Hawkins | Planet Jazz | 2152055-2
Jack Teagarden With The Red Allen Band
The Very Best Of Dixieland Jazz | Verve | 535529-2
Lionel Hampton And His Orchestra
Planet Jazz:Coleman Hawkins | Planet Jazz | 2152055-2
Planet Jazz:Ben Webster | RCA | 2165368-2
Planet Jazz:Jazz Saxophone | Planet Jazz | 2169653-2
Planet Jazz:Male Jazz Vocalists | Planet Jazz | 2169657-2
Jazz:The Essential Collection Vol.3 | IN+OUT Records | 78013-2
Louis Armstrong And Ella Fitzgerald With Bob Hagger's Orchestra
Louis Armstrong:C'est Si Bon | Dreyfus Jazz Line | FDM 36730-2
Louis Armstrong And His All Stars
Planet Jazz:Louis Armstrong | Planet Jazz | 2152052-2
Planet Jazz:Jack Teagarden | Planet Jazz | 2161236-2
Planet Jazz:Male Jazz Vocalists | Planet Jazz | 2169657-2
Best Of The Complete RCA Victor Recordings | RCA | 2663636-2
Louis Armstrong:A 100th Birthday Celebration | RCA | 2663694-2
I Love Jazz | Verve | 543747-2
Satchmo Serenaders | Verve | 543792-2
Louis Armstrong:C'est Si Bon | Dreyfus Jazz Line | FDM 36730-2
Louis Armstrong-My Greatest Songs | MCA | MCD 18347
Swing Legends:Louis Armstrong | Nimbus Records | NI 2012
Louis Armstrong And His Orchestra
Satchmo Serenaders | Verve | 543792-2
Louis Armstrong:C'est Si Bon | Dreyfus Jazz Line | FDM 36730-2
Swing Legends:Louis Armstrong | Nimbus Records | NI 2012
Louis Armstrong With Gordon Jenkins And His Orchestra And Choir
Satchmo In Style | Verve | 549594-2
Louis Armstrong With Sy Oliver And His Orchestra
Satchmo Serenaders | Verve | 543792-2
Louis Armstrong With The Gordon Jenkins Orchestra
Ambassador Louis Armstrong Vol.17:Moments To Remember(1952-1956) | Ambassador | CLA 1917
Sarah Vaughan The The Joe Lippman Orchestra
Sarah Vaughan:Lover Man | Dreyfus Jazz Line | FDM 36739-2
Teddy Wilson And His All Stars
Jazz:The Essential Collection Vol.3 | IN+OUT Records | 78013-2
Teddy Wilson And His Orchestra
Jazz:The Essential Collection Vol.3 | IN+OUT Records | 78013-2
V-Disc All Star Jam Session
Louis Armstrong-Jack Teagarden-Woody Herman:Midnights At V-Disc | Jazz Unlimited | JUCD 2048
V-Disc All Stars
Jazz:The Essential Collection Vol.3 | IN+OUT Records | 78013-2
Willie Bryant And His Orchestra
Planet Jazz:Ben Webster | RCA | 2165368-2
Wingy Mannone And His Orchestra
Planet Jazz:Jazz Trumpet | Planet Jazz | 2169654-2
Planet Jazz:Male Jazz Vocalists | Planet Jazz | 2169657-2

Coleman,Anthony | (keyboards,keyboard-sampler,org,p)
John Zorn Group
Spillane | Nonesuch | 7559-79172-2
Marc Ribot Y Los Cubanos Postizos
The Prosthetic Cubans | Atlantic | 7567-83116-2
Nuy Divertido(Very Entertaining) | Atlantic | 7567-83293-2

Coleman,Bill | (b,voc,fl-htp)
Alix Combelle Et Son Orchestre
Americans Swinging In Paris:Bill Coleman-The Elegance | EMI Records | 539662-2
Bill Coleman And His Orchestra
Don Byas:Laura | Dreyfus Jazz Line | FDM 36714-2
Bill Coleman Et Son Orchestre
Americans Swinging In Paris:Bill Coleman-The Elegance | EMI Records | 539662-2
Bill Coleman Quintet
Americans Swinging In Paris:Don Byas | EMI Records | 539655-2
Americans Swinging In Paris:Bill Coleman-The Elegance | EMI Records | 539662-2
Bill Coleman Septet
Jazz In Paris:Bill Coleman-From Boogie To Funk | EmArCy | 549401-2 PMS
Bill Coleman Sextet
Americans Swinging In Paris:Bill Coleman | EMI Records | 539663-2
Bill Coleman-Django Reinhardt Duo
Americans Swinging In Paris:Bill Coleman-The Elegance | EMI Records | 539662-2
Bill Ramsey With Eric Krans Dixieland Pipers And Guests
Caldonia And More... | Bear Family Records | BCD 16151 AH
Coleman Hawkins And His Orchestra
Jazz:The Essential Collection Vol.3 | IN+OUT Records | 78013-2
Dicky Wells And His Orchestra
Americans Swinging In Paris:Dicky Wells | EMI Records | 539664-2
Jazz:The Essential Collection Vol.3 | IN+OUT Records | 78013-2
Eddie Brunner And His Orchestra
Americans Swinging In Paris:Bill Coleman-The Elegance | EMI Records | 539662-2
Kansas City Six
Lester Young:Blue Lester | Dreyfus Jazz Line | FDM 36729-2
The Capitol Jazzmen
The Hollywood Session:The Capitol Jazzmen | Jazz Unlimited | JUCD 2044

Coleman,Dave | (dr)
Billie Holiday With The JATP All Stars
Billie Holiday Story Vol.1:Jazz At The Philharmonic | Verve | 521642-2
The Complete Jazz At The Philharmonic On Verve 1944-1949 | Verve | 523893-2
Verve Jazz Masters 47:Billie Holiday Sings Standards | Verve | 527650-2
JATP All Stars
The Complete Jazz At The Philharmonic On Verve 1944-1949 | Verve | 523893-2

Coleman,Denardo | (dr,perc,programming,keyboards)
Pat Metheny/Ornette Coleman Group
Song X | Geffen Records | GED 24096

Coleman,Earl | (voc)
Elmo Hope Ensemble
Sounds From Rikers Island | Fresh Sound Records | FSR CD 338
Sonny Rollins Quartet
Tour De Force | Original Jazz Classics | OJCCD 095-2

Coleman,Eddie | (b)
Cal Tjader Quartet
Our Blues | Fantasy | FCD 24771-2
Cal Tjader Quintet
Our Blues | Fantasy | FCD 24771-2
Concerts In The Sun | Fantasy | FCD 9688-2

Coleman,Gary | (percvib)
Dee Dee Bridgewater With Band
Dee Dee Bridgewater | Atlantic | 7567-80760-2
Grant Green Septet
Live At The Lighthouse | Blue Note | 493381-2
Stanley Turrentine And His Orchestra
Pieces Of Dream | Original Jazz Classics | OJCCD 831-2(F 9465)

Coleman,George | (as,ts,cl,ssvoc)
Ahmad Jamal Quartet
Ahmad Jamal À L'Olympia | Dreyfus Jazz Line | FDM 36629-2
Ahmad Jamal Quintet
The Essence Part 1 | Dreyfus Jazz Line | FDM 37007-2
Ahmad Jamal Septet
Live In Paris 1996 | Dreyfus Jazz Line | FDM 37020-2
Charles Mingus Orchestra
Three Or Four Shades Of Blues | Atlantic | 7567-81403-2
Chet Baker Quintet
The Jazz Giants Play Rodgers & Hart:Blue Moon | Prestige | PCD 24205-2
Groovin' With The Chet Baker Quintet | Prestige | PR20 7460-2
Comin' On With The Chet Baker Quintet | Prestige | PR20 7478-2
Cool Burnin' With The Chet Baker Quintet | Prestige | PR20 7496-2
Boppin' With The Chet Baker Quintet | Prestige | PR20 7512-2
Smokin' With The Chet Baker Quintet | Prestige | PR20 7749-2
Frank Stozier Sextet
Long Night | Milestone | MCD 47095-2
Herbie Hancock Quintet
Maiden Voyage | Blue Note | 495331-2
Herbie Hancock:The Complete Blue Note Sixties Sessions | Blue Note | 495569-2
The Best Of Blue Note | Blue Note | 796110-2
Cantaloupe Island | Blue Note | 829331-2
Horace Silver Quintet
Horace Silver Retrospective | Blue Note | 495576-2
Blue Velvet: Crooners, Swooners And Velvet Vocals | Blue Note | 521153-2
Jimmy Smith All Stars
House Party | Blue Note | 524542-2
John Patton Quartet
Accent On The Blues | Blue Note | 853924-2
Lee Morgan Sextet
Deep Blue-The United States Of Mind | Blue Note | 521152-2
Sonic Boom | Blue Note | 590414-2
Max Roach Plus Four
Clifford Brown-Max Roach:Alone Together-The Best Of The Mercury Years | Verve | 526373-2
Max Roach Quintet
Clifford Brown-Max Roach:Alone Together-The Best Of The Mercury Years | Verve | 526373-2
Deeds Not Words | Original Jazz Classics | OJC20 304-2(RLP 1122)
The Jazz Giants Play Sammy Cahn:It's Magic | Prestige | PCD 24226-2
Max Roach Sextet
Deeds Not Words | Original Jazz Classics | OJC20 304-2(RLP 1122)
Miles Davis Quintet
Ballads | CBS | 461099-2
The Complete Concert 1964:My Funny Valentine+Four & More | CBS | 471246-2
Seven Steps To Heaven | CBS | CK 48827
Reuben Wilson Sextet
The Lost Grooves | Blue Note | 831883-2
Wynton Kelly-George Coleman Quartet
Live at The Left Bank Jazz Society,Baltimore,1968 | Fresh Sound Records | FSCD 1032

Coleman,Gloria | (org)
Gloria Coleman Quartet
Soul Sisters | Impulse(MCA) | 8961048

Coleman,Ira | (b)
Antonio Farao Trio
Black Inside | Enja | ENJ-9345 2
Byron Stripling Quartet
Byron,Get On Free | Nagel-Heyer | CD 2016
Byron Stripling Quintet
Byron,Get On Free | Nagel-Heyer | CD 2016
Byron Stripling Sextet
Byron,Get On Free | Nagel-Heyer | CD 2016
David Klein Quintet
My Marilyn | Enja | ENJ-9422 2
Dee Dee Bridgewater With Band
This Is New | Verve | 016884-2
Dee Dee Bridgewater Sings Kurt Weill | EmArCy | 9809601
Franco Ambrosetti Quintet
Live At The Blue Note | Enja | ENJ-7065 2
Joe Chambers Quartet
Mirrors | Blue Note | 496685-2
Joe Chambers Quintet
Mirrors | Blue Note | 496685-2
Joe Chambers Trio
Mirrors | Blue Note | 496685-2
Klaus Doldinger Group
Back In New York:Blind Date | Atlantic | 3984-26922-2

Coleman,Jerry | (dr)
Singers Unlimited
The Singers Unlimited:Magic Voices | MPS | 539130-2

Coleman,Montez | (dr)
Claus Raible Sextet
Loopin' With Lea | Organic Music | ORGM 9724

Coleman,Ornette | (as,ts,v,tpcomp)
Charlie Haden-Ornette Coleman
Closeness Duets | Verve | 397000-2
Gunther Schuller Ensemble
Beauty Is A Rare Thing:Ornette Coleman-The Complete Atlantic Recordings | Atlantic | 8122-71410-2
Ornette Coleman Double Quartet
Beauty Is A Rare Thing:Ornette Coleman-The Complete Atlantic Recordings | Atlantic | 8122-71410-2
Free Jazz | Atlantic | 8122-75208-2
Ornette Coleman Quartet
This Is Our Music | Atlantic | 7567-80767-2
Change Of The Century | Atlantic | 7567-81341-2
Atlantic Saxophones | Rhino | 8122-71256-2
Rhino Presents The Atlantic Jazz Gallery | Atlantic | 8122-71257-2
Beauty Is A Rare Thing:Ornette Coleman-The Complete Atlantic Recordings | Atlantic | 8122-71410-2
Ornette On Tenor | Atlantic | 8122-71455-2
Tomorrow Is The Question | Original Jazz Classics | OJC20 342-2(S 7569)
Ornette Coleman Quintet
The Music Of Ornette Coleman:Something Else!! | Original Jazz Classics | OJC20 163-2
Ornette Coleman Trio
At The Golden Circle Vol.One | Blue Note | 535518-2
Pat Metheny/Ornette Coleman Group
Song X | Geffen Records | GED 24096
Rolf Kühn And Friends
Affairs:Rolf Kühn & Friends | Intuition Records | INT 3211-2

Coleman,Steve | (as,perc,voc,fl,cl,ssp)
Abbey Lincoln With Her Band
Who Used To Dance | Verve | 533559-2
Cassandra Wilson And Her Quintet
Point Of View | JMT Edition | 919004-2
Cassandra Wilson Group
Traveling Miles | Blue Note | 854123-2
Dave Holland Qartet
Extensions | ECM | 1410(841778-2)
Dave Holland Quintet
Jumpin' In | ECM | 1269
Seeds Of Time | ECM | 1292
The Razor's Edge | ECM | 1353
Dave Holland Trio
Triplicate | ECM | 1373
Steve Coleman And Five Elements
Curves Of Life | Novus | 2131693-2
Genesis & The Opening Of The Way | RCA | 2152934-2
The Sonic Language Of Myth | RCA | 2164123-2
On The Edge Of Tomorrow | JMT Edition | 919005-2
Steve Coleman And Metrics
A Tale Of 3 Cities,The EP | Novus | 2124747-2
The Way Of The Cipher | Novus | 2131690-2
Steve Coleman And The Council Of Balance
Genesis & The Opening Of The Way | RCA | 2152934-2
Steve Coleman Group
Motherland Pulse | JMT Edition | 919001-2

Coleman,Thomas 'Beale Street' | (dr)
Mose Vinson Band
Joe Hill Louis: The Be-Bop Boy | Bear Family Records | BCD 15524 AH

Coleridge Perkinson Choir,The |
Donald Byrd Orchestra With Voices
The Best Of Blue Note | Blue Note | 796110-2

Coles,Elmer | (tp)
Charles Earland Septet
Charles Earland In Concert | Prestige | PRCD 24267-2

Coles,Johnny | (fl-htp)
Astrud Gilberto With The Al Cohn Orchestra
Verve Jazz Masters 9:Astrud Gilberto | Verve | 519824-2
Astrud Gilberto With The Gil Evans Orchestra
Verve Jazz Masters 9:Astrud Gilberto | Verve | 519824-2
Verve Jazz Masters 23:Gil Evans | Verve | 521860-2
Charles Mingus Sextet
Eric Dolphy Birthday Celebration | Fantasy | FANCD 6085-2
Town Hall Concert 1964, Vol.1 | Original Jazz Classics | OJCCD 042-2
Duke Ellington And His Orchestra
Highlights From The Duke Ellington Centennial Edition | RCA | 2663672-2
The Ellington Suites | Original Jazz Classics | OJC20 446-2(2310762)
Geri Allen And The Jazzpar 1996 Nonet
Some Aspects Of Water | Storyville | STCD 4212
Geri Allen Trio With Johny Coles
Some Aspects Of Water | Storyville | STCD 4212
Gil Evans Orchestra
Verve Jazz Masters 23:Gil Evans | Verve | 521860-2
The Individualism Of Gil Evans | Verve | 833804-2
Out Of The Cool | Impulse(MCA) | 951186-2
Blues In Orbit | Enja | ENJ-3069 2
Grant Green Quintet
Am I Blue | Blue Note | 535564-2
Herbie Hancock Orchestra
Herbie Hancock:The Complete Blue Note Sixties Sessions | Blue Note | 495569-2
The Prisoner | Blue Note | 525649-2
James Moody Orchestra
The Blues And Other Colors | Original Jazz Classics | OJCCD 954-2(M 9023)
Johnny Coles Sextet
True Blue | Blue Note | 534032-2
Kenny Burrell With The Gil Evans Orchestra
Guitar Forms | Verve | 521403-2
Verve Jazz Masters 23:Gil Evans | Verve | 521860-2
Verve Jazz Masters 45:Kenny Burrell | Verve | 527652-2
Verve Jazz Masters Vol.60:The Collection | Verve | 529866-2
Miles Davis With Gil Evans & His Orchestra
Miles Davis At Carnegie Hall | CBS | CK 65027
This Is Jazz:Miles Davis Plays Ballads | CBS | CK 65038
Porgy And Bess | CBS | CK 65141
Sketches Of Spain | CBS | CK 65142
Quiet Nights | CBS | CK 65293
Ray Crawford Sextet
Smooth Groove | Candid | CCD 79028
Tina Brooks Quintet
The Waiting Game | Blue Note | 540536-2

Coletta,Francis | (g)
Francis Coletta Trio + One
Cris De Balaines | IN+OUT Records | 77030-2

Coletta,Harold | (viola)
Phil Woods Quartet With Orchestra & Strings
Round Trip | Verve | 559804-2
Wes Montgomery With The Don Sebesky Orchestra
Verve Jazz Masters 14:Wes Montgomery | Verve | 519826-2
Talkin' Jazz:Roots Of Acid Jazz | Verve | 529580-2
Bumpin' | Verve | 539062-2

Colianni,John | (p,ldp-solo)
John Colianni
Prime Cuts | Jazz Connaisseur | JCCD 9935-2

Colin,Lois | (harp)
Tom Harrell Group
Paradise | RCA | 2663738-2

Collaza,Michael | (perctimbales)
Earl Klugh Group
Late Night Guitar | Blue Note | 498573-2

Collazo,Julio | (african-drtimbales)
Machito And His Orchestra
Afro-Cuban Jazz Moods | Original Jazz Classics | OJC20 447-2

Collective 3 +,The |
The Collective 3 +
The Collective 3 + | true muze | TUMU CD 9802

Collett,Dave | (p)
Mr.Acker Bilk And His Paramount Jazz Band
The Very Best Of Dixieland Jazz | Verve | 535529-2

Colletta,Harold | (v)
Ben Webster With Orchestra And Strings
Music For Loving:Ben Webster With Strings | Verve | 527774-2
Ultimate Ben Webster selected by James Carter | Verve | 557537-2

Collette,Buddy | (alto-cl,soprano-cl,as,bs,cl,fl)
Barney Kessel And His Orchestra
Barney Kessel Plays Carmen | Original Jazz Classics | OJC 269(C 7563)
The Jazz Giants Play Rodgers & Hart:Blue Moon | Prestige | PCD 24205-2
Benny Carter And His Orchestra
Aspects | Capitol | 852677-2
Further Definitions/Additions To Further Definotions | Impulse(MCA) | 951229-2
Billy Eckstine With The Billy May Orchestra
Once More With Feeling | Roulette | 581862-2
Charles Mingus And His Orchestra
The Complete Town Hall Concert | Blue Note | 828353-2
Chico Hamilton Orchestra
With Strings Attached/The Three Faces Of Chico | Warner | 9362-47874-2
Ella Fitzgerald With Frank De Vol And His Orchestra
Get Happy! | Verve | 523321-2
Ella Fitzgerald With The Nelson Riddle Orchestra
The Best Of The Song Books:The Ballads | Verve | 521867-2
Oh Lady Be Good:The Best Of The Gershwin Songbook | Verve | 529581-2
Love Songs:The Best Of The Song Books | Verve | 531762-2
Ella Fitzgerald Sings The Johnny Mercer Songbook | Verve | 539057-2
Horace Silver Quintet With Brass
Horace Silver Retrospective | Blue Note | 495576-2
Howard Rumsey's Lighthouse All-Stars
Oboe/Flute | Original Jazz Classics | OJCCD 154-2(C 3520)
June Christy With The Pete Rugolo Orchestra
Something Cool(The Complete Mono & Stereo Versions) | Capitol | 534069-2
Peggy Lee With The Quincy Jones Orchestra
Blues Cross Country | Capitol | 520088-2
Pete Rugolo And His Orchestra
Thriller/Richard Diamon(Original Jazz Scores From 2 Classics TV Series) | Fresh Sound Records | FSCD 2015
Red Norvo Sextet
Music To Listen To Red Norvo By | Original Jazz Classics | OJCCD 1015-2(C 7534)
Zoot Sims With Orchestra
Passion Flower | Original Jazz Classics | OJCCD 939-2(2312120)

Colley,Scott | (bperc)
Chris Potter & Jazzpar Septet
This Will Be | Storyville | STCD 4245
Chris Potter Group
Traveling Mercies | Verve | 018243-2
Chris Potter Quartet
Gratitude | Verve | 549433-2
This Will Be | Storyville | STCD 4245
David Binney Group
South | ACT | 9279-2
Greg Osby Quartet With String Quartet
Symbols Of Light(A Solution) | Blue Note | 531395-2
Jam Session

Jam Session Vol.2 | Steeplechase | SCCD 31523
Joachim Kühn Group
Universal Time | EmArCy | 016671-2
Josh Roseman Unit
Cherry | Enja | ENJ-9392 2
Renee Rosnes Quartet
Art & Soul | Blue Note | 499997-2
Renee Rosnes Trio
Art & Soul | Blue Note | 499997-2
Roy Hargrove Quintet
Planet Jazz:Jazz Trumpet | Planet Jazz | 2169654-2
Willie Williams Trio
WW3 | Enja | ENJ-8060 2

Collier,Clarence | (b)
Buddy Johnson And His Orchestra
Buddy And Ella Johnson 1953-1964 | Bear Family Records | BCD 15479 DH

Collier,Earl | (tpvoc)
Stan Kenton And His Orchestra
Stan Kenton-The Formative Years | Decca | 589489-2

Collier,Kathy | (voc)
Les McCann Group
Another Beginning | Atlantic | 7567-80790-2

Collier,Ralph | (congasdr)
Peggy Lee With Benny Goodman And His Quintet
Peggy Lee & Benny Goodman:The Complete Recordings 1941-1947 | CBS | C2K 65686
Peggy Lee With Benny Goodman And His Sextet
Peggy Lee & Benny Goodman:The Complete Recordings 1941-1947 | CBS | C2K 65686
Peggy Lee With The Benny Goodman Orchestra
Peggy Lee & Benny Goodman:The Complete Recordings 1941-1947 | CBS | C2K 65686

Collier,Robert | (congas)
Wardell Gray Quartet
Wardell Gray Memorial Vol.2 | Original Jazz Classics | OJCCD 051-2(P 7009)
Wardell Gray Quintet
Wardell Gray Memorial Vol.2 | Original Jazz Classics | OJCCD 051-2(P 7009)

Colligan,George | (dr,ensoniq ASR,org,p,el-p,tpp-solo)
Alex Norris Quintet
A New Beginning | Fresh Sound Records | FSNT 081 CD
Andrew Rathbun Group
True Stories | Fresh Sound Records | FSNT 099 CD
Dave Ballou Quartet
Rothko | Steeplechase | SCCD 31525
Gary Thomas Group
Found On Sordid Street | Winter&Winter | 910002-2
George Colligan
Return To Copenhagen | Steeplechase | SCCD 31519
George Colligan Group
Unresolved | Fresh Sound Records | FSNT 054 CD
George Colligan Quartet
Desire | Fresh Sound Records | FSNT 071 CD
Ingrid Jensen Quintet
Here On Earth | Enja | ENJ-9313 2
Jam Session
Jam Session Vol.4 | Steeplechase | SCCD 31527
Jam Session Vol.6 | Steeplechase | SCCD 31537
Johannes Enders Quintet
Bright Nights | Enja | ENJ-9352 2
Marcus Printup Sextet
The New Boogaloo | Nagel-Heyer | CD 2019
Mark Turner-Chris Cheek Quintet
The Music Of Mercedes Rossy | Fresh Sound Records | FSNT 043 CD

Collignon,Médéric | (pocket-co,fl-h,voice,pocket-tp,horn)
Louis Sclavis Group
Napoli's Walls | ECM | 1857(038504-2)
Orchestre National De Jazz
Charmediterranéen | ECM | 1828(018493-2)

Collings,Bruce | (tb)
Klaus König Orchestra
Times Of Devastation/Poco A Poco | Enja | ENJ-6014 22
Klaus König Orchestra & Guests
The Song Of Songs:Oratorio For Two Solo Voices,Choir And Orchestra | Enja | ENJ-7057 2

Collins,Albert | (gvoc)
John Zorn Group
Spillane | Nonesuch | 7559-79172-2

Collins,Bert | (tpfl-h)
Grant Green With Orchestra
The Final Comedown(Soundtrack) | Blue Note | 581678-2
J.J.Johnson And His Orchestra
Planet Jazz:J.J.Johnson | Planet Jazz | 2159974-2
Jimmy McGriff Orchestra
Swingin' The Blues-Jumpin' The Blues | Laserlight | 24654
Oliver Nelson And His Orchestra
Verve Jazz Masters Vol.60:The Collection | Verve | 529866-2

Collins,Bob | (tb)
Cal Tjader Quartet
Cal Tjader Plays Jazz | Original Jazz Classics | OJCCD 986-2(F 3-211)
Dave Brubeck Octet
The Dave Brubeck Octet | Original Jazz Classics | OJCCD 101-2(F 3239)

Collins,Burt | (fl-h,tb,tppiccolo-tp)
Blue Mitchell And His Orchestra
Blue Breaks Beats Vol.2 | Blue Note | 789907-2
Jack McDuff Quartet With Orchestra
Prelude:Jack McDuff Big Band | Prestige | PRCD 24283-2
Stanley Turrentine And His Orchestra
The Lost Grooves | Blue Note | 831883-2

Collins,Cal | (gg-solo)
Benny Goodman And His Orchestra
40th Anniversary Concert-Live At Carnegie Hall | London | 820349-2
Verve Jazz Masters 33:Benny Goodman | Verve | 844410-2
Benny Goodman Quartet
Verve Jazz Masters 33:Benny Goodman | Verve | 844410-2
Benny Goodman Septet
Verve Jazz Masters 33:Benny Goodman | Verve | 844410-2
Benny Goodman Sextet
Verve Jazz Masters 33:Benny Goodman | Verve | 844410-2

Collins,Dick | (tp)
Cal Tjader's Orchestra
Tjader Plays Mambo | Original Jazz Classics | OJCCD 274-2(F 3221)
Charlie Mariano Sextet
The Jazz Scene:San Francisco | Fantasy | FCD 24760-2
Dave Brubeck Octet
The Dave Brubeck Octet | Original Jazz Classics | OJCCD 101-2(F 3239)
Nat Pierce/Dick Collins Nonet
Nat Pierce-Dick Collins-Ralph Burns & The Herdsmen Play Paris | Fantasy | FCD 24759-2
Paul Desmond Quintet
Desmond | Original Jazz Classics | OJCCD 712-2(F 3235/8082)
The Herdsmen
Nat Pierce-Dick Collins-Ralph Burns & The Herdsmen Play Paris | Fantasy | FCD 24759-2

Collins,Howard | (g)
Bobby Timmons Orchestra
Quartet And Orchestra | Milestone | MCD 47091-2
Coleman Hawkins Septet
Desafinado | Impulse(MCA) | 951227-2
Coleman Hawkins Sextet
Desafinado | Impulse(MCA) | 951227-2
John Lewis Quartet
Eviolution II | Atlantic | 7567-83313-2
Modern Jazz Quartet And Orchestra
MJQ 40 | Atlantic | 7567-82330-2

Collins,Jay | (flts)
Jacky Terrasson Group
What It Is | Blue Note | 498756-2

Collins,John | (el-gg)
Benny Carter And His Orchestra
Further Definitions/Additions To Further Definotions | Impulse(MCA) | 951229-2
Billie Holiday With Eddie Heywood And His Orchestra
Billie's Love Songs | Nimbus Records | NI 2000
Billie Holiday With The JATP All Stars
The Complete Jazz At The Philharmonic On Verve 1944-1949 | Verve | 523893-2
Coleman Hawkins All Stars
Verve Jazz Masters 43:Coleman Hawkins | Verve | 521856-2
Dizzy Gillespie And His Orchestra
Planet Jazz:Dizzy Gillespie | Planet Jazz | 2152069-2
Planet Jazz:Bebop | RCA | 2169650-2
Ella Fitzgerald With Benny Carter's Magnificent Seven
30 By Ella | Capitol | 520090-2
Ella Fitzgerald With The Billy May Orchestra
Ella Fitzgerald-First Lady Of Song | Verve | 517898-2
The Best Of The Song Books | Verve | 519804-2
Verve Jazz Masters 6:Ella Fitzgerald | Verve | 519822-2
Verve Jazz Masters 46:Ella Fitzgerald-The Jazz Sides | Verve | 527655-2
Ella Fitzgerald Sings The Harold Arlen Song Book | Verve | 589108-2
For The Love Of Ella Fitzgerald | Verve | 841765-2
Esquire All-American Award Winners
Planet Jazz:Jazz Trumpet | Planet Jazz | 2169654-2
Ike Quebec Swing Seven
The Blue Note Swingtets | Blue Note | 495697-2
JATP All Stars
The Complete Jazz At The Philharmonic On Verve 1944-1949 | Verve | 523893-2
Kenny Clarke And His 52nd Street Boys
Planet Jazz:Bebop | RCA | 2169650-2
Fats Navarro:Nostalgia | Dreyfus Jazz Line | FDM 36736-2
Louis Jordan And His Tympany Five
Louis Jordan-Let The Good Times Roll: The Complete Decca Recordings 1938-1954 | Bear Family Records | BCD 15557 IH
Milt Jackson And His Colleagues
Bag's Bag | Original Jazz Classics | OJCCD 935-2(2310842)
Nat King Cole Quartet
Penthouse Serenade | Capitol | 494504-2
Nat King Cole Quintet
Penthouse Serenade | Capitol | 494504-2
After Midnight | Capitol | 520087-2
Nat King Cole Sextet
After Midnight | Capitol | 520087-2
Nat King Cole Trio
Penthouse Serenade | Capitol | 494504-2
Sarah Vaughan With The Gerald Wilson Orchestra
Ballads | Roulette | 537561-2
Sarah Vaughan With The Jimmy Jones Quartet
Sarah Vaughan:Lover Man | Dreyfus Jazz Line | FDM 36739-2
Slam Stewart Trio
The Small Black Groups | Storyville | 4960523
Una Mae Carlisle Septet
Planet Jazz:Female Jazz Vocalists | Planet Jazz | 2169656-2
Zoot Sims With Orchestra
Passion Flower | Original Jazz Classics | OJCCD 939-2(2312120)

Collins,John or Tiny Grimes | (g)
Billie Holiday With The JATP All Stars
Billie Holiday Story Vol.1:Jazz At The Philharmonic | Verve | 521642-2
The Complete Jazz At The Philharmonic On Verve 1944-1949 | Verve | 523893-2

Collins,Junior | (fr-h)
Charlie Parker And His Orchestra
Charlie Parker:The Best Of The Verve Years | Verve | 527815-2
The Cole Porter Songbook | Verve | 823250-2
Bird: The Complete Charlie Parker On Verve | Verve | 837141-2
Charlie Parker With Orchestra
Charlie Parker Big Band | Verve | 559835-2
Charlie Parker With Orchestra & The Dave Lambert Singers
Verve Jazz Masters 28:Charlie Parker Plays Standards | Verve | 521854-2
Miles Davis And His Orchestra
The Complete Birth Of The Cool | Capitol | 494550-2
Birth Of The Cool | Capitol | 530117-2
Miles Davis:The Best Of The Capitol/Blue Note Years | Blue Note | 798287-2
Miles Davis:Milestones | Dreyfus Jazz Line | FDM 36731-2

Collins,K. | (viola)
Artie Shaw And His Orchestra
Planet JazzArtie Shaw | Planet Jazz | 2152057-2
Planet Jazz:Big Bands | Planet Jazz | 2169649-2

Collins,Lester 'Shad' | (tp)
Big Al Sears Band
Sear-iously | Bear Family Records | BCD 15668 AH
Billie Holiday With Eddie Heywood And His Orchestra
Billie's Love Songs | Nimbus Records | NI 2000
Count Basie And His Orchestra
Jazz:The Essential Collection Vol.3 | IN+OUT Records | 78013-2
From Spiritual To Swing | Vanguard | VCD 169/71
Count Basie Sextet
Jazz:The Essential Collection Vol.3 | IN+OUT Records | 78013-2
Dicky Wells And His Orchestra
Americans Swinging In Paris:Dicky Wells | EMI Records | 539664-2
Helen Humes With James P. Johnson And The Count Basie Orchestra
From Spiritual To Swing | Vanguard | VCD 169/71
Ida Cox With The James P. Johnson Septet
From Spiritual To Swing | Vanguard | VCD 169/71
Ike Quebec Swing Seven
The Blue Note Swingtets | Blue Note | 495697-2
Jimmy Rushing With Count Basie And His Orchestra
From Spiritual To Swing | Vanguard | VCD 169/71
Sammy Price Septet
Jazz:The Essential Collection Vol.3 | IN+OUT Records | 78013-2
Una Mae Carlisle Quintet
Jazz:The Essential Collection Vol.3 | IN+OUT Records | 78013-2
Una Mae Carlisle Septet
Planet Jazz:Female Jazz Vocalists | Planet Jazz | 2169656-2
Vic Dickenson Septet With Ruby Braff
Nice Work | Vanguard | VCD 79610-2

Collins,Michael | (tp)
Jazz Africa All Nations Big Band
Jadu(Jazz Africa Down Under) | Enja | ENJ-9339 2

Collins,Oliver | (psynth)
Monnette Sudler Sextet
Brighter Days For You | Steeplechase | SCCD 31087

Collins,Paul | (dr)
Jack Teagarden And His Orchestra
Jazz:The Essential Collection Vol.3 | IN+OUT Records | 78013-2

Collins,Rudy | (drperc)
Ahmed Abdul-Malik Orchestra
Jazz Sounds Of Africa | Prestige | PRCD 24279-2
Dave Pike Quintet
Carnavals | Prestige | PCD 24248-2
Dave Pike Sextet
Carnavals | Prestige | PCD 24248-2
Dizzy Gillespie And His Orchestra
Talking Verve:Dizzy Gillespie | Verve | 533846-2
Ultimate Dizzy Gillespie | Verve | 557535-2
Dizzy Gillespie Quintet
Dizzie Gillespie: Salle Pleyel/Olympia | Laserlight | 36132
Verve Jazz Masters 10:Dizzy Gillespie | Verve | 516319-2
Talking Verve:Dizzy Gillespie | Verve | 533846-2
Ultimate Dizzy Gillespie | Verve | 557535-2
Something Old Something New | Verve | 558079-2
Dizzy Gillespie Septet
The Antonio Carlos Jobim Songbook | Verve | 525472-2
Dizzy Gillespie Sextet
Verve Jazz Masters 10:Dizzy Gillespie | Verve | 516319-2
Talking Verve:Dizzy Gillespie | Verve | 533846-2
Jambo Caribe | Verve | 557492-2
Ultimate Dizzy Gillespie | Verve | 557535-2
Gene Ammons Quartet
Gentle Jug Vol.3 | Prestige | PCD 24249-2
A Stranger In Town | Prestige | PRCD 24266-2
Gene Ammons Quintet
A Stranger In Town | Prestige | PRCD 24266-2
Herbie Mann And His Orchestra
The Best Of Herbie Mann | Atlantic | 7567-81369-2
Herbie Mann Group
The Best Of Herbie Mann | Atlantic | 7567-81369-2
Rhino Presents The Atlantic Jazz Gallery | Atlantic | 8122-71257-2
Herbie Mann Septet
Herbie Mann At The Village Gate | Atlantic | 7567-81350-2
Herbie Mann Sextet
Herbie Mann At The Village Gate | Atlantic | 7567-81350-2
Herbie Mann's Cuban Band
Verve Jazz Masters 56:Herbie Mann | Verve | 529901-2
Lalo Schifrin And His Orchestra
Tin Tin Deo | Fresh Sound Records | FSR-CD 319
Lalo Schifrin Sextet
Tin Tin Deo | Fresh Sound Records | FSR-CD 319
Quincy Jones And His Orchestra
Big Band Bossa Nova | Verve | 557913-2
Rahsaan/The Complete Mercury Recordings Of Roland Kirk | Mercury | 846630-2

Collins,William 'Bootsy' | (b-g,g,b,drvoc)
Maceo Parker Group
Roots Revisited | Minor Music | 801015

Collucci,Tonny | (g)
Sidney Bechet And The Chamber Music Society Of Lower Basin Street
Sidney Bechet:Summertime | Dreyfus Jazz Line | FDM 36712-2

Collymore,Winston | (v)
Louis Armstrong And His Friends
Planet Jazz:Louis Armstrong | Planet Jazz | 2152052-2
Planet Jazz Sampler | Planet Jazz | 2152326-2
Louis Armstrong And His Friends | Bluebird | 2663961-2
Wes Montgomery With The Jimmy Jones Orchestra
Wes Montgomery-The Complete Riverside Recordings | Riverside | 12 RCD 4408-2
The Jazz Giants Play Rodgers & Hart:Blue Moon | Prestige | PCD 24205-2

Colombo,Eugenio | (as,bs,fl,b-clss)
Giessen-Köln-Nonett
Some Other Tapes | Fish Music | FM 009/10 CD
Italian Instabile Orchestra
Skies Of Europe | ECM | 1543
Transalpin Express Orchestra
Some Other Tapes | Fish Music | FM 009/10 CD

Colombo,Lou | (tpfl-h)
George Masso Sextet
C'Est Magnifique! | Nagel-Heyer | CD 060

Colon,Eddie | (perc,roto-tomstimbales)
Hal Di Meola Group
Casino | CBS | 468215-2

Colon,Ernesto | (dr,congas,bongosbells)
Pucho & His Latin Soul Brothers
Jazzin' With The Soul Brothers | Fantasy | FANCD 6086-2
Rip A Dip | Milestone | MCD 9247-2

Colon,Frank | (congas,bongos,maracas,castanets)
Barbara Dennerlein Group
Junkanoo | Verve | 537122-2
Ivo Perlman Group
Children Of Ibeji | Enja | ENJ-7005 2
Michel Petrucciani Group
Michel Petrucciani:The Blue Note Years | Blue Note | 789916-2
Ray Anderson Alligatory Band
Don't Mow Your Lawn | Enja | ENJ-8070 2
Heads And Tales | Enja | ENJ-9055 2

Colours Of Chloe,The |
Eberhard Weber Group
The Colours Of Chloe | ECM | 1042

Coltrane John | (voice)
Alice Coltrane Quartet
A Monastic Trio | Impulse(MCA) | 951267-2
Alice Coltrane Trio
A Monastic Trio | Impulse(MCA) | 951267-2

Coltrane,Alice | (harp,tamboura,p,harmonium,org,perc)
Alice Coltrane
A Monastic Trio | Impulse(MCA) | 951267-2
Alice Coltrane Quartet
A Monastic Trio | Impulse(MCA) | 951267-2
Alice Coltrane Quintet
Joe Henderson:The Milestone Years | Milestone | 8MCD 4413-2
Ptah The El Daoud | Impulse(MCA) | 951201-2
Journey In Satchidananda | Impulse(MCA) | 951228-2
Alice Coltrane Sextet
Joe Henderson:The Milestone Years | Milestone | 8MCD 4413-2
Journey In Satchidananda | Impulse(MCA) | 951228-2
Alice Coltrane Trio
A Monastic Trio | Impulse(MCA) | 951267-2
Charlie Haden-Alice Coltrane
Closeness Duets | Verve | 397000-2
John Coltrane Group
The Olatunji Concert:The Last Live Recording | Impulse(MCA) | 589120-2
John Coltrane Quartet
Coltrane Spiritual | Impulse(MCA) | 589099-2
Stellar Regions | Impulse(MCA) | 951169-2
John Coltrane Quintet
Live At The Village Vanguard Again | Impulse(MCA) | 951213-2
McCoy Tyner Sextet
Extensions | Blue Note | 837646-2

Coltrane,John | (as,ts,b-cl,ss,perc,fl,sax,bellsvoc)
Cannonball Adderley Quintet
Verve Jazz Masters 31:Cannonball Adderley | Verve | 522651-2
Cannonball Adderley Quintet In Chicago
Cannonball & Coltrane | Verve | 559770-2
Cecil Taylor Quintet
Trane's Blues | Blue Note | 498240-2
Elmo Hope Sextet
John Coltrane-The Prestige Recordings | Prestige | 16 PCD 4405-2
Gene Ammons And His All Stars
John Coltrane-The Prestige Recordings | Prestige | 16 PCD 4405-2
The Big Sound | Original Jazz Classics | OJCCD 651-2(P 7132)
Groove Blues | Original Jazz Classics | OJCCD 723-2(PR 7201)
The Prestige Legacy Vol.2:Battles Of Saxes | Prestige | PCD 24252-2
George Russell And His Orchestra
Geogre Russell New York N.Y. | Impulse(MCA) | 951278-2
John Coltrane All Stars
Dakar | Original Jazz Classics | OJC20 393-2(P 7280)
The Believer | Original Jazz Classics | OJCCD 876-2(P 7292)
Stardust | Original Jazz Classics | OJCCD 920-2(P 7268)
John Coltrane And His Orchestra
Kulu Se Mama | Impulse(MCA) | 543412-2
Ascension | Impulse(MCA) | 543413-2
John Coltrane:Standards | Impulse(MCA) | 549914-2
Meditations | Impulse(MCA) | 951199-2
John Coltrane Group
The Olatunji Concert:The Last Live Recording | Impulse(MCA) | 589120-2

INTERPRETENVERZEICHNIS

Olé Coltrane | Atlantic | 7567-81349-2
Olé Coltrane | Rhino | 8122-73699-2

John Coltrane Quartet
John Coltrane-The Prestige Recordings | Prestige | 16 PCD 4405-2
Afro Blue Impressions | Pablo | 2PACD 2620101
Trane's Blues | Blue Note | 498240-2
Kulu Se Mama | Impulse(MCA) | 543412-2
Impressions | Impulse(MCA) | 543416-2
John Coltrane:Standards | Impulse(MCA) | 549914-2
Cannonball & Coltrane | Verve | 559770-2
Coltrane Spiritual | Impulse(MCA) | 589099-2
Ballads | Impulse(MCA) | 589548-2
Coltrane | Impulse(MCA) | 589567-2
A Love Supreme | Impulse(MCA) | 589596-2
A Love Supreme | Impulse(MCA) | 589945-2
Coltrane Jazz | Atlantic | 7567-81344-2
Coltrane Plays The Blues | Atlantic | 7567-81351-2
Coltrane's Sound | Atlantic | 7567-81358-2
The Best Of John Coltrane | Atlantic | 7567-81366-2
John Coltrane-Live Trane:The European Tours | Pablo | 7PACD 4433-2
Atlantic Saxophones | Rhino | 8122-71256-2
Rhino Presents The Atlantic Jazz Gallery | Atlantic | 8122-71257-2
John Coltrane-The Heavyweight Champion:The Complete Atlantic Recordings | Atlantic | 8122-71984-2
Giant Steps | Atlantic | 8122-75203-2
My Favorite Things | Atlantic | 8122-75204-2
The Very Best Of John Coltrane | Rhino | 8122-79778-2
Coltrane Plays The Blues | Rhino | 8122-79966-2
The Gentle Side Of John Coltrane | Impulse(MCA) | 951107-2
Sun Ship | Impulse(MCA) | 951166-2
Stellar Regions | Impulse(MCA) | 951169-2
Live At Birdland | Impulse(MCA) | 951198-2
Crescent | Impulse(MCA) | 951200-2
The Coltrane Quartet Plays | Impulse(MCA) | 951214-2
Living Space | Impulse(MCA) | 951246-2
Live At The Village Vanguard:The Master Takes | Impulse(MCA) | 951251-2
John Coltrane:The Classic Quartet-Complete Impulse Studio Recordings | Impulse(MCA) | 951280-2
John Coltrane:The Complete 1961 Village Vanguard Recordings | Impulse(MCA) | 954322-2
The Other Village Vanguard Tapes | Impulse(MCA) | MCD 04137
Coltrane | Original Jazz Classics | OJC20 020-2
Soultrane | Original Jazz Classics | OJC20 021-2
Lush Life | Original Jazz Classics | OJC20 131-2
Bye Bye Blackbird | Original Jazz Classics | OJC20 681-2(2308227)
The Paris Concert | Original Jazz Classics | OJC20 781-2(2308217)
Bahia | Original Jazz Classics | OJCCD 415-2
Stardust | Original Jazz Classics | OJCCD 920-2(P 7268)
The Jazz Giants Play Sammy Cahn:It's Magic | Prestige | PCD 24226-2
The Prestige Legacy Vol.1:The High Priests | Prestige | PCD 24251-2

John Coltrane Quartet With Brass
The Complete Africa/Brass Sessions | Impulse(MCA) | 952168-2

John Coltrane Quartet With Eric Dolphy
John Coltrane:The Complete 1961 Village Vanguard Recordings | Impulse(MCA) | 954322-2

John Coltrane Quartet With Johnny Hartman
The Gentle Side Of John Coltrane | Impulse(MCA) | 951107-2

John Coltrane Quintet
John Coltrane-The Prestige Recordings | Prestige | 16 PCD 4405-2
Impressions | Impulse(MCA) | 543416-2
John Coltrane:Standards | Impulse(MCA) | 549914-2
Live At The Village Vanguard Again | Impulse(MCA) | 951213-2
Live At The Village Vanguard:The Master Takes | Impulse(MCA) | 951251-2
Eric Dolphy Birthday Celebration | Fantasy | FANCD 6085-2
Black Pearls | Original Jazz Classics | OJC 352(P 7316)
The Last Trane | Original Jazz Classics | OJC 394(P 7378)
Coltrane | Original Jazz Classics | OJC20 020-2
Lush Life | Original Jazz Classics | OJC20 131-2
Standard Coltrane | Original Jazz Classics | OJCCD 246-2
Bahia | Original Jazz Classics | OJCCD 415-2
The Believer | Original Jazz Classics | OJCCD 876-2(P 7292)
Stardust | Original Jazz Classics | OJCCD 920-2(P 7268)
The Jazz Giants Play Harold Arlen:Blues In The Night | Prestige | PCD 24201-2
The Jazz Giants Play Rodgers & Hammerstein:My Favorite Things | Prestige | PCD 24223-2
The Mal Waldron Memorial Album:Soul Eyes | Prestige | PRCD 11024-2

John Coltrane Quintet With Eric Dolphy
Coltrane Spiritual | Impulse(MCA) | 589099-2
John Coltrane-Live Trane:The European Tours | Pablo | 7PACD 4433-2
John Coltrane-The Heavyweight Champion:The Complete Atlantic Recordings | Atlantic | 8122-71984-2
John Coltrane:The Complete 1961 Village Vanguard Recordings | Impulse(MCA) | 954322-2
The Other Village Vanguard Tapes | Impulse(MCA) | MCD 04137

John Coltrane Septet With Eric Dolphy
John Coltrane:The Complete 1961 Village Vanguard Recordings | Impulse(MCA) | 954322-2
The Other Village Vanguard Tapes | Impulse(MCA) | MCD 04137

John Coltrane Sextet
John Coltrane-The Prestige Recordings | Prestige | 16 PCD 4405-2
Trane's Blues | Blue Note | 498240-2
Impressions | Impulse(MCA) | 543416-2
A Love Supreme | Impulse(MCA) | 589945-2
Blue Train | Blue Note | 591721-2
The Best Of Blue Note | Blue Note | 796110-2
Blue Train(The Ultimate Blue Train) | Blue Note | 853428-0
Live At The Village Vanguard:The Master Takes | Impulse(MCA) | 951251-2
John Coltrane:The Complete 1961 Village Vanguard Recordings | Impulse(MCA) | 954322-2
Coltrane | Original Jazz Classics | OJC20 020-2
The Prestige Legacy Vol.1:The High Priests | Prestige | PCD 24251-2
The Mal Waldron Memorial Album:Soul Eyes | Prestige | PRCD 11024-2

John Coltrane Sextet With Eric Dolphy
John Coltrane-The Heavyweight Champion:The Complete Atlantic Recordings | Atlantic | 8122-71984-2

John Coltrane Trio
John Coltrane-The Prestige Recordings | Prestige | 16 PCD 4405-2
Coltrane | Impulse(MCA) | 589567-2
Coltrane Plays The Blues | Atlantic | 7567-81351-2
Coltrane's Sound | Atlantic | 7567-81358-2
Coltrane Plays The Blues | Rhino | 8122-79966-2
Live At The Village Vanguard:The Master Takes | Impulse(MCA) | 951251-2
John Coltrane:The Classic Quartet-Complete Impulse Studio Recordings | Impulse(MCA) | 951280-2
John Coltrane:The Complete 1961 Village Vanguard Recordings | Impulse(MCA) | 954322-2
The Last Trane | Original Jazz Classics | OJC 394(P 7378)
Lush Life | Original Jazz Classics | OJC20 131-2
Bahia | Original Jazz Classics | OJCCD 415-2
The Jazz Giants Play Cole Porter:Night And Day | Prestige | PCD 24203-2

John Coltrane With The Red Garland Trio
John Coltrane-The Prestige Recordings | Prestige | 16 PCD 4405-2
The Last Trane | Original Jazz Classics | OJC 394(P 7378)
Settin' The Pace | Original Jazz Classics | OJC20 078-2
Dig It | Original Jazz Classics | OJC20 392-2(PR 7229)
Traning In | Original Jazz Classics | OJCCD 189-2

John Coltrane-Don Cherry Quartet
The Avant-Garde | Atlantic | 7567-90041-2
John Coltrane-The Heavyweight Champion:The Complete Atlantic Recordings | Atlantic | 8122-71984-2
The Avantgarde | Rhino | 8122-79892-2

John Coltrane-Duke Ellington Quartet
The Gentle Side Of John Coltrane | Impulse(MCA) | 951107-2
Duke Ellington & John Coltrane | Impulse(MCA) | 951166-2

John Coltrane-Elvin Jones
John Coltrane:The Classic Quartet-Complete Impulse Studio Recordings | Impulse(MCA) | 951280-2

John Coltrane-Eric Dolphy Quartet
John Coltrane:The Complete 1961 Village Vanguard Recordings | Impulse(MCA) | 954322-2
The Other Village Vanguard Tapes | Impulse(MCA) | MCD 04137

John Coltrane-McCoy Tyner
Ballads | Impulse(MCA) | 589548-2

John Coltrane-Milt Jackson Quintet
John Coltrane-The Heavyweight Champion:The Complete Atlantic Recordings | Atlantic | 8122-71984-2
Bags & Trane | Rhino | 8122-73685-2

John Coltrane-Paul Quinichette Quintet
John Coltrane-The Prestige Recordings | Prestige | 16 PCD 4405-2
Cattin' | Original Jazz Classics | OJCCD 460-2

John Coltrane-Rashied Ali Duo
Interstellar Space | Impulse(MCA) | 543415-2

John Coltrane-Tadd Dameron Quartet
Mating Call | Original Jazz Classics | OJCCD 212-2(P 7070)

Johnny Griffin Septet
A Blowing Session | Blue Note | 0677191
Trane's Blues | Blue Note | 498240-2

Johnny Hartman With The John Coltrane Quartet
John Coltrane:Standards | Impulse(MCA) | 549914-2
John Coltrane And Johnny Hartman | Impulse(MCA) | 951157-2

Kenny Burrell Quintet
John Coltrane-The Prestige Recordings | Prestige | 16 PCD 4405-2

Kenny Burrell-John Coltrane Duo
Kenny Burrell & John Coltrane | New Jazz | NJSA 8276-2
Kenny Burrell & John Coltrane | Original Jazz Classics | OJC20 300-2

Kenny Burrell-John Coltrane Quintet
Kenny Burrell & John Coltrane | New Jazz | NJSA 8276-2
Kenny Burrell & John Coltrane | Original Jazz Classics | OJC20 300-2

Mal Waldron Sextet
John Coltrane-The Prestige Recordings | Prestige | 16 PCD 4405-2
The Jazz Giants Play Jerome Kern:Yesterdays | Prestige | PCD 24202-2
The Mal Waldron Memorial Album:Soul Eyes | Prestige | PRCD 11024-2

Miles Davis New Quintet
Workin',Steamin',Cookin',Relaxin' With The Miles Davis Quintet | Original Jazz Classics | OJCCD 8805-2

Miles Davis Quintet
Miles Davis: Olympia, March 29th,1960 | Laserlight | 36130
Circle In The Round | CBS | 467898-2
Kind Of Blue | CBS | 480410-2
Kind Of Blue | CBS | CK 64935
This Is Jazz:Miles Davis Plays Ballads | CBS | CK 65038
Someday My Prince Will Come | CBS | CK 65919
Newport Jazz Festival 1958,July 3rd-6th,Vol.1:Mostly Miles | Phontastic | NCD 8813
Cookin' With The Miles Davis Quintet | Original Jazz Classics | OJC20 128-2
Relaxin' | Original Jazz Classics | OJC20 190-2
Miles Davis And The Modern Jazz Giants | Original Jazz Classics | OJC20 347-2(P 7150)
Steamin' | Original Jazz Classics | OJC20 391-2
The Jazz Giants Play Rodgers & Hammerstein:My Favorite Things | Prestige | PCD 24223-2
The Jazz Giants Play Duke Ellington:Caravan | Prestige | PCD 24227-2
Relaxin' | Prestige | PRSA 7129-6

Miles Davis Sextet
Circle In The Round | CBS | 467898-2
Kind Of Blue | CBS | 480410-2
Kind Of Blue | CBS | CK 64935
This Is Jazz:Miles Davis Plays Ballads | CBS | CK 65038
Someday My Prince Will Come | CBS | CK 65919

Paul Chambers Sextet
Trane's Blues | Blue Note | 498240-2

Prestige All Stars
John Coltrane-The Prestige Recordings | Prestige | 16 PCD 4405-2
The Cats | Original Jazz Classics | OJCCD 079-2(NJ 8217)
Tenor Conclave | Original Jazz Classics | OJCCD 127-2
Wheelin' & Dealin' | Original Jazz Classics | OJCCD 672-2(P7131)
The Prestige Legacy Vol.1:The High Priests | Prestige | PCD 24251-2
The Mal Waldron Memorial Album:Soul Eyes | Prestige | PRCD 11024-2

Quartet
Monk's Music | Original Jazz Classics | OJC20 084-2

Ray Draper Quintet
John Coltrane-The Prestige Recordings | Prestige | 16 PCD 4405-2

Red Garland Quintet
John Coltrane-The Prestige Recordings | Prestige | 16 PCD 4405-2
All Mornin' Long | Original Jazz Classics | OJC20 293-2(P-7130)
Dig It | Original Jazz Classics | OJC20 392-2(PR 7229)
Soul Junction | Original Jazz Classics | OJCCD 481-2
The Jazz Giants Play Duke Ellington:Caravan | Prestige | PCD 24227-2

Red Garland Quintet feat.John Coltrane
High Pressure | Original Jazz Classics | OJCCD 349-2(P 7209)

Sonny Clark Sextet
Trane's Blues | Blue Note | 498240-2

Sonny Rollins Quintet
John Coltrane-The Prestige Recordings | Prestige | 16 PCD 4405-2
Tenor Madness | Original Jazz Classics | OJC20 124-2
The Prestige Legacy Vol.2:Battles Of Saxes | Prestige | PCD 24252-2
Tenor Madness | Prestige | PRSA 7047-6

Tadd Dameron Quartet
John Coltrane-The Prestige Recordings | Prestige | 16 PCD 4405-2

Taylor's Wailers
John Coltrane-The Prestige Recordings | Prestige | 16 PCD 4405-2

The New Miles Davis Quintet
Miles | Original Jazz Classics | OJC20 006-2(P 7014)

Thelonious Monk Quartet
Jazz Profile:Thelonious Monk | Blue Note | 823518-2
Thelonious Monk:85th Birthday Celebration | zyx records | FANCD 6076-2
Thelonious Monk With John Coltrane | Jazzland | JZSA 946-6
Thelonious Monk With John Coltrane | Original Jazz Classics | OJC20 039-2
Thelonious Himself | Original Jazz Classics | OJCCD 254-2

Thelonious Monk Septet
Thelonious Monk:85th Birthday Celebration | zyx records | FANCD 6076-2
Thelonious Monk With John Coltrane | Jazzland | JZSA 946-6
Thelonious Monk With John Coltrane | Original Jazz Classics | OJC20 039-2
Monk's Music | Original Jazz Classics | OJC20 084-2

Thelonious Monk Trio
Thelonious Monk:85th Birthday Celebration | zyx records | FANCD 6076-2

Wilbur Harden Quintet
The Art Of Saxophone | Laserlight | 24652

Coltrane,Ravi | (ssts)

Bruce Cox Quartet With Guests
Stick To It | Minor Music | 801055

Elvin Jones Jazz Machine
In Europe | Enja | ENJ-7009 2
Going Home | Enja | ENJ-7095 2

Steve Coleman And Five Elements
The Sonic Language Of Myth | RCA | 2164123-2

Steve Coleman And Metrics
A Tale Of 3 Cities,The EP | Novus | 2124747-2

Steve Coleman And The Council Of Balance
Genesis & The Opening Of The Way | RCA | 2152934-2

Colucci,Michael 'Rocky' | (p)

Vic Lewis Jam Session
Vic Lewis:The Golden Years | Candid | CCD 79754

Colucci,Tony | (bjg)

Dr. Henry Levine's Barefoot Dixieland Philharmonic feat.Prof. Sidney Bechet
Planet Jazz | Planet Jazz | 2169652-2

Red And Miff's Stompers
Planet Jazz:Jazz Trumpet | Planet Jazz | 2169654-2

Roger Wolfe Kahn And His Orchestra
Planet Jazz:Jack Teagarden | Planet Jazz | 2161236-2

Colyer,Ken | (co,voc,gtp)

Ken Colyer Trio
The Golden Years Of Revival Jazz.Vol.3 | Storyville | STCD 5508

Ken Colyer's Jazzmen
The Very Best Of Dixieland Jazz | Verve | 535529-2
The Golden Years Of Revival Jazz,Vol 1 | Storyville | STCD 5506
The Golden Years Of Revival Jazz,Vol.7 | Storyville | STCD 5512
The Golden Years Of Revival Jazz,Vol.11 | Storyville | STCD 5516
The Golden Years Of Revival Jazz,Vol.13 | Storyville | STCD 5518
The Golden Years Of Revival Jazz,Vol.14 | Storyville | STCD 5519
The Golden Years Of Revibal Jazz,Vol.15 | Storyville | STCD 5520

Combe,Stuff | (dr)

Stan Getz With The Kurt Edelhagen Orchestra
Stan Getz In Europe | Laserlight | 24657

Combelle,Alix | (as,bs,cl,chimes,tsarr)

Alix Combelle Et Son Orchestre
Americans Swinging In Paris:Bill Coleman-The Elegance | EMI Records | 539662-2

Benny Carter And His Orchestra
Django Reinhardt All Star Sessions | Capitol | 531577-2
Americans Swinging In Paris:Benny Carter | EMI Records | 539647-2

Coleman Hawkins And His All Star Jam Band
Americans Swinging In Paris:Benny Carter | EMI Records | 539647-2

Coleman Hawkins With Michel Warlop And His Orchestra
Django Reinhardt All Star Sessions | Capitol | 531577-2

Eddie Brunner And His Orchestra
Americans Swinging In Paris:Bill Coleman-The Elegance | EMI Records | 539662-2

Lionel Hampton And His Orchestra
Lionel Hampton's Paris All Stars | Vogue | 21511502

Michel Warlop Et Son Orchestre
Jazz In Paris:Django Reinhardt-Django Et Compagnie | EmArCy | 549241-2 PMS

Quintet Du Hot Club De France
Django Reinhardt:Echoes Of France | Dreyfus Jazz Line | FDM 36726-2

Wal-Berg Et Son Jazz Francais
Jazz In Paris:Django Reinhardt-Django Et Compagnie | EmArCy | 549241-2 PMS

Combelle,Philippe | (drvoc)

Sonny Criss Quartet
Jazz In Paris:Saxophones Á Saint-Germain Des Prés | EmArCy | 014060-2

Sonny Criss Quintet
Jazz In Paris:Saxophones Á Saint-Germain Des Prés | EmArCy | 014060-2
Jazz In Paris:Sonny Criss-Mr.Blues Pour Flirter | EmArCy | 549231-2 PMS

Toots Thielemans Quartet
Jazz In Paris:Toots Thielemans-Blues Pour Flirter | EmArCy | 549403-2 PMS

Combine,Buddy | (dr)

Harry James And His Orchestra
Trumpet Blues:The Best Of Harry James | Capitol | 521224-2

Comegys,Leon | (tb)

Dizzy Gillespie And His Orchestra
Afro | Verve | 517052-2

Louis Jordan And His Tympany Five
Louis Jordan-Let The Good Times Roll: The Complete Decca Recordings 1938-1954 | Bear Family Records | BCD 15557 IH

Comer,Chris | (fr-h)

David Matthews & The Manhattan Jazz Orchestra
Hey Duke! | Milestone | MCD 9320-2

Comerford,Jane | (voc)

Bernard Purdie's Soul To Jazz
Bernard Purdie's Soul To Jazz | ACT | 9242-2

Comfort,Joe | (b)

Benny Carter And His Orchestra
Aspects | Capitol | 852677-2

Ella Fitzgerald With The Duke Ellington Orchestra
The Stockholm Concert 1966 | Pablo | 2308242-2

Ella Fitzgerald With The Nelson Riddle Orchestra
The Best Of The Song Books:The Ballads | Verve | 521867-2
Oh Lady Be Good:The Best Of The Gershwin Songbook | Verve | 529581-2
Love Songs:The Best Of The Song Books | Verve | 531762-2
Ella Fitzgerald Sings The Johnny Mercer Songbook | Verve | 539057-2

Harry Edison Quartet
The Complete Unedited 'Sweets At The Haig' 1953 Recordings | Fresh Sound Records | FSR CD 345

Harry James And His Orchestra
Trumpet Blues:The Best Of Harry James | Capitol | 521224-2

Lionel Hampton And His Orchestra
Lionel Hampton:Flying Home | Dreyfus Jazz Line | FDM 36735-2

Louis Armstrong With The Hal Mooney Orchestra
Ambassador Louis Armstrong Vol.17:Moments To Remember(1952-1956) | Ambassador | CLA 1917

Nat King Cole And His Trio
Nat King Cole:The Snader Telescriptions | Storyville | 4960103

Nat King Cole And His Trio With Strings
Nat King Cole:The Snader Telescriptions | Storyville | 4960103

Nat King Cole Quartet
The Instrumental Classics | Capitol | 798288-2
Nat King Cole:For Sentimental Reasons | Dreyfus Jazz Line | FDM 36740-2

Nat King Cole Quartet With The Pete Rugolo Orchestra
The Instrumental Classics | Capitol | 798288-2

Nat King Cole Quartet With The Stan Kenton Orchestra
Nat King Cole:For Sentimental Reasons | Dreyfus Jazz Line | FDM 36740-2

Nat King Cole Trio
Nat King Cole:The Snader Telescriptions | Storyville | 4960103

Nat King Cole Trio With Pete Rugolo's Orchestra
Nat King Cole:For Sentimental Reasons | Dreyfus Jazz Line | FDM 36740-2

Nat King Cole Trio With Strings
Nat King Cole:For Sentimental Reasons | Dreyfus Jazz Line | FDM 36740-2

Sarah Vaughan Plus Two
Ballads | Roulette | 537561-2

Sarah Vaughan With Barney Kessel And Joe Comfort
Jazz Profile | Blue Note | 823517-2

Sarah Vaughan With The Benny Carter Orchestra
Jazz Profile | Blue Note | 823517-2

T-Bone Walker And His Band
Atlantic Jazz: Kansas City | Atlantic | 7567-81701-2

Van Alexander Orchestra
Home Of Happy Feet/Swing! Staged For Sound! | Capitol | 535211-2

Conaway,Lincoln | (g)

Bessie Smith And Her Band
Jazz:The Essential Collection Vol.1 | IN+OUT Records | 78011-2

Concepcion,Ray | (p)

Dizzy Gillespie And His Orchestra
Afro | Verve | 517052-2

Concerto Köln |

Uri Caine With The Concerto Köln
Concerto Köln | Winter&Winter | 910086-2

Condé,Djely-Moussa | (kora)

Hank Jones Meets Cheik-Tidiana Seck

Sarala | Verve | 528783-2

Condon,Eddie | (bj,voc,gpresence)
Bud Freeman All Stars
The Bud Freeman All-Star Sessions | Prestige | PRCD 24286-2
Bud Freeman And His Famous Chicagoans
Jazz:The Essential Collection Vol.3 | IN+OUT Records | 78013-2
Bud Freeman And His Summa Cum Laude Orchestra
Planet Jazz:Bud Freeman | Planet Jazz | 2161240-2
Planet Jazz:Jazz Saxophone | Planet Jazz | 2169653-2
Eddie Condon All Stars
Jazz Festival Vol.1 | Storyville | 4960733
Eddie Condon And His Boys
The Very Best Of Dixieland Jazz | Verve | 535529-2
Eddie Condon And His Chicagoans
The Very Best Of Dixieland Jazz | Verve | 535529-2
Eddie Condon And His Orchestra
Jazz:The Essential Collection Vol.3 | IN+OUT Records | 78013-2
Eddie Condon's Hot Shots
Jazz:The Essential Collection Vol.3 | IN+OUT Records | 78013-2
Eddie's Hot Shots
Planet Jazz:Jack Teagarden | Planet Jazz | 2161236-2
Fats Waller And His Buddies
Planet Jazz:Jack Teagarden | Planet Jazz | 2161236-2
Louis Armstrong And His Savoy Ballroom Five
Jazz:The Essential Collection Vol.2 | IN+OUT Records | 78012-2
Mound City Blue Blowers
Planet Jazz:Jack Teagarden | Planet Jazz | 2161236-2
Jazz:The Essential Collection Vol.3 | IN+OUT Records | 78013-2

Condon,Eddie prob. | (g)
Max Kaminsky And His Dixieland Bashers
Planet Jazz | Planet Jazz | 2169652-2

Condouant,André | (g)
Annie Ross & PonyPoindexter With The Berlin All Stars
Annie Ross & Pony Poindexter with The Berlin All Stars | MPS | 9811257

Conexion Latina |
Conexion Latina
Calorcito | Enja | ENJ-4072 2
Mambo 2000 | Enja | ENJ-7055 2
La Conexión | Enja | ENJ-9065 2
Mambo Nights | Enja | ENJ-9402 2

Conger,Al | (btuba)
Turk Murphy And His Jazz Band
The Very Best Of Dixieland Jazz | Verve | 535529-2

Conger,Larry | (tp)

Connell,Tuey | (gvoc)
Tuey Connell Group
Songs For Joy And Sadness | Minor Music | 801095

Connick Jr.,Harry | (pvoc)
Harry Connick Jr. Quartet
We Are In Love | CBS | 466736-2
Harry Connick Jr. Quartet With Branford Marsalis
We Are In Love | CBS | 466736-2
Wynton Marsalis Group
Standard Time Vol.6:Mr.Jelly Lord | CBS | CK 69872

Connie's Inn Orchestra |
Connie's Inn Orchestra
Planet Jazz:Coleman Hawkins | Planet Jazz | 2152055-2

Conniff,Ray | (arrtb)
Artie Shaw And His Orchestra
Planet JazzArtie Shaw | Planet Jazz | 2152057-2
Planet Jazz:Male Jazz Vocalists | Planet Jazz | 2169657-2

Connor,Chris | (voc)
Chris Connor With Band
Chris Connor | Atlantic | 7567-80769-2
Chris Connor With The Hank Jones Trio
As Time Goes By | Enja | ENJ-7061 2
Chris Connor With The John Lewis Quartet
Chris Connor | Atlantic | 7567-80769-2
Chris Connor With The Ralph Burns Orchestra
Chris Connor | Atlantic | 7567-80769-2
Maynard Ferguson Orchestra With Chris Connor
Two's Company | Roulette | 837201-2
Stan Kenton And His Orchestra
Stan Kenton Portraits On Standards | Capitol | 531571-2

Connor,Ray | (tb)
Dizzy Gillespie And His Orchestra
Dizzy Gillespie:Birks Works-The Verve Big Band Sessions | Verve | 527900-2

Connors,Bill | (g,el-gg-solo)
Bill Connors
Theme To The Gaurdian | ECM | 1057
Swimming With A Hole In My Body | ECM | 1158
Bill Connors Quartet
Of Mist And Melting | ECM | 1120(847324-2)
Jan Garbarek Group
Photo With Blue Skie, White Clouds, Wires, Windows And A Red Roof | ECM | 1135 (843168-2)
Jan Garbarek Quartet
Places | ECM | 1118(829195-2)
Return To Forever
Return To The 7th Galaxy-Return To Forever:The Anthology | Verve | 533108-2
Hymn Of The Seventh Galaxy | Polydor | 825336-2

Connors,Charles | (b-tbtb)
Duke Ellington And His Orchestra
Ella Fitzgerald And Duke Ellington:Cote D'Azure Concerts on Verve | Verve | 539033-2
The Afro-Eurasian Eclipse-A Suite In Eight Parts | Original Jazz Classics | OJCCD 645-2(F 9498)
Ella Fitzgerald With The Duke Ellington Orchestra And Jimmy Jones Trio
Ella Fitzgerald And Duke Ellington:Cote D'Azure Concerts on Verve | Verve | 539033-2

Connors,Chuck | (b-tb,maracastb)
Billy Strayhorn Orchestra
Johnny Hodges With Billy Strayhorn And The Orchestra | Verve | 557543-2
Dizzy Gillespie And His Orchestra
Ultimate Dizzy Gillespie | Verve | 557535-2
Duke Ellington And His Orchestra
Planet Jazz:Johnny Hodges | Planet Jazz | 2152065-2
Duke Ellington's Far East Suite | RCA | 2174797-2
The Art Of Saxophone | Laserlight | 24652
Highlights From The Duke Ellington Centennial Edition | RCA | 2663672-2
The Popular Duke Ellington | RCA | 2663880-2
Duke Ellington: The Champs-Elysees Theater January 29-30th,1965 | Laserlight | 36131
Jazz Festival Vol.2 | Storyville | 4960743
Verve Jazz Masters 4:Duke Ellington | Verve | 516338-2
Verve Jazz Masters 20:Introducing | Verve | 519853-2
Ella & Duke At The Cote D'Azur | Verve | 539030-2
Ella Fitzgerald And Duke Ellington:Cote D'Azure Concerts on Verve | Verve | 539033-2
Soul Call | Verve | 539785-2
The Great Paris Concert | Atlantic | 7567-81303-2
New Orleans Suite | Rhino | 812273670-2
Afro-Bossa | Reprise | 9362-47876-2
Welcome To Jazz At The Philharmonic | Fantasy | FANCD 6081-2
The Ellington Suites | Original Jazz Classics | OJC20 446-2(2310762)
Latin America Suite | Original Jazz Classics | OJC20 469-2
Duke Ellington And His Orchestra feat. Paul Gonsalves | Original Jazz Classics | OJCCD 623-2
Yale Concert | Original Jazz Classics | OJCCD 664-2
Jazz At The Philharmonis Berlin '65/Paris '67 | Pablo | PACD 5304-2
The Jazz Giants Play Duke Ellington:Caravan | Prestige | PCD 24227-2
Togo Brava Swuite | Storyville | STCD 8323
Duke Ellington Orchestra
Continuum | Fantasy | FCD 24765-2
Ella Fitzgerald With The Duke Ellington Orchestra
The Stockholm Concert 1966 | Pablo | 2308242-2
Ella Fitzgerald-First Lady Of Song | Verve | 517898-2
Verve Jazz Masters 46:Ella Fitzgerald-The Jazz Sides | Verve | 527655-2
Ella At Duke's Place | Verve | 529700-2
Ella & Duke At The Cote D'Azur | Verve | 539030-2
Ella Fitzgerald And Duke Ellington:Cote D'Azure Concerts on Verve | Verve | 539033-2
Ella Fitzgerald With The Duke Ellington Orchestra And Jimmy Jones Trio
Ella & Duke At The Cote D'Azur | Verve | 539030-2
Ella Fitzgerald With The Jimmy Jones Trio
Ella Fitzgerald And Duke Ellington:Cote D'Azure Concerts on Verve | Verve | 539033-2
Johnny Hodges With Billy Strayhorn And The Duke Ellington Orchestra
Verve Jazz Masters 35:Johnny Hodges | Verve | 521857-2
Oscar Peterson With The Duke Ellington Orchestra
Oscar Peterson Plays Duke Ellington | Pablo | 2310966-2

Connors,Clare | (v)
Michael Mantler Quintet With The Balanescu Quartet
Folly Seeing All This | ECM | 1485
Rabih Abou-Khalil Group
Arabian Waltz | Enja | ENJ-9059 2

Connors,Norman | (dr,perctympani)
Pharoah Sanders Group
Black Unity | Impulse(MCA) | 951219-2

Connors,Ray | (tb)
Dizzy Gillespie Orchestra
Verve Jazz Masters 10:Dizzy Gillespie | Verve | 516319-2

Connors,Roland | (tp)
Lionel Hampton And His All Star Jazz Inner Circle
Lionel Hampton: Salle Pleyel, March 9th, 1971 | Laserlight | 36133

Conrad,Eddie | (percvoice)
Akili
Maasai Mara | M.A Music | A 802-2
Akili | M.A Music | NU 730-2
Stochelo Rosenberg Group
Gypsy Swing | Verve | 527806-2
Stochelo Rosenberg Group With Strings
Gypsy Swing | Verve | 527806-2
The Rosenberg Trio
The Rosenberg Trio:The Collection | Verve | 537152-2
The Rosenberg Trio With Frits Landesbergen
Gypsy Swing | Verve | 527806-2
The Rosenberg Trio:The Collection | Verve | 537152-2
The Rosenberg Trio With Orchestra
Noches Calientes | Verve | 557022-2
The Rosenberg Trio With Stephane Grappelli
The Rosenberg Trio:The Collection | Verve | 537152-2

Conray,Reg | (vib)
Stephane Grappelli And His Musicians
Grapelli Story | Verve | 515807-2

Conroy,Greg | (drperc)
John Stein Quartet
Conversation Pieces | Jardis Records | JRCD 20140
John Stein Quintet
Portraits And Landscapes | Jardis Records | JRCD 20029
Jazz Guitar Highlights 1 | Jardis Records | JRCD 20141

Conrozier,Jean-Louis | (voc)
Les Double Six
Les Double Six | RCA | 2164314-2

Conselman,Bob | (dr,tpvib)
Tommy Dorsey And His Orchestra
Planet Jazz:Frank Sinatra & Tommy Dorsey | Planet Jazz | 2152067-2

Console,Hector | (b)
Astor Piazzolla-Gary Burton Sextet
The New Tango | Warner | 2292-55069-2

Contanzaro,Agostino | (dr)
Omar Belmonte's Latin Lover
Vamos A Ver | EGO | 96170

Conte,Cinzia | (p)
Richard Galliano With Orchestra
Passatori | Dreyfus Jazz Line | FDM 36601-2

Conte,Luis | (bata,finger-cymbals,triangle,bongos)
Dianne Reeves With Band
I Remember | Blue Note | 790264-2
Etta James & The Roots Band
Burnin' Down he House | RCA | 3411633-2
Pat Metheny Group
We Live Here | Geffen Records | GED 24729
Richard Elliot Sextet
City Speak | Blue Note | 832620-2

Contemporary String Quartet: |
Gunther Schuller Ensemble
Beauty Is A Rare Thing:Ornette Coleman-The Complete Atlantic Recordings | Atlantic | 8122-71410-2

Conti,Ivan | (dr,perc,vocsynth)
Ithamara Koorax With Band
Love Dance:The Ballad Album | Milestone | MCD 9327-2

Conti,Sergio | (dr)
Helen Merrill And Her Band
Planet Jazz:Female Jazz Vocalists | Planet Jazz | 2169656-2
Helen Merrill With The Piero Umilliani Group
Parole E Musica | RCA | 2174798-2

Contrafouris,George | (p)
Dimitrios Vassilakis Daedalus Project
Labyrinth | Candid | CCD 79776

Coock,Willie | (tp)
Duke Ellington And His Orchestra
The Big Bands Vol.1.The Snader Telescriptions | Storyville | 4960043

Cook,George or Charles Crosby | (dr)
Eddie Baccus Quartet
Rahsaan/The Complete Mercury Recordings Of Roland Kirk | Mercury | 846630-2

Cook,Jerry | (ts)
Woody Herman And His Orchestra
Songs For Hip Lovers | Verve | 559872-2

Cook,Junior | (ts)
Bill Henderson With The Horace Silver Quintet
Horace Silver Retrospective | Blue Note | 495576-2
Blue Mitchell And His Orchestra
Blue Breaks Beats Vol.2 | Blue Note | 789907-2
Blue Mitchell Quintet
Down With It | Blue Note | 854327-2
Freddie Hubbard Quintet
This Is Jazz:Freddie Hubbard | CBS | CK 65041
Horace Silver Quintet
Blowin' The Blues Away | Blue Note | 495342-2
Horace Silver Retrospective | Blue Note | 495576-2
Song For My Father | Blue Note | 499002-2
Blue Velvet: Crooners, Swooners And Velvet Vocals | Blue Note | 521153-2
True Blue | Blue Note | 534032-2
Finger Poppin' | Blue Note | 542304-2
Silver's Serenade | Blue Note | 821288-2
The Tokyo Blues | Blue Note | 853355-2
Newport Jazz Festival 1958,July 3rd-6th,Vol.1:Mostly Miles | Phontastic | NCD 8813
Paris Blues | Pablo | PACD 5316-2
Kenny Burrell Septet
Blue Lights Vol.1&2 | Blue Note | 857184-2
McCoy Tyner Big Band
The Best Of McCoy Tyner Big Band | Dreyfus Jazz Line | FDM 37012-2

Cook,Marty | (tbvoice)
Gunter Hampel And His Galaxie Dream Band
Journey To The Song Within | Birth | 0017
Marty Cook Conspiracy
Phases Of The Moon | Tutu Records | 888160-2*
Marty Cook Group feat. Jim Pepper
Internationales Jazzfestival Münster | Tutu Records | 888110-2*
Red,White,Black & Blue | Tutu Records | 888174-2*
Marty Cook Group feat. Monty Waters
Borderlines | Tutu Records | 888122-2*
Marty Cook Quintet
Marty Cook Trio/Quintet | Tutu Records | 888210-2*
Marty Cook Trio
Marty Cook Trio/Quintet | Tutu Records | 888210-2*

Cook,Willie | (tpfl-h)
Dizzy Gillespie And His Orchestra
Planet Jazz:Dizzy Gillespie | Planet Jazz | 2152069-2
Planet Jazz:Bebop | RCA | 2169650-2
Planet Jazz:Male Jazz Vocalists | Planet Jazz | 2169657-2
Duke Ellington And Count Basie With Their Orchestras
First Time! | CBS | CK 65571
Duke Ellington And His Orchestra
The Legends Of Swing | Laserlight | 24659
100 Years Duke | Laserlight | 24906
Highlights From The Duke Ellington Centennial Edition | RCA | 2663672-2
Greatest Hits | CBS | 462959-2
Verve Jazz Masters 4:Duke Ellington | Verve | 516338-2
Ellington '55 | Capitol | 520135-2
Great Swing Classics In Hi-Fi | Capitol | 521223-2
Ellington At Newport 1956(Complete) | CBS | CK 64932
Such Sweet Thunder | CBS | CK 65568
Latin America Suite | Original Jazz Classics | OJC20 469-2
Duke Ellington Small Band
The Intimacy Of The Blues | Original Jazz Classics | OJCCD 624-2
Ella Fitzgerald With The Duke Ellington Orchestra
Ella Fitzgerald-First Lady Of Song | Verve | 517898-2
The Best Of The Song Books | Verve | 519804-2
Verve Jazz Masters 6:Ella Fitzgerald | Verve | 519822-2
The Best Of The Song Books:The Ballads | Verve | 521867-2
Verve Jazz Masters 46:Ella Fitzgerald-The Jazz Sides | Verve | 527655-2
Love Songs:The Best Of The Song Books | Verve | 531762-2
Ella Fitzgerald Sings The Duke Ellington Songbook | Verve | 559248-2
For The Love Of Ella Fitzgerald | Verve | 841765-2
Johnny Hodges And The Ellington Men
Verve Jazz Masters 35:Johnny Hodges | Verve | 521857-2
Kansas City 6
Count Basie:Kansas City 6 | Original Jazz Classics | OJC20 449-2(2310871)
Rosemary Clooney With The Duke Ellington Orchestra
Blue Rose | CBS | CK 65506
Sarah Vaughan And The Count Basie Orchestra
Sarah Vaughan Birthday Celebration | Fantasy | FANCD 6090-2

Cool Blue |
Cool Blue
House In The Country | Foolish Music | FM 211591

Coolman,Todd | (b)
Ahmad Jamal Trio
Live In Paris 1992 | Dreyfus Jazz Line | FDM 37019-2
Bobby Watson Quartet
Advance | Enja | ENJ-9075 2
David Fathead Newman Quintet Plus Clifford Jordan
Blue Head | Candid | CCD 79041

Coombes,Nigel | (v)
John Stevens Trio
4,4,4, | Konnex Records | KCD 5049

Cooper,Alan | (bcl)
Graham Stewart And His New Orleans Band
The Golden Years Of Revival Jazz,Vol.4 | Storyville | STCD 5509

Cooper,Bob | (arr,as,ts,b-cl,bs,cl,oboe,engl-h,fl)
Anita O'Day With The Buddy Bregman Orchestra
Pick Yourself Up | Verve | 517329-2
Barney Kessel Quintet
Barney Kessel Plays Standards | Original Jazz Classics | OJCCD 238-2
Bud Shank And Trombones
Cool Fool | Fresh Sound Records | FSR CD 507
Buddy Bregman And His Orchestra
Swinging Kicks | Verve | 559514-2
Chet Baker And The Lighthouse All Stars
Witch Doctor | Original Jazz Classics | OJCCD 609-2
The Jazz Giants Play Harry Warren:Lullaby Of Broadway | Prestige | PCD 24204-2
Ella Fitzgerald With Orchestra
The Best Is Yet To Come | Original Jazz Classics | OJCCD 889-2(2312138)
Ella Fitzgerald With The Buddy Bregman Orchestra
Ella Fitzgerald-First Lady Of Song | Verve | 517898-2
The Best Of The Song Books:The Ballads | Verve | 521867-2
Love Songs:The Best Of The Song Books | Verve | 531762-2
Ella Fitzgerald Sings The Cole Porter Songbook | Verve | 537257-2
Ella Fitzgerald Sings The Rodgers And Hart Song Book | Verve | 537258-2
Ella Fitzgerald With The Nelson Riddle Orchestra
Ella Fitzgerald-First Lady Of Song | Verve | 517898-2
The Best Of The Song Books | Verve | 519804-2
For The Love Of Ella Fitzgerald | Verve | 841765-2
Howard Rumsey's Lighthouse All-Stars
Oboe/Flute | Original Jazz Classics | OJCCD 154-2(C 3520)
Howard Rumsey's Lighthouse All-Stars Vol.6 | Original Jazz Classics | OJCCD 386-2(C 3504)
Sunday Jazz A La Lighthouse Vol.2 | Original Jazz Classics | OJCCD 972-2(S 2501)
Jackie Cain-Roy Kral Group
Full Circle | Fantasy | FCD 24768-2
June Christy With The Pete Rugolo Orchestra
Something Cool(The Complete Mono & Stereo Versions) | Capitol | 534069-2
June Christy With The Shorty Rogers Orchestra
June Christy Big Band Special | Capitol | 498319-2
Maynard Ferguson Band
Verve Jazz Masters 52:Maynard Ferguson | Verve | 529905-2
Miles Davis And The Lighthouse All Stars
At Last! | Original Jazz Classics | OJCCD 480-2
Nat King Cole Quartet With The Stan Kenton Orchestra
Nat King Cole:For Sentimental Reasons | Dreyfus Jazz Line | FDM 36740-2
Peggy Lee With The Quincy Jones Orchestra
Blues Cross Country | Capitol | 520088-2
Pete Rugolo And His Orchestra
Thriller/Richard Diamon(Original Jazz Scores From 2 Classics TV Series) | Fresh Sound Records | FSCD 2015
Shelly Manne And His Hollywood All Stars
Art Pepper:The Hollywood All-Star Sessions | Galaxy | 5GCD 4431-2
Shorty Rogers And His Orchestra Feat. The Giants
PLanet Jazz:Shorty Rogers | Planet Jazz | 2159976-2
Stan Kenton And His Orchestra
Swing Vol.1 | Storyville | 4960343
Stan Kenton Portraits On Standards | Capitol | 531571-2
One Night Stand | Choice | CHCD 71051
Vic Lewis West Coast All Stars
Vic Lewis Presenting A Celebration Of Contemporary West Coast Jazz | Candid | CCD 79711/12

Cooper,Chris | (fr-h)
Canadian Brass
Take The A Train | RCA | 2663455-2

Cooper,Frank 'Buster' | (clavestb)
Arnett Cobb Quintet
Smooth Sailing | Original Jazz Classics | OJCCD 323-2
Buddy Johnson And His Orchestra
Buddy And Ella Johnson 1953-1964 | Bear Family Records | BCD 15479 DH

Cat Anderson And His All Stars
Americans Swinging In Paris:Cat Anderson | EMI Records | 539658-2
Duke Ellington And His Orchestra
Planet Jazz:Johnny Hodges | Planet Jazz | 2152065-2
Duke Ellington's Far East Suite | RCA | 2174797-2
The Art Of Saxophone | Laserlight | 24652
Highlights From The Duke Ellington Centennial Edition | RCA | 2663672-2
The Popular Duke Ellington | RCA | 2663880-2
Duke Ellington: The Champs-Elysees Theater January 29-30th,1965 | Laserlight | 36131
Verve Jazz Masters 4:Duke Ellington | Verve | 516338-2
Verve Jazz Masters 20:Introducing | Verve | 519853-2
Ella & Duke At The Cote D'Azur | Verve | 539030-2
Ella Fitzgerald And Duke Ellington:Cote D'Azure Concerts on Verve | Verve | 539033-2
Soul Call | Verve | 539785-2
The Great Paris Concert | Atlantic | 7567-81303-2
Afro-Bossa | Reprise | 9362-47876-2
Latin America Suite | Original Jazz Classics | OJC20 469-2
Yale Concert | Original Jazz Classics | OJCCD 664-2
Jazz At The Philharmonis Berlin '65/Paris '67 | Pablo | PACD 5304-2
The Jazz Giants Play Duke Ellington:Caravan | Prestige | PCD 24227-2
Ella Fitzgerald With The Duke Ellington Orchestra
The Stockholm Concert 1966 | Pablo | 2308242-2
Ella Fitzgerald-First Lady Of Song | Verve | 517898-2
Verve Jazz Masters 46:Ella Fitzgerald-The Jazz Sides | Verve | 527655-2
Ella At Duke's Place | Verve | 529700-2
Ella & Duke At The Cote D'Azur | Verve | 539030-2
Ella Fitzgerald And Duke Ellington:Cote D'Azure Concerts on Verve | Verve | 539033-2
Ella Fitzgerald With The Duke Ellington Orchestra And Jimmy Jones Trio
Ella & Duke At The Cote D'Azur | Verve | 539030-2
Ella Fitzgerald And Duke Ellington:Cote D'Azure Concerts on Verve | Verve | 539033-2
Ella Fitzgerald With The Jimmy Jones Trio
Ella Fitzgerald And Duke Ellington:Cote D'Azure Concerts on Verve | Verve | 539033-2
Jack McDuff Orchestra
The Last Goodun' | Prestige | PRCD 24274-2
Oscar Peterson With The Duke Ellington Orchestra
Oscar Peterson Plays Duke Ellington | Pablo | 2310966-2
Prestige Blues-Swingers
Soul Street | Original Jazz Classics | OJCCD 987-2(NJ 8293)
Ruth Brown With Orchestra
Fine And Mellow | Fantasy | FCD 9663-2

Cooper,George 'Buster' | (tb)
Duke Ellington And His Orchestra
Welcome To Jazz At The Philharmonic | Fantasy | FANCD 6081-2

Cooper,Herbert | (voc)
Al Sears And His Orchestra
Sear-iously | Bear Family Records | BCD 15668 AH

Cooper,Leroy 'Hog' | (bs)
Buster Smith Orchestra
Atlantic Jazz: Kansas City | Atlantic | 7567-81701-2
Hank Crawford And His Orchestra
Atlantic Saxophones | Rhino | 8122-71256-2
Hank Crawford Septet
More Soul | Atlantic | 8122-73709-2

Cooper,Lindsay | (as,bassoon,sopranino-sax)
Creative Works Orchestra
Willisau And More Live | Creative Works Records | CW CD 1020-2

Cooper,Nick | (cello,clvoc)
Graham Stewart And His New Orleans Band
The Golden Years Of Revival Jazz,Vol.12 | Storyville | STCD 5517
The Golden Years Of Revival Jazz,Vol.14 | Storyville | STCD 5519
John Surman With String Quartet
Coruscating | ECM | 1702(543033-2)

Cooper,Ron | (cello)
Milt Jackson With Strings
To Bags...With Love:Memorial Album | Pablo | 2310967-2

Cooper,Sid | (as,fl,cl,b-cl,oboe,reedssax)
Duke Ellington With Tommy Dorsey And His Orchestra
Highlights From The Duke Ellington Centennial Edition | RCA | 2663672-2
Ella Fitzgerald With Sy Oliver And His Orchestra
Ella Fitzgerald:Mr.Paganini | Dreyfus Jazz Line | FDM 36741-2
Ella Fitzgerald With Sy Oliver And His Orchestra
Ella Fitzgerald:The Decca Years 1949-1954 | Decca | 050668-2
Joe Williams With The Frank Hunter Orchestra
Planet Jazz:Joe Williams | Planet Jazz | 2165370-2
Louis Armstrong And Billie Holiday With Sy Oliver's Orchestra
Louis Armstrong:C'est Si Bon | Dreyfus Jazz Line | FDM 36730-2
Miles Davis + 19
Miles Ahead | CBS | CK 65121
Miles Davis With Gil Evans & His Orchestra
This Is Jazz:Miles Davis Plays Ballads | CBS | CK 65038
Sarah Vaughan With The Hugo Winterhalter Orchestra
Sarah Vaughan:Lover Man | Dreyfus Jazz Line | FDM 36739-2
Tommy Dorsey And His Orchestra
Planet Jazz:Tommy Dorsey | Planet Jazz | 2159972-2
Planet Jazz:Jazz Greatest Hits | Planet Jazz | 2169648-2

Cooper,Steve | (b)
Johnny Lytle Quartet
Got That Feeling/Moon Child | Milestone | MCD 47093-2
Johnny Lytle Quintet
Got That Feeling/Moon Child | Milestone | MCD 47093-2

Copeland,Alan | (vocdir)
Horace Silver Quintet With Vocals
Horace Silver Retrospective | Blue Note | 495576-2

Copeland,Johnny | (gvoc)
Klaus Doldinger's Passport With Johnny 'Clyde' Copeland
Blues Roots | Warner | 9031-75417-2

Copeland,Joyce | (voc)
Horace Silver Quintet With Vocals
Horace Silver Retrospective | Blue Note | 495576-2

Copeland,Keith | (drperc)
Chris Connor With The Hank Jones Trio
As Time Goes By | Enja | ENJ-7061 2
Jam Session
Jam Session Vol.2 | Steeplechase | SCCD 31523
Markus Fleischer Quartet
Let's Call It A Day | Village | WLCD 1017-2
The Upper Manhattan Jazz Society
The Upper Manhattan Jazz Society | Enja | ENJ-4090 2

Copeland,Ray | (tpfl-h)
Ella Fitzgerald With The Bill Doggett Orchestra
Ella Fitzgerald-First Lady Of Song | Verve | 517898-2
Rhythm Is My Business | Verve | 559513-2
Frankie Laine With Buck Clayton And His Orchestra
Jazz Spectacular | CBS | CK 65507
Jimmy Witherspoon With Jay McShann And His Band
Planet Jazz:Male Jazz Vocalists | Planet Jazz | 2169657-2
Quartet
Monk's Music | Original Jazz Classics | OJC20 084-2
Thelonious Monk Quintet
Thelonious Monk:The Complete Prestige Recordings | Prestige | 3 PRCD 4428-2
Thelonious Monk:85th Birthday Celebration | zyx records | FANCD 6076-2
MONK | Original Jazz Classics | OJCCD 016-2
The Jazz Giants Play Jerome Kern:Yesterdays | Prestige | PCD 24202-2
The Prestige Legacy Vol.1:The High Priests | Prestige | PCD 24251-2
Thelonious Monk Septet
Thelonious Monk:85th Birthday Celebration | zyx records | FANCD 6076-2
Thelonious Monk With John Coltrane | Jazzland | JZSA 946-6
Thelonious Monk With John Coltrane | Original Jazz Classics | OJC20 039-2
Monk's Music | Original Jazz Classics | OJC20 084-2

Copeland,Rudy | (voc)
Charles Earland Septet
Charlie's Greatest Hits | Prestige | PCD 24250-2

Copeland,Stewart | (dr)
Stanley Clarke Group
If This Bass Could Only Talk | CBS | 460883-2

Copenhagen Art Ensemble |
Copenhagen Art Ensemble
Shape To Twelve | dacapo | DCCD 9430
Angels' Share | dacapo | DCCD 9452
Marilyn Mazur With Ars Nova And The Copenhagen Art Ensemble
Jordsange | dacapo | DCCD 9454

Copinha | (flagogo)
Baden Powell Solo/Group
Three Originals:Tristeza On Guitar/Poema On Guitar/Apaixonado | MPS | 519216-2

Copland,Marc | (keyboardsp)
Marc Copland-Greg Osby
Round And Round | Nagel-Heyer | CD 2035
Peter Herbert Group
B-A-C-H A Chromatic Universe | Between The Lines | btl 013(Efa 10183)

Copolla,John | (tp)
Vince Guaraldi Group
Charlie Brown's Holiday Hits | Fantasy | FCD 9682-2

Coppieters,Francis | (p)
Stan Getz With The Kurt Edelhagen Orchestra
Stan Getz In Europe | Laserlight | 24657

Coppola,John | (tp)
Stan Kenton And His Orchestra
Stan Kenton Portraits On Standards | Capitol | 531571-2

Cora,Tom | (accordeon,cello,perccellodax)
The Remedy
The Remedy | Jazz Haus Musik | JHM 0069 CD

Corado,Donald | (fr-h)
Gil Evans Orchestra
The Individualism Of Gil Evans | Verve | 833804-2

Corb,Morty | (bg)
Henry Red Allen Band
The Very Best Of Dixieland Jazz | Verve | 535529-2
Kid Ory's Creole Jazz Band
This Kid's The Greatest! | Good Time Jazz | GTCD 12045-2

Corbett,Larry | (cello)
Charlie Haden Quartet West With Strings
The Art Of The Song | Verve | 547403-2
Charlie Haden With String Quartet
The Art Of The Song | Verve | 547403-2
Milt Jackson And His Orchestra
Reverence And Compassion | Reprise | 9362-45204-2

Corcoran,Corky | (ts)
Harry James And His Orchestra
Great Swing Classics In Hi-Fi | Capitol | 521223-2
Trumpet Blues:The Best Of Harry James | Capitol | 521224-2
JATP All Stars
The Complete Jazz At The Philharmonic On Verve 1944-1949 | Verve | 523893-2
Lionel Hampton All Stars
Lionel Hampton:Flying Home | Dreyfus Jazz Line | FDM 36735-2

Cordaro,Jack | (clreeds)
Paul Whiteman And His Orchestra
Planet Jazz:Jack Teagarden | Planet Jazz | 2161236-2
The Three T's
Jazz:The Essential Collection Vol.3 | IN+OUT Records | 78013-2

Cordaro,Joe | (clas)
Paul Whiteman And His Orchestra
Jazz:The Essential Collection Vol.3 | IN+OUT Records | 78013-2

Cordaro,John | (cl,b-cl,asbs)
Planet Jazz:Jack Teagarden | Planet Jazz | 2161236-2

Cordes,Daniel 'Danda' | (b)
Jazz Indeed
Under Water | Traumton Records | 2415-2
Ute Kannenberg Quartet
Kannenberg On Purpose | Jazz Haus Musik | JHM 0109 CD
Ute Kannenberg Quartet With Guests
Kannenberg On Purpose | Jazz Haus Musik | JHM 0109 CD
Welcome To The Maze
Welcome To The Maze:Puzzle | Nabel Records:Jazz Network | CD 4671

Cordovani,Renato | (b-cl)
Klaus König Orchestra
Times Of Devastation/Poco A Poco | Enja | ENJ-6014 22

Cords,Nick | (viola)
Kevin Mahogany With The Bob James Trio, Kirk Whalum And Strings
My Romance | Warner | 9362-47025-2

Corea,Chick | (el-p,org,synth,cowbell,cymbal)
Al Di Meola-Chick Corea
Land Of The Midnight Sun | CBS | 468214-2
Blue Mitchell Quintet
Down With It | Blue Note | 854327-2
Bobby McFerrin-Chick Corea
Play | Blue Note | 795477-2
Cal Tjader Quintet
Talkin Verve/Roots Of Acid Jazz:Cal Tjader | Verve | 531562-2
Cal Tjader's Orchestra
Verve Jazz Masters 39:Cal Tjader | Verve | 521858-2
Talkin Verve/Roots Of Acid Jazz:Cal Tjader | Verve | 531562-2
Soul Burst | Verve | 557446-2
Chick Corea
Piano Improvisations-Vol.1 | ECM | 1014(811979-2)
Piano Improvisations-Vol.2 | ECM | 1020(829190-2)
Trio Music | ECM | 1232/33(159454-2)
Children's Songs | ECM | 1267(815680-2)
Verve Jazz Masters 3:Chick Corea | Verve | 519820-2
Expressions | GRP | GRP 97732
Chick Corea And His Orchestra
My Spanish Heart | Polydor | 543303-3
Chick Corea And Return To Forever
Light As A Feather | Polydor | 557115-2
Chick Corea Electric Band
The Chick Corea Electric Band | GRP | GRP 95352
Light Years | GRP | GRP 95462
Eye Of The Beholder | GRP | GRP 95642
Beneath The Mask | GRP | GRP 96492
Chick Corea Group
Verve Jazz Masters 3:Chick Corea | Verve | 519820-2
Chick Corea Quartet
Return To Forever | ECM | 1022(811978-2)
Verve Jazz Masters 3:Chick Corea | Verve | 519820-2
Verve Jazz Masters 20:Introducing | Verve | 519853-2
My Spanish Heart | Polydor | 543303-3
Inner Space | Atlantic | 7567-81304-2
Chick Corea Quintet
Inner Space | Atlantic | 7567-81304-2
Chick Corea-Herbie Hancock-Keith Jarrett-McCoy Tyner | Atlantic | 7567-81402-2
Chick Corea Septet
The Complete 'Is' Sessions | Blue Note | 540532-2
Chick Corea Trio
A.R.C. | ECM | 1009
Trio Music | ECM | 1232/33(159454-2)
Trio Music,Live In Europe | ECM | 1310(827769-2)
The Story Of Jazz Piano | Laserlight | 24653
Verve Jazz Masters 3:Chick Corea | Verve | 519820-2
Inner Space | Atlantic | 7567-81304-2
Chick Corea-Herbie Hancock-Keith Jarrett-McCoy Tyner | Atlantic | 7567-81402-2
Akoustic Band | GRP | GRP 95822
Chick Corea With String Quartet
Verve Jazz Masters 3:Chick Corea | Verve | 519820-2
Chick Corea With String Quartet,Flute And French Horn
Septet | ECM | 1297
Chick Corea/Gary Burton
Crystal Silence | ECM | 1024(831331-2)
Chick Corea-Gary Burton
In Concert, Zürich, October 28, 1979 | ECM | 1182/83
Chick Corea-Herbie Hancock Duo
An Evening Wirh Chick Corea & Herbie Hancock | Polydor | 835680-2
Chick Corea-Miroslav Vitous
Trio Music | ECM | 1232/33(159454-2)
Chick Corea's Return To Forever
Verve Jazz Masters 3:Chick Corea | Verve | 519820-2
Chick Corea-Stanley Clarke
Verve Jazz Masters 3:Chick Corea | Verve | 519820-2
Chick Corea-Steve Kujala
Voyage | ECM | 1282
Circle
Paris Concert | ECM | 1018/19(843163-2)
Dave Weckl Group
Master Plan | GRP | GRP 96192
Gary Burton-Chick Corea
Duet | ECM | 1140(829941-2)
GRP All-Star Big Band
All Blues | GRP | GRP 98002
Herbie Mann Group
The Best Of Herbie Mann | Atlantic | 7567-81369-2
Hubert Laws Quartet
The Laws Of Jazz | Atlantic | 8122-71636-2
Joe Henderson Quartet
Relaxin' At Camarillo | Original Jazz Classics | OJCCD 776-2(C 14006)
Katia Labeque-Chick Corea
Little Girl Blue | Dreyfus Jazz Line | FDM 36186-2
Lenny White Group
Present Tense | Hip Bop | HIBD 8004
Makoto Ozone Group
Treasure | Verve | 021906-2
Marion Brown Orchestra
Afternoon Of A Georgia Faun | ECM | 1004
Miles Davis Group
Circle In The Round | CBS | 467898-2
In A Silent Way | CBS | 86556-2
Live-Evil | CBS | C2K 65135
Live At The Fillmore East | CBS | C2K 65139
Bitches Brew | CBS | C2K 65774
On The Corner | CBS | CK 63980
Miles Davis Quintet
Black Beauty-Miles Davis At Filmore West | CBS | C2K 65138
Miles Davis Sextet
Black Beauty-Miles Davis At Filmore West | CBS | C2K 65138
Miroslav Vitous Group
Universal Syncopations | ECM | 1863(038506-2)
Return To Forever
Return To The 7th Galaxy-Return To Forever:The Anthology | Verve | 533108-2
Where Have I Known You Before | Polydor | 825206-2
Hymn Of The Seventh Galaxy | Polydor | 825336-2
Ron Carter Orchestra
Parade | Original Jazz Classics | OJCCD 1047-2(M 9088)
Ron Carter Quartet
Parade | Original Jazz Classics | OJCCD 1047-2(M 9088)
Stan Getz Quartet
Sony Jazz Collection:Stan Getz | CBS | 488623-2
Stan Getz Highlights:The Best Of The Verve Years Vol.2 | Verve | 517330-2
Verve Jazz Masters 8:Stan Getz | Verve | 519823-2
Verve Jazz Masters 53:Stan Getz-Bossa Nova | Verve | 529904-2
A Life In Jazz:A Musical Biography | Verve | 535119-2
Ultimate Stan Getz selected by Joe Henderson | Verve | 557532-2
Stan Getz Highlights | Verve | 847430-2
Stan Getz With The Richard Evans Orchestra
What The World Needs Now-Stan Getz Plays Bacharach And David | Verve | 557450-2
Wayne Shorter Sextet
Wayne Shorter:The Classic Blue Note Recordings | Blue Note | 540856-2

Cores,Alex | (v)
Grover Washington Jr. Orchestra
Jazzrock-Anthology Vol.3:Fusion | Zounds | CD 27100555

Corimbi,Martino | (voc)
Ernst Reijseger & Tenore E Cuncordu De Orosei
Colla Voche | Winter&Winter | 910037-2

Cornelius,Corky | (tp)
Benny Goodman And His Orchestra
Camel Caravan Broadcast 1939 Vol.3 | Phontastic | NCD 8819
More Camel Caravans | Phontastic | NCD 8845/6

Cornell,Butch | (org)
Boogaloo Joe Jones Quintet
Discovery:Grover Washington Jr.-The First Recordings | Prestige | PCD 11020-2
Boogaloo Joe Jones Sextet
Jazzin' With The Soul Brothers | Fantasy | FANCD 6086-2
Discovery:Grover Washington Jr.-The First Recordings | Prestige | PCD 11020-2

Cornuchet,Sonia | (keyboardsvoc)
Lazaro Ros Con Mezcla
Cantos | Intuition Records | INT 3080-2

Corrado,Donald | (fr-h)
Carmen McRae With The Ralph Burns Orchetra
Birds Of A Feather | Decca | 589515-2
Grover Washington Jr. Orchestra
Jazzrock-Anthology Vol.3:Fusion | Zounds | CD 27100555
Jimmy Smith With The Billy Byers Orchestra
Jimmy Smith:Best Of The Verve Years | Verve | 527950-2
Jimmy Smith With The Oliver Nelson Orchestra
Verve Jazz Masters 29:Jimmy Smith | Verve | 521855-2
Jimmy Smith:Best Of The Verve Years | Verve | 527950-2
Jimmy Smith-Talkin' Verve | Verve | 531563-2
John Coltrane And His Orchestra
John Coltrane:Standards | Impulse(MCA) | 549914-2
John Coltrane Quartet With Brass
The Complete Africa/Brass Sessions | Impulse(MCA) | 952168-2
Machito And His Orchestra
Afro-Cuban Jazz Moods | Original Jazz Classics | OJC20 447-2

Corrao,Vinnie | (g)
Eric Kloss Quartet
About Time | Prestige | PRCD 24268-2
Les McCann Quartet
Talkin' Verve:Les McCann | Verve | 557351-2

Corre,Jay | (cl,ts,fl,saxreeds)
Buddy Rich And His Orchestra
Swingin' New Big Band | Pacific Jazz | 835232-2
Big Swing Face | Pacific Jazz | 837989-2
Buddy Rich Big Band
The New One! | Pacific Jazz | 494507-2
Ella Fitzgerald With The Marty Paich Orchestra
Get Happy! | Verve | 523321-2
Jack Costanzo Group
Latin Fever:The Wild Rhythms Of Jack Costanza | Capitol | 590955-2

Correa,Benjamin 'Chamin' | (g)
Dave Brubeck Sextet
Bravo! Brubeck! | CBS | CK 65723

Correa,Bill | (fr-h)
Jimmy Smith With The Lalo Schifrin Orchestra
Jimmy Smith:Best Of The Verve Years | Verve | 527950-2
Jimmy Smith-Talkin' Verve | Verve | 531563-2

The Cat | Verve | 539756-2
Correa,Christine | (voc)
Frank Carlberg Group
Variations On A Summer Day | Fresh Sound Records | FSNT 083 CD
Correa,Djalma | (perc,agogo,atabaques,pinicos)
The New Dave Pike Set & Grupo Baiafra De Bahia
Dave Pike Set:Masterpieces | MPS | 531848-2
Correa,Fernando | (g)
Maximilian Geller Group
Maximilian Geller Goes Bossa | Edition Collage | EC 496-2
Maimilian Geller Goes Bossa Encore | Edition Collage | EC 505-2
Maximilian Geller Quartet feat. Melanie Bong
Maimilian Geller Goes Bossa Encore | Edition Collage | EC 505-2
Maximilian Geller Quartet feat. Sabina Sciubba
Maimilian Geller Goes Bossa Encore | Edition Collage | EC 505-2
Maximilian Geller Quartet feat. Susan Tobocman
Maimilian Geller Goes Bossa Encore | Edition Collage | EC 505-2
Melanie Bong With Band
Fantasia | Jazz 4 Ever Records:Jazz Network | J4E 4755
Correa,Mayuto | (congas,perctriangle)
Donald Byrd Orchestra
Places And Spaces | Blue Note | 854326-2
Gato Barbieri Orchestra
Latino America | Impulse(MCA) | 952236-2
Correa,William | (bongodr)
Dave Pike Quintet
Carnavals | Prestige | PCD 24248-2
Dave Pike Sextet
Carnavals | Prestige | PCD 24248-2
Tito Puente Orchestra
Planet Jazz:Tito Puente | Planet Jazz | 2165369-2
Correro,Joe | (dr)
Al Jarreau With Band
We Got By | Reprise | 7599-27222-2
All Fly Home | Warner | 7599-27362-2
Corsen,Randal | (pkeyboards)
The Rosenberg Trio
Suenos Gitanos | Polydor | 549581-2
Cortadellas,Jaume | (fl,bass-flpiccolo)
Dave Liebman And The Lluis Vidal Trio With The Orquestra De Cambra Theatre Lliure
Dave Liebman And The Lluis Vidal Trio | Fresh Sound Records | FSNT 026 CD
Orquestra De Cambra Teatre Lliure
Orquestra De Cambra Teatre Lliure and Lluis Vidal Trio feat.Dave Liebman | Fresh Sound Records | FSNT 027 CD
Porgy And Bess | Fresh Sound Records | FSNT 066 CD
Orquestra De Cambra Teatre Lliure feat. Dave Liebman
Orquestra De Cambra Teatre Lliure and Lluis Vidal Trio feat.Dave Liebman | Fresh Sound Records | FSNT 027 CD
Cortese,Dominic | (accordeon)
The Sidewalks Of New York
Tin Pan Alley:The Sidewalks Of New York | Winter&Winter | 910038-2
Uri Caine Ensemble
Wagner E Venezia | Winter&Winter | 910013-2
Cortez,Dean | (el-b)
Caldera
Jazzrock-Anthology Vol.3:Fusion | Zounds | CD 27100555
Cortijo,José | (perc)
Abdullah Ibrahim With The NDR Big Band
Ekapa Lodumo | TipToe | TIP-888840 2
We Three
The Drivin' Beat | Organic Music | ORGM 9707
Corwin,Bob | (p)
Chet Baker Septet
Chet Baker Plays The Best Of Lerner And Loewe | Original Jazz Classics | OJC20 137-2
Corwin,Bob or Lonnie Hewitt | (p)
Anita O'Day With The Cal Tjader Quartet
Verve Jazz Masters 49:Anita O'Day | Verve | 527653-2
Time For 2 | Verve | 559808-2
Coryell,Larry | (12-string-g,el-g,g,b,voc,g-solo)
Bireli Lagrene Group
Bireli Lagrene 'Highlights' | Jazzpoint | JP 1027 CD
Bireli Lagrene | Jazzpoint | JP 1049 CD
Charles Mingus Orchestra
Three Or Four Shades Of Blues | Atlantic | 7567-81403-2
Chet Baker-Wolfgang Lackerschmid Quintet
Chet Baker:The Legacy Vol.3:Why Shouldn't You Cry | Enja | ENJ-9337 2
Chico Hamilton Quartet
The Dealer | Impulse(MCA) | 547958-2
Chico Hamilton Quintet
The Dealer | Impulse(MCA) | 547958-2
The Roots Of Acid Jazz | Impulse(MCA) | IMP 12042
Gary Burton Quartet
Planet Jazz:Gary Burton | RCA | 2165367-2
Gary Burton Quartet With Orchestra
A Genuine Tong Funeral(Dark Opera Without Words) | RCA | 2119255-2
Herbie Mann Group
Memphis Underground | Atlantic | 7567-81364-2
The Best Of Herbie Mann | Atlantic | 7567-81369-2
Larry Coryell Quartet
Air Dancing | Jazzpoint | JP 1025 CD
Larry Coryell-Alphonse Mouzon Quartet
Atlantic Jazz: Fusion | Atlantic | 7567-81711-2
Larry Coryell-Miroslav Vitous
Dedicated To Bill Evans And Scott LaFaro | Jazzpoint | JP 1021 CD
Michael Mantler Group
Movies | Watt | 7 (2313107)
Movies/More Movies | Watt | 7/10(543377-2)
Sonny Rollins Sextet
Don't Ask | Original Jazz Classics | OJCCD 915-2(M 9090)
Sonny Rollins-Larry Coryell Duo
Don't Ask | Original Jazz Classics | OJCCD 915-2(M 9090)
Stephane Grappelli Quartet
Grapelli Story | Verve | 515807-2
Verve Jazz Masters 11:Stéphane Grappelli | Verve | 516758-2
The Jazz Composer's Orchestra
Comminications | JCOA | 1001/2
Coscia,Gianni | (accordeon)
Gianluigi Trovesi-Gianni Coscia
In Cerca Di Cibo | ECM | 1703(543034-2)
Cosey,Pete | (el-g,g,synthperc)
Miles Davis Group
Paris Jazz Concert:Miles Davis | Laserlight | 17445
Pangaea | CBS | 467087-2
Agharta | CBS | 467897-2
Dark Magus | CBS | C2K 65137
Costa,Carmen | (cabassa,vocperc)
Bola Sete Quintet
Tour De Force:The Bola Sete Trios | Fantasy | FCD 24766-2
Dizzy Gillespie And His Orchestra
Ultimate Dizzy Gillespie | Verve | 557535-2
Stan Getz With The Gary McFarland Orchestra
Stan Getz Highlights:The Best Of The Verve Years Vol.2 | Verve | 517330-2
Verve Jazz Masters 53:Stan Getz-Bossa Nova | Verve | 529904-2
Big Band Bossa Nova | Verve | 825771-2 PMS
Stan Getz Highlights | Verve | 847430-2
Costa,Don | (arrcond)
Dinah Washington With Orchestra
Ballads | Roulette | 537559-2
Sarah Vaughan With Orchestra
Ballads | Roulette | 537561-2
Sarah Vaughan With The Don Costa Orchestra
Jazz Profile | Blue Note | 823517-2
Costa,Eddie | (p,vibperc)
Bobby Jaspar Quintet
Flute Flight | Original Jazz Classics | OJCCD 1084-2(P 2124)
Eddie Costa Quartet
Guys And Dolls Like Vives | Verve | 549366-2
Gunther Schuller Ensemble
Beauty Is A Rare Thing:Ornette Coleman-The Complete Atlantic Recordings | Atlantic | 8122-71410-2
J.R. Monterose Sextet
Jaywalkin' | Fresh Sound Records | FSR-CD 320
Tal Farlow Quartet
Verve Jazz Masters 41:Tal Farlow | Verve | 527365-2
Tal Farlow Trio
Verve Jazz Masters 41:Tal Farlow | Verve | 527365-2
The Swinging Guitar Of Tal Farlow | Verve | 559515-2
Costa,Gal | (voc)
Antonio Carlos Jobim Group
Antonio Carlos Jobim And Friends | Verve | 531556-2
Antonio Carlos Jobim-Gal Costa Septet
Antonio Carlos Jobim And Friends | Verve | 531556-2
Gal Costa With The Herbie Hancock Sextet
Antonio Carlos Jobim And Friends | Verve | 531556-2
Gal Costa-Herbie Hancock
Antonio Carlos Jobim And Friends | Verve | 531556-2
Costa,Max | (arr)
John McLaughlin Group
The Promise | Verve | 529828-2
Costanza,Jack | (bongos)
Jack Costanzo Group
Latin Fever:The Wild Rhythms Of Jack Costanza | Capitol | 590955-2
Nat King Cole And His Trio
Nat King Cole:The Snader Telescriptions | Storyville | 4960103
Nat King Cole And His Trio With Strings
Nat King Cole:The Snader Telescriptions | Storyville | 4960103
Nat King Cole Duo
Nat King Cole:The Snader Telescriptions | Storyville | 4960103
Costanzo,Jack | (bongos,congasperc)
Nat King Cole And His Trio
Nat King Cole:Route 66 | Dreyfus Jazz Line | FDM 36716-2
Nat King Cole Quartet
Penthouse Serenade | Capitol | 494504-2
The Instrumental Classics | Capitol | 798288-2
Nat King Cole:For Sentimental Reasons | Dreyfus Jazz Line | FDM 36740-2
Nat King Cole Quartet With The Pete Rugolo Orchestra
The Instrumental Classics | Capitol | 798288-2
Nat King Cole Quartet With The Stan Kenton Orchestra
Nat King Cole:For Sentimental Reasons | Dreyfus Jazz Line | FDM 36740-2
Nat King Cole Quintet
Penthouse Serenade | Capitol | 494504-2
Nat King Cole Sextet
After Midnight | Capitol | 520087-2
Nat King Cole Trio With Pete Rugolo's Orchestra
Nat King Cole:For Sentimental Reasons | Dreyfus Jazz Line | FDM 36740-2
Costello,Elvis | (voc)
Charles Mingus Orchestra
Tonight At Noon...Three Or Four Shades Of Love | Dreyfus Jazz Line | FDM 36633-2
Costello,Gary | (b)
Vince Jones Group
For All Colours | Intuition Records | INT 3071-2
Tell Me A Secret | Intuition Records | INT 3072-2
Vince Jones Septet
On The Brink Of It | Intuition Records | INT 3068-2
Coster Jr.,Tom | (keyboards)
Steve Smith & Vital Information
Vitalive! | VeraBra Records | CDVBR 2051-2
Coster,Tom | (el-p,org,accordeonkeyboards)
Vital Information
Ray Of Hope | VeraBra Records | CDVBR 2161-2
Where We Come From | Intuition Records | INT 3218-2
Live Around The World Where We Come From Tour '98-'99 | Intuition Records | INT 3296-2
Show 'Em Where You Live | Intuition Records | INT 3306-2
Costi,Al | (g)
Stan Kenton And His Orchestra
Stan Kenton-The Formative Years | Decca | 589489-2
Cottler,Irv | (drperc)
Anita O'Day With The Billy May Orchestra
Verve Jazz Masters 49:Anita O'Day | Verve | 527653-2
Barney Kessel And His Quintet
To Swing Or Not To Swing | Original Jazz Classics | OJCCD 317-2
Barney Kessel And His Septet
To Swing Or Not To Swing | Original Jazz Classics | OJCCD 317-2
Billy Eckstine With The Billy May Orchestra
Once More With Feeling | Roulette | 581862-2
Ella Fitzgerald With The Nelson Riddle Orchestra
The Best Of The Song Books:The Ballads | Verve | 521867-2
Love Songs:The Best Of The Song Books | Verve | 531762-2
Ella Fitzgerald Sings The Johnny Mercer Songbook | Verve | 539057-2
Louis Armstrong With The Hal Mooney Orchestra
Ambassador Louis Armstrong Vol.17:Moments To Remember(1952-1956) | Ambassador | CLA 1917
Van Alexander Orchestra
Home Of Happy Feet/Swing! Staged For Sound! | Capitol | 535211-2
Cotton,Chuck | (dr)
Billy Boy Arnold Group
Eldorado Cadillac | Alligator Records | ALCD 4836
Cotton,James | (harmvoc)
James Cotton Group
Deep In The Blues | Verve | 529849-2
Muddy Waters Blues Band
Muddy Waters-The Collection | MCA | MCD 18961
Otis Spann Band
The Blues Never Die! | Original Blues Classics | OBCCD 530-2(P 7391)
Windy City Blues | Stax | SCD 8612-2
Cotton,Mike | (tp,covoc)
Great British Jazz Band
The Great British Jazz Band:Jubilee | Candid | CCD 79720
The Great British Jazz Band
A British Jazz Odyssey | Candid | CCD 79740
Cottrell Jr.,Louis | (clts)
Jim Robinson's New Orleans Band
Atlantic Jazz: New Orleans | Atlantic | 7567-81700-2
Couch Ensemble |
Couch Ensemble
Winnetou | Jazz 'n' Arts Records | JNA 1503
Coulber,Dunstan | (cl)
Dunstan Coulber Quartet
Standards For A New Century | Nagel-Heyer | CD 081
Coulibaly,Soungalo | (fl,maracas,vocperc)
Jon Hassell & Farafina
Flash Of The Spirit | Intuition Records | INT 3009-2
Coulon,Cornell | (voc)
First Revolution Singers
First Revolution Gospel Singers:A Capella | Laserlight | 24338
Coulson,Victor | (tp)
Charlie Christian All Stars
Charlie Christian-Jazz Immortal/Dizzy Gillespie 1944 | Original Jazz Classics | OJCCD 1932-2(ES 548)
Coleman Hawkins And His Orchestra
Jazz:The Essential Collection Vol.3 | IN+OUT Records | 78013-2
Minton's Playhouse All Stars
Charlie Christian:Swing To Bop | Dreyfus Jazz Line | FDM 36715-2
Coulter,Butch | (harm)
Marty Hall Band
Tried & True | Blues Beacon | BLU-1030 2
Who's Been Talkin'?s | Blues Beacon | BLU-1033 2
Coulter,Cliff | (el-b,el-pg)
John Lee Hooker Group
Endless Boogie | MCA | MCD 10413
Counce,Curtis | (b)
Chet Baker Sextet
The Best Of Chet Baker Plays | Pacific Jazz | 797161-2
Chet Baker-Art Pepper-Phil Urso Sextet
Picture Of Heath | Pacific Jazz | 494106-2
Clifford Brown All Stars
Verve Jazz Masters 44:Clifford Brown and Max Roach | Verve | 528109-2
Brownie-The Complete EmArCy Recordings Of Clifford Brown | EmArCy | 838306-2
Lester Young And His Band
Jazz Gallery:Lester Young Vol.2(1946-59) | RCA | 2119541-2
Lester Young:The Complete Aladdin Sessions | Blue Note | 832787-2
Maynard Ferguson Band
Verve Jazz Masters 52:Maynard Ferguson | Verve | 529905-2
Shorty Rogers And His Orchestra Feat. The Giants
PLanet Jazz:Shorty Rogers | Planet Jazz | 2159976-2
Count Basie Orchestra,The |
George Benson Group/Orchestra
George Benson Anthology | Warner | 8122-79934-2
Courance,Edgar | (clts)
Bill Coleman Quintet
Americans Swinging In Paris:Bill Coleman-The Elegance | EMI Records | 539662-2
Courbois,Pierre | (dr,cymbals,gongs,live-electronics)
Gunter Hampel Quintet
Legendary: The 27th Of May 1997 | Birth | CD 045
Courthaliac,Laurent | (p)
Gäel Horellou-David Sauzay Quintet
Gäel Horellou Versus David Sauzay | Fresh Sound Records | FSNT 068 CD
Courtois,Vincent | (celloelectronics)
Louis Sclavis Group
Dans La Nuit | ECM | 1805(589524-2)
Napoli's Walls | ECM | 1857(038504-2)
Louis Sclavis Quartet
L'Affrontement Des Prétendants | ECM | 1705(159927-2)
Michael Riessler & Singer Pur with Vincent Courtois
Ahi Vita | ACT | 9417-2
Michel Godard Ensemble
Castel Del Monte II | Enja | ENJ-9431 2
Michel Petrucciani With The Graffiti String Quartet
Marvellous | Dreyfus Jazz Line | FDM 36564-2
Rabih Abou-Khalil Group
Yara | Enja | ENJ-9360 2
The Cactus Of Knowledge | Enja | ENJ-9401 2
Vincent Courtois Quartet
Translucide | Enja | ENJ-9380 2
Vincent Courtois Trio
The Fitting Room | Enja | ENJ-9411 2
Yves Robert Trio
In Touch | ECM | 1787(016375-2)
Courvoisier,Sylvie | (pprepared-p)
Sylvie Courvoisier Group
Abaton | ECM | 1838/39(157628-2)
Ocre | Enja | ENJ-9323 2
Y2K | Enja | ENJ-9383 2
Cousins,Lorraine | (voc)
Charles Mingus Orchestra
Charles Mingus:Pre-Bird(Mingus Revisited) | Verve | 538636-2
Couturier,Francois | (el-p,synthp)
Anouar Brahem Group
Khomsa | ECM | 1561(527093-2)
Anouar Brahem Trio
Le Pas Du Chat Noir | ECM | 1792(016373-2)
Dominique Pifarély-Francois Couturier
Poros | ECM | 1647
Couvert,Francoise | (v)
Renaud Garcia-Fons
Navigatore | Enja | ENJ-9418 2
Renaud Garcia-Fons Group
Navigatore | Enja | ENJ-9418 2
Couvert,Philippe | (v)
Renaud Garcia-Fons
Navigatore | Enja | ENJ-9418 2
Renaud Garcia-Fons Group
Navigatore | Enja | ENJ-9418 2
Covelli,Larry | (as,saxts)
Woody Herman And His Orchestra
Verve Jazz Masters 54:Woody Herman | Verve | 529903-2
Woody Herman-1963 | Philips | 589490-2
Covey,Arnold | (g)
Benny Goodman And His Orchestra
More Camel Caravans | Phontastic | NCD 8845/6
Covington,Charles | (org)
George Benson With The Don Sebesky Orchestra
Verve Jazz Masters 21:George Benson | Verve | 521861-2
Covington,Kirk | (dr)
Allan Holdsworth Group
None Too Soon | Cream Records | CR 400-2
Covington,Warren | (tb)
Gene Krupa And His Orchestra
Mullenium | CBS | CK 65678
Cowell,Stanley | (el-p,p,org,arr,chimes,kalimba)
Art Pepper Quartet
Art Pepper:The Complete Galaxy Recordings | Galaxy | 16GCD 1016-2
The Jazz Giants Play Harry Warren:Lullaby Of Broadway | Prestige | PCD 24204-2
Art Pepper Quintet
Art Pepper:The Complete Galaxy Recordings | Galaxy | 16GCD 1016-2
Art Pepper Quintet With Strings
Art Pepper:The Complete Galaxy Recordings | Galaxy | 16GCD 1016-2
Winter Moon | Original Jazz Classics | OJC20 677-2(GXY 5140)
Gary Bartz Quartet
Libra/Another Earth | Milestone | MCD 47077-2
Gary Bartz Sextet
Libra/Another Earth | Milestone | MCD 47077-2
Jack DeJohnette Quartet
The DeJohnette Complex | Original Jazz Classics | OJCCD 617-2
Jack DeJohnette Quintet
The DeJohnette Complex | Original Jazz Classics | OJCCD 617-2
Jack DeJohnette Sextet
The DeJohnette Complex | Original Jazz Classics | OJCCD 617-2
Larry Coryell Quartet
Air Dancing | Jazzpoint | JP 1025 CD
Sonny Rollins Sextet
The Cutting Edge | Original Jazz Classics | OJC 468(M 9059)
Sonny Rollins Sextet With Rufus Harley
The Cutting Edge | Original Jazz Classics | OJC 468(M 9059)
Stan Getz Quartet
The Art Of Saxophone | Laserlight | 24652
Cowherd,Jon | (pwurlitzer)
Brian Blade Group
Fellowship | Blue Note | 859417-2
Cox,Anthony | (b,el-b,voc,b-gperc)
Christoph Lauer Quintet
Fragile Network | ACT | 9266-2
Cornelius Claudio Kreusch Group
Scoop | ACT | 9255-2
Craig Harris And Tailgater's Tales
Shelter | JMT Edition | 919008-2
Blackout In The Square Root Of Soul | JMT Edition | 919015-2
David Friedman Quartet

INTERPRETENVERZEICHNIS

Other Worlds | Intuition Records | INT 3210-2
David Friedman Trio
Other Worlds | Intuition Records | INT 3210-2
Dino Saluzzi-Anthony Cox-David Friedman
Rios | VeraBra Records | CDVBR 2156-2
Erica Lindsay Quintet
Dreamers | Candid | CCD 79040
Erica Lindsay Sextet
Dreamers | Candid | CCD 79040
Fred Wesley Group
New Friends | Minor Music | 801016
Herb Robertson Group
The Little Trumpet | JMT Edition | 919007-2
Joe Lovano Quartet
Live At The Village Vanguard | Blue Note | 829125-2

Cox,Baby | (voc)
Duke Ellington And His Cotton Club Orchestra
Planet Jazz:Duke Ellington | Planet Jazz | 2152053-2

Cox,Bruce | (dr,voctambourine)
Annette Lowman With Three Of A Kind, Fred Wesley And Rodney Jones
Brown Baby:A Tribute To Oscar Brown Jr. | Minor Music | 801061
Bruce Cox Quartet With Guests
Stick To It | Minor Music | 801055
Craig Bailey Band
A New Journey | Candid | CCD 79725
Fred Wesley Group
Swing & Be Funky | Minor Music | 801027
Amalgamation | Minor Music | 801045
Pee Wee Ellis Trio
Twelve And More Blues | Minor Music | 801034
Three Of A Kind
Drip Some Grease | Minor Music | 801056

Cox,Ida | (voc)
Ida Cox With Jesse Crump
The Blues | Storyville | 4960323
Ida Cox With The James P. Johnson Septet
From Spiritual To Swing | Vanguard | VCD 169/71

Cox,John | (dr)
Benny Waters Quartet
Hurry On Down | Storyville | STCD 8264

Cox,Kenny | (p)
Etta Jones And Her Band
Love Shout | Original Jazz Classics | OJCCD 941-2(P 7272)

Cox,Leon | (tb)
Anita O'Day With Gene Krupa And His Orchestra
Let Me Off Uptown:Anita O'Day With Gene Krupa | CBS | CK 65625
Duke Ellington And His Orchestra
Jazz Festival Vol.2 | Storyville | 4960743
Duke Ellington And His Orchestra feat. Paul Gonsalves | Original Jazz Classics | OJCCD 623-2
The Jazz Giants Play Duke Ellington:Caravan | Prestige | PCD 24227-2

Cox,Luuk | (drperc)
Dogs Don't Sing In The Rain
Bones For Breakfast | Edition Collage | EC 472-2
Vocal Moments | Take Twelve On CD | TT 008-2
Wind Moments | Take Twelve On CD | TT 009-2

Cox,Marion | (voc)
Duke Ellington And His Orchestra
Planet Jazz:Duke Ellington | Planet Jazz | 2152053-2

Coyne,Kevin | (voice)
Michael Mantler Group
Michael Mantler: No Answer/Silence | Watt | 2/5(543374-2)
Silence | Watt | 5 (2313105)

Cozeneau,Coz | (dr)
Muggsy Spanier And His Dixieland All Stars
Muggsy Spanier At Club Hangover 1953/54 | Storyville | STCD 6033

Cozier,Jimmy | (as,bs,cfl)
Abdullah Ibrahim Septet
No Fear, No Die(S'en Fout La Mort):Original Soundtrack | TipToe | TIP-888815 2

Crabtree,Richie | (p)
The Mastersounds
The Mastersounds | Prestige | PRCD 24770-2

Cracov,Dave | (v)
Artie Shaw And His Orchestra
Planet JazzArtie Shaw | Planet Jazz | 2152057-2
Planet Jazz:Jazz Greatest Hits | Planet Jazz | 2169648-2

Craig,Al | (dr)
Django Reinhardt And His Quintet
Peche À La Mode-The Great Blue Star Sessions 1947/1953 | Verve | 835418-2
Django's Music
Peche À La Mode-The Great Blue Star Sessions 1947/1953 | Verve | 835418-2

Craig,Charles | (el-p,mini-moog,voicep)
Christian McBride Group
A Family Affair | Verve | 557554-2
Teodross Avery Quartet
My Generation | Impulse(MCA) | 951181-2
Teodross Avery Quintet
My Generation | Impulse(MCA) | 951181-2

Craig,Debi | (voc)
Benny Goodman And His Orchestra
40th Anniversary Concert-Live At Carnegie Hall | London | 820349-2

Craig,James | (p)
Dinah Washington With The Eddie Chamblee Orchestra
Dinah Sings Bessie Smith | Verve | 538635-2

Cramer,Dylan | (as)
Dylan Cramer Quartet
All Night Long | Nagel-Heyer | CD 073

Cramer,Heinz | (g)
Helmut Zacharias mit Kleiner Tanz-Besetzung
Ich Habe Rhythmus | Bear Family Records | BCD 15642 AH
Helmut Zacharias Sextett
Ich Habe Rhythmus | Bear Family Records | BCD 15642 AH
Inge Brandenburg And Her All-Stars
Why Don't You Take All Of Me | Bear Family Records | BCD 15614 AH

Cramer,Ingo | (g)
Harry Allen And Randy Sandke Meets The RIAS Big Band Berlin
The Music Of The Trumpet Kings | Nagel-Heyer | CD 037

Craney,Mark | (drperc)
Jean-Luc Ponty Quintet
The Very Best Of Jean-Luc Ponty | Rhino | 8122-79862-2

Cranshaw,Bob | (b,el-bfender-b)
Betty Carter And The Harold Mabern Trio
Misty Blue:Sweet Sisters Swing Songs Of Sorrow And Sadness | Blue Note | 521151-2
Bobby Hutcherson Quartet
Herbie Hancock:The Complete Blue Note Sixties Sessions | Blue Note | 495569-2
Bobby Timmons Quartet
Quartet And Orchestra | Milestone | MCD 47091-2
Bobby Timmons Trio
Quartet And Orchestra | Milestone | MCD 47091-2
Buddy Rich Septet
Swingin' The Blues-Jumpin' The Blues | Laserlight | 24654
Coleman Hawkins Quartet
The Art Of Saxophone | Laserlight | 24652
Jazz Dance | Original Jazz Classics | OJCCD 1002-2(1210890)
Sirius | Original Jazz Classics | OJCCD 861-2(2310707)
Dexter Gordon Quartet
Dexter Gordon Birthday Celebration | Fantasy | FANCD 6082-2
Dexter Gordon Quintet
Dexter Gordon:Ballads | Blue Note | 796579-2
Jazz Profile:Dexter Gordon | Blue Note | 823514-2
Duke Pearson Orchestra
Deep Blue-The United States Of Mind | Blue Note | 521152-2
Blue Bossa | Blue Note | 795590-2
Duke Pearson Sextet
Deep Blue-The United States Of Mind | Blue Note | 521152-2
Eddie Harris Group
Here Comes The Judge | CBS | 492533-2
Freddie Hubbard Quintet
Bossa Nova Bacchanal | Blue Note | 593875-2
Gene Ammons And His All Stars
Dexter Gordon Birthday Celebration | Fantasy | FANCD 6082-2
George Benson And His Orchestra
Giblet Gravy | Verve | 543754-2
Talkin' Verve:George Benson | Verve | 553780-2
George Benson Quartet
Talkin' Verve:George Benson | Verve | 553780-2
George Benson Quartet With The Sweet Inspirations
Talkin' Verve:George Benson | Verve | 553780-2
Grant Green Sextet
Idle Moments | Blue Note | 499003-2
True Blue | Blue Note | 534032-2
Hampton Hawes Trio
Northern Windows Plus | Prestige | PRCD 24278-2
Hank Mobley Quintet
Deep Blue-The United States Of Mind | Blue Note | 521152-2
Herbie Hancock Septet
Herbie Hancock:The Complete Blue Note Sixties Sessions | Blue Note | 495569-2
Horace Silver Quartet
Horace Silver Retrospective | Blue Note | 495576-2
Horace Silver Quintet
Horace Silver Retrospective | Blue Note | 495576-2
Blue Velvet: Crooners, Swooners And Velvet Vocals | Blue Note | 521153-2
The Cape Verdean Blues | Blue Note | 576753-2
Blue Bossa | Blue Note | 795590-2
Horace Silver Sextet
Horace Silver Retrospective | Blue Note | 495576-2
Deep Blue-The United States Of Mind | Blue Note | 521152-2
The Cape Verdean Blues | Blue Note | 576753-2
Horace Silver Sextet With Vocals
Horace Silver Retrospective | Blue Note | 495576-2
Houston Person Quintet
Trust In Me | Prestige | PCD 24264-2
Houston Person Sextet
Blue Odyssey | Original Jazz Classics | OJCCD 1045-2(P 7566)
J.J.Johnson And His Orchestra
Planet Jazz:J.J.Johnson | Planet Jazz | 2159974-2
Jack Wilson Sextet
Blue N' Groovy | Blue Note | 780679-2
Jackie McLean Quartet
Right Now | Blue Note | 595972-2
JATP All Stars
J.A.T.P. In London 1969 | Pablo | 2CD 2620119
Welcome To Jazz At The Philharmonic | Fantasy | FANCD 6081-2
Jimmy Smith With The Oliver Nelson Orchestra
Verve Jazz Masters 29:Jimmy Smith | Verve | 521855-2
Jimmy Smith:Best Of The Verve Years | Verve | 527950-2
Jimmy Smith-Talkin' Verve | Verve | 531563-2
Joe Henderson Quartet
The Blue Note Years-The Best Of Joe Henderson | Blue Note | 795627-2
Joe Williams And Friends
Planet Jazz:Male Jazz Vocalists | Planet Jazz | 2169657-2
At Newport '63 | RCA | 2663919-2
Joe Williams And His Band
Planet Jazz:Joe Williams | Planet Jazz | 2165370-2
Johnny Coles Sextet
True Blue | Blue Note | 534032-2
Johnny 'Hammond' Smith Septet
Open House | Milestone | MCD 47089-2
Johnny 'Hammond' Smith Sextet
Open House | Milestone | MCD 47089-2
Johnny Lytle Quintet
The Village Caller | Original Jazz Classics | OJCCD 110-2(R 9480)
Junior Mance Quartet
That Lovin' Feelin' | Milestone | MCD 47097-2
Junior Mance Trio
Junior's Blues | Original Jazz Classics | OJCCD 1000-2(RLP 9447)
Lee Morgan Quintet
The Sidewinder | Blue Note | 495332-2
Blue N' Groovy | Blue Note | 780679-2
The Best Of Blue Note | Blue Note | 796110-2
Take Twelve | Original Jazz Classics | OJCCD 310-2
Mary Lou Williams Quartet
The Story Of Jazz Piano | Laserlight | 24653
McCoy Tyner Quintet
Live At Newport | Impulse(MCA) | 547980-2
McCoy Tyner Trio
Live At Newport | Impulse(MCA) | 547980-2
Milt Jackson Quartet
In A New Setting | Verve | 538620-2
Milt Jackson Birthday Celebration | Fantasy | FANCD 6079-2
The Jazz Giants Play Harold Arlen:Blues In The Night | Prestige | PCD 24201-2
Milt Jackson Quintet
In A New Setting | Verve | 538620-2
At The Village Gate | Original Jazz Classics | OJCCD 309-2
Nat Adderley With Jim Hall And The Junior Mance Trio
Little Big Horn! | Original Jazz Classics | OJCCD 1001-2(R 9474)
Nat Adderley With Kenny Burrell And The Junior Mance Trio
Little Big Horn! | Original Jazz Classics | OJCCD 1001-2(R 9474)
Quincy Jones Big Band
Rahsaan/The Complete Mercury Recordings Of Roland Kirk | Mercury | 846630-2
Ruth Brown With Orchestra
Fine And Mellow | Fantasy | FCD 9663-2
Sal Nistico Quartet
Heavyweights | Milestone | MCD 47096-2
Sal Nistico Quintet
Heavyweights | Milestone | MCD 47096-2
Shirley Scott Quartet
Blue Flames | Original Jazz Classics | OJCCD 328-2(P 7338)
Queen Of The Organ-Shirley Scott Memorial Album | Prestige | PRCD 11027-2
Sonny Criss Quartet
Sonny Criss Quartet Feat. Wynton Kelly | Fresh Sound Records | FSR-CD 318
The Beat Goes On! | Original Jazz Classics | OJCCD 1051-2(P 7558)
Sonny Criss Quintet
Sonny Criss Quartet Feat. Wynton Kelly | Fresh Sound Records | FSR-CD 318
Sonny Rollins Group
What's New? | RCA | 2179626-2
Sonny Rollins Plus 3
Sonny Rollins + 3 | Milestone | MCD 9250-2
Sonny Rollins Quartet
Planet Jazz:Sonny Rollins | Planet Jazz | 2152062-2
Planet Jazz:Jazz Greatest Hits | Planet Jazz | 2169648-2
The Standard Sonny Rollins | RCA | 2174801-2
The Bridge | RCA | 2179625-2
What's New? | RCA | 2179626-2
Global Warming | Milestone | MCD 9280-2
This Is What I Do | Milestone | MCD 9310-2
Next Album | Original Jazz Classics | OJC 312 (M 9042)
Sonny Rollins Quintet
Here's To The People | Milestone | MCD 9194-2
Old Flames | Milestone | MCD 9215-2
This Is What I Do | Milestone | MCD 9310-2
Next Album | Original Jazz Classics | OJC 312 (M 9042)
No Problem | Original Jazz Classics | OJCCD 1014-2(M 9104)
Sonny Rollins Quintet With Brass
Old Flames | Milestone | MCD 9215-2
Sonny Rollins Sextet
Here's To The People | Milestone | MCD 9194-2
Global Warming | Milestone | MCD 9280-2
The Cutting Edge | Original Jazz Classics | OJC 468(M 9059)
Sonny Rollins Sextet With Rufus Harley
The Cutting Edge | Original Jazz Classics | OJC 468(M 9059)
Sonny Rollins Trio
Planet Jazz:Sonny Rollins | Planet Jazz | 2152062-2
Planet Jazz:Jazz Saxophone | Planet Jazz | 2169653-2
The Standard Sonny Rollins | RCA | 2174801-2
Sonny Rollins-Coleman Hawkins Quintet
Sonny Meets Hawk! | RCA | 2174800-2
Stanley Turrentine And His Orchestra
The Lost Grooves | Blue Note | 831883-2
Stanley Turrentine Orchestra
Rough 'N' Tumble | Blue Note | 524552-2
The Spoiler | Blue Note | 853359-2
Stanley Turrentine Quartet
Blue N' Groovy | Blue Note | 780679-2
Stanley Turrentine Quintet
Hustlin' | Blue Note | 540036-2
Teddy Wilson Trio
J.A.T.P. In London 1969 | Pablo | 2CD 2620119
Wes Montgomery Orchestra
Movin' Wes | Verve | 521433-2
Wes Montgomery Quartet
Bumpin' | Verve | 539062-2
Wes Montgomery With The Don Sebesky Orchestra
Verve Jazz Masters 14:Wes Montgomery | Verve | 519826-2
Talkin' Jazz:Roots Of Acid Jazz | Verve | 529580-2
Bumpin' | Verve | 539062-2
Wes Montgomery With The Johnny Pate Orchestra
Verve Jazz Masters 14:Wes Montgomery | Verve | 519826-2
Wes Montgomery:The Verve Jazz Sides | Verve | 521690-2
Talkin' Jazz:Roots Of Acid Jazz | Verve | 529580-2
Yusef Lateef Orchestra
The Blue Yusef Lateef | Rhino | 8122-73717-2
Zoot Sims Quartet
Getting Sentimental | Choice | CHCD 71006
The Jazz Giants Play Cole Porter:Night And Day | Prestige | PCD 24203-2

Craven,Luther 'Sonny' | (tb)
Lionel Hampton And His Orchestra
Lionel Hampton:Flying Home | Dreyfus Jazz Line | FDM 36735-2

Crawdy,Julian | (fl,alto-flpiccolo)
Miles Davis With Gil Evans Orchestra, The George Gruntz Concert Jazz Band And Guests
Miles & Quincy Live At Montreux | Warner | 9362-45221-2

Crawford,Bennie | (bs)
David Fathead Newman Sextet
Fathead:Ray Charles Presents David Newman | Atlantic | 8122-73708-2
Ray Charles And His Orchestra
Ray Charles At Newport | Atlantic | 7567-80765-2
Ray Charles Sextet With The Raylets
Newport Jazz Festival 1958,July 3rd-6th Vol.4:Blues In The Night No.2 | Phontastic | NCD 8816

Crawford,Hank | (as,arr,el-p,p,vocbs)
(Little)Jimmy Scott And His Band
Mood Indigo | Milestone | MCD 9305-2
Bernard Purdie's Soul To Jazz
Bernard Purdie's Soul To Jazz II | ACT | 9253-2
David Fathead Newman Sextet
Atlantic Saxophones | Rhino | 8122-71256-2
Rhino Presents The Atlantic Jazz Gallery | Atlantic | 8122-71257-2
Hank Crawford And His Orchestra
Atlantic Saxophones | Rhino | 8122-71256-2
Roadhouse Symphony | Original Jazz Classics | OJCCD 1048-2(M 9140)
Hank Crawford Orchestra
Rhino Presents The Atlantic Jazz Gallery | Atlantic | 8122-71257-2
Hank Crawford Quartet
The World Of Hank Crawford | Milestone | MCD 9304-2
Hank Crawford Quintet
After Dark | Milestone | MCD 9279-2
The World Of Hank Crawford | Milestone | MCD 9304-2
The Jazz Giants Play Sammy Cahn:It's Magic | Prestige | PCD 24226-2
Hank Crawford Septet
More Soul | Atlantic | 8122-73709-2
The World Of Hank Crawford | Milestone | MCD 9304-2
Hank Crawford-Jimmy McGriff Quartet
Jazzin' With The Soul Brothers | Fantasy | FANCD 6086-2
Jimmy Scott With Band
Moon Glow | Milestone | MCD 9332-2

Crawford,James | (dr)
Louis Armstrong And Billie Holiday With Sy Oliver's Orchestra
Louis Armstrong:C'est Si Bon | Dreyfus Jazz Line | FDM 36730-2

Crawford,James 'Jimmy' | (dr,percvib)
Benny Goodman Trio
Benny Goodman-The Complete Capitol Trios | Capitol | 521225-2
Coleman Hawkins Sextet
Body And Soul Revisited | GRP | GRP 16272
Count Basie All Stars
The Legends Of Swing | Laserlight | 24659
Ella Fitzgerald With Sy Oliver And His Orchestra
Ella Fitzgerald:Mr.Paganini | Dreyfus Jazz Line | FDM 36741-2
Ella Fitzgerald And Louis Armstrong With Sy Oliver And His Orchestra
Ella Fitzgerald:Mr.Paganini | Dreyfus Jazz Line | FDM 36741-2
Ella Fitzgerald With The Hank Jones Quartet
Ella Fitzgerald:Mr.Paganini | Dreyfus Jazz Line | FDM 36741-2
Juanita Hall With The Claude Hopkins All Stars
Juanita Hall Sings The Blues | Original Jazz Classics | OJCCD 1928-2(CPST 556)

Crawford,Jim | (tp)
Count Basie And His Orchestra
88 Basie Street | Original Jazz Classics | OJC 808(2310901)
Fancy Pants | Original Jazz Classics | OJCCD 1038-2(2310920)

Crawford,Jimmy | (dr)
Dinah Washington With The Quincy Jones Orchestra
The Swingin' Miss 'D' | Verve | 558074-2
Ella Fitzgerald With Sy Oliver And His Orchestra
Ella Fitzgerald:The Decca Years 1949-1954 | Decca | 050668-2
Jimmy Lunceford And His Orchestra
Planet Jazz:Swing | Planet Jazz | 2169651-2
Lena Horne With The Lennie Hayton Orchestra
Planet Jazz:Lena Horne | Planet Jazz | 2165373-2

Crawford,Ray | (bg)
Babs Gonzales And His Band
Voilà | Fresh Sound Records | FSR CD 340
Gil Evans Orchestra
Out Of The Cool | Impulse(MCA) | 951186-2
Jimmy Smith With Orchestra
Verve Jazz Masters 29:Jimmy Smith | Verve | 521855-2
Ray Crawford Sextet
Smooth Groove | Candid | CCD 79028

Crawford,Virdia | (voc)
Nina Simone Quintet
Planet Jazz:Nina Simone | Planet Jazz | 2165372-2

Crayton,Connie C. | (g)
Dizzy Gillespie's Trumpet Kings
The Trumpet Kings Meet Joe Turner | Original Jazz Classics | OJCCD 497-2

Crayton,Pee Wee | (gvoc)
Sarah Vaughan And Her Band
Duke Ellington Song Book Two | Pablo | CD 2312116
Sarah Vaughan Birthday Celebration | Fantasy | FANCD 6090-2

Crea,Bob | (ts)

Buddy Rich Big Band
Backwoods Siseman/Pieces Of Dream | Laserlight | 24655
Creason,Sammy | (drperc)
Jack McDuff Group
So Blue So Funky-Heroes Of The Hammond | Blue Note | 796563-2
Creative Works Orchestra |
Creative Works Orchestra
Willisau And More Live | Creative Works Records | CW CD 1020-2
Creese,Malcolm | (b)
Laura Fygi With Band
Bewitched | Verve | 514724-2
Crego,Jose M. | (tb)
Gonzalo Rubalcaba & Cuban Quartet
Antiguo | Blue Note | 837717-2
Cremer,Thomas | (cl,percdr)
Axis
Axis | Jazz 4 Ever Records:Jazz Network | J4E 4735
Creque,Neal Earl | (orgp)
Grant Green Sextet
Alive! | Blue Note | 525650-2
Leon Thomas With Band
Super Black Blues Vol.II | RCA | 2663874-2
Cress,Curt | (dr,berimbau,percel-perc)
Klaus Doldinger's Passport
Man In The Mirror | Warner | 2292-40253-2
Running In Real Time | Warner | 2292-40633-2
Heavy Nights | Warner | 2292-42006-2
Earthborn | Atlantic | 2292-46477-2
Atlantic Jazz: Fusion | Atlantic | 7567-81711-2
Passport
Handmade | Atlantic | 2292-42172-2
Looking Thru | Atlantic | 2292-44144-2
Cross-Collateral | Atlantic | 2292-44145-2
Infinity Machine | Atlantic | 2292-44146-2
Iguacu | Atlantic | 2292-46031-2
Passport And Guests
Doldinger Jubilee Concert | Atlantic | 2292-44175-2
Doldinger's Best | ACT | 9224-2
Cressey,Jack | (as)
Billie Holiday With Toots Camarata And His Orchestra
Billie's Love Songs | Nimbus Records | NI 2000
Cressman,Jeff | (tb,bar-h,slide-whistle,pyramid-bell)
Don Cherry Group
Multi Kulti | A&M Records | 395323-2
Crettien,Philippe | (ts)
Bill Lowe/Philippe Crettien Quintet
Sunday Train | Konnex Records | KCD 5051
Creutzburg,Ekkehard | (fl)
Bernd Konrad Jazz Group With Symphonie Orchestra
Wen Die Götter Lieben | Creative Works Records | CW CD 1010-1
Crews,Felton | (el-b)
Miles Davis Group
The Man With The Horn | CBS | 468701-2
Crigger,Dave | (drperc)
Klaus Doldinger & Passport
Lifelike | Warner | 2292-46478-2
Klaus Doldinger's Passport
Blue Tattoo | Atlantic | 2292-42178-2
Oceanliner | Warner | 2292-46479-2
Criner,Clyde | (keyboards,psynth)
Cold Sweat
Cold Sweat Plays J.B. | JMT Edition | 919025-2
Craig Harris And Tailgater's Tales
Blackout In The Square Root Of Soul | JMT Edition | 919015-2
Crisby,Elena | (vvoc)
Toto Blanke Group
Fools Paradise | ALISO Records | AL 1019
Crispell,Marilyn | (pp-solo)
Greetje Bijma Trio
Barefoot | Enja | ENJ-8038 2
Lotte Anker-Marilyn Crispell-Marilyn Mazur
Poetic Justice | dacapo | DCCD 9460
Marilyn Crispell Trio
Nothing Ever Was,Anyway.Music Of Annette Peacock | ECM | 1626/27(537222-2)
Story Teller | ECM | 1847(0381192)
Marilyn Crispell-Gary Peacock-Paul Motian
Amaryllis | ECM | 1742(013400-2)
Criss,Sonny | (asss)
Sonny Criss Quartet
Jazz In Paris:Saxophones À Saint-Germain Des Prés | EmArCy | 014060-2
Sonny Criss Quartet Feat. Wynton Kelly | Fresh Sound Records | FSR-CD 318
The Beat Goes On! | Original Jazz Classics | OJCCD 1051-2(P 7558)
This Is Criss | Original Jazz Classics | OJCCD 430-2(P 7511)
Sonny Criss Quintet
Jazz In Paris:Saxophones À Saint-Germain Des Prés | EmArCy | 014060-2
Jazz In Paris:Sonny Criss-Mr.Blues Pour Flirter | EmArCy | 549231-2 PMS
Sonny Criss Quartet Feat. Wynton Kelly | Fresh Sound Records | FSR-CD 318
Wardell Gray Sextet
The Prestige Legacy Vol.2:Battles Of Saxes | Prestige | PCD 24252-2
Wardell Gray's Los Angeles All Stars
Dexter Gordon Birthday Celebration | Fantasy | FANCD 6082-2
Wardell Gray Memorial Vol.2 | Original Jazz Classics | OJCCD 051-2(P 7009)
Crocker,John | (as,ts,cl,voc,sax,harmcl-overdubbed)
Chris Barber's Jazz And Blues Band
Chris Barber On The Road:A Jazz Documentary | Storyville | 4960683
Chris Barber:40 Years Jubilee Concert | Storyville | 4990013
Chris Barber's Jazzband & das Große Rundfunkorchester Berlin,DDR
Jazz Zounds: Chris Barber | Zounds | CD 2720007
Lennie Baldwin's Dauphin Street Six
The Golden Years Of Revival Jazz,Sampler | Storyville | 109 1001
The Golden Years Of Revival Jazz,Vol 1 | Storyville | STCD 5506
The Golden Years Of Revival Jazz,Vol.3 | Storyville | STCD 5508
The Golden Years Of Revival Jazz,Vol.6 | Storyville | STCD 5511
The Golden Years Of Revival Jazz,Vol.9 | Storyville | STCD 5514
The Golden Years Of Revival Jazz,Vol.10 | Storyville | STCD 5515
The Golden Years Of Revival Jazz,Vol.13 | Storyville | STCD 5518
Croes,Steve | (keyboardssynclavier)
Yellowjackets
Live Wires | GRP | GRP 96672
Run For Your Life | GRP | GRP 97542
Crolla,Henri | (g)
Henri Crolla Quartet
Jazz In Paris:Henri Crolla-Quand Refleuriront Les Lilas Blancs? | EmArCy | 018418-2
Henri Crolla Sextet
Jazz In Paris:Henri Crolla-Quand Refleuriront Les Lilas Blancs? | EmArCy | 018418-2
Cromer,Austin | (voc)
Dizzy Gillespie And His Orchestra
Dizzy Gillespie:Birks Works-The Verve Big Band Sessions | Verve | 527900-2
Crona,Claes | (p)
Rolf Kühn Group
Internal Eyes | Intuition Records | INT 3328-2
The Three Sopranos With The HR Big Band
The Three Sopranos | hr music.de | hrmj 001-01 CD
Cronck,Billy | (p)
Louis Armstrong And His All Stars
Jazz Festival Vol.1 | Storyville | 4960733
Cronholm,Josefine | (voc)
Lotte Anker-Marilyn Crispell-Marilyn Mazur
Poetic Justice | dacapo | DCCD 9460
Pierre Dorge's New Jungle Orchestra
Giraf | dacapo | DCCD 9440
Cronkhite,Glenn | (drperc)
Art Lande Quartet
Rubisa Patrol | ECM | 1081
Vince Guaraldi Group
Charlie Brown's Holiday Hits | Fantasy | FCD 9682-2
Crosby,Anthony | (dr)
Jimmy Smith Trio
Paris Jazz Concert:Jimmy Smith And The Trio | Laserlight | 36159
Crosby,Bing | (voc)
Bing Crosby And Rosemarie Clooney With The Billy May Orchestra
Fancy Meeting You Here | RCA | 2663859-2
Louis Armstrong And Bing Crosby With Orchestra
The Very Best Of Dixieland Jazz | Verve | 535529-2
Louis Jordan And His Tympany Five
Louis Jordan-Let The Good Times Roll: The Complete Decca Recordings 1938-1954 | Bear Family Records | BCD 15557 IH
Crosby,Bob | (ldvoc)
Bob Crosby And His Orchestra
Swing Legens:Bob Crosby | Nimbus Records | NI 2011
Bob Crosby's Bobcats
Swing Legens:Bob Crosby | Nimbus Records | NI 2011
Crosby,Gary | (bvoc)
Louis Armstrong And Gary Crosby With Sonny Burke's Orchestra
Louis Armstrong-My Greatest Songs | MCA | MCD 18347
Louis Armstrong And His All Stars With Sonny Burke's Orchestra
Ambassador Louis Armstrong Vol.17:Moments To Remember(1952-1956) | Ambassador | CLA 1917
Crosby,Harper | (b)
Wardell Gray Quartet
Wardell Gray Memorial Vol.2 | Original Jazz Classics | OJCCD 051-2(P 7009)
Wardell Gray Quintet
Wardell Gray Memorial Vol.2 | Original Jazz Classics | OJCCD 051-2(P 7009)
Crosby,Israel | (b)
Ahmad Jamal Trio
At The Pershing-But Not For Me | Chess | 940910-2
Benny Morton's All Stars
The Blue Note Swingtets | Blue Note | 495697-2
Jazz:The Essential Collection Vol.3 | IN+OUT Records | 78013-2
Coleman Hawkins Quartet
Verve Jazz Masters 43:Coleman Hawkins | Verve | 521856-2
Ultimate Coleman Hawkins selected by Sonny Rollins | Verve | 557538-2
Edmond Hall's Blue Note Jazzmen
The Blue Note Jazzmen | Blue Note | 821262-2
Fletcher Henderson And His Orchestra
Jazz:The Essential Collection Vol.1 | IN+OUT Records | 78011-2
Jazz:The Essential Collection Vol.3 | IN+OUT Records | 78013-2
Gene Krupa's Swing Band
Planet Jazz:Swing | Planet Jazz | 2169651-2
Crosse,Jon | (cl,b-cl,ss,ts,fl,aspiccolo)
John Patitucci Group
Sketchbook | GRP | GRP 96172
Crossover Ensemble,The |
The Crossover Ensemble
The River:Image Of Time And Life | dacapo | DCCD 9434
The Crossover Ensemble With The Zapolski Quartet
Helios Suite | dacapo | DCCD 9459
Crothers,Scat Man | (drvoc)
Slim Gaillard Trio
The Small Black Groups | Storyville | 4960523
Crotty,Ron | (b)
Dave Brubeck Octet
The Dave Brubeck Octet | Original Jazz Classics | OJCCD 101-2(F 3239)
Dave Brubeck Quartet
The Dave Brubeck Quartet feat. Paul Desmond In Concert | Fantasy | FCD 60-013
Jazz At The College Of The Pacific | Original Jazz Classics | OJC20 047-2(F 3223)
Jazz At Oberlin | Original Jazz Classics | OJCCD 046-2
Jazz At The College Of The Pacific Vol.2 | Original Jazz Classics | OJCCD 1076-2
Ron Crotty Trio
The Jazz Scene:San Francisco | Fantasy | FCD 24760-2
Crow,Bill | (b)
Al Haig Trio
Al Haig Trio And Sextets | Original Jazz Classics | OJCCD 1929-2(SPL 1118)
Benny Goodman And His Orchestra
The Legends Of Swing | Laserlight | 24659
Gerry Mulligan Concert Jazz Band
Verve Jazz Masters 36:Gerry Mulligan | Verve | 523342-2
Verve Jazz Masters Vol.60:The Collection | Verve | 529866-2
Gerry Mulligan And The Concert Band At The Village Vanguard | Verve | 589488-2
The Complete Verve Gerry Mulligan Concert Band | Verve | 9860613
Gerry Mulligan Quartet
Paris Jazz Concert:Gerry Mulligan And His Quartet | Laserlight | 17433
Jazz At The Philharmonic: The Gerry Mulligan Quartets In Concert | Pablo | PACD 5309-2
Stan Getz Quintet
Stan Getz Highlights:The Best Of The Verve Years Vol.2 | Verve | 517330-2
Verve Jazz Masters 8:Stan Getz | Verve | 519823-2
A Life In Jazz:A Musical Biography | Verve | 535119-2
Stan Getz And The 'Cool' Sounds | Verve | 547317-2
Ultimate Stan Getz selected by Joe Henderson | Verve | 557532-2
Stan Getz Plays | Verve | 833535-2
Stan Getz Highlights | Verve | 847430-2
Stan Getz-The Complete Roost Sessions | EMI Records | 859622-2
Crowder,Robert | (perc,tsarr)
Art Blakey And The Afro Drum Ensemble
The African Beat | Blue Note | 522666-2
Earl Hines And His Orchestra
Planet Jazz:Earl Hines | Planet Jazz | 2159973-2
The Legends Of Swing | Laserlight | 24659
Jazz:The Essential Collection Vol.2 | IN+OUT Records | 78012-2
Crowdy,Andy | (bperc)
Lillian Boutté And Her Group
You've Gotta Love Pops:Lillian Bouté Sings Louis Armstrong | ART BY HEART | ABH 2005 2
Crowley,Andrew | (tp)
John Surman-Jack DeJohnette With The London Brass
Printed In Germany | ECM | 1802(017065-2)
Crozier,Jimmy | (fl,asbs)
Mongo Santamaria And His Band
Brazilian Sunset | Candid | CCD 79703
Crumbley,Elmer | (tb)
Louis Armstrong And His Orchestra
I Love Jazz | Verve | 543747-2
Louis Armstrong With Sy Oliver And His Orchestra
Louis Armstrong-My Greatest Songs | MCA | MCD 18347
Crumley,Elmer | (tb)
Louis Armstrong And Omer Simeon With The Sy Oliver Orchestra
Ambassador Louis Armstrong Vol.17:Moments To Remember(1952-1956) | Ambassador | CLA 1917
Crump,Jesse 'Tiny' | (p)
Ida Cox With Jesse Crump
The Blues | Storyville | 4960323
Crump,William 'Bill' | (bs)
Buddy Johnson And His Orchestra
Buddy And Ella Johnson 1953-1964 | Bear Family Records | BCD 15479 DH
Cruz,Adam | (cowbell,drsteel-dr)
Bruce Barth Quartet
Where Eagles Fly | Fresh Sound Records | FSNT 090 CD
Tom Harrell Group
Paradise | RCA | 2663738-2
Cruz,Celia | (voc)
Arturo Sandoval And The Latin Train Band
Arturo Sandoval & The Latin Train | GRP | GRP 98202
Cruz,Hectir | (el-b)
Conexion Latina
Calorcito | Enja | ENJ-4072 2
Cruz,Julie | (perc)
Clark Terry & Chico O Farril Orchestra
Spanish Rice | Verve | 9861050
Cruz,Rafael | (perc)
Klaus Doldinger With Orchestra
Lifelike | Warner | 2292-46478-2
McCoy Tyner Quartet
The Story Of Jazz Piano | Laserlight | 24653
The Brecker Brothers
Heavy Metal Be-Bop | RCA | 2119257-2
Cuadrada,Ramon | (tp)
Big Band Bellaterra
Don't Git Sassy | Fresh Sound Records | FSNT 048 CD
Cuadrado,Alexis | (b)
Alguimia
Alguimia 'U' | Fresh Sound Records | FSNT 023 CD
Alguimia:Standards | Fresh Sound Records | FSNT 049 CD
Alguimia Dos | Fresh Sound Records | FSNT 050 CD
Orquestra De Cambra Teatre Lliure
Tributes To Duke Ellington | Fresh Sound Records | FSNT 084 CD
The Waltzer-McHenry Quartet
Jazz Is Where You Find It | Fresh Sound Records | FSNT 021 CD
Cuber,Ronnie | (bs,cl,b-cl,fl,as,ts,saxss)
Earl Klugh Group
Late Night Guitar | Blue Note | 498573-2
George Benson Quartet
It's Uptown | CBS | 502469-2
The George Benson Cookbook | CBS | 502470-2
George Benson Quartet + Guests
The George Benson Cookbook | CBS | 502470-2
George Benson Quintet
It's Uptown | CBS | 502469-2
Hank Crawford Septet
The World Of Hank Crawford | Milestone | MCD 9304-2
Jimmy McGriff Septet
McGriff Avenue | Milestone | MCD 9325-2
Jimmy McGriff Sextet
Feelin' It | Milestone | MCD 9313-2
Lonnie Smith Quintet
Deep Blue-The United States Of Mind | Blue Note | 521152-2
The Lost Grooves | Blue Note | 831883-2
Mingus Big Band
Tonight At Noon...Three Or Four Shades Of Love | Dreyfus Jazz Line | FDM 36633-2
Mingus Big Band 93
Nostalgia In Times Square | Dreyfus Jazz Line | FDM 36559-2
'Cucurel.La',Josep | (el-bfretless-b)
Elisabet Raspall Quintet
Triangles | Fresh Sound Records | FSNT 018 CD
Pep O'Callaghan Grup
Tot Just | Fresh Sound Records | FSNT 017 CD
Cuenca,Sylvia | (dr)
Clark Terry Quintet
The Hymn | Candid | CCD 79770
Herr Ober | Nagel-Heyer | CD 068
Cuesta,Carmen | (voc)
Till Brönner Group
Chattin' With Chet | Verve | 157534-2
Love | Verve | 559058-2
Cuesta,Henry | (clbs)
Jack Teagarden And His Sextet
Mis'ry And The Blues | Verve | 9860310
Cuffee,Ed | (tbvoc)
Fletcher Henderson And His Orchestra
Jazz:The Essential Collection Vol.1 | IN+OUT Records | 78011-2
Jazz:The Essential Collection Vol.3 | IN+OUT Records | 78013-2
Cuffey,Allen C. | (rap-voc)
Klaus Doldinger & Passport
Down To Earth | Warner | 4509-93207-2
Cugny,Laurent | (string-arr)
Abbey Lincoln With The Rodney Kendrick Trio And Guests
A Turtle's Dream | Verve | 527382-2
Culasso,Nino | (tp)
Helen Merrill With The Piero Umilliani Group
Parole E Musica | RCA | 2174798-2
Cullaz,Alby | (b)
Hank Mobley Sextet
The Flip | Blue Note | 593872-2
Cullaz,Pierre | (el-gg)
Golden Gate Quartet
Americans Swinging In Paris:Golden Gate Quartet | EMI Records | 539659-2
From Spriritual To Swing Vol.2 | EMI Records | 780573-2
Spirituals To Swing 1955-69 | EMI Records | 791569-2
Golden Gate Quartet With The Martial Solal Orchestra
From Spriritual To Swing Vol.2 | EMI Records | 780573-2
Raymond Fol Big Band
Jazz In Paris:Raymond Fol-Les 4 Saisons | EmArCy | 548791-2
Sarah Vaughan With The Quincy Jones Orchestra
Jazz In Paris:Sarah Vaughan-Vaughan And Violins | EmArCy | 065004-2
4 By 4:Ella Fitzgerald/Sarah Vaughan/Billie Holiday/Dinah Washington | Verve | 559693-2
Cullen,Boyce | (tb)
Hoagy Carmichael And His Orchestra
Planet Jazz:Bud Freeman | Planet Jazz | 2161240-2
Cullen,David | (keyboards)
Barbara Thompson Group
Heavenly Bodies | VeraBra Records | CDVBR 2015-2
Culley,Wendell | (tp)
Count Basie And His Orchestra
Jazz Gallery:Lester Young Vol.2(1946-59) | RCA | 2119541-2
Jazz Collection:Count Basie | Laserlight | 24368
The Legends Of Swing | Laserlight | 24659
Atomic Swing | Roulette | 497871-2
Verve Jazz Masters 2:Count Basie | Verve | 519819-2
Count Basie Swings-Joe Williams Sings | Verve | 519852-2
Verve Jazz Masters 20:Introducing | Verve | 519853-2
April In Paris | Verve | 521402-2
Breakfast Dance And Barbecue | Roulette | 531791-2
One O'Clock Jump | Verve | 559806-2
Chairman Of The Board | Roulette | 581664-2
The Complete Atomic Basie | Roulette | 828635-2
King Of Swing | Verve | 837433-2
Count Basie At Newport | Verve | 9861761
Count On The Coast Vol.1 | Phontastic | NCD 7555
Count On The Coast Vol.2 | Phontastic | NCD 7575
Ella Fitzgerald With The Count Basie Orchestra
Ella Fitzgerald-First Lady Of Song | Verve | 517898-2
Lionel Hampton And His Orchestra
Lionel Hampton:Flying Home | Dreyfus Jazz Line | FDM 36735-2
Lionel Hampton And His Septet
Lionel Hampton:Flying Home | Dreyfus Jazz Line | FDM 36735-2
Sarah Vaughan And The Thad Jones Orchestra
Verve Jazz Masters 42:Sarah Vaughan-The Jazz Sides | Verve | 526817-2
Cullum,Jamie | (pvoc)

Jamie Cullum Group
Pointless Nostalgic | Candid | CCD 79782

Cully,Billy | (tb)
Anita O'Day With Gene Krupa And His Orchestra
Let Me Off Uptown:Anita O'Day With Gene Krupa | CBS | CK 65625

Culver,Eric | (tb)
Paulinho Da Costa Orchestra
Happy People | Original Jazz Classics | OJCCD 783-2(2312102)

Cumberbache,Williams | (perc)
David Jean-Baptiste Group
The Nature Suite | Laika Records | 35101632

Cumming,Ian | (tbrecitation)
Jan Jankeje Septet
A' Portrait Of Jan Jankeje | Jazzpoint | JP 1054 CD
SWR Big Band
Jazz In Concert | Hänssler Classics | CD 93.004

Cummings,Diana | (cellov)
Dee Dee Bridgewater With Orchestra
Dear Ella | Verve | 539102-2

Cummings,Genovia | (v)
Jim Snidero Quartet With Strings
Strings | Milestone | MCD 9326-2
Lee Konitz With Strings
Strings For Holiday:A Tribute To Billie Holiday | Enja | ENJ-9304 2
Mark Feldman Quartet
Book Of Tells | Enja | ENJ-9385 2
Tom Harrell Group
Paradise | RCA | 2663738-2

Cummings,Robert | (b-cl,perc,woodblocksvoc)
Sun Ra And His Intergalactic Research Arkestra
Black Myth/Out In Space | MPS | 557656-2

Cummings,Stephanie | (cello)
Steve Kuhn With Strings
Promises Kept | ECM | 1815(0675222)

Cunliffe,Bill | (p,arrorg)
Jacintha With Band And Strings
Lush Life | Groove Note | GRV 1011-2(Gold CD 2011)
Terell Stafford Quintet
Fields Of Gold | Nagel-Heyer | CD 2005
The Clayton Brothers Quintet
Siblingity | Warner | 9362-47813-2

Cunliffe,David | (cello)
Rabih Abou-Khalil Group
Arabian Waltz | Enja | ENJ-9059 2

Cunningham,Bob | (b)
Dizzy Gillespie Quintet
An Electrifying Evening With The Dizzy Gillespie Quintet | Verve | 557544-2
Frank Foster Quintet
Soul Outing! | Original Jazz Classics | OJCCD 984-2(7479)
The Jazz Composer's Orchestra
Comminications | JCOA | 1001/2
Yusef Lateef Orchestra
Rhino Presents The Atlantic Jazz Gallery | Atlantic | 8122-71257-2

Cunningham,Bradley | (perc)
Charles Mingus Orchestra
Cumbia & Jazz Fusion | Atlantic | 8122-71785-2

Cuntz,Uwe | (dr)
Freddy Christman Quartet
Deutsches Jazz Fesival 1954/1955 | Bear Family Records | BCD 15430

Cuome,Frank | (drperc)
Wayne Shorter Orchestra
Wayne Shorter:The Classic Blue Note Recordings | Blue Note | 540856-2

Cuomo,Brian | (p)
Bill Perkins Quartet
Swing Spring | Candid | CCD 79752

Cura,Domingo | (bombo indian)
Gato Barbieri Orchestra
Latino America | Impulse(MCA) | 952236-2

Curry,Bert | (as)
Carroll Dickerson's Savoyagers
Louis Armstrong:Fireworks | Dreyfus Jazz Line | FDM 36710-2
Louis Armstrong And His Orchestra
Satch Plays Fats(Complete) | CBS | CK 64927

Curry,Ted | (dr)
Rex Stewart Quintet
Peche Á La Mode-The Great Blue Star Sessions 1947/1953 | Verve | 835418-2

Curschellas,Corina | (dulcimer,voice,fl,accordeon,dr)
Corina Curschellas-John Wolf Brennan
Entupadas | Creative Works Records | CW CD 1013-1
Willisau And More Live | Creative Works Records | CW CD 1020-2
Creative Works Orchestra
Willisau And More Live | Creative Works Records | CW CD 1020-2
Nguyen Le Trio With Guests
Purple:Celebrating Jimi Hendrix | ACT | 9410-2

Curson,Ted | (tp,fl-h,cowbell,piccolo-tp,perc)
Archie Shepp Sextet
Fire Music | Impulse(MCA) | 951158-2
Cecil Taylor Quintet
Love For Sale | Blue Note | 494107-2
Cecil Taylor Unit
Mixed | Impulse(MCA) | IMP 12702
Charles Mingus Group
The Jazz Life! | Candid | CCD 79019
Candid Dolphy | Candid | CCD 79033
Mysterious Blues | Candid | CCD 79042
Charles Mingus Orchestra
Charles Mingus:Pre-Bird(Mingus Revisited) | Verve | 538636-2
Mingus | Candid | CCD 79021
Charles Mingus Quartet
Mingus At Antibes | Atlantic | 7567-90532-2
Charles Mingus Presents Charles Mingus | Candid | CCD 79005
Mingus | Candid | CCD 79021
Charles Mingus Quintet
Mingus At Antibes | Atlantic | 7567-90532-2
Charles Mingus-Passion Of A Man:The Complete Atlantic Recordings 1956-1961 | Atlantic | 8122-72871-2
Charles Mingus Quintet With Bud Powell
Mingus At Antibes | Atlantic | 7567-90532-2
Charles Mingus-Passion Of A Man:The Complete Atlantic Recordings 1956-1961 | Atlantic | 8122-72871-2

Curtis,Gale | (asts)
Tommy Dorsey And His Orchestra
Planet Jazz:Tommy Dorsey | Planet Jazz | 2159972-2
Planet Jazz:Jazz Greatest Hits | Planet Jazz | 2169648-2

Curtis,Howard | (dr)
Gary Thomas Group
Found On Sordid Street | Winter&Winter | 910002-2
George Colligan Group
Unresolved | Fresh Sound Records | FSNT 054 CD
Johannes Enders Quintet
Bright Nights | Enja | ENJ-9352 2

Curtis,Jual | (congasdr)
Brew Moore Quartet
No More Brew | Storyville | STCD 8275
Dexter Gordon-Benny Bailey Quintet
Revelation | Steeplechase | SCCD 31373
The Rainbow People | Steeplechase | SCCD 31521

Curtis,King | (as,g,voc,ts,el-ts,saxello,ss)
Al Smith With The King Curtis Quintet
Midnight Special | Original Blues Classics | OBCCD 583-2(BV 1013)
Eddie Harris Group
The Best Of Eddie Harris | Atlantic | 7567-81370-2
George Benson Quartet + Guests
The George Benson Cookbook | CBS | 502470-2
Herbie Mann And His Orchestra
The Best Of Herbie Mann | Atlantic | 7567-81369-2
King Curtis Band
King Curtis-Blow Man Blow | Bear Family Records | BCD 15670 CI
King Curtis Quartet
The New Scene Of King Curtis | Original Jazz Classics | OJC 198(NJ 8237)
King Curtis Quintet
The New Scene Of King Curtis | Original Jazz Classics | OJC 198(NJ 8237)
Oliver Nelson Sextet
Soul Street | Original Jazz Classics | OJCCD 987-2(NJ 8293)
Sunnyland Slim Band
Windy City Blues | Stax | SCD 8612-2

Curtis,Larry | (perc)
Marion Brown Orchestra
Afternoon Of A Georgia Faun | ECM | 1004

Curtis,Stuart | (ts)
Joe Pass With The NDR Big Band
NDR Big Band-Bravissimo | ACT | 9232-2

Cussac,Jean | (voc)
Modern Jazz Quartet And The Swingle Singers
MJQ 40 | Atlantic | 7567-82330-2
Swingle Singers
Jazz Sebastian Bach | Philips | 542552-2
Jazz Sebastian Bach Vol.2 | Philips | 542553-2
Swingle Singers Going Baroque | Philips | 546746-2
Swingle Singers Singing Mozart | Philips | 548538-2
Swingling Telemann | Philips | 586735-2
Swingle Singers Getting Romantic | Philips | 586736-2

Cusumano,Bob | (tp)
Louis Armstrong And His Orchestra
Louis Armstrong:Swing That Music | Laserlight | 36056
Tommy Dorsey And His Orchestra
Planet Jazz:Tommy Dorsey | Planet Jazz | 2159972-2
Planet Jazz:Big Bands | Planet Jazz | 2169649-2
Planet Jazz:Swing | Planet Jazz | 2169651-2

Cutlan,Paul | (b-cl)
Wanderlust + Guests
Full Bronte | Laika Records | 35101412

Cutler,Rick | (drperc)
Steve Lampert Group
Venus Perplexed | Steeplechase | SCCD 31557

Cutler,Stewart | (el-g)
Bobby Previte's Latin For Travelers
Dangerous Rip | Enja | ENJ-9324-2

Cutshall,Cutty | (tb)
Benny Goodman And His Orchestra
Great Swing Classics In Hi-Fi | Capitol | 521223-2
Charlie Christian:Swing To Bop | Dreyfus Jazz Line | FDM 36715-2
Eddie Condon All Stars
Jazz Festival Vol.1 | Storyville | 4960733
Eddie Condon And His Boys
The Very Best Of Dixieland Jazz | Verve | 535529-2
Jimmy McPartland And His Dixielanders
Planet Jazz | Planet Jazz | 2169652-2
Lee Wiley With The Dean Kincaide Dixieland Band
Planet Jazz:Female Jazz Vocalists | Planet Jazz | 2169656-2
Louis Armstrong And The Commanders under the Direction of Camarata
Satchmo Serenaders | Verve | 543792-2
Louis Armstrong With Sy Oliver And His Orchestra
Satchmo Serenaders | Verve | 543792-2
Louis Armstrong-My Greatest Songs | MCA | MCD 18347
Louis Armstrong With The Commanders
Ambassador Louis Armstrong Vol.17:Moments To Remember(1952-1956) | Ambassador | CLA 1917
Peggy Lee With Benny Goodman And His Sextet
Peggy Lee & Benny Goodman:The Complete Recordings 1941-1947 | CBS | C2K 65686
Peggy Lee With The Benny Goodman Orchestra
Peggy Lee & Benny Goodman:The Complete Recordings 1941-1947 | CBS | C2K 65686

Cuttillo,Norberto | (dr,percberimbao)
Pino Distaso/Roberto Gotta/Beto Cutillo
Tell Her It's All Right | Edition Collage | EC 463-2

Cykman,Harry | (v)
Bob James And His Orchestra
Jazzrock-Anthology Vol.3:Fusion | Zounds | CD 27100555
Earl Klugh Group With Strings
Late Night Guitar | Blue Note | 498573-2
Freddie Hubbard Orchestra
The Body And The Soul | Impulse(MCA) | 951183-2
Les McCann Group
Another Beginning | Atlantic | 7567-80790-2
Ron Carter Quintet With Strings
Pick 'Em/Super Strings | Milestone | MCD 47090-2

Cyrille,Andrew | (dr,bells,gongs,sansa,voice,conga)
Ahmed Abdullah Sextet
Jazz Sounds Of Africa | Prestige | PRCD 24279-2
Carla Bley Band
European Tour 1977 | Watt | 8
Cecil Taylor Sextet
A Blue Conception | Blue Note | 534254-2
Conquistador | Blue Note | 576749-2
Charlie Haden's Liberation Music Orchestra
Liberation Music Orchestra | Impulse(MCA) | 951188-2
Coleman Hawkins Quintet
The Hawk Relaxes | Original Jazz Classics | OJCCD 709-2(MV 15)
Ivo Perlman Group
Children Of Ibeji | Enja | ENJ-7005 2
Jean-Paul Bourelly Group
Jungle Cowboy | JMT Edition | 919009-2
John Lindberg Ensemble
A Tree Frog Tonality | Between The Lines | btl 008(Efa 10178-2)
Marion Brown Orchestra
Afternoon Of A Georgia Faun | ECM | 1004
Roswell Rudd-Archie Shepp Group
Live In New York | EmArCy | 013482-2
The Jazz Composer's Orchestra
Comminications | JCOA | 1001/2

Czabancyk,Ladislas | (b)
Django Reinhardt And The Quintet Du Hot Club De France
Peche Á La Mode-The Great Blue Star Sessions 1947/1953 | Verve | 835418-2
Quintet Du Hot Club De France
Verve Jazz Masters 38:Django Reinhardt | Verve | 516931-2
Django Reinhardt:Souveniers | Dreyfus Jazz Line | FDM 36744-2
Rex Stewart Quintet
Peche Á La Mode-The Great Blue Star Sessions 1947/1953 | Verve | 835418-2

Czelusta,Wolfgang | (tb)
Eberhard Weber Orchestra
Orchestra | ECM | 1374

D.J.A.D. | (scratch)
George Gruntz Concert Jazz Band
Blues 'N Dues Et Cetera | Enja | ENJ-6072 2

D.J.Logic[Jason Kibler] | (turntable)
Uri Caine Trio
Bedrock | Winter&Winter | 910068-2

Da Costa,Noel | (v)
Archie Shepp Orchestra
The Cry Of My People | Impulse(MCA) | 9861488

Da Costa,Paulinho | (a-go-go,berimbau,cuica,pandeiro)
Al Jarreau With Band
Tenderness | i.e. Music | 557853-2
All Fly Home | Warner | 7599-27362-2
Bobby Lyle Group
The Journey | Atlantic | 7567-82138-2
Chico Freeman Septet
Destiny's Dance | Original Jazz Classics | OJCCD 799-2(C 14008)
Dave Grusin Orchestra
Two For The Road:The Music Of Henry Mancini | GRP | GRP 98652
Dizzy Gillespie With The Lalo Schifrin Orchestra
Free Ride | Original Jazz Classics | OJCCD 784-2(2310794)
Ella Fitzgerald With Orchestra
Ella Abraca Jobim | Pablo | 2630201-2
Herbie Hancock Group
Magic Window | CBS | 486572-2
Jean-Luc Ponty Group
Mystical Adventures | Atlantic | 19333-2
Jean-Luc Ponty Sextet
The Very Best Of Jean-Luc Ponty | Rhino | 8122-79862-2
Joe Pass Sextet
Joe Pass:Guitar Virtuoso | Pablo | 4 PACD 4423-2
Jazzin' Vol.2: The Music Of Stevie Wonder | Fantasy | FANCD 6088-2
John Patitucci Group
Sketchbook | GRP | GRP 96172
Larry Carlton Group
The Gift | GRP | GRP 98542
Lee Ritenour Group
Festival | GRP | GRP 95702
Marcus Miller Group
The Sun Don't Lie | Dreyfus Jazz Line | FDM 36560-2
Miles Davis Group
Tutu | Warner | 7599-25490-2
Amandla | Warner | 7599-25873-2
Milt Jackson With Strings
To Bags...With Love:Memorial Album | Pablo | 2310967-2
Paulinho Da Costa Orchestra
Agora | Original Jazz Classics | OJCCD 630-2(2310785)
Happy People | Original Jazz Classics | OJCCD 783-2(2312102)
Stan Getz With Orchestra
Apasionado | A&M Records | 395297-2
Stanley Clarke Group
If This Bass Could Only Talk | CBS | 460883-2
The Quincy Jones-Sammy Nestico Orchestra
Basie & Beyond | Warner | 9362-47792-2
Yellowjackets
Live Wires | GRP | GRP 96672

Da Fonseca,Duduka | (drperc)
John Scofield Groups
Quiet | Verve | 533185-2

Da Silva,Jorge Ferreira | (fl)
Baden Powell Ensemble
Three Originals:Tristeza On Guitar/Poema On Guitar/Apaixonado | MPS | 519216-2

Da Silva,Jose | (perc)
Lee Ritenour Group
Rio | GRP | GRP 95242

Da Silva,Roberto | (perc)
Caldera
Jazzrock-Anthology Vol.3:Fusion | Zounds | CD 27100555

Daawood,Talib | (tp)
Dizzy Gillespie And His Orchestra
Dizzy Gillespie:Birks Works-The Verve Big Band Sessions | Verve | 527900-2

Dabbert,Harald | (fl,cl,didgeridoo,mouth-dr)
Das Obertontrio Und Toto Blanke
Energy Fields | ALISO Records | AL 1029
Toto Blanke-Rudolf Dasek With The Overtontrio
Meditation | ALISO Records | AL 1026

D'Abbico,Dario | (voice)
Michel Godard Ensemble
Castel Del Monte II | Enja | ENJ-9431 2

Dacco,Filippo | (el-gg)
Gerry Mulligan With Astor Piazzolla And His Orchestra
Tango Nuevo | Atlantic | 2292-42145-2

Daellenbach,Chuck | (tuba)
Canadian Brass
Take The A Train | RCA | 2663455-2

Daerr,Carsten | (p)
Carsten Daerr Trio
PurpleCoolCarSleep | Traumton Records | 4472-2
Matzeit-Daerr
September | Jazz Haus Musik | JHM 0125 CD

Dagley,Chris | (dr)
Gerard Presencer Group
Chasing Reality | ACT | 9422-2

D'Agostino,John | (tb)
Lena Horne With The Lennie Hayton Orchestra
Planet Jazz:Lena Horne | Planet Jazz | 2165373-2
Sarah Vaughan With The Hugo Winterhalter Orchestra
Sarah Vaughan:Lover Man | Dreyfus Jazz Line | FDM 36739-2
Sarah Vaughan With The Joe Lippman Orchestra
Sarah Vaughan:Lover Man | Dreyfus Jazz Line | FDM 36739-2

D'Agostino,Roberto | (dr)
Bernd Konrad Jazz Group With Symphonie Orchestra
Wen Die Götter Lieben | Creative Works Records | CW CD 1010-1

Dagradi,Tony | (cl,ts,fl,b-clss)
Carla Bley Band
Live! | Watt | 12(815730-2)
The Carla Bley Band
Social Studies | Watt | 11(831831-2)
I Hate To Sing | Watt | 12,5

Dahinden,Roland | (tb,bass-dr,voc,mouth-percvoice)
Cadavre Exquis
Cadavre Exquis | Creative Works Records | CW CD 1014-1
Miles Davis With Gil Evans Orchestra, The George Gruntz Concert Jazz Band And Guests
Miles & Quincy Live At Montreux | Warner | 9362-45221-2

Dahl,Carsten | (porg)
Carsten Dahl Trio
Will You Make My Soup Hot & Silver | Storyville | STCD 4203
Christina Nielsen-Carsten Dahl Duo
Lys Pa Himlen | dacapo | DCCD 9458

Dahl,Jimmy | (tb)
Chubby Jackson And His All Star Big Band
Chubby Takes Over | Fresh Sound Records | FSR-CD 324
Elliot Lawrence And His Orchestra
The Elliot Lawrence Big Band Swings Cohn & Kahn | Fantasy | FCD 24761-2
Gerry Mulligan And His Orchestra
Mullenium | CBS | CK 65678

Dahlander,Nils-Bertil | (dr)
Chet Baker Quartet
Jazz In Paris:Chet Baker Quartet Plays Standards | EmArCy | 014378-2 PMS
Verve Jazz Masters Vol.60:The Collection | Verve | 529866-2
Lars Gullin Octet
Lars Gullin 1951/52 Vol.5:First Walk | Dragon | DRCD 380
Lars Gullin Quartet
Lars Gullin 1955/56 Vol.1 | Dragon | DRCD 224

Dahlgren,Peter | (tb)
Tim Hagans With Norrbotten Big Band
Future Miles | ACT | 9235-2

Dahm,Stefan | (drperc)
booMbooM meets Uli Beckerhoff
Resurection Lounge | Laika Records | 35101512

Dähn,Fried | (el-cello)
Müller-Svoboda-Dähn-Kniel
9Q | Edition Musikat | EDM 064

Dahner,Manuel | (asts)
Ralph Schweizer Big Band
DAY Dream | Chaos | CACD 8177
Sax Mal Anders
Kontraste | Chaos | CACD 8185

Dailey,Albert | (p)

Gary Bartz Quintet
Libra/Another Earth | Milestone | MCD 47077-2
Oliver Nelson And His Orchestra
Verve Jazz Masters Vol.60:The Collection | Verve | 529866-2
Stan Getz-Joao Gilberto Orchestra
Sony Jazz Collection:Stan Getz | CBS | 488623-2
The Upper Manhattan Jazz Society
The Upper Manhattan Jazz Society | Enja | ENJ-4090 2

Dailey,Joe | (euphonium,tbtuba)
Sam Rivers Orchestra
Crystals | Impulse(MCA) | 589760-2

Dalal,Yair | (oud)
SheshBesh
SheshBesh | TipToe | TIP-888830 2

Dale,James | (pel-p)
Singers Unlimited With Rob McConnell And The Boss Brass
The Singers Unlimited:Magic Voices | MPS | 539130-2

Dale,Joe | (tp)
Anita O'Day With Gene Krupa And His Orchestra
Let Me Off Uptown:Anita O'Day With Gene Krupa | CBS | CK 65625

Dale,Larry | (gvoc)
Cootie Williams Quintet
Jazz In Paris:Joe Newman-Jazz At Midnight-Cootie Williams | EmArCy | 018446-2

Dale,Rollice | (viola)
Milt Jackson With Strings
To Bags...With Love:Memorial Album | Pablo | 2310967-2

Daley,Joe | (bar-horn,tuba,euphonium,perc,bar-h)
Charlie Haden And The Liberation Music Orchestra
The Montreal Tapes:Liberation Music Orchestra | Verve | 527469-2
Dave Douglas Group
Witness | RCA | 2663763-2
Gil Evans Orchestra
There Comes A Time | RCA | 2131392-2
Svengali | Rhino | 8122-73720-2
The Carla Bley Band
Social Studies | Watt | 11(831831-2)

Dallas,Sonny | (b)
Lee Konitz Trio
Motion | Verve | 065510-2

Dallinger,Michael | (cellovoc)
Motus Quartett
Grimson Flames | Creative Works Records | CW CD 1023-2

Dallmayer,Klaus | (tp)
Association Urbanetique
Ass Bedient | Jazz 4 Ever Records:Jazz Network | J4E 4723

Dalto,George | (p,el-pclavinet)
Gato Barbieri Group
Planet Jazz:Gato Barbieri | RCA | 2165364-2
Gato Barbieri Septet
Yesterdays | RCA | 2147797-2
George Benson Group
Breezin' | Warner | 8122-76713-2

Dalto,Jorge | (el-p,perc,keyboards,grand-p,pvoc)
Jerry Gonzalez & Fort Apache Band
The River Is Deep | Enja | ENJ-4040 2
Machito And His Orchestra
Afro-Cuban Jazz Moods | Original Jazz Classics | OJC20 447-2

Daly,Geo | (vib)
Guy Lafitte Sextet
Jazz In Paris:Guy Lafitte-Blue And Sentimental | EmArCy | 159852-2 PMS
Guy Lafitte-Peanuts Holland And Their Orchestra
Jazz In Paris:Guy Lafitte-Blue And Sentimental | EmArCy | 159852-2 PMS
Michel Attenoux And His Dream Band
Great Traditionalists | Jazzpoint | JP 1046 CD
Michel De Villers Octet
Jazz In Paris:Saxophones À Saint-Germain Des Prés | EmArCy | 014060-2

D'Amato,Chappie | (as,gvoc)
Arthur Young And Hatchett's Swingtette
Grapelli Story | Verve | 515807-2

D'Amatta,Cinho | (gvoice)
Pata Masters
Pata-Bahia | Pata Musik | PATA 11 CD

Damba,Manian | (voc)
Hank Jones Meets Cheik-Tidiana Seck
Sarala | Verve | 528783-2

D'Ambra,Annibale | (fr-h)
Banda Cittá Ruvo Di Puglia
La Banda/Banda And Jazz | Enja | ENJ-9326 2

Dameron,Tadd | (arr,ldp)
Carmen McRae With The Tadd Dameron Orchestra
Blue Moon | Verve | 543829-2
Clifford Brown-Max Roach Quintet
Verve Jazz Masters 44:Clifford Brown and Max Roach | Verve | 528109-2
Clifford Brown And Max Roach At Basin Street | Verve | 589826-2
Brownie-The Complete EmArCy Recordings Of Clifford Brown | EmArCy | 838306-2
Dexter Gordon Quintet
The Art Of Saxophone | Laserlight | 24652
Fats Navarro:Nostalgia | Dreyfus Jazz Line | FDM 36736-2
Dizzy Gillespie And His Orchestra
Planet Jazz:Dizzy Gillespie | Planet Jazz | 2152069-2
Fats Navarro Quintet
Fats Navarro:Nostalgia | Dreyfus Jazz Line | FDM 36736-2
Miles Davis Sextet
Miles Davis:Milestones | Dreyfus Jazz Line | FDM 36731-2
Miles Davis/Tadd Dameron Quintet
Miles Davis:Milestones | Dreyfus Jazz Line | FDM 36731-2
Milt Jackson Orchestra
To Bags...With Love:Memorial Album | Pablo | 2310967-2
Milt Jackson Birthday Celebration | Fantasy | FANCD 6079-2
Big Bags | Original Jazz Classics | OJCCD 366-2(RLP 9429)
Sarah Vaughan With Dizzy Gillespie And His Septet
Sarah Vaughan:Lover Man | Dreyfus Jazz Line | FDM 36739-2
Tadd Dameron And His Orchestra
Clifford Brown Memorial | Original Jazz Classics | OJC20 017-2(P 7055)
Fontainebleau | Original Jazz Classics | OJCCD 055-2
Tadd Dameron Quartet
John Coltrane-The Prestige Recordings | Prestige | 16 PCD 4405-2
Tadd Dameron Septet
The Fabulous Fats Navarro Vol.2 | Blue Note | 0677208
Fats Navarro:Nostalgia | Dreyfus Jazz Line | FDM 36736-2
Tadd Dameron Sextet
The Fabulous Fats Navarro Vol.1 | Blue Note | 0677207
Tadd Dameron Tentet
Jazz Profile:Dexter Gordon | Blue Note | 823514-2
Tadd Dameron-Fats Navarro Quintet
Fats Navarro:Nostalgia | Dreyfus Jazz Line | FDM 36736-2
Tadd Dameron-Fats Navarro Sextet
Fats Navarro:Nostalgia | Dreyfus Jazz Line | FDM 36736-2

Damiani,Paolo | (b,cello,el-b,vocld)
Italian Instabile Orchestra
Skies Of Europe | ECM | 1543
Orchestre National De Jazz
Charmediterranéen | ECM | 1828(018493-2)

D'Amico,Hank | (clas)
Bob Crosby And His Orchestra
Swing Legens:Bob Crosby | Nimbus Records | NI 2011
Ella Fitzgerald And Louis Armstrong With Sy Oliver And His Orchestra
Ella Fitzgerald:Mr.Paganini | Dreyfus Jazz Line | FDM 36741-2
Ella Fitzgerald With Sy Oliver And His Orchestra
Ella Fitzgerald:The Decca Years 1949-1954 | Decca | 050668-2
George Wettling's New Yorkers
Jazz:The Essential Collection Vol.3 | IN+OUT Records | 78013-2

Louis Armstrong And Ella Fitzgerald With Sy Oliver's Orchestra
Louis Armstrong:C'est Si Bon | Dreyfus Jazz Line | FDM 36730-2
Louis Armstrong With Sy Oliver's Choir And Orchestra
Jazz Collection:Louis Armstrong | Laserlight | 24366
Louis And The Good Book | Verve | 549593-2
Louis And The Good Book | Verve | 940130-0
Max Kaminsky And His Dixieland Bashers
Planet Jazz | Planet Jazz | 2169652-2

Damm,Jean | (tb)
Django Reinhardt With Stan Brenders Et Son Grand Orchestre
Verve Jazz Masters 38:Django Reinhardt | Verve | 516931-2

Dan Lube | (v)
Anita O'Day With The Buddy Bregman Orchestra
Verve Jazz Masters 49:Anita O'Day | Verve | 527653-2

Dandanell,Lise | (voc)
The Danish Radio Jazz Orchestra
This Train:The Danish Radio Jazz Orchestra Plays The Music Of Ray Pitts | dacapo | DCCD 9428

D'Andre,Dan | (reeds)
Billie Holiday With The Paul Whiteman Orchestra
Billie's Blues | Blue Note | 748786-2

D'Andrea,Dan | (as,sax,tsv)
Louis Armstrong With The Casa Loma Orchestra
Louis Armstrong:Swing That Music | Laserlight | 36056

Dane,Barbara | (voc)
Lu Watters' Jazz Band
Blues Over Bodega | Good Time Jazz | GTCD 12066-2

Daneck,Matthias | (dr,percxyl)
Cécile Verny Quartet
Métisse | double moon | CHRDM 71010
Got A Ticket | double moon | DMCD 1002-2
Horstmann-Wiedmann-Danek
Billy The Kid | Factory Outlet Records | FOR 2001-3 CD
Matthias Stich Sevensenses
...mehrschichtig | Satin Doll Productions | SDP 1038-1 CD
Thomas Horstmann-Martin Wiedmann Group
Decade | Factory Outlet Records | WO 95001

Danemo,Peter | (dr)
The Crossover Ensemble With The Zapolski Quartet
Helios Suite | dacapo | DCCD 9459

D'Angelis,Joseph | (fr-h)
Bill Evans Quartet With Orchestra
The Complete Bill Evans On Verve | Verve | 527953-2
From Left To Right | Verve | 557451-2

D'Angelo,Andrew | (b-cl,asvoice)
Ed Schuller Group feat. Dewey Redman
The Force | Tutu Records | 888166-2*
Frank Carlberg Group
Variations On A Summer Day | Fresh Sound Records | FSNT 083 CD

Dangerfield,Allen | (keyboardssynclavier)
Terje Rypdal Quartet
The Singles Collection | ECM | 1383(837749-2)

Daniel,Ted | (fl-h,hunting-horn,tp)
Sam Rivers Orchestra
Crystals | Impulse(MCA) | 589760-2

Danielian,Barry | (tpfl-h)
Spyro Gyra & Guests
Love & Other Obsessions | GRP | GRP 98112

Daniels,Andrew | (congas,bongos,timbalesperc)
Teodross Avery Quintet
My Generation | Impulse(MCA) | 951181-2

Daniels,Dee | (voc)
Three Of A Kind
Drip Some Grease | Minor Music | 801056

Daniels,Eddie | (alto-fl,cl,b-cl,piccolo,ts,fl,sax)
Bob James And His Orchestra
Jazzrock-Anthology Vol.3:Fusion | Zounds | CD 27100555
GRP All-Star Big Band
GRP All-Star Big Band:Live! | GRP | GRP 97402
Rolf Kühn And Friends
Affairs:Rolf Kühn & Friends | Intuition Records | INT 3211-2
Thad Jones-Mel Lewis Orchestra
The Groove Merchant/The Second Race | Laserlight | 24656
The Three Sopranos With The HR Big Band
The Three Sopranos | hr music.de | hrmj 001-01 CD

Daniels,Jim | (b-tb)
Woody Herman And The New Thundering Herd
Planet Jazz:Big Bands | Planet Jazz | 2169649-2
Woody Herman's Thundering Herd
Planet Jazz:Jazz Saxophone | Planet Jazz | 2169653-2

Daniels,Marcelle | (voc)
Elmo Hope Ensemble
Sounds From Rikers Island | Fresh Sound Records | FSR CD 338

Daniels,Warren | (ts)
Bernard Purdie Group
Jazzin' With The Soul Brothers | Fantasy | FANCD 6086-2

Danielsson,Lars | (b,cello,el-bsynth)
Caecilie Norby With Band
My Corner Of The Sky | Blue Note | 853422-2
Jazz Baltica Ensemble
The Birth+Rebirth Of Swedish Folk Jazz | ACT | 9254-2
Niels Landgren Funk Unit
Live In Stockholm | ACT | 9223-2
Nils Landgren Funk Unit
Paint It Blue:A Tribute To Cannonball Adderley | ACT | 9243-2
Nils Landgren Group
Sentimental Journey | ACT | 9409-2
Rigmor Gustafsson With The Nils Landgren Quartet And The Fleshquartet
I Will Wait For You | ACT | 9418-2
Viktoria Tolstoy Group & Strings
Shining On You | ACT | 9701-2

Danielsson,Lars Danmark | (b)
Nils Landgren First Unit And Guests
Nils Landgren-The First Unit | ACT | 9292-2

Danielsson,Palle | (bperc)
Agneta Baumann Group
Sentimental Lady | Touché Music | TMcCD 017
Albert Mangelsdorff Trio
Three Originals:The Wide Point/Trilogue/Albert Live In Montreux | MPS | 519213-2
Anouar Brahem Group
Khomsa | ECM | 1561(527093-2)
Caecilie Norby With Band
My Corner Of The Sky | Blue Note | 853422-2
Charles Lloyd Quartet
Fish Out Of Water | ECM | 1398
Collin Walcott Group
Grazing Dreams | ECM | 1096
Dino Saluzzi Trio
Responsorium | ECM | 1816(017069-2)
Eje Thelin Quartet
Ejs Thelin 1966 With Barney Wilen | Dragon | DRCD 366
Enrico Rava Quartet
The Pilgrim And The Stars | ECM | 1063(847322-2)
The Plot | ECM | 1078
Geri Allen And The Jazzpar 1996 Nonet
Some Aspects Of Water | Storyville | STCD 4212
Geri Allen Trio
Some Aspects Of Water | Storyville | STCD 4212
Geri Allen Trio With Johny Coles
Some Aspects Of Water | Storyville | STCD 4212
Jan Garbarek-Bobo Stenson Quartet
Witchi-Tai-To | ECM | 1041(833330-2)
Dansere | ECM | 1075(829193-2)
Keith Jarrett Quartet
Belonging | ECM | 1050(829115-2)
My Song | ECM | 1115(821406-2)
Nude Ants | ECM | 1171/72(829119-2)
Personal Mountains | ECM | 1382(837361-2)

Lena Willemark-Ale Möller Group
Nordan | ECM | 1536(523161-2)
Agram | ECM | 1610
Michel Petrucciani Trio
Live At The Village Vanguard | Blue Note | 540382-2
Pianism | Blue Note | 746295-2
Michel Petrucciani:The Blue Note Years | Blue Note | 789916-2
Mingus By Five
Mingus By Five | Touché Music | TMcCD 019
Monk By Five
Monk By Five | Touché Music | TMcCD 012
Nils Landgren Group
Ballads | ACT | 9268-2
Palle Danielsson Quartet
Contra Post | Caprice | CAP 21440
Palle Danielsson Quintet
Contra Post | Caprice | CAP 21440
Peter Erskine Trio
You Never Know | ECM | 1497(517353-2)
Time Being | ECM | 1532
As It Is | ECM | 1594
Juni | ECM | 1657(539726-2)
Richard Galliano Group
Laurita | Dreyfus Jazz Line | FDM 36572-9
Richard Galliano Quartet
Gallianissimo! The Best Of Richard Galliano | Dreyfus Jazz Line | FDM 36616-2
Richard Galliano Trio
Gallianissimo! The Best Of Richard Galliano | Dreyfus Jazz Line | FDM 36616-2
Tomasz Stanko Septet
Litania | ECM | 1636(537551-2)
Tomasz Stanko Sextet
Litania | ECM | 1636(537551-2)
Ulf Adaker Quartet
Reflections | Touché Music | TMcCD 016
Wolfgang Lackerschmid Sextet
One More Life | Bhakti Jazz | BR 29

Danish Radio Big Band,The |
Miles Davis With The Danish Radio Big Band
Aura | CBS | CK 63962
Mona Larsen And The Danish Radio Big Band Plus Soloists
Michael Mantler:Cerco Un Paese Innocente | ECM | 1556
Stan Getz With The Danish Radio Big Band
Stan Getz In Europe | Laserlight | 24657
The Danish Radio Big Band
Aura | CBS | CK 63962

Danish Radio Concert Orchestra |
Michael Mantler Group With The Danish Concert Radio Orchestra
Many Have No Speech | Watt | 19(835580-2)
The Danish Radio Concert Orchestra
Symphonies Vol.2 | dacapo | DCCD 9441

Danish Radio Concert Orchestra Strings,The |
Michael Mantler Group With The Danish Radio Concert Orchestra Strings
The School Of Understanding(Sort-Of-An-Opera) | ECM | 1648/49(537963-2)

Danish Radio Jazz Orchestra |
Jens Winther And The Danish Radio Jazz Orchestra
Angels | dacapo | DCCD 9442
The Danish Radio Jazz Orchestra
This Train:The Danish Radio Jazz Orchestra Plays The Music Of Ray Pitts | dacapo | DCCD 9428
Nice Work | dacapo | DCCD 9446

Danish,Silvia | (voc)
Jazzensemble Des Hessischen Rundfunks
Jazz Messe-Messe Für Unsere Zeit | hr music.de | hrmj 003-01 CD

Danko,Harold | (el-p,pp-solo)
Chet Baker Quintet
Once Upon A Summertime | Original Jazz Classics | OJCCD 405-2
Harold Danko Trio
Fantasy Exit | Steeplechase | SCCD 31530
Trilix | Steeplechase | SCCD 31551
Lee Konitz-Harold Danko Duo
Wild As Springtime | Candid | CCD 79734
Rich Perry Quintet
At Eastman | Steeplechase | SCCD 31533
Ted Brown Quartet
Preservation | Steeplechase | SCCD 31539
Woody Herman And His Orchestra
The Raven Speaks | Original Jazz Classics | OJCCD 663-2(F 9416)

Danko,Rick | (voc)
Hans Theessink Group
Call Me | Minor Music | 801022

D'Anna,Stefano | (ssts)
Orchestra Jazz Siciliana
Orchestra Jazz Siciliana Plays The Music Of Carla Bley | Watt | XtraWatt/4

Dannemann,Werner | (g)
Katie Kern Group
Still Young | Jazzpoint | JP 1070 CD
Katie Kern-Werner Dannemann
Still Young | Jazzpoint | JP 1070 CD

Danner,Michael | (tbtuba)
Abdullah Ibrahim With The NDR Big Band
Ekapa Lodumo | TipToe | TIP-888840 2
Heinz Sauer Quartet With The NDR Big Band
NDR Big Band-Bravissimo | ACT | 9232-2
Vlatko Kucan Group
Vlatko Kucan Group | true muze | TUMU CD 9803

D'Annolfo,Frank | (tb)
Glenn Miller And His Orchestra
Planet Jazz:Glenn Miller | Planet Jazz | 2152056-2
Planet Jazz:Jazz Greatest Hits | Planet Jazz | 2169648-2
Planet Jazz:Big Bands | Planet Jazz | 2169649-2
The Chesterfield Broadcasts Vol.1 | RCA | 2663113-2
The Andrew Sisters With The Glenn Miller Orchestra
The Chesterfield Broadcasts Vol.1 | RCA | 2663113-2

Dansgaard,Trine | (voc)
The Danish Radio Concert Orchestra
Symphonies Vol.2 | dacapo | DCCD 9441

Danstrup,Peter | (b,b-synth,synthb-g)
Simon Spang-Hanssen & Maneklar
Wondering | dacapo | DCCD 9436

Dantas,Rubém | (cajon,handclapping,tinajaperc)
Los Jovenes Flamencos
Jazzpana | ACT | 9212-2
Los Jovenes Flamencos With The WDR Big Band And Guests
Jazzpana | ACT | 9212-2

Danzer,Corinna | (fl,asreeds)
The United Women's Orchestra
The Blue One | Jazz Haus Musik | JHM 0099 CD
United Women's Orchestra
Virgo Supercluster | Jazz Haus Musik | JHM 0123 CD

Danzinger,Zachary | (cymbals,hi-hat,dr,sampled-perc)
Leni Stern Group
Closer To The Light | Enja | ENJ-6034 2
Michael 'Patches' Stewart Group
Penetration | Hip Bop | HIBD 8018
Till Brönner Group
Chattin' With Chet | Verve | 157534-2
Uri Caine Trio
Bedrock | Winter&Winter | 910068-2
Wayne Krantz Trio
Long To Be Loose | Enja | ENJ-7099 2
2 Drinks Minimum | Enja | ENJ-9043 2

Danzizen,Bill | (tp)
Elliot Lawrence And His Orchestra
Mullenium | CBS | CK 65678

Dapper,Frank | (drcongas)
Jo Ambros Group
Wanderlust | dml-records | CD 016
Dara,Olu | (african-fl,co,beribau,voice,voc,tp)
Cassandra Wilson Group
Blue Light 'Til Dawn | Blue Note | 781357-2
Traveling Miles | Blue Note | 854123-2
Cold Sweat
Cold Sweat Plays J.B. | JMT Edition | 919025-2
Jean-Paul Bourelly Trance Atlantic
Boom Bop II | double moon | CHRDM 71023
Darby,Ron | (dr)
Dick Charlesworth And His City Gents
The Golden Years Of Revival Jazz,Vol.4 | Storyville | STCD 5509
The Golden Years Of Revival Jazz,Vol.11 | Storyville | STCD 5516
Graham Stewart And His New Orleans Band
The Golden Years Of Revival Jazz,Vol.12 | Storyville | STCD 5517
The Golden Years Of Revival Jazz,Vol.14 | Storyville | STCD 5519
D'Arcy Jones,Brian | (voc)
The Sidewalks Of New York
Tin Pan Alley:The Sidewalks Of New York | Winter&Winter | 910038-2
Darensbourg,Joe | (cl,ssvoc)
Louis Armstrong And His All Stars
Jazz Festival Vol.1 | Storyville | 4960733
Darling,David | (cello,8-string-el-cello,perc,bells)
David Darling
Cello | ECM | 1464(511982-2)
Dark Wood | ECM | 1519(523750-2)
David Darling Group
Cycles | ECM | 1219
Ketil Bjornstad Group
The Sea | ECM | 1545(521718-2)
The Sea II | ECM | 1633(537341-2)
Ketil Bjornstad-David Darling
The River | ECM | 1593(531170-2)
Epigraphs | ECM | 1684(543159-2)
Pierre Favre Quintet
Window-Steps | ECM | 1584(529348-2)
Ralph Towner Quintet
Old Friends New Friends | ECM | 1153
Sidsel Endresen Sextet
Exile | ECM | 1524(521721-2)
Terje Rypdal Group
Skywards | ECM | 1608(533768-2)
Terje Rypdal-David Darling Duo
Eos | ECM | 1263
Darling,Wayne | (b)
Wayne Darling Group
The Art Of The Bass Vol.1 | Laika Records | 35101652
Darouiche,Biboul Ferkouzad | (kalimba,perc,voc,african-harp)
Jenny Evans And Her Quintet
Gonna Go Fishin' | ESM Records | ESM 9307
Klaus Doldinger's Passport
Klaus Doldinger Passport Live | Warner | 8573-84132-2
Darr,Jerome | (el-gg)
Charlie Parker Quintet
The Cole Porter Songbook | Verve | 823250-2
Bird: The Complete Charlie Parker On Verve | Verve | 837141-2
Dart,Bill | (dr)
Lu Watters' Yerba Buena Jazz Band
The Very Best Of Dixieland Jazz | Verve | 535529-2
Yerba Buena Jazz Band
Bunk & Lu | Good Time Jazz | GTCD 12024-2
Darvas,Julius | (b)
Bernd Konrad Jazz Group With Symphonie Orchestra
Wen Die Götter Lieben | Creative Works Records | CW CD 1010-1
Das Neves,Wilson | (atapaques,pandeiro,drperc)
Passport
Iguacu | Atlantic | 2292-46031-2
Sarah Vaughan And Her Band
Sarah Vaughan Birthday Celebration | Fantasy | FANCD 6090-2
Sarah Vaughan With Orchestra
I Love Brazil | Pablo | 2312101-2
Sarah Vaughan Birthday Celebration | Fantasy | FANCD 6090-2
dAs ptOjekT |
dAs prOjekT
dAs prOjekT | Foolish Music | FM 211288
Das,Sandeep | (tabla)
Kayhan Kalhor Trio
The Rain | ECM | 1840(066627-2)
Dasek,Rudolf | (g,el-g,vocwhistling)
Toto Blanke-Rudolf Dasek
Talking Hands:Live | ALISO Records | AL 1021
Two Much Guitar! | ALISO Records | AL 1022
Meditation | ALISO Records | AL 1026
Mona Lisa | ALISO Records | AL 1037
Toto Blanke-Rudolf Dasek With The Overtontrio
Meditation | ALISO Records | AL 1026
Dash,Julian | (ts)
Erskine Hawkins And His Orchestra
Planet Jazz:Big Bands | Planet Jazz | 2169649-2
Daskoff,Isabelle | (v)
Milt Jackson And His Orchestra
Reverence And Compassion | Reprise | 9362-45204-2
Dato,Carlo Actis | (b-cl,bs,ts,voiceperc)
Italian Instabile Orchestra
Skies Of Europe | ECM | 1543
Dato,Daniel | (v)
Charlie Haden Quartet West With Strings
Now Is The Hour | Verve | 527827-2
Dauber,Werner | (ts)
Art Van Damme Group
State Of Art | MPS | 841413-2
Daucher,Elmar | (resonating-stones)
Stephan Micus
The Muisc Of Stones | ECM | 1384(837750-2)
Dauelsberg,Claudio | (pteclados)
Duo Fenix
Karai-Eté | IN+OUT Records | 7009-2
Dauner,Wolfgang | (keyboards,p,clavinet,ringmodulator)
Albert Mangelsdorff-Wolfgang Dauner
Albert Mangelsdorff And His Friends | MPS | 067375-2
Hans Koller Quintet
Kunstkopfindianer | MPS | 9813439
Jon Hiseman With The United Jazz & Rock Ensemble And Babara Thompson's Paraphernalia
About Time Too! | VeraBra Records | CDVBR 2014-2
The German Jazz Masters
Old Friends | ACT | 9278-2
Wolfgang Dauner Trio
Music Zounds | MPS | 9808190
Dautel,Fritz | (bassoon,fl,asts)
Bernd Konrad With Erwin Lehn und sein Südfunk Orchester Stuttgart
Wen Die Götter Lieben | Creative Works Records | CW CD 1010-1
Erwin Lehn Und Sein Südfunk-Tanzorchester
Deutsches Jazz Fesival 1954/1955 | Bear Family Records | BCD 15430
Dave Lambert Singers,The |
Charlie Parker And His Orchestra
The Cole Porter Songbook | Verve | 823250-2
Bird: The Complete Charlie Parker On Verve | Verve | 837141-2
Charlie Parker With Orchestra
Charlie Parker Big Band | Verve | 559835-2
John Hendricks WithThe Dave Lambert Singers
Sing A Song Of Basie | Verve | 543827-2
Dave,Chris | (dr)
Kenny Garrett Quartet
KG Standard Of Language | Warner | 9362-48404-2
Davenport,Cow Cow | (pspeech)
Cow Cow Davenport
Boogie Woogie | Laserlight | 24321
Davenport,Pete | (voc)
Uri Caine Trio
Bedrock | Winter&Winter | 910068-2
Davenport,Wallace | (tp)
Count Basie And His Orchestra
Basie Meets Bond | Capitol | 538225-2
Basie's Beatle Bag | Verve | 557455-2
Live at The Sands | Reprise | 9362-45946-2
Frank Sinatra With The Count Basie Orchestra
It Might As Well Be Spring | Reprise | 7599-27027-2
Lionel Hampton And His Orchestra
Planet Jazz:Big Bands | Planet Jazz | 2169649-2
Davern,Kenny | (cl,ss,c-mel-saxtalking)
Byron Stripling And Friends
If I Could Be With You | Nagel-Heyer | NH 1010
George Masso Allstars
The Wonderful World Of George Gershwin | Nagel-Heyer | CD 001
One Two Three | Nagel-Heyer | CD 008
The First Sampler | Nagel-Heyer | NHR SP 5
Jack Teagarden And His Band
Meet Me Where They Play The Blues | Good Time Jazz | GTCD 12063-2
Randy Sandke And The New York Allstars
The Re-Discovered Louis And Bix | Nagel-Heyer | CD 058
Randy Sandke-Dick Hyman
The Re-Discovered Louis And Bix | Nagel-Heyer | CD 058
Summit Reunion
Jazz Im Amerikahaus,Vol.5 | Nagel-Heyer | CD 015
The First Sampler | Nagel-Heyer | NHR SP 5
The New York Allstars
We Love You,Louis! | Nagel-Heyer | CD 029
The Second Sampler | Nagel-Heyer | NHR SP 6
DaVersa,Jay | (tp)
Herbie Hancock Group
Man-Child | CBS | 471235-2
Davey,Arthur | (as)
Louis Armstrong And His Orchestra
Planet Jazz:Louis Armstrong | Planet Jazz | 2152052-2
Louis Armstrong:A 100th Birthday Celebration | RCA | 2663694-2
David,Jacques | (dr)
Henri Crolla Quartet
Jazz In Paris:Henri Crolla-Quand Refleuriront Les Lilas Blancs? | EmArCy | 018418-2
Henri Crolla Sextet
Jazz In Paris:Henri Crolla-Quand Refleuriront Les Lilas Blancs? | EmArCy | 018418-2
Sidney Bechet With Michel Attenoux And His Orchestra
Planet Jazz:Sidney Bechet | Planet Jazz | 2152063-2
David,Louis | (voc)
Mitchell's Christian Singers
From Spiritual To Swing | Vanguard | VCD 169/71
Davidoff,Thomas | (percdr-computer)
Toto Blanke Group
Fools Paradise | ALISO Records | AL 1019
Davidsen,Jakob | (p,condkeyboards)
The Crossover Ensemble
The River:Image Of Time And Life | dacapo | DCCD 9434
The Crossover Ensemble With The Zapolski Quartet
Helios Suite | dacapo | DCCD 9459
Davidsen,Nils | (b)
Copenhagen Art Ensemble
Shape To Twelve | dacapo | DCCD 9430
Angels' Share | dacapo | DCCD 9452
Marilyn Mazur With Ars Nova And The Copenhagen Art Ensemble
Jordsange | dacapo | DCCD 9454
Ok Nok...Kongo
Moonstone Journey | dacapo | DCCD 9444
The Crossover Ensemble
The River:Image Of Time And Life | dacapo | DCCD 9434
When Granny Sleeps
Welcome | dacapo | DCCD 9447
Davidson,Don | (bs)
Gerry Mulligan Tentette
Gene Norman Presents The Original Gerry Mulligan Tentet And Quartet | GNP Crescendo | GNPD 56
Davidson,Jakob | (keyboardssamples)
Takuan
Push | dacapo | DCCD 9457
Davidson,Julian | (g)
Kid Ory And His Band
The Very Best Of Dixieland Jazz | Verve | 535529-2
Kid Ory's Creole Jazz Band
This Kid's The Greatest! | Good Time Jazz | GTCD 12045-2
Davies,Howard | (dr)
Peggy Lee With The Benny Goodman Orchestra
Peggy Lee & Benny Goodman:The Complete Recordings 1941-1947 | CBS | C2K 65686
Davies,John R.T. | (as,g,org,tb,co,cornopean)
Bob Wallis Storyville Jazzmen
The Golden Years Of Revival Jazz,Vol.7 | Storyville | STCD 5512
Henrik Johansen's Jazzband
The Golden Years Of Revival Jazz,Vol.6 | Storyville | STCD 5511
The Golden Years Of Revival Jazz,Vol.7 | Storyville | STCD 5512
The Golden Years Of Revibal Jazz,Vol.15 | Storyville | STCD 5520
Mr.Acker Bilk And His Paramount Jazz Band
The Golden Years Of Revival Jazz,Vol.7 | Storyville | STCD 5512
The Golden Years Of Revival Jazz,Vol.8 | Storyville | STCD 5513
The Golden Years Of Revival Jazz,Vol.9 | Storyville | STCD 5514
The Golden Years Of Revival Jazz,Vol.10 | Storyville | STCD 5515
The Golden Years Of Revival Jazz,Vol.12 | Storyville | STCD 5517
The Golden Years Of Revival Jazz,Vol.13 | Storyville | STCD 5518
Sandy Brown's Jazz Band
The Golden Years Of Revival Jazz,Sampler | Storyville | 109 1001
The Golden Years Of Revival Jazz,Vol.6 | Storyville | STCD 5511
The Golden Years Of Revival Jazz,Vol.8 | Storyville | STCD 5513
The Golden Years Of Revival Jazz,Vol.10 | Storyville | STCD 5515
Davilla,Frank 'Paquito' | (tp)
Charlie Parker With Machito And His Orchestra
Charlie Parker:The Best Of The Verve Years | Verve | 527815-2
Talkin' Bird | Verve | 559859-2
Bird: The Complete Charlie Parker On Verve | Verve | 837141-2
Charlie Parker:April In Paris | Dreyfus Jazz Line | FDM 36737-2
Davis Jr.,Walter | (el-p,pp-solo)
Archie Shepp Sextet
The Way Ahead | Impulse(MCA) | 951272-2
Art Blakey And The Jazz Messengers
Planet Jazz:Art Blakey | Planet Jazz | 2152066-2
Planet Jazz:Lee Morgan | Planet Jazz | 2161238-2
Roots And Herbs | Blue Note | 521956-2
The Art Of Jazz | IN+OUT Records | 77028-2
Jazz In Paris:Paris Jam Session | EmArCy | 832692-2 PMS
Dizzy Gillespie And His Orchestra
Verve Jazz Masters 20:Introducing | Verve | 519853-2
Dizzy Gillespie:Birks Works-The Verve Big Band Sessions | Verve | 527900-2
Dizzy Gillespie Orchestra
Verve Jazz Masters 10:Dizzy Gillespie | Verve | 516319-2
Donald Byrd Quintet
Byrd In Paris Vol.1 | Polydor | 833394-2
Donald Byrd Sextet
Byrd In Hand | Blue Note | 542305-2
Jackie McLean Quartet
Let Freedom Ring | Blue Note | 591895-2
Walter Davis Quintet
Davis Cup | Blue Note | 0675597
Davis,Aaron | (p)
Holly Cole And Her Quartet
It Happened One Night | Metro Blue | 852699-0
Davis,Al | (tp)
Peggy Lee With The Benny Goodman Orchestra
Peggy Lee & Benny Goodman:The Complete Recordings 1941-1947 | CBS | C2K 65686
Davis,Anthony | (p,el-p,synthp-solo)
Ray Anderson Quintet
Blues Bred In The Bone | Enja | ENJ-5081 2
Davis,Art | (b,tpfl-h)
Abbey Lincoln And Her Orchestra
Straight Ahead | Candid | CCD 79015
Art Blakey Quartet
A Jazz Message | Impulse(MCA) | 547964-2
Booker Little Sextet
Out Front | Candid | CCD 79027
Candid Dolphy | Candid | CCD 79033
Buddy Childers Big Band
Just Buddy's | Candid | CCD 79761
Clifford Jordan Quintet
Mosaic | Milestone | MCD 47092-2
Count Basie And His Orchestra
Atomic Swing | Roulette | 497871-2
Dizzy Gillespie And His Orchestra
Verve Jazz Masters 10:Dizzy Gillespie | Verve | 516319-2
Gillespiana And Carnegie Hall Concert | Verve | 519809-2
Talking Verve:Dizzy Gillespie | Verve | 533846-2
Ultimate Dizzy Gillespie | Verve | 557535-2
Dizzy Gillespie Quintet
Dizzie Gillespie: Salle Pleyel/Olympia | Laserlight | 36132
Dizzy Gillespie Sextet
Dizzie Gillespie: Salle Pleyel/Olympia | Laserlight | 36132
Ernestine Anderson With Orchestra
My Kinda Swing | Mercury | 842409-2
Freddie Hubbard Sextet
Wayne Shorter:The Classic Blue Note Recordings | Blue Note | 540856-2
Holly Cole Trio
Misty Blue:Sweet Sisters Swing Songs Of Sorrow And Sadness | Blue Note | 521151-2
JATP All Stars
Stan Getz Highlights:The Best Of The Verve Years Vol.2 | Verve | 517330-2
Verve Jazz Masters 25:Stan Getz & Dizzy Gillespie | Verve | 521852-2
Jimmy Smith With The Billy Byers Orchestra
Jimmy Smith:Best Of The Verve Years | Verve | 527950-2
Jimmy Smith With The Claus Ogerman Orchestra
Verve Jazz Masters 29:Jimmy Smith | Verve | 521855-2
Any Number Can Win | Verve | 557447-2
John Coltrane And His Orchestra
Ascension | Impulse(MCA) | 543413-2
John Coltrane Group
Olé Coltrane | Atlantic | 7567-81349-2
Olé Coltrane | Rhino | 8122-73699-2
John Coltrane Quartet
The Coltrane Quartet Plays | Impulse(MCA) | 951214-2
John Coltrane:The Classic Quartet-Complete Impulse Studio Recordings | Impulse(MCA) | 951280-2
John Coltrane Quartet With Brass
The Complete Africa/Brass Sessions | Impulse(MCA) | 952168-2
John Coltrane Quintet
John Coltrane:Standards | Impulse(MCA) | 549914-2
John Coltrane Sextet
A Love Supreme | Impulse(MCA) | 589945-2
John Coltrane Sextet With Eric Dolphy
John Coltrane-The Heavyweight Champion:The Complete Atlantic Recordings | Atlantic | 8122-71984-2
Lalo Schifrin Sextet
Tin Tin Deo | Fresh Sound Records | FSR-CD 319
Max Roach All Stars
Candid Dolphy | Candid | CCD 79033
Max Roach Plus Four
Clifford Brown-Max Roach:Alone Together-The Best Of The Mercury Years | Verve | 526373-2
Max Roach Quintet
Clifford Brown-Max Roach:Alone Together-The Best Of The Mercury Years | Verve | 526373-2
Deeds Not Words | Original Jazz Classics | OJC20 304-2(RLP 1122)
The Jazz Giants Play Sammy Cahn:It's Magic | Prestige | PCD 24226-2
Max Roach Sextet
Deeds Not Words | Original Jazz Classics | OJC20 304-2(RLP 1122)
Max Roach Sextet With Choir
It's Time | Impulse(MCA) | 951185-2
McCoy Tyner Trio
Inception | Impulse(MCA) | 951220-2
Roland Kirk Quartet
Talkin' Verve-Roots Of Acid Jazz:Roland Kirk | Verve | 533101-2
Rahsaan/The Complete Mercury Recordings Of Roland Kirk | Mercury | 846630-2
Davis,Beryl | (voc)
Arthur Young And Hatchett's Swingtette
Grapelli Story | Verve | 515807-2
Stephane Grappelli Quintet
Grapelli Story | Verve | 515807-2
Davis,Bobby | (as,cl,ss,hawaiian-g-efect)
Frankie Trumbauer And His Orchestra
Jazz:The Essential Collection Vol.2 | IN+OUT Records | 78012-2
Davis,Carl | (reedsvoc)
Ella Fitzgerald With The Bill Doggett Orchestra
Rhythm Is My Business | Verve | 559513-2
Davis,Charles | (as,bs,cl,b-cl,dr,fl,alto-fl,bass-fl)
Abdullah Ibrahim And Ekaya
Water From An Ancient Well | TipToe | TIP-888812 2
Archie Shepp Septet
The Way Ahead | Impulse(MCA) | 951272-2
Cecil Taylor/Buell Neidlinger Orchestra
New York City R&B | Candid | CCD 79017
Dinah Washington With The Belford Hendricks Orchestra
Verve Jazz Masters 20:Introducing | Verve | 519853-2
What A Diff'rence A Day Makes! | Verve | 543300-2
4 By 4:Ella Fitzgerald/Sarah Vaughan/Billie Holiday/Dinah Washington | Verve | 559693-2
Dinah Washington With The Eddie Chamblee Orchestra
Verve Jazz Masters 40:Dinah Washington | Verve | 522055-2
Dinah Sings Bessie Smith | Verve | 538635-2
Ella Fitzgerald With The Bill Doggett Orchestra
Ella Fitzgerald-First Lady Of Song | Verve | 517898-2
Freddie Hubbard Orchestra
The Body And The Soul | Impulse(MCA) | 951183-2
Johnny Dyani Septet
Afrika | Steeplechase | SCS 1186(Audiophile Pressing)
Julian Priester Sextet
Out Of This World | Milestone | MCD 47087-2
Nina Simone Quintet
Planet Jazz:Nina Simone | Planet Jazz | 2165372-2
Ronnie Mathews Quintet
Ronnie Mathews-Roland Alexander-Freddie Hubbard | Prestige | PRCD 24271-2
The Jazz Composer's Orchestra
Comminications | JCOA | 1001/2
Davis,Charlie | (bstp)
Buddy Rich Big Band
Backwoods Siseman/Pieces Of Dream | Laserlight | 24655
Woody Herman And His Orchestra
The Raven Speaks | Original Jazz Classics | OJCCD 663-2(F 9416)
Davis,Danny | (alto-cl,as,perc,fl,cl,vocreeds)
Sun Ra And His Astro-Infinity Arkestra
Space Is The Place | Impulse(MCA) | 951249-2
Sun Ra And His Intergalactic Research Arkestra

Black Myth/Out In Space | MPS | 557656-2

Davis,Eddie 'Lockjaw' | (ts)

Al Smith With The Eddie Lockjaw Davis Quartet
Queen Of The Organ-Shirley Scott Memorial Album | Prestige | PRCD 11027-2
Big Joe Turner With The Count Basie Orchestra
Flip Flop And Fly | Original Jazz Classics | OJCCD 1053-2(2310937)
Big Sid Catlett And His Orchestra
The Small Black Groups | Storyville | 4960523
Coleman Hawkins With Eddie Lockjaw Davis And The Tommy Flanagan Trio
Night Hawk | Original Jazz Classics | OJC20 420-2(SV 2016)
Count Basie And His Orchestra
Jazz Gallery:Lester Young Vol.2(1946-59) | RCA | 2119541-2
Afrique | RCA | 2179618-2
Count Basie: Salle Pleyel, April 17th, 1972 | Laserlight | 36127
Atomic Swing | Roulette | 497871-2
Verve Jazz Masters 2:Count Basie | Verve | 519819-2
Basie Meets Bond | Capitol | 538225-2
Basie's Beatle Bag | Verve | 557455-2
The Complete Atomic Basie | Roulette | 828635-2
Live at The Sands | Reprise | 9362-45946-2
Count Basie And The Kansas City 7
Count Basie: Salle Pleyel, April 17th, 1972 | Laserlight | 36127
Count Basie Band
Basie Jam No. 2 | Original Jazz Classics | OJCCD 631-2(2310786)
Count Basie Kansas City 7
Count Basie Kansas City 7 | Original Jazz Classics | OJCCD 690-2(2310908)
Dinah Washington And Her Band
After Hours With Miss D | Verve | 0760562
Verve Jazz Masters 40:Dinah Washington | Verve | 522055-2
Dizzy Gillespie All Stars
Jazz At The Philharmonic:The Montreux Collection | Pablo | PACD 5306-2
Dizzy Gillespie Big 7
Dizzy-At The Montreux Jazz Festival 1975 | Original Jazz Classics | OJC20 739-2(2310749)
Eddie Lockjaw Davis And His Orchestra
Eric Dolphy:The Complete Prestige Recordings | Prestige | 9 PRCD-4418-2
Eddie Lockjaw Davis Orchestra
Afro-Jaws | Original Jazz Classics | OJCCD 403-2(RLP 9373)
Eddie Lockjaw Davis Quartet
The Art Of Saxophone | Laserlight | 24652
Jazz Legends:Eddie Lockjaw Davis Quartet Vol.1&2 | Storyville | 4960263
The Eddie Lockjaw Davis Cookbook Vol.2 | Original Jazz Classics | OJC20 653-2(P 7161)
Jaws | Original Jazz Classics | OJCCD 218-2(P 7154)
Queen Of The Organ-Shirley Scott Memorial Album | Prestige | PRCD 11027-2
Eddie Lockjaw Davis Quintet
Cookbook Vol.1 | Original Jazz Classics | OJC20 652-2(P 7141)
The Eddie Lockjaw Davis Cookbook Vol.2 | Original Jazz Classics | OJC20 653-2(P 7161)
Jaws In Orbit | Original Jazz Classics | OJCCD 322-2(P 7171)
The Jazz Giants Play Harry Warren:Lullaby Of Broadway | Prestige | PCD 24204-2
Queen Of The Organ-Shirley Scott Memorial Album | Prestige | PRCD 11027-2
Eddie Lockjaw Davis Sextet feat. Paul Gonsalves
Planet Jazz:Jazz Saxophone | Planet Jazz | 2169653-2
Eddie Lockjaw Davis With The Red Garland Trio
Prestige Moodsville Vol.1 | Original Jazz Classics | OJCCD 360-2(MV 1)
Eddie Lockjaw Davis-Johnny Griffin Quintet
Blues Up And Down | Milestone | MCD 47084-2
Battle Stations | Original Jazz Classics | OJCCD 1085(P7282)
The Jazz Giants Play Cole Porter:Night And Day | Prestige | PCD 24203-2
The Prestige Legacy Vol.2:Battles Of Saxes | Prestige | PCD 24252-2
Tough Tenors Back Again! | Storyville | STCD 8298
Eddie Lockjaw Davis-Shirley Scott Sextet
Bacalao | Original Jazz Classics | OJCCD 1090-2(P 7178)
Ella Fitzgerald And Count Basie With The JATP All Stars
Bluella:Ella Fitzgerald Sings The Blues | Pablo | 2310960-2
Ella Fitzgerald Jam
Bluella:Ella Fitzgerald Sings The Blues | Pablo | 2310960-2
Harry Edison Quintet
Edison's Light | Original Jazz Classics | OJCCD 804-2(2310780)
JATP All Stars
Welcome To Jazz At The Philharmonic | Fantasy | FANCD 6081-2
Johnny Griffin-Eddie Lockjaw Davis Quintet
Tough Tenors | Original Jazz Classics | OJCCD 1094-2(JLP 931)
Kansas City Seven
The J.J.Johnson Memorial Album | Prestige | PRCD 11025-2
Mildred Anderson With The Eddie Lockjaw Davis Quartet
Queen Of The Organ-Shirley Scott Memorial Album | Prestige | PRCD 11027-2
Milt Jackson Septet
Milt Jackson Birthday Celebration | Fantasy | FANCD 6079-2
Milt Jackson-Ray Brown Jam
Milt Jackson Birthday Celebration | Fantasy | FANCD 6079-2
Montreux '77 | Original Jazz Classics | OJC 385(2620105)
Montreux '77 | Original Jazz Classics | OJC20 375-2(2308205)
Oscar Peterson Jam
Oscar Peterson Plays Duke Ellington | Pablo | 2310966-2
Montreux '77 | Original Jazz Classics | OJC 385(2620105)
Montreux '77 | Original Jazz Classics | OJC20 378-2(2308208)
Shirley Scott All Stars
Queen Of The Organ-Shirley Scott Memorial Album | Prestige | PRCD 11027-2
Very Saxy
Very Saxy | Original Jazz Classics | OJCCD 458-2
The Prestige Legacy Vol.2:Battles Of Saxes | Prestige | PCD 24252-2

Davis,Eddy | (bj,ldvoc)

The Sidewalks Of New York
Tin Pan Alley:The Sidewalks Of New York | Winter&Winter | 910038-2
Woody Allen And His New Orleans Jazz Band
Wild Man Blues | RCA | 2663353-2
Woody Allen Trio
Wild Man Blues | RCA | 2663353-2

Davis,George | (fl,g,el-g,voc,saxts)

David Fathead Newman Septet
Jazzin' Vol.2: The Music Of Stevie Wonder | Fantasy | FANCD 6088-2
Gato Barbieri Orchestra
The Roots Of Acid Jazz | Impulse(MCA) | IMP 12042
Joe Zawinul Group
Zawinul | Atlantic | 7567-81375-2
Lee Konitz Orchestra
The Art Of Saxophone | Laserlight | 24652

Davis,Harold | (dr)

Les McCann Group
Another Beginning | Atlantic | 7567-80790-2

Davis,Henry | (b)

Dee Dee Bridgewater With Band
Dee Dee Bridgewater | Atlantic | 7567-80760-2
Herbie Hancock Group
Man-Child | CBS | 471235-2

Davis,Jackie | (org)

Dinah Washington And Her Band
After Hours With Miss D | Verve | 0760562
Verve Jazz Masters 40:Dinah Washington | Verve | 522055-2
Ella Fitzgerald With Jackie Davis And Louis Bellson
Bluella:Ella Fitzgerald Sings The Blues | Pablo | 2310960-2
Lady Time | Original Jazz Classics | OJCCD 864-2(2310825)

Davis,James | (percvoc)

Richard 'Groove' Holmes Orchestra
Comin' On Home | Blue Note | 538701-2

Davis,Jesse | (asts)

Clark Terry Quintet
The Hymn | Candid | CCD 79770
Nicholas Payton Sextet
Gumbo Nouveau | Verve | 531199-2
Roy Hargrove Quintet
Family | Verve | 527630-2
Roy Hargrove Sextet
Family | Verve | 527630-2

Davis,Jesse Edwin | (g)

Albert King Blues Band
Lovejoy | Stax | SCD 8517-2(STS 2040)
John Lee Hooker Group
Endless Boogie | MCA | MCD 10413

Davis,John Graham | (b)

LeeAnn Ledgerwood Trio
Walkin' Up | Steeplechase | SCCD 31541

Davis,Julius | (voc)

Mitchell's Christian Singers
From Spiritual To Swing | Vanguard | VCD 169/71

Davis,Kay | (voc)

Duke Ellington And His Orchestra
Planet Jazz:Duke Ellington | Planet Jazz | 2152053-2
Planet Jazz:Jazz Greatest Hits | Planet Jazz | 2169648-2
Highlights From The Duke Ellington Centennial Edition | RCA | 2663672-2
Carnegie Hall Concert December 1944 | Prestige | 2PCD 24073-2
Carnegie Hall Concert January 1946 | Prestige | 2PCD 24074-2
Carnegie Hall Concert December 1947 | Prestige | 2PCD 24075-2
Jazz:The Essential Collection Vol.2 | IN+OUT Records | 78012-2

Davis,Kenneth 'Kenny' | (bel-b)

Cassandra Wilson Group
Blue Light 'Til Dawn | Blue Note | 781357-2
Don Byron Quintet
Tuskegee Experiments | Nonesuch | 7559-79280-2
Michele Rosewoman And Quintessence
Guardians Of The Light | Enja | ENJ-9378 2
Michele Rosewoman Quintet
Harvest | Enja | ENJ-7069 2
Michele Rosewoman Sextet
Harvest | Enja | ENJ-7069 2
Rachelle Ferrell With The Terrence Blanchard Quartet
First Instrumental | Blue Note | 827820-2
Steve Coleman And The Council Of Balance
Genesis & The Opening Of The Way | RCA | 2152934-2
Tom Harrell Orchestra
Time's Mirror | RCA | 2663524-2

Davis,Lem | (as)

Billie Holiday With Eddie Heywood And His Orchestra
Billie Holiday:The Complete Commodore Recordings | GRP | 543272-2

Davis,Lenny | (viola)

A Band Of Friends
Wynton Marsalis Quartet With Strings | CBS | CK 68921

Davis,Leonard | (tp)

Eddie Condon's Hot Shots
Jazz:The Essential Collection Vol.3 | IN+OUT Records | 78013-2
Eddie's Hot Shots
Planet Jazz:Jack Teagarden | Planet Jazz | 2161236-2
Fats Waller And His Buddies
Jazz:The Essential Collection Vol.3 | IN+OUT Records | 78013-2
Louis Armstrong And His Orchestra
Louis Armstrong:Swing That Music | Laserlight | 36056
Swing Legends:Louis Armstrong | Nimbus Records | NI 2012
McKinney's Cotton Pickers
Jazz:The Essential Collection Vol.3 | IN+OUT Records | 78013-2

Davis,Lloyd | (drg)

Dave Brubeck Quartet
The Dave Brubeck Quartet feat. Paul Desmond In Concert | Fantasy | FCD 60-013
Jazz At Oberlin | Original Jazz Classics | OJCCD 046-2

Davis,Lynn | (voc)

Bobby Lyle Group
The Journey | Atlantic | 7567-82138-2

Davis,Martha | (voc)

Louis Jordan And His Tympany Five
Louis Jordan-Let The Good Times Roll: The Complete Decca Recordings 1938-1954 | Bear Family Records | BCD 15557 IH

Davis,Maxwell | (tsarr)

Helen Humes And Her All Stars
Lester Young:The Complete Aladdin Sessions | Blue Note | 832787-2
Louis Jordan With The Nelson Riddle Orchestra
Louis Jordan-Let The Good Times Roll: The Complete Decca Recordings 1938-1954 | Bear Family Records | BCD 15557 IH

Davis,Mel | (p,perc,voice,tpfl-h)

Billie Holiday With The Ray Ellis Orchestra
Lady In Satin | CBS | CK 65144
George Benson With The Don Sebesky Orchestra
Verve Jazz Masters 21:George Benson | Verve | 521861-2
Nina Simone And Orchestra
Planet Jazz:Nina Simone | Planet Jazz | 2165372-2
Wes Montgomery With The Don Sebesky Orchestra
Verve Jazz Masters 14:Wes Montgomery | Verve | 519826-2
Wes Montgomery:The Verve Jazz Sides | Verve | 521690-2
Talkin' Jazz:Roots Of Acid Jazz | Verve | 529580-2
California Dreaming | Verve | 827842-2

Davis,Melvin | (b)

Diane Schuur With Orchestra
Blues For Schuur | GRP | GRP 98632
The Best Of Diane Schuur | GRP | GRP 98882
Larry Carlton Group
The Gift | GRP | GRP 98542
Lee Ritenour Sextet
Alive In L.A. | GRP | GRP 98822

Davis,Michael | (concert-mastertb)

Laura Fygi Meets Michel Legrand
Watch What Happens | Mercury | 534598-2

Davis,Miles | (el-tp,fl-h,org,p,synth,tp,arr,bells)

Cannonball Adderley Quintet
Somethin' Else | Blue Note | 495329-2
Kind Of Blue:Blue Note Celebrate The Music Of Miles Davis | Blue Note | 534255-2
The Best Of Blue Note Vol.2 | Blue Note | 797960-2
Miles Davis:The Best Of The Capitol/Blue Note Years | Blue Note | 798287-2
Jazz Profile:Miles Davis | Blue Note | 823515-2
Ballads & Blues | Blue Note | 836633-2
Charlie Parker All Stars
Charlie Parker:Now's The Time | Dreyfus Jazz Line | FDM 36724-2
Charlie Parker And His Orchestra
Bird: The Complete Charlie Parker On Verve | Verve | 837141-2
Charlie Parker Quintet
Charlie Parker:Bird's Best Bop On Verve | Verve | 527452-2
Charlie Parker:The Best Of The Verve Years | Verve | 527815-2
Talkin' Bird | Verve | 559859-2
Charlie Parker:Now's The Time | Dreyfus Jazz Line | FDM 36724-2
Charlie Parker Septet
Charlie Parker:Now's The Time | Dreyfus Jazz Line | FDM 36724-2
Charlie Parker's Beboppers
Charlie Parker:Now's The Time | Dreyfus Jazz Line | FDM 36724-2
Marcus Miller Group
The Sun Don't Lie | Dreyfus Jazz Line | FDM 36560-2
Tales | Dreyfus Jazz Line | FDM 36571-2
Miles Davis + 19
Miles Ahead | CBS | CK 65121
Miles Davis All Star Sextet
Walkin' | Original Jazz Classics | OJC20 213-2
Miles Davis All Stars
Miles Davis Vol.1 | Blue Note | 532610-2
Miles Davis Vol.2 | Blue Note | 532611-2
Milt Jackson Birthday Celebration | Fantasy | FANCD 6079-2
Miles Davis:Milestones | Dreyfus Jazz Line | FDM 36731-2
Bags' Groove | Original Jazz Classics | OJC20 245-2
Miles Davis And The Modern Jazz Giants | Original Jazz Classics | OJC20 347-2(P 7150)
The J.J.Johnson Memorial Album | Prestige | PRCD 11025-2
Miles Davis And His Orchestra
The Complete Birth Of The Cool | Capitol | 494550-2
Birth Of The Cool | Capitol | 530117-2
Miles Davis:The Best Of The Capitol/Blue Note Years | Blue Note | 798287-2
Jazz Profile:Miles Davis | Blue Note | 823515-2
Ballads & Blues | Blue Note | 836633-2
Miles Davis:Milestones | Dreyfus Jazz Line | FDM 36731-2
Collector's Items | Original Jazz Classics | OJC20 071-2(P 7044)
Miles Davis And The Lighthouse All Stars
At Last! | Original Jazz Classics | OJCCD 480-2
Miles Davis And The Modern Jazz Giants
Thelonious Monk:85th Birthday Celebration | zyx records | FANCD 6076-2
Miles Davis Group
Paris Jazz Concert:Miles Davis | Laserlight | 17445
Miles Davis Live From His Last Concert In Avignon | Laserlight | 24327
Pangaea | CBS | 467087-2
Agharta | CBS | 467897-2
Circle In The Round | CBS | 467898-2
The Man With The Horn | CBS | 468701-2
Decoy | CBS | 468702-2
We Want Miles | CBS | 469402-2
A Tribute To Jack Johnson | CBS | 471003-2
Tutu | Warner | 7599-25490-2
Amandla | Warner | 7599-25873-2
Doo-Bop | Warner | 7599-26938-2
In A Silent Way | CBS | 86556-2
Live-Evil | CBS | C2K 65135
Dark Magus | CBS | C2K 65137
Live At The Fillmore East | CBS | C2K 65139
In Concert | CBS | C2K 65140
Bitches Brew | CBS | C2K 65774
On The Corner | CBS | CK 63980
This Is Jazz:Miles Davis Plays Ballads | CBS | CK 65038
Miles Davis New Quintet
Workin',Steamin',Cookin',Relaxin' With The Miles Davis Quintet | Original Jazz Classics | OJCCD 8805-2
Miles Davis Quartet
Miles Davis Vol.1 | Blue Note | 532610-2
Kind Of Blue:Blue Note Celebrate The Music Of Miles Davis | Blue Note | 534255-2
Miles Davis:The Best Of The Capitol/Blue Note Years | Blue Note | 798287-2
Jazz Profile:Miles Davis | Blue Note | 823515-2
Ballads & Blues | Blue Note | 836633-2
This Is Jazz:Miles Davis Plays Ballads | CBS | CK 65038
Bill Evans:Piano Player | CBS | CK 65361
Someday My Prince Will Come | CBS | CK 65919
Blue Haze | Original Jazz Classics | OJC20 093-2(P 7054)
The Musings Of Miles | Original Jazz Classics | OJCCD 004-2
The Prestige Legacy Vol.1:The High Priests | Prestige | PCD 24251-2
Miles Davis Quintet
Charles Mingus-The Complete Debut Recordings | Debut | 12 DCD 4402-2
To Bags...With Love:Memorial Album | Pablo | 2310967-2
Thelonious Monk:The Complete Prestige Recordings | Prestige | 3 PRCD 4428-2
Miles Davis: Olympia, March 29th,1960 | Laserlight | 36130
Ballads | CBS | 461099-2
Circle In The Round | CBS | 467898-2
The Complete Concert 1964:My Funny Valentine+Four & More | CBS | 471246-2
Kind Of Blue | CBS | 480410-2
Highlights From The Plugged Nickel | CBS | 481434-2
Ascenseur Pour L'Echafaud | Fontana | 836305-2
Filles De Kilimanjaro | CBS | 86555-2
Black Beauty-Miles Davis At Filmore West | CBS | C2K 65138
Miles Davis In Person-Friday Night At The Blackhawk,San Francisco,Vol.1 | CBS | C4K 87106
Miles Davis Quintet 1965-1968 | CBS | C6K 67398
Seven Steps To Heaven | CBS | CK 48827
Kind Of Blue | CBS | CK 64935
Miles Davis At Carnegie Hall | CBS | CK 65027
This Is Jazz:Miles Davis Plays Ballads | CBS | CK 65038
Sorcerer | CBS | CK 65680
Nefertiti | CBS | CK 65681
Miles Smiles | CBS | CK 65682
Miles In The Sky | CBS | CK 65684
Someday My Prince Will Come | CBS | CK 65919
E.S.P. | CBS | CK65683
Live In Stockholm | Dragon | DRCD 228
Newport Jazz Festival 1958,July 3rd-6th,Vol.1:Mostly Miles | Phontastic | NCD 8813
Blue Moods | Original Jazz Classics | OJC20 043-2(DEB 120)
Collector's Items | Original Jazz Classics | OJC20 071-2(P 7044)
Blue Haze | Original Jazz Classics | OJC20 093-2(P 7054)
Cookin' With The Miles Davis Quintet | Original Jazz Classics | OJC20 128-2
Relaxin' | Original Jazz Classics | OJC20 190-2
Walkin' | Original Jazz Classics | OJC20 213-2
Bags' Groove | Original Jazz Classics | OJC20 245-2
Miles Davis And The Modern Jazz Giants | Original Jazz Classics | OJC20 347-2(P 7150)
Steamin' | Original Jazz Classics | OJC20 391-2
The Jazz Giants Play Rodgers & Hart:Blue Moon | Prestige | PCD 24205-2
The Jazz Giants Play Rodgers & Hammerstein:My Favorite Things | Prestige | PCD 24223-2
The Jazz Giants Play Duke Ellington:Caravan | Prestige | PCD 24227-2
The Prestige Legacy Vol.1:The High Priests | Prestige | PCD 24251-2
Relaxin' | Prestige | PRSA 7129-6
Miles Davis Septet
Miles Davis And Horns | Original Jazz Classics | OJC20 053-2(P 7025)
Miles Davis Sextet
Circle In The Round | CBS | 467898-2
Kind Of Blue | CBS | 480410-2
Kind Of Blue:Blue Note Celebrate The Music Of Miles Davis | Blue Note | 534255-2
Miles Davis:The Best Of The Capitol/Blue Note Years | Blue Note | 798287-2
Jazz Profile:Miles Davis | Blue Note | 823515-2
Ballads & Blues | Blue Note | 836633-2
Black Beauty-Miles Davis At Filmore West | CBS | C2K 65138
Kind Of Blue | CBS | CK 64935
This Is Jazz:Miles Davis Plays Ballads | CBS | CK 65038
Sorcerer | CBS | CK 65680
Miles In The Sky | CBS | CK 65684
Someday My Prince Will Come | CBS | CK 65919
Miles Davis:Milestones | Dreyfus Jazz Line | FDM 36731-2
Dig | Original Jazz Classics | OJC20 005-2
Miles Davis And Horns | Original Jazz Classics | OJC20 053-2(P 7025)
The Jazz Giants Play Harold Arlen:Blues In The Night | Prestige | PCD 24201-2
The Jazz Giants Play Miles Davis:Milestones | Prestige | PCD 24225-2
The Prestige Legacy Vol.1:The High Priests | Prestige | PCD 24251-2
Miles Davis With Gil Evans & His Orchestra
Ballads | CBS | 461099-2

Miles Davis At Carnegie Hall | CBS | CK 65027
This Is Jazz:Miles Davis Plays Ballads | CBS | CK 65038
Porgy And Bess | CBS | CK 65141
Sketches Of Spain | CBS | CK 65142
Quiet Nights | CBS | CK 65293
Miles Davis With Gil Evans Orchestra, The George Gruntz Concert Jazz Band And Guests
Miles & Quincy Live At Montreux | Warner | 9362-45221-2
Miles Davis With Orchestra
Ballads | CBS | 461099-2
Miles Davis With The Danish Radio Big Band
Aura | CBS | CK 63962
Miles Davis/Tadd Dameron Quintet
Miles Davis:Milestones | Dreyfus Jazz Line | FDM 36731-2
Miles Davis-Marcus Miller Group
Siesta(Soundtrack) | Warner | 7599-25655-2
Miles Davis-Milt Jackson Quintet
Milt Jackson Birthday Celebration | Fantasy | FANCD 6079-2
Miles Davis And Milt Jackson | Original Jazz Classics | OJC20 012-2(P 7034)
Miles Davis-Milt Jackson Sextet
Miles Davis And Milt Jackson | Original Jazz Classics | OJC20 012-2(P 7034)
Sarah Vaughan With George Treadwell And His Allstars
Sarah Vaughan:Lover Man | Dreyfus Jazz Line | FDM 36739-2
Shirley Horn Trio with Miles Davis
You Won't Forget Me | Verve | 847482-2
Sonny Rollins Quartet
Sonny Rollins With The Modern Jazz Quartet | Original Jazz Classics | OJCCD 011-2
The Metronome All Stars
Planet Jazz:Dizzy Gillespie | Planet Jazz | 2152069-2
The New Miles Davis Quintet
Miles | Original Jazz Classics | OJC20 006-2(P 7014)

Davis,Nathan | (fl,ss,ts,saxas)
Roots
Salutes The Saxophone | IN+OUT Records | 7016-2
Salutes The Saxophones: Tributes To Gene Ammons, Eric Dolphy, Coleman Hawkins And Charlie Parker | IN+OUT Records | 7016-3
Jazz Unlimited | IN+OUT Records | 7017-2
Stablemates | IN+OUT Records | 7021-2
Saying Something | IN+OUT Records | 77031-2
For Diz & Bird | IN+OUT Records | 77039-2

Davis,Pat | (cl,ts,flsax)
Louis Armstrong With The Casa Loma Orchestra
Louis Armstrong:Swing That Music | Laserlight | 36056

Davis,Quin | (as,bs,fl,reedssax)
Buddy Rich And His Orchestra
Big Swing Face | Pacific Jazz | 837989-2

Davis,Quincy | (dr)
Tom Harrell Quintet
Live At The Village Vanguard | RCA | 2663910-2

Davis,Ramona | (pvoc)
Paul Whiteman And His Orchestra
Jazz:The Essential Collection Vol.3 | IN+OUT Records | 78013-2

Davis,Richard | (b,el-b,voc,percp)
Andrew Hill Quartet
A Blue Conception | Blue Note | 534254-2
Andrew Hill Sextet
Point Of Departure | Blue Note | 499007-2
Andy And The Bey Sisters
Andy Bey And The Bey Sisters | Prestige | PCD 24245-2
Ben Webster Quartet
The Jazz Giants Play Duke Ellington:Caravan | Prestige | PCD 24227-2
Bobby Hutcherson Sextet
A Blue Conception | Blue Note | 534254-2
Dialogue | Blue Note | 535586-2
Booker Ervin Quartet
The Song Book | Original Jazz Classics | OJCCD 779-2(P 7318)
The Freedom Book | Original Jazz Classics | OJCCD 845-2(P 7295)
The Space Book | Original Jazz Classics | OJCCD 896-2(PR 7386)
Heavy!!! | Original Jazz Classics | OJCCD 981-2(P 7499)
Booker Ervin Quintet
The Blues Book | Original Jazz Classics | OJCCD 780-2(P 7340)
Booker Ervin Sextet
Heavy!!! | Original Jazz Classics | OJCCD 981-2(P 7499)
Cal Tjader Sextet
Soul Bird | Verve | 549111-2
Cal Tjader's Orchestra
Verve Jazz Masters 39:Cal Tjader | Verve | 521858-2
Talkin Verve/Roots Of Acid Jazz:Cal Tjader | Verve | 531562-2
Soul Burst | Verve | 557446-2
Charlie Ventura Quintet
High On An Open Mike | Fresh Sound Records | FSR-CD 314
Chico Hamilton Quartet
The Dealer | Impulse(MCA) | 547958-2
Chico Hamilton Quintet
The Dealer | Impulse(MCA) | 547958-2
The Roots Of Acid Jazz | Impulse(MCA) | IMP 12042
Elvin Jones-Richard Davis Duo
Heavy Sounds | Impulse(MCA) | 547959-2
Elvin Jones-Richard Davis Quartet
Heavy Sounds | Impulse(MCA) | 547959-2
Elvin Jones-Richard Davis Trio
Heavy Sounds | Impulse(MCA) | 547959-2
Eric Dolphy Quintet
Out To Lunch | Blue Note | 498793-2
A Blue Conception | Blue Note | 534254-2
Eric Dolphy At The Five Spot Vol.2 | Original Jazz Classics | OJC20 247-2(P 7294)
Eric Dolphy-Booker Little Quintet
Eric Dolphy Birthday Celebration | Fantasy | FANCD 6085-2
At The Five Spot,Vol.1 | Original Jazz Classics | OJC20 133-2
Eric Dolphy Memorial Album | Original Jazz Classics | OJCCD 353-2
Eric Dophy Quintet
Eric Dolphy:The Complete Prestige Recordings | Prestige | 9 PRCD-4418-2
Frank Foster Sextet
Soul Outing! | Original Jazz Classics | OJCCD 984-2(7479)
Gary Bartz Quintet
Libra/Another Earth | Milestone | MCD 47077-2
Gary McFarland And His Orchestra
The Complete Bill Evans On Verve | Verve | 527953-2
George Benson With The Don Sebesky Orchestra
Verve Jazz Masters 21:George Benson | Verve | 521861-2
Gil Evans Orchestra
The Individualism Of Gil Evans | Verve | 833804-2
Helen Merrill With Richard Davis & Gary Bartz
A Shade Of Difference | EmArCy | 558851-2
Hubert Laws Quartet
The Laws Of Jazz | Atlantic | 8122-71636-2
J.J.Johnson Quartet
J.J.'s Broadway | Verve | 9860308
Jack McDuff Quartet With Orchestra
Prelude:Jack McDuff Big Band | Prestige | PRCD 24283-2
Jaki Byard Sextet
Jaki Byard:Solo/Strings | Prestige | PCD 24246-2
Jimmy Forrest With The Oliver Nelson Orchestra
Soul Street | Original Jazz Classics | OJCCD 987-2(NJ 8293)
Jimmy McGriff Orchestra
Swingin' The Blues-Jumpin' The Blues | Laserlight | 24654
Jimmy Smith And Wes Montgomery With Orchestra
Jimmy & Wes-The Dynamic Duo | Verve | 521445-2
Jimmy Smith And Wes Montgomery With The Oliver Nelson Orchestra
Wes Montgomery:The Verve Jazz Sides | Verve | 521690-2
Jimmy Smith:Best Of The Verve Years | Verve | 527950-2
Talkin' Jazz:Roots Of Acid Jazz | Verve | 529580-2
Jimmy Smith With The Oliver Nelson Orchestra
Verve Jazz Masters 29:Jimmy Smith | Verve | 521855-2
Jimmy Smith:Best Of The Verve Years | Verve | 527950-2
Peter & The Wolf | Verve | 547264-2
Jimmy Witherspoon And His All Stars
Blues For Easy Livers | Original Blues Classics | OBCCD 585-2(PR 7475)
Joe Henderson Quartet
Relaxin' At Camarillo | Original Jazz Classics | OJCCD 776-2(C 14006)
Joe Henderson Quintet
The Blue Note Years-The Best Of Joe Henderson | Blue Note | 795627-2
Johnny Hodges-Earl Hines Quintet
Verve Jazz Masters 35:Johnny Hodges | Verve | 521857-2
Leon Thomas With Band
Spirits Known And Unknown | RCA | 2663876-2
Louis Armstrong And His Friends
Planet Jazz:Louis Armstrong | Planet Jazz | 2152052-2
Planet Jazz Sampler | Planet Jazz | 2152326-2
Louis Armstrong And His Friends | Bluebird | 2663961-2
Milt Jackson Orchestra
Milt Jackson Birthday Celebration | Fantasy | FANCD 6079-2
Oliver Nelson And His Orchestra
More Blues And The Abstract Truth | Impulse(MCA) | 951212-2
Oscar Peterson With Orchestra
With Respect To Nat | Verve | 557486-2
Pharoah Sanders Orchestra
Karma | Impulse(MCA) | 951153-2
Jewels Of Thought | Impulse(MCA) | 951247-2
The Roots Of Acid Jazz | Impulse(MCA) | IMP 12042
Phil Woods Quartet With Orchestra & Strings
Round Trip | Verve | 559804-2
Raul De Souza Orchestra
Cannonball Adderley Birthday Celebration | Fantasy | FANCD 6087-2
Roland Kirk All Stars
Rahsaan/The Complete Mercury Recordings Of Roland Kirk | Mercury | 846630-2
Roland Kirk Quartet
Talkin' Verve-Roots Of Acid Jazz:Roland Kirk | Verve | 533101-2
Rahsaan/The Complete Mercury Recordings Of Roland Kirk | Mercury | 846630-2
Roland Kirk With The Benny Golson Orchestra
Rahsaan/The Complete Mercury Recordings Of Roland Kirk | Mercury | 846630-2
Sarah Vaughan And Her Trio
Swingin' Easy | EmArCy | 514072-2
Verve Jazz Masters 42:Sarah Vaughan-The Jazz Sides | Verve | 526817-2
Verve Jazz Masters Vol.60:The Collection | Verve | 529866-2
Sarah Vaughan And The Thad Jones Orchestra
Verve Jazz Masters 42:Sarah Vaughan-The Jazz Sides | Verve | 526817-2
Sarah Vaughan With Her Quartet
Verve Jazz Masters 42:Sarah Vaughan-The Jazz Sides | Verve | 526817-2
Sarah Vaughan With The Jimmy Jones Orchestra
Ballads | Roulette | 537561-2
Jazz Profile | Blue Note | 823517-2
Sarah Vaughan With The Jimmy Jones Trio
Linger Awhile | Pablo | 2312144-2
Sarah Vaughan Birthday Celebration | Fantasy | FANCD 6090-2
Sarah Vaughan With The Quincy Jones Orchestra
Jazz In Paris:Sarah Vaughan-Vaughan And Violins | EmArCy | 065004-2
4 By 4:Ella Fitzgerald/Sarah Vaughan/Billie Holiday/Dinah Washington | Verve | 559693-2
Sonny Stitt Quintet
Atlantic Saxophones | Rhino | 8122-71256-2
Stan Getz With The Bill Evans Trio
The Complete Bill Evans On Verve | Verve | 527953-2
Stan Getz With The Eddie Sauter Orchestra
Stan Getz Plays The Music Of Mickey One | Verve | 531232-2
Stan Getz-Bill Evans Quartet
Stan Getz Highlights:The Best Of The Verve Years Vol.2 | Verve | 517330-2
Stan Getz & Bill Evans | Verve | 833802-2
Stan Getz Highlights | Verve | 847430-2
Thad Jones-Mel Lewis Orchestra
The Groove Merchant/The Second Race | Laserlight | 24656
The Jazz Composer's Orchestra
Comminications | JCOA | 1001/2
Tony Scott Group
Tony Scott | Verve | 9861063
Tony Scott Trio
Tony Scott | Verve | 9861063
Tony Williams Lifetime
Lifetime | Blue Note | 499004-2
Wes Montgomery With The Don Sebesky Orchestra
Verve Jazz Masters 14:Wes Montgomery | Verve | 519826-2
Wes Montgomery:The Verve Jazz Sides | Verve | 521690-2
Talkin' Jazz:Roots Of Acid Jazz | Verve | 529580-2
California Dreaming | Verve | 827842-2

Davis,Richard or Bobby Rogriguez | (b)
Cal Tjader's Orchestra
Verve Jazz Masters 39:Cal Tjader | Verve | 521858-2

Davis,Ron | (bdr)
Woody Herman And The New Thundering Herd
Woody Herman:Thundering Herd | Original Jazz Classics | OJCCD 841-2

Davis,Spanky | (tpfl-h)
The Sidney Bechet Society
Jam Session Concert | Nagel-Heyer | CD 076

Davis,Stanton | (shells,tpfl-h)
Bob Stewart First Line Band
First Line | JMT Edition | 919014-2
Charlie Haden And The Liberation Music Orchestra
The Montreal Tapes:Liberation Music Orchestra | Verve | 527469-2
Fred Wesley Group
New Friends | Minor Music | 801016
Lester Bowie's Brass Fantasy
I Only Have Eyes For You | ECM | 1296(825902-2)
Avant Pop | ECM | 1326
Ray Anderson Sextet
It Just So Happens | Enja | ENJ-5037 2

Davis,Steve | (b,cl,dr,perctb)
Eddie Jefferson With The James Moody Quintet
Body And Soul | Original Jazz Classics | OJCCD 396-2(P 7619)
Eric Alexander Sextet
Man With A Horn | Milestone | MCD 9293-2
John Coltrane Quartet
Trane's Blues | Blue Note | 498240-2
Coltrane Jazz | Atlantic | 7567-81344-2
Coltrane Plays The Blues | Atlantic | 7567-81351-2
Coltrane's Sound | Atlantic | 7567-81358-2
The Best Of John Coltrane | Atlantic | 7567-81366-2
Rhino Presents The Atlantic Jazz Gallery | Atlantic | 8122-71257-2
John Coltrane-The Heavyweight Champion:The Complete Atlantic Recordings | Atlantic | 8122-71984-2
My Favorite Things | Atlantic | 8122-75204-2
The Very Best Of John Coltrane | Rhino | 8122-79778-2
Coltrane Plays The Blues | Rhino | 8122-79966-2
John Coltrane Trio
Coltrane Plays The Blues | Atlantic | 7567-81351-2
Coltrane's Sound | Atlantic | 7567-81358-2
Coltrane Plays The Blues | Rhino | 8122-79966-2
Johnny King Septet
The Meltdown | Enja | ENJ-9329 2
Lynne Arriale Trio
Arise | IN+OUT Records | 77059-2
McCoy Tyner Trio
Chick Corea-Herbie Hancock-Keith Jarrett-McCoy Tyner | Atlantic | 7567-81402-2
Nights Of Ballads And Blues | Impulse(MCA) | 951221-2
New Jazz Composers Octet
Walkin' the Line | Fresh Sound Records | FSNT 151 CD
Wolfgang Lackerschmid & Lynne Arriale Trio
You Are Here | Bhakti Jazz | BR 43

Davis,Stuart | (voc)
Vince Jones Group
Here's To The Miracles | Intuition Records | INT 3198-2

Davis,Troy | (dr)
Mark Whitfield Quartet
The Marksman | Warner | 7599-26321-2

Davis,Walter | (el-p,p,vocp-solo)
Sonny Criss Quartet
This Is Criss | Original Jazz Classics | OJCCD 430-2(P 7511)

Davis,Wild Bill | (arr,el-p,org,voc,pts)
Count Basie And His Orchestra
Verve Jazz Masters 2:Count Basie | Verve | 519819-2
Duke Ellington And His Orchestra
New Orleans Suite | Rhino | 812273670-2
Togo Brava Swuite | Storyville | STCD 8323
Duke Ellington Quartet
Togo Brava Swuite | Storyville | STCD 8323
Duke Ellington Small Band
The Intimacy Of The Blues | Original Jazz Classics | OJCCD 624-2
Ella Fitzgerald And Her All Stars
Ella Fitzgerald-First Lady Of Song | Verve | 517898-2
Verve Jazz Masters 6:Ella Fitzgerald | Verve | 519822-2
For The Love Of Ella Fitzgerald | Verve | 841765-2
Ella Fitzgerald And Her Quintet
Verve Jazz Masters 46:Ella Fitzgerald-The Jazz Sides | Verve | 527655-2
Johnny Hodges-Wild Bill Davis Sextet
Planet Jazz:Johnny Hodges | Planet Jazz | 2152065-2
Louis Jordan And His Tympany Five
Louis Jordan-Let The Good Times Roll: The Complete Decca Recordings 1938-1954 | Bear Family Records | BCD 15557 IH
Wild Bill Davis
Greatest Organ Solos Ever! | Jazz Connaisseur | JCCD 8702-2
Wild Bill Davis Group
Americans Swinging In Paris:Wild Bill Davis | EMI Records | 539665-2
Wild Bill Davis Quartet
Live At Swiss Radio Studio Zürich | Jazz Connaisseur | JCCD 8701-2
Wild Bill Davis Super Trio
That's All | Jazz Connaisseur | JCCD 9005-2

Davis,Will | (p)
Kenny Burrell Quintet
Soul Call | Original Jazz Classics | OJCCD 846-2(P 7315)

Davis,Xavier | (p)
New Jazz Composers Octet
Walkin' the Line | Fresh Sound Records | FSNT 151 CD
The New Jazz Composers Octet
First Step Into Reality | Fresh Sound Records | FSNT 059 CD
Tom Harrell Group
Paradise | RCA | 2663738-2
Tom Harrell Orchestra
Time's Mirror | RCA | 2663524-2
Tom Harrell Quintet
Live At The Village Vanguard | RCA | 2663910-2
Tom Harrell-Xavier Davis Duo
Live At The Village Vanguard | RCA | 2663910-2

Davison,Wild Bill | (co,voctp)
Eddie Condon All Stars
Jazz Festival Vol.1 | Storyville | 4960733
Sidney Bechet's Blue Note Jazzmen
Runnin' Wild | Blue Note | 821259-2

Dawson,Alan | (dr,congas,vocvib)
Booker Ervin Quartet
The Song Book | Original Jazz Classics | OJCCD 779-2(P 7318)
The Freedom Book | Original Jazz Classics | OJCCD 845-2(P 7295)
The Space Book | Original Jazz Classics | OJCCD 896-2(PR 7386)
Heavy!!! | Original Jazz Classics | OJCCD 981-2(P 7499)
Booker Ervin Quintet
The Blues Book | Original Jazz Classics | OJCCD 780-2(P 7340)
Booker Ervin Sextet
Heavy!!! | Original Jazz Classics | OJCCD 981-2(P 7499)
Booker Ervin-Dexter Gordon Quintet
Dexter Gordon Birthday Celebration | Fantasy | FANCD 6082-2
Dave Brubeck Quartet
We're All Together Again For The First Time | Atlantic | 7567-81390-2
Dave Brubeck Quartet With Gerry Mulligan
The Last Set At Newport | Atlantic | 7567-81382-2
We're All Together Again For The First Time | Atlantic | 7567-81390-2
Dave Brubeck Trio
All The Things We Are | Atlantic | 7567-81399-2
Dexter Gordon Quartet
Dexter Gordon Birthday Celebration | Fantasy | FANCD 6082-2
The Panther | Original Jazz Classics | OJCCD 770-2(P 10030)
Frank Foster Quintet
Soul Outing! | Original Jazz Classics | OJCCD 984-2(7479)
Frank Foster Sextet
Soul Outing! | Original Jazz Classics | OJCCD 984-2(7479)
Houston Person Quintet
Trust In Me | Prestige | PCD 24264-2
Jaki Byard Quartet
The Last From Lennie's | Prestige | PRCD 11029-2
Jaki Byard Sextet
Jaki Byard:Solo/Strings | Prestige | PCD 24246-2
Lionel Hampton And His Orchestra
Planet Jazz:Big Bands | Planet Jazz | 2169649-2
Sonny Criss Quartet
The Beat Goes On! | Original Jazz Classics | OJCCD 1051-2(P 7558)
This Is Criss | Original Jazz Classics | OJCCD 430-2(P 7511)
Tal Farlow Quartet
The Return Of Tal Farlow/1969 | Original Jazz Classics | OJCCD 356-2

Dawson,Colin | (tpvoc)
Bernd Lhotzky-Colin Dawson
Sophisticated | ART BY HEART | ABH 2003 2
Heiner Franz' Swing Connection
Heiner Franz' Swing Connection | Jardis Records | JRCD 9817

Dawud,Talib | (tp)
Dizzy Gillespie And His Orchestra
Ultimate Dizzy Gillespie | Verve | 557535-2
Dizzy Gillespie Orchestra
Verve Jazz Masters 10:Dizzy Gillespie | Verve | 516319-2

Day,Arita | (voc)
Herman Chittison
JazzIn Paris:Harlem Piano In Montmartre | EmArCy | 018447-2

Day,John | (b)
Clare Teal And Her Band
Orsino's Songs | Candid | CCD 79783

Day,Micheline | (voc)
Micheline Day Et Son Quatuor Swing
Jazz In Paris:Django Reinhardt-Django Et Compagnie | EmArCy | 549241-2 PMS

Dayle,Aubrey | (dr)
James Blood Ulmer Blues Experience
Live at The Bayerischer Hof | IN+OUT Records | 7018-2

De Arango,Bill | (g)
Dizzy Gillespie And His Orchestra
Planet Jazz:Dizzy Gillespie | Planet Jazz | 2152069-2
Planet Jazz Sampler | Planet Jazz | 2152326-2
Planet Jazz:Jazz Greatest Hits | Planet Jazz | 2169648-2
Planet Jazz:Bebop | RCA | 2169650-2
Dizzy Gillespie:Night In Tunisia | Dreyfus Jazz Line | FDM 36734-2

JATP All Stars
The Complete Jazz At The Philharmonic On Verve 1944-1949 | Verve | 523893-2
Sarah Vaughan With Dizzy Gillespie And His Septet
Sarah Vaughan:Lover Man | Dreyfus Jazz Line | FDM 36739-2

De Azevado,Daudeth | (cavaco)
Gato Barbieri Orchestra
Latino America | Impulse(MCA) | 952236-2

De Bellis,Robert | (b-cl,ss,bs,ts,cl,as,flalto-fl)
Marty Ehrlich Group
The Long View | Enja | ENJ-9452 2
Mongo Santamaria And His Orchestra
Jazzin' Vol.2: The Music Of Stevie Wonder | Fantasy | FANCD 6088-2
The Sidewalks Of New York
Tin Pan Alley:The Sidewalks Of New York | Winter&Winter | 910038-2

De Bie,Ivon | (p)
Quintet Du Hot Club De France
Verve Jazz Masters 38:Django Reinhardt | Verve | 516931-2

De Bruyn,Onno | (dr)
The Swingcats
Face To Face:The Swingcats Live | Nagel-Heyer | CD 072

De Caro,Lorenzo | (bs)
Banda Cittá Ruvo Di Puglia
La Banda/Banda And Jazz | Enja | ENJ-9326 2

De Carolis,Aurelio | (dr)
Django Reinhardt And The Quintet Du Hot Club De France
Planet Jazz:Stephane Grappelli | RCA | 2165366-2
Quintet Du Hot Club De France
Djangology | Bluebird | 2663957-2
Django/Django In Rome 1949-1050 | BGO Records | BGOCD 366

De Cuica,Zeca | (cuica)
Duo Fenix
Karai-Eté | IN+OUT Records | 7009-2

De Diego,Victor | (fl,ssts)
Big Band Bellaterra
Don't Git Sassy | Fresh Sound Records | FSNT 048 CD
David Mengual Quartet
Monkiana:A Tribute To Thelonious Monk | Fresh Sound Records | FSNT 019 CD
David Mengual Quintet
Monkiana:A Tribute To Thelonious Monk | Fresh Sound Records | FSNT 019 CD
Pep O'Callaghan Group
Tot Just | Fresh Sound Records | FSNT 017 CD
Ramón Diaz Group
O Si No Que? | Fresh Sound Records | FSNT 044 CD
Victor De Diego Group
Amaia | Fresh Sound Records | FSNT 012 CD

De Dominica,Robert | (fl)
Dizzy Gillespie And His Orchestra
Ultimate Dizzy Gillespie | Verve | 557535-2

De Fatto,Guy | (b)
Sidney Bechet And His Orchestra
Jazz In Paris:Sidney Bechet Et Claude Luther | EmArCy | 159821-2 PMS

De Fructa Oris |
Pierre Dorge's New Jungle Orchestra
Giraf | dacapo | DCCD 9440

de Galgoczy-Mecher,Viola | (vocvoice)
Matthias Stich & Whisper Not
Bach Lives!! | Satin Doll Productions | SDP 1018-1 CD

De Gennaro,Gianni | (ld,viellavoice)
Michel Godard Ensemble
Castel Del Monte II | Enja | ENJ-9431 2

De Groot,Ilona | (v)
Abdullah Ibrahim Trio And A String Orchestra
African Suite | TipToe | TIP-888832 2
String Orchestra
African Suite | TipToe | TIP-888832 2

De Gruyter,George | (b)
Erhard Wenig Quartet
Deutsches Jazz Fesival 1954/1955 | Bear Family Records | BCD 15430
Heinz Schönberger Quintet
Deutsches Jazz Fesival 1954/1955 | Bear Family Records | BCD 15430
Paul Kuhn Quintet
Deutsches Jazz Fesival 1954/1955 | Bear Family Records | BCD 15430
Rolf Kühn And His Quintet
Deutsches Jazz Fesival 1954/1955 | Bear Family Records | BCD 15430

De Haas,Eddie | (b)
Milton Mezz Mezzrow Sextet
Americans Swinging In Paris:Mezz Mezzrow | EMI Records | 539660-2
Milton Mezz Mezzrow-Maxim Saury Quintet
Americans Swinging In Paris:Mezz Mezzrow | EMI Records | 539660-2

De Hart,George | (dr)
Erroll Garner Trio
Erroll Garner:Trio | Dreyfus Jazz Line | FDM 36719-2

De Hollanda,Heloise Buarque | (voc)
Stan Getz-Joao Gilberto Orchestra
Sony Jazz Collection:Stan Getz | CBS | 488623-2

De Jong Cleyndert,Andrew | (b)
Stacey Kent And Her Quintet
Close Your Eyes | Candid | CCD 79737

De Karske,Karl | (b-tbtb)
Duke Ellington With Tommy Dorsey And His Orchestra
Highlights From The Duke Ellington Centennial Edition | RCA | 2663672-2
Ella Fitzgerald With The Nelson Riddle Orchestra
The Best Of The Song Books:The Ballads | Verve | 521867-2

De Kort,Bert | (co,voctp)
Dutch Swing College Band
Swinging Studio Sessons | Philips | 824256-2 PMS

De Krom,Sebastiaan | (dr)
Jamie Cullum Group
Pointless Nostalgic | Candid | CCD 79782

De La Rosa,Frank | (b)
Don Ellis Orchestra
Electric Bath | CBS | CK 65522
Ella Fitzgerald With The Tommy Flanagan Trio
Sunshine Of Your Love | MPS | 533102-2
Ella A Nice | Original Jazz Classics | OJC20 442-2
Ella Fitzgerald In Budapest | Pablo | PACD 5308-2

De Lucia,Paco | (ghand-claps)
Al Di Meola Group
Elegant Gypsy | CBS | 468213-2
John McLaughlin Group
The Promise | Verve | 529828-2
Paco De Lucia-Al Di Meola-John McLaughlin
Paco De Lucia-Al Di Meola-John McLaughlin | Verve | 533215-2

De Lussanet,Louis | (drvoc)
Dutch Swing College Band
Swinging Studio Sessons | Philips | 824256-2 PMS
Rita Reys With The Dutch Swing College Band
The Very Best Of Dixieland Jazz | Verve | 535529-2

De Martin,Maurice | (dr,perc,samplershruti-box)
For Free Hands
Eastern Moods | Laika Records | 35101502

De Melo,Gabriel Bezerra | (b)
Baden Powell Ensemble
Three Originals:Tristeza On Guitar/Poema On Guitar/Apaixonado | MPS | 519216-2

De Michele,Giuseppe | (e-flat-cl)
Banda Cittá Ruvo Di Puglia
La Banda/Banda And Jazz | Enja | ENJ-9326 2

De Mulder,J.Carlos | (archlutevihuela)
Javier Paxarino Group With Glen Velez
Temurá | ACT | 9227-2

De Munk,J. | (viola)
Stochelo Rosenberg Group With Strings
Gypsy Swing | Verve | 527806-2

De Nattes,Valérie | (v)
Stephane Grappelli With The Michel Legrand Orchestra
Grapelli Story | Verve | 515807-2

De Nordstrom,Myrna Glanz | (v)
Till Brönner Quartet & Deutsches Symphonieorchester Berlin
German Songs | Minor Music | 801057

De Oliveira,Wilson | (fl,alto-fl,cl,ss,ts,as,bssax)
HR Big Band
The American Songs Of Kurt Weill | hr music.de | hrmj 006-01 CD
Libertango:Homage An Astor Piazolla | hr music.de | hrmj 014-02 CD
HR Big Band With Marjorie Barnes And Frits Landesbergen
Swinging Christmas | hr music.de | hrmj 012-02 CD
HR Big Band With Marjorie Barnes And Frits Landesbergen And Strings
Swinging Christmas | hr music.de | hrmj 012-02 CD

De Piscopo,Tullio | (drperc)
Gerry Mulligan With Astor Piazzolla And His Orchestra
Tango Nuevo | Atlantic | 2292-42145-2

De Pourquery,Thomas | (ss,asts)
Orchestre National De Jazz
Charmediterranéen | ECM | 1828(018493-2)

De Rienzo,Allen | (tp)
Hampton Hawes Orchestra
Northern Windows Plus | Prestige | PRCD 24278-2

De Rijk,Jeroen | (perc)
The Rosenberg Trio With Orchestra
Noches Calientes | Verve | 557022-2

De Roo,Kasper | (cond)
Ensemble Modern
Elliott Sharp:Racing Hearts/Tessalation Row/Calling | hr music.de | hrmn 018-03 CD

De Rooy,Nico | (p)
Coleman Hawkins Trio
Jazz:The Essential Collection Vol.3 | IN+OUT Records | 78013-2

De Rossi,Zeno | (dr)
Palo Alto
Crash Test | Jazz 'n' Arts Records | JNA 1803

De Sah,Wanda | (voc)
Paul Desmond Quartet With The Don Sebesby Orchestra
From The Hot Afternoon | Verve | 543487-2

De Santana,Edson Emetério | (atabaquessurdo)
The New Dave Pike Set & Grupo Baiafra De Bahia
Dave Pike Set:Masterpieces | MPS | 531848-2

De Santis,Alessandro 'Alex' | (ts)
Alex De Santis Jazz Quartet
Le Canzoni Italiana | Edition Collage | EC 514-2

De Schepper,Philippe | (el-g,musical-boxg)
Claude Barthelmy Group
Moderne | Owl Records | 014739-2

De Sousa,Borel | (berimbauperc)
Lisa Wahlandt & Mulo Francel And Their Fabulous Bossa Band
Bossa Nova Affair | Edition Collage | EC 534-2
Terra Brazil
Café Com Leite | art-mode-records | AMR 2101
Thilo Kreitmeier & Group
Changes | Organic Music | ORGM 9725

De Sousa,Yorke | (p)
Stephane Grappelli Quintet
Grapelli Story | Verve | 515807-2

De Souza,Franzisco | (congasbongos)
Ella Fitzgerald With Orchestra
Ella/Things Ain't What They Used To Be | Warner | 9362-47875-2

De Souza,Raoul | (perctb)
Cal Tjader Group
Amazonas | Original Jazz Classics | OJCCD 840-2(F 9502)
Caldera
Jazzrock-Anthology Vol.3:Fusion | Zounds | CD 27100555
Raul De Souza Orchestra
Cannonball Adderley Birthday Celebration | Fantasy | FANCD 6087-2

De Souza,Yorke | (p)
Benny Carter And His Orchestra
Django Reinhardt All Star Sessions | Capitol | 531577-2
Americans Swinging In Paris:Benny Carter | EMI Records | 539647-2

De SouzamRogerio | (caxixis,chimessurdo)
Javier Paxarino Group With Glen Velez
Temurá | ACT | 9227-2

De Vega,Henri | (as,flpiccolo)
Ella Fitzgerald With Orchestra
Ella/Things Ain't What They Used To Be | Warner | 9362-47875-2

De Verteuil,Eddie | (asbs)
Kenny Clarke And His 52nd Street Boys
Planet Jazz:Bebop | RCA | 2169650-2
Fats Navarro:Nostalgia | Dreyfus Jazz Line | FDM 36736-2

De Veta,Marion | (bs)
Coleman Hawkins And His All Stars
Planet Jazz:Coleman Hawkins | Planet Jazz | 2152055-2
Planet Jazz:Bebop | RCA | 2169650-2
Jazz:The Essential Collection Vol.3 | IN+OUT Records | 78013-2

De Villers,Michel | (as,bs,b-cl,clts)
Django Reinhardt And His Quintet
Peche Á La Mode-The Great Blue Star Sessions 1947/1953 | Verve | 835418-2
Django's Music
Peche Á La Mode-The Great Blue Star Sessions 1947/1953 | Verve | 835418-2
Jack Dieval And The J.A.C.E. All-Stars
Jazz In Paris:Jack Diéval-Jazz Aux Champs Elysées | EmArCy | 018419-2
Michel De Villers Octet
Jazz In Paris:Saxophones Á Saint-Germain Des Prés | EmArCy | 014060-2

De Vriend,Jan Willem | (strings)
The Rosenberg Trio With Orchestra
Noches Calientes | Verve | 557022-2

De Waleyne,Janine | (voc)
Les Blue Stars
Jazz In Paris:Blossom Dearie-The Pianist/Les Blue Stars | EmArCy | 064784-2

De Wilde,Laurent | (el-pp)
Laurent De Wilde Sextet
Time Change | Warner | 8573-84315-2

Dean,Chris | (tb)
André Holst With Chris Dean's European Swing Orchestra
That's Swing | Nagel-Heyer | CD 079
Carla Bley Big Band
The Carla Bley Big Band Goes To Church | Watt | 27(533682-2)

Dean,Demas | (tp)
Bessie Smith And Her Band
Jazz:The Essential Collection Vol.1 | IN+OUT Records | 78011-2

Dean,Don | (el-b)
Diane Schuur With The Dave Grusin Orchestra
The Best Of Diane Schuur | GRP | GRP 98882

Dean,Donald | (drperc)
Jimmy Smith Quartet
Jimmy Smith-Talkin' Verve | Verve | 531563-2
Les McCann Group
Atlantic Jazz: Fusion | Atlantic | 7567-81711-2
Les McCann-Eddie Harris Quintet
Rhino Presents The Atlantic Jazz Gallery | Atlantic | 8122-71257-2
Swiss Movement | Atlantic | 8122-72452-2

Dean,Elton | (as,saxellowooden-fl)
Carla Bley Band
European Tour 1977 | Watt | 8

Dean,Mladen | (v)
Till Brönner Quartet & Deutsches Symphonieorchester Berlin
German Songs | Minor Music | 801057

Dean,Vinnie | (as,piccolosax)
Stan Kenton And His Orchestra
Stan Kenton Portraits On Standards | Capitol | 531571-2

Deane,J.A. | (alto-fl,perc,electronic-perc)
Jon Hassell & Farafina
Flash Of The Spirit | Intuition Records | INT 3009-2
Jon Hassell Group
Power Spot | ECM | 1327

Dearie,Blossom | (el-p,voc,keyboards,pp-solo)
Blossom Dearie Quartet
Give Him The Ooh-La-La | Verve | 517067-2
My Gentleman Friend | Verve | 519905-2
Verve Jazz Masters 51:Blossom Dearie | Verve | 529906-2
Blossom Dearie Sings Comden And Green | Verve | 589102-2
Blossom Dearie Quintet
My Gentleman Friend | Verve | 519905-2
Verve Jazz Masters 51:Blossom Dearie | Verve | 529906-2
Blossom Dearie Trio
Jazz In Paris:Blossom Dearie-The Pianist/Les Blue Stars | EmArCy | 064784-2
Verve Jazz Masters 51:Blossom Dearie | Verve | 529906-2
At Ronnie Scott's:Blossom Time | EmArCy | 558683-2
Blossom Dearie Sings Comden And Green | Verve | 589102-2
Blossom Dearie With The Russ Garcia Orchestra
Verve Jazz Masters 51:Blossom Dearie | Verve | 529906-2
Les Blue Stars
Jazz In Paris:Blossom Dearie-The Pianist/Les Blue Stars | EmArCy | 064784-2

D'Earth,John | (el-tp,tpfl-h)
George Gruntz Concert Jazz Band
Blues 'N Dues Et Cetera | Enja | ENJ-6072 2
Klaus König Orchestra
Reviews | Enja | ENJ-9061 2
Miles Davis With Gil Evans Orchestra, The George Gruntz Concert Jazz Band And Guests
Miles & Quincy Live At Montreux | Warner | 9362-45221-2

DeBarge,Darell | (voc)
Fourplay
Fourplay | Warner | 7599-26656-2

DeBarge,El | (voc)

Debenedetto,Paolo | (as)
Banda Cittá Ruvo Di Puglia
La Banda/Banda And Jazz | Enja | ENJ-9326 2

Debiossat,Alain | (ss)
Nguyen Le Group
Maghreb And Friends | ACT | 9261-2

Deblossat,Alain | (ssts)
Karim Ziad Groups
Ifrikya | ACT | 9282-2

DeBrest,Jimmy 'Spanky' | (b)
Art Blakey And The Jazz Messengers
Planet Jazz:Art Blakey | Planet Jazz | 2152066-2
Planet Jazz Sampler | Planet Jazz | 2152326-2
A Night In Tunisia | RCA | 2663896-2
Art Blakey And The Jazz Messengers With Thelonious Monk
Art Blakey's Jazz Messengers With Thelonious Monk | Atlantic | 7567-81332-2
Clifford Jordan Quartet
Spellbound | Original Jazz Classics | OJCCD 766-2(RLP 9340)
Ray Draper Quintet
John Coltrane-The Prestige Recordings | Prestige | 16 PCD 4405-2
Ray Draper Sextet
Tuba Sounds | Original Jazz Classics | OJCCD 1936-2(P 7096)

Debriano,Santi Wilson | (b)
Attila Zoller Quartet
When It's Time | Enja | ENJ-9031 2
Attila Zoller Quintet
When It's Time | Enja | ENJ-9031 2
Debriano-Hart-Blythe
3-Ology | Konnex Records | KCD 5047
Roots
Salutes The Saxophone | IN+OUT Records | 7016-2
Salutes The Saxophones: Tributes To Gene Ammons, Eric Dolphy, Coleman Hawkins And Charlie Parker | IN+OUT Records | 7016-3
Jazz Unlimited | IN+OUT Records | 7017-2
Stablemates | IN+OUT Records | 7021-2

Debrow,Leon | (tp)
Tommy Dorsey And His Orchestra
Planet Jazz:Frank Sinatra & Tommy Dorsey | Planet Jazz | 2152067-2
Planet Jazz:Big Bands | Planet Jazz | 2169649-2
Frank Sinatra And The Tommy Dorsey Orchestra | RCA | 2668701-2

Decker,James 'Jimmy' | (fr-h)
Billy May And His Orchestra
Billy May's Big Fat Brass/Bill's Bag | Capitol | 535206-2
Cal Tjader With The Clare Fischer Orchestra
Cal Tjader Plays Harold Arlen & West Side Story | Fantasy | FCD 24775-2
Ella Fitzgerald With The Nelson Riddle Orchestra
The Best Of The Song Books:The Ballads | Verve | 521867-2
Love Songs:The Best Of The Song Books | Verve | 531762-2
Ella Fitzgerald Sings The Johnny Mercer Songbook | Verve | 539057-2
Pete Rugolo And His Orchestra
Thriller/Richard Diamon(Original Jazz Scores From 2 Classics TV Series) | Fresh Sound Records | FSCD 2015

Decker,Jim | (fr-h)
Billy Eckstine With The Billy May Orchestra
Once More With Feeling | Roulette | 581862-2

Decker,Peter | (reeds,ssts)
Lee Konitz With The Oliver Strauch Group & Peter Decker
Lee Konitz With Oliver Strauch Group & Peter Decker | Edition Collage | EC 497-2

DeCoteau,Denis | (viola)
Ron Carter With Strings
Pastels | Original Jazz Classics | OJCCD 665-2(M 9073)

Decou,Walter | (p)
Bunk Johnson And His Superior Jazz Band
Authentic New Orleans Jazz | Good Time Jazz | GTCD 12048-2

Dee,Brian | (p)
George Masso Quintet
The First Sampler | Nagel-Heyer | NHR SP 5
George Masso-Ken Peplowski Quintet
Just Friends | Nagel-Heyer | CD 5001
Harry Allen Quartet
Love Songs Live! | Nagel-Heyer | NH 1014
Harry Allen Quintet
A Night At Birdland | Nagel-Heyer | CD 010
A Night At Birdland Vol. 1 | Nagel-Heyer | CD 5002
Ellington For Lovers | Nagel-Heyer | NH 1009
Love Songs Live! | Nagel-Heyer | NH 1014
The First Sampler | Nagel-Heyer | NHR SP 5
Jeanie Lambe And The Danny Moss Quartet
Three Great Concerts:Live In Hamburg 1993-1995 | Nagel-Heyer | CD 019
Oliver Jackson Orchestra
The Last Great Concert | Nagel-Heyer | CD 063
The Buck Clayton Legacy
All The Cats Join In(Buck Clayton Remembered) | Nagel-Heyer | CD 006
Encore Live | Nagel-Heyer | CD 018
The First Sampler | Nagel-Heyer | NHR SP 5
The Second Sampler | Nagel-Heyer | NHR SP 6
The Yamaha International Allstar Band
Hapy Birthday Jazzwelle Plus | Nagel-Heyer | CD 005
The First Sampler | Nagel-Heyer | NHR SP 5

Dee,Johnny | (tp)
Elliot Lawrence And His Orchestra
Mullenium | CBS | CK 65678

Deems,Barrett | (dr)
Ella Fitzgerald With Louis Armstrong And The All Stars
Ella Fitzgerald-First Lady Of Song | Verve | 517898-2
The Complete Ella Fitzgerald And Louis Armstrong On Verve | Verve | 537284-2

The Best Of Ella Fitzgerald And Louis Armstrong On Verve | Verve | 537909-2
Jack Teagarden And His Sextet
Mis'ry And The Blues | Verve | 9860310
Jack Teagarden Sextet
Newport Jazz Festival 1958,July 3rd-6th Vol.3:Blues In The Night No.1 | Phontastic | NCD 8815
Jack Teagarden Sextet With Bobby Hackett
Newport Jazz Festival 1958,July 3rd-6th Vol.3:Blues In The Night No.1 | Phontastic | NCD 8815
Louis Armstrong And Gary Crosby With Sonny Burke's Orchestra
Louis Armstrong-My Greatest Songs | MCA | MCD 18347
Louis Armstrong And His All Stars
Verve Jazz Masters 1:Louis Armstrong | Verve | 519818-2
I Love Jazz | Verve | 543747-2
Louis Armstrong:The Great Chicago Concert 1956 | CBS | C2K 65119
Louis Armstrong Plays W.C.Handy | CBS | CK 64925
Ambassador Satch | CBS | CK 64926
Satch Plays Fats(Complete) | CBS | CK 64927
Historic Barcelona Concerts At Windsor Palace 1955 | Fresh Sound Records | FSR-CD 3004
Louis Armstrong And His All Stars With Benny Carter's Orchestra
Ambassador Louis Armstrong Vol.17:Moments To Remember(1952-1956) | Ambassador | CLA 1917
Louis Armstrong And His All Stars With Sonny Burke's Orchestra
Ambassador Louis Armstrong Vol.17:Moments To Remember(1952-1956) | Ambassador | CLA 1917
Louis Armstrong And His All Stars With The Sy Oliver Orchestra
Ambassador Louis Armstrong Vol.17:Moments To Remember(1952-1956) | Ambassador | CLA 1917
Louis Armstrong And His Orchestra
I Love Jazz | Verve | 543747-2
Louis Armstrong And Omer Simeon With The Sy Oliver Orchestra
Ambassador Louis Armstrong Vol.17:Moments To Remember(1952-1956) | Ambassador | CLA 1917
Louis Armstrong With Benny Carter's Orchestra
Louis Armstrong-My Greatest Songs | MCA | MCD 18347
Louis Armstrong With Sy Oliver And His Orchestra
Louis Armstrong-My Greatest Songs | MCA | MCD 18347
Louis Armstrong With Sy Oliver's Choir And Orchestra
Jazz Collection:Louis Armstrong | Laserlight | 24366
Louis And The Good Book | Verve | 549593-2
Louis And The Good Book | Verve | 940130-0
Muggsy Spanier And His Dixieland All Stars
Muggsy Spanier At Club Hangover 1953/54 | Storyville | STCD 6033

Defense,Nene | (bongos,congas,perctambourine)
Archie Shepp Orchestra
The Cry Of My People | Impulse(MCA) | 9861488

DeFilippi,Bruno | (bj,gharm)
Lorenzo Petrocca Quartet Feat. Bruno De Filippi
Insieme | Edition Musikat | EDM 002

DeFrancesco,Joey | (keyboards,org,voc,XB2,ptp)
Essence All Stars
Hot Jazz Bisquits | Hip Bop | HIBD 8801
Illinois Jacquet With The Joey DeFrancesco Quartet
Late Night Sax | CBS | 487798-2
John McLaughlin Group
The Promise | Verve | 529828-2
John McLaughlin Trio
After The Rain | Verve | 527467-2
Katia Labeque-Joey DeFrancesco
Little Girl Blue | Dreyfus Jazz Line | FDM 36186-2
Miles Davis Group
Amandla | Warner | 7599-25873-2
Pat Martino Trio
Live At Yoshi's | Blue Note | 499749-2

DeFranco,Buddy | (b-cl,cl,asld)
Art Tatum-Buddy DeFranco Quartet
Art Tatum-The Complete Pablo Group Masterpieces | Pablo | 6 PACD 4401-2
Billie Holiday And Her All Stars
Billie's Blues | Blue Note | 748786-2
Bud Powell Orchestra
Bebop | Pablo | PACD 2310978-2
Buddy DeFranco Meets The Oscar Peterson Quartet
Hark | Original Jazz Classics | OJCCD 867-2(2310915)
Buddy DeFranco Quartet
Mr. Clarinet | Verve | 847408-2
Lush Life | Choice | CHCD 71017
Buddy DeFranco With The Oscar Peterson Trio
The Complete Lionel Hampton Quartets And Quintets With Oscar Peterson On Verve | Verve | 559797-2
Ella Fitzgerald With The Nelson Riddle Orchestra
Ella Fitzgerald-First Lady Of Song | Verve | 517898-2
The Best Of The Song Books | Verve | 519804-2
The Best Of The Song Books:The Ballads | Verve | 521867-2
Love Songs:The Best Of The Song Books | Verve | 531762-2
Ella Fitzgerald Sings The Johnny Mercer Songbook | Verve | 539057-2
For The Love Of Ella Fitzgerald | Verve | 841765-2
Glenn Miller Orchestra
Glenn Miller Serenade | CBS | 487445-2
Lionel Hampton Quartet
The Complete Lionel Hampton Quartets And Quintets With Oscar Peterson On Verve | Verve | 559797-2
Lionel Hampton Quintet
The Complete Lionel Hampton Quartets And Quintets With Oscar Peterson On Verve | Verve | 559797-2
The Lional Hampton Quintet | Verve | 589100-2
Lionel Hampton With Buddy DeFranco And The Oscar Peterson Trio
Verve Jazz Masters 26:Lionel Hampton with Oscar Peterson | Verve | 521853-2
Rolf Kühn And Friends
Affairs:Rolf Kühn & Friends | Intuition Records | INT 3211-2
The Metronome All Stars
Planet Jazz:Dizzy Gillespie | Planet Jazz | 2152069-2
The Three Sopranos With The HR Big Band
The Three Sopranos | hr music.de | hrmj 001-01 CD
Tommy Dorsey And His Orchestra
Planet Jazz:Tommy Dorsey | Planet Jazz | 2159972-2
Planet Jazz:Jazz Greatest Hits | Planet Jazz | 2169648-2

Degas,Jorge | (b,vocg)
Jorge Degas-Wolfgang Loos
Cantar A Vida | Traumton Records | 4446-2

Degen,Bob | (p,perc,prep-pp-solo)
Bob Degen
Sandcastle | free flow music | ffm 0897
Bob Degen Trio
Catability | Enja | ENJ-9332 2
Charlie Mariano Quartet
Deep In A Dream | Enja | ENJ-9423 2
Dusko Goykovich Quartet
In My Dreams | Enja | ENJ-9408 2
Fritz Krisse Quartet
Soulcolours | Laika Records | 35100782
Gabriele Hasler & Foolish Heart
God Is A She | Foolish Music | FM 111186
Heinz Sauer 4tet
Exchange 2 | free flow music | ffm 0998
Heinz Sauer Quartet With The NDR Big Band
NDR Big Band-Bravissimo | ACT | 9232-2
Heinz Sauer Trio
Exchange | free flow music | ffm 0695
Jazzensemble Des Hessischen Rundfunks
Atmosphering Conditions Permitting | ECM | 1549/50
NDR Big Band
NDR Big Band-Bravissimo | ACT | 9232-2
Peter Weiss Quartet
Personal Choice | Nabel Records:Jazz Network | CD 4669
Stefanie Schlesiger And Her Group plus String Quartet
What Love Is | Enja | ENJ-9434 2
Stefanie Schlesinger And Her Group
What Love Is | Enja | ENJ-9434 2
Wolfgang Engstfeld Quartet
Songs And Ballads | Nabel Records:Jazz Network | CD 4658

Degryse,Fabien | (gg-synth-programming)
Fabien Degryse Quintet
Medor Sadness | Edition Collage | EC 454-2

Dehnhard,Tilmann | (fl,ssts)
Jazz Indeed
Under Water | Traumton Records | 2415-2
Who The Moon Is | Traumton Records | 4427-2

Deihim,Sussan | (voc)
Heiner Goebbels Group
Shadow/Landscape With Argonauts | ECM | 1480

Deisenberger,Stefan | (soundgroove programming)
Couch Ensemble
Winnetou | Jazz 'n' Arts Records | JNA 1503

Deistler,Gaga | (g)
Kölner Saxophon Mafia With Fleisch
Kölner Saxophon Mafia Proudly Presents | Jazz Haus Musik | JHM 0046 CD

DeJohnette,Jack | (dr,african thumb-p,c-mel-sax)
Antonio Farao Quartet
Thorn | Enja | ENJ-9399 2
Antonio Farao Trio
Thorn | Enja | ENJ-9399 2
Bernard Purdie's Soul To Jazz
Bernard Purdie's Soul To Jazz II | ACT | 9253-2
Bill Connors Quartet
Of Mist And Melting | ECM | 1120(847324-2)
Bill Evans Trio
Verve Jazz Masters 5:Bill Evans | Verve | 519821-2
The Complete Bill Evans On Verve | Verve | 527953-2
The Best Of Bill Evans Live | Verve | 533825-2
At The Montreux Jazz Festival | Verve | 539758-2
Ultimate Bill Evans selected by Herbie Hancock | Verve | 557536-2
Bill Evans:The Secret Sessions | Milestone | 8MCD 4421-2
Bobby Timmons Quartet
Quartet And Orchestra | Milestone | MCD 47091-2
Bobby Timmons Trio
Quartet And Orchestra | Milestone | MCD 47091-2
Charles Lloyd Quartet
Charles Lloyd In Europe | Atlantic | 7567-80788-2
Atlantic Saxophones | Rhino | 8122-71256-2
Forest Flower:Charles Lloyd At Monterey | Atlantic | 8122-71746-2
Chick Corea Septet
The Complete 'Is' Sessions | Blue Note | 540532-2
Collin Walcott Quartet
Cloud Dance | ECM | 1062(825469-2)
Dave Holland Trio
Triplicate | ECM | 1373
Don Byron Quartet
Romance With The Unseen | Blue Note | 499545-2
Eliane Elias Trio
Blue Bossa | Blue Note | 795590-2
Freddie Hubbard With Orchestra
This Is Jazz:Freddie Hubbard | CBS | CK 65041
Gary Peacock Quartet
Voice From The Past-Paradigm | ECM | 1210(517768-2)
Gary Peacock Trio
Tales Of Another | ECM | 1101(827418-2)
Gateway
In The Moment | ECM | 1574(529346-2)
George Adams Sextet
Soung Suggestions | ECM | 1141
Gonzalo Rubalcaba Trio
The Blessing | Blue Note | 797197-2
Imagine | Blue Note | 830491-2
Herbie Hancock Group
Herbie Hancock The New Standards | Verve | 527715-2
Herbie Hancock Group With String Quartet
Herbie Hancock The New Standards | Verve | 527715-2
Herbie Hancock Group With String Quartet,Woodwinds And Brass
Herbie Hancock The New Standards | Verve | 527715-2
Herbie Hancock Group With Woodwinds And Brass
Herbie Hancock The New Standards | Verve | 527715-2
Jack DeJohnette
Pictures | ECM | 1079
Jack DeJohnette New Directions
In Europe | ECM | 1157
Jack DeJohnette Quartet
New Directions | ECM | 1128
Special Edition | ECM | 1152
Oneness | ECM | 1637(537343-2)
The DeJohnette Complex | Original Jazz Classics | OJCCD 617-2
Jack DeJohnette Quintet
The DeJohnette Complex | Original Jazz Classics | OJCCD 617-2
Jack DeJohnette Sextet
The DeJohnette Complex | Original Jazz Classics | OJCCD 617-2
Jack DeJohnette Trio
Dancing With Nature Spirits | ECM | 1558(531024-2)
Jack DeJohnette-John Abercrombie Duo
Pictures | ECM | 1079
Jack DeJohnette's Special Edition
Inflation Blues | ECM | 1244
Album Album | ECM | 1280
Jackie McLean Quintet
Jacknife | Blue Note | 540535-2
Jackie McLean Sextet
Jacknife | Blue Note | 540535-2
Jaco Pastorius With Orchestra
Word Of Mouth | Warner | 7599-23525-2
Jan Garbarek Quartet
Places | ECM | 1118(829195-2)
Joe Henderson And His Orchestra
Joe Henderson:The Milestone Years | Milestone | 8MCD 4413-2
Joe Henderson Group
Double Rainbow | Verve | 527222-2
Porgy And Bess | Verve | 539048-2
Joe Henderson Quartet
Joe Henderson:The Milestone Years | Milestone | 8MCD 4413-2
Tetragon | Original Jazz Classics | OJCCD 844-2(M 9017)
Joe Henderson Quintet
Joe Henderson:The Milestone Years | Milestone | 8MCD 4413-2
Multiple | Original Jazz Classics | OJCCD 763-2(M 9050)
Joe Henderson Sextet
Joe Henderson:The Milestone Years | Milestone | 8MCD 4413-2
Multiple | Original Jazz Classics | OJCCD 763-2(M 9050)
Joe Henderson Trio
Joe Henderson:The Milestone Years | Milestone | 8MCD 4413-2
Joe Zawinul Group
Zawinul | Atlantic | 7567-81375-2
John Abercrombie Quartet
Night | ECM | 1272(823212-2)
John Abercrombie Trio
Timeless | ECM | 1047(829114-2)
Gateway | ECM | 1061(829192-2)
Gateway 2 | ECM | 1105(847323-2)
Gateway | ECM | 1562(527637-2)
John Surman-Jack DeJohnette
The Amazing Adventures Of Simon Simon | ECM | 1193(829160-2)
Invisible Nature | ECM | 1796(016376-2)
John Surman-Jack DeJohnette With The London Brass
Printed In Germany | ECM | 1802(017065-2)
Keith Jarrett - Jack DeJohnette
Ruta + Daitya | ECM | 1021(513776-2)
Keith Jarrett Trio
Standarts Vol.1 | ECM | 1255(811966-2)
Changes | ECM | 1276(817436-2)
Standards Vol.2 | ECM | 1289(825015-2)
Standards Live | ECM | 1317(827827-2)
Still Live | ECM | 1360/61(835008-2
Changeless | ECM | 1392(839618-2)
Tribute | ECM | 1420/21
The Cure | ECM | 1440(849650-2)
Bye Bye Blackbird | ECM | 1467(513074-2)
Standards In Norway | ECM | 1542(521717-2)
Keith Jarrett At The Blue Note-The Complete Recordings | ECM | 1575/80(527638-2)
Tokyo '96 | ECM | 1666(539955-2)
Whisper Not | ECM | 1724/25(543813-2)
Inside Out | ECM | 1780(014005-2)
Always Let Me Go | ECM | 1800/01(018766-2)
Kenny Werner Trio
A Delicate Ballace | RCA | 2151694-2
Kenny Wheeler Quartet
Gnu High | ECM | 1069(825591-2)
Kenny Wheeler Quintet
Double, Double You | ECM | 1262(815675-2)
Lee Morgan Quintet
Live At The Lighthouse | Blue Note | 835228-2
Lyle Mays Trio
Fictionary | Warner | 9362-47906-2
Mark Whitfield Group
Patrice | Warner | 7599-26659-2
McCoy Tyner Group With Horns
Inner Voices | Original Jazz Classics | OJCCD 1039-2(M 9079)
McCoy Tyner Group With Horns And Voices
Inner Voices | Original Jazz Classics | OJCCD 1039-2(M 9079)
McCoy Tyner Group With Voices
Inner Voices | Original Jazz Classics | OJCCD 1039-2(M 9079)
McCoy Tyner Orchestra
13th House | Original Jazz Classics | OJCCD 1089-2(M 9102)
Michael Brecker Group
Michael Brecker | Impulse(MCA) | 950113-2
Don't Try This At Home | Impulse(MCA) | 950114-2
Tales From The Hudson | Impulse(MCA) | 951191-2
Michael Brecker Quintet
Nearness Of You-The Ballad Book | Verve | 549705-2
Michael Mantler Group
The Hapless Child | Watt | 4
Mick Goodrick Quartet
In Pas(s)ing | ECM | 1139
Mike Stern Group
Give And Take | Atlantic | 7567-83036-2
Miles Davis Group
Circle In The Round | CBS | 467898-2
Live-Evil | CBS | C2K 65135
Live At The Fillmore East | CBS | C2K 65139
Bitches Brew | CBS | C2K 65774
On The Corner | CBS | CK 63980
Miles Davis Quintet
Black Beauty-Miles Davis At Filmore West | CBS | C2K 65138
Miles Davis Sextet
Black Beauty-Miles Davis At Filmore West | CBS | C2K 65138
Miroslav Vitous Group
Universal Syncopations | ECM | 1863(038506-2)
Atlantic Jazz: Fusion | Atlantic | 7567-81711-2
Pat Metheny Quartet
80/81 | ECM | 1180/81 (843169-2)
Pat Metheny Quintet
80/81 | ECM | 1180/81 (843169-2)
Pat Metheny/Ornette Coleman Group
Song X | Geffen Records | GED 24096
Paul Desmond Orchestra
Late Night Sax | CBS | 487798-2
Skylark | CTI | ZK 65133
Ralph Towner Trio
Batik | ECM | 1121(847325-2)
Raul De Souza Orchestra
Cannonball Adderley Birthday Celebration | Fantasy | FANCD 6087-2
Ron Carter Group
Songs For You | Milestone | MCD 47099-2
Ron Carter Quintet With Strings
Pick 'Em/Super Strings | Milestone | MCD 47090-2
Sonny Rollins Plus 3
Sonny Rollins + 3 | Milestone | MCD 9250-2
Sonny Rollins Quartet
This Is What I Do | Milestone | MCD 9310-2
Next Album | Original Jazz Classics | OJC 312 (M 9042)
Sonny Rollins Quintet
Old Flames | Milestone | MCD 9215-2
This Is What I Do | Milestone | MCD 9310-2
Next Album | Original Jazz Classics | OJC 312 (M 9042)
Sonny Rollins Quintet With Brass
Old Flames | Milestone | MCD 9215-2
Sonny Rollins Sextet
Here's To The People | Milestone | MCD 9194-2
Stan Getz Quartet
The Art Of Saxophone | Laserlight | 24652
Steve Swallow Group
Real Book | Watt | XtraWatt/7(521637-2)
Terje Rypdal Trio
To Be Continued | ECM | 1192
Terje Rypdal-Miroslav Vitous-Jack DeJohnette Trio
Terje Rypdal Miroslav Vitous Jack DeJohnette | ECM | 1125(825470-2)
Wayne Shorter Sextet
Wayne Shorter:The Classic Blue Note Recordings | Blue Note | 540856-2

Dekker,Hans | (dr)
Frank Castenier Group
For You,For Me For Evermore | EmArCy | 9814976
John Goldsby Sextet
Viewpoint | Nagel-Heyer | CD 2014
NDR Big Band
NDR Big Band-Bravissimo | ACT | 9232-2
Till Brönner Quintet
My Secret Love | Minor Music | 801051
Till Brönner Quintet With Annette Lowman
My Secret Love | Minor Music | 801051

Del Barrio,Eddie | (keyboards,synth,condarr)
Caldera
Jazzrock-Anthology Vol.3:Fusion | Zounds | CD 27100555
Stan Getz With Orchestra
Apasionado | A&M Records | 395297-2

Del Bono,Anastasio | (engl-hoboe)
Charles Mingus Orchestra
Cumbia & Jazz Fusion | Atlantic | 8122-71785-2

Del Cioppo,Jorge | (voc)
Omar Belmonte's Latin Lover
Vamos A Ver | EGO | 96170

Del Fa,Alexandre | (g)
John McLaughlin With The Aighette Quartet And Yan Marez
Time Remembered:John McLaughlin Plays Bill Evans | Verve | 519861-2

Del Governatore,Al | (p)
Sandole Brothers
The Sandole Brothers | Fantasy | FCD 24763-2

Del Pedro,Mike | (p-solo)
Mike Del Pedro
Ten Piano Players,Vol.1 | Green House Music | CD 1002

Del Puerto,Carlos | (bvoc)
Irakere
Yemayá | Blue Note | 498239-2

Del Rio,Jack | (bongos,congas,tambourineperc)
Cal Tjader With The Lalo Schifrin Orchestra
Talkin Verve/Roots Of Acid Jazz:Cal Tjader | Verve | 531562-2
Dizzy Gillespie And His Orchestra
Verve Jazz Masters 10:Dizzy Gillespie | Verve | 516319-2
Gillespiana And Carnegie Hall Concert | Verve | 519809-2
Talking Verve:Dizzy Gillespie | Verve | 533846-2
Lalo Schifrin And His Orchestra
Verve Jazz Masters 39:Cal Tjader | Verve | 521858-2
Quincy Jones And His Orchestra
Rahsaan/The Complete Mercury Recordings Of Roland Kirk | Mercury | 846630-2

Delagarde,Mario | (b)
Johnny Otis And His Orchestra
Verve Jazz Masters 43:Ben Webster | Verve | 525431-2

Delbecq,Benoit | (pprepared-p)
Albrecht Maurer Trio Works
Movietalks | Jazz Haus Musik | JHM 0119 CD

Delfos,Rolf | (as,bsss)
Christian Willisohn New Band
Heart Broken Man | Blues Beacon | BLU-1026 2

Delgado,Guillermo | (b)
Dani Perez Quartet
Buenos Aires-Barcelona Connections | Fresh Sound Records | FSNT 144 CD

Delgado,Publio | (g)
Pep O'Callaghan Grup
Port O'Clock | Fresh Sound Records | FSNT 069 CD

Delhomme,Dave | (gkeyboards)
Marcus Miller Group
Live & More | Dreyfus Jazz Line | FDM 36585-2

Delin,Diane | (v)
Jens Bunge Group
Meet You In Chicago | Jazz 4 Ever Records:Jazz Network | J4E 4749

Dell,Christopher | (percvib)
Christopher Dell D.R.A.
Future Of The Smallest Form | Jazz 4 Ever Records:Jazz Network | J4E 4754

Delle,Frank | (cl,ss,tsreeds)
Abdullah Ibrahim With The NDR Big Band
Ekapa Lodumo | TipToe | TIP-888840 2
Joe Gallardo's Latino Blue
A Latin Shade Of Blue | Enja | ENJ-9421 2
Lee Konitz With The Ed Partyka Jazz Orchestra
Dreams And Realities | Laika Records | 35101642

Dell'Erba,Pasquale | (tp)
Banda Cittá Ruvo Di Puglia
La Banda/Banda And Jazz | Enja | ENJ-9326 2

Delmiro,Helio | (g,el-g,pel-p)
Antonio Carlos Jobim Group
Verve Jazz Masters 13:Antonio Carlos Jobim | Verve | 516409-2
Antonio Carlos Jobim-Elis Regina Group
The Antonio Carlos Jobim Songbook | Verve | 525472-2
Gato Barbieri Orchestra
Latino America | Impulse(MCA) | 952236-2
Sarah Vaughan And Her Band
Sarah Vaughan Birthday Celebration | Fantasy | FANCD 6090-2
Sarah Vaughan With Orchestra
I Love Brazil | Pablo | 2312101-2
Sarah Vaughan Birthday Celebration | Fantasy | FANCD 6090-2

Delmonace,Vania | (g)
Vania Delmonaco
Internationales Guitarren Festival '94 | ALISO Records | AL 1030

Delnero,Paul | (b)
Greg Abate Quintet
Dr. Jeckyll & Mr. Hyde | Candid | CCD 79715
Mitch Seidman Quartet
How 'Bout It? | Jardis Records | JRCD 20135

Deltour,Emile | (v)
Django Reinhardt With Stan Brenders Et Son Grand Orchestre
Verve Jazz Masters 38:Django Reinhardt | Verve | 516931-2

Demany,Jack | (cl,ts,arr.v)

Demming,Hajo | (gel-g)
Daniel Messina Band
Imagenes | art-mode-records | 990014

Demond,Paul | (as)
Paul Desmond-Gerry Mulligan Quartet
Two Of A Mind | RCA | 2179620-2

DeMoraes Azenha,Ana Luisa | (voc)
Ivo Perlman Group
Children Of Ibeji | Enja | ENJ-7005 2

Denard,Oscar | (p)
Lionel Hampton And His Orchestra
Planet Jazz:Lionel Hampton | Planet Jazz | 2152059-2

DeNaut,Jud | (b)
Artie Shaw And His Orchestra
Planet JazzArtie Shaw | Planet Jazz | 2152057-2
Planet Jazz:Jazz Greatest Hits | Planet Jazz | 2169648-2
Planet Jazz:Big Bands | Planet Jazz | 2169649-2

Denham,Vince | (asfl)
Joe Henderson And His Orchestra
Joe Henderson:The Milestone Years | Milestone | 8MCD 4413-2

Denia,Carlos | (g)
Carlos Denia-Uli Glaszmann
Ten Strings For Bill Evans | Edition Musikat | EDM 069

Denis,Michel | (dr)
Bill Coleman Sextet
Americans Swinging In Paris:Bill Coleman | EMI Records | 539663-2
Memphis Slim Trio
Americans Swinging In Paris:Memphis Slim | EMI Records | 539666-2

Deniz,Joe | (g)
Stephane Grappelli Quintet
Grapelli Story | Verve | 515807-2

Denizet,Manuel | (dr)
Claude Barthelmy Group
Moderne | Owl Records | 014739-2

Denjean,Jacques | (voc)
Les Double Six
Les Double Six | RCA | 2164314-2

Dennard,Kenwood | (dr,jew's-harp,vocperc)
Miles Davis With Gil Evans Orchestra, The George Gruntz Concert Jazz Band And Guests
Miles & Quincy Live At Montreux | Warner | 9362-45221-2

Dennerlein,Barbara | (org,digital-dr,synth,pgrand-p)
Barbara Dennerlein Group
Take Off | Verve | 527664-2
Junkanoo | Verve | 537122-2
Outhipped | Verve | 547503-2
Barbara Dennerlein Quartet
Hot Stuff | Enja | ENJ-6050 2
Barbara Dennerlein Quintet
That's Me | Enja | ENJ-7043 2
NDR Big Band With Guests
50 Years Of NDR Big Band:Bravissimo II | ACT | 9259-2
Russ Spiegel Group
Twilight | double moon | CHRDM 71026

Dennis,Arthur | (as,bssax)
Louis Armstrong And His Orchestra
Swing Legends:Louis Armstrong | Nimbus Records | NI 2012

Dennis,Carol | (voc)
Caldera
Jazzrock-Anthology Vol.3:Fusion | Zounds | CD 27100555

Dennis,Don | (tp)
Stan Kenton And His Orchestra
Stan Kenton Portraits On Standards | Capitol | 531571-2

Dennis,John | (p)
John Dennis Trio
Charles Mingus-The Complete Debut Recordings | Debut | 12 DCD 4402-2
Thad Jones Quartet
Charles Mingus-The Complete Debut Recordings | Debut | 12 DCD 4402-2

Dennis,Kenny | (drvoc)
Mal Waldron Trio
The Mal Waldron Memorial Album:Soul Eyes | Prestige | PRCD 11024-2
Sonny Rollins Quintet
Sonny Rollins-The Freelance Years:The Complete Riverside & Contemporary Recordings | Riverside | 5 RCD 4427-2
Sonny Stitt Quartet
Verve Jazz Masters 50:Sonny Sitt | Verve | 527651-2

Dennis,Stanley | (b)
Louis Armstrong With The Casa Loma Orchestra
Louis Armstrong:Swing That Music | Laserlight | 36056

Dennis,Willie | (tb)
Anita O'Day With The Gary McFarland Orchestra
All The Sad Youn Men | Verve | 517065-2
Verve Jazz Masters 49:Anita O'Day | Verve | 527653-2
Benny Goodman And His Orchestra
The Legends Of Swing | Laserlight | 24659
Cannonball Adderley And His Orchestra
Ballads | Blue Note | 537563-2
Charles Mingus And His Orchestra
Charles Mingus-The Complete Debut Recordings | Debut | 12 DCD 4402-2
Charles Mingus-Passion Of A Man:The Complete Atlantic Recordings 1956-1961 | Atlantic | 8122-72871-2
The Complete Town Hall Concert | Blue Note | 828353-2
Charles Mingus Group
Mingus Ah Um | CBS | CK 65512
Charles Mingus Jazz Workshop
Rhino Presents The Atlantic Jazz Gallery | Atlantic | 8122-71257-2
Blues & Roots | Atlantic | 8122-75205-2
Charles Mingus Orchestra
The Very Best Of Charles Mingus | Rhino | 8122-79988-2
Charles Mingus Septet
Charles Mingus:The Complete 1959 Columbia Recordings | CBS | C3K 65145
Four Trombones
Charles Mingus-The Complete Debut Recordings | Debut | 12 DCD 4402-2
The J.J.Johnson Memorial Album | Prestige | PRCD 11025-2
Gerry Mulligan Concert Jazz Band
Verve Jazz Masters 36:Gerry Mulligan | Verve | 523342-2
Verve Jazz Masters Vol.60:The Collection | Verve | 529866-2
Gerry Mulligan And The Concert Band At The Village Vanguard | Verve | 589488-2
The Complete Verve Gerry Mulligan Concert Band | Verve | 9860613
Jimmy Rushing And His Orchestra
Five Feet Of Soul | Roulette | 581830-2
Stan Getz With The Gary McFarland Orchestra
Verve Jazz Masters 53:Stan Getz-Bossa Nova | Verve | 529904-2
Big Band Bossa Nova | Verve | 825771-2 PMS
Stan Getz Highlights | Verve | 847430-2

Denson,Karl | (fl,ss,ts,sax,asvoc)
Fred Wesley Group
Swing & Be Funky | Minor Music | 801027
Amalgamation | Minor Music | 801045

Dent,Cedric | (voc)
Take 6
Goldmine | Reprise | 7599-25670-2
So Much To Say | Reprise | 7599-25892-2
He Is Christmas | Reprise | 7599-26665-2
Take 6 With The Yellow Jackets
He Is Christmas | Reprise | 7599-26665-2

Dentz,John | (dr)
Bill Evans Trio
Bill Evans:The Secret Sessions | Milestone | 8MCD 4421-2
Lee Konitz And His West Coast Friends
Art Pepper:The Hollywood All-Star Sessions | Galaxy | 5GCD 4431-2
Lou Levy Trio
My Old Flame | Fresh Sound Records | FSR-CD 312

Denu,Egon | (tbtp)
Wolfgang Lauth Septet
Noch Lauther | Bear Family Records | BCD 15942 AH

Deodato,Eumir | (arr,cond,el-p,g,keyboardsp)
Marcos Valle With Orchestra
Samba '68 | Verve | 559516-2

DeParis,Sidney | (co,tptuba)
Alberta Hunter With Buster Bailey's Blues Blasters
Songs We Taught Your Mother | Original Blues Classics | OBCCD 520-2
Edmond Hall's Blue Note Jazzmen
The Blue Note Jazzmen | Blue Note | 821262-2
James P.Johnson's Blue Note Jazzmen
Jazz:The Essential Collection Vol.3 | IN+OUT Records | 78013-2
The Blue Note Jazzmen | Blue Note | 821262-2
Jelly Roll Morton's New Orleans Jazzmen
Planet Jazz | Planet Jazz | 2169652-2
Planet Jazz:Male Jazz Vocalists | Planet Jazz | 2169657-2
McKinney's Cotton Pickers
Jazz:The Essential Collection Vol.3 | IN+OUT Records | 78013-2
New Orleans Feetwarmers
Jazz:The Essential Collection Vol.1 | IN+OUT Records | 78011-2
Sidney Bechet And His New Orleans Feetwarmers
Sidney Bechet:Summertime | Dreyfus Jazz Line | FDM 36712-2
Sidney Bechet's Blue Note Jazzmen
Jazz:The Essential Collection Vol.1 | IN+OUT Records | 78011-2
Sidney DeParis' Blue Note Jazzmen
The Blue Note Jazzmen | Blue Note | 821262-2
Victoria Spivey With Buster Bailey's Blues Blasters
Songs We Taught Your Mother | Original Blues Classics | OBCCD 520-2
Wilbur DeParis And His New New Orleans Band
Atlantic Jazz: New Orleans | Atlantic | 7567-81700-2

DeParis,Sidney prob. | (tp)
Bessie Smith With The James P.Johnson Orchestra And The Hal Johnson Choir
The Blues | Storyville | 4960323

DeParis,Wilbur | (dr,fl-h,tb,vocv-tb)
Django Reinhardt With Duke Ellington And His Orchestra
Django Reinhardt:Souveniers | Dreyfus Jazz Line | FDM 36744-2
Duke Ellington And His Orchestra
Planet Jazz:Duke Ellington | Planet Jazz | 2152053-2
The Legends Of Swing | Laserlight | 24659
Highlights From The Duke Ellington Centennial Edition | RCA | 2663672-2
Carnegie Hall Concert January 1946 | Prestige | 2PCD 24074-2
Jazz:The Essential Collection Vol.2 | IN+OUT Records | 78012-2
Louis Armstrong And His Orchestra
Louis Armstrong:Swing That Music | Laserlight | 36056
Jazz:The Essential Collection Vol.2 | IN+OUT Records | 78012-2
Louis Armstrong-My Greatest Songs | MCA | MCD 18347
Swing Legends:Louis Armstrong | Nimbus Records | NI 2012
Spike Hughes And His Negro Orchestra
Jazz:The Essential Collection Vol.3 | IN+OUT Records | 78013-2
Wilbur DeParis And His New New Orleans Band
Atlantic Jazz: New Orleans | Atlantic | 7567-81700-2

DePew,Art | (tp)
Harry James And His Orchestra
Trumpet Blues:The Best Of Harry James | Capitol | 521224-2
Tommy Dorsey And His Orchestra
Planet Jazz:Tommy Dorsey | Planet Jazz | 2159972-2

DePew,Bill | (as)
Benny Goodman And His Orchestra
Planet Jazz:Benny Goodman | Planet Jazz | 2152054-2
Planet Jazz Sampler | Planet Jazz | 2152326-2
Planet Jazz:Swing | Planet Jazz | 2169651-2
Planet Jazz:Female Jazz Vocalists | Planet Jazz | 2169656-2

Deponte,Reiner | (b-tb)
Bigband Der Musikschule Der Stadt Brühl Mit Gastsolisten
Pangäa | Indigo-Records | 1004 CD

Deppa,Claude | (fl-h,tp,vocvoice)
Carla Bley Band
The Very Big Carla Bley Band | Watt | 23
Big Band Theory | Watt | 25(519966-2)
Carla Bley Big Band
The Carla Bley Big Band Goes To Church | Watt | 27(533682-2)
Gail Thompson Orchestra
Gail Thompson's Jazz Africa | Enja | ENJ-9053 2

Deppenschmidt,Buddy | (drperc)
Charlie Byrd Orchestra
Latin Byrd | Milestone | MCD 47005-2
Charlie Byrd Quartet
Blues Sonata | Original Jazz Classics | OJC20 1063(RS 9453)
Charlie Byrd Quintet
Latin Byrd | Milestone | MCD 47005-2
Charlie Byrd Septet
Latin Byrd | Milestone | MCD 47005-2
Charlie Byrd Trio
Blues Sonata | Original Jazz Classics | OJC20 1063(RS 9453)
At The Village Vanguard | Original Jazz Classics | OJCCD 669-2(RLP 9452)
Stan Getz Sextet
Verve Jazz Masters 8:Stan Getz | Verve | 519823-2
Stan Getz-Charlie Byrd Sextet
Jazz Samba | Verve | 521413-2
The Antonio Carlos Jobim Songbook | Verve | 525472-2
Verve Jazz Masters 53:Stan Getz-Bossa Nova | Verve | 529904-2
Ultimate Stan Getz selected by Joe Henderson | Verve | 557532-2
Stan Getz Highlights | Verve | 847430-2

Der Rote Bereich |
Der Rote Bereich
Love Me Tender | ACT | 9286-2
Risky Business | ACT | 9407-2
Der Rote Bereich 3 | Jazz 4 Ever Records:Jazz Network | J4E 4740

Deribeaupierre,Pierre | (b-clts)
Bigband Der Musikschule Der Stadt Brühl Mit Gastsolisten
Pangäa | Indigo-Records | 1004 CD

DeRisi,Al | (tp)
Birdland Dream Band
Birdland Dream Band | RCA | 2663873-2
Elliot Lawrence And His Orchestra
The Elliot Lawrence Big Band Swings Cohn & Kahn | Fantasy | FCD 24761-2
Freddie Hubbard Orchestra
The Body And The Soul | Impulse(MCA) | 951183-2
Lena Horne With The Lennie Hayton Orchestra
Planet Jazz:Lena Horne | Planet Jazz | 2165373-2
Quincy Jones And His Orchestra
The Quintessence | Impulse(MCA) | 951222-2
The Roots Of Acid Jazz | Impulse(MCA) | IMP 12042
Ralph Burns And His Orchestra
The Complete Verve Roy Eldridge Studio Sessions | Verve | 9861278
Stan Getz With The Eddie Sauter Orchestra
Stan Getz Plays The Music Of Mickey One | Verve | 531232-2

Derlath,Dorothea | (fl)
Litschie Hrdlicka Group
Falling Lovers | EGO | 93020

Derntl,Wolfram Igor | (voc)
Franz Koglmann Group
Venus In Transit | Between The Lines | btl 017(Efa 10186)

DeRosa,Clem | (dr)
John LaPorta Octet
Theme And Variations | Fantasy | FCD 24776-2
John LaPorta Septet
Theme And Variations | Fantasy | FCD 24776-2
John LaPorta Trio
The Sandole Brothers | Fantasy | FCD 24763-2
Sandole Brothers
The Sandole Brothers | Fantasy | FCD 24763-2

DeRosa,Vince | (fr-hdescant)
Art Pepper Plus Eleven
Art Pepper + Eleven | Contemporary | CSA 7568-6
Modern Jazz Classics | Original Jazz Classics | OJC20 341-2
Billy Eckstine With The Billy May Orchestra
Once More With Feeling | Roulette | 581862-2
Billy May And His Orchestra
Billy May's Big Fat Brass/Bill's Bag | Capitol | 535206-2
Cal Tjader With The Clare Fischer Orchestra
Cal Tjader Plays Harold Arlen & West Side Story | Fantasy | FCD 24775-2
Ella Fitzgerald With Marty Paich's Dektette
Ella Swings Lightly | Verve | 517535-2
Ella Fitzgerald With The Buddy Bregman Orchestra
The Best Of The Song Books:The Ballads | Verve | 521867-2
Ella Fitzgerald Sings The Rodgers And Hart Song Book | Verve | 537258-2
Ella Fitzgerald With The Marty Paich Dek-tette
Ella Fitzgerald-First Lady Of Song | Verve | 517898-2
Verve Jazz Masters 6:Ella Fitzgerald | Verve | 519822-2
Verve Jazz Masters 46:Ella Fitzgerald-The Jazz Sides | Verve | 527655-2
Ella Fitzgerald With The Nelson Riddle Orchestra
The Best Of The Song Books:The Ballads | Verve | 521867-2
Oh Lady Be Good:The Best Of The Gershwin Songbook | Verve | 529581-2
Love Songs:The Best Of The Song Books | Verve | 531762-2
Hank Crawford Orchestra
Rhino Presents The Atlantic Jazz Gallery | Atlantic | 8122-71257-2
Horace Silver Quintet With Brass
Horace Silver Retrospective | Blue Note | 495576-2
June Christy With The Pete Rugolo Orchestra
Something Cool(The Complete Mono & Stereo Versions) | Capitol | 534069-2
Mel Tormé With The Russell Garcia Orchestra
Swingin' On The Moon | Verve | 511385-2
Pete Rugolo And His Orchestra
Thriller/Richard Diamon(Original Jazz Scores From 2 Classics TV Series) | Fresh Sound Records | FSCD 2015
Singers Unlimited With Orchestra
The Singers Unlimited:Magic Voices | MPS | 539130-2
Singers Unlimited With The Patrick Williams Orchestra
The Singers Unlimited:Magic Voices | MPS | 539130-2

Derouin,Joel | (v)
Milt Jackson And His Orchestra
Reverence And Compassion | Reprise | 9362-45204-2

Derrick,Tommy | (dr)
Reuben Wilson Quartet
Blue Breaks Beats Vol.2 | Blue Note | 789907-2

Derrien,Hervé | (cello)
Charlie Haden Quartet West With Strings
Now Is The Hour | Verve | 527827-2

Dervaux,Pierre | (tp)
Sidney Bechet With Claude Luter And His Orchestra
Planet Jazz:Sidney Bechet | Planet Jazz | 2152063-2
Sidney Bechet:Summertime | Dreyfus Jazz Line | FDM 36712-2

Derwin,Hal | (gvoc)
Ten Cats And A Mouse
The Hollywood Session:The Capitol Jazzmen | Jazz Unlimited | JUCD 2044

DeSair,Skippy | (bssax)
Woody Herman And His Orchestra
The Legends Of Swing | Laserlight | 24659
Woody Herman:Four Brother | Dreyfus Jazz Line | FDM 36722-2
Louis Armstrong-Jack Teagarden-Woody Herman:Midnights At V-Disc | Jazz Unlimited | JUCD 2048

Old Gold Rehearsals 1944 | Jazz Unlimited | JUCD 2079

Desilva,Audrey | (v)

Art Pepper Quintet With Strings
Art Pepper:The Complete Galaxy Recordings | Galaxy | 16GCD 1016-2
Winter Moon | Original Jazz Classics | OJC20 677-2(GXY 5140)

DeSilva,Ric | (perc)

Les McCann Orchestra
Talkin' Verve:Les McCann | Verve | 557351-2

Desire | (rap-voc)

George Gruntz Concert Jazz Band
Blues 'N Dues Et Cetera | Enja | ENJ-6072 2

Desmond,Paul | (as)

Dave Brubeck Octet
The Dave Brubeck Octet | Original Jazz Classics | OJCCD 101-2(F 3239)
Dave Brubeck Quartet
The Great Concerts | CBS | 462403-2
Dave Brubeck's Greatest Hits | CBS | 465703-2
We're All Together Again For The First Time | Atlantic | 7567-81390-2
Jazz:Ted Hot And Cool | CBS | CK 61468
Time Out | CBS | CK 65122
Brubeck Time | CBS | CK 65724
Buried Treasures | CBS | CK 65777
The Dave Brubeck Quartet feat. Paul Desmond In Concert | Fantasy | FCD 60-013
Jazz At The College Of The Pacific | Original Jazz Classics | OJC20 047-2(F 3223)
Jazz At Oberlin | Original Jazz Classics | OJCCD 046-2
Jazz At The College Of The Pacific Vol.2 | Original Jazz Classics | OJCCD 1076-2
Dave Brubeck Quartet With Gerry Mulligan
We're All Together Again For The First Time | Atlantic | 7567-81390-2
Dave Brubeck Quartet With Orchestra
Brandenburg Gate:Revisited | CBS | CK 65725
Dave Brubeck Quintet
Reunion | Original Jazz Classics | OJCCD 150-2
Dave Brubeck Sextet
Bravo! Brubeck! | CBS | CK 65723
Dave Brubeck-Paul Desmond Duo
1975-The Duets | Verve | 394915-2
Gerry Mulligan-Paul Desmond Quartet
Gerry Mulligan-Paul Desmond Quartet | Verve | 519850-2
Jimmy Rushing With The Dave Brubeck Quartet
Brubeck & Rushing | CBS | CK 65727
Paul Desmond And The Modern Jazz Quartet
MJQ 40 | Atlantic | 7567-82330-2
Paul Desmond Orchestra
Planet Jazz:Jazz Saxophone | Planet Jazz | 2169653-2
Late Night Sax | CBS | 487798-2
Skylark | CTI | ZK 65133
Paul Desmond Quartet
The Ballad Of Paul Desmond | RCA | 21429372
Planet Jazz:Paul Desmond | Planet Jazz | 2152061-2
Planet Jazz Sampler | Planet Jazz | 2152326-2
Bossa Antigua | RCA | 2174795-2
Easy Living | RCA | 2174796-2
Take Ten | RCA | 2179621-2
Monterey Jazz Festival 1975 | Storyville | 4960213
Live | Verve | 543501-2
Desmond | Original Jazz Classics | OJCCD 712-2(F 3235/8082)
The Jazz Giants Play Jerome Kern:Yesterdays | Prestige | PCD 24202-2
Paul Desmond Quartet With The Bill Bates Singers
Desmond | Original Jazz Classics | OJCCD 712-2(F 3235/8082)
Paul Desmond Quartet With The Don Sebesky Orchestra
From The Hot Afternoon | Verve | 543487-2
Paul Desmond Quintet
Desmond | Original Jazz Classics | OJCCD 712-2(F 3235/8082)
Paul Desmond With Different Groups
100 Ans De Jazz:Paul Desmond | RCA | 2177830-2
Paul Desmond With Strings
The Ballad Of Paul Desmond | RCA | 21429372
Planet Jazz:Paul Desmond | Planet Jazz | 2152061-2
Desmond Blue | RCA | 2663898-2
Paul Desmond-Gerry Mulligan Quartet
The Ballad Of Paul Desmond | RCA | 21429372
Planet Jazz:Paul Desmond | Planet Jazz | 2152061-2
Planet Jazz:Jazz Greatest Hits | Planet Jazz | 2169648-2

DeSouteiro,Arnaldo | (perc)

Ithamara Koorax With Band
Love Dance:The Ballad Album | Milestone | MCD 9327-2

Despot,Dalio | (keyboardsp)

Mind Games
Pretty Fonky | Edition Collage | EC 482-2
Wind Moments | Take Twelve On CD | TT 009-2
Mind Games With Philip Catherine
Pretty Fonky | Edition Collage | EC 482-2
Tom Bennecke & Space Gurilla
Wind Moments | Take Twelve On CD | TT 009-2

Dessena,Salvatore | (voc)

Ernst Reijseger & Tenore E Cuncordu De Orosei
Colla Voche | Winter&Winter | 910037-2

Destanges,Guy | (tb)

Dizzy Gillespie Orchestra And The Operatic String Orchestra
Jazz In Paris:Dizzy Gillespie And His Operatic Strings Orchestra | EmArCy | 018420-2

details not on the cover |

Al Di Meola Groups
Guitar Heroes Vol.1:Al Di Meola | Zounds | CD 2700044001
Billie Holiday
My Greatest Songs | MCA | MCD 18767
Billy May And His Orchestra With Members Of The Jimmy Lunceford Orchestra
Great Swing Classics In Hi-Fi | Capitol | 521223-2
Bobby McFerrin Group
Blue Velvet: Crooners, Swooners And Velvet Vocals | Blue Note | 521153-2
Chet Baker Group
Blue Velvet: Crooners, Swooners And Velvet Vocals | Blue Note | 521153-2
Coleman Hawkins With Different Bands
100 Ans De Jazz:Coleman Hawkins | RCA | 2177832-2
Count Basie And His Orchestra
100 Ans De Jazz:Count Basie | RCA | 2177831-2
Diane Schuur Trio With Orchestra And Strings
In Tribute | GRP | GRP 20062
Diane Schuur With Orchestra
In Tribute | GRP | GRP 20062
The Best Of Diane Schuur | GRP | GRP 98882
Diane Schuur With Orchestra And Strings
The Best Of Diane Schuur | GRP | GRP 98882
Dinah Washington With Orchestra
Mad About The Boy-The Best Of Dinah Washington | Mercury | 512214-2
Ella Fitzgerald With Orchestra
Essential Ella | Verve | 523990-2
Forever Ella | Verve | 529387-2
Fats Waller Groups
100 Ans De Jazz:Fats Waller | RCA | 2177829-2
Glen Gray And His Orchestra
Great Swing Classics In Hi-Fi | Capitol | 521223-2
Glenn Miller And His Orchestra
The Ultimate Glenn Miller-22 Original Hits From The King Of Swing | RCA | 2113137-2
Candelight Miller | RCA | 2668716-2
Glenn Miller Orchestra
Glenn Miller Serenade | CBS | 487445-2
Harry James And His Orchestra
Great Swing Classics In Hi-Fi | Capitol | 521223-2
Hoagy Carmichael And His Orchestra
Blue Velvet: Crooners, Swooners And Velvet Vocals | Blue Note | 521153-2
Illinois Jacquet With The Joey DeFrancesco Quartet
Late Night Sax | CBS | 487798-2
Jimmy Witherspoon And His Band
Blue Velvet: Crooners, Swooners And Velvet Vocals | Blue Note | 521153-2
Joe Pass With The NDR Big Band And Radio Philharmonie Hannover
Joe Pass In Hamburg | ACT | 9100-2
June Christy With Orchestra
This Is June Christy/June Christy Recalls Those Kenton Days | Capitol | 535209-2
Leon Eason Group
Blue Velvet: Crooners, Swooners And Velvet Vocals | Blue Note | 521153-2
Les Brown And His Orchestra
Great Swing Classics In Hi-Fi | Capitol | 521223-2
Louis Sclavis With The WRO Orchestra, Köln
Le Concerto Improvisé | Enja | ENJ-9397 2
Mose Allison Trio
Blue Velvet: Crooners, Swooners And Velvet Vocals | Blue Note | 521153-2
Muddy Waters Blues Band
Muddy Waters-The Collection | MCA | MCD 18961
NDR Big Band With Guests
50 Years Of NDR Big Band:Bravissimo II | ACT | 9259-2
Nina Simone Groups
Feeling Good-The Very Best Of Nina Simone | Mercury | 522747-2
Patti Austin And Her Band
Patti Austin:The Ultimate Collection | GRP | GRP 98212
Paul Desmond With Different Groups
100 Ans De Jazz:Paul Desmond | RCA | 2177830-2
Stanley Clarke Groups
Stanley Clarke Best | Zounds | CD 2700020089
Tome XX
She Could Do Nothing By Halves | Jazz Haus Musik | JHM 0084 CD
Tommy Dorsey And His Orchestra
Frank Sinatra And The Tommy Dorsey Orchestra | RCA | 2668701-2
Woody Herman And His Orchestra
Great Swing Classics In Hi-Fi | Capitol | 521223-2

details unknown |

(Little)Jimmy Scott With Orchestra
Everybody's Somebody's Fool | Decca | 050669-2
Academic Jazz Band
7.Zelt-Musik-Festival:Jazz Events | Zounds | CD 2730001
Ahmad Jamal Trio with Orchestra
Pittsburgh | Atlantic | 7567-8209-2
Al Jarreau With Band
High Crime | i.e. Music | 557848-2
Anita O'Day With The Bill Holman Orchestra
Verve Jazz Masters 49:Anita O'Day | Verve | 527653-2
Incomparable! Anita O'Day | Verve | 589516-2
Anita O'Day With The Billy May Orchestra
Verve Jazz Masters 49:Anita O'Day | Verve | 527653-2
Anita O'Day With The Buddy Bregman Orchestra
Pick Yourself Up | Verve | 517329-2
Verve Jazz Masters 49:Anita O'Day | Verve | 527653-2
Anita O'Day With The Gary McFarland Orchestra
Verve Jazz Masters 49:Anita O'Day | Verve | 527653-2
Anita O'Day With The Russ Garcia Orchestra
Verve Jazz Masters 49:Anita O'Day | Verve | 527653-2
Anthony Ortega With String Orchestra
Earth Dance | Fresh Sound Records | FSR-CD 325
Antonio Carlos Jobim Group
The Antonio Carlos Jobim Songbook | Verve | 525472-2
Antonio Carlos Jobim With The Claus Ogerman Orchestra
Verve Jazz Masters 13:Antonio Carlos Jobim | Verve | 516409-2
The Composer Of 'Desafinado' Plays | Verve | 521431-2
Astor Piazzolla With Orchestra Of St. Luke's
Concierto Para Bandoneon-Tres Tangos | Nonesuch | 7559-79174-2
Astrud Gilberto With Antonio Carlos Jobim And The Marty Paich Orchestra
The Antonio Carlos Jobim Songbook | Verve | 525472-2
Astrud Gilberto With Orchestra
This Is Astrud Gilberto | Verve | 825064-2
Astrud Gilberto With The Al Cohn Orchestra
Verve Jazz Masters 9:Astrud Gilberto | Verve | 519824-2
Astrud Gilberto With The Claus Ogerman Orchestra
Verve Jazz Masters 9:Astrud Gilberto | Verve | 519824-2
Astrud Gilberto With The Don Sebesky Orchestra
Verve Jazz Masters 9:Astrud Gilberto | Verve | 519824-2
Astrud Gilberto With The Gil Evans Orchestra
Verve Jazz Masters 9:Astrud Gilberto | Verve | 519824-2
Verve Jazz Masters 23:Gil Evans | Verve | 521860-2
Astrud Gilberto With The Marty Paich Orchestra
Verve Jazz Masters 9:Astrud Gilberto | Verve | 519824-2
Astrud Gilberto With The Walter Wanderley Trio
This Is Astrud Gilberto | Verve | 825064-2
Axel Zwingenberger With The Lionel Hampton Big Band
The Boogie Woogie Album | Vagabond | VRCD 8.88008
B.B.King Blues Band
Classic Blues | Zounds | CD 2700048
Ben Webster With Orchestra And Strings
Music For Loving:Ben Webster With Strings | Verve | 527774-2
Benny Goodman And His Orchestra
Jazz Collection:Benny Goodman | Laserlight | 24396
Bernard Purdie's Soul To Jazz
Bernard Purdie's Soul To Jazz | ACT | 9242-2
Bessie Smith And Her Band
Classic Blues | Zounds | CD 2700048
Big Joe Turner And His Orchestra
Planet Jazz:Male Jazz Vocalists | Planet Jazz | 2169657-2
Big Joe Turner With Axel Zwingenberger
Boogie Woogie Jubilee | Vagabond | VRCD 8.81010
Bill Evans Quartet With Orchestra
The Complete Bill Evans On Verve | Verve | 527953-2
From Left To Right | Verve | 557451-2
Bill Evans Trio With The Claus Ogerman Orchestra
The Complete Bill Evans On Verve | Verve | 527953-2
Bill Evans Trio With Symphony Orchestra | Verve | 821983-2
Bill Ramsey With Eric Krans Dixieland Pipers And Guests
Caldonia And More... | Bear Family Records | BCD 16151 AH
Billy Eckstine And His Orchestra
Blue Velvet: Crooners, Swooners And Velvet Vocals | Blue Note | 521153-2
Billy Eckstine With Bobby Tucker And His Orchestra
The Antonio Carlos Jobim Songbook | Verve | 525472-2
Billy Eckstine Now Singing In 12 Great Movies | Verve | 589307-2
Billy Eckstine With Hal Mooney And His Orchestra
Billy Eckstine Now Singing In 12 Great Movies | Verve | 589307-2
Billy Eckstine With The Billy May Orchestra
Once More With Feeling | Roulette | 581862-2
Billy May And His Orchestra
Billy May's Big Fat Brass/Bill's Bag | Capitol | 535206-2
Bing Crosby And Rosemarie Clooney With The Billy May Orchestra
Fancy Meeting You Here | RCA | 2663859-2
Blossom Dearie With The Russ Garcia Orchestra
Verve Jazz Masters 51:Blossom Dearie | Verve | 529906-2
Bobby McFerrin
Simple Pleasures | Manhattan | 748059-2
Bud Shank With The Len Mercer Strings
Midnight Blue(The [Be]witching Hour) | Blue Note | 854365-2
Buddy Guy Blues Band
Buddy Guy-The Complete Chess Studio Recordings | MCA | MCD 09337
Buddy Johnson And His Orchestra
Buddy And Ella Johnson 1953-1964 | Bear Family Records | BCD 15479 DH
Buddy Rich Big Band
Backwoods Siseman/Pieces Of Dream | Laserlight | 24655
Cab Calloway And His Hi De Ho Orchestra
7.Zelt-Musik-Festival:Jazz Events | Zounds | CD 2730001
Cal Tjader's Orchestra
Verve Jazz Masters 39:Cal Tjader | Verve | 521858-2
Talkin Verve/Roots Of Acid Jazz:Cal Tjader | Verve | 531562-2
Cannonball Adderley And His Orchestra
Verve Jazz Masters 31:Cannonball Adderley | Verve | 522651-2
Carmen McRae With The Jimmy Mundy Orchestra
Blue Moon | Verve | 543829-2
Carmen McRae With The Tadd Dameron Orchestra
Blue Moon | Verve | 543829-2
Charlie Christian All Stars
Charlie Christian-Jazz Immortal/Dizzy Gillespie 1944 | Original Jazz Classics | OJCCD 1932-2(ES 548)
Charlie Haden Quartet West
Always Say Goodbye | Verve | 521501-2
Charlie Haden Quartet With Orchestra
American Dreams | Verve | 064096-2
Chet Baker With String-Orchestra And Voices
Chet Baker With Fifty Italian Strings | Original Jazz Classics | OJC20 492-2(JLP 921)
Chris Connor With The Ralph Burns Orchestra
Chris Connor | Atlantic | 7567-80769-2
Clifford Brown With Strings
Clifford Brown-Max Roach:Alone Together-The Best Of The Mercury Years | Verve | 526373-2
Verve Jazz Masters 44:Clifford Brown and Max Roach | Verve | 528109-2
Brownie-The Complete EmArCy Recordings Of Clifford Brown | EmArCy | 838306-2
Coleman Hawkins Quintet With Strings
Body And Soul Revisited | GRP | GRP 16272
Coleman Hawkins With Paul Neilson's Orchestra
Body And Soul Revisited | GRP | GRP 16272
Coleman Hawkins With The Glenn Osser Orchestra
Midnight Blue(The [Be]witching Hour) | Blue Note | 854365-2
Daniel Schnyder With The NDR Radio Philharmonie Hannover
Tanatula | Enja | ENJ-9302 2
Dave Grusin Orchestra
Two For The Road:The Music Of Henry Mancini | GRP | GRP 98652
Dee Dee Bridgewater With Band
7.Zelt-Musik-Festival:Jazz Events | Zounds | CD 2730001
Della Reese With The Neal Hefti Orchestra
Della | RCA | 2663912-2
Diana Krall Group With Orchestra
When I Look In Your Eyes | Verve | 9513304
Dinah Washington And Her Orchestra
Misty Blue:Sweet Sisters Swing Songs Of Sorrow And Sadness | Blue Note | 521151-2
Verve Jazz Masters 40:Dinah Washington | Verve | 522055-2
Dinah Washington With Orchestra
Ballads | Roulette | 537559-2
Dinah Washington With The Belford Hendricks Orchestra
Verve Jazz Masters 20:Introducing | Verve | 519853-2
What A Diff'rence A Day Makes! | Verve | 543300-2
4 By 4:Ella Fitzgerald/Sarah Vaughan/Billie Holiday/Dinah Washington | Verve | 559693-2
Dinah Washington With The Jimmy Cobb Orchestra
Verve Jazz Masters 40:Dinah Washington | Verve | 522055-2
Ultimate Ben Webster selected by James Carter | Verve | 557537-2
Dinah Washington With The Quincy Jones Orchestra
The Swingin' Miss 'D' | Verve | 558074-2
4 By 4:Ella Fitzgerald/Sarah Vaughan/Billie Holiday/Dinah Washington | Verve | 559693-2
Dizzy Gillespie Orchestra And The Operatic String Orchestra
Jazz In Paris:Dizzy Gillespie And His Operatic Strings Orchestra | EmArCy | 018420-2
Dizzy Gillespie Quartet And The Operatic String Orchestra
Jazz In Paris:Dizzy Gillespie And His Operatic Strings Orchestra | EmArCy | 018420-2
Duke Ellington And His Orchestra
The Story Of Jazz Piano | Laserlight | 24653
Eddie Harris Group
Here Comes The Judge | CBS | 492533-2
Ella Fitzgerald And Barney Kessel
Jazz Collection:Ella Fitzgerald | Laserlight | 24397
Ella Fitzgerald And Her Be-Bop Boys
Jazz Collection:Ella Fitzgerald | Laserlight | 24397
Ella Fitzgerald And Her Orchestra
Jazz Collection:Ella Fitzgerald | Laserlight | 24397
Sunshine Of Your Love | MPS | 533102-2
Ella Fitzgerald And Louis Armstrong With The Russell Garcia Orchestra
Ella Fitzgerald-First Lady Of Song | Verve | 517898-2
Verve Jazz Masters 24:Ella Fitzgerald & Louis Armstrong | Verve | 521851-2
Ella Fitzgerald With Frank De Vol And His Orchestra
Like Someone In Love | Verve | 511524-2
Verve Jazz Masters 6:Ella Fitzgerald | Verve | 519822-2
Ella Fitzgerald With Orchestra
Ella Fitzgerald-First Lady Of Song | Verve | 517898-2
Misty Blue:Sweet Sisters Swing Songs Of Sorrow And Sadness | Blue Note | 521151-2
Ella/Things Ain't What They Used To Be | Warner | 9362-47875-2
Ella Fitzgerald With Paul Weston And His Orchestra
The Best Of The Song Books | Verve | 519804-2
Verve Jazz Masters 6:Ella Fitzgerald | Verve | 519822-2
Love Songs:The Best Of The Song Books | Verve | 531762-2
Ella Fitzgerald With Russell Garcia And His Orchestra
Verve Jazz Masters 6:Ella Fitzgerald | Verve | 519822-2
Ella Fitzgerald With Sy Oliver And His Orchestra
Ella Fitzgerald:The Decca Years 1949-1954 | Decca | 050668-2
Ella Fitzgerald With The Billy May Orchestra
Ella Fitzgerald-First Lady Of Song | Verve | 517898-2
The Best Of The Song Books | Verve | 519804-2
Verve Jazz Masters 6:Ella Fitzgerald | Verve | 519822-2
Verve Jazz Masters 46:Ella Fitzgerald-The Jazz Sides | Verve | 527655-2
Ella Fitzgerald Sings The Harold Arlen Song Book | Verve | 589108-2
The Silver Collection: Ella Fitzgerald-The Songbooks | Verve | 823445-2 PMS
For The Love Of Ella Fitzgerald | Verve | 841765-2
Ella Fitzgerald With The Buddy Bregman Orchestra
The Best Of The Song Books | Verve | 519804-2
The Silver Collection: Ella Fitzgerald-The Songbooks | Verve | 823445-2 PMS
For The Love Of Ella Fitzgerald | Verve | 841765-2
Ella Fitzgerald With The Frank DeVol Orchestra
Ella Fitzgerald-First Lady Of Song | Verve | 517898-2
A Life In Jazz:A Musical Biography | Verve | 535119-2
Stan Getz Highlights | Verve | 847430-2
Ella Fitzgerald Sings Sweet Songs For Swingers | Verve | 9860417
Ella Fitzgerald With The Frank DeVol Orchestra feat. Stan Getz
Ella Fitzgerald-First Lady Of Song | Verve | 517898-2
Ella Fitzgerald With The Johnny Spence Orchestra
Ella Fitzgerald-First Lady Of Song | Verve | 517898-2
Ella Fitzgerald With The Marty Paich Orchestra
Ella Fitzgerald-First Lady Of Song | Verve | 517898-2
The Antonio Carlos Jobim Songbook | Verve | 525472-2
Ella Sings Broadway | Verve | 549373-2
Whisper Not | Verve | 589947-2
For The Love Of Ella Fitzgerald | Verve | 841765-2
Ella Fitzgerald With The Nelson Riddle Orchestra
Ella Fitzgerald-First Lady Of Song | Verve | 517898-2
The Best Of The Song Books | Verve | 519804-2
Verve Jazz Masters 6:Ella Fitzgerald | Verve | 519822-2

Oh Lady Be Good:The Best Of The Gershwin Songbook | Verve | 529581-2
Love Songs:The Best Of The Song Books | Verve | 531762-2
The Silver Collection: Ella Fitzgerald-The Songbooks | Verve | 823445-2 PMS
For The Love Of Ella Fitzgerald | Verve | 841765-2
Ella Fitzgerald With The Paul Weston Orchestra
Ella Fitzgerald-First Lady Of Song | Verve | 517898-2
The Best Of The Song Books:The Ballads | Verve | 521867-2
The Silver Collection: Ella Fitzgerald-The Songbooks | Verve | 823445-2 PMS
Ferenc Snétberger With The Franz Liszt Chamber Orchestra
For My People | Enja | ENJ-9387 2
Fleurine With Band And Horn Section
Meant To Be! | EmArCy | 159085-2
Frank Sinatra With The Red Norvo Quintet(Sextet!) & Orchestra
Live In Australia,1959 | Blue Note | 837513-2
Freddie Brocksieper Und Seine Solisten
Shot Gun Boogie | Bear Family Records | BCD 16277 AH
George Benson Group
Verve Jazz Masters 21:George Benson | Verve | 521861-2
Gerald Wilson And His Orchestra
Deep Blue-The United States Of Mind | Blue Note | 521152-2
Glenn Miller And His Orchestra
Jazz Collection:Glenn Miller | Laserlight | 24367
The Glenn Miller Story Vol. 2 | RCA | ND 89221
The Glenn Miller Story Vol. 3 | RCA | ND 89222
Golden Gate Quartet
Americans Swinging In Paris:Golden Gate Quartet | EMI Records | 539659-2
Grant Green With Orchestra
Blue Break Beats | Blue Note | 799106-2
Grover Washington Jr. Orchestra
Late Night Sax | CBS | 487798-2
Harry James And His Orchestra
The Golden Trumpet Of Harry James | London | 820178-2 IMS
Helmut Zacharias mit seinen Verzauberten Geigen
Ich Habe Rhythmus | Bear Family Records | BCD 15642 AH
Helmut Zacharias mit seiner Swing-Besetzung
Ich Habe Rhythmus | Bear Family Records | BCD 15642 AH
Herbie Hancock Group
Monster | CBS | 486571-2
Inge Brandenburg
Why Don't You Take All Of Me | Bear Family Records | BCD 15614 AH
Inge Brandenburg & Otto 'Fats' Ortwein und die King Beats
Why Don't You Take All Of Me | Bear Family Records | BCD 15614 AH
Jack McDuff Group
So Blue So Funky-Heroes Of The Hammond | Blue Note | 796563-2
Jack McDuff Quartet With Orchestra
Moon Rappin' | Blue Note | 538697-2
Jaco Pastorius With Orchestra
Word Of Mouth | Warner | 7599-23525-2
Jerri Southern And The Dave Barbour Trio
The Very Thought Of You:The Decca Years 1951-1957 | Decca | 050671-2
Jerri Southern And The Frank Meriweather Orchestra
The Very Thought Of You:The Decca Years 1951-1957 | Decca | 050671-2
Jerri Southern And The Gus Levene Orchestra
The Very Thought Of You:The Decca Years 1951-1957 | Decca | 050671-2
Jerri Southern And The Norman Leyden Orchestra
The Very Thought Of You:The Decca Years 1951-1957 | Decca | 050671-2
Jerri Southern And The Ralph Burns Orchestra
The Very Thought Of You:The Decca Years 1951-1957 | Decca | 050671-2
Jerri Southern And The Sonny Burke Orchestra
The Very Thought Of You:The Decca Years 1951-1957 | Decca | 050671-2
Jerri Southern And The Toots Camarata Orchestra
The Very Thought Of You:The Decca Years 1951-1957 | Decca | 050671-2
Jerri Southern And The Victoe Young Orchestra
The Very Thought Of You:The Decca Years 1951-1957 | Decca | 050671-2
Jimmy McGriff Band
Blue Break Beats | Blue Note | 799106-2
Jimmy McGriff Orchestra
Blue Breaks Beats Vol.2 | Blue Note | 789907-2
Jimmy Smith With Orchestra
Jimmy Smith:Best Of The Verve Years | Verve | 527950-2
Jimmy Smith With The Johnny Pate Orchestra
Jimmy Smith:Best Of The Verve Years | Verve | 527950-2
Jimmy Smith With The Lalo Schifrin Orchestra
Jimmy Smith:Best Of The Verve Years | Verve | 527950-2
Jimmy Smith With The Oliver Nelson Orchestra
Jimmy Smith:Best Of The Verve Years | Verve | 527950-2
Jimmy Smith-Talkin' Verve | Verve | 531563-2
Joe Sample Group
Invitation | Warner | 9362-45209.2
Joe Williams With The Frank Hunter Orchestra
Planet Jazz:Joe Williams | Planet Jazz | 2165370-2
Joe Williams With The Harry 'Sweets' Edison Band
Together/Have A Good Time | Roulette | 531790-2
John Lee Hooker
House Of The Blues | Chess | MCD 09258
John Pisano-Billy Bean-Dennis Budimir
West Coast Sessions | String Jazz | SJRCD 1006
Johnny Hartman And The Rudy Traylor Orchestra
And I Thought About You | Blue Note | 857456-2
Juan Garcia Esquivel Orchestra
Juan's Again | RCA | 2168206-2
Julie London With Orchestra
Misty Blue:Sweet Sisters Swing Songs Of Sorrow And Sadness | Blue Note | 521151-2
Julie London With Pete King And His Orchestra
About The Blues/London By Night | Capitol | 535208-2
Julie London With Russ Garcia And His Orchestra
About The Blues/London By Night | Capitol | 535208-2
June Christy With The Pete Rugolo Orchestra
The Song Is June | Capitol | 855455-2
Kenny Burrell With The Johnny Pate Orchestra
Verve Jazz Masters 45:Kenny Burrell | Verve | 527652-2
King Curtis Band
King Curtis-Blow Man Blow | Bear Family Records | BCD 15670 CI
King Pleasure With Orchestra
Blue Velvet: Crooners, Swooners And Velvet Vocals | Blue Note | 521153-2
Koko Taylor
Classic Blues | Zounds | CD 2700048
Lajos Dudas Group
Jubilee Edition | double moon | CHRDM 71020
Laura Fygi Meets Michel Legrand
Watch What Happens | Mercury | 534598-2
Le Jazz Group De Paris
Jazz In Paris | EmArCy | 548793-2
Les Blue Stars
Jazz In Paris:Blossom Dearie-The Pianist/Les Blue Stars | EmArCy | 064784-2
Lorez Alexandria With Orchestra
Misty Blue:Sweet Sisters Swing Songs Of Sorrow And Sadness | Blue Note | 521151-2
Deep Blue-The United States Of Mind | Blue Note | 521152-2
Lou Bennett Trio With The Paris Jazz All Stars
Jazz In Paris | EmArCy | 548790-2
Louis Armstrong And Bing Crosby With Orchestra
The Very Best Of Dixieland Jazz | Verve | 535529-2
Louis Armstrong And Ella Fitzgerald With Russell Garcia's Orchestra
The Complete Ella Fitzgerald And Louis Armstrong On Verve | Verve | 537284-2
The Best Of Ella Fitzgerald And Louis Armstrong On Verve | Verve | 537909-2
Porgy And Bess | Verve | 827475-2
Louis Armstrong And His All Stars With A Studio Orchestra
What A Wonderful World | MCA | MCD 01876
Louis Armstrong With Gordon Jenkins And His Orchestra And Choir
Satchmo In Style | Verve | 549594-2
Louis Armstrong With Orchestra
Jazz Collection:Louis Armstrong | Laserlight | 24366
Louis Armstrong With The Gordon Jenkins Orchestra
Ambassador Louis Armstrong Vol.17:Moments To Remember(1952-1956) | Ambassador | CLA 1917
Louis Armstrong With The Lyn Murray Chorus
Louis And The Good Book | Verve | 549593-2
Louis Armstrong With The Russell Garcia Orchestra
Verve Jazz Masters 1:Louis Armstrong | Verve | 519818-2
The Silver Collection: Louis Armstrong | Verve | 823446-2
Louis Jordan With The Nelson Riddle Orchestra
Louis Jordan-Let The Good Times Roll: The Complete Decca Recordings 1938-1954 | Bear Family Records | BCD 15557 IH
Mahalia Jackson With Choir And Orchestra
Stille Nacht | CBS | COLCD 62130
Mahavishnu Orchestra
Visions Of The Emerald Beyond | CBS | 467904-2
Mamie Smith WithThe Lucky Millinder Orchestra
The Blues | Storyville | 4960323
Marcos Valle With Orchestra
Samba '68 | Verve | 559516-2
Margaret Whiting With Russel Garcia And His Orchestra
Margaret Whiting Sings The Jerome Kern Song Book | Verve | 559553-2
Mark Murphy With The Ralph Burns Orchestra
Crazy Rhythm:His Debut Recordings | Decca | 050670-2
Marlena Shaw With Orchestra
Deep Blue-The United States Of Mind | Blue Note | 521152-2
Mel Tormé With Orchestra
Comin' Home Baby!/Sings Sunday In New York | Warner | 8122-75438-2
Mel Tormé With The Claus Ogerman Orchestra
Comin' Home Baby!/Sings Sunday In New York | Warner | 8122-75438-2
Mel Tormé With The Geoff Love Orchestra
My Kind Of Music | Verve | 543795-2
Mel Tormé With The Jimmy Jones Orchestra
Blue Velvet: Crooners, Swooners And Velvet Vocals | Blue Note | 521153-2
Mel Tormé With The Shorty Rogers Orchestra
Comin' Home Baby!/Sings Sunday In New York | Warner | 8122-75438-2
Mel Tormé With The Tony Osborne Orchestra
My Kind Of Music | Verve | 543795-2
Mel Tormé With The Wally Stott Orchestra
My Kind Of Music | Verve | 543795-2
Miles Davis Group
A Tribute To Jack Johnson | CBS | 471003-2
Doo-Bop | Warner | 7599-26938-2
Miles Davis With Gil Evans & His Orchestra
Ballads | CBS | 461099-2
Miles Davis With Orchestra
Ballads | CBS | 461099-2
Modern Jazz Quartet And Symphony Orchestra
MJQ 40 | Atlantic | 7567-82330-2
Muddy Waters Blues Band
Classic Blues | Zounds | CD 2700048
Nancy Wilson With The Billy May Orchestra
Misty Blue:Sweet Sisters Swing Songs Of Sorrow And Sadness | Blue Note | 521151-2
Nat King Cole And George Shearing With Orchestra
Midnight Blue(The [Be]witching Hour) | Blue Note | 854365-2
Nat King Cole Quartet With The Pete Rugolo Orchestra
The Instrumental Classics | Capitol | 798288-2
Nat King Cole Trio With Frank DeVol's Orchestra
Nat King Cole:Route 66 | Dreyfus Jazz Line | FDM 36716-2
Nat King Cole Trio With Pete Rugolo's Orchestra
Nat King Cole:For Sentimental Reasons | Dreyfus Jazz Line | FDM 36740-2
Nat King Cole With Orchestra
Nat King Cole:Route 66 | Dreyfus Jazz Line | FDM 36716-2
Nelson Riddle And His Orchestra
Changing Colors | MPS | 9814794
Communication | MPS | 9814795
Nina Simone And Orchestra
Planet Jazz:Nina Simone | Planet Jazz | 2165372-2
Nina Simone With Hal Mooney's Orchestra
Verve Jazz Masters 17:Nina Simone | Verve | 518198-2
Nina Simone After Hours | Verve | 526702-2
Verve Jazz Masters Vol.58:Nina Simone Sings Nina | Verve | 529867-2
In Concert/I Put A Spell On You | Mercury | 846543-2
Nina Simone With Horace Ott's Orchestra
Verve Jazz Masters 17:Nina Simone | Verve | 518198-2
Nina Simone After Hours | Verve | 526702-2
In Concert/I Put A Spell On You | Mercury | 846543-2
Oscar Peterson Trio With The Claus Ogermann Orchestra
Three Originals:Motion&Emotions/Tristeza On Piano/Hello Herbie | MPS | 521059-2
The Antonio Carlos Jobim Songbook | Verve | 525472-2
Oscar Peterson Trio With The Nelson Riddle Orchestra
Verve Jazz Masters 16:Oscar Peterson | Verve | 516320-2
The Silver Collection: Oscar Peterson | Verve | 823447-2 PMS
Oscar Peterson Trio With The Russell Garcia Orchestra
Verve Jazz Masters 16:Oscar Peterson | Verve | 516320-2
Oscar Peterson With Orchestra
Oscar Peterson:The Composer | Pablo | 2310970-2
A Royal Wedding Suite | Original Jazz Classics | OJCCD 973-2(2312129)
Paul Desmond With Strings
The Ballad Of Paul Desmond | RCA | 21429372
Planet Jazz:Paul Desmond | Planet Jazz | 2152061-2
Desmond Blue | RCA | 2663898-2
Peggy Lee With Benny Goodman And The Paul Weston Orchestra
Peggy Lee & Benny Goodman:The Complete Recordings 1941-1947 | CBS | C2K 65686
Peggy Lee With Jack Marshall's Music
Things Are Swingin' | Capitol | 597072-2
Peggy Lee With Lou Levy's Orchestra
Pass Me By/Big Spender | Capitol | 535210-2
Peggy Lee With Orchestra
Misty Blue:Sweet Sisters Swing Songs Of Sorrow And Sadness | Blue Note | 521151-2
Pass Me By/Big Spender | Capitol | 535210-2
Peggy Lee With The Bill Holman Orchestra
Pass Me By/Big Spender | Capitol | 535210-2
Quincy Jones And His Orchestra
Talkin' Verve-Roots Of Acid Jazz:Roland Kirk | Verve | 533101-2
Rahsaan/The Complete Mercury Recordings Of Roland Kirk | Mercury | 846630-2
Richard Galliano With Orchestra
Passatori | Dreyfus Jazz Line | FDM 36601-2
Roland Kirk And His Orchestra
Talkin' Verve-Roots Of Acid Jazz:Roland Kirk | Verve | 533101-2
Rahsaan/The Complete Mercury Recordings Of Roland Kirk | Mercury | 846630-2
Roland Kirk Quartet
Rahsaan/The Complete Mercury Recordings Of Roland Kirk | Mercury | 846630-2
Ronnie Foster Group
Sweet Revival... | Blue Note | 581676-2
Roy Eldridge With The Russell Garcia Orchestra
The Complete Verve Roy Eldridge Studio Sessions | Verve | 9861278
Sarah Vaughan And The Thad Jones Orchestra
Verve Jazz Masters 42:Sarah Vaughan-The Jazz Sides | Verve | 526817-2
Sarah Vaughan With Her Quartet
Jazz Profile | Blue Note | 823517-2
Sarah Vaughan With Orchestra
Sweet 'N' Sassy | Roulette | 531793-2
Ballads | Roulette | 537561-2
Sarah Vaughan Sings The Mancini Songbook | Verve | 558401-2
Sarah Vaughan Birthday Celebration | Fantasy | FANÇD 6090-2
Sarah Vaughan With Small Group & Orchestra
Duke Ellington Song Book One | Pablo | CD 2312111
Sarah Vaughan With The Benny Carter Orchestra
Ballads | Roulette | 537561-2
Jazz Profile | Blue Note | 823517-2
Sarah Vaughan With The Billy May Orchestra
Jazz Profile | Blue Note | 823517-2
Sarah Vaughan With The Don Costa Orchestra
Jazz Profile | Blue Note | 823517-2
Sarah Vaughan With The Gerald Wilson Orchestra
Jazz Profile | Blue Note | 823517-2
Sarah Vaughan With The Hal Mooney Orchestra
Sarah Vaughan Sings Gershwin | Verve | 557567-2
4 By 4:Ella Fitzgerald/Sarah Vaughan/Billie Holiday/Dinah Washington | Verve | 559693-2
It's A Man's World | Mercury | 589487-2
Sarah Vaughan With The Jimmy Jones Orchestra
Jazz Profile | Blue Note | 823517-2
Sarah Vaughan With The Lalo Schifrin Orchestra
Jazz Profile | Blue Note | 823517-2
Sarah Vaughan With The Marty Manning Orchestra
Jazz Profile | Blue Note | 823517-2
Sarah Vaughan With The Quincy Jones Orchestra
Ballads | Roulette | 537561-2
Jazz Profile | Blue Note | 823517-2
Shirley Horn With Orchestra
Loads Of Love + Shirley Horn With Horns | Mercury | 843454-2
Shirley Horn With The Quincy Jones Orchestra
Loads Of Love + Shirley Horn With Horns | Mercury | 843454-2
Singers Unlimited With The Robert Farnon Orchestra
The Singers Unlimited:Magic Voices | MPS | 539130-2
Slim Gaillard Group
Slim Gaillard Rides Again | Dot | 589761-2
Sonny Boy Williamson Band
Classic Blues | Zounds | CD 2700048
Sonny Stitt With The Ralph Burns Orchestra
Verve Jazz Masters 50:Sonny Sitt | Verve | 527651-2
Stan Getz With Orchestra And Voices
Stan Getz Highlights | Verve | 847430-2
Stan Getz With The Eddie Sauter Orchestra
Verve Jazz Masters 8:Stan Getz | Verve | 519823-2
A Life In Jazz:A Musical Biography | Verve | 535119-2
Stan Getz Highlights | Verve | 847430-2
Stan Getz With The Michel Legrand Orchestra
Stan Getz Highlights | Verve | 847430-2
Stephane Grappelli With The Michel Legrand Orchestra
Verve Jazz Masters 11:Stéphane Grappelli | Verve | 516758-2
The Danish Radio Concert Orchestra
Symphonies Vol.2 | dacapo | DCCD 9441
The Ravens
Ultimate Ben Webster selected by James Carter | Verve | 557537-2
Tito Puente Orchestra
Planet Jazz:Tito Puente | Planet Jazz | 2165369-2
Toots Thielemans With The Ruud Bos Orchestra
The Silver Collection: Toots Thielemans | Polydor | 825086-2 PMS
Toto Blanke Group
Electric Circus' Best | ALISO Records | AL 1034
Van Alexander Orchestra
Home Of Happy Feet/Swing! Staged For Sound! | Capitol | 535211-2
Viktoria Tolstoy With The Esbjörn Svensson Trio
Viktoria Tolstoy:White Russian | Blue Note | 821220-2
Vince Jones Group
Watch What Happens | Intuition Records | INT 3070-2
Willie Bobo Group
Bobo's Beat | Roulette | 590954-2
Willie Dixon
Classic Blues | Zounds | CD 2700048
Woody Herman And His Orchestra
The Legends Of Swing | Laserlight | 24659
World Quintet With The London Mozart Players
World Quintet | TipToe | TIP-888843 2
World Quintet With The London Mozart Players And Herbert Grönemeyer
World Quintet | TipToe | TIP-888843 2
Yusef Lateef With Eternal Wind And The 'Kölner Rundfunk Orchester'
The African American Epic Suite:Music For Quintet And Orchestra | ACT | 9214-2

details unknown,Orchestra |
Miles Davis With Orchestra
Ballads | CBS | 461099-2

Deuchar,Jimmie | (mellophontp)
Kenny Clarke-Francy Boland Big Band
Three Latin Adventures | MPS | 529095-2
All Smiles | MPS | 9814790
Francy Boland-Fellini 712 | MPS | 9814805
Stan Getz With The Kurt Edelhagen Orchestra
Stan Getz In Europe | Laserlight | 24657

Deufel,Martin | (dr)
Manfred Junker Quartet
Cole Porter-Live! | Edition Collage | EC 531-2

Deutsch,Alex | (dr,body-perc,mouth-perc,vocperc)
Woody Shaw Quartet
In My Own Sweet Way | IN+OUT Records | 7003-2
Jazz Unlimited | IN+OUT Records | 7017-2

Deutsch,Silo | (dr)
Caterina Valente With The Silvio Francesco Quartet
Deutsches Jazz Fesival 1954/1955 | Bear Family Records | BCD 15430
Kurt Edelhagen All Stars
Deutsches Jazz Fesival 1954/1955 | Bear Family Records | BCD 15430
Silvio Francesco Quartet
Deutsches Jazz Fesival 1954/1955 | Bear Family Records | BCD 15430

Deutsch,Solomon | (v)
Ben Webster With Orchestra And Strings
Verve Jazz Masters 43:Ben Webster | Verve | 525431-2
Music For Loving:Ben Webster With Strings | Verve | 527774-2

Deutsche All Star Band 1953,Die |
Die Deutsche All Star Band 1953
1.Deutsches Jazz Festival 1953 Frankfurt/Main | Bear Family Records | BCD 15611 AH

Deutsches Filmorchester Babelsberg |
Frank Castenier Group
For You,For Me For Evermore | EmArCy | 9814976

Deutsches Symphonieorchester Berlin |
Till Brönner Quartet & Deutsches Symphonieorchester Berlin
German Songs | Minor Music | 801057

Deuvall,Roy | (b-tbtb)
Bob Brookmeyer Group With The WDR Big Band
Electricity | ACT | 9219-2
Eddie Harris Group With The WDR Big Band
Eddie Harris-The Last Concert | ACT | 9249-2
Jens Winther And The WDR Big Band
The Escape | dacapo | DCCD 9437
Los Jovenes Flamencos With The WDR Big Band And Guests

Jazzpana | ACT | 9212-2
Vince Mendoza With The WDR Big Band And Guests
Sketches | ACT | 9215-2

Devens,George | (perc,vibtympany.timbales)
Dizzy Gillespie And His Orchestra
Ultimate Dizzy Gillespie | Verve | 557535-2
Grant Green With Orchestra
The Final Comedown(Soundtrack) | Blue Note | 581678-2
Jimmy Smith With Orchestra
Jimmy Smith-Talkin' Verve | Verve | 531563-2
Jimmy Smith With The Billy Byers Orchestra
Jimmy Smith:Best Of The Verve Years | Verve | 527950-2
Jimmy Smith With The Claus Ogerman Orchestra
Verve Jazz Masters 29:Jimmy Smith | Verve | 521855-2
Any Number Can Win | Verve | 557447-2
Joe Williams With The Frank Hunter Orchestra
Planet Jazz:Joe Williams | Planet Jazz | 2165370-2
Rusty Bryant Group
For The Good Times | Prestige | PRCD 24269-2
Wes Montgomery Quartet
Verve Jazz Masters 14:Wes Montgomery | Verve | 519826-2
Tequila | Verve | 547769-2
Wes Montgomery Quartet With The Claus Ogerman Orchestra
Tequila | Verve | 547769-2
Wes Montgomery Quintet With The Claus Ogerman Orchestra
Talkin' Jazz:Roots Of Acid Jazz | Verve | 529580-2
Tequila | Verve | 547769-2
Wes Montgomery Sextet
Tequila | Verve | 547769-2
Wes Montgomery With The Claus Ogerman Orchestra
Verve Jazz Masters 14:Wes Montgomery | Verve | 519826-2

Devisscher,Christophe | (b)
Alexi Tuomarila Quartet
02 | Finladia Jazz | 0927-49148-2

DeVol,Frank | (arr,bcond)
Ella Fitzgerald With Frank De Vol And His Orchestra
Like Someone In Love | Verve | 511524-2
Verve Jazz Masters 6:Ella Fitzgerald | Verve | 519822-2
Get Happy! | Verve | 523321-2
Ella Fitzgerald With The Frank DeVol Orchestra
Ella Fitzgerald-First Lady Of Song | Verve | 517898-2
Get Happy! | Verve | 523321-2
A Life In Jazz:A Musical Biography | Verve | 535119-2
Stan Getz Highlights | Verve | 847430-2
Ella Fitzgerald Sings Sweet Songs For Swingers | Verve | 9860417
Ella Fitzgerald With The Frank DeVol Orchestra feat. Stan Getz
Ella Fitzgerald-First Lady Of Song | Verve | 517898-2
Herbie Mann With The Frank DeVol Orchestra
Verve Jazz Masters 56:Herbie Mann | Verve | 529901-2
Nat King Cole Trio With Frank DeVol's Orchestra
Nat King Cole:Route 66 | Dreyfus Jazz Line | FDM 36716-2
Ten Cats And A Mouse
The Hollywood Session:The Capitol Jazzmen | Jazz Unlimited | JUCD 2044

DeVos,Bob | (g)
Ron McClure Quartet
Match Point | Steeplechase | SCCD 31517

Devos,Hélène | (voc)
Swingle Singers
Jazz Sebastian Bach Vol.2 | Philips | 542553-2

DeVries,Doug | (el-gg)
Vince Jones Group
Spell | Intuition Records | INT 3067-2
It All Ends Up In Tears | Intuition Records | INT 3069-2
Watch What Happens | Intuition Records | INT 3070-2
For All Colours | Intuition Records | INT 3071-2
Tell Me A Secret | Intuition Records | INT 3072-2
Future Girl | Intuition Records | INT 3109-2
Vince Jones Septet
On The Brink Of It | Intuition Records | INT 3068-2

Dewinkel,Torsten | (g)
Russ Spiegel Group
Twilight | double moon | CHRDM 71026

DeWitt,Algie | (bata-dr)
John Coltrane Group
The Olatunji Concert:The Last Live Recording | Impulse(MCA) | 589120-2

Deyhim,Sussan | (voc)
Sotto In Su
Vanitas | Poise | Poise 04

D'Hellemmes,Eugene | (btb)
Benny Carter And His Orchestra
Americans Swinging In Paris:Benny Carter | EMI Records | 539647-2
Coleman Hawkins And His All Star Jam Band
Django Reinhardt All Star Sessions | Capitol | 531577-2
Americans Swinging In Paris:Benny Carter | EMI Records | 539647-2
Jazz:The Essential Collection Vol.3 | IN+OUT Records | 78013-2
Coleman Hawkins With Michel Warlop And His Orchestra
Django Reinhardt All Star Sessions | Capitol | 531577-2
Django Reinhardt Trio
Django/Django In Rome 1949-1050 | BGO Records | BGOCD 366
Django Reinhardt:Echoes Of France | Dreyfus Jazz Line | FDM 36726-2
Wal-Berg Et Son Jazz Francais
Jazz In Paris:Django Reinhardt-Django Et Compagnie | EmArCy | 549241-2 PMS

D'Hondt,Paul | (tp)
Django Reinhardt With Stan Brenders Et Son Grand Orchestre
Verve Jazz Masters 38:Django Reinhardt | Verve | 516931-2

Di Battista,Stefano | (asss)
Michel Petrucciani Sextet
Both Worlds | Dreyfus Jazz Line | FDM 36590-2
Nguyen Le Group
Maghreb And Friends | ACT | 9261-2

Di Benedetto,Giacomo | (voice)
La Voce-Music For Voices,Trumpet And Bass | JA & RO | JARO 4208-2

Di Castri,Furio | (b,computer-programming)
Enrico Rava-Dino Saluzzi Quintet
Volver | ECM | 1343
Paolo Fresu Angel Quartet
Metamorfosi | RCA | 2165202-2
Paolo Fresu Quartet
Angel | RCA | 2155864-2
Kind Of Porgy & Bess | RCA | 21951952
Paolo Fresu Quintet
Kind Of Porgy & Bess | RCA | 21951952
Paolo Fresu Sextet
Kind Of Porgy & Bess | RCA | 21951952
Paolo Fresu Trio
Kind Of Porgy & Bess | RCA | 21951952
Paolo Fresu-Furio Di Castri
Evening Song | Owl Records | 014733-2
Paolo Fresu-Furio Di Castri Quintet
Evening Song | Owl Records | 014733-2

Di Cintio,Vito | (cl)
Banda Città Ruvo Di Puglia
La Banda/Banda And Jazz | Enja | ENJ-9326 2

Di Domenica,Bob | (fl)
Charles Mingus Orchestra
Charles Mingus:Pre-Bird(Mingus Revisited) | Verve | 538636-2
George Russell And His Orchestra
Bill Evans:Piano Player | CBS | CK 65361
Gunther Schuller Ensemble
Beauty Is A Rare Thing:Ornette Coleman-The Complete Atlantic Recordings | Atlantic | 8122-71410-2
Modern Jazz Quartet & Guests
MJQ 40 | Atlantic | 7567-82330-2

Di Donato,Jacques | (as,cl,b-clreeds)
Double Trio(Trio De Clarinettes&Arcado)
Green Dolphy Suite | Enja | ENJ-9011 2

Di Filippi,Bruno | (el-g)
Gerry Mulligan With Astor Piazzolla And His Orchestra
Tango Nuevo | Atlantic | 2292-42145-2

Di Geraldo,Tino | (brodham,cajon,dr,perc,g,b-gdarhuka)
Javier Paxarino Group With Glen Velez
Temurá | ACT | 9227-2
Nguyen Le Trio
Bakida | ACT | 9275-2
Nguyen Le Trio With Guests
Bakida | ACT | 9275-2

Di Gioia,Roberto | (kalimba,keyboards,org,p,el-p,perc)
Al Porcino Big Band
Al Cohn Meets Al Porcino | Organic Music | ORGM 9730
Clifford Jordan Quintet
Clifford Jordan Meets Klaus Weiss | JHM Records | JHM 3617
J.C. Dook Quartet
Travelin' Man | Organic Music | ORGM 9734
Johannes Enders Quintet
Quiet Fire | Enja | ENJ-9390 2
Johnny Griffin With The NDR Big Band
NDR Big Band-Bravissimo | ACT | 9232-2
Klaus Doldinger & Passport
Down To Earth | Warner | 4509-93207-2
Klaus Doldinger's Passport
Klaus Doldinger Passport Live | Warner | 8573-84132-2
Blues Roots | Warner | 9031-75417-2
Klaus Doldinger's Passport With Johnny 'Clyde' Copeland
Blues Roots | Warner | 9031-75417-2
Klaus Weiss Quintet
A Taste Of Jazz | ATM Records | ATM 3810-AH
Pee Wee Ellis Quintet With Guests
A New Shift | Minor Music | 801060
Rigmor Gustafsson With The Nils Landgren Quartet And The Fleshquartet
I Will Wait For You | ACT | 9418-2
Till Brönner Quartet & Deutsches Symphonieorchester Berlin
German Songs | Minor Music | 801057
Wolfgang Haffner Project
Back Home | Jazz 4 Ever Records:Jazz Network | J4E 4730

Di Meola,Al | (cymbals,el-g,synth,timbales,fl,g)
Al Di Meola
Elegant Gypsy | CBS | 468213-2
Al Di Meola Group
Elegant Gypsy | CBS | 468213-2
Land Of The Midnight Sun | CBS | 468214-2
Casino | CBS | 468215-2
Jazzrock-Anthology Vol.3:Fusion | Zounds | CD 27100555
Al Di Meola Groups
Guitar Heroes Vol.1:Al Di Meola | Zounds | CD 2700044001
Al Di Meola-Chick Corea
Land Of The Midnight Sun | CBS | 468214-2
Hal Di Meola Group
Casino | CBS | 468215-2
Joe Pass
Land Of The Midnight Sun | CBS | 468214-2
John McLaughlin Group
The Promise | Verve | 529828-2
Los Jovenes Flamencos With The WDR Big Band And Guests
Jazzpana | ACT | 9212-2
Paco De Lucia-Al Di Meola-John McLaughlin
Paco De Lucia-Al Di Meola-John McLaughlin | Verve | 533215-2
Return To Forever
Where Have I Known You Before | Polydor | 825206-2

Di Muro,Pasquale | (tuba)
Banda Città Ruvo Di Puglia
La Banda/Banda And Jazz | Enja | ENJ-9326 2

Di Piazza,Dominique | (4-string-b-g,5-string-b-gel-b)
Bireli Lagrene Quartet
Standards | Blue Note | 780251-2
John McLaughlin Trio
Que Alegria | Verve | 837280-2

Di Puccio,Alessandro | (vib)
Mike Turk With The Alkaline Jazz Trio
A Little Taste Of Cannonball | Organic Music | ORGM 9708

Di Puppo,Franco | (fl)
Banda Città Ruvo Di Puglia
La Banda/Banda And Jazz | Enja | ENJ-9326 2

Di Puppo,Vincenzo | (cl)

Di Rella,Rocco | (cl)

Di Renzo,Davide | (drperc)
Gerd Baumann-Alessandro Ricciarelli Quartet
Say No More | Edition Collage | EC 489-2

Diabaté,Kassé-Mady | (voc)
Hank Jones Meets Cheik-Tidiana Seck
Sarala | Verve | 528783-2

Diabaté,Sekou | (b-g)

Diakité,Tom | (percvoc)

Dial,Harry | (dr,speech,voc,maracas,percvib)
Fats Waller And His Rhythm
Planet Jazz:Fats Waller | Planet Jazz | 2152058-2
Planet Jazz:Male Jazz Vocalists | Planet Jazz | 2169657-2
Louis Armstrong And His Orchestra
Planet Jazz:Louis Armstrong | Planet Jazz | 2152052-2
Best Of The Complete RCA Victor Recordings | RCA | 2663636-2
Louis Armstrong:A 100th Birthday Celebration | RCA | 2663694-2
Louis Jordan And His Tympany Five
Louis Jordan-Let The Good Times Roll: The Complete Decca Recordings 1938-1954 | Bear Family Records | BCD 15557 IH

Diallo,Amadou | (ts)
Antonio Hart Group
Here I Stand | Impulse(MCA) | 951208-2

Diara,Baba | (balafon,doudoum'baperc)
Jon Hassell & Farafina
Flash Of The Spirit | Intuition Records | INT 3009-2

Diara,Dra | (perc,djebevoc)
Pili-Pili
Stolen Moments | JA & RO | JARO 4159-2
Boogaloo | JA & RO | JARO 4174-2
Dance Jazz Live 1995 | JA & RO | JARO 4189-2
Jazzy World | JA & RO | JARO 4200-2
Nomans Land | JA & RO | JARO 4209-2

Diarra,Dra | (perc,konivoc)
Ballads Of Timbuktu | JA & RO | JARO 4240-2

Diaz Zayas,Miguel 'Anga' | (perc)
Steve Coleman And Five Elements
Genesis & The Opening Of The Way | RCA | 2152934-2
Steve Coleman And The Council Of Balance
Genesis & The Opening Of The Way | RCA | 2152934-2

Diaz,Candito Zayas | (voc)
Lazaro Ros Ensemble
Ori Batá (Cuban Yoruba Music) | Enja | ENJ-9381 2

Diaz,Enrique | (b,perc,voc,fl,g,charangovoice)
Markus Stockhausen Orchestra
Sol Mestizo:Markus Stockhausen Plays The Music Of Enrique Diaz | ACT | 9222-2

Diaz,Fernando | (tp)
Brocksi-Quartett
Globetrotter | Bear Family Records | BCD 15912 AH

Diaz,Joan | (p)
Joan Abril Quartet
Insomnio | Fresh Sound Records | FSNT 034 CD
Joan Abril Quintet
Insomnio | Fresh Sound Records | FSNT 034 CD
Mikel Andueza Quintet
BCN | Fresh Sound Records | FSNT 036 CD

Diaz,Luis Chico | (coro)
Conexion Latina
La Conexión | Enja | ENJ-9065 2

Diaz,Manolo | (b)
Thilo Kreitmeier Quintet
Mo' Better Blues | Organic Music | ORGM 9706

Diaz,Miguel | (congas,itotele,iya,okonkoloperc)
Danilo Perez Group
Central Avenue | Impulse(MCA) | 951281-2
Roy Hargrove's Crisol
Habana | Verve | 537563-2
Steve Coleman And Five Elements
The Sonic Language Of Myth | RCA | 2164123-2

Diaz,Ramón | (drperc)
Ramón Diaz Group
O Si No Que? | Fresh Sound Records | FSNT 044 CD

Dick,Robert | (fl,alto-fl,bass-fl,contra-bass-fl)
Klaus König Orchestra
Time Fragments:Seven Studies In Time And Motion | Enja | ENJ-8076 2
Paul Giger Trio
Vindonissa | ECM | 1836(066069-2)
Robert Dick Group With The Soldier String Quartet
Jazz Standard On Mars | Enja | ENJ-9327 2

Dickbauer,Klaus | (as,cl,reeds,sax,ts,bs)
Hans Koller Groups
Out Of The Rim | IN+OUT Records | 7014-2

Dickens,Doles | (b)
Lena Horne With The Phil Moore Four
Planet Jazz:Lena Horne | Planet Jazz | 2165373-2

Dickenson,Vic | (tbvoc)
Billie Holiday With Eddie Heywood And His Orchestra
Billie Holiday:The Complete Commodore Recordings | GRP | 543272-2
Coleman Hawkins All Stars
Coleman Hawkins All Stars | Original Jazz Classics | OJCCD 225-2(SV 2005)
Count Basie And His Orchestra
Jazz:The Essential Collection Vol.3 | IN+OUT Records | 78013-2
Count Basie Jam
Montreux '77 | Original Jazz Classics | OJC 379(2308209)
Montreux '77 | Original Jazz Classics | OJC 385(2620105)
Edmond Hall's Blue Note Jazzmen
The Blue Note Jazzmen | Blue Note | 821262-2
George Wein's Dixie Victors
The Magic Horn | RCA | 2113038-2
Planet Jazz | Planet Jazz | 2169652-2
James P.Johnson's Blue Note Jazzmen
Jazz:The Essential Collection Vol.3 | IN+OUT Records | 78013-2
The Blue Note Jazzmen | Blue Note | 821262-2
Joe Turner With Orchestra
Atlantic Jazz: Kansas City | Atlantic | 7567-81701-2
Johnny Hodges And His Band
Verve Jazz Masters 35:Johnny Hodges | Verve | 521857-2
Johnny Hodges Orchestra
The Soul Of Ben Webster | Verve | 527475-2
Lester Young And His Band
Jazz Gallery:Lester Young Vol.2(1946-59) | RCA | 2119541-2
Lester Young:The Complete Aladdin Sessions | Blue Note | 832787-2
Louis Armstrong And His Hot Seven
Planet Jazz:Louis Armstrong | Planet Jazz | 2152052-2
Best Of The Complete RCA Victor Recordings | RCA | 2663636-2
Louis Armstrong:A 100th Birthday Celebration | RCA | 2663694-2
Louis Armstrong:C'est Si Bon | Dreyfus Jazz Line | FDM 36730-2
Odetta With The Buck Clayton Sextet
Odetta And The Blues | Original Blues Classics | OBCCD 509-2(RLP 9417)
Sidney Bechet And His New Orleans Feetwarmers
Sidney Bechet:Summertime | Dreyfus Jazz Line | FDM 36712-2
Sidney Bechet's Blue Note Jazzmen
Jazz:The Essential Collection Vol.1 | IN+OUT Records | 78011-2
Sidney DeParis' Blue Note Jazzmen
The Blue Note Jazzmen | Blue Note | 821262-2
The Dixieland All Stars
The Dixieland All Stars | Jazz Unlimited | JUCD 2037
The Jazz Giants '56
Jazz Gallery:Lester Young Vol.2(1946-59) | RCA | 2119541-2
Vic Dickenson Septet
Nice Work | Vanguard | VCD 79610-2
Vic Dickenson Septet With Ruby Braff
Nice Work | Vanguard | VCD 79610-2
Vic Dickenson-Buck Clayton All Stars
Atlantic Jazz: Kansas City | Atlantic | 7567-81701-2

Dickerson,Carroll | (cond,ldv)
Carroll Dickerson's Savoyagers
Louis Armstrong:Fireworks | Dreyfus Jazz Line | FDM 36710-2
Louis Armstrong And His Orchestra
Satch Plays Fats(Complete) | CBS | CK 64927

Dickerson,Dede | (voc)
Herbie Hancock Group
Magic Window | CBS | 486572-2

Dickeson,Andrew | (drperc)
Clarion Fracture Zone
Blue Shift | VeraBra Records | CDVBR 2075-2
Mike Nock Quartet
Dark & Curious | VeraBra Records | CDVBR 2074-2

Dickler,Richard | (viola)
Ben Webster With Orchestra And Strings
Music For Loving:Ben Webster With Strings | Verve | 527774-2
Ultimate Ben Webster selected by James Carter | Verve | 557537-2
Billie Holiday With The Ray Ellis Orchestra
Lady In Satin | CBS | CK 65144
Grover Washington Jr. Orchestra
Jazzrock-Anthology Vol.3:Fusion | Zounds | CD 27100555

Dicterow,Glenn | (v)
Ron Carter Quintet With Strings
Pick 'Em/Super Strings | Milestone | MCD 47090-2

Dicterow,Harold | (v)
Ella Fitzgerald With The Frank DeVol Orchestra
Get Happy! | Verve | 523321-2

Diebetsberger,Rudolf | (fr-h)
Eberhard Weber Orchestra
Orchestra | ECM | 1374

Diehl,Eddie | (g)
Jack McDuff Orchestra
The Last Goodun' | Prestige | PRCD 24274-2
Jack McDuff Quartet
Brother Jack Meets The Boss | Original Jazz Classics | OJCCD 326-2(P 7228)
The Last Goodun' | Prestige | PRCD 24274-2
Jack McDuff Quartet With Gene Ammons
Brother Jack Meets The Boss | Original Jazz Classics | OJCCD 326-2(P 7228)
Jack McDuff Quintet
Jack McDuff:The Prestige Years | Prestige | PRCD 24387-2
Sonny Stitt-Jack McDuff Quintet
Stitt Meets Brother Jack | Original Jazz Classics | OJCCD 703-2(P 7244)

Diehl,Ray | (tb)
Max Kaminsky And His Dixieland Bashers
Planet Jazz | Planet Jazz | 2169652-2
Sidney Bechet's Blue Note Jazzmen
Runnin' Wild | Blue Note | 821259-2

Diekmann,Wolfgang | (bb-g)
Deborah Henson-Conant Trio
Just For You | Laika Records | LK 95-063
Thomas Kessler & Group
Thomas Kessler & Group | Laika Records | LK 190-015
Thomas Kessler Group
On Earth | Laika Records | 8695069
Untitled | Laika Records | LK 92-027
Ulli Bögershausen
Best Of Ulli Bögershausen | Laika Records | LK 93-045

Diener,Christian | (bel-b)

Gerwin Eisenhauer's The Gäff Gang feat. Lisa Wahland
Favorite Tunes | Edition Collage | EC 527-2
Lisa Wahland And Her Trio
Marlene | Fine Music | FM 108-2
Lisa Wahlandt & Mulo Francel And Their Fabulous Bossa Band
Bossa Nova Affair | Edition Collage | EC 534-2
Nana Mouskouri With The Berlin Radio Big Band
Nana Swings | Mercury | 074394-2
Wolfgang Haffner Project
Back Home | Jazz 4 Ever Records:Jazz Network | J4E 4730

Dieng,Aib | (congas,bells,chatan,gongsvoc)
Pharoah Sanders Orchestra
Message From Home | Verve | 529578-2

Dierksen,Uwe | (tb)
Ensemble Modern
Ensemble Modern-Fred Frith:Traffic Continues | Winter&Winter | 910044-2

Diernhammer,Carlos | (pcembalo)
Freddie Brocksieper And His Boys
Freddie's Boogie Blues | Bear Family Records | BCD 16388 AH
Freddie Brocksieper Four Stars
Freddie's Boogie Blues | Bear Family Records | BCD 16388 AH
Freddie Brocksieper Orchester
Shot Gun Boogie | Bear Family Records | BCD 16277 AH

Diers,Lisbeth | (perc)
Jazz Baltica Ensemble
The Birth+Rebirth Of Swedish Folk Jazz | ACT | 9254-2

Dierstein,Christian | (marimbaperc)
Peter Kleindienst Group
Zeitwärts:Reime Vor Pisin | double moon | DMCD 1001-2

Dies,Werner | (clel-b)
Joe Turner And Friends
The Giant Of Stride Piano In Switzerland | Jazz Connaisseur | JCCD 9106-2
Two Beat Stompers
Deutsches Jazz Fesival 1954/1955 | Bear Family Records | BCD 15430

Dieterle,Kurt | (v)
Harry James And His Orchestra
Trumpet Blues:The Best Of Harry James | Capitol | 521224-2
Paul Whiteman And His Orchestra
Planet Jazz:Jazz Trumpet | Planet Jazz | 2169654-2

Dietrich,Brigitte | (co-ld)
Brigitte Dietrich-Joe Haider Jazz Orchestra
Consequences | JHM Records | JHM 3624

Dietz,Mike | (gg-synth)
Gunter Hampel Next Generation
Next Generation | Birth | CD 043
Gunter Hampel Quartet
Time Is Now-Live At The Eldena Jazz Festival 1992 | Birth | CD 042

Dieval,Jack | (p)
Don Byas And His Orchestra
Don Byas:Laura | Dreyfus Jazz Line | FDM 36714-2
Jack Dieval And His Quartet
Americans Swinging In Paris:James Moody | EMI Records | 539653-2
Jack Dieval And The J.A.C.E. All-Stars
Jazz In Paris:Jack Diéval-Jazz Aux Champs Elysées | EmArCy | 018419-2
Jack Dieval Trio
Jazz In Paris:Jack Diéval-Jazz Aux Champs Elysées | EmArCy | 018419-2

Diez,Stephan | (gel-g)
Abdullah Ibrahim With The NDR Big Band
Ekapa Lodumo | TipToe | TIP-888840 2
Albert Mangelsdorff With The NDR Big Band
NDR Big Band-Bravissimo | ACT | 9232-2
Heinz Sauer Quartet With The NDR Big Band
NDR Big Band-Bravissimo | ACT | 9232-2
Johnny Griffin With The NDR Big Band
NDR Big Band-Bravissimo | ACT | 9232-2
NDR Big Band
NDR Big Band-Bravissimo | ACT | 9232-2
The Theatre Of Kurt Weil | ACT | 9234-2
NDR Big Band With Guests
50 Years Of NDR Big Band:Bravissimo II | ACT | 9259-2
Oscar Brown Jr. And His Group
Live Every Minute | Minor Music | 801071
Oscar Brown Jr. with The NDR Big Band
Live Every Minute | Minor Music | 801071
Stephan Dietz Quartet
Jazz Portraits | EGO | 95080

DiFalco,Ernie | (tp)
Stan Getz With The Eddie Sauter Orchestra
Stan Getz Plays The Music Of Mickey One | Verve | 531232-2

Diggs,Elmore | (b)
Chuck Brown And The Second Chapter Band
Timeless | Minor Music | 801068

Dillard,Bill | (tpvoc)
Dicky Wells And His Orchestra
Americans Swinging In Paris:Dicky Wells | EMI Records | 539664-2

Dillard,John | (tp)
Tommy Dorsey And His Orchestra
Planet Jazz:Frank Sinatra & Tommy Dorsey | Planet Jazz | 2152067-2
Planet Jazz:Male Jazz Vocalists | Planet Jazz | 2169657-2

Dillmann,Klaus | (b)
Helmut Zacharias Quintet
Ich Habe Rhythmus | Bear Family Records | BCD 15642 AH

DiMaggio,Charlie | (as,bscl)
Artie Shaw And His Orchestra
Planet JazzArtie Shaw | Planet Jazz | 2152057-2
Planet Jazz:Male Jazz Vocalists | Planet Jazz | 2169657-2
June Christy With The Johnny Guarnieri Quintet
June Christy And The Johnny Guarnieri Quintet (1949) | Jazz Unlimited | JUCD 2084

DiMaio,Nick | (tb)
June Christy With The Pete Rugolo Orchestra
Something Cool(The Complete Mono & Stereo Versions) | Capitol | 534069-2
Tommy Dorsey And His Orchestra
Planet Jazz:Tommy Dorsey | Planet Jazz | 2159972-2

DiMartino,Bobby | (p)
Ray Barretto Orchestra
Portraits In Jazz And Clave | RCA | 2168452-2

Dimusio,Jerry | (sax)
Buddy Childers Big Band
Just Buddy's | Candid | CCD 79761

Dinken,Alvin | (viola)
Ella Fitzgerald With The Billy May Orchestra
Ella Fitzgerald Sings The Harold Arlen Song Book | Verve | 589108-2

Dinkin,Alvin | (vviola)
Cal Tjader With The Clare Fischer Orchestra
Cal Tjader Plays Harold Arlen & West Side Story | Fantasy | FCD 24775-2
Ella Fitzgerald With The Billy May Orchestra
The Best Of The Song Books:The Ballads | Verve | 521867-2
Ella Fitzgerald With The Nelson Riddle Orchestra
The Best Of The Song Books:The Ballads | Verve | 521867-2
Oh Lady Be Good! The Best Of The Gershwin Songbook | Verve | 529581-2
Love Songs:The Best Of The Song Books | Verve | 531762-2
Frank Sinatra With The Count Basie Orchestra
It Might As Well Be Spring | Reprise | 7599-27027-2

Dinné,Ignaz | (as)
Ed Kröger Quartet plus Guests
Movin' On | Laika Records | 35101332

DiNovi,Gene | (cond,arr,p,vocp-solo)
Gene DiNovi Trio
Renaissance Of A Jazz Master | Candid | CCD 79708
Live At The Montreal Bistro | Candid | CCD 79726

Jubilee All Stars
Jazz Gallery:Lester Young Vol.2(1946-59) | RCA | 2119541-2
Lena Horne With The Lennie Hayton Orchestra
Planet Jazz:Lena Horne | Planet Jazz | 2165373-2
Lester Young And His Band
Lester Young:The Complete Aladdin Sessions | Blue Note | 832787-2

Dioko |
Dioko
Helix | Jazz Haus Musik | JHM 0029 CD

Diop,Abdourahmane | (drvoc)
Jean-Paul Bourelly Trance Atlantic
Boom Bop II | double moon | CHRDM 71023

DiPasqua,Michael | (drperc)
Eberhard Weber Group
Endless Days | ECM | 1748(013420-2)
Eberhard Weber Quintet
Later That Evening | ECM | 1231(829382-2)
Jan Garbarek Group
It's OK To Listen To The Gray Voice | ECM | 1294(825406-2)
Jan Garbarek Quartet
Wayfarer | ECM | 1259(811968-2)
Ralph Towner Quintet
Old Friends New Friends | ECM | 1153

Directions In Music |
Directions In Music
Live at Massey Hall:Celebrating Miles Davis & John Coltrane | Verve | 589654-2

Directors |
Directors
Directors | Jazz Haus Musik | JHM 0040 CD

DiRisi,Al | (tp)
Ralph Burns And His Orchestra
The Complete Verve Roy Eldridge Studio Sessions | Verve | 9861278

DiRubbo,Mike | (as)
Andrew Adair Group
States | Fresh Sound Records | FSNT 061 CD

Diry,Roland | (cl)
Ensemble Modern
Ensemble Modern-Fred Frith:Traffic Continues | Winter&Winter | 910044-2

Disch,Wolfgang | (drperc)
Ralph Schweizer Big Band
DAY Dream | Chaos | CACD 8177
Sax Mal Anders
Kontraste | Chaos | CACD 8185

Disley,Terry | (keyboardssynth-b)
Acoustic Alchemy
Against The Grain | GRP | GRP 97832
Dee Dee Bridgewater With Band
Victim Of Love | Verve | 841199-2

Disley,William 'Diz' | (bj,gvoc)
Bireli Lagrene Ensemble
Live | Jazzpoint | JP 1047 CD
Bireli Lagrene Group
A' Portrait Of Jan Jankeje | Jazzpoint | JP 1054 CD
A Tribute To Django Reinhardt | Jazzpoint | JP 1061 CD
Bireli Lagrene Trio
Live At The Carnegie Hall: A Tribute To Django Reinhardt | Jazzpoint | JP 1040 CD
Henrik Johansen's Jazzband
The Golden Years Of Revival Jazz,Vol.6 | Storyville | STCD 5511
The Golden Years Of Revival Jazz,Vol.7 | Storyville | STCD 5512
The Golden Years Of Revibal Jazz,Vol.15 | Storyville | STCD 5520
Stephane Grappelli And Friends
Grapelli Story | Verve | 515807-2
Stephane Grappelli Group
Stephane Grappelli:Live In San Francisco | Storyville | 4960723
Stephane Grappelli Quartet
Verve Jazz Masters 11:Stéphane Grappelli | Verve | 516758-2
Stephane Grappelli With The Diz Disley Trio
Grapelli Story | Verve | 515807-2
Stephane Grappelli-David Grisman Group
Stephane Grappelli:Live In San Francisco | Storyville | 4960723

Distaso,Pino | (g)
Pino Distaso/Roberto Gotta/Beto Cutillo
Tell Her It's All Right | Edition Collage | EC 463-2

Distel,Sacha | (g)
Bobby Jaspar Quintet
Jazz In Paris | EmArCy | 159941-2 PMS
Jack Dieval And The J.A.C.E. All-Stars
Jazz In Paris:Jack Diéval-Jazz Aux Champs Elysées | EmArCy | 018419-2
Lionel Hampton All Stars
Jazz In Paris:Lionel Hampton And His French New Sound Vol.1 | EmArCy | 549405-2 PMS
Jazz In Paris:Lionel Hampton And His French New Sound Vol.2 | EmArCy | 549406-2 PMS

Ditano,Giuseppe | (tuba)
Banda Cittá Ruvo Di Puglia
La Banda/Banda And Jazz | Enja | ENJ-9326 2

Ditmas,Bruce | (dr,electronic-perc,special-effects)
Enrico Rava-Dino Saluzzi Quintet
Volver | ECM | 1343
Gil Evans Orchestra
There Comes A Time | RCA | 2131392-2
PLay The Music Of Jimi Hendrix | RCA | 2663872-2
Svengali | Rhino | 8122-73720-2
Ku-umba Frank Lacy & The Poker Bigband
Songs From The Musical 'Poker' | Tutu Records | 888150-2*

Dittberner,Heidrun | (v)
Till Brönner Quartet & Deutsches Symphonieorchester Berlin
German Songs | Minor Music | 801057

Ditullio,Joseph | (cello)
Johnny Hartman And His Orchestra
Unforgettable | Impulse(MCA) | IMP 11522

DiTullio,Justin | (cello)
Ella Fitzgerald With The Frank DeVol Orchestra
Get Happy! | Verve | 523321-2
Herbie Mann With The Frank DeVol Orchestra
Verve Jazz Masters 56:Herbie Mann | Verve | 529901-2
Pete Rugolo And His Orchestra
Thriller/Richard Diamon(Original Jazz Scores From 2 Classics TV Series) | Fresh Sound Records | FSCD 2015

Ditzner,Erwin | (dr)
Ax Genrich Group
Psychedelic Guitar | ATM Records | ATM 3809-AH

Divigard,Jala | (voc)
Leon Thomas With Orchestra
Spirits Known And Unknown | RCA | 2663876-2

Divjak,Ratko | (dr)
Dusko Goykovich Big Band
Balkan Connection | Enja | ENJ-9047 2

Dixieland All Stars,The |
The Dixieland All Stars
The Dixieland All Stars | Jazz Unlimited | JUCD 2037

Dixon,Ben | (dr)
Baby Face Willette Quartet
So Blue So Funky-Heroes Of The Hammond | Blue Note | 796563-2
Big John Patton Quintet
So Blue So Funky-Heroes Of The Hammond | Blue Note | 796563-2
Grant Green Quartet
Ballads | Blue Note | 537560-2
Grant Green Quintet
Am I Blue | Blue Note | 535564-2
Grant Green Trio
Grant's First Stand | Blue Note | 521959-2
Jack McDuff Quartet
The Honeydripper | Original Jazz Classics | OJCCD 222-2(P 7199)

Jack McDuff:The Prestige Years | Prestige | PRCD 24387-2
John Patton Quintet
Along Came John | Blue Note | 0675614
Along Came John | Blue Note | 831915-2
Lou Donaldson Quartet
Good Gracious | Blue Note | 854325-2
Lou Donaldson Quintet
The Natural Soul | Blue Note | 542307-2
Ray Draper Sextet
Tuba Sounds | Original Jazz Classics | OJCCD 1936-2(P 7096)

Dixon,Bill | (bj,p,tpfl-h)
Cecil Taylor Sextet
A Blue Conception | Blue Note | 534254-2
Conquistador | Blue Note | 576749-2
Dick Charlesworth And His City Gents
The Golden Years Of Révival Jazz,Vol.4 | Storyville | STCD 5509
The Golden Years Of Revival Jazz,Vol.6 | Storyville | STCD 5511
The Golden Years Of Revival Jazz,Vol.11 | Storyville | STCD 5516
Franz Koglmann Quintet
Opium | Between The Lines | btl 011(Efa 10181-2)

Dixon,Charlie | (b,tuba,bjg)
Bessie Smith And Her Band
Jazz:The Essential Collection Vol.1 | IN+OUT Records | 78011-2
Bessie Smith With The James P.Johnson Orchestra And The Hal Johnson Choir
The Blues | Storyville | 4960323
Fletcher Henderson And His Orchestra
Jazz:The Essential Collection Vol.1 | IN+OUT Records | 78011-2
Henderson's Hot Six
Jazz:The Essential Collection Vol.1 | IN+OUT Records | 78011-2
The Lousiana Stompers
Jazz:The Essential Collection Vol.1 | IN+OUT Records | 78011-2

Dixon,Eric | (as,ts,cl,fl,arr,reedssax)
Ahmed Abdullah Sextet
Jazz Sounds Of Africa | Prestige | PRCD 24279-2
Big Joe Turner With The Count Basie Orchestra
Flip Flop And Fly | Original Jazz Classics | OJCCD 1053-2(2310937)
Count Basie And His Orchestra
Afrique | RCA | 2179618-2
Fun Time | Pablo | 2310945-2
Jazz Collection:Count Basie | Laserlight | 24368
The Legends Of Swing | Laserlight | 24659
Count Basie: Salle Pleyel, April 17th, 1972 | Laserlight | 36127
Atomic Swing | Roulette | 497871-2
Verve Jazz Masters 2:Count Basie | Verve | 519819-2
Basie Meets Bond | Capitol | 538225-2
Basie's Beatle Bag | Verve | 557455-2
Live at The Sands | Reprise | 9362-45946-2
88 Basie Street | Original Jazz Classics | OJC 808(2310901)
Jazz Dance | Original Jazz Classics | OJCCD 1002-2(1210890)
Fancy Pants | Original Jazz Classics | OJCCD 1038-2(2310920)
I Told You So | Original Jazz Classics | OJCCD 824-2(2310767)
Digital III At Montreux | Original Jazz Classics | OJCCD 996-2(2308223)
The Jazz Giants Play Harry Warren:Lullaby Of Broadway | Prestige | PCD 24204-2
Count Basie And The Kansas City 7
Count Basie And The Kansas City 7 | Impulse(MCA) | 951202-2
Count Basie Big Band
Montreux '77 | Original Jazz Classics | OJCCD 377-2
Farmers Market Barbecue | Original Jazz Classics | OJCCD 732-2(2310874)
Diane Schuur With The Count Basie Orchestra
The Best Of Diane Schuur | GRP | GRP 98882
Ella Fitzgerald With Count Basie And His Orchestra
Digital III At Montreux | Original Jazz Classics | OJCCD 996-2(2308223)
Ella Fitzgerald With The Count Basie Orchestra
Bluella:Ella Fitzgerald Sings The Blues | Pablo | 2310960-2
Ella Fitzgerald-First Lady Of Song | Verve | 517898-2
Ella And Basie | Verve | 539059-2
For The Love Of Ella Fitzgerald | Verve | 841765-2
Frank Sinatra With The Count Basie Orchestra
Sinatra-Basie:An Historic Musical First | Reprise | 7599-27023-2
It Might As Well Be Spring | Reprise | 7599-27027-2
Milt Jackson Orchestra
Sarah Vaughan Birthday Celebration | Fantasy | FANCD 6090-2
Milt Jackson With The Count Basie Orchestra
To Bags...With Love:Memorial Album | Pablo | 2310967-2
Milt Jackson Birthday Celebration | Fantasy | FANCD 6079-2
Milt Jackson + Count Basie + Big Band Vol.1 | Original Jazz Classics | OJCCD 740-2(2310822)
Milt Jackson + Count Basie + Big Band Vol.2 | Original Jazz Classics | OJCCD 741-2(2310823)
Quincy Jones And His Orchestra
The Quintessence | Impulse(MCA) | 951222-2
The Roots Of Acid Jazz | Impulse(MCA) | IMP 12042
Sarah Vaughan And The Count Basie Orchestra
Sarah Vaughan Birthday Celebration | Fantasy | FANCD 6090-2

Dixon,Fostina | (sax)
Grant Calvin Weston Group
Dance Romance | IN+OUT Records | 7002-2

Dixon,Gayle | (v)
Archie Shepp Orchestra
The Cry Of My People | Impulse(MCA) | 9861488

Dixon,George | (tb,as,tp,bs,vvoc)
Earl Hines And His Orchestra
Planet Jazz:Earl Hines | Planet Jazz | 2159973-2
The Legends Of Swing | Laserlight | 24659
Jazz:The Essential Collection Vol.2 | IN+OUT Records | 78012-2

Dixon,Gus | (tb)
Artie Shaw And His Orchestra
Planet Jazz:Jazz Trumpet | Planet Jazz | 2169654-2

Dixon,Iain | (cl,b-cl,ssts)
David Newton Quartet
DNA | Candid | CCD 79742
Michael Brecker Quindectet
Wide Angles | Verve | 076142-2

Dixon,Joe | (clas)
Tommy Dorsey And His Clambake Seven
Planet Jazz:Bud Freeman | Planet Jazz | 2161240-2
Tommy Dorsey And His Orchestra
Planet Jazz:Tommy Dorsey | Planet Jazz | 2159972-2
Planet Jazz:Big Bands | Planet Jazz | 2169649-2
Planet Jazz:Swing | Planet Jazz | 2169651-2

Dixon,Kenny | (dr)
Jimmy Smith With Orchestra
Verve Jazz Masters 29:Jimmy Smith | Verve | 521855-2
Jimmy Smith-Eddie Harris Trio
All The Way | Milestone | MCD 9251-2

Dixon,Lawrence | (bj,garr)
Earl Hines And His Orchestra
Jazz:The Essential Collection Vol.2 | IN+OUT Records | 78012-2

Dixon,Lucille | (b)
Ella Fitzgerald With The Bill Doggett Orchestra
Ella Fitzgerald-First Lady Of Song | Verve | 517898-2
Rhythm Is My Business | Verve | 559513-2

Dixon,Pat | (cello)
Archie Shepp Orchestra
The Cry Of My People | Impulse(MCA) | 9861488

Dixon,Tony | (tp)
André Holst With Chris Dean's European Swing Orchestra
That's Swing | Nagel-Heyer | CD 079

Dixon,Willie | (b,voc,whistling,gp)
Muddy Waters Blues Band
Muddy Waters-The Collection | MCA | MCD 18961
Willie Dixon
Classic Blues | Zounds | CD 2700048
Willie Dixon-Memphis Slim Quintet
Windy City Blues | Stax | SCD 8612-2

DJ Apollo | (turntables)
Russel Gunn Group
Ethnomusicology Vol.1 | Atlantic | 7567-83165-2
DJ Kaspar | (turntablesperc)
Balance
Elements | double moon | DMCHR 71033
DJ Olive | (turntables)
Uri Caine Group
Urlicht/Primal Light | Winter&Winter | 910004-2
DJ Pogo | (turntables)
Courtney Pine Group
Modern Day Jazz Stories | Verve | 529028-2
DJ Strangefruit | (beats,samplesambience)
Nils Petter Molvaer Group
Solid Ether | ECM | 1722(543365-2)
Djebate,Boubakar | (koravoc)
Heiner Goebbels Group
Ou Bien Le Debarquement Desastreux | ECM | 1552
Djebate,Sira | (voc)
Djemai,Abdenour | (bj,mandolavoc)
Karim Ziad Groups
Ifrikya | ACT | 9282-2
D'Leon,Oscar | (voc)
Arturo Sandoval And The Latin Train Band
Arturo Sandoval & The Latin Train | GRP | GRP 98202
Do O,Fernando | (perccabassa)
Raiz De Pedra
Diario De Bordo | TipToe | TIP-888822 2
Raiz De Pedra feat. Egberto Gismonti
Diario De Bordo | TipToe | TIP-888822 2
Dobbins,Bill | (condp)
Kevin Mahogany With The WDR Big Band And Guests
Pussy Cat Dues:The Music Of Charles Mingus | Enja | ENJ-9316 2
Rolf Römer Quartet
Tesoro | Jazz 4 Ever Records:Jazz Network | J4E 4743
Rolf Römer-Bill Dobbins Quartet
A Tribute To B.A.C.H. | Edition Collage | EC 520-2
Dobler,Thomas | (vib)
Peter A. Schmid Trio With Guests
Profound Sounds In An Empty Reservoir | Creative Works Records | CW CD 1033
Doblies,Günther | (g)
Asita Hamidi & Arcobaleno
Mosaic | Laika Records | 8695067
Dobrzynski,Walter | (b)
Brocksi-Quartett
Globetrotter | Bear Family Records | BCD 15912 AH
Dockery,Sam | (p)
Art Blakey And The Jazz Messengers
Planet Jazz:Art Blakey | Planet Jazz | 2152066-2
Planet Jazz Sampler | Planet Jazz | 2152326-2
A Night In Tunisia | RCA | 2663896-2
Doctor,Marcio | (perchand-dr)
Claudio Puntin Quartet
Mondo | Jazz Haus Musik | JHM 0134 CD
Gabriel Pérez Group
La Chipaca | Green House Music | CD 1011
Heinz Sauer Quartet With The NDR Big Band
NDR Big Band-Bravissimo | ACT | 9232-2
NDR Big Band
NDR Big Band-Bravissimo | ACT | 9232-2
The Theatre Of Kurt Weil | ACT | 9234-2
Nils Landgren Funk Unit
Paint It Blue:A Tribute To Cannonball Adderley | ACT | 9243-2
Peter Bolte-Marcio Doctor
Zeitraum | Jazz Haus Musik | JHM 0113 CD
Stefan Bauer-Claudio Puntin-Marcio Doctor
Lingo | Jazz Haus Musik | JHM 0116 CD
Wolfgang Haffner Project
Back Home | Jazz 4 Ever Records:Jazz Network | J4E 4730
Dodds,Johnny | (cl,asvoc)
Jelly Roll Morton Trio
Jazz:The Essential Collection Vol.1 | IN+OUT Records | 78011-2
Jelly Roll Morton's Red Hot Peppers
Planet Jazz:Jelly Roll Morton | Planet Jazz | 2152060-2
Jazz:The Essential Collection Vol.1 | IN+OUT Records | 78011-2
King Oliver's Creole Jazz Band
Jazz:The Essential Collection Vol.1 | IN+OUT Records | 78011-2
King Oliver's Jazz Band
Jazz:The Essential Collection Vol.1 | IN+OUT Records | 78011-2
Lil's Hot Shots
Jazz:The Essential Collection Vol.2 | IN+OUT Records | 78012-2
Louis Armstrong And His Hot Five
Jazz:The Essential Collection Vol.2 | IN+OUT Records | 78012-2
Louis Armstrong And His Hot Seven
Jazz:The Essential Collection Vol.2 | IN+OUT Records | 78012-2
Dodds,Roy | (dr)
Nicki Leighton-Thomas Group
Forbidden Games | Candid | CCD 79778
Dodds,Warren 'Baby' | (dr,swanee-whistle)
Bunk Johnson And His New Orleans Band
Planet Jazz:Jazz Trumpet | Planet Jazz | 2169654-2
Jelly Roll Morton Trio
Jazz:The Essential Collection Vol.1 | IN+OUT Records | 78011-2
Jelly Roll Morton's Red Hot Peppers
Planet Jazz:Jelly Roll Morton | Planet Jazz | 2152060-2
Jazz:The Essential Collection Vol.1 | IN+OUT Records | 78011-2
King Oliver's Creole Jazz Band
Jazz:The Essential Collection Vol.1 | IN+OUT Records | 78011-2
King Oliver's Jazz Band
Jazz:The Essential Collection Vol.1 | IN+OUT Records | 78011-2
Louis Armstrong And His Hot Seven
Jazz:The Essential Collection Vol.2 | IN+OUT Records | 78012-2
Sidney Bechet And His New Orleans Feetwarmers
Sidney Bechet:Summertime | Dreyfus Jazz Line | FDM 36712-2
Sidney Bechet Trio
Jazz:The Essential Collection Vol.1 | IN+OUT Records | 78011-2
This Is Jazz All Stars
Sidney Bechet:Summertime | Dreyfus Jazz Line | FDM 36712-2
Dodge,Joe | (dr)
Dave Brubeck Quartet
Jazz:Ted Hot And Cool | CBS | CK 61468
Brubeck Time | CBS | CK 65724
The Dave Brubeck Quartet feat. Paul Desmond In Concert | Fantasy | FCD 60-013
Jazz At The College Of The Pacific | Original Jazz Classics | OJC20 047-2(F 3223)
Jazz At The College Of The Pacific Vol.2 | Original Jazz Classics | OJCCD 1076-2
Paul Desmond Quartet
Desmond | Original Jazz Classics | OJCCD 712-2(F 3235/8082)
The Jazz Giants Play Jerome Kern:Yesterdays | Prestige | PCD 24202-2
Paul Desmond Quartet With The Bill Bates Singers
Desmond | Original Jazz Classics | OJCCD 712-2(F 3235/8082)
Paul Desmond Quintet
Desmond | Original Jazz Classics | OJCCD 712-2(F 3235/8082)
Dodgion,Jerry | (alto-fl,as,cl,fl,piccolo,ss,ts)
Abbey Lincoln And Her All Stars
The World Is Falling Down | Verve | 843476-2
Benny Goodman And His Orchestra
The Legends Of Swing | Laserlight | 24659
Blue Mitchell And His Orchestra
Blue Breaks Beats Vol.2 | Blue Note | 789907-2
Bob James And His Orchestra
Jazzrock-Anthology Vol.3:Fusion | Zounds | CD 27100555
Buck Clayton Swing Band
Swing's The Village | Nagel-Heyer | CD 5004
Blues Of Summer | Nagel-Heyer | NH 1011
Cal Tjader's Orchestra
Talkin Verve/Roots Of Acid Jazz:Cal Tjader | Verve | 531562-2
Soul Burst | Verve | 557446-2
Duke Pearson Orchestra
Blue N' Groovy | Blue Note | 780679-2
Ella Fitzgerald With The Bill Doggett Orchestra
Ella Fitzgerald-First Lady Of Song | Verve | 517898-2
Rhythm Is My Business | Verve | 559513-2
Frank Sinatra With The Red Norvo Quintet(Sextet!)
Live In Australia,1959 | Blue Note | 837513-2
Frank Sinatra With The Red Norvo Quintet(Sextet!) & Orchestra
Live In Australia,1959 | Blue Note | 837513-2
Hank Jones With Oliver Nelson's Orchestra
The Roots Of Acid Jazz | Impulse(MCA) | IMP 12042
Herbie Hancock Sextet
Herbie Hancock:The Complete Blue Note Sixties Sessions | Blue Note | 495569-2
Speak Like A Child | Blue Note | 746136-2
J.J.Johnson And His Orchestra
Planet Jazz:J.J.Johnson | Planet Jazz | 2159974-2
Jerry Dodgion Quartet
The Jazz Scene:San Francisco | Fantasy | FCD 24760-2
Jimmy Smith And Wes Montgomery With Orchestra
Jimmy & Wes-The Dynamic Duo | Verve | 521445-2
Jimmy Smith And Wes Montgomery With The Oliver Nelson Orchestra
Wes Montgomery:The Verve Jazz Sides | Verve | 521690-2
Jimmy Smith:Best Of The Verve Years | Verve | 527950-2
Talkin' Jazz:Roots Of Acid Jazz | Verve | 529580-2
Jimmy Smith With Orchestra
Jimmy Smith-Talkin' Verve | Verve | 531563-2
Jimmy Smith With The Claus Ogerman Orchestra
Verve Jazz Masters 29:Jimmy Smith | Verve | 521855-2
Any Number Can Win | Verve | 557447-2
Jimmy Smith With The Oliver Nelson Orchestra
Verve Jazz Masters 29:Jimmy Smith | Verve | 521855-2
Jimmy Smith:Best Of The Verve Years | Verve | 527950-2
Jimmy Smith-Talkin' Verve | Verve | 531563-2
Peter & The Wolf | Verve | 547264-2
Klaus Weiss Septet
All Night Through | ATM Records | ATM 3816 AH
Klaus Weiss Sextet
All Night Through | ATM Records | ATM 3816 AH
Louis Armstrong And His Friends
Louis Armstrong And His Friends | Bluebird | 2663961-2
McCoy Tyner Group With Horns
Inner Voices | Original Jazz Classics | OJCCD 1039-2(M 9079)
McCoy Tyner Group With Horns And Voices
Inner Voices | Original Jazz Classics | OJCCD 1039-2(M 9079)
Oliver Nelson And His Orchestra
Verve Jazz Masters Vol.60:The Collection | Verve | 529866-2
Oscar Peterson With Orchestra
With Respect To Nat | Verve | 557486-2
Phil Woods Quartet With Orchestra & Strings
Round Trip | Verve | 559804-2
Quincy Jones Big Band
Rahsaan/The Complete Mercury Recordings Of Roland Kirk | Mercury | 846630-2
Red Norvo Sextet
Live In Australia,1959 | Blue Note | 837513-2
Ron Carter Group
Peg Leg | Original Jazz Classics | OJCCD 621-2
Ron Carter Orchestra
Parade | Original Jazz Classics | OJCCD 1047-2(M 9088)
Stanley Turrentine And His Orchestra
The Lost Grooves | Blue Note | 831883-2
Thad Jones-Mel Lewis Orchestra
The Groove Merchant/The Second Race | Laserlight | 24656
Vince Guaraldi Quartet
The Jazz Scene:San Francisco | Fantasy | FCD 24760-2
Wes Montgomery With The Oliver Nelson Orchestra
Verve Jazz Masters 14:Wes Montgomery | Verve | 519826-2
Wes Montgomery:The Verve Jazz Sides | Verve | 521690-2
Talkin' Jazz:Roots Of Acid Jazz | Verve | 529580-2
Dodgion,Jerry or Jerome Richardson | (fl)
Cal Tjader's Orchestra
Verve Jazz Masters 39:Cal Tjader | Verve | 521858-2
Doepke,Christian | (p,keyboardsp-solo)
Christian Doepke
Ten Piano Players,Vol.1 | Green House Music | CD 1002
William Galison-Mulo Franzl Group
Midnight Sun | Edition Collage | EC 508-2
Doggett,Bill | (arr,ld,org,el-pp)
Coleman Hawkins Sextet
Body And Soul Revisited | GRP | GRP 16272
Ella Fitzgerald With Bill Doggett's Orchestra
Ella Fitzgerald:Mr.Paganini | Dreyfus Jazz Line | FDM 36741-2
Ella Fitzgerald With Louis Jordan And His Tympany Five
Ella Fitzgerald:Mr.Paganini | Dreyfus Jazz Line | FDM 36741-2
Ella Fitzgerald With Sy Oliver And His Orchestra
Ella Fitzgerald:The Decca Years 1949-1954 | Decca | 050668-2
Ella Fitzgerald With The Bill Doggett Orchestra
Ella Fitzgerald-First Lady Of Song | Verve | 517898-2
Rhythm Is My Business | Verve | 559513-2
Lionel Hampton And His Orchestra
Lionel Hampton:Flying Home | Dreyfus Jazz Line | FDM 36735-2
Louis Armstrong With Louis Jordan And His Tympany Five
Louis Armstrong:C'est Si Bon | Dreyfus Jazz Line | FDM 36730-2
Louis Jordan And His Tympany Five
Louis Jordan-Let The Good Times Roll: The Complete Decca Recordings 1938-1954 | Bear Family Records | BCD 15557 IH
Dogs Don't Sing In The Rain |
Dogs Don't Sing In The Rain
Bones For Breakfast | Edition Collage | EC 472-2
Vocal Moments | Take Twelve On CD | TT 008-2
Wind Moments | Take Twelve On CD | TT 009-2
Dogslyde |
Dogslyde
Hair Of The Dog | Intuition Records | INT 3223-2
Dohnke,Heinz | (cl)
Bernd Konrad Jazz Group With Symphonie Orchestra
Wen Die Götter Lieben | Creative Works Records | CW CD 1010-1
Dohrmann,Florian | (b)
Rainer Tempel Band
Suite Ellington | Jazz 'n' Arts Records | JNA 0401
Doky,Christian Minh | (bvoice)
Bireli Lagrene Quartet
Blue Eyes | Dreyfus Jazz Line | FDM 36591-2
Doky,Niels Lan | (p)
Tom Harrell Quintet
Visions | Contemporary | CCD 14063-2
Doldinger,Klaus | (arr,cembalo,comp,as,ts,keyboards)
Joachim Kühn And The Radio Philharmonie Hannover NDR With Jazz Soloists
Europeana | ACT | 9220-2
Klaus Doldinger
Constellation | Warner | 2292-40132-2
Klaus Doldinger & Passport
Lifelike | Warner | 2292-46478-2
Down To Earth | Warner | 4509-93207-2
Klaus Doldinger Group
Back In New York:Blind Date | Atlantic | 3984-26922-2
Klaus Doldinger Jubilee
Doldinger's Best | ACT | 9224-2
Klaus Doldinger Quartet
Doldinger's Best | ACT | 9224-2
Klaus Doldinger Quintet
Doldinger's Best | ACT | 9224-2
Klaus Doldinger Septet
Doldinger's Best | ACT | 9224-2
Klaus Doldinger With Orchestra
Lifelike | Warner | 2292-46478-2
Klaus Doldinger With Orchestra And Etta James
Lifelike | Warner | 2292-46478-2
Klaus Doldinger-Peter Trunk
Doldinger's Best | ACT | 9224-2
Klaus Doldinger's Passport
Man In The Mirror | Warner | 2292-40253-2
Running In Real Time | Warner | 2292-40633-2
Heavy Nights | Warner | 2292-42006-2
Blue Tattoo | Atlantic | 2292-42178-2
Earthborn | Atlantic | 2292-46477-2
Oceanliner | Warner | 2292-46479-2
Atlantic Jazz: Fusion | Atlantic | 7567-81711-2
Klaus Doldinger Passport Live | Warner | 8573-84132-2
Balance Of Happiness | Warner | 9031-71233-2
Blues Roots | Warner | 9031-75417-2
Klaus Doldinger's Passport With Johnny 'Clyde' Copeland
Blues Roots | Warner | 9031-75417-2
NDR-Workshop
Doldinger's Best | ACT | 9224-2
Passport
Ataraxia | Atlantic | 2292-42148-2
Handmade | Atlantic | 2292-42172-2
Uranus | Atlantic | 2292-44142-2
Second Passport | Atlantic | 2292-44143-2
Looking Thru | Atlantic | 2292-44144-2
Cross-Collateral | Atlantic | 2292-44145-2
Infinity Machine | Atlantic | 2292-44146-2
Garden Of Eden | Atlantic | 2292-44147-2
Iguacu | Atlantic | 2292-46031-2
Passport And Guests
Doldinger Jubilee Concert | Atlantic | 2292-44175-2
Doldinger's Best | ACT | 9224-2
Paul Nero Sound
Doldinger's Best | ACT | 9224-2
The German Jazz Masters
Old Friends | ACT | 9278-2
Döling,Florian | (bel-b)
Peter Kleindienst Group
Zeitwärts:Reime Vor Pisin | double moon | DMCD 1001-2
Dollarhide,Richard | (congas)
Woody Herman And The New Thundering Herd
Woody Herman:Thundering Herd | Original Jazz Classics | OJCCD 841-2
Dollmann,Jürgen | (pkeyboards)
All That Jazz & Helena Paul
All That Jazz & Helena Paul | Satin Doll Productions | SDP 1031-1 CD
Dolne,Chas | (gv)
Django Reinhardt With Stan Brenders Et Son Grand Orchestre
Verve Jazz Masters 38:Django Reinhardt | Verve | 516931-2
Dolphin,Dwayne | (b,el-bvoc)
Annette Lowman With Three Of A Kind, Fred Wesley And Rodney Jones
Brown Baby:A Tribute To Oscar Brown Jr. | Minor Music | 801061
Bruce Cox Quartet With Guests
Stick To It | Minor Music | 801055
Fred Wesley Group
Swing & Be Funky | Minor Music | 801027
Amalgamation | Minor Music | 801045
Pee Wee Ellis Trio
Twelve And More Blues | Minor Music | 801034
Three Of A Kind
Drip Some Grease | Minor Music | 801056
Dolphy,Eric | (as,arr,as-solo,b-cl,cond,b-cl-solo)
Abbey Lincoln And Her All Stars(Newport Rebels)
Candid Dolphy | Candid | CCD 79033
Abbey Lincoln And Her Orchestra
Straight Ahead | Candid | CCD 79015
Andrew Hill Sextet
Point Of Departure | Blue Note | 499007-2
Booker Little Quintet
Eric Dolphy Birthday Celebration | Fantasy | FANCD 6085-2
Booker Little Sextet
Out Front | Candid | CCD 79027
Candid Dolphy | Candid | CCD 79033
Charles Mingus And His Orchestra
The Complete Town Hall Concert | Blue Note | 828353-2
Charles Mingus Group
The Jazz Life! | Candid | CCD 79019
Candid Dolphy | Candid | CCD 79033
Mysterious Blues | Candid | CCD 79042
Charles Mingus Orchestra
Charles Mingus:Pre-Bird(Mingus Revisited) | Verve | 538636-2
Mingus Mingus Mingus | Impulse(MCA) | 951170-2
Mingus | Candid | CCD 79021
Charles Mingus Quartet
Mingus At Antibes | Atlantic | 7567-90532-2
Charles Mingus Presents Charles Mingus | Candid | CCD 79005
Mingus | Candid | CCD 79021
Charles Mingus Quintet
Mingus At Antibes | Atlantic | 7567-90532-2
Charles Mingus-Passion Of A Man:The Complete Atlantic Recordings 1956-1961 | Atlantic | 8122-72871-2
Charles Mingus Quintet With Bud Powell
Mingus At Antibes | Atlantic | 7567-90532-2
Charles Mingus-Passion Of A Man:The Complete Atlantic Recordings 1956-1961 | Atlantic | 8122-72871-2
Charles Mingus Sextet
Eric Dolphy Birthday Celebration | Fantasy | FANCD 6085-2
Town Hall Concert 1964, Vol.1 | Original Jazz Classics | OJCCD 042-2
Chico Hamilton Orchestra
With Strings Attached/The Three Faces Of Chico | Warner | 9362-47874-2
Chico Hamilton Quintet
The Original Ellington Suite | Pacific Jazz | 524567-2
With Strings Attached/The Three Faces Of Chico | Warner | 9362-47874-2
Newport Jazz Festival 1958,July 3rd-6th Vol.2:Mulligan The Main Man | Phontastic | NCD 8814
Chico Hamilton Quintet With Strings
With Strings Attached/The Three Faces Of Chico | Warner | 9362-47874-2
Eddie Lockjaw Davis And His Orchestra
Eric Dolphy:The Complete Prestige Recordings | Prestige | 9 PRCD-4418-2
Eric Dolphy
The Illinois Concert | Blue Note | 499826-2
Eric Dolphy:The Complete Prestige Recordings | Prestige | 9 PRCD-4418-2
Eric Dolphy Birthday Celebration | Fantasy | FANCD 6085-2
Eric Dolphy in Europe, Vol.1 | Original Jazz Classics | OJC 413(P 7304)
Eric Dolphy Duo
Eric Dolphy in Europe, Vol.1 | Original Jazz Classics | OJC 413(P 7304)
Eric Dolphy Quartet
The Illinois Concert | Blue Note | 499826-2
Eric Dolphy:The Complete Prestige Recordings | Prestige | 9 PRCD-4418-2
Eric Dolphy Birthday Celebration | Fantasy | FANCD 6085-2
Out There | New Jazz | NJSA 8252-6
Out There | Original Jazz Classics | OJC20 023-2(NJ 8252)
Eric Dolphy Quartet With The University Of Illinois Big Band
The Illinois Concert | Blue Note | 499826-2
Eric Dolphy Quartet With The University Of Illinois Brass Ensemble
The Illinois Concert | Blue Note | 499826-2
Eric Dolphy Quintet
Out To Lunch | Blue Note | 498793-2
A Blue Conception | Blue Note | 534254-2

Eric Dolphy:The Complete Prestige Recordings | Prestige | 9 PRCD-4418-2
Eric Dolphy Birthday Celebration | Fantasy | FANCD 6085-2
Eric Dolphy At The Five Spot Vol.2 | Original Jazz Classics | OJC20 247-2(P 7294)
Far Cry | Original Jazz Classics | OJC20 400-2
Eric Dolphy With Erik Moseholm's Trio
Eric Dolphy:The Complete Prestige Recordings | Prestige | 9 PRCD-4418-2
Eric Dolphy in Europe, Vol.1 | Original Jazz Classics | OJC 413(P 7304)
Eric Dolphy In Europe, Vol.2 | Original Jazz Classics | OJCCD 414-2
Eric Dolphy In Europe, Vol.3 | Original Jazz Classics | OJCCD 416-2
Eric Dolphy-Booker Little Quintet
Eric Dolphy:The Complete Prestige Recordings | Prestige | 9 PRCD-4418-2
Eric Dolphy Birthday Celebration | Fantasy | FANCD 6085-2
At The Five Spot,Vol.1 | Original Jazz Classics | OJC20 133-2
Eric Dolphy Memorial Album | Original Jazz Classics | OJCCD 353-2
Eric Dolphy-Chuck Israels
Eric Dolphy:The Complete Prestige Recordings | Prestige | 9 PRCD-4418-2
Eric Dophy Quintet
Eric Dolphy:The Complete Prestige Recordings | Prestige | 9 PRCD-4418-2
Freddie Hubbard Orchestra
The Body And The Soul | Impulse(MCA) | 951183-2
Freddie Hubbard Septet
The Body And The Soul | Impulse(MCA) | 951183-2
George Russell Sextet
Eric Dolphy Birthday Celebration | Fantasy | FANCD 6085-2
Ezz-thetics | Original Jazz Classics | OJCCD 070-2(RLP 9375)
The Jazz Giants Play Miles Davis:Milestones | Prestige | PCD 24225-2
Gil Evans Orchestra
Verve Jazz Masters 23:Gil Evans | Verve | 521860-2
The Individualism Of Gil Evans | Verve | 833804-2
Gunther Schuller Ensemble
Beauty Is A Rare Thing:Ornette Coleman-The Complete Atlantic Recordings | Atlantic | 8122-71410-2
Jazz Artists Guild
Newport Rebels-Jazz Artists Guild | Candid | CCD 79022
John Coltrane And His Orchestra
John Coltrane:Standards | Impulse(MCA) | 549914-2
John Coltrane Quartet With Brass
The Complete Africa/Brass Sessions | Impulse(MCA) | 952168-2
John Coltrane Quartet With Eric Dolphy
John Coltrane:The Complete 1961 Village Vanguard Recordings | Impulse(MCA) | 954322-2
John Coltrane Quintet
Live At The Village Vanguard:The Master Takes | Impulse(MCA) | 951251-2
Eric Dolphy Birthday Celebration | Fantasy | FANCD 6085-2
John Coltrane Quintet With Eric Dolphy
Coltrane Spiritual | Impulse(MCA) | 589099-2
John Coltrane-Live Trane:The European Tours | Pablo | 7PACD 4433-2
John Coltrane:The Complete 1961 Village Vanguard Recordings | Impulse(MCA) | 954322-2
The Other Village Vanguard Tapes | Impulse(MCA) | MCD 04137
John Coltrane Septet With Eric Dolphy
John Coltrane:The Complete 1961 Village Vanguard Recordings | Impulse(MCA) | 954322-2
The Other Village Vanguard Tapes | Impulse(MCA) | MCD 04137
John Coltrane Sextet
Impressions | Impulse(MCA) | 543416-2
Live At The Village Vanguard:The Master Takes | Impulse(MCA) | 951251-2
John Coltrane:The Complete 1961 Village Vanguard Recordings | Impulse(MCA) | 954322-2
John Coltrane-Eric Dolphy Quartet
John Coltrane:The Complete 1961 Village Vanguard Recordings | Impulse(MCA) | 954322-2
The Other Village Vanguard Tapes | Impulse(MCA) | MCD 04137
Ken McIntyre Quintet feat.Eric Dolphy
Eric Dolphy:The Complete Prestige Recordings | Prestige | 9 PRCD-4418-2
Eric Dolphy Birthday Celebration | Fantasy | FANCD 6085-2
Mal Waldron Sextet
Eric Dolphy:The Complete Prestige Recordings | Prestige | 9 PRCD-4418-2
Eric Dolphy Birthday Celebration | Fantasy | FANCD 6085-2
The Quest | Original Jazz Classics | OJCCD 082-2(NJ 8269)
The Mal Waldron Memorial Album:Soul Eyes | Prestige | PRCD 11024-2
Max Roach All Stars
Candid Dolphy | Candid | CCD 79033
Newport Rebels
Candid Dolphy | Candid | CCD 79033
Oliver Nelson And His Orchestra
Blues And The Abstract Truth | Impulse(MCA) | 951154-2
The Roots Of Acid Jazz | Impulse(MCA) | IMP 12042
Oliver Nelson Quintet
Eric Dolphy:The Complete Prestige Recordings | Prestige | 9 PRCD-4418-2
Eric Dolphy Birthday Celebration | Fantasy | FANCD 6085-2
Straight Ahead | Original Jazz Classics | OJCCD 099-2
Oliver Nelson Sextet
Eric Dolphy:The Complete Prestige Recordings | Prestige | 9 PRCD-4418-2
Eric Dolphy Birthday Celebration | Fantasy | FANCD 6085-2
Screamin' The Blues | Original Jazz Classics | OJC 080(NJ 8243)
The Prestige Legacy Vol.2:Battles Of Saxes | Prestige | PCD 24252-2
Ornette Coleman Double Quartet
Beauty Is A Rare Thing:Ornette Coleman-The Complete Atlantic Recordings | Atlantic | 8122-71410-2
Free Jazz | Atlantic | 8122-75208-2
Ron Carter Quintet
Eric Dolphy:The Complete Prestige Recordings | Prestige | 9 PRCD-4418-2
Eric Dolphy Birthday Celebration | Fantasy | FANCD 6085-2
Where | Original Jazz Classics | OJCCD 432-2
The Latin Jazz Quintet Plus Guest: Eric Dolphy
Eric Dolphy:The Complete Prestige Recordings | Prestige | 9 PRCD-4418-2
Eric Dolphy Birthday Celebration | Fantasy | FANCD 6085-2

Dolphy,Eric[as George Lane] | (asfl)
John Coltrane Group
Olé Coltrane | Atlantic | 7567-81349-2
Olé Coltrane | Rhino | 8122-73699-2
John Coltrane Quintet With Eric Dolphy
John Coltrane-The Heavyweight Champion:The Complete Atlantic Recordings | Atlantic | 8122-71984-2
John Coltrane Sextet With Eric Dolphy
John Coltrane-The Heavyweight Champion:The Complete Atlantic Recordings | Atlantic | 8122-71984-2

Domanico,Chuck | (bel-b)
Bobby Hutcherson Orchestra
Montara | Blue Note | 590956-2
Diane Schuur Trio
In Tribute | GRP | GRP 20062
Diane Schuur With Orchestra
Love Songs | GRP | GRP 97032
The Best Of Diane Schuur | GRP | GRP 98882
Joe Sample Group
Spellbound | Rhino | 81273726-2
Roger Kellaway Cello Quartet With The A&M Symphony Orchestra
Roger Kellaway Cello Quartet | A&M Records | 9861062
Singers Unlimited With The Roger Kellaway Cello Quartet
The Singers Unlimited:Magic Voices | MPS | 539130-2

Sonny Stitt And His West Coast Friends
Art Pepper:The Hollywood All-Star Sessions | Galaxy | 5GCD 4431-2

Dominguez,Chano | (p)
Javier Paxarino Group With Glen Velez
Temurá | ACT | 9227-2
Joaquin Chacón Group
San | Fresh Sound Records | FSNT 015 CD
Markus Stockhausen Orchestra
Sol Mestizo:Markus Stockhausen Plays The Music Of Enrique Diaz | ACT | 9222-2

Dominguez,Juanjo | (g)
Juanjo Dominguez
Che Guitarra | ALISO Records | AL 1025
Internationales Guitarren Festival '94 | ALISO Records | AL 1030

Dominguez,Rodrigo | (cl,as,ssts)
Dani Perez Quartet
Buenos Aires-Barcelona Connections | Fresh Sound Records | FSNT 144 CD
Hernan Merlo Quintet
Consin | Fresh Sound Records | FSNT 150 CD

Dömling,Norbert | (computer-programming,el-bg)
Norbert Dömling
Internationales Guitarren Festival '99 | ALISO Records | AL 1038
Toto Blanke Group
Electric Circus' Best | ALISO Records | AL 1034

Domnerus,Arne | (as,bs,cl,ssts)
Arne Domnerus Quartet
Sugar Fingers | Phontastic | NCD 8831
Arne Domnerus Quintet
Sugar Fingers | Phontastic | NCD 8831
Bengt Hallberg Quartet
Hallberg's Hot Accordion In The Foreground | Phontastic | NCD 7532
Bengt-Arne Wallin Orchestra
The Birth+Rebirth Of Swedish Folk Jazz | ACT | 9254-2
Clifford Brown And Art Farmer With The Swedish All Stars
Clifford Brown Memorial | Original Jazz Classics | OJC20 017-2(P 7055)
Coleman Hawkins With The Thore Ehrlings Orchestra
Coleman Hawkins At The Golden Circle | Dragon | DRCD 265
Lars Gullin Octet
Lars Gullin 1955/56 Vol.1 | Dragon | DRCD 224
Svend Asmussen Sextet
Svend Asmussen At Slukafter | Phontastic | NCD 8804

Donahue,Sam | (tsld)
Cab Calloway And His Orchestra
Planet Jazz:Cab Calloway | Planet Jazz | 2161237-2
Planet Jazz:Male Jazz Vocalists | Planet Jazz | 2169657-2
Stan Kenton And His Orchestra
Adventures In Blues | Capitol | 520089-2
Adventures In Jazz | Capitol | 521222-2
Vic Lewis Jam Session
Vic Lewis:The Golden Years | Candid | CCD 79754
Woody Herman And His Orchestra
The Legends Of Swing | Laserlight | 24659

Donaldson,Bobby | (drperc)
Al Smith With The King Curtis Quintet
Midnight Special | Original Blues Classics | OBCCD 583-2(BV 1013)
Benny Goodman Trio
Benny Goodman-The Complete Capitol Trios | Capitol | 521225-2
Bobby Jaspar Quintet
Flute Flight | Original Jazz Classics | OJCCD 1084-2(P 2124)
Della Reese With The Sy Oliver Orchestra
Misty Blue:Sweet Sisters Swing Songs Of Sorrow And Sadness | Blue Note | 521151-2
Etta Jones And Her Band
Love Shout | Original Jazz Classics | OJCCD 941-2(P 7272)
Etta Jones With The Jerome Richardson Sextet
Hollar! | Original Jazz Classics | OJCCD 1061(PR 7284)
Frankie Laine With Buck Clayton And His Orchestra
Jazz Spectacular | CBS | CK 65507
Helen Merrill With The Quincy Jones Orchestra
Verve Jazz Masters 44:Clifford Brown and Max Roach | Verve | 528109-2
Brownie-The Complete EmArCy Recordings Of Clifford Brown | EmArCy | 838306-2
Herbie Mann-Bobby Jaspar Sextet
Flute Flight | Original Jazz Classics | OJCCD 1084-2(P 2124)
Flute Souflé | Original Jazz Classics | OJCCD 760-2(P 7101)
Jimmy Smith With The Claus Ogerman Orchestra
Any Number Can Win | Verve | 557447-2
Louis Armstrong With Sy Oliver And His Orchestra
Satchmo Serenaders | Verve | 543792-2
Sarah Vaughan With Orchestra
!Viva! Vaughan | Mercury | 549374-2
Sarah Vaughan Sings The Mancini Songbook | Verve | 558401-2
Sarah Vaughan With The Frank Foster Orchestra
The Antonio Carlos Jobim Songbook | Verve | 525472-2
Willis Jackson Sextet
At Large | Prestige | PCD 24243-2

Donaldson,Don | (p)
Sidney Bechet And His New Orleans Feetwarmers
Sidney Bechet:Summertime | Dreyfus Jazz Line | FDM 36712-2

Donaldson,Lou | (asvoc)
Art Blakey And The Jazz Messengers
A Night At Birdland Vol. 1 | Blue Note | 532146-2
A Night At Birdland Vol. 2 | Blue Note | 532147-2
Jimmy Smith All Stars
House Party | Blue Note | 524542-2
Jimmy Smith Quartet
Cool Blues | Blue Note | 535587-2
Midnight Blue(The [Be]witching Hour) | Blue Note | 854365-2
Jimmy Smith Quintet
Cool Blues | Blue Note | 535587-2
Rockin' the Boat | Blue Note | 576755-2
Lou Donaldson Orchestra
Blue Breaks Beats Vol.2 | Blue Note | 789907-2
Lou Donaldson Quartet
Mr.Shing-A-Ling | Blue Note | 784271-2
Good Gracious | Blue Note | 854325-2
Lou Donaldson Quintet
Blue Note Plays Gershwin | Blue Note | 520808-2
Midnight Creeper | Blue Note | 524546-2
Clifford Brown Memorial Album | Blue Note | 532141-2
The Natural Soul | Blue Note | 542307-2
Mr.Shing-A-Ling | Blue Note | 784271-2
Blue Bossa | Blue Note | 795590-2
The Best Of Blue Note | Blue Note | 796110-2
Blue Break Beats | Blue Note | 799106-2
The Lost Grooves | Blue Note | 831883-2
Gravy Train | Blue Note | 853357-2
Lou Donaldson Sextet
So Blue So Funky-Heroes Of The Hammond | Blue Note | 796563-2
Milt Jackson Quintet
Wizard Of The Vibes | Blue Note | 532140-2
Thelonious Monk Sextet
Genius Of Modern Music,Vol.2 | Blue Note | 532139-2
Jazz Profile:Thelonious Monk | Blue Note | 823518-2

Donaldson,Robert | (dr)
Benny Goodman And His Orchestra
Great Swing Classics In Hi-Fi | Capitol | 521223-2

Donato,Joao | (harpsichord,keyboards,org,p,cond)
Astrud Gilberto With Antonio Carlos Jobim And The Marty Paich Orchestra
The Antonio Carlos Jobim Songbook | Verve | 525472-2
Astrud Gilberto With The Marty Paich Orchestra
Verve Jazz Masters 9:Astrud Gilberto | Verve | 519824-2
Cal Tjader's Orchestra
Talkin Verve/Roots Of Acid Jazz:Cal Tjader | Verve | 531562-2

Donato,Michel | (b)

Buddy DeFranco Quartet
Lush Life | Choice | CHCD 71017

Donderer,Georg | (cello)
Till Brönner Quartet & Deutsches Symphonieorchester Berlin
German Songs | Minor Music | 801057

Donderer,Mathias | (cello)

Donegan,Dorothy | (pp-solo)
Dorothy Donegan Trio
The Many Faces Of Dorothy Donegan | Storyville | STCD 8362

Donegan,Martin | (v)
Ben Webster With Orchestra And Strings
Music For Loving:Ben Webster With Strings | Verve | 527774-2
Ultimate Ben Webster selected by James Carter | Verve | 557537-2
Harry Carney And His Orchestra With Strings
Music For Loving:Ben Webster With Strings | Verve | 527774-2

Donegan,Tony 'Lonnie' | (bj,vocg)
Chris Barber Original Jazzband Of 1954
Chris Barber:40 Years Jubilee Concert | Storyville | 4990013
Chris Barber's Jazz Band
The Very Best Of Dixieland Jazz | Verve | 535529-2
The Best Of Dixieland-Live in 1954/55 | London | 820878-2
The Golden Years Of Revival Jazz,Vol 1 | Storyville | STCD 5506
The Golden Years Of Revival Jazz,Vol.2 | Storyville | STCD 5507
The Golden Years Of Revival Jazz.Vol.3 | Storyville | STCD 5508
The Golden Years Of Revival Jazz,Vol.4 | Storyville | STCD 5509
The Golden Years Of Revival Jazz,Vol.7 | Storyville | STCD 5512
The Golden Years Of Revival Jazz,Vol.9 | Storyville | STCD 5514
The Golden Years Of Revival Jazz,Vol.11 | Storyville | STCD 5516
The Golden Years Of Revival Jazz,Vol.13 | Storyville | STCD 5518
The Golden Years Of Revival Jazz.Vol.14 | Storyville | STCD 5519
The Golden Years Of Revibal Jazz,Vol.15 | Storyville | STCD 5520
Ken Colyer Trio
The Golden Years Of Revival Jazz.Vol.3 | Storyville | STCD 5508
Ken Colyer's Jazzmen
The Very Best Of Dixieland Jazz | Verve | 535529-2
The Golden Years Of Revival Jazz,Vol 1 | Storyville | STCD 5506
The Golden Years Of Revival Jazz,Vol.7 | Storyville | STCD 5512
The Golden Years Of Revival Jazz,Vol.11 | Storyville | STCD 5516
The Golden Years Of Revival Jazz,Vol.13 | Storyville | STCD 5518
The Golden Years Of Revival Jazz.Vol.14 | Storyville | STCD 5519
The Golden Years Of Revibal Jazz,Vol.15 | Storyville | STCD 5520
Lonnie Donegan Skiffle Group
The Best Of Dixieland-Live in 1954/55 | London | 820878-2
Monty Sunshine Trio
The Very Best Of Dixieland Jazz | Verve | 535529-2
The Golden Years Of Revival Jazz.Vol.3 | Storyville | STCD 5508
The Golden Years Of Revival Jazz,Vol.11 | Storyville | STCD 5516
The Golden Years Of Revival Jazz,Vol.13 | Storyville | STCD 5518
The Golden Years Of Revibal Jazz,Vol.15 | Storyville | STCD 5520

Donelly,Ted | (tb)
Count Basie And His Orchestra
Jazz Collection:Count Basie | Laserlight | 24368
Jazz:The Essential Collection Vol.3 | IN+OUT Records | 78013-2

Donnelly,Ted | (tb)
Planet Jazz:Count Basie | Planet Jazz | 2152068-2
Planet Jazz Sampler | Planet Jazz | 2152326-2
Planet Jazz:Jimmy Rushing | RCA | 2165371-2
Planet Jazz:Jazz Greatest Hits | Planet Jazz | 2169648-2
Planet Jazz:Big Bands | Planet Jazz | 2169649-2
Jazz:The Essential Collection Vol.3 | IN+OUT Records | 78013-2

Donovan,Bob | (asfl)
Gerry Mulligan Concert Jazz Band
Verve Jazz Masters 36:Gerry Mulligan | Verve | 523342-2
Gerry Mulligan And The Concert Band At The Village Vanguard | Verve | 589488-2
The Complete Verve Gerry Mulligan Concert Band | Verve | 9860613
The Jazz Composer's Orchestra
Comminications | JCOA | 1001/2

Doof,Sal | (as)
Coleman Hawkins Trio
Jazz:The Essential Collection Vol.3 | IN+OUT Records | 78013-2

Dook Joint |
Dook Joint
Who's Been Talkin'... | Organic Music | ORGM 9728

Dook,J.C. | (g,el-gvoc)
J.C. Dook Quartet
Travelin' Man | Organic Music | ORGM 9734

Doran,Christy | (el-g,g,12-string-g,slide-gg-synth)
Albert Mangelsdorff Quartet
Shake,Shuttle And Blow | Enja | ENJ-9374 2
Christy Doran-Fredy Studer-Stephan Wittwer
Red Twist & Tuned Arrow | ECM | 1342
Christy Doran's New Bag With Muthuswamy Balasubramoniam
Black Box | double moon | CHRDM 71022
Doran/Studer/Burri/Magnenat
Musik Für Zwei Kontrabässe, Elektrische Gitarre & Schlagzeug | ECM | 1436
Freddy Studer Orchestra
Seven Songs | VeraBra Records | CDVBR 2056-2

Dörfler,Hugo | (tb)
Helmut Zacharias mit dem Orchester Frank Folken
Ich Habe Rhythmus | Bear Family Records | BCD 15642 AH

Dorge,Pierre | (comp,ld,g,arr,gong,balafon,voice)
Chinese Compass
Chinese Compass | dacapo | DCCD 9443
European Jazz Youth Orchestra
Swinging Europe 1 | dacapo | DCCD 9449
Swinging Europe 2 | dacapo | DCCD 9450
Pierre Dorge's New Jungle Orchestra
Giraf | dacapo | DCCD 9440

Dorge,Vern | (fl,asts)
Hugh Marsh Duo/Quartet/Orchestra
The Bear Walks | VeraBra Records | CDVBR 2011-2

Dorham,Kenny | (p,tpvoc)
Abbey Lincoln And Her All Stars(Newport Rebels)
Candid Dolphy | Candid | CCD 79033
Abbey Lincoln With Her Quartet
That's Him! | Original Jazz Classics | OJCCD 085-2
Abbey Lincoln With Her Quintet
Sonny Rollins-The Freelance Years:The Complete Riverside & Contemporary Recordings | Riverside | 5 RCD 4427-2
That's Him! | Original Jazz Classics | OJCCD 085-2
Abbey Lincoln With The Benny Golson Quintet
It's Magic | Original Jazz Classics | OJCCD 205-2
Abbey Lincoln With The Benny Golson Septet
It's Magic | Original Jazz Classics | OJCCD 205-2
Abbey Lincoln With The Kenny Dorham Quintet
Abbey Is Blue | Original Jazz Classics | OJC20 069-2(RLP 1153)
Andrew Hill Sextet
Point Of Departure | Blue Note | 499007-2
Art Blakey And The Jazz Messengers
Horace Silver Retrospective | Blue Note | 495576-2
At The Cafe Bohemia Vol.1 | Blue Note | 532148-2
At The Cafe Bohemia Vol.2 | Blue Note | 532149-2
Barney Wilen Quintet
Jazz In Paris:Jazz & Cinéma Vol.1 | EmArCy | 548318-2 PMS
Barry Harris Sextet
Bull's Eye! | Original Jazz Classics | OJCCD 1082-2(P 7600)
Benny Golson Sextet
The J.J.Johnson Memorial Album | Prestige | PRCD 11025-2
Cecil Taylor Quintet
Trane's Blues | Blue Note | 498240-2
Charlie Parker And His Orchestra
Charlie Parker:The Best Of The Verve Years | Verve | 527815-2
Bird: The Complete Charlie Parker On Verve | Verve | 837141-2
Charlie Parker Quintet
Charlie Parker:Bird's Best Bop On Verve | Verve | 527452-2
Charlie Parker:The Best Of The Verve Years | Verve | 527815-2

INTERPRETENVERZEICHNIS

Dorham, Kenny | (p, tpvoc)
Charlie Parker Septet
    Charlie Parker | Verve | 539757-2
Clifford Jordan Quintet
    Mosaic | Milestone | MCD 47092-2
J.J.Johnson Sextet
    The J.J.Johnson Memorial Album | Prestige | PRCD 11025-2
Jackie McLean Quintet
    Vertigo | Blue Note | 522669-2
Jazz Artists Guild
    Newport Rebels-Jazz Artists Guild | Candid | CCD 79022
Joe Henderson Quintet
    Page One | Blue Note | 498795-2
    Our Thing | Blue Note | 525647-2
    The Blue Note Years-The Best Of Joe Henderson | Blue Note | 795627-2
Kenny Clarke And His 52nd Street Boys
    Planet Jazz:Bebop | RCA | 2169650-2
Fats Navarro:Nostalgia | Dreyfus Jazz Line | FDM 36736-2
Kenny Dorham Octet
    Afro-Cuban | Blue Note | 0675619
Kenny Dorham Orchestra
    Blue Bossa | Blue Note | 795590-2
Kenny Dorham Quartet
    The Jazz Giants Play Harry Warren:Lullaby Of Broadway | Prestige | PCD 24204-2
Kenny Dorham Quintet
    Sonny Rollins-The Freelance Years:The Complete Riverside & Contemporary Recordings | Riverside | 5 RCD 4427-2
    Una Mas | Blue Note | 521228-2
    Whistle Stop | Blue Note | 525646-2
    Jazz Contrast | Original Jazz Classics | OJCCD 028-2(RLP 239)
    The Jazz Giants Play Sammy Cahn:It's Magic | Prestige | PCD 24226-2
Kenny Dorham Septet
    Cannonball Adderley Birthday Celebration | Fantasy | FANCD 6087-2
Kenny Dorham Sextet
    The Complete Round About Midnight At The Cafe Bohemia | Blue Note | 533775-2
    Jazz Contrast | Original Jazz Classics | OJCCD 028-2(RLP 239)
Matthew Gee All-Stars
    Jazz By Gee! | Original Jazz Classics | OJCCD 1884-2(RLP 221)
Max Roach Plus Four
    Clifford Brown-Max Roach:Alone Together-The Best Of The Mercury Years | Verve | 526373-2
Max Roach Quartet
    Clifford Brown-Max Roach:Alone Together-The Best Of The Mercury Years | Verve | 526373-2
Max Roach Quintet
    Dizzy Gillespie:Pleyel Jazz Concert 1948 + Max Roach Quintet 1949 | Vogue | 21409412
    Clifford Brown-Max Roach:Alone Together-The Best Of The Mercury Years | Verve | 526373-2
Max Roach Septet
    The Jazz Life! | Candid | CCD 79019
Milt Jackson Sextet
    Milt Jackson Birthday Celebration | Fantasy | FANCD 6079-2
Oliver Nelson Quintet
    Oliver Nelson Feat. Kenny Dorham | Original Jazz Classics | OJCCD 227-2(NJ 8224)
Sonny Rollins Quintet
    Sonny Rollins Plays For Bird | Original Jazz Classics | OJCCD 214-2
    Sonny Boy | Original Jazz Classics | OJCCD 348-2(P 7207)
Tadd Dameron And His Orchestra
    Fontainebleau | Original Jazz Classics | OJCCD 055-2
Thelonious Monk Sextet
    Genius Of Modern Music,Vol.2 | Blue Note | 532139-2
    Jazz Profile:Thelonious Monk | Blue Note | 823518-2

Döring, Stefan | (b-cl, as, flss)
Matthias Petzold Group With Choir
    Psalmen und Lobgesänge für Chor und Jazz-Ensemble | Indigo-Records | 1002 CD
Matthias Petzold Septett
    Ulysses | Indigo-Records | 1003 CD

Doriz, Danny | (vib)
Bill Coleman Sextet
    Americans Swinging In Paris:Bill Coleman | EMI Records | 539663-2
Lionel Hampton All Stars
    Jazz In Paris:Lionel Hampton-Ring Dem Bells | EmArCy | 159825-2 PMS
Wild Bill Davis Group
    Americans Swinging In Paris:Wild Bill Davis | EMI Records | 539665-2

Dörner, Axel | (tp)
Brass Attack
    Brecht Songs | Tutu Records | 888190-2*
Matthias Petzold Esperanto-Music
    Lifelines | Indigo-Records | 1001 CD
Matthias Petzold Group With Choir
    Psalmen und Lobgesänge für Chor und Jazz-Ensemble | Indigo-Records | 1002 CD
The Remedy
    The Remedy | Jazz Haus Musik | JHM 0069 CD

Dorothy, Rod | (el-vv)
Barbara Thompson Group
    Heavenly Bodies | VeraBra Records | CDVBR 2015-2
Barbara Thompson's Paraphernalia
    Barbara Thompson's Special Edition | VeraBra Records | CDVBR 2017-2
Jon Hiseman With The United Jazz & Rock Ensemble And Babara Thompson's Paraphernalia
    About Time Too! | VeraBra Records | CDVBR 2014-2

Dorough, Bob | (pvoc)
Miles Davis Sextet
    Sorcerer | CBS | CK 65680

Dorris, Red | (cl, ts, vocsax)
Stan Kenton And His Orchestra
    Stan Kenton-The Formative Years | Decca | 589489-2

Dörsam, Matthias | (b-cl, flsax)
Ax Genrich Group
    Psychedelic Guitar | ATM Records | ATM 3809-AH

Dorsey, Alec | (congas)
Gerry Mulligan Quintet
    Late Night Sax | CBS | 487798-2
Lou Donaldson Quintet
    Blue Bossa | Blue Note | 795590-2
    Gravy Train | Blue Note | 853357-2

Dorsey, Bob | (asts)
Jimmy Smith With The Oliver Nelson Orchestra
    Verve Jazz Masters 29:Jimmy Smith | Verve | 521855-2
    Jimmy Smith:Best Of The Verve Years | Verve | 527950-2

Dorsey, Fran | (voc)
McCoy Tyner Group With Horns And Voices
    Inner Voices | Original Jazz Classics | OJCCD 1039-2(M 9079)
McCoy Tyner Group With Voices
    Inner Voices | Original Jazz Classics | OJCCD 1039-2(M 9079)

Dorsey, George | (as, fl, reedssax)
Billie Holiday With Sy Oliver And His Orchestra
    Billie's Love Songs | Nimbus Records | NI 2000
Della Reese With The Sy Oliver Orchestra
    Misty Blue:Sweet Sisters Swing Songs Of Sorrow And Sadness | Blue Note | 521151-2
Dizzy Gillespie And His Orchestra
    Afro | Verve | 517052-2
Ella Fitzgerald With Sy Oliver And His Orchestra
    Ella Fitzgerald:The Decca Years 1949-1954 | Decca | 050668-2
Jimmy Smith With The Oliver Nelson Orchestra
    Jimmy Smith:Best Of The Verve Years | Verve | 527950-2
    Jimmy Smith-Talkin' Verve | Verve | 531563-2
Joe Williams With The Frank Hunter Orchestra
    Planet Jazz:Joe Williams | Planet Jazz | 2165370-2
Joe Williams,With The Oliver Nelson Orchestra
    Planet Jazz:Joe Williams | Planet Jazz | 2165370-2
King Curtis Band
    King Curtis-Blow Man Blow | Bear Family Records | BCD 15670 CI
Lionel Hampton And His Orchestra
    Planet Jazz:Big Bands | Planet Jazz | 2169649-2
    Lionel Hampton:Flying Home | Dreyfus Jazz Line | FDM 36735-2
Louis Armstrong And His All Stars With The Sy Oliver Orchestra
    Ambassador Louis Armstrong Vol.17:Moments To Remember(1952-1956) | Ambassador | CLA 1917
Louis Armstrong With Sy Oliver And His Orchestra
    Satchmo Serenaders | Verve | 543792-2
    Louis And The Angels | Verve | 549592-2
    Louis Armstrong-My Greatest Songs | MCA | MCD 18347
Milt Jackson Orchestra
    To Bags...With Love:Memorial Album | Pablo | 2310967-2
    Big Bags | Original Jazz Classics | OJCCD 366-2(RLP 9429)
Oscar Peterson With The Ernie Wilkins Orchestra
    Verve Jazz Masters 16:Oscar Peterson | Verve | 516320-2

Dorsey, Jimmy | (as, ld, cl, bs, ts, reedstp)
Frankie Trumbauer And His Orchestra
    Jazz:The Essential Collection Vol.2 | IN+OUT Records | 78012-2
Hoagy Carmichael And His Orchestra
    Planet Jazz:Bud Freeman | Planet Jazz | 2161240-2
Jack Teagarden With Orchestra
    Jazz:The Essential Collection Vol.3 | IN+OUT Records | 78013-2
Jimmy Dorsey And His Orchestra
    Swing Vol.1 | Storyville | 4960343
Louis Armstrong With Jimmy Dorsey And His Orchestra
    Louis Armstrong:Swing That Music | Laserlight | 36056
    Swing Legends: Louis Armstrong | Nimbus Records | NI 2012
Paul Whiteman And His Orchestra
    Planet Jazz:Jazz Trumpet | Planet Jazz | 2169654-2
Red And Miff's Stompers
    Planet Jazz:Jazz Trumpet | Planet Jazz | 2169654-2

Dorsey, Ralph | (congasperc)
Houston Person Quintet
    Trust In Me | Prestige | PCD 24264-2
Willis Jackson Sextet
    At Large | Prestige | PCD 24243-2

Dorsey, Tommy | (tb, ld, voctp)
A Jam Session At Victor
    Planet Jazz:Fats Waller | Planet Jazz | 2152058-2
    Planet Jazz:Jazz Greatest Hits | Planet Jazz | 2169648-2
All Star Band
    Planet Jazz:Jack Teagarden | Planet Jazz | 2161236-2
Bix And His Rhythm Jugglers
    Jazz:The Essential Collection Vol.2 | IN+OUT Records | 78012-2
Duke Ellington With Tommy Dorsey And His Orchestra
    Highlights From The Duke Ellington Centennial Edition | RCA | 2663672-2
Tommy Dorsey And His Clambake Seven
    Planet Jazz:Tommy Dorsey | Planet Jazz | 2159972-2
    Planet Jazz:Bud Freeman | Planet Jazz | 2161240-2
    Planet Jazz:Swing | Planet Jazz | 2169651-2
Tommy Dorsey And His Orchestra
    Planet Jazz:Frank Sinatra & Tommy Dorsey | Planet Jazz | 2152067-2
    Planet Jazz Sampler | Planet Jazz | 2152326-2
    Planet Jazz:Tommy Dorsey | Planet Jazz | 2159972-2
    Planet Jazz:Jazz Greatest Hits | Planet Jazz | 2169648-2
    Planet Jazz:Big Bands | Planet Jazz | 2169649-2
    Planet Jazz:Swing | Planet Jazz | 2169651-2
    Planet Jazz:Male Jazz Vocalists | Planet Jazz | 2169657-2
Frank Sinatra And The Tommy Dorsey Orchestra | RCA | 2668701-2

Dos Santos, Ricardo | (b)
David Jean-Baptiste Group
    The Nature Suite | Laika Records | 35101632

Doster, Michael | (b-g)
B.B.King And His Band
    Live At San Quentin | MCA | MCD 06103

Dotson, Dennis | (tpfl-h)
Woody Herman And His Orchestra
    Jazzin' Vol.2: The Music Of Stevie Wonder | Fantasy | FANCD 6088-2
    King Cobra | Original Jazz Classics | OJCCD 1068-2(F 9499)
Woody Herman And The New Thundering Herd
    Planet Jazz:Big Bands | Planet Jazz | 2169649-2
Woody Herman's Thundering Herd
    Planet Jazz:Jazz Saxophone | Planet Jazz | 2169653-2

Dotson, Hobart | (tp)
Charles Mingus Orchestra
    Charles Mingus:Pre-Bird(Mingus Revisited) | Verve | 538636-2
Gene Ammons And His Orchestra
    A Stranger In Town | Prestige | PRCD 24266-2

Dotson-Westphalen, Elizabeth | (voc-sample)
Chris Potter Group
    Traveling Mercies | Verve | 018243-2

Doty, Robert | (woodwinds)
Paul Desmond Orchestra
    Planet Jazz:Jazz Saxophone | Planet Jazz | 2169653-2
Paul Desmond With Strings
    Desmond Blue | RCA | 2663898-2

Double Trio | (Trio De Clarinettes&Arcado)
Double Trio(Trio De Clarinettes&Arcado)
    Green Dolphy Suite | Enja | ENJ-9011 2

Double You |
Double You
    Menschbilder | Jazz Haus Musik | JHM 0062 CD

Dougherty, Eddie | (dr)
Benny Morton's All Stars
    The Blue Note Swingtets | Blue Note | 495697-2
    Jazz:The Essential Collection Vol.3 | IN+OUT Records | 78013-2
Billie Holiday And Her Quintet
    Billie Holiday:The Complete Commodore Recordings | GRP | 543272-2
Billie Holiday With Frankie Newton And His Orchestra
    Billie Holiday:The Complete Commodore Recordings | GRP | 543272-2
    Billie's Love Songs | Nimbus Records | NI 2000

Dougherty, Jack | (tp)
Tommy Dorsey And His Orchestra
    Planet Jazz:Tommy Dorsey | Planet Jazz | 2159972-2

Douglas, Bill | (b, dr, flbamboo-fl)
Art Lande Quartet
    Rubisa Patrol | ECM | 1081
Art Tatum-Ben Webster Quartet
    The Art Tatum Group Masterpieces Vol.8 | Pablo | 2405431-2
    Art Tatum-The Complete Pablo Group Masterpieces | Pablo | 6 PACD 4401-2
    The Tatum Group Masterpieces Vol.8 | Pablo | PACD20 431-2
    The Jazz Giants Play Jerome Kern:Yesterdays | Prestige | PCD 24202-2
Art Tatum-Buddy DeFranco Quartet
    Art Tatum-The Complete Pablo Group Masterpieces | Pablo | 6 PACD 4401-2
Gus Mancuso Quartet
    Gus Mancuso & Special Friends | Fantasy | FCD 24762-2
Red Norvo Sextet
    Planet Jazz:Ben Webster | RCA | 2165368-2

Douglas, Bonnie | (v)
Frank Sinatra With The Count Basie Orchestra
    It Might As Well Be Spring | Reprise | 7599-27027-2

Douglas, Dave | (tp, keyboards, voc, processed-tp)
Dave Douglas Group
    Soul On Soul | RCA | 2663603-2
    Witness | RCA | 2663763-2
    The Infinite | RCA | 2663918-2
    Dave Douglas Freak In | Bluebird | 2664008-2
Dave Douglas Quartet
    A Thousand Evenings | RCA | 2663698-2
    Charms Of The Night Sky | Winter&Winter | 910015-2
Dave Douglas Tiny Bell Trio
    Wandering Souls | Winter&Winter | 910042-2
Fred Hersch Quartet
    Point In Time | Enja | ENJ-9035 2
Fred Hersch Quintet
    Point In Time | Enja | ENJ-9035 2
Patricia Barber Group
    Modern Cool | Blue Note | 521811-2
The Sidewalks Of New York
    Tin Pan Alley:The Sidewalks Of New York | Winter&Winter | 910038-2
Uri Caine Group
    Urlicht/Primal Light | Winter&Winter | 910004-2

Douglas, Freddie | (asss)
Elmo Hope Ensemble
    Sounds From Rikers Island | Fresh Sound Records | FSR CD 338

Douglas, Jerry | (dobro)
Acoustic Alchemy
    Against The Grain | GRP | GRP 97832

Douglas, Jim | (bjg)
A Salute To Eddie Condon
    A Salute To Eddie Condon | Nagel-Heyer | CD 004
    One Two Three | Nagel-Heyer | CD 008
    The First Sampler | Nagel-Heyer | NHR SP 5
Allan Vaché Swingtet
    Jazz Im Amerikahaus,Vol.3 | Nagel-Heyer | CD 013
    Ellington For Lovers | Nagel-Heyer | NH 1009
    The First Sampler | Nagel-Heyer | NHR SP 5
Great British Jazz Band
    The Great British Jazz Band:Jubilee | Candid | CCD 79720
The Alex Welsh Legacy Band
    The Sound Of Alex Vol.1 | Nagel-Heyer | CD 070
The Great British Jazz Band
    A British Jazz Odyssey | Candid | CCD 79740

Douilliez, Jean | (tbv)
Django Reinhardt With Stan Brenders Et Son Grand Orchestre
    Verve Jazz Masters 38:Django Reinhardt | Verve | 516931-2

Douparinova, Tatiana | (voc)
Sergey Strarostin's Vocal Family
    Journey | JA & RO | JARO 4226-2

Dove, Rebecca | (voc)
Mike Westbrook Brass Band
    Glad Day:Settings Of William Blake | Enja | ENJ-9376 2

Dow, Morris | (g)
Jimmy McGriff Trio
    So Blue So Funky-Heroes Of The Hammond | Blue Note | 796563-2

Dowdy, Bill | (dr)
Anita O'Day With The Three Sounds
    Verve Jazz Masters 49:Anita O'Day | Verve | 527653-2
Nat Adderley Quintet(incl.The Three Sounds)
    Branching Out | Original Jazz Classics | OJCCD 255-2(R 285)
Nat Adderley With The Three Sounds
    Branching Out | Original Jazz Classics | OJCCD 255-2(R 285)
Stanley Turrentine With The Three Sounds
    Blue Hour | Blue Note | 524586-2
    Midnight Blue(The [Be]witching Hour) | Blue Note | 854365-2
The Three Sounds
    Bottoms Up | Blue Note | 0675629
    Black Orchid | Blue Note | 821289-2

Downey, Alan | (fl-htp)
Kenny Wheeler Ensemble
    Muisc For Large & Small Ensembles | ECM | 1415/16

Downing, Will | (voc)
Christian McBride Group
    A Family Affair | Verve | 557554-2

Dozzler, Christian | (accordeon, vocharm)
Axel Zwingenberger With The Mojo Blues Band And Red Holloway
    Axel Zwingenberger And The Friends Of Boogie Woogie,Vol.8 | Vagabond | VRCD 8.93019
Champion Jack Dupree Group
    Champ's Housewarming | Vagabond | VRCD 8.88014
Hans Theessink Group
    Journey On | Minor Music | 801062

Dr.John [MacRebenack] | (el-p, g, p, voc, org, arr, percp-solo)
Hank Crawford And His Orchestra
    Roadhouse Symphony | Original Jazz Classics | OJCCD 1048-2(M 9140)
Jimmy Smith All Stars
    Jimmy Smith:Dot Com Blues | Blue Thumb | 543978-2

Draganic, Robin | (b)
Stephan Noel Lang Trio
    Echoes | Nagel-Heyer | CD 2033

Draganis, Robin | (b)
Lyambiko And Her Trio
    Out Of This Mood | Nagel-Heyer | CD 2021

Drage, Björn Andor | (p, org, harmoniumkeyboards)
Susanne Lundeng Quartet
    Waltz For The Red Fiddle | Laika Records | 35101402

Dragus, Rogdan | (v)
Abdullah Ibrahim Trio And A String Orchestra
    African Suite | TipToe | TIP-888832 2
String Orchestra
    African Suite | TipToe | TIP-888832 2

Drake, Hamid | (cymbals, dr, frame-dr, tablas, voc)
Pharoah Sanders Orchestra
    Message From Home | Verve | 529578-2

Drakes, Jesse | (tp)
Jubilee All Stars
    Jazz Gallery:Lester Young Vol.2(1946-59) | RCA | 2119541-2
Lester Young Quintet
    Jazz Gallery:Lester Young Vol.2(1946-59) | RCA | 2119541-2

Drakes, Jesse prob. | (tp)
Draper, Briscoe | (tp)
Jelly Roll Morton And His Orchestra
    Planet Jazz:Jelly Roll Morton | Planet Jazz | 2152060-2

Draper, Ray | (tuba)
Luis Gasca Group
    Jazzin' Vol.2: The Music Of Stevie Wonder | Fantasy | FANCD 6088-2
Max Roach Plus Four
    Clifford Brown-Max Roach:Alone Together-The Best Of The Mercury Years | Verve | 526373-2
Max Roach Quintet
    Deeds Not Words | Original Jazz Classics | OJC20 304-2(RLP 1122)
    The Jazz Giants Play Sammy Cahn:It's Magic | Prestige | PCD 24226-2
Max Roach Sextet
    Deeds Not Words | Original Jazz Classics | OJC20 304-2(RLP 1122)
Ray Draper Quintet
    John Coltrane-The Prestige Recordings | Prestige | 16 PCD 4405-2
Ray Draper Sextet
    Tuba Sounds | Original Jazz Classics | OJCCD 1936-2(P 7096)

Drayton, Charlie | (bb-g)
Ben Webster Quintet
    Jazz:The Essential Collection Vol.3 | IN+OUT Records | 78013-2
Billie Holiday With The JATP All Stars
    Billie Holiday Story Vol.1:Jazz At The Philharmonic | Verve | 521642-2
    The Complete Jazz At The Philharmonic On Verve 1944-1949 | Verve | 523893-2
Louis Jordan And His Tympany Five
    Louis Jordan-Let The Good Times Roll: The Complete Decca Recordings 1938-1954 | Bear Family Records | BCD 15557 IH
Louis Jordan's Elks Rendez-Vous Band
    Louis Jordan-Let The Good Times Roll: The Complete Decca Recordings 1938-1954 | Bear Family Records | BCD 15557 IH
Roger Sturgis With Lovie Jordan's Elks Rendez-Vous Band
    Louis Jordan-Let The Good Times Roll: The Complete Decca Recordings 1938-1954 | Bear Family Records | BCD 15557 IH

Drayton, Charlie or Henry Turner | (b)
Louis Jordan And His Tympany Five
    Louis Jordan-Let The Good Times Roll: The Complete Decca Recordings 1938-1954 | Bear Family Records | BCD 15557 IH

Drayton,Leslie | (ld,tpfl-h)
Jimmy Smith All Stars
Jimmy Smith:Dot Com Blues | Blue Thumb | 543978-2

Dreares,Al | (dr)
Frank Strozier Quartet
Long Night | Milestone | MCD 47095-2

Drecker,Anneli | (voc)
Ketil Bjornstad Group
Grace | EmArCy | 013622-2

Drellinger,Art | (reedsts)
Charlie Parker With Strings
Bird: The Complete Charlie Parker On Verve | Verve | 837141-2
Charlie Parker With The Joe Lipman Orchestra
Charlie Parker With Strings:The Master Takes | Verve | 523984-2
Charlie Parker Big Band | Verve | 559835-2
Louis Armstrong And Billie Holiday With Sy Oliver's Orchestra
Louis Armstrong:C'est Si Bon | Dreyfus Jazz Line | FDM 36730-2
Louis Armstrong And Ella Fitzgerald With Bob Hagger's Orchestra
Louis Armstrong:C'est Si Bon | Dreyfus Jazz Line | FDM 36730-2
Louis Armstrong With Gordon Jenkins And His Orchestra And Choir
Satchmo In Style | Verve | 549594-2
Louis Armstrong-My Greatest Songs | MCA | MCD 18347
Swing Legends:Louis Armstrong | Nimbus Records | NI 2012
Louis Armstrong With Sy Oliver And His Orchestra
Satchmo Serenaders | Verve | 543792-2
Louis Armstrong:C'est Si Bon | Dreyfus Jazz Line | FDM 36730-2
Louis Armstrong-My Greatest Songs | MCA | MCD 18347
Sarah Vaughan The The Joe Lippman Orchestra
Sarah Vaughan:Lover Man | Dreyfus Jazz Line | FDM 36739-2

Dresser,Mark | (b,bungygiffus)
Arcado-String Trio
Arcado-String Trio | JMT Edition | 919028-2
Double Trio(Trio De Clarinettes&Arcado)
Green Dolphy Suite | Enja | ENJ-9011 2
Eric Watson Quartet
Full Metal Quartet | Owl Records | 159572-2
Greetje Bijma Trio
Barefoot | Enja | ENJ-8038 2
Hank Roberts Group
Black Pastels | JMT Edition | 919016-2
John Zorn Group
Spy Vs. Spy-The Music Of Ornette Coleman | Nonesuch | 7559-60844-2
Klaus König Orchestra
Time Fragments:Seven Studies In Time And Motion | Enja | ENJ-8076 2
Klaus König Orchestra & Guests
The Song Of Songs:Oratorio For Two Solo Voices,Choir And Orchestra | Enja | ENJ-7057 2
Marty Ehrlich Group
The Long View | Enja | ENJ-9452 2
Ray Anderson Quintet
Blues Bred In The Bone | Enja | ENJ-5081 2
Ray Anderson Sextet
It Just So Happens | Enja | ENJ-5037 2
Robert Dick Group With The Soldier String Quartet
Jazz Standard On Mars | Enja | ENJ-9327 2

Dresslar,Len | (voc)
Singers Unlimited
The Singers Unlimited:Magic Voices | MPS | 539130-2
Singers Unlimited + The Oscar Peterson Trio
The Singers Unlimited:Magic Voices | MPS | 539130-2
Singers Unlimited With Orchestra
The Singers Unlimited:Magic Voices | MPS | 539130-2
Singers Unlimited With Rob McConnell And The Boss Brass
The Singers Unlimited:Magic Voices | MPS | 539130-2
Singers Unlimited With Roger Kellaway
The Singers Unlimited:Magic Voices | MPS | 539130-2
Singers Unlimited With The Art Van Damme Quintet
The Singers Unlimited:Magic Voices | MPS | 539130-2
Singers Unlimited With The Clare Fischer Orchestra
The Singers Unlimited:Magic Voices | MPS | 539130-2
Singers Unlimited With The Pat Williams Orchestra
The Singers Unlimited:Magic Voices | MPS | 539130-2
Singers Unlimited With The Patrick Williams Orchestra
The Singers Unlimited:Magic Voices | MPS | 539130-2
Singers Unlimited With The Robert Farnon Orchestra
The Singers Unlimited:Magic Voices | MPS | 539130-2
Singers Unlimited With The Roger Kellaway Cello Quartet
The Singers Unlimited:Magic Voices | MPS | 539130-2

Drew Jr.,Kenny | (pp-solo)
Daniel Schnyder Group
Words Within Music | Enja | ENJ-9369 2
Daniel Schnyder Quintet
Nucleus | Enja | ENJ-8068 2
Mingus Big Band 93
Nostalgia In Times Square | Dreyfus Jazz Line | FDM 36559-2
Paquito D'Rivera Group With The Absolute Ensemble
Habanera | Enja | ENJ-9395 2
Warren Vaché Quintet
Warren Plays Warrey | Nagel-Heyer | CD 033
Blues Of Summer | Nagel-Heyer | NH 1011

Drew,Kenny | (arr,p,el-p,org,keyboardsp-solo)
Ben Webster With The Kenny Drew Trio
The Art Of Saxophone | Laserlight | 24652
The Story Of Jazz Piano | Laserlight | 24653
Buddy DeFranco Quartet
Mr. Clarinet | Verve | 847408-2
Chet Baker Quartet
Sings/It Could Happen To You | Original Jazz Classics | OJC20 303-2
Clifford Brown All Stars
Verve Jazz Masters 44:Clifford Brown and Max Roach | Verve | 528109-2
Brownie-The Complete EmArCy Recordings Of Clifford Brown | EmArCy | 838306-2
Dexter Gordon Quartet
Dexter Gordon:Ballads | Blue Note | 796579-2
Jazz Profile:Dexter Gordon | Blue Note | 823514-2
Swiss Nights-Vol. 1 | Steeplechase | SCCD 31050
Swiss Nights Vol.2 | Steeplechase | SCCD 31090
Swiss Nights Vol.3 | Steeplechase | SCCD 31110
Dexter Gordon Quintet
Dexter Gordon:Ballads | Blue Note | 796579-2
Dexter Gordon With The Kenny Drew Trio
Loose Walk | Steeplechase | SCCD 36032
Dizzy Gillespie Quintet
Jazz In Paris:Dizzy Gillespie-The Giant | EmArCy | 159734-2 PMS
Gene Ammons Septet
Goodbye | Original Jazz Classics | OJCCD 1081-2(P 100939)
Grant Green Quartet
Ballads | Blue Note | 537560-2
John Coltrane Quartet
Trane's Blues | Blue Note | 498240-2
John Coltrane Sextet
Trane's Blues | Blue Note | 498240-2
Blue Train | Blue Note | 591721-2
The Best Of Blue Note | Blue Note | 796110-2
Blue Train(The Ultimate Blue Train) | Blue Note | 853428-0
Johnny Griffin-Art Taylor Quartet
Johnny Griffin/Art Taylor In Copenhagen | Storyville | STCD 8300
Kenn Drew Trio
Kenny Drew Trio At The Brewhouse | Storyville | 4960633
Kenny Dorham Quintet
Whistle Stop | Blue Note | 525646-2
Kenny Drew
Kenny Drew/Solo-Duo | Storyville | STCD 8274
Kenny Drew Trio
The Kenny Drew Trio | Original Jazz Classics | OJC20 065-2(RLP 224)
Kenny Drew/Niels-Henning Orsted-Pedersen Duo
Kenny Drew/Solo-Duo | Storyville | STCD 8274
Kenny Drew-Bo Stief Duo
Kenny Drew/Solo-Duo | Storyville | STCD 8274
Kenny Drew-Wilbur Ware
The Jazz Giants Play Harry Warren:Lullaby Of Broadway | Prestige | PCD 24204-2
Philip Catherine/Niels-Henning Orsted-Pedersen With The Royal Copenhagen Chamber Orchestra
Spanish Nights | Enja | ENJ-7023 2
Sonny Rollins Quartet
Sonny Rollins With The Modern Jazz Quartet | Original Jazz Classics | OJCCD 011-2
Tour De Force | Original Jazz Classics | OJCCD 095-2
Sonny Boy | Original Jazz Classics | OJCCD 348-2(P 7207)
The Prestige Legacy Vol.1:The High Priests | Prestige | PCD 24251-2
Sonny Stitt Quartet
Kaleidoscope | Original Jazz Classics | OJCCD 060-2(P 7077)
Tina Brooks Quintet
The Waiting Game | Blue Note | 540536-2

Drew,Kenny prob. | (p)
Chet Baker Quartet
Sings/It Could Happen To You | Original Jazz Classics | OJC20 303-2

Drew,Martin | (drperc)
Buddy DeFranco Meets The Oscar Peterson Quartet
Hark | Original Jazz Classics | OJCCD 867-2(2310915)
Davide Petrocca Quartet
Move | Edition Musikat | EDM 026
Freddie Hubbard-Oscar Peterson Quintet
Face To Face | Original Jazz Classics | OJCCD 937-2(2310876)
JATP All Stars
Welcome To Jazz At The Philharmonic | Fantasy | FANCD 6081-2
Joe Pass Trio
Eximious | Original Jazz Classics | OJCCD 1037-2(2310877)
Oscar Peterson Quartet
Oscar Peterson Live! | Pablo | 2310940-2
Time After Time | Pablo | 2310947-2
Oscar Peterson Plays Duke Ellington | Pablo | 2310966-2
Oscar Peterson:The Composer | Pablo | 2310970-2
The Jazz Giants Play Miles Davis:Milestones | Prestige | PCD 24225-2

Drewes,Billy | (as,ts,cl,sax,ssfl)
Bill Frisell Band
Before We Were Born | Nonesuch | 7559-60843-2
Blues Dream | Nonesuch | 7559-79615-2
Ed Neumeister Quintet
Ed Neumeister Quartet/Quintet | Timescrapper | TSCR 9614
John Scofield Groups
Groove Elation | Blue Note | 832801-2
Miriam Alter Quintet
Alter Ego | Intuition Records | INT 3258-2
Neal Kirkwood Octet
Neal Kirkwood Octet | Timescrapper | TSCR 9612
Paul Motian Band
Psalm | ECM | 1222

Drewing,Jörg | (tb,soprano-tbtuba)
Günther Klatt Quartet
Internationales Jazzfestival Münster | Tutu Records | 888110-2*

Drews,Glenn | (tpfl-h)
Woody Herman And His Orchestra
Verve Jazz Masters 54:Woody Herman | Verve | 529903-2

Drexler,Werner | (p)
Caterina Valente With The Silvio Francesco Quartet
Deutsches Jazz Fesival 1954/1955 | Bear Family Records | BCD 15430
Kurt Edelhagen All Stars
Deutsches Jazz Fesival 1954/1955 | Bear Family Records | BCD 15430
Kurt Edelhagen All Stars Und Solisten
Deutsches Jazz Fesival 1954/1955 | Bear Family Records | BCD 15430
Quartet Der Kurt Edelhagen All Stars
Deutsches Jazz Fesival 1954/1955 | Bear Family Records | BCD 15430
Silvio Francesco Quartet
Deutsches Jazz Fesival 1954/1955 | Bear Family Records | BCD 15430

Dreyfus All Stars |
Dreyfus All Stars
Dreyfus Night In Paris | Dreyfus Jazz Line | FDM 36652-2

Drinkard,Carl | (p)
Billie Holiday And Her All Stars
Billie Holiday Story Vol.4:Lady Sings The Blues | Verve | 521429-2
The Billie Holiday Song Book | Verve | 823246-2
Billie Holiday With The Carl Drinkard Trio
Misty Blue:Sweet Sisters Swing Songs Of Sorrow And Sadness | Blue Note | 521151-2
Billie's Blues | Blue Note | 748786-2

Driscoll,Kermit | (bel-b)
Bill Frisell Band
Before We Were Born | Nonesuch | 7559-60843-2
Where In The World | Nonesuch | 7559-61181-2
Johannes Mössinger New York Trio with Joe Lovano
Monk's Corner | double moon | DMCHR 71032
Robert Dick Group With The Soldier String Quartet
Jazz Standard On Mars | Enja | ENJ-9327 2
The Bill Frisell Band
Lookout For Hope | ECM | 1350(833495-2)

D'Rivera,Paquito | (as,arr,ts,cl,ss,voc,flbs)
Bebo Valdés Trio With Paquito D'Rivera
El Arte Del Sabor | Blue Note | 535193-2
Dizzy Gillespie And The United Nation Orchestra
7.Zelt-Musik-Festival:Jazz Events | Zounds | CD 2730001
Paquito D'Rivera Group With The Absolute Ensemble
Habanera | Enja | ENJ-9395 2
Paquito D'Rivera Orchestra
Jazzrock-Anthology Vol.3:Fusion | Zounds | CD 27100555

Drootin,Buzzy | (dr)
Eddie Condon All Stars
Jazz Festival Vol.1 | Storyville | 4960733
George Wein's Dixie Victors
The Magic Horn | RCA | 2113038-2
Planet Jazz | Planet Jazz | 2169652-2
The Chicago All Stars
Planet Jazz:Bud Freeman | Planet Jazz | 2161240-2

Drori,Assa | (vconcertmaster)
Diane Schuur With Orchestra And Strings
The Best Of Diane Schuur | GRP | GRP 98882
Milt Jackson And His Orchestra
Reverence And Compassion | Reprise | 9362-45204-2

Droste,Silvia | (voc)
HR Big Band
The American Songs Of Kurt Weill | hr music.de | hrmj 006-01 CD
Ulli Jünemann-Morton Ginnerup European Jazz Project
The Exhibition | Edition Collage | EC 518-2

Drouet,Jean-Pierre | (bongosperc)
Les Double Six
Les Double Six | RCA | 2164314-2

Drummond,Anne | (fl)
Kenny Barron Group With Trio De Paz
Canta Brazil | EmArCy | 017993-2

Drummond,Billy | (cymbalsdr)
Chris Potter & Jazzpar Septet
This Will Be | Storyville | STCD 4245
Chris Potter Quartet
This Will Be | Storyville | STCD 4245
Fleurine With Band And Horn Section
Meant To Be! | EmArCy | 159085-2
Franco Ambrosetti Quintet
Light Breeze | Enja | ENJ-9331 2
George Mraz Quartet
Duke's Place | Milestone | MCD 9292-2
George Mraz Trio
Duke's Place | Milestone | MCD 9292-2
Jam Session
Jam Session Vol.3 | Steeplechase | SCCD 31526
Jam Session Vol.5 | Steeplechase | SCCD 31536
Jam Session Vol.9 | Steeplechase | SCCD 31554
Jam Session Vol.10 | Steeplechase | SCCD 31555
Jim Snidero Quartet With Strings
Strings | Milestone | MCD 9326-2
Johnny King Quintet
Notes From The Underground | Enja | ENJ-9067 2
Johnny King Septet
The Meltdown | Enja | ENJ-9329 2
Marty Ehrlich Quartet
Song | Enja | ENJ-9396 2
Marty Ehrlich Quintet
Song | Enja | ENJ-9396 2
Nat Adderley Quintet
The Old Country | Enja | ENJ-7027 2
Renee Rosnes Quartet
Art & Soul | Blue Note | 499997-2
Renee Rosnes Trio
Art & Soul | Blue Note | 499997-2

Drummond,Ray | (bpiccolo-b)
Gary Bartz Quintet
West 42nd Street | Candid | CCD 79049
Harry Edison Sextet
Swing Summit | Candid | CCD 79050
Johnny Griffin Quartet
Jazz Life Vol.1:From Village Vanguard | Storyville | 4960753
Kenny Barron Trio
Live at Bradley's | EmArCy | 549099-2
Kevin Mahogany With Orchestra
Songs And Moments | Enja | ENJ-8072 2
Tom Harrell Quintet
Visions | Contemporary | CCD 14063-2
Sail Away | Original Jazz Classics | OJCCD 1095-2(C- 14054-2)
Tom Harrell Sextet
Visions | Contemporary | CCD 14063-2
Sail Away | Original Jazz Classics | OJCCD 1095-2(C- 14054-2)
Toots Thielemans Quartet
Toots Thielemans:The Live Takes Vol.1 | IN+OUT Records | 77041-2

Dryden,Jon | (keyboards,synthp)
Bop City
Hot Jazz Bisquits | Hip Bop | HIBD 8801
Lenny White Group
Present Tense | Hip Bop | HIBD 8004
Renderers Of Spirit | Hip Bop | HIBD 8014
Hot Jazz Bisquits | Hip Bop | HIBD 8801
Urbanator
Urbanator II | Hip Bop | HIBD 8012
Hot Jazz Bisquits | Hip Bop | HIBD 8801

Dryfus,Karen | (viola)
A Band Of Friends
Wynton Marsalis Quartet With Strings | CBS | CK 68921

Du Bois,Alain | (bg)
Benny Carter And His Orchestra
The Art Of Saxophone | Laserlight | 24652
Hot Mallets
Hot Mallets...Live! | JHM Records | JHM 3610
Lucien Barbarin With The Henri Chaix Trio
Trombone Tradition | Jazz Connaisseur | JCCD 8803-2

Du Vall,Tomas | (perc)
Max Roach Group
We Insist: Freedom Now Suite | Candid | CCD 79002

Duarte,Cassio | (perc)
Duo Fenix
Karai-Eté | IN+OUT Records | 7009-2

Dubé,Sebastién | (b)
Jonas Knutsson Quartet
Jonas Knutsson Quartet | Touché Music | TMcCD 018

DuBuclet,John | (tb)
Big Band Bellaterra
Don't Git Sassy | Fresh Sound Records | FSNT 048 CD

Dubuis,Lucien | (as)
European Jazz Youth Orchestra
Swinging Europe 1 | dacapo | DCCD 9449
Swinging Europe 2 | dacapo | DCCD 9450

Duchaussoir,Rene | (g)
Stephane Grappelli Sextet
Grapelli Story | Verve | 515807-2

Duchemin,Philippe | (p)
Frank Wess Meets The Paris-Barcelona Swing Connection
Paris-Barcelona Connection | Fresh Sound Records | FSNT 002 CD

Ducret,Marc | (12-string-g,el-g,bar-el-g)
Bobby Previte's Latin For Travelers
Dangerous Rip | Enja | ENJ-9324-2
My Man In Sidney | Enja | ENJ-9348 2
Christoph Lauer Quintet
Fragile Network | ACT | 9266-2
Hans Lüdemann Rism
Unitarism | Jazz Haus Musik | JHM 0067 CD
Hans Lüdemann Rism 7
FutuRISM | Jazz Haus Musik | JHM 0092/93 CD
Klaus König Orchestra & Guests
The Song Of Songs:Oratorio For Two Solo Voices,Choir And Orchestra | Enja | ENJ-7057 2
Louis Sclavis Quartet
Acoustic Quartet | ECM | 1526
Marc Ducret
Detail | Winter&Winter | 910003-2
Marc Ducret-Bobby Previt
In The Grass | Enja | ENJ-9343 2
Tim Berne-Marc Ducret-Tom Rainey
Big Satan | Winter&Winter | 910005-2
Vincent Courtois Trio
The Fitting Room | Enja | ENJ-9411 2

Dudas,Lajos | (as,cl,electronics,cl-solo,ssts)
Lajos Dudas Group
Jubilee Edition | double moon | CHRDM 71020
Lajos Dudas Quartet
Jubilee Edition | double moon | CHRDM 71020
Nightlight | double moon | DMCHR 71030
Lajos Dudas Quintet
Talk Of The Town | double moon | CHRDM 71012
Jubilee Edition | double moon | CHRDM 71020
Some Great Songs | double moon | DMCD 1005-2
Nightlight | double moon | DMCHR 71030
Lajos Dudas Sextet
Talk Of The Town | double moon | CHRDM 71012
Lajos Dudas Trio
Talk Of The Town | double moon | CHRDM 71012
Jubilee Edition | double moon | CHRDM 71020
Mihaly Tabany Orchestra
Jubilee Edition | double moon | CHRDM 71020
Radio Jazzgroup Frankfurt
Jubilee Edition | double moon | CHRDM 71020

Dudash,Stephan | (g,vvoc)
Dave Brubeck With The Erich Kunzel Orchestra
Truth Is Fallen | Atlantic | 7567-80761-2

Dudek,Gerd | (cl,fl,bs,bcl,ss,ts,shanai,shenai)
Berlin Contemporary Jazz Orchestra
Berlin Contemporary Jazz Orchestra | ECM | 1409
Dudek-Van Den Broek-Haurand
Pulque | Konnex Records | KCD 5055
Crossing Level | Konnex Records | KCD 5077
European Jazz Ensemble
European Jazz Ensemble At The Philharmonic Cologne | M.A Music | A 800-2
20th Anniversary Tour | Konnex Records | KCD 5078
European Jazz Ensemble 25th Anniversary | Konnex Records | KCD 5100

European Jazz Ensemble & The Khan Family feat. Joachim Kühn
European Jazz Ensemble Meets The Khan Family | M.A Music | A 807-2
Henning Wolter Trio With Gerd Dudek
Two Faces | double moon | DMCD 1003-2
Henning Wolter Trio With Guests
Years Of A Trilogy | double moon | DMCHR 71021
Knut Kiesewetter With The Dieter Reith Orchestra
Reith On! | MPS | 557423-2
Lajos Dudas Quintet
Nightlight | double moon | DMCHR 71030
Paul Eßer-Gerd Dudek-Ali Haurand-Jiri Strivin
Jazz Und Lyrik:Schinderkarren Mit Buffet | Konnex Records | KCD 5108
The Quartet
Crossing Level | Konnex Records | KCD 5077
The Quartet Live In Prague | P&J Music | P&J 101-1 CD

Dudley,Eddie | (tb)
Jack Teagarden And His Orchestra
Jazz:The Essential Collection Vol.3 | IN+OUT Records | 78013-2

Dudli,Joris | (dr,perctama-dr)
Johnny Griffin-Sal Nistico-Roman Schwaller Sextet
Three Generations Of Tenorsaxophone | JHM Records | JHM 3611
Karl Ratzer Quintet
All The Way | Enja | ENJ-9448 2
Klaus Ignatzek Group
Day For Night | Nabel Records:Jazz Network | CD 4639
Klaus Ignatzek Quintet
Today Is Tomorrow/Live In Leverkusen | Nabel Records:Jazz Network | CD 4654

Dudman,Colin | (el-p,synthkeyboards)
Barbara Thompson's Paraphernalia
Mother Earth | VeraBra Records | CDVBR 2005-2
Barbara Thompson's Special Edition | VeraBra Records | CDVBR 2017-2

Dudziak,Urszula | (perc,voc,voice,synth,electronics)
Chico Freeman And Brainstorm
Threshold | IN+OUT Records | 7022-2
Urszula Dudziak
Jazz Unlimited | IN+OUT Records | 7017-2
Urszula Dudziak And Band Walk Away
Magic Lady | IN+OUT Records | 7008-2
Walkaway With Urszula Dudziak
Saturation | IN+OUT Records | 77024-2

Duell,Shela | (voc)
Tom Browne Groups
Mo' Jamaica Funk | Hip Bop | HIBD 8002

Dufort,Russ | (dr)
Oscar Peterson Trio
This Is Oscar Peterson | RCA | 2663990-2

Dufour,Christian | (viola)
Charlie Haden Quartet West With Strings
Now Is The Hour | Verve | 527827-2

Duke T. | (rap)
Reiner Witzel Group
Passage To The Ear | Nabel Records:Jazz Network | CD 4668

Duke,David | (fr-h)
Bobby Bryant Orchestra
Deep Blue-The United States Of Mind | Blue Note | 521152-2
Ella Fitzgerald With Orchestra
The Best Is Yet To Come | Original Jazz Classics | OJCCD 889-2(2312138)
Singers Unlimited With The Patrick Williams Orchestra
The Singers Unlimited:Magic Voices | MPS | 539130-2

Duke,Douglas | (orgp)
(Little)Jimmy Scott With The Lionel Hampton Orchestra
Everybody's Somebody's Fool | Decca | 050669-2
Lionel Hampton And His Orchestra
Lionel Hampton:Flying Home | Dreyfus Jazz Line | FDM 36735-2

Duke,George | (clavinet,el-p,synth,voc,grand-p)
Billy Cobham Group
The Best Of Billy Cobham | Atlantic | 7567-81558-2
Cannonball Adderley Group
Phenix | Fantasy | FCD 79004-2
Cannonball Adderley Sextet
Cannonball Adderley Birthday Celebration | Fantasy | FANCD 6087-2
Christian McBride Group
A Family Affair | Verve | 557554-2
Eddie Henderson Orchestra
Blue Breaks Beats Vol.2 | Blue Note | 789907-2
Flora Purim And Her Quartet
Joe Henderson:The Milestone Years | Milestone | 8MCD 4413-2
Flora Purim And Her Quintet
Joe Henderson:The Milestone Years | Milestone | 8MCD 4413-2
Flora Purim And Her Sextet
Joe Henderson:The Milestone Years | Milestone | 8MCD 4413-2
Butterfly Dreams | Original Jazz Classics | OJCCD 315-2
Flora Purim With Orchestra
Joe Henderson:The Milestone Years | Milestone | 8MCD 4413-2
George Duke Group
Jazzrock-Anthology Vol.3:Fusion | Zounds | CD 27100555
Joe Henderson And His Orchestra
Joe Henderson:The Milestone Years | Milestone | 8MCD 4413-2
Joe Henderson Group
Jazzin' Vol.2: The Music Of Stevie Wonder | Fantasy | FANCD 6088-2
Joe Williams With The Cannonball Adderley Sextet
Cannonball Adderley Birthday Celebration | Fantasy | FANCD 6087-2
Lenny White Group
Renderers Of Spirit | Hip Bop | HIBD 8014
Miles Davis Group
Tutu | Warner | 7599-25490-2
Amandla | Warner | 7599-25873-2
Nat Adderley Group
Soul Of The Bible | Capitol | 358257-2
Sonny Rollins Quartet
Easy Living | Original Jazz Classics | OJCCD 893-2
Sonny Rollins Quintet
Easy Living | Original Jazz Classics | OJCCD 893-2
Sonny Rollins Sextet
Jazzin' Vol.2: The Music Of Stevie Wonder | Fantasy | FANCD 6088-2
Easy Living | Original Jazz Classics | OJCCD 893-2
Stanley Clarke Group
If This Bass Could Only Talk | CBS | 460883-2

Duke,John | (b)
Bobby Bryant Orchestra
Deep Blue-The United States Of Mind | Blue Note | 521152-2
Count Basie And His Orchestra
Fun Time | Pablo | 2310945-2
Jazz Dance | Original Jazz Classics | OJCCD 1002-2(1210890)
I Told You So | Original Jazz Classics | OJCCD 824-2(2310767)
The Jazz Giants Play Harry Warren:Lullaby Of Broadway | Prestige | PCD 24204-2
Count Basie Big Band
Montreux '77 | Original Jazz Classics | OJCCD 377-2

Dukes,Joe | (dr)
George Benson With The Jack McDuff Quartet
The New Boss Guitar | Original Jazz Classics | OJCCD 461-2
Jack McDuff Orchestra
The Last Goodun' | Prestige | PRCD 24274-2
Jack McDuff Quartet
Brother Jack Meets The Boss | Original Jazz Classics | OJCCD 326-2(P 7228)
Screamin' | Original Jazz Classics | OJCCD 875-2(P 7259)
Silken Soul | Prestige | PCD 24242-2
The Soulful Drums | Prestige | PCD 24256-2
The Concert McDuff | Prestige | PRCD 24270-2
The Last Goodun' | Prestige | PRCD 24274-2
Jack McDuff:The Prestige Years | Prestige | PRCD 24387-2
Jack McDuff Quartet With Gene Ammons
Brother Jack Meets The Boss | Original Jazz Classics | OJCCD 326-2(P 7228)
Jack McDuff Quartet With Orchestra
Moon Rappin' | Blue Note | 538697-2
Prelude:Jack McDuff Big Band | Prestige | PRCD 24283-2
Jack McDuff Quintet
Silken Soul | Prestige | PCD 24242-2
The Last Goodun' | Prestige | PRCD 24274-2
Jack McDuff:The Prestige Years | Prestige | PRCD 24387-2
Jack McDuff Sextet
Silken Soul | Prestige | PCD 24242-2
The Soulful Drums | Prestige | PCD 24256-2
Jack McDuff Trio
The Last Goodun' | Prestige | PRCD 24274-2
Lonnie Smith Quintet
Deep Blue-The United States Of Mind | Blue Note | 521152-2

Dulisch,Frank | (tp)
Bigband Der Musikschule Der Stadt Brühl Mit Gastsolisten
Pangäa | Indigo-Records | 1004 CD

Dumas,Tony | (b,el-bdr)
Art Pepper Quartet
Art Pepper:The Complete Galaxy Recordings | Galaxy | 16GCD 1016-2
No Limit | Original Jazz Classics | OJCCD 411-2
Art Pepper Trio
Art Pepper:The Complete Galaxy Recordings | Galaxy | 16GCD 1016-2
Frank Morgan Quartet
Easy Living | Original Jazz Classics | OJCCD 833-2(C 14013)
J.J.Johnson-Nat Adderley Quintet
Yokohama Concert Vol.2:Chain Reaction | Pablo | PACD 2620121-2
The J.J.Johnson Memorial Album | Prestige | PRCD 11025-2
Jack Sheldon And His West Coast Friends
Art Pepper:The Hollywood All-Star Sessions | Galaxy | 5GCD 4431-2
Joe Henderson Quartet
Relaxin' At Camarillo | Original Jazz Classics | OJCCD 776-2(C 14006)

Dumont,Jack | (ascl)
Ella Fitzgerald And Louis Armstrong With Dave Barbour And His Orchestra
Ella Fitzgerald:Mr.Paganini | Dreyfus Jazz Line | FDM 36741-2
Peggy Lee With The Benny Goodman Orchestra
Peggy Lee & Benny Goodman:The Complete Recordings 1941-1947 | CBS | C2K 65686

Dumont,John | (asts)
Louis Armstrong With The Hal Mooney Orchestra
Ambassador Louis Armstrong Vol.17:Moments To Remember(1952-1956) | Ambassador | CLA 1917

Dumont,Pierre | (fr-h)
Raymond Fol Big Band
Jazz In Paris:Raymond Fol-Les 4 Saisons | EmArCy | 548791-2

Dunbar,Ted | (g)
Bernard Purdie Group
Jazzin' With The Soul Brothers | Fantasy | FANCD 6086-2
David Fathead Newman Quintet Plus Clifford Jordan
Blue Head | Candid | CCD 79041
Gil Evans Orchestra
Svengali | Rhino | 8122-73720-2
Tony Williams Lifetime
Ego | Verve | 559512-2

Duncan,Al | (dr)
Buddy Guy Blues Band
Buddy Guy-The Complete Chess Studio Recordings | MCA | MCD 09337

Duncan,Christine | (voc)
The United Women's Orchestra
The Blue One | Jazz Haus Musik | JHM 0099 CD

Duncan,Hank | (p)
New Orleans Feetwarmers
Planet Jazz | Planet Jazz | 2169652-2
Jazz:The Essential Collection Vol.1 | IN+OUT Records | 78011-2

Duncan,Henry | (drp)
Roland Kirk Quartet
Domino | Verve | 543833-2
Rahsaan/The Complete Mercury Recordings Of Roland Kirk | Mercury | 846630-2

Duncan,Molly | (ts)
Klaus Doldinger With Orchestra
Lifelike | Warner | 2292-46478-2

Dunham,Sonny | (tptb)
All Star Band
Planet Jazz:Jack Teagarden | Planet Jazz | 2161236-2
Louis Armstrong With The Casa Loma Orchestra
Louis Armstrong:Swing That Music | Laserlight | 36056

Dunlap,Gene | (dr)
Earl Klugh Trio
The Earl Klugh Trio Volume One | Warner | 7599-26750-2

Dunlop,Frankie | (drperc)
Charles Mingus Orchestra
Tijuana Moods(The Complete Edition) | RCA | 2663840-2
Joe Zawinul Quartet
To You With Love | Fresh Sound Records | Strand SLS CD 1007
Joe Zawinul Trio
To You With Love | Fresh Sound Records | Strand SLS CD 1007
Ray Crawford Sextet
Smooth Groove | Candid | CCD 79028
Sonny Rollins Orchestra
Alfie | Impulse(MCA) | 951224-2
Thelonious Monk And His Orchestra
Greatest Hits | CBS | CK 65422
Thelonious Monk Quartet
Monk At Newport 1963 & 1965 | CBS | C2K 63905
Monk's Dream | CBS | CK 63536
Greatest Hits | CBS | CK 65422
Thelonious Monk:85th Birthday Celebration | zyx records | FANCD 6076-2
Thelonious Monk In Italy | Original Jazz Classics | OJCCD 488-2(RLP 9443)
Monk In France | Original Jazz Classics | OJCCD 670-2
Thelonious Monk In Copenhagen | Storyville | STCD 8283
Thelonious Monk Quartet With Pee Wee Russell
Monk At Newport 1963 & 1965 | CBS | C2K 63905

Dunmall,Paul | (cl,ss,ts,border-pipes,ocarina)
Robin Williamson Group
Skirting The River Road | ECM | 1785(016372-2

Dunn,Donald 'Duck' | (bb-g)
Albert King Blues Band
Lovejoy | Stax | SCD 8517-2(STS 2040)

Dunne,Paul | (el-gg)
Barbara Thompson Group
Heavenly Bodies | VeraBra Records | CDVBR 2015-2
Barbara Thompson's Paraphernalia
A Cry From The Heart | VeraBra Records | CDVBR 2021-2

Dunson,Claude | (btp)
Joe Turner-Claude Dunson
The Giant Of Stride Piano In Switzerland | Jazz Connaisseur | JCCD 9106-2

Dunstan,Wayne | (as,bass-sax,bsts)
Stan Kenton And His Orchestra
Adventures In Blues | Capitol | 520089-2
Adventures In Jazz | Capitol | 521222-2
Stan Kenton Orchestra
Stompin' At Newport | Pablo | PACD 5312-2

Dunwoodie,Colin | (fl,b-cl,ss,asts)
Colin Dunwoodie Quartet
Glad To See You | Edition Collage | EC 460-2
Wind Moments | Take Twelve On CD | TT 009-2

Duo Fenix |
Duo Fenix
Karai-Eté | IN+OUT Records | 7009-2

Duppler,Lars | (p)
European Jazz Youth Orchestra
Swinging Europe 3 | dacapo | DCCD 9461
Lars Duppler Quartet
Palindrome | Jazz Haus Musik | JHM 0108 CD
Lars Duppler Sextet
Palindrome 6tet | Jazz Haus Musik | JHM 0131 CD

Dupree,Champion Jack | (g,vocp)
Axel Zwingenberger With Champion Jack Dupree & Torsten Zwingenberger
Axel Zwingenberger & The Friends Of Boogie Woogie Vol.6 | Vagabond | VRLP 8.90016
Champion Jack Dupree
Champion Jack Dupree | Storyville | 4960383
Champion Jack Dupree Group
Champ's Housewarming | Vagabond | VRCD 8.88014
Champion Jack Dupree-Axel Zwingenberger Group
Axel Zwingenberger And The Friends Of Boogie Woogie Vol.7: Champion Jack Dupree Sings Blues Classics | Vagabond | VRCD 8.92018

Dupree,Cornell | (el-gg)
Archie Shepp Orchestra
The Cry Of My People | Impulse(MCA) | 9861488
Bernard Purdie's Soul To Jazz
Bernard Purdie's Soul To Jazz II | ACT | 9253-2
Billy Cobham Group
The Best Of Billy Cobham | Atlantic | 7567-81558-2
Bobby Hutcherson Orchestra
Deep Blue-The United States Of Mind | Blue Note | 521152-2
Buddy Rich Big Band
Backwoods Siseman/Pieces Of Dream | Laserlight | 24655
Carla Bley Band
Dinner Music | Watt | 6(825815-2)
Gene Harris And The Three Sounds
Deep Blue-The United States Of Mind | Blue Note | 521152-2
Grant Green Orchestra
Grant Green:Blue Breakbeat | Blue Note | 494705-2
Grant Green With Orchestra
The Final Comedown(Soundtrack) | Blue Note | 581678-2
Grover Washington Jr. Orchestra
Jazzrock-Anthology Vol.3:Fusion | Zounds | CD 27100555
Hank Crawford-Jimmy McGriff Quartet
Jazzin' With The Soul Brothers | Fantasy | FANCD 6086-2
King Curtis Band
King Curtis-Blow Man Blow | Bear Family Records | BCD 15670 CI
Les McCann Group
Atlantic Jazz: Fusion | Atlantic | 7567-81711-2
Oscar Brown Jr. And His Group
Movin' On | Rhino | 8122-73678-2
Rahsaan Roland Kirk And His Orchestra
Blacknuss | Rhino | 8122-71408-2

Dupuis,Laurence | (v)
Charlie Haden Quartet West With Strings
Now Is The Hour | Verve | 527827-2
Stephane Grappelli With The Michel Legrand Orchestra
Grapelli Story | Verve | 515807-2

Duran,Carlos | (b)
Cal Tjader Quintet
Tjader Plays Mambo | Original Jazz Classics | OJCCD 274-2(F 3221)
The Jazz Giants Play Sammy Cahn:It's Magic | Prestige | PCD 24226-2
Cal Tjader Sextet
Cal Tjader's Latin Kick | Original Jazz Classics | OJCCD 642-2(F 8033)
Cal Tjader's Modern Mambo Quintet(Sextet)
Mambo With Tjader | Original Jazz Classics | OJCCD 271-2(F 3202)
Cal Tjader's Orchestra
Tjader Plays Mambo | Original Jazz Classics | OJCCD 274-2(F 3221)

Duran,Eddie | (g)
Benny Goodman Quintet
Verve Jazz Masters 33:Benny Goodman | Verve | 844410-2
Cal Tjader Quartet
Cal Tjader Plays Jazz | Original Jazz Classics | OJCCD 986-2(F 3-211)
Earl Hines Quartet
Another Monday Date | Prestige | PRCD 24043-2
Gus Mancuso Quartet
Gus Mancuso & Special Friends | Fantasy | FCD 24762-2
Ron Crotty Trio
The Jazz Scene:San Francisco | Fantasy | FCD 24760-2
Stan Getz-Cal Tjader Sextet
Stan Getz With Cal Tjader | Original Jazz Classics | OJC20 275-2(F 3266)
Vince Guaraldi Group
Charlie Brown's Holiday Hits | Fantasy | FCD 9682-2
Vince Guaraldi Trio
Vince Guaraldi Trio | Original Jazz Classics | OJC20 149-2(F 3225)

Duran,Hilario | (pkeyboards)
Lazaro Ros Ensemble
Ori Batá (Cuban Yoruba Music) | Enja | ENJ-9381 2

Duran,Manny | (tpfl-h)
Machito And His Orchestra
Afro-Cuban Jazz Moods | Original Jazz Classics | OJC20 447-2

Duran,Manuel | (pclaves)
Cal Tjader Quintet
Tjader Plays Mambo | Original Jazz Classics | OJCCD 274-2(F 3221)
The Jazz Giants Play Sammy Cahn:It's Magic | Prestige | PCD 24226-2
Cal Tjader Sextet
Cal Tjader's Latin Kick | Original Jazz Classics | OJCCD 642-2(F 8033)
Cal Tjader's Modern Mambo Quintet(Sextet)
Mambo With Tjader | Original Jazz Classics | OJCCD 271-2(F 3202)
Cal Tjader's Orchestra
Tjader Plays Mambo | Original Jazz Classics | OJCCD 274-2(F 3221)

Duran,Modesto | (congas,bongos,percconga)
Ella Fitzgerald With Orchestra
Ella/Things Ain't What They Used To Be | Warner | 9362-47875-2
Gerald Wilson And His Orchestra
Blue Breaks Beats Vol.2 | Blue Note | 789907-2

Duret,Lea | (cello)
Abdullah Ibrahim Trio And A String Orchestra
African Suite | TipToe | TIP-888832 2
String Orchestra
African Suite | TipToe | TIP-888832 2

Durham,Allen | (tb)
Lionel Hampton And His Orchestra
Lionel Hampton:Flying Home | Dreyfus Jazz Line | FDM 36735-2

Durham,Bobby | (dr)
All Stars
Alternate Blues | Original Jazz Classics | OJCCD 744-2
Benny Carter And His Orchestra
Jazz At The Philharmonic:The Montreux Collection | Pablo | PACD 5306-2
Ella Fitzgerald And Her All Stars
All That Jazz | Pablo | 2310938-2
Ella Fitzgerald With The Tommy Flanagan Quartet
Bluella:Ella Fitzgerald Sings The Blues | Pablo | 2310960-2
Ella In London | Original Jazz Classics | OJCCD 974-2(2310711)
Ella Fitzgerald With The Tommy Flanagan Trio
Bluella:Ella Fitzgerald Sings The Blues | Pablo | 2310960-2
Jazz Collection:Ella Fitzgerald | Laserlight | 24397
Jazzin' Vol.2: The Music Of Stevie Wonder | Fantasy | FANCD 6088-2
Montreux '77 | Original Jazz Classics | OJC20 376-2(2308206)
Ella-At The Montreux Jazz Festival 1975 | Original Jazz Classics | OJC20 789-2(2310751)
Jazz At The Philharmonic:The Montreux Collection | Pablo | PACD 5306-2
Harry Edison Sextet
Swing Summit | Candid | CCD 79050
JATP All Stars
Welcome To Jazz At The Philharmonic | Fantasy | FANCD 6081-2
Joe Pass Trio
Joe Pass:Guitar Virtuoso | Pablo | 4 PACD 4423-2
Johnny Hodges-Wild Bill Davis Sextet
Planet Jazz:Johnny Hodges | Planet Jazz | 2152065-2

Oscar Peterson Jam
Oscar Peterson Plays Duke Ellington | Pablo | 2310966-2
Montreux '77 | Original Jazz Classics | OJC 385(2620105)
Montreux '77 | Original Jazz Classics | OJC20 378-2(2308208)
Oscar Peterson Quartet
Paris Jazz Concert:Oscar Peterson | Laserlight | 36155
Oscar Peterson Trio
Oscar Peterson Plays Duke Ellington | Pablo | 2310966-2
Paris Jazz Concert:Oscar Peterson | Laserlight | 36155
Three Originals:Motion&Emotions/Tristeza On Piano/Hello Herbie | MPS | 521059-2
Exclusively For My Friends-The Lost Tapes | MPS | 529096-2
Tristeza On Piano | MPS | 817489-2 PMS
Oscar Peterson Trio With Herb Ellis
Three Originals:Motion&Emotions/Tristeza On Piano/Hello Herbie | MPS | 521059-2
Hello Herbie | MPS | 821846-2
Oscar Peterson Trio With The Claus Ogermann Orchestra
Three Originals:Motion&Emotions/Tristeza On Piano/Hello Herbie | MPS | 521059-2
The Antonio Carlos Jobim Songbook | Verve | 525472-2
Pablo All Star Jam
Montreux '77 | Original Jazz Classics | OJC 385(2620105)
Roy Eldridge 4
Montreux '77 | Original Jazz Classics | OJCCD 373-2
Sonny Stitt Quartet
The Art Of Saxophone | Laserlight | 24652
The Basie Alumni
Swinging For The Count | Candid | CCD 79724
The Trumpet Summit With The Oscar Peterson Big 4
The Trumpet Summit Meets The Oscar Peterson Big 4 | Original Jazz Classics | OJCCD 603-2
Tommy Flanagan 3
Montreux '77 | Original Jazz Classics | OJC 372(2308202)

Durham,Eddie | (arr,el-gtb)
Benny Moten's Kansas City Orchestra
Planet Jazz:Ben Webster | RCA | 2165368-2
Planet Jazz:Jimmy Rushing | RCA | 2165371-2
Planet Jazz:Swing | Planet Jazz | 2169651-2
Jazz:The Essential Collection Vol.3 | IN+OUT Records | 78013-2
Count Basie And His Orchestra
Jazz:The Essential Collection Vol.3 | IN+OUT Records | 78013-2
Harry James And His Orchestra
The Legends Of Swing | Laserlight | 24659
Kansas City Six
Jazz:The Essential Collection Vol.3 | IN+OUT Records | 78013-2

Düring,Peter | (vibperc)
The Crossover Ensemble With The Zapolski Quartet
Helios Suite | dacapo | DCCD 9459

Düringer,Roland | (b)
Lilly Thornton With The Mike Hennesey Trio
Remembering Dinah-A Salute To Dinah Washington | Hot Shot Records | HSR 8313-2

Dürst,Thomas | (bperc)
Peter Schärli Quintet With Glenn Ferris
Willisau And More Live | Creative Works Records | CW CD 1020-2
Drei Seelen/Three Souls | Creative Works Records | MIWI 1014-2

Duru,Baba | (tabla)
Herbie Hancock Group
Sunlight | CBS | 486570-2

Duryea,Andy | (tb)
Dizzy Gillespie And His Orchestra
Planet Jazz:Dizzy Gillespie | Planet Jazz | 2152069-2
Planet Jazz:Bebop | RCA | 2169650-2
Planet Jazz:Male Jazz Vocalists | Planet Jazz | 2169657-2

DuShon,Jean | (voc)
Jack McDuff Quartet With Orchestra
Moon Rappin' | Blue Note | 538697-2

Duskin,Big Joe | (voc)
Axel Zwingenberger With Big Joe Duskin
Kansas City Boogie Jam | Vagabond | VRCD 8.00027

Duss,Xavier | (oboe)
Miles Davis With Gil Evans Orchestra, The George Gruntz Concert Jazz Band And Guests
Miles & Quincy Live At Montreux | Warner | 9362-45221-2

Dutch Swing College Band |
Dutch Swing College Band
Swinging Studio Sessons | Philips | 824256-2 PMS
Digital Anniversary | Philips | 824585-2 PMS
Dutch Swing College Band Live In 1960 | Philips | 838765-2
Rita Reys With The Dutch Swing College Band
The Very Best Of Dixieland Jazz | Verve | 535529-2

Dutrey,Honore | (tb)
King Oliver's Creole Jazz Band
Jazz:The Essential Collection Vol.1 | IN+OUT Records | 78011-2
King Oliver's Jazz Band
Jazz:The Essential Collection Vol.1 | IN+OUT Records | 78011-2

Dutt,Hank | (viola)
John Zorn Group With The Kronos Quartet
Spillane | Nonesuch | 7559-79172-2

Dutton,Fred | (bbassoon)
Chamber Jazz Sextet
Plays Pal Joey | Candid | CCD 79030
Miles Davis With Gil Evans & His Orchestra
Quiet Nights | CBS | CK 65293
Stan Getz With Orchestra
Stan Getz Highlights | Verve | 847430-2

DuVernay-Shipman,Kevin | (bvoc)
Dook Joint
Who's Been Talkin'... | Organic Music | ORGM 9728

Duvivier,George | (b,arrceleste)
Anita O'Day With The Gary McFarland Orchestra
All The Sad Youn Men | Verve | 517065-2
Antonio Carlos Jobim With The Claus Ogerman Orchestra
The Composer Of 'Desafinado' Plays | Verve | 521431-2
Arnett Cobb Quintet
Smooth Sailing | Original Jazz Classics | OJCCD 323-2
Ben Webster With Orchestra And Strings
Music For Loving:Ben Webster With Strings | Verve | 527774-2
Ultimate Ben Webster selected by James Carter | Verve | 557537-2
Ben Webster With The Billy Strayhorn Trio
Music For Loving:Ben Webster With Strings | Verve | 527774-2
Benny Goodman And His Orchestra
Great Swing Classics In Hi-Fi | Capitol | 521223-2
Billie Holiday With Sy Oliver And His Orchestra
Billie's Love Songs | Nimbus Records | NI 2000
Bob Scobey's Frisco Band
Planet Jazz | Planet Jazz | 2169652-2
Bud Freeman All Stars
The Bud Freeman All-Star Sessions | Prestige | PRCD 24286-2
Bud Powell Trio
Planet Jazz:Bud Powell | Planet Jazz | 2152064-2
Planet Jazz Sampler | Planet Jazz | 2152326-2
Planet Jazz:Jazz Piano | RCA | 2169655-2
The Best Of Bud Powell On Verve | Verve | 523392-2
The Amazing Bud Powell Vol.2 | Blue Note | 532137-2
Cal Tjader With The Lalo Schifrin Orchestra
Talkin Verve/Roots Of Acid Jazz:Cal Tjader | Verve | 531562-2
Cal Tjader's Orchestra
Verve Jazz Masters 39:Cal Tjader | Verve | 521858-2
Talkin Verve/Roots Of Acid Jazz:Cal Tjader | Verve | 531562-2
Clark Terry & Chico O Farril Orchestra
Spanish Rice | Verve | 9861050
Coleman Hawkins And Confreres
Coleman Hawkins And Confreres | Verve | 835255-2 PMS
Coleman Hawkins Sextet
Hawk Eyes | Original Jazz Classics | OJCCD 294-2
Coleman Hawkins-Roy Eldridge Quintet
Verve Jazz Masters 43:Coleman Hawkins | Verve | 521856-2
Count Basie All Stars
The Legends Of Swing | Laserlight | 24659
Dave Pike Sextet
Carnavals | Prestige | PCD 24248-2
Dizzy Gillespie And His Orchestra
Ultimate Dizzy Gillespie | Verve | 557535-2
Eddie Lockjaw Davis Quartet
The Eddie Lockjaw Davis Cookbook Vol.2 | Original Jazz Classics | OJC20 653-2(P 7161)
Jaws | Original Jazz Classics | OJCCD 218-2(P 7154)
Queen Of The Organ-Shirley Scott Memorial Album | Prestige | PRCD 11027-2
Eddie Lockjaw Davis Quintet
Cookbook Vol.1 | Original Jazz Classics | OJC20 652-2(P 7141)
The Eddie Lockjaw Davis Cookbook Vol.2 | Original Jazz Classics | OJC20 653-2(P 7161)
Jaws In Orbit | Original Jazz Classics | OJCCD 322-2(P 7171)
The Jazz Giants Play Harry Warren:Lullaby Of Broadway | Prestige | PCD 24204-2
Queen Of The Organ-Shirley Scott Memorial Album | Prestige | PRCD 11027-2
Eddie Lockjaw Davis-Shirley Scott Sextet
Bacalao | Original Jazz Classics | OJCCD 1090-2(P 7178)
Ella Fitzgerald With Sy Oliver And His Orchestra
Ella Fitzgerald:The Decca Years 1949-1954 | Decca | 050668-2
Ella Fitzgerald With The Bill Doggett Orchestra
Rhythm Is My Business | Verve | 559513-2
Eric Dolphy Quartet
Eric Dolphy:The Complete Prestige Recordings | Prestige | 9 PRCD-4418-2
Eric Dolphy Birthday Celebration | Fantasy | FANCD 6085-2
Out There | New Jazz | NJSA 8252-6
Out There | Original Jazz Classics | OJC20 023-2(NJ 8252)
Etta Jones And Her Quartet
Something Nice | Original Jazz Classics | OJCCD 221-2(P 7194)
Etta Jones With Her Trio
Something Nice | Original Jazz Classics | OJCCD 221-2(P 7194)
Etta Jones With The Oliver Nelson Quintet
Hollar! | Original Jazz Classics | OJCCD 1061(PR 7284)
Frank Wess And His Orchestra
The Long Road | Prestige | PCD 24247-2
Gene Ammons Quartet
Gentle Jug Vol.3 | Prestige | PCD 24249-2
A Stranger In Town | Prestige | PRCD 24266-2
Gene Ammons Quintet
A Stranger In Town | Prestige | PRCD 24266-2
George Russell And His Orchestra
Geogre Russell New York N.Y. | Impulse(MCA) | 951278-2
Gunther Schuller Ensemble
Beauty Is A Rare Thing:Ornette Coleman-The Complete Atlantic Recordings | Atlantic | 8122-71410-2
Hank Jones With Oliver Nelson's Orchestra
The Roots Of Acid Jazz | Impulse(MCA) | IMP 12042
Jimmy Rushing With Oliver Nelson And His Orchestra
Every Day I Have The Blues | Impulse(MCA) | 547967-2
Jimmy Smith Quartet
Jimmy Smith-Talkin' Verve | Verve | 531563-2
Any Number Can Win | Verve | 557447-2
Jimmy Smith With The Lalo Schifrin Orchestra
Jimmy Smith:Best Of The Verve Years | Verve | 527950-2
Jimmy Smith-Talkin' Verve | Verve | 531563-2
The Cat | Verve | 539756-2
Jimmy Smith With The Oliver Nelson Orchestra
Verve Jazz Masters 29:Jimmy Smith | Verve | 521855-2
Jimmy Smith:Best Of The Verve Years | Verve | 527950-2
Jimmy Smith-Talkin' Verve | Verve | 531563-2
Johnny Smith Quartet
The Sound Of The Johnny Smith Guitar | Roulette | 531792-2
Juanita Hall With The Claude Hopkins All Stars
Juanita Hall Sings The Blues | Original Jazz Classics | OJCCD 1928-2(CPST 556)
Junior Mance Trio & Orchestra
That Lovin' Feelin' | Milestone | MCD 47097-2
Kenny Burrell-Jimmy Smith Quartet
Blue Bash | Verve | 557453-2
Lalo Schifrin And His Orchestra
Verve Jazz Masters 39:Cal Tjader | Verve | 521858-2
Lena Horne With The Lennie Hayton Orchestra
Planet Jazz:Lena Horne | Planet Jazz | 2165373-2
Lester Young Septet
Laughin' To Keep From Cryin' | Verve | 543301-2
Lester Young-Roy Eldridge-Harry Edison Band
Jazz Gallery:Lester Young Vol.2(1946-59) | RCA | 2119541-2
Lionel Hampton And His Orchestra
Planet Jazz:Big Bands | Planet Jazz | 2169649-2
Louis Armstrong And His Friends
Planet Jazz:Louis Armstrong | Planet Jazz | 2152052-2
Planet Jazz Sampler | Planet Jazz | 2152326-2
Louis Armstrong And His Friends | Bluebird | 2663961-2
Louis Armstrong With Sy Oliver And His Orchestra
Satchmo Serenaders | Verve | 543792-2
Louis Armstrong:C'est Si Bon | Dreyfus Jazz Line | FDM 36730-2
Louis Armstrong-My Greatest Songs | MCA | MCD 18347
Mildred Anderson With The Eddie Lockjaw Davis Quartet
Queen Of The Organ-Shirley Scott Memorial Album | Prestige | PRCD 11027-2
Mundell Lowe And His All Stars
Planet Jazz:Ben Webster | RCA | 2165368-2
Oliver Nelson Quintet
Eric Dolphy:The Complete Prestige Recordings | Prestige | 9 PRCD-4418-2
Eric Dolphy Birthday Celebration | Fantasy | FANCD 6085-2
Straight Ahead | Original Jazz Classics | OJCCD 099-2
Oliver Nelson Sextet
Eric Dolphy:The Complete Prestige Recordings | Prestige | 9 PRCD-4418-2
Eric Dolphy Birthday Celebration | Fantasy | FANCD 6085-2
Screamin' The Blues | Original Jazz Classics | OJC 080(NJ 8243)
Soul Street | Original Jazz Classics | OJCCD 987-2(NJ 8293)
The Prestige Legacy Vol.2:Battles Of Saxes | Prestige | PCD 24252-2
Paul Desmond Quartet
The Ballad Of Paul Desmond | RCA | 21429372
Paul Desmond With Strings
Desmond Blue | RCA | 2663898-2
Rolf Kühn Quartet
Rolf Kühn And His Sound Of Jazz | Fresh Sound Records | FSR-CD 326
Rolf Kühn Quintet
Rolf Kühn And His Sound Of Jazz | Fresh Sound Records | FSR-CD 326
Ron Carter Quintet
Eric Dolphy:The Complete Prestige Recordings | Prestige | 9 PRCD-4418-2
Eric Dolphy Birthday Celebration | Fantasy | FANCD 6085-2
Where | Original Jazz Classics | OJCCD 432-2
Sarah Vaughan With Mundell Lowe And George Duvivier
Ballads | Roulette | 537561-2
Jazz Profile | Blue Note | 823517-2
After Hours | Roulette | 855468-2
Sarah Vaughan With Orchestra
Sarah Vaughan Sings The Mancini Songbook | Verve | 558401-2
Sarah Vaughan With The Jimmy Jones Orchestra
Ballads | Roulette | 537561-2
Jazz Profile | Blue Note | 823517-2
Shirley Horn Trio
Queen Of The Organ-Shirley Scott Memorial Album | Prestige | PRCD 11027-2
Shirley Scott All Stars
Queen Of The Organ-Shirley Scott Memorial Album | Prestige | PRCD 11027-2
Shirley Scott Quartet
Queen Of The Organ-Shirley Scott Memorial Album | Prestige | PRCD 11027-2
Shirley Scott Trio
Like Cozy | Prestige | PCD 24258-2
Queen Of The Organ-Shirley Scott Memorial Album | Prestige | PRCD 11027-2
Sonny Stitt With Orchestra
Goin' Down Slow | Prestige | PRCD 24276-2
Stan Getz Group
Verve Jazz Masters 53:Stan Getz-Bossa Nova | Verve | 529904-2
Stan Getz Group Feat.Laurindo Almeida
Stan Getz With Guest Artist Laurindo Almeida | Verve | 823149-2
Stan Getz With Strings And Voices
Reflections | Verve | 523322-2
Stan Getz-Laurindo Almeida Orchestra
Stan Getz Highlights:The Best Of The Verve Years Vol.2 | Verve | 517330-2
Verve Jazz Masters 53:Stan Getz-Bossa Nova | Verve | 529904-2
Stan Getz Highlights | Verve | 847430-2
Stan Getz-Luiz Bonfa Group
The Antonio Carlos Jobim Songbook | Verve | 525472-2
Stan Getz-Luiz Bonfa Orchestra
Verve Jazz Masters 13:Antonio Carlos Jobim | Verve | 516409-2
Jazz Samba Encore! | Verve | 823613-2
Very Saxy
Very Saxy | Original Jazz Classics | OJCCD 458-2
The Prestige Legacy Vol.2:Battles Of Saxes | Prestige | PCD 24252-2
Wes Montgomery With The Oliver Nelson Orchestra
Verve Jazz Masters 14:Wes Montgomery | Verve | 519826-2
Wes Montgomery:The Verve Jazz Sides | Verve | 521690-2
Talkin' Jazz:Roots Of Acid Jazz | Verve | 529580-2
Willie Rodriguez Jazz Quartet
Flatjacks | Milestone | MCD 9331-2

Duvivier,George or Art Davis | (b)
Mar Murphy With The Ernie Wilkins Orchestra
RAH | Original Jazz Classics | OJCCD 141-2(R 9395)

Düwer,Sönke | (dr)
Welcome To The Maze
Welcome To The Maze:Puzzle | Nabel Records:Jazz Network | CD 4671

Dwellingham,Hershel | (dr)
Weather Report
Sweetnighter | CBS | 485102-2

Dyani,Johnny | (b,bells,voc,p,tambourine,voice)
Dollar Brand-Johnny Dyani Duo
Echoes From Africa | Enja | ENJ-3047 2
Johnny Dyani Quartet
Mbizo | Steeplechase | SCCD 31163
Johnny Dyani Septet
Afrika | Steeplechase | SCS 1186(Audiophile Pressing)

Dyani,Thomas Akuru | (congas,perc,balafonvoc)

Dyer,Ada | (voc)
Barbara Dennerlein Group
Outhipped | Verve | 547503-2
Chico Freeman And Brainstorm
Threshold | IN+OUT Records | 7022-2

Dylag,Roman | (b)
Eje Thelin Quintet
At The German Jazz Festival 1964 | Dragon | DRCD 374
Remy Filipovitch Trio
All Day Long | Album | AS 22927
Toots Thielemans With Gals And Pals
Verve Jazz Masters Vol.59:Toots Thielemans | Verve | 535271-2

Dyson,Dave | (bel-b)
Chico Freeman And Brainstorm
Threshold | IN+OUT Records | 7022-2
Steve Coleman And Five Elements
Genesis & The Opening Of The Way | RCA | 2152934-2

Dziemanowsky,Udo | (el-g)
Europa String Choir
Internationales Guitarren Festival '99 | ALISO Records | AL 1038

Eager,Allen | (asts)
52nd Street All Stars
Planet Jazz:Bebop | RCA | 2169650-2
Coleman Hawkins And His 52nd Street All Stars
Jazz:The Essential Collection Vol.3 | IN+OUT Records | 78013-2
Coleman Hawkins' Fifty-Second Street All-Stars
Planet Jazz:Coleman Hawkins | Planet Jazz | 2152055-2
Gerry Mulligan And The Sax Section
The Gerry Mulligan Songbook | Pacific Jazz | 833575-2
JATP All Stars
The Complete Jazz At The Philharmonic On Verve 1944-1949 | Verve | 523893-2
Stan Getz And His Four Brothers
The Brothers | Original Jazz Classics | OJCCD 008-2
The Prestige Legacy Vol.2:Battles Of Saxes | Prestige | PCD 24252-2
Stan Getz Five Brothers Bop Tenor Sax Stars
Stan Getz:Imagination | Dreyfus Jazz Line | FDM 36733-2
Tadd Dameron Septet
The Fabulous Fats Navarro Vol.2 | Blue Note | 0677208
Fats Navarro:Nostalgia | Dreyfus Jazz Line | FDM 36736-2

Eardley,Jon | (fl-h,lipstp)
NDR-Workshop
Doldinger's Best | ACT | 9224-2
Zoot Sims Quintet
Americans Swinging In Paris:Zoot Sims | EMI Records | 539646-2

Earl,Jimmy | (b,el-b,fretless-blow-b)
Dave Weckl Group
Heads Up | GRP | GRP 96732
Stanley Clarke Group
If This Bass Could Only Talk | CBS | 460883-2
Tom Browne Groups
Mo' Jamaica Funk | Hip Bop | HIBD 8002

Earland,Charles | (org,el-p,synthkeyboards)
Boogaloo Joe Jones Quintet
Charlie's Greatest Hits | Prestige | PCD 24250-2
Charles Earland Orchestra
Charlie's Greatest Hits | Prestige | PCD 24250-2
Charles Earland Quintet
Black Talk! | Original Jazz Classics | OJCCD 335-2(P 7758)
Charles Earland Septet
Charlie's Greatest Hits | Prestige | PCD 24250-2
Charles Earland In Concert | Prestige | PRCD 24267-2
Charles Earland Sextet
Jazzin' With The Soul Brothers | Fantasy | FANCD 6086-2
Black Talk! | Original Jazz Classics | OJCCD 335-2(P 7758)
Charlie's Greatest Hits | Prestige | PCD 24250-2
Charles Earland In Concert | Prestige | PRCD 24267-2
Lou Donaldson Quintet
Blue Break Beats | Blue Note | 799106-2
The Lost Grooves | Blue Note | 831883-2

Earle,David | (congas)
Billy Cobham Group
The Best Of Billy Cobham | Atlantic | 7567-81558-2

Easley,Bill | (alto-fl,as,ts,b-cl,cl,sax,flss)
Dee Dee Bridgewater With Big Band
Dear Ella | Verve | 539102-2
Duke Ellington Orchestra
Continuum | Fantasy | FCD 24765-2
Jimmy McGriff Quartet
Feelin' It | Milestone | MCD 9313-2
Jimmy McGriff Quintet
McGriff's House Party | Milestone | MCD 9300-2
Jimmy McGriff Septet
McGriff Avenue | Milestone | MCD 9325-2

INTERPRETENVERZEICHNIS

Jimmy McGriff Sextet
Feelin' It | Milestone | MCD 9313-2
Roland Hanna Quartet
The Story Of Jazz Piano | Laserlight | 24653
Ruth Brown With Orchestra
Fine And Mellow | Fantasy | FCD 9663-2

Easley,Dave | (pedal-steel-g)
Brian Blade Group
Fellowship | Blue Note | 859417-2

Easson,Leon | (voc)
Leon Eason Group
Blue Velvet: Crooners, Swooners And Velvet Vocals | Blue Note | 521153-2

East,Nathan | (b,voc,b-synth,el-bfretless-b)
Al Jarreau With Band
High Crime | i.e. Music | 557848-2
Al Jarreau In London | i.e. Music | 557849-2
Fourplay
Heartfelt | RCA | 2663916-2
Fourplay | Warner | 7599-26656-2
Between The Sheets | Warner | 9362-45340-2
Fourplay...Yes,Please! | Warner | 9362-47694-2
Joe Sample Group
Spellbound | Rhino | 81273726-2

Eastmond,Barry | (keyboards,psynth)
Dizzy Gillespie And His Orchestra
Closer To The Source | Atlantic | 7567-80776-2

Easton,Gene | (bs)
Gene Ammons Septet
A Stranger In Town | Prestige | PRCD 24266-2

Easton,McKinley | (bs)
Dinah Washington With The Eddie Chamblee Orchestra
Dinah Sings Bessie Smith | Verve | 538635-2

Eaton,Cleveland | (b)
Count Basie And His Orchestra
88 Basie Street | Original Jazz Classics | OJC 808(2310901)
Fancy Pants | Original Jazz Classics | OJCCD 1038-2(2310920)
Count Basie's Small Band
88 Basie Street | Original Jazz Classics | OJC 808(2310901)
Gene Ammons-James Moody Quintet
Chicago Concert | Original Jazz Classics | OJCCD 1091-2(PR 10065)

Eaton,John | (pp-solo)
Stuff Smith Quartet
Cat On A Hot Fiddle | Verve | 9861487

Eaton,Steuart | (viola)
Kölner Saxophon Mafia With The Auryn Quartet
Kölner Saxophon Mafia Proudly Presents | Jazz Haus Musik | JHM 0046 CD

Eaton,William | (arrvoc)
Grover Washington Jr. Orchestra
Inside Moves | Elektra | 7559-60318-2
Oscar Brown Jr. And His Group
Movin' On | Rhino | 8122-73678-2

Eaves,Hubert | (el-p,keyboards,pperc)
Dick Griffin Septet
The Eighth Wonder & More | Konnex Records | KCD 5059

Ebah,Akh Tal | (tp,fl-h,mellophon)
Sun Ra And His Astro-Infinity Arkestra
Space Is The Place | Impulse(MCA) | 951249-2
Sun Ra And His Intergalactic Research Arkestra
Black Myth/Out In Space | MPS | 557656-2

Ebenezer,Paul | (b)
Charlie Christian All Stars
Charlie Christian-Jazz Immortal/Dizzy Gillespie 1944 | Original Jazz Classics | OJCCD 1932-2(ES 548)
Minton's Playhouse All Stars
Charlie Christian:Swing To Bop | Dreyfus Jazz Line | FDM 36715-2

Eberhard,Silke | (as,clb-cl)
The United Women's Orchestra
The Blue One | Jazz Haus Musik | JHM 0099 CD
United Women's Orchestra
Virgo Supercluster | Jazz Haus Musik | JHM 0123 CD

Eberle,Bob | (voc)
Jimmy Dorsey And His Orchestra
Swing Vol.1 | Storyville | 4960343

Eberle,Frank | (psynth)
Frank Eberle Septet
Scarlet Sunrise | Satin Doll Productions | SDP 1041-1 CD
Rainer Tempel Big Band
Melodies Of '98 | Jazz 4 Ever Records:Jazz Network | J4E 4744
Album 03 | Jazz 'n' Arts Records | JNA 1102

Eberle,Heinz | (ts)
Freddie Brocksieper Orchester
Shot Gun Boogie | Bear Family Records | BCD 16277 AH

Eberle,Ray | (voc)
Glenn Miller And His Orchestra
The Ultimate Glenn Miller-22 Original Hits From The King Of Swing | RCA | 2113137-2
Planet Jazz:Glenn Miller | Planet Jazz | 2152056-2
The Chesterfield Broadcasts Vol.1 | RCA | 2663113-2
Candlelight Miller | RCA | 2668716-2
The Glenn Miller Story Vol. 3 | RCA | ND 89222
Swing Legends | Nimbus Records | NI 2001

Eberson,Jon | (g)
Ketil Bjornstad Group
Early Years | EmArCy | 013271-2

Ebert,Ludwig | (p)
Helmut Brandt Combo
Deutsches Jazz Fesival 1954/1955 | Bear Family Records | BCD 15430

Ecay,Jean-Marie | (g)
Richard Galliano Group
French Touch | Dreyfus Jazz Line | FDM 36596-2

Echampard,Eric | (dr)
Louis Sclavis & The Bernard Struber Jazztet
La Phare | Enja | ENJ-9359 2

Eckels,Dent | (b-clts)
Louis Armstrong With Gordon Jenkins And His Orchestra
Satchmo In Style | Verve | 549594-2
Louis Armstrong With Gordon Jenkins And His Orchestra And Choir
Satchmo In Style | Verve | 549594-2

Ecker,Uwe | (dr)
Klaus Ignatzek Group Feat.Dave Liebman
The Spell | Nabel Records:Jazz Network | CD 4614

Eckert,Christian | (g)
Fritz Münzer Tentet
Blue Ideas | Jazz 'n' Arts Records | 0200

Eckert,Elke | (voc)
Jazzensemble Des Hessischen Rundfunks
Jazz Messe-Messe Für Unsere Zeit | hr music.de | hrmj 003-01 CD

Eckert,John | (fl-h,tppiccolo-tp)
Buck Clayton Swing Band
Swing's The Village | Nagel-Heyer | CD 5004
Blues Of Summer | Nagel-Heyer | NH 1011

Eckert,Rinde | (org,harm,pipe,10-string-slide-g,voc)
Jerry Granelli UFB
News From The Street | VeraBra Records | CDVBR 2146-2
Rinde Eckert Group
Story In,Story Out | Intuition Records | INT 3507-2

Eckinger,Isla | (b,arr,dr,tbvib)
Benny Bailey Quintet
Jazz Portraits | EGO | 95080
Bill Allred-Roy Williams Quintet
Absolutely | Nagel-Heyer | CD 024
Ellington For Lovers | Nagel-Heyer | NH 1009
Blues Of Summer | Nagel-Heyer | NH 1011
The Second Sampler | Nagel-Heyer | NHR SP 6
Charlie Mariano Quartet
Deep In A Dream | Enja | ENJ-9423 2

Conte Candoli With The Joe Haider Trio
Conte Candoli Meets The Joe Haider Trio | JHM Records | JHM 3602
Dusko Goykovich Quartet
In My Dreams | Enja | ENJ-9408 2
Dusko Goykovich-Joe Haider Quintet
Jazz Portraits | EGO | 95080
Four For Jazz
The Best Of Four For Jazz & Benny Bailey | JHM Records | JHM 3615
Four For Jazz & Benny Bailey
The Best Of Four For Jazz & Benny Bailey | JHM Records | JHM 3615
Fritz Pauer Trio
Jazz Portraits | EGO | 95080
Horace Parlan Quartet
Jazz Portraits | EGO | 95080
Hot Mallets
Hot Mallets...Live! | JHM Records | JHM 3610
International Chicago-Jazz Orchestra
That's A Plenty | JHM Records | JHM 3621
Jeanie Lambe And The Danny Moss Quartet
Three Great Concerts:Live In Hamburg 1993-1995 | Nagel-Heyer | CD 019
Jeanie Lambe And The Danny Moss Septet
Three Great Concerts:Live In Hamburg 1993-1995 | Nagel-Heyer | CD 019
Joe Haider Quintet
Magic Box | JHM Records | JHM 3601
Joe Haider Trio
Jazz Portraits | EGO | 95080
Katzenvilla | JHM Records | JHM 3622
Mal Waldron Trio
Free At Last | ECM | 1001
Slide Hampton-Joe Haider Jazz Orchestra
Give Me A Double | JHM Records | JHM 3627
Stefanie Schlesiger And Her Group plus String Quartet
What Love Is | Enja | ENJ-9434 2
Stefanie Schlesinger And Her Group
What Love Is | Enja | ENJ-9434 2
Stephane Grappelli Quartet
Verve Jazz Masters 11:Stéphane Grappelli | Verve | 516758-2
Stephane Grappelli With The Diz Disley Trio
Grapelli Story | Verve | 515807-2
Tom Saunders' 'Wild Bill Davison Band' & Guests
Exactly Like You | Nagel-Heyer | CD 023
The Second Sampler | Nagel-Heyer | NHR SP 6
Wolfgang Engstfeld Quartet
Songs And Ballads | Nabel Records:Jazz Network | CD 4658

Eckland,K.O. | (p)
Firehouse Five Plus Two
Dixieland Favorites | Good Time Jazz | FCD 60-008

Ecklund,Peter | (cotp)
Louis Mazetier-Peter Ecklund
A Friendly Chat | Jazz Connaisseur | JCCD 9932-2

Eckstine,Billy | (tb,voc,tpv-tb)
Billy Eckstine And His Orchestra
Blue Velvet: Crooners, Swooners And Velvet Vocals | Blue Note | 521153-2
Billy Eckstine With Bobby Tucker And His Orchestra
The Antonio Carlos Jobim Songbook | Verve | 525472-2
Billy Eckstine Now Singing In 12 Great Movies | Verve | 589307-2
Billy Eckstine With Hal Mooney And His Orchestra
Billy Eckstine Now Singing In 12 Great Movies | Verve | 589307-2
Billy Eckstine With The Billy May Orchestra
Once More With Feeling | Roulette | 581862-2
Earl Hines And His Orchestra
Planet Jazz:Earl Hines | Planet Jazz | 2159973-2
The Metronome All Stars
Jazz Gallery:Lester Young Vol.2(1946-59) | RCA | 2119541-2

Edelhagen,Kurt | (ld)
Inge Brandenburg mit Kurt Edelhaben und seinem Orchester
Why Don't You Take All Of Me | Bear Family Records | BCD 15614 AH
Kurt Edelhagen All Stars
Deutsches Jazz Fesival 1954/1955 | Bear Family Records | BCD 15430
Kurt Edelhagen All Stars Und Solisten
Deutsches Jazz Fesival 1954/1955 | Bear Family Records | BCD 15430
Quartet Der Kurt Edelhagen All Stars
Deutsches Jazz Fesival 1954/1955 | Bear Family Records | BCD 15430
Stan Getz With The Kurt Edelhagen Orchestra
Stan Getz In Europe | Laserlight | 24657

Edelmann,Samuli | (voc)
Alexi Tuomarila Quartet
02 | Finladia Jazz | 0927-49148-2

Edelstein,Walter | (v)
Ella Fitzgerald With The Nelson Riddle Orchestra
The Best Of The Song Books:The Ballads | Verve | 521867-2
Jack Teagarden With Orchestra
Jazz:The Essential Collection Vol.3 | IN+OUT Records | 78013-2

Edén,Mats | (drone-fiddle,kantele,vviola)
Lena Willemark-Ale Möller Group
Nordan | ECM | 1536(523161-2)
Agram | ECM | 1610
Mats Eden-Jonas Simonson With The Cikada String Quartet
Milvus | ECM | 1660

Edenroth,Anders | (voc)
The Real Group
One For All | ACT | 9003-2
The Real Group With Toots Thielemans
One For All | ACT | 9003-2

Edge,Norman | (b)
Gene Ammons Septet
Bad! Bossa Nova | Original Jazz Classics | OJC20 351-2(P 7257)

Edgehill,Arthur | (dr)
Al Smith With The Eddie Lockjaw Davis Quartet
Queen Of The Organ-Shirley Scott Memorial Album | Prestige | PRCD 11027-2
Eddie Lockjaw Davis Quartet
The Eddie Lockjaw Davis Cookbook Vol.2 | Original Jazz Classics | OJC20 653-2(P 7161)
Jaws | Original Jazz Classics | OJCCD 218-2(P 7154)
Queen Of The Organ-Shirley Scott Memorial Album | Prestige | PRCD 11027-2
Eddie Lockjaw Davis Quintet
Cookbook Vol.1 | Original Jazz Classics | OJC20 652-2(P 7141)
The Eddie Lockjaw Davis Cookbook Vol.2 | Original Jazz Classics | OJC20 653-2(P 7161)
Jaws In Orbit | Original Jazz Classics | OJCCD 322-2(P 7171)
Queen Of The Organ-Shirley Scott Memorial Album | Prestige | PRCD 11027-2
Eddie Lockjaw Davis-Shirley Scott Sextet
Bacalao | Original Jazz Classics | OJCCD 1090-2(P 7178)
Kenny Dorham Sextet
The Complete Round About Midnight At The Cafe Bohemia | Blue Note | 533775-2
Mildred Anderson With The Eddie Lockjaw Davis Quartet
Queen Of The Organ-Shirley Scott Memorial Album | Prestige | PRCD 11027-2
Shirley Horn Trio
Queen Of The Organ-Shirley Scott Memorial Album | Prestige | PRCD 11027-2
Shirley Scott All Stars
Queen Of The Organ-Shirley Scott Memorial Album | Prestige | PRCD 11027-2
Shirley Scott Quartet
Queen Of The Organ-Shirley Scott Memorial Album | Prestige | PRCD 11027-2
Shirley Scott Trio
Like Cozy | Prestige | PCD 24258-2
Queen Of The Organ-Shirley Scott Memorial Album | Prestige | PRCD 11027-2

Very Saxy
Very Saxy | Original Jazz Classics | OJCCD 458-2
The Prestige Legacy Vol.2:Battles Of Saxes | Prestige | PCD 24252-2

Edgehill,Guillermo | (b)
Mongo Santamaria And His Band
Brazilian Sunset | Candid | CCD 79703

Edison,Harry 'Sweets' | (tpvoc)
Anita O'Day And Her Combo
Pick Yourself Up | Verve | 517329-2
Art Tatum Sextet
Art Tatum-The Complete Pablo Group Masterpieces | Pablo | 6 PACD 4401-2
Barney Kessel And His Septet
To Swing Or Not To Swing | Original Jazz Classics | OJCCD 317-2
Ben Webster All Stars
King Of The Tenors | Verve | 519806-2
Ben Webster And His Orchestra
Verve Jazz Masters 43:Ben Webster | Verve | 525431-2
Billie Holiday And Her All Stars
Verve Jazz Masters 12:Billie Holiday | Verve | 519825-2
Verve Jazz Masters 20:Introducing | Verve | 519853-2
Songs For Distingué Lovers | Verve | 539056-2
The Billie Holiday Song Book | Verve | 823246-2
Billie Holiday And Her Band
Verve Jazz Masters 47:Billie Holiday Sings Standards | Verve | 527650-2
Billie Holiday And Her Orchestra
Billie's Love Songs | Nimbus Records | NI 2000
Billie Holiday With The Ray Ellis Orchestra
Verve Jazz Masters 47:Billie Holiday Sings Standards | Verve | 527650-2
Buddy Rich Quintet
Buddy And Sweets | Verve | 841433-2
Charlie Parker With Machito And His Orchestra
Bird: The Complete Charlie Parker On Verve | Verve | 837141-2
Count Basie And His Orchestra
Planet Jazz:Count Basie | Planet Jazz | 2152068-2
Planet Jazz Sampler | Planet Jazz | 2152326-2
Planet Jazz:Jimmy Rushing | RCA | 2165371-2
Planet Jazz:Jazz Greatest Hits | Planet Jazz | 2169648-2
Planet Jazz:Big Bands | Planet Jazz | 2169649-2
Jazz Collection:Count Basie | Laserlight | 24368
Breakfast Dance And Barbecue | Roulette | 531791-2
Jazz:The Essential Collection Vol.3 | IN+OUT Records | 78013-2
From Spiritual To Swing | Vanguard | VCD 169/71
Count Basie Octet
Planet Jazz:Count Basie | Planet Jazz | 2152068-2
Dizzy Gillespie's Trumpet Kings
The Trumpet Kings Meet Joe Turner | Original Jazz Classics | OJCCD 497-2
Duke Ellington And Johnny Hodges Orchestra
Side By Side | Verve | 521405-2
Duke Ellington-Johnny Hodges All Stars
Verve Jazz Masters 4:Duke Ellington | Verve | 516338-2
Back To Back | Verve | 521404-2
Ella Fitzgerald And Count Basie With The JATP All Stars
Bluella:Ella Fitzgerald Sings The Blues | Pablo | 2310960-2
Ella Fitzgerald And Her All Stars
All That Jazz | Pablo | 2310938-2
Ella Fitzgerald And Her Sextet
Ella Fitzgerald-First Lady Of Song | Verve | 517898-2
Ella Fitzgerald Jam
Bluella:Ella Fitzgerald Sings The Blues | Pablo | 2310960-2
Ella Fitzgerald With Benny Carter's Magnificent Seven
30 By Ella | Capitol | 520090-2
Ella Fitzgerald With Orchestra
Ella/Things Ain't What They Used To Be | Warner | 9362-47875-2
Ella Fitzgerald With Paul Weston And His Orchestra
The Best Of The Song Books | Verve | 519804-2
Ella Fitzgerald Sings The Irving Berlin Song Book | Verve | 543830-2
Ella Fitzgerald With The Buddy Bregman Orchestra
Ella Fitzgerald-First Lady Of Song | Verve | 517898-2
Love Songs:The Best Of The Song Books | Verve | 531762-2
Ella Fitzgerald Sings The Cole Porter Songbook | Verve | 537257-2
Ella Fitzgerald Sings The Rodgers And Hart Song Book | Verve | 537258-2
Ella Fitzgerald With The Frank DeVol Orchestra
Ella Fitzgerald-First Lady Of Song | Verve | 517898-2
Get Happy! | Verve | 523321-2
Ella Fitzgerald Sings Sweet Songs For Swingers | Verve | 9860417
Ella Fitzgerald With The Marty Paich Orchestra
Whisper Not | Verve | 589947-2
For The Love Of Ella Fitzgerald | Verve | 841765-2
Ella Fitzgerald With The Paul Weston Orchestra
Ella Fitzgerald-First Lady Of Song | Verve | 517898-2
Get Happy! | Verve | 523321-2
Frank Sinatra With The Count Basie Orchestra
It Might As Well Be Spring | Reprise | 7599-27027-2
Harry Edison Quartet
The Complete Unedited 'Sweets At The Haig' 1953 Recordings | Fresh Sound Records | FSR CD 345
Harry Edison Quintet
Edison's Light | Original Jazz Classics | OJCCD 804-2(2310780)
Harry Edison Sextet
Swing Summit | Candid | CCD 79050
Harry Sweets Edison Sextet
The Soul Of Ben Webster | Verve | 527475-2
Mr.Swing Harry Edison | Verve | 559868-2
Helen Humes With James P. Johnson And The Count Basie Orchestra
From Spiritual To Swing | Vanguard | VCD 169/71
James Carter Group
Conversin' With The Elders | Atlantic | 7567-82988-2
JATP All Stars
Welcome To Jazz At The Philharmonic | Fantasy | FANCD 6081-2
Jimmy Rushing With Count Basie And His Orchestra
From Spiritual To Swing | Vanguard | VCD 169/71
Joe Williams And His Band
Blue Velvet: Crooners, Swooners And Velvet Vocals | Blue Note | 521153-2
Joe Williams With The Harry 'Sweets' Edison Band
Together/Have A Good Time | Roulette | 531790-2
Joe Williams With The Harry 'Sweets' Edison Sextet
Together/Have A Good Time | Roulette | 531790-2
Lester Young Septet
Laughin' To Keep From Cryin' | Verve | 543301-2
Lester Young-Harry Edison With The Oscar Peterson Quartet
Jazz Gallery:Lester Young Vol.2(1946-59) | RCA | 2119541-2
Lester Young-Roy Eldridge-Harry Edison Band
Jazz Gallery:Lester Young Vol.2(1946-59) | RCA | 2119541-2
Milt Jackson Septet
Milt Jackson Birthday Celebration | Fantasy | FANCD 6079-2
Nat King Cole Quintet
After Midnight | Capitol | 520087-2
Oscar Peterson-Harry Edison Duo
Oscar Peterson & Harry Edison | Original Jazz Classics | OJCCD 738-2(2310741)
Red Norvo Sextet
Planet Jazz:Ben Webster | RCA | 2165368-2
Roy Eldridge-Dizzy Gillespie-Harry Edison With The Oscar Peterson Quartet
The Complete Verve Roy Eldridge Studio Sessions | Verve | 9861278
Sarah Vaughan With The Jimmy Jones Orchestra
Ballads | Roulette | 537561-2
Jazz Profile | Blue Note | 823517-2
Sarah Vaughan With The Jimmy Jones Quintet
Jazz Profile | Blue Note | 823517-2
The Basie Alumni
Swinging For The Count | Candid | CCD 79724

Woody Herman And His Sextet
Songs For Hip Lovers | Verve | 559872-2
Zoot Sims-Harry Edison Quintet
Jazz Dance | Original Jazz Classics | OJCCD 1002-2(1210890)

Edmonds,Paul | (tpfl-h)
Mike Westbrook Orchestra
Bar Utopia-A Big Band Cabaret | Enja | ENJ-9333 2

Edmondson,Bob | (arrtb)
Dinah Washington With The Eddie Chamblee Orchestra
Verve Jazz Masters 40:Dinah Washington | Verve | 522055-2
Dizzy Gillespie And His Orchestra
Talking Verve:Dizzy Gillespie | Verve | 533846-2
Eric Dolphy Quartet With The University Of Illinois Big Band
The Illinois Concert | Blue Note | 499826-2
Gerald Wilson And His Orchestra
Blue Breaks Beats Vol.2 | Blue Note | 789907-2
Harry James And His Orchestra
Trumpet Blues:The Best Of Harry James | Capitol | 521224-2
Terry Gibbs Big Band
Terry Gibbs Dream Band Vol.4:Main Stem | Contemporary | CCD 7656-2
Terry Gibbs Dream Band
Terry Gibbs Dream Band Vol.5:The Big Cat | Contemporary | CCD 7657-2

Edmonson,Robare | (arrb)
Dinah Washington With The Eddie Chamblee Orchestra
Dinah Sings Bessie Smith | Verve | 538635-2

Edström,Ulrika | (strings)
Esbjörn Svensson Trio(E.S.T) With Strings
EST Plays Monk | ACT | 9010-2

Edwards,Donald | (dr)
Andrew Adair Group
States | Fresh Sound Records | FSNT 061 CD
Marcus Printup Sextet
The New Boogaloo | Nagel-Heyer | CD 2019

Edwards,Earl | (ts)
Johnny 'Hammond' Smith Quartet
Good 'Nuff | Prestige | PRCD 24282-2

Edwards,Edwin | (tbvoc)
Original Dixieland 'Jass' Band
Planet Jazz | Planet Jazz | 2169652-2

Edwards,Gene | (g)
Eric Kloss Quartet
About Time | Prestige | PRCD 24268-2
Richard 'Groove' Holmes Trio
Somethin' Special | Pacific Jazz | 855452-2
Soul Message | Original Jazz Classics | OJC20 329-2(P 7435)
On Basie's Bandstand | Prestige | PRCD 11028-2

Edwards,Gordon | (b,b-gdr)
Bernard Purdie Group
Jazzin' With The Soul Brothers | Fantasy | FANCD 6086-2
Carla Bley Band
Dinner Music | Watt | 6(825815-2)
Grant Green Orchestra
Grant Green:Blue Breakbeat | Blue Note | 494705-2
Grant Green With Orchestra
The Final Comedown(Soundtrack) | Blue Note | 581678-2

Edwards,Gourdine | (b)
Oscar Brown Jr. And His Group
Movin' On | Rhino | 8122-73678-2

Edwards,Marc | (dr,chimes,gongstimpany)
Cecil Taylor Unit
Dark To Themselves | Enja | ENJ-2084 2

Edwards,Richard | (b-tbtb)
Carla Bley Band
The Very Big Carla Bley Band | Watt | 23
Big Band Theory | Watt | 25(519966-2)
John Surman-Jack DeJohnette With The London Brass
Printed In Germany | ECM | 1802(017065-2)
John Surman-John Warren Group
The Brass Project | ECM | 1478

Edwards,Sidney | (cello)
Harry Carney And His Orchestra With Strings
Music For Loving:Ben Webster With Strings | Verve | 527774-2

Edwards,Teddy | (cl,tsbs)
Benny Carter And His Orchestra
Further Definitions/Additions To Further Definotions | Impulse(MCA) | 951229-2
Gerald Wilson And His Orchestra
Blue Breaks Beats Vol.2 | Blue Note | 789907-2
Jimmy Smith With Orchestra
Verve Jazz Masters 29:Jimmy Smith | Verve | 521855-2
Johnny Hartman And His Orchestra
Unforgettable | Impulse(MCA) | IMP 11522
Leroy Vinnegar Sextet
The Jazz Giants Play Harry Warren:Lullaby Of Broadway | Prestige | PCD 24204-2
Lorez Alexandria With Orchestra
Deep Blue-The United States Of Mind | Blue Note | 521152-2
Milt Jackson Quintet
Milt Jackson At The Kosei Nenkin | Pablo | 2620103-2
Sarah Vaughan And Her Band
Misty Blue:Sweet Sisters Swing Songs Of Sorrow And Sadness | Blue Note | 521151-2
Sarah Vaughan With The Gerald Wilson Orchestra
Ballads | Roulette | 537561-2
Teddy Edwards-Howard McGhee Quintet
Together Again! | Original Jazz Classics | OJCCD 424-2

Efford,Bob | (b-cl,bs,cl,ts,oboesax)
Benny Goodman And His Orchestra
Verve Jazz Masters 33:Benny Goodman | Verve | 844410-2
Vic Lewis West Coast All Stars
Vic Lewis Presenting A Celebration Of Contemporary West Coast Jazz | Candid | CCD 79711/12

Egan,Mark | (b,el-b,perc,fretless-b,keyboards)
Dave Liebman Quintet
Homage To John Coltrane | Owl Records | 018357-2
George Gruntz Concert Jazz Band '83
Theatre | ECM | 1265
Lew Soloff Group
Rainbow Mountain | TipToe | TIP-888838 2
Pat Metheny Group
Pat Metheny Group | ECM | 1114(825593-2)
American Garage | ECM | 1155(827134-2)
Stan Getz Sextet
Billy Highstreet Samba | EmArCy | 838771-2

Eggen,Christian | (cond,pkeyboards)
Terje Rypdal Group
If Mountains Could Sing | ECM | 1554(523987-2)
Skywards | ECM | 1608(533768-2)
Terje Rypdal With The Borealis Ensemble
Q.E.D. | ECM | 1474
Terje Rypdal(comp)
Undisonus | ECM | 1389

Eggert,Gören | (drperc)
Jazz Fresh
Jazz Fresh | GGG-Verlag:GGG Verlag und Mailorder | CD 01.03

Eghjort,Mogens | (cotp)
Leonardo Pedersen's Jazzkapel
The Golden Years Of Revival Jazz,Sampler | Storyville | 109 1001
The Golden Years Of Revival Jazz,Vol.11 | Storyville | STCD 5516

Egilsson,Arni | (b)
Wayne Darling Group
The Art Of The Bass Vol.1 | Laika Records | 35101652

Egli,Dominik | (dr)
Domenic Landolf Quartet
Levitation | JHM Records | JHM 3616
Matthias Spillmann Septet
Something About Water | JHM Records | JHM 3620

Eglin,Jean-Claude | (tb)
Louis Sclavis & The Bernard Struber Jazztet
La Phare | Enja | ENJ-9359 2

Egri,Janos | (b)
Ferenc Snétberger Trio
Obsession | TipToe | TIP-888834 2

Ehde,John | (cello)
Chinese Compass
Chinese Compass | dacapo | DCCD 9443
Pierre Dørge's New Jungle Orchestra
Giraf | dacapo | DCCD 9440

Ehrenkranz,William | (v)
Tommy Dorsey And His Orchestra
Planet Jazz:Frank Sinatra & Tommy Dorsey | Planet Jazz | 2152067-2

Ehrhardt,Ernie | (cello)
Milt Jackson And His Orchestra
Reverence And Compassion | Reprise | 9362-45204-2

Ehrhardt,Martin | (v)
Uri Caine With The Concerto Köln
Concerto Köln | Winter&Winter | 910086-2

Ehrhardt,Werner | (v)

Ehringer,Christian | (tpfl-h)
Fritz Münzer Tentet
Blue Ideas | Jazz 'n' Arts Records | 0200
Rainer Tempel Big Band
Melodies Of '98 | Jazz 4 Ever Records:Jazz Network | J4E 4744
Album 03 | Jazz 'n' Arts Records | JNA 1102

Ehrlich,Marty | (alto-fl,ss,as,muted-as,ts,b-cl,perc)
Andy Bey Group
Tuesdays In Chinatown | Minor Music | 801099
James Emery Quartet
Standing On A Whale... | Enja | ENJ-9312 2
James Emery Septet
Spectral Domains | Enja | ENJ-9344 2
James Emery Sextet
Luminous Cycles | Between The Lines | btl 015(Efa 10185-2)
Klaus König Orchestra
Times Of Devastation/Poco A Poco | Enja | ENJ-6014 22
Marty Ehrlich Group
The Long View | Enja | ENJ-9452 2
Marty Ehrlich Quartet
Song | Enja | ENJ-9396 2
Marty Ehrlich Quintet
New York Child | Enja | ENJ-9025 2
Song | Enja | ENJ-9396 2
Marty Ehrlich-Peter Erskine-Michael Formanek
Relativity | Enja | ENJ-9341 2

Ehwald,Peter | (reeds)
Peter Ehwald Trio
Away With Words:The Music Of John Scofield | Jazz Haus Musik | JHM 0128 CD

Eichen,Bernard | (v)
George Benson With The Don Sebesky Orchestra
Verve Jazz Masters 21:George Benson | Verve | 521861-2
Grover Washington Jr. Orchestra
Jazzrock-Anthology Vol.3:Fusion | Zounds | CD 27100555
Sarah Vaughan With Orchestra
!Viva! Vaughan | Mercury | 549374-2
Sarah Vaughan Sings The Mancini Songbook | Verve | 558401-2
Stan Getz With The Eddie Sauter Orchestra
Stan Getz Plays The Music Of Mickey One | Verve | 531232-2
Wes Montgomery Quartet With The Claus Ogerman Orchestra
Tequila | Verve | 547769-2
Wes Montgomery Quintet With The Claus Ogerman Orchestra
The Antonio Carlos Jobim Songbook | Verve | 525472-2
Talkin' Jazz:Roots Of Acid Jazz | Verve | 529580-2
Tequila | Verve | 547769-2
Wes Montgomery Trio With The Claus Ogerman Orchestra
Tequila | Verve | 547769-2
Wes Montgomery With The Claus Ogerman Orchestra
Verve Jazz Masters 14:Wes Montgomery | Verve | 519826-2

Eick,Mathias | (tp)
Jacob Young Quintet
Evening Falls | ECM | 1876(9811780)

Eidens,Christoph | (vibmarimba)
Matthias Bröde Quartet
European Faces | Edition Collage | EC 517-2
Matthias Bröde Quintet
European Faces | Edition Collage | EC 517-2
Peter Fessler Quintet
Colours Of My Mind | Minor Music | 801063

Eidus,Arnold | (v)
Coleman Hawkins With Billy Byers And His Orchestra
The Hawk In Hi-Fi | RCA | 2663842-2
Freddie Hubbard Orchestra
The Body And The Soul | Impulse(MCA) | 951183-2
Lalo Schifrin And His Orchestra
Verve Jazz Masters 39:Cal Tjader | Verve | 521858-2
Wes Montgomery Quartet With The Claus Ogerman Orchestra
Tequila | Verve | 547769-2
Wes Montgomery Quintet With The Claus Ogerman Orchestra
The Antonio Carlos Jobim Songbook | Verve | 525472-2
Talkin' Jazz:Roots Of Acid Jazz | Verve | 529580-2
Tequila | Verve | 547769-2
Wes Montgomery Trio With The Claus Ogerman Orchestra
Tequila | Verve | 547769-2
Wes Montgomery With The Claus Ogerman Orchestra
Verve Jazz Masters 14:Wes Montgomery | Verve | 519826-2
Wes Montgomery With The Don Sebesky Orchestra
Verve Jazz Masters 14:Wes Montgomery | Verve | 519826-2
Talkin' Jazz:Roots Of Acid Jazz | Verve | 529580-2
Bumpin' | Verve | 539062-2
Wes Montgomery With The Jimmy Jones Orchestra
Wes Montgomery-The Complete Riverside Recordings | Riverside | 12 RCD 4408-2
The Jazz Giants Play Rodgers & Hart:Blue Moon | Prestige | PCD 24205-2

Eigensatz,Andreas | (polychordtanpura)
Asita Hamidi & Arcobaleno
Mosaic | Laika Records | 8695067

Eight Squares And A Critic |
Eight Squares And A Critic
Muggsy Spanier And Bud Freeman:V-Discs 1944-45 | Jazz Unlimited | JUCD 2049

Eilertsen,Mats | (b)
Jacob Young Quintet
Evening Falls | ECM | 1876(9811780)

Einarsdotter,Elise | (p)
Elise Einarsdotter-Olle Steinholz
Sketches Of Roses | Touché Music | TMcCD 008

Einarsen,Ketil V. | (flpiccolo)
Geir Lysne Listening Ensemble
Korall | ACT | 9236-2
Aurora Borealis-Nordic Lights | ACT | 9406-2

Einhorn,Mauricio | (harm)
Sarah Vaughan With Orchestra
I Love Brazil | Pablo | 2312101-2
Sarah Vaughan Birthday Celebration | Fantasy | FANCD 6090-2

Eisenburg,Peter | (v)
Artie Shaw And His Orchestra
Planet JazzArtie Shaw | Planet Jazz | 2152057-2
Planet Jazz:Jazz Greatest Hits | Planet Jazz | 2169648-2

Eisenhauer,Gerwin | (dr,perc,electronics,g,lapsteel-g)
Gerwin Eisenhauer's The Gäff Gang feat. Lisa Wahland
Favorite Tunes | Edition Collage | EC 527-2
Lisa Wahland And Her Trio
Marlene | Fine Music | FM 108-2
Lisa Wahlandt & Mulo Francel And Their Fabulous Bossa Band
Bossa Nova Affair | Edition Collage | EC 534-2

Eisenhauer,Rüdiger | (gtres)
Gerwin Eisenhauer's The Gäff Gang feat. Lisa Wahland
Favorite Tunes | Edition Collage | EC 527-2
Lisa Wahlandt & Mulo Francel And Their Fabulous Bossa Band
Bossa Nova Affair | Edition Collage | EC 534-2

Eisold,Peter | (dr,perc,dr-computerkeyboards)
Matthias Müller Quartet
Bhavam | Jazz Haus Musik | JHM 0126 CD
Ulla Oster Group
Beyond Janis | Jazz Haus Musik | JHM 0052 CD

Eje,Niels | (oboe)
Miles Davis With The Danish Radio Big Band
Aura | CBS | CK 63962
The Danish Radio Big Band
Aura | CBS | CK 63962

Ek,Bengt | (clts)
Tim Hagans With Norrbotten Big Band
Future Miles | ACT | 9235-2

Ekdahl,Lisa | (voc)
Lisa Ekdahl With The Peter Nordahl Trio
When Did You Leave Heaven | RCA | 2143175-2
Back To Earth | RCA | 2161463-2
Lisa Ekdahl With The Salvador Poe Quartet, Strings And Guests
Lisa Ekdahl Sings Salvadore Poe | RCA | 2179681-2

Ekdahl,Per | (perc,compld)
European Jazz Youth Orchestra
Swinging Europe 1 | dacapo | DCCD 9449
Swinging Europe 2 | dacapo | DCCD 9450

Ekeh,Frank | (djun-djunshekere)
Don Cherry Group
Multi Kulti | A&M Records | 395323-2

Ekholm,Magnus | (tpfl-h)
Tim Hagans With Norrbotten Big Band
Future Miles | ACT | 9235-2

Ekornes,Kenneth | (drperc)
Geir Lysne Listening Ensemble
Korall | ACT | 9236-2
Aurora Borealis-Nordic Lights | ACT | 9406-2

Ekorness,Oyvind | (cello)
Ketil Bjornstad Group
Early Years | EmArCy | 013271-2

Ekyan,Andre | (ascl)
Benny Carter And His Orchestra
Americans Swinging In Paris:Benny Carter | EMI Records | 539647-2
Coleman Hawkins And His All Star Jam Band
Django Reinhardt All Star Sessions | Capitol | 531577-2
Americans Swinging In Paris:Benny Carter | EMI Records | 539647-2
Jazz:The Essential Collection Vol.3 | IN+OUT Records | 78013-2
Coleman Hawkins With Michel Warlop And His Orchestra
Django Reinhardt All Star Sessions | Capitol | 531577-2
Django Reinhardt Quintet
Django/Django In Rome 1949-1050 | BGO Records | BGOCD 366
Wal-Berg Et Son Jazz Francais
Jazz In Paris:Django Reinhardt-Django Et Compagnie | EmArCy | 549241-2 PMS

El Badri,Hani | (ney)
Mahmoud Turkmani Group
Zakira | Enja | ENJ-9475 2

El Gourd,Addellah | (hag'houge,handclappingvoc)
Randy Weston African Rhythm Quintet and The Gnawa Master Musicians of Marocco
Spirit! The Power Of Music | Verve | 543256-2

El Nil Troop |
Koch-Schütz-Studer & El Nil Troop
Heavy Cairo Trafic | Intuition Records | INT 3175-2

El Sayed,Nehad | (oud)
Mahmoud Turkmani Group
Zakira | Enja | ENJ-9475 2

El-Achek,Yassin | (v)
Rabih Abou-Khalil Group
Roots & Sprouts | Enja | ENJ-9373 2

Elam,Larry | (tp)
Joe Pass With The NDR Big Band
Joe Pass In Hamburg | ACT | 9100-2

Elder,Connie | (voice)
Charles Mingus Orchestra
Tijuana Moods(The Complete Edition) | RCA | 2663840-2

Eldridge,Roy | (arr,fl-h,p overdubbed,p-solo,tp,p,b)
Anita O'Day With Gene Krupa And His Orchestra
Let Me Off Uptown:Anita O'Day With Gene Krupa | CBS | CK 65625
Art Tatum Quartet
Art Tatum-The Complete Pablo Group Masterpieces | Pablo | 6 PACD 4401-2
Artie Shaw And His Orchestra
Planet Jazz:Jazz Trumpet | Planet Jazz | 2169654-2
Ben Webster And His Associates
Verve Jazz Masters 43:Ben Webster | Verve | 525431-2
Ultimate Ben Webster selected by James Carter | Verve | 557537-2
Ben Webster And Associates | Verve | 835254-2
Benny Carter And His Orchestra
Jazz At The Philharmonic:The Montreux Collection | Pablo | PACD 5306-2
Benny Goodman And His V-Disc All Star Band
The Legends Of Swing | Laserlight | 24659
Billie Holiday And Her All Stars
The Billie Holiday Song Book | Verve | 823246-2
Billie Holiday With Teddy Wilson And His Orchestra
Billie's Love Songs | Nimbus Records | NI 2000
Buddy Rich Orchestra
Krupa And Rich | Verve | 521643-2
Buddy Rich-Gene Krupa Orchestra
Krupa And Rich | Verve | 521643-2
Charles Mingus Group
The Jazz Life! | Candid | CCD 79019
Mysterious Blues | Candid | CCD 79042
Coleman Hawkins And Confreres
Coleman Hawkins And Confreres | Verve | 835255-2 PMS
Coleman Hawkins Quintet
Verve Jazz Masters 43:Coleman Hawkins | Verve | 521856-2
Ultimate Coleman Hawkins selected by Sonny Rollins | Verve | 557538-2
Jazz:The Essential Collection Vol.3 | IN+OUT Records | 78013-2
Coleman Hawkins-Roy Eldridge Quintet
Verve Jazz Masters 43:Coleman Hawkins | Verve | 521856-2
Count Basie And His Orchestra
Verve Jazz Masters 2:Count Basie | Verve | 519819-2
Count Basie At Newport | Verve | 9861761
Count Basie And The Kansas City 7
Count Basie: Salle Pleyel, April 17th, 1972 | Laserlight | 36127
Count Basie Jam
Montreux '77 | Original Jazz Classics | OJC 379(2308209)
Montreux '77 | Original Jazz Classics | OJC 385(2620105)
Count Basie Jam Session
Count Basie Jam Session At The Montreux Jazz Festival 1975 | Original Jazz Classics | OJC20 933-2(2310750)
Count Basie Sextet
Jazz At The Philharmonic:The Montreux Collection | Pablo | PACD 5306-2
Dicky Wells And His Orchestra
Americans Swinging In Paris:Dicky Wells | EMI Records | 539664-2
Dizzy Gillespie Sextet
Verve Jazz Masters 10:Dizzy Gillespie | Verve | 516319-2
Dizzy Gillespie-Roy Eldridge Sextet
Ultimate Dizzy Gillespie | Verve | 557535-2
The Complete Verve Roy Eldridge Studio Sessions | Verve | 9861278
Dizzy Gillespie's Trumpet Kings

INTERPRETENVERZEICHNIS

The Trumpet Kings Meet Joe Turner | Original Jazz Classics | OJCCD 497-2
Ella Fitzgerald And Count Basie With The JATP All Stars
Bluella:Ella Fitzgerald Sings The Blues | Pablo | 2310960-2
Ella Fitzgerald And Her All Stars
Ella Fitzgerald-First Lady Of Song | Verve | 517898-2
Verve Jazz Masters 6:Ella Fitzgerald | Verve | 519822-2
For The Love Of Ella Fitzgerald | Verve | 841765-2
Ella Fitzgerald And Her Quintet
Verve Jazz Masters 46:Ella Fitzgerald-The Jazz Sides | Verve | 527655-2
Ella Fitzgerald With The JATP All Stars
Ella Fitzgerald-First Lady Of Song | Verve | 517898-2
For The Love Of Ella Fitzgerald | Verve | 841765-2
Esquire Metropolitan Opera House Jam Session
Jazz:The Essential Collection Vol.3 | IN+OUT Records | 78013-2
Fletcher Henderson And His Orchestra
Jazz:The Essential Collection Vol.1 | IN+OUT Records | 78011-2
Gene Krupa Orchestra
Krupa And Rich | Verve | 521643-2
Gene Krupa's Swing Band
Planet Jazz:Swing | Planet Jazz | 2169651-2
Herb Ellis Quintet
Stan Getz Highlights:The Best Of The Verve Years Vol.2 | Verve | 517330-2
Nothing But The Blues | Verve | 521674-2
JATP All Stars
JATP In Tokyo | Pablo | 2620104-2
Stan Getz Highlights:The Best Of The Verve Years Vol.2 | Verve | 517330-2
Nothing But The Blues | Verve | 521674-2
Verve Jazz Masters 28:Charlie Parker Plays Standards | Verve | 521854-2
The Complete Jazz At The Philharmonic On Verve 1944-1949 | Verve | 523893-2
Charlie Parker:The Best Of The Verve Years | Verve | 527815-2
Jazz At The Philharmonic:Best Of The 1940's Concerts | Verve | 557534-2
The Drum Battle:Gene Krupa And Buddy Rich At JATP | Verve | 559810-2
Talkin' Bird | Verve | 559859-2
Bird: The Complete Charlie Parker On Verve | Verve | 837141-2
Welcome To Jazz At The Philharmonic | Fantasy | FANCD 6081-2
Jazz At The Philharmonic-Frankfurt 1952 | Pablo | PACD 5305-2
Jazz Artists Guild
Newport Rebels-Jazz Artists Guild | Candid | CCD 79022
Johnny Hodges And His Band
Verve Jazz Masters 35:Johnny Hodges | Verve | 521857-2
Johnny Hodges Orchestra
Planet Jazz:Johnny Hodges | Planet Jazz | 2152065-2
Side By Side | Verve | 521405-2
The Soul Of Ben Webster | Verve | 527475-2
Lester Young Septet
Laughin' To Keep From Cryin' | Verve | 543301-2
Lester Young-Roy Eldridge-Harry Edison Band
Jazz Gallery:Lester Young Vol.2(1946-59) | RCA | 2119541-2
Newport Rebels
Candid Dolphy | Candid | CCD 79033
Norman Granz Jam Session
Verve Jazz Masters 26:Lionel Hampton with Oscar Peterson | Verve | 521853-2
Verve Jazz Masters Vol.60:The Collection | Verve | 529866-2
Oscar Peterson Sextet
Oscar Peterson Trio: Olympia/Theatre Des Champs-Elysees | Laserlight | 36134
Oscar Peterson Trio With Roy Eldridge
Oscar Peterson Trio: Olympia/Theatre Des Champs-Elysees | Laserlight | 36134
Oscar Peterson With The Ernie Wilkins Orchestra
Verve Jazz Masters 16:Oscar Peterson | Verve | 516320-2
Oscar Peterson-Roy Eldridge Duo
Oscar Peterson & Roy Eldridge | Original Jazz Classics | OJCCD 727-2(2310739)
Ralph Burns And His Orchestra
The Complete Verve Roy Eldridge Studio Sessions | Verve | 9861278
Roy Eldridge 4
Montreux '77 | Original Jazz Classics | OJCCD 373-2
Roy Eldridge And His Central Plaza Dixielanders
The Very Best Of Dixieland Jazz | Verve | 535529-2
The Complete Verve Roy Eldridge Studio Sessions | Verve | 9861278
Roy Eldridge And His Orchestra
The Complete Verve Roy Eldridge Studio Sessions | Verve | 9861278
Roy Eldridge And His Orchestra With Strings
The Complete Verve Roy Eldridge Studio Sessions | Verve | 9861278
Roy Eldridge And The Jimmy Ryan All Stars
Jazz Dance | Original Jazz Classics | OJCCD 1002-2(1210890)
Little Jazz And The Jimmy Ryan All-Stars | Original Jazz Classics | OJCCD 1058-2(DRE 1001)
Roy Eldridge Quintet
The Complete Verve Roy Eldridge Studio Sessions | Verve | 9861278
Decidedly | Pablo | PACD 5314-2
Roy Eldridge Septet
To Bags...With Love:Memorial Album | Pablo | 2310967-2
Roy Eldridge Sextet
The Complete Verve Roy Eldridge Studio Sessions | Verve | 9861278
Milt Jackson Birthday Celebration | Fantasy | FANCD 6079-2
Decidedly | Pablo | PACD 5314-2
Roy Eldridge With The Russell Garcia Orchestra
The Complete Verve Roy Eldridge Studio Sessions | Verve | 9861278
Roy Eldridge-Alvin Stoller
The Complete Verve Roy Eldridge Studio Sessions | Verve | 9861278
Roy Eldridge-Benny Carter Quintet
The Complete Verve Roy Eldridge Studio Sessions | Verve | 9861278
Roy Eldridge-Dizzy Gillespie With The Oscar Peterson Quartet
The Complete Verve Roy Eldridge Studio Sessions | Verve | 9861278
Jazz Maturity... Where It's Coming From | Original Jazz Classics | OJCCD 807-2(2310816)
Roy Eldridge-Dizzy Gillespie-Harry Edison With The Oscar Peterson Quartet
The Complete Verve Roy Eldridge Studio Sessions | Verve | 9861278
Roy 'Little Jazz' Eldridge Quartet
The Complete Verve Roy Eldridge Studio Sessions | Verve | 9861278
Sonny Stitt Sextet
Verve Jazz Masters 50:Sonny Stitt | Verve | 527651-2
Teddy Wilson And His All Stars
Jazz:The Essential Collection Vol.3 | IN+OUT Records | 78013-2
The Jazz Giants '56
Jazz Gallery:Lester Young Vol.2(1946-59) | RCA | 2119541-2
The Metronome All Stars
Jazz Gallery:Lester Young Vol.2(1946-59) | RCA | 2119541-2

Elefanten,Die |
Die Elefanten
Wasserwüste | Nabel Records:Jazz Network | CD 4634

Eleodori,Paolo | (dr)
Takabanda
La Leggenda Del Pescatore | Jazz 4 Ever Records:Jazz Network | J4E 4752

Eletto,Michele | (fr-h)
Paolo Fresu-Furio Di Castri Quintet
Evening Song | Owl Records | 014733-2

Eley,Lewis | (stringsv)
Bob James And His Orchestra
Jazzrock-Anthology Vol.3:Fusion | Zounds | CD 27100555
Grover Washington Jr. Orchestra
Inside Moves | Elektra | 7559-60318-2
Helen Merrill With Orchestra
Casa Forte | EmArCy | 558848-2
Paul Desmond Quartet With The Don Sebesby Orchestra
From The Hot Afternoon | Verve | 543487-2
Sarah Vaughan With Orchestra
!Viva! Vaughan | Mercury | 549374-2
Sarah Vaughan Sings The Mancini Songbook | Verve | 558401-2
Wes Montgomery With The Don Sebesky Orchestra
Verve Jazz Masters 14:Wes Montgomery | Verve | 519826-2
Talkin' Jazz:Roots Of Acid Jazz | Verve | 529580-2
Bumpin' | Verve | 539062-2

Elfenbein,Jay | (b)
Earl Klugh Group With Strings
Late Night Guitar | Blue Note | 498573-2

Elgart,Billy | (dr,perc,tb,engl-h,b-cl,as,sax,g,p)
New On The Corner
Left Handed | Jazz 4 Ever Records:Jazz Network | J4E 4758
Paul Bley Trio
Paul Bley With Gary Peacock | ECM | 1003
Sieverts-Mahall-Elgart
Goldfischgesänge | Jazz Haus Musik | JHM 0076 CD
Vlatko Kucan Group
Vlatko Kucan Group | true muze | TUMU CD 9803
Wayne Darling Group
The Art Of The Bass Vol.1 | Laika Records | 35101652
Wolfgang Lackerschmid Quartet
One More Life | Bhakti Jazz | BR 29

Elias,David | (dr)
Max Neissendorfer Trio
Staubfrei | EGO | 95100

Elias,Eliane | (el-p,keyboards,voc,p,synthp-solo)
Eliane Elias Trio
The Story Of Jazz Piano | Laserlight | 24653
Blue Bossa | Blue Note | 795590-2
Joe Henderson Group
Double Rainbow | Verve | 527222-2
Randy Brecker Group
Jazzrock-Anthology Vol.3:Fusion | Zounds | CD 27100555
Steps Ahead
Steps Ahead:Copenhagen Live | Storyville | 4960363
Steps Ahead | Elektra | 7559-60168-2
The Brecker Brothers
Out Of The Loop | GRP | GRP 97842

Eliez,Thierry | (org,pvoc)
Dee Dee Bridgewater With Band
This Is New | Verve | 016884-2
Dee Dee Bridgewater Sings Kurt Weil | EmArCy | 9809601
Dee Dee Bridgewater With Her Quintet
Love And Peace-A Tribute To Horace Silver | Verve | 527470-2
Dee Dee Bridgewater With Her Quintet With Jimmy Smith
Love And Peace-A Tribute To Horace Silver | Verve | 527470-2
Dee Dee Bridgewater With Her Trio
Keeping Tradition | Verve | 519607-2
Live At Yoshi's | Verve | 543354-2

Eliovson,Steve | (g)
Steve Eliovson-Collin Walcott
Dawn Dance | ECM | 1198

Elizalde,John | (synth)
Singers Unlimited With The Pat Williams Orchestra
The Singers Unlimited:Magic Voices | MPS | 539130-2

Eljas,Anders | (org)
Nils Landgren-Tomasz Stanko With Anders Eljas And Claus Bantzer
Gotland | ACT | 9226-2

Elkins,Marty | (voc)
Marty Elkins And Her Sextet
Fuse Blues | Nagel-Heyer | CD 062

Ellen | (voc)
Pili-Pili
Hotel Babo | JA & RO | JARO 4147-2

Ellen,Max | (stringsv)
Bob James And His Orchestra
Jazzrock-Anthology Vol.3:Fusion | Zounds | CD 27100555
Grover Washington Jr. Orchestra
Inside Moves | Elektra | 7559-60318-2
Jazzrock-Anthology Vol.3:Fusion | Zounds | CD 27100555
Les McCann Group
Another Beginning | Atlantic | 7567-80790-2
Milt Jackson And His Orchestra
Sunflower | CTI | ZK 65131
Nina Simone And Orchestra
Baltimore | Epic | 476906-2
Sonny Stitt With Orchestra
Goin' Down Slow | Prestige | PRCD 24276-2

Eller,Harald 'Haro' | (b)
René Pretschner
Story Of A Jazz Piano Vol.1 | Green House Music | CD 1013

Ellick,Roger | (tp)
Tommy Dorsey And His Orchestra
Planet Jazz:Tommy Dorsey | Planet Jazz | 2159972-2
Planet Jazz:Jazz Greatest Hits | Planet Jazz | 2169648-2

Elling,Kurt | (voc)
Kurt Elling Group
This Time Its Love | Blue Note | 493543-2
Blue Velvet: Crooners, Swooners And Velvet Vocals | Blue Note | 521153-2
Flirting With Twilight | Blue Note | 531113-2
Kurt Elling Group With Guests
Live In Chicago | Blue Note | 522211-2

Ellington II,Edward | (g)
Duke Ellington Orchestra
Continuum | Fantasy | FCD 24765-2

Ellington,Bill | (b)
The Latin Jazz Quintet Plus Guest: Eric Dolphy
Eric Dolphy:The Complete Prestige Recordings | Prestige | 9 PRCD-4418-2
Eric Dolphy Birthday Celebration | Fantasy | FANCD 6085-2

Ellington,Duke | (announcer,arr,ld,celeste,voc,p)
Barney Bigard And His Orchestra
Highlights From The Duke Ellington Centennial Edition | RCA | 2663672-2
Jazz:The Essential Collection Vol.3 | IN+OUT Records | 78013-2
Django Reinhardt With Duke Ellington And His Orchestra
Django Reinhardt:Souveniers | Dreyfus Jazz Line | FDM 36744-2
Duke Ellington
Planet Jazz:Duke Ellington | Planet Jazz | 2152053-2
Planet Jazz:Jazz Piano | RCA | 2169655-2
Duke Ellington Live At The Whitney | Impulse(MCA) | 951173-2
Duke Ellington And Count Basie With Their Orchestras
First Time! | CBS | CK 65571
Duke Ellington And His Award Winners
Greatest Hits | CBS | 462959-2
Duke Ellington And His Cotton Club Orchestra
Planet Jazz:Duke Ellington | Planet Jazz | 2152053-2
Jazz:The Essential Collection Vol.2 | IN+OUT Records | 78012-2
Duke Ellington And His Famous Orchestra
Duke Ellington:The Blanton-Webster Band | Bluebird | 21 13181-2
Planet Jazz:Duke Ellington | Planet Jazz | 2152053-2
Planet Jazz:Johnny Hodges | Planet Jazz | 2152065-2
Planet Jazz Sampler | Planet Jazz | 2152326-2
Planet Jazz:Ben Webster | RCA | 2165368-2
Planet Jazz:Big Bands | Planet Jazz | 2169649-2
Planet Jazz:Jazz Trumpet | Planet Jazz | 2169654-2
Planet Jazz:Female Jazz Vocalists | Planet Jazz | 2169656-2
Highlights From The Duke Ellington Centennial Edition | RCA | 2663672-2
Greatest Hits | CBS | 462959-2
Jazz:The Essential Collection Vol.2 | IN+OUT Records | 78012-2
Jazz:The Essential Collection Vol.3 | IN+OUT Records | 78013-2
Duke Ellington:Ko-Ko | Dreyfus Jazz Line | FDM 36717-2
Duke Ellington And His Kentucky Club Orchestra
Jazz:The Essential Collection Vol.2 | IN+OUT Records | 78012-2
Duke Ellington And His Orchestra
Planet Jazz:Duke Ellington | Planet Jazz | 2152053-2
Planet Jazz:Johnny Hodges | Planet Jazz | 2152065-2
Planet Jazz:Jazz Greatest Hits | Planet Jazz | 2169648-2
Duke Ellington's Far East Suite | RCA | 2174797-2
Jazz Collection:Duke Ellington | Laserlight | 24369
The Art Of Saxophone | Laserlight | 24652
The Story Of Jazz Piano | Laserlight | 24653
The Legends Of Swing | Laserlight | 24659
100 Years Duke | Laserlight | 24906
Highlights From The Duke Ellington Centennial Edition | RCA | 2663672-2
The Popular Duke Ellington | RCA | 2663880-2
Carnegie Hall Concert December 1944 | Prestige | 2PCD 24073-2
Carnegie Hall Concert January 1946 | Prestige | 2PCD 24074-2
Carnegie Hall Concert December 1947 | Prestige | 2PCD 24075-2
Carnegie Hall Concert January 1943 | Prestige | 2PCD 34004-2
Duke Ellington: The Champs-Elysees Theater January 29-30th,1965 | Laserlight | 36131
Greatest Hits | CBS | 462959-2
The Big Bands Vol.1.The Snader Telescriptions | Storyville | 4960043
Duke Ellington And His Orchestra 1929-1943 | Storyville | 4960333
Jazz Festival Vol.2 | Storyville | 4960743
Verve Jazz Masters 4:Duke Ellington | Verve | 516338-2
Verve Jazz Masters 20:Introducing | Verve | 519853-2
Ellington '55 | Capitol | 520135-2
Great Swing Classics In Hi-Fi | Capitol | 521223-2
Ella & Duke At The Cote D'Azur | Verve | 539030-2
Ella Fitzgerald And Duke Ellington:Cote D'Azure Concerts on Verve | Verve | 539033-2
Soul Call | Verve | 539785-2
The Great Paris Concert | Atlantic | 7567-81303-2
Jazz:The Essential Collection Vol.2 | IN+OUT Records | 78012-2
Jazz:The Essential Collection Vol.3 | IN+OUT Records | 78013-2
New Orleans Suite | Rhino | 812273670-2
Afro-Bossa | Reprise | 9362-47876-2
Ellington At Newport 1956(Complete) | CBS | CK 64932
Black Brown And Beige | CBS | CK 65566
Such Sweet Thunder | CBS | CK 65568
Anatomy Of A Murder | CBS | CK 65569
Welcome To Jazz At The Philharmonic | Fantasy | FANCD 6081-2
The Ellington Suites | Original Jazz Classics | OJC20 446-2(2310762)
Latin America Suite | Original Jazz Classics | OJC20 469-2
Duke Ellington And His Orchestra feat. Paul Gonsalves | Original Jazz Classics | OJCCD 623-2
The Afro-Eurasian Eclipse-A Suite In Eight Parts | Original Jazz Classics | OJCCD 645-2(F 9498)
Yale Concert | Original Jazz Classics | OJCCD 664-2
Jazz At The Philharmonis Berlin '65/Paris '67 | Pablo | PACD 5304-2
Duke Ellington At The Alhambra | Pablo | PACD 5313-2
The Jazz Giants Play Duke Ellington:Caravan | Prestige | PCD 24227-2
The Duke At Fargo 1940 | Storyville | STCD 8316/17
Togo Brava Swuite | Storyville | STCD 8323
At The Hurricane:Original 1943 Broadcasts | Storyville | STCD 8359
Duke Ellington And Johnny Hodges Orchestra
Side By Side | Verve | 521405-2
Duke Ellington Duo
The Ellington Suites | Original Jazz Classics | OJC20 446-2(2310762)
Duke Ellington Quartet
Joe Pass:Guitar Virtuoso | Pablo | 4 PACD 4423-2
Great Times! | Original Jazz Classics | OJC20 108-2(RLP 475)
Latin America Suite | Original Jazz Classics | OJC20 469-2
The Jazz Giants Play Duke Ellington:Caravan | Prestige | PCD 24227-2
Togo Brava Swuite | Storyville | STCD 8323
Duke Ellington Small Band
The Intimacy Of The Blues | Original Jazz Classics | OJCCD 624-2
Duke Ellington Trio
Highlights From The Duke Ellington Centennial Edition | RCA | 2663672-2
Duke Ellington Live At The Whitney | Impulse(MCA) | 951173-2
Duke Ellington Trio With The Boston Pops Orchestra
Highlights From The Duke Ellington Centennial Edition | RCA | 2663672-2
Duke Ellington With Tommy Dorsey And His Orchestra
Highlights From The Duke Ellington Centennial Edition | RCA | 2663672-2
Duke Ellington/Jimmy Blanton
Highlights From The Duke Ellington Centennial Edition | RCA | 2663672-2
Duke Ellington:Ko-Ko | Dreyfus Jazz Line | FDM 36717-2
Duke Ellington-Billy Strayhorn Duo
Planet Jazz:Duke Ellington | Planet Jazz | 2152053-2
Highlights From The Duke Ellington Centennial Edition | RCA | 2663672-2
Duke Ellington-Billy Strayhorn Quintet
Great Times! | Original Jazz Classics | OJC20 108-2(RLP 475)
Duke Ellington-Billy Strayhorn Trio
Great Times! | Original Jazz Classics | OJC20 108-2(RLP 475)
Duke Ellington-Coleman Hawkins Orchestra
Duke Ellington Meets Coleman Hawkins | Impulse(MCA) | 951162-2
Duke Ellington-Johnny Hodges All Stars
Verve Jazz Masters 4:Duke Ellington | Verve | 516338-2
Back To Back | Verve | 521404-2
Ella Fitzgerald With The Duke Ellington Orchestra
The Stockholm Concert 1966 | Pablo | 2308242-2
Ella Fitzgerald-First Lady Of Song | Verve | 517898-2
The Best Of The Song Books | Verve | 519804-2
Verve Jazz Masters 6:Ella Fitzgerald | Verve | 519822-2
Verve Jazz Masters 46:Ella Fitzgerald-The Jazz Sides | Verve | 527655-2
Ella At Duke's Place | Verve | 529700-2
Love Songs:The Best Of The Song Books | Verve | 531762-2
Ella & Duke At The Cote D'Azur | Verve | 539030-2
Ella Fitzgerald And Duke Ellington:Cote D'Azure Concerts on Verve | Verve | 539033-2
Ella Fitzgerald Sings The Duke Ellington Songbook | Verve | 559248-2
For The Love Of Ella Fitzgerald | Verve | 841765-2
Ella Fitzgerald With The Duke Ellington Orchestra And Jimmy Jones Trio
Ella Fitzgerald And Duke Ellington:Cote D'Azure Concerts on Verve | Verve | 539033-2
Ellington/Mingus/Roach Trio
Money Jungle | Blue Note | 538227-2
Esquire All-American Award Winners
Best Of The Complete RCA Victor Recordings | RCA | 2663636-2
Highlights From The Duke Ellington Centennial Edition | RCA | 2663672-2
John Coltrane-Duke Ellington Quartet
The Gentle Side Of John Coltrane | Impulse(MCA) | 951107-2
Duke Ellington & John Coltrane | Impulse(MCA) | 951166-2
Johnny Hodges Orchestra
Planet Jazz:Johnny Hodges | Planet Jazz | 2152065-2
Planet Jazz Sampler | Planet Jazz | 2152326-2
Planet Jazz:Jazz Saxophone | Planet Jazz | 2169653-2
Highlights From The Duke Ellington Centennial Edition | RCA | 2663672-2
Leonard Feather's Esquire All-Americans
Louis Armstrong:C'est Si Bon | Dreyfus Jazz Line | FDM 36730-2
Louis Armstrong And His All Stars With Duke Ellington
Louis Armstrong-Duke Ellington:The Great Summit-Complete Session | Roulette | 524546-2
Louis Armstrong-Duke Ellington Group
Blue Velvet: Crooners, Swooners And Velvet Vocals | Blue Note | 521153-2
Oscar Peterson With The Duke Ellington Orchestra
Oscar Peterson Plays Duke Ellington | Pablo | 2310966-2
Rex Stewart And His Orchestra

Planet Jazz:Jazz Trumpet | Planet Jazz | 2169654-2
Jazz:The Essential Collection Vol.3 | IN+OUT Records | 78013-2
Rosemary Clooney With The Duke Ellington Orchestra
Blue Rose | CBS | CK 65506
Sathima Bea Benjamin Group
A Morning In Paris | Enja | ENJ-9309 2

Ellington,Marie | (voc)
Duke Ellington And His Orchestra
Planet Jazz:Duke Ellington | Planet Jazz | 2152053-2
Planet Jazz:Jazz Greatest Hits | Planet Jazz | 2169648-2
Carnegie Hall Concert December 1944 | Prestige | 2PCD 24073-2

Ellington,Mercer | (cond,arr,musical-director,tpfl-h)
Planet Jazz:Johnny Hodges | Planet Jazz | 2152065-2
Duke Ellington's Far East Suite | RCA | 2174797-2
The Art Of Saxophone | Laserlight | 24652
Highlights From The Duke Ellington Centennial Edition | RCA | 2663672-2
The Popular Duke Ellington | RCA | 2663880-2
Duke Ellington: The Champs-Elysees Theater January 29-30th,1965 | Laserlight | 36131
Verve Jazz Masters 4:Duke Ellington | Verve | 516338-2
Verve Jazz Masters 20:Introducing | Verve | 519853-2
Ella & Duke At The Cote D'Azur | Verve | 539030-2
Ella Fitzgerald And Duke Ellington:Cote D'Azure Concerts on Verve | Verve | 539033-2
Soul Call | Verve | 539785-2
New Orleans Suite | Rhino | 812273670-2
Welcome To Jazz At The Philharmonic | Fantasy | FANCD 6081-2
The Ellington Suites | Original Jazz Classics | OJC20 446-2(2310762)
Latin America Suite | Original Jazz Classics | OJC20 469-2
The Afro-Eurasian Eclipse-A Suite In Eight Parts | Original Jazz Classics | OJCCD 645-2(F 9498)
Yale Concert | Original Jazz Classics | OJCCD 664-2
Jazz At The Philharmonis Berlin '65/Paris '67 | Pablo | PACD 5304-2
The Jazz Giants Play Duke Ellington:Caravan | Prestige | PCD 24227-2
Togo Brava Swuite | Storyville | STCD 8323
Duke Ellington Orchestra
Continuum | Fantasy | FCD 24765-2
Ella Fitzgerald With The Duke Ellington Orchestra
The Stockholm Concert 1966 | Pablo | 2308242-2
Ella Fitzgerald-First Lady Of Song | Verve | 517898-2
Verve Jazz Masters 46:Ella Fitzgerald-The Jazz Sides | Verve | 527655-2
Ella & Duke At The Cote D'Azur | Verve | 539030-2
Ella Fitzgerald And Duke Ellington:Cote D'Azure Concerts on Verve | Verve | 539033-2
Ella Fitzgerald With The Duke Ellington Orchestra And Jimmy Jones Trio
Ella & Duke At The Cote D'Azur | Verve | 539030-2
Ella Fitzgerald And Duke Ellington:Cote D'Azure Concerts on Verve | Verve | 539033-2
Oscar Peterson With The Duke Ellington Orchestra
Oscar Peterson Plays Duke Ellington | Pablo | 2310966-2

Ellington,Steve | (dr)
Dave Holland Quintet
Jumpin' In | ECM | 1269
Roland Kirk Quartet
Verve Jazz Masters Vol.60:The Collection | Verve | 529866-2
Talkin' Verve-Roots Of Acid Jazz:Roland Kirk | Verve | 533101-2
Rahsaan/The Complete Mercury Recordings Of Roland Kirk | Mercury | 846630-2

Elliot,Jack | (g)
Henrik Johansen With The City Ramblers
The Golden Years Of Revival Jazz,Sampler | Storyville | 109 1001

Elliot,Jerry | (tb)
Jubilee All Stars
Jazz Gallery:Lester Young Vol.2(1946-59) | RCA | 2119541-2

Elliot,Lloyd | (tb)
Anita O'Day With The Buddy Bregman Orchestra
Pick Yourself Up | Verve | 517329-2

Elliot,Louise | (flts)
Jazz Africa All Nations Big Band
Jadu(Jazz Africa Down Under) | Enja | ENJ-9339 2

Elliot,Richard | (ts)
Richard Elliot Sextet
City Speak | Blue Note | 832620-2

Elliott,Bill | (dr)
Jack McDuff Quartet
Tough 'Duff | Original Jazz Classics | OJCCD 324-2(P 7185)
Jack McDuff:The Prestige Years | Prestige | PRCD 24387-2
Willis Jackson Quintet
Together Again: Willis Jackson With Jack McDuff | Prestige | PRCD 24284-2

Elliott,Don | (bongos,mellophone,tp,voc,vib,perc)
Bill Evans Quartet
The Complete Bill Evans On Verve | Verve | 527953-2
Bill Evans-Don Elliott
Tenderly | Milestone | MCD 9317-2
Dinah Washington With The Quincy Jones Orchestra
Verve Jazz Masters 40:Dinah Washington | Verve | 522055-2
The Swingin' Miss 'D' | Verve | 558074-2
Dinah Washington With The Terry Gibbs Band
Verve Jazz Masters 40:Dinah Washington | Verve | 522055-2
Dinah Washington With The Urbie Green Sextet
Newport Jazz Festival 1958,July 3rd-6th Vol.2:Mulligan The Main Man | Phontastic | NCD 8814
George Shearing Quintet
Verve Jazz Masters 57:George Shearing | Verve | 529900-2
Mundell Lowe And His All Stars
Planet Jazz:Ben Webster | RCA | 2165368-2
Paul Desmond Quartet
Desmond | Original Jazz Classics | OJCCD 712-2(F 3235/8082)
The Jazz Giants Play Jerome Kern:Yesterdays | Prestige | PCD 24202-2
Urbie Green Sextet
Newport Jazz Festival 1958,July 3rd-6th Vol.2:Mulligan The Main Man | Phontastic | NCD 8814

Elliott,Ernest | (as,clts)
Bessie Smith And Her Band
Jazz:The Essential Collection Vol.1 | IN+OUT Records | 78011-2

Ellis,Dave | (ts)
Dave Ellis Quartet
State Of Mind | Milestone | MCD 9328-2
Dave Ellis Quintet
State Of Mind | Milestone | MCD 9328-2

Ellis,David | (ts)
Charlie Hunter Quartet
Ready...Set...Shango! | Blue Note | 837101-2

Ellis,Don | (tparr)
Charles Mingus Group
Mingus Dynasty | CBS | CK 65513
Charles Mingus Orchestra
Charles Mingus:The Complete 1959 Columbia Recordings | CBS | C3K 65145
Don Ellis Orchestra
Electric Bath | CBS | CK 65522
Don Ellis Trio
Out Of Nowhere | Candid | CCD 79032
George Russell Sextet
Eric Dolphy Birthday Celebration | Fantasy | FANCD 6085-2
Ezz-thetics | Original Jazz Classics | OJCCD 070-2(RLP 9375)
The Outer View | Original Jazz Classics | OJCCD 616-2(RLP 9440)
The Jazz Giants Play Miles Davis:Milestones | Prestige | PCD 24225-2

Ellis,Herb | (gg-solo)
Anita O'Day With The Oscar Peterson Quartet
Verve Jazz Masters 49:Anita O'Day | Verve | 527653-2
Ben Webster All Stars
King Of The Tenors | Verve | 519806-2
Ben Webster And His Orchestra
Verve Jazz Masters 43:Ben Webster | Verve | 525431-2
Ben Webster Quartet
Soulville | Verve | 521449-2
Ultimate Ben Webster selected by James Carter | Verve | 557537-2
Ben Webster Quintet
Soulville | Verve | 521449-2
Ben Webster With The Oscar Peterson Quartet
King Of The Tenors | Verve | 519806-2
Verve Jazz Masters 43:Ben Webster | Verve | 525431-2
Ultimate Ben Webster selected by James Carter | Verve | 557537-2
Billie Holiday And Her All Stars
Verve Jazz Masters 12:Billie Holiday | Verve | 519825-2
4 By 4:Ella Fitzgerald/Sarah Vaughan/Billie Holiday/Dinah Washington | Verve | 559693-2
The Billie Holiday Song Book | Verve | 823246-2
Blossom Dearie Quartet
Give Him The Ooh-La-La | Verve | 517067-2
Verve Jazz Masters 51:Blossom Dearie | Verve | 529906-2
Buddy Rich Orchestra
Krupa And Rich | Verve | 521643-2
Buddy Rich-Gene Krupa Orchestra
Krupa And Rich | Verve | 521643-2
Coleman Hawkins And Ben Webster With The Oscar Peterson Quartet
Coleman Hawkins Encounters Ben Webster | Verve | 521427-2
Verve Jazz Masters 43:Coleman Hawkins | Verve | 521856-2
Verve Jazz Masters 43:Ben Webster | Verve | 525431-2
Verve Jazz Masters Vol.60:The Collection | Verve | 529866-2
Ultimate Coleman Hawkins selected by Sonny Rollins | Verve | 557538-2
Coleman Hawkins And Confreres
Coleman Hawkins And Confreres | Verve | 835255-2 PMS
Coleman Hawkins With The Oscar Peterson Quartet
Verve Jazz Masters 43:Coleman Hawkins | Verve | 521856-2
The Genius Of Coleman Hawkins | Verve | 539065-2
Ultimate Coleman Hawkins selected by Sonny Rollins | Verve | 557538-2
Dizzy Gillespie Septet
Stan Getz Highlights:The Best Of The Verve Years Vol.2 | Verve | 517330-2
Verve Jazz Masters 25:Stan Getz & Dizzy Gillespie | Verve | 521852-2
Stan Getz Highlights | Verve | 847430-2
Dizzy Gillespie Sextet
Verve Jazz Masters 10:Dizzy Gillespie | Verve | 516319-2
Dizzy Gillespie-Roy Eldridge Sextet
Ultimate Dizzy Gillespie | Verve | 557535-2
The Complete Verve Roy Eldridge Studio Sessions | Verve | 9861278
Dizzy Gillespie-Stan Getz Sextet
Verve Jazz Masters 25:Stan Getz & Dizzy Gillespie | Verve | 521852-2
Diz And Getz | Verve | 549749-2
Ultimate Stan Getz selected by Joe Henderson | Verve | 557532-2
Stan Getz Highlights | Verve | 847430-2
Duke Robillard-Herb Ellis Quintet
Conversation In Swing Guitar | Stony Plain | SPCD 1260
More Conversations In Swing Guitar | Stony Plain | SPCD 1292
Ella Fitzgerald And Her All Stars
Ella Fitzgerald-First Lady Of Song | Verve | 517898-2
Verve Jazz Masters 6:Ella Fitzgerald | Verve | 519822-2
Love Songs:The Best Of The Song Books | Verve | 531762-2
Ella Fitzgerald Sings The Duke Ellington Songbook | Verve | 559248-2
For The Love Of Ella Fitzgerald | Verve | 841765-2
Ella Fitzgerald And Her Quintet
Verve Jazz Masters 46:Ella Fitzgerald-The Jazz Sides | Verve | 527655-2
Ella Fitzgerald And Herb Ellis
Ella Fitzgerald-First Lady Of Song | Verve | 517898-2
Ella Fitzgerald And Louis Armstrong With The Oscar Peterson Quartet
Ella Fitzgerald-First Lady Of Song | Verve | 517898-2
Verve Jazz Masters 1:Louis Armstrong | Verve | 519818-2
Verve Jazz Masters 6:Ella Fitzgerald | Verve | 519822-2
Verve Jazz Masters 24:Ella Fitzgerald & Louis Armstrong | Verve | 521851-2
Verve Jazz Masters 46:Ella Fitzgerald-The Jazz Sides | Verve | 527655-2
Verve Jazz Masters Vol.60:The Collection | Verve | 529866-2
The Complete Ella Fitzgerald And Louis Armstrong On Verve | Verve | 537284-2
The Best Of Ella Fitzgerald And Louis Armstrong On Verve | Verve | 537909-2
Ella And Louis | Verve | 543304-2
Ella & Louis | Verve | 825373-2
Ella And Louis Again | Verve | 825374-2
For The Love Of Ella Fitzgerald | Verve | 841765-2
Ella Fitzgerald With Frank De Vol And His Orchestra
Get Happy! | Verve | 523321-2
Ella Fitzgerald With Orchestra
Ella/Things Ain't What They Used To Be | Warner | 9362-47875-2
Ella Fitzgerald With The Billy May Orchestra
The Best Of The Song Books:The Ballads | Verve | 521867-2
Love Songs:The Best Of The Song Books | Verve | 531762-2
Ella Fitzgerald Sings The Harold Arlen Song Book | Verve | 589108-2
Ella Fitzgerald With The JATP All Stars
Ella Fitzgerald-First Lady Of Song | Verve | 517898-2
For The Love Of Ella Fitzgerald | Verve | 841765-2
Ella Fitzgerald With The Lou Levy Quartet
Ella Fitzgerald-First Lady Of Song | Verve | 517898-2
Verve Jazz Masters 6:Ella Fitzgerald | Verve | 519822-2
Verve Jazz Masters 46:Ella Fitzgerald-The Jazz Sides | Verve | 527655-2
Clap Hands,Here Comes Charlie! | Verve | 835646-2
For The Love Of Ella Fitzgerald | Verve | 841765-2
Ella Fitzgerald With The Marty Paich Orchestra
Get Happy! | Verve | 523321-2
Ella Fitzgerald With The Nelson Riddle Orchestra
The Best Of The Song Books:The Ballads | Verve | 521867-2
Get Happy! | Verve | 523321-2
Ella Fitzgerald With The Oscar Peterson Quartet
Verve Jazz Masters 6:Ella Fitzgerald | Verve | 519822-2
Verve Jazz Masters 24:Ella Fitzgerald & Louis Armstrong | Verve | 521851-2
For The Love Of Ella Fitzgerald | Verve | 841765-2
Ella Fitzgerald With The Oscar Peterson Quartet And Ben Webster
Verve Jazz Masters 43:Ben Webster | Verve | 525431-2
For Musicians Only
Ultimate Stan Getz selected by Joe Henderson | Verve | 557532-2
Ultimate Dizzy Gillespie | Verve | 557535-2
For Musicians Only | Verve | 837435-2
Gene Krupa Orchestra
Krupa And Rich | Verve | 521643-2
Harry Sweets Edison Sextet
The Soul Of Ben Webster | Verve | 527475-2
Herb Ellis Quintet
Stan Getz Highlights:The Best Of The Verve Years Vol.2 | Verve | 517330-2
Nothing But The Blues | Verve | 521674-2
Herb Ellis-Joe Pass
The Jazz Giants Play Cole Porter:Night And Day | Prestige | PCD 24203-2
J.J.Johnson & Stan Getz With The Oscar Peterson Quartet
Stan Getz Highlights:The Best Of The Verve Years Vol.2 | Verve | 517330-2
A Life In Jazz:A Musical Biography | Verve | 535119-2
Stan Getz Highlights | Verve | 847430-2
Jam Session
Jazz Gallery:Lester Young Vol.2(1946-59) | RCA | 2119541-2
JATP All Stars
JATP In Tokyo | Pablo | 2620104-2
Nothing But The Blues | Verve | 521674-2
Joe Pass-Herb Ellis
Joe Pass:Guitar Virtuoso | Pablo | 4 PACD 4423-2
Johnny Frigo Sextet
I Love John Frigo...He Swings | Mercury | 9861061
Johnny Hartman And His Orchestra
Unforgettable | Impulse(MCA) | IMP 11522
Lester Young Septet
Laughin' To Keep From Cryin' | Verve | 543301-2
Lester Young With The Oscar Peterson Quartet
Jazz Gallery:Lester Young Vol.2(1946-59) | RCA | 2119541-2
Lester Young-Harry Edison With The Oscar Peterson Quartet
Jazz Gallery:Lester Young Vol.2(1946-59) | RCA | 2119541-2
Lester Young-Roy Eldridge-Harry Edison Band
Jazz Gallery:Lester Young Vol.2(1946-59) | RCA | 2119541-2
Lionel Hampton Quintet
The Complete Lionel Hampton Quartets And Quintets With Oscar Peterson On Verve | Verve | 559797-2
Lionel Hampton With The Oscar Peterson Quartet
Verve Jazz Masters 26:Lionel Hampton with Oscar Peterson | Verve | 521853-2
Louis Armstrong With The Oscar Peterson Quartet
Verve Jazz Masters 1:Louis Armstrong | Verve | 519818-2
Verve Jazz Masters 20:Introducing | Verve | 519853-2
Louis Armstrong Meets Oscar Peterson | Verve | 539060-2
Mel Brown Quartet
Chicken Fat | Impulse(MCA) | 9861047
Mel Brown Quintet
Chicken Fat | Impulse(MCA) | 9861047
Oscar Peterson Sextet
Oscar Peterson Trio: Olympia/Theatre Des Champs-Elysees | Laserlight | 36134
Oscar Peterson Trio
JATP In Tokyo | Pablo | 2620104-2
At Zardis' | Pablo | 2CD 2620118
Oscar Peterson Trio: Olympia/Theatre Des Champs-Elysees | Laserlight | 36134
Gitanes Jazz 'Round Midnight: Oscar Peterson | Verve | 511036-2 PMS
At The Stratford Shakespearean Festival | Verve | 513752-2
Verve Jazz Masters 16:Oscar Peterson | Verve | 516320-2
Verve Jazz Masters 37:Oscar Peterson Plays Broadway | Verve | 516893-2
The Oscar Peterson Trio At The Concertgebouw | Verve | 521649-2
The Song Is You-The Best Of The Verve Songbooks | Verve | 531558-2
On The Town | Verve | 543834-2
With Respect To Nat | Verve | 557486-2
Oscar Peterson Plays The Harold Arlen Song Book | Verve | 589103-2
Oscar Peterson Trio With Herb Ellis
Three Originals:Motion&Emotions/Tristeza On Piano/Hello Herbie | MPS | 521059-2
Hello Herbie | MPS | 821846-2
Roy Eldridge And His Orchestra
The Complete Verve Roy Eldridge Studio Sessions | Verve | 9861278
Roy Eldridge Quintet
The Complete Verve Roy Eldridge Studio Sessions | Verve | 9861278
Roy Eldridge Sextet
The Complete Verve Roy Eldridge Studio Sessions | Verve | 9861278
Roy Eldridge-Dizzy Gillespie With The Oscar Peterson Quartet
The Complete Verve Roy Eldridge Studio Sessions | Verve | 9861278
Roy Eldridge-Dizzy Gillespie-Harry Edison With The Oscar Peterson Quartet
The Complete Verve Roy Eldridge Studio Sessions | Verve | 9861278
Sonny Stitt Sextet
Verve Jazz Masters 50:Sonny Sitt | Verve | 527651-2
Stan Getz And J.J. Johnson With The Oscar Peterson Quartet
Ultimate Stan Getz selected by Joe Henderson | Verve | 557532-2
Stan Getz And The Oscar Peterson Trio
The Silver Collection: Stan Getz And The Oscar Peterson Trio | Verve | 827826-2
Stan Getz With The Oscar Peterson Quartet
Verve Jazz Masters 8:Stan Getz | Verve | 519823-2
Ultimate Stan Getz selected by Joe Henderson | Verve | 557532-2
Stan Getz With The Oscar Peterson Trio
Stan Getz Highlights | Verve | 847430-2
V-Disc All Star Jam Session
Louis Armstrong-Jack Teagarden-Woody Herman:Midnights At V-Disc | Jazz Unlimited | JUCD 2048
V-Disc All Stars
Jazz:The Essential Collection Vol.3 | IN+OUT Records | 78013-2

Ellis,John | (dr,ssts)
Andrew Adair Group
States | Fresh Sound Records | FSNT 061 CD
Martin Schrack Quartet
Headin' Home | Storyville | STCD 4253
Martin Schrack Quintet feat.Tom Harrell
Headin' Home | Storyville | STCD 4253

Ellis,Pee Wee | (arr,voc,as,chimes,cond,ss,tsbs)
Hans Theessink Group
Call Me | Minor Music | 801022
Maceo Parker Group
Roots Revisited | Minor Music | 801015
Mo' Roots | Minor Music | 801018
Southern Exposure | Minor Music | 801033
Maceo(Soundtrack) | Minor Music | 801046
Maceo Parker With The Rebirth Brass Band
Maceo(Soundtrack) | Minor Music | 801046
Oscar Brown Jr. And His Group
Live Every Minute | Minor Music | 801071
Pee Wee Ellis & NDR Bigband
What You Like | Minor Music | 801064
Pee Wee Ellis Quartet
Sepia Tonality | Minor Music | 801040
Pee Wee Ellis Quintet
Sepia Tonality | Minor Music | 801040
Pee Wee Ellis Quintet With Guests
A New Shift | Minor Music | 801060
Pee Wee Ellis Trio
Twelve And More Blues | Minor Music | 801034
Pee Wee Ellis-Horace Parlan
Gentle Men Blue | Minor Music | 801073

Ellis,Ray | (condarr)
Billie Holiday With The Ray Ellis Orchestra
Verve Jazz Masters 47:Billie Holiday Sings Standards | Verve | 527650-2
Lady In Satin | CBS | CK 65144

Ellsworth,Ann | (fr-h)
Paquito D'Rivera Group With The Absolute Ensemble
Habanera | Enja | ENJ-9395 2

Elman,Ziggy | (tpld)
Benny Goodman And His Orchestra
Planet Jazz:Benny Goodman | Planet Jazz | 2152054-2
Planet Jazz:Jazz Greatest Hits | Planet Jazz | 2169648-2
Planet Jazz:Big Bands | Planet Jazz | 2169649-2
Planet Jazz:Swing | Planet Jazz | 2169651-2
Planet Jazz:Jazz Trumpet | Planet Jazz | 2169654-2
Planet Jazz:Female Jazz Vocalists | Planet Jazz | 2169656-2
Benny Goodman At Carnegie Hall 1938(Complete) | CBS | C2K 65143
Charlie Christian:Swing To Bop | Dreyfus Jazz Line | FDM 36715-2
Camel Caravan Broadcast 1939 Vol.1 | Phontastic | NCD 8817
Camel Caravan Broadcast 1939 Vol.2 | Phontastic | NCD 8818
Camel Caravan Broadcast 1939 Vol.3 | Phontastic | NCD 8819
More Camel Caravans | Phontastic | NCD 8841/2
More Camel Caravans | Phontastic | NCD 8843/4
More Camel Caravans | Phontastic | NCD 8845/6
Jam Session
Benny Goodman At Carnegie Hall 1938(Complete) | CBS | C2K 65143
Lionel Hampton And His Orchestra
Planet Jazz:Lionel Hampton | Planet Jazz | 2152059-2
Planet Jazz Sampler | Planet Jazz | 2152326-2
Tommy Dorsey And His Orchestra

Planet Jazz:Frank Sinatra & Tommy Dorsey | Planet Jazz | 2152067-2
Planet Jazz Sampler | Planet Jazz | 2152326-2
Planet Jazz:Tommy Dorsey | Planet Jazz | 2159972-2
Frank Sinatra And The Tommy Dorsey Orchestra | RCA | 2668701-2

Elmer,Ziggy | (tb)
Gene Krupa And His Orchestra
Mullenium | CBS | CK 65678

Elmoe,Torben | (p)
Papa Benny's Jazzband
The Golden Years Of Revival Jazz,Vol.2 | Storyville | STCD 5507

Elniff,Jorn | (dr)
Eric Dolphy Quartet
Eric Dolphy Birthday Celebration | Fantasy | FANCD 6085-2
Eric Dolphy With Erik Moseholm's Trio
Eric Dolphy:The Complete Prestige Recordings | Prestige | 9 PRCD-4418-2
Eric Dolphy in Europe, Vol.1 | Original Jazz Classics | OJC 413(P 7304)
Eric Dolphy In Europe, Vol.2 | Original Jazz Classics | OJCCD 414-2
Eric Dolphy In Europe, Vol.3 | Original Jazz Classics | OJCCD 416-2
Stan Getz With Ib Glindemann And His Orchestra
Stan Getz In Europe | Laserlight | 24657

Elphick,Steve | (b)
Clarion Fracture Zone
Blue Shift | VeraBra Records | CDVBR 2075-2
Mara!
Ruino Vino | Laika Records | 35100792
Wanderlust + Guests
Full Bronte | Laika Records | 35101412

Elsässer,Christian | (p)
Christian Elsässer Trio
Future Days | Organic Music | ORGM 9721
Venice | Organic Music | ORGM 9727

Elsässer,Urban | (gvoc)
Art De Fakt
Art De Fakt-Ray Federman:Surfiction Jazz No.2 | double moon | CHRDM 71007

Elsdon,Alan | (tpvoc)
Graham Stewart And His New Orleans Band
The Golden Years Of Revival Jazz,Sampler | Storyville | 109 1001
The Golden Years Of Revival Jazz,Vol.4 | Storyville | STCD 5509
The Golden Years Of Revival Jazz,Vol.10 | Storyville | STCD 5515
Graham Stewart Seven
The Golden Years Of Revival Jazz,Vol.8 | Storyville | STCD 5513
Marty Grosz Quartet
Just For Fun! | Nagel-Heyer | CD 039

Elsner,Felix | (pkeyboards)
Konstantin Wienstroer-Veit Lange-Felix Elsner
Unfinished Business | Green House Music | CD 1005

Elson,Steve | (b-cl,ss,as,ts,bs,accordeon,synth)
Twice A Week & Steve Elson
Play Of Colours | Edition Collage | EC 511-2

Elton,Bill | (tb)
Chubby Jackson And His All Star Big Band
Chubby Takes Over | Fresh Sound Records | FSR-CD 324

Elwenspoek,Thomas | (dr)
Alex De Santis Jazz Quartet
Le Canzoni Italiana | Edition Collage | EC 514-2
Corinne Chatel Quintet
Ma Vie En Rose | Edition Collage | EC 525-2

El'Zabar,Kahlil | (dr,earth-dr,shekere,voice,hand-dr)
Kurt Elling Group With Guests
Live In Chicago | Blue Note | 522211-2

Emanuel,Carol | (harp)
John Zorn Group
Spillane | Nonesuch | 7559-79172-2

Emberson,Norman | (bass-dr,dr,percsnare-dr)
Chris Barber's Jazz And Blues Band
Chris Barber On The Road:A Jazz Documentary | Storyville | 4960683

Emborg,Jorgen | (pkeyboards)
Per Carsten Quintet
Via | dacapo | DCCD 9462

Emer,Michel | (p)
Micheline Day Et Son Quatuor Swing
Jazz In Paris:Django Reinhardt-Django Et Compagnie | EmArCy | 549241-2 PMS
Yvonne Louis With The Orchestra Vola
Jazz In Paris:Django Reinhardt-Django Et Compagnie | EmArCy | 549241-2 PMS

Emer,Michel or Emil Stern | (p)
Micheline Day Et Son Quatuor Swing
Jazz In Paris:Django Reinhardt-Django Et Compagnie | EmArCy | 549241-2 PMS

Emery,James | (el-g,g,mand,soprano-gg-solo)
James Emery Quartet
Fourth World | Between The Lines | btl 020(Efa 10190-2)
Standing On A Whale... | Enja | ENJ-9312 2
Spectral Domains | Enja | ENJ-9344 2
James Emery Septet
Spectral Domains | Enja | ENJ-9344 2
James Emery Sextet
Luminous Cycles | Between The Lines | btl 015(Efa 10185-2)

Emmelot,H. | (v)
Toots Thielemans And His Orchestra
Verve Jazz Masters Vol.59:Toots Thielemans | Verve | 535271-2

Emmery,Harry | (bb-g)
The Rosenberg Trio With Orchestra
Noches Calientes | Verve | 557022-2

Emminger,Norbert | (b-cl,bs,flreeds)
Horst Faigle's Jazzkrement
Gans Normal | Jazz 4 Ever Records:Jazz Network | J4E 4748
Norbert Emminger Quintet
In The Park | Edition Collage | EC 521-2

Emmons,Bobby | (org)
Herbie Mann Group
Memphis Underground | Atlantic | 7567-81364-2
The Best Of Herbie Mann | Atlantic | 7567-81369-2

Emmons,Buddy | (steel-g)
Larry Carlton Group
The Gift | GRP | GRP 98542

Emory,Sonny | (dr)
Lee Ritenour Sextet
Alive In L.A. | GRP | GRP 98822

Emphrey Jr.,Calep | (dr)
B.B.King And His Band
Live At San Quentin | MCA | MCD 06103

Ende,Harald | (saxts)
Chet Baker With The NDR-Bigband
NDR Big Band-Bravissimo | ACT | 9232-2
My Favourite Songs: The Last Great Concert Vol.1 | Enja | ENJ-5097 2
The Last Concert Vol.I+II | Enja | ENJ-6074 22
Chet Baker-The Legacy Vol.1 | Enja | ENJ-9021 2
Heinz Sauer Quartet With The NDR Big Band
NDR Big Band-Bravissimo | ACT | 9232-2
Joe Pass With The NDR Big Band
Joe Pass In Hamburg | ACT | 9100-2
Joe Pass With The NDR Big Band And Radio Philharmonie Hannover
Joe Pass In Hamburg | ACT | 9100-2
NDR Big Band
NDR Big Band-Bravissimo | ACT | 9232-2

Enderlein,Siegfried | (drperc)
Helmut Zacharias & His Sax-Team
Ich Habe Rhythmus | Bear Family Records | BCD 15642 AH
Helmut Zacharias mit Kleiner Tanz-Besetzung
Ich Habe Rhythmus | Bear Family Records | BCD 15642 AH
Helmut Zacharias mit seinem Orchester
Ich Habe Rhythmus | Bear Family Records | BCD 15642 AH

Enders,Johannes | (as,ts,fl,b-cl,ss,CR-78sax)
Johannes Enders Group
Reflections Of South Africa | Jazz 4 Ever Records:Jazz Network | J4E 4729
Johannes Enders Quartet
Sandsee | Organic Music | ORGM 9720
Kyoto | Organic Music | ORGM 9726
Johannes Enders Quintet
Bright Nights | Enja | ENJ-9352 2
Quiet Fire | Enja | ENJ-9390 2
Lutz Häfner Quartet
Way In Way Out | Jazz 4 Ever Records:Jazz Network | J4E 4757
Melanie Bong With Band
Fantasia | Jazz 4 Ever Records:Jazz Network | J4E 4755
The Tough Tenors With The Antonio Farao European Trio
Tough Tenors | Jazz 4 Ever Records:Jazz Network | J4E 4761

Endresen,Sidsel | (recitationvoc)
Christof Lauer-Jens Thomas
Shadows In The Rain | ACT | 9297-2
Nils Petter Molvaer Group
Solid Ether | ECM | 1722(543365-2)
Sidsel Endresen Quartet
So I Write | ECM | 1408(841776-2)
Sidsel Endresen Sextet
Exile | ECM | 1524(521721-2)
Sidsel Endresen-Bugge Wesseltoft
Nightsong | ACT | 9004-2
Trygve Seim Group
Different Rivers | ECM | 1744(159521-2)

Endsley,Shane | (tp)
Steve Coleman And Five Elements
The Sonic Language Of Myth | RCA | 2164123-2
Steve Coleman And The Council Of Balance
Genesis & The Opening Of The Way | RCA | 2152934-2

Enevoldsen,Bob | (b,bs,b-tb,claves,tb,v-tb,tp,ts,b-cl)
Art Pepper Plus Eleven
Art Pepper + Eleven | Contemporary | CSA 7568-6
Modern Jazz Classics | Original Jazz Classics | OJC20 341-2
Bob Enevoldsen Quintet
The Complete Nocturne Recordings:Jazz In Hollywood Series Vol.1 | Fresh Sound Records | NR 3CD-101
Bob Enevoldsen Sextet
The Complete Nocturne Recordings:Jazz In Hollywood Series Vol.1 | Fresh Sound Records | NR 3CD-101
Bud Shank And Trombones
Cool Fool | Fresh Sound Records | FSR CD 507
Ella Fitzgerald With Marty Paich's Dektette
Ella Swings Lightly | Verve | 517535-2
Ella Fitzgerald With The Marty Paich Dek-tette
Ella Fitzgerald-First Lady Of Song | Verve | 517898-2
Verve Jazz Masters 6:Ella Fitzgerald | Verve | 519822-2
Verve Jazz Masters 46:Ella Fitzgerald-The Jazz Sides | Verve | 527655-2
Gerry Mulligan Tentette
Gene Norman Presents The Original Gerry Mulligan Tentet And Quartet | GNP Crescendo | GNPD 56
Harry Babasin Quintet
The Complete Nocturne Recordings:Jazz In Hollywood Series Vol.1 | Fresh Sound Records | NR 3CD-101
Shelly Manne And His Men
Vol.1:The West Coast Sound | Original Jazz Classics | OJCCD 152-2
The Jazz Giants Play Harry Warren:Lullaby Of Broadway | Prestige | PCD 24204-2
Tal Farlow Sextet
Verve Jazz Masters 41:Tal Farlow | Verve | 527365-2
Terry Gibbs Dream Band
Terry Gibbs Dream Band Vol.3:Flying Home | Contemporary | CCD 7654-2
Terry Gibbs Dream Band Vol.6:One More Time | Contemporary | CCD 7658-2
Virgil Gonsalves Sextet
The Complete Nocturne Recordings:Jazz In Hollywood Series Vol.1 | Fresh Sound Records | NR 3CD-101

Engberg,Alf | (b)
Papa Benny's Jazzband
The Golden Years Of Revival Jazz,Sampler | Storyville | 109 1001
The Golden Years Of Revival Jazz,Vol.2 | Storyville | STCD 5507

Engel,Antje | (v)
Uri Caine With The Concerto Köln
Concerto Köln | Winter&Winter | 910086-2

Engel,Benjamin | (as)
Landes Jugend Jazz Orchester Hessen
Touch Of Lips | hr music.de | hrmj 004-01 CD

Engel,Frank | (tp)
Marcus Sukiennik Big Band
A Night In Tunisia Suite(7 Variationen über Dizzy Gillespie's 'A Night In Tunisia') | Jazz Haus Musik | ohne Nummer

Engel,Holger | (pkeyboards)
Acoustic Affaire
Mira | Jazz 'n' Arts Records | JNA 1303

Engel,Jens | (b-tb)
Miles Davis With The Danish Radio Big Band
Aura | CBS | CK 63962
The Danish Radio Big Band
Aura | CBS | CK 63962

Engel,Rudi | (b)
Benny Bailey With The Bernhard Pichl Trio
On The Corner | Jazz 4 Ever Records:Jazz Network | J4E 4726
Bernhard Pichl Trio
On The Corner | Jazz 4 Ever Records:Jazz Network | J4E 4726
New On The Corner
Left Handed | Jazz 4 Ever Records:Jazz Network | J4E 4758

Engelbrecht,Viola | (tb)
The United Women's Orchestra
The Blue One | Jazz Haus Musik | JHM 0099 CD
United Women's Orchestra
Virgo Supercluster | Jazz Haus Musik | JHM 0123 CD

Engelhardt,Dirk | (ssts)
Jürgen Knieper Quintet
State Of Things | Jazz Haus Musik | JHM 0104 CD

Engelhardt,Gudrun | (v)
Uri Caine With The Concerto Köln
Concerto Köln | Winter&Winter | 910086-2

Engelhardt,Raimund | (pakawajtablas)
Konstantin Wienstroer-Veit Lange-Felix Elsner
Unfinished Business | Green House Music | CD 1005

Engelhart,Claudia | (voc)
Don Cherry Group
Multi Kulti | A&M Records | 395323-2

Engelholt,Steen | (tb)
Stan Kenton With The Danish Radio Big Band
Stan Kenton With The Danish Radio Big Band | Storyville | STCD 8340

Engelke,Anke | (voc)
Franck Band
Dufte | Jazz Haus Musik | JHM 0054 CD

Engels,Eddie | (tp)
Toots Thielemans And His Orchestra
Verve Jazz Masters Vol.59:Toots Thielemans | Verve | 535271-2

Engels,John | (dr)
Fabien Degryse Quintet
Medor Sadness | Edition Collage | EC 454-2

Engels,Jorg | (tp)
Dirk Raulf Group
Theater I (Bühnenmusik) | Poise | Poise 07
HR Big Band
Libertango:Homage An Astor Piazolla | hr music.de | hrmj 014-02 CD

Engels,Stefan | (b)
Acoustic Affaire
Mira | Jazz 'n' Arts Records | JNA 1303

Englert,Don | (fl,cl,as,ss,piccolots)
Buddy Rich Big Band
Keep The Customer Satisfied | EMI Records | 523999-2

English,Bill | (dr)
Eddie Jefferson And His Band
Dexter Gordon Birthday Celebration | Fantasy | FANCD 6082-2
Eddie Jefferson With The James Moody Quintet
Body And Soul | Original Jazz Classics | OJCCD 396-2(P 7619)
Gene Ammons And His Orchestra
A Stranger In Town | Prestige | PRCD 24266-2
Joe Newman Quintet
Good 'N' Groovy | Original Jazz Classics | OJCCD 185-2(SV 2019)
Kenny Burrell Quintet
Midnight Blue | Blue Note | 495335-2
The Best Of Blue Note | Blue Note | 796110-2
Soul Call | Original Jazz Classics | OJCCD 846-2(P 7315)
Kenny Burrell-Jimmy Smith Quartet
Blue Bash | Verve | 557453-2
Quincy Jones And His Orchestra
The Quintessence | Impulse(MCA) | 951222-2
The Roots Of Acid Jazz | Impulse(MCA) | IMP 12042

English,Jon | (tb)
Eric Dolphy Quartet With The University Of Illinois Big Band
The Illinois Concert | Blue Note | 499826-2

Englund,Gene | (b,tbtuba)
Shorty Rogers And His Giants
PLanet Jazz:Shorty Rogers | Planet Jazz | 2159976-2
Shorty Rogers And His Orchestra Feat. The Giants
PLanet Jazz:Shorty Rogers | Planet Jazz | 2159976-2

Engstfeld,Wolfgang | (ssts)
Brecker-Engstfeld-Plümer-Weiss
ToGether | Nabel Records:Jazz Network | CD 4648
Changes
Jazz Portraits | EGO | 95080
Engstfeld-Plümer-Weiss
Drivin' | Nabel Records:Jazz Network | CD 4618
Matthias Bröde Quintet
European Faces | Edition Collage | EC 517-2
Peter Weiss Orchestra
Personal Choice | Nabel Records:Jazz Network | CD 4669
Peter Weiss Quartet
Personal Choice | Nabel Records:Jazz Network | CD 4669
Randy Brecker-Wolfgang Engstfeld Quartet
Mr. Max! | Nabel Records:Jazz Network | CD 4637
Wayne Bartlett With The Thomas Hufschmidt Trio And Wolfgang Engstfeld
Senor Blues | Laika Records | LK 95-066
Wolfgang Engstfeld Quartet
Songs And Ballads | Nabel Records:Jazz Network | CD 4658

Ennett,Lucky | (ts)
Gunter Hampel New York Orchestra
Fresh Heat-Live At Sweet Basil | Birth | CD 039

Eno,Brian | (el-b)
Jon Hassell Group
Power Spot | ECM | 1327

Enoch,Tommy | (tp)
Earl Hines And His Orchestra
Planet Jazz:Earl Hines | Planet Jazz | 2159973-2

Enos,Dave | (bel-b)
Arturo Sandoval And The Latin Train Band
Arturo Sandoval & The Latin Train | GRP | GRP 98202

Enriquez,Bobby | (p)
Richie Cole Group
Jazz Life Vol.1:From Village Vanguard | Storyville | 4960753

Enriquez,Hugo | (percvoc)
Omar Belmonte's Latin Lover
Vamos A Ver | EGO | 96170

Enriquez,Luis | (percvoc)
Arturo Sandoval And The Latin Train Band
Arturo Sandoval & The Latin Train | GRP | GRP 98202

Ens,Arthur | (g)
Glenn Miller And His Orchestra
Planet Jazz:Glenn Miller | Planet Jazz | 2152056-2
Planet Jazz:Swing | Planet Jazz | 2169651-2
Candelight Miller | RCA | 2668716-2

Ensemble 13 |
Michael Riessler And The Ensemble 13
Momentum Mobile | Enja | ENJ-9003 2

Ensemble Calixtinus |
Michel Godard Ensemble
Castel Del Monte II | Enja | ENJ-9431 2

Ensemble Indigo |
Ensemble Indigo
Reflection | Enja | ENJ-9417 2

Ensemble Modern |
Ensemble Modern
Ensemble Modern-Fred Frith:Traffic Continues | Winter&Winter | 910044-2
Elliott Sharp:Racing Hearts/Tessalation Row/Calling | hr music.de | hrmn 018-03 CD

Ephron,Fima | (b,el-b,samplesfretless-b)
David Binney Group
Balance | ACT | 9411-2

Ephross,David | (b)
Jam Session
Jam Session Vol.6 | Steeplechase | SCCD 31537

Eppinger,Stephan | (drperc)
Jenny Evans And Band
Girl Talk | Enja | ENJ-9363 2
Live At The Allotria | ESM Records | ESM 9301
Girl Talk | ESM Records | ESM 9306
Litschie Hrdlicka Group
Falling Lovers | EGO | 93020
Jazz Portraits | EGO | 95080
Thilo Kreitmeier & Group
Changes | Organic Music | ORGM 9725
William Galison-Mulo Franzl Group
Midnight Sun | Edition Collage | EC 508-2

Eppy,Bernard | (p)
Chas Burchell Trio/Quartet
Unsong Hero:The Undiscovered Genius Of Chas Burchell | IN+OUT Records | 7026-2

Epstein,Ed | (as,bsts)
Johnny Dyani Quartet
Mbizo | Steeplechase | SCCD 31163
Johnny Dyani Septet
Afrika | Steeplechase | SCS 1186(Audiophile Pressing)

Epstein,Jack | (tb)
Dr. Henry Levine's Barefoot Dixieland Philharmonic feat.Prof. Sidney Bechet
Planet Jazz | Planet Jazz | 2169652-2
Sidney Bechet And The Chamber Music Society Of Lower Basin Street
Sidney Bechet:Summertime | Dreyfus Jazz Line | FDM 36712-2

Epstein,Peter | (ssts)
Michael Cain-Ralph Alessi-Peter Epstein
Circa | ECM | 1622

Epstein[Young],Al | (bs,cl,ts,engl-h,b-cl,oboe,flsax)
Ben Webster With Orchestra And Strings
Music For Loving:Ben Webster With Strings | Verve | 527774-2
Ultimate Ben Webster selected by James Carter | Verve | 557537-2
Coleman Hawkins With Many Albam And His Orchestra
Planet Jazz:Coleman Hawkins | Planet Jazz | 2152055-2
Lena Horne With The Lennie Hayton Orchestra
Planet Jazz:Lena Horne | Planet Jazz | 2165373-2

Erb,Matthias | (tb)
Ralph Schweizer Big Band
DAY Dream | Chaos | CACD 8177

Erb,Reiner | (bassoon)
Miles Davis With Gil Evans Orchestra, The George Gruntz Concert Jazz Band And Guests

Miles & Quincy Live At Montreux | Warner | 9362-45221-2

Erbetta,Marc | (bs,drperc)

Benny Carter And His Orchestra
The Art Of Saxophone | Laserlight | 24652
Erik Truffaz Quartet
The Dawn | Blue Note | 493916-2
Bending New Corners | Blue Note | 522123-2
Erik Truffaz Quartet Quintet
Out Of A Dream | Blue Note | 855855-2

Erbstösser,Christoph | (keyboards,psynth)

Martin Fredebeul Quartet
Search | Nabel Records:Jazz Network | CD 4652

Erchinger,Andreas | (p,el-psynth)

Cécile Verny Quartet
Métisse | double moon | CHRDM 71010
Kekeli | double moon | CHRDM 71028
Got A Ticket | double moon | DMCD 1002-2
Cécile Verny Quintet
Kekeli | double moon | CHRDM 71028

Ercklentz,Sabine | (tp)

The United Women's Orchestra
The Blue One | Jazz Haus Musik | JHM 0099 CD

Erdal,Bodil | (cello)

Terje Rypdal Quartet With The Bergen Chamber Ensemble
Lux Aeterna | ECM | 1818(017070-2)

Erdmann,Daniel | (ss,tsbs)

Brass Attack
Brecht Songs | Tutu Records | 888190-2*
Erdmann 2000
Recovering From y2k | Jazz 4 Ever Records:Jazz Network | J4E 4750
Eric Schaefer & Demontage
Eric Schaefer & Demontage | Jazz Haus Musik | JHM 0117 CD

Erguner,Kudsi | (frame-drney)

Anouar Brahem Quartet
Conte De L'Incroyable Amour | ECM | 1457(511959-2)
Nguyen Le Trio With Guests
Bakida | ACT | 9275-2
Renaud Garcia-Fons
Navigatore | Enja | ENJ-9418 2
Renaud Garcia-Fons Group
Navigatore | Enja | ENJ-9418 2

Erian,Michael | (fl,ssts)

Arnulf Ochs Group
In The Mean Time | Jazz 'n' Arts Records | JNA 1202
Couch Ensemble
Winnetou | Jazz 'n' Arts Records | JNA 1503

Eric Krans Dixieland Pipers |

Bill Ramsey With Eric Krans Dixieland Pipers And Guests
Caldonia And More... | Bear Family Records | BCD 16151 AH

Erickson,Eddie | (bj,gvoc)

Dan Barrett Septet
Dan Barrett's International Swing Party | Nagel-Heyer | CD 067

Erickson,Ronald | (v)

Ron Carter With Strings
Pastels | Original Jazz Classics | OJCCD 665-2(M 9073)

Ericson,King | (congas,vocperc)

Cannonball Adderley Duo
Cannonball Adderley Birthday Celebration | Fantasy | FANCD 6087-2
Cannonball Adderley Sextet
Cannonball Adderley Birthday Celebration | Fantasy | FANCD 6087-2
Joe Williams With The Cannonball Adderley Sextet
Cannonball Adderley Birthday Celebration | Fantasy | FANCD 6087-2
Nat Adderley Group
Soul Of The Bible | Capitol | 358257-2

Ericson,King prob. | (congas)

Cannonball Adderley Duo
Cannonball Adderley Birthday Celebration | Fantasy | FANCD 6087-2

Ericson,Rolf | (tpfl-h)

Charles Mingus And His Orchestra
The Complete Town Hall Concert | Blue Note | 828353-2
Charles Mingus Orchestra
Mingus Mingus Mingus | Impulse(MCA) | 951170-2
The Black Saint And The Sinner Lady | Impulse(MCA) | 951174-2
Chet Baker And The Lighthouse All Stars
Witch Doctor | Original Jazz Classics | OJCCD 609-2
Howard Rumsey's Lighthouse All-Stars
Sunday Jazz A La Lighthouse Vol.2 | Original Jazz Classics | OJCCD 972-2(S 2501)
Lars Gullin Octet
Lars Gullin 1951/52 Vol.5:First Walk | Dragon | DRCD 380
Maynard Ferguson Orchestra With Chris Connor
Two's Company | Roulette | 837201-2
Miles Davis And The Lighthouse All Stars
At Last! | Original Jazz Classics | OJCCD 480-2
Rod Levitt Orchestra
The Dynamic Sound Patterns Of The Rod Levitt Orchestra | Original Jazz Classics | OJCCD 1955-2(RS 9471)

Eriksen,Bent 'Kid' | (p)

Henrik Johansen's Jazzband
The Golden Years Of Revival Jazz,Vol.13 | Storyville | STCD 5518

Eriksson,Rune | (tb)

Bengt-Arne Wallin Orchestra
The Birth+Rebirth Of Swedish Folk Jazz | ACT | 9254-2

Eriksson,Sixter | (tp)

Erköse,Barbaros | (cl)

Anouar Brahem Quartet
Conte De L'Incroyable Amour | ECM | 1457(511959-2)
Anouar Brahem Trio
Astrakan Café | ECM | 1718(159494-2)

Erlewein,Matthias | (cl,sax,fl,as,ts,ssreeds)

All That Jazz & Helena Paul
All That Jazz & Helena Paul | Satin Doll Productions | SDP 1031-1 CD
Claus Stötter's Nevertheless
Die Entdeckung Der Banane | Jazz 'n' Arts Records | JNA 1403
Lee Konitz With The Ed Partyka Jazz Orchestra
Dreams And Realities | Laika Records | 35101642
Rainer Tempel Big Band
Melodies Of '98 | Jazz 4 Ever Records:Jazz Network | J4E 4744

Erlich,Jesser | (strings)

Gene Harris And The Three Sounds
Deep Blue-The United States Of Mind | Blue Note | 521152-2

Erlien,Audun | (belectronics)

Nils Petter Molvaer Group
Solid Ether | ECM | 1722(543365-2)

Ermacoff,Christine | (cello)

Ella Fitzgerald With Orchestra
The Best Is Yet To Come | Original Jazz Classics | OJCCD 889-2(2312138)

Ermelin,Fred | (b)

Django Reinhardt And The Quintet Du Hot Club De France
Planet Jazz:Django Reinhardt | Planet Jazz | 2152071-2
Quintet Du Hot Club De France
Django Reinhardt:Echoes Of France | Dreyfus Jazz Line | FDM 36726-2

Ernest III,Herman | (dr)

Maceo Parker Group
Southern Exposure | Minor Music | 801033

Ernesto,Don | (perc)

Klaus Doldinger Group
Back In New York:Blind Date | Atlantic | 3984-26922-2

Ernst,Peter | (g)

Trio De La Gorra
Internationales Guitarren Festival '99 | ALISO Records | AL 1038

Ernst,Thomas | (gbj)

Directors
Directors | Jazz Haus Musik | JHM 0040 CD

Ernström,Agneta | (tibetan-bells)

Don Cherry Group
Don Cherry-The Sonet Recordings:Eternal Now/Live Ankara | Verve | 533049-2

Ernszt,Georg | (tp)

Erwin Lehn Und Sein Südfunk-Tanzorchester
Deutsches Jazz Fesival 1954/1955 | Bear Family Records | BCD 15430

Erquiaga,Steve | (el-g,g,12-string-gg-synth)

Bobby McFerrin Group
Bobby McFerrin | Elektra | 7559-60023-2

Errison,King | (congas)

Donald Byrd Orchestra
Places And Spaces | Blue Note | 854326-2

Errisson,King | (congas,bongosperc)

Bobbi Humphrey
Blue Break Beats | Blue Note | 799106-2
Bobbi Humphrey Group
Blue Breaks Beats Vol.2 | Blue Note | 789907-2
Bobby Hutcherson Orchestra
Deep Blue-The United States Of Mind | Blue Note | 521152-2
Cannonball Adderley Septet
Inside Straight | Original Jazz Classics | OJCCD 750-2(F 9435)
Donald Byrd & His Orchestra
Blue Breaks Beats Vol.2 | Blue Note | 789907-2

Erskine,Les | (dr)

Mike Stern Group
Jigsaw | Atlantic | 7567-82027-2
Vic Dickenson Septet
Nice Work | Vanguard | VCD 79610-2

Erskine,Peter | (cymbals,dr,dr-computer,gongs)

Diana Krall Group
The Girl In The Other Room | Verve | 9862246
Don Grolnick Group
Hearts And Numbers | VeraBra Records | CDVBR 2016-2
Gary Peacock Quartet
Guamba | ECM | 1352
Jan Garbarek/Miroslav Vitous/Peter Erskine
Star | ECM | 1444(849649-2)
Joe Henderson Quartet
Relaxin' At Camarillo | Original Jazz Classics | OJCCD 776-2(C 14006)
John Abercrombie Quartet
Getting There | ECM | 1321(833494-2)
November | ECM | 1502(519073-2)
John Abercrombie Trio
Current Event | ECM | 1311(827770-2)
John Abercrombie-Marc Johnson-Peter Erskine
John Abercrombie/Marc Johnson/Peter Erskine | ECM | 1390(837756-2)
John Patitucci Group
Sketchbook | GRP | GRP 96172
Mistura Fina | GRP | GRP 98022
Kenny Wheeler Ensemble
Muisc For Large & Small Ensembles | ECM | 1415/16
Kenny Wheeler Quintet
The Widow In The Window | ECM | 1417(843198-2)
Kurt Elling Group
Flirting With Twilight | Blue Note | 531113-2
Los Jovenes Flamencos With The WDR Big Band And Guests
Jazzpana | ACT | 9212-2
Marc Johnson Quartet
Bass Desires | ECM | 1299(827743-2)
Marc Johnson's Bass Desires
Second Sight | ECM | 1351(833038-2)
Marty Ehrlich-Peter Erskine-Michael Formanek
Relativity | Enja | ENJ-9341 2
Michael Brecker Group
Don't Try This At Home | Impulse(MCA) | 950114-2
Mike Stern Group
Jigsaw | Atlantic | 7567-82027-2
Nguyen Le Trio
Nguyen Le:3 Trios | ACT | 9245-2
Peter Erskine Orchestra
Peter Erskine | Original Jazz Classics | OJC 610(C 14010)
Peter Erskine Trio
You Never Know | ECM | 1497(517353-2)
Time Being | ECM | 1532
As It Is | ECM | 1594
Juni | ECM | 1657(539726-2)
ELB | ACT | 9289-2
Ralph Towner-Peter Erskine
Open Letter | ECM | 1462(511980-2)
Rolf Kühn Group
Internal Eyes | Intuition Records | INT 3328-2
Steps Ahead
Steps Ahead:Copenhagen Live | Storyville | 4960363
Steps Ahead | Elektra | 7559-60168-2
Modern Times | Elektra | 7559-60351-2
Vince Mendoza With The WDR Big Band And Guests
Sketches | ACT | 9215-2
Weather Report
Mr. Gone | CBS | 468208-2
Night Passage | CBS | 468211-2

Erstrand,Lars | (vib)

Arne Domnerus Quintet
Sugar Fingers | Phontastic | NCD 8831
International Allstars
The International Allstars Play Benny Goodman:Vol.1 | Nagel-Heyer | CD 025
The Second Sampler | Nagel-Heyer | NHR SP 6
The International Allstars
The International Allstars Play Benny Goodman Vol.1 | Nagel-Heyer | CD 045
The New York Allstars
Hey Ba-Ba-Re-Bop!! The New York Allstars Play Lionel Hampton Vol.1 | Nagel-Heyer | CD 047
The New York Allstars Play Lionel Hampton,Vol.2: Stompin' At The Savoy | Nagel-Heyer | CD 077

Ertek,Shakir | (drperc)

Chris Jarrett Trio
Chris Jarrett Trio Plays New World Music | Edition Musikat | EDM 067

Ervin,Booker | (ts)

Andrew Hill Quintet
Grass Roots | Blue Note | 522672-2
Blue Bossa | Blue Note | 795590-2
Booker Ervin Quartet
That's It | Candid | CCD 79014
The Song Book | Original Jazz Classics | OJCCD 779-2(P 7318)
The Freedom Book | Original Jazz Classics | OJCCD 845-2(P 7295)
The Space Book | Original Jazz Classics | OJCCD 896-2(PR 7386)
Heavy!!! | Original Jazz Classics | OJCCD 981-2(P 7499)
Booker Ervin Quintet
The Blues Book | Original Jazz Classics | OJCCD 780-2(P 7340)
Exultation! | Original Jazz Classics | OJCCD 835-2(P 7293)
Booker Ervin Sextet
Heavy!!! | Original Jazz Classics | OJCCD 981-2(P 7499)
Booker Ervin-Dexter Gordon Quintet
Dexter Gordon Birthday Celebration | Fantasy | FANCD 6082-2
Charles Mingus And His Orchestra
Charles Mingus-Passion Of A Man:The Complete Atlantic Recordings 1956-1961 | Atlantic | 8122-72871-2
Charles Mingus Group
The Jazz Life! | Candid | CCD 79019
Mysterious Blues | Candid | CCD 79042
Mingus Ah Um | CBS | CK 65512
Mingus Dynasty | CBS | CK 65513
Charles Mingus Jazz Workshop
Rhino Presents The Atlantic Jazz Gallery | Atlantic | 8122-71257-2
Blues & Roots | Atlantic | 8122-75205-2
Charles Mingus Orchestra
Charles Mingus:Pre-Bird(Mingus Revisited) | Verve | 538636-2
Mingus Mingus Mingus | Impulse(MCA) | 951170-2
Charles Mingus:The Complete 1959 Columbia Recordings | CBS | C3K 65145
Mingus | Candid | CCD 79021
Charles Mingus Quintet
Mingus At Antibes | Atlantic | 7567-90532-2
Charles Mingus-Passion Of A Man:The Complete Atlantic Recordings 1956-1961 | Atlantic | 8122-72871-2
Charles Mingus Quintet With Bud Powell
Mingus At Antibes | Atlantic | 7567-90532-2
Charles Mingus-Passion Of A Man:The Complete Atlantic Recordings 1956-1961 | Atlantic | 8122-72871-2
Charles Mingus Quintet With Roland Kirk
Tonight At Noon | Atlantic | 7567-80793-2
Charles Mingus-Passion Of A Man:The Complete Atlantic Recordings 1956-1961 | Atlantic | 8122-72871-2
The Very Best Of Charles Mingus | Rhino | 8122-79988-2
Charles Mingus Septet
Charles Mingus:The Complete 1959 Columbia Recordings | CBS | C3K 65145
Mal Waldron Sextet
Eric Dolphy:The Complete Prestige Recordings | Prestige | 9 PRCD-4418-2
Eric Dolphy Birthday Celebration | Fantasy | FANCD 6085-2
The Quest | Original Jazz Classics | OJCCD 082-2(NJ 8269)
The Mal Waldron Memorial Album:Soul Eyes | Prestige | PRCD 11024-2
Sonny Stitt Quartet
The Prestige Legacy Vol.2:Battles Of Saxes | Prestige | PCD 24252-2

Ervin,Dee | (perc)

Gene Harris And The Three Sounds
Deep Blue-The United States Of Mind | Blue Note | 521152-2

Erwin | (Irvin)

Benny Goodman And His Orchestra
Planet Jazz:Benny Goodman | Planet Jazz | 2152054-2

Erwin,Pee Wee | (tp)

Bud Freeman All Stars
The Bud Freeman All-Star Sessions | Prestige | PRCD 24286-2
Frank Trumbauer And His Orchestra
The Hollywood Session:The Capitol Jazzmen | Jazz Unlimited | JUCD 2044
Jess Stacy And His Orchestra
Planet Jazz:Jazz Piano | RCA | 2169655-2
Tommy Dorsey And His Orchestra
Planet Jazz:Tommy Dorsey | Planet Jazz | 2159972-2

Eschke,Jan | (p)

Florian Trübsbach Quintet
Manson & Dixon | Jazz 4 Ever Records:Jazz Network | J4E 4759
Martin Auer Quintett
Martin Auer Quintett | Jazz 4 Ever Records:Jazz Network | J4E 4762
Torsten Goods Group
Manhattan Walls | Jardis Records | JRCD 20139

Escoffery,Wayne | (ssts)

David Gibson Sextet
Maya | Nagel-Heyer | CD 2018
Eric Reed Orchestra
Happiness | Nagel-Heyer | CD 2010
Mingus Big Band
Tonight At Noon...Three Or Four Shades Of Love | Dreyfus Jazz Line | FDM 36633-2
Wayne Escoffery Quartet
Time Changes | Nagel-Heyer | CD 2015
Wayne Escoffery Quintet
Intuition | Nagel-Heyer | CD 2038

Escoudé,Christian | (el-g,gg-solo)

Charlie Haden/Christian Escoudé
Duo | Dreyfus Jazz Line | FDM 36505-2

Escovedo,Juan | (perc)

Herbie Hancock Group
Magic Window | CBS | 486572-2

Escovedo,Pete | (perc,bongos,timbalesvoc)

Mongo Santamaria And His Band
Sabroso | Original Jazz Classics | OJCCD 281-2

Escovedo,Sheila | (congas,perctimbales)

George Duke Group
Jazzrock-Anthology Vol.3:Fusion | Zounds | CD 27100555
Herbie Hancock Group
Monster | CBS | 486571-2
Magic Window | CBS | 486572-2

Escuadra,Lluis | (p)

Moments Quartet
Original Moments | Fresh Sound Records | FSNT 052 CD

Escudero,Bob | (tuba)

Fletcher Henderson And His Orchestra
Jazz:The Essential Collection Vol.1 | IN+OUT Records | 78011-2

Escudero,Ralph | (tuba)

Henderson's Hot Six
Jazz:The Essential Collection Vol.1 | IN+OUT Records | 78011-2

Eskelin,Ellery | (tscabassa)

Mark Helias Group
Loopin' The Cool | Enja | ENJ-9049 2
Rabih Abou-Khalil Group
The Cactus Of Knowledge | Enja | ENJ-9401 2

Esquire All Stars |

Esquire All-American Award Winners
Planet Jazz:Jazz Trumpet | Planet Jazz | 2169654-2
Best Of The Complete RCA Victor Recordings | RCA | 2663636-2
Highlights From The Duke Ellington Centennial Edition | RCA | 2663672-2
Esquire Metropolitan Opera House Jam Session
Jazz:The Essential Collection Vol.3 | IN+OUT Records | 78013-2
Leonard Feather's Esquire All Stars
Jazz:The Essential Collection Vol.2 | IN+OUT Records | 78012-2

Esquire All-Americans,Leonard Feather's |

Leonard Feather's Esquire All-Americans
Louis Armstrong:C'est Si Bon | Dreyfus Jazz Line | FDM 36730-2

Esquivel,Juan Garcia | (arrld)

Juan Garcia Esquivel Orchestra
Juan's Again | RCA | 2168206-2

Essence All Stars |

Essence All Stars
Afro Cubano Chant | Hip Bop | HIBD 8009
Hot Jazz Bisquits | Hip Bop | HIBD 8801

Esser,Christian | (as)

Bigband Der Musikschule Der Stadt Brühl Mit Gastsolisten
Pangäa | Indigo-Records | 1004 CD

Esser,Georg | (b,lap-steelvoc)

Nick Woodland And The Magnets
Big Heart | Blues Beacon | BLU-1013 2
Nick Woodland Quartet
Live Fireworks | Blues Beacon | BLU-1027 2

Esser,Johannes | (b)

Uri Caine With The Concerto Köln
Concerto Köln | Winter&Winter | 910086-2

Eßer,Paul | (recitation)

Paul Eßer-Gerd Dudek-Ali Haurand-Jiri Stivin
Jazz Und Lyrik:Schinderkarren Mit Buffet | Konnex Records | KCD 5108

Essex,Kenneth | (viola)

Dee Dee Bridgewater With Orchestra
Dear Ella | Verve | 539102-2

Essiet,Essiet Okon | (b)

Bruce Cox Quartet With Guests
Stick To It | Minor Music | 801055

Estades,Roberto Danobeitia | (g)

European Jazz Youth Orchestra
Swinging Europe 3 | dacapo | DCCD 9461

Estager,Jean-Francois | (perc)

Barre Phillips Group
Aquarian Rain | ECM | 1451

Estell,Oscar | (as,tsbs)

Art Farmer Septet
Plays The Arrangements And Compositions Of Gigi Gryce And Quincy Jones | Original Jazz Classics | OJCCD 054-2

INTERPRETENVERZEICHNIS

Tadd Dameron And His Orchestra
Clifford Brown Memorial | Original Jazz Classics | OJC20 017-2(P 7055)

Estermann,Thomas | (g)
Mahmoud Turkmani With The Ludus Guitar Quartet
Nuqta | TipToe | TIP-888835 2

Estes,Alan | (dr,percvib)
Don Ellis Orchestra
Electric Bath | CBS | CK 65522
Gene Harris And The Three Sounds
Deep Blue-The United States Of Mind | Blue Note | 521152-2

Estes,Buff | (assax)
Benny Goodman And His Orchestra
Charlie Christian:Swing To Bop | Dreyfus Jazz Line | FDM 36715-2
More Camel Caravans | Phontastic | NCD 8845/6
Lionel Hampton And His Orchestra
Planet Jazz:Lionel Hampton | Planet Jazz | 2152059-2

Estes,Gene | (dr,perc,vibboo-bams)
Harry James And His Orchestra
Trumpet Blues:The Best Of Harry James | Capitol | 521224-2
John Pisano-Billy Bean-Dennis Budimir
West Coast Sessions | String Jazz | SJRCD 1006
Lyke Ritz Quartet
How About Uke? | Verve | 0760942
Lyke Ritz Trio
How About Uke? | Verve | 0760942
Lyle Ritz Quartet
How About Uke? | Verve | 0760942

Estevan,Pedro | (redoubling-dr)
Javier Paxarino Group With Glen Velez
Temurá | ACT | 9227-2

Estrin,Harvey | (as,fl,alto-fl,cl,piccolo,reeds)
Bill Evans Quartet With Orchestra
The Complete Bill Evans On Verve | Verve | 527953-2
From Left To Right | Verve | 557451-2
Bill Evans With Orchestra
The Complete Bill Evans On Verve | Verve | 527953-2
From Left To Right | Verve | 557451-2
J.J.Johnson And His Orchestra
Planet Jazz:J.J.Johnson | Planet Jazz | 2159974-2
Jimmy Smith With The Oliver Nelson Orchestra
Jimmy Smith:Best Of The Verve Years | Verve | 527950-2
Stan Getz With The Eddie Sauter Orchestra
Stan Getz Plays The Music Of Mickey One | Verve | 531232-2

Esty,Bob | (voc)
Les McCann Group
Another Beginning | Atlantic | 7567-80790-2

Eternal Wind |
Yusef Lateef With Eternal Wind And The 'Kölner Rundfunk Orchester'
The African American Epic Suite:Music For Quintet And Orchestra | ACT | 9214-2

Etheridge,John | (g)
Vic Juris-John Etheridge
Bohemia | Jazzpoint | JP 1023 CD
Vic Juris-John Etheridge Quartet
Bohemia | Jazzpoint | JP 1023 CD

Etri,Bus | (g)
Charlie Barnet And His Orchestra
Planet Jazz:Big Bands | Planet Jazz | 2169649-2
Planet Jazz:Swing | Planet Jazz | 2169651-2

Etzel,Hans | (tp)
Helmut Zacharias mit dem Orchester Frank Folken
Ich Habe Rhythmus | Bear Family Records | BCD 15642 AH

Eubanks,Charles | (p)
Dewey Redman Quartet
The Struggle Continues | ECM | 1225

Eubanks,Duane | (tpfl-h)
Amos Hoffman Quartet
The Dreamer | Fresh Sound Records | FSNT 060 CD
Dave Holland Big Band
What Goes Around | ECM | 1777(014002-2)

Eubanks,Kevin | (el-g,g,g-synth,g-solovoc)
Dave Holland Qartet
Extensions | ECM | 1410(841778-2)
Dianne Reeves With Band
I Remember | Blue Note | 790264-2
Kevin Eubanks Trio
Live At Bradley's | Blue Note | 830133-2
Kevin Mahogany With Orchestra
Songs And Moments | Enja | ENJ-8072 2
Terri Lyne Carrington Group
Jazz Is A Spirit | ACT | 9408-2
World Trio
World Trio | VeraBra Records | CDVBR 2052-2

Eubanks,Robin | (shells,tb,b-tb,keyboards,bells)
Antonio Hart Group
Here I Stand | Impulse(MCA) | 951208-2
Dave Holland Big Band
What Goes Around | ECM | 1777(014002-2)
Dave Holland Quintet
The Razor's Edge | ECM | 1353
Point Of View | ECM | 1663(557020-2)
Prime Directive | ECM | 1698(547950-2)
Not For Nothin' | ECM | 1758(014004-2)
Extended Play | ECM | 1864/65(038505-2)
Dollar(Abdullah Ibrahim) Brand Group
African River | Enja | ENJ-6018 2
Erica Lindsay Sextet
Dreamers | Candid | CCD 79040
Fred Wesley Group
New Friends | Minor Music | 801016
Freddie Cole
Jazzin' Vol.2: The Music Of Stevie Wonder | Fantasy | FANCD 6088-2
Freddy Cole With Band
To The End Of The Earth | Fantasy | FCD 9675-2
Hank Roberts Group
Black Pastels | JMT Edition | 919016-2
Herb Robertson Brass Ensemble
Shades Of Bud Powell | JMT Edition | 919019-2
Herb Robertson Group
The Little Trumpet | JMT Edition | 919007-2
James Hurt Group
Dark Grooves-Mystcal Rhythms | Blue Note | 495104-2
Kevin Mahogany With Orchestra
Songs And Moments | Enja | ENJ-8072 2
Michael Brecker Quindectet
Wide Angles | Verve | 076142-2

Euell,Julian | (b)
John Coltrane-Paul Quinichette Quintet
John Coltrane-The Prestige Recordings | Prestige | 16 PCD 4405-2
Cattin' | Original Jazz Classics | OJCCD 460-2
Mal Waldron Sextet
John Coltrane-The Prestige Recordings | Prestige | 16 PCD 4405-2
The Jazz Giants Play Jerome Kern:Yesterdays | Prestige | PCD 24202-2
The Mal Waldron Memorial Album:Soul Eyes | Prestige | PRCD 11024-2
Prestige All Stars
The Prestige Legacy Vol.1:The High Priests | Prestige | PCD 24251-2

Eureka Brass Band,The |
Eureka Brass Band
Atlantic Jazz: New Orleans | Atlantic | 7567-81700-2

Europa String Choir |
Europa String Choir
Internationales Guitarren Festival '99 | ALISO Records | AL 1038

European Jazz Ensemble |
European Jazz Ensemble
European Jazz Ensemble At The Philharmonic Cologne | M.A Music | A 800-2
20th Anniversary Tour | Konnex Records | KCD 5078
European Jazz Ensemble 25th Anniversary | Konnex Records | KCD 5100
European Jazz Ensemble & The Khan Family feat. Joachim Kühn
European Jazz Ensemble Meets The Khan Family | M.A Music | A 807-2

European Jazz Giants,The |
The European Jazz Ginats
Jazz Party | Nagel-Heyer | CD 009
The First Sampler | Nagel-Heyer | NHR SP 5

European Jazz Guitar Orchestra,The |
The European Jazz Guitar Orchestra
The European Jazz Guitar Orchestra | Jardis Records | JRCD 9307

European Jazz Youth Orchestra |
European Jazz Youth Orchestra
Swinging Europe 1 | dacapo | DCCD 9449
Swinging Europe 2 | dacapo | DCCD 9450
Swinging Europe 3 | dacapo | DCCD 9461

European Trumpet Summit |
European Trumpet Summit
European Trumpet Summit | Konnex Records | KCD 5064

European Tuba Quartet |
European Tuba Quartet
Low And Behold | Jazz Haus Musik | JHM 0110 CD

Evans,Alfie | (as,cl,bs,tsreeds)
Dr. Henry Levine's Barefoot Dixieland Philharmonic feat.Prof. Sidney Bechet
Planet Jazz | Planet Jazz | 2169652-2
Roger Wolfe Kahn And His Orchestra
Planet Jazz:Jack Teagarden | Planet Jazz | 2161236-2
Sidney Bechet And The Chamber Music Society Of Lower Basin Street
Sidney Bechet:Summertime | Dreyfus Jazz Line | FDM 36712-2

Evans,Belton | (dr)
Lightnin' Hopkins Trio
The Blues Of Lightnin' Hopkins | Original Blues Classics | OBCCD 532-2(BV 1019)
Lightnin' Hopkins Trio With Sonny Terry
Last Night Blues | Original Blues Classics | OBCCD 548-2(BV 1029)
St.Louis Jimmy Oden Group
Goin' Down Slow | Original Blues Classics | OBCCD 584-2(BV 1028)
Sunnyland Slim Band
Windy City Blues | Stax | SCD 8612-2

Evans,Bill | (3-p-overdubbed,as,ts,b,fl,reeds,ss)
Bill Evans
Verve Jazz Masters 5:Bill Evans | Verve | 519821-2
Verve Jazz Masters 20:Introducing | Verve | 519853-2
Conversations With Myself | Verve | 521409-2
The Complete Bill Evans On Verve | Verve | 527953-2
The Best Of Bill Evans Live | Verve | 533825-2
At The Montreux Jazz Festival | Verve | 539758-2
Ultimate Bill Evans selected by Herbie Hancock | Verve | 557536-2
Further Conversations With Myself | Verve | 559832-2
Alone | Verve | 598319-2
Bill Evans At Town Hall | Verve | 831271-2
The Complete Fantasy Recordings | Fantasy | 9FCD 1012-2
New Jazz Conceptions | Original Jazz Classics | OJC20 025-2(RLP 223)
Everybody Digs Bill Evans | Original Jazz Classics | OJC20 068-2
Alone (Again) | Original Jazz Classics | OJCCD 795-2(F 9542)
Eloquence | Original Jazz Classics | OJCCD 814-2(F 9618)
Bill Evans Duo
Intuition | Original Jazz Classics | OJCCD 470-2
Bill Evans Quartet
The Complete Bill Evans On Verve | Verve | 527953-2
From Left To Right | Verve | 557451-2
Bill Evans Quartet With Orchestra
The Complete Bill Evans On Verve | Verve | 527953-2
From Left To Right | Verve | 557451-2
Bill Evans Quintet
The Complete Fantasy Recordings | Fantasy | 9FCD 1012-2
Interplay | Original Jazz Classics | OJCCD 308-2
Quintessence | Original Jazz Classics | OJCCD 698-2(F 9529)
The Jazz Giants Play Jerome Kern:Yesterdays | Prestige | PCD 24202-2
The Jazz Giants Play Sammy Cahn:It's Magic | Prestige | PCD 24226-2
Bill Evans Trio
The Story Of Jazz Piano | Laserlight | 24653
Bill Evans:The Complete Live At The Village Vanguard 1961 | Riverside | 3RCD 1961-2
Monterey Jazz Festival 1975 | Storyville | 4960213
Verve Jazz Masters 5:Bill Evans | Verve | 519821-2
The Complete Bill Evans On Verve | Verve | 527953-2
The Best Of Bill Evans Live | Verve | 533825-2
Trio 64 | Verve | 539058-2
At The Montreux Jazz Festival | Verve | 539758-2
Ultimate Bill Evans selected by Herbie Hancock | Verve | 557536-2
You Must Believe In Spring | Rhino | 812273719-2
Bill Evans At Town Hall | Verve | 831271-2
Bill Evans:The Secret Sessions | Milestone | 8MCD 4421-2
Bill Evans Trio:The Last Waltz | Milestone | 8MCD 4430-2
The Complete Fantasy Recordings | Fantasy | 9FCD 1012-2
Bill Evans:Piano Player | CBS | CK 65361
Blue In Green | Milestone | MCD 9185-2
On Green Dolphin Street | Milestone | MCD 9235-2
Half Moon Bay | Milestone | MCD 9282-2
Homecoming | Milestone | MCD 9291-2
Getting Sentimental | Milestone | MCD 9346-2
Since We Met | Original Jazz Classics | OJC 622(F 9501)
New Jazz Conceptions | Original Jazz Classics | OJC20 025-2(RLP 223)
Explorations | Original Jazz Classics | OJC20 037-2(RLP 9351)
Everybody Digs Bill Evans | Original Jazz Classics | OJC20 068-2
Portrait In Jazz | Original Jazz Classics | OJC20 088-2
Sunday At The Village Vanguard | Original Jazz Classics | OJC20 140-2
Waltz For Debby | Original Jazz Classics | OJC20 210-2
At Shelly's Manne-Hole | Original Jazz Classics | OJC20 263-2(RLP 9487)
Moonbeams | Original Jazz Classics | OJC20 434-2(RLP 9428)
Bill Evans:From The 70's | Original Jazz Classics | OJCCD 1069-2(F 9630)
The Tokyo Concert | Original Jazz Classics | OJCCD 345-2
How My Heart Sings! | Original Jazz Classics | OJCCD 369-2
Re: Person I Knew | Original Jazz Classics | OJCCD 749-2(F 9608)
I Will Say Goodbye | Original Jazz Classics | OJCCD 761-2(F 9593)
The Jazz Giants Play Harold Arlen:Blues In The Night | Prestige | PCD 24201-2
The Jazz Giants Play Cole Porter:Night And Day | Prestige | PCD 24203-2
The Jazz Giants Play Harry Warren:Lullaby Of Broadway | Prestige | PCD 24204-2
The Jazz Giants Play Rodgers & Hart:Blue Moon | Prestige | PCD 24205-2
The Jazz Giants Play Rodgers & Hammerstein:My Favorite Things | Prestige | PCD 24223-2
The Jazz Giants Play Miles Davis:Milestones | Prestige | PCD 24225-2
Bill Evans Trio With Jeremy Steig
The Complete Bill Evans On Verve | Verve | 527953-2
Bill Evans Trio With The Claus Ogerman Orchestra
The Complete Bill Evans On Verve | Verve | 527953-2
Bill Evans Trio With Symphony Orchestra | Verve | 821983-2
Bill Evans With Orchestra
The Complete Bill Evans On Verve | Verve | 527953-2
From Left To Right | Verve | 557451-2
Bill Evans-Don Elliott
Tenderly | Milestone | MCD 9317-2
Bill Evans-Eddie Gomez Duo
The Complete Fantasy Recordings | Fantasy | 9FCD 1012-2
Bill Evans:Piano Player | CBS | CK 65361
Montreux III | Original Jazz Classics | OJC20 644-2(F 9510)
Eloquence | Original Jazz Classics | OJCCD 814-2(F 9618)
Bill Evans-Jim Hall
Verve Jazz Masters 5:Bill Evans | Verve | 519821-2
The Complete Bill Evans On Verve | Verve | 527953-2
Undercurrent | Blue Note | 538228-2
Ultimate Bill Evans selected by Herbie Hancock | Verve | 557536-2
Bill Evans-Toots Thielemans Quintet
Affinity | Warner | 7599-27387-2
Cannonball Adderley And His Orchestra
Verve Jazz Masters 31:Cannonball Adderley | Verve | 522651-2
Cannonball Adderley Quartet
Cannonball Adderley Birthday Celebration | Fantasy | FANCD 6087-2
Know What I Mean? | Original Jazz Classics | OJC 105(R 12-433)
Cannonball Adderley Quintet
Cannonball Adderley Birthday Celebration | Fantasy | FANCD 6087-2
Portrait Of Cannonball | Original Jazz Classics | OJCCD 361-2(RLP 269)
The Jazz Giants Play Rodgers & Hammerstein:My Favorite Things | Prestige | PCD 24223-2
Chet Baker Quartet
Chet | Original Jazz Classics | OJC20 087-2
Chet Baker Quintet
Chet Baker Plays The Best Of Lerner And Loewe | Original Jazz Classics | OJC20 137-2
Chet Baker Septet
Chet | Original Jazz Classics | OJC20 087-2
Chet Baker Plays The Best Of Lerner And Loewe | Original Jazz Classics | OJC20 137-2
Chet Baker Sextet
Chet | Original Jazz Classics | OJC20 087-2
Dave Pike Quartet
Pike's Peak | Epic | 489772-2
Bill Evans:Piano Player | CBS | CK 65361
David Matthews & The Manhattan Jazz Orchestra
Back To Bach | Milestone | MCD 9312-2
Eddie Costa Quartet
Guys And Dolls Like Vives | Verve | 549366-2
Gary McFarland And His Orchestra
The Complete Bill Evans On Verve | Verve | 527953-2
George Russell And His Orchestra
Gegore Russell New York N.Y. | Impulse(MCA) | 951278-2
Bill Evans:Piano Player | CBS | CK 65361
George Russell Smalltet
The RCA Victor Jazz Workshop | RCA | 2159144-2
Gunther Schuller Ensemble
Beauty Is A Rare Thing:Ornette Coleman-The Complete Atlantic Recordings | Atlantic | 8122-71410-2
Herbie Mann With The Bill Evans Trio
Nirvana | Atlantic | 7567-90141-2
Kai Winding-J.J.Johnson Quintet
The Great Kai & J.J. | Impulse(MCA) | 951225-2
Lee Ritenour Sextet
Alive In L.A. | GRP | GRP 98822
Marion McPartland-Bill Evans-John Lewis-Patrice Rushen
Monterey Jazz Festival 1975 | Storyville | 4960213
Michael 'Patches' Stewart Group
Penetration | Hip Bop | HIBD 8018
Miles Davis Group
The Man With The Horn | CBS | 468701-2
Decoy | CBS | 468702-2
We Want Miles | CBS | 469402-2
Miles Davis Quartet
Bill Evans:Piano Player | CBS | CK 65361
Miles Davis Quintet
Kind Of Blue | CBS | CK 64935
Newport Jazz Festival 1958,July 3rd-6th,Vol.1:Mostly Miles | Phontastic | NCD 8813
Miles Davis Sextet
Circle In The Round | CBS | 467898-2
Kind Of Blue | CBS | 480410-2
Kind Of Blue | CBS | CK 64935
This Is Jazz:Miles Davis Plays Ballads | CBS | CK 65038
Monica Zetterlund With The Bill Evans Trio
The Complete Bill Evans On Verve | Verve | 527953-2
Oliver Nelson And His Orchestra
Blues And The Abstract Truth | Impulse(MCA) | 951154-2
The Roots Of Acid Jazz | Impulse(MCA) | IMP 12042
Stan Getz With The Bill Evans Trio
Verve Jazz Masters 5:Bill Evans | Verve | 519821-2
The Complete Bill Evans On Verve | Verve | 527953-2
Ultimate Bill Evans selected by Herbie Hancock | Verve | 557536-2
But Beautiful | Milestone | MCD 9249-2
Stan Getz-Bill Evans Quartet
Stan Getz Highlights:The Best Of The Verve Years Vol.2 | Verve | 517330-2
Stan Getz & Bill Evans | Verve | 833802-2
Stan Getz Highlights | Verve | 847430-2
Tony Bennett-Bill Evans
The Complete Fantasy Recordings | Fantasy | 9FCD 1012-2
The Tony Bennett-Bill Evans Album | Original Jazz Classics | OJC20 439-2(F 9489)

Evans,Gil | (arr,cond,el-p,grand-p,keyboards,ld)
Astrud Gilberto With The Gil Evans Orchestra
Verve Jazz Masters 9:Astrud Gilberto | Verve | 519824-2
Verve Jazz Masters 23:Gil Evans | Verve | 521860-2
Charlie Parker And His Orchestra
Charlie Parker:The Best Of The Verve Years | Verve | 527815-2
The Cole Porter Songbook | Verve | 823250-2
Bird: The Complete Charlie Parker On Verve | Verve | 837141-2
Charlie Parker With Orchestra
Charlie Parker Big Band | Verve | 559835-2
Charlie Parker With Orchestra & The Dave Lambert Singers
Verve Jazz Masters 28:Charlie Parker Plays Standards | Verve | 521854-2
Gil Evans And Ten
Gil Evans And Ten | Original Jazz Classics | OJC 346(P 7120)
The Jazz Giants Play Cole Porter:Night And Day | Prestige | PCD 24203-2
Gil Evans And Ten | Prestige | PRSA 7120-6
Gil Evans Orchestra
There Comes A Time | RCA | 2131392-2
PLay The Music Of Jimi Hendrix | RCA | 2663872-2
Verve Jazz Masters 23:Gil Evans | Verve | 521860-2
Svengali | Rhino | 8122-73720-2
The Individualism Of Gil Evans | Verve | 833804-2
Out Of The Cool | Impulse(MCA) | 951186-2
Blues In Orbit | Enja | ENJ-3069 2
Kenny Burrell With The Gil Evans Orchestra
Verve Jazz Masters 23:Gil Evans | Verve | 521860-2
Verve Jazz Masters 45:Kenny Burrell | Verve | 527652-2
Verve Jazz Masters Vol.60:The Collection | Verve | 529866-2
Lucy Reed With Orchestra
This Is Lucy Reed | Original Jazz Classics | OJCCD 1943-2(F 3243)
Miles Davis + 19
Miles Ahead | CBS | CK 65121
Miles Davis And His Orchestra
The Complete Birth Of The Cool | Capitol | 494550-2
Birth Of The Cool | Capitol | 530117-2
Jazz Profile:Miles Davis | Blue Note | 823515-2
Ballads & Blues | Blue Note | 836633-2
Miles Davis With Gil Evans & His Orchestra
Ballads | CBS | 461099-2
Miles Davis At Carnegie Hall | CBS | CK 65027
This Is Jazz:Miles Davis Plays Ballads | CBS | CK 65038
Porgy And Bess | CBS | CK 65141
Sketches Of Spain | CBS | CK 65142
Quiet Nights | CBS | CK 65293

Evans,Greg | (fr-h)
Paquito D'Rivera Group With The Absolute Ensemble
Habanera | Enja | ENJ-9395 2

Evans,Gus | (ascl)
Lionel Hampton And His Orchestra
Lionel Hampton:Flying Home | Dreyfus Jazz Line | FDM 36735-2

Evans,Hershel | (clts)

Count Basie And His Orchestra
Jazz:The Essential Collection Vol.3 | IN+OUT Records | 78013-2
From Spiritual To Swing | Vanguard | VCD 169/71
Harry James And His Orchestra
The Legends Of Swing | Laserlight | 24659
Jimmy Rushing With Count Basie And His Orchestra
From Spiritual To Swing | Vanguard | VCD 169/71
Lionel Hampton And His Orchestra
Planet Jazz:Swing | Planet Jazz | 2169651-2
Planet Jazz:Jazz Saxophone | Planet Jazz | 2169653-2

Evans,Jenny | (voc)
Jenny Evans And Band
Girl Talk | Enja | ENJ-9363 2
Live At The Allotria | ESM Records | ESM 9301
Girl Talk | ESM Records | ESM 9306
Jenny Evans And Her Quintet
Shiny Stockings | Enja | ENJ-9317 2
Nuages | Enja | ENJ-9467 2
Shiny Stockings | ESM Records | ESM 9305
Gonna Go Fishin' | ESM Records | ESM 9307
Nuages | ESM Records | ESM 9308
Jenny Evans And The Rudi Martini Quartet
At Lloyd's | ESM Records | ESM 9302
Pee Wee Ellis & NDR Bigband
What You Like | Minor Music | 801064

Evans,Michael | (as,vib,dr,perc,bell,tabla,voc)
Karen Mantler Group
Farewell | Watt | XtraWatt/8

Evans,Miles | (tp)
Lew Soloff Group
Rainbow Mountain | TipToe | TIP-888838 2
Miles Davis With Gil Evans Orchestra, The George Gruntz Concert Jazz Band And Guests
Miles & Quincy Live At Montreux | Warner | 9362-45221-2

Evans,Paul 'Stump' | (as,bs,c-mel-saxs)
Jelly Roll Morton's Red Hot Peppers
Planet Jazz:Jelly Roll Morton | Planet Jazz | 2152060-2
Jazz:The Essential Collection Vol.1 | IN+OUT Records | 78011-2
King Oliver And His Dixie Syncopators
Jazz:The Essential Collection Vol.1 | IN+OUT Records | 78011-2
King Oliver's Creole Jazz Band
Jazz:The Essential Collection Vol.1 | IN+OUT Records | 78011-2

Evans,Rachel | (viola)
Hank Jones Trio With The Meridian String Quartet
The Story Of Jazz Piano | Laserlight | 24653

Evans,Richard | (arr,b,cond,dir,el-b,fr-h)
Ahmad Jamal Trio with Orchestra
Pittsburgh | Atlantic | 7567-8209-2
Maynard Ferguson And His Orchestra
Verve Jazz Masters 52:Maynard Ferguson | Verve | 529905-2
Stan Getz With The Richard Evans Orchestra
What The World Needs Now-Stan Getz Plays Bacharach And David | Verve | 557450-2

Evans,Sandy | (ss,tstambourine)
Clarion Fracture Zone
Blue Shift | VeraBra Records | CDVBR 2075-2
Mara!
Ruino Vino | Laika Records | 35100792
The Catholics
Simple | Laika Records | 35100802

Evans,Sticks | (drperc)
Charles Mingus Orchestra
Charles Mingus:Pre-Bird(Mingus Revisited) | Verve | 538636-2
Gunther Schuller Ensemble
Beauty Is A Rare Thing:Ornette Coleman-The Complete Atlantic Recordings | Atlantic | 8122-71410-2

Evans,Suzan 'Sue' | (dr,perc,congas,mallet-instruments)
Gil Evans Orchestra
There Comes A Time | RCA | 2131392-2
PLay The Music Of Jimi Hendrix | RCA | 2663872-2
Svengali | Rhino | 8122-73720-2
Blues In Orbit | Enja | ENJ-3069 2

Evans,Terry | (el-g,gvoc)
Hans Theessink Group
Call Me | Minor Music | 801022
Crazy Moon | Minor Music | 801052
Journey On | Minor Music | 801062

Evans,Vincent Leroy | (kalimba,keyboards,p,el-psynth)
Chico Freeman And Brainstorm
Threshold | IN+OUT Records | 7022-2
Lenny White Group
Renderers Of Spirit | Hip Bop | HIBD 8014
Michael 'Patches' Stewart Group
Blue Patches | Hip Bop | HIBD 8016

Everyman Band |
Everyman Band
Everyman Band | ECM | 1234
Without Warning | ECM | 1290

Ewell,Don | (pp-solo)
Don Ewell
Free 'N' Easy | Good Time Jazz | GTCD 10046-2
Don Ewell Quartet
Free 'N' Easy | Good Time Jazz | GTCD 10046-2
Don Ewell Trio
Free 'N' Easy | Good Time Jazz | GTCD 10046-2
Jack Teagarden And His Sextet
Mis'ry And The Blues | Verve | 9860310
Jack Teagarden Sextet
Newport Jazz Festival 1958,July 3rd-6th Vol.3:Blues In The Night No.1 | Phontastic | NCD 8815
Jack Teagarden Sextet With Bobby Hackett
Newport Jazz Festival 1958,July 3rd-6th Vol.3:Blues In The Night No.1 | Phontastic | NCD 8815
Kid Ory's Creole Jazz Band
This Kid's The Greatest! | Good Time Jazz | GTCD 12045-2

Ewing,,Mary Helen | (viola)
A Band Of Friends
Wynton Marsalis Quartet With Strings | CBS | CK 68921

Ewing,John 'Steamline' | (tb)
Bobby Bryant Orchestra
Deep Blue-The United States Of Mind | Blue Note | 521152-2
Earl Hines And His Orchestra
Planet Jazz:Earl Hines | Planet Jazz | 2159973-2
The Legends Of Swing | Laserlight | 24659
Jazz:The Essential Collection Vol.2 | IN+OUT Records | 78012-2
Johnny Hartman And His Orchestra
Unforgettable | Impulse(MCA) | IMP 11522

Exon,Willie James | (g)
Albert King Blues Band
Wednesday Night In San Francisco | Stax | SCD 8556-2

Eychmüller,Susanne | (cello)
Michael Riessler And The Ensemble 13
Momentum Mobile | Enja | ENJ-9003 2

Eye,Yamatsuka | (voc)
Batman
Naked City | Nonesuch | 7559-79238-2

Eykan,André | (cl)
Django Reinhardt And The Quintet Du Hot Club De France
Planet Jazz:Django Reinhardt | Planet Jazz | 2152071-2

Eyles,Alex | (tb)
Vic Lewis West Coast All Stars
Vic Lewis Presenting A Celebration Of Contemporary West Coast Jazz | Candid | CCD 79711/12

Eythorstdotir,Sigga | (voc)
Marilyn Mazur With Ars Nova And The Copenhagen Art Ensemble
Jordsange | dacapo | DCCD 9454

Ezell,Will | (p,vocp-solo)
Will Ezell
Boogie Woogie | Laserlight | 24321

Fabbri,Alessandro | (dr)
Mike Turk With The Alkaline Jazz Trio
A Little Taste Of Cannonball | Organic Music | ORGM 9708

Faber,Johannes | (fl-htp)
Albert Mangelsdorff With The NDR Big Band
NDR Big Band-Bravissimo | ACT | 9232-2
Bernd Konrad With Erwin Lehn und sein Südfunk Orchester Stuttgart
Wen Die Götter Lieben | Creative Works Records | CW CD 1010-1
Heinz Sauer Quartet With The NDR Big Band
NDR Big Band-Bravissimo | ACT | 9232-2
Joe Pass With The NDR Big Band
NDR Big Band-Bravissimo | ACT | 9232-2
Johnny Griffin With The NDR Big Band
NDR Big Band-Bravissimo | ACT | 9232-2
NDR Big Band
NDR Big Band-Bravissimo | ACT | 9232-2

Faberman,Irvin | (perccond)
Max Roach With The Boston Percussion Ensemble
Clifford Brown-Max Roach:Alone Together-The Best Of The Mercury Years | Verve | 526373-2

Fabianek,Andreas | (b)
Hans Theessink Group
Crazy Moon | Minor Music | 801052

Fabretti,Pier Luigi | (oboe)
Uri Caine With The Concerto Köln
Concerto Köln | Winter&Winter | 910086-2

Fadani,Mario | (b,el-bvoice)
Ax Genrich Group
Psychedelic Guitar | ATM Records | ATM 3809-AH
Wave Cut | ATM Records | ATM 3813-AH

Faddis,Jon | (co,fl-h,tp,percshells)
Bob James And His Orchestra
Jazzrock-Anthology Vol.3:Fusion | Zounds | CD 27100555
Charles Earland Septet
Charles Earland In Concert | Prestige | PRCD 24267-2
Charles Earland Sextet
Charles Earland In Concert | Prestige | PRCD 24267-2
Dizzy Gillespie Jam
Montreux '77 | Original Jazz Classics | OJC 385(2620105)
Montreux '77 | Original Jazz Classics | OJC20 381-2(2308211)
Dizzy Gillespie Sextet
The Jazz Giants Play Harold Arlen:Blues In The Night | Prestige | PCD 24201-2
George Gruntz Concert Jazz Band
Blues 'N Dues Et Cetera | Enja | ENJ-6072 2
Les McCann Group
Another Beginning | Atlantic | 7567-80790-2
McCoy Tyner Group With Horns
Inner Voices | Original Jazz Classics | OJCCD 1039-2(M 9079)
McCoy Tyner Group With Horns And Voices
Inner Voices | Original Jazz Classics | OJCCD 1039-2(M 9079)
Oscar Peterson-Jon Faddis Duo
Oscar Peterson & Jon Faddis | Original Jazz Classics | OJCCD 1036-2(2310743)
Ron Carter Orchestra
Parade | Original Jazz Classics | OJCCD 1047-2(M 9088)
Rusty Bryant Group
For The Good Times | Prestige | PRCD 24269-2
Sonny Rollins Quintet With Brass
Old Flames | Milestone | MCD 9215-2

Faerber,Achim | (drperc)
Swim Two Birds
Sweet Reliet | Laika Records | 35101182
No Regrets | Laika Records | 35101342

Fagerquist,Don | (tp)
Anita O'Day With Gene Krupa And His Orchestra
Let Me Off Uptown:Anita O'Day With Gene Krupa | CBS | CK 65625
Ella Fitzgerald With Marty Paich's Dektette
Ella Swings Lightly | Verve | 517535-2
Ella Fitzgerald With Paul Weston And His Orchestra
Love Songs:The Best Of The Song Books | Verve | 531762-2
Ella Fitzgerald Sings The Irving Berlin Song Book | Verve | 543830-2
Ella Fitzgerald With The Billy May Orchestra
Ella Fitzgerald-First Lady Of Song | Verve | 517898-2
The Best Of The Song Books | Verve | 519804-2
Verve Jazz Masters 6:Ella Fitzgerald | Verve | 519822-2
The Best Of The Song Books:The Ballads | Verve | 521867-2
Verve Jazz Masters 46:Ella Fitzgerald-The Jazz Sides | Verve | 527655-2
Love Songs:The Best Of The Song Books | Verve | 531762-2
Ella Fitzgerald Sings The Harold Arlen Song Book | Verve | 589108-2
For The Love Of Ella Fitzgerald | Verve | 841765-2
Ella Fitzgerald With The Marty Paich Dek-tette
Ella Fitzgerald-First Lady Of Song | Verve | 517898-2
Verve Jazz Masters 6:Ella Fitzgerald | Verve | 519822-2
Verve Jazz Masters 46:Ella Fitzgerald-The Jazz Sides | Verve | 527655-2
Ella Fitzgerald With The Nelson Riddle Orchestra
Ella Fitzgerald-First Lady Of Song | Verve | 517898-2
The Best Of The Song Books | Verve | 519804-2
The Best Of The Song Books:The Ballads | Verve | 521867-2
Love Songs:The Best Of The Song Books | Verve | 531762-2
For The Love Of Ella Fitzgerald | Verve | 841765-2
Ella Fitzgerald With The Paul Weston Orchestra
Get Happy! | Verve | 523321-2
Gene Krupa And His Orchestra
Mullenium | CBS | CK 65678
Mel Tormé With The Russell Garcia Orchestra
Swingin' On The Moon | Verve | 511385-2
Pete Rugolo And His Orchestra
Thriller/Richard Diamon(Original Jazz Scores From 2 Classics TV Series) | Fresh Sound Records | FSCD 2015
Red Norvo And His Orchestra
Planet Jazz:Female Jazz Vocalists | Planet Jazz | 2169656-2
Stan Kenton And His Orchestra
Stan Kenton Portraits On Standards | Capitol | 531571-2

Fahlenbock,Thomas | (sax)
Marcus Sukiennik Big Band
A Night In Tunisia Suite(7 Variationen über Dizzy Gillespie's 'A Night In Tunisia') | Jazz Haus Musik | ohne Nummer

Fahlström,Örjan | (arr)
NDR Big Band With Guests
50 Years Of NDR Big Band:Bravissimo II | ACT | 9259-2

Fahn,Mike | (tbv-tb)
Tom Harrell Orchestra
Time's Mirror | RCA | 2663524-2

Faieta,Phil | (dr)
Johnny Frigo Sextet
I Love John Frigo...He Swings | Mercury | 9861061

Faigle,Horst | (dr,pvoice)
Horst Faigle's Jazzkrement
Gans Normal | Jazz 4 Ever Records:Jazz Network | J4E 4748

Failla,Jonathan | (voc)
Jazz Fresh
Jazz Fresh | GGG-Verlag:GGG Verlag und Mailorder | CD 01.03

Fain,Paulina | (fl)
Tangata Rea
Tango Alba Baila | Winter&Winter | 910025-2

Fairclough,Peter | (dr)
Mike Westbrook Band
Off Abbey Road | TipToe | TIP-888805 2
Mike Westbrook Orchestra
Bar Utopia-A Big Band Cabaret | Enja | ENJ-9333 2
The Orchestra Of Smith's Academy | Enja | ENJ-9358 2

Fairweather,Al | (tp)
Albert Nicholas With Adrian Bentzon's Jazzband
Albert Nicholas & The Dutch Swing College Band | Storyville | STCD 5522
Cy Laurie Jazz Band
The Golden Years Of Revival Jazz,Sampler | Storyville | 109 1001
Cy Laurie's New Orleans Septet
The Golden Years Of Revival Jazz,Vol 1 | Storyville | STCD 5506
The Golden Years Of Revival Jazz,Vol.5 | Storyville | STCD 5510
The Golden Years Of Revival Jazz,Vol.6 | Storyville | STCD 5511
The Golden Years Of Revival Jazz,Vol.8 | Storyville | STCD 5513
The Golden Years Of Revival Jazz,Vol.9 | Storyville | STCD 5514
The Golden Years Of Revival Jazz,Vol.11 | Storyville | STCD 5516
Henrik Johansen's Jazzband
The Golden Years Of Revival Jazz,Vol.6 | Storyville | STCD 5511
The Golden Years Of Revival Jazz,Vol.7 | Storyville | STCD 5512
The Golden Years Of Revibal Jazz,Vol.15 | Storyville | STCD 5520
Sandy Brown's Jazz Band
The Golden Years Of Revival Jazz,Sampler | Storyville | 109 1001
The Golden Years Of Revival Jazz,Vol.5 | Storyville | STCD 5510
The Golden Years Of Revival Jazz,Vol.6 | Storyville | STCD 5511
The Golden Years Of Revival Jazz,Vol.8 | Storyville | STCD 5513
The Golden Years Of Revival Jazz,Vol.10 | Storyville | STCD 5515

Fairweather,Didby | (co,tp,echo-covoc)
Great British Jazz Band
The Great British Jazz Band:Jubilee | Candid | CCD 79720
The Great British Jazz Band
A British Jazz Odyssey | Candid | CCD 79740

Fairy Tale Trio |
Fairy Tale Trio
Jazz Across The Border | Wergo | SM 1531-2

Faist,Andre | (tbarr)
Benny Carter And His Orchestra
The Art Of Saxophone | Laserlight | 24652

Faist,Thomas | (as,tsfl)
Al Porcino Big Band
Al Porcino Big Band Live! | Organic Music | ORGM 9717
Al Cohn Meets Al Porcino | Organic Music | ORGM 9730
Thomas Faist Jazzquartet
Visionary | JHM Records | JHM 3609
Thomas Faist Sextet
Gentle | Village | VILCD 1020-2

Faithful,Marianne | (voice)
Michael Mantler Group With The Danish Concert Radio Orchestra
Many Have No Speech | Watt | 19(835580-2)

Fajarro,Osvaldo | (voccoro)
Conexion Latina
Mambo Nights | Enja | ENJ-9402 2

Faku,Fezile 'Feya' | (tpfl-h)
Abdullah Ibrahim Quartet
Cape Town Revisited | TipToe | TIP-888836 2

Falco,Gilbert | (tb)
Ella Fitzgerald With The Nelson Riddle Orchestra
Ella Fitzgerald Sings The Johnny Mercer Songbook | Verve | 539057-2

Falensby,Fred | (ts)
Anita O'Day With The Billy May Orchestra
Verve Jazz Masters 49:Anita O'Day | Verve | 527653-2
Billy Eckstine With The Billy May Orchestra
Once More With Feeling | Roulette | 581862-2
Nat King Cole With The Billy May Orchestra
Nat King Cole:For Sentimental Reasons | Dreyfus Jazz Line | FDM 36740-2

Falk,Bror | (p)
Viktoria Tolstoy Group & Strings
Shining On You | ACT | 9701-2

Falk,Dieter | (keyboards)
Wolfgang Schmid's Kick
No Filters | TipToe | TIP-888809 2

Falk,Marika | (bandir,cajon,cuica,daff,darabuka)
NuNu!
Ocean | TipToe | TIP-888837 2
Uli Trepte Group
Real Time Music | ATM Records | ATM 3820-AH

Falk,Rune | (b-clbs)
Bengt-Arne Wallin Orchestra
The Birth+Rebirth Of Swedish Folk Jazz | ACT | 9254-2

Fallensby,Fred | (ts)
June Christy With The Pete Rugolo Orchestra
Something Cool(The Complete Mono & Stereo Versions) | Capitol | 534069-2

Faller,Markus | (dr)
Thomas Siffling Jazz Quartet
Soft Winds | Satin Doll Productions | SDP 1030-1 CD
Thomas Stiffling Group
Stories | Jazz 4 Ever Records:Jazz Network | J4E 4756

Falstitch,John | (tp)
Jack Teagarden And His Orchestra
Jazz:The Essential Collection Vol.3 | IN+OUT Records | 78013-2

Falù,Juan | (g)
Juan Falù
Internationales Guitarren Festival '94 | ALISO Records | AL 1030
Ricardo Moyano-Juan Falù
Internationales Guitarren Festival '94 | ALISO Records | AL 1030

Fambrough,Charles | (bel-b)
Allan Botschinsky Quartet
I've Got Another Rhythm | M.A Music | A 916-2
Art Blakey And The Jazz Messengers
Jazz Life Vol.2:From Seventh At Avenue South | Storyville | 4960763
Kevin Mahogany With The Bob James Trio
My Romance | Warner | 9362-47025-2
Kevin Mahogany With The Bob James Trio And Kirk Whalum
My Romance | Warner | 9362-47025-2
Kevin Mahogany With The Bob James Trio And Michael Brecker
My Romance | Warner | 9362-47025-2
Kevin Mahogany With The Bob James Trio, Kirk Whalum And Strings
My Romance | Warner | 9362-47025-2
Lenny White Group
Present Tense | Hip Bop | HIBD 8004
McCoy Tyner Septet
Focal Point | Original Jazz Classics | OJCCD 1009-2(M 9072)
McCoy Tyner Sextet
Focal Point | Original Jazz Classics | OJCCD 1009-2(M 9072)
Michael 'Patches' Stewart Group
Blue Patches | Hip Bop | HIBD 8016
Wynton Marsalis Quintet
Wynton Marsalis | CBS | 468708-2

Fandel,Leo | (fl)
Bernd Konrad Jazz Group With Symphonie Orchestra
Wen Die Götter Lieben | Creative Works Records | CW CD 1010-1

Faney,Jimmy | (g)
Jimmy Raney Quintet
Early Stan | Original Jazz Classics | OJCCD 654-2(P 7255)

Fant,Edward | (tb)
Earl Hines And His Orchestra
Planet Jazz:Earl Hines | Planet Jazz | 2159973-2

Farafina |
Jon Hassell & Farafina
Flash Of The Spirit | Intuition Records | INT 3009-2

Farao,Antonio | (p)
Antonio Farao Quartet
Thorn | Enja | ENJ-9399 2
Next Stories | Enja | ENJ-9430 2
Antonio Farao Trio
Black Inside | Enja | ENJ-9345 2
Thorn | Enja | ENJ-9399 2
Next Stories | Enja | ENJ-9430 2
Dejan Terzic European Assembly
Coming Up | double moon | DMCHR 71034
Eugen Apostolidis Quartet
Imaginary Directions | Edition Collage | EC 503-2
Franco Ambrosetti Quintet
Light Breeze | Enja | ENJ-9331 2
Johannes Enders Quartet

INTERPRETENVERZEICHNIS

Sandsee | Organic Music | ORGM 9720
The Tough Tenors With The Antonio Farao European Trio
Tough Tenors | Jazz 4 Ever Records:Jazz Network | J4E 4761
Farelli,Jonathan | (perc)
Richard Galliano With Orchestra
Passatori | Dreyfus Jazz Line | FDM 36601-2
Farkas,Mihaly | (b)
Brocksi-Quartett
Drums Boogie | Bear Family Records | BCD 15988 AH
Brocksi-Quintett
Drums Boogie | Bear Family Records | BCD 15988 AH
Brocksi-Sextett
Drums Boogie | Bear Family Records | BCD 15988 AH
Shot Gun Boogie | Bear Family Records | BCD 16277 AH
Freddie Brocksieper And His Boys
Freddie's Boogie Blues | Bear Family Records | BCD 16388 AH
Freddie Brocksieper Four Stars
Freddie's Boogie Blues | Bear Family Records | BCD 16388 AH
Freddie Brocksieper Orchester
Drums Boogie | Bear Family Records | BCD 15988 AH
Shot Gun Boogie | Bear Family Records | BCD 16277 AH
Freddie Brocksieper Quartett
Shot Gun Boogie | Bear Family Records | BCD 16277 AH
Freddie Brocksieper Quintett
Shot Gun Boogie | Bear Family Records | BCD 16277 AH
Freddie Brocksieper Star-Quintett
Shot Gun Boogie | Bear Family Records | BCD 16277 AH
Freddie Brocksieper Trio
Shot Gun Boogie | Bear Family Records | BCD 16277 AH
Freddie Brocksieper Und Seine Solisten
Freddie's Boogie Blues | Bear Family Records | BCD 16388 AH
Farlanders,The |
Farlanders
The Farlander | JA & RO | JARO 4222-2
Farley,Max | (as,sl,cl,tsfl)
Jack Teagarden And His Orchestra
Jazz:The Essential Collection Vol.3 | IN+OUT Records | 78013-2
Farlow,Tal | (gg-solo)
Oscar Pettiford Sextet
The Birdlanders,Vol.2 | Original Jazz Classics | OJCCD 1931-2
Tal Farlow
Verve Jazz Masters 41:Tal Farlow | Verve | 527365-2
Tal Farlow Quartet
Verve Jazz Masters 41:Tal Farlow | Verve | 527365-2
The Return Of Tal Farlow/1969 | Original Jazz Classics | OJCCD 356-2
Tal Farlow Sextet
Verve Jazz Masters 41:Tal Farlow | Verve | 527365-2
Tal Farlow Trio
Verve Jazz Masters 41:Tal Farlow | Verve | 527365-2
The Swinging Guitar Of Tal Farlow | Verve | 559515-2
Farmer,Addison | (b)
Art Farmer Quartet
Early Art | Original Jazz Classics | OJCCD 880-2(NJ 8258)
The Jazz Giants Play Jerome Kern:Yesterdays | Prestige | PCD 24202-2
The Jazz Giants Play Sammy Cahn:It's Magic | Prestige | PCD 24226-2
Curtis Fuller And Hampton Hawes With French Horns
Curtis Fuller And Hampton Hawes With French Horns | Original Jazz Classics | OJCCD 1942-2(NJ 8305)
Curtis Fuller And Teddy Charles With French Horns
Curtis Fuller And Hampton Hawes With French Horns | Original Jazz Classics | OJCCD 1942-2(NJ 8305)
Mal Waldron Trio
The Jazz Giants Play Rodgers & Hart:Blue Moon | Prestige | PCD 24205-2
The Mal Waldron Memorial Album:Soul Eyes | Prestige | PRCD 11024-2
Mose Allison Trio
Rhino Presents The Atlantic Jazz Gallery | Atlantic | 8122-71257-2
I Don't Worry About A Thing | Rhino | 8122-71417-2
Local Color | Original Jazz Classics | OJCCD 457-2
Mose Allison:Greatest Hits | Original Jazz Classics | OJCCD 6004-2
Mose Allison Sings The 7th Son | Prestige | PR20 7279-2
Prestige Jazz Quartet
The Mal Waldron Memorial Album:Soul Eyes | Prestige | PRCD 11024-2
The Prestige Jazz Quartet
The Prestige Jazz Quartet | Original Jazz Classics | OJCCD 1937-2(P 7108)
Farmer,Art | (fl-h,flumpettp)
Abbey Lincoln With The Benny Golson Quintet
It's Magic | Original Jazz Classics | OJCCD 205-2
Abbey Lincoln With The Benny Golson Septet
It's Magic | Original Jazz Classics | OJCCD 205-2
Anthony Ortega With The Robert Zieff Orchestra
Earth Dance | Fresh Sound Records | FSR-CD 325
Art Farmer Quartet
Sing Me Softly Of The Blues | Atlantic | 7567-80773-2
Plays The Arrangements And Compositions Of Gigi Gryce And Quincy Jones | Original Jazz Classics | OJCCD 054-2
Early Art | Original Jazz Classics | OJCCD 880-2(NJ 8258)
The Jazz Giants Play Jerome Kern:Yesterdays | Prestige | PCD 24202-2
The Jazz Giants Play Sammy Cahn:It's Magic | Prestige | PCD 24226-2
Art Farmer Quintet
From Vienna With Art | MPS | 9811443
Early Art | Original Jazz Classics | OJCCD 880-2(NJ 8258)
Art Farmer Septet
Plays The Arrangements And Compositions Of Gigi Gryce And Quincy Jones | Original Jazz Classics | OJCCD 054-2
Art Farmer/Benny Golson Jazztet
The Jazztet At Birdhouse | Argo | 589762-2
Art Farmer/Slide Hampton Quintet
In Concert | Enja | ENJ-4088 2
Ben Webster Septet
The Soul Of Ben Webster | Verve | 527475-2
Cannonball Adderley Quartet
Cannonball Adderley Birthday Celebration | Fantasy | FANCD 6087-2
Clifford Brown And Art Farmer With The Swedish All Stars
Clifford Brown Memorial | Original Jazz Classics | OJC20 017-2(P 7055)
George Russell And His Orchestra
Geogre Russell New York N.Y. | Impulse(MCA) | 951278-2
Bill Evans:Piano Player | CBS | CK 65361
George Russell Smalltet
The RCA Victor Jazz Workshop | RCA | 2159144-2
Gerry Mulligan Quartet
Newport Jazz Festival 1958,July 3rd-6th Vol.2:Mulligan The Main Man | Phontastic | NCD 8814
Hank Mobley Quintet
Hank Mobley | Blue Note | 0675622
Horace Silver Quintet
Horace Silver Retrospective | Blue Note | 495576-2
Stylings Of Silver | Blue Note | 540034-2
J.J.Johnson And His Orchestra
Planet Jazz:J.J.Johnson | Planet Jazz | 2159974-2
Kenny Clarke-Francy Boland Big Band
Clark-Boland Big Band: TNP, October 29th, 1969 | Laserlight | 36129
Lucy Reed With Orchestra
This Is Lucy Reed | Original Jazz Classics | OJCCD 1943-2(F 3243)
Mundell Lowe And His All Stars
Planet Jazz:Ben Webster | RCA | 2165368-2
Prestige Blues-Swingers
Soul Street | Original Jazz Classics | OJCCD 987-2(NJ 8293)
Ron Carter Octet
New York Slick | Original Jazz Classics | OJCCD 916-2(M 9096)
Ron Carter Sextet
New York Slick | Original Jazz Classics | OJCCD 916-2(M 9096)
Sandole Brothers
The Sandole Brothers | Fantasy | FCD 24763-2
Sonny Clark All Stars
Dial S For Sonny | Blue Note | 0675621
Sonny Clark Quintet
Cool Struttin' | Blue Note | 495327-2
Wardell Gray Quintet
Wardell Gray Memorial Vol.2 | Original Jazz Classics | OJCCD 051-2(P 7009)
Farnon,Robert | (arr,voc,conddir)
Sarah Vaughan With Orchestra
Sarah Vaughan Sings The Mancini Songbook | Verve | 558401-2
Singers Unlimited With The Robert Farnon Orchestra
The Singers Unlimited:Magic Voices | MPS | 539130-2
Farnsworth,James | (bs)
The New Jazz Composers Octet
First Step Into Reality | Fresh Sound Records | FSNT 059 CD
Farnsworth,Joe | (dr)
Eric Alexander Quartet
Man With A Horn | Milestone | MCD 9293-2
The First Milestone | Milestone | MCD 9302-2
The Second Milestone | Milestone | MCD 9315-2
Summit Meeting | Milestone | MCD 9322-2
Nightlife In Tokyo | Milestone | MCD 9330-2
Eric Alexander Quintet
The First Milestone | Milestone | MCD 9302-2
The Second Milestone | Milestone | MCD 9315-2
Summit Meeting | Milestone | MCD 9322-2
Eric Alexander Sextet
Man With A Horn | Milestone | MCD 9293-2
Steve Grossman Quartet
Steve Grossman Quartet | Dreyfus Jazz Line | FDM 36602-2
Farrell,Joe | (alto-fl,as,oboe,ss,bass-fl,piccolo)
Anfrew Hill Nonet
Passing Ships | Blue Note | 593871-2
Billy Cobham Group
Spectrum | Atlantic | 7567-81428-2
Bobby Timmons Orchestra
Quartet And Orchestra | Milestone | MCD 47091-2
Charles Mingus Orchestra
Charles Mingus:Pre-Bird(Mingus Revisited) | Verve | 538636-2
Chick Corea And Return To Forever
Light As A Feather | Polydor | 557115-2
Chick Corea Quartet
Return To Forever | ECM | 1022(811978-2)
Verve Jazz Masters 3:Chick Corea | Verve | 519820-2
Verve Jazz Masters 20:Introducing | Verve | 519853-2
Chick Corea Quintet
Inner Space | Atlantic | 7567-81304-2
Chick Corea-Herbie Hancock-Keith Jarrett-McCoy Tyner | Atlantic | 7567-81402-2
Chick Corea Trio
Verve Jazz Masters 3:Chick Corea | Verve | 519820-2
Chick Corea's Return To Forever
Verve Jazz Masters 3:Chick Corea | Verve | 519820-2
Jaki Byard Quartet
The Last From Lennie's | Prestige | PRCD 11029-2
James Moody Orchestra
The Blues And Other Colors | Original Jazz Classics | OJCCD 954-2(M 9023)
Lee Konitz Orchestra
The Art Of Saxophone | Laserlight | 24652
Maynard Ferguson Orchestra With Chris Connor
Two's Company | Roulette | 837201-2
Pat Martino Quintet
Strings! | Original Jazz Classics | OJCCD 223-2(P 7547)
Pat Martino Septet
Strings! | Original Jazz Classics | OJCCD 223-2(P 7547)
Return To Forever
Return To The 7th Galaxy-Return To Forever:The Anthology | Verve | 533108-2
Stanley Turrentine And His Orchestra
The Lost Grooves | Blue Note | 831883-2
Thad Jones-Mel Lewis Orchestra
The Groove Merchant/The Second Race | Laserlight | 24656
Willie Bobo Group
Bobo's Beat | Roulette | 590954-2
Farrell,Larry | (tb)
David Matthews & The Manhattan Jazz Orchestra
Back To Bach | Milestone | MCD 9312-2
Hey Duke! | Milestone | MCD 9320-2
Joe Lovano Nonet
On This Day At The Vanguard | Blue Note | 590950-2
Farrenden,Sean | (didgeridoo)
Jazz Africa All Nations Big Band
Jadu(Jazz Africa Down Under) | Enja | ENJ-9339 2
Farrent,Karl | (fl-htp)
Bill Ramsey With Orchestra
Gettin' Back To Swing | Bear Family Records | BCD 15813 AH
SWR Big Band
Jazz In Concert | Hänssler Classics | CD 93.004
Farrer,Pvt R | (marimba)
Steve Martland Band
The Orchestra Of Smith's Academy | Enja | ENJ-9358 2
Farris,Ralph | (viola)
Jim Snidero Quartet With Strings
Strings | Milestone | MCD 9326-2
Marty Ehrlich Group
The Long View | Enja | ENJ-9452 2
Farrow,Ernie | (b,earthboardrabab)
Barry Harris Quintet
Never Than New | Original Jazz Classics | OJCCD 1062-2(RLP 9413)
Yusef Lateef Orchestra
The Centaur And The Phoenix | Original Jazz Classics | OJCCD 721-2(RLP 9337)
Yusef Lateef Quartet
Live at Pep's Vol.2 | Impulse(MCA) | 547961-2
Eastern Sounds | Original Jazz Classics | OJC20 612-2(P 7319)
Yusef Lateef Quintet
Live at Pep's Vol.2 | Impulse(MCA) | 547961-2
The Roots Of Acid Jazz | Impulse(MCA) | IMP 12042
Other Sounds | Original Jazz Classics | OJCCD 399-2(NJ 8218)
Faso,Tony | (tp)
Billie Holiday With Sy Oliver And His Orchestra
Billie's Love Songs | Nimbus Records | NI 2000
Ella Fitzgerald With Sy Oliver And His Orchestra
Ella Fitzgerald:Mr.Paganini | Dreyfus Jazz Line | FDM 36741-2
Ella Fitzgerald With Sy Oliver And His Orchestra
Ella Fitzgerald:The Decca Years 1949-1954 | Decca | 050668-2
Peggy Lee With The Benny Goodman Orchestra
Peggy Lee & Benny Goodman:The Complete Recordings 1941-1947 | CBS | C2K 65686
Fass,Helmut | (b)
Inga Lühning With Trio
Lühning | Jazz Haus Musik | JHM 0111 CD
Fatool,Nick | (dr)
Artie Shaw And His Orchestra
Planet JazzArtie Shaw | Planet Jazz | 2152057-2
Planet Jazz:Big Bands | Planet Jazz | 2169649-2
Swing Vol.1 | Storyville | 4960343
Benny Goodman And His Orchestra
Charlie Christian:Swing To Bop | Dreyfus Jazz Line | FDM 36715-2
More Camel Caravans | Phontastic | NCD 8845/6
Benny Goodman Sextet
Charlie Christian:Swing To Bop | Dreyfus Jazz Line | FDM 36715-2
More Camel Caravans | Phontastic | NCD 8845/6
From Spiritual To Swing | Vanguard | VCD 169/71
Count Basie And His Orchestra
From Spiritual To Swing | Vanguard | VCD 169/71
Lionel Hampton And His Orchestra
Planet Jazz:Lionel Hampton | Planet Jazz | 2152059-2
Louis Armstrong With Gordon Jenkins And His Orchestra
Satchmo In Style | Verve | 549594-2
Louis Armstrong With Gordon Jenkins And His Orchestra And Choir
Satchmo In Style | Verve | 549594-2
The Capitol Jazzmen
The Hollywood Session:The Capitol Jazzmen | Jazz Unlimited | JUCD 2044
Faulise,Paul | (b-tb,tbbass-tb)
Bill Evans Quartet With Orchestra
The Complete Bill Evans On Verve | Verve | 527953-2
From Left To Right | Verve | 557451-2
Cannonball Adderley And His Orchestra
Cannonball Adderley Birthday Celebration | Fantasy | FANCD 6087-2
Charles Mingus And His Orchestra
The Complete Town Hall Concert | Blue Note | 828353-2
Dizzy Gillespie And His Orchestra
Verve Jazz Masters 10:Dizzy Gillespie | Verve | 516319-2
Gillespiana And Carnegie Hall Concert | Verve | 519809-2
Talking Verve:Dizzy Gillespie | Verve | 533846-2
Ultimate Dizzy Gillespie | Verve | 557535-2
Freddie Hubbard With Orchestra
This Is Jazz:Freddie Hubbard | CBS | CK 65041
Glenn Miller And His Orchestra
The Glenn Miller Orchestra In Digital Mood | GRP | GRP 95022
Grover Washington Jr. Orchestra
Jazzrock-Anthology Vol.3:Fusion | Zounds | CD 27100555
J.J.Johnson And His Orchestra
Planet Jazz:J.J.Johnson | Planet Jazz | 2159974-2
J.J.Johnson's All Stars
J.J.'s Broadway | Verve | 9860308
Jimmy McGriff Orchestra
Swingin' The Blues-Jumpin' The Blues | Laserlight | 24654
Jimmy Smith With Orchestra
Jimmy Smith-Talkin' Verve | Verve | 531563-2
Jimmy Smith With The Billy Byers Orchestra
Jimmy Smith:Best Of The Verve Years | Verve | 527950-2
Jimmy Smith With The Claus Ogerman Orchestra
Verve Jazz Masters 29:Jimmy Smith | Verve | 521855-2
Any Number Can Win | Verve | 557447-2
Kenny Burrell With The Don Sebesky Orchestra
Verve Jazz Masters 45:Kenny Burrell | Verve | 527652-2
Blues-The Common Ground | Verve | 589101-2
Milt Jackson Orchestra
Big Bags | Original Jazz Classics | OJCCD 366-2(RLP 9429)
Oscar Peterson With The Ernie Wilkins Orchestra
Verve Jazz Masters 16:Oscar Peterson | Verve | 516320-2
Paul Desmond Quartet With The Don Sebesby Orchestra
From The Hot Afternoon | Verve | 543487-2
Quincy Jones And His Orchestra
The Quintessence | Impulse(MCA) | 951222-2
The Roots Of Acid Jazz | Impulse(MCA) | IMP 12042
Sarah Vaughan With The Frank Foster Orchestra
The Antonio Carlos Jobim Songbook | Verve | 525472-2
Faulk,Dan | (ssts)
Dan Faulk Quartet
Spirit In The Night | Fresh Sound Records | FSNT 024 CD
Dan Faulk Trio
Spirit In The Night | Fresh Sound Records | FSNT 024 CD
Eddie Allen Quintet
Summer Days | Enja | ENJ-9388 2
Eddie Allen Sextet
Summer Days | Enja | ENJ-9388 2
Faulkner,Tony | (cond)
Kenny Wheeler Brass Ensemble
A Long Time Ago | ECM | 1691
Faulks,Lucy | (voc)
Mike Westbrook Brass Band
Glad Day:Settings Of William Blake | Enja | ENJ-9376 2
Favors,Malachi | (b,bells,whistles,gongs,el-b,log-dr)
Art Ensemble Of Chicago
Nice Guys | ECM | 1126
Full Force | ECM | 1167(829197-2)
Urban Bushmen | ECM | 1211/12
The Third Decade | ECM | 1273
Tribute To Lester | ECM | 1808(017066-2)
Americans Swinging In Paris:Art Ensemble Of Chicago | EMI Records | 539667-2
Bap-Tizum | Atlantic | 7567-80757-2
Coming Home Jamaica | Dreyfus Jazz Line | FDM 37003-2
Favre,Pierre | (dr,crotales,cymbals,gongsperc)
Bill Ramsey With The Paul Kuhn Trio
Caldonia And More... | Bear Family Records | BCD 16151 AH
Dino Saluzzi Quartet
Once Upon A Time-Far Away In The South | ECM | 1309(827768-2)
Don Menza Septet
Morning Song | MPS | 9811446
Joe Haider Trio
Jazz Portraits | EGO | 95080
Katzenvilla | JHM Records | JHM 3622
John Surman Trio
Such Winters Of Memory | ECM | 1254(810621-2)
Michel Godard Ensemble
Castel Del Mónte | Enja | ENJ-9362 2
Paul Giger Trio
Alpstein | ECM | 1426(847940-2)
Pierre Favre Ensemble
Singing Drums | ECM | 1274
Pierre Favre Quintet
Window-Steps | ECM | 1584(529348-2)
Tamia/Pierre Favre
Solitudes | ECM | 1446
Favre,Yves | (tb)
Michael Riessler And The Ensemble 13
Momentum Mobile | Enja | ENJ-9003 2
Renaud Garcia-Fons
Navigatore | Enja | ENJ-9418 2
Renaud Garcia-Fons Group
Oriental Bass | Enja | ENJ-9334 2
Navigatore | Enja | ENJ-9418 2
Fay,Tom | (p)
Benny Goodman Quintet
Verve Jazz Masters 33:Benny Goodman | Verve | 844410-2
Faye,Norman | (tp)
Chet Baker Big Band
The Best Of Chet Baker Plays | Pacific Jazz | 797161-2
Fazola[Prestopnick],Irving | (clas)
Bob Crosby And His Orchestra
Swing Legens:Bob Crosby | Nimbus Records | NI 2011
Bob Crosby's Bobcats
Swing Legens:Bob Crosby | Nimbus Records | NI 2011
Fazzini,Nicola | (ssas)
Palo Alto
Crash Test | Jazz 'n' Arts Records | JNA 1803
Feather,Leonard | (cond,arr,harpsichord,ld)
Jack Teagarden And His Band
Meet Me Where They Play The Blues | Good Time Jazz | GTCD 12063-2
Louis Armstrong And His Hot Seven
Louis Armstrong:C'est Si Bon | Dreyfus Jazz Line | FDM 36730-2
Sarah Vaughan With The Allstars
Sarah Vaughan:Lover Man | Dreyfus Jazz Line | FDM 36739-2
Featonby,Chris | (b)
John Mayer's Indio-Jazz Fusions
Ragatal | Nimbus Records | NI 5569
Federer,Günther | (resonating-stones)
Stephan Micus
The Muisc Of Stones | ECM | 1384(837750-2)
Federkeil,Elmar | (dr)
Scetches
Different Places | VeraBra Records | CDVBR 2102-2

Feeman,Ben | (sax)
Anita O'Day With Gene Krupa And His Orchestra
Let Me Off Uptown:Anita O'Day With Gene Krupa | CBS | CK 65625
Feger,Fritz | (b)
Gunter Hampel Next Generation
Next Generation | Birth | CD 043
Feichtner,Dieter | (synth)
Barre Phillips Quartet
Mountainscapes | ECM | 1076
Barre Phillips Quintet
Mountainscapes | ECM | 1076
Feierman,Jack | (tp)
Count Basie And His Orchestra
I Told You So | Original Jazz Classics | OJCCD 824-2(2310767)
Feierstein,Javier | (g)
Javier Feierstein Quartet
Wysiwyg | Fresh Sound Records | FSNT 040 CD
Feig,Gabi | (voc)
Jazzensemble Des Hessischen Rundfunks
Jazz Messe-Messe Für Unsere Zeit | hr music.de | hrmj 003-01 CD
Feigl,Johnny | (bs,clsax)
Charly Antolini Orchestra
Drum Beat | MPS | 9808191
Dieter Reith Group
Reith On! | MPS | 557423-2
Helmut Zacharias mit dem Orchester Frank Folken
Ich Habe Rhythmus | Bear Family Records | BCD 15642 AH
Kurt Edelhagen All Stars
Deutsches Jazz Fesival 1954/1955 | Bear Family Records | BCD 15430
Kurt Edelhagen All Stars Und Solisten
Deutsches Jazz Fesival 1954/1955 | Bear Family Records | BCD 15430
Quartet Der Kurt Edelhagen All Stars
Deutsches Jazz Fesival 1954/1955 | Bear Family Records | BCD 15430
Feil,Peter | (tb)
Daniel Guggenheim Group
Daniel Guggenheim Group feat. Jasper van't Hof | Laika Records | LK 990-018
HR Big Band
The American Songs Of Kurt Weill | hr music.de | hrmj 006-01 CD
Libertango:Homage An Astor Piazolla | hr music.de | hrmj 014-02 CD
HR Big Band With Marjorie Barnes And Frits Landesbergen
Swinging Christmas | hr music.de | hrmj 012-02 CD
HR Big Band With Marjorie Barnes And Frits Landesbergen And Strings
Swinging Christmas | hr music.de | hrmj 012-02 CD
Kevin Mahogany With The WDR Big Band And Guests
Pussy Cat Dues:The Music Of Charles Mingus | Enja | ENJ-9316 2
The Three Sopranos With The HR Big Band
The Three Sopranos | hr music.de | hrmj 001-01 CD
Felber,Henry | (strings)
Gene Harris And The Three Sounds
Deep Blue-The United States Of Mind | Blue Note | 521152-2
Feld,Morey | (dr)
Bobby Hackett Sextet
Jazz Festival Vol.1 | Storyville | 4960733
Jazz Festival Vol.2 | Storyville | 4960743
Johnny Smith Quintet
Moonlight In Vermont | Roulette | 596593-2
Sarah Vaughan With The Allstars
Sarah Vaughan:Lover Man | Dreyfus Jazz Line | FDM 36739-2
Felder,Bobby | (v-tb)
Charlie Byrd Sextet
Byrd's Word! | Original Jazz Classics | OJCCD 1054-2(R 9448)
Felder,Wilton | (as,ts,b,el-b,saxss)
Bobby Bryant Orchestra
Deep Blue-The United States Of Mind | Blue Note | 521152-2
Charles Kynard Quintet
The Soul Brotherhood | Prestige | PCD 24257-2
Dee Dee Bridgewater With Band
Dee Dee Bridgewater | Atlantic | 7567-80760-2
Dizzy Gillespie With The Lalo Schifrin Orchestra
Free Ride | Original Jazz Classics | OJCCD 784-2(2310794)
Donald Byrd Orchestra
Black Byrd | Blue Note | 784466-2
Ethiopian Knights | Blue Note | 854328-2
Grant Green Septet
Live At The Lighthouse | Blue Note | 493381-2
Jazz Crusaders
Chile Con Soul | Pacific Jazz | 590957-2
Jimmy Smith Quintet
Root Down | Verve | 559805-2
Jimmy Smith Sextet
Jimmy Smith:Best Of The Verve Years | Verve | 527950-2
Root Down | Verve | 559805-2
The Jazz Crusaders
Kind Of Blue:Blue Note Celebrate The Music Of Miles Davis | Blue Note | 534255-2
Feldman,Harold | (bassoon,oboe,b-cl,fl,reedsts)
Miles Davis With Gil Evans & His Orchestra
Sketches Of Spain | CBS | CK 65142
Sarah Vaughan With The Hugo Winterhalter Orchestra
Sarah Vaughan:Lover Man | Dreyfus Jazz Line | FDM 36739-2
Sarah Vaughan With The Joe Lippman Orchestra
Sarah Vaughan:Lover Man | Dreyfus Jazz Line | FDM 36739-2
Feldman,Lawrence | (as,cl,ss,fl,alto-fl,ts,piccolo-fl)
David Matthews & The Manhattan Jazz Orchestra
Hey Duko! | Milestone | MCD 9320-2
John Scofield Groups
Quiet | Verve | 533185-2
Wolfgang Lackerschmid-Donald Johnston Group
New Singers-New Songs | Bhakti Jazz | BR 31
Feldman,Mark | (v,bar-v,percvoice)
Arcado-String Trio
Arcado-String Trio | JMT Edition | 919028-2
Blaufrontal With Hank Roberts & Mark Feldman
Bad Times Roll | Jazz Haus Musik | JHM 0061 CD
Craig Bailey Band
A New Journey | Candid | CCD 79725
Daniel Schnyder Quintet With String Quartet
Mythology | Enja | ENJ-7003 2
Dave Douglas Group
Witness | RCA | 2663763-2
Dave Douglas Quartet
A Thousand Evenings | RCA | 2663698-2
Charms Of The Night Sky | Winter&Winter | 910015-2
Double Trio(Trio De Clarinettes&Arcado)
Green Dolphy Suite | Enja | ENJ-9011 2
Hans Lüdemann Rism 7
FutuRISM | Jazz Haus Musik | JHM 0092/93 CD
James Emery Septet
Spectral Domains | Enja | ENJ-9344 2
Jim Snidero Quartet With Strings
Strings | Milestone | MCD 9326-2
John Abercrombie Quartet
Cat 'N' Mouse | ECM | 1770(014001-2)
Class Trip | ECM | 1846(0381182)
John Abercrombie Sextet
Open Land | ECM | 1683(557652-2)
Karl Berger-Marc Feldman Duo
Conversations | IN+OUT Records | 77027-2
Klaus König Orchestra
Time Fragments:Seven Studies In Time And Motion | Enja | ENJ-8076 2
Reviews | Enja | ENJ-9061 2
Lee Konitz With Strings
Strings For Holiday:A Tribute To Billie Holiday | Enja | ENJ-9304 2
Mark Feldman Quartet
Book Of Tells | Enja | ENJ-9385 2
Marty Ehrlich Group
The Long View | Enja | ENJ-9452 2
Michael Brecker Quindectet
Wide Angles | Verve | 076142-2
Sylvie Courvoisier Group
Abaton | ECM | 1838/39(157628-2)
The Chromatic Persuaders
The Chromatic Persuaders | Timescrapper | TSCR 9617
The Sidewalks Of New York
Tin Pan Alley:The Sidewalks Of New York | Winter&Winter | 910038-2
Uri Caine Ensemble
Wagner E Venezia | Winter&Winter | 910013-2
Uri Caine Group
Urlicht/Primal Light | Winter&Winter | 910004-2
Feldman,Stu | (b)
Bobby McFerrin Group
Bobby McFerrin | Elektra | 7559-60023-2
Feldman,Victor | (dr,el-p,perc,synt,keyboards,p,arr)
Art Pepper Quartet
Art 'N' Zoot | Pablo | 2310957-2
Art Pepper-Zoot Sims Quintet
Art 'N' Zoot | Pablo | 2310957-2
Barney Kessel And His Quintet
Barney Kessel Plays Carmen | Original Jazz Classics | OJC 269(C 7563)
Bobby McFerrin Group
Bobby McFerrin | Elektra | 7559-60023-2
Cannonball Adderley And The Poll Winners
Cannonball Adderley And The Poll Winners | Capitol | 520086-2
Cannonball Adderley Quintet
Wes Montgomery-The Complete Riverside Recordings | Riverside | 12 RCD 4408-2
Julian Cannonball Adderlry: Salle Pleyel/Olympia | Laserlight | 36126
At The Lighthouse | Capitol | 531572-2
Cannonball Adderley Birthday Celebration | Fantasy | FANCD 6087-2
Cannonball Adderley Quintet Plus | Original Jazz Classics | OJC20 306-2
The Cannonball Adderley Quintet:Paris 1960 | Pablo | PACD 5303-2
Cannonball Adderley Quintet Plus
Cannonball Adderley Birthday Celebration | Fantasy | FANCD 6087-2
Cannonball Adderley Quintet Plus | Original Jazz Classics | OJC20 306-2
Cannonball Adderley Sextet
Julian Cannonball Adderlry: Salle Pleyel/Olympia | Laserlight | 36126
Cannonball Adderley-Nat Adderley Quintet
What Is This Thing Called Soul:In Europe-Live! | Original Jazz Classics | OJCCD 801-2(2308238)
Ella Fitzgerald With Frank De Vol And His Orchestra
Get Happy! | Verve | 523321-2
Ella Fitzgerald With Orchestra
Ella/Things Ain't What They Used To Be | Warner | 9362-47875-2
Hank Crawford Orchestra
Rhino Presents The Atlantic Jazz Gallery | Atlantic | 8122-71257-2
Leroy Vinnegar Sextet
The Jazz Giants Play Harry Warren:Lullaby Of Broadway | Prestige | PCD 24204-2
Miles Davis Quartet
This Is Jazz:Miles Davis Plays Ballads | CBS | CK 65038
Miles Davis Quintet
Ballads | CBS | 461099-2
Seven Steps To Heaven | CBS | CK 48827
Nat Adderley Quintet
A Little New York Midtown Music | Original Jazz Classics | OJCCD 1008-2(GXY 5120)
Sam Jones Plus 10
Cannonball Adderley Birthday Celebration | Fantasy | FANCD 6087-2
Shelly Manne And His Men
At The Black Hawk Vol.1 | Original Jazz Classics | OJCCD 656-2(S 7577)
At The Black Hawk Vol.2 | Original Jazz Classics | OJCCD 657-2(S 7578)
At The Black Hawk Vol.3 | Original Jazz Classics | OJCCD 658-2(S 7579)
At The Black Hawk Vol.4 | Original Jazz Classics | OJCCD 659-2(S 7580)
At The Black Hawk Vol.5 | Original Jazz Classics | OJCCD 660-2
Shelly Manne Trio
At The Black Hawk Vol.5 | Original Jazz Classics | OJCCD 660-2
Singers Unlimited With The Clare Fischer Orchestra
The Singers Unlimited:Magic Voices | MPS | 539130-2
Singers Unlimited With The Pat Williams Orchestra
The Singers Unlimited:Magic Voices | MPS | 539130-2
Sonny Rollins & The Contemporary Leaders
Sonny Rollins & The Contemporary Leaders | Original Jazz Classics | OJCCD 340-2
Victor Feldman Orchestra
Latinsville | Contemporary | CCD 9005-2
Wes Montgomery Quartet
Wes Montgomery-The Complete Riverside Recordings | Riverside | 12 RCD 4408-2
Movin' Along | Original Jazz Classics | OJC20 089-2
Wes Montgomery Quintet
Wes Montgomery-The Complete Riverside Recordings | Riverside | 12 RCD 4408-2
Movin' Along | Original Jazz Classics | OJC20 089-2
Zoot Sims Quartet
Art 'N' Zoot | Pablo | 2310957-2
Zoot Sims Quintet
Art 'N' Zoot | Pablo | 2310957-2
Quietly There-Zoot Sims Plays Johnny Mandel | Original Jazz Classics | OJCCD 787-2(2310903)
Felix,Delbert | (b)
Branford Marsalis Trio
Trio Jeepy | CBS | 465134-2
Felkay,Laszlo | (bassoon)
Bernd Konrad Jazz Group With Symphonie Orchestra
Wen Die Götter Lieben | Creative Works Records | CW CD 1010-1
Feller,Al | (v)
Charlie Parker With Strings
Verve Jazz Masters 28:Charlie Parker Plays Standards | Verve | 521854-2
Feller,Sid | (arr,ldtp)
Ella Fitzgerald With Orchestra
Misty Blue:Sweet Sisters Swing Songs Of Sorrow And Sadness | Blue Note | 521151-2
Jack Teagarden And His Orchestra
Jazz:The Essential Collection Vol.3 | IN+OUT Records | 78013-2
Felsch,Fiete | (as,fl,ssreeds)
Abdullah Ibrahim With The NDR Big Band
Ekapa Lodumo | TipToe | TIP-888840 2
NDR Big Band
The Theatre Of Kurt Weil | ACT | 9234-2
Oscar Brown Jr. with The NDR Big Band
Live Every Minute | Minor Music | 801071
Pee Wee Ellis & NDR Bigband
What You Like | Minor Music | 801064
Feman,Ben | (as)
Glenn Miller And His Orchestra
Planet Jazz:Glenn Miller | Planet Jazz | 2152056-2
Fen,Min Xiao | (gongpipa)
Randy Weston African Rhythm
Khepera | Verve | 557821-2
Fenchel,Reiner | (tp)
Jazzensemble Des Hessischen Rundfunks
Jazz Messe-Messe Für Unsere Zeit | hr music.de | hrmj 003-01 CD
Fenelly,Kate | (voc)
Kevin Mahogany With Orchestra
Songs And Moments | Enja | ENJ-8072 2
Fenger,Sos | (voc)
Nils Landgren First Unit And Guests
Nils Landgren-The First Unit | ACT | 9292-2
Fenn,Rick | (g)
Michael Mantler Group With The Danish Concert Radio Orchestra
Many Have No Speech | Watt | 19(835580-2)
Michael Mantler Quintet
Live | Watt | 18
Michael Mantler Quintet With The Balanescu Quartet
Folly Seeing All This | ECM | 1485
Fennell,Munner Bernhard | (cello,perc,balafonvoc)
Muneer B.Fennell & The Rhythm String Band
An Encounter With Higher Forces | double moon | CHRDM 71019
Fenton,Jane | (cello)
Michael Mantler Quintet With The Balanescu Quartet
Folly Seeing All This | ECM | 1485
Fenton,Nick | (b)
Charlie Christian All Stars
Thelonious Monk:85th Birthday Celebration | zyx records | FANCD 6076-2
Charlie Christian-Jazz Immortal/Dizzy Gillespie 1944 | Original Jazz Classics | OJCCD 1932-2(ES 548)
Minton's Playhouse All Stars
Charlie Christian:Swing To Bop | Dreyfus Jazz Line | FDM 36715-2
Una Mae Carlisle Quintet
Jazz:The Essential Collection Vol.3 | IN+OUT Records | 78013-2
Una Mae Carlisle Septet
Planet Jazz:Female Jazz Vocalists | Planet Jazz | 2169656-2
Ferall,Joe | (tb)
Jack Teagarden And His Orchestra
Jazz:The Essential Collection Vol.3 | IN+OUT Records | 78013-2
Ferber,Henry | (v)
Milt Jackson And His Orchestra
Reverence And Compassion | Reprise | 9362-45204-2
Ferchen,Tim | (marimbatubular-bells)
Edward Vesala Ensemble
Ode Of The Death Of Jazz | ECM | 1413(843196-2)
Ferdinando,Joe | (as,reedssax)
Jack Teagarden And His Orchestra
Jazz:The Essential Collection Vol.3 | IN+OUT Records | 78013-2
Ferelli,Tonino | (b)
Helen Merrill With The Piero Umilliani Group
Parole E Musica | RCA | 2174798-2
Féret,Philippe | (cello)
Charlie Haden Quartet West With Strings
Now Is The Hour | Verve | 527827-2
Feretti,Chet | (tp)
Maynard Ferguson Orchestra With Chris Connor
Two's Company | Roulette | 837201-2
Ferguson,Allyn | (fr-h,parr)
Chamber Jazz Sextet
Plays Pal Joey | Candid | CCD 79030
Ferguson,Audrey | (arrvoc)
Sarah Vaughan And The Count Basie Orchestra
Sarah Vaughan Birthday Celebration | Fantasy | FANCD 6090-2
Ferguson,Dan | (g)
Singers Unlimited With The Patrick Williams Orchestra
The Singers Unlimited:Magic Voices | MPS | 539130-2
Ferguson,Joe | (fl,ss,asts)
Sam Rivers Orchestra
Crystals | Impulse(MCA) | 589760-2
Ferguson,Matt | (b)
Tuey Connell Group
Songs For Joy And Sadness | Minor Music | 801095
Ferguson,Maynard | (announcement,claves,euphonium,tp)
All Star Live Jam Session
Brownie-The Complete EmArCy Recordings Of Clifford Brown | EmArCy | 838306-2
Ben Webster Sextet
Verve Jazz Masters 43:Ben Webster | Verve | 525431-2
Verve Jazz Masters 52:Maynard Ferguson | Verve | 529905-2
Birdland Dream Band
Birdland Dream Band | RCA | 2663873-2
Bud Shank And Trombones
Cool Fool | Fresh Sound Records | FSR CD 507
Buddy Bregman And His Orchestra
Swinging Kicks | Verve | 559514-2
Clifford Brown All Stars With Dinah Washington
Verve Jazz Masters 40:Dinah Washington | Verve | 522055-2
Dinah Washington And Her Band
Verve Jazz Masters 40:Dinah Washington | Verve | 522055-2
Ella Fitzgerald With The Buddy Bregman Orchestra
Love Songs:The Best Of The Song Books | Verve | 531762-2
Ella Fitzgerald Sings The Cole Porter Songbook | Verve | 537257-2
Ella Fitzgerald Sings The Rodgers And Hart Song Book | Verve | 537258-2
June Christy With The Pete Rugolo Orchestra
Something Cool(The Complete Mono & Stereo Versions) | Capitol | 534069-2
Maynard Ferguson And His Big Bop Nouveau Band
Maynard Ferguson '93-Footpath Café | Hot Shot Records | HSR 8312-2
Maynard Ferguson And His Orchestra
Verve Jazz Masters 52:Maynard Ferguson | Verve | 529905-2
Maynard Ferguson Band
Verve Jazz Masters 52:Maynard Ferguson | Verve | 529905-2
Maynard Ferguson Orchestra With Chris Connor
Two's Company | Roulette | 837201-2
Nat King Cole Quartet With The Stan Kenton Orchestra
Nat King Cole:For Sentimental Reasons | Dreyfus Jazz Line | FDM 36740-2
Pete Rugolo And His Orchestra
Verve Jazz Masters 52:Maynard Ferguson | Verve | 529905-2
Shorty Rogers And His Orchestra Feat. The Giants
PLanet Jazz:Shorty Rogers | Planet Jazz | 2159976-2
Stan Kenton And His Orchestra
Great Swing Classics In Hi-Fi | Capitol | 521223-2
Stan Kenton Portraits On Standards | Capitol | 531571-2
One Night Stand | Choice | CHCD 71051
Ferguson,Sherman | (dr,bellsvoc)
Bill Perkins-Bud Shank Quintet
The Jazz Giants Play Harold Arlen:Blues In The Night | Prestige | PCD 24201-2
Bud Shank Sextet
New Gold! | Candid | CCD 79707
Leon Thomas With Band
Super Black Blues Vol.II | RCA | 2663874-2
Pat Martino Quartet
Desperado | Original Jazz Classics | OJCCD 397-2(P 7795)
Pat Martino Quintet
Desperado | Original Jazz Classics | OJCCD 397-2(P 7795)
Ruth Brown With Orchestra
Fine And Mellow | Fantasy | FCD 9663-2
Ferguson,Stitz | (ts)
Louis Armstrong With Gordon Jenkins And His Orchestra And Choir
Satchmo In Style | Verve | 549594-2
Louis Armstrong With The Gordon Jenkins Orchestra
Ambassador Louis Armstrong Vol.17:Moments To Remember(1952-1956) | Ambassador | CLA 1917
Ferguson,Tim | (b)
Don Friedman Quartet
My Foolish Heart | Steeplechase | SCCD 31534
My Foolish Heart | Steeplechase | SCCD 31545
Ferianto,Djaduk | (srompet,kendang,beduk,klunthung)
Norbert Stein Pata Masters meets Djaduk Ferianto Kua Etnika
Pata Java | Pata Musik | PATA 16 CD
Ferina,Tony | (bs)
Stan Kenton And His Orchestra
Stan Kenton Portraits On Standards | Capitol | 531571-2
Fernandez,Agusti | (pprep-p)
Evan Parker Electro-Acoustic Ensemble

Memory/Vision | ECM | 1852(0381172)

Fernandez,Julio | (g)
Spyro Gyra & Guests
Love & Other Obsessions | GRP | GRP 98112

Fernandez,Mario | (tp)
Irakere
Yemayá | Blue Note | 498239-2

Fernandez,Nono | (b)
Mitchell-Terraza Group
Shell Blues | Fresh Sound Records | FSNT 005 CD

Fernandez,Rene | (p)
Charlie Parker With Machito And His Orchestra
Charlie Parker:The Best Of The Verve Years | Verve | 527815-2
Talkin' Bird | Verve | 559859-2
Charlie Parker:April In Paris | Dreyfus Jazz Line | FDM 36737-2

Ferngut,Leon | (viola)
Stan Getz With The Eddie Sauter Orchestra
Stan Getz Plays The Music Of Mickey One | Verve | 531232-2

Fernow,Wolfgang | (bvoc)
Matthias Stich & Whisper Not
Bach Lives!! | Satin Doll Productions | SDP 1018-1 CD

Ferra,Bebo | (g)
John Stowell-Bebo Ferra
Elle | Jardis Records | JRCD 20028
Jazz Guitar Highlights 1 | Jardis Records | JRCD 20141

Ferran,Francesca | (voc)
Mike Westbrook Brass Band
Glad Day:Settings Of William Blake | Enja | ENJ-9376 2

Ferrante,Joe | (tp)
Birdland Dream Band
Birdland Dream Band | RCA | 2663873-2
Chubby Jackson And His All Star Big Band
Chubby Takes Over | Fresh Sound Records | FSR-CD 324
George Russell And His Orchestra
Geogre Russell New York N.Y. | Impulse(MCA) | 951278-2
Joe Williams With The Frank Hunter Orchestra
Planet Jazz:Joe Williams | Planet Jazz | 2165370-2
Peggy Lee With The Benny Goodman Orchestra
Peggy Lee & Benny Goodman:The Complete Recordings 1941-1947 | CBS | C2K 65686
Stan Getz With The Eddie Sauter Orchestra
Stan Getz Plays The Music Of Mickey One | Verve | 531232-2
Stan Getz With The Gary McFarland Orchestra
Verve Jazz Masters 53:Stan Getz-Bossa Nova | Verve | 529904-2
Big Band Bossa Nova | Verve | 825771-2 PMS
Stan Getz Highlights | Verve | 847430-2

Ferrante,Russell | (el-p,keyboards,org,psynth)
GRP All-Star Big Band
GRP All-Star Big Band:Live! | GRP | GRP 97402
All Blues | GRP | GRP 98002
Robben Ford & The Blue Line
Handful Of Blues | Blue Thumb | BTR 70042
Spyro Gyra & Guests
Love & Other Obsessions | GRP | GRP 98112
Take 6 With The Yellow Jackets
He Is Christmas | Reprise | 7599-26665-2
Yellowjackets
Live Wires | GRP | GRP 96672
Run For Your Life | GRP | GRP 97542

Ferrara,Don | (tp)
Chubby Jackson Big Band
Gerry Mulligan Quartet feat.Chet Baker | Original Jazz Classics | OJCCD 711-2(F 8082/P 7641)
Gerry Mulligan And His Orchestra
Mullenium | CBS | CK 65678
Gerry Mulligan Concert Jazz Band
Verve Jazz Masters 36:Gerry Mulligan | Verve | 523342-2
Verve Jazz Masters Vol.60:The Collection | Verve | 529866-2
Gerry Mulligan And The Concert Band At The Village Vanguard | Verve | 589488-2
The Complete Verve Gerry Mulligan Concert Band | Verve | 9860613

Ferraro,Ralph | (dr)
Helen Merrill With The Piero Umilliani Group
Parole E Musica | RCA | 2174798-2

Ferreira,Dorio | (g)
Paul Desmond Quartet With The Don Sebesby Orchestra
From The Hot Afternoon | Verve | 543487-2

Ferreira,Durval | (g)
Cannonball Adderley With Sergio Mendes And The Bossa Rio Quartet
Cannonball's Bossa Nova | Blue Note | 522667-2
Cannonball Adderley With Sergio Mendes And The Bossa Rio Sextet
Cannonball's Bossa Nova | Blue Note | 522667-2
Ballads | Blue Note | 537563-2

Ferreira,Nice | (voc)
Terra Brazil
Café Com Leite | art-mode-records | AMR 2101

Ferreira,Paulo | (dr)
Stan Getz Group
Verve Jazz Masters 53:Stan Getz-Bossa Nova | Verve | 529904-2
Stan Getz Quartet
Verve Jazz Masters 53:Stan Getz-Bossa Nova | Verve | 529904-2
Stan Getz-Luiz Bonfa Group
The Antonio Carlos Jobim Songbook | Verve | 525472-2
Stan Getz-Luiz Bonfa Orchestra
Verve Jazz Masters 13:Antonio Carlos Jobim | Verve | 516409-2
Jazz Samba Encore! | Verve | 823613-2
Stan Getz-Luiz Bonfa Quartet
Jazz Samba Encore! | Verve | 823613-2
Stan Getz-Luiz Bonfa Quintet
Jazz Samba Encore! | Verve | 823613-2

Ferrell,Rachelle | (pvoc)
Rachelle Ferrell
First Instrumental | Blue Note | 827820-2
Rachelle Ferrell With The Eddie Green Trio
First Instrumental | Blue Note | 827820-2
Rachelle Ferrell With The Eddie Green Trio And Alex Foster
First Instrumental | Blue Note | 827820-2
Rachelle Ferrell With The Terrence Blanchard Quartet
First Instrumental | Blue Note | 827820-2
Rachelle Ferrell With The Wayne Shorter Sextet
First Instrumental | Blue Note | 827820-2
Rachelle Ferrell-Doug Nally
First Instrumental | Blue Note | 827820-2

Ferrer,Raimon 'Rai' | (b)
Carme Canela With The Joan Monné Trio
Introducing Carme Canela | Fresh Sound Records | FSNT 014 CD
David Xirgu Quartet
Idolents | Fresh Sound Records | FSNT 077 CD
Gorka Benitez Quartet
Gorka Benitez Trio | Fresh Sound Records | FSNT 073 CD
Gorka Benitez Quintet
Gorka Benitez Trio | Fresh Sound Records | FSNT 073 CD
Gorka Benitez Trio
Gorka Benitez Trio | Fresh Sound Records | FSNT 073 CD
Joan Monné Trio
Mireia | Fresh Sound Records | FSNT 100 CD
José Luis Gámez Quintet
Rumbo Dorte | Fresh Sound Records | FSNT 089 CD
Mikel Andueza Quintet
BCN | Fresh Sound Records | FSNT 036 CD
Pep O'Callaghan Grup
Tot Just | Fresh Sound Records | FSNT 017 CD
Port O'Clock | Fresh Sound Records | FSNT 069 CD
Victor De Diego Group
Amaia | Fresh Sound Records | FSNT 012 CD

Ferreri,Pat | (gel-g)
Singers Unlimited
The Singers Unlimited:Magic Voices | MPS | 539130-2

Ferret,Challin | (g)
Quintet Du Hot Club De France
Django Reinhardt:Souvenirs | Dreyfus Jazz Line | FDM 36744-2

Ferret,Etienne | (g)
Django Reinhardt Trio
Django Reinhardt:Souvenirs | Dreyfus Jazz Line | FDM 36744-2

Ferret,Pierre | (g)
Django Reinhardt Quartet
Django/Django In Rome 1949-1050 | BGO Records | BGOCD 366
Quintet Du Hot Club De France
Jazz In Paris:Django Reinhardt-Swing From Paris | EmArCy | 159853-2 PMS
Jazz In Paris:Django Reinhardt-Swing 39 | EmArCy | 159854-2 PMS
Verve Jazz Masters 38:Django Reinhardt | Verve | 516931-2
Django/Django In Rome 1949-1050 | BGO Records | BGOCD 366
Django Reinhardt:Echoes Of France | Dreyfus Jazz Line | FDM 36726-2
Django Reinhardt:Souvenirs | Dreyfus Jazz Line | FDM 36744-2
Stephane Grappelli And His Hot Four
Jazz In Paris:Django Reinhardt-Swing From Paris | EmArCy | 159853-2 PMS

Ferretti,Andy | (tbtp)
Bob Crosby And His Orchestra
Swing Legens:Bob Crosby | Nimbus Records | NI 2011
Louis Armstrong And The Commanders under the Direction of Camarata
Satchmo Serenaders | Verve | 543792-2
Louis Armstrong With The Commanders
Ambassador Louis Armstrong Vol.17:Moments To Remember(1952-1956) | Ambassador | CLA 1917
Sarah Vaughan With The Hugo Winterhalter Orchestra
Sarah Vaughan:Lover Man | Dreyfus Jazz Line | FDM 36739-2
Tommy Dorsey And His Orchestra
Planet Jazz:Tommy Dorsey | Planet Jazz | 2159972-2

Ferris,Glenn | (tbb-tb)
Billy Cobham Group
The Best Of Billy Cobham | Atlantic | 7567-81558-2
Palatino
Palationo Chap.3 | EmArCy | 013610-2
Peter Schärli Quintet With Glenn Ferris
Willisau And More Live | Creative Works Records | CW CD 1020-2
Drei Seelen/Three Souls | Creative Works Records | MIWI 1014-2

Ferrone,Steve | (drperc)
Klaus Doldinger With Orchestra
Lifelike | Warner | 2292-46478-2
Marcus Miller Group
The Sun Don't Lie | Dreyfus Jazz Line | FDM 36560-2

Ferstl,Henrik | (dr)
Nick Woodland And The Magnets
Big Heart | Blues Beacon | BLU-1013 2

Fessele,Joe | (keyboards)
Uli Binetsch's Own Bone
Boone Up Blues | Rockwerk Records | CD 011001

Fessler,Peter | (gvoc)
Peter Fessler Group
Eastside Moments | Minor Music | 801078
Peter Fessler Quartet
Foot Prints | Minor Music | 801058
Colours Of My Mind | Minor Music | 801063
Peter Fessler Quintet
Colours Of My Mind | Minor Music | 801063

Fetterer,Gus | (cl)
Wingy Mannone And His Orchestra
Planet Jazz:Male Jazz Vocalists | Planet Jazz | 2169657-2

Feucht,Jochen | (alto-fl,ss,ts,basset-h,clss-solo)
Jo Ambros Group
Wanderlust | dml-records | CD 016
Jochen Feucht
Signs On Lines | Satin Doll Productions | SDP 1019-1 CD
Jochen Feucht Quartet
Signs On Lines | Satin Doll Productions | SDP 1019-1 CD
Jochen Feucht Trio
Signs On Lines | Satin Doll Productions | SDP 1019-1 CD
Rainer Tempel Big Band
Album 03 | Jazz 'n' Arts Records | JNA 1102

Feuerstein,Adi | (as,fl,tsvib)
Inge Brandenburg And Her All-Stars
Why Don't You Take All Of Me | Bear Family Records | BCD 15614 AH
Wolfgang Lauth Septet
Noch Lauther | Bear Family Records | BCD 15942 AH

Fey,Martin | (p)
Brocksi-Quintett
Drums Boogie | Bear Family Records | BCD 15988 AH

Fialho,Tavinho | (b)
Duo Fenix
Karai-Eté | IN+OUT Records | 7009-2

Fichter,Thomas | (bel-b)
Ensemble Modern
Ensemble Modern-Fred Frith:Traffic Continues | Winter&Winter | 910044-2

Fickelscher,Hans | (dr)
Rade Soric Trio
Piano Moments | Take Twelve On CD | TT 007-2
Ull Möck Trio
Drilling | Satin Doll Productions | SDP 1023-1 CD

Fidler,Manny | (v)
Charlie Parker With Strings
Charlie Parker With Strings:The Master Takes | Verve | 523984-2
Charlie Parker With The Neal Hefti Orchestra
Charlie Parker:The Best Of The Verve Years | Verve | 527815-2
Bird: The Complete Charlie Parker On Verve | Verve | 837141-2

Fiedler,Arthur | (cond)
Duke Ellington Trio With The Boston Pops Orchestra
Highlights From The Duke Ellington Centennial Edition | RCA | 2663672-2

Fiedler,Frank | (b)
Tok Tok Tok
Love Again | Einstein Music | EM 01081
It Took So Long | Einstein Music | EM 21103
50 Ways To Leave Your Lover | Einstein Music | EM 91051

Field,Gregg | (dr,shakertambourine)
Buddy Childers With The Russ Garcia Strings
Artistry In Jazz | Candid | CCD 79735
Count Basie Big Band
Farmers Market Barbecue | Original Jazz Classics | OJCCD 732-2(2310874)

Fieldes,Mat | (b)
Absolute Ensemble
African Symphony | Enja | ENJ-9410 2
Paquito D'Rivera Group With The Absolute Ensemble
Habanera | Enja | ENJ-9395 2

Fields,Brandon | (as,fl,ss,ts,sax,bs,keyboardsWX5)
The Rippingtons
Tourist In Paradise | GRP | GRP 95882

Fields,Ernie | (bs,saxts)
Diane Schuur And Her Band
The Best Of Diane Schuur | GRP | GRP 98882

Fields,Geechie | (tb)
Jelly Roll Morton's Red Hot Peppers
Planet Jazz:Jelly Roll Morton | Planet Jazz | 2152060-2
Jazz:The Essential Collection Vol.1 | IN+OUT Records | 78011-2

Fields,Gene | (g)
Billie Holiday With Teddy Wilson And His Orchestra
Billie's Love Songs | Nimbus Records | NI 2000
Mildred Bailey With The Ellis Larkins Trio
Planet Jazz:Female Jazz Vocalists | Planet Jazz | 2169656-2

Fields,Herbie | (as,tscl)
Lionel Hampton And His Orchestra
Lionel Hampton:Flying Home | Dreyfus Jazz Line | FDM 36735-2
Lionel Hampton And His Septet
Lionel Hampton:Flying Home | Dreyfus Jazz Line | FDM 36735-2
Woody Herman And The Vanderbilt All Stars
Louis Armstrong-Jack Teagarden-Woody Herman:Midnights At V-Disc | Jazz Unlimited | JUCD 2048

Fields,Jackie | (as)
Coleman Hawkins And His Orchestra
Planet Jazz:Coleman Hawkins | Planet Jazz | 2152055-2
Planet Jazz Sampler | Planet Jazz | 2152326-2
Planet Jazz:Jazz Greatest Hits | Planet Jazz | 2169648-2
Jazz:The Essential Collection Vol.3 | IN+OUT Records | 78013-2

Fields,John | (b)
Stan Getz Quintet
Stan Getz-The Complete Roost Sessions | EMI Records | 859622-2

Fields,Kansas | (dr,voc,percsurdo)
Bud Powell Trio
Bud Powell Paris Sessions | Pablo | PACD 2310972-2
Dizzy Gillespie Sextet
Talking Verve:Dizzy Gillespie | Verve | 533846-2
Jambo Caribe | Verve | 557492-2
Ultimate Dizzy Gillespie | Verve | 557535-2
Kid Ory And His Band
The Very Best Of Dixieland Jazz | Verve | 535529-2
Milton Mezz Mezzrow Sextet
Americans Swinging In Paris:Mezz Mezzrow | EMI Records | 539660-2
Milton Mezz Mezzrow-Maxim Saury Quintet
Americans Swinging In Paris:Mezz Mezzrow | EMI Records | 539660-2
Sarah Vaughan With The Quincy Jones Orchestra
Jazz In Paris:Sarah Vaughan-Vaughan And Violins | EmArCy | 065004-2
Sidney Bechet-Teddy Buckner Sextet
Planet Jazz:Sidney Bechet | Planet Jazz | 2152063-2

Fields,Linda | (voc)
Jan Harrington And Friends
I Feel The Spirit | Nagel-Heyer | NHR SP 7
Jan Harrington Sextet
Jan Harrington's Christmas In New Orleans | Nagel-Heyer | NHR SP 4

Fields,Ted | (drvoc)
Bill Coleman Et Son Orchestre
Americans Swinging In Paris:Bill Coleman-The Elegance | EMI Records | 539662-2
Willie Lewis And His Entertainers
Americans Swinging In Paris:Benny Carter | EMI Records | 539647-2

Figelski,Cecil | (viola)
Ben Webster With Strings
The Warm Moods-With Strings | Rhino | 8122-73721-2
Phineas Newborn Jr. With Dennis Farnon And His Orchestra
While My Lady Sleeps | RCA | 2185157-2

Figuer,Narcisco | (v)
A Band Of Friends
Wynton Marsalis Quartet With Strings | CBS | CK 68921

Figueroa,Sammy | (congas,perc,balavoc)
Klaus Doldinger With Orchestra
Lifelike | Warner | 2292-46478-2
Miles Davis Group
The Man With The Horn | CBS | 468701-2
Paquito D'Rivera Orchestra
Jazzrock-Anthology Vol.3:Fusion | Zounds | CD 27100555
The Brecker Brothers
Heavy Metal Be-Bop | RCA | 2119257-2

Figuerola,Xavier | (as,cl,b-cl,ts,saxss)
Big Band Bellaterra
Don't Git Sassy | Fresh Sound Records | FSNT 048 CD
Dave Liebman And The Lluis Vidal Trio With The Orquestra De Cambra Theatre Lliure
Dave Liebman And The Lluis Vidal Trio | Fresh Sound Records | FSNT 026 CD
Manel Camp & Matthew Simon Acustic Jazz Quintet
Rosebud | Fresh Sound Records | FSNT 011 CD
Orquestra De Cambra Teatre Lliure
Orquestra De Cambra Teatre Lliure and Lluis Vidal Trip feat.Dave Liebman | Fresh Sound Records | FSNT 027 CD
Porgy And Bess | Fresh Sound Records | FSNT 066 CD
Tributes To Duke Ellington | Fresh Sound Records | FSNT 084 CD
Orquestra De Cambra Teatre Lliure feat. Dave Liebman
Orquestra De Cambra Teatre Lliure and Lluis Vidal Trio feat.Dave Liebman | Fresh Sound Records | FSNT 027 CD

Fila,Alex | (tp)
Benny Goodman And His Orchestra
Charlie Christian:Swing To Bop | Dreyfus Jazz Line | FDM 36715-2
Glenn Miller And His Orchestra
Planet Jazz:Glenn Miller | Planet Jazz | 2152056-2

Filano,Ken | (b)
Vinny Golia Quintet
Regards From Norma Desmond | Fresh Sound Records | FSNT 008 CD

Filho,Braz Limoge | (oboe)
Baden Powell Ensemble
Three Originals:Tristeza On Guitar/Poema On Guitar/Apaixonado | MPS | 519216-2

Filipovitch,Remy | (fl,alto-fl,cl,b-cl,ss,as,ts,bs)
Remy Filipovitch Quartet
All Night Long | Album | AS 11806
Remy Filipovitch Trio
All Day Long | Album | AS 22927
Remy Filipovitch-Gediminas Laurinavicius
Open Your Eyes | Album | AS 331108 CD
Remy Filipovitch-Will Boulware
Alone Together | Album | AS 55417 CD
Ron Marvin & Remy Filipovitch
Mysterious Traveler | Album | AS 44677 CD
Zbigniew Namyslowski-Remy Filipovitch Quintet
Go! | Album | AS 66919 CD

Filu,Roman | (as)
Gonzalo Rubalcaba & Cuban Quartet
Antiguo | Blue Note | 837717-2

Finch,Barnaby | (keyboards,psynth)
Lee Ritenour Sextet
Alive In L.A. | GRP | GRP 98822

Finch,Otis 'Candy' | (drvoc)
Billy Mitchell Quintet
This Is Billy Mitchell | Smash | 065507-2
Billy Mitchell Sextet
This Is Billy Mitchell | Smash | 065507-2
Dizzy Gillespie And His Orchestra
Talking Verve:Dizzy Gillespie | Verve | 533846-2
Dizzy Gillespie Quintet
Swing Low, Sweet Cadillac | Impulse(MCA) | 951178-2
The Roots Of Acid Jazz | Impulse(MCA) | IMP 12042
Shirley Scott Quartet
Blue Flames | Original Jazz Classics | OJCCD 328-2(P 7338)
Queen Of The Organ-Shirley Scott Memorial Album | Prestige | PRCD 11027-2
Shirley Scott Trio
Queen Of The Organ-Shirley Scott Memorial Album | Prestige | PRCD 11027-2
Stanley Turrentine Quintet
Hustlin' | Blue Note | 540036-2

Finck,David | (bstring-contractor)
Steve Kuhn Trio
Remembering Tomorrow | ECM | 1573(529035-2)
Steve Kuhn With Strings
Promises Kept | ECM | 1815(0675222)

Finclair,Barry | (strings,vviola)
A Band Of Friends
Wynton Marsalis Quartet With Strings | CBS | CK 68921
Andy Bey Group
Tuesdays In Chinatown | Minor Music | 801099
Earl Klugh Group With Strings
Late Night Guitar | Blue Note | 498573-2

Helen Merrill With Orchestra
Casa Forte | EmArCy | 558848-2
Nina Simone And Orchestra
Baltimore | Epic | 476906-2
Steve Kuhn With Strings
Promises Kept | ECM | 1815(0675222)

Finders,Matt | (b-tb,tubatb)
Buck Clayton Swing Band
Swing's The Village | Nagel-Heyer | CD 5004
Blues Of Summer | Nagel-Heyer | NH 1011
Diane Schuur With Orchestra
Blues For Schuur | GRP | GRP 98632
The Best Of Diane Schuur | GRP | GRP 98882

Findley,Charles | (tp,fl-harr)
Buddy Rich And His Orchestra
Big Swing Face | Pacific Jazz | 837989-2
Paulinho Da Costa Orchestra
Happy People | Original Jazz Classics | OJCCD 783-2(2312102)

Findley,Chuck | (fl-h,tbtp)
Al Jarreau With Band
Jarreau | i.e. Music | 557847-2
Buddy Rich Big Band
The New One! | Pacific Jazz | 494507-2
Diane Schuur With Orchestra
Blues For Schuur | GRP | GRP 98632
The Best Of Diane Schuur | GRP | GRP 98882
GRP All-Star Big Band
GRP All-Star Big Band:Live! | GRP | GRP 97402
All Blues | GRP | GRP 98002
Jaco Pastorius With Orchestra
Word Of Mouth | Warner | 7599-23525-2
Klaus Weiss Orchestra
Live At The Domicile | ATM Records | ATM 3805-AH
Lee Ritenour Group
Jazzrock-Anthology Vol.3:Fusion | Zounds | CD 27100555
Singers Unlimited With Orchestra
The Singers Unlimited:Magic Voices | MPS | 539130-2
Singers Unlimited With The Clare Fischer Orchestra
The Singers Unlimited:Magic Voices | MPS | 539130-2
Singers Unlimited With The Pat Williams Orchestra
The Singers Unlimited:Magic Voices | MPS | 539130-2

Fine,Mitch | (dr)
Pat Martino Sextet
El Hombre | Original Jazz Classics | OJCCD 195-2(P 7513)

Fine,Yossi | (bel-b)
Stanley Jordan Quartet
Live In New York | Blue Note | 497810-2

Finegan,Bill | (arrld)
Glenn Miller And His Orchestra
Planet Jazz:Glenn Miller | Planet Jazz | 2152056-2
Planet Jazz:Swing | Planet Jazz | 2169651-2
Candelight Miller | RCA | 2668716-2
The Glenn Miller Story Vol. 3 | RCA | ND 89222

Finetti,Joe Bob | (voc)
Klaus König Orchestra
Reviews | Enja | ENJ-9061 2

Fink,Achim | (tb,el-brass,flugabone,tuba)
Hugo Read Group
Songs Of A Wayfarer | Nabel Records:Jazz Network | CD 4653
Jazz Orchester Rheinland-Pfalz
Kazzou | Jazz Haus Musik | LJBB 9104
Norbert Stein Pata Orchester
Ritual Life | Pata Musik | PATA 5(JHM 50) CD
The Secret Act Of Painting | Pata Musik | PATA 7 CD

Fink,Gerd | (tb)
Al Porcino Big Band
Al Cohn Meets Al Porcino | Organic Music | ORGM 9730

Fink,Gerhard | (tb)
Al Porcino Big Band Live! | Organic Music | ORGM 9717

Fink,Johannes | (b)
Erdmann 2000
Recovering From y2k | Jazz 4 Ever Records:Jazz Network | J4E 4750
Eric Schaefer & Demontage
Eric Schaefer & Demontage | Jazz Haus Musik | JHM 0117 CD

Finkelstein,Seymor | (v)
Stan Getz With The Eddie Sauter Orchestra
Stan Getz Plays The Music Of Mickey One | Verve | 531232-2

Finkler,Markus | (tp)
Michael Riessler And The Ensemble 13
Momentum Mobile | Enja | ENJ-9003 2

Finnerty,Barry | (el-g,g,g-synthvoc)
Miles Davis Group
The Man With The Horn | CBS | 468701-2
Randy Brecker Group
Jazzrock-Anthology Vol.3:Fusion | Zounds | CD 27100555
The Brecker Brothers
Heavy Metal Be-Bop | RCA | 2119257-2

Finney,Garland | (p)
JATP All Stars
The Complete Jazz At The Philharmonic On Verve 1944-1949 | Verve | 523893-2

Finnigan,Mike | (org)
Etta James & The Roots Band
Burnin' Down he House | RCA | 3411633-2

Fint,Eckehard | (engl-hoboe)
Terje Rypdal Sextet
Terje Rypdal | ECM | 1016(527645-2)

Fioravanti,Ettore | (drperc)
Paolo Fresu Quintet
Night On The City | Owl Records | 013425-2
Melos | RCA | 2178289-2

Firehouse Five Plus Two |
Firehouse Five Plus Two
Dixieland Favorites | Good Time Jazz | FCD 60-008
Crashes A Party | Good Time Jazz | GTCD 10038-2
Goes To A Fire | Good Time Jazz | GTCD 10052-2
Goes South | Good Time Jazz | GTCD 12018-2

Firman,David | (cond)
The Danish Radio Concert Orchestra
Symphonies Vol.2 | dacapo | DCCD 9441

Firmatura,Sam | (ts)
Harry James And His Orchestra
Trumpet Blues:The Best Of Harry James | Capitol | 521224-2

First Avenue |
First Avenue
First Avenue | ECM | 1194

First Brass |
First Brass
First Brass | M.A Music | NU 158-3

First House |
First House
Erendira | ECM | 1307
Cantilena | ECM | 1393

First Revolution Singers,The |
First Revolution Singers
First Revolution Gospel Singers:A Capella | Laserlight | 24338

Firth,Everett | (perc)
Max Roach With The Boston Percussion Ensemble
Clifford Brown-Max Roach:Alone Together-The Best Of The Mercury Years | Verve | 526373-2

Firth,Pat | (b)
Vince Guaraldi Group
Charlie Brown's Holiday Hits | Fantasy | FCD 9682-2

Fisch,Burt | (viola)
Ben Webster With Orchestra And Strings
Verve Jazz Masters 43:Ben Webster | Verve | 525431-2
Music For Loving:Ben Webster With Strings | Verve | 527774-2
Wes Montgomery With The Jimmy Jones Orchestra
Wes Montgomery-The Complete Riverside Recordings | Riverside | 12 RCD 4408-2

The Jazz Giants Play Rodgers & Hart:Blue Moon | Prestige | PCD 24205-2

Fischer,Armin | (dr)
Lorenzo Petrocca Organ Trio
Milan In Minor | Jardis Records | JRCD 20136
Jazz Guitar Highlights 1 | Jardis Records | JRCD 20141
Lorenzo Petrocca Quartet Feat. Bruno De Filippi
Insieme | Edition Musikat | EDM 002
Lozenzo Petrocca Quartet
Stop It | Edition Musikat | EDM 018

Fischer,Bernd | (as)
Charly Antolini Orchestra
Drum Beat | MPS | 9808191
Dieter Reith Group
Reith On! | MPS | 557423-2

Fischer,Clare | (el-p,arr,el-org,org,bass-rec)
Cal Tjader Quintet
Talkin Verve/Roots Of Acid Jazz:Cal Tjader | Verve | 531562-2
Cal Tjader Sextet
Cuban Fantasy | Fantasy | FCD 24777-2
Cal Tjader With The Clare Fischer Orchestra
Cal Tjader Plays Harold Arlen & West Side Story | Fantasy | FCD 24775-2
Jazz Crusaders
Chile Con Soul | Pacific Jazz | 590957-2
Singers Unlimited With The Clare Fischer Orchestra
The Singers Unlimited:Magic Voices | MPS | 539130-2
Singers Unlimited With The Pat Williams Orchestra
The Singers Unlimited:Magic Voices | MPS | 539130-2
Singers Unlimited With The Patrick Williams Orchestra
The Singers Unlimited:Magic Voices | MPS | 539130-2
Vic Lewis West Coast All Stars
Vic Lewis Presenting A Celebration Of Contemporary West Coast Jazz | Candid | CCD 79711/12

Fischer,Claus | (b,voc,el-brh-g)
Franck Band
Dufte | Jazz Haus Musik | JHM 0054 CD
Peter Weiss-Claus Fischer
Personal Choice | Nabel Records:Jazz Network | CD 4669

Fischer,Delia | (p)
Duo Fenix
Karai-Eté | IN+OUT Records | 7009-2

Fischer,Dieter | (g)
Dieter Fischer Trio
Jazz Guitar Highlights 1 | Jardis Records | JRCD 20141
Trio Music | Jardis Records | JRCD 9925
Jan Jankeje Septet
A' Portrait Of Jan Jankeje | Jazzpoint | JP 1054 CD
Stuttgarter Gitarren Trio
Stuttgarter Gitarren Trio Vol.2 | Edition Musikat | EDM 034

Fischer,Franz-Peter | (v)
Bernd Konrad Jazz Group With Symphonie Orchestra
Wen Die Götter Lieben | Creative Works Records | CW CD 1010-1

Fischer,Harold | (dr)
Laura Fygi With Band
Bewitched | Verve | 514724-2

Fischer,Horst | (tp)
Erwin Lehn Und Sein Südfunk-Tanzorchester
Deutsches Jazz Fesival 1954/1955 | Bear Family Records | BCD 15430

Fischer,Jacob | (g)
Anders Lindskog Trio
Fine Together | Touché Music | TMcCD 010
Chris Potter & Jazzpar Septet
This Will Be | Storyville | STCD 4245
Kristian Jorgensen Quartet With Monty Alexander
Meeting Monty | Stunt Records | STUCD 01212
Svend Asmussen Quartet
Fit As A Fiddle | dacapo | DCCD 9429
Still Fiddling | Storyville | STCD 4252

Fischer,Johnny | (b)
Hans Koller New Jazz Stars
Deutsches Jazz Fesival 1954/1955 | Bear Family Records | BCD 15430
Helmut Weglinski Quintet
Deutsches Jazz Fesival 1954/1955 | Bear Family Records | BCD 15430
Stan Getz With The Kurt Edelhagen Orchestra
Stan Getz In Europe | Laserlight | 24657

Fischer,Jörg | (dr)
Christoph Thewes-Rudi Mahall Quartet
Quartetto Pazzo | Jazz Haus Musik | JHM 0122 CD
Uwe Oberg Quartet
Dedicated | Jazz 'n' Arts Records | JNA 1603

Fischer,Karl Albrecht | (pviola)
Tango Five feat. Raul Jaurena
Obsecion | Satin Doll Productions | SDP 1027-1 CD

Fischer,Kay | (ss)
Mathias Götz-Windstärke 4
Lunar Oder Solar? | Jazz 'n' Arts Records | JNA 1002

Fischer,Nina | (voc)
Marilyn Mazur With Ars Nova And The Copenhagen Art Ensemble
Jordsange | dacapo | DCCD 9454

Fischer,Peter | (dr)
Twice A Week & Steve Elson
Play Of Colours | Edition Collage | EC 511-2

Fischer,Sören | (tbvoc)
Harry Allen And Randy Sandke Meets The RIAS Big Band Berlin
The Music Of The Trumpet Kings | Nagel-Heyer | CD 037
Nana Mouskouri With The Berlin Radio Big Band
Nana Swings | Mercury | 074394-2
Nils Petter Molvaer Group
Elegy For Africa | Nabel Records:Jazz Network | CD 4678
Sören Fischer Quartet
Don't Change Your Hair For Me | Edition Collage | EC 513-2
Thärichens Tentett
Lady Moon | Minor Music | 801094
Welcome To The Maze
Welcome To The Maze:Puzzle | Nabel Records:Jazz Network | CD 4671

Fischer,Tony | (tp)
Kenny Clarke-Francy Boland Big Band
More Smiles | MPS | 9814789

Fischer,Vera | (fl)
Bernd Konrad Jazz Group With Symphonie Orchestra
Wen Die Götter Lieben | Creative Works Records | CW CD 1010-1

Fischer,Xaver | (keybords,pwurlitzer-p)
Hipsters In The Zone
Into The Afro-Latin Bag | Nabel Records:Jazz Network | CD 4663

Fischötter,Hardy | (dr)
Franck Band
Dufte | Jazz Haus Musik | JHM 0054 CD
Susan Weinert Band
Mysterious Stories | VeraBra Records | CDVBR 2111-2
The Bottom Line | VeraBra Records | CDVBR 2177-2
Point Of View | Intuition Records | INT 3272-2

Fish,Bert | (viola)
Ben Webster With Orchestra And Strings
Music For Loving:Ben Webster With Strings | Verve | 527774-2
Ultimate Ben Webster selected by James Carter | Verve | 557537-2
Coleman Hawkins With Billy Byers And His Orchestra
The Hawk In Hi-Fi | RCA | 2663842-2

Fishelson,Stan | (condtp)
Elliot Lawrence And His Orchestra
The Elliot Lawrence Big Band Swings Cohn & Kahn | Fantasy | FCD 24761-2
Woody Herman And His Orchestra
The Legends Of Swing | Laserlight | 24659
Woody Herman:Four Brother | Dreyfus Jazz Line | FDM 36722-2

Fisher,Glen | (b)
Nicolas Simion Trio
Back To The Roots | Tutu Records | 888176-2

Fisher,Harold | (drperc)
Laura Fygi Meets Michel Legrand
Watch What Happens | Mercury | 534598-2

Fisher,Larry | (b-tb)
Buddy Rich Big Band
Keep The Customer Satisfied | EMI Records | 523999-2

Fisher,Michael | (djembe,tambourine,pandeiro,skaker)
Dave Grusin Group
Migration | GRP | GRP 95922
Diane Schuur With Orchestra
The Best Of Diane Schuur | GRP | GRP 98882
Larry Carlton Group
The Gift | GRP | GRP 98542

Fisher,Ralph | (dr)
Chuck Brown And The Second Chapter Band
Timeless | Minor Music | 801068

Fisher,Richard | (g)
Glenn Miller And His Orchestra
Planet Jazz:Glenn Miller | Planet Jazz | 2152056-2
Planet Jazz Sampler | Planet Jazz | 2152326-2
Planet Jazz:Big Bands | Planet Jazz | 2169649-2
Planet Jazz:Swing | Planet Jazz | 2169651-2
The Chesterfield Broadcasts Vol.1 | RCA | 2663113-2
Swing Legends | Nimbus Records | NI 2001
The Andrew Sisters With The Glenn Miller Orchestra
The Chesterfield Broadcasts Vol.1 | RCA | 2663113-2

Fisher,Rob | (bel-b)
Cal Tjader Sextet
Cuban Fantasy | Fantasy | FCD 24777-2

Fisherman's Break |
Fisherman's Break
Fisherman's Break | Edition Collage | EC 450-2

Fishkin,Arnold | (bdr)
Birdland Dream Band
Birdland Dream Band | RCA | 2663873-2
Coleman Hawkins With Many Albam And His Orchestra
Planet Jazz:Coleman Hawkins | Planet Jazz | 2152055-2
Ella Fitzgerald With Bill Doggett's Orchestra
Ella Fitzgerald:Mr.Paganini | Dreyfus Jazz Line | FDM 36741-2
Jack Teagarden And His Orchestra
Jazz:The Essential Collection Vol.3 | IN+OUT Records | 78013-2
Johnny Smith Quartet
Moonlight In Vermont | Roulette | 596593-2
Johnny Smith Quintet
Moonlight In Vermont | Roulette | 596593-2
Johnny Smith Trio
Moonlight In Vermont | Roulette | 596593-2
Lee Konitz Quartet
Subconcious-Lee | Original Jazz Classics | OJCCD 186-2(P 7004)
Lee Konitz Quintet
Subconcious-Lee | Original Jazz Classics | OJCCD 186-2(P 7004)
Lenny Tristano Quartet
Subconcious-Lee | Original Jazz Classics | OJCCD 186-2(P 7004)
Lenny Tristano Quintet
Subconcious-Lee | Original Jazz Classics | OJCCD 186-2(P 7004)

Fishkind,Larry | (C-tubatuba)
European Tuba Quartet
Low And Behold | Jazz Haus Musik | JHM 0110 CD

Fishman,Greg | (ts)
Jens Bunge Group
Meet You In Chicago | Jazz 4 Ever Records:Jazz Network | J4E 4749

Fishwick,Stephen | (tp)
European Jazz Youth Orchestra
Swinging Europe 1 | dacapo | DCCD 9449
Swinging Europe 2 | dacapo | DCCD 9450

Fiszman,Nicolas | (b,g,dr-programmingb-g)
Jasper Van't Hof Group
Blue Corner | ACT | 9228-2
Philippe Caillat Group
Stream Of Time | Laika Records | LK 92-030
Philippe Caillat Special Project
Melodic Travel | Laika Records | LK 689-012
Pili-Pili
Jakko | JA & RO | JARO 4131-2
Pili-Pili Live 88 | JA & RO | JARO 4139-2
Pili-Pili | JA & RO | JARO 4141-2
Hotel Babo | JA & RO | JARO 4147-2
Hoomba-Hoomba | JA & RO | JARO 4192-2

Fitch,Bill | (congasperc)
Cal Tjader Quintet
Talkin Verve/Roots Of Acid Jazz:Cal Tjader | Verve | 531562-2
Vince Guaraldi Group
Charlie Brown's Holiday Hits | Fantasy | FCD 9682-2

Fitch,Otis | (dr)
Big John Patton Quartet
Blue Bossa | Blue Note | 795590-2

Fitzgerald,Andy | (cl,engl-h,flreeds)
Coleman Hawkins And His Orchestra
Jazz:The Essential Collection Vol.3 | IN+OUT Records | 78013-2
Gil Evans Orchestra
Verve Jazz Masters 23:Gil Evans | Verve | 521860-2
The Individualism Of Gil Evans | Verve | 833804-2
Kenny Burrell With The Gil Evans Orchestra
Guitar Forms | Verve | 521403-2
Verve Jazz Masters 23:Gil Evans | Verve | 521860-2
Verve Jazz Masters 45:Kenny Burrell | Verve | 527652-2
Verve Jazz Masters Vol.60:The Collection | Verve | 529866-2

Fitzgerald,Ella | (ldvoc)
Benny Goodman And His Orchestra
Planet Jazz:Benny Goodman | Planet Jazz | 2152054-2
Planet Jazz:Female Jazz Vocalists | Planet Jazz | 2169656-2
Count Basie And His Orchestra
One O'Clock Jump | Verve | 559806-2
Duke Ellington And His Orchestra
Verve Jazz Masters 4:Duke Ellington | Verve | 516338-2
Ella Fitzgerald And Duke Ellington:Cote D'Azure Concerts on Verve | Verve | 539033-2
Ella Fitzgerald With Sy Oliver And His Orchestra
Ella Fitzgerald:Mr.Paganini | Dreyfus Jazz Line | FDM 36741-2
Ella Fitzgerald And Barney Kessel
Jazz Collection:Ella Fitzgerald | Laserlight | 24397
Ella Fitzgerald-First Lady Of Song | Verve | 517898-2
Love Songs:The Best Of The Song Books | Verve | 531762-2
Ella Fitzgerald Sings The Rodgers And Hart Song Book | Verve | 537258-2
For The Love Of Ella Fitzgerald | Verve | 841765-2
Ella Fitzgerald And Count Basie With The JATP All Stars
Bluella:Ella Fitzgerald Sings The Blues | Pablo | 2310960-2
Ella Fitzgerald And Her All Stars
All That Jazz | Pablo | 2310938-2
Ella Fitzgerald-First Lady Of Song | Verve | 517898-2
Verve Jazz Masters 6:Ella Fitzgerald | Verve | 519822-2
The Best Of The Song Books:The Ballads | Verve | 521867-2
Love Songs:The Best Of The Song Books | Verve | 531762-2
Ella Fitzgerald Sings The Duke Ellington Songbook | Verve | 559248-2
For The Love Of Ella Fitzgerald | Verve | 841765-2
Ella Fitzgerald:Mr.Paganini | Dreyfus Jazz Line | FDM 36741-2
Ella Fitzgerald And Her Be-Bop Boys
Jazz Collection:Ella Fitzgerald | Laserlight | 24397
Ella Fitzgerald And Her Famous Orchestra
The Radio Years 1940 | Jazz Unlimited | JUCD 2065
Ella Fitzgerald And Her Orchestra
Jazz Collection:Ella Fitzgerald | Laserlight | 24397
Sunshine Of Your Love | MPS | 533102-2
Ella Fitzgerald And Her Quintet
Verve Jazz Masters 46:Ella Fitzgerald-The Jazz Sides | Verve | 527655-2
Ella Fitzgerald And Her Sextet

Ella Fitzgerald-First Lady Of Song | Verve | 517898-2
The Best Of The Song Books | Verve | 519804-2
Ella Fitzgerald And Herb Ellis
Ella Fitzgerald-First Lady Of Song | Verve | 517898-2
Ella Fitzgerald And Joe Williams With The Count Basie Octet
For The Love Of Ella Fitzgerald | Verve | 841765-2
Ella Fitzgerald And Louis Armstrong With Dave Barbour And His Orchestra
Ella Fitzgerald:Mr.Paganini | Dreyfus Jazz Line | FDM 36741-2
Ella Fitzgerald And Louis Armstrong With Sy Oliver And His Orchestra
Ella Fitzgerald:Mr.Paganini | Dreyfus Jazz Line | FDM 36741-2
Ella Fitzgerald And Louis Armstrong With The Oscar Peterson Quartet
Ella Fitzgerald-First Lady Of Song | Verve | 517898-2
Verve Jazz Masters 1:Louis Armstrong | Verve | 519818-2
Verve Jazz Masters 6:Ella Fitzgerald | Verve | 519822-2
Verve Jazz Masters 24:Ella Fitzgerald & Louis Armstrong | Verve | 521851-2
Verve Jazz Masters 46:Ella Fitzgerald-The Jazz Sides | Verve | 527655-2
Verve Jazz Masters Vol.60:The Collection | Verve | 529866-2
The Complete Ella Fitzgerald And Louis Armstrong On Verve | Verve | 537284-2
The Best Of Ella Fitzgerald And Louis Armstrong On Verve | Verve | 537909-2
Ella And Louis | Verve | 543304-2
Ella & Louis | Verve | 825373-2
Ella And Louis Again | Verve | 825374-2
For The Love Of Ella Fitzgerald | Verve | 841765-2
Ella Fitzgerald And Louis Armstrong With The Russell Garcia Orchestra
Ella Fitzgerald-First Lady Of Song | Verve | 517898-2
Verve Jazz Masters 24:Ella Fitzgerald & Louis Armstrong | Verve | 521851-2
Ella Fitzgerald And Oscar Peterson
Ella Fitzgerald-First Lady Of Song | Verve | 517898-2
Ella Fitzgerald And Paul Smith
Ella Fitzgerald-First Lady Of Song | Verve | 517898-2
Verve Jazz Masters 46:Ella Fitzgerald-The Jazz Sides | Verve | 527655-2
The Intimate Ella | Verve | 839838-2
Ella Fitzgerald And The Paul Smith Quartet
The Best Of The Song Books | Verve | 519804-2
Verve Jazz Masters 6:Ella Fitzgerald | Verve | 519822-2
Verve Jazz Masters 46:Ella Fitzgerald-The Jazz Sides | Verve | 527655-2
Ella Fitzgerald Jam
Bluella:Ella Fitzgerald Sings The Blues | Pablo | 2310960-2
Ella Fitzgerald With Benny Carter's Magnificent Seven
30 By Ella | Capitol | 520090-2
Ella Fitzgerald With Bill Doggett's Orchestra
Ella Fitzgerald:Mr.Paganini | Dreyfus Jazz Line | FDM 36741-2
Ella Fitzgerald With Count Basie And His Orchestra
Digital III At Montreux | Original Jazz Classics | OJCCD 996-2(2308223)
Ella Fitzgerald With Ellis Larkins
Ella Fitzgerald:Mr.Paganini | Dreyfus Jazz Line | FDM 36741-2
Pure Ella | GRP | GRP 16362
Ella Fitzgerald With Frank De Vol And His Orchestra
Like Someone In Love | Verve | 511524-2
Verve Jazz Masters 6:Ella Fitzgerald | Verve | 519822-2
Get Happy! | Verve | 523321-2
Ella Fitzgerald With Jackie Davis And Louis Bellson
Bluella:Ella Fitzgerald Sings The Blues | Pablo | 2310960-2
Lady Time | Original Jazz Classics | OJCCD 864-2(2310825)
Ella Fitzgerald With Joe Pass
Speak Love | Pablo | 2310888
Joe Pass:Guitar Virtuoso | Pablo | 4 PACD 4423-2
Sophisticated Lady | Pablo | PACD 5310-2
Ella Fitzgerald With Louis Armstrong And The All Stars
Ella Fitzgerald-First Lady Of Song | Verve | 517898-2
The Complete Ella Fitzgerald And Louis Armstrong On Verve | Verve | 537284-2
The Best Of Ella Fitzgerald And Louis Armstrong On Verve | Verve | 537909-2
Ella Fitzgerald With Louis Jordan And His Tympany Five
Ella Fitzgerald:Mr.Paganini | Dreyfus Jazz Line | FDM 36741-2
Ella Fitzgerald With Marty Paich's Dektette
Ella Swings Lightly | Verve | 517535-2
Ella Fitzgerald With Orchestra
Ella Abraca Jobim | Pablo | 2630201-2
Ella Fitzgerald-First Lady Of Song | Verve | 517898-2
Misty Blue:Sweet Sisters Swing Songs Of Sorrow And Sadness | Blue Note | 521151-2
Essential Ella | Verve | 523990-2
Forever Ella | Verve | 529387-2
Ella/Things Ain't What They Used To Be | Warner | 9362-47875-2
The Best Is Yet To Come | Original Jazz Classics | OJCCD 889-2(2312138)
Ella Fitzgerald With Paul Weston And His Orchestra
The Best Of The Song Books | Verve | 519804-2
Verve Jazz Masters 6:Ella Fitzgerald | Verve | 519822-2
Love Songs:The Best Of The Song Books | Verve | 531762-2
Ella Fitzgerald Sings The Irving Berlin Song Book | Verve | 543830-2
Ella Fitzgerald With Russell Garcia And His Orchestra
Verve Jazz Masters 6:Ella Fitzgerald | Verve | 519822-2
Ella Fitzgerald With Sy Oliver And His Orchestra
Ella Fitzgerald:The Decca Years 1949-1954 | Decca | 050668-2
Ella Fitzgerald With The Bill Doggett Orchestra
Ella Fitzgerald-First Lady Of Song | Verve | 517898-2
Rhythm Is My Business | Verve | 559513-2
Ella Fitzgerald With The Billy May Orchestra
Ella Fitzgerald-First Lady Of Song | Verve | 517898-2
The Best Of The Song Books | Verve | 519804-2
Verve Jazz Masters 6:Ella Fitzgerald | Verve | 519822-2
The Best Of The Song Books:The Ballads | Verve | 521867-2
Verve Jazz Masters 46:Ella Fitzgerald-The Jazz Sides | Verve | 527655-2
Love Songs:The Best Of The Song Books | Verve | 531762-2
Ella Fitzgerald Sings The Harold Arlen Song Book | Verve | 589108-2
The Silver Collection: Ella Fitzgerald-The Songbooks | Verve | 823445-2 PMS
For The Love Of Ella Fitzgerald | Verve | 841765-2
Ella Fitzgerald With The Buddy Bregman Orchestra
Ella Fitzgerald-First Lady Of Song | Verve | 517898-2
The Best Of The Song Books | Verve | 519804-2
The Best Of The Song Books:The Ballads | Verve | 521867-2
Love Songs:The Best Of The Song Books | Verve | 531762-2
Ella Fitzgerald Sings The Cole Porter Songbook | Verve | 537257-2
Ella Fitzgerald Sings The Rodgers And Hart Song Book | Verve | 537258-2
The Silver Collection: Ella Fitzgerald-The Songbooks | Verve | 823445-2 PMS
For The Love Of Ella Fitzgerald | Verve | 841765-2
Ella Fitzgerald With The Chick Webb Orchestra
Jazz Collection:Ella Fitzgerald | Laserlight | 24397
Ella Fitzgerald With The Count Basie Orchestra
Bluella:Ella Fitzgerald Sings The Blues | Pablo | 2310960-2
Ella Fitzgerald-First Lady Of Song | Verve | 517898-2
Verve Jazz Masters 46:Ella Fitzgerald-The Jazz Sides | Verve | 527655-2
Ella And Basie | Verve | 539059-2
For The Love Of Ella Fitzgerald | Verve | 841765-2
Ella Fitzgerald With The Count Basie Septet
Ella And Basie | Verve | 539059-2
Ella Fitzgerald With The Dizzy Gillespie Orchestra
Ella Fitzgerald:Mr.Paganini | Dreyfus Jazz Line | FDM 36741-2
Ella Fitzgerald With The Don Abney Trio
Ella Fitzgerald-First Lady Of Song | Verve | 517898-2
Ella Fitzgerald With The Duke Ellington Orchestra
The Stockholm Concert 1966 | Pablo | 2308242-2
Ella Fitzgerald-First Lady Of Song | Verve | 517898-2
The Best Of The Song Books | Verve | 519804-2
Verve Jazz Masters 6:Ella Fitzgerald | Verve | 519822-2
The Best Of The Song Books:The Ballads | Verve | 521867-2
Verve Jazz Masters 46:Ella Fitzgerald-The Jazz Sides | Verve | 527655-2
Ella At Duke's Place | Verve | 529700-2
Love Songs:The Best Of The Song Books | Verve | 531762-2
Ella & Duke At The Cote D'Azur | Verve | 539030-2
Ella Fitzgerald And Duke Ellington:Cote D'Azure Concerts on Verve | Verve | 539033-2
Ella Fitzgerald Sings The Duke Ellington Songbook | Verve | 559248-2
For The Love Of Ella Fitzgerald | Verve | 841765-2
Ella Fitzgerald With The Duke Ellington Orchestra And Jimmy Jones Trio
Ella & Duke At The Cote D'Azur | Verve | 539030-2
Ella Fitzgerald And Duke Ellington:Cote D'Azure Concerts on Verve | Verve | 539033-2
Ella Fitzgerald With The Frank DeVol Orchestra
Ella Fitzgerald-First Lady Of Song | Verve | 517898-2
Get Happy! | Verve | 523321-2
A Life In Jazz:A Musical Biography | Verve | 535119-2
Stan Getz Highlights | Verve | 847430-2
Ella Fitzgerald Sings Sweet Songs For Swingers | Verve | 9860417
Ella Fitzgerald With The Frank DeVol Orchestra feat. Stan Getz
Ella Fitzgerald-First Lady Of Song | Verve | 517898-2
Ella Fitzgerald With The Hank Jones Quartet
Ella Fitzgerald:Mr.Paganini | Dreyfus Jazz Line | FDM 36741-2
Ella Fitzgerald With The Hank Jones Trio
The Complete Jazz At The Philharmonic On Verve 1944-1949 | Verve | 523893-2
Ella Fitzgerald:Mr.Paganini | Dreyfus Jazz Line | FDM 36741-2
Ella Fitzgerald With The JATP All Stars
Ella Fitzgerald-First Lady Of Song | Verve | 517898-2
For The Love Of Ella Fitzgerald | Verve | 841765-2
Ella Fitzgerald With The Jimmy Jones Trio
Ella Fitzgerald-First Lady Of Song | Verve | 517898-2
Ella & Duke At The Cote D'Azur | Verve | 539030-2
Ella Fitzgerald And Duke Ellington:Cote D'Azure Concerts on Verve | Verve | 539033-2
Ella Fitzgerald With The Johnny Spence Orchestra
Ella Fitzgerald-First Lady Of Song | Verve | 517898-2
Ella Fitzgerald With The Lou Levy Quartet
Ella Fitzgerald-First Lady Of Song | Verve | 517898-2
Verve Jazz Masters 6:Ella Fitzgerald | Verve | 519822-2
Verve Jazz Masters 46:Ella Fitzgerald-The Jazz Sides | Verve | 527655-2
4 By 4:Ella Fitzgerald/Sarah Vaughan/Billie Holiday/Dinah Washington | Verve | 559693-2
Clap Hands,Here Comes Charlie! | Verve | 835646-2
For The Love Of Ella Fitzgerald | Verve | 841765-2
Ella Fitzgerald With The Lou Levy Trio
Ella Fitzgerald-First Lady Of Song | Verve | 517898-2
For The Love Of Ella Fitzgerald | Verve | 841765-2
Ella Fitzgerald With The Marty Paich Dek-tette
Ella Fitzgerald-First Lady Of Song | Verve | 517898-2
Verve Jazz Masters 6:Ella Fitzgerald | Verve | 519822-2
Verve Jazz Masters 46:Ella Fitzgerald-The Jazz Sides | Verve | 527655-2
Ella Fitzgerald With The Marty Paich Orchestra
Ella Fitzgerald-First Lady Of Song | Verve | 517898-2
Get Happy! | Verve | 523321-2
The Antonio Carlos Jobim Songbook | Verve | 525472-2
Ella Sings Broadway | Verve | 549373-2
Whisper Not | Verve | 589947-2
For The Love Of Ella Fitzgerald | Verve | 841765-2
Ella Fitzgerald With The Nelson Riddle Orchestra
Ella Fitzgerald-First Lady Of Song | Verve | 517898-2
The Best Of The Song Books | Verve | 519804-2
Verve Jazz Masters 6:Ella Fitzgerald | Verve | 519822-2
The Best Of The Song Books:The Ballads | Verve | 521867-2
Get Happy! | Verve | 523321-2
Oh Lady Be Good:The Best Of The Gershwin Songbook | Verve | 529581-2
Love Songs:The Best Of The Song Books | Verve | 531762-2
Ella Fitzgerald Sings The Johnny Mercer Songbook | Verve | 539057-2
The Silver Collection: Ella Fitzgerald-The Songbooks | Verve | 823445-2 PMS
For The Love Of Ella Fitzgerald | Verve | 841765-2
Dream Dancing | Original Jazz Classics | OJCCD 1072-2(2310814)
Ella Fitzgerald With The Oscar Peterson Quartet
Verve Jazz Masters 6:Ella Fitzgerald | Verve | 519822-2
Verve Jazz Masters 24:Ella Fitzgerald & Louis Armstrong | Verve | 521851-2
For The Love Of Ella Fitzgerald | Verve | 841765-2
Ella Fitzgerald With The Oscar Peterson Quartet And Ben Webster
Verve Jazz Masters 43:Ben Webster | Verve | 525431-2
Ella Fitzgerald With The Paul Smith Quartet
Ella Fitzgerald-First Lady Of Song | Verve | 517898-2
Mack The Knife-The Complete Ella In Berlin | Verve | 519564-2
Verve Jazz Masters 6:Ella Fitzgerald | Verve | 519822-2
Verve Jazz Masters 20:Introducing | Verve | 519853-2
The Best Of The Song Books:The Ballads | Verve | 521867-2
Ella Fitzgerald Sings The Rodgers And Hart Song Book | Verve | 537258-2
4 By 4:Ella Fitzgerald/Sarah Vaughan/Billie Holiday/Dinah Washington | Verve | 559693-2
For The Love Of Ella Fitzgerald | Verve | 841765-2
Ella Fitzgerald With The Paul Weston Orchestra
Ella Fitzgerald-First Lady Of Song | Verve | 517898-2
The Best Of The Song Books:The Ballads | Verve | 521867-2
Get Happy! | Verve | 523321-2
The Silver Collection: Ella Fitzgerald-The Songbooks | Verve | 823445-2 PMS
Ella Fitzgerald With The Tommy Flanagan Quartet
Bluella:Ella Fitzgerald Sings The Blues | Pablo | 2310960-2
Ella In London | Original Jazz Classics | OJCCD 974-2(2310711)
Ella Fitzgerald With The Tommy Flanagan Trio
Bluella:Ella Fitzgerald Sings The Blues | Pablo | 2310960-2
Jazz Collection:Ella Fitzgerald | Laserlight | 24397
Ella Fitzgerald-First Lady Of Song | Verve | 517898-2
Sunshine Of Your Love | MPS | 533102-2
Jazzin' Vol.2: The Music Of Stevie Wonder | Fantasy | FANCD 6088-2
Montreux '77 | Original Jazz Classics | OJC20 376-2(2308206)
Ella A Nice | Original Jazz Classics | OJC20 442-2
Ella-At The Montreux Jazz Festival 1975 | Original Jazz Classics | OJC20 789-2(2310751)
Jazz At The Philharmonic:The Montreux Collection | Pablo | PACD 5306-2
Ella Fitzgerald In Budapest | Pablo | PACD 5308-2
Ella Fitzgerald-Barney Kessel
Ella Fitzgerald Sings The Duke Ellington Songbook | Verve | 559248-2
Ella Fitzgerald-Joe Pass Duo
Take Love Easy | Pablo | 2310702
Fitzgerald & Pass... Again | Original Jazz Classics | OJCCD 1052-2(2310772)
Joe Pass:A Man And His Guitar | Original Jazz Classics | OJCCD 8806-2
Ella Fitzgerald-Oscar Peterson Duo
Ella And Oscar | Pablo | 2310759-2
Ella Fitzgerald-Oscar Peterson Trio
Ella And Oscar | Pablo | 2310759-2
JATP All Stars
JATP In Tokyo | Pablo | 2620104-2
Verve Jazz Masters 28:Charlie Parker Plays Standards | Verve | 521854-2
The Complete Jazz At The Philharmonic On Verve 1944-1949 | Verve | 523893-2
The Drum Battle:Gene Krupa And Buddy Rich At JATP | Verve | 559810-2
Bird: The Complete Charlie Parker On Verve | Verve | 837141-2
Welcome To Jazz At The Philharmonic | Fantasy | FANCD 6081-2
Louis Armstrong And Ella Fitzgerald With Bob Haggert's Orchestra
Louis Armstrong:C'est Si Bon | Dreyfus Jazz Line | FDM 36730-2
Louis Armstrong And Ella Fitzgerald With Russell Garcia's Orchestra
The Complete Ella Fitzgerald And Louis Armstrong On Verve | Verve | 537284-2
The Best Of Ella Fitzgerald And Louis Armstrong On Verve | Verve | 537909-2
Porgy And Bess | Verve | 827475-2
Louis Armstrong And Ella Fitzgerald With Sy Oliver's Orchestra
Louis Armstrong:C'est Si Bon | Dreyfus Jazz Line | FDM 36730-2
Louis Jordan And His Tympany Five
Louis Jordan-Let The Good Times Roll: The Complete Decca Recordings 1938-1954 | Bear Family Records | BCD 15557 IH

Fitzgibbon,Mark | (p)
Vince Jones Group
Spell | Intuition Records | INT 3067-2

Fitzpatrick,Bob | (tb)
June Christy With The Pete Rugolo Orchestra
Something Cool(The Complete Mono & Stereo Versions) | Capitol | 534069-2
Nat King Cole Quartet With The Stan Kenton Orchestra
Nat King Cole:For Sentimental Reasons | Dreyfus Jazz Line | FDM 36740-2
Stan Kenton And His Orchestra
Adventures In Blues | Capitol | 520089-2
Adventures In Jazz | Capitol | 521222-2
Great Swing Classics In Hi-Fi | Capitol | 521223-2
Stan Kenton Portraits On Standards | Capitol | 531571-2
One Night Stand | Choice | CHCD 71051

Fitzpatrick,Francis | (tb)
Pete Rugolo And His Orchestra
Thriller/Richard Diamon(Original Jazz Scores From 2 Classics TV Series) | Fresh Sound Records | FSCD 2015

Fiuczynski,Dave | (grh-g)
Bop City
Hot Jazz Bisquits | Hip Bop | HIBD 8801
Franz Koglmann Group
Venus In Transit | Between The Lines | btl 017(Efa 10186)
Josh Roseman Unit
Cherry | Enja | ENJ-9392 2

Five Elements |
Steve Coleman And Five Elements
On The Edge Of Tomorrow | JMT Edition | 919005-2

Flanagan,Tommy | (arr,ld,claves,el-p,p,celeste)
Arnett Cobb Quintet
Movin' Right Along | Original Jazz Classics | OJCCD 1074-2(P 7216)
More Party Time | Original Jazz Classics | OJCCD 979-2(P 7175)
Art Pepper Quartet
Art Pepper:The Complete Galaxy Recordings | Galaxy | 16GCD 1016-2
Straight Life | Original Jazz Classics | OJCCD 475-2
Art Pepper Quintet
Art Pepper:The Complete Galaxy Recordings | Galaxy | 16GCD 1016-2
Straight Life | Original Jazz Classics | OJCCD 475-2
Benny Bailey Septet
Big Brass | Candid | CCD 79011
Benny Carter And His Orchestra
Jazz At The Philharmonic:The Montreux Collection | Pablo | PACD 5306-2
Benny Carter Sextet
To Bags...With Love:Memorial Album | Pablo | 2310967-2
Milt Jackson Birthday Celebration | Fantasy | FANCD 6079-2
Bobby Jaspar Quintet
Flute Flight | Original Jazz Classics | OJCCD 1084-2(P 2124)
Booker Ervin Quartet
The Song Book | Original Jazz Classics | OJCCD 779-2(P 7318)
Charles Mingus Group
The Jazz Life! | Candid | CCD 79019
Mysterious Blues | Candid | CCD 79042
Clark Terry Orchestra
Color Changes | Candid | CCD 79009
Clifford Jordan Quintet
Mosaic | Milestone | MCD 47092-2
Coleman Hawkins All Stars
Coleman Hawkins All Stars | Original Jazz Classics | OJCCD 225-2(SV 2005)
Coleman Hawkins Quartet
Verve Jazz Masters 43:Coleman Hawkins | Verve | 521856-2
Today And Now | Impulse(MCA) | 951184-2
The Roots Of Acid Jazz | Impulse(MCA) | IMP 12042
At Easy | Original Jazz Classics | OJC20 181-2(MV 7)
The Jazz Giants Play Rodgers & Hammerstein:My Favorite Things | Prestige | PCD 24223-2
Coleman Hawkins Septet
Desafinado | Impulse(MCA) | 951227-2
Coleman Hawkins Sextet
Desafinado | Impulse(MCA) | 951227-2
Coleman Hawkins With Eddie Lockjaw Davis And The Tommy Flanagan Trio
Night Hawk | Original Jazz Classics | OJC20 420-2(SV 2016)
Dave Pike Quintet
Carnavals | Prestige | PCD 24248-2
Dexter Gordon Quartet
Dexter Gordon Birthday Celebration | Fantasy | FANCD 6082-2
The Panther | Original Jazz Classics | OJCCD 770-2(P 10030)
Dizzy Gillespie All Stars
Jazz At The Philharmonic:The Montreux Collection | Pablo | PACD 5306-2
Dizzy Gillespie Big 7
Dizzy-At The Montreux Jazz Festival 1975 | Original Jazz Classics | OJC20 739-2(2310749)
Dusko Goykovich Quartet
Soul Connection | Enja | ENJ-8044 2
Dusko Goykovich Quintet
Soul Connection | Enja | ENJ-8044 2
Ella Fitzgerald And Her All Stars
Ella Fitzgerald-First Lady Of Song | Verve | 517898-2
Ella Fitzgerald And Her Orchestra
Sunshine Of Your Love | MPS | 533102-2
Ella Fitzgerald Jam
Bluella:Ella Fitzgerald Sings The Blues | Pablo | 2310960-2
Ella Fitzgerald With Orchestra
Ella/Things Ain't What They Used To Be | Warner | 9362-47875-2
Ella Fitzgerald With The Tommy Flanagan Quartet
Bluella:Ella Fitzgerald Sings The Blues | Pablo | 2310960-2
Ella In London | Original Jazz Classics | OJCCD 974-2(2310711)
Ella Fitzgerald With The Tommy Flanagan Trio
Bluella:Ella Fitzgerald Sings The Blues | Pablo | 2310960-2
Jazz Collection:Ella Fitzgerald | Laserlight | 24397
Ella Fitzgerald-First Lady Of Song | Verve | 517898-2
Sunshine Of Your Love | MPS | 533102-2
Jazzin' Vol.2: The Music Of Stevie Wonder | Fantasy | FANCD 6088-2
Montreux '77 | Original Jazz Classics | OJC20 376-2(2308206)
Ella A Nice | Original Jazz Classics | OJC20 442-2
Ella-At The Montreux Jazz Festival 1975 | Original Jazz Classics | OJC20 789-2(2310751)
Jazz At The Philharmonic:The Montreux Collection | Pablo | PACD 5306-2
Ella Fitzgerald In Budapest | Pablo | PACD 5308-2
Frank Wess And His Orchestra
The Long Road | Prestige | PCD 24247-2
Gary Burton Sextet
Planet Jazz:Gary Burton | RCA | 2165367-2
Gene Ammons Quintet

Boss Tenor | Original Jazz Classics | OJC20 297-2(P-7180)
Gerry Mulligan Quintet
Late Night Sax | CBS | 487798-2
Herbie Mann-Bobby Jaspar Sextet
Flute Flight | Original Jazz Classics | OJCCD 1084-2(P 2124)
Flute Souflé | Original Jazz Classics | OJCCD 760-2(P 7101)
J.J.Johnson Quintet
The J.J.Johnson Memorial Album | Prestige | PRCD 11025-2
Jazz Artists Guild
Newport Rebels-Jazz Artists Guild | Candid | CCD 79022
Jimmy Heath Orchestra
Cannonball Adderley Birthday Celebration | Fantasy | FANCD 6087-2
Joe Henderson Group
Porgy And Bess | Verve | 539048-2
Joe Newman Quintet
Good 'N' Groovy | Original Jazz Classics | OJCCD 185-2(SV 2019)
John Coltrane Quartet
The Best Of John Coltrane | Atlantic | 7567-81366-2
Atlantic Saxophones | Rhino | 8122-71256-2
John Coltrane-The Heavyweight Champion:The Complete Atlantic Recordings | Atlantic | 8122-71984-2
Giant Steps | Atlantic | 8122-75203-2
The Very Best Of John Coltrane | Rhino | 8122-79778-2
Kenny Burrell Quintet
Kenny Burrell | Original Jazz Classics | OJCCD 019-2(P 7088)
Kenny Burrell-John Coltrane Quintet
Kenny Burrell & John Coltrane | New Jazz | NJSA 8276-2
Kenny Burrell & John Coltrane | Original Jazz Classics | OJC20 300-2
Kenny Dorham Quartet
The Jazz Giants Play Harry Warren:Lullaby Of Broadway | Prestige | PCD 24204-2
Les Spann Quintet
Gemini | Original Jazz Classics | OJCCD 1948-2(JLP 9355)
Miles Davis Quintet
Collector's Items | Original Jazz Classics | OJC20 071-2(P 7044)
Milt Jackson Sextet
Milt Jackson Birthday Celebration | Fantasy | FANCD 6079-2
Milt Jackson With Strings
To Bags...With Love:Memorial Album | Pablo | 2310967-2
Newport Rebels
Candid Dolphy | Candid | CCD 79033
Prestige All Stars
John Coltrane-The Prestige Recordings | Prestige | 16 PCD 4405-2
All Day Long | Original Jazz Classics | OJC20 456-2(P 7081)
The Cats | Original Jazz Classics | OJCCD 079-2(NJ 8217)
Roy Haynes Quartet
Out Of The Afternoon | Impulse(MCA) | 951180-2
Sonny Rollins Plus 3
Sonny Rollins + 3 | Milestone | MCD 9250-2
Sonny Rollins Quartet
Saxophone Colossus | Original Jazz Classics | OJC20 291-2
Sonny Rollins Quintet
Old Flames | Milestone | MCD 9215-2
Sonny Rollins Quintet With Brass
Old Flames | Milestone | MCD 9215-2
Tommy Flanagan
Thelonica | Enja | ENJ-4052 2
Tommy Flanagan 3
Montreux '77 | Original Jazz Classics | OJC 372(2308202)
Tommy Flanagan Trio
Sunset And The Mockingbird-The Birthday Concert | Blue Note | 493155-2
Confirmation | Enja | ENJ-4014 2
Thelonica | Enja | ENJ-4052 2
The Cats | Original Jazz Classics | OJCCD 079-2(NJ 8217)
Overseas | Original Jazz Classics | OJCCD 1033-2(P 7134)
Tommy Flanagan/George Mraz
Confirmation | Enja | ENJ-4014 2
Tommy Flanagan/Kenny Barron
The Story Of Jazz Piano | Laserlight | 24653
Tony Scott And The All Stars
Body And Soul Revisited | GRP | GRP 16272
Wes Montgomery Quartet
Wes Montgomery-The Complete Riverside Recordings | Riverside | 12 RCD 4408-2
The Incredible Guitar Of Wes Montgomery | Original Jazz Classics | OJC20 036-2
Wilbur Harden Quintet
The Art Of Saxophone | Laserlight | 24652
Willis Jackson Group
At Large | Prestige | PCD 24243-2

Flanigan,Phil | (b)
Allan Vaché Big Four
Revisited! | Nagel-Heyer | CD 044
Allan Vaché-Harry Allen Quintet
Allan And Allan | Nagel-Heyer | CD 074
Bob Wilber And Friends
What Swing Is All About | Nagel-Heyer | CD 035
Blues Of Summer | Nagel-Heyer | NH 1011
Eddie Metz And His Gang
Tough Assignment:A Tribute To Dave Tough | Nagel-Heyer | CD 053
George Masso Sextet
C'Est Magnifique! | Nagel-Heyer | CD 060
Mark Shane-Terry Blaine Group
With Thee I Swing! | Nagel-Heyer | CD 040
Warren Vaché-Allen Vaché Sextet
Mrs.Vaché's Boys | Nagel-Heyer | CD 050
Ellington For Lovers | Nagel-Heyer | NH 1009

Flarrington,Norman | (drperc)
Jean-Luc Ponty Quintet
Aurora | Atlantic | 7567-81543-2
The Very Best Of Jean-Luc Ponty | Rhino | 8122-79862-2

Flax,Marty | (bs,fl,cl,ts,reedssax)
Buddy Rich And His Orchestra
Swingin' New Big Band | Pacific Jazz | 835232-2
Big Swing Face | Pacific Jazz | 837989-2
Dizzy Gillespie And His Orchestra
Verve Jazz Masters 20:Introducing | Verve | 519853-2
Dizzy Gillespie:Birks Works-The Verve Big Band Sessions | Verve | 527900-2
Dizzy Gillespie Orchestra
Verve Jazz Masters 10:Dizzy Gillespie | Verve | 516319-2
Louis Jordan And His Tympany Five
Louis Jordan-Let The Good Times Roll: The Complete Decca Recordings 1938-1954 | Bear Family Records | BCD 15557 IH

Fleagle,Brick | (arrg)
Jack Teagarden's Big Eight
Jazz:The Essential Collection Vol.3 | IN+OUT Records | 78013-2

Fleisch: |
Kölner Saxophon Mafia With Fleisch
Kölner Saxophon Mafia Proudly Presents | Jazz Haus Musik | JHM 0046 CD

Fleischer,Markus | (g)
Markus Fleischer Quartet
Let's Call It A Day | Village | WLCD 1017-2

Fleisig,Cal | (viola)
Phil Woods Quartet With Orchestra & Strings
Round Trip | Verve | 559804-2

Fleming,George | (accordeon)
Buddy DeFranco Quartet
Lush Life | Choice | CHCD 71017

Fleming,Herb | (tb)
Great Traditionalists In Europe
Great Traditionalists | Jazzpoint | JP 1046 CD

Fleming,Michael | (b)
Chet Baker Quartet
Baby Breeze | Verve | 538328-2
Chet Baker Sextet
Baby Breeze | Verve | 538328-2
Roland Kirk And His Orchestra
Talkin' Verve-Roots Of Acid Jazz:Roland Kirk | Verve | 533101-2
Roland Kirk Group
I Talk With The Spirits | Verve | 558076-2
Roland Kirk Quartet
Verve Jazz Masters Vol.60:The Collection | Verve | 529866-2
Talkin' Verve-Roots Of Acid Jazz:Roland Kirk | Verve | 533101-2
Rahsaan/The Complete Mercury Recordings Of Roland Kirk | Mercury | 846630-2
Roland Kirk Quintet
Rahsaan/The Complete Mercury Recordings Of Roland Kirk | Mercury | 846630-2

Fleming,Peter | (tp)
Buddy Childers Big Band
Just Buddy's | Candid | CCD 79761

Flemming,Leopoldo F. | (perc)
David Murray Group
Speaking In Togues | Enja | ENJ-9370 2

Flesh Quartet | (strings)
Rigmor Gustafsson With The Nils Landgren Quartet And The Fleshquartet
I Will Wait For You | ACT | 9418-2

Flesh Quartet: |
Nils Landgren Group
Sentimental Journey | ACT | 9409-2

Fletcher,Mark | (dr)
Ian Shaw With Band
Soho Stories | Milestone | MCD 9316-2

Fletcher,Milton | (tp)
Earl Hines And His Orchestra
Planet Jazz:Earl Hines | Planet Jazz | 2159973-2
The Legends Of Swing | Laserlight | 24659
Jazz:The Essential Collection Vol.2 | IN+OUT Records | 78012-2

Fletcher,Stan | (tuba)
Stan Kenton And His Orchestra
Stan Kenton Portraits On Standards | Capitol | 531571-2

Fletcher,Wilby | (drcowbell)
Ron Carter Quartet
Songs For You | Milestone | MCD 47099-2

Fleurine | (voc)
Fleurine With Band And Horn Section
Meant To Be! | EmArCy | 159085-2

Flex,Britta-Ann | (voc)
Welcome To The Maze
Welcome To The Maze:Puzzle | Nabel Records:Jazz Network | CD 4671

Fliegauf,Johannes 'Hans' | (harm)
Al Jones Blues Band
Sharper Than A Tack | Blues Beacon | BLU-1034 2

Flierl,Rudi | (bs,clts)
Freddie Brocksieper And His Boys
Freddie's Boogie Blues | Bear Family Records | BCD 16388 AH
Hans Koller Nonet
Exclusiv | MPS | 9813440

Flolo,Jon | (v)
Terje Rypdal Quartet With The Bergen Chamber Ensemble
Lux Aeterna | ECM | 1818(017070-2)

Flood,Bernard | (tp)
Louis Armstrong And His Orchestra
Louis Armstrong:Swing That Music | Laserlight | 36056
Jazz:The Essential Collection Vol.2 | IN+OUT Records | 78012-2
Swing Legends:Louis Armstrong | Nimbus Records | NI 2012

Flood,Kenny | (ss)
Bobby Lyle Group
The Journey | Atlantic | 7567-82138-2

Flor De Tango |
Flor De Tango
Armenonville | Minor Music | 801097

Flor,Kristian | (voc)
Marilyn Mazur With Ars Nova And The Copenhagen Art Ensemble
Jordsange | dacapo | DCCD 9454

Florence,Bob | (arr,cond,keyboards,p,ldel-p)
Vic Lewis West Coast All Stars
Vic Lewis Presenting A Celebration Of Contemporary West Coast Jazz | Candid | CCD 79711/12

Flores,Chuck | (drperc)
Bud Shank Quartet
Live At The Haig | Choice | CHCD 71030
The Herdsmen
Nat Pierce-Dick Collins-Ralph Burns & The Herdsmen Play Paris | Fantasy | FCD 24759-2

Floreska,Roger | (b-tb)
Wycliffe Gordon Group
The Search | Nagel-Heyer | CD 2007

Flors,Daniel | (gg-solo)
Daniel Flors Group
When Least Expected | Fresh Sound Records | FSNT 080 CD

Flory,Med | (as,ts,arr,voc,bs,reedssax)
Art Pepper Plus Eleven
Art Pepper + Eleven | Contemporary | CSA 7568-6
Modern Jazz Classics | Original Jazz Classics | OJC20 341-2
Ella Fitzgerald With Marty Paich's Dektette
Ella Swings Lightly | Verve | 517535-2
Ella Fitzgerald With The Marty Paich Dek-tette
Ella Fitzgerald-First Lady Of Song | Verve | 517898-2
Verve Jazz Masters 6:Ella Fitzgerald | Verve | 519822-2
Verve Jazz Masters 46:Ella Fitzgerald-The Jazz Sides | Verve | 527655-2
Terry Gibbs Dream Band
Terry Gibbs Dream Band Vol.2:The Sundown Sessions | Contemporary | CCD 7652-2
Terry Gibbs Dream Band Vol.3:Flying Home | Contemporary | CCD 7654-2
Terry Gibbs Dream Band Vol.6:One More Time | Contemporary | CCD 7658-2
The Jazz Giants Play Jerome Kern:Yesterdays | Prestige | PCD 24202-2

Flowers,Herman | (p)
Buster Smith Orchestra
Atlantic Jazz: Kansas City | Atlantic | 7567-81701-2

Floyd,Babi | (voc)
Nina Simone And Orchestra
Baltimore | Epic | 476906-2

Floyd,Derek | (oboeengl-h)
Paquito D'Rivera Group With The Absolute Ensemble
Habanera | Enja | ENJ-9395 2

Floyd,Frank | (voc)
Grover Washington Jr. Orchestra
Inside Moves | Elektra | 7559-60318-2
Nina Simone And Orchestra
Baltimore | Epic | 476906-2

Floyd,Tony | (cymbals,dr,percimbales)
Vince Jones Group
It All Ends Up In Tears | Intuition Records | INT 3069-2

Flubacher,Jan | (b)
Lirico
Sussurro | Jazz Haus Musik | JHM 0129 CD

Flügel,Michael | (p,el-pmelodica)
Enrico Rava With The Michael Flügel Quartet
Live At Birdland Neuburg | double moon | CHRDM 71011
Horst Faigle's Jazzkrement
Gans Normal | Jazz 4 Ever Records:Jazz Network | J4E 4748
Norbert Emminger Quintet
In The Park | Edition Collage | EC 521-2

Fluitt,Keith | (voc)
Spyro Gyra & Guests
Love & Other Obsessions | GRP | GRP 98112

Flynn,Bridget | (dr)
Mary Lou Williams Trio
Planet Jazz:Jazz Piano | RCA | 2169655-2

Flynn,Frank | (percvib)
Ella Fitzgerald With The Nelson Riddle Orchestra
Ella Fitzgerald-First Lady Of Song | Verve | 517898-2
The Best Of The Song Books | Verve | 519804-2
For The Love Of Ella Fitzgerald | Verve | 841765-2
Pete Rugolo And His Orchestra
Thriller/Richard Diamon(Original Jazz Scores From 2 Classics TV Series) | Fresh Sound Records | FSCD 2015

Flynn,Fred | (drperc)
Ella Fitzgerald With The Nelson Riddle Orchestra
The Best Of The Song Books:The Ballads | Verve | 521867-2
Oh Lady Be Good:The Best Of The Gershwin Songbook | Verve | 529581-2
Love Songs:The Best Of The Song Books | Verve | 531762-2
Ella Fitzgerald Sings The Johnny Mercer Songbook | Verve | 539057-2

Fogel,Marty | (cl,ss,ts,flsax)
Everyman Band
Everyman Band | ECM | 1234
Without Warning | ECM | 1290

Fol,Hubert | (as,ts,arr,bscl)
Coleman Hawkins And His Rhythm
Coleman Hawkins/Johnny Hodges:The Vogue Recordings | Vogue | 21559712
Django Reinhardt And His Quintet
Django Reinhardt:Souveniers | Dreyfus Jazz Line | FDM 36744-2
Django Reinhardt Quintet
Jazz In Paris:Django Reinhardt-Nuits De Saint-Germain-Des-Prés | EmArCy | 018427-2
Django Reinhardt Sextet
Jazz In Paris:Django Reinhardt-Nuits De Saint-Germain-Des-Prés | EmArCy | 018427-2
Ernie Royal And The Duke Knights
Americans Swinging In Paris:James Moody | EMI Records | 539653-2
Hubert Fol And His Be-Bop Minstrels
Americans Swinging In Paris:Kenny Clarke | EMI Records | 539652-2
Hubert Fol Quartet
Jazz In Paris:Saxophones Á Saint-Germain Des Prés | EmArCy | 014060-2
James Moody Boptet
Americans Swinging In Paris:James Moody | EMI Records | 539653-2
Kenny Clarke 8
Americans Swinging In Paris:Kenny Clarke | EMI Records | 539652-2
Kenny Clarke And His Orchestra
Americans Swinging In Paris:James Moody | EMI Records | 539653-2
Michel De Villers Octet
Jazz In Paris:Saxophones Á Saint-Germain Des Prés | EmArCy | 014060-2

Fol,Raimond | (p,celeste,compld)
Clark Terry And His Orchestra
Clark Terry And His Orchestra Feat. Paul Gonsalves | Storyville | STCD 8322
Django Reinhardt And His Quintet
Django Reinhardt:Souveniers | Dreyfus Jazz Line | FDM 36744-2
Django Reinhardt Quintet
Jazz In Paris:Django Reinhardt-Nuits De Saint-Germain-Des-Prés | EmArCy | 018427-2
Django Reinhardt Sextet
Jazz In Paris:Django Reinhardt-Nuits De Saint-Germain-Des-Prés | EmArCy | 018427-2
Ernie Royal And The Duke Knights
Americans Swinging In Paris:James Moody | EMI Records | 539653-2
Gérard Badini Quartet
Jazz In Paris:Gérard Badini-The Swing Machine | EmArCy | 018417-2
Guy Lafitte Sextet
Jazz In Paris:Guy Lafitte-Blue And Sentimental | EmArCy | 159852-2 PMS
Hubert Fol And His Be-Bop Minstrels
Americans Swinging In Paris:Kenny Clarke | EMI Records | 539652-2
James Moody Boptet
Americans Swinging In Paris:James Moody | EMI Records | 539653-2
Johnny Hodges Orchestra
Coleman Hawkins/Johnny Hodges:The Vogue Recordings | Vogue | 21559712
Kenny Clarke 8
Americans Swinging In Paris:Kenny Clarke | EMI Records | 539652-2
Lionel Hampton All Stars
Jazz In Paris:Lionel Hampton-Ring Dem Bells | EmArCy | 159825-2 PMS
Raymond Fol Big Band
Jazz In Paris:Raymond Fol-Les 4 Saisons | EmArCy | 548791-2
Sidney Bechet With Claude Luter And His Orchestra
Planet Jazz:Sidney Bechet | Planet Jazz | 2152063-2
Stephane Grappelli Quartet
Grapelli Story | Verve | 515807-2
Stephane Grappelli Quintet
Planet Jazz:Stephane Grappelli | RCA | 2165366-2

Folami,James Ola | (perc)
Art Blakey And The Afro Drum Ensemble
The African Beat | Blue Note | 522666-2

Foley | (4-string-g,b,el-bel-g)
Lenny White Group
Renderers Of Spirit | Hip Bop | HIBD 8014
Miles Davis Group
Miles Davis Live From His Last Concert In Avignon | Laserlight | 24327

Foley,Keith | (g,keyboardssynth)
Amandla | Warner | 7599-25873-2

Foley,Ken | (g)
Nicki Leighton-Thomas Group
Forbidden Games | Candid | CCD 79778

Folkesson,Margaretha | (voc)
Nils Landgren First Unit And Guests
Nils Landgren-The First Unit | ACT | 9292-2

Folkesson,Mija | (voc)

Folleso,Annar | (v)
Terje Rypdal Quartet With The Bergen Chamber Ensemble
Lux Aeterna | ECM | 1818(017070-2)

Folmer,Nicolas | (tp)
Dee Dee Bridgewater With Band
This Is New | Verve | 016884-2
Dee Dee Bridgewater Sings Kurt Weil | EmArCy | 9809601

Folsom,Jerry | (fr-h)
The Quincy Jones-Sammy Nestico Orchestra
Basie & Beyond | Warner | 9362-47792-2

Folson,Eileen M. | (cello)
Freddy Cole With Band
Le Grand Freddy:Freddy Cole Sings The Music Of Michel Legrand | Fantasy | FCD 9683-2
Max Roach Double Quartet
To The Max! | Enja | ENJ-7021 22

Foltynowicz,Jens | (b,el-bvoc)
Hipsters In The Zone
Into The Afro-Latin Bag | Nabel Records:Jazz Network | CD 4663
René Pretschner Quartet
Floating Pictures | Green House Music | CD 1001
René Pretschner Trio
Floating Pictures | Green House Music | CD 1001
Tim Sund Quartet
About Time | Laika Records | LK 93-043
Wayne Bartlett With The Thomas Hufschmidt Group
Tokyo Blues | Laika Records | 35101212
Wayne Bartlett With The Thomas Hufschmidt Trio And Wolfgang Engstfeld
Senor Blues | Laika Records | LK 95-066

Folus,Mickey | (b-clts)
Artie Shaw And His Orchestra
Planet JazzArtie Shaw | Planet Jazz | 2152057-2
Planet Jazz:Male Jazz Vocalists | Planet Jazz | 2169657-2

Woody Herman And His Orchestra
The Legends Of Swing | Laserlight | 24659
Woody Herman:Four Brother | Dreyfus Jazz Line | FDM 36722-2
Woody Herman And The Herd
Woody Herman (And The Herd) At Carnegie Hall | Verve | 559833-2

Folwell,Bill | (b)
Albert Ayler Group
Albert Ayler Live In Greenwich Village:The Complete Impulse Recordings | Impulse(MCA) | IMP 22732
Albert Ayler Sextet
Albert Ayler Live In Greenwich Village:The Complete Impulse Recordings | Impulse(MCA) | IMP 22732

Fonlev,Kurt | (b)
Adrian Bentzon's Jazzband
The Golden Years Of Revival Jazz.Vol.3 | Storyville | STCD 5508
The Golden Years Of Revival Jazz,Vol.13 | Storyville | STCD 5518
The Golden Years Of Revival Jazz.Vol.14 | Storyville | STCD 5519

Fonnesbaek,Thomas | (b)
Kristian Jorgensen Quartet With Monty Alexander
Meeting Monty | Stunt Records | STUCD 01212

Fonseca,Duduca | (drperc)
Kenny Barron Group With Trio De Paz
Canta Brazil | EmArCy | 017993-2

Fontaine,Paul | (tp)
Woody Herman And His Orchestra
Verve Jazz Masters 54:Woody Herman | Verve | 529903-2
Woody Herman-1963 | Philips | 589490-2

Fontana,Carl | (tb)
Conte Candoli-Carl Fontana Quintet
The Complete Phoenix Recordings Vol.1 | Woofy Productions | WPCD 121
The Complete Phoenix Recordings Vol.2 | Woofy Productions | WPCD 122
The Complete Phoenix Recordings Vol.3 | Woofy Productions | WPCD 123
The Complete Phoenix Recordings Vol.4 | Woofy Productions | WPCD 124
The Complete Phoenix Recordings Vol.5 | Woofy Productions | WPCD 125
The Complete Phoenix Recordings Vol.6 | Woofy Productions | WPCD 126
Stan Kenton And His Orchestra
Great Swing Classics In Hi-Fi | Capitol | 521223-2

Fontanarosa,Guillaume | (v)
Stephane Grappelli With The Michel Legrand Orchestra
Grapelli Story | Verve | 515807-2

Fonville,Benny | (b)
JATP All Stars
The Complete Jazz At The Philharmonic On Verve 1944-1949 | Verve | 523893-2
Jazz At The Philharmonic:Best Of The 1940's Concerts | Verve | 557534-2
Kenny Kersey Trio
The Complete Jazz At The Philharmonic On Verve 1944-1949 | Verve | 523893-2

For Free Hands |
For Free Hands
Eastern Moods | Laika Records | 35101502

Forbes,Harry | (b,tbtp)
Stan Kenton And His Orchestra
Swing Vol.1 | Storyville | 4960343
Stan Kenton-The Formative Years | Decca | 589489-2

Forbes,Joel | (b)
Dan Barrett Septet
Dan Barrett's International Swing Party | Nagel-Heyer | CD 067
Wayne Escoffery Quartet
Time Changes | Nagel-Heyer | CD 2015

Forchetti,Vinvent | (tb)
Lena Horne With The Lennie Hayton Orchestra
Planet Jazz:Lena Horne | Planet Jazz | 2165373-2

Forcione,Antonio | (g)
Eduardo Niebla-Antonio Forcione Group
Poema | Jazzpoint | JP 1035 CD

Ford Jr.,Clarence | (voc)
Paulinho Da Costa Orchestra
Happy People | Original Jazz Classics | OJCCD 783-2(2312102)

Ford,Andrew | (tp)
Duke Ellington And His Orchestra
Greatest Hits | CBS | 462959-2
Louis Armstrong And His Orchestra
Louis Armstrong:C'est Si Bon | Dreyfus Jazz Line | FDM 36730-2

Ford,Fats | (tp)
Duke Ellington And Count Basie With Their Orchestras
First Time! | CBS | CK 65571
Duke Ellington And His Orchestra
Verve Jazz Masters 4:Duke Ellington | Verve | 516338-2
Louis Armstrong And His Orchestra
Best Of The Complete RCA Victor Recordings | RCA | 2663636-2
Louis Armstrong:A 100th Birthday Celebration | RCA | 2663694-2
Louis Armstrong:C'est Si Bon | Dreyfus Jazz Line | FDM 36730-2

Ford,Jimmy | (asvoc)
Maynard Ferguson And His Orchestra
Verve Jazz Masters 52:Maynard Ferguson | Verve | 529905-2
Red Rodney Quintet
The Red Rodney Quintets | Fantasy | FCD 24758-2

Ford,Joe | (as,flss)
Freddy Cole With Band
A Circle Of Love | Fantasy | FCD 9674-2
To The End Of The Earth | Fantasy | FCD 9675-2
McCoy Tyner Big Band
The Best Of McCoy Tyner Big Band | Dreyfus Jazz Line | FDM 37012-2
McCoy Tyner Group With Horns
Inner Voices | Original Jazz Classics | OJCCD 1039-2(M 9079)
McCoy Tyner Group With Horns And Voices
Inner Voices | Original Jazz Classics | OJCCD 1039-2(M 9079)
McCoy Tyner Orchestra
13th House | Original Jazz Classics | OJCCD 1089-2(M 9102)
McCoy Tyner Septet
Focal Point | Original Jazz Classics | OJCCD 1009-2(M 9072)
McCoy Tyner Sextet
Focal Point | Original Jazz Classics | OJCCD 1009-2(M 9072)

Ford,Larry | (tp)
Woody Herman And His Orchestra
Verve Jazz Masters 54:Woody Herman | Verve | 529903-2

Ford,Mark | (harmvoc)
Robben Ford & The Blue Line
Handful Of Blues | Blue Thumb | BTR 70042

Ford,Ricky | (as,ts,sax,ssperc)
Abdullah Ibrahim And Ekaya
Water From An Ancient Well | TipToe | TIP-888812 2
Abdullah Ibrahim Septet
No Fear, No Die(S'en Fout La Mort):Original Soundtrack | TipToe | TIP-888815 2
Abdullah Ibrahim Sextet
Mindif | Enja | ENJ-5073 2
Axel Zwingenberger With The Lionel Hampton Big Band
The Boogie Woogie Album | Vagabond | VRCD 8.88008
Candid Jazz Masters
The Candid Jazz Masters:For Miles | Candid | CCD 79710
Charles Mingus Orchestra
Three Or Four Shades Of Blues | Atlantic | 7567-81403-2
Cumbia & Jazz Fusion | Atlantic | 8122-71785-2
Duke Ellington Orchestra
Continuum | Fantasy | FCD 24765-2
McCoy Tyner Orchestra
13th House | Original Jazz Classics | OJCCD 1089-2(M 9102)
Ricky Ford Quartet
Manhattan Blues | Candid | CCD 79036
Ebony Rhapsody | Candid | CCD 79053

Ford,Robben | (el-g,vocg)
Robben Ford & The Blue Line
Handful Of Blues | Blue Thumb | BTR 70042
Yellowjackets
Run For Your Life | GRP | GRP 97542

Ford,Valli | (voc)
Louis Jordan And His Tympany Five
Louis Jordan-Let The Good Times Roll: The Complete Decca Recordings 1938-1954 | Bear Family Records | BCD 15557 IH

Forde,Cecily | (voc)
Freddie Brocksieper And His Boys
Freddie's Boogie Blues | Bear Family Records | BCD 16388 AH

Forde,Helge | (tbvoc)
The Brazz Brothers
Ngoma | Laika Records | 35101562

Förde,Helge | (tb)
Misha Alperin Group With The Brazz Brothers
Portrait | JA & RO | JARO 4227-2

Forde,Jan Magne | (tp,fl-h,kalimbamarimba)
The Brazz Brothers
Ngoma | Laika Records | 35101562

Förde,Jan Magne | (tpfl-h)
Misha Alperin Group With The Brazz Brothers
Portrait | JA & RO | JARO 4227-2

Forde,Jarle | (tpvoc)
The Brazz Brothers
Ngoma | Laika Records | 35101562

Förde,Jarle | (tpfl-h)
Misha Alperin Group With The Brazz Brothers
Portrait | JA & RO | JARO 4227-2

Forenbach,Jean-Claude | (ts)
Django's Music
Peche À La Mode-The Great Blue Star Sessions 1947/1953 | Verve | 835418-2

Forest,Helen | (voc)
Artie Shaw And His Orchestra
Planet JazzArtie Shaw | Planet Jazz | 2152057-2
Swing Vol.1 | Storyville | 4960343
Harry James And His Orchestra
Trumpet Blues:The Best Of Harry James | Capitol | 521224-2

Forman,Bruce | (g)
Richie Cole Group
Jazz Life Vol.1:From Village Vanguard | Storyville | 4960753

Forman,James | (pceleste)
Dizzy Gillespie And His Orchestra
Planet Jazz:Dizzy Gillespie | Planet Jazz | 2152069-2
Planet Jazz:Bebop | RCA | 2169650-2
Planet Jazz:Male Jazz Vocalists | Planet Jazz | 2169657-2

Forman,Mitchel | (keyboards,p,el-p,synth,orgp-solo)
Stan Getz Sextet
Billy Highstreet Samba | EmArCy | 838771-2

Forman,Steve | (perc,congassynth)
Lee Ritenour Group
Rio | GRP | GRP 95242
Sarah Vaughan And Her Band
Songs Of The Beatles | Atlantic | 16037-2

Formanek,Michael | (bel-b)
Art Pepper Quartet
San Francisco Samba | Contemporary | CCD 14086-2
Bob Degen Trio
Catability | Enja | ENJ-9332 2
Daniel Schnyder Group
Tanatula | Enja | ENJ-9302 2
Daniel Schnyder Quintet
Nucleus | Enja | ENJ-8068 2
Daniel Schnyder Quintet With String Quartet
Mythology | Enja | ENJ-7003 2
Dave Ballou Quartet
Dancing Foot | Steeplechase | SCCD 31556
Dave Liebman Quintet
Jazz Portraits | EGO | 95080
Gary Thomas Quartet
Pariah's Pariah | Winter&Winter | 910033-2
Harold Danko Trio
Fantasy Exit | Steeplechase | SCCD 31530
Trilix | Steeplechase | SCCD 31551
James Emery Quartet
Standing On A Whale... | Enja | ENJ-9312 2
James Emery Septet
Spectral Domains | Enja | ENJ-9344 2
Lee Konitz With Strings
Strings For Holiday:A Tribute To Billie Holiday | Enja | ENJ-9304 2
Marty Ehrlich Quartet
Song | Enja | ENJ-9396 2
Marty Ehrlich Quintet
New York Child | Enja | ENJ-9025 2
Song | Enja | ENJ-9396 2
Marty Ehrlich-Peter Erskine-Michael Formanek
Relativity | Enja | ENJ-9341 2
Mingus Big Band 93
Nostalgia In Times Square | Dreyfus Jazz Line | FDM 36559-2
Paquito D'Rivera Group With The Absolute Ensemble
Habanera | Enja | ENJ-9395 2
Rez Abbasi Group
Modern Memory | String Jazz | SJRCD 102
Uri Caine Group
Urlicht/Primal Light | Winter&Winter | 910004-2
Vic Juris Trio
Songbook 2 | Steeplechase | SCCD 31516

Forrest,Eddie | (dr)
Firehouse Five Plus Two
Dixieland Favorites | Good Time Jazz | FCD 60-008
Crashes A Party | Good Time Jazz | GTCD 10038-2
Goes To A Fire | Good Time Jazz | GTCD 10052-2

Forrest,Helen | (voc)
Artie Shaw And His Orchestra
Planet JazzArtie Shaw | Planet Jazz | 2152057-2
Harry James And His Orchestra
Great Swing Classics In Hi-Fi | Capitol | 521223-2

Forrest,Jimmy | (ts)
Big Joe Turner With The Count Basie Orchestra
Flip Flop And Fly | Original Jazz Classics | OJCCD 1053-2(2310937)
Count Basie And His Orchestra
Fun Time | Pablo | 2310945-2
Jazz Dance | Original Jazz Classics | OJCCD 1002-2(1210890)
I Told You So | Original Jazz Classics | OJCCD 824-2(2310767)
The Jazz Giants Play Harry Warren:Lullaby Of Broadway | Prestige | PCD 24204-2
Count Basie Big Band
Montreux '77 | Original Jazz Classics | OJCCD 377-2
Harry Sweets Edison Sextet
Mr.Swing Harry Edison | Verve | 559868-2
Jack McDuff Quartet
The Honeydripper | Original Jazz Classics | OJCCD 222-2(P 7199)
Tough 'Duff | Original Jazz Classics | OJCCD 324-2(P 7185)
Jack McDuff:The Prestige Years | Prestige | PRCD 24387-2
Jimmy Forrest Quartet
Forest Fire | Original Jazz Classics | OJCCD 199-2
Jimmy Forrest Quintet
Soul Street | Original Jazz Classics | OJCCD 987-2(NJ 8293)
Jimmy Forrest With The Oliver Nelson Orchestra
Soul Street | Original Jazz Classics | OJCCD 987-2(NJ 8293)
Joe Williams With The Harry 'Sweets' Edison Sextet
Together/Have A Good Time | Roulette | 531790-2
Oliver Nelson Sextet
Soul Street | Original Jazz Classics | OJCCD 987-2(NJ 8293)
Prestige Blues-Swingers
Soul Street | Original Jazz Classics | OJCCD 987-2(NJ 8293)

Forrest,Norman | (viola)
Bill Evans Quartet With Orchestra
The Complete Bill Evans On Verve | Verve | 527953-2
From Left To Right | Verve | 557451-2
Bill Evans With Orchestra
The Complete Bill Evans On Verve | Verve | 527953-2
From Left To Right | Verve | 557451-2

Forrest,Vince | (tb)
Elliot Lawrence And His Orchestra
Mullenium | CBS | CK 65678

Forrester,Bobby | (keyboards,org,pld)
Lena Horne With The George Benson Quintet
Misty Blue:Sweet Sisters Swing Songs Of Sorrow And Sadness | Blue Note | 521151-2
Ruth Brown With Orchestra
Fine And Mellow | Fantasy | FCD 9663-2

Forsberg,Uli | (concertmasterstrings)
Esbjörn Svensson Trio(E.S.T.) With Strings
EST Plays Monk | ACT | 9010-2
Viktoria Tolstoy Group & Strings
Shining On You | ACT | 9701-2

Försch,Ferdinand | (perc)
Bernd Konrad Jazz Group With Symphonie Orchestra
Wen Die Götter Lieben | Creative Works Records | CW CD 1010-1
Bernd Konrad With Erwin Lehn und sein Südfunk Orchester Stuttgart
Wen Die Götter Lieben | Creative Works Records | CW CD 1010-1

Forsman,Alf | (dr)
Krakatau
Volition | ECM | 1466

Forté,Serge | (pp-solo)
Serge Forté
Vaina | Laika Records | LK 90-021
Serge Forté Trio
Vaina | Laika Records | LK 90-021
Serge Forté-Michel Petrucciani
Vaina | Laika Records | LK 90-021

Fortune,Sonny | (alto-fl,ss,as,fl,sax,tsreeds)
Alphonse Mouzon Group
Deep Blue-The United States Of Mind | Blue Note | 521152-2
Charles Mingus Orchestra
Three Or Four Shades Of Blues | Atlantic | 7567-81403-2
Dizzy Gillespie And His Orchestra
Closer To The Source | Atlantic | 7567-80776-2
Elvin Jones Jazz Machine
In Europe | Enja | ENJ-7009 2
George Benson With The Don Sebesky Orchestra
Verve Jazz Masters 21:George Benson | Verve | 521861-2
Klaus Doldinger With Orchestra
Lifelike | Warner | 2292-46478-2
McCoy Tyner Quartet
Sahara | Original Jazz Classics | OJC20 311-2
Song For My Lady | Original Jazz Classics | OJCCD 313-2
McCoy Tyner Septet
Song For My Lady | Original Jazz Classics | OJCCD 313-2
Miles Davis Group
Pangaea | CBS | 467087-2
Agharta | CBS | 467897-2
Rabih Abou-Khalil Group
Al-Jadida | Enja | ENJ-6090 2
Bukra | Enja | ENJ-9372 2
Sonny Fortune Quartet
Monk's Mood | Konnex Records | KCD 5048

Forward,Steve | (voc)
Dee Dee Bridgewater With Band
Victim Of Love | Verve | 841199-2

Fosk,John | (tp)
Benny Goodman And His Orchestra
The Legends Of Swing | Laserlight | 24659

Fossati,Ramon | (gel-g)
Frank Wess Meets The Paris-Barcelona Swing Connection
Paris-Barcelona Connection | Fresh Sound Records | FSNT 002 CD

Fosset,Marc | (g,el-gvoc)
Stephane Grappelli Quartet
Verve Jazz Masters 11:Stéphane Grappelli | Verve | 516758-2
Stephane Grappelli 1992 Live | Dreyfus Jazz Line | FDM 37006-2
Stephane Grappelli Trio
7.Zelt-Musik-Festival:Jazz Events | Zounds | CD 2730001

Foster,Abbey | (dr,swannee-whistlevoc)
Joseph 'Dee Dee' Pierce And His Band
Atlantic Jazz: New Orleans | Atlantic | 7567-81700-2
Punch Miller's Bunch & George Lewis
Atlantic Jazz: New Orleans | Atlantic | 7567-81700-2

Foster,Al | (drperc)
Al Foster Quartet
Brandyn | Laika Records | 35100832
Art Pepper Quartet
Art Pepper:The Complete Galaxy Recordings | Galaxy | 16GCD 1016-2
Blue Mitchell And His Orchestra
Blue Breaks Beats Vol.2 | Blue Note | 789907-2
Blue Mitchell Quintet
Down With It | Blue Note | 854327-2
Bobby Hutcherson Group
Skyline | Verve | 559616-2
Buster Williams Quintet
Something More | IN+OUT Records | 7004-2
Jazz Unlimited | IN+OUT Records | 7017-2
Carmen McRae And Her Quartet
Carmen Sings Monk | RCA | 2663841-2
Carmen McRae with the Clifford Jordan Quartet
The Collected Carmen McRae | RCA | 2668713-2
Charlie Haden-Joe Henderson-Al Foster
The Montreal Tapes | Verve | 9813132
Christoph Sänger Trio
Imagination | Laika Records | 35100752
Frank Morgan All Stars
Reflections | Original Jazz Classics | OJCCD 1046-2(C 14052)
Frank Morgan Quartet
Yardbird Suite | Original Jazz Classics | OJCCD 1060-2(C 14045)
Gary Bartz Quintet
West 42nd Street | Candid | CCD 79049
George Mraz Quartet
Bottom Line | Milestone | MCD 9272-2
Horace Silver Quintet
Horace Silver Retrospective | Blue Note | 495576-2
Horace Silver Quintet With Brass
Horace Silver Retrospective | Blue Note | 495576-2
Horace Silver Quintet With Vocals
Horace Silver Retrospective | Blue Note | 495576-2
Joe Henderson Trio
The Blue Note Years-The Best Of Joe Henderson | Blue Note | 795627-2
The State Of The Tenor Vol.1&2 | Blue Note | 828879-2
Joe Lovano Orchestra
Blue Note Plays Gershwin | Blue Note | 520808-2
McCoy Tyner Trio
McCoy Tyner Plays John Coltrane | Impulse(MCA) | 589183-2
Michel Petrucciani Quartet
Michel Plays Petrucciani | Blue Note | 748679-2
Michel Petrucciani:The Blue Note Years | Blue Note | 789916-2
Michel Petrucciani Trio
Michel Plays Petrucciani | Blue Note | 748679-2
Michel Petrucciani:The Blue Note Years | Blue Note | 789916-2
Mike Stern Group
Standards(And Other Songs) | Atlantic | 7567-82419-2
Miles Davis Group
Paris Jazz Concert:Miles Davis | Laserlight | 17445
Pangaea | CBS | 467087-2
Agharta | CBS | 467897-2

The Man With The Horn | CBS | 468701-2
Decoy | CBS | 468702-2
We Want Miles | CBS | 469402-2
Amandla | Warner | 7599-25873-2
In Concert | CBS | C2K 65140
On The Corner | CBS | CK 63980
This Is Jazz:Miles Davis Plays Ballads | CBS | CK 65038
Richard Galliano Quartet
New York Tango | Dreyfus Jazz Line | FDM 36581-2
Gallianissimo! The Best Of Richard Galliano | Dreyfus Jazz Line | FDM 36616-2
Roy Hargrove Quintet
Planet Jazz:Jazz Trumpet | Planet Jazz | 2169654-2
Scolohofo
Oh! | Blue Note | 542081-2
Sonny Rollins Plus 3
Sonny Rollins + 3 | Milestone | MCD 9250-2
Sonny Rollins Quintet
Here's To The People | Milestone | MCD 9194-2
Don't Ask | Original Jazz Classics | OJCCD 915-2(M 9090)
Sonny Rollins Sextet
Don't Ask | Original Jazz Classics | OJCCD 915-2(M 9090)
Tony Lakatos Quartet
Live In Budapest | Laika Records | 35100742

Foster,Alan | (voc)
Miles Davis Group
Dark Magus | CBS | C2K 65137

Foster,Alex | (as,cl,ss,ts,piccolo,fl,piccolo-fl)
Charles Mingus Orchestra
Tonight At Noon...Three Or Four Shades Of Love | Dreyfus Jazz Line | FDM 36633-2
George Gruntz Concert Jazz Band
Blues 'N Dues Et Cetera | Enja | ENJ-6072 2
McCoy Tyner Group With Horns
Inner Voices | Original Jazz Classics | OJCCD 1039-2(M 9079)
McCoy Tyner Group With Horns And Voices
Inner Voices | Original Jazz Classics | OJCCD 1039-2(M 9079)
Miles Davis With Gil Evans Orchestra, The George Gruntz Concert Jazz Band And Guests
Miles & Quincy Live At Montreux | Warner | 9362-45221-2
Mingus Big Band
Tonight At Noon...Three Or Four Shades Of Love | Dreyfus Jazz Line | FDM 36633-2
Mingus Big Band 93
Nostalgia In Times Square | Dreyfus Jazz Line | FDM 36559-2
Rachelle Ferrell With The Eddie Green Trio And Alex Foster
First Instrumental | Blue Note | 827820-2
Tom Harrell Orchestra
Time's Mirror | RCA | 2663524-2

Foster,Artie | (tb)
Bob Crosby And His Orchestra
Swing Legens:Bob Crosby | Nimbus Records | NI 2011

Foster,Clifton | (v)
Art Pepper Quintet With Strings
Art Pepper:The Complete Galaxy Recordings | Galaxy | 16GCD 1016-2
Winter Moon | Original Jazz Classics | OJC20 677-2(GXY 5140)

Foster,David | (psynth)
Al Jarreau With Band
High Crime | i.e. Music | 557848-2

Foster,Frank | (alto-cl,ss,as,ts,arr,ld,cl,fl,reeds)
Count Basie And His Orchestra
Jazz Gallery:Lester Young Vol.2(1946-59) | RCA | 2119541-2
Jazz Collection:Count Basie | Laserlight | 24368
The Legends Of Swing | Laserlight | 24659
Atomic Swing | Roulette | 497871-2
Verve Jazz Masters 2:Count Basie | Verve | 519819-2
Count Basie Swings-Joe Williams Sings | Verve | 519852-2
Verve Jazz Masters 20:Introducing | Verve | 519853-2
April In Paris | Verve | 521402-2
Breakfast Dance And Barbecue | Roulette | 531791-2
One O'Clock Jump | Verve | 559806-2
Chairman Of The Board | Roulette | 581664-2
The Complete Atomic Basie | Roulette | 828635-2
King Of Swing | Verve | 837433-2
Count Basie At Newport | Verve | 9861761
Count On The Coast Vol.1 | Phontastic | NCD 7555
Count On The Coast Vol.2 | Phontastic | NCD 7575
Count Basie And The Kansas City 7
Count Basie And The Kansas City 7 | Impulse(MCA) | 951202-2
Diane Schuur With The Count Basie Orchestra
The Best Of Diane Schuur | GRP | GRP 98882
Donald Byrd Orchestra
Blue Break Beats | Blue Note | 799106-2
Duke Ellington And Count Basie With Their Orchestras
First Time! | CBS | CK 65571
Duke Ellington And His Orchestra
Verve Jazz Masters 4:Duke Ellington | Verve | 516338-2
Ella Fitzgerald With The Count Basie Orchestra
Ella Fitzgerald-First Lady Of Song | Verve | 517898-2
Verve Jazz Masters 46:Ella Fitzgerald-The Jazz Sides | Verve | 527655-2
Ella And Basie | Verve | 539059-2
Ella Fitzgerald With The Count Basie Septet
Ella And Basie | Verve | 539059-2
Ella Fitzgerald With The Duke Ellington Orchestra
Verve Jazz Masters 6:Ella Fitzgerald | Verve | 519822-2
The Best Of The Song Books:The Ballads | Verve | 521867-2
Verve Jazz Masters 46:Ella Fitzgerald-The Jazz Sides | Verve | 527655-2
Love Songs:The Best Of The Song Books | Verve | 531762-2
Ella Fitzgerald Sings The Duke Ellington Songbook | Verve | 559248-2
For The Love Of Ella Fitzgerald | Verve | 841765-2
Elvin Jones-Richard Davis Quartet
Heavy Sounds | Impulse(MCA) | 547959-2
Elvin Jones-Richard Davis Trio
Heavy Sounds | Impulse(MCA) | 547959-2
Frank Foster Quintet
Soul Outing! | Original Jazz Classics | OJCCD 984-2(7479)
Frank Foster Sextet
Soul Outing! | Original Jazz Classics | OJCCD 984-2(7479)
Frank Sinatra With The Count Basie Orchestra
Sinatra-Basie:An Historic Musical First | Reprise | 7599-27023-2
It Might As Well Be Spring | Reprise | 7599-27027-2
Jimmy McGriff Orchestra
Swingin' The Blues-Jumpin' The Blues | Laserlight | 24654
Joe Newman Quintet
Good 'N' Groovy | Original Jazz Classics | OJCCD 185-2(SV 2019)
Lionel Hampton And His Orchestra
Planet Jazz:Big Bands | Planet Jazz | 2169649-2
Matthew Gee All-Stars
Jazz By Gee! | Original Jazz Classics | OJCCD 1884-2(RLP 221)
McCoy Tyner Orchestra
13th House | Original Jazz Classics | OJCCD 1089-2(M 9102)
Prestige All Stars
All Day Long | Original Jazz Classics | OJC20 456-2(P 7081)
Sarah Vaughan And Joe Williams With The Count Basie Orchestra
Jazz Profile | Blue Note | 823517-2
Sarah Vaughan And The Count Basie Orchestra
Ballads | Roulette | 537561-2
Sarah Vaughan And The Thad Jones Orchestra
Verve Jazz Masters 42:Sarah Vaughan-The Jazz Sides | Verve | 526817-2
Sarah Vaughan With Band
Linger Awhile | Pablo | 2312144-2
Sarah Vaughan With Orchestra
!Viva! Vaughan | Mercury | 549374-2
Sarah Vaughan Sings The Mancini Songbook | Verve | 558401-2
Sarah Vaughan Birthday Celebration | Fantasy | FANCD 6090-2
Sarah Vaughan With Small Group & Orchestra
Duke Ellington Song Book One | Pablo | CD 2312111
Sarah Vaughan With The Benny Carter Orchestra
Jazz Profile | Blue Note | 823517-2
Sarah Vaughan With The Count Basie Band
Jazz Profile | Blue Note | 823517-2
Sarah Vaughan With The Frank Foster Orchestra
The Antonio Carlos Jobim Songbook | Verve | 525472-2
Thelonious Monk Quintet
Thelonious Monk:The Complete Prestige Recordings | Prestige | 3 PRCD 4428-2
Thelonious Monk:85th Birthday Celebration | zyx records | FANCD 6076-2
MONK | Original Jazz Classics | OJCCD 016-2
The Jazz Giants Play Jerome Kern:Yesterdays | Prestige | PCD 24202-2
The Prestige Legacy Vol.1:The High Priests | Prestige | PCD 24251-2

Foster,Gary | (as,ts,cl,fl,alto-fl,recorder)
Diane Schuur With Orchestra And Strings
The Best Of Diane Schuur | GRP | GRP 98882
Milt Jackson And His Orchestra
Reverence And Compassion | Reprise | 9362-45204-2
Singers Unlimited With The Clare Fischer Orchestra
The Singers Unlimited:Magic Voices | MPS | 539130-2
The Quincy Jones-Sammy Nestico Orchestra
Basie & Beyond | Warner | 9362-47792-2

Foster,George 'Pops' | (btuba)
Bunk Johnson-Sidney Bechet Sextet
Jazz:The Essential Collection Vol.1 | IN+OUT Records | 78011-2
Don Ewell Quartet
Free 'N' Easy | Good Time Jazz | GTCD 10046-2
Don Ewell Trio
Free 'N' Easy | Good Time Jazz | GTCD 10046-2
Earl Hines-Muggsy Spanier All Stars
Earl Hines/Muggsy Spanier All Stars:The Chicago Dates | Storyville | STCD 6037
Emmett Berry-Sammy Price Orchestra
Americans Swinging In Paris:Sammy Price | EMI Records | 539650-2
Fats Waller And His Buddies
Jazz:The Essential Collection Vol.3 | IN+OUT Records | 78013-2
Henry Allen Jr. And His New York Orchestra
Planet Jazz:Jazz Saxophone | Planet Jazz | 2169653-2
Planet Jazz:Jazz Trumpet | Planet Jazz | 2169654-2
Louis Armstrong And His Orchestra
Louis Armstrong:Swing That Music | Laserlight | 36056
Jazz:The Essential Collection Vol.2 | IN+OUT Records | 78012-2
Satch Plays Fats(Complete) | CBS | CK 64927
Louis Armstrong-My Greatest Songs | MCA | MCD 18347
Swing Legends:Louis Armstrong | Nimbus Records | NI 2012
Louis Armstrong And His Savoy Ballroom Five
Jazz:The Essential Collection Vol.2 | IN+OUT Records | 78012-2
Mezzrow-Ladnier Quintet
Planet Jazz:Jazz Trumpet | Planet Jazz | 2169654-2
Mound City Blue Blowers
Planet Jazz:Jack Teagarden | Planet Jazz | 2161236-2
Sidney Bechet With Sammy Price's Bluesicians
Planet Jazz:Sidney Bechet | Planet Jazz | 2152063-2
Sidney Bechet's Blue Note Jazzmen
Jazz:The Essential Collection Vol.1 | IN+OUT Records | 78011-2
Runnin' Wild | Blue Note | 821259-2
Sidney Bechet:Summertime | Dreyfus Jazz Line | FDM 36712-2
This Is Jazz All Stars
Sidney Bechet:Summertime | Dreyfus Jazz Line | FDM 36712-2

Foster,Herman | (bjp)
Lou Donaldson Quintet
Blue Bossa | Blue Note | 795590-2
The Best Of Blue Note | Blue Note | 796110-2
Gravy Train | Blue Note | 853357-2

Foster,JD | (b)
Marc Ribot Y Los Cubanos Postizos
Nuy Divertido(Very Entertaining) | Atlantic | 7567-83293-2

Foster,Marquis | (dr)
George Shearing Quintet
Verve Jazz Masters 57:George Shearing | Verve | 529900-2
Stan Getz Quintet
Stan Getz-The Complete Roost Sessions | EMI Records | 859622-2
Vic Dickenson-Buck Clayton All Stars
Atlantic Jazz: Kansas City | Atlantic | 7567-81701-2

Foster,Ronnie | (el-p,synth,keyboards,linn-dr,voc)
George Benson Group
Breezin' | Warner | 8122-76713-2
Grant Green Sextet
Grant Green:Blue Breakbeat | Blue Note | 494705-2
Alive! | Blue Note | 525650-2
Blue Break Beats | Blue Note | 799106-2
The Lost Grooves | Blue Note | 831883-2
Ronnie Foster Group
Sweet Revival... | Blue Note | 581676-2

Fouad,Pierre | (dr)
Quintet Du Hot Club De France
Django Reinhardt:Echoes Of France | Dreyfus Jazz Line | FDM 36726-2
Django Reinhardt:Souveniers | Dreyfus Jazz Line | FDM 36744-2

Fountain,Eli | (bass-dr,bells,concert-snare-dr)
M'Boom
To The Max! | Enja | ENJ-7021 22

Fouquey,Jean-Pierre | (pel-p)
Aldo Romano Group
AlmaLatina | Owl Records | 018364-2

Four Brothers,The |
The Four Brothers
Planet Jazz:Jazz Saxophone | Planet Jazz | 2169653-2
Together Again! | RCA | 2179623-2

Four Esquires,The | (voc)
Tommy Dorsey And His Orchestra
Planet Jazz:Tommy Dorsey | Planet Jazz | 2159972-2

Four For Jazz |
Four For Jazz
The Best Of Four For Jazz & Benny Bailey | JHM Records | JHM 3615
Four For Jazz & Benny Bailey
The Best Of Four For Jazz & Benny Bailey | JHM Records | JHM 3615

Four Trombones |
Four Trombones
Charles Mingus-The Complete Debut Recordings | Debut | 12 DCD 4402-2

Four Wanderers,The | (voc)
Fats Waller And His Buddies
Planet Jazz:Jack Teagarden | Planet Jazz | 2161236-2

Fournes,Rainer | (v)
Till Brönner Quartet & Deutsches Symphonieorchester Berlin
German Songs | Minor Music | 801057

Fournier,Denis | (clas)
Raymond Fol Big Band
Jazz In Paris:Raymond Fol-Les 4 Saisons | EmArCy | 548791-2

Fournier,Vernell | (dr)
Ahmad Jamal Trio
At The Pershing-But Not For Me | Chess | 940910-2
Gary Burton Quartet
Planet Jazz:Gary Burton | RCA | 2165367-2
George Shearing And His Quintet
The Swingin's Mutual | Capitol | 799190-2
Nancy Wilson With George Shearing And His Quintet
The Swingin's Mutual | Capitol | 799190-2

Fourplay |
Fourplay
Heartfelt | RCA | 2663916-2
Fourplay | Warner | 7599-26656-2
Between The Sheets | Warner | 9362-45340-2
Fourplay...Yes,Please! | Warner | 9362-47694-2

Fowler,Bob | (tp)
Peggy Lee With The Quincy Jones Orchestra
Blues Cross Country | Capitol | 520088-2

Fowler,Mose | (g)
Eddie Baccus Quartet
Rahsaan/The Complete Mercury Recordings Of Roland Kirk | Mercury | 846630-2

Fowler,Tom | (bb-g)
Jean-Luc Ponty Quintet
Aurora | Atlantic | 7567-81543-2
The Very Best Of Jean-Luc Ponty | Rhino | 8122-79862-2

Fowler,Walt | (fl-htp)
Allan Holdsworth Group
The Sixteen Man Of Tain | Cream Records | CR 610-2

Fowlkes,Charlie | (b-cl,bs,bar-fl,flreeds)
Count Basie And His Orchestra
Jazz Gallery:Lester Young Vol.2(1946-59) | RCA | 2119541-2
Fun Time | Pablo | 2310945-2
Jazz Collection:Count Basie | Laserlight | 24368
The Legends Of Swing | Laserlight | 24659
Atomic Swing | Roulette | 497871-2
Verve Jazz Masters 2:Count Basie | Verve | 519819-2
Count Basie Swings-Joe Williams Sings | Verve | 519852-2
Verve Jazz Masters 20:Introducing | Verve | 519853-2
April In Paris | Verve | 521402-2
Breakfast Dance And Barbecue | Roulette | 531791-2
Basie Meets Bond | Capitol | 538225-2
Basie's Beatle Bag | Verve | 557455-2
One O'Clock Jump | Verve | 559806-2
Chairman Of The Board | Roulette | 581664-2
The Complete Atomic Basie | Roulette | 828635-2
King Of Swing | Verve | 837433-2
Live at The Sands | Reprise | 9362-45946-2
Count Basie At Newport | Verve | 9861761
Count On The Coast Vol.1 | Phontastic | NCD 7555
Count On The Coast Vol.2 | Phontastic | NCD 7575
Jazz Dance | Original Jazz Classics | OJCCD 1002-2(1210890)
I Told You So | Original Jazz Classics | OJCCD 824-2(2310767)
Digital III At Montreux | Original Jazz Classics | OJCCD 996-2(2308223)
The Jazz Giants Play Harry Warren:Lullaby Of Broadway | Prestige | PCD 24204-2
Count Basie Big Band
Montreux '77 | Original Jazz Classics | OJCCD 377-2
Duke Ellington And Count Basie With Their Orchestras
First Time! | CBS | CK 65571
Ella Fitzgerald With Count Basie And His Orchestra
Digital III At Montreux | Original Jazz Classics | OJCCD 996-2(2308223)
Ella Fitzgerald With The Count Basie Orchestra
Bluella:Ella Fitzgerald Sings The Blues | Pablo | 2310960-2
Ella Fitzgerald-First Lady Of Song | Verve | 517898-2
Ella And Basie | Verve | 539059-2
For The Love Of Ella Fitzgerald | Verve | 841765-2
Frank Sinatra With The Count Basie Orchestra
Sinatra-Basie:An Historic Musical First | Reprise | 7599-27023-2
It Might As Well Be Spring | Reprise | 7599-27027-2
Lionel Hampton And His Orchestra
Lionel Hampton:Flying Home | Dreyfus Jazz Line | FDM 36735-2
Milt Jackson Orchestra
Sarah Vaughan Birthday Celebration | Fantasy | FANCD 6090-2
Milt Jackson With The Count Basie Orchestra
To Bags...With Love:Memorial Album | Pablo | 2310967-2
Milt Jackson Birthday Celebration | Fantasy | FANCD 6079-2
Milt Jackson + Count Basie + Big Band Vol.1 | Original Jazz Classics | OJCCD 740-2(2310822)
Milt Jackson + Count Basie + Big Band Vol.2 | Original Jazz Classics | OJCCD 741-2(2310823)
Sarah Vaughan And Joe Williams With The Count Basie Orchestra
Jazz Profile | Blue Note | 823517-2
Sarah Vaughan And The Count Basie Orchestra
Ballads | Roulette | 537561-2
Sarah Vaughan And The Thad Jones Orchestra
Verve Jazz Masters 42:Sarah Vaughan-The Jazz Sides | Verve | 526817-2
Sarah Vaughan With The Count Basie Band
Jazz Profile | Blue Note | 823517-2

Fowlkes,Curtis | (tbvoc)
Bill Frisell Band
Blues Dream | Nonesuch | 7559-79615-2
Gunter Hampel New York Orchestra
Fresh Heat-Live At Sweet Basil | Birth | CD 039

Fox,Max | (dulcimer)
Nicki Leighton-Thomas Group
Forbidden Games | Candid | CCD 79778

Fracchiolla,Antonio | (fr-h)
Banda Cittá Ruvo Di Puglia
La Banda/Banda And Jazz | Enja | ENJ-9326 2

Frahm,Joel | (ssts)
Avishai Cohen Quartet
The Trumpet Player | Fresh Sound Records | FSNT 161 CD
Jam Session
Jam Session Vol.6 | Steeplechase | SCCD 31537
Joel Frahm Quintet
The Rains From A Cloud Do Not Wet The Sky | Nabel Records:Jazz Network | CD 4686
Tim Sund Quintet
In The Midst Of Change | Nabel Records:Jazz Network | CD 4679

France,Martin | (drperc)
First House
Erendira | ECM | 1307
Cantilena | ECM | 1393
Flemming Agerskov Quintet
Face To Face | dacapo | DCCD 9445
Kölner Saxophon Mafia With Guests
Kölner Saxophon Mafia: 20 Jahre Saxuelle Befreiung | Jazz Haus Musik | JHM 0115 CD

France,Percy | (ts)
Jimmy Smith Quartet
Home Cookin' | Blue Note | 853360-2

Francel,Mulo | (b-cl,sax,ss,tsmand)
Jenny Evans And Her Quintet
Nuages | Enja | ENJ-9467 2
Nuages | ESM Records | ESM 9308
Lisa Wahlandt & Mulo Francel And Their Fabulous Bossa Band
Bossa Nova Affair | Edition Collage | EC 534-2
Mind Games
Mind Games Plays The Music Of Stan Getz & Astrud Gilberto | Edition Collage | EC 515-2

Franceschini,Romulus | (cond,cond.synth)
Archie Shepp Orchestra
The Cry Of My People | Impulse(MCA) | 9861488

Francesco,Silvio | (cl,g,pamdeirotambourine)
Caterina Valente With The Silvio Francesco Quartet
Deutsches Jazz Fesival 1954/1955 | Bear Family Records | BCD 15430
Caterina Valente-Catherine Michel
Girltalk | Nagel-Heyer | NH 1015
Silvio Francesco Quartet
Deutsches Jazz Fesival 1954/1955 | Bear Family Records | BCD 15430

Francis,Cleve | (voc)
Patti Austin And Her Band
Patti Austin:The Ultimate Collection | GRP | GRP 98212

Francis,David 'Panama' | (dr,percvoc)
Buddy Johnson And His Orchestra
Buddy And Ella Johnson 1953-1964 | Bear Family Records | BCD 15479 DH
Dizzy Gillespie And His Orchestra
Talking Verve:Dizzy Gillespie | Verve | 533846-2
Sister Rosetta Tharpe And Her Group
Gospel Train | Mercury | 841134-2
Sister Rosetta Tharpe And Her Group With The Harmonizing Four

Gospel Train | Mercury | 841134-2
Francis,John | (v)
Joe Temperley Quartet With Strings
Easy To Remember | Hep | CD 2083
Joe Temperley Quintet With Strings
Easy To Remember | Hep | CD 2083
Francis,Panama | (dr)
Al Sears And His Orchestra
Sear-iously | Bear Family Records | BCD 15668 AH
Axel Zwingenberger With The Lionel Hampton Big Band
The Boogie Woogie Album | Vagabond | VRCD 8.88008
Cab Calloway And His Cab Jivers
Planet Jazz:Cab Calloway | Planet Jazz | 2161237-2
Dinah Washington With The Belford Hendricks Orchestra
Verve Jazz Masters 20:Introducing | Verve | 519853-2
What A Diff'rence A Day Makes! | Verve | 543300-2
4 By 4:Ella Fitzgerald/Sarah Vaughan/Billie Holiday/Dinah Washington | Verve | 559693-2
Dorothy Donegan Trio
The Many Faces Of Dorothy Donegan | Storyville | STCD 8362
Ella Fitzgerald With Benny Carter's Magnificent Seven
30 By Ella | Capitol | 520090-2
Francis,Susie | (voc)
Dieter Antritter And His Traveling Jazz Band
Great Traditionalists | Jazzpoint | JP 1046 CD
Franck,Arnaud | (perc)
Antoine Hervé Quintet
Invention Is You | Enja | ENJ-9398 2
Franck,Hinrich | (computer-programming,keyboards,voc)
Dirk Berger Quartet
Garagenjazz | Jazz Haus Musik | JHM 0090 CD
Dirk Raulf Group
Theater I (Bühnenmusik) | Poise | Poise 07
Franck Band
Dufte | Jazz Haus Musik | JHM 0054 CD
Wollie Kaiser Timeghost
Tust Du Fühlen Gut | Jazz Haus Musik | JHM 0060 CD
Post Art Core | Jazz Haus Musik | JHM 0077 CD
Franck,Tomas | (reeds,sax,ssts)
Jens Winther And The Danish Radio Jazz Orchestra
Angels | dacapo | DCCD 9442
The Danish Radio Jazz Orchestra
This Train:The Danish Radio Jazz Orchestra Plays The Music Of Ray Pitts | dacapo | DCCD 9428
Nice Work | dacapo | DCCD 9446
Francke,Andreas | (as,cl,vocss)
Frank Eberle Septet
Scarlet Sunrise | Satin Doll Productions | SDP 1041-1 CD
Rainer Tempel Big Band
Album 03 | Jazz 'n' Arts Records | JNA 1102
Ralph Abelein Group
Mr. B's Time Machine | Satin Doll Productions | SDP 1042-1 CD
Franco,Guilherme | (agogo,ganza,guica,pandeiro,tablas)
Archie Shepp Orchestra
The Cry Of My People | Impulse(MCA) | 9861488
Ivo Perlman Group
Children Of Ibeji | Enja | ENJ-7005 2
Keith Jarrett Quintet
The Roots Of Acid Jazz | Impulse(MCA) | IMP 12042
McCoy Tyner Group With Horns And Voices
Inner Voices | Original Jazz Classics | OJCCD 1039-2(M 9079)
McCoy Tyner Orchestra
Sama Layuca | Original Jazz Classics | OJCCD 1071-2(M 9056)
McCoy Tyner Septet
Focal Point | Original Jazz Classics | OJCCD 1009-2(M 9072)
Franco,Renato | (flsax)
Duo Fenix
Karai-Eté | IN+OUT Records | 7009-2
Francois,Jean-Charles | (perc)
Ekkehard Jost Quartet
Some Other Tapes | Fish Music | FM 009/10 CD
Francois,Michel | (v)
Toots Thielemans And His Orchestra
Verve Jazz Masters Vol.59:Toots Thielemans | Verve | 535271-2
Frang,Arne | (ts)
Jon Balke w/Oslo 13
Nonsentration | ECM | 1445
Frank,Edward | (porg)
Lillian Boutté And Her Group
The Gospel Book | Blues Beacon | BLU-1017 2
Lillian Boutté And Her Group & The Soulful Heavenly Stars
The Gospel Book | Blues Beacon | BLU-1017 2
Franke-Blom,Jonas | (cello)
Jon Balke w/Magnetic North Orchestra
Further | ECM | 1517
Franken,Rob | (el-p,org,synth,grand-p,keyboards,p)
Toots Thielemans And His Orchestra
Verve Jazz Masters Vol.59:Toots Thielemans | Verve | 535271-2
Toots Thielemans Quintet
Verve Jazz Masters Vol.59:Toots Thielemans | Verve | 535271-2
The Silver Collection: Toots Thielemans | Polydor | 825086-2 PMS
Frankhauser,Charles | (tp)
Benny Goodman And His Orchestra
The Legends Of Swing | Laserlight | 24659
Woody Herman And His Orchestra
Louis Armstrong-Jack Teagarden-Woody Herman:Midnights At V-Disc | Jazz Unlimited | JUCD 2048
Frankhauser,Chuck | (tp)
Woody Herman:Four Brother | Dreyfus Jazz Line | FDM 36722-2
Old Gold Rehearsals 1944 | Jazz Unlimited | JUCD 2079
Franklin,Andre | (voc)
Archie Shepp Orchestra
The Cry Of My People | Impulse(MCA) | 9861488
Franklin,Aretha | (pvoc)
George Benson Group/Orchestra
George Benson Anthology | Warner | 8122-79934-2
Franklin,Gordon | (dir)
Dave Brubeck With The Erich Kunzel Orchestra
Truth Is Fallen | Atlantic | 7567-80761-2
Franklin,Israel | (drhand-clappings)
Mose Vinson Band
Joe Hill Louis: The Be-Bop Boy | Bear Family Records | BCD 15524 AH
Franklin,Larry | (tp)
Eric Dolphy Quartet With The University Of Illinois Big Band
The Illinois Concert | Blue Note | 499826-2
Franklin,William | (tb)
Earl Hines And His Orchestra
Jazz:The Essential Collection Vol.2 | IN+OUT Records | 78012-2
Franks,Aubrey | (ts)
Vic Lewis Jam Session
Vic Lewis:The Golden Years | Candid | CCD 79754
Franks,Michael | (voc)
Joe Sample Group
Spellbound | Rhino | 81273726-2
Yellowjackets
Live Wires | GRP | GRP 96672
Franks,Stanley | (g,el-gvoc)
David Murray Group
Speaking In Togues | Enja | ENJ-9370 2
Don Cherry Group
Multi Kulti | A&M Records | 395323-2
Franz Liszt Chamber Orchestra |
Ferenc Snétberger With The Franz Liszt Chamber Orchestra
For My People | Enja | ENJ-9387 2
Franz,Art | (fr-h)
Billy May And His Orchestra
Billy May's Big Fat Brass/Bill's Bag | Capitol | 535206-2
Franz,Heiner | (gbj)
Heiner Franz & Friends
Let's Have A Ball | Jardis Records | JRCD 20030
Jazz Guitar Highlights 1 | Jardis Records | JRCD 20141
Heiner Franz' Swing Connection
Heiner Franz' Swing Connection | Jardis Records | JRCD 9817
Heiner Franz Trio
Jazz Guitar Highlights 1 | Jardis Records | JRCD 20141
A Window To The Soul | Jardis Records | JRCD 8801
Gouache | Jardis Records | JRCD 8904
Louis Stewart-Heiner Franz
I Wished On The Moon | Jardis Records | JRCD 20027
In A Mellow Tone | Jardis Records | JRCD 9206
Louis Stewart-Heiner Franz Quartet
I Wished On The Moon | Jardis Records | JRCD 20027
Jazz Guitar Highlights 1 | Jardis Records | JRCD 20141
Winter Song | Jardis Records | JRCD 9005
Peter Leitch-Heiner Franz
At First Sight | Jardis Records | JRCD 9611
The European Jazz Guitar Orchestra
The European Jazz Guitar Orchestra | Jardis Records | JRCD 9307
Franzetti,Carlos | (cond,el-p,synth,keyboardsp)
Steve Kuhn With Strings
Promises Kept | ECM | 1815(0675222)
Franzl,Andy Mulo | (b-cl,ss,ts,clalto-cl)
Evelyn Huber-Mulo Franzl
Rendezvous | Edition Collage | EC 512-2
Mind Games
Pretty Fonky | Edition Collage | EC 482-2
Wind Moments | Take Twelve On CD | TT 009-2
Mind Games With Claudio Roditi
Live | Edition Collage | EC 501-2
Vocal Moments | Take Twelve On CD | TT 008-2
Mind Games With Philip Catherine
Pretty Fonky | Edition Collage | EC 482-2
Tom Bennecke & Space Gurilla
Wind Moments | Take Twelve On CD | TT 009-2
William Galison-Mulo Franzl Group
Midnight Sun | Edition Collage | EC 508-2
Frasconi,Miguel | (fl)
Jon Hassell Group
Power Spot | ECM | 1327
Fraser,Hugh | (tbp)
Kenny Wheeler Ensemble
Muisc For Large & Small Ensembles | ECM | 1415/16
Frau,Gianluca | (voc)
Ernst Reijseger & Tenore E Cuncordu De Orosei
Colla Voche | Winter&Winter | 910037-2
Frauchinger,Katrin | (voc)
Horn Knox
The Song Is You | JHM Records | JHM 3625
Frazier,Charles prob. | (clts)
King Oliver And His Orchestra
Jazz:The Essential Collection Vol.1 | IN+OUT Records | 78011-2
Frazier,Josiah 'Cie' | (drsnare-dr)
Eureka Brass Band
Atlantic Jazz: New Orleans | Atlantic | 7567-81700-2
Frazier,Keith | (bass-dr,cymbal,percvoc)
Maceo Parker With The Rebirth Brass Band
Southern Exposure | Minor Music | 801033
Frazier,Philip | (tuba)
Frazier,Virginia | (viola)
Jacintha With Band And Strings
Lush Life | Groove Note | GRV 1011-2(Gold CD 2011)
Fredebeul,Martin | (as,b-cl,ss,fl,p,keyboardssax)
Maria Joao Quintet
Conversa | Nabel Records:Jazz Network | CD 4628
Martin Fredebeul Quartet
Search | Nabel Records:Jazz Network | CD 4652
Frederico,Edson | (parr)
Sarah Vaughan With Orchestra
I Love Brazil | Pablo | 2312101-2
Sarah Vaughan Birthday Celebration | Fantasy | FANCD 6090-2
Free Flight |
Free Flight
Jazzrock-Anthology Vol.3:Fusion | Zounds | CD 27100555
Free,Ronnie | (dr)
Mose Allison Trio
Mose Allison:Greatest Hits | Original Jazz Classics | OJCCD 6004-2
Mose Allison Sings The 7th Son | Prestige | PR20 7279-2
Freed,Sam | (vviola)
Ella Fitzgerald With The Frank DeVol Orchestra
Get Happy! | Verve | 523321-2
Frank Sinatra With Orchestra
Planet Jazz:Frank Sinatra & Tommy Dorsey | Planet Jazz | 2152067-2
Pete Rugolo And His Orchestra
Thriller/Richard Diamon(Original Jazz Scores From 2 Classics TV Series) | Fresh Sound Records | FSCD 2015
Freedman,Daniel | (dr)
Charles Owens Quartet
Eternal Balance | Fresh Sound Records | FSNT 067 CD
Freedman,Joel | (cello)
Albert Ayler Group
Albert Ayler Live In Greenwich Village:The Complete Impulse Recordings | Impulse(MCA) | IMP 22732
Albert Ayler Quintet
Albert Ayler Live In Greenwich Village:The Complete Impulse Recordings | Impulse(MCA) | IMP 22732
Freedman,Robert | (condarr)
A Band Of Friends
Wynton Marsalis Quartet With Strings | CBS | CK 68921
Freedman,Wulf | (el-b)
Duke Ellington And His Orchestra
The Ellington Suites | Original Jazz Classics | OJC20 446-2(2310762)
Freeman,Bo | (b)
Don Cherry Group
Multi Kulti | A&M Records | 395323-2
Freeman,Bud | (as,ts,cltalking)
Benny Goodman And His Orchestra
More Camel Caravans | Phontastic | NCD 8843/4
More Camel Caravans | Phontastic | NCD 8845/6
Billie Holiday With Teddy Wilson And His Orchestra
Billie's Love Songs | Nimbus Records | NI 2000
Bud Freeman All Stars
The Bud Freeman All-Star Sessions | Prestige | PRCD 24286-2
Bud Freeman And His Famous Chicagoans
Jazz:The Essential Collection Vol.3 | IN+OUT Records | 78013-2
Bud Freeman And His Stars
Muggsy Spanier And Bud Freeman:V-Discs 1944-45 | Jazz Unlimited | JUCD 2049
Bud Freeman And His Summa Cum Laude Orchestra
Planet Jazz:Jack Teagarden | Planet Jazz | 2161236-2
Planet Jazz:Bud Freeman | Planet Jazz | 2161240-2
Planet Jazz:Jazz Saxophone | Planet Jazz | 2169653-2
Bud Freeman And The V-Disc Jumpers
Muggsy Spanier And Bud Freeman:V-Discs 1944-45 | Jazz Unlimited | JUCD 2049
Eddie Condon And His Boys
The Very Best Of Dixieland Jazz | Verve | 535529-2
Eddie Condon And His Chicagoans
The Very Best Of Dixieland Jazz | Verve | 535529-2
Eight Squares And A Critic
Muggsy Spanier And Bud Freeman:V-Discs 1944-45 | Jazz Unlimited | JUCD 2049
Gene Gifford And His Orchestra
Planet Jazz:Bud Freeman | Planet Jazz | 2161240-2
Hoagy Carmichael And His Orchestra
Planet Jazz:Bud Freeman | Planet Jazz | 2161240-2
Louis Armstrong And His All Stars
Louis Armstrong-My Greatest Songs | MCA | MCD 18347
Mezz Mezzrow And His Orchestra
Planet Jazz:Bud Freeman | Planet Jazz | 2161240-2
Mezz Mezzrow And His Swing Band
Planet Jazz:Bud Freeman | Planet Jazz | 2161240-2
Muggsy Spanier And His V-Disc All Stars
Muggsy Spanier And Bud Freeman:V-Discs 1944-45 | Jazz Unlimited | JUCD 2049
The Chicago All Stars
Planet Jazz:Bud Freeman | Planet Jazz | 2161240-2
The Dixieland All Stars
The Dixieland All Stars | Jazz Unlimited | JUCD 2037
The Three T's
Jazz:The Essential Collection Vol.3 | IN+OUT Records | 78013-2
The V-Disc Jumpers
Muggsy Spanier And Bud Freeman:V-Discs 1944-45 | Jazz Unlimited | JUCD 2049
Tommy Dorsey And His Clambake Seven
Planet Jazz:Bud Freeman | Planet Jazz | 2161240-2
Tommy Dorsey And His Orchestra
Planet Jazz:Tommy Dorsey | Planet Jazz | 2159972-2
Planet Jazz:Big Bands | Planet Jazz | 2169649-2
Planet Jazz:Swing | Planet Jazz | 2169651-2
Freeman,Buzz | (dr)
Benny Goodman And His Orchestra
More Camel Caravans | Phontastic | NCD 8843/4
More Camel Caravans | Phontastic | NCD 8845/6
Freeman,Charlie | (g)
Jack McDuff Group
So Blue So Funky-Heroes Of The Hammond | Blue Note | 796563-2
Freeman,Chico | (b-cl,ss,as,ts,synth,voc,perc,cl,fl)
Brainstorm feat. Chico Freeman
The Mystical Dreamer | IN+OUT Records | 7006-2
Chico Freeman & Franco Ambrosetti Meet Reto Weber Percussion Orchestra
Face To Face | double moon | CHRDM 71018
Chico Freeman And Brainstorm
Sweet Explosion | IN+OUT Records | 7010-2
Jazz Unlimited | IN+OUT Records | 7017-2
Threshold | IN+OUT Records | 7022-2
Chico Freeman Quartet
Destiny's Dance | Original Jazz Classics | OJCCD 799-2(C 14008)
Chico Freeman Quintet
Destiny's Dance | Original Jazz Classics | OJCCD 799-2(C 14008)
Chico Freeman Septet
Destiny's Dance | Original Jazz Classics | OJCCD 799-2(C 14008)
Chico Freeman Sextet
Destiny's Dance | Original Jazz Classics | OJCCD 799-2(C 14008)
Jack DeJohnette's Special Edition
Inflation Blues | ECM | 1244
Roots
Salutes The Saxophone | IN+OUT Records | 7016-2
Salutes The Saxophones: Tributes To Gene Ammons, Eric Dolphy, Coleman Hawkins And Charlie Parker | IN+OUT Records | 7016-3
Jazz Unlimited | IN+OUT Records | 7017-2
Stablemates | IN+OUT Records | 7021-2
Saying Something | IN+OUT Records | 77031-2
For Diz & Bird | IN+OUT Records | 77039-2
Freeman,Ernie | (arr,ld,orgp)
Jimmy Witherspoon And His Band
Baby, Baby, Baby | Original Blues Classics | OBCCD 527-2(P 7290)
Julie London With Orchestra
Misty Blue:Sweet Sisters Swing Songs Of Sorrow And Sadness | Blue Note | 521151-2
Sarah Vaughan And Her Band
Misty Blue:Sweet Sisters Swing Songs Of Sorrow And Sadness | Blue Note | 521151-2
Sarah Vaughan With The Gerald Wilson Orchestra
Ballads | Roulette | 537561-2
Freeman,George | (g)
Buddy Rich Septet
Swingin' The Blues-Jumpin' The Blues | Laserlight | 24654
Jimmy McGriff Quintet
Swingin' The Blues-Jumpin' The Blues | Laserlight | 24654
Richard 'Groove' Holmes Sextet
Somethin' Special | Pacific Jazz | 855452-2
Freeman,Hank | (assax)
Artie Shaw And His Orchestra
Planet JazzArtie Shaw | Planet Jazz | 2152057-2
Planet Jazz Sampler | Planet Jazz | 2152326-2
Planet Jazz:Swing | Planet Jazz | 2169651-2
Planet Jazz:Female Jazz Vocalists | Planet Jazz | 2169656-2
The Legends Of Swing | Laserlight | 24659
Freeman,Lee | (voc)
Babs Gonzales And His Band
Voilà | Fresh Sound Records | FSR CD 340
Freeman,Ned | (arr)
Lena Horne With The Lou Bring Orchestra
Planet Jazz:Lena Horne | Planet Jazz | 2165373-2
Planet Jazz:Female Jazz Vocalists | Planet Jazz | 2169656-2
Freeman,Russ | (el-g,keyboards,b,g-synth,perc,g,arr)
Annie Ross With Her Quintet
Misty Blue:Sweet Sisters Swing Songs Of Sorrow And Sadness | Blue Note | 521151-2
Art Pepper Plus Eleven
Art Pepper + Eleven | Contemporary | CSA 7568-6
Modern Jazz Classics | Original Jazz Classics | OJC20 341-2
Bill Watrous And His West Coast Friends
Art Pepper:The Hollywood All-Star Sessions | Galaxy | 5GCD 4431-2
Chet Baker And The Lighthouse All Stars
Witch Doctor | Original Jazz Classics | OJCCD 609-2
The Jazz Giants Play Harry Warren:Lullaby Of Broadway | Prestige | PCD 24204-2
Chet Baker Quartet
Chet Baker Quartet Live Vol.1:This Time The Dreams's On Me | Pacific Jazz | 525248-2
Chet Baker Quartet Live Vol.3: May Old Flame | Pacific Jazz | 531573-2
Let's Get Lost: The Best Of Chet Baker Sings | Pacific Jazz | 792932-2
The Best Of Chet Baker Plays | Pacific Jazz | 797161-2
At Last! | Original Jazz Classics | OJCCD 480-2
Chet Baker Septet
The Best Of Chet Baker Plays | Pacific Jazz | 797161-2
Chet Baker Sextet
The Best Of Chet Baker Plays | Pacific Jazz | 797161-2
Howard Rumsey's Lighthouse All-Stars
Sunday Jazz A La Lighthouse Vol.2 | Original Jazz Classics | OJCCD 972-2(S 2501)
June Christy With The Pete Rugolo Orchestra
Something Cool(The Complete Mono & Stereo Versions) | Capitol | 534069-2
Maynard Ferguson Band
Verve Jazz Masters 52:Maynard Ferguson | Verve | 529905-2
Russ Freeman-Shelly Manne
One On One | Contemporary | CCD 14090-2
Shelly Manne And His Men
The Gambit | Original Jazz Classics | OJCCD 1007-2(C 7557)
Vol.1:The West Coast Sound | Original Jazz Classics | OJCCD 152-2
More Swinging Sounds | Original Jazz Classics | OJCCD 320-2(C 7519)
Live! At The Manne Hole Vol.1 | Original Jazz Classics | OJCCD 714-2(S 7593)
Live! At The Manne Hole Vol.2 | Original Jazz Classics | OJCCD 715-2(S 7594)
Jazz At The Philharmonic-Yesterdays | Pablo | PACD 5318-2
The Jazz Giants Play Harry Warren:Lullaby Of Broadway | Prestige | PCD 24204-2
Sonny Stitt And His West Coast Friends
Art Pepper:The Hollywood All-Star Sessions | Galaxy | 5GCD 4431-2

The Rippingtons
Tourist In Paradise | GRP | GRP 95882

Freeman,Sharon | (fr-h,arr,celestep)
Charlie Haden And The Liberation Music Orchestra
The Montreal Tapes:Liberation Music Orchestra | Verve | 527469-2
Charlie Haden Orchestra
The Ballad Of The Fallen | ECM | 1248(811546-2)
Gil Evans Orchestra
Svengali | Rhino | 8122-73720-2

Freeman,Stan | (p)
Charlie Parker With Strings
Verve Jazz Masters 28:Charlie Parker Plays Standards | Verve | 521854-2
Charlie Parker With Strings:The Master Takes | Verve | 523984-2
Charlie Parker:The Best Of The Verve Years | Verve | 527815-2
Bird: The Complete Charlie Parker On Verve | Verve | 837141-2
Charlie Parker:April In Paris | Dreyfus Jazz Line | FDM 36737-2
Sarah Vaughan With The Norman Leyden Orchestra
Sarah Vaughan:Lover Man | Dreyfus Jazz Line | FDM 36739-2

Freeman,Von | (tsp)
Brad Goode-Von Freeman Sextet
Inside Chicago Vol.3 | Steeplechase | SCCD 31531
Inside Chicago Vol.4 | Steeplechase | SCCD 31532
Kurt Elling Group With Guests
Live In Chicago | Blue Note | 522211-2

Frehner,Hanspeter | (fl,alto-flpiccolo)
Miles Davis With Gil Evans Orchestra, The George Gruntz Concert Jazz Band And Guests
Miles & Quincy Live At Montreux | Warner | 9362-45221-2

Freiberg,Daniel | (keyboardssynth)
Paquito D'Rivera Orchestra
Jazzrock-Anthology Vol.3:Fusion | Zounds | CD 27100555

Freivogel,Willi | (fl)
Keith Jarrett With Strings
In The Light | ECM | 1033/4

French,Jeremy | (tb)
Sandy Brown's Jazz Band
The Golden Years Of Revival Jazz,Vol.5 | Storyville | STCD 5510

French-Horns |
Chet Baker With The Radio Orchestra Hannover(NDR)
My Favourite Songs: The Last Great Concert Vol.1 | Enja | ENJ-5097 2
The Last Concert Vol.I+II | Enja | ENJ-6074 22

Fresk,Livio 'Babe' | (cl,tsreeds)
Duke Ellington With Tommy Dorsey And His Orchestra
Highlights From The Duke Ellington Centennial Edition | RCA | 2663672-2
Louis Armstrong With Sy Oliver And His Orchestra
Satchmo Serenaders | Verve | 543792-2
Tommy Dorsey And His Orchestra
Planet Jazz:Tommy Dorsey | Planet Jazz | 2159972-2

Fresu,Paolo | (fl-h,tp,co,electronic-effects)
European Jazz Ensemble
European Jazz Ensemble 25th Anniversary | Konnex Records | KCD 5100
Jens Thomas
Jens Thomas Plays Ennio Morricone | ACT | 9273-2
Nguyen Le Group
Tales From Viet-Nam | ACT | 9225-2
Maghreb And Friends | ACT | 9261-2
Nguyen Le Trio With Guests
Bakida | ACT | 9275-2
Palatino
Palationo Chap.3 | EmArCy | 013610-2
Paolo Fresu Angel Quartet
Metamorfosi | RCA | 2165202-2
Paolo Fresu Quartet
Angel | RCA | 2155864-2
Kind Of Porgy & Bess | RCA | 21951952
Paolo Fresu Quintet
Night On The City | Owl Records | 013425-2
Melos | RCA | 2178289-2
Kind Of Porgy & Bess | RCA | 21951952
Paolo Fresu Sextet
Kind Of Porgy & Bess | RCA | 21951952
Paolo Fresu Trio
Kind Of Porgy & Bess | RCA | 21951952
Paolo Fresu-Furio Di Castri
Evening Song | Owl Records | 014733-2
Paolo Fresu-Furio Di Castri Quintet
Evening Song | Owl Records | 014733-2

Freund,Joki | (arr,as,sax,ss,ts,p,ts-playbacktb)
Albert Mangelsdorff With The NDR Big Band
NDR Big Band-Bravissimo | ACT | 9232-2
Bernd Konrad With Erwin Lehn und sein Südfunk Orchester Stuttgart
Wen/Die Götter Lieben | Creative Works Records | CW CD 1010-1
Charly Antolini Orchestra
Drum Beat | MPS | 9808191
Dieter Reith Group
Reith On! | MPS | 557423-2
Hans Koller Big Band
New York City | MPS | 9813437
Heinz Sauer Quartet With The NDR Big Band
NDR Big Band-Bravissimo | ACT | 9232-2
Jazzensemble Des Hessischen Rundfunks
Atmosphering Conditions Permitting | ECM | 1549/50
Jutta Hipp Quintet
Deutsches Jazz Fesival 1954/1955 | Bear Family Records | BCD 15430
Kurt Edelhagen All Stars Und Solisten
Deutsches Jazz Fesival 1954/1955 | Bear Family Records | BCD 15430
Radio Jazzgroup Frankfurt
Jubilee Edition | double moon | CHRDM 71020
Wolfgang Lauth Septet
Noch Lauther | Bear Family Records | BCD 15942 AH

Frey,Elmar | (dr,perc,ldts)
Bigband Der Musikschule Der Stadt Brühl Mit Gastsolisten
Pangäa | Indigo-Records | 1004 CD
Sorry,It's Jazz
Sorry,It's Jazz! | Satin Doll Productions | SDP 1040-1 CD

Freytag,Guntram | (sax)
Marcus Sukiennik Big Band
A Night In Tunisia Suite(7 Variationen über Dizzy Gillespie's 'A Night In Tunisia') | Jazz Haus Musik | ohne Nummer

Fricker,Daniel | (bel-b)
World Quintet
World Quintet | TipToe | TIP-888843 2
Kol Simcha
Contemporary Klezmer | Laika Records | LK 93-048
World Quintet With The London Mozart Players
World Quintet | TipToe | TIP-888843 2
World Quintet With The London Mozart Players And Herbert Grönemeyer
World Quintet | TipToe | TIP-888843 2

Fride,Jan | (perc)
Mani Neumeir Group
Privat | ATM Records | ATM 3803-AH

Fridell,Pelle | (b-cl,bsfl)
Copenhagen Art Ensemble
Shape To Twelve | dacapo | DCCD 9430
Angels' Share | dacapo | DCCD 9452

Fried,Fred | (7-string-g)
Mitch Seidman-Fred Fried
Jazz Guitar Highlights 1 | Jardis Records | JRCD 20141
This Over That | Jardis Records | JRCD 9816
Mitch Seidman-Fred Fried-Harvie Swartz
This Over That | Jardis Records | JRCD 9816

Friedlander,Erik | (cello)
A Band Of Friends
Wynton Marsalis Quartet With Strings | CBS | CK 68921
Daniel Schnyder Quintet With String Quartet
Mythology | Enja | ENJ-7003 2
Dave Douglas Group
Witness | RCA | 2663763-2
Joe Lovano Orchestra
Blue Note Plays Gershwin | Blue Note | 520808-2
Lee Konitz With Strings
Strings For Holiday:A Tribute To Billie Holiday | Enja | ENJ-9304 2
Mark Feldman Quartet
Book Of Tells | Enja | ENJ-9385 2
Marty Ehrlich Group
The Long View | Enja | ENJ-9452 2
Michael Brecker Quindectet
Wide Angles | Verve | 076142-2
Sylvie Courvoisier Group
Abaton | ECM | 1838/39(157628-2)
Uri Caine Ensemble
Wagner E Venezia | Winter&Winter | 910013-2

Friedman,David | (perc,vib,marimba,crotales)
Chet Baker Quintet
Peace | Enja | ENJ-4016 2
David Friedman
Air Sculpture | Traumton Records | 2406-2
David Friedman Quartet
Other Worlds | Intuition Records | INT 3210-2
David Friedman Trio
Other Worlds | Intuition Records | INT 3210-2
David Friedman-Jasper Van't Hof
Birds Of A Feather | Traumton Records | 2428-2
Dino Saluzzi-Anthony Cox-David Friedman
Rios | VeraBra Records | CDVBR 2156-2
Earl Klugh Group With Strings
Late Night Guitar | Blue Note | 498573-2
Ferenc Snétberger Quartet
Signature | Enja | ENJ-9017 2
Horace Silver Quartet
Horace Silver Retrospective | Blue Note | 495576-2
Lisa Bassenge Trio With Guests
A Sight, A Song | Minor Music | 801100
Wayne Shorter Orchestra
Wayne Shorter:The Classic Blue Note Recordings | Blue Note | 540856-2

Friedman,Don | (p,celestep-solo)
Booker Little Sextet
Out Front | Candid | CCD 79027
Candid Dolphy | Candid | CCD 79033
Clark Terry Quintet
The Hymn | Candid | CCD 79770
Herr Ober | Nagel-Heyer | CD 068
Clark Terry-Max Roach Quartet
Friednship | CBS | 510886-2
Don Friedman Quartet
My Foolish Heart | Steeplechase | SCCD 31534
My Foolish Heart | Steeplechase | SCCD 31545
Jimmy Giuffre Trio
Paris Jazz Concert:Jimmy Giuffre | Laserlight | 17249
Joe Henderson Quartet
Joe Henderson:The Milestone Years | Milestone | 8MCD 4413-2
Tetragon | Original Jazz Classics | OJCCD 844-2(M 9017)

Friedman,Irving 'Izzy' | (cl,as,lsts)
Bix Beiderbecke And His Gang
Jazz:The Essential Collection Vol.2 | IN+OUT Records | 78012-2

Friedman,Jerry | (g)
Dee Dee Bridgewater With Band
Dee Dee Bridgewater | Atlantic | 7567-80760-2
Nina Simone And Orchestra
Baltimore | Epic | 476906-2

Friedman,Morty | (sax)
Lena Horne With The Lou Bring Orchestra
Planet Jazz:Lena Horne | Planet Jazz | 2165373-2
Planet Jazz:Female Jazz Vocalists | Planet Jazz | 2169656-2

Friedrich,Gerry | (clts)
Jenny Evans And The Rudi Martini Quartet
At Lloyd's | ESM Records | ESM 9302

Friedrich,Hartmut | (tb)
Jazzensemble Des Hessischen Rundfunks
Jazz Messe-Messe Für Unsere Zeit | hr music.de | hrmj 003-01 CD

Friedrich,Jürgen | (p)
Friedrich-Herbert-Moreno Trio
Voyage Out | Jazz 4 Ever Records:Jazz Network | J4E 4747
Gabriel Pérez Group
La Chipaca | Green House Music | CD 1011
Alfonsina | Jazz 4 Ever Records:Jazz Network | J4E 4751
Ithamara Koorax With Band
Love Dance:The Ballad Album | Milestone | MCD 9327-2
Matthias Petzold Septett
Ulysses | Indigo-Records | 1003 CD
Tomatic 7
Haupstrom | Jazz Haus Musik | JHM 0101 CD

Friedrich,Reihold | (tpfl-h)
NDR Radio Philharmonic Orchestra
Colossus Of Sound | Enja | ENJ-9460 2

Friend,Becky | (fl)
Paul Motian Quartet
Conception Vessel | ECM | 1028(519279-2)

Fries,Fats | (dr)
Nick Woodland And The Magnets
Big Heart | Blues Beacon | BLU-1013 2
Nick Woodland Quartet
Live Fireworks | Blues Beacon | BLU-1027 2

Friesen,David | (b,b overdub,bamboo-fl,perc)
David Friesen Trio
The Name Of A Woman | Intuition Records | INT 3334-2
Denny Zeitlin-David Friesen
Live At The Jazz Bakery | Intuition Records | INT 3257-2
Joe Henderson Sextet
Joe Henderson:The Milestone Years | Milestone | 8MCD 4413-2

Frigo,John | (v)
Johnny Frigo Duo
I Love John Frigo...He Swings | Mercury | 9861061
Johnny Frigo Quartet
I Love John Frigo...He Swings | Mercury | 9861061
Johnny Frigo Sextet
I Love John Frigo...He Swings | Mercury | 9861061
Kurt Elling Group
This Time Its Love | Blue Note | 493543-2

Frigo,Johnny | (b)
Anita O'Day And Her Combo
Verve Jazz Masters 49:Anita O'Day | Verve | 527653-2

Fris,Morton | (cond)
The Danish Radio Concert Orchestra
Symphonies Vol.2 | dacapo | DCCD 9441

Friis-Holm,Joakim | (irish-harp)
ULG
Spring | Laika Records | 35101382

Friley,Vernon | (tb)
June Christy With The Shorty Rogers Orchestra
June Christy Big Band Special | Capitol | 498319-2
Peggy Lee With The Quincy Jones Orchestra
Blues Cross Country | Capitol | 520088-2
Terry Gibbs Big Band
Terry Gibbs Dream Band Vol.4:Main Stem | Contemporary | CCD 7656-2
Terry Gibbs Dream Band
Terry Gibbs Dream Band Vol.3:Flying Home | Contemporary | CCD 7654-2
Terry Gibbs Dream Band Vol.5:The Big Cat | Contemporary | CCD 7657-2
Terry Gibbs Dream Band Vol.6:One More Time | Contemporary | CCD 7658-2

Frisaura,Vincent | (tp)
Tito Puente Orchestra
Planet Jazz:Tito Puente | Planet Jazz | 2165369-2

Frisell,Bill | (cl,g,el-g,bj,b,ukulele,balalaika)
Batman
Naked City | Nonesuch | 7559-79238-2
Bill Frisell
In Line | ECM | 1241(837019-2)
Ghost Town | Nonesuch | 7559-79583-2
Bill Frisell Band
Before We Were Born | Nonesuch | 7559-60843-2
Is That You? | Nonesuch | 7559-60956-2
Where In The World | Nonesuch | 7559-61181-2
Blues Dream | Nonesuch | 7559-79615-2
Bill Frisell Quintet
Rambler | ECM | 1287
Bill Frisell Trio
Bill Frisell With Dave Hollnad And Elvin Jones | Nonesuch | 7559-79624-2
Bill Frisell-Arild Andersen
In Line | ECM | 1241(837019-2)
Don Byron Quartet
Romance With The Unseen | Blue Note | 499545-2
Tuskegee Experiments | Nonesuch | 7559-79280-2
Don Byron Quintet
Tuskegee Experiments | Nonesuch | 7559-79280-2
Eberhard Weber Group
Fluid Rustle | ECM | 1137
Eberhard Weber Quintet
Later That Evening | ECM | 1231(829382-2)
Gunter Hampel New York Orchestra
Fresh Heat-Live At Sweet Basil | Birth | CD 039
Hank Roberts Group
Black Pastels | JMT Edition | 919016-2
Herb Robertson Group
The Little Trumpet | JMT Edition | 919007-2
Jan Garbarek Quartet
Paths, Prints | ECM | 1223(829377-2)
Wayfarer | ECM | 1259(811968-2)
Jazzensemble Des Hessischen Rundfunks
Atmosphering Conditions Permitting | ECM | 1549/50
Joey Baron Quartet
We'll Soon Find Out | Intuition Records | INT 3515-2
John Zorn Group
Spillane | Nonesuch | 7559-79172-2
Kenny Wheeler/Lee Konitz/Dave Holland/Bill Frisell
Angel Song | ECM | 1607(533098-2)
Marc Johnson Group
The Sound Of Summer Running | Verve | 539299-2
Marc Johnson Quartet
Bass Desires | ECM | 1299(827743-2)
Marc Johnson's Bass Desires
Second Sight | ECM | 1351(833038-2)
Mike Stern Group
Play | Atlantic | 7567-83219-2
Paul Bley Quartet
Fragments | ECM | 1320
The Paul Bley Quartet | ECM | 1365(835250-2)
Paul Motian Band
Psalm | ECM | 1222
Paul Motian Quartet
Monk In Motian | JMT Edition | 919020-2
Paul Motian On Broadway Vol.1 | JMT Edition | 919029-2
Paul Motian Trio
It Should've Happened A Long Time Ago | ECM | 1283
Sound Of Love | Winter&Winter | 910008-2
Monk In Motian | JMT Edition | 919020-2
The Bill Frisell Band
Lookout For Hope | ECM | 1350(833495-2)

Frishberg,Dave | (p,arrvoc)
Dave Frishberg
Live At Vine Street | Original Jazz Classics | OJCCD 832-2(F 9638)
Dickie Wells-Buddy Tate Quintet
Every Day I Have The Blues | Impulse(MCA) | 547967-2
Jimmy Rushing And His Band
Planet Jazz:Jimmy Rushing | RCA | 2165371-2
Planet Jazz:Male Jazz Vocalists | Planet Jazz | 2169657-2
Jimmy Rushing And His Orchestra
Every Day I Have The Blues | Impulse(MCA) | 547967-2
Jimmy Rushing/Dave Frishberg
Planet Jazz:Jimmy Rushing | RCA | 2165371-2

Frisina,Dave | (vconcertmaster)
Ella Fitzgerald With The Frank DeVol Orchestra
Get Happy! | Verve | 523321-2
Ella Fitzgerald With The Marty Paich Orchestra
Get Happy! | Verve | 523321-2
Herbie Mann With The Frank DeVol Orchestra
Verve Jazz Masters 56:Herbie Mann | Verve | 529901-2
Mel Tormé With The Russell Garcia Orchestra
Swingin' On The Moon | Verve | 511385-2
Milt Jackson With Strings
To Bags...With Love:Memorial Album | Pablo | 2310967-2

Frith,Fred | (b,el-g,g,perc,6-string-b,voice,v)
Batman
Naked City | Nonesuch | 7559-79238-2
Ensemble Modern
Ensemble Modern-Fred Frith:Traffic Continues | Winter&Winter | 910044-2
Fred Frith Maybe Monday
Digital Wildlife | Winter&Winter | 910071-2
Heiner Goebbels/Heiner Müller
Der Mann Im Fahrstuhl | ECM | 1369(837110-2)

Froeba,Frank | (pceleste)
Benny Goodman And His Orchestra
Planet Jazz:Benny Goodman | Planet Jazz | 2152054-2
Planet Jazz:Swing | Planet Jazz | 2169651-2

Fröhlich,Holger | (as)
Landes Jugend Jazz Orchester Hessen
Touch Of Lips | hr music.de | hrmj 004-01 CD

Froleyks,Stephan | (bambusstäbe,fötenmaschine)
Stephan Froleyks
Fine Music With New Instruments | Jazz Haus Musik | JHM 0094 CD

Fromm,Louis 'Lou' | (dr)
Artie Shaw And His Orchestra
Planet Jazz:Jazz Trumpet | Planet Jazz | 2169654-2

Frommer,Gary | (dr)
Art Pepper-Warne Marsh Quintet
The Way It Is | Original Jazz Classics | OJCCD 389-2
Maynard Ferguson Band
Verve Jazz Masters 52:Maynard Ferguson | Verve | 529905-2

Frommeyer,Heinz | (p,el-pvoc)
Al Porcino Big Band
Al Porcino Big Band Live! | Organic Music | ORGM 9717
Thilo Kreitmeier & Group
Soul Call | Organic Music | ORGM 9711
Thilo Kreitmeier Quintet
Mo' Better Blues | Organic Music | ORGM 9706

Fronlev,Kurt | (b)
Adrian Bentzon's Jazzband
The Golden Years Of Revival Jazz,Vol.7 | Storyville | STCD 5512

Fröschlin,Rolf Dieter | (b,fl,clb-cl)
Regina Büchner's Jazz 4 Fun
Jazz 4 Fun | Satin Doll Productions | SDP 1017-1 CD

Frosk,John | (tpfl-h)
Bob James And His Orchestra
Jazzrock-Anthology Vol.3:Fusion | Zounds | CD 27100555
Dizzy Gillespie And His Orchestra
Verve Jazz Masters 10:Dizzy Gillespie | Verve | 516319-2
Gillespiana And Carnegie Hall Concert | Verve | 519809-2

INTERPRETENVERZEICHNIS

Talking Verve:Dizzy Gillespie | Verve | 533846-2
Ultimate Dizzy Gillespie | Verve | 557535-2
Glenn Miller And His Orchestra
The Glenn Miller Orchestra In Digital Mood | GRP | GRP 95022
Grover Washington Jr. Orchestra
Jazzrock-Anthology Vol.3:Fusion | Zounds | CD 27100555
Oscar Peterson With Orchestra
With Respect To Nat | Verve | 557486-2
Ron Carter Orchestra
Parade | Original Jazz Classics | OJCCD 1047-2(M 9088)

Frost,Soren | (dr)
Lillian Boutté And Her Group
You've Gotta Love Pops:Lillian Bouté Sings Louis Armstrong | ART BY HEART | ABH 2005 2
The Gospel Book | Blues Beacon | BLU-1017 2
Lillian Boutté And Her Group & The Soulful Heavenly Stars
The Gospel Book | Blues Beacon | BLU-1017 2

Fruscella,Tony | (tp)
Stan Getz Quintet
Stan Getz Highlights:The Best Of The Verve Years Vol.2 | Verve | 517330-2
Stan Getz And The 'Cool' Sounds | Verve | 547317-2

Frye,Carl | (as,cl,bsreeds)
Louis Armstrong And His Orchestra
Louis Armstrong:Swing That Music | Laserlight | 36056
Jazz:The Essential Collection Vol.2 | IN+OUT Records | 78012-2
Louis Armstrong:C'est Si Bon | Dreyfus Jazz Line | FDM 36730-2

Frye,Don | (parr)
King Oliver And His Orchestra
Jazz:The Essential Collection Vol.1 | IN+OUT Records | 78011-2

Fryer,Tom | (el-g)
The Collective 3 +
The Collective 3 + | true muze | TUMU CD 9802

Fryland,Thomas | (tp)
Jens Winther And The Danish Radio Jazz Orchestra
Angels | dacapo | DCCD 9442
The Danish Radio Jazz Orchestra
Nice Work | dacapo | DCCD 9446

Fryley,Vern | (tb)
Terry Gibbs Dream Band
Terry Gibbs Dream Band Vol.2:The Sundown Sessions | Contemporary | CCD 7652-2
Terry Gibbs Dream Band Vol.6:One More Time | Contemporary | CCD 7658-2
The Jazz Giants Play Jerome Kern:Yesterdays | Prestige | PCD 24202-2

Frylmark,Bertil | (dr)
Coleman Hawkins With The Thore Ehrlings Orchestra
Coleman Hawkins At The Golden Circle | Dragon | DRCD 265

Ftati,Mejdoub | (v)
Nguyen Le Group
Maghreb And Friends | ACT | 9261-2

Fuchs,Christina | (b-cl,ss,as,ts,fl,comp,ld,reedssax)
Christian Fuchs-Romy Herzberg
KontraSax | Jazz Haus Musik | JHM 0074 CD
KontaSax
KontraSax Plays Getrude Stein | Jazz Haus Musik | JHM 0096 CD
Kontrasax
Zanshin/Kontrasax | Jazz Haus Musik | JHM 0130 CD
The United Women's Orchestra
The Blue One | Jazz Haus Musik | JHM 0099 CD
United Women's Orchestra
Virgo Supercluster | Jazz Haus Musik | JHM 0123 CD

Fuchs,Thomas Karl | (grand-pgrand-p-solo)
Thomas Karl Fuchs Trio
Colours And Standards | Edition Collage | EC 509-2

Fudoli,Ron | (b)
Buddy Rich Big Band
The New One! | Pacific Jazz | 494507-2

Fuentes,Luis | (tbarr)
Daniel Humair Soultet
Jazz In Paris | EmArCy | 548793-2

Fuesers,Rudi | (tbld)
Conexion Latina
Calorcito | Enja | ENJ-4072 2
Mambo 2000 | Enja | ENJ-7055 2
La Conexión | Enja | ENJ-9065 2
Don Menza Septet
Morning Song | MPS | 9811446

Fuglsang,Peter | (cl,alto-cl,as,fl,b-clreeds)
Chris Potter & Jazzpar Septet
This Will Be | Storyville | STCD 4245
Copenhagen Art Ensemble
Shape To Twelve | dacapo | DCCD 9430
Angels' Share | dacapo | DCCD 9452
Marilyn Mazur With Ars Nova And The Copenhagen Art Ensemble
Jordsange | dacapo | DCCD 9454
Ok Nok...Kongo
Moonstone Journey | dacapo | DCCD 9444
The Crossover Ensemble With The Zapolski Quartet
Helios Suite | dacapo | DCCD 9459
The Orchestra
New Skies | dacapo | DCCD 9463

Fuhler,Cor | (p.orgkeyolin)
Michael Moore Trio
Monitor | Between The Lines | btl 003(Efa 10173-2)

Fuhlisch,Günter | (tb)
Die Deutsche All Star Band 1953
1.Deutsches Jazz Festival 1953 Frankfurt/Main | Bear Family Records | BCD 15611 AH

Fuhr,Dietmar | (b)
Enrico Rava With The Michael Flügel Quartet
Live At Birdland Neuburg | double moon | CHRDM 71011
Frank Sackenheim Quartet
The Music Of Chance | Jazz 4 Ever Records:Jazz Network | J4E 4753
Frank Sackenheim Quintet
The Music Of Chance | Jazz 4 Ever Records:Jazz Network | J4E 4753
Lars Duppler Sextet
Palindrome 6tet | Jazz Haus Musik | JHM 0131 CD
Nils Wogram Quartet
Round Trip | Enja | ENJ-9307 2
Norbert Scholly Quartet
Norbert Scholly Quartet | Jazz Haus Musik | JHM 0086 CD

Führ,Dietmar | (b)
Steve Klink Trio
Feels Like Home | Minor Music | 801092

Fuhr,Wolfgang | (fl,ts,bsss)
Double You
Menschbilder | Jazz Haus Musik | JHM 0062 CD
Franck Band
Dufte | Jazz Haus Musik | JHM 0054 CD

Fuhrmann,Renate | (rezitation)
KontaSax
KontraSax Plays Getrude Stein | Jazz Haus Musik | JHM 0096 CD

Fujiwara,Kiyoto | (b)
Gunter Hampel New York Orchestra
Fresh Heat-Live At Sweet Basil | Birth | CD 039

Fulda,Peter | (pp-solo)
Peter Fulda Trio With Céline Rudolph
Silent Dances | Jazz 4 Ever Records:Jazz Network | J4E 4731

Fulford,Tommy | (p)
Ella Fitzgerald And Her Orchestra
Jazz Collection:Ella Fitzgerald | Laserlight | 24397
Ella Fitzgerald With The Chick Webb Orchestra
Jazz Collection:Ella Fitzgerald | Laserlight | 24397

Full Moon Trio |
Full Moon Trio
Live At Birdland Neuburg | double moon | CHRDM 71024

Fullbright,Richard | (b,arrtuba)
Dicky Wells And His Orchestra
Americans Swinging In Paris:Dicky Wells | EMI Records | 539664-2

Fuller,Curtis | (perc,tb,tambourinevoc)
Abbey Lincoln With The Benny Golson Septet
It's Magic | Original Jazz Classics | OJCCD 205-2
Ahmed Abdul-Malik Orchestra
Planet Jazz:Lee Morgan | Planet Jazz | 2161238-2
Art Blakey And The Afro Drum Ensemble
The African Beat | Blue Note | 522666-2
Art Blakey And The Jazz Messengers
True Blue | Blue Note | 534032-2
Wayne Shorter:The Classic Blue Note Recordings | Blue Note | 540856-2
The Art Of Jazz | IN+OUT Records | 77028-2
Impulse!Art Blakey!Jazz Messengers! | Impulse(MCA) | 951175-2
Caravan | Original Jazz Classics | OJC20 038-2
Ugetsu | Original Jazz Classics | OJC20 090-2(RLP 9464)
Benny Golson Quintet
Groovin' | Original Jazz Classics | OJCCD 226-2(NJ 8220)
Blue Mitchell Sextet
Blue Mitchell Big 6 | Original Jazz Classics | OJCCD 615-2(RLP 12-273)
Blue Soul | Original Jazz Classics | OJCCD 765-2(RLP 1155)
Bud Powell Quartet
The Amazing Bud Powell Vol.3:Bud! | Blue Note | 535585-2
Count Basie And His Orchestra
Fun Time | Pablo | 2310945-2
Jazz Dance | Original Jazz Classics | OJCCD 1002-2(1210890)
I Told You So | Original Jazz Classics | OJCCD 824-2(2310767)
Curtis Fuller And Hampton Hawes With French Horns
Curtis Fuller And Hampton Hawes With French Horns | Original Jazz Classics | OJCCD 1942-2(NJ 8305)
Curtis Fuller And Teddy Charles With French Horns
Curtis Fuller And Hampton Hawes With French Horns | Original Jazz Classics | OJCCD 1942-2(NJ 8305)
Freddie Hubbard Orchestra
The Body And The Soul | Impulse(MCA) | 951183-2
Freddie Hubbard Septet
The Body And The Soul | Impulse(MCA) | 951183-2
Houston Person Sextet
Blue Odyssey | Original Jazz Classics | OJCCD 1045-2(P 7566)
Jackie McLean Sextet
A Long Drink Of The Blues | Original Jazz Classics | OJCCD 253-2(NJ 8253)
Jimmy Smith All Stars
House Party | Blue Note | 524542-2
Joe Henderson Septet
Mode For Joe | Blue Note | 591894-2
The Blue Note Years-The Best Of Joe Henderson | Blue Note | 795627-2
Joe Henderson Sextet
Joe Henderson:The Milestone Years | Milestone | 8MCD 4413-2
John Coltrane Sextet
Trane's Blues | Blue Note | 498240-2
Blue Train | Blue Note | 591721-2
The Best Of Blue Note | Blue Note | 796110-2
Blue Train(The Ultimate Blue Train) | Blue Note | 853428-0
Philly Joe Jones Big Band
Cannonball Adderley Birthday Celebration | Fantasy | FANCD 6087-2
Quincy Jones And His Orchestra
The Quintessence | Impulse(MCA) | 951222-2
Quincy Jones Big Band
Rahsaan/The Complete Mercury Recordings Of Roland Kirk | Mercury | 846630-2
Sonny Clark All Stars
Dial S For Sonny | Blue Note | 0675621
Sonny Clark Sextet
Trane's Blues | Blue Note | 498240-2
Wayne Shorter Quintet
Wayne Shorter:The Classic Blue Note Recordings | Blue Note | 540856-2
Wayne Shorter Sextet
Wayne Shorter:The Classic Blue Note Recordings | Blue Note | 540856-2
Blue N' Groovy | Blue Note | 780679-2
Yusef Lateef Orchestra
The Centaur And The Phoenix | Original Jazz Classics | OJCCD 721-2(RLP 9337)

Fuller,Gil | (arr,voccond)
Dizzy Gillespie And His Orchestra
Planet Jazz:Dizzy Gillespie | Planet Jazz | 2152069-2
Dizzy Gillespie Sextet
Dizzy Gillespie:Night In Tunisia | Dreyfus Jazz Line | FDM 36734-2
Kenny Clarke And His 52nd Street Boys
Planet Jazz:Bebop | RCA | 2169650-2
Fats Navarro:Nostalgia | Dreyfus Jazz Line | FDM 36736-2

Fuller,Jerry | (cldr)
Greg Clayton Trio
Live At Boomers | String Jazz | SJRCD 1013
Jack Teagarden Sextet
Newport Jazz Festival 1958,July 3rd-6th Vol.3:Blues In The Night No.1 | Phontastic | NCD 8815
Jack Teagarden Sextet With Bobby Hackett
Newport Jazz Festival 1958,July 3rd-6th Vol.3:Blues In The Night No.1 | Phontastic | NCD 8815
Oscar Peterson Quartet
Jazz Dance | Original Jazz Classics | OJCCD 1002-2(1210890)
Oscar Peterson Quintet With Strings
Jazz Dance | Original Jazz Classics | OJCCD 1002-2(1210890)
Paul Desmond Quartet
Live | Verve | 543501-2

Fuller,Jesse | (g,harm,cymbal,footdella,kazoo,voc)
Jesse Fuller
Jesse Fuller's Favorites | Original Blues Classics | OBCCD 528-2(P 7368)

Fuller,Ray | (g)
Bobby Lyle Group
The Journey | Atlantic | 7567-82138-2

Fuller,Walter | (tpvoc)
Earl Hines And His Orchestra
Planet Jazz:Earl Hines | Planet Jazz | 2159973-2
The Legends Of Swing | Laserlight | 24659
Jazz:The Essential Collection Vol.2 | IN+OUT Records | 78012-2

Fullerton,Dave | (drvoc)
Stephane Grappelli Quartet
Grapelli Story | Verve | 515807-2
Stephane Grappelli Quintet
Grapelli Story | Verve | 515807-2

Fulton,Jack | (tbvoc)
Paul Whiteman And His Orchestra
Planet Jazz:Jack Teagarden | Planet Jazz | 2161236-2
Planet Jazz:Jazz Trumpet | Planet Jazz | 2169654-2
Jazz:The Essential Collection Vol.3 | IN+OUT Records | 78013-2

Fulton,John | (cl,tssax)
Billie Holiday With Gordon Jenkins And His Orchestra
Billie's Love Songs | Nimbus Records | NI 2000
Sarah Vaughan With The Norman Leyden Orchestra
Sarah Vaughan:Lover Man | Dreyfus Jazz Line | FDM 36739-2

Fuma,John | (tp)
Vinny Golia Quintet
Regards From Norma Desmond | Fresh Sound Records | FSNT 008 CD

Fumero,Horacio | (bp-acharangado)
Albert Bover-Horacio Fumero
Duo | Fresh Sound Records | FSNT 025 CD
Manel Camp & Matthew Simon Acustic Jazz Quintet
Rosebud | Fresh Sound Records | FSNT 011 CD
Orquestra De Cambra Teatre Lliure
Porgy And Bess | Fresh Sound Records | FSNT 066 CD

Fumero,Isoca | (charango)
Gato Barbieri Orchestra
Latino America | Impulse(MCA) | 952236-2

Fun Horns |
Fun Horns
Surprise | Jazzpoint | JP 1029 CD

Funk Inc. |
Funk Inc.
Jazzin' With The Soul Brothers | Fantasy | FANCD 6086-2

Furnace,Sam | (as,bs,ts,fl,sssax)
Marty Ehrlich Group
The Long View | Enja | ENJ-9452 2
Neal Kirkwood Octet
Neal Kirkwood Octet | Timescrapper | TSCR 9612

Furtado,Ernie | (b)
Bill Evans Quartet
The Complete Bill Evans On Verve | Verve | 527953-2
Bill Evans Trio
The Complete Bill Evans On Verve | Verve | 527953-2

Furtado,Steve | (fl-htp)
The Jazz Composer's Orchestra
Comminications | JCOA | 1001/2

Fusco,Andy | (as,fl,cl,ssreeds)
John Marshall Quintet
Dreamin' On The Hudson | Organic Music | ORGM 9713

Fuss,Martin | (ts)
Hans Koller Groups
Out Of The Rim | IN+OUT Records | 7014-2

Fygi,Laura | (voc)
Laura Fygi Meets Michel Legrand
Watch What Happens | Mercury | 534598-2
Laura Fygi With Band
Bewitched | Verve | 514724-2
Laura Fygi Live At The North Sea Jazz | Spectra | 9811207

Fymard,Frederic | (viola)
Abbey Lincoln With The Rodney Kendrick Trio And Guests
A Turtle's Dream | Verve | 527382-2

'G',Wesley | (g)
Derrick James & Wesley 'G' Quintet
Two Sides To Every Story | Jardis Records | JRCD 20137

G.,Bobby | (g)
Tom Browne Group
Hot Jazz Bisquits | Hip Bop | HIBD 8801
Tom Browne Groups
Mo' Jamaica Funk | Hip Bop | HIBD 8002

Gaardmand,Anders | (fl,b-cl,bs,reedsts)
Marilyn Mazur With Ars Nova And The Copenhagen Art Ensemble
Jordsange | dacapo | DCCD 9454
The Danish Radio Jazz Orchestra
Nice Work | dacapo | DCCD 9446

Gaardsdal,Tine | (voc)
Marilyn Mazur With Ars Nova And The Copenhagen Art Ensemble
Jordsange | dacapo | DCCD 9454

Gabor,Robert | (b)
Bernd Konrad Jazz Group With Symphonie Orchestra
Wen Die Götter Lieben | Creative Works Records | CW CD 1010-1

Gabowitz,Louis | (v)
Stan Getz With The Eddie Sauter Orchestra
Stan Getz Plays The Music Of Mickey One | Verve | 531232-2

Gabrielsson,Niklas | (dr,congasvoc)
Nils Landgren Funk Unit
Fonk Da World | ACT | 9299-2

Gabrielsson,Stig | (as)
Coleman Hawkins With The Thore Ehrlings Orchestra
Coleman Hawkins At The Golden Circle | Dragon | DRCD 265

Gad,Bo | (voc)
Marilyn Mazur With Ars Nova And The Copenhagen Art Ensemble
Jordsange | dacapo | DCCD 9454

Gadd,Per-Ola | (b)
Agneta Baumann And Her Quintet
A Time For Love | Touché Music | TMcCD 006

Gadd,Steve | (dr,perc,tambourinevoc)
Al Di Meola Group
Elegant Gypsy | CBS | 468213-2
Land Of The Midnight Sun | CBS | 468214-2
Casino | CBS | 468215-2
Jazzrock-Anthology Vol.3:Fusion | Zounds | CD 27100555
Al Jarreau With Band
Jarreau | i.e. Music | 557847-2
Tenderness | i.e. Music | 557853-2
Carla Bley Band
Dinner Music | Watt | 6(825815-2)
Chick Corea And His Orchestra
My Spanish Heart | Polydor | 543303-3
Chick Corea Group
Verve Jazz Masters 3:Chick Corea | Verve | 519820-2
Chick Corea Quartet
Verve Jazz Masters 3:Chick Corea | Verve | 519820-2
Dave Weckl Group
Master Plan | GRP | GRP 96192
Eliane Elias Trio
The Story Of Jazz Piano | Laserlight | 24653
Grover Washington Jr. Orchestra
Inside Moves | Elektra | 7559-60318-2
Hal Di Meola Group
Casino | CBS | 468215-2
Michel Petrucciani Sextet
Both Worlds | Dreyfus Jazz Line | FDM 36590-2
Michel Petrucciani Trio
Trio In Tokyo | Dreyfus Jazz Line | FDM 36605-2
Paquito D'Rivera Orchestra
Jazzrock-Anthology Vol.3:Fusion | Zounds | CD 27100555
Return To Forever
Return To The 7th Galaxy-Return To Forever:The Anthology | Verve | 533108-2
Rusty Bryant Sextet
For The Good Times | Prestige | PRCD 24269-2
Weather Report
Mr. Gone | CBS | 468208-2

Gaddison,Frances | (p)
Lionel Hampton And His Orchestra
Lionel Hampton:Flying Home | Dreyfus Jazz Line | FDM 36735-2

Gade,Per | (g)
Per Carsten Quintet
Via | dacapo | DCCD 9462
The Crossover Ensemble
The River:Image Of Time And Life | dacapo | DCCD 9434
The Orchestra
New Skies | dacapo | DCCD 9463

Gadson,James | (drvoc)
Herbie Hancock Group
Man-Child | CBS | 471235-2
Magic Window | CBS | 486572-2
Paulinho Da Costa Orchestra
Happy People | Original Jazz Classics | OJCCD 783-2(2312102)

Gaeto,William 'Billy' | (dr)
Lucy Reed With The Eddie Higgins Quartet
This Is Lucy Reed | Original Jazz Classics | OJCCD 1943-2(F 3243)
Lucy Reed With The Eddie Higgins Trio
This Is Lucy Reed | Original Jazz Classics | OJCCD 1943-2(F 3243)

Gaffa,Al | (g)
Duke Pearson Orchestra
Deep Blue-The United States Of Mind | Blue Note | 521152-2
Blue Bossa | Blue Note | 795590-2

Gagliardi,Joe | (tp)
Benny Carter And His Orchestra
The Art Of Saxophone | Laserlight | 24652

Gailing,Henning | (b)
Martin Sasse Trio
Here We Come | Nagel-Heyer | CD 2008

Steve Klink Trio
Places To Come From,Places To Go | Minor Music | 801098
Gaillard,Slim | (g,p,voc,tap-dancing,vib,talking,tp)
Slim Gaillard Group
Slim Gaillard Rides Again | Dot | 589761-2
Slim Gaillard Trio
The Small Black Groups | Storyville | 4960523
Slim Gaillard-Bam Brown
The Complete Jazz At The Philharmonic On Verve 1944-1949 | Verve | 523893-2
Gainer,Camille | (cymbal,snare-drdr)
Antonio Hart Group
Ama Tu Sonrisa | Enja | ENJ-9404 2
Cornelius Claudio Kreusch Group
Scoop | ACT | 9255-2
Gainer,James | (voc)
Max Roach Chorus & Orchestra
To The Max! | Enja | ENJ-7021 22
Gaines,Charlie | (tp)
Louis Armstrong And His Orchestra
Planet Jazz:Louis Armstrong | Planet Jazz | 2152052-2
Louis Armstrong:A 100th Birthday Celebration | RCA | 2663694-2
Gaines,Roy | (gvoc)
Les McCann Group
Another Beginning | Atlantic | 7567-80790-2
Galan,Juraj | (el-g,computer-programmingg)
Bill Ramsey & Juraj Galan
Caldonia And More... | Bear Family Records | BCD 16151 AH
Galasso,Franco | (ts)
Banda Città Ruvo Di Puglia
La Banda/Banda And Jazz | Enja | ENJ-9326 2
Galasso,Michael | (v-solo)
Michael Galasso
Scenes | ECM | 1245
Galbraith,Barry | (el-gg)
Andy And The Bey Sisters
Andy Bey And The Bey Sisters | Prestige | PCD 24245-2
Anita O'Day With The Gary McFarland Orchestra
All The Sad Youn Men | Verve | 517065-2
Verve Jazz Masters 49:Anita O'Day | Verve | 527653-2
Billie Holiday With The Ray Ellis Orchestra
Verve Jazz Masters 47:Billie Holiday Sings Standards | Verve | 527650-2
Lady In Satin | CBS | CK 65144
Cannonball Adderley And His Orchestra
Verve Jazz Masters 31:Cannonball Adderley | Verve | 522651-2
Cannonball Adderley Quartet
Cannonball Adderley Birthday Celebration | Fantasy | FANCD 6087-2
Carmen McRae With Orchestra
Birds Of A Feather | Decca | 589515-2
Chris Connor With Band
Chris Connor | Atlantic | 7567-80769-2
Chris Connor With The John Lewis Quartet
Chris Connor | Atlantic | 7567-80769-2
Clark Terry & Chico O Farril Orchestra
Spanish Rice | Verve | 9861050
Clifford Brown & The Neal Hefti Orchestra
Clifford Brown With Strings | Verve | 558078-2
Clifford Brown With Strings
Clifford Brown-Max Roach:Alone Together-The Best Of The Mercury Years | Verve | 526373-2
Verve Jazz Masters 44:Clifford Brown and Max Roach | Verve | 528109-2
Brownie-The Complete EmArCy Recordings Of Clifford Brown | EmArCy | 838306-2
Coleman Hawkins All Stars
The J.J.Johnson Memorial Album | Prestige | PRCD 11025-2
Coleman Hawkins Septet
Desafinado | Impulse(MCA) | 951227-2
Coleman Hawkins Sextet
Desafinado | Impulse(MCA) | 951227-2
Coleman Hawkins With Billy Byers And His Orchestra
Planet Jazz:Coleman Hawkins | Planet Jazz | 2152055-2
The Hawk In Hi-Fi | RCA | 2663842-2
Coleman Hawkins With Many Albam And His Orchestra
Planet Jazz:Coleman Hawkins | Planet Jazz | 2152055-2
Dinah Washington And Her Orchestra
For Those In Love | EmArCy | 514073-2
Dinah Washington With The Quincy Jones Orchestra
Verve Jazz Masters 40:Dinah Washington | Verve | 522055-2
The Swingin' Miss 'D' | Verve | 558074-2
George Russell And His Orchestra
Geogre Russell New York N.Y. | Impulse(MCA) | 951278-2
Bill Evans:Piano Player | CBS | CK 65361
George Russell Smalltet
The RCA Victor Jazz Workshop | RCA | 2159144-2
Gil Evans Orchestra
The Individualism Of Gil Evans | Verve | 833804-2
Helen Merrill With The Quincy Jones Orchestra
Clifford Brown-Max Roach:Alone Together-The Best Of The Mercury Years | Verve | 526373-2
Verve Jazz Masters 44:Clifford Brown and Max Roach | Verve | 528109-2
Brownie-The Complete EmArCy Recordings Of Clifford Brown | EmArCy | 838306-2
Jimmy McGriff Orchestra
Swingin' The Blues-Jumpin' The Blues | Laserlight | 24654
Jimmy Smith With The Oliver Nelson Orchestra
Verve Jazz Masters 29:Jimmy Smith | Verve | 521855-2
Jimmy Smith:Best Of The Verve Years | Verve | 527950-2
Jimmy Smith-Talkin' Verve | Verve | 531563-2
Peter & The Wolf | Verve | 547264-2
Joe Williams With The Jimmy Jones Orchestra
Planet Jazz:Joe Williams | Planet Jazz | 2165370-2
Lee Wiley With The Dean Kincaide Dixieland Band
Planet Jazz:Female Jazz Vocalists | Planet Jazz | 2169656-2
Lucy Reed With Orchestra
This Is Lucy Reed | Original Jazz Classics | OJCCD 1943-2(F 3243)
Oscar Peterson With Orchestra
With Respect To Nat | Verve | 557486-2
Sarah Vaughan With Orchestra
!Viva! Vaughan | Mercury | 549374-2
Sarah Vaughan Sings The Mancini Songbook | Verve | 558401-2
Sarah Vaughan With The Frank Foster Orchestra
The Antonio Carlos Jobim Songbook | Verve | 525472-2
Sarah Vaughan With The Jimmy Jones Orchestra
Ballads | Roulette | 537561-2
Jazz Profile | Blue Note | 823517-2
Stan Getz With The Eddie Sauter Orchestra
Stan Getz Plays The Music Of Mickey One | Verve | 531232-2
Tal Farlow Quartet
Verve Jazz Masters 41:Tal Farlow | Verve | 527365-2
Thad Jones-Mel Lewis Orchestra
The Groove Merchant/The Second Race | Laserlight | 24656
Tito Puente Orchestra
Planet Jazz:Tito Puente | Planet Jazz | 2165369-2
Willie Rodriguez Jazz Quartet
Flatjacks | Milestone | MCD 9331-2
Galbraith,Barry or Sam Herman | (g)
Mar Murphy With The Ernie Wilkins Orchestra
RAH | Original Jazz Classics | OJCCD 141-2(R 9395)
Galbraith,Frank | (gtp)
Louis Armstrong And His Orchestra
Louis Armstrong:Swing That Music | Laserlight | 36056
Jazz:The Essential Collection Vol.2 | IN+OUT Records | 78012-2
Louis Armstrong:C'est Si Bon | Dreyfus Jazz Line | FDM 36730-2
Gald,David | (tuba)
Trygve Seim Group
Different Rivers | ECM | 1744(159521-2)
Gale,Dave | (tp)
Woody Herman And His Orchestra
Verve Jazz Masters 54:Woody Herman | Verve | 529903-2
Woody Herman-1963 | Philips | 589490-2
Gale,Eric | (el-g,gvoice-recording)
Al Jarreau With Band
Tenderness | i.e. Music | 557853-2
Bobby Timmons Orchestra
Quartet And Orchestra | Milestone | MCD 47091-2
Carla Bley Band
Dinner Music | Watt | 6(825815-2)
Diane Schuur With Orchestra
Love Songs | GRP | GRP 97032
The Best Of Diane Schuur | GRP | GRP 98882
George Benson And His Orchestra
Giblet Gravy | Verve | 543754-2
Talkin' Verve:George Benson | Verve | 553780-2
George Benson Orchestra
Talkin' Verve:George Benson | Verve | 553780-2
George Benson Sextet
Talkin' Verve:George Benson | Verve | 553780-2
Grover Washington Jr. Orchestra
Inside Moves | Elektra | 7559-60318-2
Jazzrock-Anthology Vol.3:Fusion | Zounds | CD 27100555
Herbie Hancock Septet
Herbie Hancock:The Complete Blue Note Sixties Sessions | Blue Note | 495569-2
Jimmy Smith Quartet
Jimmy Smith:Best Of The Verve Years | Verve | 527950-2
King Curtis Band
King Curtis-Blow Man Blow | Bear Family Records | BCD 15670 CI
Marcus Miller Group
Tales | Dreyfus Jazz Line | FDM 36571-2
Nina Simone And Orchestra
Planet Jazz:Nina Simone | Planet Jazz | 2165372-2
Baltimore | Epic | 476906-2
Oliver Nelson And His Orchestra
Verve Jazz Masters Vol.60:The Collection | Verve | 529866-2
Quincy Jones And His Orchestra
Verve Jazz Masters Vol.59:Toots Thielemans | Verve | 535271-2
Yusef Lateef Ensemble
Atlantic Saxophones | Rhino | 8122-71256-2
Gale,Harry | (dr)
Bix Beiderbecke And His Gang
Jazz:The Essential Collection Vol.2 | IN+OUT Records | 78012-2
Gale,Jack | (arr,b-tbtb)
Woody Herman And His Orchestra
Verve Jazz Masters 54:Woody Herman | Verve | 529903-2
Woody Herman-1963 | Philips | 589490-2
Galeazzi,Lucilla | (voc)
Michel Godard Ensemble
Castel Del Monte | Enja | ENJ-9362 2
Willem Breuker Kollektief
La Banda/Banda And Jazz | Enja | ENJ-9326 2
Galepides,Francois 'Moustache' | (dr)
Sidney Bechet With Claude Luter And His Orchestra
Planet Jazz:Sidney Bechet | Planet Jazz | 2152063-2
Sidney Bechet:Summertime | Dreyfus Jazz Line | FDM 36712-2
Gales,Joe | (ts)
Dizzy Gillespie And His Orchestra
Planet Jazz:Male Jazz Vocalists | Planet Jazz | 2169657-2
Gales,Larry | (b,dr,el-bvoc)
Candid Jazz Masters
The Candid Jazz Masters:For Miles | Candid | CCD 79710
Charlie Rouse Orchestra
Bossa Nova Bacchanal | Blue Note | 593875-2
Duke Ellington Trio
Highlights From The Duke Ellington Centennial Edition | RCA | 2663672-2
Eddie Lockjaw Davis Orchestra
Afro-Jaws | Original Jazz Classics | OJCCD 403-2(RLP 9373)
Eddie Lockjaw Davis-Johnny Griffin Quintet
Blues Up And Down | Milestone | MCD 47084-2
Battle Stations | Original Jazz Classics | OJCCD 1085(P7282)
The Prestige Legacy Vol.2:Battles Of Saxes | Prestige | PCD 24252-2
Jack McDuff Quintet
The Last Goodun' | Prestige | PRCD 24274-2
Jack McDuff Sextet
Silken Soul | Prestige | PCD 24242-2
Johnny Griffin-Eddie Lockjaw Davis Quintet
Tough Tenors | Original Jazz Classics | OJCCD 1094-2(JLP 931)
Thelonious Monk Quartet
Paris Jazz Concert:Theloniuos Monk And His Quartet | Laserlight | 17250
Monk At Newport 1963 & 1965 | CBS | C2K 63905
Live At The Jazz Workshop-Complete | CBS | C2K 65189
Live At The It Club:Complete | CBS | C2K 65288
Greatest Hits | CBS | CK 65422
MONK. | CBS | CK 86564
Gales,Lawrence | (b)
Charlie Rouse Orchestra
Blue Bossa | Blue Note | 795590-2
Galison,William | (harm)
Michael 'Patches' Stewart Group
Penetration | Hip Bop | HIBD 8018
William Galison-Mulo Franzl Group
Midnight Sun | Edition Collage | EC 508-2
Gallardo,Joe | (ptb)
Abdullah Ibrahim With The NDR Big Band
Ekapa Lodumo | TipToe | TIP-888840 2
Albert Mangelsdorff With The NDR Big Band
NDR Big Band-Bravissimo | ACT | 9232-2
Bernd Konrad With Erwin Lehn und sein Südfunk Orchester Stuttgart
Wen Die Götter Lieben | Creative Works Records | CW CD 1010-1
Conexion Latina
Calorcito | Enja | ENJ-4072 2
Heinz Sauer Quartet With The NDR Big Band
NDR Big Band-Bravissimo | ACT | 9232-2
Joe Gallardo's Latino Blue
A Latin Shade Of Blue | Enja | ENJ-9421 2
Joe Pass With The NDR Big Band
NDR Big Band-Bravissimo | ACT | 9232-2
Joe Pass With The NDR Big Band And Radio Philharmonie Hannover
Joe Pass In Hamburg | ACT | 9100-2
Johnny Griffin With The NDR Big Band
NDR Big Band-Bravissimo | ACT | 9232-2
Nana Mouskouri With The Berlin Radio Big Band
Nana Swings | Mercury | 074394-2
NDR Big Band
NDR Big Band-Bravissimo | ACT | 9232-2
The Theatre Of Kurt Weill | ACT | 9234-2
Oscar Brown Jr. And His Group
Live Every Minute | Minor Music | 801071
Oscar Brown Jr. with The NDR Big Band
Live Every Minute | Minor Music | 801071
Pee Wee Ellis & NDR Bigband
What You Like | Minor Music | 801064
Galle,Lothar | (bel-b)
Anirahtak und die Jürgen Sturm Band
Das Kurt Weill Programm | Nabel Records:Jazz Network | CD 4638
Berlin-Paris-New York/Music By Kurt Weil | Nabel Records:Jazz Network | CD 4655
Galliano | (voc)
United Future Organizatio
United Future Organization | Talkin' Loud | 518166-2
Galliano,Richard | (accordeon,accordina,bandoneon,el-p)
Anouar Brahem Group
Khomsa | ECM | 1561(527093-2)
Chet Baker & The Boto Brasilian Quartet
Chet Baker & The Boto Brasilian Quartet | Dreyfus Jazz Line | FDM 36511-9
Galliano-Portal
Blow Up | Dreyfus Jazz Line | FDM 36589-2
Joachim Kühn And The Radio Philharmonie Hannover NDR With Jazz Soloists
Europeana | ACT | 9220-2
Michel Portal-Richard Galliano
Concerts | Dreyfus Jazz Line | FDM 36661-2
Richard Galliano Group
Laurita | Dreyfus Jazz Line | FDM 36572-9
French Touch | Dreyfus Jazz Line | FDM 36596-2
Richard Galliano Group I Solisti Dell'Orchestra Della Toscana
Gallianissimo! The Best Of Richard Galliano | Dreyfus Jazz Line | FDM 36616-2
Richard Galliano Quartet
Spleen | Dreyfus Jazz Line | FDM 36513-9
Viaggio | Dreyfus Jazz Line | FDM 36562-9
New York Tango | Dreyfus Jazz Line | FDM 36581-2
Gallianissimo! The Best Of Richard Galliano | Dreyfus Jazz Line | FDM 36616-2
Richard Galliano Quintet
Spleen | Dreyfus Jazz Line | FDM 36513-9
Richard Galliano Septet
Piazzolla Forever | Dreyfus Jazz Line | FDM 36642-2
Richard Galliano Trio
Gallianissimo! The Best Of Richard Galliano | Dreyfus Jazz Line | FDM 36616-2
Richard Galliano With Orchestra
Passatori | Dreyfus Jazz Line | FDM 36601-2
Richard Galliano-Michel Portal
Gallianissimo! The Best Of Richard Galliano | Dreyfus Jazz Line | FDM 36616-2
Ron Carter-Richard Galliano Duo
Panamanhattan | Dreyfus Jazz Line | FDM 36514-2
Gallie,John | (keyboards)
Albert King Blues Band
Lovejoy | Stax | SCD 8517-2(STS 2040)
Gallivan,Joe | (g,synth,perc,congas,bellssteel-g)
Gil Evans Orchestra
There Comes A Time | RCA | 2131392-2
Gallo,Danilo | (b)
Palo Alto
Crash Test | Jazz 'n' Arts Records | JNA 1803
Galloway,Jim | (cl,ss,bsts)
Allan Vaché-Jim Galloway Sextet
Raisin' The Roof:Allan Vaché Meets Jim Galloway | Nagel-Heyer | CD 054
Jim Galloway-Jay McShann Quartet
Christmas Jazz! | Nagel-Heyer | NH 1008
Sackville All Stars
Christmas Jazz! | Nagel-Heyer | NH 1008
Galloway,Steve | (tb)
Count Basie And His Orchestra
Afrique | RCA | 2179618-2
Galloway,Tomothy | (?)
Albert King With The Willie Dixon Band
Windy City Blues | Stax | SCD 8612-2
Galper,Hal | (el-p,pp-solo)
Cannonball Adderley Septet
Inside Straight | Original Jazz Classics | OJCCD 750-2(F 9435)
Cannonball Adderley Sextet
Cannonball Adderley Birthday Celebration | Fantasy | FANCD 6087-2
Chet Baker Quintet
Chet Baker:The Most Important Jazz Album Of 1964/65 | Roulette | 581829-2
Chet Baker Sextet
Baby Breeze | Verve | 538328-2
Phil Woods Quartet
A Tribute To Charlie Parker Vol.2 | Storyville | 4960493
Putte Wickman And The Hal Galper trio
Time To Remember | Dragon | DRCD 378
Galperin,Fay | (voc)
The Sidewalks Of New York
Tin Pan Alley:The Sidewalks Of New York | Winter&Winter | 910038-2
Galperin,Saul | (voc)
Gals And Pals | (voc-group)
Toots Thielemans With Gals And Pals
Verve Jazz Masters Vol.59:Toots Thielemans | Verve | 535271-2
Galvez,Curro | (b,el-bcl)
Joan Abril Quartet
Insomnio | Fresh Sound Records | FSNT 034 CD
Joan Abril Quintet
Insomnio | Fresh Sound Records | FSNT 034 CD
Eric | Fresh Sound Records | FSNT 092 CD
Joan Abril Sextet
Eric | Fresh Sound Records | FSNT 092 CD
Ramón Diaz Group
O Si No Que? | Fresh Sound Records | FSNT 044 CD
Gambale,Frank | (el-g,g-synth,el-sitar,12-string-g,g)
Chick Corea Electric Band
Light Years | GRP | GRP 95462
Eye Of The Beholder | GRP | GRP 95642
Beneath The Mask | GRP | GRP 96492
Steve Smith & Vital Information
Vitalive! | VeraBra Records | CDVBR 2051-2
Vital Information
Ray Of Hope | VeraBra Records | CDVBR 2161-2
Where We Come From | Intuition Records | INT 3218-2
Live Around The World Where We Come From Tour '98-'99 | Intuition Records | INT 3296-2
Show 'Em Where You Live | Intuition Records | INT 3306-2
Gambella,Vince | (bg)
Jimmy Smith Quartet
Verve Jazz Masters 45:Kenny Burrell | Verve | 527652-2
Jimmy Smith:Best Of The Verve Years | Verve | 527950-2
Jimmy Smith With The Claus Ogerman Orchestra
Any Number Can Win | Verve | 557447-2
Gambino,Tommy | (ssas)
Lionel Hampton And His All Star Jazz Inner Circle
Lionel Hampton: Salle Pleyel, March 9th, 1971 | Laserlight | 36133
Gamclans,Tavil | (steel-dr)
Mani Neumeir
Privat | ATM Records | ATM 3803-AH
Mani Neumeir Group
Privat | ATM Records | ATM 3803-AH
Gámez,José Luis | (g)
José Luis Gámez Quartet
Dr.Jeckyl | Fresh Sound Records | FSNT 006 CD
Colores | Fresh Sound Records | FSNT 028 CD
José Luis Gámez Quattro | Fresh Sound Records | FSNT 094 CD
José Luis Gámez Quintet
Dr.Jeckyl | Fresh Sound Records | FSNT 006 CD
Colores | Fresh Sound Records | FSNT 028 CD
Rumbo Dorte | Fresh Sound Records | FSNT 089 CD
José Luis Gámez Trio
Colores | Fresh Sound Records | FSNT 028 CD
Gammage,Gene | (dr)
Oscar Peterson Trio
Verve Jazz Masters 37:Oscar Peterson Plays Broadway | Verve | 516893-2
Gandela,Andreas | (dr)
Frank Eberle Septet
Scarlet Sunrise | Satin Doll Productions | SDP 1041-1 CD
Peter Fulda Trio With Céline Rudolph
Silent Dances | Jazz 4 Ever Records:Jazz Network | J4E 4731

Rainer Tempel Quintet
Blick In Die Welt | Edition Musikat | EDM 038

Gander,Andrew | (dr)
Grace Knight With Orchestra
Come In Spinner | Intuition Records | INT 3052-2
Vince Jones Group
Future Girl | Intuition Records | INT 3109-2
Here's To The Miracles | Intuition Records | INT 3198-2
Vince Jones Quartet
One Day Spent | Intuition Records | INT 3087-2
Vince Jones With Orchestra
Come In Spinner | Intuition Records | INT 3052-2

Ganley,Allan | (dr)
Great British Jazz Band
The Great British Jazz Band:Jubilee | Candid | CCD 79720
Hans Koller Nonet
Exclusiv | MPS | 9813440
The Great British Jazz Band
A British Jazz Odyssey | Candid | CCD 79740
Warren Vaché Quintet
The First Sampler | Nagel-Heyer | NHR SP 5
Warren Vaché Quintet With Special Guest Allan Vaché
Jazz Im Amerikahaus,Vol.2 | Nagel-Heyer | CD 012

Gannon,Jimmy | (b)
Buddy Rich And His Orchestra
Big Swing Face | Pacific Jazz | 837989-2
Buddy Rich Big Band
The New One! | Pacific Jazz | 494507-2

Gansch,Hans | (tp)
Hans Theessink Group
Crazy Moon | Minor Music | 801052

Gansch,Thomas | (tp)
Lee Konitz With The Ed Partyka Jazz Orchestra
Dreams And Realities | Laika Records | 35101642

Gant,Frank | (dr)
Ahmad Jamal Trio
The Awakening | Impulse(MCA) | IMP 12262
Monty Alexander Sextet
Three Originals:Love And Sunshine/Estade/Cobilimbo | MPS | 523526-2
Red Garland Trio
The Nearness Of You | Original Jazz Classics | OJCCD 1003-2(JLP 962)
Yusef Lateef Sextet
The Art Of Saxophone | Laserlight | 24652

Garay,Minino | (percvoc)
Dee Dee Bridgewater With Band
This Is New | Verve | 016884-2
Dee Dee Bridgewater Sings Kurt Weill | EmArCy | 9809601
Laurent De Wilde Sextet
Time Change | Warner | 8573-84315-2

Garbarek,Jan | (fl,cl,ts,xyl,b-sax,thumb-p,ss)
Agnes Buen Garnas-Jan Garbarek
Rosensfole-Medieval Songs From Norway | ECM | 1402(839293-2)
Art Lande-Jan Garbarek
Red Lanta | ECM | 1038(829383-2)
Bill Connors Quartet
Of Mist And Melting | ECM | 1120(847324-2)
Charlie Haden Trio
Magico | ECM | 1151(823474-2)
Folk Songs | ECM | 1170(827705-2)
David Darling Group
Cycles | ECM | 1219
Eberhard Weber Group
Chorus | ECM | 1288(823844-2)
Egberto Gismonti Group
Sol Do Meio Dia | ECM | 1116(829117-2)
Gary Peacock Quartet
Voice From The Past-Paradigm | ECM | 1210(517768-2)
Guamba | ECM | 1352
Gary Peacock-Jan Garbarek
December Poems | ECM | 1119
Jan Garbarek
All Those Born With Wings | ECM | 1324(831394-2)
Jan Garbarek Group
Photo With Blue Skie, White Clouds, Wires, Windows And A Red Roof | ECM | 1135 (843168-2)
It's OK To Listen To The Gray Voice | ECM | 1294(825406-2)
Legend Of The Seven Dreams | ECM | 1381(837344-2)
I Took Up The Runes | ECM | 1419(843850-2)
Twelve Moons | ECM | 1500(519500-2)
Visible World | ECM | 1585(529086-2)
Rites | ECM | 1685/86(559006-2)
Jan Garbarek Quartet
Places | ECM | 1118(829195-2)
Paths, Prints | ECM | 1223(829377-2)
Wayfarer | ECM | 1259(811968-2)
Jan Garbarek Quintet
Sart | ECM | 1015(839305-2)
Jan Garbarek Trio
Triptychon | ECM | 1029(847321-2)
Eventyr | ECM | 1200
Madar | ECM | 1515(519075-2)
Jan Garbarek With Ustad Fateh Ali Khan & Musicians From Pakistan
Ragas And Sagas | ECM | 1442(511263-2)
Jan Garbarek/Miroslav Vitous/Peter Erskine
Star | ECM | 1444(849649-2)
Jan Garbarek-Bobo Stenson Quartet
Witchi-Tai-To | ECM | 1041(833330-2)
Dansere | ECM | 1075(829193-2)
Jan Garbarek-Kjell Johnsen Duo
Aftenland | ECM | 1169(839304-2)
Jan Garbarek-Ralph Towner
Dis | ECM | 1093(827408-2)
Jan Garbarek-Ralph Towner Group
Dis | ECM | 1093(827408-2)
Keith Jarreett/Jan Garbarek With Strings
Luminessence | ECM | 1049(839307-2)
Keith Jarrett Quartet
Belonging | ECM | 1050(829115-2)
My Song | ECM | 1115(821406-2)
Nude Ants | ECM | 1171/72(829119-2)
Personal Mountains | ECM | 1382(837361-2)
Keith Jarrett Trio With Strings
Arbour Zena | ECM | 1070(825592-2)
Miroslav Vitous Group
Universal Syncopations | ECM | 1863(038506-2)
Miroslav Vitous/Jan Garbarek
Atmos | ECM | 1475(513373-2)
Paul Giger Trio
Alpstein | ECM | 1426(847940-2)
Ralph Towner Quartet
Solstice | ECM | 1060(825458-2)
Shankar Trio
Vision | ECM | 1261(811969-2)
Shankar/Garbarek/Hussain/Gurtu
Song For Everyone | ECM | 1286(823795-2)
Terje Rypdal Sextet
Terje Rypdal | ECM | 1016(527645-2)
Zakir Hussain Group
Making Music | ECM | 1349

Garberg,Mats | (flts)
Tim Hagans With Norrbotten Big Band
Future Miles | ACT | 9235-2

Garcera,Juanjo | (dr)
Daniel Flors Group
When Least Expected | Fresh Sound Records | FSNT 080 CD

Garcia,Albert Sanz | (p)
European Jazz Youth Orchestra
Swinging Europe 1 | dacapo | DCCD 9449
Swinging Europe 2 | dacapo | DCCD 9450

Garcia,Amadeo Dedeu | (vocperc)
Conjunto Clave Y Guaguanco
Dejala En La Puntica | TipToe | TIP-888829 2

Garcia,Dick | (g)
George Shearing And His Quintet
The Swingin's Mutual | Capitol | 799190-2
George Shearing Quintet
Verve Jazz Masters 57:George Shearing | Verve | 529900-2
Nancy Wilson With George Shearing And His Quintet
The Swingin's Mutual | Capitol | 799190-2

Garcia,Guim | (as)
Alguimia
Alguimia 'U' | Fresh Sound Records | FSNT 023 CD
Alguimia:Standards | Fresh Sound Records | FSNT 049 CD
Alguimia Dos | Fresh Sound Records | FSNT 050 CD

Garcia,Hungaria 'Carmelo' | (cowbell,timbalesdr)
Jazz Crusaders
Chile Con Soul | Pacific Jazz | 590957-2
Joe Henderson And His Orchestra
Joe Henderson:The Milestone Years | Milestone | 8MCD 4413-2

Garcia,Juan | (b)
Herbie Mann And His Orchestra
The Best Of Herbie Mann | Atlantic | 7567-81369-2

Garcia,Luis | (cond)
Conexion Latina
Calorcito | Enja | ENJ-4072 2

Garcia,Philippe | (drmegaphone)
Erik Truffaz Quartet
Mantis | Blue Note | 535101-2
Erik Truffaz Quartet Quintet
Mantis | Blue Note | 535101-2
Gäel Horellou-David Sauzay Quintet
Gäel Horellou Versus David Sauzay | Fresh Sound Records | FSNT 068 CD
Laurent De Wilde Sextet
Time Change | Warner | 8573-84315-2

Garcia,Rob | (dr)
Woody Allen And His New Orleans Jazz Band
Wild Man Blues | RCA | 2663353-2

Garcia,Russell | (arr,condvib)
Anita O'Day With The Russ Garcia Orchestra
Verve Jazz Masters 49:Anita O'Day | Verve | 527653-2
Blossom Dearie With The Russ Garcia Orchestra
Verve Jazz Masters 51:Blossom Dearie | Verve | 529906-2
Bud Shank And Trombones
Cool Fool | Fresh Sound Records | FSR CD 507
Buddy Childers With The Russ Garcia Strings
Artistry In Jazz | Candid | CCD 79735
Ella Fitzgerald And Louis Armstrong With The Russell Garcia Orchestra
Ella Fitzgerald-First Lady Of Song | Verve | 517898-2
Verve Jazz Masters 24:Ella Fitzgerald & Louis Armstrong | Verve | 521851-2
Ella Fitzgerald With Frank De Vol And His Orchestra
Get Happy! | Verve | 523321-2
Ella Fitzgerald With Russell Garcia And His Orchestra
Verve Jazz Masters 6:Ella Fitzgerald | Verve | 519822-2
Ella Fitzgerald With The Marty Paich Orchestra
Get Happy! | Verve | 523321-2
Hans Koller Nonet
Exclusiv | MPS | 9813440
Julie London With Russ Garcia And His Orchestra
About The Blues/London By Night | Capitol | 535208-2
Louis Armstrong And Ella Fitzgerald With Russell Garcia's Orchestra
The Complete Ella Fitzgerald And Louis Armstrong On Verve | Verve | 537284-2
The Best Of Ella Fitzgerald And Louis Armstrong On Verve | Verve | 537909-2
Porgy And Bess | Verve | 827475-2
Louis Armstrong With The Russell Garcia Orchestra
Verve Jazz Masters 1:Louis Armstrong | Verve | 519818-2
The Silver Collection: Louis Armstrong | Verve | 823446-2
Margaret Whiting With Russel Garcia And His Orchestra
Margaret Whiting Sings The Jerome Kern Song Book | Verve | 559553-2
Mel Tormé With The Russell Garcia Orchestra
Swingin' On The Moon | Verve | 511385-2
NDR Big Band With Guests
50 Years Of NDR Big Band:Bravissimo II | ACT | 9259-2
Oscar Peterson Trio With The Russell Garcia Orchestra
Verve Jazz Masters 16:Oscar Peterson | Verve | 516320-2
Roy Eldridge With The Russell Garcia Orchestra
The Complete Verve Roy Eldridge Studio Sessions | Verve | 9861278
Stan Getz With Orchestra
Stan Getz Highlights | Verve | 847430-2

Garcia,Silva Amaro | (voc)
Conjunto Clave Y Guaguanco
Dejala En La Puntica | TipToe | TIP-888829 2

Garcia,Xavier | (keyboards,programming,sampling)
Heiner Goebbels Group
Ou Bien Le Debarquement Desastreux | ECM | 1552
Pata Music Meets Arfi
News Of Roi Ubu | Pata Musik | PATA 10 CD

Garcia-Fons,Renaud | (5-string-b,perc,hand-clapping)
Gianluigi Trovesi Nonet
Round About A Midsummer's Dream | Enja | ENJ-9384 2
Jean-Louis Matinier Quartet
Confluences | Enja | ENJ-9454 2
Michael Riessler And The Ensemble 13
Momentum Mobile | Enja | ENJ-9003 2
Michael Riessler Group
Heloise | Wergo | WER 8008-2
Tentations D'Abélard | Wergo | WER 8009-2
Michel Godard Ensemble
Castel Del Monte | Enja | ENJ-9362 2
Nguyen Le Trio
Nguyen Le:3 Trios | ACT | 9245-2
Bakida | ACT | 9275-2
Nguyen Le Trio With Guests
Bakida | ACT | 9275-2
Renaud Garcia-Fons
Légendes | Enja | ENJ-9314 2
Navigatore | Enja | ENJ-9418 2
Entremundo | Enja | ENJ-9464 2
Renaud Garcia-Fons & Jean-Louis Matinier
Fuera | Enja | ENJ-9364 2
Renaud Garcia-Fons Group
Oriental Bass | Enja | ENJ-9334 2
Navigatore | Enja | ENJ-9418 2
Entremundo | Enja | ENJ-9464 2
Renaud Garcia-Fons Quartet
Alboreá | Enja | ENJ-9057 2

Garden,Claude | (harm)
Alain Goraguer Orchestra
Jazz In Paris:Jazz & Cinéma Vol.1 | EmArCy | 548318-2 PMS

Gardiner,Ronnie | (dr)
Lisa Ekdahl With The Peter Nordahl Trio
When Did You Leave Heaven | RCA | 2143175-2
Back To Earth | RCA | 2161463-2

Gardner,Alonzo | (b,el-bg)
Cold Sweat
Cold Sweat Plays J.B. | JMT Edition | 919025-2

Gardner,Billy | (orgp)
George Braith Quartet
So Blue So Funky-Heroes Of The Hammond | Blue Note | 796563-2

Gardner,Derrick | (tpfl-h)
Craig Bailey Band
A New Journey | Candid | CCD 79725

Gardner,Earl | (fl-htp)
Andy Bey Group
Tuesdays In Chinatown | Minor Music | 801099
Dave Holland Big Band
What Goes Around | ECM | 1777(014002-2)
McCoy Tyner Big Band
The Best Of McCoy Tyner Big Band | Dreyfus Jazz Line | FDM 37012-2
Mingus Big Band
Tonight At Noon...Three Or Four Shades Of Love | Dreyfus Jazz Line | FDM 36633-2
Tom Harrell Orchestra
Time's Mirror | RCA | 2663524-2
Zoot Sims With Orchestra
Passion Flower | Original Jazz Classics | OJCCD 939-2(2312120)

Gardner,Eric | (dr)
Peter Malick Group feat. Norah Jones
New York City | Koch Records | 238678-2

Gardner,Jack | (p)
Harry James And His Orchestra
The Legends Of Swing | Laserlight | 24659

Gardonyi,Laszlo | (pp-solo)
Benni Chaves-Laszlo Gardony
Human Bass | Laika Records | 35101042

Gareis,Benedikt | (bscl)
Ralph Schweizer Big Band
DAY Dream | Chaos | CACD 8177
Sax Mal Anders
Kontraste | Chaos | CACD 8185

Gargano,Tom | (dr)
Bix And His Rhythm Jugglers
Jazz:The Essential Collection Vol.2 | IN+OUT Records | 78012-2

Gariepy,Frank | (dr)
Oscar Peterson Trio
This Is Oscar Peterson | RCA | 2663990-2

Garisto,Frank | (dr)
June Christy With The Johnny Guarnieri Quintet
June Christy And The Johnny Guarnieri Quintet (1949) | Jazz Unlimited | JUCD 2084

Garland,Ed | (b)
Kid Ory's Creole Jazz Band
This Kid's The Greatest! | Good Time Jazz | GTCD 12045-2

Garland,Joe | (bs,cl,ts,arr,reedssax)
Jelly Roll Morton And His Orchestra
Planet Jazz:Jelly Roll Morton | Planet Jazz | 2152060-2
Jazz:The Essential Collection Vol.1 | IN+OUT Records | 78011-2
Louis Armstrong And His Orchestra
Best Of The Complete RCA Victor Recordings | RCA | 2663636-2
Louis Armstrong:A 100th Birthday Celebration | RCA | 2663694-2
Louis Armstrong:Swing That Music | Laserlight | 36056
Jazz:The Essential Collection Vol.2 | IN+OUT Records | 78012-2
Louis Armstrong:C'est Si Bon | Dreyfus Jazz Line | FDM 36730-2
Swing Legends:Louis Armstrong | Nimbus Records | NI 2012

Garland,Kent | (dance,vocpow-wow-dr)
Gunther Schuller With The WDR Radio Orchestra & Rememberance Band
Witchi Tia To, The Music Of Jim Pepper | Tutu Records | 888204-2*

Garland,Red | (p,celestep-solo)
Art Pepper Quartet
Art Pepper Meets The Rhythm Section | Original Jazz Classics | OJC20 338-2
The Way It Is | Original Jazz Classics | OJCCD 389-2
The Jazz Giants Play Cole Porter:Night And Day | Prestige | PCD 24203-2
Charlie Parker Quartet
Charlie Parker At Storyville | Blue Note | 785108-2
Coleman Hawkins With The Red Garland Trio
Coleman Hawkins With The Red Garland Trio | Original Jazz Classics | OJCCD 418-2(SV 2001)
Eddie Lockjaw Davis With The Red Garland Trio
Prestige Moodsville Vol.1 | Original Jazz Classics | OJCCD 360-2(MV 1)
John Coltrane All Stars
The Believer | Original Jazz Classics | OJCCD 876-2(P 7292)
Stardust | Original Jazz Classics | OJCCD 920-2(P 7268)
John Coltrane Quartet
John Coltrane-The Prestige Recordings | Prestige | 16 PCD 4405-2
Coltrane | Original Jazz Classics | OJC20 020-2
Soultrane | Original Jazz Classics | OJC20 021-2
Lush Life | Original Jazz Classics | OJC20 131-2
Bahia | Original Jazz Classics | OJCCD 415-2
Stardust | Original Jazz Classics | OJCCD 920-2(P 7268)
The Jazz Giants Play Sammy Cahn:It's Magic | Prestige | PCD 24226-2
The Prestige Legacy Vol.1:The High Priests | Prestige | PCD 24251-2
John Coltrane Quintet
John Coltrane-The Prestige Recordings | Prestige | 16 PCD 4405-2
Black Pearls | Original Jazz Classics | OJC 352(P 7316)
The Last Trane | Original Jazz Classics | OJC 394(P 7378)
Lush Life | Original Jazz Classics | OJC20 131-2
Standard Coltrane | Original Jazz Classics | OJCCD 246-2
Bahia | Original Jazz Classics | OJCCD 415-2
The Believer | Original Jazz Classics | OJCCD 876-2(P 7292)
Stardust | Original Jazz Classics | OJCCD 920-2(P 7268)
The Jazz Giants Play Harold Arlen:Blues In The Night | Prestige | PCD 24201-2
The Jazz Giants Play Rodgers & Hammerstein:My Favorite Things | Prestige | PCD 24223-2
John Coltrane Sextet
John Coltrane-The Prestige Recordings | Prestige | 16 PCD 4405-2
Coltrane | Original Jazz Classics | OJC20 020-2
John Coltrane With The Red Garland Trio
John Coltrane-The Prestige Recordings | Prestige | 16 PCD 4405-2
The Last Trane | Original Jazz Classics | OJC 394(P 7378)
Settin' The Pace | Original Jazz Classics | OJC20 078-2
Dig It | Original Jazz Classics | OJC20 392-2(PR 7229)
Traning In | Original Jazz Classics | OJCCD 189-2
Kenny Burrell Quintet
John Coltrane-The Prestige Recordings | Prestige | 16 PCD 4405-2
Miles Davis New Quintet
Workin',Steamin',Cookin',Relaxin' With The Miles Davis Quintet | Original Jazz Classics | OJCCD 8805-2
Miles Davis Quartet
The Musings Of Miles | Original Jazz Classics | OJCCD 004-2
Miles Davis Quintet
Circle In The Round | CBS | 467898-2
This Is Jazz:Miles Davis Plays Ballads | CBS | CK 65038
Cookin' With The Miles Davis Quintet | Original Jazz Classics | OJC20 128-2
Relaxin' | Original Jazz Classics | OJC20 190-2
Miles Davis And The Modern Jazz Giants | Original Jazz Classics | OJC20 347-2(P 7150)
Steamin' | Original Jazz Classics | OJC20 391-2
The Jazz Giants Play Rodgers & Hammerstein:My Favorite Things | Prestige | PCD 24223-2
The Jazz Giants Play Duke Ellington:Caravan | Prestige | PCD 24227-2
Relaxin' | Prestige | PRSA 7129-6
Prestige All Stars
John Coltrane-The Prestige Recordings | Prestige | 16 PCD 4405-2
Tenor Conclave | Original Jazz Classics | OJCCD 127-2
Red Garland
The Nearness Of You | Original Jazz Classics | OJCCD 1003-2(JLP 962)
Red Garland Quartet
Red Garland Revisited! | Original Jazz Classics | OJCCD 985-2(P 7658)
The Jazz Giants Play Rodgers & Hart:Blue Moon | Prestige | PCD 24205-2
Red Garland Quintet
John Coltrane-The Prestige Recordings | Prestige | 16 PCD 4405-2
All Mornin' Long | Original Jazz Classics | OJC20 293-2(P-7130)

Dig It | Original Jazz Classics | OJC20 392-2(PR 7229)
Red's Good Groove | Original Jazz Classics | OJCCD 1064-2(987)
Soul Junction | Original Jazz Classics | OJCCD 481-2
The Jazz Giants Play Duke Ellington:Caravan | Prestige | PCD 24227-2
Red Garland Quintet feat.John Coltrane
High Pressure | Original Jazz Classics | OJCCD 349-2(P 7209)
Red Garland Trio
A Garland Of Red | Original Jazz Classics | OJC 126(P 7064)
Red Garland's Piano | Original Jazz Classics | OJC20 073-2(P 7086)
Dig It | Original Jazz Classics | OJC20 392-2(PR 7229)
Groovy | Original Jazz Classics | OJCCD 061-2
The Nearness Of You | Original Jazz Classics | OJCCD 1003-2(JLP 962)
It's A Blue World | Original Jazz Classics | OJCCD 1028-2(P 7838)
Red In Bluesville | Original Jazz Classics | OJCCD 295-2
Prestige Moodsville Vol.1 | Original Jazz Classics | OJCCD 360-2(MV 1)
Can't See For Lookin' | Original Jazz Classics | OJCCD 918-2(P 7276)
Red Garland Revisited! | Original Jazz Classics | OJCCD 985-2(P 7658)
The Jazz Giants Play Harold Arlen:Blues In The Night | Prestige | PCD 24201-2
The Jazz Giants Play Harry Warren:Lullaby Of Broadway | Prestige | PCD 24204-2
The Jazz Giants Play Rodgers & Hammerstein:My Favorite Things | Prestige | PCD 24223-2
Stretching Out | Prestige | PRCD 24272-2
Red Garland Trio With Ray Barretto
Manteca | Original Jazz Classics | OJCCD 428-2(PR 7139)
Sonny Rollins Quartet
Tenor Madness | Original Jazz Classics | OJC20 124-2
Tenor Madness | Prestige | PRSA 7047-6
Sonny Rollins Quintet
John Coltrane-The Prestige Recordings | Prestige | 16 PCD 4405-2
Tenor Madness | Original Jazz Classics | OJC20 124-2
The Prestige Legacy Vol.2:Battles Of Saxes | Prestige | PCD 24252-2
Tenor Madness | Prestige | PRSA 7047-6
Taylor's Wailers
John Coltrane-The Prestige Recordings | Prestige | 16 PCD 4405-2
The New Miles Davis Quintet
Miles | Original Jazz Classics | OJC20 006-2(P 7014)

Garnas,Agnes Buen | (voc)
Jan Garbarek Group
Twelve Moons | ECM | 1500(519500-2)

Garner,Erroll | (celeste,p-solo,pharpsichord)
Don Byas Quartet
Don Byas:Laura | Dreyfus Jazz Line | FDM 36714-2
Erroll Garner
Planet Jazz:Jazz Piano | RCA | 2169655-2
Verve Jazz Masters 7:Erroll Garner | Verve | 518197-2
Erroll Garner:Trio | Dreyfus Jazz Line | FDM 36719-2
Erroll Garner Quartet
Verve Jazz Masters 7:Erroll Garner | Verve | 518197-2
Verve Jazz Masters 20:Introducing | Verve | 519853-2
Contrasts | Verve | 558077-2
Erroll Garner:Trio | Dreyfus Jazz Line | FDM 36719-2
Erroll Garner Trio
The Story Of Jazz Piano | Laserlight | 24653
Body & Soul | CBS | 467916-2
Contrasts | Verve | 558077-2
Erroll Garner:Trio | Dreyfus Jazz Line | FDM 36719-2

Garner,Linton | (arr,pceleste)
Dizzy Gillespie And His Orchestra
Planet Jazz:Dizzy Gillespie | Planet Jazz | 2152069-2

Garnett,Alvester | (dr)
Abbey Lincoln With Her Band
Who Used To Dance | Verve | 533559-2
Wholly Earth | Verve | 559538-2
Cyrus Chestnut Sextet
Earth Stories | Atlantic | 7567-82876-2
Cyrus Chestnut Trio
Earth Stories | Atlantic | 7567-82876-2

Garnett,Blind Leroy | (pp-solo)
Blind Leroy Garnett
Boogie Woogie | Laserlight | 24321

Garnett,Carlos Alfredo | (fl,ts,sax,ss,ukelele,vocbs)
Miles Davis Group
In Concert | CBS | C2K 65140
On The Corner | CBS | CK 63980
Pharoah Sanders Group
Black Unity | Impulse(MCA) | 951219-2

Garnov, |
Stan Kenton With The Danish Radio Big Band
Stan Kenton With The Danish Radio Big Band | Storyville | STCD 8340

Garrett,Donald Rafael | (b,b-cl,bs,cl,dr,nye,shakuhachi)
John Coltrane And His Orchestra
Kulu Se Mama | Impulse(MCA) | 543412-2

Garrett,Glenn | (sax,tsbs)
Buddy Childers Big Band
It's What Happening Now! | Candid | CCD 79749

Garrett,Harold | (b-tb,bar-horn,tubatb)
Woody Herman And His Orchestra
The Raven Speaks | Original Jazz Classics | OJCCD 663-2(F 9416)
Woody Herman And The New Thundering Herd
Woody Herman:Thundering Herd | Original Jazz Classics | OJCCD 841-2

Garrett,Kenny | (as,ts,as-solo,fl,saxss)
Al Jarreau With Band
Tenderness | i.e. Music | 557853-2
Bobby Hutcherson Group
Skyline | Verve | 559616-2
Dannie Richmond Quintet
Three Or Four Shades Of Dannie Richmond Quintet | Tutu Records | 888120-2*
Dreyfus All Stars
Dreyfus Night In Paris | Dreyfus Jazz Line | FDM 36652-2
Essence All Stars
Hot Jazz Bisquits | Hip Bop | HIBD 8801
Freddie Hubbard Quintet
Topsy | Enja | ENJ-7025 2
John Scofield Quintet
Works For Me | Verve | 549281-2
Kenny Garrett Quartet
KG Standard Of Language | Warner | 9362-48404-2
Lenny White Group
Present Tense | Hip Bop | HIBD 8004
Marcus Miller Group
The Sun Don't Lie | Dreyfus Jazz Line | FDM 36560-2
Tales | Dreyfus Jazz Line | FDM 36571-2
Live & More | Dreyfus Jazz Line | FDM 36585-2
Michael 'Patches' Stewart Group
Penetration | Hip Bop | HIBD 8018
Mike Clark-Paul Jackson Quartet
The Funk Stops Here | TipToe | TIP-888811 2
Miles Davis Group
Miles Davis Live From His Last Concert In Avignon | Laserlight | 24327
Amandla | Warner | 7599-25873-2
Miles Davis With Gil Evans Orchestra, The George Gruntz Concert Jazz Band And Guests
Miles & Quincy Live At Montreux | Warner | 9362-45221-2
Roy Haynes Quintet
Birds Of A Feather:A Tribute To Charlie Parker | Dreyfus Jazz Line | FDM 36625-2

Garrette,Duke | (tp)
(Little)Jimmy Scott With The Lionel Hampton Orchestra
Everybody's Somebody's Fool | Decca | 050669-2
Lionel Hampton And His Orchestra
Lionel Hampton:Flying Home | Dreyfus Jazz Line | FDM 36735-2
Lionel Hampton Orchestra
The Big Bands Vol.1:The Snader Telescriptions | Storyville | 4960043

Garrison,Arvin | (g)
Charlie Parker Septet
Charlie Parker:Now's The Time | Dreyfus Jazz Line | FDM 36724-2

Garrison,Jimmy | (b)
Alice Coltrane Quartet
A Monastic Trio | Impulse(MCA) | 951267-2
Alice Coltrane Trio
A Monastic Trio | Impulse(MCA) | 951267-2
Archie Shepp Orchestra
The Cry Of My People | Impulse(MCA) | 9861488
Benny Carter And His Orchestra
Further Definitions/Additions To Further Definotions | Impulse(MCA) | 951229-2
Cal Massey Sextet
The Jazz Life! | Candid | CCD 79019
Blues To Coltrane | Candid | CCD 79029
John Coltrane And His Orchestra
Kulu Se Mama | Impulse(MCA) | 543412-2
Ascension | Impulse(MCA) | 543413-2
Meditations | Impulse(MCA) | 951199-2
John Coltrane Group
The Olatunji Concert:The Last Live Recording | Impulse(MCA) | 589120-2
John Coltrane Quartet
Afro Blue Impressions | Pablo | 2PACD 2620101
Kulu Se Mama | Impulse(MCA) | 543412-2
Impressions | Impulse(MCA) | 543416-2
John Coltrane:Standards | Impulse(MCA) | 549914-2
Coltrane Spiritual | Impulse(MCA) | 589099-2
Ballads | Impulse(MCA) | 589548-2
Coltrane | Impulse(MCA) | 589567-2
A Love Supreme | Impulse(MCA) | 589596-2
A Love Supreme | Impulse(MCA) | 589945-2
John Coltrane-Live Trane:The European Tours | Pablo | 7PACD 4433-2
The Gentle Side Of John Coltrane | Impulse(MCA) | 951107-2
Sun Ship | Impulse(MCA) | 951166-2
Stellar Regions | Impulse(MCA) | 951169-2
Live At Birdland | Impulse(MCA) | 951198-2
Crescent | Impulse(MCA) | 951200-2
The Coltrane Quartet Plays | Impulse(MCA) | 951214-2
Living Space | Impulse(MCA) | 951246-2
John Coltrane:The Classic Quartet-Complete Impulse Studio Recordings | Impulse(MCA) | 951280-2
John Coltrane:The Complete 1961 Village Vanguard Recordings | Impulse(MCA) | 954322-2
Bye Bye Blackbird | Original Jazz Classics | OJC20 681-2(2308227)
The Paris Concert | Original Jazz Classics | OJC20 781-2(2308217)
John Coltrane Quartet With Eric Dolphy
John Coltrane:The Complete 1961 Village Vanguard Recordings | Impulse(MCA) | 954322-2
John Coltrane Quartet With Johnny Hartman
The Gentle Side Of John Coltrane | Impulse(MCA) | 951107-2
John Coltrane Quintet
Impressions | Impulse(MCA) | 543416-2
John Coltrane:Standards | Impulse(MCA) | 549914-2
Live At The Village Vanguard Again | Impulse(MCA) | 951213-2
John Coltrane Quintet With Eric Dolphy
John Coltrane:The Complete 1961 Village Vanguard Recordings | Impulse(MCA) | 954322-2
The Other Village Vanguard Tapes | Impulse(MCA) | MCD 04137
John Coltrane Septet With Eric Dolphy
John Coltrane:The Complete 1961 Village Vanguard Recordings | Impulse(MCA) | 954322-2
The Other Village Vanguard Tapes | Impulse(MCA) | MCD 04137
John Coltrane Sextet
Impressions | Impulse(MCA) | 543416-2
A Love Supreme | Impulse(MCA) | 589945-2
Live At The Village Vanguard:The Master Takes | Impulse(MCA) | 951251-2
John Coltrane:The Complete 1961 Village Vanguard Recordings | Impulse(MCA) | 954322-2
John Coltrane Trio
Coltrane | Impulse(MCA) | 589567-2
Live At The Village Vanguard:The Master Takes | Impulse(MCA) | 951251-2
John Coltrane:The Classic Quartet-Complete Impulse Studio Recordings | Impulse(MCA) | 951280-2
John Coltrane:The Complete 1961 Village Vanguard Recordings | Impulse(MCA) | 954322-2
John Coltrane-Duke Ellington Quartet
Duke Ellington & John Coltrane | Impulse(MCA) | 951166-2
Johnny Hartman With The John Coltrane Quartet
John Coltrane:Standards | Impulse(MCA) | 549914-2
John Coltrane And Johnny Hartman | Impulse(MCA) | 951157-2
McCoy Tyner Trio
McCoy Tyner Plays Ellington | Impulse(MCA) | 951216-2
McCoy Tyner Trio + Latin Percussion
McCoy Tyner Plays Ellington | Impulse(MCA) | 951216-2
Ornette Coleman Quartet
Beauty Is A Rare Thing:Ornette Coleman-The Complete Atlantic Recordings | Atlantic | 8122-71410-2
Ornette On Tenor | Atlantic | 8122-71455-2
Sonny Rollins Quartet
East Broadway Run Down | Impulse(MCA) | 951161-2
Sonny Rollins Trio
East Broadway Run Down | Impulse(MCA) | 951161-2

Garrison,Matthew | (b-g,fretles-b-gel-b)
John McLaughlin Group
The Heart Of Things | Verve | 539153-2
Live In Paris | Verve | 543536-2

Garros,Christian | (drperc)
Alain Goraguer Orchestra
Jazz In Paris:Jazz & Cinéma Vol.1 | EmArCy | 548318-2 PMS
Jazz In Paris | EmArCy | 548793-2
Andre Hodeir And His Jazz Group De Paris
Jazz In Paris:Le Jazz Groupe De Paris Joue André Hodeir | EmArCy | 548792-2
Benny Golson Quintet
Nemmy Golson And The Philadelphians | Blue Note | 494104-2
Golden Gate Quartet
Americans Swinging In Paris:Golden Gate Quartet | EMI Records | 539659-2
From Spriritual To Swing Vol.2 | EMI Records | 780573-2
Spirituals To Swing 1955-69 | EMI Records | 791569-2
Jack Dieval And The J.A.C.E. All-Stars
Jazz In Paris:Jack Diéval-Jazz Aux Champs Elysées | EmArCy | 018419-2
Jacques Loussier Trio
Play Bach No.1 | Decca | 157561-2
Play Bach No.2 | Decca | 157562-2
Play Bach No.3 | Decca | 157892-2
Play Bach No.4 | Decca | 157893-2
Play Bach No.5 | Decca | 159194-2
Play Bach Aux Champs-Élysées | Decca | 159203-2
The Best Of Play Bach | Philips | 824664-2
Les Double Six
Les Double Six | RCA | 2164314-2
Lucky Thompson And His Orchestra
Americans Swinging In Paris:Lucky Thompson | EMI Records | 539651-2
Lucky Thompson's Modern Jazz Group Quartet
Jazz In Paris:Lucky Thompson-Modern Jazz Group | EmArCy | 159823-2 PMS

Garsia,Ignazio | (p)
Orchestra Jazz Siciliana
Orchestra Jazz Siciliana Plays The Music Of Carla Bley | Watt | XtraWatt/4

Garson,Mike | (grand-p-solo,keyboards,p,synth)
Free Flight
Jazzrock-Anthology Vol.3:Fusion | Zounds | CD 27100555

Garst,Herman | (b)
Blossom Dearie Trio
Jazz In Paris:Blossom Dearie-The Pianist/Les Blue Stars | EmArCy | 064784-2

Gärtner,Chancy | (sax)
Jazz Bomberos
Naranja | Green House Music | CD 1003(Maxi)

Gartz,Tomas Mera | (dr,perc,kidi,tsv)
Beng Berger Band
Bitter Funeral Beer | ECM | 1179

Garvey,Winterton | (stringsv)
A Band Of Friends
Wynton Marsalis Quartet With Strings | CBS | CK 68921
Grover Washington Jr. Orchestra
Inside Moves | Elektra | 7559-60318-2

Garvin,Carl | (tp)
Jack Teagarden And His Orchestra
Jazz:The Essential Collection Vol.3 | IN+OUT Records | 78013-2

Garvin,Clint | (cl,as,reedssax)

Garvin,Tom | (keyboardsp)
Diane Schuur And Her Band
The Best Of Diane Schuur | GRP | GRP 98882

Garzone,George | (cl,sax,ss,ts,mouth-percvoice)
Ingrid Jensen Sextet
Vernal Fields | Enja | ENJ-9013 2
Joe Lovano Nonet
On This Day At The Vanguard | Blue Note | 590950-2

Gasama,Samson | (african-dr)
Pili-Pili
Stolen Moments | JA & RO | JARO 4159-2
Jazzy World | JA & RO | JARO 4200-2

Gasca,Luis | (tpfl-h)
Joe Henderson And His Orchestra
Joe Henderson:The Milestone Years | Milestone | 8MCD 4413-2
Luis Gasca Group
Jazzin' Vol.2: The Music Of Stevie Wonder | Fantasy | FANCD 6088-2

Gascoyne,Geoff | (b)
Jamie Cullum Group
Pointless Nostalgic | Candid | CCD 79782

Gaskin,Leonard | (bld)
Al Smith With The King Curtis Quintet
Midnight Special | Original Blues Classics | OBCCD 583-2(BV 1013)
Billie Holiday And Her All Stars
Billie Holiday Story Vol.4:Lady Sings The Blues | Verve | 521429-2
Bud Freeman All Stars
The Bud Freeman All-Star Sessions | Prestige | PRCD 24286-2
Bud Freeman And His Summa Cum Laude Orchestra
Planet Jazz:Jack Teagarden | Planet Jazz | 2161236-2
Planet Jazz:Bud Freeman | Planet Jazz | 2161240-2
Don Byas Quartet
Don Byas:Laura | Dreyfus Jazz Line | FDM 36714-2
Eddie Condon And His Boys
The Very Best Of Dixieland Jazz | Verve | 535529-2
Lightnin' Hopkins
Going Away | Original Blues Classics | OBCCD 522-2(BV 1073)
Lightnin' Hopkins Trio
The Blues Of Lightnin' Hopkins | Original Blues Classics | OBCCD 532-2(BV 1019)
Lightnin' Hopkins Trio With Sonny Terry
Last Night Blues | Original Blues Classics | OBCCD 548-2(BV 1029)
Miles Davis Septet
Miles Davis And Horns | Original Jazz Classics | OJC20 053-2(P 7025)
St.Louis Jimmy Oden Group
Goin' Down Slow | Original Blues Classics | OBCCD 584-2(BV 1028)
Stan Getz Quintet
Stan Getz-The Complete Roost Sessions | EMI Records | 859622-2
Sunnyland Slim Band
Windy City Blues | Stax | SCD 8612-2
Willis Jackson Sextet
Gravy | Prestige | PCD 24254-2

Gaskin,Victor | (b)
Cannonball Adderley Quintet
Julian Cannonball Adderlry: Salle Pleyel/Olympia | Laserlight | 36126
Ballads | Blue Note | 537563-2
The Best Of Cannonball Adderley:The Capitol Years | Capitol | 795482-2
Mercy Mercy Mercy | Capitol | 829915-2
Dexter Gordon Quartet
Dexter Gordon Birthday Celebration | Fantasy | FANCD 6082-2
L.T.D. | Prestige | PCD 11018-2
XXL | Prestige | PCD 11033-2
Duke Ellington Quartet
Latin America Suite | Original Jazz Classics | OJC20 469-2
Duke Ellington Small Band
The Intimacy Of The Blues | Original Jazz Classics | OJCCD 624-2
Les McCann Quartet
Talkin' Verve:Les McCann | Verve | 557351-2
Les McCann Trio
Talkin' Verve:Les McCann | Verve | 557351-2
Nat Adderley Quintet
Joe Henderson:The Milestone Years | Milestone | 8MCD 4413-2
Nat Adderley Sextet
Joe Henderson:The Milestone Years | Milestone | 8MCD 4413-2

Gaslini,Giorgio | (cond,comp,p,anvilp-solo)
Italian Instabile Orchestra
Skies Of Europe | ECM | 1543

Gaspar,Jordi | (b)
Dave Liebman And The Lluis Vidal Trio
Dave Liebman And The Lluis Vidal Trio | Fresh Sound Records | FSNT 026 CD
Dave Liebman And The Lluis Vidal Trio With The Orquestra De Cambra Theatre Lliure
Dave Liebman And The Lluis Vidal Trio | Fresh Sound Records | FSNT 026 CD
José Luis Gámez Quartet
Colores | Fresh Sound Records | FSNT 028 CD
José Luis Gámez Quintet
Colores | Fresh Sound Records | FSNT 028 CD
José Luis Gámez Trio
Colores | Fresh Sound Records | FSNT 028 CD
Lluis Vidal Trio
Tren Nocturn | Fresh Sound Records | FSNT 003 CD
Milikituli | Fresh Sound Records | FSNT 009 CD
Orquestra De Cambra Teatre Lliure
Orquestra De Cambra Teatre Lliure and Lluis Vidal Trio feat.Dave Liebman | Fresh Sound Records | FSNT 027 CD
Orquestra De Cambra Teatre Lliure feat. Dave Liebman
Orquestra De Cambra Teatre Lliure and Lluis Vidal Trio feat.Dave Liebman | Fresh Sound Records | FSNT 027 CD

Gassama,Malando | (perc)
Al Jarreau With Band
Al Jarreau In London | i.e. Music | 557849-2

Gassama,Samson | (bougadaboudjembe)
International Commission For The Prevention Of Musical Border Control,The
The International Commission For The Prevention Of Musical Border Control | VeraBra Records | CDVBR 2093-2

Gasselin,Jaques | (v)
Ella Fitzgerald With The Billy May Orchestra
The Best Of The Song Books:The Ballads | Verve | 521867-2
Ella Fitzgerald Sings The Harold Arlen Song Book | Verve | 589108-2
Ella Fitzgerald With The Nelson Riddle Orchestra
The Best Of The Song Books:The Ballads | Verve | 521867-2
Oh Lady Be Good:The Best Of The Gershwin Songbook | Verve | 529581-2

Love Songs:The Best Of The Song Books | Verve | 531762-2
Frank Sinatra With The Count Basie Orchestra
It Might As Well Be Spring | Reprise | 7599-27027-2
Phineas Newborn Jr. With Dennis Farnon And His Orchestra
While My Lady Sleeps | RCA | 2185157-2

Gassman,Bert | (bassoonoboe)
Ella Fitzgerald With The Frank DeVol Orchestra
Get Happy! | Verve | 523321-2

Gaste,Louis | (g)
Django Reinhardt Trio
Django/Django In Rome 1949-1050 | BGO Records | BGOCD 366
Django Reinhardt:Echoes Of France | Dreyfus Jazz Line | FDM 36726-2

Gatchell,John | (brass,tpfl-h)
Earl Klugh Group
Late Night Guitar | Blue Note | 498573-2

Gates,Pamela | (v)
Stephane Grappelli With The Michel Legrand Orchestra
Grapelli Story | Verve | 515807-2

Gateway |
Gateway
In The Moment | ECM | 1574(529346-2)

Gätjen,Achim | (as)
Swim Two Birds
Sweet Reliet | Laika Records | 35101182
No Regrets | Laika Records | 35101342

Gätjens,Manfred | (tb)
Stan Getz With The Kurt Edelhagen Orchestra
Stan Getz In Europe | Laserlight | 24657

Gatti,Angel Poncho | (p,el-porg)
Gerry Mulligan With Astor Piazzolla And His Orchestra
Tango Nuevo | Atlantic | 2292-42145-2

Gattiker,David | (cello)
Creative Works Orchestra
Willisau And More Live | Creative Works Records | CW CD 1020-2

Gatto,Roberto | (dr,digital-drdr-computer)
Enrico Rava Quintet
Easy Living | ECM | 1760(9812050)
Paolo Fresu Angel Quartet
Metamorfosi | RCA | 2165202-2
Paolo Fresu Quartet
Angel | RCA | 2155864-2
Kind Of Porgy & Bess | RCA | 21951952
Paolo Fresu Quintet
Kind Of Porgy & Bess | RCA | 21951952
Paolo Fresu Sextet
Kind Of Porgy & Bess | RCA | 21951952

Gauchel,Walter | (fl,alto-fl,cl,ts,ssreeds)
Berlin Contemporary Jazz Orchestra
Berlin Contemporary Jazz Orchestra | ECM | 1409
Harry Allen And Randy Sandke Meets The RIAS Big Band Berlin
The Music Of The Trumpet Kings | Nagel-Heyer | CD 037
Nana Mouskouri With The Berlin Radio Big Band
Nana Swings | Mercury | 074394-2
Till Brönner Quintet
My Secret Love | Minor Music | 801051
Till Brönner Quintet With Annette Lowman
My Secret Love | Minor Music | 801051

Gaudry,Michel | (b)
Gérard Badini Quartet
Jazz In Paris:Gérard Badini-The Swing Machine | EmArCy | 018417-2
Les Double Six
Les Double Six | RCA | 2164314-2
Lionel Hampton All Stars
Jazz In Paris:Lionel Hampton-Ring Dem Bells | EmArCy | 159825-2 PMS
Sonny Criss Quartet
Jazz In Paris:Saxophones Á Saint-Germain Des Prés | EmArCy | 014060-2

Gaumont,Dominique | (g)
Miles Davis Group
Dark Magus | CBS | C2K 65137

Gaup,Ingor Antte Ailu | (voice)
Jan Garbarek Group
I Took Up The Runes | ECM | 1419(843850-2)

Gauthier,Jeff | (v,violavoice)
Alex Cline Group
The Lamp And The Star | ECM | 1372

Gavillet,Christian | (b-cl,bssax)
Miles Davis With Gil Evans Orchestra, The George Gruntz Concert Jazz Band And Guests
Miles & Quincy Live At Montreux | Warner | 9362-45221-2

Gawlick,Stefan | (tympany)
Uri Caine With The Concerto Köln
Concerto Köln | Winter&Winter | 910086-2

Gaye,Sol | (dr)
Terry Gibbs Octet
Jewis Melodies In Jazztime | Mercury | 589673-2

Gayles,Joe | (ts)
Dizzy Gillespie And His Orchestra
Dizzy Gillespie:Pleyel Jazz Concert 1948 + Max Roach Quintet 1949 | Vogue | 21409412
Planet Jazz:Dizzy Gillespie | Planet Jazz | 2152069-2
Planet Jazz:Bebop | RCA | 2169650-2
Ella Fitzgerald With The Dizzy Gillespie Orchestra
Ella Fitzgerald:Mr.Paganini | Dreyfus Jazz Line | FDM 36741-2
Ella Fitzgerald With The Hank Jones Trio
Ella Fitzgerald:Mr.Paganini | Dreyfus Jazz Line | FDM 36741-2

Gaylor,Hal | (b)
Benny Goodman And His All Star Sextet
Verve Jazz Masters 33:Benny Goodman | Verve | 844410-2
Benny Goodman Quintet
Verve Jazz Masters 33:Benny Goodman | Verve | 844410-2
Chico Hamilton Quintet
The Original Ellington Suite | Pacific Jazz | 524567-2
Newport Jazz Festival 1958,July 3rd-6th Vol.2:Mulligan The Main Man | Phontastic | NCD 8814
The Trio
The Trio:Rediscovered | String Jazz | SJRCD 1007

Gaylord,Charles | (vvoc)
Paul Whiteman And His Orchestra
Planet Jazz:Jazz Trumpet | Planet Jazz | 2169654-2

Gaynair,Wilton | (fl,tsss)
Horace Parlan Quartet
Jazz Portraits | EGO | 95080
Wilton Gaynair Quintet
Alpharian | Konnex Records | KCD 5032

Gayton,Clark | (tbb-tb)
Dave Stryker Octet
Blue To The Bone III | Steeplechase | SCCD 31524
Marty Ehrlich Group
The Long View | Enja | ENJ-9452 2

Gazarov,David | (pp-solo)
David Gazarov Trio
Let's Have A Merry Christmas With The David Gazarov Trio! | Organic Music | ORGM 9712
Jenny Evans And Her Quintet
Shiny Stockings | Enja | ENJ-9317 2
Shiny Stockings | ESM Records | ESM 9305
Torsten Goods Group
Manhattan Walls | Jardis Records | JRCD 20139

Gebhard,Jörg | (dr)
Bernd Konrad With Erwin Lehn und sein Südfunk Orchester Stuttgart
Wen Die Götter Lieben | Creative Works Records | CW CD 1010-1

Gebhard,Thomas | (sax)
Marcus Sukiennik Big Band
A Night In Tunisia Suite(7 Variationen über Dizzy Gillespie's 'A Night In Tunisia') | Jazz Haus Musik | ohne Nummer

Gebhardt,Jörg | (drperc)
Bill Ramsey With Orchestra
Gettin' Back To Swing | Bear Family Records | BCD 15813 AH
Horst Jankowski Orchestra With Voices
Jankowskeynotes | MPS | 9814806
SWR Big Band
Jazz In Concert | Hänssler Classics | CD 93.004

Gee,Eddie | (dr)
Johnny 'Hammond' Smith Quintet
Discovery:Grover Washington Jr.-The First Recordings | Prestige | PCD 11020-2

Gee,Matthew | (tbvoc)
Duke Ellington And His Award Winners
Greatest Hits | CBS | 462959-2
Matthew Gee All-Stars
Jazz By Gee! | Original Jazz Classics | OJCCD 1884-2(RLP 221)

Gee,Rosco | (b,el-b,keyboardsb-g)
Freddy Studer Orchestra
Seven Songs | VeraBra Records | CDVBR 2056-2

Gehl,Stephen | (v)
Art Pepper Quintet With Strings
Art Pepper:The Complete Galaxy Recordings | Galaxy | 16GCD 1016-2
Winter Moon | Original Jazz Classics | OJC20 677-2(GXY 5140)

Geier,Gerd | (electronics)
Franz Koglmann Quintet
Opium | Between The Lines | btl 011(Efa 10181-2)

Geiger,Helmut | (v)
Terje Rypdal With Strings
When Ever I Seem To Be Far Away | ECM | 1045

Geiger,Thomi | (cl,ssts)
Brigitte Dietrich-Joe Haider Jazz Orchestra
Consequences | JHM Records | JHM 3624

Geisler,Chris | (p)
Vesna Skorija Band
Niceland | Satin Doll Productions | SDP 1037-1 CD

Geisse,Gunnar | (el-g,g,bjvoc)
Marty Cook Quintet
Marty Cook Trio/Quintet | Tutu Records | 888210-2*
Marty Cook Trio
Marty Cook Trio/Quintet | Tutu Records | 888210-2*

Geisselbrecht,Peter | (p)
Balance
Some Other Tapes | Fish Music | FM 009/10 CD

Geisser,Heinz | (dr)
Q4 Orchester Project
Yavapai | Creative Works Records | CW CD 1028-2
Rissi-Mazzola-Geisser
Fuego | Creative Works Records | CW CD 1029-2

Geissler,Werner | (tp)
Spree City Stompers
Deutsches Jazz Fesival 1954/1955 | Bear Family Records | BCD 15430

Geissman,Grant | (g)
Diane Schuur And Her Band
The Best Of Diane Schuur | GRP | GRP 98882

Geist,Judy | (celloviola)
Helen Merrill With Orchestra
Casa Forte | EmArCy | 558848-2

Geldard,Bill | (b-tbtb)
Barbara Thompson Group
Heavenly Bodies | VeraBra Records | CDVBR 2015-2

Gelinas,Gabe | (asbs)
Glenn Miller And His Orchestra
Planet Jazz:Glenn Miller | Planet Jazz | 2152056-2
Candelight Miller | RCA | 2668716-2

Geller,Harry | (tp)
Artie Shaw And His Orchestra
Planet JazzArtie Shaw | Planet Jazz | 2152057-2
The Legends Of Swing | Laserlight | 24659
Benny Goodman And His Orchestra
Planet Jazz:Benny Goodman | Planet Jazz | 2152054-2
Planet Jazz Sampler | Planet Jazz | 2152326-2
Planet Jazz:Swing | Planet Jazz | 2169651-2

Geller,Herb | (alto-fl,ss,as,arr,ts,cl,engl-h,fl)
All Star Live Jam Session
Brownie-The Complete EmArCy Recordings Of Clifford Brown | EmArCy | 838306-2
Anita O'Day With The Buddy Bregman Orchestra
Pick Yourself Up | Verve | 517329-2
Art Pepper Plus Eleven
Art Pepper + Eleven | Contemporary | CSA 7568-6
Modern Jazz Classics | Original Jazz Classics | OJC20 341-2
Barney Kessel And His Orchestra
Barney Kessel Plays Carmen | Original Jazz Classics | OJC 269(C 7563)
Birdland Dream Band
Birdland Dream Band | RCA | 2663873-2
Buddy Bregman And His Orchestra
Swinging Kicks | Verve | 559514-2
Chet Baker Quintet/NDR Big Band/Radio Orchestra Hannover
Straight From The Heart-The Last Concert Vol.2 | Enja | ENJ-6020 2
The Last Concert Vol.I+II | Enja | ENJ-6074 22
Chet Baker Septet
The Best Of Chet Baker Plays | Pacific Jazz | 797161-2
Chet Baker With The NDR-Bigband
NDR Big Band-Bravissimo | ACT | 9232-2
My Favourite Songs: The Last Great Concert Vol.1 | Enja | ENJ-5097 2
The Last Concert Vol.I+II | Enja | ENJ-6074 22
Chet Baker-The Legacy Vol.1 | Enja | ENJ-9021 2
Clifford Brown All Stars
Verve Jazz Masters 44:Clifford Brown and Max Roach | Verve | 528109-2
Brownie-The Complete EmArCy Recordings Of Clifford Brown | EmArCy | 838306-2
Clifford Brown All Stars With Dinah Washington
Verve Jazz Masters 40:Dinah Washington | Verve | 522055-2
Dinah Washington And Her Band
Verve Jazz Masters 40:Dinah Washington | Verve | 522055-2
Ella Fitzgerald With The Buddy Bregman Orchestra
Ella Fitzgerald-First Lady Of Song | Verve | 517898-2
Love Songs:The Best Of The Song Books | Verve | 531762-2
Ella Fitzgerald Sings The Cole Porter Songbook | Verve | 537257-2
Heinz Sauer Quartet With The NDR Big Band
NDR Big Band-Bravissimo | ACT | 9232-2
Herb Geller Quartet
Herb Geller Plays The Al Cohn Songbook | Hep | CD 2066
To Benny & Johnny | Hep | CD 2084
Herb Geller-Brian Kellock
Hollywood Portraits | Hep | CD 2078
Herb Geller-Chuck Berghofer
To Benny & Johnny | Hep | CD 2084
Herb Geller-Hod O'Brien
To Benny & Johnny | Hep | CD 2084
Joe Pass With The NDR Big Band
NDR Big Band-Bravissimo | ACT | 9232-2
Joe Pass With The NDR Big Band And Radio Philharmonie Hannover
Joe Pass In Hamburg | ACT | 9100-2
Johnny Griffin With The NDR Big Band
NDR Big Band-Bravissimo | ACT | 9232-2
Klaus Weiss Orchestra
Live At The Domicile | ATM Records | ATM 3805-AH
Maynard Ferguson And His Orchestra
Verve Jazz Masters 52:Maynard Ferguson | Verve | 529905-2
Maynard Ferguson Band
Verve Jazz Masters 52:Maynard Ferguson | Verve | 529905-2
NDR Big Band
NDR Big Band-Bravissimo | ACT | 9232-2
NDR Big Band With Guests
50 Years Of NDR Big Band:Bravissimo II | ACT | 9259-2

Geller,Irv | (v)
Milt Jackson And His Orchestra
Reverence And Compassion | Reprise | 9362-45204-2

Geller,J. | (v)
Milt Jackson With Strings
To Bags...With Love:Memorial Album | Pablo | 2310967-2

Geller,Lorraine | (p)
Maynard Ferguson And His Orchestra
Verve Jazz Masters 52:Maynard Ferguson | Verve | 529905-2
Maynard Ferguson Band
Verve Jazz Masters 52:Maynard Ferguson | Verve | 529905-2
Miles Davis And The Lighthouse All Stars
At Last! | Original Jazz Classics | OJCCD 480-2

Geller,Lorraine or Claude Williamson | (p)
Howard Rumsey's Lighthouse All-Stars
Sunday Jazz A La Lighthouse Vol.2 | Original Jazz Classics | OJCCD 972-2(S 2501)

Geller,Maximilian | (as,flsax)
Maximilian Geller Group
Maximilian Geller Goes Bossa | Edition Collage | EC 496-2
Maimilian Geller Goes Bossa Encore | Edition Collage | EC 505-2
Maximilian Geller Quartet feat. Melanie Bong
Smile | Edition Collage | EC 461-2
Maimilian Geller Goes Bossa Encore | Edition Collage | EC 505-2
Vocal Moments | Take Twelve On CD | TT 008-2
Maximilian Geller Quartet feat. Sabina Sciubba
Maimilian Geller Goes Bossa Encore | Edition Collage | EC 505-2
Maximilian Geller Quartet feat. Susan Tobocman
Maimilian Geller Goes Bossa Encore | Edition Collage | EC 505-2

Gellers,Alvin | (p)
Tito Puente Orchestra
Planet Jazz:Tito Puente | Planet Jazz | 2165369-2

Gellert,Joachim | (tb,accordeon,tuba,b-tb)
Norbert Stein Pata Orchester
Ritual Life | Pata Musik | PATA 5(JHM 50) CD

Gellev,Vesselin | (v)
Absolute Ensemble
African Symphony | Enja | ENJ-9410 2
Melissa Walker And Her Band
I Saw The Sky | Enja | ENJ-9409 2
Paquito D'Rivera Group With The Absolute Ensemble
Habanera | Enja | ENJ-9395 2

Genetay,Claude | (cello)
Bengt-Arne Wallin Orchestra
The Birth+Rebirth Of Swedish Folk Jazz | ACT | 9254-2

Genrich,Ax | (bj,g,el-gvoice)
Ax Genrich Group
Psychedelic Guitar | ATM Records | ATM 3809-AH
Wave Cut | ATM Records | ATM 3813-AH
Guru Guru
Guru Guru/Uli Trepte | ATM Records | ATM 3815-AH

Genta | (perc)
United Future Organizatio
United Future Organization | Talkin' Loud | 518166-2

Gentry,Charles | (bs)
Ella Fitzgerald With The Billy May Orchestra
Love Songs:The Best Of The Song Books | Verve | 531762-2
Peggy Lee With The Benny Goodman Orchestra
Peggy Lee & Benny Goodman:The Complete Recordings 1941-1947 | CBS | C2K 65686

Gentry,Chuck | (as,bass-sax,b-cl,bs,cl,conta-b-cl)
Anita O'Day With The Billy May Orchestra
Verve Jazz Masters 49:Anita O'Day | Verve | 527653-2
Artie Shaw And His Orchestra
Planet Jazz:Jazz Trumpet | Planet Jazz | 2169654-2
Barney Kessel And His Orchestra
Barney Kessel Plays Carmen | Original Jazz Classics | OJC 269(C 7563)
Benny Carter And His Orchestra
Aspects | Capitol | 852677-2
Billy Eckstine With The Billy May Orchestra
Once More With Feeling | Roulette | 581862-2
Ella Fitzgerald And Louis Armstrong With Dave Barbour And His Orchestra
Ella Fitzgerald:Mr.Paganini | Dreyfus Jazz Line | FDM 36741-2
Ella Fitzgerald With Frank De Vol And His Orchestra
Get Happy! | Verve | 523321-2
Ella Fitzgerald With Paul Weston And His Orchestra
Love Songs:The Best Of The Song Books | Verve | 531762-2
Ella Fitzgerald Sings The Irving Berlin Song Book | Verve | 543830-2
Ella Fitzgerald With The Billy May Orchestra
The Best Of The Song Books:The Ballads | Verve | 521867-2
Ella Fitzgerald Sings The Harold Arlen Song Book | Verve | 589108-2
Ella Fitzgerald With The Buddy Bregman Orchestra
Ella Fitzgerald-First Lady Of Song | Verve | 517898-2
The Best Of The Song Books:The Ballads | Verve | 521867-2
Love Songs:The Best Of The Song Books | Verve | 531762-2
Ella Fitzgerald Sings The Cole Porter Songbook | Verve | 537257-2
Ella Fitzgerald Sings The Rodgers And Hart Song Book | Verve | 537258-2
Ella Fitzgerald With The Marty Paich Orchestra
Get Happy! | Verve | 523321-2
Ella Fitzgerald With The Paul Weston Orchestra
Get Happy! | Verve | 523321-2
June Christy With The Pete Rugolo Orchestra
Something Cool(The Complete Mono & Stereo Versions) | Capitol | 534069-2
Louis Armstrong And Gary Crosby With Sonny Burke's Orchestra
Louis Armstrong-My Greatest Songs | MCA | MCD 18347
Louis Armstrong And His All Stars With Sonny Burke's Orchestra
Ambassador Louis Armstrong Vol.17:Moments To Remember(1952-1956) | Ambassador | CLA 1917
Louis Armstrong With The Hal Mooney Orchestra
Ambassador Louis Armstrong Vol.17:Moments To Remember(1952-1956) | Ambassador | CLA 1917
Mel Tormé With The Billy May Orchestra
Mel Tormé Goes South Of The Border With Billy May | Verve | 589517-2
Nat King Cole With The Billy May Orchestra
Nat King Cole:For Sentimental Reasons | Dreyfus Jazz Line | FDM 36740-2
Peggy Lee With The Benny Goodman Orchestra
Peggy Lee & Benny Goodman:The Complete Recordings 1941-1947 | CBS | C2K 65686
Pete Rugolo And His Orchestra
Thriller/Richard Diamon(Original Jazz Scores From 2 Classics TV Series) | Fresh Sound Records | FSCD 2015
Red Norvo And His Orchestra
Planet Jazz:Female Jazz Vocalists | Planet Jazz | 2169656-2
Van Alexander Orchestra
Home Of Happy Feet/Swing! Staged For Sound! | Capitol | 535211-2

Genus,James | (b,6-string-b,el-bb-g)
Barbara Dennerlein Group
Outhipped | Verve | 547503-2
Christian Scheuber Quartet
Clara's Smile | double moon | DMCHR 71025
Christian Scheuber Quintet
Clara's Smile | double moon | DMCHR 71025
Cornelius Claudio Kreusch Group
Scoop | ACT | 9255-2
Dave Douglas Group
Soul On Soul | RCA | 2663603-2
The Infinite | RCA | 2663918-2
Dave Weckl Group
Hard-Wired | GRP | GRP 97602
Jean-Michel Pilc Quartet
Cardinal Points | Dreyfus Jazz Line | FDM 36649-2
Jean-Michel Pilc Quintet
Cardinal Points | Dreyfus Jazz Line | FDM 36649-2
John McLaughlin Group

The Promise | Verve | 529828-2
Lenny White Group
Present Tense | Hip Bop | HIBD 8004
Makoto Ozone Group
Treasure | Verve | 021906-2
Makoto Ozone Trio
Pandora | Verve | 549629-2
Michael Brecker Quintet
Two Blocks From The Edge | Impulse(MCA) | 951261-2
Michael 'Patches' Stewart Group
Penetration | Hip Bop | HIBD 8018
Nat Adderley Quintet
The Old Country | Enja | ENJ-7027 2
The Brecker Brothers
Return Of The Brecker Brothers | GRP | GRP 96842
Out Of The Loop | GRP | GRP 97842
The Sidewalks Of New York
Tin Pan Alley:The Sidewalks Of New York | Winter&Winter | 910038-2
Uri Caine Trio
Blue Wail | Winter&Winter | 910034-2

Georgantones,Jimmy | (g)
Les McCann Group
Talkin' Verve:Les McCann | Verve | 557351-2
Les McCann Orchestra
Talkin' Verve:Les McCann | Verve | 557351-2

George,Karl | (tp)
Lionel Hampton And His Orchestra
Lionel Hampton:Flying Home | Dreyfus Jazz Line | FDM 36735-2

George,Marvin | (dr)
Stan Kenton And His Orchestra
Stan Kenton-The Formative Years | Decca | 589489-2

George,Russell | (b)
Pee Wee Russell Quartet
Ask Me Now! | Impulse(MCA) | 755742-2

George,Steve | (voc)
Al Jarreau With Band
Al Jarreau In London | i.e. Music | 557849-2

Georges,Dupor | (tb)
Craig Bailey Band
A New Journey | Candid | CCD 79725

Georgiadis,J. | (v)
Dee Dee Bridgewater With Orchestra
Dear Ella | Verve | 539102-2

Gerard,Fred | (tp)
Lucky Thompson With The Gerard Pochonet All-Stars
Planet Jazz:Jazz Saxophone | Planet Jazz | 2169653-2
Lucky Thompson's Modern Jazz Group Tentet
Jazz In Paris:Lucky Thompson-Modern Jazz Group | EmArCy | 159823-2 PMS
Raymond Fol Big Band
Jazz In Paris:Raymond Fol-Les 4 Saisons | EmArCy | 548791-2

Gerards,Michael | (b)
Peter Materna Quartet
Full Moon Party | Village | VILCD 1021-2

Gerasimov,Anatole | (ts)
Duke Ellington Orchestra
Continuum | Fantasy | FCD 24765-2

Geremia,Renato | (fl,cl,ts,pv)
Ekkehard Jost Trio
Some Other Tapes | Fish Music | FM 009/10 CD
Italian Instabile Orchestra
Skies Of Europe | ECM | 1543

Gerhardt,Bill | (psynth)
Jed Levy Quartet
Round And Round | Steeplechase | SCCD 31529

Gerhardt,Niels | (tb)
The Danish Radio Jazz Orchestra
This Train:The Danish Radio Jazz Orchestra Plays The Music Of Ray Pitts | dacapo | DCCD 9428
The Orchestra
New Skies | dacapo | DCCD 9463

Gering,Guido | (ts)
Bigband Der Musikschule Der Stadt Brühl Mit Gastsolisten
Pangäa | Indigo-Records | 1004 CD

Germain,Anne | (voc)
Swingle Singers
Jazz Sebastian Bach | Philips | 542552-2
Swingle Singers Going Baroque | Philips | 546746-2
Swingle Singers Singing Mozart | Philips | 548538-2

Germain,Claude | (voc)
Les Double Six
Les Double Six | RCA | 2164314-2
Swingle Singers
Jazz Sebastian Bach | Philips | 542552-2
Swingle Singers Going Baroque | Philips | 546746-2
Swingle Singers Singing Mozart | Philips | 548538-2
Swingling Telemann | Philips | 586735-2
Swingle Singers Getting Romantic | Philips | 586736-2

Germain,José | (voc)
Modern Jazz Quartet And The Swingle Singers
MJQ 40 | Atlantic | 7567-82330-2
Swingle Singers
Jazz Sebastian Bach Vol.2 | Philips | 542553-2
Swingle Singers Singing Mozart | Philips | 548538-2
Swingling Telemann | Philips | 586735-2
Swingle Singers Getting Romantic | Philips | 586736-2

German Jazz Masters,The |
The German Jazz Masters
Old Friends | ACT | 9278-2

Germanson,Rick | (pfender-rhodes)
Wayne Escoffery Quintet
Intuition | Nagel-Heyer | CD 2038

Gernas,Agnes Buen | (voice)
Agnes Buen Garnas-Jan Garbarek
Rosensfole-Medieval Songs From Norway | ECM | 1402(839293-2)

Gernhuber,Klaus | (b)
Helmut Brandt Combo
Deutsches Jazz Fesival 1954/1955 | Bear Family Records | BCD 15430

Gerrard,Ben | (v)
Harry Carney And His Orchestra With Strings
Music For Loving:Ben Webster With Strings | Verve | 527774-2

Gerrits,Angela | (viola)
Couch Ensemble
Winnetou | Jazz 'n' Arts Records | JNA 1503

Gersh,Squire | (b)
Louis Armstrong And His All Stars With The Sy Oliver Orchestra
Ambassador Louis Armstrong Vol.17:Moments To Remember(1952-1956) | Ambassador | CLA 1917
Louis Armstrong And His Orchestra
I Love Jazz | Verve | 543747-2

Gersham,Paul | (v)
Coleman Hawkins With Billy Byers And His Orchestra
The Hawk In Hi-Fi | RCA | 2663842-2
Grover Washington Jr. Orchestra
Inside Moves | Elektra | 7559-60318-2
Louis Armstrong And His Friends
Planet Jazz:Louis Armstrong | Planet Jazz | 2152052-2
Planet Jazz Sampler | Planet Jazz | 2152326-2
Louis Armstrong And His Friends | Bluebird | 2663961-2
Wes Montgomery Quartet With The Claus Ogerman Orchestra
Tequila | Verve | 547769-2
Wes Montgomery Quintet With The Claus Ogerman Orchestra
Talkin' Jazz:Roots Of Acid Jazz | Verve | 529580-2
Tequila | Verve | 547769-2
Wes Montgomery Trio With The Claus Ogerman Orchestra
Tequila | Verve | 547769-2
Wes Montgomery With The Claus Ogerman Orchestra
Verve Jazz Masters 14:Wes Montgomery | Verve | 519826-2

Gershman,Manny | (as,clsax)
Frank Sinatra With Orchestra
Planet Jazz:Frank Sinatra & Tommy Dorsey | Planet Jazz | 2152067-2
Lena Horne With The Lennie Hayton Orchestra
Planet Jazz:Lena Horne | Planet Jazz | 2165373-2
Tommy Dorsey And His Orchestra
Planet Jazz:Frank Sinatra & Tommy Dorsey | Planet Jazz | 2152067-2
Planet Jazz Sampler | Planet Jazz | 2152326-2
Frank Sinatra And The Tommy Dorsey Orchestra | RCA | 2668701-2

Gershman,Nathan | (cello,stringsviola)
Chico Hamilton Orchestra
With Strings Attached/The Three Faces Of Chico | Warner | 9362-47874-2
Chico Hamilton Quintet
The Original Ellington Suite | Pacific Jazz | 524567-2
With Strings Attached/The Three Faces Of Chico | Warner | 9362-47874-2
Newport Jazz Festival 1958,July 3rd-6th Vol.2:Mulligan The Main Man | Phontastic | NCD 8814
Chico Hamilton Quintet With Strings
With Strings Attached/The Three Faces Of Chico | Warner | 9362-47874-2

Gershman,Paul | (stringsv)
Coleman Hawkins With Billy Byers And His Orchestra
The Hawk In Hi-Fi | RCA | 2663842-2
Freddie Hubbard With Orchestra
This Is Jazz:Freddie Hubbard | CBS | CK 65041
Grover Washington Jr. Orchestra
Jazzrock-Anthology Vol.3:Fusion | Zounds | CD 27100555
Les McCann Group
Another Beginning | Atlantic | 7567-80790-2
Milt Jackson And His Orchestra
Sunflower | CTI | ZK 65131
Paul Desmond Quartet With The Don Sebesby Orchestra
From The Hot Afternoon | Verve | 543487-2
Phil Woods Quartet With Orchestra & Strings
Round Trip | Verve | 559804-2
Stan Getz With The Richard Evans Orchestra
What The World Needs Now-Stan Getz Plays Bacharach And David | Verve | 557450-2
Wes Montgomery Quintet With The Claus Ogerman Orchestra
The Antonio Carlos Jobim Songbook | Verve | 525472-2
Wes Montgomery With The Don Sebesky Orchestra
Verve Jazz Masters 14:Wes Montgomery | Verve | 519826-2
Talkin' Jazz:Roots Of Acid Jazz | Verve | 529580-2
Bumpin' | Verve | 539062-2

Gertken,Klaus | (keyboards)
Human Factor
Forbidden City | Nabel Records:Jazz Network | CD 4635

Gertze,Johnny | (b)
Sathima Bea Benjamin Group
A Morning In Paris | Enja | ENJ-9309 2

Gervais,Jacques | (dr)
Bud Powell Quartet
Bud Powell Paris Sessions | Pablo | PACD 2310972-2
Bud Powell Trio
Bebop | Pablo | PACD 2310978-2
Johnny Griffin With The Bud Powell Trio
Bebop | Pablo | PACD 2310978-2

Gessinger,Nils | (el-p,org,synth,pvoice)
Albert Mangelsdorff With The NDR Big Band
NDR Big Band-Bravissimo | ACT | 9232-2

Geßner,Volker | (keyboards)
Jamenco
Conversations | Trick Music | TM 9202 CD

Getz,Jane | (p)
Charles Mingus Quartet
Right Now | Original Jazz Classics | OJCCD 237-2
Charles Mingus Quintet
Right Now | Original Jazz Classics | OJCCD 237-2

Getz,Stan | (ss,ts,bs,digital delay,echoplex)
(Little)Jimmy Scott With The Billy Taylor Orchestra
Everybody's Somebody's Fool | Decca | 050669-2
Abbey Lincoln With The Stan Getz Quartet
You Gotta Pay The Band | Verve | 511110-2
A Life In Jazz:A Musical Biography | Verve | 535119-2
Abbey Lincoln With The Stan Getz Quintet
You Gotta Pay The Band | Verve | 511110-2
Al Haig Sextet
Al Haig Trio And Sextets | Original Jazz Classics | OJCCD 1929-2(SPL 1118)
Astrud Gilberto With The New Stan Getz Quartet
Verve Jazz Masters 9:Astrud Gilberto | Verve | 519824-2
Bob Brookmeyer Quintet
Sony Jazz Collection:Stan Getz | CBS | 488623-2
Bob Brookmeyer Sextet
Late Night Sax | CBS | 487798-2
Buddy Bregman And His Orchestra
Swinging Kicks | Verve | 559514-2
Chet Baker-Stan Getz Quintet
The Stockholm Concerts | Verve | 537555-2
Stan Meets Chet | Verve | 837436-2
Diane Schuur With Orchestra
The Best Of Diane Schuur | GRP | GRP 98882
Diane Schuur With The Dave Grusin Orchestra
The Best Of Diane Schuur | GRP | GRP 98882
Dizzy Gillespie All Stars
Verve Jazz Masters 25:Stan Getz & Dizzy Gillespie | Verve | 521852-2
Dizzy Gillespie Septet
Stan Getz Highlights:The Best Of The Verve Years Vol.2 | Verve | 517330-2
Verve Jazz Masters 25:Stan Getz & Dizzy Gillespie | Verve | 521852-2
Stan Getz Highlights | Verve | 847430-2
Dizzy Gillespie-Stan Getz Sextet
Verve Jazz Masters 25:Stan Getz & Dizzy Gillespie | Verve | 521852-2
Diz And Getz | Verve | 549749-2
Ultimate Stan Getz selected by Joe Henderson | Verve | 557532-2
Stan Getz Highlights | Verve | 847430-2
Ella Fitzgerald And Count Basie With The JATP All Stars
Bluella:Ella Fitzgerald Sings The Blues | Pablo | 2310960-2
Ella Fitzgerald With Frank De Vol And His Orchestra
Like Someone In Love | Verve | 511524-2
Ella Fitzgerald With The Frank DeVol Orchestra
A Life In Jazz:A Musical Biography | Verve | 535119-2
Stan Getz Highlights | Verve | 847430-2
Ella Fitzgerald With The Frank DeVol Orchestra feat. Stan Getz
Ella Fitzgerald-First Lady Of Song | Verve | 517898-2
Ella Fitzgerald With The JATP All Stars
Ella Fitzgerald-First Lady Of Song | Verve | 517898-2
For The Love Of Ella Fitzgerald | Verve | 841765-2
For Musicians Only
Ultimate Stan Getz selected by Joe Henderson | Verve | 557532-2
Ultimate Dizzy Gillespie | Verve | 557535-2
For Musicians Only | Verve | 837435-2
Getz-Gilberto Quintet
Verve Jazz Masters 13:Antonio Carlos Jobim | Verve | 516409-2
Stan Getz Highlights:The Best Of The Verve Years Vol.2 | Verve | 517330-2
Getz/Gilberto No.2 | Verve | 519800-2
Verve Jazz Masters 20:Introducing | Verve | 519853-2
Getz/Gilberto | Polydor | 521414-2
A Life In Jazz:A Musical Biography | Verve | 535119-2
Herb Ellis Quintet
Stan Getz Highlights:The Best Of The Verve Years Vol.2 | Verve | 517330-2
Nothing But The Blues | Verve | 521674-2
J.J.Johnson & Stan Getz With The Oscar Peterson Quartet
Stan Getz Highlights:The Best Of The Verve Years Vol.2 | Verve | 517330-2
A Life In Jazz:A Musical Biography | Verve | 535119-2
Stan Getz Highlights | Verve | 847430-2
JATP All Stars
Stan Getz Highlights:The Best Of The Verve Years Vol.2 | Verve | 517330-2
Nothing But The Blues | Verve | 521674-2
Verve Jazz Masters 25:Stan Getz & Dizzy Gillespie | Verve | 521852-2
Welcome To Jazz At The Philharmonic | Fantasy | FANCD 6081-2
Jimmy Raney Quintet
Early Stan | Original Jazz Classics | OJCCD 654-2(P 7255)
Johnny Smith Quintet
Moonlight In Vermont | Roulette | 596593-2
Johnny Smith-Stan Getz Quintet
Stan Getz-The Complete Roost Sessions | EMI Records | 859622-2
Miles Davis Sextet
Miles Davis:Milestones | Dreyfus Jazz Line | FDM 36731-2
Roy Eldridge Sextet
The Complete Verve Roy Eldridge Studio Sessions | Verve | 9861278
Stan Getz And His Four Brothers
The Brothers | Original Jazz Classics | OJCCD 008-2
The Prestige Legacy Vol.2:Battles Of Saxes | Prestige | PCD 24252-2
Stan Getz And J.J. Johnson With The Oscar Peterson Quartet
Ultimate Stan Getz selected by Joe Henderson | Verve | 557532-2
Stan Getz And The Oscar Peterson Trio
The Silver Collection: Stan Getz And The Oscar Peterson Trio | Verve | 827826-2
Stan Getz And The Swedish All Stars
Stan Getz Highlights:The Best Of The Verve Years Vol.2 | Verve | 517330-2
Stan Getz Highlights | Verve | 847430-2
Stan Getz Five Brothers Bop Tenor Sax Stars
Stan Getz:Imagination | Dreyfus Jazz Line | FDM 36733-2
Stan Getz Group
Verve Jazz Masters 53:Stan Getz-Bossa Nova | Verve | 529904-2
Stan Getz Group Feat.Laurindo Almeida
Stan Getz With Guest Artist Laurindo Almeida | Verve | 823149-2
Stan Getz New Quartet
Stan Getz Highlights:The Best Of The Verve Years Vol.2 | Verve | 517330-2
A Life In Jazz:A Musical Biography | Verve | 535119-2
Stan Getz Quartet
The Art Of Saxophone | Laserlight | 24652
Stan Getz In Europe | Laserlight | 24657
Sony Jazz Collection:Stan Getz | CBS | 488623-2
Stan Getz Highlights:The Best Of The Verve Years Vol.2 | Verve | 517330-2
Getz/Gilberto No.2 | Verve | 519800-2
Verve Jazz Masters 8:Stan Getz | Verve | 519823-2
Verve Jazz Masters 53:Stan Getz-Bossa Nova | Verve | 529904-2
A Life In Jazz:A Musical Biography | Verve | 535119-2
Best Of The West Coast Sessions | Verve | 537084-2
Award Winner | Verve | 543320-2
Stan Getz And The 'Cool' Sounds | Verve | 547317-2
The Steamer | Verve | 547771-2
Ultimate Stan Getz selected by Joe Henderson | Verve | 557532-2
West Coast Jazz | Verve | 557549-2
Stan Getz Cafe Montmartre | EmArCy | 586755-2
Stan Getz Plays | Verve | 833535-2
Anniversary ! | EmArCy | 838769-2
Serenity | EmArCy | 838770-2
Stan Getz Highlights | Verve | 847430-2
Stan Getz-The Complete Roost Sessions | EMI Records | 859622-2
The Lost Sessions | Verve | 9801098
Bossas And Ballads:The Lost Sessions | Verve | 9901098
Stan Getz:Imagination | Dreyfus Jazz Line | FDM 36733-2
Stan Getz Quartets | Original Jazz Classics | OJC20 121-2(P 7002)
The Jazz Giants Play Rodgers & Hart:Blue Moon | Prestige | PCD 24205-2
Live At Montmartre(CD=Stan's Party) | Steeplechase | SCCD 37021/22
Stan Getz Quintet
Stan Getz In Europe | Laserlight | 24657
Sony Jazz Collection:Stan Getz | CBS | 488623-2
Stan Getz Highlights:The Best Of The Verve Years Vol.2 | Verve | 517330-2
Verve Jazz Masters 8:Stan Getz | Verve | 519823-2
Verve Jazz Masters 53:Stan Getz-Bossa Nova | Verve | 529904-2
A Life In Jazz:A Musical Biography | Verve | 535119-2
Best Of The West Coast Sessions | Verve | 537084-2
Stan Getz And The 'Cool' Sounds | Verve | 547317-2
Ultimate Stan Getz selected by Joe Henderson | Verve | 557532-2
West Coast Jazz | Verve | 557549-2
Stan Getz Plays | Verve | 833535-2
Stan Getz Highlights | Verve | 847430-2
Stan Getz-The Complete Roost Sessions | EMI Records | 859622-2
Stan Getz Quintet Feat. Astrud Gilberto
Verve Jazz Masters 8:Stan Getz | Verve | 519823-2
Verve Jazz Masters 53:Stan Getz-Bossa Nova | Verve | 529904-2
Getz/Gilberto | Verve | 589595-2 SACD
Stan Getz Sextet
Verve Jazz Masters 8:Stan Getz | Verve | 519823-2
Billy Highstreet Samba | EmArCy | 838771-2
Stan Getz With Ib Glindemann And His Orchestra
Stan Getz In Europe | Laserlight | 24657
Stan Getz With Orchestra
Apasionado | A&M Records | 395297-2
Stan Getz Highlights | Verve | 847430-2
Stan Getz With Orchestra And Voices
Stan Getz Highlights | Verve | 847430-2
Stan Getz With Strings And Voices
Reflections | Verve | 523322-2
Stan Getz With The Bill Evans Trio
Verve Jazz Masters 5:Bill Evans | Verve | 519821-2
The Complete Bill Evans On Verve | Verve | 527953-2
Ultimate Bill Evans selected by Herbie Hancock | Verve | 557536-2
But Beautiful | Milestone | MCD 9249-2
Stan Getz With The Claus Ogerman Orchestra
What The World Needs Now-Stan Getz Plays Bacharach And David | Verve | 557450-2
Stan Getz With The Danish Radio Big Band
Stan Getz In Europe | Laserlight | 24657
Stan Getz With The Eddie Sauter Orchestra
Verve Jazz Masters 8:Stan Getz | Verve | 519823-2
Stan Getz Plays The Music Of Mickey One | Verve | 531232-2
A Life In Jazz:A Musical Biography | Verve | 535119-2
Ultimate Stan Getz selected by Joe Henderson | Verve | 557532-2
Stan Getz Highlights | Verve | 847430-2
Stan Getz With The Gary McFarland Orchestra
Stan Getz Highlights:The Best Of The Verve Years Vol.2 | Verve | 517330-2
Verve Jazz Masters 53:Stan Getz-Bossa Nova | Verve | 529904-2
Big Band Bossa Nova | Verve | 825771-2 PMS
Stan Getz Highlights | Verve | 847430-2
Stan Getz With The Kurt Edelhagen Orchestra
Stan Getz In Europe | Laserlight | 24657
Stan Getz With The Michel Legrand Orchestra
Stan Getz Highlights | Verve | 847430-2
Stan Getz With The Oscar Peterson Quartet
Verve Jazz Masters 8:Stan Getz | Verve | 519823-2
Ultimate Stan Getz selected by Joe Henderson | Verve | 557532-2
Stan Getz With The Oscar Peterson Trio
Stan Getz Highlights | Verve | 847430-2
Stan Getz With The Richard Evans Orchestra
What The World Needs Now-Stan Getz Plays Bacharach And David | Verve | 557450-2
Stan Getz-Bill Evans Quartet
Stan Getz Highlights:The Best Of The Verve Years Vol.2 | Verve | 517330-2
Stan Getz & Bill Evans | Verve | 833802-2

INTERPRETENVERZEICHNIS

Stan Getz Highlights | Verve | 847430-2
Stan Getz-Bob Brookmeyer Quintet
Stan Getz Highlights:The Best Of The Verve Years Vol.2 | Verve | 517330-2
A Life In Jazz:A Musical Biography | Verve | 535119-2
Stan Getz-Cal Tjader Sextet
Stan Getz With Cal Tjader | Original Jazz Classics | OJC20 275-2(F 3266)
Stan Getz-Charlie Byrd Sextet
Jazz Samba | Verve | 521413-2
The Antonio Carlos Jobim Songbook | Verve | 525472-2
Verve Jazz Masters 53:Stan Getz-Bossa Nova | Verve | 529904-2
Ultimate Stan Getz selected by Joe Henderson | Verve | 557532-2
Stan Getz Highlights | Verve | 847430-2
Stan Getz-Gerry Mulligan Quintet
Stan Getz Highlights | Verve | 847430-2
Getz Meets Mulligan In Hi-Fi | Verve | 849392-2
Stan Getz-Jimmy Rowles
Sony Jazz Collection:Stan Getz | CBS | 488623-2
Stan Getz-Joao Gilberto Orchestra
Sony Jazz Collection:Stan Getz | CBS | 488623-2
Stan Getz-Joao Gilberto Quintet
The Antonio Carlos Jobim Songbook | Verve | 525472-2
Stan Getz Highlights | Verve | 847430-2
Stan Getz-Kenny Barron
People Time | EmArCy | 510134-2
A Life In Jazz:A Musical Biography | Verve | 535119-2
Stan Getz Cafe Montmartre | EmArCy | 586755-2
Stan Getz-Laurindo Almeida Orchestra
Stan Getz Highlights:The Best Of The Verve Years Vol.2 | Verve | 517330-2
Verve Jazz Masters 53:Stan Getz-Bossa Nova | Verve | 529904-2
Stan Getz Highlights | Verve | 847430-2
Stan Getz-Lionel Hampton Quintet
Stan Getz Highlights:The Best Of The Verve Years Vol.2 | Verve | 517330-2
Hamp And Getz | Verve | 831672-2
Stan Getz-Lionel Hampton Sextet
Hamp And Getz | Verve | 831672-2
Stan Getz-Luiz Bonfa Group
The Antonio Carlos Jobim Songbook | Verve | 525472-2
Stan Getz-Luiz Bonfa Orchestra
Verve Jazz Masters 13:Antonio Carlos Jobim | Verve | 516409-2
Jazz Samba Encore! | Verve | 823613-2
Stan Getz-Luiz Bonfa Quartet
Jazz Samba Encore! | Verve | 823613-2
Stan Getz-Luiz Bonfa Quintet
Jazz Samba Encore! | Verve | 823613-2
Terry Gibbs Septet
Early Stan | Original Jazz Classics | OJCCD 654-2(P 7255)
The Modern Jazz Society
A Concert Of Contemporary Music | Verve | 559827-2
The New Stan Getz Quartet
Getz Au Go Go | Verve | 821725-2
The New Stan Getz Quartet Feat. Astrud Gilberto
Getz Au Go Go | Verve | 821725-2
The New Stan Getz Quintet Feat. Astrud Gilberto
Getz Au Go Go | Verve | 821725-2
Woody Herman And His Orchestra
The Legends Of Swing | Laserlight | 24659
Woody Herman:Four Brother | Dreyfus Jazz Line | FDM 36722-2
Woody Herman And The New Thundering Herd
Planet Jazz:Big Bands | Planet Jazz | 2169649-2
Woody Herman's Thundering Herd
Planet Jazz:Jazz Saxophone | Planet Jazz | 2169653-2

Getzoff,James | (v)
Ella Fitzgerald With The Nelson Riddle Orchestra
The Best Of The Song Books:The Ballads | Verve | 521867-2
Oh Lady Be Good:The Best Of The Gershwin Songbook | Verve | 529581-2
Love Songs:The Best Of The Song Books | Verve | 531762-2
Frank Sinatra With The Count Basie Orchestra
It Might As Well Be Spring | Reprise | 7599-27027-2
Hank Crawford Orchestra
Rhino Presents The Atlantic Jazz Gallery | Atlantic | 8122-71257-2

Gewelt,Terje | (bel-b)
Misha Alperin Group With John Surman
First Impression | ECM | 1664(557650-2)
Misha Alperin Quintet
North Story | ECM | 1596

Geyer,Auwi | (b-tbtb)
Al Porcino Big Band
Al Cohn Meets Al Porcino | Organic Music | ORGM 9730

Geyer,Renée | (voc)
Wanderlust
Border Crossing | Laika Records | 35100812

Gfrerer,Stefan | (b)
Dominik Grimm-Thomas Wallisch Trio
A Brighter Day | Edition Collage | EC 510-2
Jörg Seidel Group
I Feel So Smoochie: A Tribute To Nat King Cole | Edition Collage | EC 532-2

Ghanaim,Jack | (kanoon)
Ahmed Abdul-Malik's Middle-Eastern Music
Jazz Sahara | Original Jazz Classics | OJCCD 1820-2(R 12-287)

Ghee,Matthew | (tb)
Coleman Hawkins All Star Octet
Body And Soul Revisited | GRP | GRP 16272

Ghigliordini,Elvio | (fl)
Nicola Puglielli Group
In The Middle | Jardis Records | JRCD 9924

Ghreen,Alan | (porg)
Big Allanbik
Batuque Y Blues | Blues Beacon | BLU-1031 2

Giammarco,Maurizio | (ssts)
Aldo Romano Group
AlmaLatina | Owl Records | 018364-2

Giardina,Phil | (tb)
Louis Armstrong With The Commanders
Ambassador Louis Armstrong Vol.17:Moments To Remember(1952-1956) | Ambassador | CLA 1917

Giausserand,Eric | (fl-h)
Richard Galliano Quintet
Spleen | Dreyfus Jazz Line | FDM 36513-9

Gibbons,Al | (bs,fl,b-cl,as,reedss)
Dizzy Gillespie And His Orchestra
Planet Jazz:Bebop | RCA | 2169650-2
Stanley Turrentine And His Orchestra
The Lost Grooves | Blue Note | 831883-2
The Jazz Composer's Orchestra
Comminications | JCOA | 1001/2

Gibbons,Bobby | (g)
Benny Carter And His Orchestra
Aspects | Capitol | 852677-2
Billy Eckstine With The Billy May Orchestra
Once More With Feeling | Roulette | 581862-2
Mel Tormé With The Billy May Orchestra
Mel Tormé Goes South Of The Border With Billy May | Verve | 589517-2

Gibbons,Joe | (g)
Stan Kenton And His Orchestra
Stan Kenton Portraits On Standards | Capitol | 531571-2

Gibbs,Doc | (perc)
Al Jarreau With Band
L Is For Lover | i.e. Music | 557850-2
Earl Klugh-Dr.Gibbs
Late Night Guitar | Blue Note | 498573-2

Gibbs,Eddie | (bbj)
Wilbur DeParis And His New New Orleans Band
Atlantic Jazz: New Orleans | Atlantic | 7567-81700-2

Gibbs,Edward | (g)
Lena Horne With The Phil Moore Four
Planet Jazz:Lena Horne | Planet Jazz | 2165373-2

Gibbs,George | (b,sousaphonetuba)
Stephane Grappelli And His Musicians
Grapelli Story | Verve | 515807-2
Stephane Grappelli Quartet
Grapelli Story | Verve | 515807-2

Gibbs,Leonard | (congas,chekere,claves,perc,bongos)
Grover Washington Jr. Septet
Paradise | Elektra | 7559-60537-2

Gibbs,Melvin | (b,el-b,voc,percvoice)
Jean-Paul Bourelly Trance Atlantic
Boom Bop II | double moon | CHRDM 71023
John Zorn Group
Spillane | Nonesuch | 7559-79172-2

Gibbs,Michael | (arr,comp,ld,cond.,cond,tbp)
Joachim Kühn And The Radio Philharmonie Hannover NDR With Jazz Soloists
Europeana | ACT | 9220-2
Mahavishnu Orchestra
Apocalypse | CBS | 467092-2
Michael Mantler Quintet With The London Symphony Orchestra
Something There | Watt | 13
NDR Big Band With Guests
50 Years Of NDR Big Band:Bravissimo II | ACT | 9259-2

Gibbs,Terry | (vib,ld,marimba,pvoc)
Dinah Washington With The Terry Gibbs Band
Verve Jazz Masters 40:Dinah Washington | Verve | 522055-2
Dinah Washington With The Urbie Green Sextet
Newport Jazz Festival 1958,July 3rd-6th Vol.2:Mulligan The Main Man | Phontastic | NCD 8814
Terry Gibbs Big Band
Terry Gibbs Dream Band Vol.4:Main Stem | Contemporary | CCD 7656-2
Terry Gibbs Dream Band
Terry Gibbs Dream Band Vol.2:The Sundown Sessions | Contemporary | CCD 7652-2
Terry Gibbs Dream Band Vol.3:Flying Home | Contemporary | CCD 7654-2
Terry Gibbs Dream Band Vol.5:The Big Cat | Contemporary | CCD 7657-2
Terry Gibbs Dream Band Vol.6:One More Time | Contemporary | CCD 7658-2
The Jazz Giants Play Jerome Kern:Yesterdays | Prestige | PCD 24202-2
Terry Gibbs Octet
Jewis Melodies In Jazztime | Mercury | 589673-2
Terry Gibbs Septet
Early Stan | Original Jazz Classics | OJCCD 654-2(P 7255)
The Metronome All Stars
Jazz Gallery:Lester Young Vol.2(1946-59) | RCA | 2119541-2
Tommy Dorsey And His Orchestra
Planet Jazz:Tommy Dorsey | Planet Jazz | 2159972-2
Urbie Green Sextet
Newport Jazz Festival 1958,July 3rd-6th Vol.2:Mulligan The Main Man | Phontastic | NCD 8814
Woody Herman And His Orchestra
Woody Herman:Four Brother | Dreyfus Jazz Line | FDM 36722-2

Gibeling,Howard | (tb)
Glenn Miller And His Orchestra
The Chesterfield Broadcasts Vol.1 | RCA | 2663113-2
The Andrew Sisters With The Glenn Miller Orchestra
The Chesterfield Broadcasts Vol.1 | RCA | 2663113-2

Gibert,Alain | (perc,sampling,arrtb)
Pata Music Meets Arfi
La Belle Et La Bête | Pata Musik | PATA 14(amf 1066)

Gibson,Al | (bs,cl,asts)
Dizzy Gillespie And His Orchestra
Planet Jazz:Dizzy Gillespie | Planet Jazz | 2152069-2
Planet Jazz:Bebop | RCA | 2169650-2
Planet Jazz:Male Jazz Vocalists | Planet Jazz | 2169657-2

Gibson,Dale | (tp)
André Holst With Chris Dean's European Swing Orchestra
That's Swing | Nagel-Heyer | CD 079

Gibson,Dave | (dr)
Diane Schuur And Her Band
Music Is My Life | Atlantic | 7567-83150-2

Gibson,David 'Dave' | (tb)
David Gibson Sextet
Maya | Nagel-Heyer | CD 2018
Wycliffe Gordon Group
The Search | Nagel-Heyer | CD 2007

Gibson,Elizabeth | (v)
Art Pepper Quintet With Strings
Art Pepper:The Complete Galaxy Recordings | Galaxy | 16GCD 1016-2
Winter Moon | Original Jazz Classics | OJC20 677-2(GXY 5140)

Gibson,Henley | (congas)
Oscar Peterson Sextet
Soul Espanol | Limelight | 510439-2

Gibson,Jarrett | (saxts)
Buddy Guy Blues Band
Buddy Guy-The Complete Chess Studio Recordings | MCA | MCD 09337

Gibson,Kevin | (dr)
Johannes Enders Group
Reflections Of South Africa | Jazz 4 Ever Records:Jazz Network | J4E 4729

Gibson,Lacy | (gvoc)
Buddy Guy Blues Band
Buddy Guy-The Complete Chess Studio Recordings | MCA | MCD 09337

Gier,Thomas | (b)
Peter Fulda Trio With Céline Rudolph
Silent Dances | Jazz 4 Ever Records:Jazz Network | J4E 4731

Gierde,Jorgen | (tb)
Geir Lysne Listening Ensemble
Korall | ACT | 9236-2

Giessen-Köln-Nonet |
Giessen-Köln-Nonett
Some Other Tapes | Fish Music | FM 009/10 CD

Gifford,Charles | (tp)
Louis Armstrong With Gordon Jenkins And His Orchestra And Choir
Satchmo In Style | Verve | 549594-2

Gifford,Gene | (arr,ldg)
Gene Gifford And His Orchestra
Planet Jazz:Bud Freeman | Planet Jazz | 2161240-2

Giger,Hans-Peter | (dr,perc,marimba,balafon,cymbal)
Eberhard Weber Group
The Colours Of Chloe | ECM | 1042
Four For Jazz
The Best Of Four For Jazz & Benny Bailey | JHM Records | JHM 3615
Four For Jazz & Benny Bailey
The Best Of Four For Jazz & Benny Bailey | JHM Records | JHM 3615

Giger,Paul | (v,v-d'amore,viola-d'amore)
Paul Giger Trio
Alpstein | ECM | 1426(847940-2)
Vindonissa | ECM | 1836(066069-2)

Giger,Peter | (drperc)
Jazzensemble Des Hessischen Rundfunks
Atmosphering Conditions Permitting | ECM | 1549/50

Giglio,Felix | (v)
Billie Holiday With The Ray Ellis Orchestra
Lady In Satin | CBS | CK 65144

Gilad | (perc)
Freddie Bryant Group
Brazilian Rosewood | Fresh Sound Records | FSNT 035 CD

Gilbert,Al | (sax)
Lena Horne With The Lennie Hayton Orchestra
Planet Jazz:Lena Horne | Planet Jazz | 2165373-2

Gilbert,Eileen | (voc)
George Benson And His Orchestra
Giblet Gravy | Verve | 543754-2
Talkin' Verve:George Benson | Verve | 553780-2

Gilbert,Phil | (tp)
Stan Kenton Orchestra
Stompin' At Newport | Pablo | PACD 5312-2

Gilbert,Stanley | (bel-b)
Cal Tjader Quintet
Talkin Verve/Roots Of Acid Jazz:Cal Tjader | Verve | 531562-2
Kenny Burrell Quintet
Stormy Monday Blues | Fantasy | FCD 24767-2
Mose Allison Trio
Mose Alife!/Wild Man On The Loose | Warner | 8122-75439-2

Gilberto,Astrud | (voc)
Astrud Gilberto With Antonio Carlos Jobim And The Marty Paich Orchestra
The Antonio Carlos Jobim Songbook | Verve | 525472-2
Astrud Gilberto With Orchestra
This Is Astrud Gilberto | Verve | 825064-2
Astrud Gilberto With The Al Cohn Orchestra
Verve Jazz Masters 9:Astrud Gilberto | Verve | 519824-2
Astrud Gilberto With The Claus Ogerman Orchestra
Verve Jazz Masters 9:Astrud Gilberto | Verve | 519824-2
Astrud Gilberto With The Don Sebesky Orchestra
Verve Jazz Masters 9:Astrud Gilberto | Verve | 519824-2
Astrud Gilberto With The Gil Evans Orchestra
Verve Jazz Masters 9:Astrud Gilberto | Verve | 519824-2
Verve Jazz Masters 23:Gil Evans | Verve | 521860-2
Astrud Gilberto With The Marty Paich Orchestra
Verve Jazz Masters 9:Astrud Gilberto | Verve | 519824-2
Astrud Gilberto With The New Stan Getz Quartet
Verve Jazz Masters 9:Astrud Gilberto | Verve | 519824-2
Astrud Gilberto With The Walter Wanderley Quartet
A Certain Smile A Certain Sadness | Verve | 557449-2
Astrud Gilberto With The Walter Wanderley Quintet
A Certain Smile A Certain Sadness | Verve | 557449-2
Astrud Gilberto With The Walter Wanderley Quuitet
Verve Jazz Masters 9:Astrud Gilberto | Verve | 519824-2
Astrud Gilberto With The Walter Wanderley Trio
This Is Astrud Gilberto | Verve | 825064-2
Astrud Gilberto-Walter Wanderley
A Certain Smile A Certain Sadness | Verve | 557449-2
Getz-Gilberto Quintet
Verve Jazz Masters 13:Antonio Carlos Jobim | Verve | 516409-2
Stan Getz Highlights:The Best Of The Verve Years Vol.2 | Verve | 517330-2
Getz/Gilberto No.2 | Verve | 519800-2
Verve Jazz Masters 20:Introducing | Verve | 519853-2
Getz/Gilberto | Polydor | 521414-2
A Life In Jazz:A Musical Biography | Verve | 535119-2
Stan Getz Quintet Feat. Astrud Gilberto
Verve Jazz Masters 8:Stan Getz | Verve | 519823-2
Verve Jazz Masters 53:Stan Getz-Bossa Nova | Verve | 529904-2
Getz/Gilberto | Verve | 589595-2 SACD
Stan Getz-Joao Gilberto Quintet
The Antonio Carlos Jobim Songbook | Verve | 525472-2
Stan Getz Highlights | Verve | 847430-2
The New Stan Getz Quartet Feat. Astrud Gilberto
Getz Au Go Go | Verve | 821725-2
The New Stan Getz Quintet Feat. Astrud Gilberto
Getz Au Go Go | Verve | 821725-2

Gilberto,Joao | (cond,arr,g,percvoc)
Astrud Gilberto With The New Stan Getz Quartet
Verve Jazz Masters 9:Astrud Gilberto | Verve | 519824-2
Getz-Gilberto Quintet
Verve Jazz Masters 13:Antonio Carlos Jobim | Verve | 516409-2
Stan Getz Highlights:The Best Of The Verve Years Vol.2 | Verve | 517330-2
Getz/Gilberto No.2 | Verve | 519800-2
Verve Jazz Masters 20:Introducing | Verve | 519853-2
Getz/Gilberto | Polydor | 521414-2
A Life In Jazz:A Musical Biography | Verve | 535119-2
Joao Gilberto Trio
Getz/Gilberto No.2 | Verve | 519800-2
The Antonio Carlos Jobim Songbook | Verve | 525472-2
Stan Getz Quintet
Verve Jazz Masters 53:Stan Getz-Bossa Nova | Verve | 529904-2
Stan Getz Quintet Feat. Astrud Gilberto
Verve Jazz Masters 8:Stan Getz | Verve | 519823-2
Verve Jazz Masters 53:Stan Getz-Bossa Nova | Verve | 529904-2
Getz/Gilberto | Verve | 589595-2 SACD
Stan Getz-Joao Gilberto Orchestra
Sony Jazz Collection:Stan Getz | CBS | 488623-2
Stan Getz-Joao Gilberto Quintet
The Antonio Carlos Jobim Songbook | Verve | 525472-2
Stan Getz Highlights | Verve | 847430-2

Gilberto,Joao prob. | (g)
Astrud Gilberto With The Walter Wanderley Quintet
A Certain Smile A Certain Sadness | Verve | 557449-2

Gildner,Nancy | (tp)
United Women's Orchestra
Virgo Supercluster | Jazz Haus Musik | JHM 0123 CD

Gilet,Marc | (cello)
Abbey Lincoln With The Rodney Kendrick Trio And Guests
A Turtle's Dream | Verve | 527382-2

Gilgenberg,Andreas | (b-cl,as,falto-cl,gongs,slit-dr,fl)
Norbert Stein Pata Orchester
Ritual Life | Pata Musik | PATA 5(JHM 50) CD
The Secret Act Of Painting | Pata Musik | PATA 7 CD

Gill,Ben | (v)
Ella Fitzgerald With The Billy May Orchestra
The Best Of The Song Books:The Ballads | Verve | 521867-2
Ella Fitzgerald Sings The Harold Arlen Song Book | Verve | 589108-2
Ella Fitzgerald With The Frank DeVol Orchestra
Get Happy! | Verve | 523321-2
Ella Fitzgerald With The Nelson Riddle Orchestra
The Best Of The Song Books:The Ballads | Verve | 521867-2
Oh Lady Be Good:The Best Of The Gershwin Songbook | Verve | 529581-2
Love Songs:The Best Of The Song Books | Verve | 531762-2
Pete Rugolo And His Orchestra
Thriller/Richard Diamon(Original Jazz Scores From 2 Classics TV Series) | Fresh Sound Records | FSCD 2015
Phineas Newborn Jr. With Dennis Farnon And His Orchestra
While My Lady Sleeps | RCA | 2185157-2

Gill,Paul | (b)
Jim Snidero Quartet With Strings
Strings | Milestone | MCD 9326-2

Gill,Sam | (b)
Randy Weston Trio
Randy Weston:Solo,Duo,Trio | Milestone | MCD 47085-2
Randy Weston-Sam Gill
Randy Weston:Solo,Duo,Trio | Milestone | MCD 47085-2

Gill,Vinny | (v)
Johnny Hartman And His Orchestra
Unforgettable | Impulse(MCA) | IMP 11522

Gillblad,Per Olof | (engl-hoboe)
Bengt-Arne Wallin Orchestra
The Birth+Rebirth Of Swedish Folk Jazz | ACT | 9254-2

Gillespie,Dana | (voc)
Hans Theessink Group
Journey On | Minor Music | 801062
Oscar Klein-Lino Patruno European Jazz Stars
Live at The San Marino Jazz Festival | Jazzpoint | JP 1052 CD

Gillespie,Dizzy | (arr,congas,voc,p,talking,tp,jewharp)

All Stars
Alternate Blues | Original Jazz Classics | OJCCD 744-2
Bud Powell Quintet
Bud Powell Paris Sessions | Pablo | PACD 2310972-2
Buddy Rich Orchestra
Krupa And Rich | Verve | 521643-2
Buddy Rich-Gene Krupa Orchestra
Krupa And Rich | Verve | 521643-2
Carmen McRae With The Dizzy Gillespie Quartet
Misty Blue:Sweet Sisters Swing Songs Of Sorrow And Sadness | Blue Note | 521151-2
Charlie Christian All Stars
Charlie Christian-Jazz Immortal/Dizzy Gillespie 1944 | Original Jazz Classics | OJCCD 1932-2(ES 548)
Charlie Parker And His Orchestra
Bird: The Complete Charlie Parker On Verve | Verve | 837141-2
Charlie Parker:April In Paris | Dreyfus Jazz Line | FDM 36737-2
Charlie Parker Quintet
Verve Jazz Masters 10:Dizzy Gillespie | Verve | 516319-2
Bird And Diz | Verve | 521436-2
Charlie Parker:Bird's Best Bop On Verve | Verve | 527452-2
Charlie Parker:The Best Of The Verve Years | Verve | 527815-2
Ultimate Dizzy Gillespie | Verve | 557535-2
Talkin' Bird | Verve | 559859-2
Charlie Parker-Dizzy Gillespie Quintet
Thelonious Monk:Misterioso | Dreyfus Jazz Line | FDM 36743-2
Charlie Parker's Beboppers
Charlie Parker:Now's The Time | Dreyfus Jazz Line | FDM 36724-2
Coleman Hawkins And His Orchestra
Jazz:The Essential Collection Vol.3 | IN+OUT Records | 78013-2
Dizzy Gillespie
An Electrifying Evening With The Dizzy Gillespie Quintet | Verve | 557544-2
Dizzy Gillespie All Stars
Verve Jazz Masters 25:Stan Getz & Dizzy Gillespie | Verve | 521852-2
Milt Jackson Birthday Celebration | Fantasy | FANCD 6079-2
Dizzy Gillespie:Night In Tunisia | Dreyfus Jazz Line | FDM 36734-2
Jazz At The Philharmonic:The Montreux Collection | Pablo | PACD 5306-2
Dizzy Gillespie And His Orchestra
Dizzy Gillespie:Pleyel Jazz Concert 1948 + Max Roach Quintet 1949 | Vogue | 21409412
Planet Jazz:Dizzy Gillespie | Planet Jazz | 2152069-2
Planet Jazz Sampler | Planet Jazz | 2152326-2
Planet Jazz:Jazz Greatest Hits | Planet Jazz | 2169648-2
Planet Jazz:Bebop | RCA | 2169650-2
Planet Jazz:Male Jazz Vocalists | Planet Jazz | 2169657-2
Verve Jazz Masters 10:Dizzy Gillespie | Verve | 516319-2
Afro | Verve | 517052-2
Gillespiana And Carnegie Hall Concert | Verve | 519809-2
Verve Jazz Masters 20:Introducing | Verve | 519853-2
Dizzy Gillespie:Birks Works-The Verve Big Band Sessions | Verve | 527900-2
Talking Verve:Dizzy Gillespie | Verve | 533846-2
Ultimate Dizzy Gillespie | Verve | 557535-2
Closer To The Source | Atlantic | 7567-80776-2
Dizzy Gillespie:Night In Tunisia | Dreyfus Jazz Line | FDM 36734-2
Dizzy Gillespie And The United Nation Orchestra
7.Zelt-Musik-Festival:Jazz Events | Zounds | CD 2730001
Dizzy Gillespie Big 7
Dizzy-At The Montreux Jazz Festival 1975 | Original Jazz Classics | OJC20 739-2(2310749)
Dizzy Gillespie Group
Verve Jazz Masters 10:Dizzy Gillespie | Verve | 516319-2
Dizzy Gillespie Jam
Montreux '77 | Original Jazz Classics | OJC 385(2620105)
Montreux '77 | Original Jazz Classics | OJC20 381-2(2308211)
Dizzy Gillespie Orchestra
Monterey Jazz Festival 1975 | Storyville | 4960213
Verve Jazz Masters 10:Dizzy Gillespie | Verve | 516319-2
Dizzy Gillespie Orchestra And The Operatic String Orchestra
Jazz In Paris:Dizzy Gillespie And His Operatic Strings Orchestra | EmArCy | 018420-2
Dizzy Gillespie Quartet And The Operatic String Orchestra
Jazz In Paris:Dizzy Gillespie And His Operatic Strings Orchestra | EmArCy | 018420-2
Dizzy Gillespie Quintet
Jazz In Paris:Dizzy Gillespie-The Giant | EmArCy | 159734-2 PMS
Dizzie Gillespie: Salle Pleyel/Olympia | Laserlight | 36132
Verve Jazz Masters 10:Dizzy Gillespie | Verve | 516319-2
Talking Verve:Dizzy Gillespie | Verve | 533846-2
Diz And Getz | Verve | 549749-2
Ultimate Dizzy Gillespie | Verve | 557535-2
An Electrifying Evening With The Dizzy Gillespie Quintet | Verve | 557544-2
Something Old Something New | Verve | 558079-2
Swing Low, Sweet Cadillac | Impulse(MCA) | 951178-2
Charlie Parker:Now's The Time | Dreyfus Jazz Line | FDM 36724-2
Dizzy Gillespie:Night In Tunisia | Dreyfus Jazz Line | FDM 36734-2
The Roots Of Acid Jazz | Impulse(MCA) | IMP 12042
Dizzy Gillespie Septet
Stan Getz Highlights:The Best Of The Verve Years Vol.2 | Verve | 517330-2
Verve Jazz Masters 25:Stan Getz & Dizzy Gillespie | Verve | 521852-2
The Antonio Carlos Jobim Songbook | Verve | 525472-2
Stan Getz Highlights | Verve | 847430-2
Dizzy Gillespie Sextet
Pleyel Jazz Concert 1953 | Vogue | 21409392
Dizzie Gillespie: Salle Pleyel/Olympia | Laserlight | 36132
Verve Jazz Masters 10:Dizzy Gillespie | Verve | 516319-2
Verve Jazz Masters 50:Sonny Sitt | Verve | 527651-2
Talking Verve:Dizzy Gillespie | Verve | 533846-2
Jambo Caribe | Verve | 557492-2
Ultimate Dizzy Gillespie | Verve | 557535-2
Dizzy Gillespie:Night In Tunisia | Dreyfus Jazz Line | FDM 36734-2
The Jazz Giants Play Harold Arlen:Blues In The Night | Prestige | PCD 24201-2
Dizzy Gillespie With The Lalo Schifrin Orchestra
Free Ride | Original Jazz Classics | OJCCD 784-2(2310794)
Dizzy Gillespie-Count Basie Quartet
The Gifted Ones | Original Jazz Classics | OJCCD 886-2(2310833)
Dizzy Gillespie-Roy Eldridge Sextet
Ultimate Dizzy Gillespie | Verve | 557535-2
The Complete Verve Roy Eldridge Studio Sessions | Verve | 9861278
Dizzy Gillespie's Trumpet Kings
The Trumpet Kings Meet Joe Turner | Original Jazz Classics | OJCCD 497-2
Dizzy Gillespie-Sonny Rollins-Sonny Stitt Sextet
Sonny Side Up | Verve | 521426-2
Dizzy Gillespie-Sonny Stitt Quintet
Verve Jazz Masters 10:Dizzy Gillespie | Verve | 516319-2
Dizzy Gillespie-Stan Getz Sextet
Verve Jazz Masters 25:Stan Getz & Dizzy Gillespie | Verve | 521852-2
Diz And Getz | Verve | 549749-2
Ultimate Stan Getz selected by Joe Henderson | Verve | 557532-2
Stan Getz Highlights | Verve | 847430-2
Dizzy Gillspie And His Latin American Rhythm
Afro | Verve | 517052-2
Ella Fitzgerald With The Dizzy Gillespie Orchestra
Ella Fitzgerald:Mr.Paganini | Dreyfus Jazz Line | FDM 36741-2
Ella Fitzgerald With The Duke Ellington Orchestra
Ella Fitzgerald Sings The Duke Ellington Songbook | Verve | 559248-2
For Musicians Only
Ultimate Stan Getz selected by Joe Henderson | Verve | 557532-2
Ultimate Dizzy Gillespie | Verve | 557535-2
For Musicians Only | Verve | 837435-2
Gene Krupa Orchestra
Krupa And Rich | Verve | 521643-2
Jam Session
Jazz Gallery:Lester Young Vol.2(1946-59) | RCA | 2119541-2
JATP All Stars
J.A.T.P. In London 1969 | Pablo | 2CD 2620119
Nothing But The Blues | Verve | 521674-2
Verve Jazz Masters 25:Stan Getz & Dizzy Gillespie | Verve | 521852-2
The Complete Jazz At The Philharmonic On Verve 1944-1949 | Verve | 523893-2
Bird: The Complete Charlie Parker On Verve | Verve | 837141-2
Welcome To Jazz At The Philharmonic | Fantasy | FANCD 6081-2
Johnny Hodges With The Dizzy Gillespie Quintet
Verve Jazz Masters 35:Johnny Hodges | Verve | 521857-2
Lionel Hampton And His Orchestra
Planet Jazz:Coleman Hawkins | Planet Jazz | 2152055-2
Planet Jazz:Ben Webster | RCA | 2165368-2
Planet Jazz:Jazz Saxophone | Planet Jazz | 2169653-2
Jazz:The Essential Collection Vol.3 | IN+OUT Records | 78013-2
Machito And His Orchestra
Afro-Cuban Jazz Moods | Original Jazz Classics | OJC20 447-2
Minton's Playhouse All Stars
Charlie Christian:Swing To Bop | Dreyfus Jazz Line | FDM 36715-2
Modern Jazz Sextet
Verve Jazz Masters 50:Sonny Sitt | Verve | 527651-2
The Modern Jazz Sextet | Verve | 559834-2
Mongo Santamaria Group With Dizzy Gillespie And Toots Thielemans
Summertime-Digital At Montreux 1980 | Original Jazz Classics | OJCCD 626-2(2308229)
Montreux Heat! | Pablo | PACD 5317-2
Norman Granz Jam Session
Verve Jazz Masters 26:Lionel Hampton with Oscar Peterson | Verve | 521853-2
Verve Jazz Masters Vol.60:The Collection | Verve | 529866-2
Oscar Peterson Jam
Oscar Peterson Plays Duke Ellington | Pablo | 2310966-2
Montreux '77 | Original Jazz Classics | OJC 385(2620105)
Montreux '77 | Original Jazz Classics | OJC20 378-2(2308208)
Quincy Jones Big Band
Rahsaan/The Complete Mercury Recordings Of Roland Kirk | Mercury | 846630-2
Quintet Of The Year
Charles Mingus-The Complete Debut Recordings | Debut | 12 DCD 4402-2
The Quintet-Jazz At Massey Hall | Debut | DSA 124-6
The Quintet-Jazz At Massey Hall | Original Jazz Classics | OJC20 044-2
Roy Eldridge-Dizzy Gillespie With The Oscar Peterson Quartet
The Complete Verve Roy Eldridge Studio Sessions | Verve | 9861278
Jazz Maturity... Where It's Coming From | Original Jazz Classics | OJCCD 807-2(2310816)
Roy Eldridge-Dizzy Gillespie-Harry Edison With The Oscar Peterson Quartet
The Complete Verve Roy Eldridge Studio Sessions | Verve | 9861278
Sarah Vaughan With Dizzy Gillespie And His All Star Quintet
Sarah Vaughan:Lover Man | Dreyfus Jazz Line | FDM 36739-2
Sarah Vaughan With Dizzy Gillespie And His Orchestra
Planet Jazz:Female Jazz Vocalists | Planet Jazz | 2169656-2
Sarah Vaughan With Dizzy Gillespie And His Septet
Sarah Vaughan:Lover Man | Dreyfus Jazz Line | FDM 36739-2
Sarah Vaughan With The Allstars
Sarah Vaughan:Lover Man | Dreyfus Jazz Line | FDM 36739-2
Tempo Jazzmen
Dizzy Gillespie:Night In Tunisia | Dreyfus Jazz Line | FDM 36734-2
The Metronome All Stars
Planet Jazz:Dizzy Gillespie | Planet Jazz | 2152069-2
The Trumpet Summit With The Oscar Peterson Big 4
The Trumpet Summit Meets The Oscar Peterson Big 4 | Original Jazz Classics | OJCCD 603-2
Tony Scott And His Down Beat Club Sextet
Jazz:The Essential Collection Vol.3 | IN+OUT Records | 78013-2

Gillette,Bob | (bj)
The Wolverines
Jazz:The Essential Collection Vol.2 | IN+OUT Records | 78012-2

Gilliet,Michel | (p)
Lillian Boutté And Her Group
You've Gotta Love Pops:Lillian Bouté Sings Louis Armstrong | ART BY HEART | ABH 2005 2

Gillmann,Andy | (perc)
Peter Weiss Sextet
Personal Choice | Nabel Records:Jazz Network | CD 4669

Gillot,Albert | (cl)
Dizzy Gillespie Orchestra And The Operatic String Orchestra
Jazz In Paris:Dizzy Gillespie And His Operatic Strings Orchestra | EmArCy | 018420-2

Gillum,Charles | (tp)
Buster Smith Orchestra
Atlantic Jazz: Kansas City | Atlantic | 7567-81701-2

Gillum,William 'Bill Jazz' | (harmvoc)
Memphis Slim
Memphis Slim USA | Candid | CCD 79024

Gilmore,David | (el-b,el-g,g,g-synthvoice)
Steve Coleman And Five Elements
Genesis & The Opening Of The Way | RCA | 2152934-2
Steve Coleman And The Council Of Balance
Genesis & The Opening Of The Way | RCA | 2152934-2
Uri Caine Ensemble
Love Fugue-Robert Schumann | Winter&Winter | 910049-2
Vincent Chancey Quartet
Welcome Mr. Chancey | IN+OUT Records | 7020-1

Gilmore,John | (b-cl,ts,bells,cl,perc,timbales,voc)
Cliff Jordan-John Gilmore Quintet
Blowing In From Chicago | Blue Note | 542306-2
Elmo Hope Ensemble
Sounds From Rikers Island | Fresh Sound Records | FSR CD 338
Sun Ra And His Astro-Infinity Arkestra
Space Is The Place | Impulse(MCA) | 951249-2
Sun Ra And His Intergalactic Research Arkestra
Black Myth/Out In Space | MPS | 557656-2

Gilmore,Steve | (b)
Phil Woods Quartet
A Tribute To Charlie Parker Vol.2 | Storyville | 4960493
Putte Wickman And The Hal Galper trio
Time To Remember | Dragon | DRCD 378

Gilson,Big | (gel-g)
Big Allanbik
Batuque Y Blues | Blues Beacon | BLU-1031 2

Gilstrap,James | (voc)
Bobby Lyle Group
The Journey | Atlantic | 7567-82138-2
Dee Dee Bridgewater With Band
Dee Dee Bridgewater | Atlantic | 7567-80760-2
Les McCann Group
Another Beginning | Atlantic | 7567-80790-2
Quincy Jones And His Orchestra
Verve Jazz Masters Vol.59:Toots Thielemans | Verve | 535271-2
Sarah Vaughan And Her Band
Songs Of The Beatles | Atlantic | 16037-2

Gimpel,Bronislaw | (v)
Charlie Parker With Strings
Verve Jazz Masters 28:Charlie Parker Plays Standards | Verve | 521854-2
Charlie Parker With Strings:The Master Takes | Verve | 523984-2
Charlie Parker:The Best Of The Verve Years | Verve | 527815-2
Bird: The Complete Charlie Parker On Verve | Verve | 837141-2
Charlie Parker:April In Paris | Dreyfus Jazz Line | FDM 36737-2

Gina | (voc)
Jermaine Landsberger Trio & Gina
Samba In June | Edition Collage | EC 524-2
Jermaine Landsberger Trio With Helmut Kagerer & Gina
Samba In June | Edition Collage | EC 524-2

Ginman,Lennart V. | (bb-solo)
Caecilie Norby With Band
My Corner Of The Sky | Blue Note | 853422-2
Carsten Dahl Trio
Will You Make My Soup Hot & Silver | Storyville | STCD 4203

Ginnerup,Morten | (p)
Ulli Jünemann-Morton Ginnerup European Jazz Project
The Exhibition | Edition Collage | EC 518-2

Ginsberg,Allen | (voc)
Don Cherry Group
Multi Kulti | A&M Records | 395323-2

Ginsberg,Kerstin | (dr)
Kölner Saxophon Mafia With Bad Little Dynamos
Kölner Saxophon Mafia Proudly Presents | Jazz Haus Musik | JHM 0046 CD

Ginsburg,Josh | (b)
Andrew Adair Group
States | Fresh Sound Records | FSNT 061 CD
Martin Schrack Quartet
Headin' Home | Storyville | STCD 4253
Martin Schrack Quintet feat.Tom Harrell
Headin' Home | Storyville | STCD 4253

Ginyard,Julius Caleb | (voc)
Golden Gate Quartet
Americans Swinging In Paris:Golden Gate Quartet | EMI Records | 539659-2
From Spiritual To Swing Vol.2 | EMI Records | 780573-2
Spirituals To Swing 1955-69 | EMI Records | 791569-2
Golden Gate Quartet With The Martial Solal Orchestra
Americans Swinging In Paris:Golden Gate Quartet | EMI Records | 539659-2
From Spiritual To Swing Vol.2 | EMI Records | 780573-2

Ginzberg,Leonhard | (perc)
Frank Kirchner Group
Frank Kirchner | Laika Records | LK 93-036

Giobbe,Felix | (b)
V-Disc All Star Jam Session
Louis Armstrong-Jack Teagarden-Woody Herman:Midnights At V-Disc | Jazz Unlimited | JUCD 2048

Gioga,Bob | (b-cl,bssax)
Stan Kenton And His Orchestra
Swing Vol.1 | Storyville | 4960343
Stan Kenton Portraits On Standards | Capitol | 531571-2
Stan Kenton-The Formative Years | Decca | 589489-2

Gioia,Topo | (perccongas)
Bajazzo
Caminos | Edition Collage | EC 485-2
Harlequin Galaxy | Edition Collage | EC 519-2
Ernst Bier-Mack Goldsbury Quintet
At Night When You Go To Sleep | Timescrapper | TSCR 9611
Gunther Schuller With The WDR Radio Orchestra & Rememberance Band
Witchi Tia To, The Music Of Jim Pepper | Tutu Records | 888204-2*
Rudi Neuwirth Group
Sand | Traumton Records | 2413-2

Giordana,Suzanna | (viola)
Charlie Haden Quartet West With Strings
The Art Of The Song | Verve | 547403-2

Giordano,Charlie | (accordeon)
James Carter Group
Chasin' The Gypsy | Atlantic | 7567-83304-2

Giorgiani,Joe | (tp)
Buddy Rich Big Band
Keep The Customer Satisfied | EMI Records | 523999-2

Giorgianni,Sal | (as,tsfl)
Miles Davis With Gil Evans Orchestra, The George Gruntz Concert Jazz Band And Guests
Miles & Quincy Live At Montreux | Warner | 9362-45221-2

Giovaninni,Caesar | (p)
Pete Rugolo And His Orchestra
Thriller/Richard Diamon(Original Jazz Scores From 2 Classics TV Series) | Fresh Sound Records | FSCD 2015

Giovine,Cossimo | (voice)
Michel Godard Ensemble
Castel Del Monte II | Enja | ENJ-9431 2

Girod,Roger | (klangobjecte,pklangflügel)
ATonALL
ATonALL | Creative Works Records | CW CD 1024-2
Roger Girod-Peter A.Schmid
Windschief | Creative Works Records | CW CD 1027-2

Girotto,Javier | (ss,asbs)
Stefania Tallini Trio With Guests
New Life | yvp music | CD 3114

Giroudon,James | (perc)
Barre Phillips Group
Aquarian Rain | ECM | 1451

Girsback,Squire | (btuba)
Bunk Johnson With The Yerba Buena Jazz Band
Bunk & Lu | Good Time Jazz | GTCD 12024-2

Gisbert,Gregory 'Greg' | (tpfl-h)
Jam Session
Jam Session Vol.5 | Steeplechase | SCCD 31536

Gisinger,Nicolas | (synthel-b)
Asita Hamidi & Arcobaleno
Mosaic | Laika Records | 8695067

Gisler,Fabian | (b)
Domenic Landolf Quartet
Levitation | JHM Records | JHM 3616
Matthias Spillmann Septet
Something About Water | JHM Records | JHM 3620

Gismonti,Egberto | (8-string-g,fl,g,p,bamboo-fl,dilruba)
Cal Tjader Group
Amazonas | Original Jazz Classics | OJCCD 840-2(F 9502)
Charlie Haden Trio
Magico | ECM | 1151(823474-2)
Folk Songs | ECM | 1170(827705-2)
Charlie Haden-Egberto Gismonti
In Montreal | ECM | 1746(543813-2)
Egberto Gismonti
Danca Das Cabecas | ECM | 1089
Solo | ECM | 1136
Sanfona | ECM | 1203/04(829391-2)
Danca Dos Escravos | ECM | 1387(837753-2)
Egberto Gismonti & Academia De Dancas
Sanfona | ECM | 1203/04(829391-2)
Egberto Gismonti Group
Sol Do Meio Dia | ECM | 1116(829117-2)
Infancia | ECM | 1428
Musica De Sobrevivencia | ECM | 1509(519706-2)
Egberto Gismonti Trio
ZigZag | ECM | 1582
Egberto Gismonti With The Lithuanian State Symphony Orchestra
Meeting Point | ECM | 1586(533681-2)
Egberto Gismonti/Nana Vasconcelos
Duas Vozes | ECM | 1279
Nana Vasconcelos-Egberto Gismonti Duo And Strings
Saudades | ECM | 1147
Raiz De Pedra feat. Egberto Gismonti
Diario De Bordo | TipToe | TIP-888822 2

Giuffre,Jimmy | (arr,as,ts,bs,cl,foot-tapping,ss,voc)
Anita O'Day With The Buddy Bregman Orchestra
Pick Yourself Up | Verve | 517329-2
Anita O'Day With The Jimmy Giuffre Orchestra
Verve Jazz Masters 49:Anita O'Day | Verve | 527653-2
Buddy Bregman And His Orchestra
Swinging Kicks | Verve | 559514-2
Chet Baker And The Lighthouse All Stars

Witch Doctor | Original Jazz Classics | OJCCD 609-2
Howard Rumsey's Lighthouse All-Stars
Sunday Jazz A La Lighthouse Vol.2 | Original Jazz Classics | OJCCD 972-2(S 2501)
Jesse Price And His Blues Band
Jazz Profile:Dexter Gordon | Blue Note | 823514-2
Jimmy Giuffre
The Life Of A Trio:Saturday | Owl Records | 014731-2
The Life Of A Trio:Sunday | Owl Records | 014735-2
Jimmy Giuffre 3
Jimmy Giuffre 3, 1961 | ECM | 1438/39(849644-2)
Western Suite | Atlantic | 7567-80777-2
The Jimmy Giuffre Three | Atlantic | 7567-90981-2
Jimmy Giuffre Three
Free Fall | CBS | CK 65446
Jimmy Giuffre Trio
Paris Jazz Concert:Jimmy Giuffre | Laserlight | 17249
Night Dance | Choice | CHCD 71001
The Train And The River | Choice | CHCD 71011
Jimmy Giuffre/Steve Swallow
The Life Of A Trio:Saturday | Owl Records | 014731-2
The Life Of A Trio:Sunday | Owl Records | 014735-2
Jimmy Giuffre-Paul Bley-Steve Swallow
Fly Away Little Bird | Owl Records | 018351-2
June Christy With The Pete Rugolo Orchestra
Something Cool(The Complete Mono & Stereo Versions) | Capitol | 534069-2
Lennie Niehaus Sextet
Lennie Niehaus Vol.5:The Sextet | Original Jazz Classics | OJCCD 1944-2(C 3524)
Modern Jazz Quartet feat.Jimmy Giuffre
MJQ 40 | Atlantic | 7567-82330-2
Paul Bley/Jimmy Giuffre
The Life Of A Trio:Saturday | Owl Records | 014731-2
The Life Of A Trio:Sunday | Owl Records | 014735-2
Paul Bley/Jimmy Giuffre/Steve Swallow
The Life Of A Trio:Saturday | Owl Records | 014731-2
The Life Of A Trio:Sunday | Owl Records | 014735-2
Red Norvo Septet
Jazz Profile:Dexter Gordon | Blue Note | 823514-2
Shelly Manne And His Men
Vol.1:The West Coast Sound | Original Jazz Classics | OJCCD 152-2
The Jazz Giants Play Harry Warren:Lullaby Of Broadway | Prestige | PCD 24204-2
Shorty Rogers And His Giants
PLanet Jazz:Shorty Rogers | Planet Jazz | 2159976-2
Shorty Rogers And His Orchestra Feat. The Giants
PLanet Jazz:Shorty Rogers | Planet Jazz | 2159976-2
Sonny Stitt Orchestra
Verve Jazz Masters 50:Sonny Sitt | Verve | 527651-2
Woody Herman And His Orchestra
The Legends Of Swing | Laserlight | 24659
Woody Herman:Four Brother | Dreyfus Jazz Line | FDM 36722-2
Woody Herman And The New Thundering Herd
Planet Jazz:Big Bands | Planet Jazz | 2169649-2

Giuliani,Marcello | (bel-b)
Erik Truffaz Quartet
The Dawn | Blue Note | 493916-2
Bending New Corners | Blue Note | 522123-2
Erik Truffaz Quartet Quintet
Out Of A Dream | Blue Note | 855855-2

Giuliano,Gustavo | (b)
Omar Belmonte's Latin Lover
Vamos A Ver | EGO | 96170

Givens[Nadi Qamar],Spaulding | (arr,pp-solo)
Charles Mingus And His Orchestra
Charles Mingus-The Complete Debut Recordings | Debut | 12 DCD 4402-2
Spaulding Givens
Charles Mingus-The Complete Debut Recordings | Debut | 12 DCD 4402-2
Spaulding Givens Trio
Charles Mingus-The Complete Debut Recordings | Debut | 12 DCD 4402-2
Spaulding Givens/Charles Mingus
Charles Mingus-The Complete Debut Recordings | Debut | 12 DCD 4402-2

Gjakonovski,Martin | (boud)
Dejan Terzic European Assembly
Coming Up | double moon | DMCHR 71034
Dusko Goykovich Quartet
Samba Do Mar | Enja | ENJ-9473 2
Dusko Goykovich Quintet
Balkan Blues | Enja | ENJ-9320 2
Eda Zari With The Mark Joggerst Trio
The Art Of Time | Laika Records | 35100902
Ferenc Snétberger Quartet
Signature | Enja | ENJ-9017 2
Lajos Dudas Quartet
Nightlight | double moon | DMCHR 71030
Lajos Dudas Quintet
Nightlight | double moon | DMCHR 71030
Nicolas Simion Group
Balkan Jazz | Intuition Records | INT 3339-2
The Tough Tenors With The Antonio Farao European Trio
Tough Tenors | Jazz 4 Ever Records:Jazz Network | J4E 4761

Gjerde,Jorgen | (tb)
Geir Lysne Listening Ensemble
Aurora Borealis-Nordic Lights | ACT | 9406-2

Gladden,Eddie | (drvoc)
Dexter Gordon Quartet
Dexter Gordon:Ballads | Blue Note | 796579-2
Dexter Gordon:Atlanta Georgia May 5,1981 | Storyville | STCD 8363

Gladdish,Martin | (tb)
Jamie Cullum Group
Pointless Nostalgic | Candid | CCD 79782

Glamman,Betty | (harp)
Kenny Dorham Quintet
Jazz Contrast | Original Jazz Classics | OJCCD 028-2(RLP 239)
Kenny Dorham Sextet
Jazz Contrast | Original Jazz Classics | OJCCD 028-2(RLP 239)

Glamo,Louis | (as)
Elliot Lawrence And His Orchestra
Mullenium | CBS | CK 65678

Glasel,John | (cotp)
Sidney Bechet With Bob Wilber's Wildcats
Sidney Bechet:Summertime | Dreyfus Jazz Line | FDM 36712-2
The Six
The Very Best Of Dixieland Jazz | Verve | 535529-2

Glaser,Jamie | (el-gg)
Jean-Luc Ponty Group
Mystical Adventures | Atlantic | 19333-2
Jean-Luc Ponty Quintet
The Very Best Of Jean-Luc Ponty | Rhino | 8122-79862-2
Jean-Luc Ponty Sextet
The Very Best Of Jean-Luc Ponty | Rhino | 8122-79862-2

Glaser,Joe | (drceleste)
Johannes Rediske Quintet
Deutsches Jazz Fesival 1954/1955 | Bear Family Records | BCD 15430
Re-Disc Bounce | Bear Family Records | BCD 16119 AH
Jumpin' At The Badewanne | Bear Family Records | BCD 16172 AH
Johannes Rediske Sextet
Re-Disc Bounce | Bear Family Records | BCD 16119 AH
Johnnes Rediske Quintet
Deutsches Jazz Fesival 1954/1955 | Bear Family Records | BCD 15430

Glaser,Jutta | (voc)
Jutta Glaser & Bernhard Sperrfechter
Little Girl Blue | Jazz 'n' Arts Records | JNA 0502

Glasser,David | (as,cl,flreeds)
Byron Stripling Sextet
Striplingnow! | Nagel-Heyer | CD 2002
Clark Terry Quintet
Herr Ober | Nagel-Heyer | CD 068
The Dave Glasser/Clark Terry/Barry Harris Project
Uh! Oh! | Nagel-Heyer | CD 2003
Blues Of Summer | Nagel-Heyer | NH 1011

Glaszmann,Uli | (b)
Carlos Denia-Uli Glaszmann
Ten Strings For Bill Evans | Edition Musikat | EDM 069
Frank Eberle Septet
Scarlet Sunrise | Satin Doll Productions | SDP 1041-1 CD

Glatzel,Daniel | (b-clts)
Mathias Götz-Windstärke 4
Lunar Oder Solar? | Jazz 'n' Arts Records | JNA 1002

Glauman,Betty | (harp)
Modern Jazz Quartet & Guests
MJQ 40 | Atlantic | 7567-82330-2

Glawischnig,Dieter | (condp)
Abdullah Ibrahim With The NDR Big Band
Ekapa Lodumo | TipToe | TIP-888840 2
Albert Mangelsdorff With The NDR Big Band
NDR Big Band-Bravissimo | ACT | 9232-2
Chet Baker With The NDR-Bigband
NDR Big Band-Bravissimo | ACT | 9232-2
My Favourite Songs: The Last Great Concert Vol.1 | Enja | ENJ-5097 2
The Last Concert Vol.I+II | Enja | ENJ-6074 22
Chet Baker With The Radio Orchestra Hannover(NDR)
My Favourite Songs: The Last Great Concert Vol.1 | Enja | ENJ-5097 2
The Last Concert Vol.I+II | Enja | ENJ-6074 22
Ekkehard Jost Ensemble
Weimarer Balladen | Fish Music | FM 004 CD
Ekkehard Jost Nonet
Out Of Jost's Songbook | Fish Music | FM 006 CD
Giessen-Köln-Nonett
Some Other Tapes | Fish Music | FM 009/10 CD
Heinz Sauer Quartet With The NDR Big Band
NDR Big Band-Bravissimo | ACT | 9232-2
Joe Pass With The NDR Big Band
NDR Big Band-Bravissimo | ACT | 9232-2
Johnny Griffin With The NDR Big Band
NDR Big Band-Bravissimo | ACT | 9232-2
NDR Big Band
NDR Big Band-Bravissimo | ACT | 9232-2
NDR Big Band With Guests
50 Years Of NDR Big Band:Bravissimo II | ACT | 9259-2
Transalpin Express Orchestra
Some Other Tapes | Fish Music | FM 009/10 CD

Glazener,Lawrence | (b)
A Band Of Friends
Wynton Marsalis Quartet With Strings | CBS | CK 68921

Gleeson,Pat | (rhythm-instrumentssynth)
Bennie Maupin-Dr. Patrick Gleeson
Driving While Black... | Intuition Records | INT 3242-2
Charles Earland Septet
Charlie's Greatest Hits | Prestige | PCD 24250-2
Herbie Hancock Group
Sunlight | CBS | 486570-2
Joe Henderson Sextet
Joe Henderson:The Milestone Years | Milestone | 8MCD 4413-2

Gleghorn,Arthur | (fl)
Billy Eckstine With The Billy May Orchestra
Once More With Feeling | Roulette | 581862-2

Gleim,Ecki | (g)
Stanley Blume Quartet
Movin' Up | Organic Music | ORGM 9709
Stanley Blume Quintet
Movin' Up | Organic Music | ORGM 9709

Glenn Jr.,Tyree | (ts)
Donald Byrd Orchestra
Places And Spaces | Blue Note | 854326-2

Glenn,Lloyd | (p)
Kid Ory's Creole Jazz Band
This Kid's The Greatest! | Good Time Jazz | GTCD 12045-2
Lloyd Glenn-Axel Zwingenberger
Axel Zwingenberger And The Friends Of Boogie Woogie Vol.2 | Vagabond | VRCD 8.85005
Sarah Vaughan And Her Band
Duke Ellington Song Book Two | Pablo | CD 2312116
Sarah Vaughan Birthday Celebration | Fantasy | FANCD 6090-2

Glenn,Roger | (fl,perc,sax,vib,b-flmarimba)
Donald Byrd & His Orchestra
Blue Breaks Beats Vol.2 | Blue Note | 789907-2
Donald Byrd Orchestra
Black Byrd | Blue Note | 784466-2

Glenn,Tyree | (tb,vibvoc)
(Little)Jimmy Scott With The Billy Taylor Orchestra
Everybody's Somebody's Fool | Decca | 050669-2
Big Al Sears Band
Sear-iously | Bear Family Records | BCD 15668 AH
Bobby Hutcherson Orchestra
Deep Blue-The United States Of Mind | Blue Note | 521152-2
Bud Freeman And His Summa Cum Laude Orchestra
Planet Jazz:Bud Freeman | Planet Jazz | 2161240-2
Cab Calloway And His Cab Jivers
Planet Jazz:Cab Calloway | Planet Jazz | 2161237-2
Cozy Cole's Big Seven
Body And Soul Revisited | GRP | GRP 16272
Della Reese With The Neal Hefti Orchestra
Della | RCA | 2663912-2
Don Byas And His Orchestra
Americans Swinging In Paris:Don Byas | EMI Records | 539655-2
Duke Ellington And His Orchestra
Carnegie Hall Concert December 1947 | Prestige | 2PCD 24075-2
Ike Quebec Swingtet
The Blue Note Swingtets | Blue Note | 495697-2
Louis Armstrong And His All Stars
Jazz In Paris:Louis Armstrong:The Best Live Concer Vol.1 | EmArCy | 013030-2
Jazz In Paris:Louis Armstrong-The Best Live Concert Vol.2 | EmArCy | 013031-2
Jazz Collection:Louis Armstrong | Laserlight | 24366
Live In Berlin/Friedrichstadtpalast | Jazzpoint | JP 1062 CD
The Legendary Berlin Concert Part 2 | Jazzpoint | JP 1063 CD
What A Wonderful World | MCA | MCD 01876
Louis Armstrong And His All Stars With A Studio Orchestra
What A Wonderful World | MCA | MCD 01876
Peanuts Holland And His Orchestra
Americans Swinging In Paris:Don Byas | EMI Records | 539655-2
Tyree Glenn
Don Byas:Laura | Dreyfus Jazz Line | FDM 36714-2
Tyree Glenn And His Orchestra
Americans Swinging In Paris:Don Byas | EMI Records | 539655-2

Glerum,Ernst | (b)
Amsterdam String Trio
Winter Theme | Winter&Winter | 910060-2

Glick,Jacob | (viola)
Stan Getz With The Eddie Sauter Orchestra
Verve Jazz Masters 8:Stan Getz | Verve | 519823-2
Ultimate Stan Getz selected by Joe Henderson | Verve | 557532-2

Glickman,Harry | (v)
Nina Simone And Orchestra
Baltimore | Epic | 476906-2

Glickman,Loren | (bassoon)
Miles Davis With Gil Evans & His Orchestra
Sketches Of Spain | CBS | CK 65142

Glindemann,Ib | (condarr)
Stan Getz With Ib Glindemann And His Orchestra
Stan Getz In Europe | Laserlight | 24657
Stan Kenton With The Danish Radio Big Band
Stan Kenton With The Danish Radio Big Band | Storyville | STCD 8340

Globokar,Vinko | (tb,alphorn,didjiridoo,voice,zurle)
Ekkehard Jost Quartet
Some Other Tapes | Fish Music | FM 009/10 CD
Ekkehard Jost-Vinko Globokar
Some Other Tapes | Fish Music | FM 009/10 CD

Glöckler,Ted | (dr)
Thomas Karl Fuchs Trio
Colours And Standards | Edition Collage | EC 509-2

Glod,Roby | (ssas)
Louis Sclavis & The Bernard Struber Jazztet
La Phare | Enja | ENJ-9359 2

Glöder,Reinhard | (b)
Salut!
Green & Orange | Edition Collage | EC 488-2

Gloga,Bob | (bs)
Nat King Cole Quartet With The Stan Kenton Orchestra
Nat King Cole:For Sentimental Reasons | Dreyfus Jazz Line | FDM 36740-2

Glover,Leroy | (ldorg)
King Curtis Band
King Curtis-Blow Man Blow | Bear Family Records | BCD 15670 CI

Glover,Savion | (tap-dance)
Abbey Lincoln With Her Band
Who Used To Dance | Verve | 533559-2

Glover,W. | (voc)
Sonny Rollins Group
What's New? | RCA | 2179626-2

Glow,Bernie | (tp)
Anita O'Day With The Gary McFarland Orchestra
All The Sad Youn Men | Verve | 517065-2
Artie Shaw And His Orchestra
Planet Jazz:Jazz Trumpet | Planet Jazz | 2169654-2
Cab Calloway And His Orchestra
Planet Jazz:Cab Calloway | Planet Jazz | 2161237-2
Planet Jazz:Male Jazz Vocalists | Planet Jazz | 2169657-2
Chubby Jackson And His All Star Big Band
Chubby Takes Over | Fresh Sound Records | FSR-CD 324
Coleman Hawkins With Billy Byers And His Orchestra
The Hawk In Hi-Fi | RCA | 2663842-2
Dinah Washington With The Quincy Jones Orchestra
Verve Jazz Masters 40:Dinah Washington | Verve | 522055-2
The Swingin' Miss 'D' | Verve | 558074-2
Elliot Lawrence And His Orchestra
The Elliot Lawrence Big Band Swings Cohn & Kahn | Fantasy | FCD 24761-2
George Benson With The Don Sebesky Orchestra
Verve Jazz Masters 21:George Benson | Verve | 521861-2
Gil Evans Orchestra
Verve Jazz Masters 23:Gil Evans | Verve | 521860-2
The Individualism Of Gil Evans | Verve | 833804-2
Jimmy Rushing And His Orchestra
Five Feet Of Soul | Roulette | 581830-2
Jimmy Smith With The Billy Byers Orchestra
Jimmy Smith:Best Of The Verve Years | Verve | 527950-2
Jimmy Smith With The Lalo Schifrin Orchestra
Jimmy Smith:Best Of The Verve Years | Verve | 527950-2
Jimmy Smith-Talkin' Verve | Verve | 531563-2
The Cat | Verve | 539756-2
Joe Williams With The Frank Hunter Orchestra
Planet Jazz:Joe Williams | Planet Jazz | 2165370-2
Joe Williams,With The Oliver Nelson Orchestra
Planet Jazz:Joe Williams | Planet Jazz | 2165370-2
Kenny Burrell With The Don Sebesky Orchestra
Verve Jazz Masters 45:Kenny Burrell | Verve | 527652-2
Blues-The Common Ground | Verve | 589101-2
Lena Horne With The Lennie Hayton Orchestra
Planet Jazz:Lena Horne | Planet Jazz | 2165373-2
Mar Murphy With The Ernie Wilkins Orchestra
RAH | Original Jazz Classics | OJCCD 141-2(R 9395)
Miles Davis + 19
Miles Ahead | CBS | CK 65121
Miles Davis With Gil Evans & His Orchestra
Miles Davis At Carnegie Hall | CBS | CK 65027
This Is Jazz:Miles Davis Plays Ballads | CBS | CK 65038
Porgy And Bess | CBS | CK 65141
Sketches Of Spain | CBS | CK 65142
Quiet Nights | CBS | CK 65293
Milt Jackson Orchestra
Big Bags | Original Jazz Classics | OJCCD 366-2(RLP 9429)
Modern Jazz Quartet And Orchestra
MJQ 40 | Atlantic | 7567-82330-2
Ralph Burns And His Orchestra
The Complete Verve Roy Eldridge Studio Sessions | Verve | 9861278
Stan Getz With The Gary McFarland Orchestra
Stan Getz Highlights:The Best Of The Verve Years Vol.2 | Verve | 517330-2
Verve Jazz Masters 53:Stan Getz-Bossa Nova | Verve | 529904-2
Big Band Bossa Nova | Verve | 825771-2 PMS
Tito Puente Orchestra
Planet Jazz:Tito Puente | Planet Jazz | 2165369-2
Wes Montgomery With The Don Sebesky Orchestra
Verve Jazz Masters 14:Wes Montgomery | Verve | 519826-2
Wes Montgomery:The Verve Jazz Sides | Verve | 521690-2
Talkin' Jazz:Roots Of Acid Jazz | Verve | 529580-2
California Dreaming | Verve | 827842-2
Woody Herman And His Orchestra
The Legends Of Swing | Laserlight | 24659
Woody Herman:Four Brother | Dreyfus Jazz Line | FDM 36722-2

Glüsenkamp,Benno | (dr)
Lars Duppler Quartet
Palindrome | Jazz Haus Musik | JHM 0108 CD

Glusgal,Ilja | (drperc)
Helmut Zacharias mit seinem Orchester
Ich Habe Rhythmus | Bear Family Records | BCD 15642 AH

Gmelch,Leo | (b-tbtuba)
Al Porcino Big Band
Al Porcino Big Band Live! | Organic Music | ORGM 9717
NuNu!
Ocean | TipToe | TIP-888837 2

Gmelin,Matthias | (dr)
Jermaine Landsberger Trio
Gypsy Feeling | Edition Collage | EC 516-2
Jermaine Landsberger Trio & Gina
Samba In June | Edition Collage | EC 524-2
Jermaine Landsberger Trio With Bireli Lagrene
Gypsy Feeling | Edition Collage | EC 516-2
Jermaine Landsberger Trio With Helmut Kagerer & Gina
Samba In June | Edition Collage | EC 524-2
Rainer Tempel Big Band
Melodies Of '98 | Jazz 4 Ever Records:Jazz Network | J4E 4744
Trombonefire
Sliding Affairs | Laika Records | 35101462

Gnettner,Kartsten | (b)
Helmut Nieberle & Cordes Sauvages
Jazz Guitar Highlights 1 | Jardis Records | JRCD 20141
Salut To Django | Jardis Records | JRCD 9926
Jenny Evans And Band
Girl Talk | Enja | ENJ-9363 2
Live At The Allotria | ESM Records | ESM 9301
Girl Talk | ESM Records | ESM 9306

Gocht,Stefan | (tp,fl-htuba)
Brass Attack
Brecht Songs | Tutu Records | 888190-2*

Godard,Michel | (serpenttuba)

Christoph Lauer Quintet
Fragile Network | ACT | 9266-2
Gabriele Mirabassi Trio
Latakia Blend | Enja | ENJ-9441 2
Klaus König Orchestra
Times Of Devastation/Poco A Poco | Enja | ENJ-6014 22
Time Fragments:Seven Studies In Time And Motion | Enja | ENJ-8076 2
Klaus König Orchestra & Guests
The Song Of Songs:Oratorio For Two Solo Voices,Choir And Orchestra | Enja | ENJ-7057 2
Michael Riessler Group
Heloise | Wergo | WER 8008-2
Tentations D'Abélard | Wergo | WER 8009-2
Michel Godard Ensemble
Castel Del Monte | Enja | ENJ-9362 2
Castel Del Monte II | Enja | ENJ-9431 2
Michel Godard-Miroslav Tadic-Mark Nauseef
Loose Wires | Enja | ENJ-9071 2
Patrick Bebelaar Group
Point Of View | dml-records | CD 017
Patrick Bebelaar Quartet
You Never Lose An Island | dml-records | CD 015
Rabih Abou-Khalil Group
The Sultan's Picnic | Enja | ENJ-8078 2
Arabian Waltz | Enja | ENJ-9059 2
Odd Times | Enja | ENJ-9330 2
The Cactus Of Knowledge | Enja | ENJ-9401 2
Sylvie Courvoisier Group
Ocre | Enja | ENJ-9323 2
Y2K | Enja | ENJ-9383 2
Vincent Courtois Quartet
Translucide | Enja | ENJ-9380 2
Willem Breuker Kollektief
La Banda/Banda And Jazz | Enja | ENJ-9326 2

Godding,Brian | (el-g,gg-synth)
Mike Westbrook Band
Off Abbey Road | TipToe | TIP-888805 2
Mike Westbrook Brass Band
Glad Day:Settings Of William Blake | Enja | ENJ-9376 2

Godejohann,Karl | (dr,percsampled-perc)
Philippe Caillat Special Project
Melodic Travel | Laika Records | LK 689-012

Godfrey,John | (dr)
Freddie Redd Sextet
Redd's Blues | Blue Note | 540537-2

Godfroit,Marc | (tb)
Stochelo Rosenberg Group
Gypsy Swing | Verve | 527806-2

Godla,Dezider | (viola)
Karol Adam Ensemble
Gipsy Fascination | G&J Records | GJ 2001

Godtholdt | (tpfl-h)
Copenhagen Art Ensemble
Shape To Twelve | dacapo | DCCD 9430

Goe,Gene | (tpfl-h)
Paulinho Da Costa Orchestra
Agora | Original Jazz Classics | OJCCD 630-2(2310785)

Goebbels,Heiner | (cl,ss,ts,bass-sax,g,p,synth,cello)
Heiner Goebbels Group
Shadow/Landscape With Argonauts | ECM | 1480
Ou Bien Le Debarquement Desastreux | ECM | 1552
Heiner Goebbels/Heiner Müller
Der Mann Im Fahrstuhl | ECM | 1369(837110-2)

Goerner,F. | (celloviola)
Artie Shaw And His Orchestra
Planet JazzArtie Shaw | Planet Jazz | 2152057-2
Planet Jazz:Big Bands | Planet Jazz | 2169649-2

Goetz,Mathias | (tb)
Clark Terry With The Summit Jazz Orchestra
Clark | Edition Collage | EC 530-2
Mathias Götz-Windstärke 4
Lunar Oder Solar? | Jazz 'n' Arts Records | JNA 1002

Goff,Gerry | (tp)
Duke Ellington With Tommy Dorsey And His Orchestra
Highlights From The Duke Ellington Centennial Edition | RCA | 2663672-2

Goff,Harper | (bj)
Firehouse Five Plus Two
Goes South | Good Time Jazz | GTCD 12018-2

Goines,Lincoln | (b,el-bb-g)
Bob Berg Quintet
The Art Of Saxophone | Laserlight | 24652
Leni Stern Group
Secrets | Enja | ENJ-5093 2
Closer To The Light | Enja | ENJ-6034 2
Mike Stern Group
Odds Or Evens | Atlantic | 7567-82297-2
Play | Atlantic | 7567-83219-2
Paquito D'Rivera Orchestra
Jazzrock-Anthology Vol.3:Fusion | Zounds | CD 27100555
Wayne Krantz Trio
Long To Be Loose | Enja | ENJ-7099 2
2 Drinks Minimum | Enja | ENJ-9043 2

Goines,Victor | (cl,b-cl,ss,as,tsbs)
Lincoln Center Jazz Orchestra
Big Train | CBS | CK 69860
Ruth Brown With Orchestra
Fine And Mellow | Fantasy | FCD 9663-2
Wycliffe Gordon Group
Slidin' Home | Nagel-Heyer | CD 2001
The Search | Nagel-Heyer | CD 2007
Ellington For Lovers | Nagel-Heyer | NH 1009
Blues Of Summer | Nagel-Heyer | NH 1011
Wycliffe Gordon Quintet
The Joyride | Nagel-Heyer | CD 2032
Wynton Marsalis Group
Standard Time Vol.4:Marsalis Plays Monk | CBS | CK 67503
Standard Time Vol.6:Mr.Jelly Lord | CBS | CK 69872

Gold,David | (viola)
Steve Coleman And Five Elements
The Sonic Language Of Myth | RCA | 2164123-2

Gold,Larry | (cello)
Uri Caine Group
Urlicht/Primal Light | Winter&Winter | 910004-2

Gold,Sanford | (p)
Coleman Hawkins Quintet
Body And Soul Revisited | GRP | GRP 16272
Coleman Hawkins Quintet With Strings
Body And Soul Revisited | GRP | GRP 16272
Don Byas Quartet
Don Byas:Laura | Dreyfus Jazz Line | FDM 36714-2
Johnny Smith Quintet
Moonlight In Vermont | Roulette | 596593-2
Johnny Smith-Stan Getz Quintet
Stan Getz-The Complete Roost Sessions | EMI Records | 859622-2

Goldberg,Aaron | (psynth)
Greg Tardy Band
Serendipity | Impulse(MCA) | 951258-2
Joshua Redman Quartet
Beyond | Warner | 9362-47465-2
Passage Of Time | Warner | 9362-47997-2
Joshua Redman Quartet feat. Mark Turner
Beyond | Warner | 9362-47465-2
OAM Trio
Trilingual | Fresh Sound Records | FSNT 070 CD
Wayne Escoffery Quartet
Time Changes | Nagel-Heyer | CD 2015

Goldberg,Allan | (viola)
Gary McFarland And His Orchestra
The Complete Bill Evans On Verve | Verve | 527953-2

Goldberg,Edward 'Doc' | (b)
Glenn Miller And His Orchestra
Planet Jazz:Glenn Miller | Planet Jazz | 2152056-2

Goldberg,Morris | (asthin-whistle)
Hans Theessink Group
Call Me | Minor Music | 801022

Goldberg,Richie | (drperc)
Kenny Burrell Quartet
Stormy Monday Blues | Fantasy | FCD 24767-2
Ray Charles And His Orchestra
Ray Charles At Newport | Atlantic | 7567-80765-2
Ray Charles Sextet With The Raylets
Newport Jazz Festival 1958,July 3rd-6th Vol.4:Blues In The Night No.2 | Phontastic | NCD 8816

Goldberg,Stu | (el-p,org,synth,p,cembalo,clavinet)
Toto Blanke Group
Electric Circus' Best | ALISO Records | AL 1034

Goldblatt,David | (el-p,keyboards,psynth)
John Patitucci Group
Mistura Fina | GRP | GRP 98022

Golden Gate Quartet,The | (voc)
Golden Gate Quartet
Americans Swinging In Paris:Golden Gate Quartet | EMI Records | 539659-2
Spirituals To Swing 1955-69 | EMI Records | 791569-2
Golden Gate Quartet With The Martial Solal Orchestra
Americans Swinging In Paris:Golden Gate Quartet | EMI Records | 539659-2

Golden Gate Quartet: |
Golden Gate Quartet
From Spriritual To Swing Vol.2 | EMI Records | 780573-2
From Spiritual To Swing | Vanguard | VCD 169/71
Golden Gate Quartet With The Martial Solal Orchestra
Americans Swinging In Paris:Golden Gate Quartet | EMI Records | 539659-2
From Spriritual To Swing Vol.2 | EMI Records | 780573-2

Golden,Gene | (bata,checkere,congas,bells,chekere)
Gato Barbieri Group
Planet Jazz:Gato Barbieri | RCA | 2165364-2
Gato Barbieri:The Best Of The Early Years | RCA | 2663523-2
Jerry Gonzalez & Fort Apache Band
The River Is Deep | Enja | ENJ-4040 2
Louis Armstrong And His Friends
Planet Jazz:Louis Armstrong | Planet Jazz | 2152052-2
Louis Armstrong And His Friends | Bluebird | 2663961-2

Golden,Milt | (p)
Tommy Dorsey And His Orchestra
Planet Jazz:Tommy Dorsey | Planet Jazz | 2159972-2
Planet Jazz:Jazz Greatest Hits | Planet Jazz | 2169648-2

Goldfield,Harry | (tp)
Paul Whiteman And His Orchestra
Planet Jazz:Jack Teagarden | Planet Jazz | 2161236-2
Jazz:The Essential Collection Vol.3 | IN+OUT Records | 78013-2

Goldfinger,Seymour | (tb)
Jack Teagarden And His Orchestra
Jazz:The Essential Collection Vol.3 | IN+OUT Records | 78013-2

Goldie,Don | (tpvoc)
Jack Teagarden And His Sextet
Mis'ry And The Blues | Verve | 9860310
Jack Teagarden Sextet
Newport Jazz Festival 1958,July 3rd-6th Vol.3:Blues In The Night No.1 | Phontastic | NCD 8815
Jack Teagarden Sextet With Bobby Hackett
Newport Jazz Festival 1958,July 3rd-6th Vol.3:Blues In The Night No.1 | Phontastic | NCD 8815

Goldings,Larry | (keyboards,orgp)
Carla Bley Band
4X4 | Watt | 30(159547-2)
Jason Seizer With The Larry Goldings Trio
Sketches | Organic Music | ORGM 9710
John Scofield Groups
Groove Elation | Blue Note | 832801-2
John Scofield Sextet
Hand Jive | Blue Note | 827327-2
John Stein Quintet
Portraits And Landscapes | Jardis Records | JRCD 20029
Jazz Guitar Highlights 1 | Jardis Records | JRCD 20141
Jon Hendricks Group
A Tribute To Charlie Parker Vol.2 | Storyville | 4960493
Maceo Parker Group
Mo' Roots | Minor Music | 801018
Michael Brecker Group
Time Is Of The Essence | Verve | 547844-2
Tom Browne Quintet
Another Shade Of Browne | Hip Bop | HIBD 8011
Hot Jazz Bisquits | Hip Bop | HIBD 8801

Goldsbury,Mack | (cl,ss,ts,voc,flsax)
Ed Schuller & Mack Goldbury
Art Of The Duo: Savignyplatz | Tutu Records | 888206-2*
Ed Schuller & The Eleventh Hour Band
Snake Dancing | Tutu Records | 888188-2*
Ernst Bier-Mack Goldsbury Quartet
At Night When You Go To Sleep | Timescrapper | TSCR 9611
Ernst Bier-Mack Goldsbury Quintet
At Night When You Go To Sleep | Timescrapper | TSCR 9611
Mack Goldsbury And The New York Connection
Songs I Love To Play | Timescrapper | TSCR 9615

Goldsby,John | (b,el-bb-solo)
Eddie Harris Group With The WDR Big Band
Eddie Harris-The Last Concert | ACT | 9249-2
Frank Castenier Group
For You,For Me For Evermore | EmArCy | 9814976
Frank Vignola Sextet
Off Broadway | Nagel-Heyer | CD 2006
Gianlugi Trovesi Quartet With The WDR Big Band
Dedalo | Enja | ENJ-9419 2
Hubert Nuss Trio
The Shimmering Colours Of The Stained Glass | Green House Music | CD 1008
Jens Winther And The WDR Big Band
The Escape | dacapo | DCCD 9437
Joachim Schoenecker Quartet
In The Moment | Nagel-Heyer | CD 2009
Joachim Schoenecker-Chris Potter
In The Moment | Nagel-Heyer | CD 2009
John Goldsby Sextet
Viewpoint | Nagel-Heyer | CD 2014
John Marshall Quintet
Dreamin' On The Hudson | Organic Music | ORGM 9713
Theme Of No Repeat | Organic Music | ORGM 9719
Kevin Mahogany With The WDR Big Band And Guests
Pussy Cat Dues:The Music Of Charles Mingus | Enja | ENJ-9316 2
Louis Stewart-Heiner Franz Quartet
I Wished On The Moon | Jardis Records | JRCD 20027
Jazz Guitar Highlights 1 | Jardis Records | JRCD 20141
Rolf Römer Quartet
Tesoro | Jazz 4 Ever Records:Jazz Network | J4E 4743
Rolf Römer Trio
Tesoro | Jazz 4 Ever Records:Jazz Network | J4E 4743
Rolf Römer-Bill Dobbins Quartet
A Tribute To B.A.C.H. | Edition Collage | EC 520-2

Goldschmidt,Per | (bs,saxts)
Jazz Baltica Ensemble
The Birth+Rebirth Of Swedish Folk Jazz | ACT | 9254-2

Goldsmith,Adam | (g)
Gerard Presencer Group
Chasing Reality | ACT | 9422-2

Goldsmith,Jon | (p)
Hugh Marsh Duo/Quartet/Orchestra
The Bear Walks | VeraBra Records | CDVBR 2011-2

Goldstein,Gil | (accordeon,bass-accordeon,el-p)
Bernard Purdie's Soul To Jazz
Bernard Purdie's Soul To Jazz | ACT | 9242-2
Bob Mintzer-Gil Goldstein Duo
Longing | Owl Records | 018353-2
Eddie Harris Group With The WDR Big Band
Eddie Harris-The Last Concert | ACT | 9249-2
Lenny White Group
Present Tense | Hip Bop | HIBD 8004
Manhattan Project,The
Kind Of Blue:Blue Note Celebrate The Music Of Miles Davis | Blue Note | 534255-2
Wayne Shorter:The Classic Blue Note Recordings | Blue Note | 540856-2
Michel Petrucciani Group
Music | Blue Note | 792563-2
Mike Stern Group
Standards(And Other Songs) | Atlantic | 7567-82419-2
Give And Take | Atlantic | 7567-83036-2
Miles Davis With Gil Evans Orchestra, The George Gruntz Concert Jazz Band And Guests
Miles & Quincy Live At Montreux | Warner | 9362-45221-2
Rachelle Ferrell With The Terrence Blanchard Quartet
First Instrumental | Blue Note | 827820-2
Rachelle Ferrell With The Wayne Shorter Sextet
First Instrumental | Blue Note | 827820-2

Goldstein,Malcolm | (v)
Malcolm Goldstein-Peter Niklas Wilson
Goldstein-Wilson | true muze | TUMU CD 9801

Golia,Vinny | (alto-fl,b-cl,ts,bs,piccolo,bass-fl)
Vinny Golia Quintet
Regards From Norma Desmond | Fresh Sound Records | FSNT 008 CD

Gollehon,Joseph 'Mac' | (tp)
Al Jarreau With Band
L Is For Lover | i.e. Music | 557850-2
Lester Bowie's Brass Fantasy
The Odyssey Of Funk & Popular Music | Dreyfus Jazz Line | FDM 37004-2
When The Spitit Returns | Dreyfus Jazz Line | FDM 37016-2

Golob,Ziga | (el-b)
Steve Klink Funk Unit
Places To Come From,Places To Go | Minor Music | 801098

Goloboff,Sofia | (v)
Stephane Grappelli With The Michel Legrand Orchestra
Grapelli Story | Verve | 515807-2

Golson,Benny | (arr,ld,bass-synth,p,ss,tscond)
Abbey Lincoln With The Benny Golson Quintet
It's Magic | Original Jazz Classics | OJCCD 205-2
Abbey Lincoln With The Benny Golson Septet
It's Magic | Original Jazz Classics | OJCCD 205-2
Ahmed Abdul-Malik Orchestra
Planet Jazz:Lee Morgan | Planet Jazz | 2161238-2
Art Blakey And The Jazz Messengers
Planet Jazz:Art Blakey | Planet Jazz | 2152066-2
Planet Jazz:Lee Morgan | Planet Jazz | 2161238-2
Moanin' | Blue Note | 495324-2
The Art Of Jazz | IN+OUT Records | 77028-2
The Best Of Blue Note | Blue Note | 796110-2
The Best Of Blue Note Vol.2 | Blue Note | 797960-2
Jazz In Paris:Art Blakey-1958-Paris Olympia | EmArCy | 832659-2 PMS
At The Club St.Germain | RCA | ND 74897(2)
Art Farmer/Benny Golson Jazztet
The Jazztet At Birdhouse | Argo | 589762-2
Benny Golson Band
Benny Golson:Free | GRP | 951816-2
Benny Golson Quintet
Nemmy Golson And The Philadelphians | Blue Note | 494104-2
Groovin' | Original Jazz Classics | OJCCD 226-2(NJ 8220)
Benny Golson Sextet
The J.J.Johnson Memorial Album | Prestige | PRCD 11025-2
Blue Mitchell Quintet
Out Of The Blue | Original Jazz Classics | OJCCD 667-2(RLP 1131)
Charles Mingus Group
Mingus Dynasty | CBS | CK 65513
Charles Mingus Orchestra
Charles Mingus:The Complete 1959 Columbia Recordings | CBS | C3K 65145
Dinah Washington With The Quincy Jones Orchestra
The Swingin' Miss 'D' | Verve | 558074-2
Dizzy Gillespie And His Orchestra
Dizzy Gillespie:Birks Works-The Verve Big Band Sessions | Verve | 527900-2
Ultimate Dizzy Gillespie | Verve | 557535-2
Dizzy Gillespie Orchestra
Verve Jazz Masters 10:Dizzy Gillespie | Verve | 516319-2
George Russell And His Orchestra
Geogre Russell New York N.Y. | Impulse(MCA) | 951278-2
Jack McDuff Quartet With Orchestra
Prelude:Jack McDuff Big Band | Prestige | PRCD 24283-2
Lilly Thornton With The Benny Golson Quartet
Remembering Dinah-A Salute To Dinah Washington | Hot Shot Records | HSR 8313-2
Lilly Thornton With The Benny Golson Sextet
Remembering Dinah-A Salute To Dinah Washington | Hot Shot Records | HSR 8313-2
Philly Joe Jones Big Band
Cannonball Adderley Birthday Celebration | Fantasy | FANCD 6087-2
Quincy Jones Big Band
Rahsaan/The Complete Mercury Recordings Of Roland Kirk | Mercury | 846630-2
Roland Kirk With The Benny Golson Orchestra
Rahsaan/The Complete Mercury Recordings Of Roland Kirk | Mercury | 846630-2
Ron Carter Quintet
Stardust | somethin'else | 537813-2
Roots
Saying Something | IN+OUT Records | 77031-2
For Diz & Bird | IN+OUT Records | 77039-2
Sarah Vaughan And The Thad Jones Orchestra
Verve Jazz Masters 42:Sarah Vaughan-The Jazz Sides | Verve | 526817-2
Sarah Vaughan With The Hal Mooney Orchestra
It's A Man's World | Mercury | 589487-2
Tadd Dameron And His Orchestra
Clifford Brown Memorial | Original Jazz Classics | OJC20 017-2(P 7055)
Three Of A Kind
Drip Some Grease | Minor Music | 801056
Wynton Kelly Sextet
Kelly Blue | Original Jazz Classics | OJC20 033-2(RLP 1142)
Kelly Blue | Riverside | RISA 1142-6

Gomar,Larry | (drvib)
Jack Teagarden With Orchestra
Jazz:The Essential Collection Vol.3 | IN+OUT Records | 78013-2
Paul Whiteman And His Orchestra
Planet Jazz:Jack Teagarden | Planet Jazz | 2161236-2
Jazz:The Essential Collection Vol.3 | IN+OUT Records | 78013-2

Gomersall,Anatole | (ss,asbs)
The Groenewald Newnet
Meetings | Jazz 'n' Arts Records | JNA 0702

Gomez,Carlos 'Bala' | (congas,drperc)
Quincy Jones And His Orchestra
Rahsaan/The Complete Mercury Recordings Of Roland Kirk | Mercury | 846630-2
Steve Lampert Group
Venus Perplexed | Steeplechase | SCCD 31557

Gomez,Chico | (cl)
Muggsy Spanier And His Dixieland All Stars
Muggsy Spanier At Club Hangover 1953/54 | Storyville | STCD 6033
Gomez,David | (dr,perccajon-peruano)
Alguimia
Alguimia 'U' | Fresh Sound Records | FSNT 023 CD
Alguimia:Standards | Fresh Sound Records | FSNT 049 CD
Alguimia Dos | Fresh Sound Records | FSNT 050 CD
Gómez,David | (drperc)
Javier Feierstein Quartet
Wysiwyg | Fresh Sound Records | FSNT 040 CD
Mikel Andueza Quintet
BCN | Fresh Sound Records | FSNT 036 CD
Gomez,Eddie | (b,el-b,maracasvoc)
Bennie Wallace Quartet
Bennie Wallace Plays Monk | Enja | ENJ-3091 2
Bennie Wallace Trio
Bennie Wallace Plays Monk | Enja | ENJ-3091 2
Bill Evans Duo
Intuition | Original Jazz Classics | OJCCD 470-2
Bill Evans Quartet
The Complete Bill Evans On Verve | Verve | 527953-2
From Left To Right | Verve | 557451-2
Bill Evans Quartet With Orchestra
The Complete Bill Evans On Verve | Verve | 527953-2
From Left To Right | Verve | 557451-2
Bill Evans Quintet
The Complete Fantasy Recordings | Fantasy | 9FCD 1012-2
Bill Evans Trio
Verve Jazz Masters 5:Bill Evans | Verve | 519821-2
The Complete Bill Evans On Verve | Verve | 527953-2
The Best Of Bill Evans Live | Verve | 533825-2
At The Montreux Jazz Festival | Verve | 539758-2
Ultimate Bill Evans selected by Herbie Hancock | Verve | 557536-2
You Must Believe In Spring | Rhino | 812273719-2
Bill Evans:The Secret Sessions | Milestone | 8MCD 4421-2
The Complete Fantasy Recordings | Fantasy | 9FCD 1012-2
Bill Evans:Piano Player | CBS | CK 65361
Blue In Green | Milestone | MCD 9185-2
Half Moon Bay | Milestone | MCD 9282-2
Since We Met | Original Jazz Classics | OJC 622(F 9501)
Bill Evans:From The 70's | Original Jazz Classics | OJCCD 1069-2(F 9630)
The Tokyo Concert | Original Jazz Classics | OJCCD 345-2
Re: Person I Knew | Original Jazz Classics | OJCCD 749-2(F 9608)
I Will Say Goodbye | Original Jazz Classics | OJCCD 761-2(F 9593)
The Jazz Giants Play Harold Arlen:Blues In The Night | Prestige | PCD 24201-2
The Jazz Giants Play Miles Davis:Milestones | Prestige | PCD 24225-2
Bill Evans Trio With Jeremy Steig
The Complete Bill Evans On Verve | Verve | 527953-2
Bill Evans With Orchestra
The Complete Bill Evans On Verve | Verve | 527953-2
From Left To Right | Verve | 557451-2
Bill Evans-Eddie Gomez Duo
The Complete Fantasy Recordings | Fantasy | 9FCD 1012-2
Bill Evans:Piano Player | CBS | CK 65361
Montreux III | Original Jazz Classics | OJC20 644-2(F 9510)
Eloquence | Original Jazz Classics | OJCCD 814-2(F 9618)
Chick Corea Quartet
Verve Jazz Masters 3:Chick Corea | Verve | 519820-2
Chick Corea Trio
Verve Jazz Masters 3:Chick Corea | Verve | 519820-2
Dave Liebman Quintet
Homage To John Coltrane | Owl Records | 018357-2
Dusko Goykovich Quartet
Soul Connection | Enja | ENJ-8044 2
Dusko Goykovich Quintet
Soul Connection | Enja | ENJ-8044 2
Eliane Elias Trio
The Story Of Jazz Piano | Laserlight | 24653
Blue Bossa | Blue Note | 795590-2
Jack DeJohnette New Directions
In Europe | ECM | 1157
Jack DeJohnette Quartet
New Directions | ECM | 1128
The DeJohnette Complex | Original Jazz Classics | OJCCD 617-2
Jack DeJohnette Quintet
The DeJohnette Complex | Original Jazz Classics | OJCCD 617-2
Jack DeJohnette Sextet
The DeJohnette Complex | Original Jazz Classics | OJCCD 617-2
Michel Petrucciani Group
Michel Petrucciani:The Blue Note Years | Blue Note | 789916-2
Music | Blue Note | 792563-2
Michel Petrucciani Quartet
Michel Plays Petrucciani | Blue Note | 748679-2
Michel Petrucciani:The Blue Note Years | Blue Note | 789916-2
Michel Petrucciani Trio
Michel Plays Petrucciani | Blue Note | 748679-2
Michel Petrucciani:The Blue Note Years | Blue Note | 789916-2
Mick Goodrick Quartet
In Pas(s)ing | ECM | 1139
Mike Mainieri Group
Jazz Life Vol.2:From Seventh At Avenue South | Storyville | 4960763
Mike Nock Trio
Ondas | ECM | 1220
Peter Erskine Orchestra
Peter Erskine | Original Jazz Classics | OJC 610(C 14010)
Ralph Towner Quintet
Old Friends New Friends | ECM | 1153
Ralph Towner Trio
Batik | ECM | 1121(847325-2)
Ray Barretto Orchestra
Portraits In Jazz And Clave | RCA | 2168452-2
Stan Getz With The Bill Evans Trio
But Beautiful | Milestone | MCD 9249-2
Steps Ahead
Steps Ahead:Copenhagen Live | Storyville | 4960363
Steps Ahead | Elektra | 7559-60168-2
Modern Times | Elektra | 7559-60351-2
The Jazz Composer's Orchestra
Comminications | JCOA | 1001/2
Gomez,Edsel | (psynth)
Don Byron Quintet
Tuskegee Experiments | Nonesuch | 7559-79280-2
Gomez,Felix | (keyboards)
Arturo Sandoval Quintet
I Remember Clifford | GRP | GRP 96682
Gomez,Pere | (congas)
Eladio Reinon Quintet
Es La Historia De Un Amor | Fresh Sound Records | FSNT 004 CD
Gomez,Phil | (cl)
Kid Ory And His Band
The Very Best Of Dixieland Jazz | Verve | 535529-2
Kid Ory's Creole Jazz Band
This Kid's The Greatest! | Good Time Jazz | GTCD 12045-2
Gomez,Raymond | (el-gg)
Steps Ahead
N.Y.C. | Intuition Records | INT 3007-2
Gonga,Dawilli | (el-p,synth,clavinetkeyboards)
Cal Tjader Group
Amazonas | Original Jazz Classics | OJCCD 840-2(F 9502)
Joe Henderson And His Orchestra
Joe Henderson:The Milestone Years | Milestone | 8MCD 4413-2
Gonsalves,Paul | (ts)
Billy Strayhorn Orchestra
Johnny Hodges With Billy Strayhorn And The Orchestra | Verve | 557543-2
Cat Anderson And His All Stars
Americans Swinging In Paris:Cat Anderson | EMI Records | 539658-2
Clark Terry And His Orchestra
Clark Terry And His Orchestra Feat. Paul Gonsalves | Storyville | STCD 8322
Count Basie And His Orchestra
Planet Jazz:Count Basie | Planet Jazz | 2152068-2
Planet Jazz Sampler | Planet Jazz | 2152326-2
Planet Jazz:Jimmy Rushing | RCA | 2165371-2
Planet Jazz:Jazz Greatest Hits | Planet Jazz | 2169648-2
Planet Jazz:Big Bands | Planet Jazz | 2169649-2
Jazz:The Essential Collection Vol.3 | IN+OUT Records | 78013-2
Count Basie,His Instrumentals & Rhyhtm
Planet Jazz:Count Basie | Planet Jazz | 2152068-2
Jazz:The Essential Collection Vol.3 | IN+OUT Records | 78013-2
Dizzy Gillespie All Stars
Verve Jazz Masters 25:Stan Getz & Dizzy Gillespie | Verve | 521852-2
Duke Ellington And Count Basie With Their Orchestras
First Time! | CBS | CK 65571
Duke Ellington And His Award Winners
Greatest Hits | CBS | 462959-2
Duke Ellington And His Orchestra
Planet Jazz:Johnny Hodges | Planet Jazz | 2152065-2
Duke Ellington's Far East Suite | RCA | 2174797-2
Jazz Collection:Duke Ellington | Laserlight | 24369
The Art Of Saxophone | Laserlight | 24652
The Legends Of Swing | Laserlight | 24659
100 Years Duke | Laserlight | 24906
Highlights From The Duke Ellington Centennial Edition | RCA | 2663672-2
The Popular Duke Ellington | RCA | 2663880-2
Duke Ellington: The Champs-Elysees Theater January 29-30th,1965 | Laserlight | 36131
Greatest Hits | CBS | 462959-2
The Big Bands Vol.1.The Snader Telescriptions | Storyville | 4960043
Jazz Festival Vol.2 | Storyville | 4960743
Verve Jazz Masters 4:Duke Ellington | Verve | 516338-2
Verve Jazz Masters 20:Introducing | Verve | 519853-2
Ellington '55 | Capitol | 520135-2
Great Swing Classics In Hi-Fi | Capitol | 521223-2
Ella & Duke At The Cote D'Azur | Verve | 539030-2
Ella Fitzgerald And Duke Ellington:Cote D'Azure Concerts on Verve | Verve | 539033-2
Soul Call | Verve | 539785-2
The Great Paris Concert | Atlantic | 7567-81303-2
New Orleans Suite | Rhino | 812273670-2
Afro-Bossa | Reprise | 9362-47876-2
Ellington At Newport 1956(Complete) | CBS | CK 64932
Black Brown And Beige | CBS | CK 65566
Such Sweet Thunder | CBS | CK 65568
Anatomy Of A Murder | CBS | CK 65569
The Ellington Suites | Original Jazz Classics | OJC20 446-2(2310762)
Latin America Suite | Original Jazz Classics | OJC20 469-2
Duke Ellington And His Orchestra feat. Paul Gonsalves | Original Jazz Classics | OJCCD 623-2
The Afro-Eurasian Eclipse-A Suite In Eight Parts | Original Jazz Classics | OJCCD 645-2(F 9498)
Yale Concert | Original Jazz Classics | OJCCD 664-2
Jazz At The Philharmonis Berlin '65/Paris '67 | Pablo | PACD 5304-2
Duke Ellington At The Alhambra | Pablo | PACD 5313-2
The Jazz Giants Play Duke Ellington:Caravan | Prestige | PCD 24227-2
Togo Brava Swuite | Storyville | STCD 8323
Duke Ellington Small Band
The Intimacy Of The Blues | Original Jazz Classics | OJCCD 624-2
Eddie Lockjaw Davis Sextet feat. Paul Gonsalves
Planet Jazz:Jazz Saxophone | Planet Jazz | 2169653-2
Ella Fitzgerald With The Duke Ellington Orchestra
The Stockholm Concert 1966 | Pablo | 2308242-2
Ella Fitzgerald-First Lady Of Song | Verve | 517898-2
The Best Of The Song Books | Verve | 519804-2
Verve Jazz Masters 6:Ella Fitzgerald | Verve | 519822-2
The Best Of The Song Books:The Ballads | Verve | 521867-2
Verve Jazz Masters 46:Ella Fitzgerald-The Jazz Sides | Verve | 527655-2
Ella At Duke's Place | Verve | 529700-2
Love Songs:The Best Of The Song Books | Verve | 531762-2
Ella & Duke At The Cote D'Azur | Verve | 539030-2
Ella Fitzgerald And Duke Ellington:Cote D'Azure Concerts on Verve | Verve | 539033-2
Ella Fitzgerald Sings The Duke Ellington Songbook | Verve | 559248-2
For The Love Of Ella Fitzgerald | Verve | 841765-2
Ella Fitzgerald With The Duke Ellington Orchestra And Jimmy Jones Trio
Ella & Duke At The Cote D'Azur | Verve | 539030-2
Ella Fitzgerald And Duke Ellington:Cote D'Azure Concerts on Verve | Verve | 539033-2
JATP All Stars
Welcome To Jazz At The Philharmonic | Fantasy | FANCD 6081-2
Johnny Hodges And The Ellington Men
Verve Jazz Masters 35:Johnny Hodges | Verve | 521857-2
Johnny Hodges With Billy Strayhorn And The Duke Ellington Orchestra
Verve Jazz Masters 35:Johnny Hodges | Verve | 521857-2
Oscar Peterson With The Duke Ellington Orchestra
Oscar Peterson Plays Duke Ellington | Pablo | 2310966-2
Paul Gonsalves Quintet
Gettin' Together | Original Jazz Classics | OJCCD 203-2
Quincy Jones And His Orchestra
Big Band Bossa Nova | Verve | 557913-2
Rosemary Clooney With The Duke Ellington Orchestra
Blue Rose | CBS | CK 65506
Gonsalves,Virgil | (bs)
Virgil Gonsalves Sextet
The Complete Nocturne Recordings:Jazz In Hollywood Series Vol.1 | Fresh Sound Records | NR 3CD-101
Gonsoulin,Tommy | (tp)
Harry James And His Orchestra
The Legends Of Swing | Laserlight | 24659
Gonzales Jr.,Ramon | (tp,congas,fl-h,bells,chekkereguiro)
Machito And His Orchestra
Afro-Cuban Jazz Moods | Original Jazz Classics | OJC20 447-2
Gonzales,Babs | (voc)
Babs Gonzales And His Band
Voilà | Fresh Sound Records | FSR CD 340
Babs Gonzales With The Jimmy Smith Trio
Blue Velvet: Crooners, Swooners And Velvet Vocals | Blue Note | 521153-2
Gonzales,Daniel | (congas)
Charles Mingus Orchestra
Cumbia & Jazz Fusion | Atlantic | 8122-71785-2
Gonzales,Dave | (gtp)
Lionel Hampton And His Orchestra
Planet Jazz:Lionel Hampton | Planet Jazz | 2152059-2
Gonzales,Pedro Javier | (g)
Pedro Javier Gonzales
Internationales Guitarren Festival '94 | ALISO Records | AL 1030
Gonzales,Raul | (tpfl-h)
Machito And His Orchestra
Afro-Cuban Jazz Moods | Original Jazz Classics | OJC20 447-2
Gonzalez,Andy | (b,vocperc)
Essence All Stars
Afro Cubano Chant | Hip Bop | HIBD 8009
Hot Jazz Bisquits | Hip Bop | HIBD 8801
George Benson With Orchestra
Verve Jazz Masters 21:George Benson | Verve | 521861-2
George Benson With The Don Sebesky Orchestra
Verve Jazz Masters 21:George Benson | Verve | 521861-2
Jerry Gonzalez & Fort Apache Band
The River Is Deep | Enja | ENJ-4040 2
Lazaro Ros Ensemble
Ori Batá (Cuban Yoruba Music) | Enja | ENJ-9381 2
Gonzalez,Daniel | (v)
Herbie Mann And His Orchestra
The Best Of Herbie Mann | Atlantic | 7567-81369-2
Gonzalez,Jerry | (congas,fl-h,perc,tp,bells,conga,voc)
Abbey Lincoln And Her Trio With Guests
Over The Years | Verve | 549101-2
Jerry Gonzalez & Fort Apache Band
The River Is Deep | Enja | ENJ-4040 2
McCoy Tyner Big Band
The Best Of McCoy Tyner Big Band | Dreyfus Jazz Line | FDM 37012-2
Gonzalez,Ricardo | (p)
Mongo Santamaria And His Band
Brazilian Sunset | Candid | CCD 79703
Gonzi,Mario | (drvoc)
Claus Raible Trio
Introducing The Exciting Claus Raible Trio | Organic Music | ORGM 9714
David Gazarov Trio
Let's Have A Merry Christmas With The David Gazarov Trio! | Organic Music | ORGM 9712
Klaus Ignatzek Group
Live At Leverkusener Jazztage | Nabel Records:Jazz Network | CD 4630
Roman Schwaller Nonet
The Original Tunes | JHM Records | JHM 3629
The New Roman Schwaller Jazzquartet
Welcome Back From Outer Space | JHM Records | JHM 3605
Good,Dennis Allen | (b-tb)
Buddy Rich And His Orchestra
Swingin' New Big Band | Pacific Jazz | 835232-2
Goode,Brad | (tp)
Brad Goode-Von Freeman Sextet
Inside Chicago Vol.3 | Steeplechase | SCCD 31531
Inside Chicago Vol.4 | Steeplechase | SCCD 31532
Goode,Coleridge | (b)
Joe Harriott Quintet
Free Form | EmArCy | 538184-2
Quintet Du Hot Club De France
Grapelli Story | Verve | 515807-2
Verve Jazz Masters 38:Django Reinhardt | Verve | 516931-2
Django Reinhardt:Echoes Of France | Dreyfus Jazz Line | FDM 36726-2
Django Reinhardt:Souveniers | Dreyfus Jazz Line | FDM 36744-2
Goodhew,Denney | (as,b-cl,ss,sopranino,bs,flsax)
First Avenue
First Avenue | ECM | 1194
Nils Petter Molvaer Group
Elegy For Africa | Nabel Records:Jazz Network | CD 4678
Ralph Towner Quartet
Lost And Found | ECM | 1563(529347-2)
Goodie,Frank 'Big Boy' | (clts)
Bill Coleman Et Son Orchestre
Americans Swinging In Paris:Bill Coleman-The Elegance | EMI Records | 539662-2
Goodlette,Frank | (b)
Louis Armstrong With Sy Oliver And His Orchestra
Satchmo Serenaders | Verve | 543792-2
Goodman,Anne | (cello)
Frank Sinatra With The Count Basie Orchestra
It Might As Well Be Spring | Reprise | 7599-27027-2
Goodman,Benny | (b-cl,cl,as,bs,co,voc,ld,congas,dr)
Adrian Rollini And His Orchestra
Jazz:The Essential Collection Vol.3 | IN+OUT Records | 78013-2
All Star Band
Planet Jazz:Jack Teagarden | Planet Jazz | 2161236-2
Ben Pollack And His Park Central Orchestra
Planet Jazz:Jack Teagarden | Planet Jazz | 2161236-2
Jazz:The Essential Collection Vol.3 | IN+OUT Records | 78013-2
Benny Goodman
Benny Goodman At Carnegie Hall 1938(Complete) | CBS | C2K 65143
Benny Goodman And His All Star Sextet
Verve Jazz Masters 33:Benny Goodman | Verve | 844410-2
Charlie Christian:Swing To Bop | Dreyfus Jazz Line | FDM 36715-2
Benny Goodman And His Orchestra
Planet Jazz:Benny Goodman | Planet Jazz | 2152054-2
Planet Jazz Sampler | Planet Jazz | 2152326-2
Planet Jazz:Jazz Greatest Hits | Planet Jazz | 2169648-2
Planet Jazz:Big Bands | Planet Jazz | 2169649-2
Planet Jazz:Swing | Planet Jazz | 2169651-2
Planet Jazz:Jazz Trumpet | Planet Jazz | 2169654-2
Planet Jazz:Female Jazz Vocalists | Planet Jazz | 2169656-2
Jazz Collection:Benny Goodman | Laserlight | 24396
The Legends Of Swing | Laserlight | 24659
Swing Vol.1 | Storyville | 4960343
Great Swing Classics In Hi-Fi | Capitol | 521223-2
Jazz:The Essential Collection Vol.3 | IN+OUT Records | 78013-2
40th Anniversary Concert-Live At Carnegie Hall | London | 820349-2
Verve Jazz Masters 33:Benny Goodman | Verve | 844410-2
Benny Goodman At Carnegie Hall 1938(Complete) | CBS | C2K 65143
Charlie Christian:Swing To Bop | Dreyfus Jazz Line | FDM 36715-2
Camel Caravan Broadcast 1939 Vol.1 | Phontastic | NCD 8817
Camel Caravan Broadcast 1939 Vol.2 | Phontastic | NCD 8818
Camel Caravan Broadcast 1939 Vol.3 | Phontastic | NCD 8819
More Camel Caravans | Phontastic | NCD 8841/2
More Camel Caravans | Phontastic | NCD 8843/4
More Camel Caravans | Phontastic | NCD 8845/6
Benny Goodman And His V-Disc All Star Band
The Legends Of Swing | Laserlight | 24659
Benny Goodman Band
Benny Goodman At Carnegie Hall 1938(Complete) | CBS | C2K 65143
Benny Goodman Combo
Benny Goodman At Carnegie Hall 1938(Complete) | CBS | C2K 65143
Benny Goodman Dixieland Quintet
Benny Goodman At Carnegie Hall 1938(Complete) | CBS | C2K 65143
Benny Goodman Quartet
Planet Jazz:Benny Goodman | Planet Jazz | 2152054-2
Jazz Collection:Benny Goodman | Laserlight | 24396
Together Again! | RCA | 2663881-2
Verve Jazz Masters 33:Benny Goodman | Verve | 844410-2
Benny Goodman At Carnegie Hall 1938(Complete) | CBS | C2K 65143
Camel Caravan Broadcast 1939 Vol.1 | Phontastic | NCD 8817
Camel Caravan Broadcast 1939 Vol.2 | Phontastic | NCD 8818
Camel Caravan Broadcast 1939 Vol.3 | Phontastic | NCD 8819
More Camel Caravans | Phontastic | NCD 8841/2
More Camel Caravans | Phontastic | NCD 8843/4
More Camel Caravans | Phontastic | NCD 8845/6
Benny Goodman Quintet
Verve Jazz Masters 33:Benny Goodman | Verve | 844410-2
Benny Goodman Septet
Jazz:The Essential Collection Vol.3 | IN+OUT Records | 78013-2
Verve Jazz Masters 33:Benny Goodman | Verve | 844410-2
Charlie Christian:Swing To Bop | Dreyfus Jazz Line | FDM 36715-2
Benny Goodman Septet feat.Count Basie
Charlie Christian:Swing To Bop | Dreyfus Jazz Line | FDM 36715-2
Benny Goodman Sextet
Verve Jazz Masters 33:Benny Goodman | Verve | 844410-2
Charlie Christian:Swing To Bop | Dreyfus Jazz Line | FDM 36715-2
More Camel Caravans | Phontastic | NCD 8845/6
From Spiritual To Swing | Vanguard | VCD 169/71
Benny Goodman Trio
Planet Jazz:Benny Goodman | Planet Jazz | 2152054-2
Planet Jazz:Swing | Planet Jazz | 2169651-2
Planet Jazz:Jazz Piano | RCA | 2169655-2
Jazz Collection:Benny Goodman | Laserlight | 24396
Benny Goodman-The Complete Capitol Trios | Capitol | 521225-2
Benny Goodman At Carnegie Hall 1938(Complete) | CBS | C2K 65143
Camel Caravan Broadcast 1939 Vol.2 | Phontastic | NCD 8818
Camel Caravan Broadcast 1939 Vol.3 | Phontastic | NCD 8819

More Camel Caravans | Phontastic | NCD 8841/2
More Camel Caravans | Phontastic | NCD 8843/4
More Camel Caravans | Phontastic | NCD 8845/6
Bessie Smith And Her Band
Jazz:The Essential Collection Vol.3 | IN+OUT Records | 78013-2
Billie Holiday With Teddy Wilson And His Orchestra
Billie's Love Songs | Nimbus Records | NI 2000
Count Basie And His Orchestra
From Spiritual To Swing | Vanguard | VCD 169/71
Eddie Lang-Joe Venuti And Their Allstars Orchestra
Jazz:The Essential Collection Vol.3 | IN+OUT Records | 78013-2
Gene Krupa's Swing Band
Planet Jazz:Swing | Planet Jazz | 2169651-2
Irving Mills And His Hotsy Totsy Gang
Jazz:The Essential Collection Vol.3 | IN+OUT Records | 78013-2
Jam Session
Benny Goodman At Carnegie Hall 1938(Complete) | CBS | C2K 65143
Peggy Lee With Benny Goodman And His Quintet
Peggy Lee & Benny Goodman:The Complete Recordings 1941-1947 | CBS | C2K 65686
Peggy Lee With Benny Goodman And His Sextet
Peggy Lee & Benny Goodman:The Complete Recordings 1941-1947 | CBS | C2K 65686
Peggy Lee With Benny Goodman And The Paul Weston Orchestra
Peggy Lee & Benny Goodman:The Complete Recordings 1941-1947 | CBS | C2K 65686
Peggy Lee With The Benny Goodman Orchestra
Peggy Lee & Benny Goodman:The Complete Recordings 1941-1947 | CBS | C2K 65686
Teddy Wilson And His Orchestra
Jazz:The Essential Collection Vol.3 | IN+OUT Records | 78013-2
The Hollywood Hucksters
The Hollywood Session:The Capitol Jazzmen | Jazz Unlimited | JUCD 2044
The Metronome All-Star Nine
Jazz:The Essential Collection Vol.3 | IN+OUT Records | 78013-2

Goodman,Geoff | (el-g,g,el-mandmando-cello)
Geoff Goodman Quintet
Naked Eye | Tutu Records | 888214-2*
Marty Cook Quintet
Marty Cook Trio/Quintet | Tutu Records | 888210-2*
Marty Cook Trio
Marty Cook Trio/Quintet | Tutu Records | 888210-2*
Nicolas Simion Group
Balkan Jazz | Intuition Records | INT 3339-2
Tabla & Strings
Islands Everywhere | Tutu Records | 888208-2*

Goodman,Harry | (btuba)
Ben Pollack And His Park Central Orchestra
Planet Jazz:Jack Teagarden | Planet Jazz | 2161236-2
Jazz:The Essential Collection Vol.3 | IN+OUT Records | 78013-2
Benny Goodman And His Orchestra
Planet Jazz:Benny Goodman | Planet Jazz | 2152054-2
Planet Jazz Sampler | Planet Jazz | 2152326-2
Planet Jazz:Jazz Greatest Hits | Planet Jazz | 2169648-2
Planet Jazz:Big Bands | Planet Jazz | 2169649-2
Planet Jazz:Swing | Planet Jazz | 2169651-2
Planet Jazz:Jazz Trumpet | Planet Jazz | 2169654-2
Planet Jazz:Female Jazz Vocalists | Planet Jazz | 2169656-2
Benny Goodman At Carnegie Hall 1938(Complete) | CBS | C2K 65143
Camel Caravan Broadcast 1939 Vol.1 | Phontastic | NCD 8817
Camel Caravan Broadcast 1939 Vol.2 | Phontastic | NCD 8818
Camel Caravan Broadcast 1939 Vol.3 | Phontastic | NCD 8819
More Camel Caravans | Phontastic | NCD 8841/2
More Camel Caravans | Phontastic | NCD 8843/4
More Camel Caravans | Phontastic | NCD 8845/6
Benny Goodman Band
Benny Goodman At Carnegie Hall 1938(Complete) | CBS | C2K 65143
Benny Goodman Combo
Benny Goodman At Carnegie Hall 1938(Complete) | CBS | C2K 65143
Jam Session
Benny Goodman At Carnegie Hall 1938(Complete) | CBS | C2K 65143

Goodman,Irving | (tp)
Benny Goodman And His Orchestra
Charlie Christian:Swing To Bop | Dreyfus Jazz Line | FDM 36715-2
Camel Caravan Broadcast 1939 Vol.2 | Phontastic | NCD 8818
Camel Caravan Broadcast 1939 Vol.3 | Phontastic | NCD 8819

Goodman,Jerry | (vel-v)
Mahavishnu Orchestra
The Inner Mounting Flame | CBS | CK 65523
The Mahavishnu Orchestra
Between Nothingness & Eternity | CBS | CK 32766

Goodman,Steve | (v,b,saw,voicewhistles)
Creative Works Orchestra
Willisau And More Live | Creative Works Records | CW CD 1020-2

Goodman,Tommy | (cond,arrp)
Louis Armstrong And His Orchestra
What A Wonderful World | MCA | MCD 01876
The Six
The Very Best Of Dixieland Jazz | Verve | 535529-2

Goodman,Wayne | (tb)
Lincoln Center Jazz Orchestra
Big Train | CBS | CK 69860

Goodrick,Mick | (el-g,gg-synth)
Charlie Haden And The Liberation Music Orchestra
The Montreal Tapes:Liberation Music Orchestra | Verve | 527469-2
Charlie Haden Orchestra
The Ballad Of The Fallen | ECM | 1248(811546-2)
Ed Sarath Quintet
Last Day In May | Konnex Records | KCD 5042
Gary Burton Quartet
The New Quartet | ECM | 1030
Gary Burton Quintet
Dreams So Real | ECM | 1072
Gary Burton Quintet With Eberhard Weber
Ring | ECM | 1051
Mick Goodrick Quartet
In Pas(s)ing | ECM | 1139
Steve Swallow Group
Deconstructed | Watt | XtraWatt/9(537119-2)
Steve Swallow Quintet
Always Pack Your Uniform On Top | Watt | XtraWatt/10(543506-2)

Goods,Richie | (b)
Antonio Hart Group
Ama Tu Sonrisa | Enja | ENJ-9404 2
Eddie Allen Quintet
Summer Days | Enja | ENJ-9388 2
Eddie Allen Sextet
Summer Days | Enja | ENJ-9388 2
Russell Malone Quartet
Look Who's Here | Verve | 543543-2

Goods,Torsten | (g,el-gvoc)
Torsten Goods Group
Manhattan Walls | Jardis Records | JRCD 20139

Goodwin,Bill | (drperc)
Gary Burton-Keith Jarrett Quintet
Gary Burton & Keith Jarrett | Atlantic | 7567-81374-2
Gary Burton-Stephane Grappelli Quartet
Paris Encounter | Atlantic | 7567-80763-2
George Robert-Tom Harrell Quintet
Visions | Contemporary | CCD 14063-2
Phil Woods Quartet
A Tribute To Charlie Parker Vol.2 | Storyville | 4960493
Putte Wickman And The Hal Galper trio
Time To Remember | Dragon | DRCD 378

Goodwin,Henry | (tplaughing)
Lucille Hegamin With Willie The Lion And His Cubs
Songs We Taught Your Mother | Original Blues Classics | OBCCD 520-2

Sidney Bechet And His New Orleans Feetwarmers
Sidney Bechet:Summertime | Dreyfus Jazz Line | FDM 36712-2

'Google Eyes' | (voc)
Count Basie Octet
Planet Jazz:Count Basie | Planet Jazz | 2152068-2

Goosmann,Meike | (cl,ss,asreeds)
The United Women's Orchestra
The Blue One | Jazz Haus Musik | JHM 0099 CD
United Women's Orchestra
Virgo Supercluster | Jazz Haus Musik | JHM 0123 CD

Goraguer,Alain | (p,arrld)
Alain Goraguer Orchestra
Jazz In Paris | EmArCy | 548793-2

Goraguer,Patrick | (p,comp,arrld)
Jazz In Paris:Jazz & Cinéma Vol.1 | EmArCy | 548318-2 PMS

Gordan,Christopher | (b)
Don Menza And The Joe Haider Trio
Bilein | JHM Records | JHM 3608
Don Menza Quartet
Las Vegar Late Night Sessions:Live At Capozzoli's | Woofy Productions | WPCD 116

Gordinho | (surdotambourine)
Duo Fenix
Karai-Eté | IN+OUT Records | 7009-2

Gordner,June | (dr)
Lionel Hampton And His Orchestra
Planet Jazz:Lionel Hampton | Planet Jazz | 2152059-2
Lionel Hampton And His Quintet
Planet Jazz:Jazz Greatest Hits | Planet Jazz | 2169648-2
Lionel Hampton Quintet
Planet Jazz:Lionel Hampton | Planet Jazz | 2152059-2

Gordon Sr.,George | (voc)
Hank Jones Trio With The Gordons's
Charles Mingus-The Complete Debut Recordings | Debut | 12 DCD 4402-2

Gordon,Amos | (as,saxts)
Louis Armstrong And His Orchestra
Best Of The Complete RCA Victor Recordings | RCA | 2663636-2
Louis Armstrong:A 100th Birthday Celebration | RCA | 2663694-2
Louis Armstrong:C'est Si Bon | Dreyfus Jazz Line | FDM 36730-2
Swing Legends:Louis Armstrong | Nimbus Records | NI 2012

Gordon,Bob | (b-clbs)
Chet Baker Septet
The Best Of Chet Baker Plays | Pacific Jazz | 797161-2
Herbie Harper Quintet
The Complete Nocturne Recordings:Jazz In Hollywood Series Vol.1 | Fresh Sound Records | NR 3CD-101
June Christy With The Pete Rugolo Orchestra
Something Cool(The Complete Mono & Stereo Versions) | Capitol | 534069-2
Lennie Niehaus Quintet
Lennie Niehaus Vol.1:The Quintets | Original Jazz Classics | OJCCD 1933-2(C 3518)
Maynard Ferguson Band
Verve Jazz Masters 52:Maynard Ferguson | Verve | 529905-2
Stan Kenton And His Orchestra
Stan Kenton Portraits On Standards | Capitol | 531571-2
Tal Farlow Sextet
Verve Jazz Masters 41:Tal Farlow | Verve | 527365-2

Gordon,Dennis | (voc)
First Revolution Singers
First Revolution Gospel Singers:A Capella | Laserlight | 24338

Gordon,Dexter | (ss,ts,talking,ld,spoken lyricsvoc)
Booker Ervin-Dexter Gordon Quintet
Dexter Gordon Birthday Celebration | Fantasy | FANCD 6082-2
Dexter Gordon Quartet
Go! | Blue Note | 498794-2
Blue Note Plays Gershwin | Blue Note | 520808-2
True Blue | Blue Note | 534032-2
Our Man In Paris | Blue Note | 591722-2
Dexter Gordon:Ballads | Blue Note | 796579-2
The Best Of Blue Note Vol.2 | Blue Note | 797960-2
Jazz Profile:Dexter Gordon | Blue Note | 823514-2
Midnight Blue(The [Be]witching Hour) | Blue Note | 854365-2
Dexter Gordon Birthday Celebration | Fantasy | FANCD 6082-2
More Power | Original Jazz Classics | OJC20 815-2(P 7680)
Tangerine | Original Jazz Classics | OJCCD 1041-2(P 10091)
Tower Of Power | Original Jazz Classics | OJCCD 299-2(P 7623)
The Panther | Original Jazz Classics | OJCCD 770-2(P 10030)
The Jumpin' Blues | Original Jazz Classics | OJCCD 899-2(PR 10020)
L.T.D. | Prestige | PCD 11018-2
XXL | Prestige | PCD 11033-2
Swiss Nights-Vol. 1 | Steeplechase | SCCD 31050
Swiss Nights Vol.2 | Steeplechase | SCCD 31090
Swiss Nights Vol.3 | Steeplechase | SCCD 31110
Dexter Gordon:Atlanta Georgia May 5,1981 | Storyville | STCD 8363
Dexter Gordon Quintet
The Art Of Saxophone | Laserlight | 24652
Doin' Allright | Blue Note | 784077-2
Dexter Gordon:Ballads | Blue Note | 796579-2
Jazz Profile:Dexter Gordon | Blue Note | 823514-2
Dexter Gordon Birthday Celebration | Fantasy | FANCD 6082-2
Fats Navarro:Nostalgia | Dreyfus Jazz Line | FDM 36736-2
Tangerine | Original Jazz Classics | OJCCD 1041-2(P 10091)
Tower Of Power | Original Jazz Classics | OJCCD 299-2(P 7623)
Generation | Original Jazz Classics | OJCCD 836-2(P 10069)
The Jazz Giants Play Miles Davis:Milestones | Prestige | PCD 24225-2
Dexter Gordon With The Kenny Drew Trio
Loose Walk | Steeplechase | SCCD 36032
Dexter Gordon-Benny Bailey Quintet
Revelation | Steeplechase | SCCD 31373
The Rainbow People | Steeplechase | SCCD 31521
Dexter Gordon-James Moody Quintet
More Power | Original Jazz Classics | OJC20 815-2(P 7680)
Dizzy Gillespie Sextet
Dizzy Gillespie:Night In Tunisia | Dreyfus Jazz Line | FDM 36734-2
Gene Ammons And His All Stars
Dexter Gordon Birthday Celebration | Fantasy | FANCD 6082-2
Gene Ammons-Dexter Gordon Quintet
Dexter Gordon Birthday Celebration | Fantasy | FANCD 6082-2
Herbie Hancock Quintet
Herbie Hancock:The Complete Blue Note Sixties Sessions | Blue Note | 495569-2
The Best Of Blue Note Vol.2 | Blue Note | 797960-2
Cantaloupe Island | Blue Note | 829331-2
Takin' Off | Blue Note | 837643-2
Jesse Price And His Blues Band
Jazz Profile:Dexter Gordon | Blue Note | 823514-2
Lionel Hampton And His Orchestra
Lionel Hampton:Flying Home | Dreyfus Jazz Line | FDM 36735-2
Red Norvo Septet
Jazz Profile:Dexter Gordon | Blue Note | 823514-2
Slide Hampton-Joe Haider Jazz Orchestra
Give Me A Double | JHM Records | JHM 3627
Tadd Dameron Tentet
Jazz Profile:Dexter Gordon | Blue Note | 823514-2
Wardell Gray's Los Angeles All Stars
Dexter Gordon Birthday Celebration | Fantasy | FANCD 6082-2
Wardell Gray Memorial Vol.2 | Original Jazz Classics | OJCCD 051-2(P 7009)

Gordon,Geoffrey | (perc)
David Torn/Geoffrey Gordon
Best Laid Plans | ECM | 1284

Gordon,George | (voc)
Hank Jones Trio With The Gordons's
Charles Mingus-The Complete Debut Recordings | Debut | 12 DCD 4402-2

Gordon,Hal | (perc)
Gabor Szabo Quintet
The Roots Of Acid Jazz | Impulse(MCA) | IMP 12042
The Sorcerer | Impulse(MCA) | IMP 12112

Gordon,Honey[Honi] | (screamsvoc)
Charles Mingus Group
Mingus Dynasty | CBS | CK 65513
Charles Mingus Orchestra
Charles Mingus:The Complete 1959 Columbia Recordings | CBS | C3K 65145
Hank Jones Trio With The Gordons's
Charles Mingus-The Complete Debut Recordings | Debut | 12 DCD 4402-2

Gordon,Jim | (dr)
John Lee Hooker Group
Endless Boogie | MCA | MCD 10413

Gordon,Joe | (tp)
Benny Carter And His Orchestra
Aspects | Capitol | 852677-2
Dizzy Gillespie And His Orchestra
Verve Jazz Masters 20:Introducing | Verve | 519853-2
Dizzy Gillespie:Birks Works-The Verve Big Band Sessions | Verve | 527900-2
Dizzy Gillespie Orchestra
Verve Jazz Masters 10:Dizzy Gillespie | Verve | 516319-2
Donald Brown Quintet
Donald Byrd & Doug Watkins:The Tradition Sessions | Blue Note | 540528-2
Donald Byrd Sextet
Donald Byrd & Doug Watkins:The Tradition Sessions | Blue Note | 540528-2
Harold Land Sextet
Wes Montgomery-The Complete Riverside Recordings | Riverside | 12 RCD 4408-2
Joe Gordon Quintet
Lookin' Good | Original Jazz Classics | OJCCD 1934-2(S 7597)
Shelly Manne And His Men
At The Black Hawk Vol.1 | Original Jazz Classics | OJCCD 656-2(S 7577)
At The Black Hawk Vol.2 | Original Jazz Classics | OJCCD 657-2(S 7578)
At The Black Hawk Vol.3 | Original Jazz Classics | OJCCD 658-2(S 7579)
At The Black Hawk Vol.4 | Original Jazz Classics | OJCCD 659-2(S 7580)
At The Black Hawk Vol.5 | Original Jazz Classics | OJCCD 660-2
Jazz At The Philharmonic-Yesterdays | Pablo | PACD 5318-2
Thelonious Monk Quartet Plus Two
Thelonious Monk:85th Birthday Celebration | zyx records | FANCD 6076-2
At The Blackhawk | Original Jazz Classics | OJCCD 305-2

Gordon,Jon | (as,fl,clss)
George Colligan Group
Unresolved | Fresh Sound Records | FSNT 054 CD
Louis Smith Quintet
Louisville | Steeplechase | SCCD 31552

Gordon,Joshua 'Josh' | (cello)
Steve Kuhn With Strings
Promises Kept | ECM | 1815(0675222)

Gordon,Justin | (cl,b-cl,fl,alto-fl,reedsts)
Anita O'Day With The Billy May Orchestra
Verve Jazz Masters 49:Anita O'Day | Verve | 527653-2
Barney Kessel And His Orchestra
Barney Kessel Plays Carmen | Original Jazz Classics | OJC 269(C 7563)
The Jazz Giants Play Rodgers & Hart:Blue Moon | Prestige | PCD 24205-2
Benny Carter And His Orchestra
Aspects | Capitol | 852677-2
Billy Eckstine With The Billy May Orchestra
Once More With Feeling | Roulette | 581862-2
Ella Fitzgerald With The Billy May Orchestra
Love Songs:The Best Of The Song Books | Verve | 531762-2
Ella Fitzgerald Sings The Harold Arlen Song Book | Verve | 589108-2
Ella Fitzgerald With The Nelson Riddle Orchestra
Get Happy! | Verve | 523321-2
Mel Tormé With The Billy May Orchestra
Mel Tormé Goes South Of The Border With Billy May | Verve | 589517-2
Peggy Lee With The Quincy Jones Orchestra
Blues Cross Country | Capitol | 520088-2
Van Alexander Orchestra
Home Of Happy Feet/Swing! Staged For Sound! | Capitol | 535211-2

Gordon,Kenneth | (stringsv)
A Band Of Friends
Wynton Marsalis Quartet With Strings | CBS | CK 68921
Ron Carter Quintet With Strings
Pick 'Em/Super Strings | Milestone | MCD 47090-2

Gordon,Peter | (fr-h)
Chick Corea With String Quartet,Flute And French Horn
Septet | ECM | 1297
George Gruntz Concert Jazz Band '83
Theatre | ECM | 1265
Gil Evans Orchestra
There Comes A Time | RCA | 2131392-2
PLay The Music Of Jimi Hendrix | RCA | 2663872-2
Helen Merrill With Orchestra
Casa Forte | EmArCy | 558848-2
Michael Brecker Quindectet
Wide Angles | Verve | 076142-2

Gordon,Rebecka | (voc)
Rebecka Gordon Quartet
Yiddish'n Jazz | Touché Music | TMcCD 014

Gordon,Richard | (voc)
Hank Jones Trio With The Gordons's
Charles Mingus-The Complete Debut Recordings | Debut | 12 DCD 4402-2

Gordon,Steve | (viola)
Charlie Haden Quartet West With Strings
The Art Of The Song | Verve | 547403-2

Gordon,Wycliffe | (didgeridoo,tb,tuba,voc,tpp)
Byron Stripling Quintet
Byron,Get On Free | Nagel-Heyer | CD 2016
Byron Stripling Sextet
Byron,Get On Free | Nagel-Heyer | CD 2016
David Ostwald's Gully Low Jazz Band
Blues In Your Heart | Nagel-Heyer | CD 051
Eric Reed Orchestra
Happiness | Nagel-Heyer | CD 2010
Eric Reed Quartet
Musicale | Impulse(MCA) | 951196-2
Lincoln Center Jazz Orchestra
Big Train | CBS | CK 69860
Marcus Printup Sextet
The New Boogaloo | Nagel-Heyer | CD 2019
Randy Sandke And The New York Allstars
The Re-Discovered Louis And Bix | Nagel-Heyer | CD 058
Randy Sandke Sextet
Cliffhanger | Nagel-Heyer | CD 2037
Randy Sandke-Dick Hyman
The Re-Discovered Louis And Bix | Nagel-Heyer | CD 058
The Sidney Bechet Society
Jam Session Concert | Nagel-Heyer | CD 076
Wycliffe Gordon Group
Slidin' Home | Nagel-Heyer | CD 2001
The Search | Nagel-Heyer | CD 2007
Ellington For Lovers | Nagel-Heyer | NH 1009
Blues Of Summer | Nagel-Heyer | NH 1011
Wycliffe Gordon Quintet

The Joyride | Nagel-Heyer | CD 2032
Wycliffe Gordon-Eric Reid
We | Nagel-Heyer | CD 2023
Wynton Marsalis Group
Standard Time Vol.4:Marsalis Plays Monk | CBS | CK 67503
Standard Time Vol.6:Mr.Jelly Lord | CBS | CK 69872
Gordon-Lenox,Ian | (tp,euphonium,tubafl-h)
Cadavre Exquis
Cadavre Exquis | Creative Works Records | CW CD 1014-1
Gorgoni,Al | (g)
Herbie Mann And His Orchestra
The Best Of Herbie Mann | Atlantic | 7567-81369-2
Gorman,Tony | (cl,as,tsperc)
Clarion Fracture Zone
Blue Shift | VeraBra Records | CDVBR 2075-2
Mara!
Ruino Vino | Laika Records | 35100792
Gorn,Steve | (bamboo-fl,south-american-fl,cl,ss)
Jack DeJohnette Trio
Dancing With Nature Spirits | ECM | 1558(531024-2)
Gorrie,Alan | (b,vocg)
Klaus Doldinger With Orchestra
Lifelike | Warner | 2292-46478-2
Gorter,Arjen | (b,b-gp)
Gunter Hampel Group
The 8th Of July 1969 | Birth | CD 001
Gunter Hampel Quintet
Legendary: The 27th Of May 1997 | Birth | CD 045
Goshay,Sylvester | (dr)
Lonnie Smith Quintet
The Lost Grooves | Blue Note | 831883-2
Gosset,Andre | (tb)
Dizzy Gillespie Orchestra And The Operatic String Orchestra
Jazz In Paris:Dizzy Gillespie And His Operatic Strings Orchestra | EmArCy | 018420-2
Gossez,Pierre | (as,b-cl,sax,bs,bass-sax,flts)
Golden Gate Quartet With The Martial Solal Orchestra
Americans Swinging In Paris:Golden Gate Quartet | EMI Records | 539659-2
From Spiritual To Swing Vol.2 | EMI Records | 780573-2
Kenny Clarke 8
Americans Swinging In Paris:Kenny Clarke | EMI Records | 539652-2
Le Jazz Group De Paris
Jazz In Paris | EmArCy | 548793-2
Gott,Tommy | (tp)
Roger Wolfe Kahn And His Orchestra
Planet Jazz:Jack Teagarden | Planet Jazz | 2161236-2
Gotta,Roberto | (tp,fl,sax,percsounds)
Pino Distaso/Roberto Gotta/Beto Cutillo
Tell Her It's All Right | Edition Collage | EC 463-2
Gotthoffer,Catherine | (harp)
Cal Tjader With The Clare Fischer Orchestra
Cal Tjader Plays Harold Arlen & West Side Story | Fantasy | FCD 24775-2
Milt Jackson With Strings
To Bags...With Love:Memorial Album | Pablo | 2310967-2
Gottlieb,Dan 'Danny' | (cymbals,drperc)
Bob Brookmeyer Group With The WDR Big Band
Electricity | ACT | 9219-2
Gary Burton Quartet With Eberhard Weber
Passengers | ECM | 1092(835016-2)
Lew Soloff Group
Rainbow Mountain | TipToe | TIP-888838 2
Nguyen Le Trio
Million Waves | ACT | 9221-2
Nguyen Le:3 Trios | ACT | 9245-2
Pat Metheny Group
Pat Metheny Group | ECM | 1114(825593-2)
American Garage | ECM | 1155(827134-2)
Offramp | ECM | 1216(817138-2)
Travels | ECM | 1252/53
Pat Metheny Quartet
Watercolors | ECM | 1097(827409-2)
Gottlieb,Victor | (cello)
Cal Tjader With The Clare Fischer Orchestra
Cal Tjader Plays Harold Arlen & West Side Story | Fantasy | FCD 24775-2
Gottschalk,Norbert | (tpvoc)
Peter Weiss Orchestra
Personal Choice | Nabel Records:Jazz Network | CD 4669
Gottwald,Scotty | (snare-dr)
Helmut Nieberle & Cordes Sauvages
Salut To Django | Jardis Records | JRCD 9926
Götz,Johannes | (tb)
Landes Jugend Jazz Orchester Hessen
Touch Of Lips | hr music.de | hrmj 004-01 CD
Goubert,Estelle | (pel-p)
Aldo Romano Group
AlmaLatina | Owl Records | 018364-2
Gough,Julian | (ts)
Wanderlust
Border Crossing | Laika Records | 35100812
Gouirand,Doudou | (sax,ssas)
Philippe Caillat Special Project
Melodic Travel | Laika Records | LK 689-012
Gould,Vennette | (voc)
Les McCann Group
Another Beginning | Atlantic | 7567-80790-2
Gourley,Jimmy | (g)
Gigi Gryce-Clifford Brown Octet
Planet Jazz:Clifford Brown | Planet Jazz | 2161239-2
Gigi Gryce-Clifford Brown Sextet
Planet Jazz:Clifford Brown | Planet Jazz | 2161239-2
Lester Young Quartet
Jazz Gallery:Lester Young Vol.2(1946-59) | RCA | 2119541-2
Stan Getz Quintet
Stan Getz In Europe | Laserlight | 24657
The Herdsmen
Nat Pierce-Dick Collins-Ralph Burns & The Herdsmen Play Paris | Fantasy | FCD 24759-2
Gousset,Claude | (tb)
Lionel Hampton All Stars
Jazz In Paris:Lionel Hampton-Ring Dem Bells | EmArCy | 159825-2 PMS
Goustin,Gerard | (p)
Chet Baker Quartet
Jazz In Paris:Chet Baker Quartet Plays Standards | EmArCy | 014378-2 PMS
Verve Jazz Masters Vol.60:The Collection | Verve | 529866-2
Govan,Ila | (voc)
Louis Armstrong And His Friends
Louis Armstrong And His Friends | Bluebird | 2663961-2
Govetas,Christos | (cl,chumbushgardon)
Heiner Goebbels Group
Shadow/Landscape With Argonauts | ECM | 1480
Gowans,Brad | (cl,tbv-tb)
Bud Freeman And His Summa Cum Laude Orchestra
Planet Jazz:Bud Freeman | Planet Jazz | 2161240-2
Planet Jazz:Jazz Saxophone | Planet Jazz | 2169653-2
Goya,Francis | (g)
Laura Fygi With Band
Bewitched | Verve | 514724-2
Goykovich,Dusko | (fl-htp)
Conexion Latina
Mambo Nights | Enja | ENJ-9402 2
Dusko Goykovich Big Band
Balkan Connection | Enja | ENJ-9047 2
Dusko Goykovich Quartet
Soul Connection | Enja | ENJ-8044 2
In My Dreams | Enja | ENJ-9408 2
Samba Do Mar | Enja | ENJ-9473 2
Dusko Goykovich Quintet
Soul Connection | Enja | ENJ-8044 2
Balkan Blues | Enja | ENJ-9320 2
Dusko Goykovich Quintet With The NDR Radio-Philharmonie,Hannover
Balkan Blues | Enja | ENJ-9320 2
Dusko Goykovich-Joe Haider Quintet
Jazz Portraits | EGO | 95080
Jenny Evans And Her Quintet
Shiny Stockings | Enja | ENJ-9317 2
Shiny Stockings | ESM Records | ESM 9305
Kenny Clarke-Francy Boland Big Band
Three Latin Adventures | MPS | 529095-2
More Smiles | MPS | 9814789
Francy Boland-Fellini 712 | MPS | 9814805
Nicolas Simion Group
Balkan Jazz | Intuition Records | INT 3339-2
Paul Nero Sound
Doldinger's Best | ACT | 9224-2
Stan Getz With The Kurt Edelhagen Orchestra
Stan Getz In Europe | Laserlight | 24657
Woody Herman And His Orchestra
Verve Jazz Masters 54:Woody Herman | Verve | 529903-2
Gozzo,Conrad | (tp)
Anita O'Day With The Billy May Orchestra
Verve Jazz Masters 49:Anita O'Day | Verve | 527653-2
Anita O'Day With The Buddy Bregman Orchestra
Pick Yourself Up | Verve | 517329-2
Benny Carter And His Orchestra
Aspects | Capitol | 852677-2
Billy Eckstine With The Billy May Orchestra
Once More With Feeling | Roulette | 581862-2
Billy May And His Orchestra
Billy May's Big Fat Brass/Bill's Bag | Capitol | 535206-2
Buddy Bregman And His Orchestra
Swinging Kicks | Verve | 559514-2
Ella Fitzgerald With The Billy May Orchestra
Ella Fitzgerald Sings The Harold Arlen Song Book | Verve | 589108-2
Ella Fitzgerald With The Buddy Bregman Orchestra
Ella Fitzgerald-First Lady Of Song | Verve | 517898-2
Love Songs:The Best Of The Song Books | Verve | 531762-2
Ella Fitzgerald Sings The Cole Porter Songbook | Verve | 537257-2
Ella Fitzgerald Sings The Rodgers And Hart Song Book | Verve | 537258-2
Ella Fitzgerald With The Nelson Riddle Orchestra
Get Happy! | Verve | 523321-2
Harry James And His Orchestra
Trumpet Blues:The Best Of Harry James | Capitol | 521224-2
June Christy With The Pete Rugolo Orchestra
Something Cool(The Complete Mono & Stereo Versions) | Capitol | 534069-2
Mel Tormé With The Billy May Orchestra
Mel Tormé Goes South Of The Border With Billy May | Verve | 589517-2
Nat King Cole With The Billy May Orchestra
Nat King Cole:For Sentimental Reasons | Dreyfus Jazz Line | FDM 36740-2
Peggy Lee With The Quincy Jones Orchestra
Blues Cross Country | Capitol | 520088-2
Shorty Rogers And His Orchestra Feat. The Giants
PLanet Jazz:Shorty Rogers | Planet Jazz | 2159976-2
Van Alexander Orchestra
Home Of Happy Feet/Swing! Staged For Sound! | Capitol | 535211-2
Woody Herman And His Orchestra
The Legends Of Swing | Laserlight | 24659
Woody Herman:Four Brother | Dreyfus Jazz Line | FDM 36722-2
Woody Herman And The Herd
Woody Herman (And The Herd) At Carnegie Hall | Verve | 559833-2
Graas,John | (compfr-h)
Gerry Mulligan Tentette
Gene Norman Presents The Original Gerry Mulligan Tentet And Quartet | GNP Crescendo | GNPD 56
Shorty Rogers And His Giants
PLanet Jazz:Shorty Rogers | Planet Jazz | 2159976-2
Shorty Rogers And His Orchestra Feat. The Giants
PLanet Jazz:Shorty Rogers | Planet Jazz | 2159976-2
Grabandt,Christian | (tpfl-h)
Harry Allen And Randy Sandke Meets The RIAS Big Band Berlin
The Music Of The Trumpet Kings | Nagel-Heyer | CD 037
Nana Mouskouri With The Berlin Radio Big Band
Nana Swings | Mercury | 074394-2
Grabert,Kurt | (vibdr)
Helmut Zacharias Quintet
Ich Habe Rhythmus | Bear Family Records | BCD 15642 AH
Grabosch,Horst | (co,fr-h,tp,diversefl-h)
Directors
Directors | Jazz Haus Musik | JHM 0040 CD
Dirk Raulf Group
Theater I (Bühnenmusik) | Poise | Poise 07
Georg Ruby Group
Stange Loops | Jazz Haus Musik | JHM 0057 CD
Klaus König Orchestra
Hommage A Douglas Adams | Enja | ENJ-6078 2
Norbert Stein Pata Masters
Graffiti | Pata Musik | PATA 9 CD
Pata Music Meets Arfi
News Of Roi Ubu | Pata Musik | PATA 10 CD
Grabowsky,Paul | (p,accordeon,melodica,alt-h,bass-dr)
Johnny Griffin-Sal Nistico-Roman Schwaller Sextet
Three Generations Of Tenorsaxophone | JHM Records | JHM 3611
Marty Cook Group feat. Monty Waters
Borderlines | Tutu Records | 888122-2*
Vince Jones Group
It All Ends Up In Tears | Intuition Records | INT 3069-2
Gradischnig,Herwig 'Hank' | (bssax)
Claus Raible Sextet
Loopin' With Lea | Organic Music | ORGM 9724
Grady,Eddie | (dr)
Benny Goodman Trio
Benny Goodman-The Complete Capitol Trios | Capitol | 521225-2
Louis Armstrong And The Commanders under the Direction of Camarata
Satchmo Serenaders | Verve | 543792-2
Louis Armstrong With The Commanders
Ambassador Louis Armstrong Vol.17:Moments To Remember(1952-1956) | Ambassador | CLA 1917
Graef,Friedemann | (b-cl,ss,ts,bass-sax,bs,cl,saxas)
Friedemann Graef Group
Orlando Fragments | Nabel Records:Jazz Network | CD 4681
Graef-Schippa-Moritz
Orlando Frames | Nabel Records:Jazz Network | CD 4690
Graeser,Stefanie | (voc)
Jazzensemble Des Hessischen Rundfunks
Jazz Messe-Messe Für Unsere Zeit | hr music.de | hrmj 003-01 CD
Graf,Heinz-Peter | (b)
Bernd Konrad Jazz Group With Symphonie Orchestra
Wen Die Götter Lieben | Creative Works Records | CW CD 1010-1
Graf,Klaus | (as,cl,fl,ss,sax,ldts)
Benny Waters & Jan Jankeje
Let's Talk About Jazz | G&J Records | GJ 2009 Maxi-CD
Benny Waters Sextet
A' Portrait Of Jan Jankeje | Jazzpoint | JP 1054 CD
Geir Lysne Listening Ensemble
Korall | ACT | 9236-2
Aurora Borealis-Nordic Lights | ACT | 9406-2
Thilo Wagner Quintet
Just In Time | Satin Doll Productions | SDP 1011-1 CD
Werner Lener Quartet
My Own | Satin Doll Productions | SDP 1013-1 CD
Gräff,Willie | (accordeon)
Kölner Saxophon Mafia With Willie Gräff
Kölner Saxophon Mafia Proudly Presents | Jazz Haus Musik | JHM 0046 CD
Graffiti String Quartet |
Michel Petrucciani With The Graffiti String Quartet
Marvellous | Dreyfus Jazz Line | FDM 36564-2
Graham,Bill | (as,bs,voc,reeds,tpts)
Count Basie And His Orchestra
Jazz Gallery:Lester Young Vol.2(1946-59) | RCA | 2119541-2
Verve Jazz Masters 2:Count Basie | Verve | 519819-2
Count Basie Swings-Joe Williams Sings | Verve | 519852-2
Verve Jazz Masters 20:Introducing | Verve | 519853-2
April In Paris | Verve | 521402-2
One O'Clock Jump | Verve | 559806-2
Count Basie At Newport | Verve | 9861761
Dizzy Gillespie Sextet
Pleyel Jazz Concert 1953 | Vogue | 21409392
Duke Ellington And His Orchestra
Black Brown And Beige | CBS | CK 65566
Ella Fitzgerald With The Count Basie Orchestra
Ella Fitzgerald-First Lady Of Song | Verve | 517898-2
Joe Newman And His Band
Jazz In Paris:Joe Newman-Jazz At Midnight-Cootie Williams | EmArCy | 018446-2
Sarah Vaughan With Dizzy Gillespie And His Orchestra
Planet Jazz:Female Jazz Vocalists | Planet Jazz | 2169656-2
Tommy Dorsey And His Orchestra
Planet Jazz:Tommy Dorsey | Planet Jazz | 2159972-2
Graham,Colin | (tp)
Jazz Africa All Nations Big Band
Jadu(Jazz Africa Down Under) | Enja | ENJ-9339 2
Graham,John | (ss,as,tsviola)
Dee Dee Bridgewater With Orchestra
Dear Ella | Verve | 539102-2
Itchy Fingers
Live | Enja | ENJ-6076 2
Graham,Marilyn | (concertmasterv)
Buddy Childers With The Russ Garcia Strings
Artistry In Jazz | Candid | CCD 79735
Graham,Peter | (p)
Bob Wallis Storyville Jazzmen
The Golden Years Of Revival Jazz,Vol.7 | Storyville | STCD 5512
Graham,Ron | (as)
Dogslyde
Hair Of The Dog | Intuition Records | INT 3223-2
Graig,Gary | (drperc)
Hans Theessink Group
Call Me | Minor Music | 801022
Graillier,Michel | (el-p,p,synthp-solo)
Michel Graillier
Dream Drops | Owl Records | 013434-2
Michel Grailler Trio
Dream Drops | Owl Records | 013434-2
Michel Grailler-Chet Baker
Dream Drops | Owl Records | 013434-2
Michel Grailler-J.F. Jenny-Clark
Dream Drops | Owl Records | 013434-2
Michel Grailler-Michel Petrucciani
Dream Drops | Owl Records | 013434-2
Grainger,Porter | (p)
Bessie Smith And Her Band
Jazz:The Essential Collection Vol.1 | IN+OUT Records | 78011-2
Gräminger,Kurt | (as)
Q4 Orchester Project
Lyon's Brood | Creative Works Records | CW CD 1018-3
Yavapai | Creative Works Records | CW CD 1028-2
Gramss,Sebastian | (b,el-b,klischee-o-phon,cello,g)
Jazz Orchester Rheinland-Pfalz
Kazzou | Jazz Haus Musik | LJBB 9104
Like Life | Jazz Haus Musik | LJBB 9405
Sebastian Gramss-Lömsch Lehmann
knoM.T | Jazz Haus Musik | JHM 0107 CD
The Remedy
The Remedy | Jazz Haus Musik | JHM 0069 CD
Gran,Magnus | (dr)
Anders Lindskog Quartet
Cry Me A River | Touché Music | TMcCD 005
Gustavo Bergalli Group
Tango In Jazz | Touché Music | TMcCD 007
Granados,Cesar | (congastimbales)
Conexion Latina
Calorcito | Enja | ENJ-4072 2
Granat,Mimi | (viola)
Charlie Haden Quartet West With Strings
The Art Of The Song | Verve | 547403-2
Grande,Jürgen | (b)
Clemens Maria Peters/Reinhold Bauer
Quadru Mana/Quadru Mania | Edition Collage | EC 464-2
Granell,José Luis | (as)
Daniel Flors Group
When Least Expected | Fresh Sound Records | FSNT 080 CD
Granelli,J.Anthony | (el-b)
Jerry Granelli Group
Music Has Its Way With Me | Traumton Records | 4451-2
Granelli,Jerry | (dr,electronic-dr,perc,voice,synth)
Jay Clayton-Jerry Granelli
Sound Songs | JMT Edition | 919006-2
Jerry Granelli Group
Music Has Its Way With Me | Traumton Records | 4451-2
Jerry Granelli UFB
News From The Street | VeraBra Records | CDVBR 2146-2
Lee Konitz Quartet
Haiku | Nabel Records:Jazz Network | CD 4664
Ralph Towner Quintet
City Of Eyes | ECM | 1388
Rinde Eckert Group
Story In,Story Out | Intuition Records | INT 3507-2
Vince Guaraldi Group
Charlie Brown's Holiday Hits | Fantasy | FCD 9682-2
Vince Guaraldi-Bola Sete Quartet
Vince & Bola | Fantasy | FCD 24756-2
Graner,Ulrich | (g)
NuNu!
Ocean | TipToe | TIP-888837 2
Granger,Lawrence | (v)
Herbie Hancock Group
Sunlight | CBS | 486570-2
Granjon,Stéphane | (v)
Stephane Grappelli With The Michel Legrand Orchestra
Grapelli Story | Verve | 515807-2
Grant,Gary | (fl-htp)
Al Jarreau With Band
Jarreau | i.e. Music | 557847-2
High Crime | i.e. Music | 557848-2
Dave Grusin Orchestra
Two For The Road:The Music Of Henry Mancini | GRP | GRP 98652
Diane Schuur With Orchestra
The Best Of Diane Schuur | GRP | GRP 98882
Paulinho Da Costa Orchestra
Happy People | Original Jazz Classics | OJCCD 783-2(2312102)
Singers Unlimited With The Patrick Williams Orchestra
The Singers Unlimited:Magic Voices | MPS | 539130-2
The Quincy Jones-Sammy Nestico Orchestra
Basie & Beyond | Warner | 9362-47792-2
Grant,Jewell | (as,bs,reedsts)
Benny Carter And His Orchestra
Aspects | Capitol | 852677-2

Grant,Laura | (voc)
Mike Westbrook Brass Band
Glad Day:Settings Of William Blake | Enja | ENJ-9376 2
Grant,Mel | (p)
Muggsy Spanier And His Dixieland All Stars
Muggsy Spanier At Club Hangover 1953/54 | Storyville | STCD 6033
Grant,Rodger | (p)
Mongo Santamaria And His Band
Mongo At The Village Gate | Original Jazz Classics | OJCCD 490-2(RLP 9529)
Grant,Steve | (dr)
Katie Kern Group
Still Young | Jazzpoint | JP 1070 CD
Granz,Norman | (announcer)
JATP All Stars
Verve Jazz Masters 28:Charlie Parker Plays Standards | Verve | 521854-2
Grappelli,Stephane | (celeste,el-p,v,p,p-solo,bar-v,el-v)
Andre Pasdoc With The Orchestra Vola
Jazz In Paris:Django Reinhardt-Django Et Compagnie | EmArCy | 549241-2 PMS
Arthur Young And Hatchett's Swingtette
Grapelli Story | Verve | 515807-2
Benny Carter And His Orchestra
Americans Swinging In Paris:Benny Carter | EMI Records | 539647-2
Bill Coleman Et Son Orchestre
Americans Swinging In Paris:Bill Coleman-The Elegance | EMI Records | 539662-2
Charlie Haden Quartet West
Always Say Goodbye | Verve | 521501-2
Coleman Hawkins And His All Star Jam Band
Django Reinhardt All Star Sessions | Capitol | 531577-2
Americans Swinging In Paris:Benny Carter | EMI Records | 539647-2
Jazz:The Essential Collection Vol.3 | IN+OUT Records | 78013-2
Coleman Hawkins Trio
Jazz:The Essential Collection Vol.3 | IN+OUT Records | 78013-2
Coleman Hawkins With Michel Warlop And His Orchestra
Django Reinhardt All Star Sessions | Capitol | 531577-2
Django Reinhardt And The Quintet Du Hot Club De France
Planet Jazz:Django Reinhardt | Planet Jazz | 2152071-2
Planet Jazz:Stephane Grappelli | RCA | 2165366-2
Eddie South/Stephane Grappelli Quintet
Django/Django In Rome 1949-1050 | BGO Records | BGOCD 366
Django Reinhardt:Echoes Of France | Dreyfus Jazz Line | FDM 36726-2
Gary Burton-Stephane Grappelli Quartet
Paris Encounter | Atlantic | 7567-80763-2
Micheline Day Et Son Quatuor Swing
Jazz In Paris:Django Reinhardt-Django Et Compagnie | EmArCy | 549241-2 PMS
Nitta Rette Et Son Trio Hot
Jazz In Paris:Django Reinhardt-Django Et Compagnie | EmArCy | 549241-2 PMS
Oscar Peterson Quintet
Skol | Original Jazz Classics | OJC20 496-2
Oscar Peterson-Stephane Grappelli Quartet
Jazz In Paris:Oscar Peterson-Stephane Grappelli Quartet Vol.1 | EmArCy | 013028-2
Jazz In Paris:Oscar Peterson-Stephane Grappelli Quartet Vol.2 | EmArCy | 013029-2
Quintet Du Hot Club De France
Jazz In Paris:Django Reinhardt-Swing From Paris | EmArCy | 159853-2 PMS
Jazz In Paris:Django Reinhardt-Swing 39 | EmArCy | 159854-2 PMS
Djangology | Bluebird | 2663957-2
Grapelli Story | Verve | 515807-2
Verve Jazz Masters 38:Django Reinhardt | Verve | 516931-2
Verve Jazz Masters Vol.60:The Collection | Verve | 529866-2
Django/Django In Rome 1949-1050 | BGO Records | BGOCD 366
Django Reinhardt:Echoes Of France | Dreyfus Jazz Line | FDM 36726-2
Django Reinhardt:Souveniers | Dreyfus Jazz Line | FDM 36744-2
Rob Wasserman Duet
Duets | GRP | GRP 97122
Stephane Grappelli
7.Zelt-Musik-Festival:Jazz Events | Zounds | CD 2730001
Stephane Grappelli And Friends
Grapelli Story | Verve | 515807-2
Stephane Grappelli And His Hot Four
Jazz In Paris:Django Reinhardt-Swing From Paris | EmArCy | 159853-2 PMS
Stephane Grappelli And His Musicians
Grapelli Story | Verve | 515807-2
Stephane Grappelli Group
Stephane Grappelli:Live In San Francisco | Storyville | 4960723
Stephane Grappelli Quartet
Jazz In Paris:Stephane Grappelli-Django | EmArCy | 018421-1
Planet Jazz:Stephane Grappelli | RCA | 2165366-2
I Hear Music | RCA | 2179624-2
Grapelli Story | Verve | 515807-2
Verve Jazz Masters 11:Stéphane Grappelli | Verve | 516758-2
Jazz In Paris:Stephane Grappelli-Improvisations | EmArCy | 549242-2 PMS
Stephane Grappelli 1992 Live | Dreyfus Jazz Line | FDM 37006-2
Stephane Grappelli Quintet
Planet Jazz:Stephane Grappelli | RCA | 2165366-2
Grapelli Story | Verve | 515807-2
Feeling + Finesse = Jazz | Atlantic | 7567-90140-2
Stephane Grappelli Sextet
Grapelli Story | Verve | 515807-2
Stephane Grappelli Trio
I Hear Music | RCA | 2179624-2
Verve Jazz Masters 11:Stéphane Grappelli | Verve | 516758-2
7.Zelt-Musik-Festival:Jazz Events | Zounds | CD 2730001
Tivoli Gardens, Copenhagen, Denmark | Original Jazz Classics | OJCCD 441-2
Stephane Grappelli With The Diz Disley Trio
Grapelli Story | Verve | 515807-2
Stephane Grappelli With The George Shearing Trio
Grapelli Story | Verve | 515807-2
Verve Jazz Masters 11:Stéphane Grappelli | Verve | 516758-2
Stephane Grappelli With The Michel Legrand Orchestra
Grapelli Story | Verve | 515807-2
Verve Jazz Masters 11:Stéphane Grappelli | Verve | 516758-2
Stephane Grappelli-David Grisman Group
Stephane Grappelli:Live In San Francisco | Storyville | 4960723
Stephane Grappelli-Django Reinhard
Grapelli Story | Verve | 515807-2
Stephane Grappelli-George Shearing
Grapelli Story | Verve | 515807-2
Stephane Grappelli-Ike Isaacs
Grapelli Story | Verve | 515807-2
Stephane Grappelli-Kenny Clarke
Planet Jazz:Stephane Grappelli | RCA | 2165366-2
Stephane Grappelli-Martial Solal Duo
Happy Reunion | Owl Records | 013430-2
Stephane Grappelli-McCoy Tyner Duo
The Jazz Giants Play Rodgers & Hart:Blue Moon | Prestige | PCD 24205-2
Stephane Grappelli-Michel Petrucciani Quartet
Flamingo | Dreyfus Jazz Line | FDM 36580-2
The Rosenberg Trio With Stephane Grappelli
The Rosenberg Trio:The Collection | Verve | 537152-2
Vic Lewis Jam Session
Vic Lewis:The Golden Years | Candid | CCD 79754
Yvonne Louis With The Orchestra Vola
Jazz In Paris:Django Reinhardt-Django Et Compagnie | EmArCy | 549241-2 PMS
Grappy,Andy | (tuba)
Mike Westbrook Band
Off Abbey Road | TipToe | TIP-888805 2
Mike Westbrook Orchestra
Bar Utopia-A Big Band Cabaret | Enja | ENJ-9333 2
The Orchestra Of Smith's Academy | Enja | ENJ-9358 2
Grasset,Roger | (b)
Don Byas Quintet
Jazz In Paris:Don Byas-Laura | EmArCy | 013027-2
Eddie Brunner And His Orchestra
Americans Swinging In Paris:Bill Coleman-The Elegance | EMI Records | 539662-2
Quintet Du Hot Club De France
Jazz In Paris:Django Reinhardt-Swing From Paris | EmArCy | 159853-2 PMS
Grassi,John | (tb)
Anita O'Day With Gene Krupa And His Orchestra
Let Me Off Uptown:Anita O'Day With Gene Krupa | CBS | CK 65625
Grassner,Hans | (g)
Straight Talk
Pure | Jazz 4 Ever Records:Jazz Network | J4E 4719
Grasso,Ralph | (g)
Ella Fitzgerald With The Nelson Riddle Orchestra
Dream Dancing | Original Jazz Classics | OJCCD 1072-2(2310814)
Gratkowski,Frank | (as,b-cl,cl,fl,ss,piccolo-fl,reeds)
Ekkehard Jost Nonet
Out Of Jost's Songbook | Fish Music | FM 006 CD
Franck Band
Dufte | Jazz Haus Musik | JHM 0054 CD
Frank Gratkowski Trio
Gestalten | Jazz Haus Musik | JHM 0083 CD
Giessen-Köln-Nonett
Some Other Tapes | Fish Music | FM 009/10 CD
Joachim Ullrich Orchestra
Faces Of The Duke | Jazz Haus Musik | JHM 0045 CD
Klaus König Orchestra
Times Of Devastation/Poco A Poco | Enja | ENJ-6014 22
Hommage A Douglas Adams | Enja | ENJ-6078 2
Time Fragments:Seven Studies In Time And Motion | Enja | ENJ-8076 2
Reviews | Enja | ENJ-9061 2
The Heart Project | Enja | ENJ-9338 2
Klaus König Orchestra & Guests
The Song Of Songs:Oratorio For Two Solo Voices,Choir And Orchestra | Enja | ENJ-7057 2
Matthias Petzold Group With Choir
Psalmen und Lobgesänge für Chor und Jazz-Enseble | Indigo-Records | 1002 CD
Norbert Stein Pata Orchester
The Secret Act Of Painting | Pata Musik | PATA 7 CD
Transalpin Express Orchestra
Some Other Tapes | Fish Music | FM 009/10 CD
Grau,Jürg U. | (tp,g,truempiperc)
Peter A. Schmid Trio With Guests
Profound Sounds In An Empty Reservoir | Creative Works Records | CW CD 1033
Q4 Orchester Project
Lyon's Brood | Creative Works Records | CW CD 1018-3
Grau,Tarla | (v)
Till Brönner Quartet & Deutsches Symphonieorchester Berlin
German Songs | Minor Music | 801057
Grau,Thorsten | (dr)
Arnulf Ochs Group
In The Mean Time | Jazz 'n' Arts Records | JNA 1202
Frank Eberle Septet
Scarlet Sunrise | Satin Doll Productions | SDP 1041-1 CD
Ulli Jünemann-Morton Ginnerup European Jazz Project
The Exhibition | Edition Collage | EC 518-2
Grauso,Joe | (dr)
Muggsy Spanier And His Dixieland Band
Muggsy Spanier-Manhattan Masters,1945 | Storyville | STCD 6051
Pee Wee Russell And His Dixieland Band
Muggsy Spanier-Manhattan Masters,1945 | Storyville | STCD 6051
Gravatt,Eric | (congasdr)
Joe Henderson And His Orchestra
Joe Henderson:The Milestone Years | Milestone | 8MCD 4413-2
McCoy Tyner Group With Horns And Voices
Inner Voices | Original Jazz Classics | OJCCD 1039-2(M 9079)
McCoy Tyner Septet
Focal Point | Original Jazz Classics | OJCCD 1009-2(M 9072)
McCoy Tyner Sextet
Focal Point | Original Jazz Classics | OJCCD 1009-2(M 9072)
Weather Report
Sweetnighter | CBS | 485102-2
Weathe Report Live In Tokyo | CBS | 489208-2
Graves,Aaron | (p,orgsynth)
Oscar Brown Jr. And His Group
Live Every Minute | Minor Music | 801071
Graves,Joe | (tp)
Peggy Lee With The Quincy Jones Orchestra
Blues Cross Country | Capitol | 520088-2
Van Alexander Orchestra
Home Of Happy Feet/Swing! Staged For Sound! | Capitol | 535211-2
Gravine,Mickey | (tb)
Bill Evans Quartet With Orchestra
The Complete Bill Evans On Verve | Verve | 527953-2
From Left To Right | Verve | 557451-2
Joe Williams With The Frank Hunter Orchestra
Planet Jazz:Joe Williams | Planet Jazz | 2165370-2
Gray,Bazzi Bartholomew | (voc)
Abbey Lincoln With Her Band
Who Used To Dance | Verve | 533559-2
Gray,George | (dr)
Abdullah Ibrahim Quartet
Cape Town Revisited | TipToe | TIP-888836 2
Abdullah Ibrahim Trio
Cape Town Flowers | TipToe | TIP-888826 2
Cape Town Revisited | TipToe | TIP-888836 2
Abdullah Ibrahim Trio And A String Orchestra
African Suite | TipToe | TIP-888832 2
Abdullah Ibrahim Trio With The Munich Radio Symphony Orchestra
African Symphony | Enja | ENJ-9410 2
Gray,Glen | (fl,cl,as,ldsax)
Glen Gray And His Orchestra
Great Swing Classics In Hi-Fi | Capitol | 521223-2
Gray,Jack | (viola)
Artie Shaw And His Orchestra
Planet JazzArtie Shaw | Planet Jazz | 2152057-2
Planet Jazz:Jazz Greatest Hits | Planet Jazz | 2169648-2
Gray,Jerry | (arrld)
Planet JazzArtie Shaw | Planet Jazz | 2152057-2
Planet Jazz:Swing | Planet Jazz | 2169651-2
Glenn Miller And His Orchestra
Planet Jazz:Glenn Miller | Planet Jazz | 2152056-2
Planet Jazz:Jazz Greatest Hits | Planet Jazz | 2169648-2
Planet Jazz:Big Bands | Planet Jazz | 2169649-2
Gray,John | (bjg)
Johnny Hartman And His Orchestra
Unforgettable | Impulse(MCA) | IMP 11522
Lucy Reed With The Eddie Higgins Quartet
This Is Lucy Reed | Original Jazz Classics | OJCCD 1943-2(F 3243)
Vince Guaraldi Group
Charlie Brown's Holiday Hits | Fantasy | FCD 9682-2
Gray,Larry | (b)
Buddy Childers Big Band
Just Buddy's | Candid | CCD 79761
Gray,Louis | (tp)
Louis Armstrong And His Orchestra
Louis Armstrong:C'est Si Bon | Dreyfus Jazz Line | FDM 36730-2
Gray,Luther | (dr)
Mitch Seidman Quartet
How 'Bout It? | Jardis Records | JRCD 20135
Gray,Steve | (cond,org,parr)
Heinz Sauer Quartet With The NDR Big Band
NDR Big Band-Bravissimo | ACT | 9232-2
Oscar Brown Jr. with The NDR Big Band
Live Every Minute | Minor Music | 801071
Gray,Wardell | (ts)
Al Haig Sextet(Quintet)
Al Haig Trio And Sextets | Original Jazz Classics | OJCCD 1929-2(SPL 1118)
Charlie Parker's New Stars
Charlie Parker:Now's The Time | Dreyfus Jazz Line | FDM 36724-2
Dinah Washington With The Jimmy Cobb Orchestra
Verve Jazz Masters 40:Dinah Washington | Verve | 522055-2
Ultimate Ben Webster selected by James Carter | Verve | 557537-2
Tadd Dameron Septet
The Fabulous Fats Navarro Vol.2 | Blue Note | 0677208
Fats Navarro:Nostalgia | Dreyfus Jazz Line | FDM 36736-2
Teddy Charles' West Coasters
Wardell Gray Memorial Vol.1 | Original Jazz Classics | OJCCD 050-2(P 7008)
Wardell Gray Quartet
Wardell Gray Memorial Vol.1 | Original Jazz Classics | OJCCD 050-2(P 7008)
Wardell Gray Memorial Vol.2 | Original Jazz Classics | OJCCD 051-2(P 7009)
Wardell Gray Quintet
Wardell Gray Memorial Vol.2 | Original Jazz Classics | OJCCD 051-2(P 7009)
Wardell Gray Sextet
The Prestige Legacy Vol.2:Battles Of Saxes | Prestige | PCD 24252-2
Wardell Gray's Los Angeles All Stars
Dexter Gordon Birthday Celebration | Fantasy | FANCD 6082-2
Wardell Gray Memorial Vol.2 | Original Jazz Classics | OJCCD 051-2(P 7009)
Gray,Wardell or Illinois Jacquet or Charlie Ventura | (ts)
Billie Holiday With The JATP All Stars
Billie Holiday Story Vol.1:Jazz At The Philharmonic | Verve | 521642-2
The Complete Jazz At The Philharmonic On Verve 1944-1949 | Verve | 523893-2
Verve Jazz Masters 47:Billie Holiday Sings Standards | Verve | 527650-2
Graydon,Jay | (g,syntharr)
Al Jarreau With Band
Jarreau | i.e. Music | 557847-2
High Crime | i.e. Music | 557848-2
Flora Purim With Orchestra
Joe Henderson:The Milestone Years | Milestone | 8MCD 4413-2
Grayson,Miles | (perc)
Gene Harris And The Three Sounds
Deep Blue-The United States Of Mind | Blue Note | 521152-2
Grayson,Milt | (voc)
Duke Ellington And His Orchestra
The Great Paris Concert | Atlantic | 7567-81303-2
Nina Simone And Orchestra
Baltimore | Epic | 476906-2
Wycliffe Gordon Group
Slidin' Home | Nagel-Heyer | CD 2001
Ellington For Lovers | Nagel-Heyer | NH 1009
Grean,Charlie | (arr)
Nat King Cole With Orchestra
Nat King Cole:Route 66 | Dreyfus Jazz Line | FDM 36716-2
Great British Jazz Band,The |
Great British Jazz Band
The Great British Jazz Band:Jubilee | Candid | CCD 79720
The Great British Jazz Band
A British Jazz Odyssey | Candid | CCD 79740
Greaves,John | (p,bvoc)
Michael Mantler Group With The Danish Radio Concert Orchestra Strings
The School Of Understanding(Sort-Of-An-Opera) | ECM | 1648/49(537963-2)
Michael Mantler Quintet
Live | Watt | 18
Greco,Massimo | (tp)
Orchestra Jazz Siciliana
Orchestra Jazz Siciliana Plays The Music Of Carla Bley | Watt | XtraWatt/4
Greco,Pino | (g)
Green,Arthur | (voc)
Abbey Lincoln With Her Band
Who Used To Dance | Verve | 533559-2
Green,Bennie | (tbvoc)
Dizzy Gillespie And His Orchestra
Ultimate Dizzy Gillespie | Verve | 557535-2
Four Trombones
Charles Mingus-The Complete Debut Recordings | Debut | 12 DCD 4402-2
The J.J.Johnson Memorial Album | Prestige | PRCD 11025-2
George Benson Quartet + Guests
The George Benson Cookbook | CBS | 502470-2
Miles Davis Quintet
The Jazz Giants Play Rodgers & Hart:Blue Moon | Prestige | PCD 24205-2
Miles Davis Sextet
Miles Davis And Horns | Original Jazz Classics | OJC20 053-2(P 7025)
The Prestige Legacy Vol.1:The High Priests | Prestige | PCD 24251-2
Sarah Vaughan With George Treadwell And His Allstars
Sarah Vaughan:Lover Man | Dreyfus Jazz Line | FDM 36739-2
Green,Benny | (bs,pp-solo)
Benny Green Trio
These Are Soulful Days | Blue Note | 499527-2
Blue Note Plays Gershwin | Blue Note | 520808-2
Bernard Purdie's Soul To Jazz
Bernard Purdie's Soul To Jazz II | ACT | 9253-2
Diana Krall Quartet
All For You-A Dedication To The Nat King Cole Trio | Impulse(MCA) | 951164-2
Flip Phillips Quintet
Swing Is The Thing | Verve | 543477-2
Flip Phillips Septet
Swing Is The Thing | Verve | 543477-2
Flip Phillips Sextet
Swing Is The Thing | Verve | 543477-2
Flip Phillips Trio
Swing Is The Thing | Verve | 543477-2
Freddie Hubbard Quartet
Topsy | Enja | ENJ-7025 2
Freddie Hubbard Quintet
Topsy | Enja | ENJ-7025 2
James Morrison-Ray Brown Quartet
Two The Max | East-West | 9031-77125-2
John Pizzarelli Trio
Dear Mr.Cole | Novus | 4163182-2
Tim Hagans-Marcus Printup Septet
Hub Songs | Blue Note | 859509-2
Vince Jones With The Benny Green Quartet
One Day Spent | Intuition Records | INT 3087-2
Green,Bill | (as,bass-sax,bs,cl,fl,ss,piccolo)
Benny Carter And His Orchestra
Aspects | Capitol | 852677-2
Chico Hamilton Orchestra
With Strings Attached/The Three Faces Of Chico | Warner | 9362-47874-2
Ella Fitzgerald With Orchestra
The Best Is Yet To Come | Original Jazz Classics | OJCCD 889-2(2312138)

INTERPRETENVERZEICHNIS

Ella Fitzgerald With The Nelson Riddle Orchestra
Dream Dancing | Original Jazz Classics | OJCCD 1072-2(2310814)
Horace Silver Quintet With Brass
Horace Silver Retrospective | Blue Note | 495576-2
Johnny Hartman And His Orchestra
Unforgettable | Impulse(MCA) | IMP 11522
Peggy Lee With The Quincy Jones Orchestra
Blues Cross Country | Capitol | 520088-2

Green,Charlie | (tb)
Bessie Smith And Her Band
Jazz:The Essential Collection Vol.1 | IN+OUT Records | 78011-2
Fletcher Henderson And His Orchestra
Jazz:The Essential Collection Vol.1 | IN+OUT Records | 78011-2
Henderson's Hot Six
Jazz:The Essential Collection Vol.1 | IN+OUT Records | 78011-2
Louis Armstrong With Chick Webb's Orchestra
Best Of The Complete RCA Victor Recordings | RCA | 2663636-2
Louis Armstrong:A 100th Birthday Celebration | RCA | 2663694-2

Green,Dave | (b)
Bob Wilber's Bechet Legacy
The Hamburg Concert-Tribute To A Legend | Nagel-Heyer | CD 028
The Second Sampler | Nagel-Heyer | NHR SP 6
Ralph Sutton And Friends
Sweet Sue-The Music Of Fats Waller Vol.1 | Nagel-Heyer | CD 057
Stacey Kent And Her Quintet
The Tender Trap | Candid | CCD 79751
Summit Reunion
Jazz Im Amerikahaus,Vol.5 | Nagel-Heyer | CD 015
The First Sampler | Nagel-Heyer | NHR SP 5
The New York Allstars
Hey Ba-Ba-Re-Bop!! The New York Allstars Play Lionel Hampton Vol.1 | Nagel-Heyer | CD 047
The New York Allstars Play Lionel Hampton,Vol.2: Stompin' At The Savoy | Nagel-Heyer | CD 077
Warren Vaché Quintet
The First Sampler | Nagel-Heyer | NHR SP 5
Warren Vaché Quintet With Special Guest Allan Vaché
Jazz Im Amerikahaus,Vol.2 | Nagel-Heyer | CD 012

Green,Eddie | (el-p,perc,ptp)
Pat Martino Quartet
Desperado | Original Jazz Classics | OJCCD 397-2(P 7795)
Pat Martino Quintet
Desperado | Original Jazz Classics | OJCCD 397-2(P 7795)
Rachelle Ferrell With The Eddie Green Trio
First Instrumental | Blue Note | 827820-2
Rachelle Ferrell With The Eddie Green Trio And Alex Foster
First Instrumental | Blue Note | 827820-2

Green,Elwyn L. | (rap)
Landes Jugend Jazz Orchester Hessen
Touch Of Lips | hr music.de | hrmj 004-01 CD

Green,Emmanuel | (v)
Billie Holiday With The Ray Ellis Orchestra
Lady In Satin | CBS | CK 65144
Bob James And His Orchestra
Jazzrock-Anthology Vol.3:Fusion | Zounds | CD 27100555
Freddie Hubbard With Orchestra
This Is Jazz:Freddie Hubbard | CBS | CK 65041
Grover Washington Jr. Orchestra
Jazzrock-Anthology Vol.3:Fusion | Zounds | CD 27100555
Les McCann Group
Another Beginning | Atlantic | 7567-80790-2
Milt Jackson And His Orchestra
Sunflower | CTI | ZK 65131
Phil Woods Quartet With Orchestra & Strings
Round Trip | Verve | 559804-2
Sarah Vaughan With Orchestra
!Viva! Vaughan | Mercury | 549374-2
Sarah Vaughan Sings The Mancini Songbook | Verve | 558401-2
Wes Montgomery Quartet With The Claus Ogerman Orchestra
Tequila | Verve | 547769-2
Wes Montgomery Quintet With The Claus Ogerman Orchestra
The Antonio Carlos Jobim Songbook | Verve | 525472-2
Talkin' Jazz:Roots Of Acid Jazz | Verve | 529580-2
Tequila | Verve | 547769-2
Wes Montgomery Trio With The Claus Ogerman Orchestra
Tequila | Verve | 547769-2
Wes Montgomery With The Claus Ogerman Orchestra
Verve Jazz Masters 14:Wes Montgomery | Verve | 519826-2

Green,Freddie | (g,b,shakervoc)
Benny Goodman Septet
Jazz:The Essential Collection Vol.3 | IN+OUT Records | 78013-2
Charlie Christian:Swing To Bop | Dreyfus Jazz Line | FDM 36715-2
Big Joe Turner With The Count Basie Orchestra
Flip Flop And Fly | Original Jazz Classics | OJCCD 1053-2(2310937)
Billie Holiday And Her All Stars
Verve Jazz Masters 12:Billie Holiday | Verve | 519825-2
Verve Jazz Masters Vol.60:The Collection | Verve | 529866-2
The Billie Holiday Song Book | Verve | 823246-2
Billie Holiday And Her Band
Billie's Love Songs | Nimbus Records | NI 2000
Billie Holiday And Her Orchestra
Jazz:The Essential Collection Vol.3 | IN+OUT Records | 78013-2
Billie's Love Songs | Nimbus Records | NI 2000
Billie Holiday And Her Quintet
Verve Jazz Masters 47:Billie Holiday Sings Standards | Verve | 527650-2
Charlie Parker And His Orchestra
The Cole Porter Songbook | Verve | 823250-2
Bird: The Complete Charlie Parker On Verve | Verve | 837141-2
Charlie Parker With Orchestra
Charlie Parker:The Best Of The Verve Years | Verve | 527815-2
Charlie Parker With The Joe Lipman Orchestra
Verve Jazz Masters 28:Charlie Parker Plays Standards | Verve | 521854-2
Charlie Parker Big Band | Verve | 559835-2
Count Basie All Stars
The Legends Of Swing | Laserlight | 24659
Count Basie And His Orchestra
Jazz Gallery:Lester Young Vol.2(1946-59) | RCA | 2119541-2
Planet Jazz:Count Basie | Planet Jazz | 2152068-2
Planet Jazz Sampler | Planet Jazz | 2152326-2
Planet Jazz:Jimmy Rushing | RCA | 2165371-2
Planet Jazz:Jazz Greatest Hits | Planet Jazz | 2169648-2
Planet Jazz:Big Bands | Planet Jazz | 2169649-2
Afrique | RCA | 2179618-2
Fun Time | Pablo | 2310945-2
Jazz Collection:Count Basie | Laserlight | 24368
The Legends Of Swing | Laserlight | 24659
Count Basie: Salle Pleyel, April 17th, 1972 | Laserlight | 36127
Atomic Swing | Roulette | 497871-2
Verve Jazz Masters 2:Count Basie | Verve | 519819-2
Count Basie Swings-Joe Williams Sings | Verve | 519852-2
Verve Jazz Masters 20:Introducing | Verve | 519853-2
April In Paris | Verve | 521402-2
Breakfast Dance And Barbecue | Roulette | 531791-2
Basie Meets Bond | Capitol | 538225-2
Basie's Beatle Bag | Verve | 557455-2
One O'Clock Jump | Verve | 559806-2
Chairman Of The Board | Roulette | 581664-2
Jazz:The Essential Collection Vol.3 | IN+OUT Records | 78013-2
The Complete Atomic Basie | Roulette | 828635-2
King Of Swing | Verve | 837433-2
Live at The Sands | Reprise | 9362-45946-2
Count Basie At Newport | Verve | 9861761
Count On The Coast Vol.1 | Phontastic | NCD 7555
Count On The Coast Vol.2 | Phontastic | NCD 7575
Jazz Dance | Original Jazz Classics | OJCCD 1002-2(1210890)
Fancy Pants | Original Jazz Classics | OJCCD 1038-2(2310920)
I Told You So | Original Jazz Classics | OJCCD 824-2(2310767)
Digital III.At Montreux | Original Jazz Classics | OJCCD 996-2(2308223)
The Jazz Giants Play Harry Warren:Lullaby Of Broadway | Prestige | PCD 24204-2
From Spiritual To Swing | Vanguard | VCD 169/71
Count Basie And The Kansas City 7
Count Basie: Salle Pleyel, April 17th, 1972 | Laserlight | 36127
Count Basie And The Kansas City 7 | Impulse(MCA) | 951202-2
Count Basie Big Band
Montreux '77 | Original Jazz Classics | OJCCD 377-2
Farmers Market Barbecue | Original Jazz Classics | OJCCD 732-2(2310874)
Count Basie Octet
Planet Jazz:Count Basie | Planet Jazz | 2152068-2
Count Basie Quartet
Planet Jazz:Jazz Piano | RCA | 2169655-2
Jazz:The Essential Collection Vol.3 | IN+OUT Records | 78013-2
Count Basie Sextet
Verve Jazz Masters 2:Count Basie | Verve | 519819-2
Jazz:The Essential Collection Vol.3 | IN+OUT Records | 78013-2
Count Basie,His Instrumentals & Rhyhtm
Planet Jazz:Count Basie | Planet Jazz | 2152068-2
Jazz:The Essential Collection Vol.3 | IN+OUT Records | 78013-2
Count Basie-Oscar Peterson Quintet
Satch And Josh | Pablo | 2310722-2
Jazz Dance | Original Jazz Classics | OJCCD 1002-2(1210890)
Count Basie's Kansas City Seven
Jazz:The Essential Collection Vol.3 | IN+OUT Records | 78013-2
Diane Schuur With The Count Basie Orchestra
The Best Of Diane Schuur | GRP | GRP 98882
Dicky Wells And His Orchestra
Jazz:The Essential Collection Vol.3 | IN+OUT Records | 78013-2
Duke Ellington And Count Basie With Their Orchestras
First Time! | CBS | CK 65571
Ella Fitzgerald And Count Basie With The JATP All Stars
Bluella:Ella Fitzgerald Sings The Blues | Pablo | 2310960-2
Ella Fitzgerald And Joe Williams With The Count Basie Octet
For The Love Of Ella Fitzgerald | Verve | 841765-2
Ella Fitzgerald With Count Basie And His Orchestra
Digital III At Montreux | Original Jazz Classics | OJCCD 996-2(2308223)
Ella Fitzgerald With The Count Basie Orchestra
Bluella:Ella Fitzgerald Sings The Blues | Pablo | 2310960-2
Ella Fitzgerald-First Lady Of Song | Verve | 517898-2
Verve Jazz Masters 46:Ella Fitzgerald-The Jazz Sides | Verve | 527655-2
Ella And Basie | Verve | 539059-2
For The Love Of Ella Fitzgerald | Verve | 841765-2
Ella Fitzgerald With The Count Basie Septet
Ella And Basie | Verve | 539059-2
Frank Sinatra With The Count Basie Orchestra
Sinatra-Basie:An Historic Musical First | Reprise | 7599-27023-2
It Might As Well Be Spring | Reprise | 7599-27027-2
Gerry Mulligan And The Sax Section
The Gerry Mulligan Songbook | Pacific Jazz | 833575-2
Harry Sweets Edison Sextet
Mr.Swing Harry Edison | Verve | 559868-2
Helen Humes With James P. Johnson And The Count Basie Orchestra
From Spiritual To Swing | Vanguard | VCD 169/71
Ida Cox With The James P. Johnson Septet
From Spiritual To Swing | Vanguard | VCD 169/71
JATP All Stars
Welcome To Jazz At The Philharmonic | Fantasy | FANCD 6081-2
Jimmy Rushing And His Orchestra
Five Feet Of Soul | Roulette | 581830-2
Jimmy Rushing With Count Basie And His Orchestra
From Spiritual To Swing | Vanguard | VCD 169/71
Joe Turner With Orchestra
Atlantic Jazz: Kansas City | Atlantic | 7567-81701-2
Kansas City Five
Lester Young:Blue Lester | Dreyfus Jazz Line | FDM 36729-2
Kansas City Seven
Jazz:The Essential Collection Vol.3 | IN+OUT Records | 78013-2
Kansas City Six
Jazz:The Essential Collection Vol.3 | IN+OUT Records | 78013-2
Charlie Christian:Swing To Bop | Dreyfus Jazz Line | FDM 36715-2
From Spiritual To Swing | Vanguard | VCD 169/71
Lambert, Hendricks And Ross
Sing A Song Of Basie | Verve | 543827-2
Lester Young And His Band
Jazz:The Essential Collection Vol.3 | IN+OUT Records | 78013-2
Lester Young:The Complete Aladdin Sessions | Blue Note | 832787-2
Lester Young:Blue Lester | Dreyfus Jazz Line | FDM 36729-2
Lester Young Quintet
The Art Of Saxophone | Laserlight | 24652
Jazz:The Essential Collection Vol.3 | IN+OUT Records | 78013-2
Lester Young:Blue Lester | Dreyfus Jazz Line | FDM 36729-2
Lionel Hampton And His Orchestra
Planet Jazz:Coleman Hawkins | Planet Jazz | 2152055-2
Planet Jazz:Lionel Hampton | Planet Jazz | 2152059-2
Planet Jazz:Jazz Saxophone | Planet Jazz | 2169653-2
Jazz:The Essential Collection Vol.3 | IN+OUT Records | 78013-2
Milt Jackson Orchestra
Sarah Vaughan Birthday Celebration | Fantasy | FANCD 6090-2
Milt Jackson With The Count Basie Orchestra
To Bags...With Love:Memorial Album | Pablo | 2310967-2
Milt Jackson Birthday Celebration | Fantasy | FANCD 6079-2
Milt Jackson + Count Basie + Big Band Vol.1 | Original Jazz Classics | OJCCD 740-2(2310822)
Milt Jackson + Count Basie + Big Band Vol.2 | Original Jazz Classics | OJCCD 741-2(2310823)
Sarah Vaughan And Joe Williams With The Count Basie Orchestra
Jazz Profile | Blue Note | 823517-2
Sarah Vaughan And The Count Basie Orchestra
Ballads | Roulette | 537561-2
Sarah Vaughan Birthday Celebration | Fantasy | FANCD 6090-2
Sarah Vaughan And The Thad Jones Orchestra
Verve Jazz Masters 42:Sarah Vaughan-The Jazz Sides | Verve | 526817-2
Sarah Vaughan With George Treadwell And His Allstars
Sarah Vaughan:Lover Man | Dreyfus Jazz Line | FDM 36739-2
Sarah Vaughan With The Count Basie Band
Jazz Profile | Blue Note | 823517-2
Sir Charles Thompson Quartet
Key One Up | Vanguard | VCD 79612-2
Teddy Wilson And His Orchestra
Jazz:The Essential Collection Vol.3 | IN+OUT Records | 78013-2

Green,Grant | (g)
Baby Face Willette Quartet
So Blue So Funky-Heroes Of The Hammond | Blue Note | 796563-2
Big John Patton Quartet
Got A Good Thing Goin' | Blue Note | 580731-2
Blue Bossa | Blue Note | 795590-2
Big John Patton Quintet
So Blue So Funky-Heroes Of The Hammond | Blue Note | 796563-2
Charles Kynard Sextet
The Soul Brotherhood | Prestige | PCD 24257-2
Dodo Greene With The Ike Quebec Quintet
Misty Blue:Sweet Sisters Swing Songs Of Sorrow And Sadness | Blue Note | 521151-2
Don Wilkerson Quintet
Preach Brother! | Blue Note | 0677212
Blue N' Groovy | Blue Note | 780679-2
Frant Green Quartet
Street Of Dreams | Blue Note | 821290-2
George Braith Quartet
So Blue So Funky-Heroes Of The Hammond | Blue Note | 796563-2
Gloria Coleman Quartet
Soul Sisters | Impulse(MCA) | 8961048
Grant Green Orchestra
Grant Green:Blue Breakbeat | Blue Note | 494705-2
Blue Breaks Beats Vol.2 | Blue Note | 789907-2
So Blue So Funky-Heroes Of The Hammond | Blue Note | 796563-2
Grant Green Quartet
Ballads | Blue Note | 537560-2
Grantstand | Blue Note | 591723-2
Midnight Blue(The [Be]witching Hour) | Blue Note | 854365-2
Grant Green Quintet
Kind Of Blue:Blue Note Celebrate The Music Of Miles Davis | Blue Note | 534255-2
Am I Blue | Blue Note | 535564-2
Ballads | Blue Note | 537560-2
Feelin' The Spirit | Blue Note | 746822-2
Grant Green Septet
Live At The Lighthouse | Blue Note | 493381-2
Grant Green Sextet
Grant Green:Blue Breakbeat | Blue Note | 494705-2
Idle Moments | Blue Note | 499003-2
Alive! | Blue Note | 525650-2
True Blue | Blue Note | 534032-2
Blue Bossa | Blue Note | 795590-2
Blue Break Beats | Blue Note | 799106-2
The Lost Grooves | Blue Note | 831883-2
Grant Green Trio
Talkin' About | Blue Note | 521958-2
Grant's First Stand | Blue Note | 521959-2
Ballads | Blue Note | 537560-2
Green Street | Blue Note | 540032-2
Standards | Blue Note | 821284-2
Grant Green With Orchestra
The Final Comedown(Soundtrack) | Blue Note | 581678-2
Blue Break Beats | Blue Note | 799106-2
Hank Mobley Quintet
Workout | Blue Note | 784080-2
Herbie Hancock Septet
Herbie Hancock:The Complete Blue Note Sixties Sessions | Blue Note | 495569-2
My Point Of View | Blue Note | 521226-2
Cantaloupe Island | Blue Note | 829331-2
Houston Person Sextet
Jazzin' With The Soul Brothers | Fantasy | FANCD 6086-2
Ike Quebec Quartet
Blue And Sentimental | Blue Note | 784098-2
Ike Quebec Quintet
Blue And Sentimental | Blue Note | 784098-2
Jack McDuff Quartet
The Honeydripper | Original Jazz Classics | OJCCD 222-2(P 7199)
Jack McDuff:The Prestige Years | Prestige | PRCD 24387-2
Jimmy Smith Trio
So Blue So Funky-Heroes Of The Hammond | Blue Note | 796563-2
I'm Movin' On | Blue Note | 832750-2
John Patton Quintet
Along Came John | Blue Note | 0675614
Along Came John | Blue Note | 831915-2
Larry Young Quartet
So Blue So Funky-Heroes Of The Hammond | Blue Note | 796563-2
Lee Morgan Sextet
Search For The New Land | Blue Note | 591896-2
Lou Donaldson Quartet
Good Gracious | Blue Note | 854325-2
Lou Donaldson Quintet
The Natural Soul | Blue Note | 542307-2
Reuben Wilson Sextet
The Lost Grooves | Blue Note | 831883-2
Rusty Bryant Quintet
Rusty Bryant Returns | Original Jazz Classics | OJCCD 331-2(P 7626)
Sonny Red (Kyner) Quintet
Red,Blue & Green | Milestone | MCD 47086-2
Sonny Stitt Quartet
The Jazz Giants Play Miles Davis:Milestones | Prestige | PCD 24225-2
Brothers 4 | Prestige | PCD 24261-2
Stanley Turrentine Orchestra
Rough 'N' Tumble | Blue Note | 524552-2

Green,Henry | (dr)
Lester Young And His Band
Jazz:The Essential Collection Vol.3 | IN+OUT Records | 78013-2
Lester Young:Blue Lester | Dreyfus Jazz Line | FDM 36729-2

Green,Jack | (tb)
Billie Holiday With The Ray Ellis Orchestra
Lady In Satin | CBS | CK 65144

Green,Jeannie | (voc)
Albert King Blues Band
Lovejoy | Stax | SCD 8517-2(STS 2040)

Green,Manny | (v)
Louis Armstrong And His Friends
Planet Jazz:Louis Armstrong | Planet Jazz | 2152052-2
Planet Jazz Sampler | Planet Jazz | 2152326-2
Louis Armstrong And His Friends | Bluebird | 2663961-2

Green,Marcellus | (tp)
Erskine Hawkins And His Orchestra
Planet Jazz:Big Bands | Planet Jazz | 2169649-2

Green,Richard S. | (viola)
Herbie Hancock Group With String Quartet
Herbie Hancock The New Standards | Verve | 527715-2
Herbie Hancock Group With String Quartet,Woodwinds And Brass
Herbie Hancock The New Standards | Verve | 527715-2

Green,Robert | (drperc)
Chuck Brown And The Second Chapter Band
Timeless | Minor Music | 801068

Green,Rodney | (dr)
Eric Reed Orchestra
Happiness | Nagel-Heyer | CD 2010
Greg Osby Quartet
Banned In New York | Blue Note | 496860-2
Terell Stafford Quintet
Fields Of Gold | Nagel-Heyer | CD 2005

Green,Russell | (tp)
Jimmy Lunceford And His Orchestra
The Legends Of Swing | Laserlight | 24659

Green,Thurman | (tb)
Donald Byrd Orchestra
Ethiopian Knights | Blue Note | 854328-2
Ella Fitzgerald With Orchestra
Ella/Things Ain't What They Used To Be | Warner | 9362-47875-2
Willie Bobo Group
Jazzrock-Anthology Vol.3:Fusion | Zounds | CD 27100555

Green,Tim | (ss,tsperc)
Fred Wesley Group
New Friends | Minor Music | 801016

Green,Urbie | (tbv-tb)
Astrud Gilberto With The Claus Ogerman Orchestra
Verve Jazz Masters 9:Astrud Gilberto | Verve | 519824-2
Billie Holiday With The Ray Ellis Orchestra
Lady In Satin | CBS | CK 65144
Bobby Hackett Sextet
Jazz Festival Vol.1 | Storyville | 4960733
Jazz Festival Vol.2 | Storyville | 4960743
Cab Calloway And His Orchestra
Planet Jazz:Cab Calloway | Planet Jazz | 2161237-2
Planet Jazz:Male Jazz Vocalists | Planet Jazz | 2169657-2
Cal Tjader With The Lalo Schifrin Orchestra
Talkin Verve/Roots Of Acid Jazz:Cal Tjader | Verve | 531562-2
Coleman Hawkins With Billy Byers And His Orchestra
Planet Jazz:Coleman Hawkins | Planet Jazz | 2152055-2
The Hawk In Hi-Fi | RCA | 2663842-2
Count Basie And His Orchestra
Verve Jazz Masters 2:Count Basie | Verve | 519819-2
Della Reese With The Neal Hefti Orchestra

Della | RCA | 2663912-2
Dinah Washington With The Quincy Jones Orchestra
Verve Jazz Masters 40:Dinah Washington | Verve | 522055-2
The Swingin' Miss 'D' | Verve | 558074-2
Dinah Washington With The Terry Gibbs Band
Verve Jazz Masters 40:Dinah Washington | Verve | 522055-2
Dinah Washington With The Urbie Green Sextet
Newport Jazz Festival 1958,July 3rd-6th Vol.2:Mulligan The Main Man | Phontastic | NCD 8814
Dizzy Gillespie And His Orchestra
Verve Jazz Masters 10:Dizzy Gillespie | Verve | 516319-2
Gillespiana And Carnegie Hall Concert | Verve | 519809-2
Talking Verve:Dizzy Gillespie | Verve | 533846-2
Ella Fitzgerald With The Count Basie Orchestra
Ella Fitzgerald-First Lady Of Song | Verve | 517898-2
Verve Jazz Masters 46:Ella Fitzgerald-The Jazz Sides | Verve | 527655-2
Ella And Basie | Verve | 539059-2
Ella Fitzgerald With The Count Basie Septet
Ella And Basie | Verve | 539059-2
Elliot Lawrence And His Orchestra
The Elliot Lawrence Big Band Swings Cohn & Kahn | Fantasy | FCD 24761-2
Frankie Laine With Buck Clayton And His Orchestra
Jazz Spectacular | CBS | CK 65507
Helen Merrill With Orchestra
Casa Forte | EmArCy | 558848-2
J.J.Johnson's All Stars
J.J.'s Broadway | Verve | 9860308
Jimmy Rushing And His Orchestra
Five Feet Of Soul | Roulette | 581830-2
Jimmy Smith With The Lalo Schifrin Orchestra
Jimmy Smith:Best Of The Verve Years | Verve | 527950-2
Jimmy Smith-Talkin' Verve | Verve | 531563-2
The Cat | Verve | 539756-2
Jimmy Smith With The Oliver Nelson Orchestra
Verve Jazz Masters 29:Jimmy Smith | Verve | 521855-2
Jimmy Smith:Best Of The Verve Years | Verve | 527950-2
Jimmy Smith-Talkin' Verve | Verve | 531563-2
Joe Williams With The Frank Hunter Orchestra
Planet Jazz:Joe Williams | Planet Jazz | 2165370-2
Joe Williams With The Jimmy Jones Orchestra
Planet Jazz:Joe Williams | Planet Jazz | 2165370-2
Joe Williams,With The Oliver Nelson Orchestra
Planet Jazz:Joe Williams | Planet Jazz | 2165370-2
Kenny Burrell With The Don Sebesky Orchestra
Verve Jazz Masters 45:Kenny Burrell | Verve | 527652-2
Blues-The Common Ground | Verve | 589101-2
Lalo Schifrin And His Orchestra
Verve Jazz Masters 39:Cal Tjader | Verve | 521858-2
Louis Armstrong And His Orchestra
What A Wonderful World | MCA | MCD 01876
Mar Murphy With The Ernie Wilkins Orchestra
RAH | Original Jazz Classics | OJCCD 141-2(R 9395)
Quincy Jones And His Orchestra
Talkin' Verve-Roots Of Acid Jazz:Roland Kirk | Verve | 533101-2
Rahsaan/The Complete Mercury Recordings Of Roland Kirk | Mercury | 846630-2
Ron Carter Orchestra
Parade | Original Jazz Classics | OJCCD 1047-2(M 9088)
Trigger Alpert's Absolutely All Star Seven
East Coast Sound | Original Jazz Classics | OJCCD 1012-2(JLP 11)
Urbie Green Sextet
Newport Jazz Festival 1958,July 3rd-6th Vol.2:Mulligan The Main Man | Phontastic | NCD 8814
Wes Montgomery Orchestra
Movin' Wes | Verve | 521433-2
Wes Montgomery With The Johnny Pate Orchestra
Verve Jazz Masters 14:Wes Montgomery | Verve | 519826-2
Wes Montgomery:The Verve Jazz Sides | Verve | 521690-2
Talkin' Jazz:Roots Of Acid Jazz | Verve | 529580-2

Green,William | (as,dr,fl,alto-fl,piccolo,reeds,sax)
Ella Fitzgerald With Orchestra
Ella/Things Ain't What They Used To Be | Warner | 9362-47875-2
Hampton Hawes Orchestra
Northern Windows Plus | Prestige | PRCD 24278-2
Herbie Hancock Group With String Quartet,Woodwinds And Brass
Herbie Hancock The New Standards | Verve | 527715-2
Herbie Hancock Group With Woodwinds And Brass
Herbie Hancock The New Standards | Verve | 527715-2
Marion Brown Orchestra
Afternoon Of A Georgia Faun | ECM | 1004
Stan Getz With Orchestra
Apasionado | A&M Records | 395297-2

Greenberg,Jack | (as,reeds,tswoodwinds)
Louis Armstrong And Ella Fitzgerald With Bob Hagger's Orchestra
Louis Armstrong:C'est Si Bon | Dreyfus Jazz Line | FDM 36730-2
Louis Armstrong With Gordon Jenkins And His Orchestra And Choir
Satchmo In Style | Verve | 549594-2
Ambassador Louis Armstrong Vol.17:Moments To Remember(1952-1956) | Ambassador | CLA 1917

Greenberg,Marty | (dr)
Muggsy Spanier And His Ragtime Band
Planet Jazz | Planet Jazz | 2169652-2

Greene Jr.,Willie | (voc)
Hanc Thoessink Group
Crazy Moon | Minor Music | 801052

Greene,Billy | (p)
Elvin Jones-Richard Davis Quartet
Heavy Sounds | Impulse(MCA) | 547959-2

Greene,Charles 'Flip' | (b)
Dexter Gordon Quartet
Dexter Gordon Birthday Celebration | Fantasy | FANCD 6082-2

Greene,Dodo | (voc)
Dodo Greene With The Ike Quebec Quintet
Misty Blue:Sweet Sisters Swing Songs Of Sorrow And Sadness | Blue Note | 521151-2

Greene,Ed | (dr)
Dee Dee Bridgewater With Band
Dee Dee Bridgewater | Atlantic | 7567-80760-2
Dizzy Gillespie With The Lalo Schifrin Orchestra
Free Ride | Original Jazz Classics | OJCCD 784-2(2310794)
Donald Byrd Orchestra
Ethiopian Knights | Blue Note | 854328-2
Stanley Turrentine And His Orchestra
Pieces Of Dream | Original Jazz Classics | OJCCD 831-2(F 9465)

Greene,Hillard | (b)
(Little)Jimmy Scott And His Band
Mood Indigo | Milestone | MCD 9305-2

Greene,Jimmy | (fl,ss,tsp)
Horace Silver Quintet
Jazz Has... A Sense Of Humor | Verve | 050293-2
Jam Session
Jam Session Vol.9 | Steeplechase | SCCD 31554
New Jazz Composers Octet
Walkin' the Line | Fresh Sound Records | FSNT 151 CD
The New Jazz Composers Octet
First Step Into Reality | Fresh Sound Records | FSNT 059 CD
Tom Harrell Group
Paradise | RCA | 2663738-2
Tom Harrell Quintet
Live At The Village Vanguard | RCA | 2663910-2

Greene,Joe | (voc)
Quincy Jones And His Orchestra
Verve Jazz Masters Vol.59:Toots Thielemans | Verve | 535271-2

Greene,Norman | (tb)
Louis Armstrong And His Orchestra
Louis Armstrong:Swing That Music | Laserlight | 36056

Jazz:The Essential Collection Vol.2 | IN+OUT Records | 78012-2
Louis Armstrong:C'est Si Bon | Dreyfus Jazz Line | FDM 36730-2

Greene,Richard Bob | (voc)
Klaus König Orchestra
Reviews | Enja | ENJ-9061 2

Greene,Thurman | (tb)
Buddy Childers Big Band
It's What Happening Now! | Candid | CCD 79749

Greenfish |
Greenfish
Perfume Light... | TipToe | TIP-888831 2

Greenhouse,Bernhard | (cello)
Ben Webster With Orchestra And Strings
Verve Jazz Masters 43:Ben Webster | Verve | 525431-2
Music For Loving:Ben Webster With Strings | Verve | 527774-2
Coleman Hawkins With Billy Byers And His Orchestra
The Hawk In Hi-Fi | RCA | 2663842-2

Greening,James | (tb,didjeridupocket-tp)
The Catholics
Simple | Laika Records | 35100802
Vince Jones Group
Here's To The Miracles | Intuition Records | INT 3198-2
Wanderlust
Border Crossing | Laika Records | 35100812
Wanderlust + Guests
Full Bronte | Laika Records | 35101412

Greenleaf,Fred | (tp)
Jack Teagarden And His Band
Meet Me Where They Play The Blues | Good Time Jazz | GTCD 12063-2

Greenlee,Charles | (arr,cond,euphoniumtb)
Archie Shepp Orchestra
The Cry Of My People | Impulse(MCA) | 9861488
Charles Mingus Orchestra
Charles Mingus:Pre-Bird(Mingus Revisited) | Verve | 538636-2
Dizzy Gillespie And His Orchestra
Planet Jazz:Dizzy Gillespie | Planet Jazz | 2152069-2
John Coltrane And His Orchestra
John Coltrane:Standards | Impulse(MCA) | 549914-2
John Coltrane Quartet With Brass
The Complete Africa/Brass Sessions | Impulse(MCA) | 952168-2
Roland Kirk All Stars
Rahsaan/The Complete Mercury Recordings Of Roland Kirk | Mercury | 846630-2
Roland Kirk Sextet
Talkin' Verve-Roots Of Acid Jazz:Roland Kirk | Verve | 533101-2
Roland Kirk With The Benny Golson Orchestra
Rahsaan/The Complete Mercury Recordings Of Roland Kirk | Mercury | 846630-2
Sam Rivers Orchestra
Crystals | Impulse(MCA) | 589760-2

Greenschpoon,Elizabeth | (cello)
Ella Fitzgerald With The Nelson Riddle Orchestra
The Best Of The Song Books:The Ballads | Verve | 521867-2

Greenwood,Andrew | (tp)
André Holst With Chris Dean's European Swing Orchestra
That's Swing | Nagel-Heyer | CD 079

Greer,William 'Sonny' | (dr,bells,chimes,tambourine)
Barney Bigard And His Orchestra
Highlights From The Duke Ellington Centennial Edition | RCA | 2663672-2
Jazz:The Essential Collection Vol.3 | IN+OUT Records | 78013-2
Big Al Sears Band
Sear-iously | Bear Family Records | BCD 15668 AH
Django Reinhardt With Duke Ellington And His Orchestra
Django Reinhardt:Souveniers | Dreyfus Jazz Line | FDM 36744-2
Duke Ellington And His Cotton Club Orchestra
Planet Jazz:Duke Ellington | Planet Jazz | 2152053-2
Jazz:The Essential Collection Vol.2 | IN+OUT Records | 78012-2
Duke Ellington And His Famous Orchestra
Duke Ellington:The Blanton-Webster Band | Bluebird | 21 13181-2
Planet Jazz:Duke Ellington | Planet Jazz | 2152053-2
Planet Jazz:Johnny Hodges | Planet Jazz | 2152065-2
Planet Jazz Sampler | Planet Jazz | 2152326-2
Planet Jazz:Ben Webster | RCA | 2165368-2
Planet Jazz:Big Bands | Planet Jazz | 2169649-2
Planet Jazz:Jazz Trumpet | Planet Jazz | 2169654-2
Planet Jazz:Female Jazz Vocalists | Planet Jazz | 2169656-2
Highlights From The Duke Ellington Centennial Edition | RCA | 2663672-2
Greatest Hits | CBS | 462959-2
Jazz:The Essential Collection Vol.2 | IN+OUT Records | 78012-2
Jazz:The Essential Collection Vol.3 | IN+OUT Records | 78013-2
Duke Ellington:Ko-Ko | Dreyfus Jazz Line | FDM 36717-2
Duke Ellington And His Kentucky Club Orchestra
Jazz:The Essential Collection Vol.2 | IN+OUT Records | 78012-2
Duke Ellington And His Orchestra
Planet Jazz:Duke Ellington | Planet Jazz | 2152053-2
Planet Jazz:Jazz Greatest Hits | Planet Jazz | 2169648-2
The Legends Of Swing | Laserlight | 24659
Highlights From The Duke Ellington Centennial Edition | RCA | 2663672-2
Carnegie Hall Concert January 1946 | Prestige | 2PCD 24074-2
Carnegie Hall Concert December 1947 | Prestige | 2PCD 24075-2
Carnegie Hall Concert January 1943 | Prestige | 2PCD 34004-2
Jazz:The Essential Collection Vol.2 | IN+OUT Records | 78012-2
Jazz:The Essential Collection Vol.3 | IN+OUT Records | 78013-2
The Duke At Fargo 1940 | Storyville | STCD 8316/17
At The Hurricane:Original 1943 Broadcasts | Storyville | STCD 8359
Esquire All-American Award Winners
Best Of The Complete RCA Victor Recordings | RCA | 2663636-2
Highlights From The Duke Ellington Centennial Edition | RCA | 2663672-2
Johnny Hodges And His Band
Verve Jazz Masters 35:Johnny Hodges | Verve | 521857-2
Johnny Hodges Orchestra
Planet Jazz:Johnny Hodges | Planet Jazz | 2152065-2
Planet Jazz Sampler | Planet Jazz | 2152326-2
Coleman Hawkins/Johnny Hodges:The Vogue Recordings | Vogue | 21559712
Planet Jazz:Jazz Saxophone | Planet Jazz | 2169653-2
Highlights From The Duke Ellington Centennial Edition | RCA | 2663672-2
Leonard Feather's Esquire All-Americans
Louis Armstrong:C'est Si Bon | Dreyfus Jazz Line | FDM 36730-2
Rex Stewart And His Orchestra
Planet Jazz:Ben Webster | RCA | 2165368-2
Planet Jazz:Jazz Trumpet | Planet Jazz | 2169654-2
Jazz:The Essential Collection Vol.3 | IN+OUT Records | 78013-2

Greg,Jones | (voc)
Max Roach Chorus & Orchestra
To The Max! | Enja | ENJ-7021 22

Greger Jr.,Max | (p,el-p,org,synth,clavinet,voc)
Max Greger Quintet
Night Train | Polydor | 543393-2

Greger,Max | (ldts)
Die Deutsche All Star Band 1953
1.Deutsches Jazz Festival 1953 Frankfurt/Main | Bear Family Records | BCD 15611 AH
Max Greger Quintet
Night Train | Polydor | 543393-2

Gregg,Erwin | (tb)
Al Porcino Big Band
Al Porcino Big Band Live! | Organic Music | ORGM 9717
Al Cohn Meets Al Porcino | Organic Music | ORGM 9730

Gregg,Jack | (b,african-dr,perc,wooden-flb-g)
Gunter Hampel And His Galaxie Dream Band
Journey To The Song Within | Birth | 0017

Enfant Terrible | Birth | 0025
Marion Brown Orchestra
Afternoon Of A Georgia Faun | ECM | 1004

Gregor,Tobia | (tp)
Bigband Der Musikschule Der Stadt Brühl Mit Gastsolisten
Pangäa | Indigo-Records | 1004 CD

Gregory,Haywood J. | (voc)
Eddie Harris Group With The WDR Big Band
Eddie Harris-The Last Concert | ACT | 9249-2

Greig,Stan | (drp)
Sandy Brown's Jazz Band
The Golden Years Of Revival Jazz,Vol.5 | Storyville | STCD 5510

Greiner,Angelika | (voc)
Jazzensemble Des Hessischen Rundfunks
Jazz Messe-Messe Für Unsere Zeit | hr music.de | hrmj 003-01 CD

Greiner,Hubl | (sampler)
Mani Neumeir Group
Privat | ATM Records | ATM 3803-AH

Greiner,Paul | (cl)
Bernd Konrad Jazz Group With Symphonie Orchestra
Wen Die Götter Lieben | Creative Works Records | CW CD 1010-1

Grenadier,Larry | (bel-b)
Brad Mehldau Trio
Introducing Brad Mehldau | Warner | 9362-45997-2
The Art Of The Trio Vol.1 | Warner | 9362-46260-2
The Art Of The Trio Vol.2 | Warner | 9362-46848-2
Art Of The Trio Vol.3: Songs | Warner | 9362-47051-2
Art Of The Trio Vol.4: Back At The Vanguard | Warner | 9362-47463-2
Places | Warner | 9362-47693-2
Art Of The Trio Vol.5:Progression | Warner | 9362-48005-2
Anything Goes | Warner | 9362-48608-2
Charles Lloyd Quintet
The Water Is Wide | ECM | 1734(549043-2)
Hyperion With Higgins | ECM | 1784(014000-2)
Lift Every Voice | ECM | 1832/33(018783-2)
Charles Lloyd Sextet
Lift Every Voice | ECM | 1832/33(018783-2)
Ingrid Jensen Sextet
Vernal Fields | Enja | ENJ-9013 2
Johnny King Septet
The Meltdown | Enja | ENJ-9329 2
Joshua Redman Quartet
Timeless Tales | Warner | 9362-47052-2
Mark Turner Quartet
Ballad Session | Warner | 9362-47631-2
Mark Turner Quintet
Ballad Session | Warner | 9362-47631-2
Mark Turner Trio
Ballad Session | Warner | 9362-47631-2
Mike Stern Group
Standards(And Other Songs) | Atlantic | 7567-82419-2
Pat Metheny Trio
Trio 99-00 | Warner | 9362-47632-2
Part Metheny Trio Live | Warner | 9362-47907-2
Paul Motian Trio With Chris Potter And Larry Grenadier
Paul Motian Trio 2000 + One | Winter&Winter | 910032-2
Phil Grenadier Quintet
Sweet Transients | Fresh Sound Records | FSNT 093 CD
Seamus Blake Quartet
Stranger Things Have Happened | Fresh Sound Records | FSNT 063 CD
Seamus Blake Quintet
Stranger Things Have Happened | Fresh Sound Records | FSNT 063 CD
Steve Cárdenas Trio
Shebang | Fresh Sound Records | FSNT 079 CD
Steve Smith & Vital Information
Vitalive! | VeraBra Records | CDVBR 2051-2

Grenadier,Phil | (tpfl-h)
Phil Grenadier Quintet
Sweet Transients | Fresh Sound Records | FSNT 093 CD

Grenu,Georges | (as,cl,ts,fl,saxss)
Alain Goraguer Orchestra
Jazz In Paris:Jazz & Cinéma Vol.1 | EmArCy | 548318-2 PMS
Jazz In Paris | EmArCy | 548793-2
André Hodeir And His Jazz Group De Paris
Jazz In Paris:Le Jazz Groupe De Paris Joue André Hodeir | EmArCy | 548792-2
Kenny Clarke 8
Americans Swinging In Paris:Kenny Clarke | EMI Records | 539652-2
Raymond Fol Big Band
Jazz In Paris:Raymond Fol-Les 4 Saisons | EmArCy | 548791-2

Gress,Drew | (b)
Antonio Farao Quartet
Thorn | Enja | ENJ-9399 2
Antonio Farao Trio
Thorn | Enja | ENJ-9399 2
Dave Douglas Group
Witness | RCA | 2663763-2
Don Byron Quartet
Romance With The Unseen | Blue Note | 499545-2
Fred Hersch Quartet
Point In Time | Enja | ENJ-9035 2
Fred Hersch Quintet
Point In Time | Enja | ENJ-9035 2
Fred Hersch Trio
Point In Time | Enja | ENJ-9035 2
George Colligan Group
Unresolved | Fresh Sound Records | FSNT 054 CD
James Emery Quartet
Fourth World | Between The Lines | btl 020(Efa 10190-2)
James Emery Sextet
Luminous Cycles | Between The Lines | btl 015(Efa 10185-2)
Simon Nabatov Trio
Three Stories,One End | ACT | 9401-2
Uri Caine Ensemble
Wagner E Venezia | Winter&Winter | 910013-2

Greve,Buddy | (dr)
Gus Mancuso Quintet
Gus Mancuso & Special Friends | Fantasy | FCD 24762-2

Greve,Carl | (b)
Helmut Zacharias mit Kleiner Tanz-Besetzung
Ich Habe Rhythmus | Bear Family Records | BCD 15642 AH
Helmut Zacharias Sextet
Ich Habe Rhythmus | Bear Family Records | BCD 15642 AH

Greve,Volker | (vib)
Bajazzo
Harlequin Galaxy | Edition Collage | EC 519-2

Grex Vocalis |
Terje Rypdal(comp)
Undisonus | ECM | 1389

Grey,Al | (tbvoc)
(Little)Jimmy Scott With The Lionel Hampton Orchestra
Everybody's Somebody's Fool | Decca | 050669-2
Al Grey And His Allstars
Snap Your Fingers | Verve | 9860307
Benny Carter And His Chocolate Dandies
Planet Jazz:Ben Webster | RCA | 2165368-2
Jazz:The Essential Collection Vol.3 | IN+OUT Records | 78013-2
Big Joe Turner With The Count Basie Orchestra
Flip Flop And Fly | Original Jazz Classics | OJCCD 1053-2(2310937)
Count Basie And His Orchestra
Fun Time | Pablo | 2310945-2
Jazz Collection:Count Basie | Laserlight | 24368
The Legends Of Swing | Laserlight | 24659
Count Basie: Salle Pleyel, April 17th, 1972 | Laserlight | 36127
Atomic Swing | Roulette | 497871-2
Breakfast Dance And Barbecue | Roulette | 531791-2

Basie Meets Bond | Capitol | 538225-2
Basie's Beatle Bag | Verve | 557455-2
Chairman Of The Board | Roulette | 581664-2
The Complete Atomic Basie | Roulette | 828635-2
Live at The Sands | Reprise | 9362-45946-2
Count On The Coast Vol.1 | Phontastic | NCD 7555
Count On The Coast Vol.2 | Phontastic | NCD 7575
Jazz Dance | Original Jazz Classics | OJCCD 1002-2(1210890)
I Told You So | Original Jazz Classics | OJCCD 824-2(2310767)
The Jazz Giants Play Harry Warren:Lullaby Of Broadway | Prestige | PCD 24204-2

Count Basie And The Kansas City 7
Count Basie: Salle Pleyel, April 17th, 1972 | Laserlight | 36127

Count Basie Band
Basie Jam No. 2 | Original Jazz Classics | OJCCD 631-2(2310786)

Count Basie Big Band
Montreux '77 | Original Jazz Classics | OJCCD 377-2

Count Basie Jam
Montreux '77 | Original Jazz Classics | OJC 379(2308209)
Montreux '77 | Original Jazz Classics | OJC 385(2620105)

Dizzy Gillespie And His Orchestra
Dizzy Gillespie:Birks Works-The Verve Big Band Sessions | Verve | 527900-2
Ultimate Dizzy Gillespie | Verve | 557535-2

Dizzy Gillespie Orchestra
Verve Jazz Masters 10:Dizzy Gillespie | Verve | 516319-2

Ella Fitzgerald And Count Basie With The JATP All Stars
Bluella:Ella Fitzgerald Sings The Blues | Pablo | 2310960-2

Ella Fitzgerald And Her All Stars
All That Jazz | Pablo | 2310938-2

Ella Fitzgerald With Sy Oliver And His Orchestra
Ella Fitzgerald:The Decca Years 1949-1954 | Decca | 050668-2

J.J. Johnson-Al Grey Sextet
Things Are Getting Better All The Time | Original Jazz Classics | OJCCD 745-2(2312141)
The J.J.Johnson Memorial Album | Prestige | PRCD 11025-2

JATP All Stars
Welcome To Jazz At The Philharmonic | Fantasy | FANCD 6081-2

Lionel Hampton And His Orchestra
Planet Jazz:Big Bands | Planet Jazz | 2169649-2
Lionel Hampton:Flying Home | Dreyfus Jazz Line | FDM 36735-2

Lionel Hampton Orchestra
The Big Bands Vol.1.The Snader Telescriptions | Storyville | 4960043

Louis Armstrong And His Friends
Louis Armstrong And His Friends | Bluebird | 2663961-2

Quincy Jones And His Orchestra
Verve Jazz Masters Vol.59:Toots Thielemans | Verve | 535271-2

Sarah Vaughan And Joe Williams With The Count Basie Orchestra
Jazz Profile | Blue Note | 823517-2

Sarah Vaughan And The Count Basie Orchestra
Ballads | Roulette | 537561-2

Sarah Vaughan And The Thad Jones Orchestra
Verve Jazz Masters 42:Sarah Vaughan-The Jazz Sides | Verve | 526817-2

Sarah Vaughan With The Count Basie Band
Jazz Profile | Blue Note | 823517-2

Grey,Alex | (v)

United Future Organizatio
United Future Organization | Talkin' Loud | 518166-2

Grey,D. | (fr-h)

Dee Dee Bridgewater With Orchestra
Dear Ella | Verve | 539102-2

Grey,Sonny | (tp)

Daniel Humair Soultet
Jazz In Paris | EmArCy | 548793-2

Kenny Clarke-Francy Boland Big Band
All Smiles | MPS | 9814790

Grider,Thomas | (tp)

Louis Armstrong And His Orchestra
Swing Legends:Louis Armstrong | Nimbus Records | NI 2012

Grieder,Andreas | (fl,p,org,bassoonhorns)

Marco Cerletti Group
Random And Providence | VeraBra Records | CDVBR 2039-2

Griefingholt,Andreas | (drperc)

Joel Frahm Quintet
The Rains From A Cloud Do Not Wet The Sky | Nabel Records:Jazz Network | CD 4686

Tim Sund Quintet
In The Midst Of Change | Nabel Records:Jazz Network | CD 4679

Griener,Michael | (dr,perc,trap-setdictaphone)

Andreas Willers Group
Tin Drum Stories(inspired by the novel 'Die Blechtrommel' by Günter Grass) | Between The Lines | btl 009(Efa 10179-2)

Blue Collar
Diary Of A Working Band | Jazz Haus Musik | JHM 0089 CD

Grieshofer,Ernst | (perc)

Melanie Bong With Band
Fantasia | Jazz 4 Ever Records:Jazz Network | J4E 4755

Grievey,Buddy | (dr)

Billy Eckstine And His Orchestra
Blue Velvet: Crooners, Swooners And Velvet Vocals | Blue Note | 521153-2

Griffin,Chris | (tp)

Benny Goodman And His Orchestra
Planet Jazz:Benny Goodman | Planet Jazz | 2152054-2
Planet Jazz:Jazz Greatest Hits | Planet Jazz | 2169648-2
Planet Jazz:Big Bands | Planet Jazz | 2169649-2
Great Swing Classics In Hi-Fi | Capitol | 521223-2
Benny Goodman At Carnegie Hall 1938(Complete) | CBS | C2K 65143
Camel Caravan Broadcast 1939 Vol.1 | Phontastic | NCD 8817
Camel Caravan Broadcast 1939 Vol.2 | Phontastic | NCD 8818
Camel Caravan Broadcast 1939 Vol.3 | Phontastic | NCD 8819
More Camel Caravans | Phontastic | NCD 8841/2
More Camel Caravans | Phontastic | NCD 8843/4
More Camel Caravans | Phontastic | NCD 8845/6

Charlie Parker With Strings
Bird: The Complete Charlie Parker On Verve | Verve | 837141-2

Charlie Parker With The Joe Lipman Orchestra
Charlie Parker With Strings:The Master Takes | Verve | 523984-2
Charlie Parker Big Band | Verve | 559835-2

Jam Session
Benny Goodman At Carnegie Hall 1938(Complete) | CBS | C2K 65143

Louis Armstrong With Gordon Jenkins And His Orchestra
Satchmo In Style | Verve | 549594-2

Griffin,Dick | (tb,b-tbvoc)

Abdullah Ibrahim And Ekaya
Water From An Ancient Well | TipToe | TIP-888812 2

Dick Griffin Septet
The Eighth Wonder & More | Konnex Records | KCD 5059

McCoy Tyner Group With Horns
Inner Voices | Original Jazz Classics | OJCCD 1039-2(M 9079)

McCoy Tyner Group With Horns And Voices
Inner Voices | Original Jazz Classics | OJCCD 1039-2(M 9079)

Rahsaan Roland Kirk And His Orchestra
Blacknuss | Rhino | 8122-71408-2

Rahsaan Roland Kirk Sextet
Volunteered Slavery | Rhino | 8122-71407-2

Griffin,Fred | (fr-h)

David Matthews & The Manhattan Jazz Orchestra
Back To Bach | Milestone | MCD 9312-2
Hey Duke! | Milestone | MCD 9320-2

John Scofield Groups
Quiet | Verve | 533185-2

Griffin,Geraldine | (voc)

Dick Griffin Septet
The Eighth Wonder & More | Konnex Records | KCD 5059

Griffin,Gordon | (tp)

Benny Goodman And His Orchestra
Planet Jazz:Benny Goodman | Planet Jazz | 2152054-2
Planet Jazz:Swing | Planet Jazz | 2169651-2
Planet Jazz:Jazz Trumpet | Planet Jazz | 2169654-2
Planet Jazz:Female Jazz Vocalists | Planet Jazz | 2169656-2

Louis Armstrong With Gordon Jenkins And His Orchestra And Choir
Ambassador Louis Armstrong Vol.17:Moments To Remember(1952-1956) | Ambassador | CLA 1917

Sarah Vaughan With The Joe Lippman Orchestra
Sarah Vaughan:Lover Man | Dreyfus Jazz Line | FDM 36739-2

Griffin,Johnny | (ts,percvoc)

Ahmed Abdul-Malik Orchestra
Planet Jazz:Lee Morgan | Planet Jazz | 2161238-2

Ahmed Abdul-Malik's Middle-Eastern Music
Jazz Sahara | Original Jazz Classics | OJCCD 1820-2(R 12-287)

Art Blakey And The Jazz Messengers
Planet Jazz:Art Blakey | Planet Jazz | 2152066-2
Planet Jazz Sampler | Planet Jazz | 2152326-2
A Night In Tunisia | RCA | 2663896-2

Art Blakey And The Jazz Messengers With Thelonious Monk
Art Blakey's Jazz Messengers With Thelonious Monk | Atlantic | 7567-81332-2

Babs Gonzales And His Band
Voilà | Fresh Sound Records | FSR CD 340

Blue Mitchell Sextet
Blue Mitchell Big 6 | Original Jazz Classics | OJCCD 615-2(RLP 12-273)

Bud Powell Quartet
Bud Powell Paris Sessions | Pablo | PACD 2310972-2

Chet Baker Quintet
Chet Baker In New York | Original Jazz Classics | OJC20 207-2

Count Basie Jam Session
Count Basie Jam Session At The Montreux Jazz Festival 1975 | Original Jazz Classics | OJC20 933-2(2310750)

Count Basie Sextet
Jazz At The Philharmonic:The Montreux Collection | Pablo | PACD 5306-2

Dizzy Gillespie All Stars
Jazz At The Philharmonic:The Montreux Collection | Pablo | PACD 5306-2

Dizzy Gillespie Big 7
Dizzy-At The Montreux Jazz Festival 1975 | Original Jazz Classics | OJC20 739-2(2310749)

Dizzy Gillespie Quintet
Jazz In Paris:Dizzy Gillespie-The Giant | EmArCy | 159734-2 PMS

Don Sickler Orchestra
Tribute To Charlie Parker Vol.2 | Dreyfus Jazz Line | FDM 37015-2

Eddie Lockjaw Davis-Johnny Griffin Quintet
Blues Up And Down | Milestone | MCD 47084-2
Battle Stations | Original Jazz Classics | OJCCD 1085(P7282)
The Jazz Giants Play Cole Porter:Night And Day | Prestige | PCD 24203-2
The Prestige Legacy Vol.2:Battles Of Saxes | Prestige | PCD 24252-2
Tough Tenors Back Again! | Storyville | STCD 8298

Johnny Griffin Quartet
Jazz Life Vol.1:From Village Vanguard | Storyville | 4960753
The Kerry Dancers | Original Jazz Classics | OJCCD 1952-2(RLP 9420)

Johnny Griffin Quintet
Grab This! | Original Jazz Classics | OJCCD 1941-2(RLP 9437)

Johnny Griffin Septet
A Blowing Session | Blue Note | 0677191
Trane's Blues | Blue Note | 498240-2

Johnny Griffin With The Bud Powell Trio
Bebop | Pablo | PACD 2310978-2

Johnny Griffin With The NDR Big Band
NDR Big Band-Bravissimo | ACT | 9232-2

Johnny Griffin-Art Taylor Quartet
Johnny Griffin/Art Taylor In Copenhagen | Storyville | STCD 8300

Johnny Griffin-Eddie Lockjaw Davis Quintet
Tough Tenors | Original Jazz Classics | OJCCD 1094-2(JLP 931)

Johnny Griffin-Sal Nistico-Roman Schwaller Sextet
Three Generations Of Tenorsaxophone | JHM Records | JHM 3611

Johnny Griffin-Steve Grossman Quintet
Johnny Griffin & Steve Grossman | Dreyfus Jazz Line | FDM 36615-2

Kenny Clarke-Francy Boland Big Band
Clark-Boland Big Band: TNP, October 29th, 1969 | Laserlight | 36129
Three Latin Adventures | MPS | 529095-2
More Smiles | MPS | 9814789
All Smiles | MPS | 9814790
Francy Boland-Fellini 712 | MPS | 9814805

Laura Fygi With Band
Bewitched | Verve | 514724-2

Lionel Hampton And His Orchestra
Lionel Hampton:Flying Home | Dreyfus Jazz Line | FDM 36735-2

Mel Rhyne Sextet
Organ-izing | Original Jazz Classics | OJCCD 1055-2(JLP 916)

Nat Adderley Quintet
A Little New York Midtown Music | Original Jazz Classics | OJCCD 1008-2(GXY 5120)

Nat Adderley Quintet(incl.The Three Sounds)
Branching Out | Original Jazz Classics | OJCCD 255-2(R 285)

NDR-Workshop
Doldinger's Best | ACT | 9224-2

Niels-Henning Orsted-Pedersen Trio With Johnny Griffin
Those Who Were | Verve | 533232-2

Passport And Guests
Doldinger Jubilee Concert | Atlantic | 2292-44175-2
Doldinger's Best | ACT | 9224-2

Raymond Fol Big Band
Jazz In Paris:Raymond Fol-Les 4 Saisons | EmArCy | 548791-2

Roy Eldridge Quintet
Decidedly | Pablo | PACD 5314-2

Roy Eldridge Sextet
Decidedly | Pablo | PACD 5314-2

Roy Hargrove Quintet With Johnny Griffin
Roy Hargrove Quintet With The Tenors Of Our Time | Verve | 523019-2

Thelonious Monk Quartet
Thelonious Monk:85th Birthday Celebration | zyx records | FANCD 6076-2
Misterioso | Original Jazz Classics | OJC20 206-2
Thelonious In Action | Original Jazz Classics | OJCCD 103-2

Wes Montgomery Quintet
Wes Montgomery-The Complete Riverside Recordings | Riverside | 12 RCD 4408-2
Full House | Original Jazz Classics | OJC20 106-2

Griffin,Paul | (cello,el-p,clavinet,keyboards,org,p)

Cal Tjader Sextet
Soul Bird | Verve | 549111-2

Cal Tjader's Orchestra
Verve Jazz Masters 39:Cal Tjader | Verve | 521858-2

George Benson Orchestra
Talkin' Verve:George Benson | Verve | 553780-2

George Benson Quartet
Talkin' Verve:George Benson | Verve | 553780-2

George Benson Quartet With The Sweet Inspirations
Talkin' Verve:George Benson | Verve | 553780-2

George Benson With Orchestra
Verve Jazz Masters 21:George Benson | Verve | 521861-2

King Curtis Band
King Curtis-Blow Man Blow | Bear Family Records | BCD 15670 CI

Griffin,Rayford | (dr,dr-design,voc,keyboardsperc)

Jean-Luc Ponty Group
Mystical Adventures | Atlantic | 19333-2

Jean-Luc Ponty Quartet
The Very Best Of Jean-Luc Ponty | Rhino | 8122-79862-2

Jean-Luc Ponty Quintet
The Very Best Of Jean-Luc Ponty | Rhino | 8122-79862-2

Jean-Luc Ponty Sextet
The Very Best Of Jean-Luc Ponty | Rhino | 8122-79862-2

Jean-Luc Ponty-Raymond Griffin
The Very Best Of Jean-Luc Ponty | Rhino | 8122-79862-2

Griffith,Dick | (bjtb)

Roland Kirk Quintet
The Inflated Tear | Atlantic | 7567-90045-2
The Inflated Tear | Atlantic | 8122-75207-2

Griffith,Frank | (as,clarr)

Joe Temperley Quintet With Strings
Easy To Remember | Hep | CD 2083

Griffith,Gus | (tp)

Sarah Vaughan With The Norman Leyden Orchestra
Sarah Vaughan:Lover Man | Dreyfus Jazz Line | FDM 36739-2

Griffiths,Malcolm | (tb)

John Surman Orchestra
How Many Clouds Can You See? | Deram | 844882-2

John Surman-John Warren Group
The Brass Project | ECM | 1478

Griggs,Bernie | (b)

Charlie Parker Quartet
Charlie Parker At Storyville | Blue Note | 785108-2

Grillini,Enzo | (g)

Helen Merrill And Her Band
Planet Jazz:Female Jazz Vocalists | Planet Jazz | 2169656-2

Helen Merrill With The Piero Umilliani Group
Parole E Musica | RCA | 2174798-2

Grillo,Mario | (cond,timbales,dir,perc,congas)

Machito And His Orchestra
Afro-Cuban Jazz Moods | Original Jazz Classics | OJC20 447-2

Grimes,Henry | (b)

A Band Of Friends
The Best Of The Gerry Mulligan Quartet With Chet Baker | Pacific Jazz | 795481-2

Albert Ayler Sextet
Albert Ayler Live In Greenwich Village:The Complete Impulse Recordings | Impulse(MCA) | IMP 22732

Cecil Taylor Sextet
A Blue Conception | Blue Note | 534254-2
Conquistador | Blue Note | 576749-2

Cecil Taylor Unit
Mixed | Impulse(MCA) | IMP 12702

Charles Mingus Workshop
Charles Mingus-The Complete Debut Recordings | Debut | 12 DCD 4402-2

Don Cherry Quartet
Complete Communion | Blue Note | 522673-2

Gerry Mulligan And The Sax Section
The Gerry Mulligan Songbook | Pacific Jazz | 833575-2

Gerry Mulligan Quartet
Newport Jazz Festival 1958,July 3rd-6th Vol.2:Mulligan The Main Man | Phontastic | NCD 8814

Lee Konitz Trio
Newport Jazz Festival 1958,July 3rd-6th,Vol.1:Mostly Miles | Phontastic | NCD 8813

Rolf Kühn Quintet
Rolf Kühn And His Sound Of Jazz | Fresh Sound Records | FSR-CD 326

Rolf Kühn Sextet
Rolf Kühn And His Sound Of Jazz | Fresh Sound Records | FSR-CD 326

Roy Haynes Quartet
Out Of The Afternoon | Impulse(MCA) | 951180-2

Shirley Scott Trio
Queen Of The Organ-Shirley Scott Memorial Album | Prestige | PRCD 11027-2

Sonny Rollins & Co.
Planet Jazz:Sonny Rollins | Planet Jazz | 2152062-2

Sonny Rollins Orchestra
Sonny Rollins And The Big Brass | Verve | 557545-2

Sonny Rollins Trio
Sonny Rollins And The Big Brass | Verve | 557545-2
St.Thomas:Sonny Rollins In Stockhom 1959 | Dragon | DRCD 229

Sonny Rollins-Coleman Hawkins Quintet
Planet Jazz:Sonny Rollins | Planet Jazz | 2152062-2
Sonny Meets Hawk! | RCA | 2174800-2

Grimes,Thomas | (poetry,rap,scoop-vibvoive)

Cornelius Claudio Kreusch Group
Scoop | ACT | 9255-2

Grimes,Tiny | (gvoc)

Art Tatum Trio
Art Tatum:Over The Rainbow | Dreyfus Jazz Line | FDM 36727-2

Billie Holiday With The JATP All Stars
The Complete Jazz At The Philharmonic On Verve 1944-1949 | Verve | 523893-2

Billie Holiday With The Tiny Grimes Quintet
Billie's Blues | Blue Note | 748786-2

Coleman Hawkins Sextet
Hawk Eyes | Original Jazz Classics | OJCCD 294-2

Ike Quebec Quintet
The Blue Note Swingtets | Blue Note | 495697-2

Ike Quebec Swing Seven
The Blue Note Swingtets | Blue Note | 495697-2

Ike Quebec Swingtet
The Blue Note Swingtets | Blue Note | 495697-2

Illinois Jacquet Quintet
The Blues That's Me! | Original Jazz Classics | OJCCD 614-2(P 7731)

John Hardee Swingtet
The Blue Note Swingtets | Blue Note | 495697-2

Prestige Blues-Swingers
Soul Street | Original Jazz Classics | OJCCD 987-2(NJ 8293)

Tiny Grimes Swingtet
The Blue Note Swingtets | Blue Note | 495697-2

Grimes,Tiny prob. | (g)

Billie Holiday With The JATP All Stars
Billie Holiday Story Vol.1:Jazz At The Philharmonic | Verve | 521642-2
Verve Jazz Masters 47:Billie Holiday Sings Standards | Verve | 527650-2
Jazz At The Philharmonic:Best Of The 1940's Concerts | Verve | 557534-2

Grimm,Dominik | (voc)

Dominik Grimm-Thomas Wallisch Trio
A Brighter Day | Edition Collage | EC 510-2

Grimm,Jürgen | (keyboardsp)

HR Big Band
The American Songs Of Kurt Weill | hr music.de | hrmj 006-01 CD

Grimminger,Andreas | (tpfl-h)

Jazz Orchester Rheinland-Pfalz
Kazzou | Jazz Haus Musik | LJBB 9104

Grimoin,Olivier | (viola)

Charlie Haden Quartet West With Strings
Now Is The Hour | Verve | 527827-2

Grimshaw,Stuart | (b)

Dirk Raulf Group
Theater I (Bühnenmusik) | Poise | Poise 07

Grin,Wim | (cello)

Stochelo Rosenberg Group With Strings
Gypsy Swing | Verve | 527806-2

Grinage,Les | (b)

Mundell Lowe Quartet
A Grand Night For Swinging | Original Jazz Classics | OJCCD 1940-(RLP 238)

Mundell Lowe Quintet
A Grand Night For Swinging | Original Jazz Classics | OJCCD 1940-(RLP 238)

Grisby,Michael Wall | (perc)

Kenny Barron Group
Spirit Song | Verve | 543180-2

Grisman,David | (mand)

Stephane Grappelli-David Grisman Group

Stephane Grappelli:Live In San Francisco | Storyville | 4960723

Grissett,Danny | (p)
Rickey Woodard Quartet
California Cooking No.2 | Candid | CCD 79762

Grissom,Jimmy | (voc)
Duke Ellington And His Orchestra
Ellington At Newport 1956(Complete) | CBS | CK 64932

Grocott,Shawn | (tb)
The Groenewald Newnet
Meetings | Jazz 'n' Arts Records | JNA 0702

Groenewald,Oliver | (tpfl-h)

Grolnick,Don | (clavinet,el-p,keyboards,org,synthp)
Don Grolnick Group
Hearts And Numbers | VeraBra Records | CDVBR 2016-2
Michael Brecker Group
Don't Try This At Home | Impulse(MCA) | 950114-2
Peter Erskine Orchestra
Peter Erskine | Original Jazz Classics | OJC 610(C 14010)
Steve Khan Group
Jazzrock-Anthology Vol.3:Fusion | Zounds | CD 27100555
The Brecker Brothers
The Becker Bros | RCA | 2122103-2

Gromaire,Thomas | (g)
Stéphane Mercier Group
Flor De Luna | Fresh Sound Records | FSNT 097 CD

Grömmer,Rolf | (bj)
Old Merrytale Jazz Band
The Very Best Of Dixieland Jazz | Verve | 535529-2

Grönemeyer,Herbert | (voc)
World Quintet With The London Mozart Players And Herbert Grönemeyer
World Quintet | TipToe | TIP-888843 2

Gröning,Peter | (dr)
Maria Joao Quintet
Conversa | Nabel Records:Jazz Network | CD 4628

Gronvad,Morten | (synth,perc,dr-programming,midi-vib)
VIBrations
7.Zelt-Musik-Festival:Jazz Events | Zounds | CD 2730001

Grooveyard |
Grooveyard Meets Houston Person
Basic Instinct | Organic Music | ORGM 9701
Grooveyard Meets Red Holloway
Basic Instinct | Organic Music | ORGM 9701
Grooveyard Meets Roman Schwaller
Basic Instinct | Organic Music | ORGM 9701

Gropp,Peter | (b)
Wedeli Köhler Group
Swing & Folk | Jazzpoint | JP 1067 CD

Gross,John | (fl,clts)
Shelly Manne Sextet
Alive In London | Original Jazz Classics | OJCCD 773-2(S 7629)

Gross,Mark | (as,flss)
Antonio Hart Group
Here I Stand | Impulse(MCA) | 951208-2
Dave Holland Big Band
What Goes Around | ECM | 1777(014002-2)

Gross,Michael | (tp)
Swim Two Birds
Sweet Reliet | Laika Records | 35101182
No Regrets | Laika Records | 35101342

Grossman,Andy | (b-tbtb)
Harry Allen And Randy Sandke Meets The RIAS Big Band Berlin
The Music Of The Trumpet Kings | Nagel-Heyer | CD 037

Grossman,Steve | (sax,ssts)
Johnny Griffin-Steve Grossman Quintet
Johnny Griffin & Steve Grossman | Dreyfus Jazz Line | FDM 36615-2
Miles Davis Group
Live-Evil | CBS | C2K 65135
Live At The Fillmore East | CBS | C2K 65139
Miles Davis Sextet
Black Beauty-Miles Davis At Filmore West | CBS | C2K 65138
Steve Grossman Quartet
Steve Grossman Quartet | Dreyfus Jazz Line | FDM 36602-2

Grossmann,Manfred | (tb)
Albert Mangelsdorff With The NDR Big Band
NDR Big Band-Bravissimo | ACT | 9232-2
Chet Baker With The NDR-Bigband
NDR Big Band-Bravissimo | ACT | 9232-2
My Favourite Songs: The Last Great Concert Vol.1 | Enja | ENJ-5097 2
The Last Concert Vol.I+II | Enja | ENJ-6074 22
Chet Baker-The Legacy Vol.1 | Enja | ENJ-9021 2
Heinz Sauer Quartet With The NDR Big Band
NDR Big Band-Bravissimo | ACT | 9232-2
NDR Big Band
NDR Big Band-Bravissimo | ACT | 9232-2

Grossniklaus,Melchior | (sax)
Asita Hamidi & Arcobaleno
Mosaic | Laika Records | 8695067

Grosz,Marty | (g,arr,vocbj)
Allan Vaché Swingtet
Ellington For Lovers | Nagel-Heyer | NH 1009
Marty Grosz And His Honoris Causa Jazz Band
Hooray For Bix! | Good Time Jazz | GTCD 10065-2
Marty Grosz And His Swinging Fools
Ring Dem Bells | Nagel-Heyer | CD 022
The Second Sampler | Nagel-Heyer | NHR SP 6
Marty Grosz Quartet
Just For Fun! | Nagel-Heyer | CD 039
Ralph Sutton And Friends
Sweet Sue-The Music Of Fats Waller Vol.1 | Nagel-Heyer | CD 057
The New York Allstars
Broadway | Nagel-Heyer | CD 003
One Two Three | Nagel-Heyer | CD 008
Randy Sandke Meets Bix Beiderbecke | Nagel-Heyer | CD 3002
The First Sampler | Nagel-Heyer | NHR SP 5
Tom Saunders' 'Wild Bill Davison Band' & Guests
Exactly Like You | Nagel-Heyer | CD 023
The Second Sampler | Nagel-Heyer | NHR SP 6

Group Five | (voc)
Mark Whitfield Group
Patrice | Warner | 7599-26659-2

Groupp,Martin | (perc)
Quincy Jones And His Orchestra
Rahsaan/The Complete Mercury Recordings Of Roland Kirk | Mercury | 846630-2

Grove,Henry | (voc)
Lillian Boutté And Her Group & The Soulful Heavenly Stars
The Gospel Book | Blues Beacon | BLU-1017 2

Groves,Lani | (voc)
Dee Dee Bridgewater With Band
Dee Dee Bridgewater | Atlantic | 7567-80760-2
Grover Washington Jr. Orchestra
Inside Moves | Elektra | 7559-60318-2

GRP All Stars |
GRP All-Star Big Band
GRP All-Star Big Band:Live! | GRP | GRP 97402

GRP All-Star Big Band |
All Blues | GRP | GRP 98002

Grube,Harry | (p)
Joe Pass With The NDR Big Band And Radio Philharmonie Hannover
Joe Pass In Hamburg | ACT | 9100-2

Grünewald,Dieter | (tb,tpfl-h)
HR Big Band
Libertango:Homage An Astor Piazolla | hr music.de | hrmj 014-02 CD

Grünkorn,Isabel | (v)
Till Brönner Quartet & Deutsches Symphonieorchester Berlin
German Songs | Minor Music | 801057

Gruntz,George | (cond,el-p,synth,harp,keyboards,arr)
Daniel Schnyder With The NDR Radio Philharmonie Hannover
Tanatula | Enja | ENJ-9302 2
George Gruntz Concert Jazz Band
Blues 'N Dues Et Cetera | Enja | ENJ-6072 2
George Gruntz Concert Jazz Band '83
Theatre | ECM | 1265
Miles Davis With Gil Evans Orchestra, The George Gruntz Concert Jazz Band And Guests
Miles & Quincy Live At Montreux | Warner | 9362-45221-2
NDR Big Band With Guests
50 Years Of NDR Big Band:Bravissimo II | ACT | 9259-2
Phil Woods And His European Rhythm Machine
At The Montreux Jazz Festival | Verve | 065512-2
Americans Swinging In Paris:Phil Woods | EMI Records | 539654-2

Grupo Mezcla: |
Lazaro Ros Con Mezcla
Cantos | Intuition Records | INT 3080-2

Grupp,Martin | (perc)
Quincy Jones And His Orchestra
Verve Jazz Masters Vol.59:Toots Thielemans | Verve | 535271-2

Grusin,Dave | (el-p,perc,synth,keyboards,ld,p,cond)
Al Jarreau With Band
We Got By | Reprise | 7599-27222-2
Dave Grusin
Mountain Dance | GRP | GRP 95072
Dave Grusin Group
Mountain Dance | GRP | GRP 95072
Migration | GRP | GRP 95922
Dave Grusin Orchestra
Two For The Road:The Music Of Henry Mancini | GRP | GRP 98652
Diane Schuur With Orchestra
The Best Of Diane Schuur | GRP | GRP 98882
Diane Schuur With The Dave Grusin Orchestra
The Best Of Diane Schuur | GRP | GRP 98882
Glenn Miller And His Orchestra
The Glenn Miller Orchestra In Digital Mood | GRP | GRP 95022
GRP All-Star Big Band
GRP All-Star Big Band:Live! | GRP | GRP 97402
All Blues | GRP | GRP 98002
Lee Ritenour Group
Jazzrock-Anthology Vol.3:Fusion | Zounds | CD 27100555
Rio | GRP | GRP 95242
Festival | GRP | GRP 95702
Peggy Lee With Orchestra
Pass Me By/Big Spender | Capitol | 535210-2
Quincy Jones And His Orchestra
Verve Jazz Masters Vol.59:Toots Thielemans | Verve | 535271-2
Singers Unlimited With The Patrick Williams Orchestra
The Singers Unlimited:Magic Voices | MPS | 539130-2

Grusin,Don | (clavinet,el-p,synth,keyboards,p)
Diane Schuur With The Dave Grusin Orchestra
The Best Of Diane Schuur | GRP | GRP 98882
Joe Pass Sextet
Joe Pass:Guitar Virtuoso | Pablo | 4 PACD 4423-2
Jazzin' Vol.2: The Music Of Stevie Wonder | Fantasy | FANCD 6088-2
Lee Ritenour Group
Rio | GRP | GRP 95242
Lee Ritenour With Special Guests
Festival International De Jazz De Montreal | Spectra | 9811661

Gruvstedt,Lennart | (dr)
Miles Davis With The Danish Radio Big Band
Aura | CBS | CK 63962
NDR Big Band
NDR Big Band-Bravissimo | ACT | 9232-2
Stan Getz With The Danish Radio Big Band
Stan Getz In Europe | Laserlight | 24657
The Danish Radio Big Band
Aura | CBS | CK 63962

Gryce,Gigi | (arr,as,dr,bs,clfl)
Clifford Brown Sextet
Clifford Brown Memorial Album | Blue Note | 532141-2
Gigi Gryce-Clifford Brown Octet
Planet Jazz:Clifford Brown | Planet Jazz | 2161239-2
Gigi Gryce-Clifford Brown Sextet
Planet Jazz:Clifford Brown | Planet Jazz | 2161239-2
Gigi Gryce-Donald Byrd Jazz Laboratory
At Newport | Verve | 589764-2
Quartet
Monk's Music | Original Jazz Classics | OJC20 084-2
Tadd Dameron And His Orchestra
Clifford Brown Memorial | Original Jazz Classics | OJC20 017-2(P 7055)
Thelonious Monk Septet
Thelonious Monk:85th Birthday Celebration | zyx records | FANCD 6076-2
Thelonious Monk With John Coltrane | Jazzland | JZSA 946-6
Thelonious Monk With John Coltrane | Original Jazz Classics | OJC20 039-2
Monk's Music | Original Jazz Classics | OJC20 084-2

Grythe,Torstein | (cond)
Jan Garbarek Group
Rites | ECM | 1685/86(559006-2)

Grzyb,Grzegorz | (dr)
Zbigniew Namyslowski-Remy Filipovitch Quintet
Go! | Album | AS 66919 CD

Gschößl,Gerhard | (tb,harmonisierungsgerät)
Matthias Rosenbauer-Gerhard Gschlößl
Duo 1 | Jazz 4 Ever Records:Jazz Network | J4E 4763
Rainer Tempel Big Band
Melodies Of '98 | Jazz 4 Ever Records:Jazz Network | J4E 4744
Album 03 | Jazz 'n' Arts Records | JNA 1102

GU | (voc)
Swim Two Birds
Sweet Reliet | Laika Records | 35101182
No Regrets | Laika Records | 35101342

Guaraldi,Vince | (p)
Bill Holman Octet
The Jazz Giants Play Sammy Cahn:It's Magic | Prestige | PCD 24226-2
Cal Tjader Quartet
Our Blues | Fantasy | FCD 24771-2
Jazz At The Blackhawk | Original Jazz Classics | OJCCD 436-2(F 8096)
Cal Tjader Quintet
Cal Tjader's Latin Concert | Original Jazz Classics | OJCCD 643-2(F 8014)
Cal Tjader Sextet
Black Hawk Nights | Fantasy | FCD 24755-2
The Jazz Giants Play Cole Porter:Night And Day | Prestige | PCD 24203-2
Gus Mancuso Quintet
Gus Mancuso & Special Friends | Fantasy | FCD 24762-2
Ron Crotty Trio
The Jazz Scene:San Francisco | Fantasy | FCD 24760-2
Stan Getz-Cal Tjader Sextet
Stan Getz With Cal Tjader | Original Jazz Classics | OJC20 275-2(F 3266)
Victor Feldman Orchestra
Latinsville | Contemporary | CCD 9005-2
Vince Guaraldi Group
Charlie Brown's Holiday Hits | Fantasy | FCD 9682-2
Vince Guaraldi Quartet
The Jazz Scene:San Francisco | Fantasy | FCD 24760-2
Vince Guaraldi Trio
A Charlie Brown Christmas | Fantasy | FSA 8431-6
Vince Guaraldi Trio | Original Jazz Classics | OJC20 149-2(F 3225)
Cast Your Fate To The Wind | Original Jazz Classics | OJCCD 437-2(F 8089)
Vince Guaraldi-Bola Sete Quartet
Vince & Bola | Fantasy | FCD 24756-2

Guarente,Frank | (tpld)
Jack Teagarden With Orchestra
Jazz:The Essential Collection Vol.3 | IN+OUT Records | 78013-2

Guarnieri,Johnny | (harpsichord,pceleste)
Artie Shaw And His Orchestra
Planet JazzArtie Shaw | Planet Jazz | 2152057-2
Planet Jazz:Big Bands | Planet Jazz | 2169649-2
Planet Jazz:Male Jazz Vocalists | Planet Jazz | 2169657-2
Swing Vol.1 | Storyville | 4960343
Ben Webster Quartet
Jazz:The Essential Collection Vol.3 | IN+OUT Records | 78013-2
Benny Goodman And His All Star Sextet
Charlie Christian:Swing To Bop | Dreyfus Jazz Line | FDM 36715-2
Benny Goodman And His Orchestra
Charlie Christian:Swing To Bop | Dreyfus Jazz Line | FDM 36715-2
Cozy Cole All Stars
Jazz:The Essential Collection Vol.3 | IN+OUT Records | 78013-2
Don Byas All Star Quintet
Don Byas:Laura | Dreyfus Jazz Line | FDM 36714-2
Don Byas All Stars
Don Byas:Laura | Dreyfus Jazz Line | FDM 36714-2
Don Byas Quartet
Don Byas:Laura | Dreyfus Jazz Line | FDM 36714-2
June Christy With The Johnny Guarnieri Quintet
June Christy And The Johnny Guarnieri Quintet (1949) | Jazz Unlimited | JUCD 2084
Lester Young Quartet
Verve Jazz Masters 30:Lester Young | Verve | 521859-2
Jazz:The Essential Collection Vol.3 | IN+OUT Records | 78013-2
Lester Young:Blue Lester | Dreyfus Jazz Line | FDM 36729-2
Louis Armstrong And His All Stars
Planet Jazz:Louis Armstrong | Planet Jazz | 2152052-2
Planet Jazz:Jack Teagarden | Planet Jazz | 2161236-2
Planet Jazz:Male Jazz Vocalists | Planet Jazz | 2169657-2
Best Of The Complete RCA Victor Recordings | RCA | 2663636-2
Louis Armstrong:A 100th Birthday Celebration | RCA | 2663694-2
Louis Armstrong And His Orchestra
Louis Armstrong:C'est Si Bon | Dreyfus Jazz Line | FDM 36730-2
Swing Legends:Louis Armstrong | Nimbus Records | NI 2012
V-Disc All Star Jam Session
Louis Armstrong-Jack Teagarden-Woody Herman:Midnights At V-Disc | Jazz Unlimited | JUCD 2048
V-Disc All Stars
Jazz:The Essential Collection Vol.3 | IN+OUT Records | 78013-2

Guarnieri,Leo | (b)
June Christy With The Johnny Guarnieri Quintet
June Christy And The Johnny Guarnieri Quintet (1949) | Jazz Unlimited | JUCD 2084

Guassora,Mei Berit | (tp)
European Jazz Youth Orchestra
Swinging Europe 3 | dacapo | DCCD 9461
The Orchestra
New Skies | dacapo | DCCD 9463

Gubia,Sol | (dr)
Cal Tjader Sextet
Soul Bird | Verve | 549111-2

Gubin,Sol | (dr,perc,vib,bellsv-tb)
Bill Evans Quartet With Orchestra
The Complete Bill Evans On Verve | Verve | 527953-2
From Left To Right | Verve | 557451-2
Elliot Lawrence And His Orchestra
The Elliot Lawrence Big Band Swings Cohn & Kahn | Fantasy | FCD 24761-2
Joe Williams With The Frank Hunter Orchestra
Planet Jazz:Joe Williams | Planet Jazz | 2165370-2
Joe Williams With The Jimmy Jones Orchestra
Planet Jazz:Joe Williams | Planet Jazz | 2165370-2

Gudmundson,Per | (fiddle,octave-fiddle)
Lena Willemark-Ale Möller Group
Nordan | ECM | 1536(523161-2)
Per Gudmundson-Ale Möller-Lene Willemark
Frifot | ECM | 1690(557653-2)

Gudmundsson,Gulli | (bel-b)
European Jazz Youth Orchestra
Swinging Europe 3 | dacapo | DCCD 9461

Guedes,Gabi | (congas,atabaques,djembevoice)
Pata Masters
Pata-Bahia | Pata Musik | PATA 11 CD

Guenther,Thomas | (p)
Jens Bunge Group
Meet You In Chicago | Jazz 4 Ever Records:Jazz Network | J4E 4749

Guerault,Stephane | (ts)
Wild Bill Davis Group
Americans Swinging In Paris:Wild Bill Davis | EMI Records | 539665-2

Guerin,Christian | (tb)
Sidney Bechet-Teddy Buckner Sextet
Planet Jazz:Sidney Bechet | Planet Jazz | 2152063-2

Guerin,John | (dr)
Bobby McFerrin Group
Bobby McFerrin | Elektra | 7559-60023-2
Diane Schuur And Her Band
Music Is My Life | Atlantic | 7567-83150-2
Diane Schuur With Orchestra And Strings
The Best Of Diane Schuur | GRP | GRP 98882
John Pizzarelli Quartet
Dear Mr.Cole | Novus | 4163182-2
Peggy Lee With Lou Levy's Orchestra
Pass Me By/Big Spender | Capitol | 535210-2
Singers Unlimited With The Clare Fischer Orchestra
The Singers Unlimited:Magic Voices | MPS | 539130-2
Singers Unlimited With The Pat Williams Orchestra
The Singers Unlimited:Magic Voices | MPS | 539130-2

Guerin,Roger | (fl-h,tp,euphonium,tubavoc)
Alain Goraguer Orchestra
Jazz In Paris:Jazz & Cinéma Vol.1 | EmArCy | 548318-2 PMS
Jazz In Paris | EmArCy | 548793-2
Andre Hodeir And His Jazz Group De Paris
Jazz In Paris:Le Jazz Groupe De Paris Joue André Hodeir | EmArCy | 548792-2
Benny Golson Quintet
Nemmy Golson And The Philadelphians | Blue Note | 494104-2
Django Reinhardt Sextet
Jazz In Paris:Django Reinhardt-Nuits De Saint-Germain-Des-Prés | EmArCy | 018427-2
Jimmy Raney Quintet
Jimmy Raney Visits Paris Vol.2 | Vogue | 21434802
Kenny Clarke 8
Americans Swinging In Paris:Kenny Clarke | EMI Records | 539652-2
Kenny Clarke Quintet
Jazz In Paris:Kenny Clarke Sextet Plays André Hodair | EmArCy | 834542-2 PMS
Le Jazz Group De Paris
Jazz In Paris | EmArCy | 548793-2
Les Blue Stars
Jazz In Paris:Blossom Dearie-The Pianist/Les Blue Stars | EmArCy | 064784-2
Les Double Six
Les Double Six | RCA | 2164314-2
Lucky Thompson With The Gerard Pochonet All-Stars
Planet Jazz:Jazz Saxophone | Planet Jazz | 2169653-2
Lucky Thompson's Modern Jazz Group Tentet
Jazz In Paris:Lucky Thompson-Modern Jazz Group | EmArCy | 159823-2 PMS
Raymond Fol Big Band
Jazz In Paris:Raymond Fol-Les 4 Saisons | EmArCy | 548791-2

Guerra,Julio | (itolele)
Lazaro Ros Ensemble
Ori Batá (Cuban Yoruba Music) | Enja | ENJ-9381 2

Guerra,Vince | (congas)
Dizzy Gillespie And His Orchestra
Planet Jazz:Dizzy Gillespie | Planet Jazz | 2152069-2

INTERPRETENVERZEICHNIS

Guerrero,Frank 'Chico' | (perctimbales)
Herbie Mann Sextet
Verve Jazz Masters Vol.60:The Collection | Verve | 529866-2
Verve Jazz Masters 56:Herbie Mann | Verve | 529901-2
Herbie Mann Trio
Verve Jazz Masters 56:Herbie Mann | Verve | 529901-2
Peggy Lee With The Quincy Jones Orchestra
Blues Cross Country | Capitol | 520088-2
Van Alexander Orchestra
Home Of Happy Feet/Swing! Staged For Sound! | Capitol | 535211-2
Victor Feldman Orchestra
Latinsville | Contemporary | CCD 9005-2

Guerrero,Joe 'Chico' | (perctimbales)
Stan Kenton And His Orchestra
Great Swing Classics In Hi-Fi | Capitol | 521223-2

Guerrero,Pablo | (latin-lacutionvoice)
Javier Paxarino Group With Glen Velez
Temurá | ACT | 9227-2

Guerrero,Rolando | (congasperc)
Lincoln Center Jazz Orchestra
Big Train | CBS | CK 69860

Guerrini,Mirko | (ts)
European Jazz Youth Orchestra
Swinging Europe 1 | dacapo | DCCD 9449
Swinging Europe 2 | dacapo | DCCD 9450

Guesnon,George | (bj,voc,el-gg)
George Lewis And His New Orleans Stompers
George Lewis And His New Orleans Stompers | Blue Note | 821261-2

Guest Unit: |
Nils Landgren First Unit And Guests
Nils Landgren-The First Unit | ACT | 9292-2

Guggenheim,Daniel | (sax,ssas)
Daniel Guggenheim Group
Daniel Guggenheim Group feat. Jasper van't Hof | Laika Records | LK 990-018

Gugolz,Dani | (b,vocp-solo)
Axel Zwingenberger With The Mojo Blues Band And Red Holloway
Axel Zwingenberger And The Friends Of Boogie Woogie,Vol.8 | Vagabond | VRCD 8.93019
Axel Zwingenberger-Jay McShann Quartet
Kansas City Boogie Jam | Vagabond | VRCD 8.00027
Champion Jack Dupree Group
Champ's Housewarming | Vagabond | VRCD 8.88014

Gühlke,Lars | (b)
Ed Kröger Quartet
What's New | Laika Records | 35101172
Ed Kröger Quartet plus Guests
Movin' On | Laika Records | 35101332

Guilbeau,Phil | (tp)
Count Basie And His Orchestra
Basie Meets Bond | Capitol | 538225-2
Basie's Beatle Bag | Verve | 557455-2
Live at The Sands | Reprise | 9362-45946-2
Hank Crawford And His Orchestra
Atlantic Saxophones | Rhino | 8122-71256-2
Hank Crawford Septet
More Soul | Atlantic | 8122-73709-2

Guillemet,Eustis | (b)
Lionel Hampton And His All Star Jazz Inner Circle
Lionel Hampton: Salle Pleyel, March 9th, 1971 | Laserlight | 36133

Guillemin,Michel | (b)
Stuff Smith With The Henri Chaix Trio
Late Woman Blues | Storyville | STCD 8328

Guimaraes,Nelson Franca | (cuica)
Baden Powell Ensemble
Three Originals:Tristeza On Guitar/Poema On Guitar/Apaixonado | MPS | 519216-2

Guiot,Raymond | (flpiccolo)
Alain Goraguer Orchestra
Jazz In Paris:Jazz & Cinéma Vol.1 | EmArCy | 548318-2 PMS
Jazz In Paris | EmArCy | 548793-2

Guiterrez,Steve | (dr)
Willie Bobo Group
Jazzrock-Anthology Vol.3:Fusion | Zounds | CD 27100555

Guizien,Christian | (tb)
Raymond Fol Big Band
Jazz In Paris:Raymond Fol-Les 4 Saisons | EmArCy | 548791-2

Gulda,Friedrich | (p,alto-recorder,bass-recorder)
Friedrich Gulda Septet
Friedrich Gulda At Birdland | RCA | 2112587-2
Friedrich Gulda Trio
Friedrich Gulda At Birdland | RCA | 2112587-2

Gulden,Alfred | (voc)
Christof Thewes Little Big Band
Greyhound | Jazz Haus Musik | JHM 0133 CD

Gullin,Lars | (as,bs,arr,pts)
Clifford Brown And Art Farmer With The Swedish All Stars
Clifford Brown Memorial | Original Jazz Classics | OJC20 017-2(P 7055)
Jack Noren Quartet
Lars Gullin 1953,Vol.2:Moden Sounds | Dragon | DRCD 234
Kettil Ohlsson Quintet
Lars Gullin 1953,Vol.2:Moden Sounds | Dragon | DRCD 234
Lars Gullin American All Stars
Lars Gullin 1953,Vol.2:Moden Sounds | Dragon | DRCD 234
Lars Gullin And The Chet Baker Quartet
Lars Gullin 1955/56 Vol.1 | Dragon | DRCD 224
Lars Gullin Octet
Lars Gullin 1955/56 Vol.1 | Dragon | DRCD 224
Lars Gullin 1951/52 Vol.5:First Walk | Dragon | DRCD 380
Lars Gullin Quartet
Lars Gullin 1955/56 Vol.1 | Dragon | DRCD 224
Lars Gullin 1953,Vol.2:Moden Sounds | Dragon | DRCD 234
Lars Gullin 1951/52 Vol.5:First Walk | Dragon | DRCD 380
Lars Gullin Quintet
Lars Gullin 1955/56 Vol.1 | Dragon | DRCD 224
Lars Gullin 1953,Vol.2:Moden Sounds | Dragon | DRCD 234
Lars Gullin 1951/52 Vol.5:First Walk | Dragon | DRCD 380
Lars Gullin Septet
Lars Gullin 1951/52 Vol.5:First Walk | Dragon | DRCD 380
Lars Gullin Sextet
Lars Gullin 1951/52 Vol.5:First Walk | Dragon | DRCD 380
Lars Gullin With The Bob Laine Trio
Lars Gullin 1953,Vol.2:Moden Sounds | Dragon | DRCD 234
Lars Gullin With The Wade Legge Trio
Lars Gullin 1953,Vol.2:Moden Sounds | Dragon | DRCD 234
Rita Reys With The Lars Gullin Quartet
Lars Gullin 1953,Vol.2:Moden Sounds | Dragon | DRCD 234
Stan Getz And The Swedish All Stars
Stan Getz Highlights:The Best Of The Verve Years Vol.2 | Verve | 517330-2
Stan Getz Highlights | Verve | 847430-2

Gullotti,Bob | (dr,log-drperc)
Bill Lowe/Philippe Crettien Quintet
Sunday Train | Konnex Records | KCD 5051
Deborah Henson-Conant Trio
'Round The Corner | Laika Records | LK 87-203

Gully,Terreon | (dr)
Christian McBide Quartet
Vertcal Vision | Warner | 9362-48278-2
Stefon Harris-Jacky Terrasson Group
Kindred | Blue Note | 531868-2

Gumbs,Fernando | (b)
Nat Adderley Septet
Don't Look Back | Steeplechase | SCCD 31059

Gumbs,Onaje Allen | (keyboards,p,el-p,clavinet,synth)

Gundersen,Ashild | (ss)
Terje Rypdal Quartet With The Bergen Chamber Ensemble
Lux Aeterna | ECM | 1818(017070-2)

Gungor,Hakan | (kanoun)
Renaud Garcia-Fons
Navigatore | Enja | ENJ-9418 2
Renaud Garcia-Fons Group
Navigatore | Enja | ENJ-9418 2

Gunia,Alex | (g,g-synthvoc)
Alex Gunia-Philipp Van Endert Group
Beauty Of Silence | Laika Records | 35101052

Gunkel,Johannes | (b)
Frank Paul Schubert Quartet
Der Verkauf Geht Weiter | Jazz Haus Musik | JHM 0114 CD
Franz Bauer Quintet
Plüschtier | Jazz Haus Musik | JHM 0097 CD
Thärichens Tentett
Lady Moon | Minor Music | 801094
Yakou Tribe
Red & Blue Days | Traumton Records | 4474-2

Gunn,Russell | (tp,fl-h,perc,org-bass,tambourine)
Greg Tardy Band
Serendipity | Impulse(MCA) | 951258-2
James Hurt Group
Dark Grooves-Mystcal Rhythms | Blue Note | 495104-2
Russel Gunn Group
Ethnomusicology Vol.1 | Atlantic | 7567-83165-2

Gunnarsdóttir,Gerdur | (vvoc)
Claudio Puntin Quartet
Mondo | Jazz Haus Musik | JHM 0134 CD
Claudio Puntin/Gerdur Gunnarsdóttir
Ýlir | ECM | 1749(158570-2)

Gunnison,Eric | (p,el-psynth)
Carmen McRae And Her Quartet
Carmen Sings Monk | RCA | 2663841-2
Carmen McRae with the Clifford Jordan Quartet
The Collected Carmen McRae | RCA | 2668713-2

Gupta,Arup Sen | (tablas)
Kontrasax
Zanshin/Kontrasax | Jazz Haus Musik | JHM 0130 CD

Gursch,Max | (g)
Brocksi-Quintett
Drums Boogie | Bear Family Records | BCD 15988 AH

Gürtler,John | (ts)
Landes Jugend Jazz Orchester Hessen
Touch Of Lips | hr music.de | hrmj 004-01 CD

Gürtler,Werner | (tb)
Jan Harrington And Friends
I Feel The Spirit | Nagel-Heyer | NHR SP 7
Jan Harrington Band
Christmas Jazz! | Nagel-Heyer | NH 1008
Jan Harrington Sextet
Jan Harrington's Christmas In New Orleans | Nagel-Heyer | NHR SP 4

Gurtu,Trilok | (congas,dr,tabla,perc,balafon,voice)
Alfred Harth Quintet
This Earth! | ECM | 1264
Freddy Studer Orchestra
Seven Songs | VeraBra Records | CDVBR 2056-2
Jan Garbarek Group
Visible World | ECM | 1585(529086-2)
John McLaughlin Group
The Promise | Verve | 529828-2
John McLaughlin Trio
Que Alegria | Verve | 837280-2
Ketil Bjornstad Group
Grace | EmArCy | 013622-2
Nguyen Le Group
Tales From Viet-Nam | ACT | 9225-2
Oregon
Ecotopia | ECM | 1354
45th Parallel | VeraBra Records | CDVBR 2048-2
Always,Never And Forever | Intuition Records | INT 2073-2
Pharoah Sanders Group
Save Our Children | Verve | 557297-2
Shankar/Garbarek/Hussain/Gurtu
Song For Everyone | ECM | 1286(823795-2)
Toto Blanke Group
Electric Circus' Best | ALISO Records | AL 1034

Guru Guru |
Guru Guru
Guru Guru/Uli Trepte | ATM Records | ATM 3815-AH

Gusmano,Manuel | (b)
Ithamara Koorax With Band
Love Dance:The Ballad Album | Milestone | MCD 9327-2

Gustafsson,Christer | (tp)
The Orchestra
New Skies | dacapo | DCCD 9463

Gustafsson,Gus | (dr)
Brew Moore Quintet
The Brew Moore Quintet | Original Jazz Classics | OJCCD 100-2(F 3-222)
Nat Pierce/Dick Collins Nonet
Nat Pierce-Dick Collins-Ralph Burns & The Herdsmen Play Paris | Fantasy | FCD 24759-2

Gustafsson,Rigmor | (voc)
Nils Landgren Group
Sentimental Journey | ACT | 9409-2
Rigmor Gustafsson With The Nils Landgren Quartet And The Fleshquartet
I Will Wait For You | ACT | 9418-2

Gustafsson,Rune | (g)
Bengt Hallberg Quartet
Hallberg's Hot Accordion In The Foreground | Phontastic | NCD 7532
Bengt-Arne Wallin Orchestra
The Birth+Rebirth Of Swedish Folk Jazz | ACT | 9254-2
Svend Asmussen Sextet
Svend Asmussen At Slukafter | Phontastic | NCD 8804

Gustafsson,Thoams | (reeds,ssts)
The Crossover Ensemble
The River:Image Of Time And Life | dacapo | DCCD 9434

Gustavsen,Tord | (p,fender-rhodesp-solo)
Silje Nergard Group with Strings
Nightwatch | EmArCy | 9865648
Tord Gustavsen
Changing Places | ECM | 1834(016397-2)
Tord Gustavsen Trio
Changing Places | ECM | 1834(016397-2)

Gustofson,Gus | (dr)
Brew Moore Quartet
The Brew Moore Quintet | Original Jazz Classics | OJCCD 100-2(F 3-222)
Brew Moore Quintet
The Brew Moore Quintet | Original Jazz Classics | OJCCD 100-2(F 3-222)

Gutbucket |
Gutbucket
Dry Humping The American Dream | Enja | ENJ-9466 2

Gutesha,Mladen | (cond)
Keith Jarrett Trio With Strings
Arbour Zena | ECM | 1070(825592-2)
Nana Vasconcelos-Egberto Gismonti Duo And Strings
Saudades | ECM | 1147

Guthrie,Gwen | (voc)
Dee Dee Bridgewater With Band
Dee Dee Bridgewater | Atlantic | 7567-80760-2

Gutierrez,Jose | (tb)
Jack Teagarden And His Orchestra
Jazz:The Essential Collection Vol.3 | IN+OUT Records | 78013-2

Gutiérrez,José Luis | (ssts)
José Luis Gutiérrez Trio
Núcleo | Fresh Sound Records | FSNT 039 CD

Gutmann,Pit | (dr,klangobjecte,perc,klangschalen)
ATonALL
ATonALL | Creative Works Records | CW CD 1024-2
Peter A. Schmid Duos
Duets,Dialogues & Duels | Creative Works Records | CW CD 1034
Q4 Orchester Project
Lyon's Brood | Creative Works Records | CW CD 1018-3

Gutscher,Uli | (tb,bass-fl-h,pel-p)
Uli Gutscher Quintet
Wind Moments | Take Twelve On CD | TT 009-2

Guttilla,Giovanni | (tp)
Orchestra Jazz Siciliana
Orchestra Jazz Siciliana Plays The Music Of Carla Bley | Watt | XtraWatt/4

Guttormsen,Finn | (b)
Trygve Seim-Oyvind Braekke-Per Oddvar Johansen Orchestra
The Source And Different Cikadas | ECM | 1764(014432-2)

Gützkow,Dieter | (b)
Buddy Tate With The Torsten Swingenberger Swintet
Tate Live | Nagel-Heyer | CD 080

Guy,Barry | (b,comp,ld,electronicspiccolo-b)
Evan Parker Electro-Acoustic Ensemble
Toward The Margins | ECM | 1612(453514-2)
Drawn Inward | ECM | 1693
Memory/Vision | ECM | 1852(0381172)
Evan Parker-Paul Rutherford-Barry Guy-John Stevens
4,4,4, | Konnex Records | KCD 5049
Howard Riley Trio
The Day Will Come | CBS | 494434-2
John Stevens Quartet
Re-Touch & Quartet | Konnex Records | KCD 5027
Mahmoud Turkmani
Fayka | Enja | ENJ-9447 2

Guy,Buddy | (b,b-g,g,12-string-gvoc)
Buddy Guy Blues Band
Buddy Guy-The Complete Chess Studio Recordings | MCA | MCD 09337
Passport And Guests
Doldinger's Best | ACT | 9224-2

Guy,Fred | (b,bj,g,whistlep)
Django Reinhardt With Duke Ellington And His Orchestra
Django Reinhardt:Souveniers | Dreyfus Jazz Line | FDM 36744-2
Duke Ellington And His Cotton Club Orchestra
Planet Jazz:Duke Ellington | Planet Jazz | 2152053-2
Jazz:The Essential Collection Vol.2 | IN+OUT Records | 78012-2
Duke Ellington And His Famous Orchestra
Duke Ellington:The Blanton-Webster Band | Bluebird | 21 13181-2
Planet Jazz:Duke Ellington | Planet Jazz | 2152053-2
Planet Jazz:Johnny Hodges | Planet Jazz | 2152065-2
Planet Jazz Sampler | Planet Jazz | 2152326-2
Planet Jazz:Ben Webster | RCA | 2165368-2
Planet Jazz:Big Bands | Planet Jazz | 2169649-2
Planet Jazz:Jazz Trumpet | Planet Jazz | 2169654-2
Planet Jazz:Female Jazz Vocalists | Planet Jazz | 2169656-2
Highlights From The Duke Ellington Centennial Edition | RCA | 2663672-2
Greatest Hits | CBS | 462959-2
Jazz:The Essential Collection Vol.2 | IN+OUT Records | 78012-2
Jazz:The Essential Collection Vol.3 | IN+OUT Records | 78013-2
Duke Ellington:Ko-Ko | Dreyfus Jazz Line | FDM 36717-2
Duke Ellington And His Kentucky Club Orchestra
Jazz:The Essential Collection Vol.2 | IN+OUT Records | 78012-2
Duke Ellington And His Orchestra
Planet Jazz:Duke Ellington | Planet Jazz | 2152053-2
Planet Jazz:Jazz Greatest Hits | Planet Jazz | 2169648-2
The Legends Of Swing | Laserlight | 24659
Highlights From The Duke Ellington Centennial Edition | RCA | 2663672-2
Carnegie Hall Concert December 1944 | Prestige | 2PCD 24073-2
Carnegie Hall Concert December 1947 | Prestige | 2PCD 24075-2
Carnegie Hall Concert January 1943 | Prestige | 2PCD 34004-2
Jazz:The Essential Collection Vol.2 | IN+OUT Records | 78012-2
Jazz:The Essential Collection Vol.3 | IN+OUT Records | 78013-2
The Duke At Fargo 1940 | Storyville | STCD 8316/17
At The Hurricane:Original 1943 Broadcasts | Storyville | STCD 8359

Guy,Joe | (tp)
Billie Holiday With The JATP All Stars
Billie Holiday Story Vol.1:Jazz At The Philharmonic | Verve | 521642-2
The Complete Jazz At The Philharmonic On Verve 1944-1949 | Verve | 523893-2
Verve Jazz Masters 47:Billie Holiday Sings Standards | Verve | 527650-2
Jazz At The Philharmonic:Best Of The 1940's Concerts | Verve | 557534-2
Charlie Christian All Stars
Thelonious Monk:85th Birthday Celebration | zyx records | FANCD 6076-2
Charlie Christian-Jazz Immortal/Dizzy Gillespie 1944 | Original Jazz Classics | OJCCD 1932-2(ES 548)
Coleman Hawkins And His Orchestra
Planet Jazz:Coleman Hawkins | Planet Jazz | 2152055-2
Planet Jazz Sampler | Planet Jazz | 2152326-2
Planet Jazz:Jazz Greatest Hits | Planet Jazz | 2169648-2
Jazz:The Essential Collection Vol.3 | IN+OUT Records | 78013-2
JATP All Stars
The Complete Jazz At The Philharmonic On Verve 1944-1949 | Verve | 523893-2
Lester Young Quintet
The Complete Jazz At The Philharmonic On Verve 1944-1949 | Verve | 523893-2
Minton's Playhouse All Stars
Charlie Christian:Swing To Bop | Dreyfus Jazz Line | FDM 36715-2

Guy,Raymond | (fl)
Raymond Fol Big Band
Jazz In Paris:Raymond Fol-Les 4 Saisons | EmArCy | 548791-2

Gwaltney,Tommy | (cl,as,vibxyl)
Charlie Byrd Septet
Latin Byrd | Milestone | MCD 47005-2
Nancy Harrow And The Buck Clayton All Stars
Wild Women Don't Have The Blues | Candid | CCD 79008

Haanstra,Jurre | (p,el-p,dr,condarr)
The Rosenberg Trio With Orchestra
Noches Calientes | Verve | 557022-2

Haarla,Iro | (accordeon,keyboards,harp,org,pkoto)
Edward Vesala Ensemble
Ode Of The Death Of Jazz | ECM | 1413(843196-2)
Edward Vesala Group
Lumi | ECM | 1339
Edward Vesala Nordic Gallery
Sound & Fury | ECM | 1541
Edward Vesala Sound And Fury
Invisible Strom | ECM | 1461

Haas,Alex | (b)
Tabla & Strings
Islands Everywhere | Tutu Records | 888208-2*

Haas,Arno | (ssas)
Sorry.It's Jazz
Sorry,It's Jazz! | Satin Doll Productions | SDP 1040-1 CD

Haas,Matthias | (tp)
Ralph Schweizer Big Band
DAY Dream | Chaos | CACD 8177

Haas,Stefan | (tp)

Haass,Lothar | (viola)
Uri Caine With The Concerto Köln
Concerto Köln | Winter&Winter | 910086-2

Habao,Joe | (perc)
Rahsaan Roland Kirk Sextet
Atlantic Saxophones | Rhino | 8122-71256-2

Haber,Louis | (v)

Wes Montgomery With The Don Sebesky Orchestra
Verve Jazz Masters 14:Wes Montgomery | Verve | 519826-2
Talkin' Jazz:Roots Of Acid Jazz | Verve | 529580-2
Bumpin' | Verve | 539062-2

Haberer,Christoph | (dr,electronics,perc,voc,keyboards)

Christoph Haberer Group
Pulsation | Jazz Haus Musik | JHM 0066 CD
Lee Konitz-Frank Wunsch Quartet
S'Nice | Nabel Records:Jazz Network | CD 4641
Pata Music Meets Arfi
News Of Roi Ubu | Pata Musik | PATA 10 CD

Habermann,Heinz | (tp)

Chet Baker With The NDR-Bigband
NDR Big Band-Bravissimo | ACT | 9232-2
My Favourite Songs: The Last Great Concert Vol.1 | Enja | ENJ-5097 2
The Last Concert Vol.I+II | Enja | ENJ-6074 22
Chet Baker-The Legacy Vol.1 | Enja | ENJ-9021 2
Heinz Sauer Quartet With The NDR Big Band
NDR Big Band-Bravissimo | ACT | 9232-2
Joe Pass With The NDR Big Band
Joe Pass In Hamburg | ACT | 9100-2

Habokyan,Anna | (v)

Couch Ensemble
Winnetou | Jazz 'n' Arts Records | JNA 1503

Hackbarth,Joe | (dr)

Wolfgang Lauth Quartet
Deutsches Jazz Fesival 1954/1955 | Bear Family Records | BCD 15430
Lauther | Bear Family Records | BCD 15717 AH
Noch Lauther | Bear Family Records | BCD 15942 AH
Wolfgang Lauth Septet
Noch Lauther | Bear Family Records | BCD 15942 AH

Hackett,Bobby | (co,gtp)

Artie Shaw And His Orchestra
Swing Vol.1 | Storyville | 4960343
Benny Goodman Band
Benny Goodman At Carnegie Hall 1938(Complete) | CBS | C2K 65143
Benny Goodman Combo
Benny Goodman At Carnegie Hall 1938(Complete) | CBS | C2K 65143
Benny Goodman Dixieland Quintet
Benny Goodman At Carnegie Hall 1938(Complete) | CBS | C2K 65143
Billie Holiday With Gordon Jenkins And His Orchestra
Billie's Love Songs | Nimbus Records | NI 2000
Billie Holiday With Teddy Wilson And His Orchestra
Billie's Love Songs | Nimbus Records | NI 2000
Bobby Hackett Sextet
Jazz Festival Vol.1 | Storyville | 4960733
Jazz Festival Vol.2 | Storyville | 4960743
Eddie Condon And His Orchestra
Jazz:The Essential Collection Vol.3 | IN+OUT Records | 78013-2
Glenn Miller And His Orchestra
Planet Jazz:Glenn Miller | Planet Jazz | 2152056-2
Swing Legends | Nimbus Records | NI 2001
Glenn Miller Orchestra
Glenn Miller Serenade | CBS | 487445-2
Jack Teagarden Sextet With Bobby Hackett
Newport Jazz Festival 1958,July 3rd-6th Vol.3:Blues In The Night No.1 | Phontastic | NCD 8815
Louis Armstrong And His All Stars
Planet Jazz:Louis Armstrong | Planet Jazz | 2152052-2
Planet Jazz:Jack Teagarden | Planet Jazz | 2161236-2
Planet Jazz:Male Jazz Vocalists | Planet Jazz | 2169657-2
Best Of The Complete RCA Victor Recordings | RCA | 2663636-2
Louis Armstrong:A 100th Birthday Celebration | RCA | 2663694-2
Louis Armstrong:Wintergarden 1947/Blue Note 1948 | Storyville | STCD 8242
Louis Armstrong And His Orchestra
Louis Armstrong:C'est Si Bon | Dreyfus Jazz Line | FDM 36730-2
Swing Legends:Louis Armstrong | Nimbus Records | NI 2012
V-Disc All Star Jam Session
Louis Armstrong-Jack Teagarden-Woody Herman:Midnights At V-Disc | Jazz Unlimited | JUCD 2048
V-Disc All Stars
Jazz:The Essential Collection Vol.3 | IN+OUT Records | 78013-2

Hackett,Bobby prob. | (co)

Benny Goodman Combo
Benny Goodman At Carnegie Hall 1938(Complete) | CBS | C2K 65143
Benny Goodman Dixieland Quintet
Benny Goodman At Carnegie Hall 1938(Complete) | CBS | C2K 65143

Hackney,Lou | (b)

Dizzy Gillespie And His Orchestra
Afro | Verve | 517052-2
Dizzy Gillespie Quartet And The Operatic String Orchestra
Jazz In Paris:Dizzy Gillespie And His Operatic Strings Orchestra | EmArCy | 018420-2
Dizzy Gillespie Quintet
Diz And Getz | Verve | 549749-2
Dizzy Gillespie Sextet
Pleyel Jazz Concert 1953 | Vogue | 21409392
Lars Gullin With The Wade Legge Trio
Lars Gullin 1953,Vol.2:Moden Sounds | Dragon | DRCD 234
Sarah Vaughan With Dizzy Gillespie And His Orchestra
Planet Jazz:Female Jazz Vocalists | Planet Jazz | 2169656-2

Haddad,Amir | (g)

Pepe Justicia-Amir Haddad Duo
Internationales Guitarren Festival '99 | ALISO Records | AL 1038

Haddad,Jamey | (dr,perc,frame-drvoc)

Andy Middleton Group
Nomad's Notebook | Intuition Records | INT 3264-2
Dimitrios Vassilakis Daedalus Project
Labyrinth | Candid | CCD 79776
Ed Neumeister Quintet
Ed Neumeister Quartet/Quintet | Timescrapper | TSCR 9614
Nicolas Simion Quartet feat. Tomasz Stanko
Viaggio Imaginario | Tutu Records | 888192-2*

Haden,Charlie | (b,congas,clappers,steel-dr)

Abbey Lincoln And Her All Stars
The World Is Falling Down | Verve | 843476-2
Abbey Lincoln With The Rodney Kendrick Trio And Guests
A Turtle's Dream | Verve | 527382-2
Abbey Lincoln With The Stan Getz Quartet
You Gotta Pay The Band | Verve | 511110-2
A Life In Jazz:A Musical Biography | Verve | 535119-2
Abbey Lincoln With The Stan Getz Quintet
You Gotta Pay The Band | Verve | 511110-2
Alice Coltrane Quintet
Joe Henderson:The Milestone Years | Milestone | 8MCD 4413-2
Journey In Satchidananda | Impulse(MCA) | 951228-2
Alice Coltrane Sextet
Joe Henderson:The Milestone Years | Milestone | 8MCD 4413-2
Archie Shepp Orchestra
Mama Too Tight | Impulse(MCA) | 951248-2
Art Pepper Quartet
Art Pepper:The Complete Galaxy Recordings | Galaxy | 16GCD 1016-2
Art 'N' Zoot | Pablo | 2310957-2
Living Legend | Original Jazz Classics | OJCCD 408-2
Carla Bley Band
Musique Mecanique | Watt | 9
Charlie Haden
Deep In The Blues | Verve | 529849-2
Quartet West | Verve | 831673-2
Charlie Haden And The Liberation Music Orchestra
The Montreal Tapes:Liberation Music Orchestra | Verve | 527469-2
Charlie Haden Orchestra
The Ballad Of The Fallen | ECM | 1248(811546-2)
Charlie Haden Quartet West
Haunted Heart | Verve | 513078-2
Always Say Goodbye | Verve | 521501-2
Now Is The Hour | Verve | 527827-2
Quartet West | Verve | 831673-2
In Angel City | Verve | 837031-2
Charlie Haden Quartet West With Strings
Now Is The Hour | Verve | 527827-2
The Art Of The Song | Verve | 547403-2
Charlie Haden Quartet With Orchestra
American Dreams | Verve | 064096-2
Charlie Haden Trio
Magico | ECM | 1151(823474-2)
Folk Songs | ECM | 1170(827705-2)
The Montreal Tapes Vol.1 | Verve | 523260-2
The Montreal Tapes | Verve | 537483-2
The Montreal Tapes | Verve | 537670-2
Quartet West | Verve | 831673-2
Charlie Haden With String Quartet
The Art Of The Song | Verve | 547403-2
Charlie Haden/Christian Escoudé
Duo | Dreyfus Jazz Line | FDM 36505-2
Charlie Haden-Alice Coltrane
Closeness Duets | Verve | 397000-2
Charlie Haden-Egberto Gismonti
In Montreal | ECM | 1746(543813-2)
Charlie Haden-Hank Jones
Steal Away | Verve | 527249-2
Charlie Haden-Joe Henderson-Al Foster
The Montreal Tapes | Verve | 9813132
Charlie Haden-Keith Jarrett
Closeness Duets | Verve | 397000-2
Charlie Haden-Kenny Barron
Night And The City | Verve | 539961-2
Charlie Haden-Ornette Coleman
Closeness Duets | Verve | 397000-2
Charlie Haden-Pat Metheny
Beyond The Missouri Sky | Verve | 537130-2
Charlie Haden-Paul Motian
Closeness Duets | Verve | 397000-2
Charlie Haden's Liberation Music Orchestra
Liberation Music Orchestra | Impulse(MCA) | 951188-2
Denny Zeitlin-Charlie Haden Duo
Time Remembers One Time Once | ECM | 1239
Dino Saluzzi Quartet
Once Upon A Time-Far Away In The South | ECM | 1309(827768-2)
Gato Barbieri Sextet
The Third World | RCA | 2179617-2
Geri Allen/Charlie Haden/Paul Motian
In The Year Of The Dragon | JMT Edition | 919027-2
Geri Allen/Charlie Haden/Paul Motian & Guest
In The Year Of The Dragon | JMT Edition | 919027-2
Gonzalo Rubalcaba Trio
The Blessing | Blue Note | 797197-2
Imagine | Blue Note | 830491-2
James Cotton Group
Deep In The Blues | Verve | 529849-2
John Coltrane-Don Cherry Quartet
The Avant-Garde | Atlantic | 7567-90041-2
John Coltrane-The Heavyweight Champion:The Complete Atlantic Recordings | Atlantic | 8122-71984-2
The Avantgarde | Rhino | 8122-79892-2
Joshua Redman Quartet
Wish | Warner | 9362-45365-2
Keith Jarrett Group
Expectations | CBS | C2K 65900
Keith Jarrett Group With Brass
Expectations | CBS | C2K 65900
Keith Jarrett Group With Strings
Expectations | CBS | C2K 65900
Keith Jarrett Quartet
The Survivor's Suite | ECM | 1085(827131-2)
Eyes Of The Heart | ECM | 1150(825476-2)
El Juicio(The Judgement) | Atlantic | 7567-80783-2
Byablue | Impulse(MCA) | MCD 10648
Keith Jarrett Quintet
Fort Yawuh | Impulse(MCA) | 547966-2
The Roots Of Acid Jazz | Impulse(MCA) | IMP 12042
Keith Jarrett Trio
Chick Corea-Herbie Hancock-Keith Jarrett-McCoy Tyner | Atlantic | 7567-81402-2
Somewhere Before | Atlantic | 7567-81455-2
The Mourning Of A Star | Atlantic | 8122-75355-2
Byablue | Impulse(MCA) | MCD 10648
Keith Jarrett Trio With Strings
Arbour Zena | ECM | 1070(825592-2)
Lee Konitz Trio
Another Shade Of Blue | Blue Note | 498222-2
Leo Smith Group
Devine Love | ECM | 1143
Michael Brecker Group
Michael Brecker | Impulse(MCA) | 950113-2
Don't Try This At Home | Impulse(MCA) | 950114-2
Michael Brecker Quintet
Nearness Of You-The Ballad Book | Verve | 549705-2
Old And New Dreams
Old And New Dreams | ECM | 1154
Playing | ECM | 1205
Ornette Coleman Double Quartet
Beauty Is A Rare Thing:Ornette Coleman-The Complete Atlantic Recordings | Atlantic | 8122-71410-2
Free Jazz | Atlantic | 8122-75208-2
Ornette Coleman Quartet
This Is Our Music | Atlantic | 7567-80767-2
Change Of The Century | Atlantic | 7567-81341-2
Atlantic Saxophones | Rhino | 8122-71256-2
Rhino Presents The Atlantic Jazz Gallery | Atlantic | 8122-71257-2
Beauty Is A Rare Thing:Ornette Coleman-The Complete Atlantic Recordings | Atlantic | 8122-71410-2
Pat Metheny Quartet
80/81 | ECM | 1180/81 (843169-2)
Pat Metheny Quintet
80/81 | ECM | 1180/81 (843169-2)
Pat Metheny Trio
Rejoicing | ECM | 1271(817795-2)
Pat Metheny/Ornette Coleman Group
Song X | Geffen Records | GED 24096
Paul Motian Quartet
Conception Vessel | ECM | 1028(519279-2)
Paul Motian On Broadway Vol.1 | JMT Edition | 919029-2
Paul Motian Quintet
Tribute | ECM | 1048
Paul Motian Trio
Conception Vessel | ECM | 1028(519279-2)
Roswell Rudd Sextet
Mixed | Impulse(MCA) | IMP 12702
The Jazz Composer's Orchestra
Comminications | JCOA | 1001/2
Tom Harrell Quintet
Form | Contemporary | CCD 14059-2
Visions | Contemporary | CCD 14063-2
Tom Harrell Sextet
Visions | Contemporary | CCD 14063-2

Haderer,Andreas 'Andy' | (tp,fl-h,bass-tpv-tb)

Bob Brookmeyer Group With The WDR Big Band
Electricity | ACT | 9219-2
Eddie Harris Group With The WDR Big Band
Eddie Harris-The Last Concert | ACT | 9249-2
Gianluigi Trovesi Quartet With The WDR Big Band
Dedalo | Enja | ENJ-9419 2
Jens Winther And The WDR Big Band
The Escape | dacapo | DCCD 9437
Kevin Mahogany With The WDR Big Band And Guests
Pussy Cat Dues:The Music Of Charles Mingus | Enja | ENJ-9316 2
Los Jovenes Flamencos With The WDR Big Band And Guests
Jazzpana | ACT | 9212-2
Vince Mendoza With The WDR Big Band And Guests
Sketches | ACT | 9215-2

Hadi [Curtis Porter],Shafti | (asts)

Charles Mingus Group
Mingus Ah Um | CBS | CK 65512
Charles Mingus Jazz Workshop
Tonight At Noon | Atlantic | 7567-80793-2
The Clown | Atlantic | 8122-75358-2
Charles Mingus Orchestra
Tijuana Moods(The Complete Edition) | RCA | 2663840-2
Charles Mingus Quintet
Charles Mingus-Passion Of A Man:The Complete Atlantic Recordings 1956-1961 | Atlantic | 8122-72871-2
The Very Best Of Charles Mingus | Rhino | 8122-79988-2
Charles Mingus Septet
Charles Mingus:The Complete 1959 Columbia Recordings | CBS | C3K 65145
Charles Mingus Workshop
Charles Mingus-The Complete Debut Recordings | Debut | 12 DCD 4402-2

Hadi [Curtis Porter],Shafti prob. | (fl)

Hadi,Kwame | (tp,perc,vibcongas)

Sun Ra And His Astro-Infinity Arkestra
Space Is The Place | Impulse(MCA) | 951249-2
Sun Ra And His Intergalactic Research Arkestra
Black Myth/Out In Space | MPS | 557656-2

Hadley,Steve | (b)

Vince Jones Group
It All Ends Up In Tears | Intuition Records | INT 3069-2

Hadnott,Billy | (b)

JATP All Stars
Jazz Gallery:Lester Young Vol.2(1946-59) | RCA | 2119541-2
Verve Jazz Masters 28:Charlie Parker Plays Standards | Verve | 521854-2
The Complete Jazz At The Philharmonic On Verve 1944-1949 | Verve | 523893-2
Charlie Parker:The Best Of The Verve Years | Verve | 527815-2
Jazz At The Philharmonic:Best Of The 1940's Concerts | Verve | 557534-2
Bird: The Complete Charlie Parker On Verve | Verve | 837141-2
Jubilee All Stars
Jazz Gallery:Lester Young Vol.2(1946-59) | RCA | 2119541-2
Louis Jordan And His Tympany Five
Louis Jordan-Let The Good Times Roll: The Complete Decca Recordings 1938-1954 | Bear Family Records | BCD 15557 IH
Wardell Gray Sextet
The Prestige Legacy Vol.2:Battles Of Saxes | Prestige | PCD 24252-2
Wardell Gray's Los Angeles All Stars
Dexter Gordon Birthday Celebration | Fantasy | FANCD 6082-2
Wardell Gray Memorial Vol.2 | Original Jazz Classics | OJCCD 051-2(P 7009)

Hadrick,Joe | (dr)

Willis Jackson Quintet
Gravy | Prestige | PCD 24254-2
Soul Night Live! | Prestige | PRCD 24273-2
Willis Jackson Sextet
Gravy | Prestige | PCD 24254-2
Nuther'n Like Thuther'n | Prestige | PRCD 24265-2

Haenning,Gitte | (voc)

Wolfgang Schmid's Kick
No Filters | TipToe | TIP-888809 2

Haensch,Delle | (as,bscl)

Delle Haensch Jump Combo
Deutsches Jazz Fesival 1954/1955 | Bear Family Records | BCD 15430
Freddie Brocksieper Orchester
Shot Gun Boogie | Bear Family Records | BCD 16277 AH

Hafer,John 'Dick' | (b-cl,cl,as,ts,flreeds)

Anthony Ortega With The Nat Pierce Orchestra
Earth Dance | Fresh Sound Records | FSR-CD 325
Anthony Ortega With The Robert Zieff Orchestra
Earth Dance | Fresh Sound Records | FSR-CD 325
Charles Mingus Orchestra
Mingus Mingus Mingus | Impulse(MCA) | 951170-2
The Black Saint And The Sinner Lady | Impulse(MCA) | 951174-2
Nat Pierce/Dick Collins Nonet
Nat Pierce-Dick Collins-Ralph Burns & The Herdsmen Play Paris | Fantasy | FCD 24759-2
The Herdsmen
Nat Pierce-Dick Collins-Ralph Burns & The Herdsmen Play Paris | Fantasy | FCD 24759-2

Haffner,Jon | (as)

David Binney Group
Balance | ACT | 9411-2

Haffner,Juliet | (viola)

Tom Harrell Group
Paradise | RCA | 2663738-2

Haffner,Wolfgang | (dr)

Al Porcino Big Band
Al Cohn Meets Al Porcino | Organic Music | ORGM 9730
Albert Mangelsdorff With The NDR Big Band
NDR Big Band-Bravissimo | ACT | 9232-2
Conte Candoli With The Joe Haider Trio
Conte Candoli Meets The Joe Haider Trio | JHM Records | JHM 3602
Heinz Sauer Quartet With The NDR Big Band
NDR Big Band-Bravissimo | ACT | 9232-2
HR Big Band
Libertango:Homage An Astor Piazolla | hr music.de | hrmj 014-02 CD
Joe Haider Quintet
Magic Box | JHM Records | JHM 3601
Joe Pass With The NDR Big Band And Radio Philharmonie Hannover
Joe Pass In Hamburg | ACT | 9100-2
Klaus Doldinger & Passport
Down To Earth | Warner | 4509-93207-2
Klaus Doldinger's Passport
Klaus Doldinger Passport Live | Warner | 8573-84132-2
Balance Of Happiness | Warner | 9031-71233-2
Blues Roots | Warner | 9031-75417-2
Klaus Doldinger's Passport With Johnny 'Clyde' Copeland
Blues Roots | Warner | 9031-75417-2
NDR Big Band
The Theatre Of Kurt Weil | ACT | 9234-2
Nils Landgren Group
Sentimental Journey | ACT | 9409-2
Rigmor Gustafsson With The Nils Landgren Quartet And The Fleshquartet
I Will Wait For You | ACT | 9418-2
Rolf Kühn And Friends
Affairs:Rolf Kühn & Friends | Intuition Records | INT 3211-2
Rolf Kühn Group
Inside Out | Intuition Records | INT 3276-2
Internal Eyes | Intuition Records | INT 3328-2
The German Jazz Masters
Old Friends | ACT | 9278-2
Till Brönner Group
Chattin' With Chet | Verve | 157534-2
Love | Verve | 559058-2
Viktoria Tolstoy Group & Strings
Shining On You | ACT | 9701-2
Wolfgang Haffner International Jazz Quintet
Whatever It Is | Jazz 4 Ever Records:Jazz Network | J4E 4714
Wolfgang Haffner Project
Back Home | Jazz 4 Ever Records:Jazz Network | J4E 4730

Hafid,Moulay Ali | (dumbeg)

Gato Barbieri Group
Planet Jazz:Gato Barbieri | RCA | 2165364-2

Gato Barbieri:The Best Of The Early Years | RCA | 2663523-2

Häfner,Lutz | (as,fl,b-cl,ss,ts,talk-box,reedsbs)

Conexion Latina
Mambo Nights | Enja | ENJ-9402 2
Horst Faigle's Jazzkrement
Gans Normal | Jazz 4 Ever Records:Jazz Network | J4E 4748
Lutz Häfner Quartet
Way In Way Out | Jazz 4 Ever Records:Jazz Network | J4E 4757

Hagans,Tim | (fl-htp)

Gregor Hübner Quintet
Panonien | Satin Doll Productions | SDP 1015-1 CD
Januschke's Time | Satin Doll Productions | SDP 1034-1 CD
Marco Piludu International Quartet
New York Travels | Jazz 4 Ever Records:Jazz Network | J4E 4733
Nils Landgren Funk Unit With Guests
5000 Miles | ACT | 9271-2
Rez Abbasi Group
Modern Memory | String Jazz | SJRCD 102
Tim Hagans With Norrbotten Big Band
Future Miles | ACT | 9235-2
Tim Hagans-Marcus Printup Septet
Hub Songs | Blue Note | 859509-2
Vic Juris Quartet
For The Music | Jazzpoint | JP 1034 CD

Hagberg,Garry | (el-gg)

The Atlantic Jazz Trio
Some Other Time | Factory Outlet Records | FOR 2002-1 CD
The Atlantic String Trio
First Meeting | Factory Outlet Records | FOR 2501-1 CD

Hagemann,Per | (cl)

Papa Benny's Jazzband
The Golden Years Of Revival Jazz,Sampler | Storyville | 109 1001

Hagen,Earle | (tb)

Tommy Dorsey And His Orchestra
Planet Jazz:Tommy Dorsey | Planet Jazz | 2159972-2

Hagen,Hans Gunnar | (viola)

Terje Rypdal Quartet With The Bergen Chamber Ensemble
Lux Aeterna | ECM | 1818(017070-2)

Haggag,Ismail | (duff)

Koch-Schütz-Studer & El Nil Troop
Heavy Cairo Trafic | Intuition Records | INT 3175-2

Haggart,Bob | (b,arr,ld,whistlingcond)

A Salute To Eddie Condon
A Salute To Eddie Condon | Nagel-Heyer | CD 004
One Two Three | Nagel-Heyer | CD 008
The First Sampler | Nagel-Heyer | NHR SP 5
All Star Band
Planet Jazz:Jack Teagarden | Planet Jazz | 2161236-2
Allan Vaché's Florida Jazz Allstars
Allan Vaché's Floridy Jazz Allstars | Nagel-Heyer | CD 032
Bob Crosby And His Orchestra
Swing Legens:Bob Crosby | Nimbus Records | NI 2011
Bob Crosby's Bobcats
Swing Legens:Bob Crosby | Nimbus Records | NI 2011
Bob Haggart/Ray Bauduc
Swing Legens:Bob Crosby | Nimbus Records | NI 2011
Byron Stripling And Friends
If I Could Be With You | Nagel-Heyer | NH 1010
Charlie Parker With Strings
Bird: The Complete Charlie Parker On Verve | Verve | 837141-2
Charlie Parker With The Joe Lipman Orchestra
Charlie Parker With Strings:The Master Takes | Verve | 523984-2
Charlie Parker Big Band | Verve | 559835-2
Duke Ellington And His Orchestra
Planet Jazz:Duke Ellington | Planet Jazz | 2152053-2
Planet Jazz:Jazz Greatest Hits | Planet Jazz | 2169648-2
Eddie Condon And His Chicagoans
The Very Best Of Dixieland Jazz | Verve | 535529-2
Eddie Condon And His Orchestra
Jazz:The Essential Collection Vol.3 | IN+OUT Records | 78013-2
Frank Trumbauer And His Orchestra
The Hollywood Session:The Capitol Jazzmen | Jazz Unlimited | JUCD 2044
Jess Stacy And His Orchestra
Planet Jazz:Jazz Piano | RCA | 2169655-2
Joe Ascione Octet
My Buddy:A Tribute To Buddy Rich | Nagel-Heyer | CD 036
Lee Wiley With The Dean Kincaide Dixieland Band
Planet Jazz:Female Jazz Vocalists | Planet Jazz | 2169656-2
Louis Armstrong And Ella Fitzgerald With Bob Hagger's Orchestra
Louis Armstrong:C'est Si Bon | Dreyfus Jazz Line | FDM 36730-2
Louis Armstrong And His All Stars
Planet Jazz:Louis Armstrong | Planet Jazz | 2152052-2
Planet Jazz:Jack Teagarden | Planet Jazz | 2161236-2
Planet Jazz:Male Jazz Vocalists | Planet Jazz | 2169657-2
Best Of The Complete RCA Victor Recordings | RCA | 2663636-2
Louis Armstrong:A 100th Birthday Celebration | RCA | 2663694-2
Louis Armstrong And His Orchestra
Louis Armstrong:Swing That Music | Laserlight | 36056
Louis Armstrong:C'est Si Bon | Dreyfus Jazz Line | FDM 36730-2
Muggsy Spanier And His Dixieland Band
Muggsy Spanier-Manhattan Masters,1945 | Storyville | STCD 6051
Muggsy Spanier And His V-Disc All Stars
Muggsy Spanier And Bud Freeman:V-Discs 1944-45 | Jazz Unlimited | JUCD 2049
Sarah Vaughan With The Hugo Winterhalter Orchestra
Sarah Vaughan:Lover Man | Dreyfus Jazz Line | FDM 36739-2
Sarah Vaughan With The Joe Lippman Orchestra
Sarah Vaughan:Lover Man | Dreyfus Jazz Line | FDM 36739-2
The Chicago All Stars
Planet Jazz:Bud Freeman | Planet Jazz | 2161240-2
The Metronome All-Star Nine
Jazz:The Essential Collection Vol.3 | IN+OUT Records | 78013-2
The New York Allstars
Count Basie Remembered | Nagel-Heyer | CD 031
Count Basie Remembered Vol.2 | Nagel-Heyer | CD 041
Oh,Yeah! The New York Allstars Play More Music Of Louis Armstrong | Nagel-Heyer | CD 046
V-Disc All Star Jam Session
Louis Armstrong-Jack Teagarden-Woody Herman:Midnights At V-Disc | Jazz Unlimited | JUCD 2048

Haggerty,Frank | (g)

Henry Red Allen Band
The Very Best Of Dixieland Jazz | Verve | 535529-2
Kid Ory And His Band
The Very Best Of Dixieland Jazz | Verve | 535529-2

Hagood,Kenny | (voc)

Dizzy Gillespie And His Orchestra
Dizzy Gillespie:Pleyel Jazz Concert 1948 + Max Roach Quintet 1949 | Vogue | 21409412
Planet Jazz:Dizzy Gillespie | Planet Jazz | 2152069-2
Miles Davis And His Orchestra
The Complete Birth Of The Cool | Capitol | 494550-2
Birth Of The Cool | Capitol | 530117-2
Thelonious Monk Quartet
Wizard Of The Vibes | Blue Note | 532140-2

Hahn,Jerry | (g)

Bennie Wallace Quartet
The Talk Of The Town | Enja | ENJ-7091 2

Hahn,Jürgen | (tpfl-h)

Edith Steyer... Posterity Quintet
...On The Right Track | Jazz 4 Ever Records:Jazz Network | J4E 4745
Norbert Emminger Quintet
In The Park | Edition Collage | EC 521-2

Hahn,Sepp | (tb)

Freddie Brocksieper Orchester
Drums Boogie | Bear Family Records | BCD 15988 AH

Hahne,Dorothee | (electronic-voice,samplestp)

KontaSax
KontraSax Plays Getrude Stein | Jazz Haus Musik | JHM 0096 CD

Haider,Joe | (pel-p)

Benny Bailey Quintet
Jazz Portraits | EGO | 95080
Brigitte Dietrich-Joe Haider Jazz Orchestra
Consequences | JHM Records | JHM 3624
Conte Candoli With The Joe Haider Trio
Conte Candoli Meets The Joe Haider Trio | JHM Records | JHM 3602
Don Menza And The Joe Haider Trio
Bilein | JHM Records | JHM 3608
Dusko Goykovich-Joe Haider Quintet
Jazz Portraits | EGO | 95080
Four For Jazz
The Best Of Four For Jazz & Benny Bailey | JHM Records | JHM 3615
Four For Jazz & Benny Bailey
The Best Of Four For Jazz & Benny Bailey | JHM Records | JHM 3615
Fritz Münzer Quintet
Jazz für junge Leute:Live im HR 1962 | Jazz 'n' Arts Records | C 01
Joe Haider Quintet
Magic Box | JHM Records | JHM 3601
Joe Haider Trio
Jazz Portraits | EGO | 95080
Grandfather's Garden | JHM Records | JHM 3619
Katzenvilla | JHM Records | JHM 3622
A Magyar-The Hungarian-Die Ungarische | JHM Records | JHM 3626
Slide Hampton-Joe Haider Jazz Orchestra
Give Me A Double | JHM Records | JHM 3627

Haig,Al | (p,el-p,vocp-solo)

Al Haig Sextet
Al Haig Trio And Sextets | Original Jazz Classics | OJCCD 1929-2(SPL 1118)
Al Haig Sextet(Quintet)
Al Haig Trio And Sextets | Original Jazz Classics | OJCCD 1929-2(SPL 1118)
Al Haig Trio
Al Haig Trio And Sextets | Original Jazz Classics | OJCCD 1929-2(SPL 1118)
Charlie Parker And His Orchestra
Charlie Parker:The Best Of The Verve Years | Verve | 527815-2
Bird: The Complete Charlie Parker On Verve | Verve | 837141-2
Charlie Parker Quartet
Verve Jazz Masters 28:Charlie Parker Plays Standards | Verve | 521854-2
Charlie Parker:Bird's Best Bop On Verve | Verve | 527452-2
Charlie Parker:The Best Of The Verve Years | Verve | 527815-2
Charlie Parker | Verve | 539757-2
Talkin' Bird | Verve | 559859-2
Bird: The Complete Charlie Parker On Verve | Verve | 837141-2
Charlie Parker Quintet
Charlie Parker:Bird's Best Bop On Verve | Verve | 527452-2
Charlie Parker:The Best Of The Verve Years | Verve | 527815-2
Bird At St. Nick's | Original Jazz Classics | OJC20 041-2(JWS 500)
Charlie Parker Septet
Charlie Parker | Verve | 539757-2
Charlie Parker With Strings
Verve Jazz Masters 28:Charlie Parker Plays Standards | Verve | 521854-2
Charlie Parker With Strings:The Master Takes | Verve | 523984-2
Bird: The Complete Charlie Parker On Verve | Verve | 837141-2
Chet Baker Quartet
Chet Baker In New York | Original Jazz Classics | OJC20 207-2
The Jazz Giants Play Miles Davis:Milestones | Prestige | PCD 24225-2
Chet Baker Quintet
Chet Baker In New York | Original Jazz Classics | OJC20 207-2
Coleman Hawkins All Stars
Verve Jazz Masters 43:Coleman Hawkins | Verve | 521856-2
Dizzy Gillespie All Stars
Dizzy Gillespie:Night In Tunisia | Dreyfus Jazz Line | FDM 36734-2
Dizzy Gillespie And His Orchestra
Planet Jazz:Dizzy Gillespie | Planet Jazz | 2152069-2
Planet Jazz Sampler | Planet Jazz | 2152326-2
Planet Jazz:Jazz Greatest Hits | Planet Jazz | 2169648-2
Planet Jazz:Bebop | RCA | 2169650-2
Dizzy Gillespie:Night In Tunisia | Dreyfus Jazz Line | FDM 36734-2
Dizzy Gillespie Sextet
Dizzy Gillespie:Night In Tunisia | Dreyfus Jazz Line | FDM 36734-2
Don Lanphere Quintet
Fats Navarro:Nostalgia | Dreyfus Jazz Line | FDM 36736-2
Max Roach Quintet
Dizzy Gillespie:Pleyel Jazz Concert 1948 + Max Roach Quintet 1949 | Vogue | 21409412
Miles Davis And His Orchestra
The Complete Birth Of The Cool | Capitol | 494550-2
Birth Of The Cool | Capitol | 530117-2
Miles Davis:The Best Of The Capitol/Blue Note Years | Blue Note | 798287-2
Miles Davis:Milestones | Dreyfus Jazz Line | FDM 36731-2
Sarah Vaughan With Dizzy Gillespie And His All Star Quintet
Sarah Vaughan:Lover Man | Dreyfus Jazz Line | FDM 36739-2
Stan Getz Quartet
Stan Getz-The Complete Roost Sessions | EMI Records | 859622-2
Stan Getz:Imagination | Dreyfus Jazz Line | FDM 36733-2
Stan Getz Quartets | Original Jazz Classics | OJC20 121-2(P 7002)
The Jazz Giants Play Rodgers & Hart:Blue Moon | Prestige | PCD 24205-2
Stan Getz Quintet
Stan Getz-The Complete Roost Sessions | EMI Records | 859622-2
Tempo Jazzmen
Dizzy Gillespie:Night In Tunisia | Dreyfus Jazz Line | FDM 36734-2
Wardell Gray Quartet
Wardell Gray Memorial Vol.1 | Original Jazz Classics | OJCCD 050-2(P 7008)

Haindl,Hermann | (narration)

Okschila Tatanka
Wounded Knee-Lyrik Und Jazz | Wergo | SM 1088-2

Haines,Jamal | (tb)

Steve Coleman And The Council Of Balance
Genesis & The Opening Of The Way | RCA | 2152934-2

Haisma,Yelke | (timbales)

Pili-Pili
Stolen Moments | JA & RO | JARO 4159-2
Jazzy World | JA & RO | JARO 4200-2

Haith,Kay | (voc)

Donald Byrd Orchestra
Places And Spaces | Blue Note | 854326-2

Häkä | (b)

Edward Vesala Group
Lumi | ECM | 1339

Hakim,Omar | (dr,percvoc)

Dave Grusin Group
Migration | GRP | GRP 95922
Joe Sample Group
Ashes To Ashes | Warner | 7599-26318-2
Spellbound | Rhino | 81273726-2
Lee Ritenour Group
Festival | GRP | GRP 95702
Marcus Miller Group
The Sun Don't Lie | Dreyfus Jazz Line | FDM 36560-2
Michael Brecker Group
Now You See It...(Now You Don't) | GRP | GRP 96222
Michel Petrucciani Group
Michel Petrucciani:The Blue Note Years | Blue Note | 789916-2
Playground | Blue Note | 795480-2
Mike Mainieri Group
Jazz Life Vol.2:From Seventh At Avenue South | Storyville | 4960763
Miles Davis Group
Tutu | Warner | 7599-25490-2
Amandla | Warner | 7599-25873-2
Miles Davis-Marcus Miller Group
Siesta(Soundtrack) | Warner | 7599-25655-2

Hakim,Sadik[Argonne Thornton] | (p)

Jubilee All Stars
Jazz Gallery:Lester Young Vol.2(1946-59) | RCA | 2119541-2
Lester Young And His Band
Lester Young:The Complete Aladdin Sessions | Blue Note | 832787-2
Lester Young:Blue Lester | Dreyfus Jazz Line | FDM 36729-2

Hakin,A. | (perc)

Dee Dee Bridgewater With Orchestra
Dear Ella | Verve | 539102-2

Halbeisen,Raymond | (fl,clas)

Louis Sclavis & The Bernard Struber Jazztet
La Phare | Enja | ENJ-9359 2

Halcox,Pat | (b,co,voc,p,tb,tp,cl,asfl-h)

Chris Barber Original Jazzband Of 1954
Chris Barber:40 Years Jubilee Concert | Storyville | 4990013
Chris Barber's Jazz And Blues Band
Chris Barber On The Road:A Jazz Documentary | Storyville | 4960683
Chris Barber:40 Years Jubilee Concert | Storyville | 4990013
Chris Barber's Jazz Band
The Very Best Of Dixieland Jazz | Verve | 535529-2
The Best Of Dixieland-Live in 1954/55 | London | 820878-2
The Golden Years Of Revival Jazz,Vol 1 | Storyville | STCD 5506
The Golden Years Of Revival Jazz,Vol.2 | Storyville | STCD 5507
The Golden Years Of Revival Jazz,Vol.3 | Storyville | STCD 5508
The Golden Years Of Revival Jazz,Vol.4 | Storyville | STCD 5509
The Golden Years Of Revival Jazz,Vol.7 | Storyville | STCD 5512
The Golden Years Of Revival Jazz,Vol.9 | Storyville | STCD 5514
The Golden Years Of Revival Jazz,Vol.11 | Storyville | STCD 5516
The Golden Years Of Révival Jazz,Vol.13 | Storyville | STCD 5518
The Golden Years Of Revival Jazz,Vol.14 | Storyville | STCD 5519
The Golden Years Of Revibal Jazz,Vol.15 | Storyville | STCD 5520
Chris Barber's Jazzband & das Große Rundfunkorchester Berlin,DDR
Jazz Zounds: Chris Barber | Zounds | CD 2720007
Lonnie Donegan Skiffle Group
The Best Of Dixieland-Live in 1954/55 | London | 820878-2

Hale,Corky | (harp)

Anita O'Day With The Buddy Bregman Orchestra
Verve Jazz Masters 49:Anita O'Day | Verve | 527653-2
Ella Fitzgerald With The Buddy Bregman Orchestra
The Best Of The Song Books:The Ballads | Verve | 521867-2
Love Songs:The Best Of The Song Books | Verve | 531762-2
Ella Fitzgerald Sings The Cole Porter Songbook | Verve | 537257-2

Hale,Lee | (voc)

Leon Thomas With Orchestra
Spirits Known And Unknown | RCA | 2663876-2

Halen,Carl | (co)

Marty Grosz And His Honoris Causa Jazz Band
Hooray For Bix! | Good Time Jazz | GTCD 10065-2

Haliba,Kadija | (percvoc)

Nguyen Le Group
Maghreb And Friends | ACT | 9261-2

Hall Johnson Choir,The |

Bessie Smith With The James P.Johnson Orchestra And The Hal Johnson Choir
The Blues | Storyville | 4960323

Hall,Adelaide | (voc)

Duke Ellington And His Orchestra
Jazz:The Essential Collection Vol.2 | IN+OUT Records | 78012-2

Hall,Al | (btb)

Bud Freeman And His Summa Cum Laude Orchestra
Planet Jazz:Bud Freeman | Planet Jazz | 2161240-2
Dicky Wells And His Orchestra
Jazz:The Essential Collection Vol.3 | IN+OUT Records | 78013-2
Duke Ellington And Johnny Hodges Orchestra
Side By Side | Verve | 521405-2
Duke Ellington-Johnny Hodges All Stars
Back To Back | Verve | 521404-2
George Benson Quartet + Guests
The George Benson Cookbook | CBS | 502470-2
Kenny Clarke And His 52nd Street Boys
Planet Jazz:Bebop | RCA | 2169650-2
Fats Navarro:Nostalgia | Dreyfus Jazz Line | FDM 36736-2
Louis Armstrong And His All Stars
Planet Jazz:Louis Armstrong | Planet Jazz | 2152052-2
Planet Jazz:Jack Teagarden | Planet Jazz | 2161236-2
Planet Jazz:Male Jazz Vocalists | Planet Jazz | 2169657-2
Best Of The Complete RCA Victor Recordings | RCA | 2663636-2
Louis Armstrong:A 100th Birthday Celebration | RCA | 2663694-2
Louis Armstrong And His Orchestra
Louis Armstrong:C'est Si Bon | Dreyfus Jazz Line | FDM 36730-2
Swing Legends:Louis Armstrong | Nimbus Records | NI 2012
Pete Johnson's Housewarmin'
Jazz:The Essential Collection Vol.3 | IN+OUT Records | 78013-2
Ralph Sutton Quartet
Live At Sunnie's Rendezvous Vol.1 | Storyville | STCD 8280
Super Black Blues Band
Super Black Blues Vol.II | RCA | 2663874-2
V-Disc All Star Jam Session
Louis Armstrong-Jack Teagarden-Woody Herman:Midnights At V-Disc | Jazz Unlimited | JUCD 2048

Hall,Barry Lee | (tpfl-h)

Duke Ellington Orchestra
Highlights From The Duke Ellington Centennial Edition | RCA | 2663672-2
Duke Ellington Orchestra
Continuum | Fantasy | FCD 24765-2

Hall,Ben | (tb)

Charlie Barnet And His Orchestra
Planet Jazz:Big Bands | Planet Jazz | 2169649-2
Planet Jazz:Swing | Planet Jazz | 2169651-2

Hall,Bobbye Porter | (congas,tambourineperc)

Donald Byrd Orchestra
Black Byrd | Blue Note | 784466-2
Ethiopian Knights | Blue Note | 854328-2
Grant Green Septet
Live At The Lighthouse | Blue Note | 493381-2
Sarah Vaughan And Her Band
Songs Of The Beatles | Atlantic | 16037-2

Hall,Bruce | (dr)

Rez Abbasi Group
Out Of Body | String Jazz | SJRCD 1021

Hall,Carl | (voc)

Louis Armstrong And His Friends
Louis Armstrong And His Friends | Bluebird | 2663961-2

Hall,Carlyle | (arr)

Nat King Cole Trio With Strings
Nat King Cole:For Sentimental Reasons | Dreyfus Jazz Line | FDM 36740-2

Hall,Dana | (dr)

Tuey Connell Group
Songs For Joy And Sadness | Minor Music | 801095

Hall,Edmond | (cl,as,bsvoc)

Billie Holiday And Her Orchestra
Jazz:The Essential Collection Vol.3 | IN+OUT Records | 78013-2
Buddy Tate With The Marlow Morris Quintet
Late Night Sax | CBS | 487798-2
Edmond Hall With The Ralph Sutton Group
Edmond Hall With The Ralph Sutton Group | Storyville | STCD 6052
Edmond Hall's Blue Note Jazzmen
The Blue Note Jazzmen | Blue Note | 821262-2
Ella Fitzgerald With Louis Armstrong And The All Stars
Ella Fitzgerald-First Lady Of Song | Verve | 517898-2
The Complete Ella Fitzgerald And Louis Armstrong On Verve | Verve | 537284-2
The Best Of Ella Fitzgerald And Louis Armstrong On Verve | Verve | 537909-2

Jack Teagarden And His Band
Meet Me Where They Play The Blues | Good Time Jazz | GTCD 12063-2
James P.Johnson's Blue Note Jazzmen
The Blue Note Jazzmen | Blue Note | 821262-2
Leonard Feather's Esquire All Stars
Jazz:The Essential Collection Vol.2 | IN+OUT Records | 78012-2
Lionel Hampton And His Orchestra
Planet Jazz:Coleman Hawkins | Planet Jazz | 2152055-2
Planet Jazz:Lionel Hampton | Planet Jazz | 2152059-2
Planet Jazz:Jazz Saxophone | Planet Jazz | 2169653-2
Jazz:The Essential Collection Vol.3 | IN+OUT Records | 78013-2
Louis Armstrong And His All Stars
Verve Jazz Masters 1:Louis Armstrong | Verve | 519818-2
Louis Armstrong:The Great Chicago Concert 1956 | CBS | C2K 65119
Ambassador Satch | CBS | CK 64926
Historic Barcelona Concerts At Windsor Palace 1955 | Fresh Sound Records | FSR-CD 3004
Louis Armstrong And His All Stars With The Sy Oliver Orchestra
Ambassador Louis Armstrong Vol.17:Moments To Remember(1952-1956) | Ambassador | CLA 1917
Louis Armstrong And His Orchestra
I Love Jazz | Verve | 543747-2
Louis Armstrong With Sy Oliver's Choir And Orchestra
Louis And The Good Book | Verve | 549593-2
Louis And The Good Book | Verve | 940130-0
Sidney DeParis' Blue Note Jazzmen
The Blue Note Jazzmen | Blue Note | 821262-2
Teddy Wilson Sextet
The Complete Associated Transcriptions,1944 | Storyville | STCD 8236
Vic Dickenson Septet
Nice Work | Vanguard | VCD 79610-2
Vic Dickenson Septet With Ruby Braff
Nice Work | Vanguard | VCD 79610-2

Hall,Herb | (cl)
Bud Freeman All Stars
The Bud Freeman All-Star Sessions | Prestige | PRCD 24286-2
Eddie Condon And His Boys
The Very Best Of Dixieland Jazz | Verve | 535529-2
Odetta With The Buck Clayton Sextet
Odetta And The Blues | Original Blues Classics | OBCCD 509-2(RLP 9417)
Sidney Bechet With Sammy Price's Bluesicians
Planet Jazz:Sidney Bechet | Planet Jazz | 2152063-2
Vic Dickenson-Buck Clayton All Stars
Atlantic Jazz: Kansas City | Atlantic | 7567-81701-2

Hall,Howard | (pv)
Louis Armstrong With The Casa Loma Orchestra
Louis Armstrong:Swing That Music | Laserlight | 36056

Hall,Jim | (dr,el-g,g,g-solo)
Annie Ross With Her Quintet
Misty Blue:Sweet Sisters Swing Songs Of Sorrow And Sadness | Blue Note | 521151-2
Ben Webster Quintet
At The Renaissance | Original Jazz Classics | OJC 390(C 7646)
Bill Evans Quintet
Interplay | Original Jazz Classics | OJCCD 308-2
Bill Evans-Jim Hall
Verve Jazz Masters 5:Bill Evans | Verve | 519821-2
The Complete Bill Evans On Verve | Verve | 527953-2
Undercurrent | Blue Note | 538228-2
Ultimate Bill Evans selected by Herbie Hancock | Verve | 557536-2
Bill Smith Quartet
Folk Jazz U.S.A. | Original Jazz Classics | OJCCD 1956-2(S 7591)
Ella Fitzgerald With The Lou Levy Quartet
4 By 4:Ella Fitzgerald/Sarah Vaughan/Billie Holiday/Dinah Washington | Verve | 559693-2
For The Love Of Ella Fitzgerald | Verve | 841765-2
Ella Fitzgerald With The Paul Smith Quartet
Ella Fitzgerald-First Lady Of Song | Verve | 517898-2
Mack The Knife-The Complete Ella In Berlin | Verve | 519564-2
Verve Jazz Masters 6:Ella Fitzgerald | Verve | 519822-2
4 By 4:Ella Fitzgerald/Sarah Vaughan/Billie Holiday/Dinah Washington | Verve | 559693-2
For The Love Of Ella Fitzgerald | Verve | 841765-2
Gary McFarland And His Orchestra
The Complete Bill Evans On Verve | Verve | 527953-2
Gerry Mulligan Concert Jazz Band
Verve Jazz Masters 36:Gerry Mulligan | Verve | 523342-2
Verve Jazz Masters Vol.60:The Collection | Verve | 529866-2
The Complete Verve Gerry Mulligan Concert Band | Verve | 9860613
Gunther Schuller Ensemble
Beauty Is A Rare Thing:Ornette Coleman-The Complete Atlantic Recordings | Atlantic | 8122-71410-2
Helen Merrill With The Dick Katz Group
The Feeling Is Mutual | EmArCy | 558849-2
A Shade Of Difference | EmArCy | 558851-2
Helen Merrill-Jim Hall Duo
The Feeling Is Mutual | EmArCy | 558849-2
Jim Hall Jazzpar Quartet
Jazzpar 98 | Storyville | STCD 4230
Jim Hall Jazzpar Quartet +4
Jazzpar 98 | Storyville | STCD 4230
Jim Hall With The Bill Charlap Trio
Stardust | Blue Note | 535985-2
Jim Hall With The Zapolski Quartet
Jazzpar 98 | Storyville | STCD 4230
Jim Hall-Ron Carter Duo
Alone Together | Original Jazz Classics | OJC 467(M 9045)
Jimmy Giuffre 3
Western Suite | Atlantic | 7567-80777-2
The Jimmy Giuffre Three | Atlantic | 7567-90981-2
Jimmy Giuffre Trio
Paris Jazz Concert:Jimmy Giuffre | Laserlight | 17249
Joe Turner With Orchestra
Atlantic Jazz: Kansas City | Atlantic | 7567-81701-2
Michel Petrucciani feat. Jim Hall and Wayne Shorter
Wayne Shorter:The Classic Blue Note Recordings | Blue Note | 540856-2
Power Of Three-Live At Montreux | Blue Note | 746427-2
Michel Petrucciani:The Blue Note Years | Blue Note | 789916-2
Nat Adderley And The Big Sax Section
Cannonball Adderley Birthday Celebration | Fantasy | FANCD 6087-2
That's Right | Original Jazz Classics | OJCCD 791-2(RLP 9330)
Nat Adderley With Jim Hall And The Junior Mance Trio
Little Big Horn! | Original Jazz Classics | OJCCD 1001-2(R 9474)
Paul Desmond Orchestra
Planet Jazz:Jazz Saxophone | Planet Jazz | 2169653-2
Paul Desmond Quartet
The Ballad Of Paul Desmond | RCA | 21429372
Planet Jazz:Paul Desmond | Planet Jazz | 2152061-2
Planet Jazz Sampler | Planet Jazz | 2152326-2
Bossa Antigua | RCA | 2174795-2
Easy Living | RCA | 2174796-2
Take Ten | RCA | 2179621-2
Paul Desmond With Strings
Planet Jazz:Paul Desmond | Planet Jazz | 2152061-2
Desmond Blue | RCA | 2663898-2
Paul Desmond-Gerry Mulligan Quartet
The Ballad Of Paul Desmond | RCA | 21429372
Quincy Jones And His Orchestra
Verve Jazz Masters Vol.59:Toots Thielemans | Verve | 535271-2
Big Band Bossa Nova | Verve | 557913-2
Rahsaan/The Complete Mercury Recordings Of Roland Kirk | Mercury | 846630-2
Rolf Kühn Quintet
Rolf Kühn And His Sound Of Jazz | Fresh Sound Records | FSR-CD 326

Sonny Rollins Group
What's New? | RCA | 2179626-2
Sonny Rollins Quartet
Planet Jazz:Sonny Rollins | Planet Jazz | 2152062-2
Planet Jazz:Jazz Greatest Hits | Planet Jazz | 2169648-2
The Standard Sonny Rollins | RCA | 2174801-2
The Bridge | RCA | 2179625-2
What's New? | RCA | 2179626-2
Sonny Rollins Sextet
The Standard Sonny Rollins | RCA | 2174801-2
Sonny Stitt Quintet
Atlantic Saxophones | Rhino | 8122-71256-2
Stan Getz With Orchestra And Voices
Stan Getz Highlights | Verve | 847430-2
Stan Getz With The Claus Ogerman Orchestra
What The World Needs Now-Stan Getz Plays Bacharach And David | Verve | 557450-2
Stan Getz With The Gary McFarland Orchestra
Stan Getz Highlights:The Best Of The Verve Years Vol.2 | Verve | 517330-2
Verve Jazz Masters 53:Stan Getz-Bossa Nova | Verve | 529904-2
Big Band Bossa Nova | Verve | 825771-2 PMS
Stan Getz Highlights | Verve | 847430-2

Hall,Jim or Kenny Burrell | (g)
Johnny Hartman And His Quintet
I Just Dropped By To Say Hello | MCA | 951176-2

Hall,Juanita | (voc)
Juanita Hall With The Claude Hopkins All Stars
Juanita Hall Sings The Blues | Original Jazz Classics | OJCCD 1928-2(CPST 556)

Hall,Larry | (g,tb,tpfl-h)
Buddy Rich Big Band
Backwoods Siseman/Pieces Of Dream | Laserlight | 24655

Hall,Marty | (g,el-g,12-string-gvoc)
Marty Hall Band
Tried & True | Blues Beacon | BLU-1030 2
Who's Been Talkin'?s | Blues Beacon | BLU-1033 2

Hall,Minor 'Ram' | (dr)
Don Ewell Quartet
Free 'N' Easy | Good Time Jazz | GTCD 10046-2
Don Ewell Trio
Free 'N' Easy | Good Time Jazz | GTCD 10046-2
Kid Ory's Creole Jazz Band
This Kid's The Greatest! | Good Time Jazz | GTCD 12045-2
Louis Armstrong And His Dixieland Seven
Planet Jazz:Louis Armstrong | Planet Jazz | 2152052-2
Planet Jazz:Jazz Greatest Hits | Planet Jazz | 2169648-2
Planet Jazz:Jazz Trumpet | Planet Jazz | 2169654-2
Planet Jazz:Male Jazz Vocalists | Planet Jazz | 2169657-2
Best Of The Complete RCA Victor Recordings | RCA | 2663636 2
Louis Armstrong:A 100th Birthday Celebration | RCA | 2663694-2
Louis Armstrong:C'est Si Bon | Dreyfus Jazz Line | FDM 36730-2
Swing Legends:Louis Armstrong | Nimbus Records | NI 2012

Hall,Nolan | (dr)
Joe Hill Louis
Joe Hill Louis: The Be-Bop Boy | Bear Family Records | BCD 15524 AH

Hall,Randy | (g,synth,celestevoc)
Miles Davis Group
The Man With The Horn | CBS | 468701-2

Hall,Toby | (dr,surdotimbales)
The Catholics
Simple | Laika Records | 35100802

Hall,Tubby | (dr)
Louis Armstrong And His Orchestra
Satch Plays Fats(Complete) | CBS | CK 64927

Hall,Wilbur | (gtb)
Paul Whiteman And His Orchestra
Planet Jazz:Jazz Trumpet | Planet Jazz | 2169654-2

Halladay,Marvin | (bsreeds)
Jimmy Smith With Orchestra
Jimmy Smith-Talkin' Verve | Verve | 531563-2
Jimmy Smith With The Claus Ogerman Orchestra
Verve Jazz Masters 29:Jimmy Smith | Verve | 521855-2
Any Number Can Win | Verve | 557447-2
Oscar Peterson With Orchestra
With Respect To Nat | Verve | 557486-2

Hallberg,Bengt | (accordeon,p,arrel-p)
Bengt Hallberg Quartet
Hallberg's Hot Accordion In The Foreground | Phontastic | NCD 7532
Clifford Brown And Art Farmer With The Swedish All Stars
Clifford Brown Memorial | Original Jazz Classics | OJC20 017-2(P 7055)
Lars Gullin Quartet
Lars Gullin 1951/52 Vol.5:First Walk | Dragon | DRCD 380
Stan Getz Quartet
Stan Getz Highlights | Verve | 847430-2
Svend Asmussen Sextet
Svend Asmussen At Slukafter | Phontastic | NCD 8804

Halle,Morton | (as,fl,saxss)
Geir Lysne Listening Ensemble
Korall | ACT | 9236-2
Aurora Borealis-Nordic Lights | ACT | 9406-2
Jon Balke w/Magnetic North Orchestra
Further | ECM | 1517
Kyanos | ECM | 1822(017278-2)
Jon Balke w/Oslo 13
Nonsentration | ECM | 1445

Hallgren,Staffan | (fl)
Agneta Baumann And Her Quintet
A Time For Love | Touché Music | TMcCD 006

Halliburton,John | (b-tbtb)
June Christy With The Pete Rugolo Orchestra
Something Cool(The Complete Mono & Stereo Versions) | Capitol | 534069-2
June Christy With The Shorty Rogers Orchestra
June Christy Big Band Special | Capitol | 498319-2
Nat King Cole Quartet With The Stan Kenton Orchestra
Nat King Cole:For Sentimental Reasons | Dreyfus Jazz Line | FDM 36740-2
Shorty Rogers And His Orchestra Feat. The Giants
PLanet Jazz:Shorty Rogers | Planet Jazz | 2159976-2
Stan Kenton And His Orchestra
Stan Kenton Portraits On Standards | Capitol | 531571-2

Halling,Patrick | (v)
Barbara Thompson Group
Heavenly Bodies | VeraBra Records | CDVBR 2015-2

Halopoff,Gary | (tpfl-h)
Buddy Childers Big Band
It's What Happening Now! | Candid | CCD 79749

Halprin,Diana | (v)
Earl Klugh Group With Strings
Late Night Guitar | Blue Note | 498573-2

Halten,Torg | (tp)
Anita O'Day With Gene Krupa And His Orchestra
Let Me Off Uptown:Anita O'Day With Gene Krupa | CBS | CK 65625

Haltli,Frode | (b-tbaccordeon)
Trygve Seim-Oyvind Braekke-Per Oddvar Johansen Orchestra
The Source And Different Cikadas | ECM | 1764(014432-2)

Haltli,Marius | (tpfl-h)
Christoph Lauer & Norwegian Brass
Heaven | ACT | 9420-2
Geir Lysne Listening Ensemble
Korall | ACT | 9236-2
Aurora Borealis-Nordic Lights | ACT | 9406-2

Halversen,Tom | (el-p)
Terje Rypdal Sextet
Terje Rypdal | ECM | 1016(527645-2)

Hamdy,Ahmad | (cello)
Mahmoud Turkmani Group

Zakira | Enja | ENJ-9475 2

Hameline,Teddy | (as)
Lucky Thompson With The Gerard Pochonet All-Stars
Planet Jazz:Jazz Saxophone | Planet Jazz | 2169653-2
Lucky Thompson's Modern Jazz Group Tentet
Jazz In Paris:Lucky Thompson-Modern Jazz Group | EmArCy | 159823-2 PMS

Hamer,Ian | (fl-htp)
Kenny Wheeler Brass Ensemble
A Long Time Ago | ECM | 1691
Kenny Wheeler Ensemble
Muisc For Large & Small Ensembles | ECM | 1415/16

Hamid,Abdul | (tb)
Lionel Hampton And His Orchestra
Lionel Hampton:Flying Home | Dreyfus Jazz Line | FDM 36735-2

Hamidi,Asita | (harp)
Asita Hamidi & Arcobaleno
Mosaic | Laika Records | 8695067

Hamilton,Anthony | (voice)
Don Cherry Group
Multi Kulti | A&M Records | 395323-2

Hamilton,Bobby | (dr)
Nina Simone Quartet
Verve Jazz Masters 17:Nina Simone | Verve | 518198-2
Verve Jazz Masters 20:Introducing | Verve | 519853-2
Misty Blue:Sweet Sisters Swing Songs Of Sorrow And Sadness | Blue Note | 521151-2
Nina Simone After Hours | Verve | 526702-2
In Concert/I Put A Spell On You | Mercury | 846543-2
Nina Simone Quintet
Nina Simone After Hours | Verve | 526702-2
Nina Simone Trio
Nina Simone After Hours | Verve | 526702-2
Nina Simone With Horace Ott's Orchestra
Nina Simone After Hours | Verve | 526702-2
Nina Simone-Bobby Hamilton
Verve Jazz Masters Vol.58:Nina Simone Sings Nina | Verve | 529867-2

Hamilton,Dick | (tb)
Buddy Childers Big Band
It's What Happening Now! | Candid | CCD 79749

Hamilton,Ed | (g,p,keyboards,bel-b)
Urbanator
Urbanator II | Hip Bop | HIBD 8012

Hamilton,Forrest 'Chico' | (dr,perc,gong,slapaphone,tambourine)
A Band Of Friends
The Best Of The Gerry Mulligan Quartet With Chet Baker | Pacific Jazz | 795481-2
Billie Holiday And Her All Stars
Verve Jazz Masters 12:Billie Holiday | Verve | 519825-2
The Billie Holiday Song Book | Verve | 823246-2
Chico Hamilton
The Dealer | Impulse(MCA) | 547958-2
With Strings Attached/The Three Faces Of Chico | Warner | 9362-47874-2
Chico Hamilton Orchestra
With Strings Attached/The Three Faces Of Chico | Warner | 9362-47874-2
Chico Hamilton Quartet
The Dealer | Impulse(MCA) | 547958-2
Chico Hamilton Quintet
The Original Ellington Suite | Pacific Jazz | 524567-2
The Dealer | Impulse(MCA) | 547958-2
With Strings Attached/The Three Faces Of Chico | Warner | 9362-47874-2
The Roots Of Acid Jazz | Impulse(MCA) | IMP 12042
Newport Jazz Festival 1958,July 3rd-6th Vol.2:Mulligan The Main Man | Phontastic | NCD 8814
Chico Hamilton Quintet With Strings
With Strings Attached/The Three Faces Of Chico | Warner | 9362-47874-2
Chico Hamilton Sextet
The Dealer | Impulse(MCA) | 547958-2
Gerry Mulligan Quartet
Gerry Mulligan Quartet feat.Chet Baker | Original Jazz Classics | OJCCD 711-2(F 8082/P 7641)
The Jazz Giants Play Rodgers & Hart:Blue Moon | Prestige | PCD 24205-2
Gerry Mulligan Tentette
Gene Norman Presents The Original Gerry Mulligan Tentet And Quartet | GNP Crescendo | GNPD 56
Lester Young And His Band
Jazz:The Essential Collection Vol.3 | IN+OUT Records | 78013-2
Lester Young:The Complete Aladdin Sessions | Blue Note | 832787-2
Lester Young:Blue Lester | Dreyfus Jazz Line | FDM 36729-2
Tal Farlow Quartet
Verve Jazz Masters 41:Tal Farlow | Verve | 527365-2

Hamilton,Jeff | (dr,ld,percp)
Dan Barrett Septet
Dan Barrett's International Swing Party | Nagel-Heyer | CD 067
Diana Krall Group
When I Look In Your Eyes | Verve | 9513304
The Girl In The Other Room | Verve | 9862246
Diana Krall Group With Orchestra
When I Look In Your Eyes | Verve | 9513304
Diane Schuur Trio With Orchestra And Strings
In Tribute | GRP | GRP 20062
Diane Schuur With Orchestra
In Tribute | GRP | GRP 20062
The Best Of Diane Schuur | GRP | GRP 98882
Jackie Cain-Roy Kral Group
Full Circle | Fantasy | FCD 24768-2
James Morrison-Ray Brown Quartet
Two The Max | East-West | 9031-77125-2
Milt Jackson With The Monty Alexander Trio
To Bags...With Love:Memorial Album | Pablo | 2310967-2
Soul Fusion | Original Jazz Classics | OJCCD 731-2(2310804)
Monty Alexander Trio
Montreux Alexander-Live! At The Montreux Festival | MPS | 817487-2
Stacey Kent And Her Quintet
The Tender Trap | Candid | CCD 79751
The Clayton Brothers Quintet
Siblingity | Warner | 9362-47813-2
Till Brönner-Gregoire Peters Quintet
Generations Of Jazz | Minor Music | 801037
Vic Lewis West Coast All Stars
Me And You! | Candid | CCD 79739

Hamilton,Jimmy | (as,b,cl,arr,ss,tssax)
Ben Webster With Orchestra And Strings
Verve Jazz Masters 43:Ben Webster | Verve | 525431-2
Music For Loving:Ben Webster With Strings | Verve | 527774-2
Billie Holiday With Teddy Wilson And His Orchestra
Billie's Love Songs | Nimbus Records | NI 2000
Billy Strayhorn Orchestra
Johnny Hodges With Billy Strayhorn And The Orchestra | Verve | 557543-2
Django Reinhardt With Duke Ellington And His Orchestra
Django Reinhardt:Souveniers | Dreyfus Jazz Line | FDM 36744-2
Duke Ellington And Count Basie With Their Orchestras
First Time! | CBS | CK 65571
Duke Ellington And His Award Winners
Greatest Hits | CBS | 462959-2
Duke Ellington And His Famous Orchestra
Planet Jazz:Johnny Hodges | Planet Jazz | 2152065-2
Duke Ellington And His Orchestra
Planet Jazz:Duke Ellington | Planet Jazz | 2152053-2
Planet Jazz:Johnny Hodges | Planet Jazz | 2152065-2
Planet Jazz:Jazz Greatest Hits | Planet Jazz | 2169648-2
Duke Ellington's Far East Suite | RCA | 2174797-2

Jazz Collection:Duke Ellington | Laserlight | 24369
The Art Of Saxophone | Laserlight | 24652
The Legends Of Swing | Laserlight | 24659
100 Years Duke | Laserlight | 24906
Highlights From The Duke Ellington Centennial Edition | RCA | 2663672-2
The Popular Duke Ellington | RCA | 2663880-2
Carnegie Hall Concert December 1944 | Prestige | 2PCD 24073-2
Carnegie Hall Concert January 1946 | Prestige | 2PCD 24074-2
Carnegie Hall Concert December 1947 | Prestige | 2PCD 24075-2
Duke Ellington: The Champs-Elysees Theater January 29-30th,1965 | Laserlight | 36131
Greatest Hits | CBS | 462959-2
The Big Bands Vol.1.The Snader Telescriptions | Storyville | 4960043
Jazz Festival Vol.2 | Storyville | 4960743
Verve Jazz Masters 4:Duke Ellington | Verve | 516338-2
Verve Jazz Masters 20:Introducing | Verve | 519853-2
Ellington '55 | Capitol | 520135-2
Great Swing Classics In Hi-Fi | Capitol | 521223-2
Ella & Duke At The Cote D'Azur | Verve | 539030-2
Ella Fitzgerald And Duke Ellington:Cote D'Azure Concerts on Verve | Verve | 539033-2
Soul Call | Verve | 539785-2
The Great Paris Concert | Atlantic | 7567-81303-2
Jazz:The Essential Collection Vol.2 | IN+OUT Records | 78012-2
Afro-Bossa | Reprise | 9362-47876-2
Ellington At Newport 1956(Complete) | CBS | CK 64932
Black Brown And Beige | CBS | CK 65566
Such Sweet Thunder | CBS | CK 65568
Anatomy Of A Murder | CBS | CK 65569
The Ellington Suites | Original Jazz Classics | OJC20 446-2(2310762)
Duke Ellington And His Orchestra feat. Paul Gonsalves | Original Jazz Classics | OJCCD 623-2
Yale Concert | Original Jazz Classics | OJCCD 664-2
Jazz At The Philharmonis Berlin '65/Paris '67 | Pablo | PACD 5304-2
Duke Ellington At The Alhambra | Pablo | PACD 5313-2
The Jazz Giants Play Duke Ellington:Caravan | Prestige | PCD 24227-2
At The Hurricane:Original 1943 Broadcasts | Storyville | STCD 8359

Ella Fitzgerald With The Duke Ellington Orchestra
The Stockholm Concert 1966 | Pablo | 2308242-2
Ella Fitzgerald-First Lady Of Song | Verve | 517898-2
The Best Of The Song Books | Verve | 519804-2
Verve Jazz Masters 6:Ella Fitzgerald | Verve | 519822-2
The Best Of The Song Books:The Ballads | Verve | 521867-2
Verve Jazz Masters 46:Ella Fitzgerald-The Jazz Sides | Verve | 527655-2
Ella At Duke's Place | Verve | 529700-2
Love Songs:The Best Of The Song Books | Verve | 531762-2
Ella & Duke At The Cote D'Azur | Verve | 539030-2
Ella Fitzgerald And Duke Ellington:Cote D'Azure Concerts on Verve | Verve | 539033-2
Ella Fitzgerald Sings The Duke Ellington Songbook | Verve | 559248-2
For The Love Of Ella Fitzgerald | Verve | 841765-2

Ella Fitzgerald With The Duke Ellington Orchestra And Jimmy Jones Trio
Ella & Duke At The Cote D'Azur | Verve | 539030-2
Ella Fitzgerald And Duke Ellington:Cote D'Azure Concerts on Verve | Verve | 539033-2

Esquire All-American Award Winners
Best Of The Complete RCA Victor Recordings | RCA | 2663636-2
Highlights From The Duke Ellington Centennial Edition | RCA | 2663672-2

Harry Carney And His Orchestra With Strings
Music For Loving:Ben Webster With Strings | Verve | 527774-2

Jimmy Hamilton And The Duke's Men
The Blue Note Swingtets | Blue Note | 495697-2

Johnny Hodges And His Band
Verve Jazz Masters 35:Johnny Hodges | Verve | 521857-2

Johnny Hodges And The Ellington All-Stars Without Duke
Verve Jazz Masters 35:Johnny Hodges | Verve | 521857-2

Johnny Hodges And The Ellington Men
Verve Jazz Masters 35:Johnny Hodges | Verve | 521857-2

Johnny Hodges Orchestra
Coleman Hawkins/Johnny Hodges:The Vogue Recordings | Vogue | 21559712
Verve Jazz Masters 35:Johnny Hodges | Verve | 521857-2
Verve Jazz Masters 43:Ben Webster | Verve | 525431-2

Johnny Hodges With Billy Strayhorn And The Duke Ellington Orchestra
Verve Jazz Masters 35:Johnny Hodges | Verve | 521857-2

Leonard Feather's Esquire All-Americans
Louis Armstrong:C'est Si Bon | Dreyfus Jazz Line | FDM 36730-2

Oscar Peterson With The Duke Ellington Orchestra
Oscar Peterson Plays Duke Ellington | Pablo | 2310966-2

Rosemary Clooney With The Duke Ellington Orchestra
Blue Rose | CBS | CK 65506

Hamilton,John | (tp)

Fats Waller And His Rhythm
Planet Jazz:Fats Waller | Planet Jazz | 2152058-2
Fats Waller:The Complete Associated Transcription Sessions 1935-1939 | Jazz Unlimited | JUCD 2076

Hamilton,Milton | (p)

Mongo Santamaria And His Band
Montreux Heat! | Pablo | PACD 5317-2

Mongo Santamaria Group With Dizzy Gillespie And Toots Thielemans
Summertime-Digital At Montreux 1980 | Original Jazz Classics | OJCCD 626-2(2308229)
Montreux Heat! | Pablo | PACD 5317-2

Hamilton,Scott | (ts)

Benny Goodman Septet
Verve Jazz Masters 33:Benny Goodman | Verve | 844410-2

Hamilton,Steve | (p,synthsax)

Steve Martland Band
The Orchestra Of Smith's Academy | Enja | ENJ-9358 2

Hamlin,Bob | (voc)

Louis Armstrong With The Hal Mooney Orchestra
Ambassador Louis Armstrong Vol.17:Moments To Remember(1952-1956) | Ambassador | CLA 1917

Hammann,Joyce | (vviola)

Jim Snidero Quartet With Strings
Strings | Milestone | MCD 9326-2

Mark Feldman Quartet
Book Of Tells | Enja | ENJ-9385 2

Michael Brecker Quindectet
Wide Angles | Verve | 076142-2

Uri Caine Ensemble
Wagner E Venezia | Winter&Winter | 910013-2

Hammar,Karin | (tb)

Nils Landgren Group
Sentimental Journey | ACT | 9409-2

Hammar,Mimmi | (tb)

Hammer,Bob | (arrp)

Charles Mingus And His Orchestra
The Complete Town Hall Concert | Blue Note | 828353-2

Woody Herman And His Orchestra
Verve Jazz Masters 54:Woody Herman | Verve | 529903-2

Hammer,Jan | (dr,el-p,chinese,gongs,gong,synth)

Al Di Meola Group
Elegant Gypsy | CBS | 468213-2

Billy Cobham Group
Spectrum | Atlantic | 7567-81428-2
The Best Of Billy Cobham | Atlantic | 7567-81558-2

Billy Cobham Quartet
Atlantic Jazz: Fusion | Atlantic | 7567-81711-2

John Abercrombie Quartet
Night | ECM | 1272(823212-2)

John Abercrombie Trio
Timeless | ECM | 1047(829114-2)

Mahavishnu Orchestra
The Inner Mounting Flame | CBS | CK 65523

The Mahavishnu Orchestra
Between Nothingness & Eternity | CBS | CK 32766

Hammer,Tardo | (p)

John Marshall Quintet
Dreamin' On The Hudson | Organic Music | ORGM 9713
Theme Of No Repeat | Organic Music | ORGM 9719

Marty Elkins And Her Sextet
Fuse Blues | Nagel-Heyer | CD 062

Hammer,Thomas | (drperc)

Acoustic Affaire
Mira | Jazz 'n' Arts Records | JNA 1303

Rainer Tempel Big Band
Melodies Of '98 | Jazz 4 Ever Records:Jazz Network | J4E 4744
Album 03 | Jazz 'n' Arts Records | JNA 1102

Hämmerli,Urs 'Hämi' | (b)

Cadavre Exquis
Cadavre Exquis | Creative Works Records | CW CD 1014-1

Hammerschmid,Hans | (arrp)

Albert Mangelsdorff With The NDR Big Band
NDR Big Band-Bravissimo | ACT | 9232-2

Hammes,Ernie | (tp)

Derrick James & Wesley 'G' Quintet
Two Sides To Every Story | Jardis Records | JRCD 20137

Hammond,B.G. | (as)

Hot Lips Page And His Orchestra
Don Byas:Laura | Dreyfus Jazz Line | FDM 36714-2

Hammond,Don | (fl,asreeds)

Paul Desmond Quartet With The Don Sebesby Orchestra
From The Hot Afternoon | Verve | 543487-2

Hammond,Doug | (dr,perc,marimba,balafon,jal)

James Blood Ulmer Quartet
Revealing | IN+OUT Records | 7007-2
Jazz Unlimited | IN+OUT Records | 7017-2

Ku-Umba Frank Lacy & His Quartet
Settegast Strut | Tutu Records | 888162-2*

Hammond,Gary | (perc)

Nicki Leighton-Thomas Group
Forbidden Games | Candid | CCD 79778

Hammond,John | (announcements,g,vochand-clapping)

Count Basie And His Orchestra
Jazz Gallery:Lester Young Vol.2(1946-59) | RCA | 2119541-2

Hamner,Curley | (dr)

Lionel Hampton And His Orchestra
Lionel Hampton's Paris All Stars | Vogue | 21511502

Lionel Hampton Quintet
Americans Swinging In Paris:Lionel Hampton | EMI Records | 539649-2

Lionel Hampton Sextet
Americans Swinging In Paris:Lionel Hampton | EMI Records | 539649-2

Lionel Hampton Trio
Americans Swinging In Paris:Lionel Hampton | EMI Records | 539649-2

Hamon,Pierre | (bagpipesrecorder)

Renaud Garcia-Fons
Navigatore | Enja | ENJ-9418 2

Renaud Garcia-Fons Group
Navigatore | Enja | ENJ-9418 2

Hampel,Gunter | (b-cl,bs,vib,voice,ss,p,bongos)

Gunter Hampel All Stars
Jubilation | Birth | 0038

Gunter Hampel And His Galaxie Dream Band
Journey To The Song Within | Birth | 0017
Enfant Terrible | Birth | 0025
Live At The Berlin Jazzfestival 1978 | Birth | 0027
All Is Real | Birth | 0028
All The Things You Could Be If Charles Mingus Was Your Daddy | Birth | CD 031
Celestial Glory-Live At The Knitting Factory New York | Birth | CD 040

Gunter Hampel Group
Familie | Birth | 008
The 8th Of July 1969 | Birth | CD 001

Gunter Hampel Jazz Sextet
Gunter Hampel: The 8th Of Sept.1999 | Birth | CD 049

Gunter Hampel New York Orchestra
Fresh Heat-Live At Sweet Basil | Birth | CD 039

Gunter Hampel Next Generation
Next Generation | Birth | CD 043
Köln Concert Part 1 | Birth | CD 047
Köln Concert Part 2 | Birth | CD 048

Gunter Hampel Quartet
Time Is Now-Live At The Eldena Jazz Festival 1992 | Birth | CD 042

Gunter Hampel Quintet
Legendary: The 27th Of May 1997 | Birth | CD 045

Gunter Hampel-Christian Weider
Gunter Hampel: The 8th Of Sept.1999 | Birth | CD 049

Gunter Hampel-Christian Weider Duo
Solid Fun | Birth | CD 044

Gunter Hampel-Matthias Schubert Duo
Dialog-Live At The Eldena Jazz Festival 1992 | Birth | CD 041

Gunter Hampel-Nils Wogram
Gunter Hampel: The 8th Of Sept.1999 | Birth | CD 049

Jeanne Lee Group
Natural Affinities | Owl Records | 018352-2

Marion Brown-Gunter Hampel Duo
Gemini | Birth | CD 037

Hamperian,Ralph | (b)

Axel Zwingenberger With The Lionel Hampton Big Band
The Boogie Woogie Album | Vagabond | VRCD 8.88008

Hampton Rhythm Boys,The | (voc)

Lionel Hampton And His Orchestra
Planet Jazz:Lionel Hampton | Planet Jazz | 2152059-2

Hampton,Lionel | (brushes on suitcase,dr,voc,p,vib)

(Little)Jimmy Scott With The Lionel Hampton Orchestra
Everybody's Somebody's Fool | Decca | 050669-2

Art Tatum Sextet
Art Tatum-The Complete Pablo Group Masterpieces | Pablo | 6 PACD 4401-2

Axel Zwingenberger With The Lionel Hampton Big Band
The Boogie Woogie Album | Vagabond | VRCD 8.88008

Benny Goodman And His Orchestra
Swing Vol.1 | Storyville | 4960343
40th Anniversary Concert-Live At Carnegie Hall | London | 820349-2
Camel Caravan Broadcast 1939 Vol.1 | Phontastic | NCD 8817
Camel Caravan Broadcast 1939 Vol.2 | Phontastic | NCD 8818
Camel Caravan Broadcast 1939 Vol.3 | Phontastic | NCD 8819

Benny Goodman Quartet
Planet Jazz:Benny Goodman | Planet Jazz | 2152054-2
Jazz Collection:Benny Goodman | Laserlight | 24396
Together Again! | RCA | 2663881-2
Benny Goodman At Carnegie Hall 1938(Complete) | CBS | C2K 65143
Camel Caravan Broadcast 1939 Vol.1 | Phontastic | NCD 8817
Camel Caravan Broadcast 1939 Vol.2 | Phontastic | NCD 8818
Camel Caravan Broadcast 1939 Vol.3 | Phontastic | NCD 8819
More Camel Caravans | Phontastic | NCD 8841/2
More Camel Caravans | Phontastic | NCD 8843/4
More Camel Caravans | Phontastic | NCD 8845/6

Benny Goodman Sextet
Charlie Christian:Swing To Bop | Dreyfus Jazz Line | FDM 36715-2
More Camel Caravans | Phontastic | NCD 8845/6
From Spiritual To Swing | Vanguard | VCD 169/71

Benny Goodman Trio
Camel Caravan Broadcast 1939 Vol.2 | Phontastic | NCD 8818
Camel Caravan Broadcast 1939 Vol.3 | Phontastic | NCD 8819
More Camel Caravans | Phontastic | NCD 8843/4
More Camel Caravans | Phontastic | NCD 8845/6

Count Basie And His Orchestra
From Spiritual To Swing | Vanguard | VCD 169/71

Lionel Hampton All Stars
Jazz In Paris:Lionel Hampton-Ring Dem Bells | EmArCy | 159825-2 PMS
Jazz In Paris:Lionel Hampton And His French New Sound Vol.1 | EmArCy | 549405-2 PMS
Jazz In Paris:Lionel Hampton And His French New Sound Vol.2 | EmArCy | 549406-2 PMS
Lionel Hampton:Flying Home | Dreyfus Jazz Line | FDM 36735-2

Lionel Hampton And His All Star Jazz Inner Circle
Lionel Hampton: Salle Pleyel, March 9th, 1971 | Laserlight | 36133

Lionel Hampton And His Orchestra
Lionel Hampton's Paris All Stars | Vogue | 21511502
Planet Jazz:Coleman Hawkins | Planet Jazz | 2152055-2
Planet Jazz:Lionel Hampton | Planet Jazz | 2152059-2
Planet Jazz Sampler | Planet Jazz | 2152326-2
Planet Jazz:Ben Webster | RCA | 2165368-2
Planet Jazz:Big Bands | Planet Jazz | 2169649-2
Planet Jazz:Swing | Planet Jazz | 2169651-2
Planet Jazz:Jazz Saxophone | Planet Jazz | 2169653-2
Planet Jazz:Male Jazz Vocalists | Planet Jazz | 2169657-2
Jazz:The Essential Collection Vol.3 | IN+OUT Records | 78013-2
Lionel Hampton:Flying Home | Dreyfus Jazz Line | FDM 36735-2

Lionel Hampton And His Quintet
Planet Jazz:Jazz Greatest Hits | Planet Jazz | 2169648-2

Lionel Hampton And His Septet
Lionel Hampton:Flying Home | Dreyfus Jazz Line | FDM 36735-2

Lionel Hampton Orchestra
The Big Bands Vol.1.The Snader Telescriptions | Storyville | 4960043

Lionel Hampton Quartet
The Complete Lionel Hampton Quartets And Quintets With Oscar Peterson On Verve | Verve | 559797-2
The Lional Hampton Quintet | Verve | 589100-2
Lionel Hampton:Flying Home | Dreyfus Jazz Line | FDM 36735-2

Lionel Hampton Quintet
Planet Jazz:Lionel Hampton | Planet Jazz | 2152059-2
Americans Swinging In Paris:Lionel Hampton | EMI Records | 539649-2
The Complete Lionel Hampton Quartets And Quintets With Oscar Peterson On Verve | Verve | 559797-2
The Lional Hampton Quintet | Verve | 589100-2

Lionel Hampton Sextet
Americans Swinging In Paris:Lionel Hampton | EMI Records | 539649-2

Lionel Hampton Trio
Lionel Hampton's Paris All Stars | Vogue | 21511502
Americans Swinging In Paris:Lionel Hampton | EMI Records | 539649-2

Lionel Hampton With Buddy DeFranco And The Oscar Peterson Trio
Verve Jazz Masters 26:Lionel Hampton with Oscar Peterson | Verve | 521853-2

Lionel Hampton With The Oscar Peterson Quartet
Verve Jazz Masters 26:Lionel Hampton with Oscar Peterson | Verve | 521853-2

Lionel Hampton With The Oscar Peterson Trio
Verve Jazz Masters 26:Lionel Hampton with Oscar Peterson | Verve | 521853-2

Lionel Hampton/Jess Stacy
More Camel Caravans | Phontastic | NCD 8845/6

Lionel Hampton-Oscar Peterson Duo
The Complete Lionel Hampton Quartets And Quintets With Oscar Peterson On Verve | Verve | 559797-2

Norman Granz Jam Session
Verve Jazz Masters 26:Lionel Hampton with Oscar Peterson | Verve | 521853-2
Verve Jazz Masters Vol.60:The Collection | Verve | 529866-2

Stan Getz Quintet
Verve Jazz Masters 8:Stan Getz | Verve | 519823-2

Stan Getz-Lionel Hampton Quintet
Stan Getz Highlights:The Best Of The Verve Years Vol.2 | Verve | 517330-2
Hamp And Getz | Verve | 831672-2

Stan Getz-Lionel Hampton Sextet
Hamp And Getz | Verve | 831672-2

Tatum-Hampton-Rich Trio
Art Tatum-The Complete Pablo Group Masterpieces | Pablo | 6 PACD 4401-2

Hampton,Slide | (arr,ld,tb,p,trombiniumtuba)

Art Farmer/Slide Hampton Quintet
In Concert | Enja | ENJ-4088 2

Buddy Johnson And His Orchestra
Buddy And Ella Johnson 1953-1964 | Bear Family Records | BCD 15479 DH

Charles Mingus Orchestra
Charles Mingus:Pre-Bird(Mingus Revisited) | Verve | 538636-2

Dee Dee Bridgewater With Her Septet
Dear Ella | Verve | 539102-2

Dizzy Gillespie And The United Nation Orchestra
7.Zelt-Musik-Festival:Jazz Events | Zounds | CD 2730001

Hank Mobley Sextet
The Flip | Blue Note | 593872-2

Klaus Weiss Orchestra
Live At The Domicile | ATM Records | ATM 3805-AH

McCoy Tyner Big Band
The Best Of McCoy Tyner Big Band | Dreyfus Jazz Line | FDM 37012-2

McCoy Tyner Orchestra
13th House | Original Jazz Classics | OJCCD 1089-2(M 9102)

Nat Adderley Sextet
Much Brass | Original Jazz Classics | OJCCD 848-2(R 1143)

Oscar Peterson With The Ernie Wilkins Orchestra
Verve Jazz Masters 16:Oscar Peterson | Verve | 516320-2

Slide Hampton Quartet
Americans Swinging In Paris:Slide Hampton | EMI Records | 539648-2

Slide Hampton-Joe Haider Jazz Orchestra
Give Me A Double | JHM Records | JHM 3627

Hamway,Mike | (darabeka)

Ahmed Abdul-Malik Orchestra
Planet Jazz:Lee Morgan | Planet Jazz | 2161238-2

Ahmed Abdul-Malik's Middle-Eastern Music
Jazz Sahara | Original Jazz Classics | OJCCD 1820-2(R 12-287)

Hancock,Herbie | (celeste,el-harpsichord,el-p,synth)

Al Grey And His Allstars
Snap Your Fingers | Verve | 9860307

Antonio Carlos Jobim Group
Antonio Carlos Jobim And Friends | Verve | 531556-2

Antonio Carlos Jobim With The Herbie Hancock Sextet
Antonio Carlos Jobim And Friends | Verve | 531556-2

Blue Note All Stars
Town Hall Concert | Blue Note | 497811-2

Bob Brookmeyer Quintet
Sony Jazz Collection:Stan Getz | CBS | 488623-2

Bob Brookmeyer Sextet
Late Night Sax | CBS | 487798-2

Bobby Hutcherson Quartet
Herbie Hancock:The Complete Blue Note Sixties Sessions | Blue Note | 495569-2

Bobby McFerrin Groups
Spontaneous Inventions | Blue Note | 746298-2

Buster Williams Quintet
Something More | IN+OUT Records | 7004-2
Jazz Unlimited | IN+OUT Records | 7017-2

Cal Tjader's Orchestra
Verve Jazz Masters 39:Cal Tjader | Verve | 521858-2

Chick Corea-Herbie Hancock Duo
An Evening Wirh Chick Corea & Herbie Hancock | Polydor | 835680-2

Directions In Music
Live at Massey Hall:Celebrating Miles Davis & John Coltrane | Verve | 589654-2

Donald Byrd Orchestra With Voices
True Blue | Blue Note | 534032-2
The Best Of Blue Note | Blue Note | 796110-2

Donald Byrd Quintet
Herbie Hancock:The Complete Blue Note Sixties Sessions | Blue Note | 495569-2

Free Form | Blue Note | 595961-2
Donald Byrd Septet + Voices
A New Perspective | Blue Note | 499006-2
Eric Dolphy Quartet
The Illinois Concert | Blue Note | 499826-2
Eric Dolphy Quartet With The University Of Illinois Big Band
The Illinois Concert | Blue Note | 499826-2
Eric Dolphy Quartet With The University Of Illinois Brass Ensemble
The Illinois Concert | Blue Note | 499826-2
Freddie Hubbard Quintet
Hub-Tones | Blue Note | 499008-2
Freddie Hubbard Septet
This Is Jazz:Freddie Hubbard | CBS | CK 65041
Gal Costa With The Herbie Hancock Sextet
Antonio Carlos Jobim And Friends | Verve | 531556-2
Gal Costa-Herbie Hancock
Antonio Carlos Jobim And Friends | Verve | 531556-2
George Benson And His Orchestra
Giblet Gravy | Verve | 543754-2
Talkin' Verve:George Benson | Verve | 553780-2
George Benson Orchestra
Verve Jazz Masters 21:George Benson | Verve | 521861-2
Talkin' Verve:George Benson | Verve | 553780-2
George Benson Quintet
Verve Jazz Masters 21:George Benson | Verve | 521861-2
Giblet Gravy | Verve | 543754-2
George Benson Sextet
Talkin' Verve:George Benson | Verve | 553780-2
George Benson With The Don Sebesky Orchestra
Verve Jazz Masters 21:George Benson | Verve | 521861-2
Gonzalo Rubalcaba-Herbie Hancock Quintet
Antonio Carlos Jobim And Friends | Verve | 531556-2
Grachan Moncur III Quintet
A Blue Conception | Blue Note | 534254-2
Grant Green Quintet
Feelin' The Spirit | Blue Note | 746822-2
Hank Mobley Quintet
No Room For Squares | Blue Note | 524539-2
Harbie Hancock/Ron Carter
Lifetime | Blue Note | 499004-2
Herbie Hancock
V.S.O.P. Herbie Hancock-Live At The City Center N.Y. | CBS | 486569-2
Antonio Carlos Jobim And Friends | Verve | 531556-2
Herbie Hancock Group
Man-Child | CBS | 471235-2
Sunlight | CBS | 486570-2
Monster | CBS | 486571-2
Magic Window | CBS | 486572-2
Herbie Hancock The New Standards | Verve | 527715-2
Sextant | CBS | CK 64983
Thrust | CBS | CK 64984
Head Hunters | CBS | CK 65123
Herbie Hancock Group With String Quartet
Herbie Hancock The New Standards | Verve | 527715-2
Herbie Hancock Group With String Quartet,Woodwinds And Brass
Herbie Hancock The New Standards | Verve | 527715-2
Herbie Hancock Group With Woodwinds And Brass
Herbie Hancock The New Standards | Verve | 527715-2
Herbie Hancock Orchestra
Herbie Hancock:The Complete Blue Note Sixties Sessions | Blue Note | 495569-2
The Prisoner | Blue Note | 525649-2
Herbie Hancock Quartet
Herbie Hancock:The Complete Blue Note Sixties Sessions | Blue Note | 495569-2
Empyrean Isles | Blue Note | 498796-2
Antonio Carlos Jobim And Friends | Verve | 531556-2
Blue N' Groovy | Blue Note | 780679-2
Blue Break Beats | Blue Note | 799106-2
Cantaloupe Island | Blue Note | 829331-2
Herbie Hancock Quintet
V.S.O.P. Herbie Hancock-Live At The City Center N.Y. | CBS | 486569-2
Maiden Voyage | Blue Note | 495331-2
Herbie Hancock:The Complete Blue Note Sixties Sessions | Blue Note | 495569-2
The Best Of Blue Note | Blue Note | 796110-2
The Best Of Blue Note Vol.2 | Blue Note | 797960-2
Cantaloupe Island | Blue Note | 829331-2
Takin' Off | Blue Note | 837643-2
Herbie Hancock Septet
V.S.O.P. Herbie Hancock-Live At The City Center N.Y. | CBS | 486569-2
Herbie Hancock:The Complete Blue Note Sixties Sessions | Blue Note | 495569-2
My Point Of View | Blue Note | 521226-2
Cantaloupe Island | Blue Note | 829331-2
Herbie Hancock Sextet
V.S.O.P. Herbie Hancock-Live At The City Center N.Y. | CBS | 486569-2
Herbie Hancock:The Complete Blue Note Sixties Sessions | Blue Note | 495569-2
Speak Like A Child | Blue Note | 746136-2
Herbie Hancock Trio
Herbie Hancock:The Complete Blue Note Sixties Sessions | Blue Note | 495569-2
Chick Corea-Herbie Hancock-Keith Jarrett-McCoy Tyner | Atlantic | 7567-81402-2
Jackie McLean Quintet
Herbie Hancock:The Complete Blue Note Sixties Sessions | Blue Note | 495569-2
Vertigo | Blue Note | 522669-2
Jaco Pastorius With Orchestra
Word Of Mouth | Warner | 7599-23525-2
Joe Henderson Group
Double Rainbow | Verve | 527222-2
Joe Henderson Quartet
Joe Henderson:The Milestone Years | Milestone | 8MCD 4413-2
Joe Henderson Quintet
Joe Henderson:The Milestone Years | Milestone | 8MCD 4413-2
Joe Zawinul Group
Zawinul | Atlantic | 7567-81375-2
Jon Hendricks With The Herbie Hancock Quintet
Antonio Carlos Jobim And Friends | Verve | 531556-2
Katia Labeque-Herbie Hancock
Little Girl Blue | Dreyfus Jazz Line | FDM 36186-2
Kenny Burrell Quartet
Verve Jazz Masters 45:Kenny Burrell | Verve | 527652-2
Blues-The Common Ground | Verve | 589101-2
Kenny Burrell With The Don Sebesky Orchestra
Verve Jazz Masters 45:Kenny Burrell | Verve | 527652-2
Blues-The Common Ground | Verve | 589101-2
Kenny Dorham Quintet
Una Mas | Blue Note | 521228-2
Lee Morgan Orchestra
Standards | Blue Note | 823213-2
Lee Morgan Sextet
Wayne Shorter:The Classic Blue Note Recordings | Blue Note | 540856-2
Search For The New Land | Blue Note | 591896-2
Michael Brecker Group
Don't Try This At Home | Impulse(MCA) | 950114-2
Michael Brecker Quintet
Nearness Of You-The Ballad Book | Verve | 549705-2
Miles Davis Group
Circle In The Round | CBS | 467898-2
In A Silent Way | CBS | 86556-2
Live-Evil | CBS | C2K 65135
On The Corner | CBS | CK 63980
Miles Davis Quintet
Circle In The Round | CBS | 467898-2
The Complete Concert 1964:My Funny Valentine+Four & More | CBS | 471246-2
Highlights From The Plugged Nickel | CBS | 481434-2
Filles De Kilimanjaro | CBS | 86555-2
Miles Davis Quintet 1965-1968 | CBS | C6K 67398
Seven Steps To Heaven | CBS | CK 48827
This Is Jazz:Miles Davis Plays Ballads | CBS | CK 65038
Sorcerer | CBS | CK 65680
Nefertiti | CBS | CK 65681
Miles Smiles | CBS | CK 65682
Miles In The Sky | CBS | CK 65684
E.S.P. | CBS | CK65683
Miles Davis Sextet
Circle In The Round | CBS | 467898-2
Miles In The Sky | CBS | CK 65684
Miles Davis With Gil Evans & His Orchestra
Quiet Nights | CBS | CK 65293
Milt Jackson And His Orchestra
Sunflower | CTI | ZK 65131
Miroslav Vitous Group
Atlantic Jazz: Fusion | Atlantic | 7567-81711-2
Phil Woods Quartet With Orchestra & Strings
Round Trip | Verve | 559804-2
Roland Kirk Quartet
Domino | Verve | 543833-2
Ron Carter Trio
Third Plane | Original Jazz Classics | OJCC20 754-2(M 9105)
Shirley Horn Sextet
Antonio Carlos Jobim And Friends | Verve | 531556-2
Sonny Rollins Quartet
Planet Jazz:Sonny Rollins | Planet Jazz | 2152062-2
The Standard Sonny Rollins | RCA | 2174801-2
Sonny Rollins Sextet
The Standard Sonny Rollins | RCA | 2174801-2
Stan Getz With The Claus Ogerman Orchestra
What The World Needs Now-Stan Getz Plays Bacharach And David | Verve | 557450-2
Stan Getz With The Richard Evans Orchestra
What The World Needs Now-Stan Getz Plays Bacharach And David | Verve | 557450-2
Terri Lyne Carrington Group
Jazz Is A Spirit | ACT | 9408-2
Tony Williams Lifetime
Lifetime | Blue Note | 499004-2
Wayne Shorter Quartet
Herbie Hancock:The Complete Blue Note Sixties Sessions | Blue Note | 495569-2
Kind Of Blue:Blue Note Celebrate The Music Of Miles Davis | Blue Note | 534255-2
Wayne Shorter:The Classic Blue Note Recordings | Blue Note | 540856-2
Adams Apple | Blue Note | 591901-2
Sorcerer | CBS | CK 65680
Wayne Shorter Quintet
Speak No Evil | Blue Note | 499001-2
Wayne Shorter:The Classic Blue Note Recordings | Blue Note | 540856-2
Wayne Shorter Sextet
Wayne Shorter:The Classic Blue Note Recordings | Blue Note | 540856-2
Blue N' Groovy | Blue Note | 780679-2
Wayne Shorter-Herbie Hancock
1+1:Herbie Hancock Wayne Shorter | Verve | 537564-2
Wes Montgomery With The Don Sebesky Orchestra
Wes Montgomery:The Verve Jazz Sides | Verve | 521690-2
Wes Montgomery With The Oliver Nelson Orchestra
Verve Jazz Masters 14:Wes Montgomery | Verve | 519826-2
Wes Montgomery:The Verve Jazz Sides | Verve | 521690-2
Talkin' Jazz:Roots Of Acid Jazz | Verve | 529580-2
Wynton Marsalis Quartet
Wynton Marsalis | CBS | 468708-2
Wynton Marsalis Quintet
Wynton Marsalis | CBS | 468708-2

Handy,Craig | (as,ts,fl,sax,ssbs)
Abdullah Ibrahim Sextet
Mindif | Enja | ENJ-5073 2
Barbara Dennerlein Group
Outhipped | Verve | 547503-2
Essence All Stars
Hot Jazz Bisquits | Hip Bop | HIBD 8801
Michele Rosewoman And Quintessence
Guardians Of The Light | Enja | ENJ-9378 2
Mingus Big Band
Tonight At Noon...Three Or Four Shades Of Love | Dreyfus Jazz Line | FDM 36633-2
Mingus Big Band 93
Nostalgia In Times Square | Dreyfus Jazz Line | FDM 36559-2
New Jazz Composers Octet
Walkin' the Line | Fresh Sound Records | FSNT 151 CD
Steve Coleman And Five Elements
The Sonic Language Of Myth | RCA | 2164123-2

Handy,John | (as,perc,saxello,voc,ts,cldr)
Charles Mingus And His Orchestra
Charles Mingus-Passion Of A Man:The Complete Atlantic Recordings 1956-1961 | Atlantic | 8122-72871-2
Charles Mingus Group
Mingus Ah Um | CBS | CK 65512
Mingus Dynasty | CBS | CK 65513
Charles Mingus Jazz Workshop
Rhino Presents The Atlantic Jazz Gallery | Atlantic | 8122-71257-2
Blues & Roots | Atlantic | 8122-75205-2
Charles Mingus Orchestra
The Very Best Of Charles Mingus | Rhino | 8122-79988-2
Charles Mingus:The Complete 1959 Columbia Recordings | CBS | C3K 65145
Charles Mingus Quintet
Right Now | Original Jazz Classics | OJCCD 237-2
Charles Mingus Septet
Charles Mingus:The Complete 1959 Columbia Recordings | CBS | C3K 65145
John Handy-Ali Akbar Khan Group
Two Originals:Karuna Supreme/Rainbow | MPS | 519195-2
Rainbow
Two Originals:Karuna Supreme/Rainbow | MPS | 519195-2

Handy,W.C. | (arrtalking)
Bessie Smith With The James P.Johnson Orchestra And The Hal Johnson Choir
The Blues | Storyville | 4960323
Louis Armstrong And His All Stars
Louis Armstrong Plays W.C.Handy | CBS | CK 64925

Hanell,Robert | (ld)
Chris Barber's Jazzband & das Große Rundfunkorchester Berlin,DDR
Jazz Zounds: Chris Barber | Zounds | CD 2720007

Hangen,Gesa | (cello)
Ensemble Indigo
Reflection | Enja | ENJ-9417 2

Hängsel,Björn | (b-tbb-tb.tuba)
Tim Hagans With Norrbotten Big Band
Future Miles | ACT | 9235-2

Hanke,Maria | (voc)
Marilyn Mazur With Ars Nova And The Copenhagen Art Ensemble
Jordsange | dacapo | DCCD 9454

Hanlon,Allen | (g)
Louis Armstrong And His Orchestra
What A Wonderful World | MCA | MCD 01876
Miff Mole And His Dixieland Band
Muggsy Spanier-Manhattan Masters,1945 | Storyville | STCD 6051

Hanlon,Bob | (bs,fl,as,ts,vocreeds)
Gunter Hampel New York Orchestra
Fresh Heat-Live At Sweet Basil | Birth | CD 039

Hann,Eberhard | (pan-fl)
Daniel Messina Band
Imagenes | art-mode-records | 990014

Hanna,Jake | (dr)
Allan Vaché-Jim Galloway Sextet
Raisin' The Roof:Allan Vaché Meets Jim Galloway | Nagel-Heyer | CD 054
Benny Carter Sextet
To Bags...With Love:Memorial Album | Pablo | 2310967-2
Milt Jackson Birthday Celebration | Fantasy | FANCD 6079-2
Count Basie Kansas City 7
Count Basie Kansas City 7 | Original Jazz Classics | OJCCD 690-2(2310908)
George Masso Allstars
The Wonderful World Of George Gershwin | Nagel-Heyer | CD 001
One Two Three | Nagel-Heyer | CD 008
The First Sampler | Nagel-Heyer | NHR SP 5
George Masso Quintet
The First Sampler | Nagel-Heyer | NHR SP 5
George Masso Sextet
C'Est Magnifique! | Nagel-Heyer | CD 060
George Masso-Ken Peplowski Quintet
Just Friends | Nagel-Heyer | CD 5001
Kansas City Seven
The J.J.Johnson Memorial Album | Prestige | PRCD 11025-2
Oscar Peterson Trio
Oscar Peterson In Russia | Pablo | 2CD 2625711
Warren Vaché And The New York City All-Star Big Band
Swingtime! | Nagel-Heyer | CD 059
Woody Herman And His Orchestra
Verve Jazz Masters 54:Woody Herman | Verve | 529903-2
Woody Herman-1963 | Philips | 589490-2
Woody Herman And The New Thundering Herd
Planet Jazz:Big Bands | Planet Jazz | 2169649-2
Woody Herman's Thundering Herd
Planet Jazz:Jazz Saxophone | Planet Jazz | 2169653-2

Hanna,Ken | (tp)
Stan Kenton And His Orchestra
Swing Vol.1 | Storyville | 4960343

Hanna,Sir Roland | (el-p,p,celeste,p-solotack-p)
Charles Mingus Group
Mingus Dynasty | CBS | CK 65513
Charles Mingus Orchestra
Charles Mingus:Pre-Bird(Mingus Revisited) | Verve | 538636-2
Charles Mingus:The Complete 1959 Columbia Recordings | CBS | C3K 65145
Eddie Lockjaw Davis Sextet feat. Paul Gonsalves
Planet Jazz:Jazz Saxophone | Planet Jazz | 2169653-2
Frank Vignola Sextet
Off Broadway | Nagel-Heyer | CD 2006
Phil Woods Quartet With Orchestra & Strings
Round Trip | Verve | 559804-2
Roland Hanna Quartet
The Story Of Jazz Piano | Laserlight | 24653
Ron Carter Quartet
Stardust | somethin'else | 537813-2
Ron Carter Quintet
Stardust | somethin'else | 537813-2
Ron Carter Trio
Stardust | somethin'else | 537813-2
Ron Carter-Roland Hanna
Stardust | somethin'else | 537813-2
Sarah Vaughan With The Joe Pass Quartet
Linger Awhile | Pablo | 2312144-2
Joe Pass:Guitar Virtuoso | Pablo | 4 PACD 4423-2
Sarah Vaughan With The Roland Hanna Quartet
Sarah Vaughan Birthday Celebration | Fantasy | FANCD 6090-2
Thad Jones-Mel Lewis Orchestra
The Groove Merchant/The Second Race | Laserlight | 24656
The Basie Alumni
Swinging For The Count | Candid | CCD 79724

Hannan,Nick | (voc)
Clare Teal And Her Band
Orsino's Songs | Candid | CCD 79783

Hanne,Willi | (dr)
Klaus Spencker Trio
Invisible | Jardis Records | JRCD 9409

Hannisdal,Henrik | (v)
Annette Peacock With The Cikada String Quartet
An Acrobat's Heart | ECM | 1733(159496-2)
Arild Andersen Quintet With The Cikada String Quartet
Hyperborean | ECM | 1631(537342-2)
Christof Lauer-Jens Thomas With The Cikada String Quartet
Shadows In The Rain | ACT | 9297-2
Mats Eden-Jonas Simonson With The Cikada String Quartet
Milvus | ECM | 1660
Trygve Seim-Oyvind Braekke-Per Oddvar Johansen Orchestra
The Source And Different Cikadas | ECM | 1764(014432-2)

Hannisdal,Morten | (cello)
Annette Peacock With The Cikada String Quartet
An Acrobat's Heart | ECM | 1733(159496-2)
Arild Andersen Quintet With The Cikada String Quartet
Hyperborean | ECM | 1631(537342-2)
Mats Eden-Jonas Simonson With The Cikada String Quartet
Milvus | ECM | 1660
Trygve Seim Group
Different Rivers | ECM | 1744(159521-2)
Trygve Seim-Oyvind Braekke-Per Oddvar Johansen Orchestra
The Source And Different Cikadas | ECM | 1764(014432-2)

Hannisdal,Odd | (v)
Annette Peacock With The Cikada String Quartet
An Acrobat's Heart | ECM | 1733(159496-2)
Arild Andersen Quintet With The Cikada String Quartet
Hyperborean | ECM | 1631(537342-2)
Christof Lauer-Jens Thomas With The Cikada String Quartet
Shadows In The Rain | ACT | 9297-2
Mats Eden-Jonas Simonson With The Cikada String Quartet
Milvus | ECM | 1660
Trygve Seim-Oyvind Braekke-Per Oddvar Johansen Orchestra
The Source And Different Cikadas | ECM | 1764(014432-2)

Hannisdal,Per | (bassoon)
Terje Rypdal With The Borealis Ensemble
Q.E.D. | ECM | 1474

Hannover,Radio Orchestra | (NDR)
Chet Baker With The Radio Orchestra Hannover(NDR)
My Favourite Songs: The Last Great Concert Vol.1 | Enja | ENJ-5097 2
The Last Concert Vol.I+II | Enja | ENJ-6074 22

Hanschel,Roger | (alto-cl,as,sopranino,alto-fl)
Blaufrontal
Blaufrontal | Jazz Haus Musik | JHM 0037 CD
Blaufrontal With Hank Roberts & Mark Feldman
Bad Times Roll | Jazz Haus Musik | JHM 0061 CD
Dirk Raulf Group
Theater I (Bühnenmusik) | Poise | Poise 07
Gabriele Hasler-Roger Hanschel Duo
Love Songs | Foolish Music | FM 211003
Pigeon | Jazz Haus Musik | JHM 0120 CD
Hanschel-Hübsch-Schipper
Planet Blow Chill | Jazz Haus Musik | JHM 0087 CD
Kölner Saxophon Mafia

INTERPRETENVERZEICHNIS

Saxfiguren | Jazz Haus Musik | JHM 0036 CD
Mafia Years 1982-86 | Jazz Haus Musik | JHM 0058 CD
Go Commercial... | Jazz Haus Musik | JHM 0065 CD
Place For Lovers | Jazz Haus Musik | JHM 0082 CD
Licence To Thrill | Jazz Haus Musik | JHM 0100 CD
Space Player | Jazz Haus Musik | JHM 0132 CD

Kölner Saxophon Mafia With Arno Steffen
Kölner Saxophon Mafia Proudly Presents | Jazz Haus Musik | JHM 0046 CD

Kölner Saxophon Mafia With Bad Little Dynamos
Kölner Saxophon Mafia Proudly Presents | Jazz Haus Musik | JHM 0046 CD

Kölner Saxophon Mafia With Blasorchester Dicke Luft
Kölner Saxophon Mafia Proudly Presents | Jazz Haus Musik | JHM 0046 CD

Kölner Saxophon Mafia With Clarence Barlow
Kölner Saxophon Mafia Proudly Presents | Jazz Haus Musik | JHM 0046 CD

Kölner Saxophon Mafia With Dieter Wellershoff
Kölner Saxophon Mafia Proudly Presents | Jazz Haus Musik | JHM 0046 CD

Kölner Saxophon Mafia With Fleisch
Kölner Saxophon Mafia Proudly Presents | Jazz Haus Musik | JHM 0046 CD

Kölner Saxophon Mafia With Guests
Kölner Saxophon Mafia: 20 Jahre Saxuelle Befreiung | Jazz Haus Musik | JHM 0115 CD

Kölner Saxophon Mafia With Hans Süper
Kölner Saxophon Mafia Proudly Presents | Jazz Haus Musik | JHM 0046 CD

Kölner Saxophon Mafia With Ina Stachelhaus And Erik Schneider
Kölner Saxophon Mafia Proudly Presents | Jazz Haus Musik | JHM 0046 CD

Kölner Saxophon Mafia With Ingo Kümmel And Frank Köllges
Kölner Saxophon Mafia Proudly Presents | Jazz Haus Musik | JHM 0046 CD

Kölner Saxophon Mafia With Irene Lorenz
Kölner Saxophon Mafia Proudly Presents | Jazz Haus Musik | JHM 0046 CD

Kölner Saxophon Mafia With Jacki Liebezeit
Kölner Saxophon Mafia Proudly Presents | Jazz Haus Musik | JHM 0046 CD

Kölner Saxophon Mafia With Klaus Der Geiger
Kölner Saxophon Mafia Proudly Presents | Jazz Haus Musik | JHM 0046 CD

Kölner Saxophon Mafia With Kristina Würminghausen
Kölner Saxophon Mafia Proudly Presents | Jazz Haus Musik | JHM 0046 CD

Kölner Saxophon Mafia With Lydie Auvray
Kölner Saxophon Mafia Proudly Presents | Jazz Haus Musik | JHM 0046 CD

Kölner Saxophon Mafia With Nedim Hazar And Orhan Temur
Kölner Saxophon Mafia Proudly Presents | Jazz Haus Musik | JHM 0046 CD

Kölner Saxophon Mafia With Ramesh Shotham
Kölner Saxophon Mafia Proudly Presents | Jazz Haus Musik | JHM 0046 CD

Kölner Saxophon Mafia With Rick E. Loef
Kölner Saxophon Mafia Proudly Presents | Jazz Haus Musik | JHM 0046 CD

Kölner Saxophon Mafia With The Auryn Quartet
Kölner Saxophon Mafia Proudly Presents | Jazz Haus Musik | JHM 0046 CD

Kölner Saxophon Mafia With Triviatas(1.Schwuler Männerchor Köln)
Kölner Saxophon Mafia Proudly Presents | Jazz Haus Musik | JHM 0046 CD

Kölner Saxophon Mafia With V.Nick Nikitakis
Kölner Saxophon Mafia Proudly Presents | Jazz Haus Musik | JHM 0046 CD

Kölner Saxophon Mafia With Willie Gräff
Kölner Saxophon Mafia Proudly Presents | Jazz Haus Musik | JHM 0046 CD

Planet Blow
Alien Lunatic | Jazz Haus Musik | JHM 0071 CD

Roger Hanschel/Gabriele Hasler
Go In Green | Jazz Haus Musik | JHM 0073 CD

Hansen,Claus K. | (voc)
Marilyn Mazur With Ars Nova And The Copenhagen Art Ensemble
Jordsange | dacapo | DCCD 9454

Hansen,Finn Otto | (cotp)
Papa Benny's Jazzband
The Golden Years Of Revival Jazz,Vol.2 | Storyville | STCD 5507
The Golden Years Of Revival Jazz,Vol.12 | Storyville | STCD 5517
Papa Bue's Viking Jazzband
The Golden Years Of Revival Jazz,Sampler | Storyville | 109 1001
The Golden Years Of Revival Jazz,Vol.1 | Storyville | STCD 5506
The Golden Years Of Revival Jazz,Vol.3 | Storyville | STCD 5508
The Golden Years Of Revival Jazz,Vol.5 | Storyville | STCD 5510
The Golden Years Of Revival Jazz,Vol.7 | Storyville | STCD 5512
The Golden Years Of Revival Jazz,Vol.9 | Storyville | STCD 5514
The Golden Years Of Revival Jazz,Vol.10 | Storyville | STCD 5515
The Golden Years Of Revival Jazz,Vol.11 | Storyville | STCD 5516
The Golden Years Of Revival Jazz,Vol.12 | Storyville | STCD 5517
The Golden Years Of Revival Jazz,Vol.13 | Storyville | STCD 5518
The Golden Years Of Revival Jazz,Vol.14 | Storyville | STCD 5519
The Golden Years Of Revibal Jazz,Vol.15 | Storyville | STCD 5520

Hansen,Frans | (perc)
Chinese Compass
Chinese Compass | dacapo | DCCD 9443

Hansen,Hans Borge | (tp)
Bohana Jazzband
The Golden Years Of Revival Jazz,Vol.6 | Storyville | STCD 5511
The Golden Years Of Revival Jazz,Vol.10 | Storyville | STCD 5515
Henrik Johansen's Jazzband
The Golden Years Of Revival Jazz,Vol.14 | Storyville | STCD 5519

Hansen,Hans J. | (clas)
Leonardo Pedersen's Jazzkapel
The Golden Years Of Revival Jazz,Sampler | Storyville | 109 1001
The Golden Years Of Revival Jazz,Vol.11 | Storyville | STCD 5516

Hansen,Helmuth Hjort | (tb)
Stan Kenton With The Danish Radio Big Band
Stan Kenton With The Danish Radio Big Band | Storyville | STCD 8340

Hansen,Ivan | (gangsa,gongvoc)
Marilyn Mazur With Ars Nova And The Copenhagen Art Ensemble
Jordsange | dacapo | DCCD 9454

Hansen,Morten | (b)
Earl Hines Trio
Earl Hines Live! | Storyville | STCD 8222

Hansen,Niels Richard | (bj)
Bohana Jazzband
The Golden Years Of Revival Jazz,Vol.6 | Storyville | STCD 5511
The Golden Years Of Revival Jazz,Vol.10 | Storyville | STCD 5515
Papa Benny's Jazzband
The Golden Years Of Revival Jazz,Vol.12 | Storyville | STCD 5517
Ricardo's Jazzmen
The Golden Years Of Revival Jazz,Sampler | Storyville | 109 1001

Hansen,Ole | (tb)
Sonny Criss Quintet
Sonny Criss Quartet Feat. Wynton Kelly | Fresh Sound Records | FSR-CD 318

Hansen,Ole Kock | (arr,keyboards,ld,p,el-psynth)
Ben Webster Quartet
My Man-Live At The Montmartre | Steeplechase | SCCD 31008
Miles Davis With The Danish Radio Big Band
Aura | CBS | CK 63962
Mona Larsen And The Danish Radio Big Band Plus Soloists
Michael Mantler:Cerco Un Paese Innocente | ECM | 1556
Philip Catherine/Niels-Henning Orsted-Pedersen With The Royal Copenhagen Chamber Orchestra
Spanish Nights | Enja | ENJ-7023 2
Stan Getz With The Danish Radio Big Band
Stan Getz In Europe | Laserlight | 24657
The Danish Radio Big Band
Aura | CBS | CK 63962

Hansen,Randy | (g)
Herbie Hancock Group
Monster | CBS | 486571-2

Hansen,Ricardo | (bj)
Ricardo's Jazzmen
The Golden Years Of Revival Jazz,Vol.4 | Storyville | STCD 5509
The Golden Years Of Revival Jazz,Vol.5 | Storyville | STCD 5510

Hansen,Simon S. | (fl,sax,african-flbass-fl)
Nguyen Le Group
Tales From Viet-Nam | ACT | 9225-2

Hansen,Steen | (tb)
Jens Winther And The Danish Radio Jazz Orchestra
Angels | dacapo | DCCD 9442
Mona Larsen And The Danish Radio Big Band Plus Soloists
Michael Mantler:Cerco Un Paese Innocente | ECM | 1556
The Danish Radio Jazz Orchestra
This Train:The Danish Radio Jazz Orchestra Plays The Music Of Ray Pitts | dacapo | DCCD 9428
Nice Work | dacapo | DCCD 9446

Hansen,Steen Vig | (ssts)
Arne Birger's Jazzsjak
The Golden Years Of Revival Jazz,Vol.8 | Storyville | STCD 5513
The Golden Years Of Revival Jazz,Vol.10 | Storyville | STCD 5515

Hanson,Bengt | (b)
Knud Jorgensen-Bengt Hanson
Skiss | Touché Music | TMcCD 001
Bojangles | Touché Music | TMcCD 002
Knud Jorgensen-Bengt Hanson-Gustavo Bergalli
Skiss | Touché Music | TMcCD 001
Day Dream | Touché Music | TMcCD 003

Hanzer,Boris | (recordingsound-effects)
Sotto In Su
Südamerika Sept. 90 | Jazz Haus Musik | JHM 0051 CD

Harari,Vened | (voc)
International Commission For The Prevention Of Musical Border Control,The
The International Commission For The Prevention Of Musical Border Control | VeraBra Records | CDVBR 2093-2

Hard,Warren | (perc)
Louis Armstrong And His Orchestra
What A Wonderful World | MCA | MCD 01876

Hardee,John | (ts)
John Hardee Sextet
The Blue Note Swingtets | Blue Note | 495697-2
John Hardee Swingtet
The Blue Note Swingtets | Blue Note | 495697-2
Tiny Grimes Swingtet
The Blue Note Swingtets | Blue Note | 495697-2

Harden,Wilbur | (fl-h,balloontp)
John Coltrane Quintet
John Coltrane-The Prestige Recordings | Prestige | 16 PCD 4405-2
Standard Coltrane | Original Jazz Classics | OJCCD 246-2
Bahia | Original Jazz Classics | OJCCD 415-2
Stardust | Original Jazz Classics | OJCCD 920-2(P 7268)
Wilbur Harden Quintet
The Art Of Saxophone | Laserlight | 24652
Yusef Lateef Quintet
Other Sounds | Original Jazz Classics | OJCCD 399-2(NJ 8218)

Harding,Al | (ts)
Anita O'Day With The Jimmy Giuffre Orchestra
Verve Jazz Masters 49:Anita O'Day | Verve | 527653-2

Harding,Buster | (arr,ld,pvoc)
Artie Shaw And His Orchestra
Planet Jazz:Jazz Trumpet | Planet Jazz | 2169654-2
Benny Goodman And His Orchestra
Charlie Christian:Swing To Bop | Dreyfus Jazz Line | FDM 36715-2
Stan Getz Quintet
Stan Getz-The Complete Roost Sessions | EMI Records | 859622-2

Hardman,Bill | (tp,fl-hperc)
Art Blakey And The Jazz Messengers
Planet Jazz:Art Blakey | Planet Jazz | 2152066-2
Planet Jazz Sampler | Planet Jazz | 2152326-2
A Night In Tunisia | RCA | 2663896-2
Art Blakey And The Jazz Messengers With Thelonious Monk
Art Blakey's Jazz Messengers With Thelonious Monk | Atlantic | 7567-81332-2
Eddie Jefferson And His Band
Dexter Gordon Birthday Celebration | Fantasy | FANCD 6082-2
Lou Donaldson Quintet
Blue Note Plays Gershwin | Blue Note | 520808-2
Mal Waldron Sextet
John Coltrane-The Prestige Recordings | Prestige | 16 PCD 4405-2
The Mal Waldron Memorial Album:Soul Eyes | Prestige | PRCD 11024-2

Hardwicke,Otto | (as,bass-s,bs,v,cl,ss,reedsts)
Duke Ellington And His Famous Orchestra
Duke Ellington:The Blanton-Webster Band | Bluebird | 21 13181-2
Planet Jazz:Duke Ellington | Planet Jazz | 2152053-2
Planet Jazz:Johnny Hodges | Planet Jazz | 2152065-2
Planet Jazz Sampler | Planet Jazz | 2152326-2
Planet Jazz:Ben Webster | RCA | 2165368-2
Planet Jazz:Big Bands | Planet Jazz | 2169649-2
Planet Jazz:Jazz Trumpet | Planet Jazz | 2169654-2
Planet Jazz:Female Jazz Vocalists | Planet Jazz | 2169656-2
Highlights From The Duke Ellington Centennial Edition | RCA | 2663672-2
Greatest Hits | CBS | 462959-2
Jazz:The Essential Collection Vol.2 | IN+OUT Records | 78012-2
Jazz:The Essential Collection Vol.3 | IN+OUT Records | 78013-2
Duke Ellington:Ko-Ko | Dreyfus Jazz Line | FDM 36717-2
Duke Ellington And His Kentucky Club Orchestra
Jazz:The Essential Collection Vol.2 | IN+OUT Records | 78012-2
Duke Ellington And His Orchestra
Planet Jazz:Duke Ellington | Planet Jazz | 2152053-2
Planet Jazz:Jazz Greatest Hits | Planet Jazz | 2169648-2
Highlights From The Duke Ellington Centennial Edition | RCA | 2663672-2
Carnegie Hall Concert December 1944 | Prestige | 2PCD 24073-2
Carnegie Hall Concert January 1946 | Prestige | 2PCD 24074-2
Carnegie Hall Concert January 1943 | Prestige | 2PCD 34004-2
Jazz:The Essential Collection Vol.2 | IN+OUT Records | 78012-2
Jazz:The Essential Collection Vol.3 | IN+OUT Records | 78013-2
The Duke At Fargo 1940 | Storyville | STCD 8316/17
Fats Waller And His Buddies
Planet Jazz:Jack Teagarden | Planet Jazz | 2161236-2
Jimmy Hamilton And The Duke's Men
The Blue Note Swingtets | Blue Note | 495697-2

Hardy,Earl | (tb)
Coleman Hawkins And His Orchestra
Planet Jazz:Coleman Hawkins | Planet Jazz | 2152055-2
Planet Jazz Sampler | Planet Jazz | 2152326-2
Planet Jazz:Jazz Greatest Hits | Planet Jazz | 2169648-2
Jazz:The Essential Collection Vol.3 | IN+OUT Records | 78013-2

Hardy,Hagood | (vib)
Herbie Mann Group
The Best Of Herbie Mann | Atlantic | 7567-81369-2
Rhino Presents The Atlantic Jazz Gallery | Atlantic | 8122-71257-2
Herbie Mann Septet
Herbie Mann At The Village Gate | Atlantic | 7567-81350-2
Herbie Mann Sextet
Herbie Mann At The Village Gate | Atlantic | 7567-81350-2

Hare,Pat | (g)
Walter Horton Band
Joe Hill Louis: The Be-Bop Boy | Bear Family Records | BCD 15524 AH

Harewood,Al | (dr)
Ahmed Abdul-Malik Orchestra
Planet Jazz:Lee Morgan | Planet Jazz | 2161238-2
Ahmed Abdul-Malik's Middle-Eastern Music
Jazz Sahara | Original Jazz Classics | OJCCD 1820-2(R 12-287)
Booker Ervin Quartet
That's It | Candid | CCD 79014
Dexter Gordon Quintet
Doin' Allright | Blue Note | 784077-2
Dexter Gordon:Ballads | Blue Note | 796579-2
Jazz Profile:Dexter Gordon | Blue Note | 823514-2
Dodo Greene With The Ike Quebec Quintet
Misty Blue:Sweet Sisters Swing Songs Of Sorrow And Sadness | Blue Note | 521151-2
Grant Green Quartet
Ballads | Blue Note | 537560-2
Grantstand | Blue Note | 591723-2
Grant Green Sextet
Idle Moments | Blue Note | 499003-2
Grant Green Trio
Standards | Blue Note | 821284-2
Horace Parlan Quartet
Blue Bossa | Blue Note | 795590-2
Horace Parlan Quintet
The Best Of Blue Note Vol.2 | Blue Note | 797960-2
Horace Parlan Trio
Movin' And Groovin' | Blue Note | 0677187
J.J.Johnson-Kai Winding Quintet (Jay&Kai)
The J.J.Johnson Memorial Album | Prestige | PRCD 11025-2
Lisle Atkinson Quartet
Bass Contra Bass | Storyville | STCD 8270
Lisle Atkinson Quintet
Bass Contra Bass | Storyville | STCD 8270
Lou Donaldson Quintet
Blue Note Plays Gershwin | Blue Note | 520808-2
Stanley Turrentine Quintet
Never Let Me Go | Blue Note | 576750-2

Hargrove,Roy | (fl-h,tptp-solo)
Abbey Lincoln With The Rodney Kendrick Trio And Guests
A Turtle's Dream | Verve | 527382-2
Barbara Dennerlein Group
Take Off | Verve | 527664-2
Christian McBride Group
Gettin' To It | Verve | 523989-2
Directions In Music
Live at Massey Hall:Celebrating Miles Davis & John Coltrane | Verve | 589654-2
Jimmy Smith Sextet
Angel Eyes-Ballads & Slow Jams | Verve | 527632-2
Nicholas Payton Quintet
Payton's Place | Verve | 557327-2
Nicholas Payton Sextet
Payton's Place | Verve | 557327-2
Nils Landgren Funk Unit With Guests
5000 Miles | ACT | 9271-2
Roy Hargrove
Parker's Mood | Verve | 527907-2
Roy Hargrove Quartet
Family | Verve | 527630-2
Roy Hargrove Quintet
Planet Jazz:Jazz Trumpet | Planet Jazz | 2169654-2
Roy Hargrove Quintet With The Tenors Of Our Time | Verve | 523019-2
Family | Verve | 527630-2
Roy Hargrove Quintet With Branford Marsalis
Roy Hargrove Quintet With The Tenors Of Our Time | Verve | 523019-2
Roy Hargrove Quintet With Joe Henderson
Roy Hargrove Quintet With The Tenors Of Our Time | Verve | 523019-2
Roy Hargrove Quintet With Johnny Griffin
Roy Hargrove Quintet With The Tenors Of Our Time | Verve | 523019-2
Roy Hargrove Quintet With Joshua Redman
Roy Hargrove Quintet With The Tenors Of Our Time | Verve | 523019-2
Roy Hargrove Quintet With Stanley Turrentine
Roy Hargrove Quintet With The Tenors Of Our Time | Verve | 523019-2
Roy Hargrove Sextet
Family | Verve | 527630-2
Roy Hargrove Trio
Parker's Mood | Verve | 527907-2
Roy Hargrove-Christian McBride
Parker's Mood | Verve | 527907-2
Roy Hargrove's Crisol
Habana | Verve | 537563-2
Roy Hargrove-Stephen Scott
Parker's Mood | Verve | 527907-2
Roy Hargrove-Walter Booker
Family | Verve | 527630-2
Roy Haynes Quintet
Birds Of A Feather:A Tribute To Charlie Parker | Dreyfus Jazz Line | FDM 36625-2
Shirley Horn And Her Quartet
May The Music Never End | Verve | 076028-2
Shirley Horn Quartet
The Main Ingredient | Verve | 529555-2
Sonny Rollins Quintet
Here's To The People | Milestone | MCD 9194-2
The Dave Glasser/Clark Terry/Barry Harris Project
Uh! Oh! | Nagel-Heyer | CD 2003

Harich,Matthias | (tpfl-h)
Jürgen Knieper Quintet
State Of Things | Jazz Haus Musik | JHM 0104 CD

Harland,Eric | (dr)
Greg Osby Quintet
Inner Circle | Blue Note | 499871-2
Greg Tardy Band
Serendipity | Impulse(MCA) | 951258-2
Jacky Terrasson Trio
Smile | Blue Note | 542413-2
Kenny Garrett Quartet
KG Standard Of Language | Warner | 9362-48404-2
Stefon Harris Group
Black Action Figure | Blue Note | 499546-2

Harley,Rufus | (bagpipesss)
Sonny Rollins Sextet With Rufus Harley
The Cutting Edge | Original Jazz Classics | OJC 468(M 9059)

Harmon,Bob | (tp)
Don Ellis Orchestra
Electric Bath | CBS | CK 65522

Harmonizing Four,The |
Sister Rosetta Tharpe And Her Group With The Harmonizing Four
Gospel Train | Mercury | 841134-2

Harp,Everett | (as,ssts)
Marcus Miller Group
The Sun Don't Lie | Dreyfus Jazz Line | FDM 36560-2
Live & More | Dreyfus Jazz Line | FDM 36585-2

Harper,Arthur | (b)
Shirley Scott Quintet
A Wakin' Thing | Candid | CCD 79719
Shirley Scott Trio
Skylark | Candid | CCD 79705

Harper,Billy | (cl,ts,fl,ss,as,sax,cowbellvoc)
Charles Earland Orchestra
Charlie's Greatest Hits | Prestige | PCD 24250-2
Gil Evans Orchestra
There Comes A Time | RCA | 2131392-2
PLay The Music Of Jimi Hendrix | RCA | 2663872-2
Svengali | Rhino | 8122-73720-2

Blues In Orbit | Enja | ENJ-3069 2
Klaus Weiss Septet
All Night Through | ATM Records | ATM 3816 AH
Klaus Weiss Sextet
All Night Through | ATM Records | ATM 3816 AH
Lee Morgan Orchestra
The Last Sessin | Blue Note | 493401-2
Louis Armstrong And His Friends
Louis Armstrong And His Friends | Bluebird | 2663961-2
Max Roach Sextet With The J.C.White Singers
Lift Every Voice And Sing | Atlantic | 7567-80798-2
McCoy Tyner Big Band
The Best Of McCoy Tyner Big Band | Dreyfus Jazz Line | FDM 37012-2
Thad Jones-Mel Lewis Orchestra
The Groove Merchant/The Second Race | Laserlight | 24656

Harper,George | (saxts)
Buddy Childers Big Band
It's What Happening Now! | Candid | CCD 79749

Harper,Herbie | (tbld)
Benny Carter And His Orchestra
Aspects | Capitol | 852677-2
Harry James And His Orchestra
Trumpet Blues:The Best Of Harry James | Capitol | 521224-2
Herbie Harper Quartet
The Complete Nocturne Recordings:Jazz In Hollywood Series Vol.1 | Fresh Sound Records | NR 3CD-101
Herbie Harper Quintet
The Complete Nocturne Recordings:Jazz In Hollywood Series Vol.1 | Fresh Sound Records | NR 3CD-101
June Christy With The Pete Rugolo Orchestra
Something Cool(The Complete Mono & Stereo Versions) | Capitol | 534069-2
Maynard Ferguson Band
Verve Jazz Masters 52:Maynard Ferguson | Verve | 529905-2
Nat King Cole Quartet With The Stan Kenton Orchestra
Nat King Cole:For Sentimental Reasons | Dreyfus Jazz Line | FDM 36740-2
Stan Kenton And His Orchestra
Stan Kenton Portraits On Standards | Capitol | 531571-2

Harper,Lee | (fl-htp)
Jörg Seidel Group
I Feel So Smoochie: A Tribute To Nat King Cole | Edition Collage | EC 532-2
Ray Charles And His Orchestra
Ray Charles At Newport | Atlantic | 7567-80765-2
Ray Charles Sextet With The Raylets
Newport Jazz Festival 1958,July 3rd-6th Vol.4:Blues In The Night No.2 | Phontastic | NCD 8816

Harper,Phillip | (fl-htp)
Amanda Sedgwick Quintet
Reunion | Touché Music | TMcCD 021

Harper,Rick | (tpvoc)
Buddy Johnson And His Orchestra
Buddy And Ella Johnson 1953-1964 | Bear Family Records | BCD 15479 DH

Harper,Winard | (dr,perc,jimbé-drsit-dr)
Wycliffe Gordon Group
The Search | Nagel-Heyer | CD 2007

Harrell,Tom | (fl-h,fl-h-solo,tpp)
Charlie Haden And The Liberation Music Orchestra
The Montreal Tapes:Liberation Music Orchestra | Verve | 527469-2
Fleurine With Band And Horn Section
Meant To Be! | EmArCy | 159085-2
George Gruntz Concert Jazz Band '83
Theatre | ECM | 1265
George Robert-Tom Harrell Quintet
Visions | Contemporary | CCD 14063-2
Greg Tardy Band
Serendipity | Impulse(MCA) | 951258-2
Horace Silver Quintet
Horace Silver Retrospective | Blue Note | 495576-2
Horace Silver Quintet With Brass
Horace Silver Retrospective | Blue Note | 495576-2
Horace Silver Quintet With Vocals
Horace Silver Retrospective | Blue Note | 495576-2
Joe Lovano Quartet
Live At The Village Vanguard | Blue Note | 829125-2
Martin Schrack Quintet feat.Tom Harrell
Headin' Home | Storyville | STCD 4253
Steve Swallow Group
Real Book | Watt | XtraWatt/7(521637-2)
Tom Harrell Group
Paradise | RCA | 2663738-2
Tom Harrell Orchestra
Time's Mirror | RCA | 2663524-2
Tom Harrell Quintet
Live At The Village Vanguard | RCA | 2663910-2
Form | Contemporary | CCD 14059-2
Visions | Contemporary | CCD 14063-2
Sail Away | Original Jazz Classics | OJCCD 1095-2(C- 14054-2)
Tom Harrell Sextet
Visions | Contemporary | CCD 14063-2
Sail Away | Original Jazz Classics | OJCCD 1095-2(C- 14054-2)
Tom Harrell With The Mulgrew Miller Trio
Trumpet Legacy | Milestone | MCD 9286-2
Tom Harrell-Xavier Davis Duo
Live At The Village Vanguard | RCA | 2663910-2
Vince Guaraldi Group
Charlie Brown's Holiday Hits | Fantasy | FCD 9682-2
Woody Herman And His Orchestra
Brand New | Original Jazz Classics | OJCCD 1044-2(F 8414)

Harrell,Vivian | (voc)
Eddie Harris Group
The Best Of Eddie Harris | Atlantic | 7567-81370-2

Harrell,Ziggy | (tp)
Woody Herman And His Orchestra
Verve Jazz Masters 54:Woody Herman | Verve | 529903-2
Woody Herman-1963 | Philips | 589490-2

Harriman,Paul | (b)
Acoustic Alchemy
Against The Grain | GRP | GRP 97832
Katie Kern Group
Still Young | Jazzpoint | JP 1070 CD

Harrington,David | (v)
John Zorn Group With The Kronos Quartet
Spillane | Nonesuch | 7559-79172-2

Harrington,Jan | (ldvoc)
Jan Harrington And Friends
I Feel The Spirit | Nagel-Heyer | NHR SP 7
Jan Harrington Band
Christmas-Jazz! | Nagel-Heyer | NH 1008
Jan Harrington Sextet
Jan Harrington's Christmas In New Orleans | Nagel-Heyer | NHR SP 4
Jan Harrington With The Arthur Blythe Quartet
Remembering Dinah-A Salute To Dinah Washington | Hot Shot Records | HSR 8313-2
Jan Harrington With The Mike Hennesey Trio
Remembering Dinah-A Salute To Dinah Washington | Hot Shot Records | HSR 8313-2
Jan Harrington With The Nat Adderley Quintet
Remembering Dinah-A Salute To Dinah Washington | Hot Shot Records | HSR 8313-2

Harriott,Joe | (as)
Joe Harriott Quintet
Free Form | EmArCy | 538184-2

Harris Jr.,John | (dr)
Horace Silver Quintet
The Tokyo Blues | Blue Note | 853355-2

Harris,Arville | (as,clts)
Cab Calloway And His Orchestra
Planet Jazz:Cab Calloway | Planet Jazz | 2161237-2

Harris,Barry | (p,p-solotack-p)
Art Farmer Quartet
Plays The Arrangements And Compositions Of Gigi Gryce And Quincy Jones | Original Jazz Classics | OJCCD 054-2
Barry Harris Quintet
Never Than New | Original Jazz Classics | OJCCD 1062-2(RLP 9413)
Barry Harris Sextet
Bull's Eye! | Original Jazz Classics | OJCCD 1082-2(P 7600)
Barry Harris Trio
Magnificent! | Original Jazz Classics | OJCCD 1026-2(P 7733)
Bull's Eye! | Original Jazz Classics | OJCCD 1082-2(P 7600)
Cannonball Adderley Quartet
Ballads | Blue Note | 537563-2
Cannonball Adderley Quintet
Them Dirty Blues | Blue Note | 495447-2
Them Dirty Blues | Capitol | 495447-2
Them Dirty Blues | Blue Note | 495447-2
Carmel Jones Quartet
Jay Hawk Talk | Original Jazz Classics | OJCCD 1938-2(P7401)
Carmel Jones Quintet
Jay Hawk Talk | Original Jazz Classics | OJCCD 1938-2(P7401)
Charles McPherson Quartet
Jazzin' Vol.2: The Music Of Stevie Wonder | Fantasy | FANCD 6088-2
McPherson's Mood | Original Jazz Classics | OJCCD 1947-2(PR 7743)
Charles McPherson Quintet
The Jazz Giants Play Rodgers & Hammerstein:My Favorite Things | Prestige | PCD 24223-2
Charlie Byrd Quartet
Blues Sonata | Original Jazz Classics | OJC20 1063(RS 9453)
Coleman Hawkins Quartet
Jazz Dance | Original Jazz Classics | OJCCD 1002-2(1210890)
Sirius | Original Jazz Classics | OJCCD 861-2(2310707)
Dave Pike Quartet
It's Time For Dave Pike | Original Jazz Classics | OJCCD 1951-2(RLP 9360)
Dexter Gordon Quartet
Dexter Gordon Birthday Celebration | Fantasy | FANCD 6082-2
More Power | Original Jazz Classics | OJC20 815-2(P 7680)
Tower Of Power | Original Jazz Classics | OJCCD 299-2(P 7623)
Dexter Gordon Quintet
Dexter Gordon:Ballads | Blue Note | 796579-2
Jazz Profile:Dexter Gordon | Blue Note | 823514-2
Tower Of Power | Original Jazz Classics | OJCCD 299-2(P 7623)
Dexter Gordon-James Moody Quintet
More Power | Original Jazz Classics | OJC20 815-2(P 7680)
Don Wilkerson Quartet
The Texas Twister | Original Jazz Classics | OJCCD 1950-2(RLP 1186)
Don Wilkerson Quintet
The Texas Twister | Original Jazz Classics | OJCCD 1950-2(RLP 1186)
Eddie Jefferson And His Band
Dexter Gordon Birthday Celebration | Fantasy | FANCD 6082-2
Eddie Jefferson With The James Moody Quintet
Body And Soul | Original Jazz Classics | OJCCD 396-2(P 7619)
Hank Mobley Quintet
The Art Of Saxophone | Laserlight | 24652
The Tumaround | Blue Note | 524540-2
Harold Land Sextet
Wes Montgomery-The Complete Riverside Recordings | Riverside | 12 RCD 4408-2
Johnny Griffin Quartet
The Kerry Dancers | Original Jazz Classics | OJCCD 1952-2(RLP 9420)
Lee Konitz Quartet
Lullaby Of Birdland | Candid | CCD 79709
Lee Morgan Quintet
The Sidewinder | Blue Note | 495332-2
Blue N' Groovy | Blue Note | 780679-2
The Best Of Blue Note | Blue Note | 796110-2
Take Twelve | Original Jazz Classics | OJCCD 310-2
Sal Nistico Quartet
Heavyweights | Milestone | MCD 47096-2
Sal Nistico Quintet
Heavyweights | Milestone | MCD 47096-2
Sonny Red (Kyner) Quartet
Red,Blue & Green | Milestone | MCD 47086-2
Sonny Red (Kyner) Quintet
Red,Blue & Green | Milestone | MCD 47086-2
The Dave Glasser/Clark Terry/Barry Harris Project
Uh! Oh! | Nagel-Heyer | CD 2003
Blues Of Summer | Nagel-Heyer | NH 1011
Yusef Lateef Orchestra
The Centaur And The Phoenix | Original Jazz Classics | OJCCD 721-2(RLP 9337)
Yusef Lateef Quartet
Eastern Sounds | Original Jazz Classics | OJC20 612-2(P 7319)
Into Something | Original Jazz Classics | OJCCD 700-2(NJ 8272)
Yusef Lateef Sextet
The Art Of Saxophone | Laserlight | 24652

Harris,Beaver | (dr,tambourinevoc)
Albert Ayler Group
Albert Ayler Live In Greenwich Village:The Complete Impulse Recordings | Impulse(MCA) | IMP 22732
Albert Ayler Sextet
Albert Ayler Live In Greenwich Village:The Complete Impulse Recordings | Impulse(MCA) | IMP 22732
Archie Shepp Orchestra
Mama Too Tight | Impulse(MCA) | 951248-2
The Cry Of My People | Impulse(MCA) | 9861488
Archie Shepp Septet
The Way Ahead | Impulse(MCA) | 951272-2
Archie Shepp Sextet
The Way Ahead | Impulse(MCA) | 951272-2
Beaver Harris
African Drums | Owl Records | 018356-2
Beaver Harris & Davis S.Ware
African Drums | Owl Records | 018356-2
Gato Barbieri Sextet
The Third World | RCA | 2179617-2
Roswell Rudd Sextet
Mixed | Impulse(MCA) | IMP 12702
The Jazz Composer's Orchestra
Comminications | JCOA | 1001/2

Harris,Benny | (tp)
Bud Powell Orchestra
Bebop | Pablo | PACD 2310978-2
Charlie Parker Quintet
Bird: The Complete Charlie Parker On Verve | Verve | 837141-2
Charlie Parker Septet
Talkin' Bird | Verve | 559859-2
Charlie Parker Sextet
Verve Jazz Masters 28:Charlie Parker Plays Standards | Verve | 521854-2
Coleman Hawkins All Star Octet
Body And Soul Revisited | GRP | GRP 16272
Dizzy Gillespie And His Orchestra
Planet Jazz:Dizzy Gillespie | Planet Jazz | 2152069-2
Planet Jazz:Bebop | RCA | 2169650-2
Earl Hines And His Orchestra
Planet Jazz:Earl Hines | Planet Jazz | 2159973-2

Harris,Bill | (tbtp)
Benny Goodman And His Orchestra
The Legends Of Swing | Laserlight | 24659
Charlie Parker And His Orchestra
The Cole Porter Songbook | Verve | 823250-2
Bird: The Complete Charlie Parker On Verve | Verve | 837141-2
Charlie Parker With Orchestra
Charlie Parker:The Best Of The Verve Years | Verve | 527815-2
Charlie Parker With Strings
Charlie Parker With Strings:The Master Takes | Verve | 523984-2
Bird: The Complete Charlie Parker On Verve | Verve | 837141-2
Charlie Parker With The Joe Lipman Orchestra
Verve Jazz Masters 28:Charlie Parker Plays Standards | Verve | 521854-2
Charlie Parker Big Band | Verve | 559835-2
Charlie Parker With The Neal Hefti Orchestra
Charlie Parker:The Best Of The Verve Years | Verve | 527815-2
Bird: The Complete Charlie Parker On Verve | Verve | 837141-2
JATP All Stars
JATP In Tokyo | Pablo | 2620104-2
The Complete Jazz At The Philharmonic On Verve 1944-1949 | Verve | 523893-2
Jazz At The Philharmonic:Best Of The 1940's Concerts | Verve | 557534-2
Welcome To Jazz At The Philharmonic | Fantasy | FANCD 6081-2
Norman Granz Jam Session
Verve Jazz Masters 26:Lionel Hampton with Oscar Peterson | Verve | 521853-2
Verve Jazz Masters Vol.60:The Collection | Verve | 529866-2
Woody Herman And His Orchestra
The Legends Of Swing | Laserlight | 24659
Songs For Hip Lovers | Verve | 559872-2
Woody Herman:Four Brother | Dreyfus Jazz Line | FDM 36722-2
Louis Armstrong-Jack Teagarden-Woody Herman:Midnights At V-Disc | Jazz Unlimited | JUCD 2048
Old Gold Rehearsals 1944 | Jazz Unlimited | JUCD 2079
Woody Herman And His Woodshoppers
Woody Herman (And The Herd) At Carnegie Hall | Verve | 559833-2
Woody Herman And The Herd
Woody Herman (And The Herd) At Carnegie Hall | Verve | 559833-2
Woody Herman And The Vanderbilt All Stars
Louis Armstrong-Jack Teagarden-Woody Herman:Midnights At V-Disc | Jazz Unlimited | JUCD 2048

Harris,Charles | (b,ptb)
Lionel Hampton And His Orchestra
Lionel Hampton:Flying Home | Dreyfus Jazz Line | FDM 36735-2
Lionel Hampton And His Septet
Lionel Hampton:Flying Home | Dreyfus Jazz Line | FDM 36735-2
Nat King Cole Quartet
Penthouse Serenade | Capitol | 494504-2
Nat King Cole Quintet
Penthouse Serenade | Capitol | 494504-2
After Midnight | Capitol | 520087-2
Nat King Cole Sextet
After Midnight | Capitol | 520087-2
Nat King Cole Trio
Penthouse Serenade | Capitol | 494504-2

Harris,Chuck | (tb)
Elliot Lawrence And His Orchestra
Mullenium | CBS | CK 65678

Harris,Corey | (gvoc)
Corey Harris
Betwen Midnight And Day | Alligator Records | ALCD 4837

Harris,Craig | (synclavier,tambourine,tb,bamboo-fl)
Cold Sweat
Cold Sweat Plays J.B. | JMT Edition | 919025-2
Craig Harris And Tailgater's Tales
Shelter | JMT Edition | 919008-2
Blackout In The Square Root Of Soul | JMT Edition | 919015-2
Lester Bowie's Brass Fantasy
I Only Have Eyes For You | ECM | 1296(825902-2)

Harris,Douglas | (fl,as,ssts)
McCoy Tyner Big Band
The Best Of McCoy Tyner Big Band | Dreyfus Jazz Line | FDM 37012-2
Mongo Santamaria And His Band
Montreux Heat! | Pablo | PACD 5317-2
Mongo Santamaria Group With Dizzy Gillespie And Toots Thielemans
Summertime-Digital At Montreux 1980 | Original Jazz Classics | OJCCD 626-2(2308229)
Montreux Heat! | Pablo | PACD 5317-2

Harris,Eddie | (as,ts,el-p,clavinet,el-sax,voc)
Bernard Purdie's Soul To Jazz
Bernard Purdie's Soul To Jazz | ACT | 9242-2
Eddie Harris Group
Here Comes The Judge | CBS | 492533-2
The Best Of Eddie Harris | Atlantic | 7567-81370-2
Eddie Harris Group With The WDR Big Band
Eddie Harris-The Last Concert | ACT | 9249-2
Eddie Harris Quartet
The Best Of Eddie Harris | Atlantic | 7567-81370-2
There Was A Time-Echo Of Harlem | Enja | ENJ-6068 2
Eddie Harris Quintet
The Best Of Eddie Harris | Atlantic | 7567-81370-2
Atlantic Saxophones | Rhino | 8122-71256-2
Jimmy Smith-Eddie Harris Trio
All The Way | Milestone | MCD 9251-2
John Scofield Sextet
Hand Jive | Blue Note | 827327-2
Les McCann-Eddie Harris Quintet
Rhino Presents The Atlantic Jazz Gallery | Atlantic | 8122-71257-2
Swiss Movement | Atlantic | 8122-72452-2

Harris,Gene | (p,el-keyboards,el-p,ldp-solo)
Anita O'Day With The Three Sounds
Verve Jazz Masters 49:Anita O'Day | Verve | 527653-2
Gene Harris And The Three Sounds
Deep Blue-The United States Of Mind | Blue Note | 521152-2
Gene Harris Group
Blue Breaks Beats Vol.2 | Blue Note | 789907-2
Mel Rhyne Sextet
Organ-izing | Original Jazz Classics | OJCCD 1055-2(JLP 916)
Milt Jackson Quartet
Soul Route | Original Jazz Classics | OJCCD 1059-2(2310900)
Nat Adderley Quintet(incl.The Three Sounds)
Branching Out | Original Jazz Classics | OJCCD 255-2(R 285)
Nat Adderley With The Three Sounds
Branching Out | Original Jazz Classics | OJCCD 255-2(R 285)
Stanley Turrentine With The Three Sounds
Blue Hour | Blue Note | 524586-2
Midnight Blue(The [Be]witching Hour) | Blue Note | 854365-2
The Three Sounds
Bottoms Up | Blue Note | 0675629
Blue Break Beats | Blue Note | 799106-2
Black Orchid | Blue Note | 821289-2

Harris,Hilda | (voc)
Grover Washington Jr. Orchestra
Inside Moves | Elektra | 7559-60318-2

Harris,James | (drtp)
Louis Armstrong And His Orchestra
Swing Legends:Louis Armstrong | Nimbus Records | NI 2012

Harris,Jerome | (b,voc,b-g,el-b,voice,el-g,gbj)
Bill Frisell Quintet
Rambler | ECM | 1287
Bobby Previte's Latin For Travelers
Dangerous Rip | Enja | ENJ-9324-2
My Man In Sidney | Enja | ENJ-9348 2
Jack DeJohnette Quartet
Oneness | ECM | 1637(537343-2)
Jeanne Lee Group
Natural Affinities | Owl Records | 018352-2
Ned Rothenberg Trio
Port Of Entry | Intuition Records | INT 3249-2
Ray Anderson Alligatory Band
Don't Mow Your Lawn | Enja | ENJ-8070 2
Heads And Tales | Enja | ENJ-9055 2
Ray Anderson Lapis Lazuli Band

INTERPRETENVERZEICHNIS

Funkorific | Enja | ENJ-9340 2
Sonny Rollins Quintet
Here's To The People | Milestone | MCD 9194-2
Don't Ask | Original Jazz Classics | OJCCD 915-2(M 9090)
The Jazz Giants Play Harry Warren:Lullaby Of Broadway | Prestige | PCD 24204-2
Sonny Rollins Sextet
Here's To The People | Milestone | MCD 9194-2
Don't Ask | Original Jazz Classics | OJCCD 915-2(M 9090)

Harris,Jerry | (el-b)
Sonny Rollins Quintet
Don't Stop The Carnival | Milestone | MCD 55005-2
Sonny Rollins Sextet
Don't Stop The Carnival | Milestone | MCD 55005-2

Harris,Jesse | (g)
Seamus Blake Quintet
Stranger Things Have Happened | Fresh Sound Records | FSNT 063 CD

Harris,Joe | (as,conga,congas,dr,perc,tb,voc)
Benny Goodman And His Orchestra
Planet Jazz:Benny Goodman | Planet Jazz | 2152054-2
Planet Jazz Sampler | Planet Jazz | 2152326-2
Planet Jazz:Swing | Planet Jazz | 2169651-2
Bill Coleman Septet
Jazz In Paris:Bill Coleman-From Boogie To Funk | EmArCy | 549401-2 PMS
Dizzy Gillespie All Stars
Milt Jackson Birthday Celebration | Fantasy | FANCD 6079-2
Dizzy Gillespie And His Orchestra
Planet Jazz:Dizzy Gillespie | Planet Jazz | 2152069-2
Planet Jazz:Bebop | RCA | 2169650-2
Dizzy Gillespie Quintet
Charlie Parker:Now's The Time | Dreyfus Jazz Line | FDM 36724-2
Dizzy Gillespie:Night In Tunisia | Dreyfus Jazz Line | FDM 36734-2
George Russell Smalltet
The RCA Victor Jazz Workshop | RCA | 2159144-2
Sonny Rollins Trio
St.Thomas:Sonny Rollins In Stockhom 1959 | Dragon | DRCD 229

Harris,John 'Ironman' | (drvoc)
Horace Silver Quintet
Horace Silver Retrospective | Blue Note | 495576-2
Johnny 'Hammond' Smith Quartet
Good 'Nuff | Prestige | PRCD 24282-2
Johnny 'Hammond' Smith Sextet
The Soulful Blues | Prestige | PCD 24244-2

Harris,Kevin Bruce | (el-b,voc,voiceperc)
Cassandra Wilson Group
After The Beginning Again | JMT Edition | 514001-2
Steve Coleman And Five Elements
On The Edge Of Tomorrow | JMT Edition | 919005-2
Vincent Chancey Quartet
Welcome Mr. Chancey | IN+OUT Records | 7020-1

Harris,Leroy | (as,voc,bj,clbs)
Earl Hines And His Orchestra
Planet Jazz:Earl Hines | Planet Jazz | 2159973-2
The Legends Of Swing | Laserlight | 24659
Jazz:The Essential Collection Vol.2 | IN+OUT Records | 78012-2

Harris,Little Benny | (tp)
Dizzy Gillespie And His Orchestra
Planet Jazz:Male Jazz Vocalists | Planet Jazz | 2169657-2

Harris,Milt | (org)
Johnny Lytle Quartet
Got That Feeling/Moon Child | Milestone | MCD 47093-2
Johnny Lytle Quintet
Got That Feeling/Moon Child | Milestone | MCD 47093-2
The Village Caller | Original Jazz Classics | OJCCD 110-2(R 9480)
Johnny Lytle Trio(Quartet)
Got That Feeling/Moon Child | Milestone | MCD 47093-2

Harris,Niels | (ts)
The Danish Radio Concert Orchestra
Symphonies Vol.2 | dacapo | DCCD 9441

Harris,Paul | (b,p,keyboards,orgvoc)
A Band Of Friends
Wynton Marsalis Quartet With Strings | CBS | CK 68921
Wollie Kaiser Timeghost
Post Art Core | Jazz Haus Musik | JHM 0077 CD

Harris,Ratzo | (b)
Mose Allison Quintet
Gimeracs And Gewgaws | Blue Note | 823211-2

Harris,Rodney | (rap)
Chico Freeman And Brainstorm
Threshold | IN+OUT Records | 7022-2

Harris,Sid | (v)
Charlie Parker With Strings
Charlie Parker With Strings:The Master Takes | Verve | 523984-2
Charlie Parker With The Neal Hefti Orchestra
Charlie Parker:The Best Of The Verve Years | Verve | 527815-2
Bird: The Complete Charlie Parker On Verve | Verve | 837141-2

Harris,Sidney | (tb)
Tommy Dorsey And His Orchestra
Planet Jazz:Tommy Dorsey | Planet Jazz | 2159972-2

Harris,Stan | (viola)
Ella Fitzgerald With The Nelson Riddle Orchestra
Oh Lady Be Good:The Best Of The Gershwin Songbook | Verve | 529581-2
Love Songs:The Best Of The Song Books | Verve | 531762-2
Frank Sinatra With The Count Basie Orchestra
It Might As Well Be Spring | Reprise | 7599-27027-2

Harris,Stefon | (marimba,balafon,gongvib)
Cassandra Wilson Group
Traveling Miles | Blue Note | 854123-2
Greg Osby Quintet
Inner Circle | Blue Note | 499871-2
Joe Henderson Group
Porgy And Bess | Verve | 539048-2
Klaus Doldinger Group
Back In New York:Blind Date | Atlantic | 3984-26922-2
Melissa Walker And Her Band
I Saw The Sky | Enja | ENJ-9409 2
Stefon Harris Group
Black Action Figure | Blue Note | 499546-2
Stefon Harris-Jacky Terrasson Group
Kindred | Blue Note | 531868-2
Steve Coleman And Five Elements
The Sonic Language Of Myth | RCA | 2164123-2

Harris,Tom | (b,fl,ssts)
Gail Thompson Orchestra
Gail Thompson's Jazz Africa | Enja | ENJ-9053 2

Harris,Tommie | (drvoc)
Dook Joint
Who's Been Talkin'... | Organic Music | ORGM 9728

Harris,Tony | (viola)
Barbara Thompson Group
Heavenly Bodies | VeraBra Records | CDVBR 2015-2

Harrison,Bob | (b)
Airto Moreira/Flora Purim Group
Jazz Unlimited | IN+OUT Records | 7017-2

Harrison,Donald | (as,ts,bs,tambourine,voc,as-solo)
Billy Cobham Group
Art Of Five | IN+OUT Records | 77063-2
Bruce Cox Quartet With Guests
Stick To It | Minor Music | 801055
Candid Jazz Masters
The Candid Jazz Masters:For Miles | Candid | CCD 79710
Donald Harrison
Nouveau Swing | Impulse(MCA) | 951209-2
Donald Harrison Quartet
Nouveau Swing | Impulse(MCA) | 951209-2
Free To Be | Impulse(MCA) | 951283-2
Donald Harrison Quintet
Free To Be | Impulse(MCA) | 951283-2
Donald Harrison Sextet
Free To Be | Impulse(MCA) | 951283-2
Kind Of New | Candid | CCD 79768
Donald Harrison Trio
Heroes | Nagel-Heyer | CD 2041
Eddie Allen Quintet
R 'N' B | Enja | ENJ-9033 2

Harrison,Frank | (pmelodica)
Gilad Atzmon & The Orient House Ensemble
Gilad Atzmon & The Orient House Ensemble | TipToe | TIP-888839 2

Harrison,Jimmy | (tb)
Bessie Smith And Her Band
Jazz:The Essential Collection Vol.1 | IN+OUT Records | 78011-2
Bessie Smith With Her Blue Boys
Jazz:The Essential Collection Vol.1 | IN+OUT Records | 78011-2
Chocolate Dandies
Jazz:The Essential Collection Vol.3 | IN+OUT Records | 78013-2
Fletcher Henderson And His Orchestra
Jazz:The Essential Collection Vol.1 | IN+OUT Records | 78011-2

Harrison,Len | (b)
Benny Carter And His Orchestra
Django Reinhardt All Star Sessions | Capitol | 531577-2
Americans Swinging In Paris:Benny Carter | EMI Records | 539647-2

Harrow,Nancy | (voc)
Nancy Harrow And The Buck Clayton All Stars
Wild Women Don't Have The Blues | Candid | CCD 79008

Harshman,Allan | (vviola)
Artie Shaw And His Orchestra
Planet JazzArtie Shaw | Planet Jazz | 2152057-2
Planet Jazz:Big Bands | Planet Jazz | 2169649-2
Mel Tormé With The Russell Garcia Orchestra
Swingin' On The Moon | Verve | 511385-2
Milt Jackson With Strings
To Bags...With Love:Memorial Album | Pablo | 2310967-2
Phineas Newborn Jr. With Dennis Farnon And His Orchestra
While My Lady Sleeps | RCA | 2185157-2

Hart,Antonio Maurice | (as,ts,synth,flss)
Antonio Hart Group
Here I Stand | Impulse(MCA) | 951208-2
Ama Tu Sonrisa | Enja | ENJ-9404 2
Barbara Dennerlein Group
Outhipped | Verve | 547503-2
Cyrus Chestnut Sextet
Earth Stories | Atlantic | 7567-82876-2
Dave Holland Big Band
What Goes Around | ECM | 1777(014002-2)
Dee Dee Bridgewater With Band
This Is New | Verve | 016884-2
Dee Dee Bridgewater With Big Band
Dear Ella | Verve | 539102-2
Dee Dee Bridgewater With Her Septet
Dear Ella | Verve | 539102-2
Freddie Cole
Jazzin' Vol.2: The Music Of Stevie Wonder | Fantasy | FANCD 6088-2
Freddy Cole With Band
To The End Of The Earth | Fantasy | FCD 9675-2
James Hurt Group
Dark Grooves-Mystcal Rhythms | Blue Note | 495104-2
McCoy Tyner Quartet
Prelude And Sonata | Milestone | MCD 9244-2
McCoy Tyner Quintet
Prelude And Sonata | Milestone | MCD 9244-2
Rabih Abou-Khalil Group
The Cactus Of Knowledge | Enja | ENJ-9401 2
Roy Hargrove Quintet
Planet Jazz:Jazz Trumpet | Planet Jazz | 2169654-2
Terell Stafford Quintet
Fields Of Gold | Nagel-Heyer | CD 2005

Hart,Bill | (dr)
Ethan Iverson Trio
The Minor Passions | Fresh Sound Records | FSNT 064 CD
Johannes Enders Quartet
Sandsee | Organic Music | ORGM 9720
Stan Getz Quintet
Sony Jazz Collection:Stan Getz | CBS | 488623-2
Stan Getz-Joao Gilberto Orchestra
Sony Jazz Collection:Stan Getz | CBS | 488623-2

Hart,Billy | (dr,perctrap-dr)
Charles Lloyd Quartet
The Call | ECM | 1522(517719-2)
All My Relations | ECM | 1557
Canto | ECM | 1635(537345-2)
Charles Lloyd Quintet
Lift Every Voice | ECM | 1832/33(018783-2)
Charles Lloyd Sextet
Lift Every Voice | ECM | 1832/33(018783-2)
Clark Terry Quintet
Jazz Dance | Original Jazz Classics | OJCCD 1002-2(1210890)
Debriano-Hart-Blythe
3-Ology | Konnex Records | KCD 5047
Dick Griffin Septet
The Eighth Wonder & More | Konnex Records | KCD 5059
Eddie Harris Quartet
The Best Of Eddie Harris | Atlantic | 7567-81370-2
Eddie Harris Quintet
The Best Of Eddie Harris | Atlantic | 7567-81370-2
Eddie Henderson Orchestra
Blue Breaks Beats Vol.2 | Blue Note | 789907-2
Blue Break Beats | Blue Note | 799106-2
George Mraz Quartet
Morava | Milestone | MCD 9309-2
Herbie Hancock Group
Sextant | CBS | CK 64983
Herbie Hancock Sextet
V.S.O.P. Herbie Hancock-Live At The City Center N.Y. | CBS | 486569-2
Jam Session
Jam Session Vol.1 | Steeplechase | SCCD 31522
Jimmy Smith Trio
Jimmy Smith Trio: Salle Pleyel, May 28th, 1965 | Laserlight | 36135
Jimmy Smith:Best Of The Verve Years | Verve | 527950-2
Joe Lovano Quartet
Live At The Village Vanguard | Blue Note | 829125-2
Joe Zawinul Group
Zawinul | Atlantic | 7567-81375-2
Kenny Barron Group
Spirit Song | Verve | 543180-2
Larry Coryell Quartet
Air Dancing | Jazzpoint | JP 1025 CD
Mack Goldsbury And The New York Connection
Songs I Love To Play | Timescrapper | TSCR 9615
McCoy Tyner Orchestra
Sama Layuca | Original Jazz Classics | OJCCD 1071-2(M 9056)
McCoy Tyner Quintet
Asante | Blue Note | 493384-2
Miles Davis Group
On The Corner | CBS | CK 63980
Niels-Henning Orsted-Pedersen Quartet
Dancing On The Tables | Steeplechase | SCS 1125(Audiophile Pressing)
Pat Martino Trio
Live At Yoshi's | Blue Note | 499749-2
Pharoah Sanders Group
Black Unity | Impulse(MCA) | 951219-2
Pharoah Sanders Orchestra
Karma | Impulse(MCA) | 951153-2
The Roots Of Acid Jazz | Impulse(MCA) | IMP 12042
Shirley Horn Quartet
You Won't Forget Me | Verve | 847482-2
Shirley Horn Trio
The Main Ingredient | Verve | 529555-2
You Won't Forget Me | Verve | 847482-2
A Lazy Afternoon | Steeplechase | SCCD 31111
Violets For Your Furs | Steeplechase | SCCD 31164
Shirley Horn Trio with Buck Hill
You Won't Forget Me | Verve | 847482-2
Simon Cato Spang-Hansen Quartet
Identified | dacapo | DCCD 9448
Stan Getz Quartet
Live At Montmartre(CD=Stan's Party) | Steeplechase | SCCD 37021/22
Tom Harrell Quintet
Visions | Contemporary | CCD 14063-2
Wayne Shorter Orchestra
Wayne Shorter:The Classic Blue Note Recordings | Blue Note | 540856-2
Wolfgang Lackerschmid Sextet
One More Life | Bhakti Jazz | BR 29

Hart,Clyde | (arr,pceleste)
Ben Webster Quintet
Jazz:The Essential Collection Vol.3 | IN+OUT Records | 78013-2
Coleman Hawkins And His Orchestra
Jazz:The Essential Collection Vol.3 | IN+OUT Records | 78013-2
Dizzy Gillespie All Stars
Dizzy Gillespie:Night In Tunisia | Dreyfus Jazz Line | FDM 36734-2
Dizzy Gillespie Sextet
Dizzy Gillespie:Night In Tunisia | Dreyfus Jazz Line | FDM 36734-2
Hot Lips Page And His Orchestra
Don Byas:Laura | Dreyfus Jazz Line | FDM 36714-2
Lionel Hampton And His Orchestra
Planet Jazz:Coleman Hawkins | Planet Jazz | 2152055-2
Planet Jazz:Lionel Hampton | Planet Jazz | 2152059-2
Planet Jazz Sampler | Planet Jazz | 2152326-2
Planet Jazz:Ben Webster | RCA | 2165368-2
Planet Jazz:Jazz Saxophone | Planet Jazz | 2169653-2
Jazz:The Essential Collection Vol.3 | IN+OUT Records | 78013-2
Una Mae Carlisle Quintet
Jazz:The Essential Collection Vol.3 | IN+OUT Records | 78013-2
Una Mae Carlisle Septet
Planet Jazz:Female Jazz Vocalists | Planet Jazz | 2169656-2

Hart,Dent | (tpb)
Chamber Jazz Sextet
Plays Pal Joey | Candid | CCD 79030

Hart,Jon | (b)
Pucho & His Latin Soul Brothers
Rip A Dip | Milestone | MCD 9247-2

Hart,Phil | (tp)
Bob Crosby And His Orchestra
Swing Legens:Bob Crosby | Nimbus Records | NI 2011

Hart,Roy | (bj)
Lennie Baldwin's Dauphin Street Six
The Golden Years Of Revival Jazz,Sampler | Storyville | 109 1001
The Golden Years Of Revival Jazz,Vol 1 | Storyville | STCD 5506
The Golden Years Of Revival Jazz,Vol.3 | Storyville | STCD 5508
The Golden Years Of Revival Jazz,Vol.6 | Storyville | STCD 5511
The Golden Years Of Revival Jazz,Vol.9 | Storyville | STCD 5514
The Golden Years Of Revival Jazz,Vol.10 | Storyville | STCD 5515
The Golden Years Of Revival Jazz,Vol.13 | Storyville | STCD 5518

Hart,Willy | (b,noiseel-b)
Swim Two Birds
Sweet Reliet | Laika Records | 35101182
No Regrets | Laika Records | 35101342

Harte,Roy | (bongosdr)
Arnold Ross Trio
Just You & He & Me | Fresh Sound Records | FSR-CD 313
Bob Enevoldsen Sextet
The Complete Nocturne Recordings:Jazz In Hollywood Series Vol.1 | Fresh Sound Records | NR 3CD-101
Bud Shank Quintet
The Complete Nocturne Recordings:Jazz In Hollywood Series Vol.1 | Fresh Sound Records | NR 3CD-101
Harry Babasin Quintet
The Complete Nocturne Recordings:Jazz In Hollywood Series Vol.1 | Fresh Sound Records | NR 3CD-101
Herbie Harper Quartet
The Complete Nocturne Recordings:Jazz In Hollywood Series Vol.1 | Fresh Sound Records | NR 3CD-101
Herbie Harper Quintet
The Complete Nocturne Recordings:Jazz In Hollywood Series Vol.1 | Fresh Sound Records | NR 3CD-101

Harth,Alfred 23 | (as,ts,b-cl,voice,sax,ss,cl,p,org)
Alfred 23 Harth Group
Sweet Paris | free flow music | ffm 0291
Alfred 23 Harth QuasarQuartet
POPending EYE | free flow music | ffm 0493
Alfred 23 Harth-John Zorn
Willisau And More Live | Creative Works Records | CW CD 1020-2
Alfred Harth Quintet
This Earth! | ECM | 1264

Hartl,Phil | (cond)
Vince Jones With Orchestra
Come In Spinner | Intuition Records | INT 3052-2

Hartley,Patrick | (tb)
Gail Thompson Orchestra
Gail Thompson's Jazz Africa | Enja | ENJ-9053 2
Jazz Africa All Nations Big Band
Jadu(Jazz Africa Down Under) | Enja | ENJ-9339 2

Hartling,Betram | (v)
Till Brönner Quartet & Deutsches Symphonieorchester Berlin
German Songs | Minor Music | 801057

Hartman,Johnny | (voc)
Dizzy Gillespie And His Orchestra
Planet Jazz:Dizzy Gillespie | Planet Jazz | 2152069-2
John Coltrane Quartet With Johnny Hartman
The Gentle Side Of John Coltrane | Impulse(MCA) | 951107-2
Johnny Hartman And His Orchestra
Unforgettable | Impulse(MCA) | IMP 11522
Johnny Hartman And His Quintet
I Just Dropped By To Say Hello | MCA | 951176-2
Johnny Hartman And The Rudy Traylor Orchestra
And I Thought About You | Blue Note | 857456-2
Johnny Hartman With The John Coltrane Quartet
John Coltrane:Standards | Impulse(MCA) | 549914-2
John Coltrane And Johnny Hartman | Impulse(MCA) | 951157-2
Johnny Hartman With The Masahiko Kikuchi Trio
Blue Velvet: Crooners, Swooners And Velvet Vocals | Blue Note | 521153-2
Johnny Hartman With The Terumasa Hino Quartet
Midnight Blue(The [Be]witching Hour) | Blue Note | 854365-2

Hartman,Leonard 'Lennie' | (reeds)
Billie Holiday With The Paul Whiteman Orchestra
Billie's Blues | Blue Note | 748786-2
Ella Fitzgerald With Paul Weston And His Orchestra
Ella Fitzgerald Sings The Irving Berlin Song Book | Verve | 543830-2
Ella Fitzgerald With The Paul Weston Orchestra
Get Happy! | Verve | 523321-2

Hartman,Peter | (b)
David Gibson Sextet
Maya | Nagel-Heyer | CD 2018

Hartmann,Achim | (b-tb,tubatb)
HR Big Band
Libertango:Homage An Astor Piazolla | hr music.de | hrmj 014-02 CD
Nana Mouskouri With The Berlin Radio Big Band
Nana Swings | Mercury | 074394-2

Hartmann,Alexander | (fl-h\1p)

Ralph Schweizer Big Band
DAY Dream | Chaos | CACD 8177
Sax Mal Anders
Kontraste | Chaos | CACD 8185
Hartmann,André | (dr)
Stephane Grappelli Quintet
Planet Jazz:Stephane Grappelli | RCA | 2165366-2
Hartmann,Ernst G. | (b-synthkeyboards)
Lajos Dudas Quartet
Jubilee Edition | double moon | CHRDM 71020
Lajos Dudas Quintet
Jubilee Edition | double moon | CHRDM 71020
Hartmann,Hans | (bchapmanstick)
For Free Hands
Eastern Moods | Laika Records | 35101502
Hartog,Jim | (bs)
Craig Bailey Band
A New Journey | Candid | CCD 79725
Hartschuh,Fritz | (vib)
Waltz For People Who Hate Waltzes
Noch Lauther | Bear Family Records | BCD 15942 AH
Wolfgang Lauth Quartet
Lauther | Bear Family Records | BCD 15717 AH
Noch Lauther | Bear Family Records | BCD 15942 AH
Hartstein,Max | (b)
Brew Moore Quartet
The Brew Moore Quintet | Original Jazz Classics | OJCCD 100-2(F 3-222)
Brew Moore Quintet
The Brew Moore Quintet | Original Jazz Classics | OJCCD 100-2(F 3-222)
Hartwell,Jimmy | (clas)
The Wolverines
Jazz:The Essential Collection Vol.2 | IN+OUT Records | 78012-2
Hartwig,Gerald Luciano | (bsitar)
Roman Bunka Group
Dein Kopf Ist Ein Schlafendes Auto | ATM Records | ATM 3818-AH
Harvey,James | (tbvoc)
Don Cherry Group
Multi Kulti | A&M Records | 395323-2
Harvey,Keith | (cello)
Dee Dee Bridgewater With Orchestra
Dear Ella | Verve | 539102-2
Hasegawa,Akiko or Juerg Daehler | (viola)
Daniel Schnyder With String Quartet
Tanatula | Enja | ENJ-9302 2
Haskins,Taylo |
Taylor Hawkins Group
Wake Up Call | Fresh Sound Records | FSCD 145 CD
Haskins,Taylor | (tpfl-h)
Andrew Rathbun Group
Jade | Fresh Sound Records | FSNT 076 CD
True Stories | Fresh Sound Records | FSNT 099 CD
Hasler,Gabriele | (vocvoice)
Andreas Willers Group
Andreas Willers & Friends Play Jimi Hendrix:Experience | Nabel Records:Jazz Network | CD 4665
Blue Room Ensemble
Solitude | Foolish Music | FM 211993
Cool Blue
House In The Country | Foolish Music | FM 211591
dAs prOjekT
dAs prOjekT | Foolish Music | FM 211288
Gabriele Hasler & Foolish Heart
God Is A She | Foolish Music | FM 111186
Gabriele Hasler Group
Gabriele Hasler's Rosensrücke | Foolish Music | FM 211096
Listening To Löbering | Foolish Music | FM 211389
Gabriele Hasler's Personal Notebook | Foolish Music | FM 211490
Gabriele Hasler-Elvira Plenar-Andreas Willers
Sonetburger-Nach Texten Von Oskar Pastior | Foolish Music | FM 211793
Gabriele Hasler-Georg Ruby
Spider's Lovesong | Foolish Music | FM 211893
Gabriele Hasler-Hans Lüdemann-Andreas Willers plus Jörn Schipper
Familienglück | Foolish Music | FM 211097
Gabriele Hasler-Roger Hanschel Duo
Love Songs | Foolish Music | FM 211003
Pigeon | Jazz Haus Musik | JHM 0120 CD
Georg Ruby Group
Stange Loops | Jazz Haus Musik | JHM 0057 CD
Roger Hanschel/Gabriele Hasler
Go In Green | Jazz Haus Musik | JHM 0073 CD
Haslip,Jimmy | (b,el-b,synclavier,keyboardsperc)
Take 6 With The Yellow Jackets
He Is Christmas | Reprise | 7599-26665-2
Terri Lyne Carrington Quartet
Structure | ACT | 9427-2
Yellowjackets
Live Wires | GRP | GRP 96672
Run For Your Life | GRP | GRP 97542
Hassan,Karim Othman | (oud)
Chris Jarrett Trio
Chris Jarrett Trio Plays New World Music | Edition Musikat | EDM 067
Hasselbring,Curtis | (tbvoice)
Frank Carlberg Group
Variations On A Summer Day | Fresh Sound Records | FSNT 083 CD
Tom Harrell Orchestra
Time's Mirror | RCA | 2663524-2
Hassell,Dave | (drperc)
Royce Campbell-Adrian Ingram Group
Hands Across The Water | String Jazz | SJRCD 1002
Hassell,Jon | (tp,keyboardssynth)
Jon Hassell & Farafina
Flash Of The Spirit | Intuition Records | INT 3009-2
Jon Hassell Group
Power Spot | ECM | 1327
Hastings,Lowell | (ts)
Louis Jordan With The Nelson Riddle Orchestra
Louis Jordan-Let The Good Times Roll: The Complete Decca Recordings 1938-1954 | Bear Family Records | BCD 15557 IH
Hatchett's Swingtette |
Arthur Young And Hatchett's Swingtette
Grapelli Story | Verve | 515807-2
Hathaway.Lalah | (voc)
Marcus Miller Group
Tales | Dreyfus Jazz Line | FDM 36571-2
Live & More | Dreyfus Jazz Line | FDM 36585-2
Hatt,Nelson | (piccolo-tp,tpfl-h)
Woody Herman And His Orchestra
Jazzin' Vol.2: The Music Of Stevie Wonder | Fantasy | FANCD 6088-2
King Cobra | Original Jazz Classics | OJCCD 1068-2(F 9499)
Woody Herman Herd At Montreux | Original Jazz Classics | OJCCD 991-2(F 9470)
Woody Herman And The New Thundering Herd
Planet Jazz:Big Bands | Planet Jazz | 2169649-2
Woody Herman's Thundering Herd
Planet Jazz:Jazz Saxophone | Planet Jazz | 2169653-2
Hatzigeorgiou,Michel | (b)
Toots Thielemans Quartet
Toots Thielemans:The Live Takes Vol.1 | IN+OUT Records | 77041-2
Hauck,Helmut | (tb)
Kurt Edelhagen All Stars
Deutsches Jazz Fesival 1954/1955 | Bear Family Records | BCD 15430
Kurt Edelhagen All Stars Und Solisten
Deutsches Jazz Fesival 1954/1955 | Bear Family Records | BCD 15430
Quartet Der Kurt Edelhagen All Stars
Deutsches Jazz Fesival 1954/1955 | Bear Family Records | BCD 15430

Stan Getz With The Kurt Edelhagen Orchestra
Stan Getz In Europe | Laserlight | 24657
Haug,Lars Andreas | (tuba)
Christoph Lauer & Norwegian Brass
Heaven | ACT | 9420-2
Haughton,Chauncey | (as,bs,cl,tsg)
Duke Ellington And His Orchestra
Carnegie Hall Concert January 1943 | Prestige | 2PCD 34004-2
Jazz:The Essential Collection Vol.3 | IN+OUT Records | 78013-2
At The Hurricane:Original 1943 Broadcasts | Storyville | STCD 8359
Ella Fitzgerald With The Chick Webb Orchestra
Jazz Collection:Ella Fitzgerald | Laserlight | 24397
Haugland,Stefan | (voc)
Marilyn Mazur With Ars Nova And The Copenhagen Art Ensemble
Jordsange | dacapo | DCCD 9454
Haurand,Ali | (bperc)
Dudek-Van Den Broek-Haurand
Pulque | Konnex Records | KCD 5055
Crossing Level | Konnex Records | KCD 5077
European Jazz Ensemble
European Jazz Ensemble At The Philharmonic Cologne | M.A Music | A 800-2
20th Anniversary Tour | Konnex Records | KCD 5078
European Jazz Ensemble 25th Anniversary | Konnex Records | KCD 5100
European Jazz Ensemble & The Khan Family feat. Joachim Kühn
European Jazz Ensemble Meets The Khan Family | M.A Music | A 807-2
European Trumpet Summit
European Trumpet Summit | Konnex Records | KCD 5064
Jiri Stivin-Ali Haurand
Just The Two Of Us | Konnex Records | KCD 5095
Lajos Dudas Quintet
Jubilee Edition | double moon | CHRDM 71020
Mariano-Humair-Haurand
Frontier Traffic | Konnex Records | KCD 5110
Paul Eßer-Gerd Dudek-Ali Haurand-Jiri Strivin
Jazz Und Lyrik:Schinderkarren Mit Buffet | Konnex Records | KCD 5108
Stivin-Van Den Broeck-Haurand
Bordertalk | Konnex Records | KCD 5068
The Quartet
Crossing Level | Konnex Records | KCD 5077
The Quartet Live In Prague | P&J Music | P&J 101-1 CD
Wilton Gaynair Quintet
Alpharian | Konnex Records | KCD 5032
Haus,Matthias | (percvib)
Hipsters In The Zone
Into The Afro-Latin Bag | Nabel Records:Jazz Network | CD 4663
HR Big Band
Libertango:Homage An Astor Piazolla | hr music.de | hrmj 014-02 CD
Hauschild,Thomas | (fr-h)
Eberhard Weber Orchestra
Orchestra | ECM | 1374
Hauser,Michael | (bel-b)
Schlothauer's Maniacs
Maniakisses | Timescrapper | TSCR 9811
Hauser,Michel | (vib)
Alain Goraguer Orchestra
Jazz In Paris:Jazz & Cinéma Vol.1 | EmArCy | 548318-2 PMS
Golden Gate Quartet With The Martial Solal Orchestra
Americans Swinging In Paris:Golden Gate Quartet | EMI Records | 539659-2
From Spriritual To Swing Vol.2 | EMI Records | 780573-2
Stephane Grappelli Sextet
Grapelli Story | Verve | 515807-2
Haushalter,Heike | (v)
Ensemble Indigo
Reflection | Enja | ENJ-9417 2
Hausmann,Hermann | (p)
Helmut Zacharias & His Sax-Team
Ich Habe Rhythmus | Bear Family Records | BCD 15642 AH
Hausmann,Iven | (tb)
Jan Von Klewitz Quintet
Bonehenge Suite | Jazz Haus Musik | JHM 0078 CD
Hausser,Michel | (vibxyl)
Bobby Jaspar Quintet
Jazz In Paris:Bobby Jaspar-Jeux De Quartes | EmArCy | 018423-2
Henri Crolla Sextet
Jazz In Paris:Henri Crolla-Quand Refleuriront Les Lilas Blancs? | EmArCy | 018418-2
Sarah Vaughan With The Quincy Jones Orchestra
Jazz In Paris:Sarah Vaughan-Vaughan And Violins | EmArCy | 065004-2
4 By 4:Ella Fitzgerald/Sarah Vaughan/Billie Holiday/Dinah Washington | Verve | 559693-2
Hauta-aho,Teppo | (bvoice)
Edward Vesala Group
Nan Madol | ECM | 1077
Havens,Bob | (tb)
A Salute To Eddie Condon
A Salute To Eddie Condon | Nagel-Heyer | CD 004
One Two Three | Nagel-Heyer | CD 008
The First Sampler | Nagel-Heyer | NHR SP 5
Havet,Didier | (sousaphonetuba)
Orchestre National De Jazz
Charmediterranéen | ECM | 1828(010493-2)
Havlicek,Franta | (clsax)
Jan Jankeje's Party And Swingband
Mobil | Jazzpoint | JP 1068 CD
Hawes,Hampton | (el-p,p,vocp-solo)
Art Pepper Quartet
Living Legend | Original Jazz Classics | OJCCD 408-2
Bill Perkins-Richie Kamuca Quintet
Midnight Blue(The [Be]witching Hour) | Blue Note | 854365-2
Curtis Fuller And Hampton Hawes With French Horns
Curtis Fuller And Hampton Hawes With French Horns | Original Jazz Classics | OJCCD 1942-2(NJ 8305)
Dexter Gordon Quartet
Dexter Gordon Birthday Celebration | Fantasy | FANCD 6082-2
Gene Ammons And His All Stars
Dexter Gordon Birthday Celebration | Fantasy | FANCD 6082-2
Hampton Hawes Orchestra
Northern Windows Plus | Prestige | PRCD 24278-2
Hampton Hawes Quartet
Four!! | Original Jazz Classics | OJCCD 165-2
Hampton Hawes Trio
The Trio-Vol.1 | Original Jazz Classics | OJC 316(C 3515)
Hampton Hawes Trio Vol.1 | Original Jazz Classics | OJC20 316-2(C 3505)
Bird Song | Original Jazz Classics | OJCCD 1035-2
The Sermon | Original Jazz Classics | OJCCD 1067-2(C 7653)
The Trio Vol.2 | Original Jazz Classics | OJCCD 318-2
The Jazz Giants Play Jerome Kern:Yesterdays | Prestige | PCD 24202-2
The Jazz Giants Play Rodgers & Hart:Blue Moon | Prestige | PCD 24205-2
The Jazz Giants Play Miles Davis:Milestones | Prestige | PCD 24225-2
Northern Windows Plus | Prestige | PRCD 24278-2
Lennie Niehaus Quintet
Lennie Niehaus Vol.1:The Quintets | Original Jazz Classics | OJCCD 1933-2(C 3518)
Shorty Rogers And His Giants
PLanet Jazz:Shorty Rogers | Planet Jazz | 2159976-2
Sonny Rollins & The Contemporary Leaders
Sonny Rollins & The Contemporary Leaders | Original Jazz Classics | OJCCD 340-2
Sonny Rollins And The Contemporary Leaders
Sonny Rollins-The Freelance Years:The Complete Riverside & Contemporary Recordings | Riverside | 5 RCD 4427-2
Sonny Stitt Quartet

Goin' Down Slow | Prestige | PRCD 24276-2
Wardell Gray Quartet
Wardell Gray Memorial Vol.2 | Original Jazz Classics | OJCCD 051-2(P 7009)
Wardell Gray Quintet
Wardell Gray Memorial Vol.2 | Original Jazz Classics | OJCCD 051-2(P 7009)
Hawes,Jeanette | (voc)
Paulinho Da Costa Orchestra
Happy People | Original Jazz Classics | OJCCD 783-2(2312102)
Hawkes,Bill | (viola)
John Surman With String Quartet
Coruscating | ECM | 1702(543033-2)
Michael Mantler Quintet With The Balanescu Quartet
Folly Seeing All This | ECM | 1485
Hawkins,Brian | (viola)
Dee Dee Bridgewater With Orchestra
Dear Ella | Verve | 539102-2
Hawkins,Coleman | (bass-s,bass-sax,cl,ts,bs,reeds,p)
Abbey Lincoln And Her Orchestra
Straight Ahead | Candid | CCD 79015
Ben Webster And His Associates
Verve Jazz Masters 43:Ben Webster | Verve | 525431-2
Ultimate Ben Webster selected by James Carter | Verve | 557537-2
Ben Webster And Associates | Verve | 835254-2
Benny Carter And His Orchestra
Americans Swinging In Paris:Benny Carter | EMI Records | 539647-2
Further Definitions/Additions To Further Definotions | Impulse(MCA) | 951229-2
Benny Carter-Coleman Hawkins-Johnny Hodges With The Oscar Peterson Trio
The Jazz Giants Play Duke Ellington:Caravan | Prestige | PCD 24227-2
Bessie Smith And Her Band
Jazz:The Essential Collection Vol.1 | IN+OUT Records | 78011-2
Billie Holiday And Her All Stars
The Billie Holiday Song Book | Verve | 823246-2
Billie Holiday With Buck Clayton And The Mal Waldron Trio
Billie Holiday Story Vol.1:Jazz At The Philharmonic | Verve | 521642-2
Billie Holiday With The JATP All Stars
Billie Holiday Story Vol.1:Jazz At The Philharmonic | Verve | 521642-2
The Complete Jazz At The Philharmonic On Verve 1944-1949 | Verve | 523893-2
Charlie Parker All Stars
Charlie Parker:The Best Of The Verve Years | Verve | 527815-2
Charlie Parker Quintet
Charlie Parker | Verve | 539757-2
Chocolate Dandies
Jazz:The Essential Collection Vol.3 | IN+OUT Records | 78013-2
Coleman Hawkins
Verve Jazz Masters 43:Coleman Hawkins | Verve | 521856-2
Ultimate Coleman Hawkins selected by Sonny Rollins | Verve | 557538-2
Jazz:The Essential Collection Vol.3 | IN+OUT Records | 78013-2
Body And Soul Revisited | GRP | GRP 16272
Coleman Hawkins All Star Octet
Planet Jazz:Coleman Hawkins | Planet Jazz | 2152055-2
Milt Jackson Birthday Celebration | Fantasy | FANCD 6079-2
Body And Soul Revisited | GRP | GRP 16272
Coleman Hawkins All Stars
Verve Jazz Masters 43:Coleman Hawkins | Verve | 521856-2
Coleman Hawkins All Stars | Original Jazz Classics | OJCCD 225-2(SV 2005)
The J.J.Johnson Memorial Album | Prestige | PRCD 11025-2
Coleman Hawkins' All-American Four
Verve Jazz Masters 43:Coleman Hawkins | Verve | 521856-2
Coleman Hawkins And Ben Webster With The Oscar Peterson Quartet
Coleman Hawkins Encounters Ben Webster | Verve | 521427-2
Verve Jazz Masters 43:Coleman Hawkins | Verve | 521856-2
Verve Jazz Masters 43:Ben Webster | Verve | 525431-2
Verve Jazz Masters Vol.60:The Collection | Verve | 529866-2
Ultimate Coleman Hawkins selected by Sonny Rollins | Verve | 557538-2
Coleman Hawkins And Confreres
Coleman Hawkins And Confreres | Verve | 835255-2 PMS
Coleman Hawkins And His 52nd Street All Stars
Jazz:The Essential Collection Vol.3 | IN+OUT Records | 78013-2
Coleman Hawkins And His All Star Jam Band
Django Reinhardt All Star Sessions | Capitol | 531577-2
Americans Swinging In Paris:Benny Carter | EMI Records | 539647-2
Jazz:The Essential Collection Vol.3 | IN+OUT Records | 78013-2
Coleman Hawkins And His All Stars
Planet Jazz:Coleman Hawkins | Planet Jazz | 2152055-2
Planet Jazz:Bebop | RCA | 2169650-2
Jazz:The Essential Collection Vol.3 | IN+OUT Records | 78013-2
Coleman Hawkins And His Orchestra
Planet Jazz:Coleman Hawkins | Planet Jazz | 2152055-2
Planet Jazz Sampler | Planet Jazz | 2152326-2
Planet Jazz:Jazz Greatest Hits | Planet Jazz | 2169648-2
Jazz:The Essential Collection Vol.3 | IN+OUT Records | 78013-2
Coleman Hawkins And His Rhythm
Coleman Hawkins/Johnny Hodges:The Vogue Recordings | Vogue | 21559712
Jazz:The Essential Collection Vol.3 | IN+OUT Records | 78013-2
Coleman Hawkins' Fifty-Second Street All-Stars
Planet Jazz:Coleman Hawkins | Planet Jazz | 2152055-2
Coleman Hawkins Quartet
The Art Of Saxophone | Laserlight | 24652
Thelonious Monk:The Complete Prestige Recordings | Prestige | 3 PRCD 4428-2
Late Night Sax | CBS | 487798-2
Verve Jazz Masters 43:Coleman Hawkins | Verve | 521856-2
The Complete Jazz At The Philharmonic On Verve 1944-1949 | Verve | 523893-2
Ultimate Coleman Hawkins selected by Sonny Rollins | Verve | 557538-2
Jazz:The Essential Collection Vol.3 | IN+OUT Records | 78013-2
Today And Now | Impulse(MCA) | 951184-2
Thelonious Monk:85th Birthday Celebration | zyx records | FANCD 6076-2
Body And Soul Revisited | GRP | GRP 16272
The Roots Of Acid Jazz | Impulse(MCA) | IMP 12042
Monk's Music | Original Jazz Classics | OJC20 084-2
At Easy | Original Jazz Classics | OJC20 181-2(MV 7)
Jazz Dance | Original Jazz Classics | OJCCD 1002-2(1210890)
Sirius | Original Jazz Classics | OJCCD 861-2(2310707)
The Jazz Giants Play Rodgers & Hammerstein:My Favorite Things | Prestige | PCD 24223-2
Coleman Hawkins Quintet
Verve Jazz Masters 43:Coleman Hawkins | Verve | 521856-2
Ultimate Coleman Hawkins selected by Sonny Rollins | Verve | 557538-2
Jazz:The Essential Collection Vol.3 | IN+OUT Records | 78013-2
Body And Soul Revisited | GRP | GRP 16272
Soul | Original Jazz Classics | OJC20 096-2(P 7149)
The Hawk Relaxes | Original Jazz Classics | OJCCD 709-2(MV 15)
The Jazz Giants Play Sammy Cahn:It's Magic | Prestige | PCD 24226-2
Coleman Hawkins Quintet With Strings
Body And Soul Revisited | GRP | GRP 16272
Coleman Hawkins Septet
Desafinado | Impulse(MCA) | 951227-2
Coleman Hawkins Sextet
Desafinado | Impulse(MCA) | 951227-2
Body And Soul Revisited | GRP | GRP 16272
Hawk Eyes | Original Jazz Classics | OJCCD 294-2
Coleman Hawkins' Swing Four
Jazz:The Essential Collection Vol.3 | IN+OUT Records | 78013-2
Coleman Hawkins Trio

Jazz:The Essential Collection Vol.3 | IN+OUT Records | 78013-2
Coleman Hawkins With Billy Byers And His Orchestra
Planet Jazz:Coleman Hawkins | Planet Jazz | 2152055-2
The Hawk In Hi-Fi | RCA | 2663842-2
Coleman Hawkins With Different Bands
100 Ans De Jazz:Coleman Hawkins | RCA | 2177832-2
Coleman Hawkins With Eddie Lockjaw Davis And The Tommy Flanagan Trio
Night Hawk | Original Jazz Classics | OJC20 420-2(SV 2016)
Coleman Hawkins With Many Albam And His Orchestra
Planet Jazz:Coleman Hawkins | Planet Jazz | 2152055-2
Coleman Hawkins With Michel Warlop And His Orchestra
Django Reinhardt All Star Sessions | Capitol | 531577-2
Coleman Hawkins With Paul Neilson's Orchestra
Body And Soul Revisited | GRP | GRP 16272
Coleman Hawkins With The Adrian Acea Trio
Coleman Hawkins At The Golden Circle | Dragon | DRCD 265
Coleman Hawkins With The Glenn Osser Orchestra
Midnight Blue(The [Be]witching Hour) | Blue Note | 854365-2
Coleman Hawkins With The Göran Lindberg Trio
Coleman Hawkins At The Golden Circle | Dragon | DRCD 265
Coleman Hawkins With The Oscar Peterson Quartet
Verve Jazz Masters 43:Coleman Hawkins | Verve | 521856-2
The Genius Of Coleman Hawkins | Verve | 539065-2
Ultimate Coleman Hawkins selected by Sonny Rollins | Verve | 557538-2
Coleman Hawkins With The Ramblers
Jazz:The Essential Collection Vol.3 | IN+OUT Records | 78013-2
Coleman Hawkins With The Red Garland Trio
Coleman Hawkins With The Red Garland Trio | Original Jazz Classics | OJCCD 418-2(SV 2001)
Coleman Hawkins With The Thore Ehrlings Orchestra
Coleman Hawkins At The Golden Circle | Dragon | DRCD 265
Coleman Hawkins-Roy Eldridge Quintet
Verve Jazz Masters 43:Coleman Hawkins | Verve | 521856-2
Connie's Inn Orchestra
Planet Jazz:Coleman Hawkins | Planet Jazz | 2152055-2
Cozy Cole All Stars
Ultimate Coleman Hawkins selected by Sonny Rollins | Verve | 557538-2
Cozy Cole's Big Seven
Body And Soul Revisited | GRP | GRP 16272
Dizzy Gillespie All Stars
Verve Jazz Masters 25:Stan Getz & Dizzy Gillespie | Verve | 521852-2
Duke Ellington-Coleman Hawkins Orchestra
Duke Ellington Meets Coleman Hawkins | Impulse(MCA) | 951162-2
Ella Fitzgerald With The JATP All Stars
Ella Fitzgerald-First Lady Of Song | Verve | 517898-2
For The Love Of Ella Fitzgerald | Verve | 841765-2
Esquire All-American Award Winners
Planet Jazz:Jazz Trumpet | Planet Jazz | 2169654-2
Esquire Metropolitan Opera House Jam Session
Jazz:The Essential Collection Vol.3 | IN+OUT Records | 78013-2
Fletcher Henderson And His Orchestra
Jazz:The Essential Collection Vol.1 | IN+OUT Records | 78011-2
Jazz:The Essential Collection Vol.3 | IN+OUT Records | 78013-2
George Wettling's New Yorkers
Jazz:The Essential Collection Vol.3 | IN+OUT Records | 78013-2
Henderson's Hot Six
Jazz:The Essential Collection Vol.1 | IN+OUT Records | 78011-2
Henry Red Allen's All Stars
Planet Jazz:Coleman Hawkins | Planet Jazz | 2152055-2
JATP All Stars
J.A.T.P. In London 1969 | Pablo | 2CD 2620119
Stan Getz Highlights:The Best Of The Verve Years Vol.2 | Verve | 517330-2
Nothing But The Blues | Verve | 521674-2
Verve Jazz Masters 28:Charlie Parker Plays Standards | Verve | 521854-2
The Complete Jazz At The Philharmonic On Verve 1944-1949 | Verve | 523893-2
Jazz At The Philharmonic:Best Of The 1940's Concerts | Verve | 557534-2
Bird: The Complete Charlie Parker On Verve | Verve | 837141-2
Welcome To Jazz At The Philharmonic | Fantasy | FANCD 6081-2
Norman Granz' JATP: Carnegie Hall 1949 | Pablo | PACD 5311-2
Joe Turner With Orchestra
Atlantic Jazz: Kansas City | Atlantic | 7567-81701-2
Joe Williams And Friends
Planet Jazz:Male Jazz Vocalists | Planet Jazz | 2169657-2
At Newport '63 | RCA | 2663919-2
Joe Williams And His Band
Planet Jazz:Joe Williams | Planet Jazz | 2165370-2
Juanita Hall With The Claude Hopkins All Stars
Juanita Hall Sings The Blues | Original Jazz Classics | OJCCD 1928-2(CPST 556)
Jubilee All Stars
Jazz Gallery:Lester Young Vol.2(1946-59) | RCA | 2119541-2
Leonard Feather's Esquire All Stars
Jazz:The Essential Collection Vol.2 | IN+OUT Records | 78012-2
Lionel Hampton And His Orchestra
Planet Jazz:Coleman Hawkins | Planet Jazz | 2152055-2
Planet Jazz:Lionel Hampton | Planet Jazz | 2152059-2
Planet Jazz:Ben Webster | RCA | 2165368-2
Planet Jazz:Jazz Saxophone | Planet Jazz | 2169653-2
Jazz:The Essential Collection Vol.3 | IN+OUT Records | 78013-2
Max Roach All Stars
Candid Dolphy | Candid | CCD 79033
Max Roach Group
We Insist: Freedom Now Suite | Candid | CCD 79002
McKinney's Cotton Pickers
Jazz:The Essential Collection Vol.3 | IN+OUT Records | 78013-2
Mound City Blue Blowers
Jazz:The Essential Collection Vol.3 | IN+OUT Records | 78013-2
Quartet
Monk's Music | Original Jazz Classics | OJC20 084-2
Shirley Scott All Stars
Queen Of The Organ-Shirley Scott Memorial Album | Prestige | PRCD 11027-2
Sonny Rollins-Coleman Hawkins Quintet
Planet Jazz:Sonny Rollins | Planet Jazz | 2152062-2
Sonny Meets Hawk! | RCA | 2174800-2
Spike Hughes And His Negro Orchestra
Jazz:The Essential Collection Vol.3 | IN+OUT Records | 78013-2
The Capitol Jazzmen
The Hollywood Session:The Capitol Jazzmen | Jazz Unlimited | JUCD 2044
The Lousiana Stompers
Jazz:The Essential Collection Vol.1 | IN+OUT Records | 78011-2
Thelonious Monk Quartet
Thelonious Monk:85th Birthday Celebration | zyx records | FANCD 6076-2
Thelonious Monk Septet
Thelonious Monk:85th Birthday Celebration | zyx records | FANCD 6076-2
Thelonious Monk With John Coltrane | Jazzland | JZSA 946-6
Thelonious Monk With John Coltrane | Original Jazz Classics | OJC20 039-2
Monk's Music | Original Jazz Classics | OJC20 084-2
Tony Scott And The All Stars
Body And Soul Revisited | GRP | GRP 16272
Very Saxy
Very Saxy | Original Jazz Classics | OJCCD 458-2
The Prestige Legacy Vol.2:Battles Of Saxes | Prestige | PCD 24252-2

Hawkins,Coleman or Georgie Auld | (ts)

Billie Holiday With Buck Clayton And The Mal Waldron Trio
Billie Holiday Story Vol.1:Jazz At The Philharmonic | Verve | 521642-2

Hawkins,Derek | (clas)

Vic Lewis Jam Session
Vic Lewis:The Golden Years | Candid | CCD 79754

Hawkins,Donald | (bsts)

Buddy Guy Blues Band
Buddy Guy-The Complete Chess Studio Recordings | MCA | MCD 09337

Hawkins,Erskine | (tparr)

Erskine Hawkins And His Orchestra
Planet Jazz:Big Bands | Planet Jazz | 2169649-2

Hawkins,Eva | (voc)

Christian Willisohn New Band
Heart Broken Man | Blues Beacon | BLU-1026 2

Hawkins,Jay | (bj)

Mr.Acker Bilk And His Paramount Jazz Band
The Golden Years Of Revival Jazz,Vol.2 | Storyville | STCD 5507
The Golden Years Of Revival Jazz,Vol.5 | Storyville | STCD 5510
The Golden Years Of Revival Jazz,Vol.6 | Storyville | STCD 5511
The Golden Years Of Revival Jazz,Vol.7 | Storyville | STCD 5512
The Golden Years Of Revival Jazz,Vol.8 | Storyville | STCD 5513
The Golden Years Of Revival Jazz,Vol.9 | Storyville | STCD 5514
The Golden Years Of Revival Jazz,Vol.10 | Storyville | STCD 5515
The Golden Years Of Revival Jazz,Vol.12 | Storyville | STCD 5517
The Golden Years Of Revival Jazz,Vol.13 | Storyville | STCD 5518
The Golden Years Of Revival Jazz,Vol.14 | Storyville | STCD 5519
The Golden Years Of Revibal Jazz,Vol.15 | Storyville | STCD 5520

Hawkins,Marshall | (b)

Richie Cole Group
Jazz Life Vol.1:From Village Vanguard | Storyville | 4960753
Shirley Horn With Band
The Roots Of Acid Jazz | Impulse(MCA) | IMP 12042

Hawkins,Michael | (b)

Cyrus Chestnut Trio
You Are My Sunshine | Warner | 9362-48445-2

Hawkins,Ralph | (dr)

Harry James And His Orchestra
The Legends Of Swing | Laserlight | 24659

Hawkins,Roger | (dr)

Albert King Blues Band
Lovejoy | Stax | SCD 8517-2(STS 2040)
Dee Dee Bridgewater With Band
Dee Dee Bridgewater | Atlantic | 7567-80760-2

Hayat,Guy | (b)

Bud Powell Quartet
Bud Powell Paris Sessions | Pablo | PACD 2310972-2
Bud Powell Trio
Bebop | Pablo | PACD 2310978-2
Johnny Griffin With The Bud Powell Trio
Bebop | Pablo | PACD 2310978-2

Haydn,Lilli R. | (v)

Herbie Hancock Group With String Quartet
Herbie Hancock The New Standards | Verve | 527715-2
Herbie Hancock Group With String Quartet,Woodwinds And Brass
Herbie Hancock The New Standards | Verve | 527715-2

Hayes,Al | (b,bongostb)

Gene Ammons Septet
Bad! Bossa Nova | Original Jazz Classics | OJC20 351-2(P 7257)

Hayes,Clancy | (bj,voc,drg)

Bob Scobey's Frisco Band
Planet Jazz | Planet Jazz | 2169652-2
Bunk Johnson With The Yerba Buena Jazz Band
Bunk & Lu | Good Time Jazz | GTCD 12024-2
Yerba Buena Jazz Band
Bunk & Lu | Good Time Jazz | GTCD 12024-2

Hayes,Danny | (tp)

Buddy Rich Big Band
Backwoods Siseman/Pieces Of Dream | Laserlight | 24655

Hayes,Ed | (btuba)

Louis Armstrong And His Orchestra
Planet Jazz:Louis Armstrong | Planet Jazz | 2152052-2
Louis Armstrong:A 100th Birthday Celebration | RCA | 2663694-2

Hayes,Ernest 'Ernie' | (el-p,orgp)

Al Sears & His Rock 'N' Rollers
Sear-iously | Bear Family Records | BCD 15668 AH
Al Sears And His Orchestra
Sear-iously | Bear Family Records | BCD 15668 AH
Billy Butler Quintet
Night Life | Prestige | PCD 24260-2
Chico Hamilton Quintet
The Dealer | Impulse(MCA) | 547958-2
Etta Jones And Her Band
Love Shout | Original Jazz Classics | OJCCD 941-2(P 7272)
Etta Jones With The Jerome Richardson Sextet
Hollar! | Original Jazz Classics | OJCCD 1061(PR 7284)
Gene Ammons Sextet
Fine And Mellow | Prestige | PRCD 24281-2
Gene Ammons Sextet With Strings
Fine And Mellow | Prestige | PRCD 24281-2
George Benson With The Don Sebesky Orchestra
Verve Jazz Masters 21:George Benson | Verve | 521861-2
King Curtis Band
King Curtis-Blow Man Blow | Bear Family Records | BCD 15670 CI
Nina Simone And Orchestra
Planet Jazz:Nina Simone | Planet Jazz | 2165372-2
Ronnie Foster Group
Sweet Revival... | Blue Note | 581676-2
Rusty Bryant Group
For The Good Times | Prestige | PRCD 24269-2
Sister Rosetta Tharpe And Her Group
Gospel Train | Mercury | 841134-2
Sister Rosetta Tharpe And Her Group With The Harmonizing Four
Gospel Train | Mercury | 841134-2

Hayes,Kevin | (p)

Mark Turner Quartet
Ballad Session | Warner | 9362-47631-2
Mark Turner Quintet
Ballad Session | Warner | 9362-47631-2

Hayes,Louis | (drperc)

Benny Carter-Coleman Hawkins-Johnny Hodges With The Oscar Peterson Trio
The Jazz Giants Play Duke Ellington:Caravan | Prestige | PCD 24227-2
Bill Henderson With The Horace Silver Quintet
Horace Silver Retrospective | Blue Note | 495576-2
Cannonball Adderley And His Orchestra
Cannonball Adderley Birthday Celebration | Fantasy | FANCD 6087-2
Cannonball Adderley And The Poll Winners
Cannonball Adderley And The Poll Winners | Capitol | 520086-2
Cannonball Adderley Group
Phenix | Fantasy | FCD 79004-2
Cannonball Adderley Quartet
Ballads | Blue Note | 537563-2
Cannonball Adderley Quintet
Wes Montgomery-The Complete Riverside Recordings | Riverside | 12 RCD 4408-2
Julian Cannonball Adderlry: Salle Pleyel/Olympia | Laserlight | 36126
Them Dirty Blues | Capitol | 495447-2
Them Dirty Blues | Blue Note | 495447-2
Them Dirty Blues | Capitol | 495447-2
Them Dirty Blues | Blue Note | 495447-2
Jazz Workshop Revisited | Capitol | 529441-2
At The Lighthouse | Capitol | 531572-2
Cannonball Adderley Birthday Celebration | Fantasy | FANCD 6087-2
Live In San Francisco | Original Jazz Classics | OJC20 035-2
Cannonball Adderley Quintet Plus | Original Jazz Classics | OJC20 306-2
The Cannonball Adderley Quintet:Paris 1960 | Pablo | PACD 5303-2
Live In San Francisco | Riverside | RISA 1157-6
Cannonball Adderley Quintet Plus
Cannonball Adderley Birthday Celebration | Fantasy | FANCD 6087-2
Cannonball Adderley Quintet Plus | Original Jazz Classics | OJC20 306-2
Cannonball Adderley Sextet
Julian Cannonball Adderlry: Salle Pleyel/Olympia | Laserlight | 36126
Jazz Workshop Revisited | Capitol | 529441-2
Ballads | Blue Note | 537563-2
Cannonball Adderley Birthday Celebration | Fantasy | FANCD 6087-2
Dizzy's Business-Live In Concert | Milestone | MCD 47069-2
Cannonball Adderley In New York | Original Jazz Classics | OJC20 142-2(RLP 9404)
Nippon Soul | Original Jazz Classics | OJC20 435-2(RLP 9477)
Cannonball Adderley-Nat Adderley Quintet
What Is This Thing Called Soul:In Europe-Live! | Original Jazz Classics | OJCCD 801-2(2308238)
Cannonball Adderley-Nat Adderley Sextet
The Best Of Cannonball Adderley:The Capitol Years | Capitol | 795482-2
Cecil Taylor Quintet
Trane's Blues | Blue Note | 498240-2
Dexter Gordon Quintet
Dexter Gordon Birthday Celebration | Fantasy | FANCD 6082-2
Tangerine | Original Jazz Classics | OJCCD 1041-2(P 10091)
Eddie Cleanhead Vinson With The Cannonball Adderley Quintet
Cannonball Adderley Birthday Celebration | Fantasy | FANCD 6087-2
Eddie 'Cleanhead' Vinson With The Cannonball Adderley Quintet | Milestone | MCD 9324-2
Freddie Hubbard Septet
The Body And The Soul | Impulse(MCA) | 951183-2
Gene Ammons Septet
Goodbye | Original Jazz Classics | OJCCD 1081-2(P 100939)
Grant Green Quartet
Ballads | Blue Note | 537560-2
Grant Green Quintet
Kind Of Blue:Blue Note Celebrate The Music Of Miles Davis | Blue Note | 534255-2
Ballads | Blue Note | 537560-2
Harold Land Sextet
Wes Montgomery-The Complete Riverside Recordings | Riverside | 12 RCD 4408-2
Horace Silver Quintet
Blowin' The Blues Away | Blue Note | 495342-2
Horace Silver Retrospective | Blue Note | 495576-2
Blue Velvet: Crooners, Swooners And Velvet Vocals | Blue Note | 521153-2
Six Pieces Of Silver | Blue Note | 525648-2
True Blue | Blue Note | 534032-2
Stylings Of Silver | Blue Note | 540034-2
Finger Poppin' | Blue Note | 542304-2
The Best Of Blue Note Vol.2 | Blue Note | 797960-2
A Prescription For The Blues | Impulse(MCA) | 951238-2
Newport Jazz Festival 1958,July 3rd-6th,Vol.1:Mostly Miles | Phontastic | NCD 8813
Jackie McLean Sextet
A Long Drink Of The Blues | Original Jazz Classics | OJCCD 253-2(NJ 8253)
Joe Henderson Quartet
Joe Henderson:The Milestone Years | Milestone | 8MCD 4413-2
The Kicker | Original Jazz Classics | OJCCD 465-2
Tetragon | Original Jazz Classics | OJCCD 844-2(M 9017)
The Jazz Giants Play Cole Porter:Night And Day | Prestige | PCD 24203-2
Joe Henderson Sextet
Joe Henderson:The Milestone Years | Milestone | 8MCD 4413-2
The Kicker | Original Jazz Classics | OJCCD 465-2
John Coltrane Quintet
John Coltrane-The Prestige Recordings | Prestige | 16 PCD 4405-2
The Last Trane | Original Jazz Classics | OJC 394(P 7378)
Lush Life | Original Jazz Classics | OJC20 131-2
The Believer | Original Jazz Classics | OJCCD 876-2(P 7292)
The Jazz Giants Play Harold Arlen:Blues In The Night | Prestige | PCD 24201-2
John Lee Hooker Trio
That's My Story | Original Blues Classics | OBCCD 538-2(RLP 12-321)
Lee Morgan Quintet
Take Twelve | Original Jazz Classics | OJCCD 310-2
Les Spann Quintet
Gemini | Original Jazz Classics | OJCCD 1948-2(JLP 9355)
Louis Hayes Sextet
The Crawl | Candid | CCD 79045
Lucky Thompson Quartet
The Art Of Saxophone | Laserlight | 24652
Milt Jackson With The Oscar Peterson Trio
Gitanes Jazz 'Round Midnight: Oscar Peterson | Verve | 511036-2 PMS
Nat Adderley Quartet
Wes Montgomery-The Complete Riverside Recordings | Riverside | 12 RCD 4408-2
Work Song | Original Jazz Classics | OJC20 363-2
Naturally! | Original Jazz Classics | OJCCD 1088-2(JLP 947)
Nat Adderley Quintet
Wes Montgomery-The Complete Riverside Recordings | Riverside | 12 RCD 4408-2
Work Song | Original Jazz Classics | OJC20 363-2
Nat Adderley Sextet
Wes Montgomery-The Complete Riverside Recordings | Riverside | 12 RCD 4408-2
Work Song | Original Jazz Classics | OJC20 363-2
Oscar Peterson Sextet
Soul Espanol | Limelight | 510439-2
Oscar Peterson Trio
Oscar Peterson Plays Duke Ellington | Pablo | 2310966-2
Paris Jazz Concert:Oscar Peterson | Laserlight | 36155
Verve Jazz Masters 16:Oscar Peterson | Verve | 516320-2
Swinging Cooperations:Reunion Blues/Great Connection | MPS | 539085-2
The Jazz Giants Play Rodgers & Hammerstein:My Favorite Things | Prestige | PCD 24223-2
Oscar Peterson-Milt Jackson Quartet
Swinging Cooperations:Reunion Blues/Great Connection | MPS | 539085-2
Phineas Newborn Jr. Trio
The Jazz Giants Play Miles Davis:Milestones | Prestige | PCD 24225-2
Prestige All Stars
John Coltrane-The Prestige Recordings | Prestige | 16 PCD 4405-2
The Cats | Original Jazz Classics | OJCCD 079-2(NJ 8217)
The Prestige Legacy Vol.2:Battles Of Saxes | Prestige | PCD 24252-2
Sam Jones Plus 10
Cannonball Adderley Birthday Celebration | Fantasy | FANCD 6087-2
Singers Unlimited + The Oscar Peterson Trio
The Singers Unlimited:Magic Voices | MPS | 539130-2
Sonny Clark All Stars
Dial S For Sonny | Blue Note | 0675621
Sonny Clark Trio
Dial S For Sonny | Blue Note | 0675621
Blue Note Plays Gershwin | Blue Note | 520808-2
Sonny Stitt-Sal Salvador Quintet
Newport Jazz Festival 1958,July 3rd-6th Vol.2:Mulligan The Main Man | Phontastic | NCD 8814
Tommy Flanagan Trio
The Cats | Original Jazz Classics | OJCCD 079-2(NJ 8217)
Tubby Hayes And The All Stars
Rahsaan/The Complete Mercury Recordings Of Roland Kirk | Mercury | 846630-2
Wes Montgomery Quartet
Wes Montgomery-The Complete Riverside Recordings | Riverside | 12 RCD 4408-2
Movin' Along | Original Jazz Classics | OJC20 089-2

Wes Montgomery Quintet
Wes Montgomery-The Complete Riverside Recordings | Riverside | 12 RCD 4408-2
Movin' Along | Original Jazz Classics | OJC20 089-2
Wilbur Harden Quintet
The Art Of Saxophone | Laserlight | 24652

Hayes,Mutt | (clts)
Jack Teagarden With Orchestra
Jazz:The Essential Collection Vol.3 | IN+OUT Records | 78013-2

Hayes,Thamon | (tbvoc)
Benny Moten's Kansas City Orchestra
Planet Jazz:Jimmy Rushing | RCA | 2165371-2

Hayes,Tubby | (fl,ts,vibtympani)
Tubby Hayes And The All Stars
Rahsaan/The Complete Mercury Recordings Of Roland Kirk | Mercury | 846630-2

Hayhurst,Alison | (fl)
Carla Bley Band
Fancy Chamber Music | Watt | 28(539937-2)

Hayhurst,Oli | (b)
Gilad Atzmon & The Orient House Ensemble
Gilad Atzmon & The Orient House Ensemble | TipToe | TIP-888839 2

Hayman,Joe | (as,ts,bscl)
Willie Lewis And His Entertainers
Americans Swinging In Paris:Benny Carter | EMI Records | 539647-2

Hayman,Richard | (arrld)
Cannonball Adderley And His Orchestra
Verve Jazz Masters 31:Cannonball Adderley | Verve | 522651-2

Haynes,Graham | (co,fl-h,keyboards,tibetan-tptp)
Abbey Lincoln With Her Band
Who Used To Dance | Verve | 533559-2
Ed Blackwell Project
Vol.1:What It Is? | Enja | ENJ-7089 2
Vol.2:What It Be Like? | Enja | ENJ-8054 2
Nicolas Simion Group
Black Sea | Tutu Records | 888134-2*
Steve Coleman And Five Elements
On The Edge Of Tomorrow | JMT Edition | 919005-2
Steve Coleman Group
Motherland Pulse | JMT Edition | 919001-2

Haynes,Jeff | (perc)
Cassandra Wilson Group
After The Beginning Again | JMT Edition | 514001-2
Blue Light 'Til Dawn | Blue Note | 781357-2
Traveling Miles | Blue Note | 854123-2
Craig Bailey Band
A New Journey | Candid | CCD 79725

Haynes,Phil | (dr,percvoice)
Ullmann-Wille-Haynes
Trad Corrosion | Nabel Records:Jazz Network | CD 4673

Haynes,Roland | (b)
Shelly Manne Sextet
Alive In London | Original Jazz Classics | OJCCD 773-2(S 7629)

Haynes,Roy | (dr,bell-tree,cabasa,perctympany)
Archie Shepp Sextet
The Way Ahead | Impulse(MCA) | 951272-2
Art Blakey And The Jazz Messengers
The Art Of Jazz | IN+OUT Records | 77028-2
Art Blakey Percussion Ensemble
Drums Around The Corner | Blue Note | 521455-2
Art Farmer Quartet
The Jazz Giants Play Jerome Kern:Yesterdays | Prestige | PCD 24202-2
Art Pepper Quartet
Art Pepper:The Complete Galaxy Recordings | Galaxy | 16GCD 1016-2
Art Pepper Quintet
Art Pepper:The Complete Galaxy Recordings | Galaxy | 16GCD 1016-2
Babs Gonzales And His Band
Voilà | Fresh Sound Records | FSR CD 340
Booker Little Quintet
Eric Dolphy Birthday Celebration | Fantasy | FANCD 6085-2
Bud Powell Quintet
The Amazing Bud Powell Vol.1 | Blue Note | 532136-2
Bud Powell:Bouncing With Bud | Dreyfus Jazz Line | FDM 36725-2
Bud Powell Trio
Bud Powell:Bouncing With Bud | Dreyfus Jazz Line | FDM 36725-2
Bud Powell's Modernists
The Fabulous Fats Navarro Vol.1 | Blue Note | 0677207
The Fabulous Fats Navarro Vol.2 | Blue Note | 0677208
Charlie Parker Quartet
Charlie Parker At Storyville | Blue Note | 785108-2
Charlie Parker Quintet
The Cole Porter Songbook | Verve | 823250-2
Bird: The Complete Charlie Parker On Verve | Verve | 837141-2
Bird At St. Nick's | Original Jazz Classics | OJC20 041-2(JWS 500)
Charlie Parker Sextet
Verve Jazz Masters 28:Charlie Parker Plays Standards | Verve | 521854-2
Charlie Parker:The Best Of The Verve Years | Verve | 527815-2
Talkin' Bird | Verve | 559859-2
Charlie Parker With Strings
Verve Jazz Masters 28:Charlie Parker Plays Standards | Verve | 521854-2
Charlie Parker With Strings:The Master Takes | Verve | 523984-2
Bird: The Complete Charlie Parker On Verve | Verve | 837141-2
Charlie Parker's Jazzers
Bird: The Complete Charlie Parker On Verve | Verve | 837141-2
Chick Corea Trio
Trio Music | ECM | 1232/33(159454-2)
Trio Music,Live In Europe | ECM | 1310(827769-2)
Coleman Hawkins Quartet
Late Night Sax | CBS | 487798-2
Dave Brubeck Quartet
All The Things We Are | Atlantic | 7567-81399-2
Dave Brubeck Quintet
All The Things We Are | Atlantic | 7567-81399-2
Don Sickler Orchestra
Tribute To Charlie Parker Vol.2 | Dreyfus Jazz Line | FDM 37015-2
Eddie Lockjaw Davis And His Orchestra
Eric Dolphy:The Complete Prestige Recordings | Prestige | 9 PRCD-4418-2
Eric Dolphy Quartet
Eric Dolphy:The Complete Prestige Recordings | Prestige | 9 PRCD-4418-2
Eric Dolphy Birthday Celebration | Fantasy | FANCD 6085-2
Out There | New Jazz | NJSA 8252-6
Out There | Original Jazz Classics | OJC20 023-2(NJ 8252)
Eric Dolphy Quintet
Eric Dolphy:The Complete Prestige Recordings | Prestige | 9 PRCD-4418-2
Eric Dolphy Birthday Celebration | Fantasy | FANCD 6085-2
Far Cry | Original Jazz Classics | OJC20 400-2
Eric Dolphy-Booker Little Quintet
Eric Dolphy:The Complete Prestige Recordings | Prestige | 9 PRCD-4418-2
Etta Jones And Her Quartet
Something Nice | Original Jazz Classics | OJCCD 221-2(P 7194)
Etta Jones With Her Trio
Something Nice | Original Jazz Classics | OJCCD 221-2(P 7194)
Etta Jones With The Oliver Nelson Quintet
Hollar! | Original Jazz Classics | OJCCD 1061(PR 7284)
Frank Wess Quintet
The Long Road | Prestige | PCD 24247-2
Gary Burton Quartet
Times Square | ECM | 1111
Planet Jazz:Gary Burton | RCA | 2165367-2
Jack DeJohnette Quintet
The DeJohnette Complex | Original Jazz Classics | OJCCD 617-2
Jack DeJohnette Sextet
The DeJohnette Complex | Original Jazz Classics | OJCCD 617-2
Jackie McLean Quintet
A Blue Conception | Blue Note | 534254-2
John Coltrane Quartet
Coltrane Spiritual | Impulse(MCA) | 589099-2
The Gentle Side Of John Coltrane | Impulse(MCA) | 951107-2
John Coltrane:The Classic Quartet-Complete Impulse Studio Recordings | Impulse(MCA) | 951280-2
John Coltrane Quintet
Impressions | Impulse(MCA) | 543416-2
John Coltrane-Eric Dolphy Quartet
John Coltrane:The Complete 1961 Village Vanguard Recordings | Impulse(MCA) | 954322-2
Jubilee All Stars
Jazz Gallery:Lester Young Vol.2(1946-59) | RCA | 2119541-2
Kai Winding-J.J.Johnson Quintet
The Great Kai & J.J. | Impulse(MCA) | 951225-2
Leon Thomas With Band
Spirits Known And Unknown | RCA | 2663876-2
Lester Young And His Band
Lester Young:The Complete Aladdin Sessions | Blue Note | 832787-2
Mark Isaacs/Dave Holland/Roy Haynes
Encounters | VeraBra Records | CDVBR 2076-2
Michel Petrucciani Quartet
Michel Plays Petrucciani | Blue Note | 748679-2
Michel Petrucciani Trio
Michel Plays Petrucciani | Blue Note | 748679-2
Michel Petrucciani:The Blue Note Years | Blue Note | 789916-2
Miles Davis Quintet
The Jazz Giants Play Rodgers & Hart:Blue Moon | Prestige | PCD 24205-2
Miles Davis Sextet
Miles Davis And Horns | Original Jazz Classics | OJC20 053-2(P 7025)
The Prestige Legacy Vol.1:The High Priests | Prestige | PCD 24251-2
Nat Adderley Quintet
Introducing Nat Adderley | Verve | 543828-2
Oliver Nelson And His Orchestra
Blues And The Abstract Truth | Impulse(MCA) | 951154-2
The Roots Of Acid Jazz | Impulse(MCA) | IMP 12042
Oliver Nelson Quintet
Eric Dolphy:The Complete Prestige Recordings | Prestige | 9 PRCD-4418-2
Eric Dolphy Birthday Celebration | Fantasy | FANCD 6085-2
Straight Ahead | Original Jazz Classics | OJCCD 099-2
The Jazz Giants Play Sammy Cahn:It's Magic | Prestige | PCD 24226-2
Oliver Nelson Sextet
Eric Dolphy:The Complete Prestige Recordings | Prestige | 9 PRCD-4418-2
Eric Dolphy Birthday Celebration | Fantasy | FANCD 6085-2
Screamin' The Blues | Original Jazz Classics | OJC 080(NJ 8243)
Soul Street | Original Jazz Classics | OJCCD 987-2(NJ 8293)
The Prestige Legacy Vol.2:Battles Of Saxes | Prestige | PCD 24252-2
Pharoah Sanders Orchestra
Jewels Of Thought | Impulse(MCA) | 951247-2
Thembi | Impulse(MCA) | 951253-2
Red Rodney All Stars
A Tribute To Charlie Parker Vol.1 | Storyville | 4960483
Red Rodney Quintet
The Red Rodney Quintets | Fantasy | FCD 24758-2
Roland Kirk Quartet
Talkin' Verve-Roots Of Acid Jazz:Roland Kirk | Verve | 533101-2
Domino | Verve | 543833-2
Rahsaan/The Complete Mercury Recordings Of Roland Kirk | Mercury | 846630-2
Roy Haynes Quartet
Out Of The Afternoon | Impulse(MCA) | 951180-2
Fountain Of Youth | Dreyfus Jazz Line | FDM 36663-2
Cymbalism | Original Jazz Classics | OJCCD 1079-2(NJ 8287)
Roy Haynes Quintet
Birds Of A Feather:A Tribute To Charlie Parker | Dreyfus Jazz Line | FDM 36625-2
Roy Haynes Trio
The Roy Haynes Trio | Verve | 543534-2
We Three | Original Jazz Classics | OJCCD 196-2(NJ 8210)
Sarah Vaughan And Her Trio
Swingin' Easy | EmArCy | 514072-2
Verve Jazz Masters 42:Sarah Vaughan-The Jazz Sides | Verve | 526817-2
Verve Jazz Masters Vol.60:The Collection | Verve | 529866-2
4 By 4:Ella Fitzgerald/Sarah Vaughan/Billie Holiday/Dinah Washington | Verve | 559693-2
Sarah Vaughan With Her Quartet
Verve Jazz Masters 42:Sarah Vaughan-The Jazz Sides | Verve | 526817-2
Sarah Vaughan With The Clifford Brown All Stars
Verve Jazz Masters 20:Introducing | Verve | 519853-2
Clifford Brown-Max Roach:Alone Together-The Best Of The Mercury Years | Verve | 526373-2
Sarah Vaughan | Verve | 543305-2
4 By 4:Ella Fitzgerald/Sarah Vaughan/Billie Holiday/Dinah Washington | Verve | 559693-2
Brownie-The Complete EmArCy Recordings Of Clifford Brown | EmArCy | 838306-2
Sarah Vaughan | EmArCy | 9860779
Sarah Vaughan With The Jimmy Jones Trio
Linger Awhile | Pablo | 2312144-2
Sarah Vaughan | Verve | 543305-2
Sarah Vaughan Birthday Celebration | Fantasy | FANCD 6090-2
Shirley Scott Quintet
Queen Of The Organ-Shirley Scott Memorial Album | Prestige | PRCD 11027-2
Sonny Rollins Orchestra
Sonny Rollins And The Big Brass | Verve | 557545-2
Sonny Rollins Quartet
Sonny Rollins-The Freelance Years:The Complete Riverside & Contemporary Recordings | Riverside | 5 RCD 4427-2
The Sound Of Sonny | Original Jazz Classics | OJC20 029-2
Sonny Rollins With The Modern Jazz Quartet | Original Jazz Classics | OJCCD 011-2
The Jazz Giants Play Jerome Kern:Yesterdays | Prestige | PCD 24202-2
The Jazz Giants Play Cole Porter:Night And Day | Prestige | PCD 24203-2
Sonny Rollins Trio
The Sound Of Sonny | Original Jazz Classics | OJC20 029-2
Stan Getz New Quartet
Stan Getz Highlights:The Best Of The Verve Years Vol.2 | Verve | 517330-2
Stan Getz Quartet
Stan Getz-The Complete Roost Sessions | EMI Records | 859622-2
Stan Getz:Imagination | Dreyfus Jazz Line | FDM 36733-2
Stan Getz Quartets | Original Jazz Classics | OJC20 121-2(P 7002)
The Jazz Giants Play Rodgers & Hart:Blue Moon | Prestige | PCD 24205-2
Stan Getz Quintet
Stan Getz-The Complete Roost Sessions | EMI Records | 859622-2
Stan Getz With The Eddie Sauter Orchestra
A Life In Jazz:A Musical Biography | Verve | 535119-2
Ultimate Stan Getz selected by Joe Henderson | Verve | 557532-2
Stan Getz Highlights | Verve | 847430-2
Stan Getz With The Richard Evans Orchestra
What The World Needs Now-Stan Getz Plays Bacharach And David | Verve | 557450-2
Stan Getz-Bob Brookmeyer Quintet
Stan Getz Highlights:The Best Of The Verve Years Vol.2 | Verve | 517330-2
A Life In Jazz:A Musical Biography | Verve | 535119-2
Stephane Grappelli-Michel Petrucciani Quartet
Flamingo | Dreyfus Jazz Line | FDM 36580-2
Thelonious Monk Quartet
Jazz Profile:Thelonious Monk | Blue Note | 823518-2
Thelonious Monk:85th Birthday Celebration | zyx records | FANCD 6076-2
Misterioso | Original Jazz Classics | OJC20 206-2
Thelonious In Action | Original Jazz Classics | OJCCD 103-2
Wardell Gray Quartet
Wardell Gray Memorial Vol.1 | Original Jazz Classics | OJCCD 050-2(P 7008)
Willis Jackson Group
At Large | Prestige | PCD 24243-2

Haynes,Stephen | (tp)
Gunter Hampel New York Orchestra
Fresh Heat-Live At Sweet Basil | Birth | CD 039

Hayres,Bill | (tb)
Doug Richford's London Jazzmen
The Golden Years Of Revival Jazz,Sampler | Storyville | 109 1001

Hays,Kevin | (p,el-b,clavinettalking)
Antonio Hart Group
Ama Tu Sonrisa | Enja | ENJ-9404 2
Chris Potter & Jazzpar Septet
This Will Be | Storyville | STCD 4245
Chris Potter Group
Traveling Mercies | Verve | 018243-2
Chris Potter Quartet
Gratitude | Verve | 549433-2
This Will Be | Storyville | STCD 4245
Joshua Redman Quartet
Joshua Redman | Warner | 9362-45242-2
Klaus Doldinger Group
Back In New York:Blind Date | Atlantic | 3984-26922-2

Hayse,Alvin | (tb)
Lionel Hampton And His Orchestra
Lionel Hampton's Paris All Stars | Vogue | 21511502
Lionel Hampton:Flying Home | Dreyfus Jazz Line | FDM 36735-2

Hayton,Lennie | (arr,ld,dr,pceleste)
Lena Horne With The Horace Henderson Orchestra
Planet Jazz:Lena Horne | Planet Jazz | 2165373-2
Lena Horne With The Lennie Hayton Orchestra
Planet Jazz:Lena Horne | Planet Jazz | 2165373-2

Hayward,Andre | (tb)
Dave Holland Big Band
What Goes Around | ECM | 1777(014002-2)

Hayward,Charles | (dr,hand-perc,tipanmetal)
Heiner Goebbels Group
Shadow/Landscape With Argonauts | ECM | 1480
Heiner Goebbels/Heiner Müller
Der Mann Im Fahrstuhl | ECM | 1369(837110-2)

Hayward,Chris | (fl)
Renaud Garcia-Fons
Navigatore | Enja | ENJ-9418 2
Renaud Garcia-Fons Group
Oriental Bass | Enja | ENJ-9334 2
Navigatore | Enja | ENJ-9418 2

Haywood,Cedric | (p)
Henry Red Allen Band
The Very Best Of Dixieland Jazz | Verve | 535529-2
Kid Ory And His Band
The Very Best Of Dixieland Jazz | Verve | 535529-2
Kid Ory's Creole Jazz Band
This Kid's The Greatest! | Good Time Jazz | GTCD 12045-2

Haywood,Marilyn | (voc)
Eddie Harris Group
The Best Of Eddie Harris | Atlantic | 7567-81370-2

Hazar,Nedim | (accordeon,voicerecitation)
Kölner Saxophon Mafia With Nedim Hazar And Orhan Temur
Kölner Saxophon Mafia Proudly Presents | Jazz Haus Musik | JHM 0046 CD

Hazard,Dick | (arr,ldp)
Jerri Southern And The Dick Hazard Quartet
Misty Blue:Sweet Sisters Swing Songs Of Sorrow And Sadness | Blue Note | 521151-2
Mel Tormé With Orchestra
Comin' Home Baby!/Sings Sunday In New York | Warner | 8122-75438-2

Hazlett,Chester | (as,b-clcl)
Jack Teagarden With Orchestra
Jazz:The Essential Collection Vol.3 | IN+OUT Records | 78013-2
Paul Whiteman And His Orchestra
Planet Jazz:Jazz Trumpet | Planet Jazz | 2169654-2

Hazoumé,Roger Aralamon | (african-perc,balafondancer)
Sun Ra And His Intergalactic Research Arkestra
Black Myth/Out In Space | MPS | 557656-2

Head,Marilyn | (flpiccolo)
Doug Sides Ensemble
Sumblo | Laika Records | 35100882

Heafner,Susan | (voc)
The Sidewalks Of New York
Tin Pan Alley:The Sidewalks Of New York | Winter&Winter | 910038-2

Heantzschel,Georg | (p)
Brocksi-Quartett
Globetrotter | Bear Family Records | BCD 15912 AH

Heard,Eugene 'Fats' | (dr)
Erroll Garner Quartet
Verve Jazz Masters 7:Erroll Garner | Verve | 518197-2
Verve Jazz Masters 20:Introducing | Verve | 519853-2
Contrasts | Verve | 558077-2
Erroll Garner Trio
Contrasts | Verve | 558077-2

Heard,J.C. | (dr)
Ben Webster With The Oscar Peterson Quartet
King Of The Tenors | Verve | 519806-2
Ultimate Ben Webster selected by James Carter | Verve | 557537-2
Billie Holiday And Her Orchestra
Solitude | Verve | 519810-2
Billie Holiday With Teddy Wilson And His Orchestra
Billie's Love Songs | Nimbus Records | NI 2000
Billie Holiday With The JATP All Stars
Billie Holiday Story Vol.1:Jazz At The Philharmonic | Verve | 521642-2
The Complete Jazz At The Philharmonic On Verve 1944-1949 | Verve | 523893-2
Verve Jazz Masters 47:Billie Holiday Sings Standards | Verve | 527650-2
Jazz At The Philharmonic:Best Of The 1940's Concerts | Verve | 557534-2
Buck Clayton Quartet
The Complete Jazz At The Philharmonic On Verve 1944-1949 | Verve | 523893-2
Bud Freeman All Stars
The Bud Freeman All-Star Sessions | Prestige | PRCD 24286-2
Cab Calloway And His Orchestra
Planet Jazz:Cab Calloway | Planet Jazz | 2161237-2
Planet Jazz:Male Jazz Vocalists | Planet Jazz | 2169657-2
Coleman Hawkins Quartet
The Complete Jazz At The Philharmonic On Verve 1944-1949 | Verve | 523893-2
Dizzy Gillespie All Stars
Verve Jazz Masters 25:Stan Getz & Dizzy Gillespie | Verve | 521852-2
Dizzy Gillespie And His Orchestra
Planet Jazz:Dizzy Gillespie | Planet Jazz | 2152069-2
Planet Jazz Sampler | Planet Jazz | 2152326-2
Planet Jazz:Jazz Greatest Hits | Planet Jazz | 2169648-2
Planet Jazz:Bebop | RCA | 2169650-2
Dizzy Gillespie:Night In Tunisia | Dreyfus Jazz Line | FDM 36734-2
Don Byas All Stars
Don Byas:Laura | Dreyfus Jazz Line | FDM 36714-2
Don Byas Quartet

Don Byas:Laura | Dreyfus Jazz Line | FDM 36714-2
Gene Ammons Quartet
The Jazz Giants Play Rodgers & Hart:Blue Moon | Prestige | PCD 24205-2
Gene Ammons Quintet
The Jazz Giants Play Jerome Kern:Yesterdays | Prestige | PCD 24202-2
The Jazz Giants Play Cole Porter:Night And Day | Prestige | PCD 24203-2
Gentle Jug Vol.3 | Prestige | PCD 24249-2
Ike Quebec Quartet
Midnight Blue(The [Be]witching Hour) | Blue Note | 854365-2
Ike Quebec Quintet
The Blue Note Swingtets | Blue Note | 495697-2
Ike Quebec Swing Seven
The Blue Note Swingtets | Blue Note | 495697-2
Ike Quebec Swingtet
The Blue Note Swingtets | Blue Note | 495697-2
JATP All Stars
JATP In Tokyo | Pablo | 2620104-2
The Complete Jazz At The Philharmonic On Verve 1944-1949 | Verve | 523893-2
Jazz At The Philharmonic:Best Of The 1940's Concerts | Verve | 557534-2
The Cole Porter Songbook | Verve | 823250-2
Kenny Kersey Trio
The Complete Jazz At The Philharmonic On Verve 1944-1949 | Verve | 523893-2
Lester Young Quintet
The Complete Jazz At The Philharmonic On Verve 1944-1949 | Verve | 523893-2
Lester Young With The Oscar Peterson Quartet
Jazz Gallery:Lester Young Vol.2(1946-59) | RCA | 2119541-2
Lester Young With The Oscar Peterson Trio | Verve | 521451-2
Verve Jazz Masters 30:Lester Young | Verve | 521859-2
New Orleans Feetwarmers
Jazz:The Essential Collection Vol.1 | IN+OUT Records | 78011-2
Norman Granz Jam Session
Verve Jazz Masters 35:Johnny Hodges | Verve | 521857-2
Charlie Parker:The Best Of The Verve Years | Verve | 527815-2
Talkin' Bird | Verve | 559859-2
Bird: The Complete Charlie Parker On Verve | Verve | 837141-2
Pete Johnson's Housewarmin'
Jazz:The Essential Collection Vol.3 | IN+OUT Records | 78013-2
Roy Eldridge Quintet
The Complete Verve Roy Eldridge Studio Sessions | Verve | 9861278
Sarah Vaughan With George Treadwell And His Allstars
Sarah Vaughan:Lover Man | Dreyfus Jazz Line | FDM 36739-2
Shorty Baker-Doc Cheatham Quintet
Shorty & Doc | Original Jazz Classics | OJCCD 839-2(SV 2021)
Slam Stewart Trio
The Complete Jazz At The Philharmonic On Verve 1944-1949 | Verve | 523893-2

Heard,John | (b,el-bdr)
Bill Perkins-Bud Shank Quintet
The Jazz Giants Play Harold Arlen:Blues In The Night | Prestige | PCD 24201-2
Count Basie Band
Basie Jam No. 2 | Original Jazz Classics | OJCCD 631-2(2310786)
Count Basie Kansas City 5
Milt Jackson Birthday Celebration | Fantasy | FANCD 6079-2
Count Basie Kansas City 7
Count Basie Kansas City 7 | Original Jazz Classics | OJCCD 690-2(2310908)
Count Basie-Oscar Peterson Quartet
The Timekeepers-Count Basie Meets Oscar Peterson | Original Jazz Classics | OJC20 790-2(2310896)
Count Basie-Zoot Sims Quartet
Basie & Zoot | Original Jazz Classics | OJCCD 822-2(2310745)
Ella Fitzgerald With The Nelson Riddle Orchestra
Dream Dancing | Original Jazz Classics | OJCCD 1072-2(2310814)
George Cables Trio
By George | Original Jazz Classics | OJCCD 1056-2(C 14030)
Harry Edison Quintet
Edison's Light | Original Jazz Classics | OJCCD 804-2(2310780)
Joe Henderson And His Orchestra
Joe Henderson:The Milestone Years | Milestone | 8MCD 4413-2
Kansas City Seven
The J.J.Johnson Memorial Album | Prestige | PRCD 11025-2
Kenny Burrell Quartet
Stormy Monday Blues | Fantasy | FCD 24767-2
Oscar Peterson Trio
The London Concert | Pablo | 2CD 2620111
The Jazz Giants Play Rodgers & Hart:Blue Moon | Prestige | PCD 24205-2
Sonny Stitt And His West Coast Friends
Art Pepper:The Hollywood All-Star Sessions | Galaxy | 5GCD 4431-2
Zoot Sims Quartet feat.Count Basie
Jazz Dance | Original Jazz Classics | OJCCD 1002-2(1210890)
Zoot Sims With Orchestra
Passion Flower | Original Jazz Classics | OJCCD 939-2(2312120)
Zoot Sims-Harry Edison Quintet
Jazz Dance | Original Jazz Classics | OJCCD 1002-2(1210890)

Heath,Albert 'Tootie' | (dr,perc,didgeridooegyptian-fl)
Art Farmer/Benny Golson Jazztet
The Jazztet At Birdhouse | Argo | 589762-2
Benny Golson Band
Benny Golson:Free | GRP | 951816-2
Blue Mitchell And His Orchestra
A Sure Thing | Original Jazz Classics | OJCCD 837-2
The Jazz Giants Play Jerome Kern:Yesterdays | Prestige | PCD 24202-2
Bobby Timmons Trio
In Person | Original Jazz Classics | OJC20 364-2(RLP 9391)
Bobby Timmons:The Prestige Trio Sessions | Prestige | PRCD 24277-2
Cannonball Adderley Quartet
Takes Charge | Blue Note | 534071-2
Cedar Walton Quintet
Soul Cycle | Original Jazz Classics | OJCCD 847-2(P 7693)
Charles McPherson Quintet
The Jazz Giants Play Rodgers & Hammerstein:My Favorite Things | Prestige | PCD 24223-2
Clifford Jordan Quartet
Spellbound | Original Jazz Classics | OJCCD 766-2(RLP 9340)
Clifford Jordan Quintet
Mosaic | Milestone | MCD 47092-2
Dexter Gordon Quartet
Dexter Gordon Birthday Celebration | Fantasy | FANCD 6082-2
More Power | Original Jazz Classics | OJC20 815-2(P 7680)
Tower Of Power | Original Jazz Classics | OJCCD 299-2(P 7623)
Dexter Gordon Quintet
Tower Of Power | Original Jazz Classics | OJCCD 299-2(P 7623)
Dexter Gordon-James Moody Quintet
More Power | Original Jazz Classics | OJC20 815-2(P 7680)
Herbie Hancock Orchestra
Herbie Hancock:The Complete Blue Note Sixties Sessions | Blue Note | 495569-2
The Prisoner | Blue Note | 525649-2
Jimmy Heath Orchestra
Cannonball Adderley Birthday Celebration | Fantasy | FANCD 6087-2
Joe Pass Quintet
Joe Pass:Guitar Virtuoso | Pablo | 4 PACD 4423-2
John Coltrane Quartet
John Coltrane-The Prestige Recordings | Prestige | 16 PCD 4405-2
Coltrane | Original Jazz Classics | OJC20 020-2
Lush Life | Original Jazz Classics | OJC20 131-2
John Coltrane Quintet
John Coltrane-The Prestige Recordings | Prestige | 16 PCD 4405-2
Coltrane | Original Jazz Classics | OJC20 020-2
The Mal Waldron Memorial Album:Soul Eyes | Prestige | PRCD 11024-2
John Coltrane Sextet
John Coltrane-The Prestige Recordings | Prestige | 16 PCD 4405-2
Coltrane | Original Jazz Classics | OJC20 020-2
The Prestige Legacy Vol.1:The High Priests | Prestige | PCD 24251-2
Kenny Clarke-Francy Boland Big Band
Three Latin Adventures | MPS | 529095-2
Les Spann Quintet
Gemini | Original Jazz Classics | OJCCD 1948-2(JLP 9355)
Mal Waldron Trio
The Jazz Giants Play Rodgers & Hart:Blue Moon | Prestige | PCD 24205-2
Mel Rhyne Sextet
Organ-izing | Original Jazz Classics | OJCCD 1055-2(JLP 916)
Milt Jackson Quartet
Milt Jackson Birthday Celebration | Fantasy | FANCD 6079-2
Milt Jackson Quintet
At The Village Gate | Original Jazz Classics | OJCCD 309-2
Nat Adderley Quintet
Much Brass | Original Jazz Classics | OJCCD 848-2(R 1143)
Nat Adderley Sextet
Much Brass | Original Jazz Classics | OJCCD 848-2(R 1143)
Niels-Henning Orsted-Pedersen/Sam Jones Quintet
Double Bass | Steeplechase | SCS 1055(Audiophile Pressing)
Roland Kirk With The Benny Golson Orchestra
Rahsaan/The Complete Mercury Recordings Of Roland Kirk | Mercury | 846630-2
Ronnie Mathews Quintet
Ronnie Mathews-Roland Alexander-Freddie Hubbard | Prestige | PRCD 24271-2
Ronnie Mathews Trio
Ronnie Mathews-Roland Alexander-Freddie Hubbard | Prestige | PRCD 24271-2
Tete Montoliu Trio
Tete! | Steeplechase | SCCD 31029
Walter Benton Quintet
Out Of This World | Milestone | MCD 47087-2
Wes Montgomery Quartet
Wes Montgomery-The Complete Riverside Recordings | Riverside | 12 RCD 4408-2
The Incredible Guitar Of Wes Montgomery | Original Jazz Classics | OJC20 036-2
Yusef Lateef Ensemble
Atlantic Saxophones | Rhino | 8122-71256-2
Yusef Lateef Orchestra
Rhino Presents The Atlantic Jazz Gallery | Atlantic | 8122-71257-2

Heath,Don | (dr)
Bob Enevoldsen Quintet
The Complete Nocturne Recordings:Jazz In Hollywood Series Vol.1 | Fresh Sound Records | NR 3CD-101
Bob Enevoldsen Sextet
The Complete Nocturne Recordings:Jazz In Hollywood Series Vol.1 | Fresh Sound Records | NR 3CD-101

Heath,Jimmy | (as,bs,ts,fl,ss,reedsarr)
Art Farmer Quintet
From Vienna With Art | MPS | 9811443
Blue Mitchell And His Orchestra
A Sure Thing | Original Jazz Classics | OJCCD 837-2
The Jazz Giants Play Jerome Kern:Yesterdays | Prestige | PCD 24202-2
Blue Mitchell Sextet
Blue Soul | Original Jazz Classics | OJCCD 765-2(RLP 1155)
Cal Tjader's Orchestra
Talkin Verve/Roots Of Acid Jazz:Cal Tjader | Verve | 531562-2
Carmel Jones Quintet
Jay Hawk Talk | Original Jazz Classics | OJCCD 1938-2(P7401)
Charles Earland Sextet
Jazzin' With The Soul Brothers | Fantasy | FANCD 6086-2
Charlie's Greatest Hits | Prestige | PCD 24250-2
Dizzy Gillespie All Stars
Milt Jackson Birthday Celebration | Fantasy | FANCD 6079-2
Don Sleet Quintet
All Members | Original Jazz Classics | OJCCD 1949-2(JLP 9455)
Dusko Goykovich Quintet
Soul Connection | Enja | ENJ-8044 2
Freddie Hubbard Sextet
Hub Cap | Blue Note | 542302-2
J.J.Johnson Sextet
The Eminent J.J.Johnson Vol.1 | Blue Note | 532143-2
Jimmy Heath Orchestra
Cannonball Adderley Birthday Celebration | Fantasy | FANCD 6087-2
Jimmy Heath Quartet
Blue Soul | Original Jazz Classics | OJCCD 765-2(RLP 1155)
Kenny Dorham Quintet
The Jazz Giants Play Sammy Cahn:It's Magic | Prestige | PCD 24226-2
Miles Davis All Stars
Miles Davis Vol.2 | Blue Note | 532611-2
Miles Davis Sextet
Kind Of Blue:Blue Note Celebrate The Music Of Miles Davis | Blue Note | 534255-2
Miles Davis:The Best Of The Capitol/Blue Note Years | Blue Note | 798287-2
Jazz Profile:Miles Davis | Blue Note | 823515-2
Ballads & Blues | Blue Note | 836633-2
Milt Jackson Orchestra
To Bags...With Love:Memorial Album | Pablo | 2310967-2
Milt Jackson Birthday Celebration | Fantasy | FANCD 6079-2
Big Bags | Original Jazz Classics | OJCCD 366-2(RLP 9429)
Milt Jackson Quartet
In A New Setting | Verve | 538620-2
Milt Jackson Quintet
In A New Setting | Verve | 538620-2
At The Village Gate | Original Jazz Classics | OJCCD 309-2
Nat Adderley And The Big Sax Section
Cannonball Adderley Birthday Celebration | Fantasy | FANCD 6087-2
That's Right | Original Jazz Classics | OJCCD 791-2(RLP 9330)
Sam Jones Plus 10
Cannonball Adderley Birthday Celebration | Fantasy | FANCD 6087-2

Heath,Percy | (b,drcello)
Art Farmer Quintet
Early Art | Original Jazz Classics | OJCCD 880-2(NJ 8258)
Art Farmer Septet
Plays The Arrangements And Compositions Of Gigi Gryce And Quincy Jones | Original Jazz Classics | OJCCD 054-2
Barney Wilen Quartet
Jazz In Paris:Barney Wilen-Jazz Sur Saine | EmArCy | 548317-2 PMS
Barney Wilen Quintet
Jazz In Paris:Barney Wilen-Jazz Sur Saine | EmArCy | 548317-2 PMS
Benny Golson Quintet
Nemmy Golson And The Philadelphians | Blue Note | 494104-2
Benny Goodman Quartet
Verve Jazz Masters 33:Benny Goodman | Verve | 844410-2
Benny Goodman Septet
Verve Jazz Masters 33:Benny Goodman | Verve | 844410-2
Benny Goodman Sextet
Verve Jazz Masters 33:Benny Goodman | Verve | 844410-2
Bill Evans Quintet
Interplay | Original Jazz Classics | OJCCD 308-2
Bud Powell Trio
The Best Of Bud Powell On Verve | Verve | 523392-2
Cannonball Adderley Quartet
Takes Charge | Blue Note | 534071-2
Cannonball Adderley Birthday Celebration | Fantasy | FANCD 6087-2
Know What I Mean? | Original Jazz Classics | OJC 105(R 12-433)
Cannonball Adderley-Milt Jackson Quintet
To Bags...With Love:Memorial Album | Pablo | 2310967-2
Milt Jackson Birthday Celebration | Fantasy | FANCD 6079-2
Cannonball Adderley Birthday Celebration | Fantasy | FANCD 6087-2
Things Are Getting Better | Original Jazz Classics | OJC20 032-2
Charlie Parker Quartet
Verve Jazz Masters 28:Charlie Parker Plays Standards | Verve | 521854-2
Charlie Parker:Bird's Best Bop On Verve | Verve | 527452-2
Charlie Parker:The Best Of The Verve Years | Verve | 527815-2
Charlie Parker | Verve | 539757-2
Talkin' Bird | Verve | 559859-2
Bird: The Complete Charlie Parker On Verve | Verve | 837141-2
Clifford Brown Sextet
Clifford Brown Memorial Album | Blue Note | 532141-2
Coleman Hawkins-Roy Eldridge Quintet
Verve Jazz Masters 43:Coleman Hawkins | Verve | 521856-2
Dizzy Gillespie All Stars
Milt Jackson Birthday Celebration | Fantasy | FANCD 6079-2
Horace Silver Trio
Horace Silver Retrospective | Blue Note | 495576-2
Horace Silver Trio And Spotlight On Drums:Art Blakey-Sabu | Blue Note | 591725-2
J.J.Johnson Sextet
The Eminent J.J.Johnson Vol.1 | Blue Note | 532143-2
Jimmy Heath Orchestra
Cannonball Adderley Birthday Celebration | Fantasy | FANCD 6087-2
John Coltrane-Don Cherry Quartet
The Avant-Garde | Atlantic | 7567-90041-2
The Avantgarde | Rhino | 8122-79892-2
Kenny Dorham Octet
Afro-Cuban | Blue Note | 0675619
Kenny Dorham Quintet
The Jazz Giants Play Sammy Cahn:It's Magic | Prestige | PCD 24226-2
Lou Donaldson Quintet
Clifford Brown Memorial Album | Blue Note | 532141-2
Miles Davis All Star Sextet
Walkin' | Original Jazz Classics | OJC20 213-2
Miles Davis All Stars
Miles Davis Vol.2 | Blue Note | 532611-2
Milt Jackson Birthday Celebration | Fantasy | FANCD 6079-2
Bags' Groove | Original Jazz Classics | OJC20 245-2
Miles Davis And The Modern Jazz Giants | Original Jazz Classics | OJC20 347-2(P 7150)
The J.J.Johnson Memorial Album | Prestige | PRCD 11025-2
Miles Davis And His Orchestra
Collector's Items | Original Jazz Classics | OJC20 071-2(P 7044)
Miles Davis And The Modern Jazz Giants
Thelonious Monk:85th Birthday Celebration | zyx records | FANCD 6076-2
Miles Davis Quartet
Miles Davis Vol.1 | Blue Note | 532610-2
Kind Of Blue:Blue Note Celebrate The Music Of Miles Davis | Blue Note | 534255-2
Miles Davis:The Best Of The Capitol/Blue Note Years | Blue Note | 798287-2
Jazz Profile:Miles Davis | Blue Note | 823515-2
Ballads & Blues | Blue Note | 836633-2
Blue Haze | Original Jazz Classics | OJC20 093-2(P 7054)
The Prestige Legacy Vol.1:The High Priests | Prestige | PCD 24251-2
Miles Davis Quintet
To Bags...With Love:Memorial Album | Pablo | 2310967-2
Thelonious Monk:The Complete Prestige Recordings | Prestige | 3 PRCD 4428-2
Blue Haze | Original Jazz Classics | OJC20 093-2(P 7054)
Walkin' | Original Jazz Classics | OJC20 213-2
Bags' Groove | Original Jazz Classics | OJC20 245-2
The Jazz Giants Play Rodgers & Hart:Blue Moon | Prestige | PCD 24205-2
The Prestige Legacy Vol.1:The High Priests | Prestige | PCD 24251-2
Miles Davis Sextet
Kind Of Blue:Blue Note Celebrate The Music Of Miles Davis | Blue Note | 534255-2
Miles Davis:The Best Of The Capitol/Blue Note Years | Blue Note | 798287-2
Jazz Profile:Miles Davis | Blue Note | 823515-2
Ballads & Blues | Blue Note | 836633-2
Miles Davis And Horns | Original Jazz Classics | OJC20 053-2(P 7025)
The Jazz Giants Play Miles Davis:Milestones | Prestige | PCD 24225-2
The Prestige Legacy Vol.1:The High Priests | Prestige | PCD 24251-2
Miles Davis-Milt Jackson Quintet
Milt Jackson Birthday Celebration | Fantasy | FANCD 6079-2
Miles Davis And Milt Jackson | Original Jazz Classics | OJC20 012-2(P 7034)
Miles Davis-Milt Jackson Sextet
Miles Davis And Milt Jackson | Original Jazz Classics | OJC20 012-2(P 7034)
Milt Jackson Quartet
Milt Jackson Birthday Celebration | Fantasy | FANCD 6079-2
Milt Jackson | Original Jazz Classics | OJC20 001-2(P 7003)
The Jazz Giants Play Rodgers & Hart:Blue Moon | Prestige | PCD 24205-2
The Jazz Giants Play Sammy Cahn:It's Magic | Prestige | PCD 24226-2
Milt Jackson Quintet
Wizard Of The Vibes | Blue Note | 532140-2
Milt Jackson Birthday Celebration | Fantasy | FANCD 6079-2
MJQ | Original Jazz Classics | OJCCD 125-2
Milt Jackson Septet
The Birdlanders Vol.1 | Original Jazz Classics | OJCCD 1930-2
Milt Jackson Sextet
The Birdlanders Vol.1 | Original Jazz Classics | OJCCD 1930-2
Milt Jackson Trio
Milt Jackson Birthday Celebration | Fantasy | FANCD 6079-2
Modern Jazz Quartet
To Bags...With Love:Memorial Album | Pablo | 2310967-2
The Complete Modern Jazz Quartet Prestige & Pablo Recordings | Prestige | 4PRCD 4438-2
The Modern Jazz Quartet At Music Inn With Sonny Rollins,Vol.2 | Atlantic | 7567-80794-2
Blues On Bach | Atlantic | 7567-81393-2
MJQ 40 | Atlantic | 7567-82330-2
Lonely Woman | Atlantic | 7567-90665-2
Rhino Presents The Atlantic Jazz Gallery | Atlantic | 8122-71257-2
Pyramid | Rhino | 812273679-2
Fontessa | Rhino | 8122-73687-2
Milt Jackson Birthday Celebration | Fantasy | FANCD 6079-2
Concorde | Original Jazz Classics | OJC20 002-2
Django | Original Jazz Classics | OJC20 057-2
Topsy-This One's For Basie | Original Jazz Classics | OJCCD 1073-2(2310917)
MJQ | Original Jazz Classics | OJCCD 125-2
Together Again | Pablo | PACD20 244-2(2308244)
The Jazz Giants Play Cole Porter:Night And Day | Prestige | PCD 24203-2
Modern Jazz Quartet & Guests
MJQ 40 | Atlantic | 7567-82330-2
Modern Jazz Quartet And Laurindo Almeida
MJQ 40 | Atlantic | 7567-82330-2
Modern Jazz Quartet And Orchestra
MJQ 40 | Atlantic | 7567-82330-2
Modern Jazz Quartet And Symphony Orchestra
MJQ 40 | Atlantic | 7567-82330-2
Modern Jazz Quartet And The Swingle Singers
MJQ 40 | Atlantic | 7567-82330-2
Modern Jazz Quartet feat.Jimmy Giuffre
MJQ 40 | Atlantic | 7567-82330-2
Modern Jazz Quartet With Sonny Rollins
The Modern Jazz Quartet At Music Inn With Sonny Rollins,Vol.2 | Atlantic | 7567-80794-2
MJQ 40 | Atlantic | 7567-82330-2
Modern Jazz Sextet
Verve Jazz Masters 50:Sonny Sitt | Verve | 527651-2

The Modern Jazz Sextet | Verve | 559834-2
Nat Adderley Sextet
Wes Montgomery-The Complete Riverside Recordings | Riverside | 12 RCD 4408-2
Work Song | Original Jazz Classics | OJC20 363-2
Ornette Coleman Quartet
Tomorrow Is The Question | Original Jazz Classics | OJC20 342-2(S 7569)
Paul Desmond And The Modern Jazz Quartet
MJQ 40 | Atlantic | 7567-82330-2
Paul Desmond Quartet
Planet Jazz:Paul Desmond | Planet Jazz | 2152061-2
Easy Living | RCA | 2174796-2
Ray Charles-Milt Jackson Quartet
Soul Brothers/Soul Meeting | Atlantic | 7567-81951-2
Ray Charles-Milt Jackson Quintet
Soul Brothers/Soul Meeting | Atlantic | 7567-81951-2
Sonny Rollins Quartet
Sonny Rollins-The Freelance Years:The Complete Riverside & Contemporary Recordings | Riverside | 5 RCD 4427-2
Sonny Rollins And The Big Brass | Verve | 557545-2
The Sound Of Sonny | Original Jazz Classics | OJC20 029-2
Sonny Rollins With The Modern Jazz Quartet | Original Jazz Classics | OJCCD 011-2
The Jazz Giants Play Jerome Kern:Yesterdays | Prestige | PCD 24202-2
The Jazz Giants Play Cole Porter:Night And Day | Prestige | PCD 24203-2
The Prestige Legacy Vol.1:The High Priests | Prestige | PCD 24251-2
Sonny Rollins With The Modern Jazz Quartet
The Complete Modern Jazz Quartet Prestige & Pablo Recordings | Prestige | 4PRCD 4438-2
Milt Jackson Birthday Celebration | Fantasy | FANCD 6079-2
Sonny Rollins With The Modern Jazz Quartet | Original Jazz Classics | OJCCD 011-2
The Jazz Giants Play Duke Ellington:Caravan | Prestige | PCD 24227-2
Stan Getz Quartet
Stan Getz:Imagination | Dreyfus Jazz Line | FDM 36733-2
Stan Getz Quartets | Original Jazz Classics | OJC20 121-2(P 7002)
Tadd Dameron And His Orchestra
Clifford Brown Memorial | Original Jazz Classics | OJC20 017-2(P 7055)
The Modern Jazz Society
A Concert Of Contemporary Music | Verve | 559827-2
Thelonious Monk Quintet
Thelonious Monk:The Complete Prestige Recordings | Prestige | 3 PRCD 4428-2
MONK | Original Jazz Classics | OJCCD 016-2
Thelonious Monk/Sonny Rollins | Original Jazz Classics | OJCCD 059-2
The Prestige Legacy Vol.1:The High Priests | Prestige | PCD 24251-2
Thelonious Monk Trio
Thelonious Monk:The Complete Prestige Recordings | Prestige | 3 PRCD 4428-2
Thelonious Monk | Original Jazz Classics | OJC20 010-2(P 7027)
Thelonious Monk/Sonny Rollins | Original Jazz Classics | OJCCD 059-2
Wes Montgomery Quartet
Wes Montgomery-The Complete Riverside Recordings | Riverside | 12 RCD 4408-2
The Incredible Guitar Of Wes Montgomery | Original Jazz Classics | OJC20 036-2
Zoot Sims-Al Cohn Sextet
The Brothers | Original Jazz Classics | OJCCD 008-2

Heath,Shelley | (v)
Vince Jones Group
It All Ends Up In Tears | Intuition Records | INT 3069-2

Heather,Cliff | (b-tbtb)
Louis Armstrong With Gordon Jenkins And His Orchestra And Choir
Ambassador Louis Armstrong Vol.17:Moments To Remember(1952-1956) | Ambassador | CLA 1917
Thad Jones-Mel Lewis Orchestra
The Groove Merchant/The Second Race | Laserlight | 24656

Heberer,Thomas | (tp,computer,electronics,sampling)
Berlin Contemporary Jazz Orchestra
Berlin Contemporary Jazz Orchestra | ECM | 1409
Christoph Haberer Group
Pulsation | Jazz Haus Musik | JHM 0066 CD
European Jazz Ensemble
20th Anniversary Tour | Konnex Records | KCD 5078
European Jazz Ensemble & The Khan Family feat. Joachim Kühn
European Jazz Ensemble Meets The Khan Family | M.A Music | A 807-2
European Trumpet Summit
European Trumpet Summit | Konnex Records | KCD 5064
Franck Band
Dufte | Jazz Haus Musik | JHM 0054 CD
Gabriele Hasler Group
Gabriele Hasler's Rosensrücke | Foolish Music | FM 211096
International Commission For The Prevention Of Musical Border Control,The
The International Commission For The Prevention Of Musical Border Control | VeraBra Records | CDVBR 2093-2
Jazzensemble Des Hessischen Rundfunks
Atmosphering Conditions Permitting | ECM | 1549/50
Sotto In Su
Südamerika Sept. 90 | Jazz Haus Musik | JHM 0051 CD
Vanitas | Poise | Poise 04
Thomas Heberer
Kill Yr Darlins | Poise | Poise 05
Stella | Poise | Poise 08
Mouth | Poise | Poise 09
Thomas Heberer-Dieter Manderscheid
Chicago Breakdown:The Music Of Jelly Roll Morton | Jazz Haus Musik | JHM 0038 CD
What A Wonderful World | Jazz Haus Musik | JHM 0118 CD
Tome XX
The Red Snapper | Jazz Haus Musik | JHM 0047 CD
Third Degree | Jazz Haus Musik | JHM 0063 CD

Hébert,Joseph | (cello)
Tuck And Patti
A Gift Of Love | T&P Records | 9815810

Heckel,Jürgen | (g,el-g,arr,cavaquinto,cavaquino)
Bajazzo
Caminos | Edition Collage | EC 485-2
Harlequin Galaxy | Edition Collage | EC 519-2

Heckel,Stefan | (p)
Vasilic Nenad Balkan Band
Joe-Jack | Nabel Records:Jazz Network | CD 4693

Heckscher Band,members of the Ernie |
Ella Fitzgerald And Her Orchestra
Sunshine Of Your Love | MPS | 533102-2

Hedges,Chuck | (cl)
Jeanie Lambe And The Danny Moss Septet
Three Great Concerts:Live In Hamburg 1993-1995 | Nagel-Heyer | CD 019
Tom Saunders' 'Wild Bill Davison Band' & Guests
Exactly Like You | Nagel-Heyer | CD 023
The Second Sampler | Nagel-Heyer | NHR SP 6

Hedges,Michael | (gg-solo)
Michael Hedges
Aerial Boundaries | Windham Hill | 34 11032-2

Hedman,Norman | (perccongas)
Brainstorm feat. Chico Freeman
The Mystical Dreamer | IN+OUT Records | 7006-2
Chico Freeman And Brainstorm
Sweet Explosion | IN+OUT Records | 7010-2
Jazz Unlimited | IN+OUT Records | 7017-2
Threshold | IN+OUT Records | 7022-2

Hedrich,Christian | (viola)
Terje Rypdal With Strings
When Ever I Seem To Be Far Away | ECM | 1045

Hefti,Neal | (arr,ld,condtp)
Charlie Parker With Strings
Charlie Parker With Strings:The Master Takes | Verve | 523984-2
Charlie Parker With The Neal Hefti Orchestra
Charlie Parker:The Best Of The Verve Years | Verve | 527815-2
Bird: The Complete Charlie Parker On Verve | Verve | 837141-2
Clifford Brown & The Neal Hefti Orchestra
Clifford Brown With Strings | Verve | 558078-2
Clifford Brown With Strings
Clifford Brown-Max Roach:Alone Together-The Best Of The Mercury Years | Verve | 526373-2
Verve Jazz Masters 44:Clifford Brown and Max Roach | Verve | 528109-2
Brownie-The Complete EmArCy Recordings Of Clifford Brown | EmArCy | 838306-2
Coleman Hawkins With Paul Neilson's Orchestra
Body And Soul Revisited | GRP | GRP 16272
Count Basie And His Orchestra
Verve Jazz Masters 2:Count Basie | Verve | 519819-2
The Complete Atomic Basie | Roulette | 828635-2
Della Reese With The Neal Hefti Orchestra
Della | RCA | 2663912-2
JATP All Stars
The Complete Jazz At The Philharmonic On Verve 1944-1949 | Verve | 523893-2
Lucky Thompson And His Lucky Seven
Planet Jazz:Bebop | RCA | 2169650-2
Woody Herman And His Orchestra
The Legends Of Swing | Laserlight | 24659
Woody Herman:Four Brother | Dreyfus Jazz Line | FDM 36722-2
Old Gold Rehearsals 1944 | Jazz Unlimited | JUCD 2079
Woody Herman And The Herd
Woody Herman (And The Herd) At Carnegie Hall | Verve | 559833-2

Hegamin[Nelson],Lucille | (voc)
Lucille Hegamin With Willie The Lion And His Cubs
Songs We Taught Your Mother | Original Blues Classics | OBCCD 520-2

Heggen,Henry | (harm)
Christian Willisohn Group
Blues On The World | Blues Beacon | BLU-1025 2

Hegi,Fritz | (el-p)
Bitkicks
Kickbit Information | ATM Records | ATM 3823-AH

Hehn,Hennes | (b-cl,ts,clss)
Norbert Stein Pata Orchester
Ritual Life | Pata Musik | PATA 5(JHM 50) CD

Heick,Aaron | (cl,ss,engl-h,fl,asoboe)
David Matthews & The Manhattan Jazz Orchestra
Hey Duke! | Milestone | MCD 9320-2
Michael 'Patches' Stewart Group
Penetration | Hip Bop | HIBD 8018

Heidepriem,Lucas | (tbtb-solo)
Lucas Heidepriem
Jazz Unlimited | IN+OUT Records | 7017-2
Lucas Heidepriem Quartet
Voicings | IN+OUT Records | 7011-2

Heidepriem,Thomas | (b,el-b,keyboards,fretless-b)
Bernd Konrad Jazz Group With Symphonie Orchestra
Wen Die Götter Lieben | Creative Works Records | CW CD 1010-1
dAs prOjekT
dAs prOjekT | Foolish Music | FM 211288
HR Big Band
The American Songs Of Kurt Weill | hr music.de | hrmj 006-01 CD
Libertango:Homage An Astor Piazolla | hr music.de | hrmj 014-02 CD
HR Big Band With Marjorie Barnes And Frits Landesbergen
Swinging Christmas | hr music.de | hrmj 012-02 CD
HR Big Band With Marjorie Barnes And Frits Landesbergen And Strings
Swinging Christmas | hr music.de | hrmj 012-02 CD
Jazzensemble Des Hessischen Rundfunks
Atmosphering Conditions Permitting | ECM | 1549/50
Jazz Messe-Messe Für Unsere Zeit | hr music.de | hrmj 003-01 CD

Heider,Peter | (synth,drperc)
Straight Talk
Pure | Jazz 4 Ever Records:Jazz Network | J4E 4719

Heidl,Peter | (fl)
Marcus Sukiennik Big Band
A Night In Tunisia Suite(7 Variationen über Dizzy Gillespie's 'A Night In Tunisia') | Jazz Haus Musik | ohne Nummer

Heidloff,Guido | (voc)
Michael Riessler & Singer Pur with Vincent Courtois
Ahi Vita | ACT | 9417-2

Heidrich,Peter | (viola)
Till Brönner Quartet & Deutsches Symphonieorchester Berlin
German Songs | Minor Music | 801057

Heieck,Fritz | (b)
Louis Stewart-Heiner Franz Quartet
Jazz Guitar Highlights 1 | Jardis Records | JRCD 20141
Winter Song | Jardis Records | JRCD 9005

Heikkinen,Esko | (tp,fl-hpiccolo-tp)
Edward Vesala Group
Lumi | ECM | 1339

Heimes,Martina | (tb)
Ralph Schweizer Big Band
DAY Dream | Chaos | CACD 8177

Heinilä,Kari | (cond,fl,ssts)
Edward Vesala Group
Lumi | ECM | 1339

Heinrichs,Johanna | (voc)
Jazzensemble Des Hessischen Rundfunks
Jazz Messe-Messe Für Unsere Zeit | hr music.de | hrmj 003-01 CD

Heintz,David | (gel-g)
Erika Rojo & Tim Sund
Das Lied | Nabel Records:Jazz Network | CD 4684

Heinz,Günter | (tb)
Andreas Böttcher-Günter Heinz
Ghost Busters | Organic Music | ORGM 9715

Heinze,Volker | (bel-b)
Double You
Menschbilder | Jazz Haus Musik | JHM 0062 CD
Gabriel Pérez Group
La Chipaca | Green House Music | CD 1011
Alfonsina | Jazz 4 Ever Records:Jazz Network | J4E 4751
Matthias Bröde Quartet
European Faces | Edition Collage | EC 517-2
Matthias Bröde Quintet
European Faces | Edition Collage | EC 517-2
Matthias Petzold Esperanto-Music
Lifelines | Indigo-Records | 1001 CD
Reiner Witzel Group
Passage To The Ear | Nabel Records:Jazz Network | CD 4668

Heitbaum,Gerold | (gb)
Salut!
Green & Orange | Edition Collage | EC 488-2

Heitz,Uwe | (dr)
Heiner Franz Trio
Jazz Guitar Highlights 1 | Jardis Records | JRCD 20141
A Window To The Soul | Jardis Records | JRCD 8801
Gouache | Jardis Records | JRCD 8904

Heitzler,Bernd | (b)
Cécile Verny Quartet
Got A Ticket | double moon | DMCD 1002-2

Heitzler,Michael | (cl)
World Quintet
World Quintet | TipToe | TIP-888843 2
Kol Simcha
Contemporary Klezmer | Laika Records | LK 93-048
World Quintet With The London Mozart Players
World Quintet | TipToe | TIP-888843 2
World Quintet With The London Mozart Players And Herbert Grönemeyer
World Quintet | TipToe | TIP-888843 2

Heizler,Bernd | (b)
Cécile Verny Quartet
Métisse | double moon | CHRDM 71010
Kekeli | double moon | CHRDM 71028
Cécile Verny Quintet
Kekeli | double moon | CHRDM 71028

Held,Julius | (v)
Freddie Hubbard Orchestra
The Body And The Soul | Impulse(MCA) | 951183-2
Phil Woods Quartet With Orchestra & Strings
Round Trip | Verve | 559804-2
Wes Montgomery Quartet With The Claus Ogerman Orchestra
Tequila | Verve | 547769-2
Wes Montgomery Quintet With The Claus Ogerman Orchestra
The Antonio Carlos Jobim Songbook | Verve | 525472-2
Talkin' Jazz:Roots Of Acid Jazz | Verve | 529580-2
Tequila | Verve | 547769-2
Wes Montgomery Trio With The Claus Ogerman Orchestra
Tequila | Verve | 547769-2
Wes Montgomery With The Claus Ogerman Orchestra
Verve Jazz Masters 14:Wes Montgomery | Verve | 519826-2
Wes Montgomery With The Don Sebesky Orchestra
Verve Jazz Masters 14:Wes Montgomery | Verve | 519826-2
Talkin' Jazz:Roots Of Acid Jazz | Verve | 529580-2
Bumpin' | Verve | 539062-2

Helfrich,Anke | (p)
Anke Helfrich Trio With Mark Turner
You'll See | double moon | CHRDM 71013

Helias,Mark | (b,b-g,el-b,cello,collegno battuto)
Dewey Redman Quartet
The Struggle Continues | ECM | 1225
Ed Blackwell Project
Vol.1:What It Is? | Enja | ENJ-7089 2
Vol.2:What It Be Like? | Enja | ENJ-8054 2
Marilyn Crispell Trio
Story Teller | ECM | 1847(0381192)
Mark Helias Group
Loopin' The Cool | Enja | ENJ-9049 2
Mark Helias' Open Loose
New School | Enja | ENJ-9413 2
Mark Helias/Gerry Hemingway/Ray Anderson
Bassdrumbone(Hence The Reason) | Enja | ENJ-9322 2
Marty Ehrlich Group
The Long View | Enja | ENJ-9452 2

Hellden,Matthias | (cello,percdondos)
Beng Berger Band
Bitter Funeral Beer | ECM | 1179
Nils Landgren Group
Sentimental Journey | ACT | 9409-2

Helleny,Joel | (tb)
Byron Stripling And Friends
If I Could Be With You | Nagel-Heyer | NH 1010
The New York Allstars
We Love You,Louis! | Nagel-Heyer | CD 029
Oh,Yeah! The New York Allstars Play More Music Of Louis Armstrong | Nagel-Heyer | CD 046
The Second Sampler | Nagel-Heyer | NHR SP 6

Heller,Benny 'Ben' | (g)
Benny Goodman And His Orchestra
Camel Caravan Broadcast 1939 Vol.1 | Phontastic | NCD 8817
Camel Caravan Broadcast 1939 Vol.2 | Phontastic | NCD 8818
Camel Caravan Broadcast 1939 Vol.3 | Phontastic | NCD 8819
More Camel Caravans | Phontastic | NCD 8843/4
More Camel Caravans | Phontastic | NCD 8845/6
Tommy Dorsey And His Orchestra
Planet Jazz:Frank Sinatra & Tommy Dorsey | Planet Jazz | 2152067-2

Heller,Ingmar | (bel-b)
Achim Kaufmann Trio
Weave | Jazz 4 Ever Records:Jazz Network | J4E 4737
Ansgar Striepens Quintet
Dreams And Realities | Laika Records | 35101642
HR Big Band With Marjorie Barnes And Frits Landesbergen
Swinging Christmas | hr music.de | hrmj 012-02 CD
HR Big Band With Marjorie Barnes And Frits Landesbergen And Strings
Swinging Christmas | hr music.de | hrmj 012-02 CD
Jenny Evans And Her Quintet
Gonna Go Fishin' | ESM Records | ESM 9307
John Abercrombie With The Ansgar Striepens Quintet
Dreams And Realities | Laika Records | 35101642
Lee Konitz With The Ed Partyka Jazz Orchestra
Dreams And Realities | Laika Records | 35101642
Olaf Polziehn Trio
American Songbook | Satin Doll Productions | SDP 1032-1 CD
Peter Bolte Trio
Trio | Jazz Haus Musik | JHM 0095 CD
Peter Bolte-Imgmar Heller
Trio | Jazz Haus Musik | JHM 0095 CD
Peter Bolte-Marcio Doctor
Zeitraum | Jazz Haus Musik | JHM 0113 CD
Till Brönner Quintet
My Secret Love | Minor Music | 801051
Till Brönner Quintet With Annette Lowman
My Secret Love | Minor Music | 801051

Heller,Volker | (fl,ss,tskeyboards)
Human Factor
Forbidden City | Nabel Records:Jazz Network | CD 4635

Hellhund,Herbert | (tp,fl-hzither)
Amman Boutz
Some Other Tapes | Fish Music | FM 009/10 CD
Ekkehard Jost Ensemble
Weimarer Balladen | Fish Music | FM 004 CD

Hellman,Marc | (dr)
The New Dave Pike Set & Grupo Baiafra De Bahia
Dave Pike Set:Masterpieces | MPS | 531848-2

Helm,Bob | (cl,alto-cl,as,voc,b-clss)
Lu Watters' Jazz Band
Blues Over Bodega | Good Time Jazz | GTCD 12066-2
Lu Watters' Yerba Buena Jazz Band
The Very Best Of Dixieland Jazz | Verve | 535529-2
Turk Murphy And His Jazz Band
Planet Jazz | Planet Jazz | 2169652-2
The Very Best Of Dixieland Jazz | Verve | 535529-2

Helm,Lenora | (voc)
Antonio Hart Group
Ama Tu Sonrisa | Enja | ENJ-9404 2

Helsing,E. | (g)
Helmut Zacharias mit dem Orchester Frank Folken
Ich Habe Rhythmus | Bear Family Records | BCD 15642 AH

Hemeler,Marc | (p)
Stephane Grappelli Quartet
Grapelli Story | Verve | 515807-2

Hemingway,Gerry | (dr,electronic-dr,glockenspiel,perc)
Frank Gratkowski Trio
Gestalten | Jazz Haus Musik | JHM 0083 CD
James Emery Quartet
Standing On A Whale... | Enja | ENJ-9312 2
Spectral Domains | Enja | ENJ-9344 2
James Emery Septet
Spectral Domains | Enja | ENJ-9344 2
James Emery Sextet
Luminous Cycles | Between The Lines | btl 015(Efa 10185-2)
Klaus König Orchestra
Time Fragments:Seven Studies In Time And Motion | Enja | ENJ-8076 2
Reviews | Enja | ENJ-9061 2
Mark Helias/Gerry Hemingway/Ray Anderson
Bassdrumbone(Hence The Reason) | Enja | ENJ-9322 2
Michel Wintsch & Road Movie

INTERPRETENVERZEICHNIS

Michel Wintsch & Road Movie featuring Gerry Hemingway | Between The Lines | btl 002(Efa 10172-2)

Hemmeler,Marc | (org,pel-p)
Stephane Grappelli And Friends
Grapelli Story | Verve | 515807-2
Stephane Grappelli Quartet
Planet Jazz:Stephane Grappelli | RCA | 2165366-2
I Hear Music | RCA | 2179624-2
Verve Jazz Masters 11:Stéphane Grappelli | Verve | 516758-2

Hempel,Thomas | (dr)
Lothar Müller Trio
Müller Q[kju] | JA & RO | JARO 4251-2

Hemphill,Julius | (as,ts,comp,ld,flss)
Bill Frisell Band
Before We Were Born | Nonesuch | 7559-60843-2
Jean-Paul Bourelly Group
Jungle Cowboy | JMT Edition | 919009-2
World Saxophone Quartet
Plays Duke Ellington | Nonesuch | 7559-79137-2
Dances And Ballads | Nonesuch | 7559-79164-2

Hemphill,Shelton | (tp)
Django Reinhardt With Duke Ellington And His Orchestra
Django Reinhardt:Souveniers | Dreyfus Jazz Line | FDM 36744-2
Duke Ellington And His Famous Orchestra
Planet Jazz:Johnny Hodges | Planet Jazz | 2152065-2
Duke Ellington And His Orchestra
Planet Jazz:Duke Ellington | Planet Jazz | 2152053-2
Planet Jazz:Jazz Greatest Hits | Planet Jazz | 2169648-2
The Legends Of Swing | Laserlight | 24659
Highlights From The Duke Ellington Centennial Edition | RCA | 2663672-2
Carnegie Hall Concert December 1944 | Prestige | 2PCD 24073-2
Carnegie Hall Concert January 1946 | Prestige | 2PCD 24074-2
Carnegie Hall Concert December 1947 | Prestige | 2PCD 24075-2
Jazz:The Essential Collection Vol.2 | IN+OUT Records | 78012-2
Louis Armstrong And His Orchestra
Louis Armstrong:Swing That Music | Laserlight | 36056
Jazz:The Essential Collection Vol.2 | IN+OUT Records | 78012-2
Louis Armstrong:C'est Si Bon | Dreyfus Jazz Line | FDM 36730-2
Louis Armstrong-My Greatest Songs | MCA | MCD 18347
Swing Legends:Louis Armstrong | Nimbus Records | NI 2012

Henck,Herbert | (klavierp-solo)
Herbert Henck
Improvisation IV | Wergo | SM 1067/68-50

Hendal,Karin | (v)
HR Big Band With Marjorie Barnes And Frits Landesbergen And Strings
Swinging Christmas | hr music.de | hrmj 012-02 CD

Henderson,Barringtn | (voc)
Spyro Gyra & Guests
Love & Other Obsessions | GRP | GRP 98112

Henderson,Bill | (pvoc)
Bill Henderson With The Horace Silver Quintet
Horace Silver Retrospective | Blue Note | 495576-2
Charlie Haden Quartet West With Strings
The Art Of The Song | Verve | 547403-2
Count Basie And His Orchestra
Basie's Beatle Bag | Verve | 557455-2
Horace Silver Quintet
Blue Velvet: Crooners, Swooners And Velvet Vocals | Blue Note | 521153-2

Henderson,Bob | (tb)
Bengt-Arne Wallin Orchestra
The Birth+Rebirth Of Swedish Folk Jazz | ACT | 9254-2

Henderson,Bobby | (fr-h,pp-solo)
Bobby Henderson
Key One Up | Vanguard | VCD 79612-2
Singers Unlimited With The Patrick Williams Orchestra
The Singers Unlimited:Magic Voices | MPS | 539130-2

Henderson,Eddie | (fl-h,tpel-tp)
Charles Earland Septet
Charlie's Greatest Hits | Prestige | PCD 24250-2
Courtney Pine Group
Modern Day Jazz Stories | Verve | 529028-2
Eddie Henderson Orchestra
Blue Breaks Beats Vol.2 | Blue Note | 789907-2
Blue Break Beats | Blue Note | 799106-2
Eddie Henderson With The Mulgrew Miller Trio
Trumpet Legacy | Milestone | MCD 9286-2
Essence All Stars
Hot Jazz Bisquits | Hip Bop | HIBD 8801
Herbie Hancock Group
Sextant | CBS | CK 64983
Herbie Hancock Sextet
V.S.O.P. Herbie Hancock-Live At The City Center N.Y. | CBS | 486569-2
Joe Chambers Quintet
Mirrors | Blue Note | 496685-2
Kenny Barron Group
Spirit Song | Verve | 543180-2
Kenny Barron Quintet
Live At Fat Tuesdays | Enja | ENJ-5071 2
Quickstep | Enja | ENJ-6084 2
McCoy Tyner Big Band
The Best Of McCoy Tyner Big Band | Dreyfus Jazz Line | FDM 37012-2

Henderson,Fletcher | (arr,ld,p,announcingvib)
All Star Band
Planet Jazz:Jack Teagarden | Planet Jazz | 2161236-2
Benny Goodman And His Orchestra
Planet Jazz:Benny Goodman | Planet Jazz | 2152054-2
Planet Jazz:Swing | Planet Jazz | 2169651-2
Charlie Christian:Swing To Bop | Dreyfus Jazz Line | FDM 36715-2
More Camel Caravans | Phontastic | NCD 8845/6
Benny Goodman Sextet
Charlie Christian:Swing To Bop | Dreyfus Jazz Line | FDM 36715-2
More Camel Caravans | Phontastic | NCD 8845/6
From Spiritual To Swing | Vanguard | VCD 169/71
Bessie Smith And Her Band
Jazz:The Essential Collection Vol.1 | IN+OUT Records | 78011-2
Bessie Smith With Her Blue Boys
Jazz:The Essential Collection Vol.1 | IN+OUT Records | 78011-2
Connie's Inn Orchestra
Planet Jazz:Coleman Hawkins | Planet Jazz | 2152055-2
Count Basie And His Orchestra
From Spiritual To Swing | Vanguard | VCD 169/71
Fletcher Henderson And His Orchestra
Jazz:The Essential Collection Vol.1 | IN+OUT Records | 78011-2
Jazz:The Essential Collection Vol.3 | IN+OUT Records | 78013-2
Henderson's Hot Six
Jazz:The Essential Collection Vol.1 | IN+OUT Records | 78011-2
The Lousiana Stompers
Jazz:The Essential Collection Vol.1 | IN+OUT Records | 78011-2

Henderson,Horace | (arr,ldp)
Benny Goodman And His Orchestra
Planet Jazz:Benny Goodman | Planet Jazz | 2152054-2
Billie Holiday With Sy Oliver And His Orchestra
Billie's Love Songs | Nimbus Records | NI 2000
Chocolate Dandies
Jazz:The Essential Collection Vol.3 | IN+OUT Records | 78013-2
Coleman Hawkins And His Orchestra
Jazz:The Essential Collection Vol.3 | IN+OUT Records | 78013-2
Fletcher Henderson And His Orchestra
Jazz:The Essential Collection Vol.1 | IN+OUT Records | 78011-2
Lena Horne With The Horace Henderson Orchestra
Planet Jazz:Lena Horne | Planet Jazz | 2165373-2
Louis Armstrong With Sy Oliver And His Orchestra
Satchmo Serenaders | Verve | 543792-2

Henderson,Joe | (alto-fl,ts,fl,ss,perc-overdubbing)
Alice Coltrane Quintet
Joe Henderson:The Milestone Years | Milestone | 8MCD 4413-2
Ptah The El Daoud | Impulse(MCA) | 951201-2
Alice Coltrane Sextet
Joe Henderson:The Milestone Years | Milestone | 8MCD 4413-2
Andrew Hill Sextet
Point Of Departure | Blue Note | 499007-2
Antonio Carlos Jobim Group
Antonio Carlos Jobim And Friends | Verve | 531556-2
Blue Note All Stars
Town Hall Concert | Blue Note | 497811-2
Bobby Hutcherson Quintet
Blue N' Groovy | Blue Note | 780679-2
Charles Earland Septet
Charlie's Greatest Hits | Prestige | PCD 24250-2
Charlie Haden-Joe Henderson-Al Foster
The Montreal Tapes | Verve | 9813132
Duke Pearson Quintet
Sweet Honey Bee | Blue Note | 595974-2
Duke Pearson Sextet
Deep Blue-The United States Of Mind | Blue Note | 521152-2
Sweet Honey Bee | Blue Note | 595974-2
Midnight Blue(The [Be]witching Hour) | Blue Note | 854365-2
Flora Purim And Her Quartet
Joe Henderson:The Milestone Years | Milestone | 8MCD 4413-2
Flora Purim And Her Quintet
Joe Henderson:The Milestone Years | Milestone | 8MCD 4413-2
Flora Purim And Her Sextet
Joe Henderson:The Milestone Years | Milestone | 8MCD 4413-2
Butterfly Dreams | Original Jazz Classics | OJCCD 315-2
Flora Purim With Orchestra
Joe Henderson:The Milestone Years | Milestone | 8MCD 4413-2
Frank Morgan All Stars
Reflections | Original Jazz Classics | OJCCD 1046-2(C 14052)
Freddie Hubbard Septet
This Is Jazz:Freddie Hubbard | CBS | CK 65041
Freddie Hubbard Sextet
Keystone Bop Vol.2:Friday/Saturday | Prestige | PCD 24163-2
Freddie Roach Quartet
So Blue So Funky-Heroes Of The Hammond | Blue Note | 796563-2
Grant Green Quintet
Am I Blue | Blue Note | 535564-2
Grant Green Sextet
Idle Moments | Blue Note | 499003-2
True Blue | Blue Note | 534032-2
Herbie Hancock Orchestra
Herbie Hancock:The Complete Blue Note Sixties Sessions | Blue Note | 495569-2
The Prisoner | Blue Note | 525649-2
Horace Silver Quintet
Horace Silver Retrospective | Blue Note | 495576-2
Song For My Father | Blue Note | 499002-2
The Cape Verdean Blues | Blue Note | 576753-2
Blue Bossa | Blue Note | 795590-2
The Best Of Blue Note | Blue Note | 796110-2
Horace Silver Sextet
Horace Silver Retrospective | Blue Note | 495576-2
The Cape Verdean Blues | Blue Note | 576753-2
J.J.Johnson Quintet
The J.J.Johnson Memorial Album | Prestige | PRCD 11025-2
Joe Henderson
Lush Life-The Music Of Billy Strayhorn | Verve | 511779-2
Joe Henderson And His Orchestra
Joe Henderson:The Milestone Years | Milestone | 8MCD 4413-2
Joe Henderson Group
Double Rainbow | Verve | 527222-2
Porgy And Bess | Verve | 539048-2
Jazzin' Vol.2: The Music Of Stevie Wonder | Fantasy | FANCD 6088-2
Joe Henderson Quartet
Lush Life-The Music Of Billy Strayhorn | Verve | 511779-2
The Blue Note Years-The Best Of Joe Henderson | Blue Note | 795627-2
Joe Henderson:The Milestone Years | Milestone | 8MCD 4413-2
Joe Henderson In Japan | Original Jazz Classics | OJCCD 1040-2(M 9047)
The Kicker | Original Jazz Classics | OJCCD 465-2
Relaxin' At Camarillo | Original Jazz Classics | OJCCD 776-2(C 14006)
Tetragon | Original Jazz Classics | OJCCD 844-2(M 9017)
Keystone Bop Vol.2:Friday/Saturday | Prestige | PCD 24163-2
The Jazz Giants Play Cole Porter:Night And Day | Prestige | PCD 24203-2
Joe Henderson Quintet
Page One | Blue Note | 498795-2
Lush Life-The Music Of Billy Strayhorn | Verve | 511779-2
Our Thing | Blue Note | 525647-2
The Blue Note Years-The Best Of Joe Henderson | Blue Note | 795627-2
Joe Henderson:The Milestone Years | Milestone | 8MCD 4413-2
Multiple | Original Jazz Classics | OJCCD 763-2(M 9050)
Joe Henderson Septet
Antonio Carlos Jobim And Friends | Verve | 531556-2
Mode For Joe | Blue Note | 591894-2
The Blue Note Years-The Best Of Joe Henderson | Blue Note | 795627-2
Joe Henderson Sextet
Joe Henderson:The Milestone Years | Milestone | 8MCD 4413-2
The Kicker | Original Jazz Classics | OJCCD 465-2
Multiple | Original Jazz Classics | OJCCD 763-2(M 9050)
Joe Henderson Trio
Lush Life-The Music Of Billy Strayhorn | Verve | 511779-2
The Blue Note Years-The Best Of Joe Henderson | Blue Note | 795627-2
The State Of The Tenor Vol.1&2 | Blue Note | 828879-2
Joe Henderson:The Milestone Years | Milestone | 8MCD 4413-2
Joe Henderson/Christian McBride
Lush Life-The Music Of Billy Strayhorn | Verve | 511779-2
Joe Henderson/Gregory Hutchinson
Lush Life-The Music Of Billy Strayhorn | Verve | 511779-2
Joe Henderson/Stephen Scott
Lush Life-The Music Of Billy Strayhorn | Verve | 511779-2
Johnny Coles Sextet
True Blue | Blue Note | 534032-2
Kenny Dorham Quintet
Una Mas | Blue Note | 521228-2
Klaus Ignatzek Group
Day For Night | Nabel Records:Jazz Network | CD 4639
Larry Young Quartet
Unity | Blue Note | 497808-2
Lee Konitz-Joe Henderson
Joe Henderson:The Milestone Years | Milestone | 8MCD 4413-2
Lee Morgan Quintet
The Sidewinder | Blue Note | 495332-2
The Rumproller | Blue Note | 521229-2
Blue N' Groovy | Blue Note | 780679-2
The Best Of Blue Note | Blue Note | 796110-2
The Best Of Blue Note Vol.2 | Blue Note | 797960-2
McCoy Tyner Quartet
The Real McCoy | Blue Note | 497807-2
Miroslav Vitous Group
Atlantic Jazz: Fusion | Atlantic | 7567-81711-2
Nat Adderley Quintet
Joe Henderson:The Milestone Years | Milestone | 8MCD 4413-2
Nat Adderley Sextet
Joe Henderson:The Milestone Years | Milestone | 8MCD 4413-2
Ron Carter Orchestra
Parade | Original Jazz Classics | OJCCD 1047-2(M 9088)
Ron Carter Quartet
Parade | Original Jazz Classics | OJCCD 1047-2(M 9088)
Roy Hargrove Quintet With Joe Henderson
Roy Hargrove Quintet With The Tenors Of Our Time | Verve | 523019-2
Shirley Horn Quartet
The Main Ingredient | Verve | 529555-2
Shirley Horn Quintet
The Main Ingredient | Verve | 529555-2

Henderson,Leroy | (dr)
Richard 'Groove' Holmes Trio
Somethin' Special | Pacific Jazz | 855452-2

Henderson,Marlo | (g)
Paulinho Da Costa Orchestra
Happy People | Original Jazz Classics | OJCCD 783-2(2312102)

Henderson,Michael | (bel-b)
Miles Davis Group
Paris Jazz Concert:Miles Davis | Laserlight | 17445
Pangaea | CBS | 467087-2
Agharta | CBS | 467897-2
Live-Evil | CBS | C2K 65135
Dark Magus | CBS | C2K 65137
In Concert | CBS | C2K 65140
On The Corner | CBS | CK 63980

Henderson,Rick | (as)
Dinah Washington And Her Band
After Hours With Miss D | Verve | 0760562
Verve Jazz Masters 40:Dinah Washington | Verve | 522055-2
Duke Ellington And His Orchestra
The Legends Of Swing | Laserlight | 24659
100 Years Duke | Laserlight | 24906
Ellington '55 | Capitol | 520135-2
Great Swing Classics In Hi-Fi | Capitol | 521223-2

Henderson,Scott | (el-gg)
Chick Corea Electric Band
The Chick Corea Electric Band | GRP | GRP 95352
Jean-Luc Ponty Quartet
The Very Best Of Jean-Luc Ponty | Rhino | 8122-79862-2

Henderson,Skitch | (pld)
Frank Sinatra With Orchestra
Planet Jazz:Frank Sinatra & Tommy Dorsey | Planet Jazz | 2152067-2

Henderson,Wayne | (tbeuphonium)
Jazz Crusaders
Chile Con Soul | Pacific Jazz | 590957-2
The Jazz Crusaders
Kind Of Blue:Blue Note Celebrate The Music Of Miles Davis | Blue Note | 534255-2

Henderson,William 'Bill' | (p,el-p,voc,harmoniumsynth)
Donald Byrd Orchestra
Ethiopian Knights | Blue Note | 854328-2
Pharoah Sanders Group
Save Our Children | Verve | 557297-2
Pharoah Sanders Orchestra
Message From Home | Verve | 529578-2

Hendl,Walter | (cond)
Woody Herman And The Herd
Woody Herman (And The Herd) At Carnegie Hall | Verve | 559833-2

Hendricks,Aria | (voc)
Jon Hendricks Group
A Tribute To Charlie Parker Vol.2 | Storyville | 4960493

Hendricks,Belford | (arrld)
Dinah Washington With The Belford Hendricks Orchestra
Verve Jazz Masters 20:Introducing | Verve | 519853-2
What A Diff'rence A Day Makes! | Verve | 543300-2
4 By 4:Ella Fitzgerald/Sarah Vaughan/Billie Holiday/Dinah Washington | Verve | 559693-2

Hendricks,Jon | (narrator,vocwhistling)
Antonio Carlos Jobim Group
Antonio Carlos Jobim And Friends | Verve | 531556-2
Bobby McFerrin Groups
Spontaneous Inventions | Blue Note | 746298-2
George Russell And His Orchestra
Geogre Russell New York N.Y. | Impulse(MCA) | 951278-2
John Hendricks WithThe Dave Lambert Singers
Sing A Song Of Basie | Verve | 543827-2
Jon Hendricks Group
A Tribute To Charlie Parker Vol.2 | Storyville | 4960493
Jon Hendricks With The Herbie Hancock Quintet
Antonio Carlos Jobim And Friends | Verve | 531556-2
Kurt Elling Group With Guests
Live In Chicago | Blue Note | 522211-2
Lambert, Hendricks And Bavan
Planet Jazz:Male Jazz Vocalists | Planet Jazz | 2169657-2
Lambert, Hendricks And Ross
Sing A Song Of Basie | Verve | 543827-2
Makoto Ozone Group
Treasure | Verve | 021906-2
United Future Organizatio
United Future Organization | Talkin' Loud | 518166-2

Hendricks,Judith | (voc)
Jon Hendricks Group
A Tribute To Charlie Parker Vol.2 | Storyville | 4960493

Hendricks,Marjorie | (voc)
Ray Charles And His Orchestra
Ray Charles At Newport | Atlantic | 7567-80765-2

Hendricks,Michelle | (vocvoice)
Art Blakey And The Jazz Messengers
The Art Of Jazz | IN+OUT Records | 77028-2
Jon Hendricks Group
A Tribute To Charlie Parker Vol.2 | Storyville | 4960493

Hendricksen,Arve | (tp)
Silje Nergard Group with Strings
Nightwatch | EmArCy | 9865648

Hendrickson,Al | (el-g,g,bjb-g)
Anita O'Day With The Billy May Orchestra
Verve Jazz Masters 49:Anita O'Day | Verve | 527653-2
Anita O'Day With The Buddy Bregman Orchestra
Pick Yourself Up | Verve | 517329-2
Anita O'Day With The Russ Garcia Orchestra
Verve Jazz Masters 49:Anita O'Day | Verve | 527653-2
Artie Shaw And His Orchestra
Planet JazzArtie Shaw | Planet Jazz | 2152057-2
Planet Jazz:Big Bands | Planet Jazz | 2169649-2
Barney Kessel And His Quintet
To Swing Or Not To Swing | Original Jazz Classics | OJCCD 317-2
Barney Kessel And His Septet
To Swing Or Not To Swing | Original Jazz Classics | OJCCD 317-2
Billy May And His Orchestra
Billy May's Big Fat Brass/Bill's Bag | Capitol | 535206-2
Billy May And His Orchestra With Members Of The Jimmy Lunceford Orchestra
Great Swing Classics In Hi-Fi | Capitol | 521223-2
Buddy Bregman And His Orchestra
Swinging Kicks | Verve | 559514-2
Dizzy Gillespie And His Orchestra
Talking Verve:Dizzy Gillespie | Verve | 533846-2
Ella Fitzgerald With The Billy May Orchestra
Ella Fitzgerald-First Lady Of Song | Verve | 517898-2
The Best Of The Song Books | Verve | 519804-2
Verve Jazz Masters 6:Ella Fitzgerald | Verve | 519822-2
Verve Jazz Masters 46:Ella Fitzgerald-The Jazz Sides | Verve | 527655-2
Ella Fitzgerald Sings The Harold Arlen Song Book | Verve | 589108-2
For The Love Of Ella Fitzgerald | Verve | 841765-2
Hank Crawford Orchestra
Rhino Presents The Atlantic Jazz Gallery | Atlantic | 8122-71257-2
Herbie Harper Quartet
The Complete Nocturne Recordings:Jazz In Hollywood Series Vol.1 | Fresh Sound Records | NR 3CD-101
Louis Armstrong And His Orchestra
I Love Jazz | Verve | 543747-2
Louis Armstrong With The Hal Mooney Orchestra

Ambassador Louis Armstrong Vol.17:Moments To Remember(1952-1956) | Ambassador | CLA 1917
Peggy Lee With The Benny Goodman Orchestra
Peggy Lee & Benny Goodman:The Complete Recordings 1941-1947 | CBS | C2K 65686

Henhennick,G.R. | (viola)
Ella Fitzgerald With The Frank DeVol Orchestra
Get Happy! | Verve | 523321-2

Henke,Fred | (p)
Woody Shaw Quartet
In My Own Sweet Way | IN+OUT Records | 7003-2
Jazz Unlimited | IN+OUT Records | 7017-2

Henkel,Eugen | (ts)
Brocksi-Quartett
Globetrotter | Bear Family Records | BCD 15912 AH
Drums Boogie | Bear Family Records | BCD 15988 AH
Brocksi-Quintett
Drums Boogie | Bear Family Records | BCD 15988 AH
Brocksi-Sextett
Drums Boogie | Bear Family Records | BCD 15988 AH
Shot Gun Boogie | Bear Family Records | BCD 16277 AH
Freddie Brocksieper Orchester
Drums Boogie | Bear Family Records | BCD 15988 AH
Shot Gun Boogie | Bear Family Records | BCD 16277 AH

Henkel,Roland | (dr)
Daniel Guggenheim Group
Daniel Guggenheim Group feat. Jasper van't Hof | Laika Records | LK 990-018

Hennessey,Mike | (p)
Chas Burchell Quartet
Unsong Hero:The Undiscovered Genius Of Chas Burchell | IN+OUT Records | 7026-2
Chas Burchell Quintet
Unsong Hero:The Undiscovered Genius Of Chas Burchell | IN+OUT Records | 7026-2
Chas Burchell Sextet
Unsong Hero:The Undiscovered Genius Of Chas Burchell | IN+OUT Records | 7026-2
Clark Terry Quintet
Unsong Hero:The Undiscovered Genius Of Chas Burchell | IN+OUT Records | 7026-2
Jan Harrington With The Arthur Blythe Quartet
Remembering Dinah-A Salute To Dinah Washington | Hot Shot Records | HSR 8313-2
Jan Harrington With The Mike Hennesey Trio
Remembering Dinah-A Salute To Dinah Washington | Hot Shot Records | HSR 8313-2
Jan Harrington With The Nat Adderley Quintet
Remembering Dinah-A Salute To Dinah Washington | Hot Shot Records | HSR 8313-2
Lilly Thornton With The Benny Golson Quartet
Remembering Dinah-A Salute To Dinah Washington | Hot Shot Records | HSR 8313-2
Lilly Thornton With The Benny Golson Sextet
Remembering Dinah-A Salute To Dinah Washington | Hot Shot Records | HSR 8313-2
Lilly Thornton With The Mike Hennesey Trio
Remembering Dinah-A Salute To Dinah Washington | Hot Shot Records | HSR 8313-2
Nat Adderley Quintet
Remembering Dinah-A Salute To Dinah Washington | Hot Shot Records | HSR 8313-2
Ronnie Scott With The Chas Burchell Quintet
Unsong Hero:The Undiscovered Genius Of Chas Burchell | IN+OUT Records | 7026-2
The Mike Hennessey Chastet
Shades Of Chas Burchell | IN+OUT Records | 7025-2

Henri,Tanya | (voc)
David Binney Group
Balance | ACT | 9411-2

Henrickson,Richard | (v)
A Band Of Friends
Wynton Marsalis Quartet With Strings | CBS | CK 68921

Henriksen,Arve | (tp,trumpophonevoc)
Christian Wallumrod Ensemble
Sofienberg Variations | ECM | 1809(017067-2)
Christian Wallumrod Trio
No Birch | ECM | 1628(537344-2)
Jon Balke w/Magnetic North Orchestra
Kyanos | ECM | 1822(017278-2)
Trygve Seim Group
Different Rivers | ECM | 1744(159521-2)
Trygve Seim-Oyvind Braekke-Per Oddvar Johansen Orchestra
The Source And Different Cikadas | ECM | 1764(014432-2)

Henriques,Joaquim Paes | (dr)
Baden Powell Ensemble
Three Originals:Tristeza On Guitar/Poema On Guitar/Apaixonado | MPS | 519216-2

Henriquez,Carlos | (b)
Gonzalo Rubalcaba Quartet
Supernova | Blue Note | 531172-2
Gonzalo Rubalcaba Trio
Supernova | Blue Note | 531172-2

Henry Jones | (tb)
Louis Armstrong And His Orchestra
Louis Armstrong:Swing That Music | Laserlight | 36056
Swing Legends:Louis Armstrong | Nimbus Records | NI 2012

Henry,Ann | (voc)
Dizzy Gillespie Sextet
Jambo Caribe | Verve | 557492-2

Henry,Bruce | (voice)
Steve Tibbetts Group
Exploded View | ECM | 1335

Henry,Conrad | (b)
Coleman Hawkins All Star Octet
Body And Soul Revisited | GRP | GRP 16272

Henry,Ernie | (asvoc)
Dizzy Gillespie And His Orchestra
Planet Jazz:Dizzy Gillespie | Planet Jazz | 2152069-2
Planet Jazz:Bebop | RCA | 2169650-2
Planet Jazz:Male Jazz Vocalists | Planet Jazz | 2169657-2
Dizzy Gillespie:Birks Works-The Verve Big Band Sessions | Verve | 527900-2
Ultimate Dizzy Gillespie | Verve | 557535-2
Dizzy Gillespie Orchestra
Verve Jazz Masters 10:Dizzy Gillespie | Verve | 516319-2
Matthew Gee All-Stars
Jazz By Gee! | Original Jazz Classics | OJCCD 1884-2(RLP 221)
Tadd Dameron Sextet
The Fabulous Fats Navarro Vol.1 | Blue Note | 0677207
Tadd Dameron-Fats Navarro Quintet
Fats Navarro:Nostalgia | Dreyfus Jazz Line | FDM 36736-2
Tadd Dameron-Fats Navarro Sextet
Fats Navarro:Nostalgia | Dreyfus Jazz Line | FDM 36736-2
The McGhee-Navarro Boptet
The Fabulous Fats Navarro Vol.1 | Blue Note | 0677207
The Fabulous Fats Navarro Vol.2 | Blue Note | 0677208
Thelonious Monk Quintet
Sonny Rollins-The Freelance Years:The Complete Riverside & Contemporary Recordings | Riverside | 5 RCD 4427-2
Thelonious Monk:85th Birthday Celebration | zyx records | FANCD 6076-2
Brilliant Corners | Original Jazz Classics | OJC20 026-2

Henry,Felix | (perc)
Eddie Harris Quintet
The Best Of Eddie Harris | Atlantic | 7567-81370-2

Henry,Haywood | (bs,cl,ts,reedssax)
Al Sears & His Rock 'N' Rollers
Sear-iously | Bear Family Records | BCD 15668 AH
Al Sears And His Orchestra
Sear-iously | Bear Family Records | BCD 15668 AH
Billie Holiday With The Tiny Grimes Quintet
Billie's Blues | Blue Note | 748786-2
Buddy Johnson And His Orchestra
Buddy And Ella Johnson 1953-1964 | Bear Family Records | BCD 15479 DH
Eddie Harris Group
The Best Of Eddie Harris | Atlantic | 7567-81370-2
Erskine Hawkins And His Orchestra
Planet Jazz:Big Bands | Planet Jazz | 2169649-2
Jimmy Witherspoon With Jay McShann And His Band
Planet Jazz:Male Jazz Vocalists | Planet Jazz | 2169657-2

Henry,Oscar | (tb)
Eureka Brass Band
Atlantic Jazz: New Orleans | Atlantic | 7567-81700-2

Henry,Pamela | (voc)
Landes Jugend Jazz Orchester Hessen
Touch Of Lips | hr music.de | hrmj 004-01 CD

Henry,Richard | (b-tb)
Carla Bley Big Band
The Carla Bley Big Band Goes To Church | Watt | 27(533682-2)
Lee Konitz With The Ed Partyka Jazz Orchestra
Dreams And Realities | Laika Records | 35101642

Henry,Sonny | (g)
Willie Bobo Group
Juicy | Verve | 519857-2

Henry,Trey | (b)
Buddy Childers Big Band
It's What Happening Now! | Candid | CCD 79749
Carl Saunders-Lanny Morgan Quintet
Las Vegar Late Night Sessions:Live At Capozzoli's | Woofy Productions | WPCD 109

Henry,Vince | (as,ts,harm,sax,ssb)
Cassandra Wilson Group
Traveling Miles | Blue Note | 854123-2
Jean-Paul Bourelly Trance Atlantic
Boom Bop II | double moon | CHRDM 71023
Maceo Parker Group
Roots Revisited | Minor Music | 801015
Peter Fessler Group
Eastside Moments | Minor Music | 801078

Henryson,Svante | (cello)
Jon Balke w/Magnetic North Orchestra
Kyanos | ECM | 1822(017278-2)
Ketil Bjornstad Group
Seafarer's Song | EmArCy | 9865777

Hensch,Delle | (as)
Freddie Brocksieper And His Boys
Freddie's Boogie Blues | Bear Family Records | BCD 16388 AH

Hensel,Lothar | (bandoneon)
Eckart Runge-Jacques Ammon
Cello Tango | Edition Musikat | EDM 053
Schlothauer's Maniacs
Maniakisses | Timescrapper | TSCR 9811

Hensel,Markus | (tb)
Jazz Fresh
Jazz Fresh | GGG-Verlag:GGG Verlag und Mailorder | CD 01.03

Hensel,Ronald | (org)

Henshaw,Bill | (fr-h)
Peggy Lee With The Quincy Jones Orchestra
Blues Cross Country | Capitol | 520088-2

Hensley,Tom | (keyboards)
Dee Dee Bridgewater With Band
Dee Dee Bridgewater | Atlantic | 7567-80760-2

Henson,Nick | (reeds)
Eric Dolphy Quartet With The University Of Illinois Big Band
The Illinois Concert | Blue Note | 499826-2

Henson,Purvis | (tsvoc)
Buddy Johnson And His Orchestra
Buddy And Ella Johnson 1953-1964 | Bear Family Records | BCD 15479 DH

Henson-Conant,Deborah | (harp,voc,keyboards,synth,perc)
Deborah Henson-Conant
Alter Ego | Laika Records | 35100852
Alterd Ego | Laika Records | 35100962
The Gift:15 Weihnachtslieder der Erde | Laika Records | 35100992
The Celtic Album | Laika Records | 35101022
Naked Music | Laika Records | LK 94-051
Just For You | Laika Records | LK 95-063
Deborah Henson-Conant Group
Deborah Henson-Conant:Best Of Instrumental Music | Laika Records | 35101322
Budapest | Laika Records | LK 93-039
Deborah Henson-Conant Trio
'Round The Corner | Laika Records | LK 87-203
Just For You | Laika Records | LK 95-063

Henze,Andreas | (b)
Cool Blue
House In The Country | Foolish Music | FM 211591
Lothar Müller Trio
Müller Q[kju] | JA & RO | JARO 4251-2

Heral,Patrice | (dr,perc,live-electronics,snare-dr)
Markus Stockhausen Quartet
Karta | ECM | 1704(543035-2)
Joyosa | Enja | ENJ-9468 2
Nicolas Simion Quartet feat. Tomasz Stanko
Dinner For Don Carlos | Tutu Records | 888146-2*
Renaud Garcia-Fons
Navigatore | Enja | ENJ-9418 2
Renaud Garcia-Fons Group
Navigatore | Enja | ENJ-9418 2

Herald,Alice | (voc)
Modern Jazz Quartet And The Swingle Singers
MJQ 40 | Atlantic | 7567-82330-2
Swingle Singers
Swingle Singers Singing Mozart | Philips | 548538-2
Swingling Telemann | Philips | 586735-2
Swingle Singers Getting Romantic | Philips | 586736-2

Herbert,Arthur | (dr)
Coleman Hawkins And His Orchestra
Planet Jazz:Coleman Hawkins | Planet Jazz | 2152055-2
Planet Jazz Sampler | Planet Jazz | 2152326-2
Planet Jazz:Jazz Greatest Hits | Planet Jazz | 2169648-2
Jazz:The Essential Collection Vol.3 | IN+OUT Records | 78013-2

Herbert,Greg | (as,fl,alto-fl,ts,piccoloss)
Chet Baker Quintet
Once Upon A Summertime | Original Jazz Classics | OJCCD 405-2
Woody Herman And His Orchestra
Jazzin' Vol.2: The Music Of Stevie Wonder | Fantasy | FANCD 6088-2
King Cobra | Original Jazz Classics | OJCCD 1068-2(F 9499)
The Raven Speaks | Original Jazz Classics | OJCCD 663-2(F 9416)
Woody Herman Herd At Montreux | Original Jazz Classics | OJCCD 991-2(F 9470)
Woody Herman And The New Thundering Herd
Woody Herman:Thundering Herd | Original Jazz Classics | OJCCD 841-2

Herbert,John | (b)
Andrew Rathbun Group
True Stories | Fresh Sound Records | FSNT 099 CD
Dave Ballou Quartet
Dancing Foot | Steeplechase | SCCD 31556
Friedrich-Herbert-Moreno Trio
Voyage Out | Jazz 4 Ever Records:Jazz Network | J4E 4747
Rez Abbasi Group
Out Of Body | String Jazz | SJRCD 1021

Herbert,Mort | (bv)
Ella Fitzgerald With The Frank DeVol Orchestra
Get Happy! | Verve | 523321-2
Louis Armstrong And His All Stars With Duke Ellington
Louis Armstrong-Duke Ellington:The Great Summit-Complete Session | Roulette | 524546-2
Louis Armstrong And His Orchestra
I Love Jazz | Verve | 543747-2
Louis Armstrong With Sy Oliver's Choir And Orchestra
Jazz Collection:Louis Armstrong | Laserlight | 24366
Louis And The Good Book | Verve | 549593-2
Louis And The Good Book | Verve | 940130-0
Louis Armstrong-Duke Ellington Group
Blue Velvet: Crooners, Swooners And Velvet Vocals | Blue Note | 521153-2
Pete Rugolo And His Orchestra
Thriller/Richard Diamon(Original Jazz Scores From 2 Classics TV Series) | Fresh Sound Records | FSCD 2015

Herbert,Peter | (bel-b)
Franz Koglmann Group
Venus In Transit | Between The Lines | btl 017(Efa 10186)
Franz Koglmann Quintet
Make Believe | Between The Lines | btl 001(Efa 10171-2)
Monoblue Quartet
An Affair With Strauss | Between The Lines | btl 006(Efa 10176-2)
Peter Herbert Group
B-A-C-H A Chromatic Universe | Between The Lines | btl 013(Efa 10183)

Herbig,Gary | (alto-fl,bass-fl,ts,as,cl,b-cl,fl,ss)
Diane Schuur With Orchestra
Blues For Schuur | GRP | GRP 98632
The Best Of Diane Schuur | GRP | GRP 98882
Herbie Hancock Group With String Quartet,Woodwinds And Brass
Herbie Hancock The New Standards | Verve | 527715-2
Herbie Hancock Group With Woodwinds And Brass
Herbie Hancock The New Standards | Verve | 527715-2
Paulinho Da Costa Orchestra
Happy People | Original Jazz Classics | OJCCD 783-2(2312102)
Willie Bobo Group
Jazzrock-Anthology Vol.3:Fusion | Zounds | CD 27100555

Herbolzheimer,Peter | (arr,ld,perctb)
Hans Koller Big Band
New York City | MPS | 9813437
Horst Jankowski Orchestra With Voices
Jankowskeynotes | MPS | 9814806

Herborn,Peter | (arr,ld,tb,bar-heuphonium)
Peter Herborn's Acute Insights
Peter Herborn's Acute Insights | JMT Edition | 919017-2

Herbstleb,Vaness | (voc)
Jazzensemble Des Hessischen Rundfunks
Jazz Messe-Messe Für Unsere Zeit | hr music.de | hrmj 003-01 CD

Herdsmen,The |
The Herdsmen
Nat Pierce-Dick Collins-Ralph Burns & The Herdsmen Play Paris | Fantasy | FCD 24759-2

Herdzin,Krzysztof | (p)
Zbigniew Namyslowski-Remy Filipovitch Quintet
Go! | Album | AS 66919 CD

Herfurt,Arthur 'Skeets' | (as,ts,cl,fl,e-flat-cl,piccolo,reeds)
Ella Fitzgerald With The Frank DeVol Orchestra
Get Happy! | Verve | 523321-2
June Christy With The Pete Rugolo Orchestra
Something Cool(The Complete Mono & Stereo Versions) | Capitol | 534069-2
Louis Armstrong And His All Stars With Benny Carter's Orchestra
Ambassador Louis Armstrong Vol.17:Moments To Remember(1952-1956) | Ambassador | CLA 1917
Louis Armstrong With Benny Carter's Orchestra
Louis Armstrong-My Greatest Songs | MCA | MCD 18347
Louis Armstrong With Jimmy Dorsey And His Orchestra
Louis Armstrong:Swing That Music | Laserlight | 36056
Swing Legends:Louis Armstrong | Nimbus Records | NI 2012
Nat King Cole With The Billy May Orchestra
Nat King Cole:For Sentimental Reasons | Dreyfus Jazz Line | FDM 36740-2
Stan Kenton And His Orchestra
Great Swing Classics In Hi-Fi | Capitol | 521223-2
Tommy Dorsey And His Orchestra
Planet Jazz:Tommy Dorsey | Planet Jazz | 2159972-2

Hergenröder,Stefan | (el-b)
Jamenco
Conversations | Trick Music | TM 9202 CD

Herington,Joe | (g,el-g,mandmandolin)
Michael Brecker Group
Now You See It...(Now You Don't) | GRP | GRP 96222
Michael 'Patches' Stewart Group
Penetration | Hip Bop | HIBD 8018

Herjö,Axel | (v)
Bengt-Arne Wallin Orchestra
The Birth+Rebirth Of Swedish Folk Jazz | ACT | 9254-2

Herman,Bonnie | (voc)
Eberhard Weber Group
Fluid Rustle | ECM | 1137
Singers Unlimited
The Singers Unlimited:Magic Voices | MPS | 539130-2
Singers Unlimited + The Oscar Peterson Trio
The Singers Unlimited:Magic Voices | MPS | 539130-2
Singers Unlimited With Orchestra
The Singers Unlimited:Magic Voices | MPS | 539130-2
Singers Unlimited With Rob McConnell And The Boss Brass
The Singers Unlimited:Magic Voices | MPS | 539130-2
Singers Unlimited With Roger Kellaway
The Singers Unlimited:Magic Voices | MPS | 539130-2
Singers Unlimited With The Art Van Damme Quintet
The Singers Unlimited:Magic Voices | MPS | 539130-2
Singers Unlimited With The Clare Fischer Orchestra
The Singers Unlimited:Magic Voices | MPS | 539130-2
Singers Unlimited With The Pat Williams Orchestra
The Singers Unlimited:Magic Voices | MPS | 539130-2
Singers Unlimited With The Patrick Williams Orchestra
The Singers Unlimited:Magic Voices | MPS | 539130-2
Singers Unlimited With The Robert Farnon Orchestra
The Singers Unlimited:Magic Voices | MPS | 539130-2
Singers Unlimited With The Roger Kellaway Cello Quartet
The Singers Unlimited:Magic Voices | MPS | 539130-2

Herman,Max | (tp)
Bob Crosby And His Orchestra
Swing Legens:Bob Crosby | Nimbus Records | NI 2011

Herman,Mookie | (b)
Doug Richford's London Jazzmen
The Golden Years Of Revival Jazz,Sampler | Storyville | 109 1001

Herman,Ray | (ts)
Vic Lewis West Coast All Stars
Me And You! | Candid | CCD 79739

Herman,Ron | (b)
John Stevens Quartet
Re-Touch & Quartet | Konnex Records | KCD 5027

Herman,Sam | (gshaker)
Thad Jones-Mel Lewis Orchestra
The Groove Merchant/The Second Race | Laserlight | 24656
Tommy Dorsey And His Orchestra
Planet Jazz:Tommy Dorsey | Planet Jazz | 2159972-2

Herman,Woody | (as,cl,ld,vocss)
Woody Herman And His Orchestra
The Legends Of Swing | Laserlight | 24659
Great Swing Classics In Hi-Fi | Capitol | 521223-2
Verve Jazz Masters 54:Woody Herman | Verve | 529903-2
Songs For Hip Lovers | Verve | 559872-2

Woody Herman-1963 | Philips | 589490-2
Jazzin' Vol.2: The Music Of Stevie Wonder | Fantasy | FANCD 6088-2
Woody Herman:Four Brother | Dreyfus Jazz Line | FDM 36722-2
Louis Armstrong-Jack Teagarden-Woody Herman:Midnights At V-Disc | Jazz Unlimited | JUCD 2048
Old Gold Rehearsals 1944 | Jazz Unlimited | JUCD 2079
Brand New | Original Jazz Classics | OJCCD 1044-2(F 8414)
King Cobra | Original Jazz Classics | OJCCD 1068-2(F 9499)
The Raven Speaks | Original Jazz Classics | OJCCD 663-2(F 9416)
Woody Herman Herd At Montreux | Original Jazz Classics | OJCCD 991-2(F 9470)
Woody Herman And His Sextet
Songs For Hip Lovers | Verve | 559872-2
Woody Herman And His Woodshoppers
Woody Herman (And The Herd) At Carnegie Hall | Verve | 559833-2
Woody Herman And The Herd
Woody Herman (And The Herd) At Carnegie Hall | Verve | 559833-2
Woody Herman And The New Thundering Herd
Planet Jazz:Big Bands | Planet Jazz | 2169649-2
Woody Herman:Thundering Herd | Original Jazz Classics | OJCCD 841-2
Woody Herman And The Vanderbilt All Stars
Louis Armstrong-Jack Teagarden-Woody Herman:Midnights At V-Disc | Jazz Unlimited | JUCD 2048
Woody Herman's Thundering Herd
Planet Jazz:Jazz Saxophone | Planet Jazz | 2169653-2

Hermannsdörfer,Heinz | (tb)
Kurt Edelhagen All Stars
Deutsches Jazz Fesival 1954/1955 | Bear Family Records | BCD 15430
Kurt Edelhagen All Stars Und Solisten
Deutsches Jazz Fesival 1954/1955 | Bear Family Records | BCD 15430
Quartet Der Kurt Edelhagen All Stars
Deutsches Jazz Fesival 1954/1955 | Bear Family Records | BCD 15430

Hermo,Cinta | (g,percvoc)
Piirpauke
Zerenade | JA & RO | JARO 4142-2
Piirpauke-Global Servisi | JA & RO | JARO 4150-2
Tuku Tuku | JA & RO | JARO 4158-2

Hernandez,Amado De Jesus Dedeu | (ld)
Conjunto Clave Y Guaguanco
Dejala En La Puntica | TipToe | TIP-888829 2

Hernandez,Denis 'El Huevo' | (tp)
Big Band Bellaterra
Don't Git Sassy | Fresh Sound Records | FSNT 048 CD

Hernandez,Frank | (dr)
Mongo Santamaria And His Band
Mongo At The Village Gate | Original Jazz Classics | OJCCD 490-2(RLP 9529)

Hernandez,Hector 'Flaco' | (checkere,lya,congas,batachekere)
Jerry Gonzalez & Fort Apache Band
The River Is Deep | Enja | ENJ-4040 2

Hernandez,Horacio 'El Negro' | (dr,perc,timbales,congas,bongos)
Joachim Kühn Group
Universal Time | EmArCy | 016671-2
Ramon Valle Quintet
Ramon Valle Plays Ernesto Lecuona | ACT | 9404-2
Roy Hargrove's Crisol
Habana | Verve | 537563-2

Hernandez,Maridalia | (voc)
Gonzalo Rubalcaba & Cuban Quartet
Antiguo | Blue Note | 837717-2

Hernandez,Oscar | (keyboards,p,el-psynth)
Mongo Santamaria And His Orchestra
Jazzin' Vol.2: The Music Of Stevie Wonder | Fantasy | FANCD 6088-2

Hernandez,Philip | (voc)
The Sidewalks Of New York
Tin Pan Alley:The Sidewalks Of New York | Winter&Winter | 910038-2

Hernandez,Rene | (african-dr,p,arrconga)
Charlie Parker With Machito And His Orchestra
Bird: The Complete Charlie Parker On Verve | Verve | 837141-2
Dizzy Gillespie Group
Verve Jazz Masters 10:Dizzy Gillespie | Verve | 516319-2
Dizzy Gillspie And His Latin American Rhythm
Afro | Verve | 517052-2
Machito And His Orchestra
Afro-Cuban Jazz Moods | Original Jazz Classics | OJC20 447-2
Mongo Santamaria And His Band
Sabroso | Original Jazz Classics | OJCCD 281-2

Hernandez,Wilfredo | (perc)
Conexion Latina
Calorcito | Enja | ENJ-4072 2

Herr,Michel | (DX7,el-p,keyboards,perc,kalimba,p)
Toots Thielemans Quartet
Toots Thielemans:The Live Takes Vol.1 | IN+OUT Records | 77041-2
Toots Thielemans-Michel Herr
Toots Thielemans:The Live Takes Vol.1 | IN+OUT Records | 77041-2

Herrador,Roberto | (coro)
Conexion Latina
Mambo 2000 | Enja | ENJ-7055 2

Herring,Roy | (voc)
The Brecker Brothers
Heavy Metal Be-Bop | RCA | 2119257-2

Herring,Vincent | (as,ts,flss)
Bernard Purdie's Soul To Jazz
Bernard Purdie's Soul To Jazz II | ACT | 9253-2
Dave Ellis Quintet
State Of Mind | Milestone | MCD 9328-2
Jam Session
Jam Session Vol.3 | Steeplechase | SCCD 31526
Joe Chambers Quartet
Mirrors | Blue Note | 496685-2
Joe Chambers Quintet
Mirrors | Blue Note | 496685-2
Johannes Enders Quintet
Quiet Fire | Enja | ENJ-9390 2
Mingus Big Band
Tonight At Noon...Three Or Four Shades Of Love | Dreyfus Jazz Line | FDM 36633-2
Nat Adderley Quintet
We Remember Cannon | IN+OUT Records | 7012-2
Jazz Unlimited | IN+OUT Records | 7017-2
The Old Country | Enja | ENJ-7027 2
Tim Hagans-Marcus Printup Septet
Hub Songs | Blue Note | 859509-2

Herrlich,Johannes | (tb)
Al Porcino Big Band
Al Porcino Big Band Live! | Organic Music | ORGM 9717
Johannes Herrlich Quintet
Thinking Of You | Edition Collage | EC 499-2
Nana Mouskouri With The Berlin Radio Big Band
Nana Swings | Mercury | 074394-2
Roman Schwaller Nonet
The Original Tunes | JHM Records | JHM 3629
Thomas Faist Sextet
Gentle | Village | VILCD 1020-2
Trombonefire
Sliding Affairs | Laika Records | 35101462

Hersch,Fred | (p,synthp-solo)
Fred Hersch Quartet
Point In Time | Enja | ENJ-9035 2
Fred Hersch Quintet
Point In Time | Enja | ENJ-9035 2
Fred Hersch Trio
Point In Time | Enja | ENJ-9035 2
Jane Ira Bloom-Fred Hersch Duo
As One | JMT Edition | 919003-2

Hersh,Ralph | (viola)
Wes Montgomery With The Jimmy Jones Orchestra
Wes Montgomery-The Complete Riverside Recordings | Riverside | 12 RCD 4408-2

Herskowitz,Matt | (p)
Paquito D'Rivera Group With The Absolute Ensemble
Habanera | Enja | ENJ-9395 2

Herst,Lou | (voc)
Leon Thomas With Orchestra
Spirits Known And Unknown | RCA | 2663876-2

Herstad,Svein Olav | (p)
Jan Erik Kongshaug Group
The Other World | ACT | 9267-2

Herting,Michael | (el-p,synth,keyboards,perc,voc)
Charlie Mariano Trio
Mariano | VeraBra Records | CDVBR 2124-2
International Commission For The Prevention Of Musical Border Control,The
The International Commission For The Prevention Of Musical Border Control | VeraBra Records | CDVBR 2093-2
Lajos Dudas Quintet
Jubilee Edition | double moon | CHRDM 71020

Herting,Mike | (keyboards)
Acoustic Alchemy
Against The Grain | GRP | GRP 97832

Hervé,Antoine | (p,arr,ldvoc)
Antoine Hervé Quintet
Invention Is You | Enja | ENJ-9398 2

Hervé,Gaelle | (voc)
Karim Ziad Groups
Ifrikya | ACT | 9282-2
Nguyen Le Group
Maghreb And Friends | ACT | 9261-2

Hervé,Marielle | (voc)
Karim Ziad Groups
Ifrikya | ACT | 9282-2
Nguyen Le Group
Maghreb And Friends | ACT | 9261-2

Hervey,Clay | (tb)
Gene Krupa And His Orchestra
Mullenium | CBS | CK 65678

Herweg,Dirk | (g)
Kölner Saxophon Mafia With Bad Little Dynamos
Kölner Saxophon Mafia Proudly Presents | Jazz Haus Musik | JHM 0046 CD

Herwig,Conrad | (tb)
Charles Mingus Orchestra
Tonight At Noon...Three Or Four Shades Of Love | Dreyfus Jazz Line | FDM 36633-2
Conrad Herwig-Andy LaVerne
Shades Of Light | Steeplechase | SCCD 31520
Joe Henderson Group
Porgy And Bess | Verve | 539048-2
Miles Davis With Gil Evans Orchestra, The George Gruntz Concert Jazz Band And Guests
Miles & Quincy Live At Montreux | Warner | 9362-45221-2
Mingus Big Band
Tonight At Noon...Three Or Four Shades Of Love | Dreyfus Jazz Line | FDM 36633-2
Three Of A Kind
Drip Some Grease | Minor Music | 801056
Tom Harrell Orchestra
Time's Mirror | RCA | 2663524-2

Herzberg,Norman | (bassoon)
Ella Fitzgerald With The Frank DeVol Orchestra
Get Happy! | Verve | 523321-2
Pete Rugolo And His Orchestra
Thriller/Richard Diamon(Original Jazz Scores From 2 Classics TV Series) | Fresh Sound Records | FSCD 2015

Herzberg,Romy | (b)
Christian Fuchs-Romy Herzberg
KontraSax | Jazz Haus Musik | JHM 0074 CD
KontaSax
KontraSax Plays Getrude Stein | Jazz Haus Musik | JHM 0096 CD
Kontrasax
Zanshin/Kontrasax | Jazz Haus Musik | JHM 0130 CD

Herzinger,Willi | (g)
Klaus Kreuzeder & Willi Herzinger
Sax As Sax Can | Trick Music | TM 8712 CD

Herzog,Edgar | (b-cl,bs,flreeds)
Abdullah Ibrahim With The NDR Big Band
Ekapa Lodumo | TipToe | TIP-888840 2
HR Big Band
The American Songs Of Kurt Weill | hr music.de | hrmj 006-01 CD
Lee Konitz With The Ed Partyka Jazz Orchestra
Dreams And Realities | Laika Records | 35101642
NDR Big Band
NDR Big Band-Bravissimo | ACT | 9232-2
Pee Wee Ellis & NDR Bigband
What You Like | Minor Music | 801064

Hess,Bernd | (gel-g)
Litschie Hrdlicka Group
Falling Lovers | EGO | 93020
Tabla & Strings
Islands Everywhere | Tutu Records | 888208-2*

Hesse,Joachim | (tpfl-h)
Fun Horns
Surprise | Jazzpoint | JP 1029 CD

Hesse,Oliver | (tpfl-h)
Gabriel Pérez Group
La Chipaca | Green House Music | CD 1011

Hesse,Ralph | (tpfl-h)
Al Porcino Big Band
Al Porcino Big Band Live! | Organic Music | ORGM 9717
Florian Trübsbach Quintet
Manson & Dixon | Jazz 4 Ever Records:Jazz Network | J4E 4759
HR Big Band
The American Songs Of Kurt Weill | hr music.de | hrmj 006-01 CD
HR Big Band With Marjorie Barnes And Frits Landesbergen
Swinging Christmas | hr music.de | hrmj 012-02 CD
The Groenewald Newnet
Meetings | Jazz 'n' Arts Records | JNA 0702

Hessische Chorensemble |
Jazzensemble Des Hessischen Rundfunks
Jazz Messe-Messe Für Unsere Zeit | hr music.de | hrmj 003-01 CD

Hessler,Gene | (tb)
Elliot Lawrence And His Orchestra
Mullenium | CBS | CK 65678

Hess-Taysen,Eva | (voice)
Miles Davis With The Danish Radio Big Band
Aura | CBS | CK 63962
The Danish Radio Big Band
Aura | CBS | CK 63962

Heupel,Michael | (alto-fl,perc,b-fl,flötophone)
Christoph Haberer Group
Pulsation | Jazz Haus Musik | JHM 0066 CD
Directors
Directors | Jazz Haus Musik | JHM 0040 CD
Norbert Stein Pata Masters
Pata Maroc | Pata Musik | PATA 12(AMF 1063)
Blue Slit | Pata Musik | PATA 8 CD
Graffiti | Pata Musik | PATA 9 CD
Norbert Stein Pata Masters meets Djaduk Ferianto Kua Etnika
Pata Java | Pata Musik | PATA 16 CD
Norbert Stein Pata Orchester
The Secret Act Of Painting | Pata Musik | PATA 7 CD
Nornert Stein Pata Masters
Live In Australia | Pata Musik | PATA 15 CD
Pata Masters
Pata-Bahia | Pata Musik | PATA 11 CD
Pata Music Meets Arfi
News Of Roi Ubu | Pata Musik | PATA 10 CD
La Belle Et La Bête | Pata Musik | PATA 14(amf 1066)

Heuss,Oliver | (pkeyboards)
Dirk Raulf Group
Die Welt Ist Immer Wieder Schön | Poise | Poise 03

Heute,Rainer | (b-cl,bs,reeds,saxts)
Bill Ramsey With Orchestra
Gettin' Back To Swing | Bear Family Records | BCD 15813 AH
HR Big Band
Libertango:Homage An Astor Piazolla | hr music.de | hrmj 014-02 CD
HR Big Band With Marjorie Barnes And Frits Landesbergen
Swinging Christmas | hr music.de | hrmj 012-02 CD
HR Big Band With Marjorie Barnes And Frits Landesbergen And Strings
Swinging Christmas | hr music.de | hrmj 012-02 CD
SWR Big Band
Jazz In Concert | Hänssler Classics | CD 93.004
The Three Sopranos With The HR Big Band
The Three Sopranos | hr music.de | hrmj 001-01 CD

Hevia,Fabian | (drperc)
Vince Jones Group
Here's To The Miracles | Intuition Records | INT 3198-2
Wanderlust
Border Crossing | Laika Records | 35100812
Wanderlust + Guests
Full Bronte | Laika Records | 35101412

Hewitt,Lonnie | (el-pp)
Cal Tjader Group
Verve Jazz Masters 39:Cal Tjader | Verve | 521858-2
Verve Jazz Masters Vol.60:The Collection | Verve | 529866-2
Cal Tjader Quartet
Black Hawk Nights | Fantasy | FCD 24755-2
Our Blues | Fantasy | FCD 24771-2
Cal Tjader Quintet
Soul Bird | Verve | 549111-2
Our Blues | Fantasy | FCD 24771-2
Concerts In The Sun | Fantasy | FCD 9688-2
Cal Tjader Septet
Talkin Verve/Roots Of Acid Jazz:Cal Tjader | Verve | 531562-2
Cal Tjader Sextet
Talkin Verve/Roots Of Acid Jazz:Cal Tjader | Verve | 531562-2
Black Hawk Nights | Fantasy | FCD 24755-2
Cal Tjader's Orchestra
Verve Jazz Masters 39:Cal Tjader | Verve | 521858-2
Talkin Verve/Roots Of Acid Jazz:Cal Tjader | Verve | 531562-2

Hey,Henry | (grand-psample-programming)
Andy Middleton Group
Nomad's Notebook | Intuition Records | INT 3264-2
Michael 'Patches' Stewart Group
Penetration | Hip Bop | HIBD 8018

Hey,Jerry | (fl-h,horns-arr,synth-programming,tp)
Al Jarreau With Band
Jarreau | i.e. Music | 557847-2
High Crime | i.e. Music | 557848-2
Al Jarreau In London | i.e. Music | 557849-2
Heaven And Earth | i.e. Music | 557852-2
Dave Weckl Group
Master Plan | GRP | GRP 96192
Diane Schuur With Orchestra
The Best Of Diane Schuur | GRP | GRP 98882
George Duke Group
Jazzrock-Anthology Vol.3:Fusion | Zounds | CD 27100555
Joe Sample Group
Ashes To Ashes | Warner | 7599-26318-2
Spellbound | Rhino | 81273726-2
The Quincy Jones-Sammy Nestico Orchestra
Basie & Beyond | Warner | 9362-47792-2

Heyward,Andre | (tb)
Russel Gunn Group
Ethnomusicology Vol.1 | Atlantic | 7567-83165-2

Heywood,Eddie | (p)
Billie Holiday With Eddie Heywood And His Orchestra
Billie Holiday:The Complete Commodore Recordings | GRP | 543272-2
Billie's Love Songs | Nimbus Records | NI 2000
Coleman Hawkins' Swing Four
Jazz:The Essential Collection Vol.3 | IN+OUT Records | 78013-2

Hibbler,Al | (voc)
Duke Ellington And His Orchestra
Planet Jazz:Duke Ellington | Planet Jazz | 2152053-2
Carnegie Hall Concert December 1944 | Prestige | 2PCD 24073-2
Carnegie Hall Concert January 1946 | Prestige | 2PCD 24074-2
Carnegie Hall Concert December 1947 | Prestige | 2PCD 24075-2

Hickman,Sylvester | (b)
Gene Ammons Quartet
Preachin' | Original Jazz Classics | OJCCD 792-2(P 7270)
The Jazz Giants Play Rodgers & Hammerstein:My Favorite Things | Prestige | PCD 24223-2

Hicks,Billy | (tp)
Louis Armstrong With Chick Webb's Orchestra
Best Of The Complete RCA Victor Recordings | RCA | 2663636-2
Louis Armstrong:A 100th Birthday Celebration | RCA | 2663694-2

Hicks,Dan | (voc)
Rob Wasserman Duet
Duets | GRP | GRP 97122

Hicks,Jimmie | (voc)
First Revolution Singers
First Revolution Gospel Singers:A Capella | Laserlight | 24338

Hicks,John | (el-p,p,keyboardsp-solo)
Arthur Blythe Quartet
Retroflection | Enja | ENJ-8046 2
Calling Card | Enja | ENJ-9051 2
Eric Alexander Quartet
Solid! | Milestone | MCD 9283-2
Eric Alexander Quintet
Solid! | Milestone | MCD 9283-2
Gary Bartz Quintet
West 42nd Street | Candid | CCD 79049
Joe Lovano Nonet
On This Day At The Vanguard | Blue Note | 590950-2
Kenny Barron-John Hicks Quartet
Rhythm-A-Ning | Candid | CCD 79044
Kevin Mahogany With Orchestra
Songs And Moments | Enja | ENJ-8072 2
Lee Morgan Sextet
Taru | Blue Note | 522670-2
Roy Hargrove Quartet
Family | Verve | 527630-2
Roy Hargrove Quintet
Planet Jazz:Jazz Trumpet | Planet Jazz | 2169654-2
Roy Hargrove's Crisol
Habana | Verve | 537563-2

Hidalgo,Manenquito Giovanni | (bongos,congas,chekere,cowbell,gong)
Dizzy Gillespie And The United Nation Orchestra
7.Zelt-Musik-Festival:Jazz Events | Zounds | CD 2730001
Gonzalo Rubalcaba & Cuban Quartet
Antiguo | Blue Note | 837717-2

Hieroglyphics Ensemble,The |
Don Cherry Group
Multi Kulti | A&M Records | 395323-2

Higaki,Paul | (tb)
Lionel Hampton And His Orchestra
Lionel Hampton:Flying Home | Dreyfus Jazz Line | FDM 36735-2
Lionel Hampton Orchestra
The Big Bands Vol.1.The Snader Telescriptions | Storyville | 4960043

Higginbotham,J.C. | (tb)
Alberta Hunter With Buster Bailey's Blues Blasters
Songs We Taught Your Mother | Original Blues Classics | OBCCD 520-2
Coleman Hawkins All Star Octet

Planet Jazz:Coleman Hawkins | Planet Jazz | 2152055-2
Coleman Hawkins And His Orchestra
Jazz:The Essential Collection Vol.3 | IN+OUT Records | 78013-2
Fats Waller And His Buddies
Jazz:The Essential Collection Vol.3 | IN+OUT Records | 78013-2
Fletcher Henderson And His Orchestra
Jazz:The Essential Collection Vol.1 | IN+OUT Records | 78011-2
Henry Allen Jr. And His New York Orchestra
Planet Jazz:Jazz Saxophone | Planet Jazz | 2169653-2
Planet Jazz:Jazz Trumpet | Planet Jazz | 2169654-2
Henry Red Allen's All Stars
Planet Jazz:Coleman Hawkins | Planet Jazz | 2152055-2
Jimmy Witherspoon With Jay McShann And His Band
Planet Jazz:Male Jazz Vocalists | Planet Jazz | 2169657-2
King Oliver And His Orchestra
Planet Jazz:Jazz Trumpet | Planet Jazz | 2169654-2
Louis Armstrong And His Orchestra
Louis Armstrong:Swing That Music | Laserlight | 36056
Jazz:The Essential Collection Vol.2 | IN+OUT Records | 78012-2
Satch Plays Fats(Complete) | CBS | CK 64927
Louis Armstrong-My Greatest Songs | MCA | MCD 18347
Swing Legends:Louis Armstrong | Nimbus Records | NI 2012
Louis Armstrong And His Savoy Ballroom Five
Jazz:The Essential Collection Vol.2 | IN+OUT Records | 78012-2
New Orleans Feetwarmers
Jazz:The Essential Collection Vol.1 | IN+OUT Records | 78011-2
Victoria Spivey With Buster Bailey's Blues Blasters
Songs We Taught Your Mother | Original Blues Classics | OBCCD 520-2

Higgins,Billy | (dr,gambray,perc,tambourines,tympani)
Abbey Lincoln And Her All Stars
The World Is Falling Down | Verve | 843476-2
Abdullah Ibrahim Sextet
Mindif | Enja | ENJ-5073 2
Art Pepper Quartet
Art Pepper:The Complete Galaxy Recordings | Galaxy | 16GCD 1016-2
Art 'N' Zoot | Pablo | 2310957-2
Straight Life | Original Jazz Classics | OJCCD 475-2
Art Pepper Quintet
Art Pepper:The Complete Galaxy Recordings | Galaxy | 16GCD 1016-2
Straight Life | Original Jazz Classics | OJCCD 475-2
Art Pepper Trio
Art Pepper:The Complete Galaxy Recordings | Galaxy | 16GCD 1016-2
Art Pepper-Zoot Sims Quintet
Art 'N' Zoot | Pablo | 2310957-2
Barry Harris Sextet
Bull's Eye! | Original Jazz Classics | OJCCD 1082-2(P 7600)
Barry Harris Trio
Bull's Eye! | Original Jazz Classics | OJCCD 1082-2(P 7600)
Bobby Hutcherson Quintet
Blue N' Groovy | Blue Note | 780679-2
Bobby Timmons Orchestra
Quartet And Orchestra | Milestone | MCD 47091-2
Cecil Taylor/Buell Neidlinger Orchestra
New York City R&B | Candid | CCD 79017
Cecil Taylor/Buell Neidlinger Trio
New York City R&B | Candid | CCD 79017
Cedar Walton Quartet
The Story Of Jazz Piano | Laserlight | 24653
First Set | Steeplechase | SCCD 31085
Third Set | Steeplechase | SCCD 31179
Cedar Walton Trio
God Bless Jug And Sonny | Prestige | PCD 11019-2
Left Bank Encores | Prestige | PRCD 11022-2
Charles Lloyd Quartet
Voice In The Night | ECM | 1674(559445-2)
Charles Lloyd Quintet
The Water Is Wide | ECM | 1734(549043-2)
Hyperion With Higgins | ECM | 1784(014000-2)
Charles Lloyd-Billy Higgins
Which Way Is East | ECM | 1878/79(9811796)
Charlie Haden Quartet West
Quartet West | Verve | 831673-2
Charlie Haden Trio
Quartet West | Verve | 831673-2
Clifford Jordan Quartet
Firm Roots | Steeplechase | SCCD 31033
Cyrus Chestnut Trio
Cyrus Chestnut | Atlantic | 7567-83140-2
Dave Pike Quartet
It's Time For Dave Pike | Original Jazz Classics | OJCCD 1951-2(RLP 9360)
Dexter Gordon Quartet
Go! | Blue Note | 498794-2
Dexter Gordon:Ballads | Blue Note | 796579-2
The Best Of Blue Note Vol.2 | Blue Note | 797960-2
Jazz Profile:Dexter Gordon | Blue Note | 823514-2
Midnight Blue(The [Be]witching Hour) | Blue Note | 854365-2
Dexter Gordon Birthday Celebration | Fantasy | FANCD 6082-2
Tangerine | Original Jazz Classics | OJCCD 1041-2(P 10091)
Dexter Gordon Quintet
Dexter Gordon:Ballads | Blue Note | 796579-2
Jazz Profile:Dexter Gordon | Blue Note | 823514-2
Dexter Gordon Birthday Celebration | Fantasy | FANCD 6082-2
Tangerine | Original Jazz Classics | OJCCD 1041-2(P 10091)
Generation | Original Jazz Classics | OJCCD 836-2(P 10069)
The Jazz Giants Play Miles Davis:Milestones | Prestige | PCD 24225-2
Don Wilkerson Quartet
The Texas Twister | Original Jazz Classics | OJCCD 1950-2(RLP 1186)
Don Wilkerson Quintet
Preach Brother! | Blue Note | 0677212
Blue N' Groovy | Blue Note | 780679-2
The Texas Twister | Original Jazz Classics | OJCCD 1950-2(RLP 1186)
Donald Byrd Quintet
Herbie Hancock:The Complete Blue Note Sixties Sessions | Blue Note | 495569-2
Slow Drag | Blue Note | 535560-2
Free Form | Blue Note | 595961-2
Donald Byrd Sextet
Blue Breaks Beats Vol.2 | Blue Note | 789907-2
Blue Break Beats | Blue Note | 799106-2
Blackjack | Blue Note | 821286-2
Eddie Harris Quartet
The Best Of Eddie Harris | Atlantic | 7567-81370-2
Eddie Harris Quintet
The Best Of Eddie Harris | Atlantic | 7567-81370-2
Atlantic Saxophones | Rhino | 8122-71256-2
Frank Morgan Quartet
Easy Living | Original Jazz Classics | OJCCD 833-2(C 14013)
Freddie Hubbard Quintet
Bossa Nova Bacchanal | Blue Note | 593875-2
Gary Bartz Quintet
Libra/Another Earth | Milestone | MCD 47077-2
Gene Ammons Quartet
God Bless Jug And Sonny | Prestige | PCD 11019-2
Gene Ammons-Sonny Stitt Quintet
God Bless Jug And Sonny | Prestige | PCD 11019-2
Left Bank Encores | Prestige | PRCD 11022-2
Grant Green Quintet
Feelin' The Spirit | Blue Note | 746822-2
Hank Mobley Quintet
Deep Blue-The United States Of Mind | Blue Note | 521152-2
The Turnaround | Blue Note | 524540-2
Blue Bossa | Blue Note | 795590-2
Herbie Hancock Quintet
Herbie Hancock:The Complete Blue Note Sixties Sessions | Blue Note | 495569-2
The Best Of Blue Note Vol.2 | Blue Note | 797960-2
Cantaloupe Island | Blue Note | 829331-2
Takin' Off | Blue Note | 837643-2
J.J.Johnson Quintet
The J.J.Johnson Memorial Album | Prestige | PRCD 11025-2
Jack Wilson Sextet
Blue N' Groovy | Blue Note | 780679-2
Jackie McLean Quartet
A Fickle Sonance | Blue Note | 524544-2
Let Freedom Ring | Blue Note | 591895-2
Jackie McLean Quintet
Vertigo | Blue Note | 522669-2
A Fickle Sonance | Blue Note | 524544-2
A Blue Conception | Blue Note | 534254-2
John Coltrane-Don Cherry Quartet
John Coltrane-The Heavyweight Champion:The Complete Atlantic Recordings | Atlantic | 8122-71984-2
John Scofield Quintet
Works For Me | Verve | 549281-2
Joshua Redman Quartet
Wish | Warner | 9362-45365-2
Lee Morgan Quintet
The Sidewinder | Blue Note | 495332-2
The Rumproller | Blue Note | 521229-2
The Sixth Sense | Blue Note | 522467-2
Sonic Boom | Blue Note | 590414-2
Blue N' Groovy | Blue Note | 780679-2
The Best Of Blue Note | Blue Note | 796110-2
The Best Of Blue Note Vol.2 | Blue Note | 797960-2
Caramba! | Blue Note | 853358-2
Lee Morgan Sextet
The Sixth Sense | Blue Note | 522467-2
Taru | Blue Note | 522670-2
Wayne Shorter:The Classic Blue Note Recordings | Blue Note | 540856-2
Search For The New Land | Blue Note | 591896-2
Milt Jackson And His Colleagues
Bag's Bag | Original Jazz Classics | OJCCD 935-2(2310842)
Milt Jackson And His Orchestra
Reverence And Compassion | Reprise | 9362-45204-2
Milt Jackson Quintet
Milt Jackson At The Kosei Nenkin | Pablo | 2620103-2
Niels-Henning Orsted-Pedersen/Sam Jones Quartet
Double Bass | Steeplechase | SCS 1055(Audiophile Pressing)
Niels-Henning Orsted-Pedersen/Sam Jones Quartet
Double Bass | Steeplechase | SCS 1055(Audiophile Pressing)
Ornette Coleman Double Quartet
Beauty Is A Rare Thing:Ornette Coleman-The Complete Atlantic Recordings | Atlantic | 8122-71410-2
Free Jazz | Atlantic | 8122-75208-2
Ornette Coleman Quartet
Change Of The Century | Atlantic | 7567-81341-2
Atlantic Saxophones | Rhino | 8122-71256-2
Rhino Presents The Atlantic Jazz Gallery | Atlantic | 8122-71257-2
Beauty Is A Rare Thing:Ornette Coleman-The Complete Atlantic Recordings | Atlantic | 8122-71410-2
Ornette Coleman Quintet
The Music Of Ornette Coleman:Something Else!! | Original Jazz Classics | OJC20 163-2
Pat Metheny Trio
Rejoicing | ECM | 1271(817795-2)
Sonny Rollins & Co.
Planet Jazz:Sonny Rollins | Planet Jazz | 2152062-2
Sonny Stitt Quartet
God Bless Jug And Sonny | Prestige | PCD 11019-2
Stan Getz-Cal Tjader Sextet
Stan Getz With Cal Tjader | Original Jazz Classics | OJC20 275-2(F 3266)
Thelonious Monk Quartet Plus Two
Thelonious Monk:85th Birthday Celebration | zyx records | FANCD 6076-2
At The Blackhawk | Original Jazz Classics | OJCCD 305-2
Toots Thielemans Quintet
Verve Jazz Masters Vol.59:Toots Thielemans | Verve | 535271-2
Wayne Shorter Sextet
Wayne Shorter:The Classic Blue Note Recordings | Blue Note | 540856-2
Zoot Sims Quartet
Art 'N' Zoot | Pablo | 2310957-2
Zoot Sims Quintet
Art 'N' Zoot | Pablo | 2310957-2

Higgins,Chris | (b)
Bill McHenry Quartet
Rest Stop | Fresh Sound Records | FSNT 033 CD
Cesc Miralta Quartet
Sol De Nit | Fresh Sound Records | FSNT 098 CD
Carretera Austal | Fresh Sound Records | FSNT 149 CD
Chris Cheek Quartet
I Wish I Knew | Fresh Sound Records | FSNT 022 CD
Elisabet Raspall Grup
Lila | Fresh Sound Records | FSNT 058 CD
Grant Stewart Quartet
Buen Rollo | Fresh Sound Records | FSNT 053 CD
Matt Renzi-Jimmy Weinstein Quartet
Matt Renzi-Jimmy Weinstein Quartet | Fresh Sound Records | FSNT 045 CD

Higgins,Dan | (as,cl,b-cl,fl,ts,reedssax)
Al Jarreau With Band
Heaven And Earth | i.e. Music | 557852-2
Dave Grusin Orchestra
Two For The Road:The Music Of Henry Mancini | GRP | GRP 98652
The Quincy Jones-Sammy Nestico Orchestra
Basie & Beyond | Warner | 9362-47792-2

Higgins,Eddie | (p)
Allan Vaché-Harry Allen Quintet
Allan And Allan | Nagel-Heyer | CD 074
George Masso Allstars
The Wonderful World Of George Gershwin | Nagel-Heyer | CD 001
One Two Three | Nagel-Heyer | CD 008
The First Sampler | Nagel-Heyer | NHR SP 5
Lucy Reed With The Eddie Higgins Quartet
This Is Lucy Reed | Original Jazz Classics | OJCCD 1943-2(F 3243)
Lucy Reed With The Eddie Higgins Trio
This Is Lucy Reed | Original Jazz Classics | OJCCD 1943-2(F 3243)
Warren Vaché-Allen Vaché Sextet
Mrs.Vaché's Boys | Nagel-Heyer | CD 050
Ellington For Lovers | Nagel-Heyer | NH 1009

Higgins,Frank | (tp)
Terry Gibbs Dream Band
Terry Gibbs Dream Band Vol.2:The Sundown Sessions | Contemporary | CCD 7652-2
The Jazz Giants Play Jerome Kern:Yesterdays | Prestige | PCD 24202-2

Higgins,Monk | (arr,ld,orgperc)
Gene Harris And The Three Sounds
Deep Blue-The United States Of Mind | Blue Note | 521152-2
The Three Sounds
Blue Break Beats | Blue Note | 799106-2

Higgins,Patience | (b-cl,ts,perc,voice,bs,cl,alto-cl,fl)
Dee Dee Bridgewater With Big Band
Dear Ella | Verve | 539102-2

Hilaire,Andrew | (dr)
Jelly Roll Morton's Red Hot Peppers
Planet Jazz:Jelly Roll Morton | Planet Jazz | 2152060-2
Planet Jazz Sampler | Planet Jazz | 2152326-2
Jazz:The Essential Collection Vol.1 | IN+OUT Records | 78011-2

Hilbe,Gregor | (dr)
Melanie Bong With Band
Fantasia | Jazz 4 Ever Records:Jazz Network | J4E 4755

Hildabrand,Shaunette | (voc)
The Swingcats
Face To Face:The Swingcats Live | Nagel-Heyer | CD 072

Hildebrand,Corinna | (v)
Uri Caine With The Concerto Köln
Concerto Köln | Winter&Winter | 910086-2

Hildebrandt,Lloyd | (bassoonbs)
Ella Fitzgerald With The Nelson Riddle Orchestra
The Best Of The Song Books:The Ballads | Verve | 521867-2
Love Songs:The Best Of The Song Books | Verve | 531762-2
Ella Fitzgerald Sings The Johnny Mercer Songbook | Verve | 539057-2

Hildinger,Dave | (pperc)
Charlie Ventura Quintet
High On An Open Mike | Fresh Sound Records | FSR-CD 314

Hill,Alan | (g)
Mike Westbrook Brass Band
Glad Day:Settings Of William Blake | Enja | ENJ-9376 2

Hill,Alex | (arr,pvoc)
Mezz Mezzrow And His Orchestra
Planet Jazz:Bud Freeman | Planet Jazz | 2161240-2

Hill,Andrew | (p,celestep-solo)
Andrew Hill Orchestra
Deep Blue-The United States Of Mind | Blue Note | 521152-2
Andrew Hill Quartet
A Blue Conception | Blue Note | 534254-2
Andrew Hill Quintet
Grass Roots | Blue Note | 522672-2
Blue Bossa | Blue Note | 795590-2
Andrew Hill Sextet
Point Of Departure | Blue Note | 499007-2
Grass Roots | Blue Note | 522672-2
Anfrew Hill Nonet
Passing Ships | Blue Note | 593871-2
Bobby Hutcherson Sextet
A Blue Conception | Blue Note | 534254-2
Dialogue | Blue Note | 535586-2
Hank Mobley Quintet
No Room For Squares | Blue Note | 524539-2
True Blue | Blue Note | 534032-2
Jimmy Woods Sextet
Conflict | Original Jazz Classics | OJCCD 1954-2(S 7612)
Joe Henderson Quintet
Our Thing | Blue Note | 525647-2
The Blue Note Years-The Best Of Joe Henderson | Blue Note | 795627-2
Roland Kirk Quartet
Domino | Verve | 543833-2
Rahsaan/The Complete Mercury Recordings Of Roland Kirk | Mercury | 846630-2

Hill,Benny | (dr)
Louis Armstrong And His Orchestra
Planet Jazz:Louis Armstrong | Planet Jazz | 2152052-2
Louis Armstrong:A 100th Birthday Celebration | RCA | 2663694-2

Hill,Buck | (clts)
Charlie Byrd Group
Byrd In The Wind | Original Jazz Classics | OJCCD 1086(RS 9449)
Charlie Byrd Sextet
Byrd's Word! | Original Jazz Classics | OJCCD 1054-2(R 9448)
Shirley Horn Quartet
The Main Ingredient | Verve | 529555-2
Shirley Horn Quintet
The Main Ingredient | Verve | 529555-2
Shirley Horn Trio with Buck Hill
You Won't Forget Me | Verve | 847482-2

Hill,Calvin | (bperc)
Dick Griffin Septet
The Eighth Wonder & More | Konnex Records | KCD 5059
Gordon Lee Quartet feat. Jim Pepper
Landwhales In New York | Tutu Records | 888136-2*
Lee Konitz Quartet
Lullaby Of Birdland | Candid | CCD 79709
Louis Smith Quintet
Louisville | Steeplechase | SCCD 31552
McCoy Tyner Quartet
Sahara | Original Jazz Classics | OJC20 311-2
Song For My Lady | Original Jazz Classics | OJCCD 313-2
McCoy Tyner Septet
Song For My Lady | Original Jazz Classics | OJCCD 313-2
Michael Cochrane Quartet
Path Ways | Steeplechase | SCCD 31542

Hill,Cliff | (b)
Peggy Lee With The Benny Goodman Orchestra
Peggy Lee & Benny Goodman:The Complete Recordings 1941-1947 | CBS | C2K 65686

Hill,Don | (astp)
Louis Armstrong And His Orchestra
Best Of The Complete RCA Victor Recordings | RCA | 2663636-2
Louis Armstrong:A 100th Birthday Celebration | RCA | 2663694-2
Louis Armstrong:C'est Si Bon | Dreyfus Jazz Line | FDM 36730-2

Hill,Ernest | (btuba)
Spike Hughes And His Negro Orchestra
Jazz:The Essential Collection Vol.3 | IN+OUT Records | 78013-2
Willie Bryant And His Orchestra
Planet Jazz:Ben Webster | RCA | 2165368-2

Hill,Fred 'Freddie' | (tp)
Bobby Bryant Orchestra
Deep Blue-The United States Of Mind | Blue Note | 521152-2
Gerald Wilson And His Orchestra
Blue Breaks Beats Vol.2 | Blue Note | 789907-2
Johnny Hartman And His Orchestra
Unforgettable | Impulse(MCA) | IMP 11522

Hill,Henry | (v)
Ella Fitzgerald With The Frank DeVol Orchestra
Get Happy! | Verve | 523321-2
Ella Fitzgerald With The Nelson Riddle Orchestra
The Best Of The Song Books:The Ballads | Verve | 521867-2
Phineas Newborn Jr. With Dennis Farnon And His Orchestra
While My Lady Sleeps | RCA | 2185157-2

Hill,Roger | (b-g,gperc)
Chris Barber's Jazz And Blues Band
Chris Barber On The Road:A Jazz Documentary | Storyville | 4960683

Hill,Ruth | (harp)
Tommy Dorsey And His Orchestra
Planet Jazz:Frank Sinatra & Tommy Dorsey | Planet Jazz | 2152067-2

Hill,Teddy | (cl,tsbs)
Henry Allen Jr. And His New York Orchestra
Planet Jazz:Jazz Saxophone | Planet Jazz | 2169653-2
Planet Jazz:Jazz Trumpet | Planet Jazz | 2169654-2
King Oliver And His Orchestra
Planet Jazz:Jazz Trumpet | Planet Jazz | 2169654-2
Louis Armstrong And His Orchestra
Jazz:The Essential Collection Vol.2 | IN+OUT Records | 78012-2
Satch Plays Fats(Complete) | CBS | CK 64927
Louis Armstrong And His Savoy Ballroom Five
Jazz:The Essential Collection Vol.2 | IN+OUT Records | 78012-2

Hiller,Norbert | (fl)
Horst Faigle's Jazzkrement
Gans Normal | Jazz 4 Ever Records:Jazz Network | J4E 4748

Hillery,Art | (orgp)
Ella Fitzgerald With Orchestra
The Best Is Yet To Come | Original Jazz Classics | OJCCD 889-2(2312138)
Milt Jackson Septet
Milt Jackson Birthday Celebration | Fantasy | FANCD 6079-2

Hillestad,Per | (dr)
Ketil Bjornstad Group
Water Stories | ECM | 1503(519076-2)

Hilliam,David | (dobro)
Marty Hall Band

Tried & True | Blues Beacon | BLU-1030 2

Hilliard,John | (b)
Cal Tjader Group
Verve Jazz Masters Vol.60:The Collection | Verve | 529866-2
Cal Tjader Septet
Talkin Verve/Roots Of Acid Jazz:Cal Tjader | Verve | 531562-2
Cal Tjader's Orchestra
Verve Jazz Masters 39:Cal Tjader | Verve | 521858-2

Hillman,Roscoe | (g)
Louis Armstrong With Jimmy Dorsey And His Orchestra
Louis Armstrong:Swing That Music | Laserlight | 36056
Swing Legends:Louis Armstrong | Nimbus Records | NI 2012

Hillmann,Christoph | (dr,electronicsperc)
Eda Zari With The Mark Joggerst Trio
The Art Of Time | Laika Records | 35100902
Norbert Stein Pata Masters
Pata Maroc | Pata Musik | PATA 12(AMF 1063)
Norbert Stein Pata Masters meets Djaduk Ferianto Kua Etnika
Pata Java | Pata Musik | PATA 16 CD
Nornert Stein Pata Masters
Live In Australia | Pata Musik | PATA 15 CD
Pata Music Meets Arfi
La Belle Et La Bête | Pata Musik | PATA 14(amf 1066)
Stephan-Max Wirth Quartet
Jazzchanson 20th Century Suite | double moon | DMCD 1008-2

Hills,Clifford | (b)
Jerri Southern Quartet
The Very Thought Of You:The Decca Years 1951-1957 | Decca | 050671-2

Hillyer,Lonnie | (tp)
Barry Harris Quintet
Never Than New | Original Jazz Classics | OJCCD 1062-2(RLP 9413)
Charles Mingus And His Orchestra
The Complete Town Hall Concert | Blue Note | 828353-2
Charles Mingus Group
The Jazz Life! | Candid | CCD 79019
Candid Dolphy | Candid | CCD 79033
Mysterious Blues | Candid | CCD 79042
Charles Mingus Orchestra
Mingus | Candid | CCD 79021

Himmler,Ralf | (tpfl-h)
Jazz Orchester Rheinland-Pfalz
Kazzou | Jazz Haus Musik | LJBB 9104
Like Life | Jazz Haus Musik | LJBB 9405
Last Season | Jazz Haus Musik | LJBB 9706

Hinds,Nelson | (tb)
Woody Herman And His Orchestra
Verve Jazz Masters 54:Woody Herman | Verve | 529903-2

Hines,Earl 'Fatha' | (celeste,p,vocp-solo)
Benny Carter Quartet
The Jazz Giants Play Rodgers & Hart:Blue Moon | Prestige | PCD 24205-2
Carroll Dickerson's Savoyagers
Louis Armstrong:Fireworks | Dreyfus Jazz Line | FDM 36710-2
Cozy Cole All Stars
Ultimate Coleman Hawkins selected by Sonny Rollins | Verve | 557538-2
Earl Hines
Planet Jazz:Earl Hines | Planet Jazz | 2159973-2
The Story Of Jazz Piano | Laserlight | 24653
Americans Swinging In Paris:Earl Hines | EMI Records | 539661-2
Jazz:The Essential Collection Vol.2 | IN+OUT Records | 78012-2
Another Monday Date | Prestige | PRCD 24043-2
Earl Hines And His Orchestra
Planet Jazz:Earl Hines | Planet Jazz | 2159973-2
The Legends Of Swing | Laserlight | 24659
Jazz:The Essential Collection Vol.2 | IN+OUT Records | 78012-2
Earl Hines Quartet
Another Monday Date | Prestige | PRCD 24043-2
Earl Hines Trio
Jazz In Paris:Earl Hines-Paris One Night Stand | EmArCy | 548207-2 PMS
Earl Hines Live! | Storyville | STCD 8222
Earl Hines-Muggsy Spanier All Stars
Earl Hines/Muggsy Spanier All Stars:The Chicago Dates | Storyville | STCD 6037
Johnny Hodges-Earl Hines Quintet
Verve Jazz Masters 35:Johnny Hodges | Verve | 521857-2
Louis Armstrong And His All Stars
Jazz Collection:Louis Armstrong | Laserlight | 24366
I Love Jazz | Verve | 543747-2
Louis Armstrong:C'est Si Bon | Dreyfus Jazz Line | FDM 36730-2
Louis Armstrong-My Greatest Songs | MCA | MCD 18347
Swing Legends:Louis Armstrong | Nimbus Records | NI 2012
Louis Armstrong:Wintergarden 1947/Blue Note 1948 | Storyville | STCD 8242
Louis Armstrong And His Hot Five
Jazz:The Essential Collection Vol.2 | IN+OUT Records | 78012-2
Satch Plays Fats(Complete) | CBS | CK 64927
Louis Armstrong:Fireworks | Dreyfus Jazz Line | FDM 36710-2
Louis Armstrong And His Orchestra
Jazz:The Essential Collection Vol.2 | IN+OUT Records | 78012-2
Louis Armstrong:Fireworks | Dreyfus Jazz Line | FDM 36710-2
Louis Armstrong And His Savoy Ballroom Five
Jazz:The Essential Collection Vol.2 | IN+OUT Records | 78012-2
Louis Armstrong:Fireworks | Dreyfus Jazz Line | FDM 36710-2
Louis Armstrong With Earl Hines
Jazz:The Essential Collection Vol.2 | IN+OUT Records | 78012-2
Louis Armstrong With Sy Oliver And His Orchestra
Satchmo Serenaders | Verve | 543792-2
Louis Armstrong:C'est Si Bon | Dreyfus Jazz Line | FDM 36730-2
Louis Armstrong-My Greatest Songs | MCA | MCD 18347
Louis Armstrong-Earl Hines
Louis Armstrong:Fireworks | Dreyfus Jazz Line | FDM 36710-2
Sidney Bechet And His New Orleans Feetwarmers
Sidney Bechet:Summertime | Dreyfus Jazz Line | FDM 36712-2
Sidney Bechet Trio
Jazz:The Essential Collection Vol.1 | IN+OUT Records | 78011-2

Hines,Gregory | (tap-dancingvoc)
Stanley Clarke-Gregory Himes
If This Bass Could Only Talk | CBS | 460883-2

Hines,Roger | (p)
Diane Schuur And Her Band
Music Is My Life | Atlantic | 7567-83150-2

Hing,Kenny | (as,cl,ts,flreeds)
Count Basie And His Orchestra
Fancy Pants | Original Jazz Classics | OJCCD 1038-2(2310920)
Digital III At Montreux | Original Jazz Classics | OJCCD 996-2(2308223)
Count Basie Big Band
Farmers Market Barbecue | Original Jazz Classics | OJCCD 732-2(2310874)
Count Basie's Small Band
88 Basie Street | Original Jazz Classics | OJC 808(2310901)
Diane Schuur With The Count Basie Orchestra
The Best Of Diane Schuur | GRP | GRP 98882
Ella Fitzgerald With Count Basie And His Orchestra
Digital III At Montreux | Original Jazz Classics | OJCCD 996-2(2308223)
Ella Fitzgerald With The Count Basie Orchestra
Bluella:Ella Fitzgerald Sings The Blues | Pablo | 2310960-2
For The Love Of Ella Fitzgerald | Verve | 841765-2
Milt Jackson Orchestra
Sarah Vaughan Birthday Celebration | Fantasy | FANCD 6090-2
Milt Jackson With The Count Basie Orchestra
To Bags...With Love:Memorial Album | Pablo | 2310967-2
Milt Jackson Birthday Celebration | Fantasy | FANCD 6079-2
Milt Jackson + Count Basie + Big Band Vol.1 | Original Jazz Classics | OJCCD 740-2(2310822)
Milt Jackson + Count Basie + Big Band Vol.2 | Original Jazz Classics | OJCCD 741-2(2310823)
Sarah Vaughan And The Count Basie Orchestra
Sarah Vaughan Birthday Celebration | Fantasy | FANCD 6090-2

Hinka,Jan | (viola)
Ella Fitzgerald With The Frank DeVol Orchestra
Get Happy! | Verve | 523321-2

Hinnant,Peppy | (dr)
Johnny Lytle Quartet
Got That Feeling/Moon Child | Milestone | MCD 47093-2
Johnny Lytle Quintet
Got That Feeling/Moon Child | Milestone | MCD 47093-2
The Village Caller | Original Jazz Classics | OJCCD 110-2(R 9480)
Johnny Lytle Trio(Quartet)
Got That Feeling/Moon Child | Milestone | MCD 47093-2

Hino,Motohiko | (dr)
Joe Henderson Quartet
Joe Henderson:The Milestone Years | Milestone | 8MCD 4413-2
Joe Henderson In Japan | Original Jazz Classics | OJCCD 1040-2(M 9047)
Johnny Hartman With The Terumasa Hino Quartet
Midnight Blue(The [Be]witching Hour) | Blue Note | 854365-2

Hino,Terumasa | (co,perc,wood-fl,tpfl-h)
Mal Waldron
Moods | Enja | ENJ-3021 2
Mal Waldron Sextet
Moods | Enja | ENJ-3021 2

Hinrichs,Henk | (tp)
Coleman Hawkins With The Ramblers
Jazz:The Essential Collection Vol.3 | IN+OUT Records | 78013-2

Hinshaw,William 'Bill' | (fr-h)
Ella Fitzgerald With The Nelson Riddle Orchestra
The Best Of The Song Books:The Ballads | Verve | 521867-2
Love Songs:The Best Of The Song Books | Verve | 531762-2
Ella Fitzgerald Sings The Johnny Mercer Songbook | Verve | 539057-2
Hank Crawford Orchestra
Rhino Presents The Atlantic Jazz Gallery | Atlantic | 8122-71257-2
Miles Davis With Gil Evans & His Orchestra
Quiet Nights | CBS | CK 65293

Hinterseher,Andreas | (accordeon)
Lisa Wahlandt & Mulo Francel And Their Fabulous Bossa Band
Bossa Nova Affair | Edition Collage | EC 534-2

Hinton,Milt | (b)
Al Cohn-Zoot Sims Quintet
Planet Jazz:Jazz Saxophone | Planet Jazz | 2169653-2
Al Sears And His Orchestra
Sear-iously | Bear Family Records | BCD 15668 AH
Andy And The Bey Sisters
Andy Bey And The Bey Sisters | Prestige | PCD 24245-2
Babs Gonzales And His Band
Voilà | Fresh Sound Records | FSR CD 340
Ben Webster Septet
The Soul Of Ben Webster | Verve | 527475-2
Billie Holiday And Her All Stars
The Billie Holiday Song Book | Verve | 823246-2
Billie Holiday With Buck Clayton And The Mal Waldron Trio
Billie Holiday Story Vol.1:Jazz At The Philharmonic | Verve | 521642-2
Billie Holiday With Teddy Wilson And His Orchestra
Billie's Love Songs | Nimbus Records | NI 2000
Billie Holiday With The Ray Ellis Orchestra
Verve Jazz Masters 47:Billie Holiday Sings Standards | Verve | 527650-2
Lady In Satin | CBS | CK 65144
Billy Butterfield And His Modern Dixie Stompers
Soft Strut | Fresh Sound Records | FSR-CD 318
Birdland Dream Band
Birdland Dream Band | RCA | 2663873-2
Branford Marsalis Trio
Trio Jeepy | CBS | 465134-2
Bud Freeman And His Summa Cum Laude Orchestra
Planet Jazz:Bud Freeman | Planet Jazz | 2161240-2
Buddy DeFranco Quartet
Mr. Clarinet | Verve | 847408-2
Cab Calloway And His Cab Jivers
Planet Jazz:Cab Calloway | Planet Jazz | 2161237-2
Cab Calloway And His Orchestra
Planet Jazz:Cab Calloway | Planet Jazz | 2161237-2
Planet Jazz:Male Jazz Vocalists | Planet Jazz | 2169657-2
Cannonball Adderley And His Orchestra
Verve Jazz Masters 31:Cannonball Adderley | Verve | 522651-2
Cannonball Adderley Quartet
Cannonball Adderley Birthday Celebration | Fantasy | FANCD 6087-2
Charles Mingus And His Orchestra
The Complete Town Hall Concert | Blue Note | 828353-2
Chris Connor With Band
Chris Connor | Atlantic | 7567-80769-2
Christian McBride/Ray Brown/Milt Hinton
Gettin' To It | Verve | 523989-2
Coleman Hawkins With Billy Byers And His Orchestra
Planet Jazz:Coleman Hawkins | Planet Jazz | 2152055-2
The Hawk In Hi-Fi | RCA | 2663842-2
Dick Wellstood's Wallerites
Uptown And Lowdown | Prestige | PCD 24262-2
Dinah Washington With The Belford Hendricks Orchestra
Verve Jazz Masters 20:Introducing | Verve | 519853-2
What A Diff'rence A Day Makes! | Verve | 543300-2
4 By 4:Ella Fitzgerald/Sarah Vaughan/Billie Holiday/Dinah Washington | Verve | 559693-2
Dinah Washington With The Quincy Jones Orchestra
Verve Jazz Masters 40:Dinah Washington | Verve | 522055-2
The Swingin' Miss 'D' | Verve | 558074-2
Dodo Greene With The Ike Quebec Quintet
Misty Blue:Sweet Sisters Swing Songs Of Sorrow And Sadness | Blue Note | 521151-2
Don Senay With Orchestra And Strings
Charles Mingus-The Complete Debut Recordings | Debut | 12 DCD 4402-2
Frankie Laine With Buck Clayton And His Orchestra
Jazz Spectacular | CBS | CK 65507
George Russell And His Orchestra
George Russell New York N.Y. | Impulse(MCA) | 951278-2
George Russell Smalltet
The RCA Victor Jazz Workshop | RCA | 2159144-2
George Wein's Dixie Victors
The Magic Horn | RCA | 2113038-2
Planet Jazz | Planet Jazz | 2169652-2
Gerry Mulligan With The Marian McPartland Trio
Newport Jazz Festival 1958,July 3rd-6th Vol.2:Mulligan The Main Man | Phontastic | NCD 8814
Gil Evans Orchestra
The Individualism Of Gil Evans | Verve | 833804-2
Helen Merrill With The Quincy Jones Orchestra
Clifford Brown-Max Roach:Alone Together-The Best Of The Mercury Years | Verve | 526373-2
Brownie-The Complete EmArCy Recordings Of Clifford Brown | EmArCy | 838306-2
Ike Quebec Quartet
Blue Note Plays Gershwin | Blue Note | 520808-2
Midnight Blue(The [Be]witching Hour) | Blue Note | 854365-2
Ike Quebec Quintet
The Blue Note Swingtets | Blue Note | 495697-2
Ike Quebec Swing Seven
The Blue Note Swingtets | Blue Note | 495697-2
J.R. Monterose Sextet
Jaywalkin' | Fresh Sound Records | FSR-CD 320
Jay McShann And His Orchestra
Atlantic Jazz: Kansas City | Atlantic | 7567-81701-2
Jay McShann Orchestra
The Last Of The Blue Devils | Atlantic | 7567-80791-2
Jimmy Rushing And His Band
Planet Jazz:Jimmy Rushing | RCA | 2165371-2
Planet Jazz:Male Jazz Vocalists | Planet Jazz | 2169657-2
Jimmy Rushing And His Orchestra
Five Feet Of Soul | Roulette | 581830-2
Jimmy Smith With The Claus Ogerman Orchestra
Any Number Can Win | Verve | 557447-2
Jimmy Smith With The Oliver Nelson Orchestra
Verve Jazz Masters 29:Jimmy Smith | Verve | 521855-2
Jimmy Smith:Best Of The Verve Years | Verve | 527950-2
Joe Williams With The Jimmy Jones Orchestra
Planet Jazz:Joe Williams | Planet Jazz | 2165370-2
Joe Williams,With The Oliver Nelson Orchestra
Planet Jazz:Joe Williams | Planet Jazz | 2165370-2
Johnny Hartman And His Quintet
I Just Dropped By To Say Hello | MCA | 951176-2
Johnny Hodges Orchestra
Verve Jazz Masters 35:Johnny Hodges | Verve | 521857-2
Johnny Hodges-Wild Bill Davis Sextet
Planet Jazz:Johnny Hodges | Planet Jazz | 2152065-2
Johnny Lytle Trio(Quartet)
Got That Feeling/Moon Child | Milestone | MCD 47093-2
Kenny Burrell-Jimmy Smith Quartet
Blue Bash | Verve | 557453-2
Lionel Hampton And His Orchestra
Planet Jazz:Coleman Hawkins | Planet Jazz | 2152055-2
Planet Jazz:Ben Webster | RCA | 2165368-2
Planet Jazz:Jazz Saxophone | Planet Jazz | 2169653-2
Jazz:The Essential Collection Vol.3 | IN+OUT Records | 78013-2
Lucy Reed With Orchestra
This Is Lucy Reed | Original Jazz Classics | OJCCD 1943-2(F 3243)
Monica Zetterlund With The Zoot Sims Quartet
Planet Jazz:Female Jazz Vocalists | Planet Jazz | 2169656-2
Nancy Harrow And The Buck Clayton All Stars
Wild Women Don't Have The Blues | Candid | CCD 79008
Paul Barbarin And His Band
Atlantic Jazz: New Orleans | Atlantic | 7567-81700-2
Paul Desmond With Strings
Planet Jazz:Paul Desmond | Planet Jazz | 2152061-2
Desmond Blue | RCA | 2663898-2
Quincy Jones And His Orchestra
Talkin' Verve-Roots Of Acid Jazz:Roland Kirk | Verve | 533101-2
Verve Jazz Masters Vol.59:Toots Thielemans | Verve | 535271-2
Rahsaan/The Complete Mercury Recordings Of Roland Kirk | Mercury | 846630-2
The Quintessence | Impulse(MCA) | 951222-2
The Roots Of Acid Jazz | Impulse(MCA) | IMP 12042
Ralph Sutton Quartet
The Ralph Sutton Quartet With Ruby Braff,Vol.2 | Storyville | STCD 8246
Ricky Ford Quartet
Manhattan Blues | Candid | CCD 79036
Ebony Rhapsody | Candid | CCD 79053
Sackville All Stars
Christmas Jazz! | Nagel-Heyer | NH 1008
Sandole Brothers
The Sandole Brothers | Fantasy | FCD 24763-2
Shirley Horn With Orchestra
Loads Of Love + Shirley Horn With Horns | Mercury | 843454-2
Teddy Wilson Trio
The Story Of Jazz Piano | Laserlight | 24653
Thad Jones And His Orchestra
Charles Mingus-The Complete Debut Recordings | Debut | 12 DCD 4402-2
The Basie Alumni
Swinging For The Count | Candid | CCD 79724
Tony Scott Group
Tony Scott | Verve | 9861063
Wes Montgomery With The Jimmy Jones Orchestra
Wes Montgomery-The Complete Riverside Recordings | Riverside | 12 RCD 4408-2
The Jazz Giants Play Rodgers & Hart:Blue Moon | Prestige | PCD 24205-2
Willis Jackson Sextet
Together Again: Willis Jackson With Jack McDuff | Prestige | PRCD 24284-2
Woody Herman And His Orchestra
Songs For Hip Lovers | Verve | 559872-2

Hipp,Jutta | (p)
Hugo Strasser Combo
Deutsches Jazz Fesival 1954/1955 | Bear Family Records | BCD 15430
Jutta Hipp Quintet
Deutsches Jazz Fesival 1954/1955 | Bear Family Records | BCD 15430
Jutta Hipp Trio
Jutta Hipp At The Hickory House Vol.2 | Blue Note | 0677179

Hipsters In The Zone |
Hipsters In The Zone
Into The Afro-Latin Bag | Nabel Records:Jazz Network | CD 4663

Hiromi,Ohta | (voice)
John Zorn Group With The Kronos Quartet
Spillane | Nonesuch | 7559-79172-2

Hirschfield,Jeff | (dr)
Harold Danko Trio
Fantasy Exit | Steeplechase | SCCD 31530

Hirschi,Philip | (cellovoc)
Mahavishnu Orchestra
Apocalypse | CBS | 467092-2

Hirschman,Bob | (tb)
Chas Burchell Sextet
Unsong Hero:The Undiscovered Genius Of Chas Burchell | IN+OUT Records | 7026-2

Hirsh,Meyer | (b-clbs)
Buddy Rich Big Band
The New One! | Pacific Jazz | 494507-2

Hirsh,Paul | (g)
Mike Westbrook Brass Band
Glad Day:Settings Of William Blake | Enja | ENJ-9376 2

Hirshfield,Jeff | (dr)
Allan Botschinsky Quartet
I've Got Another Rhythm | M.A Music | A 916-2
Andrew Rathbun Group
True Stories | Fresh Sound Records | FSNT 099 CD
Daniel Schnyder Quintet With String Quartet
Mythology | Enja | ENJ-7003 2
Harold Danko Trio
Trilix | Steeplechase | SCCD 31551
Lee Konitz-Wolfgang Lackerschmid Quintet
Chet Baker:The Legacy Vol.3:Why Shouldn't You Cry | Enja | ENJ-9337 2
Loren Stillman Quartet
How Swee It Is | Nagel-Heyer | CD 2031
Louis Smith Quintet
Louisville | Steeplechase | SCCD 31552
Michael Cochrane Quartet
Path Ways | Steeplechase | SCCD 31542
Rich Perry Quartet
Hearsay | Steeplechase | SCCD 31515
Steve LaSpina Quintet
Remember When | Steeplechase | SCCD 31540
Taylor Hawkins Group
Wake Up Call | Fresh Sound Records | FSCD 145 CD
Ted Brown Quartet
Preservation | Steeplechase | SCCD 31539
Theo Bleckman & Kirk Nurock Quartet
Looking-Glass River | Traumton Records | 2412-2
Vic Juris Quartet
For The Music | Jazzpoint | JP 1034 CD
Vic Juris Trio
Songbook 2 | Steeplechase | SCCD 31516

Wolfgang Lackerschmid-Donald Johnston Group
New Singers-New Songs | Bhakti Jazz | BR 31
Hirt,Thomas | (fl,ssts)
Schlaier-Hirt Duo
Don't Walk Outside Thos Area | Chaos | CACD 8186
Hirt,Tomi | (b)
Q4 Orchester Project
Lyon's Brood | Creative Works Records | CW CD 1018-3
Yavapai | Creative Works Records | CW CD 1028-2
Hirtreiter,Andreas | (voc)
Michael Riessler & Singer Pur with Vincent Courtois
Ahi Vita | ACT | 9417-2
Hiseman,Jon | (dr,cymbals,electronic-perc,perc)
Barbara Thompson Group
Heavenly Bodies | VeraBra Records | CDVBR 2015-2
Shifting Sands | Intuition Records | INT 3174-2
Barbara Thompson's Paraphernalia
Mother Earth | VeraBra Records | CDVBR 2005-2
Barbara Thompson's Special Edition | VeraBra Records | CDVBR 2017-2
A Cry From The Heart | VeraBra Records | CDVBR 2021-2
Breathless | VeraBra Records | CDVBR 2057-2
Lady Saxophone | VeraBra Records | CDVBR 2166-2
Thompson's Tangos | Intuition Records | INT 3290-2
Jon Hiseman With The United Jazz & Rock Ensemble And Babara Thompson's Paraphernalia
About Time Too! | VeraBra Records | CDVBR 2014-2
Hisson,Dick | (tb)
Della Reese With The Sy Oliver Orchestra
Misty Blue:Sweet Sisters Swing Songs Of Sorrow And Sadness | Blue Note | 521151-2
Hitchcock,Jack | (tb)
Herbie Mann Group
The Best Of Herbie Mann | Atlantic | 7567-81369-2
Hitchcock,Nigel | (as)
Itchy Fingers
Live | Enja | ENJ-6076 2
Hittner,Frank | (b-clbs)
Maynard Ferguson Orchestra With Chris Connor
Two's Company | Roulette | 837201-2
Woody Herman And His Orchestra
Verve Jazz Masters 54:Woody Herman | Verve | 529903-2
Hixon,Richard | (tb)
Cab Calloway And His Orchestra
Planet Jazz:Cab Calloway | Planet Jazz | 2161237-2
Jimmy McGriff Orchestra
Swingin' The Blues-Jumpin' The Blues | Laserlight | 24654
Miles Davis With Gil Evans & His Orchestra
Sketches Of Spain | CBS | CK 65142
Quincy Jones And His Orchestra
Rahsaan/The Complete Mercury Recordings Of Roland Kirk | Mercury | 846630-2
Hixon,Richard 'Dick' | (b-tbtb)
Chubby Jackson And His All Star Big Band
Chubby Takes Over | Fresh Sound Records | FSR-CD 324
Jimmy Smith And Wes Montgomery With Orchestra
Jimmy & Wes-The Dynamic Duo | Verve | 521445-2
Jimmy Smith And Wes Montgomery With The Oliver Nelson Orchestra
Jimmy Smith:Best Of The Verve Years | Verve | 527950-2
Talkin' Jazz:Roots Of Acid Jazz | Verve | 529580-2
Jimmy Smith With The Oliver Nelson Orchestra
Peter & The Wolf | Verve | 547264-2
Miles Davis With Gil Evans & His Orchestra
Miles Davis At Carnegie Hall | CBS | CK 65027
This Is Jazz:Miles Davis Plays Ballads | CBS | CK 65038
Porgy And Bess | CBS | CK 65141
Quiet Nights | CBS | CK 65293
Quincy Jones And His Orchestra
Talkin' Verve-Roots Of Acid Jazz:Roland Kirk | Verve | 533101-2
Sarah Vaughan With Orchestra
!Viva! Vaughan | Mercury | 549374-2
Sarah Vaughan Sings The Mancini Songbook | Verve | 558401-2
Sarah Vaughan With The Frank Foster Orchestra
The Antonio Carlos Jobim Songbook | Verve | 525472-2
Hnilicka,Jaromir | (tp)
Hans Koller Big Band
New York City | MPS | 9813437
Hobgood,Laurence | (p)
Kurt Elling Group
This Time Its Love | Blue Note | 493543-2
Blue Velvet: Crooners, Swooners And Velvet Vocals | Blue Note | 521153-2
Flirting With Twilight | Blue Note | 531113-2
Kurt Elling Group With Guests
Live In Chicago | Blue Note | 522211-2
Hobson,Hank | (b)
Stephane Grappelli And His Musicians
Grapelli Story | Verve | 515807-2
Hobson,Homer | (tp)
Carroll Dickerson's Savoyagers
Louis Armstrong:Fireworks | Dreyfus Jazz Line | FDM 36710-2
Louis Armstrong And His Orchestra
Satch Plays Fats(Complete) | CBS | CK 64927
Hoch,Reuben | (cymbals,dr-loops,drvoice)
Jim Pepper Quartet
West End Avenue | Nabel Records:Jazz Network | CD 4633
Lance Bryant With The Christoph Spendel Trio
West End Avenue II | Nabel Records:Jazz Network | CD 4644
Höchstädter,Jean-Paul | (dr)
Clark Terry With The Summit Jazz Orchestra
Clark | Edition Collage | EC 530-2
Hochstein,Abraham | (viola)
Phineas Newborn Jr. With Dennis Farnon And His Orchestra
While My Lady Sleeps | RCA | 2185157-2
Hodeir,Andre | (arr,compcond)
Andre Hodeir And His Jazz Group De Paris
Jazz In Paris:Le Jazz Groupe De Paris Joue André Hodeir | EmArCy | 548792-2
Kenny Clarke Quartet
Jazz In Paris:Kenny Clarke Sextet Plays André Hodair | EmArCy | 834542-2 PMS
Kenny Clarke Quintet
Jazz In Paris:Kenny Clarke Sextet Plays André Hodair | EmArCy | 834542-2 PMS
Kenny Clarke Sextet
Jazz In Paris:Kenny Clarke Sextet Plays André Hodair | EmArCy | 834542-2 PMS
Le Jazz Group De Paris
Jazz In Paris | EmArCy | 548793-2
Hodes,Art | (pp-solo)
Art Hodes
Keepin' Out Of Mischief Now | Candid | CCD 79717
Sidney Bechet's Blue Note Jazzmen
Jazz:The Essential Collection Vol.1 | IN+OUT Records | 78011-2
Runnin' Wild | Blue Note | 821259-2
Sidney Bechet:Summertime | Dreyfus Jazz Line | FDM 36712-2
This Is Jazz All Stars
Sidney Bechet:Summertime | Dreyfus Jazz Line | FDM 36712-2
Hodges,Johnny | (arr,as,ld,clss)
Benny Carter-Coleman Hawkins-Johnny Hodges With The Oscar Peterson Trio
The Jazz Giants Play Duke Ellington:Caravan | Prestige | PCD 24227-2
Benny Goodman Band
Benny Goodman At Carnegie Hall 1938(Complete) | CBS | C2K 65143
Billie Holiday With Teddy Wilson And His Orchestra
Billie's Love Songs | Nimbus Records | NI 2000
Billy Strayhorn Orchestra
Johnny Hodges With Billy Strayhorn And The Orchestra | Verve | 557543-2
Django Reinhardt With Duke Ellington And His Orchestra
Django Reinhardt:Souveniers | Dreyfus Jazz Line | FDM 36744-2
Duke Ellington And Count Basie With Their Orchestras
First Time! | CBS | CK 65571
Duke Ellington And His Award Winners
Greatest Hits | CBS | 462959-2
Duke Ellington And His Cotton Club Orchestra
Planet Jazz:Duke Ellington | Planet Jazz | 2152053-2
Jazz:The Essential Collection Vol.2 | IN+OUT Records | 78012-2
Duke Ellington And His Famous Orchestra
Duke Ellington:The Blanton-Webster Band | Bluebird | 21 13181-2
Planet Jazz:Duke Ellington | Planet Jazz | 2152053-2
Planet Jazz:Johnny Hodges | Planet Jazz | 2152065-2
Planet Jazz Sampler | Planet Jazz | 2152326-2
Planet Jazz:Ben Webster | RCA | 2165368-2
Planet Jazz:Big Bands | Planet Jazz | 2169649-2
Planet Jazz:Jazz Trumpet | Planet Jazz | 2169654-2
Planet Jazz:Female Jazz Vocalists | Planet Jazz | 2169656-2
Highlights From The Duke Ellington Centennial Edition | RCA | 2663672-2
Greatest Hits | CBS | 462959-2
Jazz:The Essential Collection Vol.2 | IN+OUT Records | 78012-2
Jazz:The Essential Collection Vol.3 | IN+OUT Records | 78013-2
Duke Ellington:Ko-Ko | Dreyfus Jazz Line | FDM 36717-2
Duke Ellington And His Orchestra
Planet Jazz:Duke Ellington | Planet Jazz | 2152053-2
Planet Jazz:Johnny Hodges | Planet Jazz | 2152065-2
Planet Jazz:Jazz Greatest Hits | Planet Jazz | 2169648-2
Duke Ellington's Far East Suite | RCA | 2174797-2
Jazz Collection:Duke Ellington | Laserlight | 24369
The Art Of Saxophone | Laserlight | 24652
The Legends Of Swing | Laserlight | 24659
Highlights From The Duke Ellington Centennial Edition | RCA | 2663672-2
The Popular Duke Ellington | RCA | 2663880-2
Carnegie Hall Concert December 1944 | Prestige | 2PCD 24073-2
Carnegie Hall Concert January 1946 | Prestige | 2PCD 24074-2
Carnegie Hall Concert December 1947 | Prestige | 2PCD 24075-2
Carnegie Hall Concert January 1943 | Prestige | 2PCD 34004-2
Duke Ellington: The Champs-Elysees Theater January 29-30th,1965 | Laserlight | 36131
Greatest Hits | CBS | 462959-2
Jazz Festival Vol.2 | Storyville | 4960743
Verve Jazz Masters 4:Duke Ellington | Verve | 516338-2
Verve Jazz Masters 20:Introducing | Verve | 519853-2
Ella & Duke At The Cote D'Azur | Verve | 539030-2
Ella Fitzgerald And Duke Ellington:Cote D'Azure Concerts on Verve | Verve | 539033-2
Soul Call | Verve | 539785-2
The Great Paris Concert | Atlantic | 7567-81303-2
Jazz:The Essential Collection Vol.2 | IN+OUT Records | 78012-2
Jazz:The Essential Collection Vol.3 | IN+OUT Records | 78013-2
New Orleans Suite | Rhino | 812273670-2
Afro-Bossa | Reprise | 9362-47876-2
Ellington At Newport 1956(Complete) | CBS | CK 64932
Such Sweet Thunder | CBS | CK 65568
Anatomy Of A Murder | CBS | CK 65569
Welcome To Jazz At The Philharmonic | Fantasy | FANCD 6081-2
The Ellington Suites | Original Jazz Classics | OJC20 446-2(2310762)
Latin America Suite | Original Jazz Classics | OJC20 469-2
Duke Ellington And His Orchestra feat. Paul Gonsalves | Original Jazz Classics | OJCCD 623-2
Yale Concert | Original Jazz Classics | OJCCD 664-2
Jazz At The Philharmonis Berlin '65/Paris '67 | Pablo | PACD 5304-2
Duke Ellington At The Alhambra | Pablo | PACD 5313-2
The Jazz Giants Play Duke Ellington:Caravan | Prestige | PCD 24227-2
The Duke At Fargo 1940 | Storyville | STCD 8316/17
At The Hurricane:Original 1943 Broadcasts | Storyville | STCD 8359
Duke Ellington And Johnny Hodges Orchestra
Side By Side | Verve | 521405-2
Duke Ellington Small Band
The Intimacy Of The Blues | Original Jazz Classics | OJCCD 624-2
Duke Ellington-Coleman Hawkins Orchestra
Duke Ellington Meets Coleman Hawkins | Impulse(MCA) | 951162-2
Duke Ellington-Johnny Hodges All Stars
Verve Jazz Masters 4:Duke Ellington | Verve | 516338-2
Back To Back | Verve | 521404-2
Ella Fitzgerald With The Duke Ellington Orchestra
The Stockholm Concert 1966 | Pablo | 2308242-2
Ella Fitzgerald-First Lady Of Song | Verve | 517898-2
The Best Of The Song Books | Verve | 519804-2
Verve Jazz Masters 6:Ella Fitzgerald | Verve | 519822-2
The Best Of The Song Books:The Ballads | Verve | 521867-2
Verve Jazz Masters 46:Ella Fitzgerald-The Jazz Sides | Verve | 527655-2
Ella At Duke's Place | Verve | 529700-2
Love Songs:The Best Of The Song Books | Verve | 531762-2
Ella & Duke At The Cote D'Azur | Verve | 539030-2
Ella Fitzgerald Sings The Duke Ellington Songbook | Verve | 559248-2
For The Love Of Ella Fitzgerald | Verve | 841765-2
Ella Fitzgerald With The Duke Ellington Orchestra And Jimmy Jones Trio
Ella & Duke At The Cote D'Azur | Verve | 539030-2
Ella Fitzgerald And Duke Ellington:Cote D'Azure Concerts on Verve | Verve | 539033-2
Esquire All-American Award Winners
Best Of The Complete RCA Victor Recordings | RCA | 2663636-2
Highlights From The Duke Ellington Centennial Edition | RCA | 2663672-2
Gerry Mulligan-Johnny Hodges Quintet
Gerry Mulligan Meets Johnny Hodges | Verve | 065513-2
Verve Jazz Masters 35:Johnny Hodges | Verve | 521857-2
Jam Session
Benny Goodman At Carnegie Hall 1938(Complete) | CBS | C2K 65143
JATP All Stars
The Cole Porter Songbook | Verve | 823250-2
Johnny Hodges And His Band
Verve Jazz Masters 35:Johnny Hodges | Verve | 521857-2
Johnny Hodges And The Ellington All-Stars Without Duke
Verve Jazz Masters 35:Johnny Hodges | Verve | 521857-2
Johnny Hodges And The Ellington Men
Verve Jazz Masters 35:Johnny Hodges | Verve | 521857-2
Johnny Hodges Orchestra
Planet Jazz:Johnny Hodges | Planet Jazz | 2152065-2
Planet Jazz Sampler | Planet Jazz | 2152326-2
Coleman Hawkins/Johnny Hodges:The Vogue Recordings | Vogue | 21559712
Planet Jazz:Jazz Saxophone | Planet Jazz | 2169653-2
Highlights From The Duke Ellington Centennial Edition | RCA | 2663672-2
Johnny Hodges At The Sportpalast, Berlin | Pablo | 2CD 2620102
Side By Side | Verve | 521405-2
Verve Jazz Masters 35:Johnny Hodges | Verve | 521857-2
Verve Jazz Masters 43:Ben Webster | Verve | 525431-2
The Soul Of Ben Webster | Verve | 527475-2
The Jazz Giants Play Harry Warren:Lullaby Of Broadway | Prestige | PCD 24204-2
Johnny Hodges With Billy Strayhorn And The Duke Ellington Orchestra
Verve Jazz Masters 35:Johnny Hodges | Verve | 521857-2
Johnny Hodges With The Dizzy Gillespie Quintet
Verve Jazz Masters 35:Johnny Hodges | Verve | 521857-2
Johnny Hodges-Earl Hines Quintet
Verve Jazz Masters 35:Johnny Hodges | Verve | 521857-2
Johnny Hodges-Wild Bill Davis Sextet
Planet Jazz:Johnny Hodges | Planet Jazz | 2152065-2
Leonard Feather's Esquire All-Americans
Louis Armstrong:C'est Si Bon | Dreyfus Jazz Line | FDM 36730-2
Lionel Hampton And His Orchestra
Planet Jazz:Male Jazz Vocalists | Planet Jazz | 2169657-2
Norman Granz Jam Session
Verve Jazz Masters 35:Johnny Hodges | Verve | 521857-2
Charlie Parker:The Best Of The Verve Years | Verve | 527815-2
Talkin' Bird | Verve | 559859-2
Bird: The Complete Charlie Parker On Verve | Verve | 837141-2
Oscar Peterson With The Duke Ellington Orchestra
Oscar Peterson Plays Duke Ellington | Pablo | 2310966-2
Rosemary Clooney With The Duke Ellington Orchestra
Blue Rose | CBS | CK 65506
Hodgkiss,Allan | (g)
Quintet Du Hot Club De France
Grapelli Story | Verve | 515807-2
Verve Jazz Masters 38:Django Reinhardt | Verve | 516931-2
Django Reinhardt:Echoes Of France | Dreyfus Jazz Line | FDM 36726-2
Django Reinhardt:Souveniers | Dreyfus Jazz Line | FDM 36744-2
Hoeg,T.S. | (recitation)
Copenhagen Art Ensemble
Shape To Twelve | dacapo | DCCD 9430
Hoekstra,P.E. | (v)
Toots Thielemans And His Orchestra
Verve Jazz Masters Vol.59:Toots Thielemans | Verve | 535271-2
Hoelker,Stefan | (perc)
Andy Lumpp Trio
Ostara | Nabel Records:Jazz Network | CD 4682
Andy Lumpp Trio Feat. Andy Przybielski
Musica Ex Spiritu Sancto | Nabel Records:Jazz Network | CD 4694
Andy Lumpp Trio With Andy Przybielski
Music From Planet Earth | Nabel Records:Jazz Network | CD 4687
Hoenig,Ari | (dr)
Jacques Schwarz-Bart/James Hurt Quartet
Immersion | Fresh Sound Records | FSNT 057 CD
Jam Session
Jam Session Vol.6 | Steeplechase | SCCD 31537
James Hurt Group
Dark Grooves-Mystcal Rhythms | Blue Note | 495104-2
Jean-Michel Pilc Quartet
Cardinal Points | Dreyfus Jazz Line | FDM 36649-2
Jean-Michel Pilc Quintet
Cardinal Points | Dreyfus Jazz Line | FDM 36649-2
Jean-Michel Pilc Trio
Welcome Home | Dreyfus Jazz Line | FDM 36630-2
Cardinal Points | Dreyfus Jazz Line | FDM 36649-2
Josh Roseman Unit
Cherry | Enja | ENJ-9392 2
Höfer,Armin | (sax)
Vesna Skorija Band
Niceland | Satin Doll Productions | SDP 1037-1 CD
Höfer,Monika | (voc)
Jazzensemble Des Hessischen Rundfunks
Jazz Messe-Messe Für Unsere Zeit | hr music.de | hrmj 003-01 CD
Hoff,Brynjar | (engl-hoboe)
Rainer Brünninghaus Quartet
Freigeweht | ECM | 1187(847329-2)
Hoffbauer,Manfred | (fl,clts)
Bernd Konrad With Erwin Lehn und sein Südfunk Orchester Stuttgart
Wen Die Götter Lieben | Creative Works Records | CW CD 1010-1
Eberhard Weber Group
Chorus | ECM | 1288(823844-2)
Höffken,Manfred | (voc)
Jazzensemble Des Hessischen Rundfunks
Jazz Messe-Messe Für Unsere Zeit | hr music.de | hrmj 003-01 CD
Hoffman,Harry | (v)
Billie Holiday With The Ray Ellis Orchestra
Lady In Satin | CBS | CK 65144
Hoffman,John | (tp)
Buddy Rich Big Band
Backwoods Siseman/Pieces Of Dream | Laserlight | 24655
Grace Knight With Orchestra
Come In Spinner | Intuition Records | INT 3052-2
Vince Jones With Orchestra
Come In Spinner | Intuition Records | INT 3052-2
Woody Herman And The New Thundering Herd
Planet Jazz:Big Bands | Planet Jazz | 2169649-2
Woody Herman's Thundering Herd
Planet Jazz:Jazz Saxophone | Planet Jazz | 2169653-2
Hoffmand,Amos | (goud)
Amos Hoffman Quartet
The Dreamer | Fresh Sound Records | FSNT 060 CD
Hoffmann,Hajo | (vviola)
Joachim Ullrich Orchestra
Faces Of The Duke | Jazz Haus Musik | JHM 0045 CD
Hoffmann,Ingfried | (org,ptp)
Klaus Doldinger Quartet
Doldinger's Best | ACT | 9224-2
Klaus Doldinger Quintet
Doldinger's Best | ACT | 9224-2
Klaus Doldinger Septet
Doldinger's Best | ACT | 9224-2
NDR-Workshop
Doldinger's Best | ACT | 9224-2
Paul Nero Sound
Doldinger's Best | ACT | 9224-2
Hoffmann,Markus | (v)
Uri Caine With The Concerto Köln
Concerto Köln | Winter&Winter | 910086-2
Höfler,Karoline | (b)
Dieter Fischer Trio
Jazz Guitar Highlights 1 | Jardis Records | JRCD 20141
Trio Music | Jardis Records | JRCD 9925
Lucas Heidepriem Quartet
Voicings | IN+OUT Records | 7011-2
Ull Möck Trio
Drilling | Satin Doll Productions | SDP 1023-1 CD
Walter Lang Quintet
Tales Of 2 Cities | double moon | CHRDM 71016
Hofman,Josef | (narration)
Pata Music Meets Arfi
La Belle Et La Bête | Pata Musik | PATA 14(amf 1066)
Hofmann,Edgar | (fl,clsax)
Uli Trepte Group
Real Time Music | ATM Records | ATM 3820-AH
Hofmann,Georg | (drperc)
Georg Hofmann-Lucas Niggli Duo
Mute Songs & Drumscapes | Creative Works Records | CW CD 1022-2
Richard Carr Trio
Coast To Coast | Nabel Records:Jazz Network | CD 4675
Along The Edge | Nabel Records:Jazz Network | CD 4683
Hofseth,Bendik | (sax,programming,voc,ssts)
Arild Andersen Quintet With The Cikada String Quartet
Hyperborean | ECM | 1631(537342-2)
Arild Andersen Sextet
Sagn | ECM | 1435
Ketil Bjornstad Group
Grace | EmArCy | 013622-2
Hofstra,David | (b,el-btuba)
Bill Frisell Band
Is That You? | Nonesuch | 7559-60956-2
John Zorn Group
Spillane | Nonesuch | 7559-79172-2
Hogan,Carl | (el-gg)
Louis Jordan And His Tympany Five
Louis Jordan-Let The Good Times Roll: The Complete Decca Recordings 1938-1954 | Bear Family Records | BCD 15557 IH
Hogan,Granville T. | (dr)
Cal Massey Sextet
The Jazz Life! | Candid | CCD 79019
Blues To Coltrane | Candid | CCD 79029
Hogan,Wilbert | (dr)
Fred Jackson Quartet

So Blue So Funky-Heroes Of The Hammond | Blue Note | 796563-2
Leo Parker Sextet
True Blue | Blue Note | 534032-2

Högberg,Örjan | (viola)
Nils Landgren Group
Sentimental Journey | ACT | 9409-2

Hogendijk,Jarmo | (tp)
European Jazz Ensemble
20th Anniversary Tour | Konnex Records | KCD 5078

Hogest,Carl | (ld)
Terje Rypdal(comp)
Undisonus | ECM | 1389

Hogue,Norman | (tbvoc)
David Mengual Quartet
Monkiana:A Tribute To Thelonious Monk | Fresh Sound Records | FSNT 019 CD
David Mengual Quintet
Monkiana:A Tribute To Thelonious Monk | Fresh Sound Records | FSNT 019 CD

Hohagen,Hans | (b)
Glen Buschmann Quintet
Deutsches Jazz Fesival 1954/1955 | Bear Family Records | BCD 15430
Wolfgang Sauer With The Glen Buschmann Quintet
Deutsches Jazz Fesival 1954/1955 | Bear Family Records | BCD 15430

Höhn,Wolfgang | (dr)
Peter Ehwald Trio
Away With Words:The Music Of John Scofield | Jazz Haus Musik | JHM 0128 CD

Hoisl-Rausch,Sabine | (perc)
Omar Belmonte's Latin Lover
Vamos A Ver | EGO | 96170

Hoist,Allen | (alto-fl,bs,cello,fl,asts)
Mongo Santamaria And His Band
Montreux Heat! | Pablo | PACD 5317-2
Mongo Santamaria Group With Dizzy Gillespie And Toots Thielemans
Summertime-Digital At Montreux 1980 | Original Jazz Classics | OJCCD 626-2(2308229)
Montreux Heat! | Pablo | PACD 5317-2
Renaud Garcia-Fons Group
Entremundo | Enja | ENJ-9464 2

Holand,Ulf W.O. | (samples)
Nils Petter Molvaer Group
Khmer | ECM | 1560(537798-2)

Holbroe,Hans | (cl)
Papa Benny's Jazzband
The Golden Years Of Revival Jazz,Vol.7 | Storyville | STCD 5512
The Golden Years Of Revival Jazz,Vol.11 | Storyville | STCD 5516
Ricardo's Jazzmen
The Golden Years Of Revival Jazz,Sampler | Storyville | 109 1001
The Golden Years Of Revival Jazz,Vol.4 | Storyville | STCD 5509
The Golden Years Of Revival Jazz,Vol.5 | Storyville | STCD 5510

Holcombe,Bill | (as,bsts)
Ella Fitzgerald With Sy Oliver And His Orchestra
Ella Fitzgerald:The Decca Years 1949-1954 | Decca | 050668-2
Louis Armstrong With Sy Oliver And His Orchestra
Satchmo Serenaders | Verve | 543792-2
Louis Armstrong:C'est Si Bon | Dreyfus Jazz Line | FDM 36730-2
Louis Armstrong-My Greatest Songs | MCA | MCD 18347

Holden,Carol | (fr-h)
Eric Dolphy Quartet With The University Of Illinois Brass Ensemble
The Illinois Concert | Blue Note | 499826-2

Holder,Frank | (congasbongos)
Barbara Thompson's Paraphernalia
Breathless | VeraBra Records | CDVBR 2057-2

Holder,Mitch | (el-gg)
Ella Fitzgerald With Orchestra
Ella Abraca Jobim | Pablo | 2630201-2
Lee Ritenour Group
Stolen Moments | GRP | GRP 96152

Holderness,Lorenzo | (ts)
Johnny Otis And His Orchestra
Verve Jazz Masters 43:Ben Webster | Verve | 525431-2

Holdsworth,Allan | (el-g,g,bar-gsynthaxe)
Allan Holdsworth Group
None Too Soon | Cream Records | CR 400-2
The Sixteen Man Of Tain | Cream Records | CR 610-2
The Name Of A Woman | Cream Records | JMS 18733-2
Jean-Luc Ponty Sextet
Enigmatic Ocean | Atlantic | 19110-2
The Very Best Of Jean-Luc Ponty | Rhino | 8122-79862-2
John Stevens Quartet
Re-Touch & Quartet | Konnex Records | KCD 5027
Stanley Clarke Group
If This Bass Could Only Talk | CBS | 460883-2

Holdsworth,Dave | (tpfl-h)
John Surman Orchestra
How Many Clouds Can You See? | Deram | 844882-2

Holgersson,Jones | (dr)
Lisa Ekdahl With The Salvador Poe Quartet, Strings And Guests
Lisa Ekdahl Sings Salvadore Poe | RCA | 2179681-2
Mingus By Five
Mingus By Five | Touché Music | TMcCD 019
Monk By Five
Monk By Five | Touché Music | TMcCD 012
Tim Hagans With Norrbotten Big Band
Future Miles | ACT | 9235-2
Viktoria Tolstoy Group & Strings
Shining On You | ACT | 9701-2

Holiday,Billie | (voc)
Artie Shaw And His Orchestra
Planet JazzArtie Shaw | Planet Jazz | 2152057-2
Planet Jazz:Swing | Planet Jazz | 2169651-2
Planet Jazz:Female Jazz Vocalists | Planet Jazz | 2169656-2
Benny Goodman And His Orchestra
Jazz:The Essential Collection Vol.3 | IN+OUT Records | 78013-2
Camel Caravan Broadcast 1939 Vol.1 | Phontastic | NCD 8817
Billie Holiday
My Greatest Songs | MCA | MCD 18767
Billie Holiday And Her All Stars
Verve Jazz Masters 12:Billie Holiday | Verve | 519825-2
Verve Jazz Masters 20:Introducing | Verve | 519853-2
Billie Holiday Story Vol.4:Lady Sings The Blues | Verve | 521429-2
Verve Jazz Masters 47:Billie Holiday Sings Standards | Verve | 527650-2
Verve Jazz Masters Vol.60:The Collection | Verve | 529866-2
Songs For Distingué Lovers | Verve | 539056-2
4 By 4:Ella Fitzgerald/Sarah Vaughan/Billie Holiday/Dinah Washington | Verve | 559693-2
Billie's Blues | Blue Note | 748786-2
The Billie Holiday Song Book | Verve | 823246-2
Billie Holiday And Her Band
Verve Jazz Masters 47:Billie Holiday Sings Standards | Verve | 527650-2
Billie's Love Songs | Nimbus Records | NI 2000
Billie Holiday And Her Orchestra
Solitude | Verve | 519810-2
Jazz:The Essential Collection Vol.3 | IN+OUT Records | 78013-2
Billie's Love Songs | Nimbus Records | NI 2000
Billie Holiday And Her Quintet
Verve Jazz Masters 47:Billie Holiday Sings Standards | Verve | 527650-2
Billie Holiday:The Complete Commodore Recordings | GRP | 543272-2
Billie Holiday With Bobby Tucker
Billie Holiday Story Vol.1:Jazz At The Philharmonic | Verve | 521642-2
The Complete Jazz At The Philharmonic On Verve 1944-1949 | Verve | 523893-2
Billie Holiday With Buck Clayton And The Mal Waldron Trio
Billie Holiday Story Vol.1:Jazz At The Philharmonic | Verve | 521642-2
Billie Holiday With Eddie Heywood And His Orchestra
Billie Holiday:The Complete Commodore Recordings | GRP | 543272-2
Billie's Love Songs | Nimbus Records | NI 2000
Billie Holiday With Frankie Newton And His Orchestra
Billie Holiday:The Complete Commodore Recordings | GRP | 543272-2
Billie's Love Songs | Nimbus Records | NI 2000
Billie Holiday With Gordon Jenkins And His Orchestra
Billie's Love Songs | Nimbus Records | NI 2000
Billie Holiday With Sy Oliver And His Orchestra
Billie's Love Songs | Nimbus Records | NI 2000
Billie Holiday With Teddy Wilson And His Orchestra
Billie's Love Songs | Nimbus Records | NI 2000
Billie Holiday With The Bobby Tucker Quartet
Billie's Love Songs | Nimbus Records | NI 2000
Billie Holiday With The Carl Drinkard Trio
Misty Blue:Sweet Sisters Swing Songs Of Sorrow And Sadness | Blue Note | 521151-2
Billie's Blues | Blue Note | 748786-2
Billie Holiday With The JATP All Stars
Billie Holiday Story Vol.1:Jazz At The Philharmonic | Verve | 521642-2
The Complete Jazz At The Philharmonic On Verve 1944-1949 | Verve | 523893-2
Verve Jazz Masters 47:Billie Holiday Sings Standards | Verve | 527650-2
Jazz At The Philharmonic:Best Of The 1940's Concerts | Verve | 557534-2
Billie Holiday With The Mal Waldron Trio
Billie Holiday Story Vol.1:Jazz At The Philharmonic | Verve | 521642-2
Billie Holiday With The Paul Whiteman Orchestra
Billie's Blues | Blue Note | 748786-2
Billie Holiday With The Ray Ellis Orchestra
Verve Jazz Masters 47:Billie Holiday Sings Standards | Verve | 527650-2
Lady In Satin | CBS | CK 65144
Billie Holiday With The Tiny Grimes Quintet
Billie's Blues | Blue Note | 748786-2
Billie Holiday With Toots Camarata And His Orchestra
Billie's Love Songs | Nimbus Records | NI 2000
Billie Holiday-Oscar Peterson
Solitude | Verve | 519810-2
Count Basie And His Orchestra
Jazz:The Essential Collection Vol.3 | IN+OUT Records | 78013-2
Louis Armstrong And Billie Holiday With Sy Oliver's Orchestra
Louis Armstrong:C'est Si Bon | Dreyfus Jazz Line | FDM 36730-2
Stan Getz Quintet
Stan Getz-The Complete Roost Sessions | EMI Records | 859622-2
Teddy Wilson And His All Stars
Jazz:The Essential Collection Vol.3 | IN+OUT Records | 78013-2
Teddy Wilson And His Orchestra
Jazz:The Essential Collection Vol.3 | IN+OUT Records | 78013-2

Holiday,Clarence | (bjg)
Connie's Inn Orchestra
Planet Jazz:Coleman Hawkins | Planet Jazz | 2152055-2
Fletcher Henderson And His Orchestra
Jazz:The Essential Collection Vol.1 | IN+OUT Records | 78011-2

Holkenborg,Tom | (g)
Pili-Pili
Stolen Moments | JA & RO | JARO 4159-2

Holladay,Marvin | (bssax)
Jack McDuff Quartet With Orchestra
Prelude:Jack McDuff Big Band | Prestige | PRCD 24283-2
Stan Kenton And His Orchestra
Adventures In Blues | Capitol | 520089-2
Adventures In Jazz | Capitol | 521222-2

Holland,Dave | (b,el-b,b-solo,cello,b-g,cello-solo)
Andy Middleton Group
Nomad's Notebook | Intuition Records | INT 3264-2
Anouar Brahem Trio
Thimar | ECM | 1641(539888-2)
Bill Frisell Trio
Bill Frisell With Dave Hollnad And Elvin Jones | Nonesuch | 7559-79624-2
Carla Bley Group
Tropic Appetites | Watt | 1
Cassandra Wilson Group
Traveling Miles | Blue Note | 854123-2
Charles Lloyd Quartet
Voice In The Night | ECM | 1674(559445-2)
Chick Corea Septet
The Complete 'Is' Sessions | Blue Note | 540532-2
Chick Corea Trio
A.R.C. | ECM | 1009
The Story Of Jazz Piano | Laserlight | 24653
Circle
Paris Concert | ECM | 1018/19(843163-2)
Collin Walcott Quartet
Cloud Dance | ECM | 1062(825469-2)
Dave Holland
Emerald Tears | ECM | 1109(529087-2)
Dave Holland Big Band
What Goes Around | ECM | 1777(014002-2)
Dave Holland Qartet
Extensions | ECM | 1410(841778-2)
Dream Of The Elders | ECM | 1572(529084-2)
Dave Holland Quintet
Jumpin' In | ECM | 1269
Seeds Of Time | ECM | 1292
The Razor's Edge | ECM | 1353
Point Of View | ECM | 1663(557020-2)
Prime Directive | ECM | 1698(547950-2)
Not For Nothin' | ECM | 1758(014004-2)
Extended Play | ECM | 1864/65(038505-2)
Dave Holland Trio
Triplicate | ECM | 1373
David Holland
Life Cycle | ECM | 1238
David Holland Quartet
Conference Of The Birds | ECM | 1027(829373-2)
Gateway
In The Moment | ECM | 1574(529346-2)
George Adams Sextet
Soung Suggestions | ECM | 1141
Herbie Hancock Group
Herbie Hancock The New Standards | Verve | 527715-2
Herbie Hancock Group With String Quartet
Herbie Hancock The New Standards | Verve | 527715-2
Herbie Hancock Group With String Quartet,Woodwinds And Brass
Herbie Hancock The New Standards | Verve | 527715-2
Herbie Hancock Group With Woodwinds And Brass
Herbie Hancock The New Standards | Verve | 527715-2
James Carter Quartet
The Real Quietstorm | Atlantic | 7567-82742-2
Jeanne Lee-Dave Holland
Natural Affinities | Owl Records | 018352-2
Joe Henderson And His Orchestra
Joe Henderson:The Milestone Years | Milestone | 8MCD 4413-2
Joe Henderson Group
Porgy And Bess | Verve | 539048-2
Joe Henderson Quartet
Joe Henderson:The Milestone Years | Milestone | 8MCD 4413-2
Joe Henderson Quintet
Multiple | Original Jazz Classics | OJCCD 763-2(M 9050)
Joe Henderson Sextet
Joe Henderson:The Milestone Years | Milestone | 8MCD 4413-2
Multiple | Original Jazz Classics | OJCCD 763-2(M 9050)
Joe Lovano Quartet
From The Soul | Blue Note | 798636-2
Joe Lovano Trio
Trio Fascination | Blue Note | 833114-2
John Abercrombie Trio
Gateway | ECM | 1061(829192-2)
Gateway 2 | ECM | 1105(847323-2)
Gateway | ECM | 1562(527637-2)
Karl Berger-Dave Holland Duo
Conversations | IN+OUT Records | 77027-2
Kenny Werner Trio
A Delicate Ballace | RCA | 2151694-2
Kenny Wheeler Ensemble
Muisc For Large & Small Ensembles | ECM | 1415/16
Kenny Wheeler Quartet
Gnu High | ECM | 1069(825591-2)
Kenny Wheeler Quintet
Double, Double You | ECM | 1262(815675-2)
The Widow In The Window | ECM | 1417(843198-2)
Kenny Wheeler/Lee Konitz/Dave Holland/Bill Frisell
Angel Song | ECM | 1607(533098-2)
Mark Isaacs/Dave Holland/Roy Haynes
Encounters | VeraBra Records | CDVBR 2076-2
Michael Brecker Group
Tales From The Hudson | Impulse(MCA) | 951191-2
Michel Petrucciani With The Graffiti String Quartet
Marvellous | Dreyfus Jazz Line | FDM 36564-2
Miles Davis Group
Circle In The Round | CBS | 467898-2
In A Silent Way | CBS | 86556-2
Live-Evil | CBS | C2K 65135
Live At The Fillmore East | CBS | C2K 65139
Bitches Brew | CBS | C2K 65774
Miles Davis Quintet
Filles De Kilimanjaro | CBS | 86555-2
Black Beauty-Miles Davis At Filmore West | CBS | C2K 65138
Miles Davis Sextet
Black Beauty-Miles Davis At Filmore West | CBS | C2K 65138
Roy Haynes Quintet
Birds Of A Feather:A Tribute To Charlie Parker | Dreyfus Jazz Line | FDM 36625-2
Scolohofo
Oh! | Blue Note | 542081-2
Tomasz Stanko Quartet
Balladyna | ECM | 1071(519289-2)
World Trio
World Trio | VeraBra Records | CDVBR 2052-2

Holland,Milt | (dr,percvib)
Cal Tjader With The Clare Fischer Orchestra
Cal Tjader Plays Harold Arlen & West Side Story | Fantasy | FCD 24775-2
Ella Fitzgerald With The Buddy Bregman Orchestra
The Best Of The Song Books:The Ballads | Verve | 521867-2
Ella Fitzgerald Sings The Rodgers And Hart Song Book | Verve | 537258-2
Ella Fitzgerald With The Frank DeVol Orchestra
Get Happy! | Verve | 523321-2
Herbie Mann Sextet
Verve Jazz Masters Vol.60:The Collection | Verve | 529866-2
Verve Jazz Masters 56:Herbie Mann | Verve | 529901-2
Herbie Mann Trio
Verve Jazz Masters 56:Herbie Mann | Verve | 529901-2
Pete Rugolo And His Orchestra
Thriller/Richard Diamon(Original Jazz Scores From 2 Classics TV Series) | Fresh Sound Records | FSCD 2015
Van Alexander Orchestra
Home Of Happy Feet/Swing! Staged For Sound! | Capitol | 535211-2

Holland,Peanuts | (tpvoc)
Bud Powell Quintet
Parisian Thoroughfare | Pablo | CD 2310976-2
Don Byas And His Orchestra
Americans Swinging In Paris:Don Byas | EMI Records | 539655-2
Don Byas Ree-Boppers
Don Byas:Laura | Dreyfus Jazz Line | FDM 36714-2
Guy Lafitte-Peanuts Holland And Their Orchestra
Jazz In Paris:Guy Lafitte-Blue And Sentimental | EmArCy | 159852-2 PMS
Milton Mezz Mezzrow Sextet
Americans Swinging In Paris:Mezz Mezzrow | EMI Records | 539660-2
Peanuts Holland And His Orchestra
Americans Swinging In Paris:Don Byas | EMI Records | 539655-2
Quartier Latin Jazz Band
Great Traditionalists | Jazzpoint | JP 1046 CD
Tyree Glenn
Don Byas:Laura | Dreyfus Jazz Line | FDM 36714-2
Tyree Glenn And His Orchestra
Americans Swinging In Paris:Don Byas | EMI Records | 539655-2

Hollander,Jan | (tp)
The Rosenberg Trio With Orchestra
Noches Calientes | Verve | 557022-2

Hollander,Max | (v)
Charlie Parker With Strings
Verve Jazz Masters 28:Charlie Parker Plays Standards | Verve | 521854-2
Charlie Parker With Strings:The Master Takes | Verve | 523984-2
Charlie Parker:The Best Of The Verve Years | Verve | 527815-2
Bird: The Complete Charlie Parker On Verve | Verve | 837141-2
Charlie Parker:April In Paris | Dreyfus Jazz Line | FDM 36737-2
Coleman Hawkins With Billy Byers And His Orchestra
The Hawk In Hi-Fi | RCA | 2663842-2

Hollander,Rick | (drvoc)
Christian Willisohn Group
Live At Marians | ART BY HEART | ABH 2006 2
Blues On The World | Blues Beacon | BLU-1025 2
Christian Willisohn New Band
Heart Broken Man | Blues Beacon | BLU-1026 2
Conte Candoli Quartet
Candoli Live | Nagel-Heyer | CD 2024
David Paquette Trio
Mood Swings | ART BY HEART | ABH 2004 2
Johannes Enders Quintet
Quiet Fire | Enja | ENJ-9390 2
Johannes Herrlich Quintet
Thinking Of You | Edition Collage | EC 499-2
Thomas Faist Jazzquartet
Visionary | JHM Records | JHM 3609
Thomas Faist Sextet
Gentle | Village | VILCD 1020-2
Walter Lang Quintet
Tales Of 2 Cities | double moon | CHRDM 71016

Hollenbeck,John | (dr)
Ansgar Striepens Quintet
Dreams And Realities | Laika Records | 35101642
John Abercrombie With The Ansgar Striepens Quintet
Dreams And Realities | Laika Records | 35101642
Lee Konitz With The Ed Partyka Jazz Orchestra
Dreams And Realities | Laika Records | 35101642

Höllering,Charles | (cl)
Heiner Franz' Swing Connection
Heiner Franz' Swing Connection | Jardis Records | JRCD 9817

Holley,Major | (b,el-b,tubavoice)
Al Cohn-Zoot Sims Quintet
You 'N' Me | Verve | 589318-2
Coleman Hawkins Quartet
Verve Jazz Masters 43:Coleman Hawkins | Verve | 521856-2
Today And Now | Impulse(MCA) | 951184-2
The Roots Of Acid Jazz | Impulse(MCA) | IMP 12042
The Jazz Giants Play Rodgers & Hammerstein:My Favorite Things | Prestige | PCD 24223-2
Coleman Hawkins Septet
Desafinado | Impulse(MCA) | 951227-2

Coleman Hawkins Sextet
Desafinado | Impulse(MCA) | 951227-2
Henrik Johansen's Jazzband
The Golden Years Of Revival Jazz,Vol.6 | Storyville | STCD 5511
The Golden Years Of Revival Jazz,Vol.7 | Storyville | STCD 5512
The Golden Years Of Revibal Jazz,Vol.15 | Storyville | STCD 5520
Kenny Burrell Quintet
Midnight Blue | Blue Note | 495335-2
The Best Of Blue Note | Blue Note | 796110-2
Lee Konitz Orchestra
The Art Of Saxophone | Laserlight | 24652
Milt Jackson Orchestra
Milt Jackson Birthday Celebration | Fantasy | FANCD 6079-2
Oscar Peterson-Major Holley Duo
Oscar Peterson:Get Happy | Dreyfus Jazz Line | FDM 36738-2
Quincy Jones And His Orchestra
Talkin' Verve-Roots Of Acid Jazz:Roland Kirk | Verve | 533101-2
Verve Jazz Masters Vol.59:Toots Thielemans | Verve | 535271-2
Rahsaan/The Complete Mercury Recordings Of Roland Kirk | Mercury | 846630-2
Roy Eldridge And The Jimmy Ryan All Stars
Jazz Dance | Original Jazz Classics | OJCCD 1002-2(1210890)
Little Jazz And The Jimmy Ryan All-Stars | Original Jazz Classics | OJCCD 1058-2(DRE 1001)
Stanley Turrentine Quintet
Never Let Me Go | Blue Note | 576750-2

Holliday,Simon | (p)
Marty Hall Band
Who's Been Talkin'?s | Blues Beacon | BLU-1033 2

Hollinger,Peter | (dr,metalperc)
Mani Neumeir-Peter Hollinger
Monsters Of Drums-Live | ATM Records | ATM 3821-AH

Hollon,Kenneth | (clts)
Billie Holiday And Her Quintet
Billie Holiday:The Complete Commodore Recordings | GRP | 543272-2
Billie Holiday With Frankie Newton And His Orchestra
Billie Holiday:The Complete Commodore Recordings | GRP | 543272-2
Billie's Love Songs | Nimbus Records | NI 2000
Louis Jordan And His Tympany Five
Louis Jordan-Let The Good Times Roll: The Complete Decca Recordings 1938-1954 | Bear Family Records | BCD 15557 IH

Holloway,Red | (as,ts,bs,ld,vocfl)
Axel Zwingenberger With The Mojo Blues Band And Red Holloway
Axel Zwingenberger And The Friends Of Boogie Woogie,Vol.8 | Vagabond | VRCD 8.93019
Eddie Cleanhead Vinson With Band
The Late Show-Recorded Live At Marla's Memory Lane Supper Club Vol.2 | Fantasy | FCD 9655-2
Eddie Cleanhead Vinson With The Red Holloway Quartet
Blues In The Night-Volume One:The Early Show | Fantasy | FCD 9647-2
Etta James & Eddie Cleanhead Vinson With The Red Holloway Quartet
Blues In The Night-Volume One:The Early Show | Fantasy | FCD 9647-2
Etta James With Band
The Late Show-Recorded Live At Marla's Memory Lane Supper Club Vol.2 | Fantasy | FCD 9655-2
Etta James With The Red Holloway Quartet
Blues In The Night-Volume One:The Early Show | Fantasy | FCD 9647-2
Etta James With The Red Holloway Quintet
Blues In The Night-Volume One:The Early Show | Fantasy | FCD 9647-2
Etta James/Eddie 'Cleanhead' Vinson With Band
The Late Show-Recorded Live At Marla's Memory Lane Supper Club Vol.2 | Fantasy | FCD 9655-2
Gene Ammons And His Orchestra
A Stranger In Town | Prestige | PRCD 24266-2
George Benson With The Jack McDuff Quartet
The New Boss Guitar | Original Jazz Classics | OJCCD 461-2
Grooveyard Meets Red Holloway
Basic Instinct | Organic Music | ORGM 9701
Jack McDuff Quartet
Silken Soul | Prestige | PCD 24242-2
The Soulful Drums | Prestige | PCD 24256-2
The Concert McDuff | Prestige | PRCD 24270-2
The Last Goodun' | Prestige | PRCD 24274-2
Jack McDuff:The Prestige Years | Prestige | PRCD 24387-2
Jack McDuff Quartet With Orchestra
Prelude:Jack McDuff Big Band | Prestige | PRCD 24283-2
Jack McDuff Quintet
Silken Soul | Prestige | PCD 24242-2
The Last Goodun' | Prestige | PRCD 24274-2
Jack McDuff Sextet
Silken Soul | Prestige | PCD 24242-2
The Soulful Drums | Prestige | PCD 24256-2
Plas Johnson-Red Holloway Quintet
Keep That Groove Going! | Milestone | MCD 9319-2
Red Holloway Quintet
Coast To Coast | Milestone | MCD 9335-2
Red Holloway With The Matthias Bätzel Trio
A Night Of Blues & Ballads | JHM Records | JHM 3614

Holloway,Ron | (sax,tsbs)
Chuck Brown And The Second Chapter Band
Timeless | Minor Music | 801068
Ron Holloway-Paul Bollenback
Jazzin' Vol.2: The Music Of Stevie Wonder | Fantasy | FANCD 6088-2

Holloway,Tracey | (tbeuphonium)
Mike Westbrook Orchestra
Bar Utopia-A Big Band Cabaret | Enja | ENJ-9333 2
The Orchestra Of Smith's Academy | Enja | ENJ-9358 2

Hollstein,David | (g)
Al Jones Blues Band
Sharper Than A Tack | Blues Beacon | BLU-1034 2

Hollywood Hucksters,The |
The Hollywood Hucksters
The Hollywood Session:The Capitol Jazzmen | Jazz Unlimited | JUCD 2044

Holm,Stig | (p)
Coleman Hawkins With The Thore Ehrlings Orchestra
Coleman Hawkins At The Golden Circle | Dragon | DRCD 265

Holman,Bill | (arr,comp,ld,bass-s,bs,cond,reedsts)
Anita O'Day With The Bill Holman Orchestra
Verve Jazz Masters 49:Anita O'Day | Verve | 527653-2
Incomparable! Anita O'Day | Verve | 589516-2
Art Pepper Quintet With Strings
Art Pepper:The Complete Galaxy Recordings | Galaxy | 16GCD 1016-2
Bill Holman Octet
The Jazz Giants Play Sammy Cahn:It's Magic | Prestige | PCD 24226-2
Buddy Rich Big Band
Keep The Customer Satisfied | EMI Records | 523999-2
Chamber Jazz Sextet
Plays Pal Joey | Candid | CCD 79030
Count Basie And His Orchestra
I Told You So | Original Jazz Classics | OJCCD 824-2(2310767)
Diane Schuur And Her Band
The Best Of Diane Schuur | GRP | GRP 98882
Ella Fitzgerald With Marty Paich's Dektette
Ella Swings Lightly | Verve | 517535-2
Ella Fitzgerald With The Marty Paich Dek-tette
Ella Fitzgerald-First Lady Of Song | Verve | 517898-2
Verve Jazz Masters 6:Ella Fitzgerald | Verve | 519822-2
Verve Jazz Masters 46:Ella Fitzgerald-The Jazz Sides | Verve | 527655-2
Ella Fitzgerald With The Marty Paich Orchestra
Get Happy! | Verve | 523321-2
Gerry Mulligan And The Sax Section
The Gerry Mulligan Songbook | Pacific Jazz | 833575-2
June Christy With The Pete Rugolo Orchestra
Something Cool(The Complete Mono & Stereo Versions) | Capitol | 534069-2
Mark Murphy And His Septet
Blue Velvet: Crooners, Swooners And Velvet Vocals | Blue Note | 521153-2
Maynard Ferguson And His Orchestra
Verve Jazz Masters 52:Maynard Ferguson | Verve | 529905-2
Maynard Ferguson Band
Verve Jazz Masters 52:Maynard Ferguson | Verve | 529905-2
NDR Big Band With Guests
50 Years Of NDR Big Band:Bravissimo II | ACT | 9259-2
Peggy Lee With The Bill Holman Orchestra
Pass Me By/Big Spender | Capitol | 535210-2
Sarah Vaughan With Orchestra
Sarah Vaughan Sings The Mancini Songbook | Verve | 558401-2
Shelly Manne And His Men
Vol.1:The West Coast Sound | Original Jazz Classics | OJCCD 152-2
The Jazz Giants Play Harry Warren:Lullaby Of Broadway | Prestige | PCD 24204-2
Stan Kenton And His Orchestra
Stan Kenton Portraits On Standards | Capitol | 531571-2
Terry Gibbs Dream Band
Terry Gibbs Dream Band Vol.2:The Sundown Sessions | Contemporary | CCD 7652-2
Terry Gibbs Dream Band Vol.3:Flying Home | Contemporary | CCD 7654-2
Terry Gibbs Dream Band Vol.6:One More Time | Contemporary | CCD 7658-2
The Jazz Giants Play Jerome Kern:Yesterdays | Prestige | PCD 24202-2
Woody Herman And His Orchestra
Verve Jazz Masters 54:Woody Herman | Verve | 529903-2
Zoot Sims And His Orchestra
The Jazz Giants Play Duke Ellington:Caravan | Prestige | PCD 24227-2

Holmes,Bobby | (cl,as,ssts)
King Oliver And His Orchestra
Jazz:The Essential Collection Vol.1 | IN+OUT Records | 78011-2

Holmes,Charlie | (as,cl,ssts)
Fats Waller And His Buddies
Jazz:The Essential Collection Vol.3 | IN+OUT Records | 78013-2
Henry Allen Jr. And His New York Orchestra
Planet Jazz:Jazz Saxophone | Planet Jazz | 2169653-2
Planet Jazz:Jazz Trumpet | Planet Jazz | 2169654-2
John Kirby Band
The Small Black Groups | Storyville | 4960523
King Oliver And His Orchestra
Planet Jazz:Jazz Trumpet | Planet Jazz | 2169654-2
Louis Armstrong And His Orchestra
Louis Armstrong:Swing That Music | Laserlight | 36056
Jazz:The Essential Collection Vol.2 | IN+OUT Records | 78012-2
Satch Plays Fats(Complete) | CBS | CK 64927
Louis Armstrong-My Greatest Songs | MCA | MCD 18347
Swing Legends:Louis Armstrong | Nimbus Records | NI 2012
Louis Armstrong And His Savoy Ballroom Five
Jazz:The Essential Collection Vol.2 | IN+OUT Records | 78012-2
Louis Armstrong With Sy Oliver And His Orchestra
Satchmo Serenaders | Verve | 543792-2

Holmes,Henry | (asreeds)
Louis Armstrong And His Orchestra
Jazz:The Essential Collection Vol.2 | IN+OUT Records | 78012-2

Holmes,Martin | (sax)
Tito Puente Orchestra
Planet Jazz:Tito Puente | Planet Jazz | 2165369-2

Holmes,Norma | (voc)
Les McCann Group
Another Beginning | Atlantic | 7567-80790-2

Holmes,Richard 'Groove' | (orgsynth)
Eric Kloss Quartet
About Time | Prestige | PRCD 24268-2
Richard 'Groove' Holmes Orchestra
Comin' On Home | Blue Note | 538701-2
Richard 'Groove' Holmes Quintet
Somethin' Special | Pacific Jazz | 855452-2
Richard 'Groove' Holmes Sextet
Blue Break Beats | Blue Note | 799106-2
Somethin' Special | Pacific Jazz | 855452-2
Richard 'Groove' Holmes Trio
Somethin' Special | Pacific Jazz | 855452-2
Soul Message | Original Jazz Classics | OJC20 329-2(P 7435)
On Basie's Bandstand | Prestige | PRCD 11028-2

Holmes,Rodney | (dr)
Philip Catherine Quartet
Guitar Groove | Dreyfus Jazz Line | FDM 36599-2
The Brecker Brothers
Out Of The Loop | GRP | GRP 97842
Urbanator
Urbanator II | Hip Bop | HIBD 8012
Hot Jazz Bisquits | Hip Bop | HIBD 8801

Holmes,Terry | (g)
Duke Robillard-Herb Ellis Quintet
Conversation In Swing Guitar | Stony Plain | SPCD 1260
More Conversations In Swing Guitar | Stony Plain | SPCD 1292

Holmquist,Olle | (tb)
Bengt-Arne Wallin Orchestra
The Birth+Rebirth Of Swedish Folk Jazz | ACT | 9254-2

Holmström,Gilbert | (fl,saxts)
Kjell Jansson Quartet
Back From Where We Came | Touché Music | TMcCD 009
Kjell Jansson Quintet
Back From Where We Came | Touché Music | TMcCD 009

Holst,André | (voc)
André Holst With Chris Dean's European Swing Orchestra
That's Swing | Nagel-Heyer | CD 079

Holstein,Stephan | (as,cl,b-clsax)
Christian Willisohn New Band
Heart Broken Man | Blues Beacon | BLU-1026 2
Full Moon Trio
Live At Birdland Neuburg | double moon | CHRDM 71024
Helmut Nieberle & Cordes Sauvages
Jazz Guitar Highlights 1 | Jardis Records | JRCD 20141
Salut To Django | Jardis Records | JRCD 9926

Holt,Red | (dr)
Ramsey Lewis Trio
Down To Earth | Verve | 538329-2

Holthaus,Uschi | (vocwhistling)
Das Obertontrio Und Toto Blanke
Energy Fields | ALISO Records | AL 1029
Toto Blanke-Rudolf Dasek With The Overtontrio
Meditation | ALISO Records | AL 1026

Holtlien,Gunnvo | (v)
Terje Rypdal Quartet With The Bergen Chamber Ensemble
Lux Aeterna | ECM | 1818(017070-2)

Holton,Judith | (dancervoc)
Sun Ra And His Astro-Infinity Arkestra
Space Is The Place | Impulse(MCA) | 951249-2

Holub,Robert | (cimbal)
Karol Adam Ensemble
Gipsy Fascination | G&J Records | GJ 2001

Holub,Roman | (cl)

Holy,Steve | (b)
Dylan Cramer Quartet
All Night Long | Nagel-Heyer | CD 073

Holzman,Adam | (el-p,synth,keyboards)
Lenny White Group
Present Tense | Hip Bop | HIBD 8004
Michel Petrucciani Group
Michel Petrucciani:The Blue Note Years | Blue Note | 789916-2
Music | Blue Note | 792563-2
Playground | Blue Note | 795480-2
Michel Petrucciani Quintet
Michel Petrucciani Live | Blue Note | 780589-2
Miles Davis Group
Miles Davis Live From His Last Concert In Avignon | Laserlight | 24327
Tutu | Warner | 7599-25490-2

Home,Matt | (dr)
Stacy Kent With The Jim Tomlinson Quintet
The Boy Next Door | Candid | CCD 79797

Homesick James[William Henderson] | (b-g,g,vocharm)
Homesick James Quartet
Blues On The Southside | Original Blues Classics | OBCCD 529-2(P 7388)
Windy City Blues | Stax | SCD 8612-2

Honda,Yuka | (sampler)
Dave Douglas Group
Witness | RCA | 2663763-2

Honetschläger,Manfred | (b-tbtuba)
HR Big Band
The American Songs Of Kurt Weill | hr music.de | hrmj 006-01 CD
Libertango:Homage An Astor Piazolla | hr music.de | hrmj 014-02 CD
HR Big Band With Marjorie Barnes And Frits Landesbergen
Swinging Christmas | hr music.de | hrmj 012-02 CD
HR Big Band With Marjorie Barnes And Frits Landesbergen And Strings
Swinging Christmas | hr music.de | hrmj 012-02 CD
The Three Sopranos With The HR Big Band
The Three Sopranos | hr music.de | hrmj 001-01 CD

Honeywell,Don | (assax)
Benny Goodman And His Orchestra
Verve Jazz Masters 33:Benny Goodman | Verve | 844410-2

Honsinger,Tristan | (cello,voicecello-solo)
Michael Moore Trio
Monitor | Between The Lines | btl 003(Efa 10173-2)

Hood,Bill | (bass-s,b-cl,bs,fl,reeds,sax)
Benny Carter And His Orchestra
Further Definitions/Additions To Further Definotions | Impulse(MCA) | 951229-2
Dizzy Gillespie And His Orchestra
Talking Verve:Dizzy Gillespie | Verve | 533846-2
Johnny Hartman And His Orchestra
Unforgettable | Impulse(MCA) | IMP 11522
Zoot Sims And His Orchestra
The Jazz Giants Play Duke Ellington:Caravan | Prestige | PCD 24227-2

Hood,David | (b)
Albert King Blues Band
Lovejoy | Stax | SCD 8517-2(STS 2040)
Dee Dee Bridgewater With Band
Dee Dee Bridgewater | Atlantic | 7567-80760-2

Hood,Ernie | (gzither)
Flora Purim And Her Sextet
Joe Henderson:The Milestone Years | Milestone | 8MCD 4413-2
Butterfly Dreams | Original Jazz Classics | OJCCD 315-2

Hoogendijk,Jarmo | (tp)
European Jazz Ensemble
European Jazz Ensemble 25th Anniversary | Konnex Records | KCD 5100
European Trumpet Summit
European Trumpet Summit | Konnex Records | KCD 5064

Hoogeven,Ronald | (stings)
The Rosenberg Trio With Orchestra
Noches Calientes | Verve | 557022-2

Hooker,John Lee | (gvoc)
John Lee Hooker
John Lee Hooker Plays And Sings The Blues | Chess | MCD 09199
House Of The Blues | Chess | MCD 09258
That's My Story | Original Blues Classics | OBCCD 538-2(RLP 12-321)
The Country Blues Of John Lee Hooker | Original Blues Classics | OBCCD 542-2
Burning Hell | Original Blues Classics | OBCCD 555-2(RLP 008)
John Lee Hooker Group
Endless Boogie | MCA | MCD 10413
John Lee Hooker Trio
That's My Story | Original Blues Classics | OBCCD 538-2(RLP 12-321)

Hooks,Bob | (tb)
Big Joe Turner With The Count Basie Orchestra
Flip Flop And Fly | Original Jazz Classics | OJCCD 1053-2(2310937)

Hooper,Les | (p,el-p,condarr)
Singers Unlimited
The Singers Unlimited:Magic Voices | MPS | 539130-2
Singers Unlimited With Orchestra
The Singers Unlimited:Magic Voices | MPS | 539130-2

Hooper,Nesbert 'Stix' | (drperc)
Bobby Hutcherson Orchestra
Deep Blue-The United States Of Mind | Blue Note | 521152-2
Jazz Crusaders
Chile Con Soul | Pacific Jazz | 590957-2
The Jazz Crusaders
Kind Of Blue:Blue Note Celebrate The Music Of Miles Davis | Blue Note | 534255-2

Hope,Elmo | (pp-solo)
Elmo Hope Ensemble
Sounds From Rikers Island | Fresh Sound Records | FSR CD 338
Elmo Hope Sextet
John Coltrane-The Prestige Recordings | Prestige | 16 PCD 4405-2
Harold Land Quintet
The Fox | Original Jazz Classics | OJCCD 343-2
Lou Donaldson Quintet
Clifford Brown Memorial Album | Blue Note | 532141-2

Hope,Steven | (p)
Vince Jones Group
Tell Me A Secret | Intuition Records | INT 3072-2

Hopkins,Chris | (p)
Dan Barrett Septet
Dan Barrett's International Swing Party | Nagel-Heyer | CD 067
Engelbert Wrobel-Chris Hopkins-Dan Barrett Sextet
Harlem 2000 | Nagel-Heyer | CD 082
Wrobel-Roberscheuten-Hopkins Jam Session
Jammin' At The IAJRC Convention Hamburg 1999 | Nagel-Heyer | CD 066

Hopkins,Claude | (arr,p,ldp-solo)
Bud Freeman All Stars
The Bud Freeman All-Star Sessions | Prestige | PRCD 24286-2
Cozy Cole's Big Seven
Body And Soul Revisited | GRP | GRP 16272
Jack Teagarden With The Red Allen Band
The Very Best Of Dixieland Jazz | Verve | 535529-2
Juanita Hall With The Claude Hopkins All Stars
Juanita Hall Sings The Blues | Original Jazz Classics | OJCCD 1928-2(CPST 556)

Hopkins,David | (claves,didjeriduhorns)
Marco Cerletti Group
Random And Providence | VeraBra Records | CDVBR 2039-2

Hopkins,Fred | (b,sticks,toy-dr,voiceb-solo)
Frank Ku-Umba Lacy Group
Tonal Weights & Blue Fire | Tutu Records | 888112-2*
Hamiet Bluiett Group
...You Don't Need To Know...If You Have To Ask | Tutu Records | 888128-2*
Ivo Perlman Group
Children Of Ibeji | Enja | ENJ-7005 2

Hopkins,Greg | (tp)
Buddy Rich Big Band
Backwoods Siseman/Pieces Of Dream | Laserlight | 24655

Hopkins,Sam Lightnin' | (g,p,voc,tap-dancing,narration)
Lightnin' Hopkins
The Jazz Life! | Candid | CCD 79019
Going Away | Original Blues Classics | OBCCD 522-2(BV 1073)
Lightnin' Hopkins Trio
The Blues Of Lightnin' Hopkins | Original Blues Classics | OBCCD 532-2(BV 1019)
Lightnin' Hopkins Trio With Sonny Terry
Last Night Blues | Original Blues Classics | OBCCD 548-2(BV 1029)

Hopkins,Tim | (tsrecorder)
Mike Nock Quartet
Dark & Curious | VeraBra Records | CDVBR 2074-2
Vince Jones Group
Here's To The Miracles | Intuition Records | INT 3198-2
Hopper,Hugh | (b-drb-g)
Carla Bley Band
European Tour 1977 | Watt | 8
Höppner,Roland | (dr)
Bigband Der Musikschule Der Stadt Brühl Mit Gastsolisten
Pangäa | Indigo-Records | 1004 CD
Double You
Menschbilder | Jazz Haus Musik | JHM 0062 CD
Matthias Petzold Working Band
Elements | Indigo-Records | 1005 CD
Hopps,Jimmy | (dr)
Rahsaan Roland Kirk Quartet
Rhino Presents The Atlantic Jazz Gallery | Atlantic | 8122-71257-2
Rahsaan Roland Kirk Sextet
Volunteered Slavery | Rhino | 8122-71407-2
Roland Kirk Quartet
The Inflated Tear | Atlantic | 7567-90045-2
The Inflated Tear | Atlantic | 8122-75207-2
Roland Kirk Quintet
The Inflated Tear | Atlantic | 7567-90045-2
The Inflated Tear | Atlantic | 8122-75207-2
Horak,Bronislav | (sax)
Hans Koller Big Band
New York City | MPS | 9813437
Horan,Bill | (mellophone)
Stan Kenton And His Orchestra
Adventures In Blues | Capitol | 520089-2
Horbar,Max | (as)
Cornelius Claudio Kreusch Group
Scoop | ACT | 9255-2
Horellou,Gäel | (as)
Gäel Horellou-David Sauzay Quintet
Gäel Horellou Versus David Sauzay | Fresh Sound Records | FSNT 068 CD
Laurent De Wilde Sextet
Time Change | Warner | 8573-84315-2
Horenstein,Stephen | (alto-fl,ts,bs,p,bells,cymbals)
Franz Koglmann Quintet
Opium | Between The Lines | btl 011(Efa 10181-2)
Hörlen,Johan | (b-clas)
Tim Hagans With Norrbotten Big Band
Future Miles | ACT | 9235-2
Horler,David | (tb)
Bob Brookmeyer Group With The WDR Big Band
Electricity | ACT | 9219-2
Eddie Harris Group With The WDR Big Band
Eddie Harris-The Last Concert | ACT | 9249-2
Gianlugi Trovesi Quartet With The WDR Big Band
Dedalo | Enja | ENJ-9419 2
Jens Winther And The WDR Big Band
The Escape | dacapo | DCCD 9437
Kenny Wheeler Ensemble
Muisc For Large & Small Ensembles | ECM | 1415/16
Kevin Mahogany With The WDR Big Band And Guests
Pussy Cat Dues:The Music Of Charles Mingus | Enja | ENJ-9316 2
Los Jovenes Flamencos With The WDR Big Band And Guests
Jazzpana | ACT | 9212-2
Vince Mendoza With The WDR Big Band And Guests
Sketches | ACT | 9215-2
Hörmann,Christine | (bs,fl,reedssax)
Marcus Sukiennik Big Band
A Night In Tunisia Suite(7 Variationen über Dizzy Gillespie's 'A Night In Tunisia') | Jazz Haus Musik | ohne Nummer
The United Women's Orchestra
The Blue One | Jazz Haus Musik | JHM 0099 CD
United Women's Orchestra
Virgo Supercluster | Jazz Haus Musik | JHM 0123 CD
Horn Knox |
Horn Knox
The Song Is You | JHM Records | JHM 3625
Horn Section: |
Fleurine With Band And Horn Section
Meant To Be! | EmArCy | 159085-2
Horn,Jim | (fl,bs,reedssax)
Dizzy Gillespie With The Lalo Schifrin Orchestra
Free Ride | Original Jazz Classics | OJCCD 784-2(2310794)
Gene Harris And The Three Sounds
Deep Blue-The United States Of Mind | Blue Note | 521152-2
Herbie Hancock Group
Man-Child | CBS | 471235-2
Horn,Paul | (as,fl,alto-fl,bamboo-fl,bass-fl)
Billy May And His Orchestra
Billy May's Big Fat Brass/Bill's Bag | Capitol | 535206-2
Cal Tjader Group
Verve Jazz Masters 39:Cal Tjader | Verve | 521858-2
Cal Tjader Sextet
Talkin Verve/Roots Of Acid Jazz:Cal Tjader | Verve | 531562-2
Cal Tjader With The Clare Fischer Orchestra
Cal Tjader Plays Harold Arlen & West Side Story | Fantasy | FCD 24775-2
Chico Hamilton Orchestra
With Strings Attached/The Three Faces Of Chico | Warner | 9362-47874-2
June Christy With The Pete Rugolo Orchestra
Something Cool(The Complete Mono & Stereo Versions) | Capitol | 534069-2
Miles Davis With Gil Evans & His Orchestra
Quiet Nights | CBS | CK 65293
Pete Rugolo And His Orchestra
Thriller/Richard Diamon(Original Jazz Scores From 2 Classics TV Series) | Fresh Sound Records | FSCD 2015
Van Alexander Orchestra
Home Of Happy Feet/Swing! Staged For Sound! | Capitol | 535211-2
Horn,Sandra | (tp)
The United Women's Orchestra
The Blue One | Jazz Haus Musik | JHM 0099 CD
United Women's Orchestra
Virgo Supercluster | Jazz Haus Musik | JHM 0123 CD
Horn,Sheila | (voc)
Charlie Haden Quartet West With Strings
The Art Of The Song | Verve | 547403-2
Horn,Shirley | (p,org,vocroland-p)
Carmen McRae With The Shirley Horn Trio
Planet Jazz:Female Jazz Vocalists | Planet Jazz | 2169656-2
The Collected Carmen McRae | RCA | 2668713-2
Shirley Horn
Light Out Of Darkness(A Tribute To Ray Charles) | Verve | 519703-2
Loving You | Verve | 537022-2
Shirley Horn And Her Quartet
May The Music Never End | Verve | 076028-2
Shirley Horn And Her Trio
May The Music Never End | Verve | 076028-2
Shirley Horn Quartet
Light Out Of Darkness(A Tribute To Ray Charles) | Verve | 519703-2
The Main Ingredient | Verve | 529555-2
Loving You | Verve | 537022-2
You Won't Forget Me | Verve | 847482-2
Shirley Horn Quintet
Light Out Of Darkness(A Tribute To Ray Charles) | Verve | 519703-2
The Main Ingredient | Verve | 529555-2
Antonio Carlos Jobim And Friends | Verve | 531556-2
Loving You | Verve | 537022-2
Shirley Horn Sextet
Antonio Carlos Jobim And Friends | Verve | 531556-2
Shirley Horn Trio
Light Out Of Darkness(A Tribute To Ray Charles) | Verve | 519703-2
The Antonio Carlos Jobim Songbook | Verve | 525472-2
The Main Ingredient | Verve | 529555-2
Loving You | Verve | 537022-2
You Won't Forget Me | Verve | 847482-2
A Lazy Afternoon | Steeplechase | SCCD 31111
Violets For Your Furs | Steeplechase | SCCD 31164
Shirley Horn Trio with Branford Marsalis
You Won't Forget Me | Verve | 847482-2
Shirley Horn Trio with Buck Hill
You Won't Forget Me | Verve | 847482-2
Shirley Horn Trio with Miles Davis
You Won't Forget Me | Verve | 847482-2
Shirley Horn Trio with Toots Thielemans
You Won't Forget Me | Verve | 847482-2
Shirley Horn Trio with Wynton Marsalis
You Won't Forget Me | Verve | 847482-2
Shirley Horn With Band
The Roots Of Acid Jazz | Impulse(MCA) | IMP 12042
Shirley Horn With Orchestra
Loads Of Love + Shirley Horn With Horns | Mercury | 843454-2
Shirley Horn With Strings
Here's To Life | Verve | 511879-2
Shirley Horn With The Bill Charlap Trio
Stardust | Blue Note | 535985-2
Shirley Horn With The Quincy Jones Orchestra
Loads Of Love + Shirley Horn With Horns | Mercury | 843454-2
Shirley Horn with Toots Thielemans
You Won't Forget Me | Verve | 847482-2
Stuff Smith Quartet
Cat On A Hot Fiddle | Verve | 9861487
Toots Thielemans With The Shirley Horn Trio
Verve Jazz Masters Vol.59:Toots Thielemans | Verve | 535271-2
Horne,Ellis | (cl)
Bunk Johnson With The Yerba Buena Jazz Band
Bunk & Lu | Good Time Jazz | GTCD 12024-2
Yerba Buena Jazz Band
Bunk & Lu | Good Time Jazz | GTCD 12024-2
Horne,Lena | (voc)
Lena Horne With The George Benson Quintet
Misty Blue:Sweet Sisters Swing Songs Of Sorrow And Sadness | Blue Note | 521151-2
Lena Horne With The Horace Henderson Orchestra
Planet Jazz:Lena Horne | Planet Jazz | 2165373-2
Lena Horne With The Lennie Hayton Orchestra
Planet Jazz:Lena Horne | Planet Jazz | 2165373-2
Lena Horne With The Lou Bring Orchestra
Planet Jazz:Lena Horne | Planet Jazz | 2165373-2
Planet Jazz:Female Jazz Vocalists | Planet Jazz | 2169656-2
Lena Horne With The Phil Moore Four
Planet Jazz:Lena Horne | Planet Jazz | 2165373-2
Horne,Marvin | (g)
Pucho & His Latin Soul Brothers
Jazzin' With The Soul Brothers | Fantasy | FANCD 6086-2
Rip A Dip | Milestone | MCD 9247-2
Horner,Lindsey | (b,perc,voice,el-btin-whistle)
Herb Robertson Quintet
'X'-cerpts:Live At Willisau | JMT Edition | 919013-2
Neal Kirkwood Octet
Neal Kirkwood Octet | Timescrapper | TSCR 9612
The Chromatic Persuaders
The Chromatic Persuaders | Timescrapper | TSCR 9617
Horner,Tim | (dr)
Dave Stryker Octet
Blue To The Bone III | Steeplechase | SCCD 31524
Vic Juris Trio
While My Guitar Gently Weeps | Steeplechase | SCCD 31553
Horner,William | (saxts)
Jimmy Lunceford And His Orchestra
The Legends Of Swing | Laserlight | 24659
Hornettes,The | (background-voc)
Shirley Horn Quartet
Light Out Of Darkness(A Tribute To Ray Charles) | Verve | 519703-2
Hornung,Ludwig | (v)
Stefanie Schlesiger And Her Group plus String Quartet
What Love Is | Enja | ENJ-9434 2
Horovitz,Lila | (b)
Tangata Rea
Tango Alla Baila | Winter&Winter | 910025-2
Horowitz,David | (el-p,synth,orgp)
Gil Evans Orchestra
There Comes A Time | RCA | 2131392-2
PLay The Music Of Jimi Hendrix | RCA | 2663872-2
Svengali | Rhino | 8122-73720-2
Joe Henderson And His Orchestra
Joe Henderson:The Milestone Years | Milestone | 8MCD 4413-2
Horowitz,Irving | (oboe)
Cal Tjader With The Lalo Schifrin Orchestra
Talkin Verve/Roots Of Acid Jazz:Cal Tjader | Verve | 531562-2
Lalo Schifrin And His Orchestra
Verve Jazz Masters 39:Cal Tjader | Verve | 521858-2
Horowitz,Richard | (electronic-keyboardsnay)
Jon Hassell Group
Power Spot | ECM | 1327
Horsthuis,Maurice | (viola)
Amsterdam String Trio
Winter Theme | Winter&Winter | 910060-2
Horstmann,Thomas | (g,el-g,fretless-gsynth)
Horstmann-Wiedmann-Danek
Billy The Kid | Factory Outlet Records | FOR 2001-3 CD
The Atlantic Jazz Trio
Some Other Time | Factory Outlet Records | FOR 2002-1 CD
The Atlantic String Trio
First Meeting | Factory Outlet Records | FOR 2501-1 CD
Thomas Horstmann-Markus Zaja
Somewhere | Factory Outlet Records | 400004-2
Thomas Horstmann-Martin Wiedmann Group
Decade | Factory Outlet Records | WO 95001
Horton,Big Walter 'Shakey' | (harmvoc)
Joe Hill Louis
Joe Hill Louis: The Be-Bop Boy | Bear Family Records | BCD 15524 AH
Joe Hill Louis Band
Joe Hill Louis: The Be-Bop Boy | Bear Family Records | BCD 15524 AH
Mose Vinson Band
Joe Hill Louis: The Be-Bop Boy | Bear Family Records | BCD 15524 AH
Muddy Waters Blues Band
Muddy Waters-The Collection | MCA | MCD 18961
Walter Horton Band
Joe Hill Louis: The Be-Bop Boy | Bear Family Records | BCD 15524 AH
Horton,Pug | (voc)
Bob Wilber And Friends
What Swing Is All About | Nagel-Heyer | CD 035
Blues Of Summer | Nagel-Heyer | NH 1011
Bob Wilber's Bechet Legacy
The Hamburg Concert-Tribute To A Legend | Nagel-Heyer | CD 028
Horton,Ron | (tpfl-h)
Michael Blake Group
Drift | Intuition Records | INT 3212-2
Rez Abbasi Group
Out Of Body | String Jazz | SJRCD 1021
Horvath,Csaba | (v)
Bernd Konrad Jazz Group With Symphonie Orchestra
Wen Die Götter Lieben | Creative Works Records | CW CD 1010-1
Horvath,Kornel | (perc)
Things
Mother Nature | Jazzpoint | JP 1028 CD
Horvitz,Wayne | (7,sampler,yamaha DX,celeste)
Batman
Naked City | Nonesuch | 7559-79238-2
Bill Frisell Band
Is That You? | Nonesuch | 7559-60956-2
John Zorn Group
Spillane | Nonesuch | 7559-79172-2
Marty Ehrlich Group
The Long View | Enja | ENJ-9452 2
Wayne Horvitz Group
4+1 Ensemble | Intuition Records | INT 3224-2
Horwath,Bill | (cymbalonperc)
Stan Getz With Orchestra And Voices
Stan Getz Highlights | Verve | 847430-2
Stan Getz With The Claus Ogerman Orchestra
What The World Needs Now-Stan Getz Plays Bacharach And David | Verve | 557450-2
Hosni,Lassad | (bendir,darboukaperc)
Anouar Brahem Quartet
Conte De L'Incroyable Amour | ECM | 1457(511959-2)
Anouar Brahem Trio
Barzakh | ECM | 1432(847540-2)
Astrakan Café | ECM | 1718(159494-2)
Hot Mallets |
Hot Mallets
Hot Mallets...Live! | JHM Records | JHM 3610
Höttger,Heinz | (p)
Harald Banter Ensemble
Deutsches Jazz Fesival 1954/1955 | Bear Family Records | BCD 15430
Houariyat,B'net | (percvoc)
Nguyen Le Group
Maghreb And Friends | ACT | 9261-2
Hougaard,Erling | (dr)
Papa Benny's Jazzband
The Golden Years Of Revival Jazz,Vol.2 | Storyville | STCD 5507
Houghton,John | (tb)
Willie Bryant And His Orchestra
Planet Jazz:Ben Webster | RCA | 2165368-2
Houghton,Steve | (dr)
Freddie Hubbard And His Orchestra
Born To Be Blue | Original Jazz Classics | OJCCD 734-2(2312134)
Freddie Hubbard Sextet
Keystone Bop Vol.2:Friday/Saturday | Prestige | PCD 24163-2
Joe Henderson Quartet
Keystone Bop Vol.2:Friday/Saturday | Prestige | PCD 24163-2
Houle,Francois | (cl,b-clcomp)
Francois Houle 5
Cryptology | Between The Lines | btl 012(Efa 10182-2)
House Band |
Charlie Christian All Stars
Charlie Christian-Jazz Immortal/Dizzy Gillespie 1944 | Original Jazz Classics | OJCCD 1932-2(ES 548)
House Five |
House Five
Frank Talk | Nabel Records:Jazz Network | CD 4674
House,Danny | (asreeds)
Diane Schuur With The Count Basie Orchestra
The Best Of Diane Schuur | GRP | GRP 98882
House,Ju Ju Julius | (drtrap-dr)
Chuck Brown And The Second Chapter Band
Timeless | Minor Music | 801068
House,Son | (g,vocspeech)
Son House
Classic Blues | Zounds | CD 2700048
Houston,Cissy | (voc)
Les McCann Group
Another Beginning | Atlantic | 7567-80790-2
Oscar Brown Jr. And His Group
Movin' On | Rhino | 8122-73678-2
Rahsaan Roland Kirk Sextet
Blacknuss | Rhino | 8122-71408-2
Houston,Clint | (b,el-bg)
John Stubblefield Quartet
Morning Song | Enja | ENJ-8036 2
Louis Hayes Sextet
The Crawl | Candid | CCD 79045
Stan Getz-Joao Gilberto Orchestra
Sony Jazz Collection:Stan Getz | CBS | 488623-2
Houston,John | (p)
Gene Ammons Septet
A Stranger In Town | Prestige | PRCD 24266-2
Gene Ammons-Sonny Stitt Quintet
Gentle Jug Vol.3 | Prestige | PCD 24249-2
Sonny Stitt And His Band
Kaleidoscope | Original Jazz Classics | OJCCD 060-2(P 7077)
Sonny Stitt Quintet
Kaleidoscope | Original Jazz Classics | OJCCD 060-2(P 7077)
Houston,Tate | (bs)
Ernestine Anderson With Orchestra
My Kinda Swing | Mercury | 842409-2
King Curtis Band
King Curtis-Blow Man Blow | Bear Family Records | BCD 15670 CI
Maynard Ferguson And His Orchestra
Verve Jazz Masters 52:Maynard Ferguson | Verve | 529905-2
Milt Jackson Orchestra
To Bags...With Love:Memorial Album | Pablo | 2310967-2
Milt Jackson Birthday Celebration | Fantasy | FANCD 6079-2
Big Bags | Original Jazz Classics | OJCCD 366-2(RLP 9429)
Nat Adderley And The Big Sax Section
Cannonball Adderley Birthday Celebration | Fantasy | FANCD 6087-2
That's Right | Original Jazz Classics | OJCCD 791-2(RLP 9330)
Sam Jones Plus 10
Cannonball Adderley Birthday Celebration | Fantasy | FANCD 6087-2
Yusef Lateef Orchestra
The Centaur And The Phoenix | Original Jazz Classics | OJCCD 721-2(RLP 9337)
Hovdsveen Hagen,Eli Kristin | (voice)
Moscow Art Trio
Once Upon A Time | JA & RO | JARO 4238-2
Hove,Michael | (fl,cl,ss,reedssax)
Geri Allen And The Jazzpar 1996 Nonet
Some Aspects Of Water | Storyville | STCD 4212
Jens Winther And The Danish Radio Jazz Orchestra
Angels | dacapo | DCCD 9442
Mona Larsen And The Danish Radio Big Band Plus Soloists
Michael Mantler:Cerco Un Paese Innocente | ECM | 1556
The Danish Radio Jazz Orchestra
This Train:The Danish Radio Jazz Orchestra Plays The Music Of Ray Pitts | dacapo | DCCD 9428
Nice Work | dacapo | DCCD 9446
Hovensjo,Sveinung | (bel-b)
Terje Rypdal Quartet
Waves | ECM | 1110(827419-2)
Terje Rypdal Quintet
What Comes After | ECM | 1031
When Ever I Seem To Be Far Away | ECM | 1045
Hovland,Ketil | (b-tb)
Geir Lysne Listening Ensemble
Korall | ACT | 9236-2
Aurora Borealis-Nordic Lights | ACT | 9406-2
Hovman,Klavs | (bel-b)
Marilyn Mazur's Future Song
Small Labyrinths | ECM | 1559(533679-2)
Marilyn Mazure's Future Song | VeraBra Records | CDVBR 2105-2
Howard,Avery 'Kid' | (tpvoc)
George Lewis And His Band
Atlantic Jazz: New Orleans | Atlantic | 7567-81700-2
George Lewis And His New Orleans Ragtime Band
The Beverly Caverns Session | Good Time Jazz | GTCD 12058-2

George Lewis And His New Orleans Stompers
George Lewis And His New Orleans Stompers | Blue Note | 821261-2
George Lewis And His Original New Orleans Jazzmen
George Lewis In Stockholm,1959 | Dragon | DRCD 221

Howard,Bert | (b)
Vic Lewis Jam Session
Vic Lewis:The Golden Years | Candid | CCD 79754

Howard,Charlie | (el-gg)
Sidney Bechet And His New Orleans Feetwarmers
Planet Jazz | Planet Jazz | 2169652-2
Sidney Bechet:Summertime | Dreyfus Jazz Line | FDM 36712-2

Howard,Darnell | (cl,as,vss)
Don Ewell Quartet
Free 'N' Easy | Good Time Jazz | GTCD 10046-2
Earl Hines And His Orchestra
Jazz:The Essential Collection Vol.2 | IN+OUT Records | 78012-2
Earl Hines-Muggsy Spanier All Stars
Earl Hines/Muggsy Spanier All Stars:The Chicago Dates | Storyville | STCD 6037
Jelly Roll Morton's Red Hot Peppers
Planet Jazz:Jelly Roll Morton | Planet Jazz | 2152060-2
Jazz:The Essential Collection Vol.1 | IN+OUT Records | 78011-2
King Oliver And His Dixie Syncopators
Jazz:The Essential Collection Vol.1 | IN+OUT Records | 78011-2
Muggsy Spanier And His Dixieland All Stars
Muggsy Spanier At Club Hangover 1953/54 | Storyville | STCD 6033

Howard,Ed | (b)
Antonio Farao Quartet
Next Stories | Enja | ENJ-9430 2
Antonio Farao Trio
Next Stories | Enja | ENJ-9430 2
Ingrid Jensen Quintet
Higher Grounds | Enja | ENJ-9353 2
Johannes Enders Quartet
Sandsee | Organic Music | ORGM 9720
Shirley Horn And Her Quartet
May The Music Never End | Verve | 076028-2
Shirley Horn And Her Trio
May The Music Never End | Verve | 076028-2
Victor Lewis Sextet
Eeeyyess! | Enja | ENJ-9311 2

Howard,Erica | (b)
Benny Waters Quartet
Hurry On Down | Storyville | STCD 8264

Howard,Frank | (tb)
Ella Fitzgerald And Louis Armstrong With Dave Barbour And His Orchestra
Ella Fitzgerald:Mr.Paganini | Dreyfus Jazz Line | FDM 36741-2

Howard,George | (ewi-fl,ss,bass-synth,clavinet,bells)
Stanley Clarke Group
If This Bass Could Only Talk | CBS | 460883-2

Howard,Joe | (tb,tstuba)
Ella Fitzgerald With The Buddy Bregman Orchestra
Ella Fitzgerald-First Lady Of Song | Verve | 517898-2
Love Songs:The Best Of The Song Books | Verve | 531762-2
Ella Fitzgerald Sings The Cole Porter Songbook | Verve | 537257-2
Ella Fitzgerald Sings The Rodgers And Hart Song Book | Verve | 537258-2
Pete Rugolo And His Orchestra
Thriller/Richard Diamon(Original Jazz Scores From 2 Classics TV Series) | Fresh Sound Records | FSCD 2015
Stan Kenton And His Orchestra
Stan Kenton Portraits On Standards | Capitol | 531571-2
Van Alexander Orchestra
Home Of Happy Feet/Swing! Staged For Sound! | Capitol | 535211-2

Howard,Thomas | (b)
Duke Pearson Sextet
Dedication! | Original Jazz Classics | OJCCD 1939-2(P 7729)

Howard,Tom | (tp)
Dusko Goykovich Big Band
Balkan Connection | Enja | ENJ-9047 2

Howe,Phil | (cl)
Turk Murphy And His Jazz Band
Atlantic Jazz: New Orleans | Atlantic | 7567-81700-2

Howell,John | (tp)
Cal Tjader's Orchestra
Tjader Plays Mambo | Original Jazz Classics | OJCCD 274-2(F 3221)
Nat Pierce/Dick Collins Nonet
Nat Pierce-Dick Collins-Ralph Burns & The Herdsmen Play Paris | Fantasy | FCD 24759-2
Shorty Rogers And His Orchestra Feat. The Giants
PLanet Jazz:Shorty Rogers | Planet Jazz | 2159976-2
Stan Kenton And His Orchestra
Stan Kenton Portraits On Standards | Capitol | 531571-2
One Night Stand | Choice | CHCD 71051

Howes,Christian 'Chris' | (g,vel-v)
Greg Osby Quartet With String Quartet
Symbols Of Light(A Solution) | Blue Note | 531395-2
Lenny White Group
Renderers Of Spirit | Hip Bop | HIBD 8014

Howlin' Wolf[Chester Burnett] | (g,harmvoc)
Howlin' Wolf London Session
Howlin' Wolf:The London Sessions | Chess | MCD 09297

Hoxha,Blerim | (v)
Marcio Tubino Group
Festa Do Olho | Organic Music | ORGM 9723

Hoyer,Peter | (bj)
Papa Benny's Jazzband
The Golden Years Of Revival Jazz,Vol.2 | Storyville | STCD 5507

HR Big Band |
HR Big Band
The American Songs Of Kurt Weill | hr music.de | hrmj 006-01 CD
Libertango:Homage An Astor Piazzolla | hr music.de | hrmj 014-02 CD
HR Big Band With Marjorie Barnes And Frits Landesbergen
Swinging Christmas | hr music.de | hrmj 012-02 CD
HR Big Band With Marjorie Barnes And Frits Landesbergen And Strings
Swinging Christmas | hr music.de | hrmj 012-02 CD
The Three Sopranos With The HR Big Band
The Three Sopranos | hr music.de | hrmj 001-01 CD

Hrasko,Joe | (as,bs,clsax)
Sarah Vaughan With The Quincy Jones Orchestra
Jazz In Paris:Sarah Vaughan-Vaughan And Violins | EmArCy | 065004-2
4 By 4:Ella Fitzgerald/Sarah Vaughan/Billie Holiday/Dinah Washington | Verve | 559693-2

Hrasko,Marcel | (as,bs,saxts)
Jazz In Paris:Sarah Vaughan-Vaughan And Violins | EmArCy | 065004-2
4 By 4:Ella Fitzgerald/Sarah Vaughan/Billie Holiday/Dinah Washington | Verve | 559693-2

Hrdlicka,Litschie | (b)
Litschie Hrdlicka Group
Falling Lovers | EGO | 93020
Jazz Portraits | EGO | 95080

Hubbard,Dave | (fl,ssts)
Charles Earland Septet
Charles Earland In Concert | Prestige | PRCD 24267-2
Charles Earland Sextet
Charles Earland In Concert | Prestige | PRCD 24267-2

Hubbard,David | (ssts)
Lonnie Smith Quintet
Deep Blue-The United States Of Mind | Blue Note | 521152-2

Hubbard,Eric | (flas)
Oliver Nelson And His Orchestra
Blues And The Abstract Truth | Impulse(MCA) | 951154-2

Hubbard,Freddie | (co,fl-h,tp,recitationvoc)
Al Jarreau With Band
All Fly Home | Warner | 7599-27362-2
All Stars
Alternate Blues | Original Jazz Classics | OJCCD 744-2
Art Blakey And The Jazz Messengers
True Blue | Blue Note | 534032-2
Wayne Shorter:The Classic Blue Note Recordings | Blue Note | 540856-2
The Art Of Jazz | IN+OUT Records | 77028-2
Caravan | Original Jazz Classics | OJC20 038-2
Ugetsu | Original Jazz Classics | OJC20 090-2(RLP 9464)
Bill Evans Quintet
Interplay | Original Jazz Classics | OJCCD 308-2
Blue Note All Stars
Town Hall Concert | Blue Note | 497811-2
Bobby Hutcherson Sextet
A Blue Conception | Blue Note | 534254-2
Dialogue | Blue Note | 535586-2
Count Basie Kansas City 7
Count Basie Kansas City 7 | Original Jazz Classics | OJCCD 690-2(2310908)
Dexter Gordon Quintet
Doin' Allright | Blue Note | 784077-2
Dexter Gordon:Ballads | Blue Note | 796579-2
Jazz Profile:Dexter Gordon | Blue Note | 823514-2
Dexter Gordon Birthday Celebration | Fantasy | FANCD 6082-2
Tangerine | Original Jazz Classics | OJCCD 1041-2(P 10091)
Generation | Original Jazz Classics | OJCCD 836-2(P 10069)
The Jazz Giants Play Miles Davis:Milestones | Prestige | PCD 24225-2
Duke Pearson Orchestra
Blue N' Groovy | Blue Note | 780679-2
Duke Pearson Quintet
Sweet Honey Bee | Blue Note | 595974-2
Duke Pearson Sextet
Sweet Honey Bee | Blue Note | 595974-2
Midnight Blue(The [Be]witching Hour) | Blue Note | 854365-2
Dedication! | Original Jazz Classics | OJCCD 1939-2(P 7729)
Eric Dolphy Quintet
Out To Lunch | Blue Note | 498793-2
A Blue Conception | Blue Note | 534254-2
Eric Dolphy:The Complete Prestige Recordings | Prestige | 9 PRCD-4418-2
Eric Dolphy Birthday Celebration | Fantasy | FANCD 6085-2
Freddie Hubbard And His Orchestra
Born To Be Blue | Original Jazz Classics | OJCCD 734-2(2312134)
Freddie Hubbard Orchestra
The Body And The Soul | Impulse(MCA) | 951183-2
Freddie Hubbard Quartet
Topsy | Enja | ENJ-7025 2
Freddie Hubbard Quintet
Live At The Northsea Jazz Festival | Pablo | 2620113-2
Open Sesame | Blue Note | 495341-2
Hub-Tones | Blue Note | 499008-2
Bossa Nova Bacchanal | Blue Note | 593875-2
This Is Jazz:Freddie Hubbard | CBS | CK 65041
Topsy | Enja | ENJ-7025 2
Freddie Hubbard Septet
The Body And The Soul | Impulse(MCA) | 951183-2
This Is Jazz:Freddie Hubbard | CBS | CK 65041
Freddie Hubbard Sextet
Wayne Shorter:The Classic Blue Note Recordings | Blue Note | 540856-2
Hub Cap | Blue Note | 542302-2
Keystone Bop Vol.2:Friday/Saturday | Prestige | PCD 24163-2
Freddie Hubbard Trio
This Is Jazz:Freddie Hubbard | CBS | CK 65041
Freddie Hubbard With Orchestra
This Is Jazz:Freddie Hubbard | CBS | CK 65041
Freddie Hubbard-Oscar Peterson Quintet
Face To Face | Original Jazz Classics | OJCCD 937-2(2310876)
George Benson With The Don Sebesky Orchestra
Verve Jazz Masters 21:George Benson | Verve | 521861-2
Hank Mobley Quintet
The Turnaround | Blue Note | 524540-2
Roll Call | Blue Note | 540030-2)
Herbie Hancock Quartet
Herbie Hancock:The Complete Blue Note Sixties Sessions | Blue Note | 495569-2
Empyrean Isles | Blue Note | 498796-2
Blue N' Groovy | Blue Note | 780679-2
Blue Break Beats | Blue Note | 799106-2
Cantaloupe Island | Blue Note | 829331-2
Herbie Hancock Quintet
V.S.O.P. Herbie Hancock-Live At The City Center N.Y. | CBS | 486569-2
Maiden Voyage | Blue Note | 495331-2
Herbie Hancock:The Complete Blue Note Sixties Sessions | Blue Note | 495569-2
The Best Of Blue Note | Blue Note | 796110-2
The Best Of Blue Note Vol.2 | Blue Note | 797960-2
Cantaloupe Island | Blue Note | 829331-2
Takin' Off | Blue Note | 837643-2
John Coltrane All Stars
The Believer | Original Jazz Classics | OJCCD 876-2(P 7292)
Stardust | Original Jazz Classics | OJCCD 920-2(P 7268)
John Coltrane And His Orchestra
Ascension | Impulse(MCA) | 543413-2
John Coltrane:Standards | Impulse(MCA) | 549914-2
John Coltrane Group
Olé Coltrane | Atlantic | 7567-81349-2
Olé Coltrane | Rhino | 8122-73699-2
John Coltrane Quartet With Brass
The Complete Africa/Brass Sessions | Impulse(MCA) | 952168-2
John Coltrane Quintet
John Coltrane-The Prestige Recordings | Prestige | 16 PCD 4405-2
John Coltrane Quintet With Eric Dolphy
John Coltrane-The Heavyweight Champion:The Complete Atlantic Recordings | Atlantic | 8122-71984-2
John Coltrane Sextet With Eric Dolphy
John Coltrane-The Heavyweight Champion:The Complete Atlantic Recordings | Atlantic | 8122-71984-2
Milt Jackson And His Orchestra
Sunflower | CTI | ZK 65131
Oliver Nelson And His Orchestra
Blues And The Abstract Truth | Impulse(MCA) | 951154-2
The Roots Of Acid Jazz | Impulse(MCA) | IMP 12042
Ornette Coleman Double Quartet
Beauty Is A Rare Thing:Ornette Coleman-The Complete Atlantic Recordings | Atlantic | 8122-71410-2
Free Jazz | Atlantic | 8122-75208-2
Quincy Jones And His Orchestra
Verve Jazz Masters Vol.59:Toots Thielemans | Verve | 535271-2
The Quintessence | Impulse(MCA) | 951222-2
The Roots Of Acid Jazz | Impulse(MCA) | IMP 12042
Quincy Jones Big Band
Rahsaan/The Complete Mercury Recordings Of Roland Kirk | Mercury | 846630-2
Ronnie Mathews Quintet
Ronnie Mathews-Roland Alexander-Freddie Hubbard | Prestige | PRCD 24271-2
Sarah Vaughan And The Thad Jones Orchestra
Verve Jazz Masters 42:Sarah Vaughan-The Jazz Sides | Verve | 526817-2
Sarah Vaughan With The Hal Mooney Orchestra
It's A Man's World | Mercury | 589487-2
Sonny Rollins Quartet
East Broadway Run Down | Impulse(MCA) | 951161-2
Stanley Clarke Group
If This Bass Could Only Talk | CBS | 460883-2
The Trumpet Summit With The Oscar Peterson Big 4
The Trumpet Summit Meets The Oscar Peterson Big 4 | Original Jazz Classics | OJCCD 603-2
Tina Brooks Quintet
Blue N' Groovy | Blue Note | 780679-2
Walter Benton Quintet
Out Of This World | Milestone | MCD 47087-2
Wayne Shorter Quintet
Speak No Evil | Blue Note | 499001-2
Wayne Shorter:The Classic Blue Note Recordings | Blue Note | 540856-2
Wayne Shorter Sextet
Wayne Shorter:The Classic Blue Note Recordings | Blue Note | 540856-2

Hubbard,Gerald | (g)
Richard 'Groove' Holmes Orchestra
Comin' On Home | Blue Note | 538701-2
Richard 'Groove' Holmes Sextet
Blue Break Beats | Blue Note | 799106-2

Hubbard,Neil | (g)
Jimmy Smith All Stars
Jimmy Smith:Dot Com Blues | Blue Thumb | 543978-2

Hubbard,Tom | (b)
Freddie Cole
Jazzin' Vol.2: The Music Of Stevie Wonder | Fantasy | FANCD 6088-2
Freddy Cole With Band
A Circle Of Love | Fantasy | FCD 9674-2
To The End Of The Earth | Fantasy | FCD 9675-2

Hube,Mareike | (tb)
Swim Two Birds
No Regrets | Laika Records | 35101342

Huber,Arne | (b)
Schlosser/Weber/Böhm/Huber/Binder
L 14,16 | Jazz 4 Ever Records:Jazz Network | J4E 4760
Trio Larose
Debut | Jazz 'n' Arts Records | JNA 0802
Trio Larose With Toni Lakatos
Debut | Jazz 'n' Arts Records | JNA 0802

Huber,Evelyn | (harp)
Evelyn Huber-Mulo Franzl
Rendezvous | Edition Collage | EC 512-2

Huber,Josef | (bandoneon)
Flor De Tango
Armenonville | Minor Music | 801097

Hubion,Paul | (tp)
Bobby Bryant Orchestra
Deep Blue-The United States Of Mind | Blue Note | 521152-2
Ella Fitzgerald With Orchestra
Ella/Things Ain't What They Used To Be | Warner | 9362-47875-2

Hübner,Gregor | (pv)
Beirach-Hübner-Mraz
Round About Bartok | ACT | 9276-2
Gregor Hübner Quartet
Panonien | Satin Doll Productions | SDP 1015-1 CD
Gregor Hübner Quintet
Panonien | Satin Doll Productions | SDP 1015-1 CD
Januschke's Time | Satin Doll Productions | SDP 1034-1 CD
Joel Frahm Quintet
The Rains From A Cloud Do Not Wet The Sky | Nabel Records:Jazz Network | CD 4686
Marco Piludu International Quartet
New York Travels | Jazz 4 Ever Records:Jazz Network | J4E 4733
Richard Beirach Trio
Round About Federico Mompou | ACT | 9296-2
Schwarz-Hübner Duo
Elegie | dml-records | CD 012
Tango Five feat. Raul Jaurena
Obsecion | Satin Doll Productions | SDP 1027-1 CD
The Huebner Brothers
Memories | Satin Doll Productions | SDP 1025-1 CD
Tim Sund Quintet
In The Midst Of Change | Nabel Records:Jazz Network | CD 4679

Hübner,Hans | (clas)
Fred Bunge Star Band
Deutsches Jazz Fesival 1954/1955 | Bear Family Records | BCD 15430

Hübner,Ralf-R. | (arr,dr,p,synthcomputer-programming)
Eberhard Weber Group
The Colours Of Chloe | ECM | 1042
Chorus | ECM | 1288(823844-2)
Jazzensemble Des Hessischen Rundfunks
Atmosphering Conditions Permitting | ECM | 1549/50
NDR Big Band
NDR Big Band-Bravissimo | ACT | 9232-2
Radio Jazzgroup Frankfurt
Jubilee Edition | double moon | CHRDM 71020
Ralph R.Hübner-Christoph Lauer
Mondspinner | free flow music | ffm 0796
Ralph R.Hübner-Christoph Lauer Quartet
Mondspinner | free flow music | ffm 0796

Hübner,Veit | (b)
Tango Five feat. Raul Jaurena
Obsecion | Satin Doll Productions | SDP 1027-1 CD
The Huebner Brothers
Memories | Satin Doll Productions | SDP 1025-1 CD

Hübsch,Carl Ludwig 'Lu' | (dr,tubaEb-tuba)
Carl Ludwig Hübsch
Der Erste Bericht | IN+OUT Records | 77035-2
Carl Ludwig Hübsch Trio
Carl Ludwig Hübsch's Longrun Development Of The Universe | Jazz Haus Musik | JHM 0112 CD
European Tuba Quartet
Low And Behold | Jazz Haus Musik | JHM 0110 CD
Hanschel-Hübsch-Schipper
Planet Blow Chill | Jazz Haus Musik | JHM 0087 CD
Planet Blow
Alien Lunatic | Jazz Haus Musik | JHM 0071 CD

Huby,Régis | (v)
Orchestre National De Jazz
Charmediterranéen | ECM | 1828(018493-2)

Huchard,Stéphane | (dr)
Laurent De Wilde Sextet
Time Change | Warner | 8573-84315-2

Huchin,Thierry | (v)
Charlie Haden Quartet West With Strings
Now Is The Hour | Verve | 527827-2

Hucko,Peanuts | (bs,cl,ts,vocsax)
Bud Freeman And His Stars
Muggsy Spanier And Bud Freeman:V-Discs 1944-45 | Jazz Unlimited | JUCD 2049
Bud Freeman And His Summa Cum Laude Orchestra
Planet Jazz:Jack Teagarden | Planet Jazz | 2161236-2
Planet Jazz:Bud Freeman | Planet Jazz | 2161240-2
Bud Freeman And The V-Disc Jumpers
Muggsy Spanier And Bud Freeman:V-Discs 1944-45 | Jazz Unlimited | JUCD 2049
Eddie Condon All Stars
Jazz Festival Vol.1 | Storyville | 4960733
Eight Squares And A Critic
Muggsy Spanier And Bud Freeman:V-Discs 1944-45 | Jazz Unlimited | JUCD 2049
George Wein's Dixie Victors
The Magic Horn | RCA | 2113038-2
Jack Teagarden's Big Eight
Planet Jazz:Jack Teagarden | Planet Jazz | 2161236-2
Planet Jazz | Planet Jazz | 2169652-2
Lee Wiley With The Dean Kincaide Dixieland Band
Planet Jazz:Female Jazz Vocalists | Planet Jazz | 2169656-2
Louis Armstrong And His All Stars

Planet Jazz:Louis Armstrong | Planet Jazz | 2152052-2
Planet Jazz:Jack Teagarden | Planet Jazz | 2161236-2
Planet Jazz:Male Jazz Vocalists | Planet Jazz | 2169657-2
Best Of The Complete RCA Victor Recordings | RCA | 2663636-2
Louis Armstrong:A 100th Birthday Celebration | RCA | 2663694-2
Louis Armstrong:Wintergarden 1947/Blue Note 1948 | Storyville | STCD 8242

Louis Armstrong And His Orchestra
I Love Jazz | Verve | 543747-2
Louis Armstrong:C'est Si Bon | Dreyfus Jazz Line | FDM 36730-2
Swing Legends:Louis Armstrong | Nimbus Records | NI 2012

Muggsy Spanier And His V-Disc All Stars
Muggsy Spanier And Bud Freeman:V-Discs 1944-45 | Jazz Unlimited | JUCD 2049

The Chicago All Stars
Planet Jazz:Bud Freeman | Planet Jazz | 2161240-2

The V-Disc Jumpers
Muggsy Spanier And Bud Freeman:V-Discs 1944-45 | Jazz Unlimited | JUCD 2049

Huddleston,Floyd | (voc)
Tommy Dorsey And His Orchestra
Frank Sinatra And The Tommy Dorsey Orchestra | RCA | 2668701-2

Hudson,Bruce | (tp)
Louis Armstrong With Gordon Jenkins And His Orchestra And Choir
Satchmo In Style | Verve | 549594-2

Hudson,Garth | (accordeon)
Hans Theessink Group
Call Me | Minor Music | 801022

Hudtwalcker,Olaf | (interviews)
Fritz Münzer Quintet
Jazz für junge Leute:Live im HR 1962 | Jazz 'n' Arts Records | C 01

Huergo,Lucia | (sax,keyboards,arrvoc)
Lazaro Ros Con Mezcla
Cantos | Intuition Records | INT 3080-2

Huffington,Bob | (reeds)
Eric Dolphy Quartet With The University Of Illinois Big Band
The Illinois Concert | Blue Note | 499826-2

Huffman,'Buddha' Robert | (congas,bata,bell-tree,gongs,voc)
Don Cherry Group
Multi Kulti | A&M Records | 395323-2

Huffstadt,Charles | (dr,kalimbambirra)
Greetje Bijma Kwintet
Tales Of A Voice | TipToe | TIP-888808 2

Huffstetter,Steven | (fl-htp)
Diane Schuur And Her Band
The Best Of Diane Schuur | GRP | GRP 98882

Paulinho Da Costa Orchestra
Agora | Original Jazz Classics | OJCCD 630-2(2310785)

Stan Kenton And His Orchestra
Adventures In Blues | Capitol | 520089-2

Vic Lewis West Coast All Stars
Vic Lewis Presenting A Celebration Of Contemporary West Coast Jazz | Candid | CCD 79711/12

Hufschmidt,Thomas | (p,arr,el-p,keyboards,orgsynth)
Wayne Bartlett With The Thomas Hufschmidt Group
Tokyo Blues | Laika Records | 35101212

Wayne Bartlett With The Thomas Hufschmidt Trio And Wolfgang Engstfeld
Senor Blues | Laika Records | LK 95-066

Hug,Martin | (dr)
Lucas Heidepriem Quartet
Voicings | IN+OUT Records | 7011-2

Huggins,Frank | (tp)
Terry Gibbs Big Band
Terry Gibbs Dream Band Vol.4:Main Stem | Contemporary | CCD 7656-2

Terry Gibbs Dream Band
Terry Gibbs Dream Band Vol.3:Flying Home | Contemporary | CCD 7654-2
Terry Gibbs Dream Band Vol.5:The Big Cat | Contemporary | CCD 7657-2

Hughart,Jim | (bel-b)
Diane Schuur And Her Band
The Best Of Diane Schuur | GRP | GRP 98882

Ella Fitzgerald With Orchestra
The Best Is Yet To Come | Original Jazz Classics | OJCCD 889-2(2312138)

Ella Fitzgerald With The Duke Ellington Orchestra And Jimmy Jones Trio
Ella & Duke At The Cote D'Azur | Verve | 539030-2
Ella Fitzgerald And Duke Ellington:Cote D'Azure Concerts on Verve | Verve | 539033-2

Ella Fitzgerald With The Jimmy Jones Trio
Ella Fitzgerald-First Lady Of Song | Verve | 517898-2
Ella & Duke At The Cote D'Azur | Verve | 539030-2
Ella Fitzgerald And Duke Ellington:Cote D'Azure Concerts on Verve | Verve | 539033-2

Gato Barbieri Orchestra
Latino America | Impulse(MCA) | 952236-2

Joe Pass Quartet
Apassionato | Pablo | 2310946-2
Joe Pass:Guitar Virtuoso | Pablo | 4 PACD 4423-2
Joy Spring | Blue Note | 835222-2
Ira George And Joe-Joe Pass Loves Gershwin | Original Jazz Classics | OJCCD 828-2(2312133)
The Jazz Giants Play Duke Ellington:Caravan | Prestige | PCD 24227-2

Joe Pass Trio
Resonance | Pablo | 2310968-2
Live At Donte's | Pablo | 2620114-2
Joe Pass:Guitar Virtuoso | Pablo | 4 PACD 4423-2

Milt Jackson And His Orchestra
Reverence And Compassion | Reprise | 9362-45204-2

Singers Unlimited With The Clare Fischer Orchestra
The Singers Unlimited:Magic Voices | MPS | 539130-2

Singers Unlimited With The Pat Williams Orchestra
The Singers Unlimited:Magic Voices | MPS | 539130-2

Singers Unlimited With The Patrick Williams Orchestra
The Singers Unlimited:Magic Voices | MPS | 539130-2

Hughes,Bill | (b-tbtb)
Big Joe Turner With The Count Basie Orchestra
Flip Flop And Fly | Original Jazz Classics | OJCCD 1053-2(2310937)

Count Basie And His Orchestra
Jazz Gallery:Lester Young Vol.2(1946-59) | RCA | 2119541-2
Fun Time | Pablo | 2310945-2
Jazz Collection:Count Basie | Laserlight | 24368
Count Basie: Salle Pleyel, April 17th, 1972 | Laserlight | 36127
Verve Jazz Masters 2:Count Basie | Verve | 519819-2
Count Basie Swings-Joe Williams Sings | Verve | 519852-2
Verve Jazz Masters 20:Introducing | Verve | 519853-2
April In Paris | Verve | 521402-2
Basie Meets Bond | Capitol | 538225-2
Basie's Beatle Bag | Verve | 557455-2
One O'Clock Jump | Verve | 559806-2
King Of Swing | Verve | 837433-2
Live at The Sands | Reprise | 9362-45946-2
Count Basie At Newport | Verve | 9861761
88 Basie Street | Original Jazz Classics | OJC 808(2310901)
Jazz Dance | Original Jazz Classics | OJCCD 1002-2(1210890)
Fancy Pants | Original Jazz Classics | OJCCD 1038-2(2310920)
I Told You So | Original Jazz Classics | OJCCD 824-2(2310767)
Digital III At Montreux | Original Jazz Classics | OJCCD 996-2(2308223)
The Jazz Giants Play Harry Warren:Lullaby Of Broadway | Prestige | PCD 24204-2

Count Basie Big Band
Montreux '77 | Original Jazz Classics | OJCCD 377-2
Farmers Market Barbecue | Original Jazz Classics | OJCCD 732-2(2310874)

Diane Schuur With The Count Basie Orchestra
The Best Of Diane Schuur | GRP | GRP 98882

Ella Fitzgerald With Count Basie And His Orchestra
Digital III At Montreux | Original Jazz Classics | OJCCD 996-2(2308223)

Ella Fitzgerald With The Count Basie Orchestra
Bluella:Ella Fitzgerald Sings The Blues | Pablo | 2310960-2
Ella Fitzgerald-First Lady Of Song | Verve | 517898-2
For The Love Of Ella Fitzgerald | Verve | 841765-2

Frank Sinatra With The Count Basie Orchestra
It Might As Well Be Spring | Reprise | 7599-27027-2

Milt Jackson Orchestra
Sarah Vaughan Birthday Celebration | Fantasy | FANCD 6090-2

Milt Jackson With The Count Basie Orchestra
To Bags...With Love:Memorial Album | Pablo | 2310967-2
Milt Jackson Birthday Celebration | Fantasy | FANCD 6079-2
Milt Jackson + Count Basie + Big Band Vol.1 | Original Jazz Classics | OJCCD 740-2(2310822)
Milt Jackson + Count Basie + Big Band Vol.2 | Original Jazz Classics | OJCCD 741-2(2310823)

Sarah Vaughan And The Count Basie Orchestra
Sarah Vaughan Birthday Celebration | Fantasy | FANCD 6090-2

Hughes,Bob | (b)
Steve Tibbetts Group
Bye Bye Safe Journey | ECM | 1270
Exploded View | ECM | 1335

Hughes,Ernie | (pb)
Jack Teagarden And His Orchestra
Jazz:The Essential Collection Vol.3 | IN+OUT Records | 78013-2

Wingy Mannone And His Orchestra
Planet Jazz:Male Jazz Vocalists | Planet Jazz | 2169657-2

Hughes,George | (dr)
Sarah Vaughan And Her Trio
Verve Jazz Masters 42:Sarah Vaughan-The Jazz Sides | Verve | 526817-2

Hughes,Herman | (voc)
Fats Waller And His Buddies
Planet Jazz:Jack Teagarden | Planet Jazz | 2161236-2

Hughes,Luther | (bel-b)
The Three Sounds
Blue Break Beats | Blue Note | 799106-2

Hughes,Max | (el-b)
Bajazzo
Harlequin Galaxy | Edition Collage | EC 519-2

Sören Fischer Quartet
Don't Change Your Hair For Me | Edition Collage | EC 513-2

Hughes,Norman | (v)
Jacintha With Band And Strings
Lush Life | Groove Note | GRV 1011-2(Gold CD 2011)

Hughes,Robert | (b)
Steve Tibbetts Group
Yr | ECM | 1355(835245-2)

Hughes,Ron | (b-tb)
Singers Unlimited With Rob McConnell And The Boss Brass
The Singers Unlimited:Magic Voices | MPS | 539130-2

Hughes,Tara | (voc)
Mike Westbrook Brass Band
Glad Day:Settings Of William Blake | Enja | ENJ-9376 2

Hughes,Vince | (tp)
Anita O'Day With Gene Krupa And His Orchestra
Let Me Off Uptown:Anita O'Day With Gene Krupa | CBS | CK 65625

Hughes,William | (tb)
Count Basie And His Orchestra
Afrique | RCA | 2179618-2

Hühns,Gerd | (g)
Die Deutsche All Star Band 1953
1.Deutsches Jazz Festival 1953 Frankfurt/Main | Bear Family Records | BCD 15611 AH

Heinz Schönberger Quintet
Deutsches Jazz Fesival 1954/1955 | Bear Family Records | BCD 15430

Kurt Edelhagen All Stars Und Solisten
Deutsches Jazz Fesival 1954/1955 | Bear Family Records | BCD 15430

Paul Kuhn Quartet
Deutsches Jazz Fesival 1954/1955 | Bear Family Records | BCD 15430

Paul Kuhn Quintet
Deutsches Jazz Fesival 1954/1955 | Bear Family Records | BCD 15430

Rolf Kühn And His Quintet
Deutsches Jazz Fesival 1954/1955 | Bear Family Records | BCD 15430

Huke,Jörg | (tb,berimbaoel-tb)
Andreas Willers Group
Andreas Willers & Friends Play Jimi Hendrix:Experience | Nabel Records:Jazz Network | CD 4665

Andreas Willers Octet
The Ground Music | Enja | ENJ-9368 2

Fun Horns
Surprise | Jazzpoint | JP 1029 CD

Gabriele Hasler Group
Gabriele Hasler's Rosensrücke | Foolish Music | FM 211096

Klaus König Orchestra
Time Fragments:Seven Studies In Time And Motion | Enja | ENJ-8076 2
Reviews | Enja | ENJ-9061 2

Klaus König Orchestra & Guests
The Song Of Songs:Oratorio For Two Solo Voices,Choir And Orchestra | Enja | ENJ-7057 2

Hulin,Bernard | (tp)
Lionel Hampton All Stars
Jazz In Paris:Lionel Hampton And His French New Sound Vol.1 | EmArCy | 549405-2 PMS
Jazz In Paris:Lionel Hampton And His French New Sound Vol.2 | EmArCy | 549406-2 PMS

Hull,Gene | (as)
The Jazz Composer's Orchestra
Comminications | JCOA | 1001/2

Hull,Harry | (tuba)
Bessie Smith With The James P.Johnson Orchestra And The Hal Johnson Choir
The Blues | Storyville | 4960323

Hüllemann-Watson,Kerstin | (viola)
HR Big Band With Marjorie Barnes And Frits Landesbergen And Strings
Swinging Christmas | hr music.de | hrmj 012-02 CD

Hullin,Bernard | (tp)
Django Reinhardt And His Quintet
Django Reinhardt:Souveniers | Dreyfus Jazz Line | FDM 36744-2

Django Reinhardt Sextet
Jazz In Paris:Django Reinhardt-Nuits De Saint-Germain-Des-Prés | EmArCy | 018427-2

Kenny Clarke 8
Americans Swinging In Paris:Kenny Clarke | EMI Records | 539652-2

Hülsmann,Julia | (pfender-rhodes)
Julia Hülsmann Trio With Rebekka Bakken
Scattering Poems | ACT | 9405-2

Julia Hülsmann Trio With Anna Lauvergnac
Come Closer | ACT | 9702-2

United Women's Orchestra
Virgo Supercluster | Jazz Haus Musik | JHM 0123 CD

Hultcrantz,Torbjörn | (b)
Dexter Gordon-Benny Bailey Quintet
Revelation | Steeplechase | SCCD 31373
The Rainbow People | Steeplechase | SCCD 31521

Humair,Daniel | (dr,kettle-dr,perc,roto-tom)
Bud Powell Quartet
Parisian Thoroughfare | Pablo | CD 2310976-2

Bud Powell Trio
Parisian Thoroughfare | Pablo | CD 2310976-2

Chet Baker Sextet
Chet Baker-The Italian Sessions | Bluebird | ND 82001

Daniel Humair Soultet
Jazz In Paris | EmArCy | 548793-2

Daniel Humair Trio
Humair/Jeanneau/Texier | Owl Records | 014734-2

Elek Bacsik Quartet
Jazz In Paris:Elek Baczik | EmArCy | 542231-2

Elek Bacsik Trio
Jazz In Paris:Elek Baczik | EmArCy | 542231-2

European Jazz Ensemble
20th Anniversary Tour | Konnex Records | KCD 5078
European Jazz Ensemble 25th Anniversary | Konnex Records | KCD 5100

Golden Gate Quartet With The Martial Solal Orchestra
Americans Swinging In Paris:Golden Gate Quartet | EMI Records | 539659-2
From Spriritual To Swing Vol.2 | EMI Records | 780573-2

Jean-Luc Ponty Quartet
Jazz In Paris:Jean-Luc Ponty-Jazz Long Playing | EmArCy | 548150-2 PMS

Jean-Luc Ponty Quintet
Jazz In Paris:Jean-Luc Ponty-Jazz Long Playing | EmArCy | 548150-2 PMS

Joachim Kühn Trio
Easy To Read | Owl Records | 014802-2

Joe Henderson Quintet
Joe Henderson:The Milestone Years | Milestone | 8MCD 4413-2

Joe Henderson Sextet
Joe Henderson:The Milestone Years | Milestone | 8MCD 4413-2

Kühn/Humair/Jenny-Clark
Tripple Entente | EmArCy | 558690-2

Les Double Six
Les Double Six | RCA | 2164314-2

Mariano-Humair-Haurand
Frontier Traffic | Konnex Records | KCD 5110

Phil Woods And His European Rhythm Machine
At The Montreux Jazz Festival | Verve | 065512-2
Americans Swinging In Paris:Phil Woods | EMI Records | 539654-2

Richard Galliano Group
French Touch | Dreyfus Jazz Line | FDM 36596-2

Richard Galliano Quartet
Gallianissimo! The Best Of Richard Galliano | Dreyfus Jazz Line | FDM 36616-2

Richard Galliano Trio
Gallianissimo! The Best Of Richard Galliano | Dreyfus Jazz Line | FDM 36616-2

Stephane Grappelli Quartet
Jazz In Paris:Stephane Grappelli-Django | EmArCy | 018421-1

Stephane Grappelli Quintet
Grapelli Story | Verve | 515807-2
Feeling + Finesse = Jazz | Atlantic | 7567-90140-2

Swingle Singers
Jazz Sebastian Bach Vol.2 | Philips | 542553-2
Swingle Singers Singing Mozart | Philips | 548538-2
Swingling Telemann | Philips | 586735-2
Swingle Singers Getting Romantic | Philips | 586736-2

Human Factor |
Human Factor
Forbidden City | Nabel Records:Jazz Network | CD 4635

Humble,Derek | (as)
Kenny Clarke-Francy Boland Big Band
Clark-Boland Big Band: TNP, October 29th, 1969 | Laserlight | 36129
Three Latin Adventures | MPS | 529095-2
More Smiles | MPS | 9814789
All Smiles | MPS | 9814790
Francy Boland-Fellini 712 | MPS | 9814805

Stan Getz With The Kurt Edelhagen Orchestra
Stan Getz In Europe | Laserlight | 24657

Humes,Helen | (voc)
Count Basie And His Orchestra
Jazz:The Essential Collection Vol.3 | IN+OUT Records | 78013-2

Helen Humes And Her All Stars
Lester Young:The Complete Aladdin Sessions | Blue Note | 832787-2

Helen Humes With James P. Johnson And The Count Basie Orchestra
From Spiritual To Swing | Vanguard | VCD 169/71

Helen Humes With The Kansas City Five
From Spiritual To Swing | Vanguard | VCD 169/71

Red Norvo And His Orchestra
Planet Jazz:Female Jazz Vocalists | Planet Jazz | 2169656-2

Hummel,Markus | (org)
Al Jones Blues Band
Sharper Than A Tack | Blues Beacon | BLU-1034 2

Humphrey,Bobbi | (flvoc)
Bobbi Humphrey
Blue Break Beats | Blue Note | 799106-2

Bobbi Humphrey Group
Blue Breaks Beats Vol.2 | Blue Note | 789907-2

Lee Morgan Orchestra
The Last Sessin | Blue Note | 493401-2

Humphrey,Paul | (drperc)
Charles Kynard Quintet
The Soul Brotherhood | Prestige | PCD 24257-2

Eddie Cleanhead Vinson With Band
The Late Show-Recorded Live At Marla's Memory Lane Supper Club Vol.2 | Fantasy | FCD 9655-2

Eddie Cleanhead Vinson With The Red Holloway Quartet
Blues In The Night-Volume One:The Early Show | Fantasy | FCD 9647-2

Etta James & Eddie Cleanhead Vinson With The Red Holloway Quartet
Blues In The Night-Volume One:The Early Show | Fantasy | FCD 9647-2

Etta James With Band
The Late Show-Recorded Live At Marla's Memory Lane Supper Club Vol.2 | Fantasy | FCD 9655-2

Etta James With The Red Holloway Quartet
Blues In The Night-Volume One:The Early Show | Fantasy | FCD 9647-2

Etta James With The Red Holloway Quintet
Blues In The Night-Volume One:The Early Show | Fantasy | FCD 9647-2

Etta James/Eddie 'Cleanhead' Vinson With Band
The Late Show-Recorded Live At Marla's Memory Lane Supper Club Vol.2 | Fantasy | FCD 9655-2

Gene Harris And The Three Sounds
Deep Blue-The United States Of Mind | Blue Note | 521152-2

Jimmy Smith Quintet
Root Down | Verve | 559805-2

Jimmy Smith Sextet
Jimmy Smith:Best Of The Verve Years | Verve | 527950-2
Root Down | Verve | 559805-2

Kenny Burrel Quartet
'Round Midnight | Original Jazz Classics | OJCCD 990-2(F 9417)

Les McCann Group
Another Beginning | Atlantic | 7567-80790-2

Les McCann Quartet
Talkin' Verve:Les McCann | Verve | 557351-2

Les McCann Trio
Talkin' Verve:Les McCann | Verve | 557351-2

Mel Brown Quartet
Chicken Fat | Impulse(MCA) | 9861047

Mel Brown Quintet
Chicken Fat | Impulse(MCA) | 9861047

Red Holloway Quintet
Coast To Coast | Milestone | MCD 9335-2

The Three Sounds
Blue Break Beats | Blue Note | 799106-2

Humphrey,Percy | (tp,ldvoc)
Eureka Brass Band
Atlantic Jazz: New Orleans | Atlantic | 7567-81700-2

Humphrey,Ralph | (dr,percrepique)
Free Flight
Jazzrock-Anthology Vol.3:Fusion | Zounds | CD 27100555

Humphrey,Willie | (clvoc)
Eureka Brass Band
Atlantic Jazz: New Orleans | Atlantic | 7567-81700-2

Paul Barbarin And His Band
Atlantic Jazz: New Orleans | Atlantic | 7567-81700-2

Humphries,Charles | (voc)
Chinese Compass
Chinese Compass | dacapo | DCCD 9443
Humphries,David | (finger-snapssound-effects)
Take 6
Goldmine | Reprise | 7599-25670-2
Humphries,Lex | (dr,perc,voctympany)
Dizzy Gillespie Quintet
Verve Jazz Masters 10:Dizzy Gillespie | Verve | 516319-2
Talking Verve:Dizzy Gillespie | Verve | 533846-2
Dizzy Gillespie Sextet
Ultimate Dizzy Gillespie | Verve | 557535-2
Donald Byrd Orchestra With Voices
True Blue | Blue Note | 534032-2
The Best Of Blue Note | Blue Note | 796110-2
Donald Byrd Quintet
Blue N' Groovy | Blue Note | 780679-2
Blue Bossa | Blue Note | 795590-2
Donald Byrd Septet + Voices
A New Perspective | Blue Note | 499006-2
Duke Pearson Sextet
Dedication! | Original Jazz Classics | OJCCD 1939-2(P 7729)
John Coltrane Quartet
John Coltrane-The Heavyweight Champion:The Complete Atlantic Recordings | Atlantic | 8122-71984-2
Giant Steps | Atlantic | 8122-75203-2
Johnny Hodges With The Dizzy Gillespie Quintet
Verve Jazz Masters 35:Johnny Hodges | Verve | 521857-2
Leon Thomas With The Oliver Nelson Quintet
Leon Thomas In Berlin | RCA | 2663877-2
McCoy Tyner Trio
Nights Of Ballads And Blues | Impulse(MCA) | 951221-2
Sonny Red (Kyner) Quintet
Red,Blue & Green | Milestone | MCD 47086-2
Sun Ra And His Astro-Infinity Arkestra
Space Is The Place | Impulse(MCA) | 951249-2
Sun Ra And His Intergalactic Research Arkestra
Black Myth/Out In Space | MPS | 557656-2
Wes Montgomery Quartet
Wes Montgomery-The Complete Riverside Recordings | Riverside | 12 RCD 4408-2
The Jazz Giants Play Harold Arlen:Blues In The Night | Prestige | PCD 24201-2
Wes Montgomery Quintet
Wes Montgomery-The Complete Riverside Recordings | Riverside | 12 RCD 4408-2
So Much Guitar! | Original Jazz Classics | OJC20 233-2
The Jazz Giants Play Duke Ellington:Caravan | Prestige | PCD 24227-2
Yusef Lateef Orchestra
The Centaur And The Phoenix | Original Jazz Classics | OJCCD 721-2(RLP 9337)
Yusef Lateef Quartet
Eastern Sounds | Original Jazz Classics | OJC20 612-2(P 7319)
Humphries,Ralph | (dr)
Diane Schuur With Orchestra
Love Songs | GRP | GRP 97032
The Best Of Diane Schuur | GRP | GRP 98882
Humphries,Roger | (dr)
Carmel Jones Quartet
Jay Hawk Talk | Original Jazz Classics | OJCCD 1938-2(P7401)
Carmel Jones Quintet
Jay Hawk Talk | Original Jazz Classics | OJCCD 1938-2(P7401)
Horace Silver Quintet
Horace Silver Retrospective | Blue Note | 495576-2
Song For My Father | Blue Note | 499002-2
The Cape Verdean Blues | Blue Note | 576753-2
Blue Bossa | Blue Note | 795590-2
The Best Of Blue Note | Blue Note | 796110-2
Horace Silver Sextet
Horace Silver Retrospective | Blue Note | 495576-2
The Cape Verdean Blues | Blue Note | 576753-2
Hungate,David | (bg)
Sarah Vaughan And Her Band
Songs Of The Beatles | Atlantic | 16037-2
Hunger,Chris | (flas)
David Matthews & The Manhattan Jazz Orchestra
Back To Bach | Milestone | MCD 9312-2
Hunt,Billy | (tp)
Woody Herman And His Orchestra
Verve Jazz Masters 54:Woody Herman | Verve | 529903-2
Hunt,Cecil | (congas)
Funk Inc.
Jazzin' With The Soul Brothers | Fantasy | FANCD 6086-2
Hunt,George | (tb)
Count Basie And His Orchestra
Jazz:The Essential Collection Vol.3 | IN+OUT Records | 78013-2
Earl Hines And His Orchestra
Planet Jazz:Earl Hines | Planet Jazz | 2159973-2
Hunt,Joe | (dr)
Astrud Gilberto With The New Stan Getz Quartet
Verve Jazz Masters 9:Astrud Gilberto | Verve | 519824-2
Bill Evans Trio
Bill Evans:The Secret Sessions | Milestone | 8MCD 4421-2
George Russell Sextet
Eric Dolphy Birthday Celebration | Fantasy | FANCD 6085-2
Ezz-thetics | Original Jazz Classics | OJCCD 070-2(RLP 9375)
The Jazz Giants Play Miles Davis:Milestones | Prestige | PCD 24225-2
Getz-Gilberto Quintet
Getz/Gilberto No.2 | Verve | 519800-2
Stan Getz New Quartet
A Life In Jazz:A Musical Biography | Verve | 535119-2
Stan Getz Quintet Feat. Astrud Gilberto
Verve Jazz Masters 53:Stan Getz-Bossa Nova | Verve | 529904-2
Stan Getz With Strings And Voices
Reflections | Verve | 523322-2
Steve Rochinski Quartet
Otherwise | Jardis Records | JRCD 20133
Steve Rochinski Solo/Duo/Trio/Quartet
Jazz Guitar Highlights 1 | Jardis Records | JRCD 20141
A Bird In The Hand | Jardis Records | JRCD 9922
The New Stan Getz Quartet
Getz Au Go Go | Verve | 821725-2
The New Stan Getz Quartet Feat. Astrud Gilberto
Getz Au Go Go | Verve | 821725-2
Hunt,John | (dr,tpfl-h)
Little Jimmy Scott | Specialty | SPCD 2170-2
(Little)Jimmy Scott With The Billy Taylor Orchestra
Everybody's Somebody's Fool | Decca | 050669-2
Hank Crawford And His Orchestra
Atlantic Saxophones | Rhino | 8122-71256-2
Hank Crawford Septet
More Soul | Atlantic | 8122-73709-2
Joe Henderson And His Orchestra
Joe Henderson:The Milestone Years | Milestone | 8MCD 4413-2
Sonny Stitt And His Band
Kaleidoscope | Original Jazz Classics | OJCCD 060-2(P 7077)
Hunt,Louis | (tp)
Louis Armstrong With Chick Webb's Orchestra
Best Of The Complete RCA Victor Recordings | RCA | 2663636-2
Louis Armstrong:A 100th Birthday Celebration | RCA | 2663694-2
Hunt,Nimrod | (dr,hand-drperc)
Sun Ra And His Intergalactic Research Arkestra
Black Myth/Out In Space | MPS | 557656-2
Hunt,Pee Wee | (tbvoc)
Louis Armstrong With The Casa Loma Orchestra
Louis Armstrong:Swing That Music | Laserlight | 36056
Hunt,Steve | (keyboards,synth,vib,dr,didgeridoo)
Allan Holdsworth Group
The Name Of A Woman | Cream Records | JMS 18733-2
Hal Russell NRG Ensemble
The Finnish/Swiss Tour | ECM | 1455
The Hal Russell Story | ECM | 1498
Stanley Clarke Group
If This Bass Could Only Talk | CBS | 460883-2
Hunt,Steve 'Slash' | (b)
Billy Boy Arnold Group
Eldorado Cadillac | Alligator Records | ALCD 4836
Hunte,Stanley | (v)
Ron Carter Quintet With Strings
Pick 'Em/Super Strings | Milestone | MCD 47090-2
Hunt-Ehrlich,Madeline | (voc)
Marc Ribot Y Los Cubanos Postizos
The Proshetic Cubans | Atlantic | 7567-83116-2
Hunter,Alberta | (voc)
Alberta Hunter
Planet Jazz:Female Jazz Vocalists | Planet Jazz | 2169656-2
Alberta Hunter With Buster Bailey's Blues Blasters
Songs We Taught Your Mother | Original Blues Classics | OBCCD 520-2
Hunter,Barbara Jane | (cello)
Ella Fitzgerald With Orchestra
The Best Is Yet To Come | Original Jazz Classics | OJCCD 889-2(2312138)
Hunter,Charlie | (8-string-g)
Charlie Hunter Quartet
Ready...Set...Shango! | Blue Note | 837101-2
Charlie Hunter-Leon Parker
Duo | Blue Note | 499187-2
Hunter,Chris | (as,ts,flss)
David Matthews & The Manhattan Jazz Orchestra
Hey Duke! | Milestone | MCD 9320-2
George Gruntz Concert Jazz Band
Blues 'N Dues Et Cetera | Enja | ENJ-6072 2
Hunter,Frank | (arr,condtb)
Elliot Lawrence And His Orchestra
Mullenium | CBS | CK 65678
Joe Williams With The Frank Hunter Orchestra
Planet Jazz:Joe Williams | Planet Jazz | 2165370-2
Hunter,George | (drvoc)
First Revolution Singers
First Revolution Gospel Singers:A Capella | Laserlight | 24338
Huntington,Bill | (bbj)
Bennie Wallace Quartet
The Talk Of The Town | Enja | ENJ-7091 2
Hupfauer,Pidi | (voc)
Mind Games
Pretty Fonky | Edition Collage | EC 482-2
Wind Moments | Take Twelve On CD | TT 009-2
Mind Games With Philip Catherine
Pretty Fonky | Edition Collage | EC 482-2
Tom Bennecke & Space Gurilla
Wind Moments | Take Twelve On CD | TT 009-2
Huppertsberg,Lindy 'Lady Bass' | (bvoc)
Heiner Franz & Friends
Let's Have A Ball | Jardis Records | JRCD 20030
Jazz Guitar Highlights 1 | Jardis Records | JRCD 20141
Hurdle,Tony | (tb)
Dook Joint
Who's Been Talkin'... | Organic Music | ORGM 9728
Hurley,Clyde | (tp)
Edmond Hall With The Ralph Sutton Group
Edmond Hall With The Ralph Sutton Group | Storyville | STCD 6052
Glenn Miller And His Orchestra
Planet Jazz:Glenn Miller | Planet Jazz | 2152056-2
Planet Jazz Sampler | Planet Jazz | 2152326-2
Planet Jazz:Big Bands | Planet Jazz | 2169649-2
Planet Jazz:Swing | Planet Jazz | 2169651-2
The Chesterfield Broadcasts Vol.1 | RCA | 2663113-2
Swing Legends | Nimbus Records | NI 2001
Lena Horne With The Horace Henderson Orchestra
Planet Jazz:Lena Horne | Planet Jazz | 2165373-2
The Andrew Sisters With The Glenn Miller Orchestra
The Chesterfield Broadcasts Vol.1 | RCA | 2663113-2
Tommy Dorsey And His Orchestra
Planet Jazz:Frank Sinatra & Tommy Dorsey | Planet Jazz | 2152067-2
Hurst III,Robert Leslie | (bb-solo)
Billy Cobham Group
Art Of Five | IN+OUT Records | 77063-2
Branford Marsalis Quartet
Crazy People Music | CBS | 466870-2
Kevin Eubanks Trio
Live At Bradley's | Blue Note | 830133-2
Terri Lyne Carrington Group
Jazz Is A Spirit | ACT | 9408-2
Woody Shaw Quartet
Bemsha Swing | Blue Note | 829029-2
Hurt,James | (p,el-p,orgperc)
Abbey Lincoln With Her Band
Wholly Earth | Verve | 559538-2
Antonio Hart Group
Here I Stand | Impulse(MCA) | 951208-2
Jacques Schwarz-Bart/James Hurt Quartet
Immersion | Fresh Sound Records | FSNT 057 CD
James Hurt Group
Dark Grooves-Mystcal Rhythms | Blue Note | 495104-2
Russel Gunn Group
Ethnomusicology Vol.1 | Atlantic | 7567-83165-2
Hurt,Pete | (as,clts)
Carla Bley Band
The Very Big Carla Bley Band | Watt | 23
Big Band Theory | Watt | 25(519966-2)
Hurt,Sam | (tb)
Dizzy Gillespie And His Orchestra
Planet Jazz:Dizzy Gillespie | Planet Jazz | 2152069-2
Planet Jazz:Bebop | RCA | 2169650-2
Planet Jazz:Male Jazz Vocalists | Planet Jazz | 2169657-2
Hurtig,Uno | (b-tuba)
Bengt-Arne Wallin Orchestra
The Birth+Rebirth Of Swedish Folk Jazz | ACT | 9254-2
Hurwitz,Richard | (tp)
Buddy Rich Big Band
Backwoods Siseman/Pieces Of Dream | Laserlight | 24655
Lee Konitz Orchestra
The Art Of Saxophone | Laserlight | 24652
Husband,Gary | (dr)
Allan Holdsworth Group
The Name Of A Woman | Cream Records | JMS 18733-2
Hussain,Ustad Shaukat | (tabla)
Jan Garbarek Trio
Madar | ECM | 1515(519075-2)
Jan Garbarek With Ustad Fateh Ali Khan & Musicians From Pakistan
Ragas And Sagas | ECM | 1442(511263-2)
Hussain,Zakir | (bongos,dholak,nal triangle,tabla)
John Handy-Ali Akbar Khan Group
Two Originals:Karuna Supreme/Rainbow | MPS | 519195-2
John McLaughlin Group
The Promise | Verve | 529828-2
Remember Shakti | Verve | 559945-2
Pharoah Sanders Group
Save Our Children | Verve | 557297-2
Remember Shakti
Saturday Night In Bombay | Verve | 014184-2
Shakti
Shakti With John McLaughlin | CBS | 467905-2
Shankar
Who's To Know | ECM | 1195
Shankar Group
Nobody Told Me | ECM | 1397
Shankar Quartet
M.R.C.S. | ECM | 1403
Pancha Nadai Pallavi | ECM | 1407(841641-2)
Shankar/Garbarek/Hussain/Gurtu
Song For Everyone | ECM | 1286(823795-2)
Wolfgang Schmid's Kick
No Filters | TipToe | TIP-888809 2
Zakir Hussain Group
Making Music | ECM | 1349
Hutcherson,Bobby | (marimba,vib,bass-marimba,bells)
Abbey Lincoln With Her Band
Wholly Earth | Verve | 559538-2
Al Grey And His Allstars
Snap Your Fingers | Verve | 9860307
Andrew Hill Quartet
A Blue Conception | Blue Note | 534254-2
Big John Patton Quartet
Blue Bossa | Blue Note | 795590-2
Billy Mitchell Quintet
This Is Billy Mitchell | Smash | 065507-2
Billy Mitchell Sextet
This Is Billy Mitchell | Smash | 065507-2
Blue Note All Stars
Town Hall Concert | Blue Note | 497811-2
Bobby Hutcherson Group
Skyline | Verve | 559616-2
Bobby Hutcherson Orchestra
Deep Blue-The United States Of Mind | Blue Note | 521152-2
Montara | Blue Note | 590956-2
Bobby Hutcherson Quartet
Herbie Hancock:The Complete Blue Note Sixties Sessions | Blue Note | 495569-2
Bobby Hutcherson Quintet
Blue N' Groovy | Blue Note | 780679-2
Blue Breaks Beats Vol.2 | Blue Note | 789907-2
Bobby Hutcherson Sextet
A Blue Conception | Blue Note | 534254-2
Dialogue | Blue Note | 535586-2
Chico Freeman Quartet
Destiny's Dance | Original Jazz Classics | OJCCD 799-2(C 14008)
Chico Freeman Quintet
Destiny's Dance | Original Jazz Classics | OJCCD 799-2(C 14008)
Chico Freeman Septet
Destiny's Dance | Original Jazz Classics | OJCCD 799-2(C 14008)
Chico Freeman Sextet
Destiny's Dance | Original Jazz Classics | OJCCD 799-2(C 14008)
Dexter Gordon Quintet
Jazz Profile:Dexter Gordon | Blue Note | 823514-2
Dianne Reeves With Band
Misty Blue:Sweet Sisters Swing Songs Of Sorrow And Sadness | Blue Note | 521151-2
I Remember | Blue Note | 790264-2
Donald Byrd Orchestra
Ethiopian Knights | Blue Note | 854328-2
Eddie Henderson Orchestra
Blue Breaks Beats Vol.2 | Blue Note | 789907-2
Ella Fitzgerald With Orchestra
Ella/Things Ain't What They Used To Be | Warner | 9362-47875-2
Eric Dolphy Quintet
Out To Lunch | Blue Note | 498793-2
A Blue Conception | Blue Note | 534254-2
Frank Morgan All Stars
Reflections | Original Jazz Classics | OJCCD 1046-2(C 14052)
Frant Green Quartet
Street Of Dreams | Blue Note | 821290-2
Freddie Hubbard Sextet
Keystone Bop Vol.2:Friday/Saturday | Prestige | PCD 24163-2
Grant Green Sextet
Idle Moments | Blue Note | 499003-2
Jackie McLean Quintet
A Blue Conception | Blue Note | 534254-2
Joe Henderson Septet
Mode For Joe | Blue Note | 591894-2
The Blue Note Years-The Best Of Joe Henderson | Blue Note | 795627-2
Lee Morgan Sextet
Wayne Shorter:The Classic Blue Note Recordings | Blue Note | 540856-2
McCoy Tyner Orchestra
Sama Layuca | Original Jazz Classics | OJCCD 1071-2(M 9056)
McCoy Tyner-Bobby Hutcherson Duo
Sama Layuca | Original Jazz Classics | OJCCD 1071-2(M 9056)
Sonny Rollins Quintet
No Problem | Original Jazz Classics | OJCCD 1014-2(M 9104)
Tony Williams Lifetime
Lifetime | Blue Note | 499004-2
Hutchings,Lee | (clts)
Grace Knight With Orchestra
Come In Spinner | Intuition Records | INT 3052-2
Vince Jones With Orchestra
Come In Spinner | Intuition Records | INT 3052-2
Hutchinson,Clarence | (clas)
Louis Armstrong With The Casa Loma Orchestra
Louis Armstrong:Swing That Music | Laserlight | 36056
Hutchinson,Gregory | (drvoice)
Christian McBride Group
A Family Affair | Verve | 557554-2
Eric Reed Quartet
Musicale | Impulse(MCA) | 951196-2
Eric Reed Trio
Musicale | Impulse(MCA) | 951196-2
Pure Imagination | Impulse(MCA) | 951259-2
Jimmy Smith Sextet
Angel Eyes-Ballads & Slow Jams | Verve | 527632-2
Joe Henderson Quartet
Lush Life-The Music Of Billy Strayhorn | Verve | 511779-2
Joe Henderson Quintet
Lush Life-The Music Of Billy Strayhorn | Verve | 511779-2
Joe Henderson Trio
Lush Life-The Music Of Billy Strayhorn | Verve | 511779-2
Joe Henderson/Gregory Hutchinson
Lush Life-The Music Of Billy Strayhorn | Verve | 511779-2
Joshua Redman Quartet
Joshua Redman | Warner | 9362-45242-2
Beyond | Warner | 9362-47465-2
Passage Of Time | Warner | 9362-47997-2
Joshua Redman Quartet feat. Mark Turner
Beyond | Warner | 9362-47465-2
Roy Hargrove Quartet
Family | Verve | 527630-2
Roy Hargrove Quintet
Roy Hargrove Quintet With The Tenors Of Our Time | Verve | 523019-2
Family | Verve | 527630-2
Roy Hargrove Quintet With Branford Marsalis
Roy Hargrove Quintet With The Tenors Of Our Time | Verve | 523019-2
Roy Hargrove Quintet With Joe Henderson
Roy Hargrove Quintet With The Tenors Of Our Time | Verve | 523019-2
Roy Hargrove Quintet With Johnny Griffin
Roy Hargrove Quintet With The Tenors Of Our Time | Verve | 523019-2
Roy Hargrove Quintet With Joshua Redman
Roy Hargrove Quintet With The Tenors Of Our Time | Verve | 523019-2
Roy Hargrove Quintet With Stanley Turrentine
Roy Hargrove Quintet With The Tenors Of Our Time | Verve | 523019-2
Roy Hargrove Sextet
Family | Verve | 527630-2
Teodross Avery Quartet
My Generation | Impulse(MCA) | 951181-2

Teodross Avery Quintet
My Generation | Impulse(MCA) | 951181-2

Hutchinson,Leslie | (tp)
Vic Lewis And His Band
Vic Lewis:The Golden Years | Candid | CCD 79754

Hutchinson,Ralph | (tb)
Muggsy Spanier And His Dixieland All Stars
Muggsy Spanier At Club Hangover 1953/54 | Storyville | STCD 6033

Hutchinson,Wondress | (voc)
Spyro Gyra & Guests
Love & Other Obsessions | GRP | GRP 98112

Huth,Johannes | (b)
Muriel Zoe Group
Red And Blue | ACT | 9416-2

Hutter,Ernst | (tbbass-tp)
Bill Ramsey With Orchestra
Gettin' Back To Swing | Bear Family Records | BCD 15813 AH
SWR Big Band
Jazz In Concert | Hänssler Classics | CD 93.004

Hüttner,Raimund | (sound-sampling,synth-programmingtp)
Peter Herborn's Acute Insights
Peter Herborn's Acute Insights | JMT Edition | 919017-2

Hutton,Marion | (voc)
Glenn Miller And His Orchestra
The Ultimate Glenn Miller-22 Original Hits From The King Of Swing | RCA | 2113137-2
Planet Jazz:Glenn Miller | Planet Jazz | 2152056-2
The Chesterfield Broadcasts Vol.1 | RCA | 2663113-2
Candelight Miller | RCA | 2668716-2
The Glenn Miller Story Vol. 2 | RCA | ND 89221
The Glenn Miller Story Vol. 3 | RCA | ND 89222
Swing Legends | Nimbus Records | NI 2001

Hutton,Mick | (b)
First House
Erendira | ECM | 1307
Cantilena | ECM | 1393
Nicki Leighton-Thomas Group
Forbidden Games | Candid | CCD 79778
Robin Williamson Group
Skirting The River Road | ECM | 1785(016372-2

Huy,Volker | (tp)
Ralph Schweizer Big Band
DAY Dream | Chaos | CACD 8177

Huynen,Marc | (tp)
Dogs Don't Sing In The Rain
Bones For Breakfast | Edition Collage | EC 472-2

Hyams,Harry A. | (viola)
Phineas Newborn Jr. With Dennis Farnon And His Orchestra
While My Lady Sleeps | RCA | 2185157-2

Hyams,Marjorie | (pvib)
George Shearing Quintet
Verve Jazz Masters 57:George Shearing | Verve | 529900-2
Woody Herman And His Orchestra
Woody Herman:Four Brother | Dreyfus Jazz Line | FDM 36722-2
Old Gold Rehearsals 1944 | Jazz Unlimited | JUCD 2079
Woody Herman And The Vanderbilt All Stars
Louis Armstrong-Jack Teagarden-Woody Herman:Midnights At V-Disc | Jazz Unlimited | JUCD 2048

Hyde,Dick | (bass-tb,tuba,b-tp,b-tbtb)
Diane Schuur And Her Band
The Best Of Diane Schuur | GRP | GRP 98882
Herbie Hancock Group
Man-Child | CBS | 471235-2
Paulinho Da Costa Orchestra
Happy People | Original Jazz Classics | OJCCD 783-2(2312102)
Stan Kenton And His Orchestra
Adventures In Blues | Capitol | 520089-2

Hyhne,Mads | (tbvoc)
Ok Nok...Kongo
Moonstone Journey | dacapo | DCCD 9444
Pierre Dorge's New Jungle Orchestra
Giraf | dacapo | DCCD 9440
The Crossover Ensemble
The River:Image Of Time And Life | dacapo | DCCD 9434

Hyldgaard,Susi | (accordeon,voicevoc)
Michael Mantler Group With The Danish Radio Concert Orchestra Strings
The School Of Understanding(Sort-Of-An-Opera) | ECM | 1648/49(537963-2)
Michael Mantler Orchestra
Hide And Seek | ECM | 1738(549612-2)

Hyman,Dick | (org,p,arr,celeste,cymbals,pipe-org)
Cal Tjader's Orchestra
Talkin Verve/Roots Of Acid Jazz:Cal Tjader | Verve | 531562-2
Dick Hyman
Barrel Of Keys | Jazz Connaisseur | JCCD 0140-2
There Will Never Be Another You | Jazz Connaisseur | JCCD 9831-2
Dick Hyman-Louis Mazetier Duo
Barrel Of Keys | Jazz Connaisseur | JCCD 0140-2
Joe Williams With The Frank Hunter Orchestra
Planet Jazz:Joe Williams | Planet Jazz | 2165370-2
Randy Sandke And The New York Allstars
The Re-Discovered Louis And Bix | Nagel-Heyer | CD 058
Randy Sandke-Dick Hyman
The Re-Discovered Louis And Bix | Nagel-Heyer | CD 058
Wes Montgomery With The Jimmy Jones Orchestra
Wes Montgomery-The Complete Riverside Recordings | Riverside | 12 RCD 4408-2

Hyman,Mike | (dr)
Gary Burton Quartet
Real Life Hits | ECM | 1293

Hymas,Tony | (keyboards,pel-p)
John McLaughlin Group
The Promise | Verve | 529828-2

Hytti,Antti | (b)
Piirpauke
Piirpauke-Global Servisi | JA & RO | JARO 4150-2

I Solisti Dell'Orchestra Della Toscana |
Richard Galliano With Orchestra
Passatori | Dreyfus Jazz Line | FDM 36601-2

Iandiorio,Regis | (vconcertmaster)
Earl Klugh Group With Strings
Late Night Guitar | Blue Note | 498573-2

Ibanez,Carlos | (b)
Joaquin Chacón Group
San | Fresh Sound Records | FSNT 015 CD

Ibing,Teddy | (dr)
Axel Zwingenberger With Teddy Ibing
Boogie Woogie Breakdown | Vagabond | VRCD 8.78013

Iborra,Diego | (bongos,congasperc)
Charlie Parker With Strings
Charlie Parker With Strings:The Master Takes | Verve | 523984-2
Charlie Parker With The Neal Hefti Orchestra
Charlie Parker:The Best Of The Verve Years | Verve | 527815-2
Bird: The Complete Charlie Parker On Verve | Verve | 837141-2
Tadd Dameron Tentet
Jazz Profile:Dexter Gordon | Blue Note | 823514-2

Ibsen,John | (b)
Papa Benny's Jazzband
The Golden Years Of Revival Jazz,Vol.7 | Storyville | STCD 5512
The Golden Years Of Revival Jazz,Vol.11 | Storyville | STCD 5516

Ichikawa,Hideo | (el-pp)
Joe Henderson Quartet
Joe Henderson:The Milestone Years | Milestone | 8MCD 4413-2
Joe Henderson In Japan | Original Jazz Classics | OJCCD 1040-2(M 9047)

Ifrim,Christian | (vviola)
Javier Paxarino Group With Glen Velez
Temurá | ACT | 9227-2

Igarashi,Issel | (tp)
Urbanator
Urbanator II | Hip Bop | HIBD 8012

Iglesias,Alberto | (samplestring-arr)
Javier Paxarino Group With Glen Velez
Temurá | ACT | 9227-2

Ignatzek,Klaus | (grand-p,pp-solo)
Klaus Ignatzek
Gershwin Songs | Nabel Records:Jazz Network | CD 4631
Plays Beatles Songs | Nabel Records:Jazz Network | CD 4643
Piano Solo | Nabel Records:Jazz Network | CD 4691
Klaus Ignatzek Group
Live At Leverkusener Jazztage | Nabel Records:Jazz Network | CD 4630
Day For Night | Nabel Records:Jazz Network | CD 4639
Klaus Ignatzek Group Feat.Dave Liebman
The Spell | Nabel Records:Jazz Network | CD 4614
Klaus Ignatzek Quintet
Today Is Tomorrow/Live In Leverkusen | Nabel Records:Jazz Network | CD 4654
Son Of Gaudi | Nabel Records:Jazz Network | CD 4660
Klaus Ignatzek Trio
Airballoon | Nabel Records:Jazz Network | CD 4651
Klaus Ignatzek-Claudio Roditi Quintet
Live at Bird's Eye | Village | VILCD 1023-2

Igoe,Sonny | (dr)
Joe Williams With The Frank Hunter Orchestra
Planet Jazz:Joe Williams | Planet Jazz | 2165370-2

Ikeda,Yoshio | (b)
Johnny Hartman With The Terumasa Hino Quartet
Midnight Blue(The [Be]witching Hour) | Blue Note | 854365-2

Ikkelä,Petri | (accordeon)
Edward Vesala Nordic Gallery
Sound & Fury | ECM | 1541

Ilcken,Wessel | (dr)
Rita Reys With The Lars Gullin Quartet
Lars Gullin 1953,Vol.2:Moden Sounds | Dragon | DRCD 234

Ilett,Denny | (cog)
Lillian Boutté And Her Group
You've Gotta Love Pops:Lillian Bouté Sings Louis Armstrong | ART BY HEART | ABH 2005 2

Ilg,Arnold | (cello)
HR Big Band With Marjorie Barnes And Frits Landesbergen And Strings
Swinging Christmas | hr music.de | hrmj 012-02 CD

Ilg,Cornelia | (v)

Ilg,Dieter | (bmouth-jive)
Adam Makowicz Trio
7.Zelt-Musik-Festival:Jazz Events | Zounds | CD 2730001
Adam Makowicz Trio With The Wilanow Quartet
7.Zelt-Musik-Festival:Jazz Events | Zounds | CD 2730001
Andreas Willers Octet
The Ground Music | Enja | ENJ-9368 2
Bob Brookmeyer Group With The WDR Big Band
Electricity | ACT | 9219-2
Dhafer Youssef Group
Electric Sufi | Enja | ENJ-9412 2
Klaus Ignatzek Group
Live At Leverkusener Jazztage | Nabel Records:Jazz Network | CD 4630
Klaus Ignatzek Group Feat.Dave Liebman
The Spell | Nabel Records:Jazz Network | CD 4614
Los Jovenes Flamencos With The WDR Big Band And Guests
Jazzpana | ACT | 9212-2
Nguyen Le Trio
Million Waves | ACT | 9221-2
Nguyen Le:3 Trios | ACT | 9245-2
Rolf Kühn And Friends
Affairs:Rolf Kühn & Friends | Intuition Records | INT 3211-2
Till Brönner Group
Chattin' With Chet | Verve | 157534-2
Vince Mendoza With The WDR Big Band And Guests
Sketches | ACT | 9215-2

Ilgner,Caroline | (p)
The United Women's Orchestra
The Blue One | Jazz Haus Musik | JHM 0099 CD

Illes,E. | (v)
Stochelo Rosenberg Group With Strings
Gypsy Swing | Verve | 527806-2

Illes,J. | (v)
Toots Thielemans And His Orchestra
Verve Jazz Masters Vol.59:Toots Thielemans | Verve | 535271-2

Illori,Solomon | (percvoc)
Art Blakey And The Afro Drum Ensemble
The African Beat | Blue Note | 522666-2

Imbert,Diego | (b)
Derrick James & Wesley 'G' Quintet
Two Sides To Every Story | Jardis Records | JRCD 20137

Imhorst,Nils | (bel-b)
Bigband Der Musikschule Der Stadt Brühl Mit Gastsolisten
Pangäa | Indigo-Records | 1004 CD
Jazz Orchester Rheinland-Pfalz
Last Season | Jazz Haus Musik | LJBB 9706
Matthias Petzold Working Band
Elements | Indigo-Records | 1005 CD

Imm,Paul | (b)
Laurent De Wilde Sextet
Time Change | Warner | 8573-84315-2
Peter Bolte Quartet
Evocation | Jazz Haus Musik | JHM 0079 CD
Peter Weiss-Paul Imm
Personal Choice | Nabel Records:Jazz Network | CD 4669

Impallomeni,Nino | (tp)
Brocksieper-Jazz-Ensemble
Drums Boogie | Bear Family Records | BCD 15988 AH
Brocksieper-Solisten-Orchester
Globetrotter | Bear Family Records | BCD 15912 AH
Brocksieper-Solisten-Orchester(Brocksi-Quartet)
Drums Boogie | Bear Family Records | BCD 15988 AH
Brocksieper-Special-Ensemble
Globetrotter | Bear Family Records | BCD 15912 AH
Brocksi-Quartett
Globetrotter | Bear Family Records | BCD 15912 AH
Brocksi-Quintett
Drums Boogie | Bear Family Records | BCD 15988 AH

Impallomeni,Nino prob. | (tp)
Brocksi-Quartett
Globetrotter | Bear Family Records | BCD 15912 AH

Inaba,Kunimitsu | (b)
Joe Henderson Quartet
Joe Henderson:The Milestone Years | Milestone | 8MCD 4413-2
Joe Henderson In Japan | Original Jazz Classics | OJCCD 1040-2(M 9047)

Ind,Peter | (b)
Jutta Hipp Trio
Jutta Hipp At The Hickory House Vol.2 | Blue Note | 0677179
Lennie Tristano Trio
Requiem | Atlantic | 7567-80804-2

Inderio,Regis | (stringsv)
A Band Of Friends
Wynton Marsalis Quartet With Strings | CBS | CK 68921

Ingenhag,Harald | (bells,vase-dr,drperc)
Thomas Kessler & Group
Thomas Kessler & Group | Laika Records | LK 190-015
Thomas Kessler Group
On Earth | Laika Records | 8695069
Untitled | Laika Records | LK 92-027
Ulli Bögershausen
Best Of Ulli Bögershausen | Laika Records | LK 93-045

Ingle,Ernest 'Red' | (as)
Frankie Trumbauer And His Orchestra
Jazz:The Essential Collection Vol.2 | IN+OUT Records | 78012-2

Ingraham,Jeanne | (v)
A Band Of Friends
Wynton Marsalis Quartet With Strings | CBS | CK 68921

Ingraham,Paul | (fr-h)
Miles Davis With Gil Evans & His Orchestra
Miles Davis At Carnegie Hall | CBS | CK 65027
Quiet Nights | CBS | CK 65293
Modern Jazz Quartet & Guests
MJQ 40 | Atlantic | 7567-82330-2

Ingram,Adrian | (g)
Royce Campbell-Adrian Ingram Group
Hands Across The Water | String Jazz | SJRCD 1002

Ingram,Billy | (dr)
John Lee Hooker Group
Endless Boogie | MCA | MCD 10413

Ingram,Mattan | (voc)
Marc Ribot Y Los Cubanos Postizos
The Proshetic Cubans | Atlantic | 7567-83116-2

Ingram,Miles | (voc)

Ingram,Philip | (voc)
Bobby Lyle Group
The Journey | Atlantic | 7567-82138-2

Ingram,Roger | (tpfl-h)
Maynard Ferguson And His Big Bop Nouveau Band
Maynard Ferguson '93-Footpath Café | Hot Shot Records | HSR 8312-2

Ingram,Willy Ray | (ts)
Nick Woodland And The Magnets
Big Heart | Blues Beacon | BLU-1013 2

Ingrand,Jean-Marie | (b)
Bernard Peiffer Trio
Jazz In Paris:The Bernard Peiffer Trio Plays Standards | EmArCy | 018425-2
Hubert Fol Quartet
Jazz In Paris:Saxophones À Saint-Germain Des Prés | EmArCy | 014060-2
Jimmy Raney Quartet
Jimmy Raney Visits Paris Vol.2 | Vogue | 21434802
Jimmy Raney Quintet
Jimmy Raney Visits Paris Vol.2 | Vogue | 21434802
Lester Young Quartet
Jazz Gallery:Lester Young Vol.2(1946-59) | RCA | 2119541-2
Stan Getz Quintet
Stan Getz In Europe | Laserlight | 24657
The Herdsmen
Nat Pierce-Dick Collins-Ralph Burns & The Herdsmen Play Paris | Fantasy | FCD 24759-2

Ingrand,Jean-Marie or Benoit Quersin | (b)
Rene Thomas Quartet
Jazz In Paris:René Thomas-The Real Cat | EmArCy | 549400-2 PMS
Rene Thomas Quintet
Jazz In Paris:René Thomas-The Real Cat | EmArCy | 549400-2 PMS

Ingwersen,Kerstin | (engl-hoboe)
Till Brönner Quartet & Deutsches Symphonieorchester Berlin
German Songs | Minor Music | 801057

Innacone,Rick | (el-gg)
Red Sun/SamulNori
Then Comes The White Tiger | ECM | 1499

Innanen,Mikko | (ssas)
European Jazz Youth Orchestra
Swinging Europe 3 | dacapo | DCCD 9461

Insell-Stack,Judith | (viola)
Greg Osby Quartet With String Quartet
Symbols Of Light(A Solution) | Blue Note | 531395-2
Robert Dick Group With The Soldier String Quartet
Jazz Standard On Mars | Enja | ENJ-9327 2
Steve Coleman And The Council Of Balance
Genesis & The Opening Of The Way | RCA | 2152934-2

International Allstars |
International Allstars
The International Allstars Play Benny Goodman:Vol.1 | Nagel-Heyer | CD 025
The Second Sampler | Nagel-Heyer | NHR SP 6
The International Allstars
The International Allstars Play Benny Goodman Vol.1 | Nagel-Heyer | CD 045

International Chicago-Jazz Orchestra |
International Chicago-Jazz Orchestra
That's A Plenty | JHM Records | JHM 3621

International Commission For The Prevention Of Musical Border Control,The |
International Commission For The Prevention Of Musical Border Control,The
The International Commission For The Prevention Of Musical Border Control | VeraBra Records | CDVBR 2093-2

Inzalaco,Tony | (drperc)
Kenny Clarke-Francy Boland Big Band
Three Latin Adventures | MPS | 529095-2
Paul Nero Sound
Doldinger's Best | ACT | 9224-2

Ionescu,Sorin | (v)
HR Big Band With Marjorie Barnes And Frits Landesbergen And Strings
Swinging Christmas | hr music.de | hrmj 012-02 CD

Iovkova,Sonia | (voc)
Sergey Starostin's Vocal Family
Journey | JA & RO | JARO 4226-2

Ipsen,Kjeld | (tb)
Geri Allen And The Jazzpar 1996 Nonet
Some Aspects Of Water | Storyville | STCD 4212
Mona Larsen And The Danish Radio Big Band Plus Soloists
Michael Mantler:Cerco Un Paese Innocente | ECM | 1556

Irakere |
Irakere
Yemayá | Blue Note | 498239-2

Irby,Sherman | (asfl)
James Hurt Group
Dark Grooves-Mystcal Rhythms | Blue Note | 495104-2

Irmer,Alfred | (v)
Bernd Konrad Jazz Group With Symphonie Orchestra
Wen Die Götter Lieben | Creative Works Records | CW CD 1010-1

Irmler,Markus | (tp)
Ralph Schweizer Big Band
DAY Dream | Chaos | CACD 8177

Irvine,Weldon | (el-p,org,tambourinewords)
Lenny White Group
Renderers Of Spirit | Hip Bop | HIBD 8014
Nina Simone Quintet
Planet Jazz:Nina Simone | Planet Jazz | 2165372-2
Richard 'Groove' Holmes Orchestra
Comin' On Home | Blue Note | 538701-2
Richard 'Groove' Holmes Sextet
Blue Break Beats | Blue Note | 799106-2

Irving III,Robert | (keyboards,org,synth,p,el-p,voc)
Chris Murrell-Bobby Irving III
Christmas Jazz! | Nagel-Heyer | NH 1008
Christopher Murrell-Robert Irving III
Full Circle:Gospels And Spirituals | Nagel-Heyer | NHR SP 3
Miles Davis Group
Miles Davis Live From His Last Concert In Avignon | Laserlight | 24327
The Man With The Horn | CBS | 468701-2
Decoy | CBS | 468702-2
This Is Jazz:Miles Davis Plays Ballads | CBS | CK 65038

Irving,Nat | (computer-sequencing)
Ed Schuller & The Eleventh Hour Band
Snake Dancing | Tutu Records | 888188-2*

Irvis,Charlie | (tbspeech)

Clarence Williams' Blue Five
Jazz:The Essential Collection Vol.1 | IN+OUT Records | 78011-2
Jelly Roll Morton And His Orchestra
Planet Jazz:Jelly Roll Morton | Planet Jazz | 2152060-2

Irwin,Cecil | (cl,tsarr)
Earl Hines And His Orchestra
Jazz:The Essential Collection Vol.2 | IN+OUT Records | 78012-2

Irwin,Dennis | (b)
Art Blakey And The Jazz Messengers
Night In Tunisia | Philips | 800064-2
Ed Neumeister Quartet
Ed Neumeister Quartet/Quintet | Timescrapper | TSCR 9614
Ed Neumeister Quintet
Ed Neumeister Quartet/Quintet | Timescrapper | TSCR 9614
Harry Allen Quartet
Jazz Im Amerika Haus,Vol.1 | Nagel-Heyer | CD 011
Blues Of Summer | Nagel-Heyer | NH 1011
Love Songs Live! | Nagel-Heyer | NH 1014
The First Sampler | Nagel-Heyer | NHR SP 5
Joe Lovano Nonet
On This Day At The Vanguard | Blue Note | 590950-2
John Scofield Groups
Groove Elation | Blue Note | 832801-2
John Scofield Quartet
What We Do | Blue Note | 799586-2
John Scofield Sextet
Hand Jive | Blue Note | 827327-2
Marty Elkins And Her Sextet
Fuse Blues | Nagel-Heyer | CD 062
Rich Perry Quartet
Hearsay | Steeplechase | SCCD 31515
Ted Brown Quartet
Preservation | Steeplechase | SCCD 31539

Isaac Tagul Group,The | (percvoc)
Pili-Pili
Pili-Pili | JA & RO | JARO 4141-2

Isaacs,Ike | (bg)
Ray Bryant Trio
Ray Bryant Trio | Original Jazz Classics | OJCCD 793-2(P 7098)
Stephane Grappelli Quartet
Verve Jazz Masters 11:Stéphane Grappelli | Verve | 516758-2
Stephane Grappelli With The Diz Disley Trio
Grapelli Story | Verve | 515807-2
Stephane Grappelli-Ike Isaacs
Grapelli Story | Verve | 515807-2

Isaacs,Mark | (p)
Mark Isaacs/Dave Holland/Roy Haynes
Encounters | VeraBra Records | CDVBR 2076-2

Isenmann,Luc | (dr)
European Jazz Youth Orchestra
Swinging Europe 1 | dacapo | DCCD 9449
Swinging Europe 2 | dacapo | DCCD 9450

Isham,Mark | (fl-h,synth,tp,co,ss,p)
Art Lande Quartet
Rubisa Patrol | ECM | 1081
Dave Liebman Quintet
Jazz Portraits | EGO | 95080
David Torn Quartet
Cloud About Mercury | ECM | 1322(831108-2)
Mark Isham-Art Lande
We Begin | ECM | 1338

Isles,Nabate | (tp)
Steve Coleman And The Council Of Balance
Genesis & The Opening Of The Way | RCA | 2152934-2

Ismail,Shaker | (rababa)
Koch-Schütz-Studer & El Nil Troop
Heavy Cairo Trafic | Intuition Records | INT 3175-2

Ismailov,Enver | (el-g)
Enver Ismailov
Colours Of A Ferghana Bazar-Live At The International Jazzfestival Münster | Tutu Records | 888142-2*
Enver Ismailov & Geoff Warren
Art Of The Duo:Dancing Over The Moon | Tutu Records | 888168-2*

Isola,Frank | (dr)
Gerry Mulligan Quartet
Gerry Mulligan:Pleyel Concert Vol.1 | Vogue | 21409422
Gerry Mulligan:Pleyel Concert Vol.2 | Vogue | 21409432
Planet Jazz:Gerry Mulligan | Planet Jazz | 2152070-2
Planet Jazz Sampler | Planet Jazz | 2152326-2
Planet Jazz:Jazz Saxophone | Planet Jazz | 2169653-2
Jimmy Raney Quintet
Early Stan | Original Jazz Classics | OJCCD 654-2(P 7255)
Mose Allison Trio
Back Country Suite | Original Jazz Classics | OJC 075(P 7091)
Mose Allison:Greatest Hits | Original Jazz Classics | OJCCD 6004-2
Mose Allison Sings The 7th Son | Prestige | PR20 7279-2
Stan Getz Quintet
Stan Getz Highlights:The Best Of The Verve Years Vol.2 | Verve | 517330-2
Verve Jazz Masters 8:Stan Getz | Verve | 519823-2
A Life In Jazz:A Musical Biography | Verve | 535119-2
Stan Getz And The 'Cool' Sounds | Verve | 547317-2
Ultimate Stan Getz selected by Joe Henderson | Verve | 557532-2
Stan Getz Plays | Verve | 833535-2
Stan Getz Highlights | Verve | 847430-2
Stan Getz-The Complete Roost Sessions | EMI Records | 859622-2

Israel,Theodore | (viola)
Earl Klugh Group With Strings
Late Night Guitar | Blue Note | 498573-2
Grover Washington Jr. Orchestra
Inside Moves | Elektra | 7559-60318-2

Israel,Yoron | (cymbals,snar-dr,drperc)
Ahmad Jamal Septet
Live In Paris 1996 | Dreyfus Jazz Line | FDM 37020-2
Attila Zoller Quartet
When It's Time | Enja | ENJ-9031 2
Attila Zoller Quintet
When It's Time | Enja | ENJ-9031 2
Freddie Cole
Jazzin' Vol.2: The Music Of Stevie Wonder | Fantasy | FANCD 6088-2
Freddy Cole With Band
To The End Of The Earth | Fantasy | FCD 9675-2
Le Grand Freddy:Freddy Cole Sings The Music Of Michel Legrand | Fantasy | FCD 9683-2

Israels,Charles | (b)
Nina Simone And Orchestra
Baltimore | Epic | 476906-2

Israels,Chuck | (arr,compb)
Bill Evans Trio
Verve Jazz Masters 5:Bill Evans | Verve | 519821-2
The Complete Bill Evans On Verve | Verve | 527953-2
The Best Of Bill Evans Live | Verve | 533825-2
Ultimate Bill Evans selected by Herbie Hancock | Verve | 557536-2
Bill Evans At Town Hall | Verve | 831271-2
At Shelly's Manne-Hole | Original Jazz Classics | OJC20 263-2(RLP 9487)
Moonbeams | Original Jazz Classics | OJC20 434-2(RLP 9428)
How My Heart Sings! | Original Jazz Classics | OJCCD 369-2
The Jazz Giants Play Rodgers & Hammerstein:My Favorite Things | Prestige | PCD 24223-2
Bill Evans Trio With The Claus Ogerman Orchestra
The Complete Bill Evans On Verve | Verve | 527953-2
Bill Evans Trio With Symphony Orchestra | Verve | 821983-2
Cecil Taylor Quintet
Trane's Blues | Blue Note | 498240-2
Eric Dolphy Duo
Eric Dolphy in Europe, Vol.1 | Original Jazz Classics | OJC 413(P 7304)
Eric Dolphy-Chuck Israels
Eric Dolphy:The Complete Prestige Recordings | Prestige | 9 PRCD-4418-2
Herbie Hancock Quintet
Herbie Hancock:The Complete Blue Note Sixties Sessions | Blue Note | 495569-2
Herbie Hancock Septet
Herbie Hancock:The Complete Blue Note Sixties Sessions | Blue Note | 495569-2
My Point Of View | Blue Note | 521226-2
Cantaloupe Island | Blue Note | 829331-2
Herbie Hancock Sextet
Herbie Hancock:The Complete Blue Note Sixties Sessions | Blue Note | 495569-2
Herbie Mann With The Bill Evans Trio
Nirvana | Atlantic | 7567-90141-2
J.J.Johnson's All Stars
J.J.'s Broadway | Verve | 9860308
Monica Zetterlund With The Bill Evans Trio
The Complete Bill Evans On Verve | Verve | 527953-2
Stan Getz New Quartet
A Life In Jazz:A Musical Biography | Verve | 535119-2
The New Stan Getz Quartet
Getz Au Go Go | Verve | 821725-2
The New Stan Getz Quartet Feat. Astrud Gilberto
Getz Au Go Go | Verve | 821725-2
The New Stan Getz Quintet Feat. Astrud Gilberto
Getz Au Go Go | Verve | 821725-2

Issenhuth,Dale | (bs)
Pete Rugolo And His Orchestra
Thriller/Richard Diamon(Original Jazz Scores From 2 Classics TV Series) | Fresh Sound Records | FSCD 2015

Isso,Yukihiro | (nohkan)
Toshinori Kondo & Ima plus Guests
Human Market | JA & RO | JARO 4146-2

Italian Instabile Orchestra |
Italian Instabile Orchestra
Skies Of Europe | ECM | 1543

Itchy Fingers |
Itchy Fingers
7.Zelt-Musik-Festival:Jazz Events | Zounds | CD 2730001
Live | Enja | ENJ-6076 2
Full English Breakfast | Enja | ENJ-7085 2

Itkonen,Timo | (voc)
Piirpauke
The Wild East | JA & RO | JARO 4128-2

Itt,Frank | (el-b)
Pili-Pili
Boogaloo | JA & RO | JARO 4174-2
Dance Jazz Live 1995 | JA & RO | JARO 4189-2

Ivan,Mancinello | (perc)
Banda Città Ruvo Di Puglia
La Banda/Banda And Jazz | Enja | ENJ-9326 2

Iverson,Ethan | (pdr)
Ethan Iverson Trio
Contruction Zone(Originals) | Fresh Sound Records | FSNT 046 CD
Deconstruction Zone(Originals) | Fresh Sound Records | FSNT 047 CD
The Minor Passions | Fresh Sound Records | FSNT 064 CD
Phil Grenadier Quintet
Sweet Transients | Fresh Sound Records | FSNT 093 CD
Reid Anderson Quartet
Dirty Show Tunes | Fresh Sound Records | FSNT 030 CD
Abolish Bad Architecture | Fresh Sound Records | FSNT 062 CD
The Bad Plus
These Are The Vistas | CBS | 510666-2
The Bad Plus | Fresh Sound Records | FSNT 107 CD

Iverson,Russ | (tp)
Buddy Rich Big Band
The New One! | Pacific Jazz | 494507-2

Ivory,Jackie | (org)
Willis Jackson Sextet
At Large | Prestige | PCD 24243-2

Iyer,Vijay | (keyboardsp)
Steve Coleman And Five Elements
The Sonic Language Of Myth | RCA | 2164123-2
Steve Coleman And The Council Of Balance
Genesis & The Opening Of The Way | RCA | 2152934-2

Izenhall,Aaron | (tp)
Ella Fitzgerald With Louis Jordan And His Tympany Five
Ella Fitzgerald:Mr.Paganini | Dreyfus Jazz Line | FDM 36741-2
Louis Armstrong With Louis Jordan And His Tympany Five
Louis Armstrong:C'est Si Bon | Dreyfus Jazz Line | FDM 36730-2
Louis Jordan And His Tympany Five
Louis Jordan-Let The Good Times Roll: The Complete Decca Recordings 1938-1954 | Bear Family Records | BCD 15557 IH

Izenzon,David | (b)
Archie Shepp Trio
Fire Music | Impulse(MCA) | 951158-2
Jaki Byard Trio
Sunshine Of My Soul | Original Jazz Classics | OJCCD 1946-2(PR 7550)
Ornette Coleman Trio
At The Golden Circle Vol.One | Blue Note | 535518-2
Sonny Rollins Sextet
The Standard Sonny Rollins | RCA | 2174801-2

J.C.White Singers |
Max Roach Sextet With The J.C.White Singers
Lift Every Voice And Sing | Atlantic | 7567-80798-2

Jaboulay,Christine | (viola)
Stephane Grappelli With The Michel Legrand Orchestra
Grapelli Story | Verve | 515807-2

Jaboulay,Laurence | (viola)

Jacintha | (voc)
Jacintha With Band And Strings
Lush Life | Groove Note | GRV 1011-2(Gold CD 2011)

Jackel,Conny | (fl-htp)
Charly Antolini Orchestra
Drum Beat | MPS | 9808191
Dieter Reith Group
Reith On! | MPS | 557423-2
Helmut Brandt Combo
Deutsches Jazz Fesival 1954/1955 | Bear Family Records | BCD 15430

Jackson Jr.,Fred | (reeds)
Herbie Hancock Group
Sunlight | CBS | 486570-2

Jackson Jr.,Paul | (el-gg)
The Quincy Jones-Sammy Nestico Orchestra
Basie & Beyond | Warner | 9362-47792-2

Jackson,Alan | (dr)
Howard Riley Trio
The Day Will Come | CBS | 494434-2
John Surman Orchestra
How Many Clouds Can You See? | Deram | 844882-2

Jackson,Ali 'Muhammed' | (dr)
Dee Dee Bridgewater With Her Trio
Live At Yoshi's | Verve | 543354-2
Jacky Terrasson-Emmanuel Pahud Quartet
Into The Blue | Blue Note | 557257-2

Jackson,Alvin 'Al' | (bel-b)
Milt Jackson Quintet
Milt Jackson Birthday Celebration | Fantasy | FANCD 6079-2
Yusef Lateef Sextet
The Art Of Saxophone | Laserlight | 24652

Jackson,Anthony | (b,b-g,contra-b-g,el-b,el-contra-b-g)
Al Di Meola Group
Elegant Gypsy | CBS | 468213-2
Land Of The Midnight Sun | CBS | 468214-2
Casino | CBS | 468215-2
Jazzrock-Anthology Vol.3:Fusion | Zounds | CD 27100555
Bireli Lagrene Quartet
My Favorite Django | Dreyfus Jazz Line | FDM 36574-2
Chick Corea Quartet
Verve Jazz Masters 3:Chick Corea | Verve | 519820-2
Dave Weckl Group
Master Plan | GRP | GRP 96192
Hard-Wired | GRP | GRP 97602
Grover Washington Jr. Orchestra
Inside Moves | Elektra | 7559-60318-2
Hal Di Meola Group
Casino | CBS | 468215-2
Lee Ritenour Group
Festival | GRP | GRP 95702
Michel Petrucciani Group
Michel Petrucciani:The Blue Note Years | Blue Note | 789916-2
Music | Blue Note | 792563-2
Playground | Blue Note | 795480-2
Michel Petrucciani Sextet
Both Worlds | Dreyfus Jazz Line | FDM 36590-2
Michel Petrucciani Trio
Trio In Tokyo | Dreyfus Jazz Line | FDM 36605-2
Mike Stern Group
Odds Or Evens | Atlantic | 7567-82297-2
Wayne Krantz Quartet
Signals | Enja | ENJ-6048 2

Jackson,Benny | (bj,vocg)
Chocolate Dandies
Jazz:The Essential Collection Vol.3 | IN+OUT Records | 78013-2

Jackson,Charles 'Chip' | (bel-b)
David Matthews & The Manhattan Jazz Orchestra
Back To Bach | Milestone | MCD 9312-2
Hey Duke! | Milestone | MCD 9320-2
Elvin Jones Jazz Machine
In Europe | Enja | ENJ-7009 2
Ian Shaw With Band
Soho Stories | Milestone | MCD 9316-2
Woody Herman And His Orchestra
Woody Herman Herd At Montreux | Original Jazz Classics | OJCCD 991-2(F 9470)
Woody Herman And The New Thundering Herd
Woody Herman:Thundering Herd | Original Jazz Classics | OJCCD 841-2
Woody Herman's Thundering Herd
Planet Jazz:Jazz Saxophone | Planet Jazz | 2169653-2

Jackson,Charlie | (bass-s,tuba,bj,vocg)
King Oliver's Jazz Band
Jazz:The Essential Collection Vol.1 | IN+OUT Records | 78011-2

Jackson,Chubby | (b,ld,talkingvoc)
Chubby Jackson And His All Star Big Band
Chubby Takes Over | Fresh Sound Records | FSR-CD 324
Chubby Jackson Big Band
Gerry Mulligan Quartet feat.Chet Baker | Original Jazz Classics | OJCCD 711-2(F 8082/P 7641)
Esquire All-American Award Winners
Planet Jazz:Jazz Trumpet | Planet Jazz | 2169654-2
Best Of The Complete RCA Victor Recordings | RCA | 2663636-2
Highlights From The Duke Ellington Centennial Edition | RCA | 2663672-2
JATP All Stars
The Complete Jazz At The Philharmonic On Verve 1944-1949 | Verve | 523893-2
Leonard Feather's Esquire All-Americans
Louis Armstrong:C'est Si Bon | Dreyfus Jazz Line | FDM 36730-2
Woody Herman And His Orchestra
The Legends Of Swing | Laserlight | 24659
Woody Herman:Four Brother | Dreyfus Jazz Line | FDM 36722-2
Louis Armstrong-Jack Teagarden-Woody Herman:Midnights At V-Disc | Jazz Unlimited | JUCD 2048
Old Gold Rehearsals 1944 | Jazz Unlimited | JUCD 2079
Woody Herman And His Woodshoppers
Woody Herman (And The Herd) At Carnegie Hall | Verve | 559833-2
Woody Herman And The Herd
Woody Herman (And The Herd) At Carnegie Hall | Verve | 559833-2
Woody Herman And The New Thundering Herd
Planet Jazz:Big Bands | Planet Jazz | 2169649-2
Woody Herman And The Vanderbilt All Stars
Louis Armstrong-Jack Teagarden-Woody Herman:Midnights At V-Disc | Jazz Unlimited | JUCD 2048

Jackson,Cliff | (p,p-solosax)
Alberta Hunter With Buster Bailey's Blues Blasters
Songs We Taught Your Mother | Original Blues Classics | OBCCD 520-2
Bunk Johnson-Sidney Bechet Sextet
Jazz:The Essential Collection Vol.1 | IN+OUT Records | 78011-2
Cliff Jackson's Washboard Wanderers
Uptown And Lowdown | Prestige | PCD 24262-2
New Orleans Feetwarmers
Jazz:The Essential Collection Vol.1 | IN+OUT Records | 78011-2
Sidney Bechet And His New Orleans Feetwarmers
Sidney Bechet:Summertime | Dreyfus Jazz Line | FDM 36712-2
Tommy Ladnier And His Orchestra
Planet Jazz | Planet Jazz | 2169652-2
Jazz:The Essential Collection Vol.1 | IN+OUT Records | 78011-2
Victoria Spivey With Buster Bailey's Blues Blasters
Songs We Taught Your Mother | Original Blues Classics | OBCCD 520-2

Jackson,Darryl 'Munyungo' | (perc)
Terri Lyne Carrington Group
Jazz Is A Spirit | ACT | 9408-2

Jackson,Duffy | (dr,DX7-g-pach,voc,p,orgb)
Harry Allen Quartet
Jazz Im Amerika Haus,Vol.1 | Nagel-Heyer | CD 011
Blues Of Summer | Nagel-Heyer | NH 1011
Love Songs Live! | Nagel-Heyer | NH 1014
The First Sampler | Nagel-Heyer | NHR SP 5

Jackson,Florence | (voc)
Max Roach Chorus & Orchestra
To The Max! | Enja | ENJ-7021 22

Jackson,Franz | (cl,voc,tsarr)
Earl Hines And His Orchestra
Planet Jazz:Earl Hines | Planet Jazz | 2159973-2

Jackson,Fred | (as,ts,fl,piccolo,saxcowbell)
Baby Face Willette Quartet
So Blue So Funky-Heroes Of The Hammond | Blue Note | 796563-2
Big John Patton Quintet
So Blue So Funky-Heroes Of The Hammond | Blue Note | 796563-2
Bobby Hutcherson Orchestra
Montara | Blue Note | 590956-2
Diane Schuur And Her Band
The Best Of Diane Schuur | GRP | GRP 98882
Fred Jackson Quartet
So Blue So Funky-Heroes Of The Hammond | Blue Note | 796563-2
Horace Silver Quintet With Brass
Horace Silver Retrospective | Blue Note | 495576-2
John Patton Quintet
Along Came John | Blue Note | 0675614
Along Came John | Blue Note | 831915-2

Jackson,G. | (viola)
Dee Dee Bridgewater With Orchestra
Dear Ella | Verve | 539102-2

Jackson,Gene | (drperc)
Antonio Farao Quartet
Next Stories | Enja | ENJ-9430 2
Antonio Farao Trio
Next Stories | Enja | ENJ-9430 2
Chico Freeman And Brainstorm
Threshold | IN+OUT Records | 7022-2
Christoph Lauer Quintet

Fragile Network | ACT | 9266-2
Dave Holland Qartet
Dream Of The Elders | ECM | 1572(529084-2)
Michele Rosewoman And Quintessence
Guardians Of The Light | Enja | ENJ-9378 2
Michele Rosewoman Quintet
Harvest | Enja | ENJ-7069 2
Michele Rosewoman Sextet
Harvest | Enja | ENJ-7069 2

Jackson,Gordon | (tb)
Rosemary Clooney With The Duke Ellington Orchestra
Blue Rose | CBS | CK 65506

Jackson,Harold | (b)
Wilbur DeParis And His New New Orleans Band
Atlantic Jazz: New Orleans | Atlantic | 7567-81700-2

Jackson,Harry | (tp)
Earl Hines And His Orchestra
Planet Jazz:Earl Hines | Planet Jazz | 2159973-2

Jackson,James | (african-dr,bassoon,african-perc)
Sun Ra And His Intergalactic Research Arkestra
Black Myth/Out In Space | MPS | 557656-2

Jackson,James 'Ham' | (el-g)
Louis Jordan And His Tympany Five
Louis Jordan-Let The Good Times Roll: The Complete Decca Recordings 1938-1954 | Bear Family Records | BCD 15557 IH

Jackson,Javon | (ts)
Art Blakey And The Jazz Messengers
The Art Of Jazz | IN+OUT Records | 77028-2
Donald Harrison Sextet
Kind Of New | Candid | CCD 79768
Elvin Jones Jazz Machine
Going Home | Enja | ENJ-7095 2
Elvin Jones Quintet
Youngblood | Enja | ENJ-7051 2
Essence All Stars
Hot Jazz Bisquits | Hip Bop | HIBD 8801
Freddie Cole
Jazzin' Vol.2: The Music Of Stevie Wonder | Fantasy | FANCD 6088-2
Freddy Cole With Band
To The End Of The Earth | Fantasy | FCD 9675-2
Lenny White Group
Renderers Of Spirit | Hip Bop | HIBD 8014
Tim Hagans-Marcus Printup Septet
Hub Songs | Blue Note | 859509-2
Tom Browne Quintet
Another Shade Of Browne | Hip Bop | HIBD 8011
Hot Jazz Bisquits | Hip Bop | HIBD 8801

Jackson,Jay | (dr,percvoc)
J.C. Dook Quartet
Travelin' Man | Organic Music | ORGM 9734

Jackson,Jimmy | (org,pts)
Klaus Doldinger Jubilee
Doldinger's Best | ACT | 9224-2
Passport
Uranus | Atlantic | 2292-44142-2

Jackson,Josh | (ts)
Ella Fitzgerald With Louis Jordan And His Tympany Five
Ella Fitzgerald:Mr.Paganini | Dreyfus Jazz Line | FDM 36741-2
Louis Armstrong With Louis Jordan And His Tympany Five
Louis Armstrong:C'est Si Bon | Dreyfus Jazz Line | FDM 36730-2
Louis Jordan And His Tympany Five
Louis Jordan-Let The Good Times Roll: The Complete Decca Recordings 1938-1954 | Bear Family Records | BCD 15557 IH

Jackson,Karen | (voc)
Max Roach Chorus & Orchestra
To The Max! | Enja | ENJ-7021 22

Jackson,Lawrence | (tp)
Elmo Hope Ensemble
Sounds From Rikers Island | Fresh Sound Records | FSR CD 338

Jackson,Laymon | (btuba)
Donald Byrd Quintet
Blue N' Groovy | Blue Note | 780679-2
Lou Donaldson Quintet
Blue Note Plays Gershwin | Blue Note | 520808-2
Nat Adderley Quintet
Much Brass | Original Jazz Classics | OJCCD 848-2(R 1143)
Nat Adderley Sextet
Much Brass | Original Jazz Classics | OJCCD 848-2(R 1143)

Jackson,Leroy | (b)
Jubilee All Stars
Jazz Gallery:Lester Young Vol.2(1946-59) | RCA | 2119541-2

Jackson,Mahalia | (voc)
Duke Ellington And His Orchestra
Black Brown And Beige | CBS | CK 65566
Mahalia Jackson With Choir And Orchestra
Stille Nacht | CBS | COLCD 62130

Jackson,Melvin | (btp)
Eddie Harris Group
The Best Of Eddie Harris | Atlantic | 7567-81370-2
Eddie Harris Quartet
The Best Of Eddie Harris | Atlantic | 7567-81370-2
John Klemmer Quartet
Involvement | Chess | 076139-2

Jackson,Michael Gregory | (el-g,g,perc,bamboo-fl,el-mand,voc)
Michael Gregory
The Way We Used To Do | TipToe | TIP-888806 2

Jackson,Milt | (marimba,p,org,voc,vib,g,vib.ld)
Al Sears And His Orchestra
Sear-iously | Bear Family Records | BCD 15668 AH
Barney Wilen Quartet
Jazz In Paris:Barney Wilen-Jazz Sur Saine | EmArCy | 548317-2 PMS
Barney Wilen Quintet
Jazz In Paris:Barney Wilen-Jazz Sur Saine | EmArCy | 548317-2 PMS
Benny Carter Sextet
To Bags...With Love:Memorial Album | Pablo | 2310967-2
Milt Jackson Birthday Celebration | Fantasy | FANCD 6079-2
Cannonball Adderley-Milt Jackson Quintet
To Bags...With Love:Memorial Album | Pablo | 2310967-2
Milt Jackson Birthday Celebration | Fantasy | FANCD 6079-2
Cannonball Adderley Birthday Celebration | Fantasy | FANCD 6087-2
Things Are Getting Better | Original Jazz Classics | OJC20 032-2
Coleman Hawkins All Star Octet
Milt Jackson Birthday Celebration | Fantasy | FANCD 6079-2
Count Basie Jam Session
Count Basie Jam Session At The Montreux Jazz Festival 1975 | Original Jazz Classics | OJC20 933-2(2310750)
Count Basie Kansas City 5
Milt Jackson Birthday Celebration | Fantasy | FANCD 6079-2
Count Basie Sextet
Jazz At The Philharmonic:The Montreux Collection | Pablo | PACD 5306-2
Dee Dee Bridgewater With Her Septet
Dear Ella | Verve | 539102-2
Dizzy Gillespie All Stars
Milt Jackson Birthday Celebration | Fantasy | FANCD 6079-2
Jazz At The Philharmonic:The Montreux Collection | Pablo | PACD 5306-2
Dizzy Gillespie And His Orchestra
Planet Jazz:Dizzy Gillespie | Planet Jazz | 2152069-2
Planet Jazz Sampler | Planet Jazz | 2152326-2
Planet Jazz:Jazz Greatest Hits | Planet Jazz | 2169648-2
Planet Jazz:Bebop | RCA | 2169650-2
Dizzy Gillespie:Night In Tunisia | Dreyfus Jazz Line | FDM 36734-2
Dizzy Gillespie Big 7
Dizzy-At The Montreux Jazz Festival 1975 | Original Jazz Classics | OJC20 739-2(2310749)
Dizzy Gillespie Jam
Montreux '77 | Original Jazz Classics | OJC 385(2620105)
Montreux '77 | Original Jazz Classics | OJC20 381-2(2308211)
Dizzy Gillespie Sextet
Dizzy Gillespie:Night In Tunisia | Dreyfus Jazz Line | FDM 36734-2
The Jazz Giants Play Harold Arlen:Blues In The Night | Prestige | PCD 24201-2
John Coltrane-Milt Jackson Quintet
John Coltrane-The Heavyweight Champion:The Complete Atlantic Recordings | Atlantic | 8122-71984-2
Bags & Trane | Rhino | 8122-73685-2
Miles Davis All Stars
Milt Jackson Birthday Celebration | Fantasy | FANCD 6079-2
Bags' Groove | Original Jazz Classics | OJC20 245-2
Miles Davis And The Modern Jazz Giants | Original Jazz Classics | OJC20 347-2(P 7150)
Miles Davis And The Modern Jazz Giants
Thelonious Monk:85th Birthday Celebration | zyx records | FANCD 6076-2
Miles Davis Quintet
To Bags...With Love:Memorial Album | Pablo | 2310967-2
Thelonious Monk:The Complete Prestige Recordings | Prestige | 3 PRCD 4428-2
Miles Davis-Milt Jackson Quintet
Milt Jackson Birthday Celebration | Fantasy | FANCD 6079-2
Miles Davis And Milt Jackson | Original Jazz Classics | OJC20 012-2(P 7034)
Miles Davis-Milt Jackson Sextet
Miles Davis And Milt Jackson | Original Jazz Classics | OJC20 012-2(P 7034)
Milt Jackson
Milt Jackson Birthday Celebration | Fantasy | FANCD 6079-2
Milt Jackson And His Colleagues
Bag's Bag | Original Jazz Classics | OJCCD 935-2(2310842)
Milt Jackson And His Orchestra
Reverence And Compassion | Reprise | 9362-45204-2
Sunflower | CTI | ZK 65131
Milt Jackson Big 4
Milt Jackson At The Montreux Jazz Festival 1975 | Original Jazz Classics | OJC20 884-2(2310753)
Milt Jackson Orchestra
To Bags...With Love:Memorial Album | Pablo | 2310967-2
Milt Jackson Birthday Celebration | Fantasy | FANCD 6079-2
Sarah Vaughan Birthday Celebration | Fantasy | FANCD 6090-2
Big Bags | Original Jazz Classics | OJCCD 366-2(RLP 9429)
Milt Jackson Quartet
In A New Setting | Verve | 538620-2
Milt Jackson Birthday Celebration | Fantasy | FANCD 6079-2
Milt Jackson | Original Jazz Classics | OJC20 001-2(P 7003)
Soul Route | Original Jazz Classics | OJCCD 1059-2(2310900)
Ain't But A Few Of Us Left | Original Jazz Classics | OJCCD 785-2(2310873)
Jazz At The Philharmonic:The Montreux Collection | Pablo | PACD 5306-2
The Jazz Giants Play Harold Arlen:Blues In The Night | Prestige | PCD 24201-2
The Jazz Giants Play Rodgers & Hart:Blue Moon | Prestige | PCD 24205-2
The Jazz Giants Play Sammy Cahn:It's Magic | Prestige | PCD 24226-2
Milt Jackson Quintet
Milt Jackson At The Kosei Nenkin | Pablo | 2620103-2
Wizard Of The Vibes | Blue Note | 532140-2
In A New Setting | Verve | 538620-2
Milt Jackson Birthday Celebration | Fantasy | FANCD 6079-2
MJQ | Original Jazz Classics | OJCCD 125-2
At The Village Gate | Original Jazz Classics | OJCCD 309-2
Milt Jackson Septet
Milt Jackson Birthday Celebration | Fantasy | FANCD 6079-2
The Birdlanders Vol.1 | Original Jazz Classics | OJCCD 1930-2
Milt Jackson Sextet
Milt Jackson Birthday Celebration | Fantasy | FANCD 6079-2
The Birdlanders Vol.1 | Original Jazz Classics | OJCCD 1930-2
Milt Jackson Trio
Milt Jackson Birthday Celebration | Fantasy | FANCD 6079-2
Milt Jackson With Strings
To Bags...With Love:Memorial Album | Pablo | 2310967-2
Milt Jackson With The Count Basie Orchestra
To Bags...With Love:Memorial Album | Pablo | 2310967-2
Milt Jackson Birthday Celebration | Fantasy | FANCD 6079-2
Milt Jackson + Count Basie + Big Band Vol.1 | Original Jazz Classics | OJCCD 740-2(2310822)
Milt Jackson + Count Basie + Big Band Vol.2 | Original Jazz Classics | OJCCD 741-2(2310823)
Milt Jackson With The Monty Alexander Trio
To Bags...With Love:Memorial Album | Pablo | 2310967-2
Soul Fusion | Original Jazz Classics | OJCCD 731-2(2310804)
Milt Jackson With The Oscar Peterson Trio
Gitanes Jazz 'Round Midnight: Oscar Peterson | Verve | 511036-2 PMS
Milt Jackson-Oscar Peterson
Milt Jackson Birthday Celebration | Fantasy | FANCD 6079-2
Milt Jackson-Ray Brown Jam
Milt Jackson Birthday Celebration | Fantasy | FANCD 6079-2
Montreux '77 | Original Jazz Classics | OJC 385(2620105)
Montreux '77 | Original Jazz Classics | OJC20 375-2(2308205)
Milt Jackson-Ray Brown Quartet
It Don't Mean A Thing If You Can't Tap Your Foot To It | Original Jazz Classics | OJCCD 601-2
Milt Jackson-Wes Montgomery Quintet
Wes Montgomery-The Complete Riverside Recordings | Riverside | 12 RCD 4408-2
To Bags...With Love:Memorial Album | Pablo | 2310967-2
Milt Jackson Birthday Celebration | Fantasy | FANCD 6079-2
Bags Meets Wes! | Original Jazz Classics | OJC20 234-2(RLP 9407)
Modern Jazz Quartet
To Bags...With Love:Memorial Album | Pablo | 2310967-2
The Complete Modern Jazz Quartet Prestige & Pablo Recordings | Prestige | 4PRCD 4438-2
The Modern Jazz Quartet At Music Inn With Sonny Rollins,Vol.2 | Atlantic | 7567-80794-2
Blues On Bach | Atlantic | 7567-81393-2
MJQ 40 | Atlantic | 7567-82330-2
Lonely Woman | Atlantic | 7567-90665-2
Rhino Presents The Atlantic Jazz Gallery | Atlantic | 8122-71257-2
Pyramid | Rhino | 812273679-2
Fontessa | Rhino | 8122-73687-2
Milt Jackson Birthday Celebration | Fantasy | FANCD 6079-2
Concorde | Original Jazz Classics | OJC20 002-2
Django | Original Jazz Classics | OJC20 057-2
Topsy-This One's For Basie | Original Jazz Classics | OJCCD 1073-2(2310917)
MJQ | Original Jazz Classics | OJCCD 125-2
Together Again | Pablo | PACD20 244-2(2308244)
The Jazz Giants Play Cole Porter:Night And Day | Prestige | PCD 24203-2
Modern Jazz Quartet & Guests
MJQ 40 | Atlantic | 7567-82330-2
Modern Jazz Quartet And Laurindo Almeida
MJQ 40 | Atlantic | 7567-82330-2
Modern Jazz Quartet And Orchestra
MJQ 40 | Atlantic | 7567-82330-2
Modern Jazz Quartet And Symphony Orchestra
MJQ 40 | Atlantic | 7567-82330-2
Modern Jazz Quartet And The Swingle Singers
MJQ 40 | Atlantic | 7567-82330-2
Modern Jazz Quartet feat.Jimmy Giuffre
MJQ 40 | Atlantic | 7567-82330-2
Modern Jazz Quartet With Sonny Rollins
The Modern Jazz Quartet At Music Inn With Sonny Rollins,Vol.2 | Atlantic | 7567-80794-2
MJQ 40 | Atlantic | 7567-82330-2
Oscar Peterson All Stars
Jazz At The Philharmonic:The Montreux Collection | Pablo | PACD 5306-2
Oscar Peterson Trio With Milt Jackson
Very Tall | Verve | 559830-2
Very Tall | Verve | 827821-2
Oscar Peterson-Milt Jackson Duo
To Bags...With Love:Memorial Album | Pablo | 2310967-2
Two Of The Few | Original Jazz Classics | OJCCD 689-2(2310881)
Oscar Peterson-Milt Jackson Quartet
Swinging Cooperations:Reunion Blues/Great Connection | MPS | 539085-2
Pablo All Star Jam
Montreux '77 | Original Jazz Classics | OJC 385(2620105)
Paul Desmond And The Modern Jazz Quartet
MJQ 40 | Atlantic | 7567-82330-2
Quadrant
Milt Jackson Birthday Celebration | Fantasy | FANCD 6079-2
Quincy Jones And His Orchestra
Verve Jazz Masters Vol.59:Toots Thielemans | Verve | 535271-2
Quincy Jones Big Band
Rahsaan/The Complete Mercury Recordings Of Roland Kirk | Mercury | 846630-2
Ray Charles-Milt Jackson Quartet
Soul Brothers/Soul Meeting | Atlantic | 7567-81951-2
Ray Charles-Milt Jackson Quintet
Soul Brothers/Soul Meeting | Atlantic | 7567-81951-2
Ray Charles-Milt Jackson Sextet
Soul Brothers/Soul Meeting | Atlantic | 7567-81951-2
Roy Eldridge Septet
To Bags...With Love:Memorial Album | Pablo | 2310967-2
Roy Eldridge Sextet
Milt Jackson Birthday Celebration | Fantasy | FANCD 6079-2
Decidedly | Pablo | PACD 5314-2
Sonny Rollins With The Modern Jazz Quartet
The Complete Modern Jazz Quartet Prestige & Pablo Recordings | Prestige | 4PRCD 4438-2
Milt Jackson Birthday Celebration | Fantasy | FANCD 6079-2
Sonny Rollins With The Modern Jazz Quartet | Original Jazz Classics | OJCCD 011-2
The Jazz Giants Play Duke Ellington:Caravan | Prestige | PCD 24227-2
Sonny Stitt Sextet
Milt Jackson Birthday Celebration | Fantasy | FANCD 6079-2
Tempo Jazzmen
Dizzy Gillespie:Night In Tunisia | Dreyfus Jazz Line | FDM 36734-2
The Big Three
Milt Jackson Birthday Celebration | Fantasy | FANCD 6079-2
The Big Three | Original Jazz Classics | OJCCD 805-2(2310757)
The McGhee-Navarro Boptet
The Fabulous Fats Navarro Vol.1 | Blue Note | 0677207
The Fabulous Fats Navarro Vol.2 | Blue Note | 0677208
Thelonious Monk Quartet
Wizard Of The Vibes | Blue Note | 532140-2
The Best Of Thelonious Monk:The Blue Note Years | Blue Note | 795636-2
Thelonious Monk:Misterioso | Dreyfus Jazz Line | FDM 36743-2
Thelonious Monk Quintet
Genius Of Modern Music,Vol.2 | Blue Note | 532139-2
The Best Of Thelonious Monk:The Blue Note Years | Blue Note | 795636-2
Jazz Profile:Thelonious Monk | Blue Note | 823518-2
Thelonious Monk:Misterioso | Dreyfus Jazz Line | FDM 36743-2

Jackson,Munyungo | (perc,tambourinevoice)
Christian McBride Group
A Family Affair | Verve | 557554-2

Jackson,Oliver | (dr,earthboardgong)
Dexter Gordon Quartet
Dexter Gordon Birthday Celebration | Fantasy | FANCD 6082-2
Etta Jones And Her Band
Love Shout | Original Jazz Classics | OJCCD 941-2(P 7272)
Gene Ammons Septet
Bad! Bossa Nova | Original Jazz Classics | OJC20 351-2(P 7257)
Harry Allen Quartet
Love Songs Live! | Nagel-Heyer | NH 1014
Harry Allen Quintet
A Night At Birdland | Nagel-Heyer | CD 010
A Night At Birdland Vol. 1 | Nagel-Heyer | CD 5002
Ellington For Lovers | Nagel-Heyer | NH 1009
Love Songs Live! | Nagel-Heyer | NH 1014
The First Sampler | Nagel-Heyer | NHR SP 5
Illinois Jacquet Quintet
The Blues That's Me! | Original Jazz Classics | OJCCD 614-2(P 7731)
Jeanie Lambe And The Danny Moss Quartet
Three Great Concerts:Live In Hamburg 1993-1995 | Nagel-Heyer | CD 019
Johnny Hodges Orchestra
Planet Jazz:Johnny Hodges | Planet Jazz | 2152065-2
King Curtis Quartet
The New Scene Of King Curtis | Original Jazz Classics | OJC 198(NJ 8237)
King Curtis Quintet
The New Scene Of King Curtis | Original Jazz Classics | OJC 198(NJ 8237)
Nancy Harrow And The Buck Clayton All Stars
Wild Women Don't Have The Blues | Candid | CCD 79008
Nat Pierce Quartet
My Pal Basie | Jazz Connaisseur | JCCD 8904-2
Nat Pierce Trio
My Pal Basie | Jazz Connaisseur | JCCD 8904-2
Oliver Jackson Orchestra
The Last Great Concert | Nagel-Heyer | CD 063
Teddy Wilson Trio
The Story Of Jazz Piano | Laserlight | 24653
The Buck Clayton Legacy
All The Cats Join In(Buck Clayton Rememberd) | Nagel-Heyer | CD 006
The First Sampler | Nagel-Heyer | NHR SP 5
The Yamaha International Allstar Band
Hapy Birthday Jazzwelle Plus | Nagel-Heyer | CD 005
The First Sampler | Nagel-Heyer | NHR SP 5
Yusef Lateef Quintet
Other Sounds | Original Jazz Classics | OJCCD 399-2(NJ 8218)

Jackson,Oliver or Jimmy Lovelace | (dr)
Junior Mance Trio
That Lovin' Feelin' | Milestone | MCD 47097-2

Jackson,Paul | (b,el-b,marimbula,voc,el-g,percg)
Al Jarreau With Band
High Crime | i.e. Music | 557848-2
Tenderness | i.e. Music | 557853-2
Bobby Lyle Group
The Journey | Atlantic | 7567-82138-2
Eddie Henderson Orchestra
Blue Break Beats | Blue Note | 799106-2
Ella Fitzgerald With Orchestra
Ella Abraca Jobim | Pablo | 2630201-2
Herbie Hancock Group
Man-Child | CBS | 471235-2
Sunlight | CBS | 486570-2
Thrust | CBS | CK 64984
Head Hunters | CBS | CK 65123
Herbie Hancock Septet
V.S.O.P. Herbie Hancock-Live At The City Center N.Y. | CBS | 486569-2
Marcus Miller Group
The Sun Don't Lie | Dreyfus Jazz Line | FDM 36560-2
Mike Clark-Paul Jackson Quartet
The Funk Stops Here | TipToe | TIP-888811 2
Sonny Rollins Quartet

Easy Living | Original Jazz Classics | OJCCD 893-2
Sonny Rollins Quintet
Easy Living | Original Jazz Classics | OJCCD 893-2

Jackson,Preston | (tb)
Louis Armstrong And His Orchestra
Satch Plays Fats(Complete) | CBS | CK 64927

Jackson,Quentin | (tb,b-tbvoc)
Bill Coleman Septet
Jazz In Paris:Bill Coleman-From Boogie To Funk | EmArCy | 549401-2 PMS
Billy Strayhorn Orchestra
Johnny Hodges With Billy Strayhorn And The Orchestra | Verve | 557543-2
Cat Anderson And His Orchestra
Americans Swinging In Paris:Cat Anderson | EMI Records | 539658-2
Charles Mingus And His Orchestra
The Complete Town Hall Concert | Blue Note | 828353-2
Charles Mingus Orchestra
Mingus Mingus Mingus | Impulse(MCA) | 951170-2
The Black Saint And The Sinner Lady | Impulse(MCA) | 951174-2
Count Basie And His Orchestra
Jazz Collection:Count Basie | Laserlight | 24368
The Legends Of Swing | Laserlight | 24659
Atomic Swing | Roulette | 497871-2
Dinah Washington With The Eddie Chamblee Orchestra
Dinah Sings Bessie Smith | Verve | 538635-2
Dinah Washington With The Quincy Jones Orchestra
Verve Jazz Masters 40:Dinah Washington | Verve | 522055-2
The Swingin' Miss 'D' | Verve | 558074-2
Duke Ellington And Count Basie With Their Orchestras
First Time! | CBS | CK 65571
Duke Ellington And His Orchestra
Jazz Collection:Duke Ellington | Laserlight | 24369
The Legends Of Swing | Laserlight | 24659
100 Years Duke | Laserlight | 24906
Highlights From The Duke Ellington Centennial Edition | RCA | 2663672-2
Greatest Hits | CBS | 462959-2
The Big Bands Vol.1.The Snader Telescriptions | Storyville | 4960043
Verve Jazz Masters 4:Duke Ellington | Verve | 516338-2
Ellington '55 | Capitol | 520135-2
Great Swing Classics In Hi-Fi | Capitol | 521223-2
Ellington At Newport 1956(Complete) | CBS | CK 64932
Black Brown And Beige | CBS | CK 65566
Such Sweet Thunder | CBS | CK 65568
Anatomy Of A Murder | CBS | CK 65569
The Ellington Suites | Original Jazz Classics | OJC20 446-2(2310762)
Duke Ellington At The Alhambra | Pablo | PACD 5313-2
Ella Fitzgerald With The Duke Ellington Orchestra
Ella Fitzgerald-First Lady Of Song | Verve | 517898-2
The Best Of The Song Books | Verve | 519804-2
Verve Jazz Masters 6:Ella Fitzgerald | Verve | 519822-2
The Best Of The Song Books:The Ballads | Verve | 521867-2
Verve Jazz Masters 46:Ella Fitzgerald-The Jazz Sides | Verve | 527655-2
Love Songs:The Best Of The Song Books | Verve | 531762-2
Ella Fitzgerald Sings The Duke Ellington Songbook | Verve | 559248-2
For The Love Of Ella Fitzgerald | Verve | 841765-2
Herbie Mann And His Orchestra
The Best Of Herbie Mann | Atlantic | 7567-81369-2
Jimmy Smith And Wes Montgomery With The Oliver Nelson Orchestra
Wes Montgomery:The Verve Jazz Sides | Verve | 521690-2
Jimmy Smith:Best Of The Verve Years | Verve | 527950-2
Talkin' Jazz:Roots Of Acid Jazz | Verve | 529580-2
Jimmy Smith With The Oliver Nelson Orchestra
Verve Jazz Masters 29:Jimmy Smith | Verve | 521855-2
Jimmy Smith:Best Of The Verve Years | Verve | 527950-2
Jimmy Smith-Talkin' Verve | Verve | 531563-2
Peter & The Wolf | Verve | 547264-2
Joe Williams With The Oliver Nelson Orchestra
Planet Jazz:Joe Williams | Planet Jazz | 2165370-2
Johnny Hodges And The Ellington All-Stars Without Duke
Verve Jazz Masters 35:Johnny Hodges | Verve | 521857-2
Johnny Hodges And The Ellington Men
Verve Jazz Masters 35:Johnny Hodges | Verve | 521857-2
Johnny Hodges Orchestra
Coleman Hawkins/Johnny Hodges:The Vogue Recordings | Vogue | 21559712
Johnny Hodges With Billy Strayhorn And The Duke Ellington Orchestra
Verve Jazz Masters 35:Johnny Hodges | Verve | 521857-2
King Curtis Band
King Curtis-Blow Man Blow | Bear Family Records | BCD 15670 CI
Louis Armstrong And His Friends
Louis Armstrong And His Friends | Bluebird | 2663961-2
Milt Jackson Orchestra
Milt Jackson Birthday Celebration | Fantasy | FANCD 6079-2
Quincy Jones And His Orchestra
Talkin' Verve-Roots Of Acid Jazz:Roland Kirk | Verve | 533101-2
Rahsaan/The Complete Mercury Recordings Of Roland Kirk | Mercury | 846630-2
Wes Montgomery Orchestra
Movin' Wes | Verve | 521433-2
Wes Montgomery With The Johnny Pate Orchestra
Verve Jazz Masters 14:Wes Montgomery | Verve | 519826-2
Wes Montgomery:The Verve Jazz Sides | Verve | 521690-2
Talkin' Jazz:Roots Of Acid Jazz | Verve | 529580-2
Wes Montgomery With The Oliver Nelson Orchestra
Verve Jazz Masters 14:Wes Montgomery | Verve | 519826-2
Wes Montgomery:The Verve Jazz Sides | Verve | 521690-2
Talkin' Jazz:Roots Of Acid Jazz | Verve | 529580-2

Jackson,Quentin or John Sanders | (tb)
Johnny Hodges Orchestra
Verve Jazz Masters 43:Ben Webster | Verve | 525431-2

Jackson,Randy | (bel-b)
Bobby McFerrin Group
Bobby McFerrin | Elektra | 7559-60023-2
Jean-Luc Ponty Group
Mystical Adventures | Atlantic | 19333-2
Jean-Luc Ponty Quintet
The Very Best Of Jean-Luc Ponty | Rhino | 8122-79862-2
Jean-Luc Ponty Sextet
The Very Best Of Jean-Luc Ponty | Rhino | 8122-79862-2

Jackson,Rick | (keyboards)
Larry Carlton Group
The Gift | GRP | GRP 98542

Jackson,Rita | (voc)
Chico Freeman And Brainstorm
Threshold | IN+OUT Records | 7022-2

Jackson,Ronald Shannon | (dr,arr,perc,voice,voc,fl)
Albert Mangelsdorff Trio
Three Originals:The Wide Point/Trilogue/Albert Live In Montreux | MPS | 519213-2
John Zorn Group
Spillane | Nonesuch | 7559-79172-2

Jackson,Rudy | (cl,as,ss,ts,bsreeds)
Duke Ellington And His Orchestra
Jazz:The Essential Collection Vol.2 | IN+OUT Records | 78012-2

Jackson,Wilber 'Slim' | (dr)
The Modern Jazz Disciples
Disciples Blues | Prestige | PCD 24263-2

Jackson,Willis | (tsgator-horn)
Johnny 'Hammond' Smith Quartet
Good 'Nuff | Prestige | PRCD 24282-2
Willis Jackson Group
At Large | Prestige | PCD 24243-2
Willis Jackson Quartet
At Large | Prestige | PCD 24243-2
Willis Jackson Quintet
At Large | Prestige | PCD 24243-2
Gravy | Prestige | PCD 24254-2
Soul Night Live! | Prestige | PRCD 24273-2
Together Again: Willis Jackson With Jack McDuff | Prestige | PRCD 24284-2
Willis Jackson Sextet
At Large | Prestige | PCD 24243-2
Gravy | Prestige | PCD 24254-2
Nuther'n Like Thuther'n | Prestige | PRCD 24265-2
Together Again: Willis Jackson With Jack McDuff | Prestige | PRCD 24284-2

Jacob,Christian | (p,keyboardsp-solo)
Vic Lewis West Coast All Stars
Vic Lewis Presenting A Celebration Of Contemporary West Coast Jazz | Candid | CCD 79711/12
Me And You! | Candid | CCD 79739

Jacob,Julie | (oboe,reedssax)
Barney Kessel And His Orchestra
The Jazz Giants Play Rodgers & Hart:Blue Moon | Prestige | PCD 24205-2
Billy Eckstine With The Billy May Orchestra
Once More With Feeling | Roulette | 581862-2
Ella Fitzgerald With The Billy May Orchestra
Love Songs:The Best Of The Song Books | Verve | 531762-2
Ella Fitzgerald Sings The Harold Arlen Song Book | Verve | 589108-2
Van Alexander Orchestra
Home Of Happy Feet/Swing! Staged For Sound! | Capitol | 535211-2

Jacob,Willie | (as,bottleneck-bouzouki,steel-gvoc)
NuNu!
Ocean | TipToe | TIP-888837 2

Jacobi,Frank | (ts)
René Pretschner Quartet
Floating Pictures | Green House Music | CD 1001

Jacobs,Dave | (tb)
Tommy Dorsey And His Orchestra
Planet Jazz:Frank Sinatra & Tommy Dorsey | Planet Jazz | 2152067-2
Planet Jazz Sampler | Planet Jazz | 2152326-2
Planet Jazz:Tommy Dorsey | Planet Jazz | 2159972-2

Jacobs,Dick | (arr,ld,as,bells,cl,percts)
Anthony Ortega With String Orchestra
Earth Dance | Fresh Sound Records | FSR-CD 325
Ella Fitzgerald With Sy Oliver And His Orchestra
Ella Fitzgerald:The Decca Years 1949-1954 | Decca | 050668-2
Louis Armstrong And His Orchestra
Satchmo Serenaders | Verve | 543792-2
Louis Armstrong With Sy Oliver And His Orchestra
Satchmo Serenaders | Verve | 543792-2

Jacobs,Jules | (cl,oboe,engl-h,b-cl,ts,reedssax)
Barney Kessel And His Orchestra
Barney Kessel Plays Carmen | Original Jazz Classics | OJC 269(C 7563)
Van Alexander Orchestra
Home Of Happy Feet/Swing! Staged For Sound! | Capitol | 535211-2

Jacobs,Ruud | (bp)
Laura Fygi With Band
Bewitched | Verve | 514724-2
The Rosenberg Trio With Orchestra
Noches Calientes | Verve | 557022-2

Jacobs,Sid | (b)
Wingy Mannone And His Orchestra
Planet Jazz:Male Jazz Vocalists | Planet Jazz | 2169657-2

Jacobs,Vinnie | (fr-h)
Charlie Parker With Strings
Charlie Parker With Strings:The Master Takes | Verve | 523984-2
Charlie Parker With The Neal Hefti Orchestra
Charlie Parker:The Best Of The Verve Years | Verve | 527815-2
Bird: The Complete Charlie Parker On Verve | Verve | 837141-2

Jacobsen,Lucille J. | (voc)
Max Roach Chorus & Orchestra
To The Max! | Enja | ENJ-7021 22

Jacobson,Allen | (tb)
Russ Spiegel Group
Twilight | double moon | CHRDM 71026

Jacobson,Jack | (bdr)
Stephane Grappelli And His Musicians
Grapelli Story | Verve | 515807-2

Jacobson,Syd | (g)

Jacquet,Illinois | (as,ts,master of ceremony,bassoon)
Axel Zwingenberger With The Lionel Hampton Big Band
The Boogie Woogie Album | Vagabond | VRCD 8.88008
Billie Holiday With The JATP All Stars
Billie Holiday Story Vol.1:Jazz At The Philharmonic | Verve | 521642-2
The Complete Jazz At The Philharmonic On Verve 1944-1949 | Verve | 523893-2
Verve Jazz Masters 47:Billie Holiday Sings Standards | Verve | 527650-2
Jazz At The Philharmonic:Best Of The 1940's Concerts | Verve | 557534-2
Buddy Rich Orchestra
Krupa And Rich | Verve | 521643-2
Buddy Rich Septet
Swingin' The Blues-Jumpin' The Blues | Laserlight | 24654
Buddy Rich-Gene Krupa Orchestra
Krupa And Rich | Verve | 521643-2
Count Basie And His Orchestra
Verve Jazz Masters 2:Count Basie | Verve | 519819-2
Jazz:The Essential Collection Vol.3 | IN+OUT Records | 78013-2
Count Basie At Newport | Verve | 9861761
Ella Fitzgerald With The JATP All Stars
Ella Fitzgerald-First Lady Of Song | Verve | 517898-2
For The Love Of Ella Fitzgerald | Verve | 841765-2
Gene Krupa Orchestra
Krupa And Rich | Verve | 521643-2
Illinois Jacquet Quintet
The Blues That's Me! | Original Jazz Classics | OJCCD 614-2(P 7731)
Illinois Jacquet With The Joey DeFrancesco Quartet
Late Night Sax | CBS | 487798-2
JATP All Stars
The Complete Jazz At The Philharmonic On Verve 1944-1949 | Verve | 523893-2
Jazz At The Philharmonic:Best Of The 1940's Concerts | Verve | 557534-2
Johnny Hartman And His Quintet
I Just Dropped By To Say Hello | MCA | 951176-2
Lena Horne With The Horace Henderson Orchestra
Planet Jazz:Lena Horne | Planet Jazz | 2165373-2
Lionel Hampton And His All Star Jazz Inner Circle
Lionel Hampton: Salle Pleyel, March 9th, 1971 | Laserlight | 36133
Lionel Hampton And His Orchestra
Planet Jazz:Big Bands | Planet Jazz | 2169649-2
Lionel Hampton:Flying Home | Dreyfus Jazz Line | FDM 36735-2

Jacquet,Illinois prob. | (ts)
Billie Holiday With The JATP All Stars
Billie Holiday Story Vol.1:Jazz At The Philharmonic | Verve | 521642-2

Jacquet,Russell | (tb,tpvoc)
Sonny Stitt Sextet
Milt Jackson Birthday Celebration | Fantasy | FANCD 6079-2

Jaedig,Bent | (fl,ss,tssax)
Miles Davis With The Danish Radio Big Band
Aura | CBS | CK 63962
Stan Getz With The Danish Radio Big Band
Stan Getz In Europe | Laserlight | 24657
Stan Kenton With The Danish Radio Big Band
Stan Kenton With The Danish Radio Big Band | Storyville | STCD 8340
The Danish Radio Big Band
Aura | CBS | CK 63962

Jaeger,Harry | (dr)
Benny Goodman Septet feat.Count Basie
Charlie Christian:Swing To Bop | Dreyfus Jazz Line | FDM 36715-2
Louis Armstrong With Gordon Jenkins And His Orchestra And Choir
Satchmo In Style | Verve | 549594-2
Ambassador Louis Armstrong Vol.17:Moments To Remember(1952-1956) | Ambassador | CLA 1917

Jaegers,Marcus | (b)
Dogs Don't Sing In The Rain
Bones For Breakfast | Edition Collage | EC 472-2
Vocal Moments | Take Twelve On CD | TT 008-2
Wind Moments | Take Twelve On CD | TT 009-2

Jafet,Jean-Marc | (b,percb-g)
Richard Galliano Quartet
Spleen | Dreyfus Jazz Line | FDM 36513-9
Gallianissimo! The Best Of Richard Galliano | Dreyfus Jazz Line | FDM 36616-2
Richard Galliano Quintet
Spleen | Dreyfus Jazz Line | FDM 36513-9
Sylvain Luc-André Ceccarelli-Jean Marc Jafet
SUD | Dreyfus Jazz Line | FDM 36612-2

Jaffe,Jill | (viola)
Lee Konitz With Strings
Strings For Holiday:A Tribute To Billie Holiday | Enja | ENJ-9304 2

Jaffe,Nat | (p)
Louis Armstrong And His Orchestra
Louis Armstrong:Swing That Music | Laserlight | 36056
Sarah Vaughan With Dizzy Gillespie And His Septet
Sarah Vaughan:Lover Man | Dreyfus Jazz Line | FDM 36739-2
Woody Herman And The Vanderbilt All Stars
Louis Armstrong-Jack Teagarden-Woody Herman:Midnights At V-Disc | Jazz Unlimited | JUCD 2048

Jäger,Thomas | (orgtp)
Natascha Majevskaja-Thomas Jäger
Orgel Ist Mehr!...In Bamberg,Vol.1 | Orgel ist mehr! | OIM/BA/1999-1 CD
Orgel Ist Mehr...In Bamberg Vol.2 | Orgel ist mehr! | OIM/BA/1999-2 CD
Thomas Jäger
Orgel Ist Mehr!...In Bamberg,Vol.1 | Orgel ist mehr! | OIM/BA/1999-1 CD
Orgel Ist Mehr...In Bamberg Vol.2 | Orgel ist mehr! | OIM/BA/1999-2 CD

Jäger,Tilman | (p)
Tilman Jäger Tape 4
Abendlieder | Satin Doll Productions | SDP 1043-1 CD

Jägerhult,Christer | (marimba,chimes,vib,bongos)
Bengt-Arne Wallin Orchestra
The Birth+Rebirth Of Swedish Folk Jazz | ACT | 9254-2

Jaguaraci | (tambourine)
Duo Fenix
Karai-Eté | IN+OUT Records | 7009-2

Jahner,Mathias | (sax)
Marcus Sukiennik Big Band
A Night In Tunisia Suite(7 Variationen über Dizzy Gillespie's 'A Night In Tunisia') | Jazz Haus Musik | ohne Nummer

Jakoby,Frank | (fl,ssts)
Jazz Orchester Rheinland-Pfalz
Kazzou | Jazz Haus Musik | LJBB 9104

Jaksjo,Christian | (tbeuphonium)
Geir Lysne Listening Ensemble
Korall | ACT | 9236-2
Aurora Borealis-Nordic Lights | ACT | 9406-2
Lee Konitz With The Ed Partyka Jazz Orchestra
Dreams And Realities | Laika Records | 35101642

Jakubek,Zbigniew | (keyboards)
Urszula Dudziak And Band Walk Away
Magic Lady | IN+OUT Records | 7008-2
Walkaway With Urszula Dudziak
Saturation | IN+OUT Records | 77024-2

Jakubovic,Jaroslav | (bsss)
Klaus Doldinger With Orchestra
Lifelike | Warner | 2292-46478-2

Jalkéus,Anders | (voc)
The Real Group
One For All | ACT | 9003-2
The Real Group With Toots Thielemans
One For All | ACT | 9003-2

Jalkéus,Margareta | (voc)
The Real Group
One For All | ACT | 9003-2
The Real Group With Toots Thielemans
One For All | ACT | 9003-2

Jam Session |
Jam Session
Jazz Gallery:Lester Young Vol.2(1946-59) | RCA | 2119541-2
Benny Goodman At Carnegie Hall 1938(Complete) | CBS | C2K 65143
Jam Session Vol.1 | Steeplechase | SCCD 31522
Jam Session Vol.2 | Steeplechase | SCCD 31523
Jam Session Vol.9 | Steeplechase | SCCD 31554
Jam Session Vol.10 | Steeplechase | SCCD 31555

Jamal,Ahmad | (p,el-pkeyboards)
Ahmad Jamal Quartet
Nature(The Essence Part III) | Atlantic | 3984-23105-2
Ahmad Jamal À L'Olympia | Dreyfus Jazz Line | FDM 36629-2
The Essence Part 1 | Dreyfus Jazz Line | FDM 37007-2
Big Byrd | Dreyfus Jazz Line | FDM 37008-2
Nature | Dreyfus Jazz Line | FDM 37018-2
Ahmad Jamal Quartet With Stanley Turrentine
Nature(The Essence Part III) | Atlantic | 3984-23105-2
Nature | Dreyfus Jazz Line | FDM 37018-2
Ahmad Jamal Quintet
The Essence Part 1 | Dreyfus Jazz Line | FDM 37007-2
Big Byrd | Dreyfus Jazz Line | FDM 37008-2
Ahmad Jamal Septet
Live In Paris 1996 | Dreyfus Jazz Line | FDM 37020-2
Ahmad Jamal Trio
Picture Perfect-70th Anniversary | Warner | 8573-85268-2
At The Pershing-But Not For Me | Chess | 940910-2
In Search Of Momentum (1-10) | Dreyfus Jazz Line | FDM 36644-2
Big Byrd | Dreyfus Jazz Line | FDM 37008-2
Live In Paris 1992 | Dreyfus Jazz Line | FDM 37019-2
The Awakening | Impulse(MCA) | IMP 12262
Ahmad Jamal Trio with Orchestra
Pittsburgh | Atlantic | 7567-8209-2
Ahmad Jamal-Othello Molineaux
Nature(The Essence Part III) | Atlantic | 3984-23105-2
Shirley Horn And Her Trio
May The Music Never End | Verve | 076028-2

Jamal,Khan | (marimbavib)
Monnette Sudler Sextet
Brighter Days For You | Steeplechase | SCCD 31087

Jamenco |
Jamenco
Conversations | Trick Music | TM 9202 CD

James,Billy | (dr)
Eric Kloss Quartet
About Time | Prestige | PRCD 24268-2

James,Bob | (arr,el-p,synth,clavinet,harpsichord)
Bob James And His Orchestra
Jazzrock-Anthology Vol.3:Fusion | Zounds | CD 27100555
Bob James Trio
Bold Conceptions | Verve | 557454-2
Chet Baker Quartet
Baby Breeze | Verve | 538328-2
Chet Baker-Gerry Mulligan Group
Carnegie Hall Concert Vol. 1/2 | CTI | EPC 450554-2
Essence All Stars
Afro Cubano Chant | Hip Bop | HIBD 8009
Hot Jazz Bisquits | Hip Bop | HIBD 8801
Fourplay
Heartfelt | RCA | 2663916-2
Fourplay | Warner | 7599-26656-2
Between The Sheets | Warner | 9362-45340-2

Fourplay...Yes,Please! | Warner | 9362-47694-2
George Benson With The Don Sebesky Orchestra
Verve Jazz Masters 21:George Benson | Verve | 521861-2
Grover Washington Jr. Orchestra
Jazzrock-Anthology Vol.3:Fusion | Zounds | CD 27100555
John Zorn Group
Spillane | Nonesuch | 7559-79172-2
Kevin Mahogany With The Bob James Trio
My Romance | Warner | 9362-47025-2
Kevin Mahogany With The Bob James Trio And Kirk Whalum
My Romance | Warner | 9362-47025-2
Kevin Mahogany With The Bob James Trio And Michael Brecker
My Romance | Warner | 9362-47025-2
Kevin Mahogany With The Bob James Trio, Kirk Whalum And Strings
My Romance | Warner | 9362-47025-2
Lee Ritenour Group
Festival | GRP | GRP 95702
Paul Desmond Orchestra
Late Night Sax | CBS | 487798-2
Skylark | CTI | ZK 65133
Quincy Jones And His Orchestra
Verve Jazz Masters Vol.59:Toots Thielemans | Verve | 535271-2
Sarah Vaughan And The Thad Jones Orchestra
Verve Jazz Masters 42:Sarah Vaughan-The Jazz Sides | Verve | 526817-2
Sarah Vaughan With Orchestra
!Viva! Vaughan | Mercury | 549374-2
Sarah Vaughan Sings The Mancini Songbook | Verve | 558401-2
Sarah Vaughan With The Frank Foster Orchestra
The Antonio Carlos Jobim Songbook | Verve | 525472-2
Sarah Vaughan With The Hal Mooney Orchestra
It's A Man's World | Mercury | 589487-2

James,Clifton | (dr)
Buddy Guy Blues Band
Buddy Guy-The Complete Chess Studio Recordings | MCA | MCD 09337
Homesick James Quartet
Blues On The Southside | Original Blues Classics | OBCCD 529-2(P 7388)
Windy City Blues | Stax | SCD 8612-2

James,Derrick | (as,saxss)
Derrick James & Wesley 'G' Quintet
Two Sides To Every Story | Jardis Records | JRCD 20137
Ron Ringwood's Crosscut Bluesband
Earth Tones | Organic Music | ORGM 9722
Russ Spiegel Group
Twilight | double moon | CHRDM 71026

James,Donto | (drMVP)
Etta James & The Roots Band
Burnin' Down he House | RCA | 3411633-2

James,Elmer | (btuba)
Fletcher Henderson And His Orchestra
Jazz:The Essential Collection Vol.1 | IN+OUT Records | 78011-2
Jazz:The Essential Collection Vol.3 | IN+OUT Records | 78013-2
Louis Armstrong With Chick Webb's Orchestra
Best Of The Complete RCA Victor Recordings | RCA | 2663636-2
Louis Armstrong:A 100th Birthday Celebration | RCA | 2663694-2
Tommy Ladnier And His Orchestra
Planet Jazz | Planet Jazz | 2169652-2
Jazz:The Essential Collection Vol.1 | IN+OUT Records | 78011-2

James,Etta | (voc)
Etta James & Eddie Cleanhead Vinson With The Red Holloway Quartet
Blues In The Night-Volume One:The Early Show | Fantasy | FCD 9647-2
Etta James & The Roots Band
Burnin' Down he House | RCA | 3411633-2
Etta James And The Outlaws
Monterey Jazz Festival 1975 | Storyville | 4960213
Etta James With Band
The Late Show-Recorded Live At Marla's Memory Lane Supper Club Vol.2 | Fantasy | FCD 9655-2
Etta James With The Red Holloway Quartet
Blues In The Night-Volume One:The Early Show | Fantasy | FCD 9647-2
Etta James With The Red Holloway Quintet
Blues In The Night-Volume One:The Early Show | Fantasy | FCD 9647-2
Etta James/Eddie 'Cleanhead' Vinson With Band
The Late Show-Recorded Live At Marla's Memory Lane Supper Club Vol.2 | Fantasy | FCD 9655-2
Jimmy Smith All Stars
Jimmy Smith:Dot Com Blues | Blue Thumb | 543978-2
Klaus Doldinger Jubilee
Doldinger's Best | ACT | 9224-2
Klaus Doldinger With Orchestra And Etta James
Lifelike | Warner | 2292-46478-2

James,George | (as,bs,cl,ssreeds)
Louis Armstrong And His Orchestra
Satch Plays Fats(Complete) | CBS | CK 64927

James,Harry | (tp,arrld)
All Star Band
Planet Jazz:Jack Teagarden | Planet Jazz | 2161236-2
Benny Goodman And His Orchestra
Planet Jazz:Benny Goodman | Planet Jazz | 2152054-2
Planet Jazz:Jazz Greatest Hits | Planet Jazz | 2169648-2
Planet Jazz:Big Bands | Planet Jazz | 2169649-2
Planet Jazz:Swing | Planet Jazz | 2169651-2
Planet Jazz:Jazz Trumpet | Planet Jazz | 2169654-2
Planet Jazz:Female Jazz Vocalists | Planet Jazz | 2169656-2
Swing Vol.1 | Storyville | 4960343
Benny Goodman At Carnegie Hall 1938(Complete) | CBS | C2K 65143
More Camel Caravans | Phontastic | NCD 8841/2
More Camel Caravans | Phontastic | NCD 8843/4
More Camel Caravans | Phontastic | NCD 8845/6
Harry James And His Orchestra
The Legends Of Swing | Laserlight | 24659
Great Swing Classics In Hi-Fi | Capitol | 521223-2
Trumpet Blues:The Best Of Harry James | Capitol | 521224-2
The Golden Trumpet Of Harry James | London | 820178-2 IMS
Jam Session
Benny Goodman At Carnegie Hall 1938(Complete) | CBS | C2K 65143
Lionel Hampton And His Orchestra
Planet Jazz:Swing | Planet Jazz | 2169651-2
Planet Jazz:Jazz Saxophone | Planet Jazz | 2169653-2
The Metronome All-Star Nine
Jazz:The Essential Collection Vol.3 | IN+OUT Records | 78013-2

James,Ida | (voc)
Nat King Cole Trio
The Small Black Groups | Storyville | 4960523

James,Joy | (bj)
Mr.Acker Bilk And His Paramount Jazz Band
The Very Best Of Dixieland Jazz | Verve | 535529-2

James,Olga | (voc)
Nat Adderley Group
Soul Of The Bible | Capitol | 358257-2

James,Prince | (ts)
Gene Ammons Quintet
Brother Jug! | Prestige | PR20 7792-2

James,Ricky \'Bongo\' | (bongos)
Pucho & His Latin Soul Brothers
Jazzin' With The Soul Brothers | Fantasy | FANCD 6086-2

James,Ricky 'Bongo' | (congas,bongos,bellsdjembe)
Rip A Dip | Milestone | MCD 9247-2

James,Sametto | (b)
Etta James & The Roots Band
Burnin' Down he House | RCA | 3411633-2

James,Stafford | (b,el-bdr)
Gary Bartz Ntu Troop
Jazzin' Vol.2: The Music Of Stevie Wonder | Fantasy | FANCD 6088-2
Monty Waters Quartet
Monty Waters New York Calling Vol.2 | Tutu Records | 888182-2*

James,William 'Billy' | (drel-bongos)
Don Patterson Quartet
Boppin' & Burnin' | Original Jazz Classics | OJCCD 983-2(P 7563)
Don Patterson Quintet
Boppin' & Burnin' | Original Jazz Classics | OJCCD 983-2(P 7563)
Eddie Harris Group
The Best Of Eddie Harris | Atlantic | 7567-81370-2
Eddie Lockjaw Davis Quintet
The Jazz Giants Play Harry Warren:Lullaby Of Broadway | Prestige | PCD 24204-2
Gene Ammons-Sonny Stitt Quintet
Verve Jazz Masters 50:Sonny Sitt | Verve | 527651-2
Boss Tenors In Orbit!!! | Verve | 549371-2
Sonny Stitt Quartet
The Jazz Giants Play Miles Davis:Milestones | Prestige | PCD 24225-2
The Prestige Legacy Vol.2:Battles Of Saxes | Prestige | PCD 24252-2
Brothers 4 | Prestige | PCD 24261-2
Sonny Stitt Trio
The Boss Men | Prestige | PCD 24253-2

Janarro,Mario | (p)
Dr. Henry Levine's Barefoot Dixieland Philharmonic feat.Prof. Sidney Bechet
Planet Jazz | Planet Jazz | 2169652-2
Sidney Bechet And The Chamber Music Society Of Lower Basin Street
Sidney Bechet:Summertime | Dreyfus Jazz Line | FDM 36712-2

Janek,Klaus | (b)
Flor De Tango
Armenonville | Minor Music | 801097

Jankeje,Jan | (b,el-b,perc,b-synth,voc,v,fujara)
Al Casey Quartet
A Tribute To Fats | Jazzpoint | JP 1044 CD
A' Portrait Of Jan Jankeje | Jazzpoint | JP 1054 CD
Benny Waters & Jan Jankeje
Let's Talk About Jazz | G&J Records | GJ 2009 Maxi-CD
Benny Waters Quartet
Swinging Again | Jazzpoint | JP 1037 CD
A' Portrait Of Jan Jankeje | Jazzpoint | JP 1054 CD
Benny Waters Sextet
A' Portrait Of Jan Jankeje | Jazzpoint | JP 1054 CD
Bireli Lagrene Ensemble
Bireli Swing '81 | Jazzpoint | JP 1009 CD
Live | Jazzpoint | JP 1047 CD
Routes To Django & Bireli Swing '81 | Jazzpoint | JP 1055 CD
Routs To Django-Live At The 'Krokodil' | Jazzpoint | JP 1056 CD
Bireli Lagrene Group
Bireli Lagrene 'Highlights' | Jazzpoint | JP 1027 CD
A' Portrait Of Jan Jankeje | Jazzpoint | JP 1054 CD
A Tribute To Django Reinhardt | Jazzpoint | JP 1061 CD
Bireli Lagrene Quartet
A' Portrait Of Jan Jankeje | Jazzpoint | JP 1054 CD
Bireli Lagrene Trio
Live At The Carnegie Hall: A Tribute To Django Reinhardt | Jazzpoint | JP 1040 CD
A' Portrait Of Jan Jankeje | Jazzpoint | JP 1054 CD
Doc Cheatham Sextet
A' Portrait Of Jan Jankeje | Jazzpoint | JP 1054 CD
George Kelly Quintet
A' Portrait Of Jan Jankeje | Jazzpoint | JP 1054 CD
Hans Kumpf-Jan Jankeje
A' Portrait Of Jan Jankeje | Jazzpoint | JP 1054 CD
Jaco Pastorius Groups
Another Side Of Jaco Pastorius | Jazzpoint | JP 1064 CD
Jaco Pastorius Trio
Jaco Pastorius Heavy'n Jazz & Stuttgart Aria | Jazzpoint | JP 1058 CD
Jan Jankeje Quintet
Zum Trotz | Jazzpoint | JP 1016 CD
Jan Jankeje Septet
A' Portrait Of Jan Jankeje | Jazzpoint | JP 1054 CD
Jan Jankeje Trio
A' Portrait Of Jan Jankeje | Jazzpoint | JP 1054 CD
Jan Jankeje's Party And Swingband
Mobil | Jazzpoint | JP 1068 CD
Katie Kern Group
Still Young | Jazzpoint | JP 1070 CD
Oscar Klein & Katie Kern Group
Pick-A-Blues | Jazzpoint | JP 1065 CD
Oscar Klein Band
Pick-A-Blues Live | Jazzpoint | JP 1071
Oscar Klein-Lino Patruno European Jazz Stars
Live at The San Marino Jazz Festival | Jazzpoint | JP 1052 CD
Oscar Klein's Jazz Show
Oscar Klein's Jazz Show | Jazzpoint | JP 1043 CD
Oscar Klein's Jazz Show Vol.2 | Jazzpoint | JP 1048 CD
A' Portrait Of Jan Jankeje | Jazzpoint | JP 1054 CD
Red Richards-George Kelly Sextet With Doc Cheatham
Groove Move | Jazzpoint | JP 1045 CD
Stuttgarter Dixieland All Stars
It's The Talk Of The Town | Jazzpoint | JP 1069 CD
Wedeli Köhler Group
Swing & Folk | Jazzpoint | JP 1067 CD

Jankowski Singers,The | (voc-group)
Horst Jankowski Orchestra With Voices
Jankowskeynotes | MPS | 9814806

Jankowski,Horst | (p,cembaloclavinet)
Horst Jankowski Quartet
Jankowskinetik | MPS | 9808189

Jannotta,Roger | (as,reeds,fl,b-cl,ts,oboe,whistles)
Carla Bley Band
The Very Big Carla Bley Band | Watt | 23
Big Band Theory | Watt | 25(519966-2)
Carla Bley Big Band
The Carla Bley Big Band Goes To Church | Watt | 27(533682-2)
Michael Mantler Group With The Danish Radio Concert Orchestra Strings
The School Of Understanding(Sort-Of-An-Opera) | ECM | 1648/49(537963-2)
Michael Mantler Orchestra
Hide And Seek | ECM | 1738(549612-2)

Jansen,Hans | (keyboardsp)
Stochelo Rosenberg Group
Gypsy Swing | Verve | 527806-2
Stochelo Rosenberg Group With Strings
Gypsy Swing | Verve | 527806-2

Jansen,Nils | (bass-sax,contra-b-clsopranino)
Trygve Seim Group
Different Rivers | ECM | 1744(159521-2)

Jansen-Engelen,M. | (v)
Toots Thielemans And His Orchestra
Verve Jazz Masters Vol.59:Toots Thielemans | Verve | 535271-2

Janson,Henrik | (el-gg)
Niels Landgren Funk Unit
Live In Stockholm | ACT | 9223-2
Nils Landgren Funk Unit
Paint It Blue:A Tribute To Cannonball Adderley | ACT | 9243-2
Live In Montreux | ACT | 9265-2
Nils Landgren Funk Unit With Guests
5000 Miles | ACT | 9271-2

Janssen,Digna | (voc)
Dogs Don't Sing In The Rain
Bones For Breakfast | Edition Collage | EC 472-2
Vocal Moments | Take Twelve On CD | TT 008-2
Wind Moments | Take Twelve On CD | TT 009-2

Janssen,Huub | (dr,maracas,tambourin,wbd,voc)
Dutch Swing College Band
Swinging Studio Sessons | Philips | 824256-2 PMS
Digital Anniversary | Philips | 824585-2 PMS

Janssen,Jens | (g)
Jazz Bomberos
Naranja | Green House Music | CD 1003(Maxi)

Jansson,Henrik | (g,keyboardsvoc)
Nils Landgren First Unit And Guests
Nils Landgren-The First Unit | ACT | 9292-2

Jansson,Kjell | (b)
Anders Lindskog Quartet
Cry Me A River | Touché Music | TMcCD 005
Kjell Jansson Quartet
Back From Where We Came | Touché Music | TMcCD 009
Kjell Jansson Quintet
Back From Where We Came | Touché Music | TMcCD 009

Jansson,Lars | (p,org,synthstring-ensemble)
Caecilie Norby With Band
My Corner Of The Sky | Blue Note | 853422-2

Jansson,Lennart | (bs)
Lars Gullin Octet
Lars Gullin 1955/56 Vol.1 | Dragon | DRCD 224

Jansson,Ulrika | (strings)
Esbjörn Svensson Trio(E.S.T) With Strings
EST Plays Monk | ACT | 9010-2

Jardim,Luis | (perc)
Acoustic Alchemy
Against The Grain | GRP | GRP 97832

Jarman,Joseph | (alto-fl,ss,as,ts,bs,vib,perc)
Art Ensemble Of Chicago
Nice Guys | ECM | 1126
Full Force | ECM | 1167(829197-2)
Urban Bushmen | ECM | 1211/12
The Third Decade | ECM | 1273
Americans Swinging In Paris:Art Ensemble Of Chicago | EMI Records | 539667-2
Bap-Tizum | Atlantic | 7567-80757-2

Jaroschek,Achim | (grand-p)
Achim Jaroschek-Peter Brötzmann
Neurotransmitter | double moon | DMCD 1006-2

Jaroslawski,Christian | (b)
Gunter Hampel Next Generation
Köln Concert Part 1 | Birth | CD 047
Köln Concert Part 2 | Birth | CD 048

Jarreau,Al | (fl,percvoice)
Al Jarreau With Band
Jarreau | i.e. Music | 557847-2
High Crime | i.e. Music | 557848-2
Al Jarreau In London | i.e. Music | 557849-2
L Is For Lover | i.e. Music | 557850-2
Heart's Horizon | i.e. Music | 557851-2
Heaven And Earth | i.e. Music | 557852-2
Tenderness | i.e. Music | 557853-2
We Got By | Reprise | 7599-27222-2
All Fly Home | Warner | 7599-27362-2
Joe Sample Group
Spellbound | Rhino | 81273726-2
Michael 'Patches' Stewart Group
Penetration | Hip Bop | HIBD 8018

Jarrett,Chris | (p,p-overdubbingp-solo)
Chris Jarrett
Fire | Edition Collage | EC 443-2
Live In Tübingen | Edition Collage | EC 490-2
Short Stories For Piano | Edition Musikat | EDM 056
Piano Moments | Take Twelve On CD | TT 007-2
Chris Jarrett Trio
Chris Jarrett Trio Plays New World Music | Edition Musikat | EDM 067

Jarrett,Keith | (as,pipe-org,church-org-solo)
Charles Lloyd Quartet
Charles Lloyd In Europe | Atlantic | 7567-80788-2
Atlantic Saxophones | Rhino | 8122-71256-2
Forest Flower:Charles Lloyd At Monterey | Atlantic | 8122-71746-2
Charlie Haden-Keith Jarrett
Closeness Duets | Verve | 397000-2
Freddie Hubbard With Orchestra
This Is Jazz:Freddie Hubbard | CBS | CK 65041
Gary Burton-Keith Jarrett Quintet
Gary Burton & Keith Jarrett | Atlantic | 7567-81374-2
Gary Peacock Trio
Tales Of Another | ECM | 1101(827418-2)
Keith Jarreett/Jan Garbarek With Strings
Luminessence | ECM | 1049(839307-2)
Keith Jarrett
Facing You | ECM | 1017(827132-2)
Solo-Concerts(Bremen-Lausanne) | ECM | 1035/7(827747-2)
The Köln Concert | ECM | 1064/65(810067-2)
Hymns/Spheres | ECM | 1086/7
Staircase | ECM | 1090/91
Sun Bear Concerts | ECM | 1100(843028-2)
Eyes Of The Heart | ECM | 1150(825476-2)
Sacred Hymns Of G.I.Gurdjieff | ECM | 1174
Invocations/The Moth And The Flame | ECM | 1201/02(825473-2)
Concerts(Bregenz) | ECM | 1227(827286-2)
Concerts(Bregenz/München) | ECM | 1227/9
Spheres | ECM | 1302(827463-2)
Spirits | ECM | 1333/34(829467-2)
Book Of Ways | ECM | 1344/45(831396-2)
Dark Intervals | ECM | 1379(837342-2)
Paris Concert | ECM | 1401(839173-2)
Vienna Concert | ECM | 1481(513437-2)
La Scala | ECM | 1640(537268-2)
The Melody At Night,With You | ECM | 1675(547949-2)
El Juicio(The Judgement) | Atlantic | 7567-80783-2
Byablue | Impulse(MCA) | MCD 10648
Keith Jarrett - Jack DeJohnette
Ruta + Daitya | ECM | 1021(513776-2)
Keith Jarrett Group
Expectations | CBS | C2K 65900
Keith Jarrett Group With Brass
Expectations | CBS | C2K 65900
Keith Jarrett Group With Strings
Expectations | CBS | C2K 65900
Keith Jarrett Quartet
Belonging | ECM | 1050(829115-2)
The Survivor's Suite | ECM | 1085(827131-2)
My Song | ECM | 1115(821406-2)
Eyes Of The Heart | ECM | 1150(825476-2)
Nude Ants | ECM | 1171/72(829119-2)
Personal Mountains | ECM | 1382(837361-2)
El Juicio(The Judgement) | Atlantic | 7567-80783-2
Byablue | Impulse(MCA) | MCD 10648
Keith Jarrett Quintet
Fort Yawuh | Impulse(MCA) | 547966-2
The Roots Of Acid Jazz | Impulse(MCA) | IMP 12042
Keith Jarrett Trio
Standarts Vol.1 | ECM | 1255(811966-2)
Changes | ECM | 1276(817436-2)
Standards Vol.2 | ECM | 1289(825015-2)
Standards Live | ECM | 1317(827827-2)
Still Live | ECM | 1360/61(835008-2
Changeless | ECM | 1392(839618-2)
Tribute | ECM | 1420/21
The Cure | ECM | 1440(849650-2)
Bye Bye Blackbird | ECM | 1467(513074-2)
At The Deer Head Inn | ECM | 1531(517720-2)
Standards In Norway | ECM | 1542(521717-2)
Keith Jarrett At The Blue Note-The Complete Recordings | ECM | 1575/80(527638-2)
Tokyo '96 | ECM | 1666(539955-2)
Whisper Not | ECM | 1724/25(543813-2)
Inside Out | ECM | 1780(014005-2)
Always Let Me Go | ECM | 1800/01(018766-2)
Chick Corea-Herbie Hancock-Keith Jarrett-McCoy Tyner | Atlantic | 7567-81402-2

Somewhere Before | Atlantic | 7567-81455-2
The Mourning Of A Star | Atlantic | 8122-75355-2
Byablue | Impulse(MCA) | MCD 10648
Keith Jarrett Trio With Strings
Arbour Zena | ECM | 1070(825592-2)
Keith Jarrett With String Quartet
In The Light | ECM | 1033/4
Keith Jarrett With Strings
In The Light | ECM | 1033/4
Expectations | CBS | C2K 65900
Keith Jarrett With The American Brass Quintet
In The Light | ECM | 1033/4
Keith Jarrett With The Syracuse Symphony
The Celestial Hawk | ECM | 1175
Kenny Wheeler Quartet
Gnu High | ECM | 1069(825591-2)
Miles Davis Group
Live-Evil | CBS | C2K 65135
Live At The Fillmore East | CBS | C2K 65139
Paul Motian-Keith Jarrett
Conception Vessel | ECM | 1028(519279-2)
Ralph Towner With Strings
In The Light | ECM | 1033/4

Järvi,Kristjan | (cond)
NDR Radio Philharmonic Orchestra
Colossus Of Sound | Enja | ENJ-9460 2
Paquito D'Rivera Group With The Absolute Ensemble
Habanera | Enja | ENJ-9395 2

Jarvis,Arnold | (orgp)
Cootie Williams Quintet
Jazz In Paris:Joe Newman-Jazz At Midnight-Cootie Williams | EmArCy | 018446-2

Jarvis,Clifford | (dr,perc,bells,maracasvoice)
Barry Harris Quintet
Never Than New | Original Jazz Classics | OJCCD 1062-2(RLP 9413)
Chet Baker Quintet
Chet Baker Plays The Best Of Lerner And Loewe | Original Jazz Classics | OJC20 137-2
Chet Baker Septet
Chet Baker Plays The Best Of Lerner And Loewe | Original Jazz Classics | OJC20 137-2
Freddie Hubbard Quintet
Open Sesame | Blue Note | 495341-2
Hub-Tones | Blue Note | 499008-2
Jackie McLean Quartet
Right Now | Blue Note | 595972-2
Pharoah Sanders Orchestra
Thembi | Impulse(MCA) | 951253-2
Deaf Dumb Blind | Impulse(MCA) | 951265-2

Jasca,Diego | (g,charangometronome)
Toto Blanke-Diego Jasca
Sur | ALISO Records | AL 1035

Jascalevich,Diego | (gcharango)
Trio De La Gorra
Internationales Guitarren Festival '99 | ALISO Records | AL 1038

Jason,Neil | (b,vocel-b)
The Brecker Brothers
Heavy Metal Be-Bop | RCA | 2119257-2

Jaspar,Bobby | (fl,cl,tsreeds)
Blossom Dearie Quintet
My Gentleman Friend | Verve | 519905-2
Verve Jazz Masters 51:Blossom Dearie | Verve | 529906-2
Bobby Jaspar Quintet
Jazz In Paris:Bobby Jaspar-Jeux De Quartes | EmArCy | 018423-2
Jazz In Paris | EmArCy | 159941-2 PMS
Flute Flight | Original Jazz Classics | OJCCD 1084-2(P 2124)
Chet Baker Sextet
Chet Baker-The Italian Sessions | Bluebird | ND 82001
Donald Byrd Quintet
Byrd In Paris Vol.1 | Polydor | 833394-2
Herbie Mann-Bobby Jaspar Sextet
Flute Flight | Original Jazz Classics | OJCCD 1084-2(P 2124)
Flute Souflé | Original Jazz Classics | OJCCD 760-2(P 7101)
Jimmy Raney Quintet
Jimmy Raney Visits Paris Vol.2 | Vogue | 21434802
Prestige All Stars
John Coltrane-The Prestige Recordings | Prestige | 16 PCD 4405-2
The Mal Waldron Memorial Album:Soul Eyes | Prestige | PRCD 11024-2
Wynton Kelly Sextet
Kelly Blue | Original Jazz Classics | OJC20 033-2(RLP 1142)
Kelly Blue | Riverside | RISA 1142-6

Jasper,Lex | (cond,parr)
Joe Pass With The NDR Big Band
NDR Big Band-Bravissimo | ACT | 9232-2
NDR Big Band With Guests
50 Years Of NDR Big Band:Bravissimo II | ACT | 9259-2

Jastrzebski,Pawel Maciwoda | (el-b)
Urszula Dudziak And Band Walk Away
Magic Lady | IN+OUT Records | 7008-2

JATP All Stars |
Billie Holiday With The JATP All Stars
Billie Holiday Story Vol.1:Jazz At The Philharmonic | Verve | 521642-2
The Complete Jazz At The Philharmonic On Verve 1944-1949 | Verve | 523893-2
Verve Jazz Masters 47:Billie Holiday Sings Standards | Verve | 527650-2
Jazz At The Philharmonic:Best Of The 1940's Concerts | Verve | 557534-2
Ella Fitzgerald And Count Basie With The JATP All Stars
Bluella:Ella Fitzgerald Sings The Blues | Pablo | 2310960-2
Ella Fitzgerald With The JATP All Stars
Ella Fitzgerald-First Lady Of Song | Verve | 517898-2
For The Love Of Ella Fitzgerald | Verve | 841765-2
JATP All Stars
Jazz Gallery:Lester Young Vol.2(1946-59) | RCA | 2119541-2
JATP In Tokyo | Pablo | 2620104-2
J.A.T.P. In London 1969 | Pablo | 2CD 2620119
Stan Getz Highlights:The Best Of The Verve Years Vol.2 | Verve | 517330-2
Nothing But The Blues | Verve | 521674-2
Verve Jazz Masters 25:Stan Getz & Dizzy Gillespie | Verve | 521852-2
Verve Jazz Masters 28:Charlie Parker Plays Standards | Verve | 521854-2
The Complete Jazz At The Philharmonic On Verve 1944-1949 | Verve | 523893-2
Charlie Parker:The Best Of The Verve Years | Verve | 527815-2
Jazz At The Philharmonic:Best Of The 1940's Concerts | Verve | 557534-2
The Drum Battle:Gene Krupa And Buddy Rich At JATP | Verve | 559810-2
Talkin' Bird | Verve | 559859-2
The Cole Porter Songbook | Verve | 823250-2
Bird: The Complete Charlie Parker On Verve | Verve | 837141-2
Welcome To Jazz At The Philharmonic | Fantasy | FANCD 6081-2
Jazz At The Philharmonic-Frankfurt 1952 | Pablo | PACD 5305-2
Norman Granz' JATP: Carnegie Hall 1949 | Pablo | PACD 5311-2

Jaurena,Raul | (bandoneon)
Tango Five feat. Raul Jaurena
Obsecion | Satin Doll Productions | SDP 1027-1 CD

Jay,Thurber 'Sam Guy' | (el-b)
Louis Jordan With The Nelson Riddle Orchestra
Louis Jordan-Let The Good Times Roll: The Complete Decca Recordings 1938-1954 | Bear Family Records | BCD 15557 IH

JazzAfrica All Nations Big Band |
Jazz Africa All Nations Big Band
Jadu(Jazz Africa Down Under) | Enja | ENJ-9339 2

Jazz Artists Guild |
Jazz Artists Guild
Newport Rebels-Jazz Artists Guild | Candid | CCD 79022

Jazz Bomberos |
Jazz Bomberos
Naranja | Green House Music | CD 1003(Maxi)

Jazz Composer's Orchestra,The |
The Jazz Composer's Orchestra
Comminications | JCOA | 1001/2

Jazz Crusaders,The |
Jazz Crusaders
Chile Con Soul | Pacific Jazz | 590957-2
The Jazz Crusaders
Kind Of Blue:Blue Note Celebrate The Music Of Miles Davis | Blue Note | 534255-2

Jazz Fresh |
Jazz Fresh
Jazz Fresh | GGG-Verlag:GGG Verlag und Mailorder | CD 01.03

Jazz Giants '56,The |
The Jazz Giants '56
Jazz Gallery:Lester Young Vol.2(1946-59) | RCA | 2119541-2

Jazz Indeed |
Jazz Indeed
Under Water | Traumton Records | 2415-2
Who The Moon Is | Traumton Records | 4427-2

Jazz Orchester Rheinland-Pfalz |
Jazz Orchester Rheinland-Pfalz
Kazzou | Jazz Haus Musik | LJBB 9104
Like Life | Jazz Haus Musik | LJBB 9405
Last Season | Jazz Haus Musik | LJBB 9706

Jazz Pistols |
Jazz Pistols
Special Treatment | Lipstick Records | LIP 8971-2

Jazzensemble Des Hessischen Rundfunk |
Jazzensemble Des Hessischen Rundfunks
Atmosphering Conditions Permitting | ECM | 1549/50
Jazz Messe-Messe Für Unsere Zeit | hr music.de | hrmj 003-01 CD

Jazzpar 1996 Nonet |
Geri Allen And The Jazzpar 1996 Nonet
Some Aspects Of Water | Storyville | STCD 4212

Jean,George | (tb)
Duke Ellington And His Orchestra
Ellington '55 | Capitol | 520135-2

Jean-Baptiste,David | (as,basset-h,b-cl,contra-b-cl,b-fl)
David Jean-Baptiste Group
The Nature Suite | Laika Records | 35101632

Jean-Marie,Alain | (p)
Abbey Lincoln And Her All Stars
The World Is Falling Down | Verve | 843476-2

Jeanneau,Francois | (alto-fl,ts,fl,b-cl,ss,synth,lyricon)
Daniel Humair Trio
Humair/Jeanneau/Texier | Owl Records | 014734-2
Orchestre National De Jazz
Charmediterranéen | ECM | 1828(018493-2)

Jeanrenaud,Joan | (cello)
Fred Frith Maybe Monday
Digital Wildlife | Winter&Winter | 910071-2
John Zorn Group With The Kronos Quartet
Spillane | Nonesuch | 7559-79172-2

Jeffers,Jack | (b-tb,tubatb)
Charlie Haden Orchestra
The Ballad Of The Fallen | ECM | 1248(811546-2)
Herbie Hancock Orchestra
Herbie Hancock:The Complete Blue Note Sixties Sessions | Blue Note | 495569-2
The Prisoner | Blue Note | 525649-2
Machito And His Orchestra
Afro-Cuban Jazz Moods | Original Jazz Classics | OJC20 447-2
The Jazz Composer's Orchestra
Comminications | JCOA | 1001/2

Jefferson,Eddie | (voc)
Eddie Jefferson And His Band
Dexter Gordon Birthday Celebration | Fantasy | FANCD 6082-2
Eddie Jefferson With The James Moody Quintet
Body And Soul | Original Jazz Classics | OJCCD 396-2(P 7619)

Jefferson,Freddy | (p)
Jubilee All Stars
Jazz Gallery:Lester Young Vol.2(1946-59) | RCA | 2119541-2

Jefferson,Hilton | (as,clsax)
Cab Calloway And His Cab Jivers
Planet Jazz:Cab Calloway | Planet Jazz | 2161237-2
Coleman Hawkins And His Orchestra
Jazz:The Essential Collection Vol.3 | IN+OUT Records | 78013-2
Dizzy Gillespie And His Orchestra
Afro | Verve | 517052-2
Duke Ellington And His Orchestra
Greatest Hits | CBS | 462959-2
Ella Fitzgerald And Her Famous Orchestra
The Radio Years 1940 | Jazz Unlimited | JUCD 2065
Ella Fitzgerald And Her Orchestra
Jazz Collection:Ella Fitzgerald | Laserlight | 24397
Fletcher Henderson And His Orchestra
Jazz:The Essential Collection Vol.1 | IN+OUT Records | 78011-2
Jazz:The Essential Collection Vol.3 | IN+OUT Records | 78013-2
Frankie Laine With Buck Clayton And His Orchestra
Jazz Spectacular | CBS | CK 65507
Jimmy Witherspoon With Jay McShann And His Band
Planet Jazz:Male Jazz Vocalists | Planet Jazz | 2169657-2
King Oliver And His Orchestra
Jazz:The Essential Collection Vol.1 | IN+OUT Records | 78011-2
Louis Armstrong And His All Stars With The Sy Oliver Orchestra
Ambassador Louis Armstrong Vol.17:Moments To Remember(1952-1956) | Ambassador | CLA 1917

Jefferson,Hilton or Glyn Pacque | (as)
King Oliver And His Orchestra
Jazz:The Essential Collection Vol.1 | IN+OUT Records | 78011-2

Jefferson,Ron | (dr)
Lou Rawls With Les McCann Ltd.
Blue Velvet: Crooners, Swooners And Velvet Vocals | Blue Note | 521153-2
Stormy Monday | Blue Note | 791441-2
Richard 'Groove' Holmes Quintet
Somethin' Special | Pacific Jazz | 855452-2
Richard 'Groove' Holmes Sextet
Somethin' Special | Pacific Jazz | 855452-2
Zoot Sims With The Joe Castro Trio
Live At Falcon Lair | Pablo | PACD 2310977-2

Jefferson,Tony | (dr)
Don Friedman Quartet
My Foolish Heart | Steeplechase | SCCD 31534
My Foolish Heart | Steeplechase | SCCD 31545

Jeffrey,Paul | (alto-cl,ts,arr,bells,bs,cond,fl)
Charles Mingus Orchestra
Three Or Four Shades Of Blues | Atlantic | 7567-81403-2
Cumbia & Jazz Fusion | Atlantic | 8122-71785-2
Sam Rivers Orchestra
Crystals | Impulse(MCA) | 589760-2

Jeffries,Herb | (voc)
Duke Ellington And His Famous Orchestra
Duke Ellington:The Blanton-Webster Band | Bluebird | 21 13181-2
Duke Ellington And His Orchestra
The Duke At Fargo 1940 | Storyville | STCD 8316/17

Jeffries,Norman | (dr)
Johhny Frigo Duo
I Love John Frigo...He Swings | Mercury | 9861061
Johnny Frigo Quartet
I Love John Frigo...He Swings | Mercury | 9861061

Jekabson,Erik | (tp)
Andrew Adair Group
States | Fresh Sound Records | FSNT 061 CD

Jekowsky,Sidney | (clfl)
Coleman Hawkins With Billy Byers And His Orchestra
Planet Jazz:Coleman Hawkins | Planet Jazz | 2152055-2
The Hawk In Hi-Fi | RCA | 2663842-2

Jemmott,Jerry | (b,el-bfender-b)
George Benson With The Don Sebesky Orchestra
Verve Jazz Masters 21:George Benson | Verve | 521861-2
Lou Donaldson Orchestra
Blue Breaks Beats Vol.2 | Blue Note | 789907-2
Richard 'Groove' Holmes Orchestra
Comin' On Home | Blue Note | 538701-2
Richard 'Groove' Holmes Sextet
Blue Break Beats | Blue Note | 799106-2

Jenkins,Arthur | (cabassa,conga,keyboards,perc,congas)
Gunter Hampel New York Orchestra
Fresh Heat-Live At Sweet Basil | Birth | CD 039
Joe Henderson And His Orchestra
Joe Henderson:The Milestone Years | Milestone | 8MCD 4413-2
Joe Henderson Quintet
Multiple | Original Jazz Classics | OJCCD 763-2(M 9050)
Joe Henderson Sextet
Multiple | Original Jazz Classics | OJCCD 763-2(M 9050)
Rahsaan Roland Kirk And His Orchestra
Blacknuss | Rhino | 8122-71408-2
Sonny Rollins Quintet
Next Album | Original Jazz Classics | OJC 312 (M 9042)

Jenkins,Clarence 'Pookie' | (el-b)
David Murray Group
Speaking In Togues | Enja | ENJ-9370 2

Jenkins,Clay | (fl-htp)
Bill Perkins Quintet
Swing Spring | Candid | CCD 79752
Kurt Elling Group
Flirting With Twilight | Blue Note | 531113-2
Rich Perry Quintet
At Eastman | Steeplechase | SCCD 31533

Jenkins,Dan | (tb)
John Surman-Jack DeJohnette With The London Brass
Printed In Germany | ECM | 1802(017065-2)

Jenkins,Dechown | (g)
Lenny White Group
Renderers Of Spirit | Hip Bop | HIBD 8014
Hot Jazz Bisquits | Hip Bop | HIBD 8801

Jenkins,Freddie | (bells,tap-dancing,tpvoc)
Duke Ellington And His Cotton Club Orchestra
Planet Jazz:Duke Ellington | Planet Jazz | 2152053-2
Jazz:The Essential Collection Vol.2 | IN+OUT Records | 78012-2
Duke Ellington And His Orchestra
Highlights From The Duke Ellington Centennial Edition | RCA | 2663672-2
Jazz:The Essential Collection Vol.2 | IN+OUT Records | 78012-2

Jenkins,George | (b,cond,arrdr)
Ben Webster Sextet
Verve Jazz Masters 43:Ben Webster | Verve | 525431-2
Verve Jazz Masters 52:Maynard Ferguson | Verve | 529905-2
Lionel Hampton And His Orchestra
Lionel Hampton:Flying Home | Dreyfus Jazz Line | FDM 36735-2
Louis Armstrong With Gordon Jenkins And His Orchestra And Choir
Louis Armstrong-My Greatest Songs | MCA | MCD 18347
Swing Legends:Louis Armstrong | Nimbus Records | NI 2012

Jenkins,Gordon | (arr,condld)
Benny Goodman And His Orchestra
Planet Jazz:Benny Goodman | Planet Jazz | 2152054-2
Billie Holiday With Gordon Jenkins And His Orchestra
Billie's Love Songs | Nimbus Records | NI 2000
Louis Armstrong With Gordon Jenkins And His Orchestra
Satchmo In Style | Verve | 549594-2
Louis Armstrong With Gordon Jenkins And His Orchestra And Choir
Satchmo In Style | Verve | 549594-2
Ambassador Louis Armstrong Vol.17:Moments To Remember(1952-1956) | Ambassador | CLA 1917
Louis Armstrong With The Gordon Jenkins Orchestra
Ambassador Louis Armstrong Vol.17:Moments To Remember(1952-1956) | Ambassador | CLA 1917

Jenkins,John | (as)
Prestige All Stars
The Prestige Legacy Vol.2:Battles Of Saxes | Prestige | PCD 24252-2

Jenkins,Kenny | (b)
Art Pepper Quartet
Renascene | Galaxy | GCD 4202-2

Jenkins,Leroy | (fl,harm,v,viola,hohner-org)
Archie Shepp Orchestra
The Cry Of My People | Impulse(MCA) | 9861488
Paul Motian Quartet
Conception Vessel | ECM | 1028(519279-2)

Jenkins,Les | (tb)
Artie Shaw And His Orchestra
Planet JazzArtie Shaw | Planet Jazz | 2152057-2
The Legends Of Swing | Laserlight | 24659
Tommy Dorsey And His Orchestra
Planet Jazz:Frank Sinatra & Tommy Dorsey | Planet Jazz | 2152067-2
Planet Jazz:Tommy Dorsey | Planet Jazz | 2159972-2
Planet Jazz:Big Bands | Planet Jazz | 2169649-2
Planet Jazz:Swing | Planet Jazz | 2169651-2
Planet Jazz:Male Jazz Vocalists | Planet Jazz | 2169657-2
Frank Sinatra And The Tommy Dorsey Orchestra | RCA | 2668701-2

Jenkins,Marvin | (flp)
Barney Kessel Quartet
Barney Kessel's Swingin' Party At Contemporary | Original Jazz Classics | OJCCD 1066-2(S 7613)

Jenne,Meinhard | (dr)
Lilly Thornton With The Mike Hennesey Trio
Remembering Dinah-A Salute To Dinah Washington | Hot Shot Records | HSR 8313-2
Uli Binetsch's Own Bone
Boone Up Blues | Rockwerk Records | CD 011001

Jenney,Jack | (tbtp)
Artie Shaw And His Orchestra
Planet JazzArtie Shaw | Planet Jazz | 2152057-2
Planet Jazz:Big Bands | Planet Jazz | 2169649-2
Planet Jazz:Male Jazz Vocalists | Planet Jazz | 2169657-2

Jennings,Bill | (g)
Ella Fitzgerald With Louis Jordan And His Tympany Five
Ella Fitzgerald:Mr.Paganini | Dreyfus Jazz Line | FDM 36741-2
Jack McDuff Quartet
Brother Jack | Prestige | PR20 7174-2
The Last Goodun' | Prestige | PRCD 24274-2
Jack McDuff:The Prestige Years | Prestige | PRCD 24387-2
Louis Armstrong With Louis Jordan And His Tympany Five
Louis Armstrong:C'est Si Bon | Dreyfus Jazz Line | FDM 36730-2
Louis Jordan And His Tympany Five
Louis Jordan-Let The Good Times Roll: The Complete Decca Recordings 1938-1954 | Bear Family Records | BCD 15557 IH
Willis Jackson Quintet
Together Again: Willis Jackson With Jack McDuff | Prestige | PRCD 24284-2
Willis Jackson Sextet
At Large | Prestige | PCD 24243-2
Together Again: Willis Jackson With Jack McDuff | Prestige | PRCD 24284-2

Jennings,Jack | (congas,percvib)
George Benson Orchestra
Talkin' Verve:George Benson | Verve | 553780-2
George Benson With Orchestra
Verve Jazz Masters 21:George Benson | Verve | 521861-2
George Benson With The Don Sebesky Orchestra
Verve Jazz Masters 21:George Benson | Verve | 521861-2
Paul Desmond Quartet With The Don Sebesby Orchestra

From The Hot Afternoon | Verve | 543487-2
Wes Montgomery With The Don Sebesky Orchestra
Verve Jazz Masters 14:Wes Montgomery | Verve | 519826-2
Talkin' Jazz:Roots Of Acid Jazz | Verve | 529580-2
California Dreaming | Verve | 827842-2

Jennings,Morris | (drperc)
Albert King With The Willie Dixon Band
Windy City Blues | Stax | SCD 8612-2

Jenny-Clark,Jean-Francois | (b,el-bbasses-im playback)
Albert Mangelsdorff Trio
Three Originals:The Wide Point/Trilogue/Albert Live In Montreux | MPS | 519213-2
Aldo Romano Trio
Il Piacere | Owl Records | 013575-2
Chet Baker Quartet
Jazz In Paris:Chet Baker-Broken Wing | EmArCy | 013043-2
Enrico Rava Quartet
Enrico Rava Quartet | ECM | 1122
Gato Barbieri Group
Gato Barbieri:The Best Of The Early Years | RCA | 2663523-2
Gato Barbieri Quintet
The Art Of Saxophone | Laserlight | 24652
Joachim Kühn And The Radio Philharmonie Hannover NDR With Jazz Soloists
Europeana | ACT | 9220-2
Joachim Kühn Trio
Easy To Read | Owl Records | 014802-2
Joe Henderson Quintet
Joe Henderson:The Milestone Years | Milestone | 8MCD 4413-2
Joe Henderson Sextet
Joe Henderson:The Milestone Years | Milestone | 8MCD 4413-2
Kenny Wheeler Sextet
Around 6 | ECM | 1156
Kühn/Humair/Jenny-Clark
Tripple Entente | EmArCy | 558690-2
Michel Grailler Trio
Dream Drops | Owl Records | 013434-2
Michel Grailler-J.F. Jenny-Clark
Dream Drops | Owl Records | 013434-2
Michel Petrucciani Trio
Michel Petrucciani | Owl Records | 013431-2
Paul Motian Trio
Le Voyage | ECM | 1138
Richard Galliano Group
French Touch | Dreyfus Jazz Line | FDM 36596-2
Richard Galliano Quartet
Gallianissimo! The Best Of Richard Galliano | Dreyfus Jazz Line | FDM 36616-2
Richard Galliano Trio
Gallianissimo! The Best Of Richard Galliano | Dreyfus Jazz Line | FDM 36616-2

Jensen,Arne Bue | (tbld)
Bohana Jazzband
The Golden Years Of Revival Jazz,Vol.6 | Storyville | STCD 5511
The Golden Years Of Revival Jazz,Vol.10 | Storyville | STCD 5515
Chris Barber's Jazz Band
The Golden Years Of Revival Jazz,Vol.2 | Storyville | STCD 5507
Henrik Johansen's Jazzband
The Golden Years Of Revival Jazz.Vol.14 | Storyville | STCD 5519
Papa Bue's New Orleans Band
The Golden Years Of Revival Jazz,Vol.4 | Storyville | STCD 5509
Papa Bue's Viking Jazzband
The Golden Years Of Revival Jazz,Sampler | Storyville | 109 1001
The Golden Years Of Revival Jazz,Vol 1 | Storyville | STCD 5506
The Golden Years Of Revival Jazz.Vol.3 | Storyville | STCD 5508
The Golden Years Of Revival Jazz,Vol.5 | Storyville | STCD 5510
The Golden Years Of Revival Jazz,Vol.6 | Storyville | STCD 5511
The Golden Years Of Revival Jazz,Vol.7 | Storyville | STCD 5512
The Golden Years Of Revival Jazz,Vol.8 | Storyville | STCD 5513
The Golden Years Of Revival Jazz,Vol.9 | Storyville | STCD 5514
The Golden Years Of Revival Jazz,Vol.10 | Storyville | STCD 5515
The Golden Years Of Revival Jazz,Vol.11 | Storyville | STCD 5516
The Golden Years Of Revival Jazz,Vol.12 | Storyville | STCD 5517
The Golden Years Of Revival Jazz,Vol.13 | Storyville | STCD 5518
The Golden Years Of Revival Jazz.Vol.14 | Storyville | STCD 5519
The Golden Years Of Revibal Jazz,Vol.15 | Storyville | STCD 5520

Jensen,Bjorn | (bj)
Papa Benny's Jazzband
The Golden Years Of Revival Jazz,Vol.2 | Storyville | STCD 5507
The Golden Years Of Revival Jazz,Vol.7 | Storyville | STCD 5512
The Golden Years Of Revival Jazz,Vol.11 | Storyville | STCD 5516

Jensen,Dave | (ts)
Josh Roseman Unit
Cherry | Enja | ENJ-9392 2

Jensen,Eric | (cello)
First Avenue
First Avenue | ECM | 1194

Jensen,Flemming | (dr)
Leonardo Pedersen's Jazzkapel
The Golden Years Of Revival Jazz,Sampler | Storyville | 109 1001
The Golden Years Of Revival Jazz,Vol.11 | Storyville | STCD 5516

Jensen,Fredrik O. | (tsbs)
Geir Lysne Listening Ensemble
Korall | ACT | 9236-2
Aurora Borealis-Nordic Lights | ACT | 9406-2

Jensen,Henrik Eigil | (dr)
Adrian Bentzon's Jazzband
The Golden Years Of Revival Jazz,Sampler | Storyville | 109 1001
The Golden Years Of Revival Jazz,Vol 1 | Storyville | STCD 5506
The Golden Years Of Revival Jazz,Vol.2 | Storyville | STCD 5507
The Golden Years Of Revival Jazz.Vol.3 | Storyville | STCD 5508
The Golden Years Of Revival Jazz,Vol.4 | Storyville | STCD 5509
The Golden Years Of Revival Jazz,Vol.7 | Storyville | STCD 5512
The Golden Years Of Revival Jazz,Vol.13 | Storyville | STCD 5518
The Golden Years Of Revival Jazz.Vol.14 | Storyville | STCD 5519
Henrik Johansen's Jazzband
The Golden Years Of Revival Jazz,Vol.13 | Storyville | STCD 5518

Jensen,Ingrid | (tpfl-h)
Dan Wall Quartet
Off The Wall | Enja | ENJ-9310 2
Ingrid Jensen Quintet
Here On Earth | Enja | ENJ-9313 2
Higher Grounds | Enja | ENJ-9353 2
Ingrid Jensen Sextet
Vernal Fields | Enja | ENJ-9013 2
Jam Session
Jam Session Vol.4 | Steeplechase | SCCD 31527
Johannes Enders Quintet
Bright Nights | Enja | ENJ-9352 2
Peter Herbert Group
B-A-C-H A Chromatic Universe | Between The Lines | btl 013(Efa 10183)
United Women's Orchestra
Virgo Supercluster | Jazz Haus Musik | JHM 0123 CD

Jensen,Ole Kurt | (tbb-tb)
Miles Davis With The Danish Radio Big Band
Aura | CBS | CK 63962
Stan Getz With The Danish Radio Big Band
Stan Getz In Europe | Laserlight | 24657
Stan Kenton With The Danish Radio Big Band
Stan Kenton With The Danish Radio Big Band | Storyville | STCD 8340
The Danish Radio Big Band
Aura | CBS | CK 63962

Jensen,Peter | (tb)
Jens Winther And The Danish Radio Jazz Orchestra
Angels | dacapo | DCCD 9442
The Danish Radio Jazz Orchestra
Nice Work | dacapo | DCCD 9446

Jensen,Theis | (co,voctp)
Adrian Bentzon's Jazzband
The Golden Years Of Revival Jazz,Sampler | Storyville | 109 1001
The Golden Years Of Revival Jazz,Vol 1 | Storyville | STCD 5506
The Golden Years Of Revival Jazz,Vol.2 | Storyville | STCD 5507
The Golden Years Of Revival Jazz.Vol.3 | Storyville | STCD 5508
The Golden Years Of Revival Jazz,Vol.4 | Storyville | STCD 5509
The Golden Years Of Revival Jazz,Vol.7 | Storyville | STCD 5512
The Golden Years Of Revival Jazz,Vol.13 | Storyville | STCD 5518
The Golden Years Of Revival Jazz.Vol.14 | Storyville | STCD 5519
Henrik Johansen's Jazzband
The Golden Years Of Revival Jazz,Vol.13 | Storyville | STCD 5518
Theis/Nyegaard Jazzband
The Golden Years Of Revival Jazz,Sampler | Storyville | 109 1001
The Golden Years Of Revival Jazz.Vol.3 | Storyville | STCD 5508
The Golden Years Of Revival Jazz,Vol.5 | Storyville | STCD 5510
The Golden Years Of Revival Jazz,Vol.6 | Storyville | STCD 5511
The Golden Years Of Revival Jazz,Vol.12 | Storyville | STCD 5517
The Golden Years Of Revibal Jazz,Vol.15 | Storyville | STCD 5520

Jensson,Hilmar | (el-g,percg)
Jim Black Alasnoaxis
Splay | Winter&Winter | 910076-2
Jim Black Quartet
Alasnoaxis | Winter&Winter | 910061-2

Jerome,Jerry | (as,cl,ts,ld,reedssax)
(Little)Jimmy Scott With The Billy Taylor Orchestra
Everybody's Somebody's Fool | Decca | 050669-2
Artie Shaw And His Orchestra
Planet JazzArtie Shaw | Planet Jazz | 2152057-2
Planet Jazz:Big Bands | Planet Jazz | 2169649-2
Benny Goodman And His Orchestra
Charlie Christian:Swing To Bop | Dreyfus Jazz Line | FDM 36715-2
Camel Caravan Broadcast 1939 Vol.1 | Phontastic | NCD 8817
Camel Caravan Broadcast 1939 Vol.2 | Phontastic | NCD 8818
Camel Caravan Broadcast 1939 Vol.3 | Phontastic | NCD 8819
More Camel Caravans | Phontastic | NCD 8845/6
Ella Fitzgerald With Sy Oliver And His Orchestra
Ella Fitzgerald:Mr.Paganini | Dreyfus Jazz Line | FDM 36741-2
Ella Fitzgerald With Sy Oliver And His Orchestra
Ella Fitzgerald:The Decca Years 1949-1954 | Decca | 050668-2
Lionel Hampton And His Orchestra
Planet Jazz:Lionel Hampton | Planet Jazz | 2152059-2
Planet Jazz Sampler | Planet Jazz | 2152326-2

Jerry Hey And The Hot Band |
Dave Grusin Orchestra
Two For The Road:The Music Of Henry Mancini | GRP | GRP 98652

Jeschke,Gisela | (voc)
Jazzensemble Des Hessischen Rundfunks
Jazz Messe-Messe Für Unsere Zeit | hr music.de | hrmj 003-01 CD

Jesnkins,Lester | (dr)
Cootie Williams Quintet
Jazz In Paris:Joe Newman-Jazz At Midnight-Cootie Williams | EmArCy | 018446-2

Jevic,Marko Djord | (tp)
European Jazz Youth Orchestra
Swinging Europe 1 | dacapo | DCCD 9449
Swinging Europe 2 | dacapo | DCCD 9450

Jillich,Anton | (fl-htp)
Eberhard Weber Orchestra
Orchestra | ECM | 1374

Jillis,Jana | (voc)
Spyro Gyra & Guests
Love & Other Obsessions | GRP | GRP 98112

Jinda,George | (dr,perc,cymbal,rattles,shaker,udu)
Deborah Henson-Conant Group
Budapest | Laika Records | LK 93-039

Joao,Maria | (percvoc)
Carlos Bica Group
Azul | Traumton Records | 4425-2
Maria Joao Quintet
Conversa | Nabel Records:Jazz Network | CD 4628
NDR Big Band With Guests
50 Years Of NDR Big Band:Bravissimo II | ACT | 9259-2

Jobim,Ana Lontra | (voc)
Antonio Carlos Jobim With Orchestra
Verve Jazz Masters 13:Antonio Carlos Jobim | Verve | 516409-2

Jobim,Antonio Carlos | (birdcalls,voc,g,p,el-pperc)
Antonio Carlos Jobim
Antonio Carlos Jobim And Friends | Verve | 531556-2
Antonio Carlos Jobim Group
Verve Jazz Masters 13:Antonio Carlos Jobim | Verve | 516409-2
The Antonio Carlos Jobim Songbook | Verve | 525472-2
Antonio Carlos Jobim And Friends | Verve | 531556-2
Antonio Carlos Jobim With Orchestra
Verve Jazz Masters 13:Antonio Carlos Jobim | Verve | 516409-2
Antonio Carlos Jobim With The Claus Ogerman Orchestra
Verve Jazz Masters 13:Antonio Carlos Jobim | Verve | 516409-2
The Composer Of 'Desafinado' Plays | Verve | 521431-2
Antonio Carlos Jobim With The Herbie Hancock Sextet
Antonio Carlos Jobim And Friends | Verve | 531556-2
Antonio Carlos Jobim-Elis Regina Group
The Antonio Carlos Jobim Songbook | Verve | 525472-2
Antonio Carlos Jobim-Gal Costa Septet
Antonio Carlos Jobim And Friends | Verve | 531556-2
Astrud Gilberto With Antonio Carlos Jobim And The Marty Paich Orchestra
The Antonio Carlos Jobim Songbook | Verve | 525472-2
Astrud Gilberto With The Marty Paich Orchestra
Verve Jazz Masters 9:Astrud Gilberto | Verve | 519824-2
Getz-Gilberto Quintet
Verve Jazz Masters 13:Antonio Carlos Jobim | Verve | 516409-2
Stan Getz Highlights:The Best Of The Verve Years Vol.2 | Verve | 517330-2
Verve Jazz Masters 20:Introducing | Verve | 519853-2
Getz/Gilberto | Polydor | 521414-2
A Life In Jazz:A Musical Biography | Verve | 535119-2
Stan Getz Group
Verve Jazz Masters 53:Stan Getz-Bossa Nova | Verve | 529904-2
Stan Getz Quintet
Verve Jazz Masters 53:Stan Getz-Bossa Nova | Verve | 529904-2
Stan Getz Quintet Feat. Astrud Gilberto
Verve Jazz Masters 8:Stan Getz | Verve | 519823-2
Getz/Gilberto | Verve | 589595-2 SACD
Stan Getz-Joao Gilberto Quintet
The Antonio Carlos Jobim Songbook | Verve | 525472-2
Stan Getz Highlights | Verve | 847430-2
Stan Getz-Luiz Bonfa Group
The Antonio Carlos Jobim Songbook | Verve | 525472-2
Stan Getz-Luiz Bonfa Orchestra
Verve Jazz Masters 13:Antonio Carlos Jobim | Verve | 516409-2
Jazz Samba Encore! | Verve | 823613-2

Jobim,Elizabeth | (voc)
Antonio Carlos Jobim With Orchestra
Verve Jazz Masters 13:Antonio Carlos Jobim | Verve | 516409-2

Jobim,Paul | (g,synthvoc)

Jobim,Paulo | (flg)
Antonio Carlos Jobim Group
Antonio Carlos Jobim And Friends | Verve | 531556-2
Antonio Carlos Jobim With The Herbie Hancock Sextet
Antonio Carlos Jobim And Friends | Verve | 531556-2
Antonio Carlos Jobim-Gal Costa Septet
Antonio Carlos Jobim And Friends | Verve | 531556-2
Gal Costa With The Herbie Hancock Sextet
Antonio Carlos Jobim And Friends | Verve | 531556-2
Joe Henderson Septet
Antonio Carlos Jobim And Friends | Verve | 531556-2
Sarah Vaughan With Orchestra
I Love Brazil | Pablo | 2312101-2
Sarah Vaughan Birthday Celebration | Fantasy | FANCD 6090-2

Jobim,Tom | (el-p)
I Love Brazil | Pablo | 2312101-2
Sarah Vaughan Birthday Celebration | Fantasy | FANCD 6090-2

Joch,Micha | (perc)
Bajazzo
Harlequin Galaxy | Edition Collage | EC 519-2

Jodos,Ernesto | (p)
Hernan Merlo Quintet
Consin | Fresh Sound Records | FSNT 150 CD

Joergensen,Kjell Arne | (v)
Terje Rypdal With The Borealis Ensemble
Q.E.D. | ECM | 1474

Joggerst,Mark | (p)
Eda Zari With The Mark Joggerst Trio
The Art Of Time | Laika Records | 35100902

Johansen,Arne Birger | (btuba)
Arne Birger's Jazzsjak
The Golden Years Of Revival Jazz,Vol.8 | Storyville | STCD 5513
The Golden Years Of Revival Jazz,Vol.10 | Storyville | STCD 5515
Papa Benny's Jazzband
The Golden Years Of Revival Jazz,Vol.12 | Storyville | STCD 5517
Ricardo's Jazzmen
The Golden Years Of Revival Jazz,Sampler | Storyville | 109 1001

Johansen,Egil | (dr)
Lars Gullin Octet
Lars Gullin 1955/56 Vol.1 | Dragon | DRCD 224
NDR-Workshop
Doldinger's Best | ACT | 9224-2

Johansen,Henrik | (cl)
Adrian Bentzon's Jazzband
The Golden Years Of Revival Jazz,Sampler | Storyville | 109 1001
Albert Nicholas With Adrian Bentzon's Jazzband
The Golden Years Of Revival Jazz,Sampler | Storyville | 109 1001
Henrik Johansen With The City Ramblers
The Golden Years Of Revival Jazz,Sampler | Storyville | 109 1001
Henrik Johansen's Jazzband
The Golden Years Of Revival Jazz,Vol 1 | Storyville | STCD 5506
The Golden Years Of Revival Jazz,Vol.2 | Storyville | STCD 5507
The Golden Years Of Revival Jazz,Vol.6 | Storyville | STCD 5511
The Golden Years Of Revival Jazz,Vol.7 | Storyville | STCD 5512
The Golden Years Of Revival Jazz,Vol.13 | Storyville | STCD 5518
The Golden Years Of Revival Jazz.Vol.14 | Storyville | STCD 5519
The Golden Years Of Revibal Jazz,Vol.15 | Storyville | STCD 5520
Hylda Sims And The Citty Ramblers Skiffle Group With Henrik Johansen
The Golden Years Of Revival Jazz,Vol.9 | Storyville | STCD 5514

Johansen,Jonas | (dr)
Jens Winther And The Danish Radio Jazz Orchestra
Angels | dacapo | DCCD 9442
Mona Larsen And The Danish Radio Big Band Plus Soloists
Michael Mantler:Cerco Un Paese Innocente | ECM | 1556
Niels-Henning Orsted-Pedersen Trio
Friends Forever | Milestone | MCD 9269-2
Per Carsten Quintet
Via | dacapo | DCCD 9462
The Danish Radio Jazz Orchestra
This Train:The Danish Radio Jazz Orchestra Plays The Music Of Ray Pitts | dacapo | DCCD 9428
Nice Work | dacapo | DCCD 9446

Johansen,Per Oddvar | (dr)
Christian Wallumrod Ensemble
Sofienberg Variations | ECM | 1809(017067-2)
Jan Erik Kongshaug Group
The Other World | ACT | 9267-2
Trygve Seim Group
Different Rivers | ECM | 1744(159521-2)
Trygve Seim-Oyvind Braekke-Per Oddvar Johansen Orchestra
The Source And Different Cikadas | ECM | 1764(014432-2)

Johansen,Vidar | (b-cl,fl,ss,asbs)
Jacob Young Quintet
Evening Falls | ECM | 1876(9811780)

Johansson,Ake | (p)
Anders Lindskog Quartet
Cry Me A River | Touché Music | TMcCD 005
Kjell Jansson Quartet
Back From Where We Came | Touché Music | TMcCD 009
Kjell Jansson Quintet
Back From Where We Came | Touché Music | TMcCD 009
Stan Getz And The Swedish All Stars
Stan Getz Highlights:The Best Of The Verve Years Vol.2 | Verve | 517330-2

Johansson,Arnold | (tb,vibtp)
Coleman Hawkins With The Thore Ehrlings Orchestra
Coleman Hawkins At The Golden Circle | Dragon | DRCD 265

Johansson,Dan | (tpfl-h)
Tim Hagans With Norrbotten Big Band
Future Miles | ACT | 9235-2

Johansson,Egil | (dr)
Bengt-Arne Wallin Orchestra
The Birth+Rebirth Of Swedish Folk Jazz | ACT | 9254-2
Misha Alperin Group With The Brazz Brothers
Portrait | JA & RO | JARO 4227-2

Johansson,Jan | (p,arrorg)
Stan Getz And The Swedish All Stars
Stan Getz Highlights | Verve | 847430-2
Stan Getz Quartet
Stan Getz Highlights:The Best Of The Verve Years Vol.2 | Verve | 517330-2
Stan Getz Highlights | Verve | 847430-2
Stan Getz With Orchestra
Stan Getz Highlights | Verve | 847430-2

Johansson,Per 'Ruskträsk' | (as,wooden-fl,saxss)
Nils Landgren Funk Unit
Paint It Blue:A Tribute To Cannonball Adderley | ACT | 9243-2
Live In Montreux | ACT | 9265-2
Fonk Da World | ACT | 9299-2
Nils Landgren Funk Unit With Guests
5000 Miles | ACT | 9271-2
Viktoria Tolstoy With The Esbjörn Svensson Trio
Viktoria Tolstoy:White Russian | Blue Note | 821220-2

Johansson,Tina | (perc)
Lena Willemark-Ale Möller Group
Nordan | ECM | 1536(523161-2)
Agram | ECM | 1610

John | (bird-songs)
John McLaughlin Group
The Promise | Verve | 529828-2

John Motley Singers,The |
Max Roach Chorus & Orchestra
To The Max! | Enja | ENJ-7021 22

Johnakins,Leslie | (asbs)
Billie Holiday With Eddie Heywood And His Orchestra
Billie's Love Songs | Nimbus Records | NI 2000
Charlie Parker With Machito And His Orchestra
Charlie Parker:The Best Of The Verve Years | Verve | 527815-2
Talkin' Bird | Verve | 559859-2
Bird: The Complete Charlie Parker On Verve | Verve | 837141-2
Charlie Parker:April In Paris | Dreyfus Jazz Line | FDM 36737-2

Johns,Kenny | (dr)
Louis Armstrong And His All Stars
Louis Armstrong-My Greatest Songs | MCA | MCD 18347

Johnsen,Kjell | (pipe-org)
Jan Garbarek-Kjell Johnsen Duo
Aftenland | ECM | 1169(839304-2)

Johnson,Aaron | (shells,tbtuba)
Eric Dolphy Quartet With The University Of Illinois Brass Ensemble
The Illinois Concert | Blue Note | 499826-2

Johnson,Abdu | (conga)

Pat Martino Sextet
El Hombre | Original Jazz Classics | OJCCD 195-2(P 7513)

Johnson,Al | (dr,el-bg)

Willis Jackson Quintet
Together Again: Willis Jackson With Jack McDuff | Prestige | PRCD 24284-2
Willis Jackson Sextet
Together Again: Willis Jackson With Jack McDuff | Prestige | PRCD 24284-2
Woody Herman And His Orchestra
The Raven Speaks | Original Jazz Classics | OJCCD 663-2(F 9416)

Johnson,Alphonso | (b,taurus-bass-pedals,bass-synth)

Billy Cobham Group
The Best Of Billy Cobham | Atlantic | 7567-81558-2
Eddie Henderson Orchestra
Blue Breaks Beats Vol.2 | Blue Note | 789907-2
Flora Purim With Orchestra
Joe Henderson:The Milestone Years | Milestone | 8MCD 4413-2
Philip Catherine Quartet
Guitar Groove | Dreyfus Jazz Line | FDM 36599-2
Weather Report
Black Market | CBS | 468210-2

Johnson,Alvin | (dr)

Jack McDuff Quartet
Brother Jack | Prestige | PR20 7174-2
Jack McDuff:The Prestige Years | Prestige | PRCD 24387-2

Johnson,Alvin 'Big Al' | (voc)

Lillian Boutté And Her Group & The Soulful Heavenly Stars
The Gospel Book | Blues Beacon | BLU-1017 2

Johnson,Angeline | (voc)

Blind Willie Johnson
Classic Blues | Zounds | CD 2700048

Johnson,August | (voc)

Dee Dee Bridgewater With Band
Dee Dee Bridgewater | Atlantic | 7567-80760-2

Johnson,B. | (tb)

Woody Herman And His Orchestra
Verve Jazz Masters 54:Woody Herman | Verve | 529903-2

Johnson,Bashiri | (percperc-samples)

Al Jarreau With Band
Tenderness | i.e. Music | 557853-2
Marcus Miller Group
Tales | Dreyfus Jazz Line | FDM 36571-2
Miles Davis Group
Amandla | Warner | 7599-25873-2
Spyro Gyra & Guests
Love & Other Obsessions | GRP | GRP 98112
The Brecker Brothers
Return Of The Brecker Brothers | GRP | GRP 96842

Johnson,Ben | (gtb)

Oscar Peterson Trio
Planet Music:Oscar Peterson | RCA | 2165365-2
This Is Oscar Peterson | RCA | 2663990-2

Johnson,Bill | (as,arr,b,bj,voc,cl,g,tbtp)

Abraham Burton Quartet
The Magician | Enja | ENJ-9037 2
Count Basie And His Orchestra
Planet Jazz:Count Basie | Planet Jazz | 2152068-2
Planet Jazz Sampler | Planet Jazz | 2152326-2
Planet Jazz:Jimmy Rushing | RCA | 2165371-2
Planet Jazz:Jazz Greatest Hits | Planet Jazz | 2169648-2
Planet Jazz:Big Bands | Planet Jazz | 2169649-2
Jazz:The Essential Collection Vol.3 | IN+OUT Records | 78013-2
Erskine Hawkins And His Orchestra
Planet Jazz:Big Bands | Planet Jazz | 2169649-2
King Oliver's Creole Jazz Band
Jazz:The Essential Collection Vol.1 | IN+OUT Records | 78011-2
Sammy Price Septet
Jazz:The Essential Collection Vol.3 | IN+OUT Records | 78013-2

Johnson,Billy | (b,cymbals,dr-machine-program,dr)

Abraham Burton Quartet
Closest To The Sun | Enja | ENJ-8074 2

Johnson,Birch | (tb)

David Matthews & The Manhattan Jazz Orchestra
Back To Bach | Milestone | MCD 9312-2
Hey Duke! | Milestone | MCD 9320-2

Johnson,Blind Willie | (gvoc)

Blind Willie Johnson
Classic Blues | Zounds | CD 2700048

Johnson,Bobby | (bjg)

Bessie Smith And Her Band
Jazz:The Essential Collection Vol.3 | IN+OUT Records | 78013-2
Ella Fitzgerald With The Chick Webb Orchestra
Jazz Collection:Ella Fitzgerald | Laserlight | 24397

Johnson,Budd | (as,ts,arr,bs,cl,voc,fl,reeds,sax,ss)

Al Sears And His Orchestra
Sear-iously | Bear Family Records | BCD 15668 AH
Ben Webster And His Associates
Verve Jazz Masters 43:Ben Webster | Verve | 525431-2
Ultimate Ben Webster selected by James Carter | Verve | 557537-2
Ben Webster And Associates | Verve | 835254-2
Big Al Sears Band
Sear-iously | Bear Family Records | BCD 15668 AH
Bill Coleman Septet
Jazz In Paris:Bill Coleman-From Boogie To Funk | EmArCy | 549401-2 PMS
Billie Holiday And Her All Stars
Billie Holiday Story Vol.4:Lady Sings The Blues | Verve | 521429-2
Billie Holiday With Sy Oliver And His Orchestra
Billie's Love Songs | Nimbus Records | NI 2000
Birdland Dream Band
Birdland Dream Band | RCA | 2663873-2
Bud Powell Orchestra
Bebop | Pablo | PACD 2310978-2
Cannonball Adderley And His Orchestra
Ballads | Blue Note | 537563-2
Cannonball Adderley Quintet
Ballads | Blue Note | 537563-2
Cannonball Adderley With Sergio Mendes And The Bossa Rio Sextet
Ballads | Blue Note | 537563-2
Coleman Hawkins And His All Stars
Planet Jazz:Coleman Hawkins | Planet Jazz | 2152055-2
Planet Jazz:Bebop | RCA | 2169650-2
Jazz:The Essential Collection Vol.3 | IN+OUT Records | 78013-2
Coleman Hawkins And His Orchestra
Jazz:The Essential Collection Vol.3 | IN+OUT Records | 78013-2
Dizzy Gillespie And His Orchestra
Planet Jazz:Dizzy Gillespie | Planet Jazz | 2152069-2
Duke Ellington And Count Basie With Their Orchestras
First Time! | CBS | CK 65571
Earl Hines And His Orchestra
Planet Jazz:Earl Hines | Planet Jazz | 2159973-2
Jazz:The Essential Collection Vol.2 | IN+OUT Records | 78012-2
Frankie Laine With Buck Clayton And His Orchestra
Jazz Spectacular | CBS | CK 65507
Gil Evans Orchestra
Out Of The Cool | Impulse(MCA) | 951186-2
J.J.Johnson And His Orchestra
Planet Jazz:J.J.Johnson | Planet Jazz | 2159974-2
Jimmy McGriff Orchestra
Swingin' The Blues-Jumpin' The Blues | Laserlight | 24654
Jimmy Rushing And His Band
Planet Jazz:Jimmy Rushing | RCA | 2165371-2
Jimmy Rushing And His Orchestra
Five Feet Of Soul | Roulette | 581830-2
Jimmy Smith With Orchestra
Jimmy Smith-Talkin' Verve | Verve | 531563-2
Jimmy Smith With The Claus Ogerman Orchestra
Verve Jazz Masters 29:Jimmy Smith | Verve | 521855-2
Any Number Can Win | Verve | 557447-2
Jimmy Smith With The Oliver Nelson Orchestra
Jimmy Smith:Best Of The Verve Years | Verve | 527950-2
Lionel Hampton And His Orchestra
Planet Jazz:Lionel Hampton | Planet Jazz | 2152059-2
Louis Armstrong And His Orchestra
Planet Jazz:Louis Armstrong | Planet Jazz | 2152052-2
Best Of The Complete RCA Victor Recordings | RCA | 2663636-2
Louis Armstrong:A 100th Birthday Celebration | RCA | 2663694-2
Jazz:The Essential Collection Vol.2 | IN+OUT Records | 78012-2
Louis Armstrong With Sy Oliver And His Orchestra
Satchmo Serenaders | Verve | 543792-2
Roy Eldridge Septet
To Bags...With Love:Memorial Album | Pablo | 2310967-2
Sarah Vaughan With George Treadwell And His Allstars
Sarah Vaughan:Lover Man | Dreyfus Jazz Line | FDM 36739-2

Johnson,Buddy | (ld,org,p,arr,voctp)

Buddy Johnson And His Orchestra
Buddy And Ella Johnson 1953-1964 | Bear Family Records | BCD 15479 DH
Clark Terry Orchestra
Color Changes | Candid | CCD 79009

Johnson,Bunk | (talking,tp,voctp-solo)

Bunk Johnson
Authentic New Orleans Jazz | Good Time Jazz | GTCD 12048-2
Bunk Johnson And His New Orleans Band
Planet Jazz:Jazz Trumpet | Planet Jazz | 2169654-2
Bunk Johnson And His Superior Jazz Band
Authentic New Orleans Jazz | Good Time Jazz | GTCD 12048-2
Bunk Johnson With The Yerba Buena Jazz Band
Bunk & Lu | Good Time Jazz | GTCD 12024-2
Bunk Johnson-Sidney Bechet Sextet
Jazz:The Essential Collection Vol.1 | IN+OUT Records | 78011-2

Johnson,Charles Icarus | (gvoc)

Al Jarreau With Band
Al Jarreau In London | i.e. Music | 557849-2
Sonny Rollins Quintet
Easy Living | Original Jazz Classics | OJCCD 893-2
Sonny Rollins Sextet
Jazzin' Vol.2: The Music Of Stevie Wonder | Fantasy | FANCD 6088-2
Easy Living | Original Jazz Classics | OJCCD 893-2

Johnson,Clarence | (b,cl,as,ptaking)

Louis Jordan And His Tympany Five
Louis Jordan-Let The Good Times Roll: The Complete Decca Recordings 1938-1954 | Bear Family Records | BCD 15557 IH
Louis Jordan's Elks Rendez-Vous Band
Louis Jordan-Let The Good Times Roll: The Complete Decca Recordings 1938-1954 | Bear Family Records | BCD 15557 IH
Roger Sturgis With Lovie Jordan's Elks Rendez-Vous Band
Louis Jordan-Let The Good Times Roll: The Complete Decca Recordings 1938-1954 | Bear Family Records | BCD 15557 IH

Johnson,Danny | (perc)

Keith Jarrett Quintet
Fort Yawuh | Impulse(MCA) | 547966-2

Johnson,Dewey | (tp)

John Coltrane And His Orchestra
Ascension | Impulse(MCA) | 543413-2

Johnson,Don | (tp)

Johnny Otis And His Orchestra
Verve Jazz Masters 43:Ben Webster | Verve | 525431-2

Johnson,Doris | (cello)

Harry Carney And His Orchestra With Strings
Music For Loving:Ben Webster With Strings | Verve | 527774-2

Johnson,Eddie | (pts)

Kurt Elling Group
This Time Its Love | Blue Note | 493543-2
Kurt Elling Group With Guests
Live In Chicago | Blue Note | 522211-2
Louis Jordan And His Tympany Five
Louis Jordan-Let The Good Times Roll: The Complete Decca Recordings 1938-1954 | Bear Family Records | BCD 15557 IH

Johnson,Ella | (voc)

Buddy Johnson And His Orchestra
Buddy And Ella Johnson 1953-1964 | Bear Family Records | BCD 15479 DH

Johnson,Elyse | (voc)

Lenny White Group
Renderers Of Spirit | Hip Bop | HIBD 8014

Johnson,Floyd | (ts)

Count Basie And His Orchestra
Verve Jazz Masters 2:Count Basie | Verve | 519819-2

Johnson,Folke | (tb)

Brocksieper-Jazz-Ensemble
Drums Boogie | Bear Family Records | BCD 15988 AH
Brocksieper-Solisten-Orchester
Globetrotter | Bear Family Records | BCD 15912 AH
Brocksieper-Special-Ensemble
Globetrotter | Bear Family Records | BCD 15912 AH

Johnson,Gene | (as)

Charlie Parker With Machito And His Orchestra
Charlie Parker:The Best Of The Verve Years | Verve | 527815-2
Talkin' Bird | Verve | 559859-2
Bird: The Complete Charlie Parker On Verve | Verve | 837141-2
Charlie Parker:April In Paris | Dreyfus Jazz Line | FDM 36737-2

Johnson,George | (as,cl,dr,g,tpts)

Abdullah Ibrahim Trio
Yarona | TipToe | TIP-888820 2
Charles Earland Septet
Charles Earland In Concert | Prestige | PRCD 24267-2
Charles Earland Sextet
Charles Earland In Concert | Prestige | PRCD 24267-2
Herbie Hancock Group
Magic Window | CBS | 486572-2
The Wolverines
Jazz:The Essential Collection Vol.2 | IN+OUT Records | 78012-2
Willie Lewis And His Entertainers
Americans Swinging In Paris:Benny Carter | EMI Records | 539647-2

Johnson,Gunnar | (b)

Clifford Brown And Art Farmer With The Swedish All Stars
Clifford Brown Memorial | Original Jazz Classics | OJC20 017-2(P 7055)
Stan Getz And The Swedish All Stars
Stan Getz Highlights:The Best Of The Verve Years Vol.2 | Verve | 517330-2
Stan Getz Highlights | Verve | 847430-2
Stan Getz Quartet
Stan Getz Highlights | Verve | 847430-2

Johnson,Gus | (drvoc)

Billie Holiday And Her All Stars
Verve Jazz Masters 12:Billie Holiday | Verve | 519825-2
Verve Jazz Masters Vol.60:The Collection | Verve | 529866-2
The Billie Holiday Song Book | Verve | 823246-2
Billie Holiday And Her Quintet
Verve Jazz Masters 47:Billie Holiday Sings Standards | Verve | 527650-2
Buck Clayton-Buddy Tate Quintet
Buck & Buddy Blow The Blues | Original Jazz Classics | OJCCD 850-2(SV 2030)
Coleman Hawkins With Eddie Lockjaw Davis And The Tommy Flanagan Trio
Night Hawk | Original Jazz Classics | OJC20 420-2(SV 2016)
Count Basie And His Orchestra
Jazz Gallery:Lester Young Vol.2(1946-59) | RCA | 2119541-2
Jazz Collection:Count Basie | Laserlight | 24368
Atomic Swing | Roulette | 497871-2
Verve Jazz Masters 2:Count Basie | Verve | 519819-2
King Of Swing | Verve | 837433-2
Count Basie Octet
Planet Jazz:Count Basie | Planet Jazz | 2152068-2
Eddie Lockjaw Davis Quartet
The Art Of Saxophone | Laserlight | 24652
Ella Fitzgerald And Her All Stars
Ella Fitzgerald-First Lady Of Song | Verve | 517898-2
Verve Jazz Masters 6:Ella Fitzgerald | Verve | 519822-2
For The Love Of Ella Fitzgerald | Verve | 841765-2
Ella Fitzgerald And Her Quintet
Verve Jazz Masters 46:Ella Fitzgerald-The Jazz Sides | Verve | 527655-2
Ella Fitzgerald With The Bill Doggett Orchestra
Ella Fitzgerald-First Lady Of Song | Verve | 517898-2
Rhythm Is My Business | Verve | 559513-2
Ella Fitzgerald With The Duke Ellington Orchestra
The Stockholm Concert 1966 | Pablo | 2308242-2
Ella Fitzgerald With The Lou Levy Quartet
Ella Fitzgerald-First Lady Of Song | Verve | 517898-2
4 By 4:Ella Fitzgerald/Sarah Vaughan/Billie Holiday/Dinah Washington | Verve | 559693-2
Clap Hands,Here Comes Charlie! | Verve | 835646-2
For The Love Of Ella Fitzgerald | Verve | 841765-2
Ella Fitzgerald With The Lou Levy Trio
Ella Fitzgerald-First Lady Of Song | Verve | 517898-2
For The Love Of Ella Fitzgerald | Verve | 841765-2
Ella Fitzgerald With The Paul Smith Quartet
Ella Fitzgerald-First Lady Of Song | Verve | 517898-2
Mack The Knife-The Complete Ella In Berlin | Verve | 519564-2
Verve Jazz Masters 6:Ella Fitzgerald | Verve | 519822-2
4 By 4:Ella Fitzgerald/Sarah Vaughan/Billie Holiday/Dinah Washington | Verve | 559693-2
For The Love Of Ella Fitzgerald | Verve | 841765-2
Ella Fitzgerald With The Tommy Flanagan Trio
Ella Fitzgerald-First Lady Of Song | Verve | 517898-2
Gerry Mulligan Concert Jazz Band
Verve Jazz Masters 36:Gerry Mulligan | Verve | 523342-2
Verve Jazz Masters Vol.60:The Collection | Verve | 529866-2
The Complete Verve Gerry Mulligan Concert Band | Verve | 9860613
Gerry Mulligan Quartet
Paris Jazz Concert:Gerry Mulligan And His Quartet | Laserlight | 17433
Jazz At The Philharmonic: The Gerry Mulligan Quartets In Concert | Pablo | PACD 5309-2
Hal Singer-Charlie Shavers Quintet
Blue Stompin' | Original Jazz Classics | OJCCD 834-2(P 7153)
JATP All Stars
Nothing But The Blues | Verve | 521674-2
Jimmy Rushing And His Orchestra
Five Feet Of Soul | Roulette | 581830-2
Roy Eldridge Quintet
The Complete Verve Roy Eldridge Studio Sessions | Verve | 9861278
Roy Eldridge Sextet
The Complete Verve Roy Eldridge Studio Sessions | Verve | 9861278
Sackville All Stars
Christmas Jazz! | Nagel-Heyer | NH 1008
Willie Dixon-Memphis Slim Quintet
Windy City Blues | Stax | SCD 8612-2
Willis Jackson Quintet
At Large | Prestige | PCD 24243-2

Johnson,Harald | (b)

Jan Erik Kongshaug Group
The Other World | ACT | 9267-2
Silje Nergard Group with Strings
Nightwatch | EmArCy | 9865648
Tord Gustavsen Trio
Changing Places | ECM | 1834(016397-2)

Johnson,Harold 'Money' | (tp)

King Curtis Band
King Curtis-Blow Man Blow | Bear Family Records | BCD 15670 CI
Louis Jordan And His Tympany Five
Louis Jordan-Let The Good Times Roll: The Complete Decca Recordings 1938-1954 | Bear Family Records | BCD 15557 IH

Johnson,Howard | (alto-cl,bs,tuba,arr,as,b-cl,el-b,cl)

Albert Mangelsdorff With The NDR Big Band
NDR Big Band-Bravissimo | ACT | 9232-2
Anfrew Hill Nonet
Passing Ships | Blue Note | 593871-2
Archie Shepp Orchestra
Mama Too Tight | Impulse(MCA) | 951248-2
Barbara Dennerlein Group
Junkanoo | Verve | 537122-2
Bernard Purdie's Soul To Jazz
Bernard Purdie's Soul To Jazz II | ACT | 9253-2
Carla Bley Group
Tropic Appetites | Watt | 1
Charlie Haden's Liberation Music Orchestra
Liberation Music Orchestra | Impulse(MCA) | 951188-2
Dicky Wells And His Orchestra
Americans Swinging In Paris:Dicky Wells | EMI Records | 539664-2
Dizzy Gillespie And His Orchestra
Dizzy Gillespie:Pleyel Jazz Concert 1948 + Max Roach Quintet 1949 | Vogue | 21409412
Planet Jazz:Dizzy Gillespie | Planet Jazz | 2152069-2
Planet Jazz:Bebop | RCA | 2169650-2
Dollar(Abdullah Ibrahim) Brand Group
African River | Enja | ENJ-6018 2
Ella Fitzgerald With The Dizzy Gillespie Orchestra
Ella Fitzgerald:Mr.Paganini | Dreyfus Jazz Line | FDM 36741-2
Ella Fitzgerald With The Hank Jones Trio
Ella Fitzgerald:Mr.Paganini | Dreyfus Jazz Line | FDM 36741-2
Erica Lindsay Quintet
Dreamers | Candid | CCD 79040
Erica Lindsay Sextet
Dreamers | Candid | CCD 79040
Gary Burton Quartet With Orchestra
A Genuine Tong Funeral(Dark Opera Without Words) | RCA | 2119255-2
Gato Barbieri Orchestra
The Roots Of Acid Jazz | Impulse(MCA) | IMP 12042
George Gruntz Concert Jazz Band
Blues 'N Dues Et Cetera | Enja | ENJ-6072 2
George Gruntz Concert Jazz Band '83
Theatre | ECM | 1265
Gil Evans Orchestra
There Comes A Time | RCA | 2131392-2
PLay The Music Of Jimi Hendrix | RCA | 2663872-2
Svengali | Rhino | 8122-73720-2
Blues In Orbit | Enja | ENJ-3069 2
Hank Crawford And His Orchestra
Roadhouse Symphony | Original Jazz Classics | OJCCD 1048-2(M 9140)
Heinz Sauer Quartet With The NDR Big Band
NDR Big Band-Bravissimo | ACT | 9232-2
Jack DeJohnette's Special Edition
Album Album | ECM | 1280
Joe Pass With The NDR Big Band
NDR Big Band-Bravissimo | ACT | 9232-2
Joe Pass With The NDR Big Band And Radio Philharmonie Hannover
Joe Pass In Hamburg | ACT | 9100-2
John Scofield Groups
Quiet | Verve | 533185-2
Groove Elation | Blue Note | 832801-2
Johnny Griffin With The NDR Big Band
NDR Big Band-Bravissimo | ACT | 9232-2
McCoy Tyner Big Band
The Best Of McCoy Tyner Big Band | Dreyfus Jazz Line | FDM 37012-2
Miles Davis With Gil Evans Orchestra, The George Gruntz Concert Jazz Band And Guests
Miles & Quincy Live At Montreux | Warner | 9362-45221-2
NDR Big Band

NDR Big Band-Bravissimo | ACT | 9232-2
Pee Wee Ellis Quintet
Sepia Tonality | Minor Music | 801040
Spike Hughes And His Negro Orchestra
Jazz:The Essential Collection Vol.3 | IN+OUT Records | 78013-2
Thad Jones-Mel Lewis Orchestra
The Groove Merchant/The Second Race | Laserlight | 24656
The Jazz Composer's Orchestra
Comminications | JCOA | 1001/2

Johnson,J.C. prob. | (p)
Blind Willie Dunn's Gin Bottle Four
Jazz:The Essential Collection Vol.1 | IN+OUT Records | 78011-2

Johnson,J.J. | (arr,hand-clapping,tb,echo,synth)
Benny Golson Sextet
The J.J.Johnson Memorial Album | Prestige | PRCD 11025-2
Billie Holiday With The Ray Ellis Orchestra
Lady In Satin | CBS | CK 65144
Bud Powell Orchestra
Bebop | Pablo | PACD 2310978-2
Cal Tjader's Orchestra
Verve Jazz Masters 39:Cal Tjader | Verve | 521858-2
Cannonball Adderley And His Orchestra
Verve Jazz Masters 31:Cannonball Adderley | Verve | 522651-2
Ballads | Blue Note | 537563-2
Cannonball Adderley Group
Julian 'Cannonball' Adderley | EmArCy | 830381-2
Chubby Jackson Big Band
Gerry Mulligan Quartet feat.Chet Baker | Original Jazz Classics | OJCCD 711-2(F 8082/P 7641)
Coleman Hawkins All Star Octet
Milt Jackson Birthday Celebration | Fantasy | FANCD 6079-2
Coleman Hawkins All Stars
The J.J.Johnson Memorial Album | Prestige | PRCD 11025-2
Coleman Hawkins And His All Stars
Planet Jazz:Coleman Hawkins | Planet Jazz | 2152055-2
Planet Jazz:Bebop | RCA | 2169650-2
Jazz:The Essential Collection Vol.3 | IN+OUT Records | 78013-2
Count Basie And His Orchestra
Jazz:The Essential Collection Vol.3 | IN+OUT Records | 78013-2
Count Basie Kansas City 7
Count Basie Kansas City 7 | Original Jazz Classics | OJCCD 690-2(2310908)
Dizzy Gillespie And His Orchestra
Planet Jazz:Dizzy Gillespie | Planet Jazz | 2152069-2
Planet Jazz:Bebop | RCA | 2169650-2
Afro | Verve | 517052-2
Ella Fitzgerald With Orchestra
Ella/Things Ain't What They Used To Be | Warner | 9362-47875-2
Ella Fitzgerald With The JATP All Stars
Ella Fitzgerald-First Lady Of Song | Verve | 517898-2
For The Love Of Ella Fitzgerald | Verve | 841765-2
Ella Fitzgerald With The Nelson Riddle Orchestra
Dream Dancing | Original Jazz Classics | OJCCD 1072-2(2310814)
Esquire All-American Award Winners
Planet Jazz:Jazz Trumpet | Planet Jazz | 2169654-2
Four Trombones
Charles Mingus-The Complete Debut Recordings | Debut | 12 DCD 4402-2
The J.J.Johnson Memorial Album | Prestige | PRCD 11025-2
Frankie Laine With Buck Clayton And His Orchestra
Jazz Spectacular | CBS | CK 65507
Hank Jones With Oliver Nelson's Orchestra
The Roots Of Acid Jazz | Impulse(MCA) | IMP 12042
Horace Silver Sextet
Horace Silver Retrospective | Blue Note | 495576-2
The Cape Verdean Blues | Blue Note | 576753-2
J.J. Johnson-Al Grey Sextet
Things Are Getting Better All The Time | Original Jazz Classics | OJCCD 745-2(2312141)
The J.J.Johnson Memorial Album | Prestige | PRCD 11025-2
J.J.Johnson & Stan Getz With The Oscar Peterson Quartet
Stan Getz Highlights:The Best Of The Verve Years Vol.2 | Verve | 517330-2
A Life In Jazz:A Musical Biography | Verve | 535119-2
Stan Getz Highlights | Verve | 847430-2
J.J.Johnson And His Orchestra
Planet Jazz:J.J.Johnson | Planet Jazz | 2159974-2
J.J.Johnson Quartet
J.J.'s Broadway | Verve | 9860308
J.J.Johnson Quintet
The Eminent J.J.Johnson Vol.2 | Blue Note | 532144-2
The J.J.Johnson Memorial Album | Prestige | PRCD 11025-2
J.J.Johnson Sextet
The Eminent J.J.Johnson Vol.1 | Blue Note | 532143-2
The J.J.Johnson Memorial Album | Prestige | PRCD 11025-2
J.J.Johnson-Joe Pass
The J.J.Johnson Memorial Album | Prestige | PRCD 11025-2
J.J.Johnson-Kai Winding Quintet (Jay&Kai)
The J.J.Johnson Memorial Album | Prestige | PRCD 11025-2
J.J.Johnson-Nat Adderley Quintet
Yokohama Concert Vol.2:Chain Reaction | Pablo | PACD 2620121-2
The J.J.Johnson Memorial Album | Prestige | PRCD 11025-2
J.J.Johnson's All Stars
J.J.'s Broadway | Verve | 9860308
JATP All Stars
Verve Jazz Masters 25:Stan Getz & Dizzy Gillespie | Verve | 521852-2
The Complete Jazz At The Philharmonic On Verve 1944-1949 | Verve | 523893-2
The J.J.Johnson Memorial Album | Prestige | PRCD 11025-2
Jimmy McGriff Orchestra
Swingin' The Blues-Jumpin' The Blues | Laserlight | 24654
Joe Williams With The Frank Hunter Orchestra
Planet Jazz:Joe Williams | Planet Jazz | 2165370-2
Kai Winding-J.J.Johnson Quintet
The Great Kai & J.J. | Impulse(MCA) | 951225-2
Kansas City Seven
The J.J.Johnson Memorial Album | Prestige | PRCD 11025-2
Kenny Dorham Octet
Afro-Cuban | Blue Note | 0675619
Kenny Dorham Orchestra
Blue Bossa | Blue Note | 795590-2
Louis Armstrong And His Orchestra
What A Wonderful World | MCA | MCD 01876
Miles Davis All Star Sextet
Walkin' | Original Jazz Classics | OJC20 213-2
Miles Davis All Stars
Miles Davis Vol.1 | Blue Note | 532610-2
Miles Davis Vol.2 | Blue Note | 532611-2
The J.J.Johnson Memorial Album | Prestige | PRCD 11025-2
Miles Davis And His Orchestra
The Complete Birth Of The Cool | Capitol | 494550-2
Birth Of The Cool | Capitol | 530117-2
Jazz Profile:Miles Davis | Blue Note | 823515-2
Ballads & Blues | Blue Note | 836633-2
Miles Davis:Milestones | Dreyfus Jazz Line | FDM 36731-2
Miles Davis Sextet
Kind Of Blue:Blue Note Celebrate The Music Of Miles Davis | Blue Note | 534255-2
Miles Davis:The Best Of The Capitol/Blue Note Years | Blue Note | 798287-2
Jazz Profile:Miles Davis | Blue Note | 823515-2
Ballads & Blues | Blue Note | 836633-2
Miles Davis:Milestones | Dreyfus Jazz Line | FDM 36731-2
Milt Jackson Septet
The Birdlanders Vol.1 | Original Jazz Classics | OJCCD 1930-2
Milt Jackson Sextet
The Birdlanders Vol.1 | Original Jazz Classics | OJCCD 1930-2
Oliver Nelson And His Orchestra
Verve Jazz Masters Vol.60:The Collection | Verve | 529866-2
Oscar Peterson With Orchestra
With Respect To Nat | Verve | 557486-2
Quincy Jones Big Band
Rahsaan/The Complete Mercury Recordings Of Roland Kirk | Mercury | 846630-2
Raul De Souza Orchestra
Cannonball Adderley Birthday Celebration | Fantasy | FANCD 6087-2
Ron Carter Octet
New York Slick | Original Jazz Classics | OJCCD 916-2(M 9096)
Ron Carter Sextet
New York Slick | Original Jazz Classics | OJCCD 916-2(M 9096)
Sarah Vaughan And The Thad Jones Orchestra
Verve Jazz Masters 42:Sarah Vaughan-The Jazz Sides | Verve | 526817-2
Sarah Vaughan With Small Group & Orchestra
Duke Ellington Song Book One | Pablo | CD 2312111
Sarah Vaughan With The Hal Mooney Orchestra
It's A Man's World | Mercury | 589487-2
Sonny Rollins Orchestra
Alfie | Impulse(MCA) | 951224-2
Sonny Rollins Quintet
Sonny Rollins Vol.2 | Blue Note | 497809-2
Ballads | Blue Note | 537562-2
The Blue Note Years-The Best Of Sonny Rollins | Blue Note | 793203-2
Sonny Rollins:The Blue Note Recordings | Blue Note | 821371-2
Jazz Profile:Sonny Rollins | Blue Note | 823516-2
Sonny Rollins Sextet
Sonny Rollins Vol.2 | Blue Note | 497809-2
Sonny Rollins:The Blue Note Recordings | Blue Note | 821371-2
Sonny Stitt Quintet
Sonny Stitt | Original Jazz Classics | OJCCD 009-2
Stan Getz And J.J. Johnson With The Oscar Peterson Quartet
Ultimate Stan Getz selected by Joe Henderson | Verve | 557532-2
The Metronome All Stars
Planet Jazz:Dizzy Gillespie | Planet Jazz | 2152069-2
The Modern Jazz Society
A Concert Of Contemporary Music | Verve | 559827-2
Zoot Sims With Orchestra
Passion Flower | Original Jazz Classics | OJCCD 939-2(2312120)

Johnson,Jacqueline | (cellovoc)
Vince Jones Group
It All Ends Up In Tears | Intuition Records | INT 3069-2

Johnson,James | (bdr)
Duke Ellington And His Award Winners
Greatest Hits | CBS | 462959-2
Quincy Jones And His Orchestra
The Quintessence | Impulse(MCA) | 951222-2

Johnson,James P. | (pp-solo)
Bessie Smith With James P. Johnson
Jazz:The Essential Collection Vol.1 | IN+OUT Records | 78011-2
Bessie Smith With The James P.Johnson Orchestra And The Hal Johnson Choir
The Blues | Storyville | 4960323
Edmond Hall's Blue Note Jazzmen
The Blue Note Jazzmen | Blue Note | 821262-2
Helen Humes With James P. Johnson And The Count Basie Orchestra
From Spiritual To Swing | Vanguard | VCD 169/71
Ida Cox With The James P. Johnson Septet
From Spiritual To Swing | Vanguard | VCD 169/71
James P.Johnson
The Story Of Jazz Piano | Laserlight | 24653
From Spiritual To Swing | Vanguard | VCD 169/71
James P.Johnson's Blue Note Jazzmen
Jazz:The Essential Collection Vol.3 | IN+OUT Records | 78013-2
The Blue Note Jazzmen | Blue Note | 821262-2
Louisiana Sugar Babes
Planet Jazz:Jazz Trumpet | Planet Jazz | 2169654-2
New Orleans Feetwarmers
From Spiritual To Swing | Vanguard | VCD 169/71
Sidney DeParis' Blue Note Jazzmen
The Blue Note Jazzmen | Blue Note | 821262-2

Johnson,Jay | (voc)
Stan Kenton And His Orchestra
One Night Stand | Choice | CHCD 71051

Johnson,Jef Lee | (el-gg)
James Carter Group
Layin' In The Cut | Atlantic | 7567-83305-2

Johnson,Jimmi | (drperc)
Quincy Jones And His Orchestra
Verve Jazz Masters Vol.59:Toots Thielemans | Verve | 535271-2

Johnson,Jimmy | (b,dr,el-b,g,vocld)
Allan Holdsworth Group
The Name Of A Woman | Cream Records | JMS 18733-2
Billy Butler Quintet
Night Life | Prestige | PCD 24260-2
Dee Dee Bridgewater With Band
Dee Dee Bridgewater | Atlantic | 7567-80760-2
Duke Ellington And His Orchestra
Verve Jazz Masters 4:Duke Ellington | Verve | 516338-2
Anatomy Of A Murder | CBS | CK 65569
The Ellington Suites | Original Jazz Classics | OJC20 446-2(2310762)
George Benson Quartet
Talkin' Verve:George Benson | Verve | 553780-2
George Benson Quartet With The Sweet Inspirations
Talkin' Verve:George Benson | Verve | 553780-2
Jerome Richardson Sextet
Night Life | Prestige | PCD 24260-2
Jimmy Smith With The Oliver Nelson Orchestra
Verve Jazz Masters 29:Jimmy Smith | Verve | 521855-2
Jimmy Smith:Best Of The Verve Years | Verve | 527950-2
Oscar Brown Jr. And His Group
Movin' On | Rhino | 8122-73678-2
Stan Getz With Orchestra
Apasionado | A&M Records | 395297-2
The Quincy Jones-Sammy Nestico Orchestra
Basie & Beyond | Warner | 9362-47792-2

Johnson,John T. | (tuba)
Diane Schuur With Orchestra And Strings
The Best Of Diane Schuur | GRP | GRP 98882

Johnson,Johnnie | (pvoc)
Jay McShann Quartet
Goin' To Kansas City | Stony Plain | SPCD 1286

Johnson,Johnny | (b,fl,cl,ss,as,piccolo,ts,reedssax)
Graham Stewart And His New Orleans Band
The Golden Years Of Revival Jazz,Sampler | Storyville | 109 1001
The Golden Years Of Revival Jazz,Vol.10 | Storyville | STCD 5515
Graham Stewart Seven
The Golden Years Of Revival Jazz,Vol.8 | Storyville | STCD 5513
Hugh Marsh Duo/Quartet/Orchestra
The Bear Walks | VeraBra Records | CDVBR 2011-2

Johnson,Keg | (tb)
Fletcher Henderson And His Orchestra
Jazz:The Essential Collection Vol.1 | IN+OUT Records | 78011-2
Jazz:The Essential Collection Vol.3 | IN+OUT Records | 78013-2
Gil Evans Orchestra
Out Of The Cool | Impulse(MCA) | 951186-2
Ike Quebec Swing Seven
The Blue Note Swingtets | Blue Note | 495697-2
Louis Armstrong And His Orchestra
Planet Jazz:Louis Armstrong | Planet Jazz | 2152052-2
Best Of The Complete RCA Victor Recordings | RCA | 2663636-2
Louis Armstrong:A 100th Birthday Celebration | RCA | 2663694-2
Jazz:The Essential Collection Vol.2 | IN+OUT Records | 78012-2

Johnson,Ken | (perc,congasteel-dr)
Gene Harris Group
Blue Breaks Beats Vol.2 | Blue Note | 789907-2

Johnson,Kevin | (dr,voc,g,12-string-g,percsnare-dr)
Cassandra Wilson Group
Misty Blue:Sweet Sisters Swing Songs Of Sorrow And Sadness | Blue Note | 521151-2
Blue Light 'Til Dawn | Blue Note | 781357-2
J.J.Johnson Sextet
The J.J.Johnson Memorial Album | Prestige | PRCD 11025-2
J.J.Johnson-Nat Adderley Quintet
Yokohama Concert Vol.2:Chain Reaction | Pablo | PACD 2620121-2
The J.J.Johnson Memorial Album | Prestige | PRCD 11025-2
Jean-Paul Bourelly Group
Jungle Cowboy | JMT Edition | 919009-2

Johnson,Lamont | (pp-solo)
Essence All Stars
Hot Jazz Bisquits | Hip Bop | HIBD 8801

Johnson,Lem | (cl,tsvoc)
Louis Jordan And His Tympany Five
Louis Jordan-Let The Good Times Roll: The Complete Decca Recordings 1938-1954 | Bear Family Records | BCD 15557 IH
Louis Jordan's Elks Rendez-Vous Band
Louis Jordan-Let The Good Times Roll: The Complete Decca Recordings 1938-1954 | Bear Family Records | BCD 15557 IH
Roger Sturgis With Lovie Jordan's Elks Rendez-Vous Band
Louis Jordan-Let The Good Times Roll: The Complete Decca Recordings 1938-1954 | Bear Family Records | BCD 15557 IH

Johnson,Lennie | (tp)
Duke Ellington And Count Basie With Their Orchestras
First Time! | CBS | CK 65571

Johnson,Lonnie | (g,p,voctp)
Blind Willie Dunn's Gin Bottle Four
Jazz:The Essential Collection Vol.1 | IN+OUT Records | 78011-2
Duke Ellington And His Orchestra
Jazz:The Essential Collection Vol.2 | IN+OUT Records | 78012-2
Lonnie Johnson
Classic Blues | Zounds | CD 2700048
Lonnie Johnson Trio
Bawdy Blues | Original Blues Classics | OBCCD 544-2(BV 1055)
Lonnie Johnson With Elmer Snowden
Blues And Ballads | Original Blues Classics | OBCCD 531-2(BV 1011)
Louis Armstrong And His Savoy Ballroom Five
Jazz:The Essential Collection Vol.2 | IN+OUT Records | 78012-2
Victoria Spivey
Bawdy Blues | Original Blues Classics | OBCCD 544-2(BV 1055)

Johnson,Louis | (b,vocel-b)
Herbie Hancock Group
Man-Child | CBS | 471235-2
Magic Window | CBS | 486572-2
Lee Ritenour Group
Jazzrock-Anthology Vol.3:Fusion | Zounds | CD 27100555

Johnson,Maceo | (voc)
Fats Waller And His Buddies
Planet Jazz:Jack Teagarden | Planet Jazz | 2161236-2

Johnson,Manzie | (dr)
Bunk Johnson-Sidney Bechet Sextet
Jazz:The Essential Collection Vol.1 | IN+OUT Records | 78011-2
Jelly Roll Morton And His Orchestra
Planet Jazz:Jelly Roll Morton | Planet Jazz | 2152060-2
Jazz:The Essential Collection Vol.1 | IN+OUT Records | 78011-2
Mezzrow-Ladnier Quintet
Planet Jazz:Jazz Trumpet | Planet Jazz | 2169654-2
Sidney Bechet And His New Orleans Feetwarmers
Sidney Bechet:Summertime | Dreyfus Jazz Line | FDM 36712-2
Sidney Bechet's Blue Note Jazzmen
Jazz:The Essential Collection Vol.1 | IN+OUT Records | 78011-2
Tommy Ladnier And His Orchestra
Planet Jazz | Planet Jazz | 2169652-2
Jazz:The Essential Collection Vol.1 | IN+OUT Records | 78011-2

Johnson,Marc | (b,el-bb-g)
Bill Evans Trio
Bill Evans Trio:The Last Waltz | Milestone | 8MCD 4430-2
Homecoming | Milestone | MCD 9291-2
Bill Evans-Toots Thielemans Quintet
Affinity | Warner | 7599-27387-2
Bill Perkins Quartet
Swing Spring | Candid | CCD 79752
Charles Lloyd Quintet
Lift Every Voice | ECM | 1832/33(018783-2)
Charles Lloyd Sextet
Lift Every Voice | ECM | 1832/33(018783-2)
Chris Cheek Sextet
A Girl Named Joe | Fresh Sound Records | FSNT 032 CD
Dimitrios Vassilakis Daedalus Project
Labyrinth | Candid | CCD 79776
Dino Saluzzi Trio
Cité De La Musique | ECM | 1616(533316-2)
Heinrich Köbberling-Matt Renzi Quartet
Pisces | Nabel Records:Jazz Network | CD 4677
John Abercrombie Quartet
Getting There | ECM | 1321(833494-2)
November | ECM | 1502(519073-2)
Cat 'N' Mouse | ECM | 1770(014001-2)
Class Trip | ECM | 1846(0381182)
John Abercrombie Trio
Current Event | ECM | 1311(827770-2)
John Abercrombie-Marc Johnson-Peter Erskine
John Abercrombie/Marc Johnson/Peter Erskine | ECM | 1390(837756-2)
John Lewis Quartet
Evolution II | Atlantic | 7567-83313-2
John Taylor Trio
Rosslyn | ECM | 1751(159924-2)
Kurt Elling Group
Flirting With Twilight | Blue Note | 531113-2
Lee Konitz Quintet
Sound Of Surprise | RCA | 2169309-2
Lyle Mays Trio
Fictionary | Warner | 9362-47906-2
Marc Johnson Group
The Sound Of Summer Running | Verve | 539299-2
Marc Johnson Quartet
Bass Desires | ECM | 1299(827743-2)
Marc Johnson-Eric Longsworth
If Trees Could Fly | Intuition Records | INT 3228-2
Marc Johnson's Bass Desires
Second Sight | ECM | 1351(833038-2)
Miriam Alter Quintet
Alter Ego | Intuition Records | INT 3258-2
Nguyen Le Trio
Nguyen Le:3 Trios | ACT | 9245-2
Peter O'Mara Quartet
Symmetry | Edition Collage | EC 484-2
Wind Moments | Take Twelve On CD | TT 009-2
Ralph Towner Quartet
Lost And Found | ECM | 1563(529347-2)
Toots Thielemans-Marc Johnson
Verve Jazz Masters Vol.59:Toots Thielemans | Verve | 535271-2

Johnson,Mark | (dr,perc,fl,congas,programming,sax)
Abbey Lincoln With The Stan Getz Quintet
You Gotta Pay The Band | Verve | 511110-2
A Life In Jazz:A Musical Biography | Verve | 535119-2
Abbey Lincoln With The Stan Getz Quintet
You Gotta Pay The Band | Verve | 511110-2
Cassandra Wilson And Her Quintet
Point Of View | JMT Edition | 919004-2
Cassandra Wilson Group
After The Beginning Again | JMT Edition | 514001-2
Deborah Henson-Conant Group
Budapest | Laika Records | LK 93-039
Steve Coleman And Five Elements
On The Edge Of Tomorrow | JMT Edition | 919005-2

Steve Coleman Group
Motherland Pulse | JMT Edition | 919001-2
Urbanator
Urbanator II | Hip Bop | HIBD 8012

Johnson,Mary | (speech,tanpuravoc)
Rainbow
Two Originals:Karuna Supreme/Rainbow | MPS | 519195-2

Johnson,Money | (tp,fl-hvoc)
Duke Ellington And His Orchestra
Highlights From The Duke Ellington Centennial Edition | RCA | 2663672-2
New Orleans Suite | Rhino | 812273670-2
The Ellington Suites | Original Jazz Classics | OJC20 446-2(2310762)
The Afro-Eurasian Eclipse-A Suite In Eight Parts | Original Jazz Classics | OJCCD 645-2(F 9498)
Jazz At The Philharmonis Berlin '65/Paris '67 | Pablo | PACD 5304-2
Togo Brava Swuite | Storyville | STCD 8323
Duke Ellington Orchestra
Continuum | Fantasy | FCD 24765-2

Johnson,Oliver | (b,el-b,dr,glockenspiel,gongsperc)
Mundell Lowe And His All Stars
Planet Jazz:Ben Webster | RCA | 2165368-2

Johnson,Osie | (dr,perc,tambourinevoc)
Al Cohn-Zoot Sims Quintet
Planet Jazz:Jazz Saxophone | Planet Jazz | 2169653-2
You 'N' Me | Verve | 589318-2
Andy And The Bey Sisters
Andy Bey And The Bey Sisters | Prestige | PCD 24245-2
Arnett Cobb Quintet
Smooth Sailing | Original Jazz Classics | OJCCD 323-2
Ben Webster With Orchestra And Strings
Music For Loving:Ben Webster With Strings | Verve | 527774-2
Ultimate Ben Webster selected by James Carter | Verve | 557537-2
Billie Holiday With The Ray Ellis Orchestra
Verve Jazz Masters 47:Billie Holiday Sings Standards | Verve | 527650-2
Lady In Satin | CBS | CK 65144
Chris Connor With Band
Chris Connor | Atlantic | 7567-80769-2
Coleman Hawkins All Stars
Coleman Hawkins All Stars | Original Jazz Classics | OJCCD 225-2(SV 2005)
Coleman Hawkins Quartet
At Easy | Original Jazz Classics | OJC20 181-2(MV 7)
Coleman Hawkins Quintet
Soul | Original Jazz Classics | OJC20 096-2(P 7149)
The Jazz Giants Play Sammy Cahn:It's Magic | Prestige | PCD 24226-2
Coleman Hawkins Sextet
Hawk Eyes | Original Jazz Classics | OJCCD 294-2
Coleman Hawkins With Billy Byers And His Orchestra
Planet Jazz:Coleman Hawkins | Planet Jazz | 2152055-2
The Hawk In Hi-Fi | RCA | 2663842-2
Coleman Hawkins With Many Albam And His Orchestra
Planet Jazz:Coleman Hawkins | Planet Jazz | 2152055-2
Coleman Hawkins With The Adrian Acea Trio
Coleman Hawkins At The Golden Circle | Dragon | DRCD 265
Dinah Washington With The Quincy Jones Orchestra
Verve Jazz Masters 40:Dinah Washington | Verve | 522055-2
The Swingin' Miss 'D' | Verve | 558074-2
Frank Wess And His Orchestra
The Long Road | Prestige | PCD 24247-2
Gigi Gryce-Donald Byrd Jazz Laboratory
At Newport | Verve | 589764-2
Gil Evans Orchestra
The Individualism Of Gil Evans | Verve | 833804-2
Helen Merrill With The Quincy Jones Orchestra
Clifford Brown-Max Roach:Alone Together-The Best Of The Mercury Years | Verve | 526373-2
Brownie-The Complete EmArCy Recordings Of Clifford Brown | EmArCy | 838306-2
Joe Williams With The Jimmy Jones Orchestra
Planet Jazz:Joe Williams | Planet Jazz | 2165370-2
Johnny Hodges-Wild Bill Davis Sextet
Planet Jazz:Johnny Hodges | Planet Jazz | 2152065-2
Junior Mance Trio & Orchestra
That Lovin' Feelin' | Milestone | MCD 47097-2
Lena Horne With The Lennie Hayton Orchestra
Planet Jazz:Lena Horne | Planet Jazz | 2165373-2
Monica Zetterlund With The Zoot Sims Quartet
Planet Jazz:Female Jazz Vocalists | Planet Jazz | 2169656-2
Mose Allison Trio
Rhino Presents The Atlantic Jazz Gallery | Atlantic | 8122-71257-2
I Don't Worry About A Thing | Rhino | 8122-71417-2
Paul Desmond With Strings
Desmond Blue | RCA | 2663898-2
Prestige Blues-Swingers
Soul Street | Original Jazz Classics | OJCCD 987-2(NJ 8293)
Quincy Jones And His Orchestra
Talkin' Verve-Roots Of Acid Jazz:Roland Kirk | Verve | 533101-2
Verve Jazz Masters Vol.59:Toots Thielemans | Verve | 535271-2
Rahsaan/The Complete Mercury Recordings Of Roland Kirk | Mercury | 846630-2
Shirley Horn With Orchestra
Loads Of Love + Shirley Horn With Horns | Mercury | 843454-2
Wes Montgomery With The Jimmy Jones Orchestra
Wes Montgomery-The Complete Riverside Recordings | Riverside | 12 RCD 4408-2
The Jazz Giants Play Rodgers & Hart:Blue Moon | Prestige | PCD 24205-2

Johnson,Otis | (tp)
Louis Armstrong And His Orchestra
Louis Armstrong:Swing That Music | Laserlight | 36056
Jazz:The Essential Collection Vol.2 | IN+OUT Records | 78012-2
Satch Plays Fats(Complete) | CBS | CK 64927
Swing Legends:Louis Armstrong | Nimbus Records | NI 2012
Willie Bryant And His Orchestra
Planet Jazz:Ben Webster | RCA | 2165368-2

Johnson,Pete | (pp-solo)
Albert Ammons-Pete Johnson-Meade Lux Lewis
From Spiritual To Swing | Vanguard | VCD 169/71
Benny Goodman And His Orchestra
Camel Caravan Broadcast 1939 Vol.1 | Phontastic | NCD 8817
Big Joe Turner And Pete Johnson With The Blues Band
Newport Jazz Festival 1958,July 3rd-6th Vol.3:Blues In The Night No.1 | Phontastic | NCD 8815
Big Joe Turner With Pete Johnson
From Spiritual To Swing | Vanguard | VCD 169/71
Boogie Woogie Trio
Boogie Woogie | Laserlight | 24321
Joe Turner With Orchestra
Atlantic Jazz: Kansas City | Atlantic | 7567-81701-2
Pete Johnson's Housewarmin'
Jazz:The Essential Collection Vol.3 | IN+OUT Records | 78013-2
The Capitol Jazzmen
The Hollywood Session:The Capitol Jazzmen | Jazz Unlimited | JUCD 2044

Johnson,Plas | (as,ts,fl,reeds,saxss)
Benny Carter And His Orchestra
Aspects | Capitol | 852677-2
Bobby Hutcherson Orchestra
Montara | Blue Note | 590956-2
Ella Fitzgerald With Frank De Vol And His Orchestra
Get Happy! | Verve | 523321-2
Ella Fitzgerald With The Billy May Orchestra
Ella Fitzgerald-First Lady Of Song | Verve | 517898-2
The Best Of The Song Books | Verve | 519804-2
Verve Jazz Masters 6:Ella Fitzgerald | Verve | 519822-2
The Best Of The Song Books:The Ballads | Verve | 521867-2
Verve Jazz Masters 46:Ella Fitzgerald-The Jazz Sides | Verve | 527655-2
Ella Fitzgerald Sings The Harold Arlen Song Book | Verve | 589108-2
For The Love Of Ella Fitzgerald | Verve | 841765-2
Ella Fitzgerald With The Nelson Riddle Orchestra
Ella Fitzgerald-First Lady Of Song | Verve | 517898-2
The Best Of The Song Books | Verve | 519804-2
The Best Of The Song Books:The Ballads | Verve | 521867-2
Get Happy! | Verve | 523321-2
Love Songs:The Best Of The Song Books | Verve | 531762-2
Ella Fitzgerald Sings The Johnny Mercer Songbook | Verve | 539057-2
For The Love Of Ella Fitzgerald | Verve | 841765-2
Jimmy Smith With The Oliver Nelson Orchestra
Jimmy Smith:Best Of The Verve Years | Verve | 527950-2
Jimmy Smith-Talkin' Verve | Verve | 531563-2
Joe Pass Quintet
Joe Pass:Guitar Virtuoso | Pablo | 4 PACD 4423-2
Johnny Hartman And His Orchestra
Unforgettable | Impulse(MCA) | IMP 11522
Les McCann Group
Talkin' Verve:Les McCann | Verve | 557351-2
Les McCann Orchestra
Talkin' Verve:Les McCann | Verve | 557351-2
Peggy Lee With The Quincy Jones Orchestra
Blues Cross Country | Capitol | 520088-2
Plas Johnson-Red Holloway Quintet
Keep That Groove Going! | Milestone | MCD 9319-2
T-Bone Walker And His Band
Atlantic Jazz: Kansas City | Atlantic | 7567-81701-2
Van Alexander Orchestra
Home Of Happy Feet/Swing! Staged For Sound! | Capitol | 535211-2
Wild Bill Davis Super Trio
That's All | Jazz Connaisseur | JCCD 9005-2
Zoot Sims With Orchestra
Passion Flower | Original Jazz Classics | OJCCD 939-2(2312120)

Johnson,Ray | (bp)
T-Bone Walker And His Band
Atlantic Jazz: Kansas City | Atlantic | 7567-81701-2

Johnson,Reggie | (b)
Archie Shepp Sextet
Fire Music | Impulse(MCA) | 951158-2
George Robert-Tom Harrell Quintet
Visions | Contemporary | CCD 14063-2
Kenny Burrel Quartet
'Round Midnight | Original Jazz Classics | OJCCD 990-2(F 9417)
Sonny Stitt Quartet
Goin' Down Slow | Prestige | PRCD 24276-2
The Jazz Composer's Orchestra
Comminications | JCOA | 1001/2

Johnson,Robert | (dr,g,voctp)
Robert Johnson
Robert Johnson-King Of The Delta Blues | CBS | 493006-2
Classic Blues | Zounds | CD 2700048

Johnson,Roy | (bp)
(Little)Jimmy Scott With The Lionel Hampton Orchestra
Everybody's Somebody's Fool | Decca | 050669-2
Lionel Hampton And His Orchestra
Lionel Hampton:Flying Home | Dreyfus Jazz Line | FDM 36735-2
Lionel Hampton Orchestra
The Big Bands Vol.1.The Snader Telescriptions | Storyville | 4960043
Lionel Hampton Quartet
Lionel Hampton:Flying Home | Dreyfus Jazz Line | FDM 36735-2

Johnson,Sonny | (dr)
Art Farmer Septet
Plays The Arrangements And Compositions Of Gigi Gryce And Quincy Jones | Original Jazz Classics | OJCCD 054-2

Johnson,Sy | (arrp)
Charles Mingus Sextet
Changes Two | Rhino | 8122-71404-2
Rod Levitt Orchestra
The Dynamic Sound Patterns Of The Rod Levitt Orchestra | Original Jazz Classics | OJCCD 1955-2(RS 9471)

Johnson,Tommy | (g,voc,tbtuba)
Diane Schuur With Orchestra
The Best Of Diane Schuur | GRP | GRP 98882
Singers Unlimited With The Patrick Williams Orchestra
The Singers Unlimited:Magic Voices | MPS | 539130-2
Stan Getz With Orchestra
Apasionado | A&M Records | 395297-2
The Quincy Jones-Sammy Nestico Orchestra
Basie & Beyond | Warner | 9362-47792-2

Johnson,Vince | (reeds)
Eric Dolphy Quartet With The University Of Illinois Big Band
The Illinois Concert | Blue Note | 499826-2

Johnson,Vinnie | (drvoc)
Lester Bowie's Brass Fantasy
The Fire This Time | IN+OUT Records | 7019-2
The Odyssee Of Funk & Popular Music | Dreyfus Jazz Line | FDM 37004-2
When The Spitit Returns | Dreyfus Jazz Line | FDM 37016-2

Johnson,Walter | (dr,percp)
Coleman Hawkins All Star Octet
Planet Jazz:Coleman Hawkins | Planet Jazz | 2152055-2
Coleman Hawkins And His Orchestra
Jazz:The Essential Collection Vol.3 | IN+OUT Records | 78013-2
Connie's Inn Orchestra
Planet Jazz:Coleman Hawkins | Planet Jazz | 2152055-2
Fletcher Henderson And His Orchestra
Jazz:The Essential Collection Vol.1 | IN+OUT Records | 78011-2
Jazz:The Essential Collection Vol.3 | IN+OUT Records | 78013-2

Johnson,Will | (bjg)
Fats Waller And His Buddies
Jazz:The Essential Collection Vol.3 | IN+OUT Records | 78013-2
Henry Allen Jr. And His New York Orchestra
Planet Jazz:Jazz Saxophone | Planet Jazz | 2169653-2
Planet Jazz:Jazz Trumpet | Planet Jazz | 2169654-2
King Oliver And His Orchestra
Planet Jazz:Jazz Trumpet | Planet Jazz | 2169654-2
Louis Armstrong And His Orchestra
Satch Plays Fats(Complete) | CBS | CK 64927

Johnson,Willie | (bj,g,pvoc)
Golden Gate Quartet
From Spiritual To Swing | Vanguard | VCD 169/71
King Oliver And His Orchestra
Planet Jazz:Jazz Trumpet | Planet Jazz | 2169654-2
Louis Armstrong And His Orchestra
Jazz:The Essential Collection Vol.2 | IN+OUT Records | 78012-2

Johnsson,Fredrik | (bel-b)
Lisa Ekdahl With The Salvador Poe Quartet, Strings And Guests
Lisa Ekdahl Sings Salvadore Poe | RCA | 2179681-2

Johnsson,Gunnar | (bco)
Adrian Bentzon's Jazzband
The Golden Years Of Revival Jazz,Sampler | Storyville | 109 1001
Albert Nicholas With Adrian Bentzon's Jazzband
The Golden Years Of Revival Jazz,Sampler | Storyville | 109 1001

Johnston,Clarence | (dr)
Freddie Roach Quartet
So Blue So Funky-Heroes Of The Hammond | Blue Note | 796563-2
Freddie Roach Quintet
Good Move | Blue Note | 524551-2
Freddie Roach Trio
Good Move | Blue Note | 524551-2
Jimmy Forrest Quintet
Soul Street | Original Jazz Classics | OJCCD 987-2(NJ 8293)
Joe Williams With The Harry 'Sweets' Edison Sextet
Together/Have A Good Time | Roulette | 531790-2
Stanley Turrentine Quartet
Blue Note Plays Gershwin | Blue Note | 520808-2
Never Let Me Go | Blue Note | 576750-2

Johnston,Donald | (p)
Lee Konitz-Wolfgang Lackerschmid Quintet
Chet Baker:The Legacy Vol.3:Why Shouldn't You Cry | Enja | ENJ-9337 2
Wolfgang Lackerschmid Quartet
One More Life | Bhakti Jazz | BR 29
Wolfgang Lackerschmid-Donald Johnston Group
New Singers-New Songs | Bhakti Jazz | BR 31

Johnston,Phillip | (sax,ssas)
Guy Klucevsek-Phillip Johnston
Tales From The Cryptic | Winter&Winter | 910088-2

Johnston,Ron | (p)
Dylan Cramer Quartet
All Night Long | Nagel-Heyer | CD 073

Johnstone,Marcia | (harp)
Mel Tormé With The Russell Garcia Orchestra
Swingin' On The Moon | Verve | 511385-2

Jolly,Pete | (accordeon,keyboardsp)
Art Pepper Quintet
Smack Up | Original Jazz Classics | OJC20 176-2
Chet Baker Quartet
The Best Of Chet Baker Plays | Pacific Jazz | 797161-2
Chet Baker Sextet
The Best Of Chet Baker Plays | Pacific Jazz | 797161-2
Gus Mancuso Quintet
Gus Mancuso & Special Friends | Fantasy | FCD 24762-2
Hank Crawford Orchestra
Rhino Presents The Atlantic Jazz Gallery | Atlantic | 8122-71257-2
Mel Tormé With The Russell Garcia Orchestra
Swingin' On The Moon | Verve | 511385-2
Pete Jolly And His West Coast Friends
Art Pepper:The Hollywood All-Star Sessions | Galaxy | 5GCD 4431-2
Shelly Manne And His Hollywood All Stars
Art Pepper:The Hollywood All-Star Sessions | Galaxy | 5GCD 4431-2
Terry Gibbs Dream Band
Terry Gibbs Dream Band Vol.3:Flying Home | Contemporary | CCD 7654-2
Terry Gibbs Dream Band Vol.6:One More Time | Contemporary | CCD 7658-2

Jolobe,Churchill | (dr)
Johnny Dyani Quartet
Mbizo | Steeplechase | SCCD 31163

Jones III,Willie | (dr)
Horace Silver Quintet
Jazz Has... A Sense Of Humor | Verve | 050293-2

Jones,Al | (dr,gvoc)
Al Jones Blues Band
Sharper Than A Tack | Blues Beacon | BLU-1034 2
Dizzy Gillespie Quartet And The Operatic String Orchestra
Jazz In Paris:Dizzy Gillespie And His Operatic Strings Orchestra | EmArCy | 018420-2
Dizzy Gillespie Sextet
Pleyel Jazz Concert 1953 | Vogue | 21409392
Lars Gullin With The Wade Legge Trio
Lars Gullin 1953,Vol.2:Moden Sounds | Dragon | DRCD 234
Sarah Vaughan With Dizzy Gillespie And His Orchestra
Planet Jazz:Female Jazz Vocalists | Planet Jazz | 2169656-2

Jones,Alan | (drhandmade-dr)
Andy Middleton Group
Nomad's Notebook | Intuition Records | INT 3264-2
David Friesen Trio
The Name Of A Woman | Intuition Records | INT 3334-2
Peter Bolte Quartet
Evocation | Jazz Haus Musik | JHM 0079 CD

Jones,Bobby | (cl,tstp)
Woody Herman And His Orchestra
Verve Jazz Masters 54:Woody Herman | Verve | 529903-2

Jones,Boogaloo Joe | (g)
Boogaloo Joe Jones Quintet
Discovery:Grover Washington Jr.-The First Recordings | Prestige | PCD 11020-2
Charlie's Greatest Hits | Prestige | PCD 24250-2
Boogaloo Joe Jones Sextet
Jazzin' With The Soul Brothers | Fantasy | FANCD 6086-2
Discovery:Grover Washington Jr.-The First Recordings | Prestige | PCD 11020-2

Jones,Bradley | (b,ampeg-baby-bvoc)
Dave Douglas Group
Dave Douglas Freak In | Bluebird | 2664008-2
Elvin Jones Jazz Machine
Going Home | Enja | ENJ-7095 2
Marc Ribot Y Los Cubanos Postizos
The Proshetic Cubans | Atlantic | 7567-83116-2
Nuy Divertido(Very Entertaining) | Atlantic | 7567-83293-2

Jones,Buddy | (b)
Elliot Lawrence And His Orchestra
The Elliot Lawrence Big Band Swings Cohn & Kahn | Fantasy | FCD 24761-2
The Four Brothers
Planet Jazz:Jazz Saxophone | Planet Jazz | 2169653-2
Together Again! | RCA | 2179623-2

Jones,Calvin | (b,el-b,voctb)
Muddy Waters Band
Muddy Waters:Paris 1972 | Pablo | PACD 5302-2

Jones,Carmell | (tp)
Annie Ross & PonyPoindexter With The Berlin All Stars
Annie Ross & Pony Poindexter with The Berlin All Stars | MPS | 9811257
Booker Ervin Quintet
The Blues Book | Original Jazz Classics | OJCCD 780-2(P 7340)
Carmel Jones Quartet
Jay Hawk Talk | Original Jazz Classics | OJCCD 1938-2(P7401)
Carmel Jones Quintet
Jay Hawk Talk | Original Jazz Classics | OJCCD 1938-2(P7401)
Charles McPherson Quintet
The Jazz Giants Play Rodgers & Hammerstein:My Favorite Things | Prestige | PCD 24223-2
Gerald Wilson And His Orchestra
Blue Breaks Beats Vol.2 | Blue Note | 789907-2
Horace Silver Quintet
Horace Silver Retrospective | Blue Note | 495576-2
Song For My Father | Blue Note | 499002-2
The Best Of Blue Note | Blue Note | 796110-2
Jimmy Woods Sextet
Conflict | Original Jazz Classics | OJCCD 1954-2(S 7612)
Sarah Vaughan And Her Band
Misty Blue:Sweet Sisters Swing Songs Of Sorrow And Sadness | Blue Note | 521151-2
Sarah Vaughan With The Gerald Wilson Orchestra
Ballads | Roulette | 537561-2

Jones,Champ | (b)
The Dixieland All Stars
The Dixieland All Stars | Jazz Unlimited | JUCD 2037

Jones,Clarence | (b,drvoc)
Oscar Peterson Trio
Planet Music:Oscar Peterson | RCA | 2165365-2
Planet Jazz:Jazz Piano | RCA | 2169655-2
This Is Oscar Peterson | RCA | 2663990-2

Jones,Claude | (conga,tb,preachingvoc)
Connie's Inn Orchestra
Planet Jazz:Coleman Hawkins | Planet Jazz | 2152055-2
Django Reinhardt With Duke Ellington And His Orchestra
Django Reinhardt:Souveniers | Dreyfus Jazz Line | FDM 36744-2
Duke Ellington And His Famous Orchestra
Planet Jazz:Johnny Hodges | Planet Jazz | 2152065-2
Duke Ellington And His Orchestra
Planet Jazz:Duke Ellington | Planet Jazz | 2152053-2

Planet Jazz:Jazz Greatest Hits | Planet Jazz | 2169648-2
The Legends Of Swing | Laserlight | 24659
Highlights From The Duke Ellington Centennial Edition | RCA | 2663672-2
Carnegie Hall Concert December 1944 | Prestige | 2PCD 24073-2
Carnegie Hall Concert January 1946 | Prestige | 2PCD 24074-2
Carnegie Hall Concert December 1947 | Prestige | 2PCD 24075-2
Jazz:The Essential Collection Vol.2 | IN+OUT Records | 78012-2
Fletcher Henderson And His Orchestra
Jazz:The Essential Collection Vol.1 | IN+OUT Records | 78011-2
Jazz:The Essential Collection Vol.3 | IN+OUT Records | 78013-2
Jelly Roll Morton's New Orleans Jazzmen
Planet Jazz | Planet Jazz | 2169652-2
Planet Jazz:Male Jazz Vocalists | Planet Jazz | 2169657-2
Louis Armstrong And His Orchestra
Jazz:The Essential Collection Vol.2 | IN+OUT Records | 78012-2
Louis Armstrong:C'est Si Bon | Dreyfus Jazz Line | FDM 36730-2
Swing Legends:Louis Armstrong | Nimbus Records | NI 2012
McKinney's Cotton Pickers
Jazz:The Essential Collection Vol.3 | IN+OUT Records | 78013-2

Jones,Dale | (b)
Ella Fitzgerald With Louis Armstrong And The All Stars
Ella Fitzgerald-First Lady Of Song | Verve | 517898-2
The Complete Ella Fitzgerald And Louis Armstrong On Verve | Verve | 537284-2
The Best Of Ella Fitzgerald And Louis Armstrong On Verve | Verve | 537909-2
Louis Armstrong And His All Stars
Verve Jazz Masters 1:Louis Armstrong | Verve | 519818-2

Jones,Darryl | (bel-b)
Lenny White Group
Renderers Of Spirit | Hip Bop | HIBD 8014
Hot Jazz Bisquits | Hip Bop | HIBD 8801
Miles Davis Group
Miles Davis Live From His Last Concert In Avignon | Laserlight | 24327
Decoy | CBS | 468702-2
This Is Jazz:Miles Davis Plays Ballads | CBS | CK 65038

Jones,David | (as,co,dr,tpts)
Allan Vaché Big Four
Revisited! | Nagel-Heyer | CD 044
Allan Vaché's Florida Jazz Allstars
Allan Vaché's Floridy Jazz Allstars | Nagel-Heyer | CD 032

Jones,Dick | (arrp)
Tommy Dorsey And His Clambake Seven
Planet Jazz:Tommy Dorsey | Planet Jazz | 2159972-2
Planet Jazz:Bud Freeman | Planet Jazz | 2161240-2
Planet Jazz:Swing | Planet Jazz | 2169651-2
Tommy Dorsey And His Orchestra
Planet Jazz:Tommy Dorsey | Planet Jazz | 2159972-2
Planet Jazz:Big Bands | Planet Jazz | 2169649-2
Planet Jazz:Swing | Planet Jazz | 2169651-2

Jones,Duke | (btp)
Louis Armstrong And His All Stars
Satchmo Serenaders | Verve | 543792-2
Sammy Price Septet
Jazz:The Essential Collection Vol.3 | IN+OUT Records | 78013-2

Jones,Eddie | (b)
Count Basie And His Orchestra
Jazz Gallery:Lester Young Vol.2(1946-59) | RCA | 2119541-2
Jazz Collection:Count Basie | Laserlight | 24368
The Legends Of Swing | Laserlight | 24659
Atomic Swing | Roulette | 497871-2
Verve Jazz Masters 2:Count Basie | Verve | 519819-2
Count Basie Swings-Joe Williams Sings | Verve | 519852-2
Verve Jazz Masters 20:Introducing | Verve | 519853-2
April In Paris | Verve | 521402-2
Breakfast Dance And Barbecue | Roulette | 531791-2
One O'Clock Jump | Verve | 559806-2
Chairman Of The Board | Roulette | 581664-2
The Complete Atomic Basie | Roulette | 828635-2
King Of Swing | Verve | 837433-2
Count Basie At Newport | Verve | 9861761
Count On The Coast Vol.1 | Phontastic | NCD 7555
Count On The Coast Vol.2 | Phontastic | NCD 7575
Count Basie And The Kansas City 7
Count Basie And The Kansas City 7 | Impulse(MCA) | 951202-2
Count Basie Sextet
Verve Jazz Masters 2:Count Basie | Verve | 519819-2
Duke Ellington And Count Basie With Their Orchestras
First Time! | CBS | CK 65571
Ella Fitzgerald And Joe Williams With The Count Basie Octet
For The Love Of Ella Fitzgerald | Verve | 841765-2
Ella Fitzgerald With The Count Basie Orchestra
Ella Fitzgerald-First Lady Of Song | Verve | 517898-2
Joe Newman And His Band
Jazz In Paris:Joe Newman-Jazz At Midnight-Cootie Williams | EmArCy | 018446-2
Joe Newman Quintet
Good 'N' Groovy | Original Jazz Classics | OJCCD 185-2(SV 2019)
Lambert, Hendricks And Ross
Sing A Song Of Basie | Verve | 543827-2
Sarah Vaughan And Joe Williams With The Count Basie Orchestra
Jazz Profile | Blue Note | 823517-2
Sarah Vaughan And The Count Basie Orchestra
Ballads | Roulette | 537561-2
Sarah Vaughan With The Count Basie Band
Jazz Profile | Blue Note | 823517-2

Jones,Edmond | (dr)
King Oliver And His Orchestra
Jazz:The Essential Collection Vol.1 | IN+OUT Records | 78011-2

Jones,Elvin | (dr,perc,tympanig)
Albert Mangelsdorff Trio
Three Originals:The Wide Point/Trilogue/Albert Live In Montreux | MPS | 519213-2
Albert Mangelsdorff-Elvin Jones
Albert Mangelsdorff And His Friends | MPS | 067375-2
Art Pepper Quartet
Art Pepper:The Complete Village Vanguard Sessions | Contemporary | 9CCD-4417-2
Thursday Night At The Village Vanguard | Original Jazz Classics | OJCCD 694-2(7642)
Friday Night At The Village Vanguard | Original Jazz Classics | OJCCD 695-2(C 7643)
Saturday Night At The Village Vanguard | Original Jazz Classics | OJCCD 696-2(C 7644)
The Jazz Giants Play Harold Arlen:Blues In The Night | Prestige | PCD 24201-2
Bill Frisell Trio
Bill Frisell With Dave Hollnad And Elvin Jones | Nonesuch | 7559-79624-2
Bob Brookmeyer Quintet
Sony Jazz Collection:Stan Getz | CBS | 488623-2
Bob Brookmeyer Sextet
Late Night Sax | CBS | 487798-2
Clifford Jordan Quintet
Mosaic | Milestone | MCD 47092-2
Dewey Redman-Cecil Taylor-Elvin Jones
Momentum Space | Verve | 559944-2
Elvin Jones
Youngblood | Enja | ENJ-7051 2
Elvin Jones Jazz Machine
In Europe | Enja | ENJ-7009 2
Going Home | Enja | ENJ-7095 2
Elvin Jones Quintet
Youngblood | Enja | ENJ-7051 2
Elvin Jones Trio
Youngblood | Enja | ENJ-7051 2
Elvin Jones-George Mraz
Youngblood | Enja | ENJ-7051 2
Elvin Jones-Richard Davis Duo
Heavy Sounds | Impulse(MCA) | 547959-2
Elvin Jones-Richard Davis Quartet
Heavy Sounds | Impulse(MCA) | 547959-2
Elvin Jones-Richard Davis Trio
Heavy Sounds | Impulse(MCA) | 547959-2
Frant Green Quartet
Street Of Dreams | Blue Note | 821290-2
Freddie Hubbard Sextet
Wayne Shorter:The Classic Blue Note Recordings | Blue Note | 540856-2
Gil Evans Orchestra
Verve Jazz Masters 23:Gil Evans | Verve | 521860-2
The Individualism Of Gil Evans | Verve | 833804-2
Out Of The Cool | Impulse(MCA) | 951186-2
Blues In Orbit | Enja | ENJ-3069 2
Grant Green Sextet
True Blue | Blue Note | 534032-2
Grant Green Trio
Talkin' About | Blue Note | 521958-2
Helen Merrill With The Dick Katz Group
A Shade Of Difference | EmArCy | 558851-2
Jaki Byard Trio
Sunshine Of My Soul | Original Jazz Classics | OJCCD 1946-2(PR 7550)
Jimmy Woods Sextet
Conflict | Original Jazz Classics | OJCCD 1954-2(S 7612)
Joe Henderson Quartet
The Blue Note Years-The Best Of Joe Henderson | Blue Note | 795627-2
Joe Henderson Quintet
The Blue Note Years-The Best Of Joe Henderson | Blue Note | 795627-2
Joe Lovano Trio
Trio Fascination | Blue Note | 833114-2
John Coltrane And His Orchestra
Kulu Se Mama | Impulse(MCA) | 543412-2
Ascension | Impulse(MCA) | 543413-2
John Coltrane:Standards | Impulse(MCA) | 549914-2
Meditations | Impulse(MCA) | 951199-2
John Coltrane Group
Olé Coltrane | Atlantic | 7567-81349-2
Olé Coltrane | Rhino | 8122-73699-2
John Coltrane Quartet
Afro Blue Impressions | Pablo | 2PACD 2620101
Trane's Blues | Blue Note | 498240-2
Kulu Se Mama | Impulse(MCA) | 543412-2
Impressions | Impulse(MCA) | 543416-2
John Coltrane:Standards | Impulse(MCA) | 549914-2
Coltrane Spiritual | Impulse(MCA) | 589099-2
Ballads | Impulse(MCA) | 589548-2
Coltrane | Impulse(MCA) | 589567-2
A Love Supreme | Impulse(MCA) | 589596-2
A Love Supreme | Impulse(MCA) | 589945-2
Coltrane Jazz | Atlantic | 7567-81344-2
Coltrane Plays The Blues | Atlantic | 7567-81351-2
Coltrane's Sound | Atlantic | 7567-81358-2
The Best Of John Coltrane | Atlantic | 7567-81366-2
John Coltrane-Live Trane:The European Tours | Pablo | 7PACD 4433-2
Rhino Presents The Atlantic Jazz Gallery | Atlantic | 8122-71257-2
John Coltrane-The Heavyweight Champion:The Complete Atlantic Recordings | Atlantic | 8122-71984-2
My Favorite Things | Atlantic | 8122-75204-2
The Very Best Of John Coltrane | Rhino | 8122-79778-2
Coltrane Plays The Blues | Rhino | 8122-79966-2
The Gentle Side Of John Coltrane | Impulse(MCA) | 951107-2
Sun Ship | Impulse(MCA) | 951166-2
Live At Birdland | Impulse(MCA) | 951198-2
Crescent | Impulse(MCA) | 951200-2
The Coltrane Quartet Plays | Impulse(MCA) | 951214-2
Living Space | Impulse(MCA) | 951246-2
Live At The Village Vanguard:The Master Takes | Impulse(MCA) | 951251-2
John Coltrane:The Classic Quartet-Complete Impulse Studio Recordings | Impulse(MCA) | 951280-2
John Coltrane:The Complete 1961 Village Vanguard Recordings | Impulse(MCA) | 954322-2
The Other Village Vanguard Tapes | Impulse(MCA) | MCD 04137
Bye Bye Blackbird | Original Jazz Classics | OJC20 681-2(2308227)
The Paris Concert | Original Jazz Classics | OJC20 781-2(2308217)
John Coltrane Quartet With Brass
The Complete Africa/Brass Sessions | Impulse(MCA) | 952168-2
John Coltrane Quartet With Eric Dolphy
John Coltrane:The Complete 1961 Village Vanguard Recordings | Impulse(MCA) | 954322-2
John Coltrane Quartet With Johnny Hartman
The Gentle Side Of John Coltrane | Impulse(MCA) | 951107-2
John Coltrane Quintet
John Coltrane:Standards | Impulse(MCA) | 549914-2
Live At The Village Vanguard:The Master Takes | Impulse(MCA) | 951251-2
Eric Dolphy Birthday Celebration | Fantasy | FANCD 6085-2
John Coltrane Quintet With Eric Dolphy
Coltrane Spiritual | Impulse(MCA) | 589099-2
John Coltrane-Live Trane:The European Tours | Pablo | 7PACD 4433-2
John Coltrane-The Heavyweight Champion:The Complete Atlantic Recordings | Atlantic | 8122-71984-2
John Coltrane:The Complete 1961 Village Vanguard Recordings | Impulse(MCA) | 954322-2
The Other Village Vanguard Tapes | Impulse(MCA) | MCD 04137
John Coltrane Septet With Eric Dolphy
John Coltrane:The Complete 1961 Village Vanguard Recordings | Impulse(MCA) | 954322-2
The Other Village Vanguard Tapes | Impulse(MCA) | MCD 04137
John Coltrane Sextet
Impressions | Impulse(MCA) | 543416-2
A Love Supreme | Impulse(MCA) | 589945-2
Live At The Village Vanguard:The Master Takes | Impulse(MCA) | 951251-2
John Coltrane:The Complete 1961 Village Vanguard Recordings | Impulse(MCA) | 954322-2
John Coltrane Sextet With Eric Dolphy
John Coltrane-The Heavyweight Champion:The Complete Atlantic Recordings | Atlantic | 8122-71984-2
John Coltrane Trio
Coltrane | Impulse(MCA) | 589567-2
Coltrane Plays The Blues | Atlantic | 7567-81351-2
Coltrane's Sound | Atlantic | 7567-81358-2
Coltrane Plays The Blues | Rhino | 8122-79966-2
Live At The Village Vanguard:The Master Takes | Impulse(MCA) | 951251-2
John Coltrane:The Classic Quartet-Complete Impulse Studio Recordings | Impulse(MCA) | 951280-2
John Coltrane:The Complete 1961 Village Vanguard Recordings | Impulse(MCA) | 954322-2
John Coltrane-Duke Ellington Quartet
The Gentle Side Of John Coltrane | Impulse(MCA) | 951107-2
Duke Ellington & John Coltrane | Impulse(MCA) | 951166-2
John Coltrane-Elvin Jones
John Coltrane:The Classic Quartet-Complete Impulse Studio Recordings | Impulse(MCA) | 951280-2
John Coltrane-Eric Dolphy Quartet
John Coltrane:The Complete 1961 Village Vanguard Recordings | Impulse(MCA) | 954322-2
The Other Village Vanguard Tapes | Impulse(MCA) | MCD 04137
John McLaughlin Trio
After The Rain | Verve | 527467-2
Johnny Hartman And His Quintet
I Just Dropped By To Say Hello | MCA | 951176-2
Johnny Hartman With The John Coltrane Quartet
John Coltrane:Standards | Impulse(MCA) | 549914-2
John Coltrane And Johnny Hartman | Impulse(MCA) | 951157-2
Kenny Burrell Quintet
Kenny Burrell | Original Jazz Classics | OJCCD 019-2(P 7088)
Kenny Burrell With The Gil Evans Orchestra
Guitar Forms | Verve | 521403-2
Verve Jazz Masters 23:Gil Evans | Verve | 521860-2
Verve Jazz Masters 45:Kenny Burrell | Verve | 527652-2
Verve Jazz Masters Vol.60:The Collection | Verve | 529866-2
Larry Young Quartet
Unity | Blue Note | 497808-2
So Blue So Funky-Heroes Of The Hammond | Blue Note | 796563-2
Lee Konitz Trio
Motion | Verve | 065510-2
McCoy Tyner Quartet
The Real McCoy | Blue Note | 497807-2
McCoy Tyner Sextet
Extensions | Blue Note | 837646-2
McCoy Tyner Trio
Chick Corea-Herbie Hancock-Keith Jarrett-McCoy Tyner | Atlantic | 7567-81402-2
McCoy Tyner Plays Ellington | Impulse(MCA) | 951216-2
Inception | Impulse(MCA) | 951220-2
Trident | Original Jazz Classics | OJC20 720-2(M 9063)
McCoy Tyner Trio + Latin Percussion
McCoy Tyner Plays Ellington | Impulse(MCA) | 951216-2
Michael Brecker Group
Time Is Of The Essence | Verve | 547844-2
Miles Davis Quintet
Charles Mingus-The Complete Debut Recordings | Debut | 12 DCD 4402-2
Blue Moods | Original Jazz Classics | OJC20 043-2(DEB 120)
Miles Davis With Gil Evans & His Orchestra
Ballads | CBS | 461099-2
Sketches Of Spain | CBS | CK 65142
Quiet Nights | CBS | CK 65293
Pepper Adams Quartet
10 To 4 At The 5-Spot | Original Jazz Classics | OJCCD 031-2(RLP 265)
Pepper Adams Quintet
10 To 4 At The 5-Spot | Original Jazz Classics | OJCCD 031-2(RLP 265)
Ray Brown Trio
Something For Lester | Original Jazz Classics | OJCCD 412-2
Roland Kirk Quartet
Talkin' Verve-Roots Of Acid Jazz:Roland Kirk | Verve | 533101-2
Rahsaan/The Complete Mercury Recordings Of Roland Kirk | Mercury | 846630-2
Shirley Horn Quartet
The Main Ingredient | Verve | 529555-2
Shirley Horn Quintet
The Main Ingredient | Verve | 529555-2
Sonny Rollins Quartet
East Broadway Run Down | Impulse(MCA) | 951161-2
Sonny Rollins Trio
A Night At The Village Vanguard | Blue Note | 499795-2
Ballads | Blue Note | 537562-2
The Blue Note Years-The Best Of Sonny Rollins | Blue Note | 793203-2
Sonny Rollins:The Blue Note Recordings | Blue Note | 821371-2
Jazz Profile:Sonny Rollins | Blue Note | 823516-2
East Broadway Run Down | Impulse(MCA) | 951161-2
Stan Getz Quartet
Sony Jazz Collection:Stan Getz | CBS | 488623-2
Stan Getz With The Bill Evans Trio
Verve Jazz Masters 5:Bill Evans | Verve | 519821-2
The Complete Bill Evans On Verve | Verve | 527953-2
Ultimate Bill Evans selected by Herbie Hancock | Verve | 557536-2
Stan Getz-Bill Evans Quartet
Stan Getz Highlights:The Best Of The Verve Years Vol.2 | Verve | 517330-2
Stan Getz & Bill Evans | Verve | 833802-2
Stan Getz Highlights | Verve | 847430-2
Steve Lacy Quartet
Reflections-Steve Lacy Plays Thelonious Monk | Original Jazz Classics | OJCCD 063-2
The Mal Waldron Memorial Album:Soul Eyes | Prestige | PRCD 11024-2
Super Black Blues Band
Super Black Blues Vol.II | RCA | 2663874-2
The Prestige All Stars
Olio | Original Jazz Classics | OJCCD 1004-2(P 7084)
Tommy Flanagan Trio
Confirmation | Enja | ENJ-4014 2
Overseas | Original Jazz Classics | OJCCD 1033-2(P 7134)
Wayne Shorter Quartet
Juju | Blue Note | 499005-2
Wayne Shorter:The Classic Blue Note Recordings | Blue Note | 540856-2
Wayne Shorter Quintet
Speak No Evil | Blue Note | 499001-2
Wayne Shorter:The Classic Blue Note Recordings | Blue Note | 540856-2
Night Dreamer | Blue Note | 784173-2
Yusef Lateef Quartet
Into Something | Original Jazz Classics | OJCCD 700-2(NJ 8272)
Yusef Lateef Trio
Into Something | Original Jazz Classics | OJCCD 700-2(NJ 8272)

Jones,Etta | (voc)
Etta Jones And Her Band
Love Shout | Original Jazz Classics | OJCCD 941-2(P 7272)
Etta Jones And Her Quartet
Hollar! | Original Jazz Classics | OJCCD 1061(PR 7284)
Something Nice | Original Jazz Classics | OJCCD 221-2(P 7194)
Etta Jones With Her Trio
Something Nice | Original Jazz Classics | OJCCD 221-2(P 7194)
Etta Jones With The Jerome Richardson Sextet
Hollar! | Original Jazz Classics | OJCCD 1061(PR 7284)
Etta Jones With The Oliver Nelson Quintet
Hollar! | Original Jazz Classics | OJCCD 1061(PR 7284)
Gene Ammons-Sonny Stitt Quintet
Left Bank Encores | Prestige | PRCD 11022-2

Jones,Frankie | (dr)
Gene Ammons Quintet
Brother Jug! | Prestige | PR20 7792-2
Houston Person Quintet
Trust In Me | Prestige | PCD 24264-2
Houston Person Sextet
Goodness! | Original Jazz Classics | OJC20 332-2(P 7678)
Blue Odyssey | Original Jazz Classics | OJCCD 1045-2(P 7566)

Jones,George | (drperc)
Lionel Hampton And His Septet
Lionel Hampton:Flying Home | Dreyfus Jazz Line | FDM 36735-2

Jones,Gregory | (b-g,vocel-b)
Ray Anderson Alligatory Band
Don't Mow Your Lawn | Enja | ENJ-8070 2
Heads And Tales | Enja | ENJ-9055 2

Jones,Hank | (el-harpsichord,el-p,org,p,arr)
Abbey Lincoln With The Stan Getz Quartet
You Gotta Pay The Band | Verve | 511110-2
A Life In Jazz:A Musical Biography | Verve | 535119-2
Abbey Lincoln With The Stan Getz Quintet
You Gotta Pay The Band | Verve | 511110-2
Al Cohn-Zoot Sims Quintet
Planet Jazz:Jazz Saxophone | Planet Jazz | 2169653-2
Anita O'Day With The Gary McFarland Orchestra

All The Sad Youn Men | Verve | 517065-2
Verve Jazz Masters 49:Anita O'Day | Verve | 527653-2
Art Farmer Quartet
The Jazz Giants Play Jerome Kern:Yesterdays | Prestige | PCD 24202-2
Art Pepper Quartet
Art Pepper:The Complete Galaxy Recordings | Galaxy | 16GCD 1016-2
Babs Gonzales And His Band
Voilà | Fresh Sound Records | FSR CD 340
Ben Webster With Orchestra And Strings
Music For Loving:Ben Webster With Strings | Verve | 527774-2
Ultimate Ben Webster selected by James Carter | Verve | 557537-2
Billie Holiday With The Ray Ellis Orchestra
Verve Jazz Masters 47:Billie Holiday Sings Standards | Verve | 527650-2
Birdland Dream Band
Birdland Dream Band | RCA | 2663873-2
Cab Calloway And His Orchestra
Planet Jazz:Cab Calloway | Planet Jazz | 2161237-2
Planet Jazz:Male Jazz Vocalists | Planet Jazz | 2169657-2
Cannonball Adderley Quartet
Ballads | Blue Note | 537563-2
Cannonball Adderley Quintet
The Art Of Saxophone | Laserlight | 24652
Somethin' Else | Blue Note | 495329-2
Kind Of Blue:Blue Note Celebrate The Music Of Miles Davis | Blue Note | 534255-2
The Best Of Blue Note Vol.2 | Blue Note | 797960-2
Miles Davis:The Best Of The Capitol/Blue Note Years | Blue Note | 798287-2
Jazz Profile:Miles Davis | Blue Note | 823515-2
Ballads & Blues | Blue Note | 836633-2
Charlie Haden-Hank Jones
Steal Away | Verve | 527249-2
Charlie Parker All Stars
Charlie Parker:The Best Of The Verve Years | Verve | 527815-2
Charlie Parker Quartet
Verve Jazz Masters 20:Introducing | Verve | 519853-2
Charlie Parker:Bird's Best Bop On Verve | Verve | 527452-2
Charlie Parker:The Best Of The Verve Years | Verve | 527815-2
Charlie Parker | Verve | 539757-2
Bird: The Complete Charlie Parker On Verve | Verve | 837141-2
Charlie Parker:April In Paris | Dreyfus Jazz Line | FDM 36737-2
Charlie Parker Quintet
Charlie Parker | Verve | 539757-2
Chris Connor With The Hank Jones Trio
As Time Goes By | Enja | ENJ-7061 2
Coleman Hawkins All Star Octet
Milt Jackson Birthday Celebration | Fantasy | FANCD 6079-2
Coleman Hawkins All Stars
The J.J.Johnson Memorial Album | Prestige | PRCD 11025-2
Coleman Hawkins And Confreres
Coleman Hawkins And Confreres | Verve | 835255-2 PMS
Coleman Hawkins And His All Stars
Planet Jazz:Coleman Hawkins | Planet Jazz | 2152055-2
Planet Jazz:Bebop | RCA | 2169650-2
Jazz:The Essential Collection Vol.3 | IN+OUT Records | 78013-2
Coleman Hawkins Quartet
Verve Jazz Masters 43:Coleman Hawkins | Verve | 521856-2
The Complete Jazz At The Philharmonic On Verve 1944-1949 | Verve | 523893-2
Body And Soul Revisited | GRP | GRP 16272
Coleman Hawkins With Billy Byers And His Orchestra
Planet Jazz:Coleman Hawkins | Planet Jazz | 2152055-2
The Hawk In Hi-Fi | RCA | 2663842-2
Coleman Hawkins With Many Albam And His Orchestra
Planet Jazz:Coleman Hawkins | Planet Jazz | 2152055-2
Coleman Hawkins-Roy Eldridge Quintet
Verve Jazz Masters 43:Coleman Hawkins | Verve | 521856-2
Dexter Gordon Quintet
Dexter Gordon Birthday Celebration | Fantasy | FANCD 6082-2
Tangerine | Original Jazz Classics | OJCCD 1041-2(P 10091)
Dizzy Gillespie And His Orchestra
Ultimate Dizzy Gillespie | Verve | 557535-2
Ella Fitzgerald With Sy Oliver And His Orchestra
Ella Fitzgerald:Mr.Paganini | Dreyfus Jazz Line | FDM 36741-2
Ella Fitzgerald And Her All Stars
Ella Fitzgerald:Mr.Paganini | Dreyfus Jazz Line | FDM 36741-2
Ella Fitzgerald And Louis Armstrong With Dave Barbour And His Orchestra
Ella Fitzgerald:Mr.Paganini | Dreyfus Jazz Line | FDM 36741-2
Ella Fitzgerald And Louis Armstrong With Sy Oliver And His Orchestra
Ella Fitzgerald:Mr.Paganini | Dreyfus Jazz Line | FDM 36741-2
Ella Fitzgerald With Bill Doggett's Orchestra
Ella Fitzgerald:Mr.Paganini | Dreyfus Jazz Line | FDM 36741-2
Ella Fitzgerald With Sy Oliver And His Orchestra
Ella Fitzgerald:The Decca Years 1949-1954 | Decca | 050668-2
Ella Fitzgerald With The Bill Doggett Orchestra
Ella Fitzgerald-First Lady Of Song | Verve | 517898-2
Rhythm Is My Business | Verve | 559513-2
Ella Fitzgerald With The Hank Jones Quartet
Ella Fitzgerald:Mr.Paganini | Dreyfus Jazz Line | FDM 36741-2
Ella Fitzgerald With The Hank Jones Trio
The Complete Jazz At The Philharmonic On Verve 1944-1949 | Verve | 523893-2
Ella Fitzgerald:Mr.Paganini | Dreyfus Jazz Line | FDM 36741-2
Ella Fitzgerald With The JATP All Stars
Ella Fitzgerald-First Lady Of Song | Verve | 517898-2
Ernestine Anderson With Orchestra
My Kinda Swing | Mercury | 842409-2
Gato Barbieri Group
Planet Jazz:Gato Barbieri | RCA | 2165364-2
Gato Barbieri:The Best Of The Early Years | RCA | 2663523-2
Gene Ammons Quartet
Fine And Mellow | Prestige | PRCD 24281-2
Gene Ammons Septet
Bad! Bossa Nova | Original Jazz Classics | OJC20 351-2(P 7257)
Gene Ammons Sextet
Fine And Mellow | Prestige | PRCD 24281-2
Gene Ammons Sextet With Strings
Fine And Mellow | Prestige | PRCD 24281-2
Gene Krupa Trio
The Drum Battle:Gene Krupa And Buddy Rich At JATP | Verve | 559810-2
George Benson With The Don Sebesky Orchestra
Verve Jazz Masters 21:George Benson | Verve | 521861-2
Gigi Gryce-Donald Byrd Jazz Laboratory
At Newport | Verve | 589764-2
Hank Jones Meets Cheik-Tidiana Seck
Sarala | Verve | 528783-2
Hank Jones Trio
Charles Mingus-The Complete Debut Recordings | Debut | 12 DCD 4402-2
The Complete Jazz At The Philharmonic On Verve 1944-1949 | Verve | 523893-2
Hank Jones Trio With The Gordons's
Charles Mingus-The Complete Debut Recordings | Debut | 12 DCD 4402-2
Hank Jones Trio With The Meridian String Quartet
The Story Of Jazz Piano | Laserlight | 24653
Hank Jones With Oliver Nelson's Orchestra
The Roots Of Acid Jazz | Impulse(MCA) | IMP 12042
J.J.Johnson And His Orchestra
Planet Jazz:J.J.Johnson | Planet Jazz | 2159974-2
J.J.Johnson Quartet
J.J.'s Broadway | Verve | 9860308
J.J.Johnson's All Stars
J.J.'s Broadway | Verve | 9860308
JATP All Stars
Verve Jazz Masters 28:Charlie Parker Plays Standards | Verve | 521854-2
The Complete Jazz At The Philharmonic On Verve 1944-1949 | Verve | 523893-2
Charlie Parker:The Best Of The Verve Years | Verve | 527815-2
Jazz At The Philharmonic:Best Of The 1940's Concerts | Verve | 557534-2
Talkin' Bird | Verve | 559859-2
Bird: The Complete Charlie Parker On Verve | Verve | 837141-2
Welcome To Jazz At The Philharmonic | Fantasy | FANCD 6081-2
Jazz At The Philharmonic-Frankfurt 1952 | Pablo | PACD 5305-2
Norman Granz' JATP: Carnegie Hall 1949 | Pablo | PACD 5311-2
Jimmy Rushing With Oliver Nelson And His Orchestra
Every Day I Have The Blues | Impulse(MCA) | 547967-2
Joe Williams With The Frank Hunter Orchestra
Planet Jazz:Joe Williams | Planet Jazz | 2165370-2
Joe Williams With The Jimmy Jones Orchestra
Planet Jazz:Joe Williams | Planet Jazz | 2165370-2
Joe Williams,With The Oliver Nelson Orchestra
Planet Jazz:Joe Williams | Planet Jazz | 2165370-2
John Coltrane-Milt Jackson Quintet
John Coltrane-The Heavyweight Champion:The Complete Atlantic Recordings | Atlantic | 8122-71984-2
Bags & Trane | Rhino | 8122-73685-2
John Lewis And Hank Jones
An Evening With Two Grand Pianos | Atlantic | 7567-80787-2
Johnny Hartman And His Quintet
I Just Dropped By To Say Hello | MCA | 951176-2
Johnny Hodges Orchestra
Verve Jazz Masters 35:Johnny Hodges | Verve | 521857-2
Johnny Smith Quartet
The Sound Of The Johnny Smith Guitar | Roulette | 531792-2
Kenny Dorham Quintet
Sonny Rollins-The Freelance Years:The Complete Riverside & Contemporary Recordings | Riverside | 5 RCD 4427-2
Jazz Contrast | Original Jazz Classics | OJCCD 028-2(RLP 239)
Kenny Dorham Sextet
Jazz Contrast | Original Jazz Classics | OJCCD 028-2(RLP 239)
Lawrence Brown With The Ralph Burns Orchestra
Slide Trombone | Verve | 559930-2
Lester Young Quartet
Jazz Gallery:Lester Young Vol.2(1946-59) | RCA | 2119541-2
Verve Jazz Masters 30:Lester Young | Verve | 521859-2
Verve Jazz Masters Vol.60:The Collection | Verve | 529866-2
Lester Young:Blue Lester | Dreyfus Jazz Line | FDM 36729-2
Lester Young Septet
Laughin' To Keep From Cryin' | Verve | 543301-2
Lester Young-Roy Eldridge-Harry Edison Band
Jazz Gallery:Lester Young Vol.2(1946-59) | RCA | 2119541-2
Louis Armstrong And Ella Fitzgerald With Sy Oliver's Orchestra
Louis Armstrong:C'est Si Bon | Dreyfus Jazz Line | FDM 36730-2
Louis Armstrong And His Orchestra
What A Wonderful World | MCA | MCD 01876
Louis Jordan And His Tympany Five
Louis Jordan-Let The Good Times Roll: The Complete Decca Recordings 1938-1954 | Bear Family Records | BCD 15557 IH
Milt Jackson Orchestra
To Bags...With Love:Memorial Album | Pablo | 2310967-2
Milt Jackson Birthday Celebration | Fantasy | FANCD 6079-2
Big Bags | Original Jazz Classics | OJCCD 366-2(RLP 9429)
Milt Jackson Quartet
Milt Jackson Birthday Celebration | Fantasy | FANCD 6079-2
Milt Jackson Quintet
At The Village Gate | Original Jazz Classics | OJCCD 309-2
Oscar Peterson With Orchestra
With Respect To Nat | Verve | 557486-2
Roland Kirk Quartet
Talkin' Verve-Roots Of Acid Jazz:Roland Kirk | Verve | 533101-2
Rahsaan/The Complete Mercury Recordings Of Roland Kirk | Mercury | 846630-2
Ron Carter Quartet
Carnaval | Original Jazz Classics | OJCCD 1070-2(GXY 5144)
Rusty Bryant Sextet
For The Good Times | Prestige | PRCD 24269-2
Shirley Horn With Orchestra
Loads Of Love + Shirley Horn With Horns | Mercury | 843454-2
Sonny Stitt With Orchestra
Goin' Down Slow | Prestige | PRCD 24276-2
Stan Getz With Orchestra And Voices
Stan Getz Highlights | Verve | 847430-2
Stan Getz With The Gary McFarland Orchestra
Stan Getz Highlights:The Best Of The Verve Years Vol.2 | Verve | 517330-2
Verve Jazz Masters 53:Stan Getz-Bossa Nova | Verve | 529904-2
Big Band Bossa Nova | Verve | 825771-2 PMS
Stan Getz Highlights | Verve | 847430-2
Thad Jones Quintet
Charles Mingus-The Complete Debut Recordings | Debut | 12 DCD 4402-2
Wes Montgomery Quartet
Wes Montgomery-The Complete Riverside Recordings | Riverside | 12 RCD 4408-2
The Jazz Giants Play Harold Arlen:Blues In The Night | Prestige | PCD 24201-2
Wes Montgomery Quintet
Wes Montgomery-The Complete Riverside Recordings | Riverside | 12 RCD 4408-2
So Much Guitar! | Original Jazz Classics | OJC20 233-2
The Jazz Giants Play Duke Ellington:Caravan | Prestige | PCD 24227-2
Wes Montgomery With The Jimmy Jones Orchestra
Wes Montgomery-The Complete Riverside Recordings | Riverside | 12 RCD 4408-2
The Jazz Giants Play Rodgers & Hart:Blue Moon | Prestige | PCD 24205-2

Jones,Hank or Herbie Hancock | (p)
Stan Getz With Orchestra And Voices
Stan Getz Highlights | Verve | 847430-2

Jones,Hank or Patti Bown or Bernie Leighton | (p)
Cal Tjader's Orchestra
Verve Jazz Masters 39:Cal Tjader | Verve | 521858-2

Jones,Harold | (dr,fl,percreeds)
Count Basie And His Orchestra
Afrique | RCA | 2179618-2
Count Basie: Salle Pleyel, April 17th, 1972 | Laserlight | 36127
Count Basie And The Kansas City 7
Count Basie: Salle Pleyel, April 17th, 1972 | Laserlight | 36127
Count Basie Trio
The Story Of Jazz Piano | Laserlight | 24653
Diane Schuur And Her Band
The Best Of Diane Schuur | GRP | GRP 98882
Oscar Peterson Sextet
Soul Espanol | Limelight | 510439-2
Sarah Vaughan And The Count Basie Orchestra
Sarah Vaughan Birthday Celebration | Fantasy | FANCD 6090-2
Sarah Vaughan With The Joe Pass Quartet
Linger Awhile | Pablo | 2312144-2
Joe Pass:Guitar Virtuoso | Pablo | 4 PACD 4423-2
Sarah Vaughan With The Roland Hanna Quartet
Sarah Vaughan Birthday Celebration | Fantasy | FANCD 6090-2
The Quincy Jones-Sammy Nestico Orchestra
Basie & Beyond | Warner | 9362-47792-2

Jones,Henry | (as)
Louis Armstrong And His Orchestra
Louis Armstrong:Swing That Music | Laserlight | 36056
Swing Legends:Louis Armstrong | Nimbus Records | NI 2012

Jones,Herbie | (guiro,tpfl-h)
Duke Ellington And His Orchestra
Planet Jazz:Johnny Hodges | Planet Jazz | 2152065-2
Duke Ellington's Far East Suite | RCA | 2174797-2
The Art Of Saxophone | Laserlight | 24652
Highlights From The Duke Ellington Centennial Edition | RCA | 2663672-2
The Popular Duke Ellington | RCA | 2663880-2
Duke Ellington: The Champs-Elysees Theater January 29-30th,1965 | Laserlight | 36131
Verve Jazz Masters 4:Duke Ellington | Verve | 516338-2
Verve Jazz Masters 20:Introducing | Verve | 519853-2
Ella & Duke At The Cote D'Azur | Verve | 539030-2
Ella Fitzgerald And Duke Ellington:Cote D'Azure Concerts on Verve | Verve | 539033-2
Soul Call | Verve | 539785-2
Afro-Bossa | Reprise | 9362-47876-2
Welcome To Jazz At The Philharmonic | Fantasy | FANCD 6081-2
Latin America Suite | Original Jazz Classics | OJC20 469-2
Yale Concert | Original Jazz Classics | OJCCD 664-2
Jazz At The Philharmonics Berlin '65/Paris '67 | Pablo | PACD 5304-2
The Jazz Giants Play Duke Ellington:Caravan | Prestige | PCD 24227-2
Ella Fitzgerald With The Duke Ellington Orchestra
The Stockholm Concert 1966 | Pablo | 2308242-2
Ella Fitzgerald-First Lady Of Song | Verve | 517898-2
Verve Jazz Masters 46:Ella Fitzgerald-The Jazz Sides | Verve | 527655-2
Ella At Duke's Place | Verve | 529700-2
Ella & Duke At The Cote D'Azur | Verve | 539030-2
Ella Fitzgerald And Duke Ellington:Cote D'Azure Concerts on Verve | Verve | 539033-2
Ella Fitzgerald With The Duke Ellington Orchestra And Jimmy Jones Trio
Ella & Duke At The Cote D'Azur | Verve | 539030-2
Ella Fitzgerald And Duke Ellington:Cote D'Azure Concerts on Verve | Verve | 539033-2
Oscar Peterson With The Duke Ellington Orchestra
Oscar Peterson Plays Duke Ellington | Pablo | 2310966-2

Jones,Jessica | (ts)
Don Cherry Group
Multi Kulti | A&M Records | 395323-2

Jones,Jimmie | (p)
Billy Strayhorn Orchestra
Johnny Hodges With Billy Strayhorn And The Orchestra | Verve | 557543-2
Ella Fitzgerald With The Duke Ellington Orchestra And Jimmy Jones Trio
Ella Fitzgerald And Duke Ellington:Cote D'Azure Concerts on Verve | Verve | 539033-2
Ella Fitzgerald With The Jimmy Jones Trio
Ella Fitzgerald And Duke Ellington:Cote D'Azure Concerts on Verve | Verve | 539033-2
Jimmy Hamilton And The Duke's Men
The Blue Note Swingtets | Blue Note | 495697-2
Joe Turner With Orchestra
Atlantic Jazz: Kansas City | Atlantic | 7567-81701-2
Joe Williams With The Harry 'Sweets' Edison Band
Together/Have A Good Time | Roulette | 531790-2
Johnny Hodges Orchestra
Planet Jazz:Johnny Hodges | Planet Jazz | 2152065-2
Verve Jazz Masters 43:Ben Webster | Verve | 525431-2
Johnny Hodges With Billy Strayhorn And The Duke Ellington Orchestra
Verve Jazz Masters 35:Johnny Hodges | Verve | 521857-2
Monica Zetterlund With The Zoot Sims Quartet
Planet Jazz:Female Jazz Vocalists | Planet Jazz | 2169656-2
Sarah Vaughan And Her Trio
Swingin' Easy | EmArCy | 514072-2
Verve Jazz Masters 42:Sarah Vaughan-The Jazz Sides | Verve | 526817-2
Verve Jazz Masters Vol.60:The Collection | Verve | 529866-2
Sarah Vaughan With The Hal Mooney Orchestra
Sarah Vaughan Sings Gershwin | Verve | 557567-2
Sarah Vaughan With The Hugo Winterhalter Orchestra
Sarah Vaughan:Lover Man | Dreyfus Jazz Line | FDM 36739-2
Sarah Vaughan With The Jimmy Jones Quintet
Jazz Profile | Blue Note | 823517-2
Tony Scott And His Down Beat Club Sextet
Jazz:The Essential Collection Vol.3 | IN+OUT Records | 78013-2

Jones,Jimmy | (arr,ld,b,cond,dr,p,celestep-solo)
52nd Street All Stars
Planet Jazz:Bebop | RCA | 2169650-2
Ben Webster And His Associates
Verve Jazz Masters 43:Ben Webster | Verve | 525431-2
Ultimate Ben Webster selected by James Carter | Verve | 557537-2
Ben Webster And Associates | Verve | 835254-2
Ben Webster Septet
The Soul Of Ben Webster | Verve | 527475-2
Cannonball Adderley Duo
Cannonball Adderley Birthday Celebration | Fantasy | FANCD 6087-2
Coleman Hawkins And His 52nd Street All Stars
Jazz:The Essential Collection Vol.3 | IN+OUT Records | 78013-2
Coleman Hawkins' Fifty-Second Street All-Stars
Planet Jazz:Coleman Hawkins | Planet Jazz | 2152055-2
Ella Fitzgerald With Benny Carter's Magnificent Seven
30 By Ella | Capitol | 520090-2
Ella Fitzgerald With The Duke Ellington Orchestra
The Stockholm Concert 1966 | Pablo | 2308242-2
Ella Fitzgerald-First Lady Of Song | Verve | 517898-2
Verve Jazz Masters 46:Ella Fitzgerald-The Jazz Sides | Verve | 527655-2
Ella Fitzgerald With The Duke Ellington Orchestra And Jimmy Jones Trio
Ella & Duke At The Cote D'Azur | Verve | 539030-2
Ella Fitzgerald With The Jimmy Jones Trio
Ella Fitzgerald-First Lady Of Song | Verve | 517898-2
Ella & Duke At The Cote D'Azur | Verve | 539030-2
Harry Sweets Edison Sextet
Mr.Swing Harry Edison | Verve | 559868-2
Helen Merrill With The Quincy Jones Orchestra
Clifford Brown-Max Roach:Alone Together-The Best Of The Mercury Years | Verve | 526373-2
Verve Jazz Masters 44:Clifford Brown and Max Roach | Verve | 528109-2
Brownie-The Complete EmArCy Recordings Of Clifford Brown | EmArCy | 838306-2
Joe Williams And His Band
Blue Velvet: Crooners, Swooners And Velvet Vocals | Blue Note | 521153-2
Joe Williams With The Jimmy Jones Orchestra
Planet Jazz:Joe Williams | Planet Jazz | 2165370-2
Johnny Hodges Orchestra
Verve Jazz Masters 35:Johnny Hodges | Verve | 521857-2
Mel Tormé With The Jimmy Jones Orchestra
Blue Velvet: Crooners, Swooners And Velvet Vocals | Blue Note | 521153-2
Sarah Vaughan The The Joe Lippman Orchestra
Sarah Vaughan:Lover Man | Dreyfus Jazz Line | FDM 36739-2
Sarah Vaughan With George Treadwell And His Allstars
Sarah Vaughan:Lover Man | Dreyfus Jazz Line | FDM 36739-2
Sarah Vaughan With The Clifford Brown All Stars
Verve Jazz Masters 20:Introducing | Verve | 519853-2
Clifford Brown-Max Roach:Alone Together-The Best Of The Mercury Years | Verve | 526373-2
Sarah Vaughan | Verve | 543305-2
4 By 4:Ella Fitzgerald/Sarah Vaughan/Billie Holiday/Dinah Washington | Verve | 559693-2
Brownie-The Complete EmArCy Recordings Of Clifford Brown | EmArCy | 838306-2
Sarah Vaughan | EmArCy | 9860779
Sarah Vaughan With The Jimmy Jones Orchestra
Jazz Profile | Blue Note | 823517-2
Sarah Vaughan With The Jimmy Jones Quartet

Sarah Vaughan:Lover Man | Dreyfus Jazz Line | FDM 36739-2
Sarah Vaughan With The Jimmy Jones Trio
Linger Awhile | Pablo | 2312144-2
Sarah Vaughan | Verve | 543305-2
Sarah Vaughan Birthday Celebration | Fantasy | FANCD 6090-2
Shirley Horn With Orchestra
Loads Of Love + Shirley Horn With Horns | Mercury | 843454-2
Shirley Horn With The Quincy Jones Orchestra
Loads Of Love + Shirley Horn With Horns | Mercury | 843454-2
Sidney Bechet With Noble Sissle's Swingsters
Sidney Bechet:Summertime | Dreyfus Jazz Line | FDM 36712-2
Sonny Rollins Group
What's New? | RCA | 2179626-2
Sonny Rollins Quartet
Planet Jazz:Sonny Rollins | Planet Jazz | 2152062-2
Sonny Stitt Quartet
Verve Jazz Masters 50:Sonny Sitt | Verve | 527651-2
Wes Montgomery With The Jimmy Jones Orchestra
Wes Montgomery-The Complete Riverside Recordings | Riverside | 12 RCD 4408-2
The Jazz Giants Play Rodgers & Hart:Blue Moon | Prestige | PCD 24205-2

Jones,Jo | (drtympani)

Abbey Lincoln And Her All Stars(Newport Rebels)
Candid Dolphy | Candid | CCD 79033
Albert Ammons-Pete Johnson-Meade Lux Lewis
From Spiritual To Swing | Vanguard | VCD 169/71
Andy And The Bey Sisters
Andy Bey And The Bey Sisters | Prestige | PCD 24245-2
Art Tatum Trio
Art Tatum-The Complete Pablo Group Masterpieces | Pablo | 6 PACD 4401-2
The Jazz Giants Play Rodgers & Hart:Blue Moon | Prestige | PCD 24205-2
Ben Webster And His Associates
Verve Jazz Masters 43:Ben Webster | Verve | 525431-2
Ultimate Ben Webster selected by James Carter | Verve | 557537-2
Ben Webster And Associates | Verve | 835254-2
Ben Webster With The Teddy Wilson Trio
Verve Jazz Masters 43:Ben Webster | Verve | 525431-2
Music For Loving:Ben Webster With Strings | Verve | 527774-2
Benny Carter And His Orchestra
Further Definitions/Additions To Further Definotions | Impulse(MCA) | 951229-2
Benny Goodman Septet
Jazz:The Essential Collection Vol.3 | IN+OUT Records | 78013-2
Charlie Christian:Swing To Bop | Dreyfus Jazz Line | FDM 36715-2
Benny Goodman Septet feat.Count Basie
Charlie Christian:Swing To Bop | Dreyfus Jazz Line | FDM 36715-2
Big Joe Turner And Pete Johnson With The Blues Band
Newport Jazz Festival 1958,July 3rd-6th Vol.3:Blues In The Night No.1 | Phontastic | NCD 8815
Big Maybelle With The Blues Band
Newport Jazz Festival 1958,July 3rd-6th Vol.3:Blues In The Night No.1 | Phontastic | NCD 8815
Billie Holiday And Her Band
Billie's Love Songs | Nimbus Records | NI 2000
Billie Holiday And Her Orchestra
Jazz:The Essential Collection Vol.3 | IN+OUT Records | 78013-2
Billie's Love Songs | Nimbus Records | NI 2000
Billie Holiday With Teddy Wilson And His Orchestra
Billie's Love Songs | Nimbus Records | NI 2000
Billie Holiday With The Mal Waldron Trio
Billie Holiday Story Vol.1:Jazz At The Philharmonic | Verve | 521642-2
Blossom Dearie Quartet
Give Him The Ooh-La-La | Verve | 517067-2
Verve Jazz Masters 51:Blossom Dearie | Verve | 529906-2
Boogie Woogie Trio
Boogie Woogie | Laserlight | 24321
Buddy Tate With The Marlow Morris Quintet
Late Night Sax | CBS | 487798-2
Charles Mingus Group
The Jazz Life! | Candid | CCD 79019
Mysterious Blues | Candid | CCD 79042
Chuck Berry With The Blues Band
Newport Jazz Festival 1958,July 3rd-6th Vol.3:Blues In The Night No.1 | Phontastic | NCD 8815
Coleman Hawkins All Stars
The J.J.Johnson Memorial Album | Prestige | PRCD 11025-2
Count Basie And His Orchestra
Jazz Gallery:Lester Young Vol.2(1946-59) | RCA | 2119541-2
Planet Jazz:Count Basie | Planet Jazz | 2152068-2
Planet Jazz Sampler | Planet Jazz | 2152326-2
Planet Jazz:Jimmy Rushing | RCA | 2165371-2
Planet Jazz:Jazz Greatest Hits | Planet Jazz | 2169648-2
Planet Jazz:Big Bands | Planet Jazz | 2169649-2
Jazz Collection:Count Basie | Laserlight | 24368
Verve Jazz Masters 2:Count Basie | Verve | 519819-2
Jazz:The Essential Collection Vol.3 | IN+OUT Records | 78013-2
Count Basie At Newport | Verve | 9861761
From Spiritual To Swing | Vanguard | VCD 169/71
Count Basie Quartet
Planet Jazz:Jazz Piano | RCA | 2169655-2
Jazz:The Essential Collection Vol.3 | IN+OUT Records | 78013-2
Count Basie Sextet
Jazz:The Essential Collection Vol.3 | IN+OUT Records | 78013-2
Count Basie Trio
From Spiritual To Swing | Vanguard | VCD 169/71
Count Basie,His Instrumentals & Rhyhtm
Planet Jazz:Count Basie | Planet Jazz | 2152068-2
Jazz:The Essential Collection Vol.3 | IN+OUT Records | 78013-2
Count Basie's Kansas City Seven
Jazz:The Essential Collection Vol.3 | IN+OUT Records | 78013-2
Dicky Wells And His Orchestra
Jazz:The Essential Collection Vol.3 | IN+OUT Records | 78013-2
Duke Ellington And Johnny Hodges Orchestra
Side By Side | Verve | 521405-2
Duke Ellington Quartet
Great Times! | Original Jazz Classics | OJC20 108-2(RLP 475)
Duke Ellington-Billy Strayhorn Quintet
Great Times! | Original Jazz Classics | OJC20 108-2(RLP 475)
Duke Ellington-Johnny Hodges All Stars
Verve Jazz Masters 4:Duke Ellington | Verve | 516338-2
Back To Back | Verve | 521404-2
Ella Fitzgerald With The Don Abney Trio
Ella Fitzgerald-First Lady Of Song | Verve | 517898-2
Ella Fitzgerald With The Duke Ellington Orchestra
Ella Fitzgerald And Duke Ellington:Cote D'Azure Concerts on Verve | Verve | 539033-2
Ella Fitzgerald With The JATP All Stars
Ella Fitzgerald-First Lady Of Song | Verve | 517898-2
Frankie Laine With Buck Clayton And His Orchestra
Jazz Spectacular | CBS | CK 65507
Gene Ammons-Sonny Stitt Quintet
The Prestige Legacy Vol.2:Battles Of Saxes | Prestige | PCD 24252-2
Gil Evans And Ten
Gil Evans And Ten | Original Jazz Classics | OJC 346(P 7120)
Gil Evans And Ten | Prestige | PRSA 7120-6
Harry James And His Orchestra
The Legends Of Swing | Laserlight | 24659
Helen Humes With James P. Johnson And The Count Basie Orchestra
From Spiritual To Swing | Vanguard | VCD 169/71
Helen Humes With The Kansas City Five
From Spiritual To Swing | Vanguard | VCD 169/71
Ida Cox With The James P. Johnson Septet
From Spiritual To Swing | Vanguard | VCD 169/71
Jack Teagarden And His Band
Meet Me Where They Play The Blues | Good Time Jazz | GTCD 12063-2
JATP All Stars
Stan Getz Highlights:The Best Of The Verve Years Vol.2 | Verve | 517330-2
The Complete Jazz At The Philharmonic On Verve 1944-1949 | Verve | 523893-2
Jazz At The Philharmonic:Best Of The 1940's Concerts | Verve | 557534-2
Jazz Artists Guild
Newport Rebels-Jazz Artists Guild | Candid | CCD 79022
Jimmy Rushing With Count Basie And His Orchestra
From Spiritual To Swing | Vanguard | VCD 169/71
Jo Jones Trio
Key One Up | Vanguard | VCD 79612-2
Johnny Hodges Orchestra
Side By Side | Verve | 521405-2
Verve Jazz Masters 43:Ben Webster | Verve | 525431-2
Jones-Smith Incorporated
Jazz:The Essential Collection Vol.3 | IN+OUT Records | 78013-2
Kansas City Five
Lester Young:Blue Lester | Dreyfus Jazz Line | FDM 36729-2
From Spiritual To Swing | Vanguard | VCD 169/71
Kansas City Seven
Jazz:The Essential Collection Vol.3 | IN+OUT Records | 78013-2
Kansas City Six
Jazz:The Essential Collection Vol.3 | IN+OUT Records | 78013-2
Charlie Christian:Swing To Bop | Dreyfus Jazz Line | FDM 36715-2
Lester Young:Blue Lester | Dreyfus Jazz Line | FDM 36729-2
From Spiritual To Swing | Vanguard | VCD 169/71
Lawrence Brown With The Ralph Burns Orchestra
Slide Trombone | Verve | 559930-2
Lester Young Quartet
Jazz Gallery:Lester Young Vol.2(1946-59) | RCA | 2119541-2
Verve Jazz Masters 30:Lester Young | Verve | 521859-2
Lester Young-Teddy Wilson Quartet
Jazz Gallery:Lester Young Vol.2(1946-59) | RCA | 2119541-2
Lionel Hampton And His Orchestra
Planet Jazz:Swing | Planet Jazz | 2169651-2
Planet Jazz:Jazz Saxophone | Planet Jazz | 2169653-2
New Orleans Feetwarmers
From Spiritual To Swing | Vanguard | VCD 169/71
Newport Rebels
Candid Dolphy | Candid | CCD 79033
Oscar Peterson Sextet
Oscar Peterson Trio: Olympia/Theatre Des Champs-Elysees | Laserlight | 36134
Roy Eldridge And His Central Plaza Dixielanders
The Very Best Of Dixieland Jazz | Verve | 535529-2
The Complete Verve Roy Eldridge Studio Sessions | Verve | 9861278
Roy Eldridge Quintet
The Complete Verve Roy Eldridge Studio Sessions | Verve | 9861278
Sir Charles Thompson Quartet
Key One Up | Vanguard | VCD 79612-2
Sonny Stitt Quartet
Verve Jazz Masters 50:Sonny Sitt | Verve | 527651-2
Teddy Wilson And His Orchestra
Jazz:The Essential Collection Vol.3 | IN+OUT Records | 78013-2
The Dixieland All Stars
The Dixieland All Stars | Jazz Unlimited | JUCD 2037
The Jazz Giants '56
Jazz Gallery:Lester Young Vol.2(1946-59) | RCA | 2119541-2
Vic Dickenson Septet With Ruby Braff
Nice Work | Vanguard | VCD 79610-2
Woody Herman And His Orchestra
Songs For Hip Lovers | Verve | 559872-2

Jones,Jonah | (tpvoc)

Billie Holiday With Teddy Wilson And His Orchestra
Billie's Love Songs | Nimbus Records | NI 2000
Cab Calloway And His Cab Jivers
Planet Jazz:Cab Calloway | Planet Jazz | 2161237-2
Ike Quebec Swingtet
The Blue Note Swingtets | Blue Note | 495697-2

Jones,Josh | (clave,hand-claps,voice,dr,perc)

Don Cherry Group
Multi Kulti | A&M Records | 395323-2
Steve Coleman And Metrics
The Way Of The Cipher | Novus | 2131690-2
Steve Coleman And The Council Of Balance
Genesis & The Opening Of The Way | RCA | 2152934-2

Jones,Karen | (v)

Bill Evans Quartet With Orchestra
The Complete Bill Evans On Verve | Verve | 527953-2
From Left To Right | Verve | 557451-2
Bill Evans With Orchestra
The Complete Bill Evans On Verve | Verve | 527953-2
From Left To Right | Verve | 557451-2
Milt Jackson With Strings
To Bags...With Love:Memorial Album | Pablo | 2310967-2

Jones,Leonard | (bvoice)

Lajos Dudas Quintet
Talk Of The Town | double moon | CHRDM 71012
Some Great Songs | double moon | DMCD 1005-2
Lajos Dudas Sextet
Talk Of The Town | double moon | CHRDM 71012

Jones,Nat | (clas)

Duke Ellington And His Orchestra
At The Hurricane:Original 1943 Broadcasts | Storyville | STCD 8359

Jones,Norah | (pvoc)

Peter Malick Group feat. Norah Jones
New York City | Koch Records | 238678-2

Jones,Percy | (bel-b)

Shankar/Caroline
The Epidemics | ECM | 1308

Jones,Peter | (dr,clapsp)

Vince Jones Group
Spell | Intuition Records | INT 3067-2
For All Colours | Intuition Records | INT 3071-2
Here's To The Miracles | Intuition Records | INT 3198-2

Jones,Philly Joe | (dr,arr,tympani,dr-solo,pb)

Abbey Lincoln With The Benny Golson Quintet
It's Magic | Original Jazz Classics | OJCCD 205-2
Abbey Lincoln With The Benny Golson Septet
It's Magic | Original Jazz Classics | OJCCD 205-2
Abbey Lincoln With The Kenny Dorham Quintet
Abbey Is Blue | Original Jazz Classics | OJC20 069-2(RLP 1153)
Art Blakey Percussion Ensemble
Drums Around The Corner | Blue Note | 521455-2
Art Pepper Quartet
Art Pepper Meets The Rhythm Section | Original Jazz Classics | OJC20 338-2
The Way It Is | Original Jazz Classics | OJCCD 389-2
The Jazz Giants Play Cole Porter:Night And Day | Prestige | PCD 24203-2
Ben Webster Quartet
The Jazz Giants Play Duke Ellington:Caravan | Prestige | PCD 24227-2
Benny Golson Quintet
Nemmy Golson And The Philadelphians | Blue Note | 494104-2
Bill Evans Quintet
The Complete Fantasy Recordings | Fantasy | 9FCD 1012-2
Interplay | Original Jazz Classics | OJCCD 308-2
Quintessence | Original Jazz Classics | OJCCD 698-2(F 9529)
The Jazz Giants Play Jerome Kern:Yesterdays | Prestige | PCD 24202-2
The Jazz Giants Play Sammy Cahn:It's Magic | Prestige | PCD 24226-2
Bill Evans Trio
Verve Jazz Masters 5:Bill Evans | Verve | 519821-2
The Complete Bill Evans On Verve | Verve | 527953-2
The Best Of Bill Evans Live | Verve | 533825-2
Bill Evans:The Secret Sessions | Milestone | 8MCD 4421-2
On Green Dolphin Street | Milestone | MCD 9235-2
Getting Sentimental | Milestone | MCD 9346-2
Everybody Digs Bill Evans | Original Jazz Classics | OJC20 068-2
The Jazz Giants Play Cole Porter:Night And Day | Prestige | PCD 24203-2
The Jazz Giants Play Rodgers & Hart:Blue Moon | Prestige | PCD 24205-2
Blue Mitchell Sextet
Blue Mitchell Big 6 | Original Jazz Classics | OJCCD 615-2(RLP 12-273)
Blue Soul | Original Jazz Classics | OJCCD 765-2(RLP 1155)
Bud Powell Trio
Time Waits | Blue Note | 521227-2
Cannonball Adderley Quintet
Cannonball Adderley Birthday Celebration | Fantasy | FANCD 6087-2
Portrait Of Cannonball | Original Jazz Classics | OJCCD 361-2(RLP 269)
The Jazz Giants Play Rodgers & Hammerstein:My Favorite Things | Prestige | PCD 24223-2
Chet Baker Quartet
Chet | Original Jazz Classics | OJC20 087-2
Chet Baker In New York | Original Jazz Classics | OJC20 207-2
Sings/It Could Happen To You | Original Jazz Classics | OJC20 303-2
The Jazz Giants Play Miles Davis:Milestones | Prestige | PCD 24225-2
Chet Baker Quintet
Chet Baker In New York | Original Jazz Classics | OJC20 207-2
Chet Baker Septet
Chet | Original Jazz Classics | OJC20 087-2
Clark Terry With The Thelonious Monk Trio
Thelonious Monk:85th Birthday Celebration | zyx records | FANCD 6076-2
Clark Terry-Thelonious Monk Quartet
In Orbit | Original Jazz Classics | OJC 302(R 12-271)
Dexter Gordon Quartet
Dexter Gordon:Ballads | Blue Note | 796579-2
Jazz Profile:Dexter Gordon | Blue Note | 823514-2
Dexter Gordon Birthday Celebration | Fantasy | FANCD 6082-2
Elmo Hope Ensemble
Sounds From Rikers Island | Fresh Sound Records | FSR CD 338
Elmo Hope Sextet
John Coltrane-The Prestige Recordings | Prestige | 16 PCD 4405-2
Freddie Hubbard Orchestra
The Body And The Soul | Impulse(MCA) | 951183-2
Freddie Hubbard Sextet
Hub Cap | Blue Note | 542302-2
Hank Mobley Quartet
Workout | Blue Note | 784080-2
Hank Mobley Quintet
No Room For Squares | Blue Note | 524539-2
True Blue | Blue Note | 534032-2
Workout | Blue Note | 784080-2
Hank Mobley Sextet
The Flip | Blue Note | 593872-2
Ike Quebec Quartet
Blue And Sentimental | Blue Note | 784098-2
Ike Quebec Quintet
Blue And Sentimental | Blue Note | 784098-2
Jimmy Heath Quartet
Blue Soul | Original Jazz Classics | OJCCD 765-2(RLP 1155)
John Coltrane Quartet
Trane's Blues | Blue Note | 498240-2
John Coltrane Sextet
Trane's Blues | Blue Note | 498240-2
Blue Train | Blue Note | 591721-2
The Best Of Blue Note | Blue Note | 796110-2
Blue Train(The Ultimate Blue Train) | Blue Note | 853428-0
John Coltrane-Tadd Dameron Quartet
Mating Call | Original Jazz Classics | OJCCD 212-2(P 7070)
Johnny Pace With The Chet Baker Quintet
Chet Baker Introduces Johnny Pace | Original Jazz Classics | OJCCD 433-2(RLP 12-292)
Kenny Dorham Quintet
Whistle Stop | Blue Note | 525646-2
Kenny Dorham Septet
Cannonball Adderley Birthday Celebration | Fantasy | FANCD 6087-2
Kenny Drew Trio
The Kenny Drew Trio | Original Jazz Classics | OJC20 065-2(RLP 224)
Lee Morgan Quintet
True Blue | Blue Note | 534032-2
Lou Donaldson Quintet
Clifford Brown Memorial Album | Blue Note | 532141-2
Miles Davis And His Orchestra
Collector's Items | Original Jazz Classics | OJC20 071-2(P 7044)
Miles Davis New Quintet
Workin',Steamin',Cookin',Relaxin' With The Miles Davis Quintet | Original Jazz Classics | OJCCD 8805-2
Miles Davis Quartet
Bill Evans:Piano Player | CBS | CK 65361
The Musings Of Miles | Original Jazz Classics | OJCCD 004-2
Miles Davis Quintet
Circle In The Round | CBS | 467898-2
This Is Jazz:Miles Davis Plays Ballads | CBS | CK 65038
Cookin' With The Miles Davis Quintet | Original Jazz Classics | OJC20 128-2
Relaxin' | Original Jazz Classics | OJC20 190-2
Miles Davis And The Modern Jazz Giants | Original Jazz Classics | OJC20 347-2(P 7150)
Steamin' | Original Jazz Classics | OJC20 391-2
The Jazz Giants Play Rodgers & Hammerstein:My Favorite Things | Prestige | PCD 24223-2
The Jazz Giants Play Duke Ellington:Caravan | Prestige | PCD 24227-2
Relaxin' | Prestige | PRSA 7129-6
Miles Davis Sextet
The Jazz Giants Play Miles Davis:Milestones | Prestige | PCD 24225-2
The Prestige Legacy Vol.1:The High Priests | Prestige | PCD 24251-2
Miles Davis With Gil Evans & His Orchestra
Porgy And Bess | CBS | CK 65141
Milt Jackson Orchestra
Big Bags | Original Jazz Classics | OJCCD 366-2(RLP 9429)
Milt Jackson-Wes Montgomery Quintet
Wes Montgomery-The Complete Riverside Recordings | Riverside | 12 RCD 4408-2
To Bags...With Love:Memorial Album | Pablo | 2310967-2
Milt Jackson Birthday Celebration | Fantasy | FANCD 6079-2
Bags Meets Wes! | Original Jazz Classics | OJC20 234-2(RLP 9407)
Nat Adderley Quartet
Naturally! | Original Jazz Classics | OJCCD 1088-2(JLP 947)
Paul Chambers Sextet
Trane's Blues | Blue Note | 498240-2
Philly Joe Jones Big Band
Cannonball Adderley Birthday Celebration | Fantasy | FANCD 6087-2
Red Garland Quintet
Red's Good Groove | Original Jazz Classics | OJCCD 1064-2(987)
Serge Chaloff Quartet
Blue Serge | Capitol | 494505-2
Slide Hampton Quartet
Americans Swinging In Paris:Slide Hampton | EMI Records | 539648-2
Sonny Clark Quintet
Cool Struttin' | Blue Note | 495327-2
Sonny Clark Trio
Sonny Clark | Blue Note | 533774-2
Sonny Clark Trio | Blue Note | 533774-2
Sonny Rollins Quartet
True Blue | Blue Note | 534032-2
Ballads | Blue Note | 537562-2
Newk's Time | Blue Note | 576752-2
The Blue Note Years-The Best Of Sonny Rollins | Blue Note | 793203-2
Sonny Rollins:The Blue Note Recordings | Blue Note | 821371-2
Jazz Profile:Sonny Rollins | Blue Note | 823516-2
Tenor Madness | Original Jazz Classics | OJC20 124-2

Tenor Madness | Prestige | PRSA 7047-6
Sonny Rollins Quintet
John Coltrane-The Prestige Recordings | Prestige | 16 PCD 4405-2
Tenor Madness | Original Jazz Classics | OJC20 124-2
The Prestige Legacy Vol.2:Battles Of Saxes | Prestige | PCD 24252-2
Tenor Madness | Prestige | PRSA 7047-6
Sonny Rollins/Philly Joe Jones
Newk's Time | Blue Note | 576752-2
Sonny Rollins:The Blue Note Recordings | Blue Note | 821371-2
Tadd Dameron And His Orchestra
Clifford Brown Memorial | Original Jazz Classics | OJC20 017-2(P 7055)
Tadd Dameron Quartet
John Coltrane-The Prestige Recordings | Prestige | 16 PCD 4405-2
The New Miles Davis Quintet
Miles | Original Jazz Classics | OJC20 006-2(P 7014)
Tina Brooks Quintet
The Waiting Game | Blue Note | 540536-2
Wynton Kelly Quartet
Wynton Kelly-Piano | Original Jazz Classics | OJCCD 401-2(RLP 12-254)

Jones,Quincy | (arr,comp,ld,p,supervision,talking)

Art Farmer Septet
Plays The Arrangements And Compositions Of Gigi Gryce And Quincy Jones | Original Jazz Classics | OJCCD 054-2
Cannonball Adderley Group
Julian 'Cannonball' Adderley | EmArCy | 830381-2
Count Basie And His Orchestra
Verve Jazz Masters 2:Count Basie | Verve | 519819-2
Dinah Washington And Her Orchestra
For Those In Love | EmArCy | 514073-2
Dinah Washington With The Quincy Jones Orchestra
Verve Jazz Masters 40:Dinah Washington | Verve | 522055-2
The Swingin' Miss 'D' | Verve | 558074-2
4 By 4:Ella Fitzgerald/Sarah Vaughan/Billie Holiday/Dinah Washington | Verve | 559693-2
Dizzy Gillespie And His Orchestra
Afro | Verve | 517052-2
Verve Jazz Masters 20:Introducing | Verve | 519853-2
Dizzy Gillespie:Birks Works-The Verve Big Band Sessions | Verve | 527900-2
Dizzy Gillespie Orchestra
Verve Jazz Masters 10:Dizzy Gillespie | Verve | 516319-2
Ella Fitzgerald With The Count Basie Orchestra
Ella And Basie | Verve | 539059-2
Frank Sinatra With The Count Basie Orchestra
It Might As Well Be Spring | Reprise | 7599-27027-2
Helen Merrill With The Quincy Jones Orchestra
Clifford Brown-Max Roach:Alone Together-The Best Of The Mercury Years | Verve | 526373-2
Verve Jazz Masters 44:Clifford Brown and Max Roach | Verve | 528109-2
Brownie-The Complete EmArCy Recordings Of Clifford Brown | EmArCy | 838306-2
Lionel Hampton Orchestra
The Big Bands Vol.1.The Snader Telescriptions | Storyville | 4960043
Peggy Lee With The Quincy Jones Orchestra
Blues Cross Country | Capitol | 520088-2
Quincy Jones And His Orchestra
Talkin' Verve-Roots Of Acid Jazz:Roland Kirk | Verve | 533101-2
Verve Jazz Masters Vol.59:Toots Thielemans | Verve | 535271-2
Rahsaan/The Complete Mercury Recordings Of Roland Kirk | Mercury | 846630-2
The Quintessence | Impulse(MCA) | 951222-2
The Roots Of Acid Jazz | Impulse(MCA) | IMP 12042
Quincy Jones Big Band
Rahsaan/The Complete Mercury Recordings Of Roland Kirk | Mercury | 846630-2
Sarah Vaughan With The Quincy Jones Orchestra
Jazz In Paris:Sarah Vaughan-Vaughan And Violins | EmArCy | 065004-2
Ballads | Roulette | 537561-2
4 By 4:Ella Fitzgerald/Sarah Vaughan/Billie Holiday/Dinah Washington | Verve | 559693-2
Jazz Profile | Blue Note | 823517-2
Shirley Horn With The Quincy Jones Orchestra
Loads Of Love + Shirley Horn With Horns | Mercury | 843454-2

Jones,Ralph | (dr,fl,alto-fl,b-cl,ss,ts,clay-fl)

Yusef Lateef With Eternal Wind And The 'Kölner Rundfunk Orchester'
The African American Epic Suite:Music For Quintet And Orchestra | ACT | 9214-2

Jones,Reunald | (tp)

Count Basie And His Orchestra
Jazz Gallery:Lester Young Vol.2(1946-59) | RCA | 2119541-2
Jazz Collection:Count Basie | Laserlight | 24368
Verve Jazz Masters 2:Count Basie | Verve | 519819-2
Count Basie Swings-Joe Williams Sings | Verve | 519852-2
Verve Jazz Masters 20:Introducing | Verve | 519853-2
April In Paris | Verve | 521402-2
One O'Clock Jump | Verve | 559806-2
King Of Swing | Verve | 837433-2
Count Basie At Newport | Verve | 9861761
Ella Fitzgerald With The Count Basie Orchestra
Ella Fitzgerald-First Lady Of Song | Verve | 517898-2
Jimmy Lunceford And His Orchestra
The Legends Of Swing | Laserlight | 24659
Mezz Mezzrow And His Orchestra
Planet Jazz:Bud Freeman | Planet Jazz | 2161240-2
Sonny Rollins Orchestra
Sonny Rollins And The Big Brass | Verve | 557545-2

Jones,Rickie Lee | (gvoc)

Rob Wasserman Duet
Duets | GRP | GRP 97122

Jones,Rodney | (el-g,g,12-string-g,b-gbj)

Annette Lowman With Three Of A Kind, Fred Wesley And Rodney Jones
Brown Baby:A Tribute To Oscar Brown Jr. | Minor Music | 801061
Donald Harrison Sextet
Free To Be | Impulse(MCA) | 951283-2
Jimmy McGriff Quintet
McGriff's House Party | Milestone | MCD 9300-2
Jimmy McGriff Septet
McGriff Avenue | Milestone | MCD 9325-2
Jimmy McGriff Sextet
McGriff's House Party | Milestone | MCD 9300-2
Maceo Parker Group
Roots Revisited | Minor Music | 801015
Mo' Roots | Minor Music | 801018
Southern Exposure | Minor Music | 801033
Pee Wee Ellis Quartet
Sepia Tonality | Minor Music | 801040
Pee Wee Ellis Quintet
Sepia Tonality | Minor Music | 801040
Rodney Jones Group
Soul Manifesto | Blue Note | 530499-2
Ruth Brown With Orchestra
Fine And Mellow | Fantasy | FCD 9663-2

Jones,Rudy | (ts)

Lonnie Smith Quintet
The Lost Grooves | Blue Note | 831883-2

Jones,Rufus | (dr)

Duke Ellington And His Orchestra
Planet Jazz:Johnny Hodges | Planet Jazz | 2152065-2
Duke Ellington's Far East Suite | RCA | 2174797-2
Highlights From The Duke Ellington Centennial Edition | RCA | 2663672-2
New Orleans Suite | Rhino | 812273670-2
Welcome To Jazz At The Philharmonic | Fantasy | FANCD 6081-2
The Ellington Suites | Original Jazz Classics | OJC20 446-2(2310762)
Latin America Suite | Original Jazz Classics | OJC20 469-2
The Afro-Eurasian Eclipse-A Suite In Eight Parts | Original Jazz Classics | OJCCD 645-2(F 9498)
Jazz At The Philharmonis Berlin '65/Paris '67 | Pablo | PACD 5304-2
The Jazz Giants Play Duke Ellington:Caravan | Prestige | PCD 24227-2
Togo Brava Swuite | Storyville | STCD 8323
Duke Ellington Quartet
Latin America Suite | Original Jazz Classics | OJC20 469-2
Togo Brava Swuite | Storyville | STCD 8323
Duke Ellington Small Band
The Intimacy Of The Blues | Original Jazz Classics | OJCCD 624-2
Duke Ellington Trio
Duke Ellington Live At The Whitney | Impulse(MCA) | 951173-2
Maynard Ferguson Orchestra With Chris Connor
Two's Company | Roulette | 837201-2
Oscar Peterson With The Duke Ellington Orchestra
Oscar Peterson Plays Duke Ellington | Pablo | 2310966-2

Jones,Rusty | (drtb)

Adam Makowicz Trio
7.Zelt-Musik-Festival:Jazz Events | Zounds | CD 2730001
Adam Makowicz Trio With The Wilanow Quartet
7.Zelt-Musik-Festival:Jazz Events | Zounds | CD 2730001
Jens Bunge Group
Meet You In Chicago | Jazz 4 Ever Records:Jazz Network | J4E 4749
Stephane Grappelli With The George Shearing Trio
Grapelli Story | Verve | 515807-2
Verve Jazz Masters 11:Stéphane Grappelli | Verve | 516758-2

Jones,Sam | (b,voc,cello,dr,harmp)

Abbey Lincoln With The Benny Golson Quintet
It's Magic | Original Jazz Classics | OJCCD 205-2
Abbey Lincoln With The Benny Golson Septet
It's Magic | Original Jazz Classics | OJCCD 205-2
Abbey Lincoln With The Kenny Dorham Quintet
Abbey Is Blue | Original Jazz Classics | OJC20 069-2(RLP 1153)
Arnett Cobb Quintet
Movin' Right Along | Original Jazz Classics | OJCCD 1074-2(P 7216)
More Party Time | Original Jazz Classics | OJCCD 979-2(P 7175)
Benny Carter-Coleman Hawkins-Johnny Hodges With The Oscar Peterson Trio
The Jazz Giants Play Duke Ellington:Caravan | Prestige | PCD 24227-2
Bill Evans Trio
Everybody Digs Bill Evans | Original Jazz Classics | OJC20 068-2
The Jazz Giants Play Cole Porter:Night And Day | Prestige | PCD 24203-2
Blue Mitchell And His Orchestra
A Sure Thing | Original Jazz Classics | OJCCD 837-2
The Jazz Giants Play Jerome Kern:Yesterdays | Prestige | PCD 24202-2
Blue Mitchell Quintet
Out Of The Blue | Original Jazz Classics | OJCCD 667-2(RLP 1131)
Blue Mitchell Sextet
Blue Soul | Original Jazz Classics | OJCCD 765-2(RLP 1155)
Bobby Timmons Trio
This Here Is Bobby Timmons | Original Jazz Classics | OJC20 104-2(RLP 1164)
Born To Be Blue! | Original Jazz Classics | OJC20 873-2(R 9468)
From The Bottom | Original Jazz Classics | OJCCD 1032-2(RS 3053)
Bobby Timmons:The Prestige Trio Sessions | Prestige | PRCD 24277-2
Bud Powell Trio
Time Waits | Blue Note | 521227-2
Cannonball Adderley And His Orchestra
Cannonball Adderley Birthday Celebration | Fantasy | FANCD 6087-2
Cannonball Adderley Group
Phenix | Fantasy | FCD 79004-2
Cannonball Adderley Quartet
Ballads | Blue Note | 537563-2
Cannonball Adderley Quintet
Julian Cannonball Adderlry: Salle Pleyel/Olympia | Laserlight | 36126
Somethin' Else | Blue Note | 495329-2
Them Dirty Blues | Blue Note | 495447-2
Them Dirty Blues | Capitol | 495447-2
Them Dirty Blues | Blue Note | 495447-2
Them Dirty Blues | Capitol | 495447-2
Verve Jazz Masters 31:Cannonball Adderley | Verve | 522651-2
Cannonball Adderley:Sophisticated Swing-The EmArCy Small Group Sessions | Verve | 528408-2
Jazz Workshop Revisited | Capitol | 529441-2
At The Lighthouse | Capitol | 531572-2
Kind Of Blue:Blue Note Celebrate The Music Of Miles Davis | Blue Note | 534255-2
The Best Of Blue Note Vol.2 | Blue Note | 797960-2
Miles Davis:The Best Of The Capitol/Blue Note Years | Blue Note | 798287-2
Jazz Profile:Miles Davis | Blue Note | 823515-2
Ballads & Blues | Blue Note | 836633-2
Cannonball Adderley Birthday Celebration | Fantasy | FANCD 6087-2
Live In San Francisco | Original Jazz Classics | OJC20 035-2
Cannonball Adderley Quintet Plus | Original Jazz Classics | OJC20 306-2
Portrait Of Cannonball | Original Jazz Classics | OJCCD 361-2(RLP 269)
The Cannonball Adderley Quintet:Paris 1960 | Pablo | PACD 5303-2
At Newport | Pablo | PACD 5315-2
The Jazz Giants Play Rodgers & Hammerstein:My Favorite Things | Prestige | PCD 24223-2
Live In San Francisco | Riverside | RISA 1157-6
Cannonball Adderley Quintet Plus
Cannonball Adderley Birthday Celebration | Fantasy | FANCD 6087-2
Cannonball Adderley Quintet Plus | Original Jazz Classics | OJC20 306-2
Cannonball Adderley Sextet
Julian Cannonball Adderlry: Salle Pleyel/Olympia | Laserlight | 36126
Jazz Workshop Revisited | Capitol | 529441-2
Ballads | Blue Note | 537563-2
Cannonball Adderley Birthday Celebration | Fantasy | FANCD 6087-2
Dizzy's Business-Live In Concert | Milestone | MCD 47069-2
Cannonball Adderley In New York | Original Jazz Classics | OJC20 142-2(RLP 9404)
Nippon Soul | Original Jazz Classics | OJC20 435-2(RLP 9477)
Cannonball Adderley-Nat Adderley Quintet
What Is This Thing Called Soul:In Europe-Live! | Original Jazz Classics | OJCCD 801-2(2308238)
Cannonball Adderley-Nat Adderley Sextet
The Best Of Cannonball Adderley:The Capitol Years | Capitol | 795482-2
Cedar Walton Quartet
First Set | Steeplechase | SCCD 31085
Third Set | Steeplechase | SCCD 31179
Cedar Walton Trio
God Bless Jug And Sonny | Prestige | PCD 11019-2
Left Bank Encores | Prestige | PRCD 11022-2
Chet Baker Quartet
Sings/It Could Happen To You | Original Jazz Classics | OJC20 303-2
Clark Terry With The Thelonious Monk Trio
Thelonious Monk:85th Birthday Celebration | zyx records | FANCD 6076-2
Clark Terry-Thelonious Monk Quartet
In Orbit | Original Jazz Classics | OJC 302(R 12-271)
Clifford Jordan Quartet
Firm Roots | Steeplechase | SCCD 31033
Dexter Gordon Quartet
Dexter Gordon Birthday Celebration | Fantasy | FANCD 6082-2
The Jumpin' Blues | Original Jazz Classics | OJCCD 899-2(PR 10020)
Dizzy Gillespie Quintet
Verve Jazz Masters 10:Dizzy Gillespie | Verve | 516319-2
Talking Verve:Dizzy Gillespie | Verve | 533846-2
Dizzy Gillespie Sextet
Ultimate Dizzy Gillespie | Verve | 557535-2
Don Wilkerson Quartet
The Texas Twister | Original Jazz Classics | OJCCD 1950-2(RLP 1186)
Don Wilkerson Quintet
The Texas Twister | Original Jazz Classics | OJCCD 1950-2(RLP 1186)
Donald Byrd Sextet
Byrd In Hand | Blue Note | 542305-2
Duke Ellington-Johnny Hodges All Stars
Verve Jazz Masters 4:Duke Ellington | Verve | 516338-2
Back To Back | Verve | 521404-2
Eddie Cleanhead Vinson With The Cannonball Adderley Quintet
Cannonball Adderley Birthday Celebration | Fantasy | FANCD 6087-2
Eddie 'Cleanhead' Vinson With The Cannonball Adderley Quintet | Milestone | MCD 9324-2
Eddie Lockjaw Davis With The Red Garland Trio
Prestige Moodsville Vol.1 | Original Jazz Classics | OJCCD 360-2(MV 1)
Freddie Hubbard Quintet
Open Sesame | Blue Note | 495341-2
Gene Ammons Quartet
God Bless Jug And Sonny | Prestige | PCD 11019-2
Gene Ammons Septet
Goodbye | Original Jazz Classics | OJCCD 1081-2(P 100939)
Gene Ammons-Sonny Stitt Quintet
God Bless Jug And Sonny | Prestige | PCD 11019-2
Left Bank Encores | Prestige | PRCD 11022-2
Grant Green Quartet
Ballads | Blue Note | 537560-2
Midnight Blue(The [Be]witching Hour) | Blue Note | 854365-2
Grant Green Quintet
Kind Of Blue:Blue Note Celebrate The Music Of Miles Davis | Blue Note | 534255-2
Ballads | Blue Note | 537560-2
Harold Land Sextet
Wes Montgomery-The Complete Riverside Recordings | Riverside | 12 RCD 4408-2
Horace Parlan Trio
Movin' And Groovin' | Blue Note | 0677187
James Clay/David Fathead Newman Quintet
The Sound Of The Wide Open Spaces | Original Jazz Classics | OJCCD 1075-2(RLP 1178)
JATP All Stars
Welcome To Jazz At The Philharmonic | Fantasy | FANCD 6081-2
Jimmy Heath Quartet
Blue Soul | Original Jazz Classics | OJCCD 765-2(RLP 1155)
Jimmy Smith Quintet
Prayer Meetin' | Blue Note | 576754-2
John Lee Hooker Trio
That's My Story | Original Blues Classics | OBCCD 538-2(RLP 12-321)
Johnny Hodges With The Dizzy Gillespie Quintet
Verve Jazz Masters 35:Johnny Hodges | Verve | 521857-2
Julian Priester Sextet
Out Of This World | Milestone | MCD 47087-2
Ken McIntyre Quintet feat.Eric Dolphy
Eric Dolphy:The Complete Prestige Recordings | Prestige | 9 PRCD-4418-2
Eric Dolphy Birthday Celebration | Fantasy | FANCD 6085-2
Kenny Burrell Quartet
Blue Lights Vol.1&2 | Blue Note | 857184-2
Kenny Burrell Septet
Blue Lights Vol.1&2 | Blue Note | 857184-2
Kenny Dorham Sextet
The Complete Round About Midnight At The Cafe Bohemia | Blue Note | 533775-2
Les Spann Quintet
Gemini | Original Jazz Classics | OJCCD 1948-2(JLP 9355)
Milt Jackson-Wes Montgomery Quintet
Wes Montgomery-The Complete Riverside Recordings | Riverside | 12 RCD 4408-2
To Bags...With Love:Memorial Album | Pablo | 2310967-2
Milt Jackson Birthday Celebration | Fantasy | FANCD 6079-2
Bags Meets Wes! | Original Jazz Classics | OJC20 234-2(RLP 9407)
Nat Adderley And The Big Sax Section
Cannonball Adderley Birthday Celebration | Fantasy | FANCD 6087-2
That's Right | Original Jazz Classics | OJCCD 791-2(RLP 9330)
Nat Adderley Quartet
Cannonball Adderley:Sophisticated Swing-The EmArCy Small Group Sessions | Verve | 528408-2
Naturally! | Original Jazz Classics | OJCCD 1088-2(JLP 947)
Nat Adderley Quintet
Wes Montgomery-The Complete Riverside Recordings | Riverside | 12 RCD 4408-2
Work Song | Original Jazz Classics | OJC20 363-2
Much Brass | Original Jazz Classics | OJCCD 848-2(R 1143)
Nat Adderley Sextet
Wes Montgomery-The Complete Riverside Recordings | Riverside | 12 RCD 4408-2
Cannonball Adderley Birthday Celebration | Fantasy | FANCD 6087-2
Work Song | Original Jazz Classics | OJC20 363-2
In The Bag | Original Jazz Classics | OJCCD 648-2(JLP 975)
Much Brass | Original Jazz Classics | OJCCD 848-2(R 1143)
Nat Adderley Trio
Wes Montgomery-The Complete Riverside Recordings | Riverside | 12 RCD 4408-2
Work Song | Original Jazz Classics | OJC20 363-2
Niels-Honning Orsted-Pedersen/Sam Jones Quartet
Double Bass | Steeplechase | SCS 1055(Audiophile Pressing)
Niels-Henning Orsted-Pedersen/Sam Jones Quintet
Double Bass | Steeplechase | SCS 1055(Audiophile Pressing)
Oscar Peterson Quartet
Paris Jazz Concert:Oscar Peterson | Laserlight | 36155
Oscar Peterson Sextet
Soul Espanol | Limelight | 510439-2
Oscar Peterson Trio
Oscar Peterson Plays Duke Ellington | Pablo | 2310966-2
Paris Jazz Concert:Oscar Peterson | Laserlight | 36155
Verve Jazz Masters 16:Oscar Peterson | Verve | 516320-2
Three Originals:Motion&Emotions/Tristeza On Piano/Hello Herbie | MPS | 521059-2
Exclusively For My Friends-The Lost Tapes | MPS | 529096-2
Tristeza On Piano | MPS | 817489-2 PMS
Oscar Peterson Trio With Herb Ellis
Three Originals:Motion&Emotions/Tristeza On Piano/Hello Herbie | MPS | 521059-2
Hello Herbie | MPS | 821846-2
Oscar Peterson Trio With The Claus Ogermann Orchestra
Three Originals:Motion&Emotions/Tristeza On Piano/Hello Herbie | MPS | 521059-2
The Antonio Carlos Jobim Songbook | Verve | 525472-2
Paul Gonsalves Quintet
Gettin' Together | Original Jazz Classics | OJCCD 203-2
Philly Joe Jones Big Band
Cannonball Adderley Birthday Celebration | Fantasy | FANCD 6087-2
Phineas Newborn Jr. Trio
The Jazz Giants Play Miles Davis:Milestones | Prestige | PCD 24225-2
Ray Bryant Trio
The Jazz Giants Play Miles Davis:Milestones | Prestige | PCD 24225-2
Red Garland Quintet
Red's Good Groove | Original Jazz Classics | OJCCD 1064-2(987)
Red Garland Trio
Red In Bluesville | Original Jazz Classics | OJCCD 295-2
Prestige Moodsville Vol.1 | Original Jazz Classics | OJCCD 360-2(MV 1)
The Jazz Giants Play Harold Arlen:Blues In The Night | Prestige | PCD 24201-2
The Jazz Giants Play Harry Warren:Lullaby Of Broadway | Prestige | PCD 24204-2
Sal Nistico Quartet
Heavyweights | Milestone | MCD 47096-2
Sal Nistico Quintet

Heavyweights | Milestone | MCD 47096-2
Sam Jones Plus 10
Cannonball Adderley Birthday Celebration | Fantasy | FANCD 6087-2
Sonny Stitt Quartet
God Bless Jug And Sonny | Prestige | PCD 11019-2
Stanley Turrentine Quartet
Blue Note Plays Gershwin | Blue Note | 520808-2
Never Let Me Go | Blue Note | 576750-2
Thelonious Monk And His Orchestra
Thelonious Monk:85th Birthday Celebration | zyx records | FANCD 6076-2
At Town Hall | Original Jazz Classics | OJCCD 135-2
Thelonious Monk Quartet
Thelonious Monk:85th Birthday Celebration | zyx records | FANCD 6076-2
Thelonious Monk Quintet
Thelonious Monk:85th Birthday Celebration | zyx records | FANCD 6076-2
5 By Monk By 5 | Original Jazz Classics | OJCCD 362-2
Tina Brooks Quintet
Blue N' Groovy | Blue Note | 780679-2
Tubby Hayes And The All Stars
Rahsaan/The Complete Mercury Recordings Of Roland Kirk | Mercury | 846630-2
Walter Davis Quintet
Davis Cup | Blue Note | 0675597
Wes Montgomery Quartet
Wes Montgomery-The Complete Riverside Recordings | Riverside | 12 RCD 4408-2
Movin' Along | Original Jazz Classics | OJC20 089-2
Wes Montgomery Quintet
Wes Montgomery-The Complete Riverside Recordings | Riverside | 12 RCD 4408-2
Movin' Along | Original Jazz Classics | OJC20 089-2
Willis Jackson Sextet
Nuther'n Like Thuther'n | Prestige | PRCD 24265-2
Yusef Lateef Orchestra
Rhino Presents The Atlantic Jazz Gallery | Atlantic | 8122-71257-2

Jones,Tamiko | (voc)
Herbie Mann-Tamiko Jones
The Best Of Herbie Mann | Atlantic | 7567-81369-2

Jones,Thad | (arr,co,tp,cond,fl-h,perc,ld)
Count Basie And His Orchestra
Jazz Gallery:Lester Young Vol.2(1946-59) | RCA | 2119541-2
Jazz Collection:Count Basie | Laserlight | 24368
The Legends Of Swing | Laserlight | 24659
Atomic Swing | Roulette | 497871-2
Verve Jazz Masters 2:Count Basie | Verve | 519819-2
Count Basie Swings-Joe Williams Sings | Verve | 519852-2
Verve Jazz Masters 20:Introducing | Verve | 519853-2
April In Paris | Verve | 521402-2
Breakfast Dance And Barbecue | Roulette | 531791-2
One O'Clock Jump | Verve | 559806-2
Chairman Of The Board | Roulette | 581664-2
The Complete Atomic Basie | Roulette | 828635-2
King Of Swing | Verve | 837433-2
Count Basie At Newport | Verve | 9861761
Count On The Coast Vol.1 | Phontastic | NCD 7555
Count On The Coast Vol.2 | Phontastic | NCD 7575
Count Basie And The Kansas City 7
Count Basie And The Kansas City 7 | Impulse(MCA) | 951202-2
Dexter Gordon Quintet
Dexter Gordon Birthday Celebration | Fantasy | FANCD 6082-2
Tangerine | Original Jazz Classics | OJCCD 1041-2(P 10091)
Don Senay With Orchestra And Strings
Charles Mingus-The Complete Debut Recordings | Debut | 12 DCD 4402-2
Duke Ellington And Count Basie With Their Orchestras
First Time! | CBS | CK 65571
Ella Fitzgerald And Joe Williams With The Count Basie Octet
For The Love Of Ella Fitzgerald | Verve | 841765-2
Ella Fitzgerald With The Count Basie Orchestra
Ella Fitzgerald-First Lady Of Song | Verve | 517898-2
Frank Sinatra With The Count Basie Orchestra
Sinatra-Basie:An Historic Musical First | Reprise | 7599-27023-2
Frank Wess Quintet
The Long Road | Prestige | PCD 24247-2
Gil Evans Orchestra
Verve Jazz Masters 23:Gil Evans | Verve | 521860-2
The Individualism Of Gil Evans | Verve | 833804-2
Helen Merrill With The Dick Katz Group
The Feeling Is Mutual | EmArCy | 558849-2
A Shade Of Difference | EmArCy | 558851-2
Herbie Hancock Sextet
Herbie Hancock:The Complete Blue Note Sixties Sessions | Blue Note | 495569-2
Speak Like A Child | Blue Note | 746136-2
J.J.Johnson And His Orchestra
Planet Jazz:J.J.Johnson | Planet Jazz | 2159974-2
Jimmy McGriff Orchestra
Swingin' The Blues-Jumpin' The Blues | Laserlight | 24654
Jimmy Smith With Orchestra
Jimmy Smith:Best Of The Verve Years | Verve | 527950-2
Jimmy Smith With The Lalo Schifrin Orchestra
Jimmy Smith:Best Of The Verve Years | Verve | 527950-2
Jimmy Smith-Talkin' Verve | Verve | 531563-2
The Cat | Verve | 539756-2
Joe Williams And Friends
At Newport '63 | RCA | 2663919-2
Joe Williams With The Jimmy Jones Orchestra
Planet Jazz:Joe Williams | Planet Jazz | 2165370-2
Joe Williams,With The Oliver Nelson Orchestra
Planet Jazz:Joe Williams | Planet Jazz | 2165370-2
Johnny 'Hammond' Smith Septet
Open House | Milestone | MCD 47089-2
Johnny 'Hammond' Smith Sextet
Open House | Milestone | MCD 47089-2
Kenny Burrell With The Don Sebesky Orchestra
Verve Jazz Masters 45:Kenny Burrell | Verve | 527652-2
Blues-The Common Ground | Verve | 589101-2
Louis Armstrong And His Friends
Louis Armstrong And His Friends | Bluebird | 2663961-2
Milt Jackson Orchestra
Milt Jackson Birthday Celebration | Fantasy | FANCD 6079-2
Oliver Nelson And His Orchestra
More Blues And The Abstract Truth | Impulse(MCA) | 951212-2
Oscar Brown Jr. And His Group
Movin' On | Rhino | 8122-73678-2
Phil Woods Quartet With Orchestra & Strings
Round Trip | Verve | 559804-2
Quincy Jones And His Orchestra
The Quintessence | Impulse(MCA) | 951222-2
The Roots Of Acid Jazz | Impulse(MCA) | IMP 12042
Sarah Vaughan And Joe Williams With The Count Basie Orchestra
Jazz Profile | Blue Note | 823517-2
Sarah Vaughan And The Count Basie Orchestra
Ballads | Roulette | 537561-2
Sarah Vaughan And The Thad Jones Orchestra
Verve Jazz Masters 42:Sarah Vaughan-The Jazz Sides | Verve | 526817-2
Sarah Vaughan With The Count Basie Band
Jazz Profile | Blue Note | 823517-2
Sonny Stitt With Orchestra
Goin' Down Slow | Prestige | PRCD 24276-2
Thad Jones And His Orchestra
Charles Mingus-The Complete Debut Recordings | Debut | 12 DCD 4402-2
Thad Jones Quartet
Charles Mingus-The Complete Debut Recordings | Debut | 12 DCD 4402-2
Thad Jones Quintet
Charles Mingus-The Complete Debut Recordings | Debut | 12 DCD 4402-2
Thad Jones-Mel Lewis Orchestra
The Groove Merchant/The Second Race | Laserlight | 24656
The Prestige All Stars
Olio | Original Jazz Classics | OJCCD 1004-2(P 7084)
Thelonious Monk And His Orchestra
Greatest Hits | CBS | CK 65422
Thelonious Monk Quintet
Thelonious Monk:85th Birthday Celebration | zyx records | FANCD 6076-2
5 By Monk By 5 | Original Jazz Classics | OJCCD 362-2
Yusef Lateef Ensemble
Atlantic Saxophones | Rhino | 8122-71256-2

Jones,Tony | (percts)
Don Cherry Group
Multi Kulti | A&M Records | 395323-2

Jones,Truett | (tb)
Harry James And His Orchestra
The Legends Of Swing | Laserlight | 24659

Jones,Victor | (drvoice)
(Little)Jimmy Scott And His Band
Mood Indigo | Milestone | MCD 9305-2
Ed Schuller & Band
The Eleventh Hour | Tutu Records | 888124-2*
Jimmy Ponder Quartet
Jazzin' Vol.2: The Music Of Stevie Wonder | Fantasy | FANCD 6088-2
Mal Waldron Quartet
Mal,Verve,Black & Blue | Tutu Records | 888170-2*
Michel Petrucciani Group
Michel Petrucciani:The Blue Note Years | Blue Note | 789916-2
Music | Blue Note | 792563-2
Michel Petrucciani Quintet
Michel Petrucciani Live | Blue Note | 780589-2
Mingus Big Band 93
Nostalgia In Times Square | Dreyfus Jazz Line | FDM 36559-2
Nicolas Simion Quartet
Oriental Gates:Live In Vienna | Tutu Records | 888212-2*
Nicolas Simion Quartet feat. Tomasz Stanko
Transylvanian Dance | Tutu Records | 888164-2*
Nicolas Simion Trio
Oriental Gates:Live In Vienna | Tutu Records | 888212-2*
Uli Lenz Trio
Echoes Of Mandela | Tutu Records | 888180-2*

Jones,Vince | (perc,voc,tp,fl-hpocket-tp)
Vince Jones Group
Spell | Intuition Records | INT 3067-2
It All Ends Up In Tears | Intuition Records | INT 3069-2
Watch What Happens | Intuition Records | INT 3070-2
For All Colours | Intuition Records | INT 3071-2
Tell Me A Secret | Intuition Records | INT 3072-2
Future Girl | Intuition Records | INT 3109-2
Here's To The Miracles | Intuition Records | INT 3198-2
Vince Jones Quartet
One Day Spent | Intuition Records | INT 3087-2
Vince Jones Septet
On The Brink Of It | Intuition Records | INT 3068-2
Vince Jones With Orchestra
Come In Spinner | Intuition Records | INT 3052-2
Vince Jones With The Benny Green Quartet
One Day Spent | Intuition Records | INT 3087-2

Jones,Virgil | (dr,tpfl-h)
Charles Earland Orchestra
Charlie's Greatest Hits | Prestige | PCD 24250-2
Charles Earland Quintet
Black Talk! | Original Jazz Classics | OJCCD 335-2(P 7758)
Charles Earland Sextet
Jazzin' With The Soul Brothers | Fantasy | FANCD 6086-2
Black Talk! | Original Jazz Classics | OJCCD 335-2(P 7758)
Charlie's Greatest Hits | Prestige | PCD 24250-2
Dee Dee Bridgewater With Big Band
Dear Ella | Verve | 539102-2
Frank Foster Quintet
Soul Outing! | Original Jazz Classics | OJCCD 984-2(7479)
Frank Foster Sextet
Soul Outing! | Original Jazz Classics | OJCCD 984-2(7479)
Idris Muhammad Group
Jazzin' With The Soul Brothers | Fantasy | FANCD 6086-2
Johnny 'Hammond' Smith Quartet
Open House | Milestone | MCD 47089-2
Johnny 'Hammond' Smith Sextet
The Soulful Blues | Prestige | PCD 24244-2
Leon Spencer Sextet
Jazzin' With The Soul Brothers | Fantasy | FANCD 6086-2
Discovery:Grover Washington Jr.-The First Recordings | Prestige | PCD 11020-2
McCoy Tyner Big Band
The Best Of McCoy Tyner Big Band | Dreyfus Jazz Line | FDM 37012-2
Melvin Sparks Quintet
Jazzin' With The Soul Brothers | Fantasy | FANCD 6086-2
Milt Jackson Sextet
Milt Jackson Birthday Celebration | Fantasy | FANCD 6079-2
Roland Kirk All Stars
Rahsaan/The Complete Mercury Recordings Of Roland Kirk | Mercury | 846630-2
Roland Kirk And His Orchestra
Rahsaan/The Complete Mercury Recordings Of Roland Kirk | Mercury | 846630-2
Roland Kirk Sextet
Talkin' Verve-Roots Of Acid Jazz:Roland Kirk | Verve | 533101-2
Roland Kirk With The Benny Golson Orchestra
Rahsaan/The Complete Mercury Recordings Of Roland Kirk | Mercury | 846630-2
Ruth Brown With Orchestra
Fine And Mellow | Fantasy | FCD 9663-2

Jones,Wallace | (tp)
Duke Ellington And His Famous Orchestra
Duke Ellington:The Blanton-Webster Band | Bluebird | 21 13181-2
Planet Jazz:Duke Ellington | Planet Jazz | 2152053-2
Planet Jazz:Johnny Hodges | Planet Jazz | 2152065-2
Planet Jazz Sampler | Planet Jazz | 2152326-2
Planet Jazz:Ben Webster | RCA | 2165368-2
Planet Jazz:Big Bands | Planet Jazz | 2169649-2
Planet Jazz:Jazz Trumpet | Planet Jazz | 2169654-2
Planet Jazz:Female Jazz Vocalists | Planet Jazz | 2169656-2
Highlights From The Duke Ellington Centennial Edition | RCA | 2663672-2
Greatest Hits | CBS | 462959-2
Jazz:The Essential Collection Vol.2 | IN+OUT Records | 78012-2
Jazz:The Essential Collection Vol.3 | IN+OUT Records | 78013-2
Duke Ellington:Ko-Ko | Dreyfus Jazz Line | FDM 36717-2
Duke Ellington And His Orchestra
Highlights From The Duke Ellington Centennial Edition | RCA | 2663672-2
Carnegie Hall Concert January 1943 | Prestige | 2PCD 34004-2
Jazz:The Essential Collection Vol.3 | IN+OUT Records | 78013-2
The Duke At Fargo 1940 | Storyville | STCD 8316/17
At The Hurricane:Original 1943 Broadcasts | Storyville | STCD 8359

Jones,Warren | (b)
Conte Candoli-Carl Fontana Quintet
The Complete Phoenix Recordings Vol.1 | Woofy Productions | WPCD 121
The Complete Phoenix Recordings Vol.2 | Woofy Productions | WPCD 122
The Complete Phoenix Recordings Vol.3 | Woofy Productions | WPCD 123
The Complete Phoenix Recordings Vol.4 | Woofy Productions | WPCD 124
The Complete Phoenix Recordings Vol.5 | Woofy Productions | WPCD 125
The Complete Phoenix Recordings Vol.6 | Woofy Productions | WPCD 126

Jones,Wesley | (p)
Lester Young And His Band
Jazz Gallery:Lester Young Vol.2(1946-59) | RCA | 2119541-2
Lester Young:The Complete Aladdin Sessions | Blue Note | 832787-2

Jones,Willie | (dr,perc,gvoc)
Charles Mingus Jazz Workshop
Charles Mingus-Passion Of A Man:The Complete Atlantic Recordings 1956-1961 | Atlantic | 8122-72871-2
The Very Best Of Charles Mingus | Rhino | 8122-79988-2
Charles Mingus Quintet
Charles Mingus-The Complete Debut Recordings | Debut | 12 DCD 4402-2
Mingus At The Bohemia | Original Jazz Classics | OJC20 045-2
The Charles Mingus Quintet+Max Roach | Original Jazz Classics | OJC20 440-2(F 6009)
Fred Jackson Quartet
So Blue So Funky-Heroes Of The Hammond | Blue Note | 796563-2
Thelonious Monk Quintet
Thelonious Monk:The Complete Prestige Recordings | Prestige | 3 PRCD 4428-2
MONK | Original Jazz Classics | OJCCD 016-2
Thelonious Monk/Sonny Rollins | Original Jazz Classics | OJCCD 059-2
The Prestige Legacy Vol.1:The High Priests | Prestige | PCD 24251-2

Jones,Wilmore 'Slick' | (drvib)
Fats Waller And His Rhythm
Planet Jazz:Fats Waller | Planet Jazz | 2152058-2
Fats Waller:The Complete Associated Transcription Sessions 1935-1939 | Jazz Unlimited | JUCD 2076
Lionel Hampton And His Orchestra
Planet Jazz:Lionel Hampton | Planet Jazz | 2152059-2
Planet Jazz Sampler | Planet Jazz | 2152326-2
Louis Jordan And His Tympany Five
The Small Black Groups | Storyville | 4960523
Louis Jordan-Let The Good Times Roll: The Complete Decca Recordings 1938-1954 | Bear Family Records | BCD 15557 IH
Sidney Bechet's Blue Note Jazzmen
Runnin' Wild | Blue Note | 821259-2

Jongen,Jel | (tb)
Jürgen Sturm's Ballstars
Tango Subversivo | Nabel Records:Jazz Network | CD 4613

Jönsson,Cennet | (b-cl,ss,tsreeds)
The Crossover Ensemble
The River:Image Of Time And Life | dacapo | DCCD 9434
The Crossover Ensemble With The Zapolski Quartet
Helios Suite | dacapo | DCCD 9459

Jonsson,Fredrik | (b)
Tim Hagans With Norrbotten Big Band
Future Miles | ACT | 9235-2

Joos,Herbert | (fl,fl-h,alphorn,bar-h,double-tp)
Eberhard Weber Orchestra
Orchestra | ECM | 1374
Harry Pepl/Herbert Joos/Jon Christensen
Cracked Mirrors | ECM | 1356
Herbert Joos Trio
Ballade Noire | free flow music | ffm 0392
Herbert Joos With Strings
Daybreak/The Dark Side Of Twilight | Japo | 60015
Patrick Bebelaar Quartet
You Never Lose An Island | dml-records | CD 015
Sputnik 27
But Where's The Moon? | dml-records | CD 011
Wolfgang Lackerschmid Group
Mallet Connection | Bhakti Jazz | BR 33

Jordan,Clifford | (as,fl,ss,tscowbell)
Carmen McRae And Her Quartet
Carmen Sings Monk | RCA | 2663841-2
Carmen McRae with the Clifford Jordan Quartet
The Collected Carmen McRae | RCA | 2668713-2
Charles Mingus Quartet
Right Now | Original Jazz Classics | OJCCD 237-2
Charles Mingus Quintet
Right Now | Original Jazz Classics | OJCCD 237-2
Charles Mingus Sextet
Eric Dolphy Birthday Celebration | Fantasy | FANCD 6085-2
Town Hall Concert 1964, Vol.1 | Original Jazz Classics | OJCCD 042-2
Cliff Jordan-John Gilmore Quintet
Blowing In From Chicago | Blue Note | 542306-2
Clifford Jordan Quartet
Spellbound | Original Jazz Classics | OJCCD 766-2(RLP 9340)
Firm Roots | Steeplechase | SCCD 31033
Clifford Jordan Quintet
Clifford Jordan Meets Klaus Weiss | JHM Records | JHM 3617
Mosaic | Milestone | MCD 47092-2
David Fathead Newman Quintet Plus Clifford Jordan
Blue Head | Candid | CCD 79041
Dick Griffin Septet
The Eighth Wonder & More | Konnex Records | KCD 5059
Horace Silver Quintet
Horace Silver Retrospective | Blue Note | 495576-2
Lee Morgan Quintet
Take Twelve | Original Jazz Classics | OJCCD 310-2
Max Roach Quartet
Speak, Brother, Speak | Original Jazz Classics | OJCCD 646-2(F 86007)
Max Roach Sextet With Choir
It's Time | Impulse(MCA) | 951185-2
Sonny Clark Quintet
My Conception | Blue Note | 522674-2

Jordan,Daniel | (b,fl,ssts)
Stan Getz Quartet
Stan Getz Highlights:The Best Of The Verve Years Vol.2 | Verve | 517330-2
Stan Getz Highlights | Verve | 847430-2

Jordan,Duke | (b,p,vocp-solo)
Art Pepper With The Duke Jordan Trio
Art Pepper With Duke Jordan In Copenhagen 1981 | Galaxy | 2GCD 8201-2
Barney Wilen Quintet
Jazz In Paris:Jazz & Cinéma Vol.1 | EmArCy | 548318-2 PMS
Charlie Parker Quintet
Charlie Parker:Now's The Time | Dreyfus Jazz Line | FDM 36724-2
Clark Terry Quartet
Jazz Legends:Clark Terry-Duke Jordan | Storyville | 4960283
Coleman Hawkins All Star Octet
Body And Soul Revisited | GRP | GRP 16272
Don Sickler Orchestra
Tribute To Charlie Parker Vol.2 | Dreyfus Jazz Line | FDM 37015-2
Doug Watkins Sextet
Donald Byrd & Doug Watkins:The Tradition Sessions | Blue Note | 540528-2
Duke Jordan Trio
Jazz Legends:Clark Terry-Duke Jordan | Storyville | 4960283
The Birdlanders Vol.1 | Original Jazz Classics | OJCCD 1930-2
Flight To Norway | Steeplechase | SCCD 31543
Gene Ammons-Sonny Stitt Quintet
The Prestige Legacy Vol.2:Battles Of Saxes | Prestige | PCD 24252-2
Kenny Burrell Septet
Blue Lights Vol.1&2 | Blue Note | 857184-2
Stan Getz Quintet
Stan Getz Highlights:The Best Of The Verve Years Vol.2 | Verve | 517330-2

Verve Jazz Masters 8:Stan Getz | Verve | 519823-2
A Life In Jazz:A Musical Biography | Verve | 535119-2
Ultimate Stan Getz selected by Joe Henderson | Verve | 557532-2
Stan Getz Plays | Verve | 833535-2
Stan Getz Highlights | Verve | 847430-2
Stan Getz-The Complete Roost Sessions | EMI Records | 859622-2
Tina Brooks Quintet
Blue N' Groovy | Blue Note | 780679-2

Jordan,James | (ring cymbalsring-cimbals)
Pharoah Sanders Orchestra
Thembi | Impulse(MCA) | 951253-2

Jordan,Kent | (alto-fl,flpiccolo)
Elvin Jones Jazz Machine
Going Home | Enja | ENJ-7095 2
Wynton Marsalis Sextet
Hot House Flowers | CBS | 468710-2

Jordan,Lewis | (asvoc)
Louis Armstrong With Louis Jordan And His Tympany Five
Louis Armstrong:C'est Si Bon | Dreyfus Jazz Line | FDM 36730-2
Louis Jordan And His Tympany Five
The Small Black Groups | Storyville | 4960523

Jordan,Louis | (as,ts,voc,cl,bs,percsax)
Ella Fitzgerald With Louis Jordan And His Tympany Five
Ella Fitzgerald:Mr.Paganini | Dreyfus Jazz Line | FDM 36741-2
Ella Fitzgerald With The Chick Webb Orchestra
Jazz Collection:Ella Fitzgerald | Laserlight | 24397
Louis Armstrong And His Orchestra
Planet Jazz:Louis Armstrong | Planet Jazz | 2152052-2
Louis Armstrong:A 100th Birthday Celebration | RCA | 2663694-2
Louis Jordan And His Tympany Five
Louis Jordan-Let The Good Times Roll: The Complete Decca Recordings 1938-1954 | Bear Family Records | BCD 15557 IH
Louis Jordan With The Nelson Riddle Orchestra
Louis Jordan-Let The Good Times Roll: The Complete Decca Recordings 1938-1954 | Bear Family Records | BCD 15557 IH
Louis Jordan's Elks Rendez-Vous Band
Louis Jordan-Let The Good Times Roll: The Complete Decca Recordings 1938-1954 | Bear Family Records | BCD 15557 IH
Roger Sturgis With Lovie Jordan's Elks Rendez-Vous Band
Louis Jordan-Let The Good Times Roll: The Complete Decca Recordings 1938-1954 | Bear Family Records | BCD 15557 IH

Jordan,Ludwig | (tp)
Louis Armstrong And His Orchestra
Best Of The Complete RCA Victor Recordings | RCA | 2663636-2
Louis Armstrong:A 100th Birthday Celebration | RCA | 2663694-2
Louis Armstrong:C'est Si Bon | Dreyfus Jazz Line | FDM 36730-2

Jordan,Rodney | (b)
Russel Gunn Group
Ethnomusicology Vol.1 | Atlantic | 7567-83165-2

Jordan,Sheila | (voc)
George Gruntz Concert Jazz Band '83
Theatre | ECM | 1265
George Russell Sextet
The Outer View | Original Jazz Classics | OJCCD 616-2(RLP 9440)
Sheila Jordan-Steve Swallow
Misty Blue:Sweet Sisters Swing Songs Of Sorrow And Sadness | Blue Note | 521151-2
Steve Swallow Group
Home | ECM | 1160(513424-2)

Jordan,Stanley | (el-g,g,b-programming,dr-programming)
Stanley Jordan
Live In New York | Blue Note | 497810-2
Stanley Jordan Quartet
Live In New York | Blue Note | 497810-2
Stanley Jordan Trio
Festival International De Jazz De Montreal | Spectra | 9811660

Jordan,Steve | (dr,percg)
Benny Goodman And His Orchestra
Great Swing Classics In Hi-Fi | Capitol | 521223-2
Don Grolnick Group
Hearts And Numbers | VeraBra Records | CDVBR 2016-2
Klaus Doldinger Jubilee
Doldinger's Best | ACT | 9224-2
Klaus Doldinger With Orchestra
Lifelike | Warner | 2292-46478-2
Klaus Doldinger With Orchestra And Etta James
Lifelike | Warner | 2292-46478-2
Sonny Rollins Quintet
Here's To The People | Milestone | MCD 9194-2
Sonny Rollins Sextet
Here's To The People | Milestone | MCD 9194-2
The Brecker Brothers
Out Of The Loop | GRP | GRP 97842
Vic Dickenson Septet
Nice Work | Vanguard | VCD 79610-2
Vic Dickenson Septet With Ruby Braff
Nice Work | Vanguard | VCD 79610-2

Jordan,Taft | (tpvoc)
(Little)Jimmy Scott With The Billy Taylor Orchestra
Everybody's Somebody's Fool | Decca | 050669-2
Al Sears And His Orchestra
Sear-iously | Bear Family Records | BCD 15668 AH
Django Reinhardt With Duke Ellington And His Orchestra
Django Reinhardt:Souveniers | Dreyfus Jazz Line | FDM 36744-2
Duke Ellington And His Famous Orchestra
Planet Jazz:Johnny Hodges | Planet Jazz | 2162005-2
Duke Ellington And His Orchestra
Planet Jazz:Duke Ellington | Planet Jazz | 2152053-2
Planet Jazz:Jazz Greatest Hits | Planet Jazz | 2169648-2
The Legends Of Swing | Laserlight | 24659
Highlights From The Duke Ellington Centennial Edition | RCA | 2663672-2
Carnegie Hall Concert December 1944 | Prestige | 2PCD 24073-2
Carnegie Hall Concert January 1946 | Prestige | 2PCD 24074-2
Jazz:The Essential Collection Vol.2 | IN+OUT Records | 78012-2
At The Hurricane:Original 1943 Broadcasts | Storyville | STCD 8359
Ella Fitzgerald And Her Famous Orchestra
The Radio Years 1940 | Jazz Unlimited | JUCD 2065
Ella Fitzgerald And Her Orchestra
Jazz Collection:Ella Fitzgerald | Laserlight | 24397
Ella Fitzgerald With Sy Oliver And His Orchestra
Ella Fitzgerald:The Decca Years 1949-1954 | Decca | 050668-2
Ella Fitzgerald With The Bill Doggett Orchestra
Ella Fitzgerald-First Lady Of Song | Verve | 517898-2
Rhythm Is My Business | Verve | 559513-2
Ella Fitzgerald With The Chick Webb Orchestra
Jazz Collection:Ella Fitzgerald | Laserlight | 24397
King Curtis Band
King Curtis-Blow Man Blow | Bear Family Records | BCD 15670 CI
Louis Armstrong And His Orchestra
I Love Jazz | Verve | 543747-2
Louis Armstrong And Omer Simeon With The Sy Oliver Orchestra
Ambassador Louis Armstrong Vol.17:Moments To Remember(1952-1956) | Ambassador | CLA 1917
Louis Armstrong With Sy Oliver And His Orchestra
Louis Armstrong-My Greatest Songs | MCA | MCD 18347
Miles Davis + 19
Miles Ahead | CBS | CK 65121
Miles Davis With Gil Evans & His Orchestra
This Is Jazz:Miles Davis Plays Ballads | CBS | CK 65038
Sketches Of Spain | CBS | CK 65142
Sarah Vaughan The The Joe Lippman Orchestra
Sarah Vaughan:Lover Man | Dreyfus Jazz Line | FDM 36739-2

Jordi,Thomas 'Thomy' | (bel-b)
Rudi Neuwirth Group
Sand | Traumton Records | 2413-2

Jorge,Kleber | (voc)
John Patitucci Group
Mistura Fina | GRP | GRP 98022

Jorgensen,Hendrik | (tp)
The Orchestra
New Skies | dacapo | DCCD 9463

Jorgensen,Johannes | (asbs)
Stan Getz With Ib Glindemann And His Orchestra
Stan Getz In Europe | Laserlight | 24657

Jorgensen,John | (b)
Papa Benny's Jazzband
The Golden Years Of Revival Jazz,Vol.2 | Storyville | STCD 5507

Jorgensen,Knud | (p)
Knud Jorgensen-Bengt Hanson
Skiss | Touché Music | TMcCD 001
Bojangles | Touché Music | TMcCD 002
Knud Jorgensen-Bengt Hanson-Gustavo Bergalli
Skiss | Touché Music | TMcCD 001
Day Dream | Touché Music | TMcCD 003

Jorgensen,Kristian Bagge | (v)
Kristian Jorgensen Quartet With Monty Alexander
Meeting Monty | Stunt Records | STUCD 01212

Jorgensen,Orla Levin | (b,bjco)
Papa Benny's Jazzband
The Golden Years Of Revival Jazz,Vol.2 | Storyville | STCD 5507
Theis/Nyegaard Jazzband
The Golden Years Of Revival Jazz,Sampler | Storyville | 109 1001
The Golden Years Of Revival Jazz,Vol.3 | Storyville | STCD 5508
The Golden Years Of Revival Jazz,Vol.5 | Storyville | STCD 5510
The Golden Years Of Revival Jazz,Vol.6 | Storyville | STCD 5511
The Golden Years Of Revival Jazz,Vol.12 | Storyville | STCD 5517
The Golden Years Of Revibal Jazz,Vol.15 | Storyville | STCD 5520

Jorgensen,Per | (tpvoc)
Jon Balke w/Magnetic North Orchestra
Further | ECM | 1517
Kyanos | ECM | 1822(017278-2)
Jon Balke w/Oslo 13
Nonsentration | ECM | 1445
Michael Mantler Group With The Danish Radio Concert Orchestra Strings
The School Of Understanding(Sort-Of-An-Opera) | ECM | 1648/49(537963-2)

Jörgensmann,Theo | (cl,alto-cl,bassett-hel-cl)
Jazzensemble Des Hessischen Rundfunks
Atmosphering Conditions Permitting | ECM | 1549/50

Joris,Bert | (fl-htp)
Joe Haider Quintet
Magic Box | JHM Records | JHM 3601
Philip Catherine Quartet
Blue Prince | Dreyfus Jazz Line | FDM 36614-2
Summer Night | Dreyfus Jazz Line | FDM 36637-2
Wolfgang Haffner International Jazz Quintet
Whatever It Is | Jazz 4 Ever Records:Jazz Network | J4E 4714

Jöris,Guido | (dr,synth-programming,keyboards)
Peter Fessler Quartet
Colours Of My Mind | Minor Music | 801063
Peter Fessler Quintet
Colours Of My Mind | Minor Music | 801063

Jormin,Anders | (bb-solo)
Anders Jormin
Xieyi | ECM | 1762(013998-2)
Anders Jormin With Brass Quartet
Xieyi | ECM | 1762(013998-2)
Bobo Stenson Trio
Reflections | ECM | 1516(523160-2)
War Orphans | ECM | 1604(539723-2)
Serenity | ECM | 1740/41(543611-2)
Charles Lloyd Quartet
Notes From Big Sur | ECM | 1465(511999-2)
The Call | ECM | 1522(517719-2)
All My Relations | ECM | 1557
Canto | ECM | 1635(537345-2)
Don Cherry Group
Dona Nostra | ECM | 1448(521727-2)
Jon Balke w/Magnetic North Orchestra
Further | ECM | 1517
Kyanos | ECM | 1822(017278-2)
Thomasz Stanko Quartet
Matka Joanna | ECM | 1544(523986-2)
Tomasz Stanko Quartet
Leosia | ECM | 1603(531693-2)
Tomasz Stanko Sextet
From The Green Hill | ECM | 1680(547336-2)

Jörris,Guido | (dr)
Peter Fessler Quartet
Foot Prints | Minor Music | 801058

Joseph,Don | (tp)
Gerry Mulligan And His Orchestra
Mullenium | CBS | CK 65678

Joseph,Julian | (p)
Billy Cobham Group
Art Of Five | IN+OUT Records | 77063-2
David Jean-Baptiste Group
The Nature Suite | Laika Records | 35101632

Joseph,Papa John | (b)
Joseph 'Dee Dee' Pierce And His Band
Atlantic Jazz: New Orleans | Atlantic | 7567-81700-2
Punch Miller's Bunch & George Lewis
Atlantic Jazz: New Orleans | Atlantic | 7567-81700-2

Jospin,Mowgli | (tb)
Claude Luter Et Ses L'Orientais
Jazz In Paris:Sidney Bechet Et Claude Luther | EmArCy | 159821-2 PMS
Sidney Bechet With Claude Luter And His Orchestra
Planet Jazz:Sidney Bechet | Planet Jazz | 2152063-2
Sidney Bechet:Summertime | Dreyfus Jazz Line | FDM 36712-2

Jost,Ekkehard | (as,bs,bass-sax,b-cl,accordeon)
Amman Boutz
Some Other Tapes | Fish Music | FM 009/10 CD
Balance
Some Other Tapes | Fish Music | FM 009/10 CD
Chromatic Alarm
Some Other Tapes | Fish Music | FM 009/10 CD
Ekkehard Jost & Chromatic Alarm
Von Zeit Zu Zeit | Fish Music | FM 005 CD
Wintertango | Fish Music | FM 008 CD
Ekkehard Jost Ensemble
Weimarer Balladen | Fish Music | FM 004 CD
Ekkehard Jost Nonet
Out Of Jost's Songbook | Fish Music | FM 006 CD
Ekkehard Jost Quartet
Deep | Fish Music | FM 007 CD
Some Other Tapes | Fish Music | FM 009/10 CD
Ekkehard Jost Quintet
Some Other Tapes | Fish Music | FM 009/10 CD
Ekkehard Jost Trio
Some Other Tapes | Fish Music | FM 009/10 CD
Ekkehard Jost-Vinko Globokar
Some Other Tapes | Fish Music | FM 009/10 CD
Giessen-Köln-Nonett
Some Other Tapes | Fish Music | FM 009/10 CD
Sommer-Jost DuOh!
Some Other Tapes | Fish Music | FM 009/10 CD
Transalpin Express Orchestra
Some Other Tapes | Fish Music | FM 009/10 CD

Jost,Tizian | (pmelodica)
Günther Klatt-Tizian Jost
Art Of The Duo:Live In Mexico City | Tutu Records | 888184-2*
Helmut Kagerer 4 & Roman Schwaller
Jazz Guitar Highlights 1 | Jardis Records | JRCD 20141
Gamblin' | Jardis Records | JRCD 9714
Hugo Siegmeth Quintet
Live At The Jazzclub Unterfahrt | Edition Collage | EC 533-2
Ku-umba Frank Lacy & The Poker Bigband
Songs From The Musical 'Poker' | Tutu Records | 888150-2*
Zona Sul
Pure Love | Nagel-Heyer | CD 3039

Joule,Alain | (perc)
Alain Joule
Aquarian Rain | ECM | 1451
Barre Phillips Group
Aquarian Rain | ECM | 1451

Jourdan,Andre | (dr)
Django Reinhardt And The Quintet Du Hot Club De France
Jazz In Paris:Django Reinhardt-Django's Blues | EmArCy | 013545-2
Planet Jazz:Django Reinhardt | Planet Jazz | 2152071-2
Peche Á La Mode-The Great Blue Star Sessions 1947/1953 | Verve | 835418-2
Quintet Du Hot Club De France
Verve Jazz Masters 38:Django Reinhardt | Verve | 516931-2
Django Reinhardt:Souveniers | Dreyfus Jazz Line | FDM 36744-2
Sidney Bechet And His Orchestra
Jazz In Paris:Sidney Bechet Et Claude Luther | EmArCy | 159821-2 PMS

Jowett,J.A. | (viola)
Stochelo Rosenberg Group With Strings
Gypsy Swing | Verve | 527806-2

Jowitt,R. | (cl)
Dee Dee Bridgewater With Orchestra
Dear Ella | Verve | 539102-2

Joy,Andrew | (fr-h)
Los Jovenes Flamencos With The WDR Big Band And Guests
Jazzpana | ACT | 9212-2

Joyce,Jerry | (ldv)
Artie Shaw And His Orchestra
Planet JazzArtie Shaw | Planet Jazz | 2152057-2
Planet Jazz:Jazz Greatest Hits | Planet Jazz | 2169648-2

Juanco,Javier | (g)
Moments Quartet
Original Moments | Fresh Sound Records | FSNT 052 CD

Jubilee All Stars,The |
Jubilee All Stars
Jazz Gallery:Lester Young Vol.2(1946-59) | RCA | 2119541-2

Juchors,Dominique | (v)
Stephane Grappelli With The Michel Legrand Orchestra
Grapelli Story | Verve | 515807-2

Judd Conlin Rhythmaires,The | (voc-group)
Louis Armstrong And Gary Crosby With Sonny Burke's Orchestra
Louis Armstrong-My Greatest Songs | MCA | MCD 18347
Louis Armstrong And His All Stars With Sonny Burke's Orchestra
Ambassador Louis Armstrong Vol.17:Moments To Remember(1952-1956) | Ambassador | CLA 1917

Judd Conlon Singers,The |
Louis Armstrong And Ella Fitzgerald With Russell Garcia's Orchestra
The Complete Ella Fitzgerald And Louis Armstrong On Verve | Verve | 537284-2

Jugendchor Wellenbrecher |
Matthias Petzold Group With Choir
Psalmen und Lobgesänge für Chor und Jazz-Enseble | Indigo-Records | 1002 CD

Juhnke,Gerrit | (dr)
Gunter Hampel Next Generation
Köln Concert Part 1 | Birth | CD 047
Köln Concert Part 2 | Birth | CD 048

Julian,Mike | (tb)
Paulinho Da Costa Orchestra
Agora | Original Jazz Classics | OJCCD 630-2(2310785)

Julian,Zeb | (g)
Wingy Mannone And His Orchestra
Planet Jazz:Jazz Trumpet | Planet Jazz | 2169654-2
Planet Jazz:Male Jazz Vocalists | Planet Jazz | 2169657-2

Julien,Ivan | (tp,arrld)
Raymond Fol Big Band
Jazz In Paris:Raymond Fol-Les 4 Saisons | EmArCy | 548791-2

Julyie,Katharine 'Kathryn' | (harp)
Ella Fitzgerald With The Nelson Riddle Orchestra
The Best Of The Song Books:The Ballads | Verve | 521867-2
Oh Lady Be Good:The Best Of The Gershwin Songbook | Verve | 529581-2
Love Songs:The Best Of The Song Books | Verve | 531762-2
Ella Fitzgerald Sings The Johnny Mercer Songbook | Verve | 539057-2

Jumaily,Rania | (voc)
Mike Westbrook Brass Band
Glad Day:Settings Of William Blake | Enja | ENJ-9376 2

Jun,Yu | (gu-zeng)
Chinese Compass
Chinese Compass | dacapo | DCCD 9443

Jünemann,Uli | (asss)
Markus Fleischer Quartet
Let's Call It A Day | Village | WLCD 1017-2
Ulli Jünemann-Morton Ginnerup European Jazz Project
The Exhibition | Edition Collage | EC 518-2

Jung,Albert | (cello)
Los Jovenes Flamencos With The WDR Big Band And Guests
Jazzpana | ACT | 9212-2

Jung,Jean-Yves | (p)
Derrick James & Wesley 'G' Quintet
Two Sides To Every Story | Jardis Records | JRCD 20137
Susan Weinert Band
Point Of View | Intuition Records | INT 3272-2

Jungfer,Barbara | (g)
Barbara Jungfer Trio
Vitamin B 3 | yvp music | CD 3097

Jungmair,Stefan | (programming)
Pili-Pili
Ballads Of Timbuktu | JA & RO | JARO 4240-2

Junker,Manfred | (gg-solo)
Manfred Junker
Cole Porter-Live! | Edition Collage | EC 531-2
Manfred Junker Quartet
Cole Porter-Live! | Edition Collage | EC 531-2

Juris,Vic | (g,el-gvoc)
Benny Waters Quintet
Benny Waters Plays Songs Of Love | Jazzpoint | JP 1039 CD
Bireli Lagrene Ensemble
Live | Jazzpoint | JP 1047 CD
Bireli Lagrene Group
A Tribute To Django Reinhardt | Jazzpoint | JP 1061 CD
Bireli Lagrene Trio
Live At The Carnegie Hall: A Tribute To Django Reinhardt | Jazzpoint | JP 1040 CD
A' Portrait Of Jan Jankeje | Jazzpoint | JP 1054 CD
Bireli Lagrene-Vic Juris
Bireli Lagrene 'Highlights' | Jazzpoint | JP 1027 CD
Jam Session
Jam Session Vol.2 | Steeplechase | SCCD 31523
Steve LaSpina Quintet
Remember When | Steeplechase | SCCD 31540
Vic Juris Quartet
For The Music | Jazzpoint | JP 1034 CD
Vic Juris Trio
Songbook 2 | Steeplechase | SCCD 31516
While My Guitar Gently Weeps | Steeplechase | SCCD 31553
Vic Juris-John Etheridge
Bohemia | Jazzpoint | JP 1023 CD
Vic Juris-John Etheridge Quartet
Bohemia | Jazzpoint | JP 1023 CD

Jurkievicz,Rainer | (fr-h)
Los Jovenes Flamencos With The WDR Big Band And Guests
Jazzpana | ACT | 9212-2

Just Friends |
Just Friends
Nevertheless | IN+OUT Records | 7015-2
Jazz Unlimited | IN+OUT Records | 7017-2

Justicia,Pepe | (g)
Pepe Justicia-Amir Haddad Duo
Internationales Guitarren Festival '99 | ALISO Records | AL 1038

Jütte,Bastian | (dr)
Marc Schmolling Trio
Nostalgia Soul Ship | Organic Music | ORGM 9731
Martin Auer Quintet
Martin Auer Quintett | Jazz 4 Ever Records:Jazz Network | J4E 4762
Trio Larose
Debut | Jazz 'n' Arts Records | JNA 0802
Trio Larose With Toni Lakatos
Debut | Jazz 'n' Arts Records | JNA 0802
Victor Alcántara Trio
Stabat Mater Inspirations | Organic Music | ORGM 9716

Juul,Lars | (drperc)
Jens Skou Olsen Group
September Veje | dacapo | DCCD 9451
Takuan
Push | dacapo | DCCD 9457

Juvelier,Aaron | (cello)
Gary McFarland And His Orchestra
The Complete Bill Evans On Verve | Verve | 527953-2

Kaart,Dick | (bar-htb)
Dutch Swing College Band
Swinging Studio Sessons | Philips | 824256-2 PMS
Dutch Swing College Band Live In 1960 | Philips | 838765-2
Rita Reys With The Dutch Swing College Band
The Very Best Of Dixieland Jazz | Verve | 535529-2

Kaart,Ray | (cotp)
Dutch Swing College Band
Swinging Studio Sessons | Philips | 824256-2 PMS
Rita Reys With The Dutch Swing College Band
The Very Best Of Dixieland Jazz | Verve | 535529-2

Kabok,Louis | (b)
Gabor Szabo Quintet
The Roots Of Acid Jazz | Impulse(MCA) | IMP 12042
The Sorcerer | Impulse(MCA) | IMP 12112

Kaczynski,Ray | (drperc)
Rajesh Metha
Reconfigurations | Between The Lines | btl 010(Efa 10180-2)
Schlothauer's Maniacs
Maniakisses | Timescrapper | TSCR 9811

Kaenzig,Heiri | (b,el-bsynth)
Axis
Axis | Jazz 4 Ever Records:Jazz Network | J4E 4735

Kagerer,Helmut | (g)
Helmut Kagerer 4 & Roman Schwaller
Jazz Guitar Highlights 1 | Jardis Records | JRCD 20141
Gamblin' | Jardis Records | JRCD 9714
Helmut Kagerer/Helmut Nieberle
Wes Trane | Edition Collage | EC 453-2
Helmut Kagerer-Peter Bernstein Quartet
Jazz Guitar Highlights 1 | Jardis Records | JRCD 20141
April In New York | Jardis Records | JRCD 9818
Helmut Nieberle-Helmut Kagerer
Skyliner | ART BY HEART | ABH 2001 2
Flashes | Jardis Records | JRCD 20031
Helmut Nieberle-Helmut Kagerer Quartet
Flashes | Jardis Records | JRCD 20031
Jermaine Landsberger Trio With Helmut Kagerer & Gina
Samba In June | Edition Collage | EC 524-2
Joseph Warner Quartet
Mood Pieces | Jardis Records | JRCD 9921
Matthias Bätzel Trio
Green Dumplings | JHM Records | JHM 3618
Monk's Mood | JHM Records | JHM 3628
Red Holloway With The Matthias Bätzel Trio
A Night Of Blues & Ballads | JHM Records | JHM 3614
Roots
Stablemates | IN+OUT Records | 7021-2

Kahlenborn,Peter | (dr)
Matthias Petzold Esperanto-Music
Lifelines | Indigo-Records | 1001 CD

Kahn,Eddie | (b)
Ronnie Mathews Quintet
Ronnie Mathews-Roland Alexander-Freddie Hubbard | Prestige | PRCD 24271-2
Ronnie Mathews Trio
Ronnie Mathews-Roland Alexander-Freddie Hubbard | Prestige | PRCD 24271-2
Shirley Scott Quartet
Queen Of The Organ-Shirley Scott Memorial Album | Prestige | PRCD 11027-2

Kahn,Leo | (v)
Bill Evans Quartet With Orchestra
The Complete Bill Evans On Verve | Verve | 527953-2
From Left To Right | Verve | 557451-2
Bill Evans With Orchestra
The Complete Bill Evans On Verve | Verve | 527953-2
From Left To Right | Verve | 557451-2
Earl Klugh Group With Strings
Late Night Guitar | Blue Note | 498573-2

Kahn,Lewis | (tb)
Machito And His Orchestra
Afro-Cuban Jazz Moods | Original Jazz Classics | OJC20 447-2

Kahn,Roger Wolfe | (ld)
Roger Wolfe Kahn And His Orchestra
Planet Jazz:Jack Teagarden | Planet Jazz | 2161236-2

Kahn,Tiny | (arr,drvoc)
Jubilee All Stars
Jazz Gallery:Lester Young Vol.2(1946-59) | RCA | 2119541-2
Lester Young And His Band
Lester Young:The Complete Aladdin Sessions | Blue Note | 832787-2
Stan Getz Quintet
Stan Getz-The Complete Roost Sessions | EMI Records | 859622-2

Kaihatu,Victor | (b)
Toots Thielemans Quintet
The Silver Collection: Toots Thielemans | Polydor | 825086-2 PMS

Kail,Jerome | (tp)
Jack McDuff Quartet With Orchestra
Prelude:Jack McDuff Big Band | Prestige | PRCD 24283-2
King Curtis Band
King Curtis-Blow Man Blow | Bear Family Records | BCD 15670 CI

Kail,Jerry | (tp)
Herbie Mann's Cuban Band
Verve Jazz Masters 56:Herbie Mann | Verve | 529901-2
Quincy Jones And His Orchestra
The Quintessence | Impulse(MCA) | 951222-2

Kainar,Robert | (drperc)
Jenny Evans And Her Quintet
Nuages | Enja | ENJ-9467 2
Nuages | ESM Records | ESM 9308
Lisa Wahlandt & Mulo Francel And Their Fabulous Bossa Band
Bossa Nova Affair | Edition Collage | EC 534-2
Mind Games
Mind Games Plays The Music Of Stan Getz & Astrud Gilberto | Edition Collage | EC 515-2

Kaiser,Christoph Victor | (bel-b)
Jazz Pistols
Special Treatment | Lipstick Records | LIP 8971-2

Kaiser,Wollie | (alto-fl,b-cl,ss,ts,b-fl,cl)
Blue Room Ensemble
Solitude | Foolish Music | FM 211993
Ekkehard Jost Ensemble
Weimarer Balladen | Fish Music | FM 004 CD
Ekkehard Jost Nonet
Out Of Jost's Songbook | Fish Music | FM 006 CD
Ekkehard Jost Quartet
Some Other Tapes | Fish Music | FM 009/10 CD
Ekkehard Jost Quintet
Some Other Tapes | Fish Music | FM 009/10 CD
Gabriele Hasler Group
Gabriele Hasler's Rosensrücke | Foolish Music | FM 211096
Gabriele Hasler's Personal Notebook | Foolish Music | FM 211490
Georg Ruby Group
Stange Loops | Jazz Haus Musik | JHM 0057 CD
Giessen-Köln-Nonett
Some Other Tapes | Fish Music | FM 009/10 CD
Klaus König Orchestra
Hommage A Douglas Adams | Enja | ENJ-6078 2
Time Fragments:Seven Studies In Time And Motion | Enja | ENJ-8076 2
Reviews | Enja | ENJ-9061 2
Klaus König Orchestra & Guests
The Song Of Songs:Oratorio For Two Solo Voices,Choir And Orchestra | Enja | ENJ-7057 2
Kölner Saxophon Mafia
Saxfiguren | Jazz Haus Musik | JHM 0036 CD
Mafia Years 1982-86 | Jazz Haus Musik | JHM 0058 CD
Go Commercial... | Jazz Haus Musik | JHM 0065 CD
Place For Lovers | Jazz Haus Musik | JHM 0082 CD
Licence To Thrill | Jazz Haus Musik | JHM 0100 CD
Space Player | Jazz Haus Musik | JHM 0132 CD
Kölner Saxophon Mafia With Arno Steffen
Kölner Saxophon Mafia Proudly Presents | Jazz Haus Musik | JHM 0046 CD
Kölner Saxophon Mafia With Bad Little Dynamos
Kölner Saxophon Mafia Proudly Presents | Jazz Haus Musik | JHM 0046 CD
Kölner Saxophon Mafia With Blasorchester Dicke Luft
Kölner Saxophon Mafia Proudly Presents | Jazz Haus Musik | JHM 0046 CD
Kölner Saxophon Mafia With Clarence Barlow
Kölner Saxophon Mafia Proudly Presents | Jazz Haus Musik | JHM 0046 CD
Kölner Saxophon Mafia With Dieter Wellershoff
Kölner Saxophon Mafia Proudly Presents | Jazz Haus Musik | JHM 0046 CD
Kölner Saxophon Mafia With Fleisch
Kölner Saxophon Mafia Proudly Presents | Jazz Haus Musik | JHM 0046 CD
Kölner Saxophon Mafia With Guests
Kölner Saxophon Mafia: 20 Jahre Saxuelle Befreiung | Jazz Haus Musik | JHM 0115 CD
Kölner Saxophon Mafia With Hans Süper
Kölner Saxophon Mafia Proudly Presents | Jazz Haus Musik | JHM 0046 CD
Kölner Saxophon Mafia With Ina Stachelhaus And Erik Schneider
Kölner Saxophon Mafia Proudly Presents | Jazz Haus Musik | JHM 0046 CD
Kölner Saxophon Mafia With Ingo Kümmel And Frank Köllges
Kölner Saxophon Mafia Proudly Presents | Jazz Haus Musik | JHM 0046 CD
Kölner Saxophon Mafia With Irene Lorenz
Kölner Saxophon Mafia Proudly Presents | Jazz Haus Musik | JHM 0046 CD
Kölner Saxophon Mafia With Jacki Liebezeit
Kölner Saxophon Mafia Proudly Presents | Jazz Haus Musik | JHM 0046 CD
Kölner Saxophon Mafia With Klaus Der Geiger
Kölner Saxophon Mafia Proudly Presents | Jazz Haus Musik | JHM 0046 CD
Kölner Saxophon Mafia With Kristina Würminghausen
Kölner Saxophon Mafia Proudly Presents | Jazz Haus Musik | JHM 0046 CD
Kölner Saxophon Mafia With Lydie Auvray
Kölner Saxophon Mafia Proudly Presents | Jazz Haus Musik | JHM 0046 CD
Kölner Saxophon Mafia With Nedim Hazar And Orhan Temur
Kölner Saxophon Mafia Proudly Presents | Jazz Haus Musik | JHM 0046 CD
Kölner Saxophon Mafia With Ramesh Shotham
Kölner Saxophon Mafia Proudly Presents | Jazz Haus Musik | JHM 0046 CD
Kölner Saxophon Mafia With Rick E. Loef
Kölner Saxophon Mafia Proudly Presents | Jazz Haus Musik | JHM 0046 CD
Kölner Saxophon Mafia With The Auryn Quartet
Kölner Saxophon Mafia Proudly Presents | Jazz Haus Musik | JHM 0046 CD
Kölner Saxophon Mafia With Triviatas(1.Schwuler Männerchor Köln)
Kölner Saxophon Mafia Proudly Presents | Jazz Haus Musik | JHM 0046 CD
Kölner Saxophon Mafia With V.Nick Nikitakis
Kölner Saxophon Mafia Proudly Presents | Jazz Haus Musik | JHM 0046 CD
Kölner Saxophon Mafia With Willie Gräff
Kölner Saxophon Mafia Proudly Presents | Jazz Haus Musik | JHM 0046 CD
Peter Herborn's Acute Insights
Peter Herborn's Acute Insights | JMT Edition | 919017-2
Transalpin Express Orchestra
Some Other Tapes | Fish Music | FM 009/10 CD
Ulla Oster-Wollie Kaiser
We Can Do It On Stage Any Time! | Jazz Haus Musik | JHM 0088 CD
Wollie Kaiser Timeghost
Tust Du Fühlen Gut | Jazz Haus Musik | JHM 0060 CD
Post Art Core | Jazz Haus Musik | JHM 0077 CD
New Traces For Old Aces | Jazz Haus Musik | JHM 0102 CD

Kait,Jerome | (tp)
Bill Evans Quartet With Orchestra
The Complete Bill Evans On Verve | Verve | 527953-2
From Left To Right | Verve | 557451-2

Kaita,Salif | (voc)
Cornelius Claudio Kreusch Group
Scoop | ACT | 9255-2

KajdanJean Michael | (g)
Dee Dee Bridgewater With Band
Victim Of Love | Verve | 841199-2

Kakerbeck,Franz | (asss)
Helmut Zacharias & His Sax-Team
Ich Habe Rhythmus | Bear Family Records | BCD 15642 AH
Helmut Zacharias mit seinem Orchester
Ich Habe Rhythmus | Bear Family Records | BCD 15642 AH

Kakhidze,Jansug | (condvoc)
Jan Garbarek Group
Rites | ECM | 1685/86(559006-2)

Kalachev,Sergey | (b)
Farlanders
The Farlander | JA & RO | JARO 4222-2

Kale,Karsh | (drtabla)
Dave Douglas Group
Dave Douglas Freak In | Bluebird | 2664008-2

Kalehoff,Edd | (synth)
Quincy Jones And His Orchestra
Verve Jazz Masters Vol.59:Toots Thielemans | Verve | 535271-2

Kalhor,Kayhan | (kamancheh)
Kayhan Kalhor Trio
The Rain | ECM | 1840(066627-2)

Kalifactors |
Kalifactors
An Introduction To Kalifactors | Fresh Sound Records | FSNT 143 CD

Kalister,Izaline | (voc)
Pili-Pili
Nomans Land | JA & RO | JARO 4209-2

Kaltoft,Erik | (p)
Chinese Compass
Chinese Compass | dacapo | DCCD 9443

Kamafra |
Kamafra
Kamafra Live | Edition Musikat | EDM 072

Kamaguchi,Masa | (b)
Matt Renzi-Jimmy Weinstein-Masa Kamaguchi Trio
Lines And Ballads | Fresh Sound Records | FSNT 065 CD
Roberta Piket Trio
Speak,Memory | Fresh Sound Records | FSNT 088 CD

Kaminski,Klaus | (tp)
Bigband Der Musikschule Der Stadt Brühl Mit Gastsolisten
Pangäa | Indigo-Records | 1004 CD

Kaminsky,Anatol | (v)
Ella Fitzgerald With The Frank DeVol Orchestra
Get Happy! | Verve | 523321-2
Pete Rugolo And His Orchestra
Thriller/Richard Diamon(Original Jazz Scores From 2 Classics TV Series) | Fresh Sound Records | FSCD 2015

Kaminsky,Max | (co,tpvoc)
Artie Shaw And His Orchestra
Planet JazzArtie Shaw | Planet Jazz | 2152057-2
Planet Jazz:Male Jazz Vocalists | Planet Jazz | 2169657-2
Bud Freeman And His Summa Cum Laude Orchestra
Planet Jazz:Bud Freeman | Planet Jazz | 2161240-2
Planet Jazz:Jazz Saxophone | Planet Jazz | 2169653-2
Eddie Condon And His Orchestra
Jazz:The Essential Collection Vol.3 | IN+OUT Records | 78013-2
Jack Teagarden's Big Eight
Planet Jazz:Jack Teagarden | Planet Jazz | 2161236-2
Planet Jazz | Planet Jazz | 2169652-2
Max Kaminsky And His Dixieland Bashers
Planet Jazz | Planet Jazz | 2169652-2
Mezz Mezzrow And His Orchestra
Planet Jazz:Bud Freeman | Planet Jazz | 2161240-2
Sidney Bechet's Blue Note Jazzmen
Sidney Bechet:Summertime | Dreyfus Jazz Line | FDM 36712-2
The Chicago All Stars
Planet Jazz:Bud Freeman | Planet Jazz | 2161240-2
Tommy Dorsey And His Clambake Seven
Planet Jazz:Bud Freeman | Planet Jazz | 2161240-2
Tommy Dorsey And His Orchestra
Planet Jazz:Tommy Dorsey | Planet Jazz | 2159972-2

Kämmerling,Roland | (tpfl-h)
Jazz Orchester Rheinland-Pfalz
Like Life | Jazz Haus Musik | LJBB 9405
Last Season | Jazz Haus Musik | LJBB 9706
Marcus Sukiennik Big Band
A Night In Tunisia Suite(7 Variationen über Dizzy Gillespie's 'A Night In Tunisia') | Jazz Haus Musik | ohne Nummer

Kämpgen,Nicole | (voice)
Ed Schuller & The Eleventh Hour Band
Snake Dancing | Tutu Records | 888188-2*

Kämpgen[Schuller],Nicole | (asvoc)
Gunther Schuller With The WDR Radio Orchestra & Rememberance Band
Witchi Tia To, The Music Of Jim Pepper | Tutu Records | 888204-2*

Kamuca,Richie | (as,bs,cl,ts,engl-h,b-cl,fl,sax,oboe)
Art Pepper Plus Eleven
Art Pepper + Eleven | Contemporary | CSA 7568-6
Modern Jazz Classics | Original Jazz Classics | OJC20 341-2
Bill Holman Octet
The Jazz Giants Play Sammy Cahn:It's Magic | Prestige | PCD 24226-2
Bill Perkins-Richie Kamuca Quintet
Midnight Blue(The [Be]witching Hour) | Blue Note | 854365-2
Chet Baker Sextet
The Best Of Chet Baker Plays | Pacific Jazz | 797161-2
Gus Mancuso Quintet
Gus Mancuso & Special Friends | Fantasy | FCD 24762-2
Kenny Burrell With The Gil Evans Orchestra
Guitar Forms | Verve | 521403-2
Verve Jazz Masters 23:Gil Evans | Verve | 521860-2
Verve Jazz Masters 45:Kenny Burrell | Verve | 527652-2
Verve Jazz Masters Vol.60:The Collection | Verve | 529866-2
Modern Jazz Quartet And Orchestra
MJQ 40 | Atlantic | 7567-82330-2
Shelly Manne And His Men
At The Black Hawk Vol.1 | Original Jazz Classics | OJCCD 656-2(S 7577)
At The Black Hawk Vol.2 | Original Jazz Classics | OJCCD 657-2(S 7578)
At The Black Hawk Vol.3 | Original Jazz Classics | OJCCD 658-2(S 7579)
At The Black Hawk Vol.4 | Original Jazz Classics | OJCCD 659-2(S 7580)
At The Black Hawk Vol.5 | Original Jazz Classics | OJCCD 660-2
Live! At The Manne Hole Vol.1 | Original Jazz Classics | OJCCD 714-2(S 7593)
Live! At The Manne Hole Vol.2 | Original Jazz Classics | OJCCD 715-2(S 7594)
Jazz At The Philharmonic-Yesterdays | Pablo | PACD 5318-2
Stan Kenton And His Orchestra
Stan Kenton Portraits On Standards | Capitol | 531571-2
Terry Gibbs Big Band
Terry Gibbs Dream Band Vol.4:Main Stem | Contemporary | CCD 7656-2
Terry Gibbs Dream Band
Terry Gibbs Dream Band Vol.3:Flying Home | Contemporary | CCD 7654-2
Terry Gibbs Dream Band Vol.5:The Big Cat | Contemporary | CCD 7657-2
Thad Jones-Mel Lewis Orchestra
The Groove Merchant/The Second Race | Laserlight | 24656
Zoot Sims And His Orchestra
The Jazz Giants Play Duke Ellington:Caravan | Prestige | PCD 24227-2

Kanan,Michael 'Mike' | (p)
(Little)Jimmy Scott And His Band
Mood Indigo | Milestone | MCD 9305-2
Jill Seifers And Her Quartet
The Waiting | Fresh Sound Records | FSNT 072 CD
Jimmy Scott With Band
Over The Rainbow | Milestone | MCD 9314-2
Moon Glow | Milestone | MCD 9332-2
Michael Kanan Trio
Convergence | Fresh Sound Records | FSNT 055 CD
The Gentleman Is A Dope | Fresh Sound Records | FSNT 147 CD
Nat Su Quartet
The J.Way | Fresh Sound Records | FSNT 038 CD

Kandlberger,Helmut | (b,b-gg)
Klaus Doldinger Quartet
Doldinger's Best | ACT | 9224-2
Klaus Doldinger Septet
Doldinger's Best | ACT | 9224-2

Kandri,Driss | (percdarabuka)
Marty Hall Band
Who's Been Talkin'?s | Blues Beacon | BLU-1033 2

Kane,Artie | (keyboards,orgp)
Peggy Lee With The Quincy Jones Orchestra
Blues Cross Country | Capitol | 520088-2

Kane,Danny | (harm)
Aldo Romano Group
AlmaLatina | Owl Records | 018364-2

Kane,Shyram | (tablas)

Rainbow
Two Originals:Karuna Supreme/Rainbow | MPS | 519195-2
Kane,Sol | (asbs)
Peggy Lee With The Benny Goodman Orchestra
Peggy Lee & Benny Goodman:The Complete Recordings 1941-1947 | CBS | C2K 65686
Kane,Wally | (bs)
Modern Jazz Quartet And Orchestra
MJQ 40 | Atlantic | 7567-82330-2
Kane,Walter | (bassoon,b-cl,piccolo,cl,bs,fl,reeds)
Earl Klugh Group With Strings
Late Night Guitar | Blue Note | 498573-2
Freddie Hubbard With Orchestra
This Is Jazz:Freddie Hubbard | CBS | CK 65041
Quincy Jones And His Orchestra
Verve Jazz Masters Vol.59:Toots Thielemans | Verve | 535271-2
Ron Carter Group
Peg Leg | Original Jazz Classics | OJCCD 621-2
Stan Getz With The Eddie Sauter Orchestra
Stan Getz Plays The Music Of Mickey One | Verve | 531232-2
Wes Montgomery With The Don Sebesky Orchestra
Verve Jazz Masters 14:Wes Montgomery | Verve | 519826-2
Talkin' Jazz:Roots Of Acid Jazz | Verve | 529580-2
California Dreaming | Verve | 827842-2
Kang,Eywind | (v)
Wayne Horvitz Group
4+1 Ensemble | Intuition Records | INT 3224-2
Kanga,Skaila | (harp)
Dee Dee Bridgewater With Orchestra
Dear Ella | Verve | 539102-2
Kannenberg,Ute | (voc)
Ute Kannenberg Quartet
Kannenberg On Purpose | Jazz Haus Musik | JHM 0109 CD
Ute Kannenberg Quartet With Guests
Kannenberg On Purpose | Jazz Haus Musik | JHM 0109 CD
Kannisto,Jouni | (flts)
Edward Vesala Ensemble
Ode Of The Death Of Jazz | ECM | 1413(843196-2)
Edward Vesala Nordic Gallery
Sound & Fury | ECM | 1541
Edward Vesala Sound And Fury
Invisible Strom | ECM | 1461
Kansas City Five,The |
Helen Humes With The Kansas City Five
From Spiritual To Swing | Vanguard | VCD 169/71
Kansas City Five
Lester Young:Blue Lester | Dreyfus Jazz Line | FDM 36729-2
From Spiritual To Swing | Vanguard | VCD 169/71
Kansas City Seven,The |
Kansas City Seven
Jazz:The Essential Collection Vol.3 | IN+OUT Records | 78013-2
The J.J.Johnson Memorial Album | Prestige | PRCD 11025-2
Kansas City Six,The |
Kansas City 6
Count Basie:Kansas City 6 | Original Jazz Classics | OJC20 449-2(2310871)
Kansas City Six
Jazz:The Essential Collection Vol.3 | IN+OUT Records | 78013-2
Charlie Christian:Swing To Bop | Dreyfus Jazz Line | FDM 36715-2
Lester Young:Blue Lester | Dreyfus Jazz Line | FDM 36729-2
From Spiritual To Swing | Vanguard | VCD 169/71
Kant,Luis, | (fr-h)
Dizzy Gillespie And His Orchestra
Talking Verve:Dizzy Gillespie | Verve | 533846-2
Kanté,Manfila | (g)
Hank Jones Meets Cheik-Tidiana Seck
Sarala | Verve | 528783-2
Kantumanou,Elizabeth | (voc)
James Hurt Group
Dark Grooves-Mystcal Rhythms | Blue Note | 495104-2
Kanze,Dominic | (g)
Pharoah Sanders Orchestra
Message From Home | Verve | 529578-2
Kaper,Bob | (as,cl,ts,tambourine,vocss)
Dutch Swing College Band
Swinging Studio Sessons | Philips | 824256-2 PMS
Digital Anniversary | Philips | 824585-2 PMS
Käpernick,Guido | (bkeyboards)
Jazz Fresh
Jazz Fresh | GGG-Verlag:GGG Verlag und Mailorder | CD 01.03
Kaplan,Alan | (tb)
Buddy Rich Big Band
Backwoods Siseman/Pieces Of Dream | Laserlight | 24655
Kappe,Christian | (tpfl-h)
Ulli Jünemann-Morton Ginnerup European Jazz Project
The Exhibition | Edition Collage | EC 518-2
Käppeli,Marco | (drperc)
Hans Koch/Martin Schütz/Marco Käppeli
Accélération | ECM | 1357
Peter Schärli Quintet With Glenn Ferris
Willisau And More Live | Creative Works Records | CW CD 1020-2
Drei Seelen/Three Souls | Creative Works Records | MIWI 1014-2
Kappler,Andreas | (percvoc)
Francesca Simone Trio
Guardia Li | Minor Music | 801093
Kaproff,Armand | (cello,vviola)
Ben Webster With Strings
The Warm Moods-With Strings | Rhino | 8122-73721-2
Ella Fitzgerald With The Billy May Orchestra
The Best Of The Song Books:The Ballads | Verve | 521867-2
Ella Fitzgerald Sings The Harold Arlen Song Book | Verve | 589108-2
Ella Fitzgerald With The Frank DeVol Orchestra
Get Happy! | Verve | 523321-2
Ella Fitzgerald With The Nelson Riddle Orchestra
The Best Of The Song Books:The Ballads | Verve | 521867-2
Oh Lady Be Good:The Best Of The Gershwin Songbook | Verve | 529581-2
Love Songs:The Best Of The Song Books | Verve | 531762-2
Pete Rugolo And His Orchestra
Thriller/Richard Diamon(Original Jazz Scores From 2 Classics TV Series) | Fresh Sound Records | FSCD 2015
Karacand,Naim | (v)
Ahmed Abdul-Malik Orchestra
Planet Jazz:Lee Morgan | Planet Jazz | 2161238-2
Ahmed Abdul-Malik's Middle-Eastern Music
Jazz Sahara | Original Jazz Classics | OJCCD 1820-2(R 12-287)
Karam,Anne | (cello)
Milt Jackson And His Orchestra
Reverence And Compassion | Reprise | 9362-45204-2
Karas,Sperie | (dr)
Stan Getz With Orchestra
Stan Getz Highlights | Verve | 847430-2
Karella,Clarance | (tuba)
Billy May And His Orchestra
Billy May's Big Fat Brass/Bill's Bag | Capitol | 535206-2
Karg,Björn | (voc)
Jazzensemble Des Hessischen Rundfunks
Jazz Messe-Messe Für Unsere Zeit | hr music.de | hrmj 003-01 CD
Karle,Art | (ts)
Benny Goodman And His Orchestra
Jazz:The Essential Collection Vol.3 | IN+OUT Records | 78013-2
Karlic,Chris | (bs)
New Jazz Composers Octet
Walkin' the Line | Fresh Sound Records | FSNT 151 CD
Karlsson,Daniel | (p)
Viktoria Tolstoy Group & Strings
Shining On You | ACT | 9701-2
Karlsson,Peder | (voc)
The Real Group
One For All | ACT | 9003-2
The Real Group With Toots Thielemans
One For All | ACT | 9003-2
Karmazyn,Dennis | (cello)
Chick Corea With String Quartet
Verve Jazz Masters 3:Chick Corea | Verve | 519820-2
Ella Fitzgerald With Orchestra
The Best Is Yet To Come | Original Jazz Classics | OJCCD 889-2(2312138)
Karn,Ole | (dr)
Adrian Bentzon's Jazzband
The Golden Years Of Revival Jazz,Sampler | Storyville | 109 1001
Albert Nicholas With Adrian Bentzon's Jazzband
The Golden Years Of Revival Jazz,Sampler | Storyville | 109 1001
Albert Nicholas & The Dutch Swing College Band | Storyville | STCD 5522
Henrik Johansen's Jazzband
The Golden Years Of Revival Jazz.Vol.14 | Storyville | STCD 5519
Karnataka College of Percussion,The |
Charlie Mariano & The Karnataka College Of Percussion
Jyothi | ECM | 1256
Live | VeraBra Records | CDVBR 2034-2
Karparov,Vladimir | (flsax)
For Free Hands
Eastern Moods | Laika Records | 35101502
Karpenia,Stan | (v)
Charlie Parker With Strings
Charlie Parker With Strings:The Master Takes | Verve | 523984-2
Bird: The Complete Charlie Parker On Verve | Verve | 837141-2
Karsh,Bob | (p)
Elliot Lawrence And His Orchestra
Mullenium | CBS | CK 65678
Karsh,Ken | (g)
Bobby McFerrin Group
Bobby McFerrin | Elektra | 7559-60023-2
Karskov,Uffe | (as,ts,fl,alto-fl,clreeds)
Miles Davis With The Danish Radio Big Band
Aura | CBS | CK 63962
Stan Getz With Ib Glindemann And His Orchestra
Stan Getz In Europe | Laserlight | 24657
Stan Getz With The Danish Radio Big Band
Stan Getz In Europe | Laserlight | 24657
Stan Kenton With The Danish Radio Big Band
Stan Kenton With The Danish Radio Big Band | Storyville | STCD 8340
The Danish Radio Big Band
Aura | CBS | CK 63962
Kase,Christopher | (tpfl-h)
Mingus Big Band 93
Nostalgia In Times Square | Dreyfus Jazz Line | FDM 36559-2
Kaspar,Olivier | (viola)
Charlie Haden Quartet West With Strings
Now Is The Hour | Verve | 527827-2
Kasper,Michael M. | (cello)
Ensemble Modern
Ensemble Modern-Fred Frith:Traffic Continues | Winter&Winter | 910044-2
Los Jovenes Flamencos With The WDR Big Band And Guests
Jazzpana | ACT | 9212-2
Kassis,Jim | (vib,drperc)
Rindo Eckert Group
Story In,Story Out | Intuition Records | INT 3507-2
Kat,Wim | (tp)
Toots Thielemans And His Orchestra
Verve Jazz Masters Vol.59:Toots Thielemans | Verve | 535271-2
Katarzynski,Raymond | (tb)
Raymond Fol Big Band
Jazz In Paris:Raymond Fol-Les 4 Saisons | EmArCy | 548791-2
Katayama,Suzie | (cellov)
Milt Jackson And His Orchestra
Reverence And Compassion | Reprise | 9362-45204-2
Katché,Manu | (drwavedrum)
Jan Garbarek Group
I Took Up The Runes | ECM | 1419(843850-2)
Twelve Moons | ECM | 1500(519500-2)
Visible World | ECM | 1585(529086-2)
Jan Garbarek With Ustad Fateh Ali Khan & Musicians From Pakistan
Ragas And Sagas | ECM | 1442(511263-2)
Käthner,Ulrich | (tb)
Landes Jugend Jazz Orchester Hessen
Touch Of Lips | hr music.de | hrmj 004-01 CD
Kätkä,Ippe | (dr,percgongs)
Krakatau
Matinale | ECM | 1529
Kato,Shinichi | (b)
Shinichi Kato-Masahiko Sato
Duet | Nagel-Heyer | CD 2017
Kato,William G. | (tb)
Jelly Roll Morton And His Orchestra
Planet Jazz:Jelly Roll Morton | Planet Jazz | 2152060-2
Jazz:The Essential Collection Vol.1 | IN+OUT Records | 78011-2
Katyama,Suzy | (cello)
Charlie Haden Quartet West With Strings
The Art Of The Song | Verve | 547403-2
Katz,Alexander | (tbvoc)
Benny Waters & Jan Jankeje
Let's Talk About Jazz | G&J Records | GJ 2009 Maxi-CD
Benny Waters Sextet
A' Portrait Of Jan Jankeje | Jazzpoint | JP 1054 CD
Oscar Klein-Lino Patruno European Jazz Stars
Live at The San Marino Jazz Festival | Jazzpoint | JP 1052 CD
Stuttgarter Dixieland All Stars
It's The Talk Of The Town | Jazzpoint | JP 1069 CD
Katz,Dick | (el-p,parr)
Benny Carter And His Orchestra
Further Definitions/Additions To Further Definotions | Impulse(MCA) | 951229-2
Buck Clayton Swing Band
Swing's The Village | Nagel-Heyer | CD 5004
Blues Of Summer | Nagel-Heyer | NH 1011
Helen Merrill With The Dick Katz Group
The Feeling Is Mutual | EmArCy | 558849-2
A Shade Of Difference | EmArCy | 558851-2
Helen Merrill With The Pepper Adams Quintet
Chasin' The Bird(Gershwin) | EmArCy | 558850-2
Helen Merrill-Dick Katz Duo
The Feeling Is Mutual | EmArCy | 558849-2
J.J.Johnson-Kai Winding Quintet (Jay&Kai)
The J.J.Johnson Memorial Album | Prestige | PRCD 11025-2
James Moody Orchestra
The Blues And Other Colors | Original Jazz Classics | OJCCD 954-2(M 9023)
Lee Konitz Orchestra
The Art Of Saxophone | Laserlight | 24652
Roy Eldridge And The Jimmy Ryan All Stars
Jazz Dance | Original Jazz Classics | OJCCD 1002-2(1210890)
Little Jazz And The Jimmy Ryan All-Stars | Original Jazz Classics | OJCCD 1058-2(DRE 1001)
Sonny Rollins Orchestra
Sonny Rollins And The Big Brass | Verve | 557545-2
Katz,Dill | (b-gfretless-b-g)
Barbara Thompson's Paraphernalia
Mother Earth | VeraBra Records | CDVBR 2005-2
Barbara Thompson's Special Edition | VeraBra Records | CDVBR 2017-2
Katz,Fred | (arr,condcello)
Chico Hamilton Quintet With Strings
With Strings Attached/The Three Faces Of Chico | Warner | 9362-47874-2
Katzenbeier,Hubert | (tb)
Berlin Contemporary Jazz Orchestra
Berlin Contemporary Jazz Orchestra | ECM | 1409
Katzman,Harry | (v)
Billie Holiday With The Ray Ellis Orchestra
Lady In Satin | CBS | CK 65144
Charlie Parker With Strings
Charlie Parker With Strings:The Master Takes | Verve | 523984-2
Charlie Parker With The Neal Hefti Orchestra
Charlie Parker:The Best Of The Verve Years | Verve | 527815-2
Bird: The Complete Charlie Parker On Verve | Verve | 837141-2
Freddie Hubbard Orchestra
The Body And The Soul | Impulse(MCA) | 951183-2
Phil Woods Quartet With Orchestra & Strings
Round Trip | Verve | 559804-2
Katzman,Lee | (perctp)
Anita O'Day With The Bill Holman Orchestra
Verve Jazz Masters 49:Anita O'Day | Verve | 527653-2
June Christy With The Shorty Rogers Orchestra
June Christy Big Band Special | Capitol | 498319-2
Les McCann Orchestra
Talkin' Verve:Les McCann | Verve | 557351-2
Sonny Stitt Orchestra
Verve Jazz Masters 50:Sonny Sitt | Verve | 527651-2
Stan Kenton Orchestra
Stompin' At Newport | Pablo | PACD 5312-2
Terry Gibbs Dream Band
Terry Gibbs Dream Band Vol.3:Flying Home | Contemporary | CCD 7654-2
Terry Gibbs Dream Band Vol.6:One More Time | Contemporary | CCD 7658-2
Kauffeld,Greetje | (voc)
Paul Kuhn Trio With Greetje Kauffeld
Play It Again Paul | IN+OUT Records | 77040-2
Paul Kuhn Trio With Greetje Kauffeld And Jean 'Toots' Thielemans
Play It Again Paul | IN+OUT Records | 77040-2
Kauffman,Harold | (p)
Lester Young Quartet
Jazz Gallery:Lester Young Vol.2(1946-59) | RCA | 2119541-2
Kaufman,Bernard | (as,bs,fl,b-clreeds)
Sarah Vaughan With The Hugo Winterhalter Orchestra
Sarah Vaughan:Lover Man | Dreyfus Jazz Line | FDM 36739-2
Sarah Vaughan With The Joe Lippman Orchestra
Sarah Vaughan:Lover Man | Dreyfus Jazz Line | FDM 36739-2
Kaufman,Gilbert | (synth)
Shankar/Caroline
The Epidemics | ECM | 1308
Kaufmann,Achim | (p)
Achim Kaufmann Trio
Weave | Jazz 4 Ever Records:Jazz Network | J4E 4737
Peter Bolte Quartet
Evocation | Jazz Haus Musik | JHM 0079 CD
Peter Bolte Trio
Trio | Jazz Haus Musik | JHM 0095 CD
Peter Weiss Quartet
Personal Choice | Nabel Records:Jazz Network | CD 4669
Kaufmann,Georg | (ts)
Bill Ramsey With Orchestra
Gettin' Back To Swing | Bear Family Records | BCD 15813 AH
Kaulard,Gerd | (b)
Die Elefanten
Wasserwüste | Nabel Records:Jazz Network | CD 4634
Kaumeheiwa,Keala | (b)
John Stein Quartet
Conversation Pieces | Jardis Records | JRCD 20140
John Stein Quintet
Portraits And Landscapes | Jardis Records | JRCD 20029
Jazz Guitar Highlights 1 | Jardis Records | JRCD 20141
Kaupp,Gil | (fl-htp)
Conexion Latina
Mambo Nights | Enja | ENJ-9402 2
Dusko Goykovich Big Band
Balkan Connection | Enja | ENJ-9047 2
Maximilian Geller Group
Maximilian Geller Goes Bossa | Edition Collage | EC 496-2
Kavafian,Ida | (v)
Chick Corea With String Quartet,Flute And French Horn
Septet | ECM | 1297
Steve Swallow Group
Carla | Watt | XtraWatt/2
Kavina,Lydia | (theremin)
Kölner Saxophon Mafia With Guests
Kölner Saxophon Mafia: 20 Jahre Saxuelle Befreiung | Jazz Haus Musik | JHM 0115 CD
Kawahara,Karl | (v)
Steve Kuhn With Strings
Promises Kept | ECM | 1815(0675222)
Kawamura,Samon | (turntables)
Till Brönner Group
Chattin' With Chet | Verve | 157534-2
Kawasaki,Ryo | (el-g,g,koto-gpedals)
Gil Evans Orchestra
There Comes A Time | RCA | 2131392-2
PLay The Music Of Jimi Hendrix | RCA | 2663872-2
Kay,Connie | (drperc)
Benny Goodman And His Orchestra
40th Anniversary Concert-Live At Carnegie Hall | London | 820349-2
Verve Jazz Masters 33:Benny Goodman | Verve | 844410-2
Benny Goodman Quartet
Verve Jazz Masters 33:Benny Goodman | Verve | 844410-2
Benny Goodman Quintet
Verve Jazz Masters 33:Benny Goodman | Verve | 844410-2
Benny Goodman Septet
Verve Jazz Masters 33:Benny Goodman | Verve | 844410-2
Benny Goodman Sextet
Verve Jazz Masters 33:Benny Goodman | Verve | 844410-2
Bobby Timmons Trio
Born To Be Blue! | Original Jazz Classics | OJC20 873-2(R 9468)
Cannonball Adderley Quartet
Cannonball Adderley Birthday Celebration | Fantasy | FANCD 6087-2
Know What I Mean? | Original Jazz Classics | OJC 105(R 12-433)
Chet Baker Quartet
Chet | Original Jazz Classics | OJC20 087-2
Chet Baker Septet
Chet | Original Jazz Classics | OJC20 087-2
Chet Baker Sextet
Chet | Original Jazz Classics | OJC20 087-2
Chris Connor With The John Lewis Quartet
Chris Connor | Atlantic | 7567-80769-2
Coleman Hawkins-Roy Eldridge Quintet
Verve Jazz Masters 43:Coleman Hawkins | Verve | 521856-2
Ella Fitzgerald With The JATP All Stars
For The Love Of Ella Fitzgerald | Verve | 841765-2
J.J.Johnson & Stan Getz With The Oscar Peterson Quartet
Stan Getz Highlights:The Best Of The Verve Years Vol.2 | Verve | 517330-2
A Life In Jazz:A Musical Biography | Verve | 535119-2
Stan Getz Highlights | Verve | 847430-2
James Moody Orchestra
The Blues And Other Colors | Original Jazz Classics | OJCCD 954-2(M 9023)
John Coltrane-Milt Jackson Quintet
John Coltrane-The Heavyweight Champion:The Complete Atlantic Recordings | Atlantic | 8122-71984-2
Bags & Trane | Rhino | 8122-73685-2
Lester Young Quintet
Jazz Gallery:Lester Young Vol.2(1946-59) | RCA | 2119541-2
Milt Jackson Orchestra

To Bags...With Love:Memorial Album | Pablo | 2310967-2
Milt Jackson Birthday Celebration | Fantasy | FANCD 6079-2
Big Bags | Original Jazz Classics | OJCCD 366-2(RLP 9429)
Milt Jackson Quartet
In A New Setting | Verve | 538620-2
Milt Jackson Birthday Celebration | Fantasy | FANCD 6079-2
Milt Jackson | Original Jazz Classics | OJC20 001-2(P 7003)
The Jazz Giants Play Rodgers & Hart:Blue Moon | Prestige | PCD 24205-2
The Jazz Giants Play Sammy Cahn:It's Magic | Prestige | PCD 24226-2
Milt Jackson Quintet
In A New Setting | Verve | 538620-2
Milt Jackson Sextet
Milt Jackson Birthday Celebration | Fantasy | FANCD 6079-2
Modern Jazz Quartet
To Bags...With Love:Memorial Album | Pablo | 2310967-2
The Complete Modern Jazz Quartet Prestige & Pablo Recordings | Prestige | 4PRCD 4438-2
The Modern Jazz Quartet At Music Inn With Sonny Rollins,Vol.2 | Atlantic | 7567-80794-2
Blues On Bach | Atlantic | 7567-81393-2
MJQ 40 | Atlantic | 7567-82330-2
Lonely Woman | Atlantic | 7567-90665-2
Rhino Presents The Atlantic Jazz Gallery | Atlantic | 8122-71257-2
Pyramid | Rhino | 812273679-2
Fontessa | Rhino | 8122-73687-2
Milt Jackson Birthday Celebration | Fantasy | FANCD 6079-2
Concorde | Original Jazz Classics | OJC20 002-2
Topsy-This One's For Basie | Original Jazz Classics | OJCCD 1073-2(2310917)
Together Again | Pablo | PACD20 244-2(2308244)
The Jazz Giants Play Cole Porter:Night And Day | Prestige | PCD 24203-2
Modern Jazz Quartet & Guests
MJQ 40 | Atlantic | 7567-82330-2
Modern Jazz Quartet And Laurindo Almeida
MJQ 40 | Atlantic | 7567-82330-2
Modern Jazz Quartet And Orchestra
MJQ 40 | Atlantic | 7567-82330-2
Modern Jazz Quartet And Symphony Orchestra
MJQ 40 | Atlantic | 7567-82330-2
Modern Jazz Quartet And The Swingle Singers
MJQ 40 | Atlantic | 7567-82330-2
Modern Jazz Quartet feat.Jimmy Giuffre
MJQ 40 | Atlantic | 7567-82330-2
Modern Jazz Quartet With Sonny Rollins
The Modern Jazz Quartet At Music Inn With Sonny Rollins,Vol.2 | Atlantic | 7567-80794-2
MJQ 40 | Atlantic | 7567-82330-2
Paul Desmond And The Modern Jazz Quartet
MJQ 40 | Atlantic | 7567-82330-2
Paul Desmond Orchestra
Planet Jazz:Jazz Saxophone | Planet Jazz | 2169653-2
Paul Desmond Quartet
The Ballad Of Paul Desmond | RCA | 21429372
Planet Jazz:Paul Desmond | Planet Jazz | 2152061-2
Planet Jazz Sampler | Planet Jazz | 2152326-2
Bossa Antigua | RCA | 2174795-2
Easy Living | RCA | 2174796-2
Take Ten | RCA | 2179621-2
Paul Desmond With Strings
Desmond Blue | RCA | 2663898-2
Paul Desmond-Gerry Mulligan Quartet
The Ballad Of Paul Desmond | RCA | 21429372
Planet Jazz:Paul Desmond | Planet Jazz | 2152061-2
Planet Jazz:Jazz Greatest Hits | Planet Jazz | 2169648-2
Two Of A Mind | RCA | 2179620-2
Ray Charles-Milt Jackson Sextet
Soul Brothers/Soul Meeting | Atlantic | 7567-81951-2
Sonny Rollins Quartet
Sonny Rollins And The Big Brass | Verve | 557545-2
Sonny Stitt Quintet
Atlantic Saxophones | Rhino | 8122-71256-2
Stan Getz And J.J. Johnson With The Oscar Peterson Quartet
Ultimate Stan Getz selected by Joe Henderson | Verve | 557532-2
Stan Getz With The Oscar Peterson Quartet
Verve Jazz Masters 8:Stan Getz | Verve | 519823-2
Ultimate Stan Getz selected by Joe Henderson | Verve | 557532-2
The Modern Jazz Society
A Concert Of Contemporary Music | Verve | 559827-2

Kay,Hershy | (ld)
Stan Getz With The Eddie Sauter Orchestra
Verve Jazz Masters 8:Stan Getz | Verve | 519823-2
A Life In Jazz:A Musical Biography | Verve | 535119-2
Ultimate Stan Getz selected by Joe Henderson | Verve | 557532-2
Stan Getz Highlights | Verve | 847430-2

Kay,Howard | (v)
Charlie Parker Quartet With Strings
The Cole Porter Songbook | Verve | 823250-2
Charlie Parker With Strings
Charlie Parker:The Best Of The Verve Years | Verve | 527815-2
Bird: The Complete Charlie Parker On Verve | Verve | 837141-2
Charlie Parker:April In Paris | Dreyfus Jazz Line | FDM 36737-2
Charlie Parker With The Joe Lipman Orchestra
Verve Jazz Masters 28:Charlie Parker Plays Standards | Verve | 521854-2
Charlie Parker With Strings:The Master Takes | Verve | 523984-2
Charlie Parker Big Band | Verve | 559835-2
Harry Carney And His Orchestra With Strings
Music For Loving:Ben Webster With Strings | Verve | 527774-2

Kaye,Billy | (dr)
George Benson Quartet + Guests
The George Benson Cookbook | CBS | 502470-2

Kaye,Carol | (bel-b)
Charles Kynard Quintet
The Soul Brotherhood | Prestige | PCD 24257-2
Hampton Hawes Orchestra
Northern Windows Plus | Prestige | PRCD 24278-2
Jimmy Smith With The Oliver Nelson Orchestra
Jimmy Smith-Talkin' Verve | Verve | 531563-2
Joe Williams With The Cannonball Adderley Sextet
Cannonball Adderley Birthday Celebration | Fantasy | FANCD 6087-2

Kaye,Jeff | (tpfl-h)
Buddy Childers Big Band
It's What Happening Now! | Candid | CCD 79749

Kaye,Joel | (bass-sax,bs,piccolo,flreeds)
Stan Kenton And His Orchestra
Adventures In Blues | Capitol | 520089-2
Adventures In Jazz | Capitol | 521222-2

Kaye,Leonard | (as)
Benny Goodman And His Orchestra
The Legends Of Swing | Laserlight | 24659

Kaye,Randy | (dr,percmarimba)
Jimmy Giuffre Trio
Night Dance | Choice | CHCD 71001
The Train And The River | Choice | CHCD 71011

Kaye,Tommy | (g)
Benny Goodman And His V-Disc All Star Band
The Legends Of Swing | Laserlight | 24659

Kayser,Annette | (dr)
The United Women's Orchestra
The Blue One | Jazz Haus Musik | JHM 0099 CD

Kazebier,Nate | (tp)
Benny Goodman And His Orchestra
Planet Jazz:Benny Goodman | Planet Jazz | 2152054-2
Planet Jazz Sampler | Planet Jazz | 2152326-2
Planet Jazz:Big Bands | Planet Jazz | 2169649-2
Planet Jazz:Swing | Planet Jazz | 2169651-2

Keane,Shake | (perc,tpfl-h)
Joe Harriott Quintet
Free Form | EmArCy | 538184-2
Kenny Clarke-Francy Boland Big Band
Three Latin Adventures | MPS | 529095-2

Kearns,Joe[Joey] | (ascl)
Bob Crosby And His Orchestra
Swing Legens:Bob Crosby | Nimbus Records | NI 2011
Bob Crosby's Bobcats
Swing Legens:Bob Crosby | Nimbus Records | NI 2011

Kearsey,Mike | (tb)
Steve Martland Band
The Orchestra Of Smith's Academy | Enja | ENJ-9358 2

Keb' Mo' | (gvoc)
Jimmy Smith All Stars
Jimmy Smith:Dot Com Blues | Blue Thumb | 543978-2

Keck,Thomas 'Leo' | (dr)
Spree Cuty Stompers
Deutsches Jazz Fesival 1954/1955 | Bear Family Records | BCD 15430

Kedves,G. | (fr-h)
Vince Mendoza With The WDR Big Band And Guests
Sketches | ACT | 9215-2

Keenan,Norman | (b)
Big Joe Turner With The Count Basie Orchestra
Flip Flop And Fly | Original Jazz Classics | OJCCD 1053-2(2310937)
Count Basie And His Orchestra
Afrique | RCA | 2179618-2
Count Basie: Salle Pleyel, April 17th, 1972 | Laserlight | 36127
Basie Meets Bond | Capitol | 538225-2
Basie's Beatle Bag | Verve | 557455-2
Live at The Sands | Reprise | 9362-45946-2
Count Basie And The Kansas City 7
Count Basie: Salle Pleyel, April 17th, 1972 | Laserlight | 36127
Count Basie Trio
The Story Of Jazz Piano | Laserlight | 24653

Keene,Christopher | (cond)
Keith Jarrett With The Syracuse Symphony
The Celestial Hawk | ECM | 1175

Keezer,Geoff | (el-p,synth,p,keyboardsp-solo)
Art Blakey And The Jazz Messengers
The Art Of Jazz | IN+OUT Records | 77028-2
Christian McBide Quartet
Vertcal Vision | Warner | 9362-48278-2
Gerard Presencer Group
Chasing Reality | ACT | 9422-2

Keita,Assitan 'Mama' | (percvoc)
Hank Jones Meets Cheik-Tidiana Seck
Sarala | Verve | 528783-2

Keita,Tiawara | (doudoum'ni,tamasoucou)
Jon Hassell & Farafina
Flash Of The Spirit | Intuition Records | INT 3009-2

Kelin,Fred | (fr-h)
Carmen McRae With The Ralph Burns Orchestra
Birds Of A Feather | Decca | 589515-2

Kellaway,Roger | (el-p,p,celeste,hammerklavier)
Diane Schuur With Orchestra
Love Songs | GRP | GRP 97032
The Best Of Diane Schuur | GRP | GRP 98882
Jimmy Witherspoon And His All Stars
Blues For Easy Livers | Original Blues Classics | OBCCD 585-2(PR 7475)
Kenny Burrell Quintet
Guitar Forms | Verve | 521403-2
Verve Jazz Masters 45:Kenny Burrell | Verve | 527652-2
Kenny Clarke Quintet
Verve Jazz Masters 45:Kenny Burrell | Verve | 527652-2
Oliver Nelson And His Orchestra
More Blues And The Abstract Truth | Impulse(MCA) | 951212-2
Roger Kellaway Cello Quartet With The A&M Symphony Orchestra
Roger Kellaway Cello Quartet | A&M Records | 9861062
Singers Unlimited With Roger Kellaway
The Singers Unlimited:Magic Voices | MPS | 539130-2
Singers Unlimited With The Roger Kellaway Cello Quartet
The Singers Unlimited:Magic Voices | MPS | 539130-2
Sonny Rollins Orchestra
Alfie | Impulse(MCA) | 951224-2
Stan Getz With The Eddie Sauter Orchestra
Stan Getz Plays The Music Of Mickey One | Verve | 531232-2
Tony Coe-Roger Kellaway
British-American Blue | Between The Lines | btl 007(Efa 10177-2)
Wes Montgomery Quartet
Bumpin' | Verve | 539062-2
Wes Montgomery With The Don Sebesky Orchestra
Verve Jazz Masters 14:Wes Montgomery | Verve | 519826-2
Talkin' Jazz:Roots Of Acid Jazz | Verve | 529580-2
Bumpin' | Verve | 539062-2
Zoot Sims-Harry Edison Quintet
Jazz Dance | Original Jazz Classics | OJCCD 1002-2(1210890)

Kelleher,Jack | (b)
Tommy Dorsey And His Orchestra
Planet Jazz:Frank Sinatra & Tommy Dorsey | Planet Jazz | 2152067-2
Frank Sinatra And The Tommy Dorsey Orchestra | RCA | 2668701-2

Kellem,Butch | (tb)
Thilo Kreitmeier & Group
Changes | Organic Music | ORGM 9725

Kellens,Christian | (bar-h,b-tb,tbtuba)
Stan Getz With The Kurt Edelhagen Orchestra
Stan Getz In Europe | Laserlight | 24657

Keller,Jack | (p)
John LaPorta Trio
The Sandole Brothers | Fantasy | FCD 24763-2

Keller,Jörg Achim | (condarr)
HR Big Band
Libertango:Homage An Astor Piazolla | hr music.de | hrmj 014-02 CD
HR Big Band With Marjorie Barnes And Frits Landesbergen
Swinging Christmas | hr music.de | hrmj 012-02 CD
HR Big Band With Marjorie Barnes And Frits Landesbergen And Strings
Swinging Christmas | hr music.de | hrmj 012-02 CD
Pee Wee Ellis & NDR Bigband
What You Like | Minor Music | 801064
Till Brönner Quartet & Deutsches Symphonieorchester Berlin
German Songs | Minor Music | 801057

Keller,Paul | (b)
Diana Krall Quartet
All For You-A Dedication To The Nat King Cole Trio | Impulse(MCA) | 951164-2
Diana Krall Trio
All For You-A Dedication To The Nat King Cole Trio | Impulse(MCA) | 951164-2

Keller,Rich | (dr-programming,fl)
Litschie Hrdlicka Group
Falling Lovers | EGO | 93020
Jazz Portraits | EGO | 95080
Tom Browne Group
Hot Jazz Bisquits | Hip Bop | HIBD 8801
Tom Browne Groups
Mo' Jamaica Funk | Hip Bop | HIBD 8002

Keller,Rick | (fl,sax,ss,asts)
Al Porcino Big Band
Al Porcino Big Band Live! | Organic Music | ORGM 9717
Litschie Hrdlicka Group
Falling Lovers | EGO | 93020
Torsten Goods Group
Manhattan Walls | Jardis Records | JRCD 20139

Keller,Robert | (fl,cl,tssax)
Buddy Rich And His Orchestra
Big Swing Face | Pacific Jazz | 837989-2
Buddy Rich Big Band
The New One! | Pacific Jazz | 494507-2
Wolfgang Schmid's Kick
No Filters | TipToe | TIP-888809 2

Keller,Werner | (clvoc)
Danny Moss Meets Buddha's Gamblers
A Swingin' Affair | Nagel-Heyer | CD 034
Blues Of Summer | Nagel-Heyer | NH 1011
Oscar Klein's Anniversary Band
Moonglow | Nagel-Heyer | CD 021
Ellington For Lovers | Nagel-Heyer | NH 1009
The Second Sampler | Nagel-Heyer | NHR SP 6
The Tremble Kids All Stars
The Tremble Kids All Stars Play Chicago Jazz! | Nagel-Heyer | CD 043

Kelley,Raymond J. | (celloviola)
Charlie Haden Quartet West With Strings
The Art Of The Song | Verve | 547403-2

Kelliher,Jay | (tb)
Anita O'Day With Gene Krupa And His Orchestra
Let Me Off Uptown:Anita O'Day With Gene Krupa | CBS | CK 65625

Kellner,. |
Ella Fitzgerald With The Billy May Orchestra
Ella Fitzgerald Sings The Harold Arlen Song Book | Verve | 589108-2

Kellner,Murray | (v)
The Best Of The Song Books:The Ballads | Verve | 521867-2
Ella Fitzgerald With The Nelson Riddle Orchestra
The Best Of The Song Books:The Ballads | Verve | 521867-2
Oh Lady Be Good:The Best Of The Gershwin Songbook | Verve | 529581-2
Love Songs:The Best Of The Song Books | Verve | 531762-2

Kellock,Brian | (p)
Herb Geller-Brian Kellock
Hollywood Portraits | Hep | CD 2078

Kellso,Jon-Erik | (cotp)
Mark Shane's X-Mas Allstars
What Would Santa Say? | Nagel-Heyer | CD 055
Christmas Jazz! | Nagel-Heyer | NH 1008
Marty Grosz And His Swinging Fools
Ring Dem Bells | Nagel-Heyer | CD 022
The Second Sampler | Nagel-Heyer | NHR SP 6
Ralph Sutton And Friends
Sweet Sue-The Music Of Fats Waller Vol.1 | Nagel-Heyer | CD 057
Ralph Sutton And His Allstars
Echoes Of Spring:The Complete Hamburg Concert | Nagel-Heyer | CD 038
Randy Sandke And The New York Allstars
The Re-Discovered Louis And Bix | Nagel-Heyer | CD 058
Randy Sandke-Dick Hyman
The Re-Discovered Louis And Bix | Nagel-Heyer | CD 058

Kelly,Don | (b-tbtb)
Stan Kenton And His Orchestra
Great Swing Classics In Hi-Fi | Capitol | 521223-2

Kelly,Ed | (p,orgsynth)
Art Pepper Quartet
Renascene | Galaxy | GCD 4202-2

Kelly,Fred | (fl,piccolo,ssbs)
Sam Rivers Orchestra
Crystals | Impulse(MCA) | 589760-2

Kelly,George | (p,celestets)
Axel Zwingenberger With The Lionel Hampton Big Band
The Boogie Woogie Album | Vagabond | VRCD 8.88008
Doc Cheatham Sextet
A' Portrait Of Jan Jankeje | Jazzpoint | JP 1054 CD
George Kelly Quintet
A' Portrait Of Jan Jankeje | Jazzpoint | JP 1054 CD
Red Richards Quartet
Swingtime | Jazzpoint | JP 1041 CD
Red Richards-George Kelly Sextet With Doc Cheatham
Groove Move | Jazzpoint | JP 1045 CD
Sarah Vaughan The The Joe Lippman Orchestra
Sarah Vaughan:Lover Man | Dreyfus Jazz Line | FDM 36739-2

Kelly,Jack | (g,ldp)
Joe Hill Louis
Joe Hill Louis: The Be-Bop Boy | Bear Family Records | BCD 15524 AH
Walter Horton Band
Joe Hill Louis: The Be-Bop Boy | Bear Family Records | BCD 15524 AH

Kelly,Jemina | (voc)
Mike Westbrook Brass Band
Glad Day:Settings Of William Blake | Enja | ENJ-9376 2

Kelly,Jim | (el-gg)
Grace Knight With Orchestra
Come In Spinner | Intuition Records | INT 3052-2
Vince Jones With Orchestra
Come In Spinner | Intuition Records | INT 3052-2

Kelly,Monty | (tparr)
Billie Holiday With The Paul Whiteman Orchestra
Billie's Blues | Blue Note | 748786-2

Kelly,Paula | (voc)
Glenn Miller And His Orchestra
The Ultimate Glenn Miller-22 Original Hits From The King Of Swing | RCA | 2113137-2
Candelight Miller | RCA | 2668716-2

Kelly,Red | (bvoc)
Nat Pierce/Dick Collins Nonet
Nat Pierce-Dick Collins-Ralph Burns & The Herdsmen Play Paris | Fantasy | FCD 24759-2
Stan Kenton Orchestra
Stompin' At Newport | Pablo | PACD 5312-2
The Herdsmen
Nat Pierce-Dick Collins-Ralph Burns & The Herdsmen Play Paris | Fantasy | FCD 24759-2

Kelly,T. | (cl)
Dee Dee Bridgewater With Orchestra
Dear Ella | Verve | 539102-2

Kelly,Ted | (tb)
Dizzy Gillespie And His Orchestra
Dizzy Gillespie:Pleyel Jazz Concert 1948 + Max Roach Quintet 1949 | Vogue | 21409412
Planet Jazz:Dizzy Gillespie | Planet Jazz | 2152069-2
Planet Jazz:Bebop | RCA | 2169650-2
Ernie Royal And The Duke Knights
Americans Swinging In Paris:James Moody | EMI Records | 539653-2
Jubilee All Stars
Jazz Gallery:Lester Young Vol.2(1946-59) | RCA | 2119541-2

Kelly,William 'Hicky' | (normaphoneeuphonium)
The Modern Jazz Disciples
Disciples Blues | Prestige | PCD 24263-2

Kelly,Wynton | (p)
Abbey Lincoln With Her Quartet
That's Him! | Original Jazz Classics | OJCCD 085-2
Abbey Lincoln With Her Quintet
Sonny Rollins-The Freelance Years:The Complete Riverside & Contemporary Recordings | Riverside | 5 RCD 4427-2
That's Him! | Original Jazz Classics | OJCCD 085-2
Abbey Lincoln With The Benny Golson Quintet
It's Magic | Original Jazz Classics | OJCCD 205-2
Abbey Lincoln With The Benny Golson Septet
It's Magic | Original Jazz Classics | OJCCD 205-2
Abbey Lincoln With The Kenny Dorham Quintet
Abbey Is Blue | Original Jazz Classics | OJC20 069-2(RLP 1153)
Art Farmer Quartet
Early Art | Original Jazz Classics | OJCCD 880-2(NJ 8258)
The Jazz Giants Play Sammy Cahn:It's Magic | Prestige | PCD 24226-2
Art Pepper Quartet
Gettin' Together | Original Jazz Classics | OJCCD 169-2
The Way It Is | Original Jazz Classics | OJCCD 389-2
Art Pepper Quintet
Gettin' Together | Original Jazz Classics | OJCCD 169-2
Benny Golson Sextet

The J.J.Johnson Memorial Album | Prestige | PRCD 11025-2
Billie Holiday And Her All Stars
Verve Jazz Masters 12:Billie Holiday | Verve | 519825-2
Billie Holiday Story Vol.4:Lady Sings The Blues | Verve | 521429-2
4 By 4:Ella Fitzgerald/Sarah Vaughan/Billie Holiday/Dinah Washington | Verve | 559693-2
The Billie Holiday Song Book | Verve | 823246-2
Blue Mitchell And His Orchestra
A Sure Thing | Original Jazz Classics | OJCCD 837-2
The Jazz Giants Play Jerome Kern:Yesterdays | Prestige | PCD 24202-2
Blue Mitchell Quintet
Out Of The Blue | Original Jazz Classics | OJCCD 667-2(RLP 1131)
Blue Mitchell Sextet
Blue Mitchell Big 6 | Original Jazz Classics | OJCCD 615-2(RLP 12-273)
Blue Soul | Original Jazz Classics | OJCCD 765-2(RLP 1155)
Cannonball Adderley And His Orchestra
Cannonball Adderley Birthday Celebration | Fantasy | FANCD 6087-2
Cannonball Adderley Quartet
Takes Charge | Blue Note | 534071-2
Ballads | Blue Note | 537563-2
Cannonball & Coltrane | Verve | 559770-2
Cannonball Adderley Quintet
Verve Jazz Masters 31:Cannonball Adderley | Verve | 522651-2
Cannonball Adderley Quintet In Chicago
Cannonball & Coltrane | Verve | 559770-2
Cannonball Adderley Quintet Plus
Cannonball Adderley Birthday Celebration | Fantasy | FANCD 6087-2
Cannonball Adderley Quintet Plus | Original Jazz Classics | OJC20 306-2
Cannonball Adderley-Milt Jackson Quintet
To Bags...With Love:Memorial Album | Pablo | 2310967-2
Milt Jackson Birthday Celebration | Fantasy | FANCD 6079-2
Cannonball Adderley Birthday Celebration | Fantasy | FANCD 6087-2
Things Are Getting Better | Original Jazz Classics | OJC20 032-2
Dexter Gordon Quartet
Dexter Gordon Birthday Celebration | Fantasy | FANCD 6082-2
The Jumpin' Blues | Original Jazz Classics | OJCCD 899-2(PR 10020)
Dinah Washington And Her Orchestra
For Those In Love | EmArCy | 514073-2
Dinah Washington And Her Sextet
Newport Jazz Festival 1958,July 3rd-6th Vol.4:Blues In The Night No.2 | Phontastic | NCD 8816
Dinah Washington With The Jimmy Cobb Orchestra
Verve Jazz Masters 40:Dinah Washington | Verve | 522055-2
Ultimate Ben Webster selected by James Carter | Verve | 557537-2
Dinah Washington With The Newport All Stars
Dinah Sings Bessie Smith | Verve | 538635-2
Dinah Washington With The Terry Gibbs Band
Verve Jazz Masters 40:Dinah Washington | Verve | 522055-2
Dinah Washington With The Urbie Green Sextet
Newport Jazz Festival 1958,July 3rd-6th Vol.2:Mulligan The Main Man | Phontastic | NCD 8814
Dizzy Gillespie All Stars
Verve Jazz Masters 25:Stan Getz & Dizzy Gillespie | Verve | 521852-2
Dizzy Gillespie And His Orchestra
Dizzy Gillespie:Birks Works-The Verve Big Band Sessions | Verve | 527900-2
Ultimate Dizzy Gillespie | Verve | 557535-2
Dizzy Gillespie Orchestra
Verve Jazz Masters 10:Dizzy Gillespie | Verve | 516319-2
Don Sleet Quintet
All Members | Original Jazz Classics | OJCCD 1949-2(JLP 9455)
Gene Ammons Quartet
Gentle Jug Vol.3 | Prestige | PCD 24249-2
A Stranger In Town | Prestige | PRCD 24266-2
Gene Ammons Quintet
A Stranger In Town | Prestige | PRCD 24266-2
Hank Mobley Quartet
Soul Station | Blue Note | 495343-2
Workout | Blue Note | 784080-2
Hank Mobley Quintet
Roll Call | Blue Note | 540030-2
Workout | Blue Note | 784080-2
Illinois Jacquet Quintet
The Blues That's Me! | Original Jazz Classics | OJCCD 614-2(P 7731)
J.J.Johnson Quintet
The Eminent J.J.Johnson Vol.2 | Blue Note | 532144-2
James Clay/David Fathead Newman Quintet
The Sound Of The Wide Open Spaces | Original Jazz Classics | OJCCD 1075-2(RLP 1178)
Jimmy Heath Quartet
Blue Soul | Original Jazz Classics | OJCCD 765-2(RLP 1155)
John Coltrane Quartet
Cannonball & Coltrane | Verve | 559770-2
Coltrane Jazz | Atlantic | 7567-81344-2
The Best Of John Coltrane | Atlantic | 7567-81366-2
John Coltrane-The Heavyweight Champion:The Complete Atlantic Recordings | Atlantic | 8122-71984-2
Giant Steps | Atlantic | 8122-75203-2
The Very Best Of John Coltrane | Rhino | 8122-79778-2
Johnny Griffin Septet
A Blowing Session | Blue Note | 0677191
Trane's Blues | Blue Note | 498240-2
King Curtis Quartet
The New Scene Of King Curtis | Original Jazz Classics | OJC 198(NJ 8237)
King Curtis Quintet
The New Scene Of King Curtis | Original Jazz Classics | OJC 198(NJ 8237)
Miles Davis Quartet
Someday My Prince Will Come | CBS | CK 65919
Miles Davis Quintet
Miles Davis: Olympia, March 29th,1960 | Laserlight | 36130
Ballads | CBS | 461099-2
Circle In The Round | CBS | 467898-2
Kind Of Blue | CBS | 480410-2
Miles Davis In Person-Friday Night At The Blackhawk,San Francisco,Vol.1 | CBS | C4K 87106
Miles Davis At Carnegie Hall | CBS | CK 65027
This Is Jazz:Miles Davis Plays Ballads | CBS | CK 65038
Someday My Prince Will Come | CBS | CK 65919
Live In Stockholm | Dragon | DRCD 228
Miles Davis Sextet
Kind Of Blue | CBS | 480410-2
Kind Of Blue | CBS | CK 64935
Someday My Prince Will Come | CBS | CK 65919
Miles Davis With Gil Evans & His Orchestra
Miles Davis At Carnegie Hall | CBS | CK 65027
Milt Jackson-Wes Montgomery Quintet
Wes Montgomery-The Complete Riverside Recordings | Riverside | 12 RCD 4408-2
To Bags...With Love:Memorial Album | Pablo | 2310967-2
Milt Jackson Birthday Celebration | Fantasy | FANCD 6079-2
Bags Meets Wes! | Original Jazz Classics | OJC20 234-2(RLP 9407)
Nat Adderley Quartet
Naturally! | Original Jazz Classics | OJCCD 1088-2(JLP 947)
Nat Adderley Quintet
Much Brass | Original Jazz Classics | OJCCD 848-2(R 1143)
Nat Adderley Sextet
Much Brass | Original Jazz Classics | OJCCD 848-2(R 1143)
Paul Gonsalves Quintet
Gettin' Together | Original Jazz Classics | OJCCD 203-2
Philly Joe Jones Big Band
Cannonball Adderley Birthday Celebration | Fantasy | FANCD 6087-2
Roland Kirk Quartet
Talkin' Verve-Roots Of Acid Jazz:Roland Kirk | Verve | 533101-2
Domino | Verve | 543833-2
Rahsaan/The Complete Mercury Recordings Of Roland Kirk | Mercury | 846630-2
Sonny Criss Quartet
Sonny Criss Quartet Feat. Wynton Kelly | Fresh Sound Records | FSR-CD 318
Sonny Criss Quintet
Sonny Criss Quartet Feat. Wynton Kelly | Fresh Sound Records | FSR-CD 318
Sonny Rollins Quartet
True Blue | Blue Note | 534032-2
Ballads | Blue Note | 537562-2
Newk's Time | Blue Note | 576752-2
The Blue Note Years-The Best Of Sonny Rollins | Blue Note | 793203-2
Sonny Rollins:The Blue Note Recordings | Blue Note | 821371-2
Jazz Profile:Sonny Rollins | Blue Note | 823516-2
Sonny Rollins Quintet
Ballads | Blue Note | 537562-2
Sonny Rollins:Vol.1 | Blue Note | 591724-2
The Blue Note Years-The Best Of Sonny Rollins | Blue Note | 793203-2
The Best Of Blue Note Vol.2 | Blue Note | 797960-2
Sonny Rollins:The Blue Note Recordings | Blue Note | 821371-2
Jazz Profile:Sonny Rollins | Blue Note | 823516-2
Steve Lacy Quartet
Soprano Sax | Original Jazz Classics | OJCCD 130-2(P 7125)
Super Black Blues Band
Super Black Blues Vol.II | RCA | 2663874-2
Urbie Green Sextet
Newport Jazz Festival 1958,July 3rd-6th Vol.2:Mulligan The Main Man | Phontastic | NCD 8814
Walter Benton Quintet
Out Of This World | Milestone | MCD 47087-2
Wes Montgomery Quartet
Wes Montgomery-The Complete Riverside Recordings | Riverside | 12 RCD 4408-2
Verve Jazz Masters 14:Wes Montgomery | Verve | 519826-2
Verve Jazz Masters 20:Introducing | Verve | 519853-2
Talkin' Jazz:Roots Of Acid Jazz | Verve | 529580-2
Wes Montgomery Quartet With The Claus Ogerman Orchestra
Willow Weep For Me | Verve | 589486-2
Wes Montgomery Quintet
Wes Montgomery-The Complete Riverside Recordings | Riverside | 12 RCD 4408-2
Full House | Original Jazz Classics | OJC20 106-2
Wynton Kelly Quartet
Wynton Kelly-Piano | Original Jazz Classics | OJCCD 401-2(RLP 12-254)
Wynton Kelly Sextet
Kelly Blue | Original Jazz Classics | OJC20 033-2(RLP 1142)
Kelly Blue | Riverside | RISA 1142-6
Wynton Kelly Trio
The Story Of Jazz Piano | Laserlight | 24653
Kelly Blue | Original Jazz Classics | OJC20 033-2(RLP 1142)
Wynton Kelly-Piano | Original Jazz Classics | OJCCD 401-2(RLP 12-254)
Full View | Original Jazz Classics | OJCCD 912-2(M 9004)
Kelly Blue | Riverside | RISA 1142-6
Wynton Kelly Trio With Hank Mobley
Live at The Left Bank Jazz Society,Baltimore,1967 | Fresh Sound Records | FSCD 1031
Wynton Kelly Trio With Wes Montgomery
Wes Montgomery:The Verve Jazz Sides | Verve | 521690-2
Wynton Kelly-George Coleman Quartet
Live at The Left Bank Jazz Society,Baltimore,1968 | Fresh Sound Records | FSCD 1032

Kelly,Wynton or Bill Evans | (p)
Mar Murphy With The Ernie Wilkins Orchestra
RAH | Original Jazz Classics | OJCCD 141-2(R 9395)

Kelly,Wynton or Wade Legge | (p)
Charles Mingus Workshop
Charles Mingus-The Complete Debut Recordings | Debut | 12 DCD 4402-2

Kelso,Jack | (as,cl,fl,reeds,saxts)
Hampton Hawes Orchestra
Northern Windows Plus | Prestige | PRCD 24278-2
Lionel Hampton And His Orchestra
Lionel Hampton:Flying Home | Dreyfus Jazz Line | FDM 36735-2

Keltner,Jim | (dr)
Albert King Blues Band
Lovejoy | Stax | SCD 8517-2(STS 2040)

Kemanis,Aina | (voice)
Alex Cline Group
The Lamp And The Star | ECM | 1372
Barre Phillips Trio
Journal Violone II | ECM | 1149
Marilyn Mazur's Future Song
Small Labyrinths | ECM | 1559(533679-2)
Marilyn Mazure's Future Song | VeraBra Records | CDVBR 2105-2

Kemp,Gibson | (dr)
Paul Nero Sound
Doldinger's Best | ACT | 9224-2

Kempf,Vladi | (drperc)
Marty Hall Band
Who's Been Talkin'?s | Blues Beacon | BLU-1033 2

Kendrick,Rodney | (p)
Abbey Lincoln With Her Band
Who Used To Dance | Verve | 533559-2
Abbey Lincoln With The Rodney Kendrick Trio And Guests
A Turtle's Dream | Verve | 527382-2

Kennedy,Charlie | (as,tssax)
Anita O'Day With Gene Krupa And His Orchestra
Let Me Off Uptown:Anita O'Day With Gene Krupa | CBS | CK 65625
Art Pepper Plus Eleven
Art Pepper + Eleven | Contemporary | CSA 7568-6
Modern Jazz Classics | Original Jazz Classics | OJC20 341-2
Chubby Jackson Big Band
Gerry Mulligan Quartet feat.Chet Baker | Original Jazz Classics | OJCCD 711-2(F 8082/P 7641)
Dizzy Gillespie And His Orchestra
Talking Verve:Dizzy Gillespie | Verve | 533846-2
Gene Krupa And His Orchestra
Mullenium | CBS | CK 65678
June Christy With The Shorty Rogers Orchestra
June Christy Big Band Special | Capitol | 498319-2
Terry Gibbs Big Band
Terry Gibbs Dream Band Vol.4:Main Stem | Contemporary | CCD 7656-2
Terry Gibbs Dream Band
Terry Gibbs Dream Band Vol.2:The Sundown Sessions | Contemporary | CCD 7652-2
Terry Gibbs Dream Band Vol.3:Flying Home | Contemporary | CCD 7654-2
Terry Gibbs Dream Band Vol.5:The Big Cat | Contemporary | CCD 7657-2
Terry Gibbs Dream Band Vol.6:One More Time | Contemporary | CCD 7658-2
The Jazz Giants Play Jerome Kern:Yesterdays | Prestige | PCD 24202-2

Kennedy,Dave | (tpfl-h)
Woody Herman And His Orchestra
Verve Jazz Masters 54:Woody Herman | Verve | 529903-2

Kennedy,Joe | (v)
Ahmad Jamal Quintet
Big Byrd | Dreyfus Jazz Line | FDM 37008-2
Ahmad Jamal Septet
Live In Paris 1996 | Dreyfus Jazz Line | FDM 37020-2

Kennedy,Ray | (el-p,synthp)
Dave Weckl Group
Master Plan | GRP | GRP 96192
John Pizzarelli Quartet
Dear Mr.Cole | Novus | 4163182-2
John Pizzarelli Trio
P.S. Mr.Cole | RCA | 2663563-2
John Pizzarelli Trio With Harry Allen
P.S. Mr.Cole | RCA | 2663563-2

Kennedy,Tom | (b,el-bfretless-b)
Dave Weckl Group
Master Plan | GRP | GRP 96192
Don Grolnick Group
Hearts And Numbers | VeraBra Records | CDVBR 2016-2

Kennedy,William | (dr,background-voc,keyboardsperc)
Diane Schuur With Orchestra
Love Songs | GRP | GRP 97032
The Best Of Diane Schuur | GRP | GRP 98882
Take 6 With The Yellow Jackets
He Is Christmas | Reprise | 7599-26665-2
Yellowjackets
Run For Your Life | GRP | GRP 97542

Kennel,Hans | (alphorn,fl-h,büchel,voice,tp,voc)
Kölner Saxophon Mafia With Guests
Kölner Saxophon Mafia: 20 Jahre Saxuelle Befreiung | Jazz Haus Musik | JHM 0115 CD

Kenner,Sonny | (g)
Jay McShann Quintet
What A Wonderful World | Groove Note | GN 1005(180gr-Pressung)
What A Wonderful World | Groove Note | GRV 1005-2

Kenney,Dick | (tb)
Stan Kenton And His Orchestra
Stan Kenton Portraits On Standards | Capitol | 531571-2
Van Alexander Orchestra
Home Of Happy Feet/Swing! Staged For Sound! | Capitol | 535211-2

Kenney,William | (dr)
Yellowjackets
Live Wires | GRP | GRP 96672

Kennon,George | (as)
Tommy Dorsey And His Orchestra
Planet Jazz:Tommy Dorsey | Planet Jazz | 2159972-2

Kennon,Joe | (tp)
Eric Dolphy Quartet With The University Of Illinois Big Band
The Illinois Concert | Blue Note | 499826-2

Kenny,Dick | (tb)
Stan Kenton And His Orchestra
One Night Stand | Choice | CHCD 71051

Kent,Bryan | (g)
Harry James And His Orchestra
The Legends Of Swing | Laserlight | 24659

Kent,Oliver | (pel-p)
Karl Ratzer Quintet
All The Way | Enja | ENJ-9448 2
Marcio Tubino Group
Festa Do Olho | Organic Music | ORGM 9723
Roman Schwaller Jazz Quartet
Some Changes In Life | JHM Records | JHM 3612
The New Roman Schwaller Jazzquartet
Welcome Back From Outer Space | JHM Records | JHM 3605

Kent,Peter | (v)
Jacintha With Band And Strings
Lush Life | Groove Note | GRV 1011-2(Gold CD 2011)
Milt Jackson And His Orchestra
Reverence And Compassion | Reprise | 9362-45204-2

Kent,Stacey | (voc)
Jim Tomlinson Quintet
Only Trust Your Heart | Candid | CCD 79758
Brazilian Sketches | Candid | CCD 79769
Jim Tomlinson Sextet
Only Trust Your Heart | Candid | CCD 79758
Stacey Kent And Her Quintet
Close Your Eyes | Candid | CCD 79737
The Tender Trap | Candid | CCD 79751
Let Yourself Go-Celebrating Fred Astaire | Candid | CCD 79764
Stacey Kent With The Jim Tomlison Quintet
Dreamsville | Candid | CCD 79775
Stacy Kent With The Jim Tomlinson Quintet
In Love Again | Candid | CCD 79786
The Boy Next Door | Candid | CCD 79797

Kentendijan,Joe | (v)
Charlie Haden Quartet West With Strings
The Art Of The Song | Verve | 547403-2

Kenton,Stan | (ld,narration,p,arr,voc,ld.arr)
Nat King Cole Quartet With The Stan Kenton Orchestra
Nat King Cole:For Sentimental Reasons | Dreyfus Jazz Line | FDM 36740-2
Stan Kenton And His Orchestra
Swing Vol.1 | Storyville | 4960343
Adventures In Blues | Capitol | 520089-2
Adventures In Jazz | Capitol | 521222-2
Great Swing Classics In Hi-Fi | Capitol | 521223-2
Stan Kenton Portraits On Standards | Capitol | 531571-2
Stan Kenton-The Formative Years | Decca | 589489-2
One Night Stand | Choice | CHCD 71051
Stan Kenton Orchestra
Stompin' At Newport | Pablo | PACD 5312-2
Stan Kenton With The Danish Radio Big Band
Stan Kenton With The Danish Radio Big Band | Storyville | STCD 8340
The Hollywood Hucksters
The Hollywood Session:The Capitol Jazzmen | Jazz Unlimited | JUCD 2044

Kenyatta,Robin | (as,ts,fl,percss)
Roswell Rudd Sextet
Mixed | Impulse(MCA) | IMP 12702

Kéraudren,Jean | (sound)
Michel Wintsch & Road Movie
Michel Wintsch & Road Movie featuring Gerry Hemingway | Between The Lines | btl 002(Efa 10172-2)

Kerber,Randy | (keyboards,synthp)
Diane Schuur With Orchestra
The Best Of Diane Schuur | GRP | GRP 98882
The Quincy Jones-Sammy Nestico Orchestra
Basie & Beyond | Warner | 9362-47792-2

Kern,Katie | (el-g,voc,g)
Katie Kern
Still Young | Jazzpoint | JP 1070 CD
Katie Kern Group
Still Young | Jazzpoint | JP 1070 CD
Katie Kern-Oscar Klein
Still Young | Jazzpoint | JP 1070 CD
Katie Kern-Werner Dannemann
Still Young | Jazzpoint | JP 1070 CD
Oscar Klein & Katie Kern Group
Pick-A-Blues | Jazzpoint | JP 1065 CD
Oscar Klein Band
Pick-A-Blues Live | Jazzpoint | JP 1071

Ker-Ourio,Oliver | (harm)
Christian Scheuber Quintet
Clara's Smile | double moon | DMCHR 71025

Kerr,Anthony | (vib)
Mike Westbrook Orchestra
Bar Utopia-A Big Band Cabaret | Enja | ENJ-9333 2
The Orchestra Of Smith's Academy | Enja | ENJ-9358 2

Kerr,William | (flas)
Freddy Cole With Band
To The End Of The Earth | Fantasy | FCD 9675-2

Kerschek,Wolf | (grand-pfender-rhodes)
Ulf Meyer & Martin Wind Group
Kinnings | Storyville | STCD 8374

Kersey,Kenny | (p)
Billie Holiday With The JATP All Stars
Billie Holiday Story Vol.1:Jazz At The Philharmonic | Verve | 521642-2
The Complete Jazz At The Philharmonic On Verve 1944-1949 | Verve | 523893-2

INTERPRETENVERZEICHNIS

Verve Jazz Masters 47:Billie Holiday Sings Standards | Verve | 527650-2
Jazz At The Philharmonic:Best Of The 1940's Concerts | Verve | 557534-2
Buck Clayton Quartet
The Complete Jazz At The Philharmonic On Verve 1944-1949 | Verve | 523893-2
Charlie Christian All Stars
Charlie Christian-Jazz Immortal/Dizzy Gillespie 1944 | Original Jazz Classics | OJCCD 1932-2(ES 548)
Coleman Hawkins Quartet
The Complete Jazz At The Philharmonic On Verve 1944-1949 | Verve | 523893-2
JATP All Stars
Verve Jazz Masters 28:Charlie Parker Plays Standards | Verve | 521854-2
The Complete Jazz At The Philharmonic On Verve 1944-1949 | Verve | 523893-2
Jazz At The Philharmonic:Best Of The 1940's Concerts | Verve | 557534-2
Bird: The Complete Charlie Parker On Verve | Verve | 837141-2
Jubilee All Stars
Jazz Gallery:Lester Young Vol.2(1946-59) | RCA | 2119541-2
Kenny Kersey Trio
The Complete Jazz At The Philharmonic On Verve 1944-1949 | Verve | 523893-2
Lester Young Quartet
The Complete Jazz At The Philharmonic On Verve 1944-1949 | Verve | 523893-2
Lester Young Quintet
The Complete Jazz At The Philharmonic On Verve 1944-1949 | Verve | 523893-2
Minton's Playhouse All Stars
Charlie Christian:Swing To Bop | Dreyfus Jazz Line | FDM 36715-2
Slam Stewart Trio
The Complete Jazz At The Philharmonic On Verve 1944-1949 | Verve | 523893-2

Kersthold,Andreas | (p)
Association Urbanetique
Ass Bedient | Jazz 4 Ever Records:Jazz Network | J4E 4723

Kersting,Michael | (drperc)
All That Jazz & Helena Paul
All That Jazz & Helena Paul | Satin Doll Productions | SDP 1031-1 CD
Frank Kuruc Band
Limits No Limits | Edition Musikat | EDM 023
Marco Piludu International Quartet
New York Travels | Jazz 4 Ever Records:Jazz Network | J4E 4733
Piludu Quattro
Room 626 | Jazz 4 Ever Records:Jazz Network | J4E 4721
Tim Sund & Tom Christensen Quartet
Americana | Nabel Records:Jazz Network | CD 4697
Tim Sund Trio
Trialogue | Nabel Records:Jazz Network | CD 4692

Kesber,Dim | (cl)
Albert Nicholas With The Dutch Swing College Band
Albert Nicholas & The Dutch Swing College Band | Storyville | STCD 5522
Dutch Swing College Band
Albert Nicholas & The Dutch Swing College Band | Storyville | STCD 5522

Kessel,Barney | (g,arrg-solo)
Anita O'Day And Her Combo
Pick Yourself Up | Verve | 517329-2
Anita O'Day With The Buddy Bregman Orchestra
Verve Jazz Masters 49:Anita O'Day | Verve | 527653-2
Anita O'Day With The Russ Garcia Orchestra
Verve Jazz Masters 49:Anita O'Day | Verve | 527653-2
Art Tatum Sextet
Art Tatum-The Complete Pablo Group Masterpieces | Pablo | 6 PACD 4401-2
Artie Shaw And His Orchestra
Planet Jazz:Jazz Trumpet | Planet Jazz | 2169654-2
Barney Kessel And His Orchestra
Barney Kessel Plays Carmen | Original Jazz Classics | OJC 269(C 7563)
The Jazz Giants Play Rodgers & Hart:Blue Moon | Prestige | PCD 24205-2
Barney Kessel And His Quintet
Barney Kessel Plays Carmen | Original Jazz Classics | OJC 269(C 7563)
To Swing Or Not To Swing | Original Jazz Classics | OJCCD 317-2
Barney Kessel And His Septet
To Swing Or Not To Swing | Original Jazz Classics | OJCCD 317-2
Barney Kessel Quartet
Barney Kessel's Swingin' Party At Contemporary | Original Jazz Classics | OJCCD 1066-2(S 7613)
Barney Kessel Quintet
Easy Like | Original Jazz Classics | OJCCD 153-2
Barney Kessel Plays Standards | Original Jazz Classics | OJCCD 238-2
Ben Webster With The Oscar Peterson Quartet
King Of The Tenors | Verve | 519806-2
Ultimate Ben Webster selected by James Carter | Verve | 557537-2
Benny Carter And His Orchestra
Aspects | Capitol | 852677-2
Further Definitions/Additions To Further Definotions | Impulse(MCA) | 951229-2
Benny Carter Quintet
Jazz Giant | Original Jazz Classics | OJC20 167-2(C 7555)
Billie Holiday And Her All Stars
Verve Jazz Masters 12:Billie Holiday | Verve | 519825-2
Verve Jazz Masters 20:Introducing | Verve | 519853-2
Verve Jazz Masters 47:Billie Holiday Sings Standards | Verve | 527650-2
Songs For Distingué Lovers | Verve | 539056-2
The Billie Holiday Song Book | Verve | 823246-2
Billie Holiday And Her Band
Verve Jazz Masters 47:Billie Holiday Sings Standards | Verve | 527650-2
Billie Holiday And Her Orchestra
Solitude | Verve | 519810-2
Billie Holiday With The JATP All Stars
Billie Holiday Story Vol.1:Jazz At The Philharmonic | Verve | 521642-2
The Complete Jazz At The Philharmonic On Verve 1944-1949 | Verve | 523893-2
Buddy Rich Quintet
Buddy And Sweets | Verve | 841433-2
Charlie Parker's New Stars
Charlie Parker:Now's The Time | Dreyfus Jazz Line | FDM 36724-2
Ella Fitzgerald And Barney Kessel
Ella Fitzgerald-First Lady Of Song | Verve | 517898-2
Love Songs:The Best Of The Song Books | Verve | 531762-2
Ella Fitzgerald Sings The Rodgers And Hart Song Book | Verve | 537258-2
For The Love Of Ella Fitzgerald | Verve | 841765-2
Ella Fitzgerald And Her All Stars
The Best Of The Song Books:The Ballads | Verve | 521867-2
Love Songs:The Best Of The Song Books | Verve | 531762-2
Ella Fitzgerald Sings The Duke Ellington Songbook | Verve | 559248-2
For The Love Of Ella Fitzgerald | Verve | 841765-2
Ella Fitzgerald And Her Sextet
Ella Fitzgerald-First Lady Of Song | Verve | 517898-2
The Best Of The Song Books | Verve | 519804-2
Ella Fitzgerald And The Paul Smith Quartet
The Best Of The Song Books | Verve | 519804-2
Verve Jazz Masters 6:Ella Fitzgerald | Verve | 519822-2
Verve Jazz Masters 46:Ella Fitzgerald-The Jazz Sides | Verve | 527655-2
Ella Fitzgerald With Paul Weston And His Orchestra
Love Songs:The Best Of The Song Books | Verve | 531762-2
Ella Fitzgerald Sings The Irving Berlin Song Book | Verve | 543830-2
Ella Fitzgerald With The Buddy Bregman Orchestra
Ella Fitzgerald-First Lady Of Song | Verve | 517898-2
The Best Of The Song Books:The Ballads | Verve | 521867-2
Love Songs:The Best Of The Song Books | Verve | 531762-2
Ella Fitzgerald Sings The Cole Porter Songbook | Verve | 537257-2
Ella Fitzgerald Sings The Rodgers And Hart Song Book | Verve | 537258-2
Ella Fitzgerald With The Frank DeVol Orchestra
Get Happy! | Verve | 523321-2
Ella Fitzgerald With The Nelson Riddle Orchestra
The Best Of The Song Books:The Ballads | Verve | 521867-2
Love Songs:The Best Of The Song Books | Verve | 531762-2
Ella Fitzgerald Sings The Johnny Mercer Songbook | Verve | 539057-2
Ella Fitzgerald With The Paul Smith Quartet
Ella Fitzgerald-First Lady Of Song | Verve | 517898-2
Verve Jazz Masters 20:Introducing | Verve | 519853-2
The Best Of The Song Books:The Ballads | Verve | 521867-2
Ella Fitzgerald Sings The Rodgers And Hart Song Book | Verve | 537258-2
Ella Fitzgerald With The Paul Weston Orchestra
Get Happy! | Verve | 523321-2
Ella Fitzgerald-Barney Kessel
Ella Fitzgerald Sings The Duke Ellington Songbook | Verve | 559248-2
Hampton Hawes Quartet
Four!! | Original Jazz Classics | OJCCD 165-2
Harry Sweets Edison Sextet
The Soul Of Ben Webster | Verve | 527475-2
JATP All Stars
The Drum Battle:Gene Krupa And Buddy Rich At JATP | Verve | 559810-2
The Cole Porter Songbook | Verve | 823250-2
Jesse Price And His Blues Band
Jazz Profile:Dexter Gordon | Blue Note | 823514-2
June Christy With The Pete Rugolo Orchestra
Something Cool(The Complete Mono & Stereo Versions) | Capitol | 534069-2
Kid Ory's Creole Jazz Band
This Kid's The Greatest! | Good Time Jazz | GTCD 12045-2
Lester Young With The Oscar Peterson Quartet
Jazz Gallery:Lester Young Vol.2(1946-59) | RCA | 2119541-2
Lester Young With The Oscar Peterson Trio | Verve | 521451-2
Verve Jazz Masters 30:Lester Young | Verve | 521859-2
Lionel Hampton All Stars
Lionel Hampton:Flying Home | Dreyfus Jazz Line | FDM 36735-2
Lucky Thompson And His Lucky Seven
Planet Jazz:Bebop | RCA | 2169650-2
Nat King Cole With The Billy May Orchestra
Nat King Cole:For Sentimental Reasons | Dreyfus Jazz Line | FDM 36740-2
Norman Granz Jam Session
Verve Jazz Masters 35:Johnny Hodges | Verve | 521857-2
Charlie Parker:The Best Of The Verve Years | Verve | 527815-2
Talkin' Bird | Verve | 559859-2
Bird: The Complete Charlie Parker On Verve | Verve | 837141-2
Oscar Peterson Quartet
Verve Jazz Masters 37:Oscar Peterson Plays Broadway | Verve | 516893-2
Oscar Peterson Trio
Gitanes Jazz 'Round Midnight: Oscar Peterson | Verve | 511036-2 PMS
Verve Jazz Masters 16:Oscar Peterson | Verve | 516320-2
Verve Jazz Masters 37:Oscar Peterson Plays Broadway | Verve | 516893-2
Oscar Peterson:The Gershwin Songbooks | Verve | 529698-2
The Song Is You-The Best Of The Verve Songbooks | Verve | 531558-2
Oscar Peterson Plays The Duke Ellington Song Book | Verve | 559785-2
Paul Desmond Quartet With The Bill Bates Singers
Desmond | Original Jazz Classics | OJCCD 712-2(F 3235/8082)
Red Norvo Septet
Jazz Profile:Dexter Gordon | Blue Note | 823514-2
Red Norvo Sextet
Music To Listen To Red Norvo By | Original Jazz Classics | OJCCD 1015-2(C 7534)
Roy Eldridge Quintet
The Complete Verve Roy Eldridge Studio Sessions | Verve | 9861278
Sarah Vaughan Plus Two
Ballads | Roulette | 537561-2
Sarah Vaughan With Barney Kessel And Joe Comfort
Jazz Profile | Blue Note | 823517-2
Sonny Rollins & The Contemporary Leaders
Sonny Rollins & The Contemporary Leaders | Original Jazz Classics | OJCCD 340-2
Sonny Rollins And The Contemporary Leaders
Sonny Rollins-The Freelance Years:The Complete Riverside & Contemporary Recordings | Riverside | 5 RCD 4427-2
T-Bone Walker And His Band
Atlantic Jazz: Kansas City | Atlantic | 7567-81701-2
The Poll Winners
The Poll Winners Ride Again | Original Jazz Classics | OJC 607(C 7556)
Poll Winners Three | Original Jazz Classics | OJCCD 692-2(C 7576)
Exploring The Scene | Original Jazz Classics | OJCCD 969-2(C 7581)
The Jazz Giants Play Harry Warren:Lullaby Of Broadway | Prestige | PCD 24204-2
Van Alexander Orchestra
Home Of Happy Feet/Swing! Staged For Sound! | Capitol | 535211-2
Woody Herman And His Sextet
Songs For Hip Lovers | Verve | 559872-2
Zoot Sims Quintet
Art 'N' Zoot | Pablo | 2310957-2

Kessler,Abe | (cello)
Wes Montgomery Quartet With The Claus Ogerman Orchestra
Tequila | Verve | 547769-2
Wes Montgomery Quintet With The Claus Ogerman Orchestra
The Antonio Carlos Jobim Songbook | Verve | 525472-2
Talkin' Jazz:Roots Of Acid Jazz | Verve | 529580-2
Tequila | Verve | 547769-2
Wes Montgomery Trio With The Claus Ogerman Orchestra
Tequila | Verve | 547769-2
Wes Montgomery With The Claus Ogerman Orchestra
Verve Jazz Masters 14:Wes Montgomery | Verve | 519826-2

Kessler,Jerome | (cello)
Charlie Haden Quartet West With Strings
The Art Of The Song | Verve | 547403-2
Ella Fitzgerald With Orchestra
The Best Is Yet To Come | Original Jazz Classics | OJCCD 889-2(2312138)

Kessler,Kent | (b,b-g,didgeridoo,tb,tpg)
Hal Russell NRG Ensemble
The Finnish/Swiss Tour | ECM | 1455
The Hal Russell Story | ECM | 1498

Kessler,Maz | (g,keyboards)
The Brecker Brothers
Out Of The Loop | GRP | GRP 97842

Kessler,Thomas | (p,keyboards,synth,perc,auto-harp)
Thomas Kessler & Group
Thomas Kessler & Group | Laika Records | LK 190-015
Thomas Kessler Group
On Earth | Laika Records | 8695069
Untitled | Laika Records | LK 92-027
Ulli Bögershausen
Best Of Ulli Bögershausen | Laika Records | LK 93-045

Kettel,Gary | (perc)
Barbara Thompson's Paraphernalia
Barbara Thompson's Special Edition | VeraBra Records | CDVBR 2017-2

Ketterl,Apri | (bel-b)
Uli Binetsch's Own Bone
Boone Up Blues | Rockwerk Records | CD 011001

Ketzer,Willy | (drperc)
Passport
Ataraxia | Atlantic | 2292-42148-2
Garden Of Eden | Atlantic | 2292-44147-2
Paul Kuhn Trio
Play It Again Paul | IN+OUT Records | 77040-2
Paul Kuhn Trio With Greetje Kauffeld
Play It Again Paul | IN+OUT Records | 77040-2
Paul Kuhn Trio With Greetje Kauffeld And Jean 'Toots' Thielemans
Play It Again Paul | IN+OUT Records | 77040-2
Paul Kuhn Trio With Jean 'Toots' Thielemans
Play It Again Paul | IN+OUT Records | 77040-2

Keul,Michael | (drperc)
Al Porcino Big Band
Al Porcino Big Band Live! | Organic Music | ORGM 9717
Ed Kröger Quartet
What's New | Laika Records | 35101172
Ed Kröger Quartet plus Guests
Movin' On | Laika Records | 35101332
Fisherman's Break
Fisherman's Break | Edition Collage | EC 450-2
Grooveyard Meets Houston Person
Basic Instinct | Organic Music | ORGM 9701
Grooveyard Meets Red Holloway
Basic Instinct | Organic Music | ORGM 9701
Grooveyard Meets Roman Schwaller
Basic Instinct | Organic Music | ORGM 9701
Helmut Nieberle-Helmut Kagerer Quartet
Flashes | Jardis Records | JRCD 20031
Matthias Bätzel Trio
Green Dumplings | JHM Records | JHM 3618
Monk's Mood | JHM Records | JHM 3628
Matthias Bätzel-Michael Keul
Green Dumplings | JHM Records | JHM 3618
Red Holloway With The Matthias Bätzel Trio
A Night Of Blues & Ballads | JHM Records | JHM 3614
Thilo Kreitmeier & Group
Soul Call | Organic Music | ORGM 9711
Thilo Kreitmeier Quintet
Mo' Better Blues | Organic Music | ORGM 9706

Keuser,Josef 'Jupp' | (tp)
Harald Banter Ensemble
Deutsches Jazz Fesival 1954/1955 | Bear Family Records | BCD 15430

Kevin | (org)
Albert King Blues Band
The Lost Session | Stax | SCD 8534-2

Keyes,Joe | (tp)
Benny Moten's Kansas City Orchestra
Planet Jazz:Ben Webster | RCA | 2165368-2
Planet Jazz:Jimmy Rushing | RCA | 2165371-2
Planet Jazz:Swing | Planet Jazz | 2169651-2
Jazz:The Essential Collection Vol.3 | IN+OUT Records | 78013-2
Count Basie And His Orchestra
Jazz:The Essential Collection Vol.3 | IN+OUT Records | 78013-2

Keys,Calvin | (g)
Ahmad Jamal Septet
Live In Paris 1996 | Dreyfus Jazz Line | FDM 37020-2

Keyserling,Thomas | (as,claves,fl,alto-fl,perc,ss,ts)
Gunter Hampel All Stars
Jubilation | Birth | 0038
Gunter Hampel And His Galaxie Dream Band
Journey To The Song Within | Birth | 0017
Enfant Terrible | Birth | 0025
All Is Real | Birth | 0028
All The Things You Could Be If Charles Mingus Was Your Daddy | Birth | CD 031
Celestial Glory-Live At The Knitting Factory New York | Birth | CD 040
Gunter Hampel New York Orchestra
Fresh Heat-Live At Sweet Basil | Birth | CD 039

Khaiat,Nabil | (frame-drperc)
Rabih Abou-Khalil Group
Al-Jadida | Enja | ENJ-6090 2
Blue Camel | Enja | ENJ-7053 2
Tarab | Enja | ENJ-7083 2
The Sultan's Picnic | Enja | ENJ-8078 2
Arabian Waltz | Enja | ENJ-9059 2
Odd Times | Enja | ENJ-9330 2
Yara | Enja | ENJ-9360 2
The Cactus Of Knowledge | Enja | ENJ-9401 2

Khalfa,Dahmane | (carcabas,saguetes,tbel,derbouka)
Renaud Garcia-Fons
Navigatore | Enja | ENJ-9418 2
Renaud Garcia-Fons Group
Navigatore | Enja | ENJ-9418 2

Khalfa,Rabah | (bendir,carcabas,derbouka,tar)
Renaud Garcia-Fons
Navigatore | Enja | ENJ-9418 2
Renaud Garcia-Fons Group
Oriental Bass | Enja | ENJ-9334 2
Navigatore | Enja | ENJ-9418 2

Khalid,Drashear | (dr)
Mary Lou Williams Trio
May Lou Williams Trio At Rick's Cafe Americain,Chicago,Ill. | Storyville | STCD 8285

Khalsa,Nirankar | (drperc)
José Luis Gutiérrez Trio
Núcleo | Fresh Sound Records | FSNT 039 CD

Khan,Ali Akbar | (sarod)
John Handy-Ali Akbar Khan Group
Two Originals:Karuna Supreme/Rainbow | MPS | 519195-2
Rainbow
Two Originals:Karuna Supreme/Rainbow | MPS | 519195-2

Khan,Chaka | (voc)
Fourplay
Between The Sheets | Warner | 9362-45340-2
Joe Henderson Group
Porgy And Bess | Verve | 539048-2
Lenny White Group
Present Tense | Hip Bop | HIBD 8004
Hot Jazz Bisquits | Hip Bop | HIBD 8801

Khan,Eddie | (b)
Eric Dolphy Quartet
The Illinois Concert | Blue Note | 499826-2
Eric Dolphy Quartet With The University Of Illinois Big Band
The Illinois Concert | Blue Note | 499826-2
Eric Dolphy Quartet With The University Of Illinois Brass Ensemble
The Illinois Concert | Blue Note | 499826-2
Joe Henderson Quintet
Our Thing | Blue Note | 525647-2
The Blue Note Years-The Best Of Joe Henderson | Blue Note | 795627-2
Max Roach Quartet
Speak, Brother, Speak | Original Jazz Classics | OJCCD 646-2(F 86007)

Khan,Ishad Hussain | (tabla)
European Jazz Ensemble & The Khan Family feat. Joachim Kühn
European Jazz Ensemble Meets The Khan Family | M.A Music | A 807-2

Khan,Nishat | (sitarvoice)
John McLaughlin Group
The Promise | Verve | 529828-2

Khan,Shujaat Husain | (sitarvoc)
Kayhan Kalhor Trio
The Rain | ECM | 1840(066627-2)

Khan,Steve | (el-g,g,12-string-g,arr)
Los Jovenes Flamencos With The WDR Big Band And Guests
Jazzpana | ACT | 9212-2
Steps Ahead
N.Y.C. | Intuition Records | INT 3007-2
Steve Khan Group
Jazzrock-Anthology Vol.3:Fusion | Zounds | CD 27100555
Khan,Ustad Munir | (sarangi)
European Jazz Ensemble & The Khan Family feat. Joachim Kühn
European Jazz Ensemble Meets The Khan Family | M.A Music | A 807-2
Khan,Ustad Zamir Ahmed | (sitartablas)
Khann,Aida | (voc)
Nguyen Le Trio With Guests
Purple:Celebrating Jimi Hendrix | ACT | 9410-2
Kholossy,Mohamed | (saggat)
Koch-Schütz-Studer & El Nil Troop
Heavy Cairo Trafic | Intuition Records | INT 3175-2
Khumalo,Thulise | (voc)
Chico Freeman And Brainstorm
Threshold | IN+OUT Records | 7022-2
Kibble,Mark | (voc)
Take 6
Goldmine | Reprise | 7599-25670-2
So Much To Say | Reprise | 7599-25892-2
He Is Christmas | Reprise | 7599-26665-2
Take 6 With The Yellow Jackets
He Is Christmas | Reprise | 7599-26665-2
Kibwe,Talib | (alto-cl,as,alto-fl,fl,cl,ss,tscond)
Randy Weston African Rhythm
Khepera | Verve | 557821-2
Randy Weston African Rhythm Quintet and The Gnawa Master Musicians of Marocco
Spirit! The Power Of Music | Verve | 543256-2
Kidjo,Angelique | (dance,voice,percvoc)
Cassandra Wilson Group
Traveling Miles | Blue Note | 854123-2
Pili-Pili
Jakko | JA & RO | JARO 4131-2
Be In Two Minds | JA & RO | JARO 4134-2
Pili-Pili Live 88 | JA & RO | JARO 4139-2
Pili-Pili | JA & RO | JARO 4141-2
Hotel Babo | JA & RO | JARO 4147-2
Hoomba-Hoomba | JA & RO | JARO 4192-2
Kidon,Klaudio | (voc)
Marilyn Mazur With Ars Nova And The Copenhagen Art Ensemble
Jordsange | dacapo | DCCD 9454
Kieber,Paul | (b)
Lisa Bassenge Trio
Going Home | Minor Music | 801091
Kiefer,Ed | (tb)
Woody Herman And His Orchestra
The Legends Of Swing | Laserlight | 24659
Woody Herman:Four Brother | Dreyfus Jazz Line | FDM 36722-2
Louis Armstrong-Jack Teagarden-Woody Herman:Midnights At V-Disc | Jazz Unlimited | JUCD 2048
Old Gold Rehearsals 1944 | Jazz Unlimited | JUCD 2079
Woody Herman And The Herd
Woody Herman (And The Herd) At Carnegie Hall | Verve | 559833-2
Kiefer,Rick | (tpfl-h)
Bob Brookmeyer Group With The WDR Big Band
Electricity | ACT | 9219-2
Don Menza Septet
Morning Song | MPS | 9811446
Gianlugi Trovesi Quartet With The WDR Big Band
Dedalo | Enja | ENJ-9419 2
Jens Winther And The WDR Big Band
The Escape | dacapo | DCCD 9437
Kevin Mahogany With The WDR Big Band And Guests
Pussy Cat Dues:The Music Of Charles Mingus | Enja | ENJ-9316 2
Los Jovenes Flamencos With The WDR Big Band And Guests
Jazzpana | ACT | 9212-2
Vince Mendoza With The WDR Big Band And Guests
Sketches | ACT | 9215-2
Kiehn,Charles 'Coco' | (ts)
Willie Lewis And His Entertainers
Americans Swinging In Paris:Benny Carter | EMI Records | 539647-2
Kiek,Llew | (baglama,bouzouki,g,el-gvoc)
Mara!
Ruino Vino | Laika Records | 35100792
Kiek,Mara | (tapanvoc)
Kienastl,Max | (v)
Helmut Nieberle & Cordes Sauvages
Jazz Guitar Highlights 1 | Jardis Records | JRCD 20141
Salut To Django | Jardis Records | JRCD 9926
Kienemann,Joe | (pp-solo)
Joe Kienemann
Liedgut:Amsel,Drossel,Swing & Funk | yvp music | CD 3095
Joe Kienemann Trio
Liedgut:Amsel,Drossel,Swing & Funk | yvp music | CD 3095
Kienzle.Annette | (voc)
Acoustic Affaire
Mira | Jazz 'n' Arts Records | JNA 1303
Kiesewetter,Knut | (tb,voctp)
Knut Kiesewetter With The Dieter Reith Orchestra
Reith On! | MPS | 557423-2
Kieslich,Klaus | (g)
Jameco
Conversations | Trick Music | TM 9202 CD
Kiessling,Heinz | (p)
Helmut Zacharias mit dem Orchester Frank Folken
Ich Habe Rhythmus | Bear Family Records | BCD 15642 AH
Kieszek,Adam | (b)
Terje Rypdal Quartet With The Bergen Chamber Ensemble
Lux Aeterna | ECM | 1818(017070-2)
Kievman,Louis | (viola)
Ella Fitzgerald With The Billy May Orchestra
The Best Of The Song Books:The Ballads | Verve | 521867-2
Ella Fitzgerald Sings The Harold Arlen Song Book | Verve | 589108-2
Gene Harris And The Three Sounds
Deep Blue-The United States Of Mind | Blue Note | 521152-2
Peggy Lee With The Benny Goodman Orchestra
Peggy Lee & Benny Goodman:The Complete Recordings 1941-1947 | CBS | C2K 65686
Kikoski,David 'Dave' | (org,p,el-psynth)
Al Foster Quartet
Brandyn | Laika Records | 35100832
Bruce Cox Quartet With Guests
Stick To It | Minor Music | 801055
Caecilie Norby With Band
My Corner Of The Sky | Blue Note | 853422-2
Charles Mingus Orchestra
Tonight At Noon...Three Or Four Shades Of Love | Dreyfus Jazz Line | FDM 36633-2
Ingrid Jensen Quintet
Higher Grounds | Enja | ENJ-9353 2
Mingus Big Band
Tonight At Noon...Three Or Four Shades Of Love | Dreyfus Jazz Line | FDM 36633-2
Roy Haynes Quintet
Birds Of A Feather:A Tribute To Charlie Parker | Dreyfus Jazz Line | FDM 36625-2
Kikuchi,Masabumi | (keyboards,p,el-psynth)
Johnny Hartman With The Masahiko Kikuchi Trio
Blue Velvet: Crooners, Swooners And Velvet Vocals | Blue Note | 521153-2
Masabumi Kikuchi Trio
Tethered Moon-First Meeting | Winter&Winter | 910016-2
Paul Motian Trio With Chris Potter And Larry Grenadier
Paul Motian Trio 2000 + One | Winter&Winter | 910032-2
Tethered Moon
Chansons D'Edith Piaf | Winter&Winter | 910048-2
Kilada,Nasser | (voc)
Rodach
Himmel Und Hölle-Heaven And Hell | Traumton Records | 4434-2
Kilbert,Porter | (as)
Coleman Hawkins All Star Octet
Milt Jackson Birthday Celebration | Fantasy | FANCD 6079-2
Coleman Hawkins All Stars
The J.J.Johnson Memorial Album | Prestige | PRCD 11025-2
Kilgare,Robbie | (g,keyboards)
The Brecker Brothers
Out Of The Loop | GRP | GRP 97842
Kilgore,Robby | (keyboard-programming,keyboards,p)
Return Of The Brecker Brothers | GRP | GRP 96842
Killian,Al | (tp)
Count Basie And His Orchestra
Jazz Collection:Count Basie | Laserlight | 24368
Jazz:The Essential Collection Vol.3 | IN+OUT Records | 78013-2
Duke Ellington And His Orchestra
Carnegie Hall Concert December 1947 | Prestige | 2PCD 24075-2
JATP All Stars
Jazz Gallery:Lester Young Vol.2(1946-59) | RCA | 2119541-2
The Complete Jazz At The Philharmonic On Verve 1944-1949 | Verve | 523893-2
Charlie Parker:The Best Of The Verve Years | Verve | 527815-2
Jazz At The Philharmonic:Best Of The 1940's Concerts | Verve | 557534-2
Bird: The Complete Charlie Parker On Verve | Verve | 837141-2
Lionel Hampton And His Orchestra
Lionel Hampton:Flying Home | Dreyfus Jazz Line | FDM 36735-2
Killian,Lawrence | (congas,balafon,talking-dr,perro)
Charles Earland Septet
Charlie's Greatest Hits | Prestige | PCD 24250-2
Dick Griffin Septet
The Eighth Wonder & More | Konnex Records | KCD 5059
Pharoah Sanders Group
Black Unity | Impulse(MCA) | 951219-2
Pucho & His Latin Soul Brothers
Jazzin' With The Soul Brothers | Fantasy | FANCD 6086-2
Rip A Dip | Milestone | MCD 9247-2
Killinger,Johannes | (bel-b)
All That Jazz & Helena Paul
All That Jazz & Helena Paul | Satin Doll Productions | SDP 1031-1 CD
Thomas Horstmann-Martin Wiedmann Group
Decade | Factory Outlet Records | WO 95001
Kilpatrick Jr.,Jesse | (dr)
Charles Earland Sextet
Charlie's Greatest Hits | Prestige | PCD 24250-2
Kilson,Billy | (dr)
Bop City
Hot Jazz Bisquits | Hip Bop | HIBD 8801
Dave Holland Big Band
What Goes Around | ECM | 1777(014002-2)
Dave Holland Quintet
Point Of View | ECM | 1663(557020-2)
Prime Directive | ECM | 1698(547950-2)
Not For Nothin' | ECM | 1758(014004-2)
Extended Play | ECM | 1864/65(038505-2)
Dianne Reeves With Band
I Remember | Blue Note | 790264-2
Kevin Mahogany With The Bob James Trio
My Romance | Warner | 9362-47025-2
Kevin Mahogany With The Bob James Trio And Kirk Whalum
My Romance | Warner | 9362-47025-2
Kevin Mahogany With The Bob James Trio And Michael Brecker
My Romance | Warner | 9362-47025-2
Kevin Mahogany With The Bob James Trio, Kirk Whalum And Strings
My Romance | Warner | 9362-47025-2
Kim,Ann | (cello)
Absolute Ensemble
African Symphony | Enja | ENJ-9410 2
Melissa Walker And Her Band
I Saw The Sky | Enja | ENJ-9409 2
Paquito D'Rivera Group With The Absolute Ensemble
Habanera | Enja | ENJ-9395 2
Kim,Helen | (v)
Steve Kuhn With Strings
Promises Kept | ECM | 1815(0675222)
Kimball,Ward | (tb,firebell,gongs,sirentambourine)
Firehouse Five Plus Two
Dixieland Favorites | Good Time Jazz | FCD 60-008
Crashes A Party | Good Time Jazz | GTCD 10038-2
Goes To A Fire | Good Time Jazz | GTCD 10052-2
Goes South | Good Time Jazz | GTCD 12018-2
Kimbrough,Frank | (p)
Michael Blake Group
Drift | Intuition Records | INT 3212-2
Kime,Warren | (tp)
Buddy Childers Big Band
Just Buddy's | Candid | CCD 79761
Kimpel,Larry | (bp)
Bobby Lyle Group
The Journey | Atlantic | 7667-02138-2
Larry Carlton Group
The Gift | GRP | GRP 98542
Kincaide,Dean | (arr,as,bs,sax,tbts)
Bob Crosby And His Orchestra
Swing Legens:Bob Crosby | Nimbus Records | NI 2011
Lee Wiley With The Dean Kincaide Dixieland Band
Planet Jazz:Female Jazz Vocalists | Planet Jazz | 2169656-2
Tommy Dorsey And His Orchestra
Planet Jazz:Frank Sinatra & Tommy Dorsey | Planet Jazz | 2152067-2
Kinch,Don | (b,tubatp)
Firehouse Five Plus Two
Dixieland Favorites | Good Time Jazz | FCD 60-008
Crashes A Party | Good Time Jazz | GTCD 10038-2
Goes To A Fire | Good Time Jazz | GTCD 10052-2
Kinder,Rhiannon | (voc)
Mike Westbrook Brass Band
Glad Day:Settings Of William Blake | Enja | ENJ-9376 2
Kindred,Bob | (clts)
Ian Shaw With Band
Soho Stories | Milestone | MCD 9316-2
Jimmy Scott With Band
Over The Rainbow | Milestone | MCD 9314-2
But Beautiful | Milestone | MCD 9321-2
Moon Glow | Milestone | MCD 9332-2
King Beats |
Inge Brandenburg & Otto 'Fats' Ortwein und die King Beats
Why Don't You Take All Of Me | Bear Family Records | BCD 15614 AH
King,Al | (b,percts)
Bill Ramsey & His Trio
Caldonia And More... | Bear Family Records | BCD 16151 AH
Tom Browne Groups
Mo' Jamaica Funk | Hip Bop | HIBD 8002
King,Albert | (b,gvoc)
Albert King Blues Band
Lovejoy | Stax | SCD 8517-2(STS 2040)
The Lost Session | Stax | SCD 8534-2
Wednesday Night In San Francisco | Stax | SCD 8556-2
Albert King With The Willie Dixon Band
Windy City Blues | Stax | SCD 8612-2
Oscar Peterson Trio
Planet Music:Oscar Peterson | RCA | 2165365-2
This Is Oscar Peterson | RCA | 2663990-2
King,Alphonso | (tb)
Jimmy Lunceford And His Orchestra
The Legends Of Swing | Laserlight | 24659
King,B.B. | (gvoc)
B.B.King And His Band
Live At San Quentin | MCA | MCD 06103
B.B.King Blues Band
Classic Blues | Zounds | CD 2700048
Diane Schuur Quintet With B.B.King
The Best Of Diane Schuur | GRP | GRP 98882
GRP All-Star Big Band
All Blues | GRP | GRP 98002
Jimmy Smith All Stars
Jimmy Smith:Dot Com Blues | Blue Thumb | 543978-2
King,Bertie | (as,clts)
Benny Carter And His Orchestra
Django Reinhardt All Star Sessions | Capitol | 531577-2
Americans Swinging In Paris:Benny Carter | EMI Records | 539647-2
Chris Barber's Jazz Band
The Best Of Dixieland-Live in 1954/55 | London | 820878-2
Vic Lewis And His Band
Vic Lewis:The Golden Years | Candid | CCD 79754
King,Bobby | (voc)
Hans Theessink Group
Call Me | Minor Music | 801022
King,Dave | (b,dr,el-b,gb-g)
Akili
Akili | M.A Music | NU 730-2
Bernard Purdie's Soul To Jazz
Bernard Purdie's Soul To Jazz | ACT | 9242-2
Bill Carrothers Quartet
The Electric Bill | Dreyfus Jazz Line | FDM 36631-2
Eddie Harris Group With The WDR Big Band
Eddie Harris-The Last Concert | ACT | 9249-2
The Bad Plus
These Are The Vistas | CBS | 510666-2
King,David | (drperc)
The Bad Plus | Fresh Sound Records | FSNT 107 CD
King,Fred | (concert-bells,cowbell,tympanivib)
M'Boom
To The Max! | Enja | ENJ-7021 22
King,Gary | (bel-b)
Bob James And His Orchestra
Jazzrock-Anthology Vol.3:Fusion | Zounds | CD 27100555
Nina Simone And Orchestra
Baltimore | Epic | 476906-2
King,Geoff | (b)
Graham Stewart And His New Orleans Band
The Golden Years Of Revival Jazz,Vol.12 | Storyville | STCD 5517
The Golden Years Of Revival Jazz,Vol.14 | Storyville | STCD 5519
King,Gerryck | (dr)
Rickey Woodard Quartet
California Cooking No.2 | Candid | CCD 79762
King,Howard | (drperc)
Gary Bartz Ntu Troop
Jazzin' Vol.2: The Music Of Stevie Wonder | Fantasy | FANCD 6088-2
King,Jonny | (p)
Johnny King Quintet
Notes From The Underground | Enja | ENJ-9067 2
Johnny King Septet
The Meltdown | Enja | ENJ-9329 2
King,Lee | (g)
Albert King Blues Band
The Lost Session | Stax | SCD 8534-2
King,Nancy | (vocwhinnies)
Oregon
45th Parallel | VeraBra Records | CDVBR 2048-2
King,Pete | (arr,cond,as,cl,tsvoc)
Julie London With Pete King And His Orchestra
About The Blues/London By Night | Capitol | 535208-2
King,Peter | (asss)
Doug Sides Ensemble
Sumblo | Laika Records | 35100882
King,Ron | (tpfl-h)
Buddy Childers Big Band
It's What Happening Now! | Candid | CCD 79749
Willie Bobo Group
Jazzrock-Anthology Vol.3:Fusion | Zounds | CD 27100555
King,Stan | (dr,kazoo,vocvib)
Adrian Rollini And His Orchestra
Jazz:The Essential Collection Vol.3 | IN+OUT Records | 78013-2
Jack Teagarden And His Orchestra
Jazz:The Essential Collection Vol.3 | IN+OUT Records | 78013-2
Louis Armstrong And His Orchestra
Louis Armstrong:Swing That Music | Laserlight | 36056
King,Teddi | (voc)
George Shearing Quintet
Verve Jazz Masters 57:George Shearing | Verve | 529900-2
King,Vernon | (b)
Lionel Hampton And His Orchestra
Lionel Hampton:Flying Home | Dreyfus Jazz Line | FDM 36735-2
King,Walter | (dr,voc,saxld)
B.B.King And His Band
Live At San Quentin | MCA | MCD 06103
Kingue,J.C. Doo | (gvoc)
Dook Joint
Who's Been Talkin'... | Organic Music | ORGM 9728
Ron Ringwood's Crosscut Bluesband
Earth Tones | Organic Music | ORGM 9722
Kinnamon,Larry | (p)
Harry James And His Orchestra
Trumpet Blues:The Best Of Harry James | Capitol | 521224-2
Kinney Nina Mae | (voc)
Garland Wilson
JazzIn Paris:Harlem Piano In Montmartre | EmArCy | 018447-2
Kinney,Michelle | (cello)
Steve Tibbetts Group
Big Map Idea | ECM | 1380
Kinsey,Gene | (asreeds)
Artie Shaw And His Orchestra
Planet Jazz:Male Jazz Vocalists | Planet Jazz | 2169657-2
Charlie Barnet And His Orchestra
Planet Jazz:Big Bands | Planet Jazz | 2169649-2
Planet Jazz:Swing | Planet Jazz | 2169651-2
Kinsey,Scott | (keyboards,programmingp)
Kurt Rosenwinkel Quintet
The Enemies Of Energy | Verve | 543042-2
Tim Hagans With Norrbotten Big Band
Future Miles | ACT | 9235-2
Kinzler,Jule | (fl)
Ella Fitzgerald With The Buddy Bregman Orchestra
Ella Fitzgerald Sings The Rodgers And Hart Song Book | Verve | 537258-2
Kirby,Freya | (v)
Ensemble Modern
Ensemble Modern-Fred Frith:Traffic Continues | Winter&Winter | 910044-2
Kirby,John | (b,ldtuba)
Ben Webster Sextet
Verve Jazz Masters 43:Ben Webster | Verve | 525431-2
Verve Jazz Masters 52:Maynard Ferguson | Verve | 529905-2
Billie Holiday With Teddy Wilson And His Orchestra
Billie's Love Songs | Nimbus Records | NI 2000
Chocolate Dandies
Jazz:The Essential Collection Vol.3 | IN+OUT Records | 78013-2
Coleman Hawkins' All-American Four
Verve Jazz Masters 43:Coleman Hawkins | Verve | 521856-2
Coleman Hawkins And His Orchestra
Jazz:The Essential Collection Vol.3 | IN+OUT Records | 78013-2
Coleman Hawkins And His Rhythm
Jazz:The Essential Collection Vol.3 | IN+OUT Records | 78013-2

Coleman Hawkins Quartet
Ultimate Coleman Hawkins selected by Sonny Rollins | Verve | 557538-2
Connie's Inn Orchestra
Planet Jazz:Coleman Hawkins | Planet Jazz | 2152055-2
Fletcher Henderson And His Orchestra
Jazz:The Essential Collection Vol.1 | IN+OUT Records | 78011-2
Jazz:The Essential Collection Vol.3 | IN+OUT Records | 78013-2
John Kirby Band
The Small Black Groups | Storyville | 4960523
Lionel Hampton And His Orchestra
Planet Jazz:Swing | Planet Jazz | 2169651-2
Planet Jazz:Jazz Saxophone | Planet Jazz | 2169653-2
Planet Jazz:Male Jazz Vocalists | Planet Jazz | 2169657-2
Mezz Mezzrow And His Orchestra
Planet Jazz:Bud Freeman | Planet Jazz | 2161240-2
Sarah Vaughan With John Kirby And His Orchestra
Sarah Vaughan Birthday Celebration | Fantasy | FANCD 6090-2
Sarah Vaughan:Lover Man | Dreyfus Jazz Line | FDM 36739-2
Teddy Wilson And His All Stars
Jazz:The Essential Collection Vol.3 | IN+OUT Records | 78013-2
Teddy Wilson And His Orchestra
Jazz:The Essential Collection Vol.3 | IN+OUT Records | 78013-2
The Capitol Jazzmen
The Hollywood Session:The Capitol Jazzmen | Jazz Unlimited | JUCD 2044

Kirby,Steve | (b)
Cyrus Chestnut Sextet
Earth Stories | Atlantic | 7567-82876-2
Cyrus Chestnut Trio
Earth Stories | Atlantic | 7567-82876-2
James Carter Group
Chasin' The Gypsy | Atlantic | 7567-83304-2

Kirchenchor St. Margareta |
Matthias Petzold Group With Choir
Psalmen und Lobgesänge für Chor und Jazz-Ensemble | Indigo-Records | 1002 CD

Kirchgässner,Helmut | (p)
Bernd Konrad With Erwin Lehn und sein Südfunk Orchester Stuttgart
Wen Die Götter Lieben | Creative Works Records | CW CD 1010-1

Kirchner,Frank | (sax,ss,tsbs)
Frank Kirchner Group
Frank Kirchner | Laika Records | LK 93-036
Ulli Bögershausen
Best Of Ulli Bögershausen | Laika Records | LK 93-045

Kirk,Rahsaan Roland | (cl,org,narration,ts,kirkbam)
Charles Mingus Quintet With Roland Kirk
Tonight At Noon | Atlantic | 7567-80793-2
Charles Mingus-Passion Of A Man:The Complete Atlantic Recordings 1956-1961 | Atlantic | 8122-72871-2
The Very Best Of Charles Mingus | Rhino | 8122-79988-2
Eddie Baccus Quartet
Rahsaan/The Complete Mercury Recordings Of Roland Kirk | Mercury | 846630-2
Quincy Jones And His Orchestra
Talkin' Verve-Roots Of Acid Jazz:Roland Kirk | Verve | 533101-2
Big Band Bossa Nova | Verve | 557913-2
Rahsaan/The Complete Mercury Recordings Of Roland Kirk | Mercury | 846630-2
Quincy Jones Big Band
Rahsaan/The Complete Mercury Recordings Of Roland Kirk | Mercury | 846630-2
Rahsaan Roland Kirk And His Orchestra
Blacknuss | Rhino | 8122-71408-2
Rahsaan Roland Kirk Quartet
Rhino Presents The Atlantic Jazz Gallery | Atlantic | 8122-71257-2
Rahsaan Roland Kirk Sextet
Atlantic Saxophones | Rhino | 8122-71256-2
Volunteered Slavery | Rhino | 8122-71407-2
Blacknuss | Rhino | 8122-71408-2
Roland Kirk
Rahsaan/The Complete Mercury Recordings Of Roland Kirk | Mercury | 846630-2
Roland Kirk All Stars
Rahsaan/The Complete Mercury Recordings Of Roland Kirk | Mercury | 846630-2
Roland Kirk And His Orchestra
Talkin' Verve-Roots Of Acid Jazz:Roland Kirk | Verve | 533101-2
Rahsaan/The Complete Mercury Recordings Of Roland Kirk | Mercury | 846630-2
Roland Kirk Group
I Talk With The Spirits | Verve | 558076-2
Roland Kirk Quartet
Verve Jazz Masters Vol.60:The Collection | Verve | 529866-2
Talkin' Verve-Roots Of Acid Jazz:Roland Kirk | Verve | 533101-2
Domino | Verve | 543833-2
The Inflated Tear | Atlantic | 7567-90045-2
The Inflated Tear | Atlantic | 8122-75207-2
Rahsaan/The Complete Mercury Recordings Of Roland Kirk | Mercury | 846630-2
Roland Kirk Quartet With Sonny Boy Williamson
Talkin' Verve-Roots Of Acid Jazz:Roland Kirk | Verve | 533101-2
Roland Kirk Quintet
The Inflated Tear | Atlantic | 7567-90045-2
The Inflated Tear | Atlantic | 8122-75207-2
Rahsaan/The Complete Mercury Recordings Of Roland Kirk | Mercury | 846630-2
Roland Kirk Sextet
Talkin' Verve-Roots Of Acid Jazz:Roland Kirk | Verve | 533101-2
Roland Kirk With The Benny Golson Orchestra
Rahsaan/The Complete Mercury Recordings Of Roland Kirk | Mercury | 846630-2
Roland Kirk With The Jack McDuff Trio
Kirk's Work | Original Jazz Classics | OJC20 459-2(P 7210)
Roy Haynes Quartet
Out Of The Afternoon | Impulse(MCA) | 951180-2
Tubby Hayes And The All Stars
Rahsaan/The Complete Mercury Recordings Of Roland Kirk | Mercury | 846630-2

Kirk,Wilbert | (dr,harmtambourine)
Al Sears And His Orchestra
Sear-iously | Bear Family Records | BCD 15668 AH
Sidney Bechet With Noble Sissle's Swingsters
Sidney Bechet:Summertime | Dreyfus Jazz Line | FDM 36712-2
Wilbur DeParis And His New New Orleans Band
Atlantic Jazz: New Orleans | Atlantic | 7567-81700-2

Kirkland,Dale | (tb)
Woody Herman And His Orchestra
Jazzin' Vol.2: The Music Of Stevie Wonder | Fantasy | FANCD 6088-2
King Cobra | Original Jazz Classics | OJCCD 1068-2(F 9499)
Woody Herman Herd At Montreux | Original Jazz Classics | OJCCD 991-2(F 9470)
Woody Herman And The New Thundering Herd
Planet Jazz:Big Bands | Planet Jazz | 2169649-2
Woody Herman's Thundering Herd
Planet Jazz:Jazz Saxophone | Planet Jazz | 2169653-2

Kirkland,Eddie | (b-g,g,harm,vocorg)
John Lee Hooker
John Lee Hooker Plays And Sings The Blues | Chess | MCD 09199
House Of The Blues | Chess | MCD 09258

Kirkland,Jesse | (voc)
Quincy Jones And His Orchestra
Verve Jazz Masters Vol.59:Toots Thielemans | Verve | 535271-2

Kirkland,Kenny | (el-p,synth,keyboards,pclavinet)
Arturo Sandoval Quartet
I Remember Clifford | GRP | GRP 96682
Arturo Sandoval Quintet
I Remember Clifford | GRP | GRP 96682
Branford Marsalis Quartet
Crazy People Music | CBS | 466870-2
Reqiem | CBS | 69655-2
Carla Bley Band
Heavy Heart | Watt | 14
Dizzy Gillespie And His Orchestra
Closer To The Source | Atlantic | 7567-80776-2
Michael Brecker Group
Michael Brecker | Impulse(MCA) | 950113-2
Miroslav Vitous Quartet
First Meeting | ECM | 1145
Peter Erskine Orchestra
Peter Erskine | Original Jazz Classics | OJC 610(C 14010)
Stanley Jordan Quartet
Live In New York | Blue Note | 497810-2
Wynton Marsalis Quintet
Wynton Marsalis | CBS | 468708-2
Wynton Marsalis Sextet
Hot House Flowers | CBS | 468710-2

Kirkpatrick,Don | (p)
Louis Armstrong With Chick Webb's Orchestra
Best Of The Complete RCA Victor Recordings | RCA | 2663636-2
Louis Armstrong:A 100th Birthday Celebration | RCA | 2663694-2
Wilbur DeParis And His New New Orleans Band
Atlantic Jazz: New Orleans | Atlantic | 7567-81700-2

Kirkwood,Johnny | (dr)
Louis Jordan With The Nelson Riddle Orchestra
Louis Jordan-Let The Good Times Roll: The Complete Decca Recordings 1938-1954 | Bear Family Records | BCD 15557 IH

Kirkwood,Neal | (p)
Neal Kirkwood Octet
Neal Kirkwood Octet | Timescrapper | TSCR 9612
The Chromatic Persuaders
The Chromatic Persuaders | Timescrapper | TSCR 9617

Kirschbaum,Morris | (cello)
Charlie Byrd Orchestra
Latin Byrd | Milestone | MCD 47005-2

Kirschbaum,Rolf | (g)
Swim Two Birds
Sweet Relief | Laika Records | 35101182

Kischkat,Boris | (g)
Kelm 3
Per Anno | dml-records | CD 013

Kiskalt,Fritz | (cello)
Keith Jarrett With String Quartet
In The Light | ECM | 1033/4

Kisor,Ryan | (tp)
David Matthews & The Manhattan Jazz Orchestra
Back To Bach | Milestone | MCD 9312-2
Hey Duke! | Milestone | MCD 9320-2
Horace Silver Quintet
Jazz Has... A Sense Of Humor | Verve | 050293-2
Lincoln Center Jazz Orchestra
Big Train | CBS | CK 69860
Mingus Big Band 93
Nostalgia In Times Square | Dreyfus Jazz Line | FDM 36559-2
Steve Swallow Group
Deconstructed | Watt | XtraWatt/9(537119-2)

Kistner,Udo | (bel-b)
Daniel Guggenheim Group
Daniel Guggenheim Group feat. Jasper van't Hof | Laika Records | LK 990-018

Kitagawa,Kiyoshi | (b)
Melissa Walker And Her Band
I Saw The Sky | Enja | ENJ-9409 2
Terell Stafford Quintet
Fields Of Gold | Nagel-Heyer | CD 2005

Kitschenberg,Heinz | (b-gg)
Dieter Reith Quartet
Reith On! | MPS | 557423-2
Knut Kiesewetter With The Dieter Reith Orchestra
Reith On! | MPS | 557423-2
New Jazz Group Hannover
Deutsches Jazz Fesival 1954/1955 | Bear Family Records | BCD 15430

Kitsis,Bob | (p)
Anita O'Day With Gene Krupa And His Orchestra
Let Me Off Uptown:Anita O'Day With Gene Krupa | CBS | CK 65625
Artie Shaw And His Orchestra
Planet JazzArtie Shaw | Planet Jazz | 2152057-2
The Legends Of Swing | Laserlight | 24659
Tommy Dorsey And His Orchestra
Planet Jazz:Frank Sinatra & Tommy Dorsey | Planet Jazz | 2152067-2

Kittig,Rex | (sax)
Anita O'Day With Gene Krupa And His Orchestra
Let Me Off Uptown:Anita O'Day With Gene Krupa | CBS | CK 65625

Kitzmiller,John | (btuba)
Ella Fitzgerald With Marty Paich's Dektette
Ella Swings Lightly | Verve | 517535-2
Ella Fitzgerald With The Marty Paich Dek-tette
Ella Fitzgerald-First Lady Of Song | Verve | 517898-2
Verve Jazz Masters 6:Ella Fitzgerald | Verve | 519822-2
Verve Jazz Masters 46:Ella Fitzgerald-The Jazz Sides | Verve | 527655-2
Jerri Southern And The Dick Hazard Quartet
Misty Blue:Sweet Sisters Swing Songs Of Sorrow And Sadness | Blue Note | 521151-2

Kjaeldgaard,Poul | (tb)
Stan Kenton With The Danish Radio Big Band
Stan Kenton With The Danish Radio Big Band | Storyville | STCD 8340

Kjellberg,Anders | (drperc)
Don Cherry Group
Dona Nostra | ECM | 1448(521727-2)
Jazz Baltica Ensemble
The Birth+Rebirth Of Swedish Folk Jazz | ACT | 9254-2
Nils Landgren Group
Ballads | ACT | 9268-2
Palle Danielsson Quartet
Contra Post | Caprice | CAP 21440
Palle Danielsson Quintet
Contra Post | Caprice | CAP 21440

Kjellemyr,Bjorn | (bel-b)
Ketil Bjornstad Group
Water Stories | ECM | 1503(519076-2)
Seafarer's Song | EmArCy | 9865777
Terje Rypdal And The Chasers
Blue | ECM | 1346(831516-2)
Terje Rypdal Group
If Mountains Could Sing | ECM | 1554(523987-2)
Terje Rypdal Quartet
The Singles Collection | ECM | 1383(837749-2)
Terje Rypdal Trio
Chaser | ECM | 1303
Terje Rypdal With The Borealis Ensemble
Q.E.D. | ECM | 1474

Kjos Sorensen,Hans-Kristian | (marimba,percvoice)
Christian Wallumrod Trio
No Birch | ECM | 1628(537344-2)
Misha Alperin Trio
Night After Night | ECM | 1769(014431-2)

Kjuus,Birgit | (tp)
European Jazz Youth Orchestra
Swinging Europe 3 | dacapo | DCCD 9461

Klages,T. | (v)
Artie Shaw And His Orchestra
Planet JazzArtie Shaw | Planet Jazz | 2152057-2
Planet Jazz:Big Bands | Planet Jazz | 2169649-2

Klaiber,German | (b)
Johannes Mössinger New York Trio
Monk's Corner | double moon | DMCHR 71032
Johannes Mössinger New York Trio with Joe Lovano
Monk's Corner | double moon | DMCHR 71032
Sorry.It's Jazz
Sorry,It's Jazz! | Satin Doll Productions | SDP 1040-1 CD
Stuttgarter Gitarren Trio
Stuttgarter Gitarren Trio Vol.2 | Edition Musikat | EDM 034

Klammer,Sven | (tpfl-h)
Clark Terry With The Summit Jazz Orchestra
Clark | Edition Collage | EC 530-2
European Jazz Youth Orchestra
Swinging Europe 1 | dacapo | DCCD 9449
Swinging Europe 2 | dacapo | DCCD 9450
Thärichens Tentett
Lady Moon | Minor Music | 801094

Klare,Jan | (as,cl,electronics,fl,bssax)
Joachim Raffel Sextet
...In Motion | Jazz 4 Ever Records:Jazz Network | J4E 4746
Matthias Müller Quartet
Bhavam | Jazz Haus Musik | JHM 0126 CD

Klass,Lou | (v)
Pete Rugolo And His Orchestra
Thriller/Richard Diamon(Original Jazz Scores From 2 Classics TV Series) | Fresh Sound Records | FSCD 2015

Klatka,Tony | (fl-htp)
Woody Herman And His Orchestra
Brand New | Original Jazz Classics | OJCCD 1044-2(F 8414)
Woody Herman And The New Thundering Herd
Woody Herman:Thundering Herd | Original Jazz Classics | OJCCD 841-2

Klatt,Günther | (ss,ts,p,percvoc)
Gunther Klatt & Aki Takase
Art Of The Duo: Plays Ballads Of Duke Ellington: | Tutu Records | 888116-2*
Gunther Klatt & New York Razzmatazz
Volume One:Fa Mozzo | Tutu Records | 888158-2*
Günther Klatt Quartet
Internationales Jazzfestival Münster | Tutu Records | 888110-2*
Günther Klatt-Tizian Jost
Art Of The Duo:Live In Mexico City | Tutu Records | 888184-2*

Klaus Der Geiger | (vvoc)
Kölner Saxophon Mafia With Klaus Der Geiger
Kölner Saxophon Mafia Proudly Presents | Jazz Haus Musik | JHM 0046 CD

Kleber,Jorge | (gvoc)
John Patitucci Group
Mistura Fina | GRP | GRP 98022

Kleber,Paul | (b)
Jazz Indeed
Who The Moon Is | Traumton Records | 4427-2
Lisa Bassenge Trio
A Sight, A Song | Minor Music | 801100
Lisa Bassenge Trio With Guests
A Sight, A Song | Minor Music | 801100

Klee,Harry | (as,bass-fl,b-cl,fl,piccolo,cl,ts)
Ella Fitzgerald With The Nelson Riddle Orchestra
The Best Of The Song Books:The Ballads | Verve | 521867-2
Oh Lady Be Good:The Best Of The Gershwin Songbook | Verve | 529581-2
Love Songs:The Best Of The Song Books | Verve | 531762-2
Ella Fitzgerald Sings The Johnny Mercer Songbook | Verve | 539057-2
Dream Dancing | Original Jazz Classics | OJCCD 1072-2(2310814)
June Christy With The Pete Rugolo Orchestra
Something Cool(The Complete Mono & Stereo Versions) | Capitol | 534069-2
Louis Armstrong And His All Stars With Benny Carter's Orchestra
Ambassador Louis Armstrong Vol.17:Moments To Remember(1952-1956) | Ambassador | CLA 1917
Louis Armstrong With Benny Carter's Orchestra
Louis Armstrong-My Greatest Songs | MCA | MCD 18347
Peggy Lee With The Quincy Jones Orchestra
Blues Cross Country | Capitol | 520088-2
Pete Rugolo And His Orchestra
Thriller/Richard Diamon(Original Jazz Scores From 2 Classics TV Series) | Fresh Sound Records | FSCD 2015
Stan Kenton And His Orchestra
Stan Kenton Portraits On Standards | Capitol | 531571-2

Klein,Dave | (cotp)
Adrian Rollini And His Orchestra
Jazz:The Essential Collection Vol.3 | IN+OUT Records | 78013-2

Klein,David | (as,drsax)
World Quintet
World Quintet | TipToe | TIP-888843 2
David Klein Quintet
My Marilyn | Enja | ENJ-9422 2
Kol Simcha
Contemporary Klezmer | Laika Records | LK 93-048
World Quintet With The London Mozart Players
World Quintet | TipToe | TIP-888843 2
World Quintet With The London Mozart Players And Herbert Grönemeyer
World Quintet | TipToe | TIP-888843 2

Klein,Emanuel | (tp)
Vince Guaraldi Group
Charlie Brown's Holiday Hits | Fantasy | FCD 9682-2

Klein,Ferdy | (b)
Harald Banter Ensemble
Deutsches Jazz Fesival 1954/1955 | Bear Family Records | BCD 15430

Klein,Fred | (fr-h)
Grover Washington Jr. Orchestra
Jazzrock-Anthology Vol.3:Fusion | Zounds | CD 27100555

Klein,Gary | (saxts)
Woody Herman And His Orchestra
Verve Jazz Masters 54:Woody Herman | Verve | 529903-2

Klein,Guillermo | (arr,ldp)
Taylor Hawkins Group
Wake Up Call | Fresh Sound Records | FSCD 145 CD

Klein,Günter | (v)
Keith Jarrett With String Quartet
In The Light | ECM | 1033/4

Klein,Larry | (bel-b)
Bobby McFerrin Group
Bobby McFerrin | Elektra | 7559-60023-2
Freddie Hubbard And His Orchestra
Born To Be Blue | Original Jazz Classics | OJCCD 734-2(2312134)
Freddie Hubbard Quintet
Live At The Northsea Jazz Festival | Pablo | 2620113-2
Freddie Hubbard Sextet
Keystone Bop Vol.2:Friday/Saturday | Prestige | PCD 24163-2
Joe Henderson Quartet
Keystone Bop Vol.2:Friday/Saturday | Prestige | PCD 24163-2

Klein,Manny | (tp)
Adrian Rollini And His Orchestra
Jazz:The Essential Collection Vol.3 | IN+OUT Records | 78013-2
Artie Shaw And His Orchestra
Planet JazzArtie Shaw | Planet Jazz | 2152057-2
Planet Jazz:Jazz Greatest Hits | Planet Jazz | 2169648-2
Benny Goodman And His Orchestra
Planet Jazz:Benny Goodman | Planet Jazz | 2152054-2
Billy May And His Orchestra
Billy May's Big Fat Brass/Bill's Bag | Capitol | 535206-2
Ella Fitzgerald With Paul Weston And His Orchestra
Ella Fitzgerald Sings The Irving Berlin Song Book | Verve | 543830-2
Ella Fitzgerald With The Nelson Riddle Orchestra
The Best Of The Song Books:The Ballads | Verve | 521867-2
Ella Fitzgerald With The Paul Weston Orchestra
Get Happy! | Verve | 523321-2
Lena Horne With The Lou Bring Orchestra

Planet Jazz:Lena Horne | Planet Jazz | 2165373-2
Planet Jazz:Female Jazz Vocalists | Planet Jazz | 2169656-2
Louis Armstrong And His All Stars With Benny Carter's Orchestra
Ambassador Louis Armstrong Vol.17:Moments To Remember(1952-1956) | Ambassador | CLA 1917
Louis Armstrong With Benny Carter's Orchestra
Louis Armstrong-My Greatest Songs | MCA | MCD 18347
Louis Armstrong With The Hal Mooney Orchestra
Ambassador Louis Armstrong Vol.17:Moments To Remember(1952-1956) | Ambassador | CLA 1917
Mel Tormé With The Billy May Orchestra
Mel Tormé Goes South Of The Border With Billy May | Verve | 589517-2
Nat King Cole With The Billy May Orchestra
Nat King Cole:For Sentimental Reasons | Dreyfus Jazz Line | FDM 36740-2
Roger Wolfe Kahn And His Orchestra
Planet Jazz:Jack Teagarden | Planet Jazz | 2161236-2
Van Alexander Orchestra
Home Of Happy Feet/Swing! Staged For Sound! | Capitol | 535211-2

Klein,Marlon | (clay-bongos,darabuka,djembe,shaker)
Pili-Pili
Jakko | JA & RO | JARO 4131-2
Be In Two Minds | JA & RO | JARO 4134-2
Boogaloo | JA & RO | JARO 4174-2
Dance Jazz Live 1995 | JA & RO | JARO 4189-2
Thomas Kessler Group
On Earth | Laika Records | 8695069

Klein,Matthias | (bel-b)
Jo Ambros Group
Wanderlust | dml-records | CD 016

Klein,Miriam | (voc)
David Klein Quintet
My Marilyn | Enja | ENJ-9422 2

Klein,Morton | (ts,gmouth-dr)
Tok Tok Tok
Love Again | Einstein Music | EM 01081
It Took So Long | Einstein Music | EM 21103
50 Ways To Leave Your Lover | Einstein Music | EM 91051

Klein,Niels | (clts)
Lars Duppler Sextet
Palindrome 6tet | Jazz Haus Musik | JHM 0131 CD

Klein,Oscar | (cl,co,g,harm,voc,el-g,recorderette)
Dutch Swing College Band
Swinging Studio Sessons | Philips | 824256-2 PMS
Dutch Swing College Band Live In 1960 | Philips | 838765-2
Katie Kern-Oscar Klein
Still Young | Jazzpoint | JP 1070 CD
Oscar Klein
Blues Of Summer | Nagel-Heyer | NH 1011
Oscar Klein & Katie Kern Group
Pick-A-Blues | Jazzpoint | JP 1065 CD
Oscar Klein Band
Pick-A-Blues Live | Jazzpoint | JP 1071
Oscar Klein-Lino Patruno European Jazz Stars
Live at The San Marino Jazz Festival | Jazzpoint | JP 1052 CD
Oscar Klein's Anniversary Band
Moonglow | Nagel-Heyer | CD 021
Ellington For Lovers | Nagel-Heyer | NH 1009
The Second Sampler | Nagel-Heyer | NHR SP 6
Oscar Klein's Jazz Show
Oscar Klein's Jazz Show | Jazzpoint | JP 1043 CD
Oscar Klein's Jazz Show Vol.2 | Jazzpoint | JP 1048 CD
A' Portrait Of Jan Jankeje | Jazzpoint | JP 1054 CD
The European Jazz Ginats
Jazz Party | Nagel-Heyer | CD 009
The First Sampler | Nagel-Heyer | NHR SP 5

Klein,Poldi | (cl)
Spree Cuty Stompers
Deutsches Jazz Fesival 1954/1955 | Bear Family Records | BCD 15430

Klein,Richard G. | (fr-h)
Ella Fitzgerald With Orchestra
The Best Is Yet To Come | Original Jazz Classics | OJCCD 889-2(2312138)

Kleinbub,Wieland | (p-solo)
Wieland Kleinbub
Sirkle | Edition Musikat | EDM 071

Kleindienst,Peter | (g)
Peter Kleindienst Group
Zeitwärts:Reime Vor Pisin | double moon | DMCD 1001-2

Kleindin,Franz | (ts)
Brocksi-Quartett
Globetrotter | Bear Family Records | BCD 15912 AH

Kleindin,Teddy | (cl,tsarr)
Freddie Brocksieper Orchester
Drums Boogie | Bear Family Records | BCD 15988 AH

Kleive,Audun | (dr,percsnare-dr)
Arild Andersen Quartet
If You Look Far Enough | ECM | 1493(513902-2)
Jon Balke w/Magnetic North Orchestra
Further | ECM | 1517
Kyanos | ECM | 1822(017278-2)
Jon Balke w/Oslo 13
Nonsentration | ECM | 1445
Marilyn Mazur's Future Song
Small Labyrinths | ECM | 1559(533679-2)
Marilyn Mazure's Future Song | VeraBra Records | CDVBR 2105-2
Terje Rypdal And The Chasers
Blue | ECM | 1346(831516-2)
Terje Rypdal Group
If Mountains Could Sing | ECM | 1554(523987-2)
Terje Rypdal Quartet
The Singles Collection | ECM | 1383(837749-2)
Terje Rypdal Trio
Chaser | ECM | 1303

Kleive,Iver | (org)
Terje Rypdal Quartet With The Bergen Chamber Ensemble
Lux Aeterna | ECM | 1818(017070-2)

Kleiveland,Gunn Berit | (cello)

Klemm,Thomas | (fl,ts,kalimbavoc)
Fun Horns
Surprise | Jazzpoint | JP 1029 CD
Karl Scharnweber Trio
Choral Concert | Nabel Records:Jazz Network | CD 4642
Coral Concert II/Another View | Nabel Records:Jazz Network | CD 4650

Klemmer,John | (alto-fl,ts,echoplex,fl,ss,el-p,perc)
John Klemmer Quartet
Involvement | Chess | 076139-2

Klentze,Thorsten | (gel-g)
Fisherman's Break
Fisherman's Break | Edition Collage | EC 450-2

Klevensky,Sergey | (reeds)
Farlanders
The Farlander | JA & RO | JARO 4222-2

Klevman,Louis | (viola)
Phineas Newborn Jr. With Dennis Farnon And His Orchestra
While My Lady Sleeps | RCA | 2185157-2

Klimes,Mirko | (bj)
Jan Jankeje's Party And Swingband
Mobil | Jazzpoint | JP 1068 CD

Klimm,Joe | (p)
Fred Bunge Star Band
Deutsches Jazz Fesival 1954/1955 | Bear Family Records | BCD 15430

Kline,Jonathan | (v)
Gunter Hampel And His Galaxie Dream Band
Journey To The Song Within | Birth | 0017

Kling,Schmitto | (v)
Bireli Lagrene Ensemble
Routes To Django & Bireli Swing '81 | Jazzpoint | JP 1055 CD
Routs To Django-Live At The 'Krokodil' | Jazzpoint | JP 1056 CD
Bireli Lagrene Quartet
A' Portrait Of Jan Jankeje | Jazzpoint | JP 1054 CD

Klingelhöfer,Bodo | (b)
Remy Filipovitch Quartet
All Night Long | Album | AS 11806

Klinger,Ezra | (v)
Charlie Haden Quartet West With Strings
The Art Of The Song | Verve | 547403-2

Klinghagen,Göran | (gsynth)
Palle Danielsson Quintet
Contra Post | Caprice | CAP 21440

Klink,Al | (as,b-cl,ts,bs,fl,reedssax)
Benny Goodman And His Orchestra
The Legends Of Swing | Laserlight | 24659
Great Swing Classics In Hi-Fi | Capitol | 521223-2
Ella Fitzgerald With Sy Oliver And His Orchestra
Ella Fitzgerald:Mr.Paganini | Dreyfus Jazz Line | FDM 36741-2
Ella Fitzgerald With Sy Oliver And His Orchestra
Ella Fitzgerald:The Decca Years 1949-1954 | Decca | 050668-2
Glenn Miller And His Orchestra
Planet Jazz:Glenn Miller | Planet Jazz | 2152056-2
Planet Jazz Sampler | Planet Jazz | 2152326-2
Planet Jazz:Jazz Greatest Hits | Planet Jazz | 2169648-2
Planet Jazz:Big Bands | Planet Jazz | 2169649-2
Planet Jazz:Swing | Planet Jazz | 2169651-2
The Chesterfield Broadcasts Vol.1 | RCA | 2663113-2
Candlelight Miller | RCA | 2668716-2
Swing Legends | Nimbus Records | NI 2001
Louis Armstrong And The Commanders under the Direction of Camarata
Satchmo Serenaders | Verve | 543792-2
Louis Armstrong With Sy Oliver And His Orchestra
Satchmo Serenaders | Verve | 543792-2
Louis Armstrong-My Greatest Songs | MCA | MCD 18347
Louis Armstrong With The Commanders
Ambassador Louis Armstrong Vol.17:Moments To Remember(1952-1956) | Ambassador | CLA 1917
The Andrew Sisters With The Glenn Miller Orchestra
The Chesterfield Broadcasts Vol.1 | RCA | 2663113-2
Tommy Dorsey And His Orchestra
Planet Jazz:Tommy Dorsey | Planet Jazz | 2159972-2
Planet Jazz:Jazz Greatest Hits | Planet Jazz | 2169648-2

Klink,Steve | (p,el-porg)
Steve Klink Funk Unit
Places To Come From,Places To Go | Minor Music | 801098
Steve Klink Trio
Feels Like Home | Minor Music | 801092
Places To Come From,Places To Go | Minor Music | 801098
Steve Klink-Alex Olivari
Feels Like Home | Minor Music | 801092
Steve Klink-Barbara Boyle
Places To Come From,Places To Go | Minor Music | 801098
Steve Klink-Mia Znidaric
Feels Like Home | Minor Music | 801092
Steve Klink-Sasa Olenjuk
Places To Come From,Places To Go | Minor Music | 801098

Klopfenstein,Jim | (b)
Nick Woodland And The Magnets
Big Heart | Blues Beacon | BLU-1013 2

Klorby,Thoams | (voc)
Marilyn Mazur With Ars Nova And The Copenhagen Art Ensemble
Jordsange | dacapo | DCCD 9454

Klose,Markus | (perc)
Bigband Der Musikschule Der Stadt Brühl Mit Gastsolisten
Pangäa | Indigo-Records | 1004 CD

Kloss,Eric | (as,tsss)
Eric Kloss Quartet
About Time | Prestige | PRCD 24268-2
Pat Martino Quintet
Desperado | Original Jazz Classics | OJCCD 397-2(P 7795)

Klossek,Marcus | (gel-g)
Marcus Klossek Imagination
As We Are | Jardis Records | JRCD 20134
Jazz Guitar Highlights 1 | Jardis Records | JRCD 20141

Klucevsek,Guy | (accordeonbodysounds)
Dave Douglas Quartet
A Thousand Evenings | RCA | 2663698-2
Charms Of The Night Sky | Winter&Winter | 910015-2
Guy Klucevsek-Alan Bern
Accordance | Winter&Winter | 910058-2
Guy Klucevsek-Phillip Johnston
Tales From The Cryptic | Winter&Winter | 910088-2

Kluger,Irv | (dr)
Dizzy Gillespie Sextet
Dizzy Gillespie:Night In Tunisia | Dreyfus Jazz Line | FDM 36734-2
Pete Rugolo And His Orchestra
Thriller/Richard Diamon(Original Jazz Scores From 2 Classics TV Series) | Fresh Sound Records | FSCD 2015

Klugh,Earl | (g,12-string-gg-solo)
Earl Klugh
Late Night Guitar | Blue Note | 498573-2
Earl Klugh Group
Late Night Guitar | Blue Note | 498573-2
Earl Klugh Group With Strings
Late Night Guitar | Blue Note | 498573-2
Earl Klugh Trio
The Earl Klugh Trio Volume One | Warner | 7599-26750-2
Earl Klugh-Dr.Gibbs
Late Night Guitar | Blue Note | 498573-2
Earl Klugh-Gloria Agostine
Late Night Guitar | Blue Note | 498573-2
George Benson Group/Orchestra
George Benson Anthology | Warner | 8122-79934-2
McCoy Tyner Group With Horns
Inner Voices | Original Jazz Classics | OJCCD 1039-2(M 9079)
McCoy Tyner Group With Horns And Voices
Inner Voices | Original Jazz Classics | OJCCD 1039-2(M 9079)
McCoy Tyner Group With Voices
Inner Voices | Original Jazz Classics | OJCCD 1039-2(M 9079)
Miles Davis-Marcus Miller Group
Siesta(Soundtrack) | Warner | 7599-25655-2

Knapp,Herfried | (b)
Karl Ratzer Quintet
All The Way | Enja | ENJ-9448 2

Knapp,James | (tp,fl-hwaterphone)
First Avenue
First Avenue | ECM | 1194

Knapper,Jean Louis | (gcomputer-programming)
Pili-Pili
Hotel Babo | JA & RO | JARO 4147-2

Knauer,Rocky | (b,el-bvoc)
Christian Willisohn Group
Live At Marians | ART BY HEART | ABH 2006 2
Blues On The World | Blues Beacon | BLU-1025 2
Christian Willisohn New Band
Heart Broken Man | Blues Beacon | BLU-1026 2
David Paquette Trio
Mood Swings | ART BY HEART | ABH 2004 2
Max Greger Quintet
Night Train | Polydor | 543393-2
Thilo Kreitmeier & Group
Soul Call | Organic Music | ORGM 9711
Changes | Organic Music | ORGM 9725
Thilo Kreitmeier Quintet
Mo' Better Blues | Organic Music | ORGM 9706
Wolfgang Lackerschmid Group
Mallet Connection | Bhakti Jazz | BR 33
Wolfgang Lackerschmid Quartet
One More Life | Bhakti Jazz | BR 29

Knepper,Jimmy | (perc,tb,b-tbld)
Bennie Wallace Quartet
Bennie Wallace Plays Monk | Enja | ENJ-3091 2
Benny Goodman And His Orchestra
The Legends Of Swing | Laserlight | 24659
Charles Mingus And His Orchestra
Charles Mingus-Passion Of A Man:The Complete Atlantic Recordings 1956-1961 | Atlantic | 8122-72871-2
Charles Mingus Group
The Jazz Life! | Candid | CCD 79019
Mysterious Blues | Candid | CCD 79042
Mingus Ah Um | CBS | CK 65512
Mingus Dynasty | CBS | CK 65513
Charles Mingus Jazz Workshop
Tonight At Noon | Atlantic | 7567-80793-2
Rhino Presents The Atlantic Jazz Gallery | Atlantic | 8122-71257-2
Blues & Roots | Atlantic | 8122-75205-2
The Clown | Atlantic | 8122-75358-2
Charles Mingus Orchestra
Tijuana Moods(The Complete Edition) | RCA | 2663840-2
Charles Mingus:Pre-Bird(Mingus Revisited) | Verve | 538636-2
Cumbia & Jazz Fusion | Atlantic | 8122-71785-2
The Very Best Of Charles Mingus | Rhino | 8122-79988-2
Charles Mingus:The Complete 1959 Columbia Recordings | CBS | C3K 65145
Mingus | Candid | CCD 79021
Charles Mingus Quintet
Charles Mingus-Passion Of A Man:The Complete Atlantic Recordings 1956-1961 | Atlantic | 8122-72871-2
The Very Best Of Charles Mingus | Rhino | 8122-79988-2
Charles Mingus Quintet With Roland Kirk
Tonight At Noon | Atlantic | 7567-80793-2
Charles Mingus-Passion Of A Man:The Complete Atlantic Recordings 1956-1961 | Atlantic | 8122-72871-2
The Very Best Of Charles Mingus | Rhino | 8122-79988-2
Charles Mingus Septet
Charles Mingus:The Complete 1959 Columbia Recordings | CBS | C3K 65145
Charles Mingus Workshop
Charles Mingus-The Complete Debut Recordings | Debut | 12 DCD 4402-2
Clark Terry Orchestra
Color Changes | Candid | CCD 79009
Gary Burton Quartet With Orchestra
A Genuine Tong Funeral(Dark Opera Without Words) | RCA | 2119255-2
George Russell And His Orchestra
Bill Evans:Piano Player | CBS | CK 65361
Gil Evans Orchestra
Verve Jazz Masters 23:Gil Evans | Verve | 521860-2
The Individualism Of Gil Evans | Verve | 833804-2
Out Of The Cool | Impulse(MCA) | 951186-2
Blues In Orbit | Enja | ENJ-3069 2
Jazz Artists Guild
Newport Rebels-Jazz Artists Guild | Candid | CCD 79022
Jimmy Knepper Quintet
Charles Mingus-The Complete Debut Recordings | Debut | 12 DCD 4402-2
Kenny Burrell With The Gil Evans Orchestra
Guitar Forms | Verve | 521403-2
Verve Jazz Masters 23:Gil Evans | Verve | 521860-2
Verve Jazz Masters 45:Kenny Burrell | Verve | 527652-2
Verve Jazz Masters Vol.60:The Collection | Verve | 529866-2
Kevin Mahogany With The WDR Big Band And Guests
Pussy Cat Dues:The Music Of Charles Mingus | Enja | ENJ-9316 2
Miles Davis With Gil Evans & His Orchestra
Miles Davis At Carnegie Hall | CBS | CK 65027
Quiet Nights | CBS | CK 65293
Newport Rebels
Candid Dolphy | Candid | CCD 79033
Thad Jones-Mel Lewis Orchestra
The Groove Merchant/The Second Race | Laserlight | 24656
The Jazz Composer's Orchestra
Comminications | JCOA | 1001/2
Tony Scott And The All Stars
Body And Soul Revisited | GRP | GRP 16272

Knie,Walter | (reeds)
Wes Montgomery With The Don Sebesky Orchestra
Wes Montgomery:The Verve Jazz Sides | Verve | 521690-2

Kniel,Manfred | (drperc)
Müller-Svoboda-Dahn-Kniel
9Q | Edition Musikat | EDM 064

Knieper,Jürgen | (parr)
Jürgen Knieper Quintet
State Of Things | Jazz Haus Musik | JHM 0104 CD

Knieps,Reinhold | (videotraces)
Pata Blue Chip
Pata Blue Chip | Pata Musik | PATA 13(amf 1064)

Knight,Bobby | (b-tbtb)
Gerald Wilson And His Orchestra
Blue Breaks Beats Vol.2 | Blue Note | 789907-2
Peggy Lee With The Quincy Jones Orchestra
Blues Cross Country | Capitol | 520088-2
Stan Kenton And His Orchestra
Adventures In Blues | Capitol | 520089-2

Knight,Caren | (voc)
Don Cherry Group
Multi Kulti | A&M Records | 395323-2

Knight,Grace | (voc)
Grace Knight With Orchestra
Come In Spinner | Intuition Records | INT 3052-2

Knight,Joe | (p)
Matthew Gee All-Stars
Jazz By Gee! | Original Jazz Classics | OJCCD 1884-2(RLP 221)

Knight,Susan | (viola)
Ensemble Modern
Ensemble Modern-Fred Frith:Traffic Continues | Winter&Winter | 910044-2

Knight[Pepper],Caren | (vocperc)
Gunther Schuller With The WDR Radio Orchestra & Rememberance Band
Witchi Tia To, The Music Of Jim Pepper | Tutu Records | 888204-2*

Knitzer,Jack | (bassoon)
Miles Davis With Gil Evans & His Orchestra
Sketches Of Spain | CBS | CK 65142

Knowles,Legh | (tp)
Glenn Miller And His Orchestra
Planet Jazz:Glenn Miller | Planet Jazz | 2152056-2
Planet Jazz Sampler | Planet Jazz | 2152326-2
Planet Jazz:Big Bands | Planet Jazz | 2169649-2
Planet Jazz:Swing | Planet Jazz | 2169651-2
The Chesterfield Broadcasts Vol.1 | RCA | 2663113-2
Candelight Miller | RCA | 2668716-2
Swing Legends | Nimbus Records | NI 2001
The Andrew Sisters With The Glenn Miller Orchestra
The Chesterfield Broadcasts Vol.1 | RCA | 2663113-2

Knox,Bertell | (dr)
Charlie Byrd Group
Byrd In The Wind | Original Jazz Classics | OJCCD 1086(RS 9449)
Charlie Byrd Sextet
Byrd's Word! | Original Jazz Classics | OJCCD 1054-2(R 9448)
Charlie Byrd Trio
Mr. Guitar Charlie Byrd | Original Jazz Classics | OJCCD 998-2(R 9450)

Knudsen,Kenneth | (keyboards,perc,synth,pel-p)
Arild Andersen Quintet With The Cikada String Quartet
Hyperborean | ECM | 1631(537342-2)
Kenneth Knudsen-Christian Skeel
Music For Eyes | dacapo | DCCD 9433

INTERPRETENVERZEICHNIS

Miles Davis With The Danish Radio Big Band
Aura | CBS | CK 63962
The Danish Radio Big Band
Aura | CBS | CK 63962

Knudsen,Niklas | (g)
Ok Nok...Kongo
Moonstone Journey | dacapo | DCCD 9444
When Granny Sleeps
Welcome | dacapo | DCCD 9447

Knudsen,Perry | (tpfl-h)
Miles Davis With The Danish Radio Big Band
Aura | CBS | CK 63962
Stan Getz With The Danish Radio Big Band
Stan Getz In Europe | Laserlight | 24657
The Danish Radio Big Band
Aura | CBS | CK 63962
The Danish Radio Jazz Orchestra
This Train:The Danish Radio Jazz Orchestra Plays The Music Of Ray Pitts | dacapo | DCCD 9428

Knutsen,Pete | (el-p,mellotrong)
Ketil Bjornstad Group
Early Years | EmArCy | 013271-2
Terje Rypdal Quintet
When Ever I Seem To Be Far Away | ECM | 1045

Knutsson,Jones | (sax,perc,ssbs)
Jonas Knutsson Quartet
Jonas Knutsson Quartet | Touché Music | TMcCD 018
Lena Willemark-Ale Möller Group
Nordan | ECM | 1536(523161-2)
Agram | ECM | 1610

Köbberling,Heinrich | (dr)
Christof Sänger Trio
Chorinho | Laika Records | LK 93-033
Christoph Sänger Trio
Caprice | Laika Records | LK 94-057
Florian Poser Group
Say Yes! | Edition Collage | EC 452-2
Gunter Hampel Quartet
Time Is Now-Live At The Eldena Jazz Festival 1992 | Birth | CD 042
Heinrich Köbberling-Matt Renzi Quartet
Pisces | Nabel Records:Jazz Network | CD 4677
Julia Hülsman Trio With Rebekka Bakken
Scattering Poems | ACT | 9405-2
Julia Hülsmann Trio With Anna Lauvergnac
Come Closer | ACT | 9702-2
Rolf Zielke Trio Feat. Mustafa Boztüy
Rolf Zielke Trio Feat. Mustafa Boztüy | Jazz 'n' Arts Records | JNA 0602
The Huebner Brothers
Memories | Satin Doll Productions | SDP 1025-1 CD

Kobialka,Daniel | (v)
Ron Carter With Strings
Pastels | Original Jazz Classics | OJCCD 665-2(M 9073)

Kobialka,Reinhard | (drperc)
Dioko
Helix | Jazz Haus Musik | JHM 0029 CD
Wollie Kaiser Timeghost
Tust Du Fühlen Gut | Jazz Haus Musik | JHM 0060 CD
Post Art Core | Jazz Haus Musik | JHM 0077 CD

Koblenz,Arnold | (engl-hoboe)
Ella Fitzgerald With The Buddy Bregman Orchestra
The Best Of The Song Books:The Ballads | Verve | 521867-2
Ella Fitzgerald Sings The Rodgers And Hart Song Book | Verve | 537258-2
Ella Fitzgerald With The Frank DeVol Orchestra
Get Happy! | Verve | 523321-2

Koch,Claus | (ts)
Al Porcino Big Band
Al Porcino Big Band Live! | Organic Music | ORGM 9717

Koch,Hans | (b-cl,ss,ts,cl,contra-b-cl,sax)
Hans Koch/Martin Schütz/Marco Käppeli
Accélération | ECM | 1357
Koch-Schütz-Studer & El Nil Troop
Heavy Cairo Trafic | Intuition Records | INT 3175-2

Koch,Joe | (bs,reedssax)
Ella Fitzgerald With The Frank DeVol Orchestra
Get Happy! | Verve | 523321-2
Ella Fitzgerald With The Nelson Riddle Orchestra
The Best Of The Song Books:The Ballads | Verve | 521867-2
Get Happy! | Verve | 523321-2
Oh Lady Be Good:The Best Of The Gershwin Songbook | Verve | 529581-2
Love Songs:The Best Of The Song Books | Verve | 531762-2
Ella Fitzgerald Sings The Johnny Mercer Songbook | Verve | 539057-2
Louis Armstrong And Gary Crosby With Sonny Burke's Orchestra
Louis Armstrong-My Greatest Songs | MCA | MCD 18347

Koch,Jos'Cook' | (as)
Louis Armstrong And His All Stars With Sonny Burke's Orchestra
Ambassador Louis Armstrong Vol.17:Moments To Remember(1952-1956) | Ambassador | CLA 1917

Koch,Klaus | (b,b-solodr)
Klaus Koch
Basse Partout | Creative Works Records | CW CD 1011-1
Willisau And More Live | Creative Works Records | CW CD 1020-2
Trio KoKoKo
Willisau And More Live | Creative Works Records | CW CD 1020-2

Koch,Mark | (p)
Twice A Week & Steve Elson
Play Of Colours | Edition Collage | EC 511-2

Koch,Michael | (keyboardsel-p)
Balance
Elements | double moon | DMCHR 71033

Kochbeck,Georg | (el-p,synth,keyboardsp)
Philippe Caillat Group
Stream Of Time | Laika Records | LK 92-030

Kock,Joe | (bs)
The Hollywood Hucksters
The Hollywood Session:The Capitol Jazzmen | Jazz Unlimited | JUCD 2044

Kodexx Sentimental |
Kodexx Sentimental
Das Digitale Herz | Poise | Poise 02

Koehler,Trevor | (fl,as,ts,ssbs)
Gil Evans Orchestra
PLay The Music Of Jimi Hendrix | RCA | 2663872-2
Svengali | Rhino | 8122-73720-2

Koenders,Dennis | (v)
Stochelo Rosenberg Group With Strings
Gypsy Swing | Verve | 527806-2

Koenig,George | (as,cl,reeds,saxts)
Benny Goodman And His Orchestra
Planet Jazz:Benny Goodman | Planet Jazz | 2152054-2
Planet Jazz:Jazz Greatest Hits | Planet Jazz | 2169648-2
Planet Jazz:Big Bands | Planet Jazz | 2169649-2
Planet Jazz:Swing | Planet Jazz | 2169651-2
Planet Jazz:Jazz Trumpet | Planet Jazz | 2169654-2
Planet Jazz:Female Jazz Vocalists | Planet Jazz | 2169656-2
Benny Goodman At Carnegie Hall 1938(Complete) | CBS | C2K 65143
More Camel Caravans | Phontastic | NCD 8841/2
More Camel Caravans | Phontastic | NCD 8843/4
Benny Goodman Band
Benny Goodman At Carnegie Hall 1938(Complete) | CBS | C2K 65143
Jam Session
Benny Goodman At Carnegie Hall 1938(Complete) | CBS | C2K 65143
Louis Armstrong And Ella Fitzgerald With Bob Hagger's Orchestra
Louis Armstrong:C'est Si Bon | Dreyfus Jazz Line | FDM 36730-2

Koenig,Klaus | (comp,ld,el-p,keyboards,p,perctb)
Klaus König Orchestra
Times Of Devastation/Poco A Poco | Enja | ENJ-6014 22
Hommage A Douglas Adams | Enja | ENJ-6078 2
Time Fragments:Seven Studies In Time And Motion | Enja | ENJ-8076 2
Reviews | Enja | ENJ-9061 2
The Heart Project | Enja | ENJ-9338 2
Klaus König Orchestra & Guests
The Song Of Songs:Oratorio For Two Solo Voices,Choir And Orchestra | Enja | ENJ-7057 2

Koffman,Moe | (alto-fl,ss,as,fl,cl,piccolo,ts)
Singers Unlimited With Rob McConnell And The Boss Brass
The Singers Unlimited:Magic Voices | MPS | 539130-2

Kogan,Greg | (p)
Buddy Rich Big Band
Backwoods Siseman/Pieces Of Dream | Laserlight | 24655

Kögel,Christian | (gel-g)
Jerry Granelli Group
Music Has Its Way With Me | Traumton Records | 4451-2
Jerry Granelli UFB
News From The Street | VeraBra Records | CDVBR 2146-2
Rinde Eckert Group
Story In,Story Out | Intuition Records | INT 3507-2

Koglmann,Franz | (fl-h,tpcomp)
Franz Koglmann Group
Venus In Transit | Between The Lines | btl 017(Efa 10186)
Franz Koglmann Quintet
Make Believe | Between The Lines | btl 001(Efa 10171-2)
Opium | Between The Lines | btl 011(Efa 10181-2)
Monoblue Quartet
An Affair With Strauss | Between The Lines | btl 006(Efa 10176-2)
Trio KoKoKo
Willisau And More Live | Creative Works Records | CW CD 1020-2

Kohlbacher,Steve | (tb)
Woody Herman And The New Thundering Herd
Woody Herman:Thundering Herd | Original Jazz Classics | OJCCD 841-2

Köhler,Benjamin | (pv)
Wedeli Köhler Group
Swing & Folk | Jazzpoint | JP 1067 CD

Köhler,Michael | (tb)
Dusko Goykovich Big Band
Balkan Connection | Enja | ENJ-9047 2

Köhler,Sascha | (g)
Wedeli Köhler Group
Swing & Folk | Jazzpoint | JP 1067 CD

Köhler,Wedeli | (gv)

Köhler,Wolfgang | (p)
Nana Mouskouri With The Berlin Radio Big Band
Nana Swings | Mercury | 074394-2

Kohlin,Jan | (tpfl-h)
Mona Larsen And The Danish Radio Big Band Plus Soloists
Michael Mantler:Cerco Un Paese Innocente | ECM | 1556

Kohlman,Andy | (perc)
Uli Trepte Group
Real Time Music | ATM Records | ATM 3820-AH

Kohon,Harold | (stringsv)
Bob James And His Orchestra
Jazzrock-Anthology Vol.3:Fusion | Zounds | CD 27100555
Freddie Hubbard With Orchestra
This Is Jazz:Freddie Hubbard | CBS | CK 65041
Grover Washington Jr. Orchestra
Jazzrock-Anthology Vol.3:Fusion | Zounds | CD 27100555

Koi Simcha |
Kol Simcha
Contemporary Klezmer | Laika Records | LK 93-048

Koinzer,Joe | (dr,perc,ballaphon,steel-dr,tabla)
Herbert Joos Trio
Ballade Noire | free flow music | ffm 0392

Koita,Moriba | (n'goni)
Hank Jones Meets Cheik-Tidiana Seck
Sarala | Verve | 528783-2

Koivukoski,Karri | (v)
Piirpauke
Piirpauke-Global Servisi | JA & RO | JARO 4150-2

Koivulehto,Jorma | (b)
Live In Der Balver Höhle | JA & RO | JARO 4101-2
Piirpauke-Global Servisi | JA & RO | JARO 4150-2
Jazzy World | JA & RO | JARO 4200-2

Kojeder,Erich | (tb)
Hans Theessink Group
Crazy Moon | Minor Music | 801052

Kokayi | (lyricist)
Steve Coleman And Five Elements
Curves Of Life | Novus | 2131693-2

Kolb,Philip | (as,tsfl)
Stochelo Rosenberg Group
Gypsy Swing | Verve | 527806-2
Stochelo Rosenberg Group With Strings
Gypsy Swing | Verve | 527806-2

Kolber,Ron | (bs)
Buddy Childers Big Band
Just Buddy's | Candid | CCD 79761

Koleva,Youlia | (voc)
Sergey Strarostin's Vocal Family
Journey | JA & RO | JARO 4226-2

Kolker,Adam | (cl,ss,ts,flb-cl)
Ray Barretto Orchestra
Portraits In Jazz And Clave | RCA | 2168452-2

Kolkowski,Aleksander | (stroh-v,violav)
Rajesh Metha
Reconfigurations | Between The Lines | btl 010(Efa 10180-2)

Koll,Michael | (ld)
Matthias Petzold Group With Choir
Psalmen und Lobgesänge für Chor und Jazz-Enseble | Indigo-Records | 1002 CD

Koller,Hans | (as,ts,bs,cl,cond,sax,ss,sopranino)
Attila Zoller-Hans Koller
Zoller-Koller-Solal | MPS | 8431072
Freddie Brocksieper Orchester
Shot Gun Boogie | Bear Family Records | BCD 16277 AH
Freddie Brocksieper Quartett
Shot Gun Boogie | Bear Family Records | BCD 16277 AH
Hans Koller Big Band
New York City | MPS | 9813437
Hans Koller Free Sound
Phoenix | MPS | 9813438
Hans Koller Groups
Out Of The Rim | IN+OUT Records | 7014-2
Hans Koller New Jazz Stars
Deutsches Jazz Fesival 1954/1955 | Bear Family Records | BCD 15430
Hans Koller Nonet
Exclusiv | MPS | 9813440
Hans Koller Quartet
Exclusiv | MPS | 9813440
Hans Koller Quintet
Kunstkopfindianer | MPS | 9813439
Hans Koller Trio
Relax With My Horns | MPS | 9813445
NDR-Workshop
Doldinger's Best | ACT | 9224-2
Warne Marsh/Hans Koller
Jazz Unlimited | IN+OUT Records | 7017-2
Zoller-Koller-Solal Trio
Zoller-Koller-Solal | MPS | 8431072

Koller,Martin | (g,el-g,fretless-g,g-synth)
Martin Koller's Third Movement
Right Now | Traumton Records | 4430-2

Köllges,Frank | (dir,dr,electronics,voc,perc,tympani)
Dirk Raulf Group
Die Welt Ist Immer Wieder Schön | Poise | Poise 03
Franck Band
Dufte | Jazz Haus Musik | JHM 0054 CD
Klaus König Orchestra
Times Of Devastation/Poco A Poco | Enja | ENJ-6014 22
Kölner Saxophon Mafia With Ingo Kümmel And Frank Köllges
Kölner Saxophon Mafia Proudly Presents | Jazz Haus Musik | JHM 0046 CD
Norbert Stein Pata Orchester
Ritual Life | Pata Musik | PATA 5(JHM 50) CD
The Secret Act Of Painting | Pata Musik | PATA 7 CD
Pata Music Meets Arfi
News Of Roi Ubu | Pata Musik | PATA 10 CD

Kolm 3 |
Kelm 3
Per Anno | dml-records | CD 013

Kölner Rundfunkorchester |
Yusef Lateef With Eternal Wind And The 'Kölner Rundfunk Orchester'
The African American Epic Suite:Music For Quintet And Orchestra | ACT | 9214-2

Kölner Saxophon Mafia |
Kölner Saxophon Mafia
Saxfiguren | Jazz Haus Musik | JHM 0036 CD
Mafia Years 1982-86 | Jazz Haus Musik | JHM 0058 CD
Go Commercial... | Jazz Haus Musik | JHM 0065 CD
Place For Lovers | Jazz Haus Musik | JHM 0082 CD
Licence To Thrill | Jazz Haus Musik | JHM 0100 CD
Space Player | Jazz Haus Musik | JHM 0132 CD
Kölner Saxophon Mafia With Arno Steffen
Kölner Saxophon Mafia Proudly Presents | Jazz Haus Musik | JHM 0046 CD
Kölner Saxophon Mafia With Bad Little Dynamos
Kölner Saxophon Mafia Proudly Presents | Jazz Haus Musik | JHM 0046 CD
Kölner Saxophon Mafia With Blasorchester Dicke Luft
Kölner Saxophon Mafia Proudly Presents | Jazz Haus Musik | JHM 0046 CD
Kölner Saxophon Mafia With Clarence Barlow
Kölner Saxophon Mafia Proudly Presents | Jazz Haus Musik | JHM 0046 CD
Kölner Saxophon Mafia With Dieter Wellershoff
Kölner Saxophon Mafia Proudly Presents | Jazz Haus Musik | JHM 0046 CD
Kölner Saxophon Mafia With Fleisch
Kölner Saxophon Mafia Proudly Presents | Jazz Haus Musik | JHM 0046 CD
Kölner Saxophon Mafia With Guests
Kölner Saxophon Mafia: 20 Jahre Saxuelle Befreiung | Jazz Haus Musik | JHM 0115 CD
Kölner Saxophon Mafia With Hans Süper
Kölner Saxophon Mafia Proudly Presents | Jazz Haus Musik | JHM 0046 CD
Kölner Saxophon Mafia With Ina Stachelhaus And Erik Schneider
Kölner Saxophon Mafia Proudly Presents | Jazz Haus Musik | JHM 0046 CD
Kölner Saxophon Mafia With Ingo Kümmel And Frank Köllges
Kölner Saxophon Mafia Proudly Presents | Jazz Haus Musik | JHM 0046 CD
Kölner Saxophon Mafia With Irene Lorenz
Kölner Saxophon Mafia Proudly Presents | Jazz Haus Musik | JHM 0046 CD
Kölner Saxophon Mafia With Jacki Liebezeit
Kölner Saxophon Mafia Proudly Presents | Jazz Haus Musik | JHM 0046 CD
Kölner Saxophon Mafia With Klaus Der Geiger
Kölner Saxophon Mafia Proudly Presents | Jazz Haus Musik | JHM 0046 CD
Kölner Saxophon Mafia With Kristina Würminghausen
Kölner Saxophon Mafia Proudly Presents | Jazz Haus Musik | JHM 0046 CD
Kölner Saxophon Mafia With Lydie Auvray
Kölner Saxophon Mafia Proudly Presents | Jazz Haus Musik | JHM 0046 CD
Kölner Saxophon Mafia With Nedim Hazar And Orhan Temur
Kölner Saxophon Mafia Proudly Presents | Jazz Haus Musik | JHM 0046 CD
Kölner Saxophon Mafia With Ramesh Shotham
Kölner Saxophon Mafia Proudly Presents | Jazz Haus Musik | JHM 0046 CD
Kölner Saxophon Mafia With Rick E. Loef
Kölner Saxophon Mafia Proudly Presents | Jazz Haus Musik | JHM 0046 CD
Kölner Saxophon Mafia With The Auryn Quartet
Kölner Saxophon Mafia Proudly Presents | Jazz Haus Musik | JHM 0046 CD
Kölner Saxophon Mafia With Triviatas(1.Schwuler Männerchor Köln)
Kölner Saxophon Mafia Proudly Presents | Jazz Haus Musik | JHM 0046 CD
Kölner Saxophon Mafia With V.Nick Nikitakis
Kölner Saxophon Mafia Proudly Presents | Jazz Haus Musik | JHM 0046 CD
Kölner Saxophon Mafia With Willie Gräff
Kölner Saxophon Mafia Proudly Presents | Jazz Haus Musik | JHM 0046 CD

Kölsch,Dirk Peter | (dr)
Jazz Orchester Rheinland-Pfalz
Kazzou | Jazz Haus Musik | LJBB 9104
Like Life | Jazz Haus Musik | LJBB 9405

Kolstee,Wim | (tb)
Albert Nicholas With The Dutch Swing College Band
Albert Nicholas & The Dutch Swing College Band | Storyville | STCD 5522
Dutch Swing College Band
Albert Nicholas & The Dutch Swing College Band | Storyville | STCD 5522

Koltermann,Eckard | (b-cl,bsss)
Creative Works Orchestra
Willisau And More Live | Creative Works Records | CW CD 1020-2
Trio KoKoKo
Willisau And More Live | Creative Works Records | CW CD 1020-2

Kolve,Ivar | (perc)
Terje Rypdal Quartet With The Bergen Chamber Ensemble
Lux Aeterna | ECM | 1818(017070-2)

Komagata,Hiroyuki | (g)
United Future Organizatio
United Future Organization | Talkin' Loud | 518166-2

Komer,Chris | (fr-h)
Andrew Rathbun Group
Jade | Fresh Sound Records | FSNT 076 CD

Komkommer,Joel | (computer-programming)
Pili-Pili
Hotel Babo | JA & RO | JARO 4147-2

Konate,Mahama | (balafonvoc)
Jon Hassell & Farafina
Flash Of The Spirit | Intuition Records | INT 3009-2

Kondakov,Andrei | (condp)
Christian Scheuber Quartet
Clara's Smile | double moon | DMCHR 71025
Christian Scheuber Quintet
Clara's Smile | double moon | DMCHR 71025

Kondo,Toshinori | (el-tp,keyboard-b,voc,speaker,synth)
Toshinori Kondo
Touchstone | JA & RO | JARO 4172-2
Jazzy World | JA & RO | JARO 4200-2
Toshinori Kondo & Ima
Red City Smoke | JA & RO | JARO 4173-2
Toshinori Kondo & Ima plus Guests

Human Market | JA & RO | JARO 4146-2

Kondor,Robbie | (synthorg-synth)

Michel Petrucciani Group
Michel Petrucciani:The Blue Note Years | Blue Note | 789916-2
Music | Blue Note | 792563-2

Kondziela,Paul | (b)

Duke Ellington Quartet
Latin America Suite | Original Jazz Classics | OJC20 469-2
Duke Ellington Small Band
The Intimacy Of The Blues | Original Jazz Classics | OJCCD 624-2

Kongshaug,Jan Erik | (g)

Jan Erik Kongshaug Group
The Other World | ACT | 9267-2

Konietzny,Jürgen | (tp)

Marcus Sukiennik Big Band
A Night In Tunisia Suite(7 Variationen über Dizzy Gillespie's 'A Night In Tunisia') | Jazz Haus Musik | ohne Nummer

König,Klaus | (ts)

Klaus König Orchestra
Times Of Devastation/Poco A Poco | Enja | ENJ-6014 22

Konikoff,Ross | (tp)

Buddy Rich Big Band
Backwoods Siseman/Pieces Of Dream | Laserlight | 24655

Konikoff,Sandy | (perc)

Albert King Blues Band
Lovejoy | Stax | SCD 8517-2(STS 2040)

Konitz,Lee | (as,bs,overdubbed in 1 to 4 lines,ts)

Albert Mangelsdorff-Lee Konitz
Albert Mangelsdorff And His Friends | MPS | 067375-2
Attila Zoller Quartet
When It's Time | Enja | ENJ-9031 2
Attila Zoller Quintet
When It's Time | Enja | ENJ-9031 2
Attila Zoller-Lee Konitz
When It's Time | Enja | ENJ-9031 2
Bill Evans Quintet
The Complete Fantasy Recordings | Fantasy | 9FCD 1012-2
Bob Benton With The Charles Mingus Quintet
Charles Mingus-The Complete Debut Recordings | Debut | 12 DCD 4402-2
Bud Powell Orchestra
Bebop | Pablo | PACD 2310978-2
Charles Mingus Quintet
Charles Mingus-The Complete Debut Recordings | Debut | 12 DCD 4402-2
Dave Brubeck Quartet
All The Things We Are | Atlantic | 7567-81399-2
Dave Brubeck Quintet
All The Things We Are | Atlantic | 7567-81399-2
Dave Brubeck-Lee Konitz Duo
All The Things We Are | Atlantic | 7567-81399-2
Gerry Mulligan And His Orchestra
Mullenium | CBS | CK 65678
Gerry Mulligan And The Sax Section
The Gerry Mulligan Songbook | Pacific Jazz | 833575-2
Gil Evans And Ten
The Jazz Giants Play Cole Porter:Night And Day | Prestige | PCD 24203-2
Jackie Paris With The Charles Mingus Quintet
Charles Mingus-The Complete Debut Recordings | Debut | 12 DCD 4402-2
Jazzensemble Des Hessischen Rundfunks
Atmosphering Conditions Permitting | ECM | 1549/50
Kenny Burrell With The Gil Evans Orchestra
Guitar Forms | Verve | 521403-2
Verve Jazz Masters 23:Gil Evans | Verve | 521860-2
Verve Jazz Masters 45:Kenny Burrell | Verve | 527652-2
Verve Jazz Masters Vol.60:The Collection | Verve | 529866-2
Kenny Wheeler/Lee Konitz/Dave Holland/Bill Frisell
Angel Song | ECM | 1607(533098-2)
Lars Gullin American All Stars
Lars Gullin 1953,Vol.2:Moden Sounds | Dragon | DRCD 234
Lee Konitz
Tenorlee | Choice | CHCD 71019
Lee Konitz & The Gerry Mulligan Quartet
Konitz Meets Mulligan | Pacific Jazz | 746847-2
Lee Konitz And His West Coast Friends
Art Pepper:The Hollywood All-Star Sessions | Galaxy | 5GCD 4431-2
Lee Konitz Orchestra
The Art Of Saxophone | Laserlight | 24652
Lee Konitz Quartet
Lullaby Of Birdland | Candid | CCD 79709
Haiku | Nabel Records:Jazz Network | CD 4664
Subconcious-Lee | Original Jazz Classics | OJCCD 186-2(P 7004)
Lee Konitz Quintet
Sound Of Surprise | RCA | 2169309-2
Subconcious-Lee | Original Jazz Classics | OJCCD 186-2(P 7004)
Lee Konitz Trio
Motion | Verve | 065510-2
Another Shade Of Blue | Blue Note | 498222-2
Tenorlee | Choice | CHCD 71019
Three Guys | Enja | ENJ-9351 2
Newport Jazz Festival 1958,July 3rd-6th,Vol.1:Mostly Miles | Phontastic | NCD 8813
Lee Konitz With Alan Broadbent
Live-Lee | Milestone | MCD 9329-2
Lee Konitz With Strings
Strings For Holiday:A Tribute To Billie Holiday | Enja | ENJ-9304 2
Lee Konitz With The Ed Partyka Jazz Orchestra
Dreams And Realities | Laika Records | 35101642
Lee Konitz With The Oliver Strauch Group & Peter Decker
Lee Konitz With Oliver Strauch Group & Peter Decker | Edition Collage | EC 497-2
Lee Konitz-Billy Bauer Duo
Subconcious-Lee | Original Jazz Classics | OJCCD 186-2(P 7004)
Lee Konitz-Frank Wunsch Quartet
S'Nice | Nabel Records:Jazz Network | CD 4641
Lee Konitz-Harold Danko Duo
Wild As Springtime | Candid | CCD 79734
Lee Konitz-Joe Henderson
Joe Henderson:The Milestone Years | Milestone | 8MCD 4413-2
Lee Konitz-Kenny Werner
Unleemited | Owl Records | 014727-2
Lee Konitz-Kenny Wheeler Quartet
Live At Birdland Neuburg | double moon | CHRDM 71014
Lee Konitz-Matt Wilson
Gone With The Wind | Steeplechase | SCCD 31528
Lee Konitz-Michel Petrucciani Duo
Toot Sweet | Owl Records | 013432-2
Lee Konitz-Warne Marsh Quintet
Lee Konitz With Warne Marsh | Atlantic | 8122-75356-2
Lee Konitz-Warne Marsh Sextet
Lee Konitz With Warne Marsh | Atlantic | 8122-75356-2
Lee Konitz-Wolfgang Lackerschmid Quintet
Chet Baker:The Legacy Vol.3:Why Shouldn't You Cry | Enja | ENJ-9337 2
Lennie Tristano Quartet
Requiem | Atlantic | 7567-80804-2
Lenny Tristano Quartet
Subconcious-Lee | Original Jazz Classics | OJCCD 186-2(P 7004)
Lenny Tristano Quintet
Subconcious-Lee | Original Jazz Classics | OJCCD 186-2(P 7004)
Miles Davis + 19
Miles Ahead | CBS | CK 65121
Miles Davis And His Orchestra
The Complete Birth Of The Cool | Capitol | 494550-2
Birth Of The Cool | Capitol | 530117-2
Miles Davis:The Best Of The Capitol/Blue Note Years | Blue Note | 798287-2
Jazz Profile:Miles Davis | Blue Note | 823515-2
Ballads & Blues | Blue Note | 836633-2
Miles Davis:Milestones | Dreyfus Jazz Line | FDM 36731-2
Miles Davis With Gil Evans & His Orchestra
This Is Jazz:Miles Davis Plays Ballads | CBS | CK 65038
Rolf Kühn Group
Inside Out | Intuition Records | INT 3276-2
Stan Kenton And His Orchestra
Stan Kenton Portraits On Standards | Capitol | 531571-2
Wolfgang Lackerschmid-Donald Johnston Group
New Singers-New Songs | Bhakti Jazz | BR 31

Konitz,Lee[as Zeke Tolin] | (as)

Gil Evans And Ten
Gil Evans And Ten | Original Jazz Classics | OJC 346(P 7120)
Gil Evans And Ten | Prestige | PRSA 7120-6

Konkova,Olga | (pp-solo)

Olga Konkova
Her Point Of View | Candid | CCD 79757
Olga Konkova Trio
Her Point Of View | Candid | CCD 79757
Olga Konkova-Per Mathisen Quartet
Northern Crossing | Candid | CCD 79766

Konopasek,Jan | (bs,flsax)

Hans Koller Big Band
New York City | MPS | 9813437
Woody Herman And His Orchestra
Woody Herman Herd At Montreux | Original Jazz Classics | OJCCD 991-2(F 9470)
Woody Herman And The New Thundering Herd
Woody Herman:Thundering Herd | Original Jazz Classics | OJCCD 841-2

Konrad,Bernd | (as,bass-sax,bs,b-cl,contra-b-cl,sax)

Bernd Konrad Jazz Group With Symphonie Orchestra
Wen Die Götter Lieben | Creative Works Records | CW CD 1010-1
Bernd Konrad With Erwin Lehn und sein Südfunk Orchester Stuttgart
Wen Die Götter Lieben | Creative Works Records | CW CD 1010-1
Creative Works Orchestra
Willisau And More Live | Creative Works Records | CW CD 1020-2
Hans Koller Groups
Out Of The Rim | IN+OUT Records | 7014-2

Konstantinou,Kostas | (b)

Kostas Konstantinou-Vassilis Tsabropoulos
Concentric Cycles | Nabel Records:Jazz Network | CD 4698

Konstantynowicz,Marek | (viola)

Annette Peacock With The Cikada String Quartet
An Acrobat's Heart | ECM | 1733(159496-2)
Arild Andersen Quintet With The Cikada String Quartet
Hyperborean | ECM | 1631(537342-2)
Christof Lauer-Jens Thomas With The Cikada String Quartet
Shadows In The Rain | ACT | 9297-2
Mats Eden-Jonas Simonson With The Cikada String Quartet
Milvus | ECM | 1660
Trygve Seim-Oyvind Braekke-Per Oddvar Johansen Orchestra
The Source And Different Cikadas | ECM | 1764(014432-2)

Kontomanon,Elisabeth | (voc)

Cornelius Claudio Kreusch Group
Scoop | ACT | 9255-2

Kontrasax |

Kontrasax
Zanshin/Kontrasax | Jazz Haus Musik | JHM 0130 CD

Koono | (keyboards,psynth)

Biréli Lagrene Quartet
My Favorite Django | Dreyfus Jazz Line | FDM 36574-2

Koorax,Ithamara | (voc)

Ithamara Koorax With Band
Love Dance:The Ballad Album | Milestone | MCD 9327-2

Kooymans,George | (g)

Pili-Pili
Jakko | JA & RO | JARO 4131-2

Kopf,Tobias | (b)

Marty Hall Band
Tried & True | Blues Beacon | BLU-1030 2

Kordel,Guido | (tpfl-h)

Jazz Orchester Rheinland-Pfalz
Like Life | Jazz Haus Musik | LJBB 9405
Last Season | Jazz Haus Musik | LJBB 9706

Kordus,Tom | (tb)

Buddy Childers Big Band
Just Buddy's | Candid | CCD 79761

Korner,Alexis | (g,mand,mandolinvoc)

Passport And Guests
Doldinger Jubilee Concert | Atlantic | 2292-44175-2

Kornmaier,Mathias | (dr)

Frank Sackenheim Quartet
The Music Of Chance | Jazz 4 Ever Records:Jazz Network | J4E 4753
Frank Sackenheim Quintet
The Music Of Chance | Jazz 4 Ever Records:Jazz Network | J4E 4753

Korosi,Yancey | (p)

Zoot Sims Quartet
Zoot Sims | Storyville | STCD 8367
Zoot Sims Quintet
Zoot Sims | Storyville | STCD 8367

Kortchmar,Danny | (g)

Robben Ford & The Blue Line
Handful Of Blues | Blue Thumb | BTR 70042

Korthals Altes,Erica | (v)

Stochelo Rosenberg Group With Strings
Gypsy Swing | Verve | 527806-2

Kosazana,Noma | (voc)

Noma Kosazana & Uli Lenz
Art Of The Duo: Trouble In Paradise | Tutu Records | 888144-2*

Koslowski,Jan | (g)

Landes Jugend Jazz Orchester Hessen
Touch Of Lips | hr music.de | hrmj 004-01 CD

Kostelnik,Dan | (org)

We Three
East Coasting | Organic Music | ORGM 9702
The Drivin' Beat | Organic Music | ORGM 9707
We Three With Roman Schwaller
East Coasting | Organic Music | ORGM 9702

Kostur,Glenn | (bs)

Maynard Ferguson And His Big Bop Nouveau Band
Maynard Ferguson '93-Footpath Café | Hot Shot Records | HSR 8312-2

Köszegi,Imre | (dr)

Al Casey Quartet
A Tribute To Fats | Jazzpoint | JP 1044 CD
A' Portrait Of Jan Jankeje | Jazzpoint | JP 1054 CD
Doc Cheatham Sextet
A' Portrait Of Jan Jankeje | Jazzpoint | JP 1054 CD
George Kelly Quintet
A' Portrait Of Jan Jankeje | Jazzpoint | JP 1054 CD
Hannes Beckmann Quartet
Violin Tales | Tutu Records | 888202-2*
Lajos Dudas Quartet
Jubilee Edition | double moon | CHRDM 71020
Lajos Dudas Quintet
Jubilee Edition | double moon | CHRDM 71020
Red Richards-George Kelly Sextet With Doc Cheatham
Groove Move | Jazzpoint | JP 1045 CD

Koszorski,Siegfried | (dr)

Glen Buschmann Quintet
Deutsches Jazz Fesival 1954/1955 | Bear Family Records | BCD 15430
Wolfgang Sauer With The Glen Buschmann Quintet
Deutsches Jazz Fesival 1954/1955 | Bear Family Records | BCD 15430

Kothe,Hans | (tp)

Uri Caine With The Concerto Köln
Concerto Köln | Winter&Winter | 910086-2

Kotick,Teddy | (b)

Al Cohn Quintet feat. Zoot Sims
Al And Zoot | GRP | 951827-2
Bill Evans Trio
Bill Evans:The Secret Sessions | Milestone | 8MCD 4421-2
New Jazz Conceptions | Original Jazz Classics | OJC20 025-2(RLP 223)
Charlie Parker And His Orchestra
Bird: The Complete Charlie Parker On Verve | Verve | 837141-2
Charlie Parker Quartet
Charlie Parker:Bird's Best Bop On Verve | Verve | 527452-2
Charlie Parker:The Best Of The Verve Years | Verve | 527815-2
Charlie Parker | Verve | 539757-2
Bird: The Complete Charlie Parker On Verve | Verve | 837141-2
Charlie Parker Quintet
Verve Jazz Masters 28:Charlie Parker Plays Standards | Verve | 521854-2
Charlie Parker:Bird's Best Bop On Verve | Verve | 527452-2
Charlie Parker:The Best Of The Verve Years | Verve | 527815-2
Talkin' Bird | Verve | 559859-2
The Cole Porter Songbook | Verve | 823250-2
Bird: The Complete Charlie Parker On Verve | Verve | 837141-2
Charlie Parker Septet
Talkin' Bird | Verve | 559859-2
Charlie Parker Sextet
Verve Jazz Masters 28:Charlie Parker Plays Standards | Verve | 521854-2
Charlie Parker:The Best Of The Verve Years | Verve | 527815-2
Talkin' Bird | Verve | 559859-2
The Cole Porter Songbook | Verve | 823250-2
Charlie Parker's Jazzers
Bird: The Complete Charlie Parker On Verve | Verve | 837141-2
George Russell Smalltet
The RCA Victor Jazz Workshop | RCA | 2159144-2
Herbie Nichols Trio
Blue Note Plays Gershwin | Blue Note | 520808-2
Herbie Nichols:The Complete Blue Note Recordings | Blue Note | 859352-2
Horace Silver Quintet
Horace Silver Retrospective | Blue Note | 495576-2
Stylings Of Silver | Blue Note | 540034-2
Martial Solal Trio
Martial Solal At Newport '63 | RCA | 2174803-2
Phil Woods Quartet
Woodlore | Original Jazz Classics | OJCCD 052-2
Stan Getz Quintet
Stan Getz-The Complete Roost Sessions | EMI Records | 859622-2

Kott,Alois | (b,el-b,psynth)

Ensemble Indigo
Reflection | Enja | ENJ-9417 2
Greenfish
Perfume Light... | TipToe | TIP-888831 2
Jazzensemble Des Hessischen Rundfunks
Atmosphering Conditions Permitting | ECM | 1549/50

Kottenhahn,Volker | (p)

Céline Rudolph And Her Trio
Paintings | Nabel Records:Jazz Network | CD 4661
Book Of Travels | Nabel Records:Jazz Network | CD 4672
Volker Kottenhahn Trio
Out Of Print | Nabel Records:Jazz Network | CD 4680
Welcome To The Maze
Welcome To The Maze:Puzzle | Nabel Records:Jazz Network | CD 4671

Koutzen,George | (cello)

Bob Benton With The Charles Mingus Quintet
Charles Mingus-The Complete Debut Recordings | Debut | 12 DCD 4402-2
Charles Mingus Quintet
Charles Mingus-The Complete Debut Recordings | Debut | 12 DCD 4402-2
Jackie Paris With The Charles Mingus Quintet
Charles Mingus-The Complete Debut Recordings | Debut | 12 DCD 4402-2

Kouyaté,Diely-Moussa | (g)

Hank Jones Meets Cheik-Tidiana Seck
Sarala | Verve | 528783-2

Kouyaté,Lansine | (balafon)

Kouyaté,Ousmane | (g)

Kouyaté,Soriba | (kora)

Soriba Kouyaté Quartet
Live In Montreux | ACT | 9414-2

Kovac,Gyola | (dr)

Mihaly Tabany Orchestra
Jubilee Edition | double moon | CHRDM 71020

Kovac,Roland | (p)

Hans Koller New Jazz Stars
Deutsches Jazz Fesival 1954/1955 | Bear Family Records | BCD 15430

Kovacev,Branislav | (dr)

Art Van Damme Group
State Of Art | MPS | 841413-2
Horst Jankowski Orchestra With Voices
Jankowskeynotes | MPS | 9814806
Horst Jankowski Quartet
Jankowskinetik | MPS | 9808189
Mihaly Tabany Orchestra
Jubilee Edition | double moon | CHRDM 71020

Kovacev,Lala | (drperc)

NDR Big Band With Guests
50 Years Of NDR Big Band:Bravissimo II | ACT | 9259-2

Koven,Jack | (tp)

Gil Evans And Ten
Gil Evans And Ten | Original Jazz Classics | OJC 346(P 7120)
The Jazz Giants Play Cole Porter:Night And Day | Prestige | PCD 24203-2
Gil Evans And Ten | Prestige | PRSA 7120-6

Koven,Renita | (viola)

Jacintha With Band And Strings
Lush Life | Groove Note | GRV 1011-2(Gold CD 2011)

Koverhult,Tommy | (flts)

Lisa Ekdahl With The Peter Nordahl Trio
When Did You Leave Heaven | RCA | 2143175-2

Kowald,Peter | (alphorn,tuba,b,voice,b-solocond)

Alfred 23 Harth Group
Sweet Paris | free flow music | ffm 0291
Elvira Plenar Trio
I Was Just... | free flow music | ffm 0191
Jazzensemble Des Hessischen Rundfunks
Atmosphering Conditions Permitting | ECM | 1549/50
The Remedy
The Remedy | Jazz Haus Musik | JHM 0069 CD

Kowalsky,Alexander | (tb)

Jazzensemble Des Hessischen Rundfunks
Jazz Messe-Messe Für Unsere Zeit | hr music.de | hrmj 003-01 CD

Koyaté,Fatoumata 'Mama' | (voc)

Hank Jones Meets Cheik-Tidiana Seck
Sarala | Verve | 528783-2

Kozlov,Boris | (b)

Charles Mingus Orchestra
Tonight At Noon...Three Or Four Shades Of Love | Dreyfus Jazz Line | FDM 36633-2
Mingus Big Band
Tonight At Noon...Three Or Four Shades Of Love | Dreyfus Jazz Line | FDM 36633-2

Krachmalnick,Jacob | (vconcert-master)

Milt Jackson With Strings
To Bags...With Love:Memorial Album | Pablo | 2310967-2

Kracht,Hartmut | (b,big-muff,ethno-beat,el-bb-solo)

La Voce-Music For Voices,Trumpet And Bass | JA & RO | JARO 4208-2
Hans Lüdemann Rism
Aph-o-Rism's | Jazz Haus Musik | JHM 0049 CD
Unitarism | Jazz Haus Musik | JHM 0067 CD
Hans Lüdemann Rism 7

INTERPRETENVERZEICHNIS

FutuRISM | Jazz Haus Musik | JHM 0092/93 CD
Hartmut Kracht
Kontrabass Pur | Jazz Haus Musik | JHM 0103 CD
Peter Weiss Orchestra
Personal Choice | Nabel Records:Jazz Network | CD 4669
Peter Weiss Quartet
Personal Choice | Nabel Records:Jazz Network | CD 4669

Kraft,Stan | (vviola)
Charlie Parker With Strings
Verve Jazz Masters 28:Charlie Parker Plays Standards | Verve | 521854-2
Coleman Hawkins With Billy Byers And His Orchestra
The Hawk In Hi-Fi | RCA | 2663842-2

Kragerup,Peder | (cond)
Michael Mantler Group With The Danish Concert Radio Orchestra
Many Have No Speech | Watt | 19(835580-2)

Krahmer,Carlo | (drvib)
Vic Lewis And His Band
Vic Lewis:The Golden Years | Candid | CCD 79754
Vic Lewis Jam Session
Vic Lewis:The Golden Years | Candid | CCD 79754

Krakatau |
Krakatau
Volition | ECM | 1466
Matinale | ECM | 1529

Kral,Irene | (voc)
Irene Kral With Alan Broadbent
Where Is Love? | Choice | CHCD 71012
Maynard Ferguson And His Orchestra
Verve Jazz Masters 52:Maynard Ferguson | Verve | 529905-2

Kral,Petri | (ts)
Al Porcino Big Band
Al Cohn Meets Al Porcino | Organic Music | ORGM 9730

Kral,Roy | (p,arrvoc)
Anita O'Day And Her Combo
Verve Jazz Masters 49:Anita O'Day | Verve | 527653-2
Jackie Cain/Roy Kral Quartet
Full Circle | Fantasy | FCD 24768-2
Jackie Cain-Roy Kral Group
Full Circle | Fantasy | FCD 24768-2

Krall,Diana | (keyboards,pvoc)
Dave Grusin Orchestra
Two For The Road:The Music Of Henry Mancini | GRP | GRP 98652
Diana Krall Group
When I Look In Your Eyes | Verve | 9513304
The Girl In The Other Room | Verve | 9862246
Diana Krall Group With Orchestra
When I Look In Your Eyes | Verve | 9513304
Diana Krall Quartet
All For You-A Dedication To The Nat King Cole Trio | Impulse(MCA) | 951164-2
Diana Krall Trio
All For You-A Dedication To The Nat King Cole Trio | Impulse(MCA) | 951164-2
Love Scenes | Impulse(MCA) | 951234-2

Krämer,Bernd | (gtp)
Wayne Bartlett With The Thomas Hufschmidt Group
Tokyo Blues | Laika Records | 35101212

Krämer,Oliver | (electronics)
Digital Masters Feat. Bryan Steele
Sun Dance | Edition Musikat | EDM 038

Kramer,Raphael | (cello)
Ella Fitzgerald With The Frank DeVol Orchestra
Get Happy! | Verve | 523321-2
Milt Jackson With Strings
To Bags...With Love:Memorial Album | Pablo | 2310967-2
Pete Rugolo And His Orchestra
Thriller/Richard Diamon(Original Jazz Scores From 2 Classics TV Series) | Fresh Sound Records | FSCD 2015
Phineas Newborn Jr. With Dennis Farnon And His Orchestra
While My Lady Sleeps | RCA | 2185157-2

Kramer,Ray | (cello)
Ella Fitzgerald With The Billy May Orchestra
The Best Of The Song Books:The Ballads | Verve | 521867-2
Ella Fitzgerald Sings The Harold Arlen Song Book | Verve | 589108-2
Ella Fitzgerald With The Nelson Riddle Orchestra
The Best Of The Song Books:The Ballads | Verve | 521867-2
Love Songs:The Best Of The Song Books | Verve | 531762-2

Kramer,Viola | (synthlive-electronics)
Norbert Stein Pata Orchester
Ritual Life | Pata Musik | PATA 5(JHM 50) CD
The Secret Act Of Painting | Pata Musik | PATA 7 CD

Kramis,Herbert | (b)
Schmilz
Schmilz | Creative Works Records | CW CD 1041

Kranenburg,Cornelius 'Cees' | (dr)
Coleman Hawkins Trio
Jazz:The Essential Collection Vol.3 | IN+OUT Records | 78013-2
Coleman Hawkins With The Ramblers
Jazz:The Essential Collection Vol.3 | IN+OUT Records | 78013-2
Rhoda Scott Trio
Jazz In Paris:Rhoda Scott-Live At The Olympia | EmArCy | 549879-2 PMS

Krantz,Sigge | (el-g,b,b-g,perckagan)
Beng Berger Band
Bitter Funeral Beer | ECM | 1179

Krantz,Wayne | (g,el-grh-g)
David Binney Group
Balance | ACT | 9411-2
Jasper Van't Hof Group
Blue Corner | ACT | 9228-2
Leni Stern Group
Secrets | Enja | ENJ-5093 2
Closer To The Light | Enja | ENJ-6034 2
Wayne Krantz
Signals | Enja | ENJ-6048 2
Wayne Krantz Duo
Signals | Enja | ENJ-6048 2
Wayne Krantz Quartet
Signals | Enja | ENJ-6048 2
Wayne Krantz Trio
Long To Be Loose | Enja | ENJ-7099 2
2 Drinks Minimum | Enja | ENJ-9043 2

Krassik,Nicolas | (v)
Michel Petrucciani With The Graffiti String Quartet
Marvellous | Dreyfus Jazz Line | FDM 36564-2

Kraus,Phil | (bells,marimba,celeste,perc,vib)
Cal Tjader With The Lalo Schifrin Orchestra
Talkin Verve/Roots Of Acid Jazz:Cal Tjader | Verve | 531562-2
Coleman Hawkins With Billy Byers And His Orchestra
The Hawk In Hi-Fi | RCA | 2663842-2
Freddie Hubbard With Orchestra
This Is Jazz:Freddie Hubbard | CBS | CK 65041
Jimmy Smith With The Lalo Schifrin Orchestra
Jimmy Smith:Best Of The Verve Years | Verve | 527950-2
Jimmy Smith-Talkin' Verve | Verve | 531563-2
The Cat | Verve | 539756-2
Lalo Schifrin And His Orchestra
Verve Jazz Masters 39:Cal Tjader | Verve | 521858-2
Oliver Nelson And His Orchestra
Verve Jazz Masters Vol.60:The Collection | Verve | 529866-2
Quincy Jones And His Orchestra
Talkin' Verve-Roots Of Acid Jazz:Roland Kirk | Verve | 533101-2
Rahsaan/The Complete Mercury Recordings Of Roland Kirk | Mercury | 846630-2
Stan Getz With The Eddie Sauter Orchestra
Stan Getz Plays The Music Of Mickey One | Verve | 531232-2

Krause,Jo | (dr)
Benny Bailey Quartet
Angel Eyes | Laika Records | 8695068
David Mengual Quartet
Monkiana:A Tribute To Thelonious Monk | Fresh Sound Records | FSNT 019 CD
David Mengual Quintet
Monkiana:A Tribute To Thelonious Monk | Fresh Sound Records | FSNT 019 CD
José Luis Gámez Quartet
Colores | Fresh Sound Records | FSNT 028 CD
José Luis Gámez Quattro | Fresh Sound Records | FSNT 094 CD
José Luis Gámez Quintet
Colores | Fresh Sound Records | FSNT 028 CD
José Luis Gámez Trio
Colores | Fresh Sound Records | FSNT 028 CD
The Waltzer-McHenry Quartet
Jazz Is Where You Find It | Fresh Sound Records | FSNT 021 CD

Krause,Kurt | (tb)
Bernd Konrad With Erwin Lehn und sein Südfunk Orchester Stuttgart
Wen Die Götter Lieben | Creative Works Records | CW CD 1010-1
Erwin Lehn Und Sein Südfunk-Tanzorchester
Deutsches Jazz Fesival 1954/1955 | Bear Family Records | BCD 15430

Krause,Ralf | (tb)
Jazzensemble Des Hessischen Rundfunks
Jazz Messe-Messe Für Unsere Zeit | hr music.de | hrmj 003-01 CD

Krause,Uwe | (tp)

Krauss,Briggan | (asbs)
Michael Blake Group
Drift | Intuition Records | INT 3212-2

Krautgartner,Karel | (cl)
Jazzensemble Des Hessischen Rundfunks
Atmosphering Conditions Permitting | ECM | 1549/50

Kreamen,David | (g)
Miles Davis Group
On The Corner | CBS | CK 63980

Krebs,Klaus | (el-b)
Jazz Bomberos
Naranja | Green House Music | CD 1003(Maxi)

Krechter,Joe | (b-cl)
Artie Shaw And His Orchestra
Planet JazzArtie Shaw | Planet Jazz | 2152057-2
Planet Jazz:Jazz Greatest Hits | Planet Jazz | 2169648-2

Kreibich,Paul | (dr)
Don Menza And The Joe Haider Trio
Bilein | JHM Records | JHM 3608
Herb Geller Quartet
Herb Geller Plays The Al Cohn Songbook | Hep | CD 2066
To Benny & Johnny | Hep | CD 2084
Vic Lewis West Coast All Stars
Vic Lewis Presenting A Celebration Of Contemporary West Coast Jazz | Candid | CCD 79711/12

Kreitmeier,Thilo | (as,ts,fl,varitone,reedsarr)
Al Jones Blues Band
Sharper Than A Tack | Blues Beacon | BLU-1034 2
Alberto Marsico Quintet
Them That's Got | Organic Music | ORGM 9705
Thilo Kreitmeier & Group
Soul Call | Organic Music | ORGM 9711
Changes | Organic Music | ORGM 9725
Thilo Kreitmeier Quintet
Mo' Better Blues | Organic Music | ORGM 9706

Kreitzer,Scott | (fl,alto-fl,b-clsax)
Spyro Gyra & Guests
Love & Other Obsessions | GRP | GRP 98112

Kremer,Stefan | (dr)
John Thomas & Lifeforce
Devil Dance | Nabel Records:Jazz Network | CD 4601

Kress,Carl | (bj,gg-solo)
Billie Holiday With Toots Camarata And His Orchestra
Billie's Love Songs | Nimbus Records | NI 2000
Frank Trumbauer And His Orchestra
The Hollywood Session:The Capitol Jazzmen | Jazz Unlimited | JUCD 2044
Jack Teagarden And His Band
Meet Me Where They Play The Blues | Good Time Jazz | GTCD 12063-2
Louis Armstrong And His Orchestra
Louis Armstrong:Swing That Music | Laserlight | 36056
Louis Armstrong:C'est Si Bon | Dreyfus Jazz Line | FDM 36730-2
Louis Armstrong With Gordon Jenkins And His Orchestra And Choir
Satchmo In Style | Verve | 549594-2
Louis Armstrong-My Greatest Songs | MCA | MCD 18347
Swing Legends:Louis Armstrong | Nimbus Records | NI 2012
Muggsy Spanier And His Dixieland Band
Muggsy Spanier-Manhattan Masters,1945 | Storyville | STCD 6051
The Three T's
Jazz:The Essential Collection Vol.3 | IN+OUT Records | 78013-2

Kresse,Hans | (b)
Hugo Strasser Combo
Deutsches Jazz Fesival 1954/1955 | Bear Family Records | BCD 15430
Jutta Hipp Quintet
Deutsches Jazz Fesival 1954/1955 | Bear Family Records | BCD 15430
Wolfgang Lauth Quartet
Deutsches Jazz Fesival 1954/1955 | Bear Family Records | BCD 15430
Lauther | Bear Family Records | BCD 15717 AH

Kretz,Julia-Maria | (v)
Lisa Bassenge Trio With Guests
A Sight, A Song | Minor Music | 801100

Kretzschmar,Hermann | (psampler)
Ensemble Modern
Ensemble Modern-Fred Frith:Traffic Continues | Winter&Winter | 910044-2

Kretzschmar,Robert | (ts)
Joachim Raffel Sextet
...In Motion | Jazz 4 Ever Records:Jazz Network | J4E 4746

Kreusch,Cornelius Claudio | (muted-p,p,kalimba,melodicap-solo)
Cornelius Claudio Kreusch
Talking To A Goblin | Edition Collage | EC 441-2
Piano Moments | Take Twelve On CD | TT 007-2
Cornelius Claudio Kreusch Group
Scoop | ACT | 9255-2
Cornelius Claudio Kreusch/Hans Poppel
Music For Two Pianos | Edition Collage | EC 465-2
Piano Moments | Take Twelve On CD | TT 007-2

Kreusch,Johannes Tonio | (african-vib,prepared-gg)
Cornelius Claudio Kreusch Group
Scoop | ACT | 9255-2

Kreuzeder,Klaus | (fl,ss,as,sax,lyriconsopranino)
Klaus Kreuzeder & Franz Benton
Big little Gigs: First Takes Live | Trick Music | TM 0112 CD
Klaus Kreuzeder & Henry Sincigno
Saxappeal | Trick Music | TM 9013 MC
Sax As Sax Can-Alive | Trick Music | TM 9312 CD
Klaus Kreuzeder & Willi Herzinger
Sax As Sax Can | Trick Music | TM 8712 CD

Kreuzer,Marion | (voc)
Jazzensemble Des Hessischen Rundfunks
Jazz Messe-Messe Für Unsere Zeit | hr music.de | hrmj 003-01 CD

Kricker,John | (b-tb)
Maynard Ferguson And His Big Bop Nouveau Band
Maynard Ferguson '93-Footpath Café | Hot Shot Records | HSR 8312-2

Kriegel,Volker | (fl,g,bj,el-b,voice,el-g,perc,sitar)
Dave Pike Set
Dave Pike Set:Masterpieces | MPS | 531848-2
Jazzensemble Des Hessischen Rundfunks
Atmosphering Conditions Permitting | ECM | 1549/50
Jon Hiseman With The United Jazz & Rock Ensemble And Babara Thompson's Paraphernalia
About Time Too! | VeraBra Records | CDVBR 2014-2
Klaus Doldinger Septet
Doldinger's Best | ACT | 9224-2
Passport And Guests
Doldinger Jubilee Concert | Atlantic | 2292-44175-2
The New Dave Pike Set & Grupo Baiafra De Bahia
Dave Pike Set:Masterpieces | MPS | 531848-2
Volker Kriegel Quintet
Spectrum | MPS | 9808699

Krieger,Andreas | (dr)
Günther Klatt Quartet
Internationales Jazzfestival Münster | Tutu Records | 888110-2*

Kriener,Wolfgang | (b)
Helmut Nieberle-Helmut Kagerer Quartet
Flashes | Jardis Records | JRCD 20031

Krill,Torsten | (dr)
Cécile Verny Quartet
Kekeli | double moon | CHRDM 71028
Cécile Verny Quintet
Kekeli | double moon | CHRDM 71028
Rainer Tempel Band
Suite Ellington | Jazz 'n' Arts Records | JNA 0401
Stuttgarter Gitarren Trio
Stuttgarter Gitarren Trio Vol.2 | Edition Musikat | EDM 034

Krimsky,Katrina | (p)
Katrina Krimsky-Trevor Watts
Stella Malu | ECM | 1199

Kris,Ira | (g)
Hans Koller Nonet
Exclusiv | MPS | 9813440

Krisch,Dizzy | (vib,keyboards,midi-vib)
Claus Stötter's Nevertheless
Die Entdeckung Der Banane | Jazz 'n' Arts Records | JNA 1403

Krisch,Thomas | (b)
Heiner Franz Trio
Jazz Guitar Highlights 1 | Jardis Records | JRCD 20141
A Window To The Soul | Jardis Records | JRCD 8801
Gouache | Jardis Records | JRCD 8904
Uli Gutscher Quintet
Wind Moments | Take Twelve On CD | TT 009-2
Werner Lener Quartet
My Own | Satin Doll Productions | SDP 1013-1 CD
Personal Moments | Satin Doll Productions | SDP 1026-1 CD
Colours | Satin Doll Productions | SDP 1033-1 CD
Werner Lener Trio
My Own | Satin Doll Productions | SDP 1013-1 CD
Personal Moments | Satin Doll Productions | SDP 1026-1 CD
Colours | Satin Doll Productions | SDP 1033-1 CD

Krisse,Fritz | (b)
Benny Bailey Quartet
I Thought About You | Laika Records | 35100762
Angel Eyes | Laika Records | 8695068
Benny Bailey Quartet With Wayne Bartlett
I Thought About You | Laika Records | 35100762
Fritz Krisse Quartet
Soulcolours | Laika Records | 35100782
Philippe Caillat Group
Stream Of Time | Laika Records | LK 92-030

Kristensen,Kim | (fl,keyboards,electronic-perc)
Kim Kristensen
Pulse Of Time | dacapo | DCCD 9435
Michael Mantler Group
Songs And One Symphony | ECM | 1721
Michael Mantler Group With The Danish Radio Concert Orchestra Strings
The School Of Understanding(Sort-Of-An-Opera) | ECM | 1648/49(537963-2)
Mona Larsen And The Danish Radio Big Band Plus Soloists
Michael Mantler:Cerco Un Paese Innocente | ECM | 1556

Kristensen,Niels Jakob 'Filt' | (reeds)
The Orchestra
New Skies | dacapo | DCCD 9463

Krog,Karin | (ring-modulator,tamboura,voice,voc)
John Surman Trio
Such Winters Of Memory | ECM | 1254(810621-2)
NDR Big Band With Guests
50 Years Of NDR Big Band:Bravissimo II | ACT | 9259-2
Nordic Quartet
Nordic Quartet | ECM | 1553

Kröger,Ed | (ptb)
Changes
Jazz Portraits | EGO | 95080
Ed Kröger Quartet
What's New | Laika Records | 35101172
Ed Kröger Quartet plus Guests
Movin' On | Laika Records | 35101332

Krogh,Per | (bj)
Henrik Johansen's Jazzband
The Golden Years Of Revival Jazz,Vol 1 | Storyville | STCD 5506
The Golden Years Of Revival Jazz,Vol.2 | Storyville | STCD 5507

Krokfors,Uffe | (bperc)
Edward Vesala Ensemble
Ode Of The Death Of Jazz | ECM | 1413(843196-2)
Krakatau
Volition | ECM | 1466
Matinale | ECM | 1529

Kroll,Frank | (b-cl,sax,cl,ssas)
Daniel Messina Band
Imagenes | art-mode-records | 990014
Patrick Bebelaar Group
Point Of View | dml-records | CD 017
Patrick Bebelaar Quartet
Never Thought It Could Happen | dml-records | CD 007
You Never Lose An Island | dml-records | CD 015
Sputnik 27
But Where's The Moon? | dml-records | CD 011

Kroll,Heribert | (saxss)
Frank Kroll Quintet
Landscape | dml-records | CD 014

Kronberg,Günther | (as,bs,bs-playbackreeds)
Jazzensemble Des Hessischen Rundfunks
Atmosphering Conditions Permitting | ECM | 1549/50
Klaus Weiss Orchestra
Live At The Domicile | ATM Records | ATM 3805-AH

Kroner,Erling | (tb)
Stan Getz With The Danish Radio Big Band
Stan Getz In Europe | Laserlight | 24657

Kronos Quartet |
John Zorn Group With The Kronos Quartet
Spillane | Nonesuch | 7559-79172-2

Kronstadt,Gina | (concertmasterv)
Charlie Haden Quartet West With Strings
The Art Of The Song | Verve | 547403-2
Jacintha With Band And Strings
Lush Life | Groove Note | GRV 1011-2(Gold CD 2011)

Kroon,F. | (v)
Toots Thielemans And His Orchestra
Verve Jazz Masters Vol.59:Toots Thielemans | Verve | 535271-2

Kroon,Steve | (congasperc)
Diana Krall Quartet
All For You-A Dedication To The Nat King Cole Trio | Impulse(MCA) | 951164-2
Helen Merrill With Orchestra
Casa Forte | EmArCy | 558848-2
Russell Malone Quintet
Sweet Georgia Peach | Impulse(MCA) | 951282-2
Stephen Scott Quartet
Vision Quest | Enja | ENJ-9347 2

Kropp,Wolfgang | (perccongas)
Marion Brown & Jazz Cussion

Echoes Of Blue | double moon | CHRDM 71015

Kroyt | (band)
Kölner Saxophon Mafia With Guests
Kölner Saxophon Mafia: 20 Jahre Saxuelle Befreiung | Jazz Haus Musik | JHM 0115 CD

Krückel,Jörg | (p)
Jörg Krückel-Brad Leali Quartet
Cookin' Good | Edition Collage | EC 507-2

Kruczek,Leo | (vviola)
Ben Webster With Orchestra And Strings
Verve Jazz Masters 43:Ben Webster | Verve | 525431-2
Music For Loving:Ben Webster With Strings | Verve | 527774-2
Ultimate Ben Webster selected by James Carter | Verve | 557537-2
Billie Holiday With The Ray Ellis Orchestra
Lady In Satin | CBS | CK 65144
Cannonball Adderley And His Orchestra
Verve Jazz Masters 31:Cannonball Adderley | Verve | 522651-2
Coleman Hawkins With Billy Byers And His Orchestra
The Hawk In Hi-Fi | RCA | 2663842-2
Lalo Schifrin And His Orchestra
Verve Jazz Masters 39:Cal Tjader | Verve | 521858-2
Sarah Vaughan With Orchestra
!Viva! Vaughan | Mercury | 549374-2
Sarah Vaughan Sings The Mancini Songbook | Verve | 558401-2
Stan Getz With The Eddie Sauter Orchestra
Stan Getz Plays The Music Of Mickey One | Verve | 531232-2
Wes Montgomery With The Jimmy Jones Orchestra
Wes Montgomery-The Complete Riverside Recordings | Riverside | 12 RCD 4408-2
The Jazz Giants Play Rodgers & Hart:Blue Moon | Prestige | PCD 24205-2

Krug,Peter | (b)
Marion Brown & Jazz Cussion
Echoes Of Blue | double moon | CHRDM 71015

Krug,Uli | (el-bsousaphone)
Ax Genrich Group
Psychedelic Guitar | ATM Records | ATM 3809-AH

Krüger,Erich | (viola)
Till Brönner Quartet & Deutsches Symphonieorchester Berlin
German Songs | Minor Music | 801057

Krüger,Olaf | (tp)
Wayne Bartlett With The Thomas Hufschmidt Group
Tokyo Blues | Laika Records | 35101212

Kruger,Stefan | (dr)
Lotz Of Music
Puasong Daffriek | Laika Records | LK 94-054

Krupa,Gene | (dr,ldvoc)
Anita O'Day With Gene Krupa And His Orchestra
Let Me Off Uptown:Anita O'Day With Gene Krupa | CBS | CK 65625
Benny Goodman And His Orchestra
Planet Jazz:Benny Goodman | Planet Jazz | 2152054-2
Planet Jazz Sampler | Planet Jazz | 2152326-2
Planet Jazz:Jazz Greatest Hits | Planet Jazz | 2169648-2
Planet Jazz:Big Bands | Planet Jazz | 2169649-2
Planet Jazz:Swing | Planet Jazz | 2169651-2
Planet Jazz:Jazz Trumpet | Planet Jazz | 2169654-2
Planet Jazz:Female Jazz Vocalists | Planet Jazz | 2169656-2
The Legends Of Swing | Laserlight | 24659
Swing Vol.1 | Storyville | 4960343
Jazz:The Essential Collection Vol.3 | IN+OUT Records | 78013-2
Benny Goodman At Carnegie Hall 1938(Complete) | CBS | C2K 65143
More Camel Caravans | Phontastic | NCD 8841/2
More Camel Caravans | Phontastic | NCD 8843/4
Benny Goodman Band
Benny Goodman At Carnegie Hall 1938(Complete) | CBS | C2K 65143
Benny Goodman Combo
Benny Goodman At Carnegie Hall 1938(Complete) | CBS | C2K 65143
Benny Goodman Dixieland Quintet
Benny Goodman At Carnegie Hall 1938(Complete) | CBS | C2K 65143
Benny Goodman Quartet
Planet Jazz:Benny Goodman | Planet Jazz | 2152054-2
Jazz Collection:Benny Goodman | Laserlight | 24396
Together Again! | RCA | 2663881-2
Benny Goodman At Carnegie Hall 1938(Complete) | CBS | C2K 65143
More Camel Caravans | Phontastic | NCD 8841/2
More Camel Caravans | Phontastic | NCD 8843/4
Benny Goodman Trio
Planet Jazz:Benny Goodman | Planet Jazz | 2152054-2
Planet Jazz:Swing | Planet Jazz | 2169651-2
Planet Jazz:Jazz Piano | Planet Jazz | 2169655-2
Jazz Collection:Benny Goodman | Laserlight | 24396
Benny Goodman At Carnegie Hall 1938(Complete) | CBS | C2K 65143
More Camel Caravans | Phontastic | NCD 8841/2
More Camel Caravans | Phontastic | NCD 8843/4
Big Sid Catlett And His Orchestra
The Small Black Groups | Storyville | 4960523
Buddy Rich-Gene Krupa Orchestra
Krupa And Rich | Verve | 521643-2
Eddie Condon And His Chicagoans
The Very Best Of Dixieland Jazz | Verve | 535529-2
Fats Waller And His Buddies
Planet Jazz:Jack Teagarden | Planet Jazz | 2161236-2
Gene Krupa & Buddy Rich
The Drum Battle:Gene Krupa And Buddy Rich At JATP | Verve | 559810-2
Gene Krupa And His Orchestra
Mullenium | CBS | CK 65678
Gene Krupa Orchestra
Krupa And Rich | Verve | 521643-2
Gene Krupa Trio
The Complete Jazz At The Philharmonic On Verve 1944-1949 | Verve | 523893-2
Jazz At The Philharmonic:Best Of The 1940's Concerts | Verve | 557534-2
The Drum Battle:Gene Krupa And Buddy Rich At JATP | Verve | 559810-2
Gene Krupa's Swing Band
Planet Jazz:Swing | Planet Jazz | 2169651-2
Irving Mills And His Hotsy Totsy Gang
Jazz:The Essential Collection Vol.3 | IN+OUT Records | 78013-2
Jam Session
Benny Goodman At Carnegie Hall 1938(Complete) | CBS | C2K 65143
JATP All Stars
JATP In Tokyo | Pablo | 2620104-2
The Complete Jazz At The Philharmonic On Verve 1944-1949 | Verve | 523893-2
The Drum Battle:Gene Krupa And Buddy Rich At JATP | Verve | 559810-2
Mound City Blue Blowers
Jazz:The Essential Collection Vol.3 | IN+OUT Records | 78013-2
The Metronome All-Star Nine
Jazz:The Essential Collection Vol.3 | IN+OUT Records | 78013-2
Tommy Dorsey And His Orchestra
Planet Jazz:Jazz Greatest Hits | Planet Jazz | 2169648-2

Krupa,Jen | (tb)
Wycliffe Gordon Group
The Search | Nagel-Heyer | CD 2007

Kruse,Dietmar | (tb)
Marcus Sukiennik Big Band
A Night In Tunisia Suite(7 Variationen über Dizzy Gillespie's 'A Night In Tunisia') | Jazz Haus Musik | ohne Nummer
Matthias Petzold Septett
Ulysses | Indigo-Records | 1003 CD

Kruse,Nicola | (v)
String Thing
String Thing:Alles Wird Gut | MicNic Records | MN 2
String Thing:Turtifix | MicNic Records | MN 4

Kryvenko-Fandel,Olga | (v)
Bernd Konrad Jazz Group With Symphonie Orchestra
Wen Die Götter Lieben | Creative Works Records | CW CD 1010-1

Kua Etnika |
Norbert Stein Pata Masters meets Djaduk Ferianto Kua Etnika
Pata Java | Pata Musik | PATA 16 CD

Kubach,Gerhard | (bel-b)
Bajazzo
Caminos | Edition Collage | EC 485-2
Harlequin Galaxy | Edition Collage | EC 519-2

Kubatsch,Paul | (tp)
Chet Baker With The NDR-Bigband
Chet Baker-The Legacy Vol.1 | Enja | ENJ-9021 2
Heinz Sauer Quartet With The NDR Big Band
NDR Big Band-Bravissimo | ACT | 9232-2

Kübert,Martin | (keyboardssampling)
Ulla Oster Group
Beyond Janis | Jazz Haus Musik | JHM 0052 CD

Kübler,Olaf | (flts)
Klaus Doldinger Jubilee
Doldinger's Best | ACT | 9224-2
Olaf Kübler Quartet
When I'm 64 | Village | VILCD 1016-2
Midnight Soul | Village | VILCD 1024-2
Passport
Uranus | Atlantic | 2292-44142-2
Paul Nero Sound
Doldinger's Best | ACT | 9224-2

Kucan,Vlatko | (b-cl,ssts)
Florian Poser Group
Say Yes! | Edition Collage | EC 452-2
Vlatko Kucan Group
Vlatko Kucan Group | true muze | TUMU CD 9803

Kuchenbuch,Ludolf | (ss,tsg)
Ekkehard Jost Quartet
Some Other Tapes | Fish Music | FM 009/10 CD

Kudykowski,Miroslaw | (g)
Les McCann Group
Another Beginning | Atlantic | 7567-80790-2

Kuen,Stefan | (g)
Mahmoud Turkmani With The Ludus Guitar Quartet
Nuqta | TipToe | TIP-888835 2

Kugan,Vlatko | (cl,b-cl,ss,tsmelodica)
Rajesh Metha
Reconfigurations | Between The Lines | btl 010(Efa 10180-2)

Kügler,Joachim | (voc)
Jazzensemble Des Hessischen Rundfunks
Jazz Messe-Messe Für Unsere Zeit | hr music.de | hrmj 003-01 CD

Kühn,Axel | (as,fl,cl,tssax)
Al Porcino Big Band
Al Porcino Big Band Live! | Organic Music | ORGM 9717
Bill Ramsey With Orchestra
Gettin' Back To Swing | Bear Family Records | BCD 15813 AH
SWR Big Band
Jazz In Concert | Hänssler Classics | CD 93.004

Kühn,Joachim | (as,p,el-p,synth,el-g,keyboards)
European Jazz Ensemble
20th Anniversary Tour | Konnex Records | KCD 5078
European Jazz Ensemble 25th Anniversary | Konnex Records | KCD 5100
European Jazz Ensemble & The Khan Family feat. Joachim Kühn
European Jazz Ensemble Meets The Khan Family | M.A Music | A 807-2
Joachim Kühn
The Diminished Augmented System | EmArCy | 542320-2
Joachim Kühn And The Radio Philharmonie Hannover NDR With Jazz Soloists
Europeana | ACT | 9220-2
Joachim Kühn Group
Universal Time | EmArCy | 016671-2
Joachim Kühn Trio
Easy To Read | Owl Records | 014802-2
Joachim Kühn-Rolf Kühn
Love Stories | IN+OUT Records | 77061-2
Joe Henderson Quintet
Joe Henderson:The Milestone Years | Milestone | 8MCD 4413-2
Joe Henderson Sextet
Joe Henderson:The Milestone Years | Milestone | 8MCD 4413-2
Kühn/Humair/Jenny-Clark
Tripple Entente | EmArCy | 558690-2
Rolf Kühn Group
Inside Out | Intuition Records | INT 3276-2
Rolf Kühn-Joachim Kühn
Brothers | VeraBra Records | CDVBR 2184-2
Slide Hampton Quartet
Americans Swinging In Paris:Slide Hampton | EMI Records | 539648-2
Wolfgang Lackerschmid Sextet
One More Life | Bhakti Jazz | BR 29

Kuhn,Karsten | (b)
Leonardo Pedersen's Jazzkapel
The Golden Years Of Revival Jazz,Sampler | Storyville | 109 1001
The Golden Years Of Revival Jazz,Vol.11 | Storyville | STCD 5516

Kuhn,Paul | (p,arrvoc)
Bill Ramsey With The Paul Kuhn Trio
Caldonia And More... | Bear Family Records | BCD 16151 AH
Die Deutsche All Star Band 1953
1.Deutsches Jazz Festival 1953 Frankfurt/Main | Bear Family Records | BCD 15611 AH
Freddie Brocksieper Star-Quintett
Shot Gun Boogie | Bear Family Records | BCD 16277 AH
Kurt Edelhagen All Stars Und Solisten
Deutsches Jazz Fesival 1954/1955 | Bear Family Records | BCD 15430
Paul Kuhn Quartet
Deutsches Jazz Fesival 1954/1955 | Bear Family Records | BCD 15430
Paul Kuhn Quintet
Deutsches Jazz Fesival 1954/1955 | Bear Family Records | BCD 15430
Paul Kuhn Trio
Play It Again Paul | IN+OUT Records | 77040-2
Paul Kuhn Trio With Greetje Kauffeld
Play It Again Paul | IN+OUT Records | 77040-2
Paul Kuhn Trio With Greetje Kauffeld And Jean 'Toots' Thielemans
Play It Again Paul | IN+OUT Records | 77040-2
Paul Kuhn Trio With Jean 'Toots' Thielemans
Play It Again Paul | IN+OUT Records | 77040-2
Rolf Kühn All Stars
Deutsches Jazz Fesival 1954/1955 | Bear Family Records | BCD 15430
Rolf Kühn And His Quintet
Deutsches Jazz Fesival 1954/1955 | Bear Family Records | BCD 15430

Kühn,Rolf | (cl,arr,as,synth,tscond)
European Jazz Ensemble
20th Anniversary Tour | Konnex Records | KCD 5078
Helmut Zacharias Sextet
Ich Habe Rhythmus | Bear Family Records | BCD 15642 AH
Joachim Kühn-Rolf Kühn
Love Stories | IN+OUT Records | 77061-2
NDR-Workshop
Doldinger's Best | ACT | 9224-2
Rolf Kühn All Stars
Deutsches Jazz Fesival 1954/1955 | Bear Family Records | BCD 15430
Rolf Kühn And Friends
Affairs:Rolf Kühn & Friends | Intuition Records | INT 3211-2
Rolf Kühn And His Quintet
Deutsches Jazz Fesival 1954/1955 | Bear Family Records | BCD 15430
Rolf Kühn Group
Inside Out | Intuition Records | INT 3276-2
Internal Eyes | Intuition Records | INT 3328-2
Rolf Kühn Quartet
Rolf Kühn And His Sound Of Jazz | Fresh Sound Records | FSR-CD 326
Rolf Kühn Quintet
Rolf Kühn And His Sound Of Jazz | Fresh Sound Records | FSR-CD 326
Rolf Kühn Sextet
Rolf Kühn And His Sound Of Jazz | Fresh Sound Records | FSR-CD 326
Rolf Kühn-Joachim Kühn
Brothers | VeraBra Records | CDVBR 2184-2
The Three Sopranos With The HR Big Band
The Three Sopranos | hr music.de | hrmj 001-01 CD

Kuhn,Steve | (p,el-p,percp-solo)
Art Farmer Quartet
Sing Me Softly Of The Blues | Atlantic | 7567-80773-2
David Darling Group
Cycles | ECM | 1219
Stan Getz Quartet
Stan Getz Highlights:The Best Of The Verve Years Vol.2 | Verve | 517330-2
Stan Getz-Bob Brookmeyer Quintet
Stan Getz Highlights:The Best Of The Verve Years Vol.2 | Verve | 517330-2
A Life In Jazz:A Musical Biography | Verve | 535119-2
Stan Getz-Laurindo Almeida Orchestra
Stan Getz Highlights:The Best Of The Verve Years Vol.2 | Verve | 517330-2
Verve Jazz Masters 53:Stan Getz-Bossa Nova | Verve | 529904-2
Stan Getz Highlights | Verve | 847430-2
Steve Kuhn Trio
Oceans In The Sky | Owl Records | 013428-2
Remembering Tomorrow | ECM | 1573(529035-2)
Steve Kuhn With Strings
Promises Kept | ECM | 1815(0675222)
Steve Swallow Group
Home | ECM | 1160(513424-2)
Swallow | Watt | XtraWatt/6

Kühnl,Peter | (b)
Florian Bührich Quintet
endlich Jazz...? | Jazz 4 Ever Records:Jazz Network | J4E 4764

Kuhr,Hagen | (cello)
String Thing
String Thing:Alles Wird Gut | MicNic Records | MN 2
String Thing:Turtifix | MicNic Records | MN 4

Kuiper,Jan | (g)
Greetje Bijma Kwintet
Tales Of A Voice | TipToe | TIP-888808 2

Kujack,Götz | (dr)
Duo Fenix
Karai-Eté | IN+OUT Records | 7009-2

Kujala,Steve | (fl,ssts)
Chick Corea With String Quartet,Flute And French Horn
Septet | ECM | 1297
Chick Corea-Steve Kujala
Voyage | ECM | 1282

Kukko,Sakari | (fl,p,sax,keyboards,perc,kantele,voc)
Edward Vesala Group
Nan Madol | ECM | 1077
Piirpauke
Live In Der Balver Höhle | JA & RO | JARO 4101-2
The Wild East | JA & RO | JARO 4128-2
Zerenade | JA & RO | JARO 4142-2
Piirpauke-Global Servisi | JA & RO | JARO 4150-2
Tuku Tuku | JA & RO | JARO 4158-2
Jazzy World | JA & RO | JARO 4200-2

Kulenkampff,Heiko | (paccordeon)
Stephan Meinberg VITAMINE
Horizontal | Jazz Haus Musik | JHM 0106 CD

Kulowitch,Jack | (b)
Earl Klugh Group With Strings
Late Night Guitar | Blue Note | 498573-2

Kümmel,Ingo | (recitation)
Kölner Saxophon Mafia With Ingo Kümmel And Frank Köllges
Kölner Saxophon Mafia Proudly Presents | Jazz Haus Musik | JHM 0046 CD

Kummer,Vinzenz | (b)
Danny Moss Meets Buddha's Gamblers
A Swingin' Affair | Nagel-Heyer | CD 034
Blues Of Summer | Nagel-Heyer | NH 1011
The Tremble Kids All Stars
The Tremble Kids All Stars Play Chicago Jazz! | Nagel-Heyer | CD 043

Kummert,Nicolas | (sax)
Alexi Tuomarila Quartet
02 | Finladia Jazz | 0927-49148-2

Kümpel,Kurt | (flsax)
Art Van Damme Group
State Of Art | MPS | 841413-2

Kumpf,Hans | (cl)
Hans Kumpf-Jan Jankeje
A' Portrait Of Jan Jankeje | Jazzpoint | JP 1054 CD

Kundell,Barnard | (v)
Milt Jackson With Strings
To Bags...With Love:Memorial Album | Pablo | 2310967-2

Kunene,Sipho | (v)
Abdullah Ibrahim Trio
African Magic | TipToe | TIP-888845 2

Kunkel,Jan | (cello)
Uri Caine With The Concerto Köln
Concerto Köln | Winter&Winter | 910086-2

Künstner,Martin | (engl-hoboe)
Eberhard Weber Group
Chorus | ECM | 1288(823844-2)

Kunzel,Erich | (ld)
Dave Brubeck With The Erich Kunzel Orchestra
Truth Is Fallen | Atlantic | 7567-80761-2

Kupke,Connie | (v)
Chick Corea And His Orchestra
My Spanish Heart | Polydor | 543303-3

Kurasch,William | (v)
Gene Harris And The Three Sounds
Deep Blue-The United States Of Mind | Blue Note | 521152-2

Kuratli,Fabian | (drperc)
Christy Doran's New Bag With Muthuswamy Balasubramoniam
Black Box | double moon | CHRDM 71022

Kureer,Jorgen | (dr)
Earl Hines Trio
Earl Hines Live! | Storyville | STCD 8222

Kurek,Natasza | (voc)
Arnulf Ochs Group
In The Mean Time | Jazz 'n' Arts Records | JNA 1202

Kurkiewicz,Slawomir | (b)
Thomas Stanko Quartet
Suspended Night | ECM | 1868(9811244)
Tomasz Stanko Quartet
Soul Of Things | ECM | 1788(016374-2)

Kurmann,Stephan | (b)
Willy Bischof Jazztet
Swiss Air | Jazz Connaisseur | JCCD 9523-2
Willy Bischof Trio
Swiss Air | Jazz Connaisseur | JCCD 9523-2

Kurstin,Greg | (keyboardsp)
Terri Lyne Carrington Group
Jazz Is A Spirit | ACT | 9408-2

Kurtis-Stewart,Elektra | (v)
Steve Coleman And The Council Of Balance
Genesis & The Opening Of The Way | RCA | 2152934-2

Kurtzer,Dave | (bassoon,bssax)
Gil Evans And Ten
Gil Evans And Ten | Original Jazz Classics | OJC 346(P 7120)
The Jazz Giants Play Cole Porter:Night And Day | Prestige | PCD 24203-2

INTERPRETENVERZEICHNIS

Gil Evans And Ten | Prestige | PRSA 7120-6
Lucy Reed With Orchestra
This Is Lucy Reed | Original Jazz Classics | OJCCD 1943-2(F 3243)
Tito Puente Orchestra
Planet Jazz:Tito Puente | Planet Jazz | 2165369-2

Kuruc,Frank | (g)
Cécile Verny Quintet
Kekeli | double moon | CHRDM 71028
Frank Kuruc Band
Limits No Limits | Edition Musikat | EDM 023
Stuttgarter Gitarren Trio
Stuttgarter Gitarren Trio Vol.2 | Edition Musikat | EDM 034

Kurz,Andreas | (b)
Martin Auer Quintett
Martin Auer Quintett | Jazz 4 Ever Records:Jazz Network | J4E 4762
Torsten Goods Group
Manhattan Walls | Jardis Records | JRCD 20139

Kusby,Eddie | (tb)
Anita O'Day With The Billy May Orchestra
Verve Jazz Masters 49:Anita O'Day | Verve | 527653-2
Billy Eckstine With The Billy May Orchestra
Once More With Feeling | Roulette | 581862-2
Billy May And His Orchestra
Billy May's Big Fat Brass/Bill's Bag | Capitol | 535206-2
Ella Fitzgerald With Paul Weston And His Orchestra
Ella Fitzgerald Sings The Irving Berlin Song Book | Verve | 543830-2
Ella Fitzgerald With The Billy May Orchestra
Ella Fitzgerald Sings The Harold Arlen Song Book | Verve | 589108-2
Ella Fitzgerald With The Paul Weston Orchestra
Get Happy! | Verve | 523321-2
Louis Armstrong With The Hal Mooney Orchestra
Ambassador Louis Armstrong Vol.17:Moments To Remember(1952-1956) | Ambassador | CLA 1917
Mel Tormé With The Billy May Orchestra
Mel Tormé Goes South Of The Border With Billy May | Verve | 589517-2
Nat King Cole With The Billy May Orchestra
Nat King Cole:For Sentimental Reasons | Dreyfus Jazz Line | FDM 36740-2
Peggy Lee With The Benny Goodman Orchestra
Peggy Lee & Benny Goodman:The Complete Recordings 1941-1947 | CBS | C2K 65686
Van Alexander Orchestra
Home Of Happy Feet/Swing! Staged For Sound! | Capitol | 535211-2

Kusur,Selim | (nayvoice)
Rabih Abou-Khalil Group
Nafas | ECM | 1359(835781-2)
Tarab | Enja | ENJ-7083 2
Roots & Sprouts | Enja | ENJ-9373 2

Kutcher,Sam | (tb)
Terry Gibbs Octet
Jewis Melodies In Jazztime | Mercury | 589673-2

Kutschke,Jürgen | (dr)
Tony Lakatos With The Martin Sasse Trio
Feel Alright | Edition Collage | EC 494-2

Küttner,Michael | (dr,perc,voiceafrican-dr)
Alex Gunia-Philipp Van Endert Group
Beauty Of Silence | Laika Records | 35101052
Lumpp-Read-Küttner Trio
Midnight Sun | Nabel Records:Jazz Network | CD 4612
Maria Joao Quintet
Conversa | Nabel Records:Jazz Network | CD 4628
Paul Shigihara-Charlie Mariano Quartet
Tears Of Sound | Nabel Records:Jazz Network | CD 4616
Peter Weiss Orchestra
Personal Choice | Nabel Records:Jazz Network | CD 4669
Tomato Kiss
Tomato Kiss | Nabel Records:Jazz Network | CD 4624

Kuuskmann,Martin | (bassoon)
Paquito D'Rivera Group With The Absolute Ensemble
Habanera | Enja | ENJ-9395 2

Kviberg,Jasper | (dr)
Stacey Kent With The Jim Tomlinson Quintet
Dreamsville | Candid | CCD 79775
Stacy Kent With The Jim Tomlinson Quintet
In Love Again | Candid | CCD 79786

Kwame-Bell,Khalil | (perc)
Antonio Hart Group
Ama Tu Sonrisa | Enja | ENJ-9404 2

Kwock,Robbie | (tpfl-h)
Pucho & His Latin Soul Brothers
Rip A Dip | Milestone | MCD 9247-2

Kyle,Billy | (pceleste)
Ella Fitzgerald With Louis Armstrong And The All Stars
Ella Fitzgerald-First Lady Of Song | Verve | 517898-2
The Complete Ella Fitzgerald And Louis Armstrong On Verve | Verve | 537284-2
The Best Of Ella Fitzgerald And Louis Armstrong On Verve | Verve | 537909-2
Ella Fitzgerald With Sy Oliver And His Orchestra
Ella Fitzgerald:The Decca Years 1949-1954 | Decca | 050668-2
Jack Teagarden's Big Eight
Jazz:The Essential Collection Vol.3 | IN+OUT Records | 78013-2
John Kirby Band
The Small Black Groups | Storyville | 4960523
Lionel Hampton And His Orchestra
Planet Jazz:Swing | Planet Jazz | 2169651-2
Planet Jazz:Jazz Saxophone | Planet Jazz | 2169653-2
Louis Armstrong And Billie Holiday With Sy Oliver's Orchestra
Louis Armstrong:C'est Si Bon | Dreyfus Jazz Line | FDM 36730-2
Louis Armstrong And Gary Crosby With Sonny Burke's Orchestra
Louis Armstrong-My Greatest Songs | MCA | MCD 18347
Louis Armstrong And His All Stars
Jazz In Paris:Louis Armstrong:The Best Live Concer Vol.1 | EmArCy | 013030-2
Jazz In Paris:Louis Armstrong-The Best Live Concert Vol.2 | EmArCy | 013031-2
Jazz Festival Vol.1 | Storyville | 4960733
Verve Jazz Masters 1:Louis Armstrong | Verve | 519818-2
I Love Jazz | Verve | 543747-2
Louis Armstrong:The Great Chicago Concert 1956 | CBS | C2K 65119
Louis Armstrong Plays W.C.Handy | CBS | CK 64925
Ambassador Satch | CBS | CK 64926
Satch Plays Fats(Complete) | CBS | CK 64927
Historic Barcelona Concerts At Windsor Palace 1955 | Fresh Sound Records | FSR-CD 3004
Live In Berlin/Friedrichstadtpalast | Jazzpoint | JP 1062 CD
The Legendary Berlin Concert Part 2 | Jazzpoint | JP 1063 CD
Louis Armstrong-My Greatest Songs | MCA | MCD 18347
Louis Armstrong And His All Stars With Benny Carter's Orchestra
Ambassador Louis Armstrong Vol.17:Moments To Remember(1952-1956) | Ambassador | CLA 1917
Louis Armstrong And His All Stars With Sonny Burke's Orchestra
Ambassador Louis Armstrong Vol.17:Moments To Remember(1952-1956) | Ambassador | CLA 1917
Louis Armstrong And His All Stars With The Sy Oliver Orchestra
Ambassador Louis Armstrong Vol.17:Moments To Remember(1952-1956) | Ambassador | CLA 1917
Louis Armstrong And His Orchestra
I Love Jazz | Verve | 543747-2
Louis Armstrong With Benny Carter's Orchestra
Louis Armstrong-My Greatest Songs | MCA | MCD 18347
Louis Armstrong With Sy Oliver And His Orchestra
Satchmo Serenaders | Verve | 543792-2
Louis And The Angels | Verve | 549592-2
Louis Armstrong-My Greatest Songs | MCA | MCD 18347
Louis Armstrong With Sy Oliver's Choir And Orchestra
Jazz Collection:Louis Armstrong | Laserlight | 24366
Louis And The Good Book | Verve | 549593-2
Louis And The Good Book | Verve | 940130-0
Sarah Vaughan With John Kirby And His Orchestra
Sarah Vaughan Birthday Celebration | Fantasy | FANCD 6090-2
Sarah Vaughan:Lover Man | Dreyfus Jazz Line | FDM 36739-2

Kyle,Janet | (voc)
Hans Theessink Group
Crazy Moon | Minor Music | 801052

Kynard,Ben | (as,bscl)
Lionel Hampton And His Orchestra
Lionel Hampton:Flying Home | Dreyfus Jazz Line | FDM 36735-2
Lionel Hampton Orchestra
The Big Bands Vol.1.The Snader Telescriptions | Storyville | 4960043

Kynard,Charles | (org)
Charles Kynard Quintet
The Soul Brotherhood | Prestige | PCD 24257-2
Charles Kynard Sextet
The Soul Brotherhood | Prestige | PCD 24257-2

La Duca,Paul | (b)
Joshua Redman Quartet
Joshua Redman | Warner | 9362-45242-2

La Gaia Scienza |
La Gaia Scienza
Love Fugue-Robert Schumann | Winter&Winter | 910049-2

La Magna,Carl | (v)
Mel Tormé With The Russell Garcia Orchestra
Swingin' On The Moon | Verve | 511385-2
Phineas Newborn Jr. With Dennis Farnon And His Orchestra
While My Lady Sleeps | RCA | 2185157-2

La Marchina,Robert 'Bob' | (cello)
Ella Fitzgerald With The Buddy Bregman Orchestra
The Best Of The Song Books:The Ballads | Verve | 521867-2
Love Songs:The Best Of The Song Books | Verve | 531762-2
Ella Fitzgerald Sings The Cole Porter Songbook | Verve | 537257-2
Ella Fitzgerald Sings The Rodgers And Hart Song Book | Verve | 537258-2

La Rocca,Nick | (covoc)
Original Dixieland 'Jass' Band
Planet Jazz | Planet Jazz | 2169652-2

La Rocca,Sal | (b)
Toots Thielemans Quartet
Toots Thielemans:The Live Takes Vol.1 | IN+OUT Records | 77041-2

La Rosa,Julius | (voc)
Glenn Miller And His Orchestra
The Glenn Miller Orchestra In Digital Mood | GRP | GRP 95022

La Zazzera,Massimi | (recorder)
Michel Godard Ensemble
Castel Del Monte II | Enja | ENJ-9431 2

La Zazzera,Massimo | (recorder)

Laade,Wolfgang | (b)
Spree Cuty Stompers
Deutsches Jazz Fesival 1954/1955 | Bear Family Records | BCD 15430

LaBarbera,Joe | (dr)
Bill Evans Trio
Bill Evans Trio:The Last Waltz | Milestone | 8MCD 4430-2
Homecoming | Milestone | MCD 9291-2
Carol Sloane With The Norris Turney Quartet
Something Cool | Choice | CHCD 71025
Diane Schuur Trio
In Tribute | GRP | GRP 20062
Jacintha With Band And Strings
Lush Life | Groove Note | GRV 1011-2(Gold CD 2011)
Woody Herman And His Orchestra
The Raven Speaks | Original Jazz Classics | OJCCD 663-2(F 9416)

LaBarbera,Pat | (fl,cl,ss,tsas)
Buddy Rich Big Band
Backwoods Siseman/Pieces Of Dream | Laserlight | 24655
The New One! | Pacific Jazz | 494507-2
Keep The Customer Satisfied | EMI Records | 523999-2

LaBelle,Patti | (voc)
Fourplay
Fourplay | Warner | 7599-26656-2

Labeque,Katia | (p,synth,p-solosynclavier)
Katia Labeque
Little Girl Blue | Dreyfus Jazz Line | FDM 36186-2
Katia Labeque-Chick Corea
Little Girl Blue | Dreyfus Jazz Line | FDM 36186-2
Katia Labeque-Gonzalo Rubalcaba
Little Girl Blue | Dreyfus Jazz Line | FDM 36186-2
Katia Labeque-Herbie Hancock
Little Girl Blue | Dreyfus Jazz Line | FDM 36186-2
Katia Labeque-Joe Zawinul
Little Girl Blue | Dreyfus Jazz Line | FDM 36186-2
Katia Labeque-Joey DeFrancesco
Little Girl Blue | Dreyfus Jazz Line | FDM 36186-2
Katia Labeque-Marielle Labeque
Little Girl Blue | Dreyfus Jazz Line | FDM 36186-2
Katia Labeque-Michel Camilo
Little Girl Blue | Dreyfus Jazz Line | FDM 36186-2

Labeque,Marielle | (p)
Katia Labeque-Marielle Labeque
Little Girl Blue | Dreyfus Jazz Line | FDM 36186-2

Laboriel,Abe | (b,8-string-b,hand-claps,el-b,el-g,g)
Al Jarreau With Band
Jarreau | i.e. Music | 557847-2
Dave Grusin Group
Migration | GRP | GRP 95922
Ella Fitzgerald With Orchestra
Ella Abraca Jobim | Pablo | 2630201-2
Gary Burton Quartet
The New Quartet | ECM | 1030
Joe Pass Sextet
Jazzin' Vol.2: The Music Of Stevie Wonder | Fantasy | FANCD 6088-2
Lee Ritenour Group
Rio | GRP | GRP 95242
Lee Ritenour With Special Guests
Festival International De Jazz De Montreal | Spectra | 9811661

Labutis,Vytautas | (ss,asbs)
Jazz Baltica Ensemble
The Birth+Rebirth Of Swedish Folk Jazz | ACT | 9254-2

Lacefield,Jim | (b,el-boregon-b)
Free Flight
Jazzrock-Anthology Vol.3:Fusion | Zounds | CD 27100555

Lacey,Fred | (g)
Jubilee All Stars
Jazz Gallery:Lester Young Vol.2(1946-59) | RCA | 2119541-2
Lester Young And His Band
Jazz:The Essential Collection Vol.3 | IN+OUT Records | 78013-2
Lester Young:The Complete Aladdin Sessions | Blue Note | 832787-2

Lacey,Jack | (tb)
Benny Goodman And His Orchestra
Planet Jazz:Benny Goodman | Planet Jazz | 2152054-2
Planet Jazz:Swing | Planet Jazz | 2169651-2
Frank Trumbauer And His Orchestra
The Hollywood Session:The Capitol Jazzmen | Jazz Unlimited | JUCD 2044

Lachmann,Gerhard | (tb)
Charly Antolini Orchestra
Drum Beat | MPS | 9808191
Dieter Reith Group
Reith On! | MPS | 557423-2

Lachotta,Chris | (b)
Jenny Evans And Her Quintet
Nuages | Enja | ENJ-9467 2
Nuages | ESM Records | ESM 9308

Lackerschmid,Wolfgang | (el-p,synth,perc,marimba,timpany,vib)
Attila Zoller-Wolfgang Lackerschmid
Live Highlights '92 | Bhakti Jazz | BR 28
Bireli Lagrene Ensemble
Routes To Django & Bireli Swing '81 | Jazzpoint | JP 1055 CD
Routs To Django-Live At The 'Krokodil' | Jazzpoint | JP 1056 CD
Chet Baker-Wolfgang Lackerschmid Duo
Chet Baker:The Legacy Vol.3:Why Shouldn't You Cry | Enja | ENJ-9337 2
Chet Baker-Wolfgang Lackerschmid Quintet
Chet Baker:The Legacy Vol.3:Why Shouldn't You Cry | Enja | ENJ-9337 2
Chet Baker-Wolfgang Lackerschmid Trio
Chet Baker:The Legacy Vol.3:Why Shouldn't You Cry | Enja | ENJ-9337 2
Dieter Bihlmaier Selection
Mallet Connection | Bhakti Jazz | BR 33
Full Moon Trio
Live At Birdland Neuburg | double moon | CHRDM 71024
Johannes Mössinger-Wolfgang Lackerschmid
Joana's Dance | double moon | CHRDM 71017
Lee Konitz-Wolfgang Lackerschmid Quintet
Chet Baker:The Legacy Vol.3:Why Shouldn't You Cry | Enja | ENJ-9337 2
Ray Pizzi Trio
One More Life | Bhakti Jazz | BR 29
Stefanie Schlesiger And Her Group plus String Quartet
What Love Is | Enja | ENJ-9434 2
Stefanie Schlesinger And Her Group
What Love Is | Enja | ENJ-9434 2
Terra Brazil
Café Com Leite | art-mode-records | AMR 2101
Wolfgang Lackerschmid & Lynne Arriale Trio
You Are Here | Bhakti Jazz | BR 43
Wolfgang Lackerschmid Group
Mallet Connection | Bhakti Jazz | BR 33
Wolfgang Lackerschmid Quartet
One More Life | Bhakti Jazz | BR 29
Wolfgang Lackerschmid Sextet
One More Life | Bhakti Jazz | BR 29
Wolfgang Lackerschmid-Donald Johnston Group
New Singers-New Songs | Bhakti Jazz | BR 31

Lackner,Marko | (as,b-cl,ss,fl,cl,reedssax)
Bigband Der Musikschule Der Stadt Brühl Mit Gastsolisten
Pangäa | Indigo-Records | 1004 CD
European Jazz Youth Orchestra
Swinging Europe 3 | dacapo | DCCD 9461
Lee Konitz With The Ed Partyka Jazz Orchestra
Dreams And Realities | Laika Records | 35101642
The Groenewald Newnet
Meetings | Jazz 'n' Arts Records | JNA 0702

Lacrouts,Cyrille | (cello)
Charlie Haden Quartet West With Strings
Now Is The Hour | Verve | 527827-2

Lacy Sr.,Frank | (g)
Frank Ku-Umba Lacy Group
Tonal Weights & Blue Fire | Tutu Records | 888112-2*

Lacy,Ku-umba Frank | (fl-h,fr-h,tb,p,org,voc,shells)
Abdullah Ibrahim Septet
No Fear, No Die(S'en Fout La Mort):Original Soundtrack | TipToe | TIP-888815 2
Art Blakey And The Jazz Messengers
The Art Of Jazz | IN+OUT Records | 77028-2
Barbara Dennerlein Group
Junkanoo | Verve | 537122-2
Carla Bley Band
Fleur Carnivore | Watt | 21
Frank Ku-Umba Lacy Group
Tonal Weights & Blue Fire | Tutu Records | 888112-2*
Gunther Klatt & New York Razzmatazz
Volume One:Fa Mozzo | Tutu Records | 888158-2*
Ku-Umba Frank Lacy & His Quartet
Settegast Strut | Tutu Records | 888162-2*
Ku-umba Frank Lacy & The Poker Bigband
Songs From The Musical 'Poker' | Tutu Records | 888150-2*
Lester Bowie's Brass Fantasy
Avant Pop | ECM | 1326
The Fire This Time | IN+OUT Records | 7019-2
McCoy Tyner Big Band
The Best Of McCoy Tyner Big Band | Dreyfus Jazz Line | FDM 37012-2
Mingus Big Band
Tonight At Noon...Three Or Four Shades Of Love | Dreyfus Jazz Line | FDM 36633-2
Mingus Big Band 93
Nostalgia In Times Square | Dreyfus Jazz Line | FDM 36559-2
Roy Hargrove's Crisol
Habana | Verve | 537563-2

Lacy,Steve | (fl,ss,ts,bells,footgong,voice,comp)
Cecil Taylor Quartet
At Newport | Verve | 589764-2
Cecil Taylor/Buell Neidlinger Orchestra
New York City R&B | Candid | CCD 79017
Franz Koglmann Quintet
Opium | Between The Lines | btl 011(Efa 10181-2)
Gary Burton Quartet With Orchestra
A Genuine Tong Funeral(Dark Opera Without Words) | RCA | 2119255-2
Gil Evans And Ten
Gil Evans And Ten | Original Jazz Classics | OJC 346(P 7120)
The Jazz Giants Play Cole Porter:Night And Day | Prestige | PCD 24203-2
Gil Evans And Ten | Prestige | PRSA 7120-6
Gil Evans Orchestra
Verve Jazz Masters 23:Gil Evans | Verve | 521860-2
The Individualism Of Gil Evans | Verve | 833804-2
Kenny Burrell With The Gil Evans Orchestra
Guitar Forms | Verve | 521403-2
Verve Jazz Masters 23:Gil Evans | Verve | 521860-2
Verve Jazz Masters 45:Kenny Burrell | Verve | 527652-2
Verve Jazz Masters Vol.60:The Collection | Verve | 529866-2
Mal Waldron
Moods | Enja | ENJ-3021 2
Mal Waldron Sextet
Moods | Enja | ENJ-3021 2
Miles Davis With Gil Evans & His Orchestra
Quiet Nights | CBS | CK 65293
Miles Davis With Orchestra
Ballads | CBS | 461099-2
Steve Lacy Quartet
Reflections-Steve Lacy Plays Thelonious Monk | Original Jazz Classics | OJCCD 063-2
Soprano Sax | Original Jazz Classics | OJCCD 130-2(P 7125)
The Mal Waldron Memorial Album:Soul Eyes | Prestige | PRCD 11024-2
Steve Lacy-Roswell Rudd Quartet
Monk's Dream | Verve | 543090-2
Subroto Roy Chowdhury-Steve Lacy Group
Explorations | Jazzpoint | JP 1020 CD
The Jazz Composer's Orchestra
Comminications | JCOA | 1001/2
Thelonious Monk And His Orchestra
Greatest Hits | CBS | CK 65422

Lada,Tony | (tb)
Buddy Rich Big Band
Keep The Customer Satisfied | EMI Records | 523999-2

Ladner,Calvin | (tp)
Duke Ellington Orchestra
Continuum | Fantasy | FCD 24765-2

Ladnier,Tommy | (cotp)
Bessie Smith And Her Band
Jazz:The Essential Collection Vol.1 | IN+OUT Records | 78011-2
Mezzrow-Ladnier Quintet
Planet Jazz:Jazz Trumpet | Planet Jazz | 2169654-2
New Orleans Feetwarmers

Planet Jazz | Planet Jazz | 2169652-2
Jazz:The Essential Collection Vol.1 | IN+OUT Records | 78011-2
From Spiritual To Swing | Vanguard | VCD 169/71
Tommy Ladnier And His Orchestra
Planet Jazz | Planet Jazz | 2169652-2
Jazz:The Essential Collection Vol.1 | IN+OUT Records | 78011-2

LaFargue,Taylor | (b)
Mose Allison Trio
Back Country Suite | Original Jazz Classics | OJC 075(P 7091)
Mose Allison:Greatest Hits | Original Jazz Classics | OJCCD 6004-2
Mose Allison Sings The 7th Son | Prestige | PR20 7279-2

LaFaro,Scott | (b)
Bill Evans Trio
The Story Of Jazz Piano | Laserlight | 24653
Bill Evans:The Complete Live At The Village Vanguard 1961 | Riverside | 3RCD 1961-2
On Green Dolphin Street | Milestone | MCD 9235-2
Explorations | Original Jazz Classics | OJC20 037-2(RLP 9351)
Portrait In Jazz | Original Jazz Classics | OJC20 088-2
Sunday At The Village Vanguard | Original Jazz Classics | OJC20 140-2
Waltz For Debby | Original Jazz Classics | OJC20 210-2
The Jazz Giants Play Harry Warren:Lullaby Of Broadway | Prestige | PCD 24204-2
Gunther Schuller Ensemble
Beauty Is A Rare Thing:Ornette Coleman-The Complete Atlantic Recordings | Atlantic | 8122-71410-2
Ornette Coleman Double Quartet
Beauty Is A Rare Thing:Ornette Coleman-The Complete Atlantic Recordings | Atlantic | 8122-71410-2
Free Jazz | Atlantic | 8122-75208-2
Ornette Coleman Quartet
Beauty Is A Rare Thing:Ornette Coleman-The Complete Atlantic Recordings | Atlantic | 8122-71410-2
Stan Getz Quartet
Stan Getz Highlights:The Best Of The Verve Years Vol.2 | Verve | 517330-2
Stan Getz-Cal Tjader Sextet
Stan Getz With Cal Tjader | Original Jazz Classics | OJC20 275-2(F 3266)
Victor Feldman Orchestra
Latinsville | Contemporary | CCD 9005-2

LaFaro,Scott prob. | (b)
Hampton Hawes Trio
Bird Song | Original Jazz Classics | OJCCD 1035-2

Lafitte,Guy | (tsrecitation)
Emmett Berry-Sammy Price Orchestra
Americans Swinging In Paris:Sammy Price | EMI Records | 539650-2
Golden Gate Quartet
Americans Swinging In Paris:Golden Gate Quartet | EMI Records | 539659-2
Spirituals To Swing 1955-69 | EMI Records | 791569-2
Golden Gate Quartet With The Martial Solal Orchestra
From Sprîritual To Swing Vol.2 | EMI Records | 780573-2
Guy Lafitte Sextet
Jazz In Paris:Guy Lafitte-Blue And Sentimental | EmArCy | 159852-2 PMS
Guy Lafitte-Peanuts Holland And Their Orchestra
Jazz In Paris:Guy Lafitte-Blue And Sentimental | EmArCy | 159852-2 PMS
Jack Dieval And The J.A.C.E. All-Stars
Jazz In Paris:Jack Diéval-Jazz Aux Champs Elysées | EmArCy | 018419-2
Lionel Hampton Sextet
Americans Swinging In Paris:Lionel Hampton | EMI Records | 539649-2
Lucky Thompson Quintet
Americans Swinging In Paris:Lucky Thompson | EMI Records | 539651-2

Lafosse,André | (tb)
Django's Music
Peche Á La Mode-The Great Blue Star Sessions 1947/1953 | Verve | 835418-2

Laginha,Mario | (arrp)
NDR Big Band With Guests
50 Years Of NDR Big Band:Bravissimo II | ACT | 9259-2

Lagrene,Bireli | (el-g,voc,g,b,el-bg-solo)
Bireli Lagrene
Bireli Lagrene 'Highlights' | Jazzpoint | JP 1027 CD
Bireli Lagrene Ensemble
Bireli Swing '81 | Jazzpoint | JP 1009 CD
Live | Jazzpoint | JP 1047 CD
Routes To Django & Bireli Swing '81 | Jazzpoint | JP 1055 CD
Routs To Django-Live At The 'Krokodil' | Jazzpoint | JP 1056 CD
Bireli Lagrene Group
Bireli Lagrene 'Highlights' | Jazzpoint | JP 1027 CD
Bireli Lagrene | Jazzpoint | JP 1049 CD
A' Portrait Of Jan Jankeje | Jazzpoint | JP 1054 CD
A Tribute To Django Reinhardt | Jazzpoint | JP 1061 CD
Bireli Lagrene Quartet
Standards | Blue Note | 780251-2
My Favorite Django | Dreyfus Jazz Line | FDM 36574-2
Blue Eyes | Dreyfus Jazz Line | FDM 36591-2
A' Portrait Of Jan Jankeje | Jazzpoint | JP 1054 CD
Bireli Lagrene Trio
Standards | Blue Note | 780251-2
Live At The Carnegie Hall: A Tribute To Django Reinhardt | Jazzpoint | JP 1040 CD
A' Portrait Of Jan Jankeje | Jazzpoint | JP 1054 CD
Bireli Lagrene-Philip Catherine
Bireli Lagrene 'Highlights' | Jazzpoint | JP 1027 CD
Bireli Lagrene-Vic Juris
Bireli Lagrene 'Highlights' | Jazzpoint | JP 1027 CD
Didier Lockwood Trio
Tribute To Stépane Grappelli | Dreyfus Jazz Line | FDM 36611-2
Dreyfus All Stars
Dreyfus Night In Paris | Dreyfus Jazz Line | FDM 36652-2
Duo Fenix
Karai-Eté | IN+OUT Records | 7009-2
Jaco Pastorius Groups
Another Side Of Jaco Pastorius | Jazzpoint | JP 1064 CD
Jaco Pastorius Trio
Live In Italy | Jazzpoint | JP 1031 CD
Heavy'n Jazz | Jazzpoint | JP 1036 CD
Jaco Pastorius Broadway Blues & Theresa | Jazzpoint | JP 1053 CD
Jaco Pastorius Heavy'n Jazz & Stuttgart Aria | Jazzpoint | JP 1058 CD
Live In Italy & Honestly | Jazzpoint | JP 1059 CD
Jan Jankeje Quintet
Zum Trotz | Jazzpoint | JP 1016 CD
Jermaine Landsberger Trio With Bireli Lagrene
Gypsy Feeling | Edition Collage | EC 516-2
Richard Galliano Quartet
Viaggio | Dreyfus Jazz Line | FDM 36562-9
New York Tango | Dreyfus Jazz Line | FDM 36581-2
Gallianissimo! The Best Of Richard Galliano | Dreyfus Jazz Line | FDM 36616-2
Sylvain Luc-Biréli Lagrène
Duet | Dreyfus Jazz Line | FDM 36604-2

Lagrene,Gaiti | (g)
Bireli Lagrene Ensemble
Bireli Swing '81 | Jazzpoint | JP 1009 CD
Live | Jazzpoint | JP 1047 CD
Routes To Django & Bireli Swing '81 | Jazzpoint | JP 1055 CD
Routs To Django-Live At The 'Krokodil' | Jazzpoint | JP 1056 CD
Bireli Lagrene Group
Bireli Lagrene 'Highlights' | Jazzpoint | JP 1027 CD
A Tribute To Django Reinhardt | Jazzpoint | JP 1061 CD
Bireli Lagrene Quartet
A' Portrait Of Jan Jankeje | Jazzpoint | JP 1054 CD

Laguillo | (p,keyboardsvoice)
Javier Paxarino Group With Glen Velez
Temurá | ACT | 9227-2

Lahey,Bill | (as,clsax)
Stan Kenton And His Orchestra
Stan Kenton-The Formative Years | Decca | 589489-2

Lahota,A. | (v)
Toots Thielemans And His Orchestra
Verve Jazz Masters Vol.59:Toots Thielemans | Verve | 535271-2

Lahti,Marja-Sisko | (v)
Piirpauke
Tuku Tuku | JA & RO | JARO 4158-2

Lahti,Pentti | (b-cl,fl,as,bsss)
Edward Vesala Group
Nan Madol | ECM | 1077
Lumi | ECM | 1339

Laila | (dance)
Steve Coleman And Metrics
The Way Of The Cipher | Novus | 2131690-2

Laine,Bob | (p)
Lars Gullin With The Bob Laine Trio
Lars Gullin 1953,Vol.2:Moden Sounds | Dragon | DRCD 234

Laine,Frankie | (voc)
Frankie Laine With Buck Clayton And His Orchestra
Jazz Spectacular | CBS | CK 65507

Laing,Andy | (v)
Joe Temperley Quartet With Strings
Easy To Remember | Hep | CD 2083
Joe Temperley Quintet With Strings
Easy To Remember | Hep | CD 2083

Laird,Rick | (b,el-b,vocb-g)
Buddy Rich Big Band
Keep The Customer Satisfied | EMI Records | 523999-2
Mahavishnu Orchestra
The Inner Mounting Flame | CBS | CK 65523
The Mahavishnu Orchestra
Between Nothingness & Eternity | CBS | CK 32766

Lais,Detlev | (ts)
Brocksi-Quartett
Globetrotter | Bear Family Records | BCD 15912 AH

Laizeau,Francois | (bdr)
Claus Stötter's Nevertheless
Die Entdeckung Der Banane | Jazz 'n' Arts Records | JNA 1403

Lakatos Toni | (ts)
Trio Larose With Toni Lakatos
Debut | Jazz 'n' Arts Records | JNA 0802

Lakatos,Ferenc | (tb)
Erwin Lehn Und Sein Südfunk-Tanzorchester
Deutsches Jazz Fesival 1954/1955 | Bear Family Records | BCD 15430

Lakatos,Tony | (fl,ss,ts,saxsynth)
Christoph Sänger Trio
Imagination | Laika Records | 35100752
Dejan Terzic European Assembly
Coming Up | double moon | DMCHR 71034
Dusko Goykovich Big Band
Balkan Connection | Enja | ENJ-9047 2
European Jazz Ensemble
20th Anniversary Tour | Konnex Records | KCD 5078
Fritz Krisse Quartet
Soulcolours | Laika Records | 35100782
HR Big Band
The American Songs Of Kurt Weill | hr music.de | hrmj 006-01 CD
Libertango:Homage An Astor Piazolla | hr music.de | hrmj 014-02 CD
HR Big Band With Marjorie Barnes And Frits Landesbergen
Swinging Christmas | hr music.de | hrmj 012-02 CD
HR Big Band With Marjorie Barnes And Frits Landesbergen And Strings
Swinging Christmas | hr music.de | hrmj 012-02 CD
Litschie Hrdlicka Group
Falling Lovers | EGO | 93020
Philippe Caillat Group
Stream Of Time | Laika Records | LK 92-030
Pili-Pili
Pili-Pili Live 88 | JA & RO | JARO 4139-2
Hotel Babo | JA & RO | JARO 4147-2
Stolen Moments | JA & RO | JARO 4159-2
Boogaloo | JA & RO | JARO 4174-2
Dance Jazz Live 1995 | JA & RO | JARO 4189-2
Jazzy World | JA & RO | JARO 4200-2
Nomans Land | JA & RO | JARO 4209-2
The Three Sopranos With The HR Big Band
The Three Sopranos | hr music.de | hrmj 001-01 CD
Things
Mother Nature | Jazzpoint | JP 1028 CD
Tony Lakatos Quartet
Live In Budapest | Laika Records | 35100742
Tony Lakatos With The Martin Sasse Trio
Feel Alright | Edition Collage | EC 494-2
Torsten Goods Group
Manhattan Walls | Jardis Records | JRCD 20139
Toto Blanke Group
Electric Circus' Best | ALISO Records | AL 1034

Lake,Gene | (drperc)
Steve Coleman And Five Elements
Curves Of Life | Novus | 2131693-2
Steve Coleman And Metrics
A Tale Of 3 Cities,The EP | Novus | 2124747-2
The Way Of The Cipher | Novus | 2131690-2
Steve Coleman And The Council Of Balance
Genesis & The Opening Of The Way | RCA | 2152934-2
Till Brönner Group
Chattin' With Chet | Verve | 157534-2

Lake,Oliver | (as,narration,as-solo,fl,bells,voice)
Abbey Lincoln With Her Band
Who Used To Dance | Verve | 533559-2
World Saxophone Quartet
Plays Duke Ellington | Nonesuch | 7559-79137-2
Dances And Ballads | Nonesuch | 7559-79164-2

Lakey,Claude | (as,ts,saxtp)
Harry James And His Orchestra
The Legends Of Swing | Laserlight | 24659

Lakshminarayana,V. | (cond tala keeping,v,double-vvoc)
Shankar
Who's To Know | ECM | 1195
Shankar Group
Nobody Told Me | ECM | 1397

Lal,Shankar | (tablasvoc)
Tabla & Strings
Islands Everywhere | Tutu Records | 888208-2*

Lalama,Dave | (p)
Woody Herman And His Orchestra
Verve Jazz Masters 54:Woody Herman | Verve | 529903-2

Lalama,Ralph | (fl,clts)
Joe Lovano Nonet
On This Day At The Vanguard | Blue Note | 590950-2
Mitchell-Terraza Group
Shell Blues | Fresh Sound Records | FSNT 005 CD

Lallemand,Ariane | (cello)
Absolute Ensemble
African Symphony | Enja | ENJ-9410 2

Lalue,Georges | (perc)
Raymond Fol Big Band
Jazz In Paris:Raymond Fol-Les 4 Saisons | EmArCy | 548791-2

Lamare,Hilton Napoleon 'Nappy' | (gvoc)
Bob Crosby And His Orchestra
Swing Legens:Bob Crosby | Nimbus Records | NI 2011
Bob Crosby's Bobcats
Swing Legens:Bob Crosby | Nimbus Records | NI 2011
Jack Teagarden And His Orchestra
Jazz:The Essential Collection Vol.3 | IN+OUT Records | 78013-2

The Capitol Jazzmen
The Hollywood Session:The Capitol Jazzmen | Jazz Unlimited | JUCD 2044

Lamare,Jimmy | (as,bsts)
Charlie Barnet And His Orchestra
Planet Jazz:Big Bands | Planet Jazz | 2169649-2
Planet Jazz:Swing | Planet Jazz | 2169651-2

Lamas,E. | (v)
Artie Shaw And His Orchestra
Planet JazzArtie Shaw | Planet Jazz | 2152057-2
Planet Jazz:Big Bands | Planet Jazz | 2169649-2

Lamask,Milton | (v)
Charlie Parker With Strings
Charlie Parker:The Best Of The Verve Years | Verve | 527815-2
Charlie Parker:April In Paris | Dreyfus Jazz Line | FDM 36737-2

Lamb,John | (b)
Duke Ellington And His Orchestra
Planet Jazz:Johnny Hodges | Planet Jazz | 2152065-2
Duke Ellington's Far East Suite | RCA | 2174797-2
The Art Of Saxophone | Laserlight | 24652
Highlights From The Duke Ellington Centennial Edition | RCA | 2663672-2
The Popular Duke Ellington | RCA | 2663880-2
Duke Ellington: The Champs-Elysees Theater January 29-30th,1965 | Laserlight | 36131
Verve Jazz Masters 4:Duke Ellington | Verve | 516338-2
Verve Jazz Masters 20:Introducing | Verve | 519853-2
Ella & Duke At The Cote D'Azur | Verve | 539030-2
Ella Fitzgerald And Duke Ellington:Cote D'Azure Concerts on Verve | Verve | 539033-2
Soul Call | Verve | 539785-2
Welcome To Jazz At The Philharmonic | Fantasy | FANCD 6081-2
Jazz At The Philharmonis Berlin '65/Paris '67 | Pablo | PACD 5304-2
The Jazz Giants Play Duke Ellington:Caravan | Prestige | PCD 24227-2
Duke Ellington Small Band
The Intimacy Of The Blues | Original Jazz Classics | OJCCD 624-2
Duke Ellington Trio With The Boston Pops Orchestra
Highlights From The Duke Ellington Centennial Edition | RCA | 2663672-2
Ella Fitzgerald With The Duke Ellington Orchestra
The Stockholm Concert 1966 | Pablo | 2308242-2
Ella Fitzgerald-First Lady Of Song | Verve | 517898-2
Verve Jazz Masters 46:Ella Fitzgerald-The Jazz Sides | Verve | 527655-2
Ella At Duke's Place | Verve | 529700-2
Ella & Duke At The Cote D'Azur | Verve | 539030-2
Ella Fitzgerald And Duke Ellington:Cote D'Azure Concerts on Verve | Verve | 539033-2
Oscar Peterson With The Duke Ellington Orchestra
Oscar Peterson Plays Duke Ellington | Pablo | 2310966-2

Lambe,Jeanie | (voc)
Jeanie Lambe And The Danny Moss Quartet
Three Great Concerts:Live In Hamburg 1993-1995 | Nagel-Heyer | CD 019
The Blue Noise Session | Nagel-Heyer | CD 052
The Second Sampler | Nagel-Heyer | NHR SP 6
Jeanie Lambe And The Danny Moss Septet
Three Great Concerts:Live In Hamburg 1993-1995 | Nagel-Heyer | CD 019
Oliver Jackson Orchestra
The Last Great Concert | Nagel-Heyer | CD 063
The Yamaha International Allstar Band
Happy Birthday Jazzwelle Plus | Nagel-Heyer | CD 005
Tom Saunders' 'Wild Bill Davison Band' & Guests
Exactly Like You | Nagel-Heyer | CD 023

Lambert Singers,The Dave |
Charlie Parker And His Orchestra
Charlie Parker:The Best Of The Verve Years | Verve | 527815-2
Charlie Parker With Orchestra & The Dave Lambert Singers
Verve Jazz Masters 28:Charlie Parker Plays Standards | Verve | 521854-2

Lambert,Dave | (voc)
Charlie Parker And His Orchestra
Bird: The Complete Charlie Parker On Verve | Verve | 837141-2
John Hendricks WithThe Dave Lambert Singers
Sing A Song Of Basie | Verve | 543827-2
Lambert, Hendricks And Bavan
Planet Jazz:Male Jazz Vocalists | Planet Jazz | 2169657-2
Lambert, Hendricks And Ross
Sing A Song Of Basie | Verve | 543827-2

Lambert,Hendricks & Ross |

Lambert,Lloyd | (b)
Lillian Boutté And Her Group
The Gospel Book | Blues Beacon | BLU-1017 2
Lillian Boutté And Her Group & The Soulful Heavenly Stars
The Gospel Book | Blues Beacon | BLU-1017 2

Lambert,Max | (p)
Grace Knight With Orchestra
Come In Spinner | Intuition Records | INT 3052-2
Vince Jones With Orchestra
Come In Spinner | Intuition Records | INT 3052-2

Lambooy,H.D. | (cello)
Toots Thielemans And His Orchestra
Verve Jazz Masters Vol.59:Toots Thielemans | Verve | 535271-2

Lamkin,John | (dr)
Donald Harrison Quartet
Free To Be | Impulse(MCA) | 951283-2
Donald Harrison Sextet
Free To Be | Impulse(MCA) | 951283-2

Lammi,Dick | (b,tubabj)
Lu Watters' Yerba Buena Jazz Band
The Very Best Of Dixieland Jazz | Verve | 535529-2
Turk Murphy And His Jazz Band
The Very Best Of Dixieland Jazz | Verve | 535529-2
Yerba Buena Jazz Band
Bunk & Lu | Good Time Jazz | GTCD 12024-2

Lamond,Don | (dr,perctympani)
Billie Holiday And Her All Stars
The Billie Holiday Song Book | Verve | 823246-2
Billie Holiday With Buck Clayton And The Mal Waldron Trio
Billie Holiday Story Vol.1:Jazz At The Philharmonic | Verve | 521642-2
Billie Holiday With The Ray Ellis Orchestra
Lady In Satin | CBS | CK 65144
Billy Butterfield And His Modern Dixie Stompers
Soft Strut | Fresh Sound Records | FSR-CD 318
Birdland Dream Band
Birdland Dream Band | RCA | 2663873-2
Carmen McRae With Orchestra
Birds Of A Feather | Decca | 589515-2
Charlie Parker And His Orchestra
The Cole Porter Songbook | Verve | 823250-2
Bird: The Complete Charlie Parker On Verve | Verve | 837141-2
Charlie Parker With Orchestra
Charlie Parker:The Best Of The Verve Years | Verve | 527815-2
Charlie Parker With Strings
Bird: The Complete Charlie Parker On Verve | Verve | 837141-2
Charlie Parker With The Joe Lipman Orchestra
Verve Jazz Masters 28:Charlie Parker Plays Standards | Verve | 521854-2
Charlie Parker With Strings:The Master Takes | Verve | 523984-2
Charlie Parker Big Band | Verve | 559835-2
Charlie Parker's New Stars
Charlie Parker:Now's The Time | Dreyfus Jazz Line | FDM 36724-2
Chubby Jackson And His All Star Big Band
Chubby Takes Over | Fresh Sound Records | FSR-CD 324
Chubby Jackson Big Band
Gerry Mulligan Quartet feat.Chet Baker | Original Jazz Classics | OJCCD 711-2(F 8082/P 7641)

Johnny Smith Quartet
Moonlight In Vermont | Roulette | 596593-2
Johnny Smith Quintet
Moonlight In Vermont | Roulette | 596593-2
Johnny Smith Trio
Moonlight In Vermont | Roulette | 596593-2
Johnny Smith-Stan Getz Quintet
Stan Getz-The Complete Roost Sessions | EMI Records | 859622-2
Lena Horne With The Lennie Hayton Orchestra
Planet Jazz:Lena Horne | Planet Jazz | 2165373-2
Rolf Kühn Quartet
Rolf Kühn And His Sound Of Jazz | Fresh Sound Records | FSR-CD 326
Rolf Kühn Quintet
Rolf Kühn And His Sound Of Jazz | Fresh Sound Records | FSR-CD 326
Stan Getz Quartet
Stan Getz:Imagination | Dreyfus Jazz Line | FDM 36733-2
Stan Getz Quartets | Original Jazz Classics | OJC20 121-2(P 7002)
The Four Brothers
Planet Jazz:Jazz Saxophone | Planet Jazz | 2169653-2
Together Again! | RCA | 2179623-2
Woody Herman And His Orchestra
The Legends Of Swing | Laserlight | 24659
Woody Herman:Four Brother | Dreyfus Jazz Line | FDM 36722-2
Woody Herman And His Woodshoppers
Woody Herman (And The Herd) At Carnegie Hall | Verve | 559833-2
Woody Herman And The Herd
Woody Herman (And The Herd) At Carnegie Hall | Verve | 559833-2
Woody Herman And The New Thundering Herd
Planet Jazz:Big Bands | Planet Jazz | 2169649-2
Woody Herman's Thundering Herd
Planet Jazz:Jazz Saxophone | Planet Jazz | 2169653-2
Zoot Sims Quartet
Zoot Sims Quartets | Original Jazz Classics | OJCCD 242-2(P 7026)

Lamont,Duncan | (fl,tssax)
Kenny Wheeler Ensemble
Muisc For Large & Small Ensembles | ECM | 1415/16

Lamory,Andre | (ascl)
Wal-Berg Et Son Jazz Francais
Jazz In Paris:Django Reinhardt-Django Et Compagnie | EmArCy | 549241-2 PMS

LaMotte,Keith | (mellophonetp)
Stan Kenton And His Orchestra
Adventures In Blues | Capitol | 520089-2
Adventures In Jazz | Capitol | 521222-2

Lamparter,Jochen | (g,bj,vocp)
Stuttgarter Dixieland All Stars
It's The Talk Of The Town | Jazzpoint | JP 1069 CD

Lamparter,Peter | (cl,asvoc)

Lampert,Steve | (p,synth,samplestp)
Rich Perry Quartet
Hearsay | Steeplechase | SCCD 31515
Steve Lampert Group
Venus Perplexed | Steeplechase | SCCD 31557

Lampkin,Chuck | (dr)
Dizzy Gillespie And His Orchestra
Verve Jazz Masters 10:Dizzy Gillespie | Verve | 516319-2
Gillespiana And Carnegie Hall Concert | Verve | 519809-2
Talking Verve:Dizzy Gillespie | Verve | 533846-2
Ultimate Dizzy Gillespie | Verve | 557535-2
Dizzy Gillespie Quintet
Dizzie Gillespie: Salle Pleyel/Olympia | Laserlight | 36132
An Electrifying Evening With The Dizzy Gillespie Quintet | Verve | 557544-2
Dizzy Gillespie Sextet
Dizzie Gillespie: Salle Pleyel/Olympia | Laserlight | 36132
JATP All Stars
Verve Jazz Masters 25:Stan Getz & Dizzy Gillespie | Verve | 521852-2

Lams,John | (b)
Duke Ellington And His Orchestra
Afro-Bossa | Reprise | 9362-47876-2

Lamy,Gerald | (tp)
Woody Herman And His Orchestra
Verve Jazz Masters 54:Woody Herman | Verve | 529903-2
Woody Herman-1963 | Philips | 589490-2

Land,Harold | (fl,ts,oboe,reedsss)
All Star Live Jam Session
Brownie-The Complete EmArCy Recordings Of Clifford Brown | EmArCy | 838306-2
Bill Evans Quintet
The Complete Fantasy Recordings | Fantasy | 9FCD 1012-2
Quintessence | Original Jazz Classics | OJCCD 698-2(F 9529)
The Jazz Giants Play Jerome Kern:Yesterdays | Prestige | PCD 24202-2
The Jazz Giants Play Sammy Cahn:It's Magic | Prestige | PCD 24226-2
Bobby Hutcherson Quintet
Blue Breaks Beats Vol.2 | Blue Note | 789907-2
Clifford Brown All Stars With Dinah Washington
Verve Jazz Masters 40:Dinah Washington | Verve | 522055-2
Clifford Brown-Max Roach Quintet
Clifford Brown-Max Roach:Alone Together-The Best Of The Mercury Years | Verve | 526373-2
Verve Jazz Masters 44:Clifford Brown and Max Roach | Verve | 528109-2
Verve Jazz Masters Vol.60:The Collection | Verve | 529866-2
Clifford Brown And Max Roach | Verve | 543306-2
Study In Brown | EmArCy | 814646-2
Brownie-The Complete EmArCy Recordings Of Clifford Brown | EmArCy | 838306-2
Donald Byrd Orchestra
Ethiopian Knights | Blue Note | 854328-2
Ella Fitzgerald With Orchestra
Ella/Things Ain't What They Used To Be | Warner | 9362-47875-2
Freddie Hubbard And His Orchestra
Born To Be Blue | Original Jazz Classics | OJCCD 734-2(2312134)
Gerald Wilson And His Orchestra
Blue Breaks Beats Vol.2 | Blue Note | 789907-2
Harold Land Quintet
The Fox | Original Jazz Classics | OJCCD 343-2
Harold Land Sextet
Wes Montgomery-The Complete Riverside Recordings | Riverside | 12 RCD 4408-2
Jimmy Smith With Orchestra
Verve Jazz Masters 29:Jimmy Smith | Verve | 521855-2
Jimmy Woods Sextet
Conflict | Original Jazz Classics | OJCCD 1954-2(S 7612)
Johnny Hartman And His Orchestra
Unforgettable | Impulse(MCA) | IMP 11522
Red Norvo And His Orchestra
Planet Jazz:Female Jazz Vocalists | Planet Jazz | 2169656-2
Thelonious Monk Quartet Plus Two
Thelonious Monk:85th Birthday Celebration | zyx records | FANCD 6076-2
At The Blackhawk | Original Jazz Classics | OJCCD 305-2

Landau,Michael | (el-gg)
Joe Sample Group
Ashes To Ashes | Warner | 7599-26318-2
Spellbound | Rhino | 81273726-2
Miles Davis Group
Amandla | Warner | 7599-25873-2
Stan Getz With Orchestra
Apasionado | A&M Records | 395297-2

Lande,Art | (p,percsynth)
Art Lande Quartet
Rubisa Patrol | ECM | 1081
Art Lande Trio
Skylight | ECM | 1208
Art Lande-Jan Garbark
Red Lanta | ECM | 1038(829383-2)
Gary Peacock Trio
Shift In The Wind | ECM | 1165
Mark Isham-Art Lande
We Begin | ECM | 1338

Landeck,Detlef | (tb)
Chromatic Alarm
Some Other Tapes | Fish Music | FM 009/10 CD
Ekkehard Jost & Chromatic Alarm
Von Zeit Zu Zeit | Fish Music | FM 005 CD
Wintertango | Fish Music | FM 008 CD
Ekkehard Jost Ensemble
Weimarer Balladen | Fish Music | FM 004 CD
Ekkehard Jost Nonet
Out Of Jost's Songbook | Fish Music | FM 006 CD
Giessen-Köln-Nonett
Some Other Tapes | Fish Music | FM 009/10 CD
Transalpin Express Orchestra
Some Other Tapes | Fish Music | FM 009/10 CD

Landers,Wes | (drperc)
Sonny Clark Trio
Standards | Blue Note | 821283-2

Landes Jugend Jazz Orchester Hessen |
Landes Jugend Jazz Orchester Hessen
Touch Of Lips | hr music.de | hrmj 004-01 CD

Landesbergen,Frits | (dr,percvib)
HR Big Band With Marjorie Barnes And Frits Landesbergen
Swinging Christmas | hr music.de | hrmj 012-02 CD
HR Big Band With Marjorie Barnes And Frits Landesbergen And Strings
Swinging Christmas | hr music.de | hrmj 012-02 CD
Laura Fygi With Band
Bewitched | Verve | 514724-2
Stochelo Rosenberg Group
Gypsy Swing | Verve | 527806-2
The Rosenberg Trio With Frits Landesbergen
Gypsy Swing | Verve | 527806-2
The Rosenberg Trio:The Collection | Verve | 537152-2

Landgren,Nils | (tb,fl-h,voc,keyboardstp)
Bernard Purdie's Soul To Jazz
Bernard Purdie's Soul To Jazz | ACT | 9242-2
Eddie Harris Group With The WDR Big Band
Eddie Harris-The Last Concert | ACT | 9249-2
Jazz Baltica Ensemble
The Birth+Rebirth Of Swedish Folk Jazz | ACT | 9254-2
Joe Gallardo's Latino Blue
A Latin Shade Of Blue | Enja | ENJ-9421 2
Kölner Saxophon Mafia With Guests
Kölner Saxophon Mafia: 20 Jahre Saxuelle Befreiung | Jazz Haus Musik | JHM 0115 CD
NDR Big Band With Guests
50 Years Of NDR Big Band:Bravissimo II | ACT | 9259-2
Niels Landgren Funk Unit
Live In Stockholm | ACT | 9223-2
Nils Landgren First Unit And Guests
Nils Landgren-The First Unit | ACT | 9292-2
Nils Landgren Funk Unit
Paint It Blue:A Tribute To Cannonball Adderley | ACT | 9243-2
Live In Montreux | ACT | 9265-2
Fonk Da World | ACT | 9299-2
Nils Landgren Funk Unit With Guests
5000 Miles | ACT | 9271-2
Nils Landgren Group
Ballads | ACT | 9268-2
Sentimental Journey | ACT | 9409-2
Nils Landgren With The Esbjörn Svensson Trio
Ballads | ACT | 9268-2
Nils Landgren-Esbjörn Svensson
Layers Of Light | ACT | 9281-2
Swedish Folk Modern | ACT | 9428-2
Nils Landgren-Tomasz Stanko
Gotland | ACT | 9226-2
Nils Landgren-Tomasz Stanko With Anders Eljas And Claus Bantzer
Gotland | ACT | 9226-2
Oscar Brown Jr. with The NDR Big Band
Live Every Minute | Minor Music | 801071
Rigmor Gustafsson With The Nils Landgren Quartet And The Fleshquartet
I Will Wait For You | ACT | 9418-2
Viktoria Tolstoy Group & Strings
Shining On You | ACT | 9701-2
Viktoria Tolstoy With The Esbjörn Svensson Trio
Viktoria Tolstoy:White Russian | Blue Note | 821220-2

Landham,Byron | (drwind-chimes)
Russell Malone Quartet
Look Who's Here | Verve | 543543-2

Landis,Wesley | (dr)
Little Jimmy Scott | Specialty | SPCD 2170-2

Lando,Vadim | (cl)
Paquito D'Rivera Group With The Absolute Ensemble
Habanera | Enja | ENJ-9395 2

Landolf,Domenic | (b-cl,ss,tsfl)
Brigitte Dietrich-Joe Haider Jazz Orchestra
Consequences | JHM Records | JHM 3624
Domenic Landolf Quartet
Levitation | JHM Records | JHM 3616
Matthias Spillmann Septet
Something About Water | JHM Records | JHM 3620
Roman Schwaller Nonet
The Original Tunes | JHM Records | JHM 3629

Landon,Carol | (viola)
A Band Of Friends
Wynton Marsalis Quartet With Strings | CBS | CK 68921

Landrum,Richard 'Pablo' | (bongos,congasperc)
Big John Patton Quartet
Got A Good Thing Goin' | Blue Note | 580731-2
Count Basie And His Orchestra
Afrique | RCA | 2179618-2
Gato Barbieri Sextet
The Third World | RCA | 2179617-2
Grant Green Orchestra
Grant Green:Blue Breakbeat | Blue Note | 494705-2
Blue Breaks Beats Vol.2 | Blue Note | 789907-2
So Blue So Funky-Heroes Of The Hammond | Blue Note | 796563-2
Leon Thomas With Band
Super Black Blues Vol.II | RCA | 2663874-2
Spirits Known And Unknown | RCA | 2663876-2
Leon Thomas In Berlin | RCA | 2663877-2
Rahsaan Roland Kirk Sextet
Blacknuss | Rhino | 8122-71408-2
Stanley Turrentine And His Orchestra
The Lost Grooves | Blue Note | 831883-2

Landsberger,Jermaine | (pkeyboards)
Jermaine Landsberger Trio
Gypsy Feeling | Edition Collage | EC 516-2
Jermaine Landsberger Trio & Gina
Samba In June | Edition Collage | EC 524-2
Jermaine Landsberger Trio With Bireli Lagrene
Gypsy Feeling | Edition Collage | EC 516-2
Jermaine Landsberger Trio With Helmut Kagerer & Gina
Samba In June | Edition Collage | EC 524-2

Lane,Adrian | (tb)
Mike Westbrook Orchestra
Bar Utopia-A Big Band Cabaret | Enja | ENJ-9333 2
The Orchestra Of Smith's Academy | Enja | ENJ-9358 2

Lane,Chester | (p)
Louis Jordan With The Nelson Riddle Orchestra
Louis Jordan-Let The Good Times Roll: The Complete Decca Recordings 1938-1954 | Bear Family Records | BCD 15557 IH

Lane,Gordon | (dr)
Ahmad Jamal Trio
Live In Paris 1992 | Dreyfus Jazz Line | FDM 37019-2

Lane,Mildred | (voc)
Archie Shepp Orchestra
The Cry Of My People | Impulse(MCA) | 9861488

Lane,Morris | (ts)
Lionel Hampton And His Orchestra
Lionel Hampton:Flying Home | Dreyfus Jazz Line | FDM 36735-2

Lane,Nick | (synthtb)
Diane Schuur With Orchestra
Blues For Schuur | GRP | GRP 98632
The Best Of Diane Schuur | GRP | GRP 98882

Laneri,Roberto | (b-cl)
Charles Mingus Orchestra
Cumbia & Jazz Fusion | Atlantic | 8122-71785-2

Lanese,Bob | (tpfl-h)
Chet Baker With The NDR-Bigband
NDR Big Band-Bravissimo | ACT | 9232-2
My Favourite Songs: The Last Great Concert Vol.1 | Enja | ENJ-5097 2
The Last Concert Vol.I+II | Enja | ENJ-6074 22
Joe Pass With The NDR Big Band And Radio Philharmonie Hannover
Joe Pass In Hamburg | ACT | 9100-2
Klaus Weiss Orchestra
Live At The Domicile | ATM Records | ATM 3805-AH

Lang,Billy | (g)
Klaus Doldinger's Passport
Running In Real Time | Warner | 2292-40633-2

Lang,Eddie | (bj,g,g-solov)
Blind Willie Dunn's Gin Bottle Four
Jazz:The Essential Collection Vol.1 | IN+OUT Records | 78011-2
Eddie Lang-Joe Venuti And Their Allstars Orchestra
Jazz:The Essential Collection Vol.3 | IN+OUT Records | 78013-2
Frankie Trumbauer And His Orchestra
Jazz:The Essential Collection Vol.2 | IN+OUT Records | 78012-2
Hoagy Carmichael And His Orchestra
Planet Jazz:Bud Freeman | Planet Jazz | 2161240-2
Louis Armstrong And His Orchestra
Jazz:The Essential Collection Vol.3 | IN+OUT Records | 78013-2
Roger Wolfe Kahn And His Orchestra
Planet Jazz:Jack Teagarden | Planet Jazz | 2161236-2

Lang,Evelyn | (voc)
Peter Kleindienst Group
Zeitwärts:Reime Vor Pisin | double moon | DMCD 1001-2

Lang,Irving | (b)
Anita O'Day With Gene Krupa And His Orchestra
Let Me Off Uptown:Anita O'Day With Gene Krupa | CBS | CK 65625

Lang,Jorgen | (?)
Champion Jack Dupree
Champion Jack Dupree | Storyville | 4960383

Lang,Mike | (el-p,synth,keyboards,pclavinet)
Diane Schuur With Orchestra
The Best Of Diane Schuur | GRP | GRP 98882
Don Ellis Orchestra
Electric Bath | CBS | CK 65522
Ella Fitzgerald With Orchestra
Ella Abraca Jobim | Pablo | 2630201-2
Lee Konitz And His West Coast Friends
Art Pepper:The Hollywood All-Star Sessions | Galaxy | 5GCD 4431-2
Sarah Vaughan And Her Band
Songs Of The Beatles | Atlantic | 16037-2
Stan Getz With Orchestra
Apasionado | A&M Records | 395297-2

Lang,Ronnie | (alto-fl,bs,as,piccolo,fl,piccolo-fl)
Ella Fitzgerald With The Nelson Riddle Orchestra
Ella Fitzgerald-First Lady Of Song | Verve | 517898-2
Verve Jazz Masters 6:Ella Fitzgerald | Verve | 510822-2
Henry Mancini And His Orchestra
Combo! | RCA | 2147794-2
Pete Rugolo And His Orchestra
Thriller/Richard Diamon(Original Jazz Scores From 2 Classics TV Series) | Fresh Sound Records | FSCD 2015
Stan Kenton And His Orchestra
Stan Kenton Portraits On Standards | Capitol | 531571-2
Van Alexander Orchestra
Home Of Happy Feet/Swing! Staged For Sound! | Capitol | 535211-2

Lang,Stephan Noel | (p)
Stephan Noel Lang Trio
Echoes | Nagel-Heyer | CD 2033

Lang,Sunny | (b)
Joe Turner And Friends
The Giant Of Stride Piano In Switzerland | Jazz Connaisseur | JCCD 9106-2

Lang,Walter | (el-p,claviola,arr,p,tblotus-fl)
Full Moon Trio
Live At Birdland Neuburg | double moon | CHRDM 71024
Jenny Evans And Her Quintet
Nuages | Enja | ENJ-9467 2
Gonna Go Fishin' | ESM Records | ESM 9307
Nuages | ESM Records | ESM 9308
Johannes Herrlich Quintet
Thinking Of You | Edition Collage | EC 499-2
Lisa Wahland And Her Trio
Marlene | Fine Music | FM 108-2
Lisa Wahlandt & Mulo Francel And Their Fabulous Bossa Band
Bossa Nova Affair | Edition Collage | EC 534-2
Thomas Faist Jazzquartet
Visionary | JHM Records | JHM 3609
Thomas Faist Sextet
Gentle | Village | VILCD 1020-2
Trombonefire
Sliding Affairs | Laika Records | 35101462
Walter Lang Quintet
Tales Of 2 Cities | double moon | CHRDM 71016

Lange,Hajo | (b)
Harry Allen And Randy Sandke Meets The RIAS Big Band Berlin
The Music Of The Trumpet Kings | Nagel-Heyer | CD 037

Lange,Peter | (tp,vocarr)
Stuttgarter Dixieland All Stars
It's The Talk Of The Town | Jazzpoint | JP 1069 CD
The Tremble Kids All Stars
The Tremble Kids All Stars Play Chicago Jazz! | Nagel-Heyer | CD 043

Lange,Rainer | (cello)
Los Jovenes Flamencos With The WDR Big Band And Guests
Jazzpana | ACT | 9212-2

Lange,Uwe | (b,cellog)
Sputnik 27
But Where's The Moon? | dml-records | CD 011
Thomas Siffling Jazz Quartet
Soft Winds | Satin Doll Productions | SDP 1030-1 CD
Thomas Stiffling Group
Stories | Jazz 4 Ever Records:Jazz Network | J4E 4756

Lange,Veit | (b-clts)
Konstantin Wienstroer-Veit Lange-Felix Elsner
Unfinished Business | Green House Music | CD 1005

Langer,Ameli | (voc)
Jazz Orchester Rheinland-Pfalz
Last Season | Jazz Haus Musik | LJBB 9706

Langereis,Rob | (bel-b)
Toots Thielemans And His Orchestra
Verve Jazz Masters Vol.59:Toots Thielemans | Verve | 535271-2

Langford,William | (voc)
Golden Gate Quartet
From Spiritual To Swing | Vanguard | VCD 169/71

Langguth,Tobias | (g,bpiccolo-g)
Tobias Langguth Band
One Note Bossa | Jardis Records | JRCD 9510

Langinger,Ronald | (as,flreeds)
Ella Fitzgerald With Frank De Vol And His Orchestra
Get Happy! | Verve | 523321-2
Ella Fitzgerald With Orchestra

The Best Is Yet To Come | Original Jazz Classics | OJCCD 889-2(2312138)
Louis Armstrong With The Hal Mooney Orchestra
Ambassador Louis Armstrong Vol.17:Moments To Remember(1952-1956) | Ambassador | CLA 1917

Langley,Noel | (tp)
Barbara Thompson's Paraphernalia
Breathless | VeraBra Records | CDVBR 2057-2
Mike Westbrook Orchestra
Bar Utopia-A Big Band Cabaret | Enja | ENJ-9333 2
The Orchestra Of Smith's Academy | Enja | ENJ-9358 2

Lanham,Gene | (voc)
Louis Armstrong With The Hal Mooney Orchestra
Ambassador Louis Armstrong Vol.17:Moments To Remember(1952-1956) | Ambassador | CLA 1917

Lano,Joe | (g)
Don Menza Quartet
Las Vegar Late Night Sessions:Live At Capozzoli's | Woofy Productions | WPCD 116

Lanois,Daniel | (mando-gwhite-mustang)
Brian Blade Group
Fellowship | Blue Note | 859417-2

Lanoue,Conrad | (p)
Wingy Mannone And His Orchestra
Planet Jazz:Jazz Trumpet | Planet Jazz | 2169654-2

Lanphere,Don | (as,tss)
Don Lanphere Quintet
Fats Navarro:Nostalgia | Dreyfus Jazz Line | FDM 36736-2

Lanphier,Bill | (b)
Buddy Childers Big Band
Just Buddy's | Candid | CCD 79761

Lansing,Dennis | (horns,tsbs)
Howlin' Wolf London Session
Howlin' Wolf:The London Sessions | Chess | MCD 09297

Lanzara,Reno | (dr)
John Lee Hooker Group
Endless Boogie | MCA | MCD 10413

Lanzerath,Paul | (tpfl-h)
HR Big Band
The American Songs Of Kurt Weill | hr music.de | hrmj 006-01 CD
Libertango:Homage An Astor Piazolla | hr music.de | hrmj 014-02 CD
HR Big Band With Marjorie Barnes And Frits Landesbergen
Swinging Christmas | hr music.de | hrmj 012-02 CD
HR Big Band With Marjorie Barnes And Frits Landesbergen And Strings
Swinging Christmas | hr music.de | hrmj 012-02 CD
The Three Sopranos With The HR Big Band
The Three Sopranos | hr music.de | hrmj 001-01 CD

Lapcikova,Zuzana | (cymbalonvoc)
George Mraz Quartet
Morava | Milestone | MCD 9309-2

LaPolla,Ralph | (as,cl,flsax)
Vic Lewis Jam Session
Vic Lewis:The Golden Years | Candid | CCD 79754

LaPorta,John | (arr,as,bs,cl,tswoodwinds)
Charles Mingus Orchestra
Charles Mingus:Pre-Bird(Mingus Revisited) | Verve | 538636-2
Charlie Parker With Strings
Charlie Parker With Strings:The Master Takes | Verve | 523984-2
Charlie Parker With The Neal Hefti Orchestra
Charlie Parker:The Best Of The Verve Years | Verve | 527815-2
Bird: The Complete Charlie Parker On Verve | Verve | 837141-2
Don Senay With Orchestra And Strings
Charles Mingus-The Complete Debut Recordings | Debut | 12 DCD 4402-2
George Russell And His Orchestra
Bill Evans:Piano Player | CBS | CK 65361
John LaPorta Octet
Theme And Variations | Fantasy | FCD 24776-2
John LaPorta Septet
Theme And Variations | Fantasy | FCD 24776-2
John LaPorta Trio
The Sandole Brothers | Fantasy | FCD 24763-2
Sandole Brothers
The Sandole Brothers | Fantasy | FCD 24763-2
Thad Jones And His Orchestra
Charles Mingus-The Complete Debut Recordings | Debut | 12 DCD 4402-2
The Metronome All Stars
Jazz Gallery:Lester Young Vol.2(1946-59) | RCA | 2119541-2
Woody Herman And His Orchestra
The Legends Of Swing | Laserlight | 24659
Woody Herman:Four Brother | Dreyfus Jazz Line | FDM 36722-2
Louis Armstrong-Jack Teagarden-Woody Herman:Midnights At V-Disc | Jazz Unlimited | JUCD 2048
Old Gold Rehearsals 1944 | Jazz Unlimited | JUCD 2079
Woody Herman And The Herd
Woody Herman (And The Herd) At Carnegie Hall | Verve | 559833-2

Lapuble,Pocho | (dr)
Gato Barbieri Orchestra
Latino America | Impulse(MCA) | 952236-2

Lara,Leonardo Planches | (percvoc)
Conjunto Clave Y Guaguanco
Dejala En La Puntica | TipToe | TIP-888829 2

Larché,Jean-Marc | (as,ssbs)
Anouar Brahem Group
Khomsa | ECM | 1561(527093-2)
Orchestre National De Jazz
Charmediterranéen | ECM | 1828(018493-2)

Larkin,Tippy | (tp)
Bernard Purdie Group
Jazzin' With The Soul Brothers | Fantasy | FANCD 6086-2

Larkins,Ellis | (pp-solo)
Coleman Hawkins And His Orchestra
Jazz:The Essential Collection Vol.3 | IN+OUT Records | 78013-2
Dicky Wells And His Orchestra
Jazz:The Essential Collection Vol.3 | IN+OUT Records | 78013-2
Ella Fitzgerald With Ellis Larkins
Ella Fitzgerald:Mr.Paganini | Dreyfus Jazz Line | FDM 36741-2
Pure Ella | GRP | GRP 16362
Mildred Bailey With The Ellis Larkins Trio
Planet Jazz:Female Jazz Vocalists | Planet Jazz | 2169656-2
Ruby Braff-Ellis Larkins
Duets Vol.1 | Vanguard | VCD 79609-2
Duets Vol.2 | Vanguard | VCD 79611-2

LaRoca,Pete | (dr)
Art Farmer Quartet
Sing Me Softly Of The Blues | Atlantic | 7567-80773-2
George Russell Sextet
The Outer View | Original Jazz Classics | OJCCD 616-2(RLP 9440)
Helen Merrill With The Dick Katz Group
The Feeling Is Mutual | EmArCy | 558849-2
Joe Henderson Quintet
Page One | Blue Note | 498795-2
Our Thing | Blue Note | 525647-2
The Blue Note Years-The Best Of Joe Henderson | Blue Note | 795627-2
Paul Bley Trio
The Story Of Jazz Piano | Laserlight | 24653
Sonny Clark Quintet
My Conception | Blue Note | 522674-2
Sonny Rollins Trio
A Night At The Village Vanguard | Blue Note | 499795-2
Sonny Rollins:The Blue Note Recordings | Blue Note | 821371-2
St.Thomas:Sonny Rollins In Stockhom 1959 | Dragon | DRCD 229
Stan Getz Quartet
Stan Getz Highlights:The Best Of The Verve Years Vol.2 | Verve | 517330-2

Larsen,Erik Niord | (oboe)
Terje Rypdal Quintet
What Comes After | ECM | 1031

Larsen,Frank | (?)
Champion Jack Dupree
Champion Jack Dupree | Storyville | 4960383

Larsen,Jeppe Esper | (covoc)
Chris Barber & The Ramblers
The Golden Years Of Revival Jazz,Vol.12 | Storyville | STCD 5517

Larsen,John | (sousaphone,tbtuba)
Leonardo Pedersen's Jazzkapel
The Golden Years Of Revival Jazz,Sampler | Storyville | 109 1001
The Golden Years Of Revival Jazz,Vol.11 | Storyville | STCD 5516

Larsen,Kent | (b-tb,tbvoc)
Stan Kenton And His Orchestra
Great Swing Classics In Hi-Fi | Capitol | 521223-2
Stan Kenton Orchestra
Stompin' At Newport | Pablo | PACD 5312-2

Larsen,Mona | (voc)
Copenhagen Art Ensemble
Shape To Twelve | dacapo | DCCD 9430
Michael Mantler Group
Songs And One Symphony | ECM | 1721
Michael Mantler Group With The Danish Radio Concert Orchestra Strings
The School Of Understanding(Sort-Of-An-Opera) | ECM | 1648/49(537963-2)
Mona Larsen And The Danish Radio Big Band Plus Soloists
Michael Mantler:Cerco Un Paese Innocente | ECM | 1556

Larsen,Neil | (org)
Al Jarreau With Band
Tenderness | i.e. Music | 557853-2
Diana Krall Group
The Girl In The Other Room | Verve | 9862246

Larsen,Per | (fr-h)
Stan Kenton With The Danish Radio Big Band
Stan Kenton With The Danish Radio Big Band | Storyville | STCD 8340

Larsen,Sverre | (wind-harp)
Ketil Bjornstad Group
Early Years | EmArCy | 013271-2

Larsen,Ture | (cond,tbtenor-h)
Copenhagen Art Ensemble
Shape To Twelve | dacapo | DCCD 9430
Angels' Share | dacapo | DCCD 9452
Marilyn Mazur With Ars Nova And The Copenhagen Art Ensemble
Jordsange | dacapo | DCCD 9454
Miles Davis With The Danish Radio Big Band
Aura | CBS | CK 63962
The Danish Radio Big Band
Aura | CBS | CK 63962
The Danish Radio Jazz Orchestra
This Train:The Danish Radio Jazz Orchestra Plays The Music Of Ray Pitts | dacapo | DCCD 9428

Larue,Lester | (g)
Dan Wall Quartet
Off The Wall | Enja | ENJ-9310 2

Lascarro,Juanita | (voc)
Markus Stockhausen Orchestra
Sol Mestizo:Markus Stockhausen Plays The Music Of Enrique Diaz | ACT | 9222-2

Lasha,Prince | (fl,ascl)
Prince Lasha Quartet
The Cry | Original Jazz Classics | OJCCD 1945-2(S 7610)
Prince Lasha Quintet
The Cry | Original Jazz Classics | OJCCD 1945-2(S 7610)

Lask,Ulrich P. | (as,synth,ts,computer programming,fl)
Ulrich P. Lask Group
Lask | ECM | 1217

LaSpina,Steve | (b)
Jam Session
Jam Session Vol.9 | Steeplechase | SCCD 31554
Jam Session Vol.10 | Steeplechase | SCCD 31555
Karl Schloz Quartet
A Mooth One | Nagel-Heyer | CD 2012
Steve LaSpina Quintet
Remember When | Steeplechase | SCCD 31540

Lassen,Helmuth | (tbvoc)
Papa Bue's Viking Jazzband
The Golden Years Of Revival Jazz,Vol.6 | Storyville | STCD 5511

Lassus,Francis | (dr)
Louis Sclavis Sextet
Les Violences De Rameau | ECM | 1588(533128-2)

Last,Hans | (b)
Die Deutsche All Star Band 1953
1.Deutsches Jazz Festival 1953 Frankfurt/Main | Bear Family Records | BCD 15611 AH
Helmut Zacharias & His Sax-Team
Ich Habe Rhythmus | Bear Family Records | BCD 15642 AH
Paul Kuhn Quartet
Deutsches Jazz Fesival 1954/1955 | Bear Family Records | BCD 15430
Rolf Kühn All Stars
Deutsches Jazz Fesival 1954/1955 | Bear Family Records | BCD 15430

Laster,Andy | (as,bs,cl,fl,manhasset-light-clip)
Marty Ehrlich Group
The Long View | Enja | ENJ-9452 2

Laster,Shelton | (org)
Grant Green Septet
Live At The Lighthouse | Blue Note | 493381-2

Lastie,Melvin | (cotp)
Eddie Harris Group
The Best Of Eddie Harris | Atlantic | 7567-81370-2
Herbie Hancock Septet
Herbie Hancock:The Complete Blue Note Sixties Sessions | Blue Note | 495569-2
Willie Bobo Group
Juicy | Verve | 519857-2

Lastra,Carlos | (ssas)
Hernan Merlo Quintet
Consin | Fresh Sound Records | FSNT 150 CD

Laszlo,Attila | (g)
Things
Mother Nature | Jazzpoint | JP 1028 CD

Latatos,Tony | (ssts)
The Tough Tenors With The Antonio Farao European Trio
Tough Tenors | Jazz 4 Ever Records:Jazz Network | J4E 4761

Lateef,Yusef | (engl-h,fl,ts,oboe,alto-fl,ss,p)
Art Blakey And The Afro Drum Ensemble
The African Beat | Blue Note | 522666-2
Cannonball Adderley Sextet
Jazz Workshop Revisited | Capitol | 529441-2
Cannonball Adderley Birthday Celebration | Fantasy | FANCD 6087-2
Dizzy's Business-Live In Concert | Milestone | MCD 47069-2
Cannonball Adderley In New York | Original Jazz Classics | OJC20 142-2(RLP 9404)
Nippon Soul | Original Jazz Classics | OJC20 435-2(RLP 9477)
Cannonball Adderley-Nat Adderley Sextet
The Best Of Cannonball Adderley:The Capitol Years | Capitol | 795482-2
Charles Mingus Orchestra
Charles Mingus:Pre-Bird(Mingus Revisited) | Verve | 538636-2
Clark Terry Orchestra
Color Changes | Candid | CCD 79009
Dizzy Gillespie And His Orchestra
Planet Jazz:Dizzy Gillespie | Planet Jazz | 2152069-2
Planet Jazz:Bebop | RCA | 2169650-2
Planet Jazz:Male Jazz Vocalists | Planet Jazz | 2169657-2
Ernestine Anderson With Orchestra
My Kinda Swing | Mercury | 842409-2
Grant Green Quartet
Ballads | Blue Note | 537560-2
Grantstand | Blue Note | 591723-2
Les McCann Group
Atlantic Jazz: Fusion | Atlantic | 7567-81711-2
Nat Adderley And The Big Sax Section
Cannonball Adderley Birthday Celebration | Fantasy | FANCD 6087-2
That's Right | Original Jazz Classics | OJCCD 791-2(RLP 9330)
Yusef Lateef Ensemble
Nocturnes | Atlantic | 7567-81977-2
Atlantic Saxophones | Rhino | 8122-71256-2
Yusef Lateef Orchestra
Rhino Presents The Atlantic Jazz Gallery | Atlantic | 8122-71257-2
The Blue Yusef Lateef | Rhino | 8122-73717-2
The Centaur And The Phoenix | Original Jazz Classics | OJCCD 721-2(RLP 9337)
Yusef Lateef Quartet
Live at Pep's Vol.2 | Impulse(MCA) | 547961-2
The Golden Flute | Impulse(MCA) | 9681049
Eastern Sounds | Original Jazz Classics | OJC20 612-2(P 7319)
Into Something | Original Jazz Classics | OJCCD 700-2(NJ 8272)
Yusef Lateef Quintet
Live at Pep's Vol.2 | Impulse(MCA) | 547961-2
The Roots Of Acid Jazz | Impulse(MCA) | IMP 12042
Other Sounds | Original Jazz Classics | OJCCD 399-2(NJ 8218)
Yusef Lateef Sextet
The Art Of Saxophone | Laserlight | 24652
Yusef Lateef Trio
Into Something | Original Jazz Classics | OJCCD 700-2(NJ 8272)
Yusef Lateef With Eternal Wind And The 'Kölner Rundfunk Orchester'
The African American Epic Suite:Music For Quintet And Orchestra | ACT | 9214-2

Latham,Karl | (dr)
Johannes Mössinger New York Trio
Monk's Corner | double moon | DMCHR 71032
Johannes Mössinger New York Trio with Joe Lovano
Monk's Corner | double moon | DMCHR 71032

Lathrop,Jack | (gvoc)
Glenn Miller And His Orchestra
Planet Jazz:Glenn Miller | Planet Jazz | 2152056-2
Planet Jazz:Jazz Greatest Hits | Planet Jazz | 2169648-2
Planet Jazz:Big Bands | Planet Jazz | 2169649-2

Latin Jazz Quintet,The |
The Latin Jazz Quintet Plus Guest: Eric Dolphy
Eric Dolphy:The Complete Prestige Recordings | Prestige | 9 PRCD-4418-2
Eric Dolphy Birthday Celebration | Fantasy | FANCD 6085-2

Lattmann,Bela | (b)
Things
Mother Nature | Jazzpoint | JP 1028 CD

Laubach,Jack H. | (tp)
Dizzy Gillespie With The Lalo Schifrin,Orchestra
Free Ride | Original Jazz Classics | OJCCD 784-2(2310794)

Lauber,Frank | (as,b-clreeds)
Cafe Du Sport Jazzquartett
Cafe Du Sport Jazzquartett | Minor Music | 801096
Enrico Rava With The Michael Flügel Quartet
Live At Birdland Neuburg | double moon | CHRDM 71011
Rainer Tempel Big Band
Melodies Of '98 | Jazz 4 Ever Records:Jazz Network | J4E 4744

Lauer,Christof | (reeds,ss,tsstrings)
Albert Mangelsdorff With The NDR Big Band
NDR Big Band-Bravissimo | ACT | 9232-2
Carla Bley Band
Fleur Carnivore | Watt | 21
Christof Lauer-Jens Thomas
Shadows In The Rain | ACT | 9297-2
Christof Lauer-Jens Thomas With The Cikada String Quartet
Shadows In The Rain | ACT | 9297-2
Christoph Lauer & Norwegian Brass
Heaven | ACT | 9420-2
Christoph Lauer Quintet
Fragile Network | ACT | 9266-2
Heinz Sauer Quartet With The NDR Big Band
NDR Big Band-Bravissimo | ACT | 9232-2
Jazzensemble Des Hessischen Rundfunks
Atmosphering Conditions Permitting | ECM | 1549/50
Joachim Kühn And The Radio Philharmonie Hannover NDR With Jazz Soloists
Europeana | ACT | 9220-2
NDR Big Band
NDR Big Band-Bravissimo | ACT | 9232-2
The Theatre Of Kurt Weill | ACT | 9234-2
NDR Big Band With Guests
50 Years Of NDR Big Band:Bravissimo II | ACT | 9259-2
Oscar Brown Jr. with The NDR Big Band
Live Every Minute | Minor Music | 801071
Radio Jazzgroup Frankfurt
Jubilee Edition | double moon | CHRDM 71020
Ralph R.Hübner-Christoph Lauer
Mondspinner | free flow music | ffm 0796
Ralph R.Hübner-Christoph Lauer Quartet
Mondspinner | free flow music | ffm 0796
Wolfgang Lackerschmid Sextet
One More Life | Bhakti Jazz | BR 29

Lauer,Wolfgang | (b)
Dieter Bihlmaier Selection
Mallet Connection | Bhakti Jazz | BR 33

Laufer,Heinrich | (ts)
Harald Banter Ensemble
Deutsches Jazz Fesival 1954/1955 | Bear Family Records | BCD 15430

Laugart,Xiomara | (voc)
Jacky Terrasson Group
What It Is | Blue Note | 498756-2

Laughlin,Richard | (arr,cond,tpfl-h)
Al Porcino Big Band
Al Porcino Big Band Live! | Organic Music | ORGM 9717
Benny Bailey Quartet With Strings
I Remember Love | Laika Records | 35101752
Conexion Latina
Mambo 2000 | Enja | ENJ-7055 2
Thilo Kreitmeier & Group
Changes | Organic Music | ORGM 9725

Laukamp,Bernt | (b-tbtb)
Bob Brookmeyer Group With The WDR Big Band
Electricity | ACT | 9219-2
Eddie Harris Group With The WDR Big Band
Eddie Harris-The Last Concert | ACT | 9249-2
Gianlugi Trovesi Quartet With The WDR Big Band
Dedalo | Enja | ENJ-9419 2
Jens Winther And The WDR Big Band
The Escape | dacapo | DCCD 9437
Kevin Mahogany With The WDR Big Band And Guests
Pussy Cat Dues:The Music Of Charles Mingus | Enja | ENJ-9316 2
Los Jovenes Flamencos With The WDR Big Band And Guests
Jazzpana | ACT | 9212-2
Vince Mendoza With The WDR Big Band And Guests
Sketches | ACT | 9215-2

Laurence,Chris | (bel-b)
Dee Dee Bridgewater With Orchestra
Dear Ella | Verve | 539102-2
John Surman Quartet
Stranger Than Fiction | ECM | 1534
John Surman With String Quartet
Coruscating | ECM | 1702(543033-2)
John Surman-John Warren Group
The Brass Project | ECM | 1478
Laura Fygi Meets Michel Legrand
Watch What Happens | Mercury | 534598-2

Lauridsen,Beverly | (cello)

Earl Klugh Group With Strings
Late Night Guitar | Blue Note | 498573-2
Laurie,Cy | (cl)
Cy Laurie Jazz Band
The Golden Years Of Revival Jazz,Sampler | Storyville | 109 1001
Cy Laurie's New Orleans Septet
The Golden Years Of Revival Jazz,Vol.1 | Storyville | STCD 5506
The Golden Years Of Revival Jazz,Vol.5 | Storyville | STCD 5510
The Golden Years Of Revival Jazz,Vol.6 | Storyville | STCD 5511
The Golden Years Of Revival Jazz,Vol.8 | Storyville | STCD 5513
The Golden Years Of Revival Jazz,Vol.9 | Storyville | STCD 5514
The Golden Years Of Revival Jazz,Vol.11 | Storyville | STCD 5516
Laurillard,Alan | (as,voc,fl,reeds,perc,ts,bsharm)
Greetje Bijma Kwintet
Tales Of A Voice | TipToe | TIP-888808 2
Laurinavicius,Gediminas | (synth,dr,percbalafon)
Remy Filipovitch-Gediminas Laurinavicius
Open Your Eyes | Album | AS 331108 CD
Lauritsen,Kjeld | (?)
Champion Jack Dupree
Champion Jack Dupree | Storyville | 4960383
Lauscher,Werner | (bel-b)
Scetches
Different Places | VeraBra Records | CDVBR 2102-2
Lauth,Wolfgang | (p)
Waltz For People Who Hate Waltzes
Noch Lauther | Bear Family Records | BCD 15942 AH
Wolfgang Lauth Quartet
Deutsches Jazz Fesival 1954/1955 | Bear Family Records | BCD 15430
Lauther | Bear Family Records | BCD 15717 AH
Noch Lauther | Bear Family Records | BCD 15942 AH
Wolfgang Lauth Septet
Noch Lauther | Bear Family Records | BCD 15942 AH
Lauvergnac,Anna | (voc)
Julia Hülsmann Trio With Anna Lauvergnac
Come Closer | ACT | 9702-2
Laux,Carola | (voc)
Wayne Bartlett With The Thomas Hufschmidt Group
Tokyo Blues | Laika Records | 35101212
LaVere,Charles | (p,arrvoc)
Louis Armstrong With Gordon Jenkins And His Orchestra
Satchmo In Style | Verve | 549594-2
Louis Armstrong With Gordon Jenkins And His Orchestra And Choir
Satchmo In Style | Verve | 549594-2
LaVerne,Andy | (el-p,synth,grand-p,keyboards,p)
Conrad Herwig-Andy LaVerne
Shades Of Light | Steeplechase | SCCD 31520
Jam Session
Jam Session Vol.1 | Steeplechase | SCCD 31522
Jam Session Vol.3 | Steeplechase | SCCD 31526
Jam Session Vol.5 | Steeplechase | SCCD 31536
Jam Session Vol.9 | Steeplechase | SCCD 31554
John Abercrombie-Andy LaVerne
Timeline | Steeplechase | SCCD 31538
Stan Getz Quintet
Sony Jazz Collection:Stan Getz | CBS | 488623-2
Woody Herman And His Orchestra
Jazzin' Vol.2: The Music Of Stevie Wonder | Fantasy | FANCD 6088-2
King Cobra | Original Jazz Classics | OJCCD 1068-2(F 9499)
Woody Herman Herd At Montreux | Original Jazz Classics | OJCCD 991-2(F 9470)
Woody Herman And The New Thundering Herd
Woody Herman:Thundering Herd | Original Jazz Classics | OJCCD 841-2
Law,Alex | (v)
Artie Shaw And His Orchestra
Planet JazzArtie Shaw | Planet Jazz | 2152057-2
Planet Jazz:Jazz Greatest Hits | Planet Jazz | 2169648-2
Lawless,Rudy | (dr)
Etta Jones And Her Quartet
Hollar! | Original Jazz Classics | OJCCD 1061(PR 7284)
Something Nice | Original Jazz Classics | OJCCD 221-2(P 7194)
Lawrence,Andy | (b,sousaphonetp)
Benny Waters & Jan Jankeje
Let's Talk About Jazz | G&J Records | GJ 2009 Maxi-CD
Benny Waters Sextet
A' Portrait Of Jan Jankeje | Jazzpoint | JP 1054 CD
Lawrence,Arnie | (as,reedsss)
Chico Hamilton Quartet
The Dealer | Impulse(MCA) | 547958-2
Chico Hamilton Quintet
The Dealer | Impulse(MCA) | 547958-2
The Roots Of Acid Jazz | Impulse(MCA) | IMP 12042
Lawrence,Azar | (sax,ssts)
McCoy Tyner Orchestra
Sama Layuca | Original Jazz Classics | OJCCD 1071-2(M 9056)
Miles Davis Group
Dark Magus | CBS | C2K 65137
Lawrence,Doug | (cl,tsss)
Buck Clayton Swing Band
Swing's The Village | Nagel-Heyer | CD 5004
Blues Of Summer | Nagel-Heyer | NH 1011
Lawrence,Elliot | (arr,ldp)
The Four Brothers
Planet Jazz:Jazz Saxophone | Planet Jazz | 2169653-2
Together Again! | RCA | 2179623-2
Lawrence,Elliott | (ld,parr)
Elliot Lawrence And His Orchestra
Mullenium | CBS | CK 65678
The Elliot Lawrence Big Band Swings Cohn & Kahn | Fantasy | FCD 24761-2
Lawrence,Mike | (fl-h,synth,perctp)
Gil Evans Orchestra
Blues In Orbit | Enja | ENJ-3069 2
Joe Henderson Quintet
Joe Henderson:The Milestone Years | Milestone | 8MCD 4413-2
Joe Henderson Sextet
Joe Henderson:The Milestone Years | Milestone | 8MCD 4413-2
The Kicker | Original Jazz Classics | OJCCD 465-2
Lawrence,Ronald 'Ron' | (viola)
Lee Konitz With Strings
Strings For Holiday:A Tribute To Billie Holiday | Enja | ENJ-9304 2
Lawrence,T. Ray | (voc)
Max Roach Chorus & Orchestra
To The Max! | Enja | ENJ-7021 22
Laws,Hubert | (bass-fl,piccolo,fl,alto-fl,as,reeds)
Bob James And His Orchestra
Jazzrock-Anthology Vol.3:Fusion | Zounds | CD 27100555
Bobby Timmons Orchestra
Quartet And Orchestra | Milestone | MCD 47091-2
Charles Earland Orchestra
Charlie's Greatest Hits | Prestige | PCD 24250-2
Chick Corea Quartet
Inner Space | Atlantic | 7567-81304-2
Chick Corea Septet
The Complete 'Is' Sessions | Blue Note | 540532-2
Chick Corea Trio
Inner Space | Atlantic | 7567-81304-2
Count Basie And His Orchestra
Afrique | RCA | 2179618-2
Daniel Schnyder Group
Tanatula | Enja | ENJ-9302 2
Ella Fitzgerald With Orchestra
The Best Is Yet To Come | Original Jazz Classics | OJCCD 889-2(2312138)
Freddie Hubbard With Orchestra
This Is Jazz:Freddie Hubbard | CBS | CK 65041
George Benson Group/Orchestra
George Benson Anthology | Warner | 8122-79934-2
George Benson With The Don Sebesky Orchestra
Verve Jazz Masters 21:George Benson | Verve | 521861-2
Gil Evans Orchestra
Blues In Orbit | Enja | ENJ-3069 2
Helen Merrill With The Dick Katz Group
A Shade Of Difference | EmArCy | 558851-2
Herbie Hancock Orchestra
Herbie Hancock:The Complete Blue Note Sixties Sessions | Blue Note | 495569-2
The Prisoner | Blue Note | 525649-2
Hubert Laws Quartet
The Laws Of Jazz | Atlantic | 8122-71636-2
Jaco Pastorius With Orchestra
Word Of Mouth | Warner | 7599-23525-2
Jazz Crusaders
Chile Con Soul | Pacific Jazz | 590957-2
Joe Zawinul Group
Zawinul | Atlantic | 7567-81375-2
McCoy Tyner Orchestra
13th House | Original Jazz Classics | OJCCD 1089-2(M 9102)
McCoy Tyner Sextet
Asante | Blue Note | 493384-2
Milt Jackson With Strings
To Bags...With Love:Memorial Album | Pablo | 2310967-2
Paul Desmond Quartet With The Don Sebesky Orchestra
From The Hot Afternoon | Verve | 543487-2
Quincy Jones And His Orchestra
Verve Jazz Masters Vol.59:Toots Thielemans | Verve | 535271-2
Ron Carter Octet
New York Slick | Original Jazz Classics | OJCCD 916-2(M 9096)
Ron Carter Sextet
New York Slick | Original Jazz Classics | OJCCD 916-2(M 9096)
The Quincy Jones-Sammy Nestico Orchestra
Basie & Beyond | Warner | 9362-47792-2
Laws,John | (b-clbs)
Buddy Rich Big Band
Backwoods Siseman/Pieces Of Dream | Laserlight | 24655
Laws,William | (dr)
Jelly Roll Morton And His Orchestra
Planet Jazz:Jelly Roll Morton | Planet Jazz | 2152060-2
Lawson,Bob | (bssax)
Lucky Thompson And His Lucky Seven
Planet Jazz:Bebop | RCA | 2169650-2
Lawson,Cedric | (keyboards,orgp)
Miles Davis Group
In Concert | CBS | C2K 65140
On The Corner | CBS | CK 63980
Lawson,Dorothy | (cello)
Steve Coleman And Five Elements
The Sonic Language Of Myth | RCA | 2164123-2
Lawson,Hugh | (celeste,p,bells,bottle,cymbals,el-p)
Harry Edison Sextet
Swing Summit | Candid | CCD 79050
Jimmy Forrest Quintet
Soul Street | Original Jazz Classics | OJCCD 987-2(NJ 8293)
Yusef Lateef Ensemble
Atlantic Saxophones | Rhino | 8122-71256-2
Yusef Lateef Orchestra
The Blue Yusef Lateef | Rhino | 8122-73717-2
Yusef Lateef Quartet
The Golden Flute | Impulse(MCA) | 9681049
Yusef Lateef Quintet
Other Sounds | Original Jazz Classics | OJCCD 399-2(NJ 8218)
Lawson,Ricky | (dr)
Al Jarreau With Band
Al Jarreau In London | i.e. Music | 557849-2
George Duke Group
Jazzrock-Anthology Vol.3:Fusion | Zounds | CD 27100555
Lawson,Yank | (tp)
Benny Goodman And His V-Disc All Star Band
The Legends Of Swing | Laserlight | 24659
Bob Crosby And His Orchestra
Swing Legens:Bob Crosby | Nimbus Records | NI 2011
Bob Crosby's Bobcats
Swing Legens:Bob Crosby | Nimbus Records | NI 2011
Bud Freeman And His Stars
Muggsy Spanier And Bud Freeman:V-Discs 1944-45 | Jazz Unlimited | JUCD 2049
Bud Freeman And The V-Disc Jumpers
Muggsy Spanier And Bud Freeman:V-Discs 1944-45 | Jazz Unlimited | JUCD 2049
Eight Squares And A Critic
Muggsy Spanier And Bud Freeman:V-Discs 1944-45 | Jazz Unlimited | JUCD 2049
Louis Armstrong With Gordon Jenkins And His Orchestra And Choir
Satchmo In Style | Verve | 549594-2
Ambassador Louis Armstrong Vol.17:Moments To Remember(1952-1956) | Ambassador | CLA 1917
Louis Armstrong-My Greatest Songs | MCA | MCD 18347
Swing Legends:Louis Armstrong | Nimbus Records | NI 2012
The V-Disc Jumpers
Muggsy Spanier And Bud Freeman:V-Discs 1944-45 | Jazz Unlimited | JUCD 2049
Tommy Dorsey And His Orchestra
Planet Jazz:Tommy Dorsey | Planet Jazz | 2159972-2
Lay,Ward | (b)
Eddie Lang-Joe Venuti And Their Allstars Orchestra
Jazz:The Essential Collection Vol.3 | IN+OUT Records | 78013-2
Layton,Skip | (tb)
Billie Holiday With The Paul Whiteman Orchestra
Billie's Blues | Blue Note | 748786-2
Stan Kenton And His Orchestra
Swing Vol.1 | Storyville | 4960343
Le Bars,Marie-Anne | (v)
Stephane Grappelli With The Michel Legrand Orchestra
Grapelli Story | Verve | 515807-2
Le Bevillon,Marc-Michel | (bel-b)
Verve Jazz Masters 11:Stéphane Grappelli | Verve | 516758-2
Le Flemming,Orlando | (b)
Billy Cobham Group
Art Of Five | IN+OUT Records | 77063-2
Le Jazz Group De Paris |
Le Jazz Group De Paris
Jazz In Paris | EmArCy | 548793-2
Le Tekro,Ronni | (el-g)
Terje Rypdal With The Riga Festival Orchestra
Double Concerto/5th Symphony | ECM | 1567(559964-2)
Le,Nguyen | (el-g,E-bow,fretless-g,g-synth,g)
Karim Ziad Groups
Ifrikya | ACT | 9282-2
Nguyen Le Group
Tales From Viet-Nam | ACT | 9225-2
Maghreb And Friends | ACT | 9261-2
Nguyen Le Trio
Million Waves | ACT | 9221-2
Nguyen Le:3 Trios | ACT | 9245-2
Bakida | ACT | 9275-2
Nguyen Le Trio With Guests
Bakida | ACT | 9275-2
Purple:Celebrating Jimi Hendrix | ACT | 9410-2
Paolo Fresu Angel Quartet
Metamorfosi | RCA | 2165202-2
Paolo Fresu Quartet
Angel | RCA | 2155864-2
Kind Of Porgy & Bess | RCA | 21951952
Paolo Fresu Quintet
Kind Of Porgy & Bess | RCA | 21951952
Paolo Fresu Sextet
Kind Of Porgy & Bess | RCA | 21951952
Paolo Fresu Trio
Kind Of Porgy & Bess | RCA | 21951952
Peter Erskine Trio
ELB | ACT | 9289-2
Vince Mendoza With The WDR Big Band And Guests
Sketches | ACT | 9215-2
Leach,Hazel | (fl,b-cl,ts,comp,ldreeds)
The United Women's Orchestra
The Blue One | Jazz Haus Musik | JHM 0099 CD
United Women's Orchestra
Virgo Supercluster | Jazz Haus Musik | JHM 0123 CD
Leake,Lafayette | (orgp)
Albert King With The Willie Dixon Band
Windy City Blues | Stax | SCD 8612-2
Billy Boy Arnold Group
Windy City Blues | Stax | SCD 8612-2
Buddy Guy Blues Band
Buddy Guy-The Complete Chess Studio Recordings | MCA | MCD 09337
Homesick James Quartet
Blues On The Southside | Original Blues Classics | OBCCD 529-2(P 7388)
Windy City Blues | Stax | SCD 8612-2
Howlin' Wolf London Session
Howlin' Wolf:The London Sessions | Chess | MCD 09297
Leal,Beatrice | (voc)
Mike Westbrook Brass Band
Glad Day:Settings Of William Blake | Enja | ENJ-9376 2
Leal,Frank | (as)
Chamber Jazz Sextet
Plays Pal Joey | Candid | CCD 79030
Leali,Brad | (assax)
Claus Raible Sextet
Loopin' With Lea | Organic Music | ORGM 9724
Jörg Krückel-Brad Leali Quartet
Cookin' Good | Edition Collage | EC 507-2
Leary III,James | (b)
Count Basie Big Band
Farmers Market Barbecue | Original Jazz Classics | OJCCD 732-2(2310874)
Leary,Bob | (bj,gvoc)
Allan Vaché Big Four
Revisited! | Nagel-Heyer | CD 044
Allan Vaché's Florida Jazz Allstars
Allan Vaché's Floridy Jazz Allstars | Nagel-Heyer | CD 032
Leary,Jimmy | (b)
Eddie Lockjaw Davis Quartet
The Art Of Saxophone | Laserlight | 24652
Leary,S.P. | (dr)
Otis Spann Band
The Blues Never Die! | Original Blues Classics | OBCCD 530-2(P 7391)
Windy City Blues | Stax | SCD 8612-2
Leatherbarrow,Bob | (dr)
Michael 'Patches' Stewart Group
Blue Patches | Hip Bop | HIBD 8016
Vic Lewis West Coast All Stars
Vic Lewis Presenting A Celebration Of Contemporary West Coast Jazz | Candid | CCD 79711/12
Leathers,Ann | (v)
A Band Of Friends
Wynton Marsalis Quartet With Strings | CBS | CK 68921
Leatherwood,Ray | (b)
Tommy Dorsey And His Orchestra
Planet Jazz:Frank Sinatra & Tommy Dorsey | Planet Jazz | 2152067-2
Leavitt,Sean | (g)
Eladio Reinon Quintet
Es La Historia De Un Amor | Fresh Sound Records | FSNT 004 CD
Lechner,Anja | (cello)
Misha Alperin Trio
Night After Night | ECM | 1769(014431-2)
Lechtenfeld,Bernd | (tb)
Jazz Orchester Rheinland-Pfalz
Like Life | Jazz Haus Musik | LJBB 9405
Marcus Sukiennik Big Band
A Night In Tunisia Suite(7 Variationen über Dizzy Gillespie's 'A Night In Tunisia') | Jazz Haus Musik | ohne Nummer
LeCoque,Archie | (tb)
Stan Kenton Orchestra
Stompin' At Newport | Pablo | PACD 5312-2
Ledbetter,Matthew | (voc)
Louis Armstrong And His Friends
Louis Armstrong And His Friends | Bluebird | 2663961-2
Leddy,Ed | (tp)
Bill Holman Octet
The Jazz Giants Play Sammy Cahn:It's Magic | Prestige | PCD 24226-2
Red Norvo And His Orchestra
Planet Jazz:Female Jazz Vocalists | Planet Jazz | 2169656-2
Stan Kenton And His Orchestra
Great Swing Classics In Hi-Fi | Capitol | 521223-2
Stan Kenton Orchestra
Stompin' At Newport | Pablo | PACD 5312-2
Lederer,Steve | (saxts)
Woody Herman And His Orchestra
Brand New | Original Jazz Classics | OJCCD 1044-2(F 8414)
The Raven Speaks | Original Jazz Classics | OJCCD 663-2(F 9416)
Ledford,Mark | (fl-h,voc,g,tp,whistlingkeyboards)
Lenny White Group
Present Tense | Hip Bop | HIBD 8004
Renderers Of Spirit | Hip Bop | HIBD 8014
Hot Jazz Bisquits | Hip Bop | HIBD 8801
Pat Metheny Group
Imaginary Day | Warner | 9362-46791-2
We Live Here | Geffen Records | GED 24729
The Brecker Brothers
Out Of The Loop | GRP | GRP 97842
Uri Caine Ensemble
Love Fugue-Robert Schumann | Winter&Winter | 910049-2
Ledgerwood,Lee Ann | (pp-solo)
LeeAnn Ledgerwood Trio
Walkin' Up | Steeplechase | SCCD 31541
LeDonne,Mike | (orgp)
Joshua Redman Quartet
Joshua Redman | Warner | 9362-45242-2
Lee,Bill | (bvoc)
Frank Stozier Sextet
Long Night | Milestone | MCD 47095-2
Frank Strozier Quartet
Long Night | Milestone | MCD 47095-2
Lee,Charles | (ts)
Big Al Sears And The Sparrows
Sear-iously | Bear Family Records | BCD 15668 AH
Lee,David | (dr,percp)
Joe Zawinul Group
Zawinul | Atlantic | 7567-81375-2
Lonnie Liston Smith & His Cosmic Echoes
Astral Travelling | RCA | 2663878-2
Richard Wyands Trio
Then Here And Now | Storyville | STCD 8269
Sonny Rollins Quartet
Next Album | Original Jazz Classics | OJC 312 (M 9042)
Sonny Rollins Quintet
Next Album | Original Jazz Classics | OJC 312 (M 9042)
Sonny Rollins Sextet
The Cutting Edge | Original Jazz Classics | OJC 468(M 9059)
Sonny Rollins Sextet With Rufus Harley
The Cutting Edge | Original Jazz Classics | OJC 468(M 9059)

Lee,Gordon | (p)
Gordon Lee Quartet feat. Jim Pepper
Landwhales In New York | Tutu Records | 888136-2*
Lee,Jack | (g)
Chico Freeman And Brainstorm
Threshold | IN+OUT Records | 7022-2
Lee,Jeanne | (dr-solo,voc,perc,poetry,voice)
Gunter Hampel All Stars
Jubilation | Birth | 0038
Gunter Hampel And His Galaxie Dream Band
Journey To The Song Within | Birth | 0017
Enfant Terrible | Birth | 0025
Live At The Berlin Jazzfestival 1978 | Birth | 0027
All Is Real | Birth | 0028
All The Things You Could Be If Charles Mingus Was Your Daddy | Birth | CD 031
Celestial Glory-Live At The Knitting Factory New York | Birth | CD 040
Gunter Hampel Group
Familie | Birth | 008
The 8th Of July 1969 | Birth | CD 001
Gunter Hampel New York Orchestra
Fresh Heat-Live At Sweet Basil | Birth | CD 039
Jeanne Lee Group
Natural Affinities | Owl Records | 018352-2
Jeanne Lee-Dave Holland
Natural Affinities | Owl Records | 018352-2
Jeanne Lee-Mal Waldron
After Hours | Owl Records | 013426-2
Marion Brown Orchestra
Afternoon Of A Georgia Faun | ECM | 1004
Lee,John | (b,el-b,perc,b-g,8-string-bg)
Dizzy Gillespie And The United Nation Orchestra
7.Zelt-Musik-Festival:Jazz Events | Zounds | CD 2730001
Larry Coryell-Alphonse Mouzon Quartet
Atlantic Jazz: Fusion | Atlantic | 7567-81711-2
Lee,Mel | (dr)
Mose Allison Trio
Mose Alife!/Wild Man On The Loose | Warner | 8122-75439-2
Lee,Paul[Higaki] | (tb)
(Little)Jimmy Scott With The Lionel Hampton Orchestra
Everybody's Somebody's Fool | Decca | 050669-2
Lee,Pauline | (v)
Absolute Ensemble
African Symphony | Enja | ENJ-9410 2
Lee,Peggy | (cello,drvoc)
Francois Houle 5
Cryptology | Between The Lines | btl 012(Efa 10182-2)
Peggy Lee With Benny Goodman And His Quintet
Peggy Lee & Benny Goodman:The Complete Recordings 1941-1947 | CBS | C2K 65686
Peggy Lee With Benny Goodman And His Sextet
Peggy Lee & Benny Goodman:The Complete Recordings 1941-1947 | CBS | C2K 65686
Peggy Lee With Benny Goodman And The Paul Weston Orchestra
Peggy Lee & Benny Goodman:The Complete Recordings 1941-1947 | CBS | C2K 65686
Peggy Lee With George Shearing
Beauty And The Beat | Capitol | 542308-2
Peggy Lee With Jack Marshall's Music
Things Are Swingin' | Capitol | 597072-2
Peggy Lee With Lou Levy's Orchestra
Pass Me By/Big Spender | Capitol | 535210-2
Peggy Lee With Orchestra
Misty Blue:Sweet Sisters Swing Songs Of Sorrow And Sadness | Blue Note | 521151-2
Pass Me By/Big Spender | Capitol | 535210-2
Peggy Lee With The Benny Goodman Orchestra
Peggy Lee & Benny Goodman:The Complete Recordings 1941-1947 | CBS | C2K 65686
Peggy Lee With The Bill Holman Orchestra
Pass Me By/Big Spender | Capitol | 535210-2
Peggy Lee With The George Shearing Trio
Beauty And The Beat | Capitol | 542308-2
Peggy Lee With The Quincy Jones Orchestra
Blues Cross Country | Capitol | 520088-2
Ten Cats And A Mouse
The Hollywood Session:The Capitol Jazzmen | Jazz Unlimited | JUCD 2044
The Capitol Jazzmen
The Hollywood Session:The Capitol Jazzmen | Jazz Unlimited | JUCD 2044
Lee,Phil | (el-gg)
Laura Fygi With Band
Bewitched | Verve | 514724-2
Lee,Sarah | (clglockenspiel)
Carla Bley Band
Fancy Chamber Music | Watt | 28(539937-2)
Lee,Scott | (b)
Chet Baker Quartet
Chet Baker-The Legacy Vol.4:Oh You Crazy Moon | Enja | ENJ-9453 2
Loren Stillman Quartet
How Swee It Is | Nagel-Heyer | CD 2031
Steve Rochinski Solo/Duo/Trio/Quartet
Jazz Guitar Highlights 1 | Jardis Records | JRCD 20141
A Bird In The Hand | Jardis Records | JRCD 9922
Lee,Simon | (percclapping)
Eduardo Niebla-Antonio Forcione Group
Poema | Jazzpoint | JP 1035 CD
Lee,Will | (b,background-voc,perc,vocel-b)
Don Grolnick Group
Hearts And Numbers | VeraBra Records | CDVBR 2016-2
Freddy Cole With The Eric Alexander Band
Love Makes The Changes | Fantasy | FCD 9681-2
Lew Soloff Group
Rainbow Mountain | TipToe | TIP-888838 2
Nina Simone And Orchestra
Baltimore | Epic | 476906-2
Pat Metheny Group With Orchestra
Secret Story | Geffen Records | GED 24468
Randy Brecker Group
Jazzrock-Anthology Vol.3:Fusion | Zounds | CD 27100555
Steve Khan Group
Jazzrock-Anthology Vol.3:Fusion | Zounds | CD 27100555
The Brecker Brothers
The Becker Bros | RCA | 2122103-2
Return Of The Brecker Brothers | GRP | GRP 96842
Leech,Mike | (el-b)
Herbie Mann Group
Memphis Underground | Atlantic | 7567-81364-2
The Best Of Herbie Mann | Atlantic | 7567-81369-2
Leeman,Cliff | (drp-solo)
Artie Shaw And His Orchestra
Planet JazzArtie Shaw | Planet Jazz | 2152057-2
Planet Jazz Sampler | Planet Jazz | 2152326-2
Planet Jazz:Swing | Planet Jazz | 2169651-2
Planet Jazz:Female Jazz Vocalists | Planet Jazz | 2169656-2
The Legends Of Swing | Laserlight | 24659
Joe Turner With Orchestra
Atlantic Jazz: Kansas City | Atlantic | 7567-81701-2
Lee Wiley With The Dean Kincaide Dixieland Band
Planet Jazz:Female Jazz Vocalists | Planet Jazz | 2169656-2
Leon Thomas With Orchestra
Spirits Known And Unknown | RCA | 2663876-2
Max Kaminsky And His Dixieland Bashers
Planet Jazz | Planet Jazz | 2169652-2
Ralph Sutton Quartet
Live At Sunnie's Rendezvous Vol.1 | Storyville | STCD 8280
Tommy Dorsey And His Orchestra
Planet Jazz:Tommy Dorsey | Planet Jazz | 2159972-2
Lefebvre,Tim | (b,el-bprogramming)
David Binney Group
Balance | ACT | 9411-2
Frank Castenier Group
For You,For Me For Evermore | EmArCy | 9814976
Till Brönner Group
Chattin' With Chet | Verve | 157534-2
Love | Verve | 559058-2
Uri Caine Trio
Bedrock | Winter&Winter | 910068-2
Leff,Jim | (tb)
Mitchell-Terraza Group
Shell Blues | Fresh Sound Records | FSNT 005 CD
Leftwich,John | (b)
Carmen McRae And Her Trio
The Collected Carmen McRae | RCA | 2668713-2
Carmen McRae And Her Trio With Zoot Sims
The Collected Carmen McRae | RCA | 2668713-2
Ray Walker-John Pisano Trio
Affinity | Jardis Records | JRCD 20032
Legange,Thomas | (b)
Little Jimmy Scott | Specialty | SPCD 2170-2
Legarreta,Felix | (v)
Mongo Santamaria And His Band
Sabroso | Original Jazz Classics | OJCCD 281-2
Legge,Wade | (p)
Charles Mingus Jazz Workshop
Tonight At Noon | Atlantic | 7567-80793-2
The Clown | Atlantic | 8122-75358-2
Charles Mingus Quintet
Charles Mingus-Passion Of A Man:The Complete Atlantic Recordings 1956-1961 | Atlantic | 8122-72871-2
The Very Best Of Charles Mingus | Rhino | 8122-79988-2
Dizzy Gillespie And His Orchestra
Afro | Verve | 517052-2
Dizzy Gillespie Quartet And The Operatic String Orchestra
Jazz In Paris:Dizzy Gillespie And His Operatic Strings Orchestra | EmArCy | 018420-2
Dizzy Gillespie Quintet
Diz And Getz | Verve | 549749-2
Dizzy Gillespie Sextet
Pleyel Jazz Concert 1953 | Vogue | 21409392
J.R. Monterose Quintet
Jaywalkin' | Fresh Sound Records | FSR-CD 320
Lars Gullin With The Wade Legge Trio
Lars Gullin 1953,Vol.2:Moden Sounds | Dragon | DRCD 234
Prestige All Stars
The Prestige Legacy Vol.2:Battles Of Saxes | Prestige | PCD 24252-2
Sarah Vaughan With Dizzy Gillespie And His Orchestra
Planet Jazz:Female Jazz Vocalists | Planet Jazz | 2169656-2
Sonny Rollins Quintet
Sonny Rollins Plays For Bird | Original Jazz Classics | OJCCD 214-2
Sonny Boy | Original Jazz Classics | OJCCD 348-2(P 7207)
Legnini,Eric | (pkeyboards)
Fabien Degryse Quintet
Medor Sadness | Edition Collage | EC 454-2
Legrand,Christiane | (voc)
Le Jazz Group De Paris
Jazz In Paris | EmArCy | 548793-2
Les Blue Stars
Jazz In Paris:Blossom Dearie-The Pianist/Les Blue Stars | EmArCy | 064784-2
Les Double Six
Les Double Six | RCA | 2164314-2
Modern Jazz Quartet And The Swingle Singers
MJQ 40 | Atlantic | 7567-82330-2
Swingle Singers
Jazz Sebastian Bach | Philips | 542552-2
Jazz Sebastian Bach Vol.2 | Philips | 542553-2
Swingle Singers Going Baroque | Philips | 546746-2
Swingle Singers Singing Mozart | Philips | 548538-2
Swingling Telemann | Philips | 586735-2
Swingle Singers Getting Romantic | Philips | 586736-2
Legrand,Michel | (cond,arr,vocp)
Laura Fygi Meets Michel Legrand
Watch What Happens | Mercury | 534598-2
Les Blue Stars
Jazz In Paris:Blossom Dearie-The Pianist/Les Blue Stars | EmArCy | 064784-2
Michel Legrand Trio
Jazz In Paris:Michel Legrand-Paris Jazz Piano | EmArCy | 548148-2 PMS
Stan Getz With The Michel Legrand Orchestra
Stan Getz Highlights | Verve | 847430-2
Stephane Grappelli With The Michel Legrand Orchestra
Grapelli Story | Verve | 515807-2
Verve Jazz Masters 11:Stéphane Grappelli | Verve | 516758-2
Legwabe,Joe Ditsebe | (percvoc)
Gail Thompson Orchestra
Gail Thompson's Jazz Africa | Enja | ENJ-9053 2
Jazz Africa All Nations Big Band
Jadu(Jazz Africa Down Under) | Enja | ENJ-9339 2
Lehan,Marc | (dr,perchi-hat)
Hans Lüdemann Rism
Aph-o-Rism's | Jazz Haus Musik | JHM 0049 CD
Unitarism | Jazz Haus Musik | JHM 0067 CD
Martin Fredebeul Quartet
Search | Nabel Records:Jazz Network | CD 4652
Lehel,Peter | (b-cl,ss,asts)
Peter Lehel Quartet
Heavy Rotation | Satin Doll Productions | SDP 1024-1 CD
Quique Sinesi & Daniel Messina With Guests
Prioridad A la Emoción | art-mode-records | AMR 21061
Lehman,John | (voc)
Dee Dee Bridgewater With Band
Dee Dee Bridgewater | Atlantic | 7567-80760-2
Lehmann,Bernd | (clts)
Jazz Orchester Rheinland-Pfalz
Kazzou | Jazz Haus Musik | LJBB 9104
Lehmann,Glyn | (altoniumrog)
Ronnie Taheny Group
Briefcase | Laika Records | 35101152
Lehmann,Lömsch | (cl,tsreeds)
Sebastian Gramss-Lömsch Lehmann
knoM.T | Jazz Haus Musik | JHM 0107 CD
Lehmann,Martin | (v)
Michael Riessler And The Ensemble 13
Momentum Mobile | Enja | ENJ-9003 2
Lehmann,Willy | (v)
Lehn,Erwin | (arrld)
Erwin Lehn Und Sein Südfunk-Tanzorchester
Deutsches Jazz Fesival 1954/1955 | Bear Family Records | BCD 15430
Lehrbach,Irmgard | (voc)
Jazzensemble Des Hessischen Rundfunks
Jazz Messe-Messe Für Unsere Zeit | hr music.de | hrmj 003-01 CD
Lehrfeld,Allen | (sax)
Tito Puente Orchestra
Planet Jazz:Tito Puente | Planet Jazz | 2165369-2
Lehrian,Barbara | (voc)
Jazzensemble Des Hessischen Rundfunks
Jazz Messe-Messe Für Unsere Zeit | hr music.de | hrmj 003-01 CD
Lehtimäki,Arja | (voc)
Piirpauke
Piirpauke-Global Servisi | JA & RO | JARO 4150-2
Lehtimäki,Merja | (voc)
Leibrock,Min | (bass-saxtuba)
Bix Beiderbecke And His Gang
Jazz:The Essential Collection Vol.2 | IN+OUT Records | 78012-2
Hoagy Carmichael And His Orchestra
Planet Jazz:Bud Freeman | Planet Jazz | 2161240-2
Irving Mills And His Hotsy Totsy Gang
Jazz:The Essential Collection Vol.3 | IN+OUT Records | 78013-2
The Wolverines
Jazz:The Essential Collection Vol.2 | IN+OUT Records | 78012-2
Leibundgut,Walter | (tbvoc)
The Tremble Kids All Stars
The Tremble Kids All Stars Play Chicago Jazz! | Nagel-Heyer | CD 043
Leicht,Bruno | (tp)
Matthias Petzold Group With Choir
Psalmen und Lobgesänge für Chor und Jazz-Enseble | Indigo-Records | 1002 CD
Matthias Petzold Septett
Ulysses | Indigo-Records | 1003 CD
Leicht,Oliver | (as,cl,b-cl,fl,alto-cl,ss,piccolo-fl)
Gabriel Pérez Group
La Chipaca | Green House Music | CD 1011
HR Big Band
Libertango:Homage An Astor Piazolla | hr music.de | hrmj 014-02 CD
Lee Konitz With The Ed Partyka Jazz Orchestra
Dreams And Realities | Laika Records | 35101642
Rainer Tempel Big Band
Album 03 | Jazz 'n' Arts Records | JNA 1102
The Three Sopranos With The HR Big Band
The Three Sopranos | hr music.de | hrmj 001-01 CD
Leidner,Am | (drperc)
Jürgen Sturm's Ballstars
Tango Subversivo | Nabel Records:Jazz Network | CD 4613
Leigh-Brown,Sam | (voc)
The United Women's Orchestra
The Blue One | Jazz Haus Musik | JHM 0099 CD
Leighton,Bernie | (keyboards,parr)
Billie Holiday With Gordon Jenkins And His Orchestra
Billie's Love Songs | Nimbus Records | NI 2000
Charlie Parker Quartet With Strings
The Cole Porter Songbook | Verve | 823250-2
Charlie Parker With Strings
Charlie Parker:The Best Of The Verve Years | Verve | 527815-2
Bird: The Complete Charlie Parker On Verve | Verve | 837141-2
Charlie Parker:April In Paris | Dreyfus Jazz Line | FDM 36737-2
Charlie Parker With The Joe Lipman Orchestra
Verve Jazz Masters 28:Charlie Parker Plays Standards | Verve | 521854-2
Charlie Parker With Strings:The Master Takes | Verve | 523984-2
Charlie Parker Big Band | Verve | 559835-2
Glenn Miller And His Orchestra
The Glenn Miller Orchestra In Digital Mood | GRP | GRP 95022
Joe Williams With The Jimmy Jones Orchestra
Planet Jazz:Joe Williams | Planet Jazz | 2165370-2
Leon Thomas With Orchestra
Spirits Known And Unknown | RCA | 2663876-2
Louis Armstrong And The Commanders under the Direction of Camarata
Satchmo Serenaders | Verve | 543792-2
Louis Armstrong With Gordon Jenkins And His Orchestra And Choir
Satchmo In Style | Verve | 549594-2
Ambassador Louis Armstrong Vol.17:Moments To Remember(1952-1956) | Ambassador | CLA 1917
Louis Armstrong-My Greatest Songs | MCA | MCD 18347
Swing Legends:Louis Armstrong | Nimbus Records | NI 2012
Louis Armstrong With The Commanders
Ambassador Louis Armstrong Vol.17:Moments To Remember(1952-1956) | Ambassador | CLA 1917
Leighton,Elaine | (dr)
Billie Holiday And Her All Stars
Billie's Blues | Blue Note | 748786-2
Billie Holiday With The Carl Drinkard Trio
Misty Blue:Sweet Sisters Swing Songs Of Sorrow And Sadness | Blue Note | 521151-2
Billie's Blues | Blue Note | 748786-2
Leighton-Thomas,Nicki | (voc)
Nicki Leighton-Thomas Group
Forbidden Games | Candid | CCD 79778
Leinbach,Ben | (dr)
Dogslyde
Hair Of The Dog | Intuition Records | INT 3223-2
Leininger,Ludwig | (b)
Mathias Götz-Windstärke 4
Lunar Oder Solar? | Jazz 'n' Arts Records | JNA 1002
Leis,Daniel | (gvoc)
Omar Belmonte's Latin Lover
Vamos A Ver | EGO | 96170
Leis,Detlev | (ts)
Freddie Brocksieper Und Seine Solisten
Globetrotter | Bear Family Records | BCD 15912 AH
Leistola,Elisabeth | (harp)
Edward Vesala Group
Nan Madol | ECM | 1077
Leisz,Greg | (steel-gresonator-g)
Bill Frisell Band
Blues Dream | Nonesuch | 7559-79615-2
Leitch,Peter | (gg-solo)
Oscar Peterson Quartet
Jazz Dance | Original Jazz Classics | OJCCD 1002-2(1210890)
Oscar Peterson Quintet With Strings
Jazz Dance | Original Jazz Classics | OJCCD 1002-2(1210890)
Peter Leitch-Heiner Franz
At First Sight | Jardis Records | JRCD 9611
Leith,Dick | (b-tbtb)
Miles Davis With Gil Evans & His Orchestra
Quiet Nights | CBS | CK 65293
Leitham,John | (b)
Buddy Childers With The Russ Garcia Strings
Artistry In Jazz | Candid | CCD 79735
Herb Geller Quartet
Herb Geller Plays The Al Cohn Songbook | Hep | CD 2066
Vic Lewis West Coast All Stars
Vic Lewis Presenting A Celebration Of Contemporary West Coast Jazz | Candid | CCD 79711/12
Leloup,Denis | (tb)
Dee Dee Bridgewater With Band
This Is New | Verve | 016884-2
Richard Galliano Quintet
Spleen | Dreyfus Jazz Line | FDM 36513-9
Lemarchand,Pierre | (drviola)
Django Reinhardt And His Quintet
Django Reinhardt:Souveniers | Dreyfus Jazz Line | FDM 36744-2
Django Reinhardt Quartet
Jazz In Paris:Django Reinhardt-Nuits De Saint-Germain-Des-Prés | EmArCy | 018427-2
Django Reinhardt Quintet
Jazz In Paris:Django Reinhardt-Nuits De Saint-Germain-Des-Prés | EmArCy | 018427-2
Jazz In Paris:Django Reinhardt-Nuages | EmArCy | 018428-2
Django Reinhardt Sextet
Jazz In Paris:Django Reinhardt-Nuits De Saint-Germain-Des-Prés | EmArCy | 018427-2
Michel Petrucciani With The Graffiti String Quartet
Marvellous | Dreyfus Jazz Line | FDM 36564-2
Lemer,Pete | (el-p,keyboards,synth,pvoc)
Barbara Thompson Group
Heavenly Bodies | VeraBra Records | CDVBR 2015-2
Shifting Sands | Intuition Records | INT 3174-2
Barbara Thompson's Paraphernalia
A Cry From The Heart | VeraBra Records | CDVBR 2021-2
Breathless | VeraBra Records | CDVBR 2057-2
Lady Saxophone | VeraBra Records | CDVBR 2166-2

Thompson's Tangos | Intuition Records | INT 3290-2

Lemke,Hans | (bassoon)
Till Brönner Quartet & Deutsches Symphonieorchester Berlin
German Songs | Minor Music | 801057

Lemke,Johannes | (cl,ssas)
Lirico
Sussurro | Jazz Haus Musik | JHM 0129 CD

Lemmert,Simon | (ts)
Jazz Orchester Rheinland-Pfalz
Kazzou | Jazz Haus Musik | LJBB 9104

Lemon,Brian | (p)
Danny Moss Quartet
Weaver Of Dreams | Nagel-Heyer | CD 017
The Second Sampler | Nagel-Heyer | NHR SP 6
Great British Jazz Band
The Great British Jazz Band:Jubilee | Candid | CCD 79720
Jeanie Lambe And The Danny Moss Quartet
Three Great Concerts:Live In Hamburg 1993-1995 | Nagel-Heyer | CD 019
The Second Sampler | Nagel-Heyer | NHR SP 6
The Alex Welsh Legacy Band
The Sound Of Alex Vol.1 | Nagel-Heyer | CD 070
Warren Vaché Quintet
The First Sampler | Nagel-Heyer | NHR SP 5
Warren Vaché Quintet With Special Guest Allan Vaché
Jazz Im Amerikahaus,Vol.2 | Nagel-Heyer | CD 012

Lemon,Eric | (b)
Craig Bailey Band
A New Journey | Candid | CCD 79725

Lenardt,Jörg |
Dirk Raulf Group
Theater I (Bühnenmusik) | Poise | Poise 07

Lending,Kenn | (g)
Champion Jack Dupree
Champion Jack Dupree | Storyville | 4960383

Lener,Werner | (p)
Werner Lener Quartet
My Own | Satin Doll Productions | SDP 1013-1 CD
Personal Moments | Satin Doll Productions | SDP 1026-1 CD
Colours | Satin Doll Productions | SDP 1033-1 CD
Werner Lener Trio
My Own | Satin Doll Productions | SDP 1013-1 CD
Personal Moments | Satin Doll Productions | SDP 1026-1 CD
Colours | Satin Doll Productions | SDP 1033-1 CD

Lenert,Pierre | (viola)
Stephane Grappelli With The Michel Legrand Orchestra
Grapelli Story | Verve | 515807-2

Lengenfeld,Hans | (b)
Traubeli Weiß Ensemble
Dreaming Of You | Edition Collage | EC 468-2

Lentini,Giuseppe | (cl)
Banda Città Ruvo Di Puglia
La Banda/Banda And Jazz | Enja | ENJ-9326 2

Lenz,Günter | (b,el-bg)
Berlin Contemporary Jazz Orchestra
Berlin Contemporary Jazz Orchestra | ECM | 1409
Chet Baker-Wolfgang Lackerschmid Trio
Chet Baker:The Legacy Vol.3:Why Shouldn't You Cry | Enja | ENJ-9337 2
Don Menza Septet
Morning Song | MPS | 9811446
Heinz Sauer Quartet With The NDR Big Band
NDR Big Band-Bravissimo | ACT | 9232-2
Jazzensemble Des Hessischen Rundfunks
Atmosphering Conditions Permitting | ECM | 1549/50
Leon Thomas With The Oliver Nelson Quintet
Leon Thomas In Berlin | RCA | 2663877-2
Radio Jazzgroup Frankfurt
Jubilee Edition | double moon | CHRDM 71020

Lenz,Uli | (pp-solo)
Noma Kosazana & Uli Lenz
Art Of The Duo: Trouble In Paradise | Tutu Records | 888144-2*
Nomakozasana-Uli Lenz
Tenderness | Tutu Records | 888198-2*
Uli Lenz Trio
Echoes Of Mandela | Tutu Records | 888180-2*

Leon,Pierre | (cl)
Daniel Flors Group
When Least Expected | Fresh Sound Records | FSNT 080 CD

Leon,Ruben | (fl,sax,ssas)
Don Ellis Orchestra
Electric Bath | CBS | CK 65522

Leonard,Darrell | (fl-h,tparr)
Jimmy Smith All Stars
Jimmy Smith:Dot Com Blues | Blue Thumb | 543978-2

Leonard,Gaston | (dr)
Django Reinhardt And The Quintet Du Hot Club De France
Planet Jazz:Django Reinhardt | Planet Jazz | 2152071-2
Django Reinhardt Quartet
Django Reinhardt:Echoes Of France | Dreyfus Jazz Line | FDM 36726-2

Leonard,Harlan | (cl,as,bs,ssreeds)
Benny Moten's Kansas City Orchestra
Planet Jazz:Jimmy Rushing | RCA | 2165371-2

Leonard,Jack | (voc)
Tommy Dorsey And His Orchestra
Planet Jazz:Tommy Dorsey | Planet Jazz | 2159972-2

Leonard,Mickey | (arrcond)
Bill Evans Quartet
The Complete Bill Evans On Verve | Verve | 527953-2
From Left To Right | Verve | 557451-2
Bill Evans Quartet With Orchestra
The Complete Bill Evans On Verve | Verve | 527953-2
From Left To Right | Verve | 557451-2
Bill Evans Trio
The Complete Bill Evans On Verve | Verve | 527953-2
Bill Evans With Orchestra
The Complete Bill Evans On Verve | Verve | 527953-2
From Left To Right | Verve | 557451-2

Leone,Tony | (dr)
David Gibson Sextet
Maya | Nagel-Heyer | CD 2018

Leonhart,Carolyn | (voc)
Wayne Escoffery Quintet
Intuition | Nagel-Heyer | CD 2038

Leonhart,Jay | (b,el-b,voc,gsynth)
Benny Bailey Quintet
The Satchmo Legacy | Enja | ENJ-9407 2
Glenn Miller And His Orchestra
The Glenn Miller Orchestra In Digital Mood | GRP | GRP 95022

Leonhart,Michael 'Mike' | (tp)
Ari Ambrose Quartet
Jazzmin | Steeplechase | SCCD 31535
Perico Sambeat Group
Ademuz | Fresh Sound Records | FSNT 041 CD

Leporace,Gracinha | (voc)
Lee Ritenour Group
Festival | GRP | GRP 95702

Leroi,Laurent | (accordeon)
Ax Genrich Group
Psychedelic Guitar | ATM Records | ATM 3809-AH

Leroux,Basile | (g)
Dee Dee Bridgewater With Band
Victim Of Love | Verve | 841199-2

Les Blue Stars |
Les Blue Stars
Jazz In Paris:Blossom Dearie-The Pianist/Les Blue Stars | EmArCy | 064784-2

Les Double Six |
Les Double Six
Les Double Six | RCA | 2164314-2

Lesberg,Jack | (b)
Billie Holiday With Gordon Jenkins And His Orchestra
Billie's Love Songs | Nimbus Records | NI 2000
Coleman Hawkins And His All Stars
Planet Jazz:Coleman Hawkins | Planet Jazz | 2152055-2
Planet Jazz:Bebop | RCA | 2169650-2
Jazz:The Essential Collection Vol.3 | IN+OUT Records | 78013-2
Coleman Hawkins With Billy Byers And His Orchestra
The Hawk In Hi-Fi | RCA | 2663842-2
Jack Teagarden's Big Eight
Planet Jazz:Jack Teagarden | Planet Jazz | 2161236-2
Planet Jazz | Planet Jazz | 2169652-2
Louis Armstrong And His All Stars
Louis Armstrong:Wintergarden 1947/Blue Note 1948 | Storyville | STCD 8242
Louis Armstrong With Gordon Jenkins And His Orchestra And Choir
Satchmo In Style | Verve | 549594-2
Ambassador Louis Armstrong Vol.17:Moments To Remember(1952-1956) | Ambassador | CLA 1917
Louis Armstrong-My Greatest Songs | MCA | MCD 18347
Swing Legends:Louis Armstrong | Nimbus Records | NI 2012
Max Kaminsky And His Dixieland Bashers
Planet Jazz | Planet Jazz | 2169652-2
Miff Mole And His Dixieland Band
Muggsy Spanier-Manhattan Masters,1945 | Storyville | STCD 6051
Mike Bryan Sextet
Jazz Festival Vol.2 | Storyville | 4960743
Ralph Sutton And His Allstars
Echoes Of Spring:The Complete Hamburg Concert | Nagel-Heyer | CD 038
Sarah Vaughan With The Allstars
Sarah Vaughan:Lover Man | Dreyfus Jazz Line | FDM 36739-2
The Sidney Bechet Society
Jam Session Concert | Nagel-Heyer | CD 076

Lesczak,Vito | (dr)
Maximilian Geller Group
Maximilian Geller Goes Bossa | Edition Collage | EC 496-2
Maimilian Geller Goes Bossa Encore | Edition Collage | EC 505-2
Maximilian Geller Quartet feat. Melanie Bong
Smile | Edition Collage | EC 461-2
Maimilian Geller Goes Bossa Encore | Edition Collage | EC 505-2
Vocal Moments | Take Twelve On CD | TT 008-2
Maximilian Geller Quartet feat. Sabina Sciubba
Maimilian Geller Goes Bossa Encore | Edition Collage | EC 505-2
Maximilian Geller Quartet feat. Susan Tobocman
Maimilian Geller Goes Bossa Encore | Edition Collage | EC 505-2

Lesher,Bob | (g)
Gene Krupa And His Orchestra
Mullenium | CBS | CK 65678

Leshin,Phil | (b)
Red Rodney Quintet
The Red Rodney Quintets | Fantasy | FCD 24758-2

Lesley,Kim | (voc)
Lenny White Group
Renderers Of Spirit | Hip Bop | HIBD 8014

Leslie,Chris | (v)
Ulli Bögershausen
Best Of Ulli Bögershausen | Laika Records | LK 93-045

Lessey,Bob | (g)
Fletcher Henderson And His Orchestra
Jazz:The Essential Collection Vol.1 | IN+OUT Records | 78011-2

Lestock[McKenzie],Jerry | (drperc)
Stan Kenton And His Orchestra
Adventures In Blues | Capitol | 520089-2
Adventures In Jazz | Capitol | 521222-2

Leszak,Vito | (dr)
Jörg Krückel-Brad Leali Quartet
Cookin' Good | Edition Collage | EC 507-2

L'Etienne,Thomas | (cl,asts)
Lillian Boutté And Her Group
You've Gotta Love Pops:Lillian Bouté Sings Louis Armstrong | ART BY HEART | ABH 2005 2
The Gospel Book | Blues Beacon | BLU-1017 2
Lillian Boutté And Her Group & The Soulful Heavenly Stars
The Gospel Book | Blues Beacon | BLU-1017 2

Letman,Johnny | (tpvoc)
Lena Horne With The Phil Moore Four
Planet Jazz:Lena Horne | Planet Jazz | 2165373-2

Lettau,Kevyn | (voc)
John Patitucci Group
Mistura Fina | GRP | GRP 98022

Leuchter,Heribert | (as,bs,b-cl,flld)
Jürgen Sturm's Ballstars
Tango Subversivo | Nabel Records:Jazz Network | CD 4613

Leue,Eckhard | (chairel-saw)
Kölner Saxophon Mafia With Fleisch
Kölner Saxophon Mafia Proudly Presents | Jazz Haus Musik | JHM 0046 CD

Leuschner,Michael | (tpfl-h)
Muriel Zoe Group
Red And Blue | ACT | 9416-2

Levacic,Kruno | (dr)
Dusko Goykovich Quintet
Balkan Blues | Enja | ENJ-9320 2
Ferenc Snétberger Quartet
Signature | Enja | ENJ-9017 2
Steve Klink Funk Unit
Places To Come From,Places To Go | Minor Music | 801098

Levant,Mark | (v)
Artie Shaw And His Orchestra
Planet JazzArtie Shaw | Planet Jazz | 2152057-2
Planet Jazz:Jazz Greatest Hits | Planet Jazz | 2169648-2

Levene,Gus | (cond)
Jerri Southern And The Gus Levene Orchestra
The Very Thought Of You:The Decca Years 1951-1957 | Decca | 050671-2

Leveque,Gerard | (arrcl)
Django Reinhardt And The Quintet Du Hot Club De France
Planet Jazz:Django Reinhardt | Planet Jazz | 2152071-2
Django's Music
Peche Á La Mode-The Great Blue Star Sessions 1947/1953 | Verve | 835418-2

Levey,Stan | (dr)
Ben Webster Quartet
Soulville | Verve | 521449-2
Ultimate Ben Webster selected by James Carter | Verve | 557537-2
Ben Webster Quintet
Soulville | Verve | 521449-2
Ben Webster With The Oscar Peterson Quartet
Verve Jazz Masters 43:Ben Webster | Verve | 525431-2
Ben Webster-Stan Levey
Ultimate Ben Webster selected by James Carter | Verve | 557537-2
Bill Holman Octet
The Jazz Giants Play Sammy Cahn:It's Magic | Prestige | PCD 24226-2
Buddy Bregman And His Orchestra
Swinging Kicks | Verve | 559514-2
Chet Baker Quartet
The Best Of Chet Baker Plays | Pacific Jazz | 797161-2
Chet Baker Sextet
The Best Of Chet Baker Plays | Pacific Jazz | 797161-2
Dizzy Gillespie Septet
Stan Getz Highlights:The Best Of The Verve Years Vol.2 | Verve | 517330-2
Verve Jazz Masters 25:Stan Getz & Dizzy Gillespie | Verve | 521852-2
Stan Getz Highlights | Verve | 847430-2
Dizzy Gillespie-Roy Eldridge Sextet
The Complete Verve Roy Eldridge Studio Sessions | Verve | 9861278
Ella Fitzgerald With The Lou Levy Quartet
Verve Jazz Masters 6:Ella Fitzgerald | Verve | 519822-2
Verve Jazz Masters 46:Ella Fitzgerald-The Jazz Sides | Verve | 527655-2
Clap Hands,Here Comes Charlie! | Verve | 835646-2
For The Love Of Ella Fitzgerald | Verve | 841765-2
For Musicians Only
Ultimate Stan Getz selected by Joe Henderson | Verve | 557532-2
Ultimate Dizzy Gillespie | Verve | 557535-2
For Musicians Only | Verve | 837435-2
Hampton Hawes Trio
The Sermon | Original Jazz Classics | OJCCD 1067-2(C 7653)
Herb Ellis Quintet
Stan Getz Highlights:The Best Of The Verve Years Vol.2 | Verve | 517330-2
Nothing But The Blues | Verve | 521674-2
Howard Rumsey's Lighthouse All-Stars
Oboe/Flute | Original Jazz Classics | OJCCD 154-2(C 3520)
Howard Rumsey's Lighthouse All-Stars Vol.6 | Original Jazz Classics | OJCCD 386-2(C 3504)
Johnny Hartman And His Orchestra
Unforgettable | Impulse(MCA) | IMP 11522
Lars Gullin American All Stars
Lars Gullin 1953,Vol.2:Moden Sounds | Dragon | DRCD 234
Peggy Lee With The Quincy Jones Orchestra
Blues Cross Country | Capitol | 520088-2
Sonny Stitt Quartet
Verve Jazz Masters 50:Sonny Sitt | Verve | 527651-2
Sonny Stitt Sextet
Verve Jazz Masters 50:Sonny Sitt | Verve | 527651-2
Stan Getz Quartet
Stan Getz Highlights:The Best Of The Verve Years Vol.2 | Verve | 517330-2
Best Of The West Coast Sessions | Verve | 537084-2
Award Winner | Verve | 543320-2
The Steamer | Verve | 547771-2
Stan Getz Highlights | Verve | 847430-2
Stan Getz:Imagination | Dreyfus Jazz Line | FDM 36733-2
Stan Getz Quartets | Original Jazz Classics | OJC20 121-2(P 7002)
Stan Getz-Gerry Mulligan Quintet
Stan Getz Highlights | Verve | 847430-2
Getz Meets Mulligan In Hi-Fi | Verve | 849392-2
Stan Kenton And His Orchestra
Stan Kenton Portraits On Standards | Capitol | 531571-2
Tal Farlow Quartet
Verve Jazz Masters 41:Tal Farlow | Verve | 527365-2
Tempo Jazzmen
Dizzy Gillespie:Night In Tunisia | Dreyfus Jazz Line | FDM 36734-2
Victor Feldman Orchestra
Latinsville | Contemporary | CCD 9005-2

Levi,James | (dr)
Herbie Hancock Group
Sunlight | CBS | 486570-2
Herbie Hancock Septet
V.S.O.P. Herbie Hancock-Live At The City Center N.Y. | CBS | 486569-2

Leviev,Milcho | (el-p,keyboards,p,perc,melodica)
Art Pepper Quartet
The Art Of Saxophone | Laserlight | 24652
Billy Cobham Group
The Best Of Billy Cobham | Atlantic | 7567-81558-2
Jack Sheldon And His West Coast Friends
Art Pepper:The Hollywood All-Star Sessions | Galaxy | 5GCD 4431-2
Jazzensemble Des Hessischen Rundfunks
Atmosphering Conditions Permitting | ECM | 1549/50
Wolfgang Lackerschmid Quartet
One More Life | Bhakti Jazz | BR 29

Levin,Pete | (clavinet,el-p,synth,fr-h,org)
Gil Evans Orchestra
There Comes A Time | RCA | 2131392-2
PLay The Music Of Jimi Hendrix | RCA | 2663872-2
Svengali | Rhino | 8122-73720-2
Lenny White Group
Present Tense | Hip Bop | HIBD 8004
Renderers Of Spirit | Hip Bop | HIBD 8014
Manhattan Project,The
Kind Of Blue:Blue Note Celebrate The Music Of Miles Davis | Blue Note | 534255-2
Wayne Shorter:The Classic Blue Note Recordings | Blue Note | 540856-2
Rachelle Ferrell With The Wayne Shorter Sextet
First Instrumental | Blue Note | 827820-2

Levin,Tony | (b,chapman-stick,el-b,b-g,synth-b,dr)
Buddy Rich Big Band
Backwoods Siseman/Pieces Of Dream | Laserlight | 24655
David Torn Quartet
Cloud About Mercury | ECM | 1322(831108-2)
European Jazz Ensemble
European Jazz Ensemble At The Philharmonic Cologne | M.A Music | A 800-2
20th Anniversary Tour | Konnex Records | KCD 5078
European Jazz Ensemble 25th Anniversary | Konnex Records | KCD 5100
European Jazz Ensemble & The Khan Family feat. Joachim Kühn
European Jazz Ensemble Meets The Khan Family | M.A Music | A 807-2
European Trumpet Summit
European Trumpet Summit | Konnex Records | KCD 5064
Rusty Bryant Sextet
For The Good Times | Prestige | PRCD 24269-2
Steps Ahead
Modern Times | Elektra | 7559-60351-2
N.Y.C. | Intuition Records | INT 3007-2
The Quartet
Crossing Level | Konnex Records | KCD 5077

Levine,Dave | (perc)
Pat Martino Septet
Strings! | Original Jazz Classics | OJCCD 223-2(P 7547)

Levine,Henry 'Hot Lips' | (tp)
Dr. Henry Levine's Barefoot Dixieland Philharmonic feat.Prof. Sidney Bechet
Planet Jazz | Planet Jazz | 2169652-2
Sidney Bechet And The Chamber Music Society Of Lower Basin Street
Sidney Bechet:Summertime | Dreyfus Jazz Line | FDM 36712-2

Levine,Jesse | (viola)
Ron Carter Quintet With Strings
Pick 'Em/Super Strings | Milestone | MCD 47090-2

Levine,Mark | (b,fl-h,fl,co,indian-fl,melophon)
Joe Henderson And His Orchestra
Joe Henderson:The Milestone Years | Milestone | 8MCD 4413-2

Levine,Nat | (dr)
Dr. Henry Levine's Barefoot Dixieland Philharmonic feat.Prof. Sidney Bechet
Planet Jazz | Planet Jazz | 2169652-2
Sidney Bechet And The Chamber Music Society Of Lower Basin Street
Sidney Bechet:Summertime | Dreyfus Jazz Line | FDM 36712-2

Levinsky,Walt | (as,cl,sax,fl,woodwindsreeds)
Anita O'Day With The Gary McFarland Orchestra
All The Sad Youn Men | Verve | 517065-2
Verve Jazz Masters 49:Anita O'Day | Verve | 527653-2
Cal Tjader With The Lalo Schifrin Orchestra
Talkin Verve/Roots Of Acid Jazz:Cal Tjader | Verve | 531562-2
Glenn Miller And His Orchestra
The Glenn Miller Orchestra In Digital Mood | GRP | GRP 95022
Joe Williams,With The Oliver Nelson Orchestra
Planet Jazz:Joe Williams | Planet Jazz | 2165370-2
Lalo Schifrin And His Orchestra
Verve Jazz Masters 39:Cal Tjader | Verve | 521858-2

Stan Getz With The Gary McFarland Orchestra
Verve Jazz Masters 53:Stan Getz-Bossa Nova | Verve | 529904-2
Big Band Bossa Nova | Verve | 825771-2 PMS
Stan Getz Highlights | Verve | 847430-2

Levinson,Ed | (dr)
Lee Konitz Trio
Newport Jazz Festival 1958,July 3rd-6th,Vol.1:Mostly Miles | Phontastic | NCD 8813

Levinson,Mira | (voice)
Ax Genrich Group
Psychedelic Guitar | ATM Records | ATM 3809-AH

Levister,Alonzo | (arr)
Don Senay With Orchestra And Strings
Charles Mingus-The Complete Debut Recordings | Debut | 12 DCD 4402-2
Thad Jones And His Orchestra
Charles Mingus-The Complete Debut Recordings | Debut | 12 DCD 4402-2

Levitt,Al | (dr)
Bob Benton With The Charles Mingus Quintet
Charles Mingus-The Complete Debut Recordings | Debut | 12 DCD 4402-2
Charles Mingus Quintet
Charles Mingus-The Complete Debut Recordings | Debut | 12 DCD 4402-2
Jackie Paris With The Charles Mingus Quintet
Charles Mingus-The Complete Debut Recordings | Debut | 12 DCD 4402-2
Stan Getz Quintet
Stan Getz Highlights:The Best Of The Verve Years Vol.2 | Verve | 517330-2
Stan Getz And The 'Cool' Sounds | Verve | 547317-2
Stan Getz Highlights | Verve | 847430-2
Stephane Grappelli Quartet
Grapelli Story | Verve | 515807-2
Warne Marsh Trio
The Unissued Copenhagen Studio Recordings | Storyville | STCD 8278

Levitt,Rod | (b-tb,tbarr)
Dizzy Gillespie And His Orchestra
Verve Jazz Masters 20:Introducing | Verve | 519853-2
Dizzy Gillespie:Birks Works-The Verve Big Band Sessions | Verve | 527900-2
Ultimate Dizzy Gillespie | Verve | 557535-2
Dizzy Gillespie Orchestra
Verve Jazz Masters 10:Dizzy Gillespie | Verve | 516319-2
Quincy Jones And His Orchestra
The Quintessence | Impulse(MCA) | 951222-2
The Roots Of Acid Jazz | Impulse(MCA) | IMP 12042

Levy,Hank | (bs)
Stan Kenton And His Orchestra
Stan Kenton Portraits On Standards | Capitol | 531571-2

Levy,Howard | (harmp)
Michael Riessler And The Ensemble 13
Momentum Mobile | Enja | ENJ-9003 2
Paquito D'Rivera Orchestra
Jazzrock-Anthology Vol.3:Fusion | Zounds | CD 27100555
Rabih Abou-Khalil Group
The Sultan's Picnic | Enja | ENJ-8078 2
Odd Times | Enja | ENJ-9330 2

Levy,Jed | (alto-fl,ss,tsfl)
Don Friedman Quartet
My Foolish Heart | Steeplechase | SCCD 31534
My Foolish Heart | Steeplechase | SCCD 31545
Jed Levy Quartet
Round And Round | Steeplechase | SCCD 31529
Ron McClure Quartet
Match Point | Steeplechase | SCCD 31517

Levy,Jesse | (cellostrings)
Earl Klugh Group With Strings
Late Night Guitar | Blue Note | 498573-2

Levy,John | (b)
Billie Holiday With The Bobby Tucker Quartet
Billie's Love Songs | Nimbus Records | NI 2000
Erroll Garner Trio
Erroll Garner:Trio | Dreyfus Jazz Line | FDM 36719-2
George Shearing Quintet
Verve Jazz Masters 57:George Shearing | Verve | 529900-2
Lennie Tristano Trio
The Story Of Jazz Piano | Laserlight | 24653

Levy,Lou | (porg)
Anita O'Day With The Bill Holman Orchestra
Verve Jazz Masters 49:Anita O'Day | Verve | 527653-2
Dee Dee Bridgewater With Big Band
Dear Ella | Verve | 539102-2
Dee Dee Bridgewater With Her Septet
Dear Ella | Verve | 539102-2
Dee Dee Bridgewater With Her Trio
Dear Ella | Verve | 539102-2
Dee Dee Bridgewater With Orchestra
Dear Ella | Verve | 539102-2
Ella Fitzgerald With Frank De Vol And His Orchestra
Get Happy! | Verve | 523321-2
Ella Fitzgerald With Marty Paich's Dektette
Ella Swings Lightly | Verve | 517535-2
Ella Fitzgerald With Paul Weston And His Orchestra
Love Songs:The Best Of The Song Books | Verve | 531762-2
Ella Fitzgerald With The Billy May Orchestra
The Best Of The Song Books:The Ballads | Verve | 521867-2
Love Songs:The Best Of The Song Books | Verve | 531762-2
Ella Fitzgerald Sings The Harold Arlen Song Book | Verve | 589108-2
Ella Fitzgerald With The Lou Levy Quartet
Ella Fitzgerald-First Lady Of Song | Verve | 517898-2
Verve Jazz Masters 6:Ella Fitzgerald | Verve | 519822-2
Verve Jazz Masters 46:Ella Fitzgerald-The Jazz Sides | Verve | 527655-2
4 By 4:Ella Fitzgerald/Sarah Vaughan/Billie Holiday/Dinah Washington | Verve | 559693-2
Clap Hands,Here Comes Charlie! | Verve | 835646-2
For The Love Of Ella Fitzgerald | Verve | 841765-2
Ella Fitzgerald With The Lou Levy Trio
Ella Fitzgerald-First Lady Of Song | Verve | 517898-2
For The Love Of Ella Fitzgerald | Verve | 841765-2
Ella Fitzgerald With The Marty Paich Dek-tette
Ella Fitzgerald-First Lady Of Song | Verve | 517898-2
Verve Jazz Masters 6:Ella Fitzgerald | Verve | 519822-2
Verve Jazz Masters 46:Ella Fitzgerald-The Jazz Sides | Verve | 527655-2
Lou Levy Trio
My Old Flame | Fresh Sound Records | FSR-CD 312
The Complete Nocturne Recordings:Jazz In Hollywood Series Vol.1 | Fresh Sound Records | NR 3CD-101
Peggy Lee With Lou Levy's Orchestra
Pass Me By/Big Spender | Capitol | 535210-2
Peggy Lee With The Quincy Jones Orchestra
Blues Cross Country | Capitol | 520088-2
Sonny Stitt And His West Coast Friends
Art Pepper:The Hollywood All-Star Sessions | Galaxy | 5GCD 4431-2
Sonny Stitt Quartet
Verve Jazz Masters 50:Sonny Sitt | Verve | 527651-2
Stan Getz Quartet
Stan Getz Highlights:The Best Of The Verve Years Vol.2 | Verve | 517330-2
Best Of The West Coast Sessions | Verve | 537084-2
Award Winner | Verve | 543320-2
Stan Getz And The 'Cool' Sounds | Verve | 547317-2
The Steamer | Verve | 547771-2
West Coast Jazz | Verve | 557549-2
Stan Getz Highlights | Verve | 847430-2
Stan Getz Quintet
Stan Getz Highlights:The Best Of The Verve Years Vol.2 | Verve | 517330-2
Verve Jazz Masters 8:Stan Getz | Verve | 519823-2
Best Of The West Coast Sessions | Verve | 537084-2
Ultimate Stan Getz selected by Joe Henderson | Verve | 557532-2
West Coast Jazz | Verve | 557549-2
Stan Getz Highlights | Verve | 847430-2
Stan Getz-Gerry Mulligan Quintet
Stan Getz Highlights | Verve | 847430-2
Getz Meets Mulligan In Hi-Fi | Verve | 849392-2
Stan Getz-Lionel Hampton Quintet
Stan Getz Highlights:The Best Of The Verve Years Vol.2 | Verve | 517330-2
Hamp And Getz | Verve | 831672-2
Stan Getz-Lionel Hampton Sextet
Hamp And Getz | Verve | 831672-2
Terry Gibbs Dream Band
Terry Gibbs Dream Band Vol.2:The Sundown Sessions | Contemporary | CCD 7652-2
Terry Gibbs Dream Band Vol.3:Flying Home | Contemporary | CCD 7654-2
Terry Gibbs Dream Band Vol.6:One More Time | Contemporary | CCD 7658-2
The Jazz Giants Play Jerome Kern:Yesterdays | Prestige | PCD 24202-2
Tommy Dorsey And His Orchestra
Planet Jazz:Tommy Dorsey | Planet Jazz | 2159972-2
Virgil Gonsalves Sextet
The Complete Nocturne Recordings:Jazz In Hollywood Series Vol.1 | Fresh Sound Records | NR 3CD-101
Woody Herman And His Orchestra
Woody Herman:Four Brother | Dreyfus Jazz Line | FDM 36722-2

Levy,Rob | (b)
Nicki Leighton-Thomas Group
Forbidden Games | Candid | CCD 79778

Lew,Ricardo | (el-gg)
Gato Barbieri Orchestra
Latino America | Impulse(MCA) | 952236-2

Lewalter,Rainer | (b)
Edith Steyer... Posterity Quintet
...On The Right Track | Jazz 4 Ever Records:Jazz Network | J4E 4745

Lewin,Marcus | (drperc)
The Brazz Brothers
Ngoma | Laika Records | 35101562

Lewis,Art | (drperc)
Marty Cook Group feat. Monty Waters
Borderlines | Tutu Records | 888122-2*

Lewis,Bobby | (fl-htp)
Singers Unlimited
The Singers Unlimited:Magic Voices | MPS | 539130-2

Lewis,Brandon | (dr)
LeeAnn Ledgerwood Trio
Walkin' Up | Steeplechase | SCCD 31541

Lewis,Cappy | (tp)
Ella Fitzgerald With Frank De Vol And His Orchestra
Get Happy! | Verve | 523321-2
Ella Fitzgerald With The Nelson Riddle Orchestra
Get Happy! | Verve | 523321-2
Woody Herman And His Orchestra
The Legends Of Swing | Laserlight | 24659
Woody Herman:Four Brother | Dreyfus Jazz Line | FDM 36722-2

Lewis,Carroll | (tp)
Ella Fitzgerald With The Nelson Riddle Orchestra
The Best Of The Song Books:The Ballads | Verve | 521867-2
Oh Lady Be Good:The Best Of The Gershwin Songbook | Verve | 529581-2
Love Songs:The Best Of The Song Books | Verve | 531762-2
Ella Fitzgerald Sings The Johnny Mercer Songbook | Verve | 539057-2
Dream Dancing | Original Jazz Classics | OJCCD 1072-2(2310814)

Lewis,Charles | (p,tpfl-h)
Charlie Lewis Trio
JazzIn Paris:Harlem Piano In Montmartre | EmArCy | 018447-2
Oscar Brown Jr. And His Group
Movin' On | Rhino | 8122-73678-2
Sidney Bechet All Stars
Planet Jazz:Sidney Bechet | Planet Jazz | 2152063-2
Planet Jazz Sampler | Planet Jazz | 2152326-2
Sidney Bechet And His All Stars
Sidney Bechet:Summertime | Dreyfus Jazz Line | FDM 36712-2
Sidney Bechet Quartet
Planet Jazz:Sidney Bechet | Planet Jazz | 2152063-2

Lewis,Curtis | (voc)
Babs Gonzales And His Band
Voilà | Fresh Sound Records | FSR CD 340

Lewis,Ed | (cotp)
Benny Moten's Kansas City Orchestra
Planet Jazz:Jimmy Rushing | RCA | 2165371-2
Count Basie And His Orchestra
Planet Jazz:Count Basie | Planet Jazz | 2152068-2
Planet Jazz Sampler | Planet Jazz | 2152326-2
Planet Jazz:Jimmy Rushing | RCA | 2165371-2
Planet Jazz:Jazz Greatest Hits | Planet Jazz | 2169648-2
Planet Jazz:Big Bands | Planet Jazz | 2169649-2
Jazz Collection:Count Basie | Laserlight | 24368
Jazz:The Essential Collection Vol.3 | IN+OUT Records | 78013-2
From Spiritual To Swing | Vanguard | VCD 169/71
Helen Humes With James P. Johnson And The Count Basie Orchestra
From Spiritual To Swing | Vanguard | VCD 169/71
Jimmy Rushing With Count Basie And His Orchestra
From Spiritual To Swing | Vanguard | VCD 169/71

Lewis,Eric | (p)
Cassandra Wilson Group
Traveling Miles | Blue Note | 854123-2
Craig Bailey Band
A New Journey | Candid | CCD 79725
Marcus Printup Sextet
The New Boogaloo | Nagel-Heyer | CD 2019
Wynton Marsalis Group
Standard Time Vol.6:Mr.Jelly Lord | CBS | CK 69872

Lewis,George | (cl,as,talks,voc,e-flat-cl)
Bunk Johnson And His New Orleans Band
Planet Jazz:Jazz Trumpet | Planet Jazz | 2169654-2
Bunk Johnson And His Superior Jazz Band
Authentic New Orleans Jazz | Good Time Jazz | GTCD 12048-2
George Lewis And His Band
Atlantic Jazz: New Orleans | Atlantic | 7567-81700-2
George Lewis And His New Orleans Ragtime Band
The Beverly Caverns Session | Good Time Jazz | GTCD 12058-2
George Lewis And His New Orleans Stompers
George Lewis And His New Orleans Stompers | Blue Note | 821261-2
George Lewis And His Original New Orleans Jazzmen
George Lewis In Stockholm,1959 | Dragon | DRCD 221
Heiner Goebbels/Heiner Müller
Der Mann Im Fahrstuhl | ECM | 1369(837110-2)
Joseph 'Dee Dee' Pierce And His Band
Atlantic Jazz: New Orleans | Atlantic | 7567-81700-2
Punch Miller's Bunch & George Lewis
Atlantic Jazz: New Orleans | Atlantic | 7567-81700-2
Roscoe Mitchell And The Note Factory
Nine To Get Ready | ECM | 1651(539725-2)
Steve Coleman And The Council Of Balance
Genesis & The Opening Of The Way | RCA | 2152934-2

Lewis,Herbie | (b)
Bobby Hutcherson Quintet
Blue N' Groovy | Blue Note | 780679-2
Dave Pike Quartet
Pike's Peak | Epic | 489772-2
Bill Evans:Piano Player | CBS | CK 65361
Harold Land Quintet
The Fox | Original Jazz Classics | OJCCD 343-2
Jackie McLean Quartet
Let Freedom Ring | Blue Note | 591895-2
McCoy Tyner Sextet
Asante | Blue Note | 493384-2

Lewis,Irván | (p,el-pkeyboards)
Lewis Trio With Guests
Battangó | Intuition Records | INN 1101-2

Lewis,Irving | (tp)
Woody Herman And His Orchestra
The Legends Of Swing | Laserlight | 24659
Woody Herman:Four Brother | Dreyfus Jazz Line | FDM 36722-2

Lewis,J.T. | (dr)
Stanley Jordan Quartet
Live In New York | Blue Note | 497810-2

Lewis,Jimmy | (b,el-b,fender-bg)
Billy Butler Quintet
Night Life | Prestige | PCD 24260-2
Boogaloo Joe Jones Quintet
Discovery:Grover Washington Jr.-The First Recordings | Prestige | PCD 11020-2
Charlie's Greatest Hits | Prestige | PCD 24250-2
Boogaloo Joe Jones Sextet
Jazzin' With The Soul Brothers | Fantasy | FANCD 6086-2
Discovery:Grover Washington Jr.-The First Recordings | Prestige | PCD 11020-2
Charles Kynard Sextet
The Soul Brotherhood | Prestige | PCD 24257-2
Count Basie And His Orchestra
Verve Jazz Masters 2:Count Basie | Verve | 519819-2
Grant Green Orchestra
Grant Green:Blue Breakbeat | Blue Note | 494705-2
Blue Breaks Beats Vol.2 | Blue Note | 789907-2
So Blue So Funky-Heroes Of The Hammond | Blue Note | 796563-2
Grant Green Sextet
Grant Green:Blue Breakbeat | Blue Note | 494705-2
Houston Person Sextet
Jazzin' With The Soul Brothers | Fantasy | FANCD 6086-2
Idris Muhammad Group
Jazzin' With The Soul Brothers | Fantasy | FANCD 6086-2
Johnny 'Hammond' Smith Quintet
Discovery:Grover Washington Jr.-The First Recordings | Prestige | PCD 11020-2
Johnny 'Hammond' Smith Sextet
The Soulful Blues | Prestige | PCD 24244-2
King Curtis Band
King Curtis-Blow Man Blow | Bear Family Records | BCD 15670 CI
Lou Donaldson Sextet
So Blue So Funky-Heroes Of The Hammond | Blue Note | 796563-2
Willis Jackson Quintet
Together Again: Willis Jackson With Jack McDuff | Prestige | PRCD 24284-2

Lewis,Joanna | (voc)
Motus Quartett
Grimson Flames | Creative Works Records | CW CD 1023-2

Lewis,John | (arr,musical-director,p,el-p)
Charles Mingus And His Orchestra
Charles Mingus-The Complete Debut Recordings | Debut | 12 DCD 4402-2
Charlie Parker All Stars
Charlie Parker:Now's The Time | Dreyfus Jazz Line | FDM 36724-2
Charlie Parker And His Orchestra
Bird: The Complete Charlie Parker On Verve | Verve | 837141-2
Charlie Parker Quintet
Charlie Parker:Bird's Best Bop On Verve | Verve | 527452-2
Charlie Parker:The Best Of The Verve Years | Verve | 527815-2
Chris Connor With The John Lewis Quartet
Chris Connor | Atlantic | 7567-80769-2
Clifford Brown Sextet
Clifford Brown Memorial Album | Blue Note | 532141-2
Coleman Hawkins-Roy Eldridge Quintet
Verve Jazz Masters 43:Coleman Hawkins | Verve | 521856-2
Dizzy Gillespie And His Orchestra
Dizzy Gillespie:Pleyel Jazz Concert 1948 + Max Roach Quintet 1949 | Vogue | 21409412
Planet Jazz:Dizzy Gillespie | Planet Jazz | 2152069-2
Planet Jazz:Bebop | RCA | 2169650-2
Dizzy Gillespie Quintet
Charlie Parker:Now's The Time | Dreyfus Jazz Line | FDM 36724-2
Dizzy Gillespie:Night In Tunisia | Dreyfus Jazz Line | FDM 36734-2
Dizzy Gillespie Septet
Stan Getz Highlights:The Best Of The Verve Years Vol.2 | Verve | 517330-2
Verve Jazz Masters 25:Stan Getz & Dizzy Gillespie | Verve | 521852-2
Stan Getz Highlights | Verve | 847430-2
Dizzy Gillespie-Roy Eldridge Sextet
The Complete Verve Roy Eldridge Studio Sessions | Verve | 9861278
Ella Fitzgerald With The Dizzy Gillespie Orchestra
Ella Fitzgerald:Mr.Paganini | Dreyfus Jazz Line | FDM 36741-2
Ella Fitzgerald With The Hank Jones Trio
Ella Fitzgerald:Mr.Paganini | Dreyfus Jazz Line | FDM 36741-2
For Musicians Only
Ultimate Stan Getz selected by Joe Henderson | Verve | 557532-2
Ultimate Dizzy Gillespie | Verve | 557535-2
For Musicians Only | Verve | 837435-2
Four Trombones
Charles Mingus-The Complete Debut Recordings | Debut | 12 DCD 4402-2
The J.J.Johnson Memorial Album | Prestige | PRCD 11025-2
J.J.Johnson Quintet
The J.J.Johnson Memorial Album | Prestige | PRCD 11025-2
J.J.Johnson Sextet
The Eminent J.J.Johnson Vol.1 | Blue Note | 532143-2
The J.J.Johnson Memorial Album | Prestige | PRCD 11025-2
John Lewis
Evolution | Atlantic | 7567-83211-2
John Lewis And Hank Jones
An Evening With Two Grand Pianos | Atlantic | 7567-80787-2
John Lewis Quartet
Evolution II | Atlantic | 7567-83313-2
John Lewis Sextet
Monterey Jazz Festival 1975 | Storyville | 4960213
Lester Young Quartet
Jazz Gallery:Lester Young Vol.2(1946-59) | RCA | 2119541-2
Verve Jazz Masters 30:Lester Young | Verve | 521859-2
Marion McPartland-Bill Evans-John Lewis-Patrice Rushen
Monterey Jazz Festival 1975 | Storyville | 4960213
Miles Davis All Stars
Miles Davis:Milestones | Dreyfus Jazz Line | FDM 36731-2
Miles Davis And His Orchestra
The Complete Birth Of The Cool | Capitol | 494550-2
Birth Of The Cool | Capitol | 530117-2
Miles Davis:The Best Of The Capitol/Blue Note Years | Blue Note | 798287-2
Jazz Profile:Miles Davis | Blue Note | 823515-2
Ballads & Blues | Blue Note | 836633-2
Miles Davis:Milestones | Dreyfus Jazz Line | FDM 36731-2
Miles Davis Quartet
Blue Haze | Original Jazz Classics | OJC20 093-2(P 7054)
The Prestige Legacy Vol.1:The High Priests | Prestige | PCD 24251-2
Miles Davis Quintet
The Jazz Giants Play Rodgers & Hart:Blue Moon | Prestige | PCD 24205-2
Miles Davis Septet
Miles Davis And Horns | Original Jazz Classics | OJC20 053-2(P 7025)
Miles Davis Sextet

INTERPRETENVERZEICHNIS

Miles Davis And Horns | Original Jazz Classics | OJC20 053-2(P 7025)
The Prestige Legacy Vol.1:The High Priests | Prestige | PCD 24251-2
Milt Jackson Quintet
Wizard Of The Vibes | Blue Note | 532140-2
Milt Jackson Birthday Celebration | Fantasy | FANCD 6079-2
Modern Jazz Quartet
To Bags...With Love:Memorial Album | Pablo | 2310967-2
The Complete Modern Jazz Quartet Prestige & Pablo Recordings | Prestige | 4PRCD 4438-2
The Modern Jazz Quartet At Music Inn With Sonny Rollins,Vol.2 | Atlantic | 7567-80794-2
Blues On Bach | Atlantic | 7567-81393-2
MJQ 40 | Atlantic | 7567-82330-2
Lonely Woman | Atlantic | 7567-90665-2
Rhino Presents The Atlantic Jazz Gallery | Atlantic | 8122-71257-2
Pyramid | Rhino | 812273679-2
Fontessa | Rhino | 8122-73687-2
Milt Jackson Birthday Celebration | Fantasy | FANCD 6079-2
Concorde | Original Jazz Classics | OJC20 002-2
Django | Original Jazz Classics | OJC20 057-2
Topsy-This One's For Basie | Original Jazz Classics | OJCCD 1073-2(2310917)
MJQ | Original Jazz Classics | OJCCD 125-2
Together Again | Pablo | PACD20 244-2(2308244)
The Jazz Giants Play Cole Porter:Night And Day | Prestige | PCD 24203-2
Modern Jazz Quartet & Guests
MJQ 40 | Atlantic | 7567-82330-2
Modern Jazz Quartet And Laurindo Almeida
MJQ 40 | Atlantic | 7567-82330-2
Modern Jazz Quartet And Orchestra
MJQ 40 | Atlantic | 7567-82330-2
Modern Jazz Quartet And Symphony Orchestra
MJQ 40 | Atlantic | 7567-82330-2
Modern Jazz Quartet And The Swingle Singers
MJQ 40 | Atlantic | 7567-82330-2
Modern Jazz Quartet feat.Jimmy Giuffre
MJQ 40 | Atlantic | 7567-82330-2
Modern Jazz Quartet With Sonny Rollins
The Modern Jazz Quartet At Music Inn With Sonny Rollins,Vol.2 | Atlantic | 7567-80794-2
MJQ 40 | Atlantic | 7567-82330-2
Modern Jazz Sextet
Verve Jazz Masters 50:Sonny Sitt | Verve | 527651-2
The Modern Jazz Sextet | Verve | 559834-2
Paul Desmond And The Modern Jazz Quartet
MJQ 40 | Atlantic | 7567-82330-2
Sonny Rollins Quartet
Sonny Rollins And The Big Brass | Verve | 557545-2
Sonny Rollins With The Modern Jazz Quartet
The Complete Modern Jazz Quartet Prestige & Pablo Recordings | Prestige | 4PRCD 4438-2
Milt Jackson Birthday Celebration | Fantasy | FANCD 6079-2
Sonny Rollins With The Modern Jazz Quartet | Original Jazz Classics | OJCCD 011-2
The Jazz Giants Play Duke Ellington:Caravan | Prestige | PCD 24227-2
Sonny Stitt Quintet
Atlantic Saxophones | Rhino | 8122-71256-2
Sonny Stitt | Original Jazz Classics | OJCCD 009-2
The Modern Jazz Society
A Concert Of Contemporary Music | Verve | 559827-2
Zoot Sims Quartet
Zoot Sims Quartets | Original Jazz Classics | OJCCD 242-2(P 7026)

Lewis,Juno | (percvoc)
John Coltrane And His Orchestra
Kulu Se Mama | Impulse(MCA) | 543412-2

Lewis,Meade Lux | (celeste,p-solo,harpsichord-solo,p)
Albert Ammons-Meade Lux Lewis
Boogie Woogie | Laserlight | 24321
Albert Ammons-Pete Johnson-Meade Lux Lewis
From Spiritual To Swing | Vanguard | VCD 169/71
Boogie Woogie Trio
Boogie Woogie | Laserlight | 24321
Count Basie And His Orchestra
From Spiritual To Swing | Vanguard | VCD 169/71
Meade Lux Lewis
Boogie Woogie | Laserlight | 24321
The Complete Jazz At The Philharmonic On Verve 1944-1949 | Verve | 523893-2
From Spiritual To Swing | Vanguard | VCD 169/71

Lewis,Mel | (dr,bongos,perc,dr-solop)
Anita O'Day With The Bill Holman Orchestra
Verve Jazz Masters 49:Anita O'Day | Verve | 527653-2
Anita O'Day With The Gary McFarland Orchestra
All The Sad Youn Men | Verve | 517065-2
Anita O'Day With The Jimmy Giuffre Orchestra
Verve Jazz Masters 49:Anita O'Day | Verve | 527653-2
Anita O'Day With The Russ Garcia Orchestra
Verve Jazz Masters 49:Anita O'Day | Verve | 527653-2
Annie Ross With Her Quintet
Misty Blue:Sweet Sisters Swing Songs Of Sorrow And Sadness | Blue Note | 521151-2
Art Pepper Plus Eleven
Art Pepper + Eleven | Contemporary | CSA 7568-6
Modern Jazz Classics | Original Jazz Classics | OJC20 341-2
Benny Goodman And His Orchestra
The Legends Of Swing | Laserlight | 24659
Bill Perkins-Richie Kamuca Quintet
Midnight Blue(The [Be]witching Hour) | Blue Note | 854365-2
Cal Tjader's Orchestra
Verve Jazz Masters 39:Cal Tjader | Verve | 521858-2
Chet Baker Quintet
Once Upon A Summertime | Original Jazz Classics | OJCCD 405-2
Dizzy Gillespie And His Orchestra
Talking Verve:Dizzy Gillespie | Verve | 533846-2
Ella Fitzgerald With Marty Paich's Dektette
Ella Swings Lightly | Verve | 517535-2
Ella Fitzgerald With The Marty Paich Dek-tette
Ella Fitzgerald-First Lady Of Song | Verve | 517898-2
Verve Jazz Masters 6:Ella Fitzgerald | Verve | 519822-2
Verve Jazz Masters 46:Ella Fitzgerald-The Jazz Sides | Verve | 527655-2
Gerald Wilson And His Orchestra
Blue Breaks Beats Vol.2 | Blue Note | 789907-2
Gerry Mulligan Concert Jazz Band
Verve Jazz Masters 36:Gerry Mulligan | Verve | 523342-2
Gerry Mulligan And The Concert Band At The Village Vanguard | Verve | 589488-2
The Complete Verve Gerry Mulligan Concert Band | Verve | 9860613
Gerry Mulligan Quartet
The Art Of Saxophone | Laserlight | 24652
Gerry Mulligan-Ben Webster Quintet
Verve Jazz Masters 43:Ben Webster | Verve | 525431-2
The Complete Gerry Mulligan Meets Ben Webster Sessions | Verve | 539055-2
Ultimate Ben Webster selected by James Carter | Verve | 557537-2
Gerry Mulligan-Johnny Hodges Quintet
Gerry Mulligan Meets Johnny Hodges | Verve | 065513-2
Verve Jazz Masters 35:Johnny Hodges | Verve | 521857-2
Hank Crawford Orchestra
Rhino Presents The Atlantic Jazz Gallery | Atlantic | 8122-71257-2
Helen Merrill With The Pepper Adams Quintet
Chasin' The Bird(Gershwin) | EmArCy | 558850-2
Herbie Mann Quartet
Verve Jazz Masters 56:Herbie Mann | Verve | 529901-2
Herbie Mann With The Frank DeVol Orchestra
Verve Jazz Masters 56:Herbie Mann | Verve | 529901-2
Herbie Mann's Californians
Great Ideas Of Western Man | Original Jazz Classics | OJCCD 1065-2(RLP 245)
Jack McDuff Quartet With Orchestra
Prelude:Jack McDuff Big Band | Prestige | PRCD 24283-2
Jimmy McGriff Orchestra
Swingin' The Blues-Jumpin' The Blues | Laserlight | 24654
Jimmy Rushing And His Band
Planet Jazz:Jimmy Rushing | RCA | 2165371-2
Planet Jazz:Male Jazz Vocalists | Planet Jazz | 2169657-2
Jimmy Smith Quartet
Verve Jazz Masters 45:Kenny Burrell | Verve | 527652-2
Jimmy Smith:Best Of The Verve Years | Verve | 527950-2
Jimmy Smith-Talkin' Verve | Verve | 531563-2
Any Number Can Win | Verve | 557447-2
Jimmy Witherspoon And His All Stars
Blues For Easy Livers | Original Blues Classics | OBCCD 585-2(PR 7475)
Joe Williams With The Frank Hunter Orchestra
Planet Jazz:Joe Williams | Planet Jazz | 2165370-2
June Christy With The Shorty Rogers Orchestra
June Christy Big Band Special | Capitol | 498319-2
Kenny Burrell-Jimmy Smith Quartet
Blue Bash | Verve | 557453-2
Kenny Burrell-Jimmy Smith Trio
Blue Bash | Verve | 557453-2
Mark Murphy And His Septet
Blue Velvet: Crooners, Swooners And Velvet Vocals | Blue Note | 521153-2
Mel Tormé With The Russell Garcia Orchestra
Swingin' On The Moon | Verve | 511385-2
Oscar Peterson With Orchestra
With Respect To Nat | Verve | 557486-2
Paul Desmond-Gerry Mulligan Quartet
Two Of A Mind | RCA | 2179620-2
Red Norvo And His Orchestra
Planet Jazz:Female Jazz Vocalists | Planet Jazz | 2169656-2
Sonny Stitt Quartet
Verve Jazz Masters 50:Sonny Sitt | Verve | 527651-2
Stan Getz With The Eddie Sauter Orchestra
Stan Getz Plays The Music Of Mickey One | Verve | 531232-2
Stan Kenton And His Orchestra
Great Swing Classics In Hi-Fi | Capitol | 521223-2
Terry Gibbs Big Band
Terry Gibbs Dream Band Vol.4:Main Stem | Contemporary | CCD 7656-2
Terry Gibbs Dream Band
Terry Gibbs Dream Band Vol.2:The Sundown Sessions | Contemporary | CCD 7652-2
Terry Gibbs Dream Band Vol.3:Flying Home | Contemporary | CCD 7654-2
Terry Gibbs Dream Band Vol.5:The Big Cat | Contemporary | CCD 7657-2
Terry Gibbs Dream Band Vol.6:One More Time | Contemporary | CCD 7658-2
The Jazz Giants Play Jerome Kern:Yesterdays | Prestige | PCD 24202-2
Thad Jones-Mel Lewis Orchestra
The Groove Merchant/The Second Race | Laserlight | 24656

Lewis,Mel or Grady Tate | (dr)
Jimmy McGriff Organ Blues Band
The Worm | Blue Note | 538699-2

Lewis,Mike | (b,ssts)
Bill Carrothers Quartet
The Electric Bill | Dreyfus Jazz Line | FDM 36631-2

Lewis,Mingo | (congas,cowbell,timbales,shakers)
Al Di Meola Group
Elegant Gypsy | CBS | 468213-2
Land Of The Midnight Sun | CBS | 468214-2
Jazzrock-Anthology Vol.3:Fusion | Zounds | CD 27100555
Hal Di Meola Group
Casino | CBS | 468215-2
Return To Forever
Return To The 7th Galaxy-Return To Forever:The Anthology | Verve | 533108-2

Lewis,Morty | (reedsts)
Glenn Miller And His Orchestra
The Glenn Miller Orchestra In Digital Mood | GRP | GRP 95022

Lewis,Nolan | (voc)
Buddy Johnson And His Orchestra
Buddy And Ella Johnson 1953-1964 | Bear Family Records | BCD 15479 DH

Lewis,Pete | (g)
Johnny Otis And His Orchestra
Verve Jazz Masters 43:Ben Webster | Verve | 525431-2

Lewis,Ramsey | (pvoc)
GRP All-Star Big Band
All Blues | GRP | GRP 98002
Ramsey Lewis Trio
Down To Earth | Verve | 538329-2

Lewis,Ricardo G. | (v)
Lewis Trio With Guests
Battangó | Intuition Records | INN 1101-2

Lewis,Robert 'Son' | (bass-dr)
Eureka Brass Band
Atlantic Jazz: New Orleans | Atlantic | 7567-81700-2

Lewis,Tony | (dr)
The Quartet
The Quartet Live In Prague | P&J Music | P&J 101-1 CD

Lewis,Vic | (g,voc,whistling,ldp)
The Jimmy And Marion McPartland Sessions
Vic Lewis:The Golden Years | Candid | CCD 79754
Vic Lewis And His Band
Vic Lewis:The Golden Years | Candid | CCD 79754
Vic Lewis Jam Session
Vic Lewis:The Golden Years | Candid | CCD 79754
Vic Lewis West Coast All Stars
Vic Lewis Presenting A Celebration Of Contemporary West Coast Jazz | Candid | CCD 79711/12
Me And You! | Candid | CCD 79739

Lewis,Victor | (dr,bucket,voiceperc)
Abbey Lincoln With The Rodney Kendrick Trio And Guests
A Turtle's Dream | Verve | 527382-2
Akili
Maasai Mara | M.A Music | A 802-2
Akili | M.A Music | NU 730-2
Allan Botschinsky Quartet
Last Summer | M.A Music | A 804-2
Andy Bey Group
Tuesdays In Chinatown | Minor Music | 801099
Carla Bley Band
Heavy Heart | Watt | 14
Night-Glo | Watt | 16
The Very Big Carla Bley Band | Watt | 23
4X4 | Watt | 30(159547-2)
Carla Bley Sextet
Sextet | Watt | 17
Chet Baker-Stan Getz Quintet
The Stockholm Concerts | Verve | 537555-2
Franco Ambrosetti Quintet
Live At The Blue Note | Enja | ENJ-7065 2
Ingrid Jensen Quintet
Higher Grounds | Enja | ENJ-9353 2
Joe Sample Group
Invitation | Warner | 9362-45209.2
John Stubblefield Quartet
Morning Song | Enja | ENJ-8036 2
Kenny Barron Quintet
What If | Enja | ENJ-5013 2
Live At Fat Tuesdays | Enja | ENJ-5071 2
Quickstep | Enja | ENJ-6084 2
Kenny Barron Trio
What If | Enja | ENJ-5013 2
Kenny Barron-Victor Lewis
What If | Enja | ENJ-5013 2
Klaus Doldinger Group
Back In New York:Blind Date | Atlantic | 3984-26922-2
Lew Soloff Quartet
With A Song In My Heart | Milestone | MCD 9290-2
Lew Soloff Quintet
With A Song In My Heart | Milestone | MCD 9290-2
Niels-Henning Orsted-Pedersen Trio
Those Who Were | Verve | 533232-2
Niels-Henning Orsted-Pedersen Trio With Johnny Griffin
Those Who Were | Verve | 533232-2
Randy Weston African Rhythm
Khepera | Verve | 557821-2
Stan Getz Quartet
A Life In Jazz:A Musical Biography | Verve | 535119-2
Stan Getz Cafe Montmartre | EmArCy | 586755-2
Anniversary ! | EmArCy | 838769-2
Serenity | EmArCy | 838770-2
The Lost Sessions | Verve | 9801098
Bossas And Ballads:The Lost Sessions | Verve | 9901098
Stan Getz Sextet
Billy Highstreet Samba | EmArCy | 838771-2
Stephen Scott Quartet
Vision Quest | Enja | ENJ-9347 2
Stephen Scott Trio
Vision Quest | Enja | ENJ-9347 2
Steve Swallow Group
Carla | Watt | XtraWatt/2
Victor Lewis Sextet
Eeeyyess! | Enja | ENJ-9311 2

Lewis,Willie | (as,arr,voc,clbs)
Willie Lewis And His Entertainers
Americans Swinging In Paris:Benny Carter | EMI Records | 539647-2

Lewis,Yvonne | (voc)
Grover Washington Jr. Orchestra
Inside Moves | Elektra | 7559-60318-2

Lewkovitch,Karl | (ts)
Stan Getz With Ib Glindemann And His Orchestra
Stan Getz In Europe | Laserlight | 24657

Leyden,Norm | (arrcond)
Jerri Southern And The Norman Leyden Orchestra
The Very Thought Of You:The Decca Years 1951-1957 | Decca | 050671-2

Leyh,W. | (voc)
Chico Freeman And Brainstorm
Sweet Explosion | IN+OUT Records | 7010-2

Leyland,Carl 'Sonny' | (p)
Billy Boy Arnold Group
Eldorado Cadillac | Alligator Records | ALCD 4836

Leys,John | (b-tb)
Buddy Rich Big Band
Backwoods Siseman/Pieces Of Dream | Laserlight | 24655

Lhiver,Thierry | (tb)
Frank Wess Meets The Paris-Barcelona Swing Connection
Paris-Barcelona Connection | Fresh Sound Records | FSNT 002 CD

Lhotzky,Bernd | (pp-solo)
Bernd Lhotzky
Stridewalk | Jazz Connaisseur | JCCD 0029-2
Stridin' High | Jazz Connaisseur | JCCD 9728-2
Bernd Lhotzky-Colin Dawson
Sophisticated | ART BY HEART | ABH 2003 2
Ralph Sutton-Bernd Lhotzky
Stridin' High | Jazz Connaisseur | JCCD 9728-2

Libani,Giulio | (pceleste)
Chet Baker With String-Orchestra And Voices
Chet Baker With Fifty Italian Strings | Original Jazz Classics | OJC20 492-2(JLP 921)

Libove,Charles | (v)
Earl Klugh Group With Strings
Late Night Guitar | Blue Note | 498573-2
George Benson With The Don Sebesky Orchestra
Verve Jazz Masters 21:George Benson | Verve | 521861-2
Gunther Schuller Ensemble
Beauty Is A Rare Thing:Ornette Coleman-The Complete Atlantic Recordings | Atlantic | 8122-71410-2
Helen Merrill With Orchestra
Casa Forte | EmArCy | 558848-2
Milt Jackson And His Orchestra
Sunflower | CTI | ZK 65131
Nina Simone And Orchestra
Baltimore | Epic | 476906-2
Sarah Vaughan With Orchestra
!Viva! Vaughan | Mercury | 549374-2
Sarah Vaughan Sings The Mancini Songbook | Verve | 558401-2
Stan Getz With The Eddie Sauter Orchestra
Stan Getz Plays The Music Of Mickey One | Verve | 531232-2

Lichus,Heinz | (dr)
Joe Gallardo's Latino Blue
A Latin Shade Of Blue | Enja | ENJ-9421 2

Liebezeit,Jacki | (dr)
Kölner Saxophon Mafia With Jacki Liebezeit
Kölner Saxophon Mafia Proudly Presents | Jazz Haus Musik | JHM 0046 CD

Liebman,Dave | (alto-fl,ss,ts,as,fl,bs,dida,sax,p)
Dave Liebman
Time Immemorial | Enja | ENJ-9389 2
Dave Liebman And The Lluis Vidal Trio
Dave Liebman And The Lluis Vidal Trio | Fresh Sound Records | FSNT 026 CD
Dave Liebman And The Lluis Vidal Trio With The Orquestra De Cambra Theatre Lliure
Dave Liebman And The Lluis Vidal Trio | Fresh Sound Records | FSNT 026 CD
Dave Liebman Quintet
Homage To John Coltrane | Owl Records | 018357-2
Jazz Portraits | EGO | 95080
Dimitrios Vassilakis Daedalus Project
Labyrinth | Candid | CCD 79776
Ed Sarath Quintet
Last Day In May | Konnex Records | KCD 5042
Klaus Ignatzek Group Feat.Dave Liebman
The Spell | Nabel Records:Jazz Network | CD 4614
Miles Davis Group
Paris Jazz Concert:Miles Davis | Laserlight | 17445
Dark Magus | CBS | C2K 65137
On The Corner | CBS | CK 63980
Niels-Henning Orsted-Pedersen Quartet
Dancing On The Tables | Steeplechase | SCS 1125(Audiophile Pressing)
Orquestra De Cambra Teatre Lliure feat. Dave Liebman
Orquestra De Cambra Teatre Lliure and Lluis Vidal Trio feat.Dave Liebman | Fresh Sound Records | FSNT 027 CD
Rolf Kühn And Friends
Affairs:Rolf Kühn & Friends | Intuition Records | INT 3211-2
Steve Swallow Group
Home | ECM | 1160(513424-2)
Tom Harrell Quintet
Sail Away | Original Jazz Classics | OJCCD 1095-2(C- 14054-2)
Tom Harrell Sextet
Visions | Contemporary | CCD 14063-2
Sail Away | Original Jazz Classics | OJCCD 1095-2(C- 14054-2)
Vince Mendoza With The WDR Big Band And Guests
Sketches | ACT | 9215-2

Liefland,Wilhelm | (narration)

Jazzensemble Des Hessischen Rundfunks
Atmosphering Conditions Permitting | ECM | 1549/50

Liesse,Jean | (tpvoc)
Andre Hodeir And His Jazz Group De Paris
Jazz In Paris:Le Jazz Groupe De Paris Joue André Hodeir | EmArCy | 548792-2
Kenny Clarke 8
Americans Swinging In Paris:Kenny Clarke | EMI Records | 539652-2

Lievano,Edilberto | (tb)
Conexion Latina
Mambo 2000 | Enja | ENJ-7055 2

Lievano,Joaquin | (el-g,gg-synth)
Jean-Luc Ponty Group
Atlantic Jazz: Fusion | Atlantic | 7567-81711-2
Jean-Luc Ponty Quintet
Cosmic Messenger | Atlantic | 7567-81550-2
Jean-Luc Ponty Sextet
Cosmic Messenger | Atlantic | 7567-81550-2
The Very Best Of Jean-Luc Ponty | Rhino | 8122-79862-2

Lieven,Thomas | (dr)
Art De Fakt
Art De Fakt-Ray Federman:Surfiction Jazz No.2 | double moon | CHRDM 71007

Lightcap,Chris | (b)
Ben Waltzer Quintet
In Metropolitan Motion | Fresh Sound Records | FSNT 082 CD
Chris Lightcap Quartet
Lay-Up | Fresh Sound Records | FSNT 074 CD

Lighthart,Arie | (bjg)
Dutch Swing College Band
Swinging Studio Sessons | Philips | 824256-2 PMS
Dutch Swing College Band Live In 1960 | Philips | 838765-2
Rita Reys With The Dutch Swing College Band
The Very Best Of Dixieland Jazz | Verve | 535529-2

Lightsey,Kirk | (fl,p,keyboards,celesta,el-p,voc)
Benny Bailey Quartet With Strings
I Remember Love | Laika Records | 35101752
Chet Baker Quintet
The Jazz Giants Play Rodgers & Hart:Blue Moon | Prestige | PCD 24205-2
Groovin' With The Chet Baker Quintet | Prestige | PR20 7460-2
Comin' On With The Chet Baker Quintet | Prestige | PR20 7478-2
Cool Burnin' With The Chet Baker Quintet | Prestige | PR20 7496-2
Boppin' With The Chet Baker Quintet | Prestige | PR20 7512-2
Smokin' With The Chet Baker Quintet | Prestige | PR20 7749-2
Dexter Gordon Quartet
Dexter Gordon:Atlanta Georgia May 5,1981 | Storyville | STCD 8363
Gunther Schuller With The WDR Radio Orchestra & Rememberance Band
Witchi Tia To, The Music Of Jim Pepper | Tutu Records | 888204-2*
Kenny Burrell Quintet
Stormy Monday Blues | Fantasy | FCD 24767-2
Roots
Saying Something | IN+OUT Records | 77031-2
For Diz & Bird | IN+OUT Records | 77039-2
Sonny Fortune Quartet
Monk's Mood | Konnex Records | KCD 5048

Lihocky,Markus | (ssas)
Clark Terry With The Summit Jazz Orchestra
Clark | Edition Collage | EC 530-2

Lijbaart,Joost | (dr,percamadinda)
Agog
Eat Time | Jazz Haus Musik | JHM 0072 CD

Lillich,Martin | (b,b-g,el-bshaker)
Gebhard Ullmann Quartet
Per-Dee-Doo | Nabel Records:Jazz Network | CD 4640
Ray Blue Quartet
Always With A Purpose | Ray Blue Music | JN 007(RMB 01)
Tim Sund Trio
Trialogue | Nabel Records:Jazz Network | CD 4692

Lil's Hot Shots |
Lil's Hot Shots
Jazz:The Essential Collection Vol.2 | IN+OUT Records | 78012-2

Lima,Alyrio | (perccymbals)
Franco & Lorenzo Petrocca
Italy | Edition Musikat | EDM 062

Limbach,Tonny | (b)
Coleman Hawkins With The Ramblers
Jazz:The Essential Collection Vol.3 | IN+OUT Records | 78013-2

Lim-Dutton,Elizabeth | (v)
Steve Kuhn With Strings
Promises Kept | ECM | 1815(0675222)

Limonick,Marvin | (v)
Pete Rugolo And His Orchestra
Thriller/Richard Diamon(Original Jazz Scores From 2 Classics TV Series) | Fresh Sound Records | FSCD 2015
Phineas Newborn Jr. With Dennis Farnon And His Orchestra
While My Lady Sleeps | RCA | 2185157-2

Linane,Dave | (b)
Royce Campbell-Adrian Ingram Group
Hands Across The Water | String Jazz | SJRCD 1002

Lincoln Center Jazz Orchestra,The |
Lincoln Center Jazz Orchestra
Big Train | CBS | CK 69860

Lincoln,Abbey | (vocvoc-solo)
Abbey Lincoln
That's Him! | Original Jazz Classics | OJCCD 085-2
Abbey Lincoln And Her All Stars
The World Is Falling Down | Verve | 843476-2
Abbey Lincoln And Her All Stars(Newport Rebels)
Candid Dolphy | Candid | CCD 79033
Abbey Lincoln And Her Orchestra
Straight Ahead | Candid | CCD 79015
Abbey Lincoln And Her Trio
Over The Years | Verve | 549101-2
Abbey Lincoln And Her Trio With Guests
Over The Years | Verve | 549101-2
Abbey Lincoln With Her Band
Who Used To Dance | Verve | 533559-2
Wholly Earth | Verve | 559538-2
Abbey Lincoln With Her Quartet
That's Him! | Original Jazz Classics | OJCCD 085-2
Abbey Lincoln With Her Quintet
Sonny Rollins-The Freelance Years:The Complete Riverside & Contemporary Recordings | Riverside | 5 RCD 4427-2
That's Him! | Original Jazz Classics | OJCCD 085-2
Abbey Lincoln With The Benny Golson Quintet
It's Magic | Original Jazz Classics | OJCCD 205-2
Abbey Lincoln With The Benny Golson Septet
It's Magic | Original Jazz Classics | OJCCD 205-2
Abbey Lincoln With The Kenny Dorham Quintet
Abbey Is Blue | Original Jazz Classics | OJC20 069-2(RLP 1153)
Abbey Lincoln With The Max Roach Quintet
Abbey Is Blue | Original Jazz Classics | OJC20 069-2(RLP 1153)
Abbey Lincoln With The Max Roach Sextet
Abbey Is Blue | Original Jazz Classics | OJC20 069-2(RLP 1153)
Abbey Lincoln With The Rodney Kendrick Trio And Guests
A Turtle's Dream | Verve | 527382-2
Abbey Lincoln With The Stan Getz Quartet
You Gotta Pay The Band | Verve | 511110-2
A Life In Jazz:A Musical Biography | Verve | 535119-2
Abbey Lincoln With The Stan Getz Quintet
You Gotta Pay The Band | Verve | 511110-2
Jazz Artists Guild
Newport Rebels-Jazz Artists Guild | Candid | CCD 79022
Max Roach All Stars
Candid Dolphy | Candid | CCD 79033
Max Roach Group
We Insist: Freedom Now Suite | Candid | CCD 79002
Max Roach Sextet
Clifford Brown-Max Roach:Alone Together-The Best Of The Mercury Years | Verve | 526373-2
Max Roach Sextet With Choir
It's Time | Impulse(MCA) | 951185-2
Max Roach-Abbey Lincoln
We Insist: Freedom Now Suite | Candid | CCD 79002

Lind,John | (tb)
Stan Getz With Ib Glindemann And His Orchestra
Stan Getz In Europe | Laserlight | 24657
Stan Kenton With The Danish Radio Big Band
Stan Kenton With The Danish Radio Big Band | Storyville | STCD 8340

Lindberg,Göran | (p)
Coleman Hawkins With The Göran Lindberg Trio
Coleman Hawkins At The Golden Circle | Dragon | DRCD 265

Lindberg,John | (b,el-bb-solo)
John Lindberg Ensemble
A Tree Frog Tonality | Between The Lines | btl 008(Efa 10178-2)

Lindblom,Putte | (p)
Kettil Ohlsson Quintet
Lars Gullin 1953,Vol.2:Moden Sounds | Dragon | DRCD 234
Lars Gullin Quartet
Lars Gullin 1953,Vol.2:Moden Sounds | Dragon | DRCD 234
Lars Gullin Quintet
Lars Gullin 1953,Vol.2:Moden Sounds | Dragon | DRCD 234

Lindemann,Gregor | (b)
Matthias Petzold Group With Choir
Psalmen und Lobgesänge für Chor und Jazz-Enseble | Indigo-Records | 1002 CD
Matthias Petzold Septett
Ulysses | Indigo-Records | 1003 CD

Lindemann,Jens | (tppiccolo-tp)
Canadian Brass
Take The A Train | RCA | 2663455-2

Linden,Colin | (gvoc)
Hans Theessink Group
Call Me | Minor Music | 801022

Lindenberg,Udo | (dr)
Passport
Uranus | Atlantic | 2292-44142-2

Linder,John | (tp)
Coleman Hawkins With The Thore Ehrlings Orchestra
Coleman Hawkins At The Golden Circle | Dragon | DRCD 265

Lindfors,Will | (dr)
Wedeli Köhler Group
Swing & Folk | Jazzpoint | JP 1067 CD

Lindgreen,Ole 'Fessor' | (tb)
Red Richards-George Kelly Sextet With Doc Cheatham
Groove Move | Jazzpoint | JP 1045 CD
Ricardo's Jazzmen
The Golden Years Of Revival Jazz,Sampler | Storyville | 109 1001
The Golden Years Of Revival Jazz,Vol.4 | Storyville | STCD 5509
The Golden Years Of Revival Jazz,Vol.5 | Storyville | STCD 5510

Lindgren,Carl-Eric | (ts)
Lars Gullin Septet
Lars Gullin 1951/52 Vol.5:First Walk | Dragon | DRCD 380

Lindgren,Gunnar | (ts)
Kjell Jansson Quintet
Back From Where We Came | Touché Music | TMcCD 009

Lindgren,Jonas | (v)
Nils Landgren Group
Sentimental Journey | ACT | 9409-2

Lindgren,Kurt | (b)
Coleman Hawkins With The Göran Lindberg Trio
Coleman Hawkins At The Golden Circle | Dragon | DRCD 265

Lindgren,Lars | (tpfl-h)
Jazz Baltica Ensemble
The Birth+Rebirth Of Swedish Folk Jazz | ACT | 9254-2
Jens Winther And The Danish Radio Jazz Orchestra
Angels | dacapo | DCCD 9442
The Danish Radio Jazz Orchestra
Nice Work | dacapo | DCCD 9446

Lindgren,Magnus | (fl,alto-fl,bass-fl,cl,b-cl,ts,bs,p)
Lisa Ekdahl With The Salvador Poe Quartet, Strings And Guests
Lisa Ekdahl Sings Salvadore Poe | RCA | 2179681-2
Silje Nergard Group with Strings
Nightwatch | EmArCy | 9865648

Lindholm,Lucas | (b)
Abdullah Ibrahim With The NDR Big Band
Ekapa Lodumo | TipToe | TIP-888840 2
Albert Mangelsdorff With The NDR Big Band
NDR Big Band-Bravissimo | ACT | 9232-2
Chet Baker Quintet
My Favourite Songs: The Last Great Concert Vol.1 | Enja | ENJ-5097 2
The Last Concert Vol.I+II | Enja | ENJ-6074 22
Chet Baker Quintet/NDR Big Band/Radio Orchestra Hannover
Straight From The Heart-The Last Concert Vol.2 | Enja | ENJ-6020 2
The Last Concert Vol.I+II | Enja | ENJ-6074 22
Chet Baker With The NDR-Bigband
NDR Big Band-Bravissimo | ACT | 9232-2
My Favourite Songs: The Last Great Concert Vol.1 | Enja | ENJ-5097 2
The Last Concert Vol.I+II | Enja | ENJ-6074 22
Chet Baker-The Legacy Vol.1 | Enja | ENJ-9021 2
Heinz Sauer Quartet With The NDR Big Band
NDR Big Band-Bravissimo | ACT | 9232-2
Joe Pass With The NDR Big Band
Joe Pass In Hamburg | ACT | 9100-2
NDR Big Band-Bravissimo | ACT | 9232-2
Joe Pass With The NDR Big Band And Radio Philharmonie Hannover
Joe Pass In Hamburg | ACT | 9100-2
Johnny Griffin With The NDR Big Band
NDR Big Band-Bravissimo | ACT | 9232-2
Klaus Weiss Orchestra
Live At The Domicile | ATM Records | ATM 3805-AH
NDR Big Band
NDR Big Band-Bravissimo | ACT | 9232-2
The Theatre Of Kurt Weil | ACT | 9234-2
NDR Big Band With Guests
50 Years Of NDR Big Band:Bravissimo II | ACT | 9259-2
Oscar Brown Jr. And His Group
Live Every Minute | Minor Music | 801071
Oscar Brown Jr. with The NDR Big Band
Live Every Minute | Minor Music | 801071

Lindner,Jason | (p)
Charles Owens Quartet
Eternal Balance | Fresh Sound Records | FSNT 067 CD

Lindroth,Frank | (g)
Jazz Orchester Rheinland-Pfalz
Kazzou | Jazz Haus Musik | LJBB 9104

Lindsay,Arto | (el-g,voice,gvoc)
Bill Frisell Band
Before We Were Born | Nonesuch | 7559-60843-2
Heiner Goebbels/Heiner Müller
Der Mann Im Fahrstuhl | ECM | 1369(837110-2)
Uri Caine Group
Urlicht/Primal Light | Winter&Winter | 910004-2

Lindsay,Erica | (ts)
Erica Lindsay Quintet
Dreamers | Candid | CCD 79040
Erica Lindsay Sextet
Dreamers | Candid | CCD 79040

Lindschouw,Ib | (dr)
Chris Barber's Jazz Band
The Golden Years Of Revival Jazz,Vol.2 | Storyville | STCD 5507
Papa Bue's New Orleans Band
The Golden Years Of Revival Jazz,Vol.4 | Storyville | STCD 5509
Papa Bue's Viking Jazzband
The Golden Years Of Revival Jazz,Sampler | Storyville | 109 1001
The Golden Years Of Revival Jazz,Vol.3 | Storyville | STCD 5508
The Golden Years Of Revival Jazz,Vol.7 | Storyville | STCD 5512
The Golden Years Of Revival Jazz,Vol.8 | Storyville | STCD 5513
The Golden Years Of Revival Jazz,Vol.9 | Storyville | STCD 5514
The Golden Years Of Revival Jazz,Vol.11 | Storyville | STCD 5516
The Golden Years Of Revival Jazz,Vol.12 | Storyville | STCD 5517
The Golden Years Of Revival Jazz,Vol.13 | Storyville | STCD 5518

Lindsey,Johny | (bvoc)
Jelly Roll Morton's Red Hot Peppers
Planet Jazz:Jelly Roll Morton | Planet Jazz | 2152060-2
Planet Jazz Sampler | Planet Jazz | 2152326-2
Jazz:The Essential Collection Vol.1 | IN+OUT Records | 78011-2
Louis Armstrong And His Orchestra
Satch Plays Fats(Complete) | CBS | CK 64927
Sidney Bechet And His New Orleans Feetwarmers
Sidney Bechet:Summertime | Dreyfus Jazz Line | FDM 36712-2

Lindsey,Tommy | (tp)
Coleman Hawkins And His Orchestra
Planet Jazz:Coleman Hawkins | Planet Jazz | 2152055-2
Planet Jazz Sampler | Planet Jazz | 2152326-2
Planet Jazz:Jazz Greatest Hits | Planet Jazz | 2169648-2
Jazz:The Essential Collection Vol.3 | IN+OUT Records | 78013-2

Lindskog,Anders | (ts)
Agneta Baumann And Her Quintet
A Time For Love | Touché Music | TMcCD 006
Anders Lindskog Quartet
Cry Me A River | Touché Music | TMcCD 005
Anders Lindskog Trio
Fine Together | Touché Music | TMcCD 010

Lindvall,Anders 'Chico' | (gperc)
Jens Winther And The Danish Radio Jazz Orchestra
Angels | dacapo | DCCD 9442
The Danish Radio Jazz Orchestra
This Train:The Danish Radio Jazz Orchestra Plays The Music Of Ray Pitts | dacapo | DCCD 9428
Nice Work | dacapo | DCCD 9446

Lindvall,Lars | (tp,fl-h,perc,prep-tpwhistle)
Creative Works Orchestra
Willisau And More Live | Creative Works Records | CW CD 1020-2
Gabriele Hasler Group
Gabriele Hasler's Personal Notebook | Foolish Music | FM 211490
Heinrich Von Kalnein Group
New Directions | Nabel Records:Jazz Network | CD 4670

Lindvall,Leif | (tp)
Nils Landgren First Unit And Guests
Nils Landgren-The First Unit | ACT | 9292-2

Lindvall,Per | (dr,perctp)
Ketil Bjornstad Group
Seafarer's Song | EmArCy | 9865777
Niels Landgren Funk Unit
Live In Stockholm | ACT | 9223-2
Nils Landgren First Unit And Guests
Nils Landgren-The First Unit | ACT | 9292-2
Nils Petter Molvaer Group
Solid Ether | ECM | 1722(543365-2)

Linetzky,Andres | (p)
Tangata Rea
Tango Alla Baila | Winter&Winter | 910025-2

Lingenfelder,Matthias | (v)
Kölner Saxophon Mafia With The Auryn Quartet
Kölner Saxophon Mafia Proudly Presents | Jazz Haus Musik | JHM 0046 CD

Linges,Monika | (arr,vocnarration)
Hipsters In The Zone
Into The Afro-Latin Bag | Nabel Records:Jazz Network | CD 4663
John Thomas & Lifeforce
Devil Dance | Nabel Records:Jazz Network | CD 4601
3000 Worlds | Nabel Records:Jazz Network | CD 4604
Monika Linges Quartet
Floating | Nabel Records:Jazz Network | CD 4607

Linke,Jörg | (ts)
Lozenzo Petrocca Quartet
Stop It | Edition Musikat | EDM 018

Linke,Rainer | (bel-b)
Blaufrontal
Blaufrontal | Jazz Haus Musik | JHM 0037 CD
Blaufrontal With Hank Roberts & Mark Feldman
Bad Times Roll | Jazz Haus Musik | JHM 0061 CD
Jazzensemble Des Hessischen Rundfunks
Atmosphering Conditions Permitting | ECM | 1549/50

Linn,Ray | (tparr)
Anita O'Day With The Buddy Bregman Orchestra
Pick Yourself Up | Verve | 517329-2
Barney Kessel And His Orchestra
Barney Kessel Plays Carmen | Original Jazz Classics | OJC 269(C 7563)
Buddy Bregman And His Orchestra
Swinging Kicks | Verve | 559514-2
Ella Fitzgerald With The Buddy Bregman Orchestra
Ella Fitzgerald-First Lady Of Song | Verve | 517898-2
Ella Fitzgerald Sings The Rodgers And Hart Song Book | Verve | 537258-2
Ella Fitzgerald With The Frank DeVol Orchestra
Get Happy! | Verve | 523321-2
Harry James And His Orchestra
Trumpet Blues:The Best Of Harry James | Capitol | 521224-2
JATP All Stars
The Complete Jazz At The Philharmonic On Verve 1944-1949 | Verve | 523893-2
Jesse Price And His Blues Band
Jazz Profile:Dexter Gordon | Blue Note | 823514-2
June Christy With The Pete Rugolo Orchestra
Something Cool(The Complete Mono & Stereo Versions) | Capitol | 534069-2
Maynard Ferguson And His Orchestra
Verve Jazz Masters 52:Maynard Ferguson | Verve | 529905-2
Nat King Cole With The Billy May Orchestra
Nat King Cole:For Sentimental Reasons | Dreyfus Jazz Line | FDM 36740-2
Pete Rugolo And His Orchestra
Verve Jazz Masters 52:Maynard Ferguson | Verve | 529905-2
Thriller/Richard Diamon(Original Jazz Scores From 2 Classics TV Series) | Fresh Sound Records | FSCD 2015
Red Norvo And His Orchestra
Planet Jazz:Female Jazz Vocalists | Planet Jazz | 2169656-2
Red Norvo Septet
Jazz Profile:Dexter Gordon | Blue Note | 823514-2
Tommy Dorsey And His Orchestra
Planet Jazz:Frank Sinatra & Tommy Dorsey | Planet Jazz | 2152067-2
Planet Jazz:Tommy Dorsey | Planet Jazz | 2159972-2
Planet Jazz:Big Bands | Planet Jazz | 2169649-2
Planet Jazz:Male Jazz Vocalists | Planet Jazz | 2169657-2
Frank Sinatra And The Tommy Dorsey Orchestra | RCA | 2668701-2
Woody Herman And His Orchestra
Woody Herman:Four Brother | Dreyfus Jazz Line | FDM 36722-2

Lins,Alexandre | (caxixi,cuica,djembepandeiro)
Pata Masters
Pata-Bahia | Pata Musik | PATA 11 CD

Lins,Ivan | (keyboardsvoc)
John Patitucci Group
Mistura Fina | GRP | GRP 98022

Linsner,Art | (b-tb)
Woody Herman And His Orchestra
Woody Herman Herd At Montreux | Original Jazz Classics | OJCCD 991-2(F 9470)

Linsted,Kari | (cello)
Edward Vesala Nordic Gallery
Sound & Fury | ECM | 1541

Lionberg,Red | (dr)
Anita O'Day And Her Combo
Verve Jazz Masters 49:Anita O'Day | Verve | 527653-2
Lionti,Vince | (viola)
Steve Kuhn With Strings
Promises Kept | ECM | 1815(0675222)
Lipkins,Steve | (tp)
Artie Shaw And His Orchestra
Planet JazzArtie Shaw | Planet Jazz | 2152057-2
Planet Jazz:Male Jazz Vocalists | Planet Jazz | 2169657-2
Glenn Miller And His Orchestra
Planet Jazz:Glenn Miller | Planet Jazz | 2152056-2
Lippitsch,Klaus | (perc)
Couch Ensemble
Winnetou | Jazz 'n' Arts Records | JNA 1503
Lippman,Joe | (cond,arrp)
Charlie Parker And His Orchestra
The Cole Porter Songbook | Verve | 823250-2
Bird: The Complete Charlie Parker On Verve | Verve | 837141-2
Charlie Parker Quartet With Strings
The Cole Porter Songbook | Verve | 823250-2
Charlie Parker With Orchestra
Charlie Parker:The Best Of The Verve Years | Verve | 527815-2
Charlie Parker With Strings
Charlie Parker:The Best Of The Verve Years | Verve | 527815-2
Bird: The Complete Charlie Parker On Verve | Verve | 837141-2
Charlie Parker:April In Paris | Dreyfus Jazz Line | FDM 36737-2
Charlie Parker With The Joe Lipman Orchestra
Verve Jazz Masters 28:Charlie Parker Plays Standards | Verve | 521854-2
Charlie Parker With Strings:The Master Takes | Verve | 523984-2
Charlie Parker Big Band | Verve | 559835-2
Lippmann,Horst | (dr)
Two Beat Stompers
Deutsches Jazz Fesival 1954/1955 | Bear Family Records | BCD 15430
Lipschultz,Irving | (cello)
Artie Shaw And His Orchestra
Planet JazzArtie Shaw | Planet Jazz | 2152057-2
Planet Jazz:Jazz Greatest Hits | Planet Jazz | 2169648-2
Lirico |
Lirico
Sussurro | Jazz Haus Musik | JHM 0129 CD
Lirola,Jeremy | (b)
Louis Sclavis & The Bernard Struber Jazztet
La Phare | Enja | ENJ-9359 2
Lisee,Charles | (as,bscl)
Coleman Hawkins With Michel Warlop And His Orchestra
Django Reinhardt All Star Sessions | Capitol | 531577-2
Lisiecki,Claire | (v)
Charlie Haden Quartet West With Strings
Now Is The Hour | Verve | 527827-2
List,Pip | (fr-h)
Lee Konitz With The Ed Partyka Jazz Orchestra
Dreams And Realities | Laika Records | 35101642
Listengard,Sam | (as)
Anita O'Day With Gene Krupa And His Orchestra
Let Me Off Uptown:Anita O'Day With Gene Krupa | CBS | CK 65625
Lister,William | (fr-h)
Dizzy Gillespie And His Orchestra
Gillespiana And Carnegie Hall Concert | Verve | 519809-2
Talking Verve:Dizzy Gillespie | Verve | 533846-2
Liston,Melba | (arr,cond,tbvoc)
Babs Gonzales And His Band
Voilà | Fresh Sound Records | FSR CD 340
Charles Mingus And His Orchestra
The Complete Town Hall Concert | Blue Note | 828353-2
Dinah Washington And Her Sextet
Newport Jazz Festival 1958,July 3rd-6th Vol.4:Blues In The Night No.2 | Phontastic | NCD 8816
Dinah Washington With The Newport All Stars
Dinah Sings Bessie Smith | Verve | 538635-2
Dizzy Gillespie And His Orchestra
Verve Jazz Masters 20:Introducing | Verve | 519853-2
Dizzy Gillespie:Birks Works-The Verve Big Band Sessions | Verve | 527900-2
Ultimate Dizzy Gillespie | Verve | 557535-2
Dizzy Gillespie Orchestra
Verve Jazz Masters 10:Dizzy Gillespie | Verve | 516319-2
Eddie Lockjaw Davis And His Orchestra
Eric Dolphy:The Complete Prestige Recordings | Prestige | 9 PRCD-4418-2
Ella Fitzgerald With The Bill Doggett Orchestra
Ella Fitzgerald-First Lady Of Song | Verve | 517898-2
Rhythm Is My Business | Verve | 559513-2
Freddie Hubbard Orchestra
The Body And The Soul | Impulse(MCA) | 951183-2
Jimmy Smith And Wes Montgomery With Orchestra
Jimmy & Wes-The Dynamic Duo | Verve | 521445-2
Jimmy Smith And Wes Montgomery With The Oliver Nelson Orchestra
Wes Montgomery:The Verve Jazz Sides | Verve | 521690-2
Jimmy Smith:Best Of The Verve Years | Verve | 527950-2
Talkin' Jazz:Roots Of Acid Jazz | Verve | 529580-2
Jimmy Smith With Orchestra
Jimmy Smith-Talkin' Verve | Verve | 531563-2
Jimmy Smith With The Claus Ogerman Orchestra
Verve Jazz Masters 29:Jimmy Smith | Verve | 521855-2
Any Number Can Win | Verve | 557447-2
Jimmy Smith With The Oliver Nelson Orchestra
Verve Jazz Masters 29:Jimmy Smith | Verve | 521855-2
Jimmy Smith:Best Of The Verve Years | Verve | 527950-2
Jimmy Smith-Talkin' Verve | Verve | 531563-2
Junior Mance Trio & Orchestra
That Lovin' Feelin' | Milestone | MCD 47097-2
Mar Murphy With The Ernie Wilkins Orchestra
RAH | Original Jazz Classics | OJCCD 141-2(R 9395)
Milt Jackson Orchestra
To Bags...With Love:Memorial Album | Pablo | 2310967-2
Milt Jackson Birthday Celebration | Fantasy | FANCD 6079-2
Big Bags | Original Jazz Classics | OJCCD 366-2(RLP 9429)
Oscar Peterson With The Ernie Wilkins Orchestra
Verve Jazz Masters 16:Oscar Peterson | Verve | 516320-2
Quincy Jones And His Orchestra
The Quintessence | Impulse(MCA) | 951222-2
The Roots Of Acid Jazz | Impulse(MCA) | IMP 12042
Quincy Jones Big Band
Rahsaan/The Complete Mercury Recordings Of Roland Kirk | Mercury | 846630-2
Sam Jones Plus 10
Cannonball Adderley Birthday Celebration | Fantasy | FANCD 6087-2
Lithuanian State Symphony Orchestra |
Egberto Gismonti With The Lithuanian State Symphony Orchestra
Meeting Point | ECM | 1586(533681-2)
Little Walter | (g,harmvoc)
Muddy Waters Blues Band
Muddy Waters-The Collection | MCA | MCD 18961
Little,Booker | (tp)
Abbey Lincoln And Her Orchestra
Straight Ahead | Candid | CCD 79015
Booker Little Quintet
Eric Dolphy Birthday Celebration | Fantasy | FANCD 6085-2
Booker Little Sextet
Out Front | Candid | CCD 79027
Candid Dolphy | Candid | CCD 79033
Eric Dolphy Quintet
Eric Dolphy At The Five Spot Vol.2 | Original Jazz Classics | OJC20 247-2(P 7294)
Far Cry | Original Jazz Classics | OJC20 400-2
Eric Dolphy-Booker Little Quintet
Eric Dolphy:The Complete Prestige Recordings | Prestige | 9 PRCD-4418-2
Eric Dolphy Birthday Celebration | Fantasy | FANCD 6085-2
At The Five Spot,Vol.1 | Original Jazz Classics | OJC20 133-2
Eric Dolphy Memorial Album | Original Jazz Classics | OJCCD 353-2
Eric Dophy Quintet
Eric Dolphy:The Complete Prestige Recordings | Prestige | 9 PRCD-4418-2
Jazz Artists Guild
Newport Rebels-Jazz Artists Guild | Candid | CCD 79022
John Coltrane And His Orchestra
John Coltrane:Standards | Impulse(MCA) | 549914-2
John Coltrane Quartet With Brass
The Complete Africa/Brass Sessions | Impulse(MCA) | 952168-2
Max Roach All Stars
Candid Dolphy | Candid | CCD 79033
Max Roach Group
We Insist: Freedom Now Suite | Candid | CCD 79002
Max Roach Plus Four
Clifford Brown-Max Roach:Alone Together-The Best Of The Mercury Years | Verve | 526373-2
Max Roach Quintet
Clifford Brown-Max Roach:Alone Together-The Best Of The Mercury Years | Verve | 526373-2
Deeds Not Words | Original Jazz Classics | OJC20 304-2(RLP 1122)
The Jazz Giants Play Sammy Cahn:It's Magic | Prestige | PCD 24226-2
Max Roach Sextet
Deeds Not Words | Original Jazz Classics | OJC20 304-2(RLP 1122)
Little,Jerry | (vconcertmaster)
Archie Shepp Orchestra
The Cry Of My People | Impulse(MCA) | 9861488
Little,Steve | (dr)
Duke Ellington And His Orchestra
Planet Jazz:Johnny Hodges | Planet Jazz | 2152065-2
Lionel Hampton And His Orchestra
Planet Jazz:Big Bands | Planet Jazz | 2169649-2
Little,Wilbur | (b)
Duke Jordan Trio
Flight To Norway | Steeplechase | SCCD 31543
Tommy Flanagan Trio
Overseas | Original Jazz Classics | OJCCD 1033-2(P 7134)
Littleton,Jeff | (b)
Rickey Woodard Quartet
California Cooking No.2 | Candid | CCD 79762
Littman,Peter | (dr)
Chet Baker Quartet
Let's Get Lost: The Best Of Chet Baker Sings | Pacific Jazz | 792932-2
Chet Baker Quintet
Chet Baker & Crew | Pacific Jazz | 582671-2
Chet Baker Sextet
Chet Baker & Crew | Pacific Jazz | 582671-2
The Best Of Chet Baker Plays | Pacific Jazz | 797161-2
Lars Gullin And The Chet Baker Quartet
Lars Gullin 1955/56 Vol.1 | Dragon | DRCD 224
Litton,Martin | (p)
Clare Teal And Her Band
Orsino's Songs | Candid | CCD 79783
Marty Grosz And His Swinging Fools
Ring Dem Bells | Nagel-Heyer | CD 022
The Second Sampler | Nagel-Heyer | NHR SP 6
The Great British Jazz Band
A British Jazz Odyssey | Candid | CCD 79740
Littwold,Micke | (voc)
Viktoria Tolstoy With The Esbjörn Svensson Trio
Viktoria Tolstoy:White Russian | Blue Note | 821220-2
Litty,Joachim | (b-cl,cl,aswoodwinds)
Die Elefanten
Wasserwüste | Nabel Records:Jazz Network | CD 4634
Ute Kannenberg Quartet With Guests
Kannenberg On Purpose | Jazz Haus Musik | JHM 0109 CD
Livingston,Bob | (tb)
Singers Unlimited With Rob McConnell And The Boss Brass
The Singers Unlimited:Magic Voices | MPS | 539130-2
Livingston,Fud | (as,ts,cl,arrreeds)
Louis Armstrong With Jimmy Dorsey And His Orchestra
Louis Armstrong:Swing That Music | Laserlight | 36056
Swing Legends:Louis Armstrong | Nimbus Records | NI 2012
Livingstone,Annie | (voc)
Toshinori Kondo & Ima plus Guests
Human Market | JA & RO | JARO 4146-2
Livingstone,Ulysses | (el-g,gvoc)
JATP All Stars
The Complete Jazz At The Philharmonic On Verve 1944-1949 | Verve | 523893-2
Livstrand,Anita | (axatse,sogo,bells,rattle,voice,xyl)
Beng Berger Band
Bitter Funeral Beer | ECM | 1179
Llewellyn,Jack | (grh-g)
Arthur Young And Hatchett's Swingette
Grapelli Story | Verve | 515807-2
Quintet Du Hot Club De France
Grapelli Story | Verve | 515807-2
Verve Jazz Masters 38:Django Reinhardt | Verve | 516931-2
Django Reinhardt:Echoes Of France | Dreyfus Jazz Line | FDM 36726-2
Django Reinhardt:Souveniers | Dreyfus Jazz Line | FDM 36744-2
Stephane Grappelli And His Musicians
Grapelli Story | Verve | 515807-2
Stephane Grappelli Quartet
Grapelli Story | Verve | 515807-2
Lloyd,Charles | (fl,alto-fl,bass-fl,as,ts)
Cannonball Adderley Sextet
Ballads | Blue Note | 537563-2
Cannonball Adderley-Nat Adderley Sextet
The Best Of Cannonball Adderley:The Capitol Years | Capitol | 795482-2
Charles Lloyd Quartet
Fish Out Of Water | ECM | 1398
Notes From Big Sur | ECM | 1465(511999-2)
The Call | ECM | 1522(517719-2)
All My Relations | ECM | 1557
Canto | ECM | 1635(537345-2)
Voice In The Night | ECM | 1674(559445-2)
Charles Lloyd In Europe | Atlantic | 7567-80788-2
Atlantic Saxophones | Rhino | 8122-71256-2
Forest Flower:Charles Lloyd At Monterey | Atlantic | 8122-71746-2
Charles Lloyd Quintet
The Water Is Wide | ECM | 1734(549043-2)
Hyperion With Higgins | ECM | 1784(014000-2)
Lift Every Voice | ECM | 1832/33(018783-2)
Charles Lloyd Sextet
Lift Every Voice | ECM | 1832/33(018783-2)
Charles Lloyd-Billy Higgins
Which Way Is East | ECM | 1878/79(9811796)
Chico Hamilton Quintet
The Dealer | Impulse(MCA) | 547958-2
Chico Hamilton Sextet
The Dealer | Impulse(MCA) | 547958-2
Lloyd,Frank | (fr-h)
Dee Dee Bridgewater With Orchestra
Dear Ella | Verve | 539102-2
Lloyd,Ivor | (tp)
Louis Armstrong With Sy Oliver And His Orchestra
Satchmo Serenaders | Verve | 543792-2
Lloyd,Jerry | (tp)
Gerry Mulligan And His Orchestra
Mullenium | CBS | CK 65678
Lo,Ted | (keyboards,synthp)
Ron Carter Quartet
Songs For You | Milestone | MCD 47099-2
Lobligeois,Roland | (b)
Cat Anderson And His All Stars
Americans Swinging In Paris:Cat Anderson | EMI Records | 539658-2
Toots Thielemans Quartet
Jazz In Paris:Toots Thielemans-Blues Pour Flirter | EmArCy | 549403-2 PMS
Lobo,Edu | (gvoc)
Paul Desmond Quartet With The Don Sebesby Orchestra
From The Hot Afternoon | Verve | 543487-2
Loch,Heinz | (bs)
Art Van Damme Group
State Of Art | MPS | 841413-2
Locke,Abe | (saxts)
Buddy Guy Blues Band
Buddy Guy-The Complete Chess Studio Recordings | MCA | MCD 09337
Locke,Eddie | (dr,percvoc)
Coleman Hawkins Quartet
Verve Jazz Masters 43:Coleman Hawkins | Verve | 521856-2
Today And Now | Impulse(MCA) | 951184-2
The Roots Of Acid Jazz | Impulse(MCA) | IMP 12042
Jazz Dance | Original Jazz Classics | OJCCD 1002-2(1210890)
Sirius | Original Jazz Classics | OJCCD 861-2(2310707)
The Jazz Giants Play Rodgers & Hammerstein:My Favorite Things | Prestige | PCD 24223-2
Coleman Hawkins Septet
Desafinado | Impulse(MCA) | 951227-2
Coleman Hawkins Sextet
Desafinado | Impulse(MCA) | 951227-2
Lee Konitz Orchestra
The Art Of Saxophone | Laserlight | 24652
Roy Eldridge And The Jimmy Ryan All Stars
Jazz Dance | Original Jazz Classics | OJCCD 1002-2(1210890)
Little Jazz And The Jimmy Ryan All-Stars | Original Jazz Classics | OJCCD 1058-2(DRE 1001)
Roy Eldridge Septet
To Bags...With Love:Memorial Album | Pablo | 2310967-2
Roy Eldridge Sextet
Milt Jackson Birthday Celebration | Fantasy | FANCD 6079-2
Roy 'Little Jazz' Eldridge Quartet
The Complete Verve Roy Eldridge Studio Sessions | Verve | 9861278
Warren Vaché Quartet
What Is There To Say? | Nagel-Heyer | CD 056
Warren Vaché With Joe Puma
Blues Of Summer | Nagel-Heyer | NH 1011
Locke,Joe | (midi-vib,vib,keyboardsynth)
Barbara Dennerlein Group
Take Off | Verve | 527664-2
Junkanoo | Verve | 537122-2
Eric Alexander Quintet
Solid! | Milestone | MCD 9283-2
Freddy Cole With Band
A Circle Of Love | Fantasy | FCD 9674-2
To The End Of The Earth | Fantasy | FCD 9675-2
Le Grand Freddy:Freddy Cole Sings The Music Of Michel Legrand | Fantasy | FCD 9683-2
Gerard Presencer Group
Chasing Reality | ACT | 9422-2
Jimmy Scott With Band
Over The Rainbow | Milestone | MCD 9314-2
Moon Glow | Milestone | MCD 9332-2
Johannes Enders Quartet
Kyoto | Organic Music | ORGM 9726
Mingus Big Band 93
Nostalgia In Times Square | Dreyfus Jazz Line | FDM 36559-2
Ron Carter Quartet
Stardust | somethin'else | 537813-2
Ron Carter Quintet
Stardust | somethin'else | 537813-2
Steve Lampert Group
Venus Perplexed | Steeplechase | SCCD 31557
Locker,Richard | (cello)
A Band Of Friends
Wynton Marsalis Quartet With Strings | CBS | CK 68921
Ron Carter Group
Songs For You | Milestone | MCD 47099-2
Steve Kuhn With Strings
Promises Kept | ECM | 1815(0675222)
Lockert,James | (perc)
Johnny Hartman And His Orchestra
Unforgettable | Impulse(MCA) | IMP 11522
Lockwood Jr.,Robert | (12-string-g,vocg)
Otis Spann
Walking The Blues | Candid | CCD 79025
Otis Spann/Robert Lockwood Jr.
Otis Spann Is The Blues | Candid | CCD 79001
Lockwood,Didier | (as,v,mand,b,violectra,el-vv-solo)
Didier Lockwood Trio
Tribute To Stépane Grappelli | Dreyfus Jazz Line | FDM 36611-2
Richard Galliano Group
Laurita | Dreyfus Jazz Line | FDM 36572-9
Lockwood,John | (bel-b)
Deborah Henson-Conant Trio
'Round The Corner | Laika Records | LK 87-203
Joe Maneri Quartet
In Full Cry | ECM | 1617(537048-2)
Lockwood,Willy | (b)
Django Reinhardt And His Quintet
Peche Á La Mode-The Great Blue Star Sessions 1947/1953 | Verve | 835418-2
Django's Music
Peche Á La Mode-The Great Blue Star Sessions 1947/1953 | Verve | 835418-2
Lodice,Charlie | (dr)
Edmond Hall With The Ralph Sutton Group
Edmond Hall With The Ralph Sutton Group | Storyville | STCD 6052
Lodice,Don | (cl,b-cl,contra-b-cl,ts,bs,bass-sax)
Frank Sinatra With Orchestra
Planet Jazz:Frank Sinatra & Tommy Dorsey | Planet Jazz | 2152067-2
Tommy Dorsey And His Orchestra
Planet Jazz:Frank Sinatra & Tommy Dorsey | Planet Jazz | 2152067-2
Planet Jazz Sampler | Planet Jazz | 2152326-2
Planet Jazz:Tommy Dorsey | Planet Jazz | 2159972-2
Planet Jazz:Big Bands | Planet Jazz | 2169649-2
Planet Jazz:Male Jazz Vocalists | Planet Jazz | 2169657-2
Frank Sinatra And The Tommy Dorsey Orchestra | RCA | 2668701-2
Lodwig,Ray | (tp)
Hoagy Carmichael And His Orchestra
Planet Jazz:Bud Freeman | Planet Jazz | 2161240-2
Irving Mills And His Hotsy Totsy Gang
Jazz:The Essential Collection Vol.3 | IN+OUT Records | 78013-2
Loeb,Chuck | (el-g,keyboards,dr-programming,g)
Rolf Kühn And Friends
Affairs:Rolf Kühn & Friends | Intuition Records | INT 3211-2
Rolf Kühn Group
Internal Eyes | Intuition Records | INT 3328-2
Stan Getz Sextet
Billy Highstreet Samba | EmArCy | 838771-2
Steps Ahead
Modern Times | Elektra | 7559-60351-2
Till Brönner Group
Chattin' With Chet | Verve | 157534-2
Love | Verve | 559058-2
Loef,Rick E. | (paintbrushes,pencilsharper,percil)
Kölner Saxophon Mafia With Rick E. Loef
Kölner Saxophon Mafia Proudly Presents | Jazz Haus Musik | JHM 0046 CD

Loeffler,Tschirglo | (g)
Bireli Lagrene Ensemble
Bireli Swing '81 | Jazzpoint | JP 1009 CD
Routes To Django & Bireli Swing '81 | Jazzpoint | JP 1055 CD
Routs To Django-Live At The 'Krokodil' | Jazzpoint | JP 1056 CD
Bireli Lagrene Group
Bireli Lagrene 'Highlights' | Jazzpoint | JP 1027 CD
Bireli Lagrene Quartet
A' Portrait Of Jan Jankeje | Jazzpoint | JP 1054 CD

Löfcrantz,Johan | (dr)
Agneta Baumann And Her Quartet
Comes Love... | Touché Music | TMcCD 011
Arne Domnerus Quartet
Sugar Fingers | Phontastic | NCD 8831
Arne Domnerus Quintet
Sugar Fingers | Phontastic | NCD 8831
Jan Lundgren Trio
Sugar Fingers | Phontastic | NCD 8831
Ulf Adaker Quartet
Reflections | Touché Music | TMcCD 016

Loft Line |
Loft Line
Source | Laika Records | 35101122

Lofton,Lawrence 'Tricky' | (tb)
Richard 'Groove' Holmes Sextet
Somethin' Special | Pacific Jazz | 855452-2

Logan,Alan | (p)
Terry Gibbs Octet
Jewis Melodies In Jazztime | Mercury | 589673-2

Logan,Giuseppi | (fl,b-cl,as,cl,ts,pakistani-oboe)
Roswell Rudd Sextet
Mixed | Impulse(MCA) | IMP 12702

Logan,Steve | (b,el-b,vocvoice)
Michel Petrucciani Quintet
Michel Petrucciani Live | Blue Note | 780589-2

Logerot,Stephane | (b)
Richard Galliano Septet
Piazzolla Forever | Dreyfus Jazz Line | FDM 36642-2

Loh,Jens | (b)
Arnulf Ochs Group
In The Mean Time | Jazz 'n' Arts Records | JNA 1202
Couch Ensemble
Winnetou | Jazz 'n' Arts Records | JNA 1503
Ulli Jünemann-Morton Ginnerup European Jazz Project
The Exhibition | Edition Collage | EC 518-2

Lohfink,Charly | (tb)
Heiner Franz' Swing Connection
Heiner Franz' Swing Connection | Jardis Records | JRCD 9817

Löhr,Sweet Bernhard | (loops)
Nils Landgren First Unit And Guests
Nils Landgren-The First Unit | ACT | 9292-2

Löhrer,Klaus | (b-tb,tubatb)
Copenhagen Art Ensemble
Shape To Twelve | dacapo | DCCD 9430
Angels' Share | dacapo | DCCD 9452
Jens Winther And The Danish Radio Jazz Orchestra
Angels | dacapo | DCCD 9442
Marilyn Mazur With Ars Nova And The Copenhagen Art Ensemble
Jordsange | dacapo | DCCD 9454
The Danish Radio Jazz Orchestra
Nice Work | dacapo | DCCD 9446
The Orchestra
New Skies | dacapo | DCCD 9463

Lokke,Birgit | (perc)
Kim Kristensen
Pulse Of Time | dacapo | DCCD 9435

Lokken,Herwin | (tp)
Landes Jugend Jazz Orchester Hessen
Touch Of Lips | hr music.de | hrmj 004-01 CD

Loli,Philippe | (g)
John McLaughlin Group
The Promise | Verve | 529828-2
John McLaughlin With The Aighette Quartet And Yan Marez
Time Remembered:John McLaughlin Plays Bill Evans | Verve | 519861-2

Lomask,Milt | (v)
Billie Holiday With The Ray Ellis Orchestra
Lady In Satin | CBS | CK 65144
Charlie Parker With Strings
Verve Jazz Masters 28:Charlie Parker Plays Standards | Verve | 521854-2
Charlie Parker With Strings:The Master Takes | Verve | 523984-2
Bird: The Complete Charlie Parker On Verve | Verve | 837141-2

Lombardi,Clyde | (bg)
Roy Eldridge And His Orchestra
The Complete Verve Roy Eldridge Studio Sessions | Verve | 9861278
Zoot Sims Quartet
Zoot Sims Quartets | Original Jazz Classics | OJCCD 242-2(P 7026)

Lomhoft,Aviaja | (vocvoice-samples)
Kim Kristensen
Pulse Of Time | dacapo | DCCD 9435

London Brass |
John Surman-Jack DeJohnette With The London Brass
Printed In Germany | ECM | 1802(017065-2)

London Mozart Players,The |
World Quintet With The London Mozart Players
World Quintet | TipToe | TIP-888843 2
World Quintet With The London Mozart Players And Herbert Grönemeyer
World Quintet | TipToe | TIP-888843 2

London Orchestra,The |
Pat Metheny Group With Orchestra
Secret Story | Geffen Records | GED 24468

London Philharmonia Orchestra,The |
Lalo Schifrin Trio With The London Philharmonic
Jazz Meets The Symphony | East-West | 4509-92004-2

London Studio Symphony Orchestra,The |
Laura Fygi With Band
Bewitched | Verve | 514724-2

London Symphony Orchestra,The |
Mahavishnu Orchestra
Apocalypse | CBS | 467092-2
Michael Mantler Quintet With The London Symphony Orchestra
Something There | Watt | 13

London,Art | (voc)
Peggy Lee With The Benny Goodman Orchestra
Peggy Lee & Benny Goodman:The Complete Recordings 1941-1947 | CBS | C2K 65686

London,Julie | (voc)
Julie London With Orchestra
Misty Blue:Sweet Sisters Swing Songs Of Sorrow And Sadness | Blue Note | 521151-2
Julie London With Pete King And His Orchestra
About The Blues/London By Night | Capitol | 535208-2
Julie London With Russ Garcia And His Orchestra
About The Blues/London By Night | Capitol | 535208-2

Long,Pete | (cl,as,ldts)
Itchy Fingers
Full English Breakfast | Enja | ENJ-7085 2

Longhi,Luis | (bandoneon)
Tangata Rea
Tango Alla Baila | Winter&Winter | 910025-2

Longnon,Guy | (tbtp)
Milton Mezz Mezzrow Sextet
Americans Swinging In Paris:Mezz Mezzrow | EMI Records | 539660-2
Sidney Bechet All Stars
Planet Jazz:Sidney Bechet | Planet Jazz | 2152063-2
Planet Jazz Sampler | Planet Jazz | 2152326-2
Sidney Bechet With Claude Luter And His Orchestra
Planet Jazz:Sidney Bechet | Planet Jazz | 2152063-2
Sidney Bechet With Michel Attenoux And His Orchestra
Planet Jazz:Sidney Bechet | Planet Jazz | 2152063-2

Longo,Alessandra Giura | (fl)
Paolo Fresu-Furio Di Castri Quintet
Evening Song | Owl Records | 014733-2

Longo,Michael | (keyboards,synthp)
Dizzy Gillespie Quintet
Swing Low, Sweet Cadillac | Impulse(MCA) | 951178-2
The Roots Of Acid Jazz | Impulse(MCA) | IMP 12042
Lee Konitz Orchestra
The Art Of Saxophone | Laserlight | 24652

Longshaw,Fred | (harmoniump)
Bessie Smith And Her Band
Jazz:The Essential Collection Vol.1 | IN+OUT Records | 78011-2
Bessie Smith With Louis Armstrong And Fred Longshaw
Jazz:The Essential Collection Vol.1 | IN+OUT Records | 78011-2

Longsworth,Eric | (el-cello)
Marc Johnson-Eric Longsworth
If Trees Could Fly | Intuition Records | INT 3228-2

Lookofsky,Harry | (tenor-v,v,concertmaster,volaviola)
Ben Webster With Orchestra And Strings
Music For Loving:Ben Webster With Strings | Verve | 527774-2
Ultimate Ben Webster selected by James Carter | Verve | 557537-2
Coleman Hawkins With Billy Byers And His Orchestra
The Hawk In Hi-Fi | RCA | 2663842-2
Freddie Hubbard Orchestra
The Body And The Soul | Impulse(MCA) | 951183-2
Gil Evans Orchestra
Verve Jazz Masters 23:Gil Evans | Verve | 521860-2
The Individualism Of Gil Evans | Verve | 833804-2
Grover Washington Jr. Orchestra
Inside Moves | Elektra | 7559-60318-2
Jazzrock-Anthology Vol.3:Fusion | Zounds | CD 27100555
Les McCann Group
Another Beginning | Atlantic | 7567-80790-2
Louis Armstrong And His Friends
Planet Jazz:Louis Armstrong | Planet Jazz | 2152052-2
Planet Jazz Sampler | Planet Jazz | 2152326-2
Louis Armstrong And His Friends | Bluebird | 2663961-2
Lucy Reed With Orchestra
This Is Lucy Reed | Original Jazz Classics | OJCCD 1943-2(F 3243)
Nina Simone And Orchestra
Baltimore | Epic | 476906-2
Sarah Vaughan With Orchestra
!Viva! Vaughan | Mercury | 549374-2
Sarah Vaughan Sings The Mancini Songbook | Verve | 558401-2
Wes Montgomery Quartet With The Claus Ogerman Orchestra
Tequila | Verve | 547769-2
Wes Montgomery Quintet With The Claus Ogerman Orchestra
The Antonio Carlos Jobim Songbook | Verve | 525472-2
Talkin' Jazz:Roots Of Acid Jazz | Verve | 529580-2
Tequila | Verve | 547769-2
Wes Montgomery Trio With The Claus Ogerman Orchestra
Tequila | Verve | 547769-2
Wes Montgomery With The Claus Ogerman Orchestra
Verve Jazz Masters 14:Wes Montgomery | Verve | 519826-2
Wes Montgomery With The Don Sebesky Orchestra
Verve Jazz Masters 14:Wes Montgomery | Verve | 519826-2
Talkin' Jazz:Roots Of Acid Jazz | Verve | 529580-2
Bumpin' | Verve | 539062-2
Wes Montgomery With The Jimmy Jones Orchestra
Wes Montgomery-The Complete Riverside Recordings | Riverside | 12 RCD 4408-2
The Jazz Giants Play Rodgers & Hart:Blue Moon | Prestige | PCD 24205-2

Loos,Wolfgang | (cello,el-p,org,keyboardslinn-dr)
Jorge Degas-Wolfgang Loos
Cantar A Vida | Traumton Records | 4446-2

Looser,Barbara | (cello)
HR Big Band With Marjorie Barnes And Frits Landesbergen And Strings
Swinging Christmas | hr music.de | hrmj 012-02 CD

Loper,Charles | (tb)
Al Jarreau With Band
Jarreau | i.e. Music | 557847-2
Diane Schuur And Her Band
The Best Of Diane Schuur | GRP | GRP 98882
Diane Schuur With Orchestra
The Best Of Diane Schuur | GRP | GRP 98882
The Quincy Jones-Sammy Nestico Orchestra
Basie & Beyond | Warner | 9362-47792-2

Lopez,Cesar | (as,saxss)
Irakere
Yemayá | Blue Note | 498239-2

Lopez,Charlie | (tb)
Vic Lewis West Coast All Stars
Vic Lewis Presenting A Celebration Of Contemporary West Coast Jazz | Candid | CCD 79711/12

Lopez,Israel 'Cachao' | (b)
Bebo Valdés Trio
El Arte Del Sabor | Blue Note | 535193-2
Bebo Valdés Trio With Paquito D'Rivera
El Arte Del Sabor | Blue Note | 535193-2

Lopez,Leslie | (b)
Conexion Latina
Mambo 2000 | Enja | ENJ-7055 2
La Conexión | Enja | ENJ-9065 2

Lopez,Manuel | (g,perctb)
Christian Willisohn Group
Blues On The World | Blues Beacon | BLU-1025 2

Lopez,Paul | (tp)
Jack Costanzo Group
Latin Fever:The Wild Rhythms Of Jack Costanza | Capitol | 590955-2

Lopez,Tommy | (congas,drperc)
Art Blakey And The Afrocuban Boys
Les Liaisons Dangereuses(Original Soundtrack) | Fontana | 812017-2
Cal Tjader's Orchestra
Talkin Verve/Roots Of Acid Jazz:Cal Tjader | Verve | 531562-2

LoPinto,Frank | (tp)
Tito Puente Orchestra
Planet Jazz:Tito Puente | Planet Jazz | 2165369-2

Lopo,Angela | (agogovoice)
Pata Masters
Pata-Bahia | Pata Musik | PATA 11 CD

Lorden,Herb | (as,clsax)
Harry James And His Orchestra
Trumpet Blues:The Best Of Harry James | Capitol | 521224-2

Lorentsen,Sue | (v)
Jim Snidero Quartet With Strings
Strings | Milestone | MCD 9326-2

Lorenz,Hans-Dieter | (bel-b)
Ullmann-Willers-Schäuble-Lorenz
Out To Lunch | Nabel Records:Jazz Network | CD 4623

Lorenz,Irene | (voc)
Franck Band
Dufte | Jazz Haus Musik | JHM 0054 CD
Kölner Saxophon Mafia With Irene Lorenz
Kölner Saxophon Mafia Proudly Presents | Jazz Haus Musik | JHM 0046 CD
Wollie Kaiser Timeghost
New Traces For Old Aces | Jazz Haus Musik | JHM 0102 CD

Lorenz,Marta | (fl)
Moments Quartet
Original Moments | Fresh Sound Records | FSNT 052 CD

Loriers,Natalie | (p)
Toots Thielemans Quartet
Toots Thielemans:The Live Takes Vol.1 | IN+OUT Records | 77041-2

Los Jovenes Flamencos |
Los Jovenes Flamencos
Jazzpana | ACT | 9212-2
Los Jovenes Flamencos With The WDR Big Band And Guests
Jazzpana | ACT | 9212-2

Lossing,Russ | (p)
Loren Stillman Quartet
How Swee It Is | Nagel-Heyer | CD 2031
Unit X
Rated X | Timescrapper | TSCR 9618

Lott,Carl | (dr)
Bobby Bryant Orchestra
Deep Blue-The United States Of Mind | Blue Note | 521152-2

Lott,Sinclair | (drfr-h)
Freddie Hubbard Quintet
Live At The Northsea Jazz Festival | Pablo | 2620113-2
Peggy Lee With The Benny Goodman Orchestra
Peggy Lee & Benny Goodman:The Complete Recordings 1941-1947 | CBS | C2K 65686
Peggy Lee With The Quincy Jones Orchestra
Blues Cross Country | Capitol | 520088-2

Lottermann,Stefan | (tbel-tb)
Blue Room Ensemble
Solitude | Foolish Music | FM 211993
Heinz Sauer Quintet
Lost Ends:Live at Alte Oper Frankfurt | free flow music | ffm 0594
Jan Von Klewitz Quintet
Bonehenge Suite | Jazz Haus Musik | JHM 0078 CD
Jazzensemble Des Hessischen Rundfunks
Atmosphering Conditions Permitting | ECM | 1549/50
NDR Big Band
The Theatre Of Kurt Weil | ACT | 9234-2
Oscar Brown Jr. with The NDR Big Band
Live Every Minute | Minor Music | 801071
Transalpin Express Orchestra
Some Other Tapes | Fish Music | FM 009/10 CD
Wollie Kaiser Timeghost
Post Art Core | Jazz Haus Musik | JHM 0077 CD

Lotz Of Music |
Lotz Of Music
Puasong Daffriek | Laika Records | LK 94-054

Lotz,Mark Alban | (fl,alto-fl,b-fl,piccolo,didjeridoo)
Mark Alban Lotz/Tjitze Anne Vogel
Mostly Harmless... | Edition Collage | EC 470-2

Loughbrough,Bill | (chromatic-tympani)
Chet Baker Sextet
Chet Baker & Crew | Pacific Jazz | 582671-2
The Best Of Chet Baker Plays | Pacific Jazz | 797161-2

Loughlan,Col | (clas)
Grace Knight With Orchestra
Come In Spinner | Intuition Records | INT 3052-2
Vince Jones With Orchestra
Come In Spinner | Intuition Records | INT 3052-2

Louis,Elmer | (congas,maracas,perc,bongos,cashishi)
Passport
Ataraxia | Atlantic | 2292-42148-2

Louis,Joe Hill | (dr,g,b,perc,bass-dr,harm,vochi-hat)
Joe Hill Louis
Joe Hill Louis: The Be-Bop Boy | Bear Family Records | BCD 15524 AH
Joe Hill Louis Band
Joe Hill Louis: The Be-Bop Boy | Bear Family Records | BCD 15524 AH
Mose Vinson Band
Joe Hill Louis: The Be-Bop Boy | Bear Family Records | BCD 15524 AH
Walter Horton Band
Joe Hill Louis: The Be-Bop Boy | Bear Family Records | BCD 15524 AH

Louis,Roy | (b,perc,voc,g,g-synth,mandoline)
Passport
Ataraxia | Atlantic | 2292-42148-2
Iguacu | Atlantic | 2292-46031-2

Louis,Yvonne | (voc)
Yvonne Louis With The Orchestra Vola
Jazz In Paris:Django Reinhardt-Django Et Compagnie | EmArCy | 549241-2 PMS

Louisiana Red | (dobro,voc,el-g,gharm)
Champion Jack Dupree
Champion Jack Dupree | Storyville | 4960383

Louisiana Stompers,The |
The Lousiana Stompers
Jazz:The Essential Collection Vol.1 | IN+OUT Records | 78011-2

Louisiana Sugar Babes |
Louisiana Sugar Babes
Planet Jazz:Jazz Trumpet | Planet Jazz | 2169654-2

Louiss,Eddie | (org,keyboards,p,vocvib)
Daniel Humair Soultet
Jazz In Paris | EmArCy | 548793-2
Jean-Luc Ponty Quartet
Jazz In Paris:Jean-Luc Ponty-Jazz Long Playing | EmArCy | 548150-2 PMS
Jean-Luc Ponty Quintet
Jazz In Paris:Jean-Luc Ponty-Jazz Long Playing | EmArCy | 548150-2 PMS
Les Double Six
Les Double Six | RCA | 2164314-2
Stan Getz Quartet
Stan Gotz In Europe | Laserlight | 24657
Stan Getz Highlights:The Best Of The Verve Years Vol.2 | Verve | 517330-2
Verve Jazz Masters 8:Stan Getz | Verve | 519823-2
Stan Getz Highlights | Verve | 847430-2

Lounge Lizards,The |
Lounge Lizards
Berlin 1991 Part 1 | Intuition Records | INT 2044-2
Live In Berlin 1991-Vol.2 | Intuition Records | INT 2055-2

Loup,Thomas | (tb)
Harry Allen And Randy Sandke Meets The RIAS Big Band Berlin
The Music Of The Trumpet Kings | Nagel-Heyer | CD 037

Lourau,Julien | (ssts)
Abbey Lincoln With Her Band
Who Used To Dance | Verve | 533559-2
Abbey Lincoln With The Rodney Kendrick Trio And Guests
A Turtle's Dream | Verve | 527382-2

Lourie,Vic | (clavesperc)
Louis Jordan And His Tympany Five
Louis Jordan-Let The Good Times Roll: The Complete Decca Recordings 1938-1954 | Bear Family Records | BCD 15557 IH

Louro,Vanja | (cello)
Jim Hall Jazzpar Quartet +4
Jazzpar 98 | Storyville | STCD 4230
Jim Hall With The Zapolski Quartet
Jazzpar 98 | Storyville | STCD 4230
The Crossover Ensemble With The Zapolski Quartet
Helios Suite | dacapo | DCCD 9459

Loussier,Jacques | (porg)
Jacques Loussier Trio
Play Bach No.1 | Decca | 157561-2
Play Bach No.2 | Decca | 157562-2
Play Bach No.3 | Decca | 157892-2
Play Bach No.4 | Decca | 157893-2
Play Bach No.5 | Decca | 159194-2
Play Bach Aux Champs-Élyssées | Decca | 159203-2
The Best Of Play Bach | Philips | 824664-2

Lovano,Joe | (alto-cl,as,ss,ts,c-melody-sax,bells)
Abbey Lincoln And Her Trio With Guests
Over The Years | Verve | 549101-2
Charlie Haden And The Liberation Music Orchestra
The Montreal Tapes:Liberation Music Orchestra | Verve | 527469-2
Cyrus Chestnut Trio With James Carter And Joe Lovano
Cyrus Chestnut | Atlantic | 7567-83140-2
Cyrus Chestnut Trio With Joe Lovano

INTERPRETENVERZEICHNIS

Cyrus Chestnut | Atlantic | 7567-83140-2
Flip Phillips Septet
Swing Is The Thing | Verve | 543477-2
Flip Phillips Sextet
Swing Is The Thing | Verve | 543477-2
James Emery Quartet
Fourth World | Between The Lines | btl 020(Efa 10190-2)
Joe Lovano Nonet
On This Day At The Vanguard | Blue Note | 590950-2
Joe Lovano Orchestra
Blue Note Plays Gershwin | Blue Note | 520808-2
Joe Lovano Quartet
From The Soul | Blue Note | 798636-2
Live At The Village Vanguard | Blue Note | 829125-2
Joe Lovano Sextet
Tenor Legacy | Blue Note | 827014-2
Joe Lovano Trio
Trio Fascination | Blue Note | 833114-2
Joe Lovano-Aldo Romano
Ten Tales | Owl Records | 018350-2
Joe Lovano-Gonzalo Rubalcaba
Flying Colors | Blue Note | 856092-2
Joe Lovano-Greg Osby Quintet
Friendly Fire | Blue Note | 499125-2
Johannes Mössinger New York Trio with Joe Lovano
Monk's Corner | double moon | DMCHR 71032
John Abercrombie Sextet
Open Land | ECM | 1683(557652-2)
John Scofield Quartet
What We Do | Blue Note | 799586-2
Pat Martino Quintet
Think Tank | Blue Note | 592009-2
Paul Motian Band
Psalm | ECM | 1222
Paul Motian Quartet
Monk In Motian | JMT Edition | 919020-2
Paul Motian On Broadway Vol.1 | JMT Edition | 919029-2
Paul Motian Trio
It Should've Happened A Long Time Ago | ECM | 1283
Sound Of Love | Winter&Winter | 910008-2
Monk In Motian | JMT Edition | 919020-2
Ray Barretto Orchestra
Portraits In Jazz And Clave | RCA | 2168452-2
Scolohofo
Oh! | Blue Note | 542081-2
Steve Swallow Group
Real Book | Watt | XtraWatt/7(521637-2)
Tom Harrell Quintet
Form | Contemporary | CCD 14059-2
Visions | Contemporary | CCD 14063-2
Sail Away | Original Jazz Classics | OJCCD 1095-2(C- 14054-2)
Tom Harrell Sextet
Visions | Contemporary | CCD 14063-2
Woody Herman And His Orchestra
Verve Jazz Masters 54:Woody Herman | Verve | 529903-2
Woody Herman's Thundering Herd
Planet Jazz:Jazz Saxophone | Planet Jazz | 2169653-2

Lovasz,Iren | (voc)
Ferenc Snétberger Trio
Obsession | TipToe | TIP-888834 2

Love,Geoff | (arr,condtb)
Mel Tormé With The Geoff Love Orchestra
My Kind Of Music | Verve | 543795-2

Love,Preston | (as)
Count Basie And His Orchestra
Planet Jazz:Count Basie | Planet Jazz | 2152068-2
Planet Jazz Sampler | Planet Jazz | 2152326-2
Planet Jazz:Jimmy Rushing | RCA | 2165371-2
Planet Jazz:Jazz Greatest Hits | Planet Jazz | 2169648-2
Planet Jazz:Big Bands | Planet Jazz | 2169649-2
Jazz:The Essential Collection Vol.3 | IN+OUT Records | 78013-2

Lovelace,Jimmy | (dr,bellsstell-dr)
George Benson Quartet
It's Uptown | CBS | 502469-2
The George Benson Cookbook | CBS | 502470-2
Tony Scott Group
Tony Scott | Verve | 9861063
Tony Scott Trio
Tony Scott | Verve | 9861063

Lovelle,Herbie | (dr)
(Little)Jimmy Scott With The Lucky Thompson Orchestra
Everybody's Somebody's Fool | Decca | 050669-2
Art Farmer Quartet
Early Art | Original Jazz Classics | OJCCD 880-2(NJ 8258)
The Jazz Giants Play Sammy Cahn:It's Magic | Prestige | PCD 24226-2
Bud Freeman All Stars
The Bud Freeman All-Star Sessions | Prestige | PRCD 24286-2
Jimmy Smith With Orchestra
Jimmy Smith-Talkin' Verve | Verve | 531563-2
Jimmy Smith With The Claus Ogerman Orchestra
Verve Jazz Masters 29:Jimmy Smith | Verve | 521855-2
Lightnin' Hopkins
Going Away | Original Blues Classics | OBCCD 522-2(BV 1073)
Rusty Bryant Quintet
Rusty Bryant Returns | Original Jazz Classics | OJCCD 331-2(P 7626)

Lovens,Paul | (dr,cymbals,singing-saw)
Alfred 23 Harth Group
Sweet Paris | free flow music | ffm 0291
Jazzensemble Des Hessischen Rundfunks
Atmosphering Conditions Permitting | ECM | 1549/50

Lovett,Leroy | (p,celestevoc)
Harry Carney And His Orchestra With Strings
Music For Loving:Ben Webster With Strings | Verve | 527774-2
Johnny Hodges And His Band
Verve Jazz Masters 35:Johnny Hodges | Verve | 521857-2
Johnny Hodges Orchestra
Highlights From The Duke Ellington Centennial Edition | RCA | 2663672-2
Lawrence Brown Quintet
Slide Trombone | Verve | 559930-2

Loving,Keith | (g)
Gil Evans Orchestra
PLay The Music Of Jimi Hendrix | RCA | 2663872-2

Loving,Tamiko | (voc)
Les McCann Group
Another Beginning | Atlantic | 7567-80790-2

Lovino,Simone | (fr-h)
Banda Cittá Ruvo Di Puglia
La Banda/Banda And Jazz | Enja | ENJ-9326 2

Lovitt,Lester 'Les' | (tpfl-h)
Herbie Hancock Group With String Quartet,Woodwinds And Brass
Herbie Hancock The New Standards | Verve | 527715-2
Herbie Hancock Group With Woodwinds And Brass
Herbie Hancock The New Standards | Verve | 527715-2

Lowe,Bill | (b-tb,tubatb)
Bill Lowe/Philippe Crettien Quintet
Sunday Train | Konnex Records | KCD 5051

Lowe,Curtis | (bsts)
(Little)Jimmy Scott With The Lionel Hampton Orchestra
Everybody's Somebody's Fool | Decca | 050669-2
Johnny Otis And His Orchestra
Verve Jazz Masters 43:Ben Webster | Verve | 525431-2
Lionel Hampton And His Orchestra
Planet Jazz:Lionel Hampton | Planet Jazz | 2152059-2
Lionel Hampton:Flying Home | Dreyfus Jazz Line | FDM 36735-2
Lionel Hampton Orchestra
The Big Bands Vol.1.The Snader Telescriptions | Storyville | 4960043

Lowe,Leroy | (drperc)
Kjell Jansson Quartet
Back From Where We Came | Touché Music | TMcCD 009
Kjell Jansson Quintet
Back From Where We Came | Touché Music | TMcCD 009

Lowe,Mundell | (g,arrg-solo)
Ben Webster Septet
The Soul Of Ben Webster | Verve | 527475-2
Benny Carter And His Orchestra
Further Definitions/Additions To Further Definotions | Impulse(MCA) | 951229-2
Billie Holiday With The Bobby Tucker Quartet
Billie's Love Songs | Nimbus Records | NI 2000
Blossom Dearie Quartet
Verve Jazz Masters 51:Blossom Dearie | Verve | 529906-2
Carmen McRae With Orchestra
Birds Of A Feather | Decca | 589515-2
Carmen McRae With The Ralph Burns Orchestra
Birds Of A Feather | Decca | 589515-2
Ella Fitzgerald With The Bill Doggett Orchestra
Ella Fitzgerald-First Lady Of Song | Verve | 517898-2
Rhythm Is My Business | Verve | 559513-2
Jimmy Forrest With The Oliver Nelson Orchestra
Soul Street | Original Jazz Classics | OJCCD 987-2(NJ 8293)
Joe Williams With The Frank Hunter Orchestra
Planet Jazz:Joe Williams | Planet Jazz | 2165370-2
Johnny Hodges-Wild Bill Davis Sextet
Planet Jazz:Johnny Hodges | Planet Jazz | 2152065-2
Lena Horne With The Lennie Hayton Orchestra
Planet Jazz:Lena Horne | Planet Jazz | 2165373-2
Mundell Lowe And His All Stars
Planet Jazz:Ben Webster | RCA | 2165368-2
Mundell Lowe Quartet
A Grand Night For Swinging | Original Jazz Classics | OJCCD 1940-(RLP 238)
Mundell Lowe Quintet
Mundell's Moods | Nagel-Heyer | CD 065
A Grand Night For Swinging | Original Jazz Classics | OJCCD 1940-(RLP 238)
Quincy Jones And His Orchestra
Rahsaan/The Complete Mercury Recordings Of Roland Kirk | Mercury | 846630-2
Sarah Vaughan With George Treadwell And His Allstars
Sarah Vaughan:Lover Man | Dreyfus Jazz Line | FDM 36739-2
Sarah Vaughan With Mundell Lowe And George Duvivier
Ballads | Roulette | 537561-2
Jazz Profile | Blue Note | 823517-2
After Hours | Roulette | 855468-2
Sarah Vaughan With The Norman Leyden Orchestra
Sarah Vaughan:Lover Man | Dreyfus Jazz Line | FDM 36739-2

Lowe,Sam | (tparr)
Erskine Hawkins And His Orchestra
Planet Jazz:Big Bands | Planet Jazz | 2169649-2

Lowenstein,Hugo | (assax)
Tommy Dorsey And His Orchestra
Planet Jazz:Tommy Dorsey | Planet Jazz | 2159972-2

Löwenthal,André | (el-g)
Marty Hall Band
Who's Been Talkin'?s | Blues Beacon | BLU-1033 2

Lowenthal,Marque | (p)
Lyambiko And Her Trio
Out Of This Mood | Nagel-Heyer | CD 2021

Lowka,Didi 'D.D.' | (budu-dr)
Lisa Wahlandt & Mulo Francel And Their Fabulous Bossa Band
Bossa Nova Affair | Edition Collage | EC 534-2
Mind Games
Pretty Fonky | Edition Collage | EC 482-2
Mind Games Plays The Music Of Stan Getz & Astrud Gilberto | Edition Collage | EC 515-2
Wind Moments | Take Twelve On CD | TT 009-2
Mind Games With Claudio Roditi
Live | Edition Collage | EC 501-2
Vocal Moments | Take Twelve On CD | TT 008-2
Mind Games With Philip Catherine
Pretty Fonky | Edition Collage | EC 482-2
Tom Bennecke & Space Gurilla
Wind Moments | Take Twelve On CD | TT 009-2
William Galison-Mulo Franzl Group
Midnight Sun | Edition Collage | EC 508-2

Lowman,Annette | (voc)
Annette Lowman With Three Of A Kind, Fred Wesley And Rodney Jones
Brown Baby:A Tribute To Oscar Brown Jr. | Minor Music | 801061
Bruce Cox Quartet With Guests
Stick To It | Minor Music | 801055
Till Brönner Quintet With Annette Lowman
My Secret Love | Minor Music | 801051

Lowman,Kenneth | (bassoon)
Ella Fitzgerald With The Frank DeVol Orchestra
Get Happy! | Verve | 523321-2

Lowrey,Chuck | (voc)
Tommy Dorsey And His Orchestra
Frank Sinatra And The Tommy Dorsey Orchestra | RCA | 2668701-2

Lowry,Leonard | (as)
Coleman Hawkins And His Orchestra
Jazz:The Essential Collection Vol.3 | IN+OUT Records | 78013-2

Lowther,Henry | (tpfl-h)
John Surman-John Warren Group
The Brass Project | ECM | 1478
Kenny Wheeler Brass Ensemble
A Long Time Ago | ECM | 1691
Kenny Wheeler Ensemble
Muisc For Large & Small Ensembles | ECM | 1415/16

Lowther,Quentin | (tp)
Berlin Contemporary Jazz Orchestra
Berlin Contemporary Jazz Orchestra | ECM | 1409

Lozano,Rolando | (fl)
Cal Tjader Sextet
Black Hawk Nights | Fantasy | FCD 24755-2
Mongo Santamaria And His Band
Sabroso | Original Jazz Classics | OJCCD 281-2

Lozuppone,Leonatdo | (fl-h)
Banda Cittá Ruvo Di Puglia
La Banda/Banda And Jazz | Enja | ENJ-9326 2

Lubambo,Romero | (el-g,g,cavaquinhog-synth)
Dave Douglas Group
Dave Douglas Freak In | Bluebird | 2664008-2
James Carter Group
Chasin' The Gypsy | Atlantic | 7567-83304-2
Kenny Barron Group With Trio De Paz
Canta Brazil | EmArCy | 017993-2
Michel Petrucciani Group
Music | Blue Note | 792563-2

Lubat,Bernard | (drperc)
Stan Getz Quartet
Stan Getz In Europe | Laserlight | 24657
Stan Getz Highlights:The Best Of The Verve Years Vol.2 | Verve | 517330-2
Verve Jazz Masters 8:Stan Getz | Verve | 519823-2
Stan Getz Highlights | Verve | 847430-2
Swingle Singers
Jazz Sebastian Bach Vol.2 | Philips | 542553-2

Lubbock,Jeremy | (cond)
Pat Metheny Group With Orchestra
Secret Story | Geffen Records | GED 24468

Lube,Dan | (cellov)
Ella Fitzgerald With The Billy May Orchestra
The Best Of The Song Books:The Ballads | Verve | 521867-2
Ella Fitzgerald Sings The Harold Arlen Song Book | Verve | 589108-2
Ella Fitzgerald With The Frank DeVol Orchestra
Get Happy! | Verve | 523321-2
Ella Fitzgerald With The Marty Paich Orchestra
Get Happy! | Verve | 523321-2
Ella Fitzgerald With The Nelson Riddle Orchestra
The Best Of The Song Books:The Ballads | Verve | 521867-2
Love Songs:The Best Of The Song Books | Verve | 531762-2
Harry James And His Orchestra
Trumpet Blues:The Best Of Harry James | Capitol | 521224-2
Mel Tormé With The Russell Garcia Orchestra
Swingin' On The Moon | Verve | 511385-2
Phineas Newborn Jr. With Dennis Farnon And His Orchestra
While My Lady Sleeps | RCA | 2185157-2

Lübke,Peter | (dr)
Bireli Lagrene Group
Bireli Lagrene 'Highlights' | Jazzpoint | JP 1027 CD
Francis Coletta Trio + One
Cris De Balaines | IN+OUT Records | 77030-2
Jaco Pastorius Groups
Another Side Of Jaco Pastorius | Jazzpoint | JP 1064 CD
Jaco Pastorius Trio
Jaco Pastorius Broadway Blues & Theresa | Jazzpoint | JP 1053 CD
Jaco Pastorius Heavy'n Jazz & Stuttgart Aria | Jazzpoint | JP 1058 CD

Luboff,Abe | (b)
Ella Fitzgerald With The Frank DeVol Orchestra
Get Happy! | Verve | 523321-2

Luc,Sylvain | (gg-solo)
Sylvain Luc
Solo Ambre | Dreyfus Jazz Line | FDM 36650-2
Sylvain Luc-André Ceccarelli-Jean Marc Jafet
SUD | Dreyfus Jazz Line | FDM 36612-2
Sylvain Luc-Biréli Lagrène
Duet | Dreyfus Jazz Line | FDM 36604-2

Lucas,Al | (b,el-bg)
Coleman Hawkins With The Adrian Acea Trio
Coleman Hawkins At The Golden Circle | Dragon | DRCD 265
Duke Ellington And His Orchestra
Carnegie Hall Concert January 1946 | Prestige | 2PCD 24074-2
Ellington At Newport 1956(Complete) | CBS | CK 64932
Hot Lips Page And His Orchestra
Don Byas:Laura | Dreyfus Jazz Line | FDM 36714-2
James P.Johnson's Blue Note Jazzmen
The Blue Note Jazzmen | Blue Note | 821262-2
Leo Parker Sextet
True Blue | Blue Note | 534032-2

Lucas,Boudewijn | (bb-g)
Agog
Eat Time | Jazz Haus Musik | JHM 0072 CD

Lucas,Buddy | (bs,harmts)
George Benson Orchestra
Talkin' Verve:George Benson | Verve | 553780-2
George Benson With Orchestra
Verve Jazz Masters 21:George Benson | Verve | 521861-2
Jimmy Smith With The Oliver Nelson Orchestra
Verve Jazz Masters 29:Jimmy Smith | Verve | 521855-2
Jimmy Smith:Best Of The Verve Years | Verve | 527950-2
Nina Simone And Orchestra
Planet Jazz:Nina Simone | Planet Jazz | 2165372-2
Yusef Lateef Orchestra
The Blue Yusef Lateef | Rhino | 8122-73717-2

Lucas,Cedric | (g)
Miles Davis Group
In Concert | CBS | C2K 65140

Lucas,Clyde | (dr,tbvoc)
Wild Bill Davis Quartet
Live At Swiss Radio Studio Zürich | Jazz Connaisseur | JCCD 8701-2

Lucas,Maxwell | (bs)
Buddy Johnson And His Orchestra
Buddy And Ella Johnson 1953-1964 | Bear Family Records | BCD 15479 DH

Lucas,Moyes | (dr)
Diane Schuur With The Dave Grusin Orchestra
The Best Of Diane Schuur | GRP | GRP 98882

Lucas,Ray | (drcongas)
Bobby Timmons Trio
Bobby Timmons:The Prestige Trio Sessions | Prestige | PRCD 24277-2
George Benson Quartet
It's Uptown | CBS | 502469-2
King Curtis Band
King Curtis-Blow Man Blow | Bear Family Records | BCD 15670 CI
Stanley Turrentine And His Orchestra
The Lost Grooves | Blue Note | 831883-2

Lucas,Reggie | (g)
Miles Davis Group
Paris Jazz Concert:Miles Davis | Laserlight | 17445
Pangaea | CBS | 467087-2
Agharta | CBS | 467897-2
Dark Magus | CBS | C2K 65137
On The Corner | CBS | CK 63980

Lucht,Jim | (dr)
Lester Young And Earl Swope With The Bill Potts Trio
Lester Young In Washington,DC 1956:Vol.5 | Original Jazz Classics | OJCCD 993-2
Lester Young With The Bill Potts Trio
Lester Young In Washington,DC 1956:Vol.1 | Original Jazz Classics | OJCCD 782-2(2308219)
Lester Young In Washington,DC 1956:Vol.5 | Original Jazz Classics | OJCCD 993-2
The Jazz Giants Play Harry Warren:Lullaby Of Broadway | Prestige | PCD 24204-2

Luciani,Dante | (tb)
Maynard Ferguson And His Big Bop Nouveau Band
Maynard Ferguson '93-Footpath Café | Hot Shot Records | HSR 8312-2

Lucie,Lawrence | (bj,el-gg)
Coleman Hawkins All Star Octet
Planet Jazz:Coleman Hawkins | Planet Jazz | 2152055-2
Fletcher Henderson And His Orchestra
Jazz:The Essential Collection Vol.1 | IN+OUT Records | 78011-2
Jazz:The Essential Collection Vol.3 | IN+OUT Records | 78013-2
Jelly Roll Morton's New Orleans Jazzmen
Planet Jazz | Planet Jazz | 2169652-2
Planet Jazz:Male Jazz Vocalists | Planet Jazz | 2169657-2
Louis Armstrong And His Orchestra
Louis Armstrong:Swing That Music | Laserlight | 36056
Jazz:The Essential Collection Vol.2 | IN+OUT Records | 78012-2
Louis Armstrong:C'est Si Bon | Dreyfus Jazz Line | FDM 36730-2
Spike Hughes And His Negro Orchestra
Jazz:The Essential Collection Vol.3 | IN+OUT Records | 78013-2
Super Black Blues Band
Super Black Blues Vol.II | RCA | 2663874-2

Lucien,Jon | (narrationvoc)
Grover Washington Jr. Orchestra
Inside Moves | Elektra | 7559-60318-2
Weather Report
Mr. Gone | CBS | 468208-2

Lücker,Björn | (drperc)
Triocolor
Colours Of Ghana | ACT | 9285-2

Lüdemann,Hans | (keyboards,p,bechstein-v,birds)
Blaufrontal
Blaufrontal | Jazz Haus Musik | JHM 0037 CD
Blaufrontal With Hank Roberts & Mark Feldman
Bad Times Roll | Jazz Haus Musik | JHM 0061 CD
Dirk Raulf Group
Theater I (Bühnenmusik) | Poise | Poise 07
Gabriele Hasler-Hans Lüdemann-Andreas Willers plus Jörn Schipper
Familienglück | Foolish Music | FM 211097
Hans Lüdemann
The Natural Piano | Jazz Haus Musik | JHM 0075 CD
Hans Lüdemann Rism

Aph-o-Rism's | Jazz Haus Musik | JHM 0049 CD
Unitarism | Jazz Haus Musik | JHM 0067 CD
Hans Lüdemann Rism 7
FutuRISM | Jazz Haus Musik | JHM 0092/93 CD
Jazzensemble Des Hessischen Rundfunks
Atmosphering Conditions Permitting | ECM | 1549/50

Lüderitz,Rafi | (drp)
Hans Koller Trio
Relax With My Horns | MPS | 9813445

Lüdi,Werner | (as,bssax)
Lüdi-Öcal
The Bird Who Makes The Cloud Sing As He Drums It-Live At The Montreux Jazz Festival | Creative Works Records | CW CD 1019-1
Q4 Orchester Project
Lyon's Brood | Creative Works Records | CW CD 1018-3
Werner Lüdi-Burhan Öcal
Willisau And More Live | Creative Works Records | CW CD 1020-2

Ludin,Hakim | (perc)
Frank Kroll Quintet
Landscape | dml-records | CD 014

Ludolf,Jacques | (voc)
Pili-Pili
Stolen Moments | JA & RO | JARO 4159-2

Ludolf,Jasper | (voc)

Ludus Guitar Quartet |
Mahmoud Turkmani With The Ludus Guitar Quartet
Nuqta | TipToe | TIP-888835 2

Ludvigsen,Roger | (g,percdulcimer)
Nils Petter Molvaer Group
Khmer | ECM | 1560(537798-2)

Ludwig,Frank | (ts)
Ella Fitzgerald And Louis Armstrong With Sy Oliver And His Orchestra
Ella Fitzgerald:Mr.Paganini | Dreyfus Jazz Line | FDM 36741-2
Ella Fitzgerald With Sy Oliver And His Orchestra
Ella Fitzgerald:The Decca Years 1949-1954 | Decca | 050668-2
Louis Armstrong And Ella Fitzgerald With Sy Oliver's Orchestra
Louis Armstrong:C'est Si Bon | Dreyfus Jazz Line | FDM 36730-2

Ludwig,Gene | (org)
Plas Johnson-Red Holloway Quintet
Keep That Groove Going! | Milestone | MCD 9319-2

Ludwig,Thomas Lui | (dr)
Jazz Pistols
Special Treatment | Lipstick Records | LIP 8971-2

Lueers,Tammo | (g,lap-steel6-string-b)
Swim Two Birds
Sweet Reliet | Laika Records | 35101182
No Regrets | Laika Records | 35101342

Luening,Warren | (tpfl-h)
Diane Schuur With Orchestra
The Best Of Diane Schuur | GRP | GRP 98882
Singers Unlimited With Orchestra
The Singers Unlimited:Magic Voices | MPS | 539130-2
The Quincy Jones-Sammy Nestico Orchestra
Basie & Beyond | Warner | 9362-47792-2

Lugg,George | (tb)
Sidney Bechet's Blue Note Jazzmen
Sidney Bechet:Summertime | Dreyfus Jazz Line | FDM 36712-2

Lühning,Inga | (voc)
Inga Lühning With Trio
Lühning | Jazz Haus Musik | JHM 0111 CD
Lirico
Sussurro | Jazz Haus Musik | JHM 0129 CD

Lühr,Willi | (b)
Philippe Caillat Special Project
Melodic Travel | Laika Records | LK 689-012

Luis,Ingo | (b-tbtb)
Marcus Sukiennik Big Band
A Night In Tunisia Suite(7 Variationen über Dizzy Gillespie's 'A Night In Tunisia') | Jazz Haus Musik | ohne Nummer

Luley,Jan | (pkeyboards)
Jan Harrington And Friends
I Feel The Spirit | Nagel-Heyer | NHR SP 7

Lulic,Milan | (g)
Kevin Mahogany With The WDR Big Band And Guests
Pussy Cat Dues:The Music Of Charles Mingus | Enja | ENJ-9316 2

Lumholt,Aviaja | (voc)
Marilyn Mazur With Ars Nova And The Copenhagen Art Ensemble
Jordsange | dacapo | DCCD 9454

Lumia,Guy | (v,concertmasterviola)
Earl Klugh Group With Strings
Late Night Guitar | Blue Note | 498573-2

Lumpp,Andy | (el-p,synth,pp-solo)
Andy Lumpp
Piano Solo | Nabel Records:Jazz Network | CD 4646
Dreamin' Man | Nabel Records:Jazz Network | CD 4662
Andy Lumpp Trio
Ostara | Nabel Records:Jazz Network | CD 4682
Andy Lumpp Trio Feat. Andy Przybielski
Musica Ex Spiritu Sancto | Nabel Records:Jazz Network | CD 4694
Andy Lumpp Trio With Andy Przybielski
Music From Planet Earth | Nabel Records:Jazz Network | CD 4687
John Thomas & Lifeforce
Devil Dance | Nabel Records:Jazz Network | CD 4601
3000 Worlds | Nabel Records:Jazz Network | CD 4604
Lumpp-Read-Küttner Trio
Midnight Sun | Nabel Records:Jazz Network | CD 4612
Peter Weiss Orchestra
Personal Choice | Nabel Records:Jazz Network | CD 4669
Peter Weiss Quartet
Personal Choice | Nabel Records:Jazz Network | CD 4669

Lunceford,Jimmie | (arr,ld,as,cond,flsax)
Jimmy Lunceford And His Orchestra
Planet Jazz:Swing | Planet Jazz | 2169651-2
The Legends Of Swing | Laserlight | 24659

Lund,Bernt Simen | (cello)
Trygve Seim Group
Different Rivers | ECM | 1744(159521-2)

Lund,Flemming | (fl,alto-fl,bass-flpiccolo)
The Crossover Ensemble With The Zapolski Quartet
Helios Suite | dacapo | DCCD 9459

Lund,Havard | (b-clcl)
Trygve Seim Group
Different Rivers | ECM | 1744(159521-2)

Lund,Morten | (dr)
The Orchestra
New Skies | dacapo | DCCD 9463

Lund,Tom | (gvoc)
Silje Nergard Group with Strings
Nightwatch | EmArCy | 9865648

Lundberg,Jan Olov | (tb)
The Danish Radio Jazz Orchestra
This Train:The Danish Radio Jazz Orchestra Plays The Music Of Ray Pitts | dacapo | DCCD 9428

Lundberg,Ron | (dr)
Barney Kessel Quartet
Barney Kessel's Swingin' Party At Contemporary | Original Jazz Classics | OJCCD 1066-2(S 7613)
Mose Allison Trio
The Word From Mose | Atlantic | 8122-72394-2

Lundborg,Erik | (b)
Eje Thelin Group
Ejs Thelin 1966 With Barney Wilen | Dragon | DRCD 366

Lundeng,Susanne | (vvoc)
Susanne Lundeng Quartet
Waltz For The Red Fiddle | Laika Records | 35101402

Lundgaard,Jesper | (b)
Anders Lindskog Trio
Fine Together | Touché Music | TMcCD 010
Chet Baker Quartet
Chet Baker-The Legacy Vol.2:I Remember You | Enja | ENJ-9077 2
Duke Jordan Trio
Jazz Legends:Clark Terry-Duke Jordan | Storyville | 4960283
Eddie Lockjaw Davis Quartet
Jazz Legends:Eddie Lockjaw Davis Quartet Vol.1&2 | Storyville | 4960263
Jesper Lundgaard & MadsVinding
Two Basses | Touché Music | TMcCD 020
Phineas Newborn Jr. Trio
Tivoli Encounter | Storyville | STCD 8221
Simon Cato Spang-Hansen Quartet
Identified | dacapo | DCCD 9448
Svend Asmussen Quartet
Fit As A Fiddle | dacapo | DCCD 9429
Still Fiddling | Storyville | STCD 4252

Lundgren,Jan | (pp-solo)
Arne Domnerus Quartet
Sugar Fingers | Phontastic | NCD 8831
Arne Domnerus Quintet
Sugar Fingers | Phontastic | NCD 8831
Jan Lundgren Trio
Sugar Fingers | Phontastic | NCD 8831

Lundgren,Marten | (tp)
The Orchestra
New Skies | dacapo | DCCD 9463

Lundin,Ove | (p)
Irene Sjögren Group
Song For A Willow | Touché Music | TMcCD 015

Lundvig,Svend | (tp)
Stan Getz With Ib Glindemann And His Orchestra
Stan Getz In Europe | Laserlight | 24657
Stan Kenton With The Danish Radio Big Band
Stan Kenton With The Danish Radio Big Band | Storyville | STCD 8340

Lundy,Carmen | (arr,vocvoc-playback)
Fred Wesley Group
New Friends | Minor Music | 801016

Lundy,Curtis | (bld)
Eddie Lockjaw Davis-Johnny Griffin Quintet
Tough Tenors Back Again! | Storyville | STCD 8298

Lunsford,Carl | (bjvoc)
Turk Murphy And His Jazz Band
Atlantic Jazz: New Orleans | Atlantic | 7567-81700-2

Lurie,John | (ss,asvoice)
John Zorn Group
Spillane | Nonesuch | 7559-79172-2
Lounge Lizards
Berlin 1991 Part 1 | Intuition Records | INT 2044-2
Live In Berlin 1991-Vol.2 | Intuition Records | INT 2055-2

Lussier,René | (g)
Heiner Goebbels Group
Shadow/Landscape With Argonauts | ECM | 1480

Lustgarten,Alfred | (v)
Ben Webster With Strings
The Warm Moods-With Strings | Rhino | 8122-73721-2
Ella Fitzgerald With The Frank DeVol Orchestra
Get Happy! | Verve | 523321-2
Herbie Mann With The Frank DeVol Orchestra
Verve Jazz Masters 56:Herbie Mann | Verve | 529901-2
Phineas Newborn Jr. With Dennis Farnon And His Orchestra
While My Lady Sleeps | RCA | 2185157-2

Lustgarten,Edgar 'Ed' | (cello)
Ella Fitzgerald With The Billy May Orchestra
The Best Of The Song Books:The Ballads | Verve | 521867-2
Ella Fitzgerald Sings The Harold Arlen Song Book | Verve | 589108-2
Ella Fitzgerald With The Buddy Bregman Orchestra
The Best Of The Song Books:The Ballads | Verve | 521867-2
Love Songs:The Best Of The Song Books | Verve | 531762-2
Ella Fitzgerald Sings The Cole Porter Songbook | Verve | 537257-2
Ella Fitzgerald Sings The Rodgers And Hart Song Book | Verve | 537258-2
Ella Fitzgerald With The Nelson Riddle Orchestra
The Best Of The Song Books:The Ballads | Verve | 521867-2
Frank Sinatra With The Count Basie Orchestra
It Might As Well Be Spring | Reprise | 7599-27027-2
Herbie Mann With The Frank DeVol Orchestra
Verve Jazz Masters 56:Herbie Mann | Verve | 529901-2
Jerri Southern And The Dick Hazard Quartet
Misty Blue:Sweet Sisters Swing Songs Of Sorrow And Sadness | Blue Note | 521151-2
Pete Rugolo And His Orchestra
Thriller/Richard Diamon(Original Jazz Scores From 2 Classics TV Series) | Fresh Sound Records | FSCD 2015
Phineas Newborn Jr. With Dennis Farnon And His Orchestra
While My Lady Sleeps | RCA | 2185157-2
Roger Kellaway Cello Quartet With The A&M Symphony Orchestra
Roger Kellaway Cello Quartet | A&M Records | 9861062
Singers Unlimited With The Roger Kellaway Cello Quartet
The Singers Unlimited:Magic Voices | MPS | 539130-2

Lustrea,Bob | (tb)
Buddy Childers Big Band
Just Buddy's | Candid | CCD 79761

Lutcher,Nellie or Horace Henderson | (p)
Lena Horne With The Horace Henderson Orchestra
Planet Jazz:Lena Horne | Planet Jazz | 2165373-2

Luter,Claude | (clss)
Claude Luter Et Ses L'Orientais
Jazz In Paris:Sidney Bechet Et Claude Luther | EmArCy | 159821-2 PMS
Sidney Bechet With Claude Luter And His Orchestra
Planet Jazz:Sidney Bechet | Planet Jazz | 2152063-2
Sidney Bechet:Summertime | Dreyfus Jazz Line | FDM 36712-2

Luther,Bill | (tsbs)
Harry James And His Orchestra
The Legends Of Swing | Laserlight | 24659

Lüthi,Eva | (cello)
Abdullah Ibrahim Trio And A String Orchestra
African Suite | TipToe | TIP-888832 2
String Orchestra
African Suite | TipToe | TIP-888832 2

Lüthi,Thomas | (ssts)
Matthias Spillmann Septet
Something About Water | JHM Records | JHM 3620

Lutter,Andy | (pkeyboards)
Terra Brazil
Café Com Leite | art-mode-records | AMR 2101

Lutzeier,Michael | (bs)
Al Porcino Big Band
Al Porcino Big Band Live! | Organic Music | ORGM 9717
Dusko Goykovich Big Band
Balkan Connection | Enja | ENJ-9047 2
Michael Lutzeier Quartet
Music 4 Food | Jazz 4 Ever Records:Jazz Network | J4E 4739

Luxion,Dennis | (el-pp)
Monika Linges Quartet
Floating | Nabel Records:Jazz Network | CD 4607
Tuey Connell Group
Songs For Joy And Sadness | Minor Music | 801095

Luzio,Giuseppe | (fl-h)
Banda Città Ruvo Di Puglia
La Banda/Banda And Jazz | Enja | ENJ-9326 2

Lyambiko | (voc)
Lyambiko And Her Trio
Out Of This Mood | Nagel-Heyer | CD 2021

Lychou,Gunnar | (viola)
Michael Mantler Group
Songs And One Symphony | ECM | 1721
Mona Larsen And The Danish Radio Big Band Plus Soloists
Michael Mantler:Cerco Un Paese Innocente | ECM | 1556

Lydom,Sonnich | (accordeonharm)
ULG
Spring | Laika Records | 35101382

Lyle,Bobby | (el-p,synth,clavinet,keyboards,arr)
Al Jarreau With Band
Al Jarreau In London | i.e. Music | 557849-2
Bobby Lyle Group
The Journey | Atlantic | 7567-82138-2
Pianomagic | Atlantic | 7567-82346-2
Bobby Lyle Quintet
Jazzrock-Anthology Vol.3:Fusion | Zounds | CD 27100555
Willie Bobo Group
Jazzrock-Anthology Vol.3:Fusion | Zounds | CD 27100555

Lyn Murray Choir,The |
Louis Armstrong With The Lyn Murray Chorus
Louis And The Good Book | Verve | 549593-2

Lynch,Brian | (tpfl-h)
Art Blakey And The Jazz Messengers
The Art Of Jazz | IN+OUT Records | 77028-2
Dave Stryker Octet
Blue To The Bone III | Steeplechase | SCCD 31524
Donald Harrison Quintet
Free To Be | Impulse(MCA) | 951283-2
Donald Harrison Sextet
Free To Be | Impulse(MCA) | 951283-2
Herb Robertson Brass Ensemble
Shades Of Bud Powell | JMT Edition | 919019-2

Lynch,Carl | (bg)
George Benson And His Orchestra
Giblet Gravy | Verve | 543754-2
King Curtis Band
King Curtis-Blow Man Blow | Bear Family Records | BCD 15670 CI

Lynn,Ray | (tp)
Ella Fitzgerald With The Buddy Bregman Orchestra
Love Songs:The Best Of The Song Books | Verve | 531762-2
Ella Fitzgerald Sings The Rodgers And Hart Song Book | Verve | 537258-2

Lyons,Jimmy | (as,voicetp)
Cecil Taylor Sextet
A Blue Conception | Blue Note | 534254-2
Conquistador | Blue Note | 576749-2
Cecil Taylor Unit
Dark To Themselves | Enja | ENJ-2084 2
Mixed | Impulse(MCA) | IMP 12702
The Jazz Composer's Orchestra
Comminications | JCOA | 1001/2

Lysne,Geir | (compcond)
Geir Lysne Listening Ensemble
Korall | ACT | 9236-2
Aurora Borealis-Nordic Lights | ACT | 9406-2

Lytle,Hub | (cl,tssax)
Jack Teagarden And His Orchestra
Jazz:The Essential Collection Vol.3 | IN+OUT Records | 78013-2

Lytle,Johnny | (vib)
Johnny Lytle Quartet
Got That Feeling/Moon Child | Milestone | MCD 47093-2
Johnny Lytle Quintet
Got That Feeling/Moon Child | Milestone | MCD 47093-2
The Village Caller | Original Jazz Classics | OJCCD 110-2(R 9480)
Johnny Lytle Trio(Quartet)
Got That Feeling/Moon Child | Milestone | MCD 47093-2

Lytton,Paul | (dr,electronics,perccymbals)
Evan Parker Electro-Acoustic Ensemble
Toward The Margins | ECM | 1612(453514-2)
Drawn Inward | ECM | 1693
Memory/Vision | ECM | 1852(0381172)
Philipp Wachsmann-Paul Lytton
Some Other Season | ECM | 1662

Maass,Stephan | (perc)
Mind Games With Claudio Roditi
Live | Edition Collage | EC 501-2
Vocal Moments | Take Twelve On CD | TT 008-2

Maaß,Torsten | (tpfl-h)
HR Big Band With Marjorie Barnes And Frits Landesbergen
Swinging Christmas | hr music.de | hrmj 012-02 CD
Lee Konitz With The Ed Partyka Jazz Orchestra
Dreams And Realities | Laika Records | 35101642
NDR Big Band
NDR Big Band-Bravissimo | ACT | 9232-2

Mabern,Harold | (el-p,p,vocp-solo)
Archie Shepp Orchestra
The Cry Of My People | Impulse(MCA) | 9861488
Betty Carter And The Harold Mabern Trio
Misty Blue:Sweet Sisters Swing Songs Of Sorrow And Sadness | Blue Note | 521151-2
Eric Alexander Quartet
The First Milestone | Milestone | MCD 9302-2
The Second Milestone | Milestone | MCD 9315-2
Summit Meeting | Milestone | MCD 9322-2
Nightlife In Tokyo | Milestone | MCD 9330-2
Eric Alexander Quintet
The First Milestone | Milestone | MCD 9302-2
The Second Milestone | Milestone | MCD 9315-2
Summit Meeting | Milestone | MCD 9322-2
Frank Strozier Quartet
Long Night | Milestone | MCD 47095-2
Hank Mobley Quintet
Blue Bossa | Blue Note | 795590-2
Idris Muhammad Group
Jazzin' With The Soul Brothers | Fantasy | FANCD 6086-2
Lee Morgan Orchestra
The Last Sessin | Blue Note | 493401-2
Lee Morgan Quintet
The Sixth Sense | Blue Note | 522467-2
Live At The Lighthouse | Blue Note | 835228-2
Lee Morgan Sextet
Deep Blue-The United States Of Mind | Blue Note | 521152-2
Sonic Boom | Blue Note | 590414-2
Roland Kirk All Stars
Rahsaan/The Complete Mercury Recordings Of Roland Kirk | Mercury | 846630-2
Roland Kirk Quartet
Talkin' Verve-Roots Of Acid Jazz:Roland Kirk | Verve | 533101-2
Rahsaan/The Complete Mercury Recordings Of Roland Kirk | Mercury | 846630-2
Roland Kirk Sextet
Talkin' Verve-Roots Of Acid Jazz:Roland Kirk | Verve | 533101-2
Roland Kirk With The Benny Golson Orchestra
Rahsaan/The Complete Mercury Recordings Of Roland Kirk | Mercury | 846630-2

MacClausland,Lloyd | (perc)
Max Roach With The Boston Percussion Ensemble
Clifford Brown-Max Roach:Alone Together-The Best Of The Mercury Years | Verve | 526373-2

MacDonald,Anthony | (perc)
Grover Washington Jr. Orchestra
Inside Moves | Elektra | 7559-60318-2

MacDonald,Doug | (el-gg)
Buddy Childers Big Band
It's What Happening Now! | Candid | CCD 79749

MacDonald,John | (fr-h)
Jazzensemble Des Hessischen Rundfunks
Jazz Messe-Messe Für Unsere Zeit | hr music.de | hrmj 003-01 CD

MacDonald,Ralph | (perc,congascomputer-dr)
George Benson Group
Breezin' | Warner | 8122-76713-2
Grover Washington Jr. Orchestra

MacDonald,Ralph | (perc,congascomputer-dr) Bielefelder Katalog 544 Jazz • Ausgabe 2004 Mahones,Gildo

Inside Moves | Elektra | 7559-60318-2
Joe Henderson And His Orchestra
Joe Henderson:The Milestone Years | Milestone | 8MCD 4413-2
Max Roach Sextet With The J.C.White Singers
Lift Every Voice And Sing | Atlantic | 7567-80798-2
Milt Jackson And His Orchestra
Sunflower | CTI | ZK 65131
Paul Desmond Orchestra
Late Night Sax | CBS | 487798-2
Skylark | CTI | ZK 65133
The Brecker Brothers
The Becker Bros | RCA | 2122103-2

MacDowell,Al | (b,el-b,keyboardspiccolo-b)
Urbanator
Urbanator II | Hip Bop | HIBD 8012
Hot Jazz Bisquits | Hip Bop | HIBD 8801

Mace,Tommy | (as,oboe,cl,ts,reedssax)
Charlie Parker And His Orchestra
Charlie Parker:The Best Of The Verve Years | Verve | 527815-2
The Cole Porter Songbook | Verve | 823250-2
Bird: The Complete Charlie Parker On Verve | Verve | 837141-2
Charlie Parker With Orchestra
Charlie Parker Big Band | Verve | 559835-2
Charlie Parker With Orchestra & The Dave Lambert Singers
Verve Jazz Masters 28:Charlie Parker Plays Standards | Verve | 521854-2
Charlie Parker With Strings
Verve Jazz Masters 28:Charlie Parker Plays Standards | Verve | 521854-2
Charlie Parker With Strings:The Master Takes | Verve | 523984-2
Bird: The Complete Charlie Parker On Verve | Verve | 837141-2

Macero,Teo | (arr,ld,as,bs,cl,ts,dr,keyboardssax)
Charles Mingus And His Orchestra
Charles Mingus-The Complete Debut Recordings | Debut | 12 DCD 4402-2
Miles Davis Group
On The Corner | CBS | CK 63980
Sandole Brothers
The Sandole Brothers | Fantasy | FCD 24763-2

Macey,Charlie | (g)
Herbie Mann And His Orchestra
The Best Of Herbie Mann | Atlantic | 7567-81369-2

Macey,John | (b)
Mr.Acker Bilk And His Paramount Jazz Band
The Golden Years Of Revival Jazz,Vol.2 | Storyville | STCD 5507
The Golden Years Of Revival Jazz,Vol.6 | Storyville | STCD 5511
The Golden Years Of Revival Jazz,Vol.7 | Storyville | STCD 5512
The Golden Years Of Revival Jazz,Vol.8 | Storyville | STCD 5513
The Golden Years Of Revival Jazz,Vol.9 | Storyville | STCD 5514
The Golden Years Of Revival Jazz,Vol.10 | Storyville | STCD 5515
The Golden Years Of Revival Jazz,Vol.12 | Storyville | STCD 5517
The Golden Years Of Revival Jazz,Vol.13 | Storyville | STCD 5518
The Golden Years Of Revival Jazz.Vol.14 | Storyville | STCD 5519
The Golden Years Of Revibal Jazz,Vol.15 | Storyville | STCD 5520

Macfarlane,Malcolm | (g,el-gg-synth)
Barbara Thompson's Paraphernalia
Breathless | VeraBra Records | CDVBR 2057-2

MacGregor,John Chalmers 'Chummy' | (pp.celeste)
Glenn Miller And His Orchestra
Planet Jazz:Glenn Miller | Planet Jazz | 2152056-2
Planet Jazz Sampler | Planet Jazz | 2152326-2
Planet Jazz:Jazz Greatest Hits | Planet Jazz | 2169648-2
Planet Jazz:Big Bands | Planet Jazz | 2169649-2
Planet Jazz:Swing | Planet Jazz | 2169651-2
The Chesterfield Broadcasts Vol.1 | RCA | 2663113-2
Candelight Miller | RCA | 2668716-2
Swing Legends | Nimbus Records | NI 2001
The Andrew Sisters With The Glenn Miller Orchestra
The Chesterfield Broadcasts Vol.1 | RCA | 2663113-2

Macha,Stanislav | (p)
Robert Balzar Trio
Travelling | Jazzpoint | JP 1050 CD

Machado,Cesar | (bdr)
Ithamara Koorax With Band
Love Dance:The Ballad Album | Milestone | MCD 9327-2

Machado,Edison | (drperc)
Stan Getz Group Feat.Laurindo Almeida
Stan Getz With Guest Artist Laurindo Almeida | Verve | 823149-2
Stan Getz-Laurindo Almeida Orchestra
Stan Getz Highlights:The Best Of The Verve Years Vol.2 | Verve | 517330-2
Verve Jazz Masters 53:Stan Getz-Bossa Nova | Verve | 529904-2
Stan Getz Highlights | Verve | 847430-2

Machaum | (voc)
Lenny White Group
Renderers Of Spirit | Hip Bop | HIBD 8014

Machito | (Raul Grillo)
Charlie Parker With Machito And His Orchestra
Charlie Parker:The Best Of The Verve Years | Verve | 527815-2
Talkin' Bird | Verve | 559859-2
Bird: The Complete Charlie Parker On Verve | Verve | 837141-2
Charlie Parker:April In Paris | Dreyfus Jazz Line | FDM 36737-2
Machito And His Orchestra
Afro-Cuban Jazz Moods | Original Jazz Classics | OJC20 447-2

Machwitz,Ernst | (b-cl,as,bscl)
Bernd Konrad With Erwin Lehn und sein Südfunk Orchester Stuttgart
Wen Die Götter Lieben | Creative Works Records | CW CD 1010-1
Erwin Lehn Und Sein Südfunk-Tanzorchester
Deutsches Jazz Fesival 1954/1955 | Bear Family Records | BCD 15430

MacInnes,Charles | (tb)
Joe Pass With The NDR Big Band And Radio Philharmonie Hannover
Joe Pass In Hamburg | ACT | 9100-2

Mack,Tommy | (tb)
Glenn Miller And His Orchestra
Planet Jazz:Glenn Miller | Planet Jazz | 2152056-2
The Chesterfield Broadcasts Vol.1 | RCA | 2663113-2
Swing Legends | Nimbus Records | NI 2001
The Andrew Sisters With The Glenn Miller Orchestra
The Chesterfield Broadcasts Vol.1 | RCA | 2663113-2

Mackel,Billy | (g)
Lionel Hampton All Stars
Jazz In Paris:Lionel Hampton-Ring Dem Bells | EmArCy | 159825-2 PMS
Lionel Hampton And His All Star Jazz Inner Circle
Lionel Hampton: Salle Pleyel, March 9th, 1971 | Laserlight | 36133
Lionel Hampton And His Orchestra
Lionel Hampton's Paris All Stars | Vogue | 21511502
Planet Jazz:Lionel Hampton | Planet Jazz | 2152059-2
Planet Jazz:Big Bands | Planet Jazz | 2169649-2
Lionel Hampton:Flying Home | Dreyfus Jazz Line | FDM 36735-2
Lionel Hampton And His Quintet
Planet Jazz:Jazz Greatest Hits | Planet Jazz | 2169648-2
Lionel Hampton And His Septet
Lionel Hampton:Flying Home | Dreyfus Jazz Line | FDM 36735-2
Lionel Hampton Orchestra
The Big Bands Vol.1.The Snader Telescriptions | Storyville | 4960043
Lionel Hampton Quintet
Planet Jazz:Lionel Hampton | Planet Jazz | 2152059-2
Americans Swinging In Paris:Lionel Hampton | EMI Records | 539649-2
Lionel Hampton Sextet
Americans Swinging In Paris:Lionel Hampton | EMI Records | 539649-2
Lionel Hampton Trio
Lionel Hampton's Paris All Stars | Vogue | 21511502

Macko,Joe | (el-b)
Herbie Mann And His Orchestra
The Best Of Herbie Mann | Atlantic | 7567-81369-2

Mackowiak,Alex | (b)
Inge Brandenburg And Her All-Stars
Why Don't You Take All Of Me | Bear Family Records | BCD 15614 AH

Mackrel,Dennis | (cymbalsdr)
Buck Clayton Swing Band
Swing's The Village | Nagel-Heyer | CD 5004
Blues Of Summer | Nagel-Heyer | NH 1011
Byron Stripling Quartet
Byron,Get On Free | Nagel-Heyer | CD 2016
Byron Stripling Quintet
Byron,Get On Free | Nagel-Heyer | CD 2016
Byron Stripling Sextet
Striplingnow! | Nagel-Heyer | CD 2002
Byron,Get On Free | Nagel-Heyer | CD 2016
Byron Stripling Trio
Byron,Get On Free | Nagel-Heyer | CD 2016
Carla Bley Band
Big Band Theory | Watt | 25(519966-2)
Carla Bley Big Band
The Carla Bley Big Band Goes To Church | Watt | 27(533682-2)
Count Basie And His Orchestra
88 Basie Street | Original Jazz Classics | OJC 808(2310901)
Fancy Pants | Original Jazz Classics | OJCCD 1038-2(2310920)
Count Basie's Small Band
88 Basie Street | Original Jazz Classics | OJC 808(2310901)
Diane Schuur With The Count Basie Orchestra
The Best Of Diane Schuur | GRP | GRP 98882
Hank Jones Trio With The Meridian String Quartet
The Story Of Jazz Piano | Laserlight | 24653
Kevin Mahogany With The WDR Big Band And Guests
Pussy Cat Dues:The Music Of Charles Mingus | Enja | ENJ-9316 2

Mackwell,Bob | (harp)
Gil Evans Orchestra
Verve Jazz Masters 23:Gil Evans | Verve | 521860-2
The Individualism Of Gil Evans | Verve | 833804-2

MacLaine,Margot | (viola)
Milt Jackson And His Orchestra
Reverence And Compassion | Reprise | 9362-45204-2

Madaio,Steven | (tpfl-h)
Paulinho Da Costa Orchestra
Happy People | Original Jazz Classics | OJCCD 783-2(2312102)

Madera Jr.,Jose | (congas,timbales,perccabassa)
Earl Klugh Group
Late Night Guitar | Blue Note | 498573-2
Machito And His Orchestra
Afro-Cuban Jazz Moods | Original Jazz Classics | OJC20 447-2

Madera,Jose | (clts)
Charlie Parker With Machito And His Orchestra
Charlie Parker:The Best Of The Verve Years | Verve | 527815-2
Talkin' Bird | Verve | 559859-2
Bird: The Complete Charlie Parker On Verve | Verve | 837141-2
Charlie Parker:April In Paris | Dreyfus Jazz Line | FDM 36737-2
Machito And His Orchestra
Afro-Cuban Jazz Moods | Original Jazz Classics | OJC20 447-2

Mäding-Lemmerich,Ulrike | (v)
HR Big Band With Marjorie Barnes And Frits Landesbergen And Strings
Swinging Christmas | hr music.de | hrmj 012-02 CD

Madison,Bingie | (cl,ts,reedsbs)
Louis Armstrong And His Orchestra
Louis Armstrong:Swing That Music | Laserlight | 36056
Jazz:The Essential Collection Vol.2 | IN+OUT Records | 78012-2
Louis Armstrong-My Greatest Songs | MCA | MCD 18347
Swing Legends:Louis Armstrong | Nimbus Records | NI 2012

Madison,Earl | (cello)
Charlie Haden Quartet West With Strings
The Art Of The Song | Verve | 547403-2

Madison,James | (g)
Otis Spann Band
The Blues Never Die! | Original Blues Classics | OBCCD 530-2(P 7391)
Windy City Blues | Stax | SCD 8612-2

Madison,Jimmy | (drp)
Maceo Parker Group
Mo' Roots | Minor Music | 801018
Nina Simone And Orchestra
Baltimore | Epic | 476906-2

Madrani,Saida | (percvoc)
Nguyen Le Group
Maghreb And Friends | ACT | 9261-2

Madrid,John | (tp)
Buddy Rich Big Band
Keep The Customer Satisfied | EMI Records | 523999-2

Madsen,Flemming | (cl,b-cl,bs,fl,reedssax)
Jens Winther And The Danish Radio Jazz Orchestra
Angels | dacapo | DCCD 9442
Miles Davis With The Danish Radio Big Band
Aura | CBS | CK 63962
Mona Larsen And The Danish Radio Big Band Plus Soloists
Michael Mantler:Cerco Un Paese Innocente | ECM | 1556
Stan Getz With The Danish Radio Big Band
Stan Getz In Europe | Laserlight | 24657
The Danish Radio Big Band
Aura | CBS | CK 63962
The Danish Radio Jazz Orchestra
This Train:The Danish Radio Jazz Orchestra Plays The Music Of Ray Pitts | dacapo | DCCD 9428
Nice Work | dacapo | DCCD 9446

Madsen,Knud Ryskov | (drvoc)
Papa Benny's Jazzband
The Golden Years Of Revival Jazz,Sampler | Storyville | 109 1001
The Golden Years Of Revival Jazz,Vol.2 | Storyville | STCD 5507
The Golden Years Of Revival Jazz,Vol.12 | Storyville | STCD 5517
Papa Bue's Viking Jazzband
The Golden Years Of Revival Jazz,Sampler | Storyville | 109 1001
The Golden Years Of Revival Jazz,Vol 1 | Storyville | STCD 5506
The Golden Years Of Revival Jazz,Vol.5 | Storyville | STCD 5510
The Golden Years Of Revival Jazz,Vol.6 | Storyville | STCD 5511
The Golden Years Of Revival Jazz,Vol.10 | Storyville | STCD 5515
The Golden Years Of Revival Jazz,Vol.14 | Storyville | STCD 5519
The Golden Years Of Revibal Jazz,Vol.15 | Storyville | STCD 5520

Madsen,Peter | (p,arr,voc,keyboardsorg)
Annette Lowman With Three Of A Kind, Fred Wesley And Rodney Jones
Brown Baby:A Tribute To Oscar Brown Jr. | Minor Music | 801061
Bruce Cox Quartet With Guests
Stick To It | Minor Music | 801055
Fred Wesley Group
Swing & Be Funky | Minor Music | 801027
Amalgamation | Minor Music | 801045
Three Of A Kind
Drip Some Grease | Minor Music | 801056
Uli Binetsch's Own Bone
Boone Up Blues | Rockwerk Records | CD 011001

Madsen,Thorkild Edgar | (bj)
Arne Birger's Jazzsjak
The Golden Years Of Revival Jazz,Vol.8 | Storyville | STCD 5513
The Golden Years Of Revival Jazz,Vol.10 | Storyville | STCD 5515

Maebe,Arthur | (fr-htuba)
Ella Fitzgerald With Orchestra
Ella/Things Ain't What They Used To Be | Warner | 9362-47875-2
Hank Crawford Orchestra
Rhino Presents The Atlantic Jazz Gallery | Atlantic | 8122-71257-2
Miles Davis With Gil Evans & His Orchestra
Quiet Nights | CBS | CK 65293

Maertens,Falk | (tp)
Michael Riessler And The Ensemble 13
Momentum Mobile | Enja | ENJ-9003 2

Mafali,Melo | (pp-solo)
Melo Mafali
Ten Piano Players,Vol.1 | Green House Music | CD 1002
René Pretschner & Melo Mafali
The Piano Duo:El Latino | Green House Music | CD 1006

Magadini,Pete | (drperc)
Buddy DeFranco Quartet
Lush Life | Choice | CHCD 71017

Magarelli,Gaetano | (voice)
Michel Godard Ensemble
Castel Del Monte II | Enja | ENJ-9431 2

Magdalayo,Melecio | (bs,fl,alto-fl,ssas)
Pucho & His Latin Soul Brothers
Rip A Dip | Milestone | MCD 9247-2

Mageed,Harneefan | (tb)
Dizzy Gillespie And His Orchestra
Planet Jazz:Bebop | RCA | 2169650-2

Mages,Klaus | (dr,perc,bass-slit-drberimbao)
Norbert Stein Pata Masters
Pata Maroc | Pata Musik | PATA 12(AMF 1063)
Blue Slit | Pata Musik | PATA 8 CD
Graffiti | Pata Musik | PATA 9 CD
Norbert Stein Pata Masters meets Djaduk Ferianto Kua Etnika
Pata Java | Pata Musik | PATA 16 CD
Nornert Stein Pata Masters
Live In Australia | Pata Musik | PATA 15 CD
Pata Masters
Pata-Bahia | Pata Musik | PATA 11 CD
Pata Music Meets Arfi
News Of Roi Ubu | Pata Musik | PATA 10 CD

Magis,Joe | (as,bs,tscl)
Django Reinhardt With Stan Brenders Et Son Grand Orchestre
Verve Jazz Masters 38:Django Reinhardt | Verve | 516931-2

Magnarelli,Joe | (tpfl-h)
Tom Harrell Orchestra
Time's Mirror | RCA | 2663524-2

Magnenat,Olivier | (b)
Doran/Studer/Burri/Magnenat
Musik Für Zwei Kontrabässe, Elektrische Gitarre & Schlagzeug | ECM | 1436

Magnetic North Orchestra |
Jon Balke w/Magnetic North Orchestra
Further | ECM | 1517

Magnusson,Bob | (bel-b)
Art Pepper Quartet
The Art Of Saxophone | Laserlight | 24652
Bill Watrous And His West Coast Friends
Art Pepper:The Hollywood All-Star Sessions | Galaxy | 5GCD 4431-2
Lee Konitz And His West Coast Friends
Art Pepper:The Hollywood All-Star Sessions | Galaxy | 5GCD 4431-2
Pete Jolly And His West Coast Friends
Art Pepper:The Hollywood All-Star Sessions | Galaxy | 5GCD 4431-2
Sarah Vaughan And Her Band
Songs Of The Beatles | Atlantic | 16037-2
Singers Unlimited With Orchestra
The Singers Unlimited:Magic Voices | MPS | 539130-2

Magnusson,Clarence | (cl)
The Jimmy And Marion McPartland Sessions
Vic Lewis:The Golden Years | Candid | CCD 79754

Magruder,John | (fl,b-cl,bssax)
Don Ellis Orchestra
Electric Bath | CBS | CK 65522

Mahadevan,Shankar | (voc)
Remember Shakti
Saturday Night In Bombay | Verve | 014184-2

Mahal,Taj | (dobro,voc,el-gg)
Jimmy Smith All Stars
Jimmy Smith:Dot Com Blues | Blue Thumb | 543978-2

Mahall,Rudi | (b-cl,record-player,turntablecl)
Christof Thewes-Rudi Mahall Duo
Quartetto Pazzo | Jazz Haus Musik | JHM 0122 CD
Christoph Thewes-Rudi Mahall Quartet
Quartetto Pazzo | Jazz Haus Musik | JHM 0122 CD
Der Rote Bereich
Love Me Tender | ACT | 9286-2
Risky Business | ACT | 9407-2
Der Rote Bereich 3 | Jazz 4 Ever Records:Jazz Network | J4E 4740
Geoff Goodman Quintet
Naked Eye | Tutu Records | 888214-2*
Lee Konitz Quartet
Haiku | Nabel Records:Jazz Network | CD 4664
Marty Cook Conspiracy
Phases Of The Moon | Tutu Records | 888160-2*
Sieverts-Mahall-Elgart
Goldfischgesänge | Jazz Haus Musik | JHM 0076 CD
Straight Talk
Pure | Jazz 4 Ever Records:Jazz Network | J4E 4719

Maharaj,Pandit Prakash | (tabla)
Patrick Bebelaar Group
Point Of View | dml-records | CD 017

Maharaj,Pandit Vikash | (sarod)

Maharaj,Vikash | (tambourine)

Mahavishnu Orchestra |
Mahavishnu Orchestra
Apocalypse | CBS | 467092-2
Visions Of The Emerald Beyond | CBS | 467904-2
The Inner Mounting Flame | CBS | CK 65523
The Mahavishnu Orchestra
Between Nothingness & Eternity | CBS | CK 32766

Mahdi,Kalil | (dr)
Big Al Sears Band
Sear-iously | Bear Family Records | BCD 15668 AH

Maher,Clare | (cello)
Michael Mantler Group
Michael Mantler: No Answer/Silence | Watt | 2/5(543374-2)
Silence | Watt | 5 (2313105)

Mahieu,Wiro | (b)
Rob Van Den Broeck-Wiro Mahieu
Departures | Green House Music | CD 1004

Mahieux,Jacques | (dr,pvoc)
Claude Barthelmy Group
Moderne | Owl Records | 014739-2
Renaud Garcia-Fons Quartet
Alboreá | Enja | ENJ-9057 2

Mahn,Tim | (b)
Sandy Brown's Jazz Band
The Golden Years Of Revival Jazz,Vol.5 | Storyville | STCD 5510

Mahogany,Kevin | (voc)
Kevin Mahogany With Orchestra
Songs And Moments | Enja | ENJ-8072 2
Kevin Mahogany With The Bob James Trio
My Romance | Warner | 9362-47025-2
Kevin Mahogany With The Bob James Trio And Kirk Whalum
My Romance | Warner | 9362-47025-2
Kevin Mahogany With The Bob James Trio And Michael Brecker
My Romance | Warner | 9362-47025-2
Kevin Mahogany With The Bob James Trio, Kirk Whalum And Strings
My Romance | Warner | 9362-47025-2
Kevin Mahogany With The WDR Big Band And Guests
Pussy Cat Dues:The Music Of Charles Mingus | Enja | ENJ-9316 2

Mahones,Gildo | (el-p,org,parr)
Booker Ervin Quintet
The Blues Book | Original Jazz Classics | OJCCD 780-2(P 7340)
Charlie Rouse Quartet
Late Night Sax | CBS | 487798-2
Frank Wess Quintet
The Long Road | Prestige | PCD 24247-2
Jimmy Witherspoon And His Band
Baby, Baby, Baby | Original Blues Classics | OBCCD 527-2(P 7290)
Lambert, Hendricks And Bavan
Planet Jazz:Male Jazz Vocalists | Planet Jazz | 2169657-2
Lester Young Quintet
Jazz Gallery:Lester Young Vol.2(1946-59) | RCA | 2119541-2
Sonny Stitt-Sal Salvador Quintet
Newport Jazz Festival 1958,July 3rd-6th Vol.2:Mulligan The Main Man | Phontastic | NCD 8814

Willis Jackson Sextet
At Large | Prestige | PCD 24243-2
Mahr,Monika | (voc)
Jazzensemble Des Hessischen Rundfunks
Jazz Messe-Messe Für Unsere Zeit | hr music.de | hrmj 003-01 CD
Maia,Luizao | (bel-b)
Antonio Carlos Jobim Group
Verve Jazz Masters 13:Antonio Carlos Jobim | Verve | 516409-2
Antonio Carlos Jobim-Elis Regina Group
The Antonio Carlos Jobim Songbook | Verve | 525472-2
Lee Ritenour Group
Rio | GRP | GRP 95242
Maichel,Golo | (dr)
House Five
Frank Talk | Nabel Records:Jazz Network | CD 4674
Maid,Lothar | (b-g)
Klaus Doldinger Jubilee
Doldinger's Best | ACT | 9224-2
Maiden,Willie | (arr,bs,cl,ss,tsreeds)
Maynard Ferguson And His Orchestra
Verve Jazz Masters 52:Maynard Ferguson | Verve | 529905-2
Maynard Ferguson Band
Verve Jazz Masters 52:Maynard Ferguson | Verve | 529905-2
Maynard Ferguson Orchestra With Chris Connor
Two's Company | Roulette | 837201-2
Maidman,Ian | (cora-stringsg)
Pili-Pili
Boogaloo | JA & RO | JARO 4174-2
Maihack,Jim | (tuba)
Turk Murphy And His Jazz Band
Atlantic Jazz: New Orleans | Atlantic | 7567-81700-2
Maile,Andreas 'Andi' | (cl,ss,ts,fl,assax)
Andreas Maile Quartet
Mailensteine | Satin Doll Productions | SDP 1022-1 CD
Geir Lysne Listening Ensemble
Korall | ACT | 9236-2
Aurora Borealis-Nordic Lights | ACT | 9406-2
Gregor Hübner Quartet
Panonien | Satin Doll Productions | SDP 1015-1 CD
Gregor Hübner Quintet
Panonien | Satin Doll Productions | SDP 1015-1 CD
Januschke's Time | Satin Doll Productions | SDP 1034-1 CD
SWR Big Band
Jazz In Concert | Hänssler Classics | CD 93.004
Maile,Hans | (concertmaster)
Till Brönner Quartet & Deutsches Symphonieorchester Berlin
German Songs | Minor Music | 801057
Mai-Mai,Djina | (voc)
Chinese Compass
Chinese Compass | dacapo | DCCD 9443
Main,Roy | (tb)
Harry James And His Orchestra
Trumpet Blues:The Best Of Harry James | Capitol | 521224-2
Maini,Joe | (as,tssax)
Anita O'Day With The Bill Holman Orchestra
Verve Jazz Masters 49:Anita O'Day | Verve | 527653-2
Clifford Brown All Stars
Verve Jazz Masters 44:Clifford Brown and Max Roach | Verve | 528109-2
Brownie-The Complete EmArCy Recordings Of Clifford Brown | EmArCy | 838306-2
Gerald Wilson And His Orchestra
Blue Breaks Beats Vol.2 | Blue Note | 789907-2
Jimmy Knepper Quintet
Charles Mingus-The Complete Debut Recordings | Debut | 12 DCD 4402-2
June Christy With The Shorty Rogers Orchestra
June Christy Big Band Special | Capitol | 498319-2
Shelly Manne And His Men
Vol.1:The West Coast Sound | Original Jazz Classics | OJCCD 152-2
The Jazz Giants Play Harry Warren:Lullaby Of Broadway | Prestige | PCD 24204-2
Terry Gibbs Big Band
Terry Gibbs Dream Band Vol.4:Main Stem | Contemporary | CCD 7656-2
Terry Gibbs Dream Band
Terry Gibbs Dream Band Vol.2:The Sundown Sessions | Contemporary | CCD 7652-2
Terry Gibbs Dream Band Vol.3:Flying Home | Contemporary | CCD 7654-2
Terry Gibbs Dream Band Vol.5:The Big Cat | Contemporary | CCD 7657-2
Terry Gibbs Dream Band Vol.6:One More Time | Contemporary | CCD 7658-2
The Jazz Giants Play Jerome Kern:Yesterdays | Prestige | PCD 24202-2
Mainieri,Bucky | (tb)
Billy Eckstine And His Orchestra
Blue Velvet: Crooners, Swooners And Velvet Vocals | Blue Note | 521153-2
Mainieri,Mike | (p,perc,midi-vib,synclavier,vib)
Essence All Stars
Afro Cubano Chant | Hip Bop | HIBD 8009
Hot Jazz Bisquits | Hip Bop | HIBD 8801
Kenny Burrell Sextet
Verve Jazz Masters 45:Kenny Burrell | Verve | 527652-2
Mike Mainieri Group
Jazz Life Vol.2:From Seventh At Avenue South | Storyville | 4960763
Peter Erskine Orchestra
Peter Erskine | Original Jazz Classics | OJC 610(C 14010)
Steps Ahead
Steps Ahead:Copenhagen Live | Storyville | 4960363
Steps Ahead | Elektra | 7559-60168-2
Modern Times | Elektra | 7559-60351-2
N.Y.C. | Intuition Records | INT 3007-2
Mair,Albert | (el-p)
Hans Koller Free Sound
Phoenix | MPS | 9813438
Majevskaja,Natascha | (org)
Natascha Majevskaja
Orgel Ist Mehr!...In Bamberg,Vol.1 | Orgel ist mehr! | OIM/BA/1999-1 CD
Orgel Ist Mehr...In Bamberg Vol.2 | Orgel ist mehr! | OIM/BA/1999-2 CD
Natascha Majevskaja-Thomas Jäger
Orgel Ist Mehr!...In Bamberg,Vol.1 | Orgel ist mehr! | OIM/BA/1999-1 CD
Orgel Ist Mehr...In Bamberg Vol.2 | Orgel ist mehr! | OIM/BA/1999-2 CD
Majewski,Hans-Martin | (arrld)
Inge Brandenburg mit Hans Martin Majewski und seinem Orchester
Why Don't You Take All Of Me | Bear Family Records | BCD 15614 AH
Majewski,Robert | (tp)
Jazz Baltica Ensemble
The Birth+Rebirth Of Swedish Folk Jazz | ACT | 9254-2
Majewski,Virginia | (viola)
Anita O'Day With The Buddy Bregman Orchestra
Verve Jazz Masters 49:Anita O'Day | Verve | 527653-2
Cal Tjader With The Clare Fischer Orchestra
Cal Tjader Plays Harold Arlen & West Side Story | Fantasy | FCD 24775-2
Ella Fitzgerald With The Billy May Orchestra
The Best Of The Song Books:The Ballads | Verve | 521867-2
Ella Fitzgerald Sings The Harold Arlen Song Book | Verve | 589108-2
Ella Fitzgerald With The Frank DeVol Orchestra
Get Happy! | Verve | 523321-2
Frank Sinatra With The Count Basie Orchestra
It Might As Well Be Spring | Reprise | 7599-27027-2
Makarski,Michelle | (v)
Tomasz Stanko Sextet
From The Green Hill | ECM | 1680(547336-2)
Makia,Sam | (hawaiian-g)
Coleman Hawkins Sextet
Body And Soul Revisited | GRP | GRP 16272
Makowicz,Adam | (keyboards,pp-solo)
Adam Makowicz Trio
7.Zelt-Musik-Festival:Jazz Events | Zounds | CD 2730001
Adam Makowicz Trio With The Wilanow Quartet
7.Zelt-Musik-Festival:Jazz Events | Zounds | CD 2730001
Malabe,Frankie | (congas,cowbellsperc)
Clark Terry & Chico O Farril Orchestra
Spanish Rice | Verve | 9861050
Malaby,Tony | (ssts)
Chris Lightcap Quartet
Lay-Up | Fresh Sound Records | FSNT 074 CD
Mark Helias' Open Loose
New School | Enja | ENJ-9413 2
Rez Abbasi Group
Out Of Body | String Jazz | SJRCD 1021
Malach,Bob | (as,fl,cl,ts,sax,ss,reeds,arr)
George Gruntz Concert Jazz Band
Blues 'N Dues Et Cetera | Enja | ENJ-6072 2
Jasper Van't Hof Group
Blue Corner | ACT | 9228-2
Just Friends
Nevertheless | IN+OUT Records | 7015-2
Jazz Unlimited | IN+OUT Records | 7017-2
Michael Cochrane Quartet
Path Ways | Steeplechase | SCCD 31542
Mike Stern Group
Play | Atlantic | 7567-83219-2
Miles Davis With Gil Evans Orchestra, The George Gruntz Concert Jazz Band And Guests
Miles & Quincy Live At Montreux | Warner | 9362-45221-2
Malachi,John | (parr)
Louis Jordan And His Tympany Five
Louis Jordan-Let The Good Times Roll: The Complete Decca Recordings 1938-1954 | Bear Family Records | BCD 15557 IH
Sarah Vaughan And Her Trio
Swingin' Easy | EmArCy | 514072-2
Verve Jazz Masters 42:Sarah Vaughan-The Jazz Sides | Verve | 526817-2
4 By 4:Ella Fitzgerald/Sarah Vaughan/Billie Holiday/Dinah Washington | Verve | 559693-2
Malan,Roy | (viola)
Herbie Hancock Group
Sunlight | CBS | 486570-2
Malarsky,Leonhard | (v)
Cal Tjader With The Clare Fischer Orchestra
Cal Tjader Plays Harold Arlen & West Side Story | Fantasy | FCD 24775-2
Gene Harris And The Three Sounds
Deep Blue-The United States Of Mind | Blue Note | 521152-2
Hank Crawford Orchestra
Rhino Presents The Atlantic Jazz Gallery | Atlantic | 8122-71257-2
Johnny Hartman And His Orchestra
Unforgettable | Impulse(MCA) | IMP 11522
Malek,Monika | (viola)
Ensemble Indigo
Reflection | Enja | ENJ-9417 2
Malempre,Alex | (tpfl-h)
HR Big Band
The American Songs Of Kurt Weill | hr music.de | hrmj 006-01 CD
Libertango:Homage An Astor Piazzolla | hr music.de | hrmj 014-02 CD
HR Big Band With Marjorie Barnes And Frits Landesbergen
Swinging Christmas | hr music.de | hrmj 012-02 CD
HR Big Band With Marjorie Barnes And Frits Landesbergen And Strings
Swinging Christmas | hr music.de | hrmj 012-02 CD
The Three Sopranos With The HR Big Band
The Three Sopranos | hr music.de | hrmj 001-01 CD
Maleson,Leon | (b)
Ron Carter Quartet
Songs For You | Milestone | MCD 47099-2
Ron Carter Quintet With Strings
Pick 'Em/Super Strings | Milestone | MCD 47090-2
Malet,Laurent | (fl-h)
Renaud Garcia-Fons
Navigatore | Enja | ENJ-9418 2
Renaud Garcia-Fons Group
Navigatore | Enja | ENJ-9418 2
Malheiros,Alex | (b,perc,voc,el-bg)
Azymuth
Jazzrock-Anthology Vol.3:Fusion | Zounds | CD 27100555
Ithamara Koorax With Band
Love Dance:The Ballad Album | Milestone | MCD 9327-2
Malick,Peter | (g)
Peter Malick Group feat. Norah Jones
New York City | Koch Records | 238678-2
Malignaggi,Joseph | (strings,vviola)
Wes Montgomery With The Don Sebesky Orchestra
Verve Jazz Masters 14:Wes Montgomery | Verve | 519826-2
Talkin' Jazz:Roots Of Acid Jazz | Verve | 529580-2
Bumpin' | Verve | 539062-2
Malik,Hubert | (dr)
Edith Steyer... Posterity Quintet
...On The Right Track | Jazz 4 Ever Records:Jazz Network | J4E 4745
Malik,Raphe | (tp)
Cecil Taylor Unit
Dark To Themselves | Enja | ENJ-2084 2
Malik,Sharifa Dietra | (voc)
Nils Petter Molvaer Group
Elegy For Africa | Nabel Records:Jazz Network | CD 4678
Malikova,Alisa | (ts)
Ralph Abelein Group
Mr. B's Time Machine | Satin Doll Productions | SDP 1042-1 CD
Malin,Joe | (v)
Freddie Hubbard With Orchestra
This Is Jazz:Freddie Hubbard | CBS | CK 65041
Grover Washington Jr. Orchestra
Jazzrock-Anthology Vol.3:Fusion | Zounds | CD 27100555
Les McCann Group
Another Beginning | Atlantic | 7567-80790-2
Louis Armstrong And His Friends
Planet Jazz:Louis Armstrong | Planet Jazz | 2152052-2
Planet Jazz Sampler | Planet Jazz | 2152326-2
Louis Armstrong And His Friends | Bluebird | 2663961-2
Milt Jackson And His Orchestra
Sunflower | CTI | ZK 65131
Phil Woods Quartet With Orchestra & Strings
Round Trip | Verve | 559804-2
Wes Montgomery Quartet With The Claus Ogerman Orchestra
Tequila | Verve | 547769-2
Wes Montgomery Quintet With The Claus Ogerman Orchestra
The Antonio Carlos Jobim Songbook | Verve | 525472-2
Talkin' Jazz:Roots Of Acid Jazz | Verve | 529580-2
Tequila | Verve | 547769-2
Wes Montgomery Trio With The Claus Ogerman Orchestra
Tequila | Verve | 547769-2
Wes Montgomery With The Claus Ogerman Orchestra
Verve Jazz Masters 14:Wes Montgomery | Verve | 519826-2
Malischewski,Uwe | (sax)
Scetches
Different Places | VeraBra Records | CDVBR 2102-2
Mallard,Oett 'Sax' | (ascl)
Duke Ellington And His Orchestra
At The Hurricane:Original 1943 Broadcasts | Storyville | STCD 8359
Malle,Andreas | (ts)
Bill Ramsey With Orchestra
Gettin' Back To Swing | Bear Family Records | BCD 15813 AH
Malli,Walter M. | (cymbalsperc)
Franz Koglmann Quintet
Opium | Between The Lines | btl 011(Efa 10181-2)
Mallory,Ajay | (snare-dr)
Maceo Parker With The Rebirth Brass Band
Southern Exposure | Minor Music | 801033
Malneck,Matty | (v,arrviola)
Irving Mills And His Hotsy Totsy Gang
Jazz:The Essential Collection Vol.3 | IN+OUT Records | 78013-2
Malone,Billy | (african-dr)
Marion Brown Orchestra
Afternoon Of A Georgia Faun | ECM | 1004
Malone,Kasper 'Kass' | (b)
Jack Teagarden And His Band
Meet Me Where They Play The Blues | Good Time Jazz | GTCD 12063-2
Malone,Russell | (el-g,gvoc)
Benny Green Trio
These Are Soulful Days | Blue Note | 499527-2
Christian McBride Group
A Family Affair | Verve | 557554-2
Dave Grusin Orchestra
Two For The Road:The Music Of Henry Mancini | GRP | GRP 98652
Diana Krall Group
When I Look In Your Eyes | Verve | 9513304
Diana Krall Group With Orchestra
When I Look In Your Eyes | Verve | 9513304
Diana Krall Quartet
All For You-A Dedication To The Nat King Cole Trio | Impulse(MCA) | 951164-2
Diana Krall Trio
All For You-A Dedication To The Nat King Cole Trio | Impulse(MCA) | 951164-2
Love Scenes | Impulse(MCA) | 951234-2
Harry Connick Jr. Quartet
We Are In Love | CBS | 466736-2
Harry Connick Jr. Quartet With Branford Marsalis
We Are In Love | CBS | 466736-2
Jimmy Smith All Stars
Jimmy Smith:Dot Com Blues | Blue Thumb | 543978-2
Kenny Barron Group
Spirit Song | Verve | 543180-2
Mose Allison Quintet
Gimeracs And Gewgaws | Blue Note | 823211-2
Ron Carter Trio
The Golden Striker | Blue Note | 590831-2
Roy Hargrove's Crisol
Habana | Verve | 537563-2
Russell Malone Quartet
Look Who's Here | Verve | 543543-2
Sweet Georgia Peach | Impulse(MCA) | 951282-2
Russell Malone Quintet
Sweet Georgia Peach | Impulse(MCA) | 951282-2
Malone,Tom | (b-tb,tb,fl,synthtuba)
Carla Bley Band
Night-Glo | Watt | 16
Gil Evans Orchestra
There Comes A Time | RCA | 2131392-2
PLay The Music Of Jimi Hendrix | RCA | 2663872-2
Miles Davis With Gil Evans Orchestra, The George Gruntz Concert Jazz Band And Guests
Miles & Quincy Live At Montreux | Warner | 9362-45221-2
Paulinho Da Costa Orchestra
Happy People | Original Jazz Classics | OJCCD 783-2(2312102)
Ron Carter Orchestra
Parade | Original Jazz Classics | OJCCD 1047-2(M 9088)
Malschal,Berthold | (p)
Peter Fessler Quartet
Foot Prints | Minor Music | 801058
Malta,Yoshi | (as,saxss)
Axel Zwingenberger With The Lionel Hampton Big Band
The Boogie Woogie Album | Vagabond | VRCD 8.88008
Maltoni,Quatro | (as)
Charles Mingus Orchestra
Cumbia & Jazz Fusion | Atlantic | 8122-71785-2
Malviccino,Horacio | (el-gg)
Astor Piazzolla-Gary Burton Sextet
The New Tango | Warner | 2292-55069-2
Mamao,Ivan Conte | (drsynth)
Azymuth
Jazzrock-Anthology Vol.3:Fusion | Zounds | CD 27100555
Mambretti,Sebastiano | (shaker)
Caterina Valente-Catherine Michel
Girltalk | Nagel-Heyer | NH 1015
Mami,Cheb | (accordeon-synth)
Nguyen Le Group
Maghreb And Friends | ACT | 9261-2
Mammone,Mario | (gel-g)
Inga Lühning With Trio
Lühning | Jazz Haus Musik | JHM 0111 CD
Lirico
Sussurro | Jazz Haus Musik | JHM 0129 CD
Manahan,Marie | (cello)
Pete Rugolo And His Orchestra
Thriller/Richard Diamon(Original Jazz Scores From 2 Classics TV Series) | Fresh Sound Records | FSCD 2015
Manasia,Jeremy | (p)
David Gibson Sextet
Maya | Nagel-Heyer | CD 2018
Mance,Junior[Julian C.] | (p,el-p,vocp-solo)
All Star Live Jam Session
Brownie-The Complete EmArCy Recordings Of Clifford Brown | EmArCy | 838306-2
Bernard Purdie's Soul To Jazz
Bernard Purdie's Soul To Jazz II | ACT | 9253-2
Cannonball Adderley And His Orchestra
Verve Jazz Masters 31:Cannonball Adderley | Verve | 522651-2
Cannonball Adderley Quintet
Verve Jazz Masters 31:Cannonball Adderley | Verve | 522651-2
Cannonball Adderley:Sophisticated Swing-The EmArCy Small Group Sessions | Verve | 528408-2
Cannonball Adderley Birthday Celebration | Fantasy | FANCD 6087-2
At Newport | Pablo | PACD 5315-2
Dexter Gordon Quartet
Dexter Gordon Birthday Celebration | Fantasy | FANCD 6082-2
Dinah Washington And Her Band
After Hours With Miss D | Verve | 0760562
Verve Jazz Masters 40:Dinah Washington | Verve | 522055-2
Dizzy Gillespie Quintet
Verve Jazz Masters 10:Dizzy Gillespie | Verve | 516319-2
Talking Verve:Dizzy Gillespie | Verve | 533846-2
Dizzy Gillespie Sextet
Ultimate Dizzy Gillespie | Verve | 557535-2
Eddie Lockjaw Davis-Johnny Griffin Quintet
Blues Up And Down | Milestone | MCD 47084-2
Battle Stations | Original Jazz Classics | OJCCD 1085(P7282)
The Prestige Legacy Vol.2:Battles Of Saxes | Prestige | PCD 24252-2
Gene Ammons Quintet
Brother Jug! | Prestige | PR20 7792-2
Joe Williams And Friends
Planet Jazz:Male Jazz Vocalists | Planet Jazz | 2169657-2
At Newport '63 | RCA | 2663919-2
Joe Williams And His Band
Planet Jazz:Joe Williams | Planet Jazz | 2165370-2
Johnny Griffin-Eddie Lockjaw Davis Quintet
Tough Tenors | Original Jazz Classics | OJCCD 1094-2(JLP 931)
Johnny Hodges With The Dizzy Gillespie Quintet
Verve Jazz Masters 35:Johnny Hodges | Verve | 521857-2
Jubilee All Stars
Jazz Gallery:Lester Young Vol.2(1946-59) | RCA | 2119541-2

Junior Mance Quartet
That Lovin' Feelin' | Milestone | MCD 47097-2
Junior Mance Trio
That Lovin' Feelin' | Milestone | MCD 47097-2
Junior's Blues | Original Jazz Classics | OJCCD 1000-2(RLP 9447)
Junior Mance Trio & Orchestra
That Lovin' Feelin' | Milestone | MCD 47097-2
Nat Adderley Quartet
Cannonball Adderley:Sophisticated Swing-The EmArCy Small Group Sessions | Verve | 528408-2
Nat Adderley With Jim Hall And The Junior Mance Trio
Little Big Horn! | Original Jazz Classics | OJCCD 1001-2(R 9474)
Nat Adderley With Kenny Burrell And The Junior Mance Trio
Little Big Horn! | Original Jazz Classics | OJCCD 1001-2(R 9474)
Ray Crawford Sextet
Smooth Groove | Candid | CCD 79028
Sonny Stitt Quartet
Kaleidoscope | Original Jazz Classics | OJCCD 060-2(P 7077)
Wild Bill Moore Quintet
Bottom Groove | Milestone | MCD 47098-2

Mancel,Ghislaine Benabdalla | (v)
Abdullah Ibrahim Trio And A String Orchestra
African Suite | TipToe | TIP-888832 2
String Orchestra
African Suite | TipToe | TIP-888832 2

Mancini,Henry | (arr,compcond)
Henry Mancini And His Orchestra
Combo! | RCA | 2147794-2

Mancini,Monica | (voc)
Horace Silver Quintet With Vocals
Horace Silver Retrospective | Blue Note | 495576-2

Mancuso,Gus | (bar-horntb)
Gus Mancuso Quartet
Gus Mancuso & Special Friends | Fantasy | FCD 24762-2
Gus Mancuso Quintet
Gus Mancuso & Special Friends | Fantasy | FCD 24762-2

Mandarini,Alberto | (tp)
Italian Instabile Orchestra
Skies Of Europe | ECM | 1543

Mandel,Johnny | (arr,b-tp,condtb)
Gerry Mulligan Concert Jazz Band
Verve Jazz Masters 36:Gerry Mulligan | Verve | 523342-2
Shirley Horn With Strings
Here's To Life | Verve | 511879-2

Mandell,Johnny | (arr,ldtb)
Bud Shank And Trombones
Cool Fool | Fresh Sound Records | FSR CD 507
Count Basie And His Orchestra
King Of Swing | Verve | 837433-2
Elliot Lawrence And His Orchestra
The Elliot Lawrence Big Band Swings Cohn & Kahn | Fantasy | FCD 24761-2

Manderscheid,Dieter | (b,cellovoice)
Amman Boutz
Some Other Tapes | Fish Music | FM 009/10 CD
Blue Room Ensemble
Solitude | Foolish Music | FM 211993
Chromatic Alarm
Some Other Tapes | Fish Music | FM 009/10 CD
Dioko
Helix | Jazz Haus Musik | JHM 0029 CD
Dirk Raulf Group
Die Welt Ist Immer Wieder Schön | Poise | Poise 03
Theater I (Bühnenmusik) | Poise | Poise 07
Ekkehard Jost & Chromatic Alarm
Von Zeit Zu Zeit | Fish Music | FM 005 CD
Wintertango | Fish Music | FM 008 CD
Ekkehard Jost Ensemble
Weimarer Balladen | Fish Music | FM 004 CD
Ekkehard Jost Nonet
Out Of Jost's Songbook | Fish Music | FM 006 CD
Ekkehard Jost Quartet
Some Other Tapes | Fish Music | FM 009/10 CD
Ekkehard Jost Quintet
Some Other Tapes | Fish Music | FM 009/10 CD
Ekkehard Jost Trio
Some Other Tapes | Fish Music | FM 009/10 CD
Frank Gratkowski Trio
Gestalten | Jazz Haus Musik | JHM 0083 CD
Georg Ruby Village Zone
Mackeben Revisited:The Ufa Years | Jazz Haus Musik | JHM 0121 CD
Giessen-Köln-Nonett
Some Other Tapes | Fish Music | FM 009/10 CD
Klaus König Orchestra
Hommage A Douglas Adams | Enja | ENJ-6078 2
Reviews | Enja | ENJ-9061 2
The Heart Project | Enja | ENJ-9338 2
Thomas Heberer-Dieter Manderscheid
Chicago Breakdown:The Music Of Jelly Roll Morton | Jazz Haus Musik | JHM 0038 CD
What A Wonderful World | Jazz Haus Musik | JHM 0118 CD
Tome XX
The Red Snapper | Jazz Haus Musik | JHM 0047 CD
Third Degree | Jazz Haus Musik | JHM 0063 CD
Transalpin Express Orchestra
Some Other Tapes | Fish Music | FM 009/10 CD

Mandingo,Filipe | (percvoc)
Markus Stockhausen Orchestra
Sol Mestizo:Markus Stockhausen Plays The Music Of Enrique Diaz | ACT | 9222-2

Mandinkas,The: |
Hank Jones Meets Cheik-Tidiana Seck
Sarala | Verve | 528783-2

Maneri,Joe | (as,ts,p,cl,voicereeds)
Joe Maneri Quartet
In Full Cry | ECM | 1617(537048-2)
Joe Maneri-Joe Morris-Mat Maneri
Three Men Walking | ECM | 1597
Joe Maneri-Mat Maneri
Blessed | ECM | 1661(557365-2)
Maneri/Phillips/Maneri
Tales Of Rohnlief | ECM | 1678

Maneri,Mat | (axatse,el-5-string-v,bar-v)
Franz Koglmann Group
Venus In Transit | Between The Lines | btl 017(Efa 10186)
Joe Maneri Quartet
In Full Cry | ECM | 1617(537048-2)
Joe Maneri-Joe Morris-Mat Maneri
Three Men Walking | ECM | 1597
Joe Maneri-Mat Maneri
Blessed | ECM | 1661(557365-2)
Maneri/Phillips/Maneri
Tales Of Rohnlief | ECM | 1678
Mat Maneri
Trinity | ECM | 1719
Robin Williamson Group
Skirting The River Road | ECM | 1785(016372-2

Mangano,Mickey | (tp)
Anita O'Day With Gene Krupa And His Orchestra
Let Me Off Uptown:Anita O'Day With Gene Krupa | CBS | CK 65625
Duke Ellington With Tommy Dorsey And His Orchestra
Highlights From The Duke Ellington Centennial Edition | RCA | 2663672-2
Harry James And His Orchestra
Trumpet Blues:The Best Of Harry James | Capitol | 521224-2
Tommy Dorsey And His Orchestra
Planet Jazz:Tommy Dorsey | Planet Jazz | 2159972-2
Planet Jazz:Jazz Greatest Hits | Planet Jazz | 2169648-2

Mangano,Vito | (tp)
Ella Fitzgerald With The Nelson Riddle Orchestra
The Best Of The Song Books:The Ballads | Verve | 521867-2
Get Happy! | Verve | 523321-2
Oh Lady Be Good:The Best Of The Gershwin Songbook | Verve | 529581-2
Love Songs:The Best Of The Song Books | Verve | 531762-2
Ella Fitzgerald Sings The Johnny Mercer Songbook | Verve | 539057-2
Louis Armstrong And His All Stars With Benny Carter's Orchestra
Ambassador Louis Armstrong Vol.17:Moments To Remember(1952-1956) | Ambassador | CLA 1917
Louis Armstrong With Benny Carter's Orchestra
Louis Armstrong-My Greatest Songs | MCA | MCD 18347
Pete Rugolo And His Orchestra
Thriller/Richard Diamon(Original Jazz Scores From 2 Classics TV Series) | Fresh Sound Records | FSCD 2015

Mangasuba,Fanta | (voc)
Pharoah Sanders Orchestra
Message From Home | Verve | 529578-2

Mangelsdorff,Albert | (tb,voctb-solo)
Albert Mangelsdorff Quartet
Shake,Shuttle And Blow | Enja | ENJ-9374 2
Albert Mangelsdorff Trio
Three Originals:The Wide Point/Trilogue/Albert Live In Montreux | MPS | 519213-2
Albert Mangelsdorff With The NDR Big Band
NDR Big Band-Bravissimo | ACT | 9232-2
Albert Mangelsdorff-Don Cherry
Albert Mangelsdorff And His Friends | MPS | 067375-2
Albert Mangelsdorff-Elvin Jones
Albert Mangelsdorff And His Friends | MPS | 067375-2
Albert Mangelsdorff-John Scofield
Internationales Jazzfestival Münster | Tutu Records | 888110-2*
Albert Mangelsdorff-Karl Berger
Albert Mangelsdorff And His Friends | MPS | 067375-2
Albert Mangelsdorff-Lee Konitz
Albert Mangelsdorff And His Friends | MPS | 067375-2
Albert Mangelsdorff-Reto Weber Percussion Orchestra
Live At Montreux | double moon | CHRDM 71009
Albert Mangelsdorff-Wolfgang Dauner
Albert Mangelsdorff And His Friends | MPS | 067375-2
Gunter Hampel All Stars
Jubilation | Birth | 0038
Hans Koller New Jazz Stars
Deutsches Jazz Fesival 1954/1955 | Bear Family Records | BCD 15430
Jazzensemble Des Hessischen Rundfunks
Atmosphering Conditions Permitting | ECM | 1549/50
Joachim Kühn And The Radio Philharmonie Hannover NDR With Jazz Soloists
Europeana | ACT | 9220-2
Jon Hiseman With The United Jazz & Rock Ensemble And Babara Thompson's Paraphernalia
About Time Too! | VeraBra Records | CDVBR 2014-2
Landes Jugend Jazz Orchester Hessen
Touch Of Lips | hr music.de | hrmj 004-01 CD
Mangelsdorff-Pastorius-Mouzon
Three Originals:The Wide Point/Trilogue/Albert Live In Montreux | MPS | 519213-2
NDR-Workshop
Doldinger's Best | ACT | 9224-2
Okschila Tatanka
Wounded Knee-Lyrik Und Jazz | Wergo | SM 1088-2
Radio Jazzgroup Frankfurt
Jubilee Edition | double moon | CHRDM 71020
Rolf Kühn And Friends
Affairs:Rolf Kühn & Friends | Intuition Records | INT 3211-2
The German Jazz Masters
Old Friends | ACT | 9278-2
Wolfgang Lauth Septet
Noch Lauther | Bear Family Records | BCD 15942 AH

Mangelsdorff,Emil | (as,as-playback,as-solo,cl,ss,fl,sd)
Hans Koller Big Band
New York City | MPS | 9813437
Helmut Weglinski Quintet
Deutsches Jazz Fesival 1954/1955 | Bear Family Records | BCD 15430
Jazzensemble Des Hessischen Rundfunks
Atmosphering Conditions Permitting | ECM | 1549/50
Jutta Hipp Quintet
Deutsches Jazz Fesival 1954/1955 | Bear Family Records | BCD 15430
Kurt Edelhagen All Stars Und Solisten
Deutsches Jazz Fesival 1954/1955 | Bear Family Records | BCD 15430

Mangione,Chuck | (fl-h,p,el-p,tptp.fl-h)
Chuck Mangione Quartet
Monterey Jazz Festival 1975 | Storyville | 4960213

Mangual,Jose | (3 small-kenya-dr,bongos,congas,perc)
Cal Tjader's Orchestra
Verve Jazz Masters 39:Cal Tjader | Verve | 521858-2
Talkin Verve/Roots Of Acid Jazz:Cal Tjader | Verve | 531562-2
Soul Burst | Verve | 557446-2
Charlie Parker Quintet
Bird: The Complete Charlie Parker On Verve | Verve | 837141-2
Charlie Parker Sextet
Verve Jazz Masters 28:Charlie Parker Plays Standards | Verve | 521854-2
Charlie Parker:The Best Of The Verve Years | Verve | 527815-2
Talkin' Bird | Verve | 559859-2
The Cole Porter Songbook | Verve | 823250-2
Charlie Parker With Machito And His Orchestra
Charlie Parker:The Best Of The Verve Years | Verve | 527815-2
Talkin' Bird | Verve | 559859-2
Bird: The Complete Charlie Parker On Verve | Verve | 837141-2
Charlie Parker:April In Paris | Dreyfus Jazz Line | FDM 36737-2
Charlie Parker's Jazzers
Bird: The Complete Charlie Parker On Verve | Verve | 837141-2
Dizzy Gillespie And His Orchestra
Afro | Verve | 517052-2
Gillespiana And Carnegie Hall Concert | Verve | 519809-2
Talking Verve:Dizzy Gillespie | Verve | 533846-2
Ultimate Dizzy Gillespie | Verve | 557535-2
Dizzy Gillespie Group
Verve Jazz Masters 10:Dizzy Gillespie | Verve | 516319-2
Dizzy Gillspie And His Latin American Rhythm
Afro | Verve | 517052-2
Herbie Mann Sextet
Verve Jazz Masters 56:Herbie Mann | Verve | 529901-2
Sarah Vaughan With Orchestra
!Viva! Vaughan | Mercury | 549374-2
Sarah Vaughan With The Frank Foster Orchestra
The Antonio Carlos Jobim Songbook | Verve | 525472-2

Mangual,Luis | (perc)
Gato Barbieri Orchestra
The Roots Of Acid Jazz | Impulse(MCA) | IMP 12042

Mangual,prob.Jose | (bongo)
Charlie Parker Septet
Talkin' Bird | Verve | 559859-2

Manhattan Project,The |
Manhattan Project,The
Kind Of Blue:Blue Note Celebrate The Music Of Miles Davis | Blue Note | 534255-2
Wayne Shorter:The Classic Blue Note Recordings | Blue Note | 540856-2

Manhattan Transfer,The | (voc-group)
Bobby McFerrin Groups
Spontaneous Inventions | Blue Note | 746298-2

Mani,T.A.S. | (doll,mrindangammridamgam)
Charlie Mariano & The Karnataka College Of Percussion
Jyothi | ECM | 1256
Live | VeraBra Records | CDVBR 2034-2

Mankowitz,David | (vviola)
Phil Woods Quartet With Orchestra & Strings
Round Trip | Verve | 559804-2
Stan Getz With The Eddie Sauter Orchestra
Stan Getz Plays The Music Of Mickey One | Verve | 531232-2
Stan Getz With The Richard Evans Orchestra
What The World Needs Now-Stan Getz Plays Bacharach And David | Verve | 557450-2

Mann,Bob | (g)
Don Grolnick Group
Hearts And Numbers | VeraBra Records | CDVBR 2016-2
Hugh Marsh Duo/Quartet/Orchestra
The Bear Walks | VeraBra Records | CDVBR 2011-2
The Brecker Brothers
The Becker Bros | RCA | 2122103-2

Mann,Dave | (as,ts,fl,cl,ss,slide-whistlesax)
George Gruntz Concert Jazz Band
Blues 'N Dues Et Cetera | Enja | ENJ-6072 2

Mann,Gerd | (vibp)
New Jazz Group Hannover
Deutsches Jazz Fesival 1954/1955 | Bear Family Records | BCD 15430

Mann,Herbie | (alto-fl,b-cl,cl,ts,fl,b-fl,alto-f)
Chet Baker Septet
Chet | Original Jazz Classics | OJC20 087-2
Chet Baker Plays The Best Of Lerner And Loewe | Original Jazz Classics | OJC20 137-2
Herbie Mann And His Orchestra
The Best Of Herbie Mann | Atlantic | 7567-81369-2
Herbie Mann Group
Memphis Underground | Atlantic | 7567-81364-2
The Best Of Herbie Mann | Atlantic | 7567-81369-2
Rhino Presents The Atlantic Jazz Gallery | Atlantic | 8122-71257-2
Herbie Mann Quartet
Verve Jazz Masters 56:Herbie Mann | Verve | 529901-2
Herbie Mann Septet
Herbie Mann At The Village Gate | Atlantic | 7567-81350-2
Herbie Mann Sextet
Verve Jazz Masters Vol.60:The Collection | Verve | 529866-2
Verve Jazz Masters 56:Herbie Mann | Verve | 529901-2
Herbie Mann At The Village Gate | Atlantic | 7567-81350-2
Just Wailin' | Original Jazz Classics | OJCCD 900-2(NJ 8211)
Herbie Mann Trio
Verve Jazz Masters 56:Herbie Mann | Verve | 529901-2
Herbie Mann With The Bill Evans Trio
Nirvana | Atlantic | 7567-90141-2
Herbie Mann With The Frank DeVol Orchestra
Verve Jazz Masters 56:Herbie Mann | Verve | 529901-2
Herbie Mann-Bobby Jaspar Sextet
Flute Flight | Original Jazz Classics | OJCCD 1084-2(P 2124)
Flute Souflé | Original Jazz Classics | OJCCD 760-2(P 7101)
Herbie Mann's Californians
Great Ideas Of Western Man | Original Jazz Classics | OJCCD 1065-2(RLP 245)
Herbie Mann's Cuban Band
Verve Jazz Masters 56:Herbie Mann | Verve | 529901-2
Herbie Mann-Tamiko Jones
The Best Of Herbie Mann | Atlantic | 7567-81369-2
Johnny Pace With The Chet Baker Quintet
Chet Baker Introduces Johnny Pace | Original Jazz Classics | OJCCD 433-2(RLP 12-292)
Klaus Doldinger Jubilee
Doldinger's Best | ACT | 9224-2
Klaus Doldinger With Orchestra
Lifelike | Warner | 2292-46478-2
Klaus Doldinger With Orchestra And Etta James
Lifelike | Warner | 2292-46478-2
Sarah Vaughan With The Clifford Brown All Stars
Verve Jazz Masters 20:Introducing | Verve | 519853-2
Clifford Brown-Max Roach:Alone Together-The Best Of The Mercury Years | Verve | 526373-2
Sarah Vaughan | Verve | 543305-2
4 By 4:Ella Fitzgerald/Sarah Vaughan/Billie Holiday/Dinah Washington | Verve | 559693-2
Brownie-The Complete EmArCy Recordings Of Clifford Brown | EmArCy | 838306-2
Sarah Vaughan | EmArCy | 9860779

Mann,Howie | (dr)
Elliot Lawrence And His Orchestra
Mullenium | CBS | CK 65678

Mann,Wallace | (fl)
Charlie Byrd Group
Byrd In The Wind | Original Jazz Classics | OJCCD 1086(RS 9449)

Manne,Shelly | (dr,bells,waterphone,berimbau,cuica)
52nd Street All Stars
Planet Jazz:Bebop | RCA | 2169650-2
Art Pepper Quartet
Living Legend | Original Jazz Classics | OJCCD 408-2
Barney Kessel And His Orchestra
Barney Kessel Plays Carmen | Original Jazz Classics | OJC 269(C 7563)
The Jazz Giants Play Rodgers & Hart:Blue Moon | Prestige | PCD 24205-2
Barney Kessel And His Quintet
Barney Kessel Plays Carmen | Original Jazz Classics | OJC 269(C 7563)
Barney Kessel Quintet
Easy Like | Original Jazz Classics | OJCCD 153-2
Barney Kessel Plays Standards | Original Jazz Classics | OJCCD 238-2
Benny Carter And His Orchestra
Aspects | Capitol | 852677-2
Benny Carter Quartet
The Jazz Giants Play Rodgers & Hart:Blue Moon | Prestige | PCD 24205-2
Benny Carter Quintet
Jazz Giant | Original Jazz Classics | OJC20 167-2(C 7555)
Benny Carter Sextet
Jazz Giant | Original Jazz Classics | OJC20 167-2(C 7555)
Bill Evans Trio
Verve Jazz Masters 5:Bill Evans | Verve | 519821-2
The Complete Bill Evans On Verve | Verve | 527953-2
Ultimate Bill Evans selected by Herbie Hancock | Verve | 557536-2
Bill Smith Quartet
Folk Jazz U.S.A. | Original Jazz Classics | OJCCD 1956-2(S 7591)
Bud Shank And Trombones
Cool Fool | Fresh Sound Records | FSR CD 507
Cal Tjader With The Clare Fischer Orchestra
Cal Tjader Plays Harold Arlen & West Side Story | Fantasy | FCD 24775-2
Charlie Parker Quartet
Charlie Parker | Verve | 539757-2
Bird: The Complete Charlie Parker On Verve | Verve | 837141-2
Charlie Parker With Strings
Charlie Parker With Strings:The Master Takes | Verve | 523984-2
Charlie Parker With The Neal Hefti Orchestra
Charlie Parker:The Best Of The Verve Years | Verve | 527815-2
Bird: The Complete Charlie Parker On Verve | Verve | 837141-2
Chet Baker And The Lighthouse All Stars
Witch Doctor | Original Jazz Classics | OJCCD 609-2
Chet Baker Quartet
Let's Get Lost: The Best Of Chet Baker Sings | Pacific Jazz | 792932-2
Chet Baker Septet
The Best Of Chet Baker Plays | Pacific Jazz | 797161-2
Chet Baker Sextet
The Best Of Chet Baker Plays | Pacific Jazz | 797161-2
Coleman Hawkins And His 52nd Street All Stars
Jazz:The Essential Collection Vol.3 | IN+OUT Records | 78013-2
Coleman Hawkins And His Orchestra
Jazz:The Essential Collection Vol.3 | IN+OUT Records | 78013-2

Coleman Hawkins' Fifty-Second Street All-Stars
Planet Jazz:Coleman Hawkins | Planet Jazz | 2152055-2
Coleman Hawkins' Swing Four
Jazz:The Essential Collection Vol.3 | IN+OUT Records | 78013-2
Dizzy Gillespie All Stars
Dizzy Gillespie:Night In Tunisia | Dreyfus Jazz Line | FDM 36734-2
Ella Fitzgerald With Orchestra
The Best Is Yet To Come | Original Jazz Classics | OJCCD 889-2(2312138)
Ella Fitzgerald With The Marty Paich Orchestra
Ella Fitzgerald-First Lady Of Song | Verve | 517898-2
Whisper Not | Verve | 589947-2
For The Love Of Ella Fitzgerald | Verve | 841765-2
Hampton Hawes Quartet
Four!! | Original Jazz Classics | OJCCD 165-2
Hampton Hawes Trio
The Jazz Giants Play Miles Davis:Milestones | Prestige | PCD 24225-2
Henry Mancini And His Orchestra
Combo! | RCA | 2147794-2
Howard Rumsey's Lighthouse All-Stars
Sunday Jazz A La Lighthouse Vol.2 | Original Jazz Classics | OJCCD 972-2(S 2501)
JATP All Stars
Norman Granz' JATP: Carnegie Hall 1949 | Pablo | PACD 5311-2
Joe Pass Quartet
Joe Pass:Guitar Virtuoso | Pablo | 4 PACD 4423-2
Ira George And Joe-Joe Pass Loves Gershwin | Original Jazz Classics | OJCCD 828-2(2312133)
Johnny Hartman And His Orchestra
Unforgettable | Impulse(MCA) | IMP 11522
June Christy With The Pete Rugolo Orchestra
Something Cool(The Complete Mono & Stereo Versions) | Capitol | 534069-2
Lennie Niehaus Quintet
Lennie Niehaus Vol.1:The Quintets | Original Jazz Classics | OJCCD 1933-2(C 3518)
Lennie Niehaus Sextet
Lennie Niehaus Vol.5:The Sextet | Original Jazz Classics | OJCCD 1944-2(C 3524)
Lenny Tristano Quintet
Subconcious-Lee | Original Jazz Classics | OJCCD 186-2(P 7004)
Maynard Ferguson Band
Verve Jazz Masters 52:Maynard Ferguson | Verve | 529905-2
Ornette Coleman Quartet
Tomorrow Is The Question | Original Jazz Classics | OJC20 342-2(S 7569)
Pete Rugolo And His Orchestra
Verve Jazz Masters 52:Maynard Ferguson | Verve | 529905-2
Thriller/Richard Diamon(Original Jazz Scores From 2 Classics TV Series) | Fresh Sound Records | FSCD 2015
Red Norvo Sextet
Music To Listen To Red Norvo By | Original Jazz Classics | OJCCD 1015-2(C 7534)
Russ Freeman-Shelly Manne
One On One | Contemporary | CCD 14090-2
Shelly Manne And His Friends
My Fair Lady | Original Jazz Classics | OJC 336(C 7527)
Shelly Manne And His Hollywood All Stars
Art Pepper:The Hollywood All-Star Sessions | Galaxy | 5GCD 4431-2
Shelly Manne And His Men
The Gambit | Original Jazz Classics | OJCCD 1007-2(C 7557)
Vol.1:The West Coast Sound | Original Jazz Classics | OJCCD 152-2
More Swinging Sounds | Original Jazz Classics | OJCCD 320-2(C 7519)
At The Black Hawk Vol.1 | Original Jazz Classics | OJCCD 656-2(S 7577)
At The Black Hawk Vol.2 | Original Jazz Classics | OJCCD 657-2(S 7578)
At The Black Hawk Vol.3 | Original Jazz Classics | OJCCD 658-2(S 7579)
At The Black Hawk Vol.4 | Original Jazz Classics | OJCCD 659-2(S 7580)
At The Black Hawk Vol.5 | Original Jazz Classics | OJCCD 660-2
Live! At The Manne Hole Vol.1 | Original Jazz Classics | OJCCD 714-2(S 7593)
Live! At The Manne Hole Vol.2 | Original Jazz Classics | OJCCD 715-2(S 7594)
Jazz At The Philharmonic-Yesterdays | Pablo | PACD 5318-2
The Jazz Giants Play Harry Warren:Lullaby Of Broadway | Prestige | PCD 24204-2
Shelly Manne Sextet
Alive In London | Original Jazz Classics | OJCCD 773-2(S 7629)
Shelly Manne Trio
Li'l Abner | Original Jazz Classics | OJCCD 1087-2(S 7533)
At The Black Hawk Vol.5 | Original Jazz Classics | OJCCD 660-2
Shorty Rogers And His Giants
PLanet Jazz:Shorty Rogers | Planet Jazz | 2159976-2
Shorty Rogers And His Orchestra Feat. The Giants
PLanet Jazz:Shorty Rogers | Planet Jazz | 2159976-2
Sonny Rollins & The Contemporary Leaders
Sonny Rollins & The Contemporary Leaders | Original Jazz Classics | OJCCD 340-2
Sonny Rollins And The Contemporary Leaders
Sonny Rollins-The Freelance Years:The Complete Riverside & Contemporary Recordings | Riverside | 5 RCD 4427-2
Sonny Rollins Trio
Sonny Rollins-The Freelance Years:The Complete Riverside & Contemporary Recordings | Riverside | 5 RCD 4427-2
Way Out West | Original Jazz Classics | OJC20 337-2(S 7530)
Stan Getz Quartet
Stan Getz Highlights:The Best Of The Verve Years Vol.2 | Verve | 517330-2
Best Of The West Coast Sessions | Verve | 537084-2
West Coast Jazz | Verve | 557549-2
Stan Getz Highlights | Verve | 847430-2
Stan Getz Quintet
Stan Getz Highlights:The Best Of The Verve Years Vol.2 | Verve | 517330-2
Verve Jazz Masters 8:Stan Getz | Verve | 519823-2
Best Of The West Coast Sessions | Verve | 537084-2
Ultimate Stan Getz selected by Joe Henderson | Verve | 557532-2
West Coast Jazz | Verve | 557549-2
Stan Getz Highlights | Verve | 847430-2
Stan Getz-Lionel Hampton Quintet
Stan Getz Highlights:The Best Of The Verve Years Vol.2 | Verve | 517330-2
Hamp And Getz | Verve | 831672-2
Stan Getz-Lionel Hampton Sextet
Hamp And Getz | Verve | 831672-2
Stan Kenton And His Orchestra
Swing Vol.1 | Storyville | 4960343
Stan Kenton Portraits On Standards | Capitol | 531571-2
One Night Stand | Choice | CHCD 71051
The Metronome All Stars
Planet Jazz:Dizzy Gillespie | Planet Jazz | 2152069-2
The Poll Winners
The Poll Winners Ride Again | Original Jazz Classics | OJC 607(C 7556)
Poll Winners Three | Original Jazz Classics | OJCCD 692-2(C 7576)
Exploring The Scene | Original Jazz Classics | OJCCD 969-2(C 7581)
The Jazz Giants Play Harry Warren:Lullaby Of Broadway | Prestige | PCD 24204-2
Van Alexander Orchestra
Home Of Happy Feet/Swing! Staged For Sound! | Capitol | 535211-2
Woody Herman And His Orchestra
Woody Herman:Four Brother | Dreyfus Jazz Line | FDM 36722-2
Zoot Sims With Orchestra
Passion Flower | Original Jazz Classics | OJCCD 939-2(2312120)

Manning,John | (ts)
Melvin Sparks Quintet
Jazzin' With The Soul Brothers | Fantasy | FANCD 6086-2
Reuben Wilson Quartet
Blue Breaks Beats Vol.2 | Blue Note | 789907-2

Manning,Marty | (arrld)
Dinah Washington With Orchestra
Ballads | Roulette | 537559-2
Sarah Vaughan With The Marty Manning Orchestra
Jazz Profile | Blue Note | 823517-2

Manning,P. | (v)
Dee Dee Bridgewater With Orchestra
Dear Ella | Verve | 539102-2

Manning,Rita | (v)
John Surman With String Quartet
Coruscating | ECM | 1702(543033-2)

Manno,Jack | (cond,arrvoc)
Duke Pearson Orchestra
Deep Blue-The United States Of Mind | Blue Note | 521152-2

Mannone,Joe 'Wingy' | (co,voctp)
Wingy Mannone And His Orchestra
Planet Jazz:Jazz Trumpet | Planet Jazz | 2169654-2
Planet Jazz:Male Jazz Vocalists | Planet Jazz | 2169657-2

Manns,Andreas | (b)
Landes Jugend Jazz Orchester Hessen
Touch Of Lips | hr music.de | hrmj 004-01 CD

Manreza,Jose Perez | (percvoc)
Conjunto Clave Y Guaguanco
Dejala En La Puntica | TipToe | TIP-888829 2

Manring,Michael | (b,el-b,fretless-bsynth)
Michael Hedges
Aerial Boundaries | Windham Hill | 34 11032-2

Mantilla,Ray | (bells,chimes,congas,bongos,timbales)
Charles Mingus Orchestra
Cumbia & Jazz Fusion | Atlantic | 8122-71785-2
Gato Barbieri Group
Planet Jazz:Gato Barbieri | RCA | 2165364-2
Gato Barbieri Orchestra
The Roots Of Acid Jazz | Impulse(MCA) | IMP 12042
Gato Barbieri Septet
Yesterdays | RCA | 2147797-2
Herbie Mann And His Orchestra
The Best Of Herbie Mann | Atlantic | 7567-81369-2
Herbie Mann Group
The Best Of Herbie Mann | Atlantic | 7567-81369-2
Rhino Presents The Atlantic Jazz Gallery | Atlantic | 8122-71257-2
Herbie Mann Septet
Herbie Mann At The Village Gate | Atlantic | 7567-81350-2
Herbie Mann Sextet
Herbie Mann At The Village Gate | Atlantic | 7567-81350-2
Herbie Mann's Cuban Band
Verve Jazz Masters 56:Herbie Mann | Verve | 529901-2
Max Roach Group
We Insist: Freedom Now Suite | Candid | CCD 79002
M'Boom
To The Max! | Enja | ENJ-7021 22
Mingus Big Band 93
Nostalgia In Times Square | Dreyfus Jazz Line | FDM 36559-2

Mantler,Karen | (glockenspiel,org,harm,voc,p,synth)
Carla Bley Band
Fleur Carnivore | Watt | 21
The Very Big Carla Bley Band | Watt | 23
Big Band Theory | Watt | 25(519966-2)
Musique Mecanique | Watt | 9
Carla Bley Big Band
The Carla Bley Big Band Goes To Church | Watt | 27(533682-2)
Karen Mantler Group
My Cat Arnold | Watt | XtraWatt/3
Karen Mantler And Her Cat Arnold Get The Flu | Watt | XtraWatt/5
Farewell | Watt | XtraWatt/8
Michael Mantler Group With The Danish Radio Concert Orchestra Strings
The School Of Understanding(Sort-Of-An-Opera) | ECM | 1648/49(537963-2)
Michael Mantler Quintet With The Balanescu Quartet
Folly Seeing All This | ECM | 1485
Steve Swallow Group
Swallow | Watt | XtraWatt/6

Mantler,Michael | (comp,cond,tp,ldv-tb)
Carla Bley - Michael Mantler & Orchestra
13-3/4 | Watt | 3 (2313103)
Carla Bley Band
Live! | Watt | 12(815730-2)
Heavy Heart | Watt | 14
Dinner Music | Watt | 6(825815-2)
European Tour 1977 | Watt | 8
Musique Mecanique | Watt | 9
Carla Bley Group
Tropic Appetites | Watt | 1
Charlie Haden Orchestra
The Ballad Of The Fallen | ECM | 1248(811546-2)
Charlie Haden's Liberation Music Orchestra
Liberation Music Orchestra | Impulse(MCA) | 951188-2
Gary Burton Quartet With Orchestra
A Genuine Tong Funeral(Dark Opera Without Words) | RCA | 2119255-2
Karen Mantler Group
Karen Mantler And Her Cat Arnold Get The Flu | Watt | XtraWatt/5
Michael Mantler Group
Songs And One Symphony | ECM | 1721
Michael Mantler: No Answer/Silence | Watt | 2/5(543374-2)
The Hapless Child | Watt | 4
Silence | Watt | 5 (2313105)
Movies | Watt | 7 (2313107)
Movies/More Movies | Watt | 7/10(543377-2)
Michael Mantler Group With The Danish Concert Radio Orchestra
Many Have No Speech | Watt | 19(835580-2)
Michael Mantler Group With The Danish Radio Concert Orchestra Strings
The School Of Understanding(Sort-Of-An-Opera) | ECM | 1648/49(537963-2)
Michael Mantler Orchestra
Hide And Seek | ECM | 1738(549612-2)
Michael Mantler Quintet
Live | Watt | 18
Michael Mantler Quintet With The Balanescu Quartet
Folly Seeing All This | ECM | 1485
Michael Mantler Quintet With The London Symphony Orchestra
Something There | Watt | 13
Michael Mantler Sextet
Movies/More Movies | Watt | 7/10(543377-2)
Michael Mantler-Don Preston
Alien | Watt | 15
Mona Larsen And The Danish Radio Big Band Plus Soloists
Michael Mantler:Cerco Un Paese Innocente | ECM | 1556
Radio Symphony Orchestra Frankfurt
Songs And One Symphony | ECM | 1721
The Carla Bley Band
Social Studies | Watt | 11(831831-2)
I Hate To Sing | Watt | 12,5
The Jazz Composer's Orchestra
Comminications | JCOA | 1001/2

Manzecchi,Patrick | (dr)
Andreas Maile Quartet
Mailensteine | Satin Doll Productions | SDP 1022-1 CD

Manzolini,Paolo | (g)
Gianluigi Trovesi Nonet
Round About A Midsummer's Dream | Enja | ENJ-9384 2

Maple,Tim | (g)
Steve Martland Band
The Orchestra Of Smith's Academy | Enja | ENJ-9358 2

Mapp,Gary | (b)
Thelonious Monk Trio
Thelonious Monk:The Complete Prestige Recordings | Prestige | 3 PRCD 4428-2
Thelonious Monk:85th Birthday Celebration | zyx records | FANCD 6076-2
Thelonious Monk | Original Jazz Classics | OJC20 010-2(P 7027)
The Prestige Legacy Vol.1:The High Priests | Prestige | PCD 24251-2

Mappa,Paolo | (dr)
Orchestra Jazz Siciliana
Orchestra Jazz Siciliana Plays The Music Of Carla Bley | Watt | XtraWatt/4

Mara |
Mara!
Ruino Vino | Laika Records | 35100792

Mara,Vera | (voc)
James Chirillo Quartet with Vera Mara
Sultry Serenade | Nagel-Heyer | CD 061

Marable,Lawrence | (dr)
Charlie Haden Quartet West
Haunted Heart | Verve | 513078-2
Always Say Goodbye | Verve | 521501-2
Now Is The Hour | Verve | 527827-2
In Angel City | Verve | 837031-2
Charlie Haden Quartet West With Strings
Now Is The Hour | Verve | 527827-2
The Art Of The Song | Verve | 547403-2
Chet Baker Big Band
The Best Of Chet Baker Plays | Pacific Jazz | 797161-2
Chet Baker Quartet
Let's Get Lost: The Best Of Chet Baker Sings | Pacific Jazz | 792932-2
Chet Baker Sextet
The Best Of Chet Baker Plays | Pacific Jazz | 797161-2
Chet Baker-Art Pepper-Phil Urso Sextet
Picture Of Heath | Pacific Jazz | 494106-2
Dexter Gordon Quartet
Dexter Gordon Birthday Celebration | Fantasy | FANCD 6082-2
Diane Schuur And Her Band
Music Is My Life | Atlantic | 7567-83150-2
Hampton Hawes Trio
Bird Song | Original Jazz Classics | OJCCD 1035-2
Jerry Dodgion Quartet
The Jazz Scene:San Francisco | Fantasy | FCD 24760-2
Lawrence Marable Quartet feat. James Clay
Midnight Blue(The [Be]witching Hour) | Blue Note | 854365-2
Milt Jackson Septet
Milt Jackson Birthday Celebration | Fantasy | FANCD 6079-2
Sonny Stitt Orchestra
Verve Jazz Masters 50:Sonny Sitt | Verve | 527651-2
Tal Farlow Sextet
Verve Jazz Masters 41:Tal Farlow | Verve | 527365-2
Teddy Charles' West Coasters
Wardell Gray Memorial Vol.1 | Original Jazz Classics | OJCCD 050-2(P 7008)
Wardell Gray Quartet
Wardell Gray Memorial Vol.2 | Original Jazz Classics | OJCCD 051-2(P 7009)
Wardell Gray Quintet
Wardell Gray Memorial Vol.2 | Original Jazz Classics | OJCCD 051-2(P 7009)

Marabuto,Johnny | (p)
Brew Moore Quartet
The Brew Moore Quintet | Original Jazz Classics | OJCCD 100-2(F 3-222)
Brew Moore Quintet
The Brew Moore Quintet | Original Jazz Classics | OJCCD 100-2(F 3-222)

Maras,Fulvio | (drperc)
Gianlugi Trovesi Quartet With The WDR Big Band
Dedalo | Enja | ENJ-9419 2
Gianluigi Trovesi Nonet
Round About A Midsummer's Dream | Enja | ENJ-9384 2

Marcal,Armando | (perc)
Lee Ritenour Group
Rio | GRP | GRP 95242
Pat Metheny Group
Letter From Home | Geffen Records | GED 24245
The Road To You | Geffen Records | GED 24601
Toots Thieleman And Sivuca
Verve Jazz Masters Vol.59:Toots Thielemans | Verve | 535271-2

Marcantonio,Lara | (voc)
Kevin Mahogany With Orchestra
Songs And Moments | Enja | ENJ-8072 2

Marchena,Guilhermo | (dr,perc,gong,guica,tymbales,voc)
Passport
Ataraxia | Atlantic | 2292-42148-2

Marcian,Vicente | (ts)
Daniel Flors Group
When Least Expected | Fresh Sound Records | FSNT 080 CD

Marclay,Christian | (manipulated-records,records)
John Zorn Group With The Kronos Quartet
Spillane | Nonesuch | 7559-79172-2

Marcotulli,Rita | (p)
Palle Danielsson Quartet
Contra Post | Caprice | CAP 21440
Palle Danielsson Quintet
Contra Post | Caprice | CAP 21440

Marcus,Steve | (ssts)
Buddy Rich Big Band
Backwoods Siseman/Pieces Of Dream | Laserlight | 24655
The Jazz Composer's Orchestra
Comminications | JCOA | 1001/2

Marcus,Toni | (vviola)
Carla Bley Group
Tropic Appetites | Watt | 1

Marcus,Wade | (arr,brass-arr,comp,condtb)
Grant Green With Orchestra
The Final Comedown(Soundtrack) | Blue Note | 581678-2
Horace Silver Quintet With Brass
Horace Silver Retrospective | Blue Note | 495576-2
Marlena Shaw With Orchestra
Deep Blue-The United States Of Mind | Blue Note | 521152-2

Mardigan,Art | (dr)
Dexter Gordon Quintet
Fats Navarro:Nostalgia | Dreyfus Jazz Line | FDM 36736-2
Jimmy Rowles Trio
The Complete Nocturne Recordings:Jazz In Hollywood Series Vol.1 | Fresh Sound Records | NR 3CD-101
Stan Getz Quintet
Stan Getz Highlights | Verve | 847430-2

Mardin,Arif | (arr,condorg)
Eddie Harris Group
The Best Of Eddie Harris | Atlantic | 7567-81370-2

Mardin,Joe | (synth-programming)
Joe Sample Group
Invitation | Warner | 9362-45209.2

Maresz,Yan | (arrb-g)
John McLaughlin Group
The Promise | Verve | 529828-2
John McLaughlin With The Aighette Quartet And Yan Marez
Time Remembered:John McLaughlin Plays Bill Evans | Verve | 519861-2

Maret,Gregoire | (harm)
(Little)Jimmy Scott And His Band
Mood Indigo | Milestone | MCD 9305-2
Jacky Terrasson Group

INTERPRETENVERZEICHNIS

What It Is | Blue Note | 498756-2
Jimmy Scott With Band
Over The Rainbow | Milestone | MCD 9314-2
Moon Glow | Milestone | MCD 9332-2

Marge,George | (alto-fl,oboe,recorder,alto-recorder)
Freddie Hubbard With Orchestra
This Is Jazz:Freddie Hubbard | CBS | CK 65041
George Benson Orchestra
Talkin' Verve:George Benson | Verve | 553780-2
George Benson With Orchestra
Verve Jazz Masters 21:George Benson | Verve | 521861-2
George Benson With The Don Sebesky Orchestra
Verve Jazz Masters 21:George Benson | Verve | 521861-2
Gil Evans Orchestra
Verve Jazz Masters 23:Gil Evans | Verve | 521860-2
The Individualism Of Gil Evans | Verve | 833804-2
Blues In Orbit | Enja | ENJ-3069 2
Grover Washington Jr. Orchestra
Jazzrock-Anthology Vol.3:Fusion | Zounds | CD 27100555
Jack McDuff Quartet With Orchestra
Prelude:Jack McDuff Big Band | Prestige | PRCD 24283-2
Kenny Burrell With The Gil Evans Orchestra
Guitar Forms | Verve | 521403-2
Verve Jazz Masters 23:Gil Evans | Verve | 521860-2
Verve Jazz Masters 45:Kenny Burrell | Verve | 527652-2
Verve Jazz Masters Vol.60:The Collection | Verve | 529866-2
Milt Jackson And His Orchestra
Sunflower | CTI | ZK 65131
Paul Desmond Orchestra
Planet Jazz:Jazz Saxophone | Planet Jazz | 2169653-2
Paul Desmond Quartet With The Don Sebesby Orchestra
From The Hot Afternoon | Verve | 543487-2
Paul Desmond With Strings
Desmond Blue | RCA | 2663898-2
Rod Levitt Orchestra
The Dynamic Sound Patterns Of The Rod Levitt Orchestra | Original Jazz Classics | OJCCD 1955-2(RS 9471)
Ron Carter Group
Peg Leg | Original Jazz Classics | OJCCD 621-2

Margitza,Rick | (ss,ts,pkeyboards)
Jam Session
Jam Session Vol.1 | Steeplechase | SCCD 31522
Lenny White Group
Present Tense | Hip Bop | HIBD 8004
Miles Davis Group
Amandla | Warner | 7599-25873-2

Margolin,Bob | (b,gvoc)
Billy Boy Arnold Group
Eldorado Cadillac | Alligator Records | ALCD 4836

Marguet,Christophe | (dr)
Orchestre National De Jazz
Charmediterranéen | ECM | 1828(018493-2)

Margulis,Charlie | (tp)
Artie Shaw And His Orchestra
Planet JazzArtie Shaw | Planet Jazz | 2152057-2
Planet Jazz:Jazz Greatest Hits | Planet Jazz | 2169648-2

Maria,Luizano | (b)
Toots Thieleman And Sivuca
Verve Jazz Masters Vol.59:Toots Thielemans | Verve | 535271-2

Maria,Tania | (keyboards,synth,voc,p,arrel-p)
Michel Petrucciani Group
Michel Petrucciani:The Blue Note Years | Blue Note | 789916-2
Music | Blue Note | 792563-2

Mariano,Cesar Camargo | (arr,p,keyboardsprogramming)
Antonio Carlos Jobim Group
Verve Jazz Masters 13:Antonio Carlos Jobim | Verve | 516409-2
Antonio Carlos Jobim-Elis Regina Group
The Antonio Carlos Jobim Songbook | Verve | 525472-2

Mariano,Charlie | (as,ts,bs,cl,fl,ss,indian-fl)
Charles Mingus And His Orchestra
The Complete Town Hall Concert | Blue Note | 828353-2
Charles Mingus Orchestra
Mingus Mingus Mingus | Impulse(MCA) | 951170-2
The Black Saint And The Sinner Lady | Impulse(MCA) | 951174-2
Charlie Mariano & The Karnataka College Of Percussion
Jyothi | ECM | 1256
Live | VeraBra Records | CDVBR 2034-2
Charlie Mariano Quartet
Deep In A Dream | Enja | ENJ-9423 2
The Jazz Scene:San Francisco | Fantasy | FCD 24760-2
Charlie Mariano Sextet
The Jazz Scene:San Francisco | Fantasy | FCD 24760-2
Charlie Mariano Trio
Mariano | VeraBra Records | CDVBR 2124-2
Eberhard Weber Colours
Little Movements | ECM | 1186
Eberhard Weber Quartet
Yellow Fields | ECM | 1066(843205-2)
Eberhard Weber/Colours
Silent Feet | ECM | 1107(835017-2)
Edward Vesala Group
Nan Madol | ECM | 1077
European Jazz Ensemble
20th Anniversary Tour | Konnex Records | KCD 5078
European Jazz Ensemble 25th Anniversary | Konnex Records | KCD 5100
Freddy Studer Orchestra
Seven Songs | VeraBra Records | CDVBR 2056-2
George Gruntz Concert Jazz Band '83
Theatre | ECM | 1265
International Commission For The Prevention Of Musical Border Control,The
The International Commission For The Prevention Of Musical Border Control | VeraBra Records | CDVBR 2093-2
Jasper Van't Hof-Charlie Mariano-Steve Swallow
Brutto Tempo | Intuition Records | INT 3309-2
Jon Hiseman With The United Jazz & Rock Ensemble And Babara Thompson's Paraphernalia
About Time Too! | VeraBra Records | CDVBR 2014-2
Mariano-Humair-Haurand
Frontier Traffic | Konnex Records | KCD 5110
McCoy Tyner Quintet
Live At Newport | Impulse(MCA) | 547980-2
Modern Jazz Quartet And Orchestra
MJQ 40 | Atlantic | 7567-82330-2
Paul Shigihara-Charlie Mariano Quartet
Tears Of Sound | Nabel Records:Jazz Network | CD 4616
Philippe Caillat Group
Stream Of Time | Laika Records | LK 92-030
Rabih Abou-Khalil Group
Blue Camel | Enja | ENJ-7053 2
The Sultan's Picnic | Enja | ENJ-8078 2
Rabih Abou-Khalil Quintet
Between Dusk And Dawn | Enja | ENJ-9771 2
Rabih Abou-Khalil Septet
Between Dusk And Dawn | Enja | ENJ-9771 2
Shelly Manne And His Men
The Gambit | Original Jazz Classics | OJCCD 1007-2(C 7557)
More Swinging Sounds | Original Jazz Classics | OJCCD 320-2(C 7519)
Toshiko Mariano Quartet
Toshiko Mariano Quartet | Candid | CCD 79012
Vince Mendoza With The WDR Big Band And Guests
Sketches | ACT | 9215-2

Mariano,Toquarto | (g)
Duo Fenix
Karai-Eté | IN+OUT Records | 7009-2

Maric,Davis | (p)
Steve Martland Band
The Orchestra Of Smith's Academy | Enja | ENJ-9358 2

Maricle,Sherrie | (dr)
Bill Mays Quartet
The Story Of Jazz Piano | Laserlight | 24653

Mariella,Fracesco | (b)
Maximilian Geller Quartet feat. Melanie Bong
Smile | Edition Collage | EC 461-2
Vocal Moments | Take Twelve On CD | TT 008-2

Marienthal,Eric | (as,synth,ts,saxss)
Chick Corea Electric Band
Light Years | GRP | GRP 95462
Eye Of The Beholder | GRP | GRP 95642
Beneath The Mask | GRP | GRP 96492
Dave Grusin Orchestra
Two For The Road:The Music Of Henry Mancini | GRP | GRP 98652
Dave Weckl Group
Master Plan | GRP | GRP 96192
Heads Up | GRP | GRP 96732
GRP All-Star Big Band
GRP All-Star Big Band:Live! | GRP | GRP 97402
All Blues | GRP | GRP 98002

Marillier,Daniel | (b)
Stephane Grappelli With The Michel Legrand Orchestra
Grapelli Story | Verve | 515807-2

Marillo.Tony | (dr)
Don Menza Quartet
Las Vegar Late Night Sessions:Live At Capozzoli's | Woofy Productions | WPCD 116

Marinacci,Gino | (flbs)
Helen Merrill And Her Band
Planet Jazz:Female Jazz Vocalists | Planet Jazz | 2169656-2
Helen Merrill With The Piero Umilliani Group
Parole E Musica | RCA | 2174798-2

Marini,Lou | (alto-fl,as,ts,cl,fl,saxss)
Freddy Cole With Band
Le Grand Freddy:Freddy Cole Sings The Music Of Michel Legrand | Fantasy | FCD 9683-2
Lew Soloff Group
Rainbow Mountain | TipToe | TIP-888838 2

Marino,Amerigo | (v)
Cal Tjader With The Clare Fischer Orchestra
Cal Tjader Plays Harold Arlen & West Side Story | Fantasy | FCD 24775-2
Hank Crawford Orchestra
Rhino Presents The Atlantic Jazz Gallery | Atlantic | 8122-71257-2

Marino,Jose | (b)
Astrud Gilberto With The Walter Wanderley Quartet
A Certain Smile A Certain Sadness | Verve | 557449-2
Astrud Gilberto With The Walter Wanderley Quintet
A Certain Smile A Certain Sadness | Verve | 557449-2
Astrud Gilberto With The Walter Wanderley Quuitet
Verve Jazz Masters 9:Astrud Gilberto | Verve | 519824-2

Marino,Rickey | (v)
Mel Tormé With The Russell Garcia Orchestra
Swingin' On The Moon | Verve | 511385-2

Marion,Percy | (as,bsreeds)
Duke Ellington And His Orchestra
Highlights From The Duke Ellington Centennial Edition | RCA | 2663672-2
Duke Ellington Orchestra
Continuum | Fantasy | FCD 24765-2

Marker,Gregory | (bel-b)
Sam Rivers Orchestra
Crystals | Impulse(MCA) | 589760-2

Markham,John | (dr)
Art Van Damme Group
State Of Art | MPS | 841413-2
Frank Sinatra With The Red Norvo Quintet(Sextet!)
Live In Australia,1959 | Blue Note | 837513-2
Frank Sinatra With The Red Norvo Quintet(Sextet!) & Orchestra
Live In Australia,1959 | Blue Note | 837513-2
Red Norvo Sextet
Live In Australia,1959 | Blue Note | 837513-2
Vince Guaraldi Quartet
The Jazz Scene:San Francisco | Fantasy | FCD 24760-2

Markovitz,Phil | (p)
Chet Baker Quartet
Jazz In Paris:Chet Baker-Broken Wing | EmArCy | 013043-2
Chet Baker-The Legacy Vol.4:Oh You Crazy Moon | Enja | ENJ-9453 2

Markowitz,Dave | (viola)
George Benson With The Don Sebesky Orchestra
Verve Jazz Masters 21:George Benson | Verve | 521861-2

Markowitz,Irving 'Marky' | (fl-htp)
Carmen McRae With Orchestra
Birds Of A Feather | Decca | 589515-2
Carmen McRae With The Ralph Burns Orchestra
Birds Of A Feather | Decca | 589515-2
Chubby Jackson And His All Star Big Band
Chubby Takes Over | Fresh Sound Records | FSR-CD 324
Glenn Miller And His Orchestra
The Glenn Miller Orchestra In Digital Mood | GRP | GRP 95022
Grant Green Orchestra
Grant Green:Blue Breakbeat | Blue Note | 494705-2
Grant Green With Orchestra
The Final Comedown(Soundtrack) | Blue Note | 581678-2
Grover Washington Jr. Orchestra
Jazzrock-Anthology Vol.3:Fusion | Zounds | CD 27100555
Herbie Mann And His Orchestra
The Best Of Herbie Mann | Atlantic | 7567-81369-2
Jimmy McGriff Orchestra
Swingin' The Blues-Jumpin' The Blues | Laserlight | 24654
Jimmy Rushing And His Orchestra
Five Feet Of Soul | Roulette | 581830-2
Jimmy Smith With The Johnny Pate Orchestra
Jimmy Smith-Talkin' Verve | Verve | 531563-2
Jimmy Smith With The Lalo Schifrin Orchestra
Jimmy Smith:Best Of The Verve Years | Verve | 527950-2
Jimmy Smith-Talkin' Verve | Verve | 531563-2
The Cat | Verve | 539756-2
Nina Simone And Orchestra
Planet Jazz:Nina Simone | Planet Jazz | 2165372-2
Paul Desmond Quartet With The Don Sebesby Orchestra
From The Hot Afternoon | Verve | 543487-2
Woody Herman And His Orchestra
The Legends Of Swing | Laserlight | 24659
Woody Herman:Four Brother | Dreyfus Jazz Line | FDM 36722-2
Woody Herman And The Herd
Woody Herman (And The Herd) At Carnegie Hall | Verve | 559833-2

Marks,Betty | (v)
Johnny Hartman And His Orchestra
Unforgettable | Impulse(MCA) | IMP 11522

Marks,Dennis | (bb-g)
Maynard Ferguson And His Big Bop Nouveau Band
Maynard Ferguson '93-Footpath Café | Hot Shot Records | HSR 8312-2

Marks,Jon | (p)
Jan Harrington Band
Christmas Jazz! | Nagel-Heyer | NH 1008
Jan Harrington Sextet
Jan Harrington's Christmas In New Orleans | Nagel-Heyer | NHR SP 4

Marktl,Klemens | (dr)
Couch Ensemble
Winnetou | Jazz 'n' Arts Records | JNA 1503

Markussen,Uffe | (b-cl,ts,fl,cl,ss,reeds,saxas)
Geri Allen And The Jazzpar 1996 Nonet
Some Aspects Of Water | Storyville | STCD 4212
Jens Winther And The Danish Radio Jazz Orchestra
Angels | dacapo | DCCD 9442
Joaquin Chacón Group
San | Fresh Sound Records | FSNT 015 CD
Joaquin Chacón-Uffe Markussen European Quintet
Time | Fresh Sound Records | FSNT 051 CD
Mona Larsen And The Danish Radio Big Band Plus Soloists
Michael Mantler:Cerco Un Paese Innocente | ECM | 1556
The Danish Radio Jazz Orchestra
This Train:The Danish Radio Jazz Orchestra Plays The Music Of Ray Pitts | dacapo | DCCD 9428
Nice Work | dacapo | DCCD 9446

Marmarosa,Dodo | (pp-solo)
Artie Shaw And His Orchestra
Planet Jazz:Jazz Trumpet | Planet Jazz | 2169654-2
Charlie Parker Septet
Charlie Parker:Now's The Time | Dreyfus Jazz Line | FDM 36724-2
Charlie Parker's New Stars
Charlie Parker:Now's The Time | Dreyfus Jazz Line | FDM 36724-2
Lester Young And His Band
Jazz:The Essential Collection Vol.3 | IN+OUT Records | 78013-2
Lester Young:The Complete Aladdin Sessions | Blue Note | 832787-2
Lester Young:Blue Lester | Dreyfus Jazz Line | FDM 36729-2
Lucky Thompson And His Lucky Seven
Planet Jazz:Bebop | RCA | 2169650-2
Red Norvo Septet
Jazz Profile:Dexter Gordon | Blue Note | 823514-2

Marmulla,Klaus | (ascl)
Harry Allen And Randy Sandke Meets The RIAS Big Band Berlin
The Music Of The Trumpet Kings | Nagel-Heyer | CD 037

Marocco,Frank | (accordeon,el-accordeonp)
Jacintha With Band And Strings
Lush Life | Groove Note | GRV 1011-2(Gold CD 2011)

Marotti,Art | (perc)
Jimmy Smith With The Claus Ogerman Orchestra
Any Number Can Win | Verve | 557447-2

Marowitz,Sam | (as,fl,cl,reedssax)
Cab Calloway And His Orchestra
Planet Jazz:Cab Calloway | Planet Jazz | 2161237-2
Planet Jazz:Male Jazz Vocalists | Planet Jazz | 2169657-2
Chris Connor With Band
Chris Connor | Atlantic | 7567-80769-2
Chubby Jackson And His All Star Big Band
Chubby Takes Over | Fresh Sound Records | FSR-CD 324
Coleman Hawkins With Billy Byers And His Orchestra
The Hawk In Hi-Fi | RCA | 2663842-2
Elliot Lawrence And His Orchestra
The Elliot Lawrence Big Band Swings Cohn & Kahn | Fantasy | FCD 24761-2
Lena Horne With The Lennie Hayton Orchestra
Planet Jazz:Lena Horne | Planet Jazz | 2165373-2
Louis Armstrong And His Orchestra
What A Wonderful World | MCA | MCD 01876
Ralph Burns And His Orchestra
The Complete Verve Roy Eldridge Studio Sessions | Verve | 9861278
Woody Herman And His Orchestra
The Legends Of Swing | Laserlight | 24659
Woody Herman:Four Brother | Dreyfus Jazz Line | FDM 36722-2
Louis Armstrong-Jack Teagarden-Woody Herman:Midnights At V-Disc | Jazz Unlimited | JUCD 2048
Old Gold Rehearsals 1944 | Jazz Unlimited | JUCD 2079
Woody Herman And The Herd
Woody Herman (And The Herd) At Carnegie Hall | Verve | 559833-2

Marquardt,Klaus | (v)
Katie Kern Group
Still Young | Jazzpoint | JP 1070 CD
Rainer Tempel Band
Suite Ellington | Jazz 'n' Arts Records | JNA 0401

Marquart,Bernd | (tp)
Bireli Lagrene Ensemble
Routes To Django & Bireli Swing '81 | Jazzpoint | JP 1055 CD
Routs To Django-Live At The 'Krokodil' | Jazzpoint | JP 1056 CD
Jan Jankeje Septet
A' Portrait Of Jan Jankeje | Jazzpoint | JP 1054 CD

Marquez,Basilo | (tp)
Irakere
Yemayá | Blue Note | 498239-2

Marquez,Jose Miguel | (perc)
Bajazzo
Caminos | Edition Collage | EC 485-2

Marquez,Pibo | (perc)
Antonio Farao Quartet
Next Stories | Enja | ENJ-9430 2

Marquez,Sal | (tpfl-h)
Marcus Miller Group
The Sun Don't Lie | Dreyfus Jazz Line | FDM 36560-2

Marreiro,Nicky | (congastimbales)
International Commission For The Prevention Of Musical Border Control,The
The International Commission For The Prevention Of Musical Border Control | VeraBra Records | CDVBR 2093-2

Marrero,Lawrence | (bass-dr,bjg)
Bunk Johnson And His New Orleans Band
Planet Jazz:Jazz Trumpet | Planet Jazz | 2169654-2
Bunk Johnson And His Superior Jazz Band
Authentic New Orleans Jazz | Good Time Jazz | GTCD 12048-2
George Lewis And His New Orleans Ragtime Band
The Beverly Caverns Session | Good Time Jazz | GTCD 12058-2

Marrero,Nicky | (bongos,guiro,timbales,chekere)
Conexion Latina
Mambo 2000 | Enja | ENJ-7055 2
La Conexión | Enja | ENJ-9065 2
Jerry Gonzalez & Fort Apache Band
The River Is Deep | Enja | ENJ-4040 2
Nina Simone And Orchestra
Baltimore | Epic | 476906-2

Marron,Gordon | (v)
Milt Jackson And His Orchestra
Reverence And Compassion | Reprise | 9362-45204-2

Marrow,Esther | (voc)
Duke Ellington And His Orchestra
Highlights From The Duke Ellington Centennial Edition | RCA | 2663672-2

Marsalis,Branford | (as,bs,ts,cl,ss,sax,voicewoodwinds)
Art Blakey And The Jazz Messengers
Jazz Life Vol.2:From Seventh At Avenue South | Storyville | 4960763
Branford Marsalis Quartet
Crazy People Music | CBS | 466870-2
Reqiem | CBS | 69655-2
Branford Marsalis Trio
Trio Jeepy | CBS | 465134-2
Dave Grusin Group
Migration | GRP | GRP 95922
Dizzy Gillespie And His Orchestra
Closer To The Source | Atlantic | 7567-80776-2
Essence All Stars
Hot Jazz Bisquits | Hip Bop | HIBD 8801
Harry Connick Jr. Quartet With Branford Marsalis
We Are In Love | CBS | 466736-2
Miles Davis Group
Decoy | CBS | 468702-2
Roy Hargrove Quintet With Branford Marsalis
Roy Hargrove Quintet With The Tenors Of Our Time | Verve | 523019-2
Shirley Horn Trio with Branford Marsalis
You Won't Forget Me | Verve | 847482-2
Wynton Marsalis Quartet
Wynton Marsalis | CBS | 468708-2
Wynton Marsalis Quintet
Wynton Marsalis | CBS | 468708-2
Wynton Marsalis Sextet
Hot House Flowers | CBS | 468710-2

Marsalis,Delfeayo | (tb)
Wycliffe Gordon Group
The Search | Nagel-Heyer | CD 2007

Marsalis,Ellis | (pp-solo)
Nat Adderley Sextet
Cannonball Adderley Birthday Celebration | Fantasy | FANCD 6087-2
In The Bag | Original Jazz Classics | OJCCD 648-2(JLP 975)

Marsalis,Wynton | (tp,ldvoc)
A Band Of Friends
Wynton Marsalis Quartet With Strings | CBS | CK 68921
Art Blakey And The Jazz Messengers
Jazz Life Vol.2:From Seventh At Avenue South | Storyville | 4960763
Chico Freeman Quintet
Destiny's Dance | Original Jazz Classics | OJCCD 799-2(C 14008)
Chico Freeman Septet
Destiny's Dance | Original Jazz Classics | OJCCD 799-2(C 14008)
Chico Freeman Sextet
Destiny's Dance | Original Jazz Classics | OJCCD 799-2(C 14008)
Jimmy Scott With Band
But Beautiful | Milestone | MCD 9321-2
Joe Henderson Quintet
Lush Life-The Music Of Billy Strayhorn | Verve | 511779-2
Lincoln Center Jazz Orchestra
Big Train | CBS | CK 69860
Nicholas Payton Sextet
Payton's Place | Verve | 557327-2
Roy Hargrove Sextet
Family | Verve | 527630-2
Shirley Horn Trio with Wynton Marsalis
You Won't Forget Me | Verve | 847482-2
Shirley Horn With Strings
Here's To Life | Verve | 511879-2
Wynton Marsalis Group
Standard Time Vol.4:Marsalis Plays Monk | CBS | CK 67503
Standard Time Vol.6:Mr.Jelly Lord | CBS | CK 69872
Wynton Marsalis Quartet
Wynton Marsalis | CBS | 468708-2
Wynton Marsalis Quintet
Wynton Marsalis | CBS | 468708-2
Wynton Marsalis Sextet
Hot House Flowers | CBS | 468710-2

Marsh,Fergus | (sticks)
Hugh Marsh Duo/Quartet/Orchestra
The Bear Walks | VeraBra Records | CDVBR 2011-2

Marsh,George | (dr,hand-claps,perc.remo rototoms)
Bix Beiderbecke And His Gang
Jazz:The Essential Collection Vol.2 | IN+OUT Records | 78012-2

Marsh,Hugh | (v)
Hugh Marsh Duo/Quartet/Orchestra
The Bear Walks | VeraBra Records | CDVBR 2011-2

Marsh,Jack | (bassoon)
Ella Fitzgerald With The Frank DeVol Orchestra
Get Happy! | Verve | 523321-2

Marsh,Roy | (vib)
Stephane Grappelli Quintet
Grapelli Story | Verve | 515807-2

Marsh,Warne | (ts)
Art Pepper-Warne Marsh Quintet
The Way It Is | Original Jazz Classics | OJCCD 389-2
Bill Evans Quintet
The Complete Fantasy Recordings | Fantasy | 9FCD 1012-2
Hans Koller Groups
Out Of The Rim | IN+OUT Records | 7014-2
Lee Konitz Quintet
Subconcious-Lee | Original Jazz Classics | OJCCD 186-2(P 7004)
Lee Konitz-Warne Marsh Quintet
Lee Konitz With Warne Marsh | Atlantic | 8122-75356-2
Lee Konitz-Warne Marsh Sextet
Lee Konitz With Warne Marsh | Atlantic | 8122-75356-2
The Metronome All Stars
Jazz Gallery:Lester Young Vol.2(1946-59) | RCA | 2119541-2
Warne Marsh Quintet
Jazz Of Two Cities | Fresh Sound Records | FSR-CD 342
Warne Marsh Quintet With Art Pepper
Jazz Of Two Cities | Fresh Sound Records | FSR-CD 342
Warne Marsh Trio
The Unissued Copenhagen Studio Recordings | Storyville | STCD 8278
Warne Marsh/Hans Koller
Jazz Unlimited | IN+OUT Records | 7017-2

Marshall,Eddie | (drperc)
Art Pepper Quartet
San Francisco Samba | Contemporary | CCD 14086-2
Kenny Burrell Quintet
Stormy Monday Blues | Fantasy | FCD 24767-2
Toshiko Mariano Quartet
Toshiko Mariano Quartet | Candid | CCD 79012

Marshall,Fred | (bg)
Vince Guaraldi Group
Charlie Brown's Holiday Hits | Fantasy | FCD 9682-2
Vince Guaraldi-Bola Sete Quartet
Vince & Bola | Fantasy | FCD 24756-2

Marshall,Jack | (arr,ldg)
June Christy With The Pete Rugolo Orchestra
Something Cool(The Complete Mono & Stereo Versions) | Capitol | 534069-2
Peggy Lee With Jack Marshall's Music
Things Are Swingin' | Capitol | 597072-2
Peggy Lee With Orchestra
Misty Blue:Sweet Sisters Swing Songs Of Sorrow And Sadness | Blue Note | 521151-2

Marshall,Joe | (drperc)
Al Sears And His Orchestra
Sear-iously | Bear Family Records | BCD 15668 AH
Al Sears Quintet
Swing's The Thing | Original Jazz Classics | OJCCD 838-2(SV 2018)
Count Basie And His Orchestra
Jazz:The Essential Collection Vol.3 | IN+OUT Records | 78013-2
Dickie Wells-Buddy Tate Quintet
Every Day I Have The Blues | Impulse(MCA) | 547967-2
Eberhard Weber Colours
Little Movements | ECM | 1186
Eberhard Weber/Colours
Silent Feet | ECM | 1107(835017-2)
JATP All Stars
The Complete Jazz At The Philharmonic On Verve 1944-1949 | Verve | 523893-2
Jimmy Lunceford And His Orchestra
The Legends Of Swing | Laserlight | 24659
Jimmy Rushing And His Orchestra
Every Day I Have The Blues | Impulse(MCA) | 547967-2
John Surman-John Warren Group
The Brass Project | ECM | 1478
Johnny Hodges-Earl Hines Quintet
Verve Jazz Masters 35:Johnny Hodges | Verve | 521857-2
NDR Big Band With Guests
50 Years Of NDR Big Band:Bravissimo II | ACT | 9259-2

Marshall,John | (?,dr,g,voc,tb,tpfl-h)
Al Porcino Big Band
Al Porcino Big Band Live! | Organic Music | ORGM 9717
Arild Andersen Trio
The Triangle | ECM | 1752(0381212)
Bernard Purdie's Soul To Jazz
Bernard Purdie's Soul To Jazz | ACT | 9242-2
Eddie Harris Group With The WDR Big Band
Eddie Harris-The Last Concert | ACT | 9249-2
Gianlugi Trovesi Quartet With The WDR Big Band
Dedalo | Enja | ENJ-9419 2
Harry Allen And Randy Sandke Meets The RIAS Big Band Berlin
The Music Of The Trumpet Kings | Nagel-Heyer | CD 037
Jens Winther And The WDR Big Band
The Escape | dacapo | DCCD 9437
John Goldsby Sextet
Viewpoint | Nagel-Heyer | CD 2014
John Marshall Quintet
Dreamin' On The Hudson | Organic Music | ORGM 9713
Theme Of No Repeat | Organic Music | ORGM 9719
John Surman Quartet
Stranger Than Fiction | ECM | 1534
Kevin Mahogany With The WDR Big Band And Guests
Pussy Cat Dues:The Music Of Charles Mingus | Enja | ENJ-9316 2
Los Jovenes Flamencos With The WDR Big Band And Guests
Jazzpana | ACT | 9212-2
NDR Big Band With Guests
50 Years Of NDR Big Band:Bravissimo II | ACT | 9259-2
Roy Powell Quartet
North By Northwest | Nagel-Heyer | CD 2013
Uli Beckerhoff Quartet
Secret Obsession | Nabel Records:Jazz Network | CD 4647
Uli Beckerhoff Trio
Camporondo | Nabel Records:Jazz Network | CD 4629
Vassilis Tsabropoulos Trio
Achirana | ECM | 1728(157462-2)
Vince Mendoza With The WDR Big Band And Guests
Sketches | ACT | 9215-2

Marshall,Joshi | (ts)
Dogslyde
Hair Of The Dog | Intuition Records | INT 3223-2

Marshall,Kaiser | (dr)
Bessie Smith With The James P.Johnson Orchestra And The Hal Johnson Choir
The Blues | Storyville | 4960323
Fats Waller And His Buddies
Jazz:The Essential Collection Vol.3 | IN+OUT Records | 78013-2
Fletcher Henderson And His Orchestra
Jazz:The Essential Collection Vol.1 | IN+OUT Records | 78011-2
Louis Armstrong And His Orchestra
Jazz:The Essential Collection Vol.3 | IN+OUT Records | 78013-2
McKinney's Cotton Pickers
Jazz:The Essential Collection Vol.3 | IN+OUT Records | 78013-2

Marshall,Lyndell | (dr)
Jubilee All Stars
Jazz Gallery:Lester Young Vol.2(1946-59) | RCA | 2119541-2
Lester Young And His Band
Jazz:The Essential Collection Vol.3 | IN+OUT Records | 78013-2
Lester Young:The Complete Aladdin Sessions | Blue Note | 832787-2
Lester Young:Blue Lester | Dreyfus Jazz Line | FDM 36729-2

Marshall,Mike | (g,mand,mandocello,mandola,synth)
Stephane Grappelli-David Grisman Group
Stephane Grappelli:Live In San Francisco | Storyville | 4960723

Marshall,Neil | (dr)
Eddie Lang-Joe Venuti And Their Allstars Orchestra
Jazz:The Essential Collection Vol.3 | IN+OUT Records | 78013-2

Marshall,Raymond | (voc)
First Revolution Singers
First Revolution Gospel Singers:A Capella | Laserlight | 24338

Marshall,Wende |
Duke Ellington And His Orchestra
The Big Bands Vol.1.The Snader Telescriptions | Storyville | 4960043

Marshall,Wendell | (b)
Al Sears Quintet
Swing's The Thing | Original Jazz Classics | OJCCD 838-2(SV 2018)
Al Smith With The Eddie Lockjaw Davis Quartet
Queen Of The Organ-Shirley Scott Memorial Album | Prestige | PRCD 11027-2
Ben Webster With Orchestra And Strings
Verve Jazz Masters 43:Ben Webster | Verve | 525431-2
Music For Loving:Ben Webster With Strings | Verve | 527774-2
Ultimate Ben Webster selected by James Carter | Verve | 557537-2
Coleman Hawkins All Stars
Coleman Hawkins All Stars | Original Jazz Classics | OJCCD 225-2(SV 2005)
Coleman Hawkins Quartet
Late Night Sax | CBS | 487798-2
Body And Soul Revisited | GRP | GRP 16272
At Easy | Original Jazz Classics | OJC20 181-2(MV 7)
Coleman Hawkins Quintet
Soul | Original Jazz Classics | OJC20 096-2(P 7149)
The Jazz Giants Play Sammy Cahn:It's Magic | Prestige | PCD 24226-2
Dizzy Gillespie All Stars
Verve Jazz Masters 25:Stan Getz & Dizzy Gillespie | Verve | 521852-2
Duke Ellington And His Orchestra
The Legends Of Swing | Laserlight | 24659
100 Years Duke | Laserlight | 24906
Highlights From The Duke Ellington Centennial Edition | RCA | 2663672-2
Greatest Hits | CBS | 462959-2
Ellington '55 | Capitol | 520135-2
Duke Ellington-Billy Strayhorn Trio
Great Times! | Original Jazz Classics | OJC20 108-2(RLP 475)
Eddie Costa Quartet
Guys And Dolls Like Vives | Verve | 549366-2
Eddie Lockjaw Davis And His Orchestra
Eric Dolphy:The Complete Prestige Recordings | Prestige | 9 PRCD-4418-2
Ella Fitzgerald With The Don Abney Trio
Ella Fitzgerald-First Lady Of Song | Verve | 517898-2
Gene Ammons And His Orchestra
A Stranger In Town | Prestige | PRCD 24266-2
Gene Ammons Quartet
The Mal Waldron Memorial Album:Soul Eyes | Prestige | PRCD 11024-2
A Stranger In Town | Prestige | PRCD 24266-2
Gene Ammons Sextet
Gentle Jug Vol.3 | Prestige | PCD 24249-2
Gigi Gryce-Donald Byrd Jazz Laboratory
At Newport | Verve | 589764-2
Grant Green Sextet
Blue Bossa | Blue Note | 795590-2
Hal Singer-Charlie Shavers Quintet
Blue Stompin' | Original Jazz Classics | OJCCD 834-2(P 7153)
Harry Carney And His Orchestra With Strings
Music For Loving:Ben Webster With Strings | Verve | 527774-2
Herbie Mann-Bobby Jaspar Sextet
Flute Flight | Original Jazz Classics | OJCCD 1084-2(P 2124)
Flute Souflé | Original Jazz Classics | OJCCD 760-2(P 7101)
Ike Quebec Quintet
Blue Bossa | Blue Note | 795590-2
Jack McDuff Quartet
Brother Jack | Prestige | PR20 7174-2
The Last Goodun' | Prestige | PRCD 24274-2
Jack McDuff:The Prestige Years | Prestige | PRCD 24387-2
John LaPorta Octet
Theme And Variations | Fantasy | FCD 24776-2
John LaPorta Septet
Theme And Variations | Fantasy | FCD 24776-2
Johnny Hodges Orchestra
Coleman Hawkins/Johnny Hodges:The Vogue Recordings | Vogue | 21559712
Side By Side | Verve | 521405-2
Lawrence Brown With The Ralph Burns Orchestra
Slide Trombone | Verve | 559930-2
Lonnie Johnson Trio
Bawdy Blues | Original Blues Classics | OBCCD 544-2(BV 1055)
Lonnie Johnson With Elmer Snowden
Blues And Ballads | Original Blues Classics | OBCCD 531-2(BV 1011)
Oliver Nelson Quintet
Oliver Nelson Feat. Kenny Dorham | Original Jazz Classics | OJCCD 227-2(NJ 8224)
Paul Desmond-Gerry Mulligan Quartet
The Ballad Of Paul Desmond | RCA | 21429372
Planet Jazz:Paul Desmond | Planet Jazz | 2152061-2
Planet Jazz:Jazz Greatest Hits | Planet Jazz | 2169648-2
Two Of A Mind | RCA | 2179620-2
Prestige Blues-Swingers
Soul Street | Original Jazz Classics | OJCCD 987-2(NJ 8293)
Roland Kirk Quartet
Talkin' Verve-Roots Of Acid Jazz:Roland Kirk | Verve | 533101-2
Rahsaan/The Complete Mercury Recordings Of Roland Kirk | Mercury | 846630-2
Sandole Brothers
The Sandole Brothers | Fantasy | FCD 24763-2
Shorty Baker-Doc Cheatham Quintet
Shorty & Doc | Original Jazz Classics | OJCCD 839-2(SV 2021)
Sonny Rollins Quintet
Sonny Rollins-The Freelance Years:The Complete Riverside & Contemporary Recordings | Riverside | 5 RCD 4427-2
Willis Jackson Quintet
At Large | Prestige | PCD 24243-2
Together Again: Willis Jackson With Jack McDuff | Prestige | PRCD 24284-2

Marsico,Alberto | (keyboards,org,el-pp)
Alberto Marsico Quintet
Them That's Got | Organic Music | ORGM 9705
Dook Joint
Who's Been Talkin'... | Organic Music | ORGM 9728
Lorenzo Petrocca Organ Trio
Milan In Minor | Jardis Records | JRCD 20136
Jazz Guitar Highlights 1 | Jardis Records | JRCD 20141
Lozenzo Petrocca Quartet
Stop It | Edition Musikat | EDM 018
Mike Turk With The Alkaline Jazz Trio
A Little Taste Of Cannonball | Organic Music | ORGM 9708
Ron Ringwood's Crosscut Bluesband
Earth Tones | Organic Music | ORGM 9722
Scenario
Jazz The Beatles | Organic Music | ORGM 9729
Thilo Kreitmeier & Group
Changes | Organic Music | ORGM 9725

Marstatt,German | (alto-h,tp,co,fl-hbar-horn)
Blue Room Ensemble
Solitude | Foolish Music | FM 211993
Cool Blue
House In The Country | Foolish Music | FM 211591
Jazzensemble Des Hessischen Rundfunks
Jazz Messe-Messe Für Unsere Zeit | hr music.de | hrmj 003-01 CD

Martel,Johnny | (tp)
Benny Goodman And His Orchestra
Charlie Christian:Swing To Bop | Dreyfus Jazz Line | FDM 36715-2

Martell,Arleane | (voc)
Dee Dee Bridgewater With Band
Dee Dee Bridgewater | Atlantic | 7567-80760-2

Marthe,Linley | (b)
Karim Ziad Groups
Ifrikya | ACT | 9282-2
Soriba Kouyaté Quartet
Live In Montreux | ACT | 9414-2

Martin,Adam | (tb)
Louis Armstrong And His Orchestra
Best Of The Complete RCA Victor Recordings | RCA | 2663636-2
Louis Armstrong:A 100th Birthday Celebration | RCA | 2663694-2
Louis Armstrong:C'est Si Bon | Dreyfus Jazz Line | FDM 36730-2

Martin,Alan | (v)
Stan Getz With The Eddie Sauter Orchestra
Stan Getz Plays The Music Of Mickey One | Verve | 531232-2
Ultimate Stan Getz selected by Joe Henderson | Verve | 557532-2

Martin,Allan | (stringsv)
Verve Jazz Masters 8:Stan Getz | Verve | 519823-2

Martin,Andy | (tb)
Buddy Childers Big Band
It's What Happening Now! | Candid | CCD 79749
Dave Grusin Orchestra
Two For The Road:The Music Of Henry Mancini | GRP | GRP 98652
Diane Schuur With Orchestra And Strings
The Best Of Diane Schuur | GRP | GRP 98882
Vic Lewis West Coast All Stars
Vic Lewis Presenting A Celebration Of Contemporary West Coast Jazz | Candid | CCD 79711/12
Me And You! | Candid | CCD 79739

Martin,Bill | (dr,dr-programming,perc,bell,ganza)
Lounge Lizards
Live In Berlin 1991-Vol.2 | Intuition Records | INT 2055-2

Martin,Billy | (dr,berimbau,perc,tambourinets)
John Scofield Quartet
A Go Go | Verve | 539979-2
Lounge Lizards
Berlin 1991 Part 1 | Intuition Records | INT 2044-2
Medeski Martin & Wood
Univisible | Blue Note | 535870-2
Michael Blake Group
Kingdom Of Champa | Intuition Records | INT 3189-2

Martin,Bob | (flas)
Buddy Rich Big Band
Backwoods Siseman/Pieces Of Dream | Laserlight | 24655

Martin,Bobby | (tp,vocvib)
Willie Lewis And His Entertainers
Americans Swinging In Paris:Benny Carter | EMI Records | 539647-2

Martin,Bruce | (keyboards,perc,arr)
Steps Ahead
N.Y.C. | Intuition Records | INT 3007-2

Martin,Carlos | (tb)
Big Band Bellaterra
Don't Git Sassy | Fresh Sound Records | FSNT 048 CD
Daniel Flors Group
When Least Expected | Fresh Sound Records | FSNT 080 CD
Orquestra De Cambra Teatre Lliure
Porgy And Bess | Fresh Sound Records | FSNT 066 CD

Martin,Dave | (arrld)
Leon Thomas With Orchestra
Spirits Known And Unknown | RCA | 2663876-2

Martin,David | (p)
Alix Combelle Et Son Orchestre
Americans Swinging In Paris:Bill Coleman-The Elegance | EMI Records | 539662-2
Della Reese With The Sy Oliver Orchestra
Misty Blue:Sweet Sisters Swing Songs Of Sorrow And Sadness | Blue Note | 521151-2
Ella Fitzgerald With Sy Oliver And His Orchestra
Ella Fitzgerald:The Decca Years 1949-1954 | Decca | 050668-2
Louis Armstrong And His Orchestra
I Love Jazz | Verve | 543747-2
Louis Armstrong And Omer Simeon With The Sy Oliver Orchestra
Ambassador Louis Armstrong Vol.17:Moments To Remember(1952-1956) | Ambassador | CLA 1917
Louis Armstrong With Sy Oliver And His Orchestra
Louis Armstrong-My Greatest Songs | MCA | MCD 18347

Martin,Frank | (keyboards,string-arrangements,synth)
Tuck And Patti
A Gift Of Love | T&P Records | 9815810

Martin,Frederic | (b-tb)
Jazz Orchester Rheinland-Pfalz
Like Life | Jazz Haus Musik | LJBB 9405
Last Season | Jazz Haus Musik | LJBB 9706

Martin,James | (dr)
Clark Terry Quartet
OW | Storyville | STCD 8378
Zoot Sims Quartet

Zoot Sims | Storyville | STCD 8367
Zoot Sims Quintet
Zoot Sims | Storyville | STCD 8367

Martin,Joe | (b)
Ari Ambrose Quartet
Jazmin | Steeplechase | SCCD 31535
Dan Faulk Quartet
Spirit In The Night | Fresh Sound Records | FSNT 024 CD
Dan Faulk Trio
Spirit In The Night | Fresh Sound Records | FSNT 024 CD
Jill Seifers And Her Quartet
The Waiting | Fresh Sound Records | FSNT 072 CD
Nat Su Quartet
The J.Way | Fresh Sound Records | FSNT 038 CD
Perico Sambeat Group
Ademuz | Fresh Sound Records | FSNT 041 CD

Martin,John | (cellog)
Charlie Byrd Orchestra
Latin Byrd | Milestone | MCD 47005-2

Martin,Juliana | (voc)
Mike Westbrook Brass Band
Glad Day:Settings Of William Blake | Enja | ENJ-9376 2

Martin,Kenny | (dr,voctb)
Marcus Klossek Imagination
As We Are | Jardis Records | JRCD 20134
Jazz Guitar Highlights 1 | Jardis Records | JRCD 20141
Ray Blue Quartet
Always With A Purpose | Ray Blue Music | JN 007(RMB 01)

Martin,Lloyd 'Skippy' | (arr,ld,as,bs,clreeds)
Benny Goodman And His Orchestra
Charlie Christian:Swing To Bop | Dreyfus Jazz Line | FDM 36715-2

Martin,Lois | (viola)
Absolute Ensemble
African Symphony | Enja | ENJ-9410 2
Daniel Schnyder Quintet With String Quartet
Mythology | Enja | ENJ-7003 2
Mark Feldman Quartet
Book Of Tells | Enja | ENJ-9385 2
Michael Brecker Quindectet
Wide Angles | Verve | 076142-2

Martin,Lowell | (tb)
Tommy Dorsey And His Orchestra
Planet Jazz:Frank Sinatra & Tommy Dorsey | Planet Jazz | 2152067-2
Planet Jazz Sampler | Planet Jazz | 2152326-2
Planet Jazz:Tommy Dorsey | Planet Jazz | 2159972-2
Planet Jazz:Big Bands | Planet Jazz | 2169649-2
Planet Jazz:Male Jazz Vocalists | Planet Jazz | 2169657-2
Frank Sinatra And The Tommy Dorsey Orchestra | RCA | 2668701-2

Martin,Maurice | (dr)
Wild Bill Davis Group
Americans Swinging In Paris:Wild Bill Davis | EMI Records | 539665-2

Martin,Mel | (b-cl,fl,cl,ss,as,ts,bs)
Freddy Cole With Band
A Circle Of Love | Fantasy | FCD 9674-2
To The End Of The Earth | Fantasy | FCD 9675-2
Mongo Santamaria And His Orchestra
Jazzin' Vol.2: The Music Of Stevie Wonder | Fantasy | FANCD 6088-2
Pucho & His Latin Soul Brothers
Rip A Dip | Milestone | MCD 9247-2

Martin,Patricia | (tanpura)
Subroto Roy Chowdhury Group
Serenity | Jazzpoint | JP 1017 CD
Explorations | Jazzpoint | JP 1020 CD
Subroto Roy Chowdhury-Steve Lacy Group
Explorations | Jazzpoint | JP 1020 CD

Martin,Paul | (tsviola)
Helmut Zacharias mit dem Orchester Frank Folken
Ich Habe Rhythmus | Bear Family Records | BCD 15642 AH
Kurt Edelhagen All Stars
Deutsches Jazz Fesival 1954/1955 | Bear Family Records | BCD 15430
Kurt Edelhagen All Stars Und Solisten
Deutsches Jazz Fesival 1954/1955 | Bear Family Records | BCD 15430
Quartet Der Kurt Edelhagen All Stars
Deutsches Jazz Fesival 1954/1955 | Bear Family Records | BCD 15430
Rabih Abou-Khalil Group
Arabian Waltz | Enja | ENJ-9059 2

Martin,Peter | (p)
Joshua Redman Quartet
Spirit Of The Moment:Live At The Village Vanguard | Warner | 9362-45923-2
Joshua Redman Quintet
Freedom In The Goove | Warner | 9362-46330-2

Martin,Robert L. | (cello)
Ella Fitzgerald With Orchestra
The Best Is Yet To Come | Original Jazz Classics | OJCCD 889-2(2312138)

Martin,Skippy | (as)
Glenn Miller And His Orchestra
Planet Jazz:Glenn Miller | Planet Jazz | 2152056-2
Peggy Lee With The Benny Goodman Orchestra
Peggy Lee & Benny Goodman:The Complete Recordings 1941-1947 | CBS | C2K 65686

Martin,Stu | (dr,percsynth)
Barre Phillips Quartet
Mountainscapes | ECM | 1076
Barre Phillips Quintet
Mountainscapes | ECM | 1076
Quincy Jones And His Orchestra
The Quintessence | Impulse(MCA) | 951222-2
Sonny Rollins Sextet
The Standard Sonny Rollins | RCA | 2174801-2

Martin,Till | (ts)
Till Martin Quintet
On The Trail | Nabel Records:Jazz Network | CD 4676

Martin,Vernon | (b)
Rahsaan Roland Kirk Sextet
Volunteered Slavery | Rhino | 8122-71407-2
Roland Kirk Quartet
Talkin' Verve-Roots Of Acid Jazz:Roland Kirk | Verve | 533101-2
Domino | Verve | 543833-2
Rahsaan/The Complete Mercury Recordings Of Roland Kirk | Mercury | 846630-2

Martin,Walter | (asdr)
Louis Jordan And His Tympany Five
The Small Black Groups | Storyville | 4960523
Louis Jordan-Let The Good Times Roll: The Complete Decca Recordings 1938-1954 | Bear Family Records | BCD 15557 IH
Louis Jordan's Elks Rendez-Vous Band
Louis Jordan-Let The Good Times Roll: The Complete Decca Recordings 1938-1954 | Bear Family Records | BCD 15557 IH
Roger Sturgis With Lovie Jordan's Elks Rendez-Vous Band
Louis Jordan-Let The Good Times Roll: The Complete Decca Recordings 1938-1954 | Bear Family Records | BCD 15557 IH

Martine,Tucker | (processing)
Wayne Horvitz Group
4+1 Ensemble | Intuition Records | INT 3224-2

Martinez,Alexander | (perc)
Gonzalo Rubalcaba & Cuban Quartet
Antiguo | Blue Note | 837717-2

Martinez,Anthony | (corovoc)
Conexion Latina
Mambo 2000 | Enja | ENJ-7055 2
La Conexión | Enja | ENJ-9065 2

Martinez,Baldo | (b)
José Luis Gutiérrez Trio
Núcleo | Fresh Sound Records | FSNT 039 CD

Martinez,Cesar | (dr)
Moments Quartet
Original Moments | Fresh Sound Records | FSNT 052 CD

Martinez,Eddie | (el-pp)
Gato Barbieri Orchestra
The Roots Of Acid Jazz | Impulse(MCA) | IMP 12042

Martinez,Naldo | (b)
Javier Paxarino Group With Glen Velez
Temurá | ACT | 9227-2

Martinez,Osvaldo 'Chihuahua' | (congas,bongos,percvoc)
Herbie Hancock Quartet
Herbie Hancock:The Complete Blue Note Sixties Sessions | Blue Note | 495569-2
Mongo Santamaria And His Band
Mongo At The Village Gate | Original Jazz Classics | OJCCD 490-2(RLP 9529)

Martinez,Sabu | (bongo,timbales,voc,bongos,conga)
Art Blakey-Sabu
Horace Silver Trio And Spotlight On Drums:Art Blakey-Sabu | Blue Note | 591725-2
Dizzy Gillespie And His Orchestra
Planet Jazz:Dizzy Gillespie | Planet Jazz | 2152069-2
J.J.Johnson Quintet
The Eminent J.J.Johnson Vol.2 | Blue Note | 532144-2
Kenny Clarke-Francy Boland Big Band
Three Latin Adventures | MPS | 529095-2
Sabu L. Martinez Group
Palo Congo | Blue Note | 522665-2

Martinez,Yma America | (coro)
Conexion Latina
La Conexión | Enja | ENJ-9065 2

Martini,Karl | (voc)
Jazzensemble Des Hessischen Rundfunks
Jazz Messe-Messe Für Unsere Zeit | hr music.de | hrmj 003-01 CD

Martini,Rudi | (dr)
Jenny Evans And Her Quintet
Shiny Stockings | Enja | ENJ-9317 2
Nuages | Enja | ENJ-9467 2
Shiny Stockings | ESM Records | ESM 9305
Nuages | ESM Records | ESM 9308
Jenny Evans And The Rudi Martini Quartet
At Lloyd's | ESM Records | ESM 9302

Martinier,Jean-Louis | (accordeon)
David Friedman Quartet
Other Worlds | Intuition Records | INT 3210-2
David Friedman Trio
Other Worlds | Intuition Records | INT 3210-2

Martinis,Nick | (dr)
Victor Feldman Orchestra
Latinsville | Contemporary | CCD 9005-2

Martino,Pat | (12-string-gg)
Don Patterson Quartet
Boppin' & Burnin' | Original Jazz Classics | OJCCD 983-2(P 7563)
Don Patterson Quintet
Boppin' & Burnin' | Original Jazz Classics | OJCCD 983-2(P 7563)
Eric Alexander Quintet
The First Milestone | Milestone | MCD 9302-2
Eric Kloss Quartet
About Time | Prestige | PRCD 24268-2
Jack McDuff Quartet
Silken Soul | Prestige | PCD 24242-2
The Concert McDuff | Prestige | PRCD 24270-2
Jack McDuff Quintet
Silken Soul | Prestige | PCD 24242-2
Jack McDuff Sextet
Silken Soul | Prestige | PCD 24242-2
Pat Martino Quartet
Desperado | Original Jazz Classics | OJCCD 397-2(P 7795)
Pat Martino Quintet
Think Tank | Blue Note | 592009-2
Strings! | Original Jazz Classics | OJCCD 223-2(P 7547)
Desperado | Original Jazz Classics | OJCCD 397-2(P 7795)
Pat Martino Septet
Strings! | Original Jazz Classics | OJCCD 223-2(P 7547)
Pat Martino Sextet
El Hombre | Original Jazz Classics | OJCCD 195-2(P 7513)
Pat Martino Trio
Live At Yoshi's | Blue Note | 499749-2
Willis Jackson Quintet
Gravy | Prestige | PCD 24254-2
Soul Night Live! | Prestige | PRCD 24273-2
Willis Jackson Sextet
Gravy | Prestige | PCD 24254-2
Nuther'n Like Thuther'n | Prestige | PRCD 24265-2
Woody Herman And His Orchestra
The Raven Speaks | Original Jazz Classics | OJCCD 663-2(F 9416)

Martinon,Jacques | (dr)
Django Reinhardt And The Quintet Du Hot Club De France
Planet Jazz:Django Reinhardt | Planet Jazz | 2152071-2
Planet Jazz Sampler | Planet Jazz | 2152326-2

Martinsen,Jan Olav | (fr-h)
Terje Rypdal With The Borealis Ensemble
Q.E.D. | ECM | 1474

Martland,Steve | (cond)
Steve Martland Band
The Orchestra Of Smith's Academy | Enja | ENJ-9358 2

Martlreiter,Hermann | (ssts)
Al Porcino Big Band
Al Cohn Meets Al Porcino | Organic Music | ORGM 9730

Marty,Claude | (dr)
Don Byas Quintet
Jazz In Paris:Don Byas-Laura | EmArCy | 013027-2

Maruhn,Armand | (voc)
Jazzensemble Des Hessischen Rundfunks
Jazz Messe-Messe Für Unsere Zeit | hr music.de | hrmj 003-01 CD

Marvin,Ron | (keyboards,synthelectronic-perc)
Ron Marvin & Remy Filipovitch
Mysterious Traveler | Album | AS 44677 CD

Marx,Dick | (p)
Johnny Frigo Quartet
I Love John Frigo...He Swings | Mercury | 9861061
Johnny Frigo Sextet
I Love John Frigo...He Swings | Mercury | 9861061

Marzaroli,Alfredo | (tp)
Brocksieper-Jazz-Ensemble
Drums Boogie | Bear Family Records | BCD 15988 AH
Brocksieper-Solisten-Orchester
Globetrotter | Bear Family Records | BCD 15912 AH
Brocksieper-Special-Ensemble
Globetrotter | Bear Family Records | BCD 15912 AH

Marzi,Alessandro | (dr)
Stefania Tallini Trio
New Life | yvp music | CD 3114
Stefania Tallini Trio With Guests
New Life | yvp music | CD 3114

Masaoka,Miya | (kotoelectronics)
Fred Frith Maybe Monday
Digital Wildlife | Winter&Winter | 910071-2

Mascart,Vincent | (ts)
Karim Ziad Groups
Ifrikya | ACT | 9282-2

Masekela,Hugh | (fl-h,perc,arr,cotp)
Dave Grusin Group
Migration | GRP | GRP 95922
Hugh Masekela Group
GRRR | Verve | 9860309

Maseli,Bernard | (vib)
Urszula Dudziak And Band Walk Away
Magic Lady | IN+OUT Records | 7008-2

Maseli,Marek | (synth)
Walkaway With Urszula Dudziak
Saturation | IN+OUT Records | 77024-2

Masessa,Mike | (dr)
Allan Vaché Swingtet
Jazz Im Amerikahaus,Vol.3 | Nagel-Heyer | CD 013
Ellington For Lovers | Nagel-Heyer | NH 1009
The First Sampler | Nagel-Heyer | NHR SP 5

Masetti,Glauco | (as,flss)
Chet Baker Sextet
Chet Baker In Milan | Original Jazz Classics | OJC20 370-2(JLP 18)

Masman,Theo Uden | (ldp)
Coleman Hawkins With The Ramblers
Jazz:The Essential Collection Vol.3 | IN+OUT Records | 78013-2

Mason,Ann | (harp)
Frank Sinatra With Orchestra
Planet Jazz:Frank Sinatra & Tommy Dorsey | Planet Jazz | 2152067-2

Mason,Bill | (org)
Rusty Bryant Quintet
Jazzin' With The Soul Brothers | Fantasy | FANCD 6086-2

Mason,David | (g,violavoc)
Dave Brubeck With The Erich Kunzel Orchestra
Truth Is Fallen | Atlantic | 7567-80761-2

Mason,Dick | (b)
Lennie Baldwin's Dauphin Street Six
The Golden Years Of Revival Jazz,Sampler | Storyville | 109 1001
The Golden Years Of Revival Jazz,Vol 1 | Storyville | STCD 5506
The Golden Years Of Revival Jazz,Vol.3 | Storyville | STCD 5508
The Golden Years Of Revival Jazz,Vol.6 | Storyville | STCD 5511
The Golden Years Of Revival Jazz,Vol.9 | Storyville | STCD 5514
The Golden Years Of Revival Jazz,Vol.10 | Storyville | STCD 5515
The Golden Years Of Revival Jazz,Vol.13 | Storyville | STCD 5518

Mason,Earl | (p)
Louis Armstrong And His Orchestra
Louis Armstrong:C'est Si Bon | Dreyfus Jazz Line | FDM 36730-2
Swing Legends:Louis Armstrong | Nimbus Records | NI 2012

Mason,Harold | (dr)
Bobbi Humphrey
Blue Break Beats | Blue Note | 799106-2
Bobby Hutcherson Orchestra
Montara | Blue Note | 590956-2
Bobby Lyle Quintet
Jazzrock-Anthology Vol.3:Fusion | Zounds | CD 27100555
Donald Byrd Orchestra
Black Byrd | Blue Note | 784466-2
Places And Spaces | Blue Note | 854326-2
Eddie Henderson Orchestra
Blue Breaks Beats Vol.2 | Blue Note | 789907-2
Fourplay
Fourplay | Warner | 7599-26656-2
Fourplay...Yes,Please! | Warner | 9362-47694-2
Gene Harris Group
Blue Breaks Beats Vol.2 | Blue Note | 789907-2
Joe Henderson Group
Jazzin' Vol.2: The Music Of Stevie Wonder | Fantasy | FANCD 6088-2
Lee Ritenour Group
Jazzrock-Anthology Vol.3:Fusion | Zounds | CD 27100555
Luis Gasca Group
Jazzin' Vol.2: The Music Of Stevie Wonder | Fantasy | FANCD 6088-2

Mason,Harvey | (dr,dr-program,electronic-dr,perc)
Antonio Carlos Jobim Group
Antonio Carlos Jobim And Friends | Verve | 531556-2
Antonio Carlos Jobim With The Herbie Hancock Sextet
Antonio Carlos Jobim And Friends | Verve | 531556-2
Antonio Carlos Jobim-Gal Costa Septet
Antonio Carlos Jobim And Friends | Verve | 531556-2
Bobbi Humphrey Group
Blue Breaks Beats Vol.2 | Blue Note | 789907-2
Charles Earland Septet
Charlie's Greatest Hits | Prestige | PCD 24250-2
Chet Baker-Gerry Mulligan Group
Carnegie Hall Concert Vol. 1/2 | CTI | EPC 450554-2
Dave Grusin Group
Mountain Dance | GRP | GRP 95072
Migration | GRP | GRP 95922
Dave Grusin Orchestra
Two For The Road:The Music Of Henry Mancini | GRP | GRP 98652
Diane Schuur With Orchestra
Blues For Schuur | GRP | GRP 98632
The Best Of Diane Schuur | GRP | GRP 98882
Donald Byrd & His Orchestra
Blue Breaks Beats Vol.2 | Blue Note | 789907-2
Fourplay
Heartfelt | RCA | 2663916-2
Between The Sheets | Warner | 9362-45340-2
Gal Costa With The Herbie Hancock Sextet
Antonio Carlos Jobim And Friends | Verve | 531556-2
George Benson Group
Breezin' | Warner | 8122-76713-2
Gonzalo Rubalcaba-Herbie Hancock Quintet
Antonio Carlos Jobim And Friends | Verve | 531556-2
Herbie Hancock Group
Man-Child | CBS | 471235-2
Sunlight | CBS | 486570-2
Head Hunters | CBS | CK 65123
Herbie Hancock Quartet
Antonio Carlos Jobim And Friends | Verve | 531556-2
Jimmy Smith All Stars
Jimmy Smith:Dot Com Blues | Blue Thumb | 543978-2
Joe Henderson And His Orchestra
Joe Henderson:The Milestone Years | Milestone | 8MCD 4413-2
Joe Henderson Septet
Antonio Carlos Jobim And Friends | Verve | 531556-2
Joe Pass Sextet
Jazzin' Vol.2: The Music Of Stevie Wonder | Fantasy | FANCD 6088-2
Jon Hendricks With The Herbie Hancock Quintet
Antonio Carlos Jobim And Friends | Verve | 531556-2
Lee Ritenour Group
Stolen Moments | GRP | GRP 96152
Ron Carter With Strings
Pastels | Original Jazz Classics | OJCCD 665-2(M 9073)
Shirley Horn Quintet
Antonio Carlos Jobim And Friends | Verve | 531556-2
Shirley Horn Sextet
Antonio Carlos Jobim And Friends | Verve | 531556-2
Singers Unlimited With The Clare Fischer Orchestra
The Singers Unlimited:Magic Voices | MPS | 539130-2
The Brecker Brothers
The Becker Bros | RCA | 2122103-2

Mason,Nick | (drvoice)
Michael Mantler Group
The Hapless Child | Watt | 4
Michael Mantler Quintet
Live | Watt | 18
Michael Mantler Quintet With The London Symphony Orchestra
Something There | Watt | 13

Mason,Paul | (ts)
Tommy Dorsey And His Orchestra
Planet Jazz:Frank Sinatra & Tommy Dorsey | Planet Jazz | 2152067-2
Planet Jazz Sampler | Planet Jazz | 2152326-2
Planet Jazz:Big Bands | Planet Jazz | 2169649-2
Planet Jazz:Male Jazz Vocalists | Planet Jazz | 2169657-2
Frank Sinatra And The Tommy Dorsey Orchestra | RCA | 2668701-2

Masqualero |
Masqualero
Bande A Part | ECM | 1319
Aero | ECM | 1367
Re-Enter | ECM | 1437(847939-2)

Mass,Ron | (tb)
Chick Corea And His Orchestra

My Spanish Heart | Polydor | 543303-3
Massamba | (african-dr)
Pucho & His Latin Soul Brothers
Rip A Dip | Milestone | MCD 9247-2
Massarik,Amir | (b)
SheshBesh
SheshBesh | TipToe | TIP-888830 2
Masseaux,Garvin | (chekere,perctambourine)
Art Blakey And The Afro Drum Ensemble
The African Beat | Blue Note | 522666-2
Charlie Rouse Orchestra
Bossa Nova Bacchanal | Blue Note | 593875-2
Blue Bossa | Blue Note | 795590-2
Grant Green Quintet
Feelin' The Spirit | Blue Note | 746822-2
Grant Green Sextet
Blue Bossa | Blue Note | 795590-2
Ike Quebec Quintet
Blue Bossa | Blue Note | 795590-2
Yusef Lateef Orchestra
The Centaur And The Phoenix | Original Jazz Classics | OJCCD 721-2(RLP 9337)
Masselier,Alf | (b)
Django Reinhardt Quintet
Django/Django In Rome 1949-1050 | BGO Records | BGOCD 366
Sidney Bechet All Stars
Planet Jazz:Sidney Bechet | Planet Jazz | 2152063-2
Planet Jazz Sampler | Planet Jazz | 2152326-2
Massetti,Glauco | (as)
Chet Baker With String-Orchestra And Voices
Chet Baker With Fifty Italian Strings | Original Jazz Classics | OJC20 492-2(JLP 921)
Massey,Bill | (tp)
Sonny Stitt And His Band
Kaleidoscope | Original Jazz Classics | OJCCD 060-2(P 7077)
Massey,Cal | (arr,fl-htp)
Archie Shepp Orchestra
The Cry Of My People | Impulse(MCA) | 9861488
Cal Massey Sextet
The Jazz Life! | Candid | CCD 79019
Blues To Coltrane | Candid | CCD 79029
Massey,Charles | (g)
King Curtis Band
King Curtis-Blow Man Blow | Bear Family Records | BCD 15670 CI
Massingill,Bill | (saxts)
Harry James And His Orchestra
Trumpet Blues:The Best Of Harry James | Capitol | 521224-2
Masso,George | (tbvib)
Benny Goodman And His Orchestra
40th Anniversary Concert-Live At Carnegie Hall | London | 820349-2
Verve Jazz Masters 33:Benny Goodman | Verve | 844410-2
George Masso Allstars
The Wonderful World Of George Gershwin | Nagel-Heyer | CD 001
One Two Three | Nagel-Heyer | CD 008
The First Sampler | Nagel-Heyer | NHR SP 5
George Masso Quintet
The First Sampler | Nagel-Heyer | NHR SP 5
George Masso Sextet
C'Est Magnifique! | Nagel-Heyer | CD 060
George Masso-Ken Peplowski Quintet
Just Friends | Nagel-Heyer | CD 5001
Glenn Miller And His Orchestra
The Glenn Miller Orchestra In Digital Mood | GRP | GRP 95022
Massot,Michel | (tbtuba)
Klaus König Orchestra
Hommage A Douglas Adams | Enja | ENJ-6078 2
Reviews | Enja | ENJ-9061 2
Kölner Saxophon Mafia With Guests
Kölner Saxophon Mafia: 20 Jahre Saxuelle Befreiung | Jazz Haus Musik | JHM 0115 CD
Mastandrea,Alex | (tb)
Glenn Miller And His Orchestra
The Chesterfield Broadcasts Vol.1 | RCA | 2663113-2
The Andrew Sisters With The Glenn Miller Orchestra
The Chesterfield Broadcasts Vol.1 | RCA | 2663113-2
Masters,Bob | (tp)
Dick Charlesworth And His City Gents
The Golden Years Of Revival Jazz,Vol.4 | Storyville | STCD 5509
The Golden Years Of Revival Jazz,Vol.6 | Storyville | STCD 5511
The Golden Years Of Revival Jazz,Vol.11 | Storyville | STCD 5516
Mastersounds,The |
The Mastersounds
The Mastersounds | Prestige | PRCD 24770-2
Mastren,Al | (tb)
Glenn Miller And His Orchestra
Planet Jazz:Glenn Miller | Planet Jazz | 2152056-2
Planet Jazz Sampler | Planet Jazz | 2152326-2
Planet Jazz:Big Bands | Planet Jazz | 2169649-2
Planet Jazz:Swing | Planet Jazz | 2169651-2
Candlelight Miller | RCA | 2668716-2
Swing Legends | Nimbus Records | NI 2001
Mastren,Carmen | (arrg)
All Star Band
Planet Jazz:Jack Teagarden | Planet Jazz | 2161236-2
Bechet-Spanier Big Four
Jazz:The Essential Collection Vol.1 | IN+OUT Records | 78011-2
Bud Freeman And His Stars
Muggsy Spanier And Bud Freeman:V-Discs 1944-45 | Jazz Unlimited | JUCD 2049
Bud Freeman And The V-Disc Jumpers
Muggsy Spanier And Bud Freeman:V-Discs 1944-45 | Jazz Unlimited | JUCD 2049
Eight Squares And A Critic
Muggsy Spanier And Bud Freeman:V-Discs 1944-45 | Jazz Unlimited | JUCD 2049
Louis Armstrong And The Commanders under the Direction of Camarata
Satchmo Serenaders | Verve | 543792-2
Louis Armstrong With The Commanders
Ambassador Louis Armstrong Vol.17:Moments To Remember(1952-1956) | Ambassador | CLA 1917
The V-Disc Jumpers
Muggsy Spanier And Bud Freeman:V-Discs 1944-45 | Jazz Unlimited | JUCD 2049
Tommy Dorsey And His Orchestra
Planet Jazz:Frank Sinatra & Tommy Dorsey | Planet Jazz | 2152067-2
Planet Jazz:Tommy Dorsey | Planet Jazz | 2159972-2
Planet Jazz:Big Bands | Planet Jazz | 2169649-2
Planet Jazz:Swing | Planet Jazz | 2169651-2
Mastropirro,Vincenzo | (fl)
Banda Cittá Ruvo Di Puglia
La Banda/Banda And Jazz | Enja | ENJ-9326 2
Masuda,Mikio | (keyboardsp)
Johnny Hartman With The Terumasa Hino Quartet
Midnight Blue(The [Be]witching Hour) | Blue Note | 854365-2
Masuo,Yoshiaki | (el-gg)
Sonny Rollins Sextet
The Cutting Edge | Original Jazz Classics | OJC 468(M 9059)
Sonny Rollins Sextet With Rufus Harley
The Cutting Edge | Original Jazz Classics | OJC 468(M 9059)
Mat Jr. | (org,pkeyboards)
Alex Gunia-Philipp Van Endert Group
Beauty Of Silence | Laika Records | 35101052
Mateen,Tarus | (b)
Greg Osby Quintet
Inner Circle | Blue Note | 499871-2
Jason Moran Trio
The Bandwagon | Blue Note | 591893-2
Stefon Harris Group
Black Action Figure | Blue Note | 499546-2
Stefon Harris-Jacky Terrasson Group
Kindred | Blue Note | 531868-2
Materna,Peter | (sax,ssas)
Peter Materna Quartet
Full Moon Party | Village | VILCD 1021-2
Mateus,Ricardo | (perc)
Karl Ratzer Quintet
All The Way | Enja | ENJ-9448 2
Matharu,Harjinder | (tablas)
John Mayer's Indio-Jazz Fusions
Ragatal | Nimbus Records | NI 5569
Matheeuwsen,Lucien | (b)
Henning Wolter Trio
Two Faces | double moon | DMCD 1003-2
Henning Wolter Trio With Gerd Dudek
Two Faces | double moon | DMCD 1003-2
Henning Wolter Trio With Guests
Years Of A Trilogy | double moon | DMCHR 71021
Matheny,Dmitri | (fl-h)
Jacintha With Band And Strings
Lush Life | Groove Note | GRV 1011-2(Gold CD 2011)
Mathews,Gilbert | (dr)
Johnny Dyani Septet
Afrika | Steeplechase | SCS 1186(Audiophile Pressing)
Mathews,Ronnie | (p)
Lee Morgan Quintet
The Rumproller | Blue Note | 521229-2
The Best Of Blue Note Vol.2 | Blue Note | 797960-2
Roland Alexander Quintet
Ronnie Mathews-Roland Alexander-Freddie Hubbard | Prestige | PRCD 24271-2
Ronnie Mathews Quintet
Ronnie Mathews-Roland Alexander-Freddie Hubbard | Prestige | PRCD 24271-2
Ronnie Mathews Trio
Ronnie Mathews-Roland Alexander-Freddie Hubbard | Prestige | PRCD 24271-2
Mathewson,Ron | (bb-g)
John Stevens Quartet
Re-Touch & Quartet | Konnex Records | KCD 5027
Ronnie Scott And The Band
Live At Ronnie Scott's | CBS | 494439-2
Mathias,Eddie | (bel-b)
Max Roach Sextet With The J.C.White Singers
Lift Every Voice And Sing | Atlantic | 7567-80798-2
Roland Kirk And His Orchestra
Rahsaan/The Complete Mercury Recordings Of Roland Kirk | Mercury | 846630-2
Mathiesen,Kai | (bs)
Stan Getz With Ib Glindemann And His Orchestra
Stan Getz In Europe | Laserlight | 24657
Mathieu,Konny | (b)
International Commission For The Prevention Of Musical Border Control,The
The International Commission For The Prevention Of Musical Border Control | VeraBra Records | CDVBR 2093-2
Mathis,Johnny | (voc)
Patti Austin And Her Band
Patti Austin:The Ultimate Collection | GRP | GRP 98212
Mathisen,Ole | (ssts)
Olga Konkova-Per Mathisen Quartet
Northern Crossing | Candid | CCD 79766
Mathisen.Per | (b)
Olga Konkova Trio
Her Point Of View | Candid | CCD 79757
Olga Konkova-Per Mathisen Quartet
Northern Crossing | Candid | CCD 79766
Matinier,Jean-Louis | (accordeonaccordina)
Anouar Brahem Trio
Le Pas Du Chat Noir | ECM | 1792(016373-2)
Gianluigi Trovesi Nonet
Round About A Midsummer's Dream | Enja | ENJ-9384 2
Jean-Louis Matinier Quartet
Confluences | Enja | ENJ-9454 2
Louis Sclavis Group
Dans La Nuit | ECM | 1805(589524-2)
Michael Riessler Group
Orange | ACT | 9274-2
Heloise | Wergo | WER 8008-2
Tentations D'Abélard | Wergo | WER 8009-2
Michel Godard Ensemble
Castel Del Monte | Enja | ENJ-9362 2
Philippe Caillat Group
Stream Of Time | Laika Records | LK 92-030
Renaud Garcia-Fons
Navigatore | Enja | ENJ-9418 2
Renaud Garcia-Fons & Jean-Louis Matinier
Fuera | Enja | ENJ-9364 2
Renaud Garcia-Fons Group
Oriental Bass | Enja | ENJ-9334 2
Navigatore | Enja | ENJ-9418 2
Renaud Garcia-Fons Quartet
Alboreá | Enja | ENJ-9057 2
Willem Breuker Kollektief
La Banda/Banda And Jazz | Enja | ENJ-9326 2
Matlock,Matty | (arr,as,cl,tsreeds)
Bob Crosby And His Orchestra
Swing Legens:Bob Crosby | Nimbus Records | NI 2011
Bob Crosby's Bobcats
Swing Legens:Bob Crosby | Nimbus Records | NI 2011
Ella Fitzgerald With Paul Weston And His Orchestra
Ella Fitzgerald Sings The Irving Berlin Song Book | Verve | 543830-2
Ella Fitzgerald With The Paul Weston Orchestra
Get Happy! | Verve | 523321-2
Gene Gifford And His Orchestra
Planet Jazz:Bud Freeman | Planet Jazz | 2161240-2
Matos,Bobby | (perc)
Bobby Hutcherson Orchestra
Montara | Blue Note | 590956-2
Matschat,Berthold | (p,harp,keyboardssynth-programming)
Peter Fessler Quartet
Colours Of My Mind | Minor Music | 801063
Peter Fessler Quintet
Colours Of My Mind | Minor Music | 801063
Matsuura,Toshio | (?)
United Future Organizatio
United Future Organization | Talkin' Loud | 518166-2
Matta,Nilson | (bel-b)
Kenny Barron Group With Trio De Paz
Canta Brazil | EmArCy | 017993-2
Mattar,Daniel | (percvoc)
Lisa Bassenge Trio With Guests
A Sight, A Song | Minor Music | 801100
Matteson,Richard | (btuba)
Bob Scobey's Frisco Band
Planet Jazz | Planet Jazz | 2169652-2
Matthews,Dave | (arr,as,tp,fl-hts)
Benny Goodman And His Orchestra
More Camel Caravans | Phontastic | NCD 8843/4
More Camel Caravans | Phontastic | NCD 8845/6
Harry James And His Orchestra
The Legends Of Swing | Laserlight | 24659
Jack Teagarden's Chicagoans
Jazz:The Essential Collection Vol.3 | IN+OUT Records | 78013-2
The Hollywood Session:The Capitol Jazzmen | Jazz Unlimited | JUCD 2044
Lionel Hampton And His Orchestra
Planet Jazz:Swing | Planet Jazz | 2169651-2
Planet Jazz:Jazz Saxophone | Planet Jazz | 2169653-2
The Capitol Jazzmen
Jazz:The Essential Collection Vol.3 | IN+OUT Records | 78013-2
The Hollywood Session:The Capitol Jazzmen | Jazz Unlimited | JUCD 2044
Matthews,David | (arr,cond,keyboards,psynth)
David Matthews & The Manhattan Jazz Orchestra
Back To Bach | Milestone | MCD 9312-2
Hey Duke! | Milestone | MCD 9320-2
Etta James & The Roots Band
Burnin' Down he House | RCA | 3411633-2
Nina Simone And Orchestra
Baltimore | Epic | 476906-2
Matthews,George | (fl,astb)
Cannonball Adderley And His Orchestra
Cannonball Adderley Birthday Celebration | Fantasy | FANCD 6087-2
Count Basie And His Orchestra
Planet Jazz:Count Basie | Planet Jazz | 2152068-2
Planet Jazz:Jimmy Rushing | RCA | 2165371-2
Planet Jazz:Jazz Greatest Hits | Planet Jazz | 2169648-2
Planet Jazz:Big Bands | Planet Jazz | 2169649-2
Jazz:The Essential Collection Vol.3 | IN+OUT Records | 78013-2
Count Basie,His Instrumentals & Rhyhtm
Planet Jazz:Count Basie | Planet Jazz | 2152068-2
Dizzy Gillespie And His Orchestra
Afro | Verve | 517052-2
Gillespiana And Carnegie Hall Concert | Verve | 519809-2
Talking Verve:Dizzy Gillespie | Verve | 533846-2
Ultimate Dizzy Gillespie | Verve | 557535-2
Ella Fitzgerald And Her Famous Orchestra
The Radio Years 1940 | Jazz Unlimited | JUCD 2065
Ella Fitzgerald And Her Orchestra
Jazz Collection:Ella Fitzgerald | Laserlight | 24397
Louis Armstrong And His Orchestra
Louis Armstrong:Swing That Music | Laserlight | 36056
Swing Legends:Louis Armstrong | Nimbus Records | NI 2012
Willie Bryant And His Orchestra
Planet Jazz:Ben Webster | RCA | 2165368-2
Matthews,Gilbert | (dr,perc,chimesgongs)
Amanda Sedgwick Quintet
Reunion | Touché Music | TMcCD 021
Rebecka Gordon Quartet
Yiddish'n Jazz | Touché Music | TMcCD 014
Matthews,Hal | (tb)
Paul Whiteman And His Orchestra
Planet Jazz:Jack Teagarden | Planet Jazz | 2161236-2
Matthews,Myrna | (voc)
Quincy Jones And His Orchestra
Verve Jazz Masters Vol.59:Toots Thielemans | Verve | 535271-2
Stanley Turrentine And His Orchestra
Pieces Of Dream | Original Jazz Classics | OJCCD 831-2(F 9465)
Matthews,Ronnie | (pp-solo)
Clifford Jordan Quintet
Mosaic | Milestone | MCD 47092-2
Johnny Griffin Quartet
Jazz Life Vol.1:From Village Vanguard | Storyville | 4960753
Roy Hargrove Quartet
Family | Verve | 527630-2
Roy Haynes Quartet
Cymbalism | Original Jazz Classics | OJCCD 1079-2(NJ 8287)
Matthieu,Michel | (tp)
Soriba Kouyaté Quartet
Live In Montreux | ACT | 9414-2
Mattinson,Edward | (vibperc)
Pete Rugolo And His Orchestra
Thriller/Richard Diamon(Original Jazz Scores From 2 Classics TV Series) | Fresh Sound Records | FSCD 2015
Mattison,Don | (tb,vocv-tb)
Louis Armstrong With Jimmy Dorsey And His Orchestra
Louis Armstrong:Swing That Music | Laserlight | 36056
Swing Legends:Louis Armstrong | Nimbus Records | NI 2012
Matzeit,Friedemann | (b-cl,ss,ts,flas)
Matzeit-Daerr
September | Jazz Haus Musik | JHM 0125 CD
Matzke,Werner | (cello)
Uri Caine With The Concerto Köln
Concerto Köln | Winter&Winter | 910086-2
Matzkeit,Bodo | (percwbd)
Christian Willisohn New Band
Heart Broken Man | Blues Beacon | BLU-1026 2
Martin Schmitt
Handful Of Blues | ESM Records | ESM 9303
Maubré,Jocelyne | (v)
Charlie Haden Quartet West With Strings
Now Is The Hour | Verve | 527827-2
Maugeri,Orazio | (as)
Orchestra Jazz Siciliana
Orchestra Jazz Siciliana Plays The Music Of Carla Bley | Watt | XtraWatt/4
Maunu,Peter | (el-g,gg-synth)
Bobby McFerrin Group
Bobby McFerrin | Elektra | 7559-60023-2
Jean-Luc Ponty Group
Atlantic Jazz: Fusion | Atlantic | 7567-81711-2
Jean-Luc Ponty Quintet
Cosmic Messenger | Atlantic | 7567-81550-2
Jean-Luc Ponty Sextet
Cosmic Messenger | Atlantic | 7567-81550-2
The Very Best Of Jean-Luc Ponty | Rhino | 8122-79862-2
Maunuvaara,Tapio | (tpfl-h)
Tim Hagans With Norrbotten Big Band
Future Miles | ACT | 9235-2
Maupin,Bennie | (alto-fl,b-cl,ss,ts,bass-fl,saxello)
Andrew Hill Orchestra
Deep Blue-The United States Of Mind | Blue Note | 521152-2
Bennie Maupin-Dr. Patrick Gleeson
Driving While Black... | Intuition Records | INT 3242-2
Chick Corea Septet
The Complete 'Is' Sessions | Blue Note | 540532-2
Eddie Henderson Orchestra
Blue Breaks Beats Vol.2 | Blue Note | 789907-2
Essence All Stars
Hot Jazz Bisquits | Hip Bop | HIBD 8801
Herbie Hancock Group
Man-Child | CBS | 471235-2
Sunlight | CBS | 486570-2
Sextant | CBS | CK 64983
Thrust | CBS | CK 64984
Head Hunters | CBS | CK 65123
Herbie Hancock Septet
V.S.O.P. Herbie Hancock-Live At The City Center N.Y. | CBS | 486569-2
Herbie Hancock Sextet
V.S.O.P. Herbie Hancock-Live At The City Center N.Y. | CBS | 486569-2
Horace Silver Quintet
Horace Silver Retrospective | Blue Note | 495576-2
Jack DeJohnette Quartet
The DeJohnette Complex | Original Jazz Classics | OJCCD 617-2
Jack DeJohnette Quintet
The DeJohnette Complex | Original Jazz Classics | OJCCD 617-2
Jack DeJohnette Sextet
The DeJohnette Complex | Original Jazz Classics | OJCCD 617-2
Lee Morgan Quintet
Live At The Lighthouse | Blue Note | 835228-2
Caramba! | Blue Note | 853358-2
Lee Morgan Sextet

Taru | Blue Note | 522670-2
Lenny White Group
Renderers Of Spirit | Hip Bop | HIBD 8014
Marion Brown Orchestra
Afternoon Of A Georgia Faun | ECM | 1004
Miles Davis Group
Circle In The Round | CBS | 467898-2
Bitches Brew | CBS | C2K 65774

Maur,Barry | (tb)
Buddy Rich Big Band
Backwoods Siseman/Pieces Of Dream | Laserlight | 24655
Lee Konitz Orchestra
The Art Of Saxophone | Laserlight | 24652

Maurer,Albrecht | (keyboards,v,voice,synth,computer)
Albrecht Maurer Trio Works
Movietalks | Jazz Haus Musik | JHM 0119 CD
Directors
Directors | Jazz Haus Musik | JHM 0040 CD
Norbert Stein Pata Orchester
Ritual Life | Pata Musik | PATA 5(JHM 50) CD
Pata Music Meets Arfi
News Of Roi Ubu | Pata Musik | PATA 10 CD

Maus,Carl | (dr)
Artie Shaw And His Orchestra
Planet JazzArtie Shaw | Planet Jazz | 2152057-2
Planet Jazz:Jazz Greatest Hits | Planet Jazz | 2169648-2

Maus,Georg | (b-tbtb)
Bill Ramsey With Orchestra
Gettin' Back To Swing | Bear Family Records | BCD 15813 AH
Kevin Mahogany With The WDR Big Band And Guests
Pussy Cat Dues:The Music Of Charles Mingus | Enja | ENJ-9316 2
SWR Big Band
Jazz In Concert | Hänssler Classics | CD 93.004

Mawford,Peter | (dr)
Graham Stewart And His New Orleans Band
The Golden Years Of Revival Jazz,Sampler | Storyville | 109 1001
The Golden Years Of Revival Jazz,Vol.10 | Storyville | STCD 5515
Graham Stewart Seven
The Golden Years Of Revival Jazz,Vol.8 | Storyville | STCD 5513

Maxey,Leroy | (dr)
Cab Calloway And His Orchestra
Planet Jazz:Cab Calloway | Planet Jazz | 2161237-2

Maximoff,Richard | (viola)
Earl Klugh Group With Strings
Late Night Guitar | Blue Note | 498573-2

Maxwell,Bob | (harp)
Gil Evans Orchestra
The Individualism Of Gil Evans | Verve | 833804-2

Maxwell,David | (p)
James Cotton Group
Deep In The Blues | Verve | 529849-2

Maxwell,Jimmy | (tpfl-h)
Benny Goodman And His Orchestra
The Legends Of Swing | Laserlight | 24659
Charlie Christian:Swing To Bop | Dreyfus Jazz Line | FDM 36715-2
Cab Calloway And His Orchestra
Planet Jazz:Cab Calloway | Planet Jazz | 2161237-2
Planet Jazz:Male Jazz Vocalists | Planet Jazz | 2169657-2
Cannonball Adderley And His Orchestra
Ballads | Blue Note | 537563-2
Charlie Parker And His Orchestra
The Cole Porter Songbook | Verve | 823250-2
Bird: The Complete Charlie Parker On Verve | Verve | 837141-2
Charlie Parker With Orchestra
Charlie Parker:The Best Of The Verve Years | Verve | 527815-2
Charlie Parker With The Joe Lipman Orchestra
Verve Jazz Masters 28:Charlie Parker Plays Standards | Verve | 521854-2
Charlie Parker Big Band | Verve | 559835-2
Dinah Washington With The Quincy Jones Orchestra
Verve Jazz Masters 40:Dinah Washington | Verve | 522055-2
The Swingin' Miss 'D' | Verve | 558074-2
Glenn Miller And His Orchestra
The Glenn Miller Orchestra In Digital Mood | GRP | GRP 95022
J.J.Johnson And His Orchestra
Planet Jazz:J.J.Johnson | Planet Jazz | 2159974-2
Jimmy Smith And Wes Montgomery With Orchestra
Jimmy & Wes-The Dynamic Duo | Verve | 521445-2
Jimmy Smith And Wes Montgomery With The Oliver Nelson Orchestra
Wes Montgomery:The Verve Jazz Sides | Verve | 521690-2
Jimmy Smith:Best Of The Verve Years | Verve | 527950-2
Talkin' Jazz:Roots Of Acid Jazz | Verve | 529580-2
Jimmy Smith With Orchestra
Jimmy Smith-Talkin' Verve | Verve | 531563-2
Jimmy Smith With The Claus Ogerman Orchestra
Verve Jazz Masters 29:Jimmy Smith | Verve | 521855-2
Any Number Can Win | Verve | 557447-2
Jimmy Smith With The Lalo Schifrin Orchestra
Jimmy Smith:Best Of The Verve Years | Verve | 527950-2
Jimmy Smith-Talkin' Verve | Verve | 531563-2
The Cat | Verve | 539756-2
Lena Horne With The Lennie Hayton Orchestra
Planet Jazz:Lena Horne | Planet Jazz | 2165373-2
Peggy Lee With The Benny Goodman Orchestra
Peggy Lee & Benny Goodman:The Complete Recordings 1941-1947 | CBS | C2K 65686
Quincy Jones And His Orchestra
Talkin' Verve-Roots Of Acid Jazz:Roland Kirk | Verve | 533101-2
Rahsaan/The Complete Mercury Recordings Of Roland Kirk | Mercury | 846630-2
Quincy Jones Big Band
Rahsaan/The Complete Mercury Recordings Of Roland Kirk | Mercury | 846630-2
Sarah Vaughan With The Hugo Winterhalter Orchestra
Sarah Vaughan:Lover Man | Dreyfus Jazz Line | FDM 36739-2
Sarah Vaughan With The Joe Lippman Orchestra
Sarah Vaughan:Lover Man | Dreyfus Jazz Line | FDM 36739-2
Sarah Vaughan With The Norman Leyden Orchestra
Sarah Vaughan:Lover Man | Dreyfus Jazz Line | FDM 36739-2

Maxwell,Robert | (harp)
Lalo Schifrin And His Orchestra
Verve Jazz Masters 39:Cal Tjader | Verve | 521858-2

May,Billy | (arr,ld,voc,condtp)
Anita O'Day With The Billy May Orchestra
Verve Jazz Masters 49:Anita O'Day | Verve | 527653-2
Billy Eckstine With The Billy May Orchestra
Once More With Feeling | Roulette | 581862-2
Billy May And His Orchestra
Billy May's Big Fat Brass/Bill's Bag | Capitol | 535206-2
Billy May And His Orchestra With Members Of The Jimmy Lunceford Orchestra
Great Swing Classics In Hi-Fi | Capitol | 521223-2
Bing Crosby And Rosemarie Clooney With The Billy May Orchestra
Fancy Meeting You Here | RCA | 2663859-2
Charlie Barnet And His Orchestra
Planet Jazz:Big Bands | Planet Jazz | 2169649-2
Planet Jazz:Swing | Planet Jazz | 2169651-2
Ella Fitzgerald With The Billy May Orchestra
Ella Fitzgerald-First Lady Of Song | Verve | 517898-2
The Best Of The Song Books | Verve | 519804-2
Verve Jazz Masters 6:Ella Fitzgerald | Verve | 519822-2
The Best Of The Song Books:The Ballads | Verve | 521867-2
Verve Jazz Masters 46:Ella Fitzgerald-The Jazz Sides | Verve | 527655-2
Love Songs:The Best Of The Song Books | Verve | 531762-2
Ella Fitzgerald Sings The Harold Arlen Song Book | Verve | 589108-2
The Silver Collection: Ella Fitzgerald-The Songbooks | Verve | 823445-2 PMS
For The Love Of Ella Fitzgerald | Verve | 841765-2
Glenn Miller And His Orchestra
Planet Jazz:Glenn Miller | Planet Jazz | 2152056-2
Planet Jazz:Jazz Greatest Hits | Planet Jazz | 2169648-2
Planet Jazz:Big Bands | Planet Jazz | 2169649-2
Swing Legends | Nimbus Records | NI 2001
Jack Teagarden's Chicagoans
Jazz:The Essential Collection Vol.3 | IN+OUT Records | 78013-2
The Hollywood Session:The Capitol Jazzmen | Jazz Unlimited | JUCD 2044
Louis Armstrong And Bing Crosby With Orchestra
The Very Best Of Dixieland Jazz | Verve | 535529-2
Mel Tormé With The Billy May Orchestra
Mel Tormé Goes South Of The Border With Billy May | Verve | 589517-2
Nancy Wilson With The Billy May Orchestra
Misty Blue:Sweet Sisters Swing Songs Of Sorrow And Sadness | Blue Note | 521151-2
Nat King Cole With The Billy May Orchestra
Nat King Cole:For Sentimental Reasons | Dreyfus Jazz Line | FDM 36740-2
Sarah Vaughan With The Billy May Orchestra
Jazz Profile | Blue Note | 823517-2
Ten Cats And A Mouse
The Hollywood Session:The Capitol Jazzmen | Jazz Unlimited | JUCD 2044
The Capitol Jazzmen
Jazz:The Essential Collection Vol.3 | IN+OUT Records | 78013-2
The Hollywood Session:The Capitol Jazzmen | Jazz Unlimited | JUCD 2044

May,Christof | (clb-cl)
Susanne Abbuehl Group
April | ECM | 1766(013999-2)

May,Earl | (b)
Anthony Ortega With The Nat Pierce Orchestra
Earth Dance | Fresh Sound Records | FSR-CD 325
Billy Taylor Trio
Billy Taylor Trio | Prestige | PRCD 24285-2
Chet Baker Quintet
Chet Baker Plays The Best Of Lerner And Loewe | Original Jazz Classics | OJC20 137-2
Chet Baker Septet
Chet Baker Plays The Best Of Lerner And Loewe | Original Jazz Classics | OJC20 137-2
John Coltrane Trio
John Coltrane-The Prestige Recordings | Prestige | 16 PCD 4405-2
The Last Trane | Original Jazz Classics | OJC 394(P 7378)
Lush Life | Original Jazz Classics | OJC20 131-2
The Jazz Giants Play Cole Porter:Night And Day | Prestige | PCD 24203-2
Mose Allison Trio
Mose Alife!/Wild Man On The Loose | Warner | 8122-75439-2
Prestige All Stars
The Mal Waldron Memorial Album:Soul Eyes | Prestige | PRCD 11024-2
Shirley Scott Quartet
Queen Of The Organ-Shirley Scott Memorial Album | Prestige | PRCD 11027-2

May,Guido | (dr)
Cafe Du Sport Jazzquartett
Cafe Du Sport Jazzquartett | Minor Music | 801096
Christian Elsässer Trio
Venice | Organic Music | ORGM 9727
Eckhard Weigt Quartet
Standard Moods | Organic Music | ORGM 9718
Helmut Kagerer 4 & Roman Schwaller
Jazz Guitar Highlights 1 | Jardis Records | JRCD 20141
Gamblin' | Jardis Records | JRCD 9714
Jenny Evans And Her Quintet
Gonna Go Fishin' | ESM Records | ESM 9307
Joe Kienemann Trio
Liedgut:Amsel,Drossel,Swing & Funk | yvp music | CD 3095
Pee Wee Ellis Quintet With Guests
A New Shift | Minor Music | 801060
Till Martin Quintet
On The Trail | Nabel Records:Jazz Network | CD 4676
Torsten Goods Group
Manhattan Walls | Jardis Records | JRCD 20139

Mayall,John | (harm,voc,p,org12-string-g)
Albert King Blues Band
The Lost Session | Stax | SCD 8534-2

Mayer,Capo | (b)
Francis Coletta Trio + One
Cris De Balaines | IN+OUT Records | 77030-2
Mario Neunkirchen Quintet
Long Distance | Laika Records | LK 94-060

Mayer,John | (v)
John Mayer's Indio-Jazz Fusions
Ragatal | Nimbus Records | NI 5569

Mayer,JoJo | (dr)
Olga Konkova-Per Mathisen Quartet
Northern Crossing | Candid | CCD 79766

Mayer,Jonathan | (sitar)
John Mayer's Indio-Jazz Fusions
Ragatal | Nimbus Records | NI 5569

Mayer,Marium | (viola)
Jacintha With Band And Strings
Lush Life | Groove Note | GRV 1011-2(Gold CD 2011)

Mayer,Peter | (gvoc)
Dave Weckl Group
Master Plan | GRP | GRP 96192

Mayer,Vali | (bvoc)
Häns'che Weiss-Vali Mayer Duo
The Duo Live In Concert | MMM Records | CD 1296
Just Play | MMM Records | CD 1298
Just Play II | MMM Records | CD 1303

Mayer,Wolf | (pvoc)
Matthias Stich & Whisper Not
Bach Lives!! | Satin Doll Productions | SDP 1018-1 CD
Wolf Mayer Dialects
Roots And Wings | Triptychon | 300201
Wolf Mayer Trio
I Do Believe In Spring | Triptychon | 400403

Mayerl,Andy | (b)
European Jazz Youth Orchestra
Swinging Europe 1 | dacapo | DCCD 9449
Swinging Europe 2 | dacapo | DCCD 9450

Mayers,Lloyd | (p)
Duke Ellington Orchestra
Continuum | Fantasy | FCD 24765-2
Eddie Lockjaw Davis Orchestra
Afro-Jaws | Original Jazz Classics | OJCCD 403-2(RLP 9373)
Eddie Lockjaw Davis-Johnny Griffin Quintet
Blues Up And Down | Milestone | MCD 47084-2

Mayes,Martin | (fr-h)
Italian Instabile Orchestra
Skies Of Europe | ECM | 1543

Mayfield,John | (tb)
Clarence Williams' Blue Five
Jazz:The Essential Collection Vol.1 | IN+OUT Records | 78011-2

Mayhew,Bob | (tp)
Louis Armstrong And His Orchestra
Louis Armstrong:Swing That Music | Laserlight | 36056

Mayhew,Bob or Charlie Margulis | (tp)
Paul Whiteman And His Orchestra
Planet Jazz:Jazz Trumpet | Planet Jazz | 2169654-2

Mayhew,Jack | (cl,assax)
Lena Horne With The Lou Bring Orchestra
Planet Jazz:Lena Horne | Planet Jazz | 2165373-2
Planet Jazz:Female Jazz Vocalists | Planet Jazz | 2169656-2

Mayhew,Nye | (as,ts,clvoc)
Paul Whiteman And His Orchestra
Planet Jazz:Jazz Trumpet | Planet Jazz | 2169654-2

Mayo,Scott | (voc)
John Patitucci Group
Mistura Fina | GRP | GRP 98022

Mays,Betti | (voc)
Big Sid Catlett And His Orchestra
The Small Black Groups | Storyville | 4960523

Mays,Bill | (grand-p,keyboards,p,arr,voc,el-p)
Bill Mays Quartet
The Story Of Jazz Piano | Laserlight | 24653

Mays,Lyle | (keyboards,p,el-p,autoharps,clavinet)
Eberhard Weber Quintet
Later That Evening | ECM | 1231(829382-2)
Lyle Mays
Improvisations For Expanded Piano | Warner | 9362-47284-2
Lyle Mays Trio
Fictionary | Warner | 9362-47906-2
Pat Metheny & Lyle Mays
As Falls Wichita, So Falls Wichita Falls | ECM | 1190(821416-2)
Pat Metheny Group
Pat Metheny Group | ECM | 1114(825593-2)
American Garage | ECM | 1155(827134-2)
Offramp | ECM | 1216(817138-2)
Travels | ECM | 1252/53
First Circle | ECM | 1278(823342-2)
Imaginary Day | Warner | 9362-46791-2
Letter From Home | Geffen Records | GED 24245
The Road To You | Geffen Records | GED 24601
We Live Here | Geffen Records | GED 24729
Quartet | Geffen Records | GED 24978
Pat Metheny Group With Orchestra
Secret Story | Geffen Records | GED 24468
Pat Metheny Quartet
Watercolors | ECM | 1097(827409-2)
Steve Swallow Group
Home | ECM | 1160(513424-2)

Mayuto | (perc)
Nat Adderley Group
Soul Of The Bible | Capitol | 358257-2

Maz | (keyboardsdr-programming)
The Brecker Brothers
Return Of The Brecker Brothers | GRP | GRP 96842

Maza,Diseur Diserable | (voc)
Brass Attack
Brecht Songs | Tutu Records | 888190-2*

Mazaneo,Emil | (tb)
Gene Krupa And His Orchestra
Mullenium | CBS | CK 65678

Mazelle,Kym | (voc)
Maceo Parker Group
Mo' Roots | Minor Music | 801018
Maceo(Soundtrack) | Minor Music | 801046

Mazetier,Louis | (pp-solo)
Dick Hyman-Louis Mazetier Duo
Barrel Of Keys | Jazz Connaisseur | JCCD 0140-2
Louis Mazetier
Barrel Of Keys | Jazz Connaisseur | JCCD 0140-2
The Piano Starts Talking | Jazz Connaisseur | JCCD 0243-2
Good Vibrations | Jazz Connaisseur | JCCD 9521-2
In Concert:What A Treat! | Jazz Connaisseur | JCCD 9522-2
A Friendly Chat | Jazz Connaisseur | JCCD 9932-2
Louis Mazetier-Peter Ecklund
A Friendly Chat | Jazz Connaisseur | JCCD 9932-2

Mazmanian,Greg | (v)
Art Pepper Quintet With Strings
Art Pepper:The Complete Galaxy Recordings | Galaxy | 16GCD 1016-2
Winter Moon | Original Jazz Classics | OJC20 677-2(GXY 5140)

Mazur,Marilyn | (dr,perc,balafon,voice,udop)
Copenhagen Art Ensemble
Shape To Twelve | dacapo | DCCD 9430
Jan Garbarek Group
Twelve Moons | ECM | 1500(519500-2)
Visible World | ECM | 1585(529086-2)
Rites | ECM | 1685/86(559006-2)
Jon Balke w/Magnetic North Orchestra
Further | ECM | 1517
Lotte Anker-Marilyn Crispell-Marilyn Mazur
Poetic Justice | dacapo | DCCD 9460
Marilyn Mazur With Ars Nova And The Copenhagen Art Ensemble
Jordsange | dacapo | DCCD 9454
Marilyn Mazur's Future Song
Small Labyrinths | ECM | 1559(533679-2)
Marilyn Mazure's Future Song | VeraBra Records | CDVBR 2105-2
Miles Davis With The Danish Radio Big Band
Aura | CBS | CK 63962
Simon Spang-Hanssen & Maneklar
Wondering | dacapo | DCCD 9436
The Danish Radio Big Band
Aura | CBS | CK 63962

Mazzola,Guerino | (p)
Q4 Orchester Project
Lyon's Brood | Creative Works Records | CW CD 1018-3
Yavapai | Creative Works Records | CW CD 1028-2
Rissi-Mazzola-Geisser
Fuego | Creative Works Records | CW CD 1029-2

Mazzon,Guido | (tb,tp,fl-hvoice)
Italian Instabile Orchestra
Skies Of Europe | ECM | 1543

Mazzone,Vincenzo | (dr,perctympani)
Banda Città Ruvo Di Puglia
La Banda/Banda And Jazz | Enja | ENJ-9326 2
Italian Instabile Orchestra
Skies Of Europe | ECM | 1543

M'Boom |
M'Boom
To The Max! | Enja | ENJ-7021 22

M'Boop,Abdou | (perc)
Michel Petrucciani Quintet
Michel Petrucciani Live | Blue Note | 780589-2

M'boup,Abdou | (perc,talking-drvoice)
Jean-Michel Pilc Quartet
Cardinal Points | Dreyfus Jazz Line | FDM 36649-2
Jean-Michel Pilc Quintet
Cardinal Points | Dreyfus Jazz Line | FDM 36649-2
Pharoah Sanders Group
Save Our Children | Verve | 557297-2

M'Bow,Gana | (congasperc)
Art Blakey And The Jazz Messengers
At The Club St.Germain | RCA | ND 74897(2)
Barney Wilen Quintet
Jazz In Paris:Barney Wilen-Jazz Sur Saine | EmArCy | 548317-2 PMS

McAlhany,Nancy | (v)
A Band Of Friends
Wynton Marsalis Quartet With Strings | CBS | CK 68921

McAll,Barney | (p,claps,el-p,synthorg)
Vince Jones Group
Here's To The Miracles | Intuition Records | INT 3198-2

McAll,John | (p)
Vince Jones Quartet
One Day Spent | Intuition Records | INT 3087-2

McAllister,Jay | (tuba)
Dizzy Gillespie And His Orchestra
Ultimate Dizzy Gillespie | Verve | 557535-2
Miles Davis With Gil Evans & His Orchestra
Sketches Of Spain | CBS | CK 65142
Thelonious Monk And His Orchestra
Thelonious Monk:85th Birthday Celebration | zyx records | FANCD 6076-2

At Town Hall | Original Jazz Classics | OJCCD 135-2

McAneney,Anne | (tpfl-h)
John Surman-Jack DeJohnette With The London Brass
Printed In Germany | ECM | 1802(017065-2)

McArthur,Iain | (programming)
Acoustic Alchemy
Against The Grain | GRP | GRP 97832

McBee,Cecil | (b,bird-effects,perc,finger-cymbals)
Alice Coltrane Sextet
Journey In Satchidananda | Impulse(MCA) | 951228-2
Art Pepper Quartet
Art Pepper:The Complete Galaxy Recordings | Galaxy | 16GCD 1016-2
The Jazz Giants Play Harry Warren:Lullaby Of Broadway | Prestige | PCD 24204-2
Art Pepper Quintet
Art Pepper:The Complete Galaxy Recordings | Galaxy | 16GCD 1016-2
Art Pepper Quintet With Strings
Art Pepper:The Complete Galaxy Recordings | Galaxy | 16GCD 1016-2
Winter Moon | Original Jazz Classics | OJC20 677-2(GXY 5140)
Arthur Blythe Quartet
Retroflection | Enja | ENJ-8046 2
Calling Card | Enja | ENJ-9051 2
Cecil McBee
Thembi | Impulse(MCA) | 951253-2
Charles Lloyd Quartet
Charles Lloyd In Europe | Atlantic | 7567-80788-2
Atlantic Saxophones | Rhino | 8122-71256-2
Forest Flower:Charles Lloyd At Monterey | Atlantic | 8122-71746-2
Chico Freeman Quartet
Destiny's Dance | Original Jazz Classics | OJCCD 799-2(C 14008)
Chico Freeman Quintet
Destiny's Dance | Original Jazz Classics | OJCCD 799-2(C 14008)
Chico Freeman Septet
Destiny's Dance | Original Jazz Classics | OJCCD 799-2(C 14008)
Chico Freeman Sextet
Destiny's Dance | Original Jazz Classics | OJCCD 799-2(C 14008)
Dick Griffin Septet
The Eighth Wonder & More | Konnex Records | KCD 5059
Dollar Brand Trio
The Children Of Africa | Enja | ENJ-2070 2
Eddie Harris Quartet
There Was A Time-Echo Of Harlem | Enja | ENJ-6068 2
Grachan Moncur III Quintet
A Blue Conception | Blue Note | 534254-2
Jackie McLean Quintet
A Blue Conception | Blue Note | 534254-2
James Blood Ulmer Quartet
Revealing | IN+OUT Records | 7007-2
Jazz Unlimited | IN+OUT Records | 7017-2
Joe Sample Group
Invitation | Warner | 9362-45209.2
Kenny Barron Quintet
What If | Enja | ENJ-5013 2
Live At Fat Tuesdays | Enja | ENJ-5071 2
Kenny Barron Trio
What If | Enja | ENJ-5013 2
Leon Thomas With Band
Spirits Known And Unknown | RCA | 2663876-2
Lonnie Liston Smith & His Cosmic Echoes
Astral Travelling | RCA | 2663878-2
Pharoah Sanders Group
Black Unity | Impulse(MCA) | 951219-2
Pharoah Sanders Orchestra
Jewels Of Thought | Impulse(MCA) | 951247-2
Thembi | Impulse(MCA) | 951253-2
Deaf Dumb Blind | Impulse(MCA) | 951265-2
Tony Lakatos Quartet
Live In Budapest | Laika Records | 35100742
Toots Thielemans Quartet
Images | Choice | CHCD 71007
Wayne Shorter Orchestra
Wayne Shorter:The Classic Blue Note Recordings | Blue Note | 540856-2
Wayne Shorter Quartet
Wayne Shorter:The Classic Blue Note Recordings | Blue Note | 540856-2
Wynton Kelly Trio With Hank Mobley
Live at The Left Bank Jazz Society,Baltimore,1967 | Fresh Sound Records | FSCD 1031
Yusef Lateef Ensemble
Atlantic Saxophones | Rhino | 8122-71256-2
Yusef Lateef Orchestra
The Blue Yusef Lateef | Rhino | 8122-73717-2

McBride,Christian | (b,el-b,voice,b-solo,fretless-el-b)
Abbey Lincoln With The Rodney Kendrick Trio And Guests
A Turtle's Dream | Verve | 527382-2
Benny Green Trio
These Are Soulful Days | Blue Note | 499527-2
Blue Note Plays Gershwin | Blue Note | 520808-2
Bobby Hutcherson Group
Skyline | Verve | 559616-2
Brad Mehldau Trio
Introducing Brad Mehldau | Warner | 9362-45997-2
Christian McBide Quartet
Vertcal Vision | Warner | 9362-48278-2
Christian McBride
Gettin' To It | Verve | 523989-2
Parker's Mood | Verve | 527907-2
Christian McBride Group
Gettin' To It | Verve | 523989-2
A Family Affair | Verve | 557554-2
Christian McBride/Ray Brown/Milt Hinton
Gettin' To It | Verve | 523989-2
Dave Ellis Quartet
State Of Mind | Milestone | MCD 9328-2
Diana Krall Group
The Girl In The Other Room | Verve | 9862246
Diana Krall Trio
Love Scenes | Impulse(MCA) | 951234-2
Donald Harrison Quartet
Nouveau Swing | Impulse(MCA) | 951209-2
Free To Be | Impulse(MCA) | 951283-2
Donald Harrison Quintet
Free To Be | Impulse(MCA) | 951283-2
Donald Harrison Sextet
Free To Be | Impulse(MCA) | 951283-2
Eddie Allen Quintet
R 'N' B | Enja | ENJ-9033 2
Fleurine With Band And Horn Section
Meant To Be! | EmArCy | 159085-2
Flip Phillips Quintet
Swing Is The Thing | Verve | 543477-2
Flip Phillips Septet
Swing Is The Thing | Verve | 543477-2
Flip Phillips Sextet
Swing Is The Thing | Verve | 543477-2
Flip Phillips-Christian McBride
Swing Is The Thing | Verve | 543477-2
Jimmy Smith Sextet
Angel Eyes-Ballads & Slow Jams | Verve | 527632-2
Joe Henderson Group
Double Rainbow | Verve | 527222-2
Joe Henderson Quartet
Lush Life-The Music Of Billy Strayhorn | Verve | 511779-2
Joe Henderson Quintet
Lush Life-The Music Of Billy Strayhorn | Verve | 511779-2
Joe Henderson Trio
Lush Life-The Music Of Billy Strayhorn | Verve | 511779-2
Joe Henderson/Christian McBride
Lush Life-The Music Of Billy Strayhorn | Verve | 511779-2
Joe Lovano Quartet
Live At The Village Vanguard | Blue Note | 829125-2
Joe Lovano Sextet
Tenor Legacy | Blue Note | 827014-2
John Pizzarelli Trio
Dear Mr.Cole | Novus | 4163182-2
John Scofield Quintet
Works For Me | Verve | 549281-2
Joshua Redman Quartet
Joshua Redman | Warner | 9362-45242-2
MoodSwing | Warner | 9362-45643-2
Joshua Redman Trio
Joshua Redman | Warner | 9362-45242-2
McCoy Tyner Quartet
Prelude And Sonata | Milestone | MCD 9244-2
McCoy Tyner Quintet
Prelude And Sonata | Milestone | MCD 9244-2
Pat Martino Quintet
Think Tank | Blue Note | 592009-2
Roy Hargrove Quartet
Family | Verve | 527630-2
Roy Hargrove Trio
Parker's Mood | Verve | 527907-2
Roy Hargrove-Christian McBride
Parker's Mood | Verve | 527907-2
Stephen Scott-Christian McBride
Parker's Mood | Verve | 527907-2

McBride,Reggie | (bb-g)
Al Jarreau With Band
All Fly Home | Warner | 7599-27362-2
Jimmy Smith All Stars
Jimmy Smith:Dot Com Blues | Blue Thumb | 543978-2

McBrowne,Lennie | (dr)
Billie Holiday And Her All Stars
Verve Jazz Masters 12:Billie Holiday | Verve | 519825-2
Billie Holiday Story Vol.4:Lady Sings The Blues | Verve | 521429-2
4 By 4:Ella Fitzgerald/Sarah Vaughan/Billie Holiday/Dinah Washington | Verve | 559693-2
The Billie Holiday Song Book | Verve | 823246-2
Kenny Burrel Quartet
'Round Midnight | Original Jazz Classics | OJCCD 990-2(F 9417)
Kenny Burrell Quartet
Stormy Monday Blues | Fantasy | FCD 24767-2
Sonny Stitt Quartet
Verve Jazz Masters 50:Sonny Sitt | Verve | 527651-2
Goin' Down Slow | Prestige | PRCD 24276-2

McCain,Seward | (bel-b)
Jackie Cain/Roy Kral Quartet
Full Circle | Fantasy | FCD 24768-2
Vince Guaraldi Group
Charlie Brown's Holiday Hits | Fantasy | FCD 9682-2

McCall,Barney | (p)
Vince Jones Group
It All Ends Up In Tears | Intuition Records | INT 3069-2
Future Girl | Intuition Records | INT 3109-2

McCall,Marti | (voc)
Dee Dee Bridgewater With Band
Dee Dee Bridgewater | Atlantic | 7567-80760-2
Les McCann Group
Another Beginning | Atlantic | 7567-80790-2

McCall,Steve | (dr,bells,perc,darbouka,voicep-solo)
Gunter Hampel All Stars
Jubilation | Birth | 0038
Gunter Hampel Group
The 8th Of July 1969 | Birth | CD 001

McCallum,Johnny | (bj,g,percsnare-dr)
Chris Barber's Jazzband & das Große Rundfunkorchester Berlin,DDR
Jazz Zounds: Chris Barber | Zounds | CD 2720007

McCandless,Paul | (b-cl,oboe,ss.sopranino,whistles,ss)
Al Jarreau With Band
Heaven And Earth | i.e. Music | 557852-2
Art Lande Trio
Skylight | ECM | 1208
Carla Bley Band
Night-Glo | Watt | 16
Eberhard Weber Group
Endless Days | ECM | 1748(013420-2)
Eberhard Weber Quintet
Later That Evening | ECM | 1231(829382-2)
Oregon
Oregon | ECM | 1258(811711-2)
Crossing | ECM | 1291(825323-2)
Ecotopia | ECM | 1354
45th Parallel | VeraBra Records | CDVBR 2048-2
Always,Never And Forever | Intuition Records | INT 2073-2
Northwest Passage | Intuition Records | INT 3191-2
Ralph Towner
Trios/Solos | ECM | 1025(833328-2)
Ralph Towner Quintet
City Of Eyes | ECM | 1388

McCann,Les | (el-keyboards,el-p,org,voc,keyboards)
Les McCann Group
Talkin' Verve:Les McCann | Verve | 557351-2
Another Beginning | Atlantic | 7567-80790-2
Atlantic Jazz: Fusion | Atlantic | 7567-81711-2
Les McCann Orchestra
Talkin' Verve:Les McCann | Verve | 557351-2
Les McCann Quartet
Talkin' Verve:Les McCann | Verve | 557351-2
Les McCann Trio
Talkin' Verve:Les McCann | Verve | 557351-2
Les McCann-Eddie Harris Quintet
Rhino Presents The Atlantic Jazz Gallery | Atlantic | 8122-71257-2
Swiss Movement | Atlantic | 8122-72452-2
Lou Rawls With Les McCann Ltd.
Blue Velvet: Crooners, Swooners And Velvet Vocals | Blue Note | 521153-2
Stormy Monday | Blue Note | 791441-2
Passport And Guests
Doldinger's Best | ACT | 9224-2
Richard 'Groove' Holmes Quintet
Somethin' Special | Pacific Jazz | 855452-2
Richard 'Groove' Holmes Sextet
Somethin' Special | Pacific Jazz | 855452-2

McCaslin,Donny | (cl,ts,fl,ss,tunesian-hornperc)
David Binney Group
Balance | ACT | 9411-2

McCheskie,Bob | (tb)
Vic Lewis West Coast All Stars
Vic Lewis Presenting A Celebration Of Contemporary West Coast Jazz | Candid | CCD 79711/12

McClain,Jean | (voc)
Lenny White Group
Present Tense | Hip Bop | HIBD 8004
Renderers Of Spirit | Hip Bop | HIBD 8014

McClain,Meridith | (p)
Buddy Rich Big Band
Keep The Customer Satisfied | EMI Records | 523999-2

McClellan,Bill | (drperc)
Cassandra Wilson Group
Blue Light 'Til Dawn | Blue Note | 781357-2

McClendon,Chuck | (ts)
Lionel Hampton And His All Star Jazz Inner Circle
Lionel Hampton: Salle Pleyel, March 9th, 1971 | Laserlight | 36133

McClure,Ron | (b,b-gel-b)
Art Farmer/Slide Hampton Quintet
In Concert | Enja | ENJ-4088 2
Helen Merrill With The Pepper Adams Quintet
Chasin' The Bird(Gershwin) | EmArCy | 558850-2
Jim Pepper Quartet
West End Avenue | Nabel Records:Jazz Network | CD 4633
Joe Henderson Quintet
Joe Henderson:The Milestone Years | Milestone | 8MCD 4413-2
Joe Henderson Sextet
Joe Henderson:The Milestone Years | Milestone | 8MCD 4413-2
Lee Konitz-Wolfgang Lackerschmid Quintet
Chet Baker:The Legacy Vol.3:Why Shouldn't You Cry | Enja | ENJ-9337 2
Michael Mantler Group
Michael Mantler: No Answer/Silence | Watt | 2/5(543374-2)
Silence | Watt | 5 (2313105)
Ron McClure Quartet
Match Point | Steeplechase | SCCD 31517
Wolfgang Lackerschmid-Donald Johnston Group
New Singers-New Songs | Bhakti Jazz | BR 31
Wynton Kelly Trio
Full View | Original Jazz Classics | OJCCD 912-2(M 9004)
Wynton Kelly-George Coleman Quartet
Live at The Left Bank Jazz Society,Baltimore,1968 | Fresh Sound Records | FSCD 1032

McClure,Ruby | (voc)
Max Roach Sextet With The J.C.White Singers
Lift Every Voice And Sing | Atlantic | 7567-80798-2

McColl,Bill | (cl)
Modern Jazz Quartet & Guests
MJQ 40 | Atlantic | 7567-82330-2

McConnell,John | (tb)
Fletcher Henderson And His Orchestra
Jazz:The Essential Collection Vol.3 | IN+OUT Records | 78013-2

McConnell,Maurice | (tp)
Earl Hines And His Orchestra
Planet Jazz:Earl Hines | Planet Jazz | 2159973-2

McConnell,Rob | (arr,cond,tbv-tb)
Singers Unlimited With Rob McConnell And The Boss Brass
The Singers Unlimited:Magic Voices | MPS | 539130-2

McConnell,Shorty | (tp)
Jubilee All Stars
Jazz Gallery:Lester Young Vol.2(1946-59) | RCA | 2119541-2
Lester Young And His Band
Jazz:The Essential Collection Vol.3 | IN+OUT Records | 78013-2
Lester Young:The Complete Aladdin Sessions | Blue Note | 832787-2
Lester Young:Blue Lester | Dreyfus Jazz Line | FDM 36729-2

McConney,Edmond | (dr)
Louis Armstrong And His Orchestra
Louis Armstrong:C'est Si Bon | Dreyfus Jazz Line | FDM 36730-2

McCook,Don | (ascl)
Charlie Barnet And His Orchestra
Planet Jazz:Big Bands | Planet Jazz | 2169649-2
Planet Jazz:Swing | Planet Jazz | 2169651-2

McCord,Theodore | (as,clts)
McKinney's Cotton Pickers
Jazz:The Essential Collection Vol.3 | IN+OUT Records | 78013-2

McCoy Choir,The Herman | (voc)
Duke Ellington And His Orchestra
Highlights From The Duke Ellington Centennial Edition | RCA | 2663672-2

McCoy,Roy | (tp)
Lionel Hampton And His Orchestra
Lionel Hampton:Flying Home | Dreyfus Jazz Line | FDM 36735-2

McCracken,Bob | (ascl)
Henry Red Allen Band
The Very Best Of Dixieland Jazz | Verve | 535529-2
Kid Ory's Creole Jazz Band
This Kid's The Greatest! | Good Time Jazz | GTCD 12045-2
Louis Armstrong With Gordon Jenkins And His Orchestra And Choir
Satchmo In Style | Verve | 549594-2
Louis Armstrong With The Gordon Jenkins Orchestra
Ambassador Louis Armstrong Vol.17:Moments To Remember(1952-1956) | Ambassador | CLA 1917

McCracken,Charles | (cello,stringsv)
Bob James And His Orchestra
Jazzrock-Anthology Vol.3:Fusion | Zounds | CD 27100555
Charles Mingus Orchestra
Charles Mingus:Pre-Bird(Mingus Revisited) | Verve | 538636-2
Earl Klugh Group With Strings
Late Night Guitar | Blue Note | 498573-2
Freddie Hubbard Orchestra
The Body And The Soul | Impulse(MCA) | 951183-2
Grant Green With Orchestra
The Final Comedown(Soundtrack) | Blue Note | 581678-2
Grover Washington Jr. Orchestra
Jazzrock-Anthology Vol.3:Fusion | Zounds | CD 27100555
Helen Merrill With Orchestra
Casa Forte | EmArCy | 558848-2
James Moody Orchestra
The Blues And Other Colors | Original Jazz Classics | OJCCD 954-2(M 9023)
Lalo Schifrin And His Orchestra
Verve Jazz Masters 39:Cal Tjader | Verve | 521858-2
Louis Armstrong And His Friends
Planet Jazz:Louis Armstrong | Planet Jazz | 2152052-2
Planet Jazz Sampler | Planet Jazz | 2152326-2
Louis Armstrong And His Friends | Bluebird | 2663961-2
Milt Jackson And His Orchestra
Sunflower | CTI | ZK 65131
Nina Simone And Orchestra
Baltimore | Epic | 476906-2
Paul Desmond Quartet With The Don Sebesby Orchestra
From The Hot Afternoon | Verve | 543487-2
Phil Woods Quartet With Orchestra & Strings
Round Trip | Verve | 559804-2
Ron Carter Group
Songs For You | Milestone | MCD 47099-2
Ron Carter Quintet With Strings
Pick 'Em/Super Strings | Milestone | MCD 47090-2
Stan Getz With The Eddie Sauter Orchestra
Stan Getz Plays The Music Of Mickey One | Verve | 531232-2
Stan Getz With The Richard Evans Orchestra
What The World Needs Now-Stan Getz Plays Bacharach And David | Verve | 557450-2
Wes Montgomery Quartet With The Claus Ogerman Orchestra
Tequila | Verve | 547769-2
Wes Montgomery Quintet With The Claus Ogerman Orchestra
The Antonio Carlos Jobim Songbook | Verve | 525472-2
Talkin' Jazz:Roots Of Acid Jazz | Verve | 529580-2
Tequila | Verve | 547769-2
Wes Montgomery Trio With The Claus Ogerman Orchestra
Tequila | Verve | 547769-2
Wes Montgomery With The Claus Ogerman Orchestra
Verve Jazz Masters 14:Wes Montgomery | Verve | 519826-2
Wes Montgomery With The Don Sebesky Orchestra
Verve Jazz Masters 14:Wes Montgomery | Verve | 519826-2
Talkin' Jazz:Roots Of Acid Jazz | Verve | 529580-2
Bumpin' | Verve | 539062-2
Wes Montgomery With The Jimmy Jones Orchestra
Wes Montgomery-The Complete Riverside Recordings | Riverside | 12 RCD 4408-2
The Jazz Giants Play Rodgers & Hart:Blue Moon | Prestige | PCD 24205-2

McCracken,Hugh | (g,el-gharm)
Jimmy Rushing And His Orchestra
Every Day I Have The Blues | Impulse(MCA) | 547967-2
Ron Carter With Strings
Pastels | Original Jazz Classics | OJCCD 665-2(M 9073)

INTERPRETENVERZEICHNIS

Rusty Bryant Group
For The Good Times | Prestige | PRCD 24269-2
Rusty Bryant Sextet
For The Good Times | Prestige | PRCD 24269-2
McCreary,Lou | (tb)
Dizzy Gillespie With The Lalo Schifrin Orchestra
Free Ride | Original Jazz Classics | OJCCD 784-2(2310794)
Harry James And His Orchestra
Trumpet Blues:The Best Of Harry James | Capitol | 521224-2
June Christy With The Shorty Rogers Orchestra
June Christy Big Band Special | Capitol | 498319-2
Paulinho Da Costa Orchestra
Happy People | Original Jazz Classics | OJCCD 783-2(2312102)
McCulloh,Bob | (voc)
Leon Thomas With Orchestra
Spirits Known And Unknown | RCA | 2663876-2
McCullough,Yolanda | (voc)
Grover Washington Jr. Orchestra
Inside Moves | Elektra | 7559-60318-2
McCullum,Johnny | (bj,snare-drg)
Chris Barber's Jazz And Blues Band
Chris Barber On The Road:A Jazz Documentary | Storyville | 4960683
McCune,Brandon | (p)
Abbey Lincoln And Her Trio
Over The Years | Verve | 549101-2
Abbey Lincoln And Her Trio With Guests
Over The Years | Verve | 549101-2
McCurdy,Dana | (synth)
Machito And His Orchestra
Afro-Cuban Jazz Moods | Original Jazz Classics | OJC20 447-2
McCurdy,Roy | (dr)
Betty Carter And The Harold Mabern Trio
Misty Blue:Sweet Sisters Swing Songs Of Sorrow And Sadness | Blue Note | 521151-2
Cannonball Adderley Group
Phenix | Fantasy | FCD 79004-2
Cannonball Adderley Quintet
Julian Cannonball Adderlry: Salle Pleyel/Olympia | Laserlight | 36126
Ballads | Blue Note | 537563-2
The Best Of Cannonball Adderley:The Capitol Years | Capitol | 795482-2
Mercy Mercy Mercy | Capitol | 829915-2
Cannonball Adderley Septet
Inside Straight | Original Jazz Classics | OJCCD 750-2(F 9435)
Cannonball Adderley Sextet
Cannonball Adderley Birthday Celebration | Fantasy | FANCD 6087-2
Cannonball Adderley With Sergio Mendes And The Bossa Rio Sextet
Ballads | Blue Note | 537563-2
Joe Williams With The Cannonball Adderley Sextet
Cannonball Adderley Birthday Celebration | Fantasy | FANCD 6087-2
Nat Adderley Group
Soul Of The Bible | Capitol | 358257-2
Nat Adderley Quintet
Joe Henderson:The Milestone Years | Milestone | 8MCD 4413-2
A Little New York Midtown Music | Original Jazz Classics | OJCCD 1008-2(GXY 5120)
Nat Adderley Sextet
Joe Henderson:The Milestone Years | Milestone | 8MCD 4413-2
Pete Jolly And His West Coast Friends
Art Pepper:The Hollywood All-Star Sessions | Galaxy | 5GCD 4431-2
Sarah Vaughan And Her Band
Duke Ellington Song Book Two | Pablo | CD 2312116
Sarah Vaughan With The Mike Wofford Trio
Sarah Vaughan Birthday Celebration | Fantasy | FANCD 6090-2
Sonny Rollins & Co.
Planet Jazz:Sonny Rollins | Planet Jazz | 2152062-2
Planet Jazz Sampler | Planet Jazz | 2152326-2
Sonny Rollins Quartet
Planet Jazz:Sonny Rollins | Planet Jazz | 2152062-2
Sonny Rollins Trio
Planet Jazz:Jazz Saxophone | Planet Jazz | 2169653-2
Sonny Rollins-Coleman Hawkins Quintet
Planet Jazz:Sonny Rollins | Planet Jazz | 2152062-2
Sonny Meets Hawk! | RCA | 2174800-2
The Modern Jazz Disciples
Disciples Blues | Prestige | PCD 24263-2
McDonald,Bruce | (p)
Roy Eldridge-Benny Carter Quintet
The Complete Verve Roy Eldridge Studio Sessions | Verve | 9861278
McDonald,Clarence | (keyboards)
Bobby Hutcherson Orchestra
Deep Blue-The United States Of Mind | Blue Note | 521152-2
Ella Fitzgerald With Orchestra
Ella Abraca Jobim | Pablo | 2630201-2
McDonald,Donald | (drperc)
Gil Evans Orchestra
Blues In Orbit | Enja | ENJ-3069 2
Kenny Burrell With The Don Sebesky Orchestra
Verve Jazz Masters 45:Kenny Burrell | Verve | 527652-2
Blues-The Common Ground | Verve | 589101-2
McDonald,Everett | (tp)
Harry James And His Orchestra
Trumpet Blues:The Best Of Harry James | Capitol | 521224-2
McDonald,Harold | (dr)
Bix Beiderbecke And His Gang
Jazz:The Essential Collection Vol.2 | IN+OUT Records | 78012-2
Paul Whiteman And His Orchestra
Planet Jazz:Jazz Trumpet | Planet Jazz | 2169654-2
McDonald,Jim | (dr)
Firehouse Five Plus Two
Goes South | Good Time Jazz | GTCD 12018-2
McDonald,Joe | (dr)
Charlie Mariano Quartet
The Jazz Scene:San Francisco | Fantasy | FCD 24760-2
Charlie Mariano Sextet
The Jazz Scene:San Francisco | Fantasy | FCD 24760-2
McDonald,Ralph | (congas,bongos,cow-bell,tambourine)
Bob James And His Orchestra
Jazzrock-Anthology Vol.3:Fusion | Zounds | CD 27100555
Bobby Hutcherson Orchestra
Montara | Blue Note | 590956-2
Grant Green Orchestra
Grant Green:Blue Breakbeat | Blue Note | 494705-2
Grant Green With Orchestra
The Final Comedown(Soundtrack) | Blue Note | 581678-2
Grover Washington Jr. Orchestra
Jazzrock-Anthology Vol.3:Fusion | Zounds | CD 27100555
Junior Mance Quartet
That Lovin' Feelin' | Milestone | MCD 47097-2
Les McCann Group
Atlantic Jazz: Fusion | Atlantic | 7567-81711-2
Oscar Brown Jr. And His Group
Movin' On | Rhino | 8122-73678-2
Ron Carter Group
Songs For You | Milestone | MCD 47099-2
Ron Carter Octet
New York Slick | Original Jazz Classics | OJCCD 916-2(M 9096)
Ron Carter Quintet With Strings
Pick 'Em/Super Strings | Milestone | MCD 47090-2
McDonald,Sheila | (v)
Francois Houle 5
Cryptology | Between The Lines | btl 012(Efa 10182-2)
McDonough,Dick | (bjg)
A Jam Session At Victor
Planet Jazz:Fats Waller | Planet Jazz | 2152058-2
Planet Jazz:Jazz Greatest Hits | Planet Jazz | 2169648-2
Benny Goodman And His Orchestra
Jazz:The Essential Collection Vol.3 | IN+OUT Records | 78013-2

Gene Gifford And His Orchestra
Planet Jazz:Bud Freeman | Planet Jazz | 2161240-2
McDougall,Ian | (tb)
Singers Unlimited With Rob McConnell And The Boss Brass
The Singers Unlimited:Magic Voices | MPS | 539130-2
McDowall,James | (fl)
John Mayer's Indio-Jazz Fusions
Ragatal | Nimbus Records | NI 5569
McDowell,Mississippi Fred | (gvoc)
Fred McDowell
Long Way From Home-The Blues Of Fred McDowell | Original Blues Classics | OBCCD 535-2(M 93003)
McDuff,Brother Jack | (org,keyboards,perc,vocp)
Etta James With Band
The Late Show-Recorded Live At Marla's Memory Lane Supper Club Vol.2 | Fantasy | FCD 9655-2
Etta James With The Red Holloway Quintet
Blues In The Night-Volume One:The Early Show | Fantasy | FCD 9647-2
Etta James/Eddie 'Cleanhead' Vinson With Band
The Late Show-Recorded Live At Marla's Memory Lane Supper Club Vol.2 | Fantasy | FCD 9655-2
Gene Ammons Sextet
Gentle Jug Vol.3 | Prestige | PCD 24249-2
Gene Ammons-Sonny Stitt Quartet
Gentle Jug Vol.3 | Prestige | PCD 24249-2
George Benson Group/Orchestra
George Benson Anthology | Warner | 8122-79934-2
George Benson With The Jack McDuff Quartet
The New Boss Guitar | Original Jazz Classics | OJCCD 461-2
Grant Green Quartet
Ballads | Blue Note | 537560-2
Grantstand | Blue Note | 591723-2
Jack McDuff Group
So Blue So Funky-Heroes Of The Hammond | Blue Note | 796563-2
Jack McDuff Orchestra
The Last Goodun' | Prestige | PRCD 24274-2
Jack McDuff Quartet
The Honeydripper | Original Jazz Classics | OJCCD 222-2(P 7199)
Tough 'Duff | Original Jazz Classics | OJCCD 324-2(P 7185)
Brother Jack Meets The Boss | Original Jazz Classics | OJCCD 326-2(P 7228)
Screamin' | Original Jazz Classics | OJCCD 875-2(P 7259)
Silken Soul | Prestige | PCD 24242-2
The Soulful Drums | Prestige | PCD 24256-2
Brother Jack | Prestige | PR20 7174-2
The Concert McDuff | Prestige | PRCD 24270-2
The Last Goodun' | Prestige | PRCD 24274-2
Jack McDuff:The Prestige Years | Prestige | PRCD 24387-2
Jack McDuff Quartet With Gene Ammons
Brother Jack Meets The Boss | Original Jazz Classics | OJCCD 326-2(P 7228)
Jack McDuff Quartet With Orchestra
Moon Rappin' | Blue Note | 538697-2
Prelude:Jack McDuff Big Band | Prestige | PRCD 24283-2
Jack McDuff Quintet
Silken Soul | Prestige | PCD 24242-2
The Last Goodun' | Prestige | PRCD 24274-2
Jack McDuff:The Prestige Years | Prestige | PRCD 24387-2
Jack McDuff Sextet
Silken Soul | Prestige | PCD 24242-2
The Soulful Drums | Prestige | PCD 24256-2
Jack McDuff Trio
The Last Goodun' | Prestige | PRCD 24274-2
Roland Kirk With The Jack McDuff Trio
Kirk's Work | Original Jazz Classics | OJC20 459-2(P 7210)
Sonny Stitt-Jack McDuff Quintet
Stitt Meets Brother Jack | Original Jazz Classics | OJCCD 703-2(P 7244)
Willis Jackson Quintet
Together Again: Willis Jackson With Jack McDuff | Prestige | PRCD 24284-2
Willis Jackson Sextet
Together Again: Willis Jackson With Jack McDuff | Prestige | PRCD 24284-2
McDuffie,Debbie | (voc)
Nina Simone And Orchestra
Baltimore | Epic | 476906-2
McEachern,Murray | (ld,tb,astp)
Anita O'Day With The Billy May Orchestra
Verve Jazz Masters 49:Anita O'Day | Verve | 527653-2
Benny Goodman And His Orchestra
Planet Jazz:Benny Goodman | Planet Jazz | 2152054-2
Planet Jazz:Jazz Greatest Hits | Planet Jazz | 2169648-2
Planet Jazz:Big Bands | Planet Jazz | 2169649-2
Planet Jazz:Swing | Planet Jazz | 2169651-2
Planet Jazz:Jazz Trumpet | Planet Jazz | 2169654-2
Planet Jazz:Female Jazz Vocalists | Planet Jazz | 2169656-2
More Camel Caravans | Phontastic | NCD 8841/2
Billie Holiday With The Paul Whiteman Orchestra
Billie's Blues | Blue Note | 748786-2
Ella Fitzgerald With The Marty Paich Orchestra
Get Happy! | Verve | 523321-2
Louis Armstrong With The Casa Loma Orchestra
Louis Armstrong:Swing That Music | Laserlight | 36056
Nat King Cole With The Billy May Orchestra
Nat King Cole:For Sentimental Reasons | Dreyfus Jazz Line | FDM 36740-2
McElroy,Donna | (voc)
Steve Rochinski Quartet
Otherwise | Jardis Records | JRCD 20133
McFadden,Cornell | (dr)
Nina Simone Trio
Verve Jazz Masters 17:Nina Simone | Verve | 518198-2
Verve Jazz Masters Vol.58:Nina Simone Sings Nina | Verve | 529867-2
McFadden,Eddie | (g)
Jimmy Smith All Stars
House Party | Blue Note | 524542-2
Jimmy Smith Quartet
Cool Blues | Blue Note | 535587-2
Jimmy Smith Quintet
Cool Blues | Blue Note | 535587-2
Jimmy Smith Trio
Paris Jazz Concert:Jimmy Smith And The Trio | Laserlight | 36159
Groovin' At Smalls' Paradise | Blue Note | 499777-2
Cool Blues | Blue Note | 535587-2
Johnny 'Hammond' Smith Quartet
Good 'Nuff | Prestige | PRCD 24282-2
Johnny 'Hammond' Smith Septet
Open House | Milestone | MCD 47089-2
Johnny 'Hammond' Smith Sextet
Open House | Milestone | MCD 47089-2
Johnny 'Hammond' Smith Trio
Good 'Nuff | Prestige | PRCD 24282-2
McFarland,Gary | (arr,comp,cond,vibmarimba)
Anita O'Day With The Gary McFarland Orchestra
All The Sad Youn Men | Verve | 517065-2
Verve Jazz Masters 49:Anita O'Day | Verve | 527653-2
Gary McFarland And His Orchestra
The Complete Bill Evans On Verve | Verve | 527953-2
Gerry Mulligan Concert Jazz Band
Verve Jazz Masters 36:Gerry Mulligan | Verve | 523342-2
Stan Getz With The Gary McFarland Orchestra
Stan Getz Highlights | Verve | 847430-2
McFerrin,Bobby | (el-p,voc,percvoice)
Bobby McFerrin
Simple Pleasures | Manhattan | 748059-2
The Voice | Elektra | 7559-60366-2
Bobby McFerrin Group

Blue Velvet: Crooners, Swooners And Velvet Vocals | Blue Note | 521153-2
Bobby McFerrin | Elektra | 7559-60023-2
Bobby McFerrin Groups
Spontaneous Inventions | Blue Note | 746298-2
Bobby McFerrin-Chick Corea
Play | Blue Note | 795477-2
Rob Wasserman Duet
Duets | GRP | GRP 97122
McGarity,Lou | (tbvoc)
Benny Goodman And His Orchestra
Charlie Christian:Swing To Bop | Dreyfus Jazz Line | FDM 36715-2
Billy Butterfield And His Modern Dixie Stompers
Soft Strut | Fresh Sound Records | FSR-CD 318
Charlie Parker And His Orchestra
The Cole Porter Songbook | Verve | 823250-2
Bird: The Complete Charlie Parker On Verve | Verve | 837141-2
Charlie Parker With Orchestra
Charlie Parker:The Best Of The Verve Years | Verve | 527815-2
Charlie Parker With The Joe Lipman Orchestra
Verve Jazz Masters 28:Charlie Parker Plays Standards | Verve | 521854-2
Charlie Parker Big Band | Verve | 559835-2
J.J.Johnson's All Stars
J.J.'s Broadway | Verve | 9860308
Louis Armstrong And The Commanders under the Direction of Camarata
Satchmo Serenaders | Verve | 543792-2
Louis Armstrong With Gordon Jenkins And His Orchestra And Choir
Ambassador Louis Armstrong Vol.17:Moments To Remember(1952-1956) | Ambassador | CLA 1917
Louis Armstrong With The Commanders
Ambassador Louis Armstrong Vol.17:Moments To Remember(1952-1956) | Ambassador | CLA 1917
Muggsy Spanier And His Dixieland Band
Muggsy Spanier-Manhattan Masters,1945 | Storyville | STCD 6051
Muggsy Spanier And His V-Disc All Stars
Muggsy Spanier And Bud Freeman:V-Discs 1944-45 | Jazz Unlimited | JUCD 2049
Pee Wee Russell And His Dixieland Band
Muggsy Spanier-Manhattan Masters,1945 | Storyville | STCD 6051
Peggy Lee With Benny Goodman And His Quintet
Peggy Lee & Benny Goodman:The Complete Recordings 1941-1947 | CBS | C2K 65686
Peggy Lee With Benny Goodman And His Sextet
Peggy Lee & Benny Goodman:The Complete Recordings 1941-1947 | CBS | C2K 65686
Peggy Lee With The Benny Goodman Orchestra
Peggy Lee & Benny Goodman:The Complete Recordings 1941-1947 | CBS | C2K 65686
The Chicago All Stars
Planet Jazz:Bud Freeman | Planet Jazz | 2161240-2
V-Disc All Star Jam Session
Louis Armstrong-Jack Teagarden-Woody Herman:Midnights At V-Disc | Jazz Unlimited | JUCD 2048
V-Disc All Stars
Jazz:The Essential Collection Vol.3 | IN+OUT Records | 78013-2
McGee,Charles | (tp)
Rahsaan Roland Kirk And His Orchestra
Blacknuss | Rhino | 8122-71408-2
McGee,Johnny | (tp)
Louis Armstrong And His Orchestra
Louis Armstrong:Swing That Music | Laserlight | 36056
McGee,Larry | (g)
Lonnie Smith Quintet
The Lost Grooves | Blue Note | 831883-2
McGhee,Andy | (ts)
Woody Herman And His Orchestra
Verve Jazz Masters 54:Woody Herman | Verve | 529903-2
McGhee,Brownie | (g,kazoo,vocp)
Sonny Terry & Brownie McGhee
Sonny Terry And Brownie McGhee At Suger Hill | Original Blues Classics | OBCCD 536-2(F 8091)
Just A Closer Walk With Thee | Original Blues Classics | OBCCD 541-2(F 3296)
McGhee,Charles | (tp,2-tp,fl-hvoice)
Archie Shepp Orchestra
The Cry Of My People | Impulse(MCA) | 9861488
Rahsaan Roland Kirk Sextet
Volunteered Slavery | Rhino | 8122-71407-2
McGhee,Howard | (arr,tpp)
Billie Holiday With The JATP All Stars
Billie Holiday Story Vol.1:Jazz At The Philharmonic | Verve | 521642-2
The Complete Jazz At The Philharmonic On Verve 1944-1949 | Verve | 523893-2
Verve Jazz Masters 47:Billie Holiday Sings Standards | Verve | 527650-2
Billy Strayhorn Orchestra
Johnny Hodges With Billy Strayhorn And The Orchestra | Verve | 557543-2
Charlie Parker's New Stars
Charlie Parker:Now's The Time | Dreyfus Jazz Line | FDM 36724-2
Chubby Jackson Big Band
Gerry Mulligan Quartet feat.Chet Baker | Original Jazz Classics | OJCCD 711-2(F 8082/P 7641)
Coleman Hawkins And His Orchestra
Jazz:The Essential Collection Vol.3 | IN+OUT Records | 78013-2
Don Patterson Quartet
Boppin' & Burnin' | Original Jazz Classics | OJCCD 983-2(P 7563)
Don Patterson Quintet
Boppin' & Burnin' | Original Jazz Classics | OJCCD 983-2(P 7563)
Ella Fitzgerald And Her All Stars
Ella Fitzgerald:Mr.Paganini | Dreyfus Jazz Line | FDM 36741-2
JATP All Stars
Jazz Gallery:Lester Young Vol.2(1946-59) | RCA | 2119541-2
The Complete Jazz At The Philharmonic On Verve 1944-1949 | Verve | 523893-2
Charlie Parker:The Best Of The Verve Years | Verve | 527815-2
Jazz At The Philharmonic:Best Of The 1940's Concerts | Verve | 557534-2
Bird: The Complete Charlie Parker On Verve | Verve | 837141-2
Joe Williams And Friends
Planet Jazz:Male Jazz Vocalists | Planet Jazz | 2169657-2
At Newport '63 | RCA | 2663919-2
Joe Williams And His Band
Planet Jazz:Joe Williams | Planet Jazz | 2165370-2
Lester Young And His Band
Jazz Gallery:Lester Young Vol.2(1946-59) | RCA | 2119541-2
Lester Young:The Complete Aladdin Sessions | Blue Note | 832787-2
Teddy Edwards-Howard McGhee Quintet
Together Again! | Original Jazz Classics | OJCCD 424-2
The McGhee-Navarro Boptet
The Fabulous Fats Navarro Vol.1 | Blue Note | 0677207
The Fabulous Fats Navarro Vol.2 | Blue Note | 0677208
McGhee,Howard prob. | (tp)
Billie Holiday With The JATP All Stars
Billie Holiday Story Vol.1:Jazz At The Philharmonic | Verve | 521642-2
McGhee,Larry | (g)
Lonnie Smith Quintet
Deep Blue-The United States Of Mind | Blue Note | 521152-2
McGill,Guillermo | (perc)
Perico Sambeat Group
Ademuz | Fresh Sound Records | FSNT 041 CD
McGouch,Danny | (keyboards)
Peter Malick Group feat. Norah Jones
New York City | Koch Records | 238678-2
McGrath,Fulton | (p)
Louis Armstrong And His Orchestra

Louis Armstrong:Swing That Music | Laserlight | 36056

McGreery,Lewis | (tb)

Peggy Lee With The Quincy Jones Orchestra
Blues Cross Country | Capitol | 520088-2

McGriff,Jimmy | (keyboards,org,synthp)

Buddy Rich Septet
Swingin' The Blues-Jumpin' The Blues | Laserlight | 24654
Hank Crawford-Jimmy McGriff Quartet
Jazzin' With The Soul Brothers | Fantasy | FANCD 6086-2
Jimmy McGriff Band
Blue Break Beats | Blue Note | 799106-2
Jimmy McGriff Orchestra
Swingin' The Blues-Jumpin' The Blues | Laserlight | 24654
Blue Breaks Beats Vol.2 | Blue Note | 789907-2
Jimmy McGriff Organ Blues Band
The Worm | Blue Note | 538699-2
Jimmy McGriff Quartet
Feelin' It | Milestone | MCD 9313-2
Jimmy McGriff Quintet
Swingin' The Blues-Jumpin' The Blues | Laserlight | 24654
McGriff's House Party | Milestone | MCD 9300-2
Jimmy McGriff Septet
McGriff Avenue | Milestone | MCD 9325-2
Jimmy McGriff Sextet
McGriff's House Party | Milestone | MCD 9300-2
Feelin' It | Milestone | MCD 9313-2
Jimmy McGriff Trio
So Blue So Funky-Heroes Of The Hammond | Blue Note | 796563-2

McGuffie,Bill | (pceleste)

Benny Goodman And His All Star Sextet
Verve Jazz Masters 33:Benny Goodman | Verve | 844410-2
Benny Goodman And His Orchestra
Verve Jazz Masters 33:Benny Goodman | Verve | 844410-2
Benny Goodman Quintet
Verve Jazz Masters 33:Benny Goodman | Verve | 844410-2
Benny Goodman Sextet
Verve Jazz Masters 33:Benny Goodman | Verve | 844410-2

McGuire,Larry | (tpfl-h)

Ella Fitzgerald With Orchestra
Ella/Things Ain't What They Used To Be | Warner | 9362-47875-2

McGuirk |

Jed Levy Quartet
Round And Round | Steeplechase | SCCD 31529

McHendrick,Mike | (bj)

Louis Armstrong And His Orchestra
Best Of The Complete RCA Victor Recordings | RCA | 2663636-2
Louis Armstrong:A 100th Birthday Celebration | RCA | 2663694-2

McHenry,Bill | (ts)

Ben Waltzer Quintet
In Metropolitan Motion | Fresh Sound Records | FSNT 082 CD
Bill McHenry Quartet
Rest Stop | Fresh Sound Records | FSNT 033 CD
Graphic | Fresh Sound Records | FSNT 056 CD
Chris Lightcap Quartet
Lay-Up | Fresh Sound Records | FSNT 074 CD
The Waltzer-McHenry Quartet
Jazz Is Where You Find It | Fresh Sound Records | FSNT 021 CD

McIntosh,Tom | (arr,cond,tb,b-tbtp)

Art Farmer/Benny Golson Jazztet
The Jazztet At Birdhouse | Argo | 589762-2
Eddie Harris Group
The Best Of Eddie Harris | Atlantic | 7567-81370-2
Freddy Cole With Band
Le Grand Freddy:Freddy Cole Sings The Music Of Michel Legrand | Fantasy | FCD 9683-2
George Benson And His Orchestra
Giblet Gravy | Verve | 543754-2
Jack McDuff Quartet With Orchestra
Prelude:Jack McDuff Big Band | Prestige | PRCD 24283-2
James Moody Orchestra
The Blues And Other Colors | Original Jazz Classics | OJCCD 954-2(M 9023)
Jimmy Heath Orchestra
Cannonball Adderley Birthday Celebration | Fantasy | FANCD 6087-2
Jimmy McGriff Orchestra
Swingin' The Blues-Jumpin' The Blues | Laserlight | 24654
Jimmy Smith With The Oliver Nelson Orchestra
Verve Jazz Masters 29:Jimmy Smith | Verve | 521855-2
Jimmy Smith:Best Of The Verve Years | Verve | 527950-2
Jimmy Smith-Talkin' Verve | Verve | 531563-2
Peter & The Wolf | Verve | 547264-2
King Curtis Band
King Curtis-Blow Man Blow | Bear Family Records | BCD 15670 CI
Milt Jackson Orchestra
Milt Jackson Birthday Celebration | Fantasy | FANCD 6079-2
Big Bags | Original Jazz Classics | OJCCD 366-2(RLP 9429)
Roland Kirk All Stars
Rahsaan/The Complete Mercury Recordings Of Roland Kirk | Mercury | 846630-2
Roland Kirk With The Benny Golson Orchestra
Rahsaan/The Complete Mercury Recordings Of Roland Kirk | Mercury | 846630-2
Thad Jones-Mel Lewis Orchestra
The Groove Merchant/The Second Race | Laserlight | 24656

McIntyre,Earl | (b-tb,arr,tuba,voice,euphoniumtb)

Carla Bley Band
Live! | Watt | 12(815730-2)
Heavy Heart | Watt | 14
McCoy Tyner Group With Horns
Inner Voices | Original Jazz Classics | OJCCD 1039-2(M 9079)
McCoy Tyner Group With Horns And Voices
Inner Voices | Original Jazz Classics | OJCCD 1039-2(M 9079)
Miles Davis With Gil Evans Orchestra, The George Gruntz Concert Jazz Band And Guests
Miles & Quincy Live At Montreux | Warner | 9362-45221-2
Mingus Big Band
Tonight At Noon...Three Or Four Shades Of Love | Dreyfus Jazz Line | FDM 36633-2
The Carla Bley Band
Social Studies | Watt | 11(831831-2)
I Hate To Sing | Watt | 12,5

McIntyre,Hal | (as,clsax)

Glenn Miller And His Orchestra
Planet Jazz:Glenn Miller | Planet Jazz | 2152056-2
Planet Jazz Sampler | Planet Jazz | 2152326-2
Planet Jazz:Jazz Greatest Hits | Planet Jazz | 2169648-2
Planet Jazz:Big Bands | Planet Jazz | 2169649-2
Planet Jazz:Swing | Planet Jazz | 2169651-2
The Chesterfield Broadcasts Vol.1 | RCA | 2663113-2
Candelight Miller | RCA | 2668716-2
The Glenn Miller Story Vol. 2 | RCA | ND 89221
Swing Legends | Nimbus Records | NI 2001
The Andrew Sisters With The Glenn Miller Orchestra
The Chesterfield Broadcasts Vol.1 | RCA | 2663113-2

McIntyre,Ken | (as,oboe,bassoon,b-clfl)

Charlie Haden And The Liberation Music Orchestra
The Montreal Tapes:Liberation Music Orchestra | Verve | 527469-2
Ken McIntyre Quintet feat.Eric Dolphy
Eric Dolphy:The Complete Prestige Recordings | Prestige | 9 PRCD-4418-2
Eric Dolphy Birthday Celebration | Fantasy | FANCD 6085-2
Nat Adderley Septet
Don't Look Back | Steeplechase | SCCD 31059

McIntyre,Onnie | (g)

Klaus Doldinger With Orchestra
Lifelike | Warner | 2292-46478-2

McIver,Bob | (tb)

Grace Knight With Orchestra
Come In Spinner | Intuition Records | INT 3052-2
Vince Jones With Orchestra
Come In Spinner | Intuition Records | INT 3052-2

McKay,Al | (g)

Herbie Hancock Group
Magic Window | CBS | 486572-2
Paulinho Da Costa Orchestra
Happy People | Original Jazz Classics | OJCCD 783-2(2312102)

McKay,Jim | (synth)

Gail Thompson Orchestra
Gail Thompson's Jazz Africa | Enja | ENJ-9053 2

McKay,Matthew | (tp)

Dizzy Gillespie And His Orchestra
Planet Jazz:Dizzy Gillespie | Planet Jazz | 2152069-2
Planet Jazz:Bebop | RCA | 2169650-2
Ella Fitzgerald With The Dizzy Gillespie Orchestra
Ella Fitzgerald:Mr.Paganini | Dreyfus Jazz Line | FDM 36741-2

McKay,Ron | (dr,perc,vocwbd)

Cy Laurie Jazz Band
The Golden Years Of Revival Jazz,Sampler | Storyville | 109 1001
Cy Laurie's New Orleans Septet
The Golden Years Of Revival Jazz,Vol 1 | Storyville | STCD 5506
The Golden Years Of Revival Jazz,Vol.5 | Storyville | STCD 5510
The Golden Years Of Revival Jazz,Vol.6 | Storyville | STCD 5511
The Golden Years Of Revival Jazz,Vol.8 | Storyville | STCD 5513
The Golden Years Of Revival Jazz,Vol.9 | Storyville | STCD 5514
The Golden Years Of Revival Jazz,Vol.11 | Storyville | STCD 5516
Mr.Acker Bilk And His Paramount Jazz Band
The Very Best Of Dixieland Jazz | Verve | 535529-2
The Golden Years Of Revival Jazz,Vol.5 | Storyville | STCD 5510
The Golden Years Of Revival Jazz,Vol.6 | Storyville | STCD 5511
The Golden Years Of Revival Jazz,Vol.9 | Storyville | STCD 5514
The Golden Years Of Revival Jazz,Vol.12 | Storyville | STCD 5517
The Golden Years Of Revival Jazz,Vol.13 | Storyville | STCD 5518
The Golden Years Of Revibal Jazz,Vol.15 | Storyville | STCD 5520

McKay,Stephanie | (voc)

Lenny White Group
Present Tense | Hip Bop | HIBD 8004

McKee,Andy | (b)

Daniel Schnyder Group
Tanatula | Enja | ENJ-9302 2
Michel Petrucciani Group
Michel Petrucciani:The Blue Note Years | Blue Note | 789916-2
Music | Blue Note | 792563-2
Mingus Big Band
Tonight At Noon...Three Or Four Shades Of Love | Dreyfus Jazz Line | FDM 36633-2
Mingus Big Band 93
Nostalgia In Times Square | Dreyfus Jazz Line | FDM 36559-2
Steve Grossman Quartet
Steve Grossman Quartet | Dreyfus Jazz Line | FDM 36602-2

McKee,Paul | (tb)

Brad Goode-Von Freeman Sextet
Inside Chicago Vol.3 | Steeplechase | SCCD 31531
Inside Chicago Vol.4 | Steeplechase | SCCD 31532

McKendrick,Mike | (bj,vocg)

Louis Armstrong And His Orchestra
Planet Jazz:Louis Armstrong | Planet Jazz | 2152052-2
Best Of The Complete RCA Victor Recordings | RCA | 2663636-2
Louis Armstrong:A 100th Birthday Celebration | RCA | 2663694-2
Jazz:The Essential Collection Vol.2 | IN+OUT Records | 78012-2
Satch Plays Fats(Complete) | CBS | CK 64927

McKenna,Dave | (pp-solo)

Bobby Hackett Sextet
Jazz Festival Vol.1 | Storyville | 4960733
Jazz Festival Vol.2 | Storyville | 4960743
Charlie Ventura Quintet
High On An Open Mike | Fresh Sound Records | FSR-CD 314
Frank Tate Quintet
Live In Belfast | Nagel-Heyer | CD 069
Harry Allen Quintet
Love Songs Live! | Nagel-Heyer | NH 1014

McKenna,Steve | (g)

Michael Lutzeier Quartet
Music 4 Food | Jazz 4 Ever Records:Jazz Network | J4E 4739

McKenzie,Colin | (b-g)

Trevor Watts Moiré Music Drum Orchestra
A Wider Embrace | ECM | 1449

McKenzie,Jerry | (dr)

Stan Kenton Orchestra
Stompin' At Newport | Pablo | PACD 5312-2

McKenzie,Kevan | (dr)

Hugh Marsh Duo/Quartet/Orchestra
The Bear Walks | VeraBra Records | CDVBR 2011-2

McKenzie,Red | (blue-blowing,comb,voc,ldwhistling)

Mound City Blue Blowers
Planet Jazz:Jack Teagarden | Planet Jazz | 2161236-2
Jazz:The Essential Collection Vol.3 | IN+OUT Records | 78013-2
V-Disc All Star Jam Session
Louis Armstrong-Jack Teagarden-Woody Herman:Midnights At V-Disc | Jazz Unlimited | JUCD 2048

McKerrow,Ian | (cl)

Graham Stewart And His New Orleans Band
The Golden Years Of Revival Jazz,Sampler | Storyville | 109 1001
The Golden Years Of Revival Jazz,Vol.10 | Storyville | STCD 5515
Graham Stewart Seven
The Golden Years Of Revival Jazz,Vol.8 | Storyville | STCD 5513
Papa Benny's Jazzband
The Golden Years Of Revival Jazz,Vol.2 | Storyville | STCD 5507

McKibbon,Al | (b)

52nd Street All Stars
Planet Jazz:Bebop | RCA | 2169650-2
Anita O'Day With The Russ Garcia Orchestra
Verve Jazz Masters 49:Anita O'Day | Verve | 527653-2
Benny Carter And His Orchestra
Further Definitions/Additions To Further Definotions | Impulse(MCA) | 951229-2
Billie Holiday With The JATP All Stars
Billie Holiday Story Vol.1:Jazz At The Philharmonic | Verve | 521642-2
The Complete Jazz At The Philharmonic On Verve 1944-1949 | Verve | 523893-2
Verve Jazz Masters 47:Billie Holiday Sings Standards | Verve | 527650-2
Jazz At The Philharmonic:Best Of The 1940's Concerts | Verve | 557534-2
Buck Clayton Quartet
The Complete Jazz At The Philharmonic On Verve 1944-1949 | Verve | 523893-2
Cal Tjader Group
Verve Jazz Masters 39:Cal Tjader | Verve | 521858-2
Cal Tjader Quartet
Cal Tjader Plays Harold Arlen & West Side Story | Fantasy | FCD 24775-2
Cal Tjader Plays Jazz | Original Jazz Classics | OJCCD 986-2(F 3-211)
Cal Tjader Quintet
Cal Tjader's Latin Concert | Original Jazz Classics | OJCCD 643-2(F 8014)
Cal Tjader Sextet
Talkin Verve/Roots Of Acid Jazz:Cal Tjader | Verve | 531562-2
Black Hawk Nights | Fantasy | FCD 24755-2
The Jazz Giants Play Cole Porter:Night And Day | Prestige | PCD 24203-2
Cannonball Adderley Quintet
Cannonball Adderley:Sophisticated Swing-The EmArCy Small Group Sessions | Verve | 528408-2
Coleman Hawkins And His 52nd Street All Stars
Jazz:The Essential Collection Vol.3 | IN+OUT Records | 78013-2
Coleman Hawkins' Fifty-Second Street All-Stars
Planet Jazz:Coleman Hawkins | Planet Jazz | 2152055-2
Coleman Hawkins Quartet
The Complete Jazz At The Philharmonic On Verve 1944-1949 | Verve | 523893-2
Count Basie Octet
Planet Jazz:Count Basie | Planet Jazz | 2152068-2
Dizzy Gillespie And His Orchestra
Dizzy Gillespie:Pleyel Jazz Concert 1948 + Max Roach Quintet 1949 | Vogue | 21409412
Planet Jazz:Dizzy Gillespie | Planet Jazz | 2152069-2
Planet Jazz:Bebop | RCA | 2169650-2
Planet Jazz:Male Jazz Vocalists | Planet Jazz | 2169657-2
Dizzy Gillespie Quintet
Charlie Parker:Now's The Time | Dreyfus Jazz Line | FDM 36724-2
Dizzy Gillespie:Night In Tunisia | Dreyfus Jazz Line | FDM 36734-2
Ella Fitzgerald With The Dizzy Gillespie Orchestra
Ella Fitzgerald:Mr.Paganini | Dreyfus Jazz Line | FDM 36741-2
Ella Fitzgerald With The Hank Jones Trio
Ella Fitzgerald:Mr.Paganini | Dreyfus Jazz Line | FDM 36741-2
George Shearing And His Quintet
Verve Jazz Masters 57:George Shearing | Verve | 529900-2
George Shearing Quintet
Verve Jazz Masters 57:George Shearing | Verve | 529900-2
Verve Jazz Masters Vol.59:Toots Thielemans | Verve | 535271-2
At Newport | Pablo | PACD 5315-2
George Shearing Quintet With Cannonball And Nat Adderley
At Newport | Pablo | PACD 5315-2
George Shearing Sextet
At Newport | Pablo | PACD 5315-2
Herbie Nichols Trio
Herbie Nichols:The Complete Blue Note Recordings | Blue Note | 859352-2
JATP All Stars
Jazz At The Philharmonic:Best Of The 1940's Concerts | Verve | 557534-2
Jazz Crusaders
Chile Con Soul | Pacific Jazz | 590957-2
Kenny Kersey Trio
The Complete Jazz At The Philharmonic On Verve 1944-1949 | Verve | 523893-2
Lester Young Quintet
The Complete Jazz At The Philharmonic On Verve 1944-1949 | Verve | 523893-2
Miles Davis And His Orchestra
The Complete Birth Of The Cool | Capitol | 494550-2
Birth Of The Cool | Capitol | 530117-2
Jazz Profile:Miles Davis | Blue Note | 823515-2
Ballads & Blues | Blue Note | 836633-2
Miles Davis:Milestones | Dreyfus Jazz Line | FDM 36731-2
Ruth Brown With Orchestra
Fine And Mellow | Fantasy | FCD 9663-2
Sarah Vaughan With The Gerald Wilson Orchestra
Ballads | Roulette | 537561-2
Sarah Vaughan With The Jimmy Jones Quartet
Sarah Vaughan:Lover Man | Dreyfus Jazz Line | FDM 36739-2
Thelonious Monk Quartet
Thelonious Monk:Misterioso | Dreyfus Jazz Line | FDM 36743-2
Thelonious Monk Quintet
Genius Of Modern Music,Vol.2 | Blue Note | 532139-2
The Best Of Thelonious Monk:The Blue Note Years | Blue Note | 795636-2
Jazz Profile:Thelonious Monk | Blue Note | 823518-2
Thelonious Monk:Misterioso | Dreyfus Jazz Line | FDM 36743-2
Thelonious Monk Trio
Thelonious Monk:Misterioso | Dreyfus Jazz Line | FDM 36743-2
Victor Feldman Orchestra
Latinsville | Contemporary | CCD 9005-2

McKimmey,Eddie | (b)

Artie Shaw And His Orchestra
Planet JazzArtie Shaw | Planet Jazz | 2152057-2
Planet Jazz:Male Jazz Vocalists | Planet Jazz | 2169657-2

McKinley,Ray | (dr,ldvoc)

Bud Freeman And His Stars
Muggsy Spanier And Bud Freeman:V-Discs 1944-45 | Jazz Unlimited | JUCD 2049
Bud Freeman And The V-Disc Jumpers
Muggsy Spanier And Bud Freeman:V-Discs 1944-45 | Jazz Unlimited | JUCD 2049
Eight Squares And A Critic
Muggsy Spanier And Bud Freeman:V-Discs 1944-45 | Jazz Unlimited | JUCD 2049
Glenn Miller Orchestra
Glenn Miller Serenade | CBS | 487445-2
Louis Armstrong With Jimmy Dorsey And His Orchestra
Louis Armstrong:Swing That Music | Laserlight | 36056
Swing Legends:Louis Armstrong | Nimbus Records | NI 2012
The V-Disc Jumpers
Muggsy Spanier And Bud Freeman:V-Discs 1944-45 | Jazz Unlimited | JUCD 2049

McKinney,Bernard | (bar-horn,euphonium,tbbells)

Yusef Lateef Sextet
The Art Of Saxophone | Laserlight | 24652

McKinney's Cotton Pickers |

McKinney's Cotton Pickers
Jazz:The Essential Collection Vol.3 | IN+OUT Records | 78013-2

McKinstry,Ray | (ts)

Muggsy Spanier And His Ragtime Band
Planet Jazz | Planet Jazz | 2169652-2

McKnight,Blackbird | (g)

Herbie Hancock Group
Man-Child | CBS | 471235-2

McKnight,Claude V. | (voc)

Take 6
Goldmine | Reprise | 7599-25670-2
So Much To Say | Reprise | 7599-25892-2
He Is Christmas | Reprise | 7599-26665-2
Take 6 With The Yellow Jackets
He Is Christmas | Reprise | 7599-26665-2

McKreel.Andy | (tuba)

Lee Konitz With The Ed Partyka Jazz Orchestra
Dreams And Realities | Laika Records | 35101642

McKusick,Hal | (as,b-cl,cl,ts,flreeds)

Billy Butterfield And His Modern Dixie Stompers
Soft Strut | Fresh Sound Records | FSR-CD 318
Charlie Parker And His Orchestra
Charlie Parker:The Best Of The Verve Years | Verve | 527815-2
The Cole Porter Songbook | Verve | 823250-2
Bird: The Complete Charlie Parker On Verve | Verve | 837141-2
Charlie Parker With Orchestra
Charlie Parker Big Band | Verve | 559835-2
Charlie Parker With Orchestra & The Dave Lambert Singers
Verve Jazz Masters 28:Charlie Parker Plays Standards | Verve | 521854-2
Coleman Hawkins With Billy Byers And His Orchestra
The Hawk In Hi-Fi | RCA | 2663842-2
Dinah Washington With The Quincy Jones Orchestra
Verve Jazz Masters 40:Dinah Washington | Verve | 522055-2
The Swingin' Miss 'D' | Verve | 558074-2
Elliot Lawrence And His Orchestra
The Elliot Lawrence Big Band Swings Cohn & Kahn | Fantasy | FCD 24761-2
George Russell And His Orchestra
Geogre Russell New York N.Y. | Impulse(MCA) | 951278-2
Bill Evans:Piano Player | CBS | CK 65361
George Russell Smalltet
The RCA Victor Jazz Workshop | RCA | 2159144-2
Gerry Mulligan And His Orchestra

Mullenium | CBS | CK 65678
Ralph Burns And His Orchestra
The Complete Verve Roy Eldridge Studio Sessions | Verve | 9861278
Woody Herman And His Orchestra
Songs For Hip Lovers | Verve | 559872-2

McLarand,Paul | (as)
Peggy Lee With The Benny Goodman Orchestra
Peggy Lee & Benny Goodman:The Complete Recordings 1941-1947 | CBS | C2K 65686

McLaughlin,John | (el-g,g,digital-g,ld,synclavier,bj)
Ithamara Koorax With Band
Love Dance:The Ballad Album | Milestone | MCD 9327-2
John McLaughlin Group
The Promise | Verve | 529828-2
The Heart Of Things | Verve | 539153-2
Live In Paris | Verve | 543536-2
Remember Shakti | Verve | 559945-2
John McLaughlin Quartet
Extrapolation | Polydor | 841598-2
John McLaughlin Trio
After The Rain | Verve | 527467-2
Que Alegria | Verve | 837280-2
John McLaughlin With The Aighette Quartet And Yan Marez
Time Remembered:John McLaughlin Plays Bill Evans | Verve | 519861-2
Mahavishnu Orchestra
Apocalypse | CBS | 467092-2
Visions Of The Emerald Beyond | CBS | 467904-2
The Inner Mounting Flame | CBS | CK 65523
Miles Davis Group
In A Silent Way | CBS | 86556-2
Live-Evil | CBS | C2K 65135
Bitches Brew | CBS | C2K 65774
On The Corner | CBS | CK 63980
Miles Davis With The Danish Radio Big Band
Aura | CBS | CK 63962
Miroslav Vitous Group
Universal Syncopations | ECM | 1863(038506-2)
Atlantic Jazz: Fusion | Atlantic | 7567-81711-2
Paco De Lucia-Al Di Meola-John McLaughlin
Paco De Lucia-Al Di Meola-John McLaughlin | Verve | 533215-2
Remember Shakti
Saturday Night In Bombay | Verve | 014184-2
Shakti
Shakti With John McLaughlin | CBS | 467905-2
The Mahavishnu Orchestra
Between Nothingness & Eternity | CBS | CK 32766
Wayne Shorter Sextet
Wayne Shorter:The Classic Blue Note Recordings | Blue Note | 540856-2
Zakir Hussain Group
Making Music | ECM | 1349

McLaurine,Marcus | (b)
Abdullah Ibrahim Quartet
Cape Town Revisited | TipToe | TIP-888836 2
Abdullah Ibrahim Trio
Yarona | TipToe | TIP-888820 2
Cape Town Flowers | TipToe | TIP-888826 2
Cape Town Revisited | TipToe | TIP-888836 2
Abdullah Ibrahim Trio With The Munich Radio Symphony Orchestra
African Symphony | Enja | ENJ-9410 2
Clark Terry Quintet
The Hymn | Candid | CCD 79770
Herr Ober | Nagel-Heyer | CD 068
Clark Terry-Max Roach Quartet
Friednship | CBS | 510886-2

McLean,Charlie | (reeds)
Billy Eckstine And His Orchestra
Blue Velvet: Crooners, Swooners And Velvet Vocals | Blue Note | 521153-2

McLean,Jackie | (as,perc,ts,fl,p,bells,kalimbavoice)
Abbey Lincoln And Her All Stars
The World Is Falling Down | Verve | 843476-2
Art Blakey And The Jazz Messengers
Planet Jazz:Art Blakey | Planet Jazz | 2152066-2
A Night In Tunisia | RCA | 2663896-2
The Art Of Jazz | IN+OUT Records | 77028-2
Charles Mingus And His Orchestra
Charles Mingus-Passion Of A Man:The Complete Atlantic Recordings 1956-1961 | Atlantic | 8122-72871-2
Charles Mingus Jazz Workshop
Rhino Presents The Atlantic Jazz Gallery | Atlantic | 8122-71257-2
Charles Mingus-Passion Of A Man:The Complete Atlantic Recordings 1956-1961 | Atlantic | 8122-72871-2
Blues & Roots | Atlantic | 8122-75205-2
The Very Best Of Charles Mingus | Rhino | 8122-79988-2
Charles Mingus Orchestra
The Very Best Of Charles Mingus | Rhino | 8122-79988-2
Don Sickler Orchestra
Tribute To Charlie Parker Vol.2 | Dreyfus Jazz Line | FDM 37015-2
Freddie Redd Sextet
Redd's Blues | Blue Note | 540537-2
Gene Ammons And His All Stars
Jammin' With Gene | Original Jazz Classics | OJCCD 211-2(P 7060)
Jack Wilson Sextet
Blue N' Groovy | Blue Note | 780679-2
Jackie McLean Quartet
A Fickle Sonance | Blue Note | 524544-2
Let Freedom Ring | Blue Note | 591895-2
Right Now | Blue Note | 595972-2
4, 5 And 6 | Original Jazz Classics | OJC 056(P 7048)
A Long Drink Of The Blues | Original Jazz Classics | OJCCD 253-2(NJ 8253)
The Jazz Giants Play Jerome Kern:Yesterdays | Prestige | PCD 24202-2
Jackie McLean Quintet
Herbie Hancock:The Complete Blue Note Sixties Sessions | Blue Note | 495569-2
Vertigo | Blue Note | 522669-2
A Fickle Sonance | Blue Note | 524544-2
A Blue Conception | Blue Note | 534254-2
Capuchin Swing | Blue Note | 540033-2
Jacknife | Blue Note | 540535-2
4, 5 And 6 | Original Jazz Classics | OJC 056(P 7048)
Jackie McLean Sextet
Jacknife | Blue Note | 540535-2
4, 5 And 6 | Original Jazz Classics | OJC 056(P 7048)
A Long Drink Of The Blues | Original Jazz Classics | OJCCD 253-2(NJ 8253)
Jimmy Smith Quartet
Blue Note Plays Gershwin | Blue Note | 520808-2
Lee Morgan Sextet
The Sixth Sense | Blue Note | 522467-2
Mal Waldron Sextet
John Coltrane-The Prestige Recordings | Prestige | 16 PCD 4405-2
The Mal Waldron Memorial Album:Soul Eyes | Prestige | PRCD 11024-2
Miles Davis All Stars
Miles Davis Vol.1 | Blue Note | 532610-2
Miles Davis Sextet
Miles Davis:The Best Of The Capitol/Blue Note Years | Blue Note | 798287-2
Jazz Profile:Miles Davis | Blue Note | 823515-2
Dig | Original Jazz Classics | OJC20 005-2
The Jazz Giants Play Harold Arlen:Blues In The Night | Prestige | PCD 24201-2
Miles Davis-Milt Jackson Sextet
Miles Davis And Milt Jackson | Original Jazz Classics | OJC20 012-2(P 7034)
Prestige All Stars
The Prestige Legacy Vol.2:Battles Of Saxes | Prestige | PCD 24252-2
Ray Draper Sextet
Tuba Sounds | Original Jazz Classics | OJCCD 1936-2(P 7096)
Sonny Clark Quintet
Cool Struttin' | Blue Note | 495327-2
Walter Davis Quintet
Davis Cup | Blue Note | 0675597

McLean,John | (g)
Patricia Barber Group
Modern Cool | Blue Note | 521811-2
Patricia Barber Quartet
Café Blue | Blue Note | 521810-2

McLean,Sarah | (voc)
Mike Westbrook Brass Band
Glad Day:Settings Of William Blake | Enja | ENJ-9376 2

McLemore,William | (g)
Erskine Hawkins And His Orchestra
Planet Jazz:Big Bands | Planet Jazz | 2169649-2

McLeod,Alice | (p)
Terry Gibbs Octet
Jewis Melodies In Jazztime | Mercury | 589673-2

McLeod,Raice | (dr)
Chuck Brown And The Second Chapter Band
Timeless | Minor Music | 801068

McLevy,John | (tp)
Benny Goodman And His Orchestra
Verve Jazz Masters 33:Benny Goodman | Verve | 844410-2

McLewis,Joe | (tb)
Earl Hines And His Orchestra
Planet Jazz:Earl Hines | Planet Jazz | 2159973-2
The Legends Of Swing | Laserlight | 24659
Jazz:The Essential Collection Vol.2 | IN+OUT Records | 78012-2

McLin,Jimmy | (g)
Billie Holiday And Her Quintet
Billie Holiday:The Complete Commodore Recordings | GRP | 543272-2
Billie Holiday With Frankie Newton And His Orchestra
Billie Holiday:The Complete Commodore Recordings | GRP | 543272-2
Billie's Love Songs | Nimbus Records | NI 2000

McManus,Wallace | (harp)
Charlie Parker With Strings
Verve Jazz Masters 28:Charlie Parker Plays Standards | Verve | 521854-2
Charlie Parker With Strings:The Master Takes | Verve | 523984-2
Bird: The Complete Charlie Parker On Verve | Verve | 837141-2

McMickle,Dale | (tp)
Ella Fitzgerald With The Nelson Riddle Orchestra
The Best Of The Song Books:The Ballads | Verve | 521867-2
Oh Lady Be Good:The Best Of The Gershwin Songbook | Verve | 529581-2
Love Songs:The Best Of The Song Books | Verve | 531762-2
Glenn Miller And His Orchestra
Planet Jazz:Glenn Miller | Planet Jazz | 2152056-2
Planet Jazz Sampler | Planet Jazz | 2152326-2
Planet Jazz:Jazz Greatest Hits | Planet Jazz | 2169648-2
Planet Jazz:Big Bands | Planet Jazz | 2169649-2
Planet Jazz:Swing | Planet Jazz | 2169651-2
The Chesterfield Broadcasts Vol.1 | RCA | 2663113-2
Candlelight Miller | RCA | 2668716-2
Swing Legends | Nimbus Records | NI 2001
The Andrew Sisters With The Glenn Miller Orchestra
The Chesterfield Broadcasts Vol.1 | RCA | 2663113-2

McMillan,James | (programming,tpfl-h)
Mike Westbrook Orchestra
Bar Utopia-A Big Band Cabaret | Enja | ENJ-9333 2
The Orchestra Of Smith's Academy | Enja | ENJ-9358 2

McMillan,Vic | (b)
Charlie Parker Septet
Charlie Parker:Now's The Time | Dreyfus Jazz Line | FDM 36724-2

McMullen,Craig | (g)
Donald Byrd Orchestra
Places And Spaces | Blue Note | 854326-2

McMurdo,Dave | (tb)
Singers Unlimited With Rob McConnell And The Boss Brass
The Singers Unlimited:Magic Voices | MPS | 539130-2

McMurray,David | (asts)
Bop City
Hot Jazz Bisquits | Hip Bop | HIBD 8801

McNab,Malcolm | (tp)
Singers Unlimited With The Patrick Williams Orchestra
The Singers Unlimited:Magic Voices | MPS | 539130-2

McNeal,Kevin | (gg-synth)
Greg Osby Quartet
Mindgames | JMT Edition | 919021-2
Greg Osby Quintet
Mindgames | JMT Edition | 919021-2

McNeely,Jim | (cond,p,el-p,synthp-solo)
Art Farmer/Slide Hampton Quintet
In Concert | Enja | ENJ-4088 2
Bobby Watson Quartet
Advance | Enja | ENJ-9075 2
Chet Baker-Stan Getz Quintet
The Stockholm Concerts | Verve | 537555-2
Dave Liebman Quintet
Homage To John Coltrane | Owl Records | 018357-2
Ed Neumeister Quintet
Ed Neumeister Quartet/Quintet | Timescrapper | TSCR 9614
The Danish Radio Jazz Orchestra
Nice Work | dacapo | DCCD 9446

McNeil,Chip | (sax,ssts)
Maynard Ferguson And His Big Bop Nouveau Band
Maynard Ferguson '93-Footpath Café | Hot Shot Records | HSR 8312-2

McPake,Al | (g)
Sandy Brown's Jazz Band
The Golden Years Of Revival Jazz,Vol.5 | Storyville | STCD 5510

McPartland,Jimmy | (co,voctp)
Ben Pollack And His Park Central Orchestra
Planet Jazz:Jack Teagarden | Planet Jazz | 2161236-2
Jazz:The Essential Collection Vol.3 | IN+OUT Records | 78013-2
Bud Freeman And His Summa Cum Laude Orchestra
Planet Jazz:Bud Freeman | Planet Jazz | 2161240-2
Eddie Condon And His Chicagoans
The Very Best Of Dixieland Jazz | Verve | 535529-2
George Wein's Dixie Victors
The Magic Horn | RCA | 2113038-2
Jack Teagarden And His Band
Meet Me Where They Play The Blues | Good Time Jazz | GTCD 12063-2
Jimmy McPartland And His Dixielanders
Planet Jazz | Planet Jazz | 2169652-2
The Jimmy And Marion McPartland Sessions
Vic Lewis:The Golden Years | Candid | CCD 79754

McPartland,Marian | (interviewer,pp-solo)
Bill Evans
The Complete Fantasy Recordings | Fantasy | 9FCD 1012-2
Gerry Mulligan With The Marian McPartland Trio
Newport Jazz Festival 1958,July 3rd-6th Vol.2:Mulligan The Main Man | Phontastic | NCD 8814
Marion McPartland
Monterey Jazz Festival 1975 | Storyville | 4960213
Marion McPartland-Bill Evans-John Lewis-Patrice Rushen
Monterey Jazz Festival 1975 | Storyville | 4960213
The Jimmy And Marion McPartland Sessions
Vic Lewis:The Golden Years | Candid | CCD 79754

McPhail,Jimmy | (voc)
Duke Ellington And His Orchestra
Highlights From The Duke Ellington Centennial Edition | RCA | 2663672-2

McPherson,Charles | (asts)
Barry Harris Quintet
Never Than New | Original Jazz Classics | OJCCD 1062-2(RLP 9413)
Barry Harris Sextet
Bull's Eye! | Original Jazz Classics | OJCCD 1082-2(P 7600)
Charles McPherson Quartet
Jazzin' Vol.2: The Music Of Stevie Wonder | Fantasy | FANCD 6088-2
McPherson's Mood | Original Jazz Classics | OJCCD 1947-2(PR 7743)
Charles McPherson Quintet
The Jazz Giants Play Rodgers & Hammerstein:My Favorite Things | Prestige | PCD 24223-2
Charles Mingus And His Orchestra
The Complete Town Hall Concert | Blue Note | 828353-2
Charles Mingus Group
The Jazz Life! | Candid | CCD 79019
Candid Dolphy | Candid | CCD 79033
Mysterious Blues | Candid | CCD 79042
Charles Mingus Orchestra
Mingus | Candid | CCD 79021
Della Reese With The Neal Hefti Orchestra
Della | RCA | 2663912-2
Don Patterson Quintet
Boppin' & Burnin' | Original Jazz Classics | OJCCD 983-2(P 7563)
Eddie Jefferson And His Band
Dexter Gordon Birthday Celebration | Fantasy | FANCD 6082-2
Kevin Mahogany With The WDR Big Band And Guests
Pussy Cat Dues:The Music Of Charles Mingus | Enja | ENJ-9316 2

McPherson,Eric | (dr)
Abraham Burton Quartet
Closest To The Sun | Enja | ENJ-8074 2
The Magician | Enja | ENJ-9037 2

McPherson,Norman | (tuba)
Paul Whiteman And His Orchestra
Planet Jazz:Jack Teagarden | Planet Jazz | 2161236-2
Jazz:The Essential Collection Vol.3 | IN+OUT Records | 78013-2

McRae,Carmen | (p,vocp-solo)
Carmen McRae And Her Quartet
Carmen Sings Monk | RCA | 2663841-2
Carmen McRae And Her Trio
The Collected Carmen McRae | RCA | 2668713-2
Carmen McRae And Her Trio With Zoot Sims
The Collected Carmen McRae | RCA | 2668713-2
Carmen McRae With Orchestra
Birds Of A Feather | Decca | 589515-2
Carmen McRae with the Clifford Jordan Quartet
The Collected Carmen McRae | RCA | 2668713-2
Carmen McRae With The Dizzy Gillespie Quartet
Misty Blue:Sweet Sisters Swing Songs Of Sorrow And Sadness | Blue Note | 521151-2
Carmen McRae With The Jimmy Mundy Orchestra
Blue Moon | Verve | 543829-2
Carmen McRae With The Ralph Burns Orchestra
Birds Of A Feather | Decca | 589515-2
Carmen McRae With The Shirley Horn Trio
Planet Jazz:Female Jazz Vocalists | Planet Jazz | 2169656-2
The Collected Carmen McRae | RCA | 2668713-2
Carmen McRae With The Tadd Dameron Orchestra
Blue Moon | Verve | 543829-2

McRae,Dave | (as,bs,b-cl,bass-sax,cl,saxts)
Della Reese With The Sy Oliver Orchestra
Misty Blue:Sweet Sisters Swing Songs Of Sorrow And Sadness | Blue Note | 521151-2
Ella Fitzgerald With Sy Oliver And His Orchestra
Ella Fitzgerald:The Decca Years 1949-1954 | Decca | 050668-2
Frankie Laine With Buck Clayton And His Orchestra
Jazz Spectacular | CBS | CK 65507
Louis Armstrong And His All Stars With The Sy Oliver Orchestra
Ambassador Louis Armstrong Vol.17:Moments To Remember(1952-1956) | Ambassador | CLA 1917
Louis Armstrong With Sy Oliver And His Orchestra
Satchmo Serenaders | Verve | 543792-2
Louis And The Angels | Verve | 549592-2
Louis Armstrong With Sy Oliver's Choir And Orchestra
Jazz Collection:Louis Armstrong | Laserlight | 24366
Louis And The Good Book | Verve | 549593-2
Louis And The Good Book | Verve | 940130-0

McRae,Teddy | (foot-tapping,sax,ts,bsarr)
Ella Fitzgerald And Her Famous Orchestra
The Radio Years 1940 | Jazz Unlimited | JUCD 2065
Ella Fitzgerald And Her Orchestra
Jazz Collection:Ella Fitzgerald | Laserlight | 24397
Ella Fitzgerald With The Chick Webb Orchestra
Jazz Collection:Ella Fitzgerald | Laserlight | 24397

McShann,Jay | (p,el-p,voc,talkingp-solo)
Axel Zwingenberger-Jay McShann Quartet
Kansas City Boogie Jam | Vagabond | VRCD 8.00027
Jay McShann
The Last Of The Blue Devils | Atlantic | 7567-80791-2
Jay McShann And His Orchestra
Atlantic Jazz: Kansas City | Atlantic | 7567-81701-2
Jay McShann Orchestra
The Last Of The Blue Devils | Atlantic | 7567-80791-2
Jay McShann Quartet
Goin' To Kansas City | Stony Plain | SPCD 1286
Jay McShann Quintet
What A Wonderful World | Groove Note | GN 1005(180gr-Pressung)
What A Wonderful World | Groove Note | GRV 1005-2
Jim Galloway-Jay McShann Quartet
Christmas Jazz! | Nagel-Heyer | NH 1008
Jimmy Witherspoon With Jay McShann And His Band
Planet Jazz:Male Jazz Vocalists | Planet Jazz | 2169657-2

McSticks,Chip | (dr)
Al Jarreau With Band
High Crime | i.e. Music | 557848-2

McTaggert,Steve | (v)
Vince Jones Group
It All Ends Up In Tears | Intuition Records | INT 3069-2

McTell,Blind Willie | (g,commentsvoc)
Blind Willie McTell
Last Session | Original Blues Classics | OBCCD 517-2
Bawdy Blues | Original Blues Classics | OBCCD 544-2(BV 1055)

McTier,D. | (b)
Dee Dee Bridgewater With Orchestra
Dear Ella | Verve | 539102-2

McVea,Jack | (bs,talkingts)
JATP All Stars
The Complete Jazz At The Philharmonic On Verve 1944-1949 | Verve | 523893-2
Jazz At The Philharmonic:Best Of The 1940's Concerts | Verve | 557534-2
Lionel Hampton And His Orchestra
Lionel Hampton:Flying Home | Dreyfus Jazz Line | FDM 36735-2

McVoy,Karen | (voc)
Steve Coleman And Five Elements
The Sonic Language Of Myth | RCA | 2164123-2

McWashington,Willie | (drvoc)
Benny Moten's Kansas City Orchestra
Planet Jazz:Ben Webster | RCA | 2165368-2
Planet Jazz:Jimmy Rushing | RCA | 2165371-2
Planet Jazz:Swing | Planet Jazz | 2169651-2
Jazz:The Essential Collection Vol.3 | IN+OUT Records | 78013-2

McWilliams,Paulette | (voc)
Quincy Jones And His Orchestra
Verve Jazz Masters Vol.59:Toots Thielemans | Verve | 535271-2

Mealing,John | (el-porg)
Passport
Second Passport | Atlantic | 2292-44143-2

Mears,Adrian | (tb,didgeridoo,percvoc)
Conexion Latina

Mambo Nights | Enja | ENJ-9402 2
Frank Eberle Septet
Scarlet Sunrise | Satin Doll Productions | SDP 1041-1 CD
Till Martin Quintet
On The Trail | Nabel Records:Jazz Network | CD 4676
Trombonefire
Sliding Affairs | Laika Records | 35101462
Medan,Sava | (b)
Christian Elsässer Trio
Future Days | Organic Music | ORGM 9721
Marc Schmolling Trio
Nostalgia Soul Ship | Organic Music | ORGM 9731
Zona Sul
Pure Love | Nagel-Heyer | CD 3039
Medberg,Gunnar | (tb)
Bengt-Arne Wallin Orchestra
The Birth+Rebirth Of Swedish Folk Jazz | ACT | 9254-2
Medeski,John | (el-p,org,clavinet,keyboards)
Bill Lowe/Philippe Crettien Quintet
Sunday Train | Konnex Records | KCD 5051
John Scofield Quartet
A Go Go | Verve | 539979-2
Josh Roseman Unit
Cherry | Enja | ENJ-9392 2
Marc Ribot Y Los Cubanos Postizos
The Prosthetic Cubans | Atlantic | 7567-83116-2
Medeski Martin & Wood
Univisible | Blue Note | 535870-2
Medin,Niklas | (wurlitzerorg)
Nils Landgren First Unit And Guests
Nils Landgren-The First Unit | ACT | 9292-2
Medina,Roberto | (perc)
Omar Belmonte's Latin Lover
Vamos A Ver | EGO | 96170
Medvedkjo,Georges 'Popov' | (b)
Don Byas Quintet
Jazz In Paris:Don Byas-Laura | EmArCy | 013027-2
Meek,Gary | (fl,ss,as,ts,org,keyboards)
Airto Moreira/Flora Purim Group
Jazz Unlimited | IN+OUT Records | 7017-2
Meerwald,Willi | (tb,bar-h,vocv-tb)
Oscar Klein's Anniversary Band
Moonglow | Nagel-Heyer | CD 021
Ellington For Lovers | Nagel-Heyer | NH 1009
The Second Sampler | Nagel-Heyer | NHR SP 6
Mehegan,John | (pp-solo)
Jackie Paris With The Charles Mingus Quintet
Charles Mingus-The Complete Debut Recordings | Debut | 12 DCD 4402-2
Lionel Hampton And His Septet
Lionel Hampton:Flying Home | Dreyfus Jazz Line | FDM 36735-2
Mehldau,Brad | (p,el-p,keyboardsp-solo)
Brad Mehldau
Elegiac Cycle | Warner | 9362-47357-2
Places | Warner | 9362-47693-2
Brad Mehldau Trio
Introducing Brad Mehldau | Warner | 9362-45997-2
The Art Of The Trio Vol.1 | Warner | 9362-46260-2
The Art Of The Trio Vol.2 | Warner | 9362-46848-2
Art Of The Trio Vol.3: Songs | Warner | 9362-47051-2
Art Of The Trio Vol.4: Back At The Vanguard | Warner | 9362-47463-2
Places | Warner | 9362-47693-2
Art Of The Trio Vol.5:Progression | Warner | 9362-48005-2
Anything Goes | Warner | 9362-48608-2
Brad Mehldau With The Rossy Trio
New York-Barcelona Crossing Vol.1 | Fresh Sound Records | FSNT 031 CD
New York-Barcelona Crossing Vol.2 | Fresh Sound Records | FSNT 037 CD
Charles Lloyd Quintet
The Water Is Wide | ECM | 1734(549043-2)
Hyperion With Higgins | ECM | 1784(014000-2)
Charlie Haden Quartet With Orchestra
American Dreams | Verve | 064096-2
Chris Cheek Quintet
Vine | Fresh Sound Records | FSNT 086 CD
John Scofield Quintet
Works For Me | Verve | 549281-2
Joshua Redman Quartet
MoodSwing | Warner | 9362-45643-2
Timeless Tales | Warner | 9362-47052-2
Lee Konitz Trio
Another Shade Of Blue | Blue Note | 498222-2
Mehldau & Rossy Trio
When I Fall In Love | Fresh Sound Records | FSNT 007 CD
Perico Sambeat Group
Ademuz | Fresh Sound Records | FSNT 041 CD
Perico Sambeat Quartet
Friendship | ACT | 9421-2
Perico Sambeat Quintet
Friendship | ACT | 9421-2
Mei,Shi Hong | (voc)
Chinese Compass
Chinese Compass | dacapo | DCCD 9443
Meid,Lothar | (b,b-gel-b)
Passport
Uranus | Atlantic | 2292-44142-2
Paul Nero Sound
Doldinger's Best | ACT | 9224-2
Meier,Hans | (tb)
Danny Moss Meets Buddha's Gamblers
A Swingin' Affair | Nagel-Heyer | CD 034
Blues Of Summer | Nagel-Heyer | NH 1011
Meijer,Joop | (fr-h)
Toots Thielemans And His Orchestra
Verve Jazz Masters Vol.59:Toots Thielemans | Verve | 535271-2
Meinberg,Stephan | (tp,fl-htoy-duck)
Lars Duppler Sextet
Palindrome 6tet | Jazz Haus Musik | JHM 0131 CD
Stephan Meinberg VITAMINE
Horizontal | Jazz Haus Musik | JHM 0106 CD
Tomatic 7
Haupstrom | Jazz Haus Musik | JHM 0101 CD
Meinecke,Siegfried | (viola)
Keith Jarrett With String Quartet
In The Light | ECM | 1033/4
Meinesses,Jim | (perc)
Mani Neumeir Group
Privat | ATM Records | ATM 3803-AH
Meinhold,Boris | (g)
Andreas Willers Group
Andreas Willers & Friends Play Jimi Hendrix:Experience | Nabel Records:Jazz Network | CD 4665
Meinikoff,Harry | (v)
Billie Holiday With The Ray Ellis Orchestra
Lady In Satin | CBS | CK 65144
Charlie Parker Quartet With Strings
The Cole Porter Songbook | Verve | 823250-2
Mejlvang,Jesper | (keyboards,el-pvoc)
Niels Landgren Funk Unit
Live In Stockholm | ACT | 9223-2
Nils Landgren First Unit And Guests
Nils Landgren-The First Unit | ACT | 9292-2
Meldonian,Dick | (as,reedsts)
Gerry Mulligan Concert Jazz Band
Verve Jazz Masters 36:Gerry Mulligan | Verve | 523342-2
The Complete Verve Gerry Mulligan Concert Band | Verve | 9860613
Meléndez,José Miguel | (timbales)
Irakere
Yemayá | Blue Note | 498239-2
Melian,Reinaldo | (tp)
Gonzalo Rubalcaba Quartet
Imagine | Blue Note | 830491-2
Melian,Reynaldo | (tp)
Gonzalo Rubalcaba & Cuban Quartet
Antiguo | Blue Note | 837717-2
Melito,Helcio | (dr)
Joao Gilberto Trio
The Antonio Carlos Jobim Songbook | Verve | 525472-2
Melling,Steve | (keyboards,pp-solo)
Barbara Thompson Group
Heavenly Bodies | VeraBra Records | CDVBR 2015-2
Barbara Thompson's Paraphernalia
Barbara Thompson's Special Edition | VeraBra Records | CDVBR 2017-2
Jon Hiseman With The United Jazz & Rock Ensemble And Babara Thompson's Paraphernalia
About Time Too! | VeraBra Records | CDVBR 2014-2
Mello,Chico | (g,vocperc)
Schlothauer's Maniacs
Maniakisses | Timescrapper | TSCR 9811
Mellon,Ester | (cello)
Archie Shepp Orchestra
The Cry Of My People | Impulse(MCA) | 9861488
Melnick,Mitchell | (ts)
Gene Krupa And His Orchestra
Mullenium | CBS | CK 65678
Melnikoff,Harry | (v)
Charlie Parker With Strings
Charlie Parker:The Best Of The Verve Years | Verve | 527815-2
Bird: The Complete Charlie Parker On Verve | Verve | 837141-2
Charlie Parker:April In Paris | Dreyfus Jazz Line | FDM 36737-2
Charlie Parker With The Joe Lipman Orchestra
Verve Jazz Masters 28:Charlie Parker Plays Standards | Verve | 521854-2
Charlie Parker With Strings:The Master Takes | Verve | 523984-2
Charlie Parker Big Band | Verve | 559835-2
Melo,Hernon | (b)
Hernan Merlo Quintet
Consin | Fresh Sound Records | FSNT 150 CD
Melon,Yves | (v)
Charlie Haden Quartet West With Strings
Now Is The Hour | Verve | 527827-2
Melvoin,Mike | (keyboards,pel-p)
Johnny Hartman And His Orchestra
Unforgettable | Impulse(MCA) | IMP 11522
Members of Machito's Rhythm Section) |
Ella Fitzgerald And Her All Stars
Ella Fitzgerald:Mr.Paganini | Dreyfus Jazz Line | FDM 36741-2
Members of Radio Symphony Orchestra Stuttgart | (strings)
Herbert Joos With Strings
Daybreak/The Dark Side Of Twilight | Japo | 60015
Keith Jarrett Trio With Strings
Arbour Zena | ECM | 1070(825592-2)
Members of The Banda Cittá Ruvo Di Puglia |
Willem Breuker Kollektief
La Banda/Banda And Jazz | Enja | ENJ-9326 2
Members of The Count Basie Band |
Sarah Vaughan With The Benny Carter Orchestra
Jazz Profile | Blue Note | 823517-2
Members of The Dorsey Band |
Tommy Dorsey And His Orchestra
Frank Sinatra And The Tommy Dorsey Orchestra | RCA | 2668701-2
Members of the Philharmonic Orchestra Oslo | (fr-h,cellioboe)
Eberhard Weber With Orchestra
The Following Morning | ECM | 1084(829116-2)
Members of The Youth Orchestra of The European Community |
Abdullah Ibrahim Trio And A String Orchestra
African Suite | TipToe | TIP-888832 2
String Orchestra
African Suite | TipToe | TIP-888832 2
Memphis Slim[Peter Chatman] | (p,org,voc,whistlingtalking)
Memphis Slim
Memphis Slim USA | Candid | CCD 79024
Bawdy Blues | Original Blues Classics | OBCCD 544-2(BV 1055)
Memphis Slim Trio
Americans Swinging In Paris:Memphis Slim | EMI Records | 539666-2
Willie Dixon-Memphis Slim Quintet
Windy City Blues | Stax | SCD 8612-2
Memphis Willie B.[Borum] | (g,harm,vocp)
Memphis Willie B.
Bawdy Blues | Original Blues Classics | OBCCD 544-2(BV 1055)
Mena,Antonio 'Chocolate' Diaz | (perc)
Lalo Schifrin And His Orchestra
Tin Tin Deo | Fresh Sound Records | FSR-CD 319
Menardi,Louis | (tp)
Django's Music
Peche Á La Mode-The Great Blue Star Sessions 1947/1953 | Verve | 835418-2
Mendelsoh,Danny | (cello)
Coleman Hawkins Sextet
Body And Soul Revisited | GRP | GRP 16272
Mendes,Damon | (dr)
Cold Sweat
Cold Sweat Plays J.B. | JMT Edition | 919025-2
Mendes,Sergio | (p)
Cannonball Adderley With Sergio Mendes And The Bossa Rio Quartet
Cannonball's Bossa Nova | Blue Note | 522667-2
Cannonball Adderley With Sergio Mendes And The Bossa Rio Sextet
Cannonball's Bossa Nova | Blue Note | 522667-2
Ballads | Blue Note | 537563-2
Blue Bossa | Blue Note | 795590-2
Mendolas,Juan Lazaro | (pan-pipes,wooden-flquena)
Geri Allen/Charlie Haden/Paul Motian & Guest
In The Year Of The Dragon | JMT Edition | 919027-2
Mendoza,Vince | (cond,arr,g,keyboards)
John Abercrombie Trio
Animato | ECM | 1411
Los Jovenes Flamencos With The WDR Big Band And Guests
Jazzpana | ACT | 9212-2
Vince Mendoza With The WDR Big Band And Guests
Sketches | ACT | 9215-2
Yellowjackets
Live Wires | GRP | GRP 96672
Meneghelli,Claudio | (g)
Mahmoud Turkmani With The Ludus Guitar Quartet
Nuqta | TipToe | TIP-888835 2
Menendez,Alberto | (ts)
Derrick James & Wesley 'G' Quintet
Two Sides To Every Story | Jardis Records | JRCD 20137
Russ Spiegel Group
Twilight | double moon | CHRDM 71026
Menendez,Pablo | (g,arrvoc)
Lazaro Ros Con Mezcla
Cantos | Intuition Records | INT 3080-2
Mengelberg,Misha | (pvoice)
Berlin Contemporary Jazz Orchestra
Berlin Contemporary Jazz Orchestra | ECM | 1409
Mengeon,Jean-Pierre | (p)
Coleman Hawkins And His Rhythm
Coleman Hawkins/Johnny Hodges:The Vogue Recordings | Vogue | 21559712
Mengo,Jerry | (dr)
Alix Combelle Et Son Orchestre
Americans Swinging In Paris:Bill Coleman-The Elegance | EMI Records | 539662-2
Bill Coleman Et Son Orchestre
Americans Swinging In Paris:Bill Coleman-The Elegance | EMI Records | 539662-2
Charlie Lewis Trio
JazzIn Paris:Harlem Piano In Montmartre | EmArCy | 018447-2
Dany Polo Trio
JazzIn Paris:Harlem Piano In Montmartre | EmArCy | 018447-2
Mengual,David | (b)
David Mengual Quartet
Monkiana:A Tribute To Thelonious Monk | Fresh Sound Records | FSNT 019 CD
David Mengual Quintet
Monkiana:A Tribute To Thelonious Monk | Fresh Sound Records | FSNT 019 CD
Gäel Horellou-David Sauzay Quintet
Gäel Horellou Versus David Sauzay | Fresh Sound Records | FSNT 068 CD
Georgina Weinstein With Her Quartet
Come Rain Or Come Shine | Fresh Sound Records | FSNT 020 CD
Georgina Weinstein With Her Trio
Come Rain Or Come Shine | Fresh Sound Records | FSNT 020 CD
Joan Abril Quintet
Insomnio | Fresh Sound Records | FSNT 034 CD
José Luis Gámez Quartet
José Luis Gámez Quattro | Fresh Sound Records | FSNT 094 CD
Menni,Mohamed | (percvoc)
Nguyen Le Group
Maghreb And Friends | ACT | 9261-2
Mens,Klaus | (p)
Glen Buschmann Quintet
Deutsches Jazz Fesival 1954/1955 | Bear Family Records | BCD 15430
Wolfgang Sauer With The Glen Buschmann Quintet
Deutsches Jazz Fesival 1954/1955 | Bear Family Records | BCD 15430
Mensah,Paapa J. | (african-tana-dr,ankle-bells,cabassa)
Trevor Watts Moiré Music Drum Orchestra
A Wider Embrace | ECM | 1449
Mensch,Homer | (b)
Nina Simone And Orchestra
Baltimore | Epic | 476906-2
Mensching,Fritz | (bssax)
Jamenco
Conversations | Trick Music | TM 9202 CD
Mensebach,Robert | (g,el-gvoc)
Francesca Simone Trio
Guardia Li | Minor Music | 801093
Mensing,Knud | (g)
Mind Games
Mind Games Plays The Music Of Stan Getz & Astrud Gilberto | Edition Collage | EC 515-2
Ment,Jochen | (as)
Chet Baker With The NDR-Bigband
Chet Baker-The Legacy Vol.1 | Enja | ENJ-9021 2
Heinz Sauer Quartet With The NDR Big Band
NDR Big Band-Bravissimo | ACT | 9232-2
Menza,Don | (alto-fl,b-cl,arr,as,bs,fl,ts,ss)
Buddy Rich Big Band
Keep The Customer Satisfied | EMI Records | 523999-2
Diane Schuur Trio With Orchestra And Strings
In Tribute | GRP | GRP 20062
Diane Schuur With Orchestra
In Tribute | GRP | GRP 20062
The Best Of Diane Schuur | GRP | GRP 98882
Don Menza And The Joe Haider Trio
Bilein | JHM Records | JHM 3608
Don Menza Quartet
Las Vegar Late Night Sessions:Live At Capozzoli's | Woofy Productions | WPCD 116
Don Menza Septet
Morning Song | MPS | 9811446
Klaus Weiss Orchestra
Live At The Domicile | ATM Records | ATM 3805-AH
Luis Gasca Group
Jazzin' Vol.2: The Music Of Stevie Wonder | Fantasy | FANCD 6088-2
Mercadante,Bartolo | (tb)
Banda Città Ruvo Di Puglia
La Banda/Banda And Jazz | Enja | ENJ-9326 2
Mercader,Nan | (bongosperc)
Eladio Reinon Quintet
Es La Historia De Un Amor | Fresh Sound Records | FSNT 004 CD
Manel Camp & Matthew Simon Acustic Jazz Quintet
Rosebud | Fresh Sound Records | FSNT 011 CD
Mercadier,Jean | (voc)
Les Blue Stars
Jazz In Paris:Blossom Dearie-The Pianist/Les Blue Stars | EmArCy | 064784-2
Mercado,Raul | (quena)
Gato Barbieri Orchestra
Latino America | Impulse(MCA) | 952236-2
Mercer,Johnny | (voc)
Benny Goodman And His Orchestra
Camel Caravan Broadcast 1939 Vol.1 | Phontastic | NCD 8817
Camel Caravan Broadcast 1939 Vol.2 | Phontastic | NCD 8818
Camel Caravan Broadcast 1939 Vol.3 | Phontastic | NCD 8819
Paul Whiteman And His Orchestra
Planet Jazz:Jack Teagarden | Planet Jazz | 2161236-2
Peggy Lee With Benny Goodman And The Paul Weston Orchestra
Peggy Lee & Benny Goodman:The Complete Recordings 1941-1947 | CBS | C2K 65686
Mercer,Len | (arrld)
Bud Shank With The Len Mercer Strings
Midnight Blue(The [Be]witching Hour) | Blue Note | 854365-2
Merchane,Abdelkbir | (voc)
Karim Ziad Groups
Ifrikya | ACT | 9282-2
Mercier,Stéphane | (flas)
Stéphane Mercier Group
Flor De Luna | Fresh Sound Records | FSNT 097 CD
Merck,Rüdiger | (cello)
Bernd Konrad Jazz Group With Symphonie Orchestra
Wen Die Götter Lieben | Creative Works Records | CW CD 1010-1
Mercurio,Walter | (tb)
Tommy Dorsey And His Orchestra
Planet Jazz:Frank Sinatra & Tommy Dorsey | Planet Jazz | 2152067-2
Planet Jazz:Tommy Dorsey | Planet Jazz | 2159972-2
Frank Sinatra And The Tommy Dorsey Orchestra | RCA | 2668701-2
Meredith,Mary Ann | (cello)
Art Pepper Quintet With Strings
Art Pepper:The Complete Galaxy Recordings | Galaxy | 16GCD 1016-2
Winter Moon | Original Jazz Classics | OJC20 677-2(GXY 5140)
Merendino,Sammy | (dr-programming)
Pat Metheny Group
We Live Here | Geffen Records | GED 24729
Spyro Gyra & Guests
Love & Other Obsessions | GRP | GRP 98112
Meresco,Joe | (p)
Jack Teagarden With Orchestra
Jazz:The Essential Collection Vol.3 | IN+OUT Records | 78013-2
Méreu,Jean | (tp,narrationvoice)
Pata Music Meets Arfi
News Of Roi Ubu | Pata Musik | PATA 10 CD
La Belle Et La Bête | Pata Musik | PATA 14(amf 1066)
Meridian String Quartet |
Hank Jones Trio With The Meridian String Quartet
The Story Of Jazz Piano | Laserlight | 24653
Meriweather,Frank | (condarr)
Jerri Southern And The Frank Meriweather Orchestra
The Very Thought Of You:The Decca Years 1951-1957 | Decca | 050671-2

INTERPRETENVERZEICHNIS

Merk,Heiner | (b)
Manfred Junker Quartet
Cole Porter-Live! | Edition Collage | EC 531-2
Merk,Sebastian | (dr)
Frank Paul Schubert Quartet
Der Verkauf Geht Weiter | Jazz Haus Musik | JHM 0114 CD
Landes Jugend Jazz Orchester Hessen
Touch Of Lips | hr music.de | hrmj 004-01 CD
Polyphonix
Alarm | Jazz 'n' Arts Records | 0300
Russ Spiegel Group
Twilight | double moon | CHRDM 71026
Merkelbach,Michael | (tp)
Lisa Bassenge Trio With Guests
A Sight, A Song | Minor Music | 801100
Merkin,Lester | (cl,asreeds)
Leon Thomas With Orchestra
Spirits Known And Unknown | RCA | 2663876-2
Merle,Maurice | (ssas)
Pata Music Meets Arfi
News Of Roi Ubu | Pata Musik | PATA 10 CD
Merlin,Pierre | (tp)
Claude Luter Et Ses L'Orientais
Jazz In Paris:Sidney Bechet Et Claude Luther | EmArCy | 159821-2 PMS
Merrill,Helen | (voc)
Helen Merrill And Her Band
Planet Jazz:Female Jazz Vocalists | Planet Jazz | 2169656-2
Helen Merrill With Orchestra
Casa Forte | EmArCy | 558848-2
Helen Merrill With Richard Davis & Gary Bartz
A Shade Of Difference | EmArCy | 558851-2
Helen Merrill With The Dick Katz Group
The Feeling Is Mutual | EmArCy | 558849-2
A Shade Of Difference | EmArCy | 558851-2
Helen Merrill With The Pepper Adams Quintet
Chasin' The Bird(Gershwin) | EmArCy | 558850-2
Helen Merrill With The Piero Umilliani Group
Parole E Musica | RCA | 2174798-2
Helen Merrill With The Quincy Jones Orchestra
Clifford Brown-Max Roach:Alone Together-The Best Of The Mercury Years | Verve | 526373-2
Verve Jazz Masters 44:Clifford Brown and Max Roach | Verve | 528109-2
Brownie-The Complete EmArCy Recordings Of Clifford Brown | EmArCy | 838306-2
Helen Merrill-Dick Katz Duo
The Feeling Is Mutual | EmArCy | 558849-2
Helen Merrill-Don Carter Duo
A Shade Of Difference | EmArCy | 558851-2
Helen Merrill-Gordon Beck
No Tears No Goodbyes | Owl Records | 013435-2
Helen Merrill-Jim Hall Duo
The Feeling Is Mutual | EmArCy | 558849-2
Helen Merrill-Torrie Zito Duo
Casa Forte | EmArCy | 558848-2
Merrill,Reggie | (as)
Benny Goodman And His V-Disc All Star Band
The Legends Of Swing | Laserlight | 24659
Merrill-Smolen,Sandy | (voc)
Les McCann Group
Another Beginning | Atlantic | 7567-80790-2
Merritt,Al | (dr)
Chas Burchell Quartet
Unsong Hero:The Undiscovered Genius Of Chas Burchell | IN+OUT Records | 7026-2
Chas Burchell Quintet
Unsong Hero:The Undiscovered Genius Of Chas Burchell | IN+OUT Records | 7026-2
Chas Burchell Sextet
Unsong Hero:The Undiscovered Genius Of Chas Burchell | IN+OUT Records | 7026-2
Clark Terry Quintet
Unsong Hero:The Undiscovered Genius Of Chas Burchell | IN+OUT Records | 7026-2
Geoff Carter Quintet
Unsong Hero:The Undiscovered Genius Of Chas Burchell | IN+OUT Records | 7026-2
Lilly Thornton With The Benny Golson Quartet
Remembering Dinah-A Salute To Dinah Washington | Hot Shot Records | HSR 8313-2
Lilly Thornton With The Benny Golson Sextet
Remembering Dinah-A Salute To Dinah Washington | Hot Shot Records | HSR 8313-2
Lilly Thornton With The Mike Hennesey Trio
Remembering Dinah-A Salute To Dinah Washington | Hot Shot Records | HSR 8313-2
Ronnie Scott With The Chas Burchell Quintet
Unsong Hero:The Undiscovered Genius Of Chas Burchell | IN+OUT Records | 7026-2
The Mike Hennessey Chastet
Shades Of Chas Burchell | IN+OUT Records | 7025-2
Merritt,Jymie | (bel-b)
Art Blakey And The Afrocuban Boys
Les Liaisons Dangereuses(Original Soundtrack) | Fontana | 812017-2
Art Blakey And The Jazz Messengers
Planet Jazz:Art Blakey | Planet Jazz | 2152066-2
Planet Jazz:Lee Morgan | Planet Jazz | 2161238-2
Art Blakey & The Jazz Messengers: Olympia, May 13th, 1961 | Laserlight | 36128
Paris Jazz Concert:Art Blakey & The Jazz Messengers | Laserlight | 36158
Best Of Blakey 60 | Blue Note | 493072-2
Moanin' | Blue Note | 495324-2
Roots And Herbs | Blue Note | 521956-2
The Witch Doctor | Blue Note | 521957-2
True Blue | Blue Note | 534032-2
Meet You At The Jazz Corner Of The World | Blue Note | 535565-2
Wayne Shorter:The Classic Blue Note Recordings | Blue Note | 540856-2
Blue N' Groovy | Blue Note | 780679-2
A Night In Tunisia | Blue Note | 784049-2
The Best Of Blue Note | Blue Note | 796110-2
The Best Of Blue Note Vol.2 | Blue Note | 797960-2
Les Liaisons Dangereuses(Original Soundtrack) | Fontana | 812017-2
Feedom Rider | Blue Note | 821287-2
Jazz In Paris:Art Blakey-1958-Paris Olympia | EmArCy | 832659-2 PMS
Jazz In Paris:Paris Jam Session | EmArCy | 832692-2 PMS
Impulse!Art Blakey!Jazz Messengers! | Impulse(MCA) | 951175-2
At The Club St.Germain | RCA | ND 74897(2)
Art Blakey And The Jazz Messengers With Barney Wilen And Bud Powell
Jazz In Paris:Paris Jam Session | EmArCy | 832692-2 PMS
Art Blakey Percussion Ensemble
Drums Around The Corner | Blue Note | 521455-2
Art Blakey-Barney Wilen Quartet
Les Liaisons Dangereuses(Original Soundtrack) | Fontana | 812017-2
Bobby Jaspar Quintet
Jazz In Paris:Bobby Jaspar-Jeux De Quartes | EmArCy | 018423-2
Chet Baker Quintet
Chet Baker:The Most Important Jazz Album Of 1964/65 | Roulette | 581829-2
Lee Morgan Orchestra
The Last Sessin | Blue Note | 493401-2
Lee Morgan Quintet
Live At The Lighthouse | Blue Note | 835228-2
Sonny Clark Trio
Standards | Blue Note | 821283-2
Wayne Shorter Quintet
Wayne Shorter:The Classic Blue Note Recordings | Blue Note | 540856-2
Merritt,Renzell | (dr)
David Murray Group
Speaking In Togues | Enja | ENJ-9370 2
Mertes,Wolfgang | (concertmaster)
Abdullah Ibrahim Trio And A String Orchestra
African Suite | TipToe | TIP-888832 2
String Orchestra
African Suite | TipToe | TIP-888832 2
Mertz,Paul | (parr)
Bix And His Rhythm Jugglers
Jazz:The Essential Collection Vol.2 | IN+OUT Records | 78012-2
Merville,Francois | (dr,percmarimba)
Louis Sclavis Group
Dans La Nuit | ECM | 1805(589524-2)
Louis Sclavis Quartet
L'Affrontement Des Prétendants | ECM | 1705(159927-2)
Messeder,André | (b)
André Holst With Chris Dean's European Swing Orchestra
That's Swing | Nagel-Heyer | CD 079
Messina,Daniel | (dr,percvoc)
Daniel Messina Band
Imagenes | art-mode-records | 990014
Quique Sinesi & Daniel Messina
Prioridad A la Emoción | art-mode-records | AMR 21061
Quique Sinesi & Daniel Messina With Guests
Prioridad A la Emoción | art-mode-records | AMR 21061
Messner,John | (tb)
Benny Goodman And His Orchestra
40th Anniversary Concert-Live At Carnegie Hall | London | 820349-2
Verve Jazz Masters 33:Benny Goodman | Verve | 844410-2
Bill Evans Quartet With Orchestra
The Complete Bill Evans On Verve | Verve | 527953-2
From Left To Right | Verve | 557451-2
Stan Getz With The Eddie Sauter Orchestra
Stan Getz Plays The Music Of Mickey One | Verve | 531232-2
Wes Montgomery With The Don Sebesky Orchestra
Verve Jazz Masters 14:Wes Montgomery | Verve | 519826-2
Wes Montgomery:The Verve Jazz Sides | Verve | 521690-2
Talkin' Jazz:Roots Of Acid Jazz | Verve | 529580-2
California Dreaming | Verve | 827842-2
Meßollen,Gisela | (tp)
The United Women's Orchestra
The Blue One | Jazz Haus Musik | JHM 0099 CD
Mestari,Hamid | (outarvoc)
Karim Ziad Groups
Ifrikya | ACT | 9282-2
Mesterhazy,George | (g,el-p,synth,midi-orchestrationsp)
Shirley Horn And Her Quartet
May The Music Never End | Verve | 076028-2
Shirley Horn And Her Trio
May The Music Never End | Verve | 076028-2
Shirley Horn Quartet
Loving You | Verve | 537022-2
Shirley Horn Quintet
Loving You | Verve | 537022-2
Shirley Horn Trio
Loving You | Verve | 537022-2
Meta Four | (voc-group)
The Meta Four
Jazzy World | JA & RO | JARO 4200-2
Metawee,Rehab | (voc)
Mahmoud Turkmani Group
Zakira | Enja | ENJ-9475 2
Metcalf,Louis | (cotp)
Duke Ellington And His Kentucky Club Orchestra
Jazz:The Essential Collection Vol.2 | IN+OUT Records | 78012-2
Duke Ellington And His Orchestra
Jazz:The Essential Collection Vol.2 | IN+OUT Records | 78012-2
King Oliver And His Orchestra
Planet Jazz:Jazz Trumpet | Planet Jazz | 2169654-2
Metha,Rajesh | (tp,b-tp,extensions,hybrid-tp)
Rajesh Metha
Reconfigurations | Between The Lines | btl 010(Efa 10180-2)
The Collective 3 +
The Collective 3 + | true muze | TUMU CD 9802
Metha,Uma | (lanpura)
John McLaughlin Group
Remember Shakti | Verve | 559945-2
Metha-Metric Ensemble,The |
Rajesh Metha
Reconfigurations | Between The Lines | btl 010(Efa 10180-2)
Metheny,Pat | (42-string-pikasso-g,bariton-g-solo)
Abbey Lincoln With The Rodney Kendrick Trio And Guests
A Turtle's Dream | Verve | 527382-2
Cassandra Wilson Group
Traveling Miles | Blue Note | 854123-2
Charlie Haden-Pat Metheny
Beyond The Missouri Sky | Verve | 537130-2
Gary Burton Quartet With Eberhard Weber
Passengers | ECM | 1092(835016-2)
Gary Burton Quintet
Dreams So Real | ECM | 1072
Gary Burton Quintet With Eberhard Weber
Ring | ECM | 1051
John Scofield-Pat Metheny Quartet
I Can See Your House From Here | Blue Note | 827765-2
Joshua Redman Quartet
Wish | Warner | 9362-45365-2
Marc Johnson Group
The Sound Of Summer Running | Verve | 539299-2
Michael Brecker Group
Time Is Of The Essence | Verve | 547844-2
Michael Brecker | Impulse(MCA) | 950113-2
Tales From The Hudson | Impulse(MCA) | 951191-2
Michael Brecker Quintet
Nearness Of You-The Ballad Book | Verve | 549705-2
Pat Metheny
New Chautauqua | ECM | 1131(825471-2)
One Quiet Night | Warner | 9362-48473-2
Zero Tolerance For Silence | Geffen Records | GED 24626
Pat Metheny & Lyle Mays
As Falls Wichita, So Falls Wichita Falls | ECM | 1190(821416-2)
Pat Metheny Group
Pat Metheny Group | ECM | 1114(825593-2)
American Garage | ECM | 1155(827134-2)
Offramp | ECM | 1216(817138-2)
Travels | ECM | 1252/53
First Circle | ECM | 1278(823342-2)
Imaginary Day | Warner | 9362-46791-2
Letter From Home | Geffen Records | GED 24245
The Road To You | Geffen Records | GED 24601
We Live Here | Geffen Records | GED 24729
Quartet | Geffen Records | GED 24978
Pat Metheny Group With Orchestra
Secret Story | Geffen Records | GED 24468
Pat Metheny Quartet
Watercolors | ECM | 1097(827409-2)
80/81 | ECM | 1180/81 (843169-2)
Pat Metheny Quintet
80/81 | ECM | 1180/81 (843169-2)
Pat Metheny Trio
Bright Size Life | ECM | 1073(827133-2)
Rejoicing | ECM | 1271(817795-2)
Trio 99-00 | Warner | 9362-47632-2
Part Metheny Trio Live | Warner | 9362-47907-2
Pat Metheny/Ornette Coleman Group
Song X | Geffen Records | GED 24096
Metronome All Stars,The |
The Metronome All Stars
Jazz Gallery:Lester Young Vol.2(1946-59) | RCA | 2119541-2
Planet Jazz:Dizzy Gillespie | Planet Jazz | 2152069-2
Metronome All-Star Nine |
The Metronome All-Star Nine
Jazz:The Essential Collection Vol.3 | IN+OUT Records | 78013-2
Metry-Travail,Lysiane | (v)
Charlie Haden Quartet West With Strings
Now Is The Hour | Verve | 527827-2
Mettham,John | (cocktail-drperc)
Franz Koglmann Group
Venus In Transit | Between The Lines | btl 017(Efa 10186)
Mettome,Doug | (tp)
Charlie Parker With Strings
Charlie Parker With Strings:The Master Takes | Verve | 523984-2
Charlie Parker With The Neal Hefti Orchestra
Charlie Parker:The Best Of The Verve Years | Verve | 527815-2
Bird: The Complete Charlie Parker On Verve | Verve | 837141-2
Metz Jr.,Ed 'Eddie' | (dr)
Allan Vaché's Florida Jazz Allstars
Allan Vaché's Floridy Jazz Allstars | Nagel-Heyer | CD 032
Eddie Metz And His Gang
Tough Assignment:A Tribute To Dave Tough | Nagel-Heyer | CD 053
Mark Shane-Terry Blaine Group
With Thee I Swing! | Nagel-Heyer | CD 040
The New York Allstars
Hey Ba-Ba-Re-Bop!! The New York Allstars Play Lionel Hampton Vol.1 | Nagel-Heyer | CD 047
The Vaché-Allred-Metz Family Jazz Band
Side By Side | Nagel-Heyer | CD 042
Warren Vaché-Allen Vaché Sextet
Mrs.Vaché's Boys | Nagel-Heyer | CD 050
Ellington For Lovers | Nagel-Heyer | NH 1009
Metz Sr.,Ed | (p)
The Vaché-Allred-Metz Family Jazz Band
Side By Side | Nagel-Heyer | CD 042
Metz,Eddie | (dr)
Allan Vaché-Harry Allen Quintet
Allan And Allan | Nagel-Heyer | CD 074
The New York Allstars
The New York Allstars Play Lionel Hampton,Vol.2: Stompin' At The Savoy | Nagel-Heyer | CD 077
Metzendorf,Sonja | (v)
HR Big Band With Marjorie Barnes And Frits Landesbergen And Strings
Swinging Christmas | hr music.de | hrmj 012-02 CD
Metzger,Gitta | (voc)
Jazzensemble Des Hessischen Rundfunks
Jazz Messe-Messe Für Unsere Zeit | hr music.de | hrmj 003-01 CD
Metzger,Nicole | (voc)
Ralph Schweizer Big Band
DAY Dream | Chaos | CACD 8177
Metzke,Paul | (el-b,el-g,gsynth)
Gato Barbieri Group
Planet Jazz:Gato Barbieri | RCA | 2165364-2
Gato Barbieri Orchestra
The Roots Of Acid Jazz | Impulse(MCA) | IMP 12042
Gato Barbieri Septet
Yesterdays | RCA | 2147797-2
Gil Evans Orchestra
There Comes A Time | RCA | 2131392-2
Paul Motian Quintet
Tribute | ECM | 1048
Metzler,Jochen | (fl-htp)
Ralph Abelein Group
Mr. B's Time Machine | Satin Doll Productions | SDP 1042-1 CD
Meulendijk,Bert | (g)
Laura Fygi With Band
Bewitched | Verve | 514724-2
Stochelo Rosenberg Group
Gypsy Swing | Verve | 527806-2
Stochelo Rosenberg Group With Strings
Gypsy Swing | Verve | 527806-2
The Rosenberg Trio With Orchestra
Noches Calientes | Verve | 557022-2
Meunier,Claudine | (voc)
Modern Jazz Quartet And The Swingle Singers
MJQ 40 | Atlantic | 7567-82330-2
Swingle Singers
Jazz Sebastian Bach | Philips | 542552-2
Jazz Sebastian Bach Vol.2 | Philips | 542553-2
Swingle Singers Going Baroque | Philips | 546746-2
Swingling Telemann | Philips | 586735-2
Swingle Singers Getting Romantic | Philips | 586736-2
Meunier,Maurice | (cl,asts)
Django Reinhardt And The Quintet Du Hot Club De France
Planet Jazz:Django Reinhardt | Planet Jazz | 2152071-2
Planet Jazz Sampler | Planet Jazz | 2152326-2
Henri Crolla Sextet
Jazz In Paris:Henri Crolla-Quand Refleuriront Les Lilas Blancs? | EmArCy | 018418-2
Lionel Hampton All Stars
Jazz In Paris:Lionel Hampton And His French New Sound Vol.1 | EmArCy | 549405-2 PMS
Jazz In Paris:Lionel Hampton And His French New Sound Vol.2 | EmArCy | 549406-2 PMS
Michel De Villers Octet
Jazz In Paris:Saxophones Á Saint-Germain Des Prés | EmArCy | 014060-2
Quintet Du Hot Club De France
Django Reinhardt:Souveniers | Dreyfus Jazz Line | FDM 36744-2
Meurkens,Hendrik | (harm,vib,pvoc)
Buddy Tate With The Torsten Swingenberger Swintet
Tate Live | Nagel-Heyer | CD 080
Mundell Lowe Quintet
Mundell's Moods | Nagel-Heyer | CD 065
Mewes,Oliver | (dr)
Engelbert Wrobel-Chris Hopkins-Dan Barrett Sextet
Harlem 2000 | Nagel-Heyer | CD 082
Olaf Polziehn Trio
American Songbook | Satin Doll Productions | SDP 1032-1 CD
Meyer,Alexandre | (el-g,daxophonetable-g)
Heiner Goebbels Group
Ou Bien Le Debarquement Desastreux | ECM | 1552
Meyer,Alfred | (b)
Freddy Christman Quartet
Deutsches Jazz Fesival 1954/1955 | Bear Family Records | BCD 15430
Meyer,Barbara Leah | (voc)
Landes Jugend Jazz Orchester Hessen
Touch Of Lips | hr music.de | hrmj 004-01 CD
Meyer,Bob | (dr)
Unit X
Rated X | Timescrapper | TSCR 9618
Meyer,Friedemann | (drperc)
Jazz Bomberos
Naranja | Green House Music | CD 1003(Maxi)
Meyer,Joe | (fr-h)
Ella Fitzgerald With Orchestra
The Best Is Yet To Come | Original Jazz Classics | OJCCD 889-2(2312138)
Meyer,Peter 'Banjo' | (bjvoc)
The European Jazz Ginats
Jazz Party | Nagel-Heyer | CD 009
The First Sampler | Nagel-Heyer | NHR SP 5
Meyer,Ulf | (g)
Ulf Meyer & Martin Wind Group
Kinnings | Storyville | STCD 8374

Meyers,Bumps | (ts)
Peggy Lee With The Benny Goodman Orchestra
Peggy Lee & Benny Goodman:The Complete Recordings 1941-1947 | CBS | C2K 65686
Meyers,Christian | (fl-htp)
Russ Spiegel Group
Twilight | double moon | CHRDM 71026
The Three Sopranos With The HR Big Band
The Three Sopranos | hr music.de | hrmj 001-01 CD
Meyers,Eddie | (as,sax,tpts)
Stan Kenton And His Orchestra
Swing Vol.1 | Storyville | 4960343
Meyers,Jack | (el-b)
Buddy Guy Blues Band
Buddy Guy-The Complete Chess Studio Recordings | MCA | MCD 09337
Meyers,Paul | (gbj)
Andy Bey Group
Tuesdays In Chinatown | Minor Music | 801099
Meyn,Rob | (perc)
Toots Thielemans And His Orchestra
Verve Jazz Masters Vol.59:Toots Thielemans | Verve | 535271-2
Mezzrow,Milton Mezz | (as,bells,cl,arr,speech,ts,c-mel-sax)
Ben Pollack And His Park Central Orchestra
Planet Jazz:Jack Teagarden | Planet Jazz | 2161236-2
Jazz:The Essential Collection Vol.3 | IN+OUT Records | 78013-2
Eddie Condon's Hot Shots
Jazz:The Essential Collection Vol.3 | IN+OUT Records | 78013-2
Eddie's Hot Shots
Planet Jazz:Jack Teagarden | Planet Jazz | 2161236-2
Emmett Berry-Sammy Price Orchestra
Americans Swinging In Paris:Sammy Price | EMI Records | 539650-2
Lionel Hampton And His Orchestra
Lionel Hampton's Paris All Stars | Vogue | 21511502
Mezz Mezzrow And His Orchestra
Planet Jazz:Bud Freeman | Planet Jazz | 2161240-2
Mezz Mezzrow And His Swing Band
Planet Jazz:Bud Freeman | Planet Jazz | 2161240-2
Mezzrow-Ladnier Quintet
Planet Jazz:Jazz Trumpet | Planet Jazz | 2169654-2
Milton Mezz Mezzrow Sextet
Americans Swinging In Paris:Mezz Mezzrow | EMI Records | 539660-2
Milton Mezz Mezzrow-Maxim Saury Quintet
Americans Swinging In Paris:Mezz Mezzrow | EMI Records | 539660-2
Quartier Latin Jazz Band
Great Traditionalists | Jazzpoint | JP 1046 CD
Tommy Ladnier And His Orchestra
Planet Jazz | Planet Jazz | 2169652-2
Jazz:The Essential Collection Vol.1 | IN+OUT Records | 78011-2
Mhadi,Khalil | (dr)
Rahsaan Roland Kirk Sextet
Blacknuss | Rhino | 8122-71408-2
Miano,Fabio | (p)
Grant Stewart Quartet
Buen Rollo | Fresh Sound Records | FSNT 053 CD
Micault,Gwénael | (bandoneonkeyboards)
Laura Fygi With Band
Bewitched | Verve | 514724-2
The Rosenberg Trio With Orchestra
Noches Calientes | Verve | 557022-2
Micci,Alfio | (v)
Ron Carter Quintet With Strings
Pick 'Em/Super Strings | Milestone | MCD 47090-2
Michaels,Ray | (dr)
Charlie Barnet And His Orchestra
Planet Jazz:Big Bands | Planet Jazz | 2169649-2
Planet Jazz:Swing | Planet Jazz | 2169651-2
Michailow,Peter | (dr)
Bajazzo
Caminos | Edition Collage | EC 485-2
Harlequin Galaxy | Edition Collage | EC 519-2
Michel,Catherine | (harp)
Caterina Valente-Catherine Michel
Girltalk | Nagel-Heyer | NH 1015
Michel,John | (voc)
Big Allanbik
Batuque Y Blues | Blues Beacon | BLU-1031 2
Michel,Matthieu | (fl-htp)
Axis
Axis | Jazz 4 Ever Records:Jazz Network | J4E 4735
Michelangeli,Umberto Benedetti | (v)
Gerry Mulligan With Astor Piazzolla And His Orchestra
Tango Nuevo | Atlantic | 2292-42145-2
Michelich,Peter | (p)
Dusko Goykovich Big Band
Balkan Connection | Enja | ENJ-9047 2
Dusko Goykovich Quintet
Balkan Blues | Enja | ENJ-9320 2
Michell,Billy | (ts)
Dizzy Gillespie And His Orchestra
Verve Jazz Masters 20:Introducing | Verve | 519853-2
Dizzy Gillespie:Birks Works-The Verve Big Band Sessions | Verve | 527900-2
Michelmann,Joachim | (perc)
Ekkehard Jost Quintet
Some Other Tapes | Fish Music | FM 009/10 CD
Michelot,Pierre | (barr)
Alain Goraguer Orchestra
Jazz In Paris:Jazz & Cinéma Vol.1 | EmArCy | 548318-2 PMS
Jazz In Paris | EmArCy | 548793-2
Andre Hodeir And His Jazz Group De Paris
Jazz In Paris:Le Jazz Groupe De Paris Joue André Hodeir | EmArCy | 548792-2
Benny Golson Quintet
Nemmy Golson And The Philadelphians | Blue Note | 494104-2
Bud Powell Quartet
Parisian Thoroughfare | Pablo | CD 2310976-2
Bud Powell Quintet
Parisian Thoroughfare | Pablo | CD 2310976-2
Bud Powell Paris Sessions | Pablo | PACD 2310972-2
Bud Powell Trio
Parisian Thoroughfare | Pablo | CD 2310976-2
Bud Powell Paris Sessions | Pablo | PACD 2310972-2
Bebop | Pablo | PACD 2310978-2
Clifford Brown Quartet
Planet Jazz:Clifford Brown | Planet Jazz | 2161239-2
Coleman Hawkins And His Rhythm
Coleman Hawkins/Johnny Hodges:The Vogue Recordings | Vogue | 21559712
Dexter Gordon Quartet
Blue Note Plays Gershwin | Blue Note | 520808-2
True Blue | Blue Note | 534032-2
Our Man In Paris | Blue Note | 591722-2
Dexter Gordon:Ballads | Blue Note | 796579-2
Jazz Profile:Dexter Gordon | Blue Note | 823514-2
Django Reinhardt And His Quintet
Django Reinhardt:Souveniers | Dreyfus Jazz Line | FDM 36744-2
Django Reinhardt And His Rhythm
Verve Jazz Masters 38:Django Reinhardt | Verve | 516931-2
Peche À La Mode-The Great Blue Star Sessions 1947/1953 | Verve | 835418-2
Django Reinhardt Quartet
Jazz In Paris:Django Reinhardt-Nuits De Saint-Germain-Des-Prés | EmArCy | 018427-2
Jazz In Paris:Django Reinhardt-Nuages | EmArCy | 018428-2
Django Reinhardt Quintet
Jazz In Paris:Django Reinhardt-Nuits De Saint-Germain-Des-Prés | EmArCy | 018427-2
Jazz In Paris:Django Reinhardt-Nuages | EmArCy | 018428-2
Django Reinhardt Sextet
Jazz In Paris:Django Reinhardt-Nuits De Saint-Germain-Des-Prés | EmArCy | 018427-2
Don Byas Quartet
Planet Jazz:Jazz Saxophone | Planet Jazz | 2169653-2
Don Byas-Bud Powell Quartet
A Tribute To Cannonball | CBS | CK 65186
Don Byas-Bud Powell Quintet
A Tribute To Cannonball | CBS | CK 65186
Ernie Royal And The Duke Knights
Americans Swinging In Paris:James Moody | EMI Records | 539653-2
Gigi Gryce-Clifford Brown Octet
Planet Jazz:Clifford Brown | Planet Jazz | 2161239-2
Gigi Gryce-Clifford Brown Sextet
Planet Jazz:Clifford Brown | Planet Jazz | 2161239-2
Golden Gate Quartet
Americans Swinging In Paris:Golden Gate Quartet | EMI Records | 539659-2
From Spiritual To Swing Vol.2 | EMI Records | 780573-2
Spirituals To Swing 1955-69 | EMI Records | 791569-2
Hubert Fol And His Be-Bop Minstrels
Americans Swinging In Paris:Kenny Clarke | EMI Records | 539652-2
Jacques Loussier Trio
Play Bach No.1 | Decca | 157561-2
Play Bach No.2 | Decca | 157562-2
Play Bach No.3 | Decca | 157892-2
Play Bach No.4 | Decca | 157893-2
Play Bach No.5 | Decca | 159194-2
Play Bach Aux Champs-Élyssées | Decca | 159203-2
The Best Of Play Bach | Philips | 824664-2
James Moody Quartet
Americans Swinging In Paris:James Moody | EMI Records | 539653-2
Johnny Griffin-Steve Grossman Quintet
Johnny Griffin & Steve Grossman | Dreyfus Jazz Line | FDM 36615-2
Kenny Clarke 8
Americans Swinging In Paris:Kenny Clarke | EMI Records | 539652-2
Kenny Clarke And His Orchestra
Americans Swinging In Paris:James Moody | EMI Records | 539653-2
Kenny Clarke Quartet
Americans Swinging In Paris:Kenny Clarke | EMI Records | 539652-2
Kenny Clarke Quintet
Jazz In Paris:Kenny Clarke Sextet Plays André Hodair | EmArCy | 834542-2 PMS
Les Double Six
Les Double Six | RCA | 2164314-2
Miles Davis Quintet
Ascenseur Pour LÉchafaud | Fontana | 836305-2
Richard Galliano Quartet
Viaggio | Dreyfus Jazz Line | FDM 36562-9
Gallianissimo! The Best Of Richard Galliano | Dreyfus Jazz Line | FDM 36616-2
Sammy Price Quintet
Americans Swinging In Paris:Sammy Price | EMI Records | 539650-2
Sammy Price Trio
Americans Swinging In Paris:Sammy Price | EMI Records | 539650-2
Sidney Bechet And His All Stars
Sidney Bechet:Summertime | Dreyfus Jazz Line | FDM 36712-2
Sidney Bechet And His Feetwarmers
Jazz In Paris:Sidney Bechet Et Claude Luther | EmArCy | 159821-2 PMS
Sidney Bechet:Summertime | Dreyfus Jazz Line | FDM 36712-2
Sidney Bechet Quartet
Planet Jazz:Sidney Bechet | Planet Jazz | 2152063-2
Sonny Criss Quintet
Jazz In Paris:Saxophones Á Saint-Germain Des Prés | EmArCy | 014060-2
Jazz In Paris:Sonny Criss-Mr.Blues Pour Flirter | EmArCy | 549231-2 PMS
Stan Getz Quartet
Stan Getz In Europe | Laserlight | 24657
Stephane Grappelli Quartet
Grapelli Story | Verve | 515807-2
Jazz In Paris:Stephane Grappelli-Improvisations | EmArCy | 549242-2 PMS
Swingle Singers
Jazz Sebastian Bach | Philips | 542552-2
Toots Thielemans Quintet
Verve Jazz Masters Vol.59:Toots Thielemans | Verve | 535271-2
Michels,Lloyd | (fl-htp)
Buddy Rich Big Band
Backwoods Siseman/Pieces Of Dream | Laserlight | 24655
Lee Konitz Orchestra
The Art Of Saxophone | Laserlight | 24652
The Jazz Composer's Orchestra
Comminications | JCOA | 1001/2
Michiels,Frank | (perc)
Philippe Caillat Group
Stream Of Time | Laika Records | LK 92-030
Philippe Caillat Special Project
Melodic Travel | Laika Records | LK 689-012
Michiru,Monday | (voc)
United Future Organizatio
United Future Organization | Talkin' Loud | 518166-2
Michler,Robert | (dr)
Lutz Wichert Trio
Ambiguous | Edition Musikat | EDM 068
Michler,Sarah | (v)
Till Brönner Quartet & Deutsches Symphonieorchester Berlin
German Songs | Minor Music | 801057
Michlmayr,Toni | (b)
Franz Koglmann Quintet
Opium | Between The Lines | btl 011(Efa 10181-2)
Mickle,Mickey | (tp)
Benny Goodman And His V-Disc All Star Band
The Legends Of Swing | Laserlight | 24659
Micus,Nobuko | (resonating-stones)
Stephan Micus
The Muisc Of Stones | ECM | 1384(837750-2)
Micus,Stephan | (10&14-string-g,bamboo-fl,bolombatto)
Ocean | ECM | 1318(829279-2)
Twilight Fields | ECM | 1358
The Muisc Of Stones | ECM | 1384(837750-2)
Darkness And Light | ECM | 1427(847272-2)
To The Evening Child | ECM | 1486(513780-2)
Athos-A Journey To The Holy Mountain | ECM | 1551(523292-2)
The Garden Of Mirrors | ECM | 1632(537162-2)
Desert Poems | ECM | 1757(159739-2)
Towards The Wind | ECM | 1804(159453-2)
Implosions | Japo | 60017(2360017)
Till The End Of Times | Japo | 60026(513786-2)
Wings Over Water | Japo | 60038(831058-2)
Listen To The Rain | Japo | 60040
East Of The Night | Japo | 60041(825655-2)
Koan | ECM | 804 SP
Behind Eleven Deserts | Intuition Records | INT 2042-2
Middlebrooks,Wilfred | (b)
Ella Fitzgerald With The Billy May Orchestra
The Best Of The Song Books:The Ballads | Verve | 521867-2
Ella Fitzgerald Sings The Harold Arlen Song Book | Verve | 589108-2
Ella Fitzgerald With The Lou Levy Quartet
Ella Fitzgerald-First Lady Of Song | Verve | 517898-2
4 By 4:Ella Fitzgerald/Sarah Vaughan/Billie Holiday/Dinah Washington | Verve | 559693-2
Clap Hands,Here Comes Charlie! | Verve | 835646-2
For The Love Of Ella Fitzgerald | Verve | 841765-2
Ella Fitzgerald With The Paul Smith Quartet
Ella Fitzgerald-First Lady Of Song | Verve | 517898-2
Mack The Knife-The Complete Ella In Berlin | Verve | 519564-2
Verve Jazz Masters 6:Ella Fitzgerald | Verve | 519822-2
4 By 4:Ella Fitzgerald/Sarah Vaughan/Billie Holiday/Dinah Washington | Verve | 559693-2
For The Love Of Ella Fitzgerald | Verve | 841765-2
Jimmy Giuffre Trio
Paris Jazz Concert:Jimmy Giuffre | Laserlight | 17249
Middlehoff,Barend | (ts)
Christian Willisohn New Band
Heart Broken Man | Blues Beacon | BLU-1026 2
Middleton,Andy | (sax,ssts)
Andy Middleton Group
Nomad's Notebook | Intuition Records | INT 3264-2
Middleton,Velma | (voc)
Louis Armstrong And His All Stars
Jazz Collection:Louis Armstrong | Laserlight | 24366
Louis Armstrong:The Great Chicago Concert 1956 | CBS | C2K 65119
Louis Armstrong Plays W.C.Handy | CBS | CK 64925
Satch Plays Fats(Complete) | CBS | CK 64927
Historic Barcelona Concerts At Windsor Palace 1955 | Fresh Sound Records | FSR-CD 3004
Louis Armstrong And His Orchestra
Louis Armstrong:C'est Si Bon | Dreyfus Jazz Line | FDM 36730-2
Louis Armstrong With Gordon Jenkins And His Orchestra
Satchmo In Style | Verve | 549594-2
Miehm,Heinz | (as)
Helmut Zacharias & His Sax-Team
Ich Habe Rhythmus | Bear Family Records | BCD 15642 AH
Helmut Zacharias mit seinem Orchester
Ich Habe Rhythmus | Bear Family Records | BCD 15642 AH
Mielke,Bob | (tb)
Lu Watters' Jazz Band
Blues Over Bodega | Good Time Jazz | GTCD 12066-2
Sidney Bechet With Bob Wilber's Wildcats
Sidney Bechet:Summertime | Dreyfus Jazz Line | FDM 36712-2
Mieres,Sylvia | (voc)
Human Factor
Forbidden City | Nabel Records:Jazz Network | CD 4635
Miesen,Gerhard | (v)
HR Big Band With Marjorie Barnes And Frits Landesbergen And Strings
Swinging Christmas | hr music.de | hrmj 012-02 CD
Migiani,Armand | (as,bass-s,bs,pts)
Andre Hodeir And His Jazz Group De Paris
Jazz In Paris:Le Jazz Groupe De Paris Joue André Hodeir | EmArCy | 548792-2
Kenny Clarke 8
Americans Swinging In Paris:Kenny Clarke | EMI Records | 539652-2
Kenny Clarke Quintet
Jazz In Paris:Kenny Clarke Sextet Plays André Hodair | EmArCy | 834542-2 PMS
Kenny Clarke Sextet
Jazz In Paris:Kenny Clarke Sextet Plays André Hodair | EmArCy | 834542-2 PMS
Migliori,Jay | (bs,fl,reeds,sax,ssts)
Hampton Hawes Orchestra
Northern Windows Plus | Prestige | PRCD 24278-2
Migliori,Jimmy | (asts)
Anita O'Day With Gene Krupa And His Orchestra
Let Me Off Uptown:Anita O'Day With Gene Krupa | CBS | CK 65625
Mihelich,Ed | (b)
Mihilic,Peter | (pel-p)
Maximilian Geller Group
Maximilian Geller Goes Bossa | Edition Collage | EC 496-2
Maimilian Geller Goes Bossa Encore | Edition Collage | EC 505-2
Maximilian Geller Quartet feat. Melanie Bong
Smile | Edition Collage | EC 461-2
Maimilian Geller Goes Bossa Encore | Edition Collage | EC 505-2
Vocal Moments | Take Twelve On CD | TT 008-2
Maximilian Geller Quartet feat. Sabina Sciubba
Maimilian Geller Goes Bossa Encore | Edition Collage | EC 505-2
Maximilian Geller Quartet feat. Susan Tobocman
Maimilian Geller Goes Bossa Encore | Edition Collage | EC 505-2
Mike Bryan Sextet,The |
Mike Bryan Sextet
Jazz Festival Vol.2 | Storyville | 4960743
Mikkelborg,Paile | (arr,ld,voc,fl-h,keyboards,tp,cond)
Dino Saluzzi Quartet
Once Upon A Time-Far Away In The South | ECM | 1309(827768-2)
Dusko Goykovich Quintet With The NDR Radio-Philharmonie,Hannover
Balkan Blues | Enja | ENJ-9320 2
Gary Peacock Quartet
Guamba | ECM | 1352
George Gruntz Concert Jazz Band '83
Theatre | ECM | 1265
Gert Sorensen
Gert Sorensen Plays Poul Ruders | dacapo | 8.224085 CD
Klaus Weiss Orchestra
Live At The Domicile | ATM Records | ATM 3805-AH
Miles Davis With The Danish Radio Big Band
Aura | CBS | CK 63962
NDR Big Band With Guests
50 Years Of NDR Big Band:Bravissimo II | ACT | 9259-2
Shankar Trio
Vision | ECM | 1261(811969-2)
Stan Kenton With The Danish Radio Big Band
Stan Kenton With The Danish Radio Big Band | Storyville | STCD 8340
Terje Rypdal Group
Skywards | ECM | 1608(533768-2)
Terje Rypdal Quartet
Waves | ECM | 1110(827419-2)
Terje Rypdal Quartet With The Bergen Chamber Ensemble
Lux Aeterna | ECM | 1818(017070-2)
Terje Rypdal Trio
Descendre | ECM | 1144
The Danish Radio Big Band
Aura | CBS | CK 63962
Milanez,Aloisio | (p)
Cal Tjader Group
Amazonas | Original Jazz Classics | OJCCD 840-2(F 9502)
Milder,Joakim | (arr,sax,ssts)
Mingus By Five
Mingus By Five | Touché Music | TMcCD 019
Monk By Five
Monk By Five | Touché Music | TMcCD 012
Nils Landgren Group
Ballads | ACT | 9268-2
Palle Danielsson Quartet
Contra Post | Caprice | CAP 21440
Palle Danielsson Quintet
Contra Post | Caprice | CAP 21440
Tomasz Stanko Septet
Litania | ECM | 1636(537551-2)
Tomasz Stanko Sextet
Litania | ECM | 1636(537551-2)
Milella,Pietro | (oboe)
Banda Città Ruvo Di Puglia
La Banda/Banda And Jazz | Enja | ENJ-9326 2
Miles,Barry | (el-p,synth,keyboards,marimba,porg)
Al Di Meola Group
Elegant Gypsy | CBS | 468213-2
Land Of The Midnight Sun | CBS | 468214-2
Casino | CBS | 468215-2
Hal Di Meola Group
Casino | CBS | 468215-2
Miles,Buddy | (dr)
Bill Allred-Roy Williams Quintet
Absolutely | Nagel-Heyer | CD 024
Ellington For Lovers | Nagel-Heyer | NH 1009

Blues Of Summer | Nagel-Heyer | NH 1011
The Second Sampler | Nagel-Heyer | NHR SP 6
Bob Wilber's Bechet Legacy
The Hamburg Concert-Tribute To A Legend | Nagel-Heyer | CD 028
The Second Sampler | Nagel-Heyer | NHR SP 6
Butch Miles And Friends
Blues Of Summer | Nagel-Heyer | NH 1011
Harry Allen Quintet
Love Songs Live! | Nagel-Heyer | NH 1014
Jeanie Lambe And The Danny Moss Quartet
Three Great Concerts:Live In Hamburg 1993-1995 | Nagel-Heyer | CD 019
The Second Sampler | Nagel-Heyer | NHR SP 6
Jeanie Lambe And The Danny Moss Septet
Three Great Concerts:Live In Hamburg 1993-1995 | Nagel-Heyer | CD 019
The Buck Clayton Legacy
Encore Live | Nagel-Heyer | CD 018
The Second Sampler | Nagel-Heyer | NHR SP 6
Wild Bill Davis Super Trio
That's All | Jazz Connaisseur | JCCD 9005-2

Miles,Butch | (brushes,vocdr)
A Salute To Eddie Condon
A Salute To Eddie Condon | Nagel-Heyer | CD 004
One Two Three | Nagel-Heyer | CD 008
The First Sampler | Nagel-Heyer | NHR SP 5
Butch Miles And Friends
The Second Sampler | Nagel-Heyer | NHR SP 6
Butch Miles-Howard Alden Sextet
Cookin' | Nagel-Heyer | CD 5003
Count Basie And His Orchestra
Fun Time | Pablo | 2310945-2
Jazz Dance | Original Jazz Classics | OJCCD 1002-2(1210890)
I Told You So | Original Jazz Classics | OJCCD 824-2(2310767)
Digital III At Montreux | Original Jazz Classics | OJCCD 996-2(2308223)
The Jazz Giants Play Harry Warren:Lullaby Of Broadway | Prestige | PCD 24204-2
Count Basie Big Band
Montreux '77 | Original Jazz Classics | OJCCD 377-2
Danny Moss Quartet
Weaver Of Dreams | Nagel-Heyer | CD 017
The Second Sampler | Nagel-Heyer | NHR SP 6
Ella Fitzgerald With The Count Basie Orchestra
For The Love Of Ella Fitzgerald | Verve | 841765-2
Frank Tate Quintet
Live In Belfast | Nagel-Heyer | CD 069
Milt Jackson Orchestra
Sarah Vaughan Birthday Celebration | Fantasy | FANCD 6090-2
Milt Jackson With The Count Basie Orchestra
To Bags...With Love:Memorial Album | Pablo | 2310967-2
Milt Jackson Birthday Celebration | Fantasy | FANCD 6079-2
Milt Jackson + Count Basie + Big Band Vol.1 | Original Jazz Classics | OJCCD 740-2(2310822)
Milt Jackson + Count Basie + Big Band Vol.2 | Original Jazz Classics | OJCCD 741-2(2310823)
Tom Saunders' 'Wild Bill Davison Band' & Guests
Exactly Like You | Nagel-Heyer | CD 023
The Second Sampler | Nagel-Heyer | NHR SP 6

Miles,Jason | (keyboards,programming)
Al Jarreau With Band
Tenderness | i.e. Music | 557853-2
Joe Sample Group
Ashes To Ashes | Warner | 7599-26318-2
Marcus Miller Group
The Sun Don't Lie | Dreyfus Jazz Line | FDM 36560-2
Tales | Dreyfus Jazz Line | FDM 36571-2
Michael Brecker Group
Now You See It...(Now You Don't) | GRP | GRP 96222
Miles Davis Group
Tutu | Warner | 7599-25490-2
Amandla | Warner | 7599-25873-2
Miles Davis-Marcus Miller Group
Siesta(Soundtrack) | Warner | 7599-25655-2

Miles,Matt | (b)
David Newton Quartet
DNA | Candid | CCD 79742

Miles,Ron | (tp)
Bill Frisell Band
Blues Dream | Nonesuch | 7559-79615-2
Miriam Alter Quintet
Alter Ego | Intuition Records | INT 3258-2

Miles,Victoria | (voc)
Klaus Doldinger's Passport
Running In Real Time | Warner | 2292-40633-2
Heavy Nights | Warner | 2292-42006-2

Miley,Bubber | (tp)
Duke Ellington And His Kentucky Club Orchestra
Jazz:The Essential Collection Vol.2 | IN+OUT Records | 78012-2
Duke Ellington And His Orchestra
Jazz:The Essential Collection Vol.2 | IN+OUT Records | 78012-2

Milito,Helcio | (drtamba)
Joao Gilberto Trio
Getz/Gilberto No.2 | Verve | 519800-2
Stan Getz Quartet
Getz/Gilberto No.2 | Verve | 519800-2
Stan Getz Quintet Feat. Astrud Gilberto
Verve Jazz Masters 53:Stan Getz-Bossa Nova | Verve | 529904-2
The New Stan Getz Quintet Feat. Astrud Gilberto
Getz Au Go Go | Verve | 821725-2
Wes Montgomery With The Don Sebesky Orchestra
Bumpin' | Verve | 539062-2

Milito,Helcio or Grady Tate | (dr)
Verve Jazz Masters 14:Wes Montgomery | Verve | 519826-2
Talkin' Jazz:Roots Of Acid Jazz | Verve | 529580-2

Miller,Art | (b)
Paul Whiteman And His Orchestra
Planet Jazz:Jack Teagarden | Planet Jazz | 2161236-2
Jazz:The Essential Collection Vol.3 | IN+OUT Records | 78013-2
The Three T's
Jazz:The Essential Collection Vol.3 | IN+OUT Records | 78013-2

Miller,Bill | (pv)
Charlie Barnet And His Orchestra
Planet Jazz:Big Bands | Planet Jazz | 2169649-2
Planet Jazz:Swing | Planet Jazz | 2169651-2
Ella Fitzgerald With The Frank DeVol Orchestra
Get Happy! | Verve | 523321-2
Frank Sinatra With The Red Norvo Quintet(Sextet!)
Live In Australia,1959 | Blue Note | 837513-2
Frank Sinatra With The Red Norvo Quintet(Sextet!) & Orchestra
Live In Australia,1959 | Blue Note | 837513-2
Red Norvo Sextet
Live In Australia,1959 | Blue Note | 837513-2

Miller,Bruce | (arr)
Paulinho Da Costa Orchestra
Happy People | Original Jazz Classics | OJCCD 783-2(2312102)

Miller,Byron | (b,b-synthel-b)
Flora Purim With Orchestra
Joe Henderson:The Milestone Years | Milestone | 8MCD 4413-2
George Duke Group
Jazzrock-Anthology Vol.3:Fusion | Zounds | CD 27100555
Herbie Hancock Group
Sunlight | CBS | 486570-2
Sonny Rollins Sextet
Jazzin' Vol.2: The Music Of Stevie Wonder | Fantasy | FANCD 6088-2
Easy Living | Original Jazz Classics | OJCCD 893-2
Stanley Clarke Group
If This Bass Could Only Talk | CBS | 460883-2

Miller,Daniel | (cello)
Tom Harrell Group
Paradise | RCA | 2663738-2

Miller,Denzil | (el-p,keyboards,psynth)
Urbanator
Urbanator II | Hip Bop | HIBD 8012

Miller,Eddie | (cl,tsvoc)
All Star Band
Planet Jazz:Jack Teagarden | Planet Jazz | 2161236-2
Bob Crosby And His Orchestra
Swing Legens:Bob Crosby | Nimbus Records | NI 2011
Bob Crosby's Bobcats
Swing Legens:Bob Crosby | Nimbus Records | NI 2011
Louis Armstrong And His Orchestra
I Love Jazz | Verve | 543747-2
Louis Armstrong With Gordon Jenkins And His Orchestra And Choir
Satchmo In Style | Verve | 549594-2
Ten Cats And A Mouse
The Hollywood Session:The Capitol Jazzmen | Jazz Unlimited | JUCD 2044
The Capitol Jazzmen
The Hollywood Session:The Capitol Jazzmen | Jazz Unlimited | JUCD 2044
The Metronome All-Star Nine
Jazz:The Essential Collection Vol.3 | IN+OUT Records | 78013-2

Miller,Eric | (g)
Lionel Hampton And His Orchestra
Lionel Hampton:Flying Home | Dreyfus Jazz Line | FDM 36735-2

Miller,Ernest 'Punch' | (co,tpvoc)
Punch Miller's Bunch & George Lewis
Atlantic Jazz: New Orleans | Atlantic | 7567-81700-2

Miller,Frank | (cello)
Charlie Parker With Strings
Verve Jazz Masters 28:Charlie Parker Plays Standards | Verve | 521854-2
Charlie Parker With Strings:The Master Takes | Verve | 523984-2
Charlie Parker:The Best Of The Verve Years | Verve | 527815-2
Bird: The Complete Charlie Parker On Verve | Verve | 837141-2
Charlie Parker:April In Paris | Dreyfus Jazz Line | FDM 36737-2

Miller,Glenn | (arr,ld,tbvoc)
Glenn Miller And His Orchestra
The Ultimate Glenn Miller-22 Original Hits From The King Of Swing | RCA | 2113137-2
Planet Jazz:Glenn Miller | Planet Jazz | 2152056-2
Planet Jazz Sampler | Planet Jazz | 2152326-2
Planet Jazz:Jazz Greatest Hits | Planet Jazz | 2169648-2
Planet Jazz:Big Bands | Planet Jazz | 2169649-2
Planet Jazz:Swing | Planet Jazz | 2169651-2
Jazz Collection:Glenn Miller | Laserlight | 24367
The Chesterfield Broadcasts Vol.1 | RCA | 2663113-2
Candelight Miller | RCA | 2668716-2
The Glenn Miller Story Vol. 2 | RCA | ND 89221
The Glenn Miller Story Vol. 3 | RCA | ND 89222
Swing Legends | Nimbus Records | NI 2001
Mound City Blue Blowers
Jazz:The Essential Collection Vol.3 | IN+OUT Records | 78013-2
The Andrew Sisters With The Glenn Miller Orchestra
The Chesterfield Broadcasts Vol.1 | RCA | 2663113-2

Miller,Harold | (voc)
First Revolution Singers
First Revolution Gospel Singers:A Capella | Laserlight | 24338

Miller,Harry | (bb-g)
John Surman Orchestra
How Many Clouds Can You See? | Deram | 844882-2

Miller,Jesse | (tp)
Earl Hines And His Orchestra
Planet Jazz:Earl Hines | Planet Jazz | 2159973-2

Miller,Jimmy | (drg)
Jimmy Witherspoon And His Band
Baby, Baby, Baby | Original Blues Classics | OBCCD 527-2(P 7290)
Sidney Bechet With Noble Sissle's Swingsters
Sidney Bechet:Summertime | Dreyfus Jazz Line | FDM 36712-2

Miller,Joe | (bj,hornstb)
Howlin' Wolf London Session
Howlin' Wolf:The London Sessions | Chess | MCD 09297

Miller,John | (b,keyboardsp)
Stanley Turrentine And His Orchestra
Pieces Of Dream | Original Jazz Classics | OJCCD 831-2(F 9465)

Miller,Johnny | (b,vocp)
JATP All Stars
The Complete Jazz At The Philharmonic On Verve 1944-1949 | Verve | 523893-2
Nat King Cole And His Trio
Nat King Cole:Route 66 | Dreyfus Jazz Line | FDM 36716-2
Nat King Cole Trio
The Small Black Groups | Storyville | 4960523
Live At The Circle Room | Capitol | 521859-2
The Instrumental Classics | Capitol | 798288-2
The Best Of The Nat King Cole Trio:The Vocal Classics(1942-1946) | Blue Note | 833571-2
Nat King Cole:Route 66 | Dreyfus Jazz Line | FDM 36716-2
Nat King Cole:For Sentimental Reasons | Dreyfus Jazz Line | FDM 36740-2
Love Songs | Nimbus Records | NI 2010
Nat King Cole Trio With Frank DeVol's Orchestra
Nat King Cole:Route 66 | Dreyfus Jazz Line | FDM 36716-2
Nat King Cole With Orchestra
Nat King Cole:Route 66 | Dreyfus Jazz Line | FDM 36716-2

Miller,Jonathan 'Juici' | (voice)
Marcus Miller Group
The Sun Don't Lie | Dreyfus Jazz Line | FDM 36560-2
Tales | Dreyfus Jazz Line | FDM 36571-2

Miller,Judd | (electronic-valve-instruments)
Michael Brecker Group
Don't Try This At Home | Impulse(MCA) | 950114-2
Now You See It...(Now You Don't) | GRP | GRP 96222
Yellowjackets
Run For Your Life | GRP | GRP 97542

Miller,Judy | (synth)
John Patitucci Group
Sketchbook | GRP | GRP 96172

Miller,Julian 'Juju' | (voice)
Marcus Miller Group
The Sun Don't Lie | Dreyfus Jazz Line | FDM 36560-2
Tales | Dreyfus Jazz Line | FDM 36571-2

Miller,L.Aziza | (voc)
Ahmad Jamal Trio
Picture Perfect-70th Anniversary | Warner | 8573-85268-2

Miller,Leah | (rap)
Tom Browne Groups
Mo' Jamaica Funk | Hip Bop | HIBD 8002

Miller,Marcus | (b,b-cl,b-g,dr-programming,g)
Al Jarreau With Band
Tenderness | i.e. Music | 557853-2
Dave Grusin Group
Mountain Dance | GRP | GRP 95072
Migration | GRP | GRP 95922
Don Grolnick Group
Hearts And Numbers | VeraBra Records | CDVBR 2016-2
Dreyfus All Stars
Dreyfus Night In Paris | Dreyfus Jazz Line | FDM 36652-2
Earl Klugh Group
Late Night Guitar | Blue Note | 498573-2
Grover Washington Jr. Orchestra
Inside Moves | Elektra | 7559-60318-2
Joe Sample Group
Ashes To Ashes | Warner | 7599-26318-2
Spellbound | Rhino | 81273726-2
Lee Ritenour Group
Rio | GRP | GRP 95242
Festival | GRP | GRP 95702
Lenny White Group
Present Tense | Hip Bop | HIBD 8004
Hot Jazz Bisquits | Hip Bop | HIBD 8801
Marcus Miller Group
The Sun Don't Lie | Dreyfus Jazz Line | FDM 36560-2
Tales | Dreyfus Jazz Line | FDM 36571-2
Live & More | Dreyfus Jazz Line | FDM 36585-2
Michael 'Patches' Stewart Group
Penetration | Hip Bop | HIBD 8018
Miles Davis Group
The Man With The Horn | CBS | 468701-2
We Want Miles | CBS | 469402-2
Tutu | Warner | 7599-25490-2
Amandla | Warner | 7599-25873-2
Miles Davis-Marcus Miller Group
Siesta(Soundtrack) | Warner | 7599-25655-2
Tom Browne Group
Hot Jazz Bisquits | Hip Bop | HIBD 8801
Tom Browne Groups
Mo' Jamaica Funk | Hip Bop | HIBD 8002

Miller,Mitch | (arr,ld,oboe,engl-hornprob.engl-h)
Charlie Parker With Strings
Verve Jazz Masters 28:Charlie Parker Plays Standards | Verve | 521854-2
Charlie Parker With Strings:The Master Takes | Verve | 523984-2
Charlie Parker:The Best Of The Verve Years | Verve | 527815-2
Bird: The Complete Charlie Parker On Verve | Verve | 837141-2
Charlie Parker:April In Paris | Dreyfus Jazz Line | FDM 36737-2

Miller,Mulgrew | (p,synthp-solo)
Cassandra Wilson With The Mulgrew Miller Trio
Blue Skies | JMT Edition | 919018-2
Dave Ellis Quartet
State Of Mind | Milestone | MCD 9328-2
Dave Ellis Quintet
State Of Mind | Milestone | MCD 9328-2
David Klein Quintet
My Marilyn | Enja | ENJ-9422 2
Dianne Reeves With Band
I Remember | Blue Note | 790264-2
Donald Harrison Quartet
Free To Be | Impulse(MCA) | 951283-2
Donald Harrison Quintet
Free To Be | Impulse(MCA) | 951283-2
Eddie Henderson With The Mulgrew Miller Trio
Trumpet Legacy | Milestone | MCD 9286-2
Frank Morgan All Stars
Reflections | Original Jazz Classics | OJCCD 1046-2(C 14052)
Frank Morgan Quartet
Yardbird Suite | Original Jazz Classics | OJCCD 1060-2(C 14045)
Greg Tardy Band
Serendipity | Impulse(MCA) | 951258-2
Joe Chambers Quartet
Mirrors | Blue Note | 496685-2
Joe Chambers Quintet
Mirrors | Blue Note | 496685-2
Joe Chambers Trio
Mirrors | Blue Note | 496685-2
Joe Lovano Quartet
Live At The Village Vanguard | Blue Note | 829125-2
Joe Lovano Sextet
Tenor Legacy | Blue Note | 827014-2
Lenny White Group
Present Tense | Hip Bop | HIBD 8004
Lew Soloff Quartet
With A Song In My Heart | Milestone | MCD 9290-2
Lew Soloff Quintet
With A Song In My Heart | Milestone | MCD 9290-2
Lew Soloff With The Mulgrew Miller Trio
Trumpet Legacy | Milestone | MCD 9286-2
Nicholas Payton With The Mulgrew Miller Trio
Trumpet Legacy | Milestone | MCD 9286-2
Randy Sandke Quintet
Cliffhanger | Nagel-Heyer | CD 2037
Randy Sandke Sextet
Cliffhanger | Nagel-Heyer | CD 2037
Ron Carter Trio
The Golden Striker | Blue Note | 590831-2
Steve Swallow Group
Real Book | Watt | XtraWatt/7(521637-2)
Tom Harrell With The Mulgrew Miller Trio
Trumpet Legacy | Milestone | MCD 9286-2
Toots Thielemans Quartet
Verve Jazz Masters Vol.59:Toots Thielemans | Verve | 535271-2

Miller,Paul | (g)
Art Van Damme Group
State Of Art | MPS | 841413-2

Miller,Randall | (tb)
Artie Shaw And His Orchestra
Planet JazzArtie Shaw | Planet Jazz | 2152057-2
Planet Jazz:Jazz Greatest Hits | Planet Jazz | 2169648-2
Lena Horne With The Horace Henderson Orchestra
Planet Jazz:Lena Horne | Planet Jazz | 2165373-2

Miller,Steve | (gvoc)
John Lee Hooker Group
Endless Boogie | MCA | MCD 10413

Miller,Stewart | (b)
Brad Goode-Von Freeman Sextet
Inside Chicago Vol.3 | Steeplechase | SCCD 31531
Inside Chicago Vol.4 | Steeplechase | SCCD 31532

Miller,T.prob. | (dr)
Minton's Playhouse All Stars
Charlie Christian:Swing To Bop | Dreyfus Jazz Line | FDM 36715-2

Miller,Taps | (dr,tp,ldvoc)
Charlie Christian All Stars
Charlie Christian-Jazz Immortal/Dizzy Gillespie 1944 | Original Jazz Classics | OJCCD 1932-2(ES 548)

Miller,Warren | (v)
Herbie Mann With The Frank DeVol Orchestra
Verve Jazz Masters 56:Herbie Mann | Verve | 529901-2

Miller,William | (v)
Ella Fitzgerald With The Marty Paich Orchestra
Get Happy! | Verve | 523321-2
Mel Tormé With The Russell Garcia Orchestra
Swingin' On The Moon | Verve | 511385-2
Pete Rugolo And His Orchestra
Thriller/Richard Diamon(Original Jazz Scores From 2 Classics TV Series) | Fresh Sound Records | FSCD 2015

Millet,Monica | (atabaques,djembe,udu perc)
Pata Masters
Pata-Bahia | Pata Musik | PATA 11 CD

Millikan,Robert 'Bob' | (tpfl-h)
George Gruntz Concert Jazz Band
Blues 'N Dues Et Cetera | Enja | ENJ-6072 2

Milliken,Catherine | (oboe,bass-oboeengl-h)
Ensemble Modern
Ensemble Modern-Fred Frith:Traffic Continues | Winter&Winter | 910044-2

Milliman,Linc | (btuba)
Allan Vaché Swingtet
Ellington For Lovers | Nagel-Heyer | NH 1009
The New York Allstars
Broadway | Nagel-Heyer | CD 003
One Two Three | Nagel-Heyer | CD 008
Randy Sandke Meets Bix Beiderbecke | Nagel-Heyer | CD 3002
The First Sampler | Nagel-Heyer | NHR SP 5

Millinder,Lucky | (cond,ldvoc)

Mamie Smith WithThe Lucky Millinder Orchestra
The Blues | Storyville | 4960323

Milliner,Jesse | (p)
Conexion Latina
Mambo Nights | Enja | ENJ-9402 2

Mills Brothers,The | (voc)
Louis Armstrong And The Mills Brothers
Louis Armstrong:Swing That Music | Laserlight | 36056
The Mills Brothers
The Mills Brothers Story | Storyville | 4960233

Mills Sr.,John | (gvoc)
Louis Armstrong And The Mills Brothers
Louis Armstrong:Swing That Music | Laserlight | 36056

Mills,Alvin | (el-b)
J.C. Dook Quartet
Travelin' Man | Organic Music | ORGM 9734

Mills,Dickie | (tp)
Brew Moore Quintet
The Brew Moore Quintet | Original Jazz Classics | OJCCD 100-2(F 3-222)

Mills,Donald | (voc)
Louis Armstrong And The Mills Brothers
Louis Armstrong:Swing That Music | Laserlight | 36056
The Mills Brothers
The Mills Brothers Story | Storyville | 4960233

Mills,Harry | (org,talking,tpvoc)
Louis Armstrong And The Mills Brothers
Louis Armstrong:Swing That Music | Laserlight | 36056
Louis Armstrong With Harry Mills And Choir
Louis And The Good Book | Verve | 549593-2
The Mills Brothers
The Mills Brothers Story | Storyville | 4960233

Mills,Herbert | (voc)
Louis Armstrong And The Mills Brothers
Louis Armstrong:Swing That Music | Laserlight | 36056
The Mills Brothers
The Mills Brothers Story | Storyville | 4960233

Mills,Irving | (comments,ldvoc)
Duke Ellington And His Cotton Club Orchestra
Planet Jazz:Duke Ellington | Planet Jazz | 2152053-2
Irving Mills And His Hotsy Totsy Gang
Jazz:The Essential Collection Vol.3 | IN+OUT Records | 78013-2

Mills,Jackie | (dr,perctimbales)
Billie Holiday With The JATP All Stars
Billie Holiday Story Vol.1:Jazz At The Philharmonic | Verve | 521642-2
The Complete Jazz At The Philharmonic On Verve 1944-1949 | Verve | 523893-2
Erroll Garner Quartet
Erroll Garner:Trio | Dreyfus Jazz Line | FDM 36719-2
Harry James And His Orchestra
Trumpet Blues:The Best Of Harry James | Capitol | 521224-2
Jesse Price And His Blues Band
Jazz Profile:Dexter Gordon | Blue Note | 823514-2
Jimmy McGriff Trio
So Blue So Funky-Heroes Of The Hammond | Blue Note | 796563-2
Lucky Thompson And His Lucky Seven
Planet Jazz:Bebop | RCA | 2169650-2
Red Norvo Septet
Jazz Profile:Dexter Gordon | Blue Note | 823514-2

Mills,Verley | (harp)
Billy May And His Orchestra
Billy May's Big Fat Brass/Bill's Bag | Capitol | 535206-2
Charlie Parker Quartet With Strings
The Cole Porter Songbook | Verve | 823250-2
Charlie Parker With Strings
Charlie Parker:The Best Of The Verve Years | Verve | 527815-2
Bird: The Complete Charlie Parker On Verve | Verve | 837141-2
Charlie Parker:April In Paris | Dreyfus Jazz Line | FDM 36737-2
Charlie Parker With The Joe Lipman Orchestra
Verve Jazz Masters 28:Charlie Parker Plays Standards | Verve | 521854-2
Charlie Parker With Strings:The Master Takes | Verve | 523984-2
Charlie Parker Big Band | Verve | 559835-2
Mel Tormé With The Billy May Orchestra
Mel Tormé Goes South Of The Border With Billy May | Verve | 589517-2

Millstein,Gilbert | (narration)
Billie Holiday And Her All Stars
The Billie Holiday Song Book | Verve | 823246-2

Milne,Andy | (keyboardsp)
Steve Coleman And Five Elements
Curves Of Life | Novus | 2131693-2
Genesis & The Opening Of The Way | RCA | 2152934-2
Steve Coleman And Metrics
A Tale Of 3 Cities,The EP | Novus | 2124747-2
The Way Of The Cipher | Novus | 2131690-2
Steve Coleman And The Council Of Balance
Genesis & The Opening Of The Way | RCA | 2152934-2

Milosevic,Aleksandar | (b)
Doug Sides Ensemble
Sumblo | Laika Records | 35100882

Mims,Charles | (p)
Dianne Reeves With Band
I Remember | Blue Note | 790264-2

Minafra,Pino | (tp,didjeridoo,fl-h,noise)
Italian Instabile Orchestra
Skies Of Europe | ECM | 1543
Michel Godard Ensemble
Castel Del Monte | Enja | ENJ-9362 2
Willem Breuker Kollektief
La Banda/Banda And Jazz | Enja | ENJ-9326 2

Mince,Johnny | (ascl)
Billie Holiday With Sy Oliver And His Orchestra
Billie's Love Songs | Nimbus Records | NI 2000
Louis Armstrong And Billie Holiday With Sy Oliver's Orchestra
Louis Armstrong:C'est Si Bon | Dreyfus Jazz Line | FDM 36730-2
Tommy Dorsey And His Orchestra
Planet Jazz:Frank Sinatra & Tommy Dorsey | Planet Jazz | 2152067-2
Planet Jazz:Tommy Dorsey | Planet Jazz | 2159972-2
Planet Jazz:Big Bands | Planet Jazz | 2169649-2
Planet Jazz:Male Jazz Vocalists | Planet Jazz | 2169657-2
Frank Sinatra And The Tommy Dorsey Orchestra | RCA | 2668701-2

Mind Games |
Mind Games
Pretty Fonky | Edition Collage | EC 482-2
Mind Games Plays The Music Of Stan Getz & Astrud Gilberto | Edition Collage | EC 515-2
Wind Moments | Take Twelve On CD | TT 009-2
Mind Games With Claudio Roditi
Live | Edition Collage | EC 501-2
Vocal Moments | Take Twelve On CD | TT 008-2
Mind Games With Philip Catherine
Pretty Fonky | Edition Collage | EC 482-2
Tom Bennecke & Space Gurilla
Wind Moments | Take Twelve On CD | TT 009-2

Mineau,Thierry | (el-b)
Serge Forté Trio
Vaina | Laika Records | LK 90-021

Minerve,Geezil | (asts)
Buddy Johnson And His Orchestra
Buddy And Ella Johnson 1953-1964 | Bear Family Records | BCD 15479 DH

Minerve,Harold | (as,cl,sax,flreeds)
Duke Ellington And His Orchestra
Highlights From The Duke Ellington Centennial Edition | RCA | 2663672-2
The Ellington Suites | Original Jazz Classics | OJC20 446-2(2310762)
Togo Brava Swuite | Storyville | STCD 8323
Duke Ellington Orchestra
Continuum | Fantasy | FCD 24765-2

Minger,George | (tp)
Count Basie And His Orchestra
Count Basie: Salle Pleyel, April 17th, 1972 | Laserlight | 36127

Minger,Pete | (fl-htp)
Big Joe Turner With The Count Basie Orchestra
Flip Flop And Fly | Original Jazz Classics | OJCCD 1053-2(2310937)
Count Basie And His Orchestra
Afrique | RCA | 2179618-2
Fun Time | Pablo | 2310945-2
Jazz Dance | Original Jazz Classics | OJCCD 1002-2(1210890)
I Told You So | Original Jazz Classics | OJCCD 824-2(2310767)
Digital III At Montreux | Original Jazz Classics | OJCCD 996-2(2308223)
Ella Fitzgerald With Count Basie And His Orchestra
Digital III At Montreux | Original Jazz Classics | OJCCD 996-2(2308223)
Ella Fitzgerald With The Count Basie Orchestra
Bluella:Ella Fitzgerald Sings The Blues | Pablo | 2310960-2
For The Love Of Ella Fitzgerald | Verve | 841765-2
Milt Jackson Orchestra
Sarah Vaughan Birthday Celebration | Fantasy | FANCD 6090-2
Milt Jackson With The Count Basie Orchestra
To Bags...With Love:Memorial Album | Pablo | 2310967-2
Milt Jackson Birthday Celebration | Fantasy | FANCD 6079-2
Milt Jackson + Count Basie + Big Band Vol.1 | Original Jazz Classics | OJCCD 740-2(2310822)
Milt Jackson + Count Basie + Big Band Vol.2 | Original Jazz Classics | OJCCD 741-2(2310823)

Minghetti,Lisa | (v)
Ben Webster With Strings
The Warm Moods-With Strings | Rhino | 8122-73721-2

Mingus Big Band |
Mingus Big Band
Tonight At Noon...Three Or Four Shades Of Love | Dreyfus Jazz Line | FDM 36633-2

Mingus Big Band 93 |
Mingus Big Band 93
Nostalgia In Times Square | Dreyfus Jazz Line | FDM 36559-2

Mingus By Five |
Mingus By Five
Mingus By Five | Touché Music | TMcCD 019

Mingus,Charles | (b,narration,perc,voc,cello,comp,p)
Billie Holiday With The JATP All Stars
Billie Holiday Story Vol.1:Jazz At The Philharmonic | Verve | 521642-2
The Complete Jazz At The Philharmonic On Verve 1944-1949 | Verve | 523893-2
Verve Jazz Masters 47:Billie Holiday Sings Standards | Verve | 527650-2
Billy Taylor Trio
Charles Mingus-The Complete Debut Recordings | Debut | 12 DCD 4402-2
Bob Benton With The Charles Mingus Quintet
Charles Mingus-The Complete Debut Recordings | Debut | 12 DCD 4402-2
Bud Powell Trio
Charles Mingus-The Complete Debut Recordings | Debut | 12 DCD 4402-2
Charles Mingus
Charles Mingus-Passion Of A Man:The Complete Atlantic Recordings 1956-1961 | Atlantic | 8122-72871-2
Mingus Plays Piano | Impulse(MCA) | 951217-2
Charles Mingus And His Orchestra
Charles Mingus-The Complete Debut Recordings | Debut | 12 DCD 4402-2
Charles Mingus-Passion Of A Man:The Complete Atlantic Recordings 1956-1961 | Atlantic | 8122-72871-2
The Complete Town Hall Concert | Blue Note | 828353-2
Charles Mingus Group
The Jazz Life! | Candid | CCD 79019
Candid Dolphy | Candid | CCD 79033
Mysterious Blues | Candid | CCD 79042
Mingus Ah Um | CBS | CK 65512
Mingus Dynasty | CBS | CK 65513
Charles Mingus Jazz Workshop
Tonight At Noon | Atlantic | 7567-80793-2
Rhino Presents The Atlantic Jazz Gallery | Atlantic | 8122-71257-2
Charles Mingus-Passion Of A Man:The Complete Atlantic Recordings 1956-1961 | Atlantic | 8122-72871-2
Blues & Roots | Atlantic | 8122-75205-2
The Clown | Atlantic | 8122-75358-2
The Very Best Of Charles Mingus | Rhino | 8122-79988-2
Charles Mingus Orchestra
Tijuana Moods(The Complete Edition) | RCA | 2663840-2
Charles Mingus:Pre-Bird(Mingus Revisited) | Verve | 538636-2
Three Or Four Shades Of Blues | Atlantic | 7567-81403-2
Cumbia & Jazz Fusion | Atlantic | 8122-71785-2
The Very Best Of Charles Mingus | Rhino | 8122-79988-2
Mingus Mingus Mingus | Impulse(MCA) | 951170-2
The Black Saint And The Sinner Lady | Impulse(MCA) | 951174-2
Charles Mingus:The Complete 1959 Columbia Recordings | CBS | C3K 65145
Mingus | Candid | CCD 79021
Charles Mingus Quartet
Mingus At Antibes | Atlantic | 7567-90532-2
Charles Mingus Presents Charles Mingus | Candid | CCD 79005
Mingus | Candid | CCD 79021
Right Now | Original Jazz Classics | OJCCD 237-2
Charles Mingus Quintet
Charles Mingus-The Complete Debut Recordings | Debut | 12 DCD 4402-2
Mingus At Antibes | Atlantic | 7567-90532-2
Changes One | Rhino | 8122-71403-2
Changes Two | Rhino | 8122-71404-2
Charles Mingus-Passion Of A Man:The Complete Atlantic Recordings 1956-1961 | Atlantic | 8122-72871-2
The Very Best Of Charles Mingus | Rhino | 8122-79988-2
Mingus At The Bohemia | Original Jazz Classics | OJC20 045-2
The Charles Mingus Quintet+Max Roach | Original Jazz Classics | OJC20 440-2(F 6009)
Right Now | Original Jazz Classics | OJCCD 237-2
Charles Mingus Quintet With Bud Powell
Mingus At Antibes | Atlantic | 7567-90532-2
Charles Mingus-Passion Of A Man:The Complete Atlantic Recordings 1956-1961 | Atlantic | 8122-72871-2
Charles Mingus Quintet With Roland Kirk
Tonight At Noon | Atlantic | 7567-80793-2
Charles Mingus-Passion Of A Man:The Complete Atlantic Recordings 1956-1961 | Atlantic | 8122-72871-2
The Very Best Of Charles Mingus | Rhino | 8122-79988-2
Charles Mingus Septet
Charles Mingus:The Complete 1959 Columbia Recordings | CBS | C3K 65145
Charles Mingus Sextet
Changes Two | Rhino | 8122-71404-2
Eric Dolphy Birthday Celebration | Fantasy | FANCD 6085-2
Town Hall Concert 1964, Vol.1 | Original Jazz Classics | OJCCD 042-2
Charles Mingus Workshop
Charles Mingus-The Complete Debut Recordings | Debut | 12 DCD 4402-2
Charles Mingus-Max Roach
Mingus At The Bohemia | Original Jazz Classics | OJC20 045-2
Charlie Parker And His Orchestra
Charlie Parker:The Best Of The Verve Years | Verve | 527815-2
The Cole Porter Songbook | Verve | 823250-2
Bird: The Complete Charlie Parker On Verve | Verve | 837141-2
Charlie Parker With Orchestra
Charlie Parker Big Band | Verve | 559835-2
Charlie Parker With Orchestra & The Dave Lambert Singers
Verve Jazz Masters 28:Charlie Parker Plays Standards | Verve | 521854-2
Don Senay With Orchestra And Strings
Charles Mingus-The Complete Debut Recordings | Debut | 12 DCD 4402-2
Ellington/Mingus/Roach Trio
Money Jungle | Blue Note | 538227-2
Four Trombones
Charles Mingus-The Complete Debut Recordings | Debut | 12 DCD 4402-2
The J.J.Johnson Memorial Album | Prestige | PRCD 11025-2
Hank Jones Trio
Charles Mingus-The Complete Debut Recordings | Debut | 12 DCD 4402-2
Hank Jones Trio With The Gordons's
Charles Mingus-The Complete Debut Recordings | Debut | 12 DCD 4402-2
Hazel Scott Trio
Charles Mingus-The Complete Debut Recordings | Debut | 12 DCD 4402-2
J.J.Johnson Quintet
The Eminent J.J.Johnson Vol.2 | Blue Note | 532144-2
J.R. Monterose Sextet
Jaywalkin' | Fresh Sound Records | FSR-CD 320
Jackie Paris With The Charles Mingus Quintet
Charles Mingus-The Complete Debut Recordings | Debut | 12 DCD 4402-2
JATP All Stars
The Complete Jazz At The Philharmonic On Verve 1944-1949 | Verve | 523893-2
Jazz Artists Guild
Newport Rebels-Jazz Artists Guild | Candid | CCD 79022
Jimmy Knepper Quintet
Charles Mingus-The Complete Debut Recordings | Debut | 12 DCD 4402-2
John Dennis Trio
Charles Mingus-The Complete Debut Recordings | Debut | 12 DCD 4402-2
Lionel Hampton And His Orchestra
Lionel Hampton:Flying Home | Dreyfus Jazz Line | FDM 36735-2
Miles Davis Quartet
Blue Haze | Original Jazz Classics | OJC20 093-2(P 7054)
Miles Davis Quintet
Charles Mingus-The Complete Debut Recordings | Debut | 12 DCD 4402-2
Blue Moods | Original Jazz Classics | OJC20 043-2(DEB 120)
Newport Rebels
Candid Dolphy | Candid | CCD 79033
Oscar Pettiford Sextet
Charles Mingus-The Complete Debut Recordings | Debut | 12 DCD 4402-2
Paul Bley Trio
Charles Mingus-The Complete Debut Recordings | Debut | 12 DCD 4402-2
Introducing Paul Bley | Original Jazz Classics | OJCCD 201-2(DEB 7)
Quintet Of The Year
Charles Mingus-The Complete Debut Recordings | Debut | 12 DCD 4402-2
The Quintet-Jazz At Massey Hall | Debut | DSA 124-6
The Quintet-Jazz At Massey Hall | Original Jazz Classics | OJC20 044-2
Spaulding Givens Trio
Charles Mingus-The Complete Debut Recordings | Debut | 12 DCD 4402-2
Spaulding Givens/Charles Mingus
Charles Mingus-The Complete Debut Recordings | Debut | 12 DCD 4402-2
Teddy Charles Quartet
Charles Mingus-Passion Of A Man:The Complete Atlantic Recordings 1956-1961 | Atlantic | 8122-72871-2
Thad Jones And His Orchestra
Charles Mingus-The Complete Debut Recordings | Debut | 12 DCD 4402-2
Thad Jones Quartet
Charles Mingus-The Complete Debut Recordings | Debut | 12 DCD 4402-2
Thad Jones Quintet
Charles Mingus-The Complete Debut Recordings | Debut | 12 DCD 4402-2

Mingus,Charles or Henry Grimes | (b)
Charles Mingus Workshop
Charles Mingus-The Complete Debut Recordings | Debut | 12 DCD 4402-2

Mingus,Charles prob. | (b)
Don Senay With Orchestra And Strings
Charles Mingus-The Complete Debut Recordings | Debut | 12 DCD 4402-2
Thad Jones And His Orchestra
Charles Mingus-The Complete Debut Recordings | Debut | 12 DCD 4402-2

Mingus,Eric | (voc)
Karen Mantler Group
My Cat Arnold | Watt | XtraWatt/3
Karen Mantler And Her Cat Arnold Get The Flu | Watt | XtraWatt/5

Minkkinen,Erik | (computer)
Noel Akchoté Trio
Rien | Winter&Winter | 910057-2

Minor,Dan | (tb)
Benny Moten's Kansas City Orchestra
Planet Jazz:Ben Webster | RCA | 2165368-2
Planet Jazz:Jimmy Rushing | RCA | 2165371-2
Planet Jazz:Swing | Planet Jazz | 2169651-2
Jazz:The Essential Collection Vol.3 | IN+OUT Records | 78013-2
Count Basie And His Orchestra
Jazz:The Essential Collection Vol.3 | IN+OUT Records | 78013-2
From Spiritual To Swing | Vanguard | VCD 169/71
Helen Humes With James P. Johnson And The Count Basie Orchestra
From Spiritual To Swing | Vanguard | VCD 169/71
Jimmy Rushing With Count Basie And His Orchestra
From Spiritual To Swing | Vanguard | VCD 169/71
New Orleans Feetwarmers
From Spiritual To Swing | Vanguard | VCD 169/71

Minton,Phil | (dr,p,voice,tpvoc)
Klaus König Orchestra & Guests
The Song Of Songs:Oratorio For Two Solo Voices,Choir And Orchestra | Enja | ENJ-7057 2
Mike Westbrook Band
Off Abbey Road | TipToe | TIP-888805 2

Minton's Playhouse All Stars |
Minton's Playhouse All Stars
Charlie Christian:Swing To Bop | Dreyfus Jazz Line | FDM 36715-2

Mintzer,Bob | (b-cl,sax,synth,voc,ss,ts,el-b-cl,cl)
Bob Mintzer-Gil Goldstein Duo
Longing | Owl Records | 018353-2
Buddy Rich Big Band
Backwoods Siseman/Pieces Of Dream | Laserlight | 24655
George Gruntz Concert Jazz Band
Blues 'N Dues Et Cetera | Enja | ENJ-6072 2
GRP All-Star Big Band
GRP All-Star Big Band:Live! | GRP | GRP 97402
All Blues | GRP | GRP 98002
Mike Mainieri Group
Jazz Life Vol.2:From Seventh At Avenue South | Storyville | 4960763
Peter Erskine Orchestra
Peter Erskine | Original Jazz Classics | OJC 610(C 14010)
Peter O'Mara Quartet
Symmetry | Edition Collage | EC 484-2

Wind Moments | Take Twelve On CD | TT 009-2
Rolf Kühn Group
Internal Eyes | Intuition Records | INT 3328-2
Take 6 With The Yellow Jackets
He Is Christmas | Reprise | 7599-26665-2
Yellowjackets
Live Wires | GRP | GRP 96672
Run For Your Life | GRP | GRP 97542

Minucci,Chieli | (g,el-gsynth)
Deborah Henson-Conant Group
Budapest | Laika Records | LK 93-039
Russel Gunn Group
Ethnomusicology Vol.1 | Atlantic | 7567-83165-2

Miori,Ennio | (cello)
Gerry Mulligan With Astor Piazzolla And His Orchestra
Tango Nuevo | Atlantic | 2292-42145-2

Mirabal,Linda | (voc)
Lewis Trio With Guests
Battangó | Intuition Records | INN 1101-2

Mirabassi,Gabriele | (clb-cl)
Gabriele Mirabassi Trio
Latakia Blend | Enja | ENJ-9441 2
Michel Godard Ensemble
Castel Del Monte II | Enja | ENJ-9431 2
Rabih Abou-Khalil Group
The Cactus Of Knowledge | Enja | ENJ-9401 2

Miralta,Cesc | (ssts)
Cesc Miralta Quartet
Sol De Nit | Fresh Sound Records | FSNT 098 CD
Carretera Austal | Fresh Sound Records | FSNT 149 CD
Elisabet Raspall Grup
Lila | Fresh Sound Records | FSNT 058 CD
Joan Abril Quintet
Eric | Fresh Sound Records | FSNT 092 CD
Joan Abril Sextet
Eric | Fresh Sound Records | FSNT 092 CD

Miralta,Marc | (drtablas)
Cesc Miralta Quartet
Sol De Nit | Fresh Sound Records | FSNT 098 CD
Carretera Austal | Fresh Sound Records | FSNT 149 CD
Elisabet Raspall Grup
Lila | Fresh Sound Records | FSNT 058 CD
Elisabet Raspall Quintet
Triangles | Fresh Sound Records | FSNT 018 CD
George Colligan Quartet
Desire | Fresh Sound Records | FSNT 071 CD
Grant Stewart Quartet
Buen Rollo | Fresh Sound Records | FSNT 053 CD
OAM Trio
Trilingual | Fresh Sound Records | FSNT 070 CD
Pep O'Callaghan Grup
Port O'Clock | Fresh Sound Records | FSNT 069 CD
Seamus Blake-Marc Miralta Trio
Sun Sol | Fresh Sound Records | FSNT 087 CD

Miranda,Andrés | (congas)
Irakere
Yemayá | Blue Note | 498239-2

Miranda,Edgardo | (el-g,quatro,g,coroquarto)
Jerry Gonzalez & Fort Apache Band
The River Is Deep | Enja | ENJ-4040 2

Miranda,Luis | (congas,drperc)
Cal Tjader Quintet
Tjader Plays Mambo | Original Jazz Classics | OJCCD 274-2(F 3221)
The Jazz Giants Play Sammy Cahn:It's Magic | Prestige | PCD 24226-2
Cal Tjader Sextet
Cal Tjader's Latin Kick | Original Jazz Classics | OJCCD 642-2(F 8033)
Cal Tjader's Orchestra
Tjader Plays Mambo | Original Jazz Classics | OJCCD 274-2(F 3221)
Charlie Parker Quintet
Bird: The Complete Charlie Parker On Verve | Verve | 837141-2
Charlie Parker Septet
Talkin' Bird | Verve | 559859-2
Charlie Parker Sextet
Verve Jazz Masters 28:Charlie Parker Plays Standards | Verve | 521854-2
Charlie Parker:The Best Of The Verve Years | Verve | 527815-2
Talkin' Bird | Verve | 559859-2
The Cole Porter Songbook | Verve | 823250-2
Charlie Parker With Machito And His Orchestra
Charlie Parker:The Best Of The Verve Years | Verve | 527815-2
Talkin' Bird | Verve | 559859-2
Bird: The Complete Charlie Parker On Verve | Verve | 837141-2
Charlie Parker:April In Paris | Dreyfus Jazz Line | FDM 36737-2
Charlie Parker's Jazzers
Bird: The Complete Charlie Parker On Verve | Verve | 837141-2

Miranda,Pia | (voc)
Markus Stockhausen Orchestra
Sol Mestizo:Markus Stockhausen Plays The Music Of Enrique Diaz | ACT | 9222-2

Miranda,Rafael | (congas)
Charlie Parker With Machito And His Orchestra
Bird: The Complete Charlie Parker On Verve | Verve | 837141-2

Miranda,Ralph | (perc)
Dizzy Gillespie Group
Verve Jazz Masters 10:Dizzy Gillespie | Verve | 516319-2
Dizzy Gillspie And His Latin American Rhythm
Afro | Verve | 517052-2

Miranda,Santo | (drmedium-kenya-dr)
Herbie Mann Sextet
Verve Jazz Masters 56:Herbie Mann | Verve | 529901-2

Miranda,Tony | (fr-h)
Carmen McRae With The Ralph Burns Orchetra
Birds Of A Feather | Decca | 589515-2
Elliot Lawrence And His Orchestra
The Elliot Lawrence Big Band Swings Cohn & Kahn | Fantasy | FCD 24761-2
Harry Carney And His Orchestra With Strings
Music For Loving:Ben Webster With Strings | Verve | 527774-2
Miles Davis + 19
Miles Ahead | CBS | CK 65121
Miles Davis With Gil Evans & His Orchestra
This Is Jazz:Miles Davis Plays Ballads | CBS | CK 65038
Sketches Of Spain | CBS | CK 65142
Paul Desmond With Strings
Desmond Blue | RCA | 2663898-2
Quincy Jones And His Orchestra
Rahsaan/The Complete Mercury Recordings Of Roland Kirk | Mercury | 846630-2

Miroff,Seymour | (v)
Coleman Hawkins With Billy Byers And His Orchestra
The Hawk In Hi-Fi | RCA | 2663842-2

Mironov,Jeff | (el-gg)
Bob James And His Orchestra
Jazzrock-Anthology Vol.3:Fusion | Zounds | CD 27100555
Dave Grusin Group
Mountain Dance | GRP | GRP 95072
Don Grolnick Group
Hearts And Numbers | VeraBra Records | CDVBR 2016-2
Lee Ritenour Group
Rio | GRP | GRP 95242
Steve Khan Group
Jazzrock-Anthology Vol.3:Fusion | Zounds | CD 27100555

Miskiewicz,Michal | (dr)
Thomas Stanko Quartet
Suspended Night | ECM | 1868(9811244)
Tomasz Stanko Quartet
Soul Of Things | ECM | 1788(016374-2)

Mistry,Jagdish | (v)
Kölner Saxophon Mafia With Guests
Kölner Saxophon Mafia: 20 Jahre Saxuelle Befreiung | Jazz Haus Musik | JHM 0115 CD

Mitchell,Alex | (dr)
Louis Jordan And His Tympany Five
Louis Jordan-Let The Good Times Roll: The Complete Decca Recordings 1938-1954 | Bear Family Records | BCD 15557 IH

Mitchell,Austin | (org)
Arnett Cobb Quintet
Smooth Sailing | Original Jazz Classics | OJCCD 323-2

Mitchell,Billy | (as,fl,b-cl,ts,reedsss)
Al Grey And His Allstars
Snap Your Fingers | Verve | 9860307
Billy Mitchell Quintet
This Is Billy Mitchell | Smash | 065507-2
Billy Mitchell Sextet
This Is Billy Mitchell | Smash | 065507-2
Count Basie And His Orchestra
Jazz Collection:Count Basie | Laserlight | 24368
The Legends Of Swing | Laserlight | 24659
Atomic Swing | Roulette | 497871-2
Breakfast Dance And Barbecue | Roulette | 531791-2
Chairman Of The Board | Roulette | 581664-2
Count On The Coast Vol.1 | Phontastic | NCD 7555
Count On The Coast Vol.2 | Phontastic | NCD 7575
Dizzy Gillespie And His Orchestra
Dizzy Gillespie:Birks Works-The Verve Big Band Sessions | Verve | 527900-2
Ultimate Dizzy Gillespie | Verve | 557535-2
Dizzy Gillespie Orchestra
Verve Jazz Masters 10:Dizzy Gillespie | Verve | 516319-2
Jan Harrington With The Nat Adderley Quintet
Remembering Dinah-A Salute To Dinah Washington | Hot Shot Records | HSR 8313-2
Jimmy McGriff Orchestra
Swingin' The Blues-Jumpin' The Blues | Laserlight | 24654
Joe Ascione Octet
My Buddy:A Tribute To Buddy Rich | Nagel-Heyer | CD 036
Nat Adderley Quintet
Remembering Dinah-A Salute To Dinah Washington | Hot Shot Records | HSR 8313-2
Ray Charles-Milt Jackson Sextet
Soul Brothers/Soul Meeting | Atlantic | 7567-81951-2
Sarah Vaughan And Joe Williams With The Count Basie Orchestra
Jazz Profile | Blue Note | 823517-2
Sarah Vaughan And The Count Basie Orchestra
Ballads | Roulette | 537561-2
Sarah Vaughan And The Thad Jones Orchestra
Verve Jazz Masters 42:Sarah Vaughan-The Jazz Sides | Verve | 526817-2
Sarah Vaughan With The Count Basie Band
Jazz Profile | Blue Note | 823517-2
The New York Allstars
Count Basie Remembered | Nagel-Heyer | CD 031
Count Basie Remembered Vol.2 | Nagel-Heyer | CD 041

Mitchell,Blue | (tp,cofl-h)
Albert King Blues Band
The Lost Session | Stax | SCD 8534-2
Big John Patton Quintet
So Blue So Funky-Heroes Of The Hammond | Blue Note | 796563-2
Blue Mitchell And His Orchestra
Blue Breaks Beats Vol.2 | Blue Note | 789907-2
A Sure Thing | Original Jazz Classics | OJCCD 837-2
The Jazz Giants Play Jerome Kern:Yesterdays | Prestige | PCD 24202-2
Blue Mitchell Quintet
Down With It | Blue Note | 854327-2
Out Of The Blue | Original Jazz Classics | OJCCD 667-2(RLP 1131)
Blue Mitchell Sextet
Blue Mitchell Big 6 | Original Jazz Classics | OJCCD 615-2(RLP 12-273)
Blue Soul | Original Jazz Classics | OJCCD 765-2(RLP 1155)
Bobby Hutcherson Orchestra
Deep Blue-The United States Of Mind | Blue Note | 521152-2
Montara | Blue Note | 590956-2
Cannonball Adderley Quintet
Cannonball Adderley Birthday Celebration | Fantasy | FANCD 6087-2
Portrait Of Cannonball | Original Jazz Classics | OJCCD 361-2(RLP 269)
The Jazz Giants Play Rodgers & Hammerstein:My Favorite Things | Prestige | PCD 24223-2
Charles Kynard Sextet
The Soul Brotherhood | Prestige | PCD 24257-2
Dinah Washington And Her Sextet
Newport Jazz Festival 1958,July 3rd-6th Vol.4:Blues In The Night No.2 | Phontastic | NCD 8816
Dinah Washington With The Newport All Stars
Dinah Sings Bessie Smith | Verve | 538635-2
Freddie Roach Quintet
Good Move | Blue Note | 524551-2
George Benson Quartet + Guests
The George Benson Cookbook | CBS | 502470-2
George Benson Quintet
It's Uptown | CBS | 502469-2
Grant Green Orchestra
Grant Green:Blue Breakbeat | Blue Note | 494705-2
Blue Breaks Beats Vol.2 | Blue Note | 789907-2
So Blue So Funky-Heroes Of The Hammond | Blue Note | 796563-2
Horace Silver Quintet
Blowin' The Blues Away | Blue Note | 495342-2
Horace Silver Retrospective | Blue Note | 495576-2
Song For My Father | Blue Note | 499002-2
True Blue | Blue Note | 534032-2
Finger Poppin' | Blue Note | 542304-2
Silver's Serenade | Blue Note | 821288-2
The Tokyo Blues | Blue Note | 853355-2
Paris Blues | Pablo | PACD 5316-2
Jack McDuff Orchestra
The Last Goodun' | Prestige | PRCD 24274-2
Jackie McLean Quintet
Capuchin Swing | Blue Note | 540033-2
Jimmy McGriff Organ Blues Band
The Worm | Blue Note | 538699-2
Jimmy Smith With Orchestra
Verve Jazz Masters 29:Jimmy Smith | Verve | 521855-2
Lou Donaldson Quintet
Midnight Creeper | Blue Note | 524546-2
Mr.Shing-A-Ling | Blue Note | 784271-2
The Lost Grooves | Blue Note | 831883-2
Lou Donaldson Sextet
So Blue So Funky-Heroes Of The Hammond | Blue Note | 796563-2
Louie Bellson Septet
Louie Bellson Jam | Original Jazz Classics | OJCCD 802-2(2310838)
Mar Murphy With The Ernie Wilkins Orchestra
RAH | Original Jazz Classics | OJCCD 141-2(R 9395)
Mel Rhyne Sextet
Organ-izing | Original Jazz Classics | OJCCD 1055-2(JLP 916)
Philly Joe Jones Big Band
Cannonball Adderley Birthday Celebration | Fantasy | FANCD 6087-2
Red Garland Quintet
Red's Good Groove | Original Jazz Classics | OJCCD 1064-2(987)
Sam Jones Plus 10
Cannonball Adderley Birthday Celebration | Fantasy | FANCD 6087-2
Sonny Red (Kyner) Quintet
Red,Blue & Green | Milestone | MCD 47086-2
Stanley Turrentine And His Orchestra
The Lost Grooves | Blue Note | 831883-2
Stanley Turrentine Orchestra
Rough 'N' Tumble | Blue Note | 524552-2
The Spoiler | Blue Note | 853359-2
Yusef Lateef Orchestra
The Blue Yusef Lateef | Rhino | 8122-73717-2

Mitchell,Bob | (tp)
Count Basie And His Orchestra
Fun Time | Pablo | 2310945-2
Jazz Dance | Original Jazz Classics | OJCCD 1002-2(1210890)
I Told You So | Original Jazz Classics | OJCCD 824-2(2310767)
The Jazz Giants Play Harry Warren:Lullaby Of Broadway | Prestige | PCD 24204-2
Count Basie Big Band
Montreux '77 | Original Jazz Classics | OJCCD 377-2
Jimmy Lunceford And His Orchestra
The Legends Of Swing | Laserlight | 24659
Louis Jordan And His Tympany Five
Louis Jordan-Let The Good Times Roll: The Complete Decca Recordings 1938-1954 | Bear Family Records | BCD 15557 IH
Louis Jordan With The Nelson Riddle Orchestra
Louis Jordan-Let The Good Times Roll: The Complete Decca Recordings 1938-1954 | Bear Family Records | BCD 15557 IH

Mitchell,David | (g)
Mitchell-Terraza Group
Shell Blues | Fresh Sound Records | FSNT 005 CD

Mitchell,Emily | (harp)
Lew Soloff Quintet
With A Song In My Heart | Milestone | MCD 9290-2

Mitchell,Frank | (tpts)
Andrew Hill Sextet
Grass Roots | Blue Note | 522672-2
Lee Morgan Quintet
The Sixth Sense | Blue Note | 522467-2
Lee Morgan Sextet
The Sixth Sense | Blue Note | 522467-2

Mitchell,George | (b,cotp)
Earl Hines And His Orchestra
Jazz:The Essential Collection Vol.2 | IN+OUT Records | 78012-2
Jelly Roll Morton's Red Hot Peppers
Planet Jazz:Jelly Roll Morton | Planet Jazz | 2152060-2
Planet Jazz Sampler | Planet Jazz | 2152326-2
Jazz:The Essential Collection Vol.1 | IN+OUT Records | 78011-2

Mitchell,Grover | (tb)
Count Basie And His Orchestra
Verve Jazz Masters 2:Count Basie | Verve | 519819-2
Basie Meets Bond | Capitol | 538225-2
Basie's Beatle Bag | Verve | 557455-2
Live at The Sands | Reprise | 9362-45946-2
88 Basie Street | Original Jazz Classics | OJC 808(2310901)
Fancy Pants | Original Jazz Classics | OJCCD 1038-2(2310920)
Count Basie Big Band
Farmers Market Barbecue | Original Jazz Classics | OJCCD 732-2(2310874)
Ella Fitzgerald With The Count Basie Orchestra
Ella Fitzgerald-First Lady Of Song | Verve | 517898-2
Ella And Basie | Verve | 539059-2
Frank Sinatra With The Count Basie Orchestra
It Might As Well Be Spring | Reprise | 7599-27027-2
Sarah Vaughan And The Count Basie Orchestra
Sarah Vaughan Birthday Celebration | Fantasy | FANCD 6090-2
Zoot Sims With Orchestra
Passion Flower | Original Jazz Classics | OJCCD 939-2(2312120)

Mitchell,Harold | (tp)
Louis Jordan And His Tympany Five
Louis Jordan-Let The Good Times Roll: The Complete Decca Recordings 1938-1954 | Bear Family Records | BCD 15557 IH

Mitchell,Herman | (g)
Jimmy Witherspoon And His Band
Baby, Baby, Baby | Original Blues Classics | OBCCD 527-2(P 7290)

Mitchell,Jimmy | (as,vocts)
Erskine Hawkins And His Orchestra
Planet Jazz:Big Bands | Planet Jazz | 2169649-2

Mitchell,John | (bjg)
Bill Coleman Quintet
Americans Swinging In Paris:Bill Coleman-The Elegance | EMI Records | 539662-2
Jimmy Lunceford And His Orchestra
The Legends Of Swing | Laserlight | 24659
Willie Lewis And His Entertainers
Americans Swinging In Paris:Benny Carter | EMI Records | 539647-2

Mitchell,Ollie | (tp,fl-hv)
Billy May And His Orchestra With Members Of The Jimmy Lunceford Orchestra
Great Swing Classics In Hi-Fi | Capitol | 521223-2
Buddy Rich Big Band
The New One! | Pacific Jazz | 494507-2
Harry James And His Orchestra
Trumpet Blues:The Best Of Harry James | Capitol | 521224-2
Johnny Hartman And His Orchestra
Unforgettable | Impulse(MCA) | IMP 11522
June Christy With The Pete Rugolo Orchestra
Something Cool(The Complete Mono & Stereo Versions) | Capitol | 534069-2
Pete Rugolo And His Orchestra
Thriller/Richard Diamon(Original Jazz Scores From 2 Classics TV Series) | Fresh Sound Records | FSCD 2015

Mitchell,Paul | (parr)
Tommy Dorsey And His Orchestra
Planet Jazz:Tommy Dorsey | Planet Jazz | 2159972-2

Mitchell,Red | (b,vocp)
André Previn' s Jazz Trio
King Size! | Original Jazz Classics | OJCCD 691-2(S 7570)
Art Pepper Quartet
Art Pepper:The Complete Galaxy Recordings | Galaxy | 16GCD 1016-2
Straight Life | Original Jazz Classics | OJCCD 475-2
Art Pepper Quintet
Art Pepper:The Complete Galaxy Recordings | Galaxy | 16GCD 1016-2
Straight Life | Original Jazz Classics | OJCCD 475-2
Barney Kessel And His Orchestra
The Jazz Giants Play Rodgers & Hart:Blue Moon | Prestige | PCD 24205-2
Barney Kessel And His Quintet
To Swing Or Not To Swing | Original Jazz Classics | OJCCD 317-2
Barney Kessel And His Septet
To Swing Or Not To Swing | Original Jazz Classics | OJCCD 317-2
Ben Webster Quintet
At The Renaissance | Original Jazz Classics | OJC 390(C 7646)
Bill Perkins-Richie Kamuca Quintet
Midnight Blue(The [Be]witching Hour) | Blue Note | 854365-2
Billie Holiday And Her All Stars
Verve Jazz Masters 12:Billie Holiday | Verve | 519825-2
Songs For Distingué Lovers | Verve | 539056-2
Billie's Blues | Blue Note | 748786-2
Billie Holiday And Her Band
Verve Jazz Masters 47:Billie Holiday Sings Standards | Verve | 527650-2
Billie Holiday With The Carl Drinkard Trio
Misty Blue:Sweet Sisters Swing Songs Of Sorrow And Sadness | Blue Note | 521151-2
Billie's Blues | Blue Note | 748786-2
Cal Tjader Quartet
Cal Tjader Plays Harold Arlen & West Side Story | Fantasy | FCD 24775-2
Cal Tjader With The Clare Fischer Orchestra
Cal Tjader Plays Harold Arlen & West Side Story | Fantasy | FCD 24775-2
Cal Tjader's Orchestra
Talkin Verve/Roots Of Acid Jazz:Cal Tjader | Verve | 531562-2
Clark Terry-Red Mitchell Duo
Clark Terry-Red Mitchell | Enja | ENJ-5011 2

Ella Fitzgerald And Her Sextet
Ella Fitzgerald-First Lady Of Song | Verve | 517898-2
Ella Fitzgerald With The Marty Paich Orchestra
Get Happy! | Verve | 523321-2
Gerry Mulligan Quartet
Gerry Mulligan:Pleyel Concert Vol.1 | Vogue | 21409422
Gerry Mulligan:Pleyel Concert Vol.2 | Vogue | 21409432
Planet Jazz:Gerry Mulligan | Planet Jazz | 2152070-2
Planet Jazz Sampler | Planet Jazz | 2152326-2
Planet Jazz:Jazz Saxophone | Planet Jazz | 2169653-2
Gus Mancuso Quintet
Gus Mancuso & Special Friends | Fantasy | FCD 24762-2
Hampton Hawes Quartet
Four!! | Original Jazz Classics | OJCCD 165-2
Hampton Hawes Trio
The Trio-Vol.1 | Original Jazz Classics | OJC 316(C 3515)
Hampton Hawes Trio Vol.1 | Original Jazz Classics | OJC20 316-2(C 3505)
The Trio Vol.2 | Original Jazz Classics | OJCCD 318-2
The Jazz Giants Play Jerome Kern:Yesterdays | Prestige | PCD 24202-2
The Jazz Giants Play Rodgers & Hart:Blue Moon | Prestige | PCD 24205-2
Jimmy Raney Quartet
Jimmy Raney Visits Paris Vol.1 | Vogue | 21409352
Jimmy Raney Quintet
Early Stan | Original Jazz Classics | OJCCD 654-2(P 7255)
Jimmy Rowles Trio
The Complete Nocturne Recordings:Jazz In Hollywood Series Vol.1 | Fresh Sound Records | NR 3CD-101
Lennie Niehaus Quintet
Lennie Niehaus Vol.1:The Quintets | Original Jazz Classics | OJCCD 1933-2(C 3518)
Lyke Ritz Quartet
How About Uke? | Verve | 0760942
Lyke Ritz Trio
How About Uke? | Verve | 0760942
Lyle Ritz Quartet
How About Uke? | Verve | 0760942
Maynard Ferguson Band
Verve Jazz Masters 52:Maynard Ferguson | Verve | 529905-2
Ornette Coleman Quartet
Tomorrow Is The Question | Original Jazz Classics | OJC20 342-2(S 7569)
Pete Rugolo And His Orchestra
Thriller/Richard Diamon(Original Jazz Scores From 2 Classics TV Series) | Fresh Sound Records | FSCD 2015
Red Norvo Sextet
Music To Listen To Red Norvo By | Original Jazz Classics | OJCCD 1015-2(C 7534)
Stan Kenton And His Orchestra
Adventures In Blues | Capitol | 520089-2
Adventures In Jazz | Capitol | 521222-2
Stuff Smith Quartet
Cat On A Hot Fiddle | Verve | 9861487
Tal Farlow Quartet
Verve Jazz Masters 41:Tal Farlow | Verve | 527365-2

Mitchell,Robert | (ptp)
Steve Coleman And Five Elements
The Sonic Language Of Myth | RCA | 2164123-2

Mitchell,Roscoe | (as,bass-sax,voc,piccolo,ts,as-solo)
Art Ensemble Of Chicago
Nice Guys | ECM | 1126
Full Force | ECM | 1167(829197-2)
Urban Bushmen | ECM | 1211/12
The Third Decade | ECM | 1273
Tribute To Lester | ECM | 1808(017066-2)
Americans Swinging In Paris:Art Ensemble Of Chicago | EMI Records | 539667-2
Bap-Tizum | Atlantic | 7567-80757-2
Coming Home Jamaica | Dreyfus Jazz Line | FDM 37003-2
Roscoe Mitchell And The Note Factory
Nine To Get Ready | ECM | 1651(539725-2)

Mitchell,Shedrick | (p)
Melissa Walker And Her Band
I Saw The Sky | Enja | ENJ-9409 2

Mitchell,Tom | (b-tbtb)
Billie Holiday With The Ray Ellis Orchestra
Lady In Satin | CBS | CK 65144
Cab Calloway And His Orchestra
Planet Jazz:Cab Calloway | Planet Jazz | 2161237-2
Planet Jazz:Male Jazz Vocalists | Planet Jazz | 2169657-2
Chubby Jackson And His All Star Big Band
Chubby Takes Over | Fresh Sound Records | FSR-CD 324
Coleman Hawkins With Billy Byers And His Orchestra
Planet Jazz:Coleman Hawkins | Planet Jazz | 2152055-2
The Hawk In Hi-Fi | RCA | 2663842-2
Dinah Washington With The Quincy Jones Orchestra
Verve Jazz Masters 40:Dinah Washington | Verve | 522055-2
The Swingin' Miss 'D' | Verve | 558074-2
George Russell And His Orchestra
George Russell New York N.Y. | Impulse(MCA) | 951278-2
Hank Jones With Oliver Nelson's Orchestra
The Roots Of Acid Jazz | Impulse(MCA) | IMP 12042
J.J.Johnson And His Orchestra
Planet Jazz:J.J.Johnson | Planet Jazz | 2159974-2
J.J.Johnson's All Stars
J.J.'s Broadway | Verve | 9860308
Jimmy Smith With The Billy Byers Orchestra
Jimmy Smith:Best Of The Verve Years | Verve | 527950-2
Jimmy Smith With The Oliver Nelson Orchestra
Verve Jazz Masters 29:Jimmy Smith | Verve | 521855-2
Jimmy Smith:Best Of The Verve Years | Verve | 527950-2
Leon Thomas With Orchestra
Spirits Known And Unknown | RCA | 2663876-2
Lucy Reed With Orchestra
This Is Lucy Reed | Original Jazz Classics | OJCCD 1943-2(F 3243)
Miles Davis + 19
Miles Ahead | CBS | CK 65121
Miles Davis With Gil Evans & His Orchestra
This Is Jazz:Miles Davis Plays Ballads | CBS | CK 65038
Quincy Jones And His Orchestra
The Quintessence | Impulse(MCA) | 951222-2
Stan Getz With The Eddie Sauter Orchestra
Stan Getz Plays The Music Of Mickey One | Verve | 531232-2

Mitchell,Tyler | (b)
Jon Hendricks Group
A Tribute To Charlie Parker Vol.2 | Storyville | 4960493
Shirley Horn Quartet
Light Out Of Darkness(A Tribute To Ray Charles) | Verve | 519703-2
Shirley Horn Quintet
Light Out Of Darkness(A Tribute To Ray Charles) | Verve | 519703-2
Taylor's Wailers
Mr. A.T. | Enja | ENJ-7017 2

Mitchell's Christian Singers: |
Mitchell's Christian Singers
From Spiritual To Swing | Vanguard | VCD 169/71

Mitschele,Klaus | (tp)
Kurt Edelhagen All Stars
Deutsches Jazz Fesival 1954/1955 | Bear Family Records | BCD 15430
Kurt Edelhagen All Stars Und Solisten
Deutsches Jazz Fesival 1954/1955 | Bear Family Records | BCD 15430
Quartet Der Kurt Edelhagen All Stars
Deutsches Jazz Fesival 1954/1955 | Bear Family Records | BCD 15430

Mixon,Danny | (orgp)
Charles Mingus Orchestra
Cumbia & Jazz Fusion | Atlantic | 8122-71785-2
Hank Crawford Quartet
The World Of Hank Crawford | Milestone | MCD 9304-2
Hank Crawford Quintet
After Dark | Milestone | MCD 9279-2
The World Of Hank Crawford | Milestone | MCD 9304-2
The Jazz Giants Play Sammy Cahn:It's Magic | Prestige | PCD 24226-2
Hank Crawford Septet
The World Of Hank Crawford | Milestone | MCD 9304-2

Mizell,Fonce | (clavinet,voc,keyboards,tpsolina)
Bobbi Humphrey
Blue Break Beats | Blue Note | 799106-2
Bobbi Humphrey Group
Blue Breaks Beats Vol.2 | Blue Note | 789907-2
Donald Byrd & His Orchestra
Blue Breaks Beats Vol.2 | Blue Note | 789907-2
Donald Byrd Orchestra
Black Byrd | Blue Note | 784466-2
Places And Spaces | Blue Note | 854326-2

Mizell,Larry | (arr,comp,voc,el-p,synth,cond,p)
Black Byrd | Blue Note | 784466-2
Places And Spaces | Blue Note | 854326-2

Miziallaoua,Khliff | (gvoc)
Karim Ziad Groups
Ifrikya | ACT | 9282-2

MJQ | (Modern Jazz Quartet)
Modern Jazz Quartet
To Bags...With Love:Memorial Album | Pablo | 2310967-2
The Complete Modern Jazz Quartet Prestige & Pablo Recordings | Prestige | 4PRCD 4438-2
The Modern Jazz Quartet At Music Inn With Sonny Rollins,Vol.2 | Atlantic | 7567-80794-2
Blues On Bach | Atlantic | 7567-81393-2
MJQ 40 | Atlantic | 7567-82330-2
Lonely Woman | Atlantic | 7567-90665-2
Rhino Presents The Atlantic Jazz Gallery | Atlantic | 8122-71257-2
Pyramid | Rhino | 812273679-2
Fontessa | Rhino | 8122-73687-2
Milt Jackson Birthday Celebration | Fantasy | FANCD 6079-2
Concorde | Original Jazz Classics | OJC20 002-2
Django | Original Jazz Classics | OJC20 057-2
Topsy-This One's For Basie | Original Jazz Classics | OJCCD 1073-2(2310917)
MJQ | Original Jazz Classics | OJCCD 125-2
Together Again | Pablo | PACD20 244-2(2308244)
The Jazz Giants Play Cole Porter:Night And Day | Prestige | PCD 24203-2
Modern Jazz Quartet & Guests
MJQ 40 | Atlantic | 7567-82330-2
Modern Jazz Quartet And Laurindo Almeida
MJQ 40 | Atlantic | 7567-82330-2
Modern Jazz Quartet And Orchestra
MJQ 40 | Atlantic | 7567-82330-2
Modern Jazz Quartet And Symphony Orchestra
MJQ 40 | Atlantic | 7567-82330-2
Modern Jazz Quartet And The Swingle Singers
MJQ 40 | Atlantic | 7567-82330-2
Modern Jazz Quartet feat.Jimmy Giuffre
MJQ 40 | Atlantic | 7567-82330-2
Modern Jazz Quartet With Sonny Rollins
The Modern Jazz Quartet At Music Inn With Sonny Rollins,Vol.2 | Atlantic | 7567-80794-2
MJQ 40 | Atlantic | 7567-82330-2
Paul Desmond And The Modern Jazz Quartet
MJQ 40 | Atlantic | 7567-82330-2
Sonny Rollins With The Modern Jazz Quartet
The Complete Modern Jazz Quartet Prestige & Pablo Recordings | Prestige | 4PRCD 4438-2
Milt Jackson Birthday Celebration | Fantasy | FANCD 6079-2
Sonny Rollins With The Modern Jazz Quartet | Original Jazz Classics | OJCCD 011-2
The Jazz Giants Play Duke Ellington:Caravan | Prestige | PCD 24227-2

Moberg,Per | (flbs)
Tim Hagans With Norrbotten Big Band
Future Miles | ACT | 9235-2

Mobley,Hank | (pts)
Art Blakey And The Jazz Messengers
Horace Silver Retrospective | Blue Note | 495576-2
At The Cafe Bohemia Vol.1 | Blue Note | 532148-2
At The Cafe Bohemia Vol.2 | Blue Note | 532149-2
The Jazz Messengers | CBS | CK 65265
Dizzy Gillespie And His Orchestra
Afro | Verve | 517052-2
Dizzy Gillespie Quintet
Diz And Getz | Verve | 549749-2
Donald Brown Quintet
Donald Byrd & Doug Watkins:The Tradition Sessions | Blue Note | 540528-2
Donald Byrd Orchestra With Voices
True Blue | Blue Note | 534032-2
The Best Of Blue Note | Blue Note | 796110-2
Donald Byrd Quintet
Blue Bossa | Blue Note | 795590-2
Donald Byrd Septet + Voices
A New Perspective | Blue Note | 499006-2
Donald Byrd Sextet
Donald Byrd & Doug Watkins:The Tradition Sessions | Blue Note | 540528-2
Blue Breaks Beats Vol.2 | Blue Note | 789907-2
Blue Break Beats | Blue Note | 799106-2
Blackjack | Blue Note | 821286-2
Doug Watkins Sextet
Donald Byrd & Doug Watkins:The Tradition Sessions | Blue Note | 540528-2
Elmo Hope Sextet
John Coltrane-The Prestige Recordings | Prestige | 16 PCD 4405-2
Freddie Roach Quintet
Good Move | Blue Note | 524551-2
Hank Mobley Quartet
Soul Station | Blue Note | 495343-2
Workout | Blue Note | 784080-2
Hank Mobley Quintet
Hank Mobley | Blue Note | 0675622
The Art Of Saxophone | Laserlight | 24652
Deep Blue-The United States Of Mind | Blue Note | 521152-2
No Room For Squares | Blue Note | 524539-2
The Turnaround | Blue Note | 524540-2
True Blue | Blue Note | 534032-2
Roll Call | Blue Note | 540030-2)
Workout | Blue Note | 784080-2
Blue Bossa | Blue Note | 795590-2
Hank Mobley Sextet
The Flip | Blue Note | 593872-2
Herbie Hancock Quintet
Herbie Hancock:The Complete Blue Note Sixties Sessions | Blue Note | 495569-2
Herbie Hancock Septet
Herbie Hancock:The Complete Blue Note Sixties Sessions | Blue Note | 495569-2
My Point Of View | Blue Note | 521226-2
Cantaloupe Island | Blue Note | 829331-2
Herbie Hancock Sextet
Herbie Hancock:The Complete Blue Note Sixties Sessions | Blue Note | 495569-2
Horace Silver Quintet
Horace Silver Retrospective | Blue Note | 495576-2
Six Pieces Of Silver | Blue Note | 525648-2
Stylings Of Silver | Blue Note | 540034-2
The Best Of Blue Note Vol.2 | Blue Note | 797960-2
J.J.Johnson Quintet
The Eminent J.J.Johnson Vol.2 | Blue Note | 532144-2
Jackie McLean Sextet
4, 5 And 6 | Original Jazz Classics | OJC 056(P 7048)
Johnny Griffin Septet
A Blowing Session | Blue Note | 0677191
Trane's Blues | Blue Note | 498240-2
Kenny Dorham Octet
Afro-Cuban | Blue Note | 0675619
Kenny Dorham Orchestra
Blue Bossa | Blue Note | 795590-2
Kenny Dorham Quintet
Whistle Stop | Blue Note | 525646-2
Max Roach Quartet
Clifford Brown-Max Roach:Alone Together-The Best Of The Mercury Years | Verve | 526373-2
Miles Davis Quintet
Ballads | CBS | 461099-2
Circle In The Round | CBS | 467898-2
Miles Davis In Person-Friday Night At The Blackhawk,San Francisco,Vol.1 | CBS | C4K 87106
Miles Davis At Carnegie Hall | CBS | CK 65027
This Is Jazz:Miles Davis Plays Ballads | CBS | CK 65038
Someday My Prince Will Come | CBS | CK 65919
Miles Davis Sextet
Someday My Prince Will Come | CBS | CK 65919
Prestige All Stars
John Coltrane-The Prestige Recordings | Prestige | 16 PCD 4405-2
Tenor Conclave | Original Jazz Classics | OJCCD 127-2
Sonny Clark All Stars
Dial S For Sonny | Blue Note | 0675621
Sonny Clark Quintet
My Conception | Blue Note | 522674-2
Wynton Kelly Trio With Hank Mobley
Live at The Left Bank Jazz Society,Baltimore,1967 | Fresh Sound Records | FSCD 1031

Möbus,Frank | (el-gg)
Carlos Bica & Azul
Look What They've Done To My Song | Enja | ENJ-9458 2
Carlos Bica Group
Azul | Traumton Records | 4425-2
Der Rote Bereich
Love Me Tender | ACT | 9286-2
Risky Business | ACT | 9407-2
Der Rote Bereich 3 | Jazz 4 Ever Records:Jazz Network | J4E 4740
Erdmann 2000
Recovering From y2k | Jazz 4 Ever Records:Jazz Network | J4E 4750
Ernst Bier-Mack Goldsbury Quartet
At Night When You Go To Sleep | Timescrapper | TSCR 9611
Ernst Bier-Mack Goldsbury Quintet
At Night When You Go To Sleep | Timescrapper | TSCR 9611
Horst Faigle's Jazzkrement
Gans Normal | Jazz 4 Ever Records:Jazz Network | J4E 4748
Rainer Tempel Big Band
Melodies Of '98 | Jazz 4 Ever Records:Jazz Network | J4E 4744
Album 03 | Jazz 'n' Arts Records | JNA 1102
Thomas Stiffling Group
Stories | Jazz 4 Ever Records:Jazz Network | J4E 4756

Moch,Manfred 'Mannie' | (tp)
Albert Mangelsdorff With The NDR Big Band
NDR Big Band-Bravissimo | ACT | 9232-2
Chet Baker With The NDR-Bigband
NDR Big Band-Bravissimo | ACT | 9232-2
My Favourite Songs: The Last Great Concert Vol.1 | Enja | ENJ-5097 2
The Last Concert Vol.I+II | Enja | ENJ-6074 22
Chet Baker-The Legacy Vol.1 | Enja | ENJ-9021 2
Heinz Sauer Quartet With The NDR Big Band
NDR Big Band-Bravissimo | ACT | 9232-2
Joe Pass With The NDR Big Band
Joe Pass In Hamburg | ACT | 9100-2
NDR Big Band-Bravissimo | ACT | 9232-2
Joe Pass With The NDR Big Band And Radio Philharmonie Hannover
Joe Pass In Hamburg | ACT | 9100-2
Johnny Griffin With The NDR Big Band
NDR Big Band-Bravissimo | ACT | 9232-2
NDR Big Band
NDR Big Band-Bravissimo | ACT | 9232-2

Möck,Uli 'Ull' | (keyboards,pprogramming)
Frank Kuruc Band
Limits No Limits | Edition Musikat | EDM 023
Lucas Heidepriem Quartet
Voicings | IN+OUT Records | 7011-2
Marco Piludu International Quartet
New York Travels | Jazz 4 Ever Records:Jazz Network | J4E 4733
Peter Lehel Quartet
Heavy Rotation | Satin Doll Productions | SDP 1024-1 CD
Ull Möck Trio
Drilling | Satin Doll Productions | SDP 1023-1 CD

Mockunas,Liudas | (bs)
European Jazz Youth Orchestra
Swinging Europe 1 | dacapo | DCCD 9449
Swinging Europe 2 | dacapo | DCCD 9450

Modern Jazz Disciples |
The Modern Jazz Disciples
Disciples Blues | Prestige | PCD 24263-2

Modern Jazz Sextet,The |
Modern Jazz Sextet
Verve Jazz Masters 50:Sonny Sitt | Verve | 527651-2
The Modern Jazz Sextet | Verve | 559834-2

Modern Jazz Society |
The Modern Jazz Society
A Concert Of Contemporary Music | Verve | 559827-2

Modernaires,The | (voc-group)
Glenn Miller And His Orchestra
The Ultimate Glenn Miller-22 Original Hits From The King Of Swing | RCA | 2113137-2
Planet Jazz:Glenn Miller | Planet Jazz | 2152056-2
Planet Jazz:Jazz Greatest Hits | Planet Jazz | 2169648-2
Planet Jazz:Big Bands | Planet Jazz | 2169649-2
Candlelight Miller | RCA | 2668716-2
The Glenn Miller Story Vol. 3 | RCA | ND 89222
Swing Legends | Nimbus Records | NI 2001

Moffat,Ian | (tb)
André Holst With Chris Dean's European Swing Orchestra
That's Swing | Nagel-Heyer | CD 079

Moffett,Charles | (dr,perc,orchestra-vib,tpvib)
Archie Shepp Sextet
Four For Trane | Impulse(MCA) | 951218-2
Ornette Coleman Trio
At The Golden Circle Vol.One | Blue Note | 535518-2

Moffett,Charnett | (b,el-bpiccolo-b-g)
Arturo Sandoval Quartet
I Remember Clifford | GRP | GRP 96682
Arturo Sandoval Quintet
I Remember Clifford | GRP | GRP 96682
Courtney Pine Group
Modern Day Jazz Stories | Verve | 529028-2
Dianne Reeves With Band
Misty Blue:Sweet Sisters Swing Songs Of Sorrow And Sadness | Blue Note | 521151-2
I Remember | Blue Note | 790264-2
Kenny Garrett Quartet
KG Standard Of Language | Warner | 9362-48404-2
Pharoah Sanders Orchestra
Message From Home | Verve | 529578-2
Stanley Jordan Quartet
Live In New York | Blue Note | 497810-2
Stanley Jordan Trio
Festival International De Jazz De Montreal | Spectra | 9811660

INTERPRETENVERZEICHNIS

Vince Jones With The Benny Green Quartet
One Day Spent | Intuition Records | INT 3087-2

Mogensen,Anders | (dr,perc,DW-drcymbals)
Copenhagen Art Ensemble
Shape To Twelve | dacapo | DCCD 9430
Angels' Share | dacapo | DCCD 9452
Marilyn Mazur With Ars Nova And The Copenhagen Art Ensemble
Jordsange | dacapo | DCCD 9454
The Crossover Ensemble
The River:Image Of Time And Life | dacapo | DCCD 9434
When Granny Sleeps
Welcome | dacapo | DCCD 9447

Mohamed,Menni | (percvoc)
Karim Ziad Groups
Ifrikya | ACT | 9282-2

Mohr,Hans-Jürgen | (viola)
Bernd Konrad Jazz Group With Symphonie Orchestra
Wen Die Götter Lieben | Creative Works Records | CW CD 1010-1

Mohr,Maike | (psynth)
Jazz Orchester Rheinland-Pfalz
Kazzou | Jazz Haus Musik | LJBB 9104
Like Life | Jazz Haus Musik | LJBB 9405
Last Season | Jazz Haus Musik | LJBB 9706

Möhring,Michel | (g,berimbau,balafon,perctimbales)
Marion Brown & Jazz Cussion
Echoes Of Blue | double moon | CHRDM 71015

Mojo Bluesband,The |
Axel Zwingenberger With The Mojo Blues Band And Red Holloway
Axel Zwingenberger And The Friends Of Boogie Woogie,Vol.8 | Vagabond | VRCD 8.93019

Mokatsian,Hovhannes | (v)
HR Big Band With Marjorie Barnes And Frits Landesbergen And Strings
Swinging Christmas | hr music.de | hrmj 012-02 CD

Mokross,Benny | (drperc)
Peter Materna Quartet
Full Moon Party | Village | VILCD 1021-2

Molbak,Erik | (b)
Brew Moore Quartet
No More Brew | Storyville | STCD 8275

Mole,John | (b-g)
Barbara Thompson's Paraphernalia
Barbara Thompson's Special Edition | VeraBra Records | CDVBR 2017-2

Mole,Miff | (tb)
Miff Mole And His Dixieland Band
Muggsy Spanier-Manhattan Masters,1945 | Storyville | STCD 6051
Red And Miff's Stompers
Planet Jazz:Jazz Trumpet | Planet Jazz | 2169654-2

Molgaard,Torolf | (tb)
HR Big Band
The American Songs Of Kurt Weill | hr music.de | hrmj 006-01 CD
Libertango:Homage An Astor Piazolla | hr music.de | hrmj 014-02 CD
HR Big Band With Marjorie Barnes And Frits Landesbergen
Swinging Christmas | hr music.de | hrmj 012-02 CD
HR Big Band With Marjorie Barnes And Frits Landesbergen And Strings
Swinging Christmas | hr music.de | hrmj 012-02 CD
Stan Kenton With The Danish Radio Big Band
Stan Kenton With The Danish Radio Big Band | Storyville | STCD 8340
The Three Sopranos With The HR Big Band
The Three Sopranos | hr music.de | hrmj 001-01 CD

Molin,Ole | (g)
Stan Kenton With The Danish Radio Big Band
Stan Kenton With The Danish Radio Big Band | Storyville | STCD 8340

Molineaux,Othello | (steel-dr)
Ahmad Jamal Quartet
Nature(The Essence Part III) | Atlantic | 3984-23105-2
Nature | Dreyfus Jazz Line | FDM 37018-2
Ahmad Jamal Quartet With Stanley Turrentine
Nature(The Essence Part III) | Atlantic | 3984-23105-2
Nature | Dreyfus Jazz Line | FDM 37018-2
Ahmad Jamal-Othello Molineaux
Nature(The Essence Part III) | Atlantic | 3984-23105-2

Molinetti,Armand | (dr)
Don Byas And His Orchestra
Don Byas:Laura | Dreyfus Jazz Line | FDM 36714-2
Sidney Bechet All Stars
Planet Jazz:Sidney Bechet | Planet Jazz | 2152063-2
Planet Jazz Sampler | Planet Jazz | 2152326-2

Möller,Ale | (fl,mand,perc,folk-harp)
Lena Willemark-Ale Möller Group
Nordan | ECM | 1536(523161-2)
Agram | ECM | 1610
Per Gudmundson-Ale Möller-Lene Willemark
Frifot | ECM | 1690(557653-2)
Robin Williamson Group
Skirting The River Road | ECM | 1785(016372-2

Moller,Jorgen | (co)
Leonardo Pedersen's Jazzkapel
The Golden Years Of Revival Jazz,Sampler | Storyville | 109 1001
The Golden Years Of Revival Jazz,Vol.11 | Storyville | STCD 5516
Papa Benny's Jazzband
The Golden Years Of Revival Jazz,Vol.2 | Storyville | STCD 5507

Moller,Lars | (reedsts)
The Orchestra
New Skies | dacapo | DCCD 9463

Moller,Paul Martin | (ts)
Stan Getz With Ib Glindemann And His Orchestra
Stan Getz In Europe | Laserlight | 24657

Moller,Thorkild | (dr)
Papa Benny's Jazzband
The Golden Years Of Revival Jazz,Vol.7 | Storyville | STCD 5512
The Golden Years Of Revival Jazz,Vol.11 | Storyville | STCD 5516
Ricardo's Jazzmen
The Golden Years Of Revival Jazz,Sampler | Storyville | 109 1001
The Golden Years Of Revival Jazz,Vol.4 | Storyville | STCD 5509
The Golden Years Of Revival Jazz,Vol.5 | Storyville | STCD 5510

Molster,Morten | (g)
Nils Petter Molvaer Group
Khmer | ECM | 1560(537798-2)

Möltgen,Peter | (flpiccolo)
Peter Möltgen Quartet
Mellow Acid | Edition Collage | EC 495-2

Molvaer,Nils Petter | (tp,fl-h,perc,g,b-g,samples,p,synth)
Jon Balke w/Oslo 13
Nonsentration | ECM | 1445
Ketil Bjornstad Group
Seafarer's Song | EmArCy | 9865777
Marilyn Mazur's Future Song
Small Labyrinths | ECM | 1559(533679-2)
Marilyn Mazure's Future Song | VeraBra Records | CDVBR 2105-2
Masqualero
Bande A Part | ECM | 1319
Aero | ECM | 1367
Re-Enter | ECM | 1437(847939-2)
Nils Petter Molvaer Group
Khmer | ECM | 1560(537798-2)
Solid Ether | ECM | 1722(543365-2)
Elegy For Africa | Nabel Records:Jazz Network | CD 4678
Sidsel Endresen Quartet
So I Write | ECM | 1408(841776-2)
Sidsel Endresen Sextet
Exile | ECM | 1524(521721-2)

Mombelli,Carlo | (b,clay-dr,voicefretless-b)
Raiz De Pedra
Diario De Bordo | TipToe | TIP-888822 2
Raiz De Pedra feat. Egberto Gismonti
Diario De Bordo | TipToe | TIP-888822 2

Moments Quartet |
Moments Quartet
Original Moments | Fresh Sound Records | FSNT 052 CD

Moncur III,Grachan | (tb)
Archie Shepp Orchestra
Mama Too Tight | Impulse(MCA) | 951248-2
Archie Shepp Septet
The Way Ahead | Impulse(MCA) | 951272-2
Archie Shepp Sextet
The Way Ahead | Impulse(MCA) | 951272-2
Cassandra Wilson And Her Quintet
Point Of View | JMT Edition | 919004-2
Grachan Moncur III Quintet
A Blue Conception | Blue Note | 534254-2
Herbie Hancock Septet
Herbie Hancock:The Complete Blue Note Sixties Sessions | Blue Note | 495569-2
My Point Of View | Blue Note | 521226-2
Cantaloupe Island | Blue Note | 829331-2
Herbie Hancock Sextet
Herbie Hancock:The Complete Blue Note Sixties Sessions | Blue Note | 495569-2
Jackie McLean Quintet
A Blue Conception | Blue Note | 534254-2
Joe Henderson Sextet
Joe Henderson:The Milestone Years | Milestone | 8MCD 4413-2
The Kicker | Original Jazz Classics | OJCCD 465-2
Lee Morgan Orchestra
The Last Sessin | Blue Note | 493401-2
Roswell Rudd-Archie Shepp Group
Live In New York | EmArCy | 013482-2

Moncur,Grachan | (b)
Bud Freeman All Stars
The Bud Freeman All-Star Sessions | Prestige | PRCD 24286-2
Ike Quebec Swing Seven
The Blue Note Swingtets | Blue Note | 495697-2

Mondello,Pete | (as,bs,reeds,saxts)
Benny Goodman And His Orchestra
Charlie Christian:Swing To Bop | Dreyfus Jazz Line | FDM 36715-2
Charlie Parker With Strings
Charlie Parker With Strings:The Master Takes | Verve | 523984-2
Charlie Parker With The Neal Hefti Orchestra
Charlie Parker:The Best Of The Verve Years | Verve | 527815-2
Bird: The Complete Charlie Parker On Verve | Verve | 837141-2
Chubby Jackson And His All Star Big Band
Chubby Takes Over | Fresh Sound Records | FSR-CD 324
Woody Herman And His Orchestra
The Legends Of Swing | Laserlight | 24659
Woody Herman:Four Brother | Dreyfus Jazz Line | FDM 36722-2
Louis Armstrong-Jack Teagarden-Woody Herman:Midnights At V-Disc | Jazz Unlimited | JUCD 2048
Old Gold Rehearsals 1944 | Jazz Unlimited | JUCD 2079

Mondello,Toots | (as,cl,reeds,saxts)
Benny Goodman And His Orchestra
Planet Jazz:Benny Goodman | Planet Jazz | 2152054-2
Planet Jazz Sampler | Planet Jazz | 2152326-2
Planet Jazz:Swing | Planet Jazz | 2169651-2
Charlie Christian:Swing To Bop | Dreyfus Jazz Line | FDM 36715-2
More Camel Caravans | Phontastic | NCD 8845/6
Billie Holiday With Teddy Wilson And His Orchestra
Billie's Love Songs | Nimbus Records | NI 2000
Charlie Parker With Strings
Bird: The Complete Charlie Parker On Verve | Verve | 837141-2
Charlie Parker With The Joe Lipman Orchestra
Charlie Parker With Strings:The Master Takes | Verve | 523984-2
Charlie Parker Big Band | Verve | 559835-2
Leon Thomas With Orchestra
Spirits Known And Unknown | RCA | 2663876-2
Lionel Hampton And His Orchestra
Planet Jazz:Lionel Hampton | Planet Jazz | 2152059-2
Planet Jazz Sampler | Planet Jazz | 2152326-2
Sarah Vaughan The The Joe Lippman Orchestra
Sarah Vaughan:Lover Man | Dreyfus Jazz Line | FDM 36739-2

Monder,Ben | (gel-g)
Bill McHenry Quartet
Rest Stop | Fresh Sound Records | FSNT 033 CD
Graphic | Fresh Sound Records | FSNT 056 CD
Chris Cheek Sextet
A Girl Named Joe | Fresh Sound Records | FSNT 032 CD
Gorka Benitez Quartet
Gorka Benitez Trio | Fresh Sound Records | FSNT 073 CD
Gorka Benitez Quintet
Gorka Benitez Trio | Fresh Sound Records | FSNT 073 CD
Heinrich Köbberling-Matt Renzi Quartet
Pisces | Nabel Records:Jazz Network | CD 4677
Josh Roseman Unit
Cherry | Enja | ENJ-9392 2
Matt Renzi-Jimmy Weinstein Quartet
Matt Renzi-Jimmy Weinstein Quartet | Fresh Sound Records | FSNT 045 CD
Paul Motian And The E.B.B.B.
Holiday For Strings | Winter&Winter | 910069-2
Paul Motian Electric Bebop Band
Europe | Winter&Winter | 910063-2
Taylor Hawkins Group
Wake Up Call | Fresh Sound Records | FSCD 145 CD

Mondesir,Mark | (dr)
Barbara Dennerlein Quartet
Hot Stuff | Enja | ENJ-6050 2
David Jean-Baptiste Group
The Nature Suite | Laika Records | 35101632
John McLaughlin Group
The Promise | Verve | 529828-2
Pee Wee Ellis & NDR Bigband
What You Like | Minor Music | 801064

Mondesir,Michael | (bel-b)

Mondragon,Joe | (b)
Anita O'Day And Her Combo
Pick Yourself Up | Verve | 517329-2
Anita O'Day With The Bill Holman Orchestra
Verve Jazz Masters 49:Anita O'Day | Verve | 527653-2
Anita O'Day With The Buddy Bregman Orchestra
Pick Yourself Up | Verve | 517329-2
Verve Jazz Masters 49:Anita O'Day | Verve | 527653-2
Art Pepper Plus Eleven
Art Pepper + Eleven | Contemporary | CSA 7568-6
Modern Jazz Classics | Original Jazz Classics | OJC20 341-2
Astrud Gilberto With Antonio Carlos Jobim And The Marty Paich Orchestra
The Antonio Carlos Jobim Songbook | Verve | 525472-2
Astrud Gilberto With The Marty Paich Orchestra
Verve Jazz Masters 9:Astrud Gilberto | Verve | 519824-2
Barney Kessel And His Orchestra
Barney Kessel Plays Carmen | Original Jazz Classics | OJC 269(C 7563)
Barney Kessel And His Quintet
Barney Kessel Plays Carmen | Original Jazz Classics | OJC 269(C 7563)
Billie Holiday And Her All Stars
Verve Jazz Masters 12:Billie Holiday | Verve | 519825-2
Songs For Distingué Lovers | Verve | 539056-2
Billy May And His Orchestra
Billy May's Big Fat Brass/Bill's Bag | Capitol | 535206-2
Bud Shank And Trombones
Cool Fool | Fresh Sound Records | FSR CD 507
Buddy Bregman And His Orchestra
Swinging Kicks | Verve | 559514-2
Chet Baker Quartet
Let's Get Lost: The Best Of Chet Baker Sings | Pacific Jazz | 792932-2
Chet Baker Septet
The Best Of Chet Baker Plays | Pacific Jazz | 797161-2
Ella Fitzgerald And Her All Stars
The Best Of The Song Books:The Ballads | Verve | 521867-2
Love Songs:The Best Of The Song Books | Verve | 531762-2
Ella Fitzgerald Sings The Duke Ellington Songbook | Verve | 559248-2
For The Love Of Ella Fitzgerald | Verve | 841765-2
Ella Fitzgerald And Her Sextet
Ella Fitzgerald-First Lady Of Song | Verve | 517898-2
The Best Of The Song Books | Verve | 519804-2
Ella Fitzgerald And The Paul Smith Quartet
The Best Of The Song Books | Verve | 519804-2
Verve Jazz Masters 6:Ella Fitzgerald | Verve | 519822-2
Verve Jazz Masters 46:Ella Fitzgerald-The Jazz Sides | Verve | 527655-2
Ella Fitzgerald With Frank De Vol And His Orchestra
Get Happy! | Verve | 523321-2
Ella Fitzgerald With Marty Paich's Dektette
Ella Swings Lightly | Verve | 517535-2
Ella Fitzgerald With Paul Weston And His Orchestra
Ella Fitzgerald Sings The Irving Berlin Song Book | Verve | 543830-2
Ella Fitzgerald With The Billy May Orchestra
Ella Fitzgerald-First Lady Of Song | Verve | 517898-2
The Best Of The Song Books | Verve | 519804-2
Verve Jazz Masters 6:Ella Fitzgerald | Verve | 519822-2
The Best Of The Song Books:The Ballads | Verve | 521867-2
Verve Jazz Masters 46:Ella Fitzgerald-The Jazz Sides | Verve | 527655-2
Love Songs:The Best Of The Song Books | Verve | 531762-2
Ella Fitzgerald Sings The Harold Arlen Song Book | Verve | 589108-2
For The Love Of Ella Fitzgerald | Verve | 841765-2
Ella Fitzgerald With The Buddy Bregman Orchestra
Ella Fitzgerald-First Lady Of Song | Verve | 517898-2
The Best Of The Song Books:The Ballads | Verve | 521867-2
Love Songs:The Best Of The Song Books | Verve | 531762-2
Ella Fitzgerald Sings The Cole Porter Songbook | Verve | 537257-2
Ella Fitzgerald Sings The Rodgers And Hart Song Book | Verve | 537258-2
For The Love Of Ella Fitzgerald | Verve | 841765-2
Ella Fitzgerald With The Frank DeVol Orchestra
Get Happy! | Verve | 523321-2
Ella Fitzgerald With The Lou Levy Quartet
Verve Jazz Masters 6:Ella Fitzgerald | Verve | 519822-2
Verve Jazz Masters 46:Ella Fitzgerald-The Jazz Sides | Verve | 527655-2
Clap Hands,Here Comes Charlie! | Verve | 835646-2
For The Love Of Ella Fitzgerald | Verve | 841765-2
Ella Fitzgerald With The Marty Paich Dek-tette
Ella Fitzgerald-First Lady Of Song | Verve | 517898-2
Verve Jazz Masters 6:Ella Fitzgerald | Verve | 519822-2
Verve Jazz Masters 46:Ella Fitzgerald-The Jazz Sides | Verve | 527655-2
Ella Fitzgerald With The Marty Paich Orchestra
Ella Fitzgerald-First Lady Of Song | Verve | 517898-2
Whisper Not | Verve | 589947-2
For The Love Of Ella Fitzgerald | Verve | 841765-2
Ella Fitzgerald With The Nelson Riddle Orchestra
The Best Of The Song Books:The Ballads | Verve | 521867-2
Get Happy! | Verve | 523321-2
Ella Fitzgerald With The Paul Smith Quartet
Ella Fitzgerald-First Lady Of Song | Verve | 517898-2
Verve Jazz Masters 20:Introducing | Verve | 519853-2
The Best Of The Song Books:The Ballads | Verve | 521867-2
Ella Fitzgerald Sings The Rodgers And Hart Song Book | Verve | 537258-2
Ella Fitzgerald With The Paul Weston Orchestra
Get Happy! | Verve | 523321-2
Gerry Mulligan Tentette
Gene Norman Presents The Original Gerry Mulligan Tentet And Quartet | GNP Crescendo | GNPD 56
Hank Crawford Orchestra
Rhino Presents The Atlantic Jazz Gallery | Atlantic | 8122-71257-2
Johnny Hartman And His Orchestra
Unforgettable | Impulse(MCA) | IMP 11522
June Christy With The Pete Rugolo Orchestra
Something Cool(The Complete Mono & Stereo Versions) | Capitol | 534069-2
June Christy With The Shorty Rogers Orchestra
June Christy Big Band Special | Capitol | 498319-2
Lee Konitz & The Gerry Mulligan Quartet
Konitz Meets Mulligan | Pacific Jazz | 746847-2
Mark Murphy And His Septet
Blue Velvet: Crooners, Swooners And Velvet Vocals | Blue Note | 521153-2
Pete Rugolo And His Orchestra
Verve Jazz Masters 52:Maynard Ferguson | Verve | 529905-2
Thriller/Richard Diamon(Original Jazz Scores From 2 Classics TV Series) | Fresh Sound Records | FSCD 2015
Shorty Rogers And His Giants
PLanet Jazz:Shorty Rogers | Planet Jazz | 2159976-2
Van Alexander Orchestra
Home Of Happy Feet/Swing! Staged For Sound! | Capitol | 535211-2
Woody Herman And His Orchestra
The Legends Of Swing | Laserlight | 24659
Woody Herman:Four Brother | Dreyfus Jazz Line | FDM 36722-2
Woody Herman And His Sextet
Songs For Hip Lovers | Verve | 559872-2

Monet,Kash | (perc,handclapsvoc)
The Brecker Brothers
Heavy Metal Be-Bop | RCA | 2119257-2

Monge,Luis | (p)
Conexion Latina
Calorcito | Enja | ENJ-4072 2

Monges,Amadeo | (indian harp)
Gato Barbieri Orchestra
Latino America | Impulse(MCA) | 952236-2

Monk By Five |
Monk By Five
Monk By Five | Touché Music | TMcCD 012

Monk,Thelonious | (p,celestep-solo)
Art Blakey And The Jazz Messengers With Thelonious Monk
Art Blakey's Jazz Messengers With Thelonious Monk | Atlantic | 7567-81332-2
Charlie Christian All Stars
Thelonious Monk:85th Birthday Celebration | zyx records | FANCD 6076-2
Charlie Christian-Jazz Immortal/Dizzy Gillespie 1944 | Original Jazz Classics | OJCCD 1932-2(ES 548)
Charlie Parker And His Orchestra
Bird: The Complete Charlie Parker On Verve | Verve | 837141-2
Charlie Parker:April In Paris | Dreyfus Jazz Line | FDM 36737-2
Charlie Parker Quintet
Verve Jazz Masters 10:Dizzy Gillespie | Verve | 516319-2
Bird And Diz | Verve | 521436-2
Charlie Parker:Bird's Best Bop On Verve | Verve | 527452-2
Charlie Parker:The Best Of The Verve Years | Verve | 527815-2
Ultimate Dizzy Gillespie | Verve | 557535-2
Talkin' Bird | Verve | 559859-2
Charlie Parker-Dizzy Gillespie Quintet
Thelonious Monk:Misterioso | Dreyfus Jazz Line | FDM 36743-2
Clark Terry With The Thelonious Monk Trio
Thelonious Monk:85th Birthday Celebration | zyx records | FANCD 6076-2
Clark Terry-Thelonious Monk Quartet
In Orbit | Original Jazz Classics | OJC 302(R 12-271)
Coleman Hawkins Quartet
Thelonious Monk:The Complete Prestige Recordings | Prestige | 3 PRCD 4428-2

Jazz:The Essential Collection Vol.3 | IN+OUT Records | 78013-2
Thelonious Monk:85th Birthday Celebration | zyx records | FANCD 6076-2
Monk's Music | Original Jazz Classics | OJC20 084-2
Gerry Mulligan-Thelonious Monk Quartet
Mulligan Meets Monk | Original Jazz Classics | OJC20 301-2(RLP 1106)
Miles Davis All Stars
Milt Jackson Birthday Celebration | Fantasy | FANCD 6079-2
Bags' Groove | Original Jazz Classics | OJC20 245-2
Miles Davis And The Modern Jazz Giants | Original Jazz Classics | OJC20 347-2(P 7150)
Miles Davis And The Modern Jazz Giants
Thelonious Monk:85th Birthday Celebration | zyx records | FANCD 6076-2
Miles Davis Quintet
To Bags...With Love:Memorial Album | Pablo | 2310967-2
Thelonious Monk:The Complete Prestige Recordings | Prestige | 3 PRCD 4428-2
Sonny Rollins Quartet
Thelonious Monk:The Complete Prestige Recordings | Prestige | 3 PRCD 4428-2
Sonny Rollins Vol.2 | Blue Note | 497809-2
Sonny Rollins:The Blue Note Recordings | Blue Note | 821371-2
Jazz Profile:Sonny Rollins | Blue Note | 823516-2
The Prestige Legacy Vol.1:The High Priests | Prestige | PCD 24251-2
Sonny Rollins Quartet feat.Thelonious Monk
Ballads | Blue Note | 537562-2
Thelonious Monk/Sonny Rollins | Original Jazz Classics | OJCCD 059-2
Sonny Rollins Sextet
Sonny Rollins Vol.2 | Blue Note | 497809-2
Sonny Rollins:The Blue Note Recordings | Blue Note | 821371-2
Thelonious Monk
Thelonious Monk Piano Solo | Vogue | 21409362
The Story Of Jazz Piano | Laserlight | 24653
Thelonious Monk:The Complete Prestige Recordings | Prestige | 3 PRCD 4428-2
Live At The Jazz Workshop-Complete | CBS | C2K 65189
Monk Alone:The Complete Columbia Solo Studio Recordings | CBS | C2K 65495
Monk's Dream | CBS | CK 63536
Greatest Hits | CBS | CK 65422
MONK. | CBS | CK 86564
Thelonious Monk:85th Birthday Celebration | zyx records | FANCD 6076-2
Thelonious Monk With John Coltrane | Jazzland | JZSA 946-6
Alone In San Francisco | Original Jazz Classics | OJC 231(RLP 1158)
Thelonious Monk | Original Jazz Classics | OJC20 010-2(P 7027)
Brilliant Corners | Original Jazz Classics | OJC20 026-2
Thelonious Monk With John Coltrane | Original Jazz Classics | OJC20 039-2
Misterioso | Original Jazz Classics | OJC20 206-2
The Unique Thelonious Monk | Original Jazz Classics | OJCCD 064-2
Thelonious Himself | Original Jazz Classics | OJCCD 254-2
Monk In France | Original Jazz Classics | OJCCD 670-2
The Prestige Legacy Vol.1:The High Priests | Prestige | PCD 24251-2
Thelonious Monk In Copenhagen | Storyville | STCD 8283
Thelonious Monk And His Orchestra
Greatest Hits | CBS | CK 65422
Thelonious Monk:85th Birthday Celebration | zyx records | FANCD 6076-2
At Town Hall | Original Jazz Classics | OJCCD 135-2
Thelonious Monk Quartet
Paris Jazz Concert:Theloniuos Monk And His Quartet | Laserlight | 17250
Wizard Of The Vibes | Blue Note | 532140-2
The Best Of Thelonious Monk:The Blue Note Years | Blue Note | 795636-2
Jazz Profile:Thelonious Monk | Blue Note | 823518-2
Monk At Newport 1963 & 1965 | CBS | C2K 63905
Live At The Jazz Workshop-Complete | CBS | C2K 65189
Live At The It Club:Complete | CBS | C2K 65288
Monk's Dream | CBS | CK 63536
Greatest Hits | CBS | CK 65422
MONK. | CBS | CK 86564
Thelonious Monk:85th Birthday Celebration | zyx records | FANCD 6076-2
Thelonious Monk:Misterioso | Dreyfus Jazz Line | FDM 36743-2
Thelonious Monk With John Coltrane | Jazzland | JZSA 946-6
Thelonious Monk With John Coltrane | Original Jazz Classics | OJC20 039-2
Misterioso | Original Jazz Classics | OJC20 206-2
Thelonious In Action | Original Jazz Classics | OJCCD 103-2
Thelonious Himself | Original Jazz Classics | OJCCD 254-2
Thelonious Monk In Italy | Original Jazz Classics | OJCCD 488-2(RLP 9443)
Monk In France | Original Jazz Classics | OJCCD 670-2
Thelonious Monk In Copenhagen | Storyville | STCD 8283
Thelonious Monk Quartet Plus Two
Thelonious Monk:85th Birthday Celebration | zyx records | FANCD 6076-2
At The Blackhawk | Original Jazz Classics | OJCCD 305-2
Thelonious Monk Quartet With Pee Wee Russell
Monk At Newport 1963 & 1965 | CBS | C2K 63905
Thelonious Monk Quintet
Thelonious Monk:The Complete Prestige Recordings | Prestige | 3 PRCD 4428-2
Sonny Rollins-The Freelance Years:The Complete Riverside & Contemporary Recordings | Riverside | 5 RCD 4427-2
Genius Of Modern Music,Vol.1 | Blue Note | 532138-2
Genius Of Modern Music,Vol.2 | Blue Note | 532139-2
The Best Of Thelonious Monk:The Blue Note Years | Blue Note | 795636-2
Jazz Profile:Thelonious Monk | Blue Note | 823518-2
Thelonious Monk:85th Birthday Celebration | zyx records | FANCD 6076-2
Thelonious Monk:Misterioso | Dreyfus Jazz Line | FDM 36743-2
Brilliant Corners | Original Jazz Classics | OJC20 026-2
MONK | Original Jazz Classics | OJCCD 016-2
Thelonious Monk/Sonny Rollins | Original Jazz Classics | OJCCD 059-2
5 By Monk By 5 | Original Jazz Classics | OJCCD 362-2
The Jazz Giants Play Jerome Kern:Yesterdays | Prestige | PCD 24202-2
The Prestige Legacy Vol.1:The High Priests | Prestige | PCD 24251-2
Thelonious Monk Septet
Thelonious Monk:85th Birthday Celebration | zyx records | FANCD 6076-2
Thelonious Monk With John Coltrane | Jazzland | JZSA 946-6
Thelonious Monk With John Coltrane | Original Jazz Classics | OJC20 039-2
Monk's Music | Original Jazz Classics | OJC20 084-2
Thelonious Monk Sextet
Genius Of Modern Music,Vol.1 | Blue Note | 532138-2
Genius Of Modern Music,Vol.2 | Blue Note | 532139-2
Jazz Profile:Thelonious Monk | Blue Note | 823518-2
Thelonious Monk:Misterioso | Dreyfus Jazz Line | FDM 36743-2
Thelonious Monk Trio
Thelonious Monk:The Complete Prestige Recordings | Prestige | 3 PRCD 4428-2
Genius Of Modern Music,Vol.1 | Blue Note | 532138-2
The Best Of Thelonious Monk:The Blue Note Years | Blue Note | 795636-2
Jazz Profile:Thelonious Monk | Blue Note | 823518-2
Thelonious Monk:85th Birthday Celebration | zyx records | FANCD 6076-2
Thelonious Monk:Misterioso | Dreyfus Jazz Line | FDM 36743-2
Thelonious Monk | Original Jazz Classics | OJC20 010-2(P 7027)
Plays The Music Of Duke Ellington | Original Jazz Classics | OJC20 024-2

Thelonious Monk/Sonny Rollins | Original Jazz Classics | OJCCD 059-2
The Unique Thelonious Monk | Original Jazz Classics | OJCCD 064-2
The Prestige Legacy Vol.1:The High Priests | Prestige | PCD 24251-2
Thelonious Monk-Gerry Mulligan Quartet
Thelonious Monk:85th Birthday Celebration | zyx records | FANCD 6076-2

Monné,Joan | (p)
Alguimia
Alguimia 'U' | Fresh Sound Records | FSNT 023 CD
Alguimia:Standards | Fresh Sound Records | FSNT 049 CD
Alguimia Dos | Fresh Sound Records | FSNT 050 CD
Carme Canela With The Joan Monné Trio
Introducing Carme Canela | Fresh Sound Records | FSNT 014 CD
Joan Abril Quintet
Eric | Fresh Sound Records | FSNT 092 CD
Joan Abril Sextet
Eric | Fresh Sound Records | FSNT 092 CD
Joan Monné Trio
Mireia | Fresh Sound Records | FSNT 100 CD
Pep O'Callaghan Grup
Tot Just | Fresh Sound Records | FSNT 017 CD
Port O'Clock | Fresh Sound Records | FSNT 069 CD

Monoblue Quartet |
Monoblue Quartet
An Affair With Strauss | Between The Lines | btl 006(Efa 10176-2)

Monroe,Diane | (v)
Max Roach Double Quartet
To The Max! | Enja | ENJ-7021 22

Montalbano,Claudio | (ssas)
Orchestra Jazz Siciliana
Orchestra Jazz Siciliana Plays The Music Of Carla Bley | Watt | XtraWatt/4

Montalbano,Rick | (dr)
Ari Ambrose Quartet
Jazzmin | Steeplechase | SCCD 31535

Montalvo,Mabel De La Caridad Dedeu | (vocperc)
Conjunto Clave Y Guaguanco
Dejala En La Puntica | TipToe | TIP-888829 2

Montanari,Stefano | (v)
Gianluigi Trovesi Nonet
Round About A Midsummer's Dream | Enja | ENJ-9384 2

Monte,Tony | (pld)
Karl Schloz Quartet
A Mooth One | Nagel-Heyer | CD 2012

Montego Joe | (congas,bongosdr)
Ahmed Abdul-Malik Orchestra
Jazz Sounds Of Africa | Prestige | PRCD 24279-2
Art Blakey And The Afro Drum Ensemble
The African Beat | Blue Note | 522666-2
George Benson With The Jack McDuff Quartet
The New Boss Guitar | Original Jazz Classics | OJCCD 461-2
Jack McDuff Quintet
The Last Goodun' | Prestige | PRCD 24274-2
Jack McDuff Sextet
Silken Soul | Prestige | PCD 24242-2
Roland Kirk And His Orchestra
Rahsaan/The Complete Mercury Recordings Of Roland Kirk | Mercury | 846630-2
Willis Jackson Group
At Large | Prestige | PCD 24243-2
Willis Jackson Sextet
At Large | Prestige | PCD 24243-2

Montero,Raul | (voc)
Toto Blanke Group
Fools Paradise | ALISO Records | AL 1019

Monterose,J.R. | (ssts)
Charles Mingus Jazz Workshop
Charles Mingus-Passion Of A Man:The Complete Atlantic Recordings 1956-1961 | Atlantic | 8122-72871-2
The Very Best Of Charles Mingus | Rhino | 8122-79988-2
J.R. Monterose Quintet
Jaywalkin' | Fresh Sound Records | FSR-CD 320
J.R. Monterose Sextet
Jaywalkin' | Fresh Sound Records | FSR-CD 320
Kenny Dorham Sextet
The Complete Round About Midnight At The Cafe Bohemia | Blue Note | 533775-2

Montes,Diego | (cl)
Uri Caine With The Concerto Köln
Concerto Köln | Winter&Winter | 910086-2

Montgomery Brothers,The |
Montgomery Brothers
Groove Yard | Original Jazz Classics | OJCCD 139-2(R 9362)

Montgomery William | (el-b)
Lionel Hampton And His Orchestra
Lionel Hampton's Paris All Stars | Vogue | 21511502
Lionel Hampton Trio
Lionel Hampton's Paris All Stars | Vogue | 21511502

Montgomery,Buddy | (p,synth-perc,p-solo,vibsynth)
David Fathead Newman Quintet Plus Clifford Jordan
Blue Head | Candid | CCD 79041
George Shearing With The Montgomery Brothers
Wes Montgomery-The Complete Riverside Recordings | Riverside | 12 RCD 4408-2
George Shearing And The Montgomery Brothers | Original Jazz Classics | OJCCD 040-2
Montgomery Brothers
Groove Yard | Original Jazz Classics | OJCCD 139-2(R 9362)
The Mastersounds
The Mastersounds | Prestige | PRCD 24770-2
The Montgomery Brothers
Wes Montgomery-The Complete Riverside Recordings | Riverside | 12 RCD 4408-2

Montgomery,Little Brother | (p,vocp-solo)
Buddy Guy Blues Band
Buddy Guy-The Complete Chess Studio Recordings | MCA | MCD 09337

Montgomery,Monk | (bel-b)
Art Farmer Septet
Plays The Arrangements And Compositions Of Gigi Gryce And Quincy Jones | Original Jazz Classics | OJCCD 054-2
George Shearing With The Montgomery Brothers
Wes Montgomery-The Complete Riverside Recordings | Riverside | 12 RCD 4408-2
George Shearing And The Montgomery Brothers | Original Jazz Classics | OJCCD 040-2
Montgomery Brothers
Groove Yard | Original Jazz Classics | OJCCD 139-2(R 9362)
The Mastersounds
The Mastersounds | Prestige | PRCD 24770-2
The Montgomery Brothers
Wes Montgomery-The Complete Riverside Recordings | Riverside | 12 RCD 4408-2

Montgomery,Wes | (g,b-gg-solo)
(Little)Jimmy Scott With The Lionel Hampton Orchestra
Everybody's Somebody's Fool | Decca | 050669-2
Cannonball Adderley And The Poll Winners
Cannonball Adderley And The Poll Winners | Capitol | 520086-2
Cannonball Adderley Quintet
Wes Montgomery-The Complete Riverside Recordings | Riverside | 12 RCD 4408-2
George Shearing With The Montgomery Brothers
Wes Montgomery-The Complete Riverside Recordings | Riverside | 12 RCD 4408-2
George Shearing And The Montgomery Brothers | Original Jazz Classics | OJCCD 040-2
Harold Land Sextet
Wes Montgomery-The Complete Riverside Recordings | Riverside | 12 RCD 4408-2
Jimmy Smith And Wes Montgomery With Orchestra
Jimmy & Wes-The Dynamic Duo | Verve | 521445-2
Jimmy Smith And Wes Montgomery With The Oliver Nelson Orchestra
Wes Montgomery:The Verve Jazz Sides | Verve | 521690-2
Jimmy Smith:Best Of The Verve Years | Verve | 527950-2
Talkin' Jazz:Roots Of Acid Jazz | Verve | 529580-2
Jimmy Smith Trio
Jimmy Smith:Best Of The Verve Years | Verve | 527950-2
Jimmy Smith-Wes Montgomery Quartet
Jimmy & Wes-The Dynamic Duo | Verve | 521445-2
Wes Montgomery:The Verve Jazz Sides | Verve | 521690-2
Verve Jazz Masters 29:Jimmy Smith | Verve | 521855-2
Jimmy Smith:Best Of The Verve Years | Verve | 527950-2
Talkin' Jazz:Roots Of Acid Jazz | Verve | 529580-2
Jimmy Smith-Talkin' Verve | Verve | 531563-2
Lionel Hampton And His Orchestra
Lionel Hampton:Flying Home | Dreyfus Jazz Line | FDM 36735-2
Lionel Hampton Quartet
Lionel Hampton:Flying Home | Dreyfus Jazz Line | FDM 36735-2
Milt Jackson-Wes Montgomery Quintet
Wes Montgomery-The Complete Riverside Recordings | Riverside | 12 RCD 4408-2
To Bags...With Love:Memorial Album | Pablo | 2310967-2
Milt Jackson Birthday Celebration | Fantasy | FANCD 6079-2
Bags Meets Wes! | Original Jazz Classics | OJC20 234-2(RLP 9407)
Montgomery Brothers
Groove Yard | Original Jazz Classics | OJCCD 139-2(R 9362)
Nat Adderley Quartet
Wes Montgomery-The Complete Riverside Recordings | Riverside | 12 RCD 4408-2
Work Song | Original Jazz Classics | OJC20 363-2
Nat Adderley Quintet
Wes Montgomery-The Complete Riverside Recordings | Riverside | 12 RCD 4408-2
Work Song | Original Jazz Classics | OJC20 363-2
Nat Adderley Sextet
Wes Montgomery-The Complete Riverside Recordings | Riverside | 12 RCD 4408-2
Work Song | Original Jazz Classics | OJC20 363-2
Nat Adderley Trio
Wes Montgomery-The Complete Riverside Recordings | Riverside | 12 RCD 4408-2
Work Song | Original Jazz Classics | OJC20 363-2
The Montgomery Brothers
Wes Montgomery-The Complete Riverside Recordings | Riverside | 12 RCD 4408-2
Wes Montgomery
Wes Montgomery-The Complete Riverside Recordings | Riverside | 12 RCD 4408-2
Guitar On The Go | Original Jazz Classics | OJCCD 489-2(RLP 9494)
Wes Montgomery Orchestra
Movin' Wes | Verve | 521433-2
Wes Montgomery Quartet
Wes Montgomery-The Complete Riverside Recordings | Riverside | 12 RCD 4408-2
Verve Jazz Masters 14:Wes Montgomery | Verve | 519826-2
Verve Jazz Masters 20:Introducing | Verve | 519853-2
Talkin' Jazz:Roots Of Acid Jazz | Verve | 529580-2
Bumpin' | Verve | 539062-2
Tequila | Verve | 547769-2
The Incredible Guitar Of Wes Montgomery | Original Jazz Classics | OJC20 036-2
Movin' Along | Original Jazz Classics | OJC20 089-2
The Jazz Giants Play Harold Arlen:Blues In The Night | Prestige | PCD 24201-2
Wes Montgomery Quartet With The Claus Ogerman Orchestra
Tequila | Verve | 547769-2
Willow Weep For Me | Verve | 589486-2
Wes Montgomery Quintet
Wes Montgomery-The Complete Riverside Recordings | Riverside | 12 RCD 4408-2
Movin' Along | Original Jazz Classics | OJC20 089-2
Full House | Original Jazz Classics | OJC20 106-2
So Much Guitar! | Original Jazz Classics | OJC20 233-2
The Jazz Giants Play Duke Ellington:Caravan | Prestige | PCD 24227-2
Wes Montgomery Quintet With The Claus Ogerman Orchestra
The Antonio Carlos Jobim Songbook | Verve | 525472-2
Talkin' Jazz:Roots Of Acid Jazz | Verve | 529580-2
Tequila | Verve | 547769-2
Wes Montgomery Sextet
Tequila | Verve | 547769-2
Wes Montgomery Trio
Wes Montgomery-The Complete Riverside Recordings | Riverside | 12 RCD 4408-2
Wes Montgomery:The Verve Jazz Sides | Verve | 521690-2
Tequila | Verve | 547769-2
A Dynamic New Jazz Sound | Original Jazz Classics | OJCCD 034-2
Portrait Of Wes | Original Jazz Classics | OJCCD 144-2
Boss Guitar | Original Jazz Classics | OJCCD 261-2
Guitar On The Go | Original Jazz Classics | OJCCD 489-2(RLP 9494)
The Jazz Giants Play Miles Davis:Milestones | Prestige | PCD 24225-2
Wes Montgomery Trio With The Claus Ogerman Orchestra
Tequila | Verve | 547769-2
Wes Montgomery With The Claus Ogerman Orchestra
Verve Jazz Masters 14:Wes Montgomery | Verve | 519826-2
Wes Montgomery With The Don Sebesky Orchestra
Verve Jazz Masters 14:Wes Montgomery | Verve | 519826-2
Wes Montgomery:The Verve Jazz Sides | Verve | 521690-2
Talkin' Jazz:Roots Of Acid Jazz | Verve | 529580-2
Bumpin' | Verve | 539062-2
California Dreaming | Verve | 827842-2
Wes Montgomery With The Jimmy Jones Orchestra
Wes Montgomery-The Complete Riverside Recordings | Riverside | 12 RCD 4408-2
The Jazz Giants Play Rodgers & Hart:Blue Moon | Prestige | PCD 24205-2
Wes Montgomery With The Johnny Pate Orchestra
Verve Jazz Masters 14:Wes Montgomery | Verve | 519826-2
Wes Montgomery:The Verve Jazz Sides | Verve | 521690-2
Talkin' Jazz:Roots Of Acid Jazz | Verve | 529580-2
Wes Montgomery With The Oliver Nelson Orchestra
Verve Jazz Masters 14:Wes Montgomery | Verve | 519826-2
Wes Montgomery:The Verve Jazz Sides | Verve | 521690-2
Talkin' Jazz:Roots Of Acid Jazz | Verve | 529580-2
Wynton Kelly Trio With Wes Montgomery
Wes Montgomery:The Verve Jazz Sides | Verve | 521690-2

Montmarche,Robert | (dr)
Benny Carter And His Orchestra
Django Reinhardt All Star Sessions | Capitol | 531577-2
Americans Swinging In Paris:Benny Carter | EMI Records | 539647-2

Montoliu,Tete | (pp-solo)
Eladio Reinon Quintet
Es La Historia De Un Amor | Fresh Sound Records | FSNT 004 CD
Lionel Hampton And His Quintet
Planet Jazz:Jazz Greatest Hits | Planet Jazz | 2169648-2
Lionel Hampton Quintet
Planet Jazz:Lionel Hampton | Planet Jazz | 2152059-2
Roland Kirk Quartet
Talkin' Verve-Roots Of Acid Jazz:Roland Kirk | Verve | 533101-2
Roland Kirk Quartet With Sonny Boy Williamson
Talkin' Verve-Roots Of Acid Jazz:Roland Kirk | Verve | 533101-2
Roland Kirk Quintet
Rahsaan/The Complete Mercury Recordings Of Roland Kirk | Mercury | 846630-2
Tete Montoliu

Songs For Love | Enja | ENJ-2040 2
Tete Montoliu Trio
Tete! | Steeplechase | SCCD 31029

Montreal Jubilation Gospel Choir | ()
Klaus König Orchestra & Guests
The Song Of Songs:Oratorio For Two Solo Voices,Choir And Orchestra | Enja | ENJ-7057 2

Montrose,Jack | (arr,clts)
Chet Baker Septet
The Best Of Chet Baker Plays | Pacific Jazz | 797161-2
June Christy With The Pete Rugolo Orchestra
Something Cool(The Complete Mono & Stereo Versions) | Capitol | 534069-2
Lennie Niehaus Quintet
Lennie Niehaus Vol.1:The Quintets | Original Jazz Classics | OJCCD 1933-2(C 3518)

Montz,Dick | (tp)
Eric Dolphy Quartet With The University Of Illinois Big Band
The Illinois Concert | Blue Note | 499826-2

Monville,Serge 'Bib' | (ts)
Rene Thomas Quintet
Jazz In Paris:René Thomas-The Real Cat | EmArCy | 549400-2 PMS

Moody,Bill | (dr)
Hans Koller Big Band
New York City | MPS | 9813437

Moody,Howard | (cond)
John Surman-John Taylor With Chorus
Proverbs And Songs | ECM | 1639

Moody,James | (as,ts,voc,fl,cl,ss,reedsarr)
Bobby Timmons Orchestra
Quartet And Orchestra | Milestone | MCD 47091-2
Cedar Walton Quintet
Soul Cycle | Original Jazz Classics | OJCCD 847-2(P 7693)
Dexter Gordon Quintet
Tower Of Power | Original Jazz Classics | OJCCD 299-2(P 7623)
Dexter Gordon-James Moody Quintet
More Power | Original Jazz Classics | OJC20 815-2(P 7680)
Dizzy Gillespie And His Orchestra
Planet Jazz:Dizzy Gillespie | Planet Jazz | 2152069-2
Planet Jazz:Bebop | RCA | 2169650-2
Talking Verve:Dizzy Gillespie | Verve | 533846-2
Dizzy Gillespie And The United Nation Orchestra
7.Zelt-Musik-Festival:Jazz Events | Zounds | CD 2730001
Dizzy Gillespie Quintet
Dizzie Gillespie: Salle Pleyel/Olympia | Laserlight | 36132
Verve Jazz Masters 10:Dizzy Gillespie | Verve | 516319-2
Talking Verve:Dizzy Gillespie | Verve | 533846-2
Ultimate Dizzy Gillespie | Verve | 557535-2
Something Old Something New | Verve | 558079-2
Swing Low, Sweet Cadillac | Impulse(MCA) | 951178-2
The Roots Of Acid Jazz | Impulse(MCA) | IMP 12042
Dizzy Gillespie Sextet
Talking Verve:Dizzy Gillespie | Verve | 533846-2
Jambo Caribe | Verve | 557492-2
Ultimate Dizzy Gillespie | Verve | 557535-2
Eddie Jefferson With The James Moody Quintet
Body And Soul | Original Jazz Classics | OJCCD 396-2(P 7619)
Ella Fitzgerald With The Dizzy Gillespie Orchestra
Ella Fitzgerald:Mr.Paganini | Dreyfus Jazz Line | FDM 36741-2
Ella Fitzgerald With The Hank Jones Trio
Ella Fitzgerald:Mr.Paganini | Dreyfus Jazz Line | FDM 36741-2
Ernie Royal And The Duke Knights
Americans Swinging In Paris:James Moody | EMI Records | 539653-2
Gene Ammons-James Moody Quintet
Chicago Concert | Original Jazz Classics | OJCCD 1091-2(PR 10065)
Jack Dieval And His Quartet
Americans Swinging In Paris:James Moody | EMI Records | 539653-2
James Moody Boptet
Americans Swinging In Paris:James Moody | EMI Records | 539653-2
James Moody Orchestra
The Blues And Other Colors | Original Jazz Classics | OJCCD 954-2(M 9023)
James Moody Quartet
Americans Swinging In Paris:James Moody | EMI Records | 539653-2
JATP All Stars
J.A.T.P. In London 1969 | Pablo | 2CD 2620119
Welcome To Jazz At The Philharmonic | Fantasy | FANCD 6081-2
Kenny Clarke And His Orchestra
Americans Swinging In Paris:James Moody | EMI Records | 539653-2
Max Roach Quintet
Dizzy Gillespie:Pleyel Jazz Concert 1948 + Max Roach Quintet 1949 | Vogue | 21409412
Miles Davis/Tadd Dameron Quintet
Miles Davis:Milestones | Dreyfus Jazz Line | FDM 36731-2
Milt Jackson Orchestra
To Bags...With Love:Memorial Album | Pablo | 2310967-2
Milt Jackson Birthday Celebration | Fantasy | FANCD 6079-2
Big Bags | Original Jazz Classics | OJCCD 366-2(RLP 9429)
Oscar Peterson With The Ernie Wilkins Orchestra
Verve Jazz Masters 16:Oscar Peterson | Verve | 516320-2
Quincy Jones Big Band
Rahsaan/The Complete Mercury Recordings Of Roland Kirk | Mercury | 846630-2
Tubby Hayes And The All Stars
Rahsaan/The Complete Mercury Recordings Of Roland Kirk | Mercury | 846630-2

Moody,James[as Jimmy Gloomy] | (flts)

Moon,Keith | (tb)
Stan Kenton And His Orchestra
Stan Kenton Portraits On Standards | Capitol | 531571-2

Moonan,Dennis | (cl,tsviola)
Arthur Young And Hatchett's Swingtette
Grapelli Story | Verve | 515807-2
Stephane Grappelli And His Musicians
Grapelli Story | Verve | 515807-2

Mooney,Hal | (arrld)
Billy Eckstine With Hal Mooney And His Orchestra
Billy Eckstine Now Singing In 12 Great Movies | Verve | 589307-2
Louis Armstrong With The Hal Mooney Orchestra
Ambassador Louis Armstrong Vol.17:Moments To Remember(1952-1956) | Ambassador | CLA 1917
Nina Simone With Hal Mooney's Orchestra
Verve Jazz Masters 17:Nina Simone | Verve | 518198-2
Nina Simone After Hours | Verve | 526702-2
Verve Jazz Masters Vol.58:Nina Simone Sings Nina | Verve | 529867-2
In Concert/I Put A Spell On You | Mercury | 846543-2
Sarah Vaughan With The Hal Mooney Orchestra
Sarah Vaughan Sings Gershwin | Verve | 557567-2
4 By 4:Ella Fitzgerald/Sarah Vaughan/Billie Holiday/Dinah Washington | Verve | 559693-2
It's A Man's World | Mercury | 589487-2

Moore,Alton | (tb)
Fats Waller And His Rhythm
Planet Jazz:Fats Waller | Planet Jazz | 2152058-2
Louis Armstrong And His Orchestra
Swing Legends:Louis Armstrong | Nimbus Records | NI 2012

Moore,Art | (reeds,saxts)
Jack Teagarden And His Orchestra
Jazz:The Essential Collection Vol.3 | IN+OUT Records | 78013-2

Moore,Bass | (tuba)
Jelly Roll Morton And His Orchestra
Jazz:The Essential Collection Vol.1 | IN+OUT Records | 78011-2

Moore,Bobby | (tp)
Count Basie And His Orchestra
Jazz:The Essential Collection Vol.3 | IN+OUT Records | 78013-2
Hot Lips Page Band
Planet Jazz:Jazz Trumpet | Planet Jazz | 2169654-2

Moore,Brew | (ts)
Brew Moore Quartet
The Brew Moore Quintet | Original Jazz Classics | OJCCD 100-2(F 3-222)
No More Brew | Storyville | STCD 8275
Brew Moore Quintet
The Brew Moore Quintet | Original Jazz Classics | OJCCD 100-2(F 3-222)
Cal Tjader Quintet
Cal Tjader Plays Jazz | Original Jazz Classics | OJCCD 986-2(F 3-211)
Cal Tjader Sextet
Cal Tjader's Latin Kick | Original Jazz Classics | OJCCD 642-2(F 8033)
Ella Fitzgerald And Her All Stars
Ella Fitzgerald:Mr.Paganini | Dreyfus Jazz Line | FDM 36741-2
Stan Getz And His Four Brothers
The Brothers | Original Jazz Classics | OJCCD 008-2
The Prestige Legacy Vol.2:Battles Of Saxes | Prestige | PCD 24252-2
Stan Getz Five Brothers Bop Tenor Sax Stars
Stan Getz:Imagination | Dreyfus Jazz Line | FDM 36733-2

Moore,Charles | (fl-h,conch-shells,dumbekshofar)
Yusef Lateef With Eternal Wind And The 'Kölner Rundfunk Orchester'
The African American Epic Suite:Music For Quintet And Orchestra | ACT | 9214-2

Moore,Curt | (dr)
Jackie Cain/Roy Kral Quartet
Full Circle | Fantasy | FCD 24768-2

Moore,Danny | (fl-htp)
Freddy Cole With Band
A Circle Of Love | Fantasy | FCD 9674-2
Les McCann Group
Another Beginning | Atlantic | 7567-80790-2
Oliver Nelson And His Orchestra
More Blues And The Abstract Truth | Impulse(MCA) | 951212-2
Quincy Jones And His Orchestra
Verve Jazz Masters Vol.59:Toots Thielemans | Verve | 535271-2
Thad Jones-Mel Lewis Orchestra
The Groove Merchant/The Second Race | Laserlight | 24656
Wes Montgomery With The Oliver Nelson Orchestra
Verve Jazz Masters 14:Wes Montgomery | Verve | 519826-2
Wes Montgomery:The Verve Jazz Sides | Verve | 521690-2
Talkin' Jazz:Roots Of Acid Jazz | Verve | 529580-2

Moore,Don | (btp)
Roland Kirk Quintet
Rahsaan/The Complete Mercury Recordings Of Roland Kirk | Mercury | 846630-2

Moore,Don prob. | (b)
Roland Kirk Quartet
Talkin' Verve-Roots Of Acid Jazz:Roland Kirk | Verve | 533101-2

Moore,Eddie | (cymbals,saw,dr,gongtympani)
Stanley Turrentine And His Orchestra
Pieces Of Dream | Original Jazz Classics | OJCCD 831-2(F 9465)

Moore,Eustis | (as)
Coleman Hawkins And His Orchestra
Planet Jazz:Coleman Hawkins | Planet Jazz | 2152055-2
Planet Jazz Sampler | Planet Jazz | 2152326-2
Planet Jazz:Jazz Greatest Hits | Planet Jazz | 2169648-2
Jazz:The Essential Collection Vol.3 | IN+OUT Records | 78013-2

Moore,Fred[Freddie] | (drvoc)
Emmett Berry-Sammy Price Orchestra
Americans Swinging In Paris:Sammy Price | EMI Records | 539650-2
Sidney Bechet With Sammy Price's Bluesicians
Planet Jazz:Sidney Bechet | Planet Jazz | 2152063-2
Sidney Bechet's Blue Note Jazzmen
Runnin' Wild | Blue Note | 821259-2
Sidney Bechet:Summertime | Dreyfus Jazz Line | FDM 36712-2
Wilbur DeParis And His New New Orleans Band
Atlantic Jazz: New Orleans | Atlantic | 7567-81700-2

Moore,Garfield | (cello)
Ron Carter With Strings
Pastels | Original Jazz Classics | OJCCD 665-2(M 9073)

Moore,Gerry | (p)
Vic Lewis Jam Session
Vic Lewis:The Golden Years | Candid | CCD 79754

Moore,Glen | (b,fl,p,v,el-bviola)
Glen Moore
Dragonetti's Dream | VeraBra Records | CDVBR 2154-2
Glen Moore Group
Nude Bass Ascending... | Intuition Records | INT 3192-2
Glen Moore -Rabih Abou-Khalil
Nude Bass Ascending... | Intuition Records | INT 3192-2
Glen Moore-Arto Tuncboyaciyan
Northwest Passage | Intuition Records | INT 3191-2
Oregon
Oregon | ECM | 1258(811711-2)
Crossing | ECM | 1291(825323-2)
Ecotopia | ECM | 1354
45th Parallel | VeraBra Records | CDVBR 2048-2
Always,Never And Forever | Intuition Records | INT 2073-2
Northwest Passage | Intuition Records | INT 3191-2
Rabih Abou-Khalil Group
Al-Jadida | Enja | ENJ-6090 2
Tarab | Enja | ENJ-7083 2
Bukra | Enja | ENJ-9372 2
Roots & Sprouts | Enja | ENJ-9373 2
Rabih Abou-Khalil Quintet
Between Dusk And Dawn | Enja | ENJ-9771 2
Rabih Abou-Khalil Septet
Between Dusk And Dawn | Enja | ENJ-9771 2
Ralph Towner
Trios/Solos | ECM | 1025(833328-2)
Ralph Towner-Glen Moore
Northwest Passage | Intuition Records | INT 3191-2

Moore,Jessica Care | (voc)
Antonio Hart Group
Here I Stand | Impulse(MCA) | 951208-2

Moore,Kermit | (cellostrings)
Andrew Hill Orchestra
Deep Blue-The United States Of Mind | Blue Note | 521152-2
Grover Washington Jr. Orchestra
Inside Moves | Elektra | 7559-60318-2
James Moody Orchestra
The Blues And Other Colors | Original Jazz Classics | OJCCD 954-2(M 9023)
Les McCann Group
Another Beginning | Atlantic | 7567-80790-2
Louis Armstrong And His Friends
Planet Jazz:Louis Armstrong | Planet Jazz | 2152052-2
Planet Jazz Sampler | Planet Jazz | 2152326-2
Louis Armstrong And His Friends | Bluebird | 2663961-2
Phil Woods Quartet With Orchestra & Strings
Round Trip | Verve | 559804-2
Ron Carter Group
Songs For You | Milestone | MCD 47099-2
Ron Carter Quintet With Strings
Pick 'Em/Super Strings | Milestone | MCD 47090-2
Ron Carter With Strings
Pastels | Original Jazz Classics | OJCCD 665-2(M 9073)
Wes Montgomery With The Jimmy Jones Orchestra
Wes Montgomery-The Complete Riverside Recordings | Riverside | 12 RCD 4408-2
Yusef Lateef Orchestra
The Blue Yusef Lateef | Rhino | 8122-73717-2

Moore,Laurence | (voc)
Les McCann Group
Another Beginning | Atlantic | 7567-80790-2

Moore,Malcolm | (b-g)
Steve Martland Band
The Orchestra Of Smith's Academy | Enja | ENJ-9358 2

Moore,Melvin | (tp,vvoc)
Bobby Bryant Orchestra
Deep Blue-The United States Of Mind | Blue Note | 521152-2
Johnny Hartman And His Orchestra
Unforgettable | Impulse(MCA) | IMP 11522

Moore,Michael | (as,b,el-b,b-g,cl,melodica,b-cl)
Allan Vaché-Jim Galloway Sextet
Raisin' The Roof:Allan Vaché Meets Jim Galloway | Nagel-Heyer | CD 054
Benny Goodman And His Orchestra
40th Anniversary Concert-Live At Carnegie Hall | London | 820349-2
Verve Jazz Masters 33:Benny Goodman | Verve | 844410-2
Benny Goodman Quintet
Verve Jazz Masters 33:Benny Goodman | Verve | 844410-2
Bill Evans Trio
Getting Sentimental | Milestone | MCD 9346-2
Gil Evans Orchestra
PLay The Music Of Jimi Hendrix | RCA | 2663872-2
Klaus König Orchestra & Guests
The Song Of Songs:Oratorio For Two Solo Voices,Choir And Orchestra | Enja | ENJ-7057 2
Lee Konitz Trio
Tenorlee | Choice | CHCD 71019
Michael Moore Trio
Monitor | Between The Lines | btl 003(Efa 10173-2)
Terrie Richard Alden And The Warren Vaché Quartet
Voice With Heart | Nagel-Heyer | CD 048
Zoot Sims With Orchestra
Passion Flower | Original Jazz Classics | OJCCD 939-2(2312120)

Moore,Numa 'Pee Wee' | (bs)
Dizzy Gillespie And His Orchestra
Dizzy Gillespie:Birks Works-The Verve Big Band Sessions | Verve | 527900-2
Ultimate Dizzy Gillespie | Verve | 557535-2
Dizzy Gillespie Orchestra
Verve Jazz Masters 10:Dizzy Gillespie | Verve | 516319-2
Louis Jordan And His Tympany Five
Louis Jordan-Let The Good Times Roll: The Complete Decca Recordings 1938-1954 | Bear Family Records | BCD 15557 IH

Moore,Oscar | (gvoc)
Lionel Hampton And His Orchestra
Planet Jazz:Lionel Hampton | Planet Jazz | 2152059-2
Lionel Hampton:Flying Home | Dreyfus Jazz Line | FDM 36735-2
Nat King Cole Trio
The Legends Of Swing | Laserlight | 24659
The Small Black Groups | Storyville | 4960523
Live At The Circle Room | Capitol | 521859-2
The Instrumental Classics | Capitol | 798288-2
The Best Of The Nat King Cole Trio:The Vocal Classics(1942-1946) | Blue Note | 833571-2
Nat King Cole:Route 66 | Dreyfus Jazz Line | FDM 36716-2
Nat King Cole:For Sentimental Reasons | Dreyfus Jazz Line | FDM 36740-2
Love Songs | Nimbus Records | NI 2010
Nat King Cole Trio With Frank DeVol's Orchestra
Nat King Cole:Route 66 | Dreyfus Jazz Line | FDM 36716-2
Nat King Cole With Orchestra
Nat King Cole:Route 66 | Dreyfus Jazz Line | FDM 36716-2
The Capitol Jazzmen
The Hollywood Session:The Capitol Jazzmen | Jazz Unlimited | JUCD 2044

Moore,Pat | (dance,vocpow-wow-dr)
Gunther Schuller With The WDR Radio Orchestra & Rememberance Band
Witchi Tia To, The Music Of Jim Pepper | Tutu Records | 888204-2*

Moore,Phil | (p)
Lena Horne With The Phil Moore Four
Planet Jazz:Lena Horne | Planet Jazz | 2165373-2

Moore,Ralph | (sax,ssts)
Fleurine With Band And Horn Section
Meant To Be! | EmArCy | 159085-2

Moore,Russel 'Big Chief' | (tb)
Bud Freeman All Stars
The Bud Freeman All-Star Sessions | Prestige | PRCD 24286-2
Louis Armstrong And His Orchestra
Best Of The Complete RCA Victor Recordings | RCA | 2663636-2
Louis Armstrong:A 100th Birthday Celebration | RCA | 2663694-2
Louis Armstrong:C'est Si Bon | Dreyfus Jazz Line | FDM 36730-2
Swing Legends:Louis Armstrong | Nimbus Records | NI 2012

Moore,Vic | (dr)
The Wolverines
Jazz:The Essential Collection Vol.2 | IN+OUT Records | 78012-2

Moore,'Wild' Bill | (ts)
Wild Bill Moore Quintet
Bottom Groove | Milestone | MCD 47098-2

Moore,William | (g,speech,voctuba)
Jelly Roll Morton And His Orchestra
Planet Jazz:Jelly Roll Morton | Planet Jazz | 2152060-2
King Oliver And His Orchestra
Planet Jazz:Jazz Trumpet | Planet Jazz | 2169654-2

Moorman,Dennis | (pp-solo)
Chico Freeman Septet
Destiny's Dance | Original Jazz Classics | OJCCD 799-2(C 14008)
Chico Freeman Sextet
Destiny's Dance | Original Jazz Classics | OJCCD 799-2(C 14008)

Mora,Francisco | (perc)
M'Boom
To The Max! | Enja | ENJ-7021 22

Morales,Carlos Emilio | (el-gg)
Irakere
Yemayá | Blue Note | 498239-2

Morales,Garcia | (dr)
John Thomas & Lifeforce
3000 Worlds | Nabel Records:Jazz Network | CD 4604

Morales,Humberto | (congas)
Sonny Stitt And His Band
Kaleidoscope | Original Jazz Classics | OJCCD 060-2(P 7077)
Sonny Stitt Quintet
Kaleidoscope | Original Jazz Classics | OJCCD 060-2(P 7077)

Morales,Joe | (asts)
Hans Theessink Group
Crazy Moon | Minor Music | 801052

Morales,Lloyd | (drperc)
Jerri Southern Quartet
The Very Thought Of You:The Decca Years 1951-1957 | Decca | 050671-2

Morales,Luis Cancino | (perccongas)
Steve Coleman And The Council Of Balance
Genesis & The Opening Of The Way | RCA | 2152934-2

Morales,Pancho | (congas)
Bernard Purdie's Soul To Jazz
Bernard Purdie's Soul To Jazz II | ACT | 9253-2

Morales,Rolando | (perc)
Antonio Hart Group
Ama Tu Sonrisa | Enja | ENJ-9404 2

Morales,Tony | (cymbals,hi-hat,drperc)
The Rippingtons
Tourist In Paradise | GRP | GRP 95882

Moran,Gayle | (keyboardsvoc)
Chick Corea Group
Verve Jazz Masters 3:Chick Corea | Verve | 519820-2
Mahavishnu Orchestra
Apocalypse | CBS | 467092-2

Moran,Jason | (keyboards,pmini-p)
Greg Osby Quartet
Banned In New York | Blue Note | 496860-2
Greg Osby Quartet With String Quartet
Symbols Of Light(A Solution) | Blue Note | 531395-2
Greg Osby Quintet

Inner Circle | Blue Note | 499871-2
Jason Moran
Modernistic | Blue Note | 539838-2
Jason Moran Trio
The Bandwagon | Blue Note | 591893-2
Joe Lovano-Greg Osby Quintet
Friendly Fire | Blue Note | 499125-2
Stefon Harris Group
Black Action Figure | Blue Note | 499546-2
Steve Coleman And Five Elements
The Sonic Language Of Myth | RCA | 2164123-2

Moran,Pat | (p)
Terry Gibbs Big Band
Terry Gibbs Dream Band Vol.4:Main Stem | Contemporary | CCD 7656-2
Terry Gibbs Dream Band
Terry Gibbs Dream Band Vol.3:Flying Home | Contemporary | CCD 7654-2
Terry Gibbs Dream Band Vol.5:The Big Cat | Contemporary | CCD 7657-2

Morand,Morris | (dr)
New Orleans Feetwarmers
Planet Jazz | Planet Jazz | 2169652-2
Jazz:The Essential Collection Vol.1 | IN+OUT Records | 78011-2

Morehouse,Chauncey | (dr,voc,percvib)
Bix Beiderbecke And His Gang
Jazz:The Essential Collection Vol.2 | IN+OUT Records | 78012-2
Frankie Trumbauer And His Orchestra
Jazz:The Essential Collection Vol.2 | IN+OUT Records | 78012-2
Hoagy Carmichael And His Orchestra
Planet Jazz:Bud Freeman | Planet Jazz | 2161240-2

Moreira,Airto | (congas,bongos,cuica,dr,berimbau)
Airto Moreira/Flora Purim
The Colours Of Life | IN+OUT Records | 001-2
Airto Moreira/Flora Purim Group
Jazz Unlimited | IN+OUT Records | 7017-2
Cannonball Adderley Group
Phenix | Fantasy | FCD 79004-2
Cannonball Adderley Sextet
Cannonball Adderley Birthday Celebration | Fantasy | FANCD 6087-2
Chick Corea And Return To Forever
Light As A Feather | Polydor | 557115-2
Chick Corea Quartet
Return To Forever | ECM | 1022(811978-2)
Verve Jazz Masters 20:Introducing | Verve | 519853-2
Chick Corea's Return To Forever
Verve Jazz Masters 3:Chick Corea | Verve | 519820-2
Dizzy Gillespie And The United Nation Orchestra
7.Zelt-Musik-Festival:Jazz Events | Zounds | CD 2730001
Duke Pearson Orchestra
Deep Blue-The United States Of Mind | Blue Note | 521152-2
Blue Bossa | Blue Note | 795590-2
Flora Purim And Her Quartet
Joe Henderson:The Milestone Years | Milestone | 8MCD 4413-2
Flora Purim And Her Quintet
Joe Henderson:The Milestone Years | Milestone | 8MCD 4413-2
Flora Purim And Her Sextet
Joe Henderson:The Milestone Years | Milestone | 8MCD 4413-2
Butterfly Dreams | Original Jazz Classics | OJCCD 315-2
Flora Purim With Orchestra
Joe Henderson:The Milestone Years | Milestone | 8MCD 4413-2
Freddie Hubbard With Orchestra
This Is Jazz:Freddie Hubbard | CBS | CK 65041
Gato Barbieri Group
Planet Jazz:Gato Barbieri | RCA | 2165364-2
Gato Barbieri:The Best Of The Early Years | RCA | 2663523-2
Grover Washington Jr. Orchestra
Jazzrock-Anthology Vol.3:Fusion | Zounds | CD 27100555
Joe Henderson Sextet
Joe Henderson:The Milestone Years | Milestone | 8MCD 4413-2
Keith Jarrett Group
Expectations | CBS | C2K 65900
Keith Jarrett Group With Brass
Expectations | CBS | C2K 65900
McCoy Tyner Orchestra
13th House | Original Jazz Classics | OJCCD 1089-2(M 9102)
Miles Davis Group
Circle In The Round | CBS | 467898-2
Live-Evil | CBS | C2K 65135
Live At The Fillmore East | CBS | C2K 65139
Bitches Brew | CBS | C2K 65774
Miles Davis Quintet
Black Beauty-Miles Davis At Filmore West | CBS | C2K 65138
Miles Davis Sextet
Black Beauty-Miles Davis At Filmore West | CBS | C2K 65138
Nat Adderley Group
Soul Of The Bible | Capitol | 358257-2
Nils Landgren Funk Unit
Paint It Blue:A Tribute To Cannonball Adderley | ACT | 9243-2
Paul Desmond Quartet With The Don Sebesby Orchestra
From The Hot Afternoon | Verve | 543487-2
Raul De Souza Orchestra
Cannonball Adderley Birthday Celebration | Fantasy | FANCD 6087-2
Return To Forever
Return To The 7th Galaxy-Return To Forever:The Anthology | Verve | 533108-2
Stan Getz-Joao Gilberto Orchestra
Sony Jazz Collection:Stan Getz | CBS | 488623-2

Moreira,Jurim | (dr)
Duo Fenix
Karai-Eté | IN+OUT Records | 7009-2

Moreira,Sidinho | (perc)
Ithamara Koorax With Band
Love Dance:The Ballad Album | Milestone | MCD 9327-2

Morel,Ysabel | (castanets)
Charles Mingus Orchestra
Tijuana Moods(The Complete Edition) | RCA | 2663840-2

Morelenbaum,Jacques | (cello,arrbottle)
Antonio Carlos Jobim With Orchestra
Verve Jazz Masters 13:Antonio Carlos Jobim | Verve | 516409-2
Egberto Gismonti Group
Infancia | ECM | 1428
Musica De Sobrevivencia | ECM | 1509(519706-2)

Morelenbaum,Paul | (voc)
Antonio Carlos Jobim With Orchestra
Verve Jazz Masters 13:Antonio Carlos Jobim | Verve | 516409-2

Morell,John | (g)
Shelly Manne Sextet
Alive In London | Original Jazz Classics | OJCCD 773-2(S 7629)

Morell,Marty | (dr,marimbaperc)
Bill Evans Quartet
The Complete Bill Evans On Verve | Verve | 527953-2
From Left To Right | Verve | 557451-2
Bill Evans Quartet With Orchestra
The Complete Bill Evans On Verve | Verve | 527953-2
From Left To Right | Verve | 557451-2
Bill Evans Trio
Bill Evans:The Secret Sessions | Milestone | 8MCD 4421-2
The Complete Fantasy Recordings | Fantasy | 9FCD 1012-2
Bill Evans:Piano Player | CBS | CK 65361
Blue In Green | Milestone | MCD 9185-2
Half Moon Bay | Milestone | MCD 9282-2
Since We Met | Original Jazz Classics | OJC 622(F 9501)
Bill Evans:From The 70's | Original Jazz Classics | OJCCD 1069-2(F 9630)
The Tokyo Concert | Original Jazz Classics | OJCCD 345-2
Re: Person I Knew | Original Jazz Classics | OJCCD 749-2(F 9608)
The Jazz Giants Play Harold Arlen:Blues In The Night | Prestige | PCD 24201-2
The Jazz Giants Play Miles Davis:Milestones | Prestige | PCD 24225-2
Bill Evans Trio With Jeremy Steig
The Complete Bill Evans On Verve | Verve | 527953-2
Bill Evans With Orchestra
The Complete Bill Evans On Verve | Verve | 527953-2
Gabor Szabo Quintet
The Roots Of Acid Jazz | Impulse(MCA) | IMP 12042
The Sorcerer | Impulse(MCA) | IMP 12112
Hugh Marsh Duo/Quartet/Orchestra
The Bear Walks | VeraBra Records | CDVBR 2011-2
Singers Unlimited With Rob McConnell And The Boss Brass
The Singers Unlimited:Magic Voices | MPS | 539130-2
Stan Getz With The Bill Evans Trio
But Beautiful | Milestone | MCD 9249-2

Morello,Joe | (dr)
Dave Brubeck Quartet
The Great Concerts | CBS | 462403-2
Dave Brubeck's Greatest Hits | CBS | 465703-2
Time Out | CBS | CK 65122
Buried Treasures | CBS | CK 65777
Dave Brubeck Quartet With Orchestra
Brandenburg Gate:Revisited | CBS | CK 65725
Dave Brubeck Quintet
Reunion | Original Jazz Classics | OJCCD 150-2
Dave Brubeck Sextet
Bravo! Brubeck! | CBS | CK 65723
Don Senay With Orchestra And Strings
Charles Mingus-The Complete Debut Recordings | Debut | 12 DCD 4402-2
Gary Burton Sextet
Planet Jazz:Gary Burton | RCA | 2165367-2
Gary Burton Trio
Planet Jazz:Gary Burton | RCA | 2165367-2
Jimmy Rushing With The Dave Brubeck Quartet
Brubeck & Rushing | CBS | CK 65727
Tal Farlow Quartet
Verve Jazz Masters 41:Tal Farlow | Verve | 527365-2
Thad Jones And His Orchestra
Charles Mingus-The Complete Debut Recordings | Debut | 12 DCD 4402-2

Moreno,Anthony 'Tony' | (drperc)
Friedrich-Herbert-Moreno Trio
Voyage Out | Jazz 4 Ever Records:Jazz Network | J4E 4747
Rez Abbasi Group
Modern Memory | String Jazz | SJRCD 102

Moreno,Daniel | (perc,bongoscongas)
Abbey Lincoln With Her Band
Wholly Earth | Verve | 559538-2
Conexion Latina
Mambo 2000 | Enja | ENJ-7055 2

Moreno,Luis | (b)
Piirpauke
Piirpauke-Global Servisi | JA & RO | JARO 4150-2

Morente,Enrique | (voc)
Perico Sambeat Group
Ademuz | Fresh Sound Records | FSNT 041 CD

Moret,Patrice | (b)
Gilbert Paeffgen Trio
Pedestrian Tales | Edition Musikat | EDM 061

Morgan,Albert 'Al' | (b)
Cab Calloway And His Orchestra
Planet Jazz:Cab Calloway | Planet Jazz | 2161237-2
Fats Waller And His Buddies
Planet Jazz:Jack Teagarden | Planet Jazz | 2161236-2
Louis Jordan And His Tympany Five
The Small Black Groups | Storyville | 4960523
Louis Jordan-Let The Good Times Roll: The Complete Decca Recordings 1938-1954 | Bear Family Records | BCD 15557 IH
Mound City Blue Blowers
Jazz:The Essential Collection Vol.3 | IN+OUT Records | 78013-2

Morgan,Dick | (bj,gp)
Ben Pollack And His Park Central Orchestra
Planet Jazz:Jack Teagarden | Planet Jazz | 2161236-2
Jazz:The Essential Collection Vol.3 | IN+OUT Records | 78013-2

Morgan,Eddie | (tb)
Woody Herman And His Orchestra
Verve Jazz Masters 54:Woody Herman | Verve | 529903-2
Woody Herman-1963 | Philips | 589490-2

Morgan,Frank | (as,sax,ssvoice)
Abbey Lincoln With Her Band
Who Used To Dance | Verve | 533559-2
Frank Morgan All Stars
Reflections | Original Jazz Classics | OJCCD 1046-2(C 14052)
Frank Morgan Quartet
Yardbird Suite | Original Jazz Classics | OJCCD 1060-2(C 14045)
Easy Living | Original Jazz Classics | OJCCD 833-2(C 14013)
Red Rodney All Stars
A Tribute To Charlie Parker Vol.1 | Storyville | 4960483
Teddy Charles' West Coasters
Wardell Gray Memorial Vol.1 | Original Jazz Classics | OJCCD 050-2(P 7008)

Morgan,Gary | (bs,cl,b-cl,basax)
Singers Unlimited With Rob McConnell And The Boss Brass
The Singers Unlimited:Magic Voices | MPS | 539130-2

Morgan,Gayle | (el-p,org,synth,mellotronvoc)
Chick Corea And His Orchestra
My Spanish Heart | Polydor | 543303-3

Morgan,Lanny | (as,fl,cl,ss,reeds,saxts)
Carl Saunders-Lanny Morgan Quintet
Las Vegar Late Night Sessions:Live At Capozzoli's | Woofy Productions | WPCD 109
Horace Silver Quintet With Brass
Horace Silver Retrospective | Blue Note | 495576-2
Maynard Ferguson Orchestra With Chris Connor
Two's Company | Roulette | 837201-2

Morgan,Lee | (tpfl-h)
Ahmed Abdul-Malik Orchestra
Planet Jazz:Lee Morgan | Planet Jazz | 2161238-2
Andrew Hill Quintet
Grass Roots | Blue Note | 522672-2
Blue Bossa | Blue Note | 795590-2
Art Blakey And The Jazz Messengers
Planet Jazz:Art Blakey | Planet Jazz | 2152066-2
Planet Jazz:Lee Morgan | Planet Jazz | 2161238-2
Art Blakey & The Jazz Messengers: Olympia, May 13th, 1961 | Laserlight | 36128
Paris Jazz Concert:Art Blakey & The Jazz Messengers | Laserlight | 36158
Best Of Blakey 60 | Blue Note | 493072-2
Moanin' | Blue Note | 495324-2
Roots And Herbs | Blue Note | 521956-2
The Witch Doctor | Blue Note | 521957-2
Meet You At The Jazz Corner Of The World | Blue Note | 535565-2
Wayne Shorter:The Classic Blue Note Recordings | Blue Note | 540856-2
Blue N' Groovy | Blue Note | 780679-2
A Night In Tunisia | Blue Note | 784049-2
The Best Of Blue Note | Blue Note | 796110-2
The Best Of Blue Note Vol.2 | Blue Note | 797960-2
Les Liaisons Dangereuses(Original Soundtrack) | Fontana | 812017-2
Feedom Rider | Blue Note | 821287-2
Jazz In Paris:Art Blakey-1958-Paris Olympia | EmArCy | 832659-2 PMS
Jazz In Paris:Paris Jam Session | EmArCy | 832692-2 PMS
Impulse!Art Blakey!Jazz Messengers! | Impulse(MCA) | 951175-2
At The Club St.Germain | RCA | ND 74897(2)
Art Blakey And The Jazz Messengers With Barney Wilen And Bud Powell
Jazz In Paris:Paris Jam Session | EmArCy | 832692-2 PMS
Art Blakey Percussion Ensemble
Drums Around The Corner | Blue Note | 521455-2
Benny Golson Quintet
Nemmy Golson And The Philadelphians | Blue Note | 494104-2
Charles Earland Orchestra
Charlie's Greatest Hits | Prestige | PCD 24250-2
Dizzy Gillespie And His Orchestra
Dizzy Gillespie:Birks Works-The Verve Big Band Sessions | Verve | 527900-2
Ultimate Dizzy Gillespie | Verve | 557535-2
Dizzy Gillespie Orchestra
Verve Jazz Masters 10:Dizzy Gillespie | Verve | 516319-2
Hank Mobley Quintet
Deep Blue-The United States Of Mind | Blue Note | 521152-2
No Room For Squares | Blue Note | 524539-2
True Blue | Blue Note | 534032-2
Blue Bossa | Blue Note | 795590-2
Jack Wilson Sextet
Blue N' Groovy | Blue Note | 780679-2
Jackie McLean Quintet
Jacknife | Blue Note | 540535-2
Jackie McLean Sextet
Jacknife | Blue Note | 540535-2
Jimmy Smith All Stars
House Party | Blue Note | 524542-2
Joe Henderson Septet
Mode For Joe | Blue Note | 591894-2
The Blue Note Years-The Best Of Joe Henderson | Blue Note | 795627-2
John Coltrane Sextet
Trane's Blues | Blue Note | 498240-2
Blue Train | Blue Note | 591721-2
The Best Of Blue Note | Blue Note | 796110-2
Blue Train(The Ultimate Blue Train) | Blue Note | 853428-0
Johnny Griffin Septet
A Blowing Session | Blue Note | 0677191
Trane's Blues | Blue Note | 498240-2
Lee Morgan Orchestra
The Last Sessin | Blue Note | 493401-2
Standards | Blue Note | 823213-2
Lee Morgan Quintet
The Sidewinder | Blue Note | 495332-2
The Rumproller | Blue Note | 521229-2
The Sixth Sense | Blue Note | 522467-2
True Blue | Blue Note | 534032-2
Sonic Boom | Blue Note | 590414-2
Blue N' Groovy | Blue Note | 780679-2
The Best Of Blue Note | Blue Note | 796110-2
The Best Of Blue Note Vol.2 | Blue Note | 797960-2
Live At The Lighthouse | Blue Note | 835228-2
Caramba! | Blue Note | 853358-2
Take Twelve | Original Jazz Classics | OJCCD 310-2
Lee Morgan Sextet
Deep Blue-The United States Of Mind | Blue Note | 521152-2
The Sixth Sense | Blue Note | 522467-2
Taru | Blue Note | 522670-2
Wayne Shorter:The Classic Blue Note Recordings | Blue Note | 540856-2
Sonic Boom | Blue Note | 590414-2
Search For The New Land | Blue Note | 591896-2
Philly Joe Jones Big Band
Cannonball Adderley Birthday Celebration | Fantasy | FANCD 6087-2
Reuben Wilson Sextet
The Lost Grooves | Blue Note | 831883-2
Tina Brooks Quintet
True Blue | Blue Note | 534032-2
Wayne Shorter Quintet
Wayne Shorter:The Classic Blue Note Recordings | Blue Note | 540856-2
Night Dreamer | Blue Note | 784173-2

Morgan,Perry | (voc)
Sarah Vaughan And Her Band
Songs Of The Beatles | Atlantic | 16037-2

Morgan,Richard | (oboe)
Dee Dee Bridgewater With Orchestra
Dear Ella | Verve | 539102-2

Morgan,Sonny | (bongos,congas,perc,drbells)
Charles Earland Orchestra
Charlie's Greatest Hits | Prestige | PCD 24250-2
Count Basie And His Orchestra
Afrique | RCA | 2179618-2
Gato Barbieri Group
Planet Jazz:Gato Barbieri | RCA | 2165364-2
Leon Thomas With Band
Super Black Blues Vol.II | RCA | 2663874-2
Leon Thomas In Berlin | RCA | 2663877-2
Leon Thomas With The Oliver Nelson Quintet
Leon Thomas In Berlin | RCA | 2663877-2
Lonnie Liston Smith & His Cosmic Echoes
Astral Travelling | RCA | 2663878-2

Morgan,Stanley 'Atakatun' | (congasperc)
Sun Ra And His Astro-Infinity Arkestra
Space Is The Place | Impulse(MCA) | 951249-2

Morgan,Theotis | (dr)
Albert King Blues Band
Wednesday Night In San Francisco | Stax | SCD 8556-2

Morgan,Tom | (asg)
Peggy Lee With Benny Goodman And His Quintet
Peggy Lee & Benny Goodman:The Complete Recordings 1941-1947 | CBS | C2K 65686
Peggy Lee With Benny Goodman And His Sextet
Peggy Lee & Benny Goodman:The Complete Recordings 1941-1947 | CBS | C2K 65686
Peggy Lee With The Benny Goodman Orchestra
Peggy Lee & Benny Goodman:The Complete Recordings 1941-1947 | CBS | C2K 65686

Morganelli,Mark | (fl-htp)
Mark Morganelli And The Jazz Forum All Stars
Speak Low | Candid | CCD 79054
The Basie Alumni
Swinging For The Count | Candid | CCD 79724

Morgenstern,Marvin | (stringsv)
Earl Klugh Group With Strings
Late Night Guitar | Blue Note | 498573-2
Grover Washington Jr. Orchestra
Inside Moves | Elektra | 7559-60318-2
Helen Merrill With Orchestra
Casa Forte | EmArCy | 558848-2
Nina Simone And Orchestra
Baltimore | Epic | 476906-2

Mori,Barak | (b)
Eric Reed Orchestra
Happiness | Nagel-Heyer | CD 2010

Mori,Ikue | (dr,electronic-percdr-machine)
Dave Douglas Group
Witness | RCA | 2663763-2
Dave Douglas Freak In | Bluebird | 2664008-2
Ensemble Modern
Ensemble Modern-Fred Frith:Traffic Continues | Winter&Winter | 910044-2

Moriarty,Suzette | (fr-h)
Herbie Hancock Group With String Quartet,Woodwinds And Brass
Herbie Hancock The New Standards | Verve | 527715-2
Herbie Hancock Group With Woodwinds And Brass
Herbie Hancock The New Standards | Verve | 527715-2

Mörike,Wolfgang | (b)
Thilo Wagner Quintet
Just In Time | Satin Doll Productions | SDP 1011-1 CD
Thilo Wagner Trio

Wagner,Mörike.Beck,Finally. | Nagel-Heyer | CD 078
Just In Time | Satin Doll Productions | SDP 1011-1 CD

Morillas,Charlie | (tb)
Buddy Childers Big Band
It's What Happening Now! | Candid | CCD 79749

Moritz,Ulrich | (dr,percvoc)
Die Elefanten
Wasserwüste | Nabel Records:Jazz Network | CD 4634
Friedemann Graef Group
Orlando Fragments | Nabel Records:Jazz Network | CD 4681
Graef-Schippa-Moritz
Orlando Frames | Nabel Records:Jazz Network | CD 4690
Human Factor
Forbidden City | Nabel Records:Jazz Network | CD 4635
Nils Petter Molvaer Group
Elegy For Africa | Nabel Records:Jazz Network | CD 4678

Morks,Jan | (cldr)
Dutch Swing College Band
Swinging Studio Sessons | Philips | 824256-2 PMS
Dutch Swing College Band Live In 1960 | Philips | 838765-2

Moroni,Dado | (org,p,el-pp-solo)
Dado Moroni
With Duke In Mind | Jazz Connaisseur | JCCD 9415-2
The Way I Am | Jazz Connaisseur | JCCD 9518-2
George Robert-Tom Harrell Quintet
Visions | Contemporary | CCD 14063-2
Wolfgang Haffner International Jazz Quintet
Whatever It Is | Jazz 4 Ever Records:Jazz Network | J4E 4714

Morphett,Jason | (clts)
Grace Knight With Orchestra
Come In Spinner | Intuition Records | INT 3052-2
Vince Jones With Orchestra
Come In Spinner | Intuition Records | INT 3052-2

Morrell,John | (g)
Singers Unlimited With The Clare Fischer Orchestra
The Singers Unlimited:Magic Voices | MPS | 539130-2

Morris,Cliff | (bjg)
Buddy Rich Big Band
Backwoods Siseman/Pieces Of Dream | Laserlight | 24655
Dee Dee Bridgewater With Band
Dee Dee Bridgewater | Atlantic | 7567-80760-2

Morris,Floyd | (parr)
Al Grey And His Allstars
Snap Your Fingers | Verve | 9860307

Morris,Gene | (ts)
Lionel Hampton And His Orchestra
Lionel Hampton:Flying Home | Dreyfus Jazz Line | FDM 36735-2

Morris,Joe | (b,dr,el-g,gtp)
Joe Maneri-Joe Morris-Mat Maneri
Three Men Walking | ECM | 1597
Lionel Hampton And His Orchestra
Lionel Hampton:Flying Home | Dreyfus Jazz Line | FDM 36735-2
Louis Armstrong With Louis Jordan And His Tympany Five
Louis Armstrong:C'est Si Bon | Dreyfus Jazz Line | FDM 36730-2

Morris,John | (tb)
Lionel Hampton And His Orchestra
Lionel Hampton:Flying Home | Dreyfus Jazz Line | FDM 36735-2

Morris,Marlowe | (orgp)
Buddy Tate With The Marlow Morris Quintet
Late Night Sax | CBS | 487798-2
Sidney Catlett Quartet
Jazz:The Essential Collection Vol.3 | IN+OUT Records | 78013-2
Tiny Grimes Swingtet
The Blue Note Swingtets | Blue Note | 495697-2

Morris,Scott | (drperc)
Richie Cole Group
Jazz Life Vol.1:From Village Vanguard | Storyville | 4960753

Morris,Steve | (v)
Carla Bley Band
Fancy Chamber Music | Watt | 28(539937-2)

Morris,Thomas | (co,speech,talkingtp)
Clarence Williams' Blue Five
Jazz:The Essential Collection Vol.1 | IN+OUT Records | 78011-2

Morris,Walter 'Phatz' | (tbharm)
Lionel Hampton And His Orchestra
Planet Jazz:Lionel Hampton | Planet Jazz | 2152059-2

Morris[Chris Columbus],Joe | (dr)
Ella Fitzgerald With Louis Jordan And His Tympany Five
Ella Fitzgerald:Mr.Paganini | Dreyfus Jazz Line | FDM 36741-2
Louis Jordan And His Tympany Five
Louis Jordan-Let The Good Times Roll: The Complete Decca Recordings 1938-1954 | Bear Family Records | BCD 15557 IH

Morrison,James | (dr,tb,tp,fl-h,sax,p,euphoniumv-tb)
Erskine Hawkins And His Orchestra
Planet Jazz:Big Bands | Planet Jazz | 2169649-2
James Morrison-Ray Brown Quartet
Two The Max | East-West | 9031-77125-2

Morrison,John 'Peck' | (b)
Max Roach Septet
The Jazz Life! | Candid | CCD 79019

Morrison,Peck | (b)
(Little)Jimmy Scott With The Lucky Thompson Orchestra
Everybody's Somebody's Fool | Decca | 050669-2
Abbey Lincoln And Her All Stars(Newport Rebels)
Candid Dolphy | Candid | CCD 79033
Babs Gonzales And His Band
Voilà | Fresh Sound Records | FSR CD 340
Etta Jones And Her Band
Love Shout | Original Jazz Classics | OJCCD 941-2(P 7272)
J.J.Johnson-Kai Winding Quintet (Jay&Kai)
The J.J.Johnson Memorial Album | Prestige | PRCD 11025-2
Jazz Artists Guild
Newport Rebels-Jazz Artists Guild | Candid | CCD 79022
Lou Donaldson Quintet
The Best Of Blue Note | Blue Note | 796110-2
Shirley Scott Quintet
Queen Of The Organ-Shirley Scott Memorial Album | Prestige | PRCD 11027-2
Willis Jackson Quartet
At Large | Prestige | PCD 24243-2

Morrissey,Dick | (ts)
Klaus Doldinger With Orchestra
Lifelike | Warner | 2292-46478-2

Morrow,Barry | (tb)
Machito And His Orchestra
Afro-Cuban Jazz Moods | Original Jazz Classics | OJC20 447-2

Morrow,Bob | (v)
Artie Shaw And His Orchestra
Planet JazzArtie Shaw | Planet Jazz | 2152057-2
Planet Jazz:Big Bands | Planet Jazz | 2169649-2

Morrow,Buddy | (tb)
Gato Barbieri Orchestra
The Roots Of Acid Jazz | Impulse(MCA) | IMP 12042
Joe Williams With The Frank Hunter Orchestra
Planet Jazz:Joe Williams | Planet Jazz | 2165370-2
Sarah Vaughan With The Joe Lippman Orchestra
Sarah Vaughan:Lover Man | Dreyfus Jazz Line | FDM 36739-2
Sarah Vaughan With The Norman Leyden Orchestra
Sarah Vaughan:Lover Man | Dreyfus Jazz Line | FDM 36739-2

Morrow,George | (b)
All Star Live Jam Session
Brownie-The Complete EmArCy Recordings Of Clifford Brown | EmArCy | 838306-2
Anita O'Day With The Jimmy Giuffre Orchestra
Verve Jazz Masters 49:Anita O'Day | Verve | 527653-2
Chet Baker Quartet
Sings/It Could Happen To You | Original Jazz Classics | OJC20 303-2
Clifford Brown & The Neal Hefti Orchestra
Clifford Brown With Strings | Verve | 558078-2
Clifford Brown All Stars With Dinah Washington
Verve Jazz Masters 40:Dinah Washington | Verve | 522055-2
Clifford Brown With Strings
Clifford Brown-Max Roach:Alone Together-The Best Of The Mercury Years | Verve | 526373-2
Verve Jazz Masters 44:Clifford Brown and Max Roach | Verve | 528109-2
Brownie-The Complete EmArCy Recordings Of Clifford Brown | EmArCy | 838306-2
Clifford Brown-Max Roach Quartet
Verve Jazz Masters 44:Clifford Brown and Max Roach | Verve | 528109-2
Clifford Brown-Max Roach Quintet
Clifford Brown-Max Roach:Alone Together-The Best Of The Mercury Years | Verve | 526373-2
Verve Jazz Masters 44:Clifford Brown and Max Roach | Verve | 528109-2
Verve Jazz Masters Vol.60:The Collection | Verve | 529866-2
Clifford Brown And Max Roach | Verve | 543306-2
Clifford Brown And Max Roach At Basin Street | Verve | 589826-2
Study In Brown | EmArCy | 814646-2
Brownie-The Complete EmArCy Recordings Of Clifford Brown | EmArCy | 838306-2
Dinah Washington And Her Band
Verve Jazz Masters 40:Dinah Washington | Verve | 522055-2
Max Roach Plus Four
Clifford Brown-Max Roach:Alone Together-The Best Of The Mercury Years | Verve | 526373-2
Max Roach Quartet
Clifford Brown-Max Roach:Alone Together-The Best Of The Mercury Years | Verve | 526373-2
Max Roach Quintet
Clifford Brown-Max Roach:Alone Together-The Best Of The Mercury Years | Verve | 526373-2
Max Roach Trio
Clifford Brown And Max Roach | Verve | 543306-2
Sonny Rollins Plus Four
Sonny Rollins Plus 4 | Original Jazz Classics | OJC20 243-2(P 7038)
The Prestige Legacy Vol.1:The High Priests | Prestige | PCD 24251-2
Sonny Rollins Quartet
Worktime | Original Jazz Classics | OJC20 007-2(P 7020)
Tour De Force | Original Jazz Classics | OJCCD 095-2
Sonny Boy | Original Jazz Classics | OJCCD 348-2(P 7207)
Sonny Rollins Quintet
Sonny Rollins Plays For Bird | Original Jazz Classics | OJCCD 214-2
Sonny Boy | Original Jazz Classics | OJCCD 348-2(P 7207)
Sonny Stitt Quartet
Verve Jazz Masters 50:Sonny Sitt | Verve | 527651-2

Morsey,Alexander | (bel-b)
House Five
Frank Talk | Nabel Records:Jazz Network | CD 4674
Joachim Raffel Sextet
...In Motion | Jazz 4 Ever Records:Jazz Network | J4E 4746
Joachim Raffel Trio
...In Motion | Jazz 4 Ever Records:Jazz Network | J4E 4746
Lutz Wichert Trio
Ambiguous | Edition Musikat | EDM 068

Mortensen,Finn Wellejus | (tb)
Arne Birger's Jazzsjak
The Golden Years Of Revival Jazz,Vol.8 | Storyville | STCD 5513
The Golden Years Of Revival Jazz,Vol.10 | Storyville | STCD 5515

Mortensen,John Wellejs | (co)
The Golden Years Of Revival Jazz,Vol.8 | Storyville | STCD 5513
The Golden Years Of Revival Jazz,Vol.10 | Storyville | STCD 5515

Mortimer,John | (tb)
Mr.Acker Bilk And His Paramount Jazz Band
The Golden Years Of Revival Jazz,Vol.5 | Storyville | STCD 5510
The Golden Years Of Revival Jazz,Vol.6 | Storyville | STCD 5511
The Golden Years Of Revival Jazz,Vol.9 | Storyville | STCD 5514
The Golden Years Of Revival Jazz,Vol.12 | Storyville | STCD 5517
The Golden Years Of Revival Jazz,Vol.13 | Storyville | STCD 5518
The Golden Years Of Revibal Jazz,Vol.15 | Storyville | STCD 5520

Morton,Benny | (tb)
Benny Morton's All Stars
The Blue Note Swingtets | Blue Note | 495697-2
Jazz:The Essential Collection Vol.3 | IN+OUT Records | 78013-2
Big Sid Catlett And His Orchestra
The Small Black Groups | Storyville | 4960523
Connie's Inn Orchestra
Planet Jazz:Coleman Hawkins | Planet Jazz | 2152055-2
Count Basie And His Orchestra
Jazz:The Essential Collection Vol.3 | IN+OUT Records | 78013-2
From Spiritual To Swing | Vanguard | VCD 169/71
Fletcher Henderson And His Orchestra
Jazz:The Essential Collection Vol.1 | IN+OUT Records | 78011-2
Helen Humes With James P. Johnson And The Count Basie Orchestra
From Spiritual To Swing | Vanguard | VCD 169/71
Jimmy Rushing With Count Basie And His Orchestra
From Spiritual To Swing | Vanguard | VCD 169/71
Roy Eldridge And His Central Plaza Dixielanders
The Very Best Of Dixieland Jazz | Verve | 535529-2
The Complete Verve Roy Eldridge Studio Sessions | Verve | 9861278
Teddy Wilson Sextet
The Complete Associated Transcriptions,1944 | Storyville | STCD 8236
The Lousiana Stompers
Jazz:The Essential Collection Vol.1 | IN+OUT Records | 78011-2

Morton,Benny prob. | (tb)

Morton,Jeff | (dr)
Lee Konitz Quartet
Subconcious-Lee | Original Jazz Classics | OJCCD 186-2(P 7004)
Lee Konitz Quintet
Subconcious-Lee | Original Jazz Classics | OJCCD 186-2(P 7004)
Lennie Tristano Trio
Requiem | Atlantic | 7567-80804-2
Warne Marsh Quintet
Jazz Of Two Cities | Fresh Sound Records | FSR-CD 342
Warne Marsh Quintet With Art Pepper
Jazz Of Two Cities | Fresh Sound Records | FSR-CD 342

Morton,Jelly Roll | (p,talking,voc,p-solo)
Jelly Roll Morton
The Story Of Jazz Piano | Laserlight | 24653
Jazz:The Essential Collection Vol.1 | IN+OUT Records | 78011-2
Jelly Roll Morton And His Orchestra
Planet Jazz:Jelly Roll Morton | Planet Jazz | 2152060-2
Jazz:The Essential Collection Vol.1 | IN+OUT Records | 78011-2
Jelly Roll Morton Trio
Planet Jazz:Jelly Roll Morton | Planet Jazz | 2152060-2
Jazz:The Essential Collection Vol.1 | IN+OUT Records | 78011-2
Jelly Roll Morton's New Orleans Jazzmen
Planet Jazz | Planet Jazz | 2169652-2
Planet Jazz:Male Jazz Vocalists | Planet Jazz | 2169657-2
Jelly Roll Morton's Red Hot Peppers
Planet Jazz:Jelly Roll Morton | Planet Jazz | 2152060-2
Planet Jazz Sampler | Planet Jazz | 2152326-2
Jazz:The Essential Collection Vol.1 | IN+OUT Records | 78011-2

Morway-Baker,Renae | (voc)
The Sidewalks Of New York
Tin Pan Alley:The Sidewalks Of New York | Winter&Winter | 910038-2

Mosalini,Juan Jose | (bandoneon)
Dee Dee Bridgewater With Band
This Is New | Verve | 016884-2

Mosca,Ray | (dr)
Rolf Kühn Quintet
Rolf Kühn And His Sound Of Jazz | Fresh Sound Records | FSR-CD 326
Rolf Kühn Sextet
Rolf Kühn And His Sound Of Jazz | Fresh Sound Records | FSR-CD 326

Mosca,Sal | (pp-solo)
Lee Konitz Quintet
Subconcious-Lee | Original Jazz Classics | OJCCD 186-2(P 7004)
Lee Konitz-Warne Marsh Sextet
Lee Konitz With Warne Marsh | Atlantic | 8122-75356-2

Moscardini,Carlos | (g)
Carlos Mascardini
Internationales Guitarren Festival '99 | ALISO Records | AL 1038

Mosch,Ernst | (tb)
Erwin Lehn Und Sein Südfunk-Tanzorchester
Deutsches Jazz Fesival 1954/1955 | Bear Family Records | BCD 15430

Mosch,Manfred | (tb)
Freddie Brocksieper And His Boys
Freddie's Boogie Blues | Bear Family Records | BCD 16388 AH

Moschner,Pinguin | (Bb-tuba,F-tuba,didgiridoo,tuba)
European Tuba Quartet
Low And Behold | Jazz Haus Musik | JHM 0110 CD
Jürgen Sturm's Ballstars
Tango Subversivo | Nabel Records:Jazz Network | CD 4613

Moscow Art Trio |
Mikhail Alperin's Moscow Art Trio
Hamburg Concert | JA & RO | JARO 4201-2
Moscow Art Trio
Jazzy World | JA & RO | JARO 4200-2
Music | JA & RO | JARO 4214-2
Once Upon A Time | JA & RO | JARO 4238-2

Moscow Rachmaninov Trio |
Moscow Rachmaninov Trio
Groupe Lacroix:The Composer Group | Creative Works Records | CW CD 1030-2

Moseholm,Erik | (artistic director,borganizer)
Eric Dolphy Quartet
Eric Dolphy Birthday Celebration | Fantasy | FANCD 6085-2
Eric Dolphy With Erik Moseholm's Trio
Eric Dolphy:The Complete Prestige Recordings | Prestige | 9 PRCD-4418-2
Eric Dolphy in Europe, Vol.1 | Original Jazz Classics | OJC 413(P 7304)
Eric Dolphy In Europe, Vol.2 | Original Jazz Classics | OJCCD 414-2
Eric Dolphy In Europe, Vol.3 | Original Jazz Classics | OJCCD 416-2
European Jazz Youth Orchestra
Swinging Europe 1 | dacapo | DCCD 9449
Swinging Europe 2 | dacapo | DCCD 9450

Mosele,René | (tb)
Brigitte Dietrich-Joe Haider Jazz Orchestra
Consequences | JHM Records | JHM 3624

Moses,Basil | (b)
Johannes Enders Group
Reflections Of South Africa | Jazz 4 Ever Records:Jazz Network | J4E 4729

Moses,Bobby | (claves,dr,dr-machine,log-dr,perc)
Dave Liebman Quintet
Homage To John Coltrane | Owl Records | 018357-2
Gary Burton Quartet With Orchestra
A Genuine Tong Funeral(Dark Opera Without Words) | RCA | 2119255-2
Gary Burton Quintet
Dreams So Real | ECM | 1072
Gary Burton Quintet With Eberhard Weber
Ring | ECM | 1051
George Gruntz Concert Jazz Band '83
Theatre | ECM | 1265
Gordon Lee Quartet feat. Jim Pepper
Landwhales In New York | Tutu Records | 888136-2*
Pat Metheny Trio
Bright Size Life | ECM | 1073(827133-2)
Roland Kirk Group
I Talk With The Spirits | Verve | 558076-2
Roland Kirk Quintet
Rahsaan/The Complete Mercury Recordings Of Roland Kirk | Mercury | 846630-2
Steve Swallow Group
Home | ECM | 1160(513424-2)

Moses,China | (voc)
Dee Dee Bridgewater With Band
This Is New | Verve | 016884-2

Moses,J.C. | (dr)
Archie Shepp Trio
Fire Music | Impulse(MCA) | 951158-2
Eric Dolphy Quartet
The Illinois Concert | Blue Note | 499826-2
Eric Dolphy Quartet With The University Of Illinois Big Band
The Illinois Concert | Blue Note | 499826-2
Eric Dolphy Quartet With The University Of Illinois Brass Ensemble
The Illinois Concert | Blue Note | 499826-2
Roland Kirk Quartet
Talkin' Verve-Roots Of Acid Jazz:Roland Kirk | Verve | 533101-2
Roland Kirk Quartet With Sonny Boy Williamson
Talkin' Verve-Roots Of Acid Jazz:Roland Kirk | Verve | 533101-2
Roland Kirk Quintet
Rahsaan/The Complete Mercury Recordings Of Roland Kirk | Mercury | 846630-2

Moses,Kathy | (b-fl)
Hugh Marsh Duo/Quartet/Orchestra
The Bear Walks | VeraBra Records | CDVBR 2011-2

Mosgaard,Ole Skipper | (bel-b)
Per Carsten Quintet
Via | dacapo | DCCD 9462

Mosher,Jimmy | (as,fl,clss)
Buddy Rich Big Band
The New One! | Pacific Jazz | 494507-2
Keep The Customer Satisfied | EMI Records | 523999-2

Mosher,John | (b)
Art Van Damme Group
State Of Art | MPS | 841413-2

Mosley,Don | (bdr)
Sonny Stitt Quartet
The Art Of Saxophone | Laserlight | 24652

Moss,Danny | (ts)
Danny Moss Meets Buddha's Gamblers
A Swingin' Affair | Nagel-Heyer | CD 034
Blues Of Summer | Nagel-Heyer | NH 1011
Danny Moss Quartet
Weaver Of Dreams | Nagel-Heyer | CD 017
Keeper Of The Flame | Nagel-Heyer | CD 064
The Second Sampler | Nagel-Heyer | NHR SP 6
Danny Moss-Roy Williams Quintet
Steamers! | Nagel-Heyer | CD 049
Ellington For Lovers | Nagel-Heyer | NH 1009
George Masso Allstars
The Wonderful World Of George Gershwin | Nagel-Heyer | CD 001
One Two Three | Nagel-Heyer | CD 008
The First Sampler | Nagel-Heyer | NHR SP 5
Jeanie Lambe And The Danny Moss Quartet
Three Great Concerts:Live In Hamburg 1993-1995 | Nagel-Heyer | CD 019
The Blue Noise Session | Nagel-Heyer | CD 052
The Second Sampler | Nagel-Heyer | NHR SP 6
Jeanie Lambe And The Danny Moss Septet
Three Great Concerts:Live In Hamburg 1993-1995 | Nagel-Heyer | CD 019
Oliver Jackson Orchestra
The Last Great Concert | Nagel-Heyer | CD 063
The Buck Clayton Legacy
All The Cats Join In(Buck Clayton Remembered) | Nagel-Heyer | CD 006
Encore Live | Nagel-Heyer | CD 018
The First Sampler | Nagel-Heyer | NHR SP 5
The Second Sampler | Nagel-Heyer | NHR SP 6
The Yamaha International Allstar Band

Hapy Birthday Jazzwelle Plus | Nagel-Heyer | CD 005
The First Sampler | Nagel-Heyer | NHR SP 5
Tom Saunders' 'Wild Bill Davison Band' & Guests
Exactly Like You | Nagel-Heyer | CD 023
The Second Sampler | Nagel-Heyer | NHR SP 6

Moss,David | (dr,electronics,voice,perc)
David Moss-Michael Rodach
Fragmentary Blues | Traumton Records | 4432-2
Klaus König Orchestra
Reviews | Enja | ENJ-9061 2
Uri Caine Ensemble
Love Fugue-Robert Schumann | Winter&Winter | 910049-2

Moss,Martin | (voc)
Bernard Purdie's Soul To Jazz
Bernard Purdie's Soul To Jazz | ACT | 9242-2

Moss,Ron | (tb)
Chick Corea Group
Verve Jazz Masters 3:Chick Corea | Verve | 519820-2

Moss,Steve | (perc,tsvoc)
Gary Thomas Group
Found On Sordid Street | Winter&Winter | 910002-2

Mössinger,Johannes | (pp-solo)
Johannes Mössinger
Spring In Versailles | double moon | DMCD 1004-2
Johannes Mössinger New York Trio
Monk's Corner | double moon | DMCHR 71032
Johannes Mössinger New York Trio with Joe Lovano
Monk's Corner | double moon | DMCHR 71032
Johannes Mössinger-Wolfgang Lackerschmid
Joana's Dance | double moon | CHRDM 71017

Mossman,Michel Philip | (arr,ld,fl-h,tp,tb,piccolo-tpperc)
Daniel Schnyder Group
Tanatula | Enja | ENJ-9302 2
Daniel Schnyder Quintet
Nucleus | Enja | ENJ-8068 2
Daniel Schnyder Quintet With String Quartet
Mythology | Enja | ENJ-7003 2
George Gruntz Concert Jazz Band
Blues 'N Dues Et Cetera | Enja | ENJ-6072 2
Kevin Mahogany With Orchestra
Songs And Moments | Enja | ENJ-8072 2

Most,Abe | (cl,as,reedssax)
Ella Fitzgerald With The Buddy Bregman Orchestra
Ella Fitzgerald Sings The Rodgers And Hart Song Book | Verve | 537258-2
Ella Fitzgerald With The Nelson Riddle Orchestra
Ella Fitzgerald Sings The Johnny Mercer Songbook | Verve | 539057-2
Van Alexander Orchestra
Home Of Happy Feet/Swing! Staged For Sound! | Capitol | 535211-2

Most,Sam | (cl,fl,asts)
Chubby Jackson And His All Star Big Band
Chubby Takes Over | Fresh Sound Records | FSR-CD 324

Mostafa,Amr | (req)
Mahmoud Turkmani Group
Zakira | Enja | ENJ-9475 2

Moten,Benny | (b,cl,as,ld,parr)
Benny Moten's Kansas City Orchestra
Planet Jazz:Ben Webster | RCA | 2165368-2
Planet Jazz:Jimmy Rushing | RCA | 2165371-2
Planet Jazz:Swing | Planet Jazz | 2169651-2
Jazz:The Essential Collection Vol.3 | IN+OUT Records | 78013-2
Roy 'Little Jazz' Eldridge Quartet
The Complete Verve Roy Eldridge Studio Sessions | Verve | 9861278
Wilbur DeParis And His New New Orleans Band
Atlantic Jazz: New Orleans | Atlantic | 7567-81700-2

Moten,Buster prob. | (p)
Benny Moten's Kansas City Orchestra
Planet Jazz:Jimmy Rushing | RCA | 2165371-2

Motian,Paul | (dr,calebasses,crotales,gongs)
Bill Evans Trio
The Story Of Jazz Piano | Laserlight | 24653
Bill Evans:The Complete Live At The Village Vanguard 1961 | Riverside | 3RCD 1961-2
Verve Jazz Masters 5:Bill Evans | Verve | 519821-2
The Complete Bill Evans On Verve | Verve | 527953-2
Trio 64 | Verve | 539058-2
On Green Dolphin Street | Milestone | MCD 9235-2
New Jazz Conceptions | Original Jazz Classics | OJC20 025-2(RLP 223)
Explorations | Original Jazz Classics | OJC20 037-2(RLP 9351)
Portrait In Jazz | Original Jazz Classics | OJC20 088-2
Sunday At The Village Vanguard | Original Jazz Classics | OJC20 140-2
Waltz For Debby | Original Jazz Classics | OJC20 210-2
Moonbeams | Original Jazz Classics | OJC20 434-2(RLP 9428)
How My Heart Sings! | Original Jazz Classics | OJCCD 369-2
The Jazz Giants Play Harry Warren:Lullaby Of Broadway | Prestige | PCD 24204-2
The Jazz Giants Play Rodgers & Hammerstein:My Favorite Things | Prestige | PCD 24223-2
Bill Frisell Quintet
Rambler | ECM | 1287
Carla Bley Group
Tropic Appetites | Watt | 1
Charlie Haden And The Liberation Music Orchestra
The Montreal Tapes:Liberation Music Orchestra | Verve | 527469-2
Charlie Haden Orchestra
The Ballad Of The Fallen | ECM | 1248(811546-2)
Charlie Haden Trio
The Montreal Tapes | Verve | 537483-2
The Montreal Tapes | Verve | 537670-2
Charlie Haden-Paul Motian
Closeness Duets | Verve | 397000-2
Charlie Haden's Liberation Music Orchestra
Liberation Music Orchestra | Impulse(MCA) | 951188-2
Ed Schuller Quartet feat. Dewey Redman
Mu-Point | Tutu Records | 888154-2*
Eddie Costa Quartet
Guys And Dolls Like Vives | Verve | 549366-2
George Russell Smalltet
The RCA Victor Jazz Workshop | RCA | 2159144-2
Geri Allen/Charlie Haden/Paul Motian
In The Year Of The Dragon | JMT Edition | 919027-2
Geri Allen/Charlie Haden/Paul Motian & Guest
In The Year Of The Dragon | JMT Edition | 919027-2
Herbie Mann With The Bill Evans Trio
Nirvana | Atlantic | 7567-90141-2
Keith Jarrett Group
Expectations | CBS | C2K 65900
Keith Jarrett Group With Brass
Expectations | CBS | C2K 65900
Keith Jarrett Group With Strings
Expectations | CBS | C2K 65900
Keith Jarrett Quartet
The Survivor's Suite | ECM | 1085(827131-2)
Eyes Of The Heart | ECM | 1150(825476-2)
El Juicio(The Judgement) | Atlantic | 7567-80783-2
Byablue | Impulse(MCA) | MCD 10648
Keith Jarrett Quintet
Fort Yawuh | Impulse(MCA) | 547966-2
The Roots Of Acid Jazz | Impulse(MCA) | IMP 12042
Keith Jarrett Trio
At The Deer Head Inn | ECM | 1531(517720-2)
Chick Corea-Herbie Hancock-Keith Jarrett-McCoy Tyner | Atlantic | 7567-81402-2
Somewhere Before | Atlantic | 7567-81455-2
The Mourning Of A Star | Atlantic | 8122-75355-2
Byablue | Impulse(MCA) | MCD 10648
Lee Konitz Trio
Three Guys | Enja | ENJ-9351 2

Marilyn Crispell Trio
Nothing Ever Was,Anyway.Music Of Annette Peacock | ECM | 1626/27(537222-2)
Story Teller | ECM | 1847(0381192)
Marilyn Crispell-Gary Peacock-Paul Motian
Amarylis | ECM | 1742(013400-2)
Martial Solal Trio
Martial Solal At Newport '63 | RCA | 2174803-2
Masabumi Kikuchi Trio
Tethered Moon-First Meeting | Winter&Winter | 910016-2
Mose Allison Quintet
Gimeracs And Gewgaws | Blue Note | 823211-2
Mose Allison Trio
Mose Alife!/Wild Man On The Loose | Warner | 8122-75439-2
Paul Bley Quartet
Fragments | ECM | 1320
The Paul Bley Quartet | ECM | 1365(835250-2)
Paul Bley Trio
Paul Bley With Gary Peacock | ECM | 1003
Not Two, Not One | ECM | 1670(559447-2)
Paul Motian
Conception Vessel | ECM | 1028(519279-2)
Paul Motian And The E.B.B.B.
Holiday For Strings | Winter&Winter | 910069-2
Paul Motian Band
Psalm | ECM | 1222
Paul Motian Electric Bebop Band
Flight Of The Blue Jay | Winter&Winter | 910009-2
Monk And Powell | Winter&Winter | 910045-2
Europe | Winter&Winter | 910063-2
Paul Motian Quartet
Conception Vessel | ECM | 1028(519279-2)
Monk In Motian | JMT Edition | 919020-2
Paul Motian On Broadway Vol.1 | JMT Edition | 919029-2
Paul Motian Quintet
Tribute | ECM | 1048
Paul Motian Trio
Conception Vessel | ECM | 1028(519279-2)
Le Voyage | ECM | 1138
It Should've Happened A Long Time Ago | ECM | 1283
Sound Of Love | Winter&Winter | 910008-2
Monk In Motian | JMT Edition | 919020-2
Paul Motian Trio With Chris Potter And Larry Grenadier
Paul Motian Trio 2000 + One | Winter&Winter | 910032-2
Paul Motian-Keith Jarrett
Conception Vessel | ECM | 1028(519279-2)
Pierre Favre Ensemble
Singing Drums | ECM | 1274
Stephan Oliva Trio
Fantasm | RCA | 2173925-2
Tethered Moon
Chansons D'Edith Piaf | Winter&Winter | 910048-2
Tom Harrell Quintet
Form | Contemporary | CCD 14059-2
Visions | Contemporary | CCD 14063-2
Tom Harrell Sextet
Visions | Contemporary | CCD 14063-2
Zoot Sims-Al Cohn Quintet
Jazz Alive:A Night At The Half Note | Blue Note | 494105-2
Zoot Sims-Al Cohn-Phil Woods Sextet
Jazz Alive:A Night At The Half Note | Blue Note | 494105-2

Motley,John | (ldvoc)
Max Roach Chorus & Orchestra
To The Max! | Enja | ENJ-7021 22

Motsinger,Buddy | (p)
Cal Tjader Quartet
Cal Tjader Plays Harold Arlen & West Side Story | Fantasy | FCD 24775-2

Mottola,Tony | (g)
Billie Holiday With Gordon Jenkins And His Orchestra
Billie's Love Songs | Nimbus Records | NI 2000
Lena Horne With The Lennie Hayton Orchestra
Planet Jazz:Lena Horne | Planet Jazz | 2165373-2
Sarah Vaughan With The Hugo Winterhalter Orchestra
Sarah Vaughan:Lover Man | Dreyfus Jazz Line | FDM 36739-2

Motus Quartett: |
Motus Quartett
Grimson Flames | Creative Works Records | CW CD 1023-2

Motz,Dick | (tp)
Grace Knight With Orchestra
Come In Spinner | Intuition Records | INT 3052-2
Vince Jones With Orchestra
Come In Spinner | Intuition Records | INT 3052-2

Mouncey,Arthur | (tp)
Vic Lewis Jam Session
Vic Lewis:The Golden Years | Candid | CCD 79754

Mound City Blue Blowers |
Mound City Blue Blowers
Planet Jazz:Jack Teagarden | Planet Jazz | 2161236-2
Jazz:The Essential Collection Vol.3 | IN+OUT Records | 78013-2

Mountaine,Andrea | (voc)
Mike Westbrook Brass Band
Glad Day:Settings Of William Blake | Enja | ENJ-9376 2

Mountjoy,Monte | (dr)
Firehouse Five Plus Two
Goes South | Good Time Jazz | GTCD 12018-2

Moura,Paulo | (as,clss)
Cannonball Adderley With Sergio Mendes And The Bossa Rio Sextet
Cannonball's Bossa Nova | Blue Note | 522667-2
Ballads | Blue Note | 537563-2
Blue Bossa | Blue Note | 795590-2

Mouskouri,Nana | (voc)
Nana Mouskouri With The Berlin Radio Big Band
Nana Swings | Mercury | 074394-2

Moussay,Benjamin | (p)
Louis Sclavis & The Bernard Struber Jazztet
La Phare | Enja | ENJ-9359 2

Moutin,Francois | (bel-b)
Antoine Hervé Quintet
Invention Is You | Enja | ENJ-9398 2
James Hurt Group
Dark Grooves-Mystcal Rhythms | Blue Note | 495104-2
Jean-Michel Pilc Trio
Welcome Home | Dreyfus Jazz Line | FDM 36630-2
Cardinal Points | Dreyfus Jazz Line | FDM 36649-2
Martial Solal Trio
Martial Solal NY-1 | Blue Note | 584232-2

Moutin,Louis | (dr)
Antoine Hervé Quintet
Invention Is You | Enja | ENJ-9398 2

Mouzon,Alphonse | (dr,bell-tree,perc,voc,dr-solo)
Al Di Meola Group
Land Of The Midnight Sun | CBS | 468214-2
Alphonse Mouzon Group
Deep Blue-The United States Of Mind | Blue Note | 521152-2
Gil Evans Orchestra
Blues In Orbit | Enja | ENJ-3069 2
Herbie Hancock Group
Monster | CBS | 486571-2
Magic Window | CBS | 486572-2
Just Friends
Nevertheless | IN+OUT Records | 7015-2
Jazz Unlimited | IN+OUT Records | 7017-2
Larry Coryell-Alphonse Mouzon Quartet
Atlantic Jazz: Fusion | Atlantic | 7567-81711-2
Les McCann Group
Atlantic Jazz: Fusion | Atlantic | 7567-81711-2
Mangelsdorff-Pastorius-Mouzon
Three Originals:The Wide Point/Trilogue/Albert Live In Montreux | MPS | 519213-2

McCoy Tyner Quartet
Sahara | Original Jazz Classics | OJC20 311-2
Song For My Lady | Original Jazz Classics | OJCCD 313-2
McCoy Tyner Septet
Song For My Lady | Original Jazz Classics | OJCCD 313-2
Wayne Shorter Orchestra
Wayne Shorter:The Classic Blue Note Recordings | Blue Note | 540856-2

Mower,Mike | (fl,cl,tsbs)
Itchy Fingers
Live | Enja | ENJ-6076 2
Full English Breakfast | Enja | ENJ-7085 2

Moyal,Sandrine | (v)
Stephane Grappelli With The Michel Legrand Orchestra
Grapelli Story | Verve | 515807-2

Moyano,Ricardo | (g)
Ricardo Moyano
Internationales Guitarren Festival '94 | ALISO Records | AL 1030
Ricardo Moyano-Juan Falù
Internationales Guitarren Festival '94 | ALISO Records | AL 1030

Moye,Eugene | (cellostrings)
A Band Of Friends
Wynton Marsalis Quartet With Strings | CBS | CK 68921
Kevin Mahogany With The Bob James Trio, Kirk Whalum And Strings
My Romance | Warner | 9362-47025-2
Ron Carter Quintet With Strings
Pick 'Em/Super Strings | Milestone | MCD 47090-2

Moye,Famoudou Don | (congas,bongos,balafon,bass-pan-dr)
Art Ensemble Of Chicago
Nice Guys | ECM | 1126
Full Force | ECM | 1167(829197-2)
Urban Bushmen | ECM | 1211/12
The Third Decade | ECM | 1273
Tribute To Lester | ECM | 1808(017066-2)
Americans Swinging In Paris:Art Ensemble Of Chicago | EMI Records | 539667-2
Bap-Tizum | Atlantic | 7567-80757-2
Coming Home Jamaica | Dreyfus Jazz Line | FDM 37003-2
Arthur Blythe Group
Hipmotism | Enja | ENJ-6088 2
Lester Bowie's Brass Fantasy
The Fire This Time | IN+OUT Records | 7019-2

Mr.Mad Dog | (loops)
Nils Landgren First Unit And Guests
Nils Landgren-The First Unit | ACT | 9292-2

Mraz,George 'Jiri' | (b)
(Little)Jimmy Scott And His Band
Mood Indigo | Milestone | MCD 9305-2
Allan Botschinsky Quartet
Last Summer | M.A Music | A 804-2
Art Pepper Quartet
Art Pepper:The Complete Village Vanguard Sessions | Contemporary | 9CCD-4417-2
Thursday Night At The Village Vanguard | Original Jazz Classics | OJCCD 694-2(7642)
Friday Night At The Village Vanguard | Original Jazz Classics | OJCCD 695-2(C 7643)
Saturday Night At The Village Vanguard | Original Jazz Classics | OJCCD 696-2(C 7644)
The Jazz Giants Play Harold Arlen:Blues In The Night | Prestige | PCD 24201-2
Beirach-Hübner-Mraz
Round About Bartok | ACT | 9276-2
Carmen McRae And Her Quartet
Carmen Sings Monk | RCA | 2663841-2
Carmen McRae with the Clifford Jordan Quartet
The Collected Carmen McRae | RCA | 2668713-2
Carol Sloane With The Norris Turney Quartet
Something Cool | Choice | CHCD 71025
Charles Mingus Orchestra
Three Or Four Shades Of Blues | Atlantic | 7567-81403-2
Chet Baker-Stan Getz Quintet
The Stockholm Concerts | Verve | 537555-2
Chris Connor With The Hank Jones Trio
As Time Goes By | Enja | ENJ-7061 2
Christoph Sänger Trio
Imagination | Laika Records | 35100752
Elvin Jones Quintet
Youngblood | Enja | ENJ-7051 2
Elvin Jones Trio
Youngblood | Enja | ENJ-7051 2
Elvin Jones-George Mraz
Youngblood | Enja | ENJ-7051 2
Eric Alexander Quartet
Solid! | Milestone | MCD 9283-2
Eric Alexander Quintet
Solid! | Milestone | MCD 9283-2
Freddy Cole With Band
A Circle Of Love | Fantasy | FCD 9674-2
To The End Of The Earth | Fantasy | FCD 9675-2
Le Grand Freddy:Freddy Cole Sings The Music Of Michel Legrand | Fantasy | FCD 9683-2
Freddy Cole With The Cedar Walton Trio
Love Makes The Changes | Fantasy | FCD 9681-2
Freddy Cole With The Cedar Walton Trio And Grover Washington Jr.
Love Makes The Changes | Fantasy | FCD 9681-2
Freddy Cole With The Eric Alexander Band
Love Makes The Changes | Fantasy | FCD 9681-2
George Mraz Quartet
Bottom Line | Milestone | MCD 9272-2
Duke's Place | Milestone | MCD 9292-2
Morava | Milestone | MCD 9309-2
George Mraz Trio
Duke's Place | Milestone | MCD 9292-2
Hans Koller Big Band
New York City | MPS | 9813437
Helen Merrill With Orchestra
Casa Forte | EmArCy | 558848-2
Jimmy Scott With Band
Over The Rainbow | Milestone | MCD 9314-2
But Beautiful | Milestone | MCD 9321-2
Moon Glow | Milestone | MCD 9332-2
Joe Lovano Orchestra
Blue Note Plays Gershwin | Blue Note | 520808-2
John Lewis Quartet
Eviolution II | Atlantic | 7567-83313-2
Klaus Weiss Septet
All Night Through | ATM Records | ATM 3816 AH
Klaus Weiss Sextet
All Night Through | ATM Records | ATM 3816 AH
Lew Soloff Quartet
With A Song In My Heart | Milestone | MCD 9290-2
Lew Soloff Quintet
With A Song In My Heart | Milestone | MCD 9290-2
McCoy Tyner Trio
McCoy Tyner Plays John Coltrane | Impulse(MCA) | 589183-2
Oscar Peterson Trio
Two Originals:Walking The Line/Another Day | MPS | 533549-2
Richard Beirach Trio
Round About Federico Mompou | ACT | 9296-2
Richard Galliano Quartet
New York Tango | Dreyfus Jazz Line | FDM 36581-2
Gallianissimo! The Best Of Richard Galliano | Dreyfus Jazz Line | FDM 36616-2
Singers Unlimited + The Oscar Peterson Trio
The Singers Unlimited:Magic Voices | MPS | 539130-2
Stan Getz Quartet
The Lost Sessions | Verve | 9801098

Bossas And Ballads:The Lost Sessions | Verve | 0001098
Stephane Grappelli-Michel Petrucciani Quartet
Flamingo | Dreyfus Jazz Line | FDM 36580-2
Tommy Flanagan Trio
Confirmation | Enja | ENJ-4014 2
Thelonica | Enja | ENJ-4052 2
Tommy Flanagan/George Mraz
Confirmation | Enja | ENJ-4014 2
Walter Norris-George Mraz Duo
Drifting | Enja | ENJ-2044 2
Zoot Sims Quartet
Suddenly It's Spring | Original Jazz Classics | OJCCD 742-2(2310898)
Zoot Sims Quintet
Zoot Sims And The Gershwin Brothers | Original Jazz Classics | OJC20 444-2(2310744)
Zoot Sims And The Gershwin Brothers | Pablo | PASA 2310-744-6
Zoot Sims-Jimmy Rowles Quartet
If I'm Lucky | Original Jazz Classics | OJCCD 683-2(2310803)
The Jazz Giants Play Harry Warren:Lullaby Of Broadway | Prestige | PCD 24204-2

Mt.Zion Singers | (voc)
Albert King Blues Band
Lovejoy | Stax | SCD 8517-2(STS 2040)

M'tume,James[Forman] | (congas,p,perc,rythm-boxwater-dr)
Eddie Henderson Orchestra
Blue Break Beats | Blue Note | 799106-2
Gato Barbieri Group
Planet Jazz:Gato Barbieri | RCA | 2165364-2
Gato Barbieri:The Best Of The Early Years | RCA | 2663523-2
Lonnie Liston Smith & His Cosmic Echoes
Astral Travelling | RCA | 2663878-2
McCoy Tyner Orchestra
Sama Layuca | Original Jazz Classics | OJCCD 1071-2(M 9056)
McCoy Tyner Quintet
Asante | Blue Note | 493384-2
McCoy Tyner Septet
Song For My Lady | Original Jazz Classics | OJCCD 313-2
Miles Davis Group
Paris Jazz Concert:Miles Davis | Laserlight | 17445
Pangaea | CBS | 467087-2
Agharta | CBS | 467897-2
Dark Magus | CBS | C2K 65137
In Concert | CBS | C2K 65140
On The Corner | CBS | CK 63980
Sonny Rollins Sextet
The Cutting Edge | Original Jazz Classics | OJC 468(M 9059)
Sonny Rollins Sextet With Rufus Harley
The Cutting Edge | Original Jazz Classics | OJC 468(M 9059)

Mucci,Louis | (tp)
Don Senay With Orchestra And Strings
Charles Mingus-The Complete Debut Recordings | Debut | 12 DCD 4402-2
George Russell And His Orchestra
Bill Evans:Piano Player | CBS | CK 65361
Gil Evans And Ten
Gil Evans And Ten | Original Jazz Classics | OJC 346(P 7120)
The Jazz Giants Play Cole Porter:Night And Day | Prestige | PCD 24203-2
Gil Evans And Ten | Prestige | PRSA 7120-6
Gil Evans Orchestra
Verve Jazz Masters 23:Gil Evans | Verve | 521860-2
The Individualism Of Gil Evans | Verve | 833804-2
John LaPorta Octet
Theme And Variations | Fantasy | FCD 24776-2
John LaPorta Septet
Theme And Variations | Fantasy | FCD 24776-2
Kenny Burrell With The Gil Evans Orchestra
Guitar Forms | Verve | 521403-2
Verve Jazz Masters 23:Gil Evans | Verve | 521860-2
Verve Jazz Masters 45:Kenny Burrell | Verve | 527652-2
Verve Jazz Masters Vol.60:The Collection | Verve | 529866-2
Miles Davis + 19
Miles Ahead | CBS | CK 65121
Miles Davis With Gil Evans & His Orchestra
Miles Davis At Carnegie Hall | CBS | CK 65027
This Is Jazz:Miles Davis Plays Ballads | CBS | CK 65038
Porgy And Bess | CBS | CK 65141
Sketches Of Spain | CBS | CK 65142
Quiet Nights | CBS | CK 65293
Thad Jones And His Orchestra
Charles Mingus-The Complete Debut Recordings | Debut | 12 DCD 4402-2

Muche,Matthias | (tb)
Andreas Schnerman Sextet
Welcome To My Backyard | Edition Collage | EC 535-2
Jazz Orchester Rheinland-Pfalz
Last Season | Jazz Haus Musik | LJBB 9706
Marcus Sukiennik Big Band
A Night In Tunisia Suite(7 Variationen über Dizzy Gillespie's 'A Night In Tunisia') | Jazz Haus Musik | ohne Nummer

Muckhead | (rap)
Lenny White Group
Present Tense | Hip Bop | HIBD 8004

Muddy Waters[McKinley Morganfield] | (gvoc)
Muddy Waters Band
Muddy Waters:Paris 1972 | Pablo | PACD 5302-2
Muddy Waters Blues Band
Classic Blues | Zounds | CD 2700048
Muddy Waters-The Collection | MCA | MCD 18961
Otis Spann Band
The Blues Never Die! | Original Blues Classics | OBCCD 530-2(P 7391)
Windy City Blues | Stax | SCD 8612-2

Muelbauer.Marc | (b)
Julia Hülsmann Trio With Anna Lauvergnac
Come Closer | ACT | 9702-2

Muellbauer,Marc | (b)
Julia Hülsman Trio With Rebekka Bakken
Scattering Poems | ACT | 9405-2

Muhammad,Idris[Leo Morris] | (dr,log-dr,lyrics,perctambourine)
Ahmad Jamal Quartet
Nature(The Essence Part III) | Atlantic | 3984-23105-2
Ahmad Jamal À L'Olympia | Dreyfus Jazz Line | FDM 36629-2
The Essence Part 1 | Dreyfus Jazz Line | FDM 37007-2
Big Byrd | Dreyfus Jazz Line | FDM 37008-2
Nature | Dreyfus Jazz Line | FDM 37018-2
Ahmad Jamal Quartet With Stanley Turrentine
Nature(The Essence Part III) | Atlantic | 3984-23105-2
Nature | Dreyfus Jazz Line | FDM 37018-2
Ahmad Jamal Quintet
The Essence Part 1 | Dreyfus Jazz Line | FDM 37007-2
Big Byrd | Dreyfus Jazz Line | FDM 37008-2
Ahmad Jamal Trio
Picture Perfect-70th Anniversary | Warner | 8573-85268-2
In Search Of Momentum (1-10) | Dreyfus Jazz Line | FDM 36644-2
Big Byrd | Dreyfus Jazz Line | FDM 37008-2
Andrew Hill Sextet
Grass Roots | Blue Note | 522672-2
Bob Stewart First Line Band
First Line | JMT Edition | 919014-2
Charles Earland Quintet
Black Talk! | Original Jazz Classics | OJCCD 335-2(P 7758)
Charles Earland Sextet
Black Talk! | Original Jazz Classics | OJCCD 335-2(P 7758)
Charlie's Greatest Hits | Prestige | PCD 24250-2
David Fathead Newman Septet
Jazzin' Vol.2: The Music Of Stevie Wonder | Fantasy | FANCD 6088-2
Eladio Reinon Quintet
Es La Historia De Un Amor | Fresh Sound Records | FSNT 004 CD

Eric Alexander Quartet
Solid! | Milestone | MCD 9283-2
Eric Alexander Quintet
Solid! | Milestone | MCD 9283-2
Essence All Stars
Hot Jazz Bisquits | Hip Bop | HIBD 8801
Gene Ammons Quartet
Fine And Mellow | Prestige | PRCD 24281-2
Gene Ammons Sextet
Fine And Mellow | Prestige | PRCD 24281-2
Gene Ammons Sextet With Strings
Fine And Mellow | Prestige | PRCD 24281-2
George Benson Orchestra
Talkin' Verve:George Benson | Verve | 553780-2
George Benson With Orchestra
Verve Jazz Masters 21:George Benson | Verve | 521861-2
George Benson With The Don Sebesky Orchestra
Verve Jazz Masters 21:George Benson | Verve | 521861-2
Grant Green Orchestra
Grant Green:Blue Breakbeat | Blue Note | 494705-2
Blue Breaks Beats Vol.2 | Blue Note | 789907-2
So Blue So Funky-Heroes Of The Hammond | Blue Note | 796563-2
Grant Green Sextet
Grant Green:Blue Breakbeat | Blue Note | 494705-2
Alive! | Blue Note | 525650-2
Blue Break Beats | Blue Note | 799106-2
The Lost Grooves | Blue Note | 831883-2
Hank Crawford Quintet
The Jazz Giants Play Sammy Cahn:It's Magic | Prestige | PCD 24226-2
Houston Person Sextet
Jazzin' With The Soul Brothers | Fantasy | FANCD 6086-2
Idris Muhammad Group
Jazzin' With The Soul Brothers | Fantasy | FANCD 6086-2
Joe Lovano-Greg Osby Quintet
Friendly Fire | Blue Note | 499125-2
John Scofield Groups
Groove Elation | Blue Note | 832801-2
Leon Spencer Sextet
Jazzin' With The Soul Brothers | Fantasy | FANCD 6086-2
Discovery:Grover Washington Jr.-The First Recordings | Prestige | PCD 11020-2
Lou Donaldson Orchestra
Blue Breaks Beats Vol.2 | Blue Note | 789907-2
Lou Donaldson Quartet
Mr.Shing-A-Ling | Blue Note | 784271-2
Lou Donaldson Quintet
Midnight Creeper | Blue Note | 524546-2
Mr.Shing-A-Ling | Blue Note | 784271-2
Blue Break Beats | Blue Note | 799106-2
The Lost Grooves | Blue Note | 831883-2
Lou Donaldson Sextet
So Blue So Funky-Heroes Of The Hammond | Blue Note | 796563-2
Melvin Sparks Quintet
Jazzin' With The Soul Brothers | Fantasy | FANCD 6086-2
Pharoah Sanders Orchestra
Jewels Of Thought | Impulse(MCA) | 951247-2
Reuben Wilson Sextet
The Lost Grooves | Blue Note | 831883-2
Rodney Jones Group
Soul Manifesto | Blue Note | 530499-2
Roots
Stablemates | IN+OUT Records | 7021-2
Roy Hargrove's Crisol
Habana | Verve | 537563-2
Rusty Bryant Quintet
Jazzin' With The Soul Brothers | Fantasy | FANCD 6086-2
Sonny Rollins Quartet
Global Warming | Milestone | MCD 9280-2
Sonny Stitt With Orchestra
Goin' Down Slow | Prestige | PRCD 24276-2
Stefon Harris-Jacky Terrasson Group
Kindred | Blue Note | 531868-2
Tom Browne Quintet
Another Shade Of Browne | Hip Bop | HIBD 8011
Hot Jazz Bisquits | Hip Bop | HIBD 8801

Mühlbradt,Horst | (arr,el-p,perc,keyboardsp)
Chet Baker With The NDR-Bigband
NDR Big Band-Bravissimo | ACT | 9232-2
Heinz Sauer Quartet With The NDR Big Band
NDR Big Band-Bravissimo | ACT | 9232-2
Johnny Griffin With The NDR Big Band
NDR Big Band-Bravissimo | ACT | 9232-2

Mühlnickel,Joachim | (viola)
Till Brönner Quartet & Deutsches Symphonieorchester Berlin
German Songs | Minor Music | 801057

Mukogava,Carol | (viola)
Charlie Haden Quartet West With Strings
The Art Of The Song | Verve | 547403-2
Charlie Haden With String Quartet
The Art Of The Song | Verve | 547403-2
Chick Corea And His Orchestra
My Spanish Heart | Polydor | 543303-3

Muldaur,Maria | (voc)
Jay McShann Quartet
Goin' To Kansas City | Stony Plain | SPCD 1286

Muldrow,Ronald | (g,guitorgansynth)
Eddie Harris Group
The Best Of Eddie Harris | Atlantic | 7567-81370-2

Muldrow,Sidney | (fr-h)
Gene Harris Group
Blue Breaks Beats Vol.2 | Blue Note | 789907-2

Mulford,Phil | (b-gel-b)
Barbara Thompson's Paraphernalia
A Cry From The Heart | VeraBra Records | CDVBR 2021-2
Breathless | VeraBra Records | CDVBR 2057-2

Mulia,Michael | (b)
Etta Jones And Her Quartet
Hollar! | Original Jazz Classics | OJCCD 1061(PR 7284)
Something Nice | Original Jazz Classics | OJCCD 221-2(P 7194)

Mullen,Jan | (v)
Helen Merrill With Orchestra
Casa Forte | EmArCy | 558848-2

Mullen,Jim | (b,gtuba)
Klaus Doldinger With Orchestra
Lifelike | Warner | 2292-46478-2
Mose Allison Quartet
The Mose Chronicles-Live In London,Vol.2 | Blue Note | 529748-2

Mullens,Eddie | (tp)
(Little)Jimmy Scott With The Lionel Hampton Orchestra
Everybody's Somebody's Fool | Decca | 050669-2
Billy Strayhorn Orchestra
Johnny Hodges With Billy Strayhorn And The Orchestra | Verve | 557543-2
Duke Ellington And Count Basie With Their Orchestras
First Time! | CBS | CK 65571
Duke Ellington And His Orchestra
Jazz Festival Vol.2 | Storyville | 4960743
Hot Lips Page Band
Planet Jazz:Jazz Trumpet | Planet Jazz | 2169654-2
Johnny Hodges With Billy Strayhorn And The Duke Ellington Orchestra
Verve Jazz Masters 35:Johnny Hodges | Verve | 521857-2
Lionel Hampton And His Orchestra
Lionel Hampton:Flying Home | Dreyfus Jazz Line | FDM 36735-2
Lionel Hampton Orchestra
The Big Bands Vol.1.The Snader Telescriptions | Storyville | 4960043
Louis Armstrong And His Orchestra
Best Of The Complete RCA Victor Recordings | RCA | 2663636-2
Louis Armstrong:A 100th Birthday Celebration | RCA | 2663694-2
Louis Armstrong:C'est Si Bon | Dreyfus Jazz Line | FDM 36730-2

Swing Legends:Louis Armstrong | Nimbus Records | NI 2012

Müller,Bruno | (g)
Cafe Du Sport Jazzquartett
Cafe Du Sport Jazzquartett | Minor Music | 801096

Müller,Gotthart | (viola)
Bernd Konrad Jazz Group With Symphonie Orchestra
Wen Die Götter Lieben | Creative Works Records | CW CD 1010-1

Müller,Heiner | (author)
Heiner Goebbels/Heiner Müller
Der Mann Im Fahrstuhl | ECM | 1369(837110-2)

Müller,Helmut J. | (ssts)
Müller-Svoboda-Dähn-Kniel
9Q | Edition Musikat | EDM 064

Müller,Klaus | (p,el-pkeyboards)
Daniel Messina Band
Imagenes | art-mode-records | 990014
Kamafra
Kamafra Live | Edition Musikat | EDM 072
Klaus Müller-Ekkehard Rössle
Auf Und Davon | Jazz Haus Musik | JHM 0091 CD

Müller,Lothar | (g,el-gloops)
Lothar Müller Trio
Müller Q[kju] | JA & RO | JARO 4251-2

Muller,Marc | (g)
Karen Mantler Group
My Cat Arnold | Watt | XtraWatt/3
Karen Mantler And Her Cat Arnold Get The Flu | Watt | XtraWatt/5

Müller,Matthias | (tbelectronics)
Matthias Müller Quartet
Bhavam | Jazz Haus Musik | JHM 0126 CD

Muller,Patrick | (pel-p)
Erik Truffaz Quartet
The Dawn | Blue Note | 493916-2
Bending New Corners | Blue Note | 522123-2
Erik Truffaz Quartet Quintet
Out Of A Dream | Blue Note | 855855-2

Müller,Paul | (b)
Tilman Jäger Tape 4
Abendlieder | Satin Doll Productions | SDP 1043-1 CD

Müller,Peter | (cl,as,vocdr)
Axel Zwingenberger With The Mojo Blues Band And Red Holloway
Axel Zwingenberger And The Friends Of Boogie Woogie,Vol.8 | Vagabond | VRCD 8.93019

Müller,Rainer | (tbtuba)
Dusko Goykovich Big Band
Balkan Connection | Enja | ENJ-9047 2
NDR Big Band
The Theatre Of Kurt Weil | ACT | 9234-2

Müller,Werner | (arrld)
Inge Brandenburg mit Werner Müller und seinem Orchester
Why Don't You Take All Of Me | Bear Family Records | BCD 15614 AH

Müller-Hornbach,Susanne | (cello)
Gabriele Hasler Group
Gabriele Hasler's Rosensrücke | Foolish Music | FM 211096

Mulligan,Gerry | (arr,comp,as,bs,cl,p,voc,cond,ssts)
A Band Of Friends
The Best Of The Gerry Mulligan Quartet With Chet Baker | Pacific Jazz | 795481-2
Chet Baker-Gerry Mulligan Group
Carnegie Hall Concert Vol. 1/2 | CTI | EPC 450554-2
Chubby Jackson Big Band
Gerry Mulligan Quartet feat.Chet Baker | Original Jazz Classics | OJCCD 711-2(F 8082/P 7641)
Dave Brubeck Quartet With Gerry Mulligan
The Last Set At Newport | Atlantic | 7567-81382-2
We're All Together Again For The First Time | Atlantic | 7567-81390-2
Elliot Lawrence And His Orchestra
Mullenium | CBS | CK 65678
Gene Krupa And His Orchestra
Mullenium | CBS | CK 65678
Gerry Mulligan And His Orchestra
Mullenium | CBS | CK 65678
Gerry Mulligan And The Sax Section
The Gerry Mulligan Songbook | Pacific Jazz | 833575-2
Gerry Mulligan Concert Jazz Band
Verve Jazz Masters 36:Gerry Mulligan | Verve | 523342-2
Verve Jazz Masters Vol.60:The Collection | Verve | 529866-2
Gerry Mulligan And The Concert Band At The Village Vanguard | Verve | 589488-2
The Complete Verve Gerry Mulligan Concert Band | Verve | 9860613
Gerry Mulligan Quartet
Paris Jazz Concert:Gerry Mulligan And His Quartet | Laserlight | 17433
Gerry Mulligan:Pleyel Concert Vol.1 | Vogue | 21409422
Gerry Mulligan:Pleyel Concert Vol.2 | Vogue | 21409432
Planet Jazz:Gerry Mulligan | Planet Jazz | 2152070-2
Planet Jazz Sampler | Planet Jazz | 2152326-2
Planet Jazz:Jazz Saxophone | Planet Jazz | 2169653-2
The Art Of Saxophone | Laserlight | 24652
Gene Norman Presents The Original Gerry Mulligan Tentet And Quartet | GNP Crescendo | GNPD 56
Newport Jazz Festival 1958,July 3rd-6th Vol.2:Mulligan The Main Man | Phontastic | NCD 8814
Gerry Mulligan Quartet feat.Chet Baker | Original Jazz Classics | OJCCD 711-2(F 8082/P 7641)
Jazz At The Philharmonic: The Gerry Mulligan Quartets In Concert | Pablo | PACD 5309-2
The Jazz Giants Play Rodgers & Hart:Blue Moon | Prestige | PCD 24205-2
Gerry Mulligan Quintet
Late Night Sax | CBS | 487798-2
Gerry Mulligan Sextet
The Gerry Mulligan Songbook | Pacific Jazz | 833575-2
Gerry Mulligan Tentette
Gene Norman Presents The Original Gerry Mulligan Tentet And Quartet | GNP Crescendo | GNPD 56
Gerry Mulligan With Astor Piazzolla And His Orchestra
Tango Nuevo | Atlantic | 2292-42145-2
Gerry Mulligan With The Marian McPartland Trio
Newport Jazz Festival 1958,July 3rd-6th Vol.2:Mulligan The Main Man | Phontastic | NCD 8814
Gerry Mulligan-Ben Webster Quintet
Verve Jazz Masters 43:Ben Webster | Verve | 525431-2
The Complete Gerry Mulligan Meets Ben Webster Sessions | Verve | 539055-2
Ultimate Ben Webster selected by James Carter | Verve | 557537-2
Gerry Mulligan-Johnny Hodges Quintet
Gerry Mulligan Meets Johnny Hodges | Verve | 065513-2
Verve Jazz Masters 35:Johnny Hodges | Verve | 521857-2
Gerry Mulligan-Paul Desmond Quartet
Gerry Mulligan-Paul Desmond Quartet | Verve | 519850-2
Gerry Mulligan-Thelonious Monk Quartet
Mulligan Meets Monk | Original Jazz Classics | OJC20 301-2(RLP 1106)
Lee Konitz & The Gerry Mulligan Quartet
Konitz Meets Mulligan | Pacific Jazz | 746847-2
Miles Davis And His Orchestra
The Complete Birth Of The Cool | Capitol | 494550-2
Birth Of The Cool | Capitol | 530117-2
Miles Davis:The Best Of The Capitol/Blue Note Years | Blue Note | 798287-2
Jazz Profile:Miles Davis | Blue Note | 823515-2
Ballads & Blues | Blue Note | 836633-2
Miles Davis:Milestones | Dreyfus Jazz Line | FDM 36731-2
Paul Desmond-Gerry Mulligan Quartet
The Ballad Of Paul Desmond | RCA | 21429372
Planet Jazz:Paul Desmond | Planet Jazz | 2152061-2
Planet Jazz:Jazz Greatest Hits | Planet Jazz | 2169648-2
Two Of A Mind | RCA | 2179620-2

Shirley Horn With Orchestra
Loads Of Love + Shirley Horn With Horns | Mercury | 843454-2
Stan Getz-Gerry Mulligan Quintet
Stan Getz Highlights | Verve | 847430-2
Getz Meets Mulligan In Hi-Fi | Verve | 849392-2
Thelonious Monk-Gerry Mulligan Quartet
Thelonious Monk:85th Birthday Celebration | zyx records | FANCD 6076-2

Mulligan,Kevin | (el-g,g,keyboards,synth,PPGvoc)
Klaus Doldinger & Passport
Lifelike | Warner | 2292-46478-2
Klaus Doldinger's Passport
Man In The Mirror | Warner | 2292-40253-2
Running In Real Time | Warner | 2292-40633-2
Heavy Nights | Warner | 2292-42006-2
Blue Tattoo | Atlantic | 2292-42178-2
Earthborn | Atlantic | 2292-46477-2
Oceanliner | Warner | 2292-46479-2
Passport
Garden Of Eden | Atlantic | 2292-44147-2

Mullins,Herb | (tb)
Tadd Dameron And His Orchestra
Clifford Brown Memorial | Original Jazz Classics | OJC20 017-2(P 7055)

Mullins,Reynolds | (orgp)
Lionel Hampton All Stars
Jazz In Paris:Lionel Hampton-Ring Dem Bells | EmArCy | 159825-2 PMS

Mullins,Riley | (tp)
Lincoln Center Jazz Orchestra
Big Train | CBS | CK 69860

Mullins,Rob | (keyboards,psynth)
The Rippingtons
Tourist In Paradise | GRP | GRP 95882

Mumford,Jimmy | (dr)
Funk Inc.
Jazzin' With The Soul Brothers | Fantasy | FANCD 6086-2

Mumm,Henrik | (b,el-bcello)
Frank Kroll Quintet
Landscape | dml-records | CD 014
Patrick Bebelaar Quartet
Never Thought It Could Happen | dml-records | CD 007

Mundy,Jimmy | (arr,ldts)
Benny Goodman And His Orchestra
Planet Jazz:Benny Goodman | Planet Jazz | 2152054-2
Planet Jazz:Female Jazz Vocalists | Planet Jazz | 2169656-2
Billie Holiday With The Paul Whiteman Orchestra
Billie's Blues | Blue Note | 748786-2
Carmen McRae With The Jimmy Mundy Orchestra
Blue Moon | Verve | 543829-2
Charlie Parker With Strings
Verve Jazz Masters 28:Charlie Parker Plays Standards | Verve | 521854-2
Count Basie And His Orchestra
Jazz:The Essential Collection Vol.3 | IN+OUT Records | 78013-2
The Complete Atomic Basie | Roulette | 828635-2
Dizzy Gillespie And His Orchestra
Planet Jazz:Dizzy Gillespie | Planet Jazz | 2152069-2
Earl Hines And His Orchestra
Planet Jazz:Earl Hines | Planet Jazz | 2159973-2
The Legends Of Swing | Laserlight | 24659

Munich Radio Symphony Orchestra |
Abdullah Ibrahim Trio With The Munich Radio Symphony Orchestra
African Symphony | Enja | ENJ-9410 2

Munich Saxophone Family |
Munich Saxophon Family
Balanced | Edition Collage | EC 487-2
Survival Song | JHM Records | JHM 3613

Munk,A.J. | (v)
Stochelo Rosenberg Group With Strings
Gypsy Swing | Verve | 527806-2

Munoz,Bob | (b,g,percvoc)
Gene Krupa And His Orchestra
Mullenium | CBS | CK 65678

Munson,Dick | (tp)
Woody Herman And His Orchestra
Old Gold Rehearsals 1944 | Jazz Unlimited | JUCD 2079

Münster,Jost 'Addi' | (tb)
Old Merrytale Jazz Band
The Very Best Of Dixieland Jazz | Verve | 535529-2

Münzer,Fritz | (as,compld)
Fritz Münzer Quintet
Jazz für junge Leute:Live im HR 1962 | Jazz 'n' Arts Records | C 01
Fritz Münzer Tentet
Blue Ideas | Jazz 'n' Arts Records | 0200

Mura,Patrizio,Mura | (harmvoc)
Ernst Reijseger & Tenore E Cuncordu De Orosei
Colla Voche | Winter&Winter | 910037-2

Murakami,Hiroshi | (dr)
Johnny Hartman With The Masahiko Kikuchi Trio
Blue Velvet: Crooners, Swooners And Velvet Vocals | Blue Note | 521153-2

Murakami,Yoshito | (tp)
Buddy Rich And His Orchestra
Swingin' New Big Band | Pacific Jazz | 835232-2
Big Swing Face | Pacific Jazz | 837989-2
Buddy Rich Big Band
The New One! | Pacific Jazz | 494507-2

Muranyi,Joe | (clas)
Louis Armstrong And His All Stars
Jazz Collection:Louis Armstrong | Laserlight | 24366
What A Wonderful World | MCA | MCD 01876
Louis Armstrong And His All Stars With A Studio Orchestra
What A Wonderful World | MCA | MCD 01876
Roy Eldridge And The Jimmy Ryan All Stars
Jazz Dance | Original Jazz Classics | OJCCD 1002-2(1210890)
Little Jazz And The Jimmy Ryan All-Stars | Original Jazz Classics | OJCCD 1058-2(DRE 1001)

Mure,Billy | (arr,ldg)
Jimmy Smith With The Claus Ogerman Orchestra
Any Number Can Win | Verve | 557447-2

Murphy,Mark | (voc)
Mar Murphy With The Ernie Wilkins Orchestra
RAH | Original Jazz Classics | OJCCD 141-2(R 9395)
Mark Murphy And His Septet
Blue Velvet: Crooners, Swooners And Velvet Vocals | Blue Note | 521153-2
Mark Murphy With The Ralph Burns Orchestra
Crazy Rhythm:His Debut Recordings | Decca | 050670-2

Murphy,Matt | (gvoc)
Albert King With The Willie Dixon Band
Windy City Blues | Stax | SCD 8612-2
Buddy Guy Blues Band
Buddy Guy-The Complete Chess Studio Recordings | MCA | MCD 09337

Murphy,Nipper | (tp)
Buddy Childers Big Band
Just Buddy's | Candid | CCD 79761

Murphy,Norman | (tp)
Anita O'Day With Gene Krupa And His Orchestra
Let Me Off Uptown:Anita O'Day With Gene Krupa | CBS | CK 65625

Murphy,Paul | (drg)
Buddy Childers Big Band
It's What Happening Now! | Candid | CCD 79749

Murphy,Spud | (arr)
Benny Goodman And His Orchestra
Planet Jazz:Benny Goodman | Planet Jazz | 2152054-2

Murphy,Turk | (tb,vocwbd)
Bunk Johnson With The Yerba Buena Jazz Band
Bunk & Lu | Good Time Jazz | GTCD 12024-2
Turk Murphy And His Jazz Band
Planet Jazz | Planet Jazz | 2169652-2
The Very Best Of Dixieland Jazz | Verve | 535529-2
Atlantic Jazz: New Orleans | Atlantic | 7567-81700-2
Yerba Buena Jazz Band
Bunk & Lu | Good Time Jazz | GTCD 12024-2

Murray,Alex | (v)
Pete Rugolo And His Orchestra
Thriller/Richard Diamon(Original Jazz Scores From 2 Classics TV Series) | Fresh Sound Records | FSCD 2015

Murray,Bobby | (gtb)
Etta James & The Roots Band
Burnin' Down he House | RCA | 3411633-2

Murray,Dana | (dr)
James Hurt Group
Dark Grooves-Mystcal Rhythms | Blue Note | 495104-2

Murray,David | (b-cl,sax,ts,cl,ss,vocts-solo)
Barbara Dennerlein Group
Junkanoo | Verve | 537122-2
Cold Sweat
Cold Sweat Plays J.B. | JMT Edition | 919025-2
David Murray Group
Speaking In Togues | Enja | ENJ-9370 2
Jack DeJohnette Quartet
Special Edition | ECM | 1152
Jack DeJohnette's Special Edition
Album Album | ECM | 1280
Steve Coleman And Five Elements
Curves Of Life | Novus | 2131693-2
World Saxophone Quartet
Plays Duke Ellington | Nonesuch | 7559-79137-2
Dances And Ballads | Nonesuch | 7559-79164-2

Murray,Don | (bs,cl,asts)
Bix And His Rhythm Jugglers
Jazz:The Essential Collection Vol.2 | IN+OUT Records | 78012-2
Bix Beiderbecke And His Gang
Jazz:The Essential Collection Vol.2 | IN+OUT Records | 78012-2
Frankie Trumbauer And His Orchestra
Jazz:The Essential Collection Vol.2 | IN+OUT Records | 78012-2

Murray,Fred | (p)
Dutch Swing College Band
Digital Anniversary | Philips | 824585-2 PMS

Murray,Sunny | (dr,balafon,poetry-reading,perc)
Albert Ayler Quintet
Albert Ayler Live In Greenwich Village:The Complete Impulse Recordings | Impulse(MCA) | IMP 22732
Cecil Taylor Quartet
Cecil Taylor: Air | Candid | CCD 79046
Cecil Taylor Unit
Mixed | Impulse(MCA) | IMP 12702
Gunter Hampel And His Galaxie Dream Band
Journey To The Song Within | Birth | 0017

Murrell,Christopher 'Chris' | (voc)
Chris Murrell-Bobby Irving III
Christmas Jazz! | Nagel-Heyer | NH 1008
Christopher Murrell-Robert Irving III
Full Circle:Gospels And Spirituals | Nagel-Heyer | NHR SP 3
Tom Browne Groups
Mo' Jamaica Funk | Hip Bop | HIBD 8002

Murtauch,John | (reeds)
Dizzy Gillespie And His Orchestra
Ultimate Dizzy Gillespie | Verve | 557535-2

Murugar | (drperc)
Weather Report
Sweetnighter | CBS | 485102-2

Musat,Ioana | (v)
Till Brönner Quartet & Deutsches Symphonieorchester Berlin
German Songs | Minor Music | 801057

Musiker,Ray | (cl)
Terry Gibbs Octet
Jewis Melodies In Jazztime | Mercury | 589673-2

Musiker,Sam | (cl,asts)
Anita O'Day With Gene Krupa And His Orchestra
Let Me Off Uptown:Anita O'Day With Gene Krupa | CBS | CK 65625

Muslin,Joe | (b)
Vic Lewis And His Band
Vic Lewis:The Golden Years | Candid | CCD 79754

Mussawisade,Afro | (perc)
Gabriel Pérez Group
Alfonsina | Jazz 4 Ever Records:Jazz Network | J4E 4751

Musso,Vido | (cl,tssax)
Benny Goodman And His Orchestra
Planet Jazz:Benny Goodman | Planet Jazz | 2152054-2
Planet Jazz:Jazz Greatest Hits | Planet Jazz | 2169648-2
Planet Jazz:Big Bands | Planet Jazz | 2169649-2
Planet Jazz:Swing | Planet Jazz | 2169651-2
Planet Jazz:Jazz Trumpet | Planet Jazz | 2169654-2
Planet Jazz:Female Jazz Vocalists | Planet Jazz | 2169656-2
More Camel Caravans | Phontastic | NCD 8841/2
More Camel Caravans | Phontastic | NCD 8843/4
Duke Ellington With Tommy Dorsey And His Orchestra
Highlights From The Duke Ellington Centennial Edition | RCA | 2663672 2
Peggy Lee With The Benny Goodman Orchestra
Peggy Lee & Benny Goodman:The Complete Recordings 1941-1947 | CBS | C2K 65686
Stan Kenton And His Orchestra
Swing Vol.1 | Storyville | 4960343
Great Swing Classics In Hi-Fi | Capitol | 521223-2
Teddy Wilson And His Orchestra
Jazz:The Essential Collection Vol.3 | IN+OUT Records | 78013-2

Mussolini,Romano | (p)
Oscar Klein's Anniversary Band
Moonglow | Nagel-Heyer | CD 021
Ellington For Lovers | Nagel-Heyer | NH 1009
The Second Sampler | Nagel-Heyer | NHR SP 6
Oscar Klein's Jazz Show
Oscar Klein's Jazz Show | Jazzpoint | JP 1043 CD
Oscar Klein's Jazz Show Vol.2 | Jazzpoint | JP 1048 CD
A' Portrait Of Jan Jankeje | Jazzpoint | JP 1054 CD

Mussulli,Boots | (as,bs,saxts)
Stan Kenton And His Orchestra
Swing Vol.1 | Storyville | 4960343

Mustafa,Melton | (tp)
Diane Schuur With The Count Basie Orchestra
The Best Of Diane Schuur | GRP | GRP 98882

Mustarde,Bill | (tb)
Bud Freeman And His Stars
Muggsy Spanier And Bud Freeman:V-Discs 1944-45 | Jazz Unlimited | JUCD 2049
Bud Freeman And The V-Disc Jumpers
Muggsy Spanier And Bud Freeman:V-Discs 1944-45 | Jazz Unlimited | JUCD 2049
Eight Squares And A Critic
Muggsy Spanier And Bud Freeman:V-Discs 1944-45 | Jazz Unlimited | JUCD 2049
The V-Disc Jumpers
Muggsy Spanier And Bud Freeman:V-Discs 1944-45 | Jazz Unlimited | JUCD 2049

Muthspiel,Christian | (tb,mouth-perc,voice,psynth)
Gabriele Hasler Group
Gabriele Hasler's Personal Notebook | Foolish Music | FM 211490
Nicolas Simion Quartet feat. Tomasz Stanko
Viaggio Imaginario | Tutu Records | 888192-2*

Muthspiel,Wolfgang | (g,el-g,g-synthv)
Dhafer Youssef Group
Electric Sufi | Enja | ENJ-9412 2

Mutschler,Hermann | (dr,perctimbales)
Dieter Reith Quintet
Reith On! | MPS | 557423-2
Erwin Lehn Und Sein Südfunk-Tanzorchester
Deutsches Jazz Fesival 1954/1955 | Bear Family Records | BCD 15430
VIBrations
7.Zelt-Musik-Festival:Jazz Events | Zounds | CD 2730001

Muza,Celina | (voc)
Brass Attack
Brecht Songs | Tutu Records | 888190-2*

Muzillo,Ralph | (tp)
Benny Goodman And His Orchestra
Planet Jazz:Benny Goodman | Planet Jazz | 2152054-2
Planet Jazz Sampler | Planet Jazz | 2152326-2
Planet Jazz:Swing | Planet Jazz | 2169651-2
The Legends Of Swing | Laserlight | 24659

Myers,Amina Claudine | (harpsichord,org,p,el-p,giggle-stick)
Jeanne Lee Group
Natural Affinities | Owl Records | 018352-2
Ray Anderson Lapis Lazuli Band
Funkorific | Enja | ENJ-9340 2

Myers,Bumps | (tsbs)
JATP All Stars
The Complete Jazz At The Philharmonic On Verve 1944-1949 | Verve | 523893-2

Myers,Louis | (el-g,gvoc)
Muddy Waters Band
Muddy Waters:Paris 1972 | Pablo | PACD 5302-2

Myers,Ronald | (tb)
Buddy Rich And His Orchestra
Big Swing Face | Pacific Jazz | 837989-2
Don Ellis Orchestra
Electric Bath | CBS | CK 65522

Myers,Wilson Ernest | (b,arrvoc)
Alix Combelle Et Son Orchestre
Americans Swinging In Paris:Bill Coleman-The Elegance | EMI Records | 539662-2
Bill Coleman Et Son Orchestre
Americans Swinging In Paris:Bill Coleman-The Elegance | EMI Records | 539662-2
Bill Coleman Quintet
Americans Swinging In Paris:Bill Coleman-The Elegance | EMI Records | 539662-2
Eddie South/Stephane Grappelli Quintet
Django/Django In Rome 1949-1050 | BGO Records | BGOCD 366
Django Reinhardt:Echoes Of France | Dreyfus Jazz Line | FDM 36726-2
New Orleans Feetwarmers
Planet Jazz | Planet Jazz | 2169652-2
Jazz:The Essential Collection Vol.1 | IN+OUT Records | 78011-2
Sidney Bechet And His New Orleans Feetwarmers
Planet Jazz | Planet Jazz | 2169652-2
Sidney Bechet:Summertime | Dreyfus Jazz Line | FDM 36712-2

Mygind,Jacob | (ss,asts)
Pierre Dorge's New Jungle Orchestra
Giraf | dacapo | DCCD 9440

Myklebust,Ole Jorn | (tpfl-h)
Geir Lysne Listening Ensemble
Korall | ACT | 9236-2
Aurora Borealis-Nordic Lights | ACT | 9406-2

Nabatov,Simon | (p,accordeonp-solo)
Alfred 23 Harth QuasarQuartet
POPending EYE | free flow music | ffm 0493
Klaus König Orchestra
Times Of Devastation/Poco A Poco | Enja | ENJ-6014 22
Hommage A Douglas Adams | Enja | ENJ-6078 2
Klaus König Orchestra & Guests
The Song Of Songs:Oratorio For Two Solo Voices,Choir And Orchestra | Enja | ENJ-7057 2
Nils Wogram Octet
Odd And Awkward | Enja | ENJ-9416-2
Nils Wogram Quartet
Round Trip | Enja | ENJ-9307 2
Speed Life | Enja | ENJ-9346 2
Perry Robinson Quartet
Perry Robinson Quartet | Timescrapper | TSCR 9613
Schlüter-Nabatov-Antolini
Swing Kings | ACT | 9298-2
Simon Nabatov
Ten Piano Players,Vol.1 | Green House Music | CD 1002
Simon Nabatov Trio
Three Stories,One End | ACT | 9401-2
Simon Nabatov, String Gang & Percussion
Inside Lookin' Out | Tutu Records | 888104-2*
Simon Nabatov-Ed Schuller
Inside Lookin' Out | Tutu Records | 888104-2*
Simon Nabatov-Nils Wogram
Starting A Story | ACT | 9402-2

Nadal,Philippe | (cello)
Charlie Haden Quartet West With Strings
Now Is The Hour | Verve | 527827-2

Nadien,David | (concert-master,strings,v)
Bill Evans Quartet With Orchestra
The Complete Bill Evans On Verve | Verve | 527953-2
From Left To Right | Verve | 557451-2
Bill Evans With Orchestra
The Complete Bill Evans On Verve | Verve | 527953-2
From Left To Right | Verve | 557451-2
Bob James And His Orchestra
Jazzrock-Anthology Vol.3:Fusion | Zounds | CD 27100555
Earl Klugh Group With Strings
Late Night Guitar | Blue Note | 498573-2
Freddie Hubbard With Orchestra
This Is Jazz:Freddie Hubbard | CBS | CK 65041
Grover Washington Jr. Orchestra
Inside Moves | Elektra | 7559-60318-2
Jazzrock-Anthology Vol.3:Fusion | Zounds | CD 27100555
Helen Merrill With Orchestra
Casa Forte | EmArCy | 558848-2
Les McCann Group
Another Beginning | Atlantic | 7567-80790-2
Milt Jackson And His Orchestra
Sunflower | CTI | ZK 65131
Nina Simone And Orchestra
Baltimore | Epic | 476906-2
Sarah Vaughan With Orchestra
!Viva! Vaughan | Mercury | 549374-2
Sonny Stitt With Orchestra
Goin' Down Slow | Prestige | PRCD 24276-2
Stan Getz With The Eddie Sauter Orchestra
Stan Getz Plays The Music Of Mickey One | Verve | 531232-2
Stan Getz With The Richard Evans Orchestra
What The World Needs Now-Stan Getz Plays Bacharach And David | Verve | 557450-2
Wes Montgomery With The Jimmy Jones Orchestra
Wes Montgomery-The Complete Riverside Recordings | Riverside | 12 RCD 4408-2
The Jazz Giants Play Rodgers & Hart:Blue Moon | Prestige | PCD 24205-2

Nadolny,Matthias | (tsmelodica)
Matthias Nadolny-Gunnar Plümer
You'll Never Walk Alone | Nabel Records:Jazz Network | CD 4667
Uli Beckerhoff Group
Stay | Nabel Records:Jazz Network | CD 4636
Uli Beckerhoff Quintet
Original Motion Picture Soundtrack:Das Geheimnis(Secret Of Love) | Nabel Records:Jazz Network | CD 4666
Uli Beckerhoff Septet
Private Life | Nabel Records:Jazz Network | CD 4657

Naegly,Clint | (as)
Ella Fitzgerald With The Frank DeVol Orchestra
Get Happy! | Verve | 523321-2
Naftalin,Mark | (g,keyboards,paccordeon)
John Lee Hooker Group
Endless Boogie | MCA | MCD 10413
Nagel,Norbert | (alto-fl,ss,as,cl,ts,fl,ld,saxp)
Gerwin Eisenhauer's The Gäff Gang feat. Lisa Wahland
Favorite Tunes | Edition Collage | EC 527-2
Harry Allen And Randy Sandke Meets The RIAS Big Band Berlin
The Music Of The Trumpet Kings | Nagel-Heyer | CD 037
Nagel-Heyer Allstars,The |
The Nagel-Heyer Allstars
Uptown Lowdown:A Jazz Salute To The Big Apple | Nagel-Heyer | CD 2004
Nagler,Christof | (voc)
Eckart Runge-Jacques Ammon
Cello Tango | Edition Musikat | EDM 053
Nagorski,Grzegorz 'Greg' | (tb)
Claus Raible Sextet
Loopin' With Lea | Organic Music | ORGM 9724
Nagoya,Kimiyoshi | (tp)
United Future Organizatio
United Future Organization | Talkin' Loud | 518166-2
Nagurski,K. | (reeds)
Chet Baker With The NDR-Bigband
My Favourite Songs: The Last Great Concert Vol.1 | Enja | ENJ-5097 2
The Last Concert Vol.I+II | Enja | ENJ-6074 22
Nagurski,Klaus | (bs)
NDR Big Band-Bravissimo | ACT | 9232-2
Naha,George | (el-gg)
Bernard Purdie's Soul To Jazz
Bernard Purdie's Soul To Jazz II | ACT | 9253-2
Najee | (ts)
Tom Browne Groups
Mo' Jamaica Funk | Hip Bop | HIBD 8002
Naked City |
Batman
Naked City | Nonesuch | 7559-79238-2
Nally,Doug | (dr)
Rachelle Ferrell With The Eddie Green Trio
First Instrumental | Blue Note | 827820-2
Rachelle Ferrell With The Eddie Green Trio And Alex Foster
First Instrumental | Blue Note | 827820-2
Rachelle Ferrell-Doug Nally
First Instrumental | Blue Note | 827820-2
Namyslowski,Zbigniew | (as,cello,p,sopranino,flss)
Zbigniew Namyslowski-Remy Filipovitch Quintet
Go! | Album | AS 66919 CD
Nance,Ray | (co,v,voctp)
Babs Gonzales And His Band
Voilà | Fresh Sound Records | FSR CD 340
Barney Bigard And His Orchestra
Highlights From The Duke Ellington Centennial Edition | RCA | 2663672-2
Jazz:The Essential Collection Vol.3 | IN+OUT Records | 78013-2
Django Reinhardt With Duke Ellington And His Orchestra
Django Reinhardt:Souveniers | Dreyfus Jazz Line | FDM 36744-2
Duke Ellington And Count Basie With Their Orchestras
First Time! | CBS | CK 65571
Duke Ellington And His Award Winners
Greatest Hits | CBS | 462959-2
Duke Ellington And His Famous Orchestra
Duke Ellington:The Blanton-Webster Band | Bluebird | 21 13181-2
Planet Jazz:Duke Ellington | Planet Jazz | 2152053-2
Planet Jazz:Johnny Hodges | Planet Jazz | 2152065-2
Planet Jazz:Female Jazz Vocalists | Planet Jazz | 2169656-2
Duke Ellington And His Orchestra
Planet Jazz:Duke Ellington | Planet Jazz | 2152053-2
Planet Jazz:Jazz Greatest Hits | Planet Jazz | 2169648-2
Jazz Collection:Duke Ellington | Laserlight | 24369
The Legends Of Swing | Laserlight | 24659
100 Years Duke | Laserlight | 24906
Highlights From The Duke Ellington Centennial Edition | RCA | 2663672-2
Carnegie Hall Concert December 1944 | Prestige | 2PCD 24073-2
Carnegie Hall Concert December 1947 | Prestige | 2PCD 24075-2
Carnegie Hall Concert January 1943 | Prestige | 2PCD 34004-2
Duke Ellington: The Champs-Elysees Theater January 29-30th,1965 | Laserlight | 36131
Greatest Hits | CBS | 462959-2
The Big Bands Vol.1.The Snader Telescriptions | Storyville | 4960043
Jazz Festival Vol.2 | Storyville | 4960743
Verve Jazz Masters 4:Duke Ellington | Verve | 516338-2
Verve Jazz Masters 20:Introducing | Verve | 519853-2
Ellington '55 | Capitol | 520135-2
Great Swing Classics In Hi-Fi | Capitol | 521223-2
Ella & Duke At The Cote D'Azur | Verve | 539030-2
Ella Fitzgerald And Duke Ellington:Cote D'Azure Concerts on Verve | Verve | 539033-2
The Great Paris Concert | Atlantic | 7567-81303-2
Jazz:The Essential Collection Vol.2 | IN+OUT Records | 78012-2
Jazz:The Essential Collection Vol.3 | IN+OUT Records | 78013-2
Afro-Bossa | Reprise | 9362-47876-2
Ellington At Newport 1956(Complete) | CBS | CK 64932
Black Brown And Beige | CBS | CK 65566
Such Sweet Thunder | CBS | CK 65568
Anatomy Of A Murder | CBS | CK 65569
The Ellington Suites | Original Jazz Classics | OJC20 446-2(2310762)
Duke Ellington And His Orchestra feat. Paul Gonsalves | Original Jazz Classics | OJCCD 623-2
Jazz At The Philharmonis Berlin '65/Paris '67 | Pablo | PACD 5304-2
Duke Ellington At The Alhambra | Pablo | PACD 5313-2
The Jazz Giants Play Duke Ellington:Caravan | Prestige | PCD 24227-2
The Duke At Fargo 1940 | Storyville | STCD 8316/17
At The Hurricane:Original 1943 Broadcasts | Storyville | STCD 8359
Duke Ellington-Coleman Hawkins Orchestra
Duke Ellington Meets Coleman Hawkins | Impulse(MCA) | 951162-2
Ella Fitzgerald With The Duke Ellington Orchestra
Ella Fitzgerald-First Lady Of Song | Verve | 517898-2
The Best Of The Song Books | Verve | 519804-2
Verve Jazz Masters 6:Ella Fitzgerald | Verve | 519822-2
Verve Jazz Masters 46:Ella Fitzgerald-The Jazz Sides | Verve | 527655-2
Love Songs:The Best Of The Song Books | Verve | 531762-2
Ella & Duke At The Cote D'Azur | Verve | 539030-2
Ella Fitzgerald And Duke Ellington:Cote D'Azure Concerts on Verve | Verve | 539033-2
Ella Fitzgerald Sings The Duke Ellington Songbook | Verve | 559248-2
For The Love Of Ella Fitzgerald | Verve | 841765-2
Harry Carney And His Orchestra With Strings
Music For Loving:Ben Webster With Strings | Verve | 527774-2
Jaki Byard Sextet
Jaki Byard:Solo/Strings | Prestige | PCD 24246-2
Jimmy Hamilton And The Duke's Men
The Blue Note Swingtets | Blue Note | 495697-2
Jimmy Rushing And His Band
Planet Jazz:Jimmy Rushing | RCA | 2165371-2
Planet Jazz:Male Jazz Vocalists | Planet Jazz | 2169657-2
Johnny Hodges And The Ellington All-Stars Without Duke
Verve Jazz Masters 35:Johnny Hodges | Verve | 521857-2
Johnny Hodges And The Ellington Men
Verve Jazz Masters 35:Johnny Hodges | Verve | 521857-2
Johnny Hodges Orchestra
Planet Jazz:Johnny Hodges | Planet Jazz | 2152065-2
Planet Jazz Sampler | Planet Jazz | 2152326-2
Planet Jazz:Jazz Saxophone | Planet Jazz | 2169653-2
Highlights From The Duke Ellington Centennial Edition | RCA | 2663672-2
Johnny Hodges At The Sportpalast, Berlin | Pablo | 2CD 2620102
The Jazz Giants Play Harry Warren:Lullaby Of Broadway | Prestige | PCD 24204-2
Rosemary Clooney With The Duke Ellington Orchestra
Blue Rose | CBS | CK 65506
Nandfred,Kim Glies | (voc)
Marilyn Mazur With Ars Nova And The Copenhagen Art Ensemble
Jordsange | dacapo | DCCD 9454
Nanton,Joe 'Tricky Sam' | (tbtalking)
Duke Ellington And His Cotton Club Orchestra
Planet Jazz:Duke Ellington | Planet Jazz | 2152053-2
Jazz:The Essential Collection Vol.2 | IN+OUT Records | 78012-2
Duke Ellington And His Famous Orchestra
Duke Ellington:The Blanton-Webster Band | Bluebird | 21 13181-2
Planet Jazz:Duke Ellington | Planet Jazz | 2152053-2
Planet Jazz:Johnny Hodges | Planet Jazz | 2152065-2
Planet Jazz Sampler | Planet Jazz | 2152326-2
Planet Jazz:Ben Webster | RCA | 2165368-2
Planet Jazz:Big Bands | Planet Jazz | 2169649-2
Planet Jazz:Jazz Trumpet | Planet Jazz | 2169654-2
Planet Jazz:Female Jazz Vocalists | Planet Jazz | 2169656-2
Highlights From The Duke Ellington Centennial Edition | RCA | 2663672-2
Greatest Hits | CBS | 462959-2
Jazz:The Essential Collection Vol.2 | IN+OUT Records | 78012-2
Jazz:The Essential Collection Vol.3 | IN+OUT Records | 78013-2
Duke Ellington:Ko-Ko | Dreyfus Jazz Line | FDM 36717-2
Duke Ellington And His Kentucky Club Orchestra
Jazz:The Essential Collection Vol.2 | IN+OUT Records | 78012-2
Duke Ellington And His Orchestra
Planet Jazz:Duke Ellington | Planet Jazz | 2152053-2
Planet Jazz:Jazz Greatest Hits | Planet Jazz | 2169648-2
Highlights From The Duke Ellington Centennial Edition | RCA | 2663672-2
Carnegie Hall Concert December 1944 | Prestige | 2PCD 24073-2
Carnegie Hall Concert January 1943 | Prestige | 2PCD 34004-2
Jazz:The Essential Collection Vol.2 | IN+OUT Records | 78012-2
Jazz:The Essential Collection Vol.3 | IN+OUT Records | 78013-2
The Duke At Fargo 1940 | Storyville | STCD 8316/17
At The Hurricane:Original 1943 Broadcasts | Storyville | STCD 8359
Napis,Ira | (tb)
Diane Schuur And Her Band
Music Is My Life | Atlantic | 7567-83150-2
Napoleon,Marty | (p)
Chubby Jackson And His All Star Big Band
Chubby Takes Over | Fresh Sound Records | FSR-CD 324
Gene Krupa Trio
The Complete Jazz At The Philharmonic On Verve 1944-1949 | Verve | 523893-2
Henry Red Allen's All Stars
Planet Jazz:Coleman Hawkins | Planet Jazz | 2152055-2
Louis Armstrong And His All Stars
Jazz Collection:Louis Armstrong | Laserlight | 24366
Satchmo Serenaders | Verve | 543792-2
What A Wonderful World | MCA | MCD 01876
Louis Armstrong And His All Stars With A Studio Orchestra
What A Wonderful World | MCA | MCD 01876
Louis Armstrong With Gordon Jenkins And His Orchestra And Choir
Satchmo In Style | Verve | 549594-2
Louis Armstrong With Sy Oliver And His Orchestra
Satchmo Serenaders | Verve | 543792-2
Louis Armstrong With The Gordon Jenkins Orchestra
Ambassador Louis Armstrong Vol.17:Moments To Remember(1952-1956) | Ambassador | CLA 1917
Napoleon,Teddy | (p)
Anita O'Day With Gene Krupa And His Orchestra
Let Me Off Uptown:Anita O'Day With Gene Krupa | CBS | CK 65625
Gene Krupa And His Orchestra
Mullenium | CBS | CK 65678
Gene Krupa Trio
The Complete Jazz At The Philharmonic On Verve 1944-1949 | Verve | 523893-2
Jazz At The Philharmonic:Best Of The 1940's Concerts | Verve | 557534-2
Napton,John | (tp)
Peggy Lee With The Benny Goodman Orchestra
Peggy Lee & Benny Goodman:The Complete Recordings 1941-1947 | CBS | C2K 65686
Naranjo,Albertolaures,claves,director) |
Conexion Latina
Mambo Nights | Enja | ENJ-9402 2
Naranjo,Valerie | (perc)
Robert Dick Group With The Soldier String Quartet
Jazz Standard On Mars | Enja | ENJ-9327 2
Nardy,Joe | (dr)
The Jimmy And Marion McPartland Sessions
Vic Lewis:The Golden Years | Candid | CCD 79754
Narell,Andy | (dr,steel-dr,keyboards,sequencing,p)
Marcus Miller Group
The Sun Don't Lie | Dreyfus Jazz Line | FDM 36560-2
Nascimento,Milton | (gvoc)
Sarah Vaughan With Orchestra
I Love Brazil | Pablo | 2312101-2
Sarah Vaughan Birthday Celebration | Fantasy | FANCD 6090-2
Nash,Dick | (tb)
Anita O'Day With The Russ Garcia Orchestra
Verve Jazz Masters 49:Anita O'Day | Verve | 527653-2
Art Pepper Plus Eleven
Art Pepper + Eleven | Contemporary | CSA 7568-6
Modern Jazz Classics | Original Jazz Classics | OJC20 341-2
Ella Fitzgerald With The Billy May Orchestra
Ella Fitzgerald-First Lady Of Song | Verve | 517898-2
The Best Of The Song Books | Verve | 519804-2
Verve Jazz Masters 6:Ella Fitzgerald | Verve | 519822-2
Verve Jazz Masters 46:Ella Fitzgerald-The Jazz Sides | Verve | 527655-2
Ella Fitzgerald Sings The Harold Arlen Song Book | Verve | 589108-2
For The Love Of Ella Fitzgerald | Verve | 841765-2
Ella Fitzgerald With The Nelson Riddle Orchestra
The Best Of The Song Books:The Ballads | Verve | 521867-2
Love Songs:The Best Of The Song Books | Verve | 531762-2
Ella Fitzgerald Sings The Johnny Mercer Songbook | Verve | 539057-2
Harry James And His Orchestra
Trumpet Blues:The Best Of Harry James | Capitol | 521224-2
Henry Mancini And His Orchestra
Combo! | RCA | 2147794-2
June Christy With The Shorty Rogers Orchestra
June Christy Big Band Special | Capitol | 498319-2
Mel Tormé With The Russell Garcia Orchestra
Swingin' On The Moon | Verve | 511385-2
Peggy Lee With The Quincy Jones Orchestra
Blues Cross Country | Capitol | 520088-2
Pete Rugolo And His Orchestra
Thriller/Richard Diamon(Original Jazz Scores From 2 Classics TV Series) | Fresh Sound Records | FSCD 2015
Nash,Kenneth | (congas,cowbell,reco-reco,dr,perc)
Alice Coltrane Quintet
Joe Henderson:The Milestone Years | Milestone | 8MCD 4413-2
Alice Coltrane Sextet
Joe Henderson:The Milestone Years | Milestone | 8MCD 4413-2
Art Pepper Quintet
Art Pepper:The Complete Galaxy Recordings | Galaxy | 16GCD 1016-2
Straight Life | Original Jazz Classics | OJCCD 475-2
Bobby McFerrin Group
Bobby McFerrin | Elektra | 7559-60023-2
Charles Earland Septet
Charles Earland In Concert | Prestige | PRCD 24267-2
Gene Ammons And His All Stars
Dexter Gordon Birthday Celebration | Fantasy | FANCD 6082-2
Herbie Hancock Septet
V.S.O.P. Herbie Hancock-Live At The City Center N.Y. | CBS | 486569-2
Raul De Souza Orchestra
Cannonball Adderley Birthday Celebration | Fantasy | FANCD 6087-2
Woody Herman And His Orchestra
Jazzin' Vol.2: The Music Of Stevie Wonder | Fantasy | FANCD 6088-2
King Cobra | Original Jazz Classics | OJCCD 1068-2(F 9499)
Nash,Larry | (clavinetel-p)
Bobby Hutcherson Orchestra
Montara | Blue Note | 590956-2
Lee Ritenour Group
Jazzrock-Anthology Vol.3:Fusion | Zounds | CD 27100555
Nash,Lewis | (dr)
A Band Of Friends
Wynton Marsalis Quartet With Strings | CBS | CK 68921
Christian McBride Group
Gettin' To It | Verve | 523989-2
Cyrus Chestnut Trio With Anita Baker
Cyrus Chestnut | Atlantic | 7567-83140-2
Cyrus Chestnut Trio With James Carter
Cyrus Chestnut | Atlantic | 7567-83140-2
Cyrus Chestnut Trio With James Carter And Joe Lovano
Cyrus Chestnut | Atlantic | 7567-83140-2
Cyrus Chestnut Trio With Joe Lovano
Cyrus Chestnut | Atlantic | 7567-83140-2
Dave Ellis Quartet
State Of Mind | Milestone | MCD 9328-2
Diana Krall Group With Orchestra
When I Look In Your Eyes | Verve | 9513304
Jimmy Scott With Band
But Beautiful | Milestone | MCD 9321-2
Moon Glow | Milestone | MCD 9332-2
Joe Lovano Nonet
On This Day At The Vanguard | Blue Note | 590950-2
Joe Lovano Quartet
Live At The Village Vanguard | Blue Note | 829125-2
Joe Lovano Sextet
Tenor Legacy | Blue Note | 827014-2
John Lewis Quartet
Evolution II | Atlantic | 7567-83313-2
Ken Peplowski Quartet
Lost In The Stars | Nagel-Heyer | CD 2020
Pat Martino Quintet
Think Tank | Blue Note | 592009-2
Roy Hargrove Quintet
Family | Verve | 527630-2
Russell Malone Quartet
Sweet Georgia Peach | Impulse(MCA) | 951282-2
Russell Malone Quintet
Sweet Georgia Peach | Impulse(MCA) | 951282-2
Tommy Flanagan Trio
Sunset And The Mockingbird-The Birthday Concert | Blue Note | 493155-2
Toots Thielemans Quartet
Verve Jazz Masters Vol.59:Toots Thielemans | Verve | 535271-2
Nash,Ted | (alto-fl,b-cl,ts,as,fl,cl,ss,piccolo)
Anita O'Day With The Billy May Orchestra
Verve Jazz Masters 49:Anita O'Day | Verve | 527653-2
Barney Kessel And His Orchestra
The Jazz Giants Play Rodgers & Hart:Blue Moon | Prestige | PCD 24205-2
Ella Fitzgerald With Frank De Vol And His Orchestra
Like Someone In Love | Verve | 511524-2
Ella Fitzgerald With Paul Weston And His Orchestra
Love Songs:The Best Of The Song Books | Verve | 531762-2
Ella Fitzgerald Sings The Irving Berlin Song Book | Verve | 543830-2
Ella Fitzgerald With The Billy May Orchestra
Ella Fitzgerald-First Lady Of Song | Verve | 517898-2
The Best Of The Song Books | Verve | 519804-2
Verve Jazz Masters 6:Ella Fitzgerald | Verve | 519822-2
Verve Jazz Masters 46:Ella Fitzgerald-The Jazz Sides | Verve | 527655-2
Ella Fitzgerald Sings The Harold Arlen Song Book | Verve | 589108-2
For The Love Of Ella Fitzgerald | Verve | 841765-2
Ella Fitzgerald With The Buddy Bregman Orchestra
Ella Fitzgerald-First Lady Of Song | Verve | 517898-2
The Best Of The Song Books:The Ballads | Verve | 521867-2
Love Songs:The Best Of The Song Books | Verve | 531762-2
Ella Fitzgerald Sings The Cole Porter Songbook | Verve | 537257-2
Ella Fitzgerald Sings The Rodgers And Hart Song Book | Verve | 537258-2
Ella Fitzgerald With The Marty Paich Orchestra
Get Happy! | Verve | 523321-2
Ella Fitzgerald With The Nelson Riddle Orchestra
The Best Of The Song Books:The Ballads | Verve | 521867-2
Get Happy! | Verve | 523321-2
Oh Lady Be Good:The Best Of The Gershwin Songbook | Verve | 529581-2
Love Songs:The Best Of The Song Books | Verve | 531762-2
Ella Fitzgerald With The Paul Weston Orchestra
Get Happy! | Verve | 523321-2
Henry Mancini And His Orchestra
Combo! | RCA | 2147794-2
Joe Lovano Orchestra
Blue Note Plays Gershwin | Blue Note | 520808-2
June Christy With The Pete Rugolo Orchestra
Something Cool(The Complete Mono & Stereo Versions) | Capitol | 534069-2
Lincoln Center Jazz Orchestra
Big Train | CBS | CK 69860
Mel Tormé With The Billy May Orchestra
Mel Tormé Goes South Of The Border With Billy May | Verve | 589517-2
Nat King Cole With The Billy May Orchestra
Nat King Cole:For Sentimental Reasons | Dreyfus Jazz Line | FDM 36740-2
Wycliffe Gordon Group
The Search | Nagel-Heyer | CD 2007
Nasser,Jamil[George Joyner] | (b)
Ahmad Jamal Quintet
The Essence Part 1 | Dreyfus Jazz Line | FDM 37007-2
Big Byrd | Dreyfus Jazz Line | FDM 37008-2
Ahmad Jamal Trio
Picture Perfect-70th Anniversary | Warner | 8573-85268-2
The Awakening | Impulse(MCA) | IMP 12262
Gene Ammons And His All Stars
John Coltrane-The Prestige Recordings | Prestige | 16 PCD 4405-2
The Big Sound | Original Jazz Classics | OJCCD 651-2(P 7132)
Groove Blues | Original Jazz Classics | OJCCD 723-2(PR 7201)
The Prestige Legacy Vol.2:Battles Of Saxes | Prestige | PCD 24252-2
Herbie Mann Sextet
Just Wailin' | Original Jazz Classics | OJCCD 900-2(NJ 8211)
John Coltrane With The Red Garland Trio
Dig It | Original Jazz Classics | OJC20 392-2(PR 7229)
Phineas Newborn Jr. Quartet
Fabulous Phineas | RCA | 2179622-2
Phineas Newborn Jr. Trio
Fabulous Phineas | RCA | 2179622-2
Phineas Newborn Jr. With Dennis Farnon And His Orchestra
While My Lady Sleeps | RCA | 2185157-2
Red Garland Quintet
John Coltrane-The Prestige Recordings | Prestige | 16 PCD 4405-2
All Mornin' Long | Original Jazz Classics | OJC20 293-2(P-7130)
Dig It | Original Jazz Classics | OJC20 392-2(PR 7229)
Soul Junction | Original Jazz Classics | OJCCD 481-2
The Jazz Giants Play Duke Ellington:Caravan | Prestige | PCD 24227-2
Red Garland Quintet feat.John Coltrane

High Pressure | Original Jazz Classics | OJCCD 349-2(P 7209)
Red Garland Trio
The Jazz Giants Play Rodgers & Hammerstein:My Favorite Things | Prestige | PCD 24223-2

Nathaniel,Paul | (reeds)
André Holst With Chris Dean's European Swing Orchestra
That's Swing | Nagel-Heyer | CD 079

Nathanson,Nat | (viola)
Charlie Parker With The Neal Hefti Orchestra
Charlie Parker:The Best Of The Verve Years | Verve | 527815-2
Bird: The Complete Charlie Parker On Verve | Verve | 837141-2

Natoli,Nat | (tp)
Jess Stacy And His Orchestra
Planet Jazz:Jazz Piano | RCA | 2169655-2
Paul Whiteman And His Orchestra
Planet Jazz:Jack Teagarden | Planet Jazz | 2161236-2

Naudy,Sandrine | (v)
Charlie Haden Quartet West With Strings
Now Is The Hour | Verve | 527827-2

Naughton,Bobby | (vib,bells,marimba,pclavinet)
Leo Smith Group
Devine Love | ECM | 1143

Naumann,Alexandra | (voc)
Markus Stockhausen Orchestra
Sol Mestizo:Markus Stockhausen Plays The Music Of Enrique Diaz | ACT | 9222-2

Nauseef,Mark | (aribm,balafon,chimes,chinese opera)
Edward Vesala Sound And Fury
Invisible Strom | ECM | 1461
Michel Godard-Miroslav Tadic-Mark Nauseef
Loose Wires | Enja | ENJ-9071 2
Rabih Abou-Khalil Group
The Sultan's Picnic | Enja | ENJ-8078 2
Odd Times | Enja | ENJ-9330 2
Sylvie Courvoisier Group
Ocre | Enja | ENJ-9323 2

Navalon,Santi | (p)
Daniel Flors Group
When Least Expected | Fresh Sound Records | FSNT 080 CD

Navarra,Jack | (perc)
Van Alexander Orchestra
Home Of Happy Feet/Swing! Staged For Sound! | Capitol | 535211-2

Navarrete,Banguela | (voc)
Conjunto Clave Y Guaguanco
Dejala En La Puntica | TipToe | TIP-888829 2

Navarro,Fats | (tp)
Bud Powell Quintet
The Amazing Bud Powell Vol.1 | Blue Note | 532136-2
Bud Powell:Bouncing With Bud | Dreyfus Jazz Line | FDM 36725-2
Bud Powell's Modernists
The Fabulous Fats Navarro Vol.1 | Blue Note | 0677207
The Fabulous Fats Navarro Vol.2 | Blue Note | 0677208
Coleman Hawkins All Star Octet
Milt Jackson Birthday Celebration | Fantasy | FANCD 6079-2
Coleman Hawkins All Stars
The J.J.Johnson Memorial Album | Prestige | PRCD 11025-2
Coleman Hawkins And His All Stars
Planet Jazz:Coleman Hawkins | Planet Jazz | 2152055-2
Planet Jazz:Bebop | RCA | 2169650-2
Jazz:The Essential Collection Vol.3 | IN+OUT Records | 78013-2
Dexter Gordon Quintet
Fats Navarro:Nostalgia | Dreyfus Jazz Line | FDM 36736-2
Don Lanphere Quintet
Fats Navarro:Nostalgia | Dreyfus Jazz Line | FDM 36736-2
Fats Navarro Quintet
Fats Navarro:Nostalgia | Dreyfus Jazz Line | FDM 36736-2
JATP All Stars
Norman Granz' JATP: Carnegie Hall 1949 | Pablo | PACD 5311-2
Kenny Clarke And His 52nd Street Boys
Planet Jazz:Bebop | RCA | 2169650-2
Fats Navarro:Nostalgia | Dreyfus Jazz Line | FDM 36736-2
Tadd Dameron Septet
The Fabulous Fats Navarro Vol.2 | Blue Note | 0677208
Fats Navarro:Nostalgia | Dreyfus Jazz Line | FDM 36736-2
Tadd Dameron Sextet
The Fabulous Fats Navarro Vol.1 | Blue Note | 0677207
Tadd Dameron Tentet
Jazz Profile:Dexter Gordon | Blue Note | 823514-2
Tadd Dameron-Fats Navarro Quintet
Fats Navarro:Nostalgia | Dreyfus Jazz Line | FDM 36736-2
Tadd Dameron-Fats Navarro Sextet
Fats Navarro:Nostalgia | Dreyfus Jazz Line | FDM 36736-2
The McGhee-Navarro Boptet
The Fabulous Fats Navarro Vol.1 | Blue Note | 0677207
The Fabulous Fats Navarro Vol.2 | Blue Note | 0677208
The Metronome All Stars
Planet Jazz:Dizzy Gillespie | Planet Jazz | 2152069-2

Navazio,Michele | (g)
Lounge Lizards
Berlin 1991 Part 1 | Intuition Records | INT 2044-2
Live In Berlin 1991-Vol.2 | Intuition Records | INT 2055-2

Navratil,Frantisek | (sax)
Hans Koller Big Band
New York City | MPS | 9813437

Nawothnig,Bernd | (dr)
Marion Brown & Jazz Cussion
Echoes Of Blue | double moon | CHRDM 71015

Nay,Joe | (drperc)
Annie Ross & PonyPoindexter With The Berlin All Stars
Annie Ross & Pony Poindexter with The Berlin All Stars | MPS | 9811257
Wilton Gaynair Quintet
Alpharian | Konnex Records | KCD 5032

NdegéOcello,Me'Shell | (el-b,synthvoc)
Marcus Miller Group
Tales | Dreyfus Jazz Line | FDM 36571-2
Nguyen Le Trio With Guests
Purple:Celebrating Jimi Hendrix | ACT | 9410-2

N'Diaye,Bachir | (perc)
Pili-Pili
Pili-Pili Live 88 | JA & RO | JARO 4139-2

Ndjay,Badu | (congas,talking-dr,el-g,voc,tamag)
Piirpauke
The Wild East | JA & RO | JARO 4128-2
Zerenade | JA & RO | JARO 4142-2
Piirpauke-Global Servisi | JA & RO | JARO 4150-2
Tuku Tuku | JA & RO | JARO 4158-2

N'Doye,Miki | (dr,perc,kalimbavoc)
Jon Balke w/Oslo 13
Nonsentration | ECM | 1445

NDR Big Band |
Abdullah Ibrahim With The NDR Big Band
Ekapa Lodumo | TipToe | TIP-888840 2
Albert Mangelsdorff With The NDR Big Band
NDR Big Band-Bravissimo | ACT | 9232-2
Chet Baker Quintet/NDR Big Band/Radio Orchestra Hannover
Straight From The Heart-The Last Concert Vol.2 | Enja | ENJ-6020 2
The Last Concert Vol.I+II | Enja | ENJ-6074 22
Chet Baker With The NDR-Bigband
NDR Big Band-Bravissimo | ACT | 9232-2
My Favourite Songs: The Last Great Concert Vol.1 | Enja | ENJ-5097 2
The Last Concert Vol.I+II | Enja | ENJ-6074 22
Chet Baker-The Legacy Vol.1 | Enja | ENJ-9021 2
Heinz Sauer Quartet With The NDR Big Band
NDR Big Band-Bravissimo | ACT | 9232-2
Joe Pass With The NDR Big Band
Joe Pass In Hamburg | ACT | 9100-2
NDR Big Band-Bravissimo | ACT | 9232-2
Joe Pass With The NDR Big Band And Radio Philharmonie Hannover
Joe Pass In Hamburg | ACT | 9100-2
Johnny Griffin With The NDR Big Band
NDR Big Band-Bravissimo | ACT | 9232-2
NDR Big Band
NDR Big Band-Bravissimo | ACT | 9232-2
The Theatre Of Kurt Weil | ACT | 9234-2
NDR Big Band With Guests
50 Years Of NDR Big Band:Bravissimo II | ACT | 9259-2
Oscar Brown Jr. with The NDR Big Band
Live Every Minute | Minor Music | 801071
Pee Wee Ellis & NDR Bigband
What You Like | Minor Music | 801064

NDR Radio Philharmonic Orchestra |
NDR Radio Philharmonic Orchestra
Colossus Of Sound | Enja | ENJ-9460 2

NDR Radio-Philharmonie Hannover |
Daniel Schnyder With The NDR Radio Philharmonie Hannover
Tanatula | Enja | ENJ-9302 2

NDR-Jazz-Workshop |
NDR-Workshop
Doldinger's Best | ACT | 9224-2

Ndugu[Leon Chancler] | (dr,congas,voice,perc,cymbals)
Alice Coltrane Sextet
Joe Henderson:The Milestone Years | Milestone | 8MCD 4413-2
Bobby Lyle Group
The Journey | Atlantic | 7567-82138-2
Flora Purim With Orchestra
Joe Henderson:The Milestone Years | Milestone | 8MCD 4413-2
Herbie Hancock Group
Sunlight | CBS | 486570-2
Stanley Clarke Group
If This Bass Could Only Talk | CBS | 460883-2
The Meeting
Hot Jazz Bisquits | Hip Bop | HIBD 8801

Neagley,Clint | (assax)
Anita O'Day With Gene Krupa And His Orchestra
Let Me Off Uptown:Anita O'Day With Gene Krupa | CBS | CK 65625
Peggy Lee With The Benny Goodman Orchestra
Peggy Lee & Benny Goodman:The Complete Recordings 1941-1947 | CBS | C2K 65686

Neal,Bob | (dr)
Chet Baker Quartet
Chet Baker Quartet Live Vol.3: May Old Flame | Pacific Jazz | 531573-2
Let's Get Lost: The Best Of Chet Baker Sings | Pacific Jazz | 792932-2

Neal,Buddy | (p)
Gene Krupa And His Orchestra
Mullenium | CBS | CK 65678

Neapolitan,Ray | (bsitar)
Don Ellis Orchestra
Electric Bath | CBS | CK 65522

Neary,Jerry | (tp)
Benny Goodman And His Orchestra
Planet Jazz:Benny Goodman | Planet Jazz | 2152054-2

Nederhorst,J. | (v)
Toots Thielemans And His Orchestra
Verve Jazz Masters Vol.59:Toots Thielemans | Verve | 535271-2

Neel,Bob | (dr)
Chet Baker Quartet
Chet Baker Quartet Live Vol.1:This Time The Dreams's On Me | Pacific Jazz | 525248-2

Neely,Bob | (bsts)
Buddy Guy Blues Band
Buddy Guy-The Complete Chess Studio Recordings | MCA | MCD 09337

Neely,Jimmy | (p)
Etta Jones And Her Quartet
Hollar! | Original Jazz Classics | OJCCD 1061(PR 7284)
Something Nice | Original Jazz Classics | OJCCD 221-2(P 7194)
Willis Jackson Quintet
At Large | Prestige | PCD 24243-2

Negus,John | (sax)
Buddy Childers Big Band
Just Buddy's | Candid | CCD 79761

Neidlinger,Buell | (b)
Cecil Taylor Quartet
At Newport | Verve | 589764-2
The World Of Cecil Taylor | Candid | CCD 79006
Cecil Taylor: Air | Candid | CCD 79046
Cecil Taylor Quintet
Love For Sale | Blue Note | 494107-2
Cecil Taylor Trio
Love For Sale | Blue Note | 494107-2
The World Of Cecil Taylor | Candid | CCD 79006
Cecil Taylor/Buell Neidlinger Orchestra
New York City R&B | Candid | CCD 79017
Cecil Taylor/Buell Neidlinger Quartet
New York City R&B | Candid | CCD 79017
Cecil Taylor/Buell Neidlinger Trio
New York City R&B | Candid | CCD 79017
Diane Schuur With Orchestra
The Best Of Diane Schuur | GRP | GRP 98882
Steve Lacy Quartet
Reflections-Steve Lacy Plays Thelonious Monk | Original Jazz Classics | OJCCD 063-2
Soprano Sax | Original Jazz Classics | OJCCD 130-2(P 7125)
The Mal Waldron Memorial Album:Soul Eyes | Prestige | PRCD 11024-2

Neidlinger,Sepp | (tb)
Freddie Brocksieper Und Seine Solisten
Freddie's Boogie Blues | Bear Family Records | BCD 16388 AH

Neikrug,George | (cello)
Ella Fitzgerald With The Nelson Riddle Orchestra
The Best Of The Song Books:The Ballads | Verve | 521867-2
Mel Tormé With The Russell Garcia Orchestra
Swingin' On The Moon | Verve | 511385-2
Phineas Newborn Jr. With Dennis Farnon And His Orchestra
While My Lady Sleeps | RCA | 2185157-2

Neil,Brian | (effects,gvoc)
Jazz Africa All Nations Big Band
Jadu(Jazz Africa Down Under) | Enja | ENJ-9339 2

Neil,Steve | (african-harp,bel-b)
Pharoah Sanders Orchestra
Message From Home | Verve | 529578-2

Neill,Larry | (tp)
Billie Holiday With The Paul Whiteman Orchestra
Billie's Blues | Blue Note | 748786-2
Ella Fitzgerald And Louis Armstrong With Dave Barbour And His Orchestra
Ella Fitzgerald:Mr.Paganini | Dreyfus Jazz Line | FDM 36741-2

Neilson,Chuck | (b)
Marty Grosz And His Honoris Causa Jazz Band
Hooray For Bix! | Good Time Jazz | GTCD 10065-2

Neiman,Alex | (vviola)
Ella Fitzgerald With The Nelson Riddle Orchestra
The Best Of The Song Books:The Ballads | Verve | 521867-2
Love Songs:The Best Of The Song Books | Verve | 531762-2
Mel Tormé With The Russell Garcia Orchestra
Swingin' On The Moon | Verve | 511385-2

Neissendorfer,Max | (p)
Max Neissendorfer Trio
Staubfrei | EGO | 95100

Nekljudow,Tom | (drperc)
Piirpauke
Live In Der Balver Höhle | JA & RO | JARO 4101-2
Piirpauke-Global Servisi | JA & RO | JARO 4150-2
Jazzy World | JA & RO | JARO 4200-2

Nell,Holger | (dr)
Gregor Hübner Quartet
Panonien | Satin Doll Productions | SDP 1015-1 CD
Gregor Hübner Quintet
Panonien | Satin Doll Productions | SDP 1015-1 CD
Harry Allen And Randy Sandke Meets The RIAS Big Band Berlin
The Music Of The Trumpet Kings | Nagel-Heyer | CD 037
Nana Mouskouri With The Berlin Radio Big Band
Nana Swings | Mercury | 074394-2

Nell,Thomas | (tppiccolo-tp)
Ralph Abelein Group
Mr. B's Time Machine | Satin Doll Productions | SDP 1042-1 CD

Nellums,Bob | (pp-solo)
Charles Mingus Orchestra
Three Or Four Shades Of Blues | Atlantic | 7567-81403-2
Cumbia & Jazz Fusion | Atlantic | 8122-71785-2
Dannie Richmond Quintet
Three Or Four Shades Of Dannie Richmond Quintet | Tutu Records | 888120-2*

Nelson,Davidson C.'Dave' | (co,tpvoc)
King Oliver And His Orchestra
Jazz:The Essential Collection Vol.1 | IN+OUT Records | 78011-2

Nelson,Gail | (voc)
Horace Silver Sextet With Vocals
Horace Silver Retrospective | Blue Note | 495576-2
Horace Silver-Gail Nelson
Horace Silver Retrospective | Blue Note | 495576-2

Nelson,Jimane | (org,psynth)
David Murray Group
Speaking In Togues | Enja | ENJ-9370 2

Nelson,Louis | (talkingtb)
Joseph 'Dee Dee' Pierce And His Band
Atlantic Jazz: New Orleans | Atlantic | 7567-81700-2
Punch Miller's Bunch & George Lewis
Atlantic Jazz: New Orleans | Atlantic | 7567-81700-2

Nelson,Marty | (voc)
Glenn Miller And His Orchestra
The Glenn Miller Orchestra In Digital Mood | GRP | GRP 95022

Nelson,Oliver | (arr,ld,as,ts,cl,fl,saxss)
Cal Tjader's Orchestra
Verve Jazz Masters 39:Cal Tjader | Verve | 521858-2
Talkin Verve/Roots Of Acid Jazz:Cal Tjader | Verve | 531562-2
Soul Burst | Verve | 557446-2
Cannonball Adderley And His Orchestra
Ballads | Blue Note | 537563-2
Cannonball Adderley Birthday Celebration | Fantasy | FANCD 6087-2
Cannonball Adderley Quintet
Ballads | Blue Note | 537563-2
Cannonball Adderley With Sergio Mendes And The Bossa Rio Sextet
Ballads | Blue Note | 537563-2
Count Basie And His Orchestra
Afrique | RCA | 2179618-2
Eddie Lockjaw Davis And His Orchestra
Eric Dolphy:The Complete Prestige Recordings | Prestige | 9 PRCD-4418-2
Etta Jones With The Oliver Nelson Quintet
Hollar! | Original Jazz Classics | OJCCD 1061(PR 7284)
Frank Wess And His Orchestra
The Long Road | Prestige | PCD 24247-2
Gato Barbieri Group
Planet Jazz:Gato Barbieri | RCA | 2165364-2
Gato Barbieri:The Best Of The Early Years | RCA | 2663523-2
Gene Ammons And His Orchestra
A Stranger In Town | Prestige | PRCD 24266-2
Hank Jones With Oliver Nelson's Orchestra
The Roots Of Acid Jazz | Impulse(MCA) | IMP 12042
J.J.Johnson And His Orchestra
Planet Jazz:J.J.Johnson | Planet Jazz | 2159974-2
Jimmy Forrest With The Oliver Nelson Orchestra
Soul Street | Original Jazz Classics | OJCCD 987-2(NJ 8293)
Jimmy Rushing With Oliver Nelson And His Orchestra
Every Day I Have The Blues | Impulse(MCA) | 547967-2
Jimmy Smith And Wes Montgomery With Orchestra
Jimmy & Wes-The Dynamic Duo | Verve | 521445-2
Jimmy Smith And Wes Montgomery With The Oliver Nelson Orchestra
Wes Montgomery:The Verve Jazz Sides | Verve | 521690-2
Jimmy Smith:Best Of The Verve Years | Verve | 527950-2
Talkin' Jazz:Roots Of Acid Jazz | Verve | 529580-2
Jimmy Smith With The Oliver Nelson Orchestra
Verve Jazz Masters 29:Jimmy Smith | Verve | 521855-2
Jimmy Smith:Best Of The Verve Years | Verve | 527950-2
Jimmy Smith-Talkin' Verve | Verve | 531563-2
Peter & The Wolf | Verve | 547264-2
Joe Williams,With The Oliver Nelson Orchestra
Planet Jazz:Joe Williams | Planet Jazz | 2165370-2
Leon Thomas With The Oliver Nelson Quintet
Leon Thomas In Berlin | RCA | 2663877-2
Louis Armstrong And His Friends
Planet Jazz:Louis Armstrong | Planet Jazz | 2152052-2
Louis Jordan And His Tympany Five
Louis Jordan-Let The Good Times Roll: The Complete Decca Recordings 1938-1954 | Bear Family Records | BCD 15557 IH
Oliver Nelson And His Orchestra
Verve Jazz Masters Vol.60:The Collection | Verve | 529866-2
Blues And The Abstract Truth | Impulse(MCA) | 951154-2
More Blues And The Abstract Truth | Impulse(MCA) | 951212-2
The Roots Of Acid Jazz | Impulse(MCA) | IMP 12042
Oliver Nelson Quintet
Eric Dolphy:The Complete Prestige Recordings | Prestige | 9 PRCD-4418-2
Eric Dolphy Birthday Celebration | Fantasy | FANCD 6085-2
Straight Ahead | Original Jazz Classics | OJCCD 099-2
Oliver Nelson Feat. Kenny Dorham | Original Jazz Classics | OJCCD 227-2(NJ 8224)
The Jazz Giants Play Sammy Cahn:It's Magic | Prestige | PCD 24226-2
Oliver Nelson Sextet
Eric Dolphy:The Complete Prestige Recordings | Prestige | 9 PRCD-4418-2
Eric Dolphy Birthday Celebration | Fantasy | FANCD 6085-2
Screamin' The Blues | Original Jazz Classics | OJC 080(NJ 8243)
Soul Street | Original Jazz Classics | OJCCD 987-2(NJ 8293)
The Prestige Legacy Vol.2:Battles Of Saxes | Prestige | PCD 24252-2
Quincy Jones And His Orchestra
The Quintessence | Impulse(MCA) | 951222-2
The Roots Of Acid Jazz | Impulse(MCA) | IMP 12042
Shirley Scott Quintet
Blue Seven | Original Jazz Classics | OJCCD 1050-2(P 7376)
Queen Of The Organ-Shirley Scott Memorial Album | Prestige | PRCD 11027-2
Sonny Rollins Orchestra
Alfie | Impulse(MCA) | 951224-2
Wes Montgomery With The Oliver Nelson Orchestra
Verve Jazz Masters 14:Wes Montgomery | Verve | 519826-2
Wes Montgomery:The Verve Jazz Sides | Verve | 521690-2
Talkin' Jazz:Roots Of Acid Jazz | Verve | 529580-2

Nelson,Skip | (voc)
Glenn Miller And His Orchestra
Planet Jazz:Glenn Miller | Planet Jazz | 2152056-2
Candelight Miller | RCA | 2668716-2

Nelson,Steve | (marimbavib)
Antonio Hart Group
Ama Tu Sonrisa | Enja | ENJ-9404 2
Barbara Dennerlein Group
Outhipped | Verve | 547503-2
Dave Holland Big Band
What Goes Around | ECM | 1777(014002-2)
Dave Holland Qartet
Dream Of The Elders | ECM | 1572(529084-2)
Dave Holland Quintet
Point Of View | ECM | 1663(557020-2)

Prime Directive | ECM | 1090(547050-2)
Not For Nothin' | ECM | 1758(014004-2)
Extended Play | ECM | 1864/65(038505-2)
Johnny King Quintet
Notes From The Underground | Enja | ENJ-9067 2

Nelson,Willis | (tp)
Buddy Johnson And His Orchestra
Buddy And Ella Johnson 1953-1964 | Bear Family Records | BCD 15479 DH

Nemet,Chris | (pbody-perc)
Oscar Klein & Katie Kern Group
Pick-A-Blues | Jazzpoint | JP 1065 CD
Oscar Klein Band
Pick-A-Blues Live | Jazzpoint | JP 1071

Nemeth,Eva | (cello)
Couch Ensemble
Winnetou | Jazz 'n' Arts Records | JNA 1503

Nemeth,J.S. | (v)
Toots Thielemans And His Orchestra
Verve Jazz Masters Vol.59:Toots Thielemans | Verve | 535271-2

Nemoli,Phil | (oboe)
Artie Shaw And His Orchestra
Planet JazzArtie Shaw | Planet Jazz | 2152057-2
Planet Jazz:Jazz Greatest Hits | Planet Jazz | 2169648-2

Nenad,Vasilic | (b)
Vasilic Nenad Balkan Band
Joe-Jack | Nabel Records:Jazz Network | CD 4693

Nendza,André | (b)
Alex Gunia-Philipp Van Endert Group
Beauty Of Silence | Laika Records | 35101052
Dirk Berger Quartet
Garagenjazz | Jazz Haus Musik | JHM 0090 CD
Lirico
Sussurro | Jazz Haus Musik | JHM 0129 CD
Marcus Sukiennik Big Band
A Night In Tunisia Suite(7 Variationen über Dizzy Gillespie's 'A Night In Tunisia') | Jazz Haus Musik | ohne Nummer
Olaf Kübler Quartet
When I'm 64 | Village | VILCD 1016-2
Midnight Soul | Village | VILCD 1024-2

Nene | (drperc)
Egberto Gismonti & Academia De Dancas
Sanfona | ECM | 1203/04(829391-2)

Nepus,Ira | (tb)
Woody Herman And His Orchestra
Brand New | Original Jazz Classics | OJCCD 1044-2(F 8414)

Nerem,Bjarne | (ts)
Bengt-Arne Wallin Orchestra
The Birth+Rebirth Of Swedish Folk Jazz | ACT | 9254-2
Lars Gullin Octet
Lars Gullin 1955/56 Vol.1 | Dragon | DRCD 224

Nergaard,Silje | (voc)
Silje Nergard Group with Strings
Nightwatch | EmArCy | 9865648

Nesta,Nicola | (lutevoice)
Michel Godard Ensemble
Castel Del Monte II | Enja | ENJ-9431 2

Nestico,Sam | (arr,ld,condp)
Count Basie And His Orchestra
88 Basie Street | Original Jazz Classics | OJC 808(2310901)
Sarah Vaughan And The Count Basie Orchestra
Sarah Vaughan Birthday Celebration | Fantasy | FANCD 6090-2

Neto,Sebastiao | (b)
Antonio Carlos Jobim With Orchestra
Verve Jazz Masters 13:Antonio Carlos Jobim | Verve | 516409-2

Netta,Sebastian | (dr)
Benny Bailey With The Bernhard Pichl Trio
On The Corner | Jazz 4 Ever Records:Jazz Network | J4E 4726
Bernhard Pichl Trio
On The Corner | Jazz 4 Ever Records:Jazz Network | J4E 4726

Netting,Fred | (ts)
Louis Armstrong With Sy Oliver And His Orchestra
Satchmo Serenaders | Verve | 543792-2

Neudert,Jürgen | (tb)
Abdullah Ibrahim With The NDR Big Band
Ekapa Lodumo | TipToe | TIP-888840 2
Gabriel Pérez Group
Alfonsina | Jazz 4 Ever Records:Jazz Network | J4E 4751
NDR Big Band
The Theatre Of Kurt Weil | ACT | 9234-2

Neufang,Jens | (bs,fl,cl,ss,as,reedssax)
Eddie Harris Group With The WDR Big Band
Eddie Harris-The Last Concert | ACT | 9249-2
Gianlugi Trovesi Quartet With The WDR Big Band
Dedalo | Enja | ENJ-9419 2
Jens Winther And The WDR Big Band
The Escape | dacapo | DCCD 9437
Kevin Mahogany With The WDR Big Band And Guests
Pussy Cat Dues:The Music Of Charles Mingus | Enja | ENJ-9316 2
Vince Mendoza With The WDR Big Band And Guests
Sketches | ACT | 9215-2

Neufeld,Erno | (concert-master,vconcertmaster)
Ella Fitzgerald With The Billy May Orchestra
The Best Of The Song Books:The Ballads | Verve | 521867-2
Ella Fitzgerald Sings The Harold Arlen Song Book | Verve | 589108-2
Ella Fitzgerald With The Nelson Riddle Orchestra
The Best Of The Song Books:The Ballads | Verve | 521867-2
Frank Sinatra With The Count Basie Orchestra
It Might As Well Be Spring | Reprise | 7599-27027-2
Hank Crawford Orchestra
Rhino Presents The Atlantic Jazz Gallery | Atlantic | 8122-71257-2
Milt Jackson With Strings
To Bags...With Love:Memorial Album | Pablo | 2310967-2
Pete Rugolo And His Orchestra
Thriller/Richard Diamon(Original Jazz Scores From 2 Classics TV Series) | Fresh Sound Records | FSCD 2015
Roger Kellaway Cello Quartet With The A&M Symphony Orchestra
Roger Kellaway Cello Quartet | A&M Records | 9861062

Neuffer,Annette | (voc)
Al Porcino Big Band
Al Porcino Big Band Live! | Organic Music | ORGM 9717

Neuman,Roger | (arr)
Buddy Rich Big Band
Keep The Customer Satisfied | EMI Records | 523999-2

Neumann,Irma | (v)
Pete Rugolo And His Orchestra
Thriller/Richard Diamon(Original Jazz Scores From 2 Classics TV Series) | Fresh Sound Records | FSCD 2015

Neumann,Scott | (dr)
Michael Blake Group
Kingdom Of Champa | Intuition Records | INT 3189-2

Neumann,Werner | (g,el-g,keyboards,voc,tp,g-synth)
Dirk Raulf Group
Theater I (Bühnenmusik) | Poise | Poise 07
Double You
Menschbilder | Jazz Haus Musik | JHM 0062 CD
Franck Band
Dufte | Jazz Haus Musik | JHM 0054 CD
Klaus König Orchestra
The Heart Project | Enja | ENJ-9338 2

Neumark,Andy | (dr)
Nina Simone And Orchestra
Baltimore | Epic | 476906-2

Neumeier,Mani | (dr,congas,mani-tom,cymbals,gamclans)
Guru Guru
Guru Guru/Uli Trepte | ATM Records | ATM 3815-AH
Mani Neumeir
Privat | ATM Records | ATM 3803-AH
Mani Neumeir Group
Privat | ATM Records | ATM 3803-AH
Mani Neumeir-Peter Hollinger
Monsters Of Drums-Live | ATM Records | ATM 3821-AH

Neumeister,Ed | (tb)
Ed Neumeister Quartet
Ed Neumeister Quartet/Quintet | Timescrapper | TSCR 9614
Ed Neumeister Quintet
Ed Neumeister Quartet/Quintet | Timescrapper | TSCR 9614
Neal Kirkwood Octet
Neal Kirkwood Octet | Timescrapper | TSCR 9612

Neunkirchen,Mario | (g)
Mario Neunkirchen Quintet
Long Distance | Laika Records | LK 94-060

Neuwirth,Rudi | (drwonder-tb)
Rudi Neuwirth Group
Sand | Traumton Records | 2413-2

Neves,John | (b)
Gary Burton Sextet
Planet Jazz:Gary Burton | RCA | 2165367-2
Maynard Ferguson Orchestra With Chris Connor
Two's Company | Roulette | 837201-2
Stan Getz With The Eddie Sauter Orchestra
A Life In Jazz:A Musical Biography | Verve | 535119-2
Ultimate Stan Getz selected by Joe Henderson | Verve | 557532-2
Stan Getz Highlights | Verve | 847430-2
Stan Getz-Bob Brookmeyer Quintet
Stan Getz Highlights:The Best Of The Verve Years Vol.2 | Verve | 517330-2
A Life In Jazz:A Musical Biography | Verve | 535119-2

Neves,Oscar Castro | (el-g,garr)
Antonio Carlos Jobim Group
Verve Jazz Masters 13:Antonio Carlos Jobim | Verve | 516409-2
Lee Ritenour Group
Rio | GRP | GRP 95242
Stan Getz With Orchestra
Apasionado | A&M Records | 395297-2
Stan Getz-Joao Gilberto Orchestra
Sony Jazz Collection:Stan Getz | CBS | 488623-2

Neville,Aaron | (voc)
Rob Wasserman Duet
Duets | GRP | GRP 97122

Neville,Chris | (p)
Greg Abate Quintet
Dr. Jeckyll & Mr. Hyde | Candid | CCD 79715

New Jazz Composers Octet,The |
New Jazz Composers Octet
Walkin' the Line | Fresh Sound Records | FSNT 151 CD
The New Jazz Composers Octet
First Step Into Reality | Fresh Sound Records | FSNT 059 CD

New Jazz Group Hannover |
New Jazz Group Hannover
Deutsches Jazz Fesival 1954/1955 | Bear Family Records | BCD 15430

New On The Corner |
New On The Corner
Left Handed | Jazz 4 Ever Records:Jazz Network | J4E 4758

New Orleans Feetwarmers,The |
New Orleans Feetwarmers
Planet Jazz | Planet Jazz | 2169652-2
Jazz:The Essential Collection Vol.1 | IN+OUT Records | 78011-2
From Spiritual To Swing | Vanguard | VCD 169/71

New York All Stars,The |
Allan Vaché Swingtet
Ellington For Lovers | Nagel-Heyer | NH 1009
The New York Allstars
Broadway | Nagel-Heyer | CD 003
One Two Three | Nagel-Heyer | CD 008
We Love You,Louis! | Nagel-Heyer | CD 029
Count Basie Remembered | Nagel-Heyer | CD 031
Count Basie Remembered Vol.2 | Nagel-Heyer | CD 041
Oh,Yeah! The New York Allstars Play More Music Of Louis Armstrong | Nagel-Heyer | CD 046
Hey Ba-Ba-Re-Bop!! The New York Allstars Play Lionel Hampton Vol.1 | Nagel-Heyer | CD 047
The New York Allstars Play Lionel Hampton,Vol.2: Stompin' At The Savoy | Nagel-Heyer | CD 077
Randy Sandke Meets Bix Beiderbecke | Nagel-Heyer | CD 3002
The First Sampler | Nagel-Heyer | NHR SP 5
The Second Sampler | Nagel-Heyer | NHR SP 6

New York Group Singers' Big Band |
Duke Pearson Orchestra
Deep Blue-The United States Of Mind | Blue Note | 521152-2

Newark,Andy | (dr)
Jimmy Smith All Stars
Jimmy Smith:Dot Com Blues | Blue Thumb | 543978-2

Newborn Jr.,Phineas | (p,percp-solo)
Charles Mingus Workshop
Charles Mingus-The Complete Debut Recordings | Debut | 12 DCD 4402-2
Phineas Newborn Jr.
Fabulous Phineas | RCA | 2179622-2
Phineas Newborn Jr. Quartet
Fabulous Phineas | RCA | 2179622-2
Phineas Newborn Jr. Trio
Fabulous Phineas | RCA | 2179622-2
The Jazz Giants Play Miles Davis:Milestones | Prestige | PCD 24225-2
Tivoli Encounter | Storyville | STCD 8221
Phineas Newborn Jr. With Dennis Farnon And His Orchestra
While My Lady Sleeps | RCA | 2185157-2
Roy Haynes Trio
We Three | Original Jazz Classics | OJCCD 196-2(NJ 8210)
Teddy Edwards-Howard McGhee Quintet
Together Again! | Original Jazz Classics | OJCCD 424-2

Newborn,Calvin | (g)
Jimmy Forrest Quintet
Soul Street | Original Jazz Classics | OJCCD 987-2(NJ 8293)
Phineas Newborn Jr. Quartet
Fabulous Phineas | RCA | 2179622-2
Phineas Newborn Jr. Trio
Fabulous Phineas | RCA | 2179622-2

Newcomb,Clyde | (b)
Bud Freeman And His Summa Cum Laude Orchestra
Planet Jazz:Bud Freeman | Planet Jazz | 2161240-2
Planet Jazz:Jazz Saxophone | Planet Jazz | 2169653-2

Newell,Laura | (harp)
Stan Getz With The Eddie Sauter Orchestra
Stan Getz Plays The Music Of Mickey One | Verve | 531232-2

Newman,Bill | (bjg)
Firehouse Five Plus Two
Dixieland Favorites | Good Time Jazz | FCD 60-008

Newman,Bob | (bs,saxts)
Woody Herman And His Orchestra
Songs For Hip Lovers | Verve | 559872-2

Newman,Dave | (harpv)
Billie Holiday With The Ray Ellis Orchestra
Lady In Satin | CBS | CK 65144
Coleman Hawkins With Billy Byers And His Orchestra
The Hawk In Hi-Fi | RCA | 2663842-2

Newman,David Fathead | (as,ts,bs,fl,commentary,sssax)
(Little)Jimmy Scott And His Quintet
All The Way | Warner | 7599-26955-2
Charles Kynard Sextet
The Soul Brotherhood | Prestige | PCD 24257-2
David Fathead Newman Quintet Plus Clifford Jordan
Blue Head | Candid | CCD 79041
David Fathead Newman Septet
Jazzin' Vol.2: The Music Of Stevie Wonder | Fantasy | FANCD 6088-2
David Fathead Newman Sextet
Atlantic Saxophones | Rhino | 8122-71256-2
Rhino Presents The Atlantic Jazz Gallery | Atlantic | 8122-71257-2
Fathead:Ray Charles Presents David Newman | Atlantic | 8122-73708-2
Eddie Harris Group
The Best Of Eddie Harris | Atlantic | 7567-81370-2
Hank Crawford And His Orchestra
Atlantic Saxophones | Rhino | 8122-71256-2
Roadhouse Symphony | Original Jazz Classics | OJCCD 1048-2(M 9140)
Hank Crawford Septet
More Soul | Atlantic | 8122-73709-2
James Clay/David Fathead Newman Quintet
The Sound Of The Wide Open Spaces | Original Jazz Classics | OJCCD 1075-2(RLP 1178)
Jimmy McGriff Sextet
Feelin' It | Milestone | MCD 9313-2
Jimmy Scott With Band
Over The Rainbow | Milestone | MCD 9314-2
Moon Glow | Milestone | MCD 9332-2
John Stein Quartet
Conversation Pieces | Jardis Records | JRCD 20140
Klaus Doldinger Jubilee
Doldinger's Best | ACT | 9224-2
Klaus Doldinger With Orchestra
Lifelike | Warner | 2292-46478-2
Klaus Doldinger With Orchestra And Etta James
Lifelike | Warner | 2292-46478-2
Lee Morgan Quintet
Sonic Boom | Blue Note | 590414-2
Oscar Brown Jr. And His Group
Movin' On | Rhino | 8122-73678-2
Ray Charles And His Orchestra
Ray Charles At Newport | Atlantic | 7567-80765-2
Ray Charles Sextet With The Raylets
Newport Jazz Festival 1958,July 3rd-6th Vol.4:Blues In The Night No.2 | Phontastic | NCD 8816
Roy Hargrove Quintet
Family | Verve | 527630-2
Roy Hargrove Sextet
Family | Verve | 527630-2

Newman,Joe | (fl-h,tp,condvoc)
Billie Holiday And Her All Stars
Verve Jazz Masters 12:Billie Holiday | Verve | 519825-2
Verve Jazz Masters Vol.60:The Collection | Verve | 529866-2
The Billie Holiday Song Book | Verve | 823246-2
Billie Holiday And Her Quintet
Verve Jazz Masters 47:Billie Holiday Sings Standards | Verve | 527650-2
Cannonball Adderley And His Orchestra
Cannonball Adderley Birthday Celebration | Fantasy | FANCD 6087-2
Cootie Williams Quintet
Jazz In Paris:Joe Newman-Jazz At Midnight-Cootie Williams | EmArCy | 018446-2
Count Basie And His Orchestra
Jazz Gallery:Lester Young Vol.2(1946-59) | RCA | 2119541-2
Jazz Collection:Count Basie | Laserlight | 24368
The Legends Of Swing | Laserlight | 24659
Atomic Swing | Roulette | 497871-2
Verve Jazz Masters 2:Count Basie | Verve | 519819-2
Count Basie Swings-Joe Williams Sings | Verve | 519852-2
Verve Jazz Masters 20:Introducing | Verve | 519853-2
April In Paris | Verve | 521402-2
Breakfast Dance And Barbecue | Roulette | 531791-2
One O'Clock Jump | Verve | 559806-2
Chairman Of The Board | Roulette | 581664-2
Jazz:The Essential Collection Vol.3 | IN+OUT Records | 78013-2
The Complete Atomic Basie | Roulette | 828635-2
King Of Swing | Verve | 837433-2
Count Basie At Newport | Verve | 9861761
Count On The Coast Vol.1 | Phontastic | NCD 7555
Count On The Coast Vol.2 | Phontastic | NCD 7575
Count Basie Sextet
Verve Jazz Masters 2:Count Basie | Verve | 519819-2
Eddie Harris Group
The Best Of Eddie Harris | Atlantic | 7567-81370-2
Ella Fitzgerald And Joe Williams With The Count Basie Octet
For The Love Of Ella Fitzgerald | Verve | 841765-2
Ella Fitzgerald With The Count Basie Orchestra
Ella Fitzgerald-First Lady Of Song | Verve | 517898-2
Verve Jazz Masters 46:Ella Fitzgerald-The Jazz Sides | Verve | 527655-2
Ella And Basie | Verve | 539059-2
Ella Fitzgerald With The Count Basie Septet
Ella And Basie | Verve | 539059-2
Gene Ammons Sextet
Gentle Jug Vol.3 | Prestige | PCD 24249-2
Hank Jones With Oliver Nelson's Orchestra
The Roots Of Acid Jazz | Impulse(MCA) | IMP 12042
Herbie Mann And His Orchestra
The Best Of Herbie Mann | Atlantic | 7567-81369-2
Jay McShann And His Orchestra
Atlantic Jazz: Kansas City | Atlantic | 7567-81701-2
Jay McShann Orchestra
The Last Of The Blue Devils | Atlantic | 7567-80791-2
Jimmy McGriff Orchestra
Swingin' The Blues-Jumpin' The Blues | Laserlight | 24654
Jimmy Rushing And His Orchestra
Five Feet Of Soul | Roulette | 581830-2
Jimmy Smith And Wes Montgomery With Orchestra
Jimmy & Wes-The Dynamic Duo | Verve | 521445-2
Jimmy Smith And Wes Montgomery With The Oliver Nelson Orchestra
Wes Montgomery:The Verve Jazz Sides | Verve | 521690-2
Jimmy Smith:Best Of The Verve Years | Verve | 527950-2
Talkin' Jazz:Roots Of Acid Jazz | Verve | 529580-2
Jimmy Smith With Orchestra
Jimmy Smith-Talkin' Verve | Verve | 531563-2
Jimmy Smith With The Billy Byers Orchestra
Jimmy Smith:Best Of The Verve Years | Verve | 527950-2
Jimmy Smith With The Claus Ogerman Orchestra
Verve Jazz Masters 29:Jimmy Smith | Verve | 521855-2
Any Number Can Win | Verve | 557447-2
Jimmy Smith With The Oliver Nelson Orchestra
Verve Jazz Masters 29:Jimmy Smith | Verve | 521855-2
Jimmy Smith:Best Of The Verve Years | Verve | 527950-2
Jimmy Smith-Talkin' Verve | Verve | 531563-2
Peter & The Wolf | Verve | 547264-2
Joe Newman And His Band
Jazz In Paris:Joe Newman-Jazz At Midnight-Cootie Williams | EmArCy | 018446-2
Joe Newman Quintet
Good 'N' Groovy | Original Jazz Classics | OJCCD 185-2(SV 2019)
Joe Newman With Axel Zwingenberger
Axel Zwingenberger And The Friends Of Boogie Woogie Vol.2 | Vagabond | VRCD 8.85005
Joe Turner With Orchestra
Atlantic Jazz: Kansas City | Atlantic | 7567-81701-2
King Curtis Band
King Curtis-Blow Man Blow | Bear Family Records | BCD 15670 CI
Lionel Hampton And His Orchestra
Planet Jazz:Big Bands | Planet Jazz | 2169649-2
Lionel Hampton:Flying Home | Dreyfus Jazz Line | FDM 36735-2
Modern Jazz Quartet & Guests
MJQ 40 | Atlantic | 7567-82330-2
Oliver Nelson And His Orchestra
Verve Jazz Masters Vol.60:The Collection | Verve | 529866-2
Oscar Peterson With Orchestra
With Respect To Nat | Verve | 557486-2
Quincy Jones And His Orchestra

The Quintessence | Impulse(MCA) | 951222-2
Quincy Jones Big Band
Rahsaan/The Complete Mercury Recordings Of Roland Kirk | Mercury | 846630-2
Sarah Vaughan And Joe Williams With The Count Basie Orchestra
Jazz Profile | Blue Note | 823517-2
Sarah Vaughan And The Count Basie Orchestra
Ballads | Roulette | 537561-2
Sarah Vaughan And The Thad Jones Orchestra
Verve Jazz Masters 42:Sarah Vaughan-The Jazz Sides | Verve | 526817-2
Sarah Vaughan With The Count Basie Band
Jazz Profile | Blue Note | 823517-2
Sarah Vaughan With The Hal Mooney Orchestra
It's A Man's World | Mercury | 589487-2
Shirley Horn With Band
The Roots Of Acid Jazz | Impulse(MCA) | IMP 12042
Shirley Horn With Orchestra
Loads Of Love + Shirley Horn With Horns | Mercury | 843454-2
Shirley Scott Quintet
Blue Seven | Original Jazz Classics | OJCCD 1050-2(P 7376)
Queen Of The Organ-Shirley Scott Memorial Album | Prestige | PRCD 11027-2
Sonny Stitt And His Band
Kaleidoscope | Original Jazz Classics | OJCCD 060-2(P 7077)
Wes Montgomery With The Oliver Nelson Orchestra
Verve Jazz Masters 14:Wes Montgomery | Verve | 519826-2
Wes Montgomery:The Verve Jazz Sides | Verve | 521690-2
Talkin' Jazz:Roots Of Acid Jazz | Verve | 529580-2

Newmark,Andy | (dr)
Bob James And His Orchestra
Jazzrock-Anthology Vol.3:Fusion | Zounds | CD 27100555

Newmark,Harvey | (b)
Buddy Childers Big Band
It's What Happening Now! | Candid | CCD 79749

Newport All Stars,The |
Dinah Washington With The Newport All Stars
Dinah Sings Bessie Smith | Verve | 538635-2

Newport Rebels |
Newport Rebels
Candid Dolphy | Candid | CCD 79033

Newsom,Tommy | (arr,cl,ts,flreeds)
Benny Goodman And His Orchestra
The Legends Of Swing | Laserlight | 24659
J.J.Johnson And His Orchestra
Planet Jazz:J.J.Johnson | Planet Jazz | 2159974-2

Newsome,Sam | (ssts)
Bruce Barth Quartet
Where Eagles Fly | Fresh Sound Records | FSNT 090 CD
Jam Session
Jam Session Vol.4 | Steeplechase | SCCD 31527
Jean-Michel Pilc Quartet
Cardinal Points | Dreyfus Jazz Line | FDM 36649-2
Jean-Michel Pilc Quintet
Cardinal Points | Dreyfus Jazz Line | FDM 36649-2

Newton,David | (p,keyboards,voc,synthp-solo)
David Newton
A Jazz Portrait Of Frank Sinatra | Candid | CCD 79728
David Newton Quartet
DNA | Candid | CCD 79742
Jim Tomlinson Quintet
Brazilian Sketches | Candid | CCD 79769
Stacey Kent And Her Quintet
Close Your Eyes | Candid | CCD 79737
The Tender Trap | Candid | CCD 79751
Let Yourself Go-Celebrating Fred Astaire | Candid | CCD 79764
Stacey Kent With The Jim Tomlison Quintet
Dreamsville | Candid | CCD 79775
Stacy Kent With The Jim Tomlinson Quintet
In Love Again | Candid | CCD 79786
The Boy Next Door | Candid | CCD 79797

Newton,Frankie | (tpvoc)
Bessie Smith And Her Band
Jazz:The Essential Collection Vol.3 | IN+OUT Records | 78013-2
Billie Holiday With Frankie Newton And His Orchestra
Billie Holiday:The Complete Commodore Recordings | GRP | 543272-2
Billie's Love Songs | Nimbus Records | NI 2000
Mezz Mezzrow And His Swing Band
Planet Jazz:Bud Freeman | Planet Jazz | 2161240-2

Newton,James | (fl,alto-fl,b-fl,arr,wood-fl)
Blue Note All Stars
Town Hall Concert | Blue Note | 497811-2
James Newton
Axum | ECM | 1214
7.Zelt-Musik-Festival:Jazz Events | Zounds | CD 2730001
Klaus König Orchestra & Guests
The Song Of Songs:Oratorio For Two Solo Voices,Choir And Orchestra | Enja | ENJ-7057 2

Newton,Lauren | (narration,voicevoc)
Bernd Konrad Jazz Group With Symphonie Orchestra
Wen Die Götter Lieben | Creative Works Records | CW CD 1010-1

Nhien[Pham],Hao | (dan-bau,sao-fl,sapek-clappers)
Nguyen Le Group
Tales From Viet-Nam | ACT | 9225-2
Maghreb And Friends | ACT | 9261-2
Nguyen Le Trio With Guests
Bakida | ACT | 9275-2

Nicholas,Albert | (as,cl,ss,ts,vocreeds)
Albert Nicholas With Adrian Bentzon's Jazzband
The Golden Years Of Revival Jazz,Sampler | Storyville | 109 1001
Albert Nicholas & The Dutch Swing College Band | Storyville | STCD 5522
Albert Nicholas With The Dutch Swing College Band
Albert Nicholas & The Dutch Swing College Band | Storyville | STCD 5522
Bill Ramsey With Eric Krans Dixieland Pipers And Guests
Caldonia And More... | Bear Family Records | BCD 16151 AH
Fats Waller And His Buddies
Planet Jazz:Jack Teagarden | Planet Jazz | 2161236-2
Jazz:The Essential Collection Vol.3 | IN+OUT Records | 78013-2
Henry Allen Jr. And His New York Orchestra
Planet Jazz:Jazz Saxophone | Planet Jazz | 2169653-2
Planet Jazz:Jazz Trumpet | Planet Jazz | 2169654-2
Jelly Roll Morton's New Orleans Jazzmen
Planet Jazz | Planet Jazz | 2169652-2
Planet Jazz:Male Jazz Vocalists | Planet Jazz | 2169657-2
Joe Turner-Albert Nicholas Quartet
The Giant Of Stride Piano In Switzerland | Jazz Connaisseur | JCCD 9106-2
King Oliver And His Dixie Syncopators
Jazz:The Essential Collection Vol.1 | IN+OUT Records | 78011-2
King Oliver's Jazz Band
Jazz:The Essential Collection Vol.1 | IN+OUT Records | 78011-2
Louis Armstrong And His Orchestra
Louis Armstrong:Swing That Music | Laserlight | 36056
Jazz:The Essential Collection Vol.2 | IN+OUT Records | 78012-2
Louis Armstrong-My Greatest Songs | MCA | MCD 18347
Swing Legends:Louis Armstrong | Nimbus Records | NI 2012
Louis Armstrong And His Savoy Ballroom Five
Jazz:The Essential Collection Vol.2 | IN+OUT Records | 78012-2
Pete Johnson's Housewarmin'
Jazz:The Essential Collection Vol.3 | IN+OUT Records | 78013-2

Nicholas,George 'Big Nick' | (as,tsvoc)
Dizzy Gillespie And His Orchestra
Dizzy Gillespie:Pleyel Jazz Concert 1948 + Max Roach Quintet 1949 | Vogue | 21409412
Planet Jazz:Dizzy Gillespie | Planet Jazz | 2152069-2
Planet Jazz:Bebop | RCA | 2169650-2

Ella Fitzgerald With The Dizzy Gillespie Orchestra
Ella Fitzgerald:Mr.Paganini | Dreyfus Jazz Line | FDM 36741-2
Ella Fitzgerald With The Hank Jones Trio
Ella Fitzgerald:Mr.Paganini | Dreyfus Jazz Line | FDM 36741-2
Frankie Laine With Buck Clayton And His Orchestra
Jazz Spectacular | CBS | CK 65507

Nicholas,Mickey | (assax)
Kenny Clarke 8
Americans Swinging In Paris:Kenny Clarke | EMI Records | 539652-2

Nicholas,Tom | (congas,marimba,perc,bells,conga)
Daniel Guggenheim Group
Daniel Guggenheim Group feat. Jasper van't Hof | Laika Records | LK 990-018
Monty Waters Quartet
Monty Waters New York Calling Vol.2 | Tutu Records | 888182-2*

Nichols,Billy | (g)
Bernard Purdie Group
Jazzin' With The Soul Brothers | Fantasy | FANCD 6086-2

Nichols,Bobby | (tp)
Stan Getz With The Eddie Sauter Orchestra
Stan Getz Plays The Music Of Mickey One | Verve | 531232-2

Nichols,Herbie | (p)
Herbie Nichols Trio
Blue Note Plays Gershwin | Blue Note | 520808-2
Herbie Nichols:The Complete Blue Note Recordings | Blue Note | 859352-2

Nichols,Red | (co,tpld)
Red And Miff's Stompers
Planet Jazz:Jazz Trumpet | Planet Jazz | 2169654-2

Nicholson,Edward 'Eddie' | (dr)
Tiny Grimes Swingtet
The Blue Note Swingtets | Blue Note | 495697-2
Tony Scott And His Down Beat Club Sextet
Jazz:The Essential Collection Vol.3 | IN+OUT Records | 78013-2

Nicholson,Reggie | (bells,tambourine,tap-dr,trap-dr)
Herb Robertson Group
The Little Trumpet | JMT Edition | 919007-2

Nickel,Hans | (tuba)
Los Jovenes Flamencos With The WDR Big Band And Guests
Jazzpana | ACT | 9212-2

Nickendes Perlgras |
Nickendes Perlgras
Die Hintere Vase | Jazz Haus Musik | JHM 0105 CD

Nicklaus,Friederike | (voc)
Ekkehard Jost Ensemble
Weimarer Balladen | Fish Music | FM 004 CD
Giessen-Köln-Nonett
Some Other Tapes | Fish Music | FM 009/10 CD

Nickola,Mario | (dr)
Jamenco
Conversations | Trick Music | TM 9202 CD

Nicolai,Giancarlo | (gperc)
Peter Schärli Quintet With Glenn Ferris
Willisau And More Live | Creative Works Records | CW CD 1020-2
Drei Seelen/Three Souls | Creative Works Records | MIWI 1014-2

Nicolas,Tom | (percvoc)
Monty Waters' Hot Rhythm Junction
Jazzoerty | Tutu Records | 888196-2*

Nicolau,Anca | (v)
Steve Kuhn With Strings
Promises Kept | ECM | 1815(0675222)

Nicols,Maggie | (bongos,lammer,pipe,recorder,voice)
Alfred Harth Quintet
This Earth! | ECM | 1264
Ulrich P. Lask Group
Lask | ECM | 1217

Niculescu,Florin | (v)
Florin Niculescu Quartet
Four Friends | Jardis Records | JRCD 9923

Niebergall,Buschi | (bb-tb)
Jazzensemble Des Hessischen Rundfunks
Atmosphering Conditions Permitting | ECM | 1549/50

Nieberle,Helmut | (gukelele)
Helmut Kagerer/Helmut Nieberle
Wes Trane | Edition Collage | EC 453-2
Helmut Nieberle & Cordes Sauvages
Jazz Guitar Highlights 1 | Jardis Records | JRCD 20141
Salut To Django | Jardis Records | JRCD 9926
Helmut Nieberle-Helmut Kagerer
Skyliner | ART BY HEART | ABH 2001 2
Flashes | Jardis Records | JRCD 20031
Helmut Nieberle-Helmut Kagerer Quartet
Flashes | Jardis Records | JRCD 20031
Roots
Stablemates | IN+OUT Records | 7021-2

Niebla,Eduardo | (g)
Eduardo Niebla-Antonio Forcione Group
Poema | Jazzpoint | JP 1035 CD

Niehaus,Lennie | (arras)
Lennie Niehaus Quintet
Lennie Niehaus Vol.1:The Quintets | Original Jazz Classics | OJCCD 1933-2(C 3518)
Lennie Niehaus Sextet
Lennie Niehaus Vol.5:The Sextet | Original Jazz Classics | OJCCD 1944-2(C 3524)
Stan Kenton And His Orchestra
Great Swing Classics In Hi-Fi | Capitol | 521223-2
Stan Kenton Orchestra
Stompin' At Newport | Pablo | PACD 5312-2
Terry Gibbs Dream Band
Terry Gibbs Dream Band Vol.2:The Sundown Sessions | Contemporary | CCD 7652-2

Nielsen,Benny 'Papa' | (tb)
Papa Benny's Jazzband
The Golden Years Of Revival Jazz,Sampler | Storyville | 109 1001
The Golden Years Of Revival Jazz,Vol.2 | Storyville | STCD 5507
The Golden Years Of Revival Jazz,Vol.7 | Storyville | STCD 5512
The Golden Years Of Revival Jazz,Vol.11 | Storyville | STCD 5516
The Golden Years Of Revival Jazz,Vol.12 | Storyville | STCD 5517

Nielsen,Bent | (bsreeds)
Stan Kenton With The Danish Radio Big Band
Stan Kenton With The Danish Radio Big Band | Storyville | STCD 8340

Nielsen,Christina | (reeds,ssts)
Christina Nielsen-Carsten Dahl Duo
Lys Pa Himlen | dacapo | DCCD 9458
The Orchestra
New Skies | dacapo | DCCD 9463

Nielsen,Ove | (bj)
Leonardo Pedersen's Jazzkapel
The Golden Years Of Revival Jazz,Sampler | Storyville | 109 1001
The Golden Years Of Revival Jazz,Vol.11 | Storyville | STCD 5516

Nielsen,Per | (perc)
Stan Kenton With The Danish Radio Big Band
Stan Kenton With The Danish Radio Big Band | Storyville | STCD 8340

Nielson,Elizabeth | (v)
Absolute Ensemble
African Symphony | Enja | ENJ-9410 2

Nieman,Paul | (tb)
Mike Westbrook Orchestra
The Orchestra Of Smith's Academy | Enja | ENJ-9358 2

Niemeyer,Heinz | (drbongos)
Inge Brandenburg And Her All-Stars
Why Don't You Take All Of Me | Bear Family Records | BCD 15614 AH
Johannes Rediske Quintet
Jumpin' At The Badewanne | Bear Family Records | BCD 16172 AH

Nies,Joker | (electronics)
Kölner Saxophon Mafia With Guests
Kölner Saxophon Mafia: 20 Jahre Saxuelle Befreiung | Jazz Haus Musik | JHM 0115 CD

Wollie Kaiser Timeghost
New Traces For Old Aces | Jazz Haus Musik | JHM 0102 CD

Niescier,Angelika | (ssas)
Stephan Meinberg VITAMINE
Horizontal | Jazz Haus Musik | JHM 0106 CD

Nieto,Ubaldo | (perctimbales)
Charlie Parker With Machito And His Orchestra
Charlie Parker:The Best Of The Verve Years | Verve | 527815-2
Talkin' Bird | Verve | 559859-2
Bird: The Complete Charlie Parker On Verve | Verve | 837141-2
Charlie Parker:April In Paris | Dreyfus Jazz Line | FDM 36737-2
Dizzy Gillespie And His Orchestra
Afro | Verve | 517052-2
Dizzy Gillespie Group
Verve Jazz Masters 10:Dizzy Gillespie | Verve | 516319-2
Dizzy Gillspie And His Latin American Rhythm
Afro | Verve | 517052-2

Nieve,Steve | (org)
Marc Ribot Y Los Cubanos Postizos
Nuy Divertido(Very Entertaining) | Atlantic | 7567-83293-2

Niezgoda,Manfred | (tp)
Heinz Sauer Quartet With The NDR Big Band
NDR Big Band-Bravissimo | ACT | 9232-2

Niggli,Lucas | (drperc)
Georg Hofmann-Lucas Niggli Duo
Mute Songs & Drumscapes | Creative Works Records | CW CD 1022-2
Michel Wintsch & Road Movie
Michel Wintsch & Road Movie featuring Gerry Hemingway | Between The Lines | btl 002(Efa 10172-2)

Nighthawk,Robert | (g)
Buddy Guy Blues Band
Buddy Guy-The Complete Chess Studio Recordings | MCA | MCD 09337

Nightingale,Mark | (tb)
Kenny Wheeler Brass Ensemble
A Long Time Ago | ECM | 1691

Nikitakis,V.Nick | (bouzouki)
Kölner Saxophon Mafia With V.Nick Nikitakis
Kölner Saxophon Mafia Proudly Presents | Jazz Haus Musik | JHM 0046 CD

Nilssen-Love,Paal | (dr)
Trygve Seim Group
Different Rivers | ECM | 1744(159521-2)

Nilsson,Erik | (bs,flb-cl)
Bengt-Arne Wallin Orchestra
The Birth+Rebirth Of Swedish Folk Jazz | ACT | 9254-2

Nilsson,Lisa | (voc)
Niels-Henning Orsted-Pedersen/Ulf Wakenius Duo With Lisa Nilsson
Those Who Were | Verve | 533232-2

Nilsson,Vincent | (tb)
Jens Winther And The Danish Radio Jazz Orchestra
Angels | dacapo | DCCD 9442
Michael Mantler Orchestra
Hide And Seek | ECM | 1738(549612-2)
Miles Davis With The Danish Radio Big Band
Aura | CBS | CK 63962
Mona Larsen And The Danish Radio Big Band Plus Soloists
Michael Mantler:Cerco Un Paese Innocente | ECM | 1556
Stan Getz With The Danish Radio Big Band
Stan Getz In Europe | Laserlight | 24657
The Danish Radio Big Band
Aura | CBS | CK 63962
The Danish Radio Jazz Orchestra
This Train:The Danish Radio Jazz Orchestra Plays The Music Of Ray Pitts | dacapo | DCCD 9428
Nice Work | dacapo | DCCD 9446

Nimitz,Jack | (b-cl,bs,fl,cl,bass-fl,reeds,saxts)
Bud Shank Sextet
New Gold! | Candid | CCD 79707
Diane Schuur And Her Band
The Best Of Diane Schuur | GRP | GRP 98882
Diane Schuur With Orchestra
The Best Of Diane Schuur | GRP | GRP 98882
Herbie Hancock Group
Sunlight | CBS | 486570-2
Horace Silver Quintet With Brass
Horace Silver Retrospective | Blue Note | 495576-2
Johnny Hartman And His Orchestra
Unforgettable | Impulse(MCA) | IMP 11522
June Christy With The Shorty Rogers Orchestra
June Christy Big Band Special | Capitol | 498319-2
Milt Jackson And His Orchestra
Reverence And Compassion | Reprise | 9362-45204-2
Nat Pierce/Dick Collins Nonet
Nat Pierce-Dick Collins-Ralph Burns & The Herdsmen Play Paris | Fantasy | FCD 24759-2
Peggy Lee With The Quincy Jones Orchestra
Blues Cross Country | Capitol | 520088-2
Ruth Brown With Orchestra
Fine And Mellow | Fantasy | FCD 9663-2
Singers Unlimited With The Pat Williams Orchestra
The Singers Unlimited:Magic Voices | MPS | 539130-2
Stan Kenton And His Orchestra
Great Swing Classics In Hi-Fi | Capitol | 521223-2
Terry Gibbs Big Band
Terry Gibbs Dream Band Vol.4:Main Stem | Contemporary | CCD 7656-2
Terry Gibbs Dream Band
Terry Gibbs Dream Band Vol.3:Flying Home | Contemporary | CCD 7654-2
Terry Gibbs Dream Band Vol.5:The Big Cat | Contemporary | CCD 7657-2
The Quincy Jones-Sammy Nestico Orchestra
Basie & Beyond | Warner | 9362-47792-2
Vic Lewis West Coast All Stars
Vic Lewis Presenting A Celebration Of Contemporary West Coast Jazz | Candid | CCD 79711/12
Woody Herman And His Orchestra
Great Swing Classics In Hi-Fi | Capitol | 521223-2

Nimitz,Jack or Sol Schlinger | (bs)
Songs For Hip Lovers | Verve | 559872-2

Nishizono,Mari | (gvoc)
Toshinori Kondo & Ima
Red City Smoke | JA & RO | JARO 4173-2

Nissl,Anton | (dr)
Rodach
Himmel Und Hölle-Heaven And Hell | Traumton Records | 4434-2

Nistico,Sal | (ts)
Helen Merrill With Orchestra
Casa Forte | EmArCy | 558848-2
Johnny Griffin-Sal Nistico-Roman Schwaller Sextet
Three Generations Of Tenorsaxophone | JHM Records | JHM 3611
Sal Nistico Quartet
Heavyweights | Milestone | MCD 47096-2
Sal Nistico Quintet
Heavyweights | Milestone | MCD 47096-2
Woody Herman And His Orchestra
Verve Jazz Masters 54:Woody Herman | Verve | 529903-2
Woody Herman-1963 | Philips | 589490-2
Brand New | Original Jazz Classics | OJCCD 1044-2(F 8414)

Nivison,Dick | (b)
Teddy Charles' West Coasters
Wardell Gray Memorial Vol.1 | Original Jazz Classics | OJCCD 050-2(P 7008)

Nix,Willie | (drvoc)
Joe Hill Louis
Joe Hill Louis: The Be-Bop Boy | Bear Family Records | BCD 15524 AH
Walter Horton Band

INTERPRETENVERZEICHNIS

Joe Hill Louis: The Be-Bop Boy | Bear Family Records | BCD 15524 AH

Nixon,Teddy | (tb)
New Orleans Feetwarmers
Planet Jazz | Planet Jazz | 2169652-2
Jazz:The Essential Collection Vol.1 | IN+OUT Records | 78011-2

Nizza,Pat | (tsbs)
Louis Armstrong And Billie Holiday With Sy Oliver's Orchestra
Louis Armstrong:C'est Si Bon | Dreyfus Jazz Line | FDM 36730-2

Nketia,Nana Twum | (perc)
Albert Mangelsdorff-Reto Weber Percussion Orchestra
Live At Montreux | double moon | CHRDM 71009

No Sweat Horns: |
Spyro Gyra & Guests
Love & Other Obsessions | GRP | GRP 98112

Noack,Lothar | (clts)
Johannes Rediske Quintet
Deutsches Jazz Fesival 1954/1955 | Bear Family Records | BCD 15430
Re-Disc Bounce | Bear Family Records | BCD 16119 AH
Jumpin' At The Badewanne | Bear Family Records | BCD 16172 AH
Johannes Rediske Sextet
Re-Disc Bounce | Bear Family Records | BCD 16119 AH
Johnnes Rediske Quintet
Deutsches Jazz Fesival 1954/1955 | Bear Family Records | BCD 15430

Noack,Pierre | (cello)
Till Brönner Quartet & Deutsches Symphonieorchester Berlin
German Songs | Minor Music | 801057

Nobile,Mario | (cello)
Paolo Fresu-Furio Di Castri Quintet
Evening Song | Owl Records | 014733-2

Nobili,Maurizio | (vocarr)
Melanie Bong With Band
Fantasia | Jazz 4 Ever Records:Jazz Network | J4E 4755

Nocentelli,Leo | (el-gg)
Maceo Parker Group
Southern Exposure | Minor Music | 801033

Nock,Mike | (el-p,synth,keyboards,pp-solo)
Mike Nock Quartet
Dark & Curious | VeraBra Records | CDVBR 2074-2
Mike Nock Trio
Ondas | ECM | 1220
Yusef Lateef Quartet
Live at Pep's Vol.2 | Impulse(MCA) | 547961-2
Yusef Lateef Quintet
Live at Pep's Vol.2 | Impulse(MCA) | 547961-2
The Roots Of Acid Jazz | Impulse(MCA) | IMP 12042

Nockles,Bruce | (tp)
Ensemble Modern
Ensemble Modern-Fred Frith:Traffic Continues | Winter&Winter | 910044-2

Noel,Dick | (tb)
Billy Eckstine With The Billy May Orchestra
Once More With Feeling | Roulette | 581862-2
Duke Ellington With Tommy Dorsey And His Orchestra
Highlights From The Duke Ellington Centennial Edition | RCA | 2663672-2
Ella Fitzgerald With Frank De Vol And His Orchestra
Get Happy! | Verve | 523321-2
Ella Fitzgerald With Paul Weston And His Orchestra
Ella Fitzgerald Sings The Irving Berlin Song Book | Verve | 543830-2
Ella Fitzgerald With The Nelson Riddle Orchestra
Get Happy! | Verve | 523321-2
Dream Dancing | Original Jazz Classics | OJCCD 1072-2(2310814)
Ella Fitzgerald With The Paul Weston Orchestra
Get Happy! | Verve | 523321-2
June Christy With The Pete Rugolo Orchestra
Something Cool(The Complete Mono & Stereo Versions) | Capitol | 534069-2
Tommy Dorsey And His Orchestra
Planet Jazz:Tommy Dorsey | Planet Jazz | 2159972-2

Noel,Randolph | (horn-arrstring-arr)
Abbey Lincoln With Her Band
Who Used To Dance | Verve | 533559-2
Abbey Lincoln With The Rodney Kendrick Trio And Guests
A Turtle's Dream | Verve | 527382-2

Noel,Richard | (tb)
Ella Fitzgerald With The Billy May Orchestra
Ella Fitzgerald Sings The Harold Arlen Song Book | Verve | 589108-2
Ella Fitzgerald With The Nelson Riddle Orchestra
The Best Of The Song Books:The Ballads | Verve | 521867-2
Oh Lady Be Good:The Best Of The Gershwin Songbook | Verve | 529581-2
Love Songs:The Best Of The Song Books | Verve | 531762-2

Nogueras,Yuri | (congasperc)
Lewis Trio With Guests
Battangó | Intuition Records | INN 1101-2

Noharet,Philippe | (b)
Charlie Haden Quartet West With Strings
Now Is The Hour | Verve | 527827-2
Stephane Grappelli With The Michel Legrand Orchestra
Grapelli Story | Verve | 515807-2

Nolan,D. | (v)
Dee Dee Bridgewater With Orchestra
Dear Ella | Verve | 539102-2

Nolan,John | (dr)
Dylan Cramer Quartet
All Night Long | Nagel-Heyer | CD 073

Noll,Holger | (dr)
Gregor Hübner Quintet
Januschke's Time | Satin Doll Productions | SDP 1034-1 CD

Nölle,Sebastian | (g)
Changes
Jazz Changes? | Jazz 'n' Arts Records | 0100

Nolte,Joachen | (tp)
Old Merrytale Jazz Band
The Very Best Of Dixieland Jazz | Verve | 535529-2

Nomakozasana | (keyboardsvoc)
Ku-umba Frank Lacy & The Poker Bigband
Songs From The Musical 'Poker' | Tutu Records | 888150-2*
Nomakozasana-Uli Lenz
Tenderness | Tutu Records | 888198-2*

Nonnenmacher,Horst | (b)
Andreas Willers Group
Tin Drum Stories(inspired by the novel 'Die Blechtrommel' by Günter Grass) | Between The Lines | btl 009(Efa 10179-2)
Andreas Willers & Friends Play Jimi Hendrix:Experience | Nabel Records:Jazz Network | CD 4665
Association Urbanetique
Ass Bedient | Jazz 4 Ever Records:Jazz Network | J4E 4723
Blue Collar
Diary Of A Working Band | Jazz Haus Musik | JHM 0089 CD

Noone,Jimmie | (cl,ss,tsvoc)
King Oliver's Jazz Band
Jazz:The Essential Collection Vol.1 | IN+OUT Records | 78011-2
The Capitol Jazzmen
Jazz:The Essential Collection Vol.3 | IN+OUT Records | 78013-2
The Hollywood Session:The Capitol Jazzmen | Jazz Unlimited | JUCD 2044

Noordhoek,Tineke | (vibmarimba)
Michael Mantler Group With The Danish Radio Concert Orchestra Strings
The School Of Understanding(Sort-Of-An-Opera) | ECM | 1648/49(537963-2)
Michael Mantler Orchestra
Hide And Seek | ECM | 1738(549612-2)

Norberg,Johan | (g,el-gsitar-g)
Nils Landgren Funk Unit With Guests
5000 Miles | ACT | 9271-2
Nils Landgren Group
Ballads | ACT | 9268-2

Norbo,Soren | (p)
Jens Skou Olsen Group
September Veje | dacapo | DCCD 9451

Norby,Caecilie | (voc)
Caecilie Norby With Band
My Corner Of The Sky | Blue Note | 853422-2

Norby,Louise | (voc)

Nord,Mike | (g,electronicsel-g)
Richard Carr Trio
Coast To Coast | Nabel Records:Jazz Network | CD 4675
Along The Edge | Nabel Records:Jazz Network | CD 4683

Nordahl,Peter | (p,el-pwurlitzter)
Lisa Ekdahl With The Peter Nordahl Trio
When Did You Leave Heaven | RCA | 2143175-2
Back To Earth | RCA | 2161463-2

Nordenström,Jesper | (el-p,org,synthp)
Flemming Agerskov Quintet
Face To Face | dacapo | DCCD 9445
Nils Landgren Funk Unit
Fonk Da World | ACT | 9299-2

Nordic Quartet |
Nordic Quartet
Nordic Quartet | ECM | 1553

Nordin,Sture | (b)
Brew Moore Quartet
No More Brew | Storyville | STCD 8275
Sonny Boy Williamson Group
The Blues | Storyville | 4960323

Nordsoe,Klaus | (congasperc)
Simon Spang-Hanssen & Maneklar
Wondering | dacapo | DCCD 9436

Nordstrom,Erik | (ts)
Stan Getz And The Swedish All Stars
Stan Getz Highlights:The Best Of The Verve Years Vol.2 | Verve | 517330-2
Stan Getz Highlights | Verve | 847430-2

Nordström,Katarina | (voc)
The Real Group
One For All | ACT | 9003-2
The Real Group With Toots Thielemans
One For All | ACT | 9003-2

Noren,Fredrik | (drperc)
Brew Moore Quartet
No More Brew | Storyville | STCD 8275

Noren,Jack | (dr)
Clifford Brown And Art Farmer With The Swedish All Stars
Clifford Brown Memorial | Original Jazz Classics | OJC20 017-2(P 7055)
Jack Noren Quartet
Lars Gullin 1953,Vol.2:Moden Sounds | Dragon | DRCD 234
Lars Gullin Quartet
Lars Gullin 1953,Vol.2:Moden Sounds | Dragon | DRCD 234
Lars Gullin 1951/52 Vol.5:First Walk | Dragon | DRCD 380
Lars Gullin Quintet
Lars Gullin 1953,Vol.2:Moden Sounds | Dragon | DRCD 234
Lars Gullin 1951/52 Vol.5:First Walk | Dragon | DRCD 380
Lars Gullin Septet
Lars Gullin 1951/52 Vol.5:First Walk | Dragon | DRCD 380
Lars Gullin Sextet
Lars Gullin 1951/52 Vol.5:First Walk | Dragon | DRCD 380
Lars Gullin With The Bob Laine Trio
Lars Gullin 1953,Vol.2:Moden Sounds | Dragon | DRCD 234

Noriega,Oscar | (asb-cl)
Ed Schuller Group feat. Dewey Redman
The Force | Tutu Records | 888166-2*
Unit X
Rated X | Timescrapper | TSCR 9618

Norman Granz Jam Session |
Norman Granz Jam Session
Verve Jazz Masters 26:Lionel Hampton with Oscar Peterson | Verve | 521853-2
Verve Jazz Masters Vol.60:The Collection | Verve | 529866-2
Talkin' Bird | Verve | 559859-2
Bird: The Complete Charlie Parker On Verve | Verve | 837141-2

Norman,Fred | (arr,ld,condtb)
Dinah Washington And Her Orchestra
Misty Blue:Sweet Sisters Swing Songs Of Sorrow And Sadness | Blue Note | 521151-2
Dinah Washington With Orchestra
Ballads | Roulette | 537559-2

Norman,Loulie Jean | (voc)
Paul Desmond Quartet With The Bill Bates Singers
Desmond | Original Jazz Classics | OJCCD 712-2(F 3235/8082)

Norregaard,Svend Erik | (dr)
Clark Terry Quartet
Jazz Legends:Clark Terry-Duke Jordan | Storyville | 4960283

Norris,Al | (g,vvoc)
Jimmy Lunceford And His Orchestra
Planet Jazz:Swing | Planet Jazz | 2169651-2

Norris,Alex | (tpfl-h)
Alex Norris Quintet
A New Beginning | Fresh Sound Records | FSNT 081 CD
Jam Session
Jam Session Vol.6 | Steeplechase | SCCD 31537

Norris,Bob | (congav)
Bobby Bryant Orchestra
Deep Blue-The United States Of Mind | Blue Note | 521152-2

Norris,Charles | (b)
Dizzy Gillespie's Trumpet Kings
The Trumpet Kings Meet Joe Turner | Original Jazz Classics | OJCCD 497-2

Norris,Walter | (pp-solo)
Chet Baker Quintet
My Favourite Songs: The Last Great Concert Vol.1 | Enja | ENJ-5097 2
The Last Concert Vol.I+II | Enja | ENJ-6074 22
Chet Baker Quintet/NDR Big Band/Radio Orchestra Hannover
Straight From The Heart-The Last Concert Vol.2 | Enja | ENJ-6020 2
The Last Concert Vol.I+II | Enja | ENJ-6074 22
Chet Baker With The NDR-Bigband
NDR Big Band-Bravissimo | ACT | 9232-2
My Favourite Songs: The Last Great Concert Vol.1 | Enja | ENJ-5097 2
The Last Concert Vol.I+II | Enja | ENJ-6074 22
Chet Baker-The Legacy Vol.1 | Enja | ENJ-9021 2
Chet Baker With The Radio Orchestra Hannover(NDR)
My Favourite Songs: The Last Great Concert Vol.1 | Enja | ENJ-5097 2
The Last Concert Vol.I+II | Enja | ENJ-6074 22
Heinz Sauer Quartet With The NDR Big Band
NDR Big Band-Bravissimo | ACT | 9232-2
Joe Pass With The NDR Big Band
Joe Pass In Hamburg | ACT | 9100-2
Klaus Weiss Septet
All Night Through | ATM Records | ATM 3816 AH
Klaus Weiss Sextet
All Night Through | ATM Records | ATM 3816 AH
NDR Big Band With Guests
50 Years Of NDR Big Band:Bravissimo II | ACT | 9259-2
Ornette Coleman Quintet
The Music Of Ornette Coleman:Something Else!! | Original Jazz Classics | OJC20 163-2
The Trio
The Trio:Rediscovered | String Jazz | SJRCD 1007
Walter Norris-George Mraz Duo
Drifting | Enja | ENJ-2044 2

Norske Messingsekstett,Den | (brass)
Jan Garbarek-Ralph Towner Group
Dis | ECM | 1093(827408-2)

North Sea Wind | (windharp)

Northern,Bob | (fr-h,percwhistle)
Anfrew Hill Nonet
Passing Ships | Blue Note | 593871-2
Cal Tjader With The Lalo Schifrin Orchestra
Talkin Verve/Roots Of Acid Jazz:Cal Tjader | Verve | 531562-2
Charlie Haden's Liberation Music Orchestra
Liberation Music Orchestra | Impulse(MCA) | 951188-2
Freddie Hubbard Orchestra
The Body And The Soul | Impulse(MCA) | 951183-2
Gil Evans Orchestra
The Individualism Of Gil Evans | Verve | 833804-2
Jack McDuff Quartet With Orchestra
Prelude:Jack McDuff Big Band | Prestige | PRCD 24283-2
John Coltrane And His Orchestra
John Coltrane:Standards | Impulse(MCA) | 549914-2
John Coltrane Quartet With Brass
The Complete Africa/Brass Sessions | Impulse(MCA) | 952168-2
Lalo Schifrin And His Orchestra
Verve Jazz Masters 39:Cal Tjader | Verve | 521858-2
Milt Jackson Orchestra
Milt Jackson Birthday Celebration | Fantasy | FANCD 6079-2
Quincy Jones And His Orchestra
Rahsaan/The Complete Mercury Recordings Of Roland Kirk | Mercury | 846630-2
Sun Ra And His Intergalactic Research Arkestra
Black Myth/Out In Space | MPS | 557656-2
The Jazz Composer's Orchestra
Comminications | JCOA | 1001/2
Thelonious Monk And His Orchestra
Thelonious Monk:85th Birthday Celebration | zyx records | FANCD 6076-2
At Town Hall | Original Jazz Classics | OJCCD 135-2

Northington,Audrey | (voc)
Lenny White Group
Renderers Of Spirit | Hip Bop | HIBD 8014

Norton,Kevin | (dr,samples,marimba,perc)
Dave Ballou Quartet
Dancing Foot | Steeplechase | SCCD 31556
James Emery Quartet
Spectral Domains | Enja | ENJ-9344 2
James Emery Septet
Spectral Domains | Enja | ENJ-9344 2
James Emery Sextet
Luminous Cycles | Between The Lines | btl 015(Efa 10185-2)

Norvo,Red | (marimba,xylophone,pvib)
Billie Holiday And Her All Stars
Billie's Blues | Blue Note | 748786-2
Frank Sinatra With The Red Norvo Quintet(Sextet!)
Live In Australia,1959 | Blue Note | 837513-2
Frank Sinatra With The Red Norvo Quintet(Sextet!) & Orchestra
Live In Australia,1959 | Blue Note | 837513-2
Jesse Price And His Blues Band
Jazz Profile:Dexter Gordon | Blue Note | 823514-2
Peggy Lee With The Benny Goodman Orchestra
Peggy Lee & Benny Goodman:The Complete Recordings 1941-1947 | CBS | C2K 65686
Red Norvo And His Orchestra
Planet Jazz:Female Jazz Vocalists | Planet Jazz | 2169656-2
Red Norvo Septet
Jazz Profile:Dexter Gordon | Blue Note | 823514-2
Red Norvo Sextet
Planet Jazz:Ben Webster | RCA | 2165368-2
Live In Australia,1959 | Blue Note | 837513-2
Music To Listen To Red Norvo By | Original Jazz Classics | OJCCD 1015-2(C 7534)
Ten Cats And A Mouse
The Hollywood Session:The Capitol Jazzmen | Jazz Unlimited | JUCD 2044
The Hollywood Hucksters
The Hollywood Session:The Capitol Jazzmen | Jazz Unlimited | JUCD 2044
Woody Herman And His Orchestra
Woody Herman:Four Brother | Dreyfus Jazz Line | FDM 36722-2
Woody Herman And His Woodshoppers
Woody Herman (And The Herd) At Carnegie Hall | Verve | 559833-2
Woody Herman And The Herd
Woody Herman (And The Herd) At Carnegie Hall | Verve | 559833-2

Norwegian Brass: |
Christoph Lauer & Norwegian Brass
Heaven | ACT | 9420-2

Noschke,Regine | (v)
Marcio Tubino Group
Festa Do Olho | Organic Music | ORGM 9723

Nösig,Daniel | (tp)
Couch Ensemble
Winnetou | Jazz 'n' Arts Records | JNA 1503

Noto,Sam | (tpfl-h)
Singers Unlimited With Rob McConnell And The Boss Brass
The Singers Unlimited:Magic Voices | MPS | 539130-2
Stan Kenton And His Orchestra
Adventures In Blues | Capitol | 520089-2
Great Swing Classics In Hi-Fi | Capitol | 521223-2
Stan Kenton Orchestra
Stompin' At Newport | Pablo | PACD 5312-2

Notrica,Eduardo | (gvoice)
Flor De Tango
Armenonville | Minor Music | 801097

Nottingham,Jimmy | (fl-htp)
Cannonball Adderley And His Orchestra
Ballads | Blue Note | 537563-2
Coleman Hawkins With Billy Byers And His Orchestra
Planet Jazz:Coleman Hawkins | Planet Jazz | 2152055-2
The Hawk In Hi-Fi | RCA | 2663842-2
Count Basie And His Orchestra
Planet Jazz:Count Basie | Planet Jazz | 2152068-2
Dizzy Gillespie And His Orchestra
Afro | Verve | 517052-2
Ella Fitzgerald With Sy Oliver And His Orchestra
Ella Fitzgerald:The Decca Years 1949-1954 | Decca | 050668-2
Jimmy McGriff Orchestra
Swingin' The Blues-Jumpin' The Blues | Laserlight | 24654
Joe Turner With Orchestra
Atlantic Jazz: Kansas City | Atlantic | 7567-81701-2
Joe Williams With The Frank Hunter Orchestra
Planet Jazz:Joe Williams | Planet Jazz | 2165370-2
Kenny Burrell With The Don Sebesky Orchestra
Verve Jazz Masters 45:Kenny Burrell | Verve | 527652-2
Blues-The Common Ground | Verve | 589101-2
King Curtis Band
King Curtis-Blow Man Blow | Bear Family Records | BCD 15670 Cl
Lionel Hampton And His Orchestra
Planet Jazz:Big Bands | Planet Jazz | 2169649-2
Lionel Hampton:Flying Home | Dreyfus Jazz Line | FDM 36735-2
Oscar Peterson With The Ernie Wilkins Orchestra
Verve Jazz Masters 16:Oscar Peterson | Verve | 516320-2
Quincy Jones Big Band
Rahsaan/The Complete Mercury Recordings Of Roland Kirk | Mercury | 846630-2
Thad Jones-Mel Lewis Orchestra
The Groove Merchant/The Second Race | Laserlight | 24656
Wes Montgomery With The Don Sebesky Orchestra
Verve Jazz Masters 14:Wes Montgomery | Verve | 519826-2
Wes Montgomery:The Verve Jazz Sides | Verve | 521690-2
Talkin' Jazz:Roots Of Acid Jazz | Verve | 529580-2
California Dreaming | Verve | 827842-2

Nourredine,Jacques | (b-clas)
Raymond Fol Big Band
Jazz In Paris:Raymond Fol-Les 4 Saisons | EmArCy | 548791-2

Novak,Gary | (dr,skins,sticks,keyboardsb)
Allan Holdsworth Group

The Sixteen Man Of Tain | Cream Records | CR 610-2
Dave Weckl Group
Heads Up | GRP | GRP 96732
Lee Ritenour With Special Guests
Festival International De Jazz De Montreal | Spectra | 9811661
Novak,Zdenek | (sax)
Hans Koller Big Band
New York City | MPS | 9813437
Novakov,Dusan | (dr)
Vasilic Nenad Balkan Band
Joe-Jack | Nabel Records:Jazz Network | CD 4693
Novales,David | (v)
Ben Webster With Orchestra And Strings
Music For Loving:Ben Webster With Strings | Verve | 527774-2
Ultimate Ben Webster selected by James Carter | Verve | 557537-2
Novelli | (el-b)
Gato Barbieri Orchestra
Latino America | Impulse(MCA) | 952236-2
Sarah Vaughan With Orchestra
I Love Brazil | Pablo | 2312101-2
Sarah Vaughan Birthday Celebration | Fantasy | FANCD 6090-2
Novello,John | (org,synth,pel-p)
Chick Corea Electric Band
Eye Of The Beholder | GRP | GRP 95642
November,Linda | (voc)
Dee Dee Bridgewater With Band
Dee Dee Bridgewater | Atlantic | 7567-80760-2
James Moody Orchestra
The Blues And Other Colors | Original Jazz Classics | OJCCD 954-2(M 9023)
Noves,Joseph | (voc)
Swingle Singers
Jazz Sebastian Bach Vol.2 | Philips | 542553-2
Novosel,Steve | (b)
Rahsaan Roland Kirk Quartet
Rhino Presents The Atlantic Jazz Gallery | Atlantic | 8122-71257-2
Roland Kirk Quartet
The Inflated Tear | Atlantic | 7567-90045-2
The Inflated Tear | Atlantic | 8122-75207-2
Roland Kirk Quintet
The Inflated Tear | Atlantic | 7567-90045-2
The Inflated Tear | Atlantic | 8122-75207-2
Shirley Horn Quartet
The Main Ingredient | Verve | 529555-2
Loving You | Verve | 537022-2
Shirley Horn Quintet
The Main Ingredient | Verve | 529555-2
Loving You | Verve | 537022-2
Noya,Nippy | (perc,bongos,timbaleskalimba)
Walkaway With Urszula Dudziak
Saturation | IN+OUT Records | 77024-2
Wolfgang Schmid's Kick
No Filters | TipToe | TIP-888809 2
Ntshoko,Makaya | (dr)
Mal Waldron
Moods | Enja | ENJ-3021 2
Mal Waldron Sextet
Moods | Enja | ENJ-3021 2
Sathima Bea Benjamin Group
A Morning In Paris | Enja | ENJ-9309 2
Nugier,Patrick | (accordeon)
United Future Organizatio
United Future Organization | Talkin' Loud | 518166-2
Numa-Moore,Pee Wee | (bs)
Little Jimmy Scott | Specialty | SPCD 2170-2
Nunes,William | (perc)
Joan Abril Sextet
Eric | Fresh Sound Records | FSNT 092 CD
NuNu! |
NuNu!
Ocean | TipToe | TIP-888837 2
Nur,Al Batin | (engl-h)
Sun Ra And His Intergalactic Research Arkestra
Black Myth/Out In Space | MPS | 557656-2
Nurock,Kirk | (p)
Theo Bleckman & Kirk Nurock
Looking-Glass River | Traumton Records | 2412-2
Theo Bleckman & Kirk Nurock Quartet
Looking-Glass River | Traumton Records | 2412-2
Nuß,Hubert | (pkeyboards)
Ansgar Striepens Quintet
Dreams And Realities | Laika Records | 35101642
Hubert Nuss Trio
The Shimmering Colours Of The Stained Glass | Green House Music | CD 1008
John Abercrombie With The Ansgar Striepens Quintet
Dreams And Realities | Laika Records | 35101642
Till Brönner Quintet
My Secret Love | Minor Music | 801051
Till Brönner Quintet With Annette Lowman
My Secret Love | Minor Music | 801051
Nuß,Ludwig | (tb)
All That Jazz & Helena Paul
All That Jazz & Helena Paul | Satin Doll Productions | SDP 1031-1 CD
Bill Ramsey With Orchestra
Gettin' Back To Swing | Bear Family Records | BCD 15813 AH
Gianlugi Trovesi Quartet With The WDR Big Band
Dedalo | Enja | ENJ-9419 2
Los Jovenes Flamencos With The WDR Big Band And Guests
Jazzpana | ACT | 9212-2
SWR Big Band
Jazz In Concert | Hänssler Classics | CD 93.004
Nussbaum,Adam | (drperc)
Art Farmer/Slide Hampton Quintet
In Concert | Enja | ENJ-4088 2
Bobby Watson Quartet
Advance | Enja | ENJ-9075 2
Dan Wall Quartet
Off The Wall | Enja | ENJ-9310 2
Dan Wall Trio
Off The Wall | Enja | ENJ-9310 2
Dave Liebman Quintet
Homage To John Coltrane | Owl Records | 018357-2
George Gruntz Concert Jazz Band
Blues 'N Dues Et Cetera | Enja | ENJ-6072 2
Jens Winther And The WDR Big Band
The Escape | dacapo | DCCD 9437
Joachim Schoenecker Quartet
In The Moment | Nagel-Heyer | CD 2009
Joachim Schoenecker-Chris Potter
In The Moment | Nagel-Heyer | CD 2009
John Abercrombie Sextet
Open Land | ECM | 1683(557652-2)
John Abercrombie Trio
While We're Young | ECM | 1489
Speak To The Devil | ECM | 1511
Tactics | ECM | 1623(533680-2)
Michael Brecker Group
Don't Try This At Home | Impulse(MCA) | 950114-2
Now You See It...(Now You Don't) | GRP | GRP 96222
Olga Konkova Trio
Her Point Of View | Candid | CCD 79757
Steve Swallow Group
Deconstructed | Watt | XtraWatt/9(537119-2)
Steve Swallow Quintet
Always Pack Your Uniform On Top | Watt | XtraWatt/10(543506-2)
Steve Swallow Trio
Damaged In Transit | Watt | XtraWatt/11(067792-2)
Tom Harrell Quintet
Visions | Contemporary | CCD 14063-2
Sail Away | Original Jazz Classics | OJCCD 1095-2(C- 14054-2)
Tom Harrell Sextet
Visions | Contemporary | CCD 14063-2
Sail Away | Original Jazz Classics | OJCCD 1095-2(C- 14054-2)
Toots Thielemans Quartet
Toots Thielemans:The Live Takes Vol.1 | IN+OUT Records | 77041-2
Nussbaum,Joe | (b)
Stephane Grappelli Quintet
Grapelli Story | Verve | 515807-2
Vic Lewis Jam Session
Vic Lewis:The Golden Years | Candid | CCD 79754
Nuttycomb,Wilbert | (v)
Johnny Hartman And His Orchestra
Unforgettable | Impulse(MCA) | IMP 11522
Nya | (voc)
Erik Truffaz Quartet
The Dawn | Blue Note | 493916-2
Bending New Corners | Blue Note | 522123-2
Nyberg,Lina | (voc)
Lina Nyberg-Esbjörn Svensson
Close | Touché Music | TMcCD 004
Nyegaard,Peter | (tb)
Henrik Johansen's Jazzband
The Golden Years Of Revival Jazz,Vol 1 | Storyville | STCD 5506
The Golden Years Of Revival Jazz,Vol.2 | Storyville | STCD 5507
Theis/Nyegaard Jazzband
The Golden Years Of Revival Jazz,Sampler | Storyville | 109 1001
The Golden Years Of Revival Jazz,Vol.3 | Storyville | STCD 5508
The Golden Years Of Revival Jazz,Vol.5 | Storyville | STCD 5510
The Golden Years Of Revival Jazz,Vol.12 | Storyville | STCD 5517
The Golden Years Of Revibal Jazz,Vol.15 | Storyville | STCD 5520
Nylund,Pekka | (g)
Piirpauke
Live In Der Balver Höhle | JA & RO | JARO 4101-2
Piirpauke-Global Servisi | JA & RO | JARO 4150-2
Jazzy World | JA & RO | JARO 4200-2
Nyström,Karl | (fr-h)
Bengt-Arne Wallin Orchestra
The Birth+Rebirth Of Swedish Folk Jazz | ACT | 9254-2
Nyten,Lennart | (g)
Sonny Boy Williamson Group
The Blues | Storyville | 4960323
Nyyssönen,Aku | (dr,perc,timbalesvoc)
Piirpauke
The Wild East | JA & RO | JARO 4128-2
Piirpauke-Global Servisi | JA & RO | JARO 4150-2
O,Rourke,Brian | (p)
Buddy Childers Big Band
It's What Happening Now! | Candid | CCD 79749
Oakland,Ron | (v)
A Band Of Friends
Wynton Marsalis Quartet With Strings | CBS | CK 68921
Oakley Jr.,Roy | (v)
Ron Carter With Strings
Pastels | Original Jazz Classics | OJCCD 665-2(M 9073)
Oakley,Leon | (co)
Turk Murphy And His Jazz Band
Atlantic Jazz: New Orleans | Atlantic | 7567-81700-2
OAM Trio |
OAM Trio
Trilingual | Fresh Sound Records | FSNT 070 CD
Oatts,Dick | (alto-fl,ss,as,ts,fl,cl,el-p,piccolo)
Jam Session
Jam Session Vol.3 | Steeplechase | SCCD 31526
Joe Lovano Orchestra
Blue Note Plays Gershwin | Blue Note | 520808-2
Öberg,Mats | (harm,keyboards,psynth)
Viktoria Tolstoy With The Esbjörn Svensson Trio
Viktoria Tolstoy:White Russian | Blue Note | 821220-2
Öberg,Sebastian | (cello)
Nils Landgren Group
Sentimental Journey | ACT | 9409-2
Oberg,Uwe | (pp-solo)
Uwe Oberg
Dedicated | Jazz 'n' Arts Records | JNA 1603
Uwe Oberg Quartet
Dedicated | Jazz 'n' Arts Records | JNA 1603
Oberleitner,Ewald | (b)
Ekkehard Jost Quartet
Deep | Fish Music | FM 007 CD
Some Other Tapes | Fish Music | FM 009/10 CD
Obertontrio,Das |
Das Obertontrio Und Toto Blanke
Energy Fields | ALISO Records | AL 1029
Toto Blanke-Rudolf Dasek With The Overtontrio
Meditation | ALISO Records | AL 1026
Obinata,Ayumi | (keyboardsprogramming)
United Future Organizatio
United Future Organization | Talkin' Loud | 518166-2
O'Bourke,Brian | (p)
Buddy Childers With The Russ Garcia Strings
Artistry In Jazz | Candid | CCD 79735
Ron Affif Quartet
The Jazz Giants Play Miles Davis:Milestones | Prestige | PCD 24225-2
O'Brian,Ponda | (percvoc)
Pili-Pili
Pili-Pili | JA & RO | JARO 4141-2
Hoomba-Hoomba | JA & RO | JARO 4192-2
O'Brien,Anne | (fl)
Miles Davis With Gil Evans Orchestra, The George Gruntz Concert Jazz Band And Guests
Miles & Quincy Live At Montreux | Warner | 9362-45221-2
O'Brien,Floyd | (tbarr)
Bob Crosby And His Orchestra
Swing Legens:Bob Crosby | Nimbus Records | NI 2011
Mezz Mezzrow And His Orchestra
Planet Jazz:Bud Freeman | Planet Jazz | 2161240-2
O'Brien,Hod | (p)
Herb Geller Quartet
To Benny & Johnny | Hep | CD 2084
Herb Geller-Hod O'Brien
To Benny & Johnny | Hep | CD 2084
O'Brien,Larry | (cond)
Glenn Miller And His Orchestra
The Glenn Miller Orchestra In Digital Mood | GRP | GRP 95022
O'Bryan,Ponda | (djimbe,voc,perc,african-dr,conga)
John Thomas & Lifeforce
Devil Dance | Nabel Records:Jazz Network | CD 4601
3000 Worlds | Nabel Records:Jazz Network | CD 4604
Öcal,Burhan | (bells,darbuka,dawul,gongs,kettle-dr)
Lüdi-Öcal
The Bird Who Makes The Cloud Sing As He Drums It-Live At The Montreux Jazz Festival | Creative Works Records | CW CD 1019-1
Marco Cerletti Group
Random And Providence | VeraBra Records | CDVBR 2039-2
Werner Lüdi-Burhan Öcal
Willisau And More Live | Creative Works Records | CW CD 1020-2
O'Callaghan,Pep | (gel-g)
Pep O'Callaghan Grup
Tot Just | Fresh Sound Records | FSNT 017 CD
Port O'Clock | Fresh Sound Records | FSNT 069 CD
Ochs,Arnulf | (g)
Arnulf Ochs Group
In The Mean Time | Jazz 'n' Arts Records | JNA 1202
Ochs,Larry | (as,ts,sopraninosax)
Fred Frith Maybe Monday
Digital Wildlife | Winter&Winter | 910071-2
John Lindberg Ensemble
A Tree Frog Tonality | Between The Lines | btl 008(Efa 10178-2)
Ockner,George | (cello,stringsv)
Bill Evans Quartet With Orchestra
The Complete Bill Evans On Verve | Verve | 527953-2
From Left To Right | Verve | 557451-2
Bill Evans With Orchestra
The Complete Bill Evans On Verve | Verve | 527953-2
From Left To Right | Verve | 557451-2
Billie Holiday With The Ray Ellis Orchestra
Lady In Satin | CBS | CK 65144
Paul Desmond Quartet With The Don Sebesby Orchestra
From The Hot Afternoon | Verve | 543487-2
Phil Woods Quartet With Orchestra & Strings
Round Trip | Verve | 559804-2
Stan Getz With The Eddie Sauter Orchestra
Stan Getz Plays The Music Of Mickey One | Verve | 531232-2
O'Connell,Helen | (voc)
Jimmy Dorsey And His Orchestra
Swing Vol.1 | Storyville | 4960343
O'Connor,Mark | (gv)
Michael Brecker Group
Don't Try This At Home | Impulse(MCA) | 950114-2
O'Connor,Sharon | (cello)
Art Pepper Quintet With Strings
Winter Moon | Original Jazz Classics | OJC20 677-2(GXY 5140)
Octavio | (perc)
Nat Adderley Group
Soul Of The Bible | Capitol | 358257-2
O'Day,Anita | (voc)
Anita O'Day And Her Combo
Pick Yourself Up | Verve | 517329-2
Verve Jazz Masters 49:Anita O'Day | Verve | 527653-2
Anita O'Day With Gene Krupa And His Orchestra
Let Me Off Uptown:Anita O'Day With Gene Krupa | CBS | CK 65625
Anita O'Day With The Bill Holman Orchestra
Verve Jazz Masters 49:Anita O'Day | Verve | 527653-2
Incomparable! Anita O'Day | Verve | 589516-2
Anita O'Day With The Billy May Orchestra
Verve Jazz Masters 49:Anita O'Day | Verve | 527653-2
Anita O'Day With The Buddy Bregman Orchestra
Pick Yourself Up | Verve | 517329-2
Verve Jazz Masters 49:Anita O'Day | Verve | 527653-2
Anita O'Day With The Cal Tjader Quartet
Verve Jazz Masters 49:Anita O'Day | Verve | 527653-2
Time For 2 | Verve | 559808-2
Anita O'Day With The Gary McFarland Orchestra
All The Sad Youn Men | Verve | 517065-2
Verve Jazz Masters 49:Anita O'Day | Verve | 527653-2
Anita O'Day With The Jimmy Giuffre Orchestra
Verve Jazz Masters 49:Anita O'Day | Verve | 527653-2
Anita O'Day With The Oscar Peterson Quartet
Verve Jazz Masters 49:Anita O'Day | Verve | 527653-2
Anita O'Day With The Russ Garcia Orchestra
Verve Jazz Masters 49:Anita O'Day | Verve | 527653-2
Anita O'Day With The Three Sounds
Verve Jazz Masters 49:Anita O'Day | Verve | 527653-2
Oden,Charles | (b)
Henry Red Allen Band
The Very Best Of Dixieland Jazz | Verve | 535529-2
Kid Ory And His Band
The Very Best Of Dixieland Jazz | Verve | 535529-2
Oden,James[St.Louis Jimmy] | (pvoc)
Otis Spann
Walking The Blues | Candid | CCD 79025
St.Louis Jimmy Oden Group
Goin' Down Slow | Original Blues Classics | OBCCD 584-2(BV 1028)
Odetta | (gvoc)
Odetta With The Buck Clayton Sextet
Odetta And The Blues | Original Blues Classics | OBCCD 509-2(RLP 9417)
Odges,Brian | (b)
John McLaughlin Quartet
Extrapolation | Polydor | 841598-2
Odriche,Jimmy | (sax)
Sarah Vaughan With The Norman Leyden Orchestra
Sarah Vaughan:Lover Man | Dreyfus Jazz Line | FDM 36739-2
Odun,Spencer | (p)
Lionel Hampton And His Orchestra
Planet Jazz:Lionel Hampton | Planet Jazz | 2152059-2
Oecal,Burhan | (perc)
Creative Works Orchestra
Willisau And More Live | Creative Works Records | CW CD 1020-2
Oechsner,Mic | (accordeon,vvoc)
NuNu!
Ocean | TipToe | TIP-888837 2
Oehler,Dale | (cond,arrp)
Joe Sample Group
Invitation | Warner | 9362-45209.2
Oestby,Inger-Johanne | (fl)
Terje Rypdal With The Borealis Ensemble
Q.E.D. | ECM | 1474
Oester,Bänz | (b)
Michael Beck Trio
Michael Beck Trio | JHM Records | JHM 3623
O'Farrill,Arturo | (el-p,p,orgvoice)
Carla Bley Band
Live! | Watt | 12(815730-2)
The Carla Bley Band
I Hate To Sing | Watt | 12,5
O'Farrill,Chico | (arr,dircond)
Cal Tjader Quintet
Talkin Verve/Roots Of Acid Jazz:Cal Tjader | Verve | 531562-2
Charlie Parker With Machito And His Orchestra
Bird: The Complete Charlie Parker On Verve | Verve | 837141-2
Clark Terry & Chico O Farril Orchestra
Spanish Rice | Verve | 9861050
Count Basie And His Orchestra
Basie's Beatle Bag | Verve | 557455-2
Dizzy Gillespie And His Orchestra
Afro | Verve | 517052-2
Öfwerman,Rune | (p)
Lars Gullin Quartet
Lars Gullin 1955/56 Vol.1 | Dragon | DRCD 224
Ogawa-Helferich,Rumi | (cymbalonperc)
Ensemble Modern
Ensemble Modern-Fred Frith:Traffic Continues | Winter&Winter | 910044-2
Ogerman,Claus | (arr,cond,compp)
Antonio Carlos Jobim With The Claus Ogerman Orchestra
Verve Jazz Masters 13:Antonio Carlos Jobim | Verve | 516409-2
The Composer Of 'Desafinado' Plays | Verve | 521431-2
Astrud Gilberto With The Claus Ogerman Orchestra
Verve Jazz Masters 9:Astrud Gilberto | Verve | 519824-2
Bill Evans Trio With The Claus Ogerman Orchestra
The Complete Bill Evans On Verve | Verve | 527953-2
Bill Evans Trio With Symphony Orchestra | Verve | 821983-2
Cal Tjader's Orchestra
Verve Jazz Masters 39:Cal Tjader | Verve | 521858-2
Talkin Verve/Roots Of Acid Jazz:Cal Tjader | Verve | 531562-2
Delle Haensch Jump Combo
Deutsches Jazz Fesival 1954/1955 | Bear Family Records | BCD 15430
Jimmy Smith With The Claus Ogerman Orchestra
Verve Jazz Masters 29:Jimmy Smith | Verve | 521855-2
Any Number Can Win | Verve | 557447-2
Mel Tormé With The Claus Ogerman Orchestra
Comin' Home Baby!/Sings Sunday In New York | Warner | 8122-75438-2
Oscar Peterson Trio With The Claus Ogermann Orchestra

Three Originals:Motion&Emotions/ Insteza On Piano/Hello Herbie | MPS | 521059-2
The Antonio Carlos Jobim Songbook | Verve | 525472-2
Stan Getz With Orchestra And Voices
Stan Getz Highlights | Verve | 847430-2
Stan Getz With Strings And Voices
Reflections | Verve | 523322-2
Stan Getz With The Claus Ogerman Orchestra
What The World Needs Now-Stan Getz Plays Bacharach And David | Verve | 557450-2
Wes Montgomery Quartet With The Claus Ogerman Orchestra
Tequila | Verve | 547769-2
Willow Weep For Me | Verve | 589486-2
Wes Montgomery Quintet With The Claus Ogerman Orchestra
The Antonio Carlos Jobim Songbook | Verve | 525472-2
Talkin' Jazz:Roots Of Acid Jazz | Verve | 529580-2
Tequila | Verve | 547769-2
Wes Montgomery Trio With The Claus Ogerman Orchestra
Tequila | Verve | 547769-2
Wes Montgomery With The Claus Ogerman Orchestra
Verve Jazz Masters 14:Wes Montgomery | Verve | 519826-2

Ogilvie,Brian | (cl,as,tssax)
Joe Ascione Octet
My Buddy:A Tribute To Buddy Rich | Nagel-Heyer | CD 036
Ralph Sutton And Friends
Sweet Sue-The Music Of Fats Waller Vol.1 | Nagel-Heyer | CD 057
The New York Allstars
Count Basie Remembered | Nagel-Heyer | CD 031
Count Basie Remembered Vol.2 | Nagel-Heyer | CD 041

Ohana | (percvoc)
Toots Thieleman And Sivuca
Verve Jazz Masters Vol.59:Toots Thielemans | Verve | 535271-2

Ohi,Takashi | (vib)
United Future Organizatio
United Future Organization | Talkin' Loud | 518166-2

O'Higgins,Dave | (sax,ss,as,tsbs)
Itchy Fingers
Full English Breakfast | Enja | ENJ-7085 2
Jamie Cullum Group
Pointless Nostalgic | Candid | CCD 79782
Nicki Leighton-Thomas Group
Forbidden Games | Candid | CCD 79778

Ohlsson,Kettil | (bs)
Kettil Ohlsson Quintet
Lars Gullin 1953,Vol.2:Moden Sounds | Dragon | DRCD 234

Öhman,Kjell | (p)
Toots Thielemans With Gals And Pals
Verve Jazz Masters Vol.59:Toots Thielemans | Verve | 535271-2

Ohms,Freddie | (tb)
Coleman Hawkins With Billy Byers And His Orchestra
Planet Jazz:Coleman Hawkins | Planet Jazz | 2152055-2
The Hawk In Hi-Fi | RCA | 2663842-2

Ohno,Shunzo | (tp)
Buster Williams Quintet
Something More | IN+OUT Records | 7004-2
Jazz Unlimited | IN+OUT Records | 7017-2

Oien,Jorn | (keyboards)
Geir Lysne Listening Ensemble
Korall | ACT | 9236-2

Ojeda,Bob | (tp)
Diane Schuur With The Count Basie Orchestra
The Best Of Diane Schuur | GRP | GRP 98882

Ok Nok...Kongo |
Ok Nok...Kongo
Moonstone Journey | dacapo | DCCD 9444

O'Kane,Charles | (bssax)
Cab Calloway And His Orchestra
Planet Jazz:Cab Calloway | Planet Jazz | 2161237-2
Planet Jazz:Male Jazz Vocalists | Planet Jazz | 2169657-2
Elliot Lawrence And His Orchestra
The Elliot Lawrence Big Band Swings Cohn & Kahn | Fantasy | FCD 24761-2
Lena Horne With The Lennie Hayton Orchestra
Planet Jazz:Lena Horne | Planet Jazz | 2165373-2
The Four Brothers
Together Again! | RCA | 2179623-2

Okapel,Rachel | (voc)
Mike Westbrook Brass Band
Glad Day:Settings Of William Blake | Enja | ENJ-9376 2

Okegwo,Ugonna | (b)
Jackie Terrasson Trio
Jacky Terrasson | Blue Note | 829351-2
Reach | Blue Note | 837570-2
Jacky Terrasson Group
What It Is | Blue Note | 498756-2
Jacky Terrasson Trio
Alive | Blue Note | 859651-2
Tom Harrell Group
Paradise | RCA | 2663738-2
Tom Harrell Quintet
Live At The Village Vanguard | RCA | 2663910-2

Okland,Gertrud | (v)
Jon Balke w/Magnetic North Orchestra
Further | ECM | 1517

Okland,Nils | (vfiddle)
Christian Wallumrod Ensemble
Sofienberg Variations | ECM | 1809(017067-2)

Okoshi,Tiger | (fl-h,tpel-tp)
Gary Burton Quartet
Times Square | ECM | 1111

Oksala,Timo | (g-synth)
Piirpauke
Live In Der Balver Höhle | JA & RO | JARO 4101-2
Piirpauke-Global Servisi | JA & RO | JARO 4150-2
Jazzy World | JA & RO | JARO 4200-2

Olah,E.L. | (concertmaster)
Stochelo Rosenberg Group With Strings
Gypsy Swing | Verve | 527806-2

Olah,Kalman | (keyboardsp)
Things
Mother Nature | Jazzpoint | JP 1028 CD

Olatunja,Michael | (bel-b)
David Jean-Baptiste Group
The Nature Suite | Laika Records | 35101632

Olatunji,Babatunde | (african-dr,ashiko,djembe,ngoma)
Cannonball Adderley And His Orchestra
Cannonball Adderley Birthday Celebration | Fantasy | FANCD 6087-2
Herbie Mann's Cuban Band
Verve Jazz Masters 56:Herbie Mann | Verve | 529901-2
Max Roach Group
We Insist: Freedom Now Suite | Candid | CCD 79002

Old And New Dreams |
Old And New Dreams
Old And New Dreams | ECM | 1154
Playing | ECM | 1205

Old Merrytale Jazzband |
Old Merrytale Jazz Band
The Very Best Of Dixieland Jazz | Verve | 535529-2

Oldham,Bill | (b,tubatb)
Louis Armstrong And His Orchestra
Planet Jazz:Louis Armstrong | Planet Jazz | 2152052-2
Best Of The Complete RCA Victor Recordings | RCA | 2663636-2
Louis Armstrong:A 100th Birthday Celebration | RCA | 2663694-2
Jazz:The Essential Collection Vol.2 | IN+OUT Records | 78012-2

Oldham,George | (as,clsax)
Planet Jazz:Louis Armstrong | Planet Jazz | 2152052-2
Best Of The Complete RCA Victor Recordings | RCA | 2663636-2
Louis Armstrong:A 100th Birthday Celebration | RCA | 2663694-2
Jazz:The Essential Collection Vol.2 | IN+OUT Records | 78012-2

Oldridge,Anthony | (vel-v)
Barbara Thompson's Paraphernalia
Mother Earth | VeraBra Records | CDVBR 2005-2
Barbara Thompson's Special Edition | VeraBra Records | CDVBR 2017-2

O'Leary,Pat | (b)
Bruce Barth Quartet
Where Eagles Fly | Fresh Sound Records | FSNT 090 CD
Mark Shane's X-Mas Allstars
What Would Santa Say? | Nagel-Heyer | CD 055
Christmas Jazz! | Nagel-Heyer | NH 1008
Mundell Lowe Quintet
Mundell's Moods | Nagel-Heyer | CD 065

Olenjuk,Sasa | (v)
Steve Klink-Sasa Olenjuk
Places To Come From,Places To Go | Minor Music | 801098

Oles,Darek | (b)
Jacintha With Band And Strings
Lush Life | Groove Note | GRV 1011-2(Gold CD 2011)

Oles,Lew | (tp)
Ralph Burns And His Orchestra
The Complete Verve Roy Eldridge Studio Sessions | Verve | 9861278

Oles,Louis | (tp)
Coleman Hawkins With Billy Byers And His Orchestra
The Hawk In Hi-Fi | RCA | 2663842-2

Olesen,Rune Harder | (perc)
The Orchestra
New Skies | dacapo | DCCD 9463

Oliphant,Grasselle | (dr)
Shirley Scott Quartet
Queen Of The Organ-Shirley Scott Memorial Album | Prestige | PRCD 11027-2

Oliva,Reiner | (drvoc)
Regina Büchner's Jazz 4 Fun
Jazz 4 Fun | Satin Doll Productions | SDP 1017-1 CD

Oliva,Stephan | (pp-solo)
Stephan Oliva Trio
Fantasm | RCA | 2173925-2

Olivari,Alex | (g)
Steve Klink-Alex Olivari
Feels Like Home | Minor Music | 801092

Oliver,Buford | (dr)
Don Byas And His Orchestra
Americans Swinging In Paris:Don Byas | EMI Records | 539655-2
Don Byas Quartet
Americans Swinging In Paris:Don Byas | EMI Records | 539655-2
Don Byas:Laura | Dreyfus Jazz Line | FDM 36714-2
Don Byas Ree-Boppers
Don Byas:Laura | Dreyfus Jazz Line | FDM 36714-2
Peanuts Holland And His Orchestra
Americans Swinging In Paris:Don Byas | EMI Records | 539655-2
Tyree Glenn
Don Byas:Laura | Dreyfus Jazz Line | FDM 36714-2
Tyree Glenn And His Orchestra
Americans Swinging In Paris:Don Byas | EMI Records | 539655-2

Oliver,Jay | (b,keyboards,programming,synth)
Dave Weckl Group
Master Plan | GRP | GRP 96192
Heads Up | GRP | GRP 96732
Hard-Wired | GRP | GRP 97602
Vlatko Kucan Group
Vlatko Kucan Group | true muze | TUMU CD 9803

Oliver,Jimmy | (gts)
Dizzy Gillespie All Stars
Milt Jackson Birthday Celebration | Fantasy | FANCD 6079-2

Oliver,Joseph 'King' | (co,ldtp)
Blind Willie Dunn's Gin Bottle Four
Jazz:The Essential Collection Vol.1 | IN+OUT Records | 78011-2
King Oliver And His Dixie Syncopators
Jazz:The Essential Collection Vol.1 | IN+OUT Records | 78011-2
King Oliver And His Orchestra
Planet Jazz:Jazz Trumpet | Planet Jazz | 2169654-2
Jazz:The Essential Collection Vol.1 | IN+OUT Records | 78011-2
King Oliver's Creole Jazz Band
Jazz:The Essential Collection Vol.1 | IN+OUT Records | 78011-2
King Oliver's Jazz Band
Jazz:The Essential Collection Vol.1 | IN+OUT Records | 78011-2
Sippie Wallace With King Oliver And Hersal Thomas
Jazz:The Essential Collection Vol.1 | IN+OUT Records | 78011-2

Oliver,Sy | (arr,voc,cond,ldtp)
Billie Holiday With Sy Oliver And His Orchestra
Billie's Love Songs | Nimbus Records | NI 2000
Della Reese With The Sy Oliver Orchestra
Misty Blue:Sweet Sisters Swing Songs Of Sorrow And Sadness | Blue Note | 521151-2
Duke Ellington With Tommy Dorsey And His Orchestra
Highlights From The Duke Ellington Centennial Edition | RCA | 2663672-2
Ella Fitzgerald With Sy Oliver And His Orchestra
Ella Fitzgerald:Mr.Paganini | Dreyfus Jazz Line | FDM 36741-2
Ella Fitzgerald And Louis Armstrong With Sy Oliver And His Orchestra
Ella Fitzgerald:Mr.Paganini | Dreyfus Jazz Line | FDM 36741-2
Ella Fitzgerald With Sy Oliver And His Orchestra
Ella Fitzgerald:The Decca Years 1949-1954 | Decca | 050668-2
Jimmy Lunceford And His Orchestra
Planet Jazz:Swing | Planet Jazz | 2169651-2
Louis Armstrong And Billie Holiday With Sy Oliver's Orchestra
Louis Armstrong:C'est Si Bon | Dreyfus Jazz Line | FDM 36730-2
Louis Armstrong And Ella Fitzgerald With Sy Oliver's Orchestra
Louis Armstrong:C'est Si Bon | Dreyfus Jazz Line | FDM 36730-2
Louis Armstrong And His All Stars With The Sy Oliver Orchestra
Ambassador Louis Armstrong Vol.17:Moments To Remember(1952-1956) | Ambassador | CLA 1917
Louis Armstrong And His Orchestra
I Love Jazz | Verve | 543747-2
Louis Armstrong And Omer Simeon With The Sy Oliver Orchestra
Ambassador Louis Armstrong Vol.17:Moments To Remember(1952-1956) | Ambassador | CLA 1917
Louis Armstrong With Sy Oliver And His Orchestra
Satchmo Serenaders | Verve | 543792-2
Louis And The Angels | Verve | 549592-2
Louis Armstrong:C'est Si Bon | Dreyfus Jazz Line | FDM 36730-2
Louis Armstrong-My Greatest Songs | MCA | MCD 18347
Louis Armstrong With Sy Oliver's Choir And Orchestra
Jazz Collection:Louis Armstrong | Laserlight | 24366
Louis And The Good Book | Verve | 549593-2
Louis And The Good Book | Verve | 940130-0
Tommy Dorsey And His Orchestra
Planet Jazz:Frank Sinatra & Tommy Dorsey | Planet Jazz | 2152067-2
Planet Jazz Sampler | Planet Jazz | 2152326-2
Planet Jazz:Tommy Dorsey | Planet Jazz | 2159972-2
Planet Jazz:Jazz Greatest Hits | Planet Jazz | 2169648-2
Willie Lewis And His Entertainers
Americans Swinging In Paris:Benny Carter | EMI Records | 539647-2

Ollestad,Tollak | (harm)
Dave Grusin Orchestra
Two For The Road:The Music Of Henry Mancini | GRP | GRP 98652

Ollu,Franck | (fr-hcond)
Ensemble Modern
Ensemble Modern-Fred Frith:Traffic Continues | Winter&Winter | 910044-2

Olsen,Jens Skov | (b)
Jens Skou Olsen Group
September Veje | dacapo | DCCD 9451

Olson,Mike | (synth)
Steve Tibbetts Group
The Fall Of Us All | ECM | 1527(521144-2)

Olson,Stewart | (sax)
Anita O'Day With Gene Krupa And His Orchestra
Let Me Off Uptown:Anita O'Day With Gene Krupa | CBS | CK 65625

Olsson,Chrille | (b)
Nils Landgren Group
Sentimental Journey | ACT | 9409-2

Olsson,Gordon | (tb)
Lars Gullin Octet
Lars Gullin 1955/56 Vol.1 | Dragon | DRCD 224

Olsson,Mat |
Lars Gullin 1951/52 Vol.5:First Walk | Dragon | DRCD 380

Olsson,Mats | (p)
Jack Noren Quartet
Lars Gullin 1953,Vol.2:Moden Sounds | Dragon | DRCD 234

O'Malley,Ernie | (dr)
Dick Charlesworth And His City Gents
The Golden Years Of Revival Jazz,Vol.6 | Storyville | STCD 5511

O'Mara,Peter | (el-g,gg-synth)
Jenny Evans And Her Quintet
Gonna Go Fishin' | ESM Records | ESM 9307
Klaus Doldinger & Passport
Down To Earth | Warner | 4509-93207-2
Klaus Doldinger's Passport
Klaus Doldinger Passport Live | Warner | 8573-84132-2
Blues Roots | Warner | 9031-75417-2
Klaus Doldinger's Passport With Johnny 'Clyde' Copeland
Blues Roots | Warner | 9031-75417-2
Peter O'Mara Quartet
Symmetry | Edition Collage | EC 484-2
Wind Moments | Take Twelve On CD | TT 009-2

Omoe,Elo | (b-cl,perc,bongos,fl,as)
Sun Ra And His Astro-Infinity Arkestra
Space Is The Place | Impulse(MCA) | 951249-2

Onderdonk,Dave | (g)
Kurt Elling Group
This Time Its Love | Blue Note | 493543-2

One Soul | (rap)
Gunter Hampel Next Generation
Next Generation | Birth | CD 043

O'Neal,Johnny | (p)
Clark Terry Quartet
OW | Storyville | STCD 8378

O'Neil,Buffy | (voc)
Tom Browne Groups
Mo' Jamaica Funk | Hip Bop | HIBD 8002

O'Neil,Tom | (b)
Elliot Lawrence And His Orchestra
Mullenium | CBS | CK 65678

Oosthof,Jan | (tp)
The Rosenberg Trio With Orchestra
Noches Calientes | Verve | 557022-2

Opel,Nancy | (voc)
The Sidewalks Of New York
Tin Pan Alley:The Sidewalks Of New York | Winter&Winter | 910038-2

Operatic String Orchestra,The |
Dizzy Gillespie Orchestra And The Operatic String Orchestra
Jazz In Paris:Dizzy Gillespie And His Operatic Strings Orchestra | EmArCy | 018420-2
Dizzy Gillespie Quartet And The Operatic String Orchestra
Jazz In Paris:Dizzy Gillespie And His Operatic Strings Orchestra | EmArCy | 018420-2

Opp,Joachim | (b)
Joe Bawelino Quartet
Happy Birthday Stéphane | Edition Collage | EC 458-2
Joe Bawelino Quartet & Martin Stegner
Happy Birthday Stéphane | Edition Collage | EC 458-2

Oppermann,Jens | (v)
Kölner Saxophon Mafia With The Auryn Quartet
Kölner Saxophon Mafia Proudly Presents | Jazz Haus Musik | JHM 0046 CD

Oquendo,Manny | (cowbell,guiro,timbales,dr,perc)
Cal Tjader's Orchestra
Talkin Verve/Roots Of Acid Jazz:Cal Tjader | Verve | 531562-2

O'Quinn,Keith | (tb)
Buddy Rich Big Band
Backwoods Siseman/Pieces Of Dream | Laserlight | 24655

Orange,Joseph | (tb)
Archie Shepp Sextet
Fire Music | Impulse(MCA) | 951158-2

Orchestra | (reeds,perc,brassstrings)
Anita O'Day With The Bill Holman Orchestra
Incomparable! Anita O'Day | Verve | 589516-2
Ben Webster With Orchestra And Strings
Music For Loving:Ben Webster With Strings | Verve | 527774-2
Benny Goodman And His Orchestra
Jazz Collection:Benny Goodman | Laserlight | 24396
Bill Evans Quartet With Orchestra
The Complete Bill Evans On Verve | Verve | 527953-2
From Left To Right | Verve | 557451-2
Bill Evans Trio With The Claus Ogerman Orchestra
The Complete Bill Evans On Verve | Verve | 527953-2
Bill Evans Trio With Symphony Orchestra | Verve | 821983-2
Billy Eckstine With Bobby Tucker And His Orchestra
Billy Eckstine Now Singing In 12 Great Movies | Verve | 589307-2
Billy Eckstine With Hal Mooney And His Orchestra
Billy Eckstine Now Singing In 12 Great Movies | Verve | 589307-2
Billy May And His Orchestra
Billy May's Big Fat Brass/Bill's Bag | Capitol | 535206-2
Bing Crosby And Rosemarie Clooney With The Billy May Orchestra
Fancy Meeting You Here | RCA | 2663859-2
Blossom Dearie With The Russ Garcia Orchestra
Verve Jazz Masters 51:Blossom Dearie | Verve | 529906-2
Cal Tjader's Orchestra
Verve Jazz Masters 39:Cal Tjader | Verve | 521858-2
Talkin Verve/Roots Of Acid Jazz:Cal Tjader | Verve | 531562-2
Coleman Hawkins With Paul Neilson's Orchestra
Body And Soul Revisited | GRP | GRP 16272
Dave Grusin Orchestra
Two For The Road:The Music Of Henry Mancini | GRP | GRP 98652
Diana Krall Group With Orchestra
When I Look In Your Eyes | Verve | 9513304
Dinah Washington And Her Orchestra
Verve Jazz Masters 40:Dinah Washington | Verve | 522055-2
Dinah Washington With Orchestra
Mad About The Boy-The Best Of Dinah Washington | Mercury | 512214-2
Dinah Washington With The Belford Hendricks Orchestra
What A Diff'rence A Day Makes! | Verve | 543300-2
Dinah Washington With The Quincy Jones Orchestra
4 By 4:Ella Fitzgerald/Sarah Vaughan/Billie Holiday/Dinah Washington | Verve | 559693-2
Duke Ellington And His Orchestra
The Story Of Jazz Piano | Laserlight | 24653
Highlights From The Duke Ellington Centennial Edition | RCA | 2663672-2
Duke Ellington And His Orchestra 1929-1943 | Storyville | 4960333
Duke Ellington Trio With The Boston Pops Orchestra
Highlights From The Duke Ellington Centennial Edition | RCA | 2663672-2
Ella Fitzgerald And Barney Kessel
Jazz Collection:Ella Fitzgerald | Laserlight | 24397
Ella Fitzgerald And Her Orchestra
Jazz Collection:Ella Fitzgerald | Laserlight | 24397
Ella Fitzgerald With Orchestra
Ella Fitzgerald-First Lady Of Song | Verve | 517898-2
Ella/Things Ain't What They Used To Be | Warner | 9362-47875-2
Ella Fitzgerald With The Marty Paich Orchestra
The Antonio Carlos Jobim Songbook | Verve | 525472-2

Ella Sings Broadway | Verve | 549373-2
Ella Fitzgerald With The Paul Weston Orchestra
The Best Of The Song Books:The Ballads | Verve | 521867-2
Frank Sinatra With The Red Norvo Quintet(Sextet!) & Orchestra
Live In Australia,1959 | Blue Note | 837513-2
Golden Gate Quartet
Americans Swinging In Paris:Golden Gate Quartet | EMI Records | 539659-2
Grant Green With Orchestra
Blue Break Beats | Blue Note | 799106-2
Inge Brandenburg mit Hans Martin Majewski und seinem Orchester
Why Don't You Take All Of Me | Bear Family Records | BCD 15614 AH
Inge Brandenburg mit Kurt Edelhaben und seinem Orchester
Why Don't You Take All Of Me | Bear Family Records | BCD 15614 AH
Inge Brandenburg mit Werner Müller und seinem Orchester
Why Don't You Take All Of Me | Bear Family Records | BCD 15614 AH
Jack McDuff Quartet With Orchestra
Moon Rappin' | Blue Note | 538697-2
Jerri Southern And The Frank Meriweather Orchestra
The Very Thought Of You:The Decca Years 1951-1957 | Decca | 050671-2
Jerri Southern And The Gus Levene Orchestra
The Very Thought Of You:The Decca Years 1951-1957 | Decca | 050671-2
Jerri Southern And The Norman Leyden Orchestra
The Very Thought Of You:The Decca Years 1951-1957 | Decca | 050671-2
Jerri Southern And The Ralph Burns Orchestra
The Very Thought Of You:The Decca Years 1951-1957 | Decca | 050671-2
Jerri Southern And The Sonny Burke Orchestra
The Very Thought Of You:The Decca Years 1951-1957 | Decca | 050671-2
Jerri Southern And The Toots Camarata Orchestra
The Very Thought Of You:The Decca Years 1951-1957 | Decca | 050671-2
Jerri Southern And The Victoe Young Orchestra
The Very Thought Of You:The Decca Years 1951-1957 | Decca | 050671-2
Jimmy Smith With Orchestra
Jimmy Smith:Best Of The Verve Years | Verve | 527950-2
Jimmy Smith With The Johnny Pate Orchestra
Jimmy Smith:Best Of The Verve Years | Verve | 527950-2
Joe Sample Group
Invitation | Warner | 9362-45209.2
Juan Garcia Esquivel Orchestra
Juan's Again | RCA | 2168206-2
June Christy With Orchestra
This Is June Christy/June Christy Recalls Those Kenton Days | Capitol | 535209-2
June Christy With The Pete Rugolo Orchestra
The Song Is June | Capitol | 855455-2
Kenny Burrell With The Johnny Pate Orchestra
Verve Jazz Masters 45:Kenny Burrell | Verve | 527652-2
Les Blue Stars
Jazz In Paris:Blossom Dearie-The Pianist/Les Blue Stars | EmArCy | 064784-2
Louis Armstrong And Bing Crosby With Orchestra
The Very Best Of Dixieland Jazz | Verve | 535529-2
Louis Armstrong And Ella Fitzgerald With Russell Garcia's Orchestra
The Complete Ella Fitzgerald And Louis Armstrong On Verve | Verve | 537284-2
The Best Of Ella Fitzgerald And Louis Armstrong On Verve | Verve | 537909-2
Porgy And Bess | Verve | 827475-2
Louis Armstrong With The Gordon Jenkins Orchestra
Ambassador Louis Armstrong Vol.17:Moments To Remember(1952-1956) | Ambassador | CLA 1917
Louis Jordan With The Nelson Riddle Orchestra
Louis Jordan-Let The Good Times Roll: The Complete Decca Recordings 1938-1954 | Bear Family Records | BCD 15557 IH
Mamie Smith WithThe Lucky Millinder Orchestra
The Blues | Storyville | 4960323
Mark Murphy With The Ralph Burns Orchestra
Crazy Rhythm:His Debut Recordings | Decca | 050670-2
Mel Tormé With Orchestra
Comin' Home Baby!/Sings Sunday In New York | Warner | 8122-75438-2
Mel Tormé With The Claus Ogerman Orchestra
Comin' Home Baby!/Sings Sunday In New York | Warner | 8122-75438-2
Mel Tormé With The Geoff Love Orchestra
My Kind Of Music | Verve | 543795-2
Mel Tormé With The Jimmy Jones Orchestra
Blue Velvet: Crooners, Swooners And Velvet Vocals | Blue Note | 521153-2
Mel Tormé With The Shorty Rogers Orchestra
Comin' Home Baby!/Sings Sunday In New York | Warner | 8122-75438-2
Mel Tormé With The Tony Osborne Orchestra
My Kind Of Music | Verve | 543795-2
Mel Tormé With The Wally Stott Orchestra
My Kind Of Music | Verve | 543795-2
Miles Davis Group
Doo-Bop | Warner | 7599-26938-2
Nat King Cole Trio With Pete Rugolo's Orchestra
Nat King Cole:For Sentimental Reasons | Dreyfus Jazz Line | FDM 36740-2
Nelson Riddle And His Orchestra
Changing Colors | MPS | 9814794
Communication | MPS | 9814795
Nina Simone With Hal Mooney's Orchestra
Nina Simone After Hours | Verve | 526702-2
Verve Jazz Masters Vol.58:Nina Simone Sings Nina | Verve | 529867-2
Nina Simone With Horace Ott's Orchestra
Verve Jazz Masters 17:Nina Simone | Verve | 518198-2
Nina Simone After Hours | Verve | 526702-2
Oscar Peterson Trio With The Claus Ogermann Orchestra
The Antonio Carlos Jobim Songbook | Verve | 525472-2
Oscar Peterson With Orchestra
Oscar Peterson:The Composer | Pablo | 2310970-2
A Royal Wedding Suite | Original Jazz Classics | OJCCD 973-2(2312129)
Paul Desmond With Strings
The Ballad Of Paul Desmond | RCA | 21429372
Peggy Lee With Benny Goodman And The Paul Weston Orchestra
Peggy Lee & Benny Goodman:The Complete Recordings 1941-1947 | CBS | C2K 65686
Ronnie Foster Group
Sweet Revival... | Blue Note | 581676-2
Sarah Vaughan With Orchestra
Sweet 'N' Sassy | Roulette | 531793-2
Sarah Vaughan Sings The Mancini Songbook | Verve | 558401-2
Sarah Vaughan Birthday Celebration | Fantasy | FANCD 6090-2
Sarah Vaughan With The Hal Mooney Orchestra
4 By 4:Ella Fitzgerald/Sarah Vaughan/Billie Holiday/Dinah Washington | Verve | 559693-2
Shirley Horn With Strings
Here's To Life | Verve | 511879-2
Singers Unlimited With The Robert Farnon Orchestra
The Singers Unlimited:Magic Voices | MPS | 539130-2
Woody Herman And His Orchestra
The Legends Of Swing | Laserlight | 24659

Orchestra & Chorus |
Nina Simone With Hal Mooney's Orchestra
Nina Simone After Hours | Verve | 526702-2
Stephane Grappelli With The Michel Legrand Orchestra
Verve Jazz Masters 11:Stéphane Grappelli | Verve | 516758-2

Orchestra & Strings |
Ahmad Jamal Trio with Orchestra
Pittsburgh | Atlantic | 7567-8209-2
Charlie Haden Quartet With Orchestra
American Dreams | Verve | 064096-2
Dave Brubeck Quartet With Orchestra
Brandenburg Gate:Revisited | CBS | CK 65725
Dinah Washington With Orchestra
Ballads | Roulette | 537559-2
Sarah Vaughan With The Benny Carter Orchestra
Ballads | Roulette | 537561-2

Orchestra Jazz Siciliana |
Orchestra Jazz Siciliana
Orchestra Jazz Siciliana Plays The Music Of Carla Bley | Watt | XtraWatt/4

Orchestra Of St. Luke's |
Astor Piazzolla With Orchestra Of St. Luke's
Concierto Para Bandoneon-Tres Tangos | Nonesuch | 7559-79174-2

Orchestra,The |
The Orchestra
New Skies | dacapo | DCCD 9463

Orchestre National De Jazz |
Orchestre National De Jazz
Charmediterranéen | ECM | 1828(018493-2)

Ordean,Jack | (as,clsax)
Stan Kenton And His Orchestra
Stan Kenton-The Formative Years | Decca | 589489-2

Ore,John | (b)
Hank Mobley Quintet
No Room For Squares | Blue Note | 524539-2
True Blue | Blue Note | 534032-2
Thelonious Monk Quartet
Monk's Dream | CBS | CK 63536
Greatest Hits | CBS | CK 65422
Thelonious Monk:85th Birthday Celebration | zyx records | FANCD 6076-2
Thelonious Monk In Italy | Original Jazz Classics | OJCCD 488-2(RLP 9443)
Monk In France | Original Jazz Classics | OJCCD 670-2
Thelonious Monk In Copenhagen | Storyville | STCD 8283
Thelonious Monk Quartet Plus Two
Thelonious Monk:85th Birthday Celebration | zyx records | FANCD 6076-2
At The Blackhawk | Original Jazz Classics | OJCCD 305-2

Oregon |
Oregon
Oregon | ECM | 1258(811711-2)
Crossing | ECM | 1291(825323-2)
Ecotopia | ECM | 1354
45th Parallel | VeraBra Records | CDVBR 2048-2
Always,Never And Forever | Intuition Records | INT 2073-2
Northwest Passage | Intuition Records | INT 3191-2

Orehucla,Roberto | (vib)
Tom Browne Groups
Mo' Jamaica Funk | Hip Bop | HIBD 8002

Orena,Charles | (b-cl,ss,tssax)
Buddy Childers Big Band
It's What Happening Now! | Candid | CCD 79749

Organ Jazztrio |
Organ Jazztrio & Martin Weiss
Hommage | Edition Collage | EC 492-2

Oriental Wind |
Oriental Wind
Life Road | JA & RO | JARO 4113-2
Jazzy World | JA & RO | JARO 4200-2

Orieux,Charles | (tb)
Klaus Weiss Orchestra
Live At The Domicile | ATM Records | ATM 3805-AH

Original Dixieland 'Jass' Band |
Original Dixieland 'Jass' Band
Planet Jazz | Planet Jazz | 2169652-2

Orloff,Gene | (cello,concertmaster,strings)
Ben Webster With Orchestra And Strings
Music For Loving:Ben Webster With Strings | Verve | 527774-2
Ultimate Ben Webster selected by James Carter | Verve | 557537-2
Cannonball Adderley And His Orchestra
Verve Jazz Masters 31:Cannonball Adderley | Verve | 522651-2
Charlie Parker With Strings
Charlie Parker With Strings:The Master Takes | Verve | 523984-2
Charlie Parker With The Neal Hefti Orchestra
Charlie Parker:The Best Of The Verve Years | Verve | 527815-2
Bird: The Complete Charlie Parker On Verve | Verve | 837141-2
Coleman Hawkins With Billy Byers And His Orchestra
Planet Jazz:Coleman Hawkins | Planet Jazz | 2152055-2
The Hawk In Hi-Fi | RCA | 2663842-2
Freddie Hubbard Orchestra
The Body And The Soul | Impulse(MCA) | 951183-2
Freddie Hubbard With Orchestra
This Is Jazz:Freddie Hubbard | CBS | CK 65041
Grover Washington Jr. Orchestra
Jazzrock-Anthology Vol.3:Fusion | Zounds | CD 27100555
Harry Carney And His Orchestra With Strings
Music For Loving:Ben Webster With Strings | Verve | 527774-2
Louis Armstrong And His Friends
Planet Jazz:Louis Armstrong | Planet Jazz | 2152052-2
Planet Jazz Sampler | Planet Jazz | 2152326-2
Louis Armstrong And His Friends | Bluebird | 2663961-2
Milt Jackson And His Orchestra
Sunflower | CTI | ZK 65131
Paul Desmond Quartet With The Don Sebesby Orchestra
From The Hot Afternoon | Verve | 543487-2
Sarah Vaughan With Orchestra
Sarah Vaughan Sings The Mancini Songbook | Verve | 558401-2
Shirley Horn With Orchestra
Loads Of Love + Shirley Horn With Horns | Mercury | 843454-2
Wes Montgomery Quartet With The Claus Ogerman Orchestra
Tequila | Verve | 547769-2
Wes Montgomery Quintet With The Claus Ogerman Orchestra
The Antonio Carlos Jobim Songbook | Verve | 525472-2
Talkin' Jazz:Roots Of Acid Jazz | Verve | 529580-2
Tequila | Verve | 547769-2
Wes Montgomery Trio With The Claus Ogerman Orchestra
Tequila | Verve | 547769-2
Wes Montgomery With The Claus Ogerman Orchestra
Verve Jazz Masters 14:Wes Montgomery | Verve | 519826-2
Wes Montgomery With The Don Sebesky Orchestra
Verve Jazz Masters 14:Wes Montgomery | Verve | 519826-2
Talkin' Jazz:Roots Of Acid Jazz | Verve | 529580-2
Bumpin' | Verve | 539062-2
Wes Montgomery With The Jimmy Jones Orchestra
Wes Montgomery-The Complete Riverside Recordings | Riverside | 12 RCD 4408-2
The Jazz Giants Play Rodgers & Hart:Blue Moon | Prestige | PCD 24205-2

Ormanlidis,Nikos | (v)
Bernd Konrad Jazz Group With Symphonie Orchestra
Wen Die Götter Lieben | Creative Works Records | CW CD 1010-1

Ormond,John | (b)
Abbey Lincoln And Her Trio
Over The Years | Verve | 549101-2
Abbey Lincoln And Her Trio With Guests
Over The Years | Verve | 549101-2
Abbey Lincoln With Her Band
Who Used To Dance | Verve | 533559-2
Wholly Earth | Verve | 559538-2
Antonio Hart Group
Here I Stand | Impulse(MCA) | 951208-2

Ornstein,Maarten | (b-cl,tshand-clapping)
Lotz Of Music
Puasong Daffriek | Laika Records | LK 94-054

Ornstein,Susan | (v)
A Band Of Friends
Wynton Marsalis Quartet With Strings | CBS | CK 68921

Orquestra De Cambra Teatre Lliure |
Orquestra De Cambra Teatre Lliure
Orquestra De Cambra Teatre Lliure and Lluis Vidal Trio feat.Dave Liebman | Fresh Sound Records | FSNT 027 CD
Porgy And Bess | Fresh Sound Records | FSNT 066 CD
Tributes To Duke Ellington | Fresh Sound Records | FSNT 084 CD
Orquestra De Cambra Teatre Lliure feat. Dave Liebman
Orquestra De Cambra Teatre Lliure and Lluis Vidal Trio feat.Dave Liebman | Fresh Sound Records | FSNT 027 CD

Orr,Bobby | (dr)
Benny Goodman And His Orchestra
Verve Jazz Masters 33:Benny Goodman | Verve | 844410-2
Benny Goodman Sextet
Verve Jazz Masters 33:Benny Goodman | Verve | 844410-2

Orr,Carl | (g)
Wanderlust
Border Crossing | Laika Records | 35100812

Orr,Raymond | (tp)
Buddy Johnson And His Orchestra
Buddy And Ella Johnson 1953-1964 | Bear Family Records | BCD 15479 DH
Dizzy Gillespie And His Orchestra
Planet Jazz:Dizzy Gillespie | Planet Jazz | 2152069-2
Planet Jazz:Bebop | RCA | 2169650-2
Ella Fitzgerald With The Dizzy Gillespie Orchestra
Ella Fitzgerald:Mr.Paganini | Dreyfus Jazz Line | FDM 36741-2

Orrje,Carl Fredrik | (p)
Agneta Baumann And Her Quintet
A Time For Love | Touché Music | TMcCD 006

Orselli,Mauro | (drperc)
Ekkehard Jost Trio
Some Other Tapes | Fish Music | FM 009/10 CD

Orsin,Bartil | (v)
Bengt-Arne Wallin Orchestra
The Birth+Rebirth Of Swedish Folk Jazz | ACT | 9254-2

Orsted-Pedersen,Niels-Henning | (bel-b)
Allan Botschinsky/Niels-Henning Orsted-Pedersen
Duologue | M.A Music | NU 206-3
Archie Shepp/Niels-Henning Orsted-Pedersen Duo
Looking At Bird | Steeplechase | SCS 1149(Audiophile Pressing)
Ben Webster With The Kenny Drew Trio
The Art Of Saxophone | Laserlight | 24652
The Story Of Jazz Piano | Laserlight | 24653
Benny Carter 4
Montreux '77 | Original Jazz Classics | OJC20 374-2(2308204)
Bireli Lagrene Quartet
Standards | Blue Note | 780251-2
Bireli Lagrene Trio
Standards | Blue Note | 780251-2
Buddy DeFranco Meets The Oscar Peterson Quartet
Hark | Original Jazz Classics | OJCCD 867-2(2310915)
Chet Baker Trio
The Touch Of Your Lips | Steeplechase | SCCD 31122
This Is Always | Steeplechase | SCCD 31168
Daybreak | Steeplechase | SCS 1142(Audiophile Pressing)
Count Basie Jam Session
Count Basie Jam Session At The Montreux Jazz Festival 1975 | Original Jazz Classics | OJC20 933-2(2310750)
Count Basie Sextet
Jazz At The Philharmonic:The Montreux Collection | Pablo | PACD 5306-2
Dexter Gordon Quartet
Swiss Nights-Vol. 1 | Steeplechase | SCCD 31050
Swiss Nights Vol.2 | Steeplechase | SCCD 31090
Swiss Nights Vol.3 | Steeplechase | SCCD 31110
Dexter Gordon Quintet
Dexter Gordon:Ballads | Blue Note | 796579-2
Dexter Gordon With The Kenny Drew Trio
Loose Walk | Steeplechase | SCCD 36032
Didier Lockwood Trio
Tribute To Stépane Grappelli | Dreyfus Jazz Line | FDM 36611-2
Dizzy Gillespie All Stars
Jazz At The Philharmonic:The Montreux Collection | Pablo | PACD 5306-2
Dizzy Gillespie Big 7
Dizzy-At The Montreux Jazz Festival 1975 | Original Jazz Classics | OJC20 739-2(2310749)
Dizzy Gillespie Quintet
Jazz In Paris:Dizzy Gillespie-The Giant | EmArCy | 159734-2 PMS
Don Byas Quartet
The Art Of Saxophone | Laserlight | 24652
Freddie Hubbard-Oscar Peterson Quintet
Face To Face | Original Jazz Classics | OJCCD 937-2(2310876)
JATP All Stars
Welcome To Jazz At The Philharmonic | Fantasy | FANCD 6081-2
Joe Pass Trio
Eximious | Original Jazz Classics | OJCCD 1037-2(2310877)
Joe Pass/Niels-Henning Orsted-Pedersen Duo
Joe Pass:Guitar Virtuoso | Pablo | 4 PACD 4423-2
Northsea Nights | Original Jazz Classics | OJCCD 1011-2(2308221)
Chops | Original Jazz Classics | OJCCD 786-2(2310830)
Digital III At Montreux | Original Jazz Classics | OJCCD 996-2(2308223)
Johnny Griffin-Art Taylor Quartet
Johnny Griffin/Art Taylor In Copenhagen | Storyville | STCD 8300
Kansas City 6
Count Basie:Kansas City 6 | Original Jazz Classics | OJC20 449-2(2310871)
Kenn Drew Trio
Kenny Drew Trio At The Brewhouse | Storyville | 4960633
Kenny Drew/Niels-Henning Orsted-Pedersen Duo
Kenny Drew/Solo-Duo | Storyville | STCD 8274
Miles Davis With The Danish Radio Big Band
Aura | CBS | CK 63962
Milt Jackson Big 4
Milt Jackson At The Montreux Jazz Festival 1975 | Original Jazz Classics | OJC20 884-2(2310753)
Milt Jackson Quartet
Jazz At The Philharmonic:The Montreux Collection | Pablo | PACD 5306-2
NDR-Workshop
Doldinger's Best | ACT | 9224-2
Niels-Henning Orsted-Pedersen Quartet
Dancing On The Tables | Steeplechase | SCS 1125(Audiophile Pressing)
Niels-Henning Orsted-Pedersen Trio
Those Who Were | Verve | 533232-2
Friends Forever | Milestone | MCD 9269-2
Niels-Henning Orsted-Pedersen Trio With Johnny Griffin
Those Who Were | Verve | 533232-2
Niels-Henning Orsted-Pedersen/Sam Jones Quartet
Double Bass | Steeplechase | SCS 1055(Audiophile Pressing)
Niels-Henning Orsted-Pedersen/Sam Jones Quintet
Double Bass | Steeplechase | SCS 1055(Audiophile Pressing)
Niels-Henning Orsted-Pedersen/Ulf Wakenius Duo
Those Who Were | Verve | 533232-2
Niels-Henning Orsted-Pedersen/Ulf Wakenius Duo With Lisa Nilsson
Those Who Were | Verve | 533232-2
Oscar Peterson All Stars
Jazz At The Philharmonic:The Montreux Collection | Pablo | PACD 5306-2
Oscar Peterson And The Bassists
Montreux '77 | Original Jazz Classics | OJC 383(2308213)

Oscar Peterson Duo
Oscar Peterson In Russia | Pablo | 2CD 2625711
Oscar Peterson Jam
Oscar Peterson Plays Duke Ellington | Pablo | 2310966-2
Montreux '77 | Original Jazz Classics | OJC 385(2620105)
Montreux '77 | Original Jazz Classics | OJC20 378-2(2308208)
Oscar Peterson Quartet
Oscar Peterson Plays Duke Ellington | Pablo | 2310966-2
Oscar Peterson:The Composer | Pablo | 2310970-2
Night Child | Original Jazz Classics | OJCCD 1030-2(2312108)
The Jazz Giants Play Miles Davis:Milestones | Prestige | PCD 24225-2
Oscar Peterson Quintet
Skol | Original Jazz Classics | OJC20 496-2
Oscar Peterson Trio
Nigerian Marketplace | Pablo | 2308231-2
Oscar Peterson In Russia | Pablo | 2CD 2625711
The Paris Concert | Pablo | 2PACD 2620112
Joe Pass:Guitar Virtuoso | Pablo | 4 PACD 4423-2
Swinging Cooperations:Reunion Blues/Great Connection | MPS | 539085-2
The Good Life | Original Jazz Classics | OJC 627(2308241)
The Trio | Original Jazz Classics | OJCCD 992(2310101)
The Jazz Giants Play Rodgers & Hammerstein:My Favorite Things | Prestige | PCD 24223-2
Oscar Peterson-Stephane Grappelli Quartet
Jazz In Paris:Oscar Peterson-Stephane Grappelli Quartet Vol.1 | EmArCy | 013028-2
Jazz In Paris:Oscar Peterson-Stephane Grappelli Quartet Vol.2 | EmArCy | 013029-2
Pablo All Star Jam
Montreux '77 | Original Jazz Classics | OJC 385(2620105)
Philip Catherine/Niels-Henning Orsted-Pedersen With The Royal Copenhagen Chamber Orchestra
Spanish Nights | Enja | ENJ-7023 2
Roland Kirk Quartet With Sonny Boy Williamson
Talkin' Verve-Roots Of Acid Jazz:Roland Kirk | Verve | 533101-2
Roland Kirk Quintet
Rahsaan/The Complete Mercury Recordings Of Roland Kirk | Mercury | 846630-2
Roy Eldridge 4
Montreux '77 | Original Jazz Classics | OJCCD 373-2
Roy Eldridge Quintet
Decidedly | Pablo | PACD 5314-2
Roy Eldridge Sextet
Decidedly | Pablo | PACD 5314-2
Slide Hampton Quartet
Americans Swinging In Paris:Slide Hampton | EMI Records | 539648-2
Stan Getz Quartet
Live At Montmartre(CD=Stan's Party) | Steeplechase | SCCD 37021/22
Stan Getz With The Danish Radio Big Band
Stan Getz In Europe | Laserlight | 24657
Stan Kenton With The Danish Radio Big Band
Stan Kenton With The Danish Radio Big Band | Storyville | STCD 8340
Stephane Grappelli Quartet
Grapelli Story | Verve | 515807-2
Verve Jazz Masters 11:Stéphane Grappelli | Verve | 516758-2
Stephane Grappelli 1992 Live | Dreyfus Jazz Line | FDM 37006-2
Stephane Grappelli Trio
Verve Jazz Masters 11:Stéphane Grappelli | Verve | 516758-2
Tivoli Garders, Copenhagen, Denmark | Original Jazz Classics | OJCCD 441-2
Svend Asmussen Sextet
Svend Asmussen At Slukafter | Phontastic | NCD 8804
Tete Montoliu Trio
Tete! | Steeplechase | SCCD 31029
The Danish Radio Big Band
Aura | CBS | CK 63962
Toots Thielemans Quintet
Verve Jazz Masters Vol.59:Toots Thielemans | Verve | 535271-2
The Silver Collection: Toots Thielemans | Polydor | 825086-2 PMS
Toots Thielemans Trio
Live In The Netherlands | Original Jazz Classics | OJCCD 930-2(2308233)
Warne Marsh Trio
The Unissued Copenhagen Studio Recordings | Storyville | STCD 8278
Wayne Darling Group
The Art Of The Bass Vol.1 | Laika Records | 35101652

Ortega,Anthony | (as,ts,fl,piccolo,b-clcl)
Anthony Ortega With String Orchestra
Earth Dance | Fresh Sound Records | FSR-CD 325
Anthony Ortega With The Nat Pierce Orchestra
Earth Dance | Fresh Sound Records | FSR-CD 325
Anthony Ortega With The Robert Zieff Orchestra
Earth Dance | Fresh Sound Records | FSR-CD 325
Dinah Washington With The Quincy Jones Orchestra
Verve Jazz Masters 40:Dinah Washington | Verve | 522055-2
The Swingin' Miss 'D' | Verve | 558074-2
Ella Fitzgerald With Orchestra
Ella/Things Ain't What They Used To Be | Warner | 9362-47875-2
Gerald Wilson And His Orchestra
Deep Blue-The United States Of Mind | Blue Note | 521152-2
Maynard Ferguson And His Orchestra
Verve Jazz Masters 52:Maynard Ferguson | Verve | 529905-2

Orth,Clemens | (p)
Gunter Hampel Jazz Sextet
Gunter Hampel: The 8th Of Sept.1999 | Birth | CD 049
Gunter Hampel Next Generation
Köln Concert Part 1 | Birth | CD 047
Köln Concert Part 2 | Birth | CD 048

Orth,Uli | (ssas)
Ekkehard Jost Ensemble
Weimarer Balladen | Fish Music | FM 004 CD

Ortiz,Bill | (tp,fl-hvoice)
Don Cherry Group
Multi Kulti | A&M Records | 395323-2

Ortwein,Otto 'Fats' | (voc)
Inge Brandenburg & Otto 'Fats' Ortwein und die King Beats
Why Don't You Take All Of Me | Bear Family Records | BCD 15614 AH

Ory,Edward 'Kid' | (tbvoc)
Henry Red Allen Band
The Very Best Of Dixieland Jazz | Verve | 535529-2
Jelly Roll Morton's Red Hot Peppers
Planet Jazz:Jelly Roll Morton | Planet Jazz | 2152060-2
Planet Jazz Sampler | Planet Jazz | 2152326-2
Jazz:The Essential Collection Vol.1 | IN+OUT Records | 78011-2
Kid Ory And His Band
The Very Best Of Dixieland Jazz | Verve | 535529-2
Kid Ory's Creole Jazz Band
This Kid's The Greatest! | Good Time Jazz | GTCD 12045-2
King Oliver And His Dixie Syncopators
Jazz:The Essential Collection Vol.1 | IN+OUT Records | 78011-2
King Oliver's Jazz Band
Jazz:The Essential Collection Vol.1 | IN+OUT Records | 78011-2
Lil's Hot Shots
Jazz:The Essential Collection Vol.2 | IN+OUT Records | 78012-2
Louis Armstrong And His Dixieland Seven
Planet Jazz:Louis Armstrong | Planet Jazz | 2152052-2
Planet Jazz:Jazz Greatest Hits | Planet Jazz | 2169648-2
Planet Jazz:Jazz Trumpet | Planet Jazz | 2169654-2
Planet Jazz:Male Jazz Vocalists | Planet Jazz | 2169657-2
Best Of The Complete RCA Victor Recordings | RCA | 2663636-2
Louis Armstrong:A 100th Birthday Celebration | RCA | 2663694-2
Louis Armstrong:C'est Si Bon | Dreyfus Jazz Line | FDM 36730-2
Swing Legends:Louis Armstrong | Nimbus Records | NI 2012
Louis Armstrong And His Hot Five
Jazz:The Essential Collection Vol.2 | IN+OUT Records | 78012-2

Osada,Atushi[Az'shi] | (b)
Greg Osby Quartet
Banned In New York | Blue Note | 496860-2

Osborne,Mary | (gvoc)
52nd Street All Stars
Planet Jazz:Bebop | RCA | 2169650-2
Coleman Hawkins And His 52nd Street All Stars
Jazz:The Essential Collection Vol.3 | IN+OUT Records | 78013-2
Coleman Hawkins' Fifty-Second Street All-Stars
Planet Jazz:Coleman Hawkins | Planet Jazz | 2152055-2

Osborne,Mike | (ascl)
John Surman Orchestra
How Many Clouds Can You See? | Deram | 844882-2

Osborne,Ralph | (tp)
Harry James And His Orchestra
Trumpet Blues:The Best Of Harry James | Capitol | 521224-2

Osborne,Riley | (org)
Marc Ribot Y Los Cubanos Postizos
Nuy Divertido(Very Entertaining) | Atlantic | 7567-83293-2

Osborne,Tony | (arrcond)
Mel Tormé With The Tony Osborne Orchestra
My Kind Of Music | Verve | 543795-2

Osby,Greg | (as,synth,ss,perc,voicepitchrider)
Cornelius Claudio Kreusch Group
Scoop | ACT | 9255-2
Dianne Reeves With Band
Misty Blue:Sweet Sisters Swing Songs Of Sorrow And Sadness | Blue Note | 521151-2
I Remember | Blue Note | 790264-2
Ed Schuller & Band
The Eleventh Hour | Tutu Records | 888124-2*
Gary Thomas Quartet
Pariah's Pariah | Winter&Winter | 910033-2
Greg Osby Quartet
Banned In New York | Blue Note | 496860-2
Mindgames | JMT Edition | 919021-2
Greg Osby Quartet With String Quartet
Symbols Of Light(A Solution) | Blue Note | 531395-2
Greg Osby Quintet
Inner Circle | Blue Note | 499871-2
Mindgames | JMT Edition | 919021-2
Joe Lovano-Greg Osby Quintet
Friendly Fire | Blue Note | 499125-2
Marc Copland-Greg Osby
Round And Round | Nagel-Heyer | CD 2035
Stefon Harris Group
Black Action Figure | Blue Note | 499546-2
Steve Coleman And The Council Of Balance
Genesis & The Opening Of The Way | RCA | 2152934-2
Terri Lyne Carrington Quartet
Structure | ACT | 9427-2

Osgood,Kresten | (dr)
Kristian Jorgensen Quartet With Monty Alexander
Meeting Monty | Stunt Records | STUCD 01212

O'Shea-Ramdeholl,Jacinta | (voc)
Mike Westbrook Brass Band
Glad Day:Settings Of William Blake | Enja | ENJ-9376 2

Oshun,Baba Duru | (perctabla)
Alice Coltrane Quintet
Joe Henderson:The Milestone Years | Milestone | 8MCD 4413-2
Alice Coltrane Sextet
Joe Henderson:The Milestone Years | Milestone | 8MCD 4413-2

Oslawski,John | (alto-fl,b-cl,bs,fl,assax)
The Three Sopranos With The HR Big Band
The Three Sopranos | hr music.de | hrmj 001-01 CD
Woody Herman And His Orchestra
Jazzin' Vol.2: The Music Of Stevie Wonder | Fantasy | FANCD 6088-2
King Cobra | Original Jazz Classics | OJCCD 1068-2(F 9499)
Woody Herman's Thundering Herd
Planet Jazz:Jazz Saxophone | Planet Jazz | 2169653-2

Osman,Ahmad | (b)
Mahmoud Turkmani Group
Zakira | Enja | ENJ-9475 2

Osser,Glenn | (arr,ldstrings)
Coleman Hawkins With The Glenn Osser Orchestra
Midnight Blue(The [Be]witching Hour) | Blue Note | 854365-2

Oster,Ulla | (b,el-b,samplervoc)
Ulla Oster Group
Beyond Janis | Jazz Haus Musik | JHM 0052 CD
Ulla Oster-Wollie Kaiser
We Can Do It On Stage Any Time! | Jazz Haus Musik | JHM 0088 CD
United Women's Orchestra
Virgo Supercluster | Jazz Haus Musik | JHM 0123 CD
Wollie Kaiser Timeghost
Tust Du Fühlen Gut | Jazz Haus Musik | JHM 0060 CD
Post Art Core | Jazz Haus Musik | JHM 0077 CD
New Traces For Old Aces | Jazz Haus Musik | JHM 0102 CD

Ostergren,Thomas | (b)
Johnny Dyani Septet
Afrika | Steeplechase | SCS 1186(Audiophile Pressing)

Osterloh,Klaus | (fl-h,tpvoc)
Bob Brookmeyer Group With The WDR Big Band
Electricity | ACT | 9219-2
Eddie Harris Group With The WDR Big Band
Eddie Harris-The Last Concert | ACT | 9249-2
Gianlugi Trovesi Quartet With The WDR Big Band
Dedalo | Enja | ENJ-9419 2
Jens Winther And The WDR Big Band
The Escape | dacapo | DCCD 9437
Kevin Mahogany With The WDR Big Band And Guests
Pussy Cat Dues:The Music Of Charles Mingus | Enja | ENJ-9316 2
Los Jovenes Flamencos With The WDR Big Band And Guests
Jazzpana | ACT | 9212-2
Vince Mendoza With The WDR Big Band And Guests
Sketches | ACT | 9215-2

Ostermeier,Martin | (tb)
Clark Terry With The Summit Jazz Orchestra
Clark | Edition Collage | EC 530-2

Osterwald,Hazy | (tp,vibvoc)
Willy Bischof Jazztet
Swiss Air | Jazz Connaisseur | JCCD 9523-2

Östlund,Robert | (g,org,vibsynth)
Nils Landgren Funk Unit
Fonk Da World | ACT | 9299-2
Nils Landgren Funk Unit With Guests
5000 Miles | ACT | 9271-2
Nils Landgren Group
Sentimental Journey | ACT | 9409-2

Ostrawsky,Robert | (viola)
Herbie Mann With The Frank DeVol Orchestra
Verve Jazz Masters 56:Herbie Mann | Verve | 529901-2

Öström,Magnus | (dr,perc,mohammedtablas)
Esbjörn Svensson Trio(E.S.T) With Strings
EST Plays Monk | ACT | 9010-2
Esbjörn Svensson Trio(E.S.T.)
Est-From Gagarin's Point Of View | ACT | 9005-2
Winter In Venice | ACT | 9007-2
Good Morning Susie Soho | ACT | 9009-2
EST Plays Monk | ACT | 9010-2
Strange Place For Snow | ACT | 9011-2
Seven Days Of Falling | ACT | 9012-2
E.S.T. Live | ACT | 9295-2
Nils Landgren Funk Unit
Fonk Da World | ACT | 9299-2
Nils Landgren Funk Unit With Guests
5000 Miles | ACT | 9271-2
Nils Landgren With The Esbjörn Svensson Trio
Ballads | ACT | 9268-2
Viktoria Tolstoy Group & Strings
Shining On You | ACT | 9701-2
Viktoria Tolstoy With The Esbjörn Svensson Trio
Viktoria Tolstoy:White Russian | Blue Note | 821220-2

Ostrowsky,Bob | (viola)
Ella Fitzgerald With The Frank DeVol Orchestra
Get Happy! | Verve | 523321-2

Ostwald,David | (tuba)
Byron Stripling And Friends
If I Could Be With You | Nagel-Heyer | NH 1010
David Ostwald's Gully Low Jazz Band
Blues In Your Heart | Nagel-Heyer | CD 051
Randy Sandke And The New York Allstars
The Re-Discovered Louis And Bix | Nagel-Heyer | CD 058
The New York Allstars
We Love You,Louis! | Nagel-Heyer | CD 029
The Second Sampler | Nagel-Heyer | NHR SP 6

others unknown |
Willie Bobo Group
Bobo's Beat | Roulette | 590954-2

Othman,Ahmed Ben | (karkaba,dancervoc)
Randy Weston African Rhythm Quintet and The Gnawa Master Musicians of Marocco
Spirit! The Power Of Music | Verve | 543256-2

Othman,M'Barek Ben | (karkaba,tbilvoc)

Otis,Fred | (p)
Woody Herman And His Orchestra
The Legends Of Swing | Laserlight | 24659
Woody Herman:Four Brother | Dreyfus Jazz Line | FDM 36722-2

Otis,Johnny | (dr,voc,pvib)
Johnny Otis And His Orchestra
Verve Jazz Masters 43:Ben Webster | Verve | 525431-2
Lester Young And His Band
Jazz Gallery:Lester Young Vol.2(1946-59) | RCA | 2119541-2
Lester Young:The Complete Aladdin Sessions | Blue Note | 832787-2

Otis,Jon | (perc)
David Klein Quintet
My Marilyn | Enja | ENJ-9422 2

Otis,Shuggie | (g,b,porg)
Eddie Cleanhead Vinson With Band
The Late Show-Recorded Live At Marla's Memory Lane Supper Club Vol.2 | Fantasy | FCD 9655-2
Eddie Cleanhead Vinson With The Red Holloway Quartet
Blues In The Night-Volume One:The Early Show | Fantasy | FCD 9647-2
Etta James & Eddie Cleanhead Vinson With The Red Holloway Quartet
Blues In The Night-Volume One:The Early Show | Fantasy | FCD 9647-2
Etta James With Band
The Late Show-Recorded Live At Marla's Memory Lane Supper Club Vol.2 | Fantasy | FCD 9655-2
Etta James With The Red Holloway Quartet
Blues In The Night-Volume One:The Early Show | Fantasy | FCD 9647-2
Etta James With The Red Holloway Quintet
Blues In The Night-Volume One:The Early Show | Fantasy | FCD 9647-2
Etta James/Eddie 'Cleanhead' Vinson With Band
The Late Show-Recorded Live At Marla's Memory Lane Supper Club Vol.2 | Fantasy | FCD 9655-2

Ott,Horace | (arr,clavinet,cond,el-p,keyboards,ld)
George Benson Orchestra
Talkin' Verve:George Benson | Verve | 553780-2
George Benson With Orchestra
Verve Jazz Masters 21:George Benson | Verve | 521861-2
Nina Simone With Horace Ott's Orchestra
Verve Jazz Masters 17:Nina Simone | Verve | 518198-2
Nina Simone After Hours | Verve | 526702-2
In Concert/I Put A Spell On You | Mercury | 846543-2
Rusty Bryant Group
For The Good Times | Prestige | PRCD 24269-2

Ott,Horace or Ernie Hayes | (p)
King Curtis Band
King Curtis-Blow Man Blow | Bear Family Records | BCD 15670 Cl

Ott,Horace prob. | (p)

Ott,Tobias | (ghatam,tablastanpura)
Nomakozasana-Uli Lenz
Tenderness | Tutu Records | 888198-2*
Tabla & Strings
Islands Everywhere | Tutu Records | 888208-2*

Ottaviano,Roberto | (as,b-cl,ss,sopraninosax)
Pierre Favre Quintet
Window-Steps | ECM | 1584(529348-2)

Ottaviucci,Fabrizio | (pvoice)
Markus Stockhausen Quartet
Cosi Lontano...Quasi Dentro | ECM | 1371

Ottini,Roberto | (ssbs)
Carla Bley Band
Fleur Carnivore | Watt | 21

Otto,Bernd K. | (bj,g,drld)
Alfred 23 Harth Group
Sweet Paris | free flow music | ffm 0291

Otwell,Marshall | (el-p,keyboardsp)
Carmen McRae And Her Trio
The Collected Carmen McRae | RCA | 2668713-2
Carmen McRae And Her Trio With Zoot Sims
The Collected Carmen McRae | RCA | 2668713-2
Carmen McRae With The Dizzy Gillespie Quartet
Misty Blue:Sweet Sisters Swing Songs Of Sorrow And Sadness | Blue Note | 521151-2

Oubella,Abdemedi | (handclapping,karkaba,vocdancer)
Randy Weston African Rhythm Quintet and The Gnawa Master Musicians of Marocco
Spirit! The Power Of Music | Verve | 543256-2

Oubella,Mostafa | (karkaba,dancervoc)

Ounaskari,Markku | (dr)
Piirpauke
Zerenade | JA & RO | JARO 4142-2
Piirpauke-Global Servisi | JA & RO | JARO 4150-2

Ousley,Harold | (asts)
Dinah Washington With The Newport All Stars
Dinah Sings Bessie Smith | Verve | 538635-2
Jack McDuff Quartet
Silken Soul | Prestige | PCD 24242-2
Jack McDuff Quartet With Orchestra
Prelude:Jack McDuff Big Band | Prestige | PRCD 24283-2
Jack McDuff Quintet
Silken Soul | Prestige | PCD 24242-2
Jack McDuff Sextet
Silken Soul | Prestige | PCD 24242-2

Outcalt,Al 'Chippy' | (tb)
Lionel Hampton And His Orchestra
Lionel Hampton:Flying Home | Dreyfus Jazz Line | FDM 36735-2

Outlaws,The |
Etta James And The Outlaws
Monterey Jazz Festival 1975 | Storyville | 4960213

Ouwerckx,John | (p)
Django Reinhardt With Stan Brenders Et Son Grand Orchestre
Verve Jazz Masters 38:Django Reinhardt | Verve | 516931-2

Overbeck,Pia | (bs)
Helmut Zacharias & His Sax-Team
Ich Habe Rhythmus | Bear Family Records | BCD 15642 AH

Overgaauw,Wim | (g,el-gbj)
Toots Thielemans Quintet
Verve Jazz Masters Vol.59:Toots Thielemans | Verve | 535271-2
The Silver Collection: Toots Thielemans | Polydor | 825086-2 PMS

Overton,Hal | (arr,drp)
Jimmy Raney Quintet
Early Stan | Original Jazz Classics | OJCCD 654-2(P 7255)
Teddy Charles Quartet
Charles Mingus-Passion Of A Man:The Complete Atlantic Recordings 1956-1961 | Atlantic | 8122-72871-2
Thelonious Monk And His Orchestra
Thelonious Monk:85th Birthday Celebration | zyx records | FANCD 6076-2

Overwater,Tony | (b)
Sylvie Courvoisier Group
Ocre | Enja | ENJ-9323 2
Overweg,Evert | (dr)
Toots Thielemans Quintet
The Silver Collection: Toots Thielemans | Polydor | 825086-2 PMS
Ovesen,Thomas | (b)
Jim Hall Jazzpar Quartet
Jazzpar 98 | Storyville | STCD 4230
Jim Hall Jazzpar Quartet +4
Jazzpar 98 | Storyville | STCD 4230
Joaquin Chacón-Uffe Markussen European Quintet
Time | Fresh Sound Records | FSNT 051 CD
Mona Larsen And The Danish Radio Big Band Plus Soloists
Michael Mantler:Cerco Un Paese Innocente | ECM | 1556
The Danish Radio Jazz Orchestra
This Train:The Danish Radio Jazz Orchestra Plays The Music Of Ray Pitts | dacapo | DCCD 9428
Nice Work | dacapo | DCCD 9446
Ovio,Tony | (g)
Stephane Grappelli Quintet
Planet Jazz:Stephane Grappelli | RCA | 2165366-2
Owaida,Khaled | (v)
Mahmoud Turkmani Group
Zakira | Enja | ENJ-9475 2
Owens,Charles | (as,cl,b-cl,bs,ss,oboe,engl-h,fl)
Buddy Childers Big Band
It's What Happening Now! | Candid | CCD 79749
Buddy Rich Big Band
The New One! | Pacific Jazz | 494507-2
Charles Owens Quartet
Eternal Balance | Fresh Sound Records | FSNT 067 CD
Owens,Frank | (pld)
Louis Armstrong And His Friends
Planet Jazz:Louis Armstrong | Planet Jazz | 2152052-2
Planet Jazz Sampler | Planet Jazz | 2152326-2
Louis Armstrong And His Friends | Bluebird | 2663961-2
Ruth Brown With Orchestra
Fine And Mellow | Fantasy | FCD 9663-2
Owens,Henry | (pvoc)
Golden Gate Quartet
From Spiritual To Swing | Vanguard | VCD 169/71
Owens,Jimmy | (tpfl-h)
Archie Shepp Septet
The Way Ahead | Impulse(MCA) | 951272-2
Archie Shepp Sextet
The Way Ahead | Impulse(MCA) | 951272-2
Billy Cobham Group
Spectrum | Atlantic | 7567-81428-2
Bobby Timmons Orchestra
Quartet And Orchestra | Milestone | MCD 47091-2
Booker Ervin Sextet
Heavy!!! | Original Jazz Classics | OJCCD 981-2(P 7499)
Eddie Harris Group
The Best Of Eddie Harris | Atlantic | 7567-81370-2
Gary Bartz Quintet
Libra/Another Earth | Milestone | MCD 47077-2
George Benson And His Orchestra
Giblet Gravy | Verve | 543754-2
Talkin' Verve:George Benson | Verve | 553780-2
George Benson Orchestra
Verve Jazz Masters 21:George Benson | Verve | 521861-2
Talkin' Verve:George Benson | Verve | 553780-2
Joe Zawinul Group
Zawinul | Atlantic | 7567-81375-2
Kenny Burrell With The Don Sebesky Orchestra
Verve Jazz Masters 45:Kenny Burrell | Verve | 527652-2
Blues-The Common Ground | Verve | 589101-2
Louis Armstrong And His Friends
Louis Armstrong And His Friends | Bluebird | 2663961-2
Yusef Lateef Ensemble
Atlantic Saxophones | Rhino | 8122-71256-2
Owens,Johnny | (tp)
Charlie Barnet And His Orchestra
Planet Jazz:Big Bands | Planet Jazz | 2169649-2
Planet Jazz:Swing | Planet Jazz | 2169651-2
Owens,Jon | (tp)
Maynard Ferguson And His Big Bop Nouveau Band
Maynard Ferguson '93-Footpath Café | Hot Shot Records | HSR 8312-2
Oxer,P. | (v)
Dee Dee Bridgewater With Orchestra
Dear Ella | Verve | 539102-2
Oxley,Colin | (g)
Jim Tomlinson Quartet
Brazilian Sketches | Candid | CCD 79769
Jim Tomlinson Quintet
Only Trust Your Heart | Candid | CCD 79758
Brazilian Sketches | Candid | CCD 79769
Jim Tomlinson Sextet
Only Trust Your Heart | Candid | CCD 79758
Stacey Kent And Her Quintet
Close Your Eyes | Candid | CCD 79737
The Tender Trap | Candid | CCD 79751
Let Yourself Go-Celebrating Fred Astaire | Candid | CCD 79764
Stacey Kent With The Jim Tomlison Quintet
Dreamsville | Candid | CCD 79775
Stacy Kent With The Jim Tomlinson Quintet
In Love Again | Candid | CCD 79786
The Boy Next Door | Candid | CCD 79797
Oxley,Tony | (dr,gongs,perc,electronicsv)
Ekkehard Jost Quartet
Deep | Fish Music | FM 007 CD
Some Other Tapes | Fish Music | FM 009/10 CD
John McLaughlin Quartet
Extrapolation | Polydor | 841598-2
John Surman Orchestra
How Many Clouds Can You See? | Deram | 844882-2
John Surman Quartet
Adventure Playground | ECM | 1463(511981-2)
How Many Clouds Can You See? | Deram | 844882-2
Paul Bley Quartet
In The Evenings Out There | ECM | 1488
Ronnie Scott And The Band
Live At Ronnie Scott's | CBS | 494439-2
Thomasz Stanko Quartet
Matka Joanna | ECM | 1544(523986-2)
Tomasz Stanko Quartet
Leosia | ECM | 1603(531693-2)
Tony Oxley Quintet
The Baptist Traveller | CBS | 494438-2
Tony Oxley Sextet
4 Compositions For Sextet | CBS | 494437-2
Oyeesen,Thomas | (bel-b)
Jens Winther And The Danish Radio Jazz Orchestra
Angels | dacapo | DCCD 9442
Oyewole,Abiodun | (voice)
Pharoah Sanders Group
Save Our Children | Verve | 557297-2
Ozone,Makoto | (psynth)
Gary Burton Quartet
Real Life Hits | ECM | 1293
Gary Burton Quintet
Whiz Kids | ECM | 1329
Makoto Ozone Group
Treasure | Verve | 021906-2
Makoto Ozone Trio
Pandora | Verve | 549629-2
Melissa Walker And Her Band
I Saw The Sky | Enja | ENJ-9409 2

Paak,Andy | (b-g)
Barbara Thompson Group
Heavenly Bodies | VeraBra Records | CDVBR 2015-2
Paakkunainen,Seppo 'Paroni' | (bs,fl,as,v,perc,ssts)
Edward Vesala Group
Nan Madol | ECM | 1077
George Gruntz Concert Jazz Band '83
Theatre | ECM | 1265
Pablo All Stars |
Pablo All Star Jam
Montreux '77 | Original Jazz Classics | OJC 385(2620105)
Pace,Jean | (voc)
Oscar Brown Jr. And His Group
Movin' On | Rhino | 8122-73678-2
Pace,Johnny | (voc)
Johnny Pace With The Chet Baker Quintet
Chet Baker Introduces Johnny Pace | Original Jazz Classics | OJCCD 433-2(RLP 12-292)
Pacheco,Johnny | (bongos,congas,perctambourine)
George Benson And His Orchestra
Giblet Gravy | Verve | 543754-2
George Benson Quintet
Verve Jazz Masters 21:George Benson | Verve | 521861-2
Giblet Gravy | Verve | 543754-2
George Benson Sextet
Talkin' Verve:George Benson | Verve | 553780-2
George Benson With The Don Sebesky Orchestra
Verve Jazz Masters 21:George Benson | Verve | 521861-2
Kenny Burrell With The Don Sebesky Orchestra
Verve Jazz Masters 45:Kenny Burrell | Verve | 527652-2
Blues-The Common Ground | Verve | 589101-2
McCoy Tyner Trio + Latin Percussion
McCoy Tyner Plays Ellington | Impulse(MCA) | 951216-2
Woody Herman And His Orchestra
The Raven Speaks | Original Jazz Classics | OJCCD 663-2(F 9416)
Pack,Gary | (tpfl-h)
Woody Herman Herd At Montreux | Original Jazz Classics | OJCCD 991-2(F 9470)
Packe,Rodericke | (sounds)
Dhafer Youssef Group
Electric Sufi | Enja | ENJ-9412 2
Packer,Lewis | (b)
Stuff Smith Quartet
Cat On A Hot Fiddle | Verve | 9861487
Paco[El Americano] | (handclapping)
Los Jovenes Flamencos
Jazzpana | ACT | 9212-2
Los Jovenes Flamencos With The WDR Big Band And Guests
Jazzpana | ACT | 9212-2
Pacout,Michel | (dr)
Claude Luter Et Ses L'Orientais
Jazz In Paris:Sidney Bechet Et Claude Luther | EmArCy | 159821-2 PMS
Padget,Jimmy | (tp)
Elliot Lawrence And His Orchestra
Mullenium | CBS | CK 65678
Padin,Jorge | (perc)
Gato Barbieri Orchestra
Latino America | Impulse(MCA) | 952236-2
Padovani,Jean-Marc | (ssts)
Claude Barthelmy Group
Moderne | Owl Records | 014739-2
Paeffgen,Gilbert | (drdulcimer)
Gilbert Paeffgen Trio
Pedestrian Tales | Edition Musikat | EDM 061
Paer,Lewis | (b)
Earl Klugh Group With Strings
Late Night Guitar | Blue Note | 498573-2
Page,Dave | (tp)
Lionel Hampton And His Orchestra
Lionel Hampton:Flying Home | Dreyfus Jazz Line | FDM 36735-2
Page,Drew | (tsbs)
Harry James And His Orchestra
The Legends Of Swing | Laserlight | 24659
Page,Gene | (condkeyboards)
Big Joe Turner And His Orchestra
Planet Jazz:Male Jazz Vocalists | Planet Jazz | 2169657-2
Stanley Turrentine And His Orchestra
Pieces Of Dream | Original Jazz Classics | OJCCD 831-2(F 9465)
Page,Nathan | (g)
Jimmy Smith Trio
Paris Jazz Concert:Jimmy Smith And The Trio | Laserlight | 36159
Page,Oran 'Hot Lips' | (mellophone,voctp)
Artie Shaw And His Orchestra
Planet JazzArtie Shaw | Planet Jazz | 2152057-2
Planet Jazz:Male Jazz Vocalists | Planet Jazz | 2169657-2
Ben Webster Quintet
Jazz:The Essential Collection Vol.3 | IN+OUT Records | 78013-2
Benny Moten's Kansas City Orchestra
Planet Jazz:Ben Webster | RCA | 2165368-2
Planet Jazz:Jimmy Rushing | RCA | 2165371-2
Planet Jazz:Swing | Planet Jazz | 2169651-2
Jazz:The Essential Collection Vol.3 | IN+OUT Records | 78013-2
Charlie Christian All Stars
Charlie Christian-Jazz Immortal/Dizzy Gillespie 1944 | Original Jazz Classics | OJCCD 1932-2(ES 548)
Hot Lips Page And His Orchestra
Don Byas:Laura | Dreyfus Jazz Line | FDM 36714-2
Hot Lips Page Band
Planet Jazz:Jazz Trumpet | Planet Jazz | 2169654-2
Jimmy Rushing With Count Basie And His Orchestra
From Spiritual To Swing | Vanguard | VCD 169/71
Minton's Playhouse All Stars
Charlie Christian:Swing To Bop | Dreyfus Jazz Line | FDM 36715-2
V-Disc All Star Jam Session
Louis Armstrong-Jack Teagarden-Woody Herman:Midnights At V-Disc | Jazz Unlimited | JUCD 2048
Page,Richard | (voc)
Al Jarreau With Band
Al Jarreau In London | i.e. Music | 557849-2
Horace Silver Quintet With Vocals
Horace Silver Retrospective | Blue Note | 495576-2
Page,Vernon | (tuba)
Benny Moten's Kansas City Orchestra
Planet Jazz:Jimmy Rushing | RCA | 2165371-2
Page,Walter | (b)
Albert Ammons-Pete Johnson-Meade Lux Lewis
From Spiritual To Swing | Vanguard | VCD 169/71
Benny Goodman Septet
Jazz:The Essential Collection Vol.3 | IN+OUT Records | 78013-2
Charlie Christian:Swing To Bop | Dreyfus Jazz Line | FDM 36715-2
Benny Moten's Kansas City Orchestra
Planet Jazz:Ben Webster | RCA | 2165368-2
Planet Jazz:Jimmy Rushing | RCA | 2165371-2
Planet Jazz:Swing | Planet Jazz | 2169651-2
Jazz:The Essential Collection Vol.3 | IN+OUT Records | 78013-2
Billie Holiday And Her Band
Billie's Love Songs | Nimbus Records | NI 2000
Billie Holiday And Her Orchestra
Jazz:The Essential Collection Vol.3 | IN+OUT Records | 78013-2
Billie's Love Songs | Nimbus Records | NI 2000
Boogie Woogie Trio
Boogie Woogie | Laserlight | 24321
Count Basie And His Orchestra
Planet Jazz:Count Basie | Planet Jazz | 2152068-2
Planet Jazz Sampler | Planet Jazz | 2152326-2
Planet Jazz:Jimmy Rushing | RCA | 2165371-2
Planet Jazz:Jazz Greatest Hits | Planet Jazz | 2169648-2

Planet Jazz:Big Bands | Planet Jazz | 2169649-2
Jazz:The Essential Collection Vol.3 | IN+OUT Records | 78013-2
From Spiritual To Swing | Vanguard | VCD 169/71
Count Basie Quartet
Planet Jazz:Jazz Piano | RCA | 2169655-2
Jazz:The Essential Collection Vol.3 | IN+OUT Records | 78013-2
Count Basie Sextet
Jazz:The Essential Collection Vol.3 | IN+OUT Records | 78013-2
Count Basie Trio
From Spiritual To Swing | Vanguard | VCD 169/71
Count Basie,His Instrumentals & Rhyhtm
Planet Jazz:Count Basie | Planet Jazz | 2152068-2
Jazz:The Essential Collection Vol.3 | IN+OUT Records | 78013-2
Count Basie's Kansas City Seven
Jazz:The Essential Collection Vol.3 | IN+OUT Records | 78013-2
Edmond Hall With The Ralph Sutton Group
Edmond Hall With The Ralph Sutton Group | Storyville | STCD 6052
Harry James And His Orchestra
The Legends Of Swing | Laserlight | 24659
Helen Humes With James P. Johnson And The Count Basie Orchestra
From Spiritual To Swing | Vanguard | VCD 169/71
Helen Humes With The Kansas City Five
From Spiritual To Swing | Vanguard | VCD 169/71
Ida Cox With The James P. Johnson Septet
From Spiritual To Swing | Vanguard | VCD 169/71
Jack Teagarden And His Band
Meet Me Where They Play The Blues | Good Time Jazz | GTCD 12063-2
Jimmy Rushing With Count Basie And His Orchestra
From Spiritual To Swing | Vanguard | VCD 169/71
Joe Turner With Orchestra
Atlantic Jazz: Kansas City | Atlantic | 7567-81701-2
Jones-Smith Incorporated
Jazz:The Essential Collection Vol.3 | IN+OUT Records | 78013-2
Kansas City Five
From Spiritual To Swing | Vanguard | VCD 169/71
Kansas City Six
Jazz:The Essential Collection Vol.3 | IN+OUT Records | 78013-2
Charlie Christian:Swing To Bop | Dreyfus Jazz Line | FDM 36715-2
From Spiritual To Swing | Vanguard | VCD 169/71
New Orleans Feetwarmers
From Spiritual To Swing | Vanguard | VCD 169/71
Roy Eldridge And His Central Plaza Dixielanders
The Very Best Of Dixieland Jazz | Verve | 535529-2
The Complete Verve Roy Eldridge Studio Sessions | Verve | 9861278
Sidney Bechet's Blue Note Jazzmen
Runnin' Wild | Blue Note | 821259-2
Sir Charles Thompson Quartet
Key One Up | Vanguard | VCD 79612-2
Teddy Wilson And His Orchestra
Jazz:The Essential Collection Vol.3 | IN+OUT Records | 78013-2
Vic Dickenson Septet
Nice Work | Vanguard | VCD 79610-2
Vic Dickenson Septet With Ruby Braff
Nice Work | Vanguard | VCD 79610-2
Paglia,Gustavo | (bandoneon)
Gustavo Bergalli Group
Tango In Jazz | Touché Music | TMcCD 007
Pagliarin,Vincent | (v)
Abbey Lincoln With The Rodney Kendrick Trio And Guests
A Turtle's Dream | Verve | 527382-2
Michel Petrucciani With The Graffiti String Quartet
Marvellous | Dreyfus Jazz Line | FDM 36564-2
Pahud,Emmanuel | (fl)
Jacky Terrasson-Emmanuel Pahud Quartet
Into The Blue | Blue Note | 557257-2
Paich,David | (keyboardsarr)
Sarah Vaughan And Her Band
Songs Of The Beatles | Atlantic | 16037-2
Paich,Marty | (arr,celeste,ld,comp.arr,cond,DX-7)
Art Pepper Plus Eleven
Art Pepper + Eleven | Contemporary | CSA 7568-6
Modern Jazz Classics | Original Jazz Classics | OJC20 341-2
Astrud Gilberto With Antonio Carlos Jobim And The Marty Paich Orchestra
The Antonio Carlos Jobim Songbook | Verve | 525472-2
Astrud Gilberto With The Marty Paich Orchestra
Verve Jazz Masters 9:Astrud Gilberto | Verve | 519824-2
Bob Enevoldsen Quintet
The Complete Nocturne Recordings:Jazz In Hollywood Series Vol.1 | Fresh Sound Records | NR 3CD-101
Bob Enevoldsen Sextet
The Complete Nocturne Recordings:Jazz In Hollywood Series Vol.1 | Fresh Sound Records | NR 3CD-101
Ella Fitzgerald With Marty Paich's Dektette
Ella Swings Lightly | Verve | 517535-2
Ella Fitzgerald With The Marty Paich Dek-tette
Ella Fitzgerald-First Lady Of Song | Verve | 517898-2
Verve Jazz Masters 6:Ella Fitzgerald | Verve | 519822-2
Verve Jazz Masters 46:Ella Fitzgerald-The Jazz Sides | Verve | 527655-2
Ella Fitzgerald With The Marty Paich Orchestra
Ella Fitzgerald-First Lady Of Song | Verve | 517898-2
Get Happy! | Verve | 523321-2
The Antonio Carlos Jobim Songbook | Verve | 525472-2
Ella Sings Broadway | Verve | 549373-2
Whisper Not | Verve | 589947-2
For The Love Of Ella Fitzgerald | Verve | 841765-2
Hank Crawford Orchestra
Rhino Presents The Atlantic Jazz Gallery | Atlantic | 8122-71257-2
Herbie Harper Quintet
The Complete Nocturne Recordings:Jazz In Hollywood Series Vol.1 | Fresh Sound Records | NR 3CD-101
NDR Big Band With Guests
50 Years Of NDR Big Band:Bravissimo II | ACT | 9259-2
Sarah Vaughan And Her Band
Songs Of The Beatles | Atlantic | 16037-2
Shorty Rogers And His Orchestra Feat. The Giants
PLanet Jazz:Shorty Rogers | Planet Jazz | 2159976-2
Terry Gibbs Dream Band
Terry Gibbs Dream Band Vol.2:The Sundown Sessions | Contemporary | CCD 7652-2
Woody Herman And His Orchestra
Songs For Hip Lovers | Verve | 559872-2
Paige,Billy | (as,clss)
King Oliver And His Dixie Syncopators
Jazz:The Essential Collection Vol.1 | IN+OUT Records | 78011-2
King Oliver's Jazz Band
Jazz:The Essential Collection Vol.1 | IN+OUT Records | 78011-2
Paige,Bob | (b)
Thelonious Monk Quintet
Genius Of Modern Music,Vol.1 | Blue Note | 532138-2
The Best Of Thelonious Monk:The Blue Note Years | Blue Note | 795636-2
Jazz Profile:Thelonious Monk | Blue Note | 823518-2
Thelonious Monk:Misterioso | Dreyfus Jazz Line | FDM 36743-2
Pais,Afonso | (g)
European Jazz Youth Orchestra
Swinging Europe 1 | dacapo | DCCD 9449
Swinging Europe 2 | dacapo | DCCD 9450
Päivinen,Pepa | (fl,b-cl,bs,cl,ss,tsas)
Edward Vesala Ensemble
Ode Of The Death Of Jazz | ECM | 1413(843196-2)
Päivinnen,Pepa | (fl,alto-fl,ss,ts,bs,bass-sax)
Edward Vesala Nordic Gallery
Sound & Fury | ECM | 1541
Edward Vesala Sound And Fury
Invisible Strom | ECM | 1461

Pala,Piero | (jews-harpvoc)
Ernst Reijseger & Tenore E Cuncordu De Orosei
Colla Voche | Winter&Winter | 910037-2

Palacino,Alessandro | (ssts)
Orchestra Jazz Siciliana
Orchestra Jazz Siciliana Plays The Music Of Carla Bley | Watt | XtraWatt/4

Palacios,Quelo | (g)
Gato Barbieri Orchestra
Latino America | Impulse(MCA) | 952236-2

Paladino,Don | (tp)
Harry James And His Orchestra
Trumpet Blues:The Best Of Harry James | Capitol | 521224-2
Red Norvo And His Orchestra
Planet Jazz:Female Jazz Vocalists | Planet Jazz | 2169656-2
Stan Kenton And His Orchestra
Great Swing Classics In Hi-Fi | Capitol | 521223-2
Stan Kenton Portraits On Standards | Capitol | 531571-2

Palatino |
Palatino
Palationo Chap.3 | EmArCy | 013610-2

Palet,Benet | (tp)
Big Band Bellaterra
Don't Git Sassy | Fresh Sound Records | FSNT 048 CD
Elisabet Raspall Grup
Lila | Fresh Sound Records | FSNT 058 CD
Elisabet Raspall Quintet
Triangles | Fresh Sound Records | FSNT 018 CD
Mikel Andueza Quintet
BCN | Fresh Sound Records | FSNT 036 CD
Victor De Diego Group
Amaia | Fresh Sound Records | FSNT 012 CD

Paley,Ron | (b,el-b,psynth)
Woody Herman And His Orchestra
Jazzin' Vol.2: The Music Of Stevie Wonder | Fantasy | FANCD 6088-2
King Cobra | Original Jazz Classics | OJCCD 1068-2(F 9499)

Palladino,Don | (tp)
Pete Rugolo And His Orchestra
Verve Jazz Masters 52:Maynard Ferguson | Verve | 529905-2

Palladino,Pino | (bel-b)
Jimmy Smith All Stars
Jimmy Smith:Dot Com Blues | Blue Thumb | 543978-2
John McLaughlin Group
The Promise | Verve | 529828-2

Pallanivel,A.K. | (tavil)
Remember Shakti
Saturday Night In Bombay | Verve | 014184-2

Pallemaerts,Dré | (dr,percudu)
Hans Lüdemann Rism 7
FutuRISM | Jazz Haus Musik | JHM 0092/93 CD

Pallier,Claude | (bs)
James Moody Boptet
Americans Swinging In Paris:James Moody | EMI Records | 539653-2

Palm,Beh | (bara)
Jon Hassell & Farafina
Flash Of The Spirit | Intuition Records | INT 3009-2

Palma,Joao | (drperc)
Ithamara Koorax With Band
Love Dance:The Ballad Album | Milestone | MCD 9327-2

Palmer,Chloe | (voc)
Mike Westbrook Brass Band
Glad Day:Settings Of William Blake | Enja | ENJ-9376 2

Palmer,Clarence | (b,el-p,orgvoc)
Big Al Sears And The Sparrows
Sear-iously | Bear Family Records | BCD 15668 AH
Grant Green Sextet
Grant Green:Blue Breakbeat | Blue Note | 494705-2

Palmer,Dave | (tb)
Nicki Leighton-Thomas Group
Forbidden Games | Candid | CCD 79778

Palmer,Don | (tsv)
Charlie Haden Quartet West With Strings
The Art Of The Song | Verve | 547403-2
Charlie Haden With String Quartet
The Art Of The Song | Verve | 547403-2
Lee Konitz Orchestra
The Art Of Saxophone | Laserlight | 24652
Milt Jackson And His Orchestra
Reverence And Compassion | Reprise | 9362-45204-2

Palmer,Earl | (dr)
Peggy Lee With The Quincy Jones Orchestra
Blues Cross Country | Capitol | 520088-2
T-Bone Walker And His Band
Atlantic Jazz: Kansas City | Atlantic | 7567-81701-2

Palmer,Jack | (tpvoc)
Harry James And His Orchestra
The Legends Of Swing | Laserlight | 24659

Palmer,Singleton | (btuba)
Count Basie And His Orchestra
Planet Jazz:Count Basie | Planet Jazz | 2152068-2

Palmieri,Charlie | (p)
Herbie Mann And His Orchestra
The Best Of Herbie Mann | Atlantic | 7567-81369-2

Palmieri,Eddie | (p)
Cal Tjader's Orchestra
Talkin Verve/Roots Of Acid Jazz:Cal Tjader | Verve | 531562-2
Donald Harrison Sextet
Free To Be | Impulse(MCA) | 951283-2

Palmieri,Paul | (g)
Gerry Mulligan Sextet
The Gerry Mulligan Songbook | Pacific Jazz | 833575-2

Palmieri,Remo | (g)
Dizzy Gillespie Sextet
Dizzy Gillespie:Night In Tunisia | Dreyfus Jazz Line | FDM 36734-2
Esquire All-American Award Winners
Best Of The Complete RCA Victor Recordings | RCA | 2663636-2
Highlights From The Duke Ellington Centennial Edition | RCA | 2663672-2
Lena Horne With The Phil Moore Four
Planet Jazz:Lena Horne | Planet Jazz | 2165373-2
Leonard Feather's Esquire All-Americans
Louis Armstrong:C'est Si Bon | Dreyfus Jazz Line | FDM 36730-2
Sarah Vaughan With The Teddy Wilson Quartet
Sarah Vaughan:Lover Man | Dreyfus Jazz Line | FDM 36739-2

Palmitessa,Luciano | (tp)
Banda Cittá Ruvo Di Puglia
La Banda/Banda And Jazz | Enja | ENJ-9326 2

Palmore,Eugene | (voc)
Steve Coleman And Five Elements
The Sonic Language Of Myth | RCA | 2164123-2

Palmore,Gale | (p,percvoice)
Marion Brown Orchestra
Afternoon Of A Georgia Faun | ECM | 1004

Palo Alto |
Palo Alto
Crash Test | Jazz 'n' Arts Records | JNA 1803

Palomo,Johnny | (perc)
Bobby Hutcherson Orchestra
Montara | Blue Note | 590956-2

Panayi,Andy | (fl,alto-fl,as,ssts)
Itchy Fingers
Full English Breakfast | Enja | ENJ-7085 2

Pancoast,Bob | (pkeyboards)
Johnny Smith Quartet
The Sound Of The Johnny Smith Guitar | Roulette | 531792-2

Panichi,Paul | (tp)
Grace Knight With Orchestra
Come In Spinner | Intuition Records | INT 3052-2
Vince Jones With Orchestra
Come In Spinner | Intuition Records | INT 3052-2

Pannier,Tanja | (voc)
Jazz Fresh
Jazz Fresh | GGG-Verlag:GGG Verlag und Mailorder | CD 01.03

Pantoja,Antonio | (percanapa)
Cal Tjader's Orchestra
Talkin Verve/Roots Of Acid Jazz:Cal Tjader | Verve | 531562-2
Soul Burst | Verve | 557446-2
Gato Barbieri Orchestra
Latino America | Impulse(MCA) | 952236-2
Willie Bobo Group
Jazzrock-Anthology Vol.3:Fusion | Zounds | CD 27100555

Pantoja,Rique | (keyboards,vocp)
Steps Ahead
N.Y.C. | Intuition Records | INT 3007-2

Pantoja,Victor | (bongos,voc,congas,perctimbales)
Bobby Hutcherson Orchestra
Montara | Blue Note | 590956-2
Cal Tjader's Orchestra
Verve Jazz Masters 39:Cal Tjader | Verve | 521858-2
Soul Burst | Verve | 557446-2
Jimmy Smith Quartet
Jimmy Smith-Talkin' Verve | Verve | 531563-2
Joe Henderson And His Orchestra
Joe Henderson:The Milestone Years | Milestone | 8MCD 4413-2

Paolo,Jose | (perc)
Stan Getz-Laurindo Almeida Orchestra
Stan Getz Highlights:The Best Of The Verve Years Vol.2 | Verve | 517330-2

Pap,Wolfgang | (dr)
Klaus Doldinger Jubilee
Doldinger's Best | ACT | 9224-2

Papa Bue's Viking Jazzband |
Papa Bue's Viking Jazzband
The Golden Years Of Revival Jazz,Sampler | Storyville | 109 1001
The Golden Years Of Revival Jazz,Vol 1 | Storyville | STCD 5506
The Golden Years Of Revival Jazz,Vol.5 | Storyville | STCD 5510
The Golden Years Of Revival Jazz,Vol.6 | Storyville | STCD 5511
The Golden Years Of Revival Jazz,Vol.7 | Storyville | STCD 5512
The Golden Years Of Revival Jazz,Vol.8 | Storyville | STCD 5513
The Golden Years Of Revival Jazz,Vol.9 | Storyville | STCD 5514
The Golden Years Of Revival Jazz,Vol.10 | Storyville | STCD 5515
The Golden Years Of Revival Jazz,Vol.11 | Storyville | STCD 5516
The Golden Years Of Revival Jazz,Vol.12 | Storyville | STCD 5517
The Golden Years Of Revival Jazz,Vol.13 | Storyville | STCD 5518
The Golden Years Of Revival Jazz,Vol.14 | Storyville | STCD 5519
The Golden Years Of Revibal Jazz,Vol.15 | Storyville | STCD 5520

Papa Joe Jones Speaking To Terri Lyne in 1984 |
Terri Lyne Carrington Group
Jazz Is A Spirit | ACT | 9408-2

Papademetriou,Alice | (voc)
Vince Jones Group
Here's To The Miracles | Intuition Records | INT 3198-2

Papareli,Frank | (p)
Dizzy Gillespie Sextet
Dizzy Gillespie:Night In Tunisia | Dreyfus Jazz Line | FDM 36734-2

Pape,Willi | (flsax)
Bitkicks
Kickbit Information | ATM Records | ATM 3823-AH
Uli Trepte Group
Guru Guru/Uli Trepte | ATM Records | ATM 3815-AH

Pape,Winfried | (cello)
Balance
Some Other Tapes | Fish Music | FM 009/10 CD
Ekkehard Jost Quintet
Some Other Tapes | Fish Music | FM 009/10 CD

Papetti,Fausto | (bs)
Chet Baker With String-Orchestra And Voices
Chet Baker With Fifty Italian Strings | Original Jazz Classics | OJC20 492-2(JLP 921)

Paque,Glyn | (ascl)
Willie Bryant And His Orchestra
Planet Jazz:Ben Webster | RCA | 2165368-2

Paquette,David | (pvoc)
David Paquette Trio
Mood Swings | ART BY HEART | ABH 2004 2

Paquette,Pierre | (cl,as,tsvoc)
Heiner Franz & Friends
Let's Have A Ball | Jardis Records | JRCD 20030
Jazz Guitar Highlights 1 | Jardis Records | JRCD 20141
Werner Lener Quartet
Personal Moments | Satin Doll Productions | SDP 1026-1 CD
Colours | Satin Doll Productions | SDP 1033-1 CD

Paquinet,Guy | (tbarr)
Coleman Hawkins With Michel Warlop And His Orchestra
Django Reinhardt All Star Sessions | Capitol | 531577-2
Django's Music
Peche Á La Mode-The Great Blue Star Sessions 1947/1953 | Verve | 835418-2

Paraboschi,Roger | (dr)
Bernard Peiffer Trio
Jazz In Paris:The Bernard Peiffer Trio Plays Standards | EmArCy | 018425-2
Bill Coleman And His Orchestra
Don Byas:Laura | Dreyfus Jazz Line | FDM 36714-2
Bill Coleman Quintet
Americans Swinging In Paris:Don Byas | EMI Records | 539655-2
Django Reinhardt Quintet
Django/Django In Rome 1949-1050 | BGO Records | BGOCD 366
Don Byas Quartet
Americans Swinging In Paris:Don Byas | EMI Records | 539655-2
Don Byas:Laura | Dreyfus Jazz Line | FDM 36714-2
Lucky Thompson Quartet
Americans Swinging In Paris:Lucky Thompson | EMI Records | 539651-2
Lucky Thompson Quintet
Americans Swinging In Paris:Lucky Thompson | EMI Records | 539651-2
Lucky Thompson With The Gerard Pochonet All-Stars
Planet Jazz:Jazz Saxophone | Planet Jazz | 2169653-2
Lucky Thompson's Modern Jazz Group Tentet
Jazz In Paris:Lucky Thompson-Modern Jazz Group | EmArCy | 159823-2 PMS
Sarah Vaughan With The Quincy Jones Orchestra
Jazz In Paris:Sarah Vaughan-Vaughan And Violins | EmArCy | 065004-2

Paradox |
Paradox
The First Second | TipToe | TIP-888833 2

Pardiman,Fredy | (saron,klunthung,rebana,rebabvoc)
Norbert Stein Pata Masters meets Djaduk Ferianto Kua Etnika
Pata Java | Pata Musik | PATA 16 CD

Pardini,Lou | (keyboardsvoc)
John Patitucci Group
Mistura Fina | GRP | GRP 98022

Pardo,Jorge | (fl,ssts)
Joaquin Chacón Group
San | Fresh Sound Records | FSNT 015 CD
Los Jovenes Flamencos
Jazzpana | ACT | 9212-2
Los Jovenes Flamencos With The WDR Big Band And Guests
Jazzpana | ACT | 9212-2

Pardon,Joe | (perc)
Jens Bunge Group
Meet You In Chicago | Jazz 4 Ever Records:Jazz Network | J4E 4749

Parente,Giuseppe | (tuba)
Banda Cittá Ruvo Di Puglia
La Banda/Banda And Jazz | Enja | ENJ-9326 2

Parga,Luiz | (pperc)
Stan Getz Group Feat.Laurindo Almeida
Stan Getz With Guest Artist Laurindo Almeida | Verve | 823149-2
Stan Getz-Laurindo Almeida Orchestra
Stan Getz Highlights:The Best Of The Verve Years Vol.2 | Verve | 517330-2
Verve Jazz Masters 53:Stan Getz-Bossa Nova | Verve | 529904-2
Stan Getz Highlights | Verve | 847430-2

Parghel,Anca | (pvoc)
Anca Parghel
Carpathian Colors | Nabel Records:Jazz Network | CD 4656
Klaus Ignatzek Trio
Airballoon | Nabel Records:Jazz Network | CD 4651

Parham,Charles 'Truck' | (b)
Earl Hines And His Orchestra
Planet Jazz:Earl Hines | Planet Jazz | 2159973-2
Jimmy Lunceford And His Orchestra
The Legends Of Swing | Laserlight | 24659
Muggsy Spanier And His Dixieland All Stars
Muggsy Spanier At Club Hangover 1953/54 | Storyville | STCD 6033

Paris Jazz All Stars,The |
Lou Bennett Trio With The Paris Jazz All Stars
Jazz In Paris | EmArCy | 548790-2

Paris,Jackie | (voc)
Charles Mingus Sextet
Changes Two | Rhino | 8122-71404-2
Jackie Paris With The Charles Mingus Quintet
Charles Mingus-The Complete Debut Recordings | Debut | 12 DCD 4402-2

Paris,Teddy | (dr)
Die Deutsche All Star Band 1953
1.Deutsches Jazz Festival 1953 Frankfurt/Main | Bear Family Records | BCD 15611 AH
Fred Bunge Star Band
Deutsches Jazz Fesival 1954/1955 | Bear Family Records | BCD 15430
Rolf Kühn All Stars
Deutsches Jazz Fesival 1954/1955 | Bear Family Records | BCD 15430

Paris-Barcelona Swing Connection |
Frank Wess Meets The Paris-Barcelona Swing Connection
Paris-Barcelona Connection | Fresh Sound Records | FSNT 002 CD

Park,Joe | (tuba)
Tommy Dorsey And His Orchestra
Planet Jazz:Tommy Dorsey | Planet Jazz | 2159972-2
Planet Jazz:Jazz Greatest Hits | Planet Jazz | 2169648-2

Park,Sandra | (v)
A Band Of Friends
Wynton Marsalis Quartet With Strings | CBS | CK 68921

Parke,Bernie | (voc)
Paul Desmond Quartet With The Bill Bates Singers
Desmond | Original Jazz Classics | OJCCD 712-2(F 3235/8082)

Parker Jr.,Ray | (g)
Dee Dee Bridgewater With Band
Dee Dee Bridgewater | Atlantic | 7567-80760-2
Stanley Turrentine And His Orchestra
Pieces Of Dream | Original Jazz Classics | OJCCD 831-2(F 9465)

Parker,Bill | (ts)
Count Basie And His Orchestra
Planet Jazz:Count Basie | Planet Jazz | 2152068-2

Parker,Brian | (b)
Sandy Brown's Jazz Band
The Golden Years Of Revival Jazz,Sampler | Storyville | 109 1001
The Golden Years Of Revival Jazz,Vol.6 | Storyville | STCD 5511
The Golden Years Of Revival Jazz,Vol.8 | Storyville | STCD 5513
The Golden Years Of Revival Jazz,Vol.10 | Storyville | STCD 5515

Parker,Bud | (tb)
Stan Kenton And His Orchestra
Adventures In Blues | Capitol | 520089-2
Adventures In Jazz | Capitol | 521222-2

Parker,Charlie | (as,talking,ts,vocas-solo)
Charlie Parker All Stars
Charlie Parker:The Best Of The Verve Years | Verve | 527815-2
Charlie Parker:Now's The Time | Dreyfus Jazz Line | FDM 36724-2
Charlie Parker And His Orchestra
Charlie Parker:The Best Of The Verve Years | Verve | 527815-2
The Cole Porter Songbook | Verve | 823250-2
Bird: The Complete Charlie Parker On Verve | Verve | 837141-2
Charlie Parker:April In Paris | Dreyfus Jazz Line | FDM 36737-2
Charlie Parker Quartet
Verve Jazz Masters 20:Introducing | Verve | 519853-2
Verve Jazz Masters 28:Charlie Parker Plays Standards | Verve | 521854-2
Charlie Parker:Bird's Best Bop On Verve | Verve | 527452-2
Charlie Parker:The Best Of The Verve Years | Verve | 527815-2
Charlie Parker | Verve | 539757-2
Talkin' Bird | Verve | 559859-2
Charlie Parker At Storyville | Blue Note | 785108-2
Bird: The Complete Charlie Parker On Verve | Verve | 837141-2
Charlie Parker:April In Paris | Dreyfus Jazz Line | FDM 36737-2
Charlie Parker Quartet With Strings
The Cole Porter Songbook | Verve | 823250-2
Charlie Parker Quintet
Verve Jazz Masters 10:Dizzy Gillespie | Verve | 516319-2
Bird And Diz | Verve | 521436-2
Verve Jazz Masters 28:Charlie Parker Plays Standards | Verve | 521854-2
Charlie Parker:Bird's Best Bop On Verve | Verve | 527452-2
Charlie Parker:The Best Of The Verve Years | Verve | 527815-2
Charlie Parker | Verve | 539757-2
Ultimate Dizzy Gillespie | Verve | 557535-2
Talkin' Bird | Verve | 559859-2
Charlie Parker At Storyville | Blue Note | 785108-2
The Cole Porter Songbook | Verve | 823250-2
Bird: The Complete Charlie Parker On Verve | Verve | 837141-2
Charlie Parker:Now's The Time | Dreyfus Jazz Line | FDM 36724-2
Bird At St. Nick's | Original Jazz Classics | OJC20 041-2(JWS 500)
Charlie Parker Septet
Charlie Parker | Verve | 539757-2
Talkin' Bird | Verve | 559859-2
Charlie Parker:Now's The Time | Dreyfus Jazz Line | FDM 36724-2
Charlie Parker Sextet
Verve Jazz Masters 28:Charlie Parker Plays Standards | Verve | 521854-2
Charlie Parker:The Best Of The Verve Years | Verve | 527815-2
Talkin' Bird | Verve | 559859-2
The Cole Porter Songbook | Verve | 823250-2
Charlie Parker With Machito And His Orchestra
Charlie Parker:The Best Of The Verve Years | Verve | 527815-2
Talkin' Bird | Verve | 559859-2
Bird: The Complete Charlie Parker On Verve | Verve | 837141-2
Charlie Parker:April In Paris | Dreyfus Jazz Line | FDM 36737-2
Charlie Parker With Orchestra
Charlie Parker:The Best Of The Verve Years | Verve | 527815-2
Charlie Parker Big Band | Verve | 559835-2
Charlie Parker With Orchestra & The Dave Lambert Singers
Verve Jazz Masters 28:Charlie Parker Plays Standards | Verve | 521854-2
Charlie Parker With Strings
Verve Jazz Masters 28:Charlie Parker Plays Standards | Verve | 521854-2
Charlie Parker With Strings:The Master Takes | Verve | 523984-2
Charlie Parker:The Best Of The Verve Years | Verve | 527815-2
Bird: The Complete Charlie Parker On Verve | Verve | 837141-2
Charlie Parker:April In Paris | Dreyfus Jazz Line | FDM 36737-2
Charlie Parker With The Joe Lipman Orchestra
Verve Jazz Masters 28:Charlie Parker Plays Standards | Verve | 521854-2
Charlie Parker With Strings:The Master Takes | Verve | 523984-2
Charlie Parker Big Band | Verve | 559835-2

Charlie Parker With The Neal Hefti Orchestra
Charlie Parker:The Best Of The Verve Years | Verve | 527815-2
Bird: The Complete Charlie Parker On Verve | Verve | 837141-2
Charlie Parker-Dizzy Gillespie Quintet
Thelonious Monk:Misterioso | Dreyfus Jazz Line | FDM 36743-2
Charlie Parker's Beboppers
Charlie Parker:Now's The Time | Dreyfus Jazz Line | FDM 36724-2
Charlie Parker's Jazzers
Bird: The Complete Charlie Parker On Verve | Verve | 837141-2
Charlie Parker's New Stars
Charlie Parker:Now's The Time | Dreyfus Jazz Line | FDM 36724-2
Dizzy Gillespie All Stars
Dizzy Gillespie:Night In Tunisia | Dreyfus Jazz Line | FDM 36734-2
Dizzy Gillespie Quintet
Charlie Parker:Now's The Time | Dreyfus Jazz Line | FDM 36724-2
Dizzy Gillespie:Night In Tunisia | Dreyfus Jazz Line | FDM 36734-2
Dizzy Gillespie Sextet
Dizzy Gillespie:Night In Tunisia | Dreyfus Jazz Line | FDM 36734-2
Ella Fitzgerald With The JATP All Stars
Ella Fitzgerald-First Lady Of Song | Verve | 517898-2
JATP All Stars
Jazz Gallery:Lester Young Vol.2(1946-59) | RCA | 2119541-2
Verve Jazz Masters 28:Charlie Parker Plays Standards | Verve | 521854-2
The Complete Jazz At The Philharmonic On Verve 1944-1949 | Verve | 523893-2
Charlie Parker:The Best Of The Verve Years | Verve | 527815-2
Jazz At The Philharmonic:Best Of The 1940's Concerts | Verve | 557534-2
Talkin' Bird | Verve | 559859-2
The Cole Porter Songbook | Verve | 823250-2
Bird: The Complete Charlie Parker On Verve | Verve | 837141-2
Norman Granz' JATP: Carnegie Hall 1949 | Pablo | PACD 5311-2
Miles Davis All Stars
Miles Davis:Milestones | Dreyfus Jazz Line | FDM 36731-2
Miles Davis And His Orchestra
Collector's Items | Original Jazz Classics | OJC20 071-2(P 7044)
Miles Davis Sextet
The Jazz Giants Play Miles Davis:Milestones | Prestige | PCD 24225-2
The Prestige Legacy Vol.1:The High Priests | Prestige | PCD 24251-2
Norman Granz Jam Session
Verve Jazz Masters 35:Johnny Hodges | Verve | 521857-2
Charlie Parker:The Best Of The Verve Years | Verve | 527815-2
Talkin' Bird | Verve | 559859-2
Bird: The Complete Charlie Parker On Verve | Verve | 837141-2
Quintet Of The Year
Charles Mingus-The Complete Debut Recordings | Debut | 12 DCD 4402-2
Sarah Vaughan With Dizzy Gillespie And His All Star Quintet
Sarah Vaughan:Lover Man | Dreyfus Jazz Line | FDM 36739-2
Sarah Vaughan With Dizzy Gillespie And His Septet
Sarah Vaughan:Lover Man | Dreyfus Jazz Line | FDM 36739-2
The Metronome All Stars
Planet Jazz:Dizzy Gillespie | Planet Jazz | 2152069-2

Parker,Chris | (dr)
The Brecker Brothers
The Becker Bros | RCA | 2122103-2

Parker,Doug | (p)
Harry James And His Orchestra
Trumpet Blues:The Best Of Harry James | Capitol | 521224-2

Parker,Evan | (cl,sax,reeds,ss,tapes,samples,ts)
Anliker-Parker-Schmid-Senn-Solothurnmann
September Winds | Creative Works Records | CW CD 1038/39
Evan Parker Electro-Acoustic Ensemble
Toward The Margins | ECM | 1612(453514-2)
Drawn Inward | ECM | 1693
Memory/Vision | ECM | 1852(0381172)
Evan Parker/Barre Phillips
Time Will Tell | ECM | 1537
Evan Parker-Paul Rutherford-Barry Guy-John Stevens
4,4,4, | Konnex Records | KCD 5049
Evan Parker-Peter A.Schmid
September Duos | Creative Works Records | CW CD 1036
Kenny Wheeler Ensemble
Muisc For Large & Small Ensembles | ECM | 1415/16
Kenny Wheeler Sextet
Around 6 | ECM | 1156
Paul Bley/Evan Parker
Time Will Tell | ECM | 1537
Paul Bley/Evan Parker/Barre Phillips
Time Will Tell | ECM | 1537
St.Gerold | ECM | 1609(157899-2)
Tony Oxley Quintet
The Baptist Traveller | CBS | 494438-2
Tony Oxley Sextet
4 Compositions For Sextet | CBS | 494437-2

Parker,Jack 'The Bear' | (dr)
Hot Lips Page And His Orchestra
Don Byas:Laura | Dreyfus Jazz Line | FDM 36714-2
Louis Armstrong With Sy Oliver And His Orchestra
Satchmo Serenaders | Verve | 543792-2
Nat King Cole With Orchestra
Nat King Cole:Route 66 | Dreyfus Jazz Line | FDM 36716-2

Parker,Jeff | (el-g,cow-bell,recorder,gorg)
Brian Blade Group
Fellowship | Blue Note | 859417-2

Parker,Jerry | (voc)
Charlie Parker And His Orchestra
Bird: The Complete Charlie Parker On Verve | Verve | 837141-2
Charlie Parker With Orchestra & The Dave Lambert Singers
Verve Jazz Masters 28:Charlie Parker Plays Standards | Verve | 521854-2

Parker,Johnny | (bp)
Graham Stewart And His New Orleans Band
The Golden Years Of Revival Jazz,Vol.4 | Storyville | STCD 5509
Johnny Parker Trio
The Golden Years Of Revival Jazz,Vol.5 | Storyville | STCD 5510

Parker,Leo | (as,bsvoc)
Coleman Hawkins And His Orchestra
Jazz:The Essential Collection Vol.3 | IN+OUT Records | 78013-2
Dexter Gordon Quintet
The Art Of Saxophone | Laserlight | 24652
Fats Navarro Quintet
Fats Navarro:Nostalgia | Dreyfus Jazz Line | FDM 36736-2
Leo Parker Sextet
True Blue | Blue Note | 534032-2

Parker,Leon | (congas,cowbell,cymbal,dr,perc)
Charlie Hunter-Leon Parker
Duo | Blue Note | 499187-2
Jackie Terrasson Trio
Jacky Terrasson | Blue Note | 829351-2
Reach | Blue Note | 837570-2
Jacky Terrasson Trio
Alive | Blue Note | 859651-2
James Carter Quartet
The Real Quietstorm | Atlantic | 7567-82742-2
Tom Harrell Group
Paradise | RCA | 2663738-2

Parker,Maceo | (as,perc,ts,keyboards,voc,porg)
Fred Wesley Group
New Friends | Minor Music | 801016
Hans Theessink Group
Call Me | Minor Music | 801022
Maceo Parker Group
Roots Revisited | Minor Music | 801015
Mo' Roots | Minor Music | 801018
Southern Exposure | Minor Music | 801033
Maceo(Soundtrack) | Minor Music | 801046
Maceo Parker With The Rebirth Brass Band
Southern Exposure | Minor Music | 801033
Maceo(Soundtrack) | Minor Music | 801046
Niels Landgren Funk Unit
Live In Stockholm | ACT | 9223-2
Rodney Jones Group
Soul Manifesto | Blue Note | 530499-2

Parker,Maynard | (g)
Charles Earland Orchestra
Charlie's Greatest Hits | Prestige | PCD 24250-2
Charles Earland Septet
Charles Earland In Concert | Prestige | PRCD 24267-2
Charles Earland Sextet
Jazzin' With The Soul Brothers | Fantasy | FANCD 6086-2
Charlie's Greatest Hits | Prestige | PCD 24250-2
Gene Ammons Quintet
Fine And Mellow | Prestige | PRCD 24281-2

Parker,Paul | (dr)
Wes Montgomery Trio
Wes Montgomery-The Complete Riverside Recordings | Riverside | 12 RCD 4408-2
A Dynamic New Jazz Sound | Original Jazz Classics | OJCCD 034-2
Guitar On The Go | Original Jazz Classics | OJCCD 489-2(RLP 9494)

Parker,Ray | (el-g,dr,gvoc)
Dizzy Gillespie With The Lalo Schifrin Orchestra
Free Ride | Original Jazz Classics | OJCCD 784-2(2310794)
Herbie Hancock Group
Sunlight | CBS | 486570-2
Monster | CBS | 486571-2
Magic Window | CBS | 486572-2
Herbie Hancock Septet
V.S.O.P. Herbie Hancock-Live At The City Center N.Y. | CBS | 486569-2

Parker,Sonny | (voc)
Lionel Hampton And His Orchestra
Lionel Hampton:Flying Home | Dreyfus Jazz Line | FDM 36735-2

Parker,William | (b,musette,perc,voice,cello,ts,tuba)
Roscoe Mitchell And The Note Factory
Nine To Get Ready | ECM | 1651(539725-2)

Parker[as 'Charlie Chan'],Charlie | (as)
Quintet Of The Year
The Quintet-Jazz At Massey Hall | Debut | DSA 124-6
The Quintet-Jazz At Massey Hall | Original Jazz Classics | OJC20 044-2

Parkins,Sara | (v)
Steve Coleman And Five Elements
The Sonic Language Of Myth | RCA | 2164123-2

Parkins,Zeene | (accordeon,el-harp,harp,keyboards)
Ensemble Modern
Ensemble Modern-Fred Frith:Traffic Continues | Winter&Winter | 910044-2

Parks,Dean | (el-g,gsynth-horn)
Dee Dee Bridgewater With Band
Dee Dee Bridgewater | Atlantic | 7567-80760-2
Diane Schuur And Her Band
Music Is My Life | Atlantic | 7567-83150-2
Donald Byrd Orchestra
Black Byrd | Blue Note | 784466-2
Sarah Vaughan And Her Band
Songs Of The Beatles | Atlantic | 16037-2
Stanley Turrentine And His Orchestra
Pieces Of Dream | Original Jazz Classics | OJCCD 831-2(F 9465)

Parlan,Horace | (p,celestep-solo)
Archie Shepp-Horace Parlan Duo
Goin' Home | Steeplechase | SCCD 31079
Trouble In Mind | Steeplechase | SCCD 31139
Babs Gonzales And His Band
Voilà | Fresh Sound Records | FSR CD 340
Booker Ervin Quartet
That's It | Candid | CCD 79014
Booker Ervin Quintet
Exultation! | Original Jazz Classics | OJCCD 835-2(P 7293)
Charles Mingus And His Orchestra
Charles Mingus-Passion Of A Man:The Complete Atlantic Recordings 1956-1961 | Atlantic | 8122-72871-2
Charles Mingus Group
Mingus Ah Um | CBS | CK 65512
Charles Mingus Jazz Workshop
Rhino Presents The Atlantic Jazz Gallery | Atlantic | 8122-71257-2
Blues & Roots | Atlantic | 8122-75205-2
Charles Mingus Orchestra
The Very Best Of Charles Mingus | Rhino | 8122-79988-2
Charles Mingus Septet
Charles Mingus:The Complete 1959 Columbia Recordings | CBS | C3K 65145
Dexter Gordon Quintet
Doin' Allright | Blue Note | 784077-2
Dexter Gordon:Ballads | Blue Note | 796579-2
Jazz Profile:Dexter Gordon | Blue Note | 823514-2
Eddie Lockjaw Davis-Johnny Griffin Quintet
The Jazz Giants Play Cole Porter:Night And Day | Prestige | PCD 24203-2
Horace Parlan Quartet
Blue Bossa | Blue Note | 795590-2
Jazz Portraits | EGO | 95080
Horace Parlan Quintet
The Best Of Blue Note Vol.2 | Blue Note | 797960-2
Horace Parlan Trio
Movin' And Groovin' | Blue Note | 0677187
Lou Donaldson Quintet
Blue Note Plays Gershwin | Blue Note | 520808-2
Pee Wee Ellis-Horace Parlan
Gentle Men Blue | Minor Music | 801073
Roland Kirk And His Orchestra
Rahsaan/The Complete Mercury Recordings Of Roland Kirk | Mercury | 846630-2
Roland Kirk Group
I Talk With The Spirits | Verve | 558076-2
Roland Kirk Quartet
Verve Jazz Masters Vol.60:The Collection | Verve | 529866-2
Talkin' Verve-Roots Of Acid Jazz:Roland Kirk | Verve | 533101-2
Rahsaan/The Complete Mercury Recordings Of Roland Kirk | Mercury | 846630-2
Roland Kirk Quintet
Rahsaan/The Complete Mercury Recordings Of Roland Kirk | Mercury | 846630-2

Parlan,Horace prob. | (perc)
Charles Mingus Workshop
Charles Mingus-The Complete Debut Recordings | Debut | 12 DCD 4402-2

Parlato,Dave | (bel-b)
Don Ellis Orchestra
Electric Bath | CBS | CK 65522

Parlett,Mike | (as,WX7,flts)
Gail Thompson Orchestra
Gail Thompson's Jazz Africa | Enja | ENJ-9053 2

Parran,J.D. | (alto-cl,bass-sax,contra-alto-cl)
Marty Ehrlich Group
The Long View | Enja | ENJ-9452 2

Parricelli,John | (g)
Gerard Presencer Group
Chasing Reality | ACT | 9422-2
Kenny Wheeler Brass Ensemble
A Long Time Ago | ECM | 1691

Parrish,Avery | (parr)
Erskine Hawkins And His Orchestra
Planet Jazz:Big Bands | Planet Jazz | 2169649-2

Parshley,Tom | (as,reeds,ts,woodwinds)
Billie Holiday With The Ray Ellis Orchestra
Lady In Satin | CBS | CK 65144
Louis Armstrong With Gordon Jenkins And His Orchestra And Choir
Satchmo In Style | Verve | 549594-2
Ambassador Louis Armstrong Vol.17:Moments To Remember(1952-1956) | Ambassador | CLA 1917
Louis Armstrong-My Greatest Songs | MCA | MCD 18347
Swing Legends:Louis Armstrong | Nimbus Records | NI 2012

Parson,Dion | (dr)
Donald Harrison Quartet
Nouveau Swing | Impulse(MCA) | 951209-2
Helmut Kagerer-Peter Bernstein Quartet
Jazz Guitar Highlights 1 | Jardis Records | JRCD 20141
April In New York | Jardis Records | JRCD 9818

Parsons,Bob | (bsreeds)
Dave Stryker Octet
Blue To The Bone III | Steeplechase | SCCD 31524

Parsons,John | (dobro,el-gg)
Acoustic Alchemy
Against The Grain | GRP | GRP 97832

Parsons,Karina | (voc)
Mike Westbrook Brass Band
Glad Day:Settings Of William Blake | Enja | ENJ-9376 2

Partman,Marek | (dr)
Robert Balzar Trio
Travelling | Jazzpoint | JP 1050 CD

Partyka,Edward | (b-tb,ld,tubatb)
Jens Winther And The WDR Big Band
The Escape | dacapo | DCCD 9437
Lee Konitz With The Ed Partyka Jazz Orchestra
Dreams And Realities | Laika Records | 35101642
Rainer Tempel Big Band
Melodies Of '98 | Jazz 4 Ever Records:Jazz Network | J4E 4744
Roman Schwaller Nonet
The Original Tunes | JHM Records | JHM 3629

Paschke,Stefani | (voc)
Jazzensemble Des Hessischen Rundfunks
Jazz Messe-Messe Für Unsere Zeit | hr music.de | hrmj 003-01 CD

Pascoal,Hermeto | (el-p,whistling,fl,keyboards,arr,ss)
Cal Tjader Group
Amazonas | Original Jazz Classics | OJCCD 840-2(F 9502)
Miles Davis Group
Live-Evil | CBS | C2K 65135

Pascoe,Keith | (v)
John Surman With String Quartet
Coruscating | ECM | 1702(543033-2)

Pasdoc,André | (voc)
Andre Pasdoc With The Orchestra Vola
Jazz In Paris:Django Reinhardt-Django Et Compagnie | EmArCy | 549241-2 PMS

Pasmanick,Kenneth | (bassoon)
Charlie Byrd Group
Byrd In The Wind | Original Jazz Classics | OJCCD 1086(RS 9449)
Charlie Byrd Sextet
Byrd's Word! | Original Jazz Classics | OJCCD 1054-2(R 9448)

Pasqua,Alan | (keyboards,p,el-p,orgsynth)
Lee Ritenour Sextet
Alive In L.A. | GRP | GRP 98822

Pasquall,Jerome | (as,clts)
The Lousiana Stompers
Jazz:The Essential Collection Vol.1 | IN+OUT Records | 78011-2

Pass,Joe | (el-g,el-g-solo,g-solog)
All Stars
Alternate Blues | Original Jazz Classics | OJCCD 744-2
Art Van Damme Group
State Of Art | MPS | 841413-2
Art Van Damme Quintet
Keep Going/Blue World | MPS | 529093-2
Benny Carter And His Orchestra
Jazz At The Philharmonic:The Montreux Collection | Pablo | PACD 5306-2
Benny Carter Sextet
To Bags...With Love:Memorial Album | Pablo | 2310967-2
Milt Jackson Birthday Celebration | Fantasy | FANCD 6079-2
Buddy DeFranco Meets The Oscar Peterson Quartet
Hark | Original Jazz Classics | OJCCD 867-2(2310915)
Charles Kynard Quintet
The Soul Brotherhood | Prestige | PCD 24257-2
Clark Terry Five
The Jazz Giants Play Duke Ellington:Caravan | Prestige | PCD 24227-2
Count Basie Band
Basie Jam No. 2 | Original Jazz Classics | OJCCD 631-2(2310786)
Count Basie Kansas City 5
Milt Jackson Birthday Celebration | Fantasy | FANCD 6079-2
Count Basie Kansas City 7
Count Basie Kansas City 7 | Original Jazz Classics | OJCCD 690-2(2310908)
Count Basie's Small Band
88 Basie Street | Original Jazz Classics | OJC 808(2310901)
Duke Ellington Quartet
Joe Pass:Guitar Virtuoso | Pablo | 4 PACD 4423-2
The Jazz Giants Play Duke Ellington:Caravan | Prestige | PCD 24227-2
Ella Fitzgerald Jam
Bluella:Ella Fitzgerald Sings The Blues | Pablo | 2310960-2
Ella Fitzgerald With Joe Pass
Speak Love | Pablo | 2310888
Joe Pass:Guitar Virtuoso | Pablo | 4 PACD 4423-2
Sophisticated Lady | Pablo | PACD 5310-2
Ella Fitzgerald With Orchestra
Ella Abraca Jobim | Pablo | 2630201-2
The Best Is Yet To Come | Original Jazz Classics | OJCCD 889-2(2312138)
Ella Fitzgerald With The Tommy Flanagan Quartet
Bluella:Ella Fitzgerald Sings The Blues | Pablo | 2310960-2
Ella In London | Original Jazz Classics | OJCCD 974-2(2310711)
Ella Fitzgerald-Joe Pass Duo
Take Love Easy | Pablo | 2310702
Fitzgerald & Pass... Again | Original Jazz Classics | OJCCD 1052-2(2310772)
Joe Pass:A Man And His Guitar | Original Jazz Classics | OJCCD 8806-2
Freddie Hubbard-Oscar Peterson Quintet
Face To Face | Original Jazz Classics | OJCCD 937-2(2310876)
Gerald Wilson And His Orchestra
Blue Breaks Beats Vol.2 | Blue Note | 789907-2
Herb Ellis-Joe Pass
The Jazz Giants Play Cole Porter:Night And Day | Prestige | PCD 24203-2
J.J.Johnson-Joe Pass
The J.J.Johnson Memorial Album | Prestige | PRCD 11025-2
JATP All Stars
Welcome To Jazz At The Philharmonic | Fantasy | FANCD 6081-2
The J.J.Johnson Memorial Album | Prestige | PRCD 11025-2
Joe Pass
Virtuoso | Pablo | 2310708-2
Songs For Ellen | Pablo | 2310955-2
Unforgettable | Pablo | 2310964-2
Resonance | Pablo | 2310968-2
What Is There To Say | Pablo | 2310971-2
Solo Guitar | Pablo | 2310974-2
Joe Pass:Guitar Virtuoso | Pablo | 4 PACD 4423-2
I Remember Charlie Parker | Original Jazz Classics | OJC 602(2312109)
Montreux '77 | Original Jazz Classics | OJC20 382-2(2308212)
Virtuoso No.3 | Original Jazz Classics | OJC20 684-2(2310805)
Joe Pass At The Montreux Jazz Festival 1975 | Original Jazz Classics | OJC20 934-2(2310752)
Joe Pass:A Man And His Guitar | Original Jazz Classics | OJCCD 8806-2

Digital III At Montreux | Original Jazz Classics | OJCCD 996-2(2308223)
Jazz At The Philharmonic:The Montreux Collection | Pablo | PACD 5306-2
Sophisticated Lady | Pablo | PACD 5310-2
The Jazz Giants Play Harold Arlen:Blues In The Night | Prestige | PCD 24201-2
The Jazz Giants Play Rodgers & Hart:Blue Moon | Prestige | PCD 24205-2
The Jazz Giants Play Sammy Cahn:It's Magic | Prestige | PCD 24226-2
Joe Pass Quartet
Apassionato | Pablo | 2310946-2
Nuages | Pablo | 2310961-2
Joe Pass:Guitar Virtuoso | Pablo | 4 PACD 4423-2
Joy Spring | Blue Note | 835222-2
Ira George And Joe-Joe Pass Loves Gershwin | Original Jazz Classics | OJCCD 828-2(2312133)
The Jazz Giants Play Duke Ellington:Caravan | Prestige | PCD 24227-2
Joe Pass Quintet
Joe Pass:Guitar Virtuoso | Pablo | 4 PACD 4423-2
Joe Pass Sextet
Joe Pass:Guitar Virtuoso | Pablo | 4 PACD 4423-2
Jazzin' Vol.2: The Music Of Stevie Wonder | Fantasy | FANCD 6088-2
Joe Pass Trio
Resonance | Pablo | 2310968-2
Live At Donte's | Pablo | 2620114-2
Joe Pass:Guitar Virtuoso | Pablo | 4 PACD 4423-2
Eximious | Original Jazz Classics | OJCCD 1037-2(2310877)
Joe Pass With The NDR Big Band
Joe Pass In Hamburg | ACT | 9100-2
NDR Big Band-Bravissimo | ACT | 9232-2
Joe Pass With The NDR Big Band And Radio Philharmonie Hannover
Joe Pass In Hamburg | ACT | 9100-2
Joe Pass/Niels-Henning Orsted-Pedersen Duo
Joe Pass:Guitar Virtuoso | Pablo | 4 PACD 4423-2
Northsea Nights | Original Jazz Classics | OJCCD 1011-2(2308221)
Chops | Original Jazz Classics | OJCCD 786-2(2310830)
Digital III At Montreux | Original Jazz Classics | OJCCD 996-2(2308223)
Joe Pass-Herb Ellis
Joe Pass:Guitar Virtuoso | Pablo | 4 PACD 4423-2
Joe Pass-Jimmy Rowles Duo
Joe Pass:Guitar Virtuoso | Pablo | 4 PACD 4423-2
Joe Pass:A Man And His Guitar | Original Jazz Classics | OJCCD 8806-2
Checkmate | Original Jazz Classics | OJCCD 975-2(2310865)
Joe Pass-John Pisano
Joe Pass-John Pisano:Duets | Pablo | 2310959-2
Joe Pass:Guitar Virtuoso | Pablo | 4 PACD 4423-2
Johnny Griffin Quintet
Grab This! | Original Jazz Classics | OJCCD 1941-2(RLP 9437)
Kansas City 6
Count Basie:Kansas City 6 | Original Jazz Classics | OJC20 449-2(2310871)
Kansas City Seven
The J.J.Johnson Memorial Album | Prestige | PRCD 11025-2
NDR Big Band With Guests
50 Years Of NDR Big Band:Bravissimo II | ACT | 9259-2
Oscar Peterson All Stars
Jazz At The Philharmonic:The Montreux Collection | Pablo | PACD 5306-2
Oscar Peterson Quartet
Oscar Peterson Live! | Pablo | 2310940-2
Time After Time | Pablo | 2310947-2
Oscar Peterson Plays Duke Ellington | Pablo | 2310966-2
Oscar Peterson:The Composer | Pablo | 2310970-2
Night Child | Original Jazz Classics | OJCCD 1030-2(2312108)
The Jazz Giants Play Miles Davis:Milestones | Prestige | PCD 24225-2
Oscar Peterson Quintet
Skol | Original Jazz Classics | OJC20 496-2
Oscar Peterson Trio
The Paris Concert | Pablo | 2PACD 2620112
Joe Pass:Guitar Virtuoso | Pablo | 4 PACD 4423-2
The Good Life | Original Jazz Classics | OJC 627(2308241)
The Trio | Original Jazz Classics | OJCCD 992(2310101)
Oscar Peterson-Joe Pass Duo
Oscar Pterson Et Joe Pass A La Salle Pleyel | Pablo | 2CD 2625705
Porgy And Bess | Original Jazz Classics | OJCCD 829-2(2310779)
Pablo All Star Jam
Montreux '77 | Original Jazz Classics | OJC 385(2620105)
Quadrant
Milt Jackson Birthday Celebration | Fantasy | FANCD 6079-2
Richard 'Groove' Holmes Quintet
Somethin' Special | Pacific Jazz | 855452-2
Roger Kellaway Cello Quartet With The A&M Symphony Orchestra
Roger Kellaway Cello Quartet | A&M Records | 9861062
Roy Eldridge Sextet
Decidedly | Pablo | PACD 5314-2
Sarah Vaughan And Her Band
Duke Ellington Song Book Two | Pablo | CD 2312116
Sarah Vaughan Birthday Celebration | Fantasy | FANCD 6090-2
Sarah Vaughan With Joe Pass And Mike Wofford
Sarah Vaughan Birthday Celebration | Fantasy | FANCD 6090-2
Sarah Vaughan With Small Group & Orchestra
Duke Ellington Song Book One | Pablo | CD 2312111
Sarah Vaughan With The Joe Pass Quartet
Linger Awhile | Pablo | 2312144-2
Joe Pass:Guitar Virtuoso | Pablo | 4 PACD 4423-2
Sarah Vaughan With The Oscar Peterson Quartet
How Long Has This Been Going On? | Pablo | 2310821-2
Joe Pass:Guitar Virtuoso | Pablo | 4 PACD 4423-2
Sarah Vaughan Birthday Celebration | Fantasy | FANCD 6090-2
Sarah Vaughan With The Roland Hanna Quartet
Sarah Vaughan Birthday Celebration | Fantasy | FANCD 6090-2
Sarah Vaughan-Joe Pass
Sarah Vaughan Birthday Celebration | Fantasy | FANCD 6090-2
Stephane Grappelli Trio
Tivoli Garders, Copenhagen, Denmark | Original Jazz Classics | OJCCD 441-2
The Big Three
Milt Jackson Birthday Celebration | Fantasy | FANCD 6079-2
The Big Three | Original Jazz Classics | OJCCD 805-2(2310757)
The Trumpet Summit With The Oscar Peterson Big 4
The Trumpet Summit Meets The Oscar Peterson Big 4 | Original Jazz Classics | OJCCD 603-2
Toots Thielemans Trio
Live In The Netherlands | Original Jazz Classics | OJCCD 930-2(2308233)
Zoot Sims Quintet
Zoot Sims And The Gershwin Brothers | Original Jazz Classics | OJC20 444-2(2310744)
Zoot Sims And The Gershwin Brothers | Pablo | PASA 2310-744-6
Zoot Sims-Joe Pass Duo
Joe Pass:Guitar Virtuoso | Pablo | 4 PACD 4423-2

Passport |
Klaus Doldinger & Passport
Down To Earth | Warner | 4509-93207-2
Klaus Doldinger's Passport
Man In The Mirror | Warner | 2292-40253-2
Running In Real Time | Warner | 2292-40633-2
Heavy Nights | Warner | 2292-42006-2
Blue Tattoo | Atlantic | 2292-42178-2
Earthborn | Atlantic | 2292-46477-2
Oceanliner | Warner | 2292-46479-2
Klaus Doldinger Passport Live | Warner | 8573-84132-2
Balance Of Happiness | Warner | 9031-71233-2
Blues Roots | Warner | 9031-75417-2
Klaus Doldinger's Passport With Johnny 'Clyde' Copeland
Blues Roots | Warner | 9031-75417-2
Passport
Ataraxia | Atlantic | 2292-42148-2
Handmade | Atlantic | 2292-42172-2
Uranus | Atlantic | 2292-44142-2
Second Passport | Atlantic | 2292-44143-2
Looking Thru | Atlantic | 2292-44144-2
Cross-Collateral | Atlantic | 2292-44145-2
Infinity Machine | Atlantic | 2292-44146-2
Garden Of Eden | Atlantic | 2292-44147-2
Iguacu | Atlantic | 2292-46031-2
Passport And Guests
Doldinger Jubilee Concert | Atlantic | 2292-44175-2
Doldinger's Best | ACT | 9224-2

Pastor,David | (tp)
Big Band Bellaterra
Don't Git Sassy | Fresh Sound Records | FSNT 048 CD
Daniel Flors Group
When Least Expected | Fresh Sound Records | FSNT 080 CD

Pastor,Tony | (cl,ts,vocsax)
Artie Shaw And His Orchestra
Planet JazzArtie Shaw | Planet Jazz | 2152057-2
Planet Jazz Sampler | Planet Jazz | 2152326-2
Planet Jazz:Swing | Planet Jazz | 2169651-2
Planet Jazz:Female Jazz Vocalists | Planet Jazz | 2169656-2
The Legends Of Swing | Laserlight | 24659
Swing Vol.1 | Storyville | 4960343

Pastora,Lee | (congas,bongoslatin-perc)
Billy Cobham Group
The Best Of Billy Cobham | Atlantic | 7567-81558-2

Pastorius,Jaco | (b,dr,tympani,voice,voc,el-b)
Al Di Meola Group
Land Of The Midnight Sun | CBS | 468214-2
Bireli Lagrene Group
Bireli Lagrene 'Highlights' | Jazzpoint | JP 1027 CD
Herbie Hancock Group
Sunlight | CBS | 486570-2
Jaco Pastorius
Jaco Pastorius Honestly | Jazzpoint | JP 1032 CD
Jaco Pastorius Groups
Another Side Of Jaco Pastorius | Jazzpoint | JP 1064 CD
Jaco Pastorius Trio
Live In Italy | Jazzpoint | JP 1031 CD
Heavy'n Jazz | Jazzpoint | JP 1036 CD
Jaco Pastorius Broadway Blues & Theresa | Jazzpoint | JP 1053 CD
Jaco Pastorius Heavy'n Jazz & Stuttgart Aria | Jazzpoint | JP 1058 CD
Live In Italy & Honestly | Jazzpoint | JP 1059 CD
Jaco Pastorius With Orchestra
Word Of Mouth | Warner | 7599-23525-2
Mangelsdorff-Pastorius-Mouzon
Three Originals:The Wide Point/Trilogue/Albert Live In Montreux | MPS | 519213-2
Pat Metheny Trio
Bright Size Life | ECM | 1073(827133-2)
Weather Report
Mr. Gone | CBS | 468208-2
Black Market | CBS | 468210-2
Night Passage | CBS | 468211-2
Heavy Weather | CBS | CK 65108

Pastuszyk,Regina | (reeds)
The United Women's Orchestra
The Blue One | Jazz Haus Musik | JHM 0099 CD

Pata Blue Chip |
Pata Blue Chip
Pata Blue Chip | Pata Musik | PATA 13(amf 1064)

Pata Masters |
Norbert Stein Pata Masters meets Djaduk Ferianto Kua Etnika
Pata Java | Pata Musik | PATA 16 CD
Pata Masters
Pata-Bahia | Pata Musik | PATA 11 CD

Pata Music |
Pata Music Meets Arfi
News Of Roi Ubu | Pata Musik | PATA 10 CD
La Belle Et La Bête | Pata Musik | PATA 14(amf 1066)

Pata Orchestra |
Norbert Stein Pata Orchester
The Secret Act Of Painting | Pata Musik | PATA 7 CD

Patato,Nee-Daku | (congas,bells,berimbau,brekete-dr)
Trevor Watts Moiré Music Drum Orchestra
A Wider Embrace | ECM | 1449

Pate,Don | (bel-b)
Gil Evans Orchestra
PLay The Music Of Jimi Hendrix | RCA | 2663872-2

Pate,Johnny | (arr,ld,bcond)
Jimmy Smith With The Johnny Pate Orchestra
Jimmy Smith:Best Of The Verve Years | Verve | 527950-2
Jimmy Smith-Talkin' Verve | Verve | 531563-2
Kenny Burrell With The Johnny Pate Orchestra
Verve Jazz Masters 45:Kenny Burrell | Verve | 527652-2
Shirley Horn With Band
The Roots Of Acid Jazz | Impulse(MCA) | IMP 12042
Wes Montgomery Orchestra
Movin' Wes | Verve | 521433-2
Wes Montgomery With The Johnny Pate Orchestra
Verve Jazz Masters 14:Wes Montgomery | Verve | 519826-2
Wes Montgomery:The Verve Jazz Sides | Verve | 521690-2
Talkin' Jazz:Roots Of Acid Jazz | Verve | 529580-2

Patent,Harry | (b)
Dr. Henry Levine's Barefoot Dixieland Philharmonic feat.Prof. Sidney Bechet
Planet Jazz | Planet Jazz | 2169652-2
Sidney Bechet And The Chamber Music Society Of Lower Basin Street
Sidney Bechet:Summertime | Dreyfus Jazz Line | FDM 36712-2

Patitucci,John | (5-string-b,6-string-b,arr,comp,b)
Bobby Lyle Group
The Journey | Atlantic | 7567-82138-2
Chick Corea Electric Band
The Chick Corea Electric Band | GRP | GRP 95352
Light Years | GRP | GRP 95462
Eye Of The Beholder | GRP | GRP 95642
Beneath The Mask | GRP | GRP 96492
Chick Corea Trio
Akoustic Band | GRP | GRP 95822
Danilo Perez Group
Central Avenue | Impulse(MCA) | 951281-2
Danilo Perez Trio
Central Avenue | Impulse(MCA) | 951281-2
Dave Grusin Orchestra
Two For The Road:The Music Of Henry Mancini | GRP | GRP 98652
Dave Weckl Group
Heads Up | GRP | GRP 96732
Hard-Wired | GRP | GRP 97602
Diane Schuur With Orchestra And Strings
The Best Of Diane Schuur | GRP | GRP 98882
Directions In Music
Live at Massey Hall:Celebrating Miles Davis & John Coltrane | Verve | 589654-2
GRP All-Star Big Band
GRP All-Star Big Band:Live! | GRP | GRP 97402
All Blues | GRP | GRP 98002
John Patitucci
Sketchbook | GRP | GRP 96172
John Patitucci Group
Sketchbook | GRP | GRP 96172
Mistura Fina | GRP | GRP 98022
Lee Ritenour Group
Stolen Moments | GRP | GRP 96152
Michael Brecker Quindectet
Wide Angles | Verve | 076142-2
Mike Stern Group
Civo And Toko | Atlantic | 7567-83036-2
Roy Haynes Trio
The Roy Haynes Trio | Verve | 543534-2
Wayne Shorter Quartet
Footprints Live! | Verve | 589679-2

Patrick,Pat | (as,bs,bells,solar-dr,space-lute)
Blue Mitchell And His Orchestra
A Sure Thing | Original Jazz Classics | OJCCD 837-2
Frank Stozier Sextet
Long Night | Milestone | MCD 47095-2
Jimmy Heath Orchestra
Cannonball Adderley Birthday Celebration | Fantasy | FANCD 6087-2
John Coltrane And His Orchestra
John Coltrane:Standards | Impulse(MCA) | 549914-2
John Coltrane Quartet With Brass
The Complete Africa/Brass Sessions | Impulse(MCA) | 952168-2
Mongo Santamaria And His Band
Mongo At The Village Gate | Original Jazz Classics | OJCCD 490-2(RLP 9529)
Sun Ra And His Astro-Infinity Arkestra
Space Is The Place | Impulse(MCA) | 951249-2
Sun Ra And His Intergalactic Research Arkestra
Black Myth/Out In Space | MPS | 557656-2

Patruno,Lino | (gbj)
Oscar Klein-Lino Patruno European Jazz Stars
Live at The San Marino Jazz Festival | Jazzpoint | JP 1052 CD
Oscar Klein's Anniversary Band
Moonglow | Nagel-Heyer | CD 021
Ellington For Lovers | Nagel-Heyer | NH 1009
The Second Sampler | Nagel-Heyer | NHR SP 6

Patt,Ralf-Peter | (oboe)
Bernd Konrad Jazz Group With Symphonie Orchestra
Wen Die Götter Lieben | Creative Works Records | CW CD 1010-1

Patterson,Ann | (sax)
Buddy Childers Big Band
It's What Happening Now! | Candid | CCD 79749

Patterson,Billy | (el-g,vocg)
Miles Davis Group
Amandla | Warner | 7599-25873-2

Patterson,Don | (borg)
Don Patterson Quartet
Boppin' & Burnin' | Original Jazz Classics | OJCCD 983-2(P 7563)
Don Patterson Quintet
Boppin' & Burnin' | Original Jazz Classics | OJCCD 983-2(P 7563)
Eddie Lockjaw Davis Quintet
The Jazz Giants Play Harry Warren:Lullaby Of Broadway | Prestige | PCD 24204-2
Eric Kloss Quartet
About Time | Prestige | PRCD 24268-2
Gene Ammons-Sonny Stitt Quintet
Verve Jazz Masters 50:Sonny Sitt | Verve | 527651-2
Boss Tenors In Orbit!!! | Verve | 549371-2
Sonny Stitt Quartet
The Jazz Giants Play Miles Davis:Milestones | Prestige | PCD 24225-2
The Prestige Legacy Vol.2:Battles Of Saxes | Prestige | PCD 24252-2
Brothers 4 | Prestige | PCD 24261-2
Sonny Stitt Trio
The Boss Men | Prestige | PCD 24253-2

Patterson,Ottilie | (melodica,voc,p,p-solotambourine)
Chris Barber's Jazz Band
The Best Of Dixieland-Live in 1954/55 | London | 820878-2

Pattison,Pat | (btuba)
Muggsy Spanier And His Ragtime Band
Planet Jazz | Planet Jazz | 2169652-2

Patton,Big John | (keyboards,orgtambourine)
Big John Patton Quartet
Got A Good Thing Goin' | Blue Note | 580731-2
Blue Bossa | Blue Note | 795590-2
Big John Patton Quintet
So Blue So Funky-Heroes Of The Hammond | Blue Note | 796563-2
Grant Green Quintet
Am I Blue | Blue Note | 535564-2
Jimmy Smith Quintet
Rockin' the Boat | Blue Note | 576755-2
John Patton Quartet
The Lost Grooves | Blue Note | 831883-2
Accent On The Blues | Blue Note | 853924-2
John Patton Quintet
Along Came John | Blue Note | 0675614
Along Came John | Blue Note | 831915-2
John Zorn Group
Spillane | Nonesuch | 7559-79172-2
Lou Donaldson Quartet
Good Gracious | Blue Note | 854325-2
Lou Donaldson Quintet
The Natural Soul | Blue Note | 542307-2

Patton,Julie | (narration)
Uri Caine Ensemble
Love Fugue-Robert Schumann | Winter&Winter | 910049-2

Patton,Pat | (bj)
Bunk Johnson With The Yerba Buena Jazz Band
Bunk & Lu | Good Time Jazz | GTCD 12024-2
Lu Watters' Yerba Buena Jazz Band
The Very Best Of Dixieland Jazz | Verve | 535529-2

Pattusch,Nick | (dr)
Mathias Götz-Windstärke 4
Lunar Oder Solar? | Jazz 'n' Arts Records | JNA 1002

Patumi,Daniele | (b,bodhran,perc,voiceb-solo)
Creative Works Orchestra
Willisau And More Live | Creative Works Records | CW CD 1020-2

Pauer,Fritz | (keyboards,african-fl,p,arr,el-pvoc)
Annie Ross & PonyPoindexter With The Berlin All Stars
Annie Ross & Pony Poindexter with The Berlin All Stars | MPS | 9811257
Art Farmer Quintet
From Vienna With Art | MPS | 9811443
Don Menza Septet
Morning Song | MPS | 9811446
Fritz Pauer Trio
Jazz Portraits | EGO | 95080
Live At The Berlin Jazz Galerie | MPS | 9811263
Klaus Weiss Orchestra
Live At The Domicile | ATM Records | ATM 3805-AH
NDR Big Band With Guests
50 Years Of NDR Big Band:Bravissimo II | ACT | 9259-2
Wayne Darling Group
The Art Of The Bass Vol.1 | Laika Records | 35101652

Paul Armin | (stringsraad electro-acoustic)
Jon Hassell Group
Power Spot | ECM | 1327

Paul,Emanuel | (clts)
Eureka Brass Band
Atlantic Jazz: New Orleans | Atlantic | 7567-81700-2

Paul,Helena | (voc)
All That Jazz & Helena Paul
All That Jazz & Helena Paul | Satin Doll Productions | SDP 1031-1 CD

Paul,Les | (g)
JATP All Stars
The Complete Jazz At The Philharmonic On Verve 1944-1949 | Verve | 523893-2
Jazz At The Philharmonic:Best Of The 1940's Concerts | Verve | 557534-2

Paula,J.D. | (perc)
Bola Sete Quintet
Tour De Force:The Bola Sete Trios | Fantasy | FCD 24766-2

Paula,Jose | (g,tam,percvoc)
Dizzy Gillespie And His Orchestra
Ultimate Dizzy Gillespie | Verve | 557535-2

Quincy Jones And His Orchestra
Rahsaan/The Complete Mercury Recordings Of Roland Kirk | Mercury | 846630-2

Pauli,Rebecca | (narration)
Alfred 23 Harth Group
Sweet Paris | free flow music | ffm 0291

Paulin,Roderick | (ts)
Maceo Parker With The Rebirth Brass Band
Southern Exposure | Minor Music | 801033

Paulinho,Paulo | (drperc)
Gato Barbieri Orchestra
Latino America | Impulse(MCA) | 952236-2

Paulo,Jose | (cabasa,bandero,perctambourine)
Dave Pike Quintet
Carnavals | Prestige | PCD 24248-2
Dave Pike Sextet
Carnavals | Prestige | PCD 24248-2
Stan Getz Group Feat.Laurindo Almeida
Stan Getz With Guest Artist Laurindo Almeida | Verve | 823149-2
Stan Getz With The Gary McFarland Orchestra
Stan Getz Highlights:The Best Of The Verve Years Vol.2 | Verve | 517330-2
Verve Jazz Masters 53:Stan Getz-Bossa Nova | Verve | 529904-2
Big Band Bossa Nova | Verve | 825771-2 PMS
Stan Getz Highlights | Verve | 847430-2
Stan Getz-Laurindo Almeida Orchestra
Verve Jazz Masters 53:Stan Getz-Bossa Nova | Verve | 529904-2
Stan Getz Highlights | Verve | 847430-2
Willis Jackson Group
At Large | Prestige | PCD 24243-2

Paulo,Michael, | (flsax)
Al Jarreau With Band
Al Jarreau In London | i.e. Music | 557849-2

Paulo,Pedro | (tp)
Cannonball Adderley With Sergio Mendes And The Bossa Rio Sextet
Cannonball's Bossa Nova | Blue Note | 522667-2
Ballads | Blue Note | 537563-2
Blue Bossa | Blue Note | 795590-2

Pausch,Yogo | (dr,perc,cymbalsgongs)
Brodmann-Pausch Percussion Duo
Are You Serious? | Jazz 4 Ever Records:Jazz Network | J4E 4718

Pavageau,Alcide 'Slow Drag' | (b)
Bunk Johnson And His New Orleans Band
Planet Jazz:Jazz Trumpet | Planet Jazz | 2169654-2
George Lewis And His Band
Atlantic Jazz: New Orleans | Atlantic | 7567-81700-2
George Lewis And His New Orleans Ragtime Band
The Beverly Caverns Session | Good Time Jazz | GTCD 12058-2
George Lewis And His New Orleans Stompers
George Lewis And His New Orleans Stompers | Blue Note | 821261-2
George Lewis And His Original New Orleans Jazzmen
George Lewis In Stockholm,1959 | Dragon | DRCD 221
Jim Robinson's New Orleans Band
Atlantic Jazz: New Orleans | Atlantic | 7567-81700-2

Pavlicek,Arthur | (tp)
Hans Koller Big Band
New York City | MPS | 9813437

Pavlovic,Milo | (tp)
Kenny Clarke-Francy Boland Big Band
Three Latin Adventures | MPS | 529095-2
Stan Getz With The Kurt Edelhagen Orchestra
Stan Getz In Europe | Laserlight | 24657

Paxarino,Javier | (fl,cl,ss,bass-fl,nay,shakuhachi)
Javier Paxarino Group With Glen Velez
Temurá | ACT | 9227-2

Payne,Benny | (p,celestevoc)
Cab Calloway And His Orchestra
Planet Jazz:Cab Calloway | Planet Jazz | 2161237-2

Payne,Bert | (el-gg)
Louis Jordan And His Tympany Five
Louis Jordan-Let The Good Times Roll: The Complete Decca Recordings 1938-1954 | Bear Family Records | BCD 15557 IH
Louis Jordan With The Nelson Riddle Orchestra
Louis Jordan-Let The Good Times Roll: The Complete Decca Recordings 1938-1954 | Bear Family Records | BCD 15557 IH

Payne,Cecil | (as,bsfl)
Bud Powell Orchestra
Bebop | Pablo | PACD 2310978-2
Cannonball Adderley And His Orchestra
Verve Jazz Masters 31:Cannonball Adderley | Verve | 522651-2
Cannonball Adderley Group
Julian 'Cannonball' Adderley | EmArCy | 830381-2
Coleman Hawkins All Star Octet
Body And Soul Revisited | GRP | GRP 16272
Coleman Hawkins All Stars
Verve Jazz Masters 43:Coleman Hawkins | Verve | 521856-2
Count Basie And His Orchestra
Afrique | RCA | 2179618-2
Dinah Washington And Her Orchestra
For Those In Love | EmArCy | 514073-2
Dizzy Gillespie And His Orchestra
Dizzy Gillespie:Pleyel Jazz Concert 1948 + Max Roach Quintet 1949 | Vogue | 21409412
Planet Jazz:Dizzy Gillespie | Planet Jazz | 2152069-2
Planet Jazz:Bebop | RCA | 2169650-2
Don Sickler Orchestra
Tribute To Charlie Parker Vol.2 | Dreyfus Jazz Line | FDM 37015-2
Ella Fitzgerald With The Dizzy Gillespie Orchestra
Ella Fitzgerald:Mr.Paganini | Dreyfus Jazz Line | FDM 36741-2
Ella Fitzgerald With The Hank Jones Trio
Ella Fitzgerald:Mr.Paganini | Dreyfus Jazz Line | FDM 36741-2
James Moody Orchestra
The Blues And Other Colors | Original Jazz Classics | OJCCD 954-2(M 9023)
Jimmy Smith Quartet
Six Views Of The Blues | Blue Note | 521435-2
John Coltrane All Stars
Dakar | Original Jazz Classics | OJC20 393-2(P 7280)
John Coltrane Sextet
The Mal Waldron Memorial Album:Soul Eyes | Prestige | PRCD 11024-2
Kenny Burrell Quintet
Kenny Burrell | Original Jazz Classics | OJCCD 019-2(P 7088)
Kenny Dorham Octet
Afro-Cuban | Blue Note | 0675619
Kenny Dorham Orchestra
Blue Bossa | Blue Note | 795590-2
Kenny Dorham Septet
Cannonball Adderley Birthday Celebration | Fantasy | FANCD 6087-2
Matthew Gee All-Stars
Jazz By Gee! | Original Jazz Classics | OJCCD 1884-2(RLP 221)
Max Roach Septet
The Jazz Life! | Candid | CCD 79019
Prestige All Stars
John Coltrane-The Prestige Recordings | Prestige | 16 PCD 4405-2
Ray Crawford Sextet
Smooth Groove | Candid | CCD 79028
Tadd Dameron And His Orchestra
Fontainebleau | Original Jazz Classics | OJCCD 055-2
Tadd Dameron Tentet
Jazz Profile:Dexter Gordon | Blue Note | 823514-2

Payne,Chris | (tb)
Ronnie Scott And The Band
Live At Ronnie Scott's | CBS | 494439-2

Payne,Don | (b)
Ornette Coleman Quintet
The Music Of Ornette Coleman:Something Else!! | Original Jazz Classics | OJC20 163-2
Stan Getz Quartet
Verve Jazz Masters 53:Stan Getz-Bossa Nova | Verve | 529904-2
Stan Getz-Luiz Bonfa Quartet
Jazz Samba Encore! | Verve | 823613-2
Stan Getz-Luiz Bonfa Quintet
Jazz Samba Encore! | Verve | 823613-2

Payne,Enos | (p)
Craig Bailey Band
A New Journey | Candid | CCD 79725

Payne,Sonny | (dr)
Big Joe Turner With The Count Basie Orchestra
Flip Flop And Fly | Original Jazz Classics | OJCCD 1053-2(2310937)
Count Basie And His Orchestra
Jazz Collection:Count Basie | Laserlight | 24368
The Legends Of Swing | Laserlight | 24659
Atomic Swing | Roulette | 497871-2
Verve Jazz Masters 2:Count Basie | Verve | 519819-2
Count Basie Swings-Joe Williams Sings | Verve | 519852-2
Verve Jazz Masters 20:Introducing | Verve | 519853-2
April In Paris | Verve | 521402-2
Breakfast Dance And Barbecue | Roulette | 531791-2
Basie Meets Bond | Capitol | 538225-2
Basie's Beatle Bag | Verve | 557455-2
One O'Clock Jump | Verve | 559806-2
Chairman Of The Board | Roulette | 581664-2
The Complete Atomic Basie | Roulette | 828635-2
Live at The Sands | Reprise | 9362-45946-2
Count Basie At Newport | Verve | 9861761
Count On The Coast Vol.1 | Phontastic | NCD 7555
Count On The Coast Vol.2 | Phontastic | NCD 7575
Count Basie And The Kansas City 7
Count Basie And The Kansas City 7 | Impulse(MCA) | 951202-2
Count Basie Sextet
Verve Jazz Masters 2:Count Basie | Verve | 519819-2
Duke Ellington And Count Basie With Their Orchestras
First Time! | CBS | CK 65571
Ella Fitzgerald And Joe Williams With The Count Basie Octet
For The Love Of Ella Fitzgerald | Verve | 841765-2
Ella Fitzgerald With The Count Basie Orchestra
Ella Fitzgerald-First Lady Of Song | Verve | 517898-2
Verve Jazz Masters 46:Ella Fitzgerald-The Jazz Sides | Verve | 527655-2
Ella And Basie | Verve | 539059-2
Ella Fitzgerald With The Count Basie Septet
Ella And Basie | Verve | 539059-2
Frank Sinatra With The Count Basie Orchestra
Sinatra-Basie:An Historic Musical First | Reprise | 7599-27023-2
It Might As Well Be Spring | Reprise | 7599-27027-2
Joe Newman And His Band
Jazz In Paris:Joe Newman-Jazz At Midnight-Cootie Williams | EmArCy | 018446-2
Lambert, Hendricks And Ross
Sing A Song Of Basie | Verve | 543827-2
Sarah Vaughan And Joe Williams With The Count Basie Orchestra
Jazz Profile | Blue Note | 823517-2
Sarah Vaughan And The Count Basie Orchestra
Ballads | Roulette | 537561-2
Sarah Vaughan And The Thad Jones Orchestra
Verve Jazz Masters 42:Sarah Vaughan-The Jazz Sides | Verve | 526817-2
Sarah Vaughan With The Count Basie Band
Jazz Profile | Blue Note | 823517-2

Payne,Stanley | (asts)
Billie Holiday With Frankie Newton And His Orchestra
Billie Holiday:The Complete Commodore Recordings | GRP | 543272-2
Billie's Love Songs | Nimbus Records | NI 2000
Willie Bryant And His Orchestra
Planet Jazz:Ben Webster | RCA | 2165368-2

Payton,Nicholas | (tp,fl-h,celesteharpsichord)
Abbey Lincoln With Her Band
Wholly Earth | Verve | 559538-2
Elvin Jones Jazz Machine
Going Home | Enja | ENJ-7095 2
Elvin Jones Quintet
Youngblood | Enja | ENJ-7051 2
Eric Alexander Quintet
Summit Meeting | Milestone | MCD 9322-2
Eric Reed Quintet
Musicale | Impulse(MCA) | 951196-2
Jimmy Smith Sextet
Angel Eyes-Ballads & Slow Jams | Verve | 527632-2
Nicholas Payton Quartet
Gumbo Nouveau | Verve | 531199-2
Nicholas Payton Quintet
Nick@Night | Verve | 547598-2
Payton's Place | Verve | 557327-2
Nicholas Payton Sextet
Gumbo Nouveau | Verve | 531199-2
Payton's Place | Verve | 557327-2
Nicholas Payton With The Mulgrew Miller Trio
Trumpet Legacy | Milestone | MCD 9286-2
Randy Sandke And The New York Allstars
The Re-Discovered Louis And Bix | Nagel-Heyer | CD 058

Paz,Victor | (tpfl-h)
Benny Goodman And His Orchestra
40th Anniversary Concert-Live At Carnegie Hall | London | 820349-2
Verve Jazz Masters 33:Benny Goodman | Verve | 844410-2
Machito And His Orchestra
Afro-Cuban Jazz Moods | Original Jazz Classics | OJC20 447-2

Pazant,Al | (tp)
Pucho & His Latin Soul Brothers
Jazzin' With The Soul Brothers | Fantasy | FANCD 6086-2
Rip A Dip | Milestone | MCD 9247-2

Pazant,Edward | (as,fl,tssax)
Lionel Hampton And His Orchestra
Planet Jazz:Big Bands | Planet Jazz | 2169649-2
Pucho & His Latin Soul Brothers
Rip A Dip | Milestone | MCD 9247-2

Peabody,Paul | (concertmaster,stringsv)
A Band Of Friends
Wynton Marsalis Quartet With Strings | CBS | CK 68921

Peacock,Annette | (p,vocvoice)
Annette Peacock With The Cikada String Quartet
An Acrobat's Heart | ECM | 1733(159496-2)
Marilyn Crispell Trio
Nothing Ever Was,Anyway.Music Of Annette Peacock | ECM | 1626/27(537222-2)

Peacock,Gary | (bb-solo)
Barney Kessel Quartet
Barney Kessel's Swingin' Party At Contemporary | Original Jazz Classics | OJCCD 1066-2(S 7613)
Bill Connors Quartet
Of Mist And Melting | ECM | 1120(847324-2)
Bill Evans Trio
Verve Jazz Masters 5:Bill Evans | Verve | 519821-2
The Complete Bill Evans On Verve | Verve | 527953-2
Trio 64 | Verve | 539058-2
Gary Peacock
Partners | Owl Records | 014730-2
December Poems | ECM | 1119
Gary Peacock Quartet
Voice From The Past-Paradigm | ECM | 1210(517768-2)
Guamba | ECM | 1352
Gary Peacock Trio
Tales Of Another | ECM | 1101(827418-2)
Shift In The Wind | ECM | 1165
Gary Peacock-Jan Garbarek
December Poems | ECM | 1119
Gary Peacock-Ralph Towner
Oracle | ECM | 1490(521350-2)
Gil Evans Orchestra
Verve Jazz Masters 23:Gil Evans | Verve | 521860-2
The Individualism Of Gil Evans | Verve | 833804-2
John Surman Quartet
Adventure Playground | ECM | 1463(511981-2)
Keith Jarrett Trio
Standarts Vol.1 | ECM | 1255(811966-2)
Changes | ECM | 1276(817436-2)
Standards Vol.2 | ECM | 1289(825015-2)
Standards Live | ECM | 1317(827827-2)
Still Live | ECM | 1360/61(835008-2
Changeless | ECM | 1392(839618-2)
Tribute | ECM | 1420/21
The Cure | ECM | 1440(849650-2)
Bye Bye Blackbird | ECM | 1467(513074-2)
At The Deer Head Inn | ECM | 1531(517720-2)
Standards In Norway | ECM | 1542(521717-2)
Keith Jarrett At The Blue Note-The Complete Recordings | ECM | 1575/80(527638-2)
Tokyo '96 | ECM | 1666(539955-2)
Whisper Not | ECM | 1724/25(543813-2)
Inside Out | ECM | 1780(014005-2)
Always Let Me Go | ECM | 1800/01(018766-2)
Marilyn Crispell Trio
Nothing Ever Was,Anyway.Music Of Annette Peacock | ECM | 1626/27(537222-2)
Marilyn Crispell-Gary Peacock-Paul Motian
Amaryllis | ECM | 1742(013400-2)
Markus Stockhausen Quartet
Cosi Lontano...Quasi Dentro | ECM | 1371
Masabumi Kikuchi Trio
Tethered Moon-First Meeting | Winter&Winter | 910016-2
Michel Petrucciani Quartet
Michel Plays Petrucciani | Blue Note | 748679-2
Michel Petrucciani Trio
Michel Plays Petrucciani | Blue Note | 748679-2
Michel Petrucciani:The Blue Note Years | Blue Note | 789916-2
Paul Bley Quartet
In The Evenings Out There | ECM | 1488
Paul Bley Trio
Paul Bley With Gary Peacock | ECM | 1003
Not Two, Not One | ECM | 1670(559447-2)
Paul Bley-Gary Peacock Duet
Partners | Owl Records | 014730-2
Prince Lasha Quartet
The Cry | Original Jazz Classics | OJCCD 1945-2(S 7610)
Prince Lasha Quintet
The Cry | Original Jazz Classics | OJCCD 1945-2(S 7610)
Ralph Towner Quintet
City Of Eyes | ECM | 1388
Ralph Towner-Gary Peacock
A Closer View | ECM | 1602(531623-2)
Tethered Moon
Chansons D'Edith Piaf | Winter&Winter | 910048-2
Tony Williams Lifetime
Lifetime | Blue Note | 499004-2

Peagler,Curtis | (as,ts,voc,ssbs)
Big Joe Turner With The Count Basie Orchestra
Flip Flop And Fly | Original Jazz Classics | OJCCD 1053-2(2310937)
Count Basie And His Orchestra
Count Basie: Salle Pleyel, April 17th, 1972 | Laserlight | 36127
The Modern Jazz Disciples
Disciples Blues | Prestige | PCD 24263-2

Peake,Don | (g)
Donald Byrd Orchestra
Ethiopian Knights | Blue Note | 854328-2

Pearce,John | (p)
Danny Moss Quartet
Keeper Of The Flame | Nagel-Heyer | CD 064
Danny Moss-Roy Williams Quintet
Steamers! | Nagel-Heyer | CD 049
Ellington For Lovers | Nagel-Heyer | NH 1009
Dunstan Coulber Quartet
Standards For A New Century | Nagel-Heyer | CD 081
Jeanie Lambe And The Danny Moss Quartet
The Blue Noise Session | Nagel-Heyer | CD 052
Jim Tomlinson Quintet
Only Trust Your Heart | Candid | CCD 79758
Brazilian Sketches | Candid | CCD 79769
Jim Tomlinson Sextet
Only Trust Your Heart | Candid | CCD 79758
Joe Temperley Quartet
Easy To Remember | Hep | CD 2083
Joe Temperley Quartet With Strings
Easy To Remember | Hep | CD 2083
Joe Temperley Quintet
Easy To Remember | Hep | CD 2083
Joe Temperley Quintet With Strings
Easy To Remember | Hep | CD 2083

Pearl,Rae | (voc)
Tadd Dameron Tentet
Jazz Profile:Dexter Gordon | Blue Note | 823514-2

Pearlman,David | (dobro)
Hans Theessink Group
Journey On | Minor Music | 801062

Pearson,Buddy | (as)
Duke Ellington And His Orchestra
Togo Brava Swuite | Storyville | STCD 8323

Pearson,Duke | (arr,el-p,keyboardsp)
Donald Byrd Orchestra
Blue Break Beats | Blue Note | 799106-2
Donald Byrd Orchestra With Voices
True Blue | Blue Note | 534032-2
The Best Of Blue Note | Blue Note | 796110-2
Donald Byrd Quintet
Blue N' Groovy | Blue Note | 780679-2
Blue Bossa | Blue Note | 795590-2
Donald Byrd Septet + Voices
A New Perspective | Blue Note | 499006-2
Duke Pearson Orchestra
Deep Blue-The United States Of Mind | Blue Note | 521152-2
Blue N' Groovy | Blue Note | 780679-2
Blue Bossa | Blue Note | 795590-2
Duke Pearson Quartet
Sweet Honey Bee | Blue Note | 595974-2
Duke Pearson Quintet
Sweet Honey Bee | Blue Note | 595974-2
Duke Pearson Sextet
Deep Blue-The United States Of Mind | Blue Note | 521152-2
Sweet Honey Bee | Blue Note | 595974-2
Midnight Blue(The [Be]witching Hour) | Blue Note | 854365-2
Dedication! | Original Jazz Classics | OJCCD 1939-2(P 7729)
Grant Green Sextet
Idle Moments | Blue Note | 499003-2
Johnny Coles Sextet
True Blue | Blue Note | 534032-2
Stanley Turrentine And His Orchestra
The Lost Grooves | Blue Note | 831883-2
Stanley Turrentine Orchestra
The Spoiler | Blue Note | 853359-2

Pearson,Henry 'Metathius' | (b)
Rahsaan Roland Kirk Sextet
Atlantic Saxophones | Rhino | 8122-71256-2
Blacknuss | Rhino | 8122-71408-2

Pearson,James | (p)
Ian Shaw With Band
Soho Stories | Milestone | MCD 9316-2

Pearson,Simon | (dr)

INTERPRETENVERZEICHNIS

Steve Martland Band
The Orchestra Of Smith's Academy | Enja | ENJ-9358 2

Peaston,David | (org,voc,ptambourine)
Lester Bowie Group
The Great Pretender | ECM | 1209(829369-2)

Peavey,Sister Lottie | (voc)
Bunk Johnson With The Yerba Buena Jazz Band
Bunk & Lu | Good Time Jazz | GTCD 12024-2

Peck,Bob | (tp)
Bob Crosby And His Orchestra
Swing Legens:Bob Crosby | Nimbus Records | NI 2011
Glenn Miller And His Orchestra
Planet Jazz:Glenn Miller | Planet Jazz | 2152056-2
Woody Herman And His Orchestra
The Legends Of Swing | Laserlight | 24659
Woody Herman:Four Brother | Dreyfus Jazz Line | FDM 36722-2

Peck,Nat | (tb)
Andre Hodeir And His Jazz Group De Paris
Jazz In Paris:Le Jazz Groupe De Paris Joue André Hodeir | EmArCy | 548792-2
Benny Goodman And His Orchestra
Verve Jazz Masters 33:Benny Goodman | Verve | 844410-2
Coleman Hawkins And His Rhythm
Coleman Hawkins/Johnny Hodges:The Vogue Recordings | Vogue | 21559712
Jack Dieval And His Quartet
Americans Swinging In Paris:James Moody | EMI Records | 539653-2
James Moody Boptet
Americans Swinging In Paris:James Moody | EMI Records | 539653-2
Kenny Clarke 8
Americans Swinging In Paris:Kenny Clarke | EMI Records | 539652-2
Kenny Clarke And His Orchestra
Americans Swinging In Paris:James Moody | EMI Records | 539653-2
Kenny Clarke Quintet
Jazz In Paris:Kenny Clarke Sextet Plays André Hodair | EmArCy | 834542-2 PMS
Kenny Clarke-Francy Boland Big Band
Clark-Boland Big Band: TNP, October 29th, 1969 | Laserlight | 36129
Three Latin Adventures | MPS | 529095-2
More Smiles | MPS | 9814789
All Smiles | MPS | 9814790
Francy Boland-Fellini 712 | MPS | 9814805
NDR-Workshop
Doldinger's Best | ACT | 9224-2

Pecoits,Conrado | (p,el-pvoice)
Raiz De Pedra
Diario De Bordo | TipToe | TIP-888822 2

Pecori,Carlo | (b)
Django Reinhardt And The Quintet Du Hot Club De France
Planet Jazz:Stephane Grappelli | RCA | 2165366-2
Quintet Du Hot Club De France
Djangology | Bluebird | 2663957-2
Django/Django In Rome 1949-1050 | BGO Records | BGOCD 366

Pedersen,Guy | (b)
Daniel Humair Soultet
Jazz In Paris | EmArCy | 548793-2
Earl Hines Trio
Jazz In Paris:Earl Hines-Paris One Night Stand | EmArCy | 548207-2 PMS
Elek Bacsik Quartet
Jazz In Paris:Elek Baczik | EmArCy | 542231-2
Elek Bacsik Trio
Jazz In Paris:Elek Baczik | EmArCy | 542231-2
Jean-Luc Ponty Quartet
Jazz In Paris:Jean-Luc Ponty-Jazz Long Playing | EmArCy | 548150-2 PMS
Lionel Hampton All Stars
Jazz In Paris:Lionel Hampton And His French New Sound Vol.1 | EmArCy | 549405-2 PMS
Jazz In Paris:Lionel Hampton And His French New Sound Vol.2 | EmArCy | 549406-2 PMS
Michel Legrand Trio
Jazz In Paris:Michel Legrand-Paris Jazz Piano | EmArCy | 548148-2 PMS
Stephane Grappelli Quartet
Jazz In Paris:Stephane Grappelli-Django | EmArCy | 018421-1
Stephane Grappelli Quintet
Grapelli Story | Verve | 515807-2
Feeling + Finesse = Jazz | Atlantic | 7567-90140-2
Swingle Singers
Jazz Sebastian Bach Vol.2 | Philips | 542553-2
Swingle Singers Singing Mozart | Philips | 548538-2
Swingling Telemann | Philips | 586735-2
Swingle Singers Getting Romantic | Philips | 586736-2

Pedersen,Hans Leonardo | (cl,assax)
Leonardo Pedersen's Jazzkapel
The Golden Years Of Revival Jazz,Sampler | Storyville | 109 1001

Pedersen,Helle Charlotte | (voc)
Marilyn Mazur With Ars Nova And The Copenhagen Art Ensemble
Jordsange | dacapo | DCCD 9454

Pedersen,Henrik Bolberg | (tpfl-h)
Mona Larsen And The Danish Radio Big Band Plus Soloists
Michael Mantler:Cerco Un Paese Innocente | ECM | 1556
The Danish Radio Jazz Orchestra
Nice Work | dacapo | DCCD 9446

Pedersen,Henrik Gunde | (p)
The Orchestra
New Skies | dacapo | DCCD 9463

Pedersen,Leif Arne | (cl)
Terje Rypdal With The Borealis Ensemble
Q.E.D. | ECM | 1474

Pedersen,Leonardo | (clas)
Leonardo Pedersen's Jazzkapel
The Golden Years Of Revival Jazz,Vol.11 | Storyville | STCD 5516

Pedersen,Nikolai Begelund | (tb)
The Orchestra
New Skies | dacapo | DCCD 9463

Pederson,Pullman 'Tommy' | (tb)
Anita O'Day With Gene Krupa And His Orchestra
Let Me Off Uptown:Anita O'Day With Gene Krupa | CBS | CK 65625
Anita O'Day With The Billy May Orchestra
Verve Jazz Masters 49:Anita O'Day | Verve | 527653-2
Benny Carter And His Orchestra
Aspects | Capitol | 852677-2
Billy May And His Orchestra
Billy May's Big Fat Brass/Bill's Bag | Capitol | 535206-2
Ella Fitzgerald With The Nelson Riddle Orchestra
The Best Of The Song Books:The Ballads | Verve | 521867-2
Get Happy! | Verve | 523321-2
Oh Lady Be Good:The Best Of The Gershwin Songbook | Verve | 529581-2
Love Songs:The Best Of The Song Books | Verve | 531762-2
Ella Fitzgerald Sings The Johnny Mercer Songbook | Verve | 539057-2
June Christy With The Pete Rugolo Orchestra
Something Cool(The Complete Mono & Stereo Versions) | Capitol | 534069-2
Mel Tormé With The Billy May Orchestra
Mel Tormé Goes South Of The Border With Billy May | Verve | 589517-2
Mel Tormé With The Russell Garcia Orchestra
Swingin' On The Moon | Verve | 511385-2
Nat King Cole With The Billy May Orchestra
Nat King Cole:For Sentimental Reasons | Dreyfus Jazz Line | FDM 36740-2
Van Alexander Orchestra
Home Of Happy Feet/Swing! Staged For Sound! | Capitol | 535211-2

Pedone,Antonio | (bs)
Orchestra Jazz Siciliana
Orchestra Jazz Siciliana Plays The Music Of Carla Bley | Watt | XtraWatt/4

Pedone,Pietro | (tp)

Pedretti,Jean-Jacques | (tb)
Michel Wintsch & Road Movie
Michel Wintsch & Road Movie featuring Gerry Hemingway | Between The Lines | btl 002(Efa 10172-2)

Pedroso,Miguel | (voc)
Lazaro Ros Con Mezcla
Cantos | Intuition Records | INT 3080-2

Peel,Jerry | (fr-h)
George Gruntz Concert Jazz Band
Blues 'N Dues Et Cetera | Enja | ENJ-6072 2

Peeples,William | (dr)
Ray Charles Trio
Rhino Presents The Atlantic Jazz Gallery | Atlantic | 8122-71257-2

Peer,Beverley | (b)
Ella Fitzgerald And Her Famous Orchestra
The Radio Years 1940 | Jazz Unlimited | JUCD 2065
Ella Fitzgerald And Her Orchestra
Jazz Collection:Ella Fitzgerald | Laserlight | 24397
Ella Fitzgerald With The Chick Webb Orchestra
Jazz Collection:Ella Fitzgerald | Laserlight | 24397
Mildred Bailey With The Ellis Larkins Trio
Planet Jazz:Female Jazz Vocalists | Planet Jazz | 2169656-2

Peet,Wayne | (org,synth,clavinet,p,keyboards)
Alex Cline Group
The Lamp And The Star | ECM | 1372
Vinny Golia Quintet
Regards From Norma Desmond | Fresh Sound Records | FSNT 008 CD

Peeters,Arthur | (b)
Django Reinhardt With Stan Brenders Et Son Grand Orchestre
Verve Jazz Masters 38:Django Reinhardt | Verve | 516931-2

Peeters-Goossens,G.F. | (viola)
Toots Thielemans And His Orchestra
Verve Jazz Masters Vol.59:Toots Thielemans | Verve | 535271-2

Pege,Aladar | (b)
Mihaly Tabany Orchestra
Jubilee Edition | double moon | CHRDM 71020

Pehlke,Wolf | (writer:letters from Paris)
Alfred 23 Harth Group
Sweet Paris | free flow music | ffm 0291

Peier,Marius | (perc)
Peter A. Schmid Trio With Guests
Profound Sounds In An Empty Reservoir | Creative Works Records | CW CD 1033

Peiffer,Bernard | (pp-solo)
Bernard Peiffer Trio
Jazz In Paris:The Bernard Peiffer Trio Plays Standards | EmArCy | 018425-2
Bill Coleman And His Orchestra
Don Byas:Laura | Dreyfus Jazz Line | FDM 36714-2
Bill Coleman Quintet
Americans Swinging In Paris:Don Byas | EMI Records | 539655-2
Don Byas Quartet
Americans Swinging In Paris:Don Byas | EMI Records | 539655-2
Don Byas:Laura | Dreyfus Jazz Line | FDM 36714-2

Peil,Roland | (bongos,skaker,perc,dr,keyboards)
Cafe Du Sport Jazzquartett
Cafe Du Sport Jazzquartett | Minor Music | 801096
Dirk Raulf Group
Theater I (Bühnenmusik) | Poise | Poise 07
Jens Winther And The WDR Big Band
The Escape | dacapo | DCCD 9437
Kodexx Sentimental
Das Digitale Herz | Poise | Poise 02
Matthias Petzold Working Band
Elements | Indigo-Records | 1005 CD
Reiner Witzel Group
Passage To The Ear | Nabel Records:Jazz Network | CD 4668
Scetches
Different Places | VeraBra Records | CDVBR 2102-2

Pejakovic,Branko | (b)
Jenny Evans And Her Quintet
Shiny Stockings | Enja | ENJ-9317 2
Shiny Stockings | ESM Records | ESM 9305
Jenny Evans And The Rudi Martini Quartet
At Lloyd's | ESM Records | ESM 9302
Jutta Hipp Quintet
Deutsches Jazz Fesival 1954/1955 | Bear Family Records | BCD 15430

Pelc,Josef | (tb)
Hans Koller Big Band
New York City | MPS | 9813437

Pellegrini,Al | (pld)
Mel Tormé With The Billy May Orchestra
Mel Tormé Goes South Of The Border With Billy May | Verve | 589517-2

Pelletier,Jean-Claude | (cond,orgp)
Guy Lafitte-Peanuts Holland And Their Orchestra
Jazz In Paris:Guy Lafitte-Blue And Sentimental | EmArCy | 159852-2 PMS

Pellitteri,Marcello | (dr)
David Klein Quintet
My Marilyn | Enja | ENJ-9422 2
Vic Juris-John Etheridge Quartet
Bohemia | Jazzpoint | JP 1023 CD

Pelt,Jeremy | (tpfl-h)
Mingus Big Band
Tonight At Noon...Three Or Four Shades Of Love | Dreyfus Jazz Line | FDM 36633-2
Wayne Escoffery Quintet
Intuition | Nagel-Heyer | CD 2038

Pelton,Slawn | (dr)
The Brecker Brothers
Out Of The Loop | GRP | GRP 97842

Pelzer,Jacques | (as,flss)
Rene Thomas Quintet
Jazz In Paris:René Thomas-Meeting Mister Thomas | EmArCy | 549812-2

Pemberton,Bill | (b)
Lucy Reed With Orchestra
This Is Lucy Reed | Original Jazz Classics | OJCCD 1943-2(F 3243)

Pena,John | (bel-b)
Joe Sample Group
Spellbound | Rhino | 81273726-2

Pena,Ralph | (b)
Anita O'Day With The Billy May Orchestra
Verve Jazz Masters 49:Anita O'Day | Verve | 527653-2
George Shearing And His Quintet
The Swingin's Mutual | Capitol | 799190-2
Jimmy Giuffre 3
The Jimmy Giuffre Three | Atlantic | 7567-90981-2
Mel Tormé With The Billy May Orchestra
Mel Tormé Goes South Of The Border With Billy May | Verve | 589517-2
Mel Tormé With The Russell Garcia Orchestra
Swingin' On The Moon | Verve | 511385-2
Nancy Wilson With George Shearing And His Quintet
The Swingin's Mutual | Capitol | 799190-2
Shelly Manne And His Men
Vol.1:The West Coast Sound | Original Jazz Classics | OJCCD 152-2
The Jazz Giants Play Harry Warren:Lullaby Of Broadway | Prestige | PCD 24204-2

Pendarvis,Leon | (el-p,keyboards,ld,porg)
Ron Carter Group
Songs For You | Milestone | MCD 47099-2

Pendzialek,Alfred | (tb)
Bernd Konrad With Erwin Lehn und sein Südfunk Orchester Stuttgart
Wen Die Götter Lieben | Creative Works Records | CW CD 1010-1

Penland,Ralph | (drperc)
Freddie Hubbard Quintet
This Is Jazz:Freddie Hubbard | CBS | CK 65041

George Cables Trio
By George | Original Jazz Classics | OJCCD 1056-2(C 14030)

Penman,Matt | (b)
Chris Cheek Quintet
Vine | Fresh Sound Records | FSNT 086 CD

Penn,Andrew | (tb)
Lionel Hampton And His Orchestra
Lionel Hampton:Flying Home | Dreyfus Jazz Line | FDM 36735-2

Penn,Clarence | (dr)
Dave Douglas Group
The Infinite | RCA | 2663918-2
Jimmy Scott With Band
Over The Rainbow | Milestone | MCD 9314-2
Moon Glow | Milestone | MCD 9332-2
Joshua Redman Trio
Joshua Redman | Warner | 9362-45242-2
Makoto Ozone Group
Treasure | Verve | 021906-2
Makoto Ozone Trio
Pandora | Verve | 549629-2
Melissa Walker And Her Band
I Saw The Sky | Enja | ENJ-9409 2
Paquito D'Rivera Group With The Absolute Ensemble
Habanera | Enja | ENJ-9395 2

Penner,Ed | (b,tubabass-sax)
Firehouse Five Plus Two
Goes South | Good Time Jazz | GTCD 12018-2

Penner,Ralph | (b)
Billy May And His Orchestra
Billy May's Big Fat Brass/Bill's Bag | Capitol | 535206-2

Penque,Romeo | (alto-fl,recorder,as,b-cl,ts,bs,cl)
Bill Evans Quartet With Orchestra
The Complete Bill Evans On Verve | Verve | 527953-2
From Left To Right | Verve | 557451-2
Bill Evans With Orchestra
The Complete Bill Evans On Verve | Verve | 527953-2
From Left To Right | Verve | 557451-2
Billie Holiday With The Ray Ellis Orchestra
Lady In Satin | CBS | CK 65144
Charles Mingus And His Orchestra
The Complete Town Hall Concert | Blue Note | 828353-2
Coleman Hawkins With Many Albam And His Orchestra
Planet Jazz:Coleman Hawkins | Planet Jazz | 2152055-2
Freddie Hubbard With Orchestra
This Is Jazz:Freddie Hubbard | CBS | CK 65041
Gato Barbieri Group
Planet Jazz:Gato Barbieri | RCA | 2165364-2
Gato Barbieri:The Best Of The Early Years | RCA | 2663523-2
George Benson With The Don Sebesky Orchestra
Verve Jazz Masters 21:George Benson | Verve | 521861-2
Grant Green With Orchestra
The Final Comedown(Soundtrack) | Blue Note | 581678-2
Herbie Hancock Orchestra
Herbie Hancock:The Complete Blue Note Sixties Sessions | Blue Note | 495569-2
The Prisoner | Blue Note | 525649-2
Jimmy Smith With The Oliver Nelson Orchestra
Verve Jazz Masters 29:Jimmy Smith | Verve | 521855-2
Jimmy Smith:Best Of The Verve Years | Verve | 527950-2
Joe Williams With The Frank Hunter Orchestra
Planet Jazz:Joe Williams | Planet Jazz | 2165370-2
Joe Williams,With The Oliver Nelson Orchestra
Planet Jazz:Joe Williams | Planet Jazz | 2165370-2
King Curtis Band
King Curtis-Blow Man Blow | Bear Family Records | BCD 15670 CI
Lena Horne With The Lennie Hayton Orchestra
Planet Jazz:Lena Horne | Planet Jazz | 2165373-2
Leon Thomas With Orchestra
Spirits Known And Unknown | RCA | 2663876-2
Louis Armstrong With Gordon Jenkins And His Orchestra And Choir
Satchmo In Style | Verve | 549594-2
Louis Armstrong With The Gordon Jenkins Orchestra
Ambassador Louis Armstrong Vol.17:Moments To Remember(1952-1956) | Ambassador | CLA 1917
Lucy Reed With Orchestra
This Is Lucy Reed | Original Jazz Classics | OJCCD 1943-2(F 3243)
Miles Davis + 19
Miles Ahead | CBS | CK 65121
Miles Davis With Gil Evans & His Orchestra
Miles Davis At Carnegie Hall | CBS | CK 65027
This Is Jazz:Miles Davis Plays Ballads | CBS | CK 65038
Porgy And Bess | CBS | CK 65141
Sketches Of Spain | CBS | CK 65142
Quiet Nights | CBS | CK 65293
Milt Jackson And His Orchestra
Sunflower | CTI | ZK 65131
Paul Desmond With Strings
Planet Jazz:Paul Desmond | Planet Jazz | 2152061-2
Desmond Blue | RCA | 2663898-2
Phil Woods Quartet With Orchestra & Strings
Round Trip | Verve | 559804-2
Quincy Jones And His Orchestra
Talkin' Verve-Roots Of Acid Jazz:Roland Kirk | Verve | 533101-2
Rahsaan/The Complete Mercury Recordings Of Roland Kirk | Mercury | 846630-2
Stan Getz With The Gary McFarland Orchestra
Stan Getz Highlights:The Best Of The Verve Years Vol.2 | Verve | 517330-2
Verve Jazz Masters 53:Stan Getz-Bossa Nova | Verve | 529904-2
Big Band Bossa Nova | Verve | 825771-2 PMS
Stan Getz Highlights | Verve | 847430-2
Wes Montgomery With The Oliver Nelson Orchestra
Verve Jazz Masters 14:Wes Montgomery | Verve | 519826-2
Wes Montgomery:The Verve Jazz Sides | Verve | 521690-2
Talkin' Jazz:Roots Of Acid Jazz | Verve | 529580-2

Pentoja Leite,Riqué | (el-p)
Chet Baker & The Boto Brasilian Quartet
Chet Baker & The Boto Brasilian Quartet | Dreyfus Jazz Line | FDM 36511-9

Pepito,Rietria | (perc)
Dizzy Gillespie Sextet
Verve Jazz Masters 10:Dizzy Gillespie | Verve | 516319-2

Pepl,Harry | (g,g-synthp)
Austria Drei
Jazz Portraits | EGO | 95080
Enrico Rava-Dino Saluzzi Quintet
Volver | ECM | 1343
Harry Pepl/Herbert Joos/Jon Christensen
Cracked Mirrors | ECM | 1356

Peplowski,Ken | (cl,as,tsdir)
Allan Vaché Swingtet
Ellington For Lovers | Nagel-Heyer | NH 1009
Allan Vaché-Antti Sarpila & 1 Sextet
Summit Meeting | Nagel-Heyer | CD 027
David Ostwald's Gully Low Jazz Band
Blues In Your Heart | Nagel-Heyer | CD 051
George Masso Quintet
The First Sampler | Nagel-Heyer | NHR SP 5
George Masso-Ken Peplowski Quintet
Just Friends | Nagel-Heyer | CD 5001
International Allstars
The International Allstars Play Benny Goodman:Vol.1 | Nagel-Heyer | CD 025
The Second Sampler | Nagel-Heyer | NHR SP 6
Ken Peplowski Quartet
Lost In The Stars | Nagel-Heyer | CD 2020
Randy Sandke And The New York Allstars
The Re-Discovered Louis And Bix | Nagel-Heyer | CD 058

Randy Sandke-Dick Hyman
The Re-Discovered Louis And Bix | Nagel-Heyer | CD 058
The International Allstars
The International Allstars Play Benny Goodman Vol.1 | Nagel-Heyer | CD 045
The Nagel-Heyer Allstars
Uptown Lowdown:A Jazz Salute To The Big Apple | Nagel-Heyer | CD 2004
The New York Allstars
Broadway | Nagel-Heyer | CD 003
One Two Three | Nagel-Heyer | CD 008
Randy Sandke Meets Bix Beiderbecke | Nagel-Heyer | CD 3002
The First Sampler | Nagel-Heyer | NHR SP 5

Pepper,Art | (as,bs,ts,as-solo,clfl)
Art Pepper
Art Pepper:The Complete Galaxy Recordings | Galaxy | 16GCD 1016-2
Art Pepper Plus Eleven
Art Pepper + Eleven | Contemporary | CSA 7568-6
Modern Jazz Classics | Original Jazz Classics | OJC20 341-2
Art Pepper Quartet
Art Pepper:The Complete Galaxy Recordings | Galaxy | 16GCD 1016-2
Art 'N' Zoot | Pablo | 2310957-2
The Art Of Saxophone | Laserlight | 24652
Art Pepper:The Complete Village Vanguard Sessions | Contemporary | 9CCD-4417-2
San Francisco Samba | Contemporary | CCD 14086-2
Renascene | Galaxy | GCD 4202-2
Art Pepper Meets The Rhythm Section | Original Jazz Classics | OJC20 338-2
Gettin' Together | Original Jazz Classics | OJCCD 169-2
Intensity | Original Jazz Classics | OJCCD 387-2
The Way It Is | Original Jazz Classics | OJCCD 389-2
Living Legend | Original Jazz Classics | OJCCD 408-2
No Limit | Original Jazz Classics | OJCCD 411-2
Straight Life | Original Jazz Classics | OJCCD 475-2
Arthur's Blues | Original Jazz Classics | OJCCD 680-2
Thursday Night At The Village Vanguard | Original Jazz Classics | OJCCD 694-2(7642)
Friday Night At The Village Vanguard | Original Jazz Classics | OJCCD 695-2(C 7643)
Saturday Night At The Village Vanguard | Original Jazz Classics | OJCCD 696-2(C 7644)
Roadgame | Original Jazz Classics | OJCCD 774-2(GXY 5142)
The Jazz Giants Play Harold Arlen:Blues In The Night | Prestige | PCD 24201-2
The Jazz Giants Play Jerome Kern:Yesterdays | Prestige | PCD 24202-2
The Jazz Giants Play Cole Porter:Night And Day | Prestige | PCD 24203-2
The Jazz Giants Play Harry Warren:Lullaby Of Broadway | Prestige | PCD 24204-2
Art Pepper Quintet
Art Pepper:The Complete Galaxy Recordings | Galaxy | 16GCD 1016-2
Smack Up | Original Jazz Classics | OJC20 176-2
Gettin' Together | Original Jazz Classics | OJCCD 169-2
Straight Life | Original Jazz Classics | OJCCD 475-2
Art Pepper Quintet With Strings
Art Pepper:The Complete Galaxy Recordings | Galaxy | 16GCD 1016-2
Winter Moon | Original Jazz Classics | OJC20 677-2(GXY 5140)
Art Pepper Trio
Art Pepper:The Complete Galaxy Recordings | Galaxy | 16GCD 1016-2
Art Pepper With The Duke Jordan Trio
Art Pepper With Duke Jordan In Copenhagen 1981 | Galaxy | 2GCD 8201-2
Art Pepper-George Cables Duo
Art Pepper:The Complete Galaxy Recordings | Galaxy | 16GCD 1016-2
Jazzin' Vol.2: The Music Of Stevie Wonder | Fantasy | FANCD 6088-2
Tete-A-Tete | Original Jazz Classics | OJCCD 843-2(GXY 5147)
Art Pepper-Ron Carter Duo
Art Pepper:The Complete Galaxy Recordings | Galaxy | 16GCD 1016-2
Art Pepper-Warne Marsh Quintet
The Way It Is | Original Jazz Classics | OJCCD 389-2
Art Pepper-Zoot Sims Quintet
Art 'N' Zoot | Pablo | 2310957-2
Bill Watrous And His West Coast Friends
Art Pepper:The Hollywood All-Star Sessions | Galaxy | 5GCD 4431-2
Chet Baker Big Band
The Best Of Chet Baker Plays | Pacific Jazz | 797161-2
Chet Baker Sextet
The Best Of Chet Baker Plays | Pacific Jazz | 797161-2
Chet Baker-Art Pepper-Phil Urso Sextet
Picture Of Heath | Pacific Jazz | 494106-2
Henry Mancini And His Orchestra
Combo! | RCA | 2147794-2
Jack Sheldon And His West Coast Friends
Art Pepper:The Hollywood All-Star Sessions | Galaxy | 5GCD 4431-2
Lee Konitz And His West Coast Friends
Art Pepper:The Hollywood All-Star Sessions | Galaxy | 5GCD 4431-2
Nat King Cole Quartet With The Stan Kenton Orchestra
Nat King Cole:For Sentimental Reasons | Dreyfus Jazz Line | FDM 36740-2
Pete Jolly And His West Coast Friends
Art Pepper:The Hollywood All-Star Sessions | Galaxy | 5GCD 4431-2
Shelly Manne And His Hollywood All Stars
Art Pepper:The Hollywood All-Star Sessions | Galaxy | 5GCD 4431-2
Shorty Rogers And His Giants
PLanet Jazz:Shorty Rogers | Planet Jazz | 2159976-2
Shorty Rogers And His Orchestra Feat. The Giants
PLanet Jazz:Shorty Rogers | Planet Jazz | 2159976-2
Sonny Stitt And His West Coast Friends
Art Pepper:The Hollywood All-Star Sessions | Galaxy | 5GCD 4431-2
Stan Kenton And His Orchestra
Stan Kenton Portraits On Standards | Capitol | 531571-2
One Night Stand | Choice | CHCD 71051
Warne Marsh Quintet With Art Pepper
Jazz Of Two Cities | Fresh Sound Records | FSR-CD 342

Pepper,Floy | (narration)
Gunther Schuller With The WDR Radio Orchestra & Rememberance Band
Witchi Tia To, The Music Of Jim Pepper | Tutu Records | 888204-2*

Pepper,Jack | (v)
Cal Tjader With The Clare Fischer Orchestra
Cal Tjader Plays Harold Arlen & West Side Story | Fantasy | FCD 24775-2
Pete Rugolo And His Orchestra
Thriller/Richard Diamon(Original Jazz Scores From 2 Classics TV Series) | Fresh Sound Records | FSCD 2015

Pepper,Jim | (fl,ss,ts,vocperc)
Charlie Haden Orchestra
The Ballad Of The Fallen | ECM | 1248(811546-2)
Gordon Lee Quartet feat. Jim Pepper
Landwhales In New York | Tutu Records | 888136-2*
Jim Pepper & Eagle Wing
Remembrance-Live At The International Jazzfestival Münster | Tutu Records | 888152-2*
Jim Pepper Flying Eagle
Live At New Morning,Paris | Tutu Records | 888194-2*
Jim Pepper Quartet
West End Avenue | Nabel Records:Jazz Network | CD 4633
Mal Waldron & Jim Pepper
Art Of The Duo | Tutu Records | 888106-2*
Mal Waldron Quartet feat. Jim Pepper
The Git-Go At Utopia,Volume Two | Tutu Records | 888148-2*
Mal Waldron Quartet feat.Jim Pepper
Mal, Dance And Soul | Tutu Records | 888102-2*
Quadrologue At Utopia Vol.1 | Tutu Records | 888118-2*
Marty Cook Group feat. Jim Pepper
Internationales Jazzfestival Münster | Tutu Records | 888110-2*
Red,White,Black & Blue | Tutu Records | 888174-2*

Peraza,Armando | (bongos,congasperc)
Cal Tjader Group
Verve Jazz Masters 39:Cal Tjader | Verve | 521858-2
Verve Jazz Masters Vol.60:The Collection | Verve | 529866-2
Cal Tjader Quintet
Talkin Verve/Roots Of Acid Jazz:Cal Tjader | Verve | 531562-2
Soul Bird | Verve | 549111-2
Cal Tjader Septet
Talkin Verve/Roots Of Acid Jazz:Cal Tjader | Verve | 531562-2
Cal Tjader Sextet
Talkin Verve/Roots Of Acid Jazz:Cal Tjader | Verve | 531562-2
Soul Bird | Verve | 549111-2
Cal Tjader's Orchestra
Verve Jazz Masters 39:Cal Tjader | Verve | 521858-2
Talkin Verve/Roots Of Acid Jazz:Cal Tjader | Verve | 531562-2
George Shearing And His Quintet
Verve Jazz Masters 57:George Shearing | Verve | 529900-2
Beauty And The Beat | Capitol | 542308-2
The Swingin's Mutual | Capitol | 799190-2
George Shearing Sextet
At Newport | Pablo | PACD 5315-2
George Shearing With The Montgomery Brothers
Wes Montgomery-The Complete Riverside Recordings | Riverside | 12 RCD 4408-2
George Shearing And The Montgomery Brothers | Original Jazz Classics | OJCCD 040-2
Nancy Wilson With George Shearing And His Quintet
The Swingin's Mutual | Capitol | 799190-2
Peggy Lee With George Shearing
Beauty And The Beat | Capitol | 542308-2
Victor Feldman Orchestra
Latinsville | Contemporary | CCD 9005-2

Perciful,Jack | (p)
Harry James And His Orchestra
Trumpet Blues:The Best Of Harry James | Capitol | 521224-2

Pereira,Domingo | (berimbau)
Raiz De Pedra
Diario De Bordo | TipToe | TIP-888822 2

Pereira,Ray | (bells,congas,percclaps)
Vince Jones Group
It All Ends Up In Tears | Intuition Records | INT 3069-2
Here's To The Miracles | Intuition Records | INT 3198-2
Vince Jones Septet
On The Brink Of It | Intuition Records | INT 3068-2

Perella,Harry | (p)
Paul Whiteman And His Orchestra
Planet Jazz:Jazz Trumpet | Planet Jazz | 2169654-2

Peress,Maurice | (cond)
Modern Jazz Quartet And Symphony Orchestra
MJQ 40 | Atlantic | 7567-82330-2

Perett,Judy | (cello)
Ella Fitzgerald With Orchestra
The Best Is Yet To Come | Original Jazz Classics | OJCCD 889-2(2312138)

Pereyra,Norberto | (g)
Jazzensemble Des Hessischen Rundfunks
Atmosphering Conditions Permitting | ECM | 1549/50

Pérez,Alain | (bvoc)
Lewis Trio With Guests
Battangó | Intuition Records | INN 1101-2

Perez,Alejandro | (ssts)
Joaquin Chacón Group
San | Fresh Sound Records | FSNT 015 CD

Perez,Cesar | (tb)
Conexion Latina
Mambo Nights | Enja | ENJ-9402 2

Pérez,Daniel 'Dani' | (g)
Dani Perez Quartet
Buenos Aires-Barcelona Connections | Fresh Sound Records | FSNT 144 CD
David Xirgu Quartet
Idolents | Fresh Sound Records | FSNT 077 CD
Gorka Benitez Quintet
Gorka Benitez Trio | Fresh Sound Records | FSNT 073 CD
Orquestra De Cambra Teatre Lliure
Tributes To Duke Ellington | Fresh Sound Records | FSNT 084 CD

Perez,Danilo | (p,harmonium,p-solosynth)
Danilo Perez
Panamonk | Impulse(MCA) | 951190-2
Central Avenue | Impulse(MCA) | 951281-2
Danilo Perez Group
Central Avenue | Impulse(MCA) | 951281-2
Danilo Perez Quartet
Panamonk | Impulse(MCA) | 951190-2
Danilo Perez Trio
Central Avenue | Impulse(MCA) | 951281-2
Dizzy Gillespie And The United Nation Orchestra
7.Zelt-Musik-Festival:Jazz Events | Zounds | CD 2730001
Roy Haynes Trio
The Roy Haynes Trio | Verve | 543534-2
Tom Harrell Quintet
Form | Contemporary | CCD 14059-2
Visions | Contemporary | CCD 14063-2
Tom Harrell Sextet
Visions | Contemporary | CCD 14063-2
Wayne Shorter Quartet
Footprints Live! | Verve | 589679-2
Wynton Marsalis Group
Standard Time Vol.6:Mr.Jelly Lord | CBS | CK 69872

Pérez,Gabriel | (cl,sax,flkeyboards)
Gabriel Pérez Group
La Chipaca | Green House Music | CD 1011
Alfonsina | Jazz 4 Ever Records:Jazz Network | J4E 4751
Tomatic 7
Haupstrom | Jazz Haus Musik | JHM 0101 CD

Perez,Jerry | (g)
John Lee Hooker Group
Endless Boogie | MCA | MCD 10413

Perez,Luis | (bongoscongas)
Eddie Lockjaw Davis-Shirley Scott Sextet
Bacalao | Original Jazz Classics | OJCCD 1090-2(P 7178)

Perez,Ramon Garcia | (perccongas)
Steve Coleman And The Council Of Balance
Genesis & The Opening Of The Way | RCA | 2152934-2

Perez,Raymond | (guiro)
Paquito D'Rivera Orchestra
Jazzrock-Anthology Vol.3:Fusion | Zounds | CD 27100555

Perez,Tomas | (ld,b,coroperc)
Conexion Latina
Mambo 2000 | Enja | ENJ-7055 2
Mambo Nights | Enja | ENJ-9402 2

Perfido,Peter | (dr)
Geoff Goodman Quintet
Naked Eye | Tutu Records | 888214-2*
Marty Cook Quintet
Marty Cook Trio/Quintet | Tutu Records | 888210-2*
Nicolas Simion Quartet feat. Tomasz Stanko
Viaggio Imaginario | Tutu Records | 888192-2*
Nicolas Simion Trio
Back To The Roots | Tutu Records | 888176-2

Peric |
Vasilic Nenad Balkan Band
Joe-Jack | Nabel Records:Jazz Network | CD 4693

Periera,Ray | (perc)
Vince Jones Group
Tell Me A Secret | Intuition Records | INT 3072-2
Future Girl | Intuition Records | INT 3109-2

Peris,Charles | (b-fl)
Peter A. Schmid Trio With Guests
Profound Sounds In An Empty Reservoir | Creative Works Records | CW CD 1033

Perissi,Richard 'Dick' | (fr-h)
Billy May And His Orchestra
Billy May's Big Fat Brass/Bill's Bag | Capitol | 535206-2
Cal Tjader With The Clare Fischer Orchestra
Cal Tjader Plays Harold Arlen & West Side Story | Fantasy | FCD 24775-2
Ella Fitzgerald With The Nelson Riddle Orchestra
Ella Fitzgerald Sings The Johnny Mercer Songbook | Verve | 539057-2
Miles Davis With Gil Evans & His Orchestra
Quiet Nights | CBS | CK 65293
Pete Rugolo And His Orchestra
Thriller/Richard Diamon(Original Jazz Scores From 2 Classics TV Series) | Fresh Sound Records | FSCD 2015

Perkins,Bill | (alto-fl,ss,as,ts,b-cl,bs,bj,cl,fl)
Anita O'Day With The Bill Holman Orchestra
Verve Jazz Masters 49:Anita O'Day | Verve | 527653-2
Annie Ross With Her Quintet
Misty Blue:Sweet Sisters Swing Songs Of Sorrow And Sadness | Blue Note | 521151-2
Art Pepper Plus Eleven
Art Pepper + Eleven | Contemporary | CSA 7568-6
Modern Jazz Classics | Original Jazz Classics | OJC20 341-2
Benny Carter And His Orchestra
Further Definitions/Additions To Further Definotions | Impulse(MCA) | 951229-2
Bill Perkins Quartet
Swing Spring | Candid | CCD 79752
Bill Perkins Quintet
Swing Spring | Candid | CCD 79752
Bill Perkins-Bud Shank Quintet
The Jazz Giants Play Harold Arlen:Blues In The Night | Prestige | PCD 24201-2
Bill Perkins-Richie Kamuca Quintet
Midnight Blue(The [Be]witching Hour) | Blue Note | 854365-2
Bud Shank Sextet
New Gold! | Candid | CCD 79707
Chet Baker Big Band
The Best Of Chet Baker Plays | Pacific Jazz | 797161-2
Diane Schuur With Orchestra
The Best Of Diane Schuur | GRP | GRP 98882
Dizzy Gillespie And His Orchestra
Talking Verve:Dizzy Gillespie | Verve | 533846-2
Ella Fitzgerald With The Marty Paich Orchestra
Ella Fitzgerald-First Lady Of Song | Verve | 517898-2
Whisper Not | Verve | 589947-2
Jackie Cain-Roy Kral Group
Full Circle | Fantasy | FCD 24768-2
June Christy With The Shorty Rogers Orchestra
June Christy Big Band Special | Capitol | 498319-2
Lennie Niehaus Sextet
Lennie Niehaus Vol.5:The Sextet | Original Jazz Classics | OJCCD 1944-2(C 3524)
Peggy Lee With The Quincy Jones Orchestra
Blues Cross Country | Capitol | 520088-2
Singers Unlimited With The Clare Fischer Orchestra
The Singers Unlimited:Magic Voices | MPS | 539130-2
Stan Kenton And His Orchestra
Great Swing Classics In Hi-Fi | Capitol | 521223-2
Stan Kenton Orchestra
Stompin' At Newport | Pablo | PACD 5312-2
Tal Farlow Sextet
Verve Jazz Masters 41:Tal Farlow | Verve | 527365-2
Terry Gibbs Big Band
Terry Gibbs Dream Band Vol.4:Main Stem | Contemporary | CCD 7656-2
Terry Gibbs Dream Band
Terry Gibbs Dream Band Vol.2:The Sundown Sessions | Contemporary | CCD 7652-2
Terry Gibbs Dream Band Vol.3:Flying Home | Contemporary | CCD 7654-2
Terry Gibbs Dream Band Vol.5:The Big Cat | Contemporary | CCD 7657-2
Terry Gibbs Dream Band Vol.6:One More Time | Contemporary | CCD 7658-2
The Jazz Giants Play Jerome Kern:Yesterdays | Prestige | PCD 24202-2
The Herdsmen
Nat Pierce-Dick Collins-Ralph Burns & The Herdsmen Play Paris | Fantasy | FCD 24759-2
Vic Lewis West Coast All Stars
Vic Lewis Presenting A Celebration Of Contemporary West Coast Jazz | Candid | CCD 79711/12
Me And You! | Candid | CCD 79739
Woody Herman And His Orchestra
Great Swing Classics In Hi-Fi | Capitol | 521223-2
Verve Jazz Masters 54:Woody Herman | Verve | 529903-2

Perkins,Carl | (p)
Chet Baker Sextet
The Best Of Chet Baker Plays | Pacific Jazz | 797161-2
Chet Baker-Art Pepper-Phil Urso Sextet
Picture Of Heath | Pacific Jazz | 494106-2
Leroy Vinnegar Sextet
The Jazz Giants Play Harry Warren:Lullaby Of Broadway | Prestige | PCD 24204-2

Perkins,'Pinetop' Joe | (pvoc)
Muddy Waters Band
Muddy Waters:Paris 1972 | Pablo | PACD 5302-2

Perkins,Walter | (dr)
Booker Ervin Quintet
Exultation! | Original Jazz Classics | OJCCD 835-2(P 7293)
Dave Pike Quartet
Pike's Peak | Epic | 489772-2
Bill Evans:Piano Player | CBS | CK 65361
Frank Stozier Sextet
Long Night | Milestone | MCD 47095-2
Frank Strozier Quartet
Long Night | Milestone | MCD 47095-2
Gene Ammons Quartet
A Stranger In Town | Prestige | PRCD 24266-2
Gene Ammons Sextet
Gentle Jug Vol.3 | Prestige | PCD 24249-2
George Shearing With The Montgomery Brothers
Wes Montgomery-The Complete Riverside Recordings | Riverside | 12 RCD 4408-2
George Shearing And The Montgomery Brothers | Original Jazz Classics | OJCCD 040-2
J.J.Johnson Quartet
J.J.'s Broadway | Verve | 9860308
J.J.Johnson's All Stars
J.J.'s Broadway | Verve | 9860308
Johnny Coles Sextet
True Blue | Blue Note | 534032-2
Pat Martino Quintet
Strings! | Original Jazz Classics | OJCCD 223-2(P 7547)
Pat Martino Septet
Strings! | Original Jazz Classics | OJCCD 223-2(P 7547)
Roland Kirk All Stars
Rahsaan/The Complete Mercury Recordings Of Roland Kirk | Mercury | 846630-2
Roland Kirk Group
I Talk With The Spirits | Verve | 558076-2
Roland Kirk Quintet
Rahsaan/The Complete Mercury Recordings Of Roland Kirk | Mercury | 846630-2

Roland Kirk Sextet
Talkin' Verve-Roots Of Acid Jazz:Roland Kirk | Verve | 533101-2
Sal Nistico Quartet
Heavyweights | Milestone | MCD 47096-2
Sal Nistico Quintet
Heavyweights | Milestone | MCD 47096-2
Sonny Criss Quartet
Sonny Criss Quartet Feat. Wynton Kelly | Fresh Sound Records | FSR-CD 318
Sonny Criss Quintet
Sonny Criss Quartet Feat. Wynton Kelly | Fresh Sound Records | FSR-CD 318

Perkins,Wayne | (g)
Albert King Blues Band
Lovejoy | Stax | SCD 8517-2(STS 2040)

Perkinson,Coleridge | (dirp)
Donald Byrd Orchestra With Voices
True Blue | Blue Note | 534032-2
The Best Of Blue Note | Blue Note | 796110-2
Donald Byrd Septet + Voices
A New Perspective | Blue Note | 499006-2
Max Roach Sextet With Choir
It's Time | Impulse(MCA) | 951185-2
Roland Kirk And His Orchestra
Rahsaan/The Complete Mercury Recordings Of Roland Kirk | Mercury | 846630-2

Perko,Jukka | (ssas)
Jazz Baltica Ensemble
The Birth+Rebirth Of Swedish Folk Jazz | ACT | 9254-2

Perko,Matt | (drperc)
Andreas Schnerman Quartet
4 In One | Edition Collage | EC 526-2
Welcome To My Backyard | Edition Collage | EC 535-2
Andreas Schnerman Quintet
Welcome To My Backyard | Edition Collage | EC 535-2
Andreas Schnerman Sextet
Welcome To My Backyard | Edition Collage | EC 535-2

Perla,Gene | (bel-b)
Nina Simone Quintet
Planet Jazz:Nina Simone | Planet Jazz | 2165372-2

Perlera,Ray | (perc)
Vince Jones Group
Tell Me A Secret | Intuition Records | INT 3072-2

Perlman,Ivo | (tsts-solo)
Ivo Perlman Group
Children Of Ibeji | Enja | ENJ-7005 2

Perlow,Steve | (as,bs,b-cl,reeds,saxts)
Buddy Rich And His Orchestra
Swingin' New Big Band | Pacific Jazz | 835232-2
Stan Kenton Orchestra
Stompin' At Newport | Pablo | PACD 5312-2

Perowsky,Ben | (dr,percsampling)
Mike Stern Group
Odds Or Evens | Atlantic | 7567-82297-2
Standards(And Other Songs) | Atlantic | 7567-82419-2
Play | Atlantic | 7567-83219-2
Robert Dick Group With The Soldier String Quartet
Jazz Standard On Mars | Enja | ENJ-9327 2
The Sidewalks Of New York
Tin Pan Alley:The Sidewalks Of New York | Winter&Winter | 910038-2

Perowsky,Frank | (arr,clts)
Freddy Cole With Band
To The End Of The Earth | Fantasy | FCD 9675-2

Perreiria,Durual | (g)
Cannonball Adderley With Sergio Mendes And The Bossa Rio Sextet
Blue Bossa | Blue Note | 795590-2

Perren,Fred | (el-p,synthvoc)
Bobbi Humphrey
Blue Break Beats | Blue Note | 799106-2
Donald Byrd Orchestra
Black Byrd | Blue Note | 784466-2

Perri,Danny | (g)
Leon Thomas With Orchestra
Spirits Known And Unknown | RCA | 2663876-2
Louis Armstrong And Ella Fitzgerald With Bob Hagger's Orchestra
Louis Armstrong:C'est Si Bon | Dreyfus Jazz Line | FDM 36730-2

Perrilliat,Nat | (ts)
Nat Adderley Sextet
Cannonball Adderley Birthday Celebration | Fantasy | FANCD 6087-2
In The Bag | Original Jazz Classics | OJCCD 648-2(JLP 975)

Perrillo,Ron | (p)
Brad Goode-Von Freeman Sextet
Inside Chicago Vol.3 | Steeplechase | SCCD 31531
Inside Chicago Vol.4 | Steeplechase | SCCD 31532

Perrin,Fred | (synth)
Bobbi Humphrey Group
Blue Breaks Beats Vol.2 | Blue Note | 789907-2
Donald Byrd & His Orchestra
Blue Breaks Beats Vol.2 | Blue Note | 789907-2

Perrin,Gilles | (vibperc)
Aldo Romano Group
AlmaLatina | Owl Records | 018364-2

Perrin,Mimi | (voc)
Les Double Six
Les Double Six | RCA | 2164314-2

Perrine,Matt | (sousaphone)
Ray Anderson Pocket Brass Band
Where Home Is | Enja | ENJ-9366 2

Perrotta,Ugo | (b)
Big Allanbik
Batuque Y Blues | Blues Beacon | BLU-1031 2

Perry,Bazeley | (dr)
Jimmy Smith Trio
A New Sound A New Star:Jimmy Smith At The Organ | Blue Note | 857191-2

Perry,Charlie | (dr)
Al Haig Sextet
Al Haig Trio And Sextets | Original Jazz Classics | OJCCD 1929-2(SPL 1118)
Al Haig Sextet(Quintet)
Al Haig Trio And Sextets | Original Jazz Classics | OJCCD 1929-2(SPL 1118)
Stan Getz And His Four Brothers
The Brothers | Original Jazz Classics | OJCCD 008-2
The Prestige Legacy Vol.2:Battles Of Saxes | Prestige | PCD 24252-2
Stan Getz Five Brothers Bop Tenor Sax Stars
Stan Getz:Imagination | Dreyfus Jazz Line | FDM 36733-2

Perry,Ermit V. | (tp)
Dizzy Gillespie And His Orchestra
Verve Jazz Masters 20:Introducing | Verve | 519853-2
Dizzy Gillespie:Birks Works-The Verve Big Band Sessions | Verve | 527900-2
Ultimate Dizzy Gillespie | Verve | 557535-2
Dizzy Gillespie Orchestra
Verve Jazz Masters 10:Dizzy Gillespie | Verve | 516319-2
Louis Jordan And His Tympany Five
Louis Jordan-Let The Good Times Roll: The Complete Decca Recordings 1938-1954 | Bear Family Records | BCD 15557 IH

Perry,Mario | (accordeonv)
Paul Whiteman And His Orchestra
Planet Jazz:Jazz Trumpet | Planet Jazz | 2169654-2

Perry,Ray | (as,vdr)
Lionel Hampton And His Orchestra
Lionel Hampton:Flying Home | Dreyfus Jazz Line | FDM 36735-2

Perry,Richard | (arr)
Ella Fitzgerald With Orchestra
Ella/Things Ain't What They Used To Be | Warner | 9362-47875-2

Perry,Richard 'Rich' | (fl,cl,tssax)
Fred Hersch Quartet
Point In Time | Enja | ENJ-9035 2
Fred Hersch Quintet
Point In Time | Enja | ENJ-9035 2
George Mraz Quartet
Bottom Line | Milestone | MCD 9272-2
Rich Perry Quartet
Hearsay | Steeplechase | SCCD 31515
Rich Perry Quintet
At Eastman | Steeplechase | SCCD 31533
Steve Lampert Group
Venus Perplexed | Steeplechase | SCCD 31557

Perry,Ronnie | (saxts)
Artie Shaw And His Orchestra
Planet JazzArtie Shaw | Planet Jazz | 2152057-2
Planet Jazz Sampler | Planet Jazz | 2152326-2
Planet Jazz:Swing | Planet Jazz | 2169651-2
Planet Jazz:Female Jazz Vocalists | Planet Jazz | 2169656-2
The Legends Of Swing | Laserlight | 24659

Perschke,Helmut | (dr)
New Jazz Group Hannover
Deutsches Jazz Fesival 1954/1955 | Bear Family Records | BCD 15430

Persia,Maurizio | (b-tb)
Orchestra Jazz Siciliana
Orchestra Jazz Siciliana Plays The Music Of Carla Bley | Watt | XtraWatt/4

Persiany,Andre | (p,arr,el-pld)
Michel De Villers Octet
Jazz In Paris:Saxophones Á Saint-Germain Des Prés | EmArCy | 014060-2
Sidney Bechet With Michel Attenoux And His Orchestra
Planet Jazz:Sidney Bechet | Planet Jazz | 2152063-2

Persiaux,Alain | (v)
Charlie Haden Quartet West With Strings
Now Is The Hour | Verve | 527827-2

Persing,Eric | (sound-programming)
Marcus Miller Group
The Sun Don't Lie | Dreyfus Jazz Line | FDM 36560-2

Persip,Charles | (bongos,dr,percvib)
Cannonball Adderley And His Orchestra
Cannonball Adderley Birthday Celebration | Fantasy | FANCD 6087-2
Dizzy Gillespie And His Orchestra
Afro | Verve | 517052-2
Verve Jazz Masters 20:Introducing | Verve | 519853-2
Dizzy Gillespie:Birks Works-The Verve Big Band Sessions | Verve | 527900-2
Ultimate Dizzy Gillespie | Verve | 557535-2
Dizzy Gillespie Orchestra
Verve Jazz Masters 10:Dizzy Gillespie | Verve | 516319-2
Dizzy Gillespie Quintet
Diz And Getz | Verve | 549749-2
Dizzy Gillespie Sextet
Verve Jazz Masters 50:Sonny Sitt | Verve | 527651-2
Dizzy Gillespie-Sonny Rollins-Sonny Stitt Sextet
Sonny Side Up | Verve | 521426-2
Dizzy Gillespie-Sonny Stitt Quintet
Verve Jazz Masters 10:Dizzy Gillespie | Verve | 516319-2
Ernestine Anderson With Orchestra
My Kinda Swing | Mercury | 842409-2
Gene Ammons-Sonny Stitt Quartet
Gentle Jug Vol.3 | Prestige | PCD 24249-2
George Benson Quintet
It's Uptown | CBS | 502469-2
George Russell And His Orchestra
Geogre Russell New York N.Y. | Impulse(MCA) | 951278-2
Gil Evans Orchestra
Out Of The Cool | Impulse(MCA) | 951186-2
Harry Sweets Edison Sextet
Mr.Swing Harry Edison | Verve | 559868-2
Joe Turner With Orchestra
Atlantic Jazz: Kansas City | Atlantic | 7567-81701-2
Joe Williams And His Band
Blue Velvet: Crooners, Swooners And Velvet Vocals | Blue Note | 521153-2
Joe Williams With The Harry 'Sweets' Edison Band
Together/Have A Good Time | Roulette | 531790-2
Kenny Burrell With The Gil Evans Orchestra
Guitar Forms | Verve | 521403-2
Verve Jazz Masters 23:Gil Evans | Verve | 521860-2
Verve Jazz Masters 45:Kenny Burrell | Verve | 527652-2
Verve Jazz Masters Vol.60:The Collection | Verve | 529866-2
Mal Waldron Sextet
Eric Dolphy:The Complete Prestige Recordings | Prestige | 9 PRCD-4418-2
Eric Dolphy Birthday Celebration | Fantasy | FANCD 6085-2
The Quest | Original Jazz Classics | OJCCD 082-2(NJ 8269)
The Mal Waldron Memorial Album:Soul Eyes | Prestige | PRCD 11024-2
Milt Jackson Orchestra
Milt Jackson Birthday Celebration | Fantasy | FANCD 6079-2
Modern Jazz Sextet
Verve Jazz Masters 50:Sonny Sitt | Verve | 527651-2
The Modern Jazz Sextet | Verve | 559834-2
Red Garland Trio
The Jazz Giants Play Harry Warren:Lullaby Of Broadway | Prestige | PCD 24204-2
The Jazz Giants Play Rodgers & Hammerstein:My Favorite Things | Prestige | PCD 24223-2
Roland Kirk Quartet
Talkin' Verve-Roots Of Acid Jazz:Roland Kirk | Verve | 533101-2
Rahsaan/The Complete Mercury Recordings Of Roland Kirk | Mercury | 846630-2
Ron Carter Quintet
Eric Dolphy:The Complete Prestige Recordings | Prestige | 9 PRCD-4418-2
Eric Dolphy Birthday Celebration | Fantasy | FANCD 6085-2
Where | Original Jazz Classics | OJCCD 432-2

Person,Eric | (fl,as,ss,keyboards,slave-bells)
Dave Holland Qartet
Dream Of The Elders | ECM | 1572(529084-2)

Person,Houston | (ts)
Billy Butler Quintet
Night Life | Prestige | PCD 24260-2
Charles Earland Quintet
Black Talk! | Original Jazz Classics | OJCCD 335-2(P 7758)
Charles Earland Sextet
Black Talk! | Original Jazz Classics | OJCCD 335-2(P 7758)
Charlie's Greatest Hits | Prestige | PCD 24250-2
Grooveyard Meets Houston Person
Basic Instinct | Organic Music | ORGM 9701
Hank Crawford And His Orchestra
Roadhouse Symphony | Original Jazz Classics | OJCCD 1048-2(M 9140)
Houston Person Quintet
Trust In Me | Prestige | PCD 24264-2
Houston Person Sextet
Jazzin' With The Soul Brothers | Fantasy | FANCD 6086-2
Goodness! | Original Jazz Classics | OJC20 332-2(P 7678)
Blue Odyssey | Original Jazz Classics | OJCCD 1045-2(P 7566)
Johnny 'Hammond' Smith Quartet
Open House | Milestone | MCD 47089-2
The Soulful Blues | Prestige | PCD 24244-2
Good 'Nuff | Prestige | PRCD 24282-2
Johnny 'Hammond' Smith Sextet
The Soulful Blues | Prestige | PCD 24244-2
Marty Elkins And Her Sextet
Fuse Blues | Nagel-Heyer | CD 062

personal included: |
Al Jarreau With Band
High Crime | i.e. Music | 557848-2
Alain Goraguer Orchestra
Jazz In Paris:Jazz & Cinéma Vol.1 | EmArCy | 548318-2 PMS
Artie Shaw And His Orchestra
Swing Vol.1 | Storyville | 4960343
Benny Goodman And His Orchestra
Swing Vol.1 | Storyville | 4960343
Billy May And His Orchestra With Members Of The Jimmy Lunceford Orchestra
Great Swing Classics In Hi-Fi | Capitol | 521223-2
Diane Schuur Trio With Orchestra And Strings
In Tribute | GRP | GRP 20062
Diane Schuur With Orchestra
In Tribute | GRP | GRP 20062
The Best Of Diane Schuur | GRP | GRP 98882
Diane Schuur With Orchestra And Strings
The Best Of Diane Schuur | GRP | GRP 98882
Duke Ellington And His Orchestra
Jazz Collection:Duke Ellington | Laserlight | 24369
Ella Fitzgerald With The Marty Paich Orchestra
Whisper Not | Verve | 589947-2
Freddie Brocksieper Orchester
Shot Gun Boogie | Bear Family Records | BCD 16277 AH
Glen Gray And His Orchestra
Great Swing Classics In Hi-Fi | Capitol | 521223-2
Glenn Miller And His Orchestra
The Ultimate Glenn Miller-22 Original Hits From The King Of Swing | RCA | 2113137-2
Harry James And His Orchestra
Great Swing Classics In Hi-Fi | Capitol | 521223-2
Hoagy Carmichael With Jack Teagarden And His Big Band
Swing Vol.1 | Storyville | 4960343
Jaco Pastorius With Orchestra
Word Of Mouth | Warner | 7599-23525-2
Jimmy Dorsey And His Orchestra
Swing Vol.1 | Storyville | 4960343
John Lee Hooker
House Of The Blues | Chess | MCD 09258
Les Brown And His Orchestra
Great Swing Classics In Hi-Fi | Capitol | 521223-2
Muddy Waters Blues Band
Muddy Waters-The Collection | MCA | MCD 18961
Peggy Lee With Lou Levy's Orchestra
Pass Me By/Big Spender | Capitol | 535210-2
Sarah Vaughan With The Hal Mooney Orchestra
It's A Man's World | Mercury | 589487-2
Shirley Horn With Orchestra
Loads Of Love + Shirley Horn With Horns | Mercury | 843454-2
Shirley Horn With The Quincy Jones Orchestra
Loads Of Love + Shirley Horn With Horns | Mercury | 843454-2
Stan Kenton And His Orchestra
Swing Vol.1 | Storyville | 4960343
Van Alexander Orchestra
Home Of Happy Feet/Swing! Staged For Sound! | Capitol | 535211-2
Woody Herman And His Orchestra
Great Swing Classics In Hi-Fi | Capitol | 521223-2

Persson,Ake | (tb)
Clifford Brown And Art Farmer With The Swedish All Stars
Clifford Brown Memorial | Original Jazz Classics | OJC20 017-2(P 7055)
Kenny Clarke-Francy Boland Big Band
Clark-Boland Big Band: TNP, October 29th, 1969 | Laserlight | 36129
Three Latin Adventures | MPS | 529095-2
More Smiles | MPS | 9814789
All Smiles | MPS | 9814790
Francy Boland-Fellini 712 | MPS | 9814805
Lars Gullin Octet
Lars Gullin 1951/52 Vol.5:First Walk | Dragon | DRCD 380
Lars Gullin Sextet
Lars Gullin 1951/52 Vol.5:First Walk | Dragon | DRCD 380
NDR-Workshop
Doldinger's Best | ACT | 9224-2
Stan Getz And The Swedish All Stars
Stan Getz Highlights:The Best Of The Verve Years Vol.2 | Verve | 517330-2
Stan Getz Highlights | Verve | 847430-2

Persson,Anders | (psynth)
Jonas Knutsson Quartet
Jonas Knutsson Quartet | Touché Music | TMcCD 018

Pescara,Jorge | (fretless-bstick)
Ithamara Koorax With Band
Love Dance:The Ballad Album | Milestone | MCD 9327-2

Peskin,Joel C. | (sax)
Diane Schuur And Her Band
The Best Of Diane Schuur | GRP | GRP 98882

Pet,Jacques 'Jack' | (bg)
Coleman Hawkins Trio
Jazz:The Essential Collection Vol.3 | IN+OUT Records | 78013-2
Coleman Hawkins With The Ramblers
Jazz:The Essential Collection Vol.3 | IN+OUT Records | 78013-2

Peter,Eric | (b)
Bud Powell Quartet
Parisian Thoroughfare | Pablo | CD 2310976-2
Bud Powell Quintet
The Story Of Jazz Piano | Laserlight | 24653
Bud Powell Trio
Parisian Thoroughfare | Pablo | CD 2310976-2
Fritz Münzer Quintet
Jazz für junge Leute:Live im HR 1962 | Jazz 'n' Arts Records | C 01

Peter,Klaus | (voc)
Jazzensemble Des Hessischen Rundfunks
Jazz Messe-Messe Für Unsere Zeit | hr music.de | hrmj 003-01 CD

Petereit,Dieter | (bel-b)
Atmosphering Conditions Permitting | ECM | 1549/50
Klaus Doldinger & Passport
Lifelike | Warner | 2292-46478-2
Klaus Doldinger's Passport
Man In The Mirror | Warner | 2292-40253-2
Running In Real Time | Warner | 2292-40633-2
Heavy Nights | Warner | 2292-42006-2
Blue Tattoo | Atlantic | 2292-42178-2
Earthborn | Atlantic | 2292-46477-2
Oceanliner | Warner | 2292-46479-2
Passport
Ataraxia | Atlantic | 2292-42148-2
Garden Of Eden | Atlantic | 2292-44147-2

Peters,Brock | (voc)
Duke Ellington And His Orchestra
Highlights From The Duke Ellington Centennial Edition | RCA | 2663672-2

Peters,Chie | (v)
Abdullah Ibrahim Trio And A String Orchestra
African Suite | TipToe | TIP-888832 2
String Orchestra
African Suite | TipToe | TIP-888832 2

Peters,Clemens Maria | (fl,g,hungarian-zither,mandoloncello)
Clemens Maria Peters/Reinhold Bauer
Quadru Mana/Quadru Mania | Edition Collage | EC 464-2

Peters,Gregoire | (as,bs,piccolo,b-cl,fl,alto-fl,ts)
Harry Allen And Randy Sandke Meets The RIAS Big Band Berlin
The Music Of The Trumpet Kings | Nagel-Heyer | CD 037
Till Brönner Group
Chattin' With Chet | Verve | 157534-2
Till Brönner Quartet & Deutsches Symphonieorchester Berlin
German Songs | Minor Music | 801057
Till Brönner-Gregoire Peters Quintet
Generations Of Jazz | Minor Music | 801037

Peters,Grégoire | (alto-fl,fl,cl,b-cl,contra-b-cl,ss)
Till Brönner Group

Chattin' With Chet | Verve | 157534-2

Peters,Jay | (ts)

Lionel Hampton And His Orchestra
Lionel Hampton:Flying Home | Dreyfus Jazz Line | FDM 36735-2

Peters,Jerry | (el-p,synth,keyboards,orgp)

Bobbi Humphrey
Blue Break Beats | Blue Note | 799106-2
Bobbi Humphrey Group
Blue Breaks Beats Vol.2 | Blue Note | 789907-2
Donald Byrd & His Orchestra
Blue Breaks Beats Vol.2 | Blue Note | 789907-2
Gene Harris Group
Blue Breaks Beats Vol.2 | Blue Note | 789907-2

Peters,Michael | (dr,perc,voccongas)

Remy Filipovitch Quartet
All Night Long | Album | AS 11806

Peters,Mike | (tp)

Graham Stewart And His New Orleans Band
The Golden Years Of Revival Jazz,Vol.12 | Storyville | STCD 5517
The Golden Years Of Revival Jazz,Vol.14 | Storyville | STCD 5519

Peters,Oliver | (cl,ss,ts,fl,sax,fl-halto-fl)

Gianlugi Trovesi Quartet With The WDR Big Band
Dedalo | Enja | ENJ-9419 2
John Goldsby Sextet
Viewpoint | Nagel-Heyer | CD 2014
Los Jovenes Flamencos With The WDR Big Band And Guests
Jazzpana | ACT | 9212-2

Peters,Olivier | (reeds,sax,tp,fl-h,v-tb,ssts)

Bob Brookmeyer Group With The WDR Big Band
Electricity | ACT | 9219-2
Eddie Harris Group With The WDR Big Band
Eddie Harris-The Last Concert | ACT | 9249-2
Jens Winther And The WDR Big Band
The Escape | dacapo | DCCD 9437
Kevin Mahogany With The WDR Big Band And Guests
Pussy Cat Dues:The Music Of Charles Mingus | Enja | ENJ-9316 2
Vince Mendoza With The WDR Big Band And Guests
Sketches | ACT | 9215-2

Petersen,Bjarne Liller | (bj,vocg)

Chris Barber's Jazz Band
The Golden Years Of Revival Jazz,Vol.2 | Storyville | STCD 5507
Papa Bue's New Orleans Band
The Golden Years Of Revival Jazz,Vol.4 | Storyville | STCD 5509
Papa Bue's Viking Jazzband
The Golden Years Of Revival Jazz,Sampler | Storyville | 109 1001
The Golden Years Of Revival Jazz,Vol.1 | Storyville | STCD 5506
The Golden Years Of Revival Jazz,Vol.3 | Storyville | STCD 5508
The Golden Years Of Revival Jazz,Vol.5 | Storyville | STCD 5510
The Golden Years Of Revival Jazz,Vol.6 | Storyville | STCD 5511
The Golden Years Of Revival Jazz,Vol.7 | Storyville | STCD 5512
The Golden Years Of Revival Jazz,Vol.8 | Storyville | STCD 5513
The Golden Years Of Revival Jazz,Vol.9 | Storyville | STCD 5514
The Golden Years Of Revival Jazz,Vol.10 | Storyville | STCD 5515
The Golden Years Of Revival Jazz,Vol.11 | Storyville | STCD 5516
The Golden Years Of Revival Jazz,Vol.12 | Storyville | STCD 5517
The Golden Years Of Revival Jazz,Vol.13 | Storyville | STCD 5518
The Golden Years Of Revival Jazz,Vol.14 | Storyville | STCD 5519
The Golden Years Of Revibal Jazz,Vol.15 | Storyville | STCD 5520

Petersen,Edward | (ts)

Kurt Elling Group With Guests
Live In Chicago | Blue Note | 522211-2

Petersen,Harry | (as,fl,piccolo,cl,sssax)

HR Big Band
The American Songs Of Kurt Weill | hr music.de | hrmj 006-01 CD
Libertango:Homage An Astor Piazolla | hr music.de | hrmj 014-02 CD
HR Big Band With Marjorie Barnes And Frits Landesbergen
Swinging Christmas | hr music.de | hrmj 012-02 CD
HR Big Band With Marjorie Barnes And Frits Landesbergen And Strings
Swinging Christmas | hr music.de | hrmj 012-02 CD
The Three Sopranos With The HR Big Band
The Three Sopranos | hr music.de | hrmj 001-01 CD

Petersen,Krister | (fr-h)

Anders Jormin With Brass Quartet
Xieyi | ECM | 1762(013998-2)

Petersen,Per Carsten | (fl,ssas)

Stan Getz With The Danish Radio Big Band
Stan Getz In Europe | Laserlight | 24657

Peterson,Bob | (b,orgp)

The Six
The Very Best Of Dixieland Jazz | Verve | 535529-2

Peterson,Charlie | (tp)

Tommy Dorsey And His Orchestra
Planet Jazz:Frank Sinatra & Tommy Dorsey | Planet Jazz | 2152067-2
Frank Sinatra And The Tommy Dorsey Orchestra | RCA | 2668701-2

Peterson,Chuck | (tp)

Artie Shaw And His Orchestra
Planet JazzArtie Shaw | Planet Jazz | 2152057-2
Planet Jazz Sampler | Planet Jazz | 2152326-2
Planet Jazz:Swing | Planet Jazz | 2169651-2
Planet Jazz:Female Jazz Vocalists | Planet Jazz | 2169656-2
The Legends Of Swing | Laserlight | 24659
Tommy Dorsey And His Orchestra
Planet Jazz:Frank Sinatra & Tommy Dorsey | Planet Jazz | 2152067-2
Planet Jazz Sampler | Planet Jazz | 2152326-2
Planet Jazz:Tommy Dorsey | Planet Jazz | 2159972-2
Frank Sinatra And The Tommy Dorsey Orchestra | RCA | 2668701-2
Woody Herman And His Orchestra
The Legends Of Swing | Laserlight | 24659
Woody Herman:Four Brother | Dreyfus Jazz Line | FDM 36722-2

Peterson,Hanibal Marvin | (perc,koto,tp,bell-chimes,cowbell)

Gil Evans Orchestra
There Comes A Time | RCA | 2131392-2
PLay The Music Of Jimi Hendrix | RCA | 2663872-2
Svengali | Rhino | 8122-73720-2
Pharoah Sanders Group
Black Unity | Impulse(MCA) | 951219-2

Peterson,Jimmy | (p)

Louis Jordan And His Tympany Five
Louis Jordan-Let The Good Times Roll: The Complete Decca Recordings 1938-1954 | Bear Family Records | BCD 15557 IH

Peterson,Lucky | (el-p,org,voc,g,clavinetp)

Abbey Lincoln With The Rodney Kendrick Trio And Guests
A Turtle's Dream | Verve | 527382-2

Peterson,Oscar | (clavichord,el-p,org,p,arr,comp,voc)

All Stars
Alternate Blues | Original Jazz Classics | OJCCD 744-2
Anita O'Day With The Oscar Peterson Quartet
Verve Jazz Masters 49:Anita O'Day | Verve | 527653-2
Ben Webster All Stars
King Of The Tenors | Verve | 519806-2
Ben Webster And His Orchestra
Verve Jazz Masters 43:Ben Webster | Verve | 525431-2
Ben Webster Quintet
Soulville | Verve | 521449-2
Ben Webster With The Oscar Peterson Quartet
King Of The Tenors | Verve | 519806-2
Verve Jazz Masters 43:Ben Webster | Verve | 525431-2
Ultimate Ben Webster selected by James Carter | Verve | 557537-2
Ben Webster With The Oscar Peterson Trio
Ben Webster Meets Oscar Peterson | Verve | 521448-2
Verve Jazz Masters 43:Ben Webster | Verve | 525431-2
Benny Carter-Coleman Hawkins-Johnny Hodges With The Oscar Peterson Trio
The Jazz Giants Play Duke Ellington:Caravan | Prestige | PCD 24227-2
Billie Holiday And Her All Stars
Verve Jazz Masters 12:Billie Holiday | Verve | 519825-2
Verve Jazz Masters 47:Billie Holiday Sings Standards | Verve | 527650-2
Verve Jazz Masters Vol.60:The Collection | Verve | 529866-2
4 By 4:Ella Fitzgerald/Sarah Vaughan/Billie Holiday/Dinah Washington | Verve | 559693-2
The Billie Holiday Song Book | Verve | 823246-2
Billie Holiday And Her Orchestra
Solitude | Verve | 519810-2
Billie Holiday And Her Quintet
Verve Jazz Masters 47:Billie Holiday Sings Standards | Verve | 527650-2
Billie Holiday-Oscar Peterson
Solitude | Verve | 519810-2
Buddy DeFranco Meets The Oscar Peterson Quartet
Hark | Original Jazz Classics | OJCCD 867-2(2310915)
Buddy DeFranco With The Oscar Peterson Trio
The Complete Lionel Hampton Quartets And Quintets With Oscar Peterson On Verve | Verve | 559797-2
Buddy Rich Orchestra
Krupa And Rich | Verve | 521643-2
Buddy Rich-Gene Krupa Orchestra
Krupa And Rich | Verve | 521643-2
Charlie Parker And His Orchestra
The Cole Porter Songbook | Verve | 823250-2
Bird: The Complete Charlie Parker On Verve | Verve | 837141-2
Charlie Parker With Orchestra
Charlie Parker:The Best Of The Verve Years | Verve | 527815-2
Charlie Parker With The Joe Lipman Orchestra
Verve Jazz Masters 28:Charlie Parker Plays Standards | Verve | 521854-2
Charlie Parker Big Band | Verve | 559835-2
Clark Terry Quintet
Jazz Dance | Original Jazz Classics | OJCCD 1002-2(1210890)
Clark Terry With The Oscar Peterson Trio
Verve Jazz Masters 37:Oscar Peterson Plays Broadway | Verve | 516893-2
Oscar Peterson Trio + One | Verve | 558075-2
Coleman Hawkins And Ben Webster With The Oscar Peterson Quartet
Coleman Hawkins Encounters Ben Webster | Verve | 521427-2
Verve Jazz Masters 43:Coleman Hawkins | Verve | 521856-2
Verve Jazz Masters 43:Ben Webster | Verve | 525431-2
Verve Jazz Masters Vol.60:The Collection | Verve | 529866-2
Ultimate Coleman Hawkins selected by Sonny Rollins | Verve | 557538-2
Coleman Hawkins And Confreres
Coleman Hawkins And Confreres | Verve | 835255-2 PMS
Coleman Hawkins With The Oscar Peterson Quartet
Verve Jazz Masters 43:Coleman Hawkins | Verve | 521856-2
The Genius Of Coleman Hawkins | Verve | 539065-2
Ultimate Coleman Hawkins selected by Sonny Rollins | Verve | 557538-2
Count Basie-Oscar Peterson
The Jazz Giants Play Sammy Cahn:It's Magic | Prestige | PCD 24226-2
Count Basie-Oscar Peterson Quartet
The Timekeepers-Count Basie Meets Oscar Peterson | Original Jazz Classics | OJC20 790-2(2310896)
Count Basie-Oscar Peterson Quintet
Satch And Josh | Pablo | 2310722-2
Jazz Dance | Original Jazz Classics | OJCCD 1002-2(1210890)
Dizzy Gillespie Sextet
Verve Jazz Masters 10:Dizzy Gillespie | Verve | 516319-2
Dizzy Gillespie-Roy Eldridge Sextet
Ultimate Dizzy Gillespie | Verve | 557535-2
Dizzy Gillespie-Stan Getz Sextet
Verve Jazz Masters 25:Stan Getz & Dizzy Gillespie | Verve | 521852-2
Diz And Getz | Verve | 549749-2
Ultimate Stan Getz selected by Joe Henderson | Verve | 557532-2
Stan Getz Highlights | Verve | 847430-2
Ella Fitzgerald And Her All Stars
Love Songs:The Best Of The Song Books | Verve | 531762-2
Ella Fitzgerald Sings The Duke Ellington Songbook | Verve | 559248-2
For The Love Of Ella Fitzgerald | Verve | 841765-2
Ella Fitzgerald And Her Quintet
Verve Jazz Masters 46:Ella Fitzgerald-The Jazz Sides | Verve | 527655-2
Ella Fitzgerald And Louis Armstrong With The Oscar Peterson Quartet
Ella Fitzgerald-First Lady Of Song | Verve | 517898-2
Verve Jazz Masters 1:Louis Armstrong | Verve | 519818-2
Verve Jazz Masters 6:Ella Fitzgerald | Verve | 519822-2
Verve Jazz Masters 24:Ella Fitzgerald & Louis Armstrong | Verve | 521851-2
Verve Jazz Masters 46:Ella Fitzgerald-The Jazz Sides | Verve | 527655-2
Verve Jazz Masters Vol.60:The Collection | Verve | 529866-2
The Complete Ella Fitzgerald And Louis Armstrong On Verve | Verve | 537284-2
The Best Of Ella Fitzgerald And Louis Armstrong On Verve | Verve | 537909-2
Ella And Louis | Verve | 543304-2
Ella & Louis | Verve | 825373-2
Ella And Louis Again | Verve | 825374-2
For The Love Of Ella Fitzgerald | Verve | 841765-2
Ella Fitzgerald And Oscar Peterson
Ella Fitzgerald-First Lady Of Song | Verve | 517898-2
Ella Fitzgerald With The JATP All Stars
Ella Fitzgerald-First Lady Of Song | Verve | 517898-2
For The Love Of Ella Fitzgerald | Verve | 841765-2
Ella Fitzgerald With The Oscar Peterson Quartet
Verve Jazz Masters 6:Ella Fitzgerald | Verve | 519822-2
Verve Jazz Masters 24:Ella Fitzgerald & Louis Armstrong | Verve | 521851-2
For The Love Of Ella Fitzgerald | Verve | 841765-2
Ella Fitzgerald With The Oscar Peterson Quartet And Ben Webster
Verve Jazz Masters 43:Ben Webster | Verve | 525431-2
Ella Fitzgerald-Oscar Peterson Duo
Ella And Oscar | Pablo | 2310759-2
Ella Fitzgerald-Oscar Peterson Trio
Ella And Oscar | Pablo | 2310759-2
Freddie Hubbard-Oscar Peterson Quintet
Face To Face | Original Jazz Classics | OJCCD 937-2(2310876)
Gene Krupa Orchestra
Krupa And Rich | Verve | 521643-2
Harry Sweets Edison Sextet
The Soul Of Ben Webster | Verve | 527475-2
J.J.Johnson & Stan Getz With The Oscar Peterson Quartet
Stan Getz Highlights:The Best Of The Verve Years Vol.2 | Verve | 517330-2
A Life In Jazz:A Musical Biography | Verve | 535119-2
Stan Getz Highlights | Verve | 847430-2
Jam Session
Jazz Gallery:Lester Young Vol.2(1946-59) | RCA | 2119541-2
JATP All Stars
JATP In Tokyo | Pablo | 2620104-2
Nothing But The Blues | Verve | 521674-2
The Drum Battle:Gene Krupa And Buddy Rich At JATP | Verve | 559810-2
The Cole Porter Songbook | Verve | 823250-2
Welcome To Jazz At The Philharmonic | Fantasy | FANCD 6081-2
The J.J.Johnson Memorial Album | Prestige | PRCD 11025-2
Lester Young With The Oscar Peterson Quartet
Jazz Gallery:Lester Young Vol.2(1946-59) | RCA | 2119541-2
Lester Young With The Oscar Peterson Trio | Verve | 521451-2
Verve Jazz Masters 30:Lester Young | Verve | 521859-2
Lester Young-Harry Edison With The Oscar Peterson Quartet
Jazz Gallery:Lester Young Vol.2(1946-59) | RCA | 2119541-2
Lionel Hampton Quartet
The Complete Lionel Hampton Quartets And Quintets With Oscar Peterson On Verve | Verve | 559797-2
The Lional Hampton Quintet | Verve | 589100-2
Lionel Hampton Quintet
The Complete Lionel Hampton Quartets And Quintets With Oscar Peterson On Verve | Verve | 559797-2
The Lional Hampton Quintet | Verve | 589100-2
Lionel Hampton With Buddy DeFranco And The Oscar Peterson Trio
Verve Jazz Masters 26:Lionel Hampton with Oscar Peterson | Verve | 521853-2
Lionel Hampton With The Oscar Peterson Quartet
Verve Jazz Masters 26:Lionel Hampton with Oscar Peterson | Verve | 521853-2
Lionel Hampton With The Oscar Peterson Trio
Verve Jazz Masters 26:Lionel Hampton with Oscar Peterson | Verve | 521853-2
Lionel Hampton-Oscar Peterson Duo
The Complete Lionel Hampton Quartets And Quintets With Oscar Peterson On Verve | Verve | 559797-2
Louis Armstrong With The Oscar Peterson Quartet
Verve Jazz Masters 1:Louis Armstrong | Verve | 519818-2
Verve Jazz Masters 20:Introducing | Verve | 519853-2
Louis Armstrong Meets Oscar Peterson | Verve | 539060-2
Milt Jackson Big 4
Milt Jackson At The Montreux Jazz Festival 1975 | Original Jazz Classics | OJC20 884-2(2310753)
Milt Jackson Quartet
Ain't But A Few Of Us Left | Original Jazz Classics | OJCCD 785-2(2310873)
Jazz At The Philharmonic:The Montreux Collection | Pablo | PACD 5306-2
Milt Jackson With The Oscar Peterson Trio
Gitanes Jazz 'Round Midnight: Oscar Peterson | Verve | 511036-2 PMS
Milt Jackson-Oscar Peterson
Milt Jackson Birthday Celebration | Fantasy | FANCD 6079-2
Norman Granz Jam Session
Verve Jazz Masters 26:Lionel Hampton with Oscar Peterson | Verve | 521853-2
Verve Jazz Masters 35:Johnny Hodges | Verve | 521857-2
Charlie Parker:The Best Of The Verve Years | Verve | 527815-2
Verve Jazz Masters Vol.60:The Collection | Verve | 529866-2
Talkin' Bird | Verve | 559859-2
Bird: The Complete Charlie Parker On Verve | Verve | 837141-2
Oscar Peterson
Oscar Peterson Plays Duke Ellington | Pablo | 2310966-2
Oscar Peterson:The Composer | Pablo | 2310970-2
Solo | Pablo | 2310975-2
Oscar Peterson In Russia | Pablo | 2CD 2625711
Gitanes Jazz 'Round Midnight: Oscar Peterson | Verve | 511036-2 PMS
Tracks | MPS | 523498-2
Oscar Peterson Plays The Harold Arlen Song Book | Verve | 589103-2
Jazz At The Philharmonic:The Montreux Collection | Pablo | PACD 5306-2
Oscar Peterson All Stars
Jazz At The Philharmonic:The Montreux Collection | Pablo | PACD 5306-2
Oscar Peterson And The Bassists
Montreux '77 | Original Jazz Classics | OJC 383(2308213)
Oscar Peterson Duo
Oscar Peterson In Russia | Pablo | 2CD 2625711
Oscar Peterson Jam
Oscar Peterson Plays Duke Ellington | Pablo | 2310966-2
Montreux '77 | Original Jazz Classics | OJC 385(2620105)
Montreux '77 | Original Jazz Classics | OJC20 378-2(2308208)
Oscar Peterson Quartet
Planet Music:Oscar Peterson | RCA | 2165365-2
Oscar Peterson Live! | Pablo | 2310940-2
Time After Time | Pablo | 2310947-2
Oscar Peterson Plays Duke Ellington | Pablo | 2310966-2
Oscar Peterson:The Composer | Pablo | 2310970-2
This Is Oscar Peterson | RCA | 2663990-2
Paris Jazz Concert:Oscar Peterson | Laserlight | 36155
Verve Jazz Masters 37:Oscar Peterson Plays Broadway | Verve | 516893-2
Jazz Dance | Original Jazz Classics | OJCCD 1002-2(1210890)
Night Child | Original Jazz Classics | OJCCD 1030-2(2312108)
The Jazz Giants Play Miles Davis:Milestones | Prestige | PCD 24225-2
Oscar Peterson Quintet
Skol | Original Jazz Classics | OJC20 496-2
Oscar Peterson Quintet With Strings
Jazz Dance | Original Jazz Classics | OJCCD 1002-2(1210890)
Oscar Peterson Sextet
Oscar Peterson Trio: Olympia/Theatre Des Champs-Elysees | Laserlight | 36134
Soul Espanol | Limelight | 510439-2
Oscar Peterson Trio
Planet Music:Oscar Peterson | RCA | 2165365-2
Planet Jazz:Jazz Piano | RCA | 2169655-2
Nigerian Marketplace | Pablo | 2308231-2
Oscar Peterson Plays Duke Ellington | Pablo | 2310966-2
JATP In Tokyo | Pablo | 2620104-2
This Is Oscar Peterson | RCA | 2663990-2
The London Concert | Pablo | 2CD 2620111
At Zardis' | Pablo | 2CD 2620118
Oscar Peterson In Russia | Pablo | 2CD 2625711
The Paris Concert | Pablo | 2PACD 2620112
Oscar Peterson Trio: Olympia/Theatre Des Champs-Elysees | Laserlight | 36134
Paris Jazz Concert:Oscar Peterson | Laserlight | 36155
Joe Pass:Guitar Virtuoso | Pablo | 4 PACD 4423-2
Gitanes Jazz 'Round Midnight: Oscar Peterson | Verve | 511036-2 PMS
At The Stratford Shakespearean Festival | Verve | 513752-2
Verve Jazz Masters 16:Oscar Peterson | Verve | 516320-2
Verve Jazz Masters 37:Oscar Peterson Plays Broadway | Verve | 516893-2
Porgy And Bess | Verve | 519807-2
Verve Jazz Masters 20:Introducing | Verve | 519853-2
Three Originals:Motion&Emotions/Tristeza On Piano/Hello Herbie | MPS | 521059-2
Night Train | Verve | 521440-2
We Get Request | Verve | 521442-2
The Oscar Peterson Trio At The Concertgebouw | Verve | 521649-2
Exclusively For My Friends-The Lost Tapes | MPS | 529096-2
Oscar Peterson:The Gershwin Songbooks | Verve | 529698-2
The Song Is You-The Best Of The Verve Songbooks | Verve | 531558-2
Two Originals:Walking The Line/Another Day | MPS | 533549-2
The Trio:Live From Chicago | Verve | 539063-2
Swinging Cooperations:Reunion Blues/Great Connection | MPS | 539085-2
West Side Story | Verve | 539753-2
The Sound Of The Trio | Verve | 543321-2
On The Town | Verve | 543834-2
With Respect To Nat | Verve | 557486-2
Oscar Peterson Plays The Duke Ellington Song Book | Verve | 559785-2
Oscar Peterson Plays The Harold Arlen Song Book | Verve | 589103-2
Tristeza On Piano | MPS | 817489-2 PMS
Oscar Peterson Plays The Cole Porter Song Book | Verve | 821987-2
The Silver Collection: Oscar Peterson | Verve | 823447-2 PMS
A Jazz Portrait Of Frank Sinatra | Verve | 825769-2
The Good Life | Original Jazz Classics | OJC 627(2308241)
The Trio | Original Jazz Classics | OJCCD 992(2310101)
The Jazz Giants Play Rodgers & Hart:Blue Moon | Prestige | PCD 24205-2
The Jazz Giants Play Rodgers & Hammerstein:My Favorite Things | Prestige | PCD 24223-2
Oscar Peterson Trio With Herb Ellis
Three Originals:Motion&Emotions/Tristeza On Piano/Hello Herbie | MPS | 521059-2
Hello Herbie | MPS | 821846-2

INTERPRETENVERZEICHNIS

Oscar Peterson Trio With Milt Jackson
Very Tall | Verve | 559830-2
Very Tall | Verve | 827821-2
Oscar Peterson Trio With Roy Eldridge
Oscar Peterson Trio: Olympia/Theatre Des Champs-Elysees | Laserlight | 36134
Oscar Peterson Trio With The Claus Ogermann Orchestra
Three Originals:Motion&Emotions/Tristeza On Piano/Hello Herbie | MPS | 521059-2
The Antonio Carlos Jobim Songbook | Verve | 525472-2
Oscar Peterson Trio With The Nelson Riddle Orchestra
Verve Jazz Masters 16:Oscar Peterson | Verve | 516320-2
The Silver Collection: Oscar Peterson | Verve | 823447-2 PMS
Oscar Peterson Trio With The Russell Garcia Orchestra
Verve Jazz Masters 16:Oscar Peterson | Verve | 516320-2
Oscar Peterson With Orchestra
Oscar Peterson:The Composer | Pablo | 2310970-2
With Respect To Nat | Verve | 557486-2
A Royal Wedding Suite | Original Jazz Classics | OJCCD 973-2(2312129)
Oscar Peterson With The Duke Ellington Orchestra
Oscar Peterson Plays Duke Ellington | Pablo | 2310966-2
Oscar Peterson With The Ernie Wilkins Orchestra
Verve Jazz Masters 16:Oscar Peterson | Verve | 516320-2
Oscar Peterson-Clark Terry Duo
Oscar Peterson Plays Duke Ellington | Pablo | 2310966-2
Oscar Peterson & Clark Terry | Original Jazz Classics | OJCCD 806-2(2310742)
Oscar Peterson-Harry Edison Duo
Oscar Peterson & Harry Edison | Original Jazz Classics | OJCCD 738-2(2310741)
Oscar Peterson-Joe Pass Duo
Oscar Pterson Et Joe Pass A La Salle Pleyel | Pablo | 2CD 2625705
Porgy And Bess | Original Jazz Classics | OJCCD 829-2(2310779)
Oscar Peterson-Jon Faddis Duo
Oscar Peterson & Jon Faddis | Original Jazz Classics | OJCCD 1036-2(2310743)
Oscar Peterson-Major Holley Duo
Oscar Peterson:Get Happy | Dreyfus Jazz Line | FDM 36738-2
Oscar Peterson-Milt Jackson Duo
To Bags...With Love:Memorial Album | Pablo | 2310967-2
Two Of The Few | Original Jazz Classics | OJCCD 689-2(2310881)
Oscar Peterson-Milt Jackson Quartet
Swinging Cooperations:Reunion Blues/Great Connection | MPS | 539085-2
Oscar Peterson-Ray Brown Duo
Gitanes Jazz 'Round Midnight: Oscar Peterson | Verve | 511036-2 PMS
Verve Jazz Masters 37:Oscar Peterson Plays Broadway | Verve | 516893-2
The Complete Jazz At The Philharmonic On Verve 1944-1949 | Verve | 523893-2
Oscar Peterson:Get Happy | Dreyfus Jazz Line | FDM 36738-2
Oscar Peterson-Roy Eldridge Duo
Oscar Peterson & Roy Eldridge | Original Jazz Classics | OJCCD 727-2(2310739)
Oscar Peterson-Stephane Grappelli Quartet
Jazz In Paris:Oscar Peterson-Stephane Grappelli Quartet Vol.1 | EmArCy | 013028-2
Jazz In Paris:Oscar Peterson-Stephane Grappelli Quartet Vol.2 | EmArCy | 013029-2
Pablo All Star Jam
Montreux '77 | Original Jazz Classics | OJC 385(2620105)
Ralph Burns And His Orchestra
The Complete Verve Roy Eldridge Studio Sessions | Verve | 9861278
Roy Eldridge 4
Montreux '77 | Original Jazz Classics | OJCCD 373-2
Roy Eldridge And His Orchestra
The Complete Verve Roy Eldridge Studio Sessions | Verve | 9861278
Roy Eldridge Quintet
The Complete Verve Roy Eldridge Studio Sessions | Verve | 9861278
Roy Eldridge Sextet
The Complete Verve Roy Eldridge Studio Sessions | Verve | 9861278
Roy Eldridge-Dizzy Gillespie With The Oscar Peterson Quartet
The Complete Verve Roy Eldridge Studio Sessions | Verve | 9861278
Jazz Maturity... Where It's Coming From | Original Jazz Classics | OJCCD 807-2(2310816)
Roy Eldridge-Dizzy Gillespie-Harry Edison With The Oscar Peterson Quartet
The Complete Verve Roy Eldridge Studio Sessions | Verve | 9861278
Sarah Vaughan With The Oscar Peterson Quartet
How Long Has This Been Going On? | Pablo | 2310821-2
Joe Pass:Guitar Virtuoso | Pablo | 4 PACD 4423-2
Sarah Vaughan Birthday Celebration | Fantasy | FANCD 6090-2
Singers Unlimited + The Oscar Peterson Trio
The Singers Unlimited:Magic Voices | MPS | 539130-2
Sonny Stitt Sextet
Verve Jazz Masters 50:Sonny Sitt | Verve | 527651-2
Sonny Stitt With The Oscar Peterson Trio
Verve Jazz Masters 50:Sonny Sitt | Verve | 527651-2
Stan Getz And J.J. Johnson With The Oscar Peterson Quartet
Ultimate Stan Getz selected by Joe Henderson | Verve | 557532-2
Stan Getz And The Oscar Peterson Trio
The Silver Collection: Stan Getz And The Oscar Peterson Trio | Verve | 827826-2
Stan Getz With The Oscar Peterson Quartet
Verve Jazz Masters 8:Stan Getz | Verve | 519823-2
Ultimate Stan Getz selected by Joe Henderson | Verve | 557532-2
Stan Getz With The Oscar Peterson Trio
Stan Getz Highlights | Verve | 847430-2
The Trumpet Summit With The Oscar Peterson Big 4
The Trumpet Summit Meets The Oscar Peterson Big 4 | Original Jazz Classics | OJCCD 603-2
Zoot Sims Quintet
Zoot Sims And The Gershwin Brothers | Original Jazz Classics | OJC20 444-2(2310744)
Zoot Sims And The Gershwin Brothers | Pablo | PASA 2310-744-6

Peterson,Pete | (bts)
Gene Gifford And His Orchestra
Planet Jazz:Bud Freeman | Planet Jazz | 2161240-2
Louis Armstrong And His Orchestra
Louis Armstrong:Swing That Music | Laserlight | 36056

Peterson,Ralph | (co,drtp)
Charles Lloyd Quartet
Notes From Big Sur | ECM | 1465(511999-2)
Craig Harris And Tailgater's Tales
Blackout In The Square Root Of Soul | JMT Edition | 919015-2
Dimitrios Vassilakis Daedalus Project
Labyrinth | Candid | CCD 79776
Don Byron Quartet
Tuskegee Experiments | Nonesuch | 7559-79280-2
Don Byron Quintet
Tuskegee Experiments | Nonesuch | 7559-79280-2
Uri Caine Trio
Blue Wail | Winter&Winter | 910034-2
Wayne Escoffery Quintet
Intuition | Nagel-Heyer | CD 2038

Peterson,Randy | (drperc)
Joe Maneri Quartet
In Full Cry | ECM | 1617(537048-2)

Peterson,Ricky | (keyboards,org,synth,arrvoc)
Joe Sample Group
Ashes To Ashes | Warner | 7599-26318-2
Robben Ford & The Blue Line
Handful Of Blues | Blue Thumb | BTR 70042

Peterson,Robert | (v)
Charlie Haden Quartet West With Strings
The Art Of The Song | Verve | 547403-2

Petit,Emmanuel | (cello)
Stephane Grappelli With The Michel Legrand Orchestra
Grapelli Story | Verve | 515807-2

Petit,Leo | (gbj)
Stephane Grappelli Quintet
Grapelli Story | Verve | 515807-2
Feeling + Finesse = Jazz | Atlantic | 7567-90140-2

Petit,Marie Ange | (perc)
Michel Godard Ensemble
Castel Del Monte II | Enja | ENJ-9431 2

Petit.Marie Ange | (perc)

Petrasek Epoque String Orchestra |
Benny Bailey Quartet With Strings
I Remember Love | Laika Records | 35101752

Petrella,Gianluca | (tb)
Enrico Rava Quintet
Easy Living | ECM | 1760(9812050)
Orchestre National De Jazz
Charmediterranéen | ECM | 1828(018493-2)

Petrocca,Antonio | (dr)
Antonio Petrocca Quartet
But Not For Me | Edition Musikat | EDM 047
Antonio Petrocca Trio
But Not For Me | Edition Musikat | EDM 047

Petrocca,Davide | (bel-b)
Antonio Petrocca Quartet
But Not For Me | Edition Musikat | EDM 047
Antonio Petrocca Trio
But Not For Me | Edition Musikat | EDM 047
Davide Petrocca Quartet
Move | Edition Musikat | EDM 026
Heiner Franz' Swing Connection
Heiner Franz' Swing Connection | Jardis Records | JRCD 9817
Jermaine Landsberger Trio & Gina
Samba In June | Edition Collage | EC 524-2
Jermaine Landsberger Trio With Helmut Kagerer & Gina
Samba In June | Edition Collage | EC 524-2
Lorenzo Petrocca Quartet Feat. Bruno De Filippi
Insieme | Edition Musikat | EDM 002
Patrick Tompert Trio
Hallelujah Time | Satin Doll Productions | SDP 1020-1 CD
Patrick Tompert Trio Live | Satin Doll Productions | SDP 1029-1 CD
Moche! | Satin Doll Productions | SDP 1035-1 CD
Torsten Goods Group
Manhattan Walls | Jardis Records | JRCD 20139

Petrocca,Franco | (bg)
Franco & Lorenzo Petrocca
Italy | Edition Musikat | EDM 062
Kamafra
Kamafra Live | Edition Musikat | EDM 072

Petrocca,Lorenzo | (g)
Davide Petrocca Quartet
Move | Edition Musikat | EDM 026
Franco & Lorenzo Petrocca
Italy | Edition Musikat | EDM 062
Lorenzo Petrocca Organ Trio
Milan In Minor | Jardis Records | JRCD 20136
Jazz Guitar Highlights 1 | Jardis Records | JRCD 20141
Lorenzo Petrocca Quartet Feat. Bruno De Filippi
Insieme | Edition Musikat | EDM 002
Lozenzo Petrocca Quartet
Stop It | Edition Musikat | EDM 018
Stuttgarter Gitarren Trio
Stuttgarter Gitarren Trio Vol.2 | Edition Musikat | EDM 034

Petrowsky,Ernst-Ludwig | (as,bs,ts,cl,ss,fl,p,voice,zither)
Berlin Contemporary Jazz Orchestra
Berlin Contemporary Jazz Orchestra | ECM | 1409
European Jazz Ensemble
European Jazz Ensemble At The Philharmonic Cologne | M.A Music | A 800-2
20th Anniversary Tour | Konnex Records | KCD 5078
European Jazz Ensemble & The Khan Family feat. Joachim Kühn
European Jazz Ensemble Meets The Khan Family | M.A Music | A 807-2
George Gruntz Concert Jazz Band '83
Theatre | ECM | 1265

Petrucciani,Michel | (p,org,synth,vocp-solo)
Dreyfus All Stars
Dreyfus Night In Paris | Dreyfus Jazz Line | FDM 36652-2
Joe Lovano Quartet
From The Soul | Blue Note | 798636-2
Lee Konitz-Michel Petrucciani Duo
Toot Sweet | Owl Records | 013432-2
Manhattan Project,The
Kind Of Blue:Blue Note Celebrate The Music Of Miles Davis | Blue Note | 534255-2
Wayne Shorter:The Classic Blue Note Recordings | Blue Note | 540856-2
Michel And Tony Petrucciani
Conversations | Dreyfus Jazz Line | FDM 36617-2
Michel Grailler-Michel Petrucciani
Dream Drops | Owl Records | 013434-2
Michel Petrucciani
100 Hearts | Blue Note | 538329-2
Promenade With Duke | Blue Note | 780590-2
Au Theatre Des Champ-Elysees(Paris Concert) | Dreyfus Jazz Line | FDM 36570-2
Live In Germany | Dreyfus Jazz Line | FDM 36597-2
Michel Petrucciani feat. Jim Hall and Wayne Shorter
Wayne Shorter:The Classic Blue Note Recordings | Blue Note | 540856-2
Power Of Three-Live At Montreux | Blue Note | 746427-2
Michel Petrucciani:The Blue Note Years | Blue Note | 789916-2
Michel Petrucciani Group
Michel Petrucciani:The Blue Note Years | Blue Note | 789916-2
Music | Blue Note | 792563-2
Playground | Blue Note | 795480-2
Michel Petrucciani Quartet
Michel Plays Petrucciani | Blue Note | 748679-2
Michel Petrucciani:The Blue Note Years | Blue Note | 789916-2
Michel Petrucciani Quintet
Michel Petrucciani Live | Blue Note | 780589-2
Michel Petrucciani Sextet
Both Worlds | Dreyfus Jazz Line | FDM 36590-2
Michel Petrucciani Trio
Michel Petrucciani | Owl Records | 013431-2
Live At The Village Vanguard | Blue Note | 540382-2
Pianism | Blue Note | 746295-2
Michel Plays Petrucciani | Blue Note | 748679-2
Michel Petrucciani:The Blue Note Years | Blue Note | 789916-2
Trio In Tokyo | Dreyfus Jazz Line | FDM 36605-2
Michel Petrucciani With The Graffiti String Quartet
Marvellous | Dreyfus Jazz Line | FDM 36564-2
Rachelle Ferrell With The Wayne Shorter Sextet
First Instrumental | Blue Note | 827820-2
Serge Forté-Michel Petrucciani
Vaina | Laika Records | LK 90-021
Stephane Grappelli-Michel Petrucciani Quartet
Flamingo | Dreyfus Jazz Line | FDM 36580-2
Steve Grossman Quartet
Steve Grossman Quartet | Dreyfus Jazz Line | FDM 36602-2

Petrucciani,Tony | (g)
Michel And Tony Petrucciani
Conversations | Dreyfus Jazz Line | FDM 36617-2

Pettersson,Lars | (b)
Kettil Ohlsson Quintet
Lars Gullin 1953,Vol.2:Moden Sounds | Dragon | DRCD 234

Pettiford,Oscar | (bcello)
Ben Webster Quartet
Jazz:The Essential Collection Vol.3 | IN+OUT Records | 78013-2
Chris Connor With The John Lewis Quartet
Chris Connor | Atlantic | 7567-80769-2
Coleman Hawkins All Stars
The J.J.Johnson Memorial Album | Prestige | PRCD 11025-2
Coleman Hawkins And His Orchestra
Jazz:The Essential Collection Vol.3 | IN+OUT Records | 78013-2
Coleman Hawkins' Swing Four
Jazz:The Essential Collection Vol.3 | IN+OUT Records | 78013-2
Dizzy Gillespie All Stars
Dizzy Gillespie:Night In Tunisia | Dreyfus Jazz Line | FDM 36734-2
Django Reinhardt With Duke Ellington And His Orchestra
Django Reinhardt:Souveniers | Dreyfus Jazz Line | FDM 36744-2
Duke Ellington And His Orchestra
Planet Jazz:Duke Ellington | Planet Jazz | 2152053-2
The Legends Of Swing | Laserlight | 24659
Highlights From The Duke Ellington Centennial Edition | RCA | 2663672-2
Carnegie Hall Concert January 1946 | Prestige | 2PCD 24074-2
Carnegie Hall Concert December 1947 | Prestige | 2PCD 24075-2
Jazz:The Essential Collection Vol.2 | IN+OUT Records | 78012-2
Duke Ellington Quartet
Great Times! | Original Jazz Classics | OJC20 108-2(RLP 475)
Duke Ellington-Billy Strayhorn Quintet
Great Times! | Original Jazz Classics | OJC20 108-2(RLP 475)
Esquire Metropolitan Opera House Jam Session
Jazz:The Essential Collection Vol.3 | IN+OUT Records | 78013-2
Hans Koller Quartet
Exclusiv | MPS | 9813440
Helen Merrill With The Quincy Jones Orchestra
Verve Jazz Masters 44:Clifford Brown and Max Roach | Verve | 528109-2
Brownie-The Complete EmArCy Recordings Of Clifford Brown | EmArCy | 838306-2
Ike Quebec Swingtet
The Blue Note Swingtets | Blue Note | 495697-2
Jimmy Hamilton And The Duke's Men
The Blue Note Swingtets | Blue Note | 495697-2
Kenny Dorham Octet
Afro-Cuban | Blue Note | 0675619
Kenny Dorham Orchestra
Blue Bossa | Blue Note | 795590-2
Kenny Dorham Quintet
Sonny Rollins-The Freelance Years:The Complete Riverside & Contemporary Recordings | Riverside | 5 RCD 4427-2
Jazz Contrast | Original Jazz Classics | OJCCD 028-2(RLP 239)
Kenny Dorham Sextet
Jazz Contrast | Original Jazz Classics | OJCCD 028-2(RLP 239)
Lee Konitz-Warne Marsh Quintet
Lee Konitz With Warne Marsh | Atlantic | 8122-75356-2
Lee Konitz-Warne Marsh Sextet
Lee Konitz With Warne Marsh | Atlantic | 8122-75356-2
Leonard Feather's Esquire All Stars
Jazz:The Essential Collection Vol.2 | IN+OUT Records | 78012-2
Max Roach Sextet
Deeds Not Words | Original Jazz Classics | OJC20 304-2(RLP 1122)
Miles Davis All Stars
Miles Davis Vol.1 | Blue Note | 532610-2
Miles Davis Quartet
Ballads & Blues | Blue Note | 836633-2
The Musings Of Miles | Original Jazz Classics | OJCCD 004-2
Miles Davis Sextet
Miles Davis:The Best Of The Capitol/Blue Note Years | Blue Note | 798287-2
Jazz Profile:Miles Davis | Blue Note | 823515-2
Oscar Pettiford Sextet
Charles Mingus-The Complete Debut Recordings | Debut | 12 DCD 4402-2
The Birdlanders Vol.2 | Original Jazz Classics | OJCCD 1931-2
Ray Charles-Milt Jackson Sextet
Soul Brothers/Soul Meeting | Atlantic | 7567-81951-2
Sonny Rollins Trio
Sonny Rollins-The Freelance Years:The Complete Riverside & Contemporary Recordings | Riverside | 5 RCD 4427-2
Freedom Suite | Original Jazz Classics | OJCCD 067-2
Tal Farlow Quartet
Verve Jazz Masters 41:Tal Farlow | Verve | 527365-2
Thelonious Monk Quintet
Sonny Rollins-The Freelance Years:The Complete Riverside & Contemporary Recordings | Riverside | 5 RCD 4427-2
Thelonious Monk:85th Birthday Celebration | zyx records | FANCD 6076-2
Brilliant Corners | Original Jazz Classics | OJC20 026-2
Thelonious Monk Trio
Thelonious Monk:85th Birthday Celebration | zyx records | FANCD 6076-2
Plays The Music Of Duke Ellington | Original Jazz Classics | OJC20 024-2
The Unique Thelonious Monk | Original Jazz Classics | OJCCD 064-2
Woody Herman And His Orchestra
Woody Herman:Four Brother | Dreyfus Jazz Line | FDM 36722-2

Pettigrew,John | (tb)
Johnny Otis And His Orchestra
Verve Jazz Masters 43:Ben Webster | Verve | 525431-2

Petz,Fritz | (tp)
Brocksi-Sextett
Drums Boogie | Bear Family Records | BCD 15988 AH
Shot Gun Boogie | Bear Family Records | BCD 16277 AH
Freddie Brocksieper Orchester
Shot Gun Boogie | Bear Family Records | BCD 16277 AH

Petzold,Joachim | (tb)
Matthias Petzold Esperanto-Music
Lifelines | Indigo-Records | 1001 CD
Matthias Petzold Group With Choir
Psalmen und Lobgesänge für Chor und Jazz-Enseble | Indigo-Records | 1002 CD
Matthias Petzold Septett
Ulysses | Indigo-Records | 1003 CD

Petzold,Lars | (g)
Greenfish
Perfume Light... | TipToe | TIP-888831 2

Petzold,Matthias | (cl,ts,cello,flss)
Matthias Petzold Esperanto-Music
Lifelines | Indigo-Records | 1001 CD
Matthias Petzold Group With Choir
Psalmen und Lobgesänge für Chor und Jazz-Enseble | Indigo-Records | 1002 CD
Matthias Petzold Septett
Ulysses | Indigo-Records | 1003 CD
Matthias Petzold Working Band
Elements | Indigo-Records | 1005 CD

Peucker,Paul | (reedssax)
Bob Brookmeyer Group With The WDR Big Band
Electricity | ACT | 9219-2

Peuker,Peter | (as)
Dusko Goykovich Big Band
Balkan Connection | Enja | ENJ-9047 2

Peyratoux,Michel | (b-g)
Chet Baker & The Boto Brasilian Quartet
Chet Baker & The Boto Brasilian Quartet | Dreyfus Jazz Line | FDM 36511-9

Peyton,Craig | (synth)
Steps Ahead
Modern Times | Elektra | 7559-60351-2

Pezzotta,Mario | (as)
Chet Baker With String-Orchestra And Voices
Chet Baker With Fifty Italian Strings | Original Jazz Classics | OJC20 492-2(JLP 921)

Pezzotti,Daniel | (cello)
Daniel Schnyder With String Quartet
Tanatula | Enja | ENJ-9302 2
Lee Konitz With Strings
Strings For Holiday:A Tribute To Billie Holiday | Enja | ENJ-9304 2

Pfammatter,Hans Peter | (p)
Gilbert Paeffgen Trio
Pedestrian Tales | Edition Musikat | EDM 061

Pfatt,Beate | (voc)
Jazzensemble Des Hessischen Rundfunks
Jazz Messe-Messe Für Unsere Zeit | hr music.de | hrmj 003-01 CD

Pfeffner,Ralph | (tb)
Woody Herman And His Orchestra
The Legends Of Swing | Laserlight | 24659
Woody Herman:Four Brother | Dreyfus Jazz Line | FDM 36722-2
Louis Armstrong-Jack Teagarden-Woody Herman:Midnights At V-Disc | Jazz Unlimited | JUCD 2048
Old Gold Rehearsals 1944 | Jazz Unlimited | JUCD 2079
Woody Herman And The Herd
Woody Herman (And The Herd) At Carnegie Hall | Verve | 559833-2

Pfeiffer,Fred | (engl-h)
Elliot Lawrence And His Orchestra
The Elliot Lawrence Big Band Swings Cohn & Kahn | Fantasy | FCD 24761-2

Pfeiffer,Stephan | (asreeds)
Nana Mouskouri With The Berlin Radio Big Band
Nana Swings | Mercury | 074394-2

Pfeiffer-Galilea,Stefan | (as)
Heinz Sauer Quartet With The NDR Big Band
NDR Big Band-Bravissimo | ACT | 9232-2
NDR Big Band
NDR Big Band-Bravissimo | ACT | 9232-2

Pfiffner,John | (g)
Tom Browne Groups
Mo' Jamaica Funk | Hip Bop | HIBD 8002

Pfisterer,Nicolai | (asts)
Ralph Schweizer Big Band
DAY Dream | Chaos | CACD 8177
Sax Mal Anders
Kontraste | Chaos | CACD 8185

Pfleiderer,Martin | (ssts)
Ekkehard Jost Ensemble
Weimarer Balladen | Fish Music | FM 004 CD

Philburn,Al | (tb)
Louis Armstrong And His Orchestra
Louis Armstrong:Swing That Music | Laserlight | 36056

Philcock,Al | (dr)
Stephane Grappelli And His Musicians
Grapelli Story | Verve | 515807-2

Philipp,Roland | (saxts)
Peter Schärli Quintet With Glenn Ferris
Willisau And More Live | Creative Works Records | CW CD 1020-2
Drei Seelen/Three Souls | Creative Works Records | MIWI 1014-2

Philippe,Claude | (bjtp)
Claude Luter Et Ses L'Orientais
Jazz In Paris:Sidney Bechet Et Claude Luther | EmArCy | 159821-2 PMS
Sidney Bechet With Claude Luter And His Orchestra
Planet Jazz:Sidney Bechet | Planet Jazz | 2152063-2
Sidney Bechet:Summertime | Dreyfus Jazz Line | FDM 36712-2

Philips,Peter | (b-tb)
Herbie Hancock Sextet
Herbie Hancock:The Complete Blue Note Sixties Sessions | Blue Note | 495569-2

Philips,Sonny | (el-porg)
Billy Butler Quintet
Night Life | Prestige | PCD 24260-2
Jerome Richardson Sextet
Night Life | Prestige | PCD 24260-2

Phillinganes,Gregory | (el-p,keyboards,p,orgvoc)
Paulinho Da Costa Orchestra
Agora | Original Jazz Classics | OJCCD 630-2(2310785)
Happy People | Original Jazz Classics | OJCCD 783-2(2312102)
The Quincy Jones-Sammy Nestico Orchestra
Basie & Beyond | Warner | 9362-47792-2

Phillips,Barre | (bb-solo)
Alfred Harth Quintet
This Earth! | ECM | 1264
Barre Phillips
Aquarian Rain | ECM | 1451
Barre Phillips Group
Aquarian Rain | ECM | 1451
Barre Phillips Quartet
Mountainscapes | ECM | 1076
Barre Phillips Quintet
Mountainscapes | ECM | 1076
Barre Phillips Trio
Journal Violone II | ECM | 1149
Evan Parker/Barre Phillips
Time Will Tell | ECM | 1537
Gunter Hampel All Stars
Jubilation | Birth | 0038
Jimmy Giuffre Trio
Paris Jazz Concert:Jimmy Giuffre | Laserlight | 17249
John Surman Orchestra
How Many Clouds Can You See? | Deram | 844882-2
John Surman Quartet
How Many Clouds Can You See? | Deram | 844882-2
Maneri/Phillips/Maneri
Tales Of Rohnlief | ECM | 1678
Paul Bley/Barre Phillips
Time Will Tell | ECM | 1537
Paul Bley/Evan Parker/Barre Phillips
Time Will Tell | ECM | 1537
St.Gerold | ECM | 1609(157899-2)
Terje Rypdal Quintet
What Comes After | ECM | 1031

Phillips,Bill | (fl,tsbs)
Jack McDuff Quartet With Orchestra
Moon Rappin' | Blue Note | 538697-2

Phillips,Flip | (b-cl,ssts)
Billie Holiday And Her All Stars
Verve Jazz Masters 12:Billie Holiday | Verve | 519825-2
Verve Jazz Masters 47:Billie Holiday Sings Standards | Verve | 527650-2
Billie Holiday And Her Orchestra
Solitude | Verve | 519810-2
Buddy Rich Orchestra
Krupa And Rich | Verve | 521643-2
Buddy Rich-Gene Krupa Orchestra
Krupa And Rich | Verve | 521643-2
Charlie Parker And His Orchestra
The Cole Porter Songbook | Verve | 823250-2
Bird: The Complete Charlie Parker On Verve | Verve | 837141-2
Charlie Parker With Machito And His Orchestra
Bird: The Complete Charlie Parker On Verve | Verve | 837141-2
Charlie Parker With Orchestra
Charlie Parker:The Best Of The Verve Years | Verve | 527815-2
Charlie Parker With Strings
Charlie Parker With Strings:The Master Takes | Verve | 523984-2
Charlie Parker With The Joe Lipman Orchestra
Verve Jazz Masters 28:Charlie Parker Plays Standards | Verve | 521854-2
Charlie Parker Big Band | Verve | 559835-2
Charlie Parker With The Neal Hefti Orchestra
Charlie Parker:The Best Of The Verve Years | Verve | 527815-2
Bird: The Complete Charlie Parker On Verve | Verve | 837141-2
Ella Fitzgerald And Her All Stars
Ella Fitzgerald:Mr.Paganini | Dreyfus Jazz Line | FDM 36741-2
Ella Fitzgerald With The JATP All Stars
Ella Fitzgerald-First Lady Of Song | Verve | 517898-2
For The Love Of Ella Fitzgerald | Verve | 841765-2
Flip Phillips Quintet
Swing Is The Thing | Verve | 543477-2
Flip Phillips Septet
Swing Is The Thing | Verve | 543477-2
Flip Phillips Sextet
Swing Is The Thing | Verve | 543477-2
Flip Phillips Trio
Swing Is The Thing | Verve | 543477-2
Flip Phillips-Christian McBride
Swing Is The Thing | Verve | 543477-2
Flip Phillips-Howard Alden
Swing Is The Thing | Verve | 543477-2
Gene Krupa Orchestra
Krupa And Rich | Verve | 521643-2
JATP All Stars
JATP In Tokyo | Pablo | 2620104-2
Verve Jazz Masters 28:Charlie Parker Plays Standards | Verve | 521854-2
The Complete Jazz At The Philharmonic On Verve 1944-1949 | Verve | 523893-2
Charlie Parker:The Best Of The Verve Years | Verve | 527815-2
Jazz At The Philharmonic:Best Of The 1940's Concerts | Verve | 557534-2
The Drum Battle:Gene Krupa And Buddy Rich At JATP | Verve | 559810-2
Talkin' Bird | Verve | 559859-2
The Cole Porter Songbook | Verve | 823250-2
Bird: The Complete Charlie Parker On Verve | Verve | 837141-2
Welcome To Jazz At The Philharmonic | Fantasy | FANCD 6081-2
Jazz At The Philharmonic-Frankfurt 1952 | Pablo | PACD 5305-2
Norman Granz' JATP: Carnegie Hall 1949 | Pablo | PACD 5311-2
Norman Granz Jam Session
Verve Jazz Masters 26:Lionel Hampton with Oscar Peterson | Verve | 521853-2
Verve Jazz Masters 35:Johnny Hodges | Verve | 521857-2
Charlie Parker:The Best Of The Verve Years | Verve | 527815-2
Verve Jazz Masters Vol.60:The Collection | Verve | 529866-2
Talkin' Bird | Verve | 559859-2
Bird: The Complete Charlie Parker On Verve | Verve | 837141-2
Ralph Burns And His Orchestra
The Complete Verve Roy Eldridge Studio Sessions | Verve | 9861278
Sarah Vaughan With Dizzy Gillespie And His Septet
Sarah Vaughan:Lover Man | Dreyfus Jazz Line | FDM 36739-2
Woody Herman And His Orchestra
The Legends Of Swing | Laserlight | 24659
Woody Herman:Four Brother | Dreyfus Jazz Line | FDM 36722-2
Louis Armstrong-Jack Teagarden-Woody Herman:Midnights At V-Disc | Jazz Unlimited | JUCD 2048
Old Gold Rehearsals 1944 | Jazz Unlimited | JUCD 2079
Woody Herman And His Woodshoppers
Woody Herman (And The Herd) At Carnegie Hall | Verve | 559833-2
Woody Herman And The Herd
Woody Herman (And The Herd) At Carnegie Hall | Verve | 559833-2
Woody Herman And The Vanderbilt All Stars
Louis Armstrong-Jack Teagarden-Woody Herman:Midnights At V-Disc | Jazz Unlimited | JUCD 2048

Phillips,Greg | (tb)
Anita O'Day With Gene Krupa And His Orchestra
Let Me Off Uptown:Anita O'Day With Gene Krupa | CBS | CK 65625
Tommy Dorsey And His Orchestra
Planet Jazz:Tommy Dorsey | Planet Jazz | 2159972-2

Phillips,Harvey | (tuba)
Jimmy McPartland And His Dixielanders
Planet Jazz | Planet Jazz | 2169652-2
Jimmy Smith With The Billy Byers Orchestra
Jimmy Smith:Best Of The Verve Years | Verve | 527950-2
Kenny Burrell With The Don Sebesky Orchestra
Verve Jazz Masters 45:Kenny Burrell | Verve | 527652-2
Blues-The Common Ground | Verve | 589101-2
Quincy Jones And His Orchestra
Rahsaan/The Complete Mercury Recordings Of Roland Kirk | Mercury | 846630-2
The Quintessence | Impulse(MCA) | 951222-2
Stan Getz With The Eddie Sauter Orchestra
Stan Getz Plays The Music Of Mickey One | Verve | 531232-2

Phillips,James 'Jimmy' | (b)
Leon Thomas With Band
Super Black Blues Vol.II | RCA | 2663874-2
Leon Thomas In Berlin | RCA | 2663877-2

Phillips,John | (fl,reedsts)
Jimmy Smith With Orchestra
Verve Jazz Masters 29:Jimmy Smith | Verve | 521855-2

Phillips,Nathaniel | (el-b)
Bobby Lyle Quintet
Jazzrock-Anthology Vol.3:Fusion | Zounds | CD 27100555
Willie Bobo Group
Jazzrock-Anthology Vol.3:Fusion | Zounds | CD 27100555

Phillips,Peter | (b-tb,synthtb)
Herbie Hancock Sextet
Herbie Hancock:The Complete Blue Note Sixties Sessions | Blue Note | 495569-2
Speak Like A Child | Blue Note | 746136-2

Phillips,Reuben | (ts)
Louis Jordan And His Tympany Five
Louis Jordan-Let The Good Times Roll: The Complete Decca Recordings 1938-1954 | Bear Family Records | BCD 15557 IH

Phillips,Russ | (btb)
Harry James And His Orchestra
Trumpet Blues:The Best Of Harry James | Capitol | 521224-2
Louis Armstrong And His All Stars
Satchmo Serenaders | Verve | 543792-2

Phillips,Sonny | (el-p,org,keyboardsp)
Boogaloo Joe Jones Quintet
Discovery:Grover Washington Jr.-The First Recordings | Prestige | PCD 11020-2
Gene Ammons Quartet
Gentle Jug Vol.3 | Prestige | PCD 24249-2
Brother Jug! | Prestige | PR20 7792-2
Gene Ammons Quintet
Brother Jug! | Prestige | PR20 7792-2
Fine And Mellow | Prestige | PRCD 24281-2
Houston Person Sextet
Jazzin' With The Soul Brothers | Fantasy | FANCD 6086-2
Goodness! | Original Jazz Classics | OJC20 332-2(P 7678)
Rusty Bryant Quintet
Rusty Bryant Returns | Original Jazz Classics | OJCCD 331-2(P 7626)

Phillips,Woolf | (tb)
Vic Lewis Jam Session
Vic Lewis:The Golden Years | Candid | CCD 79754

Phillips-Varjabédian | (v)
Richard Galliano Septet
Piazzolla Forever | Dreyfus Jazz Line | FDM 36642-2

Philpott | (b-g)
Eduardo Niebla-Antonio Forcione Group
Poema | Jazzpoint | JP 1035 CD

Phinnessee,Darryl | (voc)
Bobby Lyle Group
The Journey | Atlantic | 7567-82138-2

Phipps,Arthur | (b)
Jackie McLean Quartet
A Long Drink Of The Blues | Original Jazz Classics | OJCCD 253-2(NJ 8253)

Phyfe,Eddie | (dr)
Charlie Byrd Quartet
Byrd's Word! | Original Jazz Classics | OJCCD 1054-2(R 9448)
Charlie Byrd Trio
Byrd's Word! | Original Jazz Classics | OJCCD 1054-2(R 9448)
The Six
The Very Best Of Dixieland Jazz | Verve | 535529-2

Piana,Dino | (tbv-tb)
Charles Mingus Orchestra
Cumbia & Jazz Fusion | Atlantic | 8122-71785-2

Piazzolla,Astor | (arrbandoneon)
Astor Piazzolla With Orchestra Of St. Luke's
Concierto Para Bandoneon-Tres Tangos | Nonesuch | 7559-79174-2
Astor Piazzolla-Gary Burton Sextet
The New Tango | Warner | 2292-55069-2
Gerry Mulligan With Astor Piazzolla And His Orchestra
Tango Nuevo | Atlantic | 2292-42145-2

Picard,John | (tb)
Cy Laurie Jazz Band
The Golden Years Of Revival Jazz,Sampler | Storyville | 109 1001
Cy Laurie's New Orleans Septet
The Golden Years Of Revival Jazz,Vol 1 | Storyville | STCD 5506
The Golden Years Of Revival Jazz,Vol.5 | Storyville | STCD 5510
The Golden Years Of Revival Jazz,Vol.6 | Storyville | STCD 5511
The Golden Years Of Revival Jazz,Vol.8 | Storyville | STCD 5513
The Golden Years Of Revival Jazz,Vol.9 | Storyville | STCD 5514
The Golden Years Of Revival Jazz,Vol.11 | Storyville | STCD 5516

Pichl,Bernhard | (p)
Benny Bailey With The Bernhard Pichl Trio
On The Corner | Jazz 4 Ever Records:Jazz Network | J4E 4726
Bernhard Pichl Trio
On The Corner | Jazz 4 Ever Records:Jazz Network | J4E 4726
Conte Candoli Quartet
Candoli Live | Nagel-Heyer | CD 2024
New On The Corner
Left Handed | Jazz 4 Ever Records:Jazz Network | J4E 4758
Pete Yellin Quartet
Pete Yellin's European Connection:Live! | Jazz 4 Ever Records:Jazz Network | J4E 4722

Pichon,Frank | (v)
Renaud Garcia-Fons
Navigatore | Enja | ENJ-9418 2
Renaud Garcia-Fons Group
Navigatore | Enja | ENJ-9418 2

Pickens,Christopher | (voc)
Max Roach Chorus & Orchestra
To The Max! | Enja | ENJ-7021 22

Pickens,Willie | (p)
Elvin Jones Jazz Machine
In Europe | Enja | ENJ-7009 2
Going Home | Enja | ENJ-7095 2

Picker,Kai | (g)
Ekkehard Jost Quintet
Some Other Tapes | Fish Music | FM 009/10 CD

Pickering,Ben | (tb)
Tommy Dorsey And His Orchestra
Planet Jazz:Tommy Dorsey | Planet Jazz | 2159972-2

Pickins,Harry | (p)
Eddie Lockjaw Davis-Johnny Griffin Quintet
Tough Tenors Back Again! | Storyville | STCD 8298

Pico,Georvis | (dr,timbalesvoc)
Lewis Trio With Guests
Battangó | Intuition Records | INN 1101-2

Picot,Pasqual | (tuba)
Orquestra De Cambra Teatre Lliure
Porgy And Bess | Fresh Sound Records | FSNT 066 CD

Pidoux,Raphael | (cello)
Richard Galliano Septet
Piazzolla Forever | Dreyfus Jazz Line | FDM 36642-2

Pied Piepers,The | (voc)
Peggy Lee With Benny Goodman And The Paul Weston Orchestra
Peggy Lee & Benny Goodman:The Complete Recordings 1941-1947 | CBS | C2K 65686
Tommy Dorsey And His Orchestra
Planet Jazz:Frank Sinatra & Tommy Dorsey | Planet Jazz | 2152067-2
Planet Jazz:Tommy Dorsey | Planet Jazz | 2159972-2
Planet Jazz:Big Bands | Planet Jazz | 2169649-2
Frank Sinatra And The Tommy Dorsey Orchestra | RCA | 2668701-2

Pieper,Henry | (viola)
Till Brönner Quartet & Deutsches Symphonieorchester Berlin
German Songs | Minor Music | 801057

Pierce,Billie | (pvoc)
Joseph 'Dee Dee' Pierce And His Band
Atlantic Jazz: New Orleans | Atlantic | 7567-81700-2

Pierce,Billy | (sax,ssts)
Art Blakey And The Jazz Messengers
Jazz Life Vol.2:From Seventh At Avenue South | Storyville | 4960763

Pierce,Dale | (tp)
Tommy Dorsey And His Orchestra
Planet Jazz:Tommy Dorsey | Planet Jazz | 2159972-2
Planet Jazz:Jazz Greatest Hits | Planet Jazz | 2169648-2

Pierce,Joseph 'Dee Dee' | (co,voctp)
Joseph 'Dee Dee' Pierce And His Band
Atlantic Jazz: New Orleans | Atlantic | 7567-81700-2

Pierce,Nat | (arr,ld,p,celestep-solo)
Anthony Ortega With The Nat Pierce Orchestra
Earth Dance | Fresh Sound Records | FSR-CD 325
Johnny Hodges Orchestra
Planet Jazz:Johnny Hodges | Planet Jazz | 2152065-2
Lambert, Hendricks And Ross
Sing A Song Of Basie | Verve | 543827-2
Nat Pierce
My Pal Basie | Jazz Connaisseur | JCCD 8904-2
Nat Pierce Quartet
My Pal Basie | Jazz Connaisseur | JCCD 8904-2
Nat Pierce Trio
My Pal Basie | Jazz Connaisseur | JCCD 8904-2
Nat Pierce/Dick Collins Nonet
Nat Pierce-Dick Collins-Ralph Burns & The Herdsmen Play Paris | Fantasy | FCD 24759-2
Nat Pierce-Irving Stokes
My Pal Basie | Jazz Connaisseur | JCCD 8904-2
Woody Herman And His Orchestra
The Legends Of Swing | Laserlight | 24659
Great Swing Classics In Hi-Fi | Capitol | 521223-2
Verve Jazz Masters 54:Woody Herman | Verve | 529903-2
Woody Herman-1963 | Philips | 589490-2

Pierre,Catherine | (v)
Stephane Grappelli With The Michel Legrand Orchestra
Grapelli Story | Verve | 515807-2

Piestrup,Don | (arr)
Buddy Rich Big Band
Keep The Customer Satisfied | EMI Records | 523999-2

Pifarely,Dominique | (vel-v)
Andreas Willers Octet
The Ground Music | Enja | ENJ-9368 2
Dominique Pifarély-Francois Couturier
Poros | ECM | 1647
Louis Sclavis Group
Dans La Nuit | ECM | 1805(589524-2)
Louis Sclavis Quartet
Acoustic Quartet | ECM | 1526
Louis Sclavis Quintet
Rouge | ECM | 1458
Louis Sclavis Sextet
Les Violences De Rameau | ECM | 1588(533128-2)
Mike Westbrook Orchestra
The Orchestra Of Smith's Academy | Enja | ENJ-9358 2
Rabih Abou-Khalil Group
Yara | Enja | ENJ-9360 2

Vincent Courtois Trio
The Fitting Room | Enja | ENJ-9411 2

Pifferrer,Laura | (voc)
Arturo Sandoval And The Latin Train Band
Arturo Sandoval & The Latin Train | GRP | GRP 98202

Pignegny,John | (fr-h)
Dee Dee Bridgewater With Orchestra
Dear Ella | Verve | 539102-2

Piguilhem,Paul | (g)
Les Double Six
Les Double Six | RCA | 2164314-2

Pihlasviita,Rea | (voc)
Piirpauke
Tuku Tuku | JA & RO | JARO 4158-2

Piirpauke |
Live In Der Balver Höhle | JA & RO | JARO 4101-2
The Wild East | JA & RO | JARO 4128-2
Zerenade | JA & RO | JARO 4142-2
Piirpauke-Global Servisi | JA & RO | JARO 4150-2
Tuku Tuku | JA & RO | JARO 4158-2
Jazzy World | JA & RO | JARO 4200-2

Pike,Bobby | (dr)
Terry Gibbs Octet
Jewis Melodies In Jazztime | Mercury | 589673-2

Pike,Dave | (vib,el-vib,marimba,tambourine)
Dave Pike
It's Time For Dave Pike | Original Jazz Classics | OJCCD 1951-2(RLP 9360)
Dave Pike Quartet
Pike's Peak | Epic | 489772-2
Bill Evans:Piano Player | CBS | CK 65361
It's Time For Dave Pike | Original Jazz Classics | OJCCD 1951-2(RLP 9360)
Dave Pike Quintet
Carnavals | Prestige | PCD 24248-2
Dave Pike Set
Dave Pike Set:Masterpieces | MPS | 531848-2
Dave Pike Sextet
Carnavals | Prestige | PCD 24248-2
Herbie Mann Group
The Best Of Herbie Mann | Atlantic | 7567-81369-2
Kenny Clarke-Francy Boland Big Band
All Smiles | MPS | 9814790
The New Dave Pike Set & Grupo Baiafra De Bahia
Dave Pike Set:Masterpieces | MPS | 531848-2

Piket,Roberta | (p)
Roberta Piket Trio
Speak,Memory | Fresh Sound Records | FSNT 088 CD

Pilar,Milan | (b,el-b arr,perc,cond,arrel-b)
Art Van Damme Group
State Of Art | MPS | 841413-2

Pilc,Jean-Michel | (p,melodicaperc)
Jean-Michel Pilc Quartet
Cardinal Points | Dreyfus Jazz Line | FDM 36649-2
Jean-Michel Pilc Quintet
Cardinal Points | Dreyfus Jazz Line | FDM 36649-2
Jean-Michel Pilc Trio
Welcome Home | Dreyfus Jazz Line | FDM 36630-2
Cardinal Points | Dreyfus Jazz Line | FDM 36649-2

Pilet,Michel | (saxts)
Benny Carter And His Orchestra
The Art Of Saxophone | Laserlight | 24652
Hot Mallets
Hot Mallets...Live! | JHM Records | JHM 3610

Pilger,Andreas | (drperc)
Mario Neunkirchen Quintet
Long Distance | Laika Records | LK 94-060

Pili-Pili |
Pili-Pili
Jakko | JA & RO | JARO 4131-2
Be In Two Minds | JA & RO | JARO 4134-2
Pili-Pili Live 88 | JA & RO | JARO 4139-2
Pili-Pili | JA & RO | JARO 4141-2
Hotel Babo | JA & RO | JARO 4147-2
Stolen Moments | JA & RO | JARO 4159-2
Boogaloo | JA & RO | JARO 4174-2
Dance Jazz Live 1995 | JA & RO | JARO 4189-2
Hoomba-Hoomba | JA & RO | JARO 4192-2
Jazzy World | JA & RO | JARO 4200-2
Nomans Land | JA & RO | JARO 4209-2
Ballads Of Timbuktu | JA & RO | JARO 4240-2

Pillhi,Parashiyama | (tavil)
Mani Neumeir Group
Privat | ATM Records | ATM 3803-AH

Pillow,Charles | (b-cl,ts,cl,oboe,sopranino,engl-h)
John Scofield Groups
Quiet | Verve | 533185-2
Michael Brecker Quindectet
Wide Angles | Verve | 076142-2

Piltch,Dave | (b)
Bill Frisell Band
Blues Dream | Nonesuch | 7559-79615-2
Holly Cole And Her Quartet
It Happened One Night | Metro Blue | 852699-0
Holly Cole Trio
Misty Blue:Sweet Sisters Swing Songs Of Sorrow And Sadness | Blue Note | 521151-2

Piludu,Marco | (g)
Marco Piludu International Quartet
New York Travels | Jazz 4 Ever Records:Jazz Network | J4E 4733
Piludu Quattro
Room 626 | Jazz 4 Ever Records:Jazz Network | J4E 4721

Pilz,Michel | (b-cl,bs,bcl,flreeds)
Jazzensemble Des Hessischen Rundfunks
Atmosphering Conditions Permitting | ECM | 1549/50
Klaus König Orchestra
Times Of Devastation/Poco A Poco | Enja | ENJ-6014 22
Peter Weiss Sextet
Personal Choice | Nabel Records:Jazz Network | CD 4669
Schmilz
Schmilz | Creative Works Records | CW CD 1041

Pine,Courtney | (b-cl,fl,ssts)
Courtney Pine Group
Modern Day Jazz Stories | Verve | 529028-2

Pingitore,Mike | (bjg)
Billie Holiday With The Paul Whiteman Orchestra
Billie's Blues | Blue Note | 748786-2
Paul Whiteman And His Orchestra
Planet Jazz:Jack Teagarden | Planet Jazz | 2161236-2
Planet Jazz:Jazz Trumpet | Planet Jazz | 2169654-2
Jazz:The Essential Collection Vol.3 | IN+OUT Records | 78013-2

Pinheiro,Marion | (v)
Ron Carter Quintet With Strings
Pick 'Em/Super Strings | Milestone | MCD 47090-2

Pinheiro,Roberto Bastos | (percsurdo)
Lee Ritenour Group
Rio | GRP | GRP 95242
Passport
Iguacu | Atlantic | 2292-46031-2

Pini,Eugene | (v)
Stephane Grappelli And His Musicians
Grapelli Story | Verve | 515807-2

Pinkerton,Phyllis | (p)
Bob Benton With The Charles Mingus Quintet
Charles Mingus-The Complete Debut Recordings | Debut | 12 DCD 4402-2
Charles Mingus Quintet
Charles Mingus-The Complete Debut Recordings | Debut | 12 DCD 4402-2
Jackie Paris With The Charles Mingus Quintet
Charles Mingus-The Complete Debut Recordings | Debut | 12 DCD 4402-2

Pinkett,Ward | (tp)
Jelly Roll Morton's Red Hot Peppers
Planet Jazz:Jelly Roll Morton | Planet Jazz | 2152060-2
Jazz:The Essential Collection Vol.1 | IN+OUT Records | 78011-2

Pintavalle,John | (stringsv)
A Band Of Friends
Wynton Marsalis Quartet With Strings | CBS | CK 68921
Earl Klugh Group With Strings
Late Night Guitar | Blue Note | 498573-2
Grover Washington Jr. Orchestra
Jazzrock-Anthology Vol.3:Fusion | Zounds | CD 27100555
Ron Carter Quintet With Strings
Pick 'Em/Super Strings | Milestone | MCD 47090-2
Stan Getz With The Eddie Sauter Orchestra
Stan Getz Plays The Music Of Mickey One | Verve | 531232-2

Pinto,Noel Manuel | (cuica)
Passport
Iguacu | Atlantic | 2292-46031-2

Piqueras,Pasqual | (tp)
Daniel Flors Group
When Least Expected | Fresh Sound Records | FSNT 080 CD

Pirchner,Werner | (vibmarimba)
Austria Drei
Jazz Portraits | EGO | 95080
Jazzensemble Des Hessischen Rundfunks
Atmosphering Conditions Permitting | ECM | 1549/50

Pirro,Vincent | (accordeonp)
Paul Whiteman And His Orchestra
Planet Jazz:Jack Teagarden | Planet Jazz | 2161236-2

Pisani,Nick | (v)
Frank Sinatra With Orchestra
Planet Jazz:Frank Sinatra & Tommy Dorsey | Planet Jazz | 2152067-2

Pisani,Nicola | (as,bss)
Banda Città Ruvo Di Puglia
La Banda/Banda And Jazz | Enja | ENJ-9326 2

Pisano,Berto | (b)
Helen Merrill And Her Band
Planet Jazz:Female Jazz Vocalists | Planet Jazz | 2169656-2
Helen Merrill With The Piero Umilliani Group
Parole E Musica | RCA | 2174798-2

Pisano,John | (el-gg)
(Little)Jimmy Scott And His Quintet
All The Way | Warner | 7599-26955-2
Chico Hamilton Quintet
The Original Ellington Suite | Pacific Jazz | 524567-2
Newport Jazz Festival 1958,July 3rd-6th Vol.2:Mulligan The Main Man | Phontastic | NCD 8814
Diane Schuur With Orchestra
Love Songs | GRP | GRP 97032
The Best Of Diane Schuur | GRP | GRP 98882
Gato Barbieri Orchestra
Latino America | Impulse(MCA) | 952236-2
Joe Pass Quartet
Apassionato | Pablo | 2310946-2
Nuages | Pablo | 2310961-2
Joe Pass:Guitar Virtuoso | Pablo | 4 PACD 4423-2
Ira George And Joe-Joe Pass Loves Gershwin | Original Jazz Classics | OJCCD 828-2(2312133)
The Jazz Giants Play Duke Ellington:Caravan | Prestige | PCD 24227-2
Joe Pass Sextet
Jazzin' Vol.2: The Music Of Stevie Wonder | Fantasy | FANCD 6088-2
Joe Pass-John Pisano
Joe Pass-John Pisano:Duets | Pablo | 2310959-2
Joe Pass:Guitar Virtuoso | Pablo | 4 PACD 4423-2
John Pisano-Billy Bean-Dennis Budimir
West Coast Sessions | String Jazz | SJRCD 1006
Peggy Lee With Lou Levy's Orchestra
Pass Me By/Big Spender | Capitol | 535210-2
Peggy Lee With The Quincy Jones Orchestra
Blues Cross Country | Capitol | 520088-2
Ray Walker-John Pisano
Affinity | Jardis Records | JRCD 20032
Ray Walker-John Pisano Trio
Affinity | Jardis Records | JRCD 20032
Jazz Guitar Highlights 1 | Jardis Records | JRCD 20141

Pisano,Nick | (v)
Lena Horne With The Lou Bring Orchestra
Planet Jazz:Lena Horne | Planet Jazz | 2165373-2
Planet Jazz:Female Jazz Vocalists | Planet Jazz | 2169656-2

Pischel,Christian | (dr)
Hans Theessink Group
Crazy Moon | Minor Music | 801052

Pitt,Vic | (b,b-g,tubatub-b)
Chris Barber's Jazz And Blues Band
Chris Barber On The Road:A Jazz Documentary | Storyville | 4960683
Chris Barber:40 Years Jubilee Concert | Storyville | 4990013
Chris Barber's Jazzband & das Große Rundfunkorchester Berlin,DDR
Jazz Zounds: Chris Barber | Zounds | CD 2720007
The European Jazz Ginats
Jazz Party | Nagel-Heyer | CD 009
The First Sampler | Nagel-Heyer | NHR SP 5

Pittman,Bill | (g)
Peggy Lee With Lou Levy's Orchestra
Pass Me By/Big Spender | Capitol | 535210-2

Pitts,Ray | (arr,keyboards,condts)
The Danish Radio Jazz Orchestra
This Train:The Danish Radio Jazz Orchestra Plays The Music Of Ray Pitts | dacapo | DCCD 9428

Pitts,Tudy | (org)
Pat Martino Sextet
El Hombre | Original Jazz Classics | OJCCD 195-2(P 7513)

Pittson,Jeff | (keyboards)
Mike Clark-Paul Jackson Quartet
The Funk Stops Here | TipToe | TIP-888811 2

Pizzarelli,Bucky | (7-string-g,g,7-string-el-g,el-g)
Benny Bailey Quintet
The Satchmo Legacy | Enja | ENJ-9407 2
Benny Goodman And His All Star Sextet
Verve Jazz Masters 33:Benny Goodman | Verve | 844410-2
Benny Goodman And His Orchestra
Verve Jazz Masters 33:Benny Goodman | Verve | 844410-2
Benny Goodman Quintet
Verve Jazz Masters 33:Benny Goodman | Verve | 844410-2
Benny Goodman Sextet
Verve Jazz Masters 33:Benny Goodman | Verve | 844410-2
Etta Jones And Her Band
Love Shout | Original Jazz Classics | OJCCD 941-2(P 7272)
Etta Jones With The Jerome Richardson Sextet
Hollar! | Original Jazz Classics | OJCCD 1061(PR 7284)
Gene Ammons Septet
Bad! Bossa Nova | Original Jazz Classics | OJC20 351-2(P 7257)
Glenn Miller And His Orchestra
The Glenn Miller Orchestra In Digital Mood | GRP | GRP 95022
Helen Merrill With Orchestra
Casa Forte | EmArCy | 558848-2
Miles Davis Quintet
Miles Davis Quintet 1965-1968 | CBS | C6K 67398
Rex Allen's Swing Express
Keep Swingin' | Nagel-Heyer | CD 016
Ellington For Lovers | Nagel-Heyer | NH 1009
The Second Sampler | Nagel-Heyer | NHR SP 6
Sarah Vaughan And Her Band
Duke Ellington Song Book Two | Pablo | CD 2312116
Sarah Vaughan Birthday Celebration | Fantasy | FANCD 6090-2
Sarah Vaughan With Band
Linger Awhile | Pablo | 2312144-2
Sarah Vaughan With Orchestra
Sarah Vaughan Birthday Celebration | Fantasy | FANCD 6090-2
Sarah Vaughan With Small Group & Orchestra
Duke Ellington Song Book One | Pablo | CD 2312111
The Basie Alumni
Swinging For The Count | Candid | CCD 79724
Wes Montgomery With The Don Sebesky Orchestra
Verve Jazz Masters 14:Wes Montgomery | Verve | 519826-2
Wes Montgomery:The Verve Jazz Sides | Verve | 521690-2
Talkin' Jazz:Roots Of Acid Jazz | Verve | 529580-2
California Dreaming | Verve | 827842-2
Willis Jackson Sextet
At Large | Prestige | PCD 24243-2
Zoot Sims-Bucky Pizzarelli Duo
The Art Of Saxophone | Laserlight | 24652
Elegiac | Storyville | STCD 8238

Pizzarelli,John | (el-g,g,7-string-el-gvoc)
John Pizzarelli Quartet
Dear Mr.Cole | Novus | 4163182-2
John Pizzarelli Trio
P.S. Mr.Cole | RCA | 2663563-2
Dear Mr.Cole | Novus | 4163182-2
John Pizzarelli Trio With Harry Allen
P.S. Mr.Cole | RCA | 2663563-2

Pizzarelli,Martin | (b)
John Pizzarelli Quartet
Dear Mr.Cole | Novus | 4163182-2
John Pizzarelli Trio
P.S. Mr.Cole | RCA | 2663563-2
John Pizzarelli Trio With Harry Allen
P.S. Mr.Cole | RCA | 2663563-2

Pizzi,Ray | (alto-fl,ss,as,fl,bassoon,tsreeds)
Joe Henderson And His Orchestra
Joe Henderson:The Milestone Years | Milestone | 8MCD 4413-2
Ray Pizzi Trio
One More Life | Bhakti Jazz | BR 29

Pizziali,Paulo Humberto | (perc)
Baden Powell Ensemble
Three Originals:Tristeza On Guitar/Poema On Guitar/Apaixonado | MPS | 519216-2

Pizzo,Salvatore | (tb)
Orchestra Jazz Siciliana
Orchestra Jazz Siciliana Plays The Music Of Carla Bley | Watt | XtraWatt/4

Pizzurro,Salvatore | (tb)

Pla,Enrique | (dr,perctrap-dr)
Irakere
Yemayá | Blue Note | 498239-2

Planchenault,Bernard | (dr)
Blossom Dearie Trio
Jazz In Paris:Blossom Dearie-The Pianist/Les Blue Stars | EmArCy | 064784-2
Guy Lafitte Sextet
Jazz In Paris:Guy Lafitte-Blue And Sentimental | EmArCy | 159852-2 PMS
Michel De Villers Octet
Jazz In Paris:Saxophones Á Saint-Germain Des Prés | EmArCy | 014060-2

Planet Blow |
Planet Blow
Alien Lunatic | Jazz Haus Musik | JHM 0071 CD

Plasencia,Omar | (perc)
Russ Spiegel Group
Twilight | double moon | CHRDM 71026

Plater,Bobby | (as,arr,cl,sax,flts)
(Little)Jimmy Scott With The Lionel Hampton Orchestra
Everybody's Somebody's Fool | Decca | 050669-2
Big Joe Turner With The Count Basie Orchestra
Flip Flop And Fly | Original Jazz Classics | OJCCD 1053-2(2310937)
Count Basie And His Orchestra
Afrique | RCA | 2179618-2
Fun Time | Pablo | 2310945-2
Count Basie: Salle Pleyel, April 17th, 1972 | Laserlight | 36127
Basie Meets Bond | Capitol | 538225-2
Basie's Beatle Bag | Verve | 557455-2
Live at The Sands | Reprise | 9362-45946-2
Jazz Dance | Original Jazz Classics | OJCCD 1002-2(1210890)
I Told You So | Original Jazz Classics | OJCCD 824-2(2310767)
Digital III At Montreux | Original Jazz Classics | OJCCD 996-2(2308223)
The Jazz Giants Play Harry Warren:Lullaby Of Broadway | Prestige | PCD 24204-2
Count Basie Big Band
Montreux '77 | Original Jazz Classics | OJCCD 377-2
Farmers Market Barbecue | Original Jazz Classics | OJCCD 732-2(2310874)
Ella Fitzgerald With Count Basie And His Orchestra
Digital III At Montreux | Original Jazz Classics | OJCCD 996-2(2308223)
Ella Fitzgerald With The Count Basie Orchestra
Bluella:Ella Fitzgerald Sings The Blues | Pablo | 2310960-2
For The Love Of Ella Fitzgerald | Verve | 841765-2
Lionel Hampton And His Orchestra
Planet Jazz:Lionel Hampton | Planet Jazz | 2152059-2
Lionel Hampton:Flying Home | Dreyfus Jazz Line | FDM 36735-2
Lionel Hampton Orchestra
The Big Bands Vol.1.The Snader Telescriptions | Storyville | 4960043
Milt Jackson Orchestra
Sarah Vaughan Birthday Celebration | Fantasy | FANCD 6090-2
Milt Jackson With The Count Basie Orchestra
To Bags...With Love:Memorial Album | Pablo | 2310967-2
Milt Jackson Birthday Celebration | Fantasy | FANCD 6079-2
Milt Jackson + Count Basie + Big Band Vol.1 | Original Jazz Classics | OJCCD 740-2(2310822)
Milt Jackson + Count Basie + Big Band Vol.2 | Original Jazz Classics | OJCCD 741-2(2310823)
Sarah Vaughan And The Count Basie Orchestra
Sarah Vaughan Birthday Celebration | Fantasy | FANCD 6090-2

Plato,Herman | (tb)
Chet Baker With The NDR-Bigband
NDR Big Band-Bravissimo | ACT | 9232-2
My Favourite Songs: The Last Great Concert Vol.1 | Enja | ENJ-5097 2
The Last Concert Vol.I+II | Enja | ENJ-6074 22
Chet Baker-The Legacy Vol.1 | Enja | ENJ-9021 2
Heinz Sauer Quartet With The NDR Big Band
NDR Big Band-Bravissimo | ACT | 9232-2
Joe Pass With The NDR Big Band
Joe Pass In Hamburg | ACT | 9100-2

Plaxico,Lonnie | (6-string-el-b,bel-b)
Barbara Dennerlein Group
Take Off | Verve | 527664-2
Junkanoo | Verve | 537122-2
Cassandra Wilson And Her Quintet
Point Of View | JMT Edition | 919004-2
Cassandra Wilson Group
Misty Blue:Sweet Sisters Swing Songs Of Sorrow And Sadness | Blue Note | 521151-2
Blue Light 'Til Dawn | Blue Note | 781357-2
Traveling Miles | Blue Note | 854123-2
Cassandra Wilson With The Mulgrew Miller Trio
Blue Skies | JMT Edition | 919018-2
Don Byron Quartet
Tuskegee Experiments | Nonesuch | 7559-79280-2
Don Byron Quintet
Tuskegee Experiments | Nonesuch | 7559-79280-2
Greg Osby Quartet
Mindgames | JMT Edition | 919021-2
Greg Osby Quintet
Mindgames | JMT Edition | 919021-2

Lance Bryant With The Christoph Spendel Trio
West End Avenue II | Nabel Records:Jazz Network | CD 4644
Nicolas Simion Group
Black Sea | Tutu Records | 888134-2*
Ray Anderson Lapis Lazuli Band
Funkorific | Enja | ENJ-9340 2
Rodney Jones Group
Soul Manifesto | Blue Note | 530499-2
Steve Coleman Group
Motherland Pulse | JMT Edition | 919001-2

played by Steve Swallow,The bassintroduction is |
The Jazz Composer's Orchestra
Comminications | JCOA | 1001/2

Plaza,Javier | (coro,voc,maracasguira de parranda)
Conexion Latina
Mambo 2000 | Enja | ENJ-7055 2
La Conexión | Enja | ENJ-9065 2
Mambo Nights | Enja | ENJ-9402 2

Pleasant,Tim | (dr)
Michael Kanan Trio
Convergence | Fresh Sound Records | FSNT 055 CD
The Gentleman Is A Dope | Fresh Sound Records | FSNT 147 CD

Pleasure,King | (voc)
King Pleasure With Orchestra
Blue Velvet: Crooners, Swooners And Velvet Vocals | Blue Note | 521153-2

Pleeth,Anthony | (cello)
Dee Dee Bridgewater With Orchestra
Dear Ella | Verve | 539102-2

Plenar,Elvira | (p,keyboardssynth)
Elvira Plenar Trio
I Was Just... | free flow music | ffm 0191
Gabriele Hasler-Elvira Plenar-Andreas Willers
Sonetburger-Nach Texten Von Oskar Pastior | Foolish Music | FM 211793
Marilyn Mazur's Future Song
Small Labyrinths | ECM | 1559(533679-2)
Marilyn Mazure's Future Song | VeraBra Records | CDVBR 2105-2

Plettendorf,Uli | (tb)
Dusko Goykovich Big Band
Balkan Connection | Enja | ENJ-9047 2
Johnny Griffin With The NDR Big Band
NDR Big Band-Bravissimo | ACT | 9232-2

Plockyn,Michel | (fl)
Raymond Fol Big Band
Jazz In Paris:Raymond Fol-Les 4 Saisons | EmArCy | 548791-2

Plumb,Neely | (as,clbs)
Artie Shaw And His Orchestra
Planet JazzArtie Shaw | Planet Jazz | 2152057-2
Planet Jazz:Big Bands | Planet Jazz | 2169649-2
Lena Horne With The Horace Henderson Orchestra
Planet Jazz:Lena Horne | Planet Jazz | 2165373-2

Plümer,Gunnar | (b,el-bel-p)
Brecker-Engstfeld-Plümer-Weiss
ToGether | Nabel Records:Jazz Network | CD 4648
Engstfeld-Plümer-Weiss
Drivin' | Nabel Records:Jazz Network | CD 4618
Hugo Read Group
Songs Of A Wayfarer | Nabel Records:Jazz Network | CD 4653
John Thomas & Lifeforce
Devil Dance | Nabel Records:Jazz Network | CD 4601
3000 Worlds | Nabel Records:Jazz Network | CD 4604
Lee Konitz-Frank Wunsch Quartet
S'Nice | Nabel Records:Jazz Network | CD 4641
Lee Konitz-Kenny Wheeler Quartet
Live At Birdland Neuburg | double moon | CHRDM 71014
Matthias Nadolny-Gunnar Plümer
You'll Never Walk Alone | Nabel Records:Jazz Network | CD 4667
Peter Weiss Quartet
Personal Choice | Nabel Records:Jazz Network | CD 4669
Peter Weiss Sextet
Personal Choice | Nabel Records:Jazz Network | CD 4669
Randy Brecker-Wolfgang Engstfeld Quartet
Mr. Max! | Nabel Records:Jazz Network | CD 4637
Uli Beckerhoff Quintet
Original Motion Picture Soundtrack:Das Geheimnis(Secret Of Love) | Nabel Records:Jazz Network | CD 4666
Uli Beckerhoff Septet
Private Life | Nabel Records:Jazz Network | CD 4657

Plummer,Paul | (ts)
George Russell Sextet
The Outer View | Original Jazz Classics | OJCCD 616-2(RLP 9440)

Plummer,Stanley | (v)
Milt Jackson With Strings
To Bags...With Love:Memorial Album | Pablo | 2310967-2

Pocaro,Jeff | (drtom-tom)
Stan Getz With Orchestra
Apasionado | A&M Records | 395297-2

Pocaro,Joe | (drperc)
Sarah Vaughan And Her Band
Songs Of The Beatles | Atlantic | 16037-2
Singers Unlimited With The Roger Kellaway Cello Quartet
The Singers Unlimited:Magic Voices | MPS | 539130-2

Pocaro,Steve | (synth)
Sarah Vaughan And Her Band
Songs Of The Beatles | Atlantic | 16037-2

Pochonet,Gerard 'Dave' | (dr)
Jean Pierre Sasson Quartet
Americans Swinging In Paris:Lucky Thompson | EMI Records | 539651-2
Lucky Thompson Quartet
Americans Swinging In Paris:Lucky Thompson | EMI Records | 539651-2
Lucky Thompson Quintet
Americans Swinging In Paris:Lucky Thompson | EMI Records | 539651-2
Lucky Thompson Trio
Americans Swinging In Paris:Lucky Thompson | EMI Records | 539651-2
Lucky Thompson With The Gerard Pochonet All-Stars
Planet Jazz:Jazz Saxophone | Planet Jazz | 2169653-2
Wild Bill Davis Group
Americans Swinging In Paris:Wild Bill Davis | EMI Records | 539665-2

Podehl,Hans | (dr)
Heinz Schönberger Quintet
Deutsches Jazz Fesival 1954/1955 | Bear Family Records | BCD 15430
Paul Kuhn Quartet
Deutsches Jazz Fesival 1954/1955 | Bear Family Records | BCD 15430
Paul Kuhn Quintet
Deutsches Jazz Fesival 1954/1955 | Bear Family Records | BCD 15430

Poe,Salvadore | (g)
Lisa Ekdahl With The Salvador Poe Quartet, Strings And Guests
Lisa Ekdahl Sings Salvadore Poe | RCA | 2179681-2

Poffet,Joseph | (b-clas)
Q4 Orchester Project
Lyon's Brood | Creative Works Records | CW CD 1018-3

Poffet,Michael | (b)
Max Neissendorfer Trio
Staubfrei | EGO | 95100

Poffo,Christian | (keyboardsprogramming)
Mario Neunkirchen Quintet
Long Distance | Laika Records | LK 94-060

Pogoda,Matthias | (gperc)
Muriel Zoe Group
Red And Blue | ACT | 9416-2

Pöhl,Frauke | (v)
Uri Caine With The Concerto Köln
Concerto Köln | Winter&Winter | 910086-2

Pöhlert,Werner | (g)
Wolfgang Lauth Quartet
Deutsches Jazz Fesival 1954/1955 | Bear Family Records | BCD 15430
Lauther | Bear Family Records | BCD 15717 AH
Wolfgang Lauth Septet
Noch Lauther | Bear Family Records | BCD 15942 AH

Pöhnl,Oscar | (drvoc)
Al Jones Blues Band
Sharper Than A Tack | Blues Beacon | BLU-1034 2

Poindexter,Pony | (as,ssvoc)
Annie Ross & PonyPoindexter With The Berlin All Stars
Annie Ross & Pony Poindexter with The Berlin All Stars | MPS | 9811257

Pointer Sisters,The | (voc-samples)
Marcus Miller Group
Tales | Dreyfus Jazz Line | FDM 36571-2

Pointer,Roosevelt | (b)
Albert King Blues Band
Wednesday Night In San Francisco | Stax | SCD 8556-2

Poker Bigband,The |
Ku-umba Frank Lacy & The Poker Bigband
Songs From The Musical 'Poker' | Tutu Records | 888150-2*

Poland,Bob | (bs,reeds,saxts)
Harry James And His Orchestra
Trumpet Blues:The Best Of Harry James | Capitol | 521224-2
Peggy Lee With The Benny Goodman Orchestra
Peggy Lee & Benny Goodman:The Complete Recordings 1941-1947 | CBS | C2K 65686

Polcer,Ed | (co)
A Salute To Eddie Condon
A Salute To Eddie Condon | Nagel-Heyer | CD 004
One Two Three | Nagel-Heyer | CD 008
The First Sampler | Nagel-Heyer | NHR SP 5
Mark Shane-Terry Blaine Group
With Thee I Swing! | Nagel-Heyer | CD 040

Polgar,Zsolt | (cello)
Bernd Konrad Jazz Group With Symphonie Orchestra
Wen Die Götter Lieben | Creative Works Records | CW CD 1010-1

Poli,Michel | (tp)
Raymond Fol Big Band
Jazz In Paris:Raymond Fol-Les 4 Saisons | EmArCy | 548791-2

Poliakin,Raoul | (v)
Bill Evans Quartet With Orchestra
The Complete Bill Evans On Verve | Verve | 527953-2
From Left To Right | Verve | 557451-2
Bill Evans With Orchestra
The Complete Bill Evans On Verve | Verve | 527953-2
From Left To Right | Verve | 557451-2
Freddie Hubbard Orchestra
The Body And The Soul | Impulse(MCA) | 951183-2
Paul Desmond Quartet With The Don Sebesby Orchestra
From The Hot Afternoon | Verve | 543487-2
Phil Woods Quartet With Orchestra & Strings
Round Trip | Verve | 559804-2
Wes Montgomery With The Jimmy Jones Orchestra
Wes Montgomery-The Complete Riverside Recordings | Riverside | 12 RCD 4408-2
The Jazz Giants Play Rodgers & Hart:Blue Moon | Prestige | PCD 24205-2

Polifroni,Francis | (bsts)
Harry James And His Orchestra
Trumpet Blues:The Best Of Harry James | Capitol | 521224-2

Politis,James | (fl)
The Modern Jazz Society
A Concert Of Contemporary Music | Verve | 559827-2

Poll Winners,The |
The Poll Winners
The Poll Winners Ride Again | Original Jazz Classics | OJC 607(C 7556)
Poll Winners Three | Original Jazz Classics | OJCCD 692-2(C 7576)
Exploring The Scene | Original Jazz Classics | OJCCD 969-2(C 7581)
The Jazz Giants Play Harry Warren:Lullaby Of Broadway | Prestige | PCD 24204-2

Pollack,Ben | (dr,voc,ldspeech)
Ben Pollack And His Park Central Orchestra
Planet Jazz:Jack Teagarden | Planet Jazz | 2161236-2
Jazz:The Essential Collection Vol.3 | IN+OUT Records | 78013-2

Pollack,Malcolm | (background-voc)
The Brecker Brothers
Return Of The Brecker Brothers | GRP | GRP 96842

Pollakusky,Jennifer | (voc)
Kevin Mahogany With Orchestra
Songs And Moments | Enja | ENJ-8072 2

Pollan,Albert | (tuba)
Stan Kenton And His Orchestra
Adventures In Blues | Capitol | 520089-2

Pollen,Al | (tuba)
Sonny Stitt Orchestra
Verve Jazz Masters 50:Sonny Sitt | Verve | 527651-2

Pollikoff,Max | (v)
Louis Armstrong And His Friends
Planet Jazz:Louis Armstrong | Planet Jazz | 2152052-2
Planet Jazz Sampler | Planet Jazz | 2152326-2
Louis Armstrong And His Friends | Bluebird | 2663961-2
Paul Desmond Quartet With The Don Sebesby Orchestra
From The Hot Afternoon | Verve | 543487-2
Phil Woods Quartet With Orchestra & Strings
Round Trip | Verve | 559804-2

Polo,Danny | (as,cl,bs,ts,reedssax)
Coleman Hawkins All Star Octet
Planet Jazz:Coleman Hawkins | Planet Jazz | 2152055-2
Dany Polo Trio
JazzIn Paris:Harlem Piano In Montmartre | EmArCy | 018447-2
Jack Teagarden And His Orchestra
Jazz:The Essential Collection Vol.3 | IN+OUT Records | 78013-2

Polyphonix |
Polyphonix
Alarm | Jazz 'n' Arts Records | 0300

Polzer,Peter | (p)
Jörg Seidel Group
I Feel So Smoochie: A Tribute To Nat King Cole | Edition Collage | EC 532-2

Polziehn,Olaf | (keyboardsp)
Benny Waters & Jan Jankeje
Let's Talk About Jazz | G&J Records | GJ 2009 Maxi-CD
Benny Waters Sextet
A' Portrait Of Jan Jankeje | Jazzpoint | JP 1054 CD
Olaf Polziehn Trio
American Songbook | Satin Doll Productions | SDP 1032-1 CD

Pomanti,Lou | (p,synthsynclavier)
Hugh Marsh Duo/Quartet/Orchestra
The Bear Walks | VeraBra Records | CDVBR 2011-2

Pomeroy,Herb | (tp)
Anita O'Day With The Gary McFarland Orchestra
All The Sad Youn Men | Verve | 517065-2
Verve Jazz Masters 49:Anita O'Day | Verve | 527653-2
Charlie Parker Quintet
Charlie Parker At Storyville | Blue Note | 785108-2
Marty Elkins And Her Sextet
Fuse Blues | Nagel-Heyer | CD 062

Pommerenke,Eberhard | (bld)
New Jazz Group Hannover
Deutsches Jazz Fesival 1954/1955 | Bear Family Records | BCD 15430

Pompa,Anthony Michael | (voc)
Spyro Gyra & Guests
Love & Other Obsessions | GRP | GRP 98112

Pompeo,John | (dr)
Vince Guaraldi Group
Charlie Brown's Holiday Hits | Fantasy | FCD 9682-2

Ponder,Jimmy | (el-g,g,vocg-solo)
Andrew Hill Sextet
Grass Roots | Blue Note | 522672-2
Donald Byrd Orchestra
Blue Break Beats | Blue Note | 799106-2
Jimmy Ponder Quartet
Jazzin' Vol.2: The Music Of Stevie Wonder | Fantasy | FANCD 6088-2
Lou Donaldson Quartet
Mr.Shing-A-Ling | Blue Note | 784271-2
Lou Donaldson Quintet
Mr.Shing-A-Ling | Blue Note | 784271-2
The Lost Grooves | Blue Note | 831883-2
Rusty Bryant Quintet
Jazzin' With The Soul Brothers | Fantasy | FANCD 6086-2

Ponomarev,Valery | (tpfl-h)
Art Blakey And The Jazz Messengers
Night In Tunisia | Philips | 800064-2

Ponthieux,Jean-Luc | (bel-b)
Claude Barthelmy Group
Moderne | Owl Records | 014739-2

Pontieux,Loic | (dr)
Serge Forté Trio
Vaina | Laika Records | LK 90-021

Pontiggia,Claudio | (fr-h)
Miles Davis With Gil Evans Orchestra, The George Gruntz Concert Jazz Band And Guests
Miles & Quincy Live At Montreux | Warner | 9362-45221-2

Ponty,Jean-Luc | (el-v,bar-violectra,bells,grand-p)
Chick Corea Quartet
My Spanish Heart | Polydor | 543303-3
Jean-Luc Ponty
The Very Best Of Jean-Luc Ponty | Rhino | 8122-79862-2
Jean-Luc Ponty Group
Mystical Adventures | Atlantic | 19333-2
Atlantic Jazz: Fusion | Atlantic | 7567-81711-2
Jean-Luc Ponty Quartet
Jazz In Paris:Jean-Luc Ponty-Jazz Long Playing | EmArCy | 548150-2 PMS
Cosmic Messenger | Atlantic | 7567-81550-2
The Very Best Of Jean-Luc Ponty | Rhino | 8122-79862-2
Jean-Luc Ponty Quintet
Jazz In Paris:Jean-Luc Ponty-Jazz Long Playing | EmArCy | 548150-2 PMS
Aurora | Atlantic | 7567-81543-2
Cosmic Messenger | Atlantic | 7567-81550-2
The Very Best Of Jean-Luc Ponty | Rhino | 8122-79862-2
Jean-Luc Ponty Sextet
Enigmatic Ocean | Atlantic | 19110-2
Cosmic Messenger | Atlantic | 7567-81550-2
The Very Best Of Jean-Luc Ponty | Rhino | 8122-79862-2
Jean-Luc Ponty-Raymond Griffin
The Very Best Of Jean-Luc Ponty | Rhino | 8122-79862-2
Mahavishnu Orchestra
Apocalypse | CBS | 467092-2

Ponzol,Peter | (as,fl,ts,synthss)
Jazzensemble Des Hessischen Rundfunks
Atmosphering Conditions Permitting | ECM | 1549/50
Radio Jazzgroup Frankfurt
Jubilee Edition | double moon | CHRDM 71020

Pool,Carol | (v)
Steve Kuhn With Strings
Promises Kept | ECM | 1815(0675222)

Poole,Carl | (tp)
Benny Goodman And His Orchestra
Great Swing Classics In Hi-Fi | Capitol | 521223-2
Charlie Parker And His Orchestra
The Cole Porter Songbook | Verve | 823250-2
Bird: The Complete Charlie Parker On Verve | Verve | 837141-2
Charlie Parker With Orchestra
Charlie Parker:The Best Of The Verve Years | Verve | 527815-2
Charlie Parker With The Joe Lipman Orchestra
Verve Jazz Masters 28:Charlie Parker Plays Standards | Verve | 521854-2
Charlie Parker Big Band | Verve | 559835-2
Ella Fitzgerald With Sy Oliver And His Orchestra
Ella Fitzgerald:The Decca Years 1949-1954 | Decca | 050668-2
Louis Armstrong And The Commanders under the Direction of Camarata
Satchmo Serenaders | Verve | 543792-2
Louis Armstrong With Gordon Jenkins And His Orchestra And Choir
Satchmo In Style | Verve | 549594-2
Louis Armstrong-My Greatest Songs | MCA | MCD 18347
Swing Legends:Louis Armstrong | Nimbus Records | NI 2012
Louis Armstrong With The Commanders
Ambassador Louis Armstrong Vol.17:Moments To Remember(1952-1956) | Ambassador | CLA 1917

Poole,George | (cellov)
Johnny Hartman And His Orchestra
Unforgettable | Impulse(MCA) | IMP 11522

Poole,John | (dr)
Anita O'Day With The Oscar Peterson Quartet
Verve Jazz Masters 49:Anita O'Day | Verve | 527653-2

Poole,Tom | (tp)
Etta James & The Roots Band
Burnin' Down he House | RCA | 3411633-2

Popatkar,Manikrao | (tabla)
Subroto Roy Chowdhury Group
Serenity | Jazzpoint | JP 1017 CD

Pope,Odean | (fl,ts,oboevoice)
Max Roach Double Quartet
To The Max! | Enja | ENJ-7021 22
Max Roach Quartet
To The Max! | Enja | ENJ-7021 22

Popowycz,Roman | (tp)
Eric Dolphy Quartet With The University Of Illinois Big Band
The Illinois Concert | Blue Note | 499826-2

Poppel,Hans | (p)
Cornelius Claudio Kreusch/Hans Poppel
Music For Two Pianos | Edition Collage | EC 465-2
Piano Moments | Take Twelve On CD | TT 007-2

Poppink,Wim | (clas)
Coleman Hawkins Trio
Jazz:The Essential Collection Vol.3 | IN+OUT Records | 78013-2
Coleman Hawkins With The Ramblers
Jazz:The Essential Collection Vol.3 | IN+OUT Records | 78013-2

Poprawski,Lukasz | (as)
European Jazz Youth Orchestra
Swinging Europe 1 | dacapo | DCCD 9449
Swinging Europe 2 | dacapo | DCCD 9450

Porcelli,Bobby | (as,bs,flss)
Fleurine With Band And Horn Section
Meant To Be! | EmArCy | 159085-2

Porcino,Al | (ld,voctp)
Al Porcino Big Band
Al Porcino Big Band Live! | Organic Music | ORGM 9717
Al Cohn Meets Al Porcino | Organic Music | ORGM 9730
Anita O'Day With The Bill Holman Orchestra
Verve Jazz Masters 49:Anita O'Day | Verve | 527653-2
Art Pepper Plus Eleven
Art Pepper + Eleven | Contemporary | CSA 7568-6
Modern Jazz Classics | Original Jazz Classics | OJC20 341-2
Benny Carter And His Orchestra
Aspects | Capitol | 852677-2
Cal Tjader's Orchestra
Tjader Plays Mambo | Original Jazz Classics | OJCCD 274-2(F 3221)
Charlie Parker And His Orchestra
The Cole Porter Songbook | Verve | 823250-2
Bird: The Complete Charlie Parker On Verve | Verve | 837141-2

Charlie Parker With Orchestra
Charlie Parker:The Best Of The Verve Years | Verve | 527815-2
Charlie Parker With Strings
Charlie Parker With Strings:The Master Takes | Verve | 523984-2
Bird: The Complete Charlie Parker On Verve | Verve | 837141-2
Charlie Parker With The Joe Lipman Orchestra
Verve Jazz Masters 28:Charlie Parker Plays Standards | Verve | 521854-2
Charlie Parker With Strings:The Master Takes | Verve | 523984-2
Charlie Parker Big Band | Verve | 559835-2
Charlie Parker With The Neal Hefti Orchestra
Charlie Parker:The Best Of The Verve Years | Verve | 527815-2
Bird: The Complete Charlie Parker On Verve | Verve | 837141-2
Chubby Jackson Big Band
Gerry Mulligan Quartet feat.Chet Baker | Original Jazz Classics | OJCCD 711-2(F 8082/P 7641)
Dizzy Gillespie And His Orchestra
Talking Verve:Dizzy Gillespie | Verve | 533846-2
Ella Fitzgerald With Frank De Vol And His Orchestra
Get Happy! | Verve | 523321-2
Ella Fitzgerald With Marty Paich's Dektette
Ella Swings Lightly | Verve | 517535-2
Ella Fitzgerald With The Marty Paich Dek-tette
Ella Fitzgerald-First Lady Of Song | Verve | 517898-2
Verve Jazz Masters 6:Ella Fitzgerald | Verve | 519822-2
Verve Jazz Masters 46:Ella Fitzgerald-The Jazz Sides | Verve | 527655-2
Frank Sinatra With The Count Basie Orchestra
Sinatra-Basie:An Historic Musical First | Reprise | 7599-27023-2
It Might As Well Be Spring | Reprise | 7599-27027-2
Gene Krupa And His Orchestra
Mullenium | CBS | CK 65678
Johnny Hartman And His Orchestra
Unforgettable | Impulse(MCA) | IMP 11522
June Christy With The Shorty Rogers Orchestra
June Christy Big Band Special | Capitol | 498319-2
Peggy Lee With The Quincy Jones Orchestra
Blues Cross Country | Capitol | 520088-2
Ralph Burns And His Orchestra
The Complete Verve Roy Eldridge Studio Sessions | Verve | 9861278
Terry Gibbs Big Band
Terry Gibbs Dream Band Vol.4:Main Stem | Contemporary | CCD 7656-2
Terry Gibbs Dream Band
Terry Gibbs Dream Band Vol.3:Flying Home | Contemporary | CCD 7654-2
Terry Gibbs Dream Band Vol.5:The Big Cat | Contemporary | CCD 7657-2
Terry Gibbs Dream Band Vol.6:One More Time | Contemporary | CCD 7658-2
Thad Jones-Mel Lewis Orchestra
The Groove Merchant/The Second Race | Laserlight | 24656
Woody Herman And His Orchestra
The Legends Of Swing | Laserlight | 24659
Woody Herman:Four Brother | Dreyfus Jazz Line | FDM 36722-2
The Raven Speaks | Original Jazz Classics | OJCCD 663-2(F 9416)

Porecki,Benji | (org)
Chuck Brown And The Second Chapter Band
Timeless | Minor Music | 801068

Poree,Greg | (g)
Donald Byrd Orchestra
Ethiopian Knights | Blue Note | 854328-2

Porrello,Tom | (tp)
Woody Herman And His Orchestra
King Cobra | Original Jazz Classics | OJCCD 1068-2(F 9499)

Portal,Michel | (as,b-cl,sax,bandoneon,cl,ts)
Aldo Romano Duo
Il Piacere | Owl Records | 013575-2
Galliano-Portal
Blow Up | Dreyfus Jazz Line | FDM 36589-2
Jean-Luc Ponty Quintet
Jazz In Paris:Jean-Luc Ponty-Jazz Long Playing | EmArCy | 548150-2 PMS
Joachim Kühn Group
Universal Time | EmArCy | 016671-2
Michel Portal-Martial Solal
Fast Mood | RCA | 2169310-2
Michel Portal-Richard Galliano
Concerts | Dreyfus Jazz Line | FDM 36661-2
Richard Galliano Group
Laurita | Dreyfus Jazz Line | FDM 36572-9
French Touch | Dreyfus Jazz Line | FDM 36596-2
Richard Galliano Quartet
Gallianissimo! The Best Of Richard Galliano | Dreyfus Jazz Line | FDM 36616-2
Richard Galliano-Michel Portal
Gallianissimo! The Best Of Richard Galliano | Dreyfus Jazz Line | FDM 36616-2

Porter Jr.,George | (bel-b)
Maceo Parker Group
Southern Exposure | Minor Music | 801033

Porter,Bobby | (perc)
The Three Sounds
Blue Break Beats | Blue Note | 799106-2

Porter,Charles | (tp)
Paquito D'Rivera Group With The Absolute Ensemble
Habanera | Enja | ENJ-9395 2

Porter,Curtis[Shafi Hadi] | (asts)
Charles Mingus Orchestra
Tijuana Moods(The Complete Edition) | RCA | 2663840-2

Porter,Gene | (bs,cl,asts)
Fats Waller And His Rhythm
Planet Jazz:Fats Waller | Planet Jazz | 2152058-2

Porter,Jake | (tp)
Lena Horne With The Horace Henderson Orchestra
Planet Jazz:Lena Horne | Planet Jazz | 2165373-2

Porter,John | (b-gg)
Jimmy Smith All Stars
Jimmy Smith:Dot Com Blues | Blue Thumb | 543978-2

Porter,Karl | (bassoon)
Chick Corea Trio
Inner Space | Atlantic | 7567-81304-2

Porter,Larry | (p,celesta,el-p,percvoc)
Marty Cook Conspiracy
Phases Of The Moon | Tutu Records | 888160-2*
Monty Waters Quartet
Monty Waters New York Calling Vol.2 | Tutu Records | 888182-2*
Mundell Lowe Quintet
Mundell's Moods | Nagel-Heyer | CD 065

Porter,Randy | (p)
David Friesen Trio
The Name Of A Woman | Intuition Records | INT 3334-2

Porter,Roy | (dr)
Charlie Parker Septet
Charlie Parker:Now's The Time | Dreyfus Jazz Line | FDM 36724-2

Porter,Vernon | (tb)
Lionel Hampton And His Orchestra
Lionel Hampton:Flying Home | Dreyfus Jazz Line | FDM 36735-2

Porter,Yank | (dr)
Louis Armstrong And His Orchestra
Planet Jazz:Louis Armstrong | Planet Jazz | 2152052-2
Best Of The Complete RCA Victor Recordings | RCA | 2663636-2
Louis Armstrong:A 100th Birthday Celebration | RCA | 2663694-2
Jazz:The Essential Collection Vol.2 | IN+OUT Records | 78012-2

Portinho,Thelmo Martins Porto | (dr,perc,pandeirovoc)
Gato Barbieri Orchestra
The Roots Of Acid Jazz | Impulse(MCA) | IMP 12042
Paquito D'Rivera Orchestra
Jazzrock-Anthology Vol.3:Fusion | Zounds | CD 27100555

Portugail,Manfred | (el-g)
Tomatic 7
Haupstrom | Jazz Haus Musik | JHM 0101 CD

Porz,Franz | (tb)
Harald Banter Ensemble
Deutsches Jazz Fesival 1954/1955 | Bear Family Records | BCD 15430

Poschka,Rolf | (tp)
Joe Pass With The NDR Big Band
Joe Pass In Hamburg | ACT | 9100-2

Pöschl,Sunk | (dr)
Thomas Reimer Trio
Vienna's Heardt | Edition Collage | EC 506-2

Poser,Florian | (vib,marimba,xyl,g,el-p,synth,perc)
Florian Poser
Winds | Edition Collage | EC 500-2
Florian Poser Group
Say Yes! | Edition Collage | EC 452-2

Posey,Hal | (tpfl-h)
Charlie Byrd Septet
Latin Byrd | Milestone | MCD 47005-2

Posner,Leonard | (v)
Tommy Dorsey And His Orchestra
Planet Jazz:Frank Sinatra & Tommy Dorsey | Planet Jazz | 2152067-2

Potoker,Johnny | (p)
Planet Jazz:Tommy Dorsey | Planet Jazz | 2159972-2

Potratz,Oliver | (b)
Carsten Daerr Trio
PurpleCoolCarSleep | Traumton Records | 4472-2

Potter,Chris | (alto-fl,b-cl,ss,as,ts,reed-org)
Al Foster Quartet
Brandyn | Laika Records | 35100832
Antonio Farao Quartet
Thorn | Enja | ENJ-9399 2
Chris Potter & Jazzpar Septet
This Will Be | Storyville | STCD 4245
Chris Potter Group
Traveling Mercies | Verve | 018243-2
Chris Potter Quartet
Gratitude | Verve | 549433-2
This Will Be | Storyville | STCD 4245
Dave Douglas Group
The Infinite | RCA | 2663918-2
Dave Holland Big Band
What Goes Around | ECM | 1777(014002-2)
Dave Holland Quintet
Prime Directive | ECM | 1698(547950-2)
Not For Nothin' | ECM | 1758(014004-2)
Extended Play | ECM | 1864/65(038505-2)
David Binney Group
South | ACT | 9279-2
Jam Session
Jam Session Vol.1 | Steeplechase | SCCD 31522
Jim Hall Jazzpar Quartet
Jazzpar 98 | Storyville | STCD 4230
Jim Hall Jazzpar Quartet +4
Jazzpar 98 | Storyville | STCD 4230
Joachim Kühn Group
Universal Time | EmArCy | 016671-2
Joachim Schoenecker Quartet
In The Moment | Nagel-Heyer | CD 2009
Joachim Schoenecker-Chris Potter
In The Moment | Nagel-Heyer | CD 2009
Mingus Big Band 93
Nostalgia In Times Square | Dreyfus Jazz Line | FDM 36559-2
Nguyen Le Trio With Guests
Bakida | ACT | 9275-2
Paul Motian Electric Bebop Band
Flight Of The Blue Jay | Winter&Winter | 910009-2
Monk And Powell | Winter&Winter | 910045-2
Paul Motian Trio With Chris Potter And Larry Grenadier
Paul Motian Trio 2000 + One | Winter&Winter | 910032-2
Steve Swallow Group
Deconstructed | Watt | XtraWatt/9(537119-2)
Steve Swallow Quintet
Always Pack Your Uniform On Top | Watt | XtraWatt/10(543506-2)
Steve Swallow Trio
Damaged In Transit | Watt | XtraWatt/11(067792-2)

Potter,Jerry | (dr)
Willis Jackson Sextet
At Large | Prestige | PCD 24243-2

Potter,John | (bj)
Cy Laurie Jazz Band
The Golden Years Of Revival Jazz,Sampler | Storyville | 109 1001
Cy Laurie's New Orleans Septet
The Golden Years Of Revival Jazz,Vol 1 | Storyville | STCD 5506
The Golden Years Of Revival Jazz,Vol.5 | Storyville | STCD 5510
The Golden Years Of Revival Jazz,Vol.6 | Storyville | STCD 5511
The Golden Years Of Revival Jazz,Vol.8 | Storyville | STCD 5513
The Golden Years Of Revival Jazz,Vol.9 | Storyville | STCD 5514
The Golden Years Of Revival Jazz,Vol.11 | Storyville | STCD 5516

Potter,Roger | (g)
Mike Westbrook Brass Band
Glad Day:Settings Of William Blake | Enja | ENJ-9376 2

Potter,Tommy | (b)
Al Haig Sextet(Quintet)
Al Haig Trio And Sextets | Original Jazz Classics | OJCCD 1929-2(SPL 1118)
Bud Powell Quintet
The Amazing Bud Powell Vol.1 | Blue Note | 532136-2
Bud Powell:Bouncing With Bud | Dreyfus Jazz Line | FDM 36725-2
Bud Powell Trio
Bud Powell:Bouncing With Bud | Dreyfus Jazz Line | FDM 36725-2
Bud Powell's Modernists
The Fabulous Fats Navarro Vol.1 | Blue Note | 0677207
The Fabulous Fats Navarro Vol.2 | Blue Note | 0677208
Charlie Parker And His Orchestra
Charlie Parker:The Best Of The Verve Years | Verve | 527815-2
Bird: The Complete Charlie Parker On Verve | Verve | 837141-2
Charlie Parker Quintet
Charlie Parker:Bird's Best Bop On Verve | Verve | 527452-2
Charlie Parker:The Best Of The Verve Years | Verve | 527815-2
Charlie Parker:Now's The Time | Dreyfus Jazz Line | FDM 36724-2
Bird At St. Nick's | Original Jazz Classics | OJC20 041-2(JWS 500)
Charlie Parker Septet
Charlie Parker | Verve | 539757-2
Charlie Parker With Strings
Verve Jazz Masters 28:Charlie Parker Plays Standards | Verve | 521854-2
Charlie Parker With Strings:The Master Takes | Verve | 523984-2
Bird: The Complete Charlie Parker On Verve | Verve | 837141-2
Don Lanphere Quintet
Fats Navarro:Nostalgia | Dreyfus Jazz Line | FDM 36736-2
Gene Ammons-Sonny Stitt Quintet
The Prestige Legacy Vol.2:Battles Of Saxes | Prestige | PCD 24252-2
Jimmy Forrest Quintet
Soul Street | Original Jazz Classics | OJCCD 987-2(NJ 8293)
Joe Williams With The Harry 'Sweets' Edison Sextet
Together/Have A Good Time | Roulette | 531790-2
Max Roach Quintet
Dizzy Gillespie:Pleyel Jazz Concert 1948 + Max Roach Quintet 1949 | Vogue | 21409412
Miles Davis Sextet
Dig | Original Jazz Classics | OJC20 005-2
The Jazz Giants Play Harold Arlen:Blues In The Night | Prestige | PCD 24201-2
Prestige All Stars
The Prestige Legacy Vol.2:Battles Of Saxes | Prestige | PCD 24252-2
Sonny Rollins Quartet
Thelonious Monk:The Complete Prestige Recordings | Prestige | 3 PRCD 4428-2
The Prestige Legacy Vol.1:The High Priests | Prestige | PCD 24251-2
Sonny Rollins Quartet feat.Thelonious Monk
Thelonious Monk/Sonny Rollins | Original Jazz Classics | OJCCD 059-2
Sonny Stitt Quartet
Kaleidoscope | Original Jazz Classics | OJCCD 060-2(P 7077)
Stan Getz Quartet
Stan Getz-The Complete Roost Sessions | EMI Records | 859622-2
Stan Getz:Imagination | Dreyfus Jazz Line | FDM 36733-2
Stan Getz Quartets | Original Jazz Classics | OJC20 121-2(P 7002)
The Jazz Giants Play Rodgers & Hart:Blue Moon | Prestige | PCD 24205-2
Thelonious Monk Quartet
Thelonious Monk:85th Birthday Celebration | zyx records | FANCD 6076-2
Wardell Gray Quartet
Wardell Gray Memorial Vol.1 | Original Jazz Classics | OJCCD 050-2(P 7008)
Willis Jackson Quintet
Together Again: Willis Jackson With Jack McDuff | Prestige | PRCD 24284-2

Pottle,Benny | (btuba)
Jack Teagarden And His Orchestra
Jazz:The Essential Collection Vol.3 | IN+OUT Records | 78013-2

Potts,Bill | (arr,ldp)
Lester Young And Earl Swope With The Bill Potts Trio
Lester Young In Washington,DC 1956:Vol.5 | Original Jazz Classics | OJCCD 993-2
Lester Young With The Bill Potts Trio
Lester Young In Washington,DC 1956:Vol.1 | Original Jazz Classics | OJCCD 782-2(2308219)
Lester Young In Washington,DC 1956:Vol.5 | Original Jazz Classics | OJCCD 993-2
The Jazz Giants Play Harry Warren:Lullaby Of Broadway | Prestige | PCD 24204-2

Poulsen,Freddy 'Freak' | (b,bj,voctb)
Adrian Bentzon's Jazzband
The Golden Years Of Revival Jazz,Sampler | Storyville | 109 1001
The Golden Years Of Revival Jazz,Vol 1 | Storyville | STCD 5506
The Golden Years Of Revival Jazz,Vol.2 | Storyville | STCD 5507
The Golden Years Of Revival Jazz,Vol.3 | Storyville | STCD 5508
The Golden Years Of Revival Jazz,Vol.4 | Storyville | STCD 5509
The Golden Years Of Revival Jazz,Vol.7 | Storyville | STCD 5512
The Golden Years Of Revival Jazz,Vol.13 | Storyville | STCD 5518
The Golden Years Of Revival Jazz,Vol.14 | Storyville | STCD 5519
Henrik Johansen's Jazzband
The Golden Years Of Revival Jazz,Vol.13 | Storyville | STCD 5518
The Golden Years Of Revival Jazz,Vol.14 | Storyville | STCD 5519
Theis/Nyegaard Jazzband
The Golden Years Of Revival Jazz,Sampler | Storyville | 109 1001
The Golden Years Of Revival Jazz,Vol.3 | Storyville | STCD 5508
The Golden Years Of Revival Jazz,Vol.5 | Storyville | STCD 5510
The Golden Years Of Revival Jazz,Vol.6 | Storyville | STCD 5511
The Golden Years Of Revival Jazz,Vol.12 | Storyville | STCD 5517
The Golden Years Of Revibal Jazz,Vol.15 | Storyville | STCD 5520

Poulsen.Hasse | (g)
Louis Sclavis Group
Napoli's Walls | ECM | 1857(038504-2)

Poutanen,Juhani | (bells,voicev)
Edward Vesala Group
Nan Madol | ECM | 1077

Povel,Ferdinand | (as,fl,sax,ss,tsreeds)
Benny Bailey Quintet
Jazz Portraits | EGO | 95080
John Marshall Quintet
Theme Of No Repeat | Organic Music | ORGM 9719
Klaus Weiss Orchestra
Live At The Domicile | ATM Records | ATM 3805-AH
Laura Fygi With Band
Bewitched | Verve | 514724-2
Slide Hampton-Joe Haider Jazz Orchestra
Give Me A Double | JHM Records | JHM 3627
Toots Thielemans And His Orchestra
Verve Jazz Masters Vol.59:Toots Thielemans | Verve | 535271-2
Toots Thielemans With The Ruud Bos Orchestra
The Silver Collection: Toots Thielemans | Polydor | 825086-2 PMS

Powe,Norman | (tb)
Louis Armstrong And His Orchestra
Best Of The Complete RCA Victor Recordings | RCA | 2663636-2
Louis Armstrong:A 100th Birthday Celebration | RCA | 2663694-2
Louis Armstrong:C'est Si Bon | Dreyfus Jazz Line | FDM 36730-2

Powell,Benny | (b-tbtb)
(Little)Jimmy Scott With The Lionel Hampton Orchestra
Everybody's Somebody's Fool | Decca | 050669-2
Abdullah Ibrahim Sextet
Mindif | Enja | ENJ-5073 2
Count Basie And His Orchestra
Jazz Gallery:Lester Young Vol.2(1946-59) | RCA | 2119541-2
Jazz Collection:Count Basie | Laserlight | 24368
The Legends Of Swing | Laserlight | 24659
Atomic Swing | Roulette | 497871-2
Verve Jazz Masters 2:Count Basie | Verve | 519819-2
Count Basie Swings-Joe Williams Sings | Verve | 519852-2
Verve Jazz Masters 20:Introducing | Verve | 519853-2
April In Paris | Verve | 521402-2
Breakfast Dance And Barbecue | Roulette | 531791-2
One O'Clock Jump | Verve | 559806-2
Chairman Of The Board | Roulette | 581664-2
The Complete Atomic Basie | Roulette | 828635-2
King Of Swing | Verve | 837433-2
Count Basie At Newport | Verve | 9861761
Count On The Coast Vol.1 | Phontastic | NCD 7555
Count On The Coast Vol.2 | Phontastic | NCD 7575
Dee Dee Bridgewater With Big Band
Dear Ella | Verve | 539102-2
Duke Ellington And Count Basie With Their Orchestras
First Time! | CBS | CK 65571
Eddie Harris Group
The Best Of Eddie Harris | Atlantic | 7567-81370-2
Ella Fitzgerald With The Count Basie Orchestra
Ella Fitzgerald-First Lady Of Song | Verve | 517898-2
Ella And Basie | Verve | 539059-2
Frank Sinatra With The Count Basie Orchestra
Sinatra-Basie:An Historic Musical First | Reprise | 7599-27023-2
J.J.Johnson And His Orchestra
Planet Jazz:J.J.Johnson | Planet Jazz | 2159974-2
Jimmy Smith With The Johnny Pate Orchestra
Jimmy Smith-Talkin' Verve | Verve | 531563-2
Johnny Hodges Orchestra
Planet Jazz:Johnny Hodges | Planet Jazz | 2152065-2
Lionel Hampton And His Orchestra
Planet Jazz:Big Bands | Planet Jazz | 2169649-2
Lionel Hampton:Flying Home | Dreyfus Jazz Line | FDM 36735-2
Lionel Hampton Orchestra
The Big Bands Vol.1.The Snader Telescriptions | Storyville | 4960043
Quincy Jones And His Orchestra
Verve Jazz Masters Vol.59:Toots Thielemans | Verve | 535271-2
Randy Weston African Rhythm
Khepera | Verve | 557821-2
Randy Weston African Rhythm Quintet and The Gnawa Master Musicians of Marocco
Spirit! The Power Of Music | Verve | 543256-2
Sarah Vaughan And Joe Williams With The Count Basie Orchestra
Jazz Profile | Blue Note | 823517-2
Sarah Vaughan And The Count Basie Orchestra
Ballads | Roulette | 537561-2

Sarah Vaughan And The Thad Jones Orchestra
Verve Jazz Masters 42:Sarah Vaughan-The Jazz Sides | Verve | 526817-2
Sarah Vaughan With Orchestra
!Viva! Vaughan | Mercury | 549374-2
Sarah Vaughan Sings The Mancini Songbook | Verve | 558401-2
Sarah Vaughan With The Count Basie Band
Jazz Profile | Blue Note | 823517-2
Stanley Turrentine And His Orchestra
The Lost Grooves | Blue Note | 831883-2
Thad Jones-Mel Lewis Orchestra
The Groove Merchant/The Second Race | Laserlight | 24656
The Dave Glasser/Clark Terry/Barry Harris Project
Uh! Oh! | Nagel-Heyer | CD 2003
Blues Of Summer | Nagel-Heyer | NH 1011
Zoot Sims With Orchestra
Passion Flower | Original Jazz Classics | OJCCD 939-2(2312120)

Powell,Bud | (p,voc,p-solotalking)
Art Blakey And The Jazz Messengers With Barney Wilen And Bud Powell
Jazz In Paris:Paris Jam Session | EmArCy | 832692-2 PMS
Bud Powell
The Best Of Bud Powell On Verve | Verve | 523392-2
Jazz Giant | Verve | 543832-2
Bud Powell Orchestra
Bebop | Pablo | PACD 2310978-2
Bud Powell Quartet
The Amazing Bud Powell Vol.3:Bud! | Blue Note | 535585-2
Parisian Thoroughfare | Pablo | CD 2310976-2
Bud Powell Paris Sessions | Pablo | PACD 2310972-2
Bud Powell Quintet
The Story Of Jazz Piano | Laserlight | 24653
The Amazing Bud Powell Vol.1 | Blue Note | 532136-2
Parisian Thoroughfare | Pablo | CD 2310976-2
Bud Powell:Bouncing With Bud | Dreyfus Jazz Line | FDM 36725-2
Bud Powell Paris Sessions | Pablo | PACD 2310972-2
Bud Powell Trio
Charles Mingus-The Complete Debut Recordings | Debut | 12 DCD 4402-2
Planet Jazz:Bud Powell | Planet Jazz | 2152064-2
Planet Jazz Sampler | Planet Jazz | 2152326-2
Planet Jazz:Jazz Piano | RCA | 2169655-2
Time Waits | Blue Note | 521227-2
The Best Of Bud Powell On Verve | Verve | 523392-2
The Amazing Bud Powell Vol.1 | Blue Note | 532136-2
The Amazing Bud Powell Vol.2 | Blue Note | 532137-2
The Amazing Bud Powell Vol.3:Bud! | Blue Note | 535585-2
Jazz Giant | Verve | 543832-2
Parisian Thoroughfare | Pablo | CD 2310976-2
Bud Powell:Bouncing With Bud | Dreyfus Jazz Line | FDM 36725-2
Bud Powell Paris Sessions | Pablo | PACD 2310972-2
Bebop | Pablo | PACD 2310978-2
Bud Powell's Modernists
The Fabulous Fats Navarro Vol.1 | Blue Note | 0677207
The Fabulous Fats Navarro Vol.2 | Blue Note | 0677208
Charles Mingus Quintet With Bud Powell
Mingus At Antibes | Atlantic | 7567-90532-2
Charles Mingus-Passion Of A Man:The Complete Atlantic Recordings 1956-1961 | Atlantic | 8122-72871-2
Charlie Parker Quintet
Charlie Parker:Now's The Time | Dreyfus Jazz Line | FDM 36724-2
Dexter Gordon Quartet
Blue Note Plays Gershwin | Blue Note | 520808-2
True Blue | Blue Note | 534032-2
Our Man In Paris | Blue Note | 591722-2
Dexter Gordon:Ballads | Blue Note | 796579-2
Jazz Profile:Dexter Gordon | Blue Note | 823514-2
Don Byas-Bud Powell Quartet
A Tribute To Cannonball | CBS | CK 65186
Don Byas-Bud Powell Quintet
A Tribute To Cannonball | CBS | CK 65186
Johnny Griffin With The Bud Powell Trio
Bebop | Pablo | PACD 2310978-2
Kenny Clarke And His 52nd Street Boys
Planet Jazz:Bebop | RCA | 2169650-2
Fats Navarro:Nostalgia | Dreyfus Jazz Line | FDM 36736-2
Quintet Of The Year
Charles Mingus-The Complete Debut Recordings | Debut | 12 DCD 4402-2
The Quintet-Jazz At Massey Hall | Debut | DSA 124-6
The Quintet-Jazz At Massey Hall | Original Jazz Classics | OJC20 044-2
Sonny Stitt Quartet
Sonny Stitt | Original Jazz Classics | OJCCD 009-2

Powell,Eddie | (fl,bsreeds)
Billie Holiday With The Ray Ellis Orchestra
Lady In Satin | CBS | CK 65144

Powell,Ernie | (as,clts)
Billie Holiday With Teddy Wilson And His Orchestra
Billie's Love Songs | Nimbus Records | NI 2000
Hot Lips Page Band
Planet Jazz:Jazz Trumpet | Planet Jazz | 2169654-2

Powell,Gordon | (drperc)
Joe Williams With The Frank Hunter Orchestra
Planet Jazz:Joe Williams | Planet Jazz | 2165370-2

Powell,Jim | (tp,fl-htuba)
Woody Herman And His Orchestra
Verve Jazz Masters 54:Woody Herman | Verve | 529903-2

Powell,Jimmy | (asts)
Count Basie And His Orchestra
Jazz Collection:Count Basie | Laserlight | 24368
Jazz:The Essential Collection Vol.3 | IN+OUT Records | 78013-2
Dizzy Gillespie And His Orchestra
Verve Jazz Masters 20:Introducing | Verve | 519853-2
Dizzy Gillespie:Birks Works-The Verve Big Band Sessions | Verve | 527900-2
Ultimate Dizzy Gillespie | Verve | 557535-2
Dizzy Gillespie Orchestra
Verve Jazz Masters 10:Dizzy Gillespie | Verve | 516319-2

Powell,Mel | (arrp)
Benny Goodman And His Orchestra
Great Swing Classics In Hi-Fi | Capitol | 521223-2
Benny Goodman Trio
Benny Goodman-The Complete Capitol Trios | Capitol | 521225-2
JATP All Stars
The Complete Jazz At The Philharmonic On Verve 1944-1949 | Verve | 523893-2
Bird: The Complete Charlie Parker On Verve | Verve | 837141-2
Peggy Lee With Benny Goodman And His Quintet
Peggy Lee & Benny Goodman:The Complete Recordings 1941-1947 | CBS | C2K 65686
Peggy Lee With Benny Goodman And His Sextet
Peggy Lee & Benny Goodman:The Complete Recordings 1941-1947 | CBS | C2K 65686
Peggy Lee With The Benny Goodman Orchestra
Peggy Lee & Benny Goodman:The Complete Recordings 1941-1947 | CBS | C2K 65686

Powell,Richie | (p)
All Star Live Jam Session
Brownie-The Complete EmArCy Recordings Of Clifford Brown | EmArCy | 838306-2
Clifford Brown & The Neal Hefti Orchestra
Clifford Brown With Strings | Verve | 558078-2
Clifford Brown All Stars With Dinah Washington
Verve Jazz Masters 40:Dinah Washington | Verve | 522055-2
Clifford Brown With Strings
Clifford Brown-Max Roach:Alone Together-The Best Of The Mercury Years | Verve | 526373-2
Verve Jazz Masters 44:Clifford Brown and Max Roach | Verve | 528109-2
Brownie-The Complete EmArCy Recordings Of Clifford Brown | EmArCy | 838306-2
Clifford Brown-Max Roach Quartet
Verve Jazz Masters 44:Clifford Brown and Max Roach | Verve | 528109-2
Clifford Brown-Max Roach Quintet
Clifford Brown-Max Roach:Alone Together-The Best Of The Mercury Years | Verve | 526373-2
Verve Jazz Masters 44:Clifford Brown and Max Roach | Verve | 528109-2
Verve Jazz Masters Vol.60:The Collection | Verve | 529866-2
Clifford Brown And Max Roach | Verve | 543306-2
Clifford Brown And Max Roach At Basin Street | Verve | 589826-2
Study In Brown | EmArCy | 814646-2
Brownie-The Complete EmArCy Recordings Of Clifford Brown | EmArCy | 838306-2
Dinah Washington And Her Band
Verve Jazz Masters 40:Dinah Washington | Verve | 522055-2
Max Roach Trio
Clifford Brown And Max Roach | Verve | 543306-2
Sonny Rollins Plus Four
Sonny Rollins Plus 4 | Original Jazz Classics | OJC20 243-2(P 7038)
The Prestige Legacy Vol.1:The High Priests | Prestige | PCD 24251-2

Powell,Robert | (tu)
Freddie Hubbard Orchestra
The Body And The Soul | Impulse(MCA) | 951183-2

Powell,Ron | (perc,congawind-chimes)
Dianne Reeves With Band
Misty Blue:Sweet Sisters Swing Songs Of Sorrow And Sadness | Blue Note | 521151-2
I Remember | Blue Note | 790264-2

Powell,Roy | (p)
Roy Powell Quartet
North By Northwest | Nagel-Heyer | CD 2013

Powell,Rudy | (as,bs,clsax)
Big Al Sears Band
Sear-iously | Bear Family Records | BCD 15668 AH
Cliff Jackson's Washboard Wanderers
Uptown And Lowdown | Prestige | PCD 24262-2
Fats Waller And His Rhythm
Planet Jazz:Fats Waller | Planet Jazz | 2152058-2
Planet Jazz:Male Jazz Vocalists | Planet Jazz | 2169657-2
Fats Waller-Rudy Powell
Fats Waller:The Complete Associated Transcription Sessions 1935-1939 | Jazz Unlimited | JUCD 2076

Powell,Seldon | (alto-fl,as,bs,piccolo,fl,ts,cl)
Billy Butler Quintet
Night Life | Prestige | PCD 24260-2
Cal Tjader's Orchestra
Verve Jazz Masters 39:Cal Tjader | Verve | 521858-2
Talkin Verve/Roots Of Acid Jazz:Cal Tjader | Verve | 531562-2
Soul Burst | Verve | 557446-2
Charlie Byrd Trio And Guests
Byrd At The Gate | Original Jazz Classics | OJC20 262-2
Clark Terry Orchestra
Color Changes | Candid | CCD 79009
Eddie Harris Group
The Best Of Eddie Harris | Atlantic | 7567-81370-2
Freddie Hubbard Orchestra
The Body And The Soul | Impulse(MCA) | 951183-2
Friedrich Gulda Septet
Friedrich Gulda At Birdland | RCA | 2112587-2
Gato Barbieri Orchestra
The Roots Of Acid Jazz | Impulse(MCA) | IMP 12042
Jimmy Forrest With The Oliver Nelson Orchestra
Soul Street | Original Jazz Classics | OJCCD 987-2(NJ 8293)
Jimmy McGriff Orchestra
Swingin' The Blues-Jumpin' The Blues | Laserlight | 24654
Jimmy Smith With Orchestra
Jimmy Smith-Talkin' Verve | Verve | 531563-2
Jimmy Smith With The Claus Ogerman Orchestra
Verve Jazz Masters 29:Jimmy Smith | Verve | 521855-2
Any Number Can Win | Verve | 557447-2
Jimmy Witherspoon With Jay McShann And His Band
Planet Jazz:Male Jazz Vocalists | Planet Jazz | 2169657-2
Joe Turner With Orchestra
Atlantic Jazz: Kansas City | Atlantic | 7567-81701-2
Joe Williams With The Jimmy Jones Orchestra
Planet Jazz:Joe Williams | Planet Jazz | 2165370-2
Johnny 'Hammond' Smith Septet
Open House | Milestone | MCD 47089-2
Johnny 'Hammond' Smith Sextet
Open House | Milestone | MCD 47089-2
King Pleasure With Orchestra
Blue Velvet: Crooners, Swooners And Velvet Vocals | Blue Note | 521153-2
Lalo Schifrin And His Orchestra
Tin Tin Deo | Fresh Sound Records | FSR-CD 319
Les McCann Group
Another Beginning | Atlantic | 7567-80790-2
Modern Jazz Quartet And Orchestra
MJQ 40 | Atlantic | 7567-82330-2
Oscar Peterson With Orchestra
With Respect To Nat | Verve | 557486-2
Oscar Peterson With The Ernie Wilkins Orchestra
Verve Jazz Masters 16:Oscar Peterson | Verve | 516320-2
Quincy Jones And His Orchestra
Talkin' Verve-Roots Of Acid Jazz:Roland Kirk | Verve | 533101-2
Rahsaan/The Complete Mercury Recordings Of Roland Kirk | Mercury | 846630-2
The Basie Alumni
Swinging For The Count | Candid | CCD 79724
Willie Rodriguez Jazz Quartet
Flatjacks | Milestone | MCD 9331-2

Powell,Seldon or Jerome Richardson | (ts)
Cal Tjader's Orchestra
Verve Jazz Masters 39:Cal Tjader | Verve | 521858-2
Les McCann Group
Talkin' Verve:Les McCann | Verve | 557351-2

Powell,Shannon | (dr)
Harry Connick Jr. Quartet
We Are In Love | CBS | 466736-2
Harry Connick Jr. Quartet With Branford Marsalis
We Are In Love | CBS | 466736-2

Powell,Specs | (dr)
Benny Goodman And His V-Disc All Star Band
The Legends Of Swing | Laserlight | 24659
Billy Butler Quintet
Night Life | Prestige | PCD 24260-2
V-Disc All Star Jam Session
Louis Armstrong-Jack Teagarden-Woody Herman:Midnights At V-Disc | Jazz Unlimited | JUCD 2048

Powers,Buddy | (fl-htp)
Woody Herman And His Orchestra
Jazzin' Vol.2: The Music Of Stevie Wonder | Fantasy | FANCD 6088-2
Brand New | Original Jazz Classics | OJCCD 1044-2(F 8414)
King Cobra | Original Jazz Classics | OJCCD 1068-2(F 9499)
Woody Herman Herd At Montreux | Original Jazz Classics | OJCCD 991-2(F 9470)
Woody Herman And The New Thundering Herd
Woody Herman:Thundering Herd | Original Jazz Classics | OJCCD 841-2

Pozar,Robert 'Bob' | (drperc)
Bob James Trio
Bold Conceptions | Verve | 557454-2

Pozar,Vlado | (cello)
Bernd Konrad Jazz Group With Symphonie Orchestra
Wen Die Götter Lieben | Creative Works Records | CW CD 1010-1

Pozo,Chano | (bongos,voccongas)
Dizzy Gillespie And His Orchestra
Dizzy Gillespie:Pleyel Jazz Concert 1948 + Max Roach Quintet 1949 | Vogue | 21409412
Planet Jazz:Dizzy Gillespie | Planet Jazz | 2152069-2
Planet Jazz:Bebop | RCA | 2169650-2
Ella Fitzgerald With The Dizzy Gillespie Orchestra
Ella Fitzgerald:Mr.Paganini | Dreyfus Jazz Line | FDM 36741-2
Ella Fitzgerald With The Hank Jones Trio
Ella Fitzgerald:Mr.Paganini | Dreyfus Jazz Line | FDM 36741-2
Milt Jackson Quintet
Milt Jackson Birthday Celebration | Fantasy | FANCD 6079-2

Pozo,Chino | (bongos,congas,vocperc)
Charlie Parker With Machito And His Orchestra
Bird: The Complete Charlie Parker On Verve | Verve | 837141-2
Clark Terry & Chico O Farril Orchestra
Spanish Rice | Verve | 9861050
Dizzy Gillespie Sextet
Ultimate Dizzy Gillespie | Verve | 557535-2
Peggy Lee With The Quincy Jones Orchestra
Blues Cross Country | Capitol | 520088-2
Tadd Dameron Septet
The Fabulous Fats Navarro Vol.2 | Blue Note | 0677208
Fats Navarro:Nostalgia | Dreyfus Jazz Line | FDM 36736-2

Pradal,Vicente | (flamenco-gpalmas)
Renaud Garcia-Fons Group
Oriental Bass | Enja | ENJ-9334 2

Praskin,Allan | (as,perc,recorder,voc,cl,flsax)
Gunter Hampel And His Galaxie Dream Band
Journey To The Song Within | Birth | 0017

Prather,Harry | (tuba)
Jelly Roll Morton And His Orchestra
Planet Jazz:Jelly Roll Morton | Planet Jazz | 2152060-2

Prati,Walter | (electronicssound processing)
Evan Parker Electro-Acoustic Ensemble
Toward The Margins | ECM | 1612(453514-2)
Drawn Inward | ECM | 1693
Memory/Vision | ECM | 1852(0381172)

Pratt,Bobby | (tbp)
Roy Eldridge And The Jimmy Ryan All Stars
Jazz Dance | Original Jazz Classics | OJCCD 1002-2(1210890)
Little Jazz And The Jimmy Ryan All-Stars | Original Jazz Classics | OJCCD 1058-2(DRE 1001)

Pratt,Gary | (bel-b)
Louie Bellson Septet
Louie Bellson Jam | Original Jazz Classics | OJCCD 802-2(2310838)

Pratt,Jimmy | (drperc)
Hans Koller Quartet
Exclusiv | MPS | 9813440

Pray,Sue | (viola)
A Band Of Friends
Wynton Marsalis Quartet With Strings | CBS | CK 68921
Kevin Mahogany With The Bob James Trio, Kirk Whalum And Strings
My Romance | Warner | 9362-47025-2
Steve Kuhn With Strings
Promises Kept | ECM | 1815(0675222)

Preinfalk,Gerald | (cl,b-cl,ss,as,bssopranino)
Martin Koller's Third Movement
Right Now | Traumton Records | 4430-2

Preisser,Cornelia | (voc)
Jazzensemble Des Hessischen Rundfunks
Jazz Messe-Messe Für Unsere Zeit | hr music.de | hrmj 003-01 CD

Preißinger,Matthias | (p)
Gerwin Eisenhauer's The Gäff Gang feat. Lisa Wahland
Favorite Tunes | Edition Collage | EC 527-2

Prell,Don | (b)
Bud Shank Quartet
Live At The Haig | Choice | CHCD 71030

Presencer,Gerard | (tp,fl-hkeyboards)
Gerard Presencer Group
Chasing Reality | ACT | 9422-2

Press,Arthur | (perc)
Max Roach With The Boston Percussion Ensemble
Clifford Brown-Max Roach:Alone Together-The Best Of The Mercury Years | Verve | 526373-2

Press,Reiny | (bel-b)
Count Basie And His Orchestra
Jazz Dance | Original Jazz Classics | OJCCD 1002-2(1210890)

Press,Seymour | (reeds)
Della Reese With The Sy Oliver Orchestra
Misty Blue:Sweet Sisters Swing Songs Of Sorrow And Sadness | Blue Note | 521151-2

Prestige All Stars |
Prestige All Stars
John Coltrane-The Prestige Recordings | Prestige | 16 PCD 4405-2
All Day Long | Original Jazz Classics | OJC20 456-2(P 7081)
The Cats | Original Jazz Classics | OJCCD 079-2(NJ 8217)
Tenor Conclave | Original Jazz Classics | OJCCD 127-2
Wheelin' & Dealin' | Original Jazz Classics | OJCCD 672-2(P7131)
The Prestige Legacy Vol.1:The High Priests | Prestige | PCD 24251-2
The Prestige Legacy Vol.2:Battles Of Saxes | Prestige | PCD 24252-2
The Mal Waldron Memorial Album:Soul Eyes | Prestige | PRCD 11024-2
The Prestige All Stars
Olio | Original Jazz Classics | OJCCD 1004-2(P 7084)

Prestige Blues-Swingers,The |
Prestige Blues-Swingers
Soul Street | Original Jazz Classics | OJCCD 987-2(NJ 8293)

Prestige Jazz Quartet,The |
Prestige Jazz Quartet
The Mal Waldron Memorial Album:Soul Eyes | Prestige | PRCD 11024-2
The Prestige Jazz Quartet
The Prestige Jazz Quartet | Original Jazz Classics | OJCCD 1937-2(P 7108)

Prestipino,Giuseppe | (el-b)
Gerry Mulligan With Astor Piazzolla And His Orchestra
Tango Nuevo | Atlantic | 2292-42145-2

Preston,Cyril | (tbvoc)
Dick Charlesworth And His City Gents
The Golden Years Of Revival Jazz,Vol.4 | Storyville | STCD 5509
The Golden Years Of Revival Jazz,Vol.6 | Storyville | STCD 5511
The Golden Years Of Revival Jazz,Vol.11 | Storyville | STCD 5516

Preston,Don | (p,synthvoc)
Michael Mantler Group With The Danish Radio Concert Orchestra Strings
The School Of Understanding(Sort-Of-An-Opera) | ECM | 1648/49(537963-2)
Michael Mantler Quintet
Live | Watt | 18
Michael Mantler-Don Preston
Alien | Watt | 15

Preston,Eddie | (tp)
Charles Mingus Orchestra
Mingus Mingus Mingus | Impulse(MCA) | 951170-2
Duke Ellington And His Orchestra
The Ellington Suites | Original Jazz Classics | OJC20 446-2(2310762)
The Afro-Eurasian Eclipse-A Suite In Eight Parts | Original Jazz Classics | OJCCD 645-2(F 9498)
Togo Brava Swuite | Storyville | STCD 8323
McCoy Tyner Group With Horns
Inner Voices | Original Jazz Classics | OJCCD 1039-2(M 9079)
McCoy Tyner Group With Horns And Voices
Inner Voices | Original Jazz Classics | OJCCD 1039-2(M 9079)

Preston,James | (dr)
Bobby McFerrin Group
Bobby McFerrin | Elektra | 7559-60023-2

Preston,Jerry | (b)
Maceo Parker Group
Maceo(Soundtrack) | Minor Music | 801046
Maceo Parker With The Rebirth Brass Band

INTERPRETENVERZEICHNIS

Maceo(Soundtrack) | Minor Music | 801046

Preston,Nik | (b)

Dunstan Coulber Quartet

Standards For A New Century | Nagel-Heyer | CD 081

Pretschner,René | (el-p,org,p,keyboardsp-solo)

Jazz Bomberos

Naranja | Green House Music | CD 1003(Maxi)

René Pretschner

Floating Pictures | Green House Music | CD 1001

Ten Piano Players,Vol.1 | Green House Music | CD 1002

Story Of A Jazz Piano Vol.1 | Green House Music | CD 1013

René Pretschner & Melo Mafali

The Piano Duo:El Latino | Green House Music | CD 1006

René Pretschner Quartet

Floating Pictures | Green House Music | CD 1001

René Pretschner Trio

Floating Pictures | Green House Music | CD 1001

Previn,André | (arr,ld,pp-solo)

André Previn

The Jazz Giants Play Harold Arlen:Blues In The Night | Prestige | PCD 24201-2

André Previn' s Jazz Trio

King Size! | Original Jazz Classics | OJCCD 691-2(S 7570)

Barney Kessel And His Orchestra

Barney Kessel Plays Carmen | Original Jazz Classics | OJC 269(C 7563)

Barney Kessel And His Quintet

Barney Kessel Plays Carmen | Original Jazz Classics | OJC 269(C 7563)

Ben Webster-André Previn

Swinging Kicks | Verve | 559514-2

Benny Carter Quintet

Jazz Giant | Original Jazz Classics | OJC20 167-2(C 7555)

Benny Carter Sextet

Jazz Giant | Original Jazz Classics | OJC20 167-2(C 7555)

Buddy Bregman And His Orchestra

Swinging Kicks | Verve | 559514-2

Shelly Manne And His Friends

My Fair Lady | Original Jazz Classics | OJC 336(C 7527)

Shelly Manne Trio

Li'l Abner | Original Jazz Classics | OJCCD 1087-2(S 7533)

Previte,Robert 'Bobby' | (dr,perc,tambourine,voice,dr-machine)

Bobby Previte's Latin For Travelers

Dangerous Rip | Enja | ENJ-9324-2

My Man In Sidney | Enja | ENJ-9348 2

John Zorn Group

Spillane | Nonesuch | 7559-79172-2

Marc Ducret-Bobby Previt

In The Grass | Enja | ENJ-9343 2

Marty Ehrlich Group

The Long View | Enja | ENJ-9452 2

Ray Anderson Pocket Brass Band

Where Home Is | Enja | ENJ-9366 2

Prevost,Eddie | (drperc)

AMM III

It Had Been An Ordinary Enough Day In Pueblo, Colorado | Japo | 60031

Price,Bob | (tp)

Glenn Miller And His Orchestra

Planet Jazz:Glenn Miller | Planet Jazz | 2152056-2

Planet Jazz:Swing | Planet Jazz | 2169651-2

Candelight Miller | RCA | 2668716-2

Price,Charles Q. | (as,voc,clts)

Count Basie And His Orchestra

Planet Jazz:Count Basie | Planet Jazz | 2152068-2

Planet Jazz Sampler | Planet Jazz | 2152326-2

Planet Jazz:Jimmy Rushing | RCA | 2165371-2

Planet Jazz:Big Bands | Planet Jazz | 2169649-2

Jazz:The Essential Collection Vol.3 | IN+OUT Records | 78013-2

Count Basie,His Instrumentals & Rhythm

Planet Jazz:Count Basie | Planet Jazz | 2152068-2

Jazz:The Essential Collection Vol.3 | IN+OUT Records | 78013-2

Price,Ernest | (b)

Mr.Acker Bilk And His Paramount Jazz Band

The Very Best Of Dixieland Jazz | Verve | 535529-2

The Golden Years Of Revival Jazz,Vol.5 | Storyville | STCD 5510

The Golden Years Of Revival Jazz,Vol.6 | Storyville | STCD 5511

The Golden Years Of Revival Jazz,Vol.9 | Storyville | STCD 5514

The Golden Years Of Revival Jazz,Vol.12 | Storyville | STCD 5517

The Golden Years Of Revival Jazz,Vol.13 | Storyville | STCD 5518

The Golden Years Of Revibal Jazz,Vol.15 | Storyville | STCD 5520

Price,George | (fr-h)

Ella Fitzgerald With The Nelson Riddle Orchestra

Ella Fitzgerald Sings The Johnny Mercer Songbook | Verve | 539057-2

Price,Gerald | (p)

Sonny Stitt Quartet

The Art Of Saxophone | Laserlight | 24652

Price,Jesse | (drvoc)

Jesse Price And His Blues Band

Jazz Profile:Dexter Gordon | Blue Note | 823514-2

Price,John L. | (dr-programming)

Don Cherry Group

Multi Kulti | A&M Records | 395323-2

Price,Magnum Coltrane | (b,voc,el-b,rapsynth)

Niels Landgren Funk Unit

Live In Stockholm | ACT | 9223-2

Nils Landgren Funk Unit

Paint It Blue:A Tribute To Cannonball Adderley | ACT | 9243-2

Live In Montreux | ACT | 9265-2

Fonk Da World | ACT | 9299-2

Nils Landgren Funk Unit With Guests

5000 Miles | ACT | 9271-2

Nils Landgren Group

Sentimental Journey | ACT | 9409-2

Price,Mike | (tp)

Buddy Rich Big Band

Keep The Customer Satisfied | EMI Records | 523999-2

Price,Ray | (dr)

Oscar Peterson Trio

Two Originals:Walking The Line/Another Day | MPS | 533549-2

Price,Ruth | (voc)

Herb Geller Quartet

Herb Geller Plays The Al Cohn Songbook | Hep | CD 2066

Price,Sammy | (p,vocp-solo)

Axel Zwingenberger-Sam Price

Kansas City Boogie Jam | Vagabond | VRCD 8.00027

Doc Cheatham And Sammy Price

Jazz In Paris:Sammy Price And Doc Cheatham Play Gershwin | EmArCy | 018426-2

Emmett Berry-Sammy Price Orchestra

Americans Swinging In Paris:Sammy Price | EMI Records | 539650-2

Sammy Price

Jazz In Paris:Sammy Price And Doc Cheatham Play Gershwin | EmArCy | 018426-2

Americans Swinging In Paris:Sammy Price | EMI Records | 539650-2

Sammy Price Quintet

Americans Swinging In Paris:Sammy Price | EMI Records | 539650-2

Sammy Price Septet

Jazz:The Essential Collection Vol.3 | IN+OUT Records | 78013-2

Sammy Price Trio

Americans Swinging In Paris:Sammy Price | EMI Records | 539650-2

Sidney Bechet With Sammy Price's Bluesicians

Planet Jazz:Sidney Bechet | Planet Jazz | 2152063-2

Price,Tony | (tptuba)

David Matthews & The Manhattan Jazz Orchestra

Back To Bach | Milestone | MCD 9312-2

Hey Duke! | Milestone | MCD 9320-2

Freddie Hubbard With Orchestra

This Is Jazz:Freddie Hubbard | CBS | CK 65041

Priddy,Jimmy | (tb)

Glenn Miller And His Orchestra

Planet Jazz:Glenn Miller | Planet Jazz | 2152056-2

Planet Jazz:Jazz Greatest Hits | Planet Jazz | 2169648-2

Planet Jazz:Big Bands | Planet Jazz | 2169649-2

The Chesterfield Broadcasts Vol.1 | RCA | 2663113-2

Nat King Cole With The Billy May Orchestra

Nat King Cole:For Sentimental Reasons | Dreyfus Jazz Line | FDM 36740-2

The Andrew Sisters With The Glenn Miller Orchestra

The Chesterfield Broadcasts Vol.1 | RCA | 2663113-2

Pride,Norman | (congasdr)

Bernard Purdie Group

Jazzin' With The Soul Brothers | Fantasy | FANCD 6086-2

Priester,Julian | (euphonium,tb,b-tb,bells,perc,bar-h)

Abbey Lincoln And Her Orchestra

Straight Ahead | Candid | CCD 79015

Abbey Lincoln With The Max Roach Quintet

Abbey Is Blue | Original Jazz Classics | OJC20 069-2(RLP 1153)

Abbey Lincoln With The Max Roach Sextet

Abbey Is Blue | Original Jazz Classics | OJC20 069-2(RLP 1153)

Anfrew Hill Nonet

Passing Ships | Blue Note | 593871-2

Blue Mitchell And His Orchestra

Blue Breaks Beats Vol.2 | Blue Note | 789907-2

Booker Little Sextet

Out Front | Candid | CCD 79027

Candid Dolphy | Candid | CCD 79033

Cal Tjader's Orchestra

Talkin Verve/Roots Of Acid Jazz:Cal Tjader | Verve | 531562-2

Dave Holland Quintet

Jumpin' In | ECM | 1269

Seeds Of Time | ECM | 1292

Dinah Washington With The Eddie Chamblee Orchestra

Verve Jazz Masters 40:Dinah Washington | Verve | 522055-2

Dinah Sings Bessie Smith | Verve | 538635-2

Donald Byrd Orchestra

Blue Break Beats | Blue Note | 799106-2

Duke Ellington And His Orchestra

New Orleans Suite | Rhino | 812273670-2

Eddie Henderson Orchestra

Blue Breaks Beats Vol.2 | Blue Note | 789907-2

Blue Break Beats | Blue Note | 799106-2

Freddie Hubbard Sextet

Hub Cap | Blue Note | 542302-2

George Gruntz Concert Jazz Band '83

Theatre | ECM | 1265

Herbie Hancock Group

Sextant | CBS | CK 64983

Herbie Hancock Sextet

V.S.O.P. Herbie Hancock-Live At The City Center N.Y. | CBS | 486569-2

Jazz Artists Guild

Newport Rebels-Jazz Artists Guild | Candid | CCD 79022

Joe Henderson And His Orchestra

Joe Henderson:The Milestone Years | Milestone | 8MCD 4413-2

John Coltrane And His Orchestra

John Coltrane:Standards | Impulse(MCA) | 549914-2

John Coltrane Quartet With Brass

The Complete Africa/Brass Sessions | Impulse(MCA) | 952168-2

Julian Priester Sextet

Out Of This World | Milestone | MCD 47087-2

Lee Morgan Sextet

Deep Blue-The United States Of Mind | Blue Note | 521152-2

Sonic Boom | Blue Note | 590414-2

Max Roach All Stars

Candid Dolphy | Candid | CCD 79033

Max Roach Group

We Insist: Freedom Now Suite | Candid | CCD 79002

Max Roach Quintet

Clifford Brown-Max Roach:Alone Together-The Best Of The Mercury Years | Verve | 526373-2

Jazz In Paris:Max Roach-Parisian Sketches | EmArCy | 589963-2

Max Roach Septet

The Jazz Life! | Candid | CCD 79019

Max Roach Sextet

Clifford Brown-Max Roach:Alone Together-The Best Of The Mercury Years | Verve | 526373-2

Max Roach Sextet With Choir

It's Time | Impulse(MCA) | 951185-2

Stanley Turrentine Orchestra

The Spoiler | Blue Note | 853359-2

Wayne Horvitz Group

4+1 Ensemble | Intuition Records | INT 3224-2

Prill,Robert | (g)

Association Urbanetique

Ass Bedient | Jazz 4 Ever Records:Jazz Network | J4E 4723

Prina,Curt | (pvib)

Joe Turner And Friends

The Giant Of Stride Piano In Switzerland | Jazz Connaisseur | JCCD 9106-2

Prince,Bob | (arr,cond,tp,vibld)

Glenn Miller And His Orchestra

Candelight Miller | RCA | 2668716-2

Paul Desmond With Strings

Planet Jazz:Paul Desmond | Planet Jazz | 2152061-2

Desmond Blue | RCA | 2663898-2

Prince,Gene | (tp)

Louis Armstrong And His Orchestra

Louis Armstrong:Swing That Music | Laserlight | 36056

Jazz:The Essential Collection Vol.2 | IN+OUT Records | 78012-2

Louis Armstrong:C'est Si Bon | Dreyfus Jazz Line | FDM 36730-2

Prince,Viv | (dr)

Lennie Baldwin's Dauphin Street Six

The Golden Years Of Revival Jazz,Sampler | Storyville | 109 1001

The Golden Years Of Revival Jazz,Vol 1 | Storyville | STCD 5506

The Golden Years Of Revival Jazz,Vol.3 | Storyville | STCD 5508

The Golden Years Of Revival Jazz,Vol.6 | Storyville | STCD 5511

The Golden Years Of Revival Jazz,Vol.9 | Storyville | STCD 5514

The Golden Years Of Revival Jazz,Vol.10 | Storyville | STCD 5515

The Golden Years Of Revival Jazz,Vol.13 | Storyville | STCD 5518

Prince,Wesley | (bvoc)

Lionel Hampton And His Orchestra

Planet Jazz:Lionel Hampton | Planet Jazz | 2152059-2

Lionel Hampton:Flying Home | Dreyfus Jazz Line | FDM 36735-2

Nat King Cole Trio

The Legends Of Swing | Laserlight | 24659

Love Songs | Nimbus Records | NI 2010

Pring,Bob | (tb)

Buck Clayton Swing Band

Swing's The Village | Nagel-Heyer | CD 5004

Blues Of Summer | Nagel-Heyer | NH 1011

Prins,Jeanfrancois | (el-gg)

Sören Fischer Quartet

Don't Change Your Hair For Me | Edition Collage | EC 513-2

Printup,Marcus | (tpvoc)

Diane Schuur And Her Band

Music Is My Life | Atlantic | 7567-83150-2

Eric Reed Orchestra

Happiness | Nagel-Heyer | CD 2010

Lincoln Center Jazz Orchestra

Big Train | CBS | CK 69860

Marcus Printup Sextet

The New Boogaloo | Nagel-Heyer | CD 2019

Tim Hagans-Marcus Printup Septet

Hub Songs | Blue Note | 859509-2

Wycliffe Gordon Group

The Search | Nagel-Heyer | CD 2007

Prinz,Rolf | (ts)

Art Van Damme Group

State Of Art | MPS | 841413-2

Prisby,Lou | (as)

Artie Shaw And His Orchestra

Planet Jazz:Jazz Trumpet | Planet Jazz | 2169654-2

Pritchard,Bill | (tb)

Sarah Vaughan With The Hugo Winterhalter Orchestra

Sarah Vaughan:Lover Man | Dreyfus Jazz Line | FDM 36739-2

Prittwitz,Andreas | (clrecorder)

Javier Paxarino Group With Glen Velez

Temurá | ACT | 9227-2

Privin,Bernie | (tp)

Artie Shaw And His Orchestra

Planet JazzArtie Shaw | Planet Jazz | 2152057-2

The Legends Of Swing | Laserlight | 24659

Benny Goodman And His Orchestra

Great Swing Classics In Hi-Fi | Capitol | 521223-2

Billie Holiday With Sy Oliver And His Orchestra

Billie's Love Songs | Nimbus Records | NI 2000

Charlie Parker And His Orchestra

The Cole Porter Songbook | Verve | 823250-2

Bird: The Complete Charlie Parker On Verve | Verve | 837141-2

Charlie Parker With Orchestra

Charlie Parker:The Best Of The Verve Years | Verve | 527815-2

Charlie Parker With Strings

Bird: The Complete Charlie Parker On Verve | Verve | 837141-2

Charlie Parker With The Joe Lipman Orchestra

Verve Jazz Masters 28:Charlie Parker Plays Standards | Verve | 521854-2

Charlie Parker With Strings:The Master Takes | Verve | 523984-2

Charlie Parker Big Band | Verve | 559835-2

Ella Fitzgerald With Sy Oliver And His Orchestra

Ella Fitzgerald:Mr.Paganini | Dreyfus Jazz Line | FDM 36741-2

Ella Fitzgerald With Sy Oliver And His Orchestra

Ella Fitzgerald:The Decca Years 1949-1954 | Decca | 050668-2

Louis Armstrong And Billie Holiday With Sy Oliver's Orchestra

Louis Armstrong:C'est Si Bon | Dreyfus Jazz Line | FDM 36730-2

Louis Armstrong With Sy Oliver And His Orchestra

Satchmo Serenaders | Verve | 543792-2

Louis Armstrong:C'est Si Bon | Dreyfus Jazz Line | FDM 36730-2

Louis Armstrong-My Greatest Songs | MCA | MCD 18347

Peggy Lee With The Benny Goodman Orchestra

Peggy Lee & Benny Goodman:The Complete Recordings 1941-1947 | CBS | C2K 65686

prob.personal incl.: |

Anita O'Day With The Bill Holman Orchestra

Verve Jazz Masters 49:Anita O'Day | Verve | 527653-2

Anita O'Day With The Buddy Bregman Orchestra

Verve Jazz Masters 49:Anita O'Day | Verve | 527653-2

Anita O'Day With The Gary McFarland Orchestra

Verve Jazz Masters 49:Anita O'Day | Verve | 527653-2

Anita O'Day With The Russ Garcia Orchestra

Verve Jazz Masters 49:Anita O'Day | Verve | 527653-2

Glenn Miller And His Orchestra

Swing Legends | Nimbus Records | NI 2001

prob.personal: |

Anita O'Day With The Buddy Bregman Orchestra

Pick Yourself Up | Verve | 517329-2

Babs Gonzales And His Band

Voilà | Fresh Sound Records | FSR CD 340

Benny Goodman And His Orchestra

The Legends Of Swing | Laserlight | 24659

Billie Holiday With The JATP All Stars

The Complete Jazz At The Philharmonic On Verve 1944-1949 | Verve | 523893-2

Brocksieper-Jazz-Ensemble

Drums Boogie | Bear Family Records | BCD 15988 AH

Brocksieper-Solisten-Orchester

Globetrotter | Bear Family Records | BCD 15912 AH

Brocksieper-Special-Ensemble

Globetrotter | Bear Family Records | BCD 15912 AH

Brocksi-Quartett

Globetrotter | Bear Family Records | BCD 15912 AH

Buddy Childers Big Band

It's What Happening Now! | Candid | CCD 79749

Coleman Hawkins With The Thore Ehrlings Orchestra

Coleman Hawkins At The Golden Circle | Dragon | DRCD 265

Count Basie And His Orchestra

The Legends Of Swing | Laserlight | 24659

Earl Hines And His Orchestra

The Legends Of Swing | Laserlight | 24659

Ella Fitzgerald And Her Sextet

Ella Fitzgerald-First Lady Of Song | Verve | 517898-2

Ella Fitzgerald With Sy Oliver And His Orchestra

Ella Fitzgerald:The Decca Years 1949-1954 | Decca | 050668-2

Ella Fitzgerald With The Buddy Bregman Orchestra

Ella Fitzgerald-First Lady Of Song | Verve | 517898-2

Gil Evans Orchestra

The Individualism Of Gil Evans | Verve | 833804-2

Glenn Miller And His Orchestra

Candelight Miller | RCA | 2668716-2

Jack McDuff Quartet With Orchestra

Prelude:Jack McDuff Big Band | Prestige | PRCD 24283-2

Louis Jordan And His Tympany Five

Louis Jordan-Let The Good Times Roll: The Complete Decca Recordings 1938-1954 | Bear Family Records | BCD 15557 IH

Mar Murphy With The Ernie Wilkins Orchestra

RAH | Original Jazz Classics | OJCCD 141-2(R 9395)

Paul Whiteman And His Orchestra

Jazz:The Essential Collection Vol.3 | IN+OUT Records | 78013-2

Phil Woods Quartet With Orchestra & Strings

Round Trip | Verve | 559804-2

Sarah Vaughan And Joe Williams With The Count Basie Orchestra

Jazz Profile | Blue Note | 823517-2

Sarah Vaughan With The Count Basie Band

Jazz Profile | Blue Note | 823517-2

Stan Getz With The Kurt Edelhagen Orchestra

Stan Getz In Europe | Laserlight | 24657

Stan Kenton And His Orchestra

Great Swing Classics In Hi-Fi | Capitol | 521223-2

Willie Bobo Group

Juicy | Verve | 519857-2

Probert,George | (cl,ssperc)

Firehouse Five Plus Two

Dixieland Favorites | Good Time Jazz | FCD 60-008

Crashes A Party | Good Time Jazz | GTCD 10038-2

Goes To A Fire | Good Time Jazz | GTCD 10052-2

Goes South | Good Time Jazz | GTCD 12018-2

Kid Ory's Creole Jazz Band

This Kid's The Greatest! | Good Time Jazz | GTCD 12045-2

Probst,Martin | (dr)

Hugo Siegmeth Quintet

Live At The Jazzclub Unterfahrt | Edition Collage | EC 533-2

Pröbstl,Peter | (gel-g)

Jamenco

Conversations | Trick Music | TM 9202 CD

Procop,Alexander | (b)

Loft Line

Source | Laika Records | 35101122

Procope,Russell | (as,voc,cl,whistle,ss,reeds,saxts)

Billy Strayhorn Orchestra

Johnny Hodges With Billy Strayhorn And The Orchestra | Verve | 557543-2

Cat Anderson And His All Stars

Americans Swinging In Paris:Cat Anderson | EMI Records | 539658-2

Cat Anderson And His Orchestra

Americans Swinging In Paris:Cat Anderson | EMI Records | 539658-2
Connie's Inn Orchestra
Planet Jazz:Coleman Hawkins | Planet Jazz | 2152055-2
Django Reinhardt With Duke Ellington And His Orchestra
Django Reinhardt:Souveniers | Dreyfus Jazz Line | FDM 36744-2
Duke Ellington And Count Basie With Their Orchestras
First Time! | CBS | CK 65571
Duke Ellington And His Award Winners
Greatest Hits | CBS | 462959-2
Duke Ellington And His Orchestra
Planet Jazz:Duke Ellington | Planet Jazz | 2152053-2
Planet Jazz:Johnny Hodges | Planet Jazz | 2152065-2
Duke Ellington's Far East Suite | RCA | 2174797-2
Jazz Collection:Duke Ellington | Laserlight | 24369
The Art Of Saxophone | Laserlight | 24652
The Legends Of Swing | Laserlight | 24659
100 Years Duke | Laserlight | 24906
Highlights From The Duke Ellington Centennial Edition | RCA | 2663672-2
The Popular Duke Ellington | RCA | 2663880-2
Carnegie Hall Concert December 1947 | Prestige | 2PCD 24075-2
Duke Ellington: The Champs-Elysees Theater January 29-30th,1965 | Laserlight | 36131
Greatest Hits | CBS | 462959-2
The Big Bands Vol.1:The Snader Telescriptions | Storyville | 4960043
Jazz Festival Vol.2 | Storyville | 4960743
Verve Jazz Masters 4:Duke Ellington | Verve | 516338-2
Verve Jazz Masters 20:Introducing | Verve | 519853-2
Ellington '55 | Capitol | 520135-2
Great Swing Classics In Hi-Fi | Capitol | 521223-2
Ella & Duke At The Cote D'Azur | Verve | 539030-2
Ella Fitzgerald And Duke Ellington:Cote D'Azure Concerts on Verve | Verve | 539033-2
Soul Call | Verve | 539785-2
The Great Paris Concert | Atlantic | 7567-81303-2
Jazz:The Essential Collection Vol.2 | IN+OUT Records | 78012-2
New Orleans Suite | Rhino | 812273670-2
Afro-Bossa | Reprise | 9362-47876-2
Ellington At Newport 1956(Complete) | CBS | CK 64932
Black Brown And Beige | CBS | CK 65566
Such Sweet Thunder | CBS | CK 65568
Anatomy Of A Murder | CBS | CK 65569
Welcome To Jazz At The Philharmonic | Fantasy | FANCD 6081-2
The Ellington Suites | Original Jazz Classics | OJC20 446-2(2310762)
Latin America Suite | Original Jazz Classics | OJC20 469-2
Duke Ellington And His Orchestra feat. Paul Gonsalves | Original Jazz Classics | OJCCD 623-2
The Afro-Eurasian Eclipse-A Suite In Eight Parts | Original Jazz Classics | OJCCD 645-2(F 9498)
Yale Concert | Original Jazz Classics | OJCCD 664-2
Jazz At The Philharmonis Berlin '65/Paris '67 | Pablo | PACD 5304-2
Duke Ellington At The Alhambra | Pablo | PACD 5313-2
The Jazz Giants Play Duke Ellington:Caravan | Prestige | PCD 24227-2
Togo Brava Swuite | Storyville | STCD 8323
Ella Fitzgerald With The Duke Ellington Orchestra
The Stockholm Concert 1966 | Pablo | 2308242-2
Ella Fitzgerald-First Lady Of Song | Verve | 517898-2
The Best Of The Song Books | Verve | 519804-2
Verve Jazz Masters 6:Ella Fitzgerald | Verve | 519822-2
The Best Of The Song Books:The Ballads | Verve | 521867-2
Verve Jazz Masters 46:Ella Fitzgerald-The Jazz Sides | Verve | 527655-2
Ella At Duke's Place | Verve | 529700-2
Love Songs:The Best Of The Song Books | Verve | 531762-2
Ella & Duke At The Cote D'Azur | Verve | 539030-2
Ella Fitzgerald And Duke Ellington:Cote D'Azure Concerts on Verve | Verve | 539033-2
Ella Fitzgerald Sings The Duke Ellington Songbook | Verve | 559248-2
For The Love Of Ella Fitzgerald | Verve | 841765-2
Ella Fitzgerald With The Duke Ellington Orchestra And Jimmy Jones Trio
Ella & Duke At The Cote D'Azur | Verve | 539030-2
Ella Fitzgerald And Duke Ellington:Cote D'Azure Concerts on Verve | Verve | 539033-2
Ernie Royal And The Duke Knights
Americans Swinging In Paris:James Moody | EMI Records | 539653-2
Fletcher Henderson And His Orchestra
Jazz:The Essential Collection Vol.1 | IN+OUT Records | 78011-2
Jazz:The Essential Collection Vol.3 | IN+OUT Records | 78013-2
Jelly Roll Morton And His Orchestra
Planet Jazz:Jelly Roll Morton | Planet Jazz | 2152060-2
Jazz:The Essential Collection Vol.1 | IN+OUT Records | 78011-2
Johnny Hodges And The Ellington Men
Verve Jazz Masters 35:Johnny Hodges | Verve | 521857-2
Johnny Hodges With Billy Strayhorn And The Duke Ellington Orchestra
Verve Jazz Masters 35:Johnny Hodges | Verve | 521857-2
Oscar Peterson With The Duke Ellington Orchestra
Oscar Peterson Plays Duke Ellington | Pablo | 2310966-2
Rosemary Clooney With The Duke Ellington Orchestra
Blue Rose | CBS | CK 65506
Sarah Vaughan With John Kirby And His Orchestra
Sarah Vaughan Birthday Celebration | Fantasy | FANCD 6090-2
Sarah Vaughan:Lover Man | Dreyfus Jazz Line | FDM 36739-2

Proctor,Mark | (b)
Prince Lasha Quintet
The Cry | Original Jazz Classics | OJCCD 1945-2(S 7610)

Proske,Markus | (b)
Art De Fakt
Art De Fakt-Ray Federman:Surfiction Jazz No.2 | double moon | CHRDM 71007

Provan,Felicity | (co,pocket-tpvoice)
The Collective 3 +
The Collective 3 + | true muze | TUMU CD 9802

Provey,Vance R. | (tp)
Gunter Hampel New York Orchestra
Fresh Heat-Live At Sweet Basil | Birth | CD 039

Pruden,Layton | (tb)
Charles Earland Sextet
Jazzin' With The Soul Brothers | Fantasy | FANCD 6086-2
Charlie's Greatest Hits | Prestige | PCD 24250-2

Prudente,Vince | (tb)
Duke Ellington And His Orchestra
Highlights From The Duke Ellington Centennial Edition | RCA | 2663672-2
The Ellington Suites | Original Jazz Classics | OJC20 446-2(2310762)
Duke Ellington Orchestra
Continuum | Fantasy | FCD 24765-2

Pruitt,Carl | (b)
George Shearing And His Quintet
Beauty And The Beat | Capitol | 542308-2
Peggy Lee With George Shearing
Beauty And The Beat | Capitol | 542308-2
Peggy Lee With The George Shearing Trio
Beauty And The Beat | Capitol | 542308-2

Pruitt,Skip | (sax)
Chuck Brown And The Second Chapter Band
Timeless | Minor Music | 801068

Pryce,Sharlie | (voc)
Bernard Purdie's Soul To Jazz
Bernard Purdie's Soul To Jazz | ACT | 9242-2

Przybielski,Andy | (tp)
Andy Lumpp Trio Feat. Andy Przybielski
Musica Ex Spiritu Sancto | Nabel Records:Jazz Network | CD 4694
Andy Lumpp Trio With Andy Przybielski
Music From Planet Earth | Nabel Records:Jazz Network | CD 4687

Psonis,Dimitri | (baglamá,santuritzuraz)
Javier Paxarino Group With Glen Velez
Temurá | ACT | 9227-2

Pucho | (cowbelltimbales)
Pucho & His Latin Soul Brothers
Jazzin' With The Soul Brothers | Fantasy | FANCD 6086-2
Rip A Dip | Milestone | MCD 9247-2

Pudel,Charlie | (novachordp)
Arthur Young And Hatchett's Swingtette
Grapelli Story | Verve | 515807-2

Puente,Tito | (ld,marimba,perc,timbales,timbalito)
Tito Puente Orchestra
Planet Jazz:Tito Puente | Planet Jazz | 2165369-2

Puerling,Gene | (arr,vocld)
Singers Unlimited
The Singers Unlimited:Magic Voices | MPS | 539130-2
Singers Unlimited + The Oscar Peterson Trio
The Singers Unlimited:Magic Voices | MPS | 539130-2
Singers Unlimited With Orchestra
The Singers Unlimited:Magic Voices | MPS | 539130-2
Singers Unlimited With Rob McConnell And The Boss Brass
The Singers Unlimited:Magic Voices | MPS | 539130-2
Singers Unlimited With Roger Kellaway
The Singers Unlimited:Magic Voices | MPS | 539130-2
Singers Unlimited With The Art Van Damme Quintet
The Singers Unlimited:Magic Voices | MPS | 539130-2
Singers Unlimited With The Clare Fischer Orchestra
The Singers Unlimited:Magic Voices | MPS | 539130-2
Singers Unlimited With The Pat Williams Orchestra
The Singers Unlimited:Magic Voices | MPS | 539130-2
Singers Unlimited With The Patrick Williams Orchestra
The Singers Unlimited:Magic Voices | MPS | 539130-2
Singers Unlimited With The Robert Farnon Orchestra
The Singers Unlimited:Magic Voices | MPS | 539130-2
Singers Unlimited With The Roger Kellaway Cello Quartet
The Singers Unlimited:Magic Voices | MPS | 539130-2

Pugh,Jim | (euphonium,tbbar-horn)
Daniel Schnyder Group
Tanatula | Enja | ENJ-9302 2
David Matthews & The Manhattan Jazz Orchestra
Back To Bach | Milestone | MCD 9312-2
Hey Duke! | Milestone | MCD 9320-2
George Gruntz Concert Jazz Band
Blues 'N Dues Et Cetera | Enja | ENJ-6072 2
Woody Herman And His Orchestra
Jazzin' Vol.2: The Music Of Stevie Wonder | Fantasy | FANCD 6088-2
King Cobra | Original Jazz Classics | OJCCD 1068-2(F 9499)
Woody Herman Herd At Montreux | Original Jazz Classics | OJCCD 991-2(F 9470)
Woody Herman And The New Thundering Herd
Planet Jazz:Big Bands | Planet Jazz | 2169649-2
Woody Herman:Thundering Herd | Original Jazz Classics | OJCCD 841-2
Woody Herman's Thundering Herd
Planet Jazz:Jazz Saxophone | Planet Jazz | 2169653-2

Puglielli,Nicola | (gg-solo)
Nicola Puglielli Group
Jazz Guitar Highlights 1 | Jardis Records | JRCD 20141
In The Middle | Jardis Records | JRCD 9924

Puig,Carlos | (tp)
Ramon Valle Quintet
Ramon Valle Plays Ernesto Lecuona | ACT | 9404-2

Pujia,Victorio | (g)
Tangata Rea
Tango Alla Baila | Winter&Winter | 910025-2

Pujol,Toni | (b)
Moments Quartet
Original Moments | Fresh Sound Records | FSNT 052 CD

Pukwana,Dudu | (as,p,perc,congas,arr,voc,tsss)
Johnny Dyani Quartet
Mbizo | Steeplechase | SCCD 31163

Pulch,Stan prob. | (b)
Jack Teagarden Sextet
Newport Jazz Festival 1958,July 3rd-6th Vol.3:Blues In The Night No.1 | Phontastic | NCD 8815
Jack Teagarden Sextet With Bobby Hackett
Newport Jazz Festival 1958,July 3rd-6th Vol.3:Blues In The Night No.1 | Phontastic | NCD 8815

Pullen,Don | (keyboards,org,voc,pp-solo)
Charles Mingus Quintet
Changes One | Rhino | 8122-71403-2
Changes Two | Rhino | 8122-71404-2
Charles Mingus Sextet
Changes Two | Rhino | 8122-71404-2
Ivo Perlman Group
Children Of Ibeji | Enja | ENJ-7005 2
Maceo Parker Group
Roots Revisited | Minor Music | 801015
Roots
Salutes The Saxophone | IN+OUT Records | 7016-2
Salutes The Saxophones: Tributes To Gene Ammons, Eric Dolphy, Coleman Hawkins And Charlie Parker | IN+OUT Records | 7016-3
Jazz Unlimited | IN+OUT Records | 7017-2
Stablemates | IN+OUT Records | 7021-2

Pulliam,Steve | (tbvoc)
Buddy Johnson And His Orchestra
Buddy And Ella Johnson 1953-1964 | Bear Family Records | BCD 15479 DH
Eddie Lockjaw Davis Quintet
Jaws In Orbit | Original Jazz Classics | OJCCD 322-2(P 7171)

Puls,Magnus | (tb)
Tim Hagans With Norrbotten Big Band
Future Miles | ACT | 9235-2

Puls,Stan | (b)
Jack Teagarden And His Sextet
Mis'ry And The Blues | Verve | 9860310

Puma,Joe | (g)
Helen Merrill With The Pepper Adams Quintet
Chasin' The Bird(Gershwin) | EmArCy | 558850-2
Herbie Mann-Bobby Jaspar Sextet
Flute Flight | Original Jazz Classics | OJCCD 1084-2(P 2124)
Flute Souflé | Original Jazz Classics | OJCCD 760-2(P 7101)
J.R. Monterose Sextet
Jaywalkin' | Fresh Sound Records | FSR-CD 320
Prestige All Stars
The Mal Waldron Memorial Album:Soul Eyes | Prestige | PRCD 11024-2
Warren Vaché Quartet
What Is There To Say? | Nagel-Heyer | CD 056
Warren Vaché With Joe Puma
Blues Of Summer | Nagel-Heyer | NH 1011

Pumila,Steve | (perc)
Tony Scott Group
Tony Scott | Verve | 9861063

Puntillo,Nicola | (b-cl)
Banda Città Ruvo Di Puglia
La Banda/Banda And Jazz | Enja | ENJ-9326 2

Puntin,Claudio | (cl,b-cl,perc,voc,reedswoodwinds)
Andreas Willers Octet
The Ground Music | Enja | ENJ-9368 2
Blue Collar
Diary Of A Working Band | Jazz Haus Musik | JHM 0089 CD
Claudio Puntin Quartet
Mondo | Jazz Haus Musik | JHM 0134 CD
Claudio Puntin/Gerdur Gunnarsdóttir
Ýlir | ECM | 1749(158570-2)
Dirk Raulf Group
Theater I (Bühnenmusik) | Poise | Poise 07
Georg Ruby Group
Stange Loops | Jazz Haus Musik | JHM 0057 CD
Joachim Ullrich Orchestra
Faces Of The Duke | Jazz Haus Musik | JHM 0045 CD
Klaus König Orchestra
Reviews | Enja | ENJ-9061 2
Stefan Bauer-Claudio Puntin-Marcio Doctor
Lingo | Jazz Haus Musik | JHM 0116 CD

Purcell,John | (alto-fl,as,bs,oboe,piccolo,cl)
Jack DeJohnette's Special Edition
Inflation Blues | ECM | 1244
Album Album | ECM | 1280

Purdie,Bernard 'Pretty' | (drperc)
Archie Shepp Orchestra
The Cry Of My People | Impulse(MCA) | 9861488
Bernard Purdie Group
Jazzin' With The Soul Brothers | Fantasy | FANCD 6086-2
Bernard Purdie's Soul To Jazz
Bernard Purdie's Soul To Jazz | ACT | 9242-2
Bernard Purdie's Soul To Jazz II | ACT | 9253-2
Boogaloo Joe Jones Quintet
Discovery:Grover Washington Jr.-The First Recordings | Prestige | PCD 11020-2
Charlie's Greatest Hits | Prestige | PCD 24250-2
Boogaloo Joe Jones Sextet
Jazzin' With The Soul Brothers | Fantasy | FANCD 6086-2
Discovery:Grover Washington Jr.-The First Recordings | Prestige | PCD 11020-2
Gato Barbieri Group
Planet Jazz:Gato Barbieri | RCA | 2165364-2
Gato Barbieri:The Best Of The Early Years | RCA | 2663523-2
Gato Barbieri Septet
Yesterdays | RCA | 2147797-2
Gene Ammons Quartet
Gentle Jug Vol.3 | Prestige | PCD 24249-2
Brother Jug! | Prestige | PR20 7792-2
Gene Ammons Quintet
Brother Jug! | Prestige | PR20 7792-2
Grant Green With Orchestra
The Final Comedown(Soundtrack) | Blue Note | 581678-2
Hank Crawford And His Orchestra
Roadhouse Symphony | Original Jazz Classics | OJCCD 1048-2(M 9140)
Hank Crawford Quintet
After Dark | Milestone | MCD 9279-2
Hank Crawford-Jimmy McGriff Quartet
Jazzin' With The Soul Brothers | Fantasy | FANCD 6086-2
Herbie Hancock Septet
Herbie Hancock:The Complete Blue Note Sixties Sessions | Blue Note | 495569-2
Herbie Mann And His Orchestra
The Best Of Herbie Mann | Atlantic | 7567-81369-2
Jimmy McGriff Quintet
McGriff's House Party | Milestone | MCD 9300-2
Jimmy McGriff Septet
McGriff Avenue | Milestone | MCD 9325-2
Jimmy McGriff Sextet
McGriff's House Party | Milestone | MCD 9300-2
Jimmy Smith Quartet
Jimmy Smith-Talkin' Verve | Verve | 531563-2
Les McCann Group
Atlantic Jazz: Fusion | Atlantic | 7567-81711-2
Louis Armstrong And His Friends
Planet Jazz:Louis Armstrong | Planet Jazz | 2152052-2
Planet Jazz Sampler | Planet Jazz | 2152326-2
Louis Armstrong And His Friends | Bluebird | 2663961-2
Nils Landgren Funk Unit
Paint It Blue:A Tribute To Cannonball Adderley | ACT | 9243-2
Nina Simone And Orchestra
Planet Jazz:Nina Simone | Planet Jazz | 2165372-2
Oscar Brown Jr. And His Group
Movin' On | Rhino | 8122-73678-2
Rahsaan Roland Kirk And His Orchestra
Blacknuss | Rhino | 8122-71408-2
Rusty Bryant Group
For The Good Times | Prestige | PRCD 24269-2
Yusef Lateef Ensemble
Atlantic Saxophones | Rhino | 8122-71256-2

Purim,Flora | (gong,vocperc)
Airto Moreira/Flora Purim
The Colours Of Life | IN+OUT Records | 001-2
Airto Moreira/Flora Purim Group
Jazz Unlimited | IN+OUT Records | 7017-2
Chick Corea And Return To Forever
Light As A Feather | Polydor | 557115-2
Chick Corea Quartet
Return To Forever | ECM | 1022(811978-2)
Verve Jazz Masters 20:Introducing | Verve | 519853-2
Chick Corea's Return To Forever
Verve Jazz Masters 3:Chick Corea | Verve | 519820-2
Dizzy Gillespie And The United Nation Orchestra
7.Zelt-Musik-Festival:Jazz Events | Zounds | CD 2730001
Duke Pearson Orchestra
Blue Bossa | Blue Note | 795590-2
Flora Purim And Her Quartet
Joe Henderson:The Milestone Years | Milestone | 8MCD 4413-2
Flora Purim And Her Quintet
Joe Henderson:The Milestone Years | Milestone | 8MCD 4413-2
Flora Purim And Her Sextet
Joe Henderson:The Milestone Years | Milestone | 8MCD 4413-2
Butterfly Dreams | Original Jazz Classics | OJCCD 315-2
Flora Purim With Orchestra
Joe Henderson:The Milestone Years | Milestone | 8MCD 4413-2
Ivo Perlman Group
Children Of Ibeji | Enja | ENJ-7005 2
Return To Forever
Return To The 7th Galaxy-Return To Forever:The Anthology | Verve | 533108-2

Purnell,Alton | (pvoc)
Bunk Johnson And His New Orleans Band
Planet Jazz:Jazz Trumpet | Planet Jazz | 2169654-2
George Lewis And His New Orleans Ragtime Band
The Beverly Caverns Session | Good Time Jazz | GTCD 12058-2
George Lewis And His New Orleans Stompers
George Lewis And His New Orleans Stompers | Blue Note | 821261-2

Purrone,Tony | (el-gg)
Essence All Stars
Hot Jazz Bisquits | Hip Bop | HIBD 8801
Jam Session
Jam Session Vol.2 | Steeplechase | SCCD 31523
Lenny White Group
Present Tense | Hip Bop | HIBD 8004
Tony Purrone Trio
Rascality | Steeplechase | SCCD 31514

Purse,Bruce | (synthtp)
Lester Bowie's Brass Fantasy
I Only Have Eyes For You | ECM | 1296(825902-2)

Purser,David | (tbeuphonium)
John Surman-Jack DeJohnette With The London Brass
Printed In Germany | ECM | 1802(017065-2)

Purtill,Maurice 'Moe' | (dr)
Glenn Miller And His Orchestra
Planet Jazz:Glenn Miller | Planet Jazz | 2152056-2
Planet Jazz Sampler | Planet Jazz | 2152326-2
Planet Jazz:Jazz Greatest Hits | Planet Jazz | 2169648-2
Planet Jazz:Big Bands | Planet Jazz | 2169649-2
Planet Jazz:Swing | Planet Jazz | 2169651-2
The Chesterfield Broadcasts Vol.1 | RCA | 2663113-2
Candelight Miller | RCA | 2668716-2
Swing Legends | Nimbus Records | NI 2001
The Andrew Sisters With The Glenn Miller Orchestra
The Chesterfield Broadcasts Vol.1 | RCA | 2663113-2

Purves,Alan | (drperc)

Ernst Reijseger & Tenore E Cuncordu De Orosei
Colla Voche | Winter&Winter | 910037-2
The Collective 3 +
The Collective 3 + | true muze | TUMU CD 9802

Purviance,Don | (b-tb,shells,tbts)
Dee Dee Bridgewater With Big Band
Dear Ella | Verve | 539102-2

Purviance,Douglas | (b-tb,tuba,tbshells)
Tom Harrell Orchestra
Time's Mirror | RCA | 2663524-2

Purwanto | (bonang,klunthung,calung,rebana)
Norbert Stein Pata Masters meets Djaduk Ferianto Kua Etnika
Pata Java | Pata Musik | PATA 16 CD

Pusch,Bastian | (pkeyboards)
Mind Games With Claudio Roditi
Live | Edition Collage | EC 501-2
Vocal Moments | Take Twelve On CD | TT 008-2

Puschnig,Wolfgang | (alto-fl,as,hojak,shakuhachi,bansuri)
AM 4
...And She Answered | ECM | 1394
Carla Bley Band
Fleur Carnivore | Watt | 21
The Very Big Carla Bley Band | Watt | 23
Big Band Theory | Watt | 25(519966-2)
4X4 | Watt | 30(159547-2)
Carla Bley Big Band
The Carla Bley Big Band Goes To Church | Watt | 27(533682-2)
Creative Works Orchestra
Willisau And More Live | Creative Works Records | CW CD 1020-2
Hans Koller Groups
Out Of The Rim | IN+OUT Records | 7014-2
Michael Mantler Quintet With The Balanescu Quartet
Folly Seeing All This | ECM | 1485
Nguyen Le Group
Maghreb And Friends | ACT | 9261-2
Red Sun/SamulNori
Then Comes The White Tiger | ECM | 1499
Wolfgang Puschnig-Uli Scherer
Puschnig-Scherer | EmArCy | 014103-2

Pusey,Bill | (tpfl-h)
George Gruntz Concert Jazz Band '83
Theatre | ECM | 1265

Putnam,Janet | (harp)
Billie Holiday With The Ray Ellis Orchestra
Lady In Satin | CBS | CK 65144
Miles Davis With Gil Evans & His Orchestra
Ballads | CBS | 461099-2
Miles Davis At Carnegie Hall | CBS | CK 65027
Sketches Of Spain | CBS | CK 65142
Quiet Nights | CBS | CK 65293
The Modern Jazz Society
A Concert Of Contemporary Music | Verve | 559827-2

Putnam,M. | (fr-h)
Vince Mendoza With The WDR Big Band And Guests
Sketches | ACT | 9215-2

Pütz,Mark | (synthgrand-p)
Dogs Don't Sing In The Rain
Bones For Breakfast | Edition Collage | EC 472-2
Vocal Moments | Take Twelve On CD | TT 008-2
Wind Moments | Take Twelve On CD | TT 009-2

Puzie,Leonard | (voc)
The Ravens
Ultimate Ben Webster selected by James Carter | Verve | 557537-2

Pye,Livia | (voc)
Mike Westbrook Brass Band
Glad Day:Settings Of William Blake | Enja | ENJ-9376 2

Pyle,Cheryl | (fl)
Tom Harrell Quintet
Sail Away | Original Jazz Classics | OJCCD 1095-2(C- 14054-2)
Tom Harrell Sextet
Visions | Contemporary | CCD 14063-2

Pyne,Chris | (tb)
John Surman Orchestra
How Many Clouds Can You See? | Deram | 844882-2
John Surman-John Warren Group
The Brass Project | ECM | 1478
Kenny Wheeler Ensemble
Muisc For Large & Small Ensembles | ECM | 1415/16

Q4 Orchester Project |
Q4 Orchester Project
Lyon's Brood | Creative Works Records | CW CD 1018-3
Yavapai | Creative Works Records | CW CD 1028-2

Qadr,Talib | (ss,asvoc)
Dollar Brand Quartet
Africa Tears And Laugher | Enja | ENJ-3039 2

Qálvez,Curro | (bel-b)
Javier Feierstein Quartet
Wysiwyg | Fresh Sound Records | FSNT 040 CD

Qien,Jorn | (keyboards)
Geir Lysne Listening Ensemble
Aurora Borealis-Nordic Lights | ACT | 9406-2

Quadrant |
Quadrant
Milt Jackson Birthday Celebration | Fantasy | FANCD 6079-2

Qualey,David | (g)
David Qualey
Talking Hands:Live | ALISO Records | AL 1021

Quarta,Alexandro | (voice)
Michel Godard Ensemble
Castel Del Monte II | Enja | ENJ-9431 2

Quartet,The |
The Quartet
The Quartet Live In Prague | P&J Music | P&J 101-1 CD

Quartier Latin Jazz Band |
Quartier Latin Jazz Band
Great Traditionalists | Jazzpoint | JP 1046 CD

Quattara,Seydou | (bara)
Jon Hassell & Farafina
Flash Of The Spirit | Intuition Records | INT 3009-2

Quaye,Russell | (kazoo,g,vocquattro)
Henrik Johansen With The City Ramblers
The Golden Years Of Revival Jazz,Sampler | Storyville | 109 1001
Hylda Sims And The City Ramblers Skiffle Group With Henrik Johansen
The Golden Years Of Revival Jazz,Vol.9 | Storyville | STCD 5514

Quaye,Terry | (tambourine,congasvoc)
Archie Shepp Orchestra
The Cry Of My People | Impulse(MCA) | 9861488

Quealey,Chelsea | (tp)
Mezz Mezzrow And His Orchestra
Planet Jazz:Bud Freeman | Planet Jazz | 2161240-2

Quebec West,Danny | (as)
Thelonious Monk Quintet
The Best Of Thelonious Monk:The Blue Note Years | Blue Note | 795636-2
Thelonious Monk Sextet
Thelonious Monk:Misterioso | Dreyfus Jazz Line | FDM 36743-2

Quebec,Ike | (ts)
Dodo Greene With The Ike Quebec Quintet
Misty Blue:Sweet Sisters Swing Songs Of Sorrow And Sadness | Blue Note | 521151-2
Grant Green Quintet
Kind Of Blue:Blue Note Celebrate The Music Of Miles Davis | Blue Note | 534255-2
Ballads | Blue Note | 537560-2
Ike Quebec Quartet
Blue Note Plays Gershwin | Blue Note | 520808-2
Blue And Sentimental | Blue Note | 784098-2
Midnight Blue(The [Be]witching Hour) | Blue Note | 854365-2
Ike Quebec Quintet
The Blue Note Swingtets | Blue Note | 495697-2
Blue And Sentimental | Blue Note | 784098-2
Blue Bossa | Blue Note | 795590-2
Ike Quebec Swing Seven
The Blue Note Swingtets | Blue Note | 495697-2
Ike Quebec Swingtet
The Blue Note Swingtets | Blue Note | 495697-2

Queck,Holger | (voc)
Dirk Raulf Group
Theater II(Bühnenmusik) | Poise | Poise 10

Queck,Roman | (ssts)
Wayne Bartlett With The Thomas Hufschmidt Group
Tokyo Blues | Laika Records | 35101212

Queen,Alvin | (dr,narration,percvoc)
Bennie Wallace Quartet
The Talk Of The Town | Enja | ENJ-7091 2
Dusko Goykovich-Joe Haider Quintet
Jazz Portraits | EGO | 95080
Johnny Griffin-Steve Grossman Quintet
Johnny Griffin & Steve Grossman | Dreyfus Jazz Line | FDM 36615-2
Kenn Drew Trio
Kenny Drew Trio At The Brewhouse | Storyville | 4960633
Leon Thomas With Band
Leon Thomas In Berlin | RCA | 2663877-2

Quersin,Benoit | (b)
Bobby Jaspar Quintet
Jazz In Paris | EmArCy | 159941-2 PMS
Chet Baker Sextet
Chet Baker-The Italian Sessions | Bluebird | ND 82001
Lucky Thompson And His Orchestra
Americans Swinging In Paris:Lucky Thompson | EMI Records | 539651-2
Lucky Thompson Quartet
Americans Swinging In Paris:Lucky Thompson | EMI Records | 539651-2
Lucky Thompson Quintet
Americans Swinging In Paris:Lucky Thompson | EMI Records | 539651-2
Lucky Thompson Trio
Americans Swinging In Paris:Lucky Thompson | EMI Records | 539651-2
Lucky Thompson With The Gerard Pochonet All-Stars
Planet Jazz:Jazz Saxophone | Planet Jazz | 2169653-2
Lucky Thompson's Modern Jazz Group Quartet
Jazz In Paris:Lucky Thompson-Modern Jazz Group | EmArCy | 159823-2 PMS
Lucky Thompson's Modern Jazz Group Tentet
Jazz In Paris:Lucky Thompson-Modern Jazz Group | EmArCy | 159823-2 PMS
Rene Thomas Quartet
Jazz In Paris:René Thomas-Meeting Mister Thomas | EmArCy | 549812-2
Rene Thomas Quintet
Jazz In Paris:René Thomas-The Real Cat | EmArCy | 549400-2 PMS
Jazz In Paris:René Thomas-Meeting Mister Thomas | EmArCy | 549812-2
Stephane Grappelli Sextet
Grapelli Story | Verve | 515807-2
Zoot Sims Quintet
Americans Swinging In Paris:Zoot Sims | EMI Records | 539646-2

Quest,John | (b)
The Jimmy And Marion McPartland Sessions
Vic Lewis:The Golden Years | Candid | CCD 79754

Quick,Joe | (g)
Klaus Doldinger Jubilee
Doldinger's Best | ACT | 9224-2

Quick,Torita | (voc)
Things
Mother Nature | Jazzpoint | JP 1028 CD

Quicksell,Howdy | (arrbj)
Bix And His Rhythm Jugglers
Jazz:The Essential Collection Vol.2 | IN+OUT Records | 78012-2
Bix Beiderbecke And His Gang
Jazz:The Essential Collection Vol.2 | IN+OUT Records | 78012-2

Quigley,Herb | (drvib)
Paul Whiteman And His Orchestra
Planet Jazz:Jack Teagarden | Planet Jazz | 2161236-2

Quill,Daniel | (clas)
Buddy Rich And His Orchestra
Swingin' New Big Band | Pacific Jazz | 835232-2

Quill,Gene | (as,cl,b-cl,saxts)
Billie Holiday With The Ray Ellis Orchestra
Verve Jazz Masters 47:Billie Holiday Sings Standards | Verve | 527650-2
Elliot Lawrence And His Orchestra
The Elliot Lawrence Big Band Swings Cohn & Kahn | Fantasy | FCD 24761-2
Gerry Mulligan Concert Jazz Band
Verve Jazz Masters 36:Gerry Mulligan | Verve | 523342-2
Verve Jazz Masters Vol.60:The Collection | Verve | 529866-2
Gerry Mulligan And The Concert Band At The Village Vanguard | Verve | 589488-2
The Complete Verve Gerry Mulligan Concert Band | Verve | 9860613
Jimmy Rushing And His Orchestra
Five Feet Of Soul | Roulette | 581830-2
Mundell Lowe Quintet
A Grand Night For Swinging | Original Jazz Classics | OJCCD 1940-(RLP 238)
Prestige All Stars
The Prestige Legacy Vol.2:Battles Of Saxes | Prestige | PCD 24252-2
Tito Puente Orchestra
Planet Jazz:Tito Puente | Planet Jazz | 2165369-2

Quine,Robert | (gvoice)
John Zorn Group
Spillane | Nonesuch | 7559-79172-2

Quinichette,Paul | (maracasts)
Billie Holiday And Her All Stars
Verve Jazz Masters 12:Billie Holiday | Verve | 519825-2
Billie Holiday Story Vol.4:Lady Sings The Blues | Verve | 521429-2
Verve Jazz Masters Vol.60:The Collection | Verve | 529866-2
4 By 4:Ella Fitzgerald/Sarah Vaughan/Billie Holiday/Dinah Washington | Verve | 559693-2
The Billie Holiday Song Book | Verve | 823246-2
Count Basie And His Orchestra
Jazz Gallery:Lester Young Vol.2(1946-59) | RCA | 2119541-2
Verve Jazz Masters 2:Count Basie | Verve | 519819-2
Count Basie Sextet
Verve Jazz Masters 2:Count Basie | Verve | 519819-2
Dinah Washington And Her Band
After Hours With Miss D | Verve | 0760562
Dinah Washington And Her Orchestra
For Those In Love | EmArCy | 514073-2
Gene Ammons And His All Stars
John Coltrane-The Prestige Recordings | Prestige | 16 PCD 4405-2
The Big Sound | Original Jazz Classics | OJCCD 651-2(P 7132)
Groove Blues | Original Jazz Classics | OJCCD 723-2(PR 7201)
The Prestige Legacy Vol.2:Battles Of Saxes | Prestige | PCD 24252-2
Jay McShann And His Orchestra
Atlantic Jazz: Kansas City | Atlantic | 7567-81701-2
Jay McShann Orchestra
The Last Of The Blue Devils | Atlantic | 7567-80791-2
John Coltrane-Paul Quinichette Quintet
John Coltrane-The Prestige Recordings | Prestige | 16 PCD 4405-2
Cattin' | Original Jazz Classics | OJCCD 460-2
Johnny Smith Quintet
Moonlight In Vermont | Roulette | 596593-2
Prestige All Stars
John Coltrane-The Prestige Recordings | Prestige | 16 PCD 4405-2
Wheelin' & Dealin' | Original Jazz Classics | OJCCD 672-2(P7131)
The Prestige Legacy Vol.1:The High Priests | Prestige | PCD 24251-2
The Mal Waldron Memorial Album:Soul Eyes | Prestige | PRCD 11024-2
Sarah Vaughan With The Clifford Brown All Stars
Verve Jazz Masters 20:Introducing | Verve | 519853-2
Clifford Brown-Max Roach:Alone Together-The Best Of The Mercury Years | Verve | 526373-2
Sarah Vaughan | Verve | 543305-2
4 By 4:Ella Fitzgerald/Sarah Vaughan/Billie Holiday/Dinah Washington | Verve | 559693-2
Brownie-The Complete EmArCy Recordings Of Clifford Brown | EmArCy | 838306-2
Sarah Vaughan | EmArCy | 9860779
Woody Herman And His Orchestra
The Legends Of Swing | Laserlight | 24659

Quinones,Cheito | (voc)
Arturo Sandoval And The Latin Train Band
Arturo Sandoval & The Latin Train | GRP | GRP 98202

Quintana,Ismael | (perc)
Cal Tjader's Orchestra
Talkin Verve/Roots Of Acid Jazz:Cal Tjader | Verve | 531562-2

Quintana,Jose Luis 'Chancuito' | (timbales)
Roy Hargrove's Crisol
Habana | Verve | 537563-2

Quintero,Luis | (timbalesguiro)
Gonzalo Rubalcaba Quartet
Supernova | Blue Note | 531172-2

Quintero,Robert | (congas)

Quintet Du Hot Club De France |
Django Reinhardt And The Quintet Du Hot Club De France
Planet Jazz:Django Reinhardt | Planet Jazz | 2152071-2
Planet Jazz:Stephane Grappelli | RCA | 2165366-2
Quintet Du Hot Club De France
Jazz In Paris:Django Reinhardt-Swing From Paris | EmArCy | 159853-2 PMS
Jazz In Paris:Django Reinhardt-Swing 39 | EmArCy | 159854-2 PMS
Djangology | Bluebird | 2663957-2
Grapelli Story | Verve | 515807-2
Verve Jazz Masters 38:Django Reinhardt | Verve | 516931-2
Verve Jazz Masters Vol.60:The Collection | Verve | 529866-2
Django/Django In Rome 1949-1050 | BGO Records | BGOCD 366
Django Reinhardt:Echoes Of France | Dreyfus Jazz Line | FDM 36726-2
Django Reinhardt:Souveniers | Dreyfus Jazz Line | FDM 36744-2

Quintet Of The Year |
Quintet Of The Year
Charles Mingus-The Complete Debut Recordings | Debut | 12 DCD 4402-2
The Quintet-Jazz At Massey Hall | Debut | DSA 124-6
The Quintet-Jazz At Massey Hall | Original Jazz Classics | OJC20 044-2

Quintones,The | (voc)
Benny Goodman And His Orchestra
Camel Caravan Broadcast 1939 Vol.1 | Phontastic | NCD 8817

Qureshi,Taufik | (clef,dafiperc)
Remember Shakti
Saturday Night In Bombay | Verve | 014184-2

Raab,Walter | (tpfl-h)
Freddie Brocksieper And His Boys
Freddie's Boogie Blues | Bear Family Records | BCD 16388 AH

Raake,Christian | (fl,ts,ssbass-fl)
Loft Line
Source | Laika Records | 35101122

Rabanit,Claude | (tp)
Claude Luter Et Ses L'Orientais
Jazz In Paris:Sidney Bechet Et Claude Luther | EmArCy | 159821-2 PMS
Sidney Bechet With Claude Luter And His Orchestra
Planet Jazz:Sidney Bechet | Planet Jazz | 2152063-2

Rabatti,Pascal | (g)
John McLaughlin With The Aighette Quartet And Yan Marez
Time Remembered:John McLaughlin Plays Bill Evans | Verve | 519861-2

Rabbia,Michele | (perc)
Stefania Tallini Trio With Guests
New Life | yvp music | CD 3114

Rabe,Bernd | (as,cl,saxss)
Bernd Konrad With Erwin Lehn und sein Südfunk Orchester Stuttgart
Wen Die Götter Lieben | Creative Works Records | CW CD 1010-1
Bill Ramsey With Orchestra
Gettin' Back To Swing | Bear Family Records | BCD 15813 AH
Bireli Lagrene Ensemble
Bireli Swing '81 | Jazzpoint | JP 1009 CD
Routes To Django & Bireli Swing '81 | Jazzpoint | JP 1055 CD
Horst Jankowski Orchestra With Voices
Jankowskeynotes | MPS | 9814806
New Jazz Group Hannover
Deutsches Jazz Fesival 1954/1955 | Bear Family Records | BCD 15430
SWR Big Band
Jazz In Concert | Hänssler Classics | CD 93.004

Rabe,Christian | (bassoon)
Miles Davis With Gil Evans Orchestra, The George Gruntz Concert Jazz Band and Guests
Miles & Quincy Live At Montreux | Warner | 9362-45221-2

Rabinowitz,Michael | (bassoon)
Charles Mingus Orchestra
Tonight At Noon...Three Or Four Shades Of Love | Dreyfus Jazz Line | FDM 36633-2
Franz Koglmann Group
Venus In Transit | Between The Lines | btl 017(Efa 10186)

Rabinowitz,Sol | (ts)
Charlie Parker With Machito And His Orchestra
Bird: The Complete Charlie Parker On Verve | Verve | 837141-2

Rabus,Kathrin | (v)
NDR Radio Philharmonic Orchestra
Colossus Of Sound | Enja | ENJ-9460 2

Rach,Corinna | (voc)
Jazzensemble Des Hessischen Rundfunks
Jazz Messe-Messe Für Unsere Zeit | hr music.de | hrmj 003-01 CD

Racine,Philippe | (fl)
James Newton
7.Zelt-Musik-Festival:Jazz Events | Zounds | CD 2730001

Racoupeau,Philippe | (el-b)
Serge Forté Trio
Vaina | Laika Records | LK 90-021

Radanovics,Michael | (vvoc)
Motus Quartett
Grimson Flames | Creative Works Records | CW CD 1023-2

Radcliffe,Fred | (dr)
Don Byas Quartet
Don Byas:Laura | Dreyfus Jazz Line | FDM 36714-2
Lionel Hampton And His Orchestra
Lionel Hampton:Flying Home | Dreyfus Jazz Line | FDM 36735-2

Rademacher,Stefan | (b,el-bfretless-b)
Frank Kirchner Group
Frank Kirchner | Laika Records | LK 93-036

Rader,Don | (fl-h,co,tparr)
Bernd Konrad With Erwin Lehn und sein Südfunk Orchester Stuttgart
Wen Die Götter Lieben | Creative Works Records | CW CD 1010-1
Conexion Latina
Calorcito | Enja | ENJ-4072 2
Count Basie And His Orchestra
Verve Jazz Masters 2:Count Basie | Verve | 519819-2
Ella Fitzgerald With The Count Basie Orchestra
Ella Fitzgerald-First Lady Of Song | Verve | 517898-2
Ella And Basie | Verve | 539059-2
Frank Sinatra With The Count Basie Orchestra
It Might As Well Be Spring | Reprise | 7599-27027-2

Raderman,Lou | (ldv)
Anita O'Day With The Buddy Bregman Orchestra
Verve Jazz Masters 49:Anita O'Day | Verve | 527653-2
Ella Fitzgerald With The Billy May Orchestra
The Best Of The Song Books:The Ballads | Verve | 521867-2
Ella Fitzgerald Sings The Harold Arlen Song Book | Verve | 589108-2
Ella Fitzgerald With The Frank DeVol Orchestra
Get Happy! | Verve | 523321-2
Ella Fitzgerald With The Nelson Riddle Orchestra
The Best Of The Song Books:The Ballads | Verve | 521867-2
Love Songs:The Best Of The Song Books | Verve | 531762-2
Frank Sinatra With The Count Basie Orchestra
It Might As Well Be Spring | Reprise | 7599-27027-2
Hank Crawford Orchestra
Rhino Presents The Atlantic Jazz Gallery | Atlantic | 8122-71257-2
Mel Tormé With The Russell Garcia Orchestra
Swingin' On The Moon | Verve | 511385-2
Pete Rugolo And His Orchestra
Thriller/Richard Diamon(Original Jazz Scores From 2 Classics TV Series) | Fresh Sound Records | FSCD 2015

Radio Jazzgroup Frankfurt |
Radio Jazzgroup Frankfurt
Jubilee Edition | double moon | CHRDM 71020

Radio Orchester Hannover |
Chet Baker Quintet/NDR Big Band/Radio Orchestra Hannover
Straight From The Heart-The Last Concert Vol.2 | Enja | ENJ-6020 2
The Last Concert Vol.I+II | Enja | ENJ-6074 22

Radio Philharmonie Hannover NDR |
Joachim Kühn And The Radio Philharmonie Hannover NDR With Jazz Soloists
Europeana | ACT | 9220-2

Radio Symphony Orchestra |
Nana Vasconcelos-Egberto Gismonti Duo And Strings
Saudades | ECM | 1147

Radio Symphony Orchestra Frankfurt/M. |
Radio Symphony Orchestra Frankfurt
Songs And One Symphony | ECM | 1721
Elliott Sharp:Racing Hearts/Tessalation Row/Calling | hr music.de | hrmn 018-03 CD

Radio-Philharmonie Hannover |
Dusko Goykovich Quintet With The NDR Radio-Philharmonie,Hannover
Balkan Blues | Enja | ENJ-9320 2
Joe Pass With The NDR Big Band And Radio Philharmonie Hannover
Joe Pass In Hamburg | ACT | 9100-2

Radle,Alois | (cello)
Bernd Konrad Jazz Group With Symphonie Orchestra
Wen Die Götter Lieben | Creative Works Records | CW CD 1010-1

Radle,Carl | (bel-b)
John Lee Hooker Group
Endless Boogie | MCA | MCD 10413

Radocchia,Emil | (perc)
Ella Fitzgerald With The Nelson Riddle Orchestra
The Best Of The Song Books:The Ballads | Verve | 521867-2
Ella Fitzgerald Sings The Johnny Mercer Songbook | Verve | 539057-2

Radochay,Karin | (v)
Bernd Konrad Jazz Group With Symphonie Orchestra
Wen Die Götter Lieben | Creative Works Records | CW CD 1010-1

Radtke,Carsten | (g,el-gmarimba)
Radtke/Bauer/Basmann
A Contrast Music | Edition Collage | EC 491-2

Radtke,Tom | (drperc)
Singers Unlimited With Orchestra
The Singers Unlimited:Magic Voices | MPS | 539130-2

Rae,John | (dr)
Bola Sete Trio
Tour De Force:The Bola Sete Trios | Fantasy | FCD 24766-2
Cal Tjader Quartet
Cal Tjader Plays Harold Arlen & West Side Story | Fantasy | FCD 24775-2

Rae,Johnny | (dr,marimba,perc,timbalesvib)
Anita O'Day With The Cal Tjader Quartet
Verve Jazz Masters 49:Anita O'Day | Verve | 527653-2
Time For 2 | Verve | 559808-2
Art Van Damme Group
State Of Art | MPS | 841413-2
Cal Tjader Group
Verve Jazz Masters 39:Cal Tjader | Verve | 521858-2
Verve Jazz Masters Vol.60:The Collection | Verve | 529866-2
Cal Tjader Quintet
Talkin Verve/Roots Of Acid Jazz:Cal Tjader | Verve | 531562-2
Soul Bird | Verve | 549111-2
Cal Tjader Septet
Talkin Verve/Roots Of Acid Jazz:Cal Tjader | Verve | 531562-2
Cal Tjader Sextet
Talkin Verve/Roots Of Acid Jazz:Cal Tjader | Verve | 531562-2
Cal Tjader With The Lalo Schifrin Orchestra
Talkin Verve/Roots Of Acid Jazz:Cal Tjader | Verve | 531562-2
Cal Tjader's Orchestra
Verve Jazz Masters 39:Cal Tjader | Verve | 521858-2
Herbie Mann Sextet
Verve Jazz Masters 56:Herbie Mann | Verve | 529901-2
Herbie Mann's Cuban Band
Verve Jazz Masters 56:Herbie Mann | Verve | 529901-2
Lalo Schifrin And His Orchestra
Verve Jazz Masters 39:Cal Tjader | Verve | 521858-2
Stan Getz With The Gary McFarland Orchestra
Stan Getz Highlights:The Best Of The Verve Years Vol.2 | Verve | 517330-2
Verve Jazz Masters 53:Stan Getz-Bossa Nova | Verve | 529904-2
Big Band Bossa Nova | Verve | 825771-2 PMS
Stan Getz Highlights | Verve | 847430-2
Woody Herman And The New Thundering Herd
Woody Herman:Thundering Herd | Original Jazz Classics | OJCCD 841-2

Rae,Roger | (tb)
André Holst With Chris Dean's European Swing Orchestra
That's Swing | Nagel-Heyer | CD 079

Raffael,Donald | (bs,cl,tssax)
Singers Unlimited With The Pat Williams Orchestra
The Singers Unlimited:Magic Voices | MPS | 539130-2

Raffaelli,Benjamin | (g)
Dee Dee Bridgewater With Band
Victim Of Love | Verve | 841199-2

Raffel,Joachim | (p)
Joachim Raffel Sextet
...In Motion | Jazz 4 Ever Records:Jazz Network | J4E 4746
Joachim Raffel Trio
...In Motion | Jazz 4 Ever Records:Jazz Network | J4E 4746

Raffell,Don | (bschinese-gong)
Gerald Wilson And His Orchestra
Blue Breaks Beats Vol.2 | Blue Note | 789907-2

Rafik,Abdullah | (b)
Roland Kirk All Stars
Rahsaan/The Complete Mercury Recordings Of Roland Kirk | Mercury | 846630-2
Roland Kirk Quartet
Talkin' Verve-Roots Of Acid Jazz:Roland Kirk | Verve | 533101-2
Rahsaan/The Complete Mercury Recordings Of Roland Kirk | Mercury | 846630-2
Roland Kirk Sextet
Talkin' Verve-Roots Of Acid Jazz:Roland Kirk | Verve | 533101-2

Ragas,Henry | (p)
Original Dixieland 'Jass' Band
Planet Jazz | Planet Jazz | 2169652-2

Raghavan,R. | (mridangam)
Shakti
Shakti With John McLaughlin | CBS | 467905-2

Ragin,Hugh | (tp,fl-h,piccolo-tp,vocpccolo-tp)
David Murray Group
Speaking In Togues | Enja | ENJ-9370 2
Fred Wesley Group
Swing & Be Funky | Minor Music | 801027
Amalgamation | Minor Music | 801045
Roscoe Mitchell And The Note Factory
Nine To Get Ready | ECM | 1651(539725-2)

Ragin,Melvin | (g)
Dee Dee Bridgewater With Band
Dee Dee Bridgewater | Atlantic | 7567-80760-2

Raglin,Alvin 'Junior' | (b)
Duke Ellington And His Famous Orchestra
Duke Ellington:The Blanton-Webster Band | Bluebird | 21 13181-2
Planet Jazz:Johnny Hodges | Planet Jazz | 2152065-2
Duke Ellington And His Orchestra
Planet Jazz:Duke Ellington | Planet Jazz | 2152053-2
Highlights From The Duke Ellington Centennial Edition | RCA | 2663672-2
Carnegie Hall Concert December 1944 | Prestige | 2PCD 24073-2
Carnegie Hall Concert December 1947 | Prestige | 2PCD 24075-2
Carnegie Hall Concert January 1943 | Prestige | 2PCD 34004-2
Jazz:The Essential Collection Vol.3 | IN+OUT Records | 78013-2
At The Hurricane:Original 1943 Broadcasts | Storyville | STCD 8359

Rahier,Manfred | (dr)
Anirahtak und die Jürgen Sturm Band
Das Kurt Weill Programm | Nabel Records:Jazz Network | CD 4638
Berlin-Paris-New York/Music By Kurt Weil | Nabel Records:Jazz Network | CD 4655
Jürgen Sturm's Ballstars
Tango Subversivo | Nabel Records:Jazz Network | CD 4613

Rahim,Emmanuel | (congasperc)
John Coltrane Quintet
Live At The Village Vanguard Again | Impulse(MCA) | 951213-2

Raible,Claus | (pp-solo)
Al Porcino Big Band
Al Porcino Big Band Live! | Organic Music | ORGM 9717
Claus Raible
Introducing The Exciting Claus Raible Trio | Organic Music | ORGM 9714
Claus Raible Sextet
Loopin' With Lea | Organic Music | ORGM 9724
Claus Raible Trio
Introducing The Exciting Claus Raible Trio | Organic Music | ORGM 9714
Roman Schwaller Nonet
The Original Tunes | JHM Records | JHM 3629

Raichov,Peter | (accordeon)
Batoru
Tree Of Sounds | Nabel Records:Jazz Network | CD 4685

Railo,Tauno | (bvoc)
Piirpauke
The Wild East | JA & RO | JARO 4128-2
Zerenade | JA & RO | JARO 4142-2
Piirpauke-Global Servisi | JA & RO | JARO 4150-2

Raimondi,Matthew | (cello,stringsv)
A Band Of Friends
Wynton Marsalis Quartet With Strings | CBS | CK 68921
Bob James And His Orchestra
Jazzrock-Anthology Vol.3:Fusion | Zounds | CD 27100555
Freddie Hubbard With Orchestra
This Is Jazz:Freddie Hubbard | CBS | CK 65041
Les McCann Group
Another Beginning | Atlantic | 7567-80790-2
Louis Armstrong And His Friends
Planet Jazz:Louis Armstrong | Planet Jazz | 2152052-2
Louis Armstrong And His Friends | Bluebird | 2663961-2
Paul Desmond Quartet With The Don Sebesby Orchestra
From The Hot Afternoon | Verve | 543487-2
Phil Woods Quartet With Orchestra & Strings
Round Trip | Verve | 559804-2
Stan Getz With The Eddie Sauter Orchestra
Stan Getz Plays The Music Of Mickey One | Verve | 531232-2

Rainbow |
Rainbow
Two Originals:Karuna Supreme/Rainbow | MPS | 519195-2

Rainbow Orchestra,The |
Terje Rypdal(comp)
Undisonus | ECM | 1389

Rainer,Tom | (tp)
Carl Saunders-Lanny Morgan Quintet
Las Vegar Late Night Sessions:Live At Capozzoli's | Woofy Productions | WPCD 109

Rainey,Chuck | (bel-b)
Bobbi Humphrey
Blue Break Beats | Blue Note | 799106-2
Bobbi Humphrey Group
Blue Breaks Beats Vol.2 | Blue Note | 789907-2
Bobby Hutcherson Orchestra
Deep Blue-The United States Of Mind | Blue Note | 521152-2
Donald Byrd & His Orchestra
Blue Breaks Beats Vol.2 | Blue Note | 789907-2
Donald Byrd Orchestra
Black Byrd | Blue Note | 784466-2
Places And Spaces | Blue Note | 854326-2
Eddie Harris Group
The Best Of Eddie Harris | Atlantic | 7567-81370-2
Gato Barbieri Group
Planet Jazz:Gato Barbieri | RCA | 2165364-2
Gene Harris Group
Blue Breaks Beats Vol.2 | Blue Note | 789907-2
George Benson Orchestra
Talkin' Verve:George Benson | Verve | 553780-2
George Benson With Orchestra
Verve Jazz Masters 21:George Benson | Verve | 521861-2
Grant Green Sextet
Grant Green:Blue Breakbeat | Blue Note | 494705-2
Jerome Richardson Sextet
Night Life | Prestige | PCD 24260-2
King Curtis Band
King Curtis-Blow Man Blow | Bear Family Records | BCD 15670 CI
Les McCann Group
Another Beginning | Atlantic | 7567-80790-2
Louis Armstrong And His Friends
Louis Armstrong And His Friends | Bluebird | 2663961-2
Quincy Jones And His Orchestra
Verve Jazz Masters Vol.59:Toots Thielemans | Verve | 535271-2
Richard 'Groove' Holmes Orchestra
Comin' On Home | Blue Note | 538701-2
Singers Unlimited With The Patrick Williams Orchestra
The Singers Unlimited:Magic Voices | MPS | 539130-2
Yusef Lateef Ensemble
Atlantic Saxophones | Rhino | 8122-71256-2

Rainey,Hugh | (bjg)
Bob Wallis Storyville Jazzmen
The Golden Years Of Revival Jazz,Vol.7 | Storyville | STCD 5512

Rainey,Tom | (drperc)
Andreas Willers Octet
The Ground Music | Enja | ENJ-9368 2
Fred Hersch Quartet
Point In Time | Enja | ENJ-9035 2
Fred Hersch Quintet
Point In Time | Enja | ENJ-9035 2
Fred Hersch Trio
Point In Time | Enja | ENJ-9035 2
Gianlugi Trovesi Quartet With The WDR Big Band
Dedalo | Enja | ENJ-9419 2
Klaus König Orchestra
Hommage A Douglas Adams | Enja | ENJ-6078 2
Klaus König Orchestra & Guests
The Song Of Songs:Oratorio For Two Solo Voices,Choir And Orchestra | Enja | ENJ-7057 2
Mark Helias Group
Loopin' The Cool | Enja | ENJ-9049 2
Mark Helias' Open Loose
New School | Enja | ENJ-9413 2
Neal Kirkwood Octet
Neal Kirkwood Octet | Timescrapper | TSCR 9612
Simon Nabatov Trio
Three Stories,One End | ACT | 9401-2
The Chromatic Persuaders
The Chromatic Persuaders | Timescrapper | TSCR 9617
Tim Berne-Marc Ducret-Tom Rainey
Big Satan | Winter&Winter | 910005-2

Rains,John | (tb)
Milt Jackson Orchestra
Milt Jackson Birthday Celebration | Fantasy | FANCD 6079-2

Raiz De Pedra |
Raiz De Pedra
Diario De Bordo | TipToe | TIP-888822 2
Raiz De Pedra feat. Egberto Gismonti
Diario De Bordo | TipToe | TIP-888822 2

Rajagopal,R.A. | (ghantam,konakkol,morsing,ghatam)
Charlie Mariano & The Karnataka College Of Percussion
Jyothi | ECM | 1256

Ralchev,Petar | (accordeon)
Dirk Strakhof & Batoru
Arabesque | Nabel Records:Jazz Network | CD 4696

Ralph,Alan | (b-tb,euphoniumtb)
Cal Tjader's Orchestra
Verve Jazz Masters 39:Cal Tjader | Verve | 521858-2
Gato Barbieri Orchestra
The Roots Of Acid Jazz | Impulse(MCA) | IMP 12042
George Benson And His Orchestra
Giblet Gravy | Verve | 543754-2
Talkin' Verve:George Benson | Verve | 553780-2
George Benson Orchestra
Verve Jazz Masters 21:George Benson | Verve | 521861-2
Talkin' Verve:George Benson | Verve | 553780-2
Gerry Mulligan Concert Jazz Band
Verve Jazz Masters 36:Gerry Mulligan | Verve | 523342-2
Gerry Mulligan And The Concert Band At The Village Vanguard | Verve | 589488-2
The Complete Verve Gerry Mulligan Concert Band | Verve | 9860613
Joe Williams With The Frank Hunter Orchestra
Planet Jazz:Joe Williams | Planet Jazz | 2165370-2
Kenny Burrell With The Don Sebesky Orchestra
Verve Jazz Masters 45:Kenny Burrell | Verve | 527652-2
Lee Konitz Orchestra
The Art Of Saxophone | Laserlight | 24652

Ralston,Art | (as,bs,clsax)
Louis Armstrong With The Casa Loma Orchestra
Louis Armstrong:Swing That Music | Laserlight | 36056
Peggy Lee With The Benny Goodman Orchestra
Peggy Lee & Benny Goodman:The Complete Recordings 1941-1947 | CBS | C2K 65686

Ram,Deepak | (bansuri)
Dhafer Youssef Group
Electric Sufi | Enja | ENJ-9412 2

Ramamani,R.A. | (kopakko,voctambboura)
Charlie Mariano & The Karnataka College Of Percussion
Jyothi | ECM | 1256
Live | VeraBra Records | CDVBR 2034-2

Rambler's Skiffle Group |
Hylda Sims And The Citty Ramblers Skiffle Group With Henrik Johansen
The Golden Years Of Revival Jazz,Vol.9 | Storyville | STCD 5514

Ramey,Gene | (b)
Al Cohn Quartet
The Birdlanders Vol.2 | Original Jazz Classics | OJCCD 1931-2
Al Haig Sextet
Al Haig Trio And Sextets | Original Jazz Classics | OJCCD 1929-2(SPL 1118)
Buck Clayton-Buddy Tate Quintet
Buck & Buddy | Original Jazz Classics | OJCCD 757-2(SV 2017)
Buck & Buddy Blow The Blues | Original Jazz Classics | OJCCD 850-2(SV 2030)
Count Basie And His Orchestra
Jazz Gallery:Lester Young Vol.2(1946-59) | RCA | 2119541-2
Count Basie Sextet
Verve Jazz Masters 2:Count Basie | Verve | 519819-2
Duke Jordan Trio
The Birdlanders Vol.1 | Original Jazz Classics | OJCCD 1930-2
Fats Navarro Quintet
Fats Navarro:Nostalgia | Dreyfus Jazz Line | FDM 36736-2
George Shearing Trio
The Story Of Jazz Piano | Laserlight | 24653
Horace Silver Trio
Horace Silver Retrospective | Blue Note | 495576-2
Horace Silver Trio And Spotlight On Drums:Art Blakey-Sabu | Blue Note | 591725-2
Jimmy Witherspoon With Jay McShann And His Band
Planet Jazz:Male Jazz Vocalists | Planet Jazz | 2169657-2
John Hardee Sextet
The Blue Note Swingtets | Blue Note | 495697-2
Lennie Tristano Quartet
Requiem | Atlantic | 7567-80804-2
Lester Young Quartet
Jazz Gallery:Lester Young Vol.2(1946-59) | RCA | 2119541-2
Verve Jazz Masters 30:Lester Young | Verve | 521859-2
Lester Young Quintet
Jazz Gallery:Lester Young Vol.2(1946-59) | RCA | 2119541-2
Lester Young-Teddy Wilson Quartet
Jazz Gallery:Lester Young Vol.2(1946-59) | RCA | 2119541-2
Miles Davis Sextet
Miles Davis:Milestones | Dreyfus Jazz Line | FDM 36731-2
Sonny Rollins Quintet
Ballads | Blue Note | 537562-2
Sonny Rollins:Vol.1 | Blue Note | 591724-2
The Blue Note Years-The Best Of Sonny Rollins | Blue Note | 793203-2
The Best Of Blue Note Vol.2 | Blue Note | 797960-2
Sonny Rollins:The Blue Note Recordings | Blue Note | 821371-2
Jazz Profile:Sonny Rollins | Blue Note | 823516-2
Stan Getz And His Four Brothers
The Brothers | Original Jazz Classics | OJCCD 008-2
The Prestige Legacy Vol.2:Battles Of Saxes | Prestige | PCD 24252-2
Stan Getz Five Brothers Bop Tenor Sax Stars
Stan Getz:Imagination | Dreyfus Jazz Line | FDM 36733-2
Stan Getz Quartet
Stan Getz:Imagination | Dreyfus Jazz Line | FDM 36733-2
Stan Getz Quartets | Original Jazz Classics | OJC20 121-2(P 7002)
The Jazz Giants '56
Jazz Gallery:Lester Young Vol.2(1946-59) | RCA | 2119541-2
Thelonious Monk Quintet
The Best Of Thelonious Monk:The Blue Note Years | Blue Note | 795636-2
Thelonious Monk Sextet
Genius Of Modern Music,Vol.1 | Blue Note | 532138-2
Jazz Profile:Thelonious Monk | Blue Note | 823518-2
Thelonious Monk:Misterioso | Dreyfus Jazz Line | FDM 36743-2
Thelonious Monk Trio
Genius Of Modern Music,Vol.1 | Blue Note | 532138-2
The Best Of Thelonious Monk:The Blue Note Years | Blue Note | 795636-2
Jazz Profile:Thelonious Monk | Blue Note | 823518-2
Thelonious Monk:Misterioso | Dreyfus Jazz Line | FDM 36743-2
Tony Scott And His Down Beat Club Sextet
Jazz:The Essential Collection Vol.3 | IN+OUT Records | 78013-2

Tony Scott And The All Stars
Body And Soul Revisited | GRP | GRP 16272
Vic Dickenson-Buck Clayton All Stars
Atlantic Jazz: Kansas City | Atlantic | 7567-81701-2

Ramey,Hurley | (g)
Earl Hines And His Orchestra
Planet Jazz:Earl Hines | Planet Jazz | 2159973-2

Ramirez,Alfredo | (congas)
Charles Mingus Orchestra
Cumbia & Jazz Fusion | Atlantic | 8122-71785-2

Ramirez,Hugo | (clts)
Jürgen Sturm's Ballstars
Tango Subversivo | Nabel Records:Jazz Network | CD 4613

Ramirez,Pablo | (bongoscow-bell)
Conexion Latina
Mambo Nights | Enja | ENJ-9402 2

Ramirez,Roger 'Ram' | (org,pperc)
Big Sid Catlett And His Orchestra
The Small Black Groups | Storyville | 4960523
Ella Fitzgerald And Her Famous Orchestra
The Radio Years 1940 | Jazz Unlimited | JUCD 2065
Ike Quebec Quintet
The Blue Note Swingtets | Blue Note | 495697-2
Ike Quebec Swing Seven
The Blue Note Swingtets | Blue Note | 495697-2
Ike Quebec Swingtet
The Blue Note Swingtets | Blue Note | 495697-2
Willie Bryant And His Orchestra
Planet Jazz:Ben Webster | RCA | 2165368-2

Rammer,Verne | (b)
Lucy Reed With The Eddie Higgins Quartet
This Is Lucy Reed | Original Jazz Classics | OJCCD 1943-2(F 3243)
Lucy Reed With The Eddie Higgins Trio
This Is Lucy Reed | Original Jazz Classics | OJCCD 1943-2(F 3243)

Ramon[El Portugues] | (voc)
Los Jovenes Flamencos
Jazzpana | ACT | 9212-2
Los Jovenes Flamencos With The WDR Big Band And Guests
Jazzpana | ACT | 9212-2

Ramond,Christian | (b)
Christopher Dell D.R.A.
Future Of The Smallest Form | Jazz 4 Ever Records:Jazz Network | J4E 4754
Engelbert Wrobel-Chris Hopkins-Dan Barrett Sextet
Harlem 2000 | Nagel-Heyer | CD 082
Henning Berg Quartet
Minnola | Jazz Haus Musik | JHM 0127 CD
Jochen Feucht Quartet
Signs On Lines | Satin Doll Productions | SDP 1019-1 CD
Jochen Feucht Trio
Signs On Lines | Satin Doll Productions | SDP 1019-1 CD

Ramos,Carlos 'Big Horn' | (ss)
Ithamara Koorax With Band
Love Dance:The Ballad Album | Milestone | MCD 9327-2

Ramos,Fedrico 'Freddy' | (g,el-ggimbre)
Yusef Lateef With Eternal Wind And The 'Kölner Rundfunk Orchester'
The African American Epic Suite:Music For Quintet And Orchestra | ACT | 9214-2

Ramos,J.C. | (fl)
Ithamara Koorax With Band
Love Dance:The Ballad Album | Milestone | MCD 9327-2

Ramos,Manny | (congas,dr,timbalesperc)
Roland Kirk And His Orchestra
Rahsaan/The Complete Mercury Recordings Of Roland Kirk | Mercury | 846630-2
The Latin Jazz Quintet Plus Guest: Eric Dolphy
Eric Dolphy:The Complete Prestige Recordings | Prestige | 9 PRCD-4418-2
Eric Dolphy Birthday Celebration | Fantasy | FANCD 6085-2

Rampton,Kenny | (tpfl-h)
Jimmy McGriff Sextet
McGriff's House Party | Milestone | MCD 9300-2
Mingus Big Band
Tonight At Noon...Three Or Four Shades Of Love | Dreyfus Jazz Line | FDM 36633-2

Ramsby,Poul Erik | (p)
Chris Barber & The Ramblers
The Golden Years Of Revival Jazz,Vol.12 | Storyville | STCD 5517

Ramsden,Mark | (asss)
Nicki Leighton-Thomas Group
Forbidden Games | Candid | CCD 79778

Ramsey,Bill | (as,bs,pvoc)
Bill Ramsey
Caldonia And More... | Bear Family Records | BCD 16151 AH
Bill Ramsey & His Trio
Caldonia And More... | Bear Family Records | BCD 16151 AH
Bill Ramsey & Juraj Galan
Caldonia And More... | Bear Family Records | BCD 16151 AH
Bill Ramsey With Eric Krans Dixieland Pipers And Guests
Caldonia And More... | Bear Family Records | BCD 16151 AH
Bill Ramsey With Orchestra
Gettin' Back To Swing | Bear Family Records | BCD 15813 AH
Bill Ramsey With The Paul Kuhn Trio
Caldonia And More... | Bear Family Records | BCD 16151 AH

Ramsey,Jeffry | (voc)
Al Jarreau With Band
Tenderness | i.e. Music | 557853-2

Ramsey,Samuel | (fr-h)
Charlie Byrd Orchestra
Latin Byrd | Milestone | MCD 47005-2

Ramthor,Horst | (harp)
Passport
Garden Of Eden | Atlantic | 2292-44147-2

Ramzy,Hossam | (perc)
Barbara Thompson's Paraphernalia
Breathless | VeraBra Records | CDVBR 2057-2

Rand,Sam | (v)
Billie Holiday With The Ray Ellis Orchestra
Lady In Satin | CBS | CK 65144
Charlie Parker Quartet With Strings
The Cole Porter Songbook | Verve | 823250-2
Charlie Parker With Strings
Charlie Parker:The Best Of The Verve Years | Verve | 527815-2
Bird: The Complete Charlie Parker On Verve | Verve | 837141-2
Charlie Parker:April In Paris | Dreyfus Jazz Line | FDM 36737-2
Charlie Parker With The Joe Lipman Orchestra
Verve Jazz Masters 28:Charlie Parker Plays Standards | Verve | 521854-2
Charlie Parker With Strings:The Master Takes | Verve | 523984-2
Charlie Parker Big Band | Verve | 559835-2
Wes Montgomery With The Jimmy Jones Orchestra
Wes Montgomery-The Complete Riverside Recordings | Riverside | 12 RCD 4408-2

Randall,Charles | (dr)
Sarah Vaughan And Her Band
Duke Ellington Song Book Two | Pablo | CD 2312116

Randall,George | (dr)
Richard 'Groove' Holmes Trio
On Basie's Bandstand | Prestige | PRCD 11028-2

Randall,William | (as,clts)
Earl Hines And His Orchestra
Planet Jazz:Earl Hines | Planet Jazz | 2159973-2

Randalu,Kritjan | (p)
Kelm 3
Per Anno | dml-records | CD 013

Randell,Charles | (dr)
Sarah Vaughan And Her Band
Sarah Vaughan Birthday Celebration | Fantasy | FANCD 6090-2

Randle,Sean | (dr)
Jazz Africa All Nations Big Band
Jadu(Jazz Africa Down Under) | Enja | ENJ-9339 2

Randle,Vicki | (voc)
Herbie Hancock Group
Magic Window | CBS | 486572-2

Rando,Arthur | (asreeds)
Bob Crosby And His Orchestra
Swing Legens:Bob Crosby | Nimbus Records | NI 2011

Randolph,Irving 'Mouse' | (tp)
Ella Fitzgerald And Her Famous Orchestra
The Radio Years 1940 | Jazz Unlimited | JUCD 2065
Fletcher Henderson And His Orchestra
Jazz:The Essential Collection Vol.1 | IN+OUT Records | 78011-2
Jazz:The Essential Collection Vol.3 | IN+OUT Records | 78013-2
Teddy Wilson And His Orchestra
Jazz:The Essential Collection Vol.3 | IN+OUT Records | 78013-2

Randolph,Zilmer | (tp,arrvoc)
Louis Armstrong And His Orchestra
Planet Jazz:Louis Armstrong | Planet Jazz | 2152052-2
Best Of The Complete RCA Victor Recordings | RCA | 2663636-2
Louis Armstrong:A 100th Birthday Celebration | RCA | 2663694-2
Jazz:The Essential Collection Vol.2 | IN+OUT Records | 78012-2
Satch Plays Fats(Complete) | CBS | CK 64927

Raney,Doug | (g)
Chet Baker Quartet
Chet Baker-The Legacy Vol.2:I Remember You | Enja | ENJ-9077 2
Chet Baker Trio
The Touch Of Your Lips | Steeplechase | SCCD 31122
This Is Always | Steeplechase | SCCD 31168
Daybreak | Steeplechase | SCS 1142(Audiophile Pressing)
Jam Session
Jam Session Vol.10 | Steeplechase | SCCD 31555
The European Jazz Guitar Orchestra
The European Jazz Guitar Orchestra | Jardis Records | JRCD 9307

Raney,Jimmy | (gvoc)
Al Haig Sextet
Al Haig Trio And Sextets | Original Jazz Classics | OJCCD 1929-2(SPL 1118)
Al Haig Sextet(Quintet)
Al Haig Trio And Sextets | Original Jazz Classics | OJCCD 1929-2(SPL 1118)
Billie Holiday And Her All Stars
Billie's Blues | Blue Note | 748786-2
Cal Tjader With The Lalo Schifrin Orchestra
Talkin Verve/Roots Of Acid Jazz:Cal Tjader | Verve | 531562-2
Dave Pike Sextet
Carnavals | Prestige | PCD 24248-2
Jimmy Raney Quartet
Jimmy Raney Visits Paris Vol.1 | Vogue | 21409352
Jimmy Raney Visits Paris Vol.2 | Vogue | 21434802
Jimmy Raney Quintet
Jimmy Raney Visits Paris Vol.2 | Vogue | 21434802
Lalo Schifrin And His Orchestra
Verve Jazz Masters 39:Cal Tjader | Verve | 521858-2
Lalo Schifrin Sextet
Tin Tin Deo | Fresh Sound Records | FSR-CD 319
Stan Getz Quintet
Stan Getz Highlights:The Best Of The Verve Years Vol.2 | Verve | 517330-2
Verve Jazz Masters 8:Stan Getz | Verve | 519823-2
A Life In Jazz:A Musical Biography | Verve | 535119-2
Ultimate Stan Getz selected by Joe Henderson | Verve | 557532-2
Stan Getz Plays | Verve | 833535-2
Stan Getz Highlights | Verve | 847430-2
Stan Getz-The Complete Roost Sessions | EMI Records | 859622-2

Raney,Sue | (voc)
Vic Lewis West Coast All Stars
Vic Lewis Presenting A Celebration Of Contemporary West Coast Jazz | Candid | CCD 79711/12

Raney,Thom | (b)
Dizzy Gillespie And His Orchestra
Closer To The Source | Atlantic | 7567-80776-2

Range,Robert | (tb)
Erskine Hawkins And His Orchestra
Planet Jazz:Big Bands | Planet Jazz | 2169649-2

Rangell,Bobby | (fl)
Jean-Louis Matinier Quartet
Confluences | Enja | ENJ-9454 2

Rangell,Nelson | (as,fl,piccolo,whistling,piccolo-fl)
GRP All-Star Big Band
GRP All-Star Big Band:Live! | GRP | GRP 97402
All Blues | GRP | GRP 98002

Ranger-Snell,Laura | (voc)
Mike Westbrook Brass Band
Glad Day:Settings Of William Blake | Enja | ENJ-9376 2

Ranglin,Ernest | (g)
Monty Alexander Quartet
Three Originals:Love And Sunshine/Estade/Cobilimbo | MPS | 523526-2
Monty Alexander Sextet
Three Originals:Love And Sunshine/Estade/Cobilimbo | MPS | 523526-2

Ranier,Tom | (as,el-p,ts,p,synth,cl,b-cl,ss)
Diane Schuur With Orchestra
Love Songs | GRP | GRP 97032
The Best Of Diane Schuur | GRP | GRP 98882
Herb Geller Quartet
Herb Geller Plays The Al Cohn Songbook | Hep | CD 2066

Rank,Bill | (tb)
Artie Shaw And His Orchestra
Planet JazzArtie Shaw | Planet Jazz | 2152057-2
Planet Jazz:Jazz Greatest Hits | Planet Jazz | 2169648-2
Bix Beiderbecke And His Gang
Jazz:The Essential Collection Vol.2 | IN+OUT Records | 78012-2
Frankie Trumbauer And His Orchestra
Jazz:The Essential Collection Vol.2 | IN+OUT Records | 78012-2
Paul Whiteman And His Orchestra
Planet Jazz:Jack Teagarden | Planet Jazz | 2161236-2
Planet Jazz:Jazz Trumpet | Planet Jazz | 2169654-2
Jazz:The Essential Collection Vol.3 | IN+OUT Records | 78013-2

Rankin,R.S. | (g)
T-Bone Walker And His Band
Atlantic Jazz: Kansas City | Atlantic | 7567-81701-2

Ranku,Lucky | (el-gg)
Gail Thompson Orchestra
Gail Thompson's Jazz Africa | Enja | ENJ-9053 2

Rao,Ganam | (voc)
Shankar Group
Nobody Told Me | ECM | 1397

Rap Artist No Name |
Gary Thomas Group
Found On Sordid Street | Winter&Winter | 910002-2

Rapetti,Gene | (tp)
Tito Puente Orchestra
Planet Jazz:Tito Puente | Planet Jazz | 2165369-2

Raph,Alan | (b-tb,bar-horn,euphoniumtb)
George Benson And His Orchestra
Giblet Gravy | Verve | 543754-2

Raphael,Phil | (p)
Red Rodney Quintet
The Red Rodney Quintets | Fantasy | FCD 24758-2

Rapp,Winfried | (b-tb)
Eberhard Weber Orchestra
Orchestra | ECM | 1374

Rasch,L. | (fr-h)
Vince Mendoza With The WDR Big Band And Guests
Sketches | ACT | 9215-2

Rasey,Uan | (tp)
Anita O'Day With The Billy May Orchestra
Verve Jazz Masters 49:Anita O'Day | Verve | 527653-2
Benny Carter And His Orchestra
Aspects | Capitol | 852677-2
Billy Eckstine With The Billy May Orchestra
Once More With Feeling | Roulette | 581862-2
Billy May And His Orchestra
Billy May's Big Fat Brass/Bill's Bag | Capitol | 535206-2
June Christy With The Pete Rugolo Orchestra
Something Cool(The Complete Mono & Stereo Versions) | Capitol | 534069-2
Pete Rugolo And His Orchestra
Thriller/Richard Diamon(Original Jazz Scores From 2 Classics TV Series) | Fresh Sound Records | FSCD 2015
Van Alexander Orchestra
Home Of Happy Feet/Swing! Staged For Sound! | Capitol | 535211-2

Rasheed[Howard Bowe],Haleem | (tb)
Buddy Johnson And His Orchestra
Buddy And Ella Johnson 1953-1964 | Bear Family Records | BCD 15479 DH

Raskin,Milt | (p)
Anita O'Day With Gene Krupa And His Orchestra
Let Me Off Uptown:Anita O'Day With Gene Krupa | CBS | CK 65625
Billie Holiday With The JATP All Stars
The Complete Jazz At The Philharmonic On Verve 1944-1949 | Verve | 523893-2
Billy Eckstine With The Billy May Orchestra
Once More With Feeling | Roulette | 581862-2
JATP All Stars
The Complete Jazz At The Philharmonic On Verve 1944-1949 | Verve | 523893-2
Tommy Dorsey And His Orchestra
Planet Jazz:Frank Sinatra & Tommy Dorsey | Planet Jazz | 2152067-2
Planet Jazz:Tommy Dorsey | Planet Jazz | 2159972-2

Raskin,Milt prob. | (p)
Billie Holiday With The JATP All Stars
Billie Holiday Story Vol.1:Jazz At The Philharmonic | Verve | 521642-2
The Complete Jazz At The Philharmonic On Verve 1944-1949 | Verve | 523893-2
Verve Jazz Masters 47:Billie Holiday Sings Standards | Verve | 527650-2

Rasmussen,Allan | (dr)
Bohana Jazzband
The Golden Years Of Revival Jazz,Vol.6 | Storyville | STCD 5511
The Golden Years Of Revival Jazz,Vol.10 | Storyville | STCD 5515

Rasmussen,Hugo | (b)
Pierre Dorge's New Jungle Orchestra
Giraf | dacapo | DCCD 9440

Rasmussen.Kai 'Satch' | (tp)
Papa Benny's Jazzband
The Golden Years Of Revival Jazz,Sampler | Storyville | 109 1001
The Golden Years Of Revival Jazz,Vol.7 | Storyville | STCD 5512
The Golden Years Of Revival Jazz,Vol.11 | Storyville | STCD 5516

Raspall,Elisabet | (p)
Elisabet Raspall Grup
Lila | Fresh Sound Records | FSNT 058 CD
Elisabet Raspall Quintet
Triangles | Fresh Sound Records | FSNT 018 CD

Rassinfosse,Jean-Louis | (b)
Chet Baker Trio
Strollin' | Enja | ENJ-5005 2
Chet Baker In Bologna | Dreyfus Jazz Line | FDM 36558-9
Fabien Degryse Quintet
Medor Sadness | Edition Collage | EC 454-2
Klaus Ignatzek Group
Day For Night | Nabel Records:Jazz Network | CD 4639
Klaus Ignatzek Quintet
Today Is Tomorrow/Live In Leverkusen | Nabel Records:Jazz Network | CD 4654
Son Of Gaudi | Nabel Records:Jazz Network | CD 4660
Klaus Ignatzek Trio
Airballoon | Nabel Records:Jazz Network | CD 4651
Klaus Ignatzek-Claudio Roditi Quintet
Live at Bird's Eye | Village | VILCD 1023-2

Ratai,Jörg | (g)
Jazz Fresh
Jazz Fresh | GGG-Verlag:GGG Verlag und Mailorder | CD 01.03

Ratajczak,Dave | (dr,percdr-machine-program)
Allan Vaché Swingtet
Ellington For Lovers | Nagel-Heyer | NH 1009
James Chirillo Quartet with Vera Mara
Sultry Serenade | Nagel-Heyer | CD 061
James Chirillo Sextet
Sultry Serenade | Nagel-Heyer | CD 061
Mark Shane's X-Mas Allstars
What Would Santa Say? | Nagel-Heyer | CD 055
Christmas Jazz! | Nagel-Heyer | NH 1008
The New York Allstars
Broadway | Nagel-Heyer | CD 003
One Two Three | Nagel-Heyer | CD 008
Randy Sandke Meets Bix Beiderbecke | Nagel-Heyer | CD 3002
The First Sampler | Nagel-Heyer | NHR SP 5

Rathbun,Andrew | (reeds,ssts)
Andrew Rathbun Group
Jade | Fresh Sound Records | FSNT 076 CD
True Stories | Fresh Sound Records | FSNT 099 CD
Steve LaSpina Quintet
Remember When | Steeplechase | SCCD 31540
Taylor Hawkins Group
Wake Up Call | Fresh Sound Records | FSCD 145 CD

Räther,Sebastian | (bel-b)
Stephan Meinberg VITAMINE
Horizontal | Jazz Haus Musik | JHM 0106 CD
Tomatic 7
Haupstrom | Jazz Haus Musik | JHM 0101 CD

Ratzer,Karl | (el-g,g,percvoc)
Dan Wall Quartet
Off The Wall | Enja | ENJ-9310 2
Dan Wall Trio
Off The Wall | Enja | ENJ-9310 2
Karl Ratzer Quintet
All The Way | Enja | ENJ-9448 2

Rauch,Russell | (tb)
Louis Armstrong With The Casa Loma Orchestra
Louis Armstrong:Swing That Music | Laserlight | 36056

Raulf,Dirk | (b-cl,sax,bs,cl,ss,ts,comp,reedsvoc)
Dirk Raulf Group
Die Welt Ist Immer Wieder Schön | Poise | Poise 03
Theater I (Bühnenmusik) | Poise | Poise 07
Theater II(Bühnenmusik) | Poise | Poise 10
Dirk Raulf-Frank Shulte
Theater III(Bühnenmusik) | Poise | Poise 11
Kodexx Sentimental
Das Digitale Herz | Poise | Poise 02
Kölner Saxophon Mafia
Saxfiguren | Jazz Haus Musik | JHM 0036 CD
Mafia Years 1982-86 | Jazz Haus Musik | JHM 0058 CD
Go Commercial... | Jazz Haus Musik | JHM 0065 CD
Kölner Saxophon Mafia With Arno Steffen
Kölner Saxophon Mafia Proudly Presents | Jazz Haus Musik | JHM 0046 CD
Kölner Saxophon Mafia With Bad Little Dynamos
Kölner Saxophon Mafia Proudly Presents | Jazz Haus Musik | JHM 0046 CD
Kölner Saxophon Mafia With Blasorchester Dicke Luft
Kölner Saxophon Mafia Proudly Presents | Jazz Haus Musik | JHM 0046 CD
Kölner Saxophon Mafia With Clarence Barlow
Kölner Saxophon Mafia Proudly Presents | Jazz Haus Musik | JHM 0046 CD

Kölner Saxophon Mafia With Dieter Wellershoff
Kölner Saxophon Mafia Proudly Presents | Jazz Haus Musik | JHM 0046 CD
Kölner Saxophon Mafia With Fleisch
Kölner Saxophon Mafia Proudly Presents | Jazz Haus Musik | JHM 0046 CD
Kölner Saxophon Mafia With Hans Süper
Kölner Saxophon Mafia Proudly Presents | Jazz Haus Musik | JHM 0046 CD
Kölner Saxophon Mafia With Ina Stachelhaus And Erik Schneider
Kölner Saxophon Mafia Proudly Presents | Jazz Haus Musik | JHM 0046 CD
Kölner Saxophon Mafia With Ingo Kümmel And Frank Köllges
Kölner Saxophon Mafia Proudly Presents | Jazz Haus Musik | JHM 0046 CD
Kölner Saxophon Mafia With Irene Lorenz
Kölner Saxophon Mafia Proudly Presents | Jazz Haus Musik | JHM 0046 CD
Kölner Saxophon Mafia With Jacki Liebezeit
Kölner Saxophon Mafia Proudly Presents | Jazz Haus Musik | JHM 0046 CD
Kölner Saxophon Mafia With Klaus Der Geiger
Kölner Saxophon Mafia Proudly Presents | Jazz Haus Musik | JHM 0046 CD
Kölner Saxophon Mafia With Kristina Würminghausen
Kölner Saxophon Mafia Proudly Presents | Jazz Haus Musik | JHM 0046 CD
Kölner Saxophon Mafia With Lydie Auvray
Kölner Saxophon Mafia Proudly Presents | Jazz Haus Musik | JHM 0046 CD
Kölner Saxophon Mafia With Nedim Hazar And Orhan Temur
Kölner Saxophon Mafia Proudly Presents | Jazz Haus Musik | JHM 0046 CD
Kölner Saxophon Mafia With Ramesh Shotham
Kölner Saxophon Mafia Proudly Presents | Jazz Haus Musik | JHM 0046 CD
Kölner Saxophon Mafia With Rick E. Loef
Kölner Saxophon Mafia Proudly Presents | Jazz Haus Musik | JHM 0046 CD
Kölner Saxophon Mafia With The Auryn Quartet
Kölner Saxophon Mafia Proudly Presents | Jazz Haus Musik | JHM 0046 CD
Kölner Saxophon Mafia With Triviatas(1.Schwuler Männerchor Köln)
Kölner Saxophon Mafia Proudly Presents | Jazz Haus Musik | JHM 0046 CD
Kölner Saxophon Mafia With V.Nick Nikitakis
Kölner Saxophon Mafia Proudly Presents | Jazz Haus Musik | JHM 0046 CD
Kölner Saxophon Mafia With Willie Gräff
Kölner Saxophon Mafia Proudly Presents | Jazz Haus Musik | JHM 0046 CD
Tome XX
The Red Snapper | Jazz Haus Musik | JHM 0047 CD
Third Degree | Jazz Haus Musik | JHM 0063 CD
Ulla Oster Group
Beyond Janis | Jazz Haus Musik | JHM 0052 CD

Raulin,Francois | (p,keyboards,synth,percmelodica)
Louis Sclavis Quintet
Rouge | ECM | 1458
Louis Sclavis Sextet
Les Violences De Rameau | ECM | 1588(533128-2)

Rautenbach,Gernot | (synth)
Jazz Orchester Rheinland-Pfalz
Last Season | Jazz Haus Musik | LJBB 9706

Rautenberg,Kai | (grand-pp)
Harry Allen And Randy Sandke Meets The RIAS Big Band Berlin
The Music Of The Trumpet Kings | Nagel-Heyer | CD 037

Rava,Enrico | (fl-h,tpvoice)
Enrico Rava Quartet
The Pilgrim And The Stars | ECM | 1063(847322-2)
The Plot | ECM | 1078
Enrico Rava Quartet | ECM | 1122
Enrico Rava Quintet
Easy Living | ECM | 1760(9812050)
Enrico Rava With The Michael Flügel Quartet
Live At Birdland Neuburg | double moon | CHRDM 71011
Enrico Rava-Dino Saluzzi Quintet
Volver | ECM | 1343
Enrico Rava-Ran Blake
Duo En Noir | Between The Lines | btl 004(Efa 10174-2)
European Jazz Ensemble
European Jazz Ensemble At The Philharmonic Cologne | M.A Music | A 800-2
20th Anniversary Tour | Konnex Records | KCD 5078
European Trumpet Summit
European Trumpet Summit | Konnex Records | KCD 5064

Ravens:,The |
The Ravens
Ultimate Ben Webster selected by James Carter | Verve | 557537-2

Ravnam,Kari | (cello)
Terje Rypdal With The Borealis Ensemble
Q.E.D. | ECM | 1474

Rawcliffe,Susan | (didjerdu)
Alex Cline Group
The Lamp And The Star | ECM | 1372

Rawls,Lou | (voc)
Lou Rawls With Les McCann Ltd.
Blue Velvet: Crooners, Swooners And Velvet Vocals | Blue Note | 521153-2
Stormy Monday | Blue Note | 791441-2

Ray Charles Singers |
Ella Fitzgerald With Bill Doggett's Orchestra
Ella Fitzgerald:Mr.Paganini | Dreyfus Jazz Line | FDM 36741-2

Ray,Aurell | (el-12-string-gg)
Charles Earland Septet
Charles Earland In Concert | Prestige | PRCD 24267-2
Charles Earland Sextet
Charles Earland In Concert | Prestige | PRCD 24267-2
Sonny Rollins Quintet
Don't Stop The Carnival | Milestone | MCD 55005-2
Sonny Rollins Sextet
Don't Stop The Carnival | Milestone | MCD 55005-2

Ray,Brian | (g)
Klaus Doldinger Jubilee
Doldinger's Best | ACT | 9224-2
Klaus Doldinger With Orchestra And Etta James
Lifelike | Warner | 2292-46478-2

Ray,Carline | (b,vocg)
Red Richards Quartet
Swingtime | Jazzpoint | JP 1041 CD

Ray,Shibsankar | (tabla)
Subroto Roy Chowdhury Group
Explorations | Jazzpoint | JP 1020 CD
Subroto Roy Chowdhury-Steve Lacy Group
Explorations | Jazzpoint | JP 1020 CD

Raylettes,The | (voc)
Ray Charles And His Orchestra
Ray Charles At Newport | Atlantic | 7567-80765-2

Rayman,Morris | (b)
Artie Shaw And His Orchestra
Planet Jazz:Jazz Trumpet | Planet Jazz | 2169654-2

Raymond,Irving | (v)
Tommy Dorsey And His Orchestra
Planet Jazz:Frank Sinatra & Tommy Dorsey | Planet Jazz | 2152067-2

Raymond,Joe | (v)
Roger Wolfe Kahn And His Orchestra
Planet Jazz:Jack Teagarden | Planet Jazz | 2161236-2

Raynor,Michael 'Mike' | (drperc)
Kurt Elling Group
This Time Its Love | Blue Note | 493543-2
Blue Velvet: Crooners, Swooners And Velvet Vocals | Blue Note | 521153-2
Kurt Elling Group With Guests
Live In Chicago | Blue Note | 522211-2

Raynsford,Helen | (voc)
Mike Westbrook Brass Band
Glad Day:Settings Of William Blake | Enja | ENJ-9376 2

Razze,Ralph | (dr)
Buddy Childers Big Band
It's What Happening Now! | Candid | CCD 79749

Re,Andrea | (voc)
Chico Freeman And Brainstorm
Threshold | IN+OUT Records | 7022-2

Read,Alan | (el-b)
Woody Herman And His Orchestra
Brand New | Original Jazz Classics | OJCCD 1044-2(F 8414)

Read,Hugo | (as,fl,ssts)
Axis
Axis | Jazz 4 Ever Records:Jazz Network | J4E 4735
dAs prOjekT
dAs prOjekT | Foolish Music | FM 211288
Hugo Read Group
Songs Of A Wayfarer | Nabel Records:Jazz Network | CD 4653
Lumpp-Read-Küttner Trio
Midnight Sun | Nabel Records:Jazz Network | CD 4612
Peter Herborn's Acute Insights
Peter Herborn's Acute Insights | JMT Edition | 919017-2
Peter Weiss Orchestra
Personal Choice | Nabel Records:Jazz Network | CD 4669
Peter Weiss Quartet
Personal Choice | Nabel Records:Jazz Network | CD 4669
Peter Weiss Sextet
Personal Choice | Nabel Records:Jazz Network | CD 4669
Wolf Mayer Dialects
Roots And Wings | Triptychon | 300201

Real Group,The: |
The Real Group
One For All | ACT | 9003-2
The Real Group With Toots Thielemans
One For All | ACT | 9003-2

Reaney,Terry | (tp)
André Holst With Chris Dean's European Swing Orchestra
That's Swing | Nagel-Heyer | CD 079

Reasinger,Clyde | (tp)
Joe Williams With The Frank Hunter Orchestra
Planet Jazz:Joe Williams | Planet Jazz | 2165370-2
Quincy Jones And His Orchestra
The Quintessence | Impulse(MCA) | 951222-2

Reber,Raphael | (viola)
Abdullah Ibrahim Trio And A String Orchestra
African Suite | TipToe | TIP-888832 2
String Orchestra
African Suite | TipToe | TIP-888832 2

Rebillard,Jean-Pierre | (b)
Frank Wess Meets The Paris-Barcelona Swing Connection
Paris-Barcelona Connection | Fresh Sound Records | FSNT 002 CD

Rebillot,Pat | (el-p,org,keyboards,arr,pgrand-p)
Frank Foster Quintet
Soul Outing! | Original Jazz Classics | OJCCD 984-2(7479)
Frank Foster Sextet
Soul Outing! | Original Jazz Classics | OJCCD 984-2(7479)
Paul Desmond Quartet With The Don Sebesby Orchestra
From The Hot Afternoon | Verve | 543487-2

Rebirth Brass Band |
Maceo Parker With The Rebirth Brass Band
Southern Exposure | Minor Music | 801033
Maceo(Soundtrack) | Minor Music | 801046

Rebmann,Rolf | (dr)
International Chicago-Jazz Orchestra
That's A Plenty | JHM Records | JHM 3621

Rechardt,Pekka | (g)
Piirpauke
The Wild East | JA & RO | JARO 4128-2
Piirpauke-Global Servisi | JA & RO | JARO 4150-2

Reck | (b,vocel-g)
Toshinori Kondo & Ima plus Guests
Human Market | JA & RO | JARO 4146-2

Rector,Milton | (bb-g)
Otis Spann Band
The Blues Never Die! | Original Blues Classics | OBCCD 530-2(P 7391)
Windy City Blues | Stax | SCD 8612-2

Red | (Kyner)
Clifford Jordan Quintet
Mosaic | Milestone | MCD 47092-2
Donald Byrd Quintet
Slow Drag | Blue Note | 535560-2
Donald Byrd Sextet
Blue Breaks Beats Vol.2 | Blue Note | 789907-2
Blue Break Beats | Blue Note | 799106-2
Blackjack | Blue Note | 821286-2
Sonny Red (Kyner) Quartet
Red,Blue & Green | Milestone | MCD 47086-2
Sonny Red (Kyner) Quintet
Red,Blue & Green | Milestone | MCD 47086-2
Yusef Lateef Orchestra
The Blue Yusef Lateef | Rhino | 8122-73717-2

Red Sun |
Red Sun/SamulNori
Then Comes The White Tiger | ECM | 1499

Redd,Alton | (drvoc)
Henry Red Allen Band
The Very Best Of Dixieland Jazz | Verve | 535529-2

Redd,Chuck | (drvib)
Mundell Lowe Quintet
Mundell's Moods | Nagel-Heyer | CD 065

Redd,Freddie | (pcomp)
Freddie Redd Sextet
Redd's Blues | Blue Note | 540537-2

Redfield,Bob | (el-g)
Cal Tjader Sextet
Cuban Fantasy | Fantasy | FCD 24777-2

Rediske,Johannes | (el-gg)
Johannes Rediske Quintet
Deutsches Jazz Fesival 1954/1955 | Bear Family Records | BCD 15430
Re-Disc Bounce | Bear Family Records | BCD 16119 AH
Jumpin' At The Badewanne | Bear Family Records | BCD 16172 AH
Johannes Rediske Sextet
Re-Disc Bounce | Bear Family Records | BCD 16119 AH
Johnnes Rediske Quintet
Deutsches Jazz Fesival 1954/1955 | Bear Family Records | BCD 15430
Rolf Kühn All Stars
Deutsches Jazz Fesival 1954/1955 | Bear Family Records | BCD 15430

Redman,Dewey | (as,ts,cl,perc,bells,chinese-musette)
Charlie Haden Orchestra
The Ballad Of The Fallen | ECM | 1248(811546-2)
Charlie Haden's Liberation Music Orchestra
Liberation Music Orchestra | Impulse(MCA) | 951188-2
Dewey Redman Quartet
The Struggle Continues | ECM | 1225
Dewey Redman-Cecil Taylor-Elvin Jones
Momentum Space | Verve | 559944-2
Ed Schuller Group feat. Dewey Redman
The Force | Tutu Records | 888166-2*
Ed Schuller Quartet feat. Dewey Redman
Mu-Point | Tutu Records | 888154-2*
Keith Jarrett Group
Expectations | CBS | C2K 65900
Keith Jarrett Group With Brass
Expectations | CBS | C2K 65900
Keith Jarrett Quartet
The Survivor's Suite | ECM | 1085(827131-2)
Eyes Of The Heart | ECM | 1150(825476-2)
El Juicio(The Judgement) | Atlantic | 7567-80783-2
Byablue | Impulse(MCA) | MCD 10648
Keith Jarrett Quintet
Fort Yawuh | Impulse(MCA) | 547966-2
The Roots Of Acid Jazz | Impulse(MCA) | IMP 12042
Keith Jarrett Trio
Byablue | Impulse(MCA) | MCD 10648
Old And New Dreams
Old And New Dreams | ECM | 1154
Playing | ECM | 1205
Pat Metheny Quartet
80/81 | ECM | 1180/81 (843169-2)
Pat Metheny Quintet
80/81 | ECM | 1180/81 (843169-2)
Paul Motian Quartet
Monk In Motian | JMT Edition | 919020-2

Redman,Don | (arr,ld,as,voc,dr,cl,bs,ts,ssspeech)
Bessie Smith And Her Band
Jazz:The Essential Collection Vol.1 | IN+OUT Records | 78011-2
Fletcher Henderson And His Orchestra
Jazz:The Essential Collection Vol.1 | IN+OUT Records | 78011-2
Louis Armstrong And His Savoy Ballroom Five
Jazz:The Essential Collection Vol.2 | IN+OUT Records | 78012-2
Louis Armstrong:Fireworks | Dreyfus Jazz Line | FDM 36710-2
McKinney's Cotton Pickers
Jazz:The Essential Collection Vol.3 | IN+OUT Records | 78013-2

Redman,Joshua | (ss,asts)
Christian McBride Group
Gettin' To It | Verve | 523989-2
Elvin Jones Quintet
Youngblood | Enja | ENJ-7051 2
Elvin Jones Trio
Youngblood | Enja | ENJ-7051 2
Joe Lovano Sextet
Tenor Legacy | Blue Note | 827014-2
Johnny King Quintet
Notes From The Underground | Enja | ENJ-9067 2
Joshua Redman Quartet
Joshua Redman | Warner | 9362-45242-2
Wish | Warner | 9362-45365-2
MoodSwing | Warner | 9362-45643-2
Spirit Of The Moment:Live At The Village Vanguard | Warner | 9362-45923-2
Timeless Tales | Warner | 9362-47052-2
Beyond | Warner | 9362-47465-2
Passage Of Time | Warner | 9362-47997-2
Joshua Redman Quartet feat. Mark Turner
Beyond | Warner | 9362-47465-2
Joshua Redman Quintet
Freedom In The Goove | Warner | 9362-46330-2
Joshua Redman Trio
Joshua Redman | Warner | 9362-45242-2
Marcus Miller Group
Tales | Dreyfus Jazz Line | FDM 36571-2
McCoy Tyner Quintet
Prelude And Sonata | Milestone | MCD 9244-2
Nicholas Payton Quintet
Payton's Place | Verve | 557327-2
Yaya 3
Yaya 3 | Loma | 936248277-2

Redmond,Jack | (tb)
Buddy Childers Big Band
It's What Happening Now! | Candid | CCD 79749

Reece,Dizzy | (tpcongas)
Anfrew Hill Nonet
Passing Ships | Blue Note | 593871-2
Hank Mobley Sextet
The Flip | Blue Note | 593872-2

Reed,Don | (tb)
Stan Kenton Orchestra
Stompin' At Newport | Pablo | PACD 5312-2

Reed,Eric | (pvoc)
A Band Of Friends
Wynton Marsalis Quartet With Strings | CBS | CK 68921
Billy Cobham Group
Art Of Five | IN+OUT Records | 77063-2
Donald Harrison Sextet
Kind Of New | Candid | CCD 79768
Eric Reed Orchestra
Happiness | Nagel-Heyer | CD 2010
Eric Reed Quartet
Musicale | Impulse(MCA) | 951196-2
Eric Reed Quintet
Musicale | Impulse(MCA) | 951196-2
Eric Reed Trio
Musicale | Impulse(MCA) | 951196-2
Pure Imagination | Impulse(MCA) | 951259-2
The Nagel-Heyer Allstars
Uptown Lowdown:A Jazz Salute To The Big Apple | Nagel-Heyer | CD 2004
Wycliffe Gordon Group
Slidin' Home | Nagel-Heyer | CD 2001
The Search | Nagel-Heyer | CD 2007
Ellington For Lovers | Nagel-Heyer | NH 1009
Blues Of Summer | Nagel-Heyer | NH 1011
Wycliffe Gordon-Eric Reid
We | Nagel-Heyer | CD 2023
Wynton Marsalis Group
Standard Time Vol.4:Marsalis Plays Monk | CBS | CK 67503
Standard Time Vol.6:Mr.Jelly Lord | CBS | CK 69872

Reed,G.T. | (ts)
Buddy Guy Blues Band
Buddy Guy-The Complete Chess Studio Recordings | MCA | MCD 09337

Reed,Lou | (gvoc)
Rob Wasserman Duet
Duets | GRP | GRP 97122

Reed,Lucy | (voc)
Lucy Reed With Orchestra
This Is Lucy Reed | Original Jazz Classics | OJCCD 1943-2(F 3243)
Lucy Reed With The Eddie Higgins Quartet
This Is Lucy Reed | Original Jazz Classics | OJCCD 1943-2(F 3243)
Lucy Reed With The Eddie Higgins Trio
This Is Lucy Reed | Original Jazz Classics | OJCCD 1943-2(F 3243)

Reed,Ray | (as,fl,reeds,saxts)
Buddy Childers Big Band
It's What Happening Now! | Candid | CCD 79749

Reed,Waymon | (tpfl-h)
Big Joe Turner With The Count Basie Orchestra
Flip Flop And Fly | Original Jazz Classics | OJCCD 1053-2(2310937)
Count Basie And His Orchestra
Afrique | RCA | 2179618-2
Count Basie: Salle Pleyel, April 17th, 1972 | Laserlight | 36127
The Jazz Giants Play Harry Warren:Lullaby Of Broadway | Prestige | PCD 24204-2
Count Basie Big Band
Montreux '77 | Original Jazz Classics | OJCCD 377-2
Milt Jackson Orchestra
Sarah Vaughan Birthday Celebration | Fantasy | FANCD 6090-2
Milt Jackson With The Count Basie Orchestra
To Bags...With Love:Memorial Album | Pablo | 2310967-2
Milt Jackson Birthday Celebration | Fantasy | FANCD 6079-2

Milt Jackson + Count Basie + Big Band Vol.1 | Original Jazz Classics | OJCCD 740-2(2310822)
Milt Jackson + Count Basie + Big Band Vol.2 | Original Jazz Classics | OJCCD 741-2(2310823)
Sarah Vaughan And Her Band
Duke Ellington Song Book Two | Pablo | CD 2312116
Sarah Vaughan Birthday Celebration | Fantasy | FANCD 6090-2
Sarah Vaughan With Band
Linger Awhile | Pablo | 2312144-2
Sarah Vaughan With Small Group & Orchestra
Duke Ellington Song Book One | Pablo | CD 2312111

Reese,Della | (voc)
Della Reese With The Neal Hefti Orchestra
Della | RCA | 2663912-2
Della Reese With The Sy Oliver Orchestra
Misty Blue:Sweet Sisters Swing Songs Of Sorrow And Sadness | Blue Note | 521151-2

Reese,Olivia | (voc)
Hans Theessink Group
Crazy Moon | Minor Music | 801052

Reese,Rostelle | (tp)
Earl Hines And His Orchestra
Planet Jazz:Earl Hines | Planet Jazz | 2159973-2

Reeves,Dianne | (voc)
Dianne Reeves With Band
Misty Blue:Sweet Sisters Swing Songs Of Sorrow And Sadness | Blue Note | 521151-2
I Remember | Blue Note | 790264-2
Renee Rosnes Quartet
Art & Soul | Blue Note | 499997-2
Renee Rosnes Trio
Art & Soul | Blue Note | 499997-2

Reeves,Gerald | (tb)
Jelly Roll Morton's Red Hot Peppers
Planet Jazz:Jelly Roll Morton | Planet Jazz | 2152060-2
Jazz:The Essential Collection Vol.1 | IN+OUT Records | 78011-2

Reffert,Hans | (danelectro-g,melobar,harp,lapsteel)
Ax Genrich Group
Psychedelic Guitar | ATM Records | ATM 3809-AH

Reffgen,Alexander | (fl,cl,ssas)
Jazz Orchester Rheinland-Pfalz
Last Season | Jazz Haus Musik | LJBB 9706

Refosco,Mauro | (perc)
Michael Blake Group
Drift | Intuition Records | INT 3212-2

Regina,Elis | (voc)
Antonio Carlos Jobim Group
Verve Jazz Masters 13:Antonio Carlos Jobim | Verve | 516409-2
Antonio Carlos Jobim-Elis Regina Group
The Antonio Carlos Jobim Songbook | Verve | 525472-2

Regina,Francesco | (voice)
Michel Godard Ensemble
Castel Del Monte II | Enja | ENJ-9431 2

Rehak,Frank | (tb)
Dizzy Gillespie And His Orchestra
Verve Jazz Masters 10:Dizzy Gillespie | Verve | 516319-2
Gillespiana And Carnegie Hall Concert | Verve | 519809-2
Verve Jazz Masters 20:Introducing | Verve | 519853-2
Dizzy Gillespie:Birks Works-The Verve Big Band Sessions | Verve | 527900-2
Talking Verve:Dizzy Gillespie | Verve | 533846-2
Dizzy Gillespie Orchestra
Verve Jazz Masters 10:Dizzy Gillespie | Verve | 516319-2
Ernestine Anderson With Orchestra
My Kinda Swing | Mercury | 842409-2
George Russell And His Orchestra
George Russell New York N.Y. | Impulse(MCA) | 951278-2
Gerry Mulligan And His Orchestra
Mullenium | CBS | CK 65678
Gil Evans Orchestra
Verve Jazz Masters 23:Gil Evans | Verve | 521860-2
The Individualism Of Gil Evans | Verve | 833804-2
Lena Horne With The Lennie Hayton Orchestra
Planet Jazz:Lena Horne | Planet Jazz | 2165373-2
Miles Davis + 19
Miles Ahead | CBS | CK 65121
Miles Davis Sextet
Sorcerer | CBS | CK 65680
Miles Davis With Gil Evans & His Orchestra
Ballads | CBS | 461099-2
Miles Davis At Carnegie Hall | CBS | CK 65027
This Is Jazz:Miles Davis Plays Ballads | CBS | CK 65038
Porgy And Bess | CBS | CK 65141
Sketches Of Spain | CBS | CK 65142
Quiet Nights | CBS | CK 65293
Sonny Rollins Orchestra
Sonny Rollins And The Big Brass | Verve | 557545-2
Woody Herman And His Orchestra
The Legends Of Swing | Laserlight | 24659

Reher,Kurt | (cello)
Ella Fitzgerald With The Nelson Riddle Orchestra
The Best Of The Song Books:The Ballads | Verve | 521867-2
Oh Lady Be Good:The Best Of The Gershwin Songbook | Verve | 529581-2
Love Songs:The Best Of The Song Books | Verve | 531762-2
Mel Tormé With The Russell Garcia Orchestra
Swingin' On The Moon | Verve | 511385-2

Rehm,Werner | (tp)
Two Beat Stompers
Deutsches Jazz Fesival 1954/1955 | Bear Family Records | BCD 15430

Reichel,Louis | (sousaphon)

Reichenbach,Bill | (b-tb,b-tp,tb,dr,perc,arrv-tb)
Al Jarreau With Band
Jarreau | i.e. Music | 557847-2
Charlie Byrd Orchestra
Latin Byrd | Milestone | MCD 47005-2
Charlie Byrd Quartet
Latin Byrd | Milestone | MCD 47005-2
Charlie Byrd Quintet
Latin Byrd | Milestone | MCD 47005-2
Charlie Byrd Septet
Latin Byrd | Milestone | MCD 47005-2
Charlie Byrd Trio
Byrd At The Gate | Original Jazz Classics | OJC20 262-2
Charlie Byrd Trio And Guests
Byrd At The Gate | Original Jazz Classics | OJC20 262-2
Charlie Byrd Trio With Voices
Byrd Song | Original Jazz Classics | OJCCD 1092-2(RS 9481)
Dave Weckl Group
Master Plan | GRP | GRP 96192
Diane Schuur With Orchestra
The Best Of Diane Schuur | GRP | GRP 98882
George Duke Group
Jazzrock-Anthology Vol.3:Fusion | Zounds | CD 27100555
Paulinho Da Costa Orchestra
Happy People | Original Jazz Classics | OJCCD 783-2(2312102)
Stan Getz Sextet
Verve Jazz Masters 8:Stan Getz | Verve | 519823-2
Stan Getz-Charlie Byrd Sextet
Jazz Samba | Verve | 521413-2
The Antonio Carlos Jobim Songbook | Verve | 525472-2
Verve Jazz Masters 53:Stan Getz-Bossa Nova | Verve | 529904-2
Ultimate Stan Getz selected by Joe Henderson | Verve | 557532-2
Stan Getz Highlights | Verve | 847430-2
The Quincy Jones-Sammy Nestico Orchestra
Basie & Beyond | Warner | 9362-47792-2

Reichert,Rolf | (tp)
Daniel Messina Band
Imagenes | art-mode-records | 990014

Reichstaller,Claus | (tpfl-h)
Al Porcino Big Band
Al Cohn Meets Al Porcino | Organic Music | ORGM 9730
Conexion Latina
Mambo 2000 | Enja | ENJ-7055 2
La Conexión | Enja | ENJ-9065 2
Mambo Nights | Enja | ENJ-9402 2
Klaus Doldinger's Passport
Running In Real Time | Warner | 2292-40633-2

Reid,Richard | (b,b-gel-b)
Eddie Cleanhead Vinson With Band
The Late Show-Recorded Live At Marla's Memory Lane Supper Club Vol.2 | Fantasy | FCD 9655-2
Eddie Cleanhead Vinson With The Red Holloway Quartet
Blues In The Night-Volume One:The Early Show | Fantasy | FCD 9647-2
Etta James & Eddie Cleanhead Vinson With The Red Holloway Quartet
Blues In The Night-Volume One:The Early Show | Fantasy | FCD 9647-2
Etta James With Band
The Late Show-Recorded Live At Marla's Memory Lane Supper Club Vol.2 | Fantasy | FCD 9655-2
Etta James With The Red Holloway Quartet
Blues In The Night-Volume One:The Early Show | Fantasy | FCD 9647-2
Etta James With The Red Holloway Quintet
Blues In The Night-Volume One:The Early Show | Fantasy | FCD 9647-2
Etta James/Eddie 'Cleanhead' Vinson With Band
The Late Show-Recorded Live At Marla's Memory Lane Supper Club Vol.2 | Fantasy | FCD 9655-2

Reid,Rufus | (bel-b)
Dexter Gordon Quartet
Dexter Gordon:Ballads | Blue Note | 796579-2
Dexter Gordon:Atlanta Georgia May 5,1981 | Storyville | STCD 8363
Eddie Harris Group
The Best Of Eddie Harris | Atlantic | 7567-81370-2
Freddie Hubbard Quartet
Topsy | Enja | ENJ-7025 2
Freddie Hubbard Quintet
Topsy | Enja | ENJ-7025 2
Gene Ammons-Dexter Gordon Quintet
Dexter Gordon Birthday Celebration | Fantasy | FANCD 6082-2
Hank Jones Trio With The Meridian String Quartet
The Story Of Jazz Piano | Laserlight | 24653
Helen Merrill With The Pepper Adams Quintet
Chasin' The Bird(Gershwin) | EmArCy | 558850-2
Jack DeJohnette's Special Edition
Inflation Blues | ECM | 1244
Album Album | ECM | 1280
Kenny Barron Group
Spirit Song | Verve | 543180-2
Red Rodney All Stars
A Tribute To Charlie Parker Vol.1 | Storyville | 4960483
Stan Getz Quartet
A Life In Jazz:A Musical Biography | Verve | 535119-2
Stan Getz Cafe Montmartre | EmArCy | 586755-2
Anniversary ! | EmArCy | 838769-2
Serenity | EmArCy | 838770-2
Toots Thielemans Quartet
Verve Jazz Masters Vol.59:Toots Thielemans | Verve | 535271-2

Reid,Steve | (dr,perc,keyboards,perc-programming)
Miles Davis Group
Tutu | Warner | 7599-25490-2
The Rippingtons
Tourist In Paradise | GRP | GRP 95882

Reid,Vernon | (el-g,bj,g-synth,synth,steel-g,g)
Marcus Miller Group
The Sun Don't Lie | Dreyfus Jazz Line | FDM 36560-2

Reider,Jimmy | (ts)
Gerry Mulligan Concert Jazz Band
Verve Jazz Masters 36:Gerry Mulligan | Verve | 523342-2
Verve Jazz Masters Vol.60:The Collection | Verve | 529866-2
Gerry Mulligan And The Concert Band At The Village Vanguard | Verve | 589488-2
The Complete Verve Gerry Mulligan Concert Band | Verve | 9860613

Reidy,Frank | (saxts)
Benny Goodman And His Orchestra
Verve Jazz Masters 33:Benny Goodman | Verve | 844410-2

Reiff,Elke | (voc)
Elke Reiff Quartett
There Is More | Laika Records | 35101112

Reijseger,Ernst | (cellovoice)
Amsterdam String Trio
Winter Theme | Winter&Winter | 910060-2
Boi Akih
Uwa I | Enja | ENJ-9472 2
Double Trio(Trio De Clarinettes&Arcado)
Green Dolphy Suite | Enja | ENJ-9011 2
Ernst Reijseger
Colla Parta | Winter&Winter | 910012-2
Ernst Reijseger & Tenore E Cuncordu De Orosei
Colla Voche | Winter&Winter | 910037-2

Reilich,Joe | (viola)
Phineas Newborn Jr. With Dennis Farnon And His Orchestra
While My Lady Sleeps | RCA | 2185157-2

Reilles,André 'Mac Kac' | (dr)
Guy Lafitte-Peanuts Holland And Their Orchestra
Jazz In Paris:Guy Lafitte-Blue And Sentimental | EmArCy | 159852-2 PMS

Reilles,Jean-Baptiste 'Mac Kac' | (dr)
Lionel Hampton All Stars
Jazz In Paris:Lionel Hampton And His French New Sound Vol.1 | EmArCy | 549405-2 PMS
Jazz In Paris:Lionel Hampton And His French New Sound Vol.2 | EmArCy | 549406-2 PMS
Sammy Price Quintet
Americans Swinging In Paris:Sammy Price | EMI Records | 539650-2
Sammy Price Trio
Americans Swinging In Paris:Sammy Price | EMI Records | 539650-2
Stephane Grappelli Quartet
Grapelli Story | Verve | 515807-2
Jazz In Paris:Stephane Grappelli-Improvisations | EmArCy | 549242-2 PMS

Reilly,Dean | (b)
Earl Hines Quartet
Another Monday Date | Prestige | PRCD 24043-2
Vince Guaraldi Trio
Vince Guaraldi Trio | Original Jazz Classics | OJC20 149-2(F 3225)

Reimann,Bruno | (viola)
Bernd Konrad Jazz Group With Symphonie Orchestra
Wen Die Götter Lieben | Creative Works Records | CW CD 1010-1

Reimer,Jan | (g,congas,yukapatu-b,el-g,cabasa)
Steve Tibbetts Group
Exploded View | ECM | 1335

Reimer,Thomas | (g)
Thomas Reimer Trio
Vienna's Heardt | Edition Collage | EC 506-2

Reina,Jesus | (dr)
Joan Abril Quartet
Insomnio | Fresh Sound Records | FSNT 034 CD
Joan Abril Quintet
Insomnio | Fresh Sound Records | FSNT 034 CD
Eric | Fresh Sound Records | FSNT 092 CD
Joan Abril Sextet
Eric | Fresh Sound Records | FSNT 092 CD

Reinders,Frits | (g)
Coleman Hawkins Trio
Jazz:The Essential Collection Vol.3 | IN+OUT Records | 78013-2

Reindl,Rudolf | (tpfl-h)
Bernd Konrad With Erwin Lehn und sein Südfunk Orchester Stuttgart
Wen Die Götter Lieben | Creative Works Records | CW CD 1010-1
Bill Ramsey With Orchestra
Gettin' Back To Swing | Bear Family Records | BCD 15813 AH
SWR Big Band
Jazz In Concert | Hänssler Classics | CD 93.004

Reinhard,Benno | (tb)
Ralph Schweizer Big Band
DAY Dream | Chaos | CACD 8177

Reinhard,Claudia | (voc)
Michael Riessler & Singer Pur with Vincent Courtois
Ahi Vita | ACT | 9417-2

Reinhardt,Bruno | (b)
Wedeli Köhler Group
Swing & Folk | Jazzpoint | JP 1067 CD

Reinhardt,Dave | (drperc)
Richard Elliot Sextet
City Speak | Blue Note | 832620-2

Reinhardt,Django | (bj,g,arr,vg-solo)
Benny Carter And His Orchestra
Django Reinhardt All Star Sessions | Capitol | 531577-2
Americans Swinging In Paris:Benny Carter | EMI Records | 539647-2
Bill Coleman Et Son Orchestre
Americans Swinging In Paris:Bill Coleman-The Elegance | EMI Records | 539662-2
Bill Coleman-Django Reinhardt Duo
Americans Swinging In Paris:Bill Coleman-The Elegance | EMI Records | 539662-2
Coleman Hawkins And His All Star Jam Band
Django Reinhardt All Star Sessions | Capitol | 531577-2
Americans Swinging In Paris:Benny Carter | EMI Records | 539647-2
Jazz:The Essential Collection Vol.3 | IN+OUT Records | 78013-2
Coleman Hawkins Trio
Jazz:The Essential Collection Vol.3 | IN+OUT Records | 78013-2
Coleman Hawkins With Michel Warlop And His Orchestra
Django Reinhardt All Star Sessions | Capitol | 531577-2
Dicky Wells And His Orchestra
Americans Swinging In Paris:Dicky Wells | EMI Records | 539664-2
Django Reinhardt
Django Reinhardt:Souveniers | Dreyfus Jazz Line | FDM 36744-2
Django Reinhardt And His Quintet
Peche Á La Mode-The Great Blue Star Sessions 1947/1953 | Verve | 835418-2
Django Reinhardt:Souveniers | Dreyfus Jazz Line | FDM 36744-2
Django Reinhardt And His Rhythm
Verve Jazz Masters 38:Django Reinhardt | Verve | 516931-2
Peche Á La Mode-The Great Blue Star Sessions 1947/1953 | Verve | 835418-2
Django Reinhardt And The Quintet Du Hot Club De France
Jazz In Paris:Django Reinhardt-Django's Blues | EmArCy | 013545-2
Planet Jazz:Django Reinhardt | Planet Jazz | 2152071-2
Planet Jazz Sampler | Planet Jazz | 2152326-2
Planet Jazz:Stephane Grappelli | RCA | 2165366-2
Peche Á La Mode-The Great Blue Star Sessions 1947/1953 | Verve | 835418-2
Django Reinhardt Quartet
Jazz In Paris:Django Reinhardt-Nuits De Saint-Germain-Des-Prés | EmArCy | 018427-2
Jazz In Paris:Django Reinhardt-Nuages | EmArCy | 018428-2
Django/Django In Rome 1949-1050 | BGO Records | BGOCD 366
Django Reinhardt:Echoes Of France | Dreyfus Jazz Line | FDM 36726-2
Django Reinhardt Quintet
Jazz In Paris:Django Reinhardt-Nuits De Saint-Germain-Des-Prés | EmArCy | 018427-2
Jazz In Paris:Django Reinhardt-Nuages | EmArCy | 018428-2
Django/Django In Rome 1949-1050 | BGO Records | BGOCD 366
Django Reinhardt Sextet
Jazz In Paris:Django Reinhardt-Nuits De Saint-Germain-Des-Prés | EmArCy | 018427-2
Django Reinhardt Trio
Django/Django In Rome 1949-1050 | BGO Records | BGOCD 366
Django Reinhardt:Echoes Of France | Dreyfus Jazz Line | FDM 36726-2
Django Reinhardt:Souveniers | Dreyfus Jazz Line | FDM 36744-2
Django Reinhardt With Duke Ellington And His Orchestra
Django Reinhardt:Souveniers | Dreyfus Jazz Line | FDM 36744-2
Django Reinhardt With Stan Brenders Et Son Grand Orchestre
Verve Jazz Masters 38:Django Reinhardt | Verve | 516931-2
Django's Music
Peche Á La Mode-The Great Blue Star Sessions 1947/1953 | Verve | 835418-2
Eddie South/Stephane Grappelli Quintet
Django/Django In Rome 1949-1050 | BGO Records | BGOCD 366
Django Reinhardt:Echoes Of France | Dreyfus Jazz Line | FDM 36726-2
Michel Warlop Et Son Orchestre
Jazz In Paris:Django Reinhardt-Django Et Compagnie | EmArCy | 549241-2 PMS
Micheline Day Et Son Quatuor Swing
Jazz In Paris:Django Reinhardt-Django Et Compagnie | EmArCy | 549241-2 PMS
Nitta Rette Et Son Trio Hot
Jazz In Paris:Django Reinhardt-Django Et Compagnie | EmArCy | 549241-2 PMS
Quintet Du Hot Club De France
Jazz In Paris:Django Reinhardt-Swing From Paris | EmArCy | 159853-2 PMS
Jazz In Paris:Django Reinhardt-Swing 39 | EmArCy | 159854-2 PMS
Djangology | Bluebird | 2663957-2
Grapelli Story | Verve | 515807-2
Verve Jazz Masters 38:Django Reinhardt | Verve | 516931-2
Verve Jazz Masters Vol.60:The Collection | Verve | 529866-2
Django/Django In Rome 1949-1050 | BGO Records | BGOCD 366
Django Reinhardt:Echoes Of France | Dreyfus Jazz Line | FDM 36726-2
Django Reinhardt:Souveniers | Dreyfus Jazz Line | FDM 36744-2
Rex Stewart And His Feetwarmers
Django Reinhardt All Star Sessions | Capitol | 531577-2
Rex Stewart Quintet
Peche Á La Mode-The Great Blue Star Sessions 1947/1953 | Verve | 835418-2
Stephane Grappelli And His Hot Four
Jazz In Paris:Django Reinhardt-Swing From Paris | EmArCy | 159853-2 PMS
Stephane Grappelli-Django Reinhard
Grapelli Story | Verve | 515807-2
Yvonne Louis With The Orchestra Vola
Jazz In Paris:Django Reinhardt-Django Et Compagnie | EmArCy | 549241-2 PMS

Reinhardt,Django or Henri Schaap | (g)
Micheline Day Et Son Quatuor Swing
Jazz In Paris:Django Reinhardt-Django Et Compagnie | EmArCy | 549241-2 PMS

Reinhardt,Helmut | (as,bscl)
Freddie Brocksieper Star-Quintett
Shot Gun Boogie | Bear Family Records | BCD 16277 AH
Hans Koller Nonet
Exclusiv | MPS | 9813440
Kurt Edelhagen All Stars
Deutsches Jazz Fesival 1954/1955 | Bear Family Records | BCD 15430
Kurt Edelhagen All Stars Und Solisten
Deutsches Jazz Fesival 1954/1955 | Bear Family Records | BCD 15430
Quartet Der Kurt Edelhagen All Stars
Deutsches Jazz Fesival 1954/1955 | Bear Family Records | BCD 15430

Reinhardt,Joseph | (g)
Andre Pasdoc With The Orchestra Vola
Jazz In Paris:Django Reinhardt-Django Et Compagnie | EmArCy | 549241-2 PMS
Bill Coleman Et Son Orchestre
Americans Swinging In Paris:Bill Coleman-The Elegance | EMI Records | 539662-2

Django Reinhardt And His Quintet
Peche Á La Mode-The Great Blue Star Sessions 1947/1953 | Verve | 835418-2
Django Reinhardt And The Quintet Du Hot Club De France
Jazz In Paris:Django Reinhardt-Django's Blues | EmArCy | 013545-2
Planet Jazz:Django Reinhardt | Planet Jazz | 2152071-2
Peche Á La Mode-The Great Blue Star Sessions 1947/1953 | Verve | 835418-2
Django Reinhardt Quartet
Django/Django In Rome 1949-1050 | BGO Records | BGOCD 366
Django's Music
Peche Á La Mode-The Great Blue Star Sessions 1947/1953 | Verve | 835418-2
Michel Warlop Et Son Orchestre
Jazz In Paris:Django Reinhardt-Django Et Compagnie | EmArCy | 549241-2 PMS
Quintet Du Hot Club De France
Jazz In Paris:Django Reinhardt-Swing From Paris | EmArCy | 159853-2 PMS
Jazz In Paris:Django Reinhardt-Swing 39 | EmArCy | 159854-2 PMS
Verve Jazz Masters 38:Django Reinhardt | Verve | 516931-2
Django/Django In Rome 1949-1050 | BGO Records | BGOCD 366
Django Reinhardt:Echoes Of France | Dreyfus Jazz Line | FDM 36726-2
Django Reinhardt:Souveniers | Dreyfus Jazz Line | FDM 36744-2
Stephane Grappelli And His Hot Four
Jazz In Paris:Django Reinhardt-Swing From Paris | EmArCy | 159853-2 PMS
Yvonne Louis With The Orchestra Vola
Jazz In Paris:Django Reinhardt-Django Et Compagnie | EmArCy | 549241-2 PMS

Reinhardt,Ron | (keyboards)
Richard Elliot Sextet
City Speak | Blue Note | 832620-2

Reinhart,Randy | (tbtp)
Warren Vaché And The New York City All-Star Big Band
Swingtime! | Nagel-Heyer | CD 059

Reinhold-Bundgaard,Kathrine | (viola)
The Crossover Ensemble With The Zapolski Quartet
Helios Suite | dacapo | DCCD 9459

Reinke,Andreas | (viola)
Till Brönner Quartet & Deutsches Symphonieorchester Berlin
German Songs | Minor Music | 801057

Reinon,Eladio | (tsld)
Big Band Bellaterra
Don't Git Sassy | Fresh Sound Records | FSNT 048 CD
Eladio Reinon Quintet
Es La Historia De Un Amor | Fresh Sound Records | FSNT 004 CD
Georgina Weinstein With Her Quartet
Come Rain Or Come Shine | Fresh Sound Records | FSNT 020 CD

Reis,Barry | (tp)
Axel Zwingenberger With The Lionel Hampton Big Band
The Boogie Woogie Album | Vagabond | VRCD 8.88008

Reis,Rosani | (voice)
La Voce-Music For Voices,Trumpet And Bass | JA & RO | JARO 4208-2

Reiser,Niki | (flss)
Kol Simcha
Contemporary Klezmer | Laika Records | LK 93-048

Reisler,Jerome | (stringsv)
Johnny Hartman And His Orchestra
Unforgettable | Impulse(MCA) | IMP 11522

Reisman,Joe | (b,ld,clts)
Cab Calloway And His Orchestra
Planet Jazz:Cab Calloway | Planet Jazz | 2161237-2
Planet Jazz:Male Jazz Vocalists | Planet Jazz | 2169657-2

Reiter,Adrian | (g)
Peter Möltgen Quartet
Mellow Acid | Edition Collage | EC 495-2

Reiter,Joerg | (fender-rhodes,p,keyboards,p-solo)
Bernd Konrad With Erwin Lehn und sein Südfunk Orchester Stuttgart
Wen Die Götter Lieben | Creative Works Records | CW CD 1010-1
Bireli Lagrene Ensemble
Routes To Django & Bireli Swing '81 | Jazzpoint | JP 1055 CD
Routs To Django-Live At The 'Krokodil' | Jazzpoint | JP 1056 CD
Bireli Lagrene Group
Bireli Lagrene 'Highlights' | Jazzpoint | JP 1027 CD
Bireli Lagrene Quartet
A' Portrait Of Jan Jankeje | Jazzpoint | JP 1054 CD
Jazzensemble Des Hessischen Rundfunks
Atmosphering Conditions Permitting | ECM | 1549/50
Katie Kern Group
Still Young | Jazzpoint | JP 1070 CD
Russ Spiegel Group
Twilight | double moon | CHRDM 71026

Reiter,Peter | (cl,keyboards,pel-p)
HR Big Band
The American Songs Of Kurt Weill | hr music.de | hrmj 006-01 CD
Libertango:Homage An Astor Piazolla | hr music.de | hrmj 014-02 CD
HR Big Band With Marjorie Barnes And Frits Landesbergen
Swinging Christmas | hr music.de | hrmj 012-02 CD
HR Big Band With Marjorie Barnes And Frits Landesbergen And Strings
Swinging Christmas | hr music.de | hrmj 012-02 CD
Jazzensemble Des Hessischen Rundfunks
Jazz Messe-Messe Für Unsere Zeit | hr music.de | hrmj 003-01 CD
Tobias Langguth Band
One Note Bossa | Jardis Records | JRCD 9510

Reith,Dieter | (arr,el-p,org,synth,keyboards,ldp)
Bill Ramsey With Orchestra
Gettin' Back To Swing | Bear Family Records | BCD 15813 AH
Charly Antolini Orchestra
Drum Beat | MPS | 9808191
Dieter Reith Group
Reith On! | MPS | 557423-2
Dieter Reith Quartet
Reith On! | MPS | 557423-2
Dieter Reith Quintet
Reith On! | MPS | 557423-2
Dieter Reith Trio
Reith On! | MPS | 557423-2
Knut Kiesewetter With The Dieter Reith Orchestra
Reith On! | MPS | 557423-2
NDR Big Band With Guests
50 Years Of NDR Big Band:Bravissimo II | ACT | 9259-2

Rek,Vitold | (b)
Alfred 23 Harth QuasarQuartet
POPending EYE | free flow music | ffm 0493
Lajos Dudas Quintet
Jubilee Edition | double moon | CHRDM 71020
Ralph R.Hübner-Christoph Lauer Quartet
Mondspinner | free flow music | ffm 0796

Rekow,Raul | (congas)
Herbie Hancock Group
Sunlight | CBS | 486570-2

Remedy,The |
The Remedy
The Remedy | Jazz Haus Musik | JHM 0069 CD

Remember Shakti |
Remember Shakti
Saturday Night In Bombay | Verve | 014184-2

Remi,Tony | (el-gg)
David Jean-Baptiste Group
The Nature Suite | Laika Records | 35101632

Remold,Michael | (pkeyboards)
Jamenco
Conversations | Trick Music | TM 9202 CD

Remsen,Dorothy | (harp)
Ella Fitzgerald With The Frank DeVol Orchestra
Get Happy! | Verve | 523321-2

Rémy,Tony | (g,el-g,keybaords,programmingvoc)
Pee Wee Ellis & NDR Bigband
What You Like | Minor Music | 801064

Renard,Alex | (tp)
Michel Warlop Et Son Orchestre
Jazz In Paris:Django Reinhardt-Django Et Compagnie | EmArCy | 549241-2 PMS
Wal-Berg Et Son Jazz Francais
Jazz In Paris:Django Reinhardt-Django Et Compagnie | EmArCy | 549241-2 PMS
Willie Lewis And His Entertainers
Americans Swinging In Paris:Benny Carter | EMI Records | 539647-2

Renard,Johnny | (tp)
NDR-Workshop
Doldinger's Best | ACT | 9224-2

Renaud,Henri | (pcomp)
Al Cohn Quartet
The Birdlanders Vol.2 | Original Jazz Classics | OJCCD 1931-2
Clifford Brown Quartet
Planet Jazz:Clifford Brown | Planet Jazz | 2161239-2
Gigi Gryce-Clifford Brown Octet
Planet Jazz:Clifford Brown | Planet Jazz | 2161239-2
Gigi Gryce-Clifford Brown Sextet
Planet Jazz:Clifford Brown | Planet Jazz | 2161239-2
Lucky Thompson Quartet
Americans Swinging In Paris:Lucky Thompson | EMI Records | 539651-2
Lucky Thompson Quintet
Americans Swinging In Paris:Lucky Thompson | EMI Records | 539651-2
Lucky Thompson's Modern Jazz Group Quartet
Jazz In Paris:Lucky Thompson-Modern Jazz Group | EmArCy | 159823-2 PMS
Lucky Thompson's Modern Jazz Group Tentet
Jazz In Paris:Lucky Thompson-Modern Jazz Group | EmArCy | 159823-2 PMS
Milt Jackson Septet
The Birdlanders Vol.1 | Original Jazz Classics | OJCCD 1930-2
Milt Jackson Sextet
The Birdlanders Vol.1 | Original Jazz Classics | OJCCD 1930-2
Oscar Pettiford Sextet
The Birdlanders Vol.2 | Original Jazz Classics | OJCCD 1931-2
Sonny Criss Quartet
Jazz In Paris:Saxophones Á Saint-Germain Des Prés | EmArCy | 014060-2
The Herdsmen
Nat Pierce-Dick Collins-Ralph Burns & The Herdsmen Play Paris | Fantasy | FCD 24759-2
Zoot Sims Quintet
Americans Swinging In Paris:Zoot Sims | EMI Records | 539646-2

Rengifo Jr.,Felipe | (timbalescampana de cumaco)
Conexion Latina
Mambo Nights | Enja | ENJ-9402 2

Rengifo Sr.,Felipe | (congas,shekerecumaco)

Renliden,Weine | (tp)
Bengt-Arne Wallin Orchestra
The Birth+Rebirth Of Swedish Folk Jazz | ACT | 9254-2
Lars Gullin Quartet
Lars Gullin 1951/52 Vol.5:First Walk | Dragon | DRCD 380
Lars Gullin Quintet
Lars Gullin 1953,Vol.2:Moden Sounds | Dragon | DRCD 234
Lars Gullin 1951/52 Vol.5:First Walk | Dragon | DRCD 380
Lars Gullin Septet
Lars Gullin 1951/52 Vol.5:First Walk | Dragon | DRCD 380

Renn,Buzz | (cl,asfl)
Rod Levitt Orchestra
The Dynamic Sound Patterns Of The Rod Levitt Orchestra | Original Jazz Classics | OJCCD 1955-2(RS 9471)

Rensey,Stewart | (fr-h)
Dizzy Gillespie And His Orchestra
Talking Verve:Dizzy Gillespie | Verve | 533846-2

Rensvik,Anders | (viola)
Terje Rypdal Quartet With The Bergen Chamber Ensemble
Lux Aeterna | ECM | 1818(017070-2)

Renteria,Jorge | (fr-h)
Orquestra De Cambra Teatre Lliure
Porgy And Bess | Fresh Sound Records | FSNT 066 CD

Renvag,Jan Olav | (b,el-btuba)
Geir Lysne Listening Ensemble
Korall | ACT | 9236-2
Aurora Borealis-Nordic Lights | ACT | 9406-2

Renzi,Matt | (saxts)
Heinrich Köbberling-Matt Renzi Quartet
Pisces | Nabel Records:Jazz Network | CD 4677
Matt Renzi-Jimmy Weinstein Quartet
Matt Renzi-Jimmy Weinstein Quartet | Fresh Sound Records | FSNT 045 CD
Matt Renzi-Jimmy Weinstein-Masa Kamaguchi Trio
Lines And Ballads | Fresh Sound Records | FSNT 065 CD
Stan Kenton And His Orchestra
Adventures In Blues | Capitol | 520089-2
Adventures In Jazz | Capitol | 521222-2

Renzi,Mike | (keybaords,p,arrkeyboards)
Freddy Cole With Band
Le Grand Freddy:Freddy Cole Sings The Music Of Michel Legrand | Fantasy | FCD 9683-2
Lena Horne With The George Benson Quintet
Misty Blue:Sweet Sisters Swing Songs Of Sorrow And Sadness | Blue Note | 521151-2

Renzi,Paul | (fl,piccolo,reedsts)
Stan Kenton And His Orchestra
Adventures In Blues | Capitol | 520089-2
Adventures In Jazz | Capitol | 521222-2

Repka,Johannes | (g)
Landes Jugend Jazz Orchester Hessen
Touch Of Lips | hr music.de | hrmj 004-01 CD

Reschauer,Werner | (voc)
Jazzensemble Des Hessischen Rundfunks
Jazz Messe-Messe Für Unsere Zeit | hr music.de | hrmj 003-01 CD

Reschke,Viktor | (drperc)
Helmut Zacharias mit seinem Orchester
Ich Habe Rhythmus | Bear Family Records | BCD 15642 AH

Resnick,Art | (p)
Nat Adderley Quintet
We Remember Cannon | IN+OUT Records | 7012-2
Jazz Unlimited | IN+OUT Records | 7017-2

Resnick,Eph | (tb)
Stan Getz With The Eddie Sauter Orchestra
Stan Getz Plays The Music Of Mickey One | Verve | 531232-2

Resnicoff,Richie | (g)
Buddy Rich And His Orchestra
Big Swing Face | Pacific Jazz | 837989-2
Buddy Rich Big Band
The New One! | Pacific Jazz | 494507-2
Horace Silver Sextet
Horace Silver Retrospective | Blue Note | 495576-2
Deep Blue-The United States Of Mind | Blue Note | 521152-2
Horace Silver Sextet With Vocals
Horace Silver Retrospective | Blue Note | 495576-2
Rusty Bryant Group
For The Good Times | Prestige | PRCD 24269-2

rest unkn. |
Buddy Guy Blues Band
Buddy Guy-The Complete Chess Studio Recordings | MCA | MCD 09337
Roland Kirk With The Benny Golson Orchestra
Rahsaan/The Complete Mercury Recordings Of Roland Kirk | Mercury | 846630-2

Rette,Nitta | (voc)
Nitta Rette Et Son Trio Hot
Jazz In Paris:Django Reinhardt-Django Et Compagnie | EmArCy | 549241-2 PMS

Rettenbacher,Hans | (b)
Hans Koller Nonet
Exclusiv | MPS | 9813440
Hans Koller Trio
Relax With My Horns | MPS | 9813445

Rettenbacher,J.A. | (bcello)
Dave Pike Set
Dave Pike Set:Masterpieces | MPS | 531848-2

Return To Forever |
Chick Corea And Return To Forever
Light As A Feather | Polydor | 557115-2
Return To Forever
Return To The 7th Galaxy-Return To Forever:The Anthology | Verve | 533108-2
Where Have I Known You Before | Polydor | 825206-2
Hymn Of The Seventh Galaxy | Polydor | 825336-2

Reuss,Allan | (bjg)
Benny Goodman And His Orchestra
Planet Jazz:Benny Goodman | Planet Jazz | 2152054-2
Planet Jazz Sampler | Planet Jazz | 2152326-2
Planet Jazz:Jazz Greatest Hits | Planet Jazz | 2169648-2
Planet Jazz:Big Bands | Planet Jazz | 2169649-2
Planet Jazz:Swing | Planet Jazz | 2169651-2
Planet Jazz:Jazz Trumpet | Planet Jazz | 2169654-2
Planet Jazz:Female Jazz Vocalists | Planet Jazz | 2169656-2
The Legends Of Swing | Laserlight | 24659
Benny Goodman At Carnegie Hall 1938(Complete) | CBS | C2K 65143
More Camel Caravans | Phontastic | NCD 8841/2
More Camel Caravans | Phontastic | NCD 8843/4
Benny Goodman Band
Benny Goodman At Carnegie Hall 1938(Complete) | CBS | C2K 65143
Benny Goodman Combo
Benny Goodman At Carnegie Hall 1938(Complete) | CBS | C2K 65143
Billie Holiday With Teddy Wilson And His Orchestra
Billie's Love Songs | Nimbus Records | NI 2000
Coleman Hawkins And His Orchestra
Jazz:The Essential Collection Vol.3 | IN+OUT Records | 78013-2
Gene Krupa's Swing Band
Planet Jazz:Swing | Planet Jazz | 2169651-2
Glenn Miller And His Orchestra
Planet Jazz:Glenn Miller | Planet Jazz | 2152056-2
Candelight Miller | RCA | 2668716-2
Harry James And His Orchestra
Great Swing Classics In Hi-Fi | Capitol | 521223-2
Trumpet Blues:The Best Of Harry James | Capitol | 521224-2
Jack Teagarden And His Orchestra
Jazz:The Essential Collection Vol.3 | IN+OUT Records | 78013-2
Jam Session
Benny Goodman At Carnegie Hall 1938(Complete) | CBS | C2K 65143
Lionel Hampton And His Orchestra
Planet Jazz:Jazz Saxophone | Planet Jazz | 2169653-2
Planet Jazz:Male Jazz Vocalists | Planet Jazz | 2169657-2
Louis Armstrong And His Hot Seven
Planet Jazz:Louis Armstrong | Planet Jazz | 2152052-2
Best Of The Complete RCA Victor Recordings | RCA | 2663636-2
Louis Armstrong:A 100th Birthday Celebration | RCA | 2663694-2
Louis Armstrong:C'est Si Bon | Dreyfus Jazz Line | FDM 36730-2
Louis Armstrong With Gordon Jenkins And His Orchestra
Satchmo In Style | Verve | 549594-2
Louis Armstrong With Gordon Jenkins And His Orchestra And Choir
Satchmo In Style | Verve | 549594-2
Teddy Wilson And His Orchestra
Jazz:The Essential Collection Vol.3 | IN+OUT Records | 78013-2

Reuter,Markus | (warr-touch-g)
Europa String Choir
Internationales Guitarren Festival '99 | ALISO Records | AL 1038

Revell,Adrian | (fl,ss,asts)
Jazz Africa All Nations Big Band
Jadu(Jazz Africa Down Under) | Enja | ENJ-9339 2

Revis,Eric | (b)
Branford Marsalis Quartet
Reqiem | CBS | 69655-2
James Hurt Group
Dark Grooves-Mystcal Rhythms | Blue Note | 495104-2

Reyes,Jorge | (b)
Roy Hargrove's Crisol
Habana | Verve | 537563-2

Reyes,Tony | (b)
Herbie Mann Sextet
Verve Jazz Masters Vol.60:The Collection | Verve | 529866-2
Verve Jazz Masters 56:Herbie Mann | Verve | 529901-2
Jack Costanzo Group
Latin Fever:The Wild Rhythms Of Jack Costanza | Capitol | 590955-2
Victor Feldman Orchestra
Latinsville | Contemporary | CCD 9005-2

Reynolds,Blake | (as)
Artie Shaw And His Orchestra
Planet JazzArtie Shaw | Planet Jazz | 2152057-2
Planet Jazz:Jazz Greatest Hits | Planet Jazz | 2169648-2

Reynolds,Dick | (arr,ldtb)
June Christy With The Pete Rugolo Orchestra
Something Cool(The Complete Mono & Stereo Versions) | Capitol | 534069-2

Reynolds,James | (p)
Hot Lips Page Band
Planet Jazz:Jazz Trumpet | Planet Jazz | 2169654-2

Reynolds,Todd | (stringsv)
Steve Coleman And Five Elements
The Sonic Language Of Myth | RCA | 2164123-2

Reynolds,Tom | (dr)
Chamber Jazz Sextet
Plays Pal Joey | Candid | CCD 79030

Reys,Rita | (voc)
Rita Reys With The Lars Gullin Quartet
Lars Gullin 1953,Vol.2:Moden Sounds | Dragon | DRCD 234

Rezanina,Lubomir | (tpfl-h)
Bernd Konrad With Erwin Lehn und sein Südfunk Orchester Stuttgart
Wen Die Götter Lieben | Creative Works Records | CW CD 1010-1
Bill Ramsey With Orchestra
Gettin' Back To Swing | Bear Family Records | BCD 15813 AH
SWR Big Band
Jazz In Concert | Hänssler Classics | CD 93.004

Rhami,Malika | (percvoc)
Nguyen Le Group
Maghreb And Friends | ACT | 9261-2

Rhue,Phanalphie | (voc)
Tom Browne Groups
Mo' Jamaica Funk | Hip Bop | HIBD 8002

Rhyne,Chris | (el-p,synth,keyboardsp)
Jean-Luc Ponty Group
Mystical Adventures | Atlantic | 19333-2
Jean-Luc Ponty Quintet
The Very Best Of Jean-Luc Ponty | Rhino | 8122-79862-2
Jean-Luc Ponty Sextet
The Very Best Of Jean-Luc Ponty | Rhino | 8122-79862-2

Rhyne,Melvin | (org)
Mel Rhyne Sextet
Organ-izing | Original Jazz Classics | OJCCD 1055-2(JLP 916)
Wes Montgomery Trio
Wes Montgomery-The Complete Riverside Recordings | Riverside | 12 RCD 4408-2
A Dynamic New Jazz Sound | Original Jazz Classics | OJCCD 034-2
Portrait Of Wes | Original Jazz Classics | OJCCD 144-2
Boss Guitar | Original Jazz Classics | OJCCD 261-2

Guitar On The Go | Original Jazz Classics | OJCCD 489-2(RLP 9494)
The Jazz Giants Play Miles Davis:Milestones | Prestige | PCD 24225-2

RIAS-Big Band |
Harry Allen And Randy Sandke Meets The RIAS Big Band Berlin
The Music Of The Trumpet Kings | Nagel-Heyer | CD 037

Ribeiro,Clelio | (berimbau)
Passport
Iguacu | Atlantic | 2292-46031-2

Ribot,Gregory | (bs)
Marc Ribot Y Los Cubanos Postizos
The Prosthetic Cubans | Atlantic | 7567-83116-2

Ribot,Marc | (el-g,g,e-flat-h,voc,g-solotp)
Dave Douglas Group
Dave Douglas Freak In | Bluebird | 2664008-2
James Carter Group
Layin' In The Cut | Atlantic | 7567-83305-2
Marc Ribot Y Los Cubanos Postizos
The Prosthetic Cubans | Atlantic | 7567-83116-2
Nuy Divertido(Very Entertaining) | Atlantic | 7567-83293-2
Noel Akchoté-Marc Ribot-Eugene Chadbourne
Lust Corner | Winter&Winter | 910019-2

Ricard,Fip | (tp)
Count Basie And His Orchestra
Atomic Swing | Roulette | 497871-2
Verve Jazz Masters 2:Count Basie | Verve | 519819-2
Dinah Washington With The Eddie Chamblee Orchestra
Verve Jazz Masters 40:Dinah Washington | Verve | 522055-2
Dinah Sings Bessie Smith | Verve | 538635-2
Ella Fitzgerald With The Count Basie Orchestra
Ella Fitzgerald-First Lady Of Song | Verve | 517898-2
Ella And Basie | Verve | 539059-2
Frank Sinatra With The Count Basie Orchestra
Sinatra-Basie:An Historic Musical First | Reprise | 7599-27023-2

Ricard,Paul | (tp)
Joe Turner With Orchestra
Atlantic Jazz: Kansas City | Atlantic | 7567-81701-2

Ricci,George | (cellostrings)
Ben Webster With Orchestra And Strings
Music For Loving:Ben Webster With Strings | Verve | 527774-2
Ultimate Ben Webster selected by James Carter | Verve | 557537-2
Bill Evans Quartet With Orchestra
The Complete Bill Evans On Verve | Verve | 527953-2
From Left To Right | Verve | 557451-2
Cannonball Adderley And His Orchestra
Verve Jazz Masters 31:Cannonball Adderley | Verve | 522651-2
Coleman Hawkins With Billy Byers And His Orchestra
The Hawk In Hi-Fi | RCA | 2663842-2
George Benson With The Don Sebesky Orchestra
Verve Jazz Masters 21:George Benson | Verve | 521861-2
Grover Washington Jr. Orchestra
Jazzrock-Anthology Vol.3:Fusion | Zounds | CD 27100555
Les McCann Group
Another Beginning | Atlantic | 7567-80790-2
Louis Armstrong And His Friends
Planet Jazz:Louis Armstrong | Planet Jazz | 2152052-2
Planet Jazz Sampler | Planet Jazz | 2152326-2
Louis Armstrong And His Friends | Bluebird | 2663961-2
Milt Jackson And His Orchestra
Sunflower | CTI | ZK 65131
Paul Desmond Orchestra
Late Night Sax | CBS | 487798-2
Skylark | CTI | ZK 65133
Paul Desmond Quartet With The Don Sebesby Orchestra
From The Hot Afternoon | Verve | 543487-2
Phil Woods Quartet With Orchestra & Strings
Round Trip | Verve | 559804-2
Stan Getz With The Eddie Sauter Orchestra
Stan Getz Plays The Music Of Mickey One | Verve | 531232-2
Wes Montgomery Quartet With The Claus Ogerman Orchestra
Tequila | Verve | 547769-2
Wes Montgomery Quintet With The Claus Ogerman Orchestra
The Antonio Carlos Jobim Songbook | Verve | 525472-2
Talkin' Jazz:Roots Of Acid Jazz | Verve | 529580-2
Tequila | Verve | 547769-2
Wes Montgomery Trio With The Claus Ogerman Orchestra
Tequila | Verve | 547769-2
Wes Montgomery With The Claus Ogerman Orchestra
Verve Jazz Masters 14:Wes Montgomery | Verve | 519826-2
Wes Montgomery With The Don Sebesky Orchestra
Verve Jazz Masters 14:Wes Montgomery | Verve | 519826-2
Talkin' Jazz:Roots Of Acid Jazz | Verve | 529580-2
Bumpin' | Verve | 539062-2
Wes Montgomery With The Jimmy Jones Orchestra
Wes Montgomery-The Complete Riverside Recordings | Riverside | 12 RCD 4408-2
The Jazz Giants Play Rodgers & Hart:Blue Moon | Prestige | PCD 24205-2

Ricci,Paul | (as,b-cl,bs,cl,reedsts)
Benny Goodman And His Orchestra
Great Swing Classics In Hi-Fi | Capitol | 521223-2
Billie Holiday With Toots Camarata And His Orchestra
Billie's Love Songs | Nimbus Records | NI 2000
Leon Thomas With Orchestra
Spirits Known And Unknown | RCA | 2663876-2
Louis Armstrong And His Orchestra
Louis Armstrong:Swing That Music | Laserlight | 36056
Louis Armstrong:C'est Si Bon | Dreyfus Jazz Line | FDM 36730-2

Ricciarelli,Alessandro | (gel-g)
Gerd Baumann-Alessandro Ricciarelli Quartet
Say No More | Edition Collage | EC 489-2

Riccio,Renato | (viola)
Gerry Mulligan With Astor Piazzolla And His Orchestra
Tango Nuevo | Atlantic | 2292-42145-2

Rice,Charlie | (dr)
Chet Baker Quartet
Baby Breeze | Verve | 538328-2
Chet Baker Quintet
Chet Baker:The Most Important Jazz Album Of 1964/65 | Roulette | 581829-2
Chet Baker Sextet
Baby Breeze | Verve | 538328-2
Louis Jordan And His Tympany Five
Louis Jordan-Let The Good Times Roll: The Complete Decca Recordings 1938-1954 | Bear Family Records | BCD 15557 IH

Rice,Marlene | (vviola)
Steve Coleman And The Council Of Balance
Genesis & The Opening Of The Way | RCA | 2152934-2

Rice-Shaw,Marlene | (v)
Greg Osby Quartet With String Quartet
Symbols Of Light(A Solution) | Blue Note | 531395-2

Rich,Buddy | (drvoc)
Art Tatum Sextet
Art Tatum-The Complete Pablo Group Masterpieces | Pablo | 6 PACD 4401-2
Artie Shaw And His Orchestra
Planet JazzArtie Shaw | Planet Jazz | 2152057-2
Swing Vol.1 | Storyville | 4960343
Bud Powell Trio
The Best Of Bud Powell On Verve | Verve | 523392-2
Buddy DeFranco With The Oscar Peterson Trio
The Complete Lionel Hampton Quartets And Quintets With Oscar Peterson On Verve | Verve | 559797-2
Buddy Rich And His Orchestra
Swingin' New Big Band | Pacific Jazz | 835232-2
Big Swing Face | Pacific Jazz | 837989-2
Buddy Rich Big Band
Backwoods Siseman/Pieces Of Dream | Laserlight | 24655
The New One! | Pacific Jazz | 494507-2
Keep The Customer Satisfied | EMI Records | 523999-2
Buddy Rich Orchestra
Krupa And Rich | Verve | 521643-2
Buddy Rich Quintet
Buddy And Sweets | Verve | 841433-2
Buddy Rich Septet
Swingin' The Blues-Jumpin' The Blues | Laserlight | 24654
Buddy Rich-Gene Krupa Orchestra
Krupa And Rich | Verve | 521643-2
Charlie Parker All Stars
Charlie Parker:The Best Of The Verve Years | Verve | 527815-2
Charlie Parker And His Orchestra
Bird: The Complete Charlie Parker On Verve | Verve | 837141-2
Charlie Parker:April In Paris | Dreyfus Jazz Line | FDM 36737-2
Charlie Parker Quartet
Verve Jazz Masters 20:Introducing | Verve | 519853-2
Charlie Parker | Verve | 539757-2
Bird: The Complete Charlie Parker On Verve | Verve | 837141-2
Charlie Parker:April In Paris | Dreyfus Jazz Line | FDM 36737-2
Charlie Parker Quartet With Strings
The Cole Porter Songbook | Verve | 823250-2
Charlie Parker Quintet
Verve Jazz Masters 10:Dizzy Gillespie | Verve | 516319-2
Bird And Diz | Verve | 521436-2
Charlie Parker:Bird's Best Bop On Verve | Verve | 527452-2
Charlie Parker:The Best Of The Verve Years | Verve | 527815-2
Charlie Parker | Verve | 539757-2
Ultimate Dizzy Gillespie | Verve | 557535-2
Talkin' Bird | Verve | 559859-2
Charlie Parker With Machito And His Orchestra
Bird: The Complete Charlie Parker On Verve | Verve | 837141-2
Charlie Parker With Strings
Verve Jazz Masters 28:Charlie Parker Plays Standards | Verve | 521854-2
Charlie Parker With Strings:The Master Takes | Verve | 523984-2
Charlie Parker:The Best Of The Verve Years | Verve | 527815-2
Bird: The Complete Charlie Parker On Verve | Verve | 837141-2
Charlie Parker:April In Paris | Dreyfus Jazz Line | FDM 36737-2
Charlie Parker With The Joe Lipman Orchestra
Verve Jazz Masters 28:Charlie Parker Plays Standards | Verve | 521854-2
Charlie Parker With Strings:The Master Takes | Verve | 523984-2
Charlie Parker Big Band | Verve | 559835-2
Charlie Parker-Dizzy Gillespie Quintet
Thelonious Monk:Misterioso | Dreyfus Jazz Line | FDM 36743-2
Coleman Hawkins Quartet
Verve Jazz Masters 43:Coleman Hawkins | Verve | 521856-2
The Complete Jazz At The Philharmonic On Verve 1944-1949 | Verve | 523893-2
Count Basie Sextet
Verve Jazz Masters 2:Count Basie | Verve | 519819-2
Duke Ellington With Tommy Dorsey And His Orchestra
Highlights From The Duke Ellington Centennial Edition | RCA | 2663672-2
Ella Fitzgerald And Louis Armstrong With The Oscar Peterson Quartet
Ella Fitzgerald-First Lady Of Song | Verve | 517898-2
Verve Jazz Masters 24:Ella Fitzgerald & Louis Armstrong | Verve | 521851-2
Verve Jazz Masters 46:Ella Fitzgerald-The Jazz Sides | Verve | 527655-2
The Complete Ella Fitzgerald And Louis Armstrong On Verve | Verve | 537284-2
The Best Of Ella Fitzgerald And Louis Armstrong On Verve | Verve | 537909-2
Ella And Louis | Verve | 543304-2
Ella & Louis | Verve | 825373-2
Ella Fitzgerald With The Hank Jones Trio
The Complete Jazz At The Philharmonic On Verve 1944-1949 | Verve | 523893-2
Ella Fitzgerald With The JATP All Stars
Ella Fitzgerald-First Lady Of Song | Verve | 517898-2
Gene Krupa & Buddy Rich
The Drum Battle:Gene Krupa And Buddy Rich At JATP | Verve | 559810-2
Hank Jones Trio
The Complete Jazz At The Philharmonic On Verve 1944-1949 | Verve | 523893-2
Jam Session
Jazz Gallery:Lester Young Vol.2(1946-59) | RCA | 2119541-2
JATP All Stars
Verve Jazz Masters 28:Charlie Parker Plays Standards | Verve | 521854-2
The Complete Jazz At The Philharmonic On Verve 1944-1949 | Verve | 523893-2
Charlie Parker:The Best Of The Verve Years | Verve | 527815-2
Jazz At The Philharmonic:Best Of The 1940's Concerts | Verve | 557534-2
The Drum Battle:Gene Krupa And Buddy Rich At JATP | Verve | 559810-2
Talkin' Bird | Verve | 559859-2
Bird: The Complete Charlie Parker On Verve | Verve | 837141-2
Kenny Kersey Trio
The Complete Jazz At The Philharmonic On Verve 1944-1949 | Verve | 523893-2
Lester Young Quartet
Jazz Gallery:Lester Young Vol.2(1946-59) | RCA | 2119541-2
Verve Jazz Masters 30:Lester Young | Verve | 521859-2
Verve Jazz Masters Vol.60:The Collection | Verve | 529866-2
Lester Young:Blue Lester | Dreyfus Jazz Line | FDM 36729-2
Lester Young Trio
Verve Jazz Masters 30:Lester Young | Verve | 521859-2
Lester Young:Blue Lester | Dreyfus Jazz Line | FDM 36729-2
Lester Young-Harry Edison With The Oscar Peterson Quartet
Jazz Gallery:Lester Young Vol.2(1946-59) | RCA | 2119541-2
Lionel Hampton Quartet
The Complete Lionel Hampton Quartets And Quintets With Oscar Peterson On Verve | Verve | 559797-2
The Lional Hampton Quintet | Verve | 589100-2
Lionel Hampton Quintet
The Complete Lionel Hampton Quartets And Quintets With Oscar Peterson On Verve | Verve | 559797-2
The Lional Hampton Quintet | Verve | 589100-2
Lionel Hampton With Buddy DeFranco And The Oscar Peterson Trio
Verve Jazz Masters 26:Lionel Hampton with Oscar Peterson | Verve | 521853-2
Lionel Hampton With The Oscar Peterson Quartet
Verve Jazz Masters 26:Lionel Hampton with Oscar Peterson | Verve | 521853-2
Lionel Hampton With The Oscar Peterson Trio
Verve Jazz Masters 26:Lionel Hampton with Oscar Peterson | Verve | 521853-2
Norman Granz Jam Session
Verve Jazz Masters 26:Lionel Hampton with Oscar Peterson | Verve | 521853-2
Verve Jazz Masters Vol.60:The Collection | Verve | 529866-2
Roy Eldridge And His Orchestra
The Complete Verve Roy Eldridge Studio Sessions | Verve | 9861278
Roy Eldridge-Dizzy Gillespie-Harry Edison With The Oscar Peterson Quartet
The Complete Verve Roy Eldridge Studio Sessions | Verve | 9861278
Tatum-Hampton-Rich Trio
Art Tatum-The Complete Pablo Group Masterpieces | Pablo | 6 PACD 4401-2
Tommy Dorsey And His Orchestra
Planet Jazz:Frank Sinatra & Tommy Dorsey | Planet Jazz | 2152067-2
Planet Jazz Sampler | Planet Jazz | 2152326-2
Planet Jazz:Tommy Dorsey | Planet Jazz | 2159972-2
Planet Jazz:Big Bands | Planet Jazz | 2169649-2
Planet Jazz:Male Jazz Vocalists | Planet Jazz | 2169657-2
Frank Sinatra And The Tommy Dorsey Orchestra | RCA | 2668701-2
Woody Herman And His Orchestra
Woody Herman:Four Brother | Dreyfus Jazz Line | FDM 36722-2

Rich,Ron | (congas)
Les McCann Group
Talkin' Verve:Les McCann | Verve | 557351-2
Les McCann Orchestra
Talkin' Verve:Les McCann | Verve | 557351-2

Rich[as 'Buddy Poor'],Buddy | (dr)
Harry James And His Orchestra
Trumpet Blues:The Best Of Harry James | Capitol | 521224-2

Richard Armin | (stringsraad electro-acoustic)
Jon Hassell Group
Power Spot | ECM | 1327

Richard,Ferdinand | (b-g)
Alfred 23 Harth Group
Sweet Paris | free flow music | ffm 0291

Richards,Carolyn | (voc)
JATP All Stars
The Complete Jazz At The Philharmonic On Verve 1944-1949 | Verve | 523893-2

Richards,Charles 'Red' | (p,vocp-solo)
Al Casey Quartet
A Tribute To Fats | Jazzpoint | JP 1044 CD
A' Portrait Of Jan Jankeje | Jazzpoint | JP 1054 CD
Benny Waters Quintet
Benny Waters Plays Songs Of Love | Jazzpoint | JP 1039 CD
Bud Freeman All Stars
The Bud Freeman All-Star Sessions | Prestige | PRCD 24286-2
Doc Cheatham Sextet
A' Portrait Of Jan Jankeje | Jazzpoint | JP 1054 CD
George Kelly Quintet
A' Portrait Of Jan Jankeje | Jazzpoint | JP 1054 CD
Muggsy Spanier And His Dixieland All Stars
Muggsy Spanier At Club Hangover 1953/54 | Storyville | STCD 6033
Red Richards
My Romance | Jazzpoint | JP 1042 CD
Red Richards Quartet
Swingtime | Jazzpoint | JP 1041 CD
Red Richards-George Kelly Sextet With Doc Cheatham
Groove Move | Jazzpoint | JP 1045 CD

Richards,Emil | (bell-tree,contra-bass-marimba)
Diane Schuur And Her Band
Music Is My Life | Atlantic | 7567-83150-2
Dizzy Gillespie And His Orchestra
Talking Verve:Dizzy Gillespie | Verve | 533846-2
Ella Fitzgerald With The Billy May Orchestra
Love Songs:The Best Of The Song Books | Verve | 531762-2
Ella Fitzgerald Sings The Harold Arlen Song Book | Verve | 589108-2
Ella Fitzgerald With The Nelson Riddle Orchestra
Love Songs:The Best Of The Song Books | Verve | 531762-2
Frank Sinatra With The Count Basie Orchestra
It Might As Well Be Spring | Reprise | 7599-27027-2
George Shearing And His Quintet
Beauty And The Beat | Capitol | 542308-2
George Shearing Quintet
At Newport | Pablo | PACD 5315-2
George Shearing Quintet With Cannonball And Nat Adderley
At Newport | Pablo | PACD 5315-2
George Shearing Sextet
At Newport | Pablo | PACD 5315-2
Louie Bellson Septet
Louie Bellson Jam | Original Jazz Classics | OJCCD 802-2(2310838)
Peggy Lee With George Shearing
Beauty And The Beat | Capitol | 542308-2
Peggy Lee With The Quincy Jones Orchestra
Blues Cross Country | Capitol | 520088-2
Roger Kellaway Cello Quartet With The A&M Symphony Orchestra
Roger Kellaway Cello Quartet | A&M Records | 9861062
Singers Unlimited With The Roger Kellaway Cello Quartet
The Singers Unlimited:Magic Voices | MPS | 539130-2
The Quincy Jones-Sammy Nestico Orchestra
Basie & Beyond | Warner | 9362-47792-2

Richards,Johnny | (arr,ldcond)
Ben Webster With Strings
The Warm Moods-With Strings | Rhino | 8122-73721-2

Richards,Land | (dr)
Larry Carlton Group
The Gift | GRP | GRP 98542

Richards,Martin | (dr)
Gary Burton Quintet
Whiz Kids | ECM | 1329

Richards,Marty | (dr)
Duke Robillard-Herb Ellis Quintet
Conversation In Swing Guitar | Stony Plain | SPCD 1260
More Conversations In Swing Guitar | Stony Plain | SPCD 1292
Peter Malick Group feat. Norah Jones
New York City | Koch Records | 238678-2

Richards,Nicki | (g,midi-gvoc)
Lenny White Group
Present Tense | Hip Bop | HIBD 8004
Renderers Of Spirit | Hip Bop | HIBD 8014

Richards[Alden],Terrie | (voc)
Butch Miles-Howard Alden Sextet
Cookin' | Nagel-Heyer | CD 5003
Rex Allen's Swing Express
Keep Swingin' | Nagel-Heyer | CD 016
Terrie Richard Alden And The Warren Vaché Quartet
Voice With Heart | Nagel-Heyer | CD 048
Terrie Richard Alden-Howard Alden
Love | Nagel-Heyer | CD 071

Richardson,Ernest | (g)
Sister Rosetta Tharpe And Her Group
Gospel Train | Mercury | 841134-2
Sister Rosetta Tharpe And Her Group With The Harmonizing Four
Gospel Train | Mercury | 841134-2

Richardson,Jerome | (alto-fl,ts,as,b-cl,bs,b-fl,b-g,cl)
(Little)Jimmy Scott With The Lionel Hampton Orchestra
Everybody's Somebody's Fool | Decca | 050669-2
Abbey Lincoln With The Benny Golson Septet
It's Magic | Original Jazz Classics | OJCCD 205-2
Ahmed Abdul-Malik Orchestra
Planet Jazz:Lee Morgan | Planet Jazz | 2161238-2
Andy And The Bey Sisters
Andy Bey And The Bey Sisters | Prestige | PCD 24245-2
Anita O'Day With The Gary McFarland Orchestra
All The Sad Youn Men | Verve | 517065-2
Verve Jazz Masters 49:Anita O'Day | Verve | 527653-2
Blue Mitchell And His Orchestra
A Sure Thing | Original Jazz Classics | OJCCD 837-2
The Jazz Giants Play Jerome Kern:Yesterdays | Prestige | PCD 24202-2
Cal Tjader's Orchestra
Verve Jazz Masters 39:Cal Tjader | Verve | 521858-2
Talkin Verve/Roots Of Acid Jazz:Cal Tjader | Verve | 531562-2
Soul Burst | Verve | 557446-2
Cannonball Adderley And His Orchestra
Verve Jazz Masters 31:Cannonball Adderley | Verve | 522651-2
Cannonball Adderley Birthday Celebration | Fantasy | FANCD 6087-2
Cannonball Adderley Group
Julian 'Cannonball' Adderley | EmArCy | 830381-2
Charles Mingus And His Orchestra
The Complete Town Hall Concert | Blue Note | 828353-2
Charles Mingus Group
Mingus Dynasty | CBS | CK 65513
Charles Mingus Orchestra
Mingus Mingus Mingus | Impulse(MCA) | 951170-2

The Black Saint And The Sinner Lady | Impulse(MCA) | 951174-2
Charles Mingus:The Complete 1959 Columbia Recordings | CBS | C3K 65145
Dinah Washington With The Belford Hendricks Orchestra
Verve Jazz Masters 20:Introducing | Verve | 519853-2
What A Diff'rence A Day Makes! | Verve | 543300-2
4 By 4:Ella Fitzgerald/Sarah Vaughan/Billie Holiday/Dinah Washington | Verve | 559693-2
Dinah Washington With The Quincy Jones Orchestra
Verve Jazz Masters 40:Dinah Washington | Verve | 522055-2
The Swingin' Miss 'D' | Verve | 558074-2
Dizzy Gillespie With The Lalo Schifrin Orchestra
Free Ride | Original Jazz Classics | OJCCD 784-2(2310794)
Eddie Lockjaw Davis And His Orchestra
Eric Dolphy:The Complete Prestige Recordings | Prestige | 9 PRCD-4418-2
Eddie Lockjaw Davis Quintet
Cookbook Vol.1 | Original Jazz Classics | OJC20 652-2(P 7141)
The Eddie Lockjaw Davis Cookbook Vol.2 | Original Jazz Classics | OJC20 653-2(P 7161)
Queen Of The Organ-Shirley Scott Memorial Album | Prestige | PRCD 11027-2
Etta Jones And Her Band
Love Shout | Original Jazz Classics | OJCCD 941-2(P 7272)
Etta Jones With The Jerome Richardson Sextet
Hollar! | Original Jazz Classics | OJCCD 1061(PR 7284)
Freddie Hubbard Orchestra
The Body And The Soul | Impulse(MCA) | 951183-2
Gene Ammons And His All Stars
John Coltrane-The Prestige Recordings | Prestige | 16 PCD 4405-2
The Big Sound | Original Jazz Classics | OJCCD 651-2(P 7132)
Groove Blues | Original Jazz Classics | OJCCD 723-2(PR 7201)
The Prestige Legacy Vol.2:Battles Of Saxes | Prestige | PCD 24252-2
George Benson With The Don Sebesky Orchestra
Verve Jazz Masters 21:George Benson | Verve | 521861-2
Gil Evans Orchestra
The Individualism Of Gil Evans | Verve | 833804-2
Hank Jones With Oliver Nelson's Orchestra
The Roots Of Acid Jazz | Impulse(MCA) | IMP 12042
Herbie Hancock Orchestra
Herbie Hancock:The Complete Blue Note Sixties Sessions | Blue Note | 495569-2
The Prisoner | Blue Note | 525649-2
Horace Silver Quintet With Brass
Horace Silver Retrospective | Blue Note | 495576-2
J.J.Johnson And His Orchestra
Planet Jazz:J.J.Johnson | Planet Jazz | 2159974-2
Jerome Richardson Sextet
Night Life | Prestige | PCD 24260-2
Jimmy McGriff Orchestra
Swingin' The Blues-Jumpin' The Blues | Laserlight | 24654
Jimmy Smith And Wes Montgomery With Orchestra
Jimmy & Wes-The Dynamic Duo | Verve | 521445-2
Jimmy Smith And Wes Montgomery With The Oliver Nelson Orchestra
Wes Montgomery:The Verve Jazz Sides | Verve | 521690-2
Jimmy Smith:Best Of The Verve Years | Verve | 527950-2
Talkin' Jazz:Roots Of Acid Jazz | Verve | 529580-2
Jimmy Smith With Orchestra
Jimmy Smith-Talkin' Verve | Verve | 531563-2
Jimmy Smith With The Claus Ogerman Orchestra
Any Number Can Win | Verve | 557447-2
Jimmy Smith With The Johnny Pate Orchestra
Jimmy Smith-Talkin' Verve | Verve | 531563-2
Jimmy Smith With The Oliver Nelson Orchestra
Verve Jazz Masters 29:Jimmy Smith | Verve | 521855-2
Jimmy Smith:Best Of The Verve Years | Verve | 527950-2
Jimmy Smith-Talkin' Verve | Verve | 531563-2
Peter & The Wolf | Verve | 547264-2
Joe Turner With Orchestra
Atlantic Jazz: Kansas City | Atlantic | 7567-81701-2
Joe Williams With The Frank Hunter Orchestra
Planet Jazz:Joe Williams | Planet Jazz | 2165370-2
Joe Williams With The Jimmy Jones Orchestra
Planet Jazz:Joe Williams | Planet Jazz | 2165370-2
Johnny Hodges Orchestra
Verve Jazz Masters 35:Johnny Hodges | Verve | 521857-2
Junior Mance Trio & Orchestra
That Lovin' Feelin' | Milestone | MCD 47097-2
Kenny Burrell Quintet
Stormy Monday Blues | Fantasy | FCD 24767-2
Kenny Burrell With The Don Sebesky Orchestra
Verve Jazz Masters 45:Kenny Burrell | Verve | 527652-2
Blues-The Common Ground | Verve | 589101-2
Lalo Schifrin And His Orchestra
Tin Tin Deo | Fresh Sound Records | FSR-CD 319
Lee Ritenour Group
Jazzrock-Anthology Vol.3:Fusion | Zounds | CD 27100555
Lionel Hampton And His Orchestra
Planet Jazz:Big Bands | Planet Jazz | 2169649-2
Lionel Hampton:Flying Home | Dreyfus Jazz Line | FDM 36735-2
Lionel Hampton Orchestra
The Big Bands Vol.1:The Snader Telescriptions | Storyville | 4960043
Louis Armstrong And His Orchestra
What A Wonderful World | MCA | MCD 01876
Miles Davis With Gil Evans & His Orchestra
Miles Davis At Carnegie Hall | CBS | CK 65027
This Is Jazz:Miles Davis Plays Ballads | CBS | CK 65038
Porgy And Bess | CBS | CK 65141
Quiet Nights | CBS | CK 65293
Milt Jackson Orchestra
To Bags...With Love:Memorial Album | Pablo | 2310967-2
Milt Jackson Birthday Celebration | Fantasy | FANCD 6079-2
Big Bags | Original Jazz Classics | OJCCD 366-2(RLP 9429)
Milt Jackson With Strings
To Bags...With Love:Memorial Album | Pablo | 2310967-2
Nina Simone And Orchestra
Planet Jazz:Nina Simone | Planet Jazz | 2165372-2
Oliver Nelson And His Orchestra
Verve Jazz Masters Vol.60:The Collection | Verve | 529866-2
Oscar Peterson With Orchestra
With Respect To Nat | Verve | 557486-2
Oscar Peterson With The Ernie Wilkins Orchestra
Verve Jazz Masters 16:Oscar Peterson | Verve | 516320-2
Phil Woods Quartet With Orchestra & Strings
Round Trip | Verve | 559804-2
Prestige Blues-Swingers
Soul Street | Original Jazz Classics | OJCCD 987-2(NJ 8293)
Quincy Jones And His Orchestra
Talkin' Verve-Roots Of Acid Jazz:Roland Kirk | Verve | 533101-2
Verve Jazz Masters Vol.59:Toots Thielemans | Verve | 535271-2
Big Band Bossa Nova | Verve | 557913-2
Rahsaan/The Complete Mercury Recordings Of Roland Kirk | Mercury | 846630-2
The Quintessence | Impulse(MCA) | 951222-2
The Roots Of Acid Jazz | Impulse(MCA) | IMP 12042
Raul De Souza Orchestra
Cannonball Adderley Birthday Celebration | Fantasy | FANCD 6087-2
Sarah Vaughan With Orchestra
!Viva! Vaughan | Mercury | 549374-2
Sarah Vaughan Sings The Mancini Songbook | Verve | 558401-2
Sarah Vaughan With The Frank Foster Orchestra
The Antonio Carlos Jobim Songbook | Verve | 525472-2
Shirley Horn With Band
The Roots Of Acid Jazz | Impulse(MCA) | IMP 12042
Shirley Horn With Orchestra
Loads Of Love + Shirley Horn With Horns | Mercury | 843454-2
Stan Getz With The Richard Evans Orchestra
What The World Needs Now-Stan Getz Plays Bacharach And David | Verve | 557450-2

Thad Jones-Mel Lewis Orchestra
The Groove Merchant/The Second Race | Laserlight | 24656
Wes Montgomery Orchestra
Movin' Wes | Verve | 521433-2
Wes Montgomery With The Johnny Pate Orchestra
Verve Jazz Masters 14:Wes Montgomery | Verve | 519826-2
Wes Montgomery:The Verve Jazz Sides | Verve | 521690-2
Talkin' Jazz:Roots Of Acid Jazz | Verve | 529580-2
Zoot Sims And His Orchestra
The Jazz Giants Play Duke Ellington:Caravan | Prestige | PCD 24227-2

Richardson,Joe | (g)
King Curtis Band
King Curtis-Blow Man Blow | Bear Family Records | BCD 15670 CI

Richardson,John | (bperc)
Donald Byrd Orchestra
Blue Break Beats | Blue Note | 799106-2

Richardson,Richard | (tb)
Freddie Brocksieper Orchester
Drums Boogie | Bear Family Records | BCD 15988 AH

Richardson,Rodney | (b)
Count Basie And His Orchestra
Planet Jazz:Count Basie | Planet Jazz | 2152068-2
Jazz:The Essential Collection Vol.3 | IN+OUT Records | 78013-2
Count Basie's Kansas City Seven
Jazz:The Essential Collection Vol.3 | IN+OUT Records | 78013-2
Jubilee All Stars
Jazz Gallery:Lester Young Vol.2(1946-59) | RCA | 2119541-2
Kansas City Five
Lester Young:Blue Lester | Dreyfus Jazz Line | FDM 36729-2
Kansas City Seven
Jazz:The Essential Collection Vol.3 | IN+OUT Records | 78013-2
Lester Young And His Band
Jazz:The Essential Collection Vol.3 | IN+OUT Records | 78013-2
Lester Young:The Complete Aladdin Sessions | Blue Note | 832787-2
Lester Young:Blue Lester | Dreyfus Jazz Line | FDM 36729-2
Lester Young Quartet
The Complete Jazz At The Philharmonic On Verve 1944-1949 | Verve | 523893-2
Lester Young Quintet
The Art Of Saxophone | Laserlight | 24652
Jazz:The Essential Collection Vol.3 | IN+OUT Records | 78013-2
Lester Young:Blue Lester | Dreyfus Jazz Line | FDM 36729-2

Richardson,Wally | (g)
Al Sears Quintet
Swing's The Thing | Original Jazz Classics | OJCCD 838-2(SV 2018)
Buddy Johnson And His Orchestra
Buddy And Ella Johnson 1953-1964 | Bear Family Records | BCD 15479 DH
Etta Jones And Her Quartet
Hollar! | Original Jazz Classics | OJCCD 1061(PR 7284)
Something Nice | Original Jazz Classics | OJCCD 221-2(P 7194)
Jimmy Rushing And His Orchestra
Every Day I Have The Blues | Impulse(MCA) | 547967-2
Shirley Scott Quintet
Queen Of The Organ-Shirley Scott Memorial Album | Prestige | PRCD 11027-2
Sonny Stitt With Orchestra
Goin' Down Slow | Prestige | PRCD 24276-2
Willie Dixon-Memphis Slim Quintet
Windy City Blues | Stax | SCD 8612-2

Richford,Doug | (clvoc)
Doug Richford's London Jazzmen
The Golden Years Of Revival Jazz,Sampler | Storyville | 109 1001

Richie | (dr)
Howlin' Wolf London Session
Howlin' Wolf:The London Sessions | Chess | MCD 09297

Richie,Paul | (reedswoodwinds)
Dizzy Gillespie And His Orchestra
Ultimate Dizzy Gillespie | Verve | 557535-2

Richman,Abe 'Boomie' | (b-cl,ts,cl,reedssax)
Benny Goodman And His Orchestra
Great Swing Classics In Hi-Fi | Capitol | 521223-2
Billy Butterfield And His Modern Dixie Stompers
Soft Strut | Fresh Sound Records | FSR-CD 318
Cab Calloway And His Orchestra
Planet Jazz:Cab Calloway | Planet Jazz | 2161237-2
Planet Jazz:Male Jazz Vocalists | Planet Jazz | 2169657-2
Lena Horne With The Lennie Hayton Orchestra
Planet Jazz:Lena Horne | Planet Jazz | 2165373-2
Tommy Dorsey And His Orchestra
Planet Jazz:Tommy Dorsey | Planet Jazz | 2159972-2

Richman,Albert | (fr-h)
Dizzy Gillespie And His Orchestra
Verve Jazz Masters 10:Dizzy Gillespie | Verve | 516319-2
Gillespiana And Carnegie Hall Concert | Verve | 519809-2
Paul Desmond Orchestra
Planet Jazz:Jazz Saxophone | Planet Jazz | 2169653-2
Paul Desmond With Strings
Planet Jazz:Paul Desmond | Planet Jazz | 2152061-2
Desmond Blue | RCA | 2663898-2

Richman,Helen | (fl)
Andrew Rathbun Group
Jade | Fresh Sound Records | FSNT 076 CD

Richman,Jeff | (g)
Terri Lyne Carrington Group
Jazz Is A Spirit | ACT | 9408-2

Richmond,Abraham | (reedsts)
Louis Armstrong With Gordon Jenkins And His Orchestra And Choir
Satchmo In Style | Verve | 549594-2
Ambassador Louis Armstrong Vol.17:Moments To Remember(1952-1956) | Ambassador | CLA 1917

Richmond,Bill | (dr)
Ella Fitzgerald With The Nelson Riddle Orchestra
The Best Of The Song Books:The Ballads | Verve | 521867-2
Get Happy! | Verve | 523321-2

Richmond,Boomie | (reedsts)
Muggsy Spanier And His V-Disc All Stars
Muggsy Spanier And Bud Freeman:V-Discs 1944-45 | Jazz Unlimited | JUCD 2049

Richmond,Dannie | (dr,vocdr-solo)
Bennie Wallace Quartet
Bennie Wallace Plays Monk | Enja | ENJ-3091 2
Bennie Wallace Trio
Bennie Wallace Plays Monk | Enja | ENJ-3091 2
Charles Mingus And His Orchestra
Charles Mingus-Passion Of A Man:The Complete Atlantic Recordings 1956-1961 | Atlantic | 8122-72871-2
The Complete Town Hall Concert | Blue Note | 828353-2
Charles Mingus Group
The Jazz Life! | Candid | CCD 79019
Candid Dolphy | Candid | CCD 79033
Mysterious Blues | Candid | CCD 79042
Mingus Ah Um | CBS | CK 65512
Mingus Dynasty | CBS | CK 65513
Charles Mingus Jazz Workshop
Tonight At Noon | Atlantic | 7567-80793-2
Rhino Presents The Atlantic Jazz Gallery | Atlantic | 8122-71257-2
Blues & Roots | Atlantic | 8122-75205-2
The Clown | Atlantic | 8122-75358-2
Charles Mingus Orchestra
Tijuana Moods(The Complete Edition) | RCA | 2663840-2
Charles Mingus:Pre-Bird(Mingus Revisited) | Verve | 538636-2
Three Or Four Shades Of Blues | Atlantic | 7567-81403-2
Cumbia & Jazz Fusion | Atlantic | 8122-71785-2
The Very Best Of Charles Mingus | Rhino | 8122-79988-2
Mingus Mingus Mingus | Impulse(MCA) | 951170-2
The Black Saint And The Sinner Lady | Impulse(MCA) | 951174-2
Charles Mingus:The Complete 1959 Columbia Recordings | CBS | C3K 65145

Mingus | Candid | CCD 79021
Charles Mingus Quartet
Mingus At Antibes | Atlantic | 7567-90532-2
Charles Mingus Presents Charles Mingus | Candid | CCD 79005
Mingus | Candid | CCD 79021
Right Now | Original Jazz Classics | OJCCD 237-2
Charles Mingus Quintet
Mingus At Antibes | Atlantic | 7567-90532-2
Changes One | Rhino | 8122-71403-2
Changes Two | Rhino | 8122-71404-2
Charles Mingus-Passion Of A Man:The Complete Atlantic Recordings 1956-1961 | Atlantic | 8122-72871-2
The Very Best Of Charles Mingus | Rhino | 8122-79988-2
Right Now | Original Jazz Classics | OJCCD 237-2
Charles Mingus Quintet With Bud Powell
Mingus At Antibes | Atlantic | 7567-90532-2
Charles Mingus-Passion Of A Man:The Complete Atlantic Recordings 1956-1961 | Atlantic | 8122-72871-2
Charles Mingus Quintet With Roland Kirk
Tonight At Noon | Atlantic | 7567-80793-2
Charles Mingus-Passion Of A Man:The Complete Atlantic Recordings 1956-1961 | Atlantic | 8122-72871-2
The Very Best Of Charles Mingus | Rhino | 8122-79988-2
Charles Mingus Septet
Charles Mingus:The Complete 1959 Columbia Recordings | CBS | C3K 65145
Charles Mingus Sextet
Changes Two | Rhino | 8122-71404-2
Eric Dolphy Birthday Celebration | Fantasy | FANCD 6085-2
Town Hall Concert 1964, Vol.1 | Original Jazz Classics | OJCCD 042-2
Charles Mingus Workshop
Charles Mingus-The Complete Debut Recordings | Debut | 12 DCD 4402-2
Chet Baker Quartet
Sings/It Could Happen To You | Original Jazz Classics | OJC20 303-2
Dannie Richmond Quintet
Three Or Four Shades Of Dannie Richmond Quintet | Tutu Records | 888120-2*
Danny Richmond
Mysterious Blues | Candid | CCD 79042
Duke Jordan Trio
Flight To Norway | Steeplechase | SCCD 31543
Jimmy Knepper Quintet
Charles Mingus-The Complete Debut Recordings | Debut | 12 DCD 4402-2

Richmond,Kim | (as,fl,cl,ss,piccolo,reeds,saxts)
Eric Dolphy Quartet With The University Of Illinois Big Band
The Illinois Concert | Blue Note | 499826-2

Richmond,Mike | (bel-b)
George Gruntz Concert Jazz Band
Blues 'N Dues Et Cetera | Enja | ENJ-6072 2
Miles Davis With Gil Evans Orchestra, The George Gruntz Concert Jazz Band And Guests
Miles & Quincy Live At Montreux | Warner | 9362-45221-2
Stan Getz Quintet
Sony Jazz Collection:Stan Getz | CBS | 488623-2
Theo Bleckman & Kirk Nurock Quartet
Looking-Glass River | Traumton Records | 2412-2

Richter,Andreas | (tb)
Eberhard Weber Orchestra
Orchestra | ECM | 1374

Richter,Gerc | (tp)
Freddie Brocksieper And His Boys
Freddie's Boogie Blues | Bear Family Records | BCD 16388 AH

Richter,Jürgen | (b)
Corinne Chatel Quintet
Ma Vie En Rose | Edition Collage | EC 525-2

Richter,Kay | (dr)
Wolfgang Schmid's Kick
No Filters | TipToe | TIP-888809 2

Richter,Otto | (v)
Bitkicks
Kickbit Information | ATM Records | ATM 3823-AH

Rickman,Patrick | (tpperc)
Antonio Hart Group
Here I Stand | Impulse(MCA) | 951208-2
Craig Bailey Band
A New Journey | Candid | CCD 79725

Rickman,Sean | (dr)
Steve Coleman And Five Elements
Genesis & The Opening Of The Way | RCA | 2152934-2
The Sonic Language Of Myth | RCA | 2164123-2
Steve Coleman And The Council Of Balance
Genesis & The Opening Of The Way | RCA | 2152934-2

Ricks,Jeanne | (voc)
Steve Coleman And Five Elements
The Sonic Language Of Myth | RCA | 2164123-2

Ricotti,Frank | (as,vib,perccongas)
Dee Dee Bridgewater With Orchestra
Dear Ella | Verve | 539102-2

Riddick,Clyde | (voc)
Golden Gate Quartet
Americans Swinging In Paris:Golden Gate Quartet | EMI Records | 539659-2
From Spriritual To Swing Vol.2 | EMI Records | 780573-2
Spirituals To Swing 1955-69 | EMI Records | 791569-2
Golden Gate Quartet With The Martial Solal Orchestra
Americans Swinging In Paris:Golden Gate Quartet | EMI Records | 539659-2
From Spriritual To Swing Vol.2 | EMI Records | 780573-2

Riddle,Christopher | (b-tb)
Ella Fitzgerald With The Nelson Riddle Orchestra
Dream Dancing | Original Jazz Classics | OJCCD 1072-2(2310814)

Riddle,Nelson | (arr,ld,cond,tbvoc)
Ella Fitzgerald-First Lady Of Song | Verve | 517898-2
The Best Of The Song Books | Verve | 519804-2
Verve Jazz Masters 6:Ella Fitzgerald | Verve | 519822-2
The Best Of The Song Books:The Ballads | Verve | 521867-2
Get Happy! | Verve | 523321-2
Oh Lady Be Good:The Best Of The Gershwin Songbook | Verve | 529581-2
Love Songs:The Best Of The Song Books | Verve | 531762-2
Ella Fitzgerald Sings The Johnny Mercer Songbook | Verve | 539057-2
The Silver Collection: Ella Fitzgerald-The Songbooks | Verve | 823445-2 PMS
For The Love Of Ella Fitzgerald | Verve | 841765-2
Dream Dancing | Original Jazz Classics | OJCCD 1072-2(2310814)
Louis Jordan With The Nelson Riddle Orchestra
Louis Jordan-Let The Good Times Roll: The Complete Decca Recordings 1938-1954 | Bear Family Records | BCD 15557 IH
Nelson Riddle And His Orchestra
Changing Colors | MPS | 9814794
Communication | MPS | 9814795
Oscar Peterson Trio With The Nelson Riddle Orchestra
Verve Jazz Masters 16:Oscar Peterson | Verve | 516320-2
The Silver Collection: Oscar Peterson | Verve | 823447-2 PMS
Tommy Dorsey And His Orchestra
Planet Jazz:Tommy Dorsey | Planet Jazz | 2159972-2
Planet Jazz:Jazz Greatest Hits | Planet Jazz | 2169648-2

Riddles,David Willard | (reeds)
Herbie Hancock Group
Sunlight | CBS | 486570-2

Ridley,Larry | (b)
Cedar Walton Quartet
The Story Of Jazz Piano | Laserlight | 24653
Dexter Gordon Quartet
Dexter Gordon Birthday Celebration | Fantasy | FANCD 6082-2

The Panther | Original Jazz Classics | OJCCD 770-2(P 10030)
Duke Ellington Orchestra
Continuum | Fantasy | FCD 24765-2
Freddie Hubbard Sextet
Hub Cap | Blue Note | 542302-2
Hank Mobley Quintet
Blue Bossa | Blue Note | 795590-2
Horace Silver Quintet
Horace Silver Retrospective | Blue Note | 495576-2
Jackie McLean Quintet
A Blue Conception | Blue Note | 534254-2
Jacknife | Blue Note | 540535-2
Jackie McLean Sextet
Jacknife | Blue Note | 540535-2
Lucky Thompson Quartet
The Art Of Saxophone | Laserlight | 24652
Red Garland Trio
The Nearness Of You | Original Jazz Classics | OJCCD 1003-2(JLP 962)
Roy Haynes Quartet
Cymbalism | Original Jazz Classics | OJCCD 1079-2(NJ 8287)

Riebeek,Peter | (voc)
Pili-Pili
Hotel Babo | JA & RO | JARO 4147-2

Rieck,Marcus | (dr)
Lars Duppler Sextet
Palindrome 6tet | Jazz Haus Musik | JHM 0131 CD
Steve Klink Trio
Feels Like Home | Minor Music | 801092
Places To Come From,Places To Go | Minor Music | 801098

Riedel,Georg | (b)
Bengt Hallberg Quartet
Hallberg's Hot Accordion In The Foreground | Phontastic | NCD 7532
Bengt-Arne Wallin Orchestra
The Birth+Rebirth Of Swedish Folk Jazz | ACT | 9254-2
Lars Gullin Octet
Lars Gullin 1955/56 Vol.1 | Dragon | DRCD 224
Lars Gullin Quartet
Lars Gullin 1955/56 Vol.1 | Dragon | DRCD 224
Lars Gullin 1953,Vol.2:Moden Sounds | Dragon | DRCD 234
Lars Gullin Quintet
Lars Gullin 1955/56 Vol.1 | Dragon | DRCD 224
Lars Gullin 1953,Vol.2:Moden Sounds | Dragon | DRCD 234

Riedl,Franz Xaver | (bs)
Fred Bunge Star Band
Deutsches Jazz Fesival 1954/1955 | Bear Family Records | BCD 15430

Riedler,Ilse | (ts)
European Jazz Youth Orchestra
Swinging Europe 3 | dacapo | DCCD 9461

Riekenberg,Dave | (bs,flts)
The New Jazz Composers Octet
First Step Into Reality | Fresh Sound Records | FSNT 059 CD

Riel,Alex | (drperc)
Abdullah Ibrahim With The NDR Big Band
Ekapa Lodumo | TipToe | TIP-888840 2
Ben Webster Quartet
My Man-Live At The Montmartre | Steeplechase | SCCD 31008
Ben Webster With The Kenny Drew Trio
The Art Of Saxophone | Laserlight | 24652
The Story Of Jazz Piano | Laserlight | 24653
Bob Brookmeyer Quartet
Old Friends | Storyville | STCD 8292
Caecilie Norby With Band
My Corner Of The Sky | Blue Note | 853422-2
Chet Baker With The NDR-Bigband
Chet Baker-The Legacy Vol.1 | Enja | ENJ-9021 2
Dexter Gordon Quartet
Swiss Nights-Vol. 1 | Steeplechase | SCCD 31050
Swiss Nights Vol.2 | Steeplechase | SCCD 31090
Swiss Nights Vol.3 | Steeplechase | SCCD 31110
Dexter Gordon With The Kenny Drew Trio
Loose Walk | Steeplechase | SCCD 36032
Joe Pass With The NDR Big Band
Joe Pass In Hamburg | ACT | 9100-2
NDR Big Band With Guests
50 Years Of NDR Big Band:Bravissimo II | ACT | 9259-2
Niels-Henning Orsted-Pedersen Trio
Those Who Were | Verve | 533232-2
Stephane Grappelli Trio
Verve Jazz Masters 11:Stéphane Grappelli | Verve | 516758-2
Thomas Clausen Trio
She Touched Me | M.A Music | A 628-2
Thomas Clausen Trio With Gary Burton
Flowers And Trees | M.A Music | A 805-2
Café Noir | M.A Music | INTCD 004
Ulf Meyer & Martin Wind Group
Kinnings | Storyville | STCD 8374

Riemer,Susanne | (tp)
The United Women's Orchestra
The Blue One | Jazz Haus Musik | JHM 0099 CD

Rieppi,Pablo | (perc)
Paquito D'Rivera Group With The Absolute Ensemble
Habanera | Enja | ENJ-9395 2

Ries,Barry | (tpfl-h)
Joe Lovano Nonet
On This Day At The Vanguard | Blue Note | 590950-2
Steve Swallow Quintet
Always Pack Your Uniform On Top | Watt | XtraWatt/10(543506-2)

Ries,Tanja | (voc)
Brass Attack
Brecht Songs | Tutu Records | 888190-2*

Rieser,Dan | (dr)
Bill McHenry Quartet
Rest Stop | Fresh Sound Records | FSNT 033 CD
Chris Cheek Sextet
A Girl Named Joe | Fresh Sound Records | FSNT 032 CD

Riessler,Michael | (alto-cl,as,b-cl,sopranino,cl)
Michael Riessler & Singer Pur with Vincent Courtois
Ahi Vita | ACT | 9417-2
Michael Riessler And The Ensemble 13
Momentum Mobile | Enja | ENJ-9003 2
Michael Riessler Group
Orange | ACT | 9274-2
Heloise | Wergo | WER 8008-2
Tentations D'Abélard | Wergo | WER 8009-2
Pata Music Meets Arfi
News Of Roi Ubu | Pata Musik | PATA 10 CD
Trio Clastrier-Riessler-Rizzo
Palude | Wergo | WER 8010-2

Riestra,Pepito | (perc)
Dizzy Gillespie Septet
The Antonio Carlos Jobim Songbook | Verve | 525472-2
Elek Bacsik Quartet
Jazz In Paris:Elek Baczik | EmArCy | 542231-2

Rifbjerk,Frands | (drperc)
Carsten Dahl Trio
Will You Make My Soup Hot & Silver | Storyville | STCD 4203
Joaquin Chacón-Uffe Markussen European Quintet
Time | Fresh Sound Records | FSNT 051 CD

Rifkin,Joshua | (p-solo)
Joshua Rifkin
Scott Joplin Piano Rags | Nonesuch | 7559-79159-2

Riga Festival Orchestra |
Terje Rypdal With The Riga Festival Orchestra
Double Concerto/5th Symphony | ECM | 1567(559964-2)

Rigert,Stephan | (drperc)
Asita Hamidi & Arcobaleno
Mosaic | Laika Records | 8695067

Riggins,Emmanuel | (el-p,clavinetorg)
Grant Green Orchestra
Grant Green:Blue Breakbeat | Blue Note | 494705-2
Blue Breaks Beats Vol.2 | Blue Note | 789907-2
So Blue So Funky-Heroes Of The Hammond | Blue Note | 796563-2
Grant Green Sextet
Grant Green:Blue Breakbeat | Blue Note | 494705-2

Riggins,Karriem | (dr)
Eric Reed Quartet
Musicale | Impulse(MCA) | 951196-2
Eric Reed Quintet
Musicale | Impulse(MCA) | 951196-2
Roy Hargrove Quartet
Family | Verve | 527630-2

Riggs,Chuck | (dr)
Marty Grosz And His Swinging Fools
Ring Dem Bells | Nagel-Heyer | CD 022
The Second Sampler | Nagel-Heyer | NHR SP 6

Rigou,Marcel | (b)
Stan Getz With Ib Glindemann And His Orchestra
Stan Getz In Europe | Laserlight | 24657

Riikonen,Matti | (tp)
Edward Vesala Ensemble
Ode Of The Death Of Jazz | ECM | 1413(843196-2)
Edward Vesala Nordic Gallery
Sound & Fury | ECM | 1541
Edward Vesala Sound And Fury
Invisible Strom | ECM | 1461

Riina,Faro | (tp)
Orchestra Jazz Siciliana
Orchestra Jazz Siciliana Plays The Music Of Carla Bley | Watt | XtraWatt/4

Riina,Nico | (tp)

Riis,Jacob | (tb)
Copenhagen Art Ensemble
Angels' Share | dacapo | DCCD 9452
The Orchestra
New Skies | dacapo | DCCD 9463

Riis,Jesper | (tpfl-h)
Copenhagen Art Ensemble
Shape To Twelve | dacapo | DCCD 9430
Angels' Share | dacapo | DCCD 9452
Jens Winther And The Danish Radio Jazz Orchestra
Angels | dacapo | DCCD 9442
The Crossover Ensemble
The River:Image Of Time And Life | dacapo | DCCD 9434
The Danish Radio Jazz Orchestra
Nice Work | dacapo | DCCD 9446

Riisnaes,Knut | (fl,ss,tssax)
Ketil Bjornstad Group
Early Years | EmArCy | 013271-2

Riley,Ben | (drperc)
Abdullah Ibrahim And Ekaya
Water From An Ancient Well | TipToe | TIP-888812 2
Abdullah Ibrahim Septet
No Fear, No Die(S'en Fout La Mort):Original Soundtrack | TipToe | TIP-888815 2
Alice Coltrane Quartet
A Monastic Trio | Impulse(MCA) | 951267-2
Alice Coltrane Quintet
Ptah The El Daoud | Impulse(MCA) | 951201-2
Duke Ellington Trio
Highlights From The Duke Ellington Centennial Edition | RCA | 2663672-2
Eddie Harris Quartet
There Was A Time-Echo Of Harlem | Enja | ENJ-6068 2
Eddie Lockjaw Davis Orchestra
Afro-Jaws | Original Jazz Classics | OJCCD 403-2(RLP 9373)
Eddie Lockjaw Davis-Johnny Griffin Quintet
Blues Up And Down | Milestone | MCD 47084-2
Battle Stations | Original Jazz Classics | OJCCD 1085(P7282)
The Jazz Giants Play Cole Porter:Night And Day | Prestige | PCD 24203-2
The Prestige Legacy Vol.2:Battles Of Saxes | Prestige | PCD 24252-2
Freddy Cole With Band
Le Grand Freddy:Freddy Cole Sings The Music Of Michel Legrand | Fantasy | FCD 9683-2
Freddy Cole With The Cedar Walton Trio
Love Makes The Changes | Fantasy | FCD 9681-2
Freddy Cole With The Cedar Walton Trio And Grover Washington Jr.
Love Makes The Changes | Fantasy | FCD 9681-2
Freddy Cole With The Eric Alexander Band
Love Makes The Changes | Fantasy | FCD 9681-2
Johnny Griffin Quartet
The Kerry Dancers | Original Jazz Classics | OJCCD 1952-2(RLP 9420)
Johnny Griffin-Eddie Lockjaw Davis Quintet
Tough Tenors | Original Jazz Classics | OJCCD 1094-2(JLP 931)
Kenny Barron Trio
Live at Bradley's | EmArCy | 549099-2
Ricky Ford Quartet
Manhattan Blues | Candid | CCD 79036
Ebony Rhapsody | Candid | CCD 79053
Ron Carter Group
Peg Leg | Original Jazz Classics | OJCCD 621-2
Ron Carter Quartet
Pick 'Em/Super Strings | Milestone | MCD 47090-2
Sonny Rollins Group
What's New? | RCA | 2179626-2
Sonny Rollins Quartet
Planet Jazz:Sonny Rollins | Planet Jazz | 2152062-2
The Bridge | RCA | 2179625-2
What's New? | RCA | 2179626-2
Thelonious Monk Quartet
Paris Jazz Concert:Theloniuos Monk And His Quartet | Laserlight | 17250
Monk At Newport 1963 & 1965 | CBS | C2K 63905
Live At The Jazz Workshop-Complete | CBS | C2K 65189
Live At The It Club:Complete | CBS | C2K 65288
Greatest Hits | CBS | CK 65422
MONK. | CBS | CK 86564
Wild Bill Moore Quintet
Bottom Groove | Milestone | MCD 47098-2

Riley,Doug | (porg)
Hugh Marsh Duo/Quartet/Orchestra
The Bear Walks | VeraBra Records | CDVBR 2011-2

Riley,Herlin | (dr,perc,voctambourine)
Bennie Wallace Quartet
Bennie Wallace In Berlin | Enja | ENJ-9425 2
David Ostwald's Gully Low Jazz Band
Blues In Your Heart | Nagel-Heyer | CD 051
Lincoln Center Jazz Orchestra
Big Train | CBS | CK 69860
Mark Whitfield Quartet
The Marksman | Warner | 7599-26321-2
Wycliffe Gordon Group
Slidin' Home | Nagel-Heyer | CD 2001
The Search | Nagel-Heyer | CD 2007
Ellington For Lovers | Nagel-Heyer | NH 1009
Blues Of Summer | Nagel-Heyer | NH 1011
Wycliffe Gordon Quintet
The Joyride | Nagel-Heyer | CD 2032
Wynton Marsalis Group
Standard Time Vol.4:Marsalis Plays Monk | CBS | CK 67503
Standard Time Vol.6:Mr.Jelly Lord | CBS | CK 69872

Riley,Herman | (alto-fl,ts,cl,fl,as,ss,bsreeds)
Bobby Bryant Orchestra
Deep Blue-The United States Of Mind | Blue Note | 521152-2
Jimmy Smith All Stars
Jimmy Smith:Dot Com Blues | Blue Thumb | 543978-2
Ruth Brown With Orchestra
Fine And Mellow | Fantasy | FCD 9663-2

Riley,Howard | (pp-solo)
Howard Riley Trio
The Day Will Come | CBS | 494434-2

Riley,Jim | (asperc)
Miles Davis Group
Bitches Brew | CBS | C2K 65774

Riley,John | (b,drperc)
Hubert Nuss Trio
The Shimmering Colours Of The Stained Glass | Green House Music | CD 1008
Miles Davis With Gil Evans Orchestra, The George Gruntz Concert Jazz Band And Guests
Miles & Quincy Live At Montreux | Warner | 9362-45221-2
Rolf Römer Quartet
Tesoro | Jazz 4 Ever Records:Jazz Network | J4E 4743
Rolf Römer Trio
Tesoro | Jazz 4 Ever Records:Jazz Network | J4E 4743
Woody Herman And His Orchestra
Verve Jazz Masters 54:Woody Herman | Verve | 529903-2

Rill,Santiago Garzon | (percvoc)
Conjunto Clave Y Guaguanco
Dejala En La Puntica | TipToe | TIP-888829 2

Riney,Sam | (as,fl,alto-fl,sax,ss,tssynth)
Herbie Hancock Group With String Quartet,Woodwinds And Brass
Herbie Hancock The New Standards | Verve | 527715-2
Herbie Hancock Group With Woodwinds And Brass
Herbie Hancock The New Standards | Verve | 527715-2

Ringkjobing,Bjorn | (tp)
Marilyn Mazur With Ars Nova And The Copenhagen Art Ensemble
Jordsange | dacapo | DCCD 9454

Ringwood,Ron | (percvoc)
Ron Ringwood's Crosscut Bluesband
Earth Tones | Organic Music | ORGM 9722

Rinkevicius,Gintaras | (cond)
Egberto Gismonti With The Lithuanian State Symphony Orchestra
Meeting Point | ECM | 1586(533681-2)

Rinkin,Alvin | (viola)
Johnny Hartman And His Orchestra
Unforgettable | Impulse(MCA) | IMP 11522

Rinne,Tapani | (cl,b-cl,ssts)
Edward Vesala Group
Lumi | ECM | 1339
Edward Vesala Nordic Gallery
Sound & Fury | ECM | 1541

Rios,Carlos | (el-g,percg)
Chick Corea Electric Band
The Chick Corea Electric Band | GRP | GRP 95352
Dave Grusin Group
Migration | GRP | GRP 95922

Ripp,Brian | (sax)
Buddy Childers Big Band
Just Buddy's | Candid | CCD 79761

Rippingtons,The |
The Rippingtons
Tourist In Paradise | GRP | GRP 95882

Risavy,Rudi | (fl)
Art Van Damme Group
State Of Art | MPS | 841413-2

Risenhoover,Max | (b,dr,perc-sequencing,cymbal)
The Brecker Brothers
Return Of The Brecker Brothers | GRP | GRP 96842

Riskin,Itzy | (p)
Frankie Trumbauer And His Orchestra
Jazz:The Essential Collection Vol.2 | IN+OUT Records | 78012-2

Riso,Pete | (dr)
Cal Tjader Sextet
Cuban Fantasy | Fantasy | FCD 24777-2

Rissanen,Antti | (tb)
European Jazz Youth Orchestra
Swinging Europe 1 | dacapo | DCCD 9449
Swinging Europe 2 | dacapo | DCCD 9450

Rissanen,Marja-Liisa | (viola)
Terje Rypdal With The Borealis Ensemble
Q.E.D. | ECM | 1474

Rissi,Mathias | (as,ldts)
Q4 Orchester Project
Lyon's Brood | Creative Works Records | CW CD 1018-3
Yavapai | Creative Works Records | CW CD 1028-2
Rissi-Mazzola-Geisser
Fuego | Creative Works Records | CW CD 1029-2

Rissmann,Gunther | (b)
Horst Faigle's Jazzkrement
Gans Normal | Jazz 4 Ever Records:Jazz Network | J4E 4748
Pete Yellin Quartet
Pete Yellin's European Connection:Live! | Jazz 4 Ever Records:Jazz Network | J4E 4722

Ritchie,Larry | (dr)
Ray Draper Quintet
John Coltrane-The Prestige Recordings | Prestige | 16 PCD 4405-2

Ritenour,Lee | (el-g,12-string-g,synth,g,b-synth)
Al Jarreau With Band
All Fly Home | Warner | 7599-27362-2
David Fathead Newman Septet
Jazzin' Vol.2: The Music Of Stevie Wonder | Fantasy | FANCD 6088-2
Diane Schuur With Orchestra
The Best Of Diane Schuur | GRP | GRP 98882
Dizzy Gillespie With The Lalo Schifrin Orchestra
Free Ride | Original Jazz Classics | OJCCD 784-2(2310794)
Fourplay
Fourplay | Warner | 7599-26656-2
Between The Sheets | Warner | 9362-45340-2
Gato Barbieri Orchestra
Latino America | Impulse(MCA) | 952236-2
Joe Henderson And His Orchestra
Joe Henderson:The Milestone Years | Milestone | 8MCD 4413-2
Lee Ritenour Group
Jazzrock-Anthology Vol.3:Fusion | Zounds | CD 27100555
Rio | GRP | GRP 95242
Festival | GRP | GRP 95702
Stolen Moments | GRP | GRP 96152
Lee Ritenour Sextet
Alive In L.A. | GRP | GRP 98822
Lee Ritenour With Special Guests
Festival International De Jazz De Montreal | Spectra | 9811661
Paulinho Da Costa Orchestra
Agora | Original Jazz Classics | OJCCD 630-2(2310785)
Sarah Vaughan And Her Band
Songs Of The Beatles | Atlantic | 16037-2

Ritscher,Karen | (viola)
Steve Kuhn With Strings
Promises Kept | ECM | 1815(0675222)

Ritter,Bertram | (dr)
Heinz Sauer 4tet
Exchange 2 | free flow music | ffm 0998

Ritz,Ellen | (voc)
Benny Waters & Jan Jankeje
Let's Talk About Jazz | G&J Records | GJ 2009 Maxi-CD
Benny Waters Sextet
A' Portrait Of Jan Jankeje | Jazzpoint | JP 1054 CD

Ritz,Lyke | (ukelele)
Lyke Ritz Quartet
How About Uke? | Verve | 0760942
Lyke Ritz Trio
How About Uke? | Verve | 0760942
Lyle Ritz Quartet
How About Uke? | Verve | 0760942

Ritzenhöff,Jörg | (org,recitation,pvoc)
Dirk Raulf Group
Die Welt Ist Immer Wieder Schön | Poise | Poise 03
Kodexx Sentimental
Das Digitale Herz | Poise | Poise 02

Rivera,Dave | (p)
Cab Calloway And His Cab Jivers
Planet Jazz:Cab Calloway | Planet Jazz | 2161237-2
Ike Quebec Quintet
The Blue Note Swingtets | Blue Note | 495697-2

Rivera,Joe | (tp)
Conexion Latina
La Conexión | Enja | ENJ-9065 2
Dusko Goykovich Big Band
Balkan Connection | Enja | ENJ-9047 2

Rivera,Joseph | (shakerstambourine)
Stanley Turrentine Orchestra
The Spoiler | Blue Note | 853359-2

Rivera,Mario | (alto-fl,ts,b-cl,bs,fl,ss,piccolo)
Dizzy Gillespie And The United Nation Orchestra
7.Zelt-Musik-Festival:Jazz Events | Zounds | CD 2730001
Machito And His Orchestra
Afro-Cuban Jazz Moods | Original Jazz Classics | OJC20 447-2

Rivera,Martin | (b)
Dexter Gordon Quartet
Dexter Gordon Birthday Celebration | Fantasy | FANCD 6082-2
Kenny Burrell Quintet
Soul Call | Original Jazz Classics | OJCCD 846-2(P 7315)
Sonny Stitt-Sal Salvador Quintet
Newport Jazz Festival 1958,July 3rd-6th Vol.2:Mulligan The Main Man | Phontastic | NCD 8814

Rivera,Ramon | (congasperc)
Henry Mancini And His Orchestra
Combo! | RCA | 2147794-2
Victor Feldman Orchestra
Latinsville | Contemporary | CCD 9005-2

Rivera,Ray | (dr,gperc)
Jack Costanzo Group
Latin Fever:The Wild Rhythms Of Jack Costanza | Capitol | 590955-2

Rivero,René Marino | (bandoneon)
René Marino Rivero
Che Bandoneon | ALISO Records | AL 1020

Rivers,Craig | (fl,tsss)
Mongo Santamaria And His Band
Brazilian Sunset | Candid | CCD 79703

Rivers,Sam | (b-cl,ts,fl,ss,reeds,arr,p,voicesax)
Bobby Hutcherson Sextet
A Blue Conception | Blue Note | 534254-2
Dialogue | Blue Note | 535586-2
David Holland Quartet
Conference Of The Birds | ECM | 1027(829373-2)
Dick Griffin Septet
The Eighth Wonder & More | Konnex Records | KCD 5059
Larry Young Quartet
So Blue So Funky-Heroes Of The Hammond | Blue Note | 796563-2
Roots
Salutes The Saxophone | IN+OUT Records | 7016-2
Salutes The Saxophones: Tributes To Gene Ammons, Eric Dolphy, Coleman Hawkins And Charlie Parker | IN+OUT Records | 7016-3
Jazz Unlimited | IN+OUT Records | 7017-2
Stablemates | IN+OUT Records | 7021-2
Sam Rivers Orchestra
Crystals | Impulse(MCA) | 589760-2
Sam Rivers Quartet
A Blue Conception | Blue Note | 534254-2
Fuchsia Swing Song | Blue Note | 593874-2
Tony Williams Lifetime
Lifetime | Blue Note | 499004-2

Rizzi,Tony | (g)
Herbie Mann Sextet
Verve Jazz Masters Vol.60:The Collection | Verve | 529866-2
Verve Jazz Masters 56:Herbie Mann | Verve | 529901-2
June Christy With The Pete Rugolo Orchestra
Something Cool(The Complete Mono & Stereo Versions) | Capitol | 534069-2

Rizzo,Carlo | (bendir,tambourin,perc,tambourello)
Gianluigi Trovesi Nonet
Round About A Midsummer's Dream | Enja | ENJ-9384 2
Michael Riessler Group
Heloise | Wergo | WER 8008-2
Tentations D'Abélard | Wergo | WER 8009-2
Trio Clastrier-Riessler-Rizzo
Palude | Wergo | WER 8010-2

Rizzo,Joe | (arr)
Stan Kenton And His Orchestra
Stan Kenton-The Formative Years | Decca | 589489-2

Rizzotto,Dalton | (tb)
Harry James And His Orchestra
The Legends Of Swing | Laserlight | 24659

Roach,Freddie | (org)
Freddie Roach Quartet
So Blue So Funky-Heroes Of The Hammond | Blue Note | 796563-2
Freddie Roach Quintet
Good Move | Blue Note | 524551-2
Freddie Roach Trio
Good Move | Blue Note | 524551-2

Roach,Max | (bass-dr,concert-snare-dr,cymbals)
Abbey Lincoln And Her Orchestra
Straight Ahead | Candid | CCD 79015
Abbey Lincoln With Her Quartet
That's Him! | Original Jazz Classics | OJCCD 085-2
Abbey Lincoln With Her Quintet
Sonny Rollins-The Freelance Years:The Complete Riverside & Contemporary Recordings | Riverside | 5 RCD 4427-2
That's Him! | Original Jazz Classics | OJCCD 085-2
Abbey Lincoln With The Max Roach Quintet
Abbey Is Blue | Original Jazz Classics | OJC20 069-2(RLP 1153)
Abbey Lincoln With The Max Roach Sextet
Abbey Is Blue | Original Jazz Classics | OJC20 069-2(RLP 1153)
Al Cohn Quartet
The Birdlanders Vol.2 | Original Jazz Classics | OJCCD 1931-2
All Star Live Jam Session
Brownie-The Complete EmArCy Recordings Of Clifford Brown | EmArCy | 838306-2
Benny Golson Sextet
The J.J.Johnson Memorial Album | Prestige | PRCD 11025-2
Billy Taylor Trio
Charles Mingus-The Complete Debut Recordings | Debut | 12 DCD 4402-2
Booker Little Sextet
Out Front | Candid | CCD 79027
Candid Dolphy | Candid | CCD 79033
Bud Powell Orchestra
Bebop | Pablo | PACD 2310978-2
Bud Powell Trio
Charles Mingus-The Complete Debut Recordings | Debut | 12 DCD 4402-2
The Best Of Bud Powell On Verve | Verve | 523392-2
The Amazing Bud Powell Vol.1 | Blue Note | 532136-2
Jazz Giant | Verve | 543832-2
Bud Powell:Bouncing With Bud | Dreyfus Jazz Line | FDM 36725-2
Cannonball Adderley Group
Julian 'Cannonball' Adderley | EmArCy | 830381-2
Charles Mingus Orchestra
Charles Mingus:Pre-Bird(Mingus Revisited) | Verve | 538636-2
Charles Mingus Quintet
Charles Mingus-The Complete Debut Recordings | Debut | 12 DCD 4402-2
The Charles Mingus Quintet+Max Roach | Original Jazz Classics | OJC20 440-2(F 6009)
Charles Mingus-Max Roach
Mingus At The Bohemia | Original Jazz Classics | OJC20 045-2
Charlie Parker All Stars
Charlie Parker:Now's The Time | Dreyfus Jazz Line | FDM 36724-2
Charlie Parker And His Orchestra
Charlie Parker:The Best Of The Verve Years | Verve | 527815-2
The Cole Porter Songbook | Verve | 823250-2
Bird: The Complete Charlie Parker On Verve | Verve | 837141-2
Charlie Parker Quartet
Verve Jazz Masters 28:Charlie Parker Plays Standards | Verve | 521854-2
Charlie Parker:Bird's Best Bop On Verve | Verve | 527452-2
Charlie Parker:The Best Of The Verve Years | Verve | 527815-2
Charlie Parker | Verve | 539757-2
Talkin' Bird | Verve | 559859-2
Bird: The Complete Charlie Parker On Verve | Verve | 837141-2
Charlie Parker Quintet
Charlie Parker:Bird's Best Bop On Verve | Verve | 527452-2
Charlie Parker:The Best Of The Verve Years | Verve | 527815-2
Talkin' Bird | Verve | 559859-2
Bird: The Complete Charlie Parker On Verve | Verve | 837141-2
Charlie Parker:Now's The Time | Dreyfus Jazz Line | FDM 36724-2
Charlie Parker Septet
Charlie Parker | Verve | 539757-2
Talkin' Bird | Verve | 559859-2
Charlie Parker Sextet
Verve Jazz Masters 28:Charlie Parker Plays Standards | Verve | 521854-2
The Cole Porter Songbook | Verve | 823250-2
Charlie Parker With Orchestra
Charlie Parker Big Band | Verve | 559835-2
Charlie Parker With Orchestra & The Dave Lambert Singers
Verve Jazz Masters 28:Charlie Parker Plays Standards | Verve | 521854-2
Charlie Parker's Beboppers
Charlie Parker:Now's The Time | Dreyfus Jazz Line | FDM 36724-2
Chet Baker And The Lighthouse All Stars
Witch Doctor | Original Jazz Classics | OJCCD 609-2
The Jazz Giants Play Harry Warren:Lullaby Of Broadway | Prestige | PCD 24204-2
Chet Baker Quartet
At Last! | Original Jazz Classics | OJCCD 480-2
Clark Terry-Max Roach Quartet
Friednship | CBS | 510886-2
Clifford Brown & The Neal Hefti Orchestra
Clifford Brown With Strings | Verve | 558078-2
Clifford Brown All Stars
Verve Jazz Masters 44:Clifford Brown and Max Roach | Verve | 528109-2
Brownie-The Complete EmArCy Recordings Of Clifford Brown | EmArCy | 838306-2
Clifford Brown All Stars With Dinah Washington
Verve Jazz Masters 40:Dinah Washington | Verve | 522055-2
Clifford Brown With Strings
Clifford Brown-Max Roach:Alone Together-The Best Of The Mercury Years | Verve | 526373-2
Verve Jazz Masters 44:Clifford Brown and Max Roach | Verve | 528109-2
Brownie-The Complete EmArCy Recordings Of Clifford Brown | EmArCy | 838306-2
Clifford Brown-Max Roach Quartet
Verve Jazz Masters 44:Clifford Brown and Max Roach | Verve | 528109-2
Clifford Brown-Max Roach Quintet
Clifford Brown-Max Roach:Alone Together-The Best Of The Mercury Years | Verve | 526373-2
Verve Jazz Masters 44:Clifford Brown and Max Roach | Verve | 528109-2
Verve Jazz Masters Vol.60:The Collection | Verve | 529866-2
Clifford Brown And Max Roach | Verve | 543306-2
Clifford Brown And Max Roach At Basin Street | Verve | 589826-2
Study In Brown | EmArCy | 814646-2
Brownie-The Complete EmArCy Recordings Of Clifford Brown | EmArCy | 838306-2
Coleman Hawkins All Star Octet
Milt Jackson Birthday Celebration | Fantasy | FANCD 6079-2
Coleman Hawkins All Stars
The J.J.Johnson Memorial Album | Prestige | PRCD 11025-2
Coleman Hawkins And His All Stars
Planet Jazz:Coleman Hawkins | Planet Jazz | 2152055-2
Planet Jazz:Bebop | RCA | 2169650-2
Jazz:The Essential Collection Vol.3 | IN+OUT Records | 78013-2
Coleman Hawkins And His Orchestra
Jazz:The Essential Collection Vol.3 | IN+OUT Records | 78013-2
Dinah Washington And Her Band
Verve Jazz Masters 40:Dinah Washington | Verve | 522055-2
Dinah Washington And Her Sextet
Newport Jazz Festival 1958,July 3rd-6th Vol.4:Blues In The Night No.2 | Phontastic | NCD 8816
Dinah Washington With The Newport All Stars
Dinah Sings Bessie Smith | Verve | 538635-2
Dinah Washington With The Terry Gibbs Band
Verve Jazz Masters 40:Dinah Washington | Verve | 522055-2
Dinah Washington With The Urbie Green Sextet
Newport Jazz Festival 1958,July 3rd-6th Vol.2:Mulligan The Main Man | Phontastic | NCD 8814
Dizzy Gillespie-Stan Getz Sextet
Verve Jazz Masters 25:Stan Getz & Dizzy Gillespie | Verve | 521852-2
Diz And Getz | Verve | 549749-2
Ultimate Stan Getz selected by Joe Henderson | Verve | 557532-2
Stan Getz Highlights | Verve | 847430-2
Don Byas Quartet
Don Byas:Laura | Dreyfus Jazz Line | FDM 36714-2
Don Lanphere Quintet
Fats Navarro:Nostalgia | Dreyfus Jazz Line | FDM 36736-2
Ellington/Mingus/Roach Trio
Money Jungle | Blue Note | 538227-2
George Russell And His Orchestra
Geogre Russell New York N.Y. | Impulse(MCA) | 951278-2
Hank Jones Trio
Charles Mingus-The Complete Debut Recordings | Debut | 12 DCD 4402-2
Hank Jones Trio With The Gordons's
Charles Mingus-The Complete Debut Recordings | Debut | 12 DCD 4402-2
Hazel Scott Trio
Charles Mingus-The Complete Debut Recordings | Debut | 12 DCD 4402-2
Herbie Nichols Trio
Blue Note Plays Gershwin | Blue Note | 520808-2
Herbie Nichols:The Complete Blue Note Recordings | Blue Note | 859352-2
Howard Rumsey's Lighthouse All-Stars
Oboe/Flute | Original Jazz Classics | OJCCD 154-2(C 3520)
Sunday Jazz A La Lighthouse Vol.2 | Original Jazz Classics | OJCCD 972-2(S 2501)
J.J.Johnson Quintet
The J.J.Johnson Memorial Album | Prestige | PRCD 11025-2
J.J.Johnson Sextet
The J.J.Johnson Memorial Album | Prestige | PRCD 11025-2
Jackie Paris With The Charles Mingus Quintet
Charles Mingus-The Complete Debut Recordings | Debut | 12 DCD 4402-2
JATP All Stars
Welcome To Jazz At The Philharmonic | Fantasy | FANCD 6081-2
Jazz At The Philharmonic-Frankfurt 1952 | Pablo | PACD 5305-2
Jazz Artists Guild
Newport Rebels-Jazz Artists Guild | Candid | CCD 79022
John Dennis Trio
Charles Mingus-The Complete Debut Recordings | Debut | 12 DCD 4402-2
Kenny Dorham Quintet
Sonny Rollins-The Freelance Years:The Complete Riverside & Contemporary Recordings | Riverside | 5 RCD 4427-2
Jazz Contrast | Original Jazz Classics | OJCCD 028-2(RLP 239)
Kenny Dorham Sextet
Jazz Contrast | Original Jazz Classics | OJCCD 028-2(RLP 239)
Max Roach
Charles Mingus-The Complete Debut Recordings | Debut | 12 DCD 4402-2
To The Max! | Enja | ENJ-7021 22
At Last! | Original Jazz Classics | OJCCD 480-2
Max Roach All Stars
Candid Dolphy | Candid | CCD 79033
Max Roach Chorus & Orchestra
To The Max! | Enja | ENJ-7021 22
Max Roach Double Quartet
To The Max! | Enja | ENJ-7021 22
Max Roach Group
We Insist: Freedom Now Suite | Candid | CCD 79002
Max Roach Plus Four
Clifford Brown-Max Roach:Alone Together-The Best Of The Mercury Years | Verve | 526373-2
Max Roach Quartet
Clifford Brown-Max Roach:Alone Together-The Best Of The Mercury Years | Verve | 526373-2
To The Max! | Enja | ENJ-7021 22
Speak, Brother, Speak | Original Jazz Classics | OJCCD 646-2(F 86007)
Max Roach Quintet
Dizzy Gillespie:Pleyel Jazz Concert 1948 + Max Roach Quintet 1949 | Vogue | 21409412
Clifford Brown-Max Roach:Alone Together-The Best Of The Mercury Years | Verve | 526373-2
Jazz In Paris:Max Roach-Parisian Sketches | EmArCy | 589963-2
Deeds Not Words | Original Jazz Classics | OJC20 304-2(RLP 1122)
The Jazz Giants Play Sammy Cahn:It's Magic | Prestige | PCD 24226-2
Max Roach Septet
The Jazz Life! | Candid | CCD 79019
Max Roach Sextet
Clifford Brown-Max Roach:Alone Together-The Best Of The Mercury Years | Verve | 526373-2
Deeds Not Words | Original Jazz Classics | OJC20 304-2(RLP 1122)
Max Roach Sextet With Choir
It's Time | Impulse(MCA) | 951185-2
Max Roach Sextet With The J.C.White Singers
Lift Every Voice And Sing | Atlantic | 7567-80798-2
Max Roach Trio
Clifford Brown And Max Roach | Verve | 543306-2
Max Roach With The Boston Percussion Ensemble
Clifford Brown-Max Roach:Alone Together-The Best Of The Mercury Years | Verve | 526373-2
Max Roach-Abbey Lincoln
We Insist: Freedom Now Suite | Candid | CCD 79002
M'Boom
To The Max! | Enja | ENJ-7021 22
Miles Davis All Stars
Miles Davis:Milestones | Dreyfus Jazz Line | FDM 36731-2
Miles Davis And His Orchestra
The Complete Birth Of The Cool | Capitol | 494550-2
Birth Of The Cool | Capitol | 530117-2
Miles Davis:The Best Of The Capitol/Blue Note Years | Blue Note | 798287-2
Jazz Profile:Miles Davis | Blue Note | 823515-2
Ballads & Blues | Blue Note | 836633-2
Miles Davis:Milestones | Dreyfus Jazz Line | FDM 36731-2
Miles Davis And The Lighthouse All Stars
At Last! | Original Jazz Classics | OJCCD 480-2
Miles Davis Quartet
Blue Haze | Original Jazz Classics | OJC20 093-2(P 7054)
The Prestige Legacy Vol.1:The High Priests | Prestige | PCD 24251-2
Oscar Pettiford Sextet
The Birdlanders Vol.2 | Original Jazz Classics | OJCCD 1931-2
Quintet Of The Year
Charles Mingus-The Complete Debut Recordings | Debut | 12 DCD 4402-2
The Quintet-Jazz At Massey Hall | Debut | DSA 124-6
The Quintet-Jazz At Massey Hall | Original Jazz Classics | OJC20 044-2
Sarah Vaughan With Dizzy Gillespie And His Septet
Sarah Vaughan:Lover Man | Dreyfus Jazz Line | FDM 36739-2
Sonny Rollins Plus Four
Sonny Rollins Plus 4 | Original Jazz Classics | OJC20 243-2(P 7038)
The Prestige Legacy Vol.1:The High Priests | Prestige | PCD 24251-2
Sonny Rollins Quartet
Worktime | Original Jazz Classics | OJC20 007-2(P 7020)
Saxophone Colossus | Original Jazz Classics | OJC20 291-2
Tour De Force | Original Jazz Classics | OJCCD 095-2
Sonny Boy | Original Jazz Classics | OJCCD 348-2(P 7207)
Sonny Rollins Quintet
Ballads | Blue Note | 537562-2
Sonny Rollins:Vol.1 | Blue Note | 591724-2
The Blue Note Years-The Best Of Sonny Rollins | Blue Note | 793203-2
The Best Of Blue Note Vol.2 | Blue Note | 797960-2
Sonny Rollins:The Blue Note Recordings | Blue Note | 821371-2
Jazz Profile:Sonny Rollins | Blue Note | 823516-2
Sonny Rollins Plays For Bird | Original Jazz Classics | OJCCD 214-2
Sonny Boy | Original Jazz Classics | OJCCD 348-2(P 7207)
Sonny Rollins Trio
Sonny Rollins-The Freelance Years:The Complete Riverside & Contemporary Recordings | Riverside | 5 RCD 4427-2
Freedom Suite | Original Jazz Classics | OJCCD 067-2
Sonny Stitt Quartet
Sonny Stitt | Original Jazz Classics | OJCCD 009-2
Sonny Stitt Quintet
Sonny Stitt | Original Jazz Classics | OJCCD 009-2
Spaulding Givens Trio
Charles Mingus-The Complete Debut Recordings | Debut | 12 DCD 4402-2
Stan Getz Quartet
Stan Getz And The 'Cool' Sounds | Verve | 547317-2
Stan Getz Plays | Verve | 833535-2
Stan Getz Highlights | Verve | 847430-2
Thad Jones Quartet
Charles Mingus-The Complete Debut Recordings | Debut | 12 DCD 4402-2
The Capitol Jazzmen
The Hollywood Session:The Capitol Jazzmen | Jazz Unlimited | JUCD 2044
The Metronome All Stars
Jazz Gallery:Lester Young Vol.2(1946-59) | RCA | 2119541-2
Thelonious Monk Quintet
Sonny Rollins-The Freelance Years:The Complete Riverside & Contemporary Recordings | Riverside | 5 RCD 4427-2
Thelonious Monk:85th Birthday Celebration | zyx records | FANCD 6076-2
Brilliant Corners | Original Jazz Classics | OJC20 026-2
Thelonious Monk Sextet
Genius Of Modern Music,Vol.2 | Blue Note | 532139-2
Jazz Profile:Thelonious Monk | Blue Note | 823518-2
Thelonious Monk Trio
Thelonious Monk:The Complete Prestige Recordings | Prestige | 3 PRCD 4428-2

Thelonious Monk:85th Birthday Celebration | zyx records | FANCD 6076-2
Thelonious Monk | Original Jazz Classics | OJC20 010-2(P 7027)
The Prestige Legacy Vol.1:The High Priests | Prestige | PCD 24251-2
Urbie Green Sextet
Newport Jazz Festival 1958,July 3rd-6th Vol.2:Mulligan The Main Man | Phontastic | NCD 8814

Roach,Max or Art Taylor | (dr)
Billy Taylor Trio
Charles Mingus-The Complete Debut Recordings | Debut | 12 DCD 4402-2

Roach,Maxine | (viola)
A Band Of Friends
Wynton Marsalis Quartet With Strings | CBS | CK 68921
Abbey Lincoln With The Stan Getz Quintet
You Gotta Pay The Band | Verve | 511110-2
Max Roach Double Quartet
To The Max! | Enja | ENJ-7021 22
Ron Carter Quintet With Strings
Pick 'Em/Super Strings | Milestone | MCD 47090-2

Roane,Eddie | (tpvoc)
Louis Jordan And His Tympany Five
The Small Black Groups | Storyville | 4960523
Louis Jordan-Let The Good Times Roll: The Complete Decca Recordings 1938-1954 | Bear Family Records | BCD 15557 IH

Robben,Rainer | (dr)
Association Urbanetique
Ass Bedient | Jazz 4 Ever Records:Jazz Network | J4E 4723

Robbins,Billy | (tp)
Woody Herman And His Orchestra
Old Gold Rehearsals 1944 | Jazz Unlimited | JUCD 2079

Roberscheuten,Frank | (cl,asts)
The Swingcats
Face To Face:The Swingcats Live | Nagel-Heyer | CD 072
Wrobel-Roberscheuten-Hopkins Jam Session
Jammin' At The IAJRC Convention Hamburg 1999 | Nagel-Heyer | CD 066

Robert,George | (as,clss)
George Robert-Tom Harrell Quintet
Visions | Contemporary | CCD 14063-2

Robert,Ives | (tb)
Heiner Goebbels Group
Ou Bien Le Debarquement Desastreux | ECM | 1552

Robert,Jean | (clts)
Brocksi-Quartett
Globetrotter | Bear Family Records | BCD 15912 AH
Brocksi-Quintett
Drums Boogie | Bear Family Records | BCD 15988 AH

Robert,Yves | (tb)
Louis Sclavis Sextet
Les Violences De Rameau | ECM | 1588(533128-2)
Vincent Courtois Quartet
Translucide | Enja | ENJ-9380 2
Yves Robert Trio
In Touch | ECM | 1787(016375-2)

Roberts,Auston | (bvoc)
Oscar Peterson Trio
Planet Music:Oscar Peterson | RCA | 2165365-2
Planet Jazz:Jazz Piano | RCA | 2169655-2
This Is Oscar Peterson | RCA | 2663990-2

Roberts,Caughey | (as,clts)
Count Basie And His Orchestra
Jazz:The Essential Collection Vol.3 | IN+OUT Records | 78013-2
Kid Ory And His Band
The Very Best Of Dixieland Jazz | Verve | 535529-2

Roberts,Claude | (bjg)
Earl Hines And His Orchestra
Planet Jazz:Earl Hines | Planet Jazz | 2159973-2
The Legends Of Swing | Laserlight | 24659
Jazz:The Essential Collection Vol.2 | IN+OUT Records | 78012-2

Roberts,Davide | (p)
Alex De Santis Jazz Quartet
Le Canzoni Italiana | Edition Collage | EC 514-2
Corinne Chatel Quintet
Ma Vie En Rose | Edition Collage | EC 525-2

Roberts,Dick | (bjg)
Firehouse Five Plus Two
Dixieland Favorites | Good Time Jazz | FCD 60-008
Crashes A Party | Good Time Jazz | GTCD 10038-2
Goes To A Fire | Good Time Jazz | GTCD 10052-2
Goes South | Good Time Jazz | GTCD 12018-2

Roberts,Frank | (keyboards,porg)
Passport
Handmade | Atlantic | 2292-42172-2

Roberts,George | (b-tb,cowbell,maracastb)
Anita O'Day With The Buddy Bregman Orchestra
Pick Yourself Up | Verve | 517329-2
Benny Carter And His Orchestra
Aspects | Capitol | 852677-2
Billy May And His Orchestra
Billy May's Big Fat Brass/Bill's Bag | Capitol | 535206-2
Buddy Bregman And His Orchestra
Swinging Kicks | Verve | 559514-2
Cal Tjader With The Clare Fischer Orchestra
Cal Tjader Plays Harold Arlen & West Side Story | Fantasy | FCD 24775-2
Ella Fitzgerald With Frank De Vol And His Orchestra
Get Happy! | Verve | 523321-2
Ella Fitzgerald With The Billy May Orchestra
Ella Fitzgerald Sings The Harold Arlen Song Book | Verve | 589108-2
Ella Fitzgerald With The Buddy Bregman Orchestra
Ella Fitzgerald-First Lady Of Song | Verve | 517898-2
Love Songs:The Best Of The Song Books | Verve | 531762-2
Ella Fitzgerald Sings The Cole Porter Songbook | Verve | 537257-2
Ella Fitzgerald Sings The Rodgers And Hart Song Book | Verve | 537258-2
Ella Fitzgerald With The Frank DeVol Orchestra
Get Happy! | Verve | 523321-2
Ella Fitzgerald With The Marty Paich Orchestra
Get Happy! | Verve | 523321-2
Ella Fitzgerald With The Nelson Riddle Orchestra
The Best Of The Song Books:The Ballads | Verve | 521867-2
Get Happy! | Verve | 523321-2
Oh Lady Be Good:The Best Of The Gershwin Songbook | Verve | 529581-2
Love Songs:The Best Of The Song Books | Verve | 531762-2
Ella Fitzgerald Sings The Johnny Mercer Songbook | Verve | 539057-2
Harry James And His Orchestra
Trumpet Blues:The Best Of Harry James | Capitol | 521224-2
June Christy With The Pete Rugolo Orchestra
Something Cool(The Complete Mono & Stereo Versions) | Capitol | 534069-2
Louis Armstrong With The Hal Mooney Orchestra
Ambassador Louis Armstrong Vol.17:Moments To Remember(1952-1956) | Ambassador | CLA 1917
Mel Tormé With The Russell Garcia Orchestra
Swingin' On The Moon | Verve | 511385-2
Peggy Lee With The Quincy Jones Orchestra
Blues Cross Country | Capitol | 520088-2
Pete Rugolo And His Orchestra
Thriller/Richard Diamon(Original Jazz Scores From 2 Classics TV Series) | Fresh Sound Records | FSCD 2015
Singers Unlimited With The Patrick Williams Orchestra
The Singers Unlimited:Magic Voices | MPS | 539130-2
Stan Kenton And His Orchestra
Stan Kenton Portraits On Standards | Capitol | 531571-2

Roberts,Glen | (b)

Roberts,H. | (voc)
Sonny Rollins Group
What's New? | RCA | 2179626-2

Roberts,Hank | (cello,electronic-processed-cello)
Alex Cline Group
The Lamp And The Star | ECM | 1372
Arcado-String Trio
Arcado-String Trio | JMT Edition | 919028-2
Bill Frisell Band
Before We Were Born | Nonesuch | 7559-60843-2
Where In The World | Nonesuch | 7559-61181-2
Blaufrontal With Hank Roberts & Mark Feldman
Bad Times Roll | Jazz Haus Musik | JHM 0061 CD
Hank Roberts Group
Black Pastels | JMT Edition | 919016-2
The Bill Frisell Band
Lookout For Hope | ECM | 1350(833495-2)

Roberts,Howard | (el-gg)
Anita O'Day With The Russ Garcia Orchestra
Verve Jazz Masters 49:Anita O'Day | Verve | 527653-2
Art Pepper Quartet
Art Pepper:The Complete Galaxy Recordings | Galaxy | 16GCD 1016-2
Art Pepper Quintet
Art Pepper:The Complete Galaxy Recordings | Galaxy | 16GCD 1016-2
Art Pepper Quintet With Strings
Art Pepper:The Complete Galaxy Recordings | Galaxy | 16GCD 1016-2
Winter Moon | Original Jazz Classics | OJC20 677-2(GXY 5140)
Bob Enevoldsen Quintet
The Complete Nocturne Recordings:Jazz In Hollywood Series Vol.1 | Fresh Sound Records | NR 3CD-101
Bob Enevoldsen Sextet
The Complete Nocturne Recordings:Jazz In Hollywood Series Vol.1 | Fresh Sound Records | NR 3CD-101
Diane Schuur With The Dave Grusin Orchestra
The Best Of Diane Schuur | GRP | GRP 98882
Herbie Mann With The Frank DeVol Orchestra
Verve Jazz Masters 56:Herbie Mann | Verve | 529901-2
Jimmy Smith With The Oliver Nelson Orchestra
Jimmy Smith:Best Of The Verve Years | Verve | 527950-2
Jimmy Smith-Talkin' Verve | Verve | 531563-2
Johnny Hartman And His Orchestra
Unforgettable | Impulse(MCA) | IMP 11522
June Christy With The Pete Rugolo Orchestra
Something Cool(The Complete Mono & Stereo Versions) | Capitol | 534069-2
Mel Tormé With The Russell Garcia Orchestra
Swingin' On The Moon | Verve | 511385-2
Peggy Lee With The Quincy Jones Orchestra
Blues Cross Country | Capitol | 520088-2
Pete Rugolo And His Orchestra
Verve Jazz Masters 52:Maynard Ferguson | Verve | 529905-2

Roberts,Judy | (pvoc)
Jens Bunge Group
Meet You In Chicago | Jazz 4 Ever Records:Jazz Network | J4E 4749

Roberts,Katy | (p)
Ku-Umba Frank Lacy & His Quartet
Settegast Strut | Tutu Records | 888162-2*

Roberts,Marcus | (as,pp-solo)
Mark Whitfield Quartet
The Marksman | Warner | 7599-26321-2

Roberts,Pola | (dr)
Gloria Coleman Quartet
Soul Sisters | Impulse(MCA) | 8961048

Roberts,Steve | (g)
Buddy Childers Big Band
Just Buddy's | Candid | CCD 79761

Robertson,Angie | (viola)
Vince Jones Group
It All Ends Up In Tears | Intuition Records | INT 3069-2

Robertson,Bill | (tb)
Charlie Barnet And His Orchestra
Planet Jazz:Big Bands | Planet Jazz | 2169649-2
Planet Jazz:Swing | Planet Jazz | 2169651-2

Robertson,Herb | (fl-h,co,pocket-tp,v-tb,tp)
Herb Robertson Brass Ensemble
Shades Of Bud Powell | JMT Edition | 919019-2
Herb Robertson Group
The Little Trumpet | JMT Edition | 919007-2
Herb Robertson Quintet
'X'-cerpts:Live At Willisau | JMT Edition | 919013-2
Klaus König Orchestra & Guests
The Song Of Songs:Oratorio For Two Solo Voices,Choir And Orchestra | Enja | ENJ-7057 2

Robertson,Jan | (dr)
Nils Landgren Funk Unit
Live In Montreux | ACT | 9265-2

Robertson,Janne | (dr)
Nils Landgren Funk Unit With Guests
5000 Miles | ACT | 9271-2
Nils Landgren Group
Sentimental Journey | ACT | 9409-2

Robertson,Lester | (tb)
Johnny Hartman And His Orchestra
Unforgettable | Impulse(MCA) | IMP 11522

Robichaux,Joe | (p)
George Lewis And His Original New Orleans Jazzmen
George Lewis In Stockholm,1959 | Dragon | DRCD 221

Robillard,Duke | (g,el-g,vocg-synth)
Duke Robillard-Herb Ellis Quintet
Conversation In Swing Guitar | Stony Plain | SPCD 1260
More Conversations In Swing Guitar | Stony Plain | SPCD 1292
Jay McShann Quartet
Goin' To Kansas City | Stony Plain | SPCD 1286

Robins,Jimmy | (porg)
Dizzy Gillespie's Trumpet Kings
The Trumpet Kings Meet Joe Turner | Original Jazz Classics | OJCCD 497-2

Robinson,Albertine | (voc)
George Benson And His Orchestra
Giblet Gravy | Verve | 543754-2
Talkin' Verve:George Benson | Verve | 553780-2
Nina Simone And Orchestra
Baltimore | Epic | 476906-2

Robinson,Billy | (as,bs,sax,tstuba)
Stan Kenton Orchestra
Stompin' At Newport | Pablo | PACD 5312-2

Robinson,Booker T. | (dr)
Les McCann Group
Talkin' Verve:Les McCann | Verve | 557351-2
Les McCann Orchestra
Talkin' Verve:Les McCann | Verve | 557351-2

Robinson,Carol | (b-cl)
Peter Herbert Group
B-A-C-H A Chromatic Universe | Between The Lines | btl 013(Efa 10183)

Robinson,Danny | (g)
Terri Lyne Carrington Group
Jazz Is A Spirit | ACT | 9408-2

Robinson,Edward 'Bass' | (b)
Coleman Hawkins Quartet
Thelonious Monk:The Complete Prestige Recordings | Prestige | 3 PRCD 4428-2
Jazz:The Essential Collection Vol.3 | IN+OUT Records | 78013-2
Thelonious Monk:85th Birthday Celebration | zyx records | FANCD 6076-2

Robinson,Eli | (tbvoc)
Big Al Sears Band
Sear-iously | Bear Family Records | BCD 15668 AH
Count Basie And His Orchestra
Planet Jazz:Count Basie | Planet Jazz | 2152068-2
Planet Jazz:Jazz Greatest Hits | Planet Jazz | 2169648-2
Jazz Collection:Count Basie | Laserlight | 24368
Jazz:The Essential Collection Vol.3 | IN+OUT Records | 78013-2

Robinson,Frank | (ptp)
Buddy Johnson And His Orchestra
Buddy And Ella Johnson 1953-1964 | Bear Family Records | BCD 15479 DH
Willis Jackson Quintet
Gravy | Prestige | PCD 24254-2
Soul Night Live! | Prestige | PRCD 24273-2
Willis Jackson Sextet
Gravy | Prestige | PCD 24254-2
Nuther'n Like Thuther'n | Prestige | PRCD 24265-2

Robinson,Fred | (tb)
Carroll Dickerson's Savoyagers
Louis Armstrong:Fireworks | Dreyfus Jazz Line | FDM 36710-2
Louis Armstrong And His Hot Five
Jazz:The Essential Collection Vol.2 | IN+OUT Records | 78012-2
Satch Plays Fats(Complete) | CBS | CK 64927
Louis Armstrong:Fireworks | Dreyfus Jazz Line | FDM 36710-2
Louis Armstrong And His Orchestra
Jazz:The Essential Collection Vol.2 | IN+OUT Records | 78012-2
Satch Plays Fats(Complete) | CBS | CK 64927
Louis Armstrong:Fireworks | Dreyfus Jazz Line | FDM 36710-2
Louis Armstrong And His Savoy Ballroom Five
Jazz:The Essential Collection Vol.2 | IN+OUT Records | 78012-2
Louis Armstrong:Fireworks | Dreyfus Jazz Line | FDM 36710-2

Robinson,Freddie | (el-gg)
The Three Sounds
Blue Break Beats | Blue Note | 799106-2

Robinson,Gale | (fr-h)
Ella Fitzgerald With Orchestra
The Best Is Yet To Come | Original Jazz Classics | OJCCD 889-2(2312138)

Robinson,James | (tb)
Lionel Hampton And His Orchestra
Lionel Hampton:Flying Home | Dreyfus Jazz Line | FDM 36735-2

Robinson,Janice | (tb)
McCoy Tyner Group With Horns
Inner Voices | Original Jazz Classics | OJCCD 1039-2(M 9079)
McCoy Tyner Group With Horns And Voices
Inner Voices | Original Jazz Classics | OJCCD 1039-2(M 9079)

Robinson,Jim | (tb)
Bunk Johnson And His New Orleans Band
Planet Jazz:Jazz Trumpet | Planet Jazz | 2169654-2
Bunk Johnson And His Superior Jazz Band
Authentic New Orleans Jazz | Good Time Jazz | GTCD 12048-2
George Lewis And His Band
Atlantic Jazz: New Orleans | Atlantic | 7567-81700-2
George Lewis And His New Orleans Ragtime Band
The Beverly Caverns Session | Good Time Jazz | GTCD 12058-2
George Lewis And His New Orleans Stompers
George Lewis And His New Orleans Stompers | Blue Note | 821261-2
George Lewis And His Original New Orleans Jazzmen
George Lewis In Stockholm,1959 | Dragon | DRCD 221
Jim Robinson's New Orleans Band
Atlantic Jazz: New Orleans | Atlantic | 7567-81700-2

Robinson,Jimmy Lee | (b-gg)
Al Smith With The King Curtis Quintet
Midnight Special | Original Blues Classics | OBCCD 583-2(BV 1013)
St.Louis Jimmy Oden Group
Goin' Down Slow | Original Blues Classics | OBCCD 584-2(BV 1028)

Robinson,John | (cello,drperc)
Abbey Lincoln With The Rodney Kendrick Trio And Guests
A Turtle's Dream | Verve | 527382-2
Herbie Hancock Group
Magic Window | CBS | 486572-2
Joe Sample Group
Spellbound | Rhino | 81273726-2
Stanley Clarke Group
If This Bass Could Only Talk | CBS | 460883-2
Stanley Clarke-John Robinson
If This Bass Could Only Talk | CBS | 460883-2

Robinson,Justin | (as)
Abbey Lincoln With Her Band
Who Used To Dance | Verve | 533559-2
Jimmy Scott With Band
Over The Rainbow | Milestone | MCD 9314-2

Robinson,Kathleen | (v)
Charlie Haden Quartet West With Strings
The Art Of The Song | Verve | 547403-2

Robinson,Lenny | (dr)
Chuck Brown And The Second Chapter Band
Timeless | Minor Music | 801068

Robinson,Les | (as,saxts)
Artie Shaw And His Orchestra
Planet JazzArtie Shaw | Planet Jazz | 2152057-2
Planet Jazz Sampler | Planet Jazz | 2152326-2
Planet Jazz:Big Bands | Planet Jazz | 2169649-2
Planet Jazz:Swing | Planet Jazz | 2169651-2
Planet Jazz:Female Jazz Vocalists | Planet Jazz | 2169656-2
Planet Jazz:Male Jazz Vocalists | Planet Jazz | 2169657-2
The Legends Of Swing | Laserlight | 24659
The Capitol Jazzmen
The Hollywood Session:The Capitol Jazzmen | Jazz Unlimited | JUCD 2044

Robinson,Lester | (tb)
Lena Horne With The Horace Henderson Orchestra
Planet Jazz:Lena Horne | Planet Jazz | 2165373-2

Robinson,Mabel | (voc)
Louis Jordan And His Tympany Five
Louis Jordan-Let The Good Times Roll: The Complete Decca Recordings 1938-1954 | Bear Family Records | BCD 15557 IH

Robinson,Orphy | (marimba)
David Jean-Baptiste Group
The Nature Suite | Laika Records | 35101632

Robinson,Perry | (cl,perc,sssopranino)
Archie Shepp Orchestra
Mama Too Tight | Impulse(MCA) | 951248-2
Charlie Haden's Liberation Music Orchestra
Liberation Music Orchestra | Impulse(MCA) | 951188-2
Gunter Hampel All Stars
Jubilation | Birth | 0038
Gunter Hampel And His Galaxie Dream Band
Journey To The Song Within | Birth | 0017
Enfant Terrible | Birth | 0025
Live At The Berlin Jazzfestival 1978 | Birth | 0027
All Is Real | Birth | 0028
All The Things You Could Be If Charles Mingus Was Your Daddy | Birth | CD 031
Celestial Glory-Live At The Knitting Factory New York | Birth | CD 040
Gunter Hampel New York Orchestra
Fresh Heat-Live At Sweet Basil | Birth | CD 039
Perry Robinson Quartet
Perry Robinson Quartet | Timescrapper | TSCR 9613
Ray Anderson Sextet
It Just So Happens | Enja | ENJ-5037 2

Robinson,Prince | (cl,as,tsreeds)
Duke Ellington And His Kentucky Club Orchestra
Jazz:The Essential Collection Vol.2 | IN+OUT Records | 78012-2
Louis Armstrong And His Orchestra
Louis Armstrong:Swing That Music | Laserlight | 36056
Jazz:The Essential Collection Vol.2 | IN+OUT Records | 78012-2
Louis Armstrong:C'est Si Bon | Dreyfus Jazz Line | FDM 36730-2

Robinson,Prince prob. | (reeds)
Duke Ellington And His Kentucky Club Orchestra
Jazz:The Essential Collection Vol.2 | IN+OUT Records | 78012-2

Robinson,Robert | (cl,tstb)
Harry James And His Orchestra
Trumpet Blues:The Best Of Harry James | Capitol | 521224-2
Robinson,Scott | (alto-cl,ts,as,bass-sax,c-mel-sax,co)
Allan Vaché Swingtet
Ellington For Lovers | Nagel-Heyer | NH 1009
Buck Clayton Swing Band
Swing's The Village | Nagel-Heyer | CD 5004
Blues Of Summer | Nagel-Heyer | NH 1011
Caecilie Norby With Band
My Corner Of The Sky | Blue Note | 853422-2
Charles Mingus Orchestra
Tonight At Noon...Three Or Four Shades Of Love | Dreyfus Jazz Line | FDM 36633-2
Dan Barrett Septet
Dan Barrett's International Swing Party | Nagel-Heyer | CD 067
James Chirillo Sextet
Sultry Serenade | Nagel-Heyer | CD 061
Joe Lovano Nonet
On This Day At The Vanguard | Blue Note | 590950-2
Marty Grosz And His Swinging Fools
Ring Dem Bells | Nagel-Heyer | CD 022
The Second Sampler | Nagel-Heyer | NHR SP 6
Randy Sandke And The New York Allstars
The Re-Discovered Louis And Bix | Nagel-Heyer | CD 058
Randy Sandke-Dick Hyman
The Re-Discovered Louis And Bix | Nagel-Heyer | CD 058
The Buck Clayton Legacy
Encore Live | Nagel-Heyer | CD 018
The Second Sampler | Nagel-Heyer | NHR SP 6
The Nagel-Heyer Allstars
Uptown Lowdown:A Jazz Salute To The Big Apple | Nagel-Heyer | CD 2004
The New York Allstars
Broadway | Nagel-Heyer | CD 003
One Two Three | Nagel-Heyer | CD 008
Randy Sandke Meets Bix Beiderbecke | Nagel-Heyer | CD 3002
The First Sampler | Nagel-Heyer | NHR SP 5
Robinson,Silivea | (voc)
Tom Browne Groups
Mo' Jamaica Funk | Hip Bop | HIBD 8002
Robinson,Wesley | (p)
Louis Armstrong And His Orchestra
Planet Jazz:Louis Armstrong | Planet Jazz | 2152052-2
Louis Armstrong:A 100th Birthday Celebration | RCA | 2663694-2
Robles,Ion | (ts)
Big Band Bellaterra
Don't Git Sassy | Fresh Sound Records | FSNT 048 CD
David Mengual Quartet
Monkiana:A Tribute To Thelonious Monk | Fresh Sound Records | FSNT 019 CD
David Mengual Quintet
Monkiana:A Tribute To Thelonious Monk | Fresh Sound Records | FSNT 019 CD
Javier Feierstein Quartet
Wysiwyg | Fresh Sound Records | FSNT 040 CD
Pep O'Callaghan Grup
Port O'Clock | Fresh Sound Records | FSNT 069 CD
Robyn,Paul | (viola)
Ella Fitzgerald With The Billy May Orchestra
The Best Of The Song Books:The Ballads | Verve | 521867-2
Ella Fitzgerald Sings The Harold Arlen Song Book | Verve | 589108-2
Ella Fitzgerald With The Nelson Riddle Orchestra
The Best Of The Song Books:The Ballads | Verve | 521867-2
Love Songs:The Best Of The Song Books | Verve | 531762-2
Frank Sinatra With The Count Basie Orchestra
It Might As Well Be Spring | Reprise | 7599-27027-2
Harry James And His Orchestra
Trumpet Blues:The Best Of Harry James | Capitol | 521224-2
Phineas Newborn Jr. With Dennis Farnon And His Orchestra
While My Lady Sleeps | RCA | 2185157-2
Roccisano,Joe | (as,synth,fl,clss)
Don Ellis Orchestra
Electric Bath | CBS | CK 65522
Roche,Betty | (voc)
Duke Ellington And His Orchestra
Carnegie Hall Concert January 1943 | Prestige | 2PCD 34004-2
Jazz:The Essential Collection Vol.3 | IN+OUT Records | 78013-2
Rochinski,Steve | (gg-solo)
Steve Rochinski
Otherwise | Jardis Records | JRCD 20133
Steve Rochinski Quartet
Otherwise | Jardis Records | JRCD 20133
Steve Rochinski Solo/Duo/Trio/Quartet
Jazz Guitar Highlights 1 | Jardis Records | JRCD 20141
A Bird In The Hand | Jardis Records | JRCD 9922
Steve Rochinski-Jim Stinnett
Otherwise | Jardis Records | JRCD 20133
Rockin' Dopsie | (accordeonvoc)
Rockin' Dopsie And The Zydeco Twisters
Rockin' Dopsie And The Zydeco Twister | Storyville | 4960423
Rockwell,Bob | (cl,ss,fl,ts,reedssax)
Mona Larsen And The Danish Radio Big Band Plus Soloists
Michael Mantler:Cerco Un Paese Innocente | ECM | 1556
Rockwin,Eric | (b)
Gutbucket
Dry Humping The American Dream | Enja | ENJ-9466 2
Rodach,Michael | (g,el-g,b,slide-g,gbkeyboards)
David Moss-Michael Rodach
Fragmentary Blues | Traumton Records | 4432-2
Die Elefanten
Wasserwüste | Nabel Records:Jazz Network | CD 4634
Gebhard Ullmann Quartet
Per-Dee-Doo | Nabel Records:Jazz Network | CD 4640
Rodach
Himmel Und Hölle-Heaven And Hell | Traumton Records | 4434-2
Rodby,Steve | (b,b-dr,b-g,b-synth,el-bpiccolo-b)
Pat Metheny Group
Offramp | ECM | 1216(817138-2)
Travels | ECM | 1252/53
First Circle | ECM | 1278(823342-2)
Imaginary Day | Warner | 9362-46791-2
Letter From Home | Geffen Records | GED 24245
The Road To You | Geffen Records | GED 24601
We Live Here | Geffen Records | GED 24729
Quartet | Geffen Records | GED 24978
Rodenkirchen,Norbert | (fl)
Dirk Raulf Group
Theater II(Bühnenmusik) | Poise | Poise 10
Rodgers,Gene | (ptp)
Coleman Hawkins All Star Octet
Planet Jazz:Coleman Hawkins | Planet Jazz | 2152055-2
Coleman Hawkins And His Orchestra
Planet Jazz:Coleman Hawkins | Planet Jazz | 2152055-2
Planet Jazz Sampler | Planet Jazz | 2152326-2
Planet Jazz:Jazz Greatest Hits | Planet Jazz | 2169648-2
Jazz:The Essential Collection Vol.3 | IN+OUT Records | 78013-2
Rodgers,George | (cond)
King Oliver And His Orchestra
Jazz:The Essential Collection Vol.1 | IN+OUT Records | 78011-2
Rodgers,Harry | (tb)
Artie Shaw And His Orchestra
Planet JazzArtie Shaw | Planet Jazz | 2152057-2
Planet Jazz Sampler | Planet Jazz | 2152326-2
Planet Jazz:Swing | Planet Jazz | 2169651-2
Planet Jazz:Jazz Trumpet | Planet Jazz | 2169654-2
Planet Jazz:Female Jazz Vocalists | Planet Jazz | 2169656-2
The Legends Of Swing | Laserlight | 24659
Rodgers,Jimmy | (gvoc)
Jimmy Rodgers With Louis And Lil Armstrong
Best Of The Complete RCA Victor Recordings | RCA | 2663636-2
Muddy Waters Blues Band
Muddy Waters-The Collection | MCA | MCD 18961
Rodgers,Nile | (gkeyboards)
Al Jarreau With Band
L Is For Lover | i.e. Music | 557850-2
Rodgers,Rueben | (b)
Donald Harrison Quartet
Nouveau Swing | Impulse(MCA) | 951209-2
Rodgers,Sarah Ann | (voc)
Max Roach Chorus & Orchestra
To The Max! | Enja | ENJ-7021 22
Rodin,Gil | (as,cl,fl,ss,bass-sax,tsbs)
Bob Crosby And His Orchestra
Swing Legens:Bob Crosby | Nimbus Records | NI 2011
Bob Crosby's Bobcats
Swing Legens:Bob Crosby | Nimbus Records | NI 2011
Roditi,Claudio | (fl-h,roraty-v-tp,rotary-v-tp,p,tp)
Candid Jazz Masters
The Candid Jazz Masters:For Miles | Candid | CCD 79710
Dizzy Gillespie And The United Nation Orchestra
7.Zelt-Musik-Festival:Jazz Events | Zounds | CD 2730001
Gary Bartz Quintet
West 42nd Street | Candid | CCD 79049
Klaus Ignatzek Quintet
Today Is Tomorrow/Live In Leverkusen | Nabel Records:Jazz Network | CD 4654
Son Of Gaudi | Nabel Records:Jazz Network | CD 4660
Klaus Ignatzek-Claudio Roditi Quintet
Live at Bird's Eye | Village | VILCD 1023-2
Mind Games With Claudio Roditi
Live | Edition Collage | EC 501-2
Vocal Moments | Take Twelve On CD | TT 008-2
Paquito D'Rivera Orchestra
Jazzrock-Anthology Vol.3:Fusion | Zounds | CD 27100555
Roots
For Diz & Bird | IN+OUT Records | 77039-2
Rodney,Phil | (oboe)
Coleman Hawkins With Billy Byers And His Orchestra
The Hawk In Hi-Fi | RCA | 2663842-2
Rodney,Red | (fl-h,talking,interview,tpvoc)
Charlie Parker And His Orchestra
Bird: The Complete Charlie Parker On Verve | Verve | 837141-2
Charlie Parker Quintet
Charlie Parker:Bird's Best Bop On Verve | Verve | 527452-2
Charlie Parker:The Best Of The Verve Years | Verve | 527815-2
Bird At St. Nick's | Original Jazz Classics | OJC20 041-2(JWS 500)
Gene Krupa And His Orchestra
Mullenium | CBS | CK 65678
Red Rodney All Stars
A Tribute To Charlie Parker Vol.1 | Storyville | 4960483
Red Rodney Quintet
The Red Rodney Quintets | Fantasy | FCD 24758-2
Woody Herman And His Orchestra
Woody Herman:Four Brother | Dreyfus Jazz Line | FDM 36722-2
Rodnon,Mel | (as)
Benny Goodman And His Orchestra
40th Anniversary Concert-Live At Carnegie Hall | London | 820349-2
Verve Jazz Masters 33:Benny Goodman | Verve | 844410-2
Rodrigues,Jay | (as,tsreeds)
Josh Roseman Unit
Cherry | Enja | ENJ-9392 2
Rodriguez Pedrosa,Mario Facundo | (vocperc)
Conjunto Clave Y Guaguanco
Dejala En La Puntica | TipToe | TIP-888829 2
Rodriguez,Alex | (tp)
Ella Fitzgerald With Orchestra
Ella/Things Ain't What They Used To Be | Warner | 9362-47875-2
Rodriguez,Arsenio | (g,congavoc)
Sabu L. Martinez Group
Palo Congo | Blue Note | 522665-2
Rodriguez,Bill | (dr)
Jimmy Smith With The Oliver Nelson Orchestra
Verve Jazz Masters 29:Jimmy Smith | Verve | 521855-2
Jimmy Smith:Best Of The Verve Years | Verve | 527950-2
Jimmy Smith-Talkin' Verve | Verve | 531563-2
Rodriguez,Bobby | (bel-b)
Cal Tjader's Orchestra
Talkin Verve/Roots Of Acid Jazz:Cal Tjader | Verve | 531562-2
Soul Burst | Verve | 557446-2
Dizzy Gillespie And His Orchestra
Afro | Verve | 517052-2
Rodriguez,Damarys Driggs | (vocperc)
Conjunto Clave Y Guaguanco
Dejala En La Puntica | TipToe | TIP-888829 2
Rodriguez,E.J. | (congas,perc,dr,bells,berimbau)
Josh Roseman Unit
Cherry | Enja | ENJ-9392 2
Marc Ribot Y Los Cubanos Postizos
The Proshetic Cubans | Atlantic | 7567-83116-2
Nuy Divertido(Very Entertaining) | Atlantic | 7567-83293-2
Rodriguez,Eddie | (percvoc)
Mongo Santamaria And His Band
Brazilian Sunset | Candid | CCD 79703
Rodriguez,Frankie | (bata,checkere,quinto,voc,chekere)
Jerry Gonzalez & Fort Apache Band
The River Is Deep | Enja | ENJ-4040 2
Rodriguez,Irwin 'Wito' | (ldvoc)
Conexion Latina
Calorcito | Enja | ENJ-4072 2
Rodriguez,Johnny | (bongos,concas,voc,congasperc)
Art Blakey And The Afrocuban Boys
Les Liaisons Dangereuses(Original Soundtrack) | Fontana | 812017-2
Gene Harris And The Three Sounds
Deep Blue-The United States Of Mind | Blue Note | 521152-2
Rodriguez,Jose | (tb)
Cal Tjader's Orchestra
Talkin Verve/Roots Of Acid Jazz:Cal Tjader | Verve | 531562-2
Rodriguez,Jose 'Papo' | (bongos,chekere,congas,percvoc)
Conexion Latina
Calorcito | Enja | ENJ-4072 2
Rodriguez,Mike | (tp)
Eric Reed Orchestra
Happiness | Nagel-Heyer | CD 2010
Rodriguez,Nicholas | (p)
Spike Hughes And His Negro Orchestra
Jazz:The Essential Collection Vol.3 | IN+OUT Records | 78013-2
Rodriguez,Octavio | (percbata-dr)
Lazaro Ros Con Mezcla
Cantos | Intuition Records | INT 3080-2
Rodriguez,Omar | (b)
Ramon Valle Quintet
Ramon Valle Plays Ernesto Lecuona | ACT | 9404-2
Rodriguez,Red | (p)
Jelly Roll Morton And His Orchestra
Planet Jazz:Jelly Roll Morton | Planet Jazz | 2152060-2
Rodriguez,Robert J. | (chekere,claves,dr,perc,voc,timbales)
Marc Ribot Y Los Cubanos Postizos
The Proshetic Cubans | Atlantic | 7567-83116-2
Nuy Divertido(Very Entertaining) | Atlantic | 7567-83293-2
Rodriguez,Roberto | (b,tpvoc)
Charlie Parker With Machito And His Orchestra
Charlie Parker:The Best Of The Verve Years | Verve | 527815-2
Talkin' Bird | Verve | 559859-2
Bird: The Complete Charlie Parker On Verve | Verve | 837141-2
Charlie Parker:April In Paris | Dreyfus Jazz Line | FDM 36737-2
Dizzy Gillespie Group
Verve Jazz Masters 10:Dizzy Gillespie | Verve | 516319-2
Dizzy Gillspie And His Latin American Rhythm
Afro | Verve | 517052-2
Sarah Vaughan With Orchestra
!Viva! Vaughan | Mercury | 549374-2
Sarah Vaughan With The Frank Foster Orchestra
The Antonio Carlos Jobim Songbook | Verve | 525472-2
Tito Puente Orchestra
Planet Jazz:Tito Puente | Planet Jazz | 2165369-2
Rodriguez,Willie | (bongos,congas,dr,perc,shakers)
Art Blakey And The Afrocuban Boys
Les Liaisons Dangereuses(Original Soundtrack) | Fontana | 812017-2
Billie Holiday With The Paul Whiteman Orchestra
Billie's Blues | Blue Note | 748786-2
Cal Tjader's Orchestra
Verve Jazz Masters 39:Cal Tjader | Verve | 521858-2
Coleman Hawkins Septet
Desafinado | Impulse(MCA) | 951227-2
Coleman Hawkins Sextet
Desafinado | Impulse(MCA) | 951227-2
Dizzy Gillespie And His Orchestra
Verve Jazz Masters 10:Dizzy Gillespie | Verve | 516319-2
Gillespiana And Carnegie Hall Concert | Verve | 519809-2
Talking Verve:Dizzy Gillespie | Verve | 533846-2
Ernestine Anderson With Orchestra
My Kinda Swing | Mercury | 842409-2
Jack McDuff Quartet With Orchestra
Prelude:Jack McDuff Big Band | Prestige | PRCD 24283-2
Joe Williams,With The Oliver Nelson Orchestra
Planet Jazz:Joe Williams | Planet Jazz | 2165370-2
Johnny Lytle Quintet
The Village Caller | Original Jazz Classics | OJCCD 110-2(R 9480)
Kenny Burrell Quintet
Guitar Forms | Verve | 521403-2
Verve Jazz Masters 45:Kenny Burrell | Verve | 527652-2
Kenny Clarke Quintet
Verve Jazz Masters 45:Kenny Burrell | Verve | 527652-2
King Curtis Band
King Curtis-Blow Man Blow | Bear Family Records | BCD 15670 CI
Lalo Schifrin Sextet
Tin Tin Deo | Fresh Sound Records | FSR-CD 319
Lena Horne With The Lennie Hayton Orchestra
Planet Jazz:Lena Horne | Planet Jazz | 2165373-2
McCoy Tyner Trio + Latin Percussion
McCoy Tyner Plays Ellington | Impulse(MCA) | 951216-2
Sarah Vaughan With Orchestra
Sarah Vaughan Sings The Mancini Songbook | Verve | 558401-2
Sonny Rollins Group
What's New? | RCA | 2179626-2
Sonny Rollins Quartet
Planet Jazz:Sonny Rollins | Planet Jazz | 2152062-2
Willie Rodriguez Jazz Quartet
Flatjacks | Milestone | MCD 9331-2
Roeder,Shorty | (b)
Hans Koller New Jazz Stars
Deutsches Jazz Fesival 1954/1955 | Bear Family Records | BCD 15430
Roelofs,Annemarie | (tb,vvoice)
The United Women's Orchestra
The Blue One | Jazz Haus Musik | JHM 0099 CD
United Women's Orchestra
Virgo Supercluster | Jazz Haus Musik | JHM 0123 CD
Rogall,Volker | (psynth)
Hugo Read Group
Songs Of A Wayfarer | Nabel Records:Jazz Network | CD 4653
Roger,Jean-Francois | (marimba,perctables)
Renaud Garcia-Fons Group
Oriental Bass | Enja | ENJ-9334 2
Roger,Stephane | (dr)
Frank Wess Meets The Paris-Barcelona Swing Connection
Paris-Barcelona Connection | Fresh Sound Records | FSNT 002 CD
Rogers,Adam | (el-gg)
Charles Mingus Orchestra
Tonight At Noon...Three Or Four Shades Of Love | Dreyfus Jazz Line | FDM 36633-2
Chris Potter Group
Traveling Mercies | Verve | 018243-2
David Binney Group
South | ACT | 9279-2
Balance | ACT | 9411-2
Jacky Terrasson Group
What It Is | Blue Note | 498756-2
Michael Brecker Quindectet
Wide Angles | Verve | 076142-2
Michael 'Patches' Stewart Group
Penetration | Hip Bop | HIBD 8018
Terri Lyne Carrington Quartet
Structure | ACT | 9427-2
Rogers,Angel | (voc)
Dizzy Gillespie And His Orchestra
Closer To The Source | Atlantic | 7567-80776-2
Rogers,Barry | (congastb)
Cal Tjader's Orchestra
Talkin Verve/Roots Of Acid Jazz:Cal Tjader | Verve | 531562-2
Rogers,Bruce | (cello)
Stan Getz With The Eddie Sauter Orchestra
Stan Getz Plays The Music Of Mickey One | Verve | 531232-2
Ultimate Stan Getz selected by Joe Henderson | Verve | 557532-2
Rogers,Buce | (cello)
Verve Jazz Masters 8:Stan Getz | Verve | 519823-2
Rogers,Chris | (tpfl-h)
Tom Harrell Orchestra
Time's Mirror | RCA | 2663524-2
Rogers,Ernest | (dr)
Bunk Johnson And His Superior Jazz Band
Authentic New Orleans Jazz | Good Time Jazz | GTCD 12048-2
Rogers,Harry | (tb)
Artie Shaw And His Orchestra
Planet JazzArtie Shaw | Planet Jazz | 2152057-2
The Legends Of Swing | Laserlight | 24659
Rogers,Kenny | (b-cl,as,bsss)
Cold Sweat
Cold Sweat Plays J.B. | JMT Edition | 919025-2
Rogers,Paul | (b)
Orchestre National De Jazz
Charmediterranéen | ECM | 1828(018493-2)
Rogers,Reuben | (b)
Donald Harrison Quartet
Free To Be | Impulse(MCA) | 951283-2
Donald Harrison Sextet
Free To Be | Impulse(MCA) | 951283-2
Eric Reed Trio
Pure Imagination | Impulse(MCA) | 951259-2
Joshua Redman Quartet
Passage Of Time | Warner | 9362-47997-2
Nicholas Payton Quartet
Gumbo Nouveau | Verve | 531199-2
Nicholas Payton Quintet
Nick@Night | Verve | 547598-2
Payton's Place | Verve | 557327-2
Nicholas Payton Sextet
Gumbo Nouveau | Verve | 531199-2
Payton's Place | Verve | 557327-2
Rogers,Ruben | (b)
Joshua Redman Quartet
Beyond | Warner | 9362-47465-2
Joshua Redman Quartet feat. Mark Turner
Beyond | Warner | 9362-47465-2
Rogers,Shorty | (arr,ld,cond,fl-h,tp,b-tpvoc)
Bud Shank Quintet

The Complete Nocturne Recordings:Jazz In Hollywood Series Vol.1 | Fresh Sound Records | NR 3CD-101
Howard Rumsey's Lighthouse All-Stars
Sunday Jazz A La Lighthouse Vol.2 | Original Jazz Classics | OJCCD 972-2(S 2501)
June Christy With The Pete Rugolo Orchestra
Something Cool(The Complete Mono & Stereo Versions) | Capitol | 534069-2
Mel Tormé With Orchestra
Comin' Home Baby!/Sings Sunday In New York | Warner | 8122-75438-2
Mel Tormé With The Shorty Rogers Orchestra
Comin' Home Baby!/Sings Sunday In New York | Warner | 8122-75438-2
Nat King Cole Quartet With The Stan Kenton Orchestra
Nat King Cole:For Sentimental Reasons | Dreyfus Jazz Line | FDM 36740-2
Peggy Lee With Orchestra
Pass Me By/Big Spender | Capitol | 535210-2
Shorty Rogers And His Giants
PLanet Jazz:Shorty Rogers | Planet Jazz | 2159976-2
Shorty Rogers And His Orchestra Feat. The Giants
PLanet Jazz:Shorty Rogers | Planet Jazz | 2159976-2
Stan Kenton And His Orchestra
One Night Stand | Choice | CHCD 71051
Terry Gibbs Septet
Early Stan | Original Jazz Classics | OJCCD 654-2(P 7255)
Woody Herman And His Orchestra
The Legends Of Swing | Laserlight | 24659
Woody Herman:Four Brother | Dreyfus Jazz Line | FDM 36722-2
Woody Herman And His Woodshoppers
Woody Herman (And The Herd) At Carnegie Hall | Verve | 559833-2
Woody Herman And The Herd
Woody Herman (And The Herd) At Carnegie Hall | Verve | 559833-2

Roggen,Live Maria | (percvoc)
European Jazz Youth Orchestra
Swinging Europe 1 | dacapo | DCCD 9449
Swinging Europe 2 | dacapo | DCCD 9450

Roggenbuck,Burkhard | (perc)
HR Big Band With Marjorie Barnes And Frits Landesbergen
Swinging Christmas | hr music.de | hrmj 012-02 CD
HR Big Band With Marjorie Barnes And Frits Landesbergen And Strings
Swinging Christmas | hr music.de | hrmj 012-02 CD

Roggenkamp,Wolfgang | (dr,percorg)
Barbara Jungfer Trio
Vitamin B 3 | yvp music | CD 3097

Rohde,Kai | (b)
Ekkehard Jost Trio
Some Other Tapes | Fish Music | FM 009/10 CD

Röhm,Jojo | (b)
Kölner Saxophon Mafia With Bad Little Dynamos
Kölner Saxophon Mafia Proudly Presents | Jazz Haus Musik | JHM 0046 CD

Rohrer,Samuel | (drperc)
Michael Beck Trio
Michael Beck Trio | JHM Records | JHM 3623
Susanne Abbuehl Group
April | ECM | 1766(013999-2)

Roidinger,Adelhard | (b,el-b,synthdr-computer)
Austria Drei
Jazz Portraits | EGO | 95080
European Jazz Ensemble
European Jazz Ensemble 25th Anniversary | Konnex Records | KCD 5100
Hans Koller Free Sound
Phoenix | MPS | 9813438
Hans Koller Quintet
Kunstkopfindianer | MPS | 9813439
Jazzensemble Des Hessischen Rundfunks
Atmosphering Conditions Permitting | ECM | 1549/50
Melanie Bong With Band
Fantasia | Jazz 4 Ever Records:Jazz Network | J4E 4755

Roither,Gerhard | (v)
Till Brönner Quartet & Deutsches Symphonieorchester Berlin
German Songs | Minor Music | 801057

Roizner,El Zurdo | (drperc)
Gato Barbieri Orchestra
Latino America | Impulse(MCA) | 952236-2

Rojas,Marcus | (perctuba)
Marc Ribot Y Los Cubanos Postizos
Nuy Divertido(Very Entertaining) | Atlantic | 7567-83293-2
Marty Ehrlich Group
The Long View | Enja | ENJ-9452 2
Michael Blake Group
Kingdom Of Champa | Intuition Records | INT 3189-2
Drift | Intuition Records | INT 3212-2

Rojas,Vicente | (voc)
Arturo Sandoval And The Latin Train Band
Arturo Sandoval & The Latin Train | GRP | GRP 98202

Rojo,Erika | (voc)
Erika Rojo & Tim Sund
Das Lied | Nabel Records:Jazz Network | CD 4684

Roker,Granville 'Mickey' | (drvoc)
Andrew Hill Orchestra
Deep Blue-The United States Of Mind | Blue Note | 521152-2
Bobby Hutcherson Quintet
Blue Breaks Beats Vol.2 | Blue Note | 789907-2
Charles Kynard Sextet
The Soul Brotherhood | Prestige | PCD 24257-2
Dizzy Gillespie All Stars
Jazz At The Philharmonic:The Montreux Collection | Pablo | PACD 5306-2
Dizzy Gillespie Big 7
Dizzy-At The Montreux Jazz Festival 1975 | Original Jazz Classics | OJC20 739-2(2310749)
Dizzy Gillespie-Count Basie Quartet
The Gifted Ones | Original Jazz Classics | OJCCD 886-2(2310833)
Duke Pearson Orchestra
Deep Blue-The United States Of Mind | Blue Note | 521152-2
Blue Bossa | Blue Note | 795590-2
Duke Pearson Quartet
Sweet Honey Bee | Blue Note | 595974-2
Duke Pearson Quintet
Sweet Honey Bee | Blue Note | 595974-2
Duke Pearson Sextet
Deep Blue-The United States Of Mind | Blue Note | 521152-2
Sweet Honey Bee | Blue Note | 595974-2
Midnight Blue(The [Be]witching Hour) | Blue Note | 854365-2
Dusko Goykovich Quartet
Soul Connection | Enja | ENJ-8044 2
Dusko Goykovich Quintet
Soul Connection | Enja | ENJ-8044 2
Ella Fitzgerald With Count Basie And His Orchestra
Digital III At Montreux | Original Jazz Classics | OJCCD 996-2(2308223)
Ella Fitzgerald With The Count Basie Orchestra
Bluella:Ella Fitzgerald Sings The Blues | Pablo | 2310960-2
Gene Ammons Sextet
Fine And Mellow | Prestige | PRCD 24281-2
Herbie Hancock Sextet
Herbie Hancock:The Complete Blue Note Sixties Sessions | Blue Note | 495569-2
Herbie Hancock Trio
Herbie Hancock:The Complete Blue Note Sixties Sessions | Blue Note | 495569-2
Horace Silver Quartet
Horace Silver Retrospective | Blue Note | 495576-2
Horace Silver Quintet
Horace Silver Retrospective | Blue Note | 495576-2
Blue Velvet: Crooners, Swooners And Velvet Vocals | Blue Note | 521153-2
Horace Silver Sextet
Horace Silver Retrospective | Blue Note | 495576-2
Deep Blue-The United States Of Mind | Blue Note | 521152-2
Horace Silver Sextet With Vocals
Horace Silver Retrospective | Blue Note | 495576-2
J.J. Johnson-Al Grey Sextet
Things Are Getting Better All The Time | Original Jazz Classics | OJCCD 745-2(2312141)
The J.J.Johnson Memorial Album | Prestige | PRCD 11025-2
Joe Williams And Friends
Planet Jazz:Male Jazz Vocalists | Planet Jazz | 2169657-2
At Newport '63 | RCA | 2663919-2
Joe Williams And His Band
Planet Jazz:Joe Williams | Planet Jazz | 2165370-2
Junior Mance Trio
Junior's Blues | Original Jazz Classics | OJCCD 1000-2(RLP 9447)
Lee Morgan Orchestra
Standards | Blue Note | 823213-2
Lee Morgan Quintet
Live At The Lighthouse | Blue Note | 835228-2
Lee Morgan Sextet
Deep Blue-The United States Of Mind | Blue Note | 521152-2
Sonic Boom | Blue Note | 590414-2
Machito And His Orchestra
Afro-Cuban Jazz Moods | Original Jazz Classics | OJC20 447-2
Mary Lou Williams Quartet
The Story Of Jazz Piano | Laserlight | 24653
McCoy Tyner Quintet
Live At Newport | Impulse(MCA) | 547980-2
McCoy Tyner Trio
Live At Newport | Impulse(MCA) | 547980-2
Milt Jackson Big 4
Milt Jackson At The Montreux Jazz Festival 1975 | Original Jazz Classics | OJC20 884-2(2310753)
Milt Jackson Quartet
Milt Jackson Birthday Celebration | Fantasy | FANCD 6079-2
Soul Route | Original Jazz Classics | OJCCD 1059-2(2310900)
Jazz At The Philharmonic:The Montreux Collection | Pablo | PACD 5306-2
The Jazz Giants Play Harold Arlen:Blues In The Night | Prestige | PCD 24201-2
Milt Jackson-Ray Brown Quartet
It Don't Mean A Thing If You Can't Tap Your Foot To It | Original Jazz Classics | OJCCD 601-2
Nat Adderley With Jim Hall And The Junior Mance Trio
Little Big Horn! | Original Jazz Classics | OJCCD 1001-2(R 9474)
Nat Adderley With Kenny Burrell And The Junior Mance Trio
Little Big Horn! | Original Jazz Classics | OJCCD 1001-2(R 9474)
Oscar Peterson Quintet
Skol | Original Jazz Classics | OJC20 496-2
Quadrant
Milt Jackson Birthday Celebration | Fantasy | FANCD 6079-2
Roy Eldridge-Dizzy Gillespie With The Oscar Peterson Quartet
Jazz Maturity... Where It's Coming From | Original Jazz Classics | OJCCD 807-2(2310816)
Shirley Scott Trio
Skylark | Candid | CCD 79705
Sonny Rollins Quartet
Planet Jazz:Sonny Rollins | Planet Jazz | 2152062-2
The Standard Sonny Rollins | RCA | 2174801-2
Sonny Rollins On Impulse | Impulse(MCA) | 951223-2
The Roots Of Acid Jazz | Impulse(MCA) | IMP 12042
Sonny Rollins Trio
Planet Jazz:Sonny Rollins | Planet Jazz | 2152062-2
The Standard Sonny Rollins | RCA | 2174801-2
Stanley Turrentine Orchestra
Rough 'N' Tumble | Blue Note | 524552-2
The Spoiler | Blue Note | 853359-2
Stanley Turrentine Quartet
Blue N' Groovy | Blue Note | 780679-2
Willis Jackson Quartet
At Large | Prestige | PCD 24243-2
Zoot Sims Quartet
Getting Sentimental | Choice | CHCD 71006
The Jazz Giants Play Cole Porter:Night And Day | Prestige | PCD 24203-2

Rokovic,Bora | (p)
Dusko Goykovich Quintet With The NDR Radio-Philharmonie,Hannover
Balkan Blues | Enja | ENJ-9320 2

Roland Kirk Spirit Choir,The | (background-voc)
Rahsaan Roland Kirk Sextet
Volunteered Slavery | Rhino | 8122-71407-2

Roland,E.J. | (g)
Jerri Southern Quartet
The Very Thought Of You:The Decca Years 1951-1957 | Decca | 050671-2

Roland,Gene | (arr,cl,mellophone,ss,tp,vocv-tb)
Charles Mingus And His Orchestra
The Complete Town Hall Concert | Blue Note | 828353-2
Stan Kenton And His Orchestra
Adventures In Blues | Capitol | 520089-2
Adventures In Jazz | Capitol | 521222-2

Roland,Joe | (vib)
George Shearing Quintet
Verve Jazz Masters 57:George Shearing | Verve | 529900-2

Roland,Larry | (b)
Gunter Hampel Jazz Sextet
Gunter Hampel: The 8th Of Sept.1999 | Birth | CD 049

Rolfe,Bob | (tp)
Harry James And His Orchestra
Trumpet Blues:The Best Of Harry James | Capitol | 521224-2
Stan Kenton And His Orchestra
Adventures In Blues | Capitol | 520089-2
Adventures In Jazz | Capitol | 521222-2

Rollet,Christian | (drperc)
Pata Music Meets Arfi
News Of Roi Ubu | Pata Musik | PATA 10 CD
La Belle Et La Bête | Pata Musik | PATA 14(amf 1066)

Rollings,Matt | (keyboards)
Larry Carlton Group
The Gift | GRP | GRP 98542

Rollini,Adrian | (bass-sax,goofus,hot-fountain-pen,ld)
Adrian Rollini And His Orchestra
Jazz:The Essential Collection Vol.3 | IN+OUT Records | 78013-2
Bix Beiderbecke And His Gang
Jazz:The Essential Collection Vol.2 | IN+OUT Records | 78012-2
Frankie Trumbauer And His Orchestra
Jazz:The Essential Collection Vol.2 | IN+OUT Records | 78012-2
Jack Teagarden And His Orchestra
Jazz:The Essential Collection Vol.3 | IN+OUT Records | 78013-2

Rollini,Arthur | (as,ts,clsax)
Adrian Rollini And His Orchestra
Jazz:The Essential Collection Vol.3 | IN+OUT Records | 78013-2
All Star Band
Planet Jazz:Jack Teagarden | Planet Jazz | 2161236-2
Benny Goodman And His Orchestra
Planet Jazz:Benny Goodman | Planet Jazz | 2152054-2
Planet Jazz Sampler | Planet Jazz | 2152326-2
Planet Jazz:Jazz Greatest Hits | Planet Jazz | 2169648-2
Planet Jazz:Big Bands | Planet Jazz | 2169649-2
Planet Jazz:Swing | Planet Jazz | 2169651-2
Planet Jazz:Jazz Trumpet | Planet Jazz | 2169654-2
Planet Jazz:Female Jazz Vocalists | Planet Jazz | 2169656-2
Benny Goodman At Carnegie Hall 1938(Complete) | CBS | C2K 65143
Camel Caravan Broadcast 1939 Vol.1 | Phontastic | NCD 8817
Camel Caravan Broadcast 1939 Vol.2 | Phontastic | NCD 8818
Camel Caravan Broadcast 1939 Vol.3 | Phontastic | NCD 8819
More Camel Caravans | Phontastic | NCD 8841/2
More Camel Caravans | Phontastic | NCD 8843/4
More Camel Caravans | Phontastic | NCD 8845/6
Benny Goodman And His V-Disc All Star Band
The Legends Of Swing | Laserlight | 24659
Benny Goodman Band
Benny Goodman At Carnegie Hall 1938(Complete) | CBS | C2K 65143
Jam Session
Benny Goodman At Carnegie Hall 1938(Complete) | CBS | C2K 65143
Louis Armstrong And His Orchestra
Louis Armstrong:Swing That Music | Laserlight | 36056
Louis Armstrong:C'est Si Bon | Dreyfus Jazz Line | FDM 36730-2

Rollins,Lucille | (cowbell)
Sonny Rollins Sextet
Sunny Days,Starry Nights | Milestone | MCD 9122-2

Rollins,Sonny | (ss,ts,talking,lyricon,pts-solo)
Abbey Lincoln With Her Quartet
That's Him! | Original Jazz Classics | OJCCD 085-2
Abbey Lincoln With Her Quintet
Sonny Rollins-The Freelance Years:The Complete Riverside & Contemporary Recordings | Riverside | 5 RCD 4427-2
That's Him! | Original Jazz Classics | OJCCD 085-2
Art Farmer Quintet
Early Art | Original Jazz Classics | OJCCD 880-2(NJ 8258)
Bud Powell Quintet
The Amazing Bud Powell Vol.1 | Blue Note | 532136-2
Bud Powell:Bouncing With Bud | Dreyfus Jazz Line | FDM 36725-2
Bud Powell's Modernists
The Fabulous Fats Navarro Vol.1 | Blue Note | 0677207
The Fabulous Fats Navarro Vol.2 | Blue Note | 0677208
Clifford Brown-Max Roach Quintet
Clifford Brown-Max Roach:Alone Together-The Best Of The Mercury Years | Verve | 526373-2
Verve Jazz Masters 44:Clifford Brown and Max Roach | Verve | 528109-2
Clifford Brown And Max Roach At Basin Street | Verve | 589826-2
Brownie-The Complete EmArCy Recordings Of Clifford Brown | EmArCy | 838306-2
Dizzy Gillespie Sextet
Verve Jazz Masters 50:Sonny Sitt | Verve | 527651-2
Dizzy Gillespie-Sonny Rollins-Sonny Stitt Sextet
Sonny Side Up | Verve | 521426-2
J.J.Johnson Sextet
The J.J.Johnson Memorial Album | Prestige | PRCD 11025-2
Kenny Dorham Quintet
Sonny Rollins-The Freelance Years:The Complete Riverside & Contemporary Recordings | Riverside | 5 RCD 4427-2
Jazz Contrast | Original Jazz Classics | OJCCD 028-2(RLP 239)
Kenny Dorham Sextet
Jazz Contrast | Original Jazz Classics | OJCCD 028-2(RLP 239)
Max Roach Plus Four
Clifford Brown-Max Roach:Alone Together-The Best Of The Mercury Years | Verve | 526373-2
Max Roach Quintet
Clifford Brown-Max Roach:Alone Together-The Best Of The Mercury Years | Verve | 526373-2
Miles Davis And His Orchestra
Collector's Items | Original Jazz Classics | OJC20 071-2(P 7044)
Miles Davis Quintet
Collector's Items | Original Jazz Classics | OJC20 071-2(P 7044)
Bags' Groove | Original Jazz Classics | OJC20 245-2
Miles Davis Sextet
Dig | Original Jazz Classics | OJC20 005-2
Miles Davis And Horns | Original Jazz Classics | OJC20 053-2(P 7025)
The Jazz Giants Play Harold Arlen:Blues In The Night | Prestige | PCD 24201-2
The Jazz Giants Play Miles Davis:Milestones | Prestige | PCD 24225-2
The Prestige Legacy Vol.1:The High Priests | Prestige | PCD 24251-2
Modern Jazz Quartet With Sonny Rollins
The Modern Jazz Quartet At Music Inn With Sonny Rollins,Vol.2 | Atlantic | 7567-80794-2
MJQ 40 | Atlantic | 7567-82330-2
Sonny Rollins
Sonny Rollins-The Freelance Years:The Complete Riverside & Contemporary Recordings | Riverside | 5 RCD 4427-2
St.Thomas:Sonny Rollins In Stockholm 1959 | Dragon | DRCD 229
Sonny Rollins & Co.
Planet Jazz:Sonny Rollins | Planet Jazz | 2152062-2
Planet Jazz Sampler | Planet Jazz | 2152326-2
Sonny Rollins & The Contemporary Leaders
Sonny Rollins & The Contemporary Leaders | Original Jazz Classics | OJCCD 340-2
Sonny Rollins And The Contemporary Leaders
Sonny Rollins-The Freelance Years:The Complete Riverside & Contemporary Recordings | Riverside | 5 RCD 4427-2
Sonny Rollins Group
What's New? | RCA | 2179626-2
Sonny Rollins Orchestra
Sonny Rollins And The Big Brass | Verve | 557545-2
Alfie | Impulse(MCA) | 951224-2
Sonny Rollins Plus 3
Sonny Rollins + 3 | Milestone | MCD 9250-2
Sonny Rollins Plus Four
Sonny Rollins Plus 4 | Original Jazz Classics | OJC20 243-2(P 7038)
The Prestige Legacy Vol.1:The High Priests | Prestige | PCD 24251-2
Sonny Rollins Quartet
Planet Jazz:Sonny Rollins | Planet Jazz | 2152062-2
Planet Jazz:Jazz Greatest Hits | Planet Jazz | 2169648-2
The Standard Sonny Rollins | RCA | 2174801-2
The Bridge | RCA | 2179625-2
What's New? | RCA | 2179626-2
Thelonious Monk:The Complete Prestige Recordings | Prestige | 3 PRCD 4428-2
Sonny Rollins Vol.2 | Blue Note | 497809-2
Sonny Rollins-The Freelance Years:The Complete Riverside & Contemporary Recordings | Riverside | 5 RCD 4427-2
True Blue | Blue Note | 534032-2
Ballads | Blue Note | 537562-2
Sonny Rollins And The Big Brass | Verve | 557545-2
Newk's Time | Blue Note | 576752-2
The Blue Note Years-The Best Of Sonny Rollins | Blue Note | 793203-2
Sonny Rollins:The Blue Note Recordings | Blue Note | 821371-2
Jazz Profile:Sonny Rollins | Blue Note | 823516-2
East Broadway Run Down | Impulse(MCA) | 951161-2
Sonny Rollins On Impulse | Impulse(MCA) | 951223-2
The Roots Of Acid Jazz | Impulse(MCA) | IMP 12042
Global Warming | Milestone | MCD 9280-2
This Is What I Do | Milestone | MCD 9310-2
Next Album | Original Jazz Classics | OJC 312 (M 9042)
Worktime | Original Jazz Classics | OJC20 007-2(P 7020)
The Sound Of Sonny | Original Jazz Classics | OJC20 029-2
Tenor Madness | Original Jazz Classics | OJC20 124-2
Saxophone Colossus | Original Jazz Classics | OJC20 291-2
Sonny Rollins With The Modern Jazz Quartet | Original Jazz Classics | OJCCD 011-2
Tour De Force | Original Jazz Classics | OJCCD 095-2
Sonny Boy | Original Jazz Classics | OJCCD 348-2(P 7207)
Easy Living | Original Jazz Classics | OJCCD 893-2
The Jazz Giants Play Jerome Kern:Yesterdays | Prestige | PCD 24202-2
The Jazz Giants Play Cole Porter:Night And Day | Prestige | PCD 24203-2
The Prestige Legacy Vol.1:The High Priests | Prestige | PCD 24251-2
Tenor Madness | Prestige | PRSA 7047-6
Sonny Rollins Quartet feat.Thelonious Monk
Ballads | Blue Note | 537562-2
Thelonious Monk/Sonny Rollins | Original Jazz Classics | OJCCD 059-2

Sonny Rollins Quintet
John Coltrane-The Prestige Recordings | Prestige | 16 PCD 4405-2
Sonny Rollins Vol.2 | Blue Note | 497809-2
Sonny Rollins-The Freelance Years:The Complete Riverside & Contemporary Recordings | Riverside | 5 RCD 4427-2
Ballads | Blue Note | 537562-2
Sonny Rollins:Vol.1 | Blue Note | 591724-2
The Blue Note Years-The Best Of Sonny Rollins | Blue Note | 793203-2
The Best Of Blue Note Vol.2 | Blue Note | 797960-2
Sonny Rollins:The Blue Note Recordings | Blue Note | 821371-2
Jazz Profile:Sonny Rollins | Blue Note | 823516-2
Don't Stop The Carnival | Milestone | MCD 55005-2
Sunny Days,Starry Nights | Milestone | MCD 9122-2
Here's To The People | Milestone | MCD 9194-2
Old Flames | Milestone | MCD 9215-2
This Is What I Do | Milestone | MCD 9310-2
Next Album | Original Jazz Classics | OJC 312 (M 9042)
Tenor Madness | Original Jazz Classics | OJC20 124-2
No Problem | Original Jazz Classics | OJCCD 1014-2(M 9104)
Sonny Rollins Plays For Bird | Original Jazz Classics | OJCCD 214-2
Sonny Boy | Original Jazz Classics | OJCCD 348-2(P 7207)
Easy Living | Original Jazz Classics | OJCCD 893-2
Don't Ask | Original Jazz Classics | OJCCD 915-2(M 9090)
The Jazz Giants Play Harry Warren:Lullaby Of Broadway | Prestige | PCD 24204-2
The Prestige Legacy Vol.2:Battles Of Saxes | Prestige | PCD 24252-2
Tenor Madness | Prestige | PRSA 7047-6
Sonny Rollins Quintet With Brass
Old Flames | Milestone | MCD 9215-2
Sonny Rollins Sextet
The Standard Sonny Rollins | RCA | 2174801-2
Sonny Rollins Vol.2 | Blue Note | 497809-2
Sonny Rollins:The Blue Note Recordings | Blue Note | 821371-2
Jazzin' Vol.2: The Music Of Stevie Wonder | Fantasy | FANCD 6088-2
Don't Stop The Carnival | Milestone | MCD 55005-2
Sunny Days,Starry Nights | Milestone | MCD 9122-2
Here's To The People | Milestone | MCD 9194-2
Global Warming | Milestone | MCD 9280-2
The Cutting Edge | Original Jazz Classics | OJC 468(M 9059)
Easy Living | Original Jazz Classics | OJCCD 893-2
Don't Ask | Original Jazz Classics | OJCCD 915-2(M 9090)
Sonny Rollins Sextet With Rufus Harley
The Cutting Edge | Original Jazz Classics | OJC 468(M 9059)
Sonny Rollins Trio
Planet Jazz:Sonny Rollins | Planet Jazz | 2152062-2
Planet Jazz:Jazz Saxophone | Planet Jazz | 2169653-2
The Standard Sonny Rollins | RCA | 2174801-2
A Night At The Village Vanguard | Blue Note | 499795-2
Sonny Rollins-The Freelance Years:The Complete Riverside & Contemporary Recordings | Riverside | 5 RCD 4427-2
Ballads | Blue Note | 537562-2
Sonny Rollins And The Big Brass | Verve | 557545-2
The Blue Note Years-The Best Of Sonny Rollins | Blue Note | 793203-2
Sonny Rollins:The Blue Note Recordings | Blue Note | 821371-2
Jazz Profile:Sonny Rollins | Blue Note | 823516-2
East Broadway Run Down | Impulse(MCA) | 951161-2
St.Thomas:Sonny Rollins In Stockholm 1959 | Dragon | DRCD 229
The Sound Of Sonny | Original Jazz Classics | OJC20 029-2
Way Out West | Original Jazz Classics | OJC20 337-2(S 7530)
Freedom Suite | Original Jazz Classics | OJCCD 067-2
Sonny Rollins With The Modern Jazz Quartet
The Complete Modern Jazz Quartet Prestige & Pablo Recordings | Prestige | 4PRCD 4438-2
Milt Jackson Birthday Celebration | Fantasy | FANCD 6079-2
Sonny Rollins With The Modern Jazz Quartet | Original Jazz Classics | OJCCD 011-2
The Jazz Giants Play Duke Ellington:Caravan | Prestige | PCD 24227-2
Sonny Rollins/Philly Joe Jones
Newk's Time | Blue Note | 576752-2
Sonny Rollins:The Blue Note Recordings | Blue Note | 821371-2
Sonny Rollins-Coleman Hawkins Quintet
Planet Jazz:Sonny Rollins | Planet Jazz | 2152062-2
Sonny Meets Hawk! | RCA | 2174800-2
Sonny Rollins-Larry Coryell Duo
Don't Ask | Original Jazz Classics | OJCCD 915-2(M 9090)
Thelonious Monk Quartet
Thelonious Monk:85th Birthday Celebration | zyx records | FANCD 6076-2
Thelonious Monk Quintet
Thelonious Monk:The Complete Prestige Recordings | Prestige | 3 PRCD 4428-2
Sonny Rollins-The Freelance Years:The Complete Riverside & Contemporary Recordings | Riverside | 5 RCD 4427-2
Thelonious Monk:85th Birthday Celebration | zyx records | FANCD 6076-2
Brilliant Corners | Original Jazz Classics | OJC20 026-2
MONK | Original Jazz Classics | OJCCD 016-2
Thelonious Monk/Sonny Rollins | Original Jazz Classics | OJCCD 059-2
The Prestige Legacy Vol.1:The High Priests | Prestige | PCD 24251-2

Roman,Olga | (vocvoice)
Danilo Perez Quartet
Panamonk | Impulse(MCA) | 951190-2

Romano,Aldo | (dr,perc,el-g,g,voc,p,voicesynth)
Aldo Romano Duo
Il Piacere | Owl Records | 013575-2
Aldo Romano Group
AlmaLatina | Owl Records | 018364-2
Aldo Romano Trio
Il Piacere | Owl Records | 013575-2
Enrico Rava Quartet
Enrico Rava Quartet | ECM | 1122
Franz Koglmann Quintet
Opium | Between The Lines | btl 011(Efa 10181-2)
Gato Barbieri Quintet
The Art Of Saxophone | Laserlight | 24652
Joe Lovano-Aldo Romano
Ten Tales | Owl Records | 018350-2
Michel Grailler Trio
Dream Drops | Owl Records | 013434-2
Michel Petrucciani Group
Playground | Blue Note | 795480-2
Michel Petrucciani Trio
Michel Petrucciani | Owl Records | 013431-2
Palatino
Palationo Chap.3 | EmArCy | 013610-2
Steve Kuhn Trio
Oceans In The Sky | Owl Records | 013428-2

Romano,Joe | (as,fl,ts,reeds,saxss)
Buddy Rich Big Band
Backwoods Siseman/Pieces Of Dream | Laserlight | 24655
Gus Mancuso Quintet
Gus Mancuso & Special Friends | Fantasy | FCD 24762-2

Romao,Dom Um | (berimbau,dr,perc,voc,bells,claves)
Cannonball Adderley With Sergio Mendes And The Bossa Rio Quartet
Cannonball's Bossa Nova | Blue Note | 522667-2
Cannonball Adderley With Sergio Mendes And The Bossa Rio Sextet
Cannonball's Bossa Nova | Blue Note | 522667-2
Ballads | Blue Note | 537563-2
Blue Bossa | Blue Note | 795590-2
Collin Walcott Group
Grazing Dreams | ECM | 1096
Freddy Studer Orchestra
Seven Songs | VeraBra Records | CDVBR 2056-2
Helen Merrill With Orchestra
Casa Forte | EmArCy | 558848-2
Ithamara Koorax With Band
Love Dance:The Ballad Album | Milestone | MCD 9327-2
McCoy Tyner Orchestra
13th House | Original Jazz Classics | OJCCD 1089-2(M 9102)
Weather Report
Sweetnighter | CBS | 485102-2
Weathe Report Live In Tokyo | CBS | 489208-2

Römer,Rainer | (perc)
Ensemble Modern
Ensemble Modern-Fred Frith:Traffic Continues | Winter&Winter | 910044-2

Römer,Rolf | (b-cl,ss,ts,cl,reedssax)
Bob Brookmeyer Group With The WDR Big Band
Electricity | ACT | 9219-2
Eddie Harris Group With The WDR Big Band
Eddie Harris-The Last Concert | ACT | 9249-2
Gianlugi Trovesi Quartet With The WDR Big Band
Dedalo | Enja | ENJ-9419 2
Jens Winther And The WDR Big Band
The Escape | dacapo | DCCD 9437
Kevin Mahogany With The WDR Big Band And Guests
Pussy Cat Dues:The Music Of Charles Mingus | Enja | ENJ-9316 2
Los Jovenes Flamencos With The WDR Big Band And Guests
Jazzpana | ACT | 9212-2
Rolf Römer Quartet
Tesoro | Jazz 4 Ever Records:Jazz Network | J4E 4743
Rolf Römer Trio
Tesoro | Jazz 4 Ever Records:Jazz Network | J4E 4743
Rolf Römer-Bill Dobbins Quartet
A Tribute To B.A.C.H. | Edition Collage | EC 520-2
Vince Mendoza With The WDR Big Band And Guests
Sketches | ACT | 9215-2

Romero,Martin | (congas)
Daniel Messina Band
Imagenes | art-mode-records | 990014

Romero,Raoul | (arrts)
Woody Herman And His Orchestra
Verve Jazz Masters 54:Woody Herman | Verve | 529903-2

Romero,Ray | (bata,bata-dr,bongosconga)
Sabu L. Martinez Group
Palo Congo | Blue Note | 522665-2

Romersa,Ernest | (reeds)
Ella Fitzgerald With The Frank DeVol Orchestra
Get Happy! | Verve | 523321-2

Romersa,Ted | (as,cl,tssax)
Stan Kenton And His Orchestra
Stan Kenton-The Formative Years | Decca | 589489-2

Romersa,Tom 'Tommy' | (dr)
Benny Goodman Trio
Benny Goodman-The Complete Capitol Trios | Capitol | 521225-2
Peggy Lee With The Benny Goodman Orchestra
Peggy Lee & Benny Goodman:The Complete Recordings 1941-1947 | CBS | C2K 65686

Romm,Ronald | (tpfl-h)
Canadian Brass
Take The A Train | RCA | 2663455-2

Romondi,Matthew | (strings)
Grover Washington Jr. Orchestra
Inside Moves | Elektra | 7559-60318-2

Ronak,Bent | (tb)
Stan Getz With Ib Glindemann And His Orchestra
Stan Getz In Europe | Laserlight | 24657

Ronan,Karl | (b-tb)
European Jazz Youth Orchestra
Swinging Europe 1 | dacapo | DCCD 9449
Swinging Europe 2 | dacapo | DCCD 9450

Ronayne,John | (v)
Dee Dee Bridgewater With Orchestra
Dear Ella | Verve | 539102-2

Ronchaud,Roland | (p)
Rene Thomas Quintet
Jazz In Paris:René Thomas-The Real Cat | EmArCy | 549400-2 PMS

Rondinelli,Bruno | (ts)
Elliot Lawrence And His Orchestra
Mullenium | CBS | CK 65678

Roney,Antoine | (ssts)
Lenny White Group
Present Tense | Hip Bop | HIBD 8004

Roney,Wallace | (tpfl-h)
George Gruntz Concert Jazz Band
Blues 'N Dues Et Cetera | Enja | ENJ-6072 2
Kenny Barron Quintet
What If | Enja | ENJ-5013 2
Miles Davis With Gil Evans Orchestra, The George Gruntz Concert Jazz Band And Guests
Miles & Quincy Live At Montreux | Warner | 9362-45221-2
Terri Lyne Carrington Group
Jazz Is A Spirit | ACT | 9408-2

Rönfeld,Werner | (bs)
Chet Baker With The NDR-Bigband
Chet Baker-The Legacy Vol.1 | Enja | ENJ-9021 2
Heinz Sauer Quartet With The NDR Big Band
NDR Big Band-Bravissimo | ACT | 9232-2

Rongetti,Nick | (p)
Muggsy Spanier And His Dixieland Band
Muggsy Spanier-Manhattan Masters,1945 | Storyville | STCD 6051

Roos,Mary | (voc)
André Holst With Chris Dean's European Swing Orchestra
That's Swing | Nagel-Heyer | CD 079

Root,Alan | (p)
Graham Stewart And His New Orleans Band
The Golden Years Of Revival Jazz,Sampler | Storyville | 109 1001
The Golden Years Of Revival Jazz,Vol.10 | Storyville | STCD 5515
Graham Stewart Seven
The Golden Years Of Revival Jazz,Vol.8 | Storyville | STCD 5513

Root,Billy | (bsts)
Dizzy Gillespie And His Orchestra
Dizzy Gillespie:Birks Works-The Verve Big Band Sessions | Verve | 527900-2
Ultimate Dizzy Gillespie | Verve | 557535-2
Dizzy Gillespie Orchestra
Verve Jazz Masters 10:Dizzy Gillespie | Verve | 516319-2

Roots |
Roots
Salutes The Saxophone | IN+OUT Records | 7016-2
Salutes The Saxophones: Tributes To Gene Ammons, Eric Dolphy, Coleman Hawkins And Charlie Parker | IN+OUT Records | 7016-3
Jazz Unlimited | IN+OUT Records | 7017-2
Stablemates | IN+OUT Records | 7021-2
Saying Something | IN+OUT Records | 77031-2
For Diz & Bird | IN+OUT Records | 77039-2

Roots Band,The |
Etta James & The Roots Band
Burnin' Down he House | RCA | 3411633-2

Ros,Lazaro | (voc)
Gonzalo Rubalcaba & Cuban Quartet
Antiguo | Blue Note | 837717-2
Lazaro Ros Con Mezcla
Cantos | Intuition Records | INT 3080-2
Lazaro Ros Ensemble
Ori Batá (Cuban Yoruba Music) | Enja | ENJ-9381 2

Rosa,Eddie | (cl,as,reedssax)
Van Alexander Orchestra
Home Of Happy Feet/Swing! Staged For Sound! | Capitol | 535211-2

Rosales,Edgard | (congasmaracas)
Cal Tjader Quintet
Tjader Plays Mambo | Original Jazz Classics | OJCCD 274-2(F 3221)

Rosales,Gerardo | (congas,guiro,maracasperc)
The Rosenberg Trio
Suenos Gitanos | Polydor | 549581-2

Rosalies,Edward | (bongo,congaperc)
Cal Tjader's Modern Mambo Quintet(Sextet)
Mambo With Tjader | Original Jazz Classics | OJCCD 271-2(F 3202)
Conexion Latina
La Conexión | Enja | ENJ-9065 2

Rosand,Aaron | (v)
Bill Evans Quartet With Orchestra
The Complete Bill Evans On Verve | Verve | 527953-2
From Left To Right | Verve | 557451-2

Rosati,Archie | (clsax)
Lena Horne With The Lou Bring Orchestra
Planet Jazz:Lena Horne | Planet Jazz | 2165373-2
Planet Jazz:Female Jazz Vocalists | Planet Jazz | 2169656-2

Rose,Adonis | (dr)
Nicholas Payton Quartet
Gumbo Nouveau | Verve | 531199-2
Nicholas Payton Quintet
Nick@Night | Verve | 547598-2
Payton's Place | Verve | 557327-2
Nicholas Payton Sextet
Gumbo Nouveau | Verve | 531199-2
Payton's Place | Verve | 557327-2

Rose,George | (g)
Louis Armstrong With Sy Oliver And His Orchestra
Satchmo Serenaders | Verve | 543792-2

Rose,Hans-Joachim | (v)
Bernd Konrad Jazz Group With Symphonie Orchestra
Wen Die Götter Lieben | Creative Works Records | CW CD 1010-1

Rose,Henri | (p)
Van Alexander Orchestra
Home Of Happy Feet/Swing! Staged For Sound! | Capitol | 535211-2

Rose,Michel | (pedal-steel-gshaker)
The Catholics
Simple | Laika Records | 35100802

Rose,Wally | (p)
Lu Watters' Jazz Band
Blues Over Bodega | Good Time Jazz | GTCD 12066-2
Lu Watters' Yerba Buena Jazz Band
The Very Best Of Dixieland Jazz | Verve | 535529-2
Yerba Buena Jazz Band
Bunk & Lu | Good Time Jazz | GTCD 12024-2

Rösel,Heinz | (dr)
Helmut Weglinski Quintet
Deutsches Jazz Fesival 1954/1955 | Bear Family Records | BCD 15430

Roseman,Joshua 'Josh' | (tb)
Dave Douglas Group
Soul On Soul | RCA | 2663603-2
Witness | RCA | 2663763-2
Dave Holland Big Band
What Goes Around | ECM | 1777(014002-2)
Josh Roseman Unit
Cherry | Enja | ENJ-9392 2
Lester Bowie's Brass Fantasy
The Odysse Of Funk & Popular Music | Dreyfus Jazz Line | FDM 37004-2
When The Spitit Returns | Dreyfus Jazz Line | FDM 37016-2
Steve Coleman And The Council Of Balance
Genesis & The Opening Of The Way | RCA | 2152934-2
The Sidewalks Of New York
Tin Pan Alley:The Sidewalks Of New York | Winter&Winter | 910038-2
Uri Caine Group
Urlicht/Primal Light | Winter&Winter | 910004-2

Rosen,Abe | (harp)
Woody Herman And The Herd
Woody Herman (And The Herd) At Carnegie Hall | Verve | 559833-2

Rosen,Adrian | (b)
Michael 'Patches' Stewart Group
Blue Patches | Hip Bop | HIBD 8016

Rosen,Meyer | (harp)
Charlie Parker With Strings
Charlie Parker:The Best Of The Verve Years | Verve | 527815-2
Bird: The Complete Charlie Parker On Verve | Verve | 837141-2
Charlie Parker:April In Paris | Dreyfus Jazz Line | FDM 36737-2

Rosen,Myoer | (harp)
Verve Jazz Masters 28:Charlie Parker Plays Standards | Verve | 521854-2
Charlie Parker With Strings:The Master Takes | Verve | 523984-2

Rosen,Sam | (dr)
Tommy Dorsey And His Orchestra
Planet Jazz:Tommy Dorsey | Planet Jazz | 2159972-2

Rosenbauer,Matthias | (drperc)
Matthias Rosenbauer-Gerhard Gschlößl
Duo 1 | Jazz 4 Ever Records:Jazz Network | J4E 4763

Rosenberg,John | (tp)
Chick Corea Group
Verve Jazz Masters 3:Chick Corea | Verve | 519820-2

Rosenberg,Nonnie | (b)
The Rosenberg Trio
Gypsy Swing | Verve | 527806-2
The Rosenberg Trio:The Collection | Verve | 537152-2
Suenos Gitanos | Polydor | 549581-2
Tribute To Django Reinhardt | EmArCy | 9811568
The Rosenberg Trio With Frits Landesbergen
Gypsy Swing | Verve | 527806-2
The Rosenberg Trio:The Collection | Verve | 537152-2
The Rosenberg Trio With Orchestra
Noches Calientes | Verve | 557022-2
The Rosenberg Trio With Stephane Grappelli
The Rosenberg Trio:The Collection | Verve | 537152-2

Rosenberg,Nou'che | (g)
The Rosenberg Trio
Gypsy Swing | Verve | 527806-2
The Rosenberg Trio:The Collection | Verve | 537152-2
Suenos Gitanos | Polydor | 549581-2
Tribute To Django Reinhardt | EmArCy | 9811568
The Rosenberg Trio With Frits Landesbergen
Gypsy Swing | Verve | 527806-2
The Rosenberg Trio:The Collection | Verve | 537152-2
The Rosenberg Trio With Orchestra
Noches Calientes | Verve | 557022-2
The Rosenberg Trio With Stephane Grappelli
The Rosenberg Trio:The Collection | Verve | 537152-2

Rosenberg,Roger | (alto-fl,b-cl,bs,bassoon,contra-b-cl)
Buddy Rich Big Band
Backwoods Siseman/Pieces Of Dream | Laserlight | 24655
David Matthews & The Manhattan Jazz Orchestra
Back To Bach | Milestone | MCD 9312-2
Hey Duke! | Milestone | MCD 9320-2
George Gruntz Concert Jazz Band
Blues 'N Dues Et Cetera | Enja | ENJ-6072 2
John Scofield Groups
Quiet | Verve | 533185-2
Miles Davis With Gil Evans Orchestra, The George Gruntz Concert Jazz Band And Guests
Miles & Quincy Live At Montreux | Warner | 9362-45221-2
Mingus Big Band 93
Nostalgia In Times Square | Dreyfus Jazz Line | FDM 36559-2

Rosenberg,Stochelo | (gg-solo)
Stochelo Rosenberg Group
Gypsy Swing | Verve | 527806-2
Stochelo Rosenberg Group With Strings
Gypsy Swing | Verve | 527806-2
The Rosenberg Trio
Gypsy Swing | Verve | 527806-2
The Rosenberg Trio:The Collection | Verve | 537152-2
Suenos Gitanos | Polydor | 549581-2
Tribute To Django Reinhardt | EmArCy | 9811568
The Rosenberg Trio With Frits Landesbergen
Gypsy Swing | Verve | 527806-2

The Rosenberg Trio:The Collection | Verve | 537152-2
The Rosenberg Trio With Orchestra
Noches Calientes | Verve | 557022-2
The Rosenberg Trio With Stephane Grappelli
The Rosenberg Trio:The Collection | Verve | 537152-2

Rosenberger,Walter | (perc)
Stan Getz With The Eddie Sauter Orchestra
Stan Getz Plays The Music Of Mickey One | Verve | 531232-2

Rosenblatt,Joel | (dr)
Spyro Gyra & Guests
Love & Other Obsessions | GRP | GRP 98112

Rosenburg,John | (tp)
Chick Corea And His Orchestra
My Spanish Heart | Polydor | 543303-3

Rosenburg,Roger | (b-cl)
Freddy Cole With Band
To The End Of The Earth | Fantasy | FCD 9675-2

Rosendal,Peter | (psynth)
ULG
Spring | Laika Records | 35101382

Rosenfeld,Benny | (tpfl-h)
Jens Winther And The Danish Radio Jazz Orchestra
Angels | dacapo | DCCD 9442
Miles Davis With The Danish Radio Big Band
Aura | CBS | CK 63962
Mona Larsen And The Danish Radio Big Band Plus Soloists
Michael Mantler:Cerco Un Paese Innocente | ECM | 1556
Stan Getz With The Danish Radio Big Band
Stan Getz In Europe | Laserlight | 24657
The Danish Radio Big Band
Aura | CBS | CK 63962
The Danish Radio Jazz Orchestra
This Train:The Danish Radio Jazz Orchestra Plays The Music Of Ray Pitts | dacapo | DCCD 9428
Nice Work | dacapo | DCCD 9446

Rosenfeld,Mindy | (fl)
Michael Hedges
Aerial Boundaries | Windham Hill | 34 11032-2

Rosengarden,Bobby | (bongos,dr,perc,p-solo,vibxylophone)
Astrud Gilberto With The Walter Wanderley Quartet
A Certain Smile A Certain Sadness | Verve | 557449-2
Astrud Gilberto With The Walter Wanderley Quintet
A Certain Smile A Certain Sadness | Verve | 557449-2
Astrud Gilberto With The Walter Wanderley Quuitet
Verve Jazz Masters 9:Astrud Gilberto | Verve | 519824-2
Billie Holiday With The Ray Ellis Orchestra
Lady In Satin | CBS | CK 65144
Cal Tjader's Orchestra
Verve Jazz Masters 39:Cal Tjader | Verve | 521858-2
Clark Terry & Chico O Farril Orchestra
Spanish Rice | Verve | 9861050
J.J.Johnson And His Orchestra
Planet Jazz:J.J.Johnson | Planet Jazz | 2159974-2
Jimmy Smith With The Oliver Nelson Orchestra
Verve Jazz Masters 29:Jimmy Smith | Verve | 521855-2
Jimmy Smith:Best Of The Verve Years | Verve | 527950-2
Jimmy Smith-Talkin' Verve | Verve | 531563-2
Peter & The Wolf | Verve | 547264-2
Miles Davis With Gil Evans & His Orchestra
Miles Davis At Carnegie Hall | CBS | CK 65027
Quiet Nights | CBS | CK 65293
Stan Getz With Orchestra And Voices
Stan Getz Highlights | Verve | 847430-2
Stan Getz With The Claus Ogerman Orchestra
What The World Needs Now-Stan Getz Plays Bacharach And David | Verve | 557450-2

Rosengren,Bernt | (alto-fl,ts,as,fl,cl,oboe,sstaragot)
Don Cherry Group
Don Cherry-The Sonet Recordings:Eternal Now/Live Ankara | Verve | 533049-2
Tomasz Stanko Septet
Litania | ECM | 1636(537551-2)
Tomasz Stanko Sextet
Litania | ECM | 1636(537551-2)

Rosenstein,Harald | (as,fl,cl,ss,reedssax)
Eddie Harris Group With The WDR Big Band
Eddie Harris-The Last Concert | ACT | 9249-2
Gianlugi Trovesi Quartet With The WDR Big Band
Dedalo | Enja | ENJ-9419 2
Jens Winther And The WDR Big Band
The Escape | dacapo | DCCD 9437
Kevin Mahogany With The WDR Big Band And Guests
Pussy Cat Dues:The Music Of Charles Mingus | Enja | ENJ-9316 2
Los Jovenes Flamencos With The WDR Big Band And Guests
Jazzpana | ACT | 9212-2
Vince Mendoza With The WDR Big Band And Guests
Sketches | ACT | 9215-2

Rosenwinkel,Kurt | (el-g,g,4-string-stella,voicep)
Chris Cheek Quartet
I Wish I Knew | Fresh Sound Records | FSNT 022 CD
Chris Cheek Quintet
Vine | Fresh Sound Records | FSNT 086 CD
George Colligan Group
Unresolved | Fresh Sound Records | FSNT 054 CD
Jill Seifers And Her Quartet
The Waiting | Fresh Sound Records | FSNT 072 CD
Kurt Rosenwinkel Quartet
The Next Stop | Verve | 549162-2
Kurt Rosenwinkel Quintet
The Enemies Of Energy | Verve | 543042-2
Kurt Rosenwinkel Trio
East Coast Love Affair | Fresh Sound Records | FSNT 016 CD
Mark Turner Quartet
Ballad Session | Warner | 9362-47631-2
Dharma Days | Warner | 9362-47998-2
Mark Turner Quintet
Ballad Session | Warner | 9362-47631-2
Paul Motian Electric Bebop Band
Flight Of The Blue Jay | Winter&Winter | 910009-2
Monk And Powell | Winter&Winter | 910045-2
Perico Sambeat Group
Ademuz | Fresh Sound Records | FSNT 041 CD
Perico Sambeat Quintet
Friendship | ACT | 9421-2
Seamus Blake Quartet
Stranger Things Have Happened | Fresh Sound Records | FSNT 063 CD
Seamus Blake Quintet
Stranger Things Have Happened | Fresh Sound Records | FSNT 063 CD

Röser,Uli | (euphoniumtb)
Rainer Tempel Big Band
Album 03 | Jazz 'n' Arts Records | JNA 1102
Ralph Abelein Group
Mr. B's Time Machine | Satin Doll Productions | SDP 1042-1 CD

Rosewoman,Michele | (p,clave,vocgankogui)
Michele Rosewoman And Quintessence
Guardians Of The Light | Enja | ENJ-9378 2
Michele Rosewoman Quintet
Harvest | Enja | ENJ-7069 2
Michele Rosewoman Sextet
Harvest | Enja | ENJ-7069 2

Rosnes,Renee | (keyboards,p,synthvoc)
Fleurine With Band And Horn Section
Meant To Be! | EmArCy | 159085-2
George Mraz Quartet
Duke's Place | Milestone | MCD 9292-2
George Mraz Trio
Duke's Place | Milestone | MCD 9292-2
Jim Snidero Quartet With Strings
Strings | Milestone | MCD 9326-2
Jimmy Scott With Band
But Beautiful | Milestone | MCD 9321-2
Moon Glow | Milestone | MCD 9332-2
Niels-Henning Orsted-Pedersen Trio
Friends Forever | Milestone | MCD 9269-2
Renee Rosnes Quartet
Art & Soul | Blue Note | 499997-2
Renee Rosnes Trio
Art & Soul | Blue Note | 499997-2

Rosning,Lasse | (piccolo-tp)
Terje Rypdal With The Borealis Ensemble
Q.E.D. | ECM | 1474

Rosoff,Elliot | (stringsv)
Milt Jackson And His Orchestra
Sunflower | CTI | ZK 65131

Rosolino,Frank | (tbvoc)
Anita O'Day With The Bill Holman Orchestra
Verve Jazz Masters 49:Anita O'Day | Verve | 527653-2
Anita O'Day With The Buddy Bregman Orchestra
Pick Yourself Up | Verve | 517329-2
Anita O'Day With The Jimmy Giuffre Orchestra
Verve Jazz Masters 49:Anita O'Day | Verve | 527653-2
Anita O'Day With The Russ Garcia Orchestra
Verve Jazz Masters 49:Anita O'Day | Verve | 527653-2
Benny Carter And His Orchestra
Aspects | Capitol | 852677-2
Benny Carter Sextet
Jazz Giant | Original Jazz Classics | OJC20 167-2(C 7555)
Bill Holman Octet
The Jazz Giants Play Sammy Cahn:It's Magic | Prestige | PCD 24226-2
Buddy Bregman And His Orchestra
Swinging Kicks | Verve | 559514-2
Chet Baker Big Band
The Best Of Chet Baker Plays | Pacific Jazz | 797161-2
Dizzy Gillespie And His Orchestra
Talking Verve:Dizzy Gillespie | Verve | 533846-2
Frank Rosolino Quartet
Frank Talks! | Storyville | STCD 8284
Horace Silver Quintet With Brass
Horace Silver Retrospective | Blue Note | 495576-2
Howard Rumsey's Lighthouse All-Stars
Howard Rumsey's Lighthouse All-Stars Vol.6 | Original Jazz Classics | OJCCD 386-2(C 3504)
June Christy With The Pete Rugolo Orchestra
Something Cool(The Complete Mono & Stereo Versions) | Capitol | 534069-2
June Christy With The Shorty Rogers Orchestra
June Christy Big Band Special | Capitol | 498319-2
Lars Gullin American All Stars
Lars Gullin 1953,Vol.2:Moden Sounds | Dragon | DRCD 234
Lee Ritenour Group
Jazzrock-Anthology Vol.3:Fusion | Zounds | CD 27100555
Luis Gasca Group
Jazzin' Vol.2: The Music Of Stevie Wonder | Fantasy | FANCD 6088-2
Paulinho Da Costa Orchestra
Agora | Original Jazz Classics | OJCCD 630-2(2310785)
Peggy Lee With The Quincy Jones Orchestra
Blues Cross Country | Capitol | 520088-2
Pete Rugolo And His Orchestra
Thriller/Richard Diamon(Original Jazz Scores From 2 Classics TV Series) | Fresh Sound Records | FSCD 2015
Quincy Jones And His Orchestra
Verve Jazz Masters Vol.59:Toots Thielemans | Verve | 535271-2
Sonny Stitt Orchestra
Verve Jazz Masters 50:Sonny Sitt | Verve | 527651-2
Stan Kenton And His Orchestra
Stan Kenton Portraits On Standards | Capitol | 531571-2
Terry Gibbs Big Band
Terry Gibbs Dream Band Vol.4:Main Stem | Contemporary | CCD 7656-2
Terry Gibbs Dream Band
Terry Gibbs Dream Band Vol.3:Flying Home | Contemporary | CCD 7654-2
Terry Gibbs Dream Band Vol.5:The Big Cat | Contemporary | CCD 7657-2
Victor Feldman Orchestra
Latinsville | Contemporary | CCD 9005-2
Zoot Sims And His Orchestra
The Jazz Giants Play Duke Ellington:Caravan | Prestige | PCD 24227-2

Ross,André | (ts)
Rene Thomas Quintet
Jazz In Paris:René Thomas-The Real Cat | EmArCy | 549400-2 PMS

Ross,Annie | (voc)
Annie Ross & PonyPoindexter With The Berlin All Stars
Annie Ross & Pony Poindexter with The Berlin All Stars | MPS | 9811257
Annie Ross With Her Quintet
Misty Blue:Sweet Sisters Swing Songs Of Sorrow And Sadness | Blue Note | 521151-2
Charlie Parker And His Orchestra
Charlie Parker:The Best Of The Verve Years | Verve | 527815-2
Bird: The Complete Charlie Parker On Verve | Verve | 837141-2
Charlie Parker With Orchestra & The Dave Lambert Singers
Verve Jazz Masters 28:Charlie Parker Plays Standards | Verve | 521854-2
Lambert, Hendricks And Ross
Sing A Song Of Basie | Verve | 543827-2

Ross,Arnold | (p)
Arnold Ross Trio
Just You & He & Me | Fresh Sound Records | FSR-CD 313
Barney Kessel Quintet
Easy Like | Original Jazz Classics | OJCCD 153-2
Benny Carter And His Orchestra
Aspects | Capitol | 852677-2
Dizzy Gillespie Orchestra And The Operatic String Orchestra
Jazz In Paris:Dizzy Gillespie And His Operatic Strings Orchestra | EmArCy | 018420-2
Ella Fitzgerald With The Frank DeVol Orchestra
Get Happy! | Verve | 523321-2
Harry Edison Quartet
The Complete Unedited 'Sweets At The Haig' 1953 Recordings | Fresh Sound Records | FSR CD 345
JATP All Stars
Jazz Gallery:Lester Young Vol.2(1946-59) | RCA | 2119541-2
The Complete Jazz At The Philharmonic On Verve 1944-1949 | Verve | 523893-2
Charlie Parker:The Best Of The Verve Years | Verve | 527815-2
Jazz At The Philharmonic:Best Of The 1940's Concerts | Verve | 557534-2
Bird: The Complete Charlie Parker On Verve | Verve | 837141-2

Ross,Barry | (arrtb)
Klaus Weiss Orchestra
Live At The Domicile | ATM Records | ATM 3805-AH

Ross,Bill | (fl,alto-fl,tspiccolo)
Woody Herman And His Orchestra
Verve Jazz Masters 54:Woody Herman | Verve | 529903-2

Ross,Brandon | (el-g,gvoc)
Cassandra Wilson Group
Misty Blue:Sweet Sisters Swing Songs Of Sorrow And Sadness | Blue Note | 521151-2
Blue Light 'Til Dawn | Blue Note | 781357-2
Midnight Blue(The [Be]witching Hour) | Blue Note | 854365-2
Cold Sweat
Cold Sweat Plays J.B. | JMT Edition | 919025-2
Ivo Perlman Group
Children Of Ibeji | Enja | ENJ-7005 2

Ross,Florian | (p)
Frank Sackenheim Quartet
The Music Of Chance | Jazz 4 Ever Records:Jazz Network | J4E 4753
Frank Sackenheim Quintet
The Music Of Chance | Jazz 4 Ever Records:Jazz Network | J4E 4753

Ross,Hank | (as,clts)
Charlie Parker And His Orchestra
The Cole Porter Songbook | Verve | 823250-2
Bird: The Complete Charlie Parker On Verve | Verve | 837141-2
Charlie Parker With Orchestra
Charlie Parker:The Best Of The Verve Years | Verve | 527815-2
Charlie Parker With Strings
Bird: The Complete Charlie Parker On Verve | Verve | 837141-2
Charlie Parker With The Joe Lipman Orchestra
Verve Jazz Masters 28:Charlie Parker Plays Standards | Verve | 521854-2
Charlie Parker With Strings:The Master Takes | Verve | 523984-2
Charlie Parker Big Band | Verve | 559835-2
Jess Stacy And His Orchestra
Planet Jazz:Jazz Piano | RCA | 2169655-2
Sarah Vaughan With The Hugo Winterhalter Orchestra
Sarah Vaughan:Lover Man | Dreyfus Jazz Line | FDM 36739-2
Sarah Vaughan With The Joe Lippman Orchestra
Sarah Vaughan:Lover Man | Dreyfus Jazz Line | FDM 36739-2

Ross,Holli | (voc)
Wolfgang Lackerschmid-Donald Johnston Group
New Singers-New Songs | Bhakti Jazz | BR 31

Ross,Margaret | (harpvoc)
Freddie Hubbard With Orchestra
This Is Jazz:Freddie Hubbard | CBS | CK 65041
George Russell And His Orchestra
Bill Evans:Piano Player | CBS | CK 65361
Gil Evans Orchestra
The Individualism Of Gil Evans | Verve | 833804-2
Grover Washington Jr. Orchestra
Jazzrock-Anthology Vol.3:Fusion | Zounds | CD 27100555
Jimmy Smith With The Billy Byers Orchestra
Jimmy Smith:Best Of The Verve Years | Verve | 527950-2
Milt Jackson And His Orchestra
Sunflower | CTI | ZK 65131
Paul Desmond Quartet With The Don Sebesby Orchestra
From The Hot Afternoon | Verve | 543487-2
Quincy Jones And His Orchestra
Rahsaan/The Complete Mercury Recordings Of Roland Kirk | Mercury | 846630-2
Wes Montgomery With The Don Sebesky Orchestra
Verve Jazz Masters 14:Wes Montgomery | Verve | 519826-2
Talkin' Jazz:Roots Of Acid Jazz | Verve | 529580-2
Bumpin' | Verve | 539062-2
Wes Montgomery With The Jimmy Jones Orchestra
Wes Montgomery-The Complete Riverside Recordings | Riverside | 12 RCD 4408-2

Ross,Matt | (p)
Geoff Carter Quintet
Unsong Hero:The Undiscovered Genius Of Chas Burchell | IN+OUT Records | 7026-2

Ross,Melinda | (cello)
Ron Carter With Strings
Pastels | Original Jazz Classics | OJCCD 665-2(M 9073)

Ross,Nathan 'Nat' | (v)
Ella Fitzgerald With The Billy May Orchestra
The Best Of The Song Books:The Ballads | Verve | 521867-2
Ella Fitzgerald Sings The Harold Arlen Song Book | Verve | 589108-2
Ella Fitzgerald With The Nelson Riddle Orchestra
The Best Of The Song Books:The Ballads | Verve | 521867-2
Oh Lady Be Good:The Best Of The Gershwin Songbook | Verve | 529581-2
Love Songs:The Best Of The Song Books | Verve | 531762-2

Ross,Ronnie | (b-cl,as,bs,clts)
Hans Koller Nonet
Exclusiv | MPS | 9813440

Ross,Sam | (vviola)
Tommy Dorsey And His Orchestra
Planet Jazz:Frank Sinatra & Tommy Dorsey | Planet Jazz | 2152067-2

Rossi,Lauro | (tb,percvoice)
Italian Instabile Orchestra
Skies Of Europe | ECM | 1543

Rossiter,Red | (tp)
Jelly Roll Morton And His Orchestra
Planet Jazz:Jelly Roll Morton | Planet Jazz | 2152060-2

Rössle,Ekkehard | (sax,ssts)
Cécile Verny Quintet
Kekeli | double moon | CHRDM 71028
Kelm 3
Per Anno | dml-records | CD 013
Klaus Müller-Ekkehard Rössle
Auf Und Davon | Jazz Haus Musik | JHM 0091 CD
The Huebner Brothers
Memories | Satin Doll Productions | SDP 1025-1 CD
Tilman Jäger Tape 4
Abendlieder | Satin Doll Productions | SDP 1043-1 CD
Walter Lang Quintet
Tales Of 2 Cities | double moon | CHRDM 71016

Rosso,Nino | (cellotp)
Ella Fitzgerald With The Frank DeVol Orchestra
Get Happy! | Verve | 523321-2
Helen Merrill And Her Band
Planet Jazz:Female Jazz Vocalists | Planet Jazz | 2169656-2
Helen Merrill With The Piero Umilliani Group
Parole E Musica | RCA | 2174798-2

Rossy,Jorge 'Jordi' | (dr)
Amos Hoffman Quartet
The Dreamer | Fresh Sound Records | FSNT 060 CD
Ben Waltzer Trio
For Good | Fresh Sound Records | FSNT 013 CD
Big Band Bellaterra
Don't Git Sassy | Fresh Sound Records | FSNT 048 CD
Brad Mehldau Trio
Introducing Brad Mehldau | Warner | 9362-45997-2
The Art Of The Trio Vol.1 | Warner | 9362-46260-2
The Art Of The Trio Vol.2 | Warner | 9362-46848-2
Art Of The Trio Vol.3: Songs | Warner | 9362-47051-2
Art Of The Trio Vol.4: Back At The Vanguard | Warner | 9362-47463-2
Places | Warner | 9362-47693-2
Art Of The Trio Vol.5:Progression | Warner | 9362-48005-2
Anything Goes | Warner | 9362-48608-2
Brad Mehldau With The Rossy Trio
New York-Barcelona Crossing Vol.1 | Fresh Sound Records | FSNT 031 CD
New York-Barcelona Crossing Vol.2 | Fresh Sound Records | FSNT 037 CD
Chris Cheek Quartet
I Wish I Knew | Fresh Sound Records | FSNT 022 CD
Chris Cheek Quintet
Vine | Fresh Sound Records | FSNT 086 CD
Chris Cheek Sextet
A Girl Named Joe | Fresh Sound Records | FSNT 032 CD
Dan Faulk Quartet
Spirit In The Night | Fresh Sound Records | FSNT 024 CD
Dan Faulk Trio
Spirit In The Night | Fresh Sound Records | FSNT 024 CD
Ethan Iverson Trio
Contruction Zone(Originals) | Fresh Sound Records | FSNT 046 CD
Decontruction Zone(Originals) | Fresh Sound Records | FSNT 047 CD
Freddie Bryant Group
Brazilian Rosewood | Fresh Sound Records | FSNT 035 CD

Georgina Weinstein With Her Quartet
Come Rain Or Come Shine | Fresh Sound Records | FSNT 020 CD
Georgina Weinstein With Her Trio
Come Rain Or Come Shine | Fresh Sound Records | FSNT 020 CD
Jill Seifers And Her Quartet
The Waiting | Fresh Sound Records | FSNT 072 CD
José Luis Gámez Quartet
Dr.Jeckyl | Fresh Sound Records | FSNT 006 CD
José Luis Gámez Quintet
Dr.Jeckyl | Fresh Sound Records | FSNT 006 CD
Rumbo Dorte | Fresh Sound Records | FSNT 089 CD
Klaus Ignatzek Quintet
Son Of Gaudi | Nabel Records:Jazz Network | CD 4660
Kurt Rosenwinkel Trio
East Coast Love Affair | Fresh Sound Records | FSNT 016 CD
Mark Turner-Chris Cheek Quintet
The Music Of Mercedes Rossy | Fresh Sound Records | FSNT 043 CD
Mehldau & Rossy Trio
When I Fall In Love | Fresh Sound Records | FSNT 007 CD
Nat Su Quartet
The J.Way | Fresh Sound Records | FSNT 038 CD
Perico Sambeat Group
Ademuz | Fresh Sound Records | FSNT 041 CD
Reid Anderson Quartet
Dirty Show Tunes | Fresh Sound Records | FSNT 030 CD
Seamus Blake Quartet
Stranger Things Have Happened | Fresh Sound Records | FSNT 063 CD
Seamus Blake Quintet
Stranger Things Have Happened | Fresh Sound Records | FSNT 063 CD
Till Brönner Quartet & Deutsches Symphonieorchester Berlin
German Songs | Minor Music | 801057

Rossy,Mario | (b)
Big Band Bellaterra
Don't Git Sassy | Fresh Sound Records | FSNT 048 CD
Brad Mehldau With The Rossy Trio
New York-Barcelona Crossing Vol.1 | Fresh Sound Records | FSNT 031 CD
New York-Barcelona Crossing Vol.2 | Fresh Sound Records | FSNT 037 CD
Daniel Flors Group
When Least Expected | Fresh Sound Records | FSNT 080 CD
Eladio Reinon Quintet
Es La Historia De Un Amor | Fresh Sound Records | FSNT 004 CD
George Colligan Quartet
Desire | Fresh Sound Records | FSNT 071 CD
José Luis Gámez Quartet
Dr.Jeckyl | Fresh Sound Records | FSNT 006 CD
José Luis Gámez Quintet
Dr.Jeckyl | Fresh Sound Records | FSNT 006 CD
Mark Turner-Chris Check Quintet
The Music Of Mercedes Rossy | Fresh Sound Records | FSNT 043 CD
Mehldau & Rossy Trio
When I Fall In Love | Fresh Sound Records | FSNT 007 CD

Rostaing,Hubert | (as,clts)
Django Reinhardt And The Quintet Du Hot Club De France
Jazz In Paris:Django Reinhardt-Django's Blues | EmArCy | 013545-2
Planet Jazz:Django Reinhardt | Planet Jazz | 2152071-2
Peche Á La Mode-The Great Blue Star Sessions 1947/1953 | Verve | 835418-2
Don Byas And His Orchestra
Americans Swinging In Paris:Don Byas | EMI Records | 539655-2
Kenny Clarke Sextet
Jazz In Paris:Kenny Clarke Sextet Plays André Hodair | EmArCy | 834542-2 PMS
Quintet Du Hot Club De France
Verve Jazz Masters 38:Django Reinhardt | Verve | 516931-2
Django Reinhardt:Echoes Of France | Dreyfus Jazz Line | FDM 36726-2
Django Reinhardt:Souveniers | Dreyfus Jazz Line | FDM 36744-2
Rex Stewart Quintet
Peche Á La Mode-The Great Blue Star Sessions 1947/1953 | Verve | 835418-2
Tyree Glenn
Don Byas:Laura | Dreyfus Jazz Line | FDM 36714-2

Rostvold,Bjarne | (congas,drsnare-dr)
Frank Rosolino Quartet
Frank Talks! | Storyville | STCD 8284
Phineas Newborn Jr. Trio
Tivoli Encounter | Storyville | STCD 8221
Stan Kenton With The Danish Radio Big Band
Stan Kenton With The Danish Radio Big Band | Storyville | STCD 8340

Rosy Rosy | (voc)
Uli Trepte Group
Guru Guru/Uli Trepte | ATM Records | ATM 3815-AH

Rotella,John | (asbs)
June Christy With The Pete Rugolo Orchestra
Something Cool(The Complete Mono & Stereo Versions) | Capitol | 534069-2

Rotenberg,June | (b)
Mary Lou Williams Trio
Planet Jazz:Jazz Piano | RCA | 2169655-2

Roth,Rudi | (dr,perc,voicecongas)
Thilo Kreitmeier & Group
Soul Call | Organic Music | ORGM 9711

Roth,Yvonne | (as)
Landes Jugend Jazz Orchester Hessen
Touch Of Lips | hr music.de | hrmj 004-01 CD

Rothchild,David | (tb)
Conexion Latina
La Conexión | Enja | ENJ-9065 2

Rothe,Gert | (cello)
Bernd Konrad Jazz Group With Symphonie Orchestra
Wen Die Götter Lieben | Creative Works Records | CW CD 1010-1

Rothenberg,Ned | (as,sampling,sequencing,ts)
Heiner Goebbels/Heiner Müller
Der Mann Im Fahrstuhl | ECM | 1369(837110-2)
Marty Ehrlich Group
The Long View | Enja | ENJ-9452 2
Ned Rothenberg Trio
Port Of Entry | Intuition Records | INT 3249-2

Rothermel,Jim | (as,clss)
Rex Allen's Swing Express
Keep Swingin' | Nagel-Heyer | CD 016
Ellington For Lovers | Nagel-Heyer | NH 1009
The Second Sampler | Nagel-Heyer | NHR SP 6

Rothstein,Jack | (vconcertmaster)
Dee Dee Bridgewater With Orchestra
Dear Ella | Verve | 539102-2
Laura Fygi With Band
Bewitched | Verve | 514724-2

Rotondi,Jim | (tpfl-h)
Eric Alexander Quintet
Solid! | Milestone | MCD 9283-2
The Second Milestone | Milestone | MCD 9315-2
Eric Alexander Sextet
Man With A Horn | Milestone | MCD 9293-2

Rotter,Thomas | (bel-b)
Daniel Messina Band
Imagenes | art-mode-records | 990014
Rade Soric Trio
Piano Moments | Take Twelve On CD | TT 007-2

Roumanis,George | (b)
Johnny Smith Quartet
The Sound Of The Johnny Smith Guitar | Roulette | 531792-2

Rounds,Clyde | (as,tscl)
Tommy Dorsey And His Orchestra
Planet Jazz:Tommy Dorsey | Planet Jazz | 2159972-2
Planet Jazz:Big Bands | Planet Jazz | 2169649-2
Planet Jazz:Swing | Planet Jazz | 2169651-2

Roupe,Bjarne | (gsynth)
Michael Mantler Group
Songs And One Symphony | ECM | 1721
Michael Mantler Group With The Danish Radio Concert Orchestra Strings
The School Of Understanding(Sort-Of-An-Opera) | ECM | 1648/49(537963-2)
Michael Mantler Orchestra
Hide And Seek | ECM | 1738(549612-2)
Miles Davis With The Danish Radio Big Band
Aura | CBS | CK 63962
Mona Larsen And The Danish Radio Big Band Plus Soloists
Michael Mantler:Cerco Un Paese Innocente | ECM | 1556
The Danish Radio Big Band
Aura | CBS | CK 63962
The Danish Radio Jazz Orchestra
This Train:The Danish Radio Jazz Orchestra Plays The Music Of Ray Pitts | dacapo | DCCD 9428

Rouse,Charlie | (b-cl,ts,fl,talkingld)
Art Farmer Septet
Plays The Arrangements And Compositions Of Gigi Gryce And Quincy Jones | Original Jazz Classics | OJCCD 054-2
Babs Gonzales And His Band
Voilà | Fresh Sound Records | FSR CD 340
Benny Carter And His Orchestra
Further Definitions/Additions To Further Definotions | Impulse(MCA) | 951229-2
Carmen McRae And Her Quartet
Carmen Sings Monk | RCA | 2663841-2
Charlie Rouse Orchestra
Bossa Nova Bacchanal | Blue Note | 593875-2
Blue Bossa | Blue Note | 795590-2
Charlie Rouse Quartet
Late Night Sax | CBS | 487798-2
Clifford Brown Sextet
Clifford Brown Memorial Album | Blue Note | 532141-2
Donald Byrd Sextet
Byrd In Hand | Blue Note | 542305-2
Fats Navarro Quintet
Fats Navarro:Nostalgia | Dreyfus Jazz Line | FDM 36736-2
Freddie Hubbard Quintet
Bossa Nova Bacchanal | Blue Note | 593875-2
Gerry Mulligan And His Orchestra
Mullenium | CBS | CK 65678
Herbie Mann Sextet
Just Wailin' | Original Jazz Classics | OJCCD 900-2(NJ 8211)
Nat Adderley And The Big Sax Section
Cannonball Adderley Birthday Celebration | Fantasy | FANCD 6087-2
That's Right | Original Jazz Classics | OJCCD 791-2(RLP 9330)
Tadd Dameron Sextet
The Fabulous Fats Navarro Vol.1 | Blue Note | 0677207
Tadd Dameron-Fats Navarro Sextet
Fats Navarro:Nostalgia | Dreyfus Jazz Line | FDM 36736-2
The Upper Manhattan Jazz Society
The Upper Manhattan Jazz Society | Enja | ENJ-4090 2
Thelonious Monk And His Orchestra
Greatest Hits | CBS | CK 65422
Thelonious Monk:85th Birthday Celebration | zyx records | FANCD 6076-2
At Town Hall | Original Jazz Classics | OJCCD 135-2
Thelonious Monk Quartet
Paris Jazz Concert:Theloniuos Monk And His Quartet | Laserlight | 17250
Monk At Newport 1963 & 1965 | CBS | C2K 63905
Live At The Jazz Workshop-Complete | CBS | C2K 65189
Live At The It Club:Complete | CBS | C2K 65288
Monk's Dream | CBS | CK 63536
Greatest Hits | CBS | CK 65422
MONK. | CBS | CK 86564
Thelonious Monk:85th Birthday Celebration | zyx records | FANCD 6076-2
Thelonious Monk In Italy | Original Jazz Classics | OJCCD 488-2(RLP 9443)
Monk In France | Original Jazz Classics | OJCCD 670-2
Thelonious Monk In Copenhagen | Storyville | STCD 8283
Thelonious Monk Quartet Plus Two
Thelonious Monk:85th Birthday Celebration | zyx records | FANCD 6076-2
At The Blackhawk | Original Jazz Classics | OJCCD 305-2
Thelonious Monk Quartet With Pee Wee Russell
Monk At Newport 1963 & 1965 | CBS | C2K 63905
Thelonious Monk Quintet
Thelonious Monk:85th Birthday Celebration | zyx records | FANCD 6076-2
5 By Monk By 5 | Original Jazz Classics | OJCCD 362-2

Routch,Bob | (fr-h)
Charles Mingus Orchestra
Tonight At Noon...Three Or Four Shades Of Love | Dreyfus Jazz Line | FDM 36633-2

Rover,Albert | (p)
Bob Sands Quartet
JumpSTART | Fresh Sound Records | FSNT 042 CD
Bob Sands Quintet
JumpSTART | Fresh Sound Records | FSNT 042 CD

Rover,Christian | (gg-synth)
Alberto Marsico Quintet
Them That's Got | Organic Music | ORGM 9705
Christian Rover Group feat. Rhoda Scott
Christian Rover Group-Live With Rhoda Scott At The Organ | Organic Music | ORGM 9704

Rovere,Gilbert 'Bibi' | (b)
Bud Powell Trio
Bud Powell Paris Sessions | Pablo | PACD 2310972-2
Jean-Luc Ponty Quartet
Jazz In Paris:Jean-Luc Ponty-Jazz Long Playing | EmArCy | 548150-2 PMS
Jean-Luc Ponty Quintet
Jazz In Paris:Jean-Luc Ponty-Jazz Long Playing | EmArCy | 548150-2 PMS
Rene Thomas Quartet
Jazz In Paris:René Thomas-Meeting Mister Thomas | EmArCy | 549812-2
Rene Thomas Quintet
Jazz In Paris:René Thomas-Meeting Mister Thomas | EmArCy | 549812-2

Rovere,Paul | (b)
Barney Wilen Quintet
Jazz In Paris:Jazz & Cinéma Vol.1 | EmArCy | 548318-2 PMS
Bobby Jaspar Quintet
Jazz In Paris:Bobby Jaspar-Jeux Dé Quartes | EmArCy | 018423-2
Golden Gate Quartet
Americans Swinging In Paris:Golden Gate Quartet | EMI Records | 539659-2
Spirituals To Swing 1955-69 | EMI Records | 791569-2
Golden Gate Quartet With The Martial Solal Orchestra
Americans Swinging In Paris:Golden Gate Quartet | EMI Records | 539659-2
From Spriritual To Swing Vol.2 | EMI Records | 780573-2
Jack Dieval And The J.A.C.E. All-Stars
Jazz In Paris:Jack Diéval-Jazz Aux Champs Elysées | EmArCy | 018419-2
Jean Pierre Sasson Quartet
Americans Swinging In Paris:Lucky Thompson | EMI Records | 539651-2
Lionel Hampton Quintet
Americans Swinging In Paris:Lionel Hampton | EMI Records | 539649-2
Lionel Hampton Sextet
Americans Swinging In Paris:Lionel Hampton | EMI Records | 539649-2
Lionel Hampton Trio
Americans Swinging In Paris:Lionel Hampton | EMI Records | 539649-2

Rovira,Tony | (b)
Quintet Du Hot Club De France
Django Reinhardt:Echoes Of France | Dreyfus Jazz Line | FDM 36726-2
Stephane Grappelli And His Hot Four
Jazz In Paris:Django Reinhardt-Swing From Paris | EmArCy | 159853-2 PMS

Rowe,John | (g)
Gene Harris Group
Blue Breaks Beats Vol.2 | Blue Note | 789907-2

Rowe,Keith | (g,prep.-ptransistor-radio)
AMM III
It Had Been An Ordinary Enough Day In Pueblo, Colorado | Japo | 60031

Rowell,Mary | (v)
Daniel Schnyder Quintet With String Quartet
Mythology | Enja | ENJ-7003 2
Steve Coleman And Five Elements
The Sonic Language Of Myth | RCA | 2164123-2

Rowin,John | (g)
Bobbi Humphrey Group
Blue Breaks Beats Vol.2 | Blue Note | 789907-2
Donald Byrd Orchestra
Places And Spaces | Blue Note | 854326-2

Rowland,Bill | (p)
Sarah Vaughan With The Joe Lippman Orchestra
Sarah Vaughan:Lover Man | Dreyfus Jazz Line | FDM 36739-2

Rowles,Jimmy | (celeste,p,arr,ld,el-pvoc)
Barney Kessel And His Quintet
To Swing Or Not To Swing | Original Jazz Classics | OJCCD 317-2
Barney Kessel And His Septet
To Swing Or Not To Swing | Original Jazz Classics | OJCCD 317-2
Ben Webster Quintet
At The Renaissance | Original Jazz Classics | OJC 390(C 7646)
Benny Carter Sextet
Jazz Giant | Original Jazz Classics | OJC20 167-2(C 7555)
Benny Goodman And His Orchestra
40th Anniversary Concert-Live At Carnegie Hall | London | 820349-2
Benny Goodman Trio
Benny Goodman-The Complete Capitol Trios | Capitol | 521225-2
Billie Holiday And Her All Stars
Verve Jazz Masters 12:Billie Holiday | Verve | 519825-2
Verve Jazz Masters 20:Introducing | Verve | 519853-2
Songs For Distingué Lovers | Verve | 539056-2
Billie Holiday And Her Band
Verve Jazz Masters 47:Billie Holiday Sings Standards | Verve | 527650-2
Billy Eckstine With The Billy May Orchestra
Once More With Feeling | Roulette | 581862-2
Bud Shank Quintet
The Complete Nocturne Recordings:Jazz In Hollywood Series Vol.1 | Fresh Sound Records | NR 3CD-101
Buddy Rich Quintet
Buddy And Sweets | Verve | 841433-2
Charles Mingus Orchestra
Three Or Four Shades Of Blues | Atlantic | 7567-81403-2
Ella Fitzgerald With Orchestra
The Best Is Yet To Come | Original Jazz Classics | OJCCD 889-2(2312138)
Ella Fitzgerald With The Marty Paich Orchestra
Ella Fitzgerald-First Lady Of Song | Verve | 517898-2
Whisper Not | Verve | 589947-2
For The Love Of Ella Fitzgerald | Verve | 841765-2
Gerry Mulligan-Ben Webster Quintet
Verve Jazz Masters 43:Ben Webster | Verve | 525431-2
The Complete Gerry Mulligan Meets Ben Webster Sessions | Verve | 539055-2
Ultimate Ben Webster selected by James Carter | Verve | 557537-2
Harry Babasin Quintet
The Complete Nocturne Recordings:Jazz In Hollywood Series Vol.1 | Fresh Sound Records | NR 3CD-101
Herbie Harper Quintet
The Complete Nocturne Recordings:Jazz In Hollywood Series Vol.1 | Fresh Sound Records | NR 3CD-101
Herbie Mann Quartet
Verve Jazz Masters 56:Herbie Mann | Verve | 529901-2
Herbie Mann With The Frank DeVol Orchestra
Verve Jazz Masters 56:Herbie Mann | Verve | 529901-2
Herbie Mann's Californians
Great Ideas Of Western Man | Original Jazz Classics | OJCCD 1065-2(RLP 245)
Jimmy Rowles
Jimmy Rowles/Subtle Legend Vol.1 | Storyville | STCD 8287
Jimmy Rowles Trio
The Complete Nocturne Recordings:Jazz In Hollywood Series Vol.1 | Fresh Sound Records | NR 3CD-101
Jimmy Rowles/Subtle Legend Vol.1 | Storyville | STCD 8287
Joe Pass-Jimmy Rowles Duo
Joe Pass:Guitar Virtuoso | Pablo | 4 PACD 4423-2
Joe Pass:A Man And His Guitar | Original Jazz Classics | OJCCD 8806-2
Checkmate | Original Jazz Classics | OJCCD 975-2(2310865)
June Christy With The Shorty Rogers Orchestra
June Christy Big Band Special | Capitol | 498319-2
Lee Konitz Trio
Tenorlee | Choice | CHCD 71019
Mark Murphy And His Septet
Blue Velvet: Crooners, Swooners And Velvet Vocals | Blue Note | 521153-2
Mel Tormé With The Billy May Orchestra
Mel Tormé Goes South Of The Border With Billy May | Verve | 589517-2
Nat King Cole With The Billy May Orchestra
Nat King Cole:For Sentimental Reasons | Dreyfus Jazz Line | FDM 36740-2
Peggy Lee With The Quincy Jones Orchestra
Blues Cross Country | Capitol | 520088-2
Pete Rugolo And His Orchestra
Thriller/Richard Diamon(Original Jazz Scores From 2 Classics TV Series) | Fresh Sound Records | FSCD 2015
Red Norvo And His Orchestra
Planet Jazz:Female Jazz Vocalists | Planet Jazz | 2169656-2
Red Norvo Sextet
Planet Jazz:Ben Webster | RCA | 2165368-2
Sarah Vaughan And Her Band
Duke Ellington Song Book Two | Pablo | CD 2312116
Sarah Vaughan Birthday Celebration | Fantasy | FANCD 6090-2
Sarah Vaughan With Small Group & Orchestra
Duke Ellington Song Book One | Pablo | CD 2312111
Sonny Stitt Orchestra
Verve Jazz Masters 50:Sonny Sitt | Verve | 527651-2
Stan Getz Quartet
Sony Jazz Collection:Stan Getz | CBS | 488623-2
Stan Getz And The 'Cool' Sounds | Verve | 547317-2
Stan Getz Plays | Verve | 833535-2
Stan Getz Highlights | Verve | 847430-2
Stan Getz-Jimmy Rowles
Sony Jazz Collection:Stan Getz | CBS | 488623-2
The Hollywood Hucksters
The Hollywood Session:The Capitol Jazzmen | Jazz Unlimited | JUCD 2044
Woody Herman And His Orchestra
The Legends Of Swing | Laserlight | 24659
Woody Herman:Four Brother | Dreyfus Jazz Line | FDM 36722-2
Woody Herman And His Sextet

Songs For Hip Lovers | Verve | 559872-2
Zoot Sims Quartet
Getting Sentimental | Choice | CHCD 71006
Suddenly It's Spring | Original Jazz Classics | OJCCD 742-2(2310898)
The Jazz Giants Play Cole Porter:Night And Day | Prestige | PCD 24203-2
Zoot Sims With Orchestra
Passion Flower | Original Jazz Classics | OJCCD 939-2(2312120)
Zoot Sims-Jimmy Rowles Quartet
If I'm Lucky | Original Jazz Classics | OJCCD 683-2(2310803)
The Jazz Giants Play Harry Warren:Lullaby Of Broadway | Prestige | PCD 24204-2

Rowser,Jimmy | (bel-b)
Les McCann Group
Another Beginning | Atlantic | 7567-80790-2
Atlantic Jazz: Fusion | Atlantic | 7567-81711-2
Red Garland Trio
Stretching Out | Prestige | PRCD 24272-2

Rox,Georg | (keyboards)
Philippe Caillat Group
Stream Of Time | Laika Records | LK 92-030

Roy,Badal | (bells,tablas,percwoodblocks)
Badal Roy & Amit Chatterjee
Art Of The Duo: Endless Radiance | Tutu Records | 888178-2*
Lonnie Liston Smith & His Cosmic Echoes
Astral Travelling | RCA | 2663878-2
Miles Davis Group
In Concert | CBS | C2K 65140
On The Corner | CBS | CK 63980

Royal Copenhagen Chamber Orchestra,The |
Philip Catherine/Niels-Henning Orsted-Pedersen With The Royal Copenhagen Chamber Orchestra
Spanish Nights | Enja | ENJ-7023 2

Royal Philharmonic Orchestra, London |
Terje Rypdal(comp)
Undisonus | ECM | 1389

Royal,Ernie | (tp,fl-hvoc)
Birdland Dream Band
Birdland Dream Band | RCA | 2663873-2
Cal Tjader With The Lalo Schifrin Orchestra
Talkin Verve/Roots Of Acid Jazz:Cal Tjader | Verve | 531562-2
Cal Tjader's Orchestra
Verve Jazz Masters 39:Cal Tjader | Verve | 521858-2
Cannonball Adderley And His Orchestra
Verve Jazz Masters 31:Cannonball Adderley | Verve | 522651-2
Cannonball Adderley Birthday Celebration | Fantasy | FANCD 6087-2
Charles Mingus And His Orchestra
Charles Mingus-The Complete Debut Recordings | Debut | 12 DCD 4402-2
The Complete Town Hall Concert | Blue Note | 828353-2
Chubby Jackson And His All Star Big Band
Chubby Takes Over | Fresh Sound Records | FSR-CD 324
Clark Terry & Chico O Farril Orchestra
Spanish Rice | Verve | 9861050
Coleman Hawkins With Billy Byers And His Orchestra
The Hawk In Hi-Fi | RCA | 2663842-2
Della Reese With The Neal Hefti Orchestra
Della | RCA | 2663912-2
Dinah Washington With The Quincy Jones Orchestra
The Swingin' Miss 'D' | Verve | 558074-2
Dizzy Gillespie And His Orchestra
Verve Jazz Masters 10:Dizzy Gillespie | Verve | 516319-2
Afro | Verve | 517052-2
Gillespiana And Carnegie Hall Concert | Verve | 519809-2
Talking Verve:Dizzy Gillespie | Verve | 533846-2
Eddie Lockjaw Davis Orchestra
Afro-Jaws | Original Jazz Classics | OJCCD 403-2(RLP 9373)
Ella Fitzgerald With The Bill Doggett Orchestra
Ella Fitzgerald-First Lady Of Song | Verve | 517898-2
Rhythm Is My Business | Verve | 559513-2
Elliot Lawrence And His Orchestra
The Elliot Lawrence Big Band Swings Cohn & Kahn | Fantasy | FCD 24761-2
Ernestine Anderson With Orchestra
My Kinda Swing | Mercury | 842409-2
Ernie Royal And The Duke Knights
Americans Swinging In Paris:James Moody | EMI Records | 539653-2
Freddie Hubbard Orchestra
The Body And The Soul | Impulse(MCA) | 951183-2
George Benson And His Orchestra
Giblet Gravy | Verve | 543754-2
Talkin' Verve:George Benson | Verve | 553780-2
George Benson Orchestra
Verve Jazz Masters 21:George Benson | Verve | 521861-2
Talkin' Verve:George Benson | Verve | 553780-2
George Russell And His Orchestra
Geogre Russell New York N.Y. | Impulse(MCA) | 951278-2
Gil Evans Orchestra
There Comes A Time | RCA | 2131392-2
The Individualism Of Gil Evans | Verve | 833804-2
Blues In Orbit | Enja | ENJ-3069 2
Grover Washington Jr. Orchestra
Jazzrock-Anthology Vol.3:Fusion | Zounds | CD 27100555
Hank Jones With Oliver Nelson's Orchestra
The Roots Of Acid Jazz | Impulse(MCA) | IMP 12042
J.J.Johnson And His Orchestra
Planet Jazz:J.J.Johnson | Planet Jazz | 2159974-2
Jimmy Forrest With The Oliver Nelson Orchestra
Soul Street | Original Jazz Classics | OJCCD 987-2(NJ 8293)
Jimmy McGriff Orchestra
Swingin' The Blues-Jumpin' The Blues | Laserlight | 24654
Jimmy Smith And Wes Montgomery With Orchestra
Jimmy & Wes-The Dynamic Duo | Verve | 521445-2
Jimmy Smith And Wes Montgomery With The Oliver Nelson Orchestra
Wes Montgomery:The Verve Jazz Sides | Verve | 521690-2
Jimmy Smith:Best Of The Verve Years | Verve | 527950-2
Talkin' Jazz:Roots Of Acid Jazz | Verve | 529580-2
Jimmy Smith With Orchestra
Jimmy Smith-Talkin' Verve | Verve | 531563-2
Jimmy Smith With The Billy Byers Orchestra
Jimmy Smith:Best Of The Verve Years | Verve | 527950-2
Jimmy Smith With The Johnny Pate Orchestra
Jimmy Smith-Talkin' Verve | Verve | 531563-2
Jimmy Smith With The Lalo Schifrin Orchestra
Jimmy Smith:Best Of The Verve Years | Verve | 527950-2
Jimmy Smith-Talkin' Verve | Verve | 531563-2
The Cat | Verve | 539756-2
Jimmy Smith With The Oliver Nelson Orchestra
Verve Jazz Masters 29:Jimmy Smith | Verve | 521855-2
Jimmy Smith:Best Of The Verve Years | Verve | 527950-2
Jimmy Smith-Talkin' Verve | Verve | 531563-2
Peter & The Wolf | Verve | 547264-2
Joe Williams With The Frank Hunter Orchestra
Planet Jazz:Joe Williams | Planet Jazz | 2165370-2
Johnny Hodges Orchestra
Verve Jazz Masters 35:Johnny Hodges | Verve | 521857-2
Junior Mance Trio & Orchestra
That Lovin' Feelin' | Milestone | MCD 47097-2
Kenny Burrell With The Don Sebesky Orchestra
Verve Jazz Masters 45:Kenny Burrell | Verve | 527652-2
Blues-The Common Ground | Verve | 589101-2
King Curtis Band
King Curtis-Blow Man Blow | Bear Family Records | BCD 15670 Cl
Lalo Schifrin And His Orchestra
Verve Jazz Masters 39:Cal Tjader | Verve | 521858-2
Lawrence Brown With The Ralph Burns Orchestra
Slide Trombone | Verve | 559930-2
Lionel Hampton And His Orchestra
Lionel Hampton:Flying Home | Dreyfus Jazz Line | FDM 36735-2
Louis Armstrong And His Friends
Louis Armstrong And His Friends | Bluebird | 2663961-2
Mar Murphy With The Ernie Wilkins Orchestra
RAH | Original Jazz Classics | OJCCD 141-2(R 9395)
McCoy Tyner Group With Horns
Inner Voices | Original Jazz Classics | OJCCD 1039-2(M 9079)
McCoy Tyner Group With Horns And Voices
Inner Voices | Original Jazz Classics | OJCCD 1039-2(M 9079)
Miles Davis + 19
Miles Ahead | CBS | CK 65121
Miles Davis With Gil Evans & His Orchestra
Ballads | CBS | 461099-2
Miles Davis At Carnegie Hall | CBS | CK 65027
This Is Jazz:Miles Davis Plays Ballads | CBS | CK 65038
Porgy And Bess | CBS | CK 65141
Sketches Of Spain | CBS | CK 65142
Quiet Nights | CBS | CK 65293
Milt Jackson Orchestra
Milt Jackson Birthday Celebration | Fantasy | FANCD 6079-2
Big Bags | Original Jazz Classics | OJCCD 366-2(RLP 9429)
Modern Jazz Quartet And Orchestra
MJQ 40 | Atlantic | 7567-82330-2
Oliver Nelson And His Orchestra
Verve Jazz Masters Vol.60:The Collection | Verve | 529866-2
Oscar Peterson With Orchestra
With Respect To Nat | Verve | 557486-2
Oscar Peterson With The Ernie Wilkins Orchestra
Verve Jazz Masters 16:Oscar Peterson | Verve | 516320-2
Quincy Jones And His Orchestra
Talkin' Verve-Roots Of Acid Jazz:Roland Kirk | Verve | 533101-2
Verve Jazz Masters Vol.59:Toots Thielemans | Verve | 535271-2
Rahsaan/The Complete Mercury Recordings Of Roland Kirk | Mercury | 846630-2
The Quintessence | Impulse(MCA) | 951222-2
Shirley Horn With Orchestra
Loads Of Love + Shirley Horn With Horns | Mercury | 843454-2
Sonny Rollins Orchestra
Sonny Rollins And The Big Brass | Verve | 557545-2
Stan Kenton And His Orchestra
Stan Kenton Portraits On Standards | Capitol | 531571-2
Wes Montgomery Orchestra
Movin' Wes | Verve | 521433-2
Wes Montgomery With The Johnny Pate Orchestra
Verve Jazz Masters 14:Wes Montgomery | Verve | 519826-2
Wes Montgomery:The Verve Jazz Sides | Verve | 521690-2
Talkin' Jazz:Roots Of Acid Jazz | Verve | 529580-2
Wes Montgomery With The Oliver Nelson Orchestra
Verve Jazz Masters 14:Wes Montgomery | Verve | 519826-2
Wes Montgomery:The Verve Jazz Sides | Verve | 521690-2
Talkin' Jazz:Roots Of Acid Jazz | Verve | 529580-2
Woody Herman And His Orchestra
The Legends Of Swing | Laserlight | 24659
Woody Herman:Four Brother | Dreyfus Jazz Line | FDM 36722-2

Royal,Marshall | (as,ld,cl,flreeds)
Cannonball Adderley And His Orchestra
Ballads | Blue Note | 537563-2
Cannonball Adderley Quintet
Ballads | Blue Note | 537563-2
Cannonball Adderley With Sergio Mendes And The Bossa Rio Sextet
Ballads | Blue Note | 537563-2
Count Basie And His Orchestra
Jazz Gallery:Lester Young Vol.2(1946-59) | RCA | 2119541-2
Jazz Collection:Count Basie | Laserlight | 24368
The Legends Of Swing | Laserlight | 24659
Atomic Swing | Roulette | 497871-2
Verve Jazz Masters 2:Count Basie | Verve | 519819-2
Count Basie Swings-Joe Williams Sings | Verve | 519852-2
Verve Jazz Masters 20:Introducing | Verve | 519853-2
April In Paris | Verve | 521402-2
Breakfast Dance And Barbecue | Roulette | 531791-2
Basie Meets Bond | Capitol | 538225-2
Basie's Beatle Bag | Verve | 557455-2
One O'Clock Jump | Verve | 559806-2
Chairman Of The Board | Roulette | 581664-2
The Complete Atomic Basie | Roulette | 828635-2
King Of Swing | Verve | 837433-2
Live at The Sands | Reprise | 9362-45946-2
Count Basie At Newport | Verve | 9861761
Count On The Coast Vol.1 | Phontastic | NCD 7555
Count On The Coast Vol.2 | Phontastic | NCD 7575
Duke Ellington And Count Basie With Their Orchestras
First Time! | CBS | CK 65571
Duke Ellington And His Orchestra
Highlights From The Duke Ellington Centennial Edition | RCA | 2663672-2
Ella Fitzgerald With Orchestra
Ella/Things Ain't What They Used To Be | Warner | 9362-47875-2
The Best Is Yet To Come | Original Jazz Classics | OJCCD 889-2(2312138)
Ella Fitzgerald With The Count Basie Orchestra
Ella Fitzgerald-First Lady Of Song | Verve | 517898-2
Ella And Basie | Verve | 539059-2
Frank Sinatra With The Count Basie Orchestra
Sinatra-Basie:An Historic Musical First | Reprise | 7599-27023-2
It Might As Well Be Spring | Reprise | 7599-27027-2
Lionel Hampton And His Orchestra
Lionel Hampton:Flying Home | Dreyfus Jazz Line | FDM 36735-2
Sarah Vaughan And Joe Williams With The Count Basie Orchestra
Jazz Profile | Blue Note | 823517-2
Sarah Vaughan And The Count Basie Orchestra
Ballads | Roulette | 537561-2
Sarah Vaughan And The Thad Jones Orchestra
Verve Jazz Masters 42:Sarah Vaughan-The Jazz Sides | Verve | 526817-2
Sarah Vaughan With The Count Basie Band
Jazz Profile | Blue Note | 823517-2
Zoot Sims With Orchestra
Passion Flower | Original Jazz Classics | OJCCD 939-2(2312120)

Roych,Massimo | (voc)
Ernst Reijseger & Tenore E Cuncordu De Orosei
Colla Voche | Winter&Winter | 910037-2

Rozanoff,Abraham | (bs)
Louis Armstrong With Sy Oliver And His Orchestra
Satchmo Serenaders | Verve | 543792-2

Rozenblatt,David | (perc)
Paquito D'Rivera Group With The Absolute Ensemble
Habanera | Enja | ENJ-9395 2

Rubalcaba,Gonzalo | (keyboards,arr,p,percp-solo)
Antonio Carlos Jobim Group
Antonio Carlos Jobim And Friends | Verve | 531556-2
Charlie Haden Trio
The Montreal Tapes | Verve | 537670-2
Gonzalo Rubalcaba
Imagine | Blue Note | 830491-2
Gonzalo Rubalcaba & Cuban Quartet
Antiguo | Blue Note | 837717-2
Gonzalo Rubalcaba Quartet
Supernova | Blue Note | 531172-2
Imagine | Blue Note | 830491-2
Gonzalo Rubalcaba Trio
The Trio | somethin'else | 494442-2
Inner Voyage | Blue Note | 499241-2
Supernova | Blue Note | 531172-2
The Blessing | Blue Note | 797197-2
Imagine | Blue Note | 830491-2
Gonzalo Rubalcaba Trio With Michael Brecker
Inner Voyage | Blue Note | 499241-2
Gonzalo Rubalcaba-Herbie Hancock Quintet
Antonio Carlos Jobim And Friends | Verve | 531556-2
Ithamara Koorax With Band
Love Dance:The Ballad Album | Milestone | MCD 9327-2
Joe Henderson Septet
Antonio Carlos Jobim And Friends | Verve | 531556-2
Joe Lovano-Gonzalo Rubalcaba
Flying Colors | Blue Note | 856092-2
Katia Labeque-Gonzalo Rubalcaba
Little Girl Blue | Dreyfus Jazz Line | FDM 36186-2
Pat Martino Quintet
Think Tank | Blue Note | 592009-2

Rüben,Bruno | (v)
Bernd Konrad Jazz Group With Symphonie Orchestra
Wen Die Götter Lieben | Creative Works Records | CW CD 1010-1

Rubenstein,Bertil | (orgp)
Tony Scott Group
Tony Scott | Verve | 9861063

Rubie,Steve | (fl)
Ian Shaw With Band
Soho Stories | Milestone | MCD 9316-2

Rubin,Alan | (tpfl-h)
Duke Ellington And His Orchestra
New Orleans Suite | Rhino | 812273670-2
Freddie Hubbard With Orchestra
This Is Jazz:Freddie Hubbard | CBS | CK 65041
Gato Barbieri Orchestra
The Roots Of Acid Jazz | Impulse(MCA) | IMP 12042
Grover Washington Jr. Orchestra
Jazzrock-Anthology Vol.3:Fusion | Zounds | CD 27100555
Hank Crawford And His Orchestra
Roadhouse Symphony | Original Jazz Classics | OJCCD 1048-2(M 9140)

Rubin,Jules | (as,clts)
Louis Armstrong And His Orchestra
Louis Armstrong:Swing That Music | Laserlight | 36056
Louis Armstrong:C'est Si Bon | Dreyfus Jazz Line | FDM 36730-2

Rubin,Mike | (b)
Billy Eckstine With The Billy May Orchestra
Once More With Feeling | Roulette | 581862-2

Rubin,Nathan | (vconcertmaster)
Art Pepper Quintet With Strings
Art Pepper:The Complete Galaxy Recordings | Galaxy | 16GCD 1016-2
Winter Moon | Original Jazz Classics | OJC20 677-2(GXY 5140)
Herbie Hancock Group
Sunlight | CBS | 486570-2
Ron Carter With Strings
Pastels | Original Jazz Classics | OJCCD 665-2(M 9073)

Rubini,Vicenco | (tb)
Banda Città Ruvo Di Puglia
La Banda/Banda And Jazz | Enja | ENJ-9326 2

Rubinowitch,Sam | (as,b-cl,bssax)
Woody Herman And His Orchestra
The Legends Of Swing | Laserlight | 24659
Woody Herman:Four Brother | Dreyfus Jazz Line | FDM 36722-2
Woody Herman And The Herd
Woody Herman (And The Herd) At Carnegie Hall | Verve | 559833-2

Ruby,Georg | (ld,p,perc,voicep-solo)
Dioko
Helix | Jazz Haus Musik | JHM 0029 CD
Gabriele Hasler-Georg Ruby
Spider's Lovesong | Foolish Music | FM 211893
Georg Ruby Group
Stange Loops | Jazz Haus Musik | JHM 0057 CD
Georg Ruby Village Zone
Mackeben Revisited:The Ufa Years | Jazz Haus Musik | JHM 0121 CD
Jazz Orchester Rheinland-Pfalz
Kazzou | Jazz Haus Musik | LJBB 9104
Like Life | Jazz Haus Musik | LJBB 9405
Last Season | Jazz Haus Musik | LJBB 9706
Marcus Sukiennik Big Band
A Night In Tunisia Suite(7 Variationen über Dizzy Gillespie's 'A Night In Tunisia') | Jazz Haus Musik | ohne Nummer

Ruck,Roland | (b)
Elke Reiff Quartett
There Is More | Laika Records | 35101112

Rucker,Washington | (dr)
Dizzy Gillespie's Trumpet Kings
The Trumpet Kings Meet Joe Turner | Original Jazz Classics | OJCCD 497-2

Rückert,Jochen | (dr)
Achim Kaufmann Trio
Weave | Jazz 4 Ever Records:Jazz Network | J4E 4737
Anke Helfrich Trio With Mark Turner
You'll See | double moon | CHRDM 71013
Dirk Berger Quartet
Garagenjazz | Jazz Haus Musik | JHM 0090 CD
Jam Session
Jam Session Vol.4 | Steeplechase | SCCD 31527
Jochen Feucht Quartet
Signs On Lines | Satin Doll Productions | SDP 1019-1 CD
Jochen Feucht Trio
Signs On Lines | Satin Doll Productions | SDP 1019-1 CD
Matthias Petzold Group With Choir
Psalmen und Lobgesänge für Chor und Jazz-Enseble | Indigo-Records | 1002 CD
Nils Wogram Octet
Odd And Awkward | Enja | ENJ-9416-2
Nils Wogram Quartet
Round Trip | Enja | ENJ-9307 2
Speed Life | Enja | ENJ-9346 2
Nils Wogram Sextet
Odd And Awkward | Enja | ENJ-9416-2
Norbert Scholly Quartet
Norbert Scholly Quartet | Jazz Haus Musik | JHM 0086 CD
Rolf Kühn Group
Inside Out | Intuition Records | INT 3276-2
The Three Sopranos With The HR Big Band
The Three Sopranos | hr music.de | hrmj 001-01 CD

Rückert,Peter | (tp)
Johannes Rediske Sextet
Re-Disc Bounce | Bear Family Records | BCD 16119 AH

Rucks,Jimmy | (bvoc)
The Ravens
Ultimate Ben Webster selected by James Carter | Verve | 557537-2

Rudd,Jimmy | (b)
Helen Humes And Her All Stars
Lester Young:The Complete Aladdin Sessions | Blue Note | 832787-2

Rudd,Roswell | (tb,chimes,fr-hvoc)
Archie Shepp Orchestra
Mama Too Tight | Impulse(MCA) | 951248-2
Archie Shepp Sextet
Four For Trane | Impulse(MCA) | 951218-2
Carla Bley Band
Dinner Music | Watt | 6(825815-2)
European Tour 1977 | Watt | 8
Musique Mecanique | Watt | 9
Cecil Taylor Unit
Mixed | Impulse(MCA) | IMP 12702
Cecil Taylor/Buell Neidlinger Orchestra
New York City R&B | Candid | CCD 79017
Charlie Haden's Liberation Music Orchestra
Liberation Music Orchestra | Impulse(MCA) | 951188-2
Enrico Rava Quartet
Enrico Rava Quartet | ECM | 1122
Gato Barbieri Sextet
The Third World | RCA | 2179617-2
Roswell Rudd Sextet

Mixed | Impulse(MCA) | IMP 12702
Roswell Rudd-Archie Shepp Group
Live In New York | EmArCy | 013482-2
Steve Lacy-Roswell Rudd Quartet
Monk's Dream | Verve | 543090-2
The Jazz Composer's Orchestra
Comminications | JCOA | 1001/2

Ruderman,Morton | (fl)
Artie Shaw And His Orchestra
Planet JazzArtie Shaw | Planet Jazz | 2152057-2
Planet Jazz:Jazz Greatest Hits | Planet Jazz | 2169648-2
Ella Fitzgerald With The Frank DeVol Orchestra
Get Happy! | Verve | 523321-2

Ruderman,Sylvia | (fl)

Ruders,Paul | (keyboards)
Gert Sorensen
Gert Sorensen Plays Poul Ruders | dacapo | 8.224085 CD

Rüdisüli,Robi | (blowing-stuff)
Peter A. Schmid Trio With Guests
Profound Sounds In An Empty Reservoir | Creative Works Records | CW CD 1033

Rudnitsky,Alvin | (v)
Coleman Hawkins With Billy Byers And His Orchestra
The Hawk In Hi-Fi | RCA | 2663842-2

Rudolph,Adam | (bell,clay-dr,cymbals,frame-dr,gongs)
Yusef Lateef With Eternal Wind And The 'Kölner Rundfunk Orchester'
The African American Epic Suite:Music For Quintet And Orchestra | ACT | 9214-2

Rudolph,Bob | (tb)
Woody Herman And His Orchestra
Verve Jazz Masters 54:Woody Herman | Verve | 529903-2

Rudolph,Céline | (voc)
Céline Rudolph And Her Trio
Paintings | Nabel Records:Jazz Network | CD 4661
Book Of Travels | Nabel Records:Jazz Network | CD 4672
Peter Fulda Trio With Céline Rudolph
Silent Dances | Jazz 4 Ever Records:Jazz Network | J4E 4731
United Women's Orchestra
Virgo Supercluster | Jazz Haus Musik | JHM 0123 CD

Rudolph,Lars | (g,tp,double-metronome,dr-machine)
Alfred 23 Harth Group
Sweet Paris | free flow music | ffm 0291

Ruede,Clay | (cello)
A Band Of Friends
Wynton Marsalis Quartet With Strings | CBS | CK 68921

Ruf,Bernd | (clcond)
Tango Five feat. Raul Jaurena
Obsecion | Satin Doll Productions | SDP 1027-1 CD

Ruff,Mitchael | (el-p,org,vocsynth-org)
Nils Landgren First Unit And Guests
Nils Landgren-The First Unit | ACT | 9292-2

Ruff,Nadia | (voc)

Ruff,Willie | (bfr-h)
Gil Evans And Ten
Gil Evans And Ten | Original Jazz Classics | OJC 346(P 7120)
The Jazz Giants Play Cole Porter:Night And Day | Prestige | PCD 24203-2
Gil Evans And Ten | Prestige | PRSA 7120-6
Jimmy Smith With The Oliver Nelson Orchestra
Verve Jazz Masters 29:Jimmy Smith | Verve | 521855-2
Jimmy Smith:Best Of The Verve Years | Verve | 527950-2
Jimmy Smith-Talkin' Verve | Verve | 531563-2
Peter & The Wolf | Verve | 547264-2
Miles Davis + 19
Miles Ahead | CBS | CK 65121
Miles Davis With Gil Evans & His Orchestra
This Is Jazz:Miles Davis Plays Ballads | CBS | CK 65038
Porgy And Bess | CBS | CK 65141
Milt Jackson Orchestra
To Bags...With Love:Memorial Album | Pablo | 2310967-2
Milt Jackson Birthday Celebration | Fantasy | FANCD 6079-2
Big Bags | Original Jazz Classics | OJCCD 366-2(RLP 9429)
Oscar Peterson With The Ernie Wilkins Orchestra
Verve Jazz Masters 16:Oscar Peterson | Verve | 516320-2

Ruffell,Donald | (bs,clts)
Louis Armstrong And Gary Crosby With Sonny Burke's Orchestra
Louis Armstrong-My Greatest Songs | MCA | MCD 18347
Louis Armstrong And His All Stars
Satchmo Serenaders | Verve | 543792-2
Louis Armstrong And His All Stars With Benny Carter's Orchestra
Ambassador Louis Armstrong Vol.17:Moments To Remember(1952-1956) | Ambassador | CLA 1917
Louis Armstrong And His All Stars With Sonny Burke's Orchestra
Ambassador Louis Armstrong Vol.17:Moments To Remember(1952-1956) | Ambassador | CLA 1917
Louis Armstrong With Benny Carter's Orchestra
Louis Armstrong-My Greatest Songs | MCA | MCD 18347
Louis Armstrong With The Hal Mooney Orchestra
Ambassador Louis Armstrong Vol.17:Moments To Remember(1952-1956) | Ambassador | CLA 1917

Ruffins,Kermit | (tp,perc,ldvoc)
Maceo Parker With The Rebirth Brass Band
Southern Exposure | Minor Music | 801033

Ruffo,Mascagni 'Musky' | (as,cl,saxts)
Anita O'Day With Gene Krupa And His Orchestra
Let Me Off Uptown:Anita O'Day With Gene Krupa | CBS | CK 65625

Ruggieri,Vinnie | (dr)
Sal Nistico Quartet
Heavyweights | Milestone | MCD 47096-2
Sal Nistico Quintet
Heavyweights | Milestone | MCD 47096-2

Rugolo,Pete | (arr,celeste,ld,condp)
June Christy With The Pete Rugolo Orchestra
Something Cool(The Complete Mono & Stereo Versions) | Capitol | 534069-2
The Song Is June | Capitol | 855455-2
Nat King Cole Quartet With The Pete Rugolo Orchestra
The Instrumental Classics | Capitol | 798288-2
Nat King Cole Quartet With The Stan Kenton Orchestra
Nat King Cole:For Sentimental Reasons | Dreyfus Jazz Line | FDM 36740-2
Nat King Cole Trio With Pete Rugolo's Orchestra
Nat King Cole:For Sentimental Reasons | Dreyfus Jazz Line | FDM 36740-2
Pete Rugolo And His Orchestra
Verve Jazz Masters 52:Maynard Ferguson | Verve | 529905-2
Thriller/Richard Diamon(Original Jazz Scores From 2 Classics TV Series) | Fresh Sound Records | FSCD 2015
The Metronome All Stars
Planet Jazz:Dizzy Gillespie | Planet Jazz | 2152069-2

Ruhland,Martin | (gongs,tam-tamperc)
Munich Saxophon Family
Balanced | Edition Collage | EC 487-2

Ruiz,Antonio 'Kiko' | (flamenco-g)
Renaud Garcia-Fons
Navigatore | Enja | ENJ-9418 2
Renaud Garcia-Fons Group
Navigatore | Enja | ENJ-9418 2
Entremundo | Enja | ENJ-9464 2

Ruiz,Hilton | (el-p,keyboards,p,arr,claves)
David Fathead Newman Septet
Jazzin' Vol.2: The Music Of Stevie Wonder | Fantasy | FANCD 6088-2

Ruiz,Otmaro | (p,keyboardssynth)
Arturo Sandoval And The Latin Train Band
Arturo Sandoval & The Latin Train | GRP | GRP 98202
John McLaughlin Group
Live In Paris | Verve | 543536-2

Rumig,Dirk | (cl,as,tsss)
Ralph Schweizer Big Band
DAY Dream | Chaos | CACD 8177
Sax Mal Anders
Kontraste | Chaos | CACD 8185

Rummage,Bob | (dr)
Brad Goode-Von Freeman Sextet
Inside Chicago Vol.3 | Steeplechase | SCCD 31531
Inside Chicago Vol.4 | Steeplechase | SCCD 31532

Rumsey,Howard | (b)
Chet Baker And The Lighthouse All Stars
Witch Doctor | Original Jazz Classics | OJCCD 609-2
The Jazz Giants Play Harry Warren:Lullaby Of Broadway | Prestige | PCD 24204-2
Chet Baker Quartet
At Last! | Original Jazz Classics | OJCCD 480-2
Howard Rumsey's Lighthouse All-Stars
Oboe/Flute | Original Jazz Classics | OJCCD 154-2(C 3520)
Howard Rumsey's Lighthouse All-Stars Vol.6 | Original Jazz Classics | OJCCD 386-2(C 3504)
Sunday Jazz A La Lighthouse Vol.2 | Original Jazz Classics | OJCCD 972-2(S 2501)
Miles Davis And The Lighthouse All Stars
At Last! | Original Jazz Classics | OJCCD 480-2
Stan Kenton And His Orchestra
Stan Kenton-The Formative Years | Decca | 589489-2

Rundel,Peter | (cond)
Radio Symphony Orchestra Frankfurt
Songs And One Symphony | ECM | 1721
Elliott Sharp:Racing Hearts/Tessalation Row/Calling | hr music.de | hrmn 018-03 CD

Rundfunkorchester Berlin |
Chris Barber's Jazzband & das Große Rundfunkorchester Berlin,DDR
Jazz Zounds: Chris Barber | Zounds | CD 2720007

Rundquist,Fred | (g)
Art Van Damme Group
State Of Art | MPS | 841413-2

Rundquist,Gösta | (p)
Agneta Baumann And Her Quartet
Comes Love... | Touché Music | TMcCD 011
Agneta Baumann Group
Sentimental Lady | Touché Music | TMcCD 017

Runge,Eckart | (cello)
Eckart Runge-Jacques Ammon
Cello Tango | Edition Musikat | EDM 053

Runov,John | (cl)
Papa Benny's Jazzband
The Golden Years Of Revival Jazz,Vol.12 | Storyville | STCD 5517

Ruocco,John | (b-cl,ts,cl,reedssax)
Akili
Maasai Mara | M.A Music | A 802-2
Dino Saluzzi Group
If | Enja | ENJ-9451 2

Ruomi | (raprecitation)
Gunter Hampel Next Generation
Next Generation | Birth | CD 043

Rupcic,Hrvoje | (perc)
Mind Games
Pretty Fonky | Edition Collage | EC 482-2
Wind Moments | Take Twelve On CD | TT 009-2
Mind Games With Philip Catherine
Pretty Fonky | Edition Collage | EC 482-2
Tom Bennecke & Space Gurilla
Wind Moments | Take Twelve On CD | TT 009-2

Rupp,Kenny | (tbtuba)
Maynard Ferguson Orchestra With Chris Connor
Two's Company | Roulette | 837201-2

Ruppersberg,Don | (tb)
Charlie Barnet And His Orchestra
Planet Jazz:Big Bands | Planet Jazz | 2169649-2
Planet Jazz:Swing | Planet Jazz | 2169651-2

Rüsenberg,Michael | (soundscapes)
Norbert Stein Pata Masters
Pata Maroc | Pata Musik | PATA 12(AMF 1063)

Rushen,Patrice | (el-p,synth,clavinet,keyboards,perc)
Eddie Henderson Orchestra
Blue Break Beats | Blue Note | 799106-2
Jean-Luc Ponty Quintet
Aurora | Atlantic | 7567-81543-2
The Very Best Of Jean-Luc Ponty | Rhino | 8122-79862-2
Lenny White Group
Renderers Of Spirit | Hip Bop | HIBD 8014
Hot Jazz Bisquits | Hip Bop | HIBD 8801
Luis Gasca Group
Jazzin' Vol.2: The Music Of Stevie Wonder | Fantasy | FANCD 6088-2
Marion McPartland-Bill Evans-John Lewis-Patrice Rushen
Monterey Jazz Festival 1975 | Storyville | 4960213
The Meeting
Hot Jazz Bisquits | Hip Bop | HIBD 8801

Rushing,Jimmy | (dr,pvoc)
Benny Moten's Kansas City Orchestra
Planet Jazz:Jimmy Rushing | RCA | 2165371-2
Count Basie And His Orchestra
Planet Jazz:Count Basie | Planet Jazz | 2152068-2
Planet Jazz:Jimmy Rushing | RCA | 2165371-2
Planet Jazz:Big Bands | Planet Jazz | 2169649-2
Verve Jazz Masters 2:Count Basie | Verve | 519819-2
Jazz:The Essential Collection Vol.3 | IN+OUT Records | 78013-2
Count Basie At Newport | Verve | 9861761
Count Basie Sextet
Jazz:The Essential Collection Vol.3 | IN+OUT Records | 78013-2
Jimmy Rushing And His Band
Planet Jazz:Jimmy Rushing | RCA | 2165371-2
Planet Jazz:Male Jazz Vocalists | Planet Jazz | 2169657-2
Jimmy Rushing And His Orchestra
Every Day I Have The Blues | Impulse(MCA) | 547967-2
Five Feet Of Soul | Roulette | 581830-2
Jimmy Rushing With Count Basie And His Orchestra
From Spiritual To Swing | Vanguard | VCD 169/71
Jimmy Rushing With Oliver Nelson And His Orchestra
Every Day I Have The Blues | Impulse(MCA) | 547967-2
Jimmy Rushing With The Dave Brubeck Quartet
Brubeck & Rushing | CBS | CK 65727
Jimmy Rushing/Dave Frishberg
Planet Jazz:Jimmy Rushing | RCA | 2165371-2
Jones-Smith Incorporated
Jazz:The Essential Collection Vol.3 | IN+OUT Records | 78013-2

Ruskin,Tommy | (dr)
Jay McShann Quartet
Goin' To Kansas City | Stony Plain | SPCD 1286

Russ Garcia Strings |
Buddy Childers With The Russ Garcia Strings
Artistry In Jazz | Candid | CCD 79735

Russell,Brenda | (background-vocvoc)
Yellowjackets
Live Wires | GRP | GRP 96672

Russell,Curly | (b)
Art Blakey And The Jazz Messengers
A Night At Birdland Vol. 1 | Blue Note | 532146-2
A Night At Birdland Vol. 2 | Blue Note | 532147-2
Billie Holiday With The JATP All Stars
The Complete Jazz At The Philharmonic On Verve 1944-1949 | Verve | 523893-2
Bud Powell Trio
The Best Of Bud Powell On Verve | Verve | 523392-2
The Amazing Bud Powell Vol.1 | Blue Note | 532136-2
Jazz Giant | Verve | 543832-2
Bud Powell:Bouncing With Bud | Dreyfus Jazz Line | FDM 36725-2
Charlie Parker All Stars
Charlie Parker:Now's The Time | Dreyfus Jazz Line | FDM 36724-2
Charlie Parker And His Orchestra
Bird: The Complete Charlie Parker On Verve | Verve | 837141-2
Charlie Parker:April In Paris | Dreyfus Jazz Line | FDM 36737-2
Charlie Parker Quintet
Verve Jazz Masters 10:Dizzy Gillespie | Verve | 516319-2
Bird And Diz | Verve | 521436-2
Charlie Parker:Bird's Best Bop On Verve | Verve | 527452-2
Charlie Parker:The Best Of The Verve Years | Verve | 527815-2
Ultimate Dizzy Gillespie | Verve | 557535-2
Talkin' Bird | Verve | 559859-2
Charlie Parker With Strings
Charlie Parker With Strings:The Master Takes | Verve | 523984-2
Charlie Parker With The Neal Hefti Orchestra
Charlie Parker:The Best Of The Verve Years | Verve | 527815-2
Bird: The Complete Charlie Parker On Verve | Verve | 837141-2
Charlie Parker-Dizzy Gillespie Quintet
Thelonious Monk:Misterioso | Dreyfus Jazz Line | FDM 36743-2
Charlie Parker's Beboppers
Charlie Parker:Now's The Time | Dreyfus Jazz Line | FDM 36724-2
Cliff Jordan-John Gilmore Quintet
Blowing In From Chicago | Blue Note | 542306-2
Coleman Hawkins All Star Octet
Milt Jackson Birthday Celebration | Fantasy | FANCD 6079-2
Coleman Hawkins All Stars
The J.J.Johnson Memorial Album | Prestige | PRCD 11025-2
Dizzy Gillespie All Stars
Dizzy Gillespie:Night In Tunisia | Dreyfus Jazz Line | FDM 36734-2
Horace Silver Trio
Horace Silver Retrospective | Blue Note | 495576-2
Horace Silver Trio And Spotlight On Drums:Art Blakey-Sabu | Blue Note | 591725-2
JATP All Stars
The Complete Jazz At The Philharmonic On Verve 1944-1949 | Verve | 523893-2
Jubilee All Stars
Jazz Gallery:Lester Young Vol.2(1946-59) | RCA | 2119541-2
Lester Young And His Band
Lester Young:The Complete Aladdin Sessions | Blue Note | 832787-2
Sarah Vaughan With Dizzy Gillespie And His All Star Quintet
Sarah Vaughan:Lover Man | Dreyfus Jazz Line | FDM 36739-2
Sarah Vaughan With Dizzy Gillespie And His Septet
Sarah Vaughan:Lover Man | Dreyfus Jazz Line | FDM 36739-2
Sonny Stitt Quartet
Sonny Stitt | Original Jazz Classics | OJCCD 009-2
Tadd Dameron Septet
The Fabulous Fats Navarro Vol.2 | Blue Note | 0677208
Fats Navarro:Nostalgia | Dreyfus Jazz Line | FDM 36736-2
Tadd Dameron Tentet
Jazz Profile:Dexter Gordon | Blue Note | 823514-2
Tadd Dameron-Fats Navarro Quintet
Fats Navarro:Nostalgia | Dreyfus Jazz Line | FDM 36736-2
Terry Gibbs Septet
Early Stan | Original Jazz Classics | OJCCD 654-2(P 7255)
The McGhee-Navarro Boptet
The Fabulous Fats Navarro Vol.1 | Blue Note | 0677207
The Fabulous Fats Navarro Vol.2 | Blue Note | 0677208
Thelonious Monk Quintet
Thelonious Monk:The Complete Prestige Recordings | Prestige | 3 PRCD 4428-2
Thelonious Monk:85th Birthday Celebration | zyx records | FANCD 6076-2
MONK | Original Jazz Classics | OJCCD 016-2
The Jazz Giants Play Jerome Kern:Yesterdays | Prestige | PCD 24202-2
The Prestige Legacy Vol.1:The High Priests | Prestige | PCD 24251-2
Zoot Sims Quartet
Zoot Sims Quartets | Original Jazz Classics | OJCCD 242-2(P 7026)

Russell,Curly or Rodney Richardson | (g)
JATP All Stars
The Complete Jazz At The Philharmonic On Verve 1944-1949 | Verve | 523893-2

Russell,Curly prob. | (b)
Billie Holiday With The JATP All Stars
Billie Holiday Story Vol.1:Jazz At The Philharmonic | Verve | 521642-2
The Complete Jazz At The Philharmonic On Verve 1944-1949 | Verve | 523893-2

Russell,George | (arr,comp,ld,b,church-org,cond,dr,p)
George Russell And His Orchestra
Geogre Russell New York N.Y. | Impulse(MCA) | 951278-2
Bill Evans:Piano Player | CBS | CK 65361
George Russell And The Living Time Orchestra
Kind Of Blue:Blue Note Celebrate The Music Of Miles Davis | Blue Note | 534255-2
George Russell Sextet
Eric Dolphy Birthday Celebration | Fantasy | FANCD 6085-2
Ezz-thetics | Original Jazz Classics | OJCCD 070-2(RLP 9375)
The Outer View | Original Jazz Classics | OJCCD 616-2(RLP 9440)
The Jazz Giants Play Miles Davis:Milestones | Prestige | PCD 24225-2
George Russell Smalltet
The RCA Victor Jazz Workshop | RCA | 2159144-2
Gerry Mulligan Concert Jazz Band
Verve Jazz Masters 36:Gerry Mulligan | Verve | 523342-2
Lucy Reed With Orchestra
This Is Lucy Reed | Original Jazz Classics | OJCCD 1943-2(F 3243)

Russell,Graham | (tp)
Mike Westbrook Orchestra
The Orchestra Of Smith's Academy | Enja | ENJ-9358 2

Russell,Hal | (tp,ss,ts,vib,dr,perc,congas)
Hal Russell
Hal's Bells | ECM | 1484
Hal Russell NRG Ensemble
The Finnish/Swiss Tour | ECM | 1455
The Hal Russell Story | ECM | 1498

Russell,Johnny | (ts)
Willie Bryant And His Orchestra
Planet Jazz:Ben Webster | RCA | 2165368-2

Russell,Luis | (p,arrceleste)
Henry Allen Jr. And His New York Orchestra
Planet Jazz:Jazz Saxophone | Planet Jazz | 2169653-2
Planet Jazz:Jazz Trumpet | Planet Jazz | 2169654-2
King Oliver And His Dixie Syncopators
Jazz:The Essential Collection Vol.1 | IN+OUT Records | 78011-2
King Oliver And His Orchestra
Planet Jazz:Jazz Trumpet | Planet Jazz | 2169654-2
King Oliver's Jazz Band
Jazz:The Essential Collection Vol.1 | IN+OUT Records | 78011-2
Louis Armstrong And His Orchestra
Louis Armstrong:Swing That Music | Laserlight | 36056
Jazz:The Essential Collection Vol.2 | IN+OUT Records | 78012-2
Satch Plays Fats(Complete) | CBS | CK 64927
Louis Armstrong:C'est Si Bon | Dreyfus Jazz Line | FDM 36730-2
Louis Armstrong-My Greatest Songs | MCA | MCD 18347
Swing Legends:Louis Armstrong | Nimbus Records | NI 2012
Louis Armstrong And His Savoy Ballroom Five
Jazz:The Essential Collection Vol.2 | IN+OUT Records | 78012-2

Russell,Mischa | (concertmasterv)
Ben Webster With Orchestra And Strings
Music For Loving:Ben Webster With Strings | Verve | 527774-2
Ultimate Ben Webster selected by James Carter | Verve | 557537-2
Ella Fitzgerald With The Billy May Orchestra
The Best Of The Song Books:The Ballads | Verve | 521867-2
Ella Fitzgerald Sings The Harold Arlen Song Book | Verve | 589108-2
Ella Fitzgerald With The Buddy Bregman Orchestra
The Best Of The Song Books:The Ballads | Verve | 521867-2
Love Songs:The Best Of The Song Books | Verve | 531762-2
Ella Fitzgerald Sings The Cole Porter Songbook | Verve | 537257-2
Ella Fitzgerald Sings The Rodgers And Hart Song Book | Verve | 537258-2

Ella Fitzgerald With The Nelson Riddle Orchestra
The Best Of The Song Books:The Ballads | Verve | 521867-2
Frank Sinatra With Orchestra
Planet Jazz:Frank Sinatra & Tommy Dorsey | Planet Jazz | 2152067-2
Harry James And His Orchestra
Trumpet Blues:The Best Of Harry James | Capitol | 521224-2
Lena Horne With The Lou Bring Orchestra
Planet Jazz:Lena Horne | Planet Jazz | 2165373-2
Planet Jazz:Female Jazz Vocalists | Planet Jazz | 2169656-2
Paul Whiteman And His Orchestra
Planet Jazz:Jazz Trumpet | Planet Jazz | 2169654-2

Russell,Pee Wee | (cl,as,tsvoc)
Bud Freeman And His Famous Chicagoans
Jazz:The Essential Collection Vol.3 | IN+OUT Records | 78013-2
Bud Freeman And His Summa Cum Laude Orchestra
Planet Jazz:Bud Freeman | Planet Jazz | 2161240-2
Planet Jazz:Jazz Saxophone | Planet Jazz | 2169653-2
Eddie Condon And His Chicagoans
The Very Best Of Dixieland Jazz | Verve | 535529-2
Eddie Condon And His Orchestra
Jazz:The Essential Collection Vol.3 | IN+OUT Records | 78013-2
Hoagy Carmichael And His Orchestra
Planet Jazz:Bud Freeman | Planet Jazz | 2161240-2
Jack Teagarden And His Orchestra
Jazz:The Essential Collection Vol.3 | IN+OUT Records | 78013-2
Miff Mole And His Dixieland Band
Muggsy Spanier-Manhattan Masters,1945 | Storyville | STCD 6051
Mound City Blue Blowers
Jazz:The Essential Collection Vol.3 | IN+OUT Records | 78013-2
Muggsy Spanier And His Dixieland Band
Muggsy Spanier-Manhattan Masters,1945 | Storyville | STCD 6051
Muggsy Spanier And His V-Disc All Stars
Muggsy Spanier And Bud Freeman:V-Discs 1944-45 | Jazz Unlimited | JUCD 2049
Pee Wee Russell And His Dixieland Band
Muggsy Spanier-Manhattan Masters,1945 | Storyville | STCD 6051
Pee Wee Russell Quartet
Ask Me Now! | Impulse(MCA) | 755742-2
The Dixieland All Stars
The Dixieland All Stars | Jazz Unlimited | JUCD 2037
Thelonious Monk Quartet With Pee Wee Russell
Monk At Newport 1963 & 1965 | CBS | C2K 63905

Russian Folk Ensemble |
Mikhail Alperin's Moscow Art Trio With The Tuva Folk & Russian Folk Ensemble
Prayer | JA & RO | JARO 4193-2

Russin,Irving 'Babe' | (reedsts)
Benny Goodman And His Orchestra
Planet Jazz:Big Bands | Planet Jazz | 2169649-2
Benny Goodman At Carnegie Hall 1938(Complete) | CBS | C2K 65143
Benny Goodman Band
Benny Goodman At Carnegie Hall 1938(Complete) | CBS | C2K 65143
Billie Holiday With Teddy Wilson And His Orchestra
Billie's Love Songs | Nimbus Records | NI 2000
Ella Fitzgerald With Paul Weston And His Orchestra
Love Songs:The Best Of The Song Books | Verve | 531762-2
Ella Fitzgerald Sings The Irving Berlin Song Book | Verve | 543830-2
Ella Fitzgerald With The Nelson Riddle Orchestra
The Best Of The Song Books:The Ballads | Verve | 521867-2
Love Songs:The Best Of The Song Books | Verve | 531762-2
Ella Fitzgerald Sings The Johnny Mercer Songbook | Verve | 539057-2
Ella Fitzgerald With The Paul Weston Orchestra
Get Happy! | Verve | 523321-2
Glen Gray And His Orchestra
Great Swing Classics In Hi-Fi | Capitol | 521223-2
Glenn Miller And His Orchestra
Swing Legends | Nimbus Records | NI 2001
Jam Session
Benny Goodman At Carnegie Hall 1938(Complete) | CBS | C2K 65143
JATP All Stars
The Complete Jazz At The Philharmonic On Verve 1944-1949 | Verve | 523893-2
Lionel Hampton And His Orchestra
Planet Jazz:Swing | Planet Jazz | 2169651-2
Planet Jazz:Jazz Saxophone | Planet Jazz | 2169653-2
Louis Armstrong And His All Stars With Benny Carter's Orchestra
Ambassador Louis Armstrong Vol.17:Moments To Remember(1952-1956) | Ambassador | CLA 1917
Louis Armstrong With Benny Carter's Orchestra
Louis Armstrong-My Greatest Songs | MCA | MCD 18347
Louis Armstrong With The Hal Mooney Orchestra
Ambassador Louis Armstrong Vol.17:Moments To Remember(1952-1956) | Ambassador | CLA 1917
Tommy Dorsey And His Orchestra
Planet Jazz:Frank Sinatra & Tommy Dorsey | Planet Jazz | 2152067-2
Planet Jazz:Tommy Dorsey | Planet Jazz | 2159972-2
Van Alexander Orchestra
Home Of Happy Feet/Swing! Staged For Sound! | Capitol | 535211-2

Russin,Jack | (p)
Irving Mills And His Hotsy Totsy Gang
Jazz:The Essential Collection Vol.3 | IN+OUT Records | 78013-2
Jack Teagarden And His Orchestra
Jazz:The Essential Collection Vol.3 | IN+OUT Records | 78013-2

Russin,Jack or Frank Signorelli | (p)
Irving Mills And His Hotsy Totsy Gang
Jazz:The Essential Collection Vol.3 | IN+OUT Records | 78013-2

Russkaja Pesnja Folk Choir |
Mikhail Alperin's Moscow Art Trio With The Russkaja Pesnja Folk Choir
Folk Dreams | JA & RO | JARO 4187-2

Russo,Ambrose | (v)
Ella Fitzgerald With The Frank DeVol Orchestra
Get Happy! | Verve | 523321-2
Pete Rugolo And His Orchestra
Thriller/Richard Diamon(Original Jazz Scores From 2 Classics TV Series) | Fresh Sound Records | FSCD 2015

Russo,Bill | (arr,condtb)
Cannonball Adderley And His Orchestra
Verve Jazz Masters 31:Cannonball Adderley | Verve | 522651-2

Russo,Charles | (b-cl,cl,reeds,saxwoodwinds)
Ron Carter Group
Peg Leg | Original Jazz Classics | OJCCD 621-2
Stan Getz With The Eddie Sauter Orchestra
Stan Getz Plays The Music Of Mickey One | Verve | 531232-2

Russo,Sonny | (tbtp)
Birdland Dream Band
Birdland Dream Band | RCA | 2663873-2
Glenn Miller And His Orchestra
The Glenn Miller Orchestra In Digital Mood | GRP | GRP 95022
John LaPorta Octet
Theme And Variations | Fantasy | FCD 24776-2
John LaPorta Septet
Theme And Variations | Fantasy | FCD 24776-2
Sandole Brothers
The Sandole Brothers | Fantasy | FCD 24763-2
Stan Getz With The Eddie Sauter Orchestra
Stan Getz Plays The Music Of Mickey One | Verve | 531232-2

Russo,Tony | (cltp)
Anita O'Day With Gene Krupa And His Orchestra
Let Me Off Uptown:Anita O'Day With Gene Krupa | CBS | CK 65625

Russo,William 'Bill' | (arr,ld,comp,condtb)
Stan Kenton And His Orchestra
Stan Kenton Portraits On Standards | Capitol | 531571-2

Ruth,Peter | (fl,harm,vocjew-harp)
Dave Brubeck With The Erich Kunzel Orchestra
Truth Is Fallen | Atlantic | 7567-80761-2

Ruther,Wyatt | (b)
Chico Hamilton Orchestra
With Strings Attached/The Three Faces Of Chico | Warner | 9362-47874-2
Chico Hamilton Quintet
With Strings Attached/The Three Faces Of Chico | Warner | 9362-47874-2
Chico Hamilton Quintet With Strings
With Strings Attached/The Three Faces Of Chico | Warner | 9362-47874-2
Erroll Garner Quartet
Verve Jazz Masters 7:Erroll Garner | Verve | 518197-2
Verve Jazz Masters 20:Introducing | Verve | 519853-2
Contrasts | Verve | 558077-2
Erroll Garner Trio
Contrasts | Verve | 558077-2

Rutherford,Paul | (euphonium,tb,tb-solovoice)
Evan Parker-Paul Rutherford-Barry Guy-John Stevens
4,4,4, | Konnex Records | KCD 5049
Kenny Wheeler Ensemble
Muisc For Large & Small Ensembles | ECM | 1415/16
Tony Oxley Sextet
4 Compositions For Sextet | CBS | 494437-2

Rutherford,Rudy | (as,bs,cl,tsreeds)
Big Joe Turner And Pete Johnson With The Blues Band
Newport Jazz Festival 1958,July 3rd-6th Vol.3:Blues In The Night No.1 | Phontastic | NCD 8815
Big Maybelle With The Blues Band
Newport Jazz Festival 1958,July 3rd-6th Vol.3:Blues In The Night No.1 | Phontastic | NCD 8815
Chuck Berry With The Blues Band
Newport Jazz Festival 1958,July 3rd-6th Vol.3:Blues In The Night No.1 | Phontastic | NCD 8815
Count Basie And His Orchestra
Planet Jazz:Count Basie | Planet Jazz | 2152068-2
Planet Jazz:Jazz Greatest Hits | Planet Jazz | 2169648-2
Jazz:The Essential Collection Vol.3 | IN+OUT Records | 78013-2

Rutkauskas,Alejandro | (v)
Daniel Schnyder With String Quartet
Tanatula | Enja | ENJ-9302 2

Rutledge,Mike | (viola)
String Thing
String Thing:Alles Wird Gut | MicNic Records | MN 2
String Thing:Turtifix | MicNic Records | MN 4

Rutz,Brigitta | (viola)
Bernd Konrad Jazz Group With Symphonie Orchestra
Wen Die Götter Lieben | Creative Works Records | CW CD 1010-1

Ruzilla,Fred | (viola)
Charlie Parker With The Neal Hefti Orchestra
Charlie Parker:The Best Of The Verve Years | Verve | 527815-2
Bird: The Complete Charlie Parker On Verve | Verve | 837141-2

Ryam,Roger | (ts)
Marcus Miller Group
Live & More | Dreyfus Jazz Line | FDM 36585-2

Ryan,Jack | (b)
Ella Fitzgerald With Paul Weston And His Orchestra
Love Songs:The Best Of The Song Books | Verve | 531762-2
Ella Fitzgerald Sings The Irving Berlin Song Book | Verve | 543830-2

Ryan,Jim | (keyboardssynth)
Al Jarreau With Band
All Fly Home | Warner | 7599-27362-2

Ryan,Joel | (computersound-processing)
Evan Parker Electro-Acoustic Ensemble
Memory/Vision | ECM | 1852(0381172)

Rydh,Niclas | (b-tb)
Anders Jormin With Brass Quartet
Xieyi | ECM | 1762(013998-2)

Rydquist,Robin | (tpfl-h)

Ryerson,Arthur 'Art' | (g)
Charlie Parker With Strings
Bird: The Complete Charlie Parker On Verve | Verve | 837141-2
Charlie Parker With The Joe Lipman Orchestra
Charlie Parker With Strings:The Master Takes | Verve | 523984-2
Charlie Parker Big Band | Verve | 559835-2
Leon Thomas With Orchestra
Spirits Known And Unknown | RCA | 2663876-2
Louis Armstrong And His All Stars
What A Wonderful World | MCA | MCD 01876
Louis Armstrong And His Orchestra
What A Wonderful World | MCA | MCD 01876
Louis Armstrong With Gordon Jenkins And His Orchestra And Choir
Satchmo In Style | Verve | 549594-2
Louis Armstrong With The Gordon Jenkins Orchestra
Ambassador Louis Armstrong Vol.17:Moments To Remember(1952-1956) | Ambassador | CLA 1917

Ryerson,Frank | (tp)
Jack Teagarden And His Orchestra
Jazz:The Essential Collection Vol.3 | IN+OUT Records | 78013-2

Rykiel,Jean-Philippe | (electronic-keyboardssynth)
Jon Hassell Group
Power Spot | ECM | 1327
Karim Ziad Groups
Ifrikya | ACT | 9282-2

Ryland,Floyd | (voc)
Buddy Johnson And His Orchestra
Buddy And Ella Johnson 1953-1964 | Bear Family Records | BCD 15479 DH

Rypdal,Inger Lise | (voc)
Terje Rypdal Sextet
Terje Rypdal | ECM | 1016(527645-2)

Rypdal,Terje | (casio mt-30,electronic-g,el-g)
Jan Garbarek Quintet
Sart | ECM | 1015(839305-2)
Ketil Bjornstad Group
Water Stories | ECM | 1503(519076-2)
The Sea | ECM | 1545(521718-2)
The Sea II | ECM | 1633(537341-2)
Markus Stockhausen Quartet
Karta | ECM | 1704(543035-2)
Michael Mantler Group
The Hapless Child | Watt | 4
Nordic Quartet
Nordic Quartet | ECM | 1553
Terje Rypdal And The Chasers
Blue | ECM | 1346(831516-2)
Terje Rypdal Group
Odyssey | ECM | 1067/8
If Mountains Could Sing | ECM | 1554(523987-2)
Skywards | ECM | 1608(533768-2)
Terje Rypdal Quartet
Waves | ECM | 1110(827419-2)
The Singles Collection | ECM | 1383(837749-2)
Terje Rypdal Quartet With The Bergen Chamber Ensemble
Lux Aeterna | ECM | 1818(017070-2)
Terje Rypdal Quintet
What Comes After | ECM | 1031
When Ever I Seem To Be Far Away | ECM | 1045
Terje Rypdal Sextet
Terje Rypdal | ECM | 1016(527645-2)
Terje Rypdal Trio
Descendre | ECM | 1144
To Be Continued | ECM | 1192
Chaser | ECM | 1303
Terje Rypdal With Strings
When Ever I Seem To Be Far Away | ECM | 1045
Terje Rypdal With The Borealis Ensemble
Q.E.D. | ECM | 1474
Terje Rypdal With The Riga Festival Orchestra
Double Concerto/5th Symphony | ECM | 1567(559964-2)
Terje Rypdal-David Darling Duo
Eos | ECM | 1263
Terje Rypdal-Miroslav Vitous-Jack DeJohnette Trio
Terje Rypdal Miroslav Vitous Jack DeJohnette | ECM | 1125(825470-2)
Tomasz Stanko Septet
Litania | ECM | 1636(537551-2)
Tomasz Stanko-Terje Rypdal
Litania | ECM | 1636(537551-2)

Ryschka,Jurij | (tpfl-h)
Jazz Orchester Rheinland-Pfalz
Like Life | Jazz Haus Musik | LJBB 9405

Saad,Antoine | (v)
Till Brönner Quartet & Deutsches Symphonieorchester Berlin
German Songs | Minor Music | 801057

Saarelaht,Mart | (p)
Vince Jones Group
Watch What Happens | Intuition Records | INT 3070-2

Saassaa.Ahmed | (hag'hougevoc)
Randy Weston African Rhythm Quintet and The Gnawa Master Musicians of Marocco
Spirit! The Power Of Music | Verve | 543256-2

Saastamoinen,Ilpo | (b)
Piirpauke
Piirpauke-Global Servisi | JA & RO | JARO 4150-2

Sabal-Lecco,Armand | (b,background-voc,piccolo-b,tenor-b)
John Patitucci Group
Mistura Fina | GRP | GRP 98022
The Brecker Brothers
Return Of The Brecker Brothers | GRP | GRP 96842
Out Of The Loop | GRP | GRP 97842

Sabatelli,Pasquale | (bassoon)
Charles Mingus Orchestra
Cumbia & Jazz Fusion | Atlantic | 8122-71785-2

Sabatés,Riqui | (g)
Big Band Bellaterra
Don't Git Sassy | Fresh Sound Records | FSNT 048 CD

Saberton,Pete | (p,el-psynth)
Mike Westbrook Orchestra
The Orchestra Of Smith's Academy | Enja | ENJ-9358 2

Sabinski,Antje | (viola)
Uri Caine With The Concerto Köln
Concerto Köln | Winter&Winter | 910086-2

Saby,Lea | (voc)
booMbooM meets Uli Beckerhoff
Resurection Lounge | Laika Records | 35101512

Saccaro,Frank | (tb)
Ella Fitzgerald With Sy Oliver And His Orchestra
Ella Fitzgerald:The Decca Years 1949-1954 | Decca | 050668-2

Sacher,Barry | (v)
Chick Corea And His Orchestra
My Spanish Heart | Polydor | 543303-3

Sacher,Buddy | (g)
Ulla Oster Group
Beyond Janis | Jazz Haus Musik | JHM 0052 CD

Sachs,Aaron | (as,bs,clts)
Sarah Vaughan With The Allstars
Sarah Vaughan:Lover Man | Dreyfus Jazz Line | FDM 36739-2
The Modern Jazz Society
A Concert Of Contemporary Music | Verve | 559827-2

Sachs,Helen | (voc)
Salut!
Green & Orange | Edition Collage | EC 488-2

Sachs,Klaus | (p)
Helmut Weglinski Quintet
Deutsches Jazz Fesival 1954/1955 | Bear Family Records | BCD 15430

Sackenheim,Frank | (as,tssax)
Frank Sackenheim Quartet
The Music Of Chance | Jazz 4 Ever Records:Jazz Network | J4E 4753
Frank Sackenheim Quintet
The Music Of Chance | Jazz 4 Ever Records:Jazz Network | J4E 4753
Lars Duppler Quartet
Palindrome | Jazz Haus Musik | JHM 0108 CD

Sackenhein,Frank | (ts)
Lars Duppler Sextet
Palindrome 6tet | Jazz Haus Musik | JHM 0131 CD

Sackville All Stars |
Sackville All Stars
Christmas Jazz! | Nagel-Heyer | NH 1008

Sadek,Ragab | (tablas)
Koch-Schütz-Studer & El Nil Troop
Heavy Cairo Trafic | Intuition Records | INT 3175-2

Sadi,Fats | (bongos,perc,vibvoc)
Andre Hodeir And His Jazz Group De Paris
Jazz In Paris:Le Jazz Groupe De Paris Joue André Hodeir | EmArCy | 548792-2
Bobby Jaspar Quintet
Jazz In Paris:Bobby Jaspar-Jeux De Quartes | EmArCy | 018423-2
Django Reinhardt Quintet
Jazz In Paris:Django Reinhardt-Nuages | EmArCy | 018428-2
Klaus Doldinger Septet
Doldinger's Best | ACT | 9224-2
Les Blue Stars
Jazz In Paris:Blossom Dearie-The Pianist/Les Blue Stars | EmArCy | 064784-2
Raymond Fol Big Band
Jazz In Paris:Raymond Fol-Les 4 Saisons | EmArCy | 548791-2

Sadiq | (dr,percrecitation)
Don Byron Quintet
Tuskegee Experiments | Nonesuch | 7559-79280-2
Gunter Hampel Jazz Sextet
Gunter Hampel: The 8th Of Sept.1999 | Birth | CD 049

Sadownick,Daniel | (congasperc)
Michael Brecker Quindectet
Wide Angles | Verve | 076142-2

Safranski,Eddie | (b)
Don Byas All Star Quintet
Don Byas:Laura | Dreyfus Jazz Line | FDM 36714-2
Don Byas All Stars
Don Byas:Laura | Dreyfus Jazz Line | FDM 36714-2
Johnny Smith Quintet
Moonlight In Vermont | Roulette | 596593-2
Johnny Smith-Stan Getz Quintet
Stan Getz-The Complete Roost Sessions | EMI Records | 859622-2
Sarah Vaughan The The Joe Lippman Orchestra
Sarah Vaughan:Lover Man | Dreyfus Jazz Line | FDM 36739-2
Stan Kenton And His Orchestra
Swing Vol.1 | Storyville | 4960343
The Metronome All Stars
Jazz Gallery:Lester Young Vol.2(1946-59) | RCA | 2119541-2
Planet Jazz:Dizzy Gillespie | Planet Jazz | 2152069-2

Safred,Gianni | (p)
Django Reinhardt And The Quintet Du Hot Club De France
Planet Jazz:Stephane Grappelli | RCA | 2165366-2
Quintet Du Hot Club De France
Djangology | Bluebird | 2663957-2
Django/Django In Rome 1949-1050 | BGO Records | BGOCD 366

Saft,Jamie | (el-p,moog,org,el-b,mini-moog)
Bobby Previte's Latin For Travelers
Dangerous Rip | Enja | ENJ-9324-2
My Man In Sidney | Enja | ENJ-9348 2
Dave Douglas Group
Dave Douglas Freak In | Bluebird | 2664008-2
Jerry Granelli Group
Music Has Its Way With Me | Traumton Records | 4451-2

Saguets,Arthur | (cl,sax,tsbars)
Django Reinhardt With Stan Brenders Et Son Grand Orchestre
Verve Jazz Masters 38:Django Reinhardt | Verve | 516931-2

Sahmaoui,Aziz | (voc)
Nguyen Le Group
Maghreb And Friends | ACT | 9261-2

Sahota,Yogish S. | (tamburatampura)

John Handy-Ali Akbar Khan Group
Two Originals:Karuna Supreme/Rainbow | MPS | 519195-2
Sailes,Jesse | (dr)
Kid Ory And His Band
The Very Best Of Dixieland Jazz | Verve | 535529-2
Saint-Arroman,Nathalie | (v)
Stephane Grappelli With The Michel Legrand Orchestra
Grapelli Story | Verve | 515807-2
Saisse,Philippe | (keyboards,dr-programming,marimba)
Al Di Meola Group
Jazzrock-Anthology Vol.3:Fusion | Zounds | CD 27100555
Al Jarreau With Band
Tenderness | i.e. Music | 557853-2
Marcus Miller Group
The Sun Don't Lie | Dreyfus Jazz Line | FDM 36560-2
Saiz,Suso | (keyboards,hypnoticsti-bow)
Javier Paxarino Group With Glen Velez
Temurá | ACT | 9227-2
Sakai,Taizo | (el-gg)
Toshinori Kondo & Ima
Red City Smoke | JA & RO | JARO 4173-2
Toshinori Kondo & Ima plus Guests
Human Market | JA & RO | JARO 4146-2
Sakho,Mabinthy | (voc)
Pili-Pili
Nomans Land | JA & RO | JARO 4209-2
Ballads Of Timbuktu | JA & RO | JARO 4240-2
Sako,Fatoumata | (voc)
Pharoah Sanders Orchestra
Message From Home | Verve | 529578-2
Salaam,Abdul[William 'Chieftie' Scott] | (tp)
Louis Armstrong With Sy Oliver And His Orchestra
Louis Armstrong-My Greatest Songs | MCA | MCD 18347
Salad,Sonny | (as)
Charlie Parker With Strings
Charlie Parker With Strings:The Master Takes | Verve | 523984-2
Charlie Parker With The Neal Hefti Orchestra
Charlie Parker:The Best Of The Verve Years | Verve | 527815-2
Bird: The Complete Charlie Parker On Verve | Verve | 837141-2
Salamon,Udo | (bs)
Landes Jugend Jazz Orchester Hessen
Touch Of Lips | hr music.de | hrmj 004-01 CD
Salazar,Marcello | (perc,congastimbales)
Passport
Iguacu | Atlantic | 2292-46031-2
Salfellner,Christian | (dr)
Christian Wegscheider Trio
Live | Village | VILCD 1015-2
Heinrich Von Kalnein Group
New Directions | Nabel Records:Jazz Network | CD 4670
Johannes Enders Quartet
Kyoto | Organic Music | ORGM 9726
Salis,Antonello | (accordeon,el-p,fisarmonica,voc)
Jens Thomas
Jens Thomas Plays Ennio Morricone | ACT | 9273-2
Paolo Fresu Angel Quartet
Metamorfosi | RCA | 2165202-2
Paolo Fresu Quartet
Kind Of Porgy & Bess | RCA | 21951952
Paolo Fresu Quintet
Kind Of Porgy & Bess | RCA | 21951952
Paolo Fresu Sextet
Kind Of Porgy & Bess | RCA | 21951952
Paolo Fresu Trio
Kind Of Porgy & Bess | RCA | 21951952
Salisbury Festival Chorus |
John Surman-John Taylor With Chorus
Proverbs And Songs | ECM | 1639
Salko, |
Nat King Cole Quartet With The Stan Kenton Orchestra
Nat King Cole:For Sentimental Reasons | Dreyfus Jazz Line | FDM 36740-2
Salko,Jim | (tp)
Pete Rugolo And His Orchestra
Thriller/Richard Diamon(Original Jazz Scores From 2 Classics TV Series) | Fresh Sound Records | FSCD 2015
Salo,Per | (p)
Michael Mantler Orchestra
Hide And Seek | ECM | 1738(549612-2)
Saloum,Abdul | (tp)
Louis Armstrong And Omer Simeon With The Sy Oliver Orchestra
Ambassador Louis Armstrong Vol.17:Moments To Remember(1952-1956) | Ambassador | CLA 1917
Salter,Bill | (bel-b)
Les McCann Group
Atlantic Jazz: Fusion | Atlantic | 7567-81711-2
Oscar Brown Jr. And His Group
Movin' On | Rhino | 8122-73678-2
Rahsaan Roland Kirk And His Orchestra
Blacknuss | Rhino | 8122-71408-2
Yusef Lateef Orchestra
Rhino Presents The Atlantic Jazz Gallery | Atlantic | 8122-71257-2
Saltzman,Larry | (g)
The Brecker Brothers
Out Of The Loop | GRP | GRP 97842
Salut! |
Salut!
Green & Orange | Edition Collage | EC 488-2
Saluzzi,Celso | (perc,bandoneonvoice)
Dino Saluzzi Group
Mojotoro | ECM | 1447
Dino Saluzzi-Anthony Cox-David Friedman
Rios | VeraBra Records | CDVBR 2156-2
Saluzzi,Dino | (bandoneon,fl,percvoice)
Dino Saluzzi
Kultrum | ECM | 1251(821407-2)
Andina | ECM | 1375(837186-2)
Dino Saluzzi Group
Mojotoro | ECM | 1447
If | Enja | ENJ-9451 2
Dino Saluzzi Quartet
Once Upon A Time-Far Away In The South | ECM | 1309(827768-2)
Dino Saluzzi Trio
Cité De La Musique | ECM | 1616(533316-2)
Responsorium | ECM | 1816(017069-2)
Enrico Rava-Dino Saluzzi Quintet
Volver | ECM | 1343
Gato Barbieri Orchestra
Latino America | Impulse(MCA) | 952236-2
George Gruntz Concert Jazz Band '83
Theatre | ECM | 1265
Tomasz Stanko Sextet
From The Green Hill | ECM | 1680(547336-2)
Saluzzi,Felix 'Cuchara' | (cl,ssts)
Dino Saluzzi Group
Mojotoro | ECM | 1447
Saluzzi,José Maria | (dr,pec,voiceg)
Dino Saluzzi Trio
Cité De La Musique | ECM | 1616(533316-2)
Responsorium | ECM | 1816(017069-2)
Salvador,Inaki | (p)
Joaquin Chacón Group
San | Fresh Sound Records | FSNT 015 CD
Salvador,Sal | (g)
Sonny Stitt-Sal Salvador Quintet
Newport Jazz Festival 1958,July 3rd-6th Vol.2:Mulligan The Main Man | Phontastic | NCD 8814
Stan Kenton And His Orchestra
Stan Kenton Portraits On Standards | Capitol | 531571-2
Salvatorelli,Simone | (perc)
Banda Città Ruvo Di Puglia
La Banda/Banda And Jazz | Enja | ENJ-9326 2
Salvatori,Anthony | (b-tb)
Buddy Rich Big Band
Backwoods Siseman/Pieces Of Dream | Laserlight | 24655
Salvo,Christopher | (cl)
Yusef Lateef Ensemble
Nocturnes | Atlantic | 7567-81977-2
Salzwedel,Martin | (voc)
Jazzensemble Des Hessischen Rundfunks
Jazz Messe-Messe Für Unsere Zeit | hr music.de | hrmj 003-01 CD
Samaroff,Tosha | (stringsv)
Ben Webster With Orchestra And Strings
Music For Loving:Ben Webster With Strings | Verve | 527774-2
Ultimate Ben Webster selected by James Carter | Verve | 557537-2
Bill Evans Quartet With Orchestra
The Complete Bill Evans On Verve | Verve | 527953-2
From Left To Right | Verve | 557451-2
Bill Evans With Orchestra
The Complete Bill Evans On Verve | Verve | 527953-2
From Left To Right | Verve | 557451-2
Coleman Hawkins With Billy Byers And His Orchestra
The Hawk In Hi-Fi | RCA | 2663842-2
Freddie Hubbard With Orchestra
This Is Jazz:Freddie Hubbard | CBS | CK 65041
Phil Woods Quartet With Orchestra & Strings
Round Trip | Verve | 559804-2
Sarah Vaughan With Orchestra
!Viva! Vaughan | Mercury | 549374-2
Sarah Vaughan Sings The Mancini Songbook | Verve | 558401-2
Samba,Math | (african-percdancer)
Sun Ra And His Intergalactic Research Arkestra
Black Myth/Out In Space | MPS | 557656-2
Sambeat,Perico | (as,fl,keyboardsss)
Bob Sands Quintet
JumpSTART | Fresh Sound Records | FSNT 042 CD
Brad Mehldau With The Rossy Trio
New York-Barcelona Crossing Vol.1 | Fresh Sound Records | FSNT 031 CD
New York-Barcelona Crossing Vol.2 | Fresh Sound Records | FSNT 037 CD
George Colligan Quartet
Desire | Fresh Sound Records | FSNT 071 CD
José Luis Gámez Quartet
Dr.Jeckyl | Fresh Sound Records | FSNT 006 CD
Colores | Fresh Sound Records | FSNT 028 CD
José Luis Gámez Quintet
Dr.Jeckyl | Fresh Sound Records | FSNT 006 CD
Colores | Fresh Sound Records | FSNT 028 CD
Rumbo Dorte | Fresh Sound Records | FSNT 089 CD
Perico Sambeat Group
Ademuz | Fresh Sound Records | FSNT 041 CD
Perico Sambeat Quartet
Friendship | ACT | 9421-2
Perico Sambeat Quintet
Friendship | ACT | 9421-2
Ramon Valle Quintet
Ramon Valle Plays Ernesto Lecuona | ACT | 9404-2
Samborski,Bob | (tb)
Buddy Childers Big Band
Just Buddy's | Candid | CCD 79761
Samp,Harry | (tp)
Inge Brandenburg And Her All-Stars
Why Don't You Take All Of Me | Bear Family Records | BCD 15614 AH
Sample,Joe | (arr,clavinet,el-p,keyboards,org,p)
Al Jarreau With Band
Tenderness | i.e. Music | 557853-2
Bobby Bryant Orchestra
Deep Blue-The United States Of Mind | Blue Note | 521152-2
Bobby Hutcherson Quintet
Blue Breaks Beats Vol.2 | Blue Note | 789907-2
Buddy Rich Big Band
Keep The Customer Satisfied | EMI Records | 523999-2
Dee Dee Bridgewater With Band
Dee Dee Bridgewater | Atlantic | 7567-80760-2
Donald Byrd Orchestra
Black Byrd | Blue Note | 784466-2
Ethiopian Knights | Blue Note | 854328-2
Ella Fitzgerald With Orchestra
Ella/Things Ain't What They Used To Be | Warner | 9362-47875-2
Jazz Crusaders
Chile Con Soul | Pacific Jazz | 590957-2
Joe Sample Group
Ashes To Ashes | Warner | 7599-26318-2
Spellbound | Rhino | 81273726-2
Invitation | Warner | 9362-45209-2
Kenny Burrel Quartet
'Round Midnight | Original Jazz Classics | OJCCD 990-2(F 9417)
Marcus Miller Group
The Sun Don't Lie | Dreyfus Jazz Line | FDM 36560-2
Miles Davis Group
Amandla | Warner | 7599-25873-2
Quincy Jones And His Orchestra
Verve Jazz Masters Vol.59:Toots Thielemans | Verve | 535271-2
The Jazz Crusaders
Kind Of Blue:Blue Note Celebrate The Music Of Miles Davis | Blue Note | 534255-2
Sample,Joe | (rap)
Marcus Miller Group
Tales | Dreyfus Jazz Line | FDM 36571-2
Sampson,Armand | (g)
Oscar Peterson Quartet
Planet Music:Oscar Peterson | RCA | 2165365-2
This Is Oscar Peterson | RCA | 2663990-2
Sampson,Beate | (voc)
Joe Bawelino Quartet
Happy Birthday Stéphane | Edition Collage | EC 458-2
Joe Bawelino Quartet & Martin Stegner
Happy Birthday Stéphane | Edition Collage | EC 458-2
Straight Talk
Pure | Jazz 4 Ever Records:Jazz Network | J4E 4719
Sampson,Devey | (b)
Clark Terry Quartet
OW | Storyville | STCD 8378
Zoot Sims Quartet
Zoot Sims | Storyville | STCD 8367
Zoot Sims Quintet
Zoot Sims | Storyville | STCD 8367
Sampson,Edgar | (arr,as,v,bs,clreeds)
Benny Goodman And His Orchestra
Planet Jazz:Benny Goodman | Planet Jazz | 2152054-2
Planet Jazz Sampler | Planet Jazz | 2152326-2
Planet Jazz:Swing | Planet Jazz | 2169651-2
Louis Armstrong With Chick Webb's Orchestra
Best Of The Complete RCA Victor Recordings | RCA | 2663636-2
Louis Armstrong:A 100th Birthday Celebration | RCA | 2663694-2
Sampson,Michael | (v)
Albert Ayler Group
Albert Ayler Live In Greenwich Village:The Complete Impulse Recordings | Impulse(MCA) | IMP 22732
Albert Ayler Sextet
Albert Ayler Live In Greenwich Village:The Complete Impulse Recordings | Impulse(MCA) | IMP 22732
Samson | (percvoc)
Pili-Pili
Jakko | JA & RO | JARO 4131-2
Pili-Pili Live 88 | JA & RO | JARO 4139-2
Samuel,Morey | (tb)
Artie Shaw And His Orchestra
Planet JazzArtie Shaw | Planet Jazz | 2152057-2
Gene Gifford And His Orchestra
Planet Jazz:Bud Freeman | Planet Jazz | 2161240-2
Samuel,Tunde | (voc)
Craig Harris And Tailgater's Tales
Shelter | JMT Edition | 919008-2
Samuels,Dave | (cymbal-rolls,marimba,steel-dr,perc)
Art Lande Trio
Skylight | ECM | 1208
Chet Baker-Gerry Mulligan Group
Carnegie Hall Concert Vol. 1/2 | CTI | EPC 450554-2
Pat Metheny Group
Imaginary Day | Warner | 9362-46791-2
We Live Here | Geffen Records | GED 24729
Spyro Gyra & Guests
Love & Other Obsessions | GRP | GRP 98112
Samuels,Morey | (tb)
Artie Shaw And His Orchestra
Planet Jazz:Male Jazz Vocalists | Planet Jazz | 2169657-2
Samuels,Paul | (drperc)
Greg Osby Quartet
Mindgames | JMT Edition | 919021-2
Greg Osby Quintet
Mindgames | JMT Edition | 919021-2
SamulNori |
Red Sun/SamulNori
Then Comes The White Tiger | ECM | 1499
Sanabria,Bobby | (dr,cascara,timbales,perccongas)
Daniel Schnyder Group
Tanatula | Enja | ENJ-9302 2
Ray Barretto Orchestra
Portraits In Jazz And Clave | RCA | 2168452-2
Sanborn,David | (as,fl,ss,sopraninots)
Al Jarreau With Band
Tenderness | i.e. Music | 557853-2
Gil Evans Orchestra
There Comes A Time | RCA | 2131392-2
PLay The Music Of Jimi Hendrix | RCA | 2663872-2
Svengali | Rhino | 8122-73720-2
John McLaughlin Group
The Promise | Verve | 529828-2
Leni Stern Group
Closer To The Light | Enja | ENJ-6034 2
Marcus Miller Group
The Sun Don't Lie | Dreyfus Jazz Line | FDM 36560-2
Mike Stern Group
Give And Take | Atlantic | 7567-83036-2
Steve Khan Group
Jazzrock-Anthology Vol.3:Fusion | Zounds | CD 27100555
The Brecker Brothers
The Becker Bros | RCA | 2122103-2
Return Of The Brecker Brothers | GRP | GRP 96842
Sanborn,Jonathan | (b)
Karen Mantler Group
My Cat Arnold | Watt | XtraWatt/3
Karen Mantler And Her Cat Arnold Get The Flu | Watt | XtraWatt/5
Sanchez,Antonio | (drperc)
Michael Brecker Quindectet
Wide Angles | Verve | 076142-2
Sanchez,David | (fl,ss,ts,perc,tbchekere)
Arturo Sandoval Quintet
I Remember Clifford | GRP | GRP 96682
Barbara Dennerlein Group
Junkanoo | Verve | 537122-2
Don Ellis Orchestra
Electric Bath | CBS | CK 65522
Johnny King Septet
The Meltdown | Enja | ENJ-9329 2
Kenny Barron Group
Spirit Song | Verve | 543180-2
Roy Hargrove's Crisol
Habana | Verve | 537563-2
Sanchez,Poncho | (congas,bata,voc,bongos,campana)
Cal Tjader Sextet
Cuban Fantasy | Fantasy | FCD 24777-2
Sanchez-Gonzalez,Angel | (palmascajon,jaleopandeiro)
Renaud Garcia-Fons Group
Entremundo | Enja | ENJ-9464 2
Sandbakken,Are | (viola)
Terje Rypdal With The Borealis Ensemble
Q.E.D. | ECM | 1474
Sandell,Bruce | (cl,voc,flts)
Vince Jones Group
It All Ends Up In Tears | Intuition Records | INT 3069-2
Tell Me A Secret | Intuition Records | INT 3072-2
Sander-Laun,Ira | (voc)
Jazzensemble Des Hessischen Rundfunks
Jazz Messe-Messe Für Unsere Zeit | hr music.de | hrmj 003-01 CD
Sanders,H. | (v)
Toots Thielemans And His Orchestra
Verve Jazz Masters Vol.59:Toots Thielemans | Verve | 535271-2
Sanders,John | (tbv-tb)
Duke Ellington And His Orchestra
Jazz Collection:Duke Ellington | Laserlight | 24369
The Legends Of Swing | Laserlight | 24659
100 Years Duke | Laserlight | 24906
Greatest Hits | CBS | 462959-2
Verve Jazz Masters 4:Duke Ellington | Verve | 516338-2
Ellington '55 | Capitol | 520135-2
Great Swing Classics In Hi-Fi | Capitol | 521223-2
Ellington At Newport 1956(Complete) | CBS | CK 64932
Black Brown And Beige | CBS | CK 65566
Such Sweet Thunder | CBS | CK 65568
Anatomy Of A Murder | CBS | CK 65569
The Ellington Suites | Original Jazz Classics | OJC20 446-2(2310762)
Duke Ellington At The Alhambra | Pablo | PACD 5313-2
Ella Fitzgerald With The Duke Ellington Orchestra
Ella Fitzgerald-First Lady Of Song | Verve | 517898-2
The Best Of The Song Books | Verve | 519804-2
Verve Jazz Masters 6:Ella Fitzgerald | Verve | 519822-2
The Best Of The Song Books:The Ballads | Verve | 521867-2
Verve Jazz Masters 46:Ella Fitzgerald-The Jazz Sides | Verve | 527655-2
Love Songs:The Best Of The Song Books | Verve | 531762-2
Ella Fitzgerald Sings The Duke Ellington Songbook | Verve | 559248-2
For The Love Of Ella Fitzgerald | Verve | 841765-2
Johnny Hodges And The Ellington Men
Verve Jazz Masters 35:Johnny Hodges | Verve | 521857-2
Rosemary Clooney With The Duke Ellington Orchestra
Blue Rose | CBS | CK 65506
Sanders,Peter | (cello)
Andy Bey Group
Tuesdays In Chinatown | Minor Music | 801099
Sanders,Pharoah | (alto-fl,ts,bailophone,brass-bell)
Alice Coltrane Quartet
A Monastic Trio | Impulse(MCA) | 951267-2
Alice Coltrane Quintet
Ptah The El Daoud | Impulse(MCA) | 951201-2
Journey In Satchidananda | Impulse(MCA) | 951228-2
Alice Coltrane Sextet
Journey In Satchidananda | Impulse(MCA) | 951228-2
Gary Bartz Sextet
Libra/Another Earth | Milestone | MCD 47077-2
John Coltrane And His Orchestra
Kulu Se Mama | Impulse(MCA) | 543412-2
Ascension | Impulse(MCA) | 543413-2

INTERPRETENVERZEICHNIS

Meditations | Impulse(MCA) | 951199-2
John Coltrane Group
The Olatunji Concert:The Last Live Recording | Impulse(MCA) | 589120-2
John Coltrane Quintet
Live At The Village Vanguard Again | Impulse(MCA) | 951213-2
Leon Thomas With Band
Spirits Known And Unknown | RCA | 2663876-2
Pharoah Sanders Group
Save Our Children | Verve | 557297-2
Black Unity | Impulse(MCA) | 951219-2
Pharoah Sanders Orchestra
Message From Home | Verve | 529578-2
Karma | Impulse(MCA) | 951153-2
Jewels Of Thought | Impulse(MCA) | 951247-2
Thembi | Impulse(MCA) | 951253-2
Deaf Dumb Blind | Impulse(MCA) | 951265-2
The Roots Of Acid Jazz | Impulse(MCA) | IMP 12042
Randy Weston African Rhythm
Khepera | Verve | 557821-2
The Jazz Composer's Orchestra
Comminications | JCOA | 1001/2

Sanders,Roger | (congasperc)
Abbey Lincoln And Her Orchestra
Straight Ahead | Candid | CCD 79015
Max Roach All Stars
Candid Dolphy | Candid | CCD 79033
Yusef Lateef Orchestra
The Centaur And The Phoenix | Original Jazz Classics | OJCCD 721-2(RLP 9337)

Sandke,Jordan | (tpco)
Buck Clayton Swing Band
Swing's The Village | Nagel-Heyer | CD 5004
Blues Of Summer | Nagel-Heyer | NH 1011
Howlin' Wolf London Session
Howlin' Wolf:The London Sessions | Chess | MCD 09297

Sandke,Randy | (co,tp,fl-h,gld)
Allan Vaché Swingtet
Ellington For Lovers | Nagel-Heyer | NH 1009
Bob Wilber's Bechet Legacy
The Hamburg Concert-Tribute To A Legend | Nagel-Heyer | CD 028
The Second Sampler | Nagel-Heyer | NHR SP 6
Butch Miles And Friends
The Second Sampler | Nagel-Heyer | NHR SP 6
Butch Miles-Howard Alden Sextet
Cookin' | Nagel-Heyer | CD 5003
Byron Stripling And Friends
If I Could Be With You | Nagel-Heyer | NH 1010
David Ostwald's Gully Low Jazz Band
Blues In Your Heart | Nagel-Heyer | CD 051
Eddie Metz And His Gang
Tough Assignment:A Tribute To Dave Tough | Nagel-Heyer | CD 053
Frank Vignola Sextet
Off Broadway | Nagel-Heyer | CD 2006
George Masso Allstars
The Wonderful World Of George Gershwin | Nagel-Heyer | CD 001
One Two Three | Nagel-Heyer | CD 008
The First Sampler | Nagel-Heyer | NHR SP 5
Harry Allen And Randy Sandke Meets The RIAS Big Band Berlin
The Music Of The Trumpet Kings | Nagel-Heyer | CD 037
Harry Allen Quintet
A Night At Birdland | Nagel-Heyer | CD 010
A Night At Birdland Vol. 1 | Nagel-Heyer | CD 5002
Ellington For Lovers | Nagel-Heyer | NH 1009
Love Songs Live! | Nagel-Heyer | NH 1014
The First Sampler | Nagel-Heyer | NHR SP 5
James Chirillo Sextet
Sultry Serenade | Nagel-Heyer | CD 061
Joe Ascione Octet
My Buddy:A Tribute To Buddy Rich | Nagel-Heyer | CD 036
Oliver Jackson Orchestra
The Last Great Concert | Nagel-Heyer | CD 063
Randy Sandke And The New York Allstars
The Re-Discovered Louis And Bix | Nagel-Heyer | CD 058
Randy Sandke Quintet
Cliffhanger | Nagel-Heyer | CD 2037
Randy Sandke Sextet
Cliffhanger | Nagel-Heyer | CD 2037
Randy Sandke-Dick Hyman
The Re-Discovered Louis And Bix | Nagel-Heyer | CD 058
Randy Sandke-Howard Alden
Ellington For Lovers | Nagel-Heyer | NH 1009
The Buck Clayton Legacy
All The Cats Join In(Buck Clayton Remembered) | Nagel-Heyer | CD 006
Encore Live | Nagel-Heyer | CD 018
The First Sampler | Nagel-Heyer | NHR SP 5
The Second Sampler | Nagel-Heyer | NHR SP 6
The Nagel-Heyer Allstars
Uptown Lowdown:A Jazz Salute To The Big Apple | Nagel-Heyer | CD 2004
The New York Allstars
Broadway | Nagel-Heyer | CD 003
One Two Three | Nagel-Heyer | CD 008
We Love You,Louis! | Nagel-Heyer | CD 029
Count Basie Remembered | Nagel-Heyer | CD 031
Count Basie Remembered Vol.2 | Nagel-Heyer | CD 041
Oh,Yeah! The New York Allstars Play More Music Of Louis Armstrong | Nagel-Heyer | CD 046
Hey Ba-Ba-Re-Bop!! The New York Allstars Play Lionel Hampton Vol.1 | Nagel-Heyer | CD 047
The New York Allstars Play Lionel Hampton,Vol.2: Stompin' At The Savoy | Nagel-Heyer | CD 077
Randy Sandke Meets Bix Beiderbecke | Nagel-Heyer | CD 3002
The First Sampler | Nagel-Heyer | NHR SP 5
The Second Sampler | Nagel-Heyer | NHR SP 6
The Yamaha International Allstar Band
Hapy Birthday Jazzwelle Plus | Nagel-Heyer | CD 005
The First Sampler | Nagel-Heyer | NHR SP 5
Warren Vaché Quintet
Warren Plays Warrey | Nagel-Heyer | CD 033
Blues Of Summer | Nagel-Heyer | NH 1011
Wycliffe Gordon Group
Slidin' Home | Nagel-Heyer | CD 2001
Blues Of Summer | Nagel-Heyer | NH 1011

Sandler,Myron | (viola)
Mel Tormé With The Russell Garcia Orchestra
Swingin' On The Moon | Verve | 511385-2

Sandole,Adolphe | (arr)
Sandole Brothers
The Sandole Brothers | Fantasy | FCD 24763-2

Sandole,Dennis | (garr)

Sandoval,Arturo | (fl-h,tp,cowbell,timbales,voc,p,perc)
Arturo Sandoval And The Latin Train Band
Arturo Sandoval & The Latin Train | GRP | GRP 98202
Arturo Sandoval Quartet
I Remember Clifford | GRP | GRP 96682
Arturo Sandoval Quintet
I Remember Clifford | GRP | GRP 96682
Dizzy Gillespie And The United Nation Orchestra
7.Zelt-Musik-Festival:Jazz Events | Zounds | CD 2730001
GRP All-Star Big Band
GRP All-Star Big Band:Live! | GRP | GRP 97402
All Blues | GRP | GRP 98002

Sands,Bobby | (ts)
Bob Sands Quartet
JumpSTART | Fresh Sound Records | FSNT 042 CD
Bob Sands Quintet
JumpSTART | Fresh Sound Records | FSNT 042 CD

Sandstrom,Brian | (b,tp,el-g,perc,toy-hornsg)
Hal Russell NRG Ensemble
The Finnish/Swiss Tour | ECM | 1455
The Hal Russell Story | ECM | 1498

Sandström,Yngve | (fl,alto-flpiccolo)
Bengt-Arne Wallin Orchestra
The Birth+Rebirth Of Swedish Folk Jazz | ACT | 9254-2

Sane,Ismaila | (percvoc)
Piirpauke
Tuku Tuku | JA & RO | JARO 4158-2

Sanfino,Gerald | (b,flts)
Sarah Vaughan With The Jimmy Jones Orchestra
Ballads | Roulette | 537561-2
Tito Puente Orchestra
Planet Jazz:Tito Puente | Planet Jazz | 2165369-2

Sanfino,Jerry | (as,ts,cl,flreeds)
(Little)Jimmy Scott With The Billy Taylor Orchestra
Everybody's Somebody's Fool | Decca | 050669-2
Sarah Vaughan With The Jimmy Jones Orchestra
Jazz Profile | Blue Note | 823517-2
Stan Getz With The Gary McFarland Orchestra
Stan Getz Highlights:The Best Of The Verve Years Vol.2 | Verve | 517330-2
Verve Jazz Masters 53:Stan Getz-Bossa Nova | Verve | 529904-2
Big Band Bossa Nova | Verve | 825771-2 PMS

Sanford,Bill | (p)
The Ravens
Ultimate Ben Webster selected by James Carter | Verve | 557537-2

Sänger,Christof | (pp-solo)
Christof Sänger Trio
Chorinho | Laika Records | LK 93-033
Christoph Sänger
Live At The Montreal Jazz Festival | Laika Records | 35100822
Christoph Sänger Trio
Imagination | Laika Records | 35100752
Caprice | Laika Records | LK 94-057
Ernie Watts-Christof Sänger
Blue Topaz | Laika Records | 35101352

Sänger,Stephan | (v)
Uri Caine With The Concerto Köln
Concerto Köln | Winter&Winter | 910086-2

Sanguinetti,Alex | (dr)
Christian Elsässer Trio
Future Days | Organic Music | ORGM 9721

Sanner,Karl | (dr)
Delle Haensch Jump Combo
Deutsches Jazz Fesival 1954/1955 | Bear Family Records | BCD 15430
Erhard Wenig Quartet
Deutsches Jazz Fesival 1954/1955 | Bear Family Records | BCD 15430
Hugo Strasser Combo
Deutsches Jazz Fesival 1954/1955 | Bear Family Records | BCD 15430
Jutta Hipp Quintet
Deutsches Jazz Fesival 1954/1955 | Bear Family Records | BCD 15430
Rolf Kühn And His Quintet
Deutsches Jazz Fesival 1954/1955 | Bear Family Records | BCD 15430

Sanner,Willie | (bs)
Hans Koller New Jazz Stars
Deutsches Jazz Fesival 1954/1955 | Bear Family Records | BCD 15430

Sanogo,Maré | (djembedoum-doum)
Hank Jones Meets Cheik-Tidiana Seck
Sarala | Verve | 528783-2

Sanou,Souleyname | (dancer,maracasdoudoum'ni)
Jon Hassell & Farafina
Flash Of The Spirit | Intuition Records | INT 3009-2

Sanow,Robert | (v)
Charlie Haden Quartet West With Strings
The Art Of The Song | Verve | 547403-2

Sansalone,Bruno | (clb-cl)
Renaud Garcia-Fons
Navigatore | Enja | ENJ-9418 2
Renaud Garcia-Fons Group
Oriental Bass | Enja | ENJ-9334 2
Navigatore | Enja | ENJ-9418 2

Sanshiro | (as,fasfl)
United Future Organizatio
United Future Organization | Talkin' Loud | 518166-2

Santamaria,Mongo | (congas,bongos,congas-soloperc)
Cal Tjader Quintet
Our Blues | Fantasy | FCD 24771-2
Concerts In The Sun | Fantasy | FCD 9688-2
Cal Tjader's Latin Concert | Original Jazz Classics | OJCCD 643-2(F 8014)
Cal Tjader Sextet
Black Hawk Nights | Fantasy | FCD 24755-2
The Jazz Giants Play Cole Porter:Night And Day | Prestige | PCD 24203-2
Mongo Santamaria And His Band
Brazilian Sunset | Candid | CCD 79703
Sabroso | Original Jazz Classics | OJCCD 281-2
Mongo At The Village Gate | Original Jazz Classics | OJCCD 490-2(RLP 9529)
Montreux Heat! | Pablo | PACD 5317-2
Mongo Santamaria And His Orchestra
Jazzin' Vol.2: The Music Of Stevie Wonder | Fantasy | FANCD 6088-2
Mongo Santamaria Group With Dizzy Gillespie And Toots Thielemans
Summertime-Digital At Montreux 1980 | Original Jazz Classics | OJCCD 626-2(2308229)
Montreux Heat! | Pablo | PACD 5317-2
Victor Feldman Orchestra
Latinsville | Contemporary | CCD 9005-2

Santamaria,Ramon | (congas)
Dizzy Gillespie And His Orchestra
Afro | Verve | 517052-2
Tito Puente Orchestra
Planet Jazz:Tito Puente | Planet Jazz | 2165369-2

Santana,Carlos | (el-gg)
Herbie Hancock Group
Monster | CBS | 486571-2

Santandreu,Jesus | (ts)
Daniel Flors Group
When Least Expected | Fresh Sound Records | FSNT 080 CD

Santiago,Freddie | (marimba,perc,bongos,conga,timbales)
Bernd Konrad With Erwin Lehn und sein Südfunk Orchester Stuttgart
Wen Die Götter Lieben | Creative Works Records | CW CD 1010-1
Los Jovenes Flamencos With The WDR Big Band And Guests
Jazzpana | ACT | 9212-2

Santiago,Lester | (p)
Paul Barbarin And His Band
Atlantic Jazz: New Orleans | Atlantic | 7567-81700-2

Santini,Simone | (sopraninoas)
Scenario
Jazz The Beatles | Organic Music | ORGM 9729

Santisi,Ray | (p)
Donald Byrd Quartet
Donald Byrd & Doug Watkins:The Tradition Sessions | Blue Note | 540528-2
Doug Watkins Trio
Donald Byrd & Doug Watkins:The Tradition Sessions | Blue Note | 540528-2

Santos,Jumma prob. | (perc)
John Coltrane Group
The Olatunji Concert:The Last Live Recording | Impulse(MCA) | 589120-2

Santos,Pedro 'Sosongo' | (percwhistles)
Passport
Iguacu | Atlantic | 2292-46031-2

Santos,Turk | (cog)
Marty Grosz And His Honoris Causa Jazz Band
Hooray For Bix! | Good Time Jazz | GTCD 10065-2

Sanz,Albert | (p)
Cesc Miralta Quartet
Sol De Nit | Fresh Sound Records | FSNT 098 CD
Carretera Austal | Fresh Sound Records | FSNT 149 CD
José Luis Gámez Quartet
José Luis Gámez Quattro | Fresh Sound Records | FSNT 094 CD
Kalifactors
An Introduction To Kalifactors | Fresh Sound Records | FSNT 143 CD

Saparoff,Albert | (v)
Ella Fitzgerald With The Frank DeVol Orchestra
Get Happy! | Verve | 523321-2

Saracco,Frank | (tb)
Della Reese With The Sy Oliver Orchestra
Misty Blue:Sweet Sisters Swing Songs Of Sorrow And Sadness | Blue Note | 521151-2
Ella Fitzgerald With Sy Oliver And His Orchestra
Ella Fitzgerald:The Decca Years 1949-1954 | Decca | 050668-2

Sarath,Ed | (fl-h)
Ed Sarath Quintet
Last Day In May | Konnex Records | KCD 5042

Sarcer,David | (v)
Billie Holiday With The Ray Ellis Orchestra
Lady In Satin | CBS | CK 65144

Sardjoi,Chander | (dr)
Mark Zubeck Quartet
Horse With A Broken Leg | Fresh Sound Records | FSNT 078 CD
Mark Zubeck Quintet
Horse With A Broken Leg | Fresh Sound Records | FSNT 078 CD

Sargeant,Emmet | (cello)
Johnny Hartman And His Orchestra
Unforgettable | Impulse(MCA) | IMP 11522

Sargent,Gene | (g)
Woody Herman And His Orchestra
The Legends Of Swing | Laserlight | 24659
Woody Herman:Four Brother | Dreyfus Jazz Line | FDM 36722-2

Sargent,Kenny | (as,bs,cl,vocsax)
Louis Armstrong With The Casa Loma Orchestra
Louis Armstrong:Swing That Music | Laserlight | 36056

Saridakis,Emmanuel | (porg)
Dimitrios Vassilakis Daedalus Project
Labyrinth | Candid | CCD 79776

Sarin,Michael | (dr,perc,cowbellswhistles)
Dave Ballou Quartet
Rothko | Steeplechase | SCCD 31525
Dave Douglas Group
Witness | RCA | 2663763-2
Dave Douglas Freak In | Bluebird | 2664008-2
Marty Ehrlich Group
The Long View | Enja | ENJ-9452 2

Sarkissian,Setrak | (daraboukka)
Rabih Abou-Khalil Group
Nafas | ECM | 1359(835781-2)

Sarmanto,Pekka | (b)
Edward Vesala Nordic Gallery
Sound & Fury | ECM | 1541

Sarmato,Pekka | (b)
Edward Vesala Sound And Fury
Invisible Strom | ECM | 1461

Sarpila,Antti | (cl,sax,ssts)
Allan Vaché-Antti Sarpila & 1 Sextet
Summit Meeting | Nagel-Heyer | CD 027
Allan Vaché-Antti Sarpila Quintet
Swing Is Here | Nagel-Heyer | CD 026
Blues Of Summer | Nagel-Heyer | NH 1011
The Second Sampler | Nagel-Heyer | NHR SP 6
Bob Wilber And Friends
What Swing Is All About | Nagel-Heyer | CD 035
Blues Of Summer | Nagel-Heyer | NH 1011
International Allstars
The International Allstars Play Benny Goodman:Vol.1 | Nagel-Heyer | CD 025
Oliver Jackson Orchestra
The Last Great Concert | Nagel-Heyer | CD 063
Ralph Sutton And His Allstars
Echoes Of Spring:The Complete Hamburg Concert | Nagel-Heyer | CD 038
The Buck Clayton Legacy
All The Cats Join In(Buck Clayton Remembered) | Nagel-Heyer | CD 006
Encore Live | Nagel-Heyer | CD 018
The First Sampler | Nagel-Heyer | NHR SP 5
The Second Sampler | Nagel-Heyer | NHR SP 6
The European Jazz Ginats
Jazz Party | Nagel-Heyer | CD 009
The First Sampler | Nagel-Heyer | NHR SP 5
The International Allstars
The International Allstars Play Benny Goodman Vol.1 | Nagel-Heyer | CD 045
The New York Allstars
Hey Ba-Ba-Re-Bop!! The New York Allstars Play Lionel Hampton Vol.1 | Nagel-Heyer | CD 047
The New York Allstars Play Lionel Hampton,Vol.2: Stompin' At The Savoy | Nagel-Heyer | CD 077
The Yamaha International Allstar Band
Hapy Birthday Jazzwelle Plus | Nagel-Heyer | CD 005
The First Sampler | Nagel-Heyer | NHR SP 5

Sarser,Dave | (vviola)
Coleman Hawkins With Billy Byers And His Orchestra
The Hawk In Hi-Fi | RCA | 2663842-2

Sass,Jon | (tuba)
Hans Theessink Group
Call Me | Minor Music | 801022
Crazy Moon | Minor Music | 801052
Journey On | Minor Music | 801062

Sasse,Martin | (p)
Martin Sasse Trio
Here We Come | Nagel-Heyer | CD 2008
Tony Lakatos With The Martin Sasse Trio
Feel Alright | Edition Collage | EC 494-2

Sasse,Philippe | (keyboards)
Al Jarreau With Band
L Is For Lover | i.e. Music | 557850-2

Sassenroth,Thomas | (tb)
Jazz Orchester Rheinland-Pfalz
Kazzou | Jazz Haus Musik | LJBB 9104
Like Life | Jazz Haus Musik | LJBB 9405
Last Season | Jazz Haus Musik | LJBB 9706

Sassetti,Bernardo | (p)
José Luis Gámez Quintet
Rumbo Dorte | Fresh Sound Records | FSNT 089 CD

Sasson,Jean-Pierre | (g)
Don Byas Quintet
Jazz In Paris:Don Byas-Laura | EmArCy | 013027-2
Jean Pierre Sasson Quartet
Americans Swinging In Paris:Lucky Thompson | EMI Records | 539651-2
Sidney Bechet And His Orchestra
Jazz In Paris:Sidney Bechet Et Claude Luther | EmArCy | 159821-2 PMS

Sasson,Marshall | (v)
Ella Fitzgerald With The Billy May Orchestra
Ella Fitzgerald Sings The Harold Arlen Song Book | Verve | 589108-2
Harry James And His Orchestra
Trumpet Blues:The Best Of Harry James | Capitol | 521224-2

Sato,Masahiko | (cond,arr,el-p,p,modulatorsynth)
Shinichi Kato-Masahiko Sato
Duet | Nagel-Heyer | CD 2017

Sattar,Saber Ardel | (qanoun)

Mahmoud Turkmani Group
Zakira | Enja | ENJ-9475 2
Satterfield,Jack | (tb)
Coleman Hawkins With Billy Byers And His Orchestra
Planet Jazz:Coleman Hawkins | Planet Jazz | 2152055-2
The Hawk In Hi-Fi | RCA | 2663842-2
Ella Fitzgerald With Sy Oliver And His Orchestra
Ella Fitzgerald:The Decca Years 1949-1954 | Decca | 050668-2
Jess Stacy And His Orchestra
Planet Jazz:Jazz Piano | RCA | 2169655-2
Louis Armstrong With The Commanders
Ambassador Louis Armstrong Vol.17:Moments To Remember(1952-1956) | Ambassador | CLA 1917
Sarah Vaughan With The Norman Leyden Orchestra
Sarah Vaughan:Lover Man | Dreyfus Jazz Line | FDM 36739-2
Satterfield,Tommy | (arr,pceleste)
Bix Beiderbecke And His Gang
Jazz:The Essential Collection Vol.2 | IN+OUT Records | 78012-2
Satterwhite,Tex | (tb)
Duke Ellington With Tommy Dorsey And His Orchestra
Highlights From The Duke Ellington Centennial Edition | RCA | 2663672-2
Tommy Dorsey And His Orchestra
Planet Jazz:Tommy Dorsey | Planet Jazz | 2159972-2
Planet Jazz:Jazz Greatest Hits | Planet Jazz | 2169648-2
Saturino,Pernell | (perccongas)
Antonio Hart Group
Here I Stand | Impulse(MCA) | 951208-2
Saturnino | (b)
Michael 'Patches' Stewart Group
Penetration | Hip Bop | HIBD 8018
Saturnino,Pernell | (congas,clave,okonkolo,shekereguiro)
Danilo Perez Group
Central Avenue | Impulse(MCA) | 951281-2
Saudan,Nathalie | (v)
Michel Wintsch & Road Movie
Michel Wintsch & Road Movie featuring Gerry Hemingway | Between The Lines | btl 002(Efa 10172-2)
Saudrais,Charles | (dr)
Zoot Sims Quintet
Americans Swinging In Paris:Zoot Sims | EMI Records | 539646-2
Sauer,Heinz | (as,sequencer,synth,dr-computer,ts)
George Adams Sextet
Soung Suggestions | ECM | 1141
Heinz Sauer 4tet
Exchange 2 | free flow music | ffm 0998
Heinz Sauer Quartet With The NDR Big Band
NDR Big Band-Bravissimo | ACT | 9232-2
Heinz Sauer Quintet
Lost Ends:Live at Alte Oper Frankfurt | free flow music | ffm 0594
Heinz Sauer Trio
Exchange | free flow music | ffm 0695
Jazzensemble Des Hessischen Rundfunks
Atmosphering Conditions Permitting | ECM | 1549/50
NDR Big Band With Guests
50 Years Of NDR Big Band:Bravissimo II | ACT | 9259-2
Radio Jazzgroup Frankfurt
Jubilee Edition | double moon | CHRDM 71020
Sauer,Wolfgang | (voc)
Wolfgang Sauer With The Glen Buschmann Quintet
Deutsches Jazz Fesival 1954/1955 | Bear Family Records | BCD 15430
Sauerborn,Hans Dieter | (as,fl,alto-fl,cl,ssts)
HR Big Band
The American Songs Of Kurt Weill | hr music.de | hrmj 006-01 CD
Libertango:Homage An Astor Piazolla | hr music.de | hrmj 014-02 CD
HR Big Band With Marjorie Barnes And Frits Landesbergen
Swinging Christmas | hr music.de | hrmj 012-02 CD
HR Big Band With Marjorie Barnes And Frits Landesbergen And Strings
Swinging Christmas | hr music.de | hrmj 012-02 CD
The Three Sopranos With The HR Big Band
The Three Sopranos | hr music.de | hrmj 001-01 CD
Saulesco,Mirecea | (v)
Bengt-Arne Wallin Orchestra
The Birth+Rebirth Of Swedish Folk Jazz | ACT | 9254-2
Saunders,Carl | (mellophone,tpfl-h)
Carl Saunders-Lanny Morgan Quintet
Las Vegar Late Night Sessions:Live At Capozzoli's | Woofy Productions | WPCD 109
Stan Kenton And His Orchestra
Adventures In Blues | Capitol | 520089-2
Adventures In Jazz | Capitol | 521222-2
Vic Lewis West Coast All Stars
Me And You! | Candid | CCD 79739
Saunders,Fernando | (b,el-b,vocg)
Jacky Terrasson Group
What It Is | Blue Note | 498756-2
Saunders,Harry | (dr)
Sonny Rollins Quartet
Planet Jazz:Jazz Greatest Hits | Planet Jazz | 2169648-2
The Bridge | RCA | 2179625-2
Stuff Smith Quartet
Cat On A Hot Fiddle | Verve | 9861487
Saunders,John | (tb)
(Little)Jimmy Scott With The Lucky Thompson Orchestra
Everybody's Somebody's Fool | Decca | 050669-2
Saunders,Russ | (b)
Elliot Lawrence And His Orchestra
The Elliot Lawrence Big Band Swings Cohn & Kahn | Fantasy | FCD 24761-2
Saunders,Tom | (b,voice,co,voctuba)
International Chicago-Jazz Orchestra
That's A Plenty | JHM Records | JHM 3621
Jeanie Lambe And The Danny Moss Septet
Three Great Concerts:Live In Hamburg 1993-1995 | Nagel-Heyer | CD 019
The Alex Welsh Legacy Band
The Sound Of Alex Vol.1 | Nagel-Heyer | CD 070
Tom Saunders' 'Wild Bill Davison Band' & Guests
Exactly Like You | Nagel-Heyer | CD 023
The Second Sampler | Nagel-Heyer | NHR SP 6
Saunders,Zack | (voc)
Grover Washington Jr. Orchestra
Inside Moves | Elektra | 7559-60318-2
Saury,Maxim | (cl)
Milton Mezz Mezzrow-Maxim Saury Quintet
Americans Swinging In Paris:Mezz Mezzrow | EMI Records | 539660-2
Sammy Price Quintet
Americans Swinging In Paris:Sammy Price | EMI Records | 539650-2
Sauter,Eddie | (arr,ldtp)
Stan Getz With The Eddie Sauter Orchestra
Verve Jazz Masters 8:Stan Getz | Verve | 519823-2
Stan Getz Plays The Music Of Mickey One | Verve | 531232-2
A Life In Jazz:A Musical Biography | Verve | 535119-2
Ultimate Stan Getz selected by Joe Henderson | Verve | 557532-2
Stan Getz Highlights | Verve | 847430-2
Sauter,Thomas | (tb)
Fritz Münzer Tentet
Blue Ideas | Jazz 'n' Arts Records | 0200
Sauvaire,Alexandre | (v)
Abdullah Ibrahim Trio And A String Orchestra
African Suite | TipToe | TIP-888832 2
String Orchestra
African Suite | TipToe | TIP-888832 2
Sauzay,David | (ts)
Gäel Horellou-David Sauzay Quintet
Gäel Horellou Versus David Sauzay | Fresh Sound Records | FSNT 068 CD
Savakus,Russell | (b)
Chet Baker Trio
Embraceable You | Pacific Jazz | 831676-2
Louis Armstrong And His Orchestra
What A Wonderful World | MCA | MCD 01876
Savery,Uffe | (marimba)
The Danish Radio Concert Orchestra
Symphonies Vol.2 | dacapo | DCCD 9441
Savino,Santo | (dr)
Carl Saunders-Lanny Morgan Quintet
Las Vegar Late Night Sessions:Live At Capozzoli's | Woofy Productions | WPCD 109
Savinova,Natalia | (cello)
Moscow Rachmaninov Trio
Groupe Lacroix:The Composer Group | Creative Works Records | CW CD 1030-2
Savitt,Buddy | (ts)
Woody Herman And His Orchestra
Woody Herman:Four Brother | Dreyfus Jazz Line | FDM 36722-2
Sawkins,Jeremy | (gel-g)
Wanderlust + Guests
Full Bronte | Laika Records | 35101412
Sawyer,Dan | (el-gg)
Jean-Luc Ponty Quintet
The Very Best Of Jean-Luc Ponty | Rhino | 8122-79862-2
Sawyer,Jaz | (dr)
Abbey Lincoln And Her Trio
Over The Years | Verve | 549101-2
Abbey Lincoln And Her Trio With Guests
Over The Years | Verve | 549101-2
Jacky Terrasson Group
What It Is | Blue Note | 498756-2
Sax Mal Anders |
Sax Mal Anders
Kontraste | Chaos | CACD 8185
Saxon,Joseph | (cello)
Pete Rugolo And His Orchestra
Thriller/Richard Diamon(Original Jazz Scores From 2 Classics TV Series) | Fresh Sound Records | FSCD 2015
Saxton,Bill | (bs,fl,ts,sax,ssvoc)
Dick Griffin Septet
The Eighth Wonder & More | Konnex Records | KCD 5059
Sayer,Cynthia | (p)
Woody Allen And His New Orleans Jazz Band
Wild Man Blues | RCA | 2663353-2
Sayles,Emanuel | (bj,vocg)
George Lewis And His Band
Atlantic Jazz: New Orleans | Atlantic | 7567-81700-2
Jim Robinson's New Orleans Band
Atlantic Jazz: New Orleans | Atlantic | 7567-81700-2
Joseph 'Dee Dee' Pierce And His Band
Atlantic Jazz: New Orleans | Atlantic | 7567-81700-2
Punch Miller's Bunch & George Lewis
Atlantic Jazz: New Orleans | Atlantic | 7567-81700-2
Sbarbaro,Tony | (dr,kazoovoc)
Original Dixieland 'Jass' Band
Planet Jazz | Planet Jazz | 2169652-2
Scafe,Bruce | (tp)
Eric Dolphy Quartet With The University Of Illinois Big Band
The Illinois Concert | Blue Note | 499826-2
Scaglione,Nunzio | (ascl)
Maynard Ferguson And His Big Bop Nouveau Band
Maynard Ferguson '93-Footpath Café | Hot Shot Records | HSR 8312-2
Scales,Martin | (el-g,el-gg,gg-synth)
Joseph Warner Quartet
Mood Pieces | Jardis Records | JRCD 9921
Pee Wee Ellis Quintet With Guests
A New Shift | Minor Music | 801060
Scales,Patrick | (bel-b)
Klaus Doldinger's Passport
Klaus Doldinger Passport Live | Warner | 8573-84132-2
Pee Wee Ellis Quintet With Guests
A New Shift | Minor Music | 801060
Scalise,Ron | (reeds)
Eric Dolphy Quartet With The University Of Illinois Big Band
The Illinois Concert | Blue Note | 499826-2
Scannapieco,Daniele | (flas)
Dee Dee Bridgewater With Band
This Is New | Verve | 016884-2
Dee Dee Bridgewater Sings Kurt Weil | EmArCy | 9809601
Scarborough,Skip | (el-p,synth,pclavinet)
Donald Byrd Orchestra
Places And Spaces | Blue Note | 854326-2
Scarpantoni,Jane | (cello)
Lounge Lizards
Berlin 1991 Part 1 | Intuition Records | INT 2044-2
Live In Berlin 1991-Vol.2 | Intuition Records | INT 2055-2
Scenario |
Scenario
Jazz The Beatles | Organic Music | ORGM 9729
Scetches |
Scetches
Different Places | VeraBra Records | CDVBR 2102-2
Schaab,Bruno | (voice)
Ax Genrich Group
Psychedelic Guitar | ATM Records | ATM 3809-AH
Schachter,Julius | (v)
Ben Webster With Orchestra And Strings
Verve Jazz Masters 43:Ben Webster | Verve | 525431-2
Music For Loving:Ben Webster With Strings | Verve | 527774-2
Phil Woods Quartet With Orchestra & Strings
Round Trip | Verve | 559804-2
Schackman,Al | (g,ptambourine)
Nina Simone And Orchestra
Baltimore | Epic | 476906-2
Schädlich,Johannes | (b)
Jazzensemble Des Hessischen Rundfunks
Jazz Messe-Messe Für Unsere Zeit | hr music.de | hrmj 003-01 CD
Lee Konitz With The Oliver Strauch Group & Peter Decker
Lee Konitz With Oliver Strauch Group & Peter Decker | Edition Collage | EC 497-2
Markus Fleischer Quartet
Let's Call It A Day | Village | WLCD 1017-2
The European Jazz Guitar Orchestra
The European Jazz Guitar Orchestra | Jardis Records | JRCD 9307
Schaefer,Bill | (tb)
Anita O'Day With The Billy May Orchestra
Verve Jazz Masters 49:Anita O'Day | Verve | 527653-2
Billy Eckstine With The Billy May Orchestra
Once More With Feeling | Roulette | 581862-2
Ella Fitzgerald With Paul Weston And His Orchestra
Ella Fitzgerald Sings The Irving Berlin Song Book | Verve | 543830-2
Ella Fitzgerald With The Paul Weston Orchestra
Get Happy! | Verve | 523321-2
Schaefer,Frank | (cello)
Mike Westbrook Orchestra
The Orchestra Of Smith's Academy | Enja | ENJ-9358 2
Nicki Leighton-Thomas Group
Forbidden Games | Candid | CCD 79778
Schaeffer,Jack | (tp)
Harry James And His Orchestra
The Legends Of Swing | Laserlight | 24659
Schaeffer,Paul | (el-p)
The Brecker Brothers
Heavy Metal Be-Bop | RCA | 2119257-2
Schaeffer,Ralph | (vviola)
Milt Jackson With Strings
To Bags...With Love:Memorial Album | Pablo | 2310967-2
Phineas Newborn Jr. With Dennis Farnon And His Orchestra
While My Lady Sleeps | RCA | 2185157-2
Schaeffer,Steve | (dr)
Diane Schuur With Orchestra
The Best Of Diane Schuur | GRP | GRP 98882
Singers Unlimited With The Patrick Williams Orchestra
The Singers Unlimited:Magic Voices | MPS | 539130-2
Schäfer,Brigitta | (sax)
Art De Fakt
Art De Fakt-Ray Federman:Surfiction Jazz No.2 | double moon | CHRDM 71007
Schäfer,Eric | (dr)
Carsten Daerr Trio
PurpleCoolCarSleep | Traumton Records | 4472-2
Eric Schaefer & Demontage
Eric Schaefer & Demontage | Jazz Haus Musik | JHM 0117 CD
Nickendes Perlgras
Die Hintere Vase | Jazz Haus Musik | JHM 0105 CD
Schäfer,Stefen Ivan | (g)
Jazz Pistols
Special Treatment | Lipstick Records | LIP 8971-2
Schäfers,Michael | (b)
Balance
Elements | double moon | DMCHR 71033
Schaffer,William | (g)
Tommy Dorsey And His Clambake Seven
Planet Jazz:Tommy Dorsey | Planet Jazz | 2159972-2
Planet Jazz:Bud Freeman | Planet Jazz | 2161240-2
Planet Jazz:Swing | Planet Jazz | 2169651-2
Tommy Dorsey And His Orchestra
Planet Jazz:Tommy Dorsey | Planet Jazz | 2159972-2
Schaffner,Dani | (drperc)
Q4 Orchester Project
Lyon's Brood | Creative Works Records | CW CD 1018-3
Schaper,Hendrik | (el-p,synthkeyboards)
Klaus Doldinger & Passport
Lifelike | Warner | 2292-46478-2
Klaus Doldinger's Passport
Blue Tattoo | Atlantic | 2292-42178-2
Oceanliner | Warner | 2292-46479-2
Passport
Ataraxia | Atlantic | 2292-42148-2
Garden Of Eden | Atlantic | 2292-44147-2
Schappert,Axel | (tb)
Landes Jugend Jazz Orchester Hessen
Touch Of Lips | hr music.de | hrmj 004-01 CD
Scharf,Hans Kaspar | (tb)
Jazzensemble Des Hessischen Rundfunks
Jazz Messe-Messe Für Unsere Zeit | hr music.de | hrmj 003-01 CD
Scharf,Harry | (b)
Hugo Siegmeth Quintet
Live At The Jazzclub Unterfahrt | Edition Collage | EC 533-2
Scharf,Monika | (voc)
Jazzensemble Des Hessischen Rundfunks
Jazz Messe-Messe Für Unsere Zeit | hr music.de | hrmj 003-01 CD
Scharfenberger,Werner | (paccordeon)
Freddie Brocksieper Quintett
Shot Gun Boogie | Bear Family Records | BCD 16277 AH
Schärli,Peter | (tp,fl-hhalf-tp)
Creative Works Orchestra
Willisau And More Live | Creative Works Records | CW CD 1020-2
Michel Wintsch & Road Movie
Michel Wintsch & Road Movie featuring Gerry Hemingway | Between The Lines | btl 002(Efa 10172-2)
Peter Schärli Quintet With Glenn Ferris
Willisau And More Live | Creative Works Records | CW CD 1020-2
Drei Seelen/Three Souls | Creative Works Records | MIWI 1014-2
Scharnweber,Karl | (church-org)
Karl Scharnweber Trio
Choral Concert | Nabel Records:Jazz Network | CD 4642
Coral Concert II/Another View | Nabel Records:Jazz Network | CD 4650
Schatz,Ziggy | (tp)
Herbie Mann's Cuban Band
Verve Jazz Masters 56:Herbie Mann | Verve | 529901-2
Schaub,Brigitte | (cello)
Joachim Ullrich Orchestra
Faces Of The Duke | Jazz Haus Musik | JHM 0045 CD
Schäuble,Nikolaus 'Niko' | (dr,keyboardsperc)
Andreas Willers Group
Andreas Willers & Friends Play Jimi Hendrix:Experience | Nabel Records:Jazz Network | CD 4665
Die Elefanten
Wasserwüste | Nabel Records:Jazz Network | CD 4634
Gebhard Ullmann Quartet
Per-Dee-Doo | Nabel Records:Jazz Network | CD 4640
Ullmann-Willers-Schäuble-Lorenz
Out To Lunch | Nabel Records:Jazz Network | CD 4623
Schecroun,Ralph | (p)
Django Reinhardt Quintet
Django/Django In Rome 1949-1050 | BGO Records | BGOCD 366
James Moody Quartet
Americans Swinging In Paris:James Moody | EMI Records | 539653-2
Scheffers,Pi | (arr)
Brocksieper-Jazz-Ensemble
Drums Boogie | Bear Family Records | BCD 15988 AH
Brocksieper-Solisten-Orchester
Globetrotter | Bear Family Records | BCD 15912 AH
Brocksieper-Special-Ensemble
Globetrotter | Bear Family Records | BCD 15912 AH
Scheib,Stefan | (b)
Christoph Thewes-Rudi Mahall Quartet
Quartetto Pazzo | Jazz Haus Musik | JHM 0122 CD
Scheibe,Mark | (p)
Swim Two Birds
No Regrets | Laika Records | 35101342
Scheidegger,Buddha | (p)
Danny Moss Meets Buddha's Gamblers
A Swingin' Affair | Nagel-Heyer | CD 034
Blues Of Summer | Nagel-Heyer | NH 1011
Schell,Harry | (b)
Delle Haensch Jump Combo
Deutsches Jazz Fesival 1954/1955 | Bear Family Records | BCD 15430
Schellekens,Shell | (dr)
Jasper Van't Hof
Pili-Pili | Warner | 2292-40458-2
Pili-Pili
Pili-Pili | JA & RO | JARO 4141-2
Schellenschötter |
Paul Giger Trio
Alpstein | ECM | 1426(847940-2)
Schemmler,Günter | (paccordeon)
Freddie Brocksieper Quartett
Shot Gun Boogie | Bear Family Records | BCD 16277 AH
Freddie Brocksieper Trio
Shot Gun Boogie | Bear Family Records | BCD 16277 AH
Inge Brandenburg And Her All-Stars
Why Don't You Take All Of Me | Bear Family Records | BCD 15614 AH
Schenderlein,Peter | (p,keyboardssynth)
Loft Line
Source | Laika Records | 35101122
Schenk,James | (b)
Max Roach Group
We Insist: Freedom Now Suite | Candid | CCD 79002
Schenker,Daniel 'Dani' | (tpfl-h)
Brigitte Dietrich-Joe Haider Jazz Orchestra
Consequences | JHM Records | JHM 3624
Q4 Orchester Project
Yavapai | Creative Works Records | CW CD 1028-2
Scherer,Peter | (keyboards,dr-programming,org)

INTERPRETENVERZEICHNIS

Al Jarreau With Band
L Is For Lover | i.e. Music | 557850-2
Bill Frisell Band
Before We Were Born | Nonesuch | 7559-60843-2

Scherer,Uli | (keyboards,face-perc,melodica,p,el-p)
AM 4
...And She Answered | ECM | 1394
Wolfgang Puschnig-Uli Scherer
Puschnig-Scherer | EmArCy | 014103-2

Scherr,Tony | (b,el-b,moonlute,el-g,g,b-gdobro)
Marco Piludu International Quartet
New York Travels | Jazz 4 Ever Records:Jazz Network | J4E 4733
Michael Blake Group
Kingdom Of Champa | Intuition Records | INT 3189-2
Drift | Intuition Records | INT 3212-2
Slow Poke
Redemption | Intuition Records | INT 3260-2

Scherrer,Andy | (p,reeds,sax,ssts)
Hot Mallets
Hot Mallets...Live! | JHM Records | JHM 3610
Slide Hampton-Joe Haider Jazz Orchestra
Give Me A Double | JHM Records | JHM 3627

Schertzer,Hymie | (as,bs,b-cl,cl,reedssax)
All Star Band
Planet Jazz:Jack Teagarden | Planet Jazz | 2161236-2
Benny Goodman And His Orchestra
Planet Jazz:Benny Goodman | Planet Jazz | 2152054-2
Planet Jazz Sampler | Planet Jazz | 2152326-2
Planet Jazz:Jazz Greatest Hits | Planet Jazz | 2169648-2
Planet Jazz:Big Bands | Planet Jazz | 2169649-2
Planet Jazz:Swing | Planet Jazz | 2169651-2
Planet Jazz:Jazz Trumpet | Planet Jazz | 2169654-2
Planet Jazz:Female Jazz Vocalists | Planet Jazz | 2169656-2
The Legends Of Swing | Laserlight | 24659
Great Swing Classics In Hi-Fi | Capitol | 521223-2
Benny Goodman At Carnegie Hall 1938(Complete) | CBS | C2K 65143
Camel Caravan Broadcast 1939 Vol.1 | Phontastic | NCD 8817
Camel Caravan Broadcast 1939 Vol.2 | Phontastic | NCD 8818
Camel Caravan Broadcast 1939 Vol.3 | Phontastic | NCD 8819
More Camel Caravans | Phontastic | NCD 8841/2
More Camel Caravans | Phontastic | NCD 8843/4
Benny Goodman And His V-Disc All Star Band
The Legends Of Swing | Laserlight | 24659
Benny Goodman Band
Benny Goodman At Carnegie Hall 1938(Complete) | CBS | C2K 65143
Billie Holiday With Teddy Wilson And His Orchestra
Billie's Love Songs | Nimbus Records | NI 2000
Billie Holiday With Toots Camarata And His Orchestra
Billie's Love Songs | Nimbus Records | NI 2000
Ella Fitzgerald With Sy Oliver And His Orchestra
Ella Fitzgerald:The Decca Years 1949-1954 | Decca | 050668-2
Jam Session
Benny Goodman At Carnegie Hall 1938(Complete) | CBS | C2K 65143
Jess Stacy And His Orchestra
Planet Jazz:Jazz Piano | RCA | 2169655-2
Louis Armstrong And The Commanders under the Direction of Camarata
Satchmo Serenaders | Verve | 543792-2
Louis Armstrong With Gordon Jenkins And His Orchestra And Choir
Satchmo In Style | Verve | 549594-2
Louis Armstrong-My Greatest Songs | MCA | MCD 18347
Swing Legends:Louis Armstrong | Nimbus Records | NI 2012
Louis Armstrong With Sy Oliver And His Orchestra
Satchmo Serenaders | Verve | 543792-2
Louis Armstrong:C'est Si Bon | Dreyfus Jazz Line | FDM 36730-2
Louis Armstrong-My Greatest Songs | MCA | MCD 18347
Louis Armstrong With The Commanders
Ambassador Louis Armstrong Vol.17:Moments To Remember(1952-1956) | Ambassador | CLA 1917
Peggy Lee With The Benny Goodman Orchestra
Peggy Lee & Benny Goodman:The Complete Recordings 1941-1947 | CBS | C2K 65686
Sarah Vaughan The The Joe Lippman Orchestra
Sarah Vaughan:Lover Man | Dreyfus Jazz Line | FDM 36739-2
Tommy Dorsey And His Orchestra
Planet Jazz:Frank Sinatra & Tommy Dorsey | Planet Jazz | 2152067-2
Planet Jazz:Tommy Dorsey | Planet Jazz | 2159972-2
Planet Jazz:Big Bands | Planet Jazz | 2169649-2
Planet Jazz:Male Jazz Vocalists | Planet Jazz | 2169657-2
Frank Sinatra And The Tommy Dorsey Orchestra | RCA | 2668701-2

Scherzer,Derek | (dr)
Jazz Orchester Rheinland-Pfalz
Last Season | Jazz Haus Musik | LJBB 9706

Scheu,Joachim | (p)
Lorenzo Petrocca Quartet Feat. Bruno De Filippi
Insieme | Edition Musikat | EDM 002

Scheuber,Christian | (dr)
Christian Scheuber Quartet
Clara's Smile | double moon | DMCHR 71025
Christian Scheuber Quintet
Clara's Smile | double moon | DMCHR 71025

Scheuermann,Michael | (tb)
Bigband Der Musikschule Der Stadt Brühl Mit Gastsolisten
Pangäa | Indigo-Records | 1004 CD

Scheunemann,Karsten | (sax)
Mario Neunkirchen Quintet
Long Distance | Laika Records | LK 94-060

Scheurell,Casey | (dr,gongperc)
Jean-Luc Ponty Quartet
Cosmic Messenger | Atlantic | 7567-81550-2
The Very Best Of Jean-Luc Ponty | Rhino | 8122-79862-2
Jean-Luc Ponty Sextet
Cosmic Messenger | Atlantic | 7567-81550-2
The Very Best Of Jean-Luc Ponty | Rhino | 8122-79862-2

Schiaffini,Giancarlo | (tb,b-tb,euphonium,tapestuba)
Italian Instabile Orchestra
Skies Of Europe | ECM | 1543

Schiano,Mario | (as,org,sax,voicess)

Schiba,Reda | (voc)
Koch-Schütz-Studer & El Nil Troop
Heavy Cairo Trafic | Intuition Records | INT 3175-2

Schick,Hugh | (fl-h)
Yusef Lateef Ensemble
Nocturnes | Atlantic | 7567-81977-2

Schickentanz,Andreas | (tb)
Bigband Der Musikschule Der Stadt Brühl Mit Gastsolisten
Pangäa | Indigo-Records | 1004 CD
Matthias Petzold Working Band
Elements | Indigo-Records | 1005 CD

Schiefel,Michael | (electronics,voicevoc)
Batoru
Tree Of Sounds | Nabel Records:Jazz Network | CD 4685
Dirk Strakhof & Batoru
Arabesque | Nabel Records:Jazz Network | CD 4696
Jazz Indeed
Under Water | Traumton Records | 2415-2
Who The Moon Is | Traumton Records | 4427-2
Michael Schiefel
I Don't Belong | Traumton Records | 4433-2
Susan Weinert Band
Point Of View | Intuition Records | INT 3272-2
Thärichens Tentett
Lady Moon | Minor Music | 801094

Schieferdecker,Markus | (b)
Clark Terry With The Summit Jazz Orchestra
Clark | Edition Collage | EC 530-2
Lutz Häfner Quartet
Way In Way Out | Jazz 4 Ever Records:Jazz Network | J4E 4757
Norbert Emminger Quintet
In The Park | Edition Collage | EC 521-2

Schießl,Rudi | (b)
Alex De Santis Jazz Quartet
Le Canzoni Italiana | Edition Collage | EC 514-2

Schifano,Frank | (b,vocel-b)
Dizzy Gillespie And His Orchestra
Talking Verve:Dizzy Gillespie | Verve | 533846-2
Dizzy Gillespie Quintet
Swing Low, Sweet Cadillac | Impulse(MCA) | 951178-2
The Roots Of Acid Jazz | Impulse(MCA) | IMP 12042
Lalo Schifrin And His Orchestra
Tin Tin Deo | Fresh Sound Records | FSR-CD 319

Schiff,Bobby | (p)
Buddy Childers Big Band
Just Buddy's | Candid | CCD 79761

Schifrin,Lalo | (arr,cond,el-keyboards,harpsichordp)
Astor Piazzolla With Orchestra Of St. Luke's
Concierto Para Bandoneon-Tres Tangos | Nonesuch | 7559-79174-2
Cal Tjader With The Lalo Schifrin Orchestra
Talkin Verve/Roots Of Acid Jazz:Cal Tjader | Verve | 531562-2
Dizzy Gillespie And His Orchestra
Verve Jazz Masters 10:Dizzy Gillespie | Verve | 516319-2
Gillespiana And Carnegie Hall Concert | Verve | 519809-2
Talking Verve:Dizzy Gillespie | Verve | 533846-2
Ultimate Dizzy Gillespie | Verve | 557535-2
Dizzy Gillespie Quintet
Dizzie Gillespie: Salle Pleyel/Olympia | Laserlight | 36132
An Electrifying Evening With The Dizzy Gillespie Quintet | Verve | 557544-2
Dizzy Gillespie Septet
The Antonio Carlos Jobim Songbook | Verve | 525472-2
Dizzy Gillespie Sextet
Dizzie Gillespie: Salle Pleyel/Olympia | Laserlight | 36132
Verve Jazz Masters 10:Dizzy Gillespie | Verve | 516319-2
Dizzy Gillespie With The Lalo Schifrin Orchestra
Free Ride | Original Jazz Classics | OJCCD 784-2(2310794)
JATP All Stars
Stan Getz Highlights:The Best Of The Verve Years Vol.2 | Verve | 517330-2
Verve Jazz Masters 25:Stan Getz & Dizzy Gillespie | Verve | 521852-2
Jimmy Smith With The Lalo Schifrin Orchestra
Jimmy Smith:Best Of The Verve Years | Verve | 527950-2
Jimmy Smith-Talkin' Verve | Verve | 531563-2
The Cat | Verve | 539756-2
Lalo Schifrin And His Orchestra
Verve Jazz Masters 39:Cal Tjader | Verve | 521858-2
Tin Tin Deo | Fresh Sound Records | FSR-CD 319
Lalo Schifrin Sextet
Tin Tin Deo | Fresh Sound Records | FSR-CD 319
Lalo Schifrin Trio With The London Philharmonic
Jazz Meets The Symphony | East-West | 4509-92004-2
Quincy Jones And His Orchestra
Big Band Bossa Nova | Verve | 557913-2
Rahsaan/The Complete Mercury Recordings Of Roland Kirk | Mercury | 846630-2
Sarah Vaughan With Orchestra
Sweet 'N' Sassy | Roulette | 531793-2
Sarah Vaughan With The Lalo Schifrin Orchestra
Jazz Profile | Blue Note | 823517-2
Stan Getz With Strings And Voices
Reflections | Verve | 523322-2

Schilder,Hilton | (p)
Johannes Enders Group
Reflections Of South Africa | Jazz 4 Ever Records:Jazz Network | J4E 4729

Schildkraut,Dave | (asts)
Miles Davis Quintet
Blue Haze | Original Jazz Classics | OJC20 093-2(P 7054)
Walkin' | Original Jazz Classics | OJC20 213-2
The Prestige Legacy Vol.1:The High Priests | Prestige | PCD 24251-2

Schildkraut,David | (reeds,saxts)
Tito Puente Orchestra
Planet Jazz:Tito Puente | Planet Jazz | 2165369-2

Schilgen,Dirik | (dr)
Jobias Langguth Band
One Note Bossa | Jardis Records | JRCD 9510
Wayne Bartlett With The Thomas Hufschmidt Trio And Wolfgang Engstfeld
Senor Blues | Laika Records | LK 95-066
Wolf Mayer Dialects
Roots And Wings | Triptychon | 300201
Wolf Mayer Trio
I Do Believe In Spring | Triptychon | 400403

Schilling,Andreas | (cubesmetal-plate)
Kölner Saxophon Mafia With Fleisch
Kölner Saxophon Mafia Proudly Presents | Jazz Haus Musik | JHM 0046 CD

Schilperoort,Peter | (bs,p,cl,ss,dr,voc,ts,bj,gclaves)
Albert Nicholas With The Dutch Swing College Band
Albert Nicholas & The Dutch Swing College Band | Storyville | STCD 5522
Dutch Swing College Band
Swinging Studio Sessons | Philips | 824256-2 PMS
Digital Anniversary | Philips | 824585-2 PMS
Dutch Swing College Band Live In 1960 | Philips | 838765-2
Albert Nicholas & The Dutch Swing College Band | Storyville | STCD 5522
Rita Reys With The Dutch Swing College Band
The Very Best Of Dixieland Jazz | Verve | 535529-2

Schiltknecht,Roland | (swiss-hammered-dulcimer)
Peter A. Schmid Duos
Duets,Dialogues & Duels | Creative Works Records | CW CD 1034

Schimer,Jonathan | (cello)
Jo Ambros Group
Wanderlust | dml-records | CD 016

Schimmelpfennig,Frank | (g)
Association Urbanetique
Ass Bedient | Jazz 4 Ever Records:Jazz Network | J4E 4723

Schimmeroth,Alex | (p,el-psynth)
House Five
Frank Talk | Nabel Records:Jazz Network | CD 4674

Schimscheimer,Marcel | (dr-programming)
The Rosenberg Trio
The Rosenberg Trio:The Collection | Verve | 537152-2

Schindler,Xenia | (harp)
Miles Davis With Gil Evans Orchestra, The George Gruntz Concert Jazz Band And Guests
Miles & Quincy Live At Montreux | Warner | 9362-45221-2

Schinkopf,Matthias | (sax)
booMbooM meets Uli Beckerhoff
Resurection Lounge | Laika Records | 35101512

Schiöppfe,William | (dr)
Don Byas Quartet
The Art Of Saxophone | Laserlight | 24652
Stan Getz And The Swedish All Stars
Stan Getz Highlights:The Best Of The Verve Years Vol.2 | Verve | 517330-2
Stan Getz Highlights | Verve | 847430-2
Stan Getz Quartet
Stan Getz Highlights:The Best Of The Verve Years Vol.2 | Verve | 517330-2
Stan Getz Highlights | Verve | 847430-2

Schiorring,Erik | (bj)
Papa Benny's Jazzband
The Golden Years Of Revival Jazz,Sampler | Storyville | 109 1001

Schippa,Jörg | (gelectronics)
Andreas Willers Group
Andreas Willers & Friends Play Jimi Hendrix:Experience | Nabel Records:Jazz Network | CD 4665

Friedemann Graef Group
Orlando Fragments | Nabel Records:Jazz Network | CD 4681
Graef-Schippa-Moritz
Orlando Frames | Nabel Records:Jazz Network | CD 4690

Schipper,Jörn | (dr,euphonium,glockenspiel,perctuba)
Blue Room Ensemble
Solitude | Foolish Music | FM 211993
Cool Blue
House In The Country | Foolish Music | FM 211591
dAs prOjekT
dAs prOjekT | Foolish Music | FM 211288
Gabriele Hasler & Foolish Heart
God Is A She | Foolish Music | FM 111186
Gabriele Hasler Group
Gabriele Hasler's Rosensrücke | Foolish Music | FM 211096
Listening To Löbering | Foolish Music | FM 211389
Gabriele Hasler's Personal Notebook | Foolish Music | FM 211490
Gabriele Hasler-Hans Lüdemann-Andreas Willers plus Jörn Schipper
Familienglück | Foolish Music | FM 211097
Hanschel-Hübsch-Schipper
Planet Blow Chill | Jazz Haus Musik | JHM 0087 CD
Planet Blow
Alien Lunatic | Jazz Haus Musik | JHM 0071 CD

Schirmer,Rouven | (cello)
Lisa Bassenge Trio With Guests
A Sight, A Song | Minor Music | 801100

Schirmsheimer,Marcel | (b)
Akili
Maasai Mara | M.A Music | A 802-2

Schläger,Ralph | (dr)
Matthias Petzold Septett
Ulysses | Indigo-Records | 1003 CD

Schlaier,Manne | (gpolysub-b)
Schlaier-Hirt Duo
Don't Walk Outside Thos Area | Chaos | CACD 8186

Schlamminger,Sam | (daf)
Renaud Garcia-Fons Group
Oriental Bass | Enja | ENJ-9334 2

Schläppi,Daniel | (b)
Twice A Week & Steve Elson
Play Of Colours | Edition Collage | EC 511-2

Schlemmer,Christoph | (dr)
Barbara Jungfer Trio
Vitamin B 3 | yvp music | CD 3097

Schlesinger,Stefanie | (voc)
Stefanie Schlesiger And Her Group plus String Quartet
What Love Is | Enja | ENJ-9434 2
Stefanie Schlesinger And Her Group
What Love Is | Enja | ENJ-9434 2

Schlick,Frederic | (accordeon)
Helmut Nieberle & Cordes Sauvages
Jazz Guitar Highlights 1 | Jardis Records | JRCD 20141
Salut To Django | Jardis Records | JRCD 9926

Schlinger,Sol | (b-cl,bs,reeds,saxts)
Benny Goodman And His Orchestra
Great Swing Classics In Hi-Fi | Capitol | 521223-2
40th Anniversary Concert-Live At Carnegie Hall | London | 820349-2
Verve Jazz Masters 33:Benny Goodman | Verve | 844410-2
Coleman Hawkins With Billy Byers And His Orchestra
The Hawk In Hi-Fi | RCA | 2663842-2
George Russell And His Orchestra
Geogre Russell New York N.Y. | Impulse(MCA) | 951278-2
Glenn Miller And His Orchestra
The Glenn Miller Orchestra In Digital Mood | GRP | GRP 95022
Jimmy Rushing And His Orchestra
Five Feet Of Soul | Roulette | 581830-2
John LaPorta Octet
Theme And Variations | Fantasy | FCD 24776-2
Lucy Reed With Orchestra
This Is Lucy Reed | Original Jazz Classics | OJCCD 1943-2(F 3243)

Schlosser,Axel | (tp,co,fl-hharmon mute fills)
Clark Terry With The Summit Jazz Orchestra
Clark | Edition Collage | EC 530-2
Frank Eberle Septet
Scarlet Sunrise | Satin Doll Productions | SDP 1041-1 CD
Mathias Götz-Windstärke 4
Lunar Oder Solar? | Jazz 'n' Arts Records | JNA 1002
Rainer Tempel Big Band
Melodies Of '98 | Jazz 4 Ever Records:Jazz Network | J4E 4744
Album 03 | Jazz 'n' Arts Records | JNA 1102
Rainer Tempel Quintet
Blick In Die Welt | Edition Musikat | EDM 038
Schlosser/Weber/Böhm/Huber/Binder
L 14,16 | Jazz 4 Ever Records:Jazz Network | J4E 4760

Schlothauer,Burkhard | (v,violavoc)
Schlothauer's Maniacs
Maniakisses | Timescrapper | TSCR 9811

Schlott,Volker | (as,bamboo-fl,fl,alto-fl,ss,perc)
Bajazzo
Harlequin Galaxy | Edition Collage | EC 519-2
Fun Horns
Surprise | Jazzpoint | JP 1029 CD

Schloz,Karl | (grh-g)
Karl Schloz Quartet
A Mooth One | Nagel-Heyer | CD 2012
Till Brönner Group
Chattin' With Chet | Verve | 157534-2

Schlumpf,Martin | (b,b-cl,as,gongs,ld,manzello)
Cadavre Exquis
Cadavre Exquis | Creative Works Records | CW CD 1014-1

Schlunck,Anke | (voc)
Jazzensemble Des Hessischen Rundfunks
Jazz Messe-Messe Für Unsere Zeit | hr music.de | hrmj 003-01 CD

Schlüter,Wolfgang | (perc,tympani,vib,marimbacongas)
Albert Mangelsdorff With The NDR Big Band
NDR Big Band-Bravissimo | ACT | 9232-2
Chet Baker With The NDR-Bigband
NDR Big Band-Bravissimo | ACT | 9232-2
My Favourite Songs: The Last Great Concert Vol.1 | Enja | ENJ-5097 2
The Last Concert Vol.I+II | Enja | ENJ-6074 22
Dusko Goykovich Quintet With The NDR Radio-Philharmonie,Hannover
Balkan Blues | Enja | ENJ-9320 2
Heinz Sauer Quartet With The NDR Big Band
NDR Big Band-Bravissimo | ACT | 9232-2
Jazz Baltica Ensemble
The Birth+Rebirth Of Swedish Folk Jazz | ACT | 9254-2
Joe Pass With The NDR Big Band
Joe Pass In Hamburg | ACT | 9100-2
Joe Pass With The NDR Big Band And Radio Philharmonie Hannover
Joe Pass In Hamburg | ACT | 9100-2
Johnny Griffin With The NDR Big Band
NDR Big Band-Bravissimo | ACT | 9232-2
NDR Big Band
NDR Big Band-Bravissimo | ACT | 9232-2
NDR Big Band With Guests
50 Years Of NDR Big Band:Bravissimo II | ACT | 9259-2
Schlüter-Nabatov-Antolini
Swing Kings | ACT | 9298-2

Schmalhofer,Ludwig | (viola)
Stefanie Schlesiger And Her Group plus String Quartet
What Love Is | Enja | ENJ-9434 2

Schmalzried,Dieter | (b)
Thomas Karl Fuchs Trio
Colours And Standards | Edition Collage | EC 509-2

Schmauch,Davis | (tpfl-h)
Jazz Orchester Rheinland-Pfalz
Last Season | Jazz Haus Musik | LJBB 9706

Schmeisser,Uwe | (cello)
Los Jovenes Flamencos With The WDR Big Band And Guests

Jazzpana | ACT | 9212-2
Schmid,Alfa | (tp)
Hans Koller Big Band
New York City | MPS | 9813437
Schmid,Andreas | (p)
Lisa Bassenge Trio
A Sight, A Song | Minor Music | 801100
Lisa Bassenge Trio With Guests
A Sight, A Song | Minor Music | 801100
Schmid,Lucas | (b-tb,tuba,tbvoc)
Gianlugi Trovesi Quartet With The WDR Big Band
Dedalo | Enja | ENJ-9419 2
Heinz Sauer Quartet With The NDR Big Band
NDR Big Band-Bravissimo | ACT | 9232-2
NDR Big Band
NDR Big Band-Bravissimo | ACT | 9232-2
Pee Wee Ellis & NDR Bigband
What You Like | Minor Music | 801064
Schmid,Peter | (b,b-cl,ssbs)
Al Jones Blues Band
Sharper Than A Tack | Blues Beacon | BLU-1034 2
Q4 Orchester Project
Lyon's Brood | Creative Works Records | CW CD 1018-3
Schmid,Peter A. | (b-cl,contra-b-cl,ss,as,alto-fl)
Anliker-Parker-Schmid-Senn-Solothurnmann
September Winds | Creative Works Records | CW CD 1038/39
ATonALL
ATonALL | Creative Works Records | CW CD 1024-2
Evan Parker-Peter A.Schmid
September Duos | Creative Works Records | CW CD 1036
Peter A. Schmid Duos
Duets,Dialogues & Duels | Creative Works Records | CW CD 1034
Peter A. Schmid Trio With Guests
Profound Sounds In An Empty Reservoir | Creative Works Records | CW CD 1033
Roger Girod-Peter A.Schmid
Windschief | Creative Works Records | CW CD 1027-2
Schmilz
Schmilz | Creative Works Records | CW CD 1041
Schmid,Ralf | (psampling)
Nana Mouskouri With The Berlin Radio Big Band
Nana Swings | Mercury | 074394-2
Schmid,Stefan | (p,keaboards,perchand-clapping)
Lotz Of Music
Puasong Daffriek | Laika Records | LK 94-054
Till Martin Quintet
On The Trail | Nabel Records:Jazz Network | CD 4676
Schmid,Willy | (clvoc)
Willy Bischof Jazztet
Swiss Air | Jazz Connaisseur | JCCD 9523-2
Schmid,Wolfgang | (b,b-g,ld,voc,el-b,el-g,12-string-g)
Klaus Doldinger's Passport
Atlantic Jazz: Fusion | Atlantic | 7567-81711-2
Paradox
The First Second | TipToe | TIP-888833 2
Passport
Handmade | Atlantic | 2292-42172-2
Second Passport | Atlantic | 2292-44143-2
Looking Thru | Atlantic | 2292-44144-2
Cross-Collateral | Atlantic | 2292-44145-2
Infinity Machine | Atlantic | 2292-44146-2
Iguacu | Atlantic | 2292-46031-2
Passport And Guests
Doldinger Jubilee Concert | Atlantic | 2292-44175-2
Doldinger's Best | ACT | 9224-2
Wolfgang Schmid's Kick
No Filters | TipToe | TIP-888809 2
Schmidger,Chris | (b)
Dutch Swing College Band
Swinging Studio Sessons | Philips | 824256-2 PMS
Schmidl,Marcus | (arrvoc)
Michael Riessler & Singer Pur with Vincent Courtois
Ahi Vita | ACT | 9417-2
Schmidli,Peter | (g)
Danny Moss Meets Buddha's Gamblers
A Swingin' Affair | Nagel-Heyer | CD 034
Blues Of Summer | Nagel-Heyer | NH 1011
Hot Mallets
Hot Mallets...Live! | JHM Records | JHM 3610
The Tremble Kids All Stars
The Tremble Kids All Stars Play Chicago Jazz! | Nagel-Heyer | CD 043
Schmidlin,Peter | (drperc)
Willy Bischof Jazztet
Swiss Air | Jazz Connaisseur | JCCD 9523-2
Willy Bischof Trio
Swiss Air | Jazz Connaisseur | JCCD 9523-2
Schmidt,Andreas | (pvoice)
Lee Konitz Quartet
Haiku | Nabel Records:Jazz Network | CD 4664
Lisa Bassenge Trio
Going Home | Minor Music | 801091
Schmidt,Arthur | (p,ld,synthCD-sounds)
Ute Kannenberg Quartet
Kannenberg On Purpose | Jazz Haus Musik | JHM 0109 CD
Ute Kannenberg Quartet With Guests
Kannenberg On Purpose | Jazz Haus Musik | JHM 0109 CD
Schmidt,Bobby | (dr)
Helmut Zacharias mit dem Orchester Frank Folken
Ich Habe Rhythmus | Bear Family Records | BCD 15642 AH
Kurt Edelhagen All Stars Und Solisten
Deutsches Jazz Fesival 1954/1955 | Bear Family Records | BCD 15430
Quartet Der Kurt Edelhagen All Stars
Deutsches Jazz Fesival 1954/1955 | Bear Family Records | BCD 15430
Schmidt,Christian | (b)
Till Brönner Quartet & Deutsches Symphonieorchester Berlin
German Songs | Minor Music | 801057
Schmidt,Claudia | (voice)
Steve Tibbetts Group
Exploded View | ECM | 1335
The Fall Of Us All | ECM | 1527(521144-2)
Schmidt,Eckart | (p)
Spree Cuty Stompers
Deutsches Jazz Fesival 1954/1955 | Bear Family Records | BCD 15430
Schmidt,Jochen | (b,el-b,vib,marimbasynth)
Klaus Doldinger & Passport
Down To Earth | Warner | 4509-93207-2
Klaus Doldinger's Passport
Balance Of Happiness | Warner | 9031-71233-2
Blues Roots | Warner | 9031-75417-2
Klaus Doldinger's Passport With Johnny 'Clyde' Copeland
Blues Roots | Warner | 9031-75417-2
Markus Stockhausen Orchestra
Sol Mestizo:Markus Stockhausen Plays The Music Of Enrique Diaz | ACT | 9222-2
Peter Weiss Sextet
Personal Choice | Nabel Records:Jazz Network | CD 4669
Schmidt,Peter | (dr)
Frieder Berlin Trio
Soul Fingers | Satin Doll Productions | SDP 1039-1 CD
Schmidt,Stefan | (viola)
Uri Caine With The Concerto Köln
Concerto Köln | Winter&Winter | 910086-2
Schmidt,Sylvio prob. | (v)
Yvonne Louis With The Orchestra Vola
Jazz In Paris:Django Reinhardt-Django Et Compagnie | EmArCy | 549241-2 PMS
Schmidt.Markus | (dr)
Kamafra
Kamafra Live | Edition Musikat | EDM 072
Schmidt-Relenberg,Markus | (saxts)
Joe Pass With The NDR Big Band
Joe Pass In Hamburg | ACT | 9100-2
Schmidt-Relenberg,Tobias | (ts)
NDR Big Band
NDR Big Band-Bravissimo | ACT | 9232-2
Schmidt-Schulz,Eberhardt | (tp)
Brocksieper-Jazz-Ensemble
Drums Boogie | Bear Family Records | BCD 15988 AH
Brocksieper-Solisten-Orchester
Globetrotter | Bear Family Records | BCD 15912 AH
Brocksieper-Special-Ensemble
Globetrotter | Bear Family Records | BCD 15912 AH
Schmiedt,Wolfgang | (g,el-g6-string-g)
Karl Scharnweber Trio
Choral Concert | Nabel Records:Jazz Network | CD 4642
Coral Concert II/Another View | Nabel Records:Jazz Network | CD 4650
Schmilz |
Schmilz
Schmilz | Creative Works Records | CW CD 1041
Schmit,Lucien | (cello)
Ben Webster With Orchestra And Strings
Music For Loving:Ben Webster With Strings | Verve | 527774-2
Ultimate Ben Webster selected by James Carter | Verve | 557537-2
Wes Montgomery With The Jimmy Jones Orchestra
Wes Montgomery-The Complete Riverside Recordings | Riverside | 12 RCD 4408-2
Schmit.Lyonal | (v)
Richard Galliano Septet
Piazzolla Forever | Dreyfus Jazz Line | FDM 36642-2
Schmitt,Martin | (p,vocreeds)
Martin Schmitt
Handful Of Blues | ESM Records | ESM 9303
Schmitt,Uwe | (drtom-tom)
Alfred 23 Harth Group
Sweet Paris | free flow music | ffm 0291
Schmitz,Bobby | (clas)
Harald Banter Ensemble
Deutsches Jazz Fesival 1954/1955 | Bear Family Records | BCD 15430
Schmitz,Csaba | (dr)
Mind Games
Pretty Fonky | Edition Collage | EC 482-2
Mind Games Plays The Music Of Stan Getz & Astrud Gilberto | Edition Collage | EC 515-2
Wind Moments | Take Twelve On CD | TT 009-2
Mind Games With Claudio Roditi
Live | Edition Collage | EC 501-2
Vocal Moments | Take Twelve On CD | TT 008-2
Mind Games With Philip Catherine
Pretty Fonky | Edition Collage | EC 482-2
Tom Bennecke & Space Gurilla
Wind Moments | Take Twelve On CD | TT 009-2
Schmitz,Marion | (fl)
Matthias Petzold Working Band
Elements | Indigo-Records | 1005 CD
Schmitz-Schulz,Eberhard | (tp)
Erwin Lehn Und Sein Südfunk-Tanzorchester
Deutsches Jazz Fesival 1954/1955 | Bear Family Records | BCD 15430
Schmitz-Steinberg,Christian | (parr)
Brocksi-Quartett
Drums Boogie | Bear Family Records | BCD 15988 AH
Brocksi-Sextett
Drums Boogie | Bear Family Records | BCD 15988 AH
Shot Gun Boogie | Bear Family Records | BCD 16277 AH
Freddie Brocksieper Orchester
Shot Gun Boogie | Bear Family Records | BCD 16277 AH
Schmolck,Stefan | (bsound-processing)
Heinz Sauer 4tet
Exchange 2 | free flow music | ffm 0998
Heinz Sauer Quintet
Lost Ends:Live at Alte Oper Frankfurt | free flow music | ffm 0594
Heinz Sauer Trio
Exchange | free flow music | ffm 0695
Jazzensemble Des Hessischen Rundfunks
Atmosphering Conditions Permitting | ECM | 1549/50
Wolf Mayer Dialects
Roots And Wings | Triptychon | 300201
Wolf Mayer Trio
I Do Believe In Spring | Triptychon | 400403
Schmolling,Marc | (p)
Marc Schmolling Trio
Nostalgia Soul Ship | Organic Music | ORGM 9731
Mathias Götz-Windstärke 4
Lunar Oder Solar? | Jazz 'n' Arts Records | JNA 1002
Wanja Slavin-Matc Schmolling
Off Minor | Organic Music | ORGM 9732
Schneebiegl,Rolf | (tpvib)
Freddie Brocksieper Quintett
Shot Gun Boogie | Bear Family Records | BCD 16277 AH
Kurt Edelhagen All Stars
Deutsches Jazz Fesival 1954/1955 | Bear Family Records | BCD 15430
Kurt Edelhagen All Stars Und Solisten
Deutsches Jazz Fesival 1954/1955 | Bear Family Records | BCD 15430
Quartet Der Kurt Edelhagen All Stars
Deutsches Jazz Fesival 1954/1955 | Bear Family Records | BCD 15430
Schneer,Charlie | (p)
Charlie Byrd Group
Byrd In The Wind | Original Jazz Classics | OJCCD 1086(RS 9449)
Charlie Byrd Quartet
Byrd's Word! | Original Jazz Classics | OJCCD 1054-2(R 9448)
Schneider Essleben,Florian | (fl)
Paul Nero Sound
Doldinger's Best | ACT | 9224-2
Schneider Heermann | (tampura)
Munich Saxophon Family
Balanced | Edition Collage | EC 487-2
Schneider,Eric | (fl,tssax)
Count Basie And His Orchestra
88 Basie Street | Original Jazz Classics | OJC 808(2310901)
Schneider,Erik | (p)
Kölner Saxophon Mafia With Ina Stachelhaus And Erik Schneider
Kölner Saxophon Mafia Proudly Presents | Jazz Haus Musik | JHM 0046 CD
Schneider,Florian | (fl,cl,ss,tsbs)
Kölner Saxophon Mafia
Mafia Years 1982-86 | Jazz Haus Musik | JHM 0058 CD
Schneider,Hans Wolf 'Hawe' | (tb)
Quartier Latin Jazz Band
Great Traditionalists | Jazzpoint | JP 1046 CD
Spree Cuty Stompers
Deutsches Jazz Fesival 1954/1955 | Bear Family Records | BCD 15430
Schneider,Heinrich | (ts)
Helmut Zacharias & His Sax-Team
Ich Habe Rhythmus | Bear Family Records | BCD 15642 AH
Helmut Zacharias mit seinem Orchester
Ich Habe Rhythmus | Bear Family Records | BCD 15642 AH
Schneider,Helmut | (v)
Bernd Konrad Jazz Group With Symphonie Orchestra
Wen Die Götter Lieben | Creative Works Records | CW CD 1010-1
Schneider,Hermine | (tp)
United Women's Orchestra
Virgo Supercluster | Jazz Haus Musik | JHM 0123 CD
Schneider,Larry | (alto-fl,ss,ts,fl,cl,oboesax)
Bill Evans-Toots Thielemans Quintet
Affinity | Warner | 7599-27387-2
Horace Silver Quintet
Horace Silver Retrospective | Blue Note | 495576-2
Jam Session
Jam Session Vol.1 | Steeplechase | SCCD 31522
Miles Davis With Gil Evans Orchestra, The George Gruntz Concert Jazz Band And Guests
Miles & Quincy Live At Montreux | Warner | 9362-45221-2
Steve Smith & Vital Information
Vitalive! | VeraBra Records | CDVBR 2051-2
Schneider,Susanne | (voc)
Joachim Ullrich Orchestra
Faces Of The Duke | Jazz Haus Musik | JHM 0045 CD
Schneider,Ubald | (tp)
Freddie Brocksieper Orchester
Drums Boogie | Bear Family Records | BCD 15988 AH
Schneider-Hollek,Matthias | (electronics)
Digital Masters Feat. Bryan Steele
Sun Dance | Edition Musikat | EDM 038
Schneier,Harold | (cello)
Pete Rugolo And His Orchestra
Thriller/Richard Diamon(Original Jazz Scores From 2 Classics TV Series) | Fresh Sound Records | FSCD 2015
Schnelle,Rainer | (p,synthsequencer-programming)
Tomato Kiss
Tomato Kiss | Nabel Records:Jazz Network | CD 4624
Schnermann,Andreas | (p)
Andreas Schnerman Quartet
4 In One | Edition Collage | EC 526-2
Welcome To My Backyard | Edition Collage | EC 535-2
Andreas Schnerman Quintet
Welcome To My Backyard | Edition Collage | EC 535-2
Andreas Schnerman Sextet
Welcome To My Backyard | Edition Collage | EC 535-2
Schnitter,David | (ss,tsvoc)
Art Blakey And The Jazz Messengers
Night In Tunisia | Philips | 800064-2
Freddie Hubbard Quintet
Live At The Northsea Jazz Festival | Pablo | 2620113-2
Schnittjer,Günther | (voc)
Helmut Zacharias & His Sax-Team
Ich Habe Rhythmus | Bear Family Records | BCD 15642 AH
Schnyder,Daniel | (arr,comp,fl,ss,tssax)
Abdullah Ibrahim Trio And A String Orchestra
African Suite | TipToe | TIP-888832 2
Abdullah Ibrahim Trio With The Munich Radio Symphony Orchestra
African Symphony | Enja | ENJ-9410 2
Daniel Schnyder Group
Tanatula | Enja | ENJ-9302 2
Words Within Music | Enja | ENJ-9369 2
Daniel Schnyder Quintet
Nucleus | Enja | ENJ-8068 2
Daniel Schnyder Quintet With String Quartet
Mythology | Enja | ENJ-7003 2
Daniel Schnyder With String Quartet
Tanatula | Enja | ENJ-9302 2
Daniel Schnyder With The NDR Radio Philharmonie Hannover
Tanatula | Enja | ENJ-9302 2
NDR Radio Philharmonic Orchestra
Colossus Of Sound | Enja | ENJ-9460 2
String Orchestra
African Suite | TipToe | TIP-888832 2
Schober,Andreas | (v)
Bernd Konrad Jazz Group With Symphonie Orchestra
Wen Die Götter Lieben | Creative Works Records | CW CD 1010-1
Schoen,Jeff | (keyboardsvoc)
The Brecker Brothers
Heavy Metal Be-Bop | RCA | 2119257-2
Schoen,Jonas | (flsax)
Andreas Schnerman Sextet
Welcome To My Backyard | Edition Collage | EC 535-2
Schoenberg,Gordon | (oboe)
Ella Fitzgerald With The Frank DeVol Orchestra
Get Happy! | Verve | 523321-2
Ella Fitzgerald With The Nelson Riddle Orchestra
Dream Dancing | Original Jazz Classics | OJCCD 1072-2(2310814)
Schoenecker,Joachim | (gg-solo)
Joachim Schoenecker
In The Moment | Nagel-Heyer | CD 2009
Joachim Schoenecker Quartet
In The Moment | Nagel-Heyer | CD 2009
Joachim Schoenecker-Chris Potter
In The Moment | Nagel-Heyer | CD 2009
Schoenefeld,Christian | (congas,drperc)
Joachim Raffel Sextet
...In Motion | Jazz 4 Ever Records:Jazz Network | J4E 4746
Joachim Raffel Trio
...In Motion | Jazz 4 Ever Records:Jazz Network | J4E 4746
The Groenewald Newnet
Meetings | Jazz 'n' Arts Records | JNA 0702
Schoeppach,Brad | (el-g,g12-string-g)
Paul Motian Electric Bebop Band
Flight Of The Blue Jay | Winter&Winter | 910009-2
Schollmeyer,Harald | (tb)
Marcus Sukiennik Big Band
A Night In Tunisia Suite(7 Variationen über Dizzy Gillespie's 'A Night In Tunisia') | Jazz Haus Musik | ohne Nummer
Scholly,Norbert | (gwaldzither)
Nicolas Simion Group
Balkan Jazz | Intuition Records | INT 3339-2
Norbert Scholly Quartet
Norbert Scholly Quartet | Jazz Haus Musik | JHM 0086 CD
Scholten,Joop | (g)
Toots Thielemans Quintet
The Silver Collection: Toots Thielemans | Polydor | 825086-2 PMS
Scholtes,Gene | (bassoon)
Charles Mingus Orchestra
Cumbia & Jazz Fusion | Atlantic | 8122-71785-2
Scholz,Martin | (p)
Peter Materna Quartet
Full Moon Party | Village | VILCD 1021-2
Schomisch,Markus | (perc)
Jazz Orchester Rheinland-Pfalz
Kazzou | Jazz Haus Musik | LJBB 9104
Like Life | Jazz Haus Musik | LJBB 9405
Schön,Arnold | (tb)
Joe Pass With The NDR Big Band
Joe Pass In Hamburg | ACT | 9100-2
NDR Big Band-Bravissimo | ACT | 9232-2
Joe Pass With The NDR Big Band And Radio Philharmonie Hannover
Joe Pass In Hamburg | ACT | 9100-2
Johnny Griffin With The NDR Big Band
NDR Big Band-Bravissimo | ACT | 9232-2
NDR Big Band
NDR Big Band-Bravissimo | ACT | 9232-2
Schön,Peter | (keyboardsp)
Akili
Maasai Mara | M.A Music | A 802-2
Akili | M.A Music | NU 730-2
Schonbach,Sanford | (viola)
Ella Fitzgerald With The Frank DeVol Orchestra
Get Happy! | Verve | 523321-2
Schönberger,Heinz | (clarr)
Heinz Schönberger Quintet
Deutsches Jazz Fesival 1954/1955 | Bear Family Records | BCD 15430
Kurt Edelhagen All Stars Und Solisten
Deutsches Jazz Fesival 1954/1955 | Bear Family Records | BCD 15430
Schönborn,Olaf | (assax)
Acoustic Affaire
Mira | Jazz 'n' Arts Records | JNA 1303
Changes

Jazz Changes? | Jazz 'n' Arts Records | 0100
Fritz Münzer Tentet
Blue Ideas | Jazz 'n' Arts Records | 0200

Schönburg,Kai | (dr)
Erika Rojo & Tim Sund
Das Lied | Nabel Records:Jazz Network | CD 4684
René Pretschner Quartet
Floating Pictures | Green House Music | CD 1001
René Pretschner Trio
Floating Pictures | Green House Music | CD 1001
Thärichens Tentett
Lady Moon | Minor Music | 801094
Tim Sund Quartet
About Time | Laika Records | LK 93-043

Schoneberg,Gordon | (oboe)
Ella Fitzgerald With The Nelson Riddle Orchestra
Dream Dancing | Original Jazz Classics | OJCCD 1072-2(2310814)

Schoneberg,Seymour | (oboe)
The Best Of The Song Books:The Ballads | Verve | 521867-2
Love Songs:The Best Of The Song Books | Verve | 531762-2
Ella Fitzgerald Sings The Johnny Mercer Songbook | Verve | 539057-2

Schöneich,Michael | (b)
Jürgen Sturm's Ballstars
Tango Subversivo | Nabel Records:Jazz Network | CD 4613
Monika Linges Quartet
Floating | Nabel Records:Jazz Network | CD 4607

Schönenberg,Detlef | (drperc)
Jazzensemble Des Hessischen Rundfunks
Atmosphering Conditions Permitting | ECM | 1549/50

Schönfeld,Peter | (b,b-gfretless-b)
The Atlantic Jazz Trio
Some Other Time | Factory Outlet Records | FOR 2002-1 CD
The Atlantic String Trio
First Meeting | Factory Outlet Records | FOR 2501-1 CD

Schoof,Manfred | (co,flh,fl-h,tptp-solo)
European Jazz Ensemble
European Jazz Ensemble At The Philharmonic Cologne | M.A Music | A 800-2
20th Anniversary Tour | Konnex Records | KCD 5078
European Jazz Ensemble & The Khan Family feat. Joachim Kühn
European Jazz Ensemble Meets The Khan Family | M.A Music | A 807-2
Fritz Münzer Quintet
Jazz für junge Leute:Live im HR 1962 | Jazz 'n' Arts Records | C 01
Gunter Hampel All Stars
Jubilation | Birth | 0038
Gunter Hampel Quintet
Legendary: The 27th Of May 1997 | Birth | CD 045
Jasper Van't Hof
Pili-Pili | Warner | 2292-40458-2
Manfred Schoof/Rainer Brünninghaus
Shadows & Smiles | Wergo | WER 80007-50
Miles Davis With Gil Evans Orchestra, The George Gruntz Concert Jazz Band And Guests
Miles & Quincy Live At Montreux | Warner | 9362-45221-2
Pili-Pili
Jakko | JA & RO | JARO 4131-2
Pili-Pili | JA & RO | JARO 4141-2
Stolen Moments | JA & RO | JARO 4159-2
Hoomba-Hoomba | JA & RO | JARO 4192-2
The German Jazz Masters
Old Friends | ACT | 9278-2

Schöpfer,Klaus | (g)
Bernd Konrad With Erwin Lehn und sein Südfunk Orchester Stuttgart
Wen Die Götter Lieben | Creative Works Records | CW CD 1010-1
SWR Big Band
Jazz In Concert | Hänssler Classics | CD 93.004

Schöpper,Klaus-Peter | (g)
Bill Ramsey With Orchestra
Gettin' Back To Swing | Bear Family Records | BCD 15813 AH

Schorn,Steffen | (alto-fl,b-cl,contra-b-cl,bs,cl)
Kölner Saxophon Mafia
Place For Lovers | Jazz Haus Musik | JHM 0082 CD
Licence To Thrill | Jazz Haus Musik | JHM 0100 CD
Space Player | Jazz Haus Musik | JHM 0132 CD
Kölner Saxophon Mafia With Guests
Kölner Saxophon Mafia: 20 Jahre Saxuelle Befreiung | Jazz Haus Musik | JHM 0115 CD
Los Jovenes Flamencos With The WDR Big Band And Guests
Jazzpana | ACT | 9212-2
Nils Landgren Funk Unit
Paint It Blue:A Tribute To Cannonball Adderley | ACT | 9243-2
Nils Wogram Octet
Odd And Awkward | Enja | ENJ-9416-2
Nils Wogram Sextet
Odd And Awkward | Enja | ENJ-9416-2
Oscar Brown Jr. with The NDR Big Band
Live Every Minute | Minor Music | 801071
Pee Wee Ellis & NDR Bigband
What You Like | Minor Music | 801064

Schott,Simon | (p-solo)
Simon Schott
Bar Piano: Simon Schott Plays Your Favorite Evergreens Vol.1 | Organic Music | ORGM 9733
Bar Piano: Simon Schott Plays Your Favorite Evergreens Vol.2 | Organic Music | ORGM 9735

Schou,Jens | (cl)
Chinese Compass
Chinese Compass | dacapo | DCCD 9443

Schouten,K. | (viola)
Toots Thielemans And His Orchestra
Verve Jazz Masters Vol.59:Toots Thielemans | Verve | 535271-2

Schoyble,Niko | (dr-machine)
Gebhard Ullmann-Andreas Willers
Playful '93 | Nabel Records:Jazz Network | CD 4659

Schrack,Martin | (grand-p,keyboardsp)
Eckhard Weigt Quartet
Standard Moods | Organic Music | ORGM 9718
Martin Schrack Quartet
Headin' Home | Storyville | STCD 4253
Martin Schrack Quintet feat.Tom Harrell
Headin' Home | Storyville | STCD 4253
SWR Big Band
Jazz In Concert | Hänssler Classics | CD 93.004
Uli Gutscher Quintet
Wind Moments | Take Twelve On CD | TT 009-2

Schrama,Cees | (metronome,tambourine,pperc)
The Rosenberg Trio With Frits Landesbergen
Gypsy Swing | Verve | 527806-2
Toots Thielemans-Cees Schrama
Verve Jazz Masters Vol.59:Toots Thielemans | Verve | 535271-2

Schreiber,Freddy | (b)
Anita O'Day With The Cal Tjader Quartet
Verve Jazz Masters 49:Anita O'Day | Verve | 527653-2
Time For 2 | Verve | 559808-2
Cal Tjader Quintet
Talkin Verve/Roots Of Acid Jazz:Cal Tjader | Verve | 531562-2

Schrieber,Fred | (b)
Bola Sete Trio
Tour De Force:The Bola Sete Trios | Fantasy | FCD 24766-2

Schrier,Joop | (p)
Albert Nicholas With The Dutch Swing College Band
Albert Nicholas & The Dutch Swing College Band | Storyville | STCD 5522
Dutch Swing College Band
Albert Nicholas & The Dutch Swing College Band | Storyville | STCD 5522

Schröck,Marie-Christine | (cl,tsreeds)
The United Women's Orchestra
The Blue One | Jazz Haus Musik | JHM 0099 CD
United Women's Orchestra
Virgo Supercluster | Jazz Haus Musik | JHM 0123 CD

Schröder,Eberhard | (b)
Frank Kuruc Band
Limits No Limits | Edition Musikat | EDM 023

Schröder,Else Torp | (voc)
Marilyn Mazur With Ars Nova And The Copenhagen Art Ensemble
Jordsange | dacapo | DCCD 9454

Schröder,John | (dr,gp)
Chet Baker Quintet
My Favourite Songs: The Last Great Concert Vol.1 | Enja | ENJ-5097 2
The Last Concert Vol.I+II | Enja | ENJ-6074 22
Chet Baker Quintet/NDR Big Band/Radio Orchestra Hannover
Straight From The Heart-The Last Concert Vol.2 | Enja | ENJ-6020 2
The Last Concert Vol.I+II | Enja | ENJ-6074 22
Chet Baker With The NDR-Bigband
NDR Big Band-Bravissimo | ACT | 9232-2
My Favourite Songs: The Last Great Concert Vol.1 | Enja | ENJ-5097 2
The Last Concert Vol.I+II | Enja | ENJ-6074 22
Chet Baker-The Legacy Vol.1 | Enja | ENJ-9021 2
Chet Baker With The Radio Orchestra Hannover(NDR)
My Favourite Songs: The Last Great Concert Vol.1 | Enja | ENJ-5097 2
The Last Concert Vol.I+II | Enja | ENJ-6074 22
Clifford Jordan Quintet
Clifford Jordan Meets Klaus Weiss | JHM Records | JHM 3617
Der Rote Bereich
Love Me Tender | ACT | 9286-2
Der Rote Bereich 3 | Jazz 4 Ever Records:Jazz Network | J4E 4740
Erdmann 2000
Recovering From y2k | Jazz 4 Ever Records:Jazz Network | J4E 4750
Jan Von Klewitz Quintet
Bonehenge Suite | Jazz Haus Musik | JHM 0078 CD
Jazzensemble Des Hessischen Rundfunks
Atmosphering Conditions Permitting | ECM | 1549/50
Klaus Weiss Quintet
A Taste Of Jazz | ATM Records | ATM 3810-AH
NDR Big Band
NDR Big Band-Bravissimo | ACT | 9232-2
Rolf Kühn Group
Inside Out | Intuition Records | INT 3276-2

Schroeder,Gene | (p)
Bob Scobey's Frisco Band
Planet Jazz | Planet Jazz | 2169652-2
Bud Freeman And His Summa Cum Laude Orchestra
Planet Jazz:Jack Teagarden | Planet Jazz | 2161236-2
Planet Jazz:Bud Freeman | Planet Jazz | 2161240-2
Eddie Condon And His Boys
The Very Best Of Dixieland Jazz | Verve | 535529-2
Eddie Condon And His Orchestra
Jazz:The Essential Collection Vol.3 | IN+OUT Records | 78013-2
Jack Teagarden's Big Eight
Planet Jazz:Jack Teagarden | Planet Jazz | 2161236-2
Planet Jazz | Planet Jazz | 2169652-2
Miff Mole And His Dixieland Band
Muggsy Spanier-Manhattan Masters,1945 | Storyville | STCD 6051
Muggsy Spanier And His Dixieland Band
Muggsy Spanier-Manhattan Masters,1945 | Storyville | STCD 6051
Pee Wee Russell And His Dixieland Band
Muggsy Spanier-Manhattan Masters,1945 | Storyville | STCD 6051

Schroeder,Marianne | (pp-solo)
John Wolf Brennan-Marianne Schroeder
The Well-Prepared Clavier/Das Wohlpräparierte Klavier | Creative Works Records | CW CD 1032-2

Schroeder,Wiebke | (voice)
Till Brönner Group
Chattin' With Chet | Verve | 157534-2

Schröteler,Daniel 'Danny' | (drperc)
Henning Berg Quartet
Minnola | Jazz Haus Musik | JHM 0127 CD
Rolf Römer-Bill Dobbins Quartet
A Tribute To B.A.C.H. | Edition Collage | EC 520-2

Schröter,Achim | (as)
Jazz Orchester Rheinland-Pfalz
Last Season | Jazz Haus Musik | LJBB 9706

Schrouder,Charles | (voc)
Louis Armstrong With The Hal Mooney Orchestra
Ambassador Louis Armstrong Vol.17:Moments To Remember(1952-1956) | Ambassador | CLA 1917

Schubert,Frank Paul | (ssas)
Frank Paul Schubert Quartet
Der Verkauf Geht Weiter | Jazz Haus Musik | JHM 0114 CD

Schubert,Matthias | (sax,tsoboe)
Andreas Willers Octet
The Ground Music | Enja | ENJ-9368 2
Carl Ludwig Hübsch Trio
Carl Ludwig Hübsch's Longrun Development Of The Universe | Jazz Haus Musik | JHM 0112 CD
Gunter Hampel-Matthias Schubert Duo
Dialog-Live At The Eldena Jazz Festival 1992 | Birth | CD 041
Joachim Ullrich Orchestra
Faces Of The Duke | Jazz Haus Musik | JHM 0045 CD
Klaus König Orchestra
Times Of Devastation/Poco A Poco | Enja | ENJ-6014 22
Hommage A Douglas Adams | Enja | ENJ-6078 2
Time Fragments:Seven Studies In Time And Motion | Enja | ENJ-8076 2
Reviews | Enja | ENJ-9061 2
Klaus König Orchestra & Guests
The Song Of Songs:Oratorio For Two Solo Voices,Choir And Orchestra | Enja | ENJ-7057 2
The Remedy
The Remedy | Jazz Haus Musik | JHM 0069 CD
Uwe Oberg Quartet
Dedicated | Jazz 'n' Arts Records | JNA 1603

Schubert,Peter | (cl)
Old Merrytale Jazz Band
The Very Best Of Dixieland Jazz | Verve | 535529-2

Schuchman,Harry | (as,cl,oboe,saxreeds)
Tommy Dorsey And His Orchestra
Planet Jazz:Frank Sinatra & Tommy Dorsey | Planet Jazz | 2152067-2
Planet Jazz:Tommy Dorsey | Planet Jazz | 2159972-2

Schuh,Michael | (tpfl-h)
Jazz Orchester Rheinland-Pfalz
Kazzou | Jazz Haus Musik | LJBB 9104
Like Life | Jazz Haus Musik | LJBB 9405
Last Season | Jazz Haus Musik | LJBB 9706
Marcus Sukiennik Big Band
A Night In Tunisia Suite(7 Variationen über Dizzy Gillespie's 'A Night In Tunisia') | Jazz Haus Musik | ohne Nummer

Schuller,Ed | (b,tuning-forkvoc)
Ed Schuller & Band
The Eleventh Hour | Tutu Records | 888124-2*
Ed Schuller & Mack Goldbury
Art Of The Duo: Savignyplatz | Tutu Records | 888206-2*
Ed Schuller & The Eleventh Hour Band
Snake Dancing | Tutu Records | 888188-2*
Ed Schuller Group feat. Dewey Redman
The Force | Tutu Records | 888166-2*
Ed Schuller Quartet feat. Dewey Redman
Mu-Point | Tutu Records | 888154-2*
Ernst Bier-Mack Goldsbury Quartet
At Night When You Go To Sleep | Timescrapper | TSCR 9611
Ernst Bier-Mack Goldsbury Quintet
At Night When You Go To Sleep | Timescrapper | TSCR 9611
Gunther Klatt & New York Razzmatazz
Volume One:Fa Mozzo | Tutu Records | 888158-2*
Gunther Schuller With The WDR Radio Orchestra & Rememberance Band
Witchi Tia To, The Music Of Jim Pepper | Tutu Records | 888204-2*
Jim Pepper & Eagle Wing
Remembrance-Live At The International Jazzfestival Münster | Tutu Records | 888152-2*
Jim Pepper Flying Eagle
Live At New Morning,Paris | Tutu Records | 888194-2*
Ku-umba Frank Lacy & The Poker Bigband
Songs From The Musical 'Poker' | Tutu Records | 888150-2*
Mack Goldsbury And The New York Connection
Songs I Love To Play | Timescrapper | TSCR 9615
Mal Waldron Quartet
Mal,Verve,Black & Blue | Tutu Records | 888170-2*
Mal Waldron Quartet feat. Jim Pepper
The Git-Go At Utopia,Volume Two | Tutu Records | 888148-2*
Mal Waldron Quartet feat.Jim Pepper
Mal, Dance And Soul | Tutu Records | 888102-2*
Quadrologue At Utopia Vol.1 | Tutu Records | 888118-2*
Mal Waldron Trio
Mal, Dance And Soul | Tutu Records | 888102-2*
Marty Cook Conspiracy
Phases Of The Moon | Tutu Records | 888160-2*
Marty Cook Group feat. Jim Pepper
Internationales Jazzfestival Münster | Tutu Records | 888110-2*
Red,White,Black & Blue | Tutu Records | 888174-2*
Marty Cook Group feat. Monty Waters
Borderlines | Tutu Records | 888122-2*
Marty Cook Quintet
Marty Cook Trio/Quintet | Tutu Records | 888210-2*
Nicolas Simion Quartet
Oriental Gates:Live In Vienna | Tutu Records | 888212-2*
Nicolas Simion Quartet feat. Tomasz Stanko
Dinner For Don Carlos | Tutu Records | 888146-2*
Transylvanian Dance | Tutu Records | 888164-2*
Viaggio Imaginario | Tutu Records | 888192-2*
Nicolas Simion Trio
Oriental Gates:Live In Vienna | Tutu Records | 888212-2*
Paul Motian Band
Psalm | ECM | 1222
Perry Robinson Quartet
Perry Robinson Quartet | Timescrapper | TSCR 9613
Simon Nabatov, String Gang & Percussion
Inside Lookin' Out | Tutu Records | 888104-2*
Simon Nabatov-Ed Schuller
Inside Lookin' Out | Tutu Records | 888104-2*
Uli Lenz Trio
Echoes Of Mandela | Tutu Records | 888180-2*
Unit X
Rated X | Timescrapper | TSCR 9618

Schuller,George | (drperc)
Andrew Rathbun Group
Jade | Fresh Sound Records | FSNT 076 CD
Gunther Schuller With The WDR Radio Orchestra & Rememberance Band
Witchi Tia To, The Music Of Jim Pepper | Tutu Records | 888204-2*
Tom Beckham Quartet
Suspicions | Fresh Sound Records | FSNT 075 CD

Schuller,Gunther | (cond,arrfr-h)
Charles Mingus Orchestra
Charles Mingus:Pre-Bird(Mingus Revisited) | Verve | 538636-2
Dizzy Gillespie And His Orchestra
Verve Jazz Masters 10:Dizzy Gillespie | Verve | 516319-2
Gillespiana And Carnegie Hall Concert | Verve | 519809-2
Talking Verve:Dizzy Gillespie | Verve | 533846-2
Ultimate Dizzy Gillespie | Verve | 557535-2
Gunther Schuller Ensemble
Beauty Is A Rare Thing:Ornette Coleman-The Complete Atlantic Recordings | Atlantic | 8122-71410-2
Gunther Schuller With The WDR Radio Orchestra & Rememberance Band
Witchi Tia To, The Music Of Jim Pepper | Tutu Records | 888204-2*
Miles Davis And His Orchestra
The Complete Birth Of The Cool | Capitol | 494550-2
Birth Of The Cool | Capitol | 530117-2
Jazz Profile:Miles Davis | Blue Note | 823515-2
Ballads & Blues | Blue Note | 836633-2
Miles Davis:Milestones | Dreyfus Jazz Line | FDM 36731-2
Miles Davis With Gil Evans & His Orchestra
This Is Jazz:Miles Davis Plays Ballads | CBS | CK 65038
Porgy And Bess | CBS | CK 65141
Modern Jazz Quartet & Guests
MJQ 40 | Atlantic | 7567-82330-2
Modern Jazz Quartet And Symphony Orchestra
MJQ 40 | Atlantic | 7567-82330-2
The Modern Jazz Society
A Concert Of Contemporary Music | Verve | 559827-2

Schuller,Hansi | (b)
Frieder Berlin Trio
Soul Fingers | Satin Doll Productions | SDP 1039-1 CD

Schulman,Allan | (cello)
Louis Armstrong And His Friends
Planet Jazz:Louis Armstrong | Planet Jazz | 2152052-2
Planet Jazz Sampler | Planet Jazz | 2152326-2
Louis Armstrong And His Friends | Bluebird | 2663961-2

Schulman,Harry | (oboe)
Charles Mingus Orchestra
Charles Mingus:Pre-Bird(Mingus Revisited) | Verve | 538636-2

Schulmann,Bill | (cello)
Ben Pollack And His Park Central Orchestra
Planet Jazz:Jack Teagarden | Planet Jazz | 2161236-2
Jazz:The Essential Collection Vol.3 | IN+OUT Records | 78013-2

Schulte,Frank | (comp,electronics,records,sampling)
Dirk Raulf Group
Die Welt Ist Immer Wieder Schön | Poise | Poise 03
Theater I (Bühnenmusik) | Poise | Poise 07
Dirk Raulf-Frank Shulte
Theater III(Bühnenmusik) | Poise | Poise 11
Sotto In Su
Südamerika Sept. 90 | Jazz Haus Musik | JHM 0051 CD
Vanitas | Poise | Poise 04

Schultz,Ekkart | (prep-tapessampling)
Toto Blanke Group
Fools Paradise | ALISO Records | AL 1019

Schultz,Nicolai | (reeds)
Jens Winther And The Danish Radio Jazz Orchestra
Angels | dacapo | DCCD 9442
The Danish Radio Jazz Orchestra
Nice Work | dacapo | DCCD 9446

Schultze,Heinz | (g)
Heinz Sauer Quartet With The NDR Big Band
NDR Big Band-Bravissimo | ACT | 9232-2

Schultze,Kristian | (el-p,mellotron,org,keyboards,synth)
Klaus Doldinger's Passport
Atlantic Jazz: Fusion | Atlantic | 7567-81711-2
Passport
Looking Thru | Atlantic | 2292-44144-2
Cross-Collateral | Atlantic | 2292-44145-2
Infinity Machine | Atlantic | 2292-44146-2
Iguacu | Atlantic | 2292-46031-2
Passport And Guests
Doldinger Jubilee Concert | Atlantic | 2292-44175-2

Schultze,Werner | (b)
Caterina Valente With The Silvio Francesco Quartet
Deutsches Jazz Fesival 1954/1955 | Bear Family Records | BCD 15430
Kurt Edelhagen All Stars
Deutsches Jazz Fesival 1954/1955 | Bear Family Records | BCD 15430
Kurt Edelhagen All Stars Und Solisten
Deutsches Jazz Fesival 1954/1955 | Bear Family Records | BCD 15430
Quartet Der Kurt Edelhagen All Stars

Deutsches Jazz Fesival 1954/1955 | Bear Family Records | BCD 15430
Silvio Francesco Quartet
Deutsches Jazz Fesival 1954/1955 | Bear Family Records | BCD 15430

Schulz,Helmuth | (b)
Christian Elsässer Trio
Future Days | Organic Music | ORGM 9721

Schulz,Mini | (b)
Peter Lehel Quartet
Heavy Rotation | Satin Doll Productions | SDP 1024-1 CD

Schulze,Fritz | (p)
Brocksi-Quartett
Globetrotter | Bear Family Records | BCD 15912 AH

Schulze,Kristian | (org)
Passport And Guests
Doldinger's Best | ACT | 9224-2

Schulze,Nicolas | (accordeon)
Jo Ambros Group
Wanderlust | dml-records | CD 016

Schumacher,Dave | (b-clbs)
Tom Harrell Orchestra
Time's Mirror | RCA | 2663524-2

Schumacher,Dieter | (bongos,b-dr,bells,glasses,triangle)
Dieter Fischer Trio
Jazz Guitar Highlights 1 | Jardis Records | JRCD 20141
Trio Music | Jardis Records | JRCD 9925
Peter Lehel Quartet
Heavy Rotation | Satin Doll Productions | SDP 1024-1 CD

Schumacher,Nils | (voc)
Kölner Saxophon Mafia With Bad Little Dynamos
Kölner Saxophon Mafia Proudly Presents | Jazz Haus Musik | JHM 0046 CD

Schuman,Mark | (cello)
A Band Of Friends
Wynton Marsalis Quartet With Strings | CBS | CK 68921

Schuman,Tom | (el-p,synth,prepared-p,keyboardsp)
Spyro Gyra & Guests
Love & Other Obsessions | GRP | GRP 98112

Schumann,Andreas | (v)
Till Brönner Quartet & Deutsches Symphonieorchester Berlin
German Songs | Minor Music | 801057

Schumann,Coco | (g)
Helmut Zacharias Quintet
Ich Habe Rhythmus | Bear Family Records | BCD 15642 AH

Schünemann,Uli | (tpfl-h)
Jazz Orchester Rheinland-Pfalz
Kazzou | Jazz Haus Musik | LJBB 9104

Schutt,Arthur | (harmonium,pceleste)
Red And Miff's Stompers
Planet Jazz:Jazz Trumpet | Planet Jazz | 2169654-2
Roger Wolfe Kahn And His Orchestra
Planet Jazz:Jack Teagarden | Planet Jazz | 2161236-2

Schüttrumpf,Gerd | (bj)
Two Beat Stompers
Deutsches Jazz Fesival 1954/1955 | Bear Family Records | BCD 15430

Schutz,Buddy | (dr)
Benny Goodman And His Orchestra
Camel Caravan Broadcast 1939 Vol.1 | Phontastic | NCD 8817
Camel Caravan Broadcast 1939 Vol.2 | Phontastic | NCD 8818
Camel Caravan Broadcast 1939 Vol.3 | Phontastic | NCD 8819
Benny Goodman Quartet
Camel Caravan Broadcast 1939 Vol.1 | Phontastic | NCD 8817
Camel Caravan Broadcast 1939 Vol.2 | Phontastic | NCD 8818
Camel Caravan Broadcast 1939 Vol.3 | Phontastic | NCD 8819

Schütz,Martin | (cello,b,el-5-string-cello)
Hans Koch/Martin Schütz/Marco Käppeli
Accélération | ECM | 1357
Koch-Schütz-Studer & El Nil Troop
Heavy Cairo Trafic | Intuition Records | INT 3175-2
Michel Wintsch & Road Movie
Michel Wintsch & Road Movie featuring Gerry Hemingway | Between The Lines | btl 002(Efa 10172-2)

Schuur,Diane | (el-p,voc,keyboardsp)
Diane Schuur
Music Is My Life | Atlantic | 7567-83150-2
Diane Schuur And Her Band
Music Is My Life | Atlantic | 7567-83150-2
The Best Of Diane Schuur | GRP | GRP 98882
Diane Schuur Quintet With B.B.King
The Best Of Diane Schuur | GRP | GRP 98882
Diane Schuur Trio
In Tribute | GRP | GRP 20062
Diane Schuur Trio With Orchestra And Strings
In Tribute | GRP | GRP 20062
Diane Schuur With Orchestra
In Tribute | GRP | GRP 20062
Love Songs | GRP | GRP 97032
Blues For Schuur | GRP | GRP 98632
The Best Of Diane Schuur | GRP | GRP 98882
Diane Schuur With Orchestra And Strings
The Best Of Diane Schuur | GRP | GRP 98882
Diane Schuur With The Count Basie Orchestra
The Best Of Diane Schuur | GRP | GRP 98882
Diane Schuur With The Dave Grusin Orchestra
The Best Of Diane Schuur | GRP | GRP 98882

Schwab,Guido | (bel-b)
Jazz Orchester Rheinland-Pfalz
Like Life | Jazz Haus Musik | LJBB 9405
Last Season | Jazz Haus Musik | LJBB 9706

Schwab,Sigi | (g,el-g,el-b,g-synth,12-string-g)
Art Van Damme Group
State Of Art | MPS | 841413-2
Paul Nero Sound
Doldinger's Best | ACT | 9224-2
Singers Unlimited With The Art Van Damme Quintet
The Singers Unlimited:Magic Voices | MPS | 539130-2

Schwaiger,Herman | (b)
Vince Jones Group
Spell | Intuition Records | INT 3067-2

Schwalke,Dagmar | (v)
Till Brönner Quartet & Deutsches Symphonieorchester Berlin
German Songs | Minor Music | 801057

Schwaller,Roman | (cl,tssax)
Dusko Goykovich-Joe Haider Quintet
Jazz Portraits | EGO | 95080
Grooveyard Meets Roman Schwaller
Basic Instinct | Organic Music | ORGM 9701
Heinz Sauer Quartet With The NDR Big Band
NDR Big Band-Bravissimo | ACT | 9232-2
Helmut Kagerer 4 & Roman Schwaller
Jazz Guitar Highlights 1 | Jardis Records | JRCD 20141
Gamblin' | Jardis Records | JRCD 9714
Joe Haider Quintet
Magic Box | JHM Records | JHM 3601
Joe Pass With The NDR Big Band
NDR Big Band-Bravissimo | ACT | 9232-2
Joe Pass With The NDR Big Band And Radio Philharmonie Hannover
Joe Pass In Hamburg | ACT | 9100-2
Johnny Griffin With The NDR Big Band
NDR Big Band-Bravissimo | ACT | 9232-2
Johnny Griffin-Sal Nistico-Roman Schwaller Sextet
Three Generations Of Tenorsaxophone | JHM Records | JHM 3611
Klaus Ignatzek Group
Live At Leverkusener Jazztage | Nabel Records:Jazz Network | CD 4630
Munich Saxophon Family
Balanced | Edition Collage | EC 487-2
Survival Song | JHM Records | JHM 3613
Roman Schwaller Jazz Quartet
Some Changes In Life | JHM Records | JHM 3612
Roman Schwaller Nonet
The Original Tunes | JHM Records | JHM 3629
The New Roman Schwaller Jazzquartet
Welcome Back From Outer Space | JHM Records | JHM 3605
We Three With Roman Schwaller
East Coasting | Organic Music | ORGM 9702
Wolfgang Haffner International Jazz Quintet
Whatever It Is | Jazz 4 Ever Records:Jazz Network | J4E 4714

Schwamm,Klaus | (v)
HR Big Band With Marjorie Barnes And Frits Landesbergen And Strings
Swinging Christmas | hr music.de | hrmj 012-02 CD

Schwanitz,Bernie | (tp)
Marcus Sukiennik Big Band
A Night In Tunisia Suite(7 Variationen über Dizzy Gillespie's 'A Night In Tunisia') | Jazz Haus Musik | ohne Nummer

Schwartz,Brian | (tpfl-h)
Buddy Childers Big Band
It's What Happening Now! | Candid | CCD 79749

Schwartz,Christine | (viola)
Bernd Konrad Jazz Group With Symphonie Orchestra
Wen Die Götter Lieben | Creative Works Records | CW CD 1010-1

Schwartz,Curtis | (voc)
Stacy Kent With The Jim Tomlinson Quintet
The Boy Next Door | Candid | CCD 79797

Schwartz,Daniel | (el-b)
Jon Hassell & Farafina
Flash Of The Spirit | Intuition Records | INT 3009-2

Schwartz,David | (vviola)
Bill Evans Quartet With Orchestra
The Complete Bill Evans On Verve | Verve | 527953-2
From Left To Right | Verve | 557451-2
Bill Evans With Orchestra
The Complete Bill Evans On Verve | Verve | 527953-2
From Left To Right | Verve | 557451-2
Cannonball Adderley And His Orchestra
Verve Jazz Masters 31:Cannonball Adderley | Verve | 522651-2
Louis Armstrong And His Friends
Planet Jazz:Louis Armstrong | Planet Jazz | 2152052-2
Planet Jazz Sampler | Planet Jazz | 2152326-2
Louis Armstrong And His Friends | Bluebird | 2663961-2
Milt Jackson With Strings
To Bags...With Love:Memorial Album | Pablo | 2310967-2
Wes Montgomery With The Don Sebesky Orchestra
Verve Jazz Masters 14:Wes Montgomery | Verve | 519826-2
Talkin' Jazz:Roots Of Acid Jazz | Verve | 529580-2
Bumpin' | Verve | 539062-2

Schwartz,George | (tp)
Artie Shaw And His Orchestra
Planet Jazz:Jazz Trumpet | Planet Jazz | 2169654-2

Schwartz,Jack | (bsts)
Gene Krupa And His Orchestra
Mullenium | CBS | CK 65678
Terry Gibbs Dream Band
Terry Gibbs Dream Band Vol.2:The Sundown Sessions | Contemporary | CCD 7652-2
Terry Gibbs Dream Band Vol.3:Flying Home | Contemporary | CCD 7654-2
Terry Gibbs Dream Band Vol.6:One More Time | Contemporary | CCD 7658-2
The Jazz Giants Play Jerome Kern:Yesterdays | Prestige | PCD 24202-2

Schwartz,Jerry | (p)
The Jimmy And Marion McPartland Sessions
Vic Lewis:The Golden Years | Candid | CCD 79754

Schwartz,Julie | (as)
Peggy Lee With The Benny Goodman Orchestra
Peggy Lee & Benny Goodman:The Complete Recordings 1941-1947 | CBS | C2K 65686

Schwartz,Thornel | (g)
Babs Gonzales With The Jimmy Smith Trio
Blue Velvet: Crooners, Swooners And Velvet Vocals | Blue Note | 521153-2
Jimmy Forrest Quartet
Forest Fire | Original Jazz Classics | OJCCD 199-2
Jimmy McGriff Orchestra
Swingin' The Blues-Jumpin' The Blues | Laserlight | 24654
Jimmy McGriff Organ Blues Band
The Worm | Blue Note | 538699-2
Jimmy Smith Quartet
Jimmy Smith-Talkin' Verve | Verve | 531563-2
Jimmy Smith Trio
A New Sound A New Star:Jimmy Smith At The Organ | Blue Note | 857191-2
Johnny 'Hammond' Smith Sextet
The Soulful Blues | Prestige | PCD 24244-2

Schwartz,Wilbur | (as,bs,cl,sax,fl,e-flat-cl,piccolo)
Anita O'Day With The Billy May Orchestra
Verve Jazz Masters 49:Anita O'Day | Verve | 527653-2
Billy Eckstine With The Billy May Orchestra
Once More With Feeling | Roulette | 581862-2
Ella Fitzgerald With Orchestra
The Best Is Yet To Come | Original Jazz Classics | OJCCD 889-2(2312138)
Ella Fitzgerald With The Billy May Orchestra
Ella Fitzgerald Sings The Harold Arlen Song Book | Verve | 589108-2
Ella Fitzgerald With The Buddy Bregman Orchestra
The Best Of The Song Books:The Ballads | Verve | 521867-2
Ella Fitzgerald With The Nelson Riddle Orchestra
The Best Of The Song Books:The Ballads | Verve | 521867-2
Love Songs:The Best Of The Song Books | Verve | 531762-2
Ella Fitzgerald Sings The Johnny Mercer Songbook | Verve | 539057-2
Dream Dancing | Original Jazz Classics | OJCCD 1072-2(2310814)
Glenn Miller And His Orchestra
Planet Jazz:Glenn Miller | Planet Jazz | 2152056-2
Planet Jazz Sampler | Planet Jazz | 2152326-2
Planet Jazz:Jazz Greatest Hits | Planet Jazz | 2169648-2
Planet Jazz:Big Bands | Planet Jazz | 2169649-2
Planet Jazz:Swing | Planet Jazz | 2169651-2
The Chesterfield Broadcasts Vol.1 | RCA | 2663113-2
Candelight Miller | RCA | 2668716-2
Swing Legends | Nimbus Records | NI 2001
June Christy With The Pete Rugolo Orchestra
Something Cool(The Complete Mono & Stereo Versions) | Capitol | 534069-2
The Andrew Sisters With The Glenn Miller Orchestra
The Chesterfield Broadcasts Vol.1 | RCA | 2663113-2

Schwartz,Willie | (as,clfl)
Ella Fitzgerald With The Buddy Bregman Orchestra
Ella Fitzgerald Sings The Rodgers And Hart Song Book | Verve | 537258-2
Nat King Cole With The Billy May Orchestra
Nat King Cole:For Sentimental Reasons | Dreyfus Jazz Line | FDM 36740-2

Schwartz-Bart,Jacques | (ts)
James Hurt Group
Dark Grooves-Mystcal Rhythms | Blue Note | 495104-2

Schwartzberg,Alan | (dr)
Dee Dee Bridgewater With Band
Dee Dee Bridgewater | Atlantic | 7567-80760-2
The Brecker Brothers
Heavy Metal Be-Bop | RCA | 2119257-2

Schwarz,Paul | (clavinet,el-p,org,p,keyboards,perc)
Bernd Konrad Jazz Group With Symphonie Orchestra
Wen Die Götter Lieben | Creative Works Records | CW CD 1010-1
Herbert Joos Trio
Ballade Noire | free flow music | ffm 0392
Schwarz-Hübner Duo
Elegie | dml-records | CD 012

Schwarz,Richard | (marimba)
Don Byron Quintet
Tuskegee Experiments | Nonesuch | 7559-79280-2

Schwarz,Terry | (v)
Bernd Konrad Jazz Group With Symphonie Orchestra
Wen Die Götter Lieben | Creative Works Records | CW CD 1010-1

Schwarz,Thomas | (oboe)
Herbert Joos With Strings
Daybreak/The Dark Side Of Twilight | Japo | 60015

Schwarz,Ulrich C. | (cl,ssfl)
Jan Jankeje Septet
A' Portrait Of Jan Jankeje | Jazzpoint | JP 1054 CD

Schwarz-Bart,Jacques | (ts)
Jacques Schwarz-Bart/James Hurt Quartet
Immersion | Fresh Sound Records | FSNT 057 CD

Schwatlo,Peter | (tb)
Conexion Latina
Mambo Nights | Enja | ENJ-9402 2
Wayne Bartlett With The Thomas Hufschmidt Group
Tokyo Blues | Laika Records | 35101212

Schweitzer,Christoph | (tb)
Oscar Brown Jr. with The NDR Big Band
Live Every Minute | Minor Music | 801071

Schweizer,Christoph | (tbb-tb)
Abdullah Ibrahim With The NDR Big Band
Ekapa Lodumo | TipToe | TIP-888840 2

Schweizer,Mike | (ss,tssopranino)
Matthias Stich Sevensenses
...mehrschichtig | Satin Doll Productions | SDP 1038-1 CD
Peter Kleindienst Group
Zeitwärts:Reime Vor Pisin | double moon | DMCD 1001-2

Schweizer,Ralph | (cl,b-clld)
Ralph Schweizer Big Band
DAY Dream | Chaos | CACD 8177

Schwer,Harald | (p)
Stuttgarter Dixieland All Stars
It's The Talk Of The Town | Jazzpoint | JP 1069 CD

Schwickerath,Dany | (g)
Lee Konitz With The Oliver Strauch Group & Peter Decker
Lee Konitz With Oliver Strauch Group & Peter Decker | Edition Collage | EC 497-2

Schwidewski,Uwe | (bel-b)
NuNu!
Ocean | TipToe | TIP-888837 2

Schwingenschlögl,Paul | (tpfl-h)
Takabanda
La Leggenda Del Pescatore | Jazz 4 Ever Records:Jazz Network | J4E 4752

Sciommeri,Armando | (dr)
Nicola Puglielli Group
In The Middle | Jardis Records | JRCD 9924

Sciubba,Sabina | (voc)
Maximilian Geller Group
Maximilian Geller Goes Bossa | Edition Collage | EC 496-2
Maximilian Geller Quartet feat. Sabina Sciubba
Maimilian Geller Goes Bossa Encore | Edition Collage | EC 505-2
Sabina Sciubba-Paulo Cardoso
VoceBasso | Organic Music | ORGM 9703

Sciubbia,Sabina | (voc)
Sabina Sciubbia
VoceBasso | Organic Music | ORGM 9703

Sclavis,Louis | (b-cl,ss,cl,bssax)
Double Trio(Trio De Clarinettes&Arcado)
Green Dolphy Suite | Enja | ENJ-9011 2
Klaus König Orchestra
Hommage A Douglas Adams | Enja | ENJ-6078 2
Louis Sclavis & The Bernard Struber Jazztet
La Phare | Enja | ENJ-9359 2
Louis Sclavis Group
Dans La Nuit | ECM | 1805(589524-2)
Napoli's Walls | ECM | 1857(038504-2)
Louis Sclavis Quartet
Acoustic Quartet | ECM | 1526
L'Affrontement Des Prétendants | ECM | 1705(159927-2)
Louis Sclavis Quintet
Rouge | ECM | 1458
Louis Sclavis Sextet
Les Violences De Rameau | ECM | 1588(533128-2)
Louis Sclavis With The WRO Orchestra, Köln
Le Concerto Improvisé | Enja | ENJ-9397 2

Scobey,Bob | (cotp)
Bob Scobey's Frisco Band
Planet Jazz | Planet Jazz | 2169652-2
Yerba Buena Jazz Band
Bunk & Lu | Good Time Jazz | GTCD 12024-2

Scofield,John | (el-g,perc,g,el-b,el-sitar,steel-g)
Albert Mangelsdorff-John Scofield
Internationales Jazzfestival Münster | Tutu Records | 888110-2*
Billy Cobham Group
The Best Of Billy Cobham | Atlantic | 7567-81558-2
Charles Mingus Orchestra
Three Or Four Shades Of Blues | Atlantic | 7567-81403-2
Chet Baker-Gerry Mulligan Group
Carnegie Hall Concert Vol. 1/2 | CTI | EPC 450554-2
Chris Potter Group
Traveling Mercies | Verve | 018243-2
George Gruntz Concert Jazz Band
Blues 'N Dues Et Cetera | Enja | ENJ-6072 2
Herbie Hancock Group
Herbie Hancock The New Standards | Verve | 527715-2
Herbie Hancock Group With String Quartet
Herbie Hancock The New Standards | Verve | 527715-2
Herbie Hancock Group With String Quartet,Woodwinds And Brass
Herbie Hancock The New Standards | Verve | 527715-2
Herbie Hancock Group With Woodwinds And Brass
Herbie Hancock The New Standards | Verve | 527715-2
Jay McShann And His Orchestra
Atlantic Jazz: Kansas City | Atlantic | 7567-81701-2
Jay McShann Orchestra
The Last Of The Blue Devils | Atlantic | 7567-80791-2
Joe Henderson Group
Porgy And Bess | Verve | 539048-2
John Patitucci Group
Sketchbook | GRP | GRP 96172
John Scofield Groups
Quiet | Verve | 533185-2
Groove Elation | Blue Note | 832801-2
John Scofield Quartet
A Go Go | Verve | 539979-2
What We Do | Blue Note | 799586-2
John Scofield Quintet
Works For Me | Verve | 549281-2
John Scofield Sextet
Hand Jive | Blue Note | 827327-2
John Scofield Trio
En Route | Verve | 9861357
John Scofield-Pat Metheny Quartet
I Can See Your House From Here | Blue Note | 827765-2
Lenny White Group
Present Tense | Hip Bop | HIBD 8004
Marc Johnson Quartet
Bass Desires | ECM | 1299(827743-2)
Marc Johnson's Bass Desires
Second Sight | ECM | 1351(833038-2)
Mike Stern Group
Play | Atlantic | 7567-83219-2
Miles Davis Group
Decoy | CBS | 468702-2
This Is Jazz:Miles Davis Plays Ballads | CBS | CK 65038

Miles Davis-Marcus Miller Group
Siesta(Soundtrack) | Warner | 7599-25655-2
Niels-Henning Orsted-Pedersen Quartet
Dancing On The Tables | Steeplechase | SCS 1125(Audiophile Pressing)
Ray Anderson Quintet
Blues Bred In The Bone | Enja | ENJ-5081 2
Scolohofo
Oh! | Blue Note | 542081-2
Steve Swallow Group
Swallow | Watt | XtraWatt/6
Teodross Avery Quartet
My Generation | Impulse(MCA) | 951181-2

Scott,Aaron | (dr)
McCoy Tyner Big Band
The Best Of McCoy Tyner Big Band | Dreyfus Jazz Line | FDM 37012-2
McCoy Tyner Quartet
The Story Of Jazz Piano | Laserlight | 24653
McCoy Tyner Trio
Remembering John | Enja | ENJ-6080 2

Scott,Bessye Ruth | (voc)
McCoy Tyner Group With Horns And Voices
Inner Voices | Original Jazz Classics | OJCCD 1039-2(M 9079)
McCoy Tyner Group With Voices
Inner Voices | Original Jazz Classics | OJCCD 1039-2(M 9079)

Scott,Bobby | (p,arr,vocvib)
Chet Baker With Bobby Scott
Baby Breeze | Verve | 538328-2
Chet Baker With Bobby Scott And Kenny Burrell
Baby Breeze | Verve | 538328-2
Quincy Jones And His Orchestra
Talkin' Verve-Roots Of Acid Jazz:Roland Kirk | Verve | 533101-2
Verve Jazz Masters Vol.59:Toots Thielemans | Verve | 535271-2
Rahsaan/The Complete Mercury Recordings Of Roland Kirk | Mercury | 846630-2
The Quintessence | Impulse(MCA) | 951222-2
Quincy Jones Big Band
Rahsaan/The Complete Mercury Recordings Of Roland Kirk | Mercury | 846630-2
Wes Montgomery Orchestra
Movin' Wes | Verve | 521433-2
Wes Montgomery With The Johnny Pate Orchestra
Verve Jazz Masters 14:Wes Montgomery | Verve | 519826-2
Wes Montgomery:The Verve Jazz Sides | Verve | 521690-2
Talkin' Jazz:Roots Of Acid Jazz | Verve | 529580-2

Scott,Buck | (tb)
Wingy Mannone And His Orchestra
Planet Jazz:Male Jazz Vocalists | Planet Jazz | 2169657-2

Scott,Bud | (bj,vocg)
Jelly Roll Morton's Red Hot Peppers
Planet Jazz:Jelly Roll Morton | Planet Jazz | 2152060-2
Jazz:The Essential Collection Vol.1 | IN+OUT Records | 78011-2
King Oliver And His Dixie Syncopators
Jazz:The Essential Collection Vol.1 | IN+OUT Records | 78011-2
King Oliver's Creole Jazz Band
Jazz:The Essential Collection Vol.1 | IN+OUT Records | 78011-2
King Oliver's Jazz Band
Jazz:The Essential Collection Vol.1 | IN+OUT Records | 78011-2
Louis Armstrong And His Dixieland Seven
Planet Jazz:Louis Armstrong | Planet Jazz | 2152052-2
Planet Jazz:Jazz Greatest Hits | Planet Jazz | 2169648-2
Planet Jazz:Jazz Trumpet | Planet Jazz | 2169654-2
Planet Jazz:Male Jazz Vocalists | Planet Jazz | 2169657-2
Best Of The Complete RCA Victor Recordings | RCA | 2663636-2
Louis Armstrong:A 100th Birthday Celebration | RCA | 2663694-2
Louis Armstrong:C'est Si Bon | Dreyfus Jazz Line | FDM 36730-2
Swing Legends:Louis Armstrong | Nimbus Records | NI 2012

Scott,Calo | (cellov)
Ahmed Abdullah Sextet
Jazz Sounds Of Africa | Prestige | PRCD 24279-2
Ahmed Abdul-Malik Orchestra
Jazz Sounds Of Africa | Prestige | PRCD 24279-2
Gerry Mulligan Sextet
The Gerry Mulligan Songbook | Pacific Jazz | 833575-2

Scott,Carl | (voc)
McCoy Tyner Group With Horns And Voices
Inner Voices | Original Jazz Classics | OJCCD 1039-2(M 9079)
McCoy Tyner Group With Voices
Inner Voices | Original Jazz Classics | OJCCD 1039-2(M 9079)

Scott,Cecil | (bs,cl,tsbass-sax)
Lucille Hegamin With Willie The Lion And His Cubs
Songs We Taught Your Mother | Original Blues Classics | OBCCD 520-2

Scott,Christian | (tpfl-h)
Donald Harrison Sextet
Kind Of New | Candid | CCD 79768

Scott,Clifford | (as,ts,flsax)
Lionel Hampton And His Orchestra
Lionel Hampton's Paris All Stars | Vogue | 21511502
Richard 'Groove' Holmes Quintet
Somethin' Special | Pacific Jazz | 855452-2
Wild Bill Davis Quartet
Live At Swiss Radio Studio Zürich | Jazz Connaisseur | JCCD 8701-2

Scott,Duck | (dr)
We Three
East Coasting | Organic Music | ORGM 9702
The Drivin' Beat | Organic Music | ORGM 9707
We Three With Roman Schwaller
East Coasting | Organic Music | ORGM 9702

Scott,George | (cl,as,perc,tpvoc)
Charles Mingus Orchestra
Charles Mingus:Pre-Bird(Mingus Revisited) | Verve | 538636-2

Scott,Gracie | (voc)
The Jimmy And Marion McPartland Sessions
Vic Lewis:The Golden Years | Candid | CCD 79754

Scott,Hazel | (p)
Hazel Scott Trio
Charles Mingus-The Complete Debut Recordings | Debut | 12 DCD 4402-2

Scott,Howard | (co,tbtp)
Fletcher Henderson And His Orchestra
Jazz:The Essential Collection Vol.1 | IN+OUT Records | 78011-2

Scott,Howard or Bill Dillard | (tp)
Spike Hughes And His Negro Orchestra
Jazz:The Essential Collection Vol.3 | IN+OUT Records | 78013-2

Scott,Janie Bob | (voc)
Klaus König Orchestra
Reviews | Enja | ENJ-9061 2

Scott,Jeff | (fr-h)
Freddy Cole With Band
To The End Of The Earth | Fantasy | FCD 9675-2

Scott,Jimmy[Little] | (voc)
Little Jimmy Scott | Specialty | SPCD 2170-2
(Little)Jimmy Scott And His Band
Mood Indigo | Milestone | MCD 9305-2
(Little)Jimmy Scott And His Quintet
All The Way | Warner | 7599-26955-2
(Little)Jimmy Scott With Orchestra
Everybody's Somebody's Fool | Decca | 050669-2
(Little)Jimmy Scott With The Billy Taylor Orchestra
Everybody's Somebody's Fool | Decca | 050669-2
(Little)Jimmy Scott With The Lionel Hampton Orchestra
Everybody's Somebody's Fool | Decca | 050669-2
(Little)Jimmy Scott With The Lucky Thompson Orchestra
Everybody's Somebody's Fool | Decca | 050669-2
Jimmy Scott
But Beautiful | Milestone | MCD 9321-2
Jimmy Scott With Band
Over The Rainbow | Milestone | MCD 9314-2
But Beautiful | Milestone | MCD 9321-2
Moon Glow | Milestone | MCD 9332-2

Scott,Johnny | (fl,cl,as,saxts)
NDR-Workshop
Doldinger's Best | ACT | 9224-2

Scott,Kendrick | (dr)
Kalifactors
An Introduction To Kalifactors | Fresh Sound Records | FSNT 143 CD

Scott,Kermit | (ts)
Charlie Christian All Stars
Charlie Christian-Jazz Immortal/Dizzy Gillespie 1944 | Original Jazz Classics | OJCCD 1932-2(ES 548)
Minton's Playhouse All Stars
Charlie Christian:Swing To Bop | Dreyfus Jazz Line | FDM 36715-2

Scott,Marilyn | (background-vocvoc)
Yellowjackets
Live Wires | GRP | GRP 96672

Scott,Mike | (dr)
Chas Burchell Quintet
Unsong Hero:The Undiscovered Genius Of Chas Burchell | IN+OUT Records | 7026-2

Scott,Morris | (fr-h)
Dizzy Gillespie And His Orchestra
Gillespiana And Carnegie Hall Concert | Verve | 519809-2
Talking Verve:Dizzy Gillespie | Verve | 533846-2

Scott,Rhoda | (orgvoc)
Christian Rover Group feat. Rhoda Scott
Christian Rover Group-Live With Rhoda Scott At The Organ | Organic Music | ORGM 9704
Rhoda Scott Trio
Jazz In Paris:Rhoda Scott-Live At The Olympia | EmArCy | 549879-2 PMS
Rhoda Scott-Kenny Clarke
Jazz In Paris:Rhoda Scott + Kenny Clarke | EmArCy | 549287-2 PMS

Scott,Robert | (drtb)
Count Basie And His Orchestra
Jazz:The Essential Collection Vol.3 | IN+OUT Records | 78013-2

Scott,Ronnie | (bs,reeds,ssts)
Kenny Clarke-Francy Boland Big Band
Clark-Boland Big Band: TNP, October 29th, 1969 | Laserlight | 36129
Three Latin Adventures | MPS | 529095-2
More Smiles | MPS | 9814789
All Smiles | MPS | 9814790
Francy Boland-Fellini 712 | MPS | 9814805
Pablo All Star Jam
Montreux '77 | Original Jazz Classics | OJC 385(2620105)
Ronnie Scott And The Band
Live At Ronnie Scott's | CBS | 494439-2
Ronnie Scott With The Chas Burchell Quintet
Unsong Hero:The Undiscovered Genius Of Chas Burchell | IN+OUT Records | 7026-2

Scott,Sarah | (cl)
David Jean-Baptiste Group
The Nature Suite | Laika Records | 35101632

Scott,Shirley | (orgp)
Al Smith With The Eddie Lockjaw Davis Quartet
Queen Of The Organ-Shirley Scott Memorial Album | Prestige | PRCD 11027-2
Antonio Hart Group
Here I Stand | Impulse(MCA) | 951208-2
Eddie Lockjaw Davis Quartet
The Eddie Lockjaw Davis Cookbook Vol.2 | Original Jazz Classics | OJC20 653-2(P 7161)
Jaws | Original Jazz Classics | OJCCD 218-2(P 7154)
Queen Of The Organ-Shirley Scott Memorial Album | Prestige | PRCD 11027-2
Eddie Lockjaw Davis Quintet
Cookbook Vol.1 | Original Jazz Classics | OJC20 652-2(P 7141)
The Eddie Lockjaw Davis Cookbook Vol.2 | Original Jazz Classics | OJC20 653-2(P 7161)
Jaws In Orbit | Original Jazz Classics | OJCCD 322-2(P 7171)
Queen Of The Organ-Shirley Scott Memorial Album | Prestige | PRCD 11027-2
Eddie Lockjaw Davis-Shirley Scott Sextet
Bacalao | Original Jazz Classics | OJCCD 1090-2(P 7178)
Jimmy Rushing With Oliver Nelson And His Orchestra
Every Day I Have The Blues | Impulse(MCA) | 547967-2
Mildred Anderson With The Eddie Lockjaw Davis Quartet
Queen Of The Organ-Shirley Scott Memorial Album | Prestige | PRCD 11027-2
Shirley Horn Trio
Queen Of The Organ-Shirley Scott Memorial Album | Prestige | PRCD 11027-2
Shirley Scott All Stars
Queen Of The Organ-Shirley Scott Memorial Album | Prestige | PRCD 11027-2
Shirley Scott Quartet
Blue Flames | Original Jazz Classics | OJCCD 328-2(P 7338)
Queen Of The Organ-Shirley Scott Memorial Album | Prestige | PRCD 11027-2
Shirley Scott Quintet
A Wakin' Thing | Candid | CCD 79719
Blue Seven | Original Jazz Classics | OJCCD 1050-2(P 7376)
Queen Of The Organ-Shirley Scott Memorial Album | Prestige | PRCD 11027-2
Shirley Scott Trio
Skylark | Candid | CCD 79705
Like Cozy | Prestige | PCD 24258-2
Queen Of The Organ-Shirley Scott Memorial Album | Prestige | PRCD 11027-2
Stanley Turrentine Quartet
Blue Note Plays Gershwin | Blue Note | 520808-2
Never Let Me Go | Blue Note | 576750-2
The Roots Of Acid Jazz | Impulse(MCA) | IMP 12042
Stanley Turrentine Quintet
Hustlin' | Blue Note | 540036-2
Never Let Me Go | Blue Note | 576750-2
Very Saxy
Very Saxy | Original Jazz Classics | OJCCD 458-2
The Prestige Legacy Vol.2:Battles Of Saxes | Prestige | PCD 24252-2

Scott,Stephen | (p,kalimba,keyboardsp-solo)
Joe Henderson Quartet
Lush Life-The Music Of Billy Strayhorn | Verve | 511779-2
Joe Henderson Quintet
Lush Life-The Music Of Billy Strayhorn | Verve | 511779-2
Joe Henderson Trio
Lush Life-The Music Of Billy Strayhorn | Verve | 511779-2
Joe Henderson/Stephen Scott
Lush Life-The Music Of Billy Strayhorn | Verve | 511779-2
Roy Hargrove Quartet
Family | Verve | 527630-2
Roy Hargrove Quintet
Family | Verve | 527630-2
Roy Hargrove Sextet
Family | Verve | 527630-2
Roy Hargrove Trio
Parker's Mood | Verve | 527907-2
Roy Hargrove-Stephen Scott
Parker's Mood | Verve | 527907-2
Sonny Rollins Plus 3
Sonny Rollins + 3 | Milestone | MCD 9250-2
Sonny Rollins Quartet
Global Warming | Milestone | MCD 9280-2
This Is What I Do | Milestone | MCD 9310-2
Sonny Rollins Quintet
This Is What I Do | Milestone | MCD 9310-2
Sonny Rollins Sextet
Global Warming | Milestone | MCD 9280-2
Stephen Scott
Parker's Mood | Verve | 527907-2
Stephen Scott Quartet
Vision Quest | Enja | ENJ-9347 2
Stephen Scott Trio
Vision Quest | Enja | ENJ-9347 2
Stephen Scott-Christian McBride
Parker's Mood | Verve | 527907-2
Victor Lewis Sextet
Eeeyyess! | Enja | ENJ-9311 2

Scott,Tom | (as,ts,bs,keyboards,ld,string-synth)
Dave Grusin Orchestra
Two For The Road:The Music Of Henry Mancini | GRP | GRP 98652
Diane Schuur With Orchestra
Love Songs | GRP | GRP 97032
The Best Of Diane Schuur | GRP | GRP 98882
GRP All-Star Big Band
GRP All-Star Big Band:Live! | GRP | GRP 97402
All Blues | GRP | GRP 98002
Jaco Pastorius With Orchestra
Word Of Mouth | Warner | 7599-23525-2
Jimmy Smith With The Oliver Nelson Orchestra
Jimmy Smith:Best Of The Verve Years | Verve | 527950-2
Jimmy Smith-Talkin' Verve | Verve | 531563-2
Lee Ritenour Group
Jazzrock-Anthology Vol.3:Fusion | Zounds | CD 27100555
Singers Unlimited With The Patrick Williams Orchestra
The Singers Unlimited:Magic Voices | MPS | 539130-2

Scott,Tony | (bongos,bs,bs-solo,cl,arr,as,b-cl,p)
Ben Webster With Orchestra And Strings
Music For Loving:Ben Webster With Strings | Verve | 527774-2
Ultimate Ben Webster selected by James Carter | Verve | 557537-2
Big Joe Turner And Pete Johnson With The Blues Band
Newport Jazz Festival 1958,July 3rd-6th Vol.3:Blues In The Night No.1 | Phontastic | NCD 8815
Big Maybelle With The Blues Band
Newport Jazz Festival 1958,July 3rd-6th Vol.3:Blues In The Night No.1 | Phontastic | NCD 8815
Billie Holiday And Her All Stars
Verve Jazz Masters 12:Billie Holiday | Verve | 519825-2
Billie Holiday Story Vol.4:Lady Sings The Blues | Verve | 521429-2
4 By 4:Ella Fitzgerald/Sarah Vaughan/Billie Holiday/Dinah Washington | Verve | 559693-2
The Billie Holiday Song Book | Verve | 823246-2
Chuck Berry With The Blues Band
Newport Jazz Festival 1958,July 3rd-6th Vol.3:Blues In The Night No.1 | Phontastic | NCD 8815
Jazzensemble Des Hessischen Rundfunks
Atmosphering Conditions Permitting | ECM | 1549/50
Kenny Clarke 8
Americans Swinging In Paris:Kenny Clarke | EMI Records | 539652-2
Mundell Lowe And His All Stars
Planet Jazz:Ben Webster | RCA | 2165368-2
Sarah Vaughan With George Treadwell And His Allstars
Sarah Vaughan:Lover Man | Dreyfus Jazz Line | FDM 36739-2
The Modern Jazz Society
A Concert Of Contemporary Music | Verve | 559827-2
Tony Scott And His Down Beat Club Sextet
Jazz:The Essential Collection Vol.3 | IN+OUT Records | 78013-2
Tony Scott And The All Stars
Body And Soul Revisited | GRP | GRP 16272
Tony Scott Group
Tony Scott | Verve | 9861063
Tony Scott Trio
Music For Zen Meditation | Verve | 521444-2
Tony Scott | Verve | 9861063
Tony Scott-Collin Walcott
Music For Yoga Meditation And Other Joys | Verve | 835371-2
Trigger Alpert's Absolutely All Star Seven
East Coast Sound | Original Jazz Classics | OJCCD 1012-2(JLP 11)

Scott,Ulysses | (as)
Hot Lips Page Band
Planet Jazz:Jazz Trumpet | Planet Jazz | 2169654-2

Scott,Wally | (arrcond)
Mel Tormé With The Wally Stott Orchestra
My Kind Of Music | Verve | 543795-2

Scott,William | (tp)
Jimmy Lunceford And His Orchestra
The Legends Of Swing | Laserlight | 24659
Louis Armstrong And His Orchestra
Best Of The Complete RCA Victor Recordings | RCA | 2663636-2
Louis Armstrong:A 100th Birthday Celebration | RCA | 2663694-2
Louis Armstrong:C'est Si Bon | Dreyfus Jazz Line | FDM 36730-2
Swing Legends:Louis Armstrong | Nimbus Records | NI 2012

Scott,William 'Chiefie'[Abdul Salaam] | (tp)
I Love Jazz | Verve | 543747-2

Scottile,John | (tp)
Buddy Rich And His Orchestra
Swingin' New Big Band | Pacific Jazz | 835232-2
Big Swing Face | Pacific Jazz | 837989-2

Scrima,Mickey | (dr)
Harry James And His Orchestra
The Legends Of Swing | Laserlight | 24659

Scriven,Tony | (drwbd)
Graham Stewart And His New Orleans Band
The Golden Years Of Revival Jazz,Vol.4 | Storyville | STCD 5509
Johnny Parker Trio
The Golden Years Of Revival Jazz,Vol.5 | Storyville | STCD 5510

Scully,John | (p)
Tal Farlow Quartet
The Return Of Tal Farlow/1969 | Original Jazz Classics | OJCCD 356-2

Seaberg,George | (tp)
Duke Ellington With Tommy Dorsey And His Orchestra
Highlights From The Duke Ellington Centennial Edition | RCA | 2663672-2
Ella Fitzgerald With The Nelson Riddle Orchestra
The Best Of The Song Books:The Ballads | Verve | 521867-2
Love Songs:The Best Of The Song Books | Verve | 531762-2
Ella Fitzgerald Sings The Johnny Mercer Songbook | Verve | 539057-2
Tommy Dorsey And His Orchestra
Planet Jazz:Tommy Dorsey | Planet Jazz | 2159972-2
Planet Jazz:Jazz Greatest Hits | Planet Jazz | 2169648-2

Sealey,Milton | (p)
Milton Mezz Mezzrow Sextet
Americans Swinging In Paris:Mezz Mezzrow | EMI Records | 539660-2
Milton Mezz Mezzrow-Maxim Saury Quintet
Americans Swinging In Paris:Mezz Mezzrow | EMI Records | 539660-2

Sealey,Paul | (bjg)
Benny Waters Quartet
Hurry On Down | Storyville | STCD 8264
Chris Barber's Jazz And Blues Band
Chris Barber:40 Years Jubilee Concert | Storyville | 4990013
Doug Richford's London Jazzmen
The Golden Years Of Revival Jazz,Sampler | Storyville | 109 1001

Seaman,Ben | (tb)
Gene Krupa And His Orchestra
Mullenium | CBS | CK 65678

Seamen,Phil | (dr)
Golden Gate Quartet
Americans Swinging In Paris:Golden Gate Quartet | EMI Records | 539659-2
Spirituals To Swing 1955-69 | EMI Records | 791569-2
Joe Harriott Quintet
Free Form | EmArCy | 538184-2

Sears,Al | (as,bs,ts,arr,tambourinevoc)
Al Sears & His Rock 'N' Rollers

Sear-iously | Bear Family Records | BCD 15668 AH
Al Sears And His Orchestra
Sear-iously | Bear Family Records | BCD 15668 AH
Al Sears Quintet
Swing's The Thing | Original Jazz Classics | OJCCD 838-2(SV 2018)
Big Al Sears And The Sparrows
Sear-iously | Bear Family Records | BCD 15668 AH
Big Al Sears Band
Sear-iously | Bear Family Records | BCD 15668 AH
Django Reinhardt With Duke Ellington And His Orchestra
Django Reinhardt:Souveniers | Dreyfus Jazz Line | FDM 36744-2
Duke Ellington And His Famous Orchestra
Planet Jazz:Johnny Hodges | Planet Jazz | 2152065-2
Duke Ellington And His Orchestra
Planet Jazz:Duke Ellington | Planet Jazz | 2152053-2
Planet Jazz:Jazz Greatest Hits | Planet Jazz | 2169648-2
The Legends Of Swing | Laserlight | 24659
Highlights From The Duke Ellington Centennial Edition | RCA | 2663672-2
Carnegie Hall Concert December 1944 | Prestige | 2PCD 24073-2
Carnegie Hall Concert January 1946 | Prestige | 2PCD 24074-2
Carnegie Hall Concert December 1947 | Prestige | 2PCD 24075-2
Jazz:The Essential Collection Vol.2 | IN+OUT Records | 78012-2
Frankie Laine With Buck Clayton And His Orchestra
Jazz Spectacular | CBS | CK 65507
Johnny Hodges And His Band
Verve Jazz Masters 35:Johnny Hodges | Verve | 521857-2
Johnny Hodges Orchestra
Highlights From The Duke Ellington Centennial Edition | RCA | 2663672-2
Lionel Hampton And His Orchestra
Lionel Hampton:Flying Home | Dreyfus Jazz Line | FDM 36735-2

Seaton,Laura | (v)
A Band Of Friends
Wynton Marsalis Quartet With Strings | CBS | CK 68921
Andy Bey Group
Tuesdays In Chinatown | Minor Music | 801099
Jim Snidero Quartet With Strings
Strings | Milestone | MCD 9326-2
Kevin Mahogany With The Bob James Trio, Kirk Whalum And Strings
My Romance | Warner | 9362-47025-2

Seaton,Lynn | (b,el-bvoc)
Bill Mays Quartet
The Story Of Jazz Piano | Laserlight | 24653
Buck Clayton Swing Band
Swing's The Village | Nagel-Heyer | CD 5004
Blues Of Summer | Nagel-Heyer | NH 1011
Diane Schuur With The Count Basie Orchestra
The Best Of Diane Schuur | GRP | GRP 98882

Seattle,Matt | (bagpipe)
Kölner Saxophon Mafia With Guests
Kölner Saxophon Mafia: 20 Jahre Saxuelle Befreiung | Jazz Haus Musik | JHM 0115 CD

Seay,Clarence | (b)
Wynton Marsalis Quintet
Wynton Marsalis | CBS | 468708-2

Sebbag,Raphael | (?voc)
United Future Organizatio
United Future Organization | Talkin' Loud | 518166-2

Sebesky,Don | (arr,cond,el-p,ptb)
Astrud Gilberto With The Don Sebesky Orchestra
Verve Jazz Masters 9:Astrud Gilberto | Verve | 519824-2
Freddie Hubbard With Orchestra
This Is Jazz:Freddie Hubbard | CBS | CK 65041
George Benson With The Don Sebesky Orchestra
Verve Jazz Masters 21:George Benson | Verve | 521861-2
Kenny Burrell With The Don Sebesky Orchestra
Verve Jazz Masters 45:Kenny Burrell | Verve | 527652-2
Blues-The Common Ground | Verve | 589101-2
Paul Desmond Orchestra
Late Night Sax | CBS | 487798-2
Skylark | CTI | ZK 65133
Paul Desmond Quartet With The Don Sebesby Orchestra
From The Hot Afternoon | Verve | 543487-2
Ron Carter With Strings
Pastels | Original Jazz Classics | OJCCD 665-2(M 9073)
Wes Montgomery With The Don Sebesky Orchestra
Verve Jazz Masters 14:Wes Montgomery | Verve | 519826-2
Wes Montgomery:The Verve Jazz Sides | Verve | 521690-2
Talkin' Jazz:Roots Of Acid Jazz | Verve | 529580-2
Bumpin' | Verve | 539062-2

Seck,Cheick-Tidiane | (org,perc,ldvoc)
Hank Jones Meets Cheik-Tidiana Seck
Sarala | Verve | 528783-2

Secon,Morris | (fr-h)
Jimmy Smith With The Billy Byers Orchestra
Jimmy Smith:Best Of The Verve Years | Verve | 527950-2

Sedgwick,Amanda | (as)
Amanda Sedgwick Quintet
Reunion | Touché Music | TMcCD 021

Sedler,Jimmy | (tp)
Jimmy Smith With The Claus Ogerman Orchestra
Any Number Can Win | Verve | 557447-2

Sedric,Gene | (clts)
Dick Wellstood's Wallerites
Uptown And Lowdown | Prestige | PCD 24262-2
Fats Waller And His Rhythm
Planet Jazz:Fats Waller | Planet Jazz | 2152058-2
Planet Jazz Sampler | Planet Jazz | 2152326-2
Fats Waller:The Complete Associated Transcription Sessions 1935-1939 | Jazz Unlimited | JUCD 2076
Lena Horne With The Phil Moore Four
Planet Jazz:Lena Horne | Planet Jazz | 2165373-2

See Yuen,Victor | (perc)
Lester Bowie's Brass Fantasy
The Odysse Of Funk & Popular Music | Dreyfus Jazz Line | FDM 37004-2
When The Spitit Returns | Dreyfus Jazz Line | FDM 37016-2
Nat Adderley Septet
Don't Look Back | Steeplechase | SCCD 31059
Sonny Rollins Sextet
Global Warming | Milestone | MCD 9280-2

See,Cees | (dr,perc,flvoice)
Klaus Doldinger Quartet
Doldinger's Best | ACT | 9224-2
Klaus Doldinger Quintet
Doldinger's Best | ACT | 9224-2
Klaus Doldinger Septet
Doldinger's Best | ACT | 9224-2
Volker Kriegel Quintet
Spectrum | MPS | 9808699

Seed,Lenny | (congas)
George Benson Quartet + Guests
The George Benson Cookbook | CBS | 502470-2

Seefelder,Jürgen | (fl,ss,sax,tsreeds)
Munich Saxophon Family
Balanced | Edition Collage | EC 487-2
Survival Song | JHM Records | JHM 3613
Piludu Quattro
Room 626 | Jazz 4 Ever Records:Jazz Network | J4E 4721
Russ Spiegel Group
Twilight | double moon | CHRDM 71026

Seegel,Stefan | (dr)
Florian Bührich Quintet
endlich Jazz...? | Jazz 4 Ever Records:Jazz Network | J4E 4764

Seelig,Norman | (b)
Tommy Dorsey And His Orchestra
Planet Jazz:Tommy Dorsey | Planet Jazz | 2159972-2

Segal,Jerry | (drperc)
Curtis Fuller And Hampton Hawes With French Horns
Curtis Fuller And Hampton Hawes With French Horns | Original Jazz Classics | OJCCD 1942-2(NJ 8305)
Curtis Fuller And Teddy Charles With French Horns
Curtis Fuller And Hampton Hawes With French Horns | Original Jazz Classics | OJCCD 1942-2(NJ 8305)
Mal Waldron Trio
The Mal Waldron Memorial Album:Soul Eyes | Prestige | PRCD 11024-2
Prestige Jazz Quartet
The Mal Waldron Memorial Album:Soul Eyes | Prestige | PRCD 11024-2
The Prestige Jazz Quartet
The Prestige Jazz Quartet | Original Jazz Classics | OJCCD 1937-2(P 7108)

Seghezzo,Dave | (oboe)
Miles Davis With Gil Evans Orchestra, The George Gruntz Concert Jazz Band And Guests
Miles & Quincy Live At Montreux | Warner | 9362-45221-2

Sehring,Rudi | (dr)
Hans Koller New Jazz Stars
Deutsches Jazz Fesival 1954/1955 | Bear Family Records | BCD 15430

Seidel,Jörg | (g)
Jörg Seidel Group
I Feel So Smoochie: A Tribute To Nat King Cole | Edition Collage | EC 532-2
Organ Jazztrio & Martin Weiss
Hommage | Edition Collage | EC 492-2

Seidelin,Mogens 'Basse' | (b,sousaphonsousaphone)
Champion Jack Dupree-Axel Zwingenberger Group
Axel Zwingenberger And The Friends Of Boogie Woogie Vol.7: Champion Jack Dupree Sings Blues Classics | Vagabond | VRCD 8.92018
Chris Barber's Jazz Band
The Golden Years Of Revival Jazz,Vol.2 | Storyville | STCD 5507
Papa Bue's New Orleans Band
The Golden Years Of Revival Jazz,Vol.4 | Storyville | STCD 5509
Papa Bue's Viking Jazzband
The Golden Years Of Revival Jazz,Vol.1 | Storyville | STCD 5506
The Golden Years Of Revival Jazz,Vol.3 | Storyville | STCD 5508
The Golden Years Of Revival Jazz,Vol.5 | Storyville | STCD 5510
The Golden Years Of Revival Jazz,Vol.6 | Storyville | STCD 5511
The Golden Years Of Revival Jazz,Vol.7 | Storyville | STCD 5512
The Golden Years Of Revival Jazz,Vol.8 | Storyville | STCD 5513
The Golden Years Of Revival Jazz,Vol.9 | Storyville | STCD 5514
The Golden Years Of Revival Jazz,Vol.10 | Storyville | STCD 5515
The Golden Years Of Revival Jazz,Vol.11 | Storyville | STCD 5516
The Golden Years Of Revival Jazz,Vol.12 | Storyville | STCD 5517
The Golden Years Of Revival Jazz,Vol.13 | Storyville | STCD 5518
The Golden Years Of Revival Jazz,Vol.14 | Storyville | STCD 5519
The Golden Years Of Revibal Jazz,Vol.15 | Storyville | STCD 5520

Seidelmann,Horst | (dr)
Waltz For People Who Hate Waltzes
Noch Lauther | Bear Family Records | BCD 15942 AH

Seidemann,Johannes | (fl,alto-fl,cl,ss,as,ts,bssax)
Cool Blue
House In The Country | Foolish Music | FM 211591
Jazzensemble Des Hessischen Rundfunks
Jazz Messe-Messe Für Unsere Zeit | hr music.de | hrmj 003-01 CD

Seiden,Paul | (tb)
Louis Armstrong And His Orchestra
I Love Jazz | Verve | 543747-2

Seidman,Mitch | (gel-g)
Mitch Seidman Quartet
How 'Bout It? | Jardis Records | JRCD 20135
Mitch Seidman-Fred Fried
Jazz Guitar Highlights 1 | Jardis Records | JRCD 20141
This Over That | Jardis Records | JRCD 9816
Mitch Seidman-Fred Fried-Harvie Swartz
This Over That | Jardis Records | JRCD 9816

Seifers,Jill | (voc)
Ingrid Jensen Quintet
Here On Earth | Enja | ENJ-9313 2
Jill Seifers And Her Quartet
The Waiting | Fresh Sound Records | FSNT 072 CD

Seifert,Zbigniew | (as,v,el-vv-solo)
Hans Koller Quintet
Kunstkopfindianer | MPS | 9813439

Seim,Kjell | (cond)
Terje Rypdal Quartet With The Bergen Chamber Ensemble
Lux Aeterna | ECM | 1818(017070-2)

Seim,Trygve | (ssts)
Christian Wallumrod Ensemble
Sofienberg Variations | ECM | 1809(017067-2)
Trygve Seim Group
Different Rivers | ECM | 1744(159521-2)
Trygve Seim-Oyvind Braekke-Per Oddvar Johansen Orchestra
The Source And Different Cikadas | ECM | 1764(014432-2)

Seitz,Ernst | (clp)
Colin Dunwoodie Quartet
Glad To See You | Edition Collage | EC 460-2
Wind Moments | Take Twelve On CD | TT 009-2

Seitz,Joseph | (ts)
Freddie Brocksieper Orchester
Drums Boogie | Bear Family Records | BCD 15988 AH

Seiver,Sarah | (cello)
Kevin Mahogany With The Bob James Trio, Kirk Whalum And Strings
My Romance | Warner | 9362-47025-2

Seizer,Jason | (ssts)
Jason Seizer With The Larry Goldings Trio
Sketches | Organic Music | ORGM 9710
Johannes Herrlich Quintet
Thinking Of You | Edition Collage | EC 499-2

Seland,Bernhard | (b-clbs)
Geir Lysne Listening Ensemble
Korall | ACT | 9236-2
Aurora Borealis-Nordic Lights | ACT | 9406-2

Selby,Sidney 'Guitar Crusher' | (voc)
Marty Hall Band
Who's Been Talkin'?s | Blues Beacon | BLU-1033 2

Selden,Paul F. | (tb)
Elliot Lawrence And His Orchestra
The Elliot Lawrence Big Band Swings Cohn & Kahn | Fantasy | FCD 24761-2
Louis Armstrong And Omer Simeon With The Sy Oliver Orchestra
Ambassador Louis Armstrong Vol.17:Moments To Remember(1952-1956) | Ambassador | CLA 1917

Seldon,Paul | (tb)
Louis Armstrong With Sy Oliver And His Orchestra
Louis Armstrong-My Greatest Songs | MCA | MCD 18347

Selico,Ron | (dr)
Albert King Blues Band
The Lost Session | Stax | SCD 8534-2

Sell,Rainer | (tb)
Horst Faigle's Jazzkrement
Gans Normal | Jazz 4 Ever Records:Jazz Network | J4E 4748
Rainer Tempel Big Band
Melodies Of '98 | Jazz 4 Ever Records:Jazz Network | J4E 4744
Album 03 | Jazz 'n' Arts Records | JNA 1102

Sellani,Renato | (p)
Chet Baker Quartet
Chet Baker In Milan | Original Jazz Classics | OJC20 370-2(JLP 18)
Chet Baker Sextet
Chet Baker In Milan | Original Jazz Classics | OJC20 370-2(JLP 18)

Selle,Elna Foleide | (v)
Terje Rypdal Quartet With The Bergen Chamber Ensemble
Lux Aeterna | ECM | 1818(017070-2)

Sellin,Hervé | (p)
Dee Dee Bridgewater With Her Trio
Live In Paris | Verve | 014317-2
Richard Galliano Septet
Piazzolla Forever | Dreyfus Jazz Line | FDM 36642-2

Selmi,Bechir | (v)
Anouar Brahem Group
Khomsa | ECM | 1561(527093-2)
Anouar Brahem Trio
Barzakh | ECM | 1432(847540-2)

Seltzer,Mike | (tb)
Paquito D'Rivera Group With The Absolute Ensemble
Habanera | Enja | ENJ-9395 2

Selvaganesh | (kanjira,ghatammridangam)
Remember Shakti
Saturday Night In Bombay | Verve | 014184-2

Sembritzki,Semel | (ssts)
Jürgen Sturm's Ballstars
Tango Subversivo | Nabel Records:Jazz Network | CD 4613

Semeya,Kyphus | (voc)
Bobby Lyle Group
The Journey | Atlantic | 7567-82138-2

Senatore,Pat | (b)
Stan Kenton And His Orchestra
Adventures In Blues | Capitol | 520089-2
Adventures In Jazz | Capitol | 521222-2

Senay,Don | (voc)
Don Senay With Orchestra And Strings
Charles Mingus-The Complete Debut Recordings | Debut | 12 DCD 4402-2

Sendecki,Vladislaw | (keyboards,synth,orgp)
Bireli Lagrene Group
Bireli Lagrene 'Highlights' | Jazzpoint | JP 1027 CD
Jaco Pastorius Groups
Another Side Of Jaco Pastorius | Jazzpoint | JP 1064 CD
Jaco Pastorius Trio
Jaco Pastorius Heavy'n Jazz & Stuttgart Aria | Jazzpoint | JP 1058 CD
Klaus Doldinger's Passport
Balance Of Happiness | Warner | 9031-71233-2
NDR Big Band
NDR Big Band-Bravissimo | ACT | 9232-2
The Theatre Of Kurt Weil | ACT | 9234-2
NDR Big Band With Guests
50 Years Of NDR Big Band:Bravissimo II | ACT | 9259-2
Oscar Brown Jr. with The NDR Big Band
Live Every Minute | Minor Music | 801071
Ralph R.Hübner-Christoph Lauer Quartet
Mondspinner | free flow music | ffm 0796

Senior Girls Choir Of Blackheath Conservatoire Of Music And The Arts |
Mike Westbrook Brass Band
Glad Day:Settings Of William Blake | Enja | ENJ-9376 2

Senior,George | (b)
Arthur Young And Hatchett's Swingtette
Grapelli Story | Verve | 515807-2

Senise,Mauro | (fl,ss,assax)
Duo Fenix
Karai-Eté | IN+OUT Records | 7009-2
Egberto Gismonti & Academia De Dancas
Sanfona | ECM | 1203/04(829391-2)

Senn,Reto | (cl,b-cltaragot)
Anliker-Parker-Schmid-Senn-Solothurnmann
September Winds | Creative Works Records | CW CD 1038/39

Senst,Ingo | (b)
The Groenewald Newnet
Meetings | Jazz 'n' Arts Records | JNA 0702

Seok,Kang Min | (bara,ching,chnaggo,voicebuk)
Red Sun/SamulNori
Then Comes The White Tiger | ECM | 1499

Serafine,Frank | (synth)
Don Cherry Group
Multi Kulti | A&M Records | 395323-2

Serfaty,Aaron | (dr)
Arturo Sandoval And The Latin Train Band
Arturo Sandoval & The Latin Train | GRP | GRP 98202

Sergio | (b)
Baden Powell Solo/Group
Three Originals:Tristeza On Guitar/Poema On Guitar/Apaixonado | MPS | 519216-2

Serierse,Marcel | (dr)
Stochelo Rosenberg Group
Gypsy Swing | Verve | 527806-2
Stochelo Rosenberg Group With Strings
Gypsy Swing | Verve | 527806-2

Serri,Franco | (b)
Chet Baker Quartet
Chet Baker In Milan | Original Jazz Classics | OJC20 370-2(JLP 18)
Chet Baker Sextet
Chet Baker In Milan | Original Jazz Classics | OJC20 370-2(JLP 18)

Sertso,Ingrid | (vocvoc.perc)
Don Cherry Group
Multi Kulti | A&M Records | 395323-2
Karl Berger-Ingrid Sertso Duo
Conversations | IN+OUT Records | 77027-2

Sete,Bola | (g)
Bola Sete Quintet
Tour De Force:The Bola Sete Trios | Fantasy | FCD 24766-2
Bola Sete Trio
Tour De Force:The Bola Sete Trios | Fantasy | FCD 24766-2
Dizzy Gillespie And His Orchestra
Ultimate Dizzy Gillespie | Verve | 557535-2
Vince Guaraldi-Bola Sete Quartet
Vince & Bola | Fantasy | FCD 24756-2

Settelmeyer,Bernd | (dr,marimbaperc)
Jo Ambros Group
Wanderlust | dml-records | CD 016
Sputnik 27
But Where's The Moon? | dml-records | CD 011
Vesna Skorija Band
Niceland | Satin Doll Productions | SDP 1037-1 CD

Setz,Freddy | (org,dr,perc,string-ensemblep)
Roman Bunka Group
Dein Kopf Ist Ein Schlafendes Auto | ATM Records | ATM 3818-AH

Setzer,Markus | (b)
Sabine&Markus Setzer
Between The Words | Lipstick Records | LIP 8970

Setzer,Sabine | (voice)

Seuss,Ludwig | (keyboards,org,accordeonp)
Christian Willisohn New Band
Heart Broken Man | Blues Beacon | BLU-1026 2
Christian Willisohn-Boris Vanderlek-Ludwig Seuss
Blues News | Blues Beacon | BLU-1019 2
Nick Woodland And The Magnets
Big Heart | Blues Beacon | BLU-1013 2
Nick Woodland Quartet
Live Fireworks | Blues Beacon | BLU-1027 2

Severin,Chris | (b)
Dianne Reeves With Band
I Remember | Blue Note | 790264-2

Severino,Frank | (dr)
Clark Terry Five
The Jazz Giants Play Duke Ellington:Caravan | Prestige | PCD 24227-2
Joe Pass Trio
Resonance | Pablo | 2310968-2
Live At Donte's | Pablo | 2620114-2
Joe Pass:Guitar Virtuoso | Pablo | 4 PACD 4423-2
Les McCann Trio
Talkin' Verve:Les McCann | Verve | 557351-2
Milt Jackson And His Colleagues
Bag's Bag | Original Jazz Classics | OJCCD 935-2(2310842)

Severinsen,Doc | (tpfl-h)
Anita O'Day With The Gary McFarland Orchestra
All The Sad Youn Men | Verve | 517065-2
Benny Goodman And His Orchestra
The Legends Of Swing | Laserlight | 24659
Cab Calloway And His Orchestra
Planet Jazz:Cab Calloway | Planet Jazz | 2161237-2
Dinah Washington With The Quincy Jones Orchestra
Verve Jazz Masters 40:Dinah Washington | Verve | 522055-2
The Swingin' Miss 'D' | Verve | 558074-2
George Russell And His Orchestra
Geogre Russell New York N.Y. | Impulse(MCA) | 951278-2
Gerry Mulligan Concert Jazz Band
Verve Jazz Masters 36:Gerry Mulligan | Verve | 523342-2
Verve Jazz Masters Vol.60:The Collection | Verve | 529866-2
The Complete Verve Gerry Mulligan Concert Band | Verve | 9860613
Jimmy Smith With The Oliver Nelson Orchestra
Verve Jazz Masters 29:Jimmy Smith | Verve | 521855-2
Jimmy Smith:Best Of The Verve Years | Verve | 527950-2
Lena Horne With The Lennie Hayton Orchestra
Planet Jazz:Lena Horne | Planet Jazz | 2165373-2
Mike Bryan Sextet
Jazz Festival Vol.2 | Storyville | 4960743
Milt Jackson Orchestra
To Bags...With Love:Memorial Album | Pablo | 2310967-2
Big Bags | Original Jazz Classics | OJCCD 366-2(RLP 9429)
Stan Getz With The Gary McFarland Orchestra
Stan Getz Highlights:The Best Of The Verve Years Vol.2 | Verve | 517330-2
Verve Jazz Masters 53:Stan Getz-Bossa Nova | Verve | 529904-2
Big Band Bossa Nova | Verve | 825771-2 PMS
Stan Getz Highlights | Verve | 847430-2

Sewell,Marvin | (el-g,g,bozoukidobro)
Cassandra Wilson Group
Traveling Miles | Blue Note | 854123-2

Sewing,Jack | (b)
Stephane Grappelli Group
Stephane Grappelli:Live In San Francisco | Storyville | 4960723
Stephane Grappelli Quartet
Planet Jazz:Stephane Grappelli | RCA | 2165366-2
I Hear Music | RCA | 2179624-2
Stephane Grappelli Quintet
Planet Jazz:Stephane Grappelli | RCA | 2165366-2
Stephane Grappelli Trio
I Hear Music | RCA | 2179624-2
7.Zelt-Musik-Festival:Jazz Events | Zounds | CD 2730001
Stephane Grappelli-David Grisman Group
Stephane Grappelli:Live In San Francisco | Storyville | 4960723

Seykora,Frederick | (cello)
Ella Fitzgerald With Orchestra
The Best Is Yet To Come | Original Jazz Classics | OJCCD 889-2(2312138)
Milt Jackson And His Orchestra
Reverence And Compassion | Reprise | 9362-45204-2

Seyler,Jürgen | (tbvoc)
Ralph Abelein Group
Mr. B's Time Machine | Satin Doll Productions | SDP 1042-1 CD

Seymour,Earl | (fl,alto-fl,cl,b-cl,bsts)
Hugh Marsh Duo/Quartet/Orchestra
The Bear Walks | VeraBra Records | CDVBR 2011-2

Shabazz,Majid | (bells,tambouraperc)
Alice Coltrane Sextet
Journey In Satchidananda | Impulse(MCA) | 951228-2
Pharoah Sanders Orchestra
Thembi | Impulse(MCA) | 951253-2

Shackman,Al | (gharm)
Nina Simone Quartet
Misty Blue:Sweet Sisters Swing Songs Of Sorrow And Sadness | Blue Note | 521151-2
Nina Simone Quintet
Planet Jazz:Nina Simone | Planet Jazz | 2165372-2
Nina Simone After Hours | Verve | 526702-2

Shaffer,Paul | (keyboards,orgp)
Lew Soloff Group
Rainbow Mountain | TipToe | TIP-888838 2

Shaheen,Ibrahim | (gaula)
Koch-Schütz-Studer & El Nil Troop
Heavy Cairo Trafic | Intuition Records | INT 3175-2

Shahid,Jaribu | (b,congas,el-b,voice,vocperc)
James Carter Group
Conversin' With The Elders | Atlantic | 7567-82988-2
James Carter Quartet
The Real Quietstorm | Atlantic | 7567-82742-2
James Carter-Shahid Jaribu
The Real Quietstorm | Atlantic | 7567-82742-2
Roscoe Mitchell And The Note Factory
Nine To Get Ready | ECM | 1651(539725-2)

Shaier,Julius | (viola)
Stan Getz With The Eddie Sauter Orchestra
Stan Getz Plays The Music Of Mickey One | Verve | 531232-2

Shakesnider,Wilmer | (reeds)
Ella Fitzgerald With The Bill Doggett Orchestra
Ella Fitzgerald-First Lady Of Song | Verve | 517898-2
Rhythm Is My Business | Verve | 559513-2

Shakespeare,Bill | (tp)
Arthur Young And Hatchett's Swingtette
Grapelli Story | Verve | 515807-2

Shakti |
Shakti
Shakti With John McLaughlin | CBS | 467905-2

Shamban,David | (cello)
Milt Jackson And His Orchestra
Reverence And Compassion | Reprise | 9362-45204-2

Shamban,Kwihee | (v)

Shams El Dine,Adel | (riq)
Renaud Garcia-Fons
Navigatore | Enja | ENJ-9418 2
Renaud Garcia-Fons Group
Navigatore | Enja | ENJ-9418 2

Shane,Mark | (pvoc)
Allan Vaché Swingtet
Ellington For Lovers | Nagel-Heyer | NH 1009
Allan Vaché-Antti Sarpila & 1 Sextet
Summit Meeting | Nagel-Heyer | CD 027
Allan Vaché-Antti Sarpila Quintet
Swing Is Here | Nagel-Heyer | CD 026
Blues Of Summer | Nagel-Heyer | NH 1011
The Second Sampler | Nagel-Heyer | NHR SP 6
Bob Wilber And Friends
What Swing Is All About | Nagel-Heyer | CD 035
Blues Of Summer | Nagel-Heyer | NH 1011
Bob Wilber's Bechet Legacy
The Hamburg Concert-Tribute To A Legend | Nagel-Heyer | CD 028
The Second Sampler | Nagel-Heyer | NHR SP 6
Byron Stripling And Friends
If I Could Be With You | Nagel-Heyer | NH 1010
David Ostwald's Gully Low Jazz Band
Blues In Your Heart | Nagel-Heyer | CD 051
International Allstars
The International Allstars Play Benny Goodman:Vol.1 | Nagel-Heyer | CD 025
The Second Sampler | Nagel-Heyer | NHR SP 6
Joe Ascione Octet
My Buddy:A Tribute To Buddy Rich | Nagel-Heyer | CD 036
Mark Shane's X-Mas Allstars
What Would Santa Say? | Nagel-Heyer | CD 055
Christmas Jazz! | Nagel-Heyer | NH 1008
Mark Shane-Terry Blaine Group
With Thee I Swing! | Nagel-Heyer | CD 040
Rex Allen's Swing Express
Keep Swingin' | Nagel-Heyer | CD 016
Ellington For Lovers | Nagel-Heyer | NH 1009
The Second Sampler | Nagel-Heyer | NHR SP 6
The International Allstars
The International Allstars Play Benny Goodman Vol.1 | Nagel-Heyer | CD 045
The Nagel-Heyer Allstars
Uptown Lowdown:A Jazz Salute To The Big Apple | Nagel-Heyer | CD 2004
The New York Allstars
Broadway | Nagel-Heyer | CD 003
One Two Three | Nagel-Heyer | CD 008
We Love You,Louis! | Nagel-Heyer | CD 029
Count Basie Remembered | Nagel-Heyer | CD 031
Count Basie Remembered Vol.2 | Nagel-Heyer | CD 041
Randy Sandke Meets Bix Beiderbecke | Nagel-Heyer | CD 3002
The First Sampler | Nagel-Heyer | NHR SP 5
The Second Sampler | Nagel-Heyer | NHR SP 6
The Sidney Bechet Society
Jam Session Concert | Nagel-Heyer | CD 076

Shank,Bud | (alto-fl,as,bs,ts,woodwinds,bass-s)
Anita O'Day With The Buddy Bregman Orchestra
Pick Yourself Up | Verve | 517329-2
Anita O'Day With The Jimmy Giuffre Orchestra
Verve Jazz Masters 49:Anita O'Day | Verve | 527653-2
Anita O'Day With The Russ Garcia Orchestra
Verve Jazz Masters 49:Anita O'Day | Verve | 527653-2
Art Pepper Plus Eleven
Art Pepper + Eleven | Contemporary | CSA 7568-6
Modern Jazz Classics | Original Jazz Classics | OJC20 341-2
Astrud Gilberto With Antonio Carlos Jobim And The Marty Paich Orchestra
The Antonio Carlos Jobim Songbook | Verve | 525472-2
Astrud Gilberto With The Marty Paich Orchestra
Verve Jazz Masters 9:Astrud Gilberto | Verve | 519824-2
Barney Kessel Quintet
Easy Like | Original Jazz Classics | OJCCD 153-2
Benny Carter And His Orchestra
Further Definitions/Additions To Further Definotions | Impulse(MCA) | 951229-2
Bill Perkins-Bud Shank Quintet
The Jazz Giants Play Harold Arlen:Blues In The Night | Prestige | PCD 24201-2
Bud Shank And Trombones
Cool Fool | Fresh Sound Records | FSR CD 507
Bud Shank Quartet
Live At The Haig | Choice | CHCD 71030
Bud Shank Quintet
The Complete Nocturne Recordings:Jazz In Hollywood Series Vol.1 | Fresh Sound Records | NR 3CD-101
Bud Shank Sextet
New Gold! | Candid | CCD 79707
Bud Shank With The Len Mercer Strings
Midnight Blue(The [Be]witching Hour) | Blue Note | 854365-2
Buddy Bregman And His Orchestra
Swinging Kicks | Verve | 559514-2
Chet Baker And The Lighthouse All Stars
Witch Doctor | Original Jazz Classics | OJCCD 609-2
The Jazz Giants Play Harry Warren:Lullaby Of Broadway | Prestige | PCD 24204-2
Chet Baker Big Band
The Best Of Chet Baker Plays | Pacific Jazz | 797161-2
Chet Baker Sextet
The Best Of Chet Baker Plays | Pacific Jazz | 797161-2
Ella Fitzgerald With Marty Paich's Dektette
Ella Swings Lightly | Verve | 517535-2
Ella Fitzgerald With The Buddy Bregman Orchestra
Ella Fitzgerald-First Lady Of Song | Verve | 517898-2
The Best Of The Song Books:The Ballads | Verve | 521867-2
Love Songs:The Best Of The Song Books | Verve | 531762-2
Ella Fitzgerald Sings The Cole Porter Songbook | Verve | 537257-2
Ella Fitzgerald Sings The Rodgers And Hart Song Book | Verve | 537258-2
Ella Fitzgerald With The Marty Paich Dek-tette
Ella Fitzgerald-First Lady Of Song | Verve | 517898-2
Verve Jazz Masters 6:Ella Fitzgerald | Verve | 519822-2
Verve Jazz Masters 46:Ella Fitzgerald-The Jazz Sides | Verve | 527655-2
Gerald Wilson And His Orchestra
Blue Breaks Beats Vol.2 | Blue Note | 789907-2
Gerry Mulligan Tentette
Gene Norman Presents The Original Gerry Mulligan Tentet And Quartet | GNP Crescendo | GNPD 56
Herbie Harper Quintet
The Complete Nocturne Recordings:Jazz In Hollywood Series Vol.1 | Fresh Sound Records | NR 3CD-101
Howard Rumsey's Lighthouse All-Stars
Oboe/Flute | Original Jazz Classics | OJCCD 154-2(C 3520)
Howard Rumsey's Lighthouse All-Stars Vol.6 | Original Jazz Classics | OJCCD 386-2(C 3504)
Sunday Jazz A La Lighthouse Vol.2 | Original Jazz Classics | OJCCD 972-2(S 2501)
June Christy With The Pete Rugolo Orchestra
Something Cool(The Complete Mono & Stereo Versions) | Capitol | 534069-2
June Christy With The Shorty Rogers Orchestra
June Christy Big Band Special | Capitol | 498319-2
Margaret Whiting With Russel Garcia And His Orchestra
Margaret Whiting Sings The Jerome Kern Song Book | Verve | 559553-2
Maynard Ferguson And His Orchestra
Verve Jazz Masters 52:Maynard Ferguson | Verve | 529905-2
Maynard Ferguson Band
Verve Jazz Masters 52:Maynard Ferguson | Verve | 529905-2
Mel Tormé With The Billy May Orchestra
Mel Tormé Goes South Of The Border With Billy May | Verve | 589517-2
Mel Tormé With The Russell Garcia Orchestra
Swingin' On The Moon | Verve | 511385-2
Miles Davis And The Lighthouse All Stars
At Last! | Original Jazz Classics | OJCCD 480-2
Nat King Cole Quartet With The Stan Kenton Orchestra
Nat King Cole:For Sentimental Reasons | Dreyfus Jazz Line | FDM 36740-2
Peggy Lee With The Quincy Jones Orchestra
Blues Cross Country | Capitol | 520088-2
Pete Rugolo And His Orchestra
Thriller/Richard Diamon(Original Jazz Scores From 2 Classics TV Series) | Fresh Sound Records | FSCD 2015
Sarah Vaughan With Orchestra
Sarah Vaughan Sings The Mancini Songbook | Verve | 558401-2
Shorty Rogers And His Orchestra Feat. The Giants
PLanet Jazz:Shorty Rogers | Planet Jazz | 2159976-2
Singers Unlimited With Orchestra
The Singers Unlimited:Magic Voices | MPS | 539130-2
Stan Kenton And His Orchestra
Stan Kenton Portraits On Standards | Capitol | 531571-2
One Night Stand | Choice | CHCD 71051

Shank,Kendra | (g,vocvoice)
Abbey Lincoln And Her Trio With Guests
Over The Years | Verve | 549101-2

Shankar | (double-v,tamboura,voc,perc)
Shakti
Shakti With John McLaughlin | CBS | 467905-2
Shankar
Who's To Know | ECM | 1195
Shankar Group
Nobody Told Me | ECM | 1397
Shankar Quartet
M.R.C.S. | ECM | 1403
Pancha Nadai Pallavi | ECM | 1407(841641-2)
Shankar Trio
Vision | ECM | 1261(811969-2)
Shankar/Caroline
The Epidemics | ECM | 1308

Shankar,Bhavani | (cholakpakhawaj)
Remember Shakti
Saturday Night In Bombay | Verve | 014184-2

Shanley,Brian | (cl)
Bob Scobey's Frisco Band
Planet Jazz | Planet Jazz | 2169652-2

Shapiro,Artie | (b)
Billie Holiday With The Paul Whiteman Orchestra
Billie's Blues | Blue Note | 748786-2
Jack Teagarden's Chicagoans
Jazz:The Essential Collection Vol.3 | IN+OUT Records | 78013-2
The Hollywood Session:The Capitol Jazzmen | Jazz Unlimited | JUCD 2044
Peggy Lee With The Benny Goodman Orchestra
Peggy Lee & Benny Goodman:The Complete Recordings 1941-1947 | CBS | C2K 65686
The Capitol Jazzmen
Jazz:The Essential Collection Vol.3 | IN+OUT Records | 78013-2
The Hollywood Session:The Capitol Jazzmen | Jazz Unlimited | JUCD 2044

Shapiro,Eunice | (v)
Ella Fitzgerald With The Marty Paich Orchestra
Get Happy! | Verve | 523321-2
Ella Fitzgerald With The Nelson Riddle Orchestra
Oh Lady Be Good:The Best Of The Gershwin Songbook | Verve | 529581-2
Love Songs:The Best Of The Song Books | Verve | 531762-2

Shapiro,Harvey | (celloharp)
Stan Getz With The Eddie Sauter Orchestra
Stan Getz Plays The Music Of Mickey One | Verve | 531232-2
Wes Montgomery Quartet With The Claus Ogerman Orchestra
Tequila | Verve | 547769-2
Wes Montgomery Quintet With The Claus Ogerman Orchestra
The Antonio Carlos Jobim Songbook | Verve | 525472-2
Talkin' Jazz:Roots Of Acid Jazz | Verve | 529580-2
Tequila | Verve | 547769-2
Wes Montgomery Trio With The Claus Ogerman Orchestra
Tequila | Verve | 547769-2
Wes Montgomery With The Claus Ogerman Orchestra
Verve Jazz Masters 14:Wes Montgomery | Verve | 519826-2

Shapiro,Michael | (dr,percvoc)
Airto Moreira/Flora Purim Group
Jazz Unlimited | IN+OUT Records | 7017-2
John Patitucci Group
Mistura Fina | GRP | GRP 98022

Shapiro,Sol | (v)
Freddie Hubbard Orchestra
The Body And The Soul | Impulse(MCA) | 951183-2
Wes Montgomery With The Don Sebesky Orchestra
Verve Jazz Masters 14:Wes Montgomery | Verve | 519826-2
Talkin' Jazz:Roots Of Acid Jazz | Verve | 529580-2
Bumpin' | Verve | 539062-2

Sharfe,Mike | (b)
Wolfgang Lackerschmid & Lynne Arriale Trio
You Are Here | Bhakti Jazz | BR 43

Sharma,Shiv Kumar | (santur)
Remember Shakti
Saturday Night In Bombay | Verve | 014184-2

Sha'Ron | (voc)
Lillian Boutté And Her Group
The Gospel Book | Blues Beacon | BLU-1017 2

Sharon,Ralph | (cond,arr,pceleste)
J.R. Monterose Sextet
Jaywalkin' | Fresh Sound Records | FSR-CD 320

Sharp,Fred | (g)
Miff Mole And His Dixieland Band
Muggsy Spanier-Manhattan Masters,1945 | Storyville | STCD 6051

Sharp,Sidney 'Sid' | (concertmasterv)
Ella Fitzgerald With The Nelson Riddle Orchestra
The Best Of The Song Books:The Ballads | Verve | 521867-2
Sarah Vaughan And Her Band
Songs Of The Beatles | Atlantic | 16037-2

Sharpe,Avery | (b,el-bvoc)
McCoy Tyner Big Band
The Best Of McCoy Tyner Big Band | Dreyfus Jazz Line | FDM 37012-2
McCoy Tyner Quartet
The Story Of Jazz Piano | Laserlight | 24653
McCoy Tyner Trio
Remembering John | Enja | ENJ-6080 2

Sharpe,D. | (drvoice)
Carla Bley Band
Live! | Watt | 12(815730-2)
Musique Mecanique | Watt | 9
Michael Mantler Sextet
Movies/More Movies | Watt | 7/10(543377-2)
The Carla Bley Band
Social Studies | Watt | 11(831831-2)
I Hate To Sing | Watt | 12,5

Sharpley,Andrew | (samplerturntable)
Noel Akchoté Trio
Rien | Winter&Winter | 910057-2

Sharrock,Linda | (voc)
AM 4
...And She Answered | ECM | 1394
Red Sun/SamulNori
Then Comes The White Tiger | ECM | 1499

Sharrock,Sonny | (el-g,g,slide-whistlevoc)
Herbie Mann Group
Memphis Underground | Atlantic | 7567-81364-2
The Best Of Herbie Mann | Atlantic | 7567-81369-2
Wayne Shorter Sextet
Wayne Shorter:The Classic Blue Note Recordings | Blue Note | 540856-2

Shashikumar,T.N. | (kanjeera,kanjirakonakkol)
Charlie Mariano & The Karnataka College Of Percussion
Jyothi | ECM | 1256
Live | VeraBra Records | CDVBR 2034-2

Shaughnessy,Ed | (dr,percvib)
Billie Holiday And Her All Stars
Verve Jazz Masters 12:Billie Holiday | Verve | 519825-2
4 By 4:Ella Fitzgerald/Sarah Vaughan/Billie Holiday/Dinah Washington | Verve | 559693-2
The Billie Holiday Song Book | Verve | 823246-2
Cal Tjader With The Lalo Schifrin Orchestra
Talkin Verve/Roots Of Acid Jazz:Cal Tjader | Verve | 531562-2
Cal Tjader's Orchestra
Verve Jazz Masters 39:Cal Tjader | Verve | 521858-2
Clark Terry Orchestra
Color Changes | Candid | CCD 79009
Freddie Hubbard Septet
This Is Jazz:Freddie Hubbard | CBS | CK 65041
Gary McFarland And His Orchestra
The Complete Bill Evans On Verve | Verve | 527953-2
George Benson With The Don Sebesky Orchestra
Verve Jazz Masters 21:George Benson | Verve | 521861-2
Gerry Mulligan With The Marian McPartland Trio
Newport Jazz Festival 1958,July 3rd-6th Vol.2:Mulligan The Main Man | Phontastic | NCD 8814
Jimmy Forrest With The Oliver Nelson Orchestra

Soul Street | Original Jazz Classics | OJCCD 987-2(NJ 8293)
Jimmy Smith With The Claus Ogerman Orchestra
Any Number Can Win | Verve | 557447-2
Jimmy Smith With The Oliver Nelson Orchestra
Verve Jazz Masters 29:Jimmy Smith | Verve | 521855-2
Jimmy Smith:Best Of The Verve Years | Verve | 527950-2
Johnny Smith Quartet
The Sound Of The Johnny Smith Guitar | Roulette | 531792-2
Lalo Schifrin And His Orchestra
Verve Jazz Masters 39:Cal Tjader | Verve | 521858-2
Mundell Lowe And His All Stars
Planet Jazz:Ben Webster | RCA | 2165368-2
Teddy Charles Quartet
Charles Mingus-Passion Of A Man:The Complete Atlantic Recordings 1956-1961 | Atlantic | 8122-72871-2
Trigger Alpert's Absolutely All Star Seven
East Coast Sound | Original Jazz Classics | OJCCD 1012-2(JLP 11)

Shavers,Charlie | (tp,arrvoc)
Billie Holiday And Her All Stars
Verve Jazz Masters 12:Billie Holiday | Verve | 519825-2
Billie Holiday Story Vol.4:Lady Sings The Blues | Verve | 521429-2
Verve Jazz Masters 47:Billie Holiday Sings Standards | Verve | 527650-2
4 By 4:Ella Fitzgerald/Sarah Vaughan/Billie Holiday/Dinah Washington | Verve | 559693-2
The Billie Holiday Song Book | Verve | 823246-2
Billie Holiday And Her Orchestra
Solitude | Verve | 519810-2
Carmen McRae With The Tadd Dameron Orchestra
Blue Moon | Verve | 543829-2
Coleman Hawkins And His 52nd Street All Stars
Jazz:The Essential Collection Vol.3 | IN+OUT Records | 78013-2
Coleman Hawkins' Fifty-Second Street All-Stars
Planet Jazz:Coleman Hawkins | Planet Jazz | 2152055-2
Coleman Hawkins Sextet
Hawk Eyes | Original Jazz Classics | OJCCD 294-2
Coleman Hawkins With Billy Byers And His Orchestra
The Hawk In Hi-Fi | RCA | 2663842-2
Count Basie And His Orchestra
Verve Jazz Masters 2:Count Basie | Verve | 519819-2
Della Reese With The Sy Oliver Orchestra
Misty Blue:Sweet Sisters Swing Songs Of Sorrow And Sadness | Blue Note | 521151-2
Dinah Washington With The Quincy Jones Orchestra
Verve Jazz Masters 40:Dinah Washington | Verve | 522055-2
The Swingin' Miss 'D' | Verve | 558074-2
Duke Ellington With Tommy Dorsey And His Orchestra
Highlights From The Duke Ellington Centennial Edition | RCA | 2663672-2
Ella Fitzgerald With Sy Oliver And His Orchestra
Ella Fitzgerald:The Decca Years 1949-1954 | Decca | 050668-2
Esquire All-American Award Winners
Planet Jazz:Jazz Trumpet | Planet Jazz | 2169654-2
Best Of The Complete RCA Victor Recordings | RCA | 2663636-2
Highlights From The Duke Ellington Centennial Edition | RCA | 2663672-2
Hal Singer-Charlie Shavers Quintet
Blue Stompin' | Original Jazz Classics | OJCCD 834-2(P 7153)
JATP All Stars
JATP In Tokyo | Pablo | 2620104-2
The Complete Jazz At The Philharmonic On Verve 1944-1949 | Verve | 523893-2
The Drum Battle:Gene Krupa And Buddy Rich At JATP | Verve | 559810-2
The Cole Porter Songbook | Verve | 823250-2
Jimmy McPartland And His Dixielanders
Planet Jazz | Planet Jazz | 2169652-2
Jimmy Smith With The Claus Ogerman Orchestra
Verve Jazz Masters 29:Jimmy Smith | Verve | 521855-2
Any Number Can Win | Verve | 557447-2
John Kirby Band
The Small Black Groups | Storyville | 4960523
Leonard Feather's Esquire All-Americans
Louis Armstrong:C'est Si Bon | Dreyfus Jazz Line | FDM 36730-2
Lionel Hampton All Stars
Lionel Hampton:Flying Home | Dreyfus Jazz Line | FDM 36735-2
Louis Armstrong And His Orchestra
I Love Jazz | Verve | 543747-2
Louis Armstrong And Omer Simeon With The Sy Oliver Orchestra
Ambassador Louis Armstrong Vol.17:Moments To Remember(1952-1956) | Ambassador | CLA 1917
Louis Armstrong With Sy Oliver And His Orchestra
Louis Armstrong-My Greatest Songs | MCA | MCD 18347
Norman Granz Jam Session
Verve Jazz Masters 35:Johnny Hodges | Verve | 521857-2
Charlie Parker:The Best Of The Verve Years | Verve | 527815-2
Talkin' Bird | Verve | 559859-2
Bird: The Complete Charlie Parker On Verve | Verve | 837141-2
Sarah Vaughan And The Thad Jones Orchestra
Verve Jazz Masters 42:Sarah Vaughan-The Jazz Sides | Verve | 526817-2
Sarah Vaughan With The Hal Mooney Orchestra
It's A Man's World | Mercury | 589487-2
Sidney Bechet And His New Orleans Feetwarmers
Planet Jazz | Planet Jazz | 2169652-2
Sidney Bechet:Summertime | Dreyfus Jazz Line | FDM 36712-2
The Hollywood Hucksters
The Hollywood Session:The Capitol Jazzmen | Jazz Unlimited | JUCD 2044
Tommy Dorsey And His Orchestra
Planet Jazz:Tommy Dorsey | Planet Jazz | 2159972-2
V-Disc All Star Jam Session
Louis Armstrong-Jack Teagarden-Woody Herman:Midnights At V-Disc | Jazz Unlimited | JUCD 2048
Woody Herman And His Orchestra
Songs For Hip Lovers | Verve | 559872-2
Woody Herman And The Vanderbilt All Stars
Louis Armstrong-Jack Teagarden-Woody Herman:Midnights At V-Disc | Jazz Unlimited | JUCD 2048

Shaw,Artie | (cl,arras)
Artie Shaw And His Orchestra
Planet JazzArtie Shaw | Planet Jazz | 2152057-2
Planet Jazz Sampler | Planet Jazz | 2152326-2
Planet Jazz:Jazz Greatest Hits | Planet Jazz | 2169648-2
Planet Jazz:Big Bands | Planet Jazz | 2169649-2
Planet Jazz:Swing | Planet Jazz | 2169651-2
Planet Jazz:Jazz Trumpet | Planet Jazz | 2169654-2
Planet Jazz:Female Jazz Vocalists | Planet Jazz | 2169656-2
Planet Jazz:Male Jazz Vocalists | Planet Jazz | 2169657-2
The Legends Of Swing | Laserlight | 24659
Swing Vol.1 | Storyville | 4960343

Shaw,Arvell | (bvoc)
Axel Zwingenberger With The Lionel Hampton Big Band
The Boogie Woogie Album | Vagabond | VRCD 8.88008
Cozy Cole's Big Seven
Body And Soul Revisited | GRP | GRP 16272
Dorothy Donegan Trio
The Many Faces Of Dorothy Donegan | Storyville | STCD 8362
Jack Teagarden With The Red Allen Band
The Very Best Of Dixieland Jazz | Verve | 535529-2
Louis Armstrong And His All Stars
Jazz Collection:Louis Armstrong | Laserlight | 24366
I Love Jazz | Verve | 543747-2
Louis Armstrong Plays W.C.Handy | CBS | CK 64925
Ambassador Satch | CBS | CK 64926
Satch Plays Fats(Complete) | CBS | CK 64927
Louis Armstrong:C'est Si Bon | Dreyfus Jazz Line | FDM 36730-2
Historic Barcelona Concerts At Windsor Palace 1955 | Fresh Sound Records | FSR-CD 3004
Live In Berlin/Friedrichstadtpalast | Jazzpoint | JP 1062 CD
The Legendary Berlin Concert Part 2 | Jazzpoint | JP 1063 CD
Louis Armstrong-My Greatest Songs | MCA | MCD 18347
Swing Legends:Louis Armstrong | Nimbus Records | NI 2012
Louis Armstrong:Wintergarden 1947/Blue Note 1948 | Storyville | STCD 8242
Louis Armstrong And His All Stars With Benny Carter's Orchestra
Ambassador Louis Armstrong Vol.17:Moments To Remember(1952-1956) | Ambassador | CLA 1917
Louis Armstrong And His All Stars With Sonny Burke's Orchestra
Ambassador Louis Armstrong Vol.17:Moments To Remember(1952-1956) | Ambassador | CLA 1917
Louis Armstrong And His Orchestra
Best Of The Complete RCA Victor Recordings | RCA | 2663636-2
Louis Armstrong:A 100th Birthday Celebration | RCA | 2663694-2
I Love Jazz | Verve | 543747-2
Satchmo Serenaders | Verve | 543792-2
Louis Armstrong:C'est Si Bon | Dreyfus Jazz Line | FDM 36730-2
Swing Legends:Louis Armstrong | Nimbus Records | NI 2012
Louis Armstrong And Omer Simeon With The Sy Oliver Orchestra
Ambassador Louis Armstrong Vol.17:Moments To Remember(1952-1956) | Ambassador | CLA 1917
Louis Armstrong With Benny Carter's Orchestra
Louis Armstrong-My Greatest Songs | MCA | MCD 18347
Louis Armstrong With Gordon Jenkins And His Orchestra And Choir
Satchmo In Style | Verve | 549594-2
Louis Armstrong With Sy Oliver And His Orchestra
Satchmo Serenaders | Verve | 543792-2
Louis Armstrong-My Greatest Songs | MCA | MCD 18347
Louis Armstrong With The Gordon Jenkins Orchestra
Ambassador Louis Armstrong Vol.17:Moments To Remember(1952-1956) | Ambassador | CLA 1917

Shaw,Clarence | (perctp)
Charles Mingus Orchestra
Tijuana Moods(The Complete Edition) | RCA | 2663840-2
Charles Mingus Workshop
Charles Mingus-The Complete Debut Recordings | Debut | 12 DCD 4402-2

Shaw,Ian | (pvoc)
Clare Teal And Her Band
Orsino's Songs | Candid | CCD 79783
Ian Shaw With Band
Soho Stories | Milestone | MCD 9316-2
Ian Shaw With The Cedar Walton Trio
In A New York Minute | Milestone | MCD 9297-2
Nicki Leighton-Thomas Group
Forbidden Games | Candid | CCD 79778

Shaw,Jaleel | (as)
Mingus Big Band
Tonight At Noon...Three Or Four Shades Of Love | Dreyfus Jazz Line | FDM 36633-2

Shaw,Lonnie | (bs,fl,saxts)
(Little)Jimmy Scott With The Lionel Hampton Orchestra
Everybody's Somebody's Fool | Decca | 050669-2
Lionel Hampton And His Orchestra
Lionel Hampton:Flying Home | Dreyfus Jazz Line | FDM 36735-2

Shaw,Mack prob. | (tuba)
Duke Ellington And His Kentucky Club Orchestra
Jazz:The Essential Collection Vol.2 | IN+OUT Records | 78012-2

Shaw,Marlena | (voc)
Marlena Shaw With Orchestra
Deep Blue-The United States Of Mind | Blue Note | 521152-2

Shaw,Martin | (tp)
Jamie Cullum Group
Pointless Nostalgic | Candid | CCD 79782

Shaw,Robert | (v)
Steve Kuhn With Strings
Promises Kept | ECM | 1815(0675222)

Shaw,Woody | (co,fl-h,tp,maracasyodeling)
Andrew Hill Sextet
Grass Roots | Blue Note | 522672-2
Anfrew Hill Nonet
Passing Ships | Blue Note | 593871-2
Chick Corea Quintet
Inner Space | Atlantic | 7567-81304-2
Chick Corea-Herbie Hancock-Keith Jarrett-McCoy Tyner | Atlantic | 7567-81402-2
Chick Corea Septet
The Complete 'Is' Sessions | Blue Note | 540532-2
Horace Silver Quintet
Horace Silver Retrospective | Blue Note | 495576-2
The Cape Verdean Blues | Blue Note | 576753-2
Blue Bossa | Blue Note | 795590-2
Horace Silver Sextet
Horace Silver Retrospective | Blue Note | 495576-2
The Cape Verdean Blues | Blue Note | 576753-2
Joe Henderson Quintet
Joe Henderson:The Milestone Years | Milestone | 8MCD 4413-2
Joe Henderson Sextet
Joe Henderson:The Milestone Years | Milestone | 8MCD 4413-2
Joe Zawinul Group
Zawinul | Atlantic | 7567-81375-2
Larry Young Quartet
Unity | Blue Note | 497808-2
Pharoah Sanders Orchestra
Deaf Dumb Blind | Impulse(MCA) | 951265-2
Woody Shaw Quartet
In My Own Sweet Way | IN+OUT Records | 7003-2
Jazz Unlimited | IN+OUT Records | 7017-2
Bemsha Swing | Blue Note | 829029-2

Shawker,Norris 'Bunny' | (dr)
Billie Holiday With Gordon Jenkins And His Orchestra
Billie's Love Songs | Nimbus Records | NI 2000
Coleman Hawkins Quintet
Body And Soul Revisited | GRP | GRP 16272
Coleman Hawkins Quintet With Strings
Body And Soul Revisited | GRP | GRP 16272
Louis Armstrong With Sy Oliver And His Orchestra
Satchmo Serenaders | Verve | 543792-2
Louis Armstrong-My Greatest Songs | MCA | MCD 18347
Nat King Cole Quartet
Penthouse Serenade | Capitol | 494504-2
Nat King Cole Quintet
Penthouse Serenade | Capitol | 494504-2
Sarah Vaughan With The Joe Lippman Orchestra
Sarah Vaughan:Lover Man | Dreyfus Jazz Line | FDM 36739-2

Shea,Frank | (dr)
Willis Jackson Quintet
Together Again: Willis Jackson With Jack McDuff | Prestige | PRCD 24284-2

Sheahan,John | (fiddlethin-whistle)
Hans Theessink Group
Crazy Moon | Minor Music | 801052

Shearing,George | (accordeon,p,vocp-solo)
George Shearing
Verve Jazz Masters 57:George Shearing | Verve | 529900-2
The Shearing Piano | Capitol | 531574-2
George Shearing And His Quintet
Verve Jazz Masters 57:George Shearing | Verve | 529900-2
Beauty And The Beat | Capitol | 542308-2
The Swingin's Mutual | Capitol | 799190-2
George Shearing Quintet
Verve Jazz Masters 57:George Shearing | Verve | 529900-2
Verve Jazz Masters Vol.59:Toots Thielemans | Verve | 535271-2
At Newport | Pablo | PACD 5315-2
George Shearing Quintet With Cannonball And Nat Adderley
At Newport | Pablo | PACD 5315-2
George Shearing Sextet
At Newport | Pablo | PACD 5315-2
George Shearing Trio
The Story Of Jazz Piano | Laserlight | 24653
George Shearing With The Montgomery Brothers
Wes Montgomery-The Complete Riverside Recordings | Riverside | 12 RCD 4408-2
George Shearing And The Montgomery Brothers | Original Jazz Classics | OJCCD 040-2
Nancy Wilson With George Shearing And His Quintet
The Swingin's Mutual | Capitol | 799190-2
Nat King Cole And George Shearing With Orchestra
Midnight Blue(The [Be]witching Hour) | Blue Note | 854365-2
Peggy Lee With George Shearing
Beauty And The Beat | Capitol | 542308-2
Peggy Lee With The George Shearing Trio
Beauty And The Beat | Capitol | 542308-2
Stephane Grappelli And His Musicians
Grapelli Story | Verve | 515807-2
Stephane Grappelli Quartet
Grapelli Story | Verve | 515807-2
Stephane Grappelli Quintet
Grapelli Story | Verve | 515807-2
Stephane Grappelli With The George Shearing Trio
Grapelli Story | Verve | 515807-2
Verve Jazz Masters 11:Stéphane Grappelli | Verve | 516758-2
Stephane Grappelli-George Shearing
Grapelli Story | Verve | 515807-2
Vic Lewis And His Band
Vic Lewis:The Golden Years | Candid | CCD 79754

Sheen,Mickey | (dr)
Coleman Hawkins And Confreres
Coleman Hawkins And Confreres | Verve | 835255-2 PMS
Coleman Hawkins-Roy Eldridge Quintet
Verve Jazz Masters 43:Coleman Hawkins | Verve | 521856-2
Lester Young Septet
Laughin' To Keep From Cryin' | Verve | 543301-2
Lester Young-Roy Eldridge-Harry Edison Band
Jazz Gallery:Lester Young Vol.2(1946-59) | RCA | 2119541-2

Sheet,Walter | (arr)
Ella Fitzgerald With The Billy May Orchestra
The Best Of The Song Books:The Ballads | Verve | 521867-2
Ella Fitzgerald Sings The Harold Arlen Song Book | Verve | 589108-2

Sheffield,Roosevelt | (b)
Ray Charles Trio
Rhino Presents The Atlantic Jazz Gallery | Atlantic | 8122-71257-2

Sheldon,Jack | (tpvoc)
Art Pepper Plus Eleven
Art Pepper + Eleven | Contemporary | CSA 7568-6
Modern Jazz Classics | Original Jazz Classics | OJC20 341-2
Art Pepper Quintet
Smack Up | Original Jazz Classics | OJC20 176-2
Benny Goodman And His Orchestra
40th Anniversary Concert-Live At Carnegie Hall | London | 820349-2
Verve Jazz Masters 33:Benny Goodman | Verve | 844410-2
Diane Schuur With Orchestra
Love Songs | GRP | GRP 97032
The Best Of Diane Schuur | GRP | GRP 98882
Diane Schuur With Orchestra And Strings
The Best Of Diane Schuur | GRP | GRP 98882
Gary Burton Quartet
Planet Jazz:Gary Burton | RCA | 2165367-2
Herbie Mann's Californians
Great Ideas Of Western Man | Original Jazz Classics | OJCCD 1065-2(RLP 245)
Jack Sheldon And His West Coast Friends
Art Pepper:The Hollywood All-Star Sessions | Galaxy | 5GCD 4431-2
Peggy Lee With The Quincy Jones Orchestra
Blues Cross Country | Capitol | 520088-2
Rolf Kühn Sextet
Rolf Kühn And His Sound Of Jazz | Fresh Sound Records | FSR-CD 326
Sonny Stitt Orchestra
Verve Jazz Masters 50:Sonny Sitt | Verve | 527651-2

Sheller,Marty | (cond,guiro,tpperc)
Mongo Santamaria And His Band
Mongo At The Village Gate | Original Jazz Classics | OJCCD 490-2(RLP 9529)

Shelton,Abraham | (voc)
Max Roach Chorus & Orchestra
To The Max! | Enja | ENJ-7021 22

Shelton,Don | (as,bs,cl,voc,fl,alto-fl,ts,piccolo)
Lyke Ritz Quartet
How About Uke? | Verve | 0760942
Lyle Ritz Quartet
How About Uke? | Verve | 0760942
Singers Unlimited
The Singers Unlimited:Magic Voices | MPS | 539130-2
Singers Unlimited + The Oscar Peterson Trio
The Singers Unlimited:Magic Voices | MPS | 539130-2
Singers Unlimited With Orchestra
The Singers Unlimited:Magic Voices | MPS | 539130-2
Singers Unlimited With Rob McConnell And The Boss Brass
The Singers Unlimited:Magic Voices | MPS | 539130-2
Singers Unlimited With Roger Kellaway
The Singers Unlimited:Magic Voices | MPS | 539130-2
Singers Unlimited With The Art Van Damme Quintet
The Singers Unlimited:Magic Voices | MPS | 539130-2
Singers Unlimited With The Clare Fischer Orchestra
The Singers Unlimited:Magic Voices | MPS | 539130-2
Singers Unlimited With The Pat Williams Orchestra
The Singers Unlimited:Magic Voices | MPS | 539130-2
Singers Unlimited With The Patrick Williams Orchestra
The Singers Unlimited:Magic Voices | MPS | 539130-2
Singers Unlimited With The Robert Farnon Orchestra
The Singers Unlimited:Magic Voices | MPS | 539130-2
Singers Unlimited With The Roger Kellaway Cello Quartet
The Singers Unlimited:Magic Voices | MPS | 539130-2
Vic Lewis West Coast All Stars
Vic Lewis Presenting A Celebration Of Contemporary West Coast Jazz | Candid | CCD 79711/12

Shelton,Louie | (g)
Big Joe Turner And His Orchestra
Planet Jazz:Male Jazz Vocalists | Planet Jazz | 2169657-2
Sarah Vaughan And Her Band
Songs Of The Beatles | Atlantic | 16037-2

Shelvin,Tommy | (el-b)
Jack McDuff Sextet
The Soulful Drums | Prestige | PCD 24256-2

Shepard,Ernie | (bvoc)
Duke Ellington And His Orchestra
The Great Paris Concert | Atlantic | 7567-81303-2
Afro-Bossa | Reprise | 9362-47876-2
Sonny Stitt And His Band
Kaleidoscope | Original Jazz Classics | OJCCD 060-2(P 7077)
Sonny Stitt Quintet
Kaleidoscope | Original Jazz Classics | OJCCD 060-2(P 7077)

Shepard,Tom | (tb)
Anita O'Day With The Billy May Orchestra
Verve Jazz Masters 49:Anita O'Day | Verve | 527653-2
Ella Fitzgerald With The Marty Paich Orchestra
Get Happy! | Verve | 523321-2
Ella Fitzgerald With The Nelson Riddle Orchestra
The Best Of The Song Books:The Ballads | Verve | 521867-2
Love Songs:The Best Of The Song Books | Verve | 531762-2
Ella Fitzgerald Sings The Johnny Mercer Songbook | Verve | 539057-2
Mel Tormé With The Russell Garcia Orchestra

Swingin' On The Moon | Verve | 511385-2
Peggy Lee With The Quincy Jones Orchestra
Blues Cross Country | Capitol | 520088-2
Stan Kenton And His Orchestra
Stan Kenton Portraits On Standards | Capitol | 531571-2

Shepherd,Dave | (cl)
Great British Jazz Band
The Great British Jazz Band:Jubilee | Candid | CCD 79720
The Alex Welsh Legacy Band
The Sound Of Alex Vol.1 | Nagel-Heyer | CD 070
The Great British Jazz Band
A British Jazz Odyssey | Candid | CCD 79740

Shepherd,Jean | (narration)
Charles Mingus Jazz Workshop
The Clown | Atlantic | 8122-75358-2
Charles Mingus Quintet
Charles Mingus-Passion Of A Man:The Complete Atlantic Recordings 1956-1961 | Atlantic | 8122-72871-2

Shepherd,Leo | (tp)
(Little)Jimmy Scott With The Lionel Hampton Orchestra
Everybody's Somebody's Fool | Decca | 050669-2
Lionel Hampton Orchestra
The Big Bands Vol.1.The Snader Telescriptions | Storyville | 4960043

Shepherd,Shep | (dr)
Odetta With The Buck Clayton Sextet
Odetta And The Blues | Original Blues Classics | OBCCD 509-2(RLP 9417)

Shepherd,William 'Bill' | (tb)
Dizzy Gillespie And His Orchestra
Dizzy Gillespie:Pleyel Jazz Concert 1948 + Max Roach Quintet 1949 | Vogue | 21409412
Planet Jazz:Dizzy Gillespie | Planet Jazz | 2152069-2
Planet Jazz:Bebop | RCA | 2169650-2
Ella Fitzgerald With The Dizzy Gillespie Orchestra
Ella Fitzgerald:Mr.Paganini | Dreyfus Jazz Line | FDM 36741-2
Ella Fitzgerald With The Hank Jones Trio
Ella Fitzgerald:Mr.Paganini | Dreyfus Jazz Line | FDM 36741-2

Shepik,Brad | (el-gg)
Dave Douglas Tiny Bell Trio
Wandering Souls | Winter&Winter | 910042-2
Franz Koglmann Quintet
Make Believe | Between The Lines | btl 001(Efa 10171-2)

Shepley,Joe | (tpfl-h)
David Matthews & The Manhattan Jazz Orchestra
Back To Bach | Milestone | MCD 9312-2
Hey Duke! | Milestone | MCD 9320-2
Earl Klugh Group
Late Night Guitar | Blue Note | 498573-2
Kenny Burrell With The Don Sebesky Orchestra
Verve Jazz Masters 45:Kenny Burrell | Verve | 527652-2
Ron Carter Orchestra
Parade | Original Jazz Classics | OJCCD 1047-2(M 9088)
Rusty Bryant Group
For The Good Times | Prestige | PRCD 24269-2

Shepp,Archie | (as,ts,voc,fl,ss,p,recitationbs)
Archie Sheep-Jasper Van't Hof Duo
Mama Rose | Steeplechase | SCCD 31169
Archie Shepp Orchestra
Mama Too Tight | Impulse(MCA) | 951248-2
The Cry Of My People | Impulse(MCA) | 9861488
Archie Shepp Septet
The Way Ahead | Impulse(MCA) | 951272-2
Archie Shepp Sextet
Fire Music | Impulse(MCA) | 951158-2
Four For Trane | Impulse(MCA) | 951218-2
The Way Ahead | Impulse(MCA) | 951272-2
Archie Shepp Trio
Fire Music | Impulse(MCA) | 951158-2
Archie Shepp/Niels-Henning Orsted-Pedersen Duo
Looking At Bird | Steeplechase | SCS 1149(Audiophile Pressing)
Archie Shepp-Dollar Brand Duo
The Art Of Saxophone | Laserlight | 24652
Archie Shepp-Horace Parlan Duo
Goin' Home | Steeplechase | SCCD 31079
Trouble In Mind | Steeplechase | SCCD 31139
Cecil Taylor Quartet
The World Of Cecil Taylor | Candid | CCD 79006
Cecil Taylor: Air | Candid | CCD 79046
Cecil Taylor Unit
Mixed | Impulse(MCA) | IMP 12702
Cecil Taylor/Buell Neidlinger Orchestra
New York City R&B | Candid | CCD 79017
Cecil Taylor/Buell Neidlinger Quartet
New York City R&B | Candid | CCD 79017
Chico Hamilton Quintet
The Dealer | Impulse(MCA) | 547958-2
The Roots Of Acid Jazz | Impulse(MCA) | IMP 12042
John Coltrane And His Orchestra
Ascension | Impulse(MCA) | 543413-2
John Coltrane Sextet
A Love Supreme | Impulse(MCA) | 589945-2
Roswell Rudd-Archie Shepp Group
Live In New York | EmArCy | 013482-2

Sheppard,Andy | (cl,tsss)
Barbara Dennerlein Quartet
Hot Stuff | Enja | ENJ-6050 2
Carla Bley Band
Fleur Carnivore | Watt | 21
Carla Bley Big Band
The Carla Bley Big Band Goes To Church | Watt | 27(533682-2)
Carla Bley/Andy Sheppard/Steve Swallow
Song With Legs | Watt | 26(527069)
Dimitrios Vassilakis Daedalus Project
Labyrinth | Candid | CCD 79776

Sheppard,Bob | (as,cl,b-cl,fl,alto-fl,ssts)
Carla Bley Band
The Very Big Carla Bley Band | Watt | 23
Big Band Theory | Watt | 25(519966-2)
4X4 | Watt | 30(159547-2)
Kurt Elling Group
Flirting With Twilight | Blue Note | 531113-2

Sheppard,Harry | (vib)
Mike Bryan Sextet
Jazz Festival Vol.2 | Storyville | 4960743

Sheppard,Leo | (tp)
Lionel Hampton And His Orchestra
Lionel Hampton:Flying Home | Dreyfus Jazz Line | FDM 36735-2

Sherba,John | (v)
John Zorn Group With The Kronos Quartet
Spillane | Nonesuch | 7559-79172-2

Sherman,James | (p)
Billie Holiday And Her Orchestra
Jazz:The Essential Collection Vol.3 | IN+OUT Records | 78013-2

Sherman,Ray | (keyboardsp)
Glen Gray And His Orchestra
Great Swing Classics In Hi-Fi | Capitol | 521223-2
Van Alexander Orchestra
Home Of Happy Feet/Swing! Staged For Sound! | Capitol | 535211-2

Sherock,Shorty | (tp)
Anita O'Day With Gene Krupa And His Orchestra
Let Me Off Uptown:Anita O'Day With Gene Krupa | CBS | CK 65625
Benny Carter And His Orchestra
Aspects | Capitol | 852677-2
Ella Fitzgerald With The Nelson Riddle Orchestra
The Best Of The Song Books:The Ballads | Verve | 521867-2
Get Happy! | Verve | 523321-2
Oh Lady Be Good:The Best Of The Gershwin Songbook | Verve | 529581-2
Love Songs:The Best Of The Song Books | Verve | 531762-2
Ella Fitzgerald Sings The Johnny Mercer Songbook | Verve | 539057-2
Dream Dancing | Original Jazz Classics | OJCCD 1072-2(2310814)
Glen Gray And His Orchestra
Great Swing Classics In Hi-Fi | Capitol | 521223-2
JATP All Stars
The Complete Jazz At The Philharmonic On Verve 1944-1949 | Verve | 523893-2
Jazz At The Philharmonic:Best Of The 1940's Concerts | Verve | 557534-2
The Capitol Jazzmen
The Hollywood Session:The Capitol Jazzmen | Jazz Unlimited | JUCD 2044
Tommy Dorsey And His Orchestra
Planet Jazz:Frank Sinatra & Tommy Dorsey | Planet Jazz | 2152067-2
Frank Sinatra And The Tommy Dorsey Orchestra | RCA | 2668701-2
Van Alexander Orchestra
Home Of Happy Feet/Swing! Staged For Sound! | Capitol | 535211-2

Sherree | (voc)
Fourplay
Fourplay...Yes,Please! | Warner | 9362-47694-2

Sherrill,Joya | (voc)
Duke Ellington And His Orchestra
Planet Jazz:Duke Ellington | Planet Jazz | 2152053-2
Planet Jazz:Jazz Greatest Hits | Planet Jazz | 2169648-2
Highlights From The Duke Ellington Centennial Edition | RCA | 2663672-2
Carnegie Hall Concert January 1946 | Prestige | 2PCD 24074-2

Sherry,Claude | (fr-h)
Pete Rugolo And His Orchestra
Thriller/Richard Diamon(Original Jazz Scores From 2 Classics TV Series) | Fresh Sound Records | FSCD 2015

Sherry,Fred | (cello)
Chick Corea With String Quartet,Flute And French Horn
Septet | ECM | 1297
Steve Swallow Group
Carla | Watt | XtraWatt/2

Sherwood,Bobby | (gtp)
Artie Shaw And His Orchestra
Planet JazzArtie Shaw | Planet Jazz | 2152057-2
Planet Jazz:Jazz Greatest Hits | Planet Jazz | 2169648-2
Ten Cats And A Mouse
The Hollywood Session:The Capitol Jazzmen | Jazz Unlimited | JUCD 2044

SheshBesh |
SheshBesh
SheshBesh | TipToe | TIP-888830 2

Shew,Bobby | (tp,fl-h,coshew-horn)
Buddy Rich And His Orchestra
Swingin' New Big Band | Pacific Jazz | 835232-2
Big Swing Face | Pacific Jazz | 837989-2
Conexion Latina
Mambo Nights | Enja | ENJ-9402 2
Herbie Hancock Group
Sunlight | CBS | 486570-2
Hugo Siegmeth Quintet
Live At The Jazzclub Unterfahrt | Edition Collage | EC 533-2
Singers Unlimited With The Pat Williams Orchestra
The Singers Unlimited:Magic Voices | MPS | 539130-2

Shezbie,Derrick | (tpperc)
Maceo Parker With The Rebirth Brass Band
Southern Exposure | Minor Music | 801033

Shields,Larry | (clvoc)
Original Dixieland 'Jass' Band
Planet Jazz | Planet Jazz | 2169652-2

Shiffman,Bud | (as)
Peggy Lee With The Benny Goodman Orchestra
Peggy Lee & Benny Goodman:The Complete Recordings 1941-1947 | CBS | C2K 65686

Shigihara,Paul | (g,el-gg-synth)
Charlie Mariano Trio
Mariano | VeraBra Records | CDVBR 2124-2
Gianlugi Trovesi Quartet With The WDR Big Band
Dedalo | Enja | ENJ-9419 2
International Commission For The Prevention Of Musical Border Control,The
The International Commission For The Prevention Of Musical Border Control | VeraBra Records | CDVBR 2093-2
Jens Winther And The WDR Big Band
The Escape | dacapo | DCCD 9437
Klaus Doldinger's Passport
Balance Of Happiness | Warner | 9031-71233-2
Paul Shigihara-Charlie Mariano Quartet
Tears Of Sound | Nabel Records:Jazz Network | CD 4616

Shihab,Sahib | (alto-fl,ss,bs,as,fl,tambourine,ts)
Abbey Lincoln With The Benny Golson Septet
It's Magic | Original Jazz Classics | OJCCD 205-2
Bengt-Arne Wallin Orchestra
The Birth+Rebirth Of Swedish Folk Jazz | ACT | 9254-2
Curtis Fuller And Hampton Hawes With French Horns
Curtis Fuller And Hampton Hawes With French Horns | Original Jazz Classics | OJCCD 1942-2(NJ 8305)
Curtis Fuller And Teddy Charles With French Horns
Curtis Fuller And Hampton Hawes With French Horns | Original Jazz Classics | OJCCD 1942-2(NJ 8305)
Dinah Washington And Her Sextet
Newport Jazz Festival 1958,July 3rd-6th Vol.4:Blues In The Night No.2 | Phontastic | NCD 8816
Dinah Washington With The Newport All Stars
Dinah Sings Bessie Smith | Verve | 538635-2
John Coltrane Sextet
John Coltrane-The Prestige Recordings | Prestige | 16 PCD 4405-2
Coltrane | Original Jazz Classics | OJC20 020-2
The Prestige Legacy Vol.1:The High Priests | Prestige | PCD 24251-2
Kenny Clarke-Francy Boland Big Band
Clark-Boland Big Band: TNP, October 29th, 1969 | Laserlight | 36129
Three Latin Adventures | MPS | 529095-2
More Smiles | MPS | 9814789
All Smiles | MPS | 9814790
Francy Boland-Fellini 712 | MPS | 9814805
Mal Waldron Sextet
John Coltrane-The Prestige Recordings | Prestige | 16 PCD 4405-2
The Jazz Giants Play Jerome Kern:Yesterdays | Prestige | PCD 24202-2
NDR-Workshop
Doldinger's Best | ACT | 9224-2
Paul Nero Sound
Doldinger's Best | ACT | 9224-2
Philly Joe Jones Big Band
Cannonball Adderley Birthday Celebration | Fantasy | FANCD 6087-2
Prestige All Stars
The Prestige Legacy Vol.2:Battles Of Saxes | Prestige | PCD 24252-2
Raul De Souza Orchestra
Cannonball Adderley Birthday Celebration | Fantasy | FANCD 6087-2
Tadd Dameron And His Orchestra
Fontainebleau | Original Jazz Classics | OJCCD 055-2
Tadd Dameron Tentet
Jazz Profile:Dexter Gordon | Blue Note | 823514-2
Thelonious Monk Quintet
Genius Of Modern Music,Vol.1 | Blue Note | 532138-2
Genius Of Modern Music,Vol.2 | Blue Note | 532139-2
The Best Of Thelonious Monk:The Blue Note Years | Blue Note | 795636-2
Jazz Profile:Thelonious Monk | Blue Note | 823518-2
Thelonious Monk:Misterioso | Dreyfus Jazz Line | FDM 36743-2

Shilansky,Mark | (p)
Mitch Seidman Quartet
How 'Bout It? | Jardis Records | JRCD 20135

Shilkloper,Arkady | (fl-h,fr-h,alphorn,voicejagdhorn)
Andreas Willers Octet
The Ground Music | Enja | ENJ-9368 2
Mikhail Alperin/Arkady Shilkloper
Wave Over Sorrow | ECM | 1396
Mikhail Alperin's Moscow Art Trio
Folk Dreams | JA & RO | JARO 4187-2
Prayer | JA & RO | JARO 4193-2
Hamburg Concert | JA & RO | JARO 4201-2
Mikhail Alperin's Moscow Art Trio With The Russkaja Pesnja Folk Choir
Folk Dreams | JA & RO | JARO 4187-2
Mikhail Alperin's Moscow Art Trio With The Tuva Folk & Russian Folk Ensemble
Prayer | JA & RO | JARO 4193-2
Misha Alperin Group With John Surman
First Impression | ECM | 1664(557650-2)
Misha Alperin Quintet
North Story | ECM | 1596
Moscow Art Trio
Music | JA & RO | JARO 4214-2
Portrait | JA & RO | JARO 4227-2
Once Upon A Time | JA & RO | JARO 4238-2
Moscow Art Trio And The Bulgarian Voices Angelite
Portrait | JA & RO | JARO 4227-2

Shim,Mark | (clts)
Mose Allison Quintet
Gimeracs And Gewgaws | Blue Note | 823211-2

Shimada,Nariko | (bassooncontra-bassoon)
Ensemble Modern
Ensemble Modern-Fred Frith:Traffic Continues | Winter&Winter | 910044-2

Shine,Bill | (as,saxts)
Woody Herman And His Orchestra
Old Gold Rehearsals 1944 | Jazz Unlimited | JUCD 2079

Shiner,Ray | (engl-h,cl,tsoboe)
Stan Getz With The Eddie Sauter Orchestra
Stan Getz Plays The Music Of Mickey One | Verve | 531232-2

Shipinsky,Murray | (b)
Dizzy Gillespie Sextet
Dizzy Gillespie:Night In Tunisia | Dreyfus Jazz Line | FDM 36734-2

Shipp,Matthew | (p,percp-solo)
Roscoe Mitchell And The Note Factory
Nine To Get Ready | ECM | 1651(539725-2)

Shirasaka,Nobuyuki | (ohtsuzumi)
Toshinori Kondo & Ima plus Guests
Human Market | JA & RO | JARO 4146-2

Shirley,Jimmy | (g)
Edmond Hall's Blue Note Jazzmen
The Blue Note Jazzmen | Blue Note | 821262-2
James P.Johnson's Blue Note Jazzmen
Jazz:The Essential Collection Vol.3 | IN+OUT Records | 78013-2
The Blue Note Jazzmen | Blue Note | 821262-2
John Hardee Sextet
The Blue Note Swingtets | Blue Note | 495697-2
Pete Johnson's Housewarmin'
Jazz:The Essential Collection Vol.3 | IN+OUT Records | 78013-2
Sidney DeParis' Blue Note Jazzmen
The Blue Note Jazzmen | Blue Note | 821262-2

Shirnian,Harry | (viola)
Charlie Haden Quartet West With Strings
The Art Of The Song | Verve | 547403-2

Shive,Carol | (vvoc)
Mahavishnu Orchestra
Apocalypse | CBS | 467092-2

Shlomo,Absholom Ben | (fl,cl,asperc)
Sun Ra And His Intergalactic Research Arkestra
Black Myth/Out In Space | MPS | 557656-2

Shoffner,Bob | (cotp)
Blind Willie Dunn's Gin Bottle Four
Jazz:The Essential Collection Vol.1 | IN+OUT Records | 78011-2
King Oliver And His Dixie Syncopators
Jazz:The Essential Collection Vol.1 | IN+OUT Records | 78011-2
King Oliver's Jazz Band
Jazz:The Essential Collection Vol.1 | IN+OUT Records | 78011-2

Shore,Paul | (v)
Harry James And His Orchestra
Trumpet Blues:The Best Of Harry James | Capitol | 521224-2

Short,Bob | (b,tubaco)
Lu Watters' Jazz Band
Blues Over Bodega | Good Time Jazz | GTCD 12066-2
Turk Murphy And His Jazz Band
Planet Jazz | Planet Jazz | 2169652-2

Shorter,Alan | (fl-h,tptambourine)
Archie Shepp Sextet
Four For Trane | Impulse(MCA) | 951218-2

Shorter,Wayne | (arr,as,ts,cl,lyricon,sax,ss,bs,p)
Art Blakey And The Jazz Messengers
Planet Jazz:Art Blakey | Planet Jazz | 2152066-2
Planet Jazz:Lee Morgan | Planet Jazz | 2161238-2
Art Blakey & The Jazz Messengers: Olympia, May 13th, 1961 | Laserlight | 36128
Paris Jazz Concert:Art Blakey & The Jazz Messengers | Laserlight | 36158
Best Of Blakey 60 | Blue Note | 493072-2
Roots And Herbs | Blue Note | 521956-2
The Witch Doctor | Blue Note | 521957-2
True Blue | Blue Note | 534032-2
Meet You At The Jazz Corner Of The World | Blue Note | 535565-2
Wayne Shorter:The Classic Blue Note Recordings | Blue Note | 540856-2
The Art Of Jazz | IN+OUT Records | 77028-2
Blue N' Groovy | Blue Note | 780679-2
A Night In Tunisia | Blue Note | 784049-2
Feedom Rider | Blue Note | 821287-2
Jazz In Paris:Paris Jam Session | EmArCy | 832692-2 PMS
Impulse!Art Blakey!Jazz Messengers! | Impulse(MCA) | 951175-2
Caravan | Original Jazz Classics | OJC20 038-2
Ugetsu | Original Jazz Classics | OJC20 090-2(RLP 9464)
Art Blakey And The Jazz Messengers With Barney Wilen And Bud Powell
Jazz In Paris:Paris Jam Session | EmArCy | 832692-2 PMS
Bobby McFerrin Groups
Spontaneous Inventions | Blue Note | 746298-2
Buster Williams Quintet
Something More | IN+OUT Records | 7004-2
Jazz Unlimited | IN+OUT Records | 7017-2
Donald Byrd Quintet
Herbie Hancock:The Complete Blue Note Sixties Sessions | Blue Note | 495569-2
Freddie Hubbard Orchestra
The Body And The Soul | Impulse(MCA) | 951183-2
Freddie Hubbard Septet
The Body And The Soul | Impulse(MCA) | 951183-2
Freddie Hubbard Sextet
Wayne Shorter:The Classic Blue Note Recordings | Blue Note | 540856-2
Gil Evans Orchestra
Verve Jazz Masters 23:Gil Evans | Verve | 521860-2
The Individualism Of Gil Evans | Verve | 833804-2
Grachan Moncur III Quintet
A Blue Conception | Blue Note | 534254-2
Herbie Hancock Group
Man-Child | CBS | 471235-2
Herbie Hancock Quintet
V.S.O.P. Herbie Hancock-Live At The City Center N.Y. | CBS | 486569-2
Jaco Pastorius With Orchestra
Word Of Mouth | Warner | 7599-23525-2
Joe Zawinul Group

Zawinul | Atlantic | 7567-81375-2
John Scofield Groups
Quiet | Verve | 533185-2
Lee Morgan Orchestra
Standards | Blue Note | 823213-2
Lee Morgan Sextet
Wayne Shorter:The Classic Blue Note Recordings | Blue Note | 540856-2
Search For The New Land | Blue Note | 591896-2
Manhattan Project,The
Kind Of Blue:Blue Note Celebrate The Music Of Miles Davis | Blue Note | 534255-2
Wayne Shorter:The Classic Blue Note Recordings | Blue Note | 540856-2
Marcus Miller Group
The Sun Don't Lie | Dreyfus Jazz Line | FDM 36560-2
McCoy Tyner Sextet
Extensions | Blue Note | 837646-2
Michel Petrucciani feat. Jim Hall and Wayne Shorter
Wayne Shorter:The Classic Blue Note Recordings | Blue Note | 540856-2
Power Of Three-Live At Montreux | Blue Note | 746427-2
Michel Petrucciani:The Blue Note Years | Blue Note | 789916-2
Miles Davis Group
Circle In The Round | CBS | 467898-2
In A Silent Way | CBS | 86556-2
Live-Evil | CBS | C2K 65135
Bitches Brew | CBS | C2K 65774
Miles Davis Quintet
Circle In The Round | CBS | 467898-2
Highlights From The Plugged Nickel | CBS | 481434-2
Filles De Kilimanjaro | CBS | 86555-2
Miles Davis Quintet 1965-1968 | CBS | C6K 67398
This Is Jazz:Miles Davis Plays Ballads | CBS | CK 65038
Sorcerer | CBS | CK 65680
Nefertiti | CBS | CK 65681
Miles Smiles | CBS | CK 65682
Miles In The Sky | CBS | CK 65684
E.S.P. | CBS | CK65683
Miles Davis Sextet
Circle In The Round | CBS | 467898-2
Sorcerer | CBS | CK 65680
Miles In The Sky | CBS | CK 65684
Rachelle Ferrell With The Wayne Shorter Sextet
First Instrumental | Blue Note | 827820-2
Stanley Clarke Group
If This Bass Could Only Talk | CBS | 460883-2
Wayne Shorter Orchestra
Wayne Shorter:The Classic Blue Note Recordings | Blue Note | 540856-2
Wayne Shorter Quartet
Herbie Hancock:The Complete Blue Note Sixties Sessions | Blue Note | 495569-2
Juju | Blue Note | 499005-2
Kind Of Blue:Blue Note Celebrate The Music Of Miles Davis | Blue Note | 534255-2
Wayne Shorter:The Classic Blue Note Recordings | Blue Note | 540856-2
Footprints Live! | Verve | 589679-2
Adams Apple | Blue Note | 591901-2
Sorcerer | CBS | CK 65680
Wayne Shorter Quintet
Speak No Evil | Blue Note | 499001-2
Wayne Shorter:The Classic Blue Note Recordings | Blue Note | 540856-2
Night Dreamer | Blue Note | 784173-2
Wayne Shorter Sextet
Wayne Shorter:The Classic Blue Note Recordings | Blue Note | 540856-2
Blue N' Groovy | Blue Note | 780679-2
Wayne Shorter-Herbie Hancock
1+1:Herbie Hancock-Wayne Shorter | Verve | 537564-2
Weather Report
Mr. Gone | CBS | 468208-2
Black Market | CBS | 468210-2
Night Passage | CBS | 468211-2
Sweetnighter | CBS | 485102-2
Weathe Report Live In Tokyo | CBS | 489208-2
Heavy Weather | CBS | CK 65108

Shotham,Ramesh | (cymbals,ghatam,kanjira,milkpot)
Charlie Mariano & The Karnataka College Of Percussion
Live | VeraBra Records | CDVBR 2034-2
Christoph Haberer Group
Pulsation | Jazz Haus Musik | JHM 0066 CD
Dirk Raulf Group
Theater I (Bühnenmusik) | Poise | Poise 07
Kölner Saxophon Mafia With Ramesh Shotham
Kölner Saxophon Mafia Proudly Presents | Jazz Haus Musik | JHM 0046 CD
Nicolas Simion Group
Balkan Jazz | Intuition Records | INT 3339-2
Rabih Abou-Khalil Group
Al-Jadida | Enja | ENJ-6090 2
Blue Camel | Enja | ENJ-7053 2
Tarab | Enja | ENJ-7083 2
Bukra | Enja | ENJ-9372 2
Rabih Abou-Khalil Quintet
Between Dusk And Dawn | Enja | ENJ-9771 2
Rabih Abou-Khalil Septet
Between Dusk And Dawn | Enja | ENJ-9771 2

Shrinivas,U. | (mand)
Remember Shakti
Saturday Night In Bombay | Verve | 014184-2

Shroyer,Kenny | (b-tbtb)
Anita O'Day With The Russ Garcia Orchestra
Verve Jazz Masters 49:Anita O'Day | Verve | 527653-2
Buddy Childers Big Band
It's What Happening Now! | Candid | CCD 79749
Dizzy Gillespie And His Orchestra
Talking Verve:Dizzy Gillespie | Verve | 533846-2
Frank Sinatra With The Count Basie Orchestra
It Might As Well Be Spring | Reprise | 7599-27027-2
June Christy With The Shorty Rogers Orchestra
June Christy Big Band Special | Capitol | 498319-2
Stan Kenton Orchestra
Stompin' At Newport | Pablo | PACD 5312-2
Van Alexander Orchestra
Home Of Happy Feet/Swing! Staged For Sound! | Capitol | 535211-2

Shterev,Simeon | (fl)
Jazzensemble Des Hessischen Rundfunks
Atmosphering Conditions Permitting | ECM | 1549/50

Shu,Eddie | (cl,sax,harm,tpts)
Louis Armstrong And His All Stars
Jazz In Paris:Louis Armstrong:The Best Live Concer Vol.1 | EmArCy | 013030-2
Jazz In Paris:Louis Armstrong-The Best Live Concert Vol.2 | EmArCy | 013031-2
Live In Berlin/Friedrichstadtpalast | Jazzpoint | JP 1062 CD
The Legendary Berlin Concert Part 2 | Jazzpoint | JP 1063 CD

Shubring,Clarence | (v)
Mel Tormé With The Russell Garcia Orchestra
Swingin' On The Moon | Verve | 511385-2

Shulman,Alan | (cello)
Bob James And His Orchestra
Jazzrock-Anthology Vol.3:Fusion | Zounds | CD 27100555
Coleman Hawkins With Billy Byers And His Orchestra
The Hawk In Hi-Fi | RCA | 2663842-2

Grant Green With Orchestra
The Final Comedown(Soundtrack) | Blue Note | 581678-2
Harry Carney And His Orchestra With Strings
Music For Loving:Ben Webster With Strings | Verve | 527774-2
Milt Jackson And His Orchestra
Sunflower | CTI | ZK 65131
Nina Simone And Orchestra
Baltimore | Epic | 476906-2

Shulman,Amy | (harp)
Jacintha With Band And Strings
Lush Life | Groove Note | GRV 1011-2(Gold CD 2011)

Shulman,Ira | (fl,cl,tspiccolo)
Don Ellis Orchestra
Electric Bath | CBS | CK 65522

Shulman,Joe | (b)
Lester Young Quartet
Jazz Gallery:Lester Young Vol.2(1946-59) | RCA | 2119541-2
Miles Davis And His Orchestra
The Complete Birth Of The Cool | Capitol | 494550-2
Birth Of The Cool | Capitol | 530117-2
Miles Davis:The Best Of The Capitol/Blue Note Years | Blue Note | 798287-2
Miles Davis:Milestones | Dreyfus Jazz Line | FDM 36731-2

Shulman,Matt | (tp)
Josh Roseman Unit
Cherry | Enja | ENJ-9392 2

Shulman,Sylvan | (cond,arrv)
Harry Carney And His Orchestra With Strings
Music For Loving:Ben Webster With Strings | Verve | 527774-2
Paul Desmond Quartet With The Don Sebesby Orchestra
From The Hot Afternoon | Verve | 543487-2
Wes Montgomery With The Jimmy Jones Orchestra
Wes Montgomery-The Complete Riverside Recordings | Riverside | 12 RCD 4408-2

Shulman,Sylvan prob. | (v)
Charlie Parker With The Joe Lipman Orchestra
Charlie Parker With Strings:The Master Takes | Verve | 523984-2
Charlie Parker Big Band | Verve | 559835-2

Shunk,Larry | (b-tbtb)
Woody Herman And His Orchestra
Verve Jazz Masters 54:Woody Herman | Verve | 529903-2

Shure,Paul | (concertmaster,ldv)
Charlie Haden Quartet West With Strings
The Art Of The Song | Verve | 547403-2
Ella Fitzgerald With The Nelson Riddle Orchestra
The Best Of The Song Books:The Ballads | Verve | 521867-2
Frank Sinatra With The Count Basie Orchestra
It Might As Well Be Spring | Reprise | 7599-27027-2
Hank Crawford Orchestra
Rhino Presents The Atlantic Jazz Gallery | Atlantic | 8122-71257-2

Shy,Robert | (dr)
Rahsaan Roland Kirk Sextet
Atlantic Saxophones | Rhino | 8122-71256-2

Sickler,Don | (fl-h,ld,tparr)
Don Sickler Orchestra
Tribute To Charlie Parker Vol.2 | Dreyfus Jazz Line | FDM 37015-2
Fleurine With Band And Horn Section
Meant To Be! | EmArCy | 159085-2

Siclair,Ted | (b)
Lionel Hampton And His Orchestra
Lionel Hampton:Flying Home | Dreyfus Jazz Line | FDM 36735-2

Sida,Rafael | (perc)
Jonas Knutsson Quartet
Jonas Knutsson Quartet | Touché Music | TMcCD 018

Siddik,Rasul | (tp)
Lester Bowie's Brass Fantasy
Avant Pop | ECM | 1326

Sidell,Al | (dr)
Muggsy Spanier And His Ragtime Band
Planet Jazz | Planet Jazz | 2169652-2
Planet Jazz:Jazz Trumpet | Planet Jazz | 2169654-2

Sides,Douglas 'Doug' | (dr)
Doug Sides Ensemble
Sumblo | Laika Records | 35100882
Fritz Krisse Quartet
Soulcolours | Laika Records | 35100782
John Marshall Quintet
Theme Of No Repeat | Organic Music | ORGM 9719
Johnny Griffin Quintet
Grab This! | Original Jazz Classics | OJCCD 1941-2(RLP 9437)

Sidewalks Of New York Choir,The | (crowd)
The Sidewalks Of New York
Tin Pan Alley:The Sidewalks Of New York | Winter&Winter | 910038-2

Sidney Bechet Society,The |
The Sidney Bechet Society
Jam Session Concert | Nagel-Heyer | CD 076

Sieb,Lothar | (b)
Vesna Skorija Band
Niceland | Satin Doll Productions | SDP 1037-1 CD

Siebert,Stephan | (b-g)
Human Factor
Forbidden City | Nabel Records:Jazz Network | CD 4635

Siegel,Bill | (tb)
Tommy Dorsey And His Orchestra
Planet Jazz:Tommy Dorsey | Planet Jazz | 2159972-2

Siegel,Eileen | (v)
Terje Rypdal With The Borealis Ensemble
Q.E.D. | ECM | 14/4

Siegel,Ray | (btuba)
Gerry Mulligan Tentette
Gene Norman Presents The Original Gerry Mulligan Tentet And Quartet | GNP Crescendo | GNPD 56

Siegelstein,Sandy | (fr-h)
Miles Davis And His Orchestra
The Complete Birth Of The Cool | Capitol | 494550-2
Birth Of The Cool | Capitol | 530117-2
Jazz Profile:Miles Davis | Blue Note | 823515-2
Miles Davis:Milestones | Dreyfus Jazz Line | FDM 36731-2

Siegler,John | (b)
Bobby McFerrin Group
Bobby McFerrin | Elektra | 7559-60023-2

Siegmeth,Hugo | (ts)
Clark Terry With The Summit Jazz Orchestra
Clark | Edition Collage | EC 530-2
Hugo Siegmeth Quintet
Live At The Jazzclub Unterfahrt | Edition Collage | EC 533-2

Sierra,Rafael | (perc)
Sarah Vaughan With Orchestra
!Viva! Vaughan | Mercury | 549374-2
Sarah Vaughan With The Frank Foster Orchestra
The Antonio Carlos Jobim Songbook | Verve | 525472-2

Sieverts,Henning | (bcello)
Florian Trübsbach Quintet
Manson & Dixon | Jazz 4 Ever Records:Jazz Network | J4E 4759
Geoff Goodman Quintet
Naked Eye | Tutu Records | 888214-2*
Heinrich Von Kalnein Group
New Directions | Nabel Records:Jazz Network | CD 4670
Horst Faigle's Jazzkrement
Gans Normal | Jazz 4 Ever Records:Jazz Network | J4E 4748
Joe Kienemann Trio
Liedgut:Amsel,Drossel,Swing & Funk | yvp music | CD 3095
Michael Lutzeier Quartet
Music 4 Food | Jazz 4 Ever Records:Jazz Network | J4E 4739
Nils Wogram Octet
Odd And Awkward | Enja | ENJ-9416-2
Sieverts-Mahall-Elgart
Goldfischgesänge | Jazz Haus Musik | JHM 0076 CD

Wolfgang Lackerschmid Quartet
One More Life | Bhakti Jazz | BR 29

Siffling,Thomas | (tpfl-h)
Polyphonix
Alarm | Jazz 'n' Arts Records | 0300
Rainer Tempel Big Band
Melodies Of '98 | Jazz 4 Ever Records:Jazz Network | J4E 4744
Album 03 | Jazz 'n' Arts Records | JNA 1102
Thomas Siffling Jazz Quartet
Soft Winds | Satin Doll Productions | SDP 1030-1 CD

Sigg,Stefan | (tp)
Corinne Chatel Quintet
Ma Vie En Rose | Edition Collage | EC 525-2

Sigismonti,Henry | (fr-h)
Peggy Lee With The Quincy Jones Orchestra
Blues Cross Country | Capitol | 520088-2

Signorelli,Frank | (pceleste)
Bix Beiderbecke And His Gang
Jazz:The Essential Collection Vol.2 | IN+OUT Records | 78012-2
Eddie Lang-Joe Venuti And Their Allstars Orchestra
Jazz:The Essential Collection Vol.3 | IN+OUT Records | 78013-2
Frankie Trumbauer And His Orchestra
Jazz:The Essential Collection Vol.2 | IN+OUT Records | 78012-2

Sikora,Ray | (tb)
Stan Kenton And His Orchestra
Adventures In Blues | Capitol | 520089-2

Silberman,R. | (v)
Toots Thielemans And His Orchestra
Verve Jazz Masters Vol.59:Toots Thielemans | Verve | 535271-2

Silloway,Ward | (tb)
Benny Goodman And His V-Disc All Star Band
The Legends Of Swing | Laserlight | 24659
Bob Crosby And His Orchestra
Swing Legens:Bob Crosby | Nimbus Records | NI 2011
Bob Crosby's Bobcats
Swing Legens:Bob Crosby | Nimbus Records | NI 2011
Tommy Dorsey And His Orchestra
Planet Jazz:Frank Sinatra & Tommy Dorsey | Planet Jazz | 2152067-2
Planet Jazz:Tommy Dorsey | Planet Jazz | 2159972-2

Silva,Alan | (b,cello,perc,voice,p,vviola)
Albert Ayler Group
Albert Ayler Live In Greenwich Village:The Complete Impulse Recordings | Impulse(MCA) | IMP 22732
Cecil Taylor Sextet
A Blue Conception | Blue Note | 534254-2
Conquistador | Blue Note | 576749-2
Franz Koglmann Quintet
Opium | Between The Lines | btl 011(Efa 10181-2)
Sun Ra And His Intergalactic Research Arkestra
Black Myth/Out In Space | MPS | 557656-2
The Jazz Composer's Orchestra
Comminications | JCOA | 1001/2

Silva,Joe | (ts)
Cal Tjader Sextet
The Jazz Giants Play Cole Porter:Night And Day | Prestige | PCD 24203-2

Silva,Jose | (perc,tsv)
Herbie Mann And His Orchestra
The Best Of Herbie Mann | Atlantic | 7567-81369-2
Mongo Santamaria And His Band
Sabroso | Original Jazz Classics | OJCCD 281-2

Silva,Jose 'Chombo' | (ts)
Cal Tjader Sextet
Black Hawk Nights | Fantasy | FCD 24755-2

Silva,Marcos | (keyboardssynth)
Airto Moreira/Flora Purim Group
Jazz Unlimited | IN+OUT Records | 7017-2

Silva,Roberto | (dr,percberimbau)
Cal Tjader Group
Amazonas | Original Jazz Classics | OJCCD 840-2(F 9502)

Silvano,Judi | (fl,voicevoc)
James Emery Quartet
Fourth World | Between The Lines | btl 020(Efa 10190-2)
Joe Lovano Orchestra
Blue Note Plays Gershwin | Blue Note | 520808-2

Silveira,Ricardo | (el-g,hand-claps,ghandclaps)
John Patitucci Group
Sketchbook | GRP | GRP 96172
Toots Thieleman And Sivuca
Verve Jazz Masters Vol.59:Toots Thielemans | Verve | 535271-2

Silver,Horace | (el-p,voc,pcomp)
Art Blakey And The Jazz Messengers
Horace Silver Retrospective | Blue Note | 495576-2
A Night At Birdland Vol. 1 | Blue Note | 532146-2
A Night At Birdland Vol. 2 | Blue Note | 532147-2
At The Cafe Bohemia Vol.1 | Blue Note | 532148-2
At The Cafe Bohemia Vol.2 | Blue Note | 532149-2
The Jazz Messengers | CBS | CK 65265
Art Farmer Quintet
Early Art | Original Jazz Classics | OJCCD 880-2(NJ 8258)
Art Farmer Septet
Plays The Arrangements And Compositions Of Gigi Gryce And Quincy Jones | Original Jazz Classics | OJCCD 054-2
Bill Henderson With The Horace Silver Quintet
Horace Silver Retrospective | Blue Note | 495576-2
Cliff Jordan-John Gilmore Quintet
Blowing In From Chicago | Blue Note | 542306-2
Dee Dee Bridgewater With Her Quartet With Horace Silver
Love And Peace-A Tribute To Horace Silver | Verve | 527470-2
Donald Brown Quintet
Donald Byrd & Doug Watkins:The Tradition Sessions | Blue Note | 540528-2
Donald Byrd Sextet
Donald Byrd & Doug Watkins:The Tradition Sessions | Blue Note | 540528-2
Hank Mobley Quintet
Hank Mobley | Blue Note | 0675622
Horace Silver Quartet
Horace Silver Retrospective | Blue Note | 495576-2
Horace Silver Quintet
Jazz Has... A Sense Of Humor | Verve | 050293-2
Blowin' The Blues Away | Blue Note | 495342-2
Horace Silver Retrospective | Blue Note | 495576-2
Song For My Father | Blue Note | 499002-2
Blue Velvet: Crooners, Swooners And Velvet Vocals | Blue Note | 521153-2
Six Pieces Of Silver | Blue Note | 525648-2
True Blue | Blue Note | 534032-2
Stylings Of Silver | Blue Note | 540034-2
Finger Poppin' | Blue Note | 542304-2
The Cape Verdean Blues | Blue Note | 576753-2
Blue Bossa | Blue Note | 795590-2
The Best Of Blue Note | Blue Note | 796110-2
The Best Of Blue Note Vol.2 | Blue Note | 797960-2
Silver's Serenade | Blue Note | 821288-2
The Tokyo Blues | Blue Note | 853355-2
A Prescription For The Blues | Impulse(MCA) | 951238-2
Newport Jazz Festival 1958,July 3rd-6th,Vol.1:Mostly Miles | Phontastic | NCD 8813
Paris Blues | Pablo | PACD 5316-2
Horace Silver Quintet With Brass
Horace Silver Retrospective | Blue Note | 495576-2
Horace Silver Quintet With Vocals
Horace Silver Retrospective | Blue Note | 495576-2
Horace Silver Sextet
The Story Of Jazz Piano | Laserlight | 24653
Horace Silver Retrospective | Blue Note | 495576-2
Deep Blue-The United States Of Mind | Blue Note | 521152-2

The Cape Verdean Blues | Blue Note | 576753-2
Horace Silver Sextet With Vocals
Horace Silver Retrospective | Blue Note | 495576-2
Horace Silver Trio
Horace Silver Retrospective | Blue Note | 495576-2
Song For My Father | Blue Note | 499002-2
Horace Silver Trio And Spotlight On Drums:Art Blakey-Sabu | Blue Note | 591725-2
Horace Silver-Gail Nelson
Horace Silver Retrospective | Blue Note | 495576-2
J.J.Johnson Quintet
The Eminent J.J.Johnson Vol.2 | Blue Note | 532144-2
Kenny Dorham Octet
Afro-Cuban | Blue Note | 0675619
Kenny Dorham Orchestra
Blue Bossa | Blue Note | 795590-2
Lester Young Quintet
Jazz Gallery:Lester Young Vol.2(1946-59) | RCA | 2119541-2
Miles Davis All Star Sextet
Walkin' | Original Jazz Classics | OJC20 213-2
Miles Davis All Stars
The J.J.Johnson Memorial Album | Prestige | PRCD 11025-2
Miles Davis Quartet
Miles Davis Vol.1 | Blue Note | 532610-2
Kind Of Blue:Blue Note Celebrate The Music Of Miles Davis | Blue Note | 534255-2
Miles Davis:The Best Of The Capitol/Blue Note Years | Blue Note | 798287-2
Jazz Profile:Miles Davis | Blue Note | 823515-2
Ballads & Blues | Blue Note | 836633-2
Blue Haze | Original Jazz Classics | OJC20 093-2(P 7054)
Miles Davis Quintet
Blue Haze | Original Jazz Classics | OJC20 093-2(P 7054)
Walkin' | Original Jazz Classics | OJC20 213-2
Bags' Groove | Original Jazz Classics | OJC20 245-2
The Prestige Legacy Vol.1:The High Priests | Prestige | PCD 24251-2
Milt Jackson Quartet
Milt Jackson Birthday Celebration | Fantasy | FANCD 6079-2
Milt Jackson | Original Jazz Classics | OJC20 001-2(P 7003)
The Jazz Giants Play Rodgers & Hart:Blue Moon | Prestige | PCD 24205-2
The Jazz Giants Play Sammy Cahn:It's Magic | Prestige | PCD 24226-2
Milt Jackson Quintet
Milt Jackson Birthday Celebration | Fantasy | FANCD 6079-2
MJQ | Original Jazz Classics | OJCCD 125-2
Nat Adderley Quintet
Introducing Nat Adderley | Verve | 543828-2
Paul Chambers Sextet
Trane's Blues | Blue Note | 498240-2
Sonny Rollins Quintet
Sonny Rollins Vol.2 | Blue Note | 497809-2
Ballads | Blue Note | 537562-2
The Blue Note Years-The Best Of Sonny Rollins | Blue Note | 793203-2
Sonny Rollins:The Blue Note Recordings | Blue Note | 821371-2
Jazz Profile:Sonny Rollins | Blue Note | 823516-2
Sonny Rollins Sextet
Sonny Rollins Vol.2 | Blue Note | 497809-2
Sonny Rollins:The Blue Note Recordings | Blue Note | 821371-2
Stan Getz Quartet
Stan Getz-The Complete Roost Sessions | EMI Records | 859622-2
Stan Getz:Imagination | Dreyfus Jazz Line | FDM 36733-2
Stan Getz Quintet
Stan Getz-The Complete Roost Sessions | EMI Records | 859622-2

Silverlight,Terry | (dr,percvoc)
David Matthews & The Manhattan Jazz Orchestra
Back To Bach | Milestone | MCD 9312-2
Hey Duke! | Milestone | MCD 9320-2

Silverman,Mike | (b)
Dogslyde
Hair Of The Dog | Intuition Records | INT 3223-2

Silvesterchlauseschuppel |
Paul Giger Trio
Alpstein | ECM | 1426(847940-2)

Silvestre,Rosangela | (dancevoc)
Steve Coleman And Five Elements
Genesis & The Opening Of The Way | RCA | 2152934-2
The Sonic Language Of Myth | RCA | 2164123-2

Silzer,Werner | (perc)
Omar Belmonte's Latin Lover
Vamos A Ver | EGO | 96170

Sim,Mike | (as,bs,sax,ssts)
Barbara Dennerlein Group
Take Off | Verve | 527664-2
Eugen Apostolidis Quartet
Imaginary Directions | Edition Collage | EC 503-2

Sim,Pierre | (b)
Golden Gate Quartet
Spirituals To Swing 1955-69 | EMI Records | 791569-2
Golden Gate Quartet With The Martial Solal Orchestra
From Spiritual To Swing Vol.2 | EMI Records | 780573-2

Sim,Pierre prob. | (b)

Simeon,Omer | (as,cl,bs,ld,b-cl,sax,ss,reedsts)
Earl Hines And His Orchestra
Planet Jazz:Earl Hines | Planet Jazz | 2159973-2
The Legends Of Swing | Laserlight | 24659
Jazz:The Essential Collection Vol.2 | IN+OUT Records | 78012-2
Fletcher Henderson And His Orchestra
Jazz:The Essential Collection Vol.1 | IN+OUT Records | 78011-2
Jelly Roll Morton's Red Hot Peppers
Planet Jazz:Jelly Roll Morton | Planet Jazz | 2152060-2
Planet Jazz Sampler | Planet Jazz | 2152326-2
Jazz:The Essential Collection Vol.1 | IN+OUT Records | 78011-2
Jimmy Lunceford And His Orchestra
The Legends Of Swing | Laserlight | 24659
Louis Armstrong And His Orchestra
I Love Jazz | Verve | 543747-2
Louis Armstrong And Omer Simeon With The Sy Oliver Orchestra
Ambassador Louis Armstrong Vol.17:Moments To Remember(1952-1956) | Ambassador | CLA 1917
Louis Armstrong With Sy Oliver And His Orchestra
Louis Armstrong-My Greatest Songs | MCA | MCD 18347
Wilbur DeParis And His New New Orleans Band
Atlantic Jazz: New Orleans | Atlantic | 7567-81700-2

similar pers. |
B.B.King And His Band
Live At San Quentin | MCA | MCD 06103

Simion,Nicolas | (b-cl,ss,ts,caval,kalimbawooden-fl)
Gunther Schuller With The WDR Radio Orchestra & Rememberance Band
Witchi Tia To, The Music Of Jim Pepper | Tutu Records | 888204-2*
Ku-umba Frank Lacy & The Poker Bigband
Songs From The Musical 'Poker' | Tutu Records | 888150-2*
Mal Waldron Quartet
Mal,Verve,Black & Blue | Tutu Records | 888170-2*
Mal Waldron-Nicolas Simion
Art Of The Duo:The Big Rochade | Tutu Records | 888186-2*
Nicolas Simion Group
Black Sea | Tutu Records | 888134-2*
Balkan Jazz | Intuition Records | INT 3339-2
Nicolas Simion Quartet
Oriental Gates:Live In Vienna | Tutu Records | 888212-2*
Nicolas Simion Quartet feat. Tomasz Stanko
Dinner For Don Carlos | Tutu Records | 888146-2*
Transylvanian Dance | Tutu Records | 888164-2*
Viaggio Imaginario | Tutu Records | 888192-2*
Nicolas Simion Trio
Back To The Roots | Tutu Records | 888176-2
Oriental Gates:Live In Vienna | Tutu Records | 888212-2*

Vasilic Nenad Balkan Band
Joe-Jack | Nabel Records:Jazz Network | CD 4693

Simmerl,Thomas | (dr,percsteel-dr)
Pili-Pili
Boogaloo | JA & RO | JARO 4174-2

Simmons,Alan | (bb-overdubbed)
Chas Burchell Quartet
Unsong Hero:The Undiscovered Genius Of Chas Burchell | IN+OUT Records | 7026-2
Chas Burchell Quintet
Unsong Hero:The Undiscovered Genius Of Chas Burchell | IN+OUT Records | 7026-2
Chas Burchell Sextet
Unsong Hero:The Undiscovered Genius Of Chas Burchell | IN+OUT Records | 7026-2
Chas Burchell Trio/Quartet
Unsong Hero:The Undiscovered Genius Of Chas Burchell | IN+OUT Records | 7026-2
Clark Terry Quintet
Unsong Hero:The Undiscovered Genius Of Chas Burchell | IN+OUT Records | 7026-2
Geoff Carter Quintet
Unsong Hero:The Undiscovered Genius Of Chas Burchell | IN+OUT Records | 7026-2
Lilly Thornton With The Benny Golson Quartet
Remembering Dinah-A Salute To Dinah Washington | Hot Shot Records | HSR 8313-2
Lilly Thornton With The Benny Golson Sextet
Remembering Dinah-A Salute To Dinah Washington | Hot Shot Records | HSR 8313-2
Lilly Thornton With The Mike Hennesey Trio
Remembering Dinah-A Salute To Dinah Washington | Hot Shot Records | HSR 8313-2
Ronnie Scott With The Chas Burchell Quintet
Unsong Hero:The Undiscovered Genius Of Chas Burchell | IN+OUT Records | 7026-2
The Mike Hennessey Chastet
Shades Of Chas Burchell | IN+OUT Records | 7025-2

Simmons,Art | (p)
Don Byas Quartet
Jazz In Paris:Don Byas-Laura | EmArCy | 013027-2
Don Byas Quintet
Jazz In Paris:Don Byas-Laura | EmArCy | 013027-2
Les Double Six
Les Double Six | RCA | 2164314-2

Simmons,James 'Sid' | (pel-p)
Grover Washington Jr. Septet
Paradise | Elektra | 7559-60537-2

Simmons,John | (bp)
(Little)Jimmy Scott With The Billy Taylor Orchestra
Everybody's Somebody's Fool | Decca | 050669-2
Art Tatum Quartet
Art Tatum-The Complete Pablo Group Masterpieces | Pablo | 6 PACD 4401-2
Benny Carter And His Chocolate Dandies
Planet Jazz:Ben Webster | RCA | 2165368-2
Jazz:The Essential Collection Vol.3 | IN+OUT Records | 78013-2
Big Sid Catlett And His Orchestra
The Small Black Groups | Storyville | 4960523
Billie Holiday And Her All Stars
Verve Jazz Masters 12:Billie Holiday | Verve | 519825-2
Verve Jazz Masters 20:Introducing | Verve | 519853-2
Billie Holiday And Her Band
Verve Jazz Masters 47:Billie Holiday Sings Standards | Verve | 527650-2
Billie Holiday With Eddie Heywood And His Orchestra
Billie Holiday:The Complete Commodore Recordings | GRP | 543272-2
Buddy Rich Quintet
Buddy And Sweets | Verve | 841433-2
Erroll Garner Trio
The Story Of Jazz Piano | Laserlight | 24653
Body & Soul | CBS | 467916-2
Erroll Garner:Trio | Dreyfus Jazz Line | FDM 36719-2
James P.Johnson's Blue Note Jazzmen
Jazz:The Essential Collection Vol.3 | IN+OUT Records | 78013-2
The Blue Note Jazzmen | Blue Note | 821262-2
John Coltrane-Tadd Dameron Quartet
Mating Call | Original Jazz Classics | OJCCD 212-2(P 7070)
John Hardee Swingtet
The Blue Note Swingtets | Blue Note | 495697-2
Kansas City Six
Lester Young:Blue Lester | Dreyfus Jazz Line | FDM 36729-2
Lena Horne With The Horace Henderson Orchestra
Planet Jazz:Lena Horne | Planet Jazz | 2165373-2
Matthew Gee All-Stars
Jazz By Gee! | Original Jazz Classics | OJCCD 1884-2(RLP 221)
Peggy Lee With The Benny Goodman Orchestra
Peggy Lee & Benny Goodman:The Complete Recordings 1941-1947 | CBS | C2K 65686
Roy Eldridge-Benny Carter Quintet
The Complete Verve Roy Eldridge Studio Sessions | Verve | 9861278
Sidney Catlett Quartet
Jazz:The Essential Collection Vol.3 | IN+OUT Records | 78013-2
Sidney DeParis' Blue Note Jazzmen
The Blue Note Jazzmen | Blue Note | 821262-2
Tadd Dameron And His Orchestra
Fontainebleau | Original Jazz Classics | OJCCD 055-2
Tadd Dameron Quartet
John Coltrane-The Prestige Recordings | Prestige | 16 PCD 4405-2
Thelonious Monk Quartet
Wizard Of The Vibes | Blue Note | 532140-2
The Best Of Thelonious Monk:The Blue Note Years | Blue Note | 795636-2
Thelonious Monk:Misterioso | Dreyfus Jazz Line | FDM 36743-2

Simmons,Norman | (pceleste)
Eddie Lockjaw Davis-Johnny Griffin Quintet
Battle Stations | Original Jazz Classics | OJCCD 1085(P7282)
Red Rodney Quintet
The Red Rodney Quintets | Fantasy | FCD 24758-2
Roy Eldridge Septet
To Bags...With Love:Memorial Album | Pablo | 2310967-2
Roy Eldridge Sextet
Milt Jackson Birthday Celebration | Fantasy | FANCD 6079-2

Simmons,Sonny | (as,oboeengl-h)
Prince Lasha Quartet
The Cry | Original Jazz Classics | OJCCD 1945-2(S 7610)
Prince Lasha Quintet
The Cry | Original Jazz Classics | OJCCD 1945-2(S 7610)

Simmons,Suzanne | (voc)
McCoy Tyner Group With Horns And Voices
Inner Voices | Original Jazz Classics | OJCCD 1039-2(M 9079)
McCoy Tyner Group With Voices
Inner Voices | Original Jazz Classics | OJCCD 1039-2(M 9079)

Simms,Edward | (tp)
Earl Hines And His Orchestra
Planet Jazz:Earl Hines | Planet Jazz | 2159973-2
Jazz:The Essential Collection Vol.2 | IN+OUT Records | 78012-2

Simms,Emmanuel | (dr)
Buddy Johnson And His Orchestra
Buddy And Ella Johnson 1953-1964 | Bear Family Records | BCD 15479 DH

Simoens,Lucien | (b)
Bill Coleman Et Son Orchestre
Americans Swinging In Paris:Bill Coleman-The Elegance | EMI Records | 539662-2
Don Byas And His Orchestra
Don Byas:Laura | Dreyfus Jazz Line | FDM 36714-2

Quintet Du Hot Club De France
Django Reinhardt:Echoes Of France | Dreyfus Jazz Line | FDM 36726-2

Simon,Alan | (p)
James Chirillo Quartet with Vera Mara
Sultry Serenade | Nagel-Heyer | CD 061
James Chirillo Sextet
Sultry Serenade | Nagel-Heyer | CD 061

Simon,Dick | (tb)
Two Beat Stompers
Deutsches Jazz Fesival 1954/1955 | Bear Family Records | BCD 15430

Simon,Eduardo | (p)
Freddie Bryant Group
Brazilian Rosewood | Fresh Sound Records | FSNT 035 CD

Simon,Edward | (keyboards,p,congassynth)
Greg Osby Quintet
Mindgames | JMT Edition | 919021-2

Simon,Fred | (bs,synth-programmingts)
Lionel Hampton And His Orchestra
Lionel Hampton:Flying Home | Dreyfus Jazz Line | FDM 36735-2
Louis Jordan And His Tympany Five
Louis Jordan-Let The Good Times Roll: The Complete Decca Recordings 1938-1954 | Bear Family Records | BCD 15557 IH

Simon,George | (drtb)
Count Basie And His Orchestra
Planet Jazz:Count Basie | Planet Jazz | 2152068-2
Planet Jazz Sampler | Planet Jazz | 2152326-2

Simon,Jan-Martin | (b)
Fritz Münzer Tentet
Blue Ideas | Jazz 'n' Arts Records | 0200

Simon,John | (p)
Howlin' Wolf London Session
Howlin' Wolf:The London Sessions | Chess | MCD 09297

Simon,Matthew L. | (tpfl-h)
Big Band Bellaterra
Don't Git Sassy | Fresh Sound Records | FSNT 048 CD
Dave Liebman And The Lluis Vidal Trio With The Orquestra De Cambra Theatre Lliure
Dave Liebman And The Lluis Vidal Trio | Fresh Sound Records | FSNT 026 CD
Eladio Reinon Quintet
Es La Historia De Un Amor | Fresh Sound Records | FSNT 004 CD
Manel Camp & Matthew Simon Acustic Jazz Quintet
Rosebud | Fresh Sound Records | FSNT 011 CD
Orquestra De Cambra Teatre Lliure
Orquestra De Cambra Teatre Lliure and Lluis Vidal Trio feat.Dave Liebman | Fresh Sound Records | FSNT 027 CD
Tributes To Duke Ellington | Fresh Sound Records | FSNT 084 CD
Orquestra De Cambra Teatre Lliure feat. Dave Liebman
Orquestra De Cambra Teatre Lliure and Lluis Vidal Trio feat.Dave Liebman | Fresh Sound Records | FSNT 027 CD

Simon,Maurice | (as,bs,saxts)
Buddy Johnson And His Orchestra
Buddy And Ella Johnson 1953-1964 | Bear Family Records | BCD 15479 DH
Duke Ellington Orchestra
Continuum | Fantasy | FCD 24765-2

Simon,Stafford | (cl,tsfl)
Louis Jordan And His Tympany Five
Louis Jordan-Let The Good Times Roll: The Complete Decca Recordings 1938-1954 | Bear Family Records | BCD 15557 IH

Simone,Francesca | (voc)
Francesca Simone Trio
Guardia Li | Minor Music | 801093

Simone,Nina | (p,harmony,harpsichord,shaker)
Nina Simone
Planet Jazz:Nina Simone | Planet Jazz | 2165372-2
Verve Jazz Masters 17:Nina Simone | Verve | 518198-2
Nina Simone After Hours | Verve | 526702-2
Verve Jazz Masters Vol.58:Nina Simone Sings Nina | Verve | 529867-2
Nina Simone And Orchestra
Planet Jazz:Nina Simone | Planet Jazz | 2165372-2
Baltimore | Epic | 476906-2
Nina Simone Groups
Feeling Good-The Very Best Of Nina Simone | Mercury | 522747-2
Nina Simone Quartet
Verve Jazz Masters 17:Nina Simone | Verve | 518198-2
Verve Jazz Masters 20:Introducing | Verve | 519853-2
Misty Blue:Sweet Sisters Swing Songs Of Sorrow And Sadness | Blue Note | 521151-2
Nina Simone After Hours | Verve | 526702-2
In Concert/I Put A Spell On You | Mercury | 846543-2
Nina Simone Quintet
Planet Jazz:Nina Simone | Planet Jazz | 2165372-2
Nina Simone After Hours | Verve | 526702-2
Verve Jazz Masters Vol.58:Nina Simone Sings Nina | Verve | 529867-2
Nina Simone Trio
Verve Jazz Masters 17:Nina Simone | Verve | 518198-2
Nina Simone After Hours | Verve | 526702-2
Verve Jazz Masters Vol.58:Nina Simone Sings Nina | Verve | 529867-2
Nina Simone With Hal Mooney's Orchestra
Verve Jazz Masters 17:Nina Simone | Verve | 518198-2
Nina Simone After Hours | Verve | 526702-2
Verve Jazz Masters Vol.58:Nina Simone Sings Nina | Verve | 529867-2
In Concert/I Put A Spell On You | Mercury | 846543-2
Nina Simone With Horace Ott's Orchestra
Verve Jazz Masters 17:Nina Simone | Verve | 518198-2
Nina Simone After Hours | Verve | 526702-2
In Concert/I Put A Spell On You | Mercury | 846543-2
Nina Simone-Bob Bushnell
Planet Jazz:Nina Simone | Planet Jazz | 2165372-2
Planet Jazz:Female Jazz Vocalists | Planet Jazz | 2169656-2
Nina Simone-Bobby Hamilton
Verve Jazz Masters Vol.58:Nina Simone Sings Nina | Verve | 529867-2
Nina Simone-Lisle Atkinson
Verve Jazz Masters Vol.58:Nina Simone Sings Nina | Verve | 529867-2

Simons,Barbara | (viola)
Ella Fitzgerald With The Nelson Riddle Orchestra
The Best Of The Song Books:The Ballads | Verve | 521867-2
Oh Lady Be Good:The Best Of The Gershwin Songbook | Verve | 529581-2
Love Songs:The Best Of The Song Books | Verve | 531762-2

Simons,Charles | (percvib)
The Latin Jazz Quintet Plus Guest: Eric Dolphy
Eric Dolphy:The Complete Prestige Recordings | Prestige | 9 PRCD-4418-2
Eric Dolphy Birthday Celebration | Fantasy | FANCD 6085-2

Simons,Ed | (v)
Stan Getz With The Eddie Sauter Orchestra
Stan Getz Plays The Music Of Mickey One | Verve | 531232-2

Simons,Franz | (tb)
Hans Koller Big Band
New York City | MPS | 9813437

Simons,Janet | (viola)
Stan Getz With The Eddie Sauter Orchestra
Stan Getz Plays The Music Of Mickey One | Verve | 531232-2

Simonsen,Annette L. | (voc)
Chinese Compass
Chinese Compass | dacapo | DCCD 9443

Simonson,Jonas | (flalto-fl)
Mats Eden-Jonas Simonson With The Cikada String Quartet
Milvus | ECM | 1660

Simpkins,Andrew | (b)
Anita O'Day With The Three Sounds
Verve Jazz Masters 49:Anita O'Day | Verve | 527653-2
Bobby Lyle Group
The Journey | Atlantic | 7567-82138-2
Gene Harris And The Three Sounds
Deep Blue-The United States Of Mind | Blue Note | 521152-2

Joe Pass Quintet
Joe Pass:Guitar Virtuoso | Pablo | 4 PACD 4423-2
Mel Rhyne Sextet
Organ-izing | Original Jazz Classics | OJCCD 1055-2(JLP 916)
Monty Alexander Quartet
Three Originals:Love And Sunshine/Estade/Cobilimbo | MPS | 523526-2
Monty Alexander Sextet
Three Originals:Love And Sunshine/Estade/Cobilimbo | MPS | 523526-2
Nat Adderley Quintet(incl.The Three Sounds)
Branching Out | Original Jazz Classics | OJCCD 255-2(R 285)
Nat Adderley With The Three Sounds
Branching Out | Original Jazz Classics | OJCCD 255-2(R 285)
Ron Affif Quartet
The Jazz Giants Play Miles Davis:Milestones | Prestige | PCD 24225-2
Sarah Vaughan And Her Band
Duke Ellington Song Book Two | Pablo | CD 2312116
Sarah Vaughan Birthday Celebration | Fantasy | FANCD 6090-2
Sarah Vaughan And The Count Basie Orchestra
Sarah Vaughan Birthday Celebration | Fantasy | FANCD 6090-2
Sarah Vaughan With Band
Linger Awhile | Pablo | 2312144-2
Sarah Vaughan With Orchestra
Sarah Vaughan Birthday Celebration | Fantasy | FANCD 6090-2
Sarah Vaughan With Small Group & Orchestra
Duke Ellington Song Book One | Pablo | CD 2312111
Sarah Vaughan With The Joe Pass Quartet
Linger Awhile | Pablo | 2312144-2
Joe Pass:Guitar Virtuoso | Pablo | 4 PACD 4423-2
Sarah Vaughan With The Mike Wofford Trio
Sarah Vaughan Birthday Celebration | Fantasy | FANCD 6090-2
Sarah Vaughan With The Roland Hanna Quartet
Sarah Vaughan Birthday Celebration | Fantasy | FANCD 6090-2
Stanley Turrentine With The Three Sounds
Blue Hour | Blue Note | 524586-2
Midnight Blue(The [Be]witching Hour) | Blue Note | 854365-2
Stephane Grappelli With The George Shearing Trio
Grapelli Story | Verve | 515807-2
Verve Jazz Masters 11:Stéphane Grappelli | Verve | 516758-2
The Three Sounds
Bottoms Up | Blue Note | 0675629
Black Orchid | Blue Note | 821289-2
Zoot Sims With Orchestra
Passion Flower | Original Jazz Classics | OJCCD 939-2(2312120)

Simpkins,Jesse | (b)
Louis Jordan And His Tympany Five
Louis Jordan-Let The Good Times Roll: The Complete Decca Recordings 1938-1954 | Bear Family Records | BCD 15557 IH

Simpkins,Mack | (dr)
Stanley Turrentine Quartet
The Roots Of Acid Jazz | Impulse(MCA) | IMP 12042

Simpson,Mike | (flts)
Johnny Frigo Sextet
I Love John Frigo...He Swings | Mercury | 9861061

Simpson,Ray | (voc)
Nina Simone And Orchestra
Baltimore | Epic | 476906-2

Simpson,Valerie | (voc)
Quincy Jones And His Orchestra
Verve Jazz Masters Vol.59:Toots Thielemans | Verve | 535271-2

Sims,Edward | (tbtp)
Erskine Hawkins And His Orchestra
Planet Jazz:Big Bands | Planet Jazz | 2169649-2

Sims,Hylda | (gvoc)
Henrik Johansen With The City Ramblers
The Golden Years Of Revival Jazz,Sampler | Storyville | 109 1001
Hylda Sims And The Citty Ramblers Skiffle Group With Henrik Johansen
The Golden Years Of Revival Jazz,Vol.9 | Storyville | STCD 5514

Sims,Mark Loudon | (b,b-g,keyboards,percorg)
Don Cherry Group
Multi Kulti | A&M Records | 395323-2

Sims,Ray | (tbvoc)
Harry James And His Orchestra
Trumpet Blues:The Best Of Harry James | Capitol | 521224-2
Red Norvo And His Orchestra
Planet Jazz:Female Jazz Vocalists | Planet Jazz | 2169656-2

Sims,Rudolph | (cello)
Ben Webster With Orchestra And Strings
Music For Loving:Ben Webster With Strings | Verve | 527774-2
Ultimate Ben Webster selected by James Carter | Verve | 557537-2

Sims,Zoot | (as,ts,cl,reeds,sax,vocss)
Al Cohn Quintet feat. Zoot Sims
Al And Zoot | GRP | 951827-2
Al Cohn-Zoot Sims Duo
You 'N' Me | Verve | 589318-2
Al Cohn-Zoot Sims Quintet
Planet Jazz:Jazz Saxophone | Planet Jazz | 2169653-2
You 'N' Me | Verve | 589318-2
Anita O'Day With The Gary McFarland Orchestra
All The Sad Youn Men | Verve | 517065-2
Verve Jazz Masters 49:Anita O'Day | Verve | 527653-2
Art Pepper-Zoot Sims Quintet
Art 'N' Zoot | Pablo | 2310957-2
Benny Carter And His Orchestra
Jazz At The Philharmonic:The Montreux Collection | Pablo | PACD 5306-2
Benny Goodman And His All Star Sextet
Verve Jazz Masters 33:Benny Goodman | Verve | 844410-2
Benny Goodman And His Orchestra
The Legends Of Swing | Laserlight | 24659
Bud Powell Quartet
Parisian Thoroughfare | Pablo | CD 2310976-2
Carmen McRae And Her Trio With Zoot Sims
The Collected Carmen McRae | RCA | 2668713-2
Charles Mingus And His Orchestra
The Complete Town Hall Concert | Blue Note | 828353-2
Chet Baker Quintet
Chet Baker Plays The Best Of Lerner And Loewe | Original Jazz Classics | OJC20 137-2
Chet Baker Septet
Chet Baker Plays The Best Of Lerner And Loewe | Original Jazz Classics | OJC20 137-2
Chris Connor With Band
Chris Connor | Atlantic | 7567-80769-2
Chubby Jackson Big Band
Gerry Mulligan Quartet feat.Chet Baker | Original Jazz Classics | OJCCD 711-2(F 8082/P 7641)
Coleman Hawkins With Billy Byers And His Orchestra
The Hawk In Hi-Fi | RCA | 2663842-2
Count Basie Jam
Montreux '77 | Original Jazz Classics | OJC 379(2308209)
Montreux '77 | Original Jazz Classics | OJC 385(2620105)
Count Basie-Zoot Sims Quartet
Basie & Zoot | Original Jazz Classics | OJCCD 822-2(2310745)
Ella Fitzgerald Jam
Bluella:Ella Fitzgerald Sings The Blues | Pablo | 2310960-2
Ella Fitzgerald With Orchestra
Ella Abraca Jobim | Pablo | 2630201-2
Elliot Lawrence And His Orchestra
The Elliot Lawrence Big Band Swings Cohn & Kahn | Fantasy | FCD 24761-2
Gerry Mulligan And His Orchestra
Mullenium | CBS | CK 65678
Gerry Mulligan And The Sax Section
The Gerry Mulligan Songbook | Pacific Jazz | 833575-2
Gerry Mulligan Concert Jazz Band
Verve Jazz Masters 36:Gerry Mulligan | Verve | 523342-2
The Complete Verve Gerry Mulligan Concert Band | Verve | 9860613
JATP All Stars
J.A.T.P. In London 1969 | Pablo | 2CD 2620119
Welcome To Jazz At The Philharmonic | Fantasy | FANCD 6081-2
Jimmy Rushing And His Band
Planet Jazz:Jimmy Rushing | RCA | 2165371-2
Planet Jazz:Male Jazz Vocalists | Planet Jazz | 2169657-2
Jimmy Rushing And His Orchestra
Five Feet Of Soul | Roulette | 581830-2
Jimmy Smith With The Oliver Nelson Orchestra
Verve Jazz Masters 29:Jimmy Smith | Verve | 521855-2
Jimmy Smith:Best Of The Verve Years | Verve | 527950-2
Jimmy Smith-Talkin' Verve | Verve | 531563-2
Joe Williams And Friends
Planet Jazz:Male Jazz Vocalists | Planet Jazz | 2169657-2
At Newport '63 | RCA | 2663919-2
Joe Williams And His Band
Planet Jazz:Joe Williams | Planet Jazz | 2165370-2
Johnny Smith Quintet
Moonlight In Vermont | Roulette | 596593-2
Lars Gullin American All Stars
Lars Gullin 1953,Vol.2:Moden Sounds | Dragon | DRCD 234
Miles Davis Septet
Miles Davis And Horns | Original Jazz Classics | OJC20 053-2(P 7025)
Monica Zetterlund With The Zoot Sims Quartet
Planet Jazz:Female Jazz Vocalists | Planet Jazz | 2169656-2
Oliver Nelson And His Orchestra
Verve Jazz Masters Vol.60:The Collection | Verve | 529866-2
Peggy Lee With The Benny Goodman Orchestra
Peggy Lee & Benny Goodman:The Complete Recordings 1941-1947 | CBS | C2K 65686
Prestige All Stars
John Coltrane-The Prestige Recordings | Prestige | 16 PCD 4405-2
Tenor Conclave | Original Jazz Classics | OJCCD 127-2
Quincy Jones And His Orchestra
Verve Jazz Masters Vol.59:Toots Thielemans | Verve | 535271-2
Sarah Vaughan And Her Band
Sarah Vaughan Birthday Celebration | Fantasy | FANCD 6090-2
Sarah Vaughan With Small Group & Orchestra
Duke Ellington Song Book One | Pablo | CD 2312111
Sarah Vaughan With The Quincy Jones Orchestra
Jazz In Paris:Sarah Vaughan-Vaughan And Violins | EmArCy | 065004-2
4 By 4:Ella Fitzgerald/Sarah Vaughan/Billie Holiday/Dinah Washington | Verve | 559693-2
Stan Getz And His Four Brothers
The Brothers | Original Jazz Classics | OJCCD 008-2
The Prestige Legacy Vol.2:Battles Of Saxes | Prestige | PCD 24252-2
Stan Getz Five Brothers Bop Tenor Sax Stars
Stan Getz:Imagination | Dreyfus Jazz Line | FDM 36733-2
Stan Kenton And His Orchestra
Stan Kenton Portraits On Standards | Capitol | 531571-2
The Four Brothers
Planet Jazz:Jazz Saxophone | Planet Jazz | 2169653-2
Together Again! | RCA | 2179623-2
Trigger Alpert's Absolutely All Star Seven
East Coast Sound | Original Jazz Classics | OJCCD 1012-2(JLP 11)
Woody Herman And His Orchestra
The Legends Of Swing | Laserlight | 24659
Woody Herman:Four Brother | Dreyfus Jazz Line | FDM 36722-2
Woody Herman And The New Thundering Herd
Planet Jazz:Big Bands | Planet Jazz | 2169649-2
Zoot Sims And His Orchestra
The Jazz Giants Play Duke Ellington:Caravan | Prestige | PCD 24227-2
Zoot Sims Quartet
Art 'N' Zoot | Pablo | 2310957-2
Getting Sentimental | Choice | CHCD 71006
Zoot Sims Quartets | Original Jazz Classics | OJCCD 242-2(P 7026)
Suddenly It's Spring | Original Jazz Classics | OJCCD 742-2(2310898)
The Jazz Giants Play Cole Porter:Night And Day | Prestige | PCD 24203-2
Zoot Sims | Storyville | STCD 8367
Zoot Sims Quartet feat.Count Basie
Jazz Dance | Original Jazz Classics | OJCCD 1002-2(1210890)
Zoot Sims Quintet
Art 'N' Zoot | Pablo | 2310957-2
Americans Swinging In Paris:Zoot Sims | EMI Records | 539646-2
Zoot Sims And The Gershwin Brothers | Original Jazz Classics | OJC20 444-2(2310744)
Quietly There-Zoot Sims Plays Johnny Mandel | Original Jazz Classics | OJCCD 787-2(2310903)
Zoot Sims And The Gershwin Brothers | Pablo | PASA 2310-744-6
Zoot Sims | Storyville | STCD 8367
Zoot Sims With Orchestra
Passion Flower | Original Jazz Classics | OJCCD 939-2(2312120)
Zoot Sims With The Joe Castro Trio
Live At Falcon Lair | Pablo | PACD 2310977-2
Zoot Sims-Al Cohn Quintet
Jazz Alive:A Night At The Half Note | Blue Note | 494105-2
Zoot Sims-Al Cohn Sextet
The Brothers | Original Jazz Classics | OJCCD 008-2
Zoot Sims-Al Cohn-Phil Woods Sextet
Jazz Alive:A Night At The Half Note | Blue Note | 494105-2
Zoot Sims-Bucky Pizzarelli Duo
The Art Of Saxophone | Laserlight | 24652
Elegiac | Storyville | STCD 8238
Zoot Sims-Harry Edison Quintet
Jazz Dance | Original Jazz Classics | OJCCD 1002-2(1210890)
Zoot Sims-Jimmy Rowles Quartet
If I'm Lucky | Original Jazz Classics | OJCCD 683-2(2310803)
The Jazz Giants Play Harry Warren:Lullaby Of Broadway | Prestige | PCD 24204-2
Zoot Sims-Joe Pass Duo
Joe Pass:Guitar Virtuoso | Pablo | 4 PACD 4423-2

Sinatra,Frank | (voc)
Frank Sinatra With Orchestra
Planet Jazz:Frank Sinatra & Tommy Dorsey | Planet Jazz | 2152067-2
Frank Sinatra With The Count Basie Orchestra
Sinatra-Basie:An Historic Musical First | Reprise | 7599-27023-2
It Might As Well Be Spring | Reprise | 7599-27027-2
Frank Sinatra With The Red Norvo Quintet(Sextet!)
Live In Australia,1959 | Blue Note | 837513-2
Frank Sinatra With The Red Norvo Quintet(Sextet!) & Orchestra
Live In Australia,1959 | Blue Note | 837513-2
Tommy Dorsey And His Orchestra
Planet Jazz:Frank Sinatra & Tommy Dorsey | Planet Jazz | 2152067-2
Planet Jazz Sampler | Planet Jazz | 2152326-2
Planet Jazz:Tommy Dorsey | Planet Jazz | 2159972-2
Planet Jazz:Big Bands | Planet Jazz | 2169649-2
Planet Jazz:Male Jazz Vocalists | Planet Jazz | 2169657-2
Frank Sinatra And The Tommy Dorsey Orchestra | RCA | 2668701-2

Sinatra,Spencer | (bs,fl,alto-fl,piccolo,reedsts)
Gary McFarland And His Orchestra
The Complete Bill Evans On Verve | Verve | 527953-2
Stan Kenton And His Orchestra
Great Swing Classics In Hi-Fi | Capitol | 521223-2

Sincigno,Henry | (g)
Klaus Kreuzeder & Henry Sincigno
Saxappeal | Trick Music | TM 9013 MC
Sax As Sax Can-Alive | Trick Music | TM 9312 CD

Sinclair,Ted | (b)
Lionel Hampton And His Orchestra
Lionel Hampton:Flying Home | Dreyfus Jazz Line | FDM 36735-2

Sinese,Quinque | (g,charangospanish-7-string-g)
Gabriel Pérez Group
La Chipaca | Green House Music | CD 1011

Sinesi,Quinque | (g,spanish-gcharango)
Alfonsina | Jazz 4 Ever Records:Jazz Network | J4E 4751
Quique Sinesi & Daniel Messina
Prioridad A la Emoción | art-mode-records | AMR 21061
Quique Sinesi & Daniel Messina With Guests
Prioridad A la Emoción | art-mode-records | AMR 21061

Singer Pur |
Michael Riessler & Singer Pur with Vincent Courtois
Ahi Vita | ACT | 9417-2

Singer,Hal | (ts)
Hal Singer-Charlie Shavers Quintet
Blue Stompin' | Original Jazz Classics | OJCCD 834-2(P 7153)
Vic Dickenson-Buck Clayton All Stars
Atlantic Jazz: Kansas City | Atlantic | 7567-81701-2

Singer,Joe | (fr-hv)
Charlie Parker With Strings
Charlie Parker:The Best Of The Verve Years | Verve | 527815-2
Bird: The Complete Charlie Parker On Verve | Verve | 837141-2
Charlie Parker:April In Paris | Dreyfus Jazz Line | FDM 36737-2
Charlie Parker With The Joe Lipman Orchestra
Verve Jazz Masters 28:Charlie Parker Plays Standards | Verve | 521854-2
Charlie Parker With Strings:The Master Takes | Verve | 523984-2
Charlie Parker Big Band | Verve | 559835-2
Dizzy Gillespie And His Orchestra
Ultimate Dizzy Gillespie | Verve | 557535-2
Miles Davis With Gil Evans & His Orchestra
Sketches Of Spain | CBS | CK 65142

Singer,Lou | (drperc)
Erroll Garner Trio
Erroll Garner:Trio | Dreyfus Jazz Line | FDM 36719-2
Mel Tormé With The Billy May Orchestra
Mel Tormé Goes South Of The Border With Billy May | Verve | 589517-2
Pete Rugolo And His Orchestra
Thriller/Richard Diamon(Original Jazz Scores From 2 Classics TV Series) | Fresh Sound Records | FSCD 2015

Singer,Ludger | (tb,el-orchestrion,keyboards,tp,p)
Anirahtak und die Jürgen Sturm Band
Das Kurt Weill Programm | Nabel Records:Jazz Network | CD 4638
Berlin-Paris-New York/Music By Kurt Weil | Nabel Records:Jazz Network | CD 4655
Art De Fakt
Art De Fakt-Ray Federman:Surfiction Jazz No.2 | double moon | CHRDM 71007

Singers Unlimited,The |
Singers Unlimited
The Singers Unlimited:Magic Voices | MPS | 539130-2
Singers Unlimited + The Oscar Peterson Trio
The Singers Unlimited:Magic Voices | MPS | 539130-2
Singers Unlimited With Orchestra
The Singers Unlimited:Magic Voices | MPS | 539130-2
Singers Unlimited With Rob McConnell And The Boss Brass
The Singers Unlimited:Magic Voices | MPS | 539130-2
Singers Unlimited With Roger Kellaway
The Singers Unlimited:Magic Voices | MPS | 539130-2
Singers Unlimited With The Art Van Damme Quintet
The Singers Unlimited:Magic Voices | MPS | 539130-2
Singers Unlimited With The Clare Fischer Orchestra
The Singers Unlimited:Magic Voices | MPS | 539130-2
Singers Unlimited With The Pat Williams Orchestra
The Singers Unlimited:Magic Voices | MPS | 539130-2
Singers Unlimited With The Patrick Williams Orchestra
The Singers Unlimited:Magic Voices | MPS | 539130-2
Singers Unlimited With The Robert Farnon Orchestra
The Singers Unlimited:Magic Voices | MPS | 539130-2
Singers Unlimited With The Roger Kellaway Cello Quartet
The Singers Unlimited:Magic Voices | MPS | 539130-2

Singleton,Willie | (tp)
Duke Ellington Orchestra
Continuum | Fantasy | FCD 24765-2

Singleton,Zutty | (dr,chimes,preachingvoc)
Alberta Hunter With Buster Bailey's Blues Blasters
Songs We Taught Your Mother | Original Blues Classics | OBCCD 520-2
Carroll Dickerson's Savoyagers
Louis Armstrong:Fireworks | Dreyfus Jazz Line | FDM 36710-2
Dick Wellstood's Wallerites
Uptown And Lowdown | Prestige | PCD 24262-2
Fats Waller And His Rhythm
Planet Jazz:Fats Waller | Planet Jazz | 2152058-2
Jack Teagarden's Chicagoans
Jazz:The Essential Collection Vol.3 | IN+OUT Records | 78013-2
The Hollywood Session:The Capitol Jazzmen | Jazz Unlimited | JUCD 2044
Jelly Roll Morton Trio
Planet Jazz:Jelly Roll Morton | Planet Jazz | 2152060-2
Jelly Roll Morton's New Orleans Jazzmen
Planet Jazz | Planet Jazz | 2169652-2
Planet Jazz:Male Jazz Vocalists | Planet Jazz | 2169657-2
Lionel Hampton And His Orchestra
Planet Jazz:Coleman Hawkins | Planet Jazz | 2152055-2
Planet Jazz:Lionel Hampton | Planet Jazz | 2152059-2
Planet Jazz:Jazz Saxophone | Planet Jazz | 2169653-2
Jazz:The Essential Collection Vol.3 | IN+OUT Records | 78013-2
Louis Armstrong And His Hot Five
Jazz:The Essential Collection Vol.2 | IN+OUT Records | 78012-2
Satch Plays Fats(Complete) | CBS | CK 64927
Louis Armstrong:Fireworks | Dreyfus Jazz Line | FDM 36710-2
Louis Armstrong And His Hot Seven
Planet Jazz:Louis Armstrong | Planet Jazz | 2152052-2
Best Of The Complete RCA Victor Recordings | RCA | 2663636-2
Louis Armstrong:A 100th Birthday Celebration | RCA | 2663694-2
Louis Armstrong:C'est Si Bon | Dreyfus Jazz Line | FDM 36730-2
Louis Armstrong And His Orchestra
Jazz:The Essential Collection Vol.2 | IN+OUT Records | 78012-2
Satch Plays Fats(Complete) | CBS | CK 64927
Louis Armstrong:Fireworks | Dreyfus Jazz Line | FDM 36710-2
Louis Armstrong:C'est Si Bon | Dreyfus Jazz Line | FDM 36730-2
Swing Legends:Louis Armstrong | Nimbus Records | NI 2012
Louis Armstrong And His Savoy Ballroom Five
Jazz:The Essential Collection Vol.2 | IN+OUT Records | 78012-2
Louis Armstrong:Fireworks | Dreyfus Jazz Line | FDM 36710-2
Sidney Bechet And His Orchestra
Sidney Bechet:Summertime | Dreyfus Jazz Line | FDM 36712-2
Sidney Bechet Trio
Planet Jazz:Sidney Bechet | Planet Jazz | 2152063-2
The Capitol Jazzmen
Jazz:The Essential Collection Vol.3 | IN+OUT Records | 78013-2
The Hollywood Session:The Capitol Jazzmen | Jazz Unlimited | JUCD 2044
Victoria Spivey With Buster Bailey's Blues Blasters
Songs We Taught Your Mother | Original Blues Classics | OBCCD 520-2

Siotto,Mario | (voc)
Ernst Reijseger & Tenore E Cuncordu De Orosei
Colla Voche | Winter&Winter | 910037-2

Sipiagin,Alex | (fl-htp)
Barbara Dennerlein Group
Outhipped | Verve | 547503-2
Charles Mingus Orchestra
Tonight At Noon...Three Or Four Shades Of Love | Dreyfus Jazz Line | FDM 36633-2
Dave Holland Big Band
What Goes Around | ECM | 1777(014002-2)
Michael Brecker Quindectet
Wide Angles | Verve | 076142-2
Mingus Big Band
Tonight At Noon...Three Or Four Shades Of Love | Dreyfus Jazz Line | FDM 36633-2

Siracusa,Gerard | (drperc)
Michael Riessler Group
Heloise | Wergo | WER 8008-2

Tentations D'Abélard | Wergo | WER 8009-2

Sircus,Joe | (congas)
Reuben Wilson Sextet
The Lost Grooves | Blue Note | 831883-2

Sireens | (voc)
Nick Woodland And The Magnets
Big Heart | Blues Beacon | BLU-1013 2

'Siri',Ricardo | (perc)
Big Allanbik
Batuque Y Blues | Blues Beacon | BLU-1031 2

Sirinian,Sebu | (v)
Hank Jones Trio With The Meridian String Quartet
The Story Of Jazz Piano | Laserlight | 24653

Sirkis,Asaf | (drbandir)
Gilad Atzmon & The Orient House Ensemble
Gilad Atzmon & The Orient House Ensemble | TipToe | TIP-888839 2

Sisi | (v)
Pili-Pili
Be In Two Minds | JA & RO | JARO 4134-2

Sissoko,Moussa | (djembetama)
Hank Jones Meets Cheik-Tidiana Seck
Sarala | Verve | 528783-2
Heiner Goebbels Group
Ou Bien Le Debarquement Desastreux | ECM | 1552

Sithole,Samila | (perc,congastimbales)
The Catholics
Simple | Laika Records | 35100802

Sitter,Primus | (g)
Couch Ensemble
Winnetou | Jazz 'n' Arts Records | JNA 1503
The Groenewald Newnet
Meetings | Jazz 'n' Arts Records | JNA 0702

Sivamani | (drperc)
Remember Shakti
Saturday Night In Bombay | Verve | 014184-2

Sivaraman,Umayalpuram K. | (Mridagam)
Shankar
Who's To Know | ECM | 1195

Sivuca | (accordeon,voc,g,porg)
Toots Thieleman And Sivuca
Verve Jazz Masters Vol.59:Toots Thielemans | Verve | 535271-2

Six | (rap)
Urbanator
Urbanator II | Hip Bop | HIBD 8012

Six,Jack | (b)
Dave Brubeck Quartet
We're All Together Again For The First Time | Atlantic | 7567-81390-2
All The Things We Are | Atlantic | 7567-81399-2
Dave Brubeck Quartet With Gerry Mulligan
The Last Set At Newport | Atlantic | 7567-81382-2
We're All Together Again For The First Time | Atlantic | 7567-81390-2
Dave Brubeck Quintet
All The Things We Are | Atlantic | 7567-81399-2
Dave Brubeck Trio
All The Things We Are | Atlantic | 7567-81399-2
Tal Farlow Quartet
The Return Of Tal Farlow/1969 | Original Jazz Classics | OJCCD 356-2

Six,The |
The Six
The Very Best Of Dixieland Jazz | Verve | 535529-2

Sjögren,Irene | (voc)
Irene Sjögren Group
Song For A Willow | Touché Music | TMcCD 015

Sjöstedt,Martin | (b)
Amanda Sedgwick Quintet
Reunion | Touché Music | TMcCD 021

Sjösten,Lars | (pld)
Brew Moore Quartet
No More Brew | Storyville | STCD 8275
Dexter Gordon-Benny Bailey Quintet
Revelation | Steeplechase | SCCD 31373
The Rainbow People | Steeplechase | SCCD 31521
Eje Thelin Group
Ejs Thelin 1966 With Barney Wilen | Dragon | DRCD 366

Skaff,Greg | (el-gg)
Marty Elkins And Her Sextet
Fuse Blues | Nagel-Heyer | CD 062

Skaggs,Chester 'Gino' | (bel-b)
John Lee Hooker Group
Endless Boogie | MCA | MCD 10413

Skar,Reidar | (sound treatment)
Nils Petter Molvaer Group
Khmer | ECM | 1560(537798-2)
Solid Ether | ECM | 1722(543365-2)

Skeat,Len | (b)
Allan Vaché-Antti Sarpila & 1 Sextet
Summit Meeting | Nagel-Heyer | CD 027
Allan Vaché-Antti Sarpila Quintet
Swing Is Here | Nagel-Heyer | CD 026
Blues Of Summer | Nagel-Heyer | NH 1011
The Second Sampler | Nagel-Heyer | NHR SP 6
Danny Moss Quartet
Weaver Of Dreams | Nagel-Heyer | CD 017
Keeper Of The Flame | Nagel-Heyer | CD 064
The Second Sampler | Nagel-Heyer | NHR SP 6
Danny Moss-Roy Williams Quintet
Steamers! | Nagel-Heyer | CD 049
Ellington For Lovers | Nagel-Heyer | NH 1009
George Masso Allstars
The Wonderful World Of George Gershwin | Nagel-Heyer | CD 001
One Two Three | Nagel-Heyer | CD 008
The First Sampler | Nagel-Heyer | NHR SP 5
George Masso Quintet
The First Sampler | Nagel-Heyer | NHR SP 5
George Masso-Ken Peplowski Quintet
Just Friends | Nagel-Heyer | CD 5001
Great British Jazz Band
The Great British Jazz Band:Jubilee | Candid | CCD 79720
Harry Allen Quartet
Love Songs Live! | Nagel-Heyer | NH 1014
Harry Allen Quintet
A Night At Birdland | Nagel-Heyer | CD 010
A Night At Birdland Vol. 1 | Nagel-Heyer | CD 5002
Ellington For Lovers | Nagel-Heyer | NH 1009
Love Songs Live! | Nagel-Heyer | NH 1014
The First Sampler | Nagel-Heyer | NHR SP 5
International Allstars
The International Allstars Play Benny Goodman:Vol.1 | Nagel-Heyer | CD 025
The Second Sampler | Nagel-Heyer | NHR SP 6
Jeanie Lambe And The Danny Moss Quartet
Three Great Concerts:Live In Hamburg 1993-1995 | Nagel-Heyer | CD 019
The Blue Noise Session | Nagel-Heyer | CD 052
The Second Sampler | Nagel-Heyer | NHR SP 6
Oliver Jackson Orchestra
The Last Great Concert | Nagel-Heyer | CD 063
The Buck Clayton Legacy
All The Cats Join In(Buck Clayton Rememberd) | Nagel-Heyer | CD 006
Encore Live | Nagel-Heyer | CD 018
The First Sampler | Nagel-Heyer | NHR SP 5
The Second Sampler | Nagel-Heyer | NHR SP 6
The Great British Jazz Band
A British Jazz Odyssey | Candid | CCD 79740
The International Allstars
The International Allstars Play Benny Goodman Vol.1 | Nagel-Heyer | CD 045
The Yamaha International Allstar Band
Hapy Birthday Jazzwelle Plus | Nagel-Heyer | CD 005
The First Sampler | Nagel-Heyer | NHR SP 5

Skeel,Christian | (computersamples)
Kenneth Knudsen-Christian Skeel
Music For Eyes | dacapo | DCCD 9433

Skeete,Frank | (b)
Don Byas Quartet
Don Byas:Laura | Dreyfus Jazz Line | FDM 36714-2
Lester Young Quintet
Jazz Gallery:Lester Young Vol.2(1946-59) | RCA | 2119541-2

Skerlecz,Gabor |
European Jazz Youth Orchestra
Swinging Europe 3 | dacapo | DCCD 9461

Skerritt,Fred | (as,clsax)
Charlie Parker With Machito And His Orchestra
Charlie Parker:The Best Of The Verve Years | Verve | 527815-2
Talkin' Bird | Verve | 559859-2
Bird: The Complete Charlie Parker On Verve | Verve | 837141-2
Charlie Parker:April In Paris | Dreyfus Jazz Line | FDM 36737-2

Skidmore,Alan | (fl,as,ts,sssax)
European Jazz Ensemble
European Jazz Ensemble 25th Anniversary | Konnex Records | KCD 5100
John Surman Orchestra
How Many Clouds Can You See? | Deram | 844882-2
NDR Big Band
NDR Big Band-Bravissimo | ACT | 9232-2

Skidmore,Jimmy | (ts)
The Jimmy And Marion McPartland Sessions
Vic Lewis:The Golden Years | Candid | CCD 79754

Skiles,Jimmy | (tb)
Tommy Dorsey And His Orchestra
Planet Jazz:Frank Sinatra & Tommy Dorsey | Planet Jazz | 2152067-2
Planet Jazz:Tommy Dorsey | Planet Jazz | 2159972-2

Skinner,Steve | (dr-programmingsynth)
Spyro Gyra & Guests
Love & Other Obsessions | GRP | GRP 98112

Skinner,Tom | (dr)
Nicolas Simion Group
Balkan Jazz | Intuition Records | INT 3339-2

Skipper,Ole | (bel-b)
VIBrations
7.Zelt-Musik-Festival:Jazz Events | Zounds | CD 2730001

Skiver,Bob | (clts)
Marty Grosz And His Honoris Causa Jazz Band
Hooray For Bix! | Good Time Jazz | GTCD 10065-2

Sklair,Josh | (gld)
Etta James & The Roots Band
Burnin' Down he House | RCA | 3411633-2

Sklair,Lee | (bel-b)
Billy Cobham Group
Spectrum | Atlantic | 7567-81428-2
The Best Of Billy Cobham | Atlantic | 7567-81558-2
Billy Cobham Quartet
Atlantic Jazz: Fusion | Atlantic | 7567-81711-2

Skoglund,Bosse | (drkagan)
Beng Berger Band
Bitter Funeral Beer | ECM | 1179

Skokann,Fritz | (ts)
Helmut Zacharias & His Sax-Team
Ich Habe Rhythmus | Bear Family Records | BCD 15642 AH
Helmut Zacharias mit seinem Orchester
Ich Habe Rhythmus | Bear Family Records | BCD 15642 AH

Skolnick,Sam | (tp)
Tommy Dorsey And His Orchestra
Planet Jazz:Tommy Dorsey | Planet Jazz | 2159972-2

Skorgan,Anita | (voc)
Dee Dee Bridgewater With Band
Victim Of Love | Verve | 841199-2

Skorija,Vesna | (voc)
Vesna Skorija Band
Niceland | Satin Doll Productions | SDP 1037-1 CD

Skrepek,Paul | (dr)
Oskar Aichinger Trio
Elelents Of Poetry | Between The Lines | btl 005(Efa 10175-2)

Skriptschinski,Frank | (b)
String Thing
String Thing:Alles Wird Gut | MicNic Records | MN 2
String Thing:Turtifix | MicNic Records | MN 4

Slade,Owen | (tuba)
John Surman-Jack DeJohnette With The London Brass
Printed In Germany | ECM | 1802(017065-2)

Slagle,Steve | (alto-cl,as,ss,bs,cl,fl,alto-fl)
Barbara Dennerlein Group
Outhipped | Verve | 547503-2
Carla Bley Band
Live! | Watt | 12(815730-2)
Heavy Heart | Watt | 14
Charlie Haden Orchestra
The Ballad Of The Fallen | ECM | 1248(811546-2)
Dave Stryker Octet
Blue To The Bone III | Steeplechase | SCCD 31524
Joe Lovano Nonet
On This Day At The Vanguard | Blue Note | 590950-2
Mingus Big Band 93
Nostalgia In Times Square | Dreyfus Jazz Line | FDM 36559-2
The Carla Bley Band
I Hate To Sing | Watt | 12,5

Slaney,Tom | (tp)
Maynard Ferguson And His Orchestra
Verve Jazz Masters 52:Maynard Ferguson | Verve | 529905-2

Slapin,Bill | (bs,cl,sax,fl,b-clreeds)
Bill Evans Quartet With Orchestra
The Complete Bill Evans On Verve | Verve | 527953-2
From Left To Right | Verve | 557451-2
Glenn Miller And His Orchestra
The Glenn Miller Orchestra In Digital Mood | GRP | GRP 95022
Les McCann Group
Another Beginning | Atlantic | 7567-80790-2

Slater,Ashley | (b-tbtb)
Barbara Thompson's Paraphernalia
Breathless | VeraBra Records | CDVBR 2057-2
Carla Bley Band
The Very Big Carla Bley Band | Watt | 23
Big Band Theory | Watt | 25(519966-2)

Slatkin,Eleanor | (cello)
Ella Fitzgerald With The Billy May Orchestra
The Best Of The Song Books:The Ballads | Verve | 521867-2
Ella Fitzgerald Sings The Harold Arlen Song Book | Verve | 589108-2
Ella Fitzgerald With The Nelson Riddle Orchestra
The Best Of The Song Books:The Ballads | Verve | 521867-2
Oh Lady Be Good:The Best Of The Gershwin Songbook | Verve | 529581-2
Love Songs:The Best Of The Song Books | Verve | 531762-2
Pete Rugolo And His Orchestra
Thriller/Richard Diamon(Original Jazz Scores From 2 Classics TV Series) | Fresh Sound Records | FSCD 2015

Slatkin,Felix | (cellov)
Ella Fitzgerald With The Marty Paich Orchestra
Get Happy! | Verve | 523321-2
Ella Fitzgerald With The Nelson Riddle Orchestra
The Best Of The Song Books:The Ballads | Verve | 521867-2
Oh Lady Be Good:The Best Of The Gershwin Songbook | Verve | 529581-2
Love Songs:The Best Of The Song Books | Verve | 531762-2

Slaughter,James | (dr)
Dinah Washington With The Eddie Chamblee Orchestra
Verve Jazz Masters 40:Dinah Washington | Verve | 522055-2
Dinah Sings Bessie Smith | Verve | 538635-2

Slaughter,John | (el-gg)
Chris Barber's Jazz And Blues Band
Chris Barber:40 Years Jubilee Concert | Storyville | 4990013
Chris Barber's Jazzband & das Große Rundfunkorchester Berlin,DDR
Jazz Zounds: Chris Barber | Zounds | CD 2720007

Slavin,Wanja | (clsax)
Wanja Slavin-Matc Schmolling
Off Minor | Organic Music | ORGM 9732

Sleet,Don | (tp)
Don Sleet Quintet
All Members | Original Jazz Classics | OJCCD 1949-2(JLP 9455)

Slessinger,Lois | (v)
Archie Shepp Orchestra
The Cry Of My People | Impulse(MCA) | 9861488

Sletten,Finn | (perc)
Jon Balke w/Oslo 13
Nonsentration | ECM | 1445
Susanne Lundeng Quartet
Waltz For The Red Fiddle | Laika Records | 35101402

Sloane,Carol | (voc)
Carol Sloane With The Norris Turney Quartet
Something Cool | Choice | CHCD 71025
Lionel Hampton And His Orchestra
Lionel Hampton:Flying Home | Dreyfus Jazz Line | FDM 36735-2

Slon,Claudio | (dr,synth,perc,timbales,vocwater-dr)
Astrud Gilberto With The Walter Wanderley Quartet
A Certain Smile A Certain Sadness | Verve | 557449-2
Astrud Gilberto With The Walter Wanderley Quintet
A Certain Smile A Certain Sadness | Verve | 557449-2
Astrud Gilberto With The Walter Wanderley Quuitet
Verve Jazz Masters 9:Astrud Gilberto | Verve | 519824-2
Joe Pass Sextet
Joe Pass:Guitar Virtuoso | Pablo | 4 PACD 4423-2
Marcos Valle With Orchestra
Samba '68 | Verve | 559516-2
Paulinho Da Costa Orchestra
Agora | Original Jazz Classics | OJCCD 630-2(2310785)

Slone,David | (b)
Milt Jackson And His Orchestra
Reverence And Compassion | Reprise | 9362-45204-2

Slovinsky,Philippe | (tp)
Renaud Garcia-Fons Group
Entremundo | Enja | ENJ-9464 2

Slow Poke |
Slow Poke
Redemption | Intuition Records | INT 3260-2

Smaak,Bert | (dr)
Acoustic Alchemy
Against The Grain | GRP | GRP 97832
International Commission For The Prevention Of Musical Border Control,The
The International Commission For The Prevention Of Musical Border Control | VeraBra Records | CDVBR 2093-2

Small Band |
Mark Murphy With The Ralph Burns Orchestra
Crazy Rhythm:His Debut Recordings | Decca | 050670-2

Small,Ernie | (bs,piccolo,tb,flts)
Harry James And His Orchestra
Trumpet Blues:The Best Of Harry James | Capitol | 521224-2

Small,Teddy | (as)
Buddy Johnson And His Orchestra
Buddy And Ella Johnson 1953-1964 | Bear Family Records | BCD 15479 DH

Smalls,Cliff | (p)
Big Al Sears Band
Sear-iously | Bear Family Records | BCD 15668 AH

Smiley,Bill | (b-tbtb)
Terry Gibbs Dream Band
Terry Gibbs Dream Band Vol.2:The Sundown Sessions | Contemporary | CCD 7652-2
Terry Gibbs Dream Band Vol.3:Flying Home | Contemporary | CCD 7654-2
Terry Gibbs Dream Band Vol.6:One More Time | Contemporary | CCD 7658-2
The Jazz Giants Play Jerome Kern:Yesterdays | Prestige | PCD 24202-2

Smiley,Dan | (v)
Art Pepper Quintet With Strings
Art Pepper:The Complete Galaxy Recordings | Galaxy | 16GCD 1016-2
Winter Moon | Original Jazz Classics | OJC20 677-2(GXY 5140)

Smirnoff,Kelly | (v)
Charlie Parker Quartet With Strings
The Cole Porter Songbook | Verve | 823250-2
Charlie Parker With Strings
Charlie Parker:The Best Of The Verve Years | Verve | 527815-2
Bird: The Complete Charlie Parker On Verve | Verve | 837141-2
Charlie Parker:April In Paris | Dreyfus Jazz Line | FDM 36737-2
Charlie Parker With The Joe Lipman Orchestra
Verve Jazz Masters 28:Charlie Parker Plays Standards | Verve | 521854-2
Charlie Parker With Strings:The Master Takes | Verve | 523984-2
Charlie Parker Big Band | Verve | 559835-2
Charlie Parker With The Neal Hefti Orchestra
Charlie Parker:The Best Of The Verve Years | Verve | 527815-2
Bird: The Complete Charlie Parker On Verve | Verve | 837141-2

Smirnoff,Ziggy | (v)
Charlie Parker With Strings
Charlie Parker With Strings:The Master Takes | Verve | 523984-2
Harry Carney And His Orchestra With Strings
Music For Loving:Ben Webster With Strings | Verve | 527774-2

Smith Jr.,Noland | (tp)
Stan Getz With Orchestra
Apasionado | A&M Records | 395297-2

Smith,Al | (voc)
Al Smith With The Eddie Lockjaw Davis Quartet
Queen Of The Organ-Shirley Scott Memorial Album | Prestige | PRCD 11027-2
Al Smith With The King Curtis Quintet
Midnight Special | Original Blues Classics | OBCCD 583-2(BV 1013)

Smith,Allan | (tp)
Ella Fitzgerald And Her Orchestra
Sunshine Of Your Love | MPS | 533102-2

Smith,André | (voc)
Barbara Dennerlein Group
Outhipped | Verve | 547503-2

Smith,Aubrey | (voc)
Taylor Hawkins Group
Wake Up Call | Fresh Sound Records | FSCD 145 CD

Smith,Ben | (as,clreeds)
Hot Lips Page Band
Planet Jazz:Jazz Trumpet | Planet Jazz | 2169654-2

Smith,Bessie | (voc)
Bessie Smith And Her Band
Jazz:The Essential Collection Vol.1 | IN+OUT Records | 78011-2
Jazz:The Essential Collection Vol.3 | IN+OUT Records | 78013-2
Classic Blues | Zounds | CD 2700048
Bessie Smith With Her Blue Boys
Jazz:The Essential Collection Vol.1 | IN+OUT Records | 78011-2
Bessie Smith With James P. Johnson
Jazz:The Essential Collection Vol.1 | IN+OUT Records | 78011-2
Bessie Smith With Louis Armstrong And Fred Longshaw
Jazz:The Essential Collection Vol.1 | IN+OUT Records | 78011-2
Bessie Smith With The James P.Johnson Orchestra And The Hal Johnson Choir
The Blues | Storyville | 4960323
Henderson's Hot Six
Jazz:The Essential Collection Vol.1 | IN+OUT Records | 78011-2

Smith,Bill | (cl,b-cl,bs,el-clcl-solo)

Barney Kessel And His Orchestra
Barney Kessel Plays Carmen | Original Jazz Classics | OJC 269(C 7563)
Bill Smith Quartet
Folk Jazz U.S.A. | Original Jazz Classics | OJCCD 1956-2(S 7591)
Dave Brubeck Octet
The Dave Brubeck Octet | Original Jazz Classics | OJCCD 101-2(F 3239)
Red Norvo Sextet
Music To Listen To Red Norvo By | Original Jazz Classics | OJCCD 1015-2(C 7534)

Smith,Billy | (dr,tp,tsvoc)
Thelonious Monk Sextet
Genius Of Modern Music,Vol.1 | Blue Note | 532138-2
Jazz Profile:Thelonious Monk | Blue Note | 823518-2
Thelonious Monk:Misterioso | Dreyfus Jazz Line | FDM 36743-2

Smith,Buster | (arr,asdr)
Buster Smith Orchestra
Atlantic Jazz: Kansas City | Atlantic | 7567-81701-2

Smith,Carl | (tp)
Count Basie And His Orchestra
Jazz:The Essential Collection Vol.3 | IN+OUT Records | 78013-2
Jones-Smith Incorporated
Jazz:The Essential Collection Vol.3 | IN+OUT Records | 78013-2

Smith,Carson | (b)
A Band Of Friends
The Best Of The Gerry Mulligan Quartet With Chet Baker | Pacific Jazz | 795481-2
Billie Holiday And Her All Stars
The Billie Holiday Song Book | Verve | 823246-2
Buddy Rich And His Orchestra
Swingin' New Big Band | Pacific Jazz | 835232-2
Chet Baker Quartet
Chet Baker Quartet Live Vol.1:This Time The Dreams's On Me | Pacific Jazz | 525248-2
Chet Baker Quartet Live Vol.3: May Old Flame | Pacific Jazz | 531573-2
Let's Get Lost: The Best Of Chet Baker Sings | Pacific Jazz | 792932-2
The Best Of Chet Baker Plays | Pacific Jazz | 797161-2
Chet Baker Sextet
The Best Of Chet Baker Plays | Pacific Jazz | 797161-2
Gerry Mulligan Quartet
Gene Norman Presents The Original Gerry Mulligan Tentet And Quartet | GNP Crescendo | GNPD 56
Gerry Mulligan Quartet feat.Chet Baker | Original Jazz Classics | OJCCD 711-2(F 8082/P 7641)
The Jazz Giants Play Rodgers & Hart:Blue Moon | Prestige | PCD 24205-2
Lee Konitz & The Gerry Mulligan Quartet
Konitz Meets Mulligan | Pacific Jazz | 746847-2

Smith,Cecilia | (marimba)
Cassandra Wilson Group
Traveling Miles | Blue Note | 854123-2

Smith,Charles | (perc)
Max Roach With The Boston Percussion Ensemble
Clifford Brown-Max Roach:Alone Together-The Best Of The Mercury Years | Verve | 526373-2

Smith,Charlie | (congas,drp)
Ella Fitzgerald And Her All Stars
Ella Fitzgerald:Mr.Paganini | Dreyfus Jazz Line | FDM 36741-2
Ella Fitzgerald With The Hank Jones Trio
Ella Fitzgerald:Mr.Paganini | Dreyfus Jazz Line | FDM 36741-2
Louis Jordan And His Tympany Five
Louis Jordan-Let The Good Times Roll: The Complete Decca Recordings 1938-1954 | Bear Family Records | BCD 15557 IH
Milt Jackson Septet
The Birdlanders Vol.1 | Original Jazz Classics | OJCCD 1930-2
Milt Jackson Sextet
The Birdlanders Vol.1 | Original Jazz Classics | OJCCD 1930-2
Milt Jackson Trio
Milt Jackson Birthday Celebration | Fantasy | FANCD 6079-2
Roy Eldridge And His Orchestra
The Complete Verve Roy Eldridge Studio Sessions | Verve | 9861278

Smith,Clinton | (tb)
Buster Smith Orchestra
Atlantic Jazz: Kansas City | Atlantic | 7567-81701-2

Smith,Dalton | (tp)
Stan Kenton And His Orchestra
Adventures In Blues | Capitol | 520089-2
Adventures In Jazz | Capitol | 521222-2

Smith,Dave | (tp)
European Jazz Youth Orchestra
Swinging Europe 3 | dacapo | DCCD 9461
John Mayer's Indio-Jazz Fusions
Ragatal | Nimbus Records | NI 5569

Smith,Derek | (p,el-p,caliopeclavichord)
Mike Bryan Sextet
Jazz Festival Vol.2 | Storyville | 4960743

Smith,Dick | (bperc)
Hugh Marsh Duo/Quartet/Orchestra
The Bear Walks | VeraBra Records | CDVBR 2011-2

Smith,Don | (fl,p,voc,tpfl-h)
Dick Griffin Septet
The Eighth Wonder & More | Konnex Records | KCD 5059
Stan Kenton And His Orchestra
Stan Kenton Portraits On Standards | Capitol | 531571-2

Smith,Donald | (fl,voc,porg)
Lester Bowie Group
The Great Pretender | ECM | 1209(829369-2)
Lester Bowie Quartet
The Great Pretender | ECM | 1209(829369-2)

Smith,Eddie | (bj,gtp)
Count Basie And His Orchestra
Jazz:The Essential Collection Vol.3 | IN+OUT Records | 78013-2
Earl Hines And His Orchestra
The Legends Of Swing | Laserlight | 24659

Smith,Floyd | (g)
Johnny 'Hammond' Smith Quartet
Good 'Nuff | Prestige | PRCD 24282-2

Smith,George | (cl,tsuba)
Ella Fitzgerald With The Nelson Riddle Orchestra
The Best Of The Song Books:The Ballads | Verve | 521867-2
Love Songs:The Best Of The Song Books | Verve | 531762-2
Ella Fitzgerald Sings The Johnny Mercer Songbook | Verve | 539057-2
John Surman Orchestra
How Many Clouds Can You See? | Deram | 844882-2

Smith,George Harmonica | (harmvoc)
Big Joe Turner And His Orchestra
Planet Jazz:Male Jazz Vocalists | Planet Jazz | 2169657-2

Smith,Harold | (dr,perc,voctb)
Jan Harrington And Friends
I Feel The Spirit | Nagel-Heyer | NHR SP 7
Jan Harrington Band
Christmas Jazz! | Nagel-Heyer | NH 1008
Jan Harrington Sextet
Jan Harrington's Christmas In New Orleans | Nagel-Heyer | NHR SP 4
Sam Rivers Orchestra
Crystals | Impulse(MCA) | 589760-2

Smith,Howard | (pvoc)
Adrian Rollini And His Orchestra
Jazz:The Essential Collection Vol.3 | IN+OUT Records | 78013-2
Tommy Dorsey And His Orchestra
Planet Jazz:Frank Sinatra & Tommy Dorsey | Planet Jazz | 2152067-2
Planet Jazz:Tommy Dorsey | Planet Jazz | 2159972-2

Smith,Jabbo | (co,tp,tbvoc)
Louisiana Sugar Babes
Planet Jazz:Jazz Trumpet | Planet Jazz | 2169654-2

Smith,Jimmie | (dr)
Benny Carter 4
Montreux '77 | Original Jazz Classics | OJC20 374-2(2308204)
Count Basie Jam
Montreux '77 | Original Jazz Classics | OJC 379(2308209)
Montreux '77 | Original Jazz Classics | OJC 385(2620105)
Dizzy Gillespie Jam
Montreux '77 | Original Jazz Classics | OJC20 381-2(2308211)
Dizzy Gillespie Sextet
The Jazz Giants Play Harold Arlen:Blues In The Night | Prestige | PCD 24201-2
Etta Jones And Her Band
Love Shout | Original Jazz Classics | OJCCD 941-2(P 7272)
Harry Edison Quintet
Edison's Light | Original Jazz Classics | OJCCD 804-2(2310780)
Jimmy Forrest Quartet
Forest Fire | Original Jazz Classics | OJCCD 199-2
Jimmy Witherspoon And His Band
Baby, Baby, Baby | Original Blues Classics | OBCCD 527-2(P 7290)
Lambert, Hendricks And Bavan
Planet Jazz:Male Jazz Vocalists | Planet Jazz | 2169657-2
Milt Jackson With Strings
To Bags...With Love:Memorial Album | Pablo | 2310967-2
Milt Jackson-Ray Brown Jam
Milt Jackson Birthday Celebration | Fantasy | FANCD 6079-2
Montreux '77 | Original Jazz Classics | OJC 385(2620105)
Montreux '77 | Original Jazz Classics | OJC20 375-2(2308205)
Richard 'Groove' Holmes Trio
Soul Message | Original Jazz Classics | OJC20 329-2(P 7435)
Zoot Sims-Harry Edison Quintet
Jazz Dance | Original Jazz Classics | OJCCD 1002-2(1210890)

Smith,Jimmy | (b,tuba,bj,g,org,arp-string-ensemble)
Babs Gonzales With The Jimmy Smith Trio
Blue Velvet: Crooners, Swooners And Velvet Vocals | Blue Note | 521153-2
Dee Dee Bridgewater With Her Quintet With Jimmy Smith
Love And Peace-A Tribute To Horace Silver | Verve | 527470-2
George Benson Group/Orchestra
George Benson Anthology | Warner | 8122-79934-2
Jimmy Smith All Stars
House Party | Blue Note | 524542-2
Jimmy Smith:Dot Com Blues | Blue Thumb | 543978-2
Jimmy Smith And Wes Montgomery With Orchestra
Jimmy & Wes-The Dynamic Duo | Verve | 521445-2
Jimmy Smith And Wes Montgomery With The Oliver Nelson Orchestra
Wes Montgomery:The Verve Jazz Sides | Verve | 521690-2
Jimmy Smith:Best Of The Verve Years | Verve | 527950-2
Talkin' Jazz:Roots Of Acid Jazz | Verve | 529580-2
Jimmy Smith Quartet
Blue Note Plays Gershwin | Blue Note | 520808-2
Six Views Of The Blues | Blue Note | 521435-2
Verve Jazz Masters 45:Kenny Burrell | Verve | 527652-2
Jimmy Smith:Best Of The Verve Years | Verve | 527950-2
Jimmy Smith-Talkin' Verve | Verve | 531563-2
Cool Blues | Blue Note | 535587-2
Any Number Can Win | Verve | 557447-2
Prayer Meetin' | Blue Note | 576754-2
Back At The Chicken Shack | Blue Note | 746402-2
The Best Of Blue Note | Blue Note | 796110-2
Home Cookin' | Blue Note | 853360-2
Midnight Blue(The [Be]witching Hour) | Blue Note | 854365-2
Fourmost Return | Milestone | MCD 9311-2
Jimmy Smith Quintet
Cool Blues | Blue Note | 535587-2
Root Down | Verve | 559805-2
Prayer Meetin' | Blue Note | 576754-2
Rockin' the Boat | Blue Note | 576755-2
Jimmy Smith Sextet
Angel Eyes-Ballads & Slow Jams | Verve | 527632-2
Jimmy Smith:Best Of The Verve Years | Verve | 527950-2
Root Down | Verve | 559805-2
Jimmy Smith Trio
Jimmy Smith Trio: Salle Pleyel, May 28th, 1965 | Laserlight | 36135
Paris Jazz Concert:Jimmy Smith And The Trio | Laserlight | 36159
Groovin' At Smalls' Paradise | Blue Note | 499777-2
Verve Jazz Masters 29:Jimmy Smith | Verve | 521855-2
Verve Jazz Masters 21:George Benson | Verve | 521861-2
Bucket! | Blue Note | 524550-2
Jimmy Smith:Best Of The Verve Years | Verve | 527950-2
Verve Jazz Masters Vol.60:The Collection | Verve | 529866-2
Jimmy Smith-Talkin' Verve | Verve | 531563-2
Cool Blues | Blue Note | 535587-2
Organ Grinder Swing | Verve | 543831-2
Talkin' Verve:George Benson | Verve | 553780-2
So Blue So Funky-Heroes Of The Hammond | Blue Note | 796563-2
Standards | Blue Note | 821282-2
I'm Movin' On | Blue Note | 832750-2
Home Cookin' | Blue Note | 853360-2
A New Sound A New Star:Jimmy Smith At The Organ | Blue Note | 857191-2
Jimmy Smith With Orchestra
Verve Jazz Masters 29:Jimmy Smith | Verve | 521855-2
Jimmy Smith:Best Of The Verve Years | Verve | 527950-2
Jimmy Smith-Talkin' Verve | Verve | 531563-2
Jimmy Smith With The Billy Byers Orchestra
Jimmy Smith:Best Of The Verve Years | Verve | 527950-2
Jimmy Smith With The Claus Ogerman Orchestra
Verve Jazz Masters 29:Jimmy Smith | Verve | 521855-2
Any Number Can Win | Verve | 557447-2
Jimmy Smith With The Johnny Pate Orchestra
Jimmy Smith:Best Of The Verve Years | Verve | 527950-2
Jimmy Smith-Talkin' Verve | Verve | 531563-2
Jimmy Smith With The Lalo Schifrin Orchestra
Jimmy Smith:Best Of The Verve Years | Verve | 527950-2
Jimmy Smith-Talkin' Verve | Verve | 531563-2
The Cat | Verve | 539756-2
Jimmy Smith With The Oliver Nelson Orchestra
Verve Jazz Masters 29:Jimmy Smith | Verve | 521855-2
Jimmy Smith:Best Of The Verve Years | Verve | 527950-2
Jimmy Smith-Talkin' Verve | Verve | 531563-2
Peter & The Wolf | Verve | 547264-2
Jimmy Smith-Eddie Harris Trio
All The Way | Milestone | MCD 9251-2
Jimmy Smith-Wes Montgomery Quartet
Jimmy & Wes-The Dynamic Duo | Verve | 521445-2
Wes Montgomery:The Verve Jazz Sides | Verve | 521690-2
Verve Jazz Masters 29:Jimmy Smith | Verve | 521855-2
Jimmy Smith:Best Of The Verve Years | Verve | 527950-2
Talkin' Jazz:Roots Of Acid Jazz | Verve | 529580-2
Jimmy Smith-Talkin' Verve | Verve | 531563-2
Kenny Burrell-Jimmy Smith Quartet
Blue Bash | Verve | 557453-2
Kenny Burrell-Jimmy Smith Trio
Blue Bash | Verve | 557453-2

Smith,Joe | (cotp)
Bessie Smith And Her Band
Jazz:The Essential Collection Vol.1 | IN+OUT Records | 78011-2
Bessie Smith With Her Blue Boys
Jazz:The Essential Collection Vol.1 | IN+OUT Records | 78011-2
Bessie Smith With The James P.Johnson Orchestra And The Hal Johnson Choir
The Blues | Storyville | 4960323
Henderson's Hot Six
Jazz:The Essential Collection Vol.1 | IN+OUT Records | 78011-2
McKinney's Cotton Pickers
Jazz:The Essential Collection Vol.3 | IN+OUT Records | 78013-2
The Lousiana Stompers
Jazz:The Essential Collection Vol.1 | IN+OUT Records | 78011-2

Smith,John | (as,dr,el-b,g,bts)
Fats Waller And His Rhythm
Planet Jazz:Fats Waller | Planet Jazz | 2152058-2
Fats Waller:The Complete Associated Transcription Sessions 1935-1939 | Jazz Unlimited | JUCD 2076
Sarah Vaughan And Her Band
Songs Of The Beatles | Atlantic | 16037-2

Smith,John 'Butch' | (ss,asvoc)
Engelbert Wrobel-Chris Hopkins-Dan Barrett Sextet
Harlem 2000 | Nagel-Heyer | CD 082

Smith,Johnny | (gg-solo)
Johnny Smith Quartet
The Sound Of The Johnny Smith Guitar | Roulette | 531792-2
Moonlight In Vermont | Roulette | 596593-2
Johnny Smith Quintet
Moonlight In Vermont | Roulette | 596593-2
Johnny Smith Trio
Moonlight In Vermont | Roulette | 596593-2
Johnny Smith-Stan Getz Quintet
Stan Getz-The Complete Roost Sessions | EMI Records | 859622-2

Smith,Johnny 'Hammond' | (keyboardsorg)
Gene Ammons Quintet
Gentle Jug Vol.3 | Prestige | PCD 24249-2
Johnny 'Hammond' Smith Quartet
Open House | Milestone | MCD 47089-2
The Soulful Blues | Prestige | PCD 24244-2
Good 'Nuff | Prestige | PRCD 24282-2
Johnny 'Hammond' Smith Quintet
Discovery:Grover Washington Jr.-The First Recordings | Prestige | PCD 11020-2
Johnny 'Hammond' Smith Septet
Open House | Milestone | MCD 47089-2
Johnny 'Hammond' Smith Sextet
Open House | Milestone | MCD 47089-2
The Soulful Blues | Prestige | PCD 24244-2
Johnny 'Hammond' Smith Trio
Good 'Nuff | Prestige | PRCD 24282-2
Oliver Nelson Quintet
The Jazz Giants Play Sammy Cahn:It's Magic | Prestige | PCD 24226-2
Wild Bill Moore Quintet
Bottom Groove | Milestone | MCD 47098-2

Smith,Josea | (b)
Buster Smith Orchestra
Atlantic Jazz: Kansas City | Atlantic | 7567-81701-2

Smith,Larry | (asrecitation)
James Carter Group
Conversin' With The Elders | Atlantic | 7567-82988-2

Smith,Lee | (b)
Mongo Santamaria And His Band
Montreux Heat! | Pablo | PACD 5317-2
Mongo Santamaria Group With Dizzy Gillespie And Toots Thielemans
Summertime-Digital At Montreux 1980 | Original Jazz Classics | OJCCD 626-2(2308229)
Montreux Heat! | Pablo | PACD 5317-2

Smith,Leo[Wadada] | (tp,fl,perc,gongs,steel-o-phone,fl-h)
Jeanne Lee Group
Natural Affinities | Owl Records | 018352-2
John Lindberg Ensemble
A Tree Frog Tonality | Between The Lines | btl 008(Efa 10178-2)
Leo Smith Group
Devine Love | ECM | 1143
Wadada Leo Smith
Kulture Jazz | ECM | 1507

Smith,Leopolodo F. | (perc)
Dick Griffin Septet
The Eighth Wonder & More | Konnex Records | KCD 5059

Smith,Leslie | (voc)
Nils Landgren First Unit And Guests
Nils Landgren-The First Unit | ACT | 9292-2

Smith,Lonnie | (keyboards,org,p,el-p,synthvoc)
George Benson Group/Orchestra
George Benson Anthology | Warner | 8122-79934-2
George Benson Quartet
It's Uptown | CBS | 502469-2
The George Benson Cookbook | CBS | 502470-2
George Benson Quartet + Guests
The George Benson Cookbook | CBS | 502470-2
George Benson Quintet
It's Uptown | CBS | 502469-2
Jimmy McGriff Sextet
McGriff's House Party | Milestone | MCD 9300-2
Lonnie Smith Quintet
Deep Blue-The United States Of Mind | Blue Note | 521152-2
The Lost Grooves | Blue Note | 831883-2
Lou Donaldson Quartet
Mr.Shing-A-Ling | Blue Note | 784271-2
Lou Donaldson Quintet
Midnight Creeper | Blue Note | 524546-2
Mr.Shing-A-Ling | Blue Note | 784271-2
Lou Donaldson Sextet
So Blue So Funky-Heroes Of The Hammond | Blue Note | 796563-2
Red Holloway Quintet
Coast To Coast | Milestone | MCD 9335-2
Rodney Jones Group
Soul Manifesto | Blue Note | 530499-2

Smith,Lonnie Liston | (org,p,bailophone,ring-cymbals)
Gato Barbieri Group
Planet Jazz:Gato Barbieri | RCA | 2165364-2
Gato Barbieri:The Best Of The Early Years | RCA | 2663523-2
Gato Barbieri Sextet
The Third World | RCA | 2179617-2
Leon Thomas With Band
Spirits Known And Unknown | RCA | 2663876-2
Leon Thomas In Berlin | RCA | 2663877-2
Lonnie Liston Smith & His Cosmic Echoes
Astral Travelling | RCA | 2663878-2
Pharoah Sanders Orchestra
Karma | Impulse(MCA) | 951153-2
Jewels Of Thought | Impulse(MCA) | 951247-2
Thembi | Impulse(MCA) | 951253-2
Deaf Dumb Blind | Impulse(MCA) | 951265-2
The Roots Of Acid Jazz | Impulse(MCA) | IMP 12042
Roland Kirk Quartet
Talkin' Verve-Roots Of Acid Jazz:Roland Kirk | Verve | 533101-2

Smith,Louis | (tpfl-h)
Horace Silver Quintet
Newport Jazz Festival 1958,July 3rd-6th,Vol.1:Mostly Miles | Phontastic | NCD 8813
Kenny Burrell Septet
Blue Lights Vol.1&2 | Blue Note | 857184-2
Louis Smith Quintet
Louisville | Steeplechase | SCCD 31552

Smith,Malcom | (tb)
Clare Teal And Her Band
Orsino's Songs | Candid | CCD 79783

Smith,Mamie | (voc)
Mamie Smith WithThe Lucky Millinder Orchestra
The Blues | Storyville | 4960323

Smith,Marvin 'Smitty' | (dr,perc,perc-sample,rap,voc,voice)
Daniel Schnyder Quintet
Nucleus | Enja | ENJ-8068 2
Dave Holland Qartet
Extensions | ECM | 1410(841778-2)
Dave Holland Quintet
Seeds Of Time | ECM | 1292
The Razor's Edge | ECM | 1353
David Fathead Newman Quintet Plus Clifford Jordan
Blue Head | Candid | CCD 79041
Dianne Reeves With Band
Misty Blue:Sweet Sisters Swing Songs Of Sorrow And Sadness | Blue Note | 521151-2

I Remember | Blue Note | 790264-2
Ed Sarath Quintet
Last Day In May | Konnex Records | KCD 5042
Eddie Allen Quintet
R 'N' B | Enja | ENJ-9033 2
Gebhard Ullmann Trio
Suite Noire | Nabel Records:Jazz Network | CD 4649
Gebhard Ullmann-Andreas Willers
Playful '93 | Nabel Records:Jazz Network | CD 4659
Gunter Hampel New York Orchestra
Fresh Heat-Live At Sweet Basil | Birth | CD 039
Kevin Mahogany With Orchestra
Songs And Moments | Enja | ENJ-8072 2
McCoy Tyner Quartet
Prelude And Sonata | Milestone | MCD 9244-2
McCoy Tyner Quintet
Prelude And Sonata | Milestone | MCD 9244-2
Mingus Big Band 93
Nostalgia In Times Square | Dreyfus Jazz Line | FDM 36559-2
Sonny Rollins Quintet
The Jazz Giants Play Harry Warren:Lullaby Of Broadway | Prestige | PCD 24204-2
Steve Coleman And Five Elements
On The Edge Of Tomorrow | JMT Edition | 919005-2
Steve Coleman Group
Motherland Pulse | JMT Edition | 919001-2

Smith,Mauricio | (fl,as,piccolo,cl,ss,ts,vocreeds)
Charles Mingus Orchestra
Cumbia & Jazz Fusion | Atlantic | 8122-71785-2
Machito And His Orchestra
Afro-Cuban Jazz Moods | Original Jazz Classics | OJC20 447-2

Smith,Mike | (as,bdr)
Buddy Childers Big Band
Just Buddy's | Candid | CCD 79761

Smith,Nadja | (newspeak)
Jeanne Lee Group
Natural Affinities | Owl Records | 018352-2

Smith,Neal | (dr)
Cyrus Chestnut Trio
You Are My Sunshine | Warner | 9362-48445-2

Smith,Nigel Portman | (b,porg)
Marty Hall Band
Who's Been Talkin'?s | Blues Beacon | BLU-1033 2

Smith,Nolan | (tpfl-h)
Diane Schuur And Her Band
The Best Of Diane Schuur | GRP | GRP 98882
Ella Fitzgerald With The Count Basie Orchestra
For The Love Of Ella Fitzgerald | Verve | 841765-2

Smith,O.C. | (voc)
Ahmad Jamal Trio
Picture Perfect-70th Anniversary | Warner | 8573-85268-2

Smith,Paul | (p,arr,celesteorg)
Anita O'Day And Her Combo
Pick Yourself Up | Verve | 517329-2
Anita O'Day With The Buddy Bregman Orchestra
Pick Yourself Up | Verve | 517329-2
Verve Jazz Masters 49:Anita O'Day | Verve | 527653-2
Billy May And His Orchestra
Billy May's Big Fat Brass/Bill's Bag | Capitol | 535206-2
Buddy Bregman And His Orchestra
Swinging Kicks | Verve | 559514-2
Ella Fitzgerald And Her All Stars
The Best Of The Song Books:The Ballads | Verve | 521867-2
Love Songs:The Best Of The Song Books | Verve | 531762-2
Ella Fitzgerald Sings The Duke Ellington Songbook | Verve | 559248-2
For The Love Of Ella Fitzgerald | Verve | 841765-2
Ella Fitzgerald And Her Sextet
Ella Fitzgerald-First Lady Of Song | Verve | 517898-2
The Best Of The Song Books | Verve | 519804-2
Ella Fitzgerald And Paul Smith
Ella Fitzgerald-First Lady Of Song | Verve | 517898-2
Verve Jazz Masters 46:Ella Fitzgerald-The Jazz Sides | Verve | 527655-2
The Intimate Ella | Verve | 839838-2
Ella Fitzgerald And The Paul Smith Quartet
The Best Of The Song Books | Verve | 519804-2
Verve Jazz Masters 6:Ella Fitzgerald | Verve | 519822-2
Verve Jazz Masters 46:Ella Fitzgerald-The Jazz Sides | Verve | 527655-2
Ella Fitzgerald With Count Basie And His Orchestra
Digital III At Montreux | Original Jazz Classics | OJCCD 996-2(2308223)
Ella Fitzgerald With Paul Weston And His Orchestra
Love Songs:The Best Of The Song Books | Verve | 531762-2
Ella Fitzgerald Sings The Irving Berlin Song Book | Verve | 543830-2
Ella Fitzgerald With The Billy May Orchestra
Ella Fitzgerald-First Lady Of Song | Verve | 517898-2
The Best Of The Song Books | Verve | 519804-2
Verve Jazz Masters 6:Ella Fitzgerald | Verve | 519822-2
Verve Jazz Masters 46:Ella Fitzgerald-The Jazz Sides | Verve | 527655-2
Ella Fitzgerald Sings The Harold Arlen Song Book | Verve | 589108-2
For The Love Of Ella Fitzgerald | Verve | 841765-2
Ella Fitzgerald With The Buddy Bregman Orchestra
Ella Fitzgerald-First Lady Of Song | Verve | 517898-2
The Best Of The Song Books:The Ballads | Verve | 521867-2
Love Songs:The Best Of The Song Books | Verve | 531762-2
Ella Fitzgerald Sings The Cole Porter Songbook | Verve | 537257-2
Ella Fitzgerald Sings The Rodgers And Hart Song Book | Verve | 537258-2
For The Love Of Ella Fitzgerald | Verve | 841765-2
Ella Fitzgerald With The Count Basie Orchestra
Bluella:Ella Fitzgerald Sings The Blues | Pablo | 2310960-2
Ella Fitzgerald With The Nelson Riddle Orchestra
Ella Fitzgerald-First Lady Of Song | Verve | 517898-2
The Best Of The Song Books | Verve | 519804-2
The Best Of The Song Books:The Ballads | Verve | 521867-2
Get Happy! | Verve | 523321-2
Oh Lady Be Good:The Best Of The Gershwin Songbook | Verve | 529581-2
Love Songs:The Best Of The Song Books | Verve | 531762-2
Ella Fitzgerald Sings The Johnny Mercer Songbook | Verve | 539057-2
For The Love Of Ella Fitzgerald | Verve | 841765-2
Dream Dancing | Original Jazz Classics | OJCCD 1072-2(2310814)
Ella Fitzgerald With The Paul Smith Quartet
Ella Fitzgerald-First Lady Of Song | Verve | 517898-2
Mack The Knife-The Complete Ella In Berlin | Verve | 519564-2
Verve Jazz Masters 6:Ella Fitzgerald | Verve | 519822-2
Verve Jazz Masters 20:Introducing | Verve | 519853-2
The Best Of The Song Books:The Ballads | Verve | 521867-2
Ella Fitzgerald Sings The Rodgers And Hart Song Book | Verve | 537258-2
4 By 4:Ella Fitzgerald/Sarah Vaughan/Billie Holiday/Dinah Washington | Verve | 559693-2
For The Love Of Ella Fitzgerald | Verve | 841765-2
Ella Fitzgerald With The Paul Weston Orchestra
Get Happy! | Verve | 523321-2
June Christy With The Pete Rugolo Orchestra
Something Cool(The Complete Mono & Stereo Versions) | Capitol | 534069-2
Stuff Smith Quartet
Cat On A Hot Fiddle | Verve | 9861487
Tommy Dorsey And His Orchestra
Planet Jazz:Tommy Dorsey | Planet Jazz | 2159972-2
Van Alexander Orchestra
Home Of Happy Feet/Swing! Staged For Sound! | Capitol | 535211-2

Smith,Richard | (drg)
Eddie Harris Group
The Best Of Eddie Harris | Atlantic | 7567-81370-2

Richard Elliot Sextet
City Speak | Blue Note | 832620-2

Smith,Roger | (gtb)
John Stevens Trio
4,4,4, | Konnex Records | KCD 5049

Smith,Rudy | (steel-dr)
Johnny Dyani Septet
Afrika | Steeplechase | SCS 1186(Audiophile Pressing)

Smith,Russell | (tb,tp,vovv-tb)
Bessie Smith With The James P.Johnson Orchestra And The Hal Johnson Choir
The Blues | Storyville | 4960323
Connie's Inn Orchestra
Planet Jazz:Coleman Hawkins | Planet Jazz | 2152055-2
Fletcher Henderson And His Orchestra
Jazz:The Essential Collection Vol.1 | IN+OUT Records | 78011-2
Jazz:The Essential Collection Vol.3 | IN+OUT Records | 78013-2
The Lousiana Stompers
Jazz:The Essential Collection Vol.1 | IN+OUT Records | 78011-2
Vince Jones Group
Spell | Intuition Records | INT 3067-2
It All Ends Up In Tears | Intuition Records | INT 3069-2

Smith,Russell prob. | (tp)
The Lousiana Stompers
Jazz:The Essential Collection Vol.1 | IN+OUT Records | 78011-2

Smith,Sean | (b)
Jacky Terrasson Trio
Smile | Blue Note | 542413-2
Jacky Terrasson-Emmanuel Pahud Quartet
Into The Blue | Blue Note | 557257-2

Smith,Sidney | (fl)
Baden Powell Quartet
Three Originals:Tristeza On Guitar/Poema On Guitar/Apaixonado | MPS | 519216-2
Sidney Smith & Eberhard Weber
Three Originals:Tristeza On Guitar/Poema On Guitar/Apaixonado | MPS | 519216-2

Smith,Sonelius | (pceleste)
Rahsaan Roland Kirk Sextet
Blacknuss | Rhino | 8122-71408-2

Smith,Steve | (dr,perc,ptp)
Jean-Luc Ponty Sextet
Enigmatic Ocean | Atlantic | 19110-2
The Very Best Of Jean-Luc Ponty | Rhino | 8122-79862-2
Steps Ahead
N.Y.C. | Intuition Records | INT 3007-2
Steve Smith & Vital Information
Vitalive! | VeraBra Records | CDVBR 2051-2
Vital Information
Ray Of Hope | VeraBra Records | CDVBR 2161-2
Where We Come From | Intuition Records | INT 3218-2
Live Around The World Where We Come From Tour '98-'99 | Intuition Records | INT 3296-2
Show 'Em Where You Live | Intuition Records | INT 3306-2

Smith,Stuff | (vvoc)
Ella Fitzgerald And Her All Stars
The Best Of The Song Books:The Ballads | Verve | 521867-2
Love Songs:The Best Of The Song Books | Verve | 531762-2
Ella Fitzgerald Sings The Duke Ellington Songbook | Verve | 559248-2
For The Love Of Ella Fitzgerald | Verve | 841765-2
Ella Fitzgerald And Her Sextet
Ella Fitzgerald-First Lady Of Song | Verve | 517898-2
The Best Of The Song Books | Verve | 519804-2
Nat King Cole Quintet
After Midnight | Capitol | 520087-2
Oscar Peterson Sextet
Oscar Peterson Trio: Olympia/Theatre Des Champs-Elysees | Laserlight | 36134
Stuff Smith Quartet
Cat On A Hot Fiddle | Verve | 9861487
Stuff Smith With The Henri Chaix Trio
Late Woman Blues | Storyville | STCD 8328

Smith,Tab | (as,tsss)
Billie Holiday With Frankie Newton And His Orchestra
Billie Holiday:The Complete Commodore Recordings | GRP | 543272-2
Billie's Love Songs | Nimbus Records | NI 2000

Smith,Teddy | (b)
Horace Silver Quintet
Horace Silver Retrospective | Blue Note | 495576-2
Song For My Father | Blue Note | 499002-2
The Best Of Blue Note | Blue Note | 796110-2
Sonny Rollins Sextet
The Standard Sonny Rollins | RCA | 2174801-2

Smith,Tommy | (fr-h,sax,tp,fl-h,ssts)
Gary Burton Quintet
Whiz Kids | ECM | 1329

Smith,Warren | (bass-marimba,bongos)
Bob Crosby And His Orchestra
Swing Legens:Bob Crosby | Nimbus Records | NI 2011
Bob Crosby's Bobcats
Swing Legens:Bob Crosby | Nimbus Records | NI 2011
Charles Mingus And His Orchestra
The Complete Town Hall Concert | Blue Note | 828353-2
Count Basie And His Orchestra
Afrique | RCA | 2179618-2
Dick Griffin Septet
The Eighth Wonder & More | Konnex Records | KCD 5059
Gil Evans Orchestra
There Comes A Time | RCA | 2131392-2
PLay The Music Of Jimi Hendrix | RCA | 2663872-2
Glenn Miller And His Orchestra
Planet Jazz:Glenn Miller | Planet Jazz | 2152056-2
Grant Green With Orchestra
The Final Comedown(Soundtrack) | Blue Note | 581678-2
Herb Robertson Group
The Little Trumpet | JMT Edition | 919007-2
Herbie Mann And His Orchestra
The Best Of Herbie Mann | Atlantic | 7567-81369-2
Jimmy Smith With The Oliver Nelson Orchestra
Jimmy Smith:Best Of The Verve Years | Verve | 527950-2
Lu Watters' Yerba Buena Jazz Band
The Very Best Of Dixieland Jazz | Verve | 535529-2
M'Boom
To The Max! | Enja | ENJ-7021 22
Sam Rivers Orchestra
Crystals | Impulse(MCA) | 589760-2
Tony Williams Lifetime
Ego | Verve | 559512-2

Smith,William Oscar | (b)
Coleman Hawkins And His Orchestra
Planet Jazz:Coleman Hawkins | Planet Jazz | 2152055-2
Planet Jazz Sampler | Planet Jazz | 2152326-2
Planet Jazz:Jazz Greatest Hits | Planet Jazz | 2169648-2
Jazz:The Essential Collection Vol.3 | IN+OUT Records | 78013-2

Smith,Willie | (as,cl,arr,voc,bs,drsax)
Billie Holiday And Her All Stars
Verve Jazz Masters 12:Billie Holiday | Verve | 519825-2
The Billie Holiday Song Book | Verve | 823246-2
Billie Holiday With The JATP All Stars
Billie Holiday Story Vol.1:Jazz At The Philharmonic | Verve | 521642-2
The Complete Jazz At The Philharmonic On Verve 1944-1949 | Verve | 523893-2
Verve Jazz Masters 47:Billie Holiday Sings Standards | Verve | 527650-2
Billy May And His Orchestra With Members Of The Jimmy Lunceford Orchestra
Great Swing Classics In Hi-Fi | Capitol | 521223-2
Duke Ellington And His Orchestra

Highlights From The Duke Ellington Centennial Edition | RCA | 2663672-2
The Big Bands Vol.1.The Snader Telescriptions | Storyville | 4960043
Ella Fitzgerald With The Nelson Riddle Orchestra
Ella Fitzgerald-First Lady Of Song | Verve | 517898-2
The Best Of The Song Books | Verve | 519804-2
The Best Of The Song Books:The Ballads | Verve | 521867-2
Love Songs:The Best Of The Song Books | Verve | 531762-2
Ella Fitzgerald Sings The Johnny Mercer Songbook | Verve | 539057-2
For The Love Of Ella Fitzgerald | Verve | 841765-2
Gene Krupa Trio
The Drum Battle:Gene Krupa And Buddy Rich At JATP | Verve | 559810-2
Harry James And His Orchestra
Great Swing Classics In Hi-Fi | Capitol | 521223-2
Trumpet Blues:The Best Of Harry James | Capitol | 521224-2
Helen Humes And Her All Stars
Lester Young:The Complete Aladdin Sessions | Blue Note | 832787-2
JATP All Stars
Jazz Gallery:Lester Young Vol.2(1946-59) | RCA | 2119541-2
JATP In Tokyo | Pablo | 2620104-2
Verve Jazz Masters 28:Charlie Parker Plays Standards | Verve | 521854-2
The Complete Jazz At The Philharmonic On Verve 1944-1949 | Verve | 523893-2
Charlie Parker:The Best Of The Verve Years | Verve | 527815-2
Jazz At The Philharmonic:Best Of The 1940's Concerts | Verve | 557534-2
Bird: The Complete Charlie Parker On Verve | Verve | 837141-2
Jimmy Lunceford And His Orchestra
Planet Jazz:Swing | Planet Jazz | 2169651-2
Lester Young And His Band
Jazz Gallery:Lester Young Vol.2(1946-59) | RCA | 2119541-2
Lester Young:The Complete Aladdin Sessions | Blue Note | 832787-2
Lionel Hampton All Stars
Lionel Hampton:Flying Home | Dreyfus Jazz Line | FDM 36735-2
Nat King Cole Quintet
After Midnight | Capitol | 520087-2
Red Norvo And His Orchestra
Planet Jazz:Female Jazz Vocalists | Planet Jazz | 2169656-2

Smith,Willie 'Big Eyes' | (dr)
Muddy Waters Band
Muddy Waters:Paris 1972 | Pablo | PACD 5302-2

Smith,Willie 'The Lion' | (celeste,p,talking,vocp-solo)
Lucille Hegamin With Willie The Lion And His Cubs
Songs We Taught Your Mother | Original Blues Classics | OBCCD 520-2
Mezz Mezzrow And His Orchestra
Planet Jazz:Bud Freeman | Planet Jazz | 2161240-2
Mezz Mezzrow And His Swing Band
Planet Jazz:Bud Freeman | Planet Jazz | 2161240-2
Sidney Bechet And His New Orleans Feetwarmers
Planet Jazz | Planet Jazz | 2169652-2
Sidney Bechet:Summertime | Dreyfus Jazz Line | FDM 36712-2
Willie 'The Lion' Smith
Planet Jazz:Jazz Piano | RCA | 2169655-2

Smithers,Elmer | (tb)
Bob Crosby And His Orchestra
Swing Legens:Bob Crosby | Nimbus Records | NI 2011
Tommy Dorsey And His Orchestra
Planet Jazz:Frank Sinatra & Tommy Dorsey | Planet Jazz | 2152067-2
Planet Jazz:Tommy Dorsey | Planet Jazz | 2159972-2

Smock,Hendrik | (dr)
Lutz Häfner Quartet
Way In Way Out | Jazz 4 Ever Records:Jazz Network | J4E 4757
Martin Sasse Trio
Here We Come | Nagel-Heyer | CD 2008

Smookler,Gene | (bs)
Woody Herman And His Orchestra
Brand New | Original Jazz Classics | OJCCD 1044-2(F 8414)

Smooth,C.L. | (voc)
Bop City
Hot Jazz Bisquits | Hip Bop | HIBD 8801

Smulyan,Gary | (b-cl,bsreeds)
Dave Holland Big Band
What Goes Around | ECM | 1777(014002-2)
Kevin Mahogany With Orchestra
Songs And Moments | Enja | ENJ-8072 2
Woody Herman And His Orchestra
Verve Jazz Masters 54:Woody Herman | Verve | 529903-2

Smythe,Pat | (el-pp)
Joe Harriott Quintet
Free Form | EmArCy | 538184-2

Snajer,Ernesto | (g)
Kim Kristensen
Pulse Of Time | dacapo | DCCD 9435

Snare,Tod | (dr)
Urbanator
Urbanator II | Hip Bop | HIBD 8012

Sne,Normunds | (cond)
Terje Rypdal With The Riga Festival Orchestra
Double Concerto/5th Symphony | ECM | 1567(559964-2)

Sneider,John | (fl-htp)
Andy Bey Group
Tuesdays In Chinatown | Minor Music | 801099
David Gibson Sextet
Maya | Nagel-Heyer | CD 2018

Snétberger,Ferenc | (gg-solo)
Dusko Goykovich Quartet
Samba Do Mar | Enja | ENJ-9473 2
Ferenc Snétberger
For My People | Enja | ENJ-9387 2
Balance | Enja | ENJ-9432 2
The Budapest Concert | TipToe | TIP-888823 2
Ferenc Snétberger Quartet
Signature | Enja | ENJ-9017 2
Ferenc Snétberger Trio
Obsession | TipToe | TIP-888834 2
Ferenc Snétberger With The Franz Liszt Chamber Orchestra
For My People | Enja | ENJ-9387 2
Ferenc Snétberger-Markus Stockhausen
For My People | Enja | ENJ-9387 2
Markus Stockhausen Quartet
Joyosa | Enja | ENJ-9468 2

Snidero,Jim | (as,fl,alto-fl,clss)
Jim Snidero Quartet With Strings
Strings | Milestone | MCD 9326-2

Snitzer,Andy | (keyboard-b-dr-programmingts)
The Brecker Brothers
Out Of The Loop | GRP | GRP 97842

Snow,Frank | (tp)
Vince Guaraldi Group
Charlie Brown's Holiday Hits | Fantasy | FCD 9682-2

Snow,Phoebe | (voc)
Bobby McFerrin Group
Bobby McFerrin | Elektra | 7559-60023-2

Snowden,Elmer | (bjg)
Cliff Jackson's Washboard Wanderers
Uptown And Lowdown | Prestige | PCD 24262-2
Lonnie Johnson Trio
Bawdy Blues | Original Blues Classics | OBCCD 544-2(BV 1055)
Lonnie Johnson With Elmer Snowden
Blues And Ballads | Original Blues Classics | OBCCD 531-2(BV 1011)

Snyder,Bob | (as,bscl)
Benny Goodman And His Orchestra
Charlie Christian:Swing To Bop | Dreyfus Jazz Line | FDM 36715-2
Lionel Hampton And His All Star Jazz Inner Circle
Lionel Hampton: Salle Pleyel, March 9th, 1971 | Laserlight | 36133

Snyder,Bruce | (ts)
Tommy Dorsey And His Orchestra
Planet Jazz:Frank Sinatra & Tommy Dorsey | Planet Jazz | 2152067-2

Snyder,Terry | (dr)
Sarah Vaughan With The Hugo Winterhalter Orchestra
Sarah Vaughan:Lover Man | Dreyfus Jazz Line | FDM 36739-2
Sarah Vaughan With The Norman Leyden Orchestra
Sarah Vaughan:Lover Man | Dreyfus Jazz Line | FDM 36739-2

Snyders,Bruce | (clas)
Tommy Dorsey And His Orchestra
Planet Jazz:Frank Sinatra & Tommy Dorsey | Planet Jazz | 2152067-2
Planet Jazz Sampler | Planet Jazz | 2152326-2

Socarras,Albert | (cl,as,ssfl)
Leon Thomas With Orchestra
Spirits Known And Unknown | RCA | 2663876-2

Socolow,Frank | (as,ts,reedsvoc)
Elliot Lawrence And His Orchestra
The Elliot Lawrence Big Band Swings Cohn & Kahn | Fantasy | FCD 24761-2

Socolow,Paul | (bel-b)
Leni Stern Group
Closer To The Light | Enja | ENJ-6034 2

Sodaro,Edgardo | (cello)
Coleman Hawkins With Billy Byers And His Orchestra
The Hawk In Hi-Fi | RCA | 2663842-2

Soderblom,Ken 'Kenny' | (ascl)
Lucy Reed With The Eddie Higgins Quartet
This Is Lucy Reed | Original Jazz Classics | OJCCD 1943-2(F 3243)

Soelberg,Jacob | (v)
Jim Hall Jazzpar Quartet +4
Jazzpar 98 | Storyville | STCD 4230
Jim Hall With The Zapolski Quartet
Jazzpar 98 | Storyville | STCD 4230
The Crossover Ensemble With The Zapolski Quartet
Helios Suite | dacapo | DCCD 9459

Soeteman,Iman | (fr-hhorn)
Toots Thielemans And His Orchestra
Verve Jazz Masters Vol.59:Toots Thielemans | Verve | 535271-2

Sohier,Martijn | (tb)
The Rosenberg Trio With Orchestra
Noches Calientes | Verve | 557022-2
Ulli Jünemann-Morton Ginnerup European Jazz Project
The Exhibition | Edition Collage | EC 518-2

Soirat,Felipe | (dr)
Bob Sands Quartet
JumpSTART | Fresh Sound Records | FSNT 042 CD
Bob Sands Quintet
JumpSTART | Fresh Sound Records | FSNT 042 CD

Sokolow,Rachel | (v)
Charlie Haden Quartet West With Strings
The Art Of The Song | Verve | 547403-2

Solal,Martial | (p,arr,el-pp-solo)
Attila Zoller-Martial Solal
Zoller-Koller-Solal | MPS | 8431072
Django Reinhardt Quintet
Jazz In Paris:Django Reinhardt-Nuages | EmArCy | 018428-2
Don Byas Quartet
Planet Jazz:Jazz Saxophone | Planet Jazz | 2169653-2
Golden Gate Quartet With The Martial Solal Orchestra
Americans Swinging In Paris:Golden Gate Quartet | EMI Records | 539659-2
From Spriritual To Swing Vol.2 | EMI Records | 780573-2
Kenny Clarke Quartet
Americans Swinging In Paris:Kenny Clarke | EMI Records | 539652-2
Jazz In Paris:Kenny Clarke Sextet Plays André Hodair | EmArCy | 834542-2 PMS
Kenny Clarke Quintet
Jazz In Paris:Kenny Clarke Sextet Plays André Hodair | EmArCy | 834542-2 PMS
Kenny Clarke Sextet
Jazz In Paris:Kenny Clarke Sextet Plays André Hodair | EmArCy | 834542-2 PMS
Lucky Thompson And His Orchestra
Americans Swinging In Paris:Lucky Thompson | EMI Records | 539651-2
Lucky Thompson Quartet
Americans Swinging In Paris:Lucky Thompson | EMI Records | 539651-2
The Jazz Life! | Candid | CCD 79019
Lucky Thompson Quintet
Americans Swinging In Paris:Lucky Thompson | EMI Records | 539651-2
Lucky Thompson With The Gerard Pochonet All-Stars
Planet Jazz:Jazz Saxophone | Planet Jazz | 2169653-2
Martial Solal
Zoller-Koller-Solal | MPS | 8431072
Martial Solal Trio
Martial Solal At Newport '63 | RCA | 2174803-2
Martial Solal NY-1 | Blue Note | 584232-2
Michel Portal-Martial Solal
Fast Mood | RCA | 2169310-2
Rolf Kühn Group
Internal Eyes | Intuition Records | INT 3328-2
Stan Getz Quartet
Stan Getz In Europe | Laserlight | 24657
Stephane Grappelli-Martial Solal Duo
Happy Reunion | Owl Records | 013430-2
Zoller-Koller-Solal Trio
Zoller-Koller-Solal | MPS | 8431072

Solal,Martial as Lalos Bing | (p)
Henri Crolla Quartet
Jazz In Paris:Henri Crolla-Quand Refleuriront Les Lilas Blancs? | EmArCy | 018418-2

Solberg,Nils | (g)
Clare Teal And Her Band
Orsino's Songs | Candid | CCD 79783

Solberg,Nils Olaf | (viola)
Terje Rypdal Quartet With The Bergen Chamber Ensemble
Lux Aeterna | ECM | 1818(017070-2)

Soldier String Quartet,The |
Robert Dick Group With The Soldier String Quartet
Jazz Standard On Mars | Enja | ENJ-9327 2

Soldier,Dave | (bj,v,gmetal-v)

Soldner,Tobias | (bass-tuba)
Michael Riessler And The Ensemble 13
Momentum Mobile | Enja | ENJ-9003 2

Soldo,Joe | (as,contractor,fl,clreeds)
Bill Evans Quartet With Orchestra
The Complete Bill Evans On Verve | Verve | 527953-2
From Left To Right | Verve | 557451-2
Bill Evans With Orchestra
The Complete Bill Evans On Verve | Verve | 527953-2
From Left To Right | Verve | 557451-2
Elliot Lawrence And His Orchestra
Mullenium | CBS | CK 65678

Solid | (rap)
Urbanator
Urbanator II | Hip Bop | HIBD 8012
Hot Jazz Bisquits | Hip Bop | HIBD 8801

Solisti Dell'Orchestra Della Toscana |
Richard Galliano Group I Solisti Dell'Orchestra Della Toscana
Gallianissimo! The Best Of Richard Galliano | Dreyfus Jazz Line | FDM 36616-2

Soll,Hendrik | (dr,keyboardsp)
Henning Berg Quartet
Minnola | Jazz Haus Musik | JHM 0127 CD
Joachim Ullrich Orchestra
Faces Of The Duke | Jazz Haus Musik | JHM 0045 CD

Marcus Sukiennik Big Band
A Night In Tunisia Suite(7 Variationen über Dizzy Gillespie's 'A Night In Tunisia') | Jazz Haus Musik | ohne Nummer

Sollesnes,Ellisiv | (v)
Terje Rypdal Quartet With The Bergen Chamber Ensemble
Lux Aeterna | ECM | 1818(017070-2)

Solodchin,Galina | (v)
Dee Dee Bridgewater With Orchestra
Dear Ella | Verve | 539102-2

Soloff,Lew | (fl-h,tp,electronic-tppiccolo-tp)
Bob James And His Orchestra
Jazzrock-Anthology Vol.3:Fusion | Zounds | CD 27100555
Carla Bley Band
Fleur Carnivore | Watt | 21
The Very Big Carla Bley Band | Watt | 23
Big Band Theory | Watt | 25(519966-2)
4X4 | Watt | 30(159547-2)
Carla Bley Big Band
The Carla Bley Big Band Goes To Church | Watt | 27(533682-2)
Daniel Schnyder Quintet With String Quartet
Mythology | Enja | ENJ-7003 2
David Matthews & The Manhattan Jazz Orchestra
Back To Bach | Milestone | MCD 9312-2
Hey Duke! | Milestone | MCD 9320-2
Freddy Cole With Band
Le Grand Freddy:Freddy Cole Sings The Music Of Michel Legrand | Fantasy | FCD 9683-2
Gil Evans Orchestra
There Comes A Time | RCA | 2131392-2
PLay The Music Of Jimi Hendrix | RCA | 2663872-2
Ian Shaw With Band
Soho Stories | Milestone | MCD 9316-2
Jimmy Scott With Band
But Beautiful | Milestone | MCD 9321-2
Moon Glow | Milestone | MCD 9332-2
Lew Soloff Group
Rainbow Mountain | TipToe | TIP-888838 2
Lew Soloff Quartet
With A Song In My Heart | Milestone | MCD 9290-2
Lew Soloff Quintet
With A Song In My Heart | Milestone | MCD 9290-2
Lew Soloff With The Mulgrew Miller Trio
Trumpet Legacy | Milestone | MCD 9286-2
Miles Davis With Gil Evans Orchestra, The George Gruntz Concert Jazz Band And Guests
Miles & Quincy Live At Montreux | Warner | 9362-45221-2
Mingus Big Band 93
Nostalgia In Times Square | Dreyfus Jazz Line | FDM 36559-2
Ray Anderson Alligatory Band
Don't Mow Your Lawn | Enja | ENJ-8070 2
Heads And Tales | Enja | ENJ-9055 2
Ray Anderson Pocket Brass Band
Where Home Is | Enja | ENJ-9366 2
Reiner Witzel Group
Passage To The Ear | Nabel Records:Jazz Network | CD 4668

Solomon,Ayi | (perc)
Pierre Dorge's New Jungle Orchestra
Giraf | dacapo | DCCD 9440

Solomon,Clifford | (as,ts,ssbs)
Albert King Blues Band
The Lost Session | Stax | SCD 8534-2
Art Farmer Septet
Plays The Arrangements And Compositions Of Gigi Gryce And Quincy Jones | Original Jazz Classics | OJCCD 054-2
Gigi Gryce-Clifford Brown Octet
Planet Jazz:Clifford Brown | Planet Jazz | 2161239-2

Solomon,D. | (v)
Dee Dee Bridgewater With Orchestra
Dear Ella | Verve | 539102-2

Solomon,Melvin | (tp)
Louis Armstrong With Sy Oliver And His Orchestra
Satchmo Serenaders | Verve | 543792-2
Louis Armstrong:C'est Si Bon | Dreyfus Jazz Line | FDM 36730-2
Louis Armstrong-My Greatest Songs | MCA | MCD 18347
Sarah Vaughan With The Joe Lippman Orchestra
Sarah Vaughan:Lover Man | Dreyfus Jazz Line | FDM 36739-2
Sarah Vaughan With The Norman Leyden Orchestra
Sarah Vaughan:Lover Man | Dreyfus Jazz Line | FDM 36739-2

Solomon,Red | (tp)
Tommy Dorsey And His Orchestra
Planet Jazz:Tommy Dorsey | Planet Jazz | 2159972-2

Solothurnmann,Jürg | (ssas)
Anliker-Parker-Schmid-Senn-Solothurnmann
September Winds | Creative Works Records | CW CD 1038/39

Solti,Janos | (dr)
Things
Mother Nature | Jazzpoint | JP 1028 CD

Solum,Bjorn | (cello)
Terje Rypdal With The Borealis Ensemble
Q.E.D. | ECM | 1474

Solund,Jens | (b)
Henrik Johansen's Jazzband
The Golden Years Of Revival Jazz,Vol 1 | Storyville | STCD 5506
The Golden Years Of Revival Jazz,Vol.2 | Storyville | STCD 5507

Sommer,Günter 'Baby' | (dr,gongs,bandoneon,darabuka,harm)
Ekkehard Jost Trio
Some Other Tapes | Fish Music | FM 009/10 CD
Sommer-Jost DuOh!
Some Other Tapes | Fish Music | FM 009/10 CD

Sommer,Ted | (drperc)
Carmen McRae With The Ralph Burns Orchestra
Birds Of A Feather | Decca | 589515-2
Tito Puente Orchestra
Planet Jazz:Tito Puente | Planet Jazz | 2165369-2

Sommers,Avery | (voc)
Horace Silver Quintet With Vocals
Horace Silver Retrospective | Blue Note | 495576-2

Songai | (voc)
McCoy Tyner Quintet
Asante | Blue Note | 493384-2

Songer,Wayne | (ascl)
Lena Horne With The Horace Henderson Orchestra
Planet Jazz:Lena Horne | Planet Jazz | 2165373-2
Louis Armstrong With Gordon Jenkins And His Orchestra
Satchmo In Style | Verve | 549594-2

Sonnenschein,Simone | (fl,ssas)
Jazz Orchester Rheinland-Pfalz
Kazzou | Jazz Haus Musik | LJBB 9104
Like Life | Jazz Haus Musik | LJBB 9405

Sonnleitner,Fritz | (v)
Keith Jarrett With String Quartet
In The Light | ECM | 1033/4

Soo,Kim Duk | (changgo,ching,hojok,piri)
Red Sun/SamulNori
Then Comes The White Tiger | ECM | 1499

Soo,Lee Kwang | (changgo,ching,k'kwaengwarivoice)

Soorez,Jose | (drperc)
Stan Getz Group Feat.Laurindo Almeida
Stan Getz With Guest Artist Laurindo Almeida | Verve | 823149-2
Stan Getz-Laurindo Almeida Orchestra
Stan Getz Highlights:The Best Of The Verve Years Vol.2 | Verve | 517330-2
Verve Jazz Masters 53:Stan Getz-Bossa Nova | Verve | 529904-2
Stan Getz Highlights | Verve | 847430-2

Sööt,Raul | (ts)
European Jazz Youth Orchestra
Swinging Europe 1 | dacapo | DCCD 9449
Swinging Europe 2 | dacapo | DCCD 9450

Soper,Tut | (p)
Marty Grosz And His Honoris Causa Jazz Band
Hooray For Bix! | Good Time Jazz | GTCD 10065-2

Soph,Ed | (dr)
Woody Herman And His Orchestra
Brand New | Original Jazz Classics | OJCCD 1044-2(F 8414)

Sophos,Anthony | (cello)
Phil Woods Quartet With Orchestra & Strings
Round Trip | Verve | 559804-2

Sorensen,Gert | (keyboards,percsound-design)
Gert Sorensen
Gert Sorensen Plays Poul Ruders | dacapo | 8.224085 CD

Sorensen,Hans-Kristian Kjos | (marimbaperc)
Misha Alperin Group With John Surman
First Impression | ECM | 1664(557650-2)
Moscow Art Trio
Music | JA & RO | JARO 4214-2

Sorensen,Helle | (cello)
Michael Mantler Group
Songs And One Symphony | ECM | 1721
Michael Mantler Group With The Danish Radio Concert Orchestra Strings
The School Of Understanding(Sort-Of-An-Opera) | ECM | 1648/49(537963-2)
Michael Mantler Orchestra
Hide And Seek | ECM | 1738(549612-2)
Mona Larsen And The Danish Radio Big Band Plus Soloists
Michael Mantler:Cerco Un Paese Innocente | ECM | 1556

Sorensen,Marianne | (v)
Michael Mantler Group
Songs And One Symphony | ECM | 1721
Michael Mantler Group With The Danish Radio Concert Orchestra Strings
The School Of Understanding(Sort-Of-An-Opera) | ECM | 1648/49(537963-2)
Michael Mantler Orchestra
Hide And Seek | ECM | 1738(549612-2)
Mona Larsen And The Danish Radio Big Band Plus Soloists
Michael Mantler:Cerco Un Paese Innocente | ECM | 1556

Soric,Rade | (p)
Rade Soric Trio
Piano Moments | Take Twelve On CD | TT 007-2

Sorkin,Herbert | (v)
Nina Simone And Orchestra
Baltimore | Epic | 476906-2

Sorry It's Jazz |
Sorry.It's Jazz
Sorry,It's Jazz! | Satin Doll Productions | SDP 1040-1 CD

Sortomme,Richard | (v)
A Band Of Friends
Wynton Marsalis Quartet With Strings | CBS | CK 68921
Earl Klugh Group With Strings
Late Night Guitar | Blue Note | 498573-2
Nina Simone And Orchestra
Baltimore | Epic | 476906-2
Steve Kuhn With Strings
Promises Kept | ECM | 1815(0675222)

Soskin,Mark | (el-p,keyboards,p,synthclavinet)
Sonny Rollins Quintet
Don't Stop The Carnival | Milestone | MCD 55005-2
Sunny Days,Starry Nights | Milestone | MCD 9122-2
Here's To The People | Milestone | MCD 9194-2
Don't Ask | Original Jazz Classics | OJCCD 915-2(M 9090)
The Jazz Giants Play Harry Warren:Lullaby Of Broadway | Prestige | PCD 24204-2
Sonny Rollins Sextet
Don't Stop The Carnival | Milestone | MCD 55005-2
Sunny Days,Starry Nights | Milestone | MCD 9122-2
Here's To The People | Milestone | MCD 9194-2
Don't Ask | Original Jazz Classics | OJCCD 915-2(M 9090)

Sosson,Marshall | (v)
Cal Tjader With The Clare Fischer Orchestra
Cal Tjader Plays Harold Arlen & West Side Story | Fantasy | FCD 24775-2
Ella Fitzgerald With The Billy May Orchestra
The Best Of The Song Books:The Ballads | Verve | 521867-2
Ella Fitzgerald With The Nelson Riddle Orchestra
The Best Of The Song Books:The Ballads | Verve | 521867-2
Oh Lady Be Good:The Best Of The Gershwin Songbook | Verve | 529581-2
Love Songs:The Best Of The Song Books | Verve | 531762-2
Frank Sinatra With The Count Basie Orchestra
It Might As Well Be Spring | Reprise | 7599-27027-2
Hank Crawford Orchestra
Rhino Presents The Atlantic Jazz Gallery | Atlantic | 8122-71257-2

Sotille,John | (tp)
Buddy Rich Big Band
The New One! | Pacific Jazz | 494507-2

Sotto In Su |
Sotto In Su
Südamerika Sept. 90 | Jazz Haus Musik | JHM 0051 CD
Vanitas | Poise | Poise 04

Souchy,Jean-Eric | (viola)
Michael Riessler And The Ensemble 13
Momentum Mobile | Enja | ENJ-9003 2

Soudieux,Emmanuel | (b)
Charlie Lewis Trio
JazzIn Paris:Harlem Piano In Montmartre | EmArCy | 018447-2
Django Reinhardt And The Quintet Du Hot Club De France
Jazz In Paris:Django Reinhardt-Django's Blues | EmArCy | 013545-2
Planet Jazz:Django Reinhardt | Planet Jazz | 2152071-2
Planet Jazz Sampler | Planet Jazz | 2152326-2
Peche Á La Mode-The Great Blue Star Sessions 1947/1953 | Verve | 835418-2
Django Reinhardt Trio
Django Reinhardt:Souveniers | Dreyfus Jazz Line | FDM 36744-2
Henri Crolla Quartet
Jazz In Paris:Henri Crolla-Quand Refleuriront Les Lilas Blancs? | EmArCy | 018418-2
Henri Crolla Sextet
Jazz In Paris:Henri Crolla-Quand Refleuriront Les Lilas Blancs? | EmArCy | 018418-2
Jack Dieval And His Quartet
Americans Swinging In Paris:James Moody | EMI Records | 539653-2
Quintet Du Hot Club De France
Jazz In Paris:Django Reinhardt-Swing From Paris | EmArCy | 159853-2 PMS
Jazz In Paris:Django Reinhardt-Swing 39 | EmArCy | 159854-2 PMS
Verve Jazz Masters 38:Django Reinhardt | Verve | 516931-2
Django Reinhardt:Souveniers | Dreyfus Jazz Line | FDM 36744-2

Soulful Heavenly Stars,The |
Lillian Boutté And Her Group & The Soulful Heavenly Stars
The Gospel Book | Blues Beacon | BLU-1017 2

South,Eddie | (v,vocwhistling)
Eddie South/Stephane Grappelli Quintet
Django/Django In Rome 1949-1050 | BGO Records | BGOCD 366
Django Reinhardt:Echoes Of France | Dreyfus Jazz Line | FDM 36726-2

Southall,Henry | (tb)
Woody Herman And His Orchestra
Verve Jazz Masters 54:Woody Herman | Verve | 529903-2

Southcott,Derek | (tb)
André Holst With Chris Dean's European Swing Orchestra
That's Swing | Nagel-Heyer | CD 079

Southern,Jeri | (pvoc)
Jerri Southern And The Dave Barbour Trio
The Very Thought Of You:The Decca Years 1951-1957 | Decca | 050671-2
Jerri Southern And The Dick Hazard Quartet
Misty Blue:Sweet Sisters Swing Songs Of Sorrow And Sadness | Blue Note | 521151-2

INTERPRETENVERZEICHNIS

Jerri Southern And The Frank Meriweather Orchestra
The Very Thought Of You:The Decca Years 1951-1957 | Decca | 050671-2
Jerri Southern And The Gus Levene Orchestra
The Very Thought Of You:The Decca Years 1951-1957 | Decca | 050671-2
Jerri Southern And The Norman Leyden Orchestra
The Very Thought Of You:The Decca Years 1951-1957 | Decca | 050671-2
Jerri Southern And The Ralph Burns Orchestra
The Very Thought Of You:The Decca Years 1951-1957 | Decca | 050671-2
Jerri Southern And The Sonny Burke Orchestra
The Very Thought Of You:The Decca Years 1951-1957 | Decca | 050671-2
Jerri Southern And The Toots Camarata Orchestra
The Very Thought Of You:The Decca Years 1951-1957 | Decca | 050671-2
Jerri Southern And The Victoe Young Orchestra
The Very Thought Of You:The Decca Years 1951-1957 | Decca | 050671-2
Jerri Southern Quartet
The Very Thought Of You:The Decca Years 1951-1957 | Decca | 050671-2

Souza,Fernado | (b)
Duo Fenix
Karai-Eté | IN+OUT Records | 7009-2

Souza,Luciana | (voc)
Andrew Rathbun Group
Jade | Fresh Sound Records | FSNT 076 CD
True Stories | Fresh Sound Records | FSNT 099 CD
Danilo Perez Group
Central Avenue | Impulse(MCA) | 951281-2

Souze,Bebeto Jose | (b)
Duke Pearson Orchestra
Blue Bossa | Blue Note | 795590-2

Soyer,David | (cellov)
Billie Holiday With The Ray Ellis Orchestra
Lady In Satin | CBS | CK 65144

Soyer,Janet | (harp)
Sarah Vaughan With The Jimmy Jones Orchestra
Ballads | Roulette | 537561-2
Jazz Profile | Blue Note | 823517-2

Spaits,Gerald | (b)
Jay McShann Quintet
What A Wonderful World | Groove Note | GN 1005(180gr-Pressung)
What A Wonderful World | Groove Note | GRV 1005-2

Spang-Hansen,Simon | (as,ss,tsafrican-fl)
Simon Cato Spang-Hansen Quartet
Identified | dacapo | DCCD 9448
Simon Spang-Hanssen & Maneklar
Wondering | dacapo | DCCD 9436

Spangler,Bob | (dr)
Glenn Miller And His Orchestra
Planet Jazz:Glenn Miller | Planet Jazz | 2152056-2

Spangler,Charles E. | (synth)
Dizzy Gillespie With The Lalo Schifrin Orchestra
Free Ride | Original Jazz Classics | OJCCD 784-2(2310794)

Spanier,Calder | (as)
Charlie Hunter Quartet
Ready...Set...Shango! | Blue Note | 837101-2

Spanier,Francis 'Muggsy' | (cotp)
Bechet-Spanier Big Four
Jazz:The Essential Collection Vol.1 | IN+OUT Records | 78011-2
Bob Crosby And His Orchestra
Swing Legens:Bob Crosby | Nimbus Records | NI 2011
Earl Hines-Muggsy Spanier All Stars
Earl Hines/Muggsy Spanier All Stars:The Chicago Dates | Storyville | STCD 6037
Miff Mole And His Dixieland Band
Muggsy Spanier-Manhattan Masters,1945 | Storyville | STCD 6051
Muggsy Spanier And His Dixieland All Stars
Muggsy Spanier At Club Hangover 1953/54 | Storyville | STCD 6033
Muggsy Spanier And His Dixieland Band
Muggsy Spanier-Manhattan Masters,1945 | Storyville | STCD 6051
Muggsy Spanier And His Ragtime Band
Planet Jazz | Planet Jazz | 2169652-2
Planet Jazz:Jazz Trumpet | Planet Jazz | 2169654-2
Muggsy Spanier And His V-Disc All Stars
Muggsy Spanier And Bud Freeman:V-Discs 1944-45 | Jazz Unlimited | JUCD 2049
Pee Wee Russell And His Dixieland Band
Muggsy Spanier-Manhattan Masters,1945 | Storyville | STCD 6051

Spaniol,Frank | (reedsts)
Polyphonix
Alarm | Jazz 'n' Arts Records | 0300

Spann,Leon | (b)
Buddy Johnson And His Orchestra
Buddy And Ella Johnson 1953-1964 | Bear Family Records | BCD 15479 DH

Spann,Les | (fl,gvoc)
Abbey Lincoln With The Kenny Dorham Quintet
Abbey Is Blue | Original Jazz Classics | OJC20 069-2(RLP 1153)
Babs Gonzales And His Band
Voilà | Fresh Sound Records | FSR CD 340
Ben Webster And His Associates
Verve Jazz Masters 43:Ben Webster | Verve | 525431-2
Ultimate Ben Webster selected by James Carter | Verve | 557537-2
Ben Webster And Associates | Verve | 835254-2
Benny Bailey Septet
Big Brass | Candid | CCD 79011
Bill Coleman Septet
Jazz In Paris:Bill Coleman-From Boogie To Funk | EmArCy | 549401-2 PMS
Charles Mingus And His Orchestra
The Complete Town Hall Concert | Blue Note | 828353-2
Dizzy Gillespie Quintet
Verve Jazz Masters 10:Dizzy Gillespie | Verve | 516319-2
Talking Verve:Dizzy Gillespie | Verve | 533846-2
Dizzy Gillespie Sextet
Ultimate Dizzy Gillespie | Verve | 557535-2
Duke Ellington And Johnny Hodges Orchestra
Side By Side | Verve | 521405-2
Duke Ellington-Johnny Hodges All Stars
Verve Jazz Masters 4:Duke Ellington | Verve | 516338-2
Back To Back | Verve | 521404-2
Johnny Hodges Orchestra
Verve Jazz Masters 43:Ben Webster | Verve | 525431-2
Johnny Hodges With The Dizzy Gillespie Quintet
Verve Jazz Masters 35:Johnny Hodges | Verve | 521857-2
Les Spann Quintet
Gemini | Original Jazz Classics | OJCCD 1948-2(JLP 9355)
Nat Adderley And The Big Sax Section
That's Right | Original Jazz Classics | OJCCD 791-2(RLP 9330)
Sam Jones Plus 10
Cannonball Adderley Birthday Celebration | Fantasy | FANCD 6087-2

Spann,Otis | (p,vocp-solo)
Buddy Guy Blues Band
Buddy Guy-The Complete Chess Studio Recordings | MCA | MCD 09337
Muddy Waters Blues Band
Muddy Waters-The Collection | MCA | MCD 18961
Otis Spann
Otis Spann Is The Blues | Candid | CCD 79001
Walking The Blues | Candid | CCD 79025
Otis Spann Band
The Blues Never Die! | Original Blues Classics | OBCCD 530-2(P 7391)
Windy City Blues | Stax | SCD 8612-2
Otis Spann/Robert Lockwood Jr.
Otis Spann Is The Blues | Candid | CCD 79001

Spannagel,Andreas | (fl,alto-flts)
Thärichens Tentett
Lady Moon | Minor Music | 801094

Spannuth,Fred | (clts)
Freddie Brocksieper Four Stars
Freddie's Boogie Blues | Bear Family Records | BCD 16388 AH
Freddie Brocksieper Und Seine Solisten
Freddie's Boogie Blues | Bear Family Records | BCD 16388 AH

Spanyi,Emil | (p)
Heinrich Von Kalnein Group
New Directions | Nabel Records:Jazz Network | CD 4670

Sparks,Melvin | (gvoc)
Charles Earland Quintet
Black Talk! | Original Jazz Classics | OJCCD 335-2(P 7758)
Charles Earland Sextet
Black Talk! | Original Jazz Classics | OJCCD 335-2(P 7758)
Charlie's Greatest Hits | Prestige | PCD 24250-2
Hank Crawford And His Orchestra
Roadhouse Symphony | Original Jazz Classics | OJCCD 1048-2(M 9140)
Hank Crawford Quartet
The World Of Hank Crawford | Milestone | MCD 9304-2
Hank Crawford Quintet
After Dark | Milestone | MCD 9279-2
The World Of Hank Crawford | Milestone | MCD 9304-2
The Jazz Giants Play Sammy Cahn:It's Magic | Prestige | PCD 24226-2
Hank Crawford Septet
The World Of Hank Crawford | Milestone | MCD 9304-2
Idris Muhammad Group
Jazzin' With The Soul Brothers | Fantasy | FANCD 6086-2
Jimmy McGriff Septet
McGriff Avenue | Milestone | MCD 9325-2
Jimmy McGriff Sextet
Feelin' It | Milestone | MCD 9313-2
Leon Spencer Sextet
Jazzin' With The Soul Brothers | Fantasy | FANCD 6086-2
Discovery:Grover Washington Jr.-The First Recordings | Prestige | PCD 11020-2
Lou Donaldson Orchestra
Blue Breaks Beats Vol.2 | Blue Note | 789907-2
Lou Donaldson Quintet
Blue Break Beats | Blue Note | 799106-2
The Lost Grooves | Blue Note | 831883-2
Lou Donaldson Sextet
So Blue So Funky-Heroes Of The Hammond | Blue Note | 796563-2
Melvin Sparks Quintet
Jazzin' With The Soul Brothers | Fantasy | FANCD 6086-2
Plas Johnson-Red Holloway Quintet
Keep That Groove Going! | Milestone | MCD 9319-2
Pucho & His Latin Soul Brothers
Rip A Dip | Milestone | MCD 9247-2
Red Holloway Quintet
Coast To Coast | Milestone | MCD 9335-2
Reuben Wilson Quartet
Blue Breaks Beats Vol.2 | Blue Note | 789907-2

Sparla,Hans | (tb)
Lajos Dudas Quintet
Jubilee Edition | double moon | CHRDM 71020

Sparrow,Arnett | (tb)
Cannonball Adderley And His Orchestra
Cannonball Adderley Birthday Celebration | Fantasy | FANCD 6087-2
Dizzy Gillespie And His Orchestra
Gillespiana And Carnegie Hall Concert | Verve | 519809-2
Talking Verve:Dizzy Gillespie | Verve | 533846-2
Ultimate Dizzy Gillespie | Verve | 557535-2

Sparrow,John | (bs,saxts)
Lionel Hampton And His Orchestra
Lionel Hampton:Flying Home | Dreyfus Jazz Line | FDM 36735-2
Louis Armstrong And His Orchestra
Best Of The Complete RCA Victor Recordings | RCA | 2663636-2
Louis Armstrong:A 100th Birthday Celebration | RCA | 2663694-2
Louis Armstrong:C'est Si Bon | Dreyfus Jazz Line | FDM 36730-2
Swing Legends:Louis Armstrong | Nimbus Records | NI 2012

Spassov,Theodossij | (kavalvoice)
Dimitrios Vassilakis Daedalus Project
Labyrinth | Candid | CCD 79776
Fairy Tale Trio
Jazz Across The Border | Wergo | SM 1531-2
Jazzensemble Des Hessischen Rundfunks
Atmosphering Conditions Permitting | ECM | 1549/50

Spaulding,James | (alto-fl,as,bass-fl,b-fl,fl)
Duke Ellington Orchestra
Continuum | Fantasy | FCD 24765-2
Duke Pearson Orchestra
Blue N' Groovy | Blue Note | 780679-2
Duke Pearson Quartet
Sweet Honey Bee | Blue Note | 595974-2
Duke Pearson Sextet
Deep Blue-The United States Of Mind | Blue Note | 521152-2
Sweet Honey Bee | Blue Note | 595974-2
Midnight Blue(The [Be]witching Hour) | Blue Note | 854365-2
Freddie Hubbard Quintet
Hub-Tones | Blue Note | 499008-2
Grant Green Sextet
True Blue | Blue Note | 534032-2
Lee Morgan Orchestra
Standards | Blue Note | 823213-2
Leon Thomas With Band
Spirits Known And Unknown | RCA | 2663876-2
Louis Armstrong And His Friends
Planet Jazz:Louis Armstrong | Planet Jazz | 2152052-2
Planet Jazz Sampler | Planet Jazz | 2152326-2
Louis Armstrong And His Friends | Bluebird | 2663961-2
Pharoah Sanders Orchestra
Karma | Impulse(MCA) | 951153-2
The Roots Of Acid Jazz | Impulse(MCA) | IMP 12042
Stanley Turrentine And His Orchestra
The Lost Grooves | Blue Note | 831883-2
Stanley Turrentine Orchestra
Rough 'N' Tumble | Blue Note | 524552-2
The Spoiler | Blue Note | 853359-2
Wayne Shorter Sextet
Wayne Shorter:The Classic Blue Note Recordings | Blue Note | 540856-2
Blue N' Groovy | Blue Note | 780679-2

Spax | (rap)
Gunter Hampel Next Generation
Next Generation | Birth | CD 043

Spears,Louis | (bcello)
Eddie Harris Quintet
The Best Of Eddie Harris | Atlantic | 7567-81370-2

Spears,Maurice | (b-tbtb)
Diane Schuur And Her Band
The Best Of Diane Schuur | GRP | GRP 98882
Herbie Hancock Group
Sunlight | CBS | 486570-2
Herbie Hancock Group With String Quartet,Woodwinds And Brass
Herbie Hancock The New Standards | Verve | 527715-2
Herbie Hancock Group With Woodwinds And Brass
Herbie Hancock The New Standards | Verve | 527715-2
Horace Silver Quintet With Brass
Horace Silver Retrospective | Blue Note | 495576-2
Jimmy Smith All Stars
Jimmy Smith:Dot Com Blues | Blue Thumb | 543978-2

Spedding,Chris | (garr)
Michael Mantler Group
Michael Mantler: No Answer/Silence | Watt | 2/5(543374-2)
Silence | Watt | 5 (2313105)

Speed,Chris | (cl,sax,tsperc)
Dave Douglas Group
Soul On Soul | RCA | 2663603-2
Witness | RCA | 2663763-2
Dave Douglas Freak In | Bluebird | 2664008-2
Frank Carlberg Group
Variations On A Summer Day | Fresh Sound Records | FSNT 083 CD
Franz Koglmann Group
Venus In Transit | Between The Lines | btl 017(Efa 10186)
James Emery Quartet
Spectral Domains | Enja | ENJ-9344 2
James Emery Septet
Spectral Domains | Enja | ENJ-9344 2
James Emery Sextet
Luminous Cycles | Between The Lines | btl 015(Efa 10185-2)
Jim Black Alasnoaxis
Splay | Winter&Winter | 910076-2
Jim Black Quartet
Alasnoaxis | Winter&Winter | 910061-2
Nils Wogram Octet
Odd And Awkward | Enja | ENJ-9416-2
Nils Wogram Sextet
Odd And Awkward | Enja | ENJ-9416-2

Speer,Daniel | (b)
Lars Duppler Quartet
Palindrome | Jazz Haus Musik | JHM 0108 CD

Speight,Bruno | (g)
Maceo Parker Group
Maceo(Soundtrack) | Minor Music | 801046
Maceo Parker With The Rebirth Brass Band
Maceo(Soundtrack) | Minor Music | 801046

Speight,Ed | (el-g)
Maceo Parker Group
Maceo(Soundtrack) | Minor Music | 801046
Maceo Parker With The Rebirth Brass Band
Maceo(Soundtrack) | Minor Music | 801046

Speight,Martin | (p)
Stephan-Max Wirth Quartet
Jazzchanson 20th Century Suite | double moon | DMCD 1008-2

Speltz,David | (cello)
Chick Corea And His Orchestra
My Spanish Heart | Polydor | 543303-3

Spence,Alister | (p,keyboardssynth)
Clarion Fracture Zone
Blue Shift | VeraBra Records | CDVBR 2075-2
Wanderlust
Border Crossing | Laika Records | 35100812
Wanderlust + Guests
Full Bronte | Laika Records | 35101412

Spence,Johnny | (arrld)
Ella Fitzgerald With The Johnny Spence Orchestra
Ella Fitzgerald-First Lady Of Song | Verve | 517898-2

Spencer Jr.,Leon | (org)
Leon Spencer Sextet
Jazzin' With The Soul Brothers | Fantasy | FANCD 6086-2
Discovery:Grover Washington Jr.-The First Recordings | Prestige | PCD 11020-2
Lou Donaldson Orchestra
Blue Breaks Beats Vol.2 | Blue Note | 789907-2
Lou Donaldson Quintet
The Lost Grooves | Blue Note | 831883-2
Melvin Sparks Quintet
Jazzin' With The Soul Brothers | Fantasy | FANCD 6086-2

Spencer,Dick | (as,piccolo,fl,clsax)
Don Menza Septet
Morning Song | MPS | 9811446
Hans Koller Nonet
Exclusiv | MPS | 9813440

Spencer,Donnell | (dr)
Bobby Lyle Group
The Journey | Atlantic | 7567-82138-2

Spencer,Joel | (dr)
Buddy Childers Big Band
Just Buddy's | Candid | CCD 79761

Spencer,Kristin | (cello)
Abdullah Ibrahim Trio And A String Orchestra
African Suite | TipToe | TIP-888832 2
String Orchestra
African Suite | TipToe | TIP-888832 2

Spencer,Ngoh | (voc)
Herbie Hancock Group
Magic Window | CBS | 486572-2

Spencers,C. | (voc)
Sonny Rollins Group
What's New? | RCA | 2179626-2

Spencker,Klaus | (g)
Klaus Spencker Trio
Invisible | Jardis Records | JRCD 9409

Spendel,Christoph | (keyboards,synth,p,el-p,b,dr,perc)
Jim Pepper Quartet
West End Avenue | Nabel Records:Jazz Network | CD 4633
Lance Bryant With The Christoph Spendel Trio
West End Avenue II | Nabel Records:Jazz Network | CD 4644
Olaf Kübler Quartet
When I'm 64 | Village | VILCD 1016-2
Midnight Soul | Village | VILCD 1024-2

Spering,Christian | (b)
Gustavo Bergalli Group
Tango In Jazz | Touché Music | TMcCD 007
Viktoria Tolstoy Group & Strings
Shining On You | ACT | 9701-2

Sperling,Jack | (dr)
Ella Fitzgerald With The Marty Paich Orchestra
Get Happy! | Verve | 523321-2

Sperrfechter,Bernhard | (g)
Jutta Glaser & Bernhard Sperrfechter
Little Girl Blue | Jazz 'n' Arts Records | JNA 0502

Sperry,Christine | (voc)
David Matthews & The Manhattan Jazz Orchestra
Hey Duke! | Milestone | MCD 9320-2

Speth,Micha | (viola)
Jo Ambros Group
Wanderlust | dml-records | CD 016

Spice,Irving | (v)
Freddie Hubbard With Orchestra
This Is Jazz:Freddie Hubbard | CBS | CK 65041
Grover Washington Jr. Orchestra
Jazzrock-Anthology Vol.3:Fusion | Zounds | CD 27100555
Milt Jackson And His Orchestra
Sunflower | CTI | ZK 65131

Spiegel,Ray | (tablas)
Danilo Perez Group
Central Avenue | Impulse(MCA) | 951281-2

Spiegel,Russ | (el-gg)
Russ Spiegel Group
Twilight | double moon | CHRDM 71026

Spiegelberg,Martin | (g)
Edith Steyer... Posterity Quintet
...On The Right Track | Jazz 4 Ever Records:Jazz Network | J4E 4745

Spiegelman,Stanley | (viola)
Artie Shaw And His Orchestra
Planet JazzArtie Shaw | Planet Jazz | 2152057-2
Planet Jazz:Jazz Greatest Hits | Planet Jazz | 2169648-2

Spieldock,Al | (dr)
Lionel Hampton And His Orchestra
Planet Jazz:Lionel Hampton | Planet Jazz | 2152059-2

Lionel Hampton:Flying Home | Dreyfus Jazz Line | FDM 36735-2

Spieler,Barney | (b)
Miles Davis/Tadd Dameron Quintet
Miles Davis:Milestones | Dreyfus Jazz Line | FDM 36731-2

Spillmann,Matthias | (tp)
Brigitte Dietrich-Joe Haider Jazz Orchestra
Consequences | JHM Records | JHM 3624
Horn Knox
The Song Is You | JHM Records | JHM 3625
Matthias Spillmann Septet
Something About Water | JHM Records | JHM 3620

Spinney,Bradley | (xylophone)
Billie Holiday With The Ray Ellis Orchestra
Lady In Satin | CBS | CK 65144

Spinozza,David | (el-gg)
Earl Klugh Group
Late Night Guitar | Blue Note | 498573-2
Gato Barbieri Group
Planet Jazz:Gato Barbieri | RCA | 2165364-2
Gato Barbieri:The Best Of The Early Years | RCA | 2663523-2
Grover Washington Jr. Orchestra
Jazzrock-Anthology Vol.3:Fusion | Zounds | CD 27100555
Les McCann Group
Atlantic Jazz: Fusion | Atlantic | 7567-81711-2
Ronnie Foster Group
Sweet Revival... | Blue Note | 581676-2
Rusty Bryant Group
For The Good Times | Prestige | PRCD 24269-2

Spirli,Alfred | (drperc)
Pata Music Meets Arfi
News Of Roi Ubu | Pata Musik | PATA 10 CD

Spivak,Charlie | (tp)
All Star Band
Planet Jazz:Jack Teagarden | Planet Jazz | 2161236-2
Bob Crosby And His Orchestra
Swing Legens:Bob Crosby | Nimbus Records | NI 2011
Bob Crosby's Bobcats
Swing Legens:Bob Crosby | Nimbus Records | NI 2011

Spivey,Victoria | (p,vocukelele)
Victoria Spivey
Bawdy Blues | Original Blues Classics | OBCCD 544-2(BV 1055)
Victoria Spivey With Buster Bailey's Blues Blasters
Songs We Taught Your Mother | Original Blues Classics | OBCCD 520-2

Splawn,Johnny | (tp)
John Coltrane Quintet
John Coltrane-The Prestige Recordings | Prestige | 16 PCD 4405-2
Coltrane | Original Jazz Classics | OJC20 020-2
The Mal Waldron Memorial Album:Soul Eyes | Prestige | PRCD 11024-2
John Coltrane Sextet
John Coltrane-The Prestige Recordings | Prestige | 16 PCD 4405-2
Coltrane | Original Jazz Classics | OJC20 020-2
The Prestige Legacy Vol.1:The High Priests | Prestige | PCD 24251-2

Spoerri,Bruno | (as,ts,bs,el-ts,sopranino,ss)
Albert Mangelsdorff Quartet
Shake,Shuttle And Blow | Enja | ENJ-9374 2

Spooner,John | (dr)
Stephane Grappelli And Friends
Grapelli Story | Verve | 515807-2

Sporny,Dick | (tb)
Eric Dolphy Quartet With The University Of Illinois Big Band
The Illinois Concert | Blue Note | 499826-2

Sprecher,Eve | (v)
Milt Jackson And His Orchestra
Reverence And Compassion | Reprise | 9362-45204-2

Spree City Stompers |
Spree Cuty Stompers
Deutsches Jazz Fesival 1954/1955 | Bear Family Records | BCD 15430

Sprenger,Raphael | (tp)
Balance
Elements | double moon | DMCHR 71033

Spring,Bryan | (dr)
Passport
Second Passport | Atlantic | 2292-44143-2

Springer,Joe | (p)
Anita O'Day With Gene Krupa And His Orchestra
Let Me Off Uptown:Anita O'Day With Gene Krupa | CBS | CK 65625

Sproles,Victor | (b)
Chet Baker-Stan Getz Quintet
Stan Meets Chet | Verve | 837436-2
Clark Terry Quintet
Jazz Dance | Original Jazz Classics | OJCCD 1002-2(1210890)
Eddie Lockjaw Davis-Johnny Griffin Quintet
Battle Stations | Original Jazz Classics | OJCCD 1085(P7282)
Lee Morgan Quintet
The Rumproller | Blue Note | 521229-2
The Best Of Blue Note Vol.2 | Blue Note | 797960-2
Lee Morgan Sextet
The Sixth Sense | Blue Note | 522467-2
Red Rodney Quintet
The Red Rodney Quintets | Fantasy | FCD 24758-2
Stan Getz Quartet
Verve Jazz Masters 8:Stan Getz | Verve | 519823-2

Spruill,John | (porg)
Lionel Hampton And His All Star Jazz Inner Circle
Lionel Hampton: Salle Pleyel, March 9th, 1971 | Laserlight | 36133
Lionel Hampton And His Orchestra
Planet Jazz:Big Bands | Planet Jazz | 2169649-2
Pucho & His Latin Soul Brothers
Jazzin' With The Soul Brothers | Fantasy | FANCD 6086-2
Rip A Dip | Milestone | MCD 9247-2

Spruill,Stephanie | (percvoc)
Bobbi Humphrey
Blue Break Beats | Blue Note | 799106-2
Bobbi Humphrey Group
Blue Breaks Beats Vol.2 | Blue Note | 789907-2
Donald Byrd & His Orchestra
Blue Breaks Beats Vol.2 | Blue Note | 789907-2
Donald Byrd Orchestra
Black Byrd | Blue Note | 784466-2
Nat Adderley Group
Soul Of The Bible | Capitol | 358257-2

Spühler,Martin | (klangsäulenklangschalen)
ATonALL
ATonALL | Creative Works Records | CW CD 1024-2

Spurgin,Tony | (dr)
Arthur Young And Hatchett's Swingtette
Grapelli Story | Verve | 515807-2

Spurlock,Jack | (tb)
Buddy Rich Big Band
The New One! | Pacific Jazz | 494507-2
Stan Kenton And His Orchestra
Adventures In Blues | Capitol | 520089-2
Adventures In Jazz | Capitol | 521222-2

Sputh,Alexander | (g)
Sigi Busch-Alexander Sputh Duo
Jazz Portraits | EGO | 95080

Sputnik 27 |
Sputnik 27
But Where's The Moon? | dml-records | CD 011

Spychalski,Alex | (p,accordeonharpsichord)
Johannes Rediske Quintet
Deutsches Jazz Fesival 1954/1955 | Bear Family Records | BCD 15430
Re-Disc Bounce | Bear Family Records | BCD 16119 AH
Jumpin' At The Badewanne | Bear Family Records | BCD 16172 AH
Johannes Rediske Sextet
Re-Disc Bounce | Bear Family Records | BCD 16119 AH
Johnnes Rediske Quintet
Deutsches Jazz Fesival 1954/1955 | Bear Family Records | BCD 15430

Spyro Gyra |
Spyro Gyra & Guests
Love & Other Obsessions | GRP | GRP 98112

Squires,Bruce | (tb)
Benny Goodman And His Orchestra
More Camel Caravans | Phontastic | NCD 8845/6
Harry James And His Orchestra
The Legends Of Swing | Laserlight | 24659

St.Cyr,Johnny | (bj,speech,talking,voc,gturntables)
Jelly Roll Morton's Red Hot Peppers
Planet Jazz:Jelly Roll Morton | Planet Jazz | 2152060-2
Planet Jazz Sampler | Planet Jazz | 2152326-2
Jazz:The Essential Collection Vol.1 | IN+OUT Records | 78011-2
King Oliver's Creole Jazz Band
Jazz:The Essential Collection Vol.1 | IN+OUT Records | 78011-2
King Oliver's Jazz Band
Jazz:The Essential Collection Vol.1 | IN+OUT Records | 78011-2
Lil's Hot Shots
Jazz:The Essential Collection Vol.2 | IN+OUT Records | 78012-2
Louis Armstrong And His Hot Five
Jazz:The Essential Collection Vol.2 | IN+OUT Records | 78012-2
Louis Armstrong And His Hot Seven
Jazz:The Essential Collection Vol.2 | IN+OUT Records | 78012-2

St.John Assambly |
Dave Brubeck With The Erich Kunzel Orchestra
Truth Is Fallen | Atlantic | 7567-80761-2

St.John,Art | (cl,as,reedssax)
Jack Teagarden And His Orchestra
Jazz:The Essential Collection Vol.3 | IN+OUT Records | 78013-2

St.Paul | (g)
Joe Sample Group
Ashes To Ashes | Warner | 7599-26318-2

St.Peter,Frank | (as,flcl)
Klaus Weiss Septet
All Night Through | ATM Records | ATM 3816 AH

Stabenow,Thomas | (b)
Bill Ramsey With Orchestra
Gettin' Back To Swing | Bear Family Records | BCD 15813 AH
Clifford Jordan Quintet
Clifford Jordan Meets Klaus Weiss | JHM Records | JHM 3617
Eckhard Weigt Quartet
Standard Moods | Organic Music | ORGM 9718
Johannes Enders Quartet
Kyoto | Organic Music | ORGM 9726
Johnny Griffin-Sal Nistico-Roman Schwaller Sextet
Three Generations Of Tenorsaxophone | JHM Records | JHM 3611
Klaus Weiss Quintet
A Taste Of Jazz | ATM Records | ATM 3810-AH
Roman Schwaller Jazz Quartet
Some Changes In Life | JHM Records | JHM 3612
Roman Schwaller Nonet
The Original Tunes | JHM Records | JHM 3629
Russ Spiegel Group
Twilight | double moon | CHRDM 71026
SWR Big Band
Jazz In Concert | Hänssler Classics | CD 93.004
The New Roman Schwaller Jazzquartet
Welcome Back From Outer Space | JHM Records | JHM 3605
Thomas Faist Sextet
Gentle | Village | VILCD 1020-2
Till Martin Quintet
On The Trail | Nabel Records:Jazz Network | CD 4676
Trombonefire
Sliding Affairs | Laika Records | 35101462
Victor Alcántara Trio
Stabat Mater Inspirations | Organic Music | ORGM 9716
Wolfgang Haffner International Jazz Quintet
Whatever It Is | Jazz 4 Ever Records:Jazz Network | J4E 4714

Stabulas,Nick | (dr)
Al Cohn Quintet feat. Zoot Sims
Al And Zoot | GRP | 951827-2
Carmen McRae With Orchestra
Birds Of A Feather | Decca | 589515-2
Friedrich Gulda Septet
Friedrich Gulda At Birdland | RCA | 2112587-2
Friedrich Gulda Tentet
Friedrich Gulda At Birdland | RCA | 2112587-2
Gil Evans And Ten
Gil Evans And Ten | Original Jazz Classics | OJC 346(P 7120)
The Jazz Giants Play Cole Porter:Night And Day | Prestige | PCD 24203-2
Gil Evans And Ten | Prestige | PRSA 7120-6
Mose Allison Trio
Local Color | Original Jazz Classics | OJCCD 457-2
Mose Allison:Greatest Hits | Original Jazz Classics | OJCCD 6004-2
Mose Allison Sings The 7th Son | Prestige | PR20 7279-2
Phil Woods Quartet
Woodlore | Original Jazz Classics | OJCCD 052-2

Stacey,Jack | (as,cl,reedsts)
Artie Shaw And His Orchestra
Planet JazzArtie Shaw | Planet Jazz | 2152057-2
Planet Jazz:Jazz Greatest Hits | Planet Jazz | 2169648-2
Lena Horne With The Horace Henderson Orchestra
Planet Jazz:Lena Horne | Planet Jazz | 2165373-2
Louis Armstrong With Jimmy Dorsey And His Orchestra
Louis Armstrong:Swing That Music | Laserlight | 36056
Swing Legends:Louis Armstrong | Nimbus Records | NI 2012

Stacey,Paul | (g)
Nicki Leighton-Thomas Group
Forbidden Games | Candid | CCD 79778

Stachelhaus,Ina | (voc)
Kölner Saxophon Mafia With Ina Stachelhaus And Erik Schneider
Kölner Saxophon Mafia Proudly Presents | Jazz Haus Musik | JHM 0046 CD

Stacy,Jess | (pp-solo)
Benny Goodman And His Orchestra
Planet Jazz:Benny Goodman | Planet Jazz | 2152054-2
Planet Jazz Sampler | Planet Jazz | 2152326-2
Planet Jazz:Jazz Greatest Hits | Planet Jazz | 2169648-2
Planet Jazz:Big Bands | Planet Jazz | 2169649-2
Planet Jazz:Swing | Planet Jazz | 2169651-2
Planet Jazz:Jazz Trumpet | Planet Jazz | 2169654-2
Planet Jazz:Female Jazz Vocalists | Planet Jazz | 2169656-2
The Legends Of Swing | Laserlight | 24659
Benny Goodman At Carnegie Hall 1938(Complete) | CBS | C2K 65143
Camel Caravan Broadcast 1939 Vol.1 | Phontastic | NCD 8817
Camel Caravan Broadcast 1939 Vol.2 | Phontastic | NCD 8818
Camel Caravan Broadcast 1939 Vol.3 | Phontastic | NCD 8819
More Camel Caravans | Phontastic | NCD 8841/2
More Camel Caravans | Phontastic | NCD 8843/4
More Camel Caravans | Phontastic | NCD 8845/6
Benny Goodman Band
Benny Goodman At Carnegie Hall 1938(Complete) | CBS | C2K 65143
Benny Goodman Combo
Benny Goodman At Carnegie Hall 1938(Complete) | CBS | C2K 65143
Benny Goodman Dixieland Quintet
Benny Goodman At Carnegie Hall 1938(Complete) | CBS | C2K 65143
Benny Goodman Quartet
Camel Caravan Broadcast 1939 Vol.2 | Phontastic | NCD 8818
Camel Caravan Broadcast 1939 Vol.3 | Phontastic | NCD 8819
Benny Goodman Trio
Camel Caravan Broadcast 1939 Vol.3 | Phontastic | NCD 8819
Bob Crosby And His Orchestra
Swing Legens:Bob Crosby | Nimbus Records | NI 2011
Gene Krupa's Swing Band
Planet Jazz:Swing | Planet Jazz | 2169651-2
Harry James And His Orchestra
The Legends Of Swing | Laserlight | 24659
Jam Session
Benny Goodman At Carnegie Hall 1938(Complete) | CBS | C2K 65143
Jess Stacy And His Orchestra
Planet Jazz:Jazz Piano | RCA | 2169655-2
Lionel Hampton And His Orchestra
Planet Jazz:Male Jazz Vocalists | Planet Jazz | 2169657-2
Lionel Hampton/Jess Stacy
More Camel Caravans | Phontastic | NCD 8845/6
Muggsy Spanier And His V-Disc All Stars
Muggsy Spanier And Bud Freeman:V-Discs 1944-45 | Jazz Unlimited | JUCD 2049
The Metronome All-Star Nine
Jazz:The Essential Collection Vol.3 | IN+OUT Records | 78013-2

Stadler,Marcus | (tb)
Bigband Der Musikschule Der Stadt Brühl Mit Gastsolisten
Pangäa | Indigo-Records | 1004 CD

Stadt-Geräusche |
Kölner Saxophon Mafia
Mafia Years 1982-86 | Jazz Haus Musik | JHM 0058 CD

Staffa,Klaus M. | (percvoice)
Die Elefanten
Wasserwüste | Nabel Records:Jazz Network | CD 4634

Stafford,George | (dr)
Eddie Condon's Hot Shots
Jazz:The Essential Collection Vol.3 | IN+OUT Records | 78013-2
Eddie's Hot Shots
Planet Jazz:Jack Teagarden | Planet Jazz | 2161236-2
Mezz Mezzrow And His Swing Band
Planet Jazz:Bud Freeman | Planet Jazz | 2161240-2

Stafford,Jo | (voc)
Tommy Dorsey And His Orchestra
Frank Sinatra And The Tommy Dorsey Orchestra | RCA | 2668701-2

Stafford,Rennelle | (voc)
Les McCann Group
Another Beginning | Atlantic | 7567-80790-2

Stafford,Terell | (tpfl-h)
Craig Bailey Band
A New Journey | Candid | CCD 79725
Shirley Scott Quintet
A Wakin' Thing | Candid | CCD 79719
Terell Stafford Quintet
Fields Of Gold | Nagel-Heyer | CD 2005
The Clayton Brothers Quintet
Siblingity | Warner | 9362-47813-2
Victor Lewis Sextet
Eeeyyess! | Enja | ENJ-9311 2

Stagl,Franz | (tuba)
Eberhard Weber Orchestra
Orchestra | ECM | 1374

Stagnitta,Frank | (p)
Doug Sides Ensemble
Sumblo | Laika Records | 35100882

Stahl,Dave | (fl-htp)
Count Basie And His Orchestra
Fun Time | Pablo | 2310945-2
Woody Herman And His Orchestra
Jazzin' Vol.2: The Music Of Stevie Wonder | Fantasy | FANCD 6088-2
King Cobra | Original Jazz Classics | OJCCD 1068-2(F 9499)
Woody Herman Herd At Montreux | Original Jazz Classics | OJCCD 991-2(F 9470)
Woody Herman And The New Thundering Herd
Woody Herman:Thundering Herd | Original Jazz Classics | OJCCD 841-2

Stahl,Dorothy | (cello)
Charlie Byrd Orchestra
Latin Byrd | Milestone | MCD 47005-2

Staicov,Constantin | (v)
Bernd Konrad Jazz Group With Symphonie Orchestra
Wen Die Götter Lieben | Creative Works Records | CW CD 1010-1

Stainton,Chris | (bp)
Jimmy Smith All Stars
Jimmy Smith:Dot Com Blues | Blue Thumb | 543978-2

Staley,Jim | (tb,b-tbdidjeridu)
John Zorn Group
Spillane | Nonesuch | 7559-79172-2

Stallworth,Paul | (b)
Al Jarreau With Band
We Got By | Reprise | 7599-27222-2

Stalz,Petra | (vviola)
Ensemble Indigo
Reflection | Enja | ENJ-9417 2

Stamm,Marvin | (fl-h,tpco)
Bob James And His Orchestra
Jazzrock-Anthology Vol.3:Fusion | Zounds | CD 27100555
Cal Tjader's Orchestra
Verve Jazz Masters 39:Cal Tjader | Verve | 521858-2
Freddie Hubbard With Orchestra
This Is Jazz:Freddie Hubbard | CBS | CK 65041
George Benson With The Don Sebesky Orchestra
Verve Jazz Masters 21:George Benson | Verve | 521861-2
George Gruntz Concert Jazz Band
Blues 'N Dues Et Cetera | Enja | ENJ-6072 2
Glenn Miller And His Orchestra
The Glenn Miller Orchestra In Digital Mood | GRP | GRP 95022
Grant Green Orchestra
Grant Green:Blue Breakbeat | Blue Note | 494705-2
Grant Green With Orchestra
The Final Comedown(Soundtrack) | Blue Note | 581678-2
Grover Washington Jr. Orchestra
Jazzrock-Anthology Vol.3:Fusion | Zounds | CD 27100555
Kenny Burrell With The Don Sebesky Orchestra
Verve Jazz Masters 45:Kenny Burrell | Verve | 527652-2
Louis Armstrong And His Friends
Louis Armstrong And His Friends | Bluebird | 2663961-2
Miles Davis With Gil Evans Orchestra, The George Gruntz Concert Jazz Band And Guests
Miles & Quincy Live At Montreux | Warner | 9362-45221-2
Paul Desmond Quartet With The Don Sebesby Orchestra
From The Hot Afternoon | Verve | 543487-2
Quincy Jones And His Orchestra
Verve Jazz Masters Vol.59:Toots Thielemans | Verve | 535271-2
Stan Kenton And His Orchestra
Adventures In Blues | Capitol | 520089-2
Adventures In Jazz | Capitol | 521222-2
Stanley Turrentine And His Orchestra
The Lost Grooves | Blue Note | 831883-2
Thad Jones-Mel Lewis Orchestra
The Groove Merchant/The Second Race | Laserlight | 24656

Stamm,Ruppert | (vibbow-vibes)
Lisa Wahlandt & Mulo Francel And Their Fabulous Bossa Band
Bossa Nova Affair | Edition Collage | EC 534-2

Stan,Mircea | (tb)
Edward Vesala Group
Nan Madol | ECM | 1077

Stander,Bob | (g)
Big Allanbik
Batuque Y Blues | Blues Beacon | BLU-1031 2

Stanfield,Leemie | (b)
Erskine Hawkins And His Orchestra
Planet Jazz:Big Bands | Planet Jazz | 2169649-2

Stangberg,Anna | (harp)
Bengt-Arne Wallin Orchestra
The Birth+Rebirth Of Swedish Folk Jazz | ACT | 9254-2

Stangenes,Geir Atle | (v)
Terje Rypdal Quartet With The Bergen Chamber Ensemble
Lux Aeterna | ECM | 1818(017070-2)

Stangl,Burkhard | (g)
Monoblue Quartet
An Affair With Strauss | Between The Lines | btl 006(Efa 10176-2)

INTERPRETENVERZEICHNIS

Staniloi,Otto | (as,bs,fl,cl,saxts)
Al Porcino Big Band
Al Cohn Meets Al Porcino | Organic Music | ORGM 9730
Stanko,Tomasz | (tp,voicetp-solo)
Gary Peacock Quartet
Voice From The Past-Paradigm | ECM | 1210(517768-2)
Jazz Baltica Ensemble
The Birth+Rebirth Of Swedish Folk Jazz | ACT | 9254-2
NDR Big Band With Guests
50 Years Of NDR Big Band:Bravissimo II | ACT | 9259-2
Nicolas Simion Quartet feat. Tomasz Stanko
Dinner For Don Carlos | Tutu Records | 888146-2*
Transylvanian Dance | Tutu Records | 888164-2*
Viaggio Imaginario | Tutu Records | 888192-2*
Nils Landgren-Tomasz Stanko
Gotland | ACT | 9226-2
Nils Landgren-Tomasz Stanko With Anders Eljas And Claus Bantzer
Gotland | ACT | 9226-2
Thomas Stanko Quartet
Suspended Night | ECM | 1868(9811244)
Thomasz Stanko Quartet
Matka Joanna | ECM | 1544(523986-2)
Tomasz Stanko Quartet
Balladyna | ECM | 1071(519289-2)
Leosia | ECM | 1603(531693-2)
Soul Of Things | ECM | 1788(016374-2)
Tomasz Stanko Septet
Litania | ECM | 1636(537551-2)
Tomasz Stanko Sextet
Litania | ECM | 1636(537551-2)
From The Green Hill | ECM | 1680(547336-2)
Tomasz Stanko-Terje Rypdal
Litania | ECM | 1636(537551-2)
Vlatko Kucan Group
Vlatko Kucan Group | true muze | TUMU CD 9803
Stanley,Bill | (tuba)
J.J.Johnson And His Orchestra
Planet Jazz:J.J.Johnson | Planet Jazz | 2159974-2
Stanley,Emanuel | (b)
International Commission For The Prevention Of Musical Border Control,The
The International Commission For The Prevention Of Musical Border Control | VeraBra Records | CDVBR 2093-2
Stapleton,Bill | (fl-htp)
Woody Herman And His Orchestra
The Raven Speaks | Original Jazz Classics | OJCCD 663-2(F 9416)
Woody Herman And The New Thundering Herd
Woody Herman:Thundering Herd | Original Jazz Classics | OJCCD 841-2
Staringer,Richie | (fender-rhodes)
Tok Tok Tok
Love Again | Einstein Music | EM 01081
It Took So Long | Einstein Music | EM 21103
50 Ways To Leave Your Lover | Einstein Music | EM 91051
Stark,Bengt | (dr)
Agneta Baumann And Her Quintet
A Time For Love | Touché Music | TMcCD 006
Stark,Bobby | (tp)
Chocolate Dandies
Jazz:The Essential Collection Vol.3 | IN+OUT Records | 78013-2
Connie's Inn Orchestra
Planet Jazz:Coleman Hawkins | Planet Jazz | 2152055-2
Ella Fitzgerald And Her Orchestra
Jazz Collection:Ella Fitzgerald | Laserlight | 24397
Ella Fitzgerald With The Chick Webb Orchestra
Jazz Collection:Ella Fitzgerald | Laserlight | 24397
Fletcher Henderson And His Orchestra
Jazz:The Essential Collection Vol.1 | IN+OUT Records | 78011-2
Jazz:The Essential Collection Vol.3 | IN+OUT Records | 78013-2
Starling,Ray | (mellophon,p,tpmellophone)
Anthony Ortega With The Nat Pierce Orchestra
Earth Dance | Fresh Sound Records | FSR-CD 325
Buddy Rich And His Orchestra
Big Swing Face | Pacific Jazz | 837989-2
Buddy Rich Big Band
The New One! | Pacific Jazz | 494507-2
Stan Kenton And His Orchestra
Adventures In Blues | Capitol | 520089-2
Adventures In Jazz | Capitol | 521222-2
Starnes,Spencer | (b)
Hans Theessink Group
Crazy Moon | Minor Music | 801052
Starostin,Sergey | (cl,alto-cl,reedsvoc)
Farlanders
The Farlander | JA & RO | JARO 4222-2
Mikhail Alperin's Moscow Art Trio
Folk Dreams | JA & RO | JARO 4187-2
Prayer | JA & RO | JARO 4193-2
Hamburg Concert | JA & RO | JARO 4201-2
Mikhail Alperin's Moscow Art Trio With The Russkaja Pesnja Folk Choir
Folk Dreams | JA & RO | JARO 4187-2
Mikhail Alperin's Moscow Art Trio With The Tuva Folk & Russian Folk Ensemble
Prayer | JA & RO | JARO 4193-2
Moscow Art Trio
Music | JA & RO | JARO 4214-2
Portrait | JA & RO | JARO 4227-2
Once Upon A Time | JA & RO | JARO 4238-2
Moscow Art Trio And The Bulgarian Voices Angelite
Portrait | JA & RO | JARO 4227-2
Sergey Starostin's Vocal Family
Journey | JA & RO | JARO 4226-2
Starr,Kay | (voc)
The Capitol Jazzmen
The Hollywood Session:The Capitol Jazzmen | Jazz Unlimited | JUCD 2044
Starr,Ron | (fl,cl,tssax)
Don Ellis Orchestra
Electric Bath | CBS | CK 65522
Statterfield,Jack | (tb)
Louis Armstrong And The Commanders under the Direction of Camarata
Satchmo Serenaders | Verve | 543792-2
Stauss,Markus | (sax,ss,bass-sax,tsbs)
Q4 Orchester Project
Lyon's Brood | Creative Works Records | CW CD 1018-3
Yavapai | Creative Works Records | CW CD 1028-2
Steacker,Richard Lee | (gel-g)
Grover Washington Jr. Septet
Paradise | Elektra | 7559-60537-2
Steadman,Jim | (gvoc)
Tom Browne Groups
Mo' Jamaica Funk | Hip Bop | HIBD 8002
Stearns,Al | (tp)
Tommy Dorsey And His Orchestra
Planet Jazz:Frank Sinatra & Tommy Dorsey | Planet Jazz | 2152067-2
Planet Jazz Sampler | Planet Jazz | 2152326-2
Stearns,Lawrence | (tp)
Peggy Lee With The Benny Goodman Orchestra
Peggy Lee & Benny Goodman:The Complete Recordings 1941-1947 | CBS | C2K 65686
Steede,Erwin | (as)
Ahmed Abdul-Malik Orchestra
Jazz Sounds Of Africa | Prestige | PRCD 24279-2
Steele,Bryan | (sax)
Digital Masters Feat. Bryan Steele
Sun Dance | Edition Musikat | EDM 038
Steele,George | (tb)
Albert Ayler Group
Albert Ayler Live In Greenwich Village:The Complete Impulse Recordings | Impulse(MCA) | IMP 22732
Steen,Teddy | (tb)
United Women's Orchestra
Virgo Supercluster | Jazz Haus Musik | JHM 0123 CD
Stefanet,Anatol | (reedsviola)
Trigon
Oglinda | JA & RO | JARO 4215-2
Stefanski,Janusz | (drperc)
Hans Koller Quintet
Kunstkopfindianer | MPS | 9813439
Wolfgang Lackerschmid Group
Mallet Connection | Bhakti Jazz | BR 33
Steffen,Andreas | (fl,ssas)
Jazz Orchester Rheinland-Pfalz
Kazzou | Jazz Haus Musik | LJBB 9104
Steffen,Arno | (voc)
Kölner Saxophon Mafia With Arno Steffen
Kölner Saxophon Mafia Proudly Presents | Jazz Haus Musik | JHM 0046 CD
Steffens,Andreas | (fl,cl,ssas)
Jazz Orchester Rheinland-Pfalz
Like Life | Jazz Haus Musik | LJBB 9405
Last Season | Jazz Haus Musik | LJBB 9706
Steffensen,John | (congasperc)
Stan Kenton With The Danish Radio Big Band
Stan Kenton With The Danish Radio Big Band | Storyville | STCD 8340
Stegmeyer,Bill | (arr,as,cl,ts,reeds,saxtp)
Frank Trumbauer And His Orchestra
The Hollywood Session:The Capitol Jazzmen | Jazz Unlimited | JUCD 2044
George Wein's Dixie Victors
The Magic Horn | RCA | 2113038-2
Planet Jazz | Planet Jazz | 2169652-2
Glenn Miller And His Orchestra
Planet Jazz:Glenn Miller | Planet Jazz | 2152056-2
Louis Armstrong And Ella Fitzgerald With Bob Hagger's Orchestra
Louis Armstrong:C'est Si Bon | Dreyfus Jazz Line | FDM 36730-2
Louis Armstrong And His Orchestra
Louis Armstrong:Swing That Music | Laserlight | 36056
Louis Armstrong:C'est Si Bon | Dreyfus Jazz Line | FDM 36730-2
Stegner,Martin | (vviola)
Joe Bawelino Quartet & Martin Stegner
Happy Birthday Stéphane | Edition Collage | EC 458-2
Stehen,Niels Jorgen | (p)
Eddie Lockjaw Davis Quartet
Jazz Legends:Eddie Lockjaw Davis Quartet Vol.1&2 | Storyville | 4960263
Steidle,Oliver Bernd | (dr)
Der Rote Bereich
Risky Business | ACT | 9407-2
Steiff,Helen | (voc)
Leon Thomas With Orchestra
Spirits Known And Unknown | RCA | 2663876-2
Steiff,Pete | (voc)
Steig,Jeremy | (fl,alto-fl,bass-fl,electronics)
Bill Evans Trio With Jeremy Steig
The Complete Bill Evans On Verve | Verve | 527953-2
Nat Adderley Sextet
Joe Henderson:The Milestone Years | Milestone | 8MCD 4413-2
Steimberg,Mariano | (dr)
Dani Perez Quartet
Buenos Aires-Barcelona Connections | Fresh Sound Records | FSNT 144 CD
Stein Norbert | (electronic-composer)
Pata Blue Chip
Pata Blue Chip | Pata Musik | PATA 13(amf 1064)
Stein,Andy | (v)
Andy Bey Group
Tuesdays In Chinatown | Minor Music | 801099
Stein,Eddie | (v)
Jacintha With Band And Strings
Lush Life | Groove Note | GRV 1011-2(Gold CD 2011)
Stein,Gerd | (g)
Ekkehard Jost Ensemble
Weimarer Balladen | Fish Music | FM 004 CD
Stein,Hal | (as)
Prestige All Stars
The Prestige Legacy Vol.2:Battles Of Saxes | Prestige | PCD 24252-2
Stein,John | (g)
John Stein Quartet
Conversation Pieces | Jardis Records | JRCD 20140
John Stein Quintet
Portraits And Landscapes | Jardis Records | JRCD 20029
Jazz Guitar Highlights 1 | Jardis Records | JRCD 20141
Stein,Lou | (p,arrp-solo)
Charlie Parker With Strings
Bird: The Complete Charlie Parker On Verve | Verve | 837141-2
Charlie Parker With The Joe Lipman Orchestra
Charlie Parker With Strings:The Master Takes | Verve | 523984-2
Charlie Parker Big Band | Verve | 559835-2
Lee Wiley With The Dean Kincaide Dixieland Band
Planet Jazz:Female Jazz Vocalists | Planet Jazz | 2169656-2
Woody Herman And His Orchestra
Songs For Hip Lovers | Verve | 559872-2
Stein,Maurice | (as,b-clreeds)
Ella Fitzgerald With The Buddy Bregman Orchestra
Love Songs:The Best Of The Song Books | Verve | 531762-2
Ella Fitzgerald Sings The Rodgers And Hart Song Book | Verve | 537258-2
Stein,Nancy | (cello)
Ella Fitzgerald With Orchestra
The Best Is Yet To Come | Original Jazz Classics | OJCCD 889-2(2312138)
Stein,Norbert | (b-cl,ss,ts,synth,perc,cl)
Kölner Saxophon Mafia
Mafia Years 1982-86 | Jazz Haus Musik | JHM 0058 CD
Norbert Stein Pata Masters
Pata Maroc | Pata Musik | PATA 12(AMF 1063)
Blue Slit | Pata Musik | PATA 8 CD
Graffiti | Pata Musik | PATA 9 CD
Norbert Stein Pata Masters meets Djaduk Ferianto Kua Etnika
Pata Java | Pata Musik | PATA 16 CD
Norbert Stein Pata Orchester
Ritual Life | Pata Musik | PATA 5(JHM 50) CD
The Secret Act Of Painting | Pata Musik | PATA 7 CD
Nornert Stein Pata Masters
Live In Australia | Pata Musik | PATA 15 CD
Pata Masters
Pata-Bahia | Pata Musik | PATA 11 CD
Pata Music Meets Arfi
News Of Roi Ubu | Pata Musik | PATA 10 CD
La Belle Et La Bête | Pata Musik | PATA 14(amf 1066)
Stein,Rudi | (cello)
Jacintha With Band And Strings
Lush Life | Groove Note | GRV 1011-2(Gold CD 2011)
Steinberg,Albert | (strings)
Gene Harris And The Three Sounds
Deep Blue-The United States Of Mind | Blue Note | 521152-2
Steinberg,Ben | (v)
Stan Getz With The Eddie Sauter Orchestra
Stan Getz Plays The Music Of Mickey One | Verve | 531232-2
Steinberg,Lisa | (v)
A Band Of Friends
Wynton Marsalis Quartet With Strings | CBS | CK 68921
Steiner,Michael | (bsreeds)
Fritz Münzer Tentet
Blue Ideas | Jazz 'n' Arts Records | 0200
Rainer Tempel Big Band
Melodies Of '98 | Jazz 4 Ever Records:Jazz Network | J4E 4744
Steinhauer,Dietmar | (p,keyboardssynth)
Frank Kirchner Group
Frank Kirchner | Laika Records | LK 93-036
Steinholtz,Jerry | (perc)
Lee Ritenour Group
Jazzrock-Anthology Vol.3:Fusion | Zounds | CD 27100555
Steinholtz,Olle | (b)
Elise Einarsdotter-Olle Steinholz
Sketches Of Roses | Touché Music | TMcCD 008
Irene Sjögren Group
Song For A Willow | Touché Music | TMcCD 015
Stenson,Bobo | (el-p,pperc)
Bobo Stenson Trio
Reflections | ECM | 1516(523160-2)
War Orphans | ECM | 1604(539723-2)
Serenity | ECM | 1740/41(543611-2)
Charles Lloyd Quartet
Fish Out Of Water | ECM | 1398
Notes From Big Sur | ECM | 1465(511999-2)
The Call | ECM | 1522(517719-2)
All My Relations | ECM | 1557
Canto | ECM | 1635(537345-2)
Don Cherry Group
Dona Nostra | ECM | 1448(521727-2)
Jan Garbarek Quintet
Sart | ECM | 1015(839305-2)
Jan Garbarek-Bobo Stenson Quartet
Witchi-Tai-To | ECM | 1041(833330-2)
Dansere | ECM | 1075(829193-2)
Mingus By Five
Mingus By Five | Touché Music | TMcCD 019
Monk By Five
Monk By Five | Touché Music | TMcCD 012
Nils Landgren Group
Ballads | ACT | 9268-2
Terje Rypdal Sextet
Terje Rypdal | ECM | 1016(527645-2)
Thomasz Stanko Quartet
Matka Joanna | ECM | 1544(523986-2)
Tomasz Stanko Quartet
Leosia | ECM | 1603(531693-2)
Tomasz Stanko Septet
Litania | ECM | 1636(537551-2)
Tomasz Stanko Sextet
Litania | ECM | 1636(537551-2)
Ulf Adaker Quartet
Reflections | Touché Music | TMcCD 016
Stepansky,Joe | (v)
Ella Fitzgerald With The Billy May Orchestra
The Best Of The Song Books:The Ballads | Verve | 521867-2
Ella Fitzgerald Sings The Harold Arlen Song Book | Verve | 589108-2
Stephen,Phil | (tuba)
Billy Eckstine With The Billy May Orchestra
Once More With Feeling | Roulette | 581862-2
Stephens,Charles | (tb)
Archie Shepp Orchestra
The Cry Of My People | Impulse(MCA) | 9861488
McCoy Tyner Group With Horns
Inner Voices | Original Jazz Classics | OJCCD 1039-2(M 9079)
McCoy Tyner Group With Horns And Voices
Inner Voices | Original Jazz Classics | OJCCD 1039-2(M 9079)
Sam Rivers Orchestra
Crystals | Impulse(MCA) | 589760-2
Stephens,Chip | (p)
Steve Rochinski Quartet
Otherwise | Jardis Records | JRCD 20133
Stephens,Haig | (b)
Billie Holiday With Toots Camarata And His Orchestra
Billie's Love Songs | Nimbus Records | NI 2000
Bob Crosby's Bobcats
Swing Legens:Bob Crosby | Nimbus Records | NI 2011
Stephens,Mary | (voc)
Archie Shepp Orchestra
The Cry Of My People | Impulse(MCA) | 9861488
Stephens,Phil | (btuba)
Charlie Barnet And His Orchestra
Planet Jazz:Big Bands | Planet Jazz | 2169649-2
Planet Jazz:Swing | Planet Jazz | 2169651-2
Ella Fitzgerald With The Frank DeVol Orchestra
Get Happy! | Verve | 523321-2
June Christy With The Pete Rugolo Orchestra
Something Cool(The Complete Mono & Stereo Versions) | Capitol | 534069-2
Louis Armstrong With Gordon Jenkins And His Orchestra
Satchmo In Style | Verve | 549594-2
Louis Armstrong With Gordon Jenkins And His Orchestra And Choir
Satchmo In Style | Verve | 549594-2
Nat King Cole With The Billy May Orchestra
Nat King Cole:For Sentimental Reasons | Dreyfus Jazz Line | FDM 36740-2
Pete Rugolo And His Orchestra
Thriller/Richard Diamon(Original Jazz Scores From 2 Classics TV Series) | Fresh Sound Records | FSCD 2015
Tommy Dorsey And His Orchestra
Planet Jazz:Frank Sinatra & Tommy Dorsey | Planet Jazz | 2152067-2
Stephenson,Ronnie | (drperc)
Heinz Sauer Quartet With The NDR Big Band
NDR Big Band-Bravissimo | ACT | 9232-2
Joe Pass With The NDR Big Band
NDR Big Band-Bravissimo | ACT | 9232-2
NDR Big Band With Guests
50 Years Of NDR Big Band:Bravissimo II | ACT | 9259-2
Remy Filipovitch Trio
All Day Long | Album | AS 22927
Stepney,Bill | (drvoc)
Buddy Guy Blues Band
Buddy Guy-The Complete Chess Studio Recordings | MCA | MCD 09337
Steps Ahead |
Steps Ahead
Steps Ahead:Copenhagen Live | Storyville | 4960363
Steps Ahead | Elektra | 7559-60168-2
Modern Times | Elektra | 7559-60351-2
N.Y.C. | Intuition Records | INT 3007-2
Stepton,Rick | (tb)
Buddy Rich Big Band
Keep The Customer Satisfied | EMI Records | 523999-2
Woody Herman And His Orchestra
The Raven Speaks | Original Jazz Classics | OJCCD 663-2(F 9416)
Sterkin,David | (viola)
Ella Fitzgerald With The Nelson Riddle Orchestra
The Best Of The Song Books:The Ballads | Verve | 521867-2
Harry James And His Orchestra
Trumpet Blues:The Best Of Harry James | Capitol | 521224-2
Sterling,Arthur | (p)
Leon Thomas With The Oliver Nelson Quintet
Leon Thomas In Berlin | RCA | 2663877-2
Stern,Bobby | (as,ts,harm,flss)
Conexion Latina
Mambo 2000 | Enja | ENJ-7055 2
Stern,Emile | (p)
Bill Coleman Et Son Orchestre
Americans Swinging In Paris:Bill Coleman-The Elegance | EMI Records | 539662-2
Michel Warlop Et Son Orchestre
Jazz In Paris:Django Reinhardt-Django Et Compagnie | EmArCy | 549241-2 PMS

Nitta Rette Et Son Trio Hot
Jazz In Paris:Django Reinhardt-Django Et Compagnie | EmArCy | 549241-2 PMS

Stern,Hank | (btuba)
Frank Sinatra With Orchestra
Planet Jazz:Frank Sinatra & Tommy Dorsey | Planet Jazz | 2152067-2

Stern,Leni | (g,el-g,perc,slide-gvoc)
Leni Stern Group
Secrets | Enja | ENJ-5093 2
Closer To The Light | Enja | ENJ-6034 2
Wayne Krantz Duo
Signals | Enja | ENJ-6048 2

Stern,Mike | (el-gg)
Bob Berg Quintet
The Art Of Saxophone | Laserlight | 24652
Michael Brecker Group
Don't Try This At Home | Impulse(MCA) | 950114-2
Michael Mantler Quintet With The London Symphony Orchestra
Something There | Watt | 13
Mike Stern Group
Jigsaw | Atlantic | 7567-82027-2
Odds Or Evens | Atlantic | 7567-82297-2
Standards(And Other Songs) | Atlantic | 7567-82419-2
Give And Take | Atlantic | 7567-83036-2
Play | Atlantic | 7567-83219-2
Miles Davis Group
The Man With The Horn | CBS | 468701-2
We Want Miles | CBS | 469402-2
The Brecker Brothers
Return Of The Brecker Brothers | GRP | GRP 96842

Sternbach,David | (fr-h)
Stan Kenton With The Danish Radio Big Band
Stan Kenton With The Danish Radio Big Band | Storyville | STCD 8340

Sterzer,Philipp | (fl)
Mind Games
Pretty Fonky | Edition Collage | EC 482-2
Wind Moments | Take Twelve On CD | TT 009-2
Mind Games With Philip Catherine
Pretty Fonky | Edition Collage | EC 482-2
Tom Bennecke & Space Gurilla
Wind Moments | Take Twelve On CD | TT 009-2

Stetch,John | (p)
Andrew Rathbun Group
Jade | Fresh Sound Records | FSNT 076 CD

Steuberville,Ben | (b)
Gene Ammons Septet
A Stranger In Town | Prestige | PRCD 24266-2

Steudinger,Torsten | (b)
Changes
Jazz Changes? | Jazz 'n' Arts Records | 0100

Steuernagel,Rudi | (ts)
Wolfgang Lauth Septet
Noch Lauther | Bear Family Records | BCD 15942 AH

Stevens,Cathy | (viola)
Europa String Choir
Internationales Guitarren Festival '99 | ALISO Records | AL 1038

Stevens,Felicity | (voc)
Mike Westbrook Brass Band
Glad Day:Settings Of William Blake | Enja | ENJ-9376 2

Stevens,Haig | (b)
Louis Armstrong And His Orchestra
Louis Armstrong:Swing That Music | Laserlight | 36056

Stevens,John | (dr,celeste,co,mini-tp,perc,voice)
Buddy Childers Big Band
It's What Happening Now! | Candid | CCD 79749
Evan Parker-Paul Rutherford-Barry Guy-John Stevens
4,4,4, | Konnex Records | KCD 5049
John Stevens Quartet
Re-Touch & Quartet | Konnex Records | KCD 5027
John Stevens Trio
4,4,4, | Konnex Records | KCD 5049

Stevens,Leo | (dr)
Johnny 'Hammond' Smith Quartet
Good 'Nuff | Prestige | PRCD 24282-2
Johnny 'Hammond' Smith Septet
Open House | Milestone | MCD 47089-2
Johnny 'Hammond' Smith Trio
Good 'Nuff | Prestige | PRCD 24282-2

Stevens,Mark | (perc,vibtimbales)
Don Ellis Orchestra
Electric Bath | CBS | CK 65522

Stevens,Phil | (b)
Tommy Dorsey And His Orchestra
Planet Jazz:Tommy Dorsey | Planet Jazz | 2159972-2

Stevens,Sally | (voc)
Les McCann Group
Another Beginning | Atlantic | 7567-80790-2

Stevenson,Bobby | (p)
Van Alexander Orchestra
Home Of Happy Feet/Swing! Staged For Sound! | Capitol | 535211-2

Stevenson,George | (tb)
Hot Lips Page Band
Planet Jazz:Jazz Trumpet | Planet Jazz | 2169654-2
Sidney Bechet With Sammy Price's Bluesicians
Planet Jazz:Sidney Bechet | Planet Jazz | 2152063-2

Stevenson,Joe | (bj)
Graham Stewart And His New Orleans Band
The Golden Years Of Revival Jazz,Vol.12 | Storyville | STCD 5517
The Golden Years Of Revival Jazz,Vol.14 | Storyville | STCD 5519

Stevenson,Rudy | (fl,gbj)
Cedar Walton Quintet
Soul Cycle | Original Jazz Classics | OJCCD 847-2(P 7693)
Nina Simone And Orchestra
Planet Jazz:Nina Simone | Planet Jazz | 2165372-2
Nina Simone Quartet
Verve Jazz Masters 17:Nina Simone | Verve | 518198-2
Verve Jazz Masters 20:Introducing | Verve | 519853-2
Nina Simone After Hours | Verve | 526702-2
In Concert/I Put A Spell On You | Mercury | 846543-2
Nina Simone Quintet
Nina Simone After Hours | Verve | 526702-2
Nina Simone With Hal Mooney's Orchestra
Verve Jazz Masters 17:Nina Simone | Verve | 518198-2
In Concert/I Put A Spell On You | Mercury | 846543-2
Nina Simone With Horace Ott's Orchestra
Nina Simone After Hours | Verve | 526702-2
In Concert/I Put A Spell On You | Mercury | 846543-2

Stevenson,Rudy prob. | (bongos)
Nina Simone Trio
Verve Jazz Masters Vol.58:Nina Simone Sings Nina | Verve | 529867-2

Stevenson,Tommy | (tp)
Jimmy Lunceford And His Orchestra
Planet Jazz:Swing | Planet Jazz | 2169651-2

Steward,Herbie | (as,ts,cl,ss,flsax)
The Four Brothers
Planet Jazz:Jazz Saxophone | Planet Jazz | 2169653-2
Together Again! | RCA | 2179623-2

Steward,Reginald | (tb)
Maceo Parker With The Rebirth Brass Band
Southern Exposure | Minor Music | 801033

Steward,Teddy | (dr)
Dizzy Gillespie And His Orchestra
Planet Jazz:Dizzy Gillespie | Planet Jazz | 2152069-2

Stewart,Aaron | (ssts)
Steve Coleman And The Council Of Balance
Genesis & The Opening Of The Way | RCA | 2152934-2

Stewart,Al | (tp)
Birdland Dream Band
Birdland Dream Band | RCA | 2663873-2

Chubby Jackson And His All Star Big Band
Chubby Takes Over | Fresh Sound Records | FSR-CD 324
Woody Herman And His Orchestra
The Legends Of Swing | Laserlight | 24659

Stewart,Bill | (cl,sax,drp)
Bob Degen Trio
Catability | Enja | ENJ-9332 2
Chris Potter Group
Traveling Mercies | Verve | 018243-2
Fred Wesley Group
New Friends | Minor Music | 801016
Ingrid Jensen Quintet
Here On Earth | Enja | ENJ-9313 2
Jason Seizer With The Larry Goldings Trio
Sketches | Organic Music | ORGM 9710
John Scofield Groups
Quiet | Verve | 533185-2
John Scofield Quartet
What We Do | Blue Note | 799586-2
John Scofield Sextet
Hand Jive | Blue Note | 827327-2
John Scofield Trio
En Route | Verve | 9861357
John Scofield-Pat Metheny Quartet
I Can See Your House From Here | Blue Note | 827765-2
Maceo Parker Group
Mo' Roots | Minor Music | 801018
Southern Exposure | Minor Music | 801033
Martial Solal Trio
Martial Solal NY-1 | Blue Note | 584232-2
Marty Ehrlich Quintet
New York Child | Enja | ENJ-9025 2
Michael Brecker Group
Time Is Of The Essence | Verve | 547844-2
Pat Metheny Trio
Trio 99-00 | Warner | 9362-47632-2
Part Metheny Trio Live | Warner | 9362-47907-2
Phil Grenadier Quintet
Sweet Transients | Fresh Sound Records | FSNT 093 CD

Stewart,Bob | (tubavoc)
Bob Stewart First Line Band
First Line | JMT Edition | 919014-2
McCoy Tyner Orchestra
13th House | Original Jazz Classics | OJCCD 1089-2(M 9102)

Stewart,Dave | (b-tb,tpvoc)
Kenny Wheeler Brass Ensemble
A Long Time Ago | ECM | 1691

Stewart,David | (b-tb)
John Surman-Jack DeJohnette With The London Brass
Printed In Germany | ECM | 1802(017065-2)
John Surman-John Warren Group
The Brass Project | ECM | 1478

Stewart,Dee | (tp)
Benny Moten's Kansas City Orchestra
Planet Jazz:Ben Webster | RCA | 2165368-2
Planet Jazz:Jimmy Rushing | RCA | 2165371-2
Planet Jazz:Swing | Planet Jazz | 2169651-2
Jazz:The Essential Collection Vol.3 | IN+OUT Records | 78013-2

Stewart,Graham | (tbvoc)
Graham Stewart And His New Orleans Band
The Golden Years Of Revival Jazz,Sampler | Storyville | 109 1001
The Golden Years Of Revival Jazz,Vol.4 | Storyville | STCD 5509
The Golden Years Of Revival Jazz,Vol.10 | Storyville | STCD 5515
The Golden Years Of Revival Jazz,Vol.12 | Storyville | STCD 5517
The Golden Years Of Revival Jazz,Vol.14 | Storyville | STCD 5519
Graham Stewart Seven
The Golden Years Of Revival Jazz,Vol.8 | Storyville | STCD 5513

Stewart,Grant | (ts)
Grant Stewart Quartet
Buen Rollo | Fresh Sound Records | FSNT 053 CD

Stewart,Herbie | (as,tscl)
Artie Shaw And His Orchestra
Planet Jazz:Jazz Trumpet | Planet Jazz | 2169654-2
Woody Herman And His Orchestra
The Legends Of Swing | Laserlight | 24659
Woody Herman:Four Brother | Dreyfus Jazz Line | FDM 36722-2

Stewart,Ian | (p)
Howlin' Wolf London Session
Howlin' Wolf:The London Sessions | Chess | MCD 09297

Stewart,Jimmy | (g)
Gabor Szabo Quintet
The Roots Of Acid Jazz | Impulse(MCA) | IMP 12042
The Sorcerer | Impulse(MCA) | IMP 12112

Stewart,Leroy | (el-b)
Buddy Guy Blues Band
Buddy Guy-The Complete Chess Studio Recordings | MCA | MCD 09337

Stewart,Louis | (el-g,gg-solo)
Benny Goodman And His Orchestra
Verve Jazz Masters 33:Benny Goodman | Verve | 844410-2
Benny Goodman Sextet
Verve Jazz Masters 33:Benny Goodman | Verve | 844410-2
Louis Stewart
Jazz Guitar Highlights 1 | Jardis Records | JRCD 20141
In A Mellow Tone | Jardis Records | JRCD 9206
Out On His Own | Jardis Records | JRCD 9612
Louis Stewart-Heiner Franz
I Wished On The Moon | Jardis Records | JRCD 20027
In A Mellow Tone | Jardis Records | JRCD 9206
Louis Stewart-Heiner Franz Quartet
I Wished On The Moon | Jardis Records | JRCD 20027
Jazz Guitar Highlights 1 | Jardis Records | JRCD 20141
Winter Song | Jardis Records | JRCD 9005
Louis Stewart-Martin Taylor
Acoustic Guitar Duets | Jardis Records | JRCD 9613
The European Jazz Guitar Orchestra
The European Jazz Guitar Orchestra | Jardis Records | JRCD 9307

Stewart,M. | (voc)
Sonny Rollins Group
What's New? | RCA | 2179626-2

Stewart,Maeretha | (voc)
Grover Washington Jr. Orchestra
Inside Moves | Elektra | 7559-60318-2
Nina Simone And Orchestra
Baltimore | Epic | 476906-2

Stewart,Mary Ann | (voc)
Eddie Harris Group
The Best Of Eddie Harris | Atlantic | 7567-81370-2

Stewart,Michael | (tpfl-h)
Al Jarreau With Band
Al Jarreau In London | i.e. Music | 557849-2
Tenderness | i.e. Music | 557853-2
Lenny White Group
Present Tense | Hip Bop | HIBD 8004
Renderers Of Spirit | Hip Bop | HIBD 8014
Marcus Miller Group
The Sun Don't Lie | Dreyfus Jazz Line | FDM 36560-2
Tales | Dreyfus Jazz Line | FDM 36571-2
Live & More | Dreyfus Jazz Line | FDM 36585-2
Michael 'Patches' Stewart Group
Blue Patches | Hip Bop | HIBD 8016
Penetration | Hip Bop | HIBD 8018

Stewart,Rex | (co,kazoo,voctp)
Connie's Inn Orchestra
Planet Jazz:Coleman Hawkins | Planet Jazz | 2152055-2
Cozy Cole's Big Seven
Body And Soul Revisited | GRP | GRP 16272
Duke Ellington And His Famous Orchestra
Duke Ellington:The Blanton-Webster Band | Bluebird | 21 13181-2
Planet Jazz:Duke Ellington | Planet Jazz | 2152053-2
Planet Jazz:Johnny Hodges | Planet Jazz | 2152065-2
Planet Jazz Sampler | Planet Jazz | 2152326-2
Planet Jazz:Ben Webster | RCA | 2165368-2
Planet Jazz:Big Bands | Planet Jazz | 2169649-2
Planet Jazz:Jazz Trumpet | Planet Jazz | 2169654-2
Planet Jazz:Female Jazz Vocalists | Planet Jazz | 2169656-2
Highlights From The Duke Ellington Centennial Edition | RCA | 2663672-2
Greatest Hits | CBS | 462959-2
Jazz:The Essential Collection Vol.2 | IN+OUT Records | 78012-2
Jazz:The Essential Collection Vol.3 | IN+OUT Records | 78013-2
Duke Ellington:Ko-Ko | Dreyfus Jazz Line | FDM 36717-2
Duke Ellington And His Orchestra
Planet Jazz:Duke Ellington | Planet Jazz | 2152053-2
Planet Jazz:Jazz Greatest Hits | Planet Jazz | 2169648-2
Highlights From The Duke Ellington Centennial Edition | RCA | 2663672-2
Carnegie Hall Concert December 1944 | Prestige | 2PCD 24073-2
Carnegie Hall Concert January 1943 | Prestige | 2PCD 34004-2
Jazz:The Essential Collection Vol.2 | IN+OUT Records | 78012-2
Jazz:The Essential Collection Vol.3 | IN+OUT Records | 78013-2
The Duke At Fargo 1940 | Storyville | STCD 8316/17
At The Hurricane:Original 1943 Broadcasts | Storyville | STCD 8359
Eddie Condon And His Boys
The Very Best Of Dixieland Jazz | Verve | 535529-2
Fletcher Henderson And His Orchestra
Jazz:The Essential Collection Vol.1 | IN+OUT Records | 78011-2
Jack Teagarden's Big Eight
Jazz:The Essential Collection Vol.3 | IN+OUT Records | 78013-2
Rex Stewart And His Feetwarmers
Django Reinhardt All Star Sessions | Capitol | 531577-2
Rex Stewart And His Orchestra
Planet Jazz:Ben Webster | RCA | 2165368-2
Planet Jazz:Jazz Trumpet | Planet Jazz | 2169654-2
Jazz:The Essential Collection Vol.3 | IN+OUT Records | 78013-2
Rex Stewart Quintet
Peche Á La Mode-The Great Blue Star Sessions 1947/1953 | Verve | 835418-2
Sidney Bechet And His New Orleans Feetwarmers
Sidney Bechet:Summertime | Dreyfus Jazz Line | FDM 36712-2

Stewart,Robert 'Bob' | (fl-htuba)
Arthur Blythe Group
Hipmotism | Enja | ENJ-6088 2
Bill Frisell Quintet
Rambler | ECM | 1287
Carla Bley Band
Fleur Carnivore | Watt | 21
Dinner Music | Watt | 6(825815-2)
European Tour 1977 | Watt | 8
Musique Mecanique | Watt | 9
Don Cherry Group
Multi Kulti | A&M Records | 395323-2
Gebhard Ullmann Trio
Suite Noire | Nabel Records:Jazz Network | CD 4649
Gebhard Ullmann-Andreas Willers
Playful '93 | Nabel Records:Jazz Network | CD 4659
Gil Evans Orchestra
There Comes A Time | RCA | 2131392-2
Gunter Hampel New York Orchestra
Fresh Heat-Live At Sweet Basil | Birth | CD 039
Herb Robertson Brass Ensemble
Shades Of Bud Powell | JMT Edition | 919019-2
Herb Robertson Group
The Little Trumpet | JMT Edition | 919007-2
Josh Roseman Unit
Cherry | Enja | ENJ-9392 2
Lester Bowie's Brass Fantasy
I Only Have Eyes For You | ECM | 1296(825902-2)
Avant Pop | ECM | 1326
The Fire This Time | IN+OUT Records | 7019-2
The Odysse Of Funk & Popular Music | Dreyfus Jazz Line | FDM 37004-2
When The Spitit Returns | Dreyfus Jazz Line | FDM 37016-2
Machito And His Orchestra
Afro-Cuban Jazz Moods | Original Jazz Classics | OJC20 447-2
Ray Anderson Sextet
It Just So Happens | Enja | ENJ-5037 2
Sonny Rollins Quintet With Brass
Old Flames | Milestone | MCD 9215-2
The Carla Bley Band
I Hate To Sing | Watt | 12,5
The Sidewalks Of New York
Tin Pan Alley:The Sidewalks Of New York | Winter&Winter | 910038-2

Stewart,Shannon | (scratsh)
Tom Browne Groups
Mo' Jamaica Funk | Hip Bop | HIBD 8002

Stewart,Slam | (bvoice)
Art Tatum Trio
Art Tatum:Complete Capitol Recordings | Capitol | 821325-2
Art Tatum:Over The Rainbow | Dreyfus Jazz Line | FDM 36727-2
Coleman Hawkins Quintet
Ultimate Coleman Hawkins selected by Sonny Rollins | Verve | 557538-2
Dizzy Gillespie Sextet
Dizzy Gillespie:Night In Tunisia | Dreyfus Jazz Line | FDM 36734-2
Don Byas Quartet
Don Byas:Laura | Dreyfus Jazz Line | FDM 36714-2
Don Byas/Slam Stewart
Don Byas:Laura | Dreyfus Jazz Line | FDM 36714-2
Fats Waller And His Rhythm
Planet Jazz:Fats Waller | Planet Jazz | 2152058-2
Lester Young Quartet
Verve Jazz Masters 30:Lester Young | Verve | 521859-2
Jazz:The Essential Collection Vol.3 | IN+OUT Records | 78013-2
Lester Young:Blue Lester | Dreyfus Jazz Line | FDM 36729-2
Lionel Hampton All Stars
Lionel Hampton:Flying Home | Dreyfus Jazz Line | FDM 36735-2
Slam Stewart Trio
The Small Black Groups | Storyville | 4960523
The Complete Jazz At The Philharmonic On Verve 1944-1949 | Verve | 523893-2
Teddy Wilson Sextet
The Complete Associated Transcriptions,1944 | Storyville | STCD 8236

Stewart,Teddy | (dr)
Dizzy Gillespie And His Orchestra
Planet Jazz:Dizzy Gillespie | Planet Jazz | 2152069-2
Planet Jazz:Bebop | RCA | 2169650-2
Planet Jazz:Male Jazz Vocalists | Planet Jazz | 2169657-2
Sonny Stitt Quartet
Kaleidoscope | Original Jazz Classics | OJCCD 060-2(P 7077)

Steyer,Edith | (clsax)
Edith Steyer... Posterity Quintet
...On The Right Track | Jazz 4 Ever Records:Jazz Network | J4E 4745

Stibon,Franck | (p,synthvoc)
Richard Galliano Quartet
Spleen | Dreyfus Jazz Line | FDM 36513-9
Gallianissimo! The Best Of Richard Galliano | Dreyfus Jazz Line | FDM 36616-2
Richard Galliano Quintet
Spleen | Dreyfus Jazz Line | FDM 36513-9

Stich,Matthias | (as,b-cl,sopranino,ss,cl)
Matthias Stich & Whisper Not
Bach Lives!! | Satin Doll Productions | SDP 1018-1 CD
Matthias Stich Sevensenses
...mehrschichtig | Satin Doll Productions | SDP 1038-1 CD
Peter Kleindienst Group
Zeitwärts:Reime Vor Pisin | double moon | DMCD 1001-2

Sticker,Felix | (tb)
Daniel Messina Band
Imagenes | art-mode-records | 990014
Stickland,Clifton | (ts)
Jack Teagarden's Big Eight
Planet Jazz:Jack Teagarden | Planet Jazz | 2161236-2
Planet Jazz | Planet Jazz | 2169652-2
Stidham,Arbee | (gvoc)
Memphis Slim
Memphis Slim USA | Candid | CCD 79024
Stief,Bo | (b,b-gel-b)
Ben Webster Quartet
My Man-Live At The Montmartre | Steeplechase | SCCD 31008
Frank Rosolino Quartet
Frank Talks! | Storyville | STCD 8284
Just Friends
Nevertheless | IN+OUT Records | 7015-2
Jazz Unlimited | IN+OUT Records | 7017-2
Kenny Drew-Bo Stief Duo
Kenny Drew/Solo-Duo | Storyville | STCD 8274
Miles Davis With The Danish Radio Big Band
Aura | CBS | CK 63962
The Danish Radio Big Band
Aura | CBS | CK 63962
Stiffling,Thomas | (tpfl-h)
Thomas Stiffling Group
Stories | Jazz 4 Ever Records:Jazz Network | J4E 4756
Stiles,Danny | (tpfl-h)
Gerry Mulligan Concert Jazz Band
The Complete Verve Gerry Mulligan Concert Band | Verve | 9860613
J.J.Johnson And His Orchestra
Planet Jazz:J.J.Johnson | Planet Jazz | 2159974-2
Jack McDuff Quartet With Orchestra
Prelude:Jack McDuff Big Band | Prestige | PRCD 24283-2
Jimmy Smith With The Billy Byers Orchestra
Jimmy Smith:Best Of The Verve Years | Verve | 527950-2
Oscar Peterson With Orchestra
With Respect To Nat | Verve | 557486-2
Singers Unlimited With The Patrick Williams Orchestra
The Singers Unlimited:Magic Voices | MPS | 539130-2
Stillman,Loren | (as)
Loren Stillman Quartet
How Swee It Is | Nagel-Heyer | CD 2031
Stillman,Robert | (ts)
Kalifactors
An Introduction To Kalifactors | Fresh Sound Records | FSNT 143 CD
Stilo,Nicola | (alto-fl,fl,gp)
Chet Baker-Wolfgang Lackerschmid Trio
Chet Baker:The Legacy Vol.3:Why Shouldn't You Cry | Enja | ENJ-9337 2
Stimpson,George | (fr-h)
Singers Unlimited With Rob McConnell And The Boss Brass
The Singers Unlimited:Magic Voices | MPS | 539130-2
Sting | (b,el-b,vocg)
Joe Henderson Group
Porgy And Bess | Verve | 539048-2
John McLaughlin Group
The Promise | Verve | 529828-2
Stinkin' Rich | (vocturntables)
Jerry Granelli Group
Music Has Its Way With Me | Traumton Records | 4451-2
Stinnett,Jim | (b)
Steve Rochinski Quartet
Otherwise | Jardis Records | JRCD 20133
Steve Rochinski-Jim Stinnett
Otherwise | Jardis Records | JRCD 20133
Stinson,Albert | (bvoc)
Bobby Hutcherson Quartet
Herbie Hancock:The Complete Blue Note Sixties Sessions | Blue Note | 495569-2
Chico Hamilton Quintet
The Dealer | Impulse(MCA) | 547958-2
Chico Hamilton Sextet
The Dealer | Impulse(MCA) | 547958-2
Stitely,Jedd | (udu)
Patricia Barber Group
Modern Cool | Blue Note | 521811-2
Stitt,Sonny | (as,ts,bs,voc,takling,ts-solo,p)
Art Blakey Quartet
A Jazz Message | Impulse(MCA) | 547964-2
Dizzy Gillespie Septet
Stan Getz Highlights:The Best Of The Verve Years Vol.2 | Verve | 517330-2
Verve Jazz Masters 25:Stan Getz & Dizzy Gillespie | Verve | 521852-2
Stan Getz Highlights | Verve | 847430-2
Dizzy Gillespie Sextet
Verve Jazz Masters 50:Sonny Sitt | Verve | 527651-2
Dizzy Gillespie:Night In Tunisia | Dreyfus Jazz Line | FDM 36734-2
Dizzy Gillespie-Sonny Rollins-Sonny Stitt Sextet
Sonny Side Up | Verve | 521426-2
Dizzy Gillespie-Sonny Stitt Quintet
Verve Jazz Masters 10:Dizzy Gillespie | Verve | 516319-2
Ella Fitzgerald With The JATP All Stars
Ella Fitzgerald-First Lady Of Song | Verve | 517898-2
For The Love Of Ella Fitzgerald | Verve | 841765-2
For Musicians Only
Ultimate Stan Getz selected by Joe Henderson | Verve | 557532-2
Ultimate Dizzy Gillespie | Verve | 557535-2
For Musicians Only | Verve | 837435-2
Gene Ammons-Sonny Stitt Quartet
Gentle Jug Vol.3 | Prestige | PCD 24249-2
Gene Ammons-Sonny Stitt Quintet
Verve Jazz Masters 50:Sonny Sitt | Verve | 527651-2
Boss Tenors In Orbit!!! | Verve | 549371-2
God Bless Jug And Sonny | Prestige | PCD 11019-2
Gentle Jug Vol.3 | Prestige | PCD 24249-2
The Prestige Legacy Vol.2:Battles Of Saxes | Prestige | PCD 24252-2
Left Bank Encores | Prestige | PRCD 11022-2
J.J.Johnson Quintet
The J.J.Johnson Memorial Album | Prestige | PRCD 11025-2
Kenny Clarke And His 52nd Street Boys
Planet Jazz:Bebop | RCA | 2169650-2
Fats Navarro:Nostalgia | Dreyfus Jazz Line | FDM 36736-2
Miles Davis Quintet
Live In Stockholm | Dragon | DRCD 228
Modern Jazz Sextet
Verve Jazz Masters 50:Sonny Sitt | Verve | 527651-2
The Modern Jazz Sextet | Verve | 559834-2
Sonny Stitt And His Band
Kaleidoscope | Original Jazz Classics | OJCCD 060-2(P 7077)
Sonny Stitt And His West Coast Friends
Art Pepper:The Hollywood All-Star Sessions | Galaxy | 5GCD 4431-2
Sonny Stitt Orchestra
Verve Jazz Masters 50:Sonny Sitt | Verve | 527651-2
Sonny Stitt Quartet
The Art Of Saxophone | Laserlight | 24652
Verve Jazz Masters 50:Sonny Sitt | Verve | 527651-2
Sonny Stitt | Original Jazz Classics | OJCCD 009-2
Kaleidoscope | Original Jazz Classics | OJCCD 060-2(P 7077)
God Bless Jug And Sonny | Prestige | PCD 11019-2
The Jazz Giants Play Miles Davis:Milestones | Prestige | PCD 24225-2
The Prestige Legacy Vol.2:Battles Of Saxes | Prestige | PCD 24252-2
Brothers 4 | Prestige | PCD 24261-2
Goin' Down Slow | Prestige | PRCD 24276-2
Sonny Stitt Quintet
Atlantic Saxophones | Rhino | 8122-71256-2
Sonny Stitt | Original Jazz Classics | OJCCD 009-2
Kaleidoscope | Original Jazz Classics | OJCCD 060-2(P 7077)
Sonny Stitt Sextet
Verve Jazz Masters 50:Sonny Sitt | Verve | 527651-2
Milt Jackson Birthday Celebration | Fantasy | FANCD 6079-2
Sonny Stitt Trio
The Boss Men | Prestige | PCD 24253-2
Sonny Stitt With Orchestra
Goin' Down Slow | Prestige | PRCD 24276-2
Sonny Stitt With The Oscar Peterson Trio
Verve Jazz Masters 50:Sonny Sitt | Verve | 527651-2
Sonny Stitt With The Ralph Burns Orchestra
Verve Jazz Masters 50:Sonny Sitt | Verve | 527651-2
Sonny Stitt-Jack McDuff Quintet
Stitt Meets Brother Jack | Original Jazz Classics | OJCCD 703-2(P 7244)
Sonny Stitt-Sal Salvador Quintet
Newport Jazz Festival 1958,July 3rd-6th Vol.2:Mulligan The Main Man | Phontastic | NCD 8814
Stivin,Jiri | (dr,fl,as,recorder,whistle,b-cl,bs)
European Jazz Ensemble
20th Anniversary Tour | Konnex Records | KCD 5078
European Jazz Ensemble 25th Anniversary | Konnex Records | KCD 5100
Jiri Stivin-Ali Haurand
Just The Two Of Us | Konnex Records | KCD 5095
Paul Eßer-Gerd Dudek-Ali Haurand-Jiri Strivin
Jazz Und Lyrik:Schinderkarren Mit Buffet | Konnex Records | KCD 5108
Stivin-Van Den Broeck-Haurand
Bordertalk | Konnex Records | KCD 5068
Stock,Christian | (b)
Ray Pizzi Trio
One More Life | Bhakti Jazz | BR 29
Stockhausen,Markus | (fl-h,piccolo-tp,tp,fl,el-tp,synth)
Antoine Hervé Quintet
Invention Is You | Enja | ENJ-9398 2
Aparis
Aparis | ECM | 1404
Despite The Fire Fighters' Efforts... | ECM | 1496(517717-2)
Dhafer Youssef Group
Electric Sufi | Enja | ENJ-9412 2
Ferenc Snétberger-Markus Stockhausen
For My People | Enja | ENJ-9387 2
Gianlugi Trovesi Quartet With The WDR Big Band
Dedalo | Enja | ENJ-9419 2
Joachim Kühn And The Radio Philharmonie Hannover NDR With Jazz Soloists
Europeana | ACT | 9220-2
Markus Stockhausen Orchestra
Sol Mestizo:Markus Stockhausen Plays The Music Of Enrique Diaz | ACT | 9222-2
Markus Stockhausen Quartet
Cosi Lontano...Quasi Dentro | ECM | 1371
Karta | ECM | 1704(543035-2)
Joyosa | Enja | ENJ-9468 2
Rainer Brünninghaus Trio
Continuum | ECM | 1266(815679-2)
Ralph Towner Quintet
City Of Eyes | ECM | 1388
Stockhausen,Simon | (sax,synth,ss,keyboards)
Aparis
Aparis | ECM | 1404
Markus Stockhausen Orchestra
Sol Mestizo:Markus Stockhausen Plays The Music Of Enrique Diaz | ACT | 9222-2
Stockholm Session Strings |
Viktoria Tolstoy Group & Strings
Shining On You | ACT | 9701-2
Stockman,Eberhard | (ss,askeyboards)
Aparis
Despite The Fire Fighters' Efforts... | ECM | 1496(517717-2)
Stockton[Mason],Ann | (harp)
Ella Fitzgerald With The Nelson Riddle Orchestra
The Best Of The Song Books:The Ballads | Verve | 521867-2
Stöger,Dominik | (tb)
Lee Konitz With The Ed Partyka Jazz Orchestra
Dreams And Realities | Laika Records | 35101642
Stokes,Irving | (tpfl-h)
Nat Pierce Quartet
My Pal Basie | Jazz Connaisseur | JCCD 8904-2
Nat Pierce-Irving Stokes
My Pal Basie | Jazz Connaisseur | JCCD 8904-2
Stoll,Martin | (oboe)
Joachim Kühn And The Radio Philharmonie Hannover NDR With Jazz Soloists
Europeana | ACT | 9220-2
Stoller,Alvin | (bongos,drperc)
Anita O'Day And Her Combo
Pick Yourself Up | Verve | 517329-2
Anita O'Day With The Buddy Bregman Orchestra
Pick Yourself Up | Verve | 517329-2
Verve Jazz Masters 49:Anita O'Day | Verve | 527653-2
Art Tatum Quartet
Art Tatum-The Complete Pablo Group Masterpieces | Pablo | 6 PACD 4401-2
Ben Webster All Stars
King Of The Tenors | Verve | 519806-2
Ben Webster And His Orchestra
Verve Jazz Masters 43:Ben Webster | Verve | 525431-2
Ben Webster With The Oscar Peterson Quartet
King Of The Tenors | Verve | 519806-2
Ultimate Ben Webster selected by James Carter | Verve | 557537-2
Benny Carter And His Orchestra
Further Definitions/Additions To Further Definotions | Impulse(MCA) | 951229-2
Billie Holiday And Her All Stars
Verve Jazz Masters 12:Billie Holiday | Verve | 519825-2
Verve Jazz Masters 47:Billie Holiday Sings Standards | Verve | 527650-2
Songs For Distingué Lovers | Verve | 539056-2
Billie Holiday And Her Band
Verve Jazz Masters 47:Billie Holiday Sings Standards | Verve | 527650-2
Billie Holiday And Her Orchestra
Solitude | Verve | 519810-2
Billy May And His Orchestra
Billy May's Big Fat Brass/Bill's Bag | Capitol | 535206-2
Billy May And His Orchestra With Members Of The Jimmy Lunceford Orchestra
Great Swing Classics In Hi-Fi | Capitol | 521223-2
Buddy Bregman And His Orchestra
Swinging Kicks | Verve | 559514-2
Coleman Hawkins And Ben Webster With The Oscar Peterson Quartet
Coleman Hawkins Encounters Ben Webster | Verve | 521427-2
Verve Jazz Masters 43:Coleman Hawkins | Verve | 521856-2
Verve Jazz Masters 43:Ben Webster | Verve | 525431-2
Verve Jazz Masters Vol.60:The Collection | Verve | 529866-2
Ultimate Coleman Hawkins selected by Sonny Rollins | Verve | 557538-2
Coleman Hawkins And Confreres
Coleman Hawkins And Confreres | Verve | 835255-2 PMS
Coleman Hawkins With The Oscar Peterson Quartet
Verve Jazz Masters 43:Coleman Hawkins | Verve | 521856-2
The Genius Of Coleman Hawkins | Verve | 539065-2
Ultimate Coleman Hawkins selected by Sonny Rollins | Verve | 557538-2
Ella Fitzgerald And Her All Stars
The Best Of The Song Books:The Ballads | Verve | 521867-2
Love Songs:The Best Of The Song Books | Verve | 531762-2
Ella Fitzgerald Sings The Duke Ellington Songbook | Verve | 559248-2
For The Love Of Ella Fitzgerald | Verve | 841765-2
Ella Fitzgerald And Her Quintet
Verve Jazz Masters 46:Ella Fitzgerald-The Jazz Sides | Verve | 527655-2
Ella Fitzgerald And Her Sextet
Ella Fitzgerald-First Lady Of Song | Verve | 517898-2
The Best Of The Song Books | Verve | 519804-2
Ella Fitzgerald And Louis Armstrong With Dave Barbour And His Orchestra
Ella Fitzgerald:Mr.Paganini | Dreyfus Jazz Line | FDM 36741-2
Ella Fitzgerald And The Paul Smith Quartet
The Best Of The Song Books | Verve | 519804-2
Verve Jazz Masters 6:Ella Fitzgerald | Verve | 519822-2
Verve Jazz Masters 46:Ella Fitzgerald-The Jazz Sides | Verve | 527655-2
Ella Fitzgerald With Frank De Vol And His Orchestra
Get Happy! | Verve | 523321-2
Ella Fitzgerald With Paul Weston And His Orchestra
Love Songs:The Best Of The Song Books | Verve | 531762-2
Ella Fitzgerald Sings The Irving Berlin Song Book | Verve | 543830-2
Ella Fitzgerald With The Billy May Orchestra
Ella Fitzgerald-First Lady Of Song | Verve | 517898-2
The Best Of The Song Books | Verve | 519804-2
Verve Jazz Masters 6:Ella Fitzgerald | Verve | 519822-2
The Best Of The Song Books:The Ballads | Verve | 521867-2
Verve Jazz Masters 46:Ella Fitzgerald-The Jazz Sides | Verve | 527655-2
Love Songs:The Best Of The Song Books | Verve | 531762-2
Ella Fitzgerald Sings The Harold Arlen Song Book | Verve | 589108-2
For The Love Of Ella Fitzgerald | Verve | 841765-2
Ella Fitzgerald With The Buddy Bregman Orchestra
Ella Fitzgerald-First Lady Of Song | Verve | 517898-2
The Best Of The Song Books:The Ballads | Verve | 521867-2
Love Songs:The Best Of The Song Books | Verve | 531762-2
Ella Fitzgerald Sings The Cole Porter Songbook | Verve | 537257-2
Ella Fitzgerald Sings The Rodgers And Hart Song Book | Verve | 537258-2
For The Love Of Ella Fitzgerald | Verve | 841765-2
Ella Fitzgerald With The Frank DeVol Orchestra
Get Happy! | Verve | 523321-2
Ella Fitzgerald With The Nelson Riddle Orchestra
Ella Fitzgerald-First Lady Of Song | Verve | 517898-2
The Best Of The Song Books | Verve | 519804-2
The Best Of The Song Books:The Ballads | Verve | 521867-2
Oh Lady Be Good:The Best Of The Gershwin Songbook | Verve | 529581-2
Love Songs:The Best Of The Song Books | Verve | 531762-2
For The Love Of Ella Fitzgerald | Verve | 841765-2
Ella Fitzgerald With The Oscar Peterson Quartet And Ben Webster
Verve Jazz Masters 43:Ben Webster | Verve | 525431-2
Ella Fitzgerald With The Paul Smith Quartet
Ella Fitzgerald-First Lady Of Song | Verve | 517898-2
Verve Jazz Masters 20:Introducing | Verve | 519853-2
The Best Of The Song Books:The Ballads | Verve | 521867-2
Ella Fitzgerald Sings The Rodgers And Hart Song Book | Verve | 537258-2
Ella Fitzgerald With The Paul Weston Orchestra
Get Happy! | Verve | 523321-2
Erroll Garner Trio
The Story Of Jazz Piano | Laserlight | 24653
Erroll Garner:Trio | Dreyfus Jazz Line | FDM 36719-2
Harry Edison Quartet
The Complete Unedited 'Sweets At The Haig' 1953 Recordings | Fresh Sound Records | FSR CD 345
Harry Sweets Edison Sextet
The Soul Of Ben Webster | Verve | 527475-2
JATP All Stars
The Complete Jazz At The Philharmonic On Verve 1944-1949 | Verve | 523893-2
June Christy With The Pete Rugolo Orchestra
Something Cool(The Complete Mono & Stereo Versions) | Capitol | 534069-2
Maynard Ferguson And His Orchestra
Verve Jazz Masters 52:Maynard Ferguson | Verve | 529905-2
Mel Tormé With The Billy May Orchestra
Mel Tormé Goes South Of The Border With Billy May | Verve | 589517-2
Nat King Cole With The Billy May Orchestra
Nat King Cole:For Sentimental Reasons | Dreyfus Jazz Line | FDM 36740-2
Oscar Peterson Quartet
Verve Jazz Masters 37:Oscar Peterson Plays Broadway | Verve | 516893-2
Peggy Lee With The Benny Goodman Orchestra
Peggy Lee & Benny Goodman:The Complete Recordings 1941-1947 | CBS | C2K 65686
Pete Rugolo And His Orchestra
Thriller/Richard Diamon(Original Jazz Scores From 2 Classics TV Series) | Fresh Sound Records | FSCD 2015
Phineas Newborn Jr. With Dennis Farnon And His Orchestra
While My Lady Sleeps | RCA | 2185157-2
Roy Eldridge Quintet
The Complete Verve Roy Eldridge Studio Sessions | Verve | 9861278
Roy Eldridge-Alvin Stoller
The Complete Verve Roy Eldridge Studio Sessions | Verve | 9861278
Roy Eldridge-Benny Carter Quintet
The Complete Verve Roy Eldridge Studio Sessions | Verve | 9861278
Tommy Dorsey And His Orchestra
Planet Jazz:Tommy Dorsey | Planet Jazz | 2159972-2
Van Alexander Orchestra
Home Of Happy Feet/Swing! Staged For Sound! | Capitol | 535211-2
Stolterfoht,Jan | (g)
Andreas Willers Group
Andreas Willers & Friends Play Jimi Hendrix:Experience | Nabel Records:Jazz Network | CD 4665
Stone,Bob | (b)
Harry James And His Orchestra
Trumpet Blues:The Best Of Harry James | Capitol | 521224-2
Stone,Butch | (bs,reedsvoc)
Les Brown And His Orchestra
Great Swing Classics In Hi-Fi | Capitol | 521223-2
Van Alexander Orchestra
Home Of Happy Feet/Swing! Staged For Sound! | Capitol | 535211-2
Stone,Cameron L. | (cello)
Herbie Hancock Group With String Quartet
Herbie Hancock The New Standards | Verve | 527715-2
Herbie Hancock Group With String Quartet,Woodwinds And Brass
Herbie Hancock The New Standards | Verve | 527715-2
Stone,Fred | (tpfl-h)
Duke Ellington And His Orchestra
New Orleans Suite | Rhino | 812273670-2
Stone,Gene | (dr)
Prince Lasha Quartet
The Cry | Original Jazz Classics | OJCCD 1945-2(S 7610)
Prince Lasha Quintet
The Cry | Original Jazz Classics | OJCCD 1945-2(S 7610)
Stone,Jesse | (accordeon,parr)
Al Sears And His Orchestra
Sear-iously | Bear Family Records | BCD 15668 AH
Stoneburn,Sid | (ascl)
Louis Armstrong And His Orchestra
Louis Armstrong:Swing That Music | Laserlight | 36056
Louis Armstrong:C'est Si Bon | Dreyfus Jazz Line | FDM 36730-2
Tommy Dorsey And His Clambake Seven
Planet Jazz:Tommy Dorsey | Planet Jazz | 2159972-2
Planet Jazz:Swing | Planet Jazz | 2169651-2
Tommy Dorsey And His Orchestra

Planet Jazz:Tommy Dorsey | Planet Jazz | 2159972-2

Stoner,Martin | (v)
A Band Of Friends
Wynton Marsalis Quartet With Strings | CBS | CK 68921

Stonzek,Morris | (v)
Freddie Hubbard Orchestra
The Body And The Soul | Impulse(MCA) | 951183-2

Stoor,Bosse | (dr)
Kettil Ohlsson Quintet
Lars Gullin 1953,Vol.2:Moden Sounds | Dragon | DRCD 234
Lars Gullin Quartet
Lars Gullin 1953,Vol.2:Moden Sounds | Dragon | DRCD 234

Storaas,Vigleik | (p)
Nordic Quartet
Nordic Quartet | ECM | 1553

Stordahl,Axel | (arrld)
Frank Sinatra With Orchestra
Planet Jazz:Frank Sinatra & Tommy Dorsey | Planet Jazz | 2152067-2
Tommy Dorsey And His Orchestra
Planet Jazz:Frank Sinatra & Tommy Dorsey | Planet Jazz | 2152067-2
Frank Sinatra And The Tommy Dorsey Orchestra | RCA | 2668701-2

Storer,Margaret | (b)
Milt Jackson And His Orchestra
Reverence And Compassion | Reprise | 9362-45204-2

Störmer,Friedrich | (b)
Peter Ehwald Trio
Away With Words:The Music Of John Scofield | Jazz Haus Musik | JHM 0128 CD

Storne,Jean | (b)
Django Reinhardt Quartet
Django Reinhardt:Echoes Of France | Dreyfus Jazz Line | FDM 36726-2

Story,Nat | (tb)
Ella Fitzgerald And Her Famous Orchestra
The Radio Years 1940 | Jazz Unlimited | JUCD 2065
Ella Fitzgerald And Her Orchestra
Jazz Collection:Ella Fitzgerald | Laserlight | 24397
Ella Fitzgerald With The Chick Webb Orchestra
Jazz Collection:Ella Fitzgerald | Laserlight | 24397

Stötter,Claus | (fl-h,tpalt-h)
Abdullah Ibrahim With The NDR Big Band
Ekapa Lodumo | TipToe | TIP-888840 2
Axis
Axis | Jazz 4 Ever Records:Jazz Network | J4E 4735
Claus Stötter's Nevertheless
Die Entdeckung Der Banane | Jazz 'n' Arts Records | JNA 1403
Frank Kuruc Band
Limits No Limits | Edition Musikat | EDM 023
Heinz Sauer Quartet With The NDR Big Band
NDR Big Band-Bravissimo | ACT | 9232-2
Klaus König Orchestra
The Heart Project | Enja | ENJ-9338 2
NDR Big Band
The Theatre Of Kurt Weil | ACT | 9234-2
Oscar Brown Jr. with The NDR Big Band
Live Every Minute | Minor Music | 801071
Pee Wee Ellis & NDR Bigband
What You Like | Minor Music | 801064
Rainer Tempel Band
Suite Ellington | Jazz 'n' Arts Records | JNA 0401
Thomas Horstmann-Martin Wiedmann Group
Decade | Factory Outlet Records | WO 95001

Stötzler,Olaf | (g)
Andreas Maile Quartet
Mailensteine | Satin Doll Productions | SDP 1022-1 CD

Stötzner,Ernst | (voice)
Heiner Goebbels/Heiner Müller
Der Mann Im Fahrstuhl | ECM | 1369(837110-2)

Stout,Ron | (tpfl-h)
Buddy Childers Big Band
It's What Happening Now! | Candid | CCD 79749
Vic Lewis West Coast All Stars
Me And You! | Candid | CCD 79739

Stouthamer,Paul | (cello)
The Collective 3 +
The Collective 3 + | true muze | TUMU CD 9802

Stovall,Don | (as)
Big Sid Catlett And His Orchestra
The Small Black Groups | Storyville | 4960523
Sammy Price Septet
Jazz:The Essential Collection Vol.3 | IN+OUT Records | 78013-2

Stowell,John | (cymbals,log-dr,12-string-g,thumb-p)
John Stowell-Bebo Ferra
Elle | Jardis Records | JRCD 20028
Jazz Guitar Highlights 1 | Jardis Records | JRCD 20141

Stoykov,Teodossi | (b)
Lajos Dudas Quartet
Jubilee Edition | double moon | CHRDM 71020
Lajos Dudas Quintet
Jubilee Edition | double moon | CHRDM 71020
Lajos Dudas Trio
Jubilee Edition | double moon | CHRDM 71020

Strahl,Bob | (b)
Gene Krupa And His Orchestra
Mullenium | CBS | CK 65678

Straight Talk |
Straight Talk
Pure | Jazz 4 Ever Records:Jazz Network | J4E 4719

Strait,Todd | (drperc)
Jay McShann Quintet
What A Wonderful World | Groove Note | GN 1005(180gr-Pressung)
What A Wonderful World | Groove Note | GRV 1005-2

Strakhof,Dirk | (bel-b)
Batoru
Tree Of Sounds | Nabel Records:Jazz Network | CD 4685
Céline Rudolph And Her Trio
Paintings | Nabel Records:Jazz Network | CD 4661
Book Of Travels | Nabel Records:Jazz Network | CD 4672
Dirk Strakhof & Batoru
Arabesque | Nabel Records:Jazz Network | CD 4696
Erika Rojo & Tim Sund
Das Lied | Nabel Records:Jazz Network | CD 4684
Nils Petter Molvaer Group
Elegy For Africa | Nabel Records:Jazz Network | CD 4678
Volker Kottenhahn Trio
Out Of Print | Nabel Records:Jazz Network | CD 4680

Strandberg,Bo | (tpfl-h)
Tim Hagans With Norrbotten Big Band
Future Miles | ACT | 9235-2

Strange,Pete | (tb)
Great British Jazz Band
The Great British Jazz Band:Jubilee | Candid | CCD 79720
The Great British Jazz Band
A British Jazz Odyssey | Candid | CCD 79740

Strasser,Hugo | (as,bscl)
Brocksi-Sextett
Drums Boogie | Bear Family Records | BCD 15988 AH
Shot Gun Boogie | Bear Family Records | BCD 16277 AH
Delle Haensch Jump Combo
Deutsches Jazz Fesival 1954/1955 | Bear Family Records | BCD 15430
Freddie Brocksieper And His Boys
Freddie's Boogie Blues | Bear Family Records | BCD 16388 AH
Freddie Brocksieper Orchester
Shot Gun Boogie | Bear Family Records | BCD 16277 AH
Freddie Brocksieper Quintett
Shot Gun Boogie | Bear Family Records | BCD 16277 AH
Hugo Strasser Combo
Deutsches Jazz Fesival 1954/1955 | Bear Family Records | BCD 15430
Kurt Edelhagen All Stars Und Solisten
Deutsches Jazz Fesival 1954/1955 | Bear Family Records | BCD 15430

Strasser,Joe | (dr)
Alex Norris Quintet
A New Beginning | Fresh Sound Records | FSNT 081 CD

Strasser,Michael | (dr)
Axel Zwingenberger-Jay McShann Quartet
Kansas City Boogie Jam | Vagabond | VRCD 8.00027
Champion Jack Dupree Group
Champ's Housewarming | Vagabond | VRCD 8.88014
Champion Jack Dupree-Axel Zwingenberger Group
Axel Zwingenberger And The Friends Of Boogie Woogie Vol.7: Champion Jack Dupree Sings Blues Classics | Vagabond | VRCD 8.92018

Stratton,Don | (tp)
Elliot Lawrence And His Orchestra
The Elliot Lawrence Big Band Swings Cohn & Kahn | Fantasy | FCD 24761-2

Strauch,Oliver | (dr)
Derrick James & Wesley 'G' Quintet
Two Sides To Every Story | Jardis Records | JRCD 20137
Lee Konitz With The Oliver Strauch Group & Peter Decker
Lee Konitz With Oliver Strauch Group & Peter Decker | Edition Collage | EC 497-2
Louis Stewart-Heiner Franz Quartet
I Wished On The Moon | Jardis Records | JRCD 20027
Jazz Guitar Highlights 1 | Jardis Records | JRCD 20141

Strayhorn,Billy | (arr,comp,ld,celeste,p,narration)
Ben Webster With Orchestra And Strings
Music For Loving:Ben Webster With Strings | Verve | 527774-2
Ultimate Ben Webster selected by James Carter | Verve | 557537-2
Ben Webster With The Billy Strayhorn Trio
Music For Loving:Ben Webster With Strings | Verve | 527774-2
Billy Strayhorn Orchestra
Johnny Hodges With Billy Strayhorn And The Orchestra | Verve | 557543-2
Duke Ellington And Count Basie With Their Orchestras
First Time! | CBS | CK 65571
Duke Ellington And His Famous Orchestra
Duke Ellington:The Blanton-Webster Band | Bluebird | 21 13181-2
Planet Jazz:Duke Ellington | Planet Jazz | 2152053-2
Planet Jazz Sampler | Planet Jazz | 2152326-2
Planet Jazz:Big Bands | Planet Jazz | 2169649-2
Jazz:The Essential Collection Vol.2 | IN+OUT Records | 78012-2
Duke Ellington:Ko-Ko | Dreyfus Jazz Line | FDM 36717-2
Duke Ellington And His Orchestra
Carnegie Hall Concert December 1944 | Prestige | 2PCD 24073-2
Carnegie Hall Concert January 1946 | Prestige | 2PCD 24074-2
Carnegie Hall Concert December 1947 | Prestige | 2PCD 24075-2
Carnegie Hall Concert January 1943 | Prestige | 2PCD 34004-2
Ellington '55 | Capitol | 520135-2
Afro-Bossa | Reprise | 9362 47876-2
Anatomy Of A Murder | CBS | CK 65569
Duke Ellington-Billy Strayhorn Duo
Planet Jazz:Duke Ellington | Planet Jazz | 2152053-2
Highlights From The Duke Ellington Centennial Edition | RCA | 2663672-2
Duke Ellington-Billy Strayhorn Quintet
Great Times! | Original Jazz Classics | OJC20 108-2(RLP 475)
Duke Ellington-Billy Strayhorn Trio
Great Times! | Original Jazz Classics | OJC20 108-2(RLP 475)
Ella Fitzgerald With The Duke Ellington Orchestra
The Best Of The Song Books:The Ballads | Verve | 521867-2
Ella Fitzgerald Sings The Duke Ellington Songbook | Verve | 559248-2
Esquire All-American Award Winners
Best Of The Complete RCA Victor Recordings | RCA | 2663636-2
Highlights From The Duke Ellington Centennial Edition | RCA | 2663672-2
Johnny Hodges And His Band
Verve Jazz Masters 35:Johnny Hodges | Verve | 521857-2
Johnny Hodges And The Ellington All-Stars Without Duke
Verve Jazz Masters 35:Johnny Hodges | Verve | 521857-2
Johnny Hodges And The Ellington Men
Verve Jazz Masters 35:Johnny Hodges | Verve | 521857-2
Johnny Hodges Orchestra
Side By Side | Verve | 521405-2
The Soul Of Ben Webster | Verve | 527475-2
Johnny Hodges With Billy Strayhorn And The Duke Ellington Orchestra
Verve Jazz Masters 35:Johnny Hodges | Verve | 521857-2
Lena Horne With The Lennie Hayton Orchestra
Planet Jazz:Lena Horne | Planet Jazz | 2165373-2
Leonard Feather's Esquire All-Americans
Louis Armstrong:C'est Si Bon | Dreyfus Jazz Line | FDM 36730-2
Rex Stewart And His Orchestra
Planet Jazz:Ben Webster | RCA | 2165368-2
Sathima Bea Benjamin Group
A Morning In Paris | Enja | ENJ-9309 2

Strazzeri,Frank | (pp-solo)
Bill Perkins Quintet
Swing Spring | Candid | CCD 79752
Peggy Lee With The Quincy Jones Orchestra
Blues Cross Country | Capitol | 520088-2
Vic Lewis West Coast All Stars
Vic Lewis Presenting A Celebration Of Contemporary West Coast Jazz | Candid | CCD 79711/12

Street,Ben | (b)
Andrew Rathbun Group
Jade | Fresh Sound Records | FSNT 076 CD
Frank Carlberg Group
Variations On A Summer Day | Fresh Sound Records | FSNT 083 CD
Kurt Rosenwinkel Quartet
The Next Stop | Verve | 549162-2
Kurt Rosenwinkel Quintet
The Enemies Of Energy | Verve | 543042-2
Michael Kanan Trio
Convergence | Fresh Sound Records | FSNT 055 CD
The Gentleman Is A Dope | Fresh Sound Records | FSNT 147 CD
Perico Sambeat Quartet
Friendship | ACT | 9421-2
Perico Sambeat Quintet
Friendship | ACT | 9421-2
Taylor Hawkins Group
Wake Up Call | Fresh Sound Records | FSCD 145 CD

Street,Karen | (accordeon,voicets)
Mike Westbrook Orchestra
Bar Utopia-A Big Band Cabaret | Enja | ENJ-9333 2

street-noise |
Peter Bolte
Trio | Jazz Haus Musik | JHM 0095 CD

Streichergruppe des Radio-Sinfonie-Orchesters Frankfurt |
HR Big Band With Marjorie Barnes And Frits Landesbergen And Strings
Swinging Christmas | hr music.de | hrmj 012-02 CD

Strempel,Sebastian | (tpfl-h)
Al Porcino Big Band
Al Porcino Big Band Live! | Organic Music | ORGM 9717
Lee Konitz With The Ed Partyka Jazz Orchestra
Dreams And Realities | Laika Records | 35101642

Strenger,Yevgenia | (v)
Kevin Mahogany With The Bob James Trio, Kirk Whalum And Strings
My Romance | Warner | 9362-47025-2

Stricker,Felix | (tb)
Quique Sinesi & Daniel Messina With Guests
Prioridad A la Emoción | art-mode-records | AMR 21061

Strickfaden,Charles | (as,bs,cl,ts,oboereeds)
Frank Sinatra With Orchestra
Planet Jazz:Frank Sinatra & Tommy Dorsey | Planet Jazz | 2152067-2
Paul Whiteman And His Orchestra
Planet Jazz:Jack Teagarden | Planet Jazz | 2161236-2
Planet Jazz:Jazz Trumpet | Planet Jazz | 2169654-2
Jazz:The Essential Collection Vol.3 | IN+OUT Records | 78013-2

Strickland,Marcus | (b-cl,ssts)
Roy Haynes Quartet
Fountain Of Youth | Dreyfus Jazz Line | FDM 36663-2

Strickland,Stan | (fl,ts,ssvoc)
Marty Ehrlich Quintet
New York Child | Enja | ENJ-9025 2

Strien,Ary | (accordeon)
Schlothauer's Maniacs
Maniakisses | Timescrapper | TSCR 9811

Striepens,Ansgar | (tbld)
Ansgar Striepens Quintet
Dreams And Realities | Laika Records | 35101642
John Abercrombie With The Ansgar Striepens Quintet
Dreams And Realities | Laika Records | 35101642
Lee Konitz With The Ed Partyka Jazz Orchestra
Dreams And Realities | Laika Records | 35101642
Wayne Bartlett With The Thomas Hufschmidt Group
Tokyo Blues | Laika Records | 35101212

String Orchestra |
Singers Unlimited With The Robert Farnon Orchestra
The Singers Unlimited:Magic Voices | MPS | 539130-2

String Quartet |
Bud Shank And Trombones
Cool Fool | Fresh Sound Records | FSR CD 507

String Section |
Keith Jarrett Group With Strings
Expectations | CBS | C2K 65900
Keith Jarrett With Strings
Expectations | CBS | C2K 65900

String Thing |
String Thing
String Thing:Alles Wird Gut | MicNic Records | MN 2
String Thing:Turtifix | MicNic Records | MN 4

Strings |
Al Jarreau With Band
We Got By | Reprise | 7599-27222-2
Anita O'Day With The Buddy Bregman Orchestra
Pick Yourself Up | Verve | 517329-2
Anthony Ortega With String Orchestra
Earth Dance | Fresh Sound Records | FSR-CD 325
Antonio Carlos Jobim With The Claus Ogerman Orchestra
Verve Jazz Masters 13:Antonio Carlos Jobim | Verve | 516409-2
The Composer Of 'Desafinado' Plays | Verve | 521431-2
Astrud Gilberto With Antonio Carlos Jobim And The Marty Paich Orchestra
The Antonio Carlos Jobim Songbook | Verve | 525472-2
Astrud Gilberto With The Don Sebesky Orchestra
Verve Jazz Masters 9:Astrud Gilberto | Verve | 519824-2
Ben Webster With Orchestra And Strings
Music For Loving:Ben Webster With Strings | Verve | 527774-2
Billie Holiday With Gordon Jenkins And His Orchestra
Billie's Love Songs | Nimbus Records | NI 2000
Billie Holiday With Toots Camarata And His Orchestra
Billie's Love Songs | Nimbus Records | NI 2000
Bud Shank With The Len Mercer Strings
Midnight Blue(The [Be]witching Hour) | Blue Note | 854365-2
Cal Tjader's Orchestra
Verve Jazz Masters 39:Cal Tjader | Verve | 521858-2
Talkin Verve/Roots Of Acid Jazz:Cal Tjader | Verve | 531562-2
Cannonball Adderley Group
Phenix | Fantasy | FCD 79004-2
Charlie Haden Quartet West
Always Say Goodbye | Verve | 521501-2
Chet Baker With String-Orchestra And Voices
Chet Baker With Fifty Italian Strings | Original Jazz Classics | OJC20 492-2(JLP 921)
Clifford Brown With Strings
Clifford Brown-Max Roach:Alone Together-The Best Of The Mercury Years | Verve | 526373-2
Verve Jazz Masters 44:Clifford Brown and Max Roach | Verve | 528109-2
Brownie-The Complete EmArCy Recordings Of Clifford Brown | EmArCy | 838306-2
Coleman Hawkins Quintet With Strings
Body And Soul Revisited | GRP | GRP 16272
Coleman Hawkins With The Glenn Osser Orchestra
Midnight Blue(The [Be]witching Hour) | Blue Note | 854365-2
Dave Grusin Group
Migration | GRP | GRP 95922
Dave Grusin Orchestra
Two For The Road:The Music Of Henry Mancini | GRP | GRP 98652
Diane Schuur Trio With Orchestra And Strings
In Tribute | GRP | GRP 20062
Diane Schuur With Orchestra
Love Songs | GRP | GRP 97032
The Best Of Diane Schuur | GRP | GRP 98882
Diane Schuur With Orchestra And Strings
The Best Of Diane Schuur | GRP | GRP 98882
Diane Schuur With The Dave Grusin Orchestra
The Best Of Diane Schuur | GRP | GRP 98882
Dinah Washington With The Belford Hendricks Orchestra
What A Diff'rence A Day Makes! | Verve | 543300-2
Duke Ellington With Tommy Dorsey And His Orchestra
Highlights From The Duke Ellington Centennial Edition | RCA | 2663672-2
Eddie Harris Group
The Best Of Eddie Harris | Atlantic | 7567-81370-2
Ella Fitzgerald With Paul Weston And His Orchestra
Love Songs:The Best Of The Song Books | Verve | 531762-2
Ella Fitzgerald With The Nelson Riddle Orchestra
The Best Of The Song Books | Verve | 519804-2
Frank Castenier Group
For You,For Me For Evermore | EmArCy | 9814976
Gene Ammons Sextet With Strings
Fine And Mellow | Prestige | PRCD 24281-2
George Benson With Orchestra
Verve Jazz Masters 21:George Benson | Verve | 521861-2
George Benson With The Don Sebesky Orchestra
Verve Jazz Masters 21:George Benson | Verve | 521861-2
Joe Williams With The Frank Hunter Orchestra
Planet Jazz:Joe Williams | Planet Jazz | 2165370-2
Lena Horne With The Lennie Hayton Orchestra
Planet Jazz:Lena Horne | Planet Jazz | 2165373-2
Lisa Ekdahl With The Salvador Poe Quartet, Strings And Guests
Lisa Ekdahl Sings Salvadore Poe | RCA | 2179681-2
Louis Armstrong And His Orchestra
What A Wonderful World | MCA | MCD 01876
Louis Armstrong With The Gordon Jenkins Orchestra
Ambassador Louis Armstrong Vol.17:Moments To Remember(1952-1956) | Ambassador | CLA 1917
Marcos Valle With Orchestra
Samba '68 | Verve | 559516-2
Nat King Cole And George Shearing With Orchestra
Midnight Blue(The [Be]witching Hour) | Blue Note | 854365-2
Nat King Cole Trio With Strings
Nat King Cole:For Sentimental Reasons | Dreyfus Jazz Line | FDM 36740-2
Nat King Cole With Orchestra
Nat King Cole:Route 66 | Dreyfus Jazz Line | FDM 36716-2
Oscar Peterson Quintet With Strings
Jazz Dance | Original Jazz Classics | OJCCD 1002-2(1210890)
Paul Desmond Orchestra
Planet Jazz:Jazz Saxophone | Planet Jazz | 2169653-2
Paul Desmond With Strings
The Ballad Of Paul Desmond | RCA | 21429372
Planet Jazz:Paul Desmond | Planet Jazz | 2152061-2
Desmond Blue | RCA | 2663898-2
Peggy Lee With The Quincy Jones Orchestra

INTERPRETENVERZEICHNIS

Blues Cross Country | Capitol | 520088-2
Roy Eldridge And His Orchestra With Strings
The Complete Verve Roy Eldridge Studio Sessions | Verve | 9861278
Roy Eldridge With The Russell Garcia Orchestra
The Complete Verve Roy Eldridge Studio Sessions | Verve | 9861278
Sarah Vaughan And Her Band
Songs Of The Beatles | Atlantic | 16037-2
Sarah Vaughan And The Count Basie Orchestra
Ballads | Roulette | 537561-2
Sarah Vaughan With Orchestra
!Viva! Vaughan | Mercury | 549374-2
Sarah Vaughan With The Benny Carter Orchestra
Ballads | Roulette | 537561-2
Sarah Vaughan With The Hal Mooney Orchestra
It's A Man's World | Mercury | 589487-2
Sarah Vaughan With The Jimmy Jones Orchestra
Ballads | Roulette | 537561-2
Jazz Profile | Blue Note | 823517-2
Sarah Vaughan With The Quincy Jones Orchestra
Jazz In Paris:Sarah Vaughan-Vaughan And Violins | EmArCy | 065004-2
4 By 4:Ella Fitzgerald/Sarah Vaughan/Billie Holiday/Dinah Washington | Verve | 559693-2
Shirley Horn With Strings
Here's To Life | Verve | 511879-2
Silje Nergard Group with Strings
Nightwatch | EmArCy | 9865648
Stan Getz With The Eddie Sauter Orchestra
A Life In Jazz:A Musical Biography | Verve | 535119-2
Stan Getz Highlights | Verve | 847430-2
Stan Getz With The Michel Legrand Orchestra
Stan Getz Highlights | Verve | 847430-2
Tommy Dorsey And His Orchestra
Planet Jazz:Tommy Dorsey | Planet Jazz | 2159972-2
Planet Jazz:Jazz Greatest Hits | Planet Jazz | 2169648-2
Viktoria Tolstoy With The Esbjörn Svensson Trio
Viktoria Tolstoy:White Russian | Blue Note | 821220-2
Vince Jones With Orchestra
Come In Spinner | Intuition Records | INT 3052-2

Strings & Brass |
Laura Fygi Meets Michel Legrand
Watch What Happens | Mercury | 534598-2

Strings,Woodwinds |
Chet Baker With The Radio Orchestra Hannover(NDR)
My Favourite Songs: The Last Great Concert Vol.1 | Enja | ENJ-5097 2
The Last Concert Vol.I+II | Enja | ENJ-6074 22

Stripling,Byron | (fl-h,tpvoc)
Buck Clayton Swing Band
Swing's The Village | Nagel-Heyer | CD 5004
Blues Of Summer | Nagel-Heyer | NH 1011
Byron Stripling And Friends
If I Could Be With You | Nagel-Heyer | NH 1010
Byron Stripling Quartet
Byron,Get On Free | Nagel-Heyer | CD 2016
Byron Stripling Quintet
Byron,Get On Free | Nagel-Heyer | CD 2016
Byron Stripling Sextet
Striplingnow! | Nagel-Heyer | CD 2002
Byron,Get On Free | Nagel-Heyer | CD 2016
Byron Stripling Trio
Byron,Get On Free | Nagel-Heyer | CD 2016
Dee Dee Bridgewater With Big Band
Dear Ella | Verve | 539102-2
Diane Schuur With The Count Basie Orchestra
The Best Of Diane Schuur | GRP | GRP 98882
Freddie Cole
Jazzin' Vol.2: The Music Of Stevie Wonder | Fantasy | FANCD 6088-2
Freddy Cole With Band
To The End Of The Earth | Fantasy | FCD 9675-2
GRP All-Star Big Band
GRP All-Star Big Band:Live! | GRP | GRP 97402
Sonny Rollins Quintet With Brass
Old Flames | Milestone | MCD 9215-2
The New York Allstars
We Love You,Louis! | Nagel-Heyer | CD 029
Oh,Yeah! The New York Allstars Play More Music Of Louis Armstrong | Nagel-Heyer | CD 046
The Second Sampler | Nagel-Heyer | NHR SP 6

Ströble,Tim | (cello)
Rainer Tempel Band
Suite Ellington | Jazz 'n' Arts Records | JNA 0401

Ströer,Ernst | (perc)
Klaus Doldinger & Passport
Down To Earth | Warner | 4509-93207-2
Klaus Doldinger's Passport
Klaus Doldinger Passport Live | Warner | 8573-84132-2
Balance Of Happiness | Warner | 9031-71233-2
Blues Roots | Warner | 9031-75417-2
Klaus Doldinger's Passport With Johnny 'Clyde' Copeland
Blues Roots | Warner | 9031-75417-2

Stroman,Clarence 'Scoby' | (dr)
Roland Alexander Quintet
Ronnie Mathews-Roland Alexander-Freddie Hubbard | Prestige | PRCD 24271-2

Stromer,Rckhard | (drvoc)
Ralph Abelein Group
Mr. B's Time Machine | Satin Doll Productions | SDP 1042-1 CD

Strong,Dennis | (dr)
Sidney Bechet With Bob Wilber's Wildcats
Sidney Bechet:Summertime | Dreyfus Jazz Line | FDM 36712-2

Strong,Frank | (tb)
Gerald Wilson And His Orchestra
Blue Breaks Beats Vol.2 | Blue Note | 789907-2

Strong,Jimmy | (clts)
Carroll Dickerson's Savoyagers
Louis Armstrong:Fireworks | Dreyfus Jazz Line | FDM 36710-2
Louis Armstrong And His Hot Five
Jazz:The Essential Collection Vol.2 | IN+OUT Records | 78012-2
Satch Plays Fats(Complete) | CBS | CK 64927
Louis Armstrong:Fireworks | Dreyfus Jazz Line | FDM 36710-2
Louis Armstrong And His Orchestra
Jazz:The Essential Collection Vol.2 | IN+OUT Records | 78012-2
Satch Plays Fats(Complete) | CBS | CK 64927
Louis Armstrong:Fireworks | Dreyfus Jazz Line | FDM 36710-2
Louis Armstrong And His Savoy Ballroom Five
Jazz:The Essential Collection Vol.2 | IN+OUT Records | 78012-2
Louis Armstrong:Fireworks | Dreyfus Jazz Line | FDM 36710-2

Stroup,Bob | (tb)
Woody Herman And His Orchestra
Verve Jazz Masters 54:Woody Herman | Verve | 529903-2

Strozier,Frank | (asfl)
Booker Ervin Quintet
Exultation! | Original Jazz Classics | OJCCD 835-2(P 7293)
Chet Baker Sextet
Baby Breeze | Verve | 538328-2
Frank Stozier Sextet
Long Night | Milestone | MCD 47095-2
Frank Strozier Quartet
Long Night | Milestone | MCD 47095-2
Roy Haynes Quartet
Cymbalism | Original Jazz Classics | OJCCD 1079-2(NJ 8287)

Struber,Bernard | (g)
Louis Sclavis & The Bernard Struber Jazztet
La Phare | Enja | ENJ-9359 2

Struck,Frank | (fr-h,tpfl-h)
Klaus König Orchestra
Times Of Devastation/Poco A Poco | Enja | ENJ-6014 22

Struck,Stephan | (tp)
Joachim Raffel Sextet
...In Motion | Jazz 4 Ever Records:Jazz Network | J4E 4746

Strunkeit,Sven | (tb)
Michael Riessler And The Ensemble 13
Momentum Mobile | Enja | ENJ-9003 2

Struzyk,Janni | (tuba)
The United Women's Orchestra
The Blue One | Jazz Haus Musik | JHM 0099 CD
United Women's Orchestra
Virgo Supercluster | Jazz Haus Musik | JHM 0123 CD

Stryi,Wolfgang | (contra-b-clsax)
Ensemble Modern
Ensemble Modern-Fred Frith:Traffic Continues | Winter&Winter | 910044-2

Stryker,Dave | (g)
Allan Botschinsky Quartet
Last Summer | M.A Music | A 804-2
I've Got Another Rhythm | M.A Music | A 916-2
Dave Stryker Octet
Blue To The Bone III | Steeplechase | SCCD 31524
Jam Session
Jam Session Vol.2 | Steeplechase | SCCD 31523
Jam Session Vol.10 | Steeplechase | SCCD 31555

Stuart,Billy | (dr)
Maceo Parker Group
Roots Revisited | Minor Music | 801015

Stuart,Glenn | (tp)
Don Ellis Orchestra
Electric Bath | CBS | CK 65522

Stuart,Hamish | (b,bells,dr,gvoc)
Klaus Doldinger With Orchestra
Lifelike | Warner | 2292-46478-2
Vince Jones Group
Here's To The Miracles | Intuition Records | INT 3198-2

Stuart,Kirk | (p)
Sarah Vaughan And Her Trio
Verve Jazz Masters 42:Sarah Vaughan-The Jazz Sides | Verve | 526817-2

Stubblefield,John | (fl,b-cl,ts,perc,gong,ss,oboesax)
Dollar(Abdullah Ibrahim) Brand Group
African River | Enja | ENJ-6018 2
John Stubblefield Quartet
Morning Song | Enja | ENJ-8036 2
Kenny Barron Quintet
What If | Enja | ENJ-5013 2
Live At Fat Tuesdays | Enja | ENJ-5071 2
Quickstep | Enja | ENJ-6084 2
Louis Hayes Sextet
The Crawl | Candid | CCD 79045
McCoy Tyner Big Band
The Best Of McCoy Tyner Big Band | Dreyfus Jazz Line | FDM 37012-2
McCoy Tyner Orchestra
Sama Layuca | Original Jazz Classics | OJCCD 1071-2(M 9056)
Mingus Big Band
Tonight At Noon...Three Or Four Shades Of Love | Dreyfus Jazz Line | FDM 36633-2
Mingus Big Band 93
Nostalgia In Times Square | Dreyfus Jazz Line | FDM 36559-2
Nat Adderley Septet
Don't Look Back | Steeplechase | SCCD 31059

Stubbs,George | (p)
Buddy Johnson And His Orchestra
Buddy And Ella Johnson 1953-1964 | Bear Family Records | BCD 15479 DH
King Curtis Band
King Curtis-Blow Man Blow | Bear Family Records | BCD 15670 CI

Stubbs,Ken | (asss)
First House
Erendira | ECM | 1307
Cantilena | ECM | 1393

Stubenhaus,Neil | (bel-b)
The Quincy Jones-Sammy Nestico Orchestra
Basie & Beyond | Warner | 9362-47792-2

Studd,Tony | (b-tbtb)
Cannonball Adderley And His Orchestra
Ballads | Blue Note | 537563-2
Cannonball Adderley Quintet
Ballads | Blue Note | 537563-2
Cannonball Adderley With Sergio Mendes And The Bossa Rio Sextet
Ballads | Blue Note | 537563-2
Gerry Mulligan Concert Jazz Band
Verve Jazz Masters 36:Gerry Mulligan | Verve | 523342-2
Verve Jazz Masters Vol.60:The Collection | Verve | 529866-2
The Complete Verve Gerry Mulligan Concert Band | Verve | 9860613
Gil Evans Orchestra
Verve Jazz Masters 23:Gil Evans | Verve | 521860-2
The Individualism Of Gil Evans | Verve | 833804-2
Out Of The Cool | Impulse(MCA) | 951186-2
Grover Washington Jr. Orchestra
Jazzrock-Anthology Vol.3:Fusion | Zounds | CD 27100555
Herbie Hancock Orchestra
Herbie Hancock:The Complete Blue Note Sixties Sessions | Blue Note | 495569-2
The Prisoner | Blue Note | 525649-2
J.J.Johnson And His Orchestra
Planet Jazz:J.J.Johnson | Planet Jazz | 2159974-2
Jimmy McGriff Orchestra
Swingin' The Blues-Jumpin' The Blues | Laserlight | 24654
Jimmy Smith And Wes Montgomery With Orchestra
Jimmy & Wes-The Dynamic Duo | Verve | 521445-2
Jimmy Smith And Wes Montgomery With The Oliver Nelson Orchestra
Wes Montgomery:The Verve Jazz Sides | Verve | 521690-2
Jimmy Smith:Best Of The Verve Years | Verve | 527950-2
Jimmy Smith With The Lalo Schifrin Orchestra
Jimmy Smith:Best Of The Verve Years | Verve | 527950-2
The Cat | Verve | 539756-2
Jimmy Smith With The Oliver Nelson Orchestra
Peter & The Wolf | Verve | 547264-2
Johnny Hodges Orchestra
Verve Jazz Masters 35:Johnny Hodges | Verve | 521857-2
Kenny Burrell With The Don Sebesky Orchestra
Verve Jazz Masters 45:Kenny Burrell | Verve | 527652-2
Blues-The Common Ground | Verve | 589101-2
King Curtis Band
King Curtis-Blow Man Blow | Bear Family Records | BCD 15670 CI
Modern Jazz Quartet And Orchestra
MJQ 40 | Atlantic | 7567-82330-2
Oliver Nelson And His Orchestra
Verve Jazz Masters Vol.60:The Collection | Verve | 529866-2
Oscar Peterson With Orchestra
With Respect To Nat | Verve | 557486-2
Phil Woods Quartet With Orchestra & Strings
Round Trip | Verve | 559804-2
Quincy Jones And His Orchestra
Talkin' Verve-Roots Of Acid Jazz:Roland Kirk | Verve | 533101-2
Verve Jazz Masters Vol.59:Toots Thielemans | Verve | 535271-2
Rahsaan/The Complete Mercury Recordings Of Roland Kirk | Mercury | 846630-2
Stan Getz With The Gary McFarland Orchestra
Stan Getz Highlights:The Best Of The Verve Years Vol.2 | Verve | 517330-2
Verve Jazz Masters 53:Stan Getz-Bossa Nova | Verve | 529904-2
Big Band Bossa Nova | Verve | 825771-2 PMS
Stan Getz Highlights | Verve | 847430-2
Wes Montgomery With The Oliver Nelson Orchestra
Verve Jazz Masters 14:Wes Montgomery | Verve | 519826-2
Wes Montgomery:The Verve Jazz Sides | Verve | 521690-2
Talkin' Jazz:Roots Of Acid Jazz | Verve | 529580-2

Stüdemann,Barbara | (voice)
Gunter Hampel Next Generation
Next Generation | Birth | CD 043

Studenroth,Kurt | (clts)
The Groenewald Newnet
Meetings | Jazz 'n' Arts Records | JNA 0702

Student,Mariola | (v)
Klaus Müller-Ekkehard Rössle
Auf Und Davon | Jazz Haus Musik | JHM 0091 CD

Studer,Freddy | (dr,cymbals,gongs,log-drperc)
Christy Doran-Fredy Studer-Stephan Wittwer
Red Twist & Tuned Arrow | ECM | 1342
Doran/Studer/Burri/Magnenat
Musik Für Zwei Kontrabässe, Elektrische Gitarre & Schlagzeug | ECM | 1436
Freddy Studer Orchestra
Seven Songs | VeraBra Records | CDVBR 2056-2
Koch-Schütz-Studer & El Nil Troop
Heavy Cairo Trafic | Intuition Records | INT 3175-2
Pierre Favre Ensemble
Singing Drums | ECM | 1274
Rainer Brünninghaus Trio
Continuum | ECM | 1266(815679-2)

Studer,Jim | (keyboardsvoc)
Al Jarreau With Band
Al Jarreau In London | i.e. Music | 557849-2

Studio Orchestra |
Louis Armstrong With Orchestra
Jazz Collection:Louis Armstrong | Laserlight | 24366

Studnitzky,Sebastian | (tpfl-h)
Antonio Petrocca Quartet
But Not For Me | Edition Musikat | EDM 047
Jochen Feucht Quartet
Signs On Lines | Satin Doll Productions | SDP 1019-1 CD
Rainer Tempel Big Band
Melodies Of '98 | Jazz 4 Ever Records:Jazz Network | J4E 4744
Thilo Wagner Quintet
Just In Time | Satin Doll Productions | SDP 1011-1 CD

Stuermer,Daryl | (el-g,keyboards,dr-machine,el-bg)
Jean-Luc Ponty Quintet
Aurora | Atlantic | 7567-81543-2
The Very Best Of Jean-Luc Ponty | Rhino | 8122-79862-2
Jean-Luc Ponty Sextet
Enigmatic Ocean | Atlantic | 19110-2
The Very Best Of Jean-Luc Ponty | Rhino | 8122-79862-2

Stühlen,Peter | (soundsculptures)
Norbert Stein Pata Orchester
Ritual Life | Pata Musik | PATA 5(JHM 50) CD

Stuhlmaker,Mort | (b)
Bud Freeman And His Famous Chicagoans
Jazz:The Essential Collection Vol.3 | IN+OUT Records | 78013-2
Peggy Lee With The Benny Goodman Orchestra
Peggy Lee & Benny Goodman:The Complete Recordings 1941-1947 | CBS | C2K 65686

Stulce,Fred | (as,arr,cl,reedsts)
Ella Fitzgerald With Paul Weston And His Orchestra
Love Songs:The Best Of The Song Books | Verve | 531762-2
Ella Fitzgerald Sings The Irving Berlin Song Book | Verve | 543830-2
Ella Fitzgerald With The Paul Weston Orchestra
Get Happy! | Verve | 523321-2
Frank Sinatra With Orchestra
Planet Jazz:Frank Sinatra & Tommy Dorsey | Planet Jazz | 2152067-2
Tommy Dorsey And His Orchestra
Planet Jazz:Frank Sinatra & Tommy Dorsey | Planet Jazz | 2152067-2
Planet Jazz Sampler | Planet Jazz | 2152326-2
Planet Jazz:Tommy Dorsey | Planet Jazz | 2159972-2
Planet Jazz:Big Bands | Planet Jazz | 2169649-2
Planet Jazz:Swing | Planet Jazz | 2169651-2
Planet Jazz:Male Jazz Vocalists | Planet Jazz | 2169657-2
Frank Sinatra And The Tommy Dorsey Orchestra | RCA | 2668701-2

Stull,Matthew Bob | (voc)
Klaus König Orchestra
Reviews | Enja | ENJ-9061 2

Sturgis,Roger | (voc)
Roger Sturgis With Lovie Jordan's Elks Rendez-Vous Band
Louis Jordan-Let The Good Times Roll: The Complete Decca Recordings 1938-1954 | Bear Family Records | BCD 15557 IH

Sturgis,Ted | (b)
Billie Holiday With Eddie Heywood And His Orchestra
Billie's Love Songs | Nimbus Records | NI 2000
Don Byas And His Orchestra
Americans Swinging In Paris:Don Byas | EMI Records | 539655-2
Don Byas Quartet
Americans Swinging In Paris:Don Byas | EMI Records | 539655-2
Peanuts Holland And His Orchestra
Americans Swinging In Paris:Don Byas | EMI Records | 539655-2
Roy Eldridge Septet
To Bags...With Love:Memorial Album | Pablo | 2310967-2
Roy Eldridge Sextet
Milt Jackson Birthday Celebration | Fantasy | FANCD 6079-2
Tyree Glenn And His Orchestra
Americans Swinging In Paris:Don Byas | EMI Records | 539655-2

Sturkin,David | (viola)
Artie Shaw And His Orchestra
Planet JazzArtie Shaw | Planet Jazz | 2152057-2
Planet Jazz:Jazz Greatest Hits | Planet Jazz | 2169648-2

Sturm,Jürgen | (g)
Anirahtak und die Jürgen Sturm Band
Das Kurt Weill Programm | Nabel Records:Jazz Network | CD 4638
Berlin-Paris-New York/Music By Kurt Weil | Nabel Records:Jazz Network | CD 4655
Jürgen Sturm's Ballstars
Tango Subversivo | Nabel Records:Jazz Network | CD 4613

Sturt,Hilary | (v)
Ensemble Modern
Ensemble Modern-Fred Frith:Traffic Continues | Winter&Winter | 910044-2

Stuttgarter Dixieland All Stars |
Stuttgarter Dixieland All Stars
It's The Talk Of The Town | Jazzpoint | JP 1069 CD

Stuttgarter Gitarren Trio |
Stuttgarter Gitarren Trio
Stuttgarter Gitarren Trio Vol.2 | Edition Musikat | EDM 034

Su,Nat | (as)
Cadavre Exquis
Cadavre Exquis | Creative Works Records | CW CD 1014-1
Nat Su Quartet
The J.Way | Fresh Sound Records | FSNT 038 CD

Suarez-Paz,Fernando | (v)
Astor Piazzolla-Gary Burton Sextet
The New Tango | Warner | 2292-55069-2

SublettJoe | (ts)
Jimmy Smith All Stars
Jimmy Smith:Dot Com Blues | Blue Thumb | 543978-2

Subramaniam,Dr. L. | (v,perc,surmandal,tambura,violectra)
Rainbow
Two Originals:Karuna Supreme/Rainbow | MPS | 519195-2

Sub-Zero | (lyricist)
Steve Coleman And Five Elements
Curves Of Life | Novus | 2131693-2

Succi,Achille | (b-cl)
Pierre Dorge's New Jungle Orchestra
Giraf | dacapo | DCCD 9440

Suchomel,Miroslav | (ts)
European Jazz Youth Orchestra
Swinging Europe 3 | dacapo | DCCD 9461

Suchoski,Bob | (bs)
Buddy Rich Big Band

Keep The Customer Satisfied | EMI Records | 523999-2
Suchovsky,Michael | (dr)
Everyman Band
Everyman Band | ECM | 1234
Without Warning | ECM | 1290
Südfunk Symphony Orchestra Stuttgart |
Eberhard Weber Group
The Colours Of Chloe | ECM | 1042
Südfunk Symphony Orchestra,Members of the |
Terje Rypdal With Strings
When Ever I Seem To Be Far Away | ECM | 1045
Südfunk Symphony Orchestra,String Section of the |
Keith Jarrett/Jan Garbarek With Strings
Luminessence | ECM | 1049(839307-2)
Keith Jarrett With Strings
In The Light | ECM | 1033/4
Ralph Towner With Strings
In The Light | ECM | 1033/4
Sudholter,Dick | (fl-h,tpco)
Tom Saunders' 'Wild Bill Davison Band' & Guests
Exactly Like You | Nagel-Heyer | CD 023
The Second Sampler | Nagel-Heyer | NHR SP 6
Sudler,Monnette | (gvoc)
Monnette Sudler Sextet
Brighter Days For You | Steeplechase | SCCD 31087
Sudmann,Rolf | (theremin)
Blue Collar
Diary Of A Working Band | Jazz Haus Musik | JHM 0089 CD
Sugar,Henry | (v)
Cal Tjader With The Clare Fischer Orchestra
Cal Tjader Plays Harold Arlen & West Side Story | Fantasy | FCD 24775-2
Suggs,Milton | (b)
Mary Lou Williams Trio
May Lou Williams Trio At Rick's Cafe Americain,Chicago,Ill. | Storyville | STCD 8285
Suggs,Pete | (dr)
Fletcher Henderson And His Orchestra
Jazz:The Essential Collection Vol.3 | IN+OUT Records | 78013-2
Suharjono | (saron,klunthung,calung,rebana,siter)
Norbert Stein Pata Masters meets Djaduk Ferianto Kua Etnika
Pata Java | Pata Musik | PATA 16 CD
Suhner,Reto | (ss,asts)
Manfred Junker Quartet
Cole Porter-Live! | Edition Collage | EC 531-2
Sukiennik,Marcus | (parr)
Marcus Sukiennik Big Band
A Night In Tunisia Suite(7 Variationen über Dizzy Gillespie's 'A Night In Tunisia') | Jazz Haus Musik | ohne Nummer
Sukoco | (gender,kendang,calung,ketipung)
Norbert Stein Pata Masters meets Djaduk Ferianto Kua Etnika
Pata Java | Pata Musik | PATA 16 CD
Sulic,Lujo | (v)
Bernd Konrad Jazz Group With Symphonie Orchestra
Wen Die Götter Lieben | Creative Works Records | CW CD 1010-1
Sulieman[Leonard Graham],Idrees | (fl-htp)
Bengt-Arne Wallin Orchestra
The Birth+Rebirth Of Swedish Folk Jazz | ACT | 9254-2
Coleman Hawkins All Star Octet
Body And Soul Revisited | GRP | GRP 16272
Coleman Hawkins All Stars
The J.J.Johnson Memorial Album | Prestige | PRCD 11025-2
Don Byas-Bud Powell Quintet
A Tribute To Cannonball | CBS | CK 65186
Friedrich Gulda Septet
Friedrich Gulda At Birdland | RCA | 2112587-2
Gene Ammons And His All Stars
Blue Gene | Original Jazz Classics | OJC20 192-2(P 7146)
Kenny Clarke-Francy Boland Big Band
Clark-Boland Big Band: TNP, October 29th, 1969 | Laserlight | 36129
Three Latin Adventures | MPS | 529095-2
More Smiles | MPS | 9814789
All Smiles | MPS | 9814790
Francy Boland-Fellini 712 | MPS | 9814805
Louis Jordan And His Tympany Five
Louis Jordan-Let The Good Times Roll: The Complete Decca Recordings 1938-1954 | Bear Family Records | BCD 15557 IH
Mal Waldron Sextet
John Coltrane-The Prestige Recordings | Prestige | 16 PCD 4405-2
The Jazz Giants Play Jerome Kern:Yesterdays | Prestige | PCD 24202-2
Miles Davis With The Danish Radio Big Band
Aura | CBS | CK 63962
NDR-Workshop
Doldinger's Best | ACT | 9224-2
Prestige All Stars
John Coltrane-The Prestige Recordings | Prestige | 16 PCD 4405-2
The Cats | Original Jazz Classics | OJCCD 079-2(NJ 8217)
The Mal Waldron Memorial Album:Soul Eyes | Prestige | PRCD 11024-2
Prestige Blues-Swingers
Soul Street | Original Jazz Classics | OJCCD 987-2(NJ 8293)
Slide Hampton-Joe Haider Jazz Orchestra
Give Me A Double | JHM Records | JHM 3627
Stan Getz With The Danish Radio Big Band
Stan Getz In Europe | Laserlight | 24657
Stan Kenton With The Danish Radio Big Band
Stan Kenton With The Danish Radio Big Band | Storyville | STCD 8340
Tadd Dameron And His Orchestra
Clifford Brown Memorial | Original Jazz Classics | OJC20 017-2(P 7055)
The Danish Radio Big Band
Aura | CBS | CK 63962
Thelonious Monk Quintet
The Best Of Thelonious Monk:The Blue Note Years | Blue Note | 795636-2
Thelonious Monk Sextet
Genius Of Modern Music,Vol.1 | Blue Note | 532138-2
Jazz Profile:Thelonious Monk | Blue Note | 823518-2
Thelonious Monk:Misterioso | Dreyfus Jazz Line | FDM 36743-2
Sullivan,Charles | (tpfl-h)
McCoy Tyner Orchestra
13th House | Original Jazz Classics | OJCCD 1089-2(M 9102)
Sullivan,Ira | (fl,alto-fl,ss,as,perc,fl-h,shaker)
Red Rodney Quintet
The Red Rodney Quintets | Fantasy | FCD 24758-2
Sullivan,Joe | (pp-solo)
Avishai Cohen Quartet
The Trumpet Player | Fresh Sound Records | FSNT 161 CD
Avishai Cohen Trio
The Trumpet Player | Fresh Sound Records | FSNT 161 CD
Benny Goodman And His Orchestra
Jazz:The Essential Collection Vol.3 | IN+OUT Records | 78013-2
Billie Holiday And Her Orchestra
Billie's Love Songs | Nimbus Records | NI 2000
Eddie Condon And His Chicagoans
The Very Best Of Dixieland Jazz | Verve | 535529-2
Eddie Condon's Hot Shots
Jazz:The Essential Collection Vol.3 | IN+OUT Records | 78013-2
Eddie's Hot Shots
Planet Jazz:Jack Teagarden | Planet Jazz | 2161236-2
Jack Teagarden's Chicagoans
Jazz:The Essential Collection Vol.3 | IN+OUT Records | 78013-2
The Hollywood Session:The Capitol Jazzmen | Jazz Unlimited | JUCD 2044
Lionel Hampton And His Orchestra
Planet Jazz:Coleman Hawkins | Planet Jazz | 2152055-2
Planet Jazz:Lionel Hampton | Planet Jazz | 2152059-2
Planet Jazz:Jazz Saxophone | Planet Jazz | 2169653-2
Jazz:The Essential Collection Vol.3 | IN+OUT Records | 78013-2
Louis Armstrong And His Orchestra
Jazz:The Essential Collection Vol.3 | IN+OUT Records | 78013-2
Sidney Bechet's Blue Note Jazzmen
Runnin' Wild | Blue Note | 821259-2
The Capitol Jazzmen
Jazz:The Essential Collection Vol.3 | IN+OUT Records | 78013-2
The Hollywood Session:The Capitol Jazzmen | Jazz Unlimited | JUCD 2044
Sullivan,John | (b)
Roy Haynes Quartet
Fountain Of Youth | Dreyfus Jazz Line | FDM 36663-2
Sullivan,Kate | (ld)
Kevin Mahogany With Orchestra
Songs And Moments | Enja | ENJ-8072 2
Sulzman,Stan | (as,fl,alto-fl,ts,sssax)
Chet Baker With The NDR-Bigband
Chet Baker-The Legacy Vol.1 | Enja | ENJ-9021 2
European Jazz Ensemble
European Jazz Ensemble At The Philharmonic Cologne | M.A Music | A 800-2
20th Anniversary Tour | Konnex Records | KCD 5078
European Jazz Ensemble 25th Anniversary | Konnex Records | KCD 5100
European Jazz Ensemble & The Khan Family feat. Joachim Kühn
European Jazz Ensemble Meets The Khan Family | M.A Music | A 807-2
Kenny Wheeler Ensemble
Music For Large & Small Ensembles | ECM | 1415/16
Sumen,Jimi | (el-gg)
Edward Vesala Ensemble
Ode Of The Death Of Jazz | ECM | 1413(843196-2)
Edward Vesala Nordic Gallery
Sound & Fury | ECM | 1541
Edward Vesala Sound And Fury
Invisible Strom | ECM | 1461
Sümer,Irfan | (tsperc)
Don Cherry Group
Don Cherry-The Sonet Recordings:Eternal Now/Live Ankara | Verve | 533049-2
Sumlin,Hubert | (el-g,vocg)
Howlin' Wolf London Session
Howlin' Wolf:The London Sessions | Chess | MCD 09297
Summers,Bill | (congas,perc,congabalafon)
Bobby Lyle Group
The Journey | Atlantic | 7567-82138-2
Dianne Reeves With Band
I Remember | Blue Note | 790264-2
Herbie Hancock Group
Man-Child | CBS | 471235-2
Sunlight | CBS | 486570-2
Thrust | CBS | CK 64984
Head Hunters | CBS | CK 65123
Joe Henderson And His Orchestra
Joe Henderson:The Milestone Years | Milestone | 8MCD 4413-2
Joe Henderson Group
Jazzin' Vol.2: The Music Of Stevie Wonder | Fantasy | FANCD 6088-2
Joe Henderson Quintet
Joe Henderson:The Milestone Years | Milestone | 8MCD 4413-2
Joe Henderson Sextet
Joe Henderson:The Milestone Years | Milestone | 8MCD 4413-2
Joe Henderson Trio
Joe Henderson:The Milestone Years | Milestone | 8MCD 4413-2
Sonny Rollins Quintet
Don't Ask | Original Jazz Classics | OJCCD 915-2(M 9090)
Sonny Rollins Sextet
Jazzin' Vol.2: The Music Of Stevie Wonder | Fantasy | FANCD 6088-2
Easy Living | Original Jazz Classics | OJCCD 893-2
Don't Ask | Original Jazz Classics | OJCCD 915-2(M 9090)
Summers,Bob | (tp,fl-hperc)
Count Basie And His Orchestra
88 Basie Street | Original Jazz Classics | OJC 808(2310901)
Fancy Pants | Original Jazz Classics | OJCCD 1038-2(2310920)
Count Basie Big Band
Farmers Market Barbecue | Original Jazz Classics | OJCCD 732-2(2310874)
Count Basie's Small Band
88 Basie Street | Original Jazz Classics | OJC 808(2310901)
Sarah Vaughan And The Count Basie Orchestra
Sarah Vaughan Birthday Celebration | Fantasy | FANCD 6090-2
Summers,Ted | (dr)
George Russell And His Orchestra
Bill Evans:Piano Player | CBS | CK 65361
Summey Jr.,Harold | (dr)
Willie Williams Trio
WW3 | Enja | ENJ-8060 2
Summit Reunion |
Summit Reunion
Jazz Im Amerikahaus,Vol.5 | Nagel-Heyer | CD 015
The First Sampler | Nagel-Heyer | NHR SP 5
Sun Ra | (cl,p,synth,spacemaster,clavinet)
Sun Ra And His Astro-Infinity Arkestra
Space Is The Place | Impulse(MCA) | 951249-2
Sun Ra And His Intergalactic Research Arkestra
Black Myth/Out In Space | MPS | 557656-2
Sun,Selcuk | (b)
Don Cherry Group
Don Cherry-The Sonet Recordings:Eternal Now/Live Ankara | Verve | 533049-2
Sund,Tim | (p)
Erika Rojo & Tim Sund
Das Lied | Nabel Records:Jazz Network | CD 4684
Joel Frahm Quintet
The Rains From A Cloud Do Not Wet The Sky | Nabel Records:Jazz Network | CD 4686
Tim Sund & Tom Christensen Quartet
Americana | Nabel Records:Jazz Network | CD 4697
Tim Sund Quartet
About Time | Laika Records | LK 93-043
Tim Sund Quintet
In The Midst Of Change | Nabel Records:Jazz Network | CD 4679
Tim Sund Trio
Trialogue | Nabel Records:Jazz Network | CD 4692
Sunde,Helge | (tb)
Geir Lysne Listening Ensemble
Korall | ACT | 9236-2
Aurora Borealis-Nordic Lights | ACT | 9406-2
Sunde,Torbjorn | (tbvoc)
Jon Balke w/Oslo 13
Nonsentration | ECM | 1445
Terje Rypdal Group
Odyssey | ECM | 1067/8
Sundevall,Leppe | (b,b-tp,tenor-htp)
Lars Gullin Octet
Lars Gullin 1951/52 Vol.5:First Walk | Dragon | DRCD 380
Sundita,Sekou | (voc)
Cold Sweat
Cold Sweat Plays J.B. | JMT Edition | 919025-2
Sundquist,Ake | (drperc)
Nils Landgren Funk Unit With Guests
5000 Miles | ACT | 9271-2
Sundquist,Knut Eric | (b)
Abdullah Ibrahim Trio And A String Orchestra
African Suite | TipToe | TIP-888832 2
String Orchestra
African Suite | TipToe | TIP-888832 2
Sunkel,Phil | (tp)
Eddie Lockjaw Davis Orchestra
Afro-Jaws | Original Jazz Classics | OJCCD 403-2(RLP 9373)
Gerry Mulligan And His Orchestra
Mullenium | CBS | CK 65678
Gerry Mulligan Concert Jazz Band
The Complete Verve Gerry Mulligan Concert Band | Verve | 9860613
Gil Evans Orchestra
Out Of The Cool | Impulse(MCA) | 951186-2
J.R. Monterose Quintet
Jaywalkin' | Fresh Sound Records | FSR-CD 320
Lawrence Brown With The Ralph Burns Orchestra
Slide Trombone | Verve | 559930-2
Sunnyland Slim[Albert Luandrew] | (p,vocp-solo)
Sunnyland Slim Band
Windy City Blues | Stax | SCD 8612-2
Sunshine,Monty | (cl,ss,vocp)
Chris Barber Original Jazzband Of 1954
Chris Barber:40 Years Jubilee Concert | Storyville | 4990013
Chris Barber's Jazz Band
The Very Best Of Dixieland Jazz | Verve | 535529-2
The Best Of Dixieland-Live in 1954/55 | London | 820878-2
The Golden Years Of Revival Jazz,Vol 1 | Storyville | STCD 5506
The Golden Years Of Revival Jazz,Vol.2 | Storyville | STCD 5507
The Golden Years Of Revival Jazz.Vol.3 | Storyville | STCD 5508
The Golden Years Of Revival Jazz,Vol.4 | Storyville | STCD 5509
The Golden Years Of Revival Jazz,Vol.7 | Storyville | STCD 5512
The Golden Years Of Revival Jazz,Vol.9 | Storyville | STCD 5514
The Golden Years Of Revival Jazz,Vol.11 | Storyville | STCD 5516
The Golden Years Of Revival Jazz,Vol.13 | Storyville | STCD 5518
The Golden Years Of Revival Jazz.Vol.14 | Storyville | STCD 5519
The Golden Years Of Revibal Jazz,Vol.15 | Storyville | STCD 5520
Ken Colyer's Jazzmen
The Very Best Of Dixieland Jazz | Verve | 535529-2
The Golden Years Of Revival Jazz,Vol 1 | Storyville | STCD 5506
The Golden Years Of Revival Jazz,Vol.7 | Storyville | STCD 5512
The Golden Years Of Revival Jazz,Vol.11 | Storyville | STCD 5516
The Golden Years Of Revival Jazz,Vol.13 | Storyville | STCD 5518
The Golden Years Of Revival Jazz,Vol.14 | Storyville | STCD 5519
The Golden Years Of Revibal Jazz,Vol.15 | Storyville | STCD 5520
Monty Sunshine Trio
The Very Best Of Dixieland Jazz | Verve | 535529-2
The Golden Years Of Revival Jazz.Vol.3 | Storyville | STCD 5508
The Golden Years Of Revival Jazz,Vol.11 | Storyville | STCD 5516
The Golden Years Of Revival Jazz,Vol.13 | Storyville | STCD 5518
The Golden Years Of Revibal Jazz,Vol.15 | Storyville | STCD 5520
Sunship | (tympani)
Bobby Lyle Quintet
Jazzrock-Anthology Vol.3:Fusion | Zounds | CD 27100555
Suojärvi,Tauno | (b)
Jack Noren Quartet
Lars Gullin 1953,Vol.2:Moden Sounds | Dragon | DRCD 234
Super Black Blues Band |
Super Black Blues Band
Super Black Blues Vol.II | RCA | 2663874-2
Süper,Hans | (mandvoc)
Kölner Saxophon Mafia With Hans Süper
Kölner Saxophon Mafia Proudly Presents | Jazz Haus Musik | JHM 0046 CD
Supernatural | (rap)
Till Brönner Group
Chattin' With Chet | Verve | 157534-2
Suprapto,Sony | (kempul,gong,beduk,rebanavoc)
Norbert Stein Pata Masters meets Djaduk Ferianto Kua Etnika
Pata Java | Pata Musik | PATA 16 CD
Suprynowicz,Clark | (bel-b)
Rinde Eckert Group
Story In,Story Out | Intuition Records | INT 3507-2
Sur,André | (v)
Flor De Tango
Armenonville | Minor Music | 801097
Surman,John | (alto-cl,b-cl,ss,bs,keyboards)
Anouar Brahem Trio
Thimar | ECM | 1641(539888-2)
Barre Phillips Quartet
Mountainscapes | ECM | 1076
Barre Phillips Quintet
Mountainscapes | ECM | 1076
Barre Phillips Trio
Journal Violone II | ECM | 1149
John Abercrombie Quartet
November | ECM | 1502(519073-2)
John McLaughlin Quartet
Extrapolation | Polydor | 841598-2
John Surman
Upon Reflection | ECM | 1148(825472-2)
Withholding Pattern | ECM | 1295(825407-2)
Private City | ECM | 1366
Road To Saint Ives | ECM | 1418(843849-2)
A Biography Of The Rev. Absolom Dawe | ECM | 1528(523749-2)
John Surman Orchestra
How Many Clouds Can You See? | Deram | 844882-2
John Surman Quartet
Adventure Playground | ECM | 1463(511981-2)
Stranger Than Fiction | ECM | 1534
How Many Clouds Can You See? | Deram | 844882-2
John Surman Trio
Such Winters Of Memory | ECM | 1254(810621-2)
John Surman With String Quartet
Coruscating | ECM | 1702(543033-2)
John Surman-Jack DeJohnette
The Amazing Adventures Of Simon Simon | ECM | 1193(829160-2)
Invisible Nature | ECM | 1796(016376-2)
John Surman-Jack DeJohnette With The London Brass
Printed In Germany | ECM | 1802(017065-2)
John Surman-John Taylor With Chorus
Proverbs And Songs | ECM | 1639
John Surman-John Warren Group
The Brass Project | ECM | 1478
Mick Goodrick Quartet
In Pas(s)ing | ECM | 1139
Miroslav Vitous Group
Journey's End | ECM | 1242(843171-2)
Miroslav Vitous Quartet
First Meeting | ECM | 1145
Misha Alperin Group With John Surman
First Impression | ECM | 1664(557650-2)
NDR Big Band With Guests
50 Years Of NDR Big Band:Bravissimo II | ACT | 9259-2
Nordic Quartet
Nordic Quartet | ECM | 1553
Paul Bley Quartet
Fragments | ECM | 1320
The Paul Bley Quartet | ECM | 1365(835250-2)
In The Evenings Out There | ECM | 1488
Ronnie Scott And The Band
Live At Ronnie Scott's | CBS | 494439-2
Tomasz Stanko Sextet
From The Green Hill | ECM | 1680(547336-2)
Surmann,Willi | (bs)
Helmut Zacharias & His Sax-Team
Ich Habe Rhythmus | Bear Family Records | BCD 15642 AH
Helmut Zacharias mit seinem Orchester
Ich Habe Rhythmus | Bear Family Records | BCD 15642 AH
Susanna | (bird-songs)
John McLaughlin Group
The Promise | Verve | 529828-2
Sushel,Robert | (v)
Milt Jackson And His Orchestra
Reverence And Compassion | Reprise | 9362-45204-2
Suso,Jali Foday Musa | (balafon,dusungunl,dusungoni,kalimba)
Pharoah Sanders Orchestra
Message From Home | Verve | 529578-2
Suso,Miriam | (voc)

INTERPRETENVERZEICHNIS

Suso,Salie | (voc)

Sutherland,Rowland | (fl)
David Jean-Baptiste Group
The Nature Suite | Laika Records | 35101632

Suthers,Tom | (bssax)
Harry James And His Orchestra
Trumpet Blues:The Best Of Harry James | Capitol | 521224-2

Sutinen,Kirsti | (v)
Till Brönner Quartet & Deutsches Symphonieorchester Berlin
German Songs | Minor Music | 801057

Suttles,Warren | (voc)
The Ravens
Ultimate Ben Webster selected by James Carter | Verve | 557537-2

Sutton,Alan 'Little Bear' | (wbd)
Henrik Johansen With The City Ramblers
The Golden Years Of Revival Jazz,Sampler | Storyville | 109 1001
Hylda Sims And The City Ramblers Skiffle Group With Henrik Johansen
The Golden Years Of Revival Jazz,Vol.9 | Storyville | STCD 5514

Sutton,Ralph | (pp-solo)
Edmond Hall With The Ralph Sutton Group
Edmond Hall With The Ralph Sutton Group | Storyville | STCD 6052
Ralph Sutton
Stridin' High | Jazz Connaisseur | JCCD 9728-2
Ralph Sutton And Friends
Sweet Sue-The Music Of Fats Waller Vol.1 | Nagel-Heyer | CD 057
Ralph Sutton And His Allstars
Echoes Of Spring:The Complete Hamburg Concert | Nagel-Heyer | CD 038
Ralph Sutton Quartet
The Ralph Sutton Quartet With Ruby Braff,Vol.2 | Storyville | STCD 8246
Live At Sunnie's Rendezvous Vol.1 | Storyville | STCD 8280
Ralph Sutton-Bernd Lhotzky
Stridin' High | Jazz Connaisseur | JCCD 9728-2
Sackville All Stars
Christmas Jazz! | Nagel-Heyer | NH 1008

Sutton,Tierney | (voc)
Buddy Childers Big Band
It's What Happening Now! | Candid | CCD 79749

Suvarjiyo | (demung,klunthung,rebanavoc)
Norbert Stein Pata Masters meets Djaduk Ferianto Kua Etnika
Pata Java | Pata Musik | PATA 16 CD

Suyker,Willard 'Bill' | (g)
Jerome Richardson Sextet
Night Life | Prestige | PCD 24260-2
Jimmy Smith With The Oliver Nelson Orchestra
Verve Jazz Masters 29:Jimmy Smith | Verve | 521855-2
Jimmy Smith:Best Of The Verve Years | Verve | 527950-2
Jimmy Smith-Talkin' Verve | Verve | 531563-2
Louis Armstrong And His Orchestra
What A Wonderful World | MCA | MCD 01876

Suzano,Marcos | (block,caxixi,moringa,pandeirocuica)
Duo Fenix
Karai-Eté | IN+OUT Records | 7009-2

Suzuki,Michiyo | (b-cl)
Paquito D'Rivera Group With The Absolute Ensemble
Habanera | Enja | ENJ-9395 2

Suzuki,Yoshio | (b)
Johnny Hartman With The Masahiko Kikuchi Trio
Blue Velvet: Crooners, Swooners And Velvet Vocals | Blue Note | 521153-2

Svafnisson,Svenni | (?)
Champion Jack Dupree
Champion Jack Dupree | Storyville | 4960383

Svanes,Elisabeth | (v)
Terje Rypdal Quartet With The Bergen Chamber Ensemble
Lux Aeterna | ECM | 1818(017070-2)

Svanström,P-O | (tb)
Tim Hagans With Norrbotten Big Band
Future Miles | ACT | 9235-2

Svare,Jorgen | (clb-cl)
Chris Barber's Jazz Band
The Golden Years Of Revival Jazz,Vol.2 | Storyville | STCD 5507
Papa Bue's New Orleans Band
The Golden Years Of Revival Jazz,Vol.4 | Storyville | STCD 5509
Papa Bue's Viking Jazzband
The Golden Years Of Revival Jazz,Sampler | Storyville | 109 1001
The Golden Years Of Revival Jazz,Vol 1 | Storyville | STCD 5506
The Golden Years Of Revival Jazz,Vol.3 | Storyville | STCD 5508
The Golden Years Of Revival Jazz,Vol.5 | Storyville | STCD 5510
The Golden Years Of Revival Jazz,Vol.6 | Storyville | STCD 5511
The Golden Years Of Revival Jazz,Vol.7 | Storyville | STCD 5512
The Golden Years Of Revival Jazz,Vol.8 | Storyville | STCD 5513
The Golden Years Of Revival Jazz,Vol.9 | Storyville | STCD 5514
The Golden Years Of Revival Jazz,Vol.10 | Storyville | STCD 5515
The Golden Years Of Revival Jazz,Vol.11 | Storyville | STCD 5516
The Golden Years Of Revival Jazz,Vol.12 | Storyville | STCD 5517
The Golden Years Of Revival Jazz,Vol.13 | Storyville | STCD 5518
The Golden Years Of Revival Jazz.Vol.14 | Storyville | STCD 5519
The Golden Years Of Revibal Jazz,Vol.15 | Storyville | STCD 5520

Sveidahl,Jesper | (tp)
Copenhagen Art Ensemble
Angels' Share | dacapo | DCCD 9452

Svend Saaby Danish Choir |
Sarah Vaughan With Orchestra
Sarah Vaughan Sings The Mancini Songbook | Verve | 558401-2

Svensson,Esbjörn | (el-p,keyboards,grand-p,perc,p,vib)
Esbjörn Svensson Trio(E.S.T) With Strings
EST Plays Monk | ACT | 9010-2
Esbjörn Svensson Trio(E.S.T.)
Est-From Gagarin's Point Of View | ACT | 9005-2
Winter In Venice | ACT | 9007-2
Good Morning Susie Soho | ACT | 9009-2
EST Plays Monk | ACT | 9010-2
Strange Place For Snow | ACT | 9011-2
Seven Days Of Falling | ACT | 9012-2
E.S.T. Live | ACT | 9295-2
Lina Nyberg-Esbjörn Svensson
Close | Touché Music | TMcCD 004
Nils Landgren Funk Unit
Paint It Blue:A Tribute To Cannonball Adderley | ACT | 9243-2
Live In Montreux | ACT | 9265-2
Fonk Da World | ACT | 9299-2
Nils Landgren Funk Unit With Guests
5000 Miles | ACT | 9271-2
Nils Landgren Group
Sentimental Journey | ACT | 9409-2
Nils Landgren With The Esbjörn Svensson Trio
Ballads | ACT | 9268-2
Nils Landgren-Esbjörn Svensson
Layers Of Light | ACT | 9281-2
Swedish Folk Modern | ACT | 9428-2
Viktoria Tolstoy With The Esbjörn Svensson Trio
Viktoria Tolstoy:White Russian | Blue Note | 821220-2

Svensson,Gunnar | (pperc)
Lars Gullin Octet
Lars Gullin 1955/56 Vol.1 | Dragon | DRCD 224
Lars Gullin Quartet
Lars Gullin 1951/52 Vol.5:First Walk | Dragon | DRCD 380
Lars Gullin Quintet
Lars Gullin 1951/52 Vol.5:First Walk | Dragon | DRCD 380
Lars Gullin Septet
Lars Gullin 1951/52 Vol.5:First Walk | Dragon | DRCD 380
Lars Gullin Sextet
Lars Gullin 1951/52 Vol.5:First Walk | Dragon | DRCD 380
Rita Reys With The Lars Gullin Quartet
Lars Gullin 1953,Vol.2:Moden Sounds | Dragon | DRCD 234

Svensson,Harald | (el-p,keyboards,psynth)
Oriental Wind
Life Road | JA & RO | JARO 4113-2
Jazzy World | JA & RO | JARO 4200-2

Svensson,Staffan | (tp)
Rigmor Gustafsson With The Nils Landgren Quartet And The Fleshquartet
I Will Wait For You | ACT | 9418-2

Sverrisson,Skuli | (el-bperc)
Jim Black Alasnoaxis
Splay | Winter&Winter | 910076-2
Jim Black Quartet
Alasnoaxis | Winter&Winter | 910061-2

Svoboda,Michael 'Mike' | (tbsousaphone)
Müller-Svoboda-Dähn-Kniel
9Q | Edition Musikat | EDM 064

Swainson,Neil | (b)
Jim Galloway-Jay McShann Quartet
Christmas Jazz! | Nagel-Heyer | NH 1008
Woody Shaw Quartet
In My Own Sweet Way | IN+OUT Records | 7003-2
Jazz Unlimited | IN+OUT Records | 7017-2

Swallow,Steve | (b,el-b,b-g,dr,ld,voice,el-b-solo)
Art Farmer Quartet
Sing Me Softly Of The Blues | Atlantic | 7567-80773-2
Carla Bley Band
Live! | Watt | 12(815730-2)
Heavy Heart | Watt | 14
Night-Glo | Watt | 16
Fleur Carnivore | Watt | 21
The Very Big Carla Bley Band | Watt | 23
Big Band Theory | Watt | 25(519966-2)
Fancy Chamber Music | Watt | 28(539937-2)
4X4 | Watt | 30(159547-2)
Musique Mecanique | Watt | 9
Carla Bley Big Band
The Carla Bley Big Band Goes To Church | Watt | 27(533682-2)
Carla Bley Sextet
Sextet | Watt | 17
Carla Bley/Andy Sheppard/Steve Swallow
Song With Legs | Watt | 26(527069)
Carla Bley-Steve Swallow
Duets | Watt | 20(837345-2)
Go Together | Watt | 24(517673-2)
Are We There Yet? | Watt | 29(547297)
Chick Corea Quintet
Inner Space | Atlantic | 7567-81304-2
Chick Corea-Herbie Hancock-Keith Jarrett-McCoy Tyner | Atlantic | 7567-81402-2
Chick Corea Trio
Chick Corea-Herbie Hancock-Keith Jarrett-McCoy Tyner | Atlantic | 7567-81402-2
Don Ellis Trio
Out Of Nowhere | Candid | CCD 79032
Gary Burton Quartet
Times Square | ECM | 1111
Real Life Hits | ECM | 1293
Planet Jazz:Gary Burton | RCA | 2165367-2
Gary Burton Quartet With Eberhard Weber
Passengers | ECM | 1092(835016-2)
Gary Burton Quartet With Orchestra
A Genuine Tong Funeral(Dark Opera Without Words) | RCA | 2119255-2
Gary Burton Quintet
Dreams So Real | ECM | 1072
Whiz Kids | ECM | 1329
Gary Burton Quintet With Eberhard Weber
Ring | ECM | 1051
Gary Burton-Keith Jarrett Quintet
Gary Burton & Keith Jarrett | Atlantic | 7567-81374-2
Gary Burton-Stephane Grappelli Quartet
Paris Encounter | Atlantic | 7567-80763-2
Gary Burton-Steve Swallow
Hotel Hello | ECM | 1055(835586-2)
George Russell Sextet
Eric Dolphy Birthday Celebration | Fantasy | FANCD 6085-2
Ezz-thetics | Original Jazz Classics | OJCCD 070-2(RLP 9375)
The Outer View | Original Jazz Classics | OJCCD 616-2(RLP 9440)
The Jazz Giants Play Miles Davis:Milestones | Prestige | PCD 24225-2
Glen Moore Group
Nude Bass Ascending... | Intuition Records | INT 3192-2
Jasper Van't Hof-Charlie Mariano-Steve Swallow
Brutto Tempo | Intuition Records | INT 3309-2
Jimmy Giuffre 3
Jimmy Giuffre 3, 1961 | ECM | 1438/39(849644-2)
Jimmy Giuffre Three
Free Fall | CBS | CK 65446
Jimmy Giuffre/Steve Swallow
The Life Of A Trio:Saturday | Owl Records | 014731-2
The Life Of A Trio:Sunday | Owl Records | 014735-2
Jimmy Giuffre-Paul Bley-Steve Swallow
Fly Away Little Bird | Owl Records | 018351-2
John Scofield Groups
Quiet | Verve | 533185-2
John Scofield Trio
En Route | Verve | 9861357
John Scofield-Pat Metheny Quartet
I Can See Your House From Here | Blue Note | 827765-2
Karen Mantler Group
Karen Mantler And Her Cat Arnold Get The Flu | Watt | XtraWatt/5
Lee Konitz Trio
Three Guys | Enja | ENJ-9351 2
Michael Mantler Group
The Hapless Child | Watt | 4
Movies | Watt | 7 (2313107)
Movies/More Movies | Watt | 7/10(543377-2)
Michael Mantler Quintet With The London Symphony Orchestra
Something There | Watt | 13
Michael Mantler Sextet
Movies/More Movies | Watt | 7/10(543377-2)
Orchestra Jazz Siciliana
Orchestra Jazz Siciliana Plays The Music Of Carla Bley | Watt | XtraWatt/4
Paul Bley Trio
The Story Of Jazz Piano | Laserlight | 24653
Paul Bley/Jimmy Giuffre/Steve Swallow
The Life Of A Trio:Saturday | Owl Records | 014731-2
The Life Of A Trio:Sunday | Owl Records | 014735-2
Paul Bley/Steve Swallow
The Life Of A Trio:Saturday | Owl Records | 014731-2
The Life Of A Trio;Sunday | Owl Records | 014735-2
Paul Motian Electric Bebop Band
Flight Of The Blue Jay | Winter&Winter | 910009-2
Monk And Powell | Winter&Winter | 910045-2
Paul Motian Trio With Chris Potter And Larry Grenadier
Paul Motian Trio 2000 + One | Winter&Winter | 910032-2
Pierre Favre Quintet
Window-Steps | ECM | 1584(529348-2)
Rabih Abou-Khalil Group
Blue Camel | Enja | ENJ-7053 2
The Sultan's Picnic | Enja | ENJ-8078 2
Sheila Jordan-Steve Swallow
Misty Blue:Sweet Sisters Swing Songs Of Sorrow And Sadness | Blue Note | 521151-2
Stan Getz New Quartet
Stan Getz Highlights:The Best Of The Verve Years Vol.2 | Verve | 517330-2
Stan Getz-Joao Gilberto Orchestra
Sony Jazz Collection:Stan Getz | CBS | 488623-2
Steve Swallow
The Life Of A Trio:Saturday | Owl Records | 014731-2
Steve Swallow Group
Home | ECM | 1160(513424-2)
Carla | Watt | XtraWatt/2
Swallow | Watt | XtraWatt/6
Real Book | Watt | XtraWatt/7(521637-2)
Deconstructed | Watt | XtraWatt/9(537119-2)
Steve Swallow Quintet
Always Pack Your Uniform On Top | Watt | XtraWatt/10(543506-2)
Steve Swallow Trio
Damaged In Transit | Watt | XtraWatt/11(067792-2)
The Carla Bley Band
Social Studies | Watt | 11(831831-2)
I Hate To Sing | Watt | 12,5
The Jazz Composer's Orchestra
Comminications | JCOA | 1001/2

Swank,Ken | (drtambourine)
John Lee Hooker Group
Endless Boogie | MCA | MCD 10413

Swansen,Chris | (conddr)
Phil Woods Quartet With Orchestra & Strings
Round Trip | Verve | 559804-2

Swanston,Ed | (p)
(Little)Jimmy Scott With The Lucky Thompson Orchestra
Everybody's Somebody's Fool | Decca | 050669-2
Louis Armstrong And His Orchestra
Best Of The Complete RCA Victor Recordings | RCA | 2663636-2
Louis Armstrong:A 100th Birthday Celebration | RCA | 2663694-2
Louis Armstrong:C'est Si Bon | Dreyfus Jazz Line | FDM 36730-2

Swanton,Lloyd | (b,cabasa,el-b,shakertambourine)
Grace Knight With Orchestra
Come In Spinner | Intuition Records | INT 3052-2
The Catholics
Simple | Laika Records | 35100802
Vince Jones Group
Future Girl | Intuition Records | INT 3109-2
Vince Jones Quartet
One Day Spent | Intuition Records | INT 3087-2
Vince Jones With Orchestra
Come In Spinner | Intuition Records | INT 3052-2

Swartz,Harvie | (b,el-bel-g)
Ed Sarath Quintet
Last Day In May | Konnex Records | KCD 5042
Gregor Hübner Quartet
Panonien | Satin Doll Productions | SDP 1015-1 CD
Gregor Hübner Quintet
Panonien | Satin Doll Productions | SDP 1015-1 CD
Januschke's Time | Satin Doll Productions | SDP 1034-1 CD
Leni Stern Group
Secrets | Enja | ENJ-5093 2
Mitch Seidman-Fred Fried-Harvie Swartz
This Over That | Jardis Records | JRCD 9816

Swayzee,Edwin | (tp)
Cab Calloway And His Orchestra
Planet Jazz:Cab Calloway | Planet Jazz | 2161237-2
Jelly Roll Morton And His Orchestra
Planet Jazz:Jelly Roll Morton | Planet Jazz | 2152060-2
Jazz:The Essential Collection Vol.1 | IN+OUT Records | 78011-2

Swedien,Bruce | (snare)
Nils Landgren First Unit And Guests
Nils Landgren-The First Unit | ACT | 9292-2

Sweet Inspirations,The | (voc-group)
George Benson Orchestra
Talkin' Verve:George Benson | Verve | 553780-2
George Benson Quartet With The Sweet Inspirations
Talkin' Verve:George Benson | Verve | 553780-2
Yusef Lateef Orchestra
The Blue Yusef Lateef | Rhino | 8122-73717-2

Sweetney,Bernard | (dr)
Shirley Horn With Band
The Roots Of Acid Jazz | Impulse(MCA) | IMP 12042

Swift,Bob | (b-tbtb)
Artie Shaw And His Orchestra
Planet Jazz:Jazz Trumpet | Planet Jazz | 2169654-2
Woody Herman And His Orchestra
The Legends Of Swing | Laserlight | 24659
Woody Herman:Four Brother | Dreyfus Jazz Line | FDM 36722-2

Swim Two Birds |
Swim Two Birds
Sweet Relief | Laika Records | 35101182
No Regrets | Laika Records | 35101342

Swindell,Bill | (asts)
Leo Parker Sextet
True Blue | Blue Note | 534032-2

Swingcats,The |
The Swingcats
Face To Face:The Swingcats Live | Nagel-Heyer | CD 072

Swingle Singers | (voc-group)
Modern Jazz Quartet And The Swingle Singers
MJQ 40 | Atlantic | 7567-82330-2
Swingle Singers
Jazz Sebastian Bach | Philips | 542552-2
Jazz Sebastian Bach Vol.2 | Philips | 542553-2
Swingle Singers Going Baroque | Philips | 546746-2
Swingle Singers Singing Mozart | Philips | 548538-2
Swingling Telemann | Philips | 586735-2
Swingle Singers Getting Romantic | Philips | 586736-2

Swingle,Ward | (ldvoc)
Les Double Six
Les Double Six | RCA | 2164314-2
Modern Jazz Quartet And The Swingle Singers
MJQ 40 | Atlantic | 7567-82330-2
Swingle Singers
Jazz Sebastian Bach | Philips | 542552-2
Jazz Sebastian Bach Vol.2 | Philips | 542553-2
Swingle Singers Going Baroque | Philips | 546746-2
Swingle Singers Singing Mozart | Philips | 548538-2
Swingling Telemann | Philips | 586735-2
Swingle Singers Getting Romantic | Philips | 586736-2

Swisshelm,Robert | (fr-h)
John Coltrane And His Orchestra
John Coltrane:Standards | Impulse(MCA) | 549914-2
John Coltrane Quartet With Brass
The Complete Africa/Brass Sessions | Impulse(MCA) | 952168-2
Miles Davis With Gil Evans & His Orchestra
Miles Davis At Carnegie Hall | CBS | CK 65027
Quiet Nights | CBS | CK 65293

Switzer,Don | (tb)
Woody Herman And His Orchestra
Brand New | Original Jazz Classics | OJCCD 1044-2(F 8414)

Swope,Earl | (tb)
Lester Young And Earl Swope With The Bill Potts Trio
Lester Young In Washington,DC 1956:Vol.5 | Original Jazz Classics | OJCCD 993-2
Terry Gibbs Septet
Early Stan | Original Jazz Classics | OJCCD 654-2(P 7255)
Woody Herman And His Orchestra
The Legends Of Swing | Laserlight | 24659
Woody Herman:Four Brother | Dreyfus Jazz Line | FDM 36722-2

Swope,Terry | (voc)
Al Haig Sextet(Quintet)
Al Haig Trio And Sextets | Original Jazz Classics | OJCCD 1929-2(SPL 1118)

SWR Big Band |
SWR Big Band
Jazz In Concert | Hänssler Classics | CD 93.004

Sybill | (voc)
Lenny White Group
Present Tense | Hip Bop | HIBD 8004

Sydow,Joe | (b)
Helmut Zacharias mit dem Orchester Frank Folken
Ich Habe Rhythmus | Bear Family Records | BCD 15642 AH
Sylla,Kadia Tou | (voc)
Pili-Pili
Stolen Moments | JA & RO | JARO 4159-2
Jazzy World | JA & RO | JARO 4200-2
Sylla,Salifou | (percvoc)
Be In Two Minds | JA & RO | JARO 4134-2
Sylvain,Marc | (el-b)
Aldo Romano Group
AlmaLatina | Owl Records | 018364-2
Sylven,Bo | (arrg)
Pee Wee Ellis & NDR Bigband
What You Like | Minor Music | 801064
Stan Getz With The Danish Radio Big Band
Stan Getz In Europe | Laserlight | 24657
Sylvester | (voc)
Herbie Hancock Group
Magic Window | CBS | 486572-2
Sylvestre,Brigitte | (harp)
Michael Riessler Group
Heloise | Wergo | WER 8008-2
Tentations D'Abélard | Wergo | WER 8009-2
Sylvestre,Frederic | (g)
Florin Niculescu Quartet
Four Friends | Jardis Records | JRCD 9923
The European Jazz Guitar Orchestra
The European Jazz Guitar Orchestra | Jardis Records | JRCD 9307
Sylvestre,Gaston | (cymbal)
Michael Riessler Group
Heloise | Wergo | WER 8008-2
Tentations D'Abélard | Wergo | WER 8009-2
Renaud Garcia-Fons Group
Entremundo | Enja | ENJ-9464 2
Symphony Orchestra |
Modern Jazz Quartet And Symphony Orchestra
MJQ 40 | Atlantic | 7567-82330-2
Synigal,Edgar | (sax)
B.B.King And His Band
Live At San Quentin | MCA | MCD 06103
Syracuse Symphony |
Keith Jarrett With The Syracuse Symphony
The Celestial Hawk | ECM | 1175
System,Jessie | (voc)
Uri Caine Trio
Bedrock | Winter&Winter | 910068-2
Szabo,Frank | (tpfl-h)
Count Basie And His Orchestra
Fun Time | Pablo | 2310945-2
88 Basie Street | Original Jazz Classics | OJC 808(2310901)
Fancy Pants | Original Jazz Classics | OJCCD 1038-2(2310920)
Diane Schuur And Her Band
The Best Of Diane Schuur | GRP | GRP 98882
Sarah Vaughan And The Count Basie Orchestra
Sarah Vaughan Birthday Celebration | Fantasy | FANCD 6090-2
Szabo,Gabor | (gv)
Bernd Konrad Jazz Group With Symphonie Orchestra
Wen Die Götter Lieben | Creative Works Records | CW CD 1010-1
Chico Hamilton Quintet
The Dealer | Impulse(MCA) | 547958-2
Chico Hamilton Sextet
The Dealer | Impulse(MCA) | 547958-2
Gabor Szabo Quintet
The Roots Of Acid Jazz | Impulse(MCA) | IMP 12042
The Sorcerer | Impulse(MCA) | IMP 12112
Paul Desmond Orchestra
Late Night Sax | CBS | 487798-2
Skylark | CTI | ZK 65133
Szabo,Jeffrey | (cello)
Tom Harrell Group
Paradise | RCA | 2663738-2
Szameitat,Winfried |
Alfred 23 Harth Group
Sweet Paris | free flow music | ffm 0291
Szenkar,Claudio | (p,percvib)
Paul Nero Sound
Doldinger's Best | ACT | 9224-2
Szonyi,Francois | (g)
John McLaughlin With The Aighette Quartet And Yan Marez
Time Remembered:John McLaughlin Plays Bill Evans | Verve | 519861-2
Szperalski,Gerhard | (cello)
Los Jovenes Flamencos With The WDR Big Band And Guests
Jazzpana | ACT | 9212-2
Szudy,Janos | (drperc)
Lajos Dudas Quartet
Jubilee Edition | double moon | CHRDM 71020
Lajos Dudas Quintet
Jubilee Edition | double moon | CHRDM 71020
Szukalski,Tomasz | (b-cl,tsss)
Tomasz Stanko Quartet
Balladyna | ECM | 1071(519289-2)
Szurmant,Jan | (tp)
Landes Jugend Jazz Orchester Hessen
Touch Of Lips | hr music.de | hrmj 004-01 CD
Tabachnikowa,Viktoria | (p)
Belov Duo
Internationales Guitarren Festival '99 | ALISO Records | AL 1038
Tabackin,Lew | (fl,alto-fl,ts,piccolo,reedsts-solo)
Donald Byrd Orchestra
Blue Break Beats | Blue Note | 799106-2
The Jazz Composer's Orchestra
Comminications | JCOA | 1001/2
Toshiko Akiyoshi-Lew Tabackin Big Band
Monterey Jazz Festival 1975 | Storyville | 4960213
Tabal,Tani | (dr)
James Carter Group
Conversin' With The Elders | Atlantic | 7567-82988-2
James Carter Quartet
The Real Quietstorm | Atlantic | 7567-82742-2
Tabany,Mihaly | (accordinld)
Mihaly Tabany Orchestra
Jubilee Edition | double moon | CHRDM 71020
Tabatchnikowa,Viktoria | (p)
Viktoria Tabatchnikowa-Eugenij Belov
Troika | ALISO Records | AL 1036
Tabbal,Tani | (dr,bongos,voc,gembe,voice,hand-dr)
Roscoe Mitchell And The Note Factory
Nine To Get Ready | ECM | 1651(539725-2)
Tablas & Strings |
Tabla & Strings
Islands Everywhere | Tutu Records | 888208-2*
Tabor,Charlie | (tp)
Brocksi-Quintett
Drums Boogie | Bear Family Records | BCD 15988 AH
Freddie Brocksieper And His Boys
Freddie's Boogie Blues | Bear Family Records | BCD 16388 AH
Freddie Brocksieper Orchester
Drums Boogie | Bear Family Records | BCD 15988 AH
Freddie Brocksieper Star-Quintett
Shot Gun Boogie | Bear Family Records | BCD 16277 AH
Freddie Brocksieper Und Seine Solisten
Freddie's Boogie Blues | Bear Family Records | BCD 16388 AH
Taborn,Craig | (el-pp)
Dave Douglas Group
Dave Douglas Freak In | Bluebird | 2664008-2
James Carter Group
Conversin' With The Elders | Atlantic | 7567-82988-2

James Carter Quartet
The Real Quietstorm | Atlantic | 7567-82742-2
James Carter-Craig Tahorn
The Real Quietstorm | Atlantic | 7567-82742-2
Roscoe Mitchell And The Note Factory
Nine To Get Ready | ECM | 1651(539725-2)
Tacchi,Andrea | (v)
Richard Galliano Group I Solisti Dell'Orchestra Della Toscana
Gallianissimo! The Best Of Richard Galliano | Dreyfus Jazz Line | FDM 36616-2
Tachibana,Hajime | (g)
United Future Organizatio
United Future Organization | Talkin' Loud | 518166-2
Tack,Ernie | (b-tbtb)
Harry James And His Orchestra
Trumpet Blues:The Best Of Harry James | Capitol | 521224-2
Jimmy Smith With The Oliver Nelson Orchestra
Jimmy Smith:Best Of The Verve Years | Verve | 527950-2
Jimmy Smith-Talkin' Verve | Verve | 531563-2
Johnny Hartman And His Orchestra
Unforgettable | Impulse(MCA) | IMP 11522
Tacuma,Jamaaladeen | (b,b-g,el-b,handclapping,voc)
Grant Calvin Weston Group
Dance Romance | IN+OUT Records | 7002-2
James Blood Ulmer Group
Jazz Unlimited | IN+OUT Records | 7017-2
James Carter Group
Layin' In The Cut | Atlantic | 7567-83305-2
Red Sun/SamulNori
Then Comes The White Tiger | ECM | 1499
Tadic,Miroslav | (g,el-gslide-g)
Michel Godard-Miroslav Tadic-Mark Nauseef
Loose Wires | Enja | ENJ-9071 2
Tae,Kim Woon | (bara,bukching)
Red Sun/SamulNori
Then Comes The White Tiger | ECM | 1499
Taeger,Vincent | (dr)
European Jazz Youth Orchestra
Swinging Europe 3 | dacapo | DCCD 9461
Tafjord,Hild Sofie | (fr-h)
Trygve Seim Group
Different Rivers | ECM | 1744(159521-2)
Tafjord,Runar | (fr-hvoc)
Misha Alperin Group With The Brazz Brothers
Portrait | JA & RO | JARO 4227-2
The Brazz Brothers
Ngoma | Laika Records | 35101562
Tafjord,Stein Erik | (tubavoc)
Misha Alperin Group With The Brazz Brothers
Portrait | JA & RO | JARO 4227-2
The Brazz Brothers
Ngoma | Laika Records | 35101562
Taft,Jim 'Slim' | (b)
Louis Armstrong With Jimmy Dorsey And His Orchestra
Louis Armstrong:Swing That Music | Laserlight | 36056
Swing Legends:Louis Armstrong | Nimbus Records | NI 2012
Tagliani,Pedro | (g,triangle,voice,g-synthsurdo)
Raiz De Pedra
Diario De Bordo | TipToe | TIP-888822 2
Raiz De Pedra feat. Egberto Gismonti
Diario De Bordo | TipToe | TIP-888822 2
Stefanie Schlesiger And Her Group plus String Quartet
What Love Is | Enja | ENJ-9434 2
Stefanie Schlesinger And Her Group
What Love Is | Enja | ENJ-9434 2
Zona Sul
Pure Love | Nagel-Heyer | CD 3039
Tagul Group,The Isaac | (percvoc)
Jasper Van't Hof
Pili-Pili | Warner | 2292-40458-2
Taheney,Ronnie | (g,p,keyboardsvoc)
Ronnie Taheny Group
Briefcase | Laika Records | 35101152
Tahmasebi,Mohammad | (dombac)
Ulli Bögershausen
Best Of Ulli Bögershausen | Laika Records | LK 93-045
Taitt,George | (tp)
Thelonious Monk Quintet
Genius Of Modern Music,Vol.1 | Blue Note | 532138-2
The Best Of Thelonious Monk:The Blue Note Years | Blue Note | 795636-2
Jazz Profile:Thelonious Monk | Blue Note | 823518-2
Thelonious Monk:Misterioso | Dreyfus Jazz Line | FDM 36743-2
Taitt,Mel | (ts)
Ella Fitzgerald With Sy Oliver And His Orchestra
Ella Fitzgerald:The Decca Years 1949-1954 | Decca | 050668-2
Takabanda |
Takabanda
La Leggenda Del Pescatore | Jazz 4 Ever Records:Jazz Network | J4E 4752
Takahashi,Mariko | (narrationvoice)
John McLaughlin Group
The Promise | Verve | 529828-2
Uri Caine Ensemble
Love Fugue-Robert Schumann | Winter&Winter | 910049-2
Takamäki,Jone | (ss,as,ts,bass-sax,bell,krakaphone)
Krakatau
Volition | ECM | 1466
Matinale | ECM | 1529
Takas,Bill | (bel-b)
Gerry Mulligan Concert Jazz Band
The Complete Verve Gerry Mulligan Concert Band | Verve | 9860613
Takase,Aki | (p,celeste,cond,kotop-solo)
Aki Takase
Ten Piano Players,Vol.1 | Green House Music | CD 1002
Aki Takase-Alexander von Schlippenbach
Internationales Jazzfestival Münster | Tutu Records | 888110-2*
Berlin Contemporary Jazz Orchestra
Berlin Contemporary Jazz Orchestra | ECM | 1409
Gunther Klatt & Aki Takase
Art Of The Duo: Plays Ballads Of Duke Ellington: | Tutu Records | 888116-2*
Jazzensemble Des Hessischen Rundfunks
Atmosphering Conditions Permitting | ECM | 1549/50
Take 6 | (voc-group)
Joe Sample Group
Spellbound | Rhino | 81273726-2
Take 6
Goldmine | Reprise | 7599-25670-2
So Much To Say | Reprise | 7599-25892-2
He Is Christmas | Reprise | 7599-26665-2
Tonight Take 6 | Warner | 9362-47611-2
Take 6 With The Yellow Jackets
He Is Christmas | Reprise | 7599-26665-2
Yellowjackets
Live Wires | GRP | GRP 96672
Takeishi,Satoshi | (drperc)
Paul Giger Trio
Vindonissa | ECM | 1836(066069-2)
Takuan |
Takuan
Push | dacapo | DCCD 9457
Takvorian,Tak | (tb)
Vic Lewis Jam Session
Vic Lewis:The Golden Years | Candid | CCD 79754
Talamacus,Big Royal | (filtered-boom-b)
Jean-Paul Bourelly Trance Atlantic
Boom Bop II | double moon | CHRDM 71023

Tallini,Stefania | (p)
Stefania Tallini Trio
New Life | yvp music | CD 3114
Stefania Tallini Trio With Guests
New Life | yvp music | CD 3114
Tam 'Echo' Tam | (a capella voc-group)
Tam 'Echo' Tam
Jazzy World | JA & RO | JARO 4200-2
Tamia | (voice)
Freddy Studer Orchestra
Seven Songs | VeraBra Records | CDVBR 2056-2
Tamia/Pierre Favre
Solitudes | ECM | 1446
Tampa Red[Hudson Whitaker] | (g,kazoo,voc,speechg-solo)
Tampa Red
Bawdy Blues | Original Blues Classics | OBCCD 544-2(BV 1055)
Tana,Akira | (drperc)
Lena Horne With The George Benson Quintet
Misty Blue:Sweet Sisters Swing Songs Of Sorrow And Sadness | Blue Note | 521151-2
Ruth Brown With Orchestra
Fine And Mellow | Fantasy | FCD 9663-2
Zoot Sims Quartet
Suddenly It's Spring | Original Jazz Classics | OJCCD 742-2(2310898)
Tang,Achim | (b)
Oskar Aichinger Trio
Elelents Of Poetry | Between The Lines | btl 005(Efa 10175-2)
Tangata Rea |
Tangata Rea
Tango Alla Baila | Winter&Winter | 910025-2
Tanggaard,Aage | (dr)
Chet Baker Quartet
Chet Baker-The Legacy Vol.2:I Remember You | Enja | ENJ-9077 2
Chet Baker Quintet
My Favourite Songs: The Last Great Concert Vol.1 | Enja | ENJ-5097 2
The Last Concert Vol.I+II | Enja | ENJ-6074 22
Chet Baker Quintet/NDR Big Band/Radio Orchestra Hannover
Straight From The Heart-The Last Concert Vol.2 | Enja | ENJ-6020 2
The Last Concert Vol.I+II | Enja | ENJ-6074 22
Chet Baker With The NDR-Bigband
NDR Big Band-Bravissimo | ACT | 9232-2
My Favourite Songs: The Last Great Concert Vol.1 | Enja | ENJ-5097 2
The Last Concert Vol.I+II | Enja | ENJ-6074 22
Duke Jordan Trio
Jazz Legends:Clark Terry-Duke Jordan | Storyville | 4960283
Johnny Griffin With The NDR Big Band
NDR Big Band-Bravissimo | ACT | 9232-2
Svend Asmussen Quartet
Fit As A Fiddle | dacapo | DCCD 9429
Still Fiddling | Storyville | STCD 4252
Tango Five |
Tango Five feat. Raul Jaurena
Obsecion | Satin Doll Productions | SDP 1027-1 CD
Tango[Interactive Computer Program] | (keyboardsampling)
Henning Berg & John Taylor With 'Tango'
Tango & Company | Jazz Haus Musik | JHM 0085 CD
Tanksley,Francesca | (psynth)
Erica Lindsay Quintet
Dreamers | Candid | CCD 79040
Erica Lindsay Sextet
Dreamers | Candid | CCD 79040
Tannenbaum,Jules | (cello)
Artie Shaw And His Orchestra
Planet JazzArtie Shaw | Planet Jazz | 2152057-2
Planet Jazz:Jazz Greatest Hits | Planet Jazz | 2169648-2
Tannenbaum,Wolfe | (bs)
Sarah Vaughan With The Joe Lippman Orchestra
Sarah Vaughan:Lover Man | Dreyfus Jazz Line | FDM 36739-2
Tanner,Paul | (tb)
Glenn Miller And His Orchestra
Planet Jazz:Glenn Miller | Planet Jazz | 2152056-2
Planet Jazz Sampler | Planet Jazz | 2152326-2
Planet Jazz:Jazz Greatest Hits | Planet Jazz | 2169648-2
Planet Jazz:Big Bands | Planet Jazz | 2169649-2
Planet Jazz:Swing | Planet Jazz | 2169651-2
The Chesterfield Broadcasts Vol.1 | RCA | 2663113-2
Candelight Miller | RCA | 2668716-2
Swing Legends | Nimbus Records | NI 2001
The Andrew Sisters With The Glenn Miller Orchestra
The Chesterfield Broadcasts Vol.1 | RCA | 2663113-2
Tanno,Vinnie | (fl-htp)
Stan Kenton And His Orchestra
Great Swing Classics In Hi-Fi | Capitol | 521223-2
Tanza,Rudolph 'Rudy' | (as)
Artie Shaw And His Orchestra
Planet Jazz:Jazz Trumpet | Planet Jazz | 2169654-2
Tapio,Jorma | (alto-fl,alto-cl,b-cl,as,perc,flb-fl)
Edward Vesala Ensemble
Ode Of The Death Of Jazz | ECM | 1413(843196-2)
Edward Vesala Group
Lumi | ECM | 1339
Edward Vesala Nordic Gallery
Sound & Fury | ECM | 1541
Edward Vesala Sound And Fury
Invisible Strom | ECM | 1461
Tarack,Gerald | (stringsv)
Stan Getz With The Eddie Sauter Orchestra
Verve Jazz Masters 8:Stan Getz | Verve | 519823-2
Ultimate Stan Getz selected by Joe Henderson | Verve | 557532-2
Stan Getz With The Richard Evans Orchestra
What The World Needs Now-Stan Getz Plays Bacharach And David | Verve | 557450-2
Tarak,Gerald | (v)
Helen Merrill With Orchestra
Casa Forte | EmArCy | 558848-2
Tarasov,Vladimir | (dr,perc,bells,horn,instruments)
Alfred 23 Harth QuasarQuartet
POPending EYE | free flow music | ffm 0493
Lajos Dudas Quintet
Jubilee Edition | double moon | CHRDM 71020
Tardin,Léo | (p)
Matthias Spillmann Septet
Something About Water | JHM Records | JHM 3620
Tardy,Greg | (b-cl,ts,cl,flarr)
Alex Norris Quintet
A New Beginning | Fresh Sound Records | FSNT 081 CD
Dave Douglas Group
Soul On Soul | RCA | 2663603-2
Greg Tardy Band
Serendipity | Impulse(MCA) | 951258-2
James Hurt Group
Dark Grooves-Mystcal Rhythms | Blue Note | 495104-2
Russel Gunn Group
Ethnomusicology Vol.1 | Atlantic | 7567-83165-2
Steve Coleman And The Council Of Balance
Genesis & The Opening Of The Way | RCA | 2152934-2
The New Jazz Composers Octet
First Step Into Reality | Fresh Sound Records | FSNT 059 CD
Tarrant,Jesse | (tb)
Dizzy Gillespie And His Orchestra
Planet Jazz:Dizzy Gillespie | Planet Jazz | 2152069-2
Planet Jazz:Bebop | RCA | 2169650-2
Planet Jazz:Male Jazz Vocalists | Planet Jazz | 2169657-2
Tatanka,Okschila | (hand-drvoice)
Okschila Tatanka
Wounded Knee-Lyrik Und Jazz | Wergo | SM 1088-2
Tate,Buddy | (cl,ts,bs,voc,flreeds)
Benny Goodman And His Orchestra
40th Anniversary Concert-Live At Carnegie Hall | London | 820349-2

INTERPRETENVERZEICHNIS

Verve Jazz Masters 33:Benny Goodman | Verve | 844410-2
Big Joe Turner And Pete Johnson With The Blues Band
Newport Jazz Festival 1958,July 3rd-6th Vol.3:Blues In The Night No.1 | Phontastic | NCD 8815
Big Maybelle With The Blues Band
Newport Jazz Festival 1958,July 3rd-6th Vol.3:Blues In The Night No.1 | Phontastic | NCD 8815
Buck Clayton-Buddy Tate Quintet
Buck & Buddy | Original Jazz Classics | OJCCD 757-2(SV 2017)
Buck & Buddy Blow The Blues | Original Jazz Classics | OJCCD 850-2(SV 2030)
Buddy Tate With The Marlow Morris Quintet
Late Night Sax | CBS | 487798-2
Buddy Tate With The Torsten Swingenberger Swintet
Tate Live | Nagel-Heyer | CD 080
Chuck Berry With The Blues Band
Newport Jazz Festival 1958,July 3rd-6th Vol.3:Blues In The Night No.1 | Phontastic | NCD 8815
Count Basie And His Orchestra
Planet Jazz:Count Basie | Planet Jazz | 2152068-2
Planet Jazz Sampler | Planet Jazz | 2152326-2
Planet Jazz:Jimmy Rushing | RCA | 2165371-2
Planet Jazz:Jazz Greatest Hits | Planet Jazz | 2169648-2
Planet Jazz:Big Bands | Planet Jazz | 2169649-2
Jazz Collection:Count Basie | Laserlight | 24368
Jazz:The Essential Collection Vol.3 | IN+OUT Records | 78013-2
From Spiritual To Swing | Vanguard | VCD 169/71
Dickie Wells-Buddy Tate Quintet
Every Day I Have The Blues | Impulse(MCA) | 547967-2
Harry Edison Sextet
Swing Summit | Candid | CCD 79050
Helen Humes With James P. Johnson And The Count Basie Orchestra
From Spiritual To Swing | Vanguard | VCD 169/71
Ida Cox With The James P. Johnson Septet
From Spiritual To Swing | Vanguard | VCD 169/71
James Carter Group
Conversin' With The Elders | Atlantic | 7567-82988-2
Jay McShann And His Orchestra
Atlantic Jazz: Kansas City | Atlantic | 7567-81701-2
Jay McShann Orchestra
The Last Of The Blue Devils | Atlantic | 7567-80791-2
Jimmy Rushing And His Orchestra
Every Day I Have The Blues | Impulse(MCA) | 547967-2
Nancy Harrow And The Buck Clayton All Stars
Wild Women Don't Have The Blues | Candid | CCD 79008
Roy Eldridge And His Orchestra
The Complete Verve Roy Eldridge Studio Sessions | Verve | 9861278
Shirley Scott All Stars
Queen Of The Organ-Shirley Scott Memorial Album | Prestige | PRCD 11027-2
Very Saxy
Very Saxy | Original Jazz Classics | OJCCD 458-2
The Prestige Legacy Vol.2:Battles Of Saxes | Prestige | PCD 24252-2

Tate,Evan | (fl,ssas)
Munich Saxophon Family
Balanced | Edition Collage | EC 487-2

Tate,Frank | (b)
Allan Vaché Swingtet
Jazz Im Amerikahaus,Vol.3 | Nagel-Heyer | CD 013
Ellington For Lovers | Nagel-Heyer | NH 1009
The First Sampler | Nagel-Heyer | NHR SP 5
Butch Miles And Friends
Blues Of Summer | Nagel-Heyer | NH 1011
The Second Sampler | Nagel-Heyer | NHR SP 6
Butch Miles-Howard Alden Sextet
Cookin' | Nagel-Heyer | CD 5003
Frank Tate Quintet
Live In Belfast | Nagel-Heyer | CD 069
Harry Allen Quintet
Love Songs Live! | Nagel-Heyer | NH 1014
Rex Allen's Swing Express
Keep Swingin' | Nagel-Heyer | CD 016
Ellington For Lovers | Nagel-Heyer | NH 1009
The Second Sampler | Nagel-Heyer | NHR SP 6
Ruby Braff Trio
Ruby Braff Trio:In Concert | Storyville | 4960543
As Time Goes By... | Candid | CCD 79741

Tate,Grady | (dr,percvoc)
(Little)Jimmy Scott And His Band
Mood Indigo | Milestone | MCD 9305-2
(Little)Jimmy Scott And His Quintet
All The Way | Warner | 7599-26955-2
Astrud Gilberto With The Al Cohn Orchestra
Verve Jazz Masters 9:Astrud Gilberto | Verve | 519824-2
Astrud Gilberto With The Gil Evans Orchestra
Verve Jazz Masters 9:Astrud Gilberto | Verve | 519824-2
Verve Jazz Masters 23:Gil Evans | Verve | 521860-2
Benny Bailey Quintet
The Satchmo Legacy | Enja | ENJ-9407 2
Bill Evans Trio With The Claus Ogerman Orchestra
The Complete Bill Evans On Verve | Verve | 527953-2
Cal Tjader Quintet
Talkin Verve/Roots Of Acid Jazz:Cal Tjader | Verve | 531562-2
Cal Tjader Sextet
Soul Bird | Verve | 549111-2
Cal Tjader's Orchestra
Verve Jazz Masters 39:Cal Tjader | Verve | 521858-2
Talkin Verve/Roots Of Acid Jazz:Cal Tjader | Verve | 531562-2
Soul Burst | Verve | 557446-2
Charles Mingus And His Orchestra
The Complete Town Hall Concert | Blue Note | 828353-2
Chick Corea Quartet
Inner Space | Atlantic | 7567-81304-2
Clark Terry & Chico O Farril Orchestra
Spanish Rice | Verve | 9861050
Dee Dee Bridgewater With Big Band
Dear Ella | Verve | 539102-2
Dee Dee Bridgewater With Her Septet
Dear Ella | Verve | 539102-2
Duke Pearson Orchestra
Blue N' Groovy | Blue Note | 780679-2
Eddie Harris Group
The Best Of Eddie Harris | Atlantic | 7567-81370-2
Eddie Lockjaw Davis Sextet feat. Paul Gonsalves
Planet Jazz:Jazz Saxophone | Planet Jazz | 2169653-2
Ella Fitzgerald With The Duke Ellington Orchestra And Jimmy Jones Trio
Ella & Duke At The Cote D'Azur | Verve | 539030-2
Ella Fitzgerald And Duke Ellington:Cote D'Azure Concerts on Verve | Verve | 539033-2
Ella Fitzgerald With The Jimmy Jones Trio
Ella Fitzgerald-First Lady Of Song | Verve | 517898-2
Ella & Duke At The Cote D'Azur | Verve | 539030-2
Ella Fitzgerald And Duke Ellington:Cote D'Azure Concerts on Verve | Verve | 539033-2
Eric Kloss Quartet
About Time | Prestige | PRCD 24268-2
Freddy Cole With Band
Le Grand Freddy:Freddy Cole Sings The Music Of Michel Legrand | Fantasy | FCD 9683-2
Gato Barbieri Orchestra
The Roots Of Acid Jazz | Impulse(MCA) | IMP 12042
Grant Green Orchestra
Grant Green:Blue Breakbeat | Blue Note | 494705-2
Grant Green With Orchestra
The Final Comedown(Soundtrack) | Blue Note | 581678-2
Hank Jones With Oliver Nelson's Orchestra
The Roots Of Acid Jazz | Impulse(MCA) | IMP 12042
Helen Merrill With Orchestra
Casa Forte | EmArCy | 558848-2
J.J.Johnson And His Orchestra
Planet Jazz:J.J.Johnson | Planet Jazz | 2159974-2
Jimmy McGriff Orchestra
Swingin' The Blues-Jumpin' The Blues | Laserlight | 24654
Jimmy Rushing With Oliver Nelson And His Orchestra
Every Day I Have The Blues | Impulse(MCA) | 547967-2
Jimmy Scott With Band
Over The Rainbow | Milestone | MCD 9314-2
Moon Glow | Milestone | MCD 9332-2
Jimmy Smith And Wes Montgomery With Orchestra
Jimmy & Wes-The Dynamic Duo | Verve | 521445-2
Jimmy Smith And Wes Montgomery With The Oliver Nelson Orchestra
Wes Montgomery:The Verve Jazz Sides | Verve | 521690-2
Jimmy Smith:Best Of The Verve Years | Verve | 527950-2
Talkin' Jazz:Roots Of Acid Jazz | Verve | 529580-2
Jimmy Smith Quartet
Jimmy Smith:Best Of The Verve Years | Verve | 527950-2
Jimmy Smith-Talkin' Verve | Verve | 531563-2
Fourmost Return | Milestone | MCD 9311-2
Jimmy Smith Trio
Verve Jazz Masters 29:Jimmy Smith | Verve | 521855-2
Jimmy Smith:Best Of The Verve Years | Verve | 527950-2
Verve Jazz Masters Vol.60:The Collection | Verve | 529866-2
Jimmy Smith-Talkin' Verve | Verve | 531563-2
Organ Grinder Swing | Verve | 543831-2
Jimmy Smith With Orchestra
Jimmy Smith-Talkin' Verve | Verve | 531563-2
Jimmy Smith With The Billy Byers Orchestra
Jimmy Smith:Best Of The Verve Years | Verve | 527950-2
Jimmy Smith With The Lalo Schifrin Orchestra
Jimmy Smith:Best Of The Verve Years | Verve | 527950-2
Jimmy Smith-Talkin' Verve | Verve | 531563-2
The Cat | Verve | 539756-2
Jimmy Smith With The Oliver Nelson Orchestra
Verve Jazz Masters 29:Jimmy Smith | Verve | 521855-2
Jimmy Smith:Best Of The Verve Years | Verve | 527950-2
Jimmy Smith-Talkin' Verve | Verve | 531563-2
Peter & The Wolf | Verve | 547264-2
Jimmy Smith-Wes Montgomery Quartet
Jimmy & Wes-The Dynamic Duo | Verve | 521445-2
Wes Montgomery:The Verve Jazz Sides | Verve | 521690-2
Verve Jazz Masters 29:Jimmy Smith | Verve | 521855-2
Jimmy Smith:Best Of The Verve Years | Verve | 527950-2
Talkin' Jazz:Roots Of Acid Jazz | Verve | 529580-2
Jimmy Smith-Talkin' Verve | Verve | 531563-2
Johnny 'Hammond' Smith Quartet
The Soulful Blues | Prestige | PCD 24244-2
Johnny Hodges Orchestra
Verve Jazz Masters 35:Johnny Hodges | Verve | 521857-2
Kenny Burrell Quartet
Verve Jazz Masters 45:Kenny Burrell | Verve | 527652-2
Blues-The Common Ground | Verve | 589101-2
Kenny Burrell Quintet
Guitar Forms | Verve | 521403-2
Verve Jazz Masters 45:Kenny Burrell | Verve | 527652-2
Kenny Burrell Sextet
Verve Jazz Masters 45:Kenny Burrell | Verve | 527652-2
Kenny Burrell With The Don Sebesky Orchestra
Verve Jazz Masters 45:Kenny Burrell | Verve | 527652-2
Blues-The Common Ground | Verve | 589101-2
Kenny Burrell-Grover Washington Quartet
Blue Note Plays Gershwin | Blue Note | 520808-2
Kenny Clarke Quintet
Verve Jazz Masters 45:Kenny Burrell | Verve | 527652-2
Lalo Schifrin Trio With The London Philharmonic
Jazz Meets The Symphony | East-West | 4509-92004-2
Louis Armstrong And His Orchestra
What A Wonderful World | MCA | MCD 01876
Miles Davis With Gil Evans Orchestra, The George Gruntz Concert Jazz Band And Guests
Miles & Quincy Live At Montreux | Warner | 9362-45221-2
Milt Jackson Quartet
Ain't But A Few Of Us Left | Original Jazz Classics | OJCCD 785-2(2310873)
Oliver Nelson And His Orchestra
Verve Jazz Masters Vol.60:The Collection | Verve | 529866-2
More Blues And The Abstract Truth | Impulse(MCA) | 951212-2
Pee Wee Ellis Quartet
Sepia Tonality | Minor Music | 801040
Pee Wee Ellis Quintet
Sepia Tonality | Minor Music | 801040
Phil Woods Quartet With Orchestra & Strings
Round Trip | Verve | 559804-2
Quincy Jones And His Orchestra
Verve Jazz Masters Vol.59:Toots Thielemans | Verve | 535271-2
Ray Bryant Trio
The Jazz Giants Play Miles Davis:Milestones | Prestige | PCD 24225-2
Roland Kirk Quartet
Talkin' Verve-Roots Of Acid Jazz:Roland Kirk | Verve | 533101-2
Sarah Vaughan And Her Band
Duke Ellington Song Book Two | Pablo | CD 2312116
Sarah Vaughan Birthday Celebration | Fantasy | FANCD 6090-2
Sarah Vaughan With Band
Linger Awhile | Pablo | 2312144-2
Sarah Vaughan With Orchestra
Sarah Vaughan Birthday Celebration | Fantasy | FANCD 6090-2
Sarah Vaughan With Small Group & Orchestra
Duke Ellington Song Book One | Pablo | CD 2312111
Stan Getz Quartet
Stan Getz Highlights:The Best Of The Verve Years Vol.2 | Verve | 517330-2
Verve Jazz Masters 8:Stan Getz | Verve | 519823-2
Verve Jazz Masters 53:Stan Getz-Bossa Nova | Verve | 529904-2
A Life In Jazz:A Musical Biography | Verve | 535119-2
Ultimate Stan Getz selected by Joe Henderson | Verve | 557532-2
Stan Getz Highlights | Verve | 847430-2
Stan Getz With Orchestra And Voices
Stan Getz Highlights | Verve | 847430-2
Stan Getz With The Claus Ogerman Orchestra
What The World Needs Now-Stan Getz Plays Bacharach And David | Verve | 557450-2
Stan Getz With The Richard Evans Orchestra
What The World Needs Now-Stan Getz Plays Bacharach And David | Verve | 557450-2
Stan Getz-Joao Gilberto Orchestra
Sony Jazz Collection:Stan Getz | CBS | 488623-2
Stanley Turrentine And His Orchestra
The Lost Grooves | Blue Note | 831883-2
Wes Montgomery Orchestra
Movin' Wes | Verve | 521433-2
Wes Montgomery Quartet
Verve Jazz Masters 14:Wes Montgomery | Verve | 519826-2
Talkin' Jazz:Roots Of Acid Jazz | Verve | 529580-2
Bumpin' | Verve | 539062-2
Tequila | Verve | 547769-2
Wes Montgomery Quartet With The Claus Ogerman Orchestra
Tequila | Verve | 547769-2
Wes Montgomery Quintet With The Claus Ogerman Orchestra
The Antonio Carlos Jobim Songbook | Verve | 525472-2
Talkin' Jazz:Roots Of Acid Jazz | Verve | 529580-2
Tequila | Verve | 547769-2
Wes Montgomery Sextet
Tequila | Verve | 547769-2
Wes Montgomery Trio
Wes Montgomery:The Verve Jazz Sides | Verve | 521690-2
Tequila | Verve | 547769-2
Wes Montgomery Trio With The Claus Ogerman Orchestra
Tequila | Verve | 547769-2
Wes Montgomery With The Claus Ogerman Orchestra
Verve Jazz Masters 14:Wes Montgomery | Verve | 519826-2
Wes Montgomery With The Don Sebesky Orchestra
Verve Jazz Masters 14:Wes Montgomery | Verve | 519826-2
Wes Montgomery:The Verve Jazz Sides | Verve | 521690-2
Talkin' Jazz:Roots Of Acid Jazz | Verve | 529580-2
Bumpin' | Verve | 539062-2
California Dreaming | Verve | 827842-2
Wes Montgomery With The Johnny Pate Orchestra
Verve Jazz Masters 14:Wes Montgomery | Verve | 519826-2
Wes Montgomery:The Verve Jazz Sides | Verve | 521690-2
Talkin' Jazz:Roots Of Acid Jazz | Verve | 529580-2
Wes Montgomery With The Oliver Nelson Orchestra
Verve Jazz Masters 14:Wes Montgomery | Verve | 519826-2
Wes Montgomery:The Verve Jazz Sides | Verve | 521690-2
Talkin' Jazz:Roots Of Acid Jazz | Verve | 529580-2
Zoot Sims Quintet
Zoot Sims And The Gershwin Brothers | Original Jazz Classics | OJC20 444-2(2310744)
Zoot Sims And The Gershwin Brothers | Pablo | PASA 2310-744-6
Zoot Sims With Orchestra
Passion Flower | Original Jazz Classics | OJCCD 939-2(2312120)

Tate,Grady or Sol Gubin | (dr)
Cal Tjader's Orchestra
Verve Jazz Masters 39:Cal Tjader | Verve | 521858-2

Tatum,Art | (p,celeste,voc,p-solo,narration)
Art Tatum
Planet Jazz:Jazz Piano | RCA | 2169655-2
The Story Of Jazz Piano | Laserlight | 24653
Art Tatum:20th Century Piano Genius | Verve | 531763-2
Art Tatum-The Complete Pablo Solo Masterpieces | Pablo | 7 PACD 4404-2
Jazz:The Essential Collection Vol.2 | IN+OUT Records | 78012-2
Art Tatum:Complete Capitol Recordings | Capitol | 821325-2
Art Tatum:Over The Rainbow | Dreyfus Jazz Line | FDM 36727-2
The Jazz Giants Play Harold Arlen:Blues In The Night | Prestige | PCD 24201-2
The Jazz Giants Play Cole Porter:Night And Day | Prestige | PCD 24203-2
The Jazz Giants Play Harry Warren:Lullaby Of Broadway | Prestige | PCD 24204-2
The Jazz Giants Play Sammy Cahn:It's Magic | Prestige | PCD 24226-2
The Jazz Giants Play Duke Ellington:Caravan | Prestige | PCD 24227-2
Art Tatum-The Complete Jazz Chronicle Solo Session | Storyville | STCD 8253
Art Tatum Quartet
Art Tatum-The Complete Pablo Group Masterpieces | Pablo | 6 PACD 4401-2
Art Tatum Sextet
Art Tatum-The Complete Pablo Group Masterpieces | Pablo | 6 PACD 4401-2
Art Tatum Trio
Art Tatum-The Complete Pablo Group Masterpieces | Pablo | 6 PACD 4401-2
Art Tatum:Complete Capitol Recordings | Capitol | 821325-2
Art Tatum:Over The Rainbow | Dreyfus Jazz Line | FDM 36727-2
The Jazz Giants Play Rodgers & Hart:Blue Moon | Prestige | PCD 24205-2
Art Tatum-Ben Webster Quartet
The Art Tatum Group Masterpieces Vol.8 | Pablo | 2405431-2
Art Tatum-The Complete Pablo Group Masterpieces | Pablo | 6 PACD 4401-2
The Tatum Group Masterpieces Vol.8 | Pablo | PACD20 431-2
The Jazz Giants Play Jerome Kern:Yesterdays | Prestige | PCD 24202-2
Art Tatum-Buddy DeFranco Quartet
Art Tatum-The Complete Pablo Group Masterpieces | Pablo | 6 PACD 4401-2
Esquire Metropolitan Opera House Jam Session
Jazz:The Essential Collection Vol.3 | IN+OUT Records | 78013-2
Leonard Feather's Esquire All Stars
Jazz:The Essential Collection Vol.2 | IN+OUT Records | 78012-2
Tatum-Carter-Bellson Trio
Art Tatum-The Complete Pablo Group Masterpieces | Pablo | 6 PACD 4401-2
Tatum-Hampton-Rich Trio
Art Tatum-The Complete Pablo Group Masterpieces | Pablo | 6 PACD 4401-2

Tatum,Dick | (tp)
Doug Richford's London Jazzmen
The Golden Years Of Revival Jazz,Sampler | Storyville | 109 1001

Taub,Andy | (keyboards)
Marc Ribot Y Los Cubanos Postizos
Nuy Divertido(Very Entertaining) | Atlantic | 7567-83293-2

Taub,Brenda Lee | (voc)
Max Roach Chorus & Orchestra
To The Max! | Enja | ENJ-7021 22

Taubert,Hans-Dieter | (dr)
Helmut Brandt Combo
Deutsches Jazz Fesival 1954/1955 | Bear Family Records | BCD 15430

Taubitz,Adam | (v)
Daniel Schnyder With String Quartet
Tanatula | Enja | ENJ-9302 2

Tavaglione,Steve | (as,cl,ss,ts,EWI,fl,saxsynth)
Caldera
Jazzrock-Anthology Vol.3:Fusion | Zounds | CD 27100555
Dave Weckl Group
Heads Up | GRP | GRP 96732
Hard-Wired | GRP | GRP 97602
John Patitucci Group
Mistura Fina | GRP | GRP 98022

Tax,Melvin | (cl,ts,flreeds)
Louis Armstrong With Sy Oliver And His Orchestra
Satchmo Serenaders | Verve | 543792-2
Nina Simone And Orchestra
Planet Jazz:Nina Simone | Planet Jazz | 2165372-2

Taye,Wolfe | (ts)
Benny Goodman And His V-Disc All Star Band
The Legends Of Swing | Laserlight | 24659

Taylor,Alfred | (dr)
Hot Lips Page Band
Planet Jazz:Jazz Trumpet | Planet Jazz | 2169654-2

Taylor,Andy | (reeds)
André Holst With Chris Dean's European Swing Orchestra
That's Swing | Nagel-Heyer | CD 079

Taylor,Arthur 'Art' | (dr,gongrhythm-logs)
Arnett Cobb Quintet
Movin' Right Along | Original Jazz Classics | OJCCD 1074-2(P 7216)
More Party Time | Original Jazz Classics | OJCCD 979-2(P 7175)
Art Farmer Quartet
Plays The Arrangements And Compositions Of Gigi Gryce And Quincy Jones | Original Jazz Classics | OJCCD 054-2
Art Farmer Septet
Plays The Arrangements And Compositions Of Gigi Gryce And Quincy Jones | Original Jazz Classics | OJCCD 054-2
Benny Bailey Septet
Big Brass | Candid | CCD 79011
Bud Powell Quartet
The Amazing Bud Powell Vol.3:Bud! | Blue Note | 535585-2
Bud Powell Trio
Planet Jazz:Bud Powell | Planet Jazz | 2152064-2
Planet Jazz Sampler | Planet Jazz | 2152326-2
Planet Jazz:Jazz Piano | RCA | 2169655-2
The Best Of Bud Powell On Verve | Verve | 523392-2
The Amazing Bud Powell Vol.2 | Blue Note | 532137-2
The Amazing Bud Powell Vol.3:Bud! | Blue Note | 535585-2
Charlie Parker Quintet

Verve Jazz Masters 28:Charlie Parker Plays Standards | Verve | 521854-2
The Cole Porter Songbook | Verve | 823250-2
Bird: The Complete Charlie Parker On Verve | Verve | 837141-2
Charlie Rouse Quartet
Late Night Sax | CBS | 487798-2
Coleman Hawkins All Star Octet
Body And Soul Revisited | GRP | GRP 16272
Dexter Gordon Quintet
Dexter Gordon:Ballads | Blue Note | 796579-2
Donald Byrd Quintet
Byrd In Paris Vol.1 | Polydor | 833394-2
Donald Byrd Sextet
Byrd In Hand | Blue Note | 542305-2
Doug Watkins Sextet
Donald Byrd & Doug Watkins:The Tradition Sessions | Blue Note | 540528-2
Eddie Lockjaw Davis With The Red Garland Trio
Prestige Moodsville Vol.1 | Original Jazz Classics | OJCCD 360-2(MV 1)
Four Trombones
Charles Mingus-The Complete Debut Recordings | Debut | 12 DCD 4402-2
The J.J.Johnson Memorial Album | Prestige | PRCD 11025-2
Gene Ammons And His All Stars
John Coltrane-The Prestige Recordings | Prestige | 16 PCD 4405-2
Blue Gene | Original Jazz Classics | OJC20 192-2(P 7146)
Jammin' With Gene | Original Jazz Classics | OJCCD 211-2(P 7060)
The Big Sound | Original Jazz Classics | OJCCD 651-2(P 7132)
Groove Blues | Original Jazz Classics | OJCCD 723-2(PR 7201)
The Prestige Legacy Vol.2:Battles Of Saxes | Prestige | PCD 24252-2
Gene Ammons Quintet
Boss Tenor | Original Jazz Classics | OJC20 297-2(P-7180)
Gentle Jug Vol.3 | Prestige | PCD 24249-2
Herbie Mann Sextet
Just Wailin' | Original Jazz Classics | OJCCD 900-2(NJ 8211)
Jackie McLean Quartet
4, 5 And 6 | Original Jazz Classics | OJC 056(P 7048)
A Long Drink Of The Blues | Original Jazz Classics | OJCCD 253-2(NJ 8253)
The Jazz Giants Play Jerome Kern:Yesterdays | Prestige | PCD 24202-2
Jackie McLean Quintet
Capuchin Swing | Blue Note | 540033-2
4, 5 And 6 | Original Jazz Classics | OJC 056(P 7048)
Jackie McLean Sextet
4, 5 And 6 | Original Jazz Classics | OJC 056(P 7048)
James Clay/David Fathead Newman Quintet
The Sound Of The Wide Open Spaces | Original Jazz Classics | OJCCD 1075-2(RLP 1178)
John Coltrane All Stars
Dakar | Original Jazz Classics | OJC20 393-2(P 7280)
The Believer | Original Jazz Classics | OJCCD 876-2(P 7292)
Stardust | Original Jazz Classics | OJCCD 920-2(P 7268)
John Coltrane Quartet
John Coltrane-The Prestige Recordings | Prestige | 16 PCD 4405-2
The Best Of John Coltrane | Atlantic | 7567-81366-2
Atlantic Saxophones | Rhino | 8122-71256-2
John Coltrane-The Heavyweight Champion:The Complete Atlantic Recordings | Atlantic | 8122-71984-2
Giant Steps | Atlantic | 8122-75203-2
The Very Best Of John Coltrane | Rhino | 8122-79778-2
Soultrane | Original Jazz Classics | OJC20 021-2
Bahia | Original Jazz Classics | OJCCD 415-2
Stardust | Original Jazz Classics | OJCCD 920-2(P 7268)
The Jazz Giants Play Sammy Cahn:It's Magic | Prestige | PCD 24226-2
The Prestige Legacy Vol.1:The High Priests | Prestige | PCD 24251-2
John Coltrane Quintet
John Coltrane-The Prestige Recordings | Prestige | 16 PCD 4405-2
The Jazz Giants Play Rodgers & Hammerstein:My Favorite Things | Prestige | PCD 24223-2
John Coltrane Sextet
The Mal Waldron Memorial Album:Soul Eyes | Prestige | PRCD 11024-2
John Coltrane Trio
John Coltrane-The Prestige Recordings | Prestige | 16 PCD 4405-2
The Last Trane | Original Jazz Classics | OJC 394(P 7378)
Lush Life | Original Jazz Classics | OJC20 131-2
Bahia | Original Jazz Classics | OJCCD 415-2
The Jazz Giants Play Cole Porter:Night And Day | Prestige | PCD 24203-2
John Coltrane With The Red Garland Trio
John Coltrane-The Prestige Recordings | Prestige | 16 PCD 4405-2
The Last Trane | Original Jazz Classics | OJC 394(P 7378)
Settin' The Pace | Original Jazz Classics | OJC20 078-2
Dig It | Original Jazz Classics | OJC20 392-2(PR 7229)
Traning In | Original Jazz Classics | OJCCD 189-2
Johnny Griffin-Art Taylor Quartet
Johnny Griffin/Art Taylor In Copenhagen | Storyville | STCD 8300
Johnny 'Hammond' Smith Sextet
Open House | Milestone | MCD 47089-2
Julian Priester Sextet
Out Of This World | Milestone | MCD 47087-2
Kai Winding-J.J.Johnson Quintet
The Great Kai & J.J. | Impulse(MCA) | 951225-2
Ken McIntyre Quintet feat.Eric Dolphy
Eric Dolphy:The Complete Prestige Recordings | Prestige | 9 PRCD-4418-2
Eric Dolphy Birthday Celebration | Fantasy | FANCD 6085-2
Kenny Dorham Quartet
The Jazz Giants Play Harry Warren:Lullaby Of Broadway | Prestige | PCD 24204-2
Lennie Tristano Quartet
Requiem | Atlantic | 7567-80804-2
Mal Waldron Sextet
John Coltrane-The Prestige Recordings | Prestige | 16 PCD 4405-2
The Mal Waldron Memorial Album:Soul Eyes | Prestige | PRCD 11024-2
Matthew Gee All-Stars
Jazz By Gee! | Original Jazz Classics | OJCCD 1884-2(RLP 221)
Miles Davis + 19
Miles Ahead | CBS | CK 65121
Miles Davis Quintet
Collector's Items | Original Jazz Classics | OJC20 071-2(P 7044)
Miles Davis With Gil Evans & His Orchestra
This Is Jazz:Miles Davis Plays Ballads | CBS | CK 65038
Miles Davis-Milt Jackson Quintet
Milt Jackson Birthday Celebration | Fantasy | FANCD 6079-2
Miles Davis And Milt Jackson | Original Jazz Classics | OJC20 012-2(P 7034)
Miles Davis-Milt Jackson Sextet
Miles Davis And Milt Jackson | Original Jazz Classics | OJC20 012-2(P 7034)
Oliver Nelson Quintet
Oliver Nelson Feat. Kenny Dorham | Original Jazz Classics | OJCCD 227-2(NJ 8224)
Prestige All Stars
John Coltrane-The Prestige Recordings | Prestige | 16 PCD 4405-2
All Day Long | Original Jazz Classics | OJC20 456-2(P 7081)
Tenor Conclave | Original Jazz Classics | OJCCD 127-2
Wheelin' & Dealin' | Original Jazz Classics | OJCCD 672-2(P7131)
The Prestige Legacy Vol.2:Battles Of Saxes | Prestige | PCD 24252-2
The Mal Waldron Memorial Album:Soul Eyes | Prestige | PRCD 11024-2
Ray Charles-Milt Jackson Quartet
Soul Brothers/Soul Meeting | Atlantic | 7567-81951-2
Ray Charles-Milt Jackson Quintet
Soul Brothers/Soul Meeting | Atlantic | 7567-81951-2
Raymond Fol Big Band
Jazz In Paris:Raymond Fol-Les 4 Saisons | EmArCy | 548791-2
Red Garland Quartet
Red Garland Revisited! | Original Jazz Classics | OJCCD 985-2(P 7658)
The Jazz Giants Play Rodgers & Hart:Blue Moon | Prestige | PCD 24205-2
Red Garland Quintet
John Coltrane-The Prestige Recordings | Prestige | 16 PCD 4405-2
All Mornin' Long | Original Jazz Classics | OJC20 293-2(P-7130)
Dig It | Original Jazz Classics | OJC20 392-2(PR 7229)
Soul Junction | Original Jazz Classics | OJCCD 481-2
The Jazz Giants Play Duke Ellington:Caravan | Prestige | PCD 24227-2
Red Garland Quintet feat.John Coltrane
High Pressure | Original Jazz Classics | OJCCD 349-2(P 7209)
Red Garland Trio
A Garland Of Red | Original Jazz Classics | OJC 126(P 7064)
Red Garland's Piano | Original Jazz Classics | OJC20 073-2(P 7086)
Dig It | Original Jazz Classics | OJC20 392-2(PR 7229)
Groovy | Original Jazz Classics | OJCCD 061-2
It's A Blue World | Original Jazz Classics | OJCCD 1028-2(P 7838)
Red In Bluesville | Original Jazz Classics | OJCCD 295-2
Prestige Moodsville Vol.1 | Original Jazz Classics | OJCCD 360-2(MV 1)
Can't See For Lookin' | Original Jazz Classics | OJCCD 918-2(PR 7276)
Red Garland Revisited! | Original Jazz Classics | OJCCD 985-2(P 7658)
The Jazz Giants Play Harold Arlen:Blues In The Night | Prestige | PCD 24201-2
Red Garland Trio With Ray Barretto
Manteca | Original Jazz Classics | OJCCD 428-2(PR 7139)
Roland Kirk With The Jack McDuff Trio
Kirk's Work | Original Jazz Classics | OJC20 459-2(P 7210)
Sonny Clark Sextet
Trane's Blues | Blue Note | 498240-2
Sonny Rollins Quartet
Thelonious Monk:The Complete Prestige Recordings | Prestige | 3 PRCD 4428-2
The Prestige Legacy Vol.1:The High Priests | Prestige | PCD 24251-2
Sonny Rollins Quartet feat.Thelonious Monk
Thelonious Monk/Sonny Rollins | Original Jazz Classics | OJCCD 059-2
Sonny Stitt-Jack McDuff Quintet
Stitt Meets Brother Jack | Original Jazz Classics | OJCCD 703-2(P 7244)
Taylor's Wailers
John Coltrane-The Prestige Recordings | Prestige | 16 PCD 4405-2
Mr. A.T. | Enja | ENJ-7017 2
Thelonious Monk And His Orchestra
Thelonious Monk:85th Birthday Celebration | zyx records | FANCD 6076-2
At Town Hall | Original Jazz Classics | OJCCD 135-2
Thelonious Monk Quartet
Thelonious Monk:85th Birthday Celebration | zyx records | FANCD 6076-2
Thelonious Monk Quintet
Thelonious Monk:85th Birthday Celebration | zyx records | FANCD 6076-2
5 By Monk By 5 | Original Jazz Classics | OJCCD 362-2
Tina Brooks Quintet
Blue N' Groovy | Blue Note | 780679-2
Tommy Flanagan Trio
Thelonica | Enja | ENJ-4052 2
Walter Davis Quintet
Davis Cup | Blue Note | 0675597

Taylor,Arthur or Walter Jones | (bj)
King Oliver And His Orchestra
Jazz:The Essential Collection Vol.1 | IN+OUT Records | 78011-2

Taylor,Billy | (b,tuba,chimes,dr,org,pp-solo)
(Little)Jimmy Scott With The Billy Taylor Orchestra
Everybody's Somebody's Fool | Decca | 050669-2
Bessie Smith And Her Band
Jazz:The Essential Collection Vol.3 | IN+OUT Records | 78013-2
Billy Taylor Trio
Charles Mingus-The Complete Debut Recordings | Debut | 12 DCD 4402-2
Billy Taylor Trio | Prestige | PRCD 24285-2
Coleman Hawkins Quintet
Verve Jazz Masters 43:Coleman Hawkins | Verve | 521856-2
Ultimate Coleman Hawkins selected by Sonny Rollins | Verve | 557538-2
Jazz:The Essential Collection Vol.3 | IN+OUT Records | 78013-2
Cozy Cole All Stars
Ultimate Coleman Hawkins selected by Sonny Rollins | Verve | 557538-2
Jazz:The Essential Collection Vol.3 | IN+OUT Records | 78013-2
Don Byas And His Orchestra
Americans Swinging In Paris:Don Byas | EMI Records | 539655-2
Don Byas Quartet
Americans Swinging In Paris:Don Byas | EMI Records | 539655-2
Don Byas:Laura | Dreyfus Jazz Line | FDM 36714-2
Don Byas Ree-Boppers
Don Byas:Laura | Dreyfus Jazz Line | FDM 36714-2
Don Senay With Orchestra And Strings
Charles Mingus-The Complete Debut Recordings | Debut | 12 DCD 4402-2
Duke Ellington And His Famous Orchestra
Greatest Hits | CBS | 462959-2
Jazz:The Essential Collection Vol.2 | IN+OUT Records | 78012-2
Duke Ellington And His Orchestra
Jazz:The Essential Collection Vol.3 | IN+OUT Records | 78013-2
George Wettling's New Yorkers
Jazz:The Essential Collection Vol.3 | IN+OUT Records | 78013-2
Jack Teagarden's Big Eight
Jazz:The Essential Collection Vol.3 | IN+OUT Records | 78013-2
McKinney's Cotton Pickers
Jazz:The Essential Collection Vol.3 | IN+OUT Records | 78013-2
Mundell Lowe Quartet
A Grand Night For Swinging | Original Jazz Classics | OJCCD 1940-(RLP 238)
Mundell Lowe Quintet
A Grand Night For Swinging | Original Jazz Classics | OJCCD 1940-(RLP 238)
Peanuts Holland And His Orchestra
Americans Swinging In Paris:Don Byas | EMI Records | 539655-2
Rex Stewart And His Feetwarmers
Django Reinhardt All Star Sessions | Capitol | 531577-2
Sarah Vaughan With George Treadwell And His Allstars
Sarah Vaughan:Lover Man | Dreyfus Jazz Line | FDM 36739-2
Sarah Vaughan With The Teddy Wilson Quartet
Sarah Vaughan:Lover Man | Dreyfus Jazz Line | FDM 36739-2
Thad Jones And His Orchestra
Charles Mingus-The Complete Debut Recordings | Debut | 12 DCD 4402-2
Tyree Glenn
Don Byas:Laura | Dreyfus Jazz Line | FDM 36714-2
Tyree Glenn And His Orchestra
Americans Swinging In Paris:Don Byas | EMI Records | 539655-2

Taylor,Billy prob. | (p)
Woody Herman And The Vanderbilt All Stars
Louis Armstrong-Jack Teagarden-Woody Herman:Midnights At V-Disc | Jazz Unlimited | JUCD 2048

Taylor,Calvin | (el-b)
Nina Simone And Orchestra
Planet Jazz:Nina Simone | Planet Jazz | 2165372-2

Taylor,Cecil | (grand-p,p,bells,perc,voicep-solo)
Cecil Taylor Quartet
At Newport | Verve | 589764-2
The World Of Cecil Taylor | Candid | CCD 79006
Cecil Taylor: Air | Candid | CCD 79046
Cecil Taylor Quintet
Love For Sale | Blue Note | 494107-2
Trane's Blues | Blue Note | 498240-2
Cecil Taylor Sextet
A Blue Conception | Blue Note | 534254-2
Conquistador | Blue Note | 576749-2
Cecil Taylor Trio
Love For Sale | Blue Note | 494107-2
The World Of Cecil Taylor | Candid | CCD 79006
Cecil Taylor Unit
Dark To Themselves | Enja | ENJ-2084 2
Mixed | Impulse(MCA) | IMP 12702
Cecil Taylor/Buell Neidlinger Orchestra
New York City R&B | Candid | CCD 79017
Cecil Taylor/Buell Neidlinger Quartet
New York City R&B | Candid | CCD 79017
Cecil Taylor/Buell Neidlinger Trio
New York City R&B | Candid | CCD 79017
Dewey Redman-Cecil Taylor-Elvin Jones
Momentum Space | Verve | 559944-2
The Jazz Composer's Orchestra
Comminications | JCOA | 1001/2

Taylor,Dave | (b-tb,horse-whinny,mutes,tuba,voc,ld)
Bob James And His Orchestra
Jazzrock-Anthology Vol.3:Fusion | Zounds | CD 27100555
Cadavre Exquis
Cadavre Exquis | Creative Works Records | CW CD 1014-1
Carla Bley Band
Night-Glo | Watt | 16
Daniel Schnyder Group
Tanatula | Enja | ENJ-9302 2
Words Within Music | Enja | ENJ-9369 2
David Matthews & The Manhattan Jazz Orchestra
Back To Bach | Milestone | MCD 9312-2
Hey Duke! | Milestone | MCD 9320-2
Duke Ellington And His Orchestra
New Orleans Suite | Rhino | 812273670-2
George Gruntz Concert Jazz Band
Blues 'N Dues Et Cetera | Enja | ENJ-6072 2
George Gruntz Concert Jazz Band '83
Theatre | ECM | 1265
Hank Roberts Group
Black Pastels | JMT Edition | 919016-2
Miles Davis With Gil Evans Orchestra, The George Gruntz Concert Jazz Band And Guests
Miles & Quincy Live At Montreux | Warner | 9362-45221-2
Mingus Big Band
Tonight At Noon...Three Or Four Shades Of Love | Dreyfus Jazz Line | FDM 36633-2
Mingus Big Band 93
Nostalgia In Times Square | Dreyfus Jazz Line | FDM 36559-2
Paquito D'Rivera Group With The Absolute Ensemble
Habanera | Enja | ENJ-9395 2

Taylor,Dick | (tb)
Gene Krupa And His Orchestra
Mullenium | CBS | CK 65678

Taylor,Eddie | (b-g,dr,el-g,voc,g,tsmonologue)
Homesick James Quartet
Blues On The Southside | Original Blues Classics | OBCCD 529-2(P 7388)
Windy City Blues | Stax | SCD 8612-2

Taylor,Eva | (voc)
Clarence Williams' Blue Five
Jazz:The Essential Collection Vol.1 | IN+OUT Records | 78011-2

Taylor,Gene | (bel-b)
Bill Henderson With The Horace Silver Quintet
Horace Silver Retrospective | Blue Note | 495576-2
Blue Mitchell And His Orchestra
Blue Breaks Beats Vol.2 | Blue Note | 789907-2
Blue Mitchell Quintet
Down With It | Blue Note | 854327-2
Duke Pearson Orchestra
Blue N' Groovy | Blue Note | 780679-2
Eddie Jefferson And His Band
Dexter Gordon Birthday Celebration | Fantasy | FANCD 6082-2
Horace Silver Quintet
Blowin' The Blues Away | Blue Note | 495342-2
Horace Silver Retrospective | Blue Note | 495576-2
Song For My Father | Blue Note | 499002-2
Blue Velvet: Crooners, Swooners And Velvet Vocals | Blue Note | 521153-2
True Blue | Blue Note | 534032-2
Finger Poppin' | Blue Note | 542304-2
Silver's Serenade | Blue Note | 821288-2
The Tokyo Blues | Blue Note | 853355-2
Newport Jazz Festival 1958,July 3rd-6th,Vol.1:Mostly Miles | Phontastic | NCD 8813
Paris Blues | Pablo | PACD 5316-2
Horace Silver Trio
Song For My Father | Blue Note | 499002-2
Nina Simone And Orchestra
Planet Jazz:Nina Simone | Planet Jazz | 2165372-2
Roland Alexander Quintet
Ronnie Mathews-Roland Alexander-Freddie Hubbard | Prestige | PRCD 24271-2

Taylor,James | (el-p,org,keyboards,clavinet,p,perc)
Michael Brecker Quintet
Nearness Of You-The Ballad Book | Verve | 549705-2

Taylor,Jane | (bassoon)
Freddie Hubbard With Orchestra
This Is Jazz:Freddie Hubbard | CBS | CK 65041

Taylor,Joan | (voc)
McCoy Tyner Group With Horns And Voices
Inner Voices | Original Jazz Classics | OJCCD 1039-2(M 9079)
McCoy Tyner Group With Voices
Inner Voices | Original Jazz Classics | OJCCD 1039-2(M 9079)

Taylor,John | (b,bs,el-p,hohner-electra-p)
Azimuth
Azimuth '85 | ECM | 1298
How It Was Then...Never Again | ECM | 1538
Azimuth | ECM | 1546/48(523010-2)
Azimuth With Ralph Towner
Azimuth | ECM | 1546/48(523010-2)
Henning Berg & John Taylor With 'Tango'
Tango & Company | Jazz Haus Musik | JHM 0085 CD
Jan Garbarek Group
Photo With Blue Skie, White Clouds, Wires, Windows And A Red Roof | ECM | 1135 (843168-2)
Jan Garbarek Quartet
Places | ECM | 1118(829195-2)
John Surman Orchestra
How Many Clouds Can You See? | Deram | 844882-2
John Surman Quartet
Stranger Than Fiction | ECM | 1534
How Many Clouds Can You See? | Deram | 844882-2
John Surman-John Taylor With Chorus
Proverbs And Songs | ECM | 1639
John Taylor
Ten Piano Players,Vol.1 | Green House Music | CD 1002
John Taylor Trio
Rosslyn | ECM | 1751(159924-2)
Kenny Wheeler Brass Ensemble
A Long Time Ago | ECM | 1691
Kenny Wheeler Ensemble
Muisc For Large & Small Ensembles | ECM | 1415/16
Kenny Wheeler Quintet
Double, Double You | ECM | 1262(815675-2)
The Widow In The Window | ECM | 1417(843198-2)
Miroslav Vitous Group
Journey's End | ECM | 1242(843171-2)
Norma Winstone Trio
Somewhere Called Home | ECM | 1337
Peter Erskine Trio

You Never Know | ECM | 1497(517353-2)
Time Being | ECM | 1532
As It Is | ECM | 1594
Juni | ECM | 1657(539726-2)
Uli Beckerhoff Septet
Private Life | Nabel Records:Jazz Network | CD 4657
Volker Kriegel Quintet
Spectrum | MPS | 9808699

Taylor,Josea | (bassoon)
Yusef Lateef Orchestra
The Centaur And The Phoenix | Original Jazz Classics | OJCCD 721-2(RLP 9337)

Taylor,Koko | (voc)
Koko Taylor
Classic Blues | Zounds | CD 2700048

Taylor,Larry | (b)
Albert King Blues Band
The Lost Session | Stax | SCD 8534-2

Taylor,Les | (bsreeds)
Ella Fitzgerald With The Bill Doggett Orchestra
Ella Fitzgerald-First Lady Of Song | Verve | 517898-2
Rhythm Is My Business | Verve | 559513-2

Taylor,Louis | (ss,tstb)
Count Basie And His Orchestra
Jazz:The Essential Collection Vol.3 | IN+OUT Records | 78013-2
Earl Hines And His Orchestra
Jazz:The Essential Collection Vol.2 | IN+OUT Records | 78012-2

Taylor,Luis | (dr)
Johnny 'Hammond' Smith Quartet
Open House | Milestone | MCD 47089-2

Taylor,Malcolm | (tb)
Duke Ellington And His Orchestra
The Ellington Suites | Original Jazz Classics | OJC20 446-2(2310762)
The Afro-Eurasian Eclipse-A Suite In Eight Parts | Original Jazz Classics | OJCCD 645-2(F 9498)
Togo Brava Swuite | Storyville | STCD 8323

Taylor,Mark | (drfr-h)
Marty Elkins And Her Sextet
Fuse Blues | Nagel-Heyer | CD 062
Mose Allison Quartet
The Mose Chronicles-Live In London,Vol.2 | Blue Note | 529748-2
Mose Allison Trio
The Mose Chronicles-Live In London,Vol.1 | Blue Note | 529747-2

Taylor,Martin | (el-g,g,g-solog-solo & overdubbing)
Louis Stewart-Martin Taylor
Acoustic Guitar Duets | Jardis Records | JRCD 9613
Stephane Grappelli Group
Stephane Grappelli:Live In San Francisco | Storyville | 4960723
Stephane Grappelli-David Grisman Group
Stephane Grappelli:Live In San Francisco | Storyville | 4960723

Taylor,R. | (fl)
Dee Dee Bridgewater With Orchestra
Dear Ella | Verve | 539102-2

Taylor,Rudolph | (dr)
Earl Hines And His Orchestra
Planet Jazz:Earl Hines | Planet Jazz | 2159973-2

Taylor,Sam 'The Man' | (as,sax,tsvoc)
Al Sears And His Orchestra
Sear-iously | Bear Family Records | BCD 15668 AH
Buddy Johnson And His Orchestra
Buddy And Ella Johnson 1953-1964 | Bear Family Records | BCD 15479 DH
Cab Calloway And His Cab Jivers
Planet Jazz:Cab Calloway | Planet Jazz | 2161237-2
Della Reese With The Sy Oliver Orchestra
Misty Blue:Sweet Sisters Swing Songs Of Sorrow And Sadness | Blue Note | 521151-2
Ella Fitzgerald With Sy Oliver And His Orchestra
Ella Fitzgerald:The Decca Years 1949-1954 | Decca | 050668-2
Lawrence Brown Quintet
Slide Trombone | Verve | 559930-2
Louis Armstrong And His Orchestra
Satchmo Serenaders | Verve | 543792-2

Taylor,Vance | (keyboards,p,synthgrand-p)
Stanley Clarke Group
If This Bass Could Only Talk | CBS | 460883-2

Taylor,Vincent | (steel-dr)
Monty Alexander Sextet
Three Originals:Love And Sunshine/Estade/Cobilimbo | MPS | 523526-2

Taylor,Yack | (voc)
Louis Jordan And His Tympany Five
Louis Jordan-Let The Good Times Roll: The Complete Decca Recordings 1938-1954 | Bear Family Records | BCD 15557 IH

Tayo,Ife | (percdancer)
Sun Ra And His Intergalactic Research Arkestra
Black Myth/Out In Space | MPS | 557656-2

Tbilisi Symphony Orchestra |
Jan Garbarek Group
Rites | ECM | 1685/86(559006-2)

Tcheuredkjan,Jean-Claude | (v)
Charlie Haden Quartet West With Strings
Now Is The Hour | Verve | 527827-2

Tchicai,John | (as,p,dr,perc,voice,ts,voc,b-cl,ss)
Archie Shepp Sextet
Four For Trane | Impulse(MCA) | 951218-2
John Coltrane And His Orchestra
Ascension | Impulse(MCA) | 543413-2
Ok Nok...Kongo
Moonstone Journey | dacapo | DCCD 9444
Pierre Dorge's New Jungle Orchestra
Giraf | dacapo | DCCD 9440

Teagarden,Charlie | (tpvoc)
Benny Goodman And His Orchestra
Jazz:The Essential Collection Vol.3 | IN+OUT Records | 78013-2
Eddie Lang-Joe Venuti And Their Allstars Orchestra
Jazz:The Essential Collection Vol.3 | IN+OUT Records | 78013-2
Jack Teagarden And His Orchestra
Jazz:The Essential Collection Vol.3 | IN+OUT Records | 78013-2
Paul Whiteman And His Orchestra
Planet Jazz:Jack Teagarden | Planet Jazz | 2161236-2
Jazz:The Essential Collection Vol.3 | IN+OUT Records | 78013-2
The Three T's
Jazz:The Essential Collection Vol.3 | IN+OUT Records | 78013-2

Teagarden,Jack | (tbvoc)
Adrian Rollini And His Orchestra
Jazz:The Essential Collection Vol.3 | IN+OUT Records | 78013-2
All Star Band
Planet Jazz:Jack Teagarden | Planet Jazz | 2161236-2
Ben Pollack And His Park Central Orchestra
Planet Jazz:Jack Teagarden | Planet Jazz | 2161236-2
Jazz:The Essential Collection Vol.3 | IN+OUT Records | 78013-2
Benny Goodman And His Orchestra
Planet Jazz:Benny Goodman | Planet Jazz | 2152054-2
Jazz:The Essential Collection Vol.3 | IN+OUT Records | 78013-2
Camel Caravan Broadcast 1939 Vol.1 | Phontastic | NCD 8817
Bessie Smith And Her Band
Jazz:The Essential Collection Vol.3 | IN+OUT Records | 78013-2
Big Joe Turner And Pete Johnson With The Blues Band
Newport Jazz Festival 1958,July 3rd-6th Vol.3:Blues In The Night No.1 | Phontastic | NCD 8815
Big Maybelle With The Blues Band
Newport Jazz Festival 1958,July 3rd-6th Vol.3:Blues In The Night No.1 | Phontastic | NCD 8815
Bud Freeman And His Famous Chicagoans
Jazz:The Essential Collection Vol.3 | IN+OUT Records | 78013-2
Bud Freeman And His Summa Cum Laude Orchestra
Planet Jazz:Jack Teagarden | Planet Jazz | 2161236-2
Planet Jazz:Bud Freeman | Planet Jazz | 2161240-2
Chuck Berry With The Blues Band
Newport Jazz Festival 1958,July 3rd-6th Vol.3:Blues In The Night No.1 | Phontastic | NCD 8815
Eddie Condon And His Chicagoans
The Very Best Of Dixieland Jazz | Verve | 535529-2
Eddie Condon And His Orchestra
Jazz:The Essential Collection Vol.3 | IN+OUT Records | 78013-2
Eddie Condon's Hot Shots
Jazz:The Essential Collection Vol.3 | IN+OUT Records | 78013-2
Eddie Lang-Joe Venuti And Their Allstars Orchestra
Jazz:The Essential Collection Vol.3 | IN+OUT Records | 78013-2
Eddie's Hot Shots
Planet Jazz:Jack Teagarden | Planet Jazz | 2161236-2
Esquire Metropolitan Opera House Jam Session
Jazz:The Essential Collection Vol.3 | IN+OUT Records | 78013-2
Fats Waller And His Buddies
Planet Jazz:Jack Teagarden | Planet Jazz | 2161236-2
Jazz:The Essential Collection Vol.3 | IN+OUT Records | 78013-2
George Wettling's New Yorkers
Jazz:The Essential Collection Vol.3 | IN+OUT Records | 78013-2
Hoagy Carmichael And His Orchestra
Planet Jazz:Bud Freeman | Planet Jazz | 2161240-2
Hoagy Carmichael With Jack Teagarden And His Big Band
Swing Vol.1 | Storyville | 4960343
Irving Mills And His Hotsy Totsy Gang
Jazz:The Essential Collection Vol.3 | IN+OUT Records | 78013-2
Jack Teagarden And His Band
Meet Me Where They Play The Blues | Good Time Jazz | GTCD 12063-2
Jack Teagarden And His Orchestra
Jazz:The Essential Collection Vol.3 | IN+OUT Records | 78013-2
Jack Teagarden And His Sextet
Mis'ry And The Blues | Verve | 9860310
Jack Teagarden Sextet
Newport Jazz Festival 1958,July 3rd-6th Vol.3:Blues In The Night No.1 | Phontastic | NCD 8815
Jack Teagarden Sextet With Bobby Hackett
Newport Jazz Festival 1958,July 3rd-6th Vol.3:Blues In The Night No.1 | Phontastic | NCD 8815
Jack Teagarden With Orchestra
Jazz:The Essential Collection Vol.3 | IN+OUT Records | 78013-2
Jack Teagarden With The Red Allen Band
The Very Best Of Dixieland Jazz | Verve | 535529-2
Jack Teagarden's Big Eight
Planet Jazz:Jack Teagarden | Planet Jazz | 2161236-2
Planet Jazz | Planet Jazz | 2169652-2
Jazz:The Essential Collection Vol.3 | IN+OUT Records | 78013-2
Jack Teagarden's Chicagoans
Jazz:The Essential Collection Vol.3 | IN+OUT Records | 78013-2
The Hollywood Session:The Capitol Jazzmen | Jazz Unlimited | JUCD 2044
Louis Armstrong And His All Stars
Planet Jazz:Louis Armstrong | Planet Jazz | 2152052-2
Planet Jazz:Jack Teagarden | Planet Jazz | 2161236-2
Planet Jazz:Male Jazz Vocalists | Planet Jazz | 2169657-2
Jazz Collection:Louis Armstrong | Laserlight | 24366
Best Of The Complete RCA Victor Recordings | RCA | 2663636-2
Louis Armstrong:A 100th Birthday Celebration | RCA | 2663694-2
I Love Jazz | Verve | 543747-2
Louis Armstrong:C'est Si Bon | Dreyfus Jazz Line | FDM 36730-2
Louis Armstrong-My Greatest Songs | MCA | MCD 18347
Swing Legends:Louis Armstrong | Nimbus Records | NI 2012
Louis Armstrong:Wintergarden 1947/Blue Note 1948 | Storyville | STCD 8242
Louis Armstrong And His Orchestra
Jazz:The Essential Collection Vol.3 | IN+OUT Records | 78013-2
Louis Armstrong:C'est Si Bon | Dreyfus Jazz Line | FDM 36730-2
Swing Legends:Louis Armstrong | Nimbus Records | NI 2012
Mound City Blue Blowers
Planet Jazz:Jack Teagarden | Planet Jazz | 2161236-2
Paul Whiteman And His Orchestra
Planet Jazz:Jack Teagarden | Planet Jazz | 2161236-2
Jazz:The Essential Collection Vol.3 | IN+OUT Records | 78013-2
Roger Wolfe Kahn And His Orchestra
Planet Jazz:Jack Teagarden | Planet Jazz | 2161236-2
The Capitol Jazzmen
Jazz:The Essential Collection Vol.3 | IN+OUT Records | 78013-2
The Hollywood Session:The Capitol Jazzmen | Jazz Unlimited | JUCD 2044
The Metronome All-Star Nine
Jazz:The Essential Collection Vol.3 | IN+OUT Records | 78013-2
The Three T's
Jazz:The Essential Collection Vol.3 | IN+OUT Records | 78013-2
V-Disc All Star Jam Session
Louis Armstrong-Jack Teagarden-Woody Herman:Midnights At V-Disc | Jazz Unlimited | JUCD 2048
V-Disc All Stars
Jazz:The Essential Collection Vol.3 | IN+OUT Records | 78013-2

Teagarden,Norma | (p)
Jack Teagarden And His Band
Meet Me Where They Play The Blues | Good Time Jazz | GTCD 12063-2

Teague,Thurman | (b)
Harry James And His Orchestra
The Legends Of Swing | Laserlight | 24659

Teal,Clare | (voc)
Clare Teal And Her Band
Orsino's Songs | Candid | CCD 79783

Teboe,Dana | (tb)
Arturo Sandoval And The Latin Train Band
Arturo Sandoval & The Latin Train | GRP | GRP 98202

Tecco,Donna | (v)
A Band Of Friends
Wynton Marsalis Quartet With Strings | CBS | CK 68921

Techner,Joe | (tp)
Elliot Lawrence And His Orchestra
Mullenium | CBS | CK 65678

Tedesco,Tommy | (g,el-gvoc)
Ella Fitzgerald With Orchestra
The Best Is Yet To Come | Original Jazz Classics | OJCCD 889-2(2312138)

Tee,Richard | (digital-p,el-p,clavinet,org)
Carla Bley Band
Dinner Music | Watt | 6(825815-2)
Grant Green Orchestra
Grant Green:Blue Breakbeat | Blue Note | 494705-2
Grant Green With Orchestra
The Final Comedown(Soundtrack) | Blue Note | 581678-2
Grover Washington Jr. Orchestra
Inside Moves | Elektra | 7559-60318-2
Jazzrock-Anthology Vol.3:Fusion | Zounds | CD 27100555
Klaus Doldinger Jubilee
Doldinger's Best | ACT | 9224-2
Klaus Doldinger With Orchestra
Lifelike | Warner | 2292-46478-2
Klaus Doldinger With Orchestra And Etta James
Lifelike | Warner | 2292-46478-2
Oscar Brown Jr. And His Group
Movin' On | Rhino | 8122-73678-2
Rahsaan Roland Kirk And His Orchestra
Blacknuss | Rhino | 8122-71408-2

Teepe,Joris | (btalking)
Jörg Krückel-Brad Leali Quartet
Cookin' Good | Edition Collage | EC 507-2
Maximilian Geller Group
Maximilian Geller Goes Bossa | Edition Collage | EC 496-2
Maimilian Geller Goes Bossa Encore | Edition Collage | EC 505-2
Maximilian Geller Quartet feat. Melanie Bong
Maimilian Geller Goes Bossa Encore | Edition Collage | EC 505-2
Maximilian Geller Quartet feat. Sabina Sciubba
Maimilian Geller Goes Bossa Encore | Edition Collage | EC 505-2
Maximilian Geller Quartet feat. Susan Tobocman
Maimilian Geller Goes Bossa Encore | Edition Collage | EC 505-2

Tei,Adrian | (sax)
Anita O'Day With Gene Krupa And His Orchestra
Let Me Off Uptown:Anita O'Day With Gene Krupa | CBS | CK 65625

Teilmann,Iben Bramsnaes | (viola)
Jim Hall Jazzpar Quartet +4
Jazzpar 98 | Storyville | STCD 4230
Jim Hall With The Zapolski Quartet
Jazzpar 98 | Storyville | STCD 4230

Teimar,Margit | (voc)
Bengt-Arne Wallin Orchestra
The Birth+Rebirth Of Swedish Folk Jazz | ACT | 9254-2

Tekula,Joe | (cello)
Gary McFarland And His Orchestra
The Complete Bill Evans On Verve | Verve | 527953-2
Gunther Schuller Ensemble
Beauty Is A Rare Thing:Ornette Coleman-The Complete Atlantic Recordings | Atlantic | 8122-71410-2
Modern Jazz Quartet & Guests
MJQ 40 | Atlantic | 7567-82330-2

Tellemar,Hasse | (b)
Coleman Hawkins With The Thore Ehrlings Orchestra
Coleman Hawkins At The Golden Circle | Dragon | DRCD 265

Tellnes,Thorsten | (p)
Terje Rypdal Quartet With The Bergen Chamber Ensemble
Lux Aeterna | ECM | 1818(017070-2)

Temiz,Okay | (dr,bells,berimbau,sticks,talking-dr)
Don Cherry Group
Dona Nostra | ECM | 1448(521727-2)
Don Cherry-The Sonet Recordings:Eternal Now/Live Ankara | Verve | 533049-2
Oriental Wind
Life Road | JA & RO | JARO 4113-2
Jazzy World | JA & RO | JARO 4200-2

Tempel,Rainer | (arr,ldp)
Rainer Tempel Band
Suite Ellington | Jazz 'n' Arts Records | JNA 0401
Rainer Tempel Big Band
Melodies Of '98 | Jazz 4 Ever Records:Jazz Network | J4E 4744
Album 03 | Jazz 'n' Arts Records | JNA 1102
Rainer Tempel Quintet
Blick In Die Welt | Edition Musikat | EDM 038

Temperley,Joe | (as,ts,bs,b-cl,ss,bs-solo,clsax)
Buck Clayton Swing Band
Swing's The Village | Nagel-Heyer | CD 5004
Blues Of Summer | Nagel-Heyer | NH 1011
Duke Ellington Orchestra
Continuum | Fantasy | FCD 24765-2
Joe Temperley
Easy To Remember | Hep | CD 2083
Joe Temperley Quartet
Easy To Remember | Hep | CD 2083
Joe Temperley Quartet With Strings
Easy To Remember | Hep | CD 2083
Joe Temperley Quintet
Easy To Remember | Hep | CD 2083
Joe Temperley Quintet With Strings
Easy To Remember | Hep | CD 2083
Lincoln Center Jazz Orchestra
Big Train | CBS | CK 69860
Thad Jones-Mel Lewis Orchestra
The Groove Merchant/The Second Race | Laserlight | 24656
The Nagel-Heyer Allstars
Uptown Lowdown:A Jazz Salute To The Big Apple | Nagel-Heyer | CD 2004
Wycliffe Gordon Group
Slidin' Home | Nagel-Heyer | CD 2001

Tempo Jazzmen |
Tempo Jazzmen
Dizzy Gillespie:Night In Tunisia | Dreyfus Jazz Line | FDM 36734-2

Tempo,Denis | (clas)
Louis Sclavis & The Bernard Struber Jazztet
La Phare | Enja | ENJ-9359 2

Tempo,Nino | (ts)
Diane Schuur And Her Band
Music Is My Life | Atlantic | 7567-83150-2
Maynard Ferguson Band
Verve Jazz Masters 52:Maynard Ferguson | Verve | 529905-2

Temur,Orhan | (perc,saz,v,darbukaoud)
Dirk Rauff Group
Theater I (Bühnenmusik) | Poise | Poise 07
Kölner Saxophon Mafia With Nedim Hazar And Orhan Temur
Kölner Saxophon Mafia Proudly Presents | Jazz Haus Musik | JHM 0046 CD

Ten Cats And A Mouse |
Ten Cats And A Mouse
The Hollywood Session:The Capitol Jazzmen | Jazz Unlimited | JUCD 2044

TenBroek,Nicholaas | (string-arrangement,tbbs)
Joe Henderson And His Orchestra
Joe Henderson:The Milestone Years | Milestone | 8MCD 4413-2

Tenda,Toru | (alto-fl,piccolo,japanese-fl,bass-fl)
Muneer B.Fennell & The Rhythm String Band
An Encounter With Higher Forces | double moon | CHRDM 71019

Tender Loving Care | (background-voc)
Oscar Brown Jr. And His Group
Movin' On | Rhino | 8122-73678-2

Tenenbom,Steven | (viola)
Chick Corea With String Quartet,Flute And French Horn
Septet | ECM | 1297

Tenney,John | (v)
Art Pepper Quintet With Strings
Art Pepper:The Complete Galaxy Recordings | Galaxy | 16GCD 1016-2
Winter Moon | Original Jazz Classics | OJC20 677-2(GXY 5140)

Tennyson,Hal | (asbs)
Glenn Miller And His Orchestra
Planet Jazz:Glenn Miller | Planet Jazz | 2152056-2
Planet Jazz Sampler | Planet Jazz | 2152326-2
Planet Jazz:Big Bands | Planet Jazz | 2169649-2
Planet Jazz:Swing | Planet Jazz | 2169651-2

Tenore E Cuncordu De Orosei |
Ernst Reijseger & Tenore E Cuncordu De Orosei
Colla Voche | Winter&Winter | 910037-2

Terlitzky,Olga | (viola)
Absolute Ensemble
African Symphony | Enja | ENJ-9410 2
Melissa Walker And Her Band
I Saw The Sky | Enja | ENJ-9409 2
Paquito D'Rivera Group With The Absolute Ensemble
Habanera | Enja | ENJ-9395 2

Terlouw,P.M. | (v)
Stochelo Rosenberg Group With Strings
Gypsy Swing | Verve | 527806-2

Terra Brazil |
Terra Brazil
Café Com Leite | art-mode-records | AMR 2101

Terrasson,Jackie[Jacky] | (p,el-parr)
Jackie Terrasson Trio
Jacky Terrasson | Blue Note | 829351-2
Reach | Blue Note | 837570-2
Jacky Terrasson Group
What It Is | Blue Note | 498756-2
Jacky Terrasson Trio
Smile | Blue Note | 542413-2

Alive | Blue Note | 859651-2
Jacky Terrasson-Emmanuel Pahud Quartet
Into The Blue | Blue Note | 557257-2
Michael 'Patches' Stewart Group
Blue Patches | Hip Bop | HIBD 8016
Stefon Harris-Jacky Terrasson Group
Kindred | Blue Note | 531868-2

Terraza,Ignasi | (p)
Mitchell-Terraza Group
Shell Blues | Fresh Sound Records | FSNT 005 CD

Terrill,Harry | (as)
Charlie Parker And His Orchestra
The Cole Porter Songbook | Verve | 823250-2
Bird: The Complete Charlie Parker On Verve | Verve | 837141-2
Charlie Parker With Orchestra
Charlie Parker:The Best Of The Verve Years | Verve | 527815-2
Charlie Parker With The Joe Lipman Orchestra
Verve Jazz Masters 28:Charlie Parker Plays Standards | Verve | 521854-2
Charlie Parker Big Band | Verve | 559835-2
Gene Krupa And His Orchestra
Mullenium | CBS | CK 65678
Sarah Vaughan With The Joe Lippman Orchestra
Sarah Vaughan:Lover Man | Dreyfus Jazz Line | FDM 36739-2

Terry,Buddy | (ss)
Alphonse Mouzon Group
Deep Blue-The United States Of Mind | Blue Note | 521152-2

Terry,Clark | (fl-h,talking,tp,mouth-piece,voc)
Abbey Lincoln And Her All Stars
The World Is Falling Down | Verve | 843476-2
All Star Live Jam Session
Brownie-The Complete EmArCy Recordings Of Clifford Brown | EmArCy | 838306-2
All Stars
Alternate Blues | Original Jazz Classics | OJCCD 744-2
Babs Gonzales And His Band
Voilà | Fresh Sound Records | FSR CD 340
Benny Carter And His Orchestra
Jazz At The Philharmonic:The Montreux Collection | Pablo | PACD 5306-2
Benny Goodman And His Orchestra
The Legends Of Swing | Laserlight | 24659
Blue Mitchell And His Orchestra
A Sure Thing | Original Jazz Classics | OJCCD 837-2
The Jazz Giants Play Jerome Kern:Yesterdays | Prestige | PCD 24202-2
Bud Powell Quartet
Parisian Thoroughfare | Pablo | CD 2310976-2
Bud Powell Quintet
The Story Of Jazz Piano | Laserlight | 24653
Parisian Thoroughfare | Pablo | CD 2310976-2
Cal Tjader With The Lalo Schifrin Orchestra
Talkin Verve/Roots Of Acid Jazz:Cal Tjader | Verve | 531562-2
Cannonball Adderley And His Orchestra
Ballads | Blue Note | 537563-2
Cannonball Adderley Birthday Celebration | Fantasy | FANCD 6087-2
Cecil Taylor/Buell Neidlinger Orchestra
New York City R&B | Candid | CCD 79017
Charles Mingus And His Orchestra
The Complete Town Hall Concert | Blue Note | 828353-2
Charles Mingus Orchestra
Charles Mingus:Pre-Bird(Mingus Revisited) | Verve | 538636-2
Charlie Byrd Trio And Guests
Byrd At The Gate | Original Jazz Classics | OJC20 262-2
Clark Terry & Chico O Farril Orchestra
Spanish Rice | Verve | 9861050
Clark Terry And His Orchestra
Clark Terry And His Orchestra Feat. Paul Gonsalves | Storyville | STCD 8322
Clark Terry Five
The Jazz Giants Play Duke Ellington:Caravan | Prestige | PCD 24227-2
Clark Terry Orchestra
Color Changes | Candid | CCD 79009
Clark Terry Quartet
Jazz Legends:Clark Terry-Duke Jordan | Storyville | 4960283
OW | Storyville | STCD 8378
Clark Terry Quintet
Unsong Hero:The Undiscovered Genius Of Chas Burchell | IN+OUT Records | 7026-2
The Hymn | Candid | CCD 79770
Herr Ober | Nagel-Heyer | CD 068
Jazz Dance | Original Jazz Classics | OJCCD 1002-2(1210890)
Clark Terry With The Oscar Peterson Trio
Verve Jazz Masters 37:Oscar Peterson Plays Broadway | Verve | 516893-2
Oscar Peterson Trio + One | Verve | 558075-2
Clark Terry With The Summit Jazz Orchestra
Clark | Edition Collage | EC 530-2
Clark Terry With The Thelonious Monk Trio
Thelonious Monk:85th Birthday Celebration | zyx records | FANCD 6076-2
Clark Terry-Max Roach Quartet
Friednship | CBS | 510886-2
Clark Terry-Red Mitchell Duo
Clark Terry-Red Mitchell | Enja | ENJ-5011 2
Clark Terry-Thelonious Monk Quartet
In Orbit | Original Jazz Classics | OJC 302(R 12-271)
Clifford Brown All Stars With Dinah Washington
Verve Jazz Masters 40:Dinah Washington | Verve | 522055-2
Count Basie And His Orchestra
Planet Jazz:Count Basie | Planet Jazz | 2152068-2
Count Basie Band
Basie Jam No. 2 | Original Jazz Classics | OJCCD 631-2(2310786)
Dave Pike Sextet
Carnavals | Prestige | PCD 24248-2
Dinah Washington And Her Band
After Hours With Miss D | Verve | 0760562
Verve Jazz Masters 40:Dinah Washington | Verve | 522055-2
Dinah Washington And Her Orchestra
For Those In Love | EmArCy | 514073-2
Dinah Washington With The Eddie Chamblee Orchestra
Dinah Sings Bessie Smith | Verve | 538635-2
Dinah Washington With The Quincy Jones Orchestra
Verve Jazz Masters 40:Dinah Washington | Verve | 522055-2
The Swingin' Miss 'D' | Verve | 558074-2
Dizzy Gillespie And His Orchestra
Verve Jazz Masters 10:Dizzy Gillespie | Verve | 516319-2
Gillespiana And Carnegie Hall Concert | Verve | 519809-2
Talking Verve:Dizzy Gillespie | Verve | 533846-2
Ultimate Dizzy Gillespie | Verve | 557535-2
Dizzy Gillespie's Trumpet Kings
The Trumpet Kings Meet Joe Turner | Original Jazz Classics | OJCCD 497-2
Duke Ellington And His Orchestra
Jazz Collection:Duke Ellington | Laserlight | 24369
The Legends Of Swing | Laserlight | 24659
100 Years Duke | Laserlight | 24906
Highlights From The Duke Ellington Centennial Edition | RCA | 2663672-2
Greatest Hits | CBS | 462959-2
The Big Bands Vol.1.The Snader Telescriptions | Storyville | 4960043
Verve Jazz Masters 4:Duke Ellington | Verve | 516338-2
Ellington '55 | Capitol | 520135-2
Great Swing Classics In Hi-Fi | Capitol | 521223-2
Ellington At Newport 1956(Complete) | CBS | CK 64932
Black Brown And Beige | CBS | CK 65566
Such Sweet Thunder | CBS | CK 65568
Anatomy Of A Murder | CBS | CK 65569
The Ellington Suites | Original Jazz Classics | OJC20 446-2(2310762)
Duke Ellington At The Alhambra | Pablo | PACD 5313-2
Eddie Lockjaw Davis And His Orchestra
Eric Dolphy:The Complete Prestige Recordings | Prestige | 9 PRCD-4418-2
Eddie Lockjaw Davis Orchestra
Afro-Jaws | Original Jazz Classics | OJCCD 403-2(RLP 9373)
Ella Fitzgerald And Her All Stars
All That Jazz | Pablo | 2310938-2
Ella Fitzgerald Jam
Bluella:Ella Fitzgerald Sings The Blues | Pablo | 2310960-2
Ella Fitzgerald With Orchestra
Ella Abraca Jobim | Pablo | 2630201-2
Ella Fitzgerald With The Duke Ellington Orchestra
Ella Fitzgerald-First Lady Of Song | Verve | 517898-2
The Best Of The Song Books | Verve | 519804-2
Verve Jazz Masters 6:Ella Fitzgerald | Verve | 519822-2
The Best Of The Song Books:The Ballads | Verve | 521867-2
Verve Jazz Masters 46:Ella Fitzgerald-The Jazz Sides | Verve | 527655-2
Love Songs:The Best Of The Song Books | Verve | 531762-2
Ella Fitzgerald Sings The Duke Ellington Songbook | Verve | 559248-2
For The Love Of Ella Fitzgerald | Verve | 841765-2
Ernestine Anderson With Orchestra
My Kinda Swing | Mercury | 842409-2
Freddie Hubbard Orchestra
The Body And The Soul | Impulse(MCA) | 951183-2
Gary Burton Sextet
Planet Jazz:Gary Burton | RCA | 2165367-2
Gene Ammons And His Orchestra
A Stranger In Town | Prestige | PRCD 24266-2
George Benson Orchestra
Talkin' Verve:George Benson | Verve | 553780-2
George Benson With Orchestra
Verve Jazz Masters 21:George Benson | Verve | 521861-2
Gerry Mulligan Concert Jazz Band
Verve Jazz Masters 36:Gerry Mulligan | Verve | 523342-2
Verve Jazz Masters Vol.60:The Collection | Verve | 529866-2
Gerry Mulligan And The Concert Band At The Village Vanguard | Verve | 589488-2
The Complete Verve Gerry Mulligan Concert Band | Verve | 9860613
Hank Jones With Oliver Nelson's Orchestra
The Roots Of Acid Jazz | Impulse(MCA) | IMP 12042
J.J.Johnson And His Orchestra
Planet Jazz:J.J.Johnson | Planet Jazz | 2159974-2
J.J.Johnson Sextet
The J.J.Johnson Memorial Album | Prestige | PRCD 11025-2
JATP All Stars
J.A.T.P. In London 1969 | Pablo | 2CD 2620119
Welcome To Jazz At The Philharmonic | Fantasy | FANCD 6081-2
Jimmy Heath Orchestra
Cannonball Adderley Birthday Celebration | Fantasy | FANCD 6087-2
Jimmy Rushing With Oliver Nelson And His Orchestra
Every Day I Have The Blues | Impulse(MCA) | 547967-2
Jimmy Smith And Wes Montgomery With Orchestra
Jimmy & Wes-The Dynamic Duo | Verve | 521445-2
Jimmy Smith And Wes Montgomery With The Oliver Nelson Orchestra
Wes Montgomery:The Verve Jazz Sides | Verve | 521690-2
Jimmy Smith:Best Of The Verve Years | Verve | 527950-2
Talkin' Jazz:Roots Of Acid Jazz | Verve | 529580-2
Jimmy Smith With The Oliver Nelson Orchestra
Verve Jazz Masters 29:Jimmy Smith | Verve | 521855-2
Jimmy Smith:Best Of The Verve Years | Verve | 527950-2
Jimmy Smith-Talkin' Verve | Verve | 531563-2
Joe Williams And Friends
Planet Jazz:Male Jazz Vocalists | Planet Jazz | 2169657-2
At Newport '63 | RCA | 2663919-2
Joe Williams And His Band
Planet Jazz:Joe Williams | Planet Jazz | 2165370-2
Joe Williams With The Jimmy Jones Orchestra
Planet Jazz:Joe Williams | Planet Jazz | 2165370-2
Joe Williams,With The Oliver Nelson Orchestra
Planet Jazz:Joe Williams | Planet Jazz | 2165370-2
Johnny Hodges And His Band
Verve Jazz Masters 35:Johnny Hodges | Verve | 521857-2
Johnny Hodges And The Ellington All-Stars Without Duke
Verve Jazz Masters 35:Johnny Hodges | Verve | 521857-2
Johnny Hodges And The Ellington Men
Verve Jazz Masters 35:Johnny Hodges | Verve | 521857-2
Junior Mance Trio & Orchestra
That Lovin' Feelin' | Milestone | MCD 47097-2
Lalo Schifrin And His Orchestra
Verve Jazz Masters 39:Cal Tjader | Verve | 521858-2
Tin Tin Deo | Fresh Sound Records | FSR-CD 319
Laura Fygi With Band
Bewitched | Verve | 514724-2
Louis Armstrong And His Orchestra
What A Wonderful World | MCA | MCD 01876
Mar Murphy With The Ernie Wilkins Orchestra
RAH | Original Jazz Classics | OJCCD 141-2(R 9395)
McCoy Tyner Quintet
Live At Newport | Impulse(MCA) | 547980-2
Milt Jackson Orchestra
To Bags...With Love:Memorial Album | Pablo | 2310967-2
Milt Jackson Birthday Celebration | Fantasy | FANCD 6079-2
Big Bags | Original Jazz Classics | OJCCD 366-2(RLP 9429)
Milt Jackson-Ray Brown Jam
Milt Jackson Birthday Celebration | Fantasy | FANCD 6079-2
Montreux '77 | Original Jazz Classics | OJC 385(2620105)
Montreux '77 | Original Jazz Classics | OJC20 375-2(2308205)
Modern Jazz Quartet And Orchestra
MJQ 40 | Atlantic | 7567-82330-2
Oliver Nelson And His Orchestra
Verve Jazz Masters Vol.60:The Collection | Verve | 529866-2
Oscar Peterson Jam
Oscar Peterson Plays Duke Ellington | Pablo | 2310966-2
Montreux '77 | Original Jazz Classics | OJC 385(2620105)
Montreux '77 | Original Jazz Classics | OJC20 378-2(2308208)
Oscar Peterson Quintet With Strings
Jazz Dance | Original Jazz Classics | OJCCD 1002-2(1210890)
Oscar Peterson With The Ernie Wilkins Orchestra
Verve Jazz Masters 16:Oscar Peterson | Verve | 516320-2
Oscar Peterson-Clark Terry Duo
Oscar Peterson Plays Duke Ellington | Pablo | 2310966-2
Oscar Peterson & Clark Terry | Original Jazz Classics | OJCCD 806-2(2310742)
Pablo All Star Jam
Montreux '77 | Original Jazz Classics | OJC 385(2620105)
Quincy Jones And His Orchestra
Big Band Bossa Nova | Verve | 557913-2
Rahsaan/The Complete Mercury Recordings Of Roland Kirk | Mercury | 846630-2
The Quintessence | Impulse(MCA) | 951222-2
Rosemary Clooney With The Duke Ellington Orchestra
Blue Rose | CBS | CK 65506
Sarah Vaughan And The Thad Jones Orchestra
Verve Jazz Masters 42:Sarah Vaughan-The Jazz Sides | Verve | 526817-2
Sarah Vaughan With The Hal Mooney Orchestra
It's A Man's World | Mercury | 589487-2
Sonny Rollins Orchestra
Sonny Rollins And The Big Brass | Verve | 557545-2
Stan Getz With The Eddie Sauter Orchestra
Stan Getz Plays The Music Of Mickey One | Verve | 531232-2
Stan Getz With The Gary McFarland Orchestra
Stan Getz Highlights:The Best Of The Verve Years Vol.2 | Verve | 517330-2
Verve Jazz Masters 53:Stan Getz-Bossa Nova | Verve | 529904-2
Big Band Bossa Nova | Verve | 825771-2 PMS
The Basie Alumni
Swinging For The Count | Candid | CCD 79724
The Dave Glasser/Clark Terry/Barry Harris Project
Uh! Oh! | Nagel-Heyer | CD 2003
Blues Of Summer | Nagel-Heyer | NH 1011
The Trumpet Summit With The Oscar Peterson Big 4
The Trumpet Summit Meets The Oscar Peterson Big 4 | Original Jazz Classics | OJCCD 603-2
Thelonious Monk Quintet
Sonny Rollins-The Freelance Years:The Complete Riverside & Contemporary Recordings | Riverside | 5 RCD 4427-2
Brilliant Corners | Original Jazz Classics | OJC20 026-2
Toshiko Akiyoshi-Lew Tabackin Big Band
Monterey Jazz Festival 1975 | Storyville | 4960213
Wardell Gray Sextet
The Prestige Legacy Vol.2:Battles Of Saxes | Prestige | PCD 24252-2
Wardell Gray's Los Angeles All Stars
Dexter Gordon Birthday Celebration | Fantasy | FANCD 6082-2
Wardell Gray Memorial Vol.2 | Original Jazz Classics | OJCCD 051-2(P 7009)
Wes Montgomery Orchestra
Movin' Wes | Verve | 521433-2
Wes Montgomery With The Johnny Pate Orchestra
Verve Jazz Masters 14:Wes Montgomery | Verve | 519826-2
Wes Montgomery:The Verve Jazz Sides | Verve | 521690-2
Talkin' Jazz:Roots Of Acid Jazz | Verve | 529580-2
Willie Bobo Group
Bobo's Beat | Roulette | 590954-2
Yusef Lateef Orchestra
The Centaur And The Phoenix | Original Jazz Classics | OJCCD 721-2(RLP 9337)

Terry,Howard | (bassoon,bs,cl,b-clsax)
Barney Kessel And His Orchestra
The Jazz Giants Play Rodgers & Hart:Blue Moon | Prestige | PCD 24205-2
Ella Fitzgerald With The Nelson Riddle Orchestra
The Best Of The Song Books:The Ballads | Verve | 521867-2
Love Songs:The Best Of The Song Books | Verve | 531762-2
Ella Fitzgerald Sings The Johnny Mercer Songbook | Verve | 539057-2

Terry,Lesa | (v)
Freddy Cole With Band
Le Grand Freddy:Freddy Cole Sings The Music Of Michel Legrand | Fantasy | FCD 9683-2
Max Roach Double Quartet
To The Max! | Enja | ENJ-7021 22

Terry,Pete | (b-cl,bassoon,bsts)
Barney Kessel And His Orchestra
Barney Kessel Plays Carmen | Original Jazz Classics | OJC 269(C 7563)

Terry,Sonny | (harmvoc)
Lightnin' Hopkins Trio With Sonny Terry
Last Night Blues | Original Blues Classics | OBCCD 548-2(BV 1029)
Sonny Terry
From Spiritual To Swing | Vanguard | VCD 169/71
Sonny Terry & Brownie McGhee
Sonny Terry And Brownie McGhee At Suger Hill | Original Blues Classics | OBCCD 536-2(F 8091)
Just A Closer Walk With Thee | Original Blues Classics | OBCCD 541-2(F 3296)
Sonny Terry-Bull City Red
From Spiritual To Swing | Vanguard | VCD 169/71

Terry,Yosvanny | (flts)
Antonio Hart Group
Ama Tu Sonrisa | Enja | ENJ-9404 2

Terwilliger,Daryl | (v)
Johnny Hartman And His Orchestra
Unforgettable | Impulse(MCA) | IMP 11522

Terzic,Dejan | (drld)
Dejan Terzic European Assembly
Coming Up | double moon | DMCHR 71034
Enrico Rava With The Michael Flügel Quartet
Live At Birdland Neuburg | double moon | CHRDM 71011
Norbert Emminger Quintet
In The Park | Edition Collage | EC 521-2
Pete Yellin Quartet
Pete Yellin's European Connection:Live! | Jazz 4 Ever Records:Jazz Network | J4E 4722
The Tough Tenors With The Antonio Farao European Trio
Tough Tenors | Jazz 4 Ever Records:Jazz Network | J4E 4761
Torsten Goods Group
Manhattan Walls | Jardis Records | JRCD 20139

Testemiteanu,Sergiu | (b-g)
Trigon
Oglinda | JA & RO | JARO 4215-2

Tétard,Christian | (v)
Charlie Haden Quartet West With Strings
Now Is The Hour | Verve | 527827-2

Tethered Moon |
Tethered Moon
Chansons D'Edith Piaf | Winter&Winter | 910048-2

Tevelian,Meg | (g)
Brocksieper-Jazz-Ensemble
Drums Boogie | Bear Family Records | BCD 15988 AH
Brocksieper-Solisten-Orchester
Globetrotter | Bear Family Records | BCD 15912 AH
Brocksieper-Special-Ensemble
Globetrotter | Bear Family Records | BCD 15912 AH

Texidor,Joe Habad | (perc,sound-tree,tambourine)
Rahsaan Roland Kirk And His Orchestra
Blacknuss | Rhino | 8122-71408-2
Rahsaan Roland Kirk Sextet
Blacknuss | Rhino | 8122-71408-2

Texier,Henri | (b,fl,percvoc)
Daniel Humair Trio
Humair/Jeanneau/Texier | Owl Records | 014734-2
Phil Woods And His European Rhythm Machine
At The Montreux Jazz Festival | Verve | 065512-2
Americans Swinging In Paris:Phil Woods | EMI Records | 539654-2

Thaler,Manny | (bassoon)
Charlie Parker And His Orchestra
Charlie Parker:The Best Of The Verve Years | Verve | 527815-2
The Cole Porter Songbook | Verve | 823250-2
Bird: The Complete Charlie Parker On Verve | Verve | 837141-2
Charlie Parker With Orchestra
Charlie Parker Big Band | Verve | 559835-2
Charlie Parker With Orchestra & The Dave Lambert Singers
Verve Jazz Masters 28:Charlie Parker Plays Standards | Verve | 521854-2

Thanh,Huong | (voc)
Nguyen Le Group
Tales From Viet-Nam | ACT | 9225-2
Maghreb And Friends | ACT | 9261-2

Thärichen,Nicolai | (p)
Thärichens Tentett
Lady Moon | Minor Music | 801094

Tharpe,Sister Rosetta | (gvoc)
Sister Rosetta Tharpe And Her Group
Gospel Train | Mercury | 841134-2
Sister Rosetta Tharpe And Her Group With The Harmonizing Four
Gospel Train | Mercury | 841134-2
Sister Rosetta Tharpe With Albert Ammons
From Spiritual To Swing | Vanguard | VCD 169/71

Thathaal,Deepika | (voice)
Jan Garbarek With Ustad Fateh Ali Khan & Musicians From Pakistan
Ragas And Sagas | ECM | 1442(511263-2)

The Bad Plus: |
The Bad Plus
These Are The Vistas | CBS | 510666-2

INTERPRETENVERZEICHNIS

The Bad Plus | Fresh Sound Records | FSNT 107 CD

The Meeting |
The Meeting
Hot Jazz Bisquits | Hip Bop | HIBD 8801

The Romantchicks: |
The Sidewalks Of New York
Tin Pan Alley:The Sidewalks Of New York | Winter&Winter | 910038-2

The Three T's |
The Three T's
Jazz:The Essential Collection Vol.3 | IN+OUT Records | 78013-2

Thedford,Billy | (voc)
Sarah Vaughan And Her Band
Songs Of The Beatles | Atlantic | 16037-2

Theessink,Hans | (g,12-string-bj,voc,bj,jews-harp)
Hans Theessink
Hans Theessink:Solo | Minor Music | 801047
Hans Theessink Group
Call Me | Minor Music | 801022
Crazy Moon | Minor Music | 801052
Journey On | Minor Music | 801062

Theill,Ole | (dr,tables,perctablas)
Simon Spang-Hanssen & Maneklar
Wondering | dacapo | DCCD 9436

Theissing,Tscho | (v,voc,voiceperc)
Motus Quartett
Grimson Flames | Creative Works Records | CW CD 1023-2

Thelfa,Ali | (bass-dr,tambourine,dr,perc,djembe)
Hans Theessink Group
Crazy Moon | Minor Music | 801052
Journey On | Minor Music | 801062

Thelin,Eje | (tbkeyboards)
Eje Thelin Group
Ejs Thelin 1966 With Barney Wilen | Dragon | DRCD 366
Eje Thelin Quartet
Ejs Thelin 1966 With Barney Wilen | Dragon | DRCD 366
Eje Thelin Quintet
At The German Jazz Festival 1964 | Dragon | DRCD 374
Kenny Wheeler Sextet
Around 6 | ECM | 1156
NDR-Workshop
Doldinger's Best | ACT | 9224-2

Theobald,Robert | (p)
Two Beat Stompers
Deutsches Jazz Fesival 1954/1955 | Bear Family Records | BCD 15430

Theus,Fats | (ts)
Jimmy McGriff Organ Blues Band
The Worm | Blue Note | 538699-2

Theus,Son Ship | (drperc)
Eddie Henderson Orchestra
Blue Break Beats | Blue Note | 799106-2

Thewes,Christoph | (tb,condcomp)
Christof Thewes Little Big Band
Greyhound | Jazz Haus Musik | JHM 0133 CD
Christof Thewes-Rudi Mahall Duo
Quartetto Pazzo | Jazz Haus Musik | JHM 0122 CD
Christoph Thewes-Rudi Mahall Quartet
Quartetto Pazzo | Jazz Haus Musik | JHM 0122 CD

Thiam,Mor | (african-dr,voc,djembe,rainsticks)
Ivo Perlman Group
Children Of Ibeji | Enja | ENJ-7005 2

Thieke,Michael | (cl,alto-cl,assax)
Eric Schaefer & Demontage
Eric Schaefer & Demontage | Jazz Haus Musik | JHM 0117 CD
Franz Bauer Quintet
Plüschtier | Jazz Haus Musik | JHM 0097 CD
Nickendes Perlgras
Die Hintere Vase | Jazz Haus Musik | JHM 0105 CD

Thielemans,Jean 'Toots | (harm,vocwhistling)
George Shearing Quintet
Verve Jazz Masters Vol.59:Toots Thielemans | Verve | 535271-2
Quincy Jones And His Orchestra
Verve Jazz Masters Vol.59:Toots Thielemans | Verve | 535271-2
Toots Thieleman And Sivuca
Verve Jazz Masters Vol.59:Toots Thielemans | Verve | 535271-2
Toots Thielemans And His Orchestra
Verve Jazz Masters Vol.59:Toots Thielemans | Verve | 535271-2
Toots Thielemans Quartet
Verve Jazz Masters Vol.59:Toots Thielemans | Verve | 535271-2
Toots Thielemans Quintet
Verve Jazz Masters Vol.59:Toots Thielemans | Verve | 535271-2
Toots Thielemans Trio
Live In The Netherlands | Original Jazz Classics | OJCCD 930-2(2308233)
Toots Thielemans With Gals And Pals
Verve Jazz Masters Vol.59:Toots Thielemans | Verve | 535271-2
Toots Thielemans With The Shirley Horn Trio
Verve Jazz Masters Vol.59:Toots Thielemans | Verve | 535271-2
Toots Thielemans-Cees Schrama
Verve Jazz Masters Vol.59:Toots Thielemans | Verve | 535271-2
Toots Thielemans-Marc Johnson
Verve Jazz Masters Vol.59:Toots Thielemans | Verve | 535271-2

Thielemans,Jean 'Toots' | (g,harm,whistlingg-solo)
Bill Evans-Toots Thielemans Quintet
Affinity | Warner | 7599-27387-2
Diane Schuur With Orchestra
Love Songs | GRP | GRP 97032
The Best Of Diane Schuur | GRP | GRP 98882
Ella Fitzgerald With Orchestra
Ella Abraca Jobim | Pablo | 2630201-2
George Shearing And His Quintet
Verve Jazz Masters 57:George Shearing | Verve | 529900-2
Beauty And The Beat | Capitol | 542308-2
George Shearing Quintet
Verve Jazz Masters 57:George Shearing | Verve | 529900-2
Verve Jazz Masters Vol.59:Toots Thielemans | Verve | 535271-2
At Newport | Pablo | PACD 5315-2
George Shearing Quintet With Cannonball And Nat Adderley
At Newport | Pablo | PACD 5315-2
George Shearing Sextet
At Newport | Pablo | PACD 5315-2
Laura Fygi With Band
Bewitched | Verve | 514724-2
Mongo Santamaria Group With Dizzy Gillespie And Toots Thielemans
Summertime-Digital At Montreux 1980 | Original Jazz Classics | OJCCD 626-2(2308229)
Montreux Heat! | Pablo | PACD 5317-2
Oscar Peterson All Stars
Jazz At The Philharmonic:The Montreux Collection | Pablo | PACD 5306-2
Paul Kuhn Trio With Greetje Kauffeld And Jean 'Toots' Thielemans
Play It Again Paul | IN+OUT Records | 77040-2
Paul Kuhn Trio With Jean 'Toots' Thielemans
Play It Again Paul | IN+OUT Records | 77040-2
Peggy Lee With George Shearing
Beauty And The Beat | Capitol | 542308-2
Peggy Lee With The Quincy Jones Orchestra
Blues Cross Country | Capitol | 520088-2
Quincy Jones And His Orchestra
Verve Jazz Masters Vol.59:Toots Thielemans | Verve | 535271-2
Richard Galliano Group
Laurita | Dreyfus Jazz Line | FDM 36572-9
Richard Galliano Quartet
Gallianissimo! The Best Of Richard Galliano | Dreyfus Jazz Line | FDM 36616-2
Sarah Vaughan And Her Band
Songs Of The Beatles | Atlantic | 16037-2
Shirley Horn Trio with Toots Thielemans
You Won't Forget Me | Verve | 847482-2
Shirley Horn with Toots Thielemans
You Won't Forget Me | Verve | 847482-2
The Real Group With Toots Thielemans
One For All | ACT | 9003-2
The Rosenberg Trio
Suenos Gitanos | Polydor | 549581-2
Toots Thieleman And Sivuca
Verve Jazz Masters Vol.59:Toots Thielemans | Verve | 535271-2
Toots Thielemans
The Silver Collection: Toots Thielemans | Polydor | 825086-2 PMS
Toots Thielemans And His Orchestra
Verve Jazz Masters Vol.59:Toots Thielemans | Verve | 535271-2
Toots Thielemans Quartet
Verve Jazz Masters Vol.59:Toots Thielemans | Verve | 535271-2
Jazz In Paris:Toots Thielemans-Blues Pour Flirter | EmArCy | 549403-2 PMS
Toots Thielemans:The Live Takes Vol.1 | IN+OUT Records | 77041-2
Images | Choice | CHCD 71007
Toots Thielemans Quintet
Verve Jazz Masters Vol.59:Toots Thielemans | Verve | 535271-2
The Silver Collection: Toots Thielemans | Polydor | 825086-2 PMS
Toots Thielemans With Gals And Pals
Verve Jazz Masters Vol.59:Toots Thielemans | Verve | 535271-2
Toots Thielemans With The Ruud Bos Orchestra
The Silver Collection: Toots Thielemans | Polydor | 825086-2 PMS
Toots Thielemans With The Shirley Horn Trio
Verve Jazz Masters Vol.59:Toots Thielemans | Verve | 535271-2
Toots Thielemans-Cees Schrama
Verve Jazz Masters Vol.59:Toots Thielemans | Verve | 535271-2
Toots Thielemans-Kenny Werner Duo
Toots Thielemans & Kenny Werner | EmArCy | 014722-2
Toots Thielemans-Marc Johnson
Verve Jazz Masters Vol.59:Toots Thielemans | Verve | 535271-2
Toots Thielemans-Michel Herr
Toots Thielemans:The Live Takes Vol.1 | IN+OUT Records | 77041-2
Viktoria Tolstoy Group & Strings
Shining On You | ACT | 9701-2

Thielemans,Marcel | (tb)
Coleman Hawkins Trio
Jazz:The Essential Collection Vol.3 | IN+OUT Records | 78013-2
Coleman Hawkins With The Ramblers
Jazz:The Essential Collection Vol.3 | IN+OUT Records | 78013-2

Thigpen,Ed | (dr,perc,vocmarimba)
Anthony Ortega With The Nat Pierce Orchestra
Earth Dance | Fresh Sound Records | FSR-CD 325
Ben Webster With The Oscar Peterson Trio
Ben Webster Meets Oscar Peterson | Verve | 521448-2
Verve Jazz Masters 43:Ben Webster | Verve | 525431-2
Berlin Contemporary Jazz Orchestra
Berlin Contemporary Jazz Orchestra | ECM | 1409
Blossom Dearie Quartet
My Gentleman Friend | Verve | 519905-2
Verve Jazz Masters 51:Blossom Dearie | Verve | 529906-2
Blossom Dearie Sings Comden And Green | Verve | 589102-2
Blossom Dearie Quintet
My Gentleman Friend | Verve | 519905-2
Verve Jazz Masters 51:Blossom Dearie | Verve | 529906-2
Blossom Dearie Trio
Verve Jazz Masters 51:Blossom Dearie | Verve | 529906-2
Blossom Dearie Sings Comden And Green | Verve | 589102-2
Cal Tjader's Orchestra
Talkin Verve/Roots Of Acid Jazz:Cal Tjader | Verve | 531562-2
Clark Terry With The Oscar Peterson Trio
Verve Jazz Masters 37:Oscar Peterson Plays Broadway | Verve | 516893-2
Oscar Peterson Trio + One | Verve | 558075-2
Dinah Washington And Her Band
After Hours With Miss D | Verve | 0760562
Verve Jazz Masters 40:Dinah Washington | Verve | 522055-2
Eddie Lockjaw Davis Quartet
Jazz Legends:Eddie Lockjaw Davis Quartet Vol.1&2 | Storyville | 4960263
Ella Fitzgerald And Count Basie With The JATP All Stars
Bluella:Ella Fitzgerald Sings The Blues | Pablo | 2310960-2
Ella Fitzgerald With The Tommy Flanagan Trio
Sunshine Of Your Love | MPS | 533102-2
Ella A Nice | Original Jazz Classics | OJC20 442-2
Ella Fitzgerald In Budapest | Pablo | PACD 5308-2
Eric Watson Quartet
Full Metal Quartet | Owl Records | 159572-2
Gene Ammons Quartet
The Mal Waldron Memorial Album:Soul Eyes | Prestige | PRCD 11024-2
A Stranger In Town | Prestige | PRCD 24266-2
JATP All Stars
Welcome To Jazz At The Philharmonic | Fantasy | FANCD 6081-2
John Coltrane-Paul Quinichette Quintet
John Coltrane-The Prestige Recordings | Prestige | 16 PCD 4405-2
Cattin' | Original Jazz Classics | OJCCD 460-2
Johnny Pace With The Chet Baker Quintet
Chet Baker Introduces Johnny Pace | Original Jazz Classics | OJCCD 433-2(RLP 12-292)
Jutta Hipp Trio
Jutta Hipp At The Hickory House Vol.2 | Blue Note | 0677179
Mal Waldron Sextet
John Coltrane-The Prestige Recordings | Prestige | 16 PCD 4405-2
The Jazz Giants Play Jerome Kern:Yesterdays | Prestige | PCD 24202-2
Milt Jackson With The Oscar Peterson Trio
Gitanes Jazz 'Round Midnight: Oscar Peterson | Verve | 511036-2 PMS
Mundell Lowe Quartet
A Grand Night For Swinging | Original Jazz Classics | OJCCD 1940-(RLP 238)
Mundell Lowe Quintet
A Grand Night For Swinging | Original Jazz Classics | OJCCD 1940-(RLP 238)
Oscar Peterson Trio
Oscar Peterson Trio: Olympia/Theatre Des Champs-Elysees | Laserlight | 36134
Gitanes Jazz 'Round Midnight: Oscar Peterson | Verve | 511036-2 PMS
Verve Jazz Masters 16:Oscar Peterson | Verve | 516320-2
Verve Jazz Masters 37:Oscar Peterson Plays Broadway | Verve | 516893-2
Porgy And Bess | Verve | 519807-2
Verve Jazz Masters 20:Introducing | Verve | 519853-2
Night Train | Verve | 521440-2
We Get Request | Verve | 521442-2
Exclusively For My Friends-The Lost Tapes | MPS | 529096-2
Oscar Peterson:The Gershwin Songbooks | Verve | 529698-2
The Song Is You-The Best Of The Verve Songbooks | Verve | 531558-2
The Trio:Live From Chicago | Verve | 539063-2
West Side Story | Verve | 539753-2
The Sound Of The Trio | Verve | 543321-2
Oscar Peterson Plays The Duke Ellington Song Book | Verve | 559785-2
Oscar Peterson Plays The Harold Arlen Song Book | Verve | 589103-2
Oscar Peterson Plays The Cole Porter Song Book | Verve | 821987-2
The Silver Collection: Oscar Peterson | Verve | 823447-2 PMS
A Jazz Portrait Of Frank Sinatra | Verve | 825769-2
Oscar Peterson Trio With Milt Jackson
Very Tall | Verve | 559830-2
Very Tall | Verve | 827821-2
Oscar Peterson Trio With Roy Eldridge
Oscar Peterson Trio: Olympia/Theatre Des Champs-Elysees | Laserlight | 36134
Oscar Peterson Trio With The Nelson Riddle Orchestra
Verve Jazz Masters 16:Oscar Peterson | Verve | 516320-2
The Silver Collection: Oscar Peterson | Verve | 823447-2 PMS
Oscar Peterson Trio With The Russell Garcia Orchestra
Verve Jazz Masters 16:Oscar Peterson | Verve | 516320-2
Oscar Peterson With The Ernie Wilkins Orchestra
Verve Jazz Masters 16:Oscar Peterson | Verve | 516320-2
Prestige All Stars
The Prestige Legacy Vol.1:The High Priests | Prestige | PCD 24251-2
The Mal Waldron Memorial Album:Soul Eyes | Prestige | PRCD 11024-2
Roots
Saying Something | IN+OUT Records | 77031-2
For Diz & Bird | IN+OUT Records | 77039-2
Sonny Stitt With The Oscar Peterson Trio
Verve Jazz Masters 50:Sonny Sitt | Verve | 527651-2
Svend Asmussen Sextet
Svend Asmussen At Slukafter | Phontastic | NCD 8804
Teddy Edwards-Howard McGhee Quintet
Together Again! | Original Jazz Classics | OJCCD 424-2

Thilo,Jesper | (cl,ts,fl,ss,as,reeds,saxvoc)
Miles Davis With The Danish Radio Big Band
Aura | CBS | CK 63962
Stan Getz With The Danish Radio Big Band
Stan Getz In Europe | Laserlight | 24657
The Danish Radio Big Band
Aura | CBS | CK 63962
The European Jazz Ginats
Jazz Party | Nagel-Heyer | CD 009
The First Sampler | Nagel-Heyer | NHR SP 5

Things |
Things
Mother Nature | Jazzpoint | JP 1028 CD

Thirkell,John | (tp)
Barbara Thompson Group
Heavenly Bodies | VeraBra Records | CDVBR 2015-2

Thomas Jr.,Robert | (hand-dr,hand-percperc)
Stan Getz Sextet
Billy Highstreet Samba | EmArCy | 838771-2
Weather Report
Night Passage | CBS | 468211-2

Thomas,Al | (gtb)
Ella Fitzgerald With Orchestra
Ella/Things Ain't What They Used To Be | Warner | 9362-47875-2

Thomas,Alan | (p)
Cy Laurie Jazz Band
The Golden Years Of Revival Jazz,Sampler | Storyville | 109 1001
Cy Laurie's New Orleans Septet
The Golden Years Of Revival Jazz,Vol 1 | Storyville | STCD 5506
The Golden Years Of Revival Jazz,Vol.5 | Storyville | STCD 5510
The Golden Years Of Revival Jazz,Vol.6 | Storyville | STCD 5511
The Golden Years Of Revival Jazz,Vol.8 | Storyville | STCD 5513
The Golden Years Of Revival Jazz,Vol.9 | Storyville | STCD 5514
The Golden Years Of Revival Jazz,Vol.11 | Storyville | STCD 5516
Sandy Brown's Jazz Band
The Golden Years Of Revival Jazz,Sampler | Storyville | 109 1001
The Golden Years Of Revival Jazz,Vol.6 | Storyville | STCD 5511
The Golden Years Of Revival Jazz,Vol.8 | Storyville | STCD 5513
The Golden Years Of Revival Jazz,Vol.10 | Storyville | STCD 5515

Thomas,Andy | (p)
Victor Feldman Orchestra
Latinsville | Contemporary | CCD 9005-2

Thomas,Angus | (bel-b)
Hans Theessink Group
Journey On | Minor Music | 801062
Nicolas Simion Quartet feat. Tomasz Stanko
Viaggio Imaginario | Tutu Records | 888192-2*

Thomas,Arnold | (p)
Louis Jordan And His Tympany Five
The Small Black Groups | Storyville | 4960523
Louis Jordan-Let The Good Times Roll: The Complete Decca Recordings 1938-1954 | Bear Family Records | BCD 15557 IH

Thomas,Bob | (tbv)
Paul Barbarin And His Band
Atlantic Jazz: New Orleans | Atlantic | 7567-81700-2

Thomas,Bobby | (dr)
Hubert Laws Quartet
The Laws Of Jazz | Atlantic | 8122-71636-2
Montgomery Brothers
Groove Yard | Original Jazz Classics | OJCCD 139-2(R 9362)
Richard Williams Quintet
New Horn In Town | Candid | CCD 79003
The Montgomery Brothers
Wes Montgomery-The Complete Riverside Recordings | Riverside | 12 RCD 4408-2

Thomas,Bruce | (p)
Steve Rochinski Solo/Duo/Trio/Quartet
Jazz Guitar Highlights 1 | Jardis Records | JRCD 20141
A Bird In The Hand | Jardis Records | JRCD 9922

Thomas,Christopher | (b)
Brian Blade Group
Fellowship | Blue Note | 859417-2
Joshua Redman Quartet
Spirit Of The Moment:Live At The Village Vanguard | Warner | 9362-45923-2
Joshua Redman Quintet
Freedom In The Goove | Warner | 9362-46330-2

Thomas,Clarence | (fl,ss,tsperc)
Idris Muhammad Group
Jazzin' With The Soul Brothers | Fantasy | FANCD 6086-2

Thomas,Cybil | (voc)
Toshinori Kondo & Ima plus Guests
Human Market | JA & RO | JARO 4146-2

Thomas,David | (voc)
Take 6
Goldmine | Reprise | 7599-25670-2
So Much To Say | Reprise | 7599-25892-2
He Is Christmas | Reprise | 7599-26665-2
Take 6 With The Yellow Jackets
He Is Christmas | Reprise | 7599-26665-2

Thomas,Frank | (p)
Firehouse Five Plus Two
Dixieland Favorites | Good Time Jazz | FCD 60-008
Crashes A Party | Good Time Jazz | GTCD 10038-2
Goes To A Fire | Good Time Jazz | GTCD 10052-2
Goes South | Good Time Jazz | GTCD 12018-2

Thomas,Gary | (alto-fl,ts,fl,ss,rap-voc,synth)
Gary Thomas Group
Found On Sordid Street | Winter&Winter | 910002-2
Gary Thomas Quartet
Pariah's Pariah | Winter&Winter | 910033-2
Ingrid Jensen Quintet
Higher Grounds | Enja | ENJ-9353 2
John McLaughlin Group
The Heart Of Things | Verve | 539153-2
Live In Paris | Verve | 543536-2
Michele Rosewoman Quintet
Harvest | Enja | ENJ-7069 2
Michele Rosewoman Sextet
Harvest | Enja | ENJ-7069 2
Rez Abbasi Group
Modern Memory | String Jazz | SJRCD 102
Stefon Harris Group
Black Action Figure | Blue Note | 499546-2
Terri Lyne Carrington Group
Jazz Is A Spirit | ACT | 9408-2

Thomas,Hersal | (p)
Sippie Wallace With King Oliver And Hersal Thomas
Jazz:The Essential Collection Vol.1 | IN+OUT Records | 78011-2

Thomas,Jamal | (dr)
Maceo Parker Group
Maceo(Soundtrack) | Minor Music | 801046
Maceo Parker With The Rebirth Brass Band
Maceo(Soundtrack) | Minor Music | 801046

Thomas,Jens | (p,perc,voicep-solo)
Christof Lauer-Jens Thomas
Shadows In The Rain | ACT | 9297-2
Christof Lauer-Jens Thomas With The Cikada String Quartet
Shadows In The Rain | ACT | 9297-2
Gebhard Ullmann Trio
Essencia | Between The Lines | btl 017(Efa 10187-2)
Jens Thomas
Jens Thomas Plays Ennio Morricone | ACT | 9273-2
Paul Brody's Tango Toy
Klezmer Stories | Laika Records | 35101222
Triocolor
Colours Of Ghana | ACT | 9285-2
Thomas,Joe | (as,cl,ts,voc,el-b,shakers,fl,reeds)
Billy May And His Orchestra With Members Of The Jimmy Lunceford Orchestra
Great Swing Classics In Hi-Fi | Capitol | 521223-2
Coleman Hawkins All Stars
Coleman Hawkins All Stars | Original Jazz Classics | OJCCD 225-2(SV 2005)
Cozy Cole All Stars
Ultimate Coleman Hawkins selected by Sonny Rollins | Verve | 557538-2
Fletcher Henderson And His Orchestra
Jazz:The Essential Collection Vol.1 | IN+OUT Records | 78011-2
George Wettling's New Yorkers
Jazz:The Essential Collection Vol.3 | IN+OUT Records | 78013-2
JATP All Stars
The Complete Jazz At The Philharmonic On Verve 1944-1949 | Verve | 523893-2
Jelly Roll Morton And His Orchestra
Planet Jazz:Jelly Roll Morton | Planet Jazz | 2152060-2
Jimmy Lunceford And His Orchestra
Planet Jazz:Swing | Planet Jazz | 2169651-2
The Legends Of Swing | Laserlight | 24659
Rhoda Scott Trio
Jazz In Paris:Rhoda Scott-Live At The Olympia | EmArCy | 549879-2 PMS
Thomas,John | (co,g,comp,el-g,b-g,cow-bell,synth)
Chick Corea And His Orchestra
My Spanish Heart | Polydor | 543303-3
Chick Corea Group
Verve Jazz Masters 3:Chick Corea | Verve | 519820-2
Count Basie And His Orchestra
I Told You So | Original Jazz Classics | OJCCD 824-2(2310767)
Jimmy McGriff Quintet
Swingin' The Blues-Jumpin' The Blues | Laserlight | 24654
Joe Henderson And His Orchestra
Joe Henderson:The Milestone Years | Milestone | 8MCD 4413-2
Joe Henderson Sextet
Multiple | Original Jazz Classics | OJCCD 763-2(M 9050)
John Thomas & Lifeforce
Devil Dance | Nabel Records:Jazz Network | CD 4601
3000 Worlds | Nabel Records:Jazz Network | CD 4604
Louis Armstrong And His Hot Seven
Jazz:The Essential Collection Vol.2 | IN+OUT Records | 78012-2
Woody Herman And His Orchestra
The Raven Speaks | Original Jazz Classics | OJCCD 663-2(F 9416)
Thomas,Lee | (voc)
Buddy Johnson And His Orchestra
Buddy And Ella Johnson 1953-1964 | Bear Family Records | BCD 15479 DH
Thomas,Lee prob. | (voc)
Thomas,Leon | (perc,voc,wood-flvoice)
Leon Thomas
Leon Thomas In Berlin | RCA | 2663877-2
Leon Thomas With Band
Super Black Blues Vol.II | RCA | 2663874-2
Spirits Known And Unknown | RCA | 2663876-2
Leon Thomas In Berlin | RCA | 2663877-2
Leon Thomas With Orchestra
Spirits Known And Unknown | RCA | 2663876-2
Leon Thomas With The Oliver Nelson Quintet
Leon Thomas In Berlin | RCA | 2663877-2
Louis Armstrong And His Friends
Louis Armstrong And His Friends | Bluebird | 2663961-2
Pharoah Sanders Orchestra
Karma | Impulse(MCA) | 951153-2
Jewels Of Thought | Impulse(MCA) | 951247-2
The Roots Of Acid Jazz | Impulse(MCA) | IMP 12042
Thomas,Maurice | (tp)
Raymond Fol Big Band
Jazz In Paris:Raymond Fol-Les 4 Saisons | EmArCy | 548791-2
Thomas,Michael Tilson | (pcond)
Mahavishnu Orchestra
Apocalypse | CBS | 467092-2
Thomas,Milton | (viola)
Ella Fitzgerald With The Frank DeVol Orchestra
Get Happy! | Verve | 523321-2
Herbie Mann With The Frank DeVol Orchestra
Verve Jazz Masters 56:Herbie Mann | Verve | 529901-2
Thomas,Naomi | (voc)
Lou Donaldson Orchestra
Blue Breaks Beats Vol.2 | Blue Note | 789907-2
Thomas,Philip | (dr)
Buddy Guy Blues Band
Buddy Guy-The Complete Chess Studio Recordings | MCA | MCD 09337
Thomas,Philippe | (tp)
Mark Zubeck Quartet
Horse With A Broken Leg | Fresh Sound Records | FSNT 078 CD
Mark Zubeck Quintet
Horse With A Broken Leg | Fresh Sound Records | FSNT 078 CD
Stéphane Mercier Group
Flor De Luna | Fresh Sound Records | FSNT 097 CD
Thomas,Rene | (g)
Chet Baker Sextet
Chet Baker-The Italian Sessions | Bluebird | ND 82001
Lou Bennett Trio
Jazz In Paris | EmArCy | 548790-2
Lou Bennett Trio With The Paris Jazz All Stars
Jazz In Paris | EmArCy | 548790-2
Rene Thomas Quartet
Jazz In Paris:René Thomas-The Real Cat | EmArCy | 549400-2 PMS
Jazz In Paris:René Thomas-Meeting Mister Thomas | EmArCy | 549812-2
Rene Thomas Quintet
Jazz In Paris:René Thomas-The Real Cat | EmArCy | 549400-2 PMS
Jazz In Paris:René Thomas-Meeting Mister Thomas | EmArCy | 549812-2
Sonny Criss Quintet
Jazz In Paris:Saxophones À Saint-Germain Des Prés | EmArCy | 014060-2
Jazz In Paris:Sonny Criss-Mr.Blues Pour Flirter | EmArCy | 549231-2 PMS
Sonny Rollins Orchestra
Sonny Rollins And The Big Brass | Verve | 557545-2
Stan Getz Quartet
Stan Getz In Europe | Laserlight | 24657
Stan Getz Highlights:The Best Of The Verve Years Vol.2 | Verve | 517330-2
Verve Jazz Masters 8:Stan Getz | Verve | 519823-2
Stan Getz Highlights | Verve | 847430-2
Thomas,Rene prob. | (g)
Bud Powell Quintet
Parisian Thoroughfare | Pablo | CD 2310976-2
Thomas,Robert C. | (dr,hand-drperc)
Paul Desmond With Strings
Planet Jazz:Paul Desmond | Planet Jazz | 2152061-2
Desmond Blue | RCA | 2663898-2
Thomas,Sam | (g)
John Klemmer Quartet
Involvement | Chess | 076139-2
Thomas,Tamara | (voc)
Mike Westbrook Brass Band
Glad Day:Settings Of William Blake | Enja | ENJ-9376 2
Thomas,Tasha | (voc)
Louis Armstrong And His Friends
Louis Armstrong And His Friends | Bluebird | 2663961-2
Thomas,Torten | (fl,clts)
Jazz Orchester Rheinland-Pfalz
Like Life | Jazz Haus Musik | LJBB 9405
Last Season | Jazz Haus Musik | LJBB 9706
Thomas,Vaneese | (voc)
Spyro Gyra & Guests
Love & Other Obsessions | GRP | GRP 98112
Thomas,Walter 'Foots' | (as,bs,ts,cl,ss,bass-saxfl)
Cab Calloway And His Orchestra
Planet Jazz:Cab Calloway | Planet Jazz | 2161237-2
Jelly Roll Morton And His Orchestra
Planet Jazz:Jelly Roll Morton | Planet Jazz | 2152060-2
Thomé,Christian | (dr,p.voc,perc,glockenspiel)
Georg Ruby Village Zone
Mackeben Revisited:The Ufa Years | Jazz Haus Musik | JHM 0121 CD
Inga Lühning With Trio
Lühning | Jazz Haus Musik | JHM 0111 CD
Stephan Meinberg VITAMINE
Horizontal | Jazz Haus Musik | JHM 0106 CD
Tomatic 7
Haupstrom | Jazz Haus Musik | JHM 0101 CD
Thompson,Alfredo | (ts)
Gonzalo Rubalcaba & Cuban Quartet
Antiguo | Blue Note | 837717-2
Irakere
Yemayá | Blue Note | 498239-2
Thompson,Barbara | (alto-fl,ss,as,ts,piccolo,fl)
Barbara Thompson Group
Heavenly Bodies | VeraBra Records | CDVBR 2015-2
Shifting Sands | Intuition Records | INT 3174-2
Barbara Thompson's Paraphernalia
Mother Earth | VeraBra Records | CDVBR 2005-2
Barbara Thompson's Special Edition | VeraBra Records | CDVBR 2017-2
A Cry From The Heart | VeraBra Records | CDVBR 2021-2
Breathless | VeraBra Records | CDVBR 2057-2
Lady Saxophone | VeraBra Records | CDVBR 2166-2
Thompson's Tangos | Intuition Records | INT 3290-2
Jon Hiseman With The United Jazz & Rock Ensemble And Babara Thompson's Paraphernalia
About Time Too! | VeraBra Records | CDVBR 2014-2
Thompson,Bert | (b)
Lajos Dudas Quartet
Jubilee Edition | double moon | CHRDM 71020
Thompson,Bill | (fl,as,tsvoc)
John Stein Quintet
Portraits And Landscapes | Jardis Records | JRCD 20029
Jazz Guitar Highlights 1 | Jardis Records | JRCD 20141
Paul Desmond Quartet With The Bill Bates Singers
Desmond | Original Jazz Classics | OJCCD 712-2(F 3235/8082)
Thompson,Billy | (v)
Barbara Thompson Group
Shifting Sands | Intuition Records | INT 3174-2
Barbara Thompson's Paraphernalia
Thompson's Tangos | Intuition Records | INT 3290-2
Thompson,Brian | (tp)
Maynard Ferguson And His Big Bop Nouveau Band
Maynard Ferguson '93-Footpath Café | Hot Shot Records | HSR 8312-2
Thompson,Ches | (fr-h)
Dizzy Gillespie And His Orchestra
Talking Verve:Dizzy Gillespie | Verve | 533846-2
Thompson,Chester | (drkeyboards)
Weather Report
Black Market | CBS | 468210-2
Thompson,Chuck | (drsax)
Hampton Hawes Trio
The Trio-Vol.1 | Original Jazz Classics | OJC 316(C 3515)
Hampton Hawes Trio Vol.1 | Original Jazz Classics | OJC20 316-2(C 3505)
The Trio Vol.2 | Original Jazz Classics | OJCCD 318-2
The Jazz Giants Play Jerome Kern:Yesterdays | Prestige | PCD 24202-2
Wardell Gray Sextet
The Prestige Legacy Vol.2:Battles Of Saxes | Prestige | PCD 24252-2
Wardell Gray's Los Angeles All Stars
Dexter Gordon Birthday Celebration | Fantasy | FANCD 6082-2
Wardell Gray Memorial Vol.2 | Original Jazz Classics | OJCCD 051-2(P 7009)
Thompson,Danny | (as,bassoon,bs,perc,fl,bongos,voc)
Sun Ra And His Astro-Infinity Arkestra
Space Is The Place | Impulse(MCA) | 951249-2
Sun Ra And His Intergalactic Research Arkestra
Black Myth/Out In Space | MPS | 557656-2
Thompson,David | (arr,background-vocfr-h)
Dave Liebman And The Lluis Vidal Trio With The Orquestra De Cambra Theatre Lliure
Dave Liebman And The Lluis Vidal Trio | Fresh Sound Records | FSNT 026 CD
Orquestra De Cambra Teatre Lliure
Orquestra De Cambra Teatre Lliure and Lluis Vidal Trio feat.Dave Liebman | Fresh Sound Records | FSNT 027 CD
Orquestra De Cambra Teatre Lliure feat. Dave Liebman
Orquestra De Cambra Teatre Lliure and Lluis Vidal Trio feat.Dave Liebman | Fresh Sound Records | FSNT 027 CD
Thompson,Deborah | (voc)
Paulinho Da Costa Orchestra
Happy People | Original Jazz Classics | OJCCD 783-2(2312102)
Thompson,Dickie | (gvoc)
Johnny Hodges-Wild Bill Davis Sextet
Planet Jazz:Johnny Hodges | Planet Jazz | 2152065-2
Wild Bill Davis Quartet
Live At Swiss Radio Studio Zürich | Jazz Connaisseur | JCCD 8701-2
Thompson,Don | (b,el-b,perc,pvib)
Paul Desmond Quartet
Live | Verve | 543501-2
Singers Unlimited With Rob McConnell And The Boss Brass
The Singers Unlimited:Magic Voices | MPS | 539130-2
Thompson,Ernest | (bscl)
Louis Armstrong And His Orchestra
Best Of The Complete RCA Victor Recordings | RCA | 2663636-2
Louis Armstrong:A 100th Birthday Celebration | RCA | 2663694-2
Louis Armstrong:C'est Si Bon | Dreyfus Jazz Line | FDM 36730-2
Thompson,Gail | (fl)
Gail Thompson Orchestra
Gail Thompson's Jazz Africa | Enja | ENJ-9053 2
Thompson,Harold | (perc)
Max Roach With The Boston Percussion Ensemble
Clifford Brown-Max Roach:Alone Together-The Best Of The Mercury Years | Verve | 526373-2
Thompson,Ken | (as)
Gutbucket
Dry Humping The American Dream | Enja | ENJ-9466 2
Thompson,Lowell | (bongos)
Dave Brubeck With The Erich Kunzel Orchestra
Truth Is Fallen | Atlantic | 7567-80761-2
Thompson,Lucky | (bs,sax,ss,ts,arrvoc)
(Little)Jimmy Scott With The Lucky Thompson Orchestra
Everybody's Somebody's Fool | Decca | 050669-2
Cedar Walton Quartet
The Story Of Jazz Piano | Laserlight | 24653
Charlie Parker Septet
Charlie Parker:Now's The Time | Dreyfus Jazz Line | FDM 36724-2
Count Basie And His Orchestra
Jazz:The Essential Collection Vol.3 | IN+OUT Records | 78013-2
Dinah Washington With The Quincy Jones Orchestra
Verve Jazz Masters 40:Dinah Washington | Verve | 522055-2
The Swingin' Miss 'D' | Verve | 558074-2
Dizzy Gillespie And His Orchestra
Afro | Verve | 517052-2
Jean Pierre Sasson Quartet
Americans Swinging In Paris:Lucky Thompson | EMI Records | 539651-2
Kenny Clarke 8
Americans Swinging In Paris:Kenny Clarke | EMI Records | 539652-2
Kenny Clarke Quartet
Americans Swinging In Paris:Kenny Clarke | EMI Records | 539652-2
Louis Armstrong And His All Stars With The Sy Oliver Orchestra
Ambassador Louis Armstrong Vol.17:Moments To Remember(1952-1956) | Ambassador | CLA 1917
Louis Armstrong And His Orchestra
Swing Legends:Louis Armstrong | Nimbus Records | NI 2012
Louis Armstrong With Sy Oliver And His Orchestra
Louis And The Angels | Verve | 549592-2
Lucky Thompson And His Lucky Seven
Planet Jazz:Bebop | RCA | 2169650-2
Lucky Thompson And His Orchestra
Americans Swinging In Paris:Lucky Thompson | EMI Records | 539651-2
Lucky Thompson Quartet
The Art Of Saxophone | Laserlight | 24652
Americans Swinging In Paris:Lucky Thompson | EMI Records | 539651-2
The Jazz Life! | Candid | CCD 79019
Lucky Thompson Quintet
Americans Swinging In Paris:Lucky Thompson | EMI Records | 539651-2
Lucky Thompson Trio
Americans Swinging In Paris:Lucky Thompson | EMI Records | 539651-2
Lucky Thompson With The Gerard Pochonet All-Stars
Planet Jazz:Jazz Saxophone | Planet Jazz | 2169653-2
Lucky Thompson's Modern Jazz Group Quartet
Jazz In Paris:Lucky Thompson-Modern Jazz Group | EmArCy | 159823-2 PMS
Lucky Thompson's Modern Jazz Group Tentet
Jazz In Paris:Lucky Thompson-Modern Jazz Group | EmArCy | 159823-2 PMS
Miles Davis All Star Sextet
Walkin' | Original Jazz Classics | OJC20 213-2
Miles Davis All Stars
The J.J.Johnson Memorial Album | Prestige | PRCD 11025-2
Quincy Jones Big Band
Rahsaan/The Complete Mercury Recordings Of Roland Kirk | Mercury | 846630-2
Tempo Jazzmen
Dizzy Gillespie:Night In Tunisia | Dreyfus Jazz Line | FDM 36734-2
The Modern Jazz Society
A Concert Of Contemporary Music | Verve | 559827-2
Thelonious Monk Sextet
Genius Of Modern Music,Vol.2 | Blue Note | 532139-2
Jazz Profile:Thelonious Monk | Blue Note | 823518-2
Thompson,Malachi | (tprecitation)
Lester Bowie's Brass Fantasy
I Only Have Eyes For You | ECM | 1296(825902-2)
Avant Pop | ECM | 1326
Thompson,Mark | (ptp)
Buddy Childers Big Band
Just Buddy's | Candid | CCD 79761
Thompson,Marshall | (drtimbales)
Chet Baker-Stan Getz Quintet
Stan Meets Chet | Verve | 837436-2
Gene Ammons-James Moody Quintet
Chicago Concert | Original Jazz Classics | OJCCD 1091-2(PR 10065)
Oscar Peterson Sextet
Soul Espanol | Limelight | 510439-2
Stan Getz Quartet
Verve Jazz Masters 8:Stan Getz | Verve | 519823-2
Thompson,Mike | (paccordeon)
Peter Malick Group feat. Norah Jones
New York City | Koch Records | 238678-2
Thompson,Shaun | (reeds)
André Holst With Chris Dean's European Swing Orchestra
That's Swing | Nagel-Heyer | CD 079
Thompson,Sir Charles | (org,p,celeste,vocp-solo)
Buck Clayton-Buddy Tate Quintet
Buck & Buddy | Original Jazz Classics | OJCCD 757-2(SV 2017)
Buck & Buddy Blow The Blues | Original Jazz Classics | OJCCD 850-2(SV 2030)
Charlie Parker Quintet
Charlie Parker At Storyville | Blue Note | 785108-2
Coleman Hawkins And His Orchestra
Jazz:The Essential Collection Vol.3 | IN+OUT Records | 78013-2
Dodo Greene With The Ike Quebec Quintet
Misty Blue:Sweet Sisters Swing Songs Of Sorrow And Sadness | Blue Note | 521151-2
Frankie Laine With Buck Clayton And His Orchestra
Jazz Spectacular | CBS | CK 65507
Ike Quebec Quartet
Midnight Blue(The [Be]witching Hour) | Blue Note | 854365-2
Joe Williams With The Harry 'Sweets' Edison Sextet
Together/Have A Good Time | Roulette | 531790-2
Sir Charles Thompson
Playing My Way | Jazz Connaisseur | JCCD 9313-2
Sir Charles Thompson Quartet
Key One Up | Vanguard | VCD 79612-2
Sonny Stitt Sextet
Milt Jackson Birthday Celebration | Fantasy | FANCD 6079-2
Vic Dickenson Septet
Nice Work | Vanguard | VCD 79610-2
Vic Dickenson Septet With Ruby Braff
Nice Work | Vanguard | VCD 79610-2
Thompson.Rich | (dr)
Rich Perry Quintet
At Eastman | Steeplechase | SCCD 31533
Thoms,Renato | (perc)
Antonio Hart Group
Ama Tu Sonrisa | Enja | ENJ-9404 2
Eric Reed Orchestra
Happiness | Nagel-Heyer | CD 2010
Stéphane Mercier Group
Flor De Luna | Fresh Sound Records | FSNT 097 CD
Thomsen,Jorn H. | (tp)
Henrik Johansen's Jazzband
The Golden Years Of Revival Jazz,Vol 1 | Storyville | STCD 5506
The Golden Years Of Revival Jazz,Vol.2 | Storyville | STCD 5507
Thomsen,Jorn L. | (tp)
Ricardo's Jazzmen
The Golden Years Of Revival Jazz,Sampler | Storyville | 109 1001
The Golden Years Of Revival Jazz,Vol.4 | Storyville | STCD 5509
The Golden Years Of Revival Jazz,Vol.5 | Storyville | STCD 5510
Thönes,Jo | (dr,electronic-dr,music-computer)
Aparis
Aparis | ECM | 1404
Despite The Fire Fighters' Efforts... | ECM | 1496(517717-2)
Hugo Read Group
Songs Of A Wayfarer | Nabel Records:Jazz Network | CD 4653

Peter Herborn's Acute Insights
Peter Herborn's Acute Insights | JMT Edition | 919017-2
Uli Beckerhoff Quintet
Original Motion Picture Soundtrack:Das Geheimnis(Secret Of Love) | Nabel Records:Jazz Network | CD 4666
Uli Beckerhoff Septet
Private Life | Nabel Records:Jazz Network | CD 4657

Thornburg,Lee R. | (tp,fl-h,tbarr)
Etta James & The Roots Band
Burnin' Down he House | RCA | 3411633-2

Thornhill,Claude | (arr,pvib)
Benny Goodman And His Orchestra
Planet Jazz:Female Jazz Vocalists | Planet Jazz | 2169656-2
Billie Holiday And Her Band
Billie's Love Songs | Nimbus Records | NI 2000
Bud Freeman All Stars
The Bud Freeman All-Star Sessions | Prestige | PRCD 24286-2
Gene Gifford And His Orchestra
Planet Jazz:Bud Freeman | Planet Jazz | 2161240-2

Thornton,Argonne | (p)
Lester Young And His Band
Jazz:The Essential Collection Vol.3 | IN+OUT Records | 78013-2

Thornton,Lilly | (voc)
Lilly Thornton With The Benny Golson Quartet
Remembering Dinah-A Salute To Dinah Washington | Hot Shot Records | HSR 8313-2
Lilly Thornton With The Benny Golson Sextet
Remembering Dinah-A Salute To Dinah Washington | Hot Shot Records | HSR 8313-2
Lilly Thornton With The Mike Hennesey Trio
Remembering Dinah-A Salute To Dinah Washington | Hot Shot Records | HSR 8313-2

Thornton,Steve | (perc,congas,cuicasurdo)
Marcus Miller Group
The Sun Don't Lie | Dreyfus Jazz Line | FDM 36560-2
Michel Petrucciani Group
Michel Petrucciani:The Blue Note Years | Blue Note | 789916-2
Playground | Blue Note | 795480-2
Michel Petrucciani Quartet
Michel Plays Petrucciani | Blue Note | 748679-2
Michel Petrucciani:The Blue Note Years | Blue Note | 789916-2
Miles Davis Group
This Is Jazz:Miles Davis Plays Ballads | CBS | CK 65038
The Brecker Brothers
Out Of The Loop | GRP | GRP 97842

Thorpe,Simon | (b)
Jim Tomlinson Quartet
Brazilian Sketches | Candid | CCD 79769
Jim Tomlinson Quintet
Only Trust Your Heart | Candid | CCD 79758
Brazilian Sketches | Candid | CCD 79769
Jim Tomlinson Sextet
Only Trust Your Heart | Candid | CCD 79758
Stacey Kent And Her Quintet
Let Yourself Go-Celebrating Fred Astaire | Candid | CCD 79764
Stacey Kent With The Jim Tomlison Quintet
Dreamsville | Candid | CCD 79775
Stacy Kent With The Jim Tomlinson Quintet
In Love Again | Candid | CCD 79786

Thorpe,William | (bbs)
Charles Earland Orchestra
Charlie's Greatest Hits | Prestige | PCD 24250-2

Thow,George | (tp)
Artie Shaw And His Orchestra
Planet JazzArtie Shaw | Planet Jazz | 2152057-2
Planet Jazz:Jazz Greatest Hits | Planet Jazz | 2169648-2
Louis Armstrong With Gordon Jenkins And His Orchestra And Choir
Satchmo In Style | Verve | 549594-2
Louis Armstrong With Jimmy Dorsey And His Orchestra
Louis Armstrong:Swing That Music | Laserlight | 36056
Swing Legends:Louis Armstrong | Nimbus Records | NI 2012

Thowsen,Pal | (drperc)
Ketil Bjornstad Group
Early Years | EmArCy | 013271-2

Threadgill,Henry | (as,b-fl,ts,bass-fl,cl,arr,fl,bs)
Jean-Paul Bourelly Trance Atlantic
Boom Bop II | double moon | CHRDM 71023

Three Of A Kind: |
Annette Lowman With Three Of A Kind, Fred Wesley And Rodney Jones
Brown Baby:A Tribute To Oscar Brown Jr. | Minor Music | 801061
Three Of A Kind
Drip Some Grease | Minor Music | 801056

Three Sounds,The |
Anita O'Day With The Three Sounds
Verve Jazz Masters 49:Anita O'Day | Verve | 527653-2
Nat Adderley Quintet(incl.The Three Sounds)
Branching Out | Original Jazz Classics | OJCCD 255-2(R 285)
Nat Adderley With The Three Sounds
Branching Out | Original Jazz Classics | OJCCD 255-2(R 285)
Stanley Turrentine With The Three Sounds
Blue Hour | Blue Note | 524586-2
Midnight Blue(The [Be]witching Hour) | Blue Note | 854365-2
The Three Sounds
Bottoms Up | Blue Note | 0675629
Blue Break Beats | Blue Note | 799106-2
Black Orchid | Blue Note | 821289-2

Thuillier,Francois | (tuba)
Louis Sclavis & The Bernard Struber Jazztet
La Phare | Enja | ENJ-9359 2

Thurlow,Janet | (voc)
Charles Mingus And His Orchestra
Charles Mingus-The Complete Debut Recordings | Debut | 12 DCD 4402-2

Thurman,Bob | (p)
John Lee Hooker
House Of The Blues | Chess | MCD 09258

Thusek,Heribert | (flvib)
Art Van Damme Group
State Of Art | MPS | 841413-2
Art Van Damme Quintet
Keep Going/Blue World | MPS | 529093-2
Singers Unlimited With The Art Van Damme Quintet
The Singers Unlimited:Magic Voices | MPS | 539130-2

Thys,Nicolas 'Nic' | (b)
Andreas Maile Quartet
Mailensteine | Satin Doll Productions | SDP 1022-1 CD
Johannes Herrlich Quintet
Thinking Of You | Edition Collage | EC 499-2
Nils Wogram Quartet
Speed Life | Enja | ENJ-9346 2

Tibbetts,Steve | (12-string-g,g,dobro,kalimba)
Steve Tibbetts Duo
Northern Song | ECM | 1218
Steve Tibbetts Group
Bye Bye Safe Journey | ECM | 1270
Exploded View | ECM | 1335
Yr | ECM | 1355(835245-2)
Big Map Idea | ECM | 1380
The Fall Of Us All | ECM | 1527(521144-2)
Steve Tibbetts | ECM | 1814(017068-2)

Tibbs,Harvey | (tb)
Buck Clayton Swing Band
Swing's The Village | Nagel-Heyer | CD 5004
Blues Of Summer | Nagel-Heyer | NH 1011

Tiberl,Frank | (fl,cl,ss,ts,bassoon,cowbellsax)
Woody Herman And His Orchestra
Verve Jazz Masters 54:Woody Herman | Verve | 529903-2
Jazzin' Vol.2: The Music Of Stevie Wonder | Fantasy | FANCD 6088-2
Brand New | Original Jazz Classics | OJCCD 1044-2(F 8414)
King Cobra | Original Jazz Classics | OJCCD 1068-2(F 9499)
The Raven Speaks | Original Jazz Classics | OJCCD 663-2(F 9416)
Woody Herman Herd At Montreux | Original Jazz Classics | OJCCD 991-2(F 9470)
Woody Herman And The New Thundering Herd
Woody Herman:Thundering Herd | Original Jazz Classics | OJCCD 841-2
Woody Herman's Thundering Herd
Planet Jazz:Jazz Saxophone | Planet Jazz | 2169653-2

Tiberian,Mircea | (p)
Nicolas Simion Quartet
Oriental Gates:Live In Vienna | Tutu Records | 888212-2*

Tidd,Anthony | (el-b,pkeyboards)
Steve Coleman And Five Elements
The Sonic Language Of Myth | RCA | 2164123-2

Tiehuis,Peter | (g,sequencer-programmingsynth)
Wolfgang Haffner Project
Back Home | Jazz 4 Ever Records:Jazz Network | J4E 4730

Tihany,Peter | (p)
Mihaly Tabany Orchestra
Jubilee Edition | double moon | CHRDM 71020

Tilche,Jean-Jacques | (g)
Dizzy Gillespie Orchestra And The Operatic String Orchestra
Jazz In Paris:Dizzy Gillespie And His Operatic Strings Orchestra | EmArCy | 018420-2
Don Byas And His Orchestra
Don Byas:Laura | Dreyfus Jazz Line | FDM 36714-2
Don Byas Quintet
Jazz In Paris:Don Byas-Laura | EmArCy | 013027-2
Don Byas Ree-Boppers
Don Byas:Laura | Dreyfus Jazz Line | FDM 36714-2
Tyree Glenn
Don Byas:Laura | Dreyfus Jazz Line | FDM 36714-2

Tilitz,Jerry | (tb,voctb-solo)
Oliver Jackson Orchestra
The Last Great Concert | Nagel-Heyer | CD 063
The Buck Clayton Legacy
All The Cats Join In(Buck Clayton Rememberd) | Nagel-Heyer | CD 006
Encore Live | Nagel-Heyer | CD 018
The First Sampler | Nagel-Heyer | NHR SP 5
The Second Sampler | Nagel-Heyer | NHR SP 6
The Yamaha International Allstar Band
Hapy Birthday Jazzwelle Plus | Nagel-Heyer | CD 005
The First Sampler | Nagel-Heyer | NHR SP 5

Tilling,Daniel | (p)
Amanda Sedgwick Quintet
Reunion | Touché Music | TMcCD 021

Tillman,Wilbert | (sousaphone)
Eureka Brass Band
Atlantic Jazz: New Orleans | Atlantic | 7567-81700-2

Tillotson,Brooks | (brassfr-h)
Grover Washington Jr. Orchestra
Jazzrock-Anthology Vol.3:Fusion | Zounds | CD 27100555
Machito And His Orchestra
Afro-Cuban Jazz Moods | Original Jazz Classics | OJC20 447-2

Tilton,Martha | (voc)
Benny Goodman And His Orchestra
Planet Jazz:Female Jazz Vocalists | Planet Jazz | 2169656-2
40th Anniversary Concert-Live At Carnegie Hall | London | 820349-2
Benny Goodman At Carnegie Hall 1938(Complete) | CBS | C2K 65143
Camel Caravan Broadcast 1939 Vol.1 | Phontastic | NCD 8817
Camel Caravan Broadcast 1939 Vol.2 | Phontastic | NCD 8818
Camel Caravan Broadcast 1939 Vol.3 | Phontastic | NCD 8819
More Camel Caravans | Phontastic | NCD 8843/4

Timbrell,Tiny | (g)
Harry James And His Orchestra
Trumpet Blues:The Best Of Harry James | Capitol | 521224-2

Timm,Stefan | (dr)
Jürgen Knieper Quintet
State Of Things | Jazz Haus Musik | JHM 0104 CD

Timmer,Sabine | (bs)
Bigband Der Musikschule Der Stadt Brühl Mit Gastsolisten
Pangäa | Indigo-Records | 1004 CD

Timmons,Bobby | (hand-clapping,p,celeste,p-solo,vib)
Anthony Ortega With The Nat Pierce Orchestra
Earth Dance | Fresh Sound Records | FSR-CD 325
Arnett Cobb Quintet
Movin' Right Along | Original Jazz Classics | OJCCD 1074-2(P 7216)
More Party Time | Original Jazz Classics | OJCCD 979-2(P 7175)
Art Blakey And The Afrocuban Boys
Les Liaisons Dangereuses(Original Soundtrack) | Fontana | 812017-2
Art Blakey And The Jazz Messengers
Planet Jazz:Art Blakey | Planet Jazz | 2152066-2
Planet Jazz:Lee Morgan | Planet Jazz | 2161238-2
Art Blakey & The Jazz Messengers: Olympia, May 13th, 1961 | Laserlight | 36128
Paris Jazz Concert:Art Blakey & The Jazz Messengers | Laserlight | 36158
Best Of Blakey 60 | Blue Note | 493072-2
Moanin' | Blue Note | 495324-2
Roots And Herbs | Blue Note | 521956-2
The Witch Doctor | Blue Note | 521957-2
Meet You At The Jazz Corner Of The World | Blue Note | 535565-2
Wayne Shorter:The Classic Blue Note Recordings | Blue Note | 540856-2
Blue N' Groovy | Blue Note | 780679-2
A Night In Tunisia | Blue Note | 784049-2
The Best Of Blue Note | Blue Note | 796110-2
The Best Of Blue Note Vol.2 | Blue Note | 797960-2
Les Liaisons Dangereuses(Original Soundtrack) | Fontana | 812017-2
Feedom Rider | Blue Note | 821287-2
Jazz In Paris:Art Blakey-1958-Paris Olympia | EmArCy | 832659-2 PMS
Impulse!Art Blakey!Jazz Messengers! | Impulse(MCA) | 951175-2
At The Club St.Germain | RCA | ND 74897(2)
Art Blakey Percussion Ensemble
Drums Around The Corner | Blue Note | 521455-2
Art Blakey-Barney Wilen Quartet
Les Liaisons Dangereuses(Original Soundtrack) | Fontana | 812017-2
Benny Golson Quintet
Nemmy Golson And The Philadelphians | Blue Note | 494104-2
Bobby Timmons
This Here Is Bobby Timmons | Original Jazz Classics | OJC20 104-2(RLP 1164)
From The Bottom | Original Jazz Classics | OJCCD 1032-2(RS 3053)
Bobby Timmons Orchestra
Quartet And Orchestra | Milestone | MCD 47091-2
Bobby Timmons Quartet
Quartet And Orchestra | Milestone | MCD 47091-2
Bobby Timmons Trio
Quartet And Orchestra | Milestone | MCD 47091-2
This Here Is Bobby Timmons | Original Jazz Classics | OJC20 104-2(RLP 1164)
In Person | Original Jazz Classics | OJC20 364-2(RLP 9391)
Born To Be Blue! | Original Jazz Classics | OJC20 873-2(R 9468)
From The Bottom | Original Jazz Classics | OJCCD 1032-2(RS 3053)
Bobby Timmons:The Prestige Trio Sessions | Prestige | PRCD 24277-2
Cannonball Adderley Quintet
Them Dirty Blues | Blue Note | 495447-2
Them Dirty Blues | Capitol | 495447-2
Cannonball Adderley Birthday Celebration | Fantasy | FANCD 6087-2
Live In San Francisco | Original Jazz Classics | OJC20 035-2
Live In San Francisco | Riverside | RISA 1157-6
Chet Baker Big Band
The Best Of Chet Baker Plays | Pacific Jazz | 797161-2
Chet Baker Quintet
Chet Baker & Crew | Pacific Jazz | 582671-2
Chet Baker Sextet
Chet Baker & Crew | Pacific Jazz | 582671-2
The Best Of Chet Baker Plays | Pacific Jazz | 797161-2
Dexter Gordon Quartet
Dexter Gordon Birthday Celebration | Fantasy | FANCD 6082-2
L.T.D. | Prestige | PCD 11018-2
XXL | Prestige | PCD 11033-2
Kenny Burrell Quartet
Blue Lights Vol.1&2 | Blue Note | 857184-2
Kenny Burrell Septet
Blue Lights Vol.1&2 | Blue Note | 857184-2
Kenny Dorham Sextet
The Complete Round About Midnight At The Cafe Bohemia | Blue Note | 533775-2
Lee Morgan Quintet
True Blue | Blue Note | 534032-2
Maynard Ferguson And His Orchestra
Verve Jazz Masters 52:Maynard Ferguson | Verve | 529905-2
Nat Adderley Sextet
Wes Montgomery-The Complete Riverside Recordings | Riverside | 12 RCD 4408-2
Work Song | Original Jazz Classics | OJC20 363-2
Pepper Adams Quartet
10 To 4 At The 5-Spot | Original Jazz Classics | OJCCD 031-2(RLP 265)
Pepper Adams Quintet
10 To 4 At The 5-Spot | Original Jazz Classics | OJCCD 031-2(RLP 265)
Sonny Stitt Quartet
Verve Jazz Masters 50:Sonny Sitt | Verve | 527651-2

Timofeev,Pavel | (dr)
Farlanders
The Farlander | JA & RO | JARO 4222-2

Timofejev,Kirill | (cello)
Jo Ambros Group
Wanderlust | dml-records | CD 016

Tinney,Allen | (p)
Big Al Sears And The Sparrows
Sear-iously | Bear Family Records | BCD 15668 AH
Charlie Christian All Stars
Charlie Christian-Jazz Immortal/Dizzy Gillespie 1944 | Original Jazz Classics | OJCCD 1932-2(ES 548)

Tinney,William | (gdr)
Big Al Sears And The Sparrows
Sear-iously | Bear Family Records | BCD 15668 AH

Tinterow,Bernard | (v)
Tommy Dorsey And His Orchestra
Planet Jazz:Frank Sinatra & Tommy Dorsey | Planet Jazz | 2152067-2

Tinwa,Joshua | (dr)
Brass Attack
Brecht Songs | Tutu Records | 888190-2*

Tiny Bell Trio |
Dave Douglas Tiny Bell Trio
Wandering Souls | Winter&Winter | 910042-2

Tippetts,Julie | (bongos,concertina,recorder,voice,g)
Carla Bley Group
Tropic Appetites | Watt | 1
John Stevens Quartet
Re-Touch & Quartet | Konnex Records | KCD 5027

Tipton,Lisa | (v)
Hank Jones Trio With The Meridian String Quartet
The Story Of Jazz Piano | Laserlight | 24653

Tischbirek,Alexander | (ts)
Landes Jugend Jazz Orchester Hessen
Touch Of Lips | hr music.de | hrmj 004-01 CD

Tischendorf,Heinz | (ssts)
Erwin Lehn Und Sein Südfunk-Tanzorchester
Deutsches Jazz Fesival 1954/1955 | Bear Family Records | BCD 15430

Tischitz,Henri | (b)
Bill Coleman Sextet
Americans Swinging In Paris:Bill Coleman | EMI Records | 539663-2

Tittmann,Otto | (b)
Brocksieper-Jazz-Ensemble
Drums Boogie | Bear Family Records | BCD 15988 AH
Brocksieper-Solisten-Orchester
Globetrotter | Bear Family Records | BCD 15912 AH
Brocksieper-Solisten-Orchester(Brocksi-Quartet)
Drums Boogie | Bear Family Records | BCD 15988 AH
Brocksieper-Special-Ensemble
Globetrotter | Bear Family Records | BCD 15912 AH
Brocksi-Quartett
Globetrotter | Bear Family Records | BCD 15912 AH
Brocksi-Quintett
Drums Boogie | Bear Family Records | BCD 15988 AH

Titz,Christoph | (fl-h,tpkeyboards)
Scetches
Different Places | VeraBra Records | CDVBR 2102-2

Tizol,Juan | (tbv-tb)
Barney Bigard And His Orchestra
Highlights From The Duke Ellington Centennial Edition | RCA | 2663672-2
Jazz:The Essential Collection Vol.3 | IN+OUT Records | 78013-2
Duke Ellington And Count Basie With Their Orchestras
First Time! | CBS | CK 65571
Duke Ellington And His Cotton Club Orchestra
Jazz:The Essential Collection Vol.2 | IN+OUT Records | 78012-2
Duke Ellington And His Famous Orchestra
Duke Ellington:The Blanton-Webster Band | Bluebird | 21 13181-2
Planet Jazz:Duke Ellington | Planet Jazz | 2152053-2
Planet Jazz:Johnny Hodges | Planet Jazz | 2152065-2
Planet Jazz Sampler | Planet Jazz | 2152326-2
Planet Jazz:Ben Webster | RCA | 2165368-2
Planet Jazz:Big Bands | Planet Jazz | 2169649-2
Planet Jazz:Jazz Trumpet | Planet Jazz | 2169654-2
Planet Jazz:Female Jazz Vocalists | Planet Jazz | 2169656-2
Highlights From The Duke Ellington Centennial Edition | RCA | 2663672-2
Greatest Hits | CBS | 462959-2
Jazz:The Essential Collection Vol.2 | IN+OUT Records | 78012-2
Jazz:The Essential Collection Vol.3 | IN+OUT Records | 78013-2
Duke Ellington:Ko-Ko | Dreyfus Jazz Line | FDM 36717-2
Duke Ellington And His Orchestra
The Legends Of Swing | Laserlight | 24659
Highlights From The Duke Ellington Centennial Edition | RCA | 2663672-2
Carnegie Hall Concert January 1943 | Prestige | 2PCD 34004-2
Greatest Hits | CBS | 462959-2
The Big Bands Vol.1.The Snader Telescriptions | Storyville | 4960043
Jazz:The Essential Collection Vol.2 | IN+OUT Records | 78012-2
Jazz:The Essential Collection Vol.3 | IN+OUT Records | 78013-2
The Duke At Fargo 1940 | Storyville | STCD 8316/17
At The Hurricane:Original 1943 Broadcasts | Storyville | STCD 8359
Ella Fitzgerald With Paul Weston And His Orchestra
Ella Fitzgerald Sings The Irving Berlin Song Book | Verve | 543830-2
Ella Fitzgerald With The Nelson Riddle Orchestra
Get Happy! | Verve | 523321-2
Ella Fitzgerald With The Paul Weston Orchestra
Get Happy! | Verve | 523321-2
Harry James And His Orchestra
Trumpet Blues:The Best Of Harry James | Capitol | 521224-2
Nat King Cole Quintet
After Midnight | Capitol | 520087-2
Nat King Cole Sextet
After Midnight | Capitol | 520087-2

Tjader,Cal | (dr,vib,cabassa,cencero,cymbal,bongo)
Anita O'Day With The Cal Tjader Quartet
Verve Jazz Masters 49:Anita O'Day | Verve | 527653-2
Time For 2 | Verve | 559808-2
Cal Tjader Group

Verve Jazz Masters 39:Cal Tjader | Verve | 521858-2
Verve Jazz Masters Vol.60:The Collection | Verve | 529866-2
Amazonas | Original Jazz Classics | OJCCD 840-2(F 9502)
Cal Tjader Quartet
Black Hawk Nights | Fantasy | FCD 24755-2
Our Blues | Fantasy | FCD 24771-2
Cal Tjader Plays Harold Arlen & West Side Story | Fantasy | FCD 24775-2
Jazz At The Blackhawk | Original Jazz Classics | OJCCD 436-2(F 8096)
Cal Tjader Plays Jazz | Original Jazz Classics | OJCCD 986-2(F 3-211)
Cal Tjader Quintet
Talkin Verve/Roots Of Acid Jazz:Cal Tjader | Verve | 531562-2
Soul Bird | Verve | 549111-2
Our Blues | Fantasy | FCD 24771-2
Concerts In The Sun | Fantasy | FCD 9688-2
Tjader Plays Mambo | Original Jazz Classics | OJCCD 274-2(F 3221)
Cal Tjader's Latin Concert | Original Jazz Classics | OJCCD 643-2(F 8014)
Cal Tjader Plays Jazz | Original Jazz Classics | OJCCD 986-2(F 3-211)
The Jazz Giants Play Sammy Cahn:It's Magic | Prestige | PCD 24226-2
Cal Tjader Septet
Talkin Verve/Roots Of Acid Jazz:Cal Tjader | Verve | 531562-2
Cal Tjader Sextet
Talkin Verve/Roots Of Acid Jazz:Cal Tjader | Verve | 531562-2
Soul Bird | Verve | 549111-2
Black Hawk Nights | Fantasy | FCD 24755-2
Cuban Fantasy | Fantasy | FCD 24777-2
Cal Tjader's Latin Kick | Original Jazz Classics | OJCCD 642-2(F 8033)
The Jazz Giants Play Cole Porter:Night And Day | Prestige | PCD 24203-2
Cal Tjader With The Clare Fischer Orchestra
Cal Tjader Plays Harold Arlen & West Side Story | Fantasy | FCD 24775-2
Cal Tjader With The Lalo Schifrin Orchestra
Talkin Verve/Roots Of Acid Jazz:Cal Tjader | Verve | 531562-2
Cal Tjader's Modern Mambo Quintet(Sextet)
Mambo With Tjader | Original Jazz Classics | OJCCD 271-2(F 3202)
Cal Tjader's Orchestra
Verve Jazz Masters 39:Cal Tjader | Verve | 521858-2
Talkin Verve/Roots Of Acid Jazz:Cal Tjader | Verve | 531562-2
Soul Burst | Verve | 557446-2
Tjader Plays Mambo | Original Jazz Classics | OJCCD 274-2(F 3221)
Dave Brubeck Octet
The Dave Brubeck Octet | Original Jazz Classics | OJCCD 101-2(F 3239)
Dizzy Gillespie Orchestra
Monterey Jazz Festival 1975 | Storyville | 4960213
George Shearing And His Quintet
Verve Jazz Masters 57:George Shearing | Verve | 529900-2
George Shearing Quintet
Verve Jazz Masters 57:George Shearing | Verve | 529900-2
Verve Jazz Masters Vol.59:Toots Thielemans | Verve | 535271-2
Gus Mancuso Quartet
Gus Mancuso & Special Friends | Fantasy | FCD 24762-2
Gus Mancuso Quintet
Gus Mancuso & Special Friends | Fantasy | FCD 24762-2
Lalo Schifrin And His Orchestra
Verve Jazz Masters 39:Cal Tjader | Verve | 521858-2
Stan Getz-Cal Tjader Sextet
Stan Getz With Cal Tjader | Original Jazz Classics | OJC20 275-2(F 3266)

Tjong-Ayong,Georg | (sax)
Marcus Sukiennik Big Band
A Night In Tunisia Suite(7 Variationen über Dizzy Gillespie's 'A Night In Tunisia') | Jazz Haus Musik | ohne Nummer

Tobarczyk,Walter | (perc)
Max Roach With The Boston Percussion Ensemble
Clifford Brown-Max Roach:Alone Together-The Best Of The Mercury Years | Verve | 526373-2

Tobin,Louise | (voc)
Benny Goodman And His Orchestra
More Camel Caravans | Phontastic | NCD 8845/6

Tobocman,Susan | (voc)
Maximilian Geller Group
Maximilian Geller Goes Bossa | Edition Collage | EC 496-2
Maximilian Geller Quartet feat. Susan Tobocman
Maimilian Geller Goes Bossa Encore | Edition Collage | EC 505-2

Todd,Gary | (b)
Fisherman's Break
Fisherman's Break | Edition Collage | EC 450-2
Stephan Dietz Quartet
Jazz Portraits | EGO | 95080

Todd,Phil | (b-cl,ss,fl,ts,sax,assynth)
Acoustic Alchemy
Against The Grain | GRP | GRP 97832

Todd,Richard | (fr-h)
Diane Schuur With Orchestra And Strings
The Best Of Diane Schuur | GRP | GRP 98882

Todd,Steve | (perc)
Ronnie Taheny Group
Briefcase | Laika Records | 35101152

Todd,Tommy | (p)
Lionel Hampton All Stars
Lionel Hampton:Flying Home | Dreyfus Jazz Line | FDM 36735-2

Tofani,David | (alto-fl,b-cl,cl,fl,piccolo,as,ss,ts)
Earl Klugh Group
Late Night Guitar | Blue Note | 498573-2

Tofft,Claus 'Vikingo' | (congasperc)
Conexion Latina
Mambo 2000 | Enja | ENJ-7055 2
La Conexión | Enja | ENJ-9065 2

Togashi,Haruo | (keyboards,keyboard-bvoc)
Toshinori Kondo & Ima
Red City Smoke | JA & RO | JARO 4173-2
Toshinori Kondo & Ima plus Guests
Human Market | JA & RO | JARO 4146-2

Togeby,Lars | (tpfl-h)
Mona Larsen And The Danish Radio Big Band Plus Soloists
Michael Mantler:Cerco Un Paese Innocente | ECM | 1556
The Danish Radio Jazz Orchestra
This Train:The Danish Radio Jazz Orchestra Plays The Music Of Ray Pitts | dacapo | DCCD 9428

Tok Tok Tok |
Tok Tok Tok
Love Again | Einstein Music | EM 01081
It Took So Long | Einstein Music | EM 21103
50 Ways To Leave Your Lover | Einstein Music | EM 91051

Tokunaga,Kiyoshi | (b)
Jimmy Giuffre Trio
Night Dance | Choice | CHCD 71001
The Train And The River | Choice | CHCD 71011

Tole,Bill | (tb)
Bobby Bryant Orchestra
Deep Blue-The United States Of Mind | Blue Note | 521152-2
Ella Fitzgerald With Orchestra
Ella/Things Ain't What They Used To Be | Warner | 9362-47875-2

Toledo,Maria | (voc)
Stan Getz Group
Verve Jazz Masters 53:Stan Getz-Bossa Nova | Verve | 529904-2
Stan Getz Quartet
Verve Jazz Masters 53:Stan Getz-Bossa Nova | Verve | 529904-2
Stan Getz-Luiz Bonfa Orchestra
Verve Jazz Masters 13:Antonio Carlos Jobim | Verve | 516409-2
Jazz Samba Encore! | Verve | 823613-2
Stan Getz-Luiz Bonfa Quartet
Jazz Samba Encore! | Verve | 823613-2
Stan Getz-Luiz Bonfa Quintet
Jazz Samba Encore! | Verve | 823613-2

Toledo,Rene L. | (g,el-g,vocp)
Arturo Sandoval And The Latin Train Band
Arturo Sandoval & The Latin Train | GRP | GRP 98202

Tolentino,Julius | (as)
Eric Reed Orchestra
Happiness | Nagel-Heyer | CD 2010

Tölkes,Christian | (g)
Bigband Der Musikschule Der Stadt Brühl Mit Gastsolisten
Pangäa | Indigo-Records | 1004 CD

Tollin,Björn | (perc)
Lena Willemark-Ale Möller Group
Nordan | ECM | 1536(523161-2)

Tolliver,Charles | (fl-htp)
Gary Bartz Sextet
Libra/Another Earth | Milestone | MCD 47077-2
Horace Silver Quintet
Horace Silver Retrospective | Blue Note | 495576-2
Jackie McLean Quintet
A Blue Conception | Blue Note | 534254-2
Jacknife | Blue Note | 540535-2
Jackie McLean Sextet
Jacknife | Blue Note | 540535-2
Louis Hayes Sextet
The Crawl | Candid | CCD 79045
McCoy Tyner Septet
Song For My Lady | Original Jazz Classics | OJCCD 313-2

Tolliver,James | (arr,pts)
New Orleans Feetwarmers
Jazz:The Essential Collection Vol.1 | IN+OUT Records | 78011-2

Tolonen,Jukka | (el-g,perc,g,p,spinet,keyboards)
Piirpauke
Zerenade | JA & RO | JARO 4142-2

Tolstoy,Viktoria | (voc)
Nils Landgren Funk Unit With Guests
5000 Miles | ACT | 9271-2
Nils Landgren Group
Sentimental Journey | ACT | 9409-2
Viktoria Tolstoy Group & Strings
Shining On You | ACT | 9701-2
Viktoria Tolstoy With The Esbjörn Svensson Trio
Viktoria Tolstoy:White Russian | Blue Note | 821220-2

Tomato Kiss |
Tomato Kiss
Tomato Kiss | Nabel Records:Jazz Network | CD 4624

Tome XX |
Tome XX
The Red Snapper | Jazz Haus Musik | JHM 0047 CD
Third Degree | Jazz Haus Musik | JHM 0063 CD
She Could Do Nothing By Halves | Jazz Haus Musik | JHM 0084 CD

Tomlin,Bo | (p)
Al Jarreau With Band
High Crime | i.e. Music | 557848-2

Tomlinson,Jim | (cl,as,ts,fl,saxvoc)
Jim Tomlinson Quartet
Brazilian Sketches | Candid | CCD 79769
Jim Tomlinson Quintet
Only Trust Your Heart | Candid | CCD 79758
Brazilian Sketches | Candid | CCD 79769
Jim Tomlinson Sextet
Only Trust Your Heart | Candid | CCD 79758
Stacey Kent And Her Quintet
Close Your Eyes | Candid | CCD 79737
The Tender Trap | Candid | CCD 79751
Let Yourself Go-Celebrating Fred Astaire | Candid | CCD 79764
Stacey Kent With The Jim Tomlison Quintet
Dreamsville | Candid | CCD 79775
Stacy Kent With The Jim Tomlinson Quintet
In Love Again | Candid | CCD 79786
The Boy Next Door | Candid | CCD 79797

Tommasi,Amedeo | (p)
Chet Baker Sextet
Chet Baker-The Italian Sessions | Bluebird | ND 82001

Tommaso,Bruno | (arr,ldb)
Italian Instabile Orchestra
Skies Of Europe | ECM | 1543
Willem Breuker Kollektief
La Banda/Banda And Jazz | Enja | ENJ-9326 2

Tompert,Patrick | (p)
Patrick Tompert Trio
Hallelujah Time | Satin Doll Productions | SDP 1020-1 CD
Patrick Tompert Trio Live | Satin Doll Productions | SDP 1029-1 CD
Moche! | Satin Doll Productions | SDP 1035-1 CD
Sorry,It's Jazz
Sorry,It's Jazz! | Satin Doll Productions | SDP 1040-1 CD

Tompkins,Eddie | (tpvoc)
Jimmy Lunceford And His Orchestra
Planet Jazz:Swing | Planet Jazz | 2169651-2

Tompkins,Ross | (p,el-pp-solo)
Louie Bellson Septet
Louie Bellson Jam | Original Jazz Classics | OJCCD 802-2(2310838)
Zoot Sims And His Orchestra
The Jazz Giants Play Duke Ellington:Caravan | Prestige | PCD 24227-2

Tomter,Lars Anders | (viola)
Terje Rypdal Group
If Mountains Could Sing | ECM | 1554(523987-2)

Tonnesen,Terje | (v)
Skywards | ECM | 1608(533768-2)
Terje Rypdal(comp)
Undisonus | ECM | 1389

Tonolo,Pietro | (as,sax,ss,tsbs)
Paul Motian And The E.B.B.B.
Holiday For Strings | Winter&Winter | 910069-2
Paul Motian Electric Bebop Band
Europe | Winter&Winter | 910063-2

Tononi,Tiziano | (dr,perc,congas,boo-bam,cymbals)
Italian Instabile Orchestra
Skies Of Europe | ECM | 1543

Tooley,Ron | (tpfl-h)
Dee Dee Bridgewater With Big Band
Dear Ella | Verve | 539102-2

Torchinsky,Yves | (bel-b)
Claus Stötter's Nevertheless
Die Entdeckung Der Banane | Jazz 'n' Arts Records | JNA 1403
Renaud Garcia-Fons Quartet
Alboreá | Enja | ENJ-9057 2

Torge,Anna | (mand)
Trio De La Gorra
Internationales Guitarren Festival '99 | ALISO Records | AL 1038

Torkewitz,Chris | (flts)
Jazz Orchester Rheinland-Pfalz
Last Season | Jazz Haus Musik | LJBB 9706

Tormé,Mel | (drvoc)
Glenn Miller And His Orchestra
The Glenn Miller Orchestra In Digital Mood | GRP | GRP 95022
Mel Tormé With Orchestra
Comin' Home Baby!/Sings Sunday In New York | Warner | 8122-75438-2
Mel Tormé With The Billy May Orchestra
Mel Tormé Goes South Of The Border With Billy May | Verve | 589517-2
Mel Tormé With The Claus Ogerman Orchestra
Comin' Home Baby!/Sings Sunday In New York | Warner | 8122-75438-2
Mel Tormé With The Geoff Love Orchestra
My Kind Of Music | Verve | 543795-2
Mel Tormé With The Jimmy Jones Orchestra
Blue Velvet: Crooners, Swooners And Velvet Vocals | Blue Note | 521153-2
Mel Tormé With The Russell Garcia Orchestra
Swingin' On The Moon | Verve | 511385-2
Mel Tormé With The Shorty Rogers Orchestra
Comin' Home Baby!/Sings Sunday In New York | Warner | 8122-75438-2
Mel Tormé With The Tony Osborne Orchestra
My Kind Of Music | Verve | 543795-2
Mel Tormé With The Wally Stott Orchestra
My Kind Of Music | Verve | 543795-2

Torn,David | (el-g,fl,g,b,dr,g-loops,hand-perc)
David Torn Quartet
Cloud About Mercury | ECM | 1322(831108-2)
David Torn/Geoffrey Gordon
Best Laid Plans | ECM | 1284
Everyman Band
Everyman Band | ECM | 1234
Without Warning | ECM | 1290
Jan Garbarek Group
It's OK To Listen To The Gray Voice | ECM | 1294(825406-2)

Törner,Gösta | (tpld)
Coleman Hawkins With The Thore Ehrlings Orchestra
Coleman Hawkins At The Golden Circle | Dragon | DRCD 265

Tornquist,Lillian | (harp)
Miles Davis With The Danish Radio Big Band
Aura | CBS | CK 63962
The Danish Radio Big Band
Aura | CBS | CK 63962
The Danish Radio Concert Orchestra
Symphonies Vol.2 | dacapo | DCCD 9441

Tornquist,Rebecka | (voc)
Michael 'Patches' Stewart Group
Blue Patches | Hip Bop | HIBD 8016

Toro,Efrain | (perc)
Stan Getz Quintet
Sony Jazz Collection:Stan Getz | CBS | 488623-2

Torre,Al | (dr)
Cal Tjader Quartet
Jazz At The Blackhawk | Original Jazz Classics | OJCCD 436-2(F 8096)

Torrent,Shay | (org)
Jack Teagarden And His Sextet
Mis'ry And The Blues | Verve | 9860310

Torres,Al | (dr)
Cal Tjader Quartet
Our Blues | Fantasy | FCD 24771-2

Torres,Gene | (bel-b)
Steve Lampert Group
Venus Perplexed | Steeplechase | SCCD 31557

Torres,Jaime | (charango)
Jazzensemble Des Hessischen Rundfunks
Atmosphering Conditions Permitting | ECM | 1549/50

Torres,Joseph | (perc)
Les McCann Orchestra
Talkin' Verve:Les McCann | Verve | 557351-2

Torriente,Liber | (dr)
Ramon Valle Trio
No Escape | ACT | 9424-2

Tortelli,Morgan M. | (perc)
Richard Galliano With Orchestra
Passatori | Dreyfus Jazz Line | FDM 36601-2

Tortiller,Frank | (marimba,timbales,gongsvib)
Renaud Garcia-Fons
Navigatore | Enja | ENJ-9418 2
Renaud Garcia-Fons Group
Navigatore | Enja | ENJ-9418 2

Toscarelli,Mario | (dr)
Jess Stacy And His Orchestra
Planet Jazz:Jazz Piano | RCA | 2169655-2

Totah,Nabil 'Knobby' | (bfinger-cymbals)
Bobby Hackett Sextet
Jazz Festival Vol.1 | Storyville | 4960733
Jazz Festival Vol.2 | Storyville | 4960743
Herbie Mann And His Orchestra
The Best Of Herbie Mann | Atlantic | 7567-81369-2
Herbie Mann Sextet
Verve Jazz Masters 56:Herbie Mann | Verve | 529901-2
Herbie Mann's Cuban Band
Verve Jazz Masters 56:Herbie Mann | Verve | 529901-2
Zoot Sims-Al Cohn Quintet
Jazz Alive:A Night At The Half Note | Blue Note | 494105-2
Zoot Sims-Al Cohn-Phil Woods Sextet
Jazz Alive:A Night At The Half Note | Blue Note | 494105-2

Totah,Nabil 'Knobby' or Bill Takas | (b)
Tal Farlow Quartet
Verve Jazz Masters 41:Tal Farlow | Verve | 527365-2

Toth,Jerry | (fl,alto-cl,as,clsax)
Singers Unlimited With Rob McConnell And The Boss Brass
The Singers Unlimited:Magic Voices | MPS | 539130-2

Toto | (bird-songs)
John McLaughlin Group
The Promise | Verve | 529828-2

Touff,Cy | (bass-tp)
Johnny Frigo Sextet
I Love John Frigo...He Swings | Mercury | 9861061
Nat Pierce/Dick Collins Nonet
Nat Pierce-Dick Collins-Ralph Burns & The Herdsmen Play Paris | Fantasy | FCD 24759-2
The Herdsmen
Nat Pierce-Dick Collins-Ralph Burns & The Herdsmen Play Paris | Fantasy | FCD 24759-2

Tough Tenors,The |
The Tough Tenors With The Antonio Farao European Trio
Tough Tenors | Jazz 4 Ever Records:Jazz Network | J4E 4761

Tough,Dave | (dr)
Artie Shaw And His Orchestra
Planet JazzArtie Shaw | Planet Jazz | 2152057-2
Planet Jazz:Male Jazz Vocalists | Planet Jazz | 2169657-2
Benny Goodman And His All Star Sextet
Charlie Christian:Swing To Bop | Dreyfus Jazz Line | FDM 36715-2
Benny Goodman And His Orchestra
Charlie Christian:Swing To Bop | Dreyfus Jazz Line | FDM 36715-2
More Camel Caravans | Phontastic | NCD 8843/4
More Camel Caravans | Phontastic | NCD 8845/6
Benny Goodman Quartet
More Camel Caravans | Phontastic | NCD 8843/4
More Camel Caravans | Phontastic | NCD 8845/6
Bud Freeman And His Famous Chicagoans
Jazz:The Essential Collection Vol.3 | IN+OUT Records | 78013-2
Jack Teagarden And His Orchestra
Jazz:The Essential Collection Vol.3 | IN+OUT Records | 78013-2
Jack Teagarden's Big Eight
Planet Jazz:Jack Teagarden | Planet Jazz | 2161236-2
Planet Jazz | Planet Jazz | 2169652-2
Jazz:The Essential Collection Vol.3 | IN+OUT Records | 78013-2
JATP All Stars
The Complete Jazz At The Philharmonic On Verve 1944-1949 | Verve | 523893-2
Tommy Dorsey And His Clambake Seven
Planet Jazz:Bud Freeman | Planet Jazz | 2161240-2
Tommy Dorsey And His Orchestra
Planet Jazz:Tommy Dorsey | Planet Jazz | 2159972-2
Planet Jazz:Big Bands | Planet Jazz | 2169649-2
Planet Jazz:Swing | Planet Jazz | 2169651-2
Woody Herman And His Orchestra
The Legends Of Swing | Laserlight | 24659
Woody Herman:Four Brother | Dreyfus Jazz Line | FDM 36722-2
Louis Armstrong-Jack Teagarden-Woody Herman:Midnights At V-Disc | Jazz Unlimited | JUCD 2048
Old Gold Rehearsals 1944 | Jazz Unlimited | JUCD 2079

Tournier,Henri | (flbansuri)

Renaud Garcia-Fons Group
Entremundo | Enja | ENJ-9464 2

Towler,Tom | (b-gel-b)
Jean-Luc Ponty Quintet
The Very Best Of Jean-Luc Ponty | Rhino | 8122-79862-2

Towner,Ralph | (12-string-g,windharp,fl-h,g,p,perc)
Andy Middleton Group
Nomad's Notebook | Intuition Records | INT 3264-2
Arild Andersen Quartet
If You Look Far Enough | ECM | 1493(513902-2)
Azimuth With Ralph Towner
Azimuth | ECM | 1546/48(523010-2)
Egberto Gismonti Group
Sol Do Meio Dia | ECM | 1116(829117-2)
Gary Peacock-Ralph Towner
Oracle | ECM | 1490(521350-2)
Jan Garbarek-Ralph Towner
Dis | ECM | 1093(827408-2)
Jan Garbarek-Ralph Towner Group
Dis | ECM | 1093(827408-2)
John Abercrombie-Ralph Towner Duo
Sargasso Sea | ECM | 1080
Oregon
Oregon | ECM | 1258(811711-2)
Crossing | ECM | 1291(825323-2)
Ecotopia | ECM | 1354
45th Parallel | VeraBra Records | CDVBR 2048-2
Always,Never And Forever | Intuition Records | INT 2073-2
Northwest Passage | Intuition Records | INT 3191-2
Ralph Towner
Trios/Solos | ECM | 1025(833328-2)
Diary | ECM | 1032(829157-2)
Solo Concert | ECM | 1173(827268-2)
Blue Sun | ECM | 1250(829162-2)
Ana | ECM | 1611(537023-2)
Anthem | ECM | 1743(543814-2)
Ralph Towner Quartet
Solstice | ECM | 1060(825458-2)
Lost And Found | ECM | 1563(529347-2)
Ralph Towner Quintet
Old Friends New Friends | ECM | 1153
City Of Eyes | ECM | 1388
Ralph Towner Trio
Batik | ECM | 1121(847325-2)
Ralph Towner With Strings
In The Light | ECM | 1033/4
Ralph Towner-Gary Burton
Matchbook | ECM | 1056(835014-2)
Slide Show | ECM | 1306
Ralph Towner-Gary Peacock
A Closer View | ECM | 1602(531623-2)
Ralph Towner-Glen Moore
Northwest Passage | Intuition Records | INT 3191-2
Ralph Towner-Mark Walker
Northwest Passage | Intuition Records | INT 3191-2
Ralph Towner-Peter Erskine
Open Letter | ECM | 1462(511980-2)

Towns,Colin | (arrcond)
Christof Lauer-Jens Thomas With The Cikada String Quartet
Shadows In The Rain | ACT | 9297-2
NDR Big Band
The Theatre Of Kurt Weil | ACT | 9234-2

Toyfl,Markus | (gvoc)
Axel Zwingenberger With The Mojo Blues Band And Red Holloway
Axel Zwingenberger And The Friends Of Boogie Woogie,Vol.8 | Vagabond | VRCD 8.93019
Champion Jack Dupree Group
Champ's Housewarming | Vagabond | VRCD 8.88014

Tozzi,Wolfgang | (dr)
Dominik Grimm-Thomas Wallisch Trio
A Brighter Day | Edition Collage | EC 510-2

Tracanna,Tino | (sax,ss,as,tsbs)
Paolo Fresu Quintet
Night On The City | Owl Records | 013425-2
Melos | RCA | 2178289-2

Trace,Ella | (voc)
Clare Teal And Her Band
Orsino's Songs | Candid | CCD 79783

Tracey,Clark | (dr)
Heinz Sauer Quartet With The NDR Big Band
NDR Big Band-Bravissimo | ACT | 9232-2

Tracey,Stan | (p,arrsynth)
NDR Big Band
NDR Big Band-Bravissimo | ACT | 9232-2

Tracy,Jeanie | (voc)
Herbie Hancock Group
Magic Window | CBS | 486572-2

Traeger,Charles | (b)
Sidney Bechet With Bob Wilber's Wildcats
Sidney Bechet:Summertime | Dreyfus Jazz Line | FDM 36712-2

Traenor,John 'Mambo' | (perc,trianglewbd)
Hans Theessink Group
Crazy Moon | Minor Music | 801052

Trafficante,Mike | (btuba)
Paul Whiteman And His Orchestra
Planet Jazz:Jazz Trumpet | Planet Jazz | 2169654-2

Tragg,Nickie | (org)
Louis Armstrong With Sy Oliver's Choir And Orchestra
Jazz Collection:Louis Armstrong | Laserlight | 24366
Louis And The Good Book | Verve | 549593-2
Louis And The Good Book | Verve | 940130-0

Traindl,Josef | (tb)
Franz Koglmann Quintet
Opium | Between The Lines | btl 011(Efa 10181-2)

Trainer,Freddie | (tp)
Lena Horne With The Horace Henderson Orchestra
Planet Jazz:Lena Horne | Planet Jazz | 2165373-2

Tramontana,Sebi | (tbbaritone-fl-h)
Italian Instabile Orchestra
Skies Of Europe | ECM | 1543
Transalpin Express Orchestra
Some Other Tapes | Fish Music | FM 009/10 CD

Tranberg,Kasper | (co,tpfl-h)
Chris Potter & Jazzpar Septet
This Will Be | Storyville | STCD 4245
Copenhagen Art Ensemble
Shape To Twelve | dacapo | DCCD 9430
Angels' Share | dacapo | DCCD 9452
Marilyn Mazur With Ars Nova And The Copenhagen Art Ensemble
Jordsange | dacapo | DCCD 9454
Ok Nok...Kongo
Moonstone Journey | dacapo | DCCD 9444
Pierre Dørge's New Jungle Orchestra
Giraf | dacapo | DCCD 9440
When Granny Sleeps
Welcome | dacapo | DCCD 9447

Transalpin Express Orchestra |
Transalpin Express Orchestra
Some Other Tapes | Fish Music | FM 009/10 CD

Traore,Kaloga | (doundoumba,tam-tam,voicevoc)
Pili-Pili
Stolen Moments | JA & RO | JARO 4159-2
Jazzy World | JA & RO | JARO 4200-2

Trappier,Arthur | (dr)
James P.Johnson's Blue Note Jazzmen
The Blue Note Jazzmen | Blue Note | 821262-2

Trasante,Jorge 'Negrito' | (dr,congasperc)
Renaud Garcia-Fons Group
Navigatore | Enja | ENJ-9418 2

Traugott,Erich | (tpfl-h)
Singers Unlimited With Rob McConnell And The Boss Brass
The Singers Unlimited:Magic Voices | MPS | 539130-2

Trauner,Erik | (g,vocslide-g)
Axel Zwingenberger With The Mojo Blues Band And Red Holloway
Axel Zwingenberger And The Friends Of Boogie Woogie,Vol.8 | Vagabond | VRCD 8.93019
Champion Jack Dupree Group
Champ's Housewarming | Vagabond | VRCD 8.88014

Travieso,Israel Moises 'Quinque' | (conga)
Sabu L. Martinez Group
Palo Congo | Blue Note | 522665-2

Travieso,Raul 'Caesar' | (congavoc)

Travis,Nick | (tp,tbv-tb)
Birdland Dream Band
Birdland Dream Band | RCA | 2663873-2
Chris Connor With Band
Chris Connor | Atlantic | 7567-80769-2
Chubby Jackson And His All Star Big Band
Chubby Takes Over | Fresh Sound Records | FSR-CD 324
Coleman Hawkins With Billy Byers And His Orchestra
The Hawk In Hi-Fi | RCA | 2663842-2
Coleman Hawkins With Many Albam And His Orchestra
Planet Jazz:Coleman Hawkins | Planet Jazz | 2152055-2
Dinah Washington With The Quincy Jones Orchestra
Verve Jazz Masters 40:Dinah Washington | Verve | 522055-2
The Swingin' Miss 'D' | Verve | 558074-2
Dizzy Gillespie And His Orchestra
Gillespiana And Carnegie Hall Concert | Verve | 519809-2
Talking Verve:Dizzy Gillespie | Verve | 533846-2
Ultimate Dizzy Gillespie | Verve | 557535-2
Elliot Lawrence And His Orchestra
The Elliot Lawrence Big Band Swings Cohn & Kahn | Fantasy | FCD 24761-2
Gerry Mulligan Concert Jazz Band
Verve Jazz Masters 36:Gerry Mulligan | Verve | 523342-2
Verve Jazz Masters Vol.60:The Collection | Verve | 529866-2
Gerry Mulligan And The Concert Band At The Village Vanguard | Verve | 589488-2
The Complete Verve Gerry Mulligan Concert Band | Verve | 9860613
Lena Horne With The Lennie Hayton Orchestra
Planet Jazz:Lena Horne | Planet Jazz | 2165373-2
Stan Getz With The Gary McFarland Orchestra
Verve Jazz Masters 53:Stan Getz-Bossa Nova | Verve | 529904-2
Big Band Bossa Nova | Verve | 825771-2 PMS
Stan Getz Highlights | Verve | 847430-2
Thelonious Monk And His Orchestra
Greatest Hits | CBS | CK 65422
Tito Puente Orchestra
Planet Jazz:Tito Puente | Planet Jazz | 2165369-2
Woody Herman And His Orchestra
The Legends Of Swing | Laserlight | 24659

Traxler,Gene | (b)
Benny Goodman And His V-Disc All Star Band
The Legends Of Swing | Laserlight | 24659
Tommy Dorsey And His Clambake Seven
Planet Jazz:Tommy Dorsey | Planet Jazz | 2159972-2
Planet Jazz:Bud Freeman | Planet Jazz | 2161240-2
Planet Jazz:Swing | Planet Jazz | 2169651-2
Tommy Dorsey And His Orchestra
Planet Jazz:Frank Sinatra & Tommy Dorsey | Planet Jazz | 2152067-2
Planet Jazz:Tommy Dorsey | Planet Jazz | 2159972-2
Planet Jazz:Big Bands | Planet Jazz | 2169649-2
Planet Jazz:Swing | Planet Jazz | 2169651-2

Trayler,Rudy | (dr)
Louis Armstrong With Sy Oliver And His Orchestra
Louis And The Angels | Verve | 549592-2

Traylor,Rudy | (conddr)
Johnny Hartman And The Rudy Traylor Orchestra
And I Thought About You | Blue Note | 857456-2

Trcek,Blaz | (bs)
European Jazz Youth Orchestra
Swinging Europe 3 | dacapo | DCCD 9461

Treadwell,Constance | (voc)
Leon Thomas With Orchestra
Spirits Known And Unknown | RCA | 2663876-2

Trebacz,Leon | (v)
Pete Rugolo And His Orchestra
Thriller/Richard Diamon(Original Jazz Scores From 2 Classics TV Series) | Fresh Sound Records | FSCD 2015

Tremble Kids All Stars,The |
The Tremble Kids All Stars
The Tremble Kids All Stars Play Chicago Jazz! | Nagel-Heyer | CD 043

Tremontana,Sebi | (tb)
Ekkehard Jost Quintet
Some Other Tapes | Fish Music | FM 009/10 CD
Kölner Saxophon Mafia With Guests
Kölner Saxophon Mafia: 20 Jahre Saxuelle Befreiung | Jazz Haus Musik | JHM 0115 CD
Transalpin Express Orchestra
Some Other Tapes | Fish Music | FM 009/10 CD

Trenner,Don | (p)
Ben Webster With Strings
The Warm Moods-With Strings | Rhino | 8122-73721-2

Trepte,Uli | (b,vocb-g)
Bitkicks
Kickbit Information | ATM Records | ATM 3823-AH
Guru Guru
Guru Guru/Uli Trepte | ATM Records | ATM 3815-AH
Uli Trepte Group
Guru Guru/Uli Trepte | ATM Records | ATM 3815-AH
Real Time Music | ATM Records | ATM 3820-AH

Tretter,Armin | (as,sopranino,cl,alukoffer-perc,fl)
Kölner Saxophon Mafia
Mafia Years 1982-86 | Jazz Haus Musik | JHM 0058 CD

Tricarico,Bob | (bassoon,contra-bassoon,b-cl,bs,cl)
Anthony Ortega With The Robert Zieff Orchestra
Earth Dance | Fresh Sound Records | FSR-CD 325
Ella Fitzgerald With The Nelson Riddle Orchestra
Dream Dancing | Original Jazz Classics | OJCCD 1072-2(2310814)
Gil Evans Orchestra
Verve Jazz Masters 23:Gil Evans | Verve | 521860-2
The Individualism Of Gil Evans | Verve | 833804-2
Out Of The Cool | Impulse(MCA) | 951186-2
Joe Williams With The Frank Hunter Orchestra
Planet Jazz:Joe Williams | Planet Jazz | 2165370-2
Kenny Burrell With The Gil Evans Orchestra
Guitar Forms | Verve | 521403-2
Verve Jazz Masters 23:Gil Evans | Verve | 521860-2
Verve Jazz Masters 45:Kenny Burrell | Verve | 527652-2
Verve Jazz Masters Vol.60:The Collection | Verve | 529866-2
Miles Davis With Gil Evans & His Orchestra
Miles Davis At Carnegie Hall | CBS | CK 65027
Quiet Nights | CBS | CK 65293
Singers Unlimited With Orchestra
The Singers Unlimited:Magic Voices | MPS | 539130-2

Trice,Amos | (p)
Sonny Stitt Quartet
Verve Jazz Masters 50:Sonny Sitt | Verve | 527651-2

Tricolor |
Triocolor
Colours Of Ghana | ACT | 9285-2

Triffon,George | (tpfr-h)
Bill Evans Quartet With Orchestra
The Complete Bill Evans On Verve | Verve | 527953-2
From Left To Right | Verve | 557451-2

Trigg,Dave | (tpfl-h)
Buddy Childers Big Band
It's What Happening Now! | Candid | CCD 79749

Triglia,Bill | (p)
Charles Mingus Orchestra
Tijuana Moods(The Complete Edition) | RCA | 2663840-2
Jimmy Knepper Quintet
Charles Mingus-The Complete Debut Recordings | Debut | 12 DCD 4402-2

Trigon |
Trigon
Oglinda | JA & RO | JARO 4215-2

Trimble,James | (tb)
Buddy Rich And His Orchestra
Swingin' New Big Band | Pacific Jazz | 835232-2
Big Swing Face | Pacific Jazz | 837989-2
Buddy Rich Big Band
The New One! | Pacific Jazz | 494507-2

Trimboli,Dan | (flsax)
Louis Armstrong And His Orchestra
What A Wonderful World | MCA | MCD 01876

Trio De La Gorra |
Trio De La Gorra
Internationales Guitarren Festival '99 | ALISO Records | AL 1038

Trio De Paz |
Kenny Barron Group With Trio De Paz
Canta Brazil | EmArCy | 017993-2

Trio KoKoKo |
Trio KoKoKo
Willisau And More Live | Creative Works Records | CW CD 1020-2

Trio Larose |
Trio Larose
Debut | Jazz 'n' Arts Records | JNA 0802
Trio Larose With Toni Lakatos
Debut | Jazz 'n' Arts Records | JNA 0802

Trio,The |
The Trio
The Trio:Rediscovered | String Jazz | SJRCD 1007

Triscari,Joe | (tp)
Anita O'Day With Gene Krupa And His Orchestra
Let Me Off Uptown:Anita O'Day With Gene Krupa | CBS | CK 65625
Benny Carter And His Orchestra
Aspects | Capitol | 852677-2
Billy Eckstine With The Billy May Orchestra
Once More With Feeling | Roulette | 581862-2
Ella Fitzgerald With The Billy May Orchestra
Ella Fitzgerald Sings The Harold Arlen Song Book | Verve | 589108-2
Gene Krupa And His Orchestra
Mullenium | CBS | CK 65678
Peggy Lee With The Quincy Jones Orchestra
Blues Cross Country | Capitol | 520088-2
Pete Rugolo And His Orchestra
Thriller/Richard Diamon(Original Jazz Scores From 2 Classics TV Series) | Fresh Sound Records | FSCD 2015

Triscari,Mike | (g)
Gene Krupa And His Orchestra
Mullenium | CBS | CK 65678

Triscari,Ray | (astp)
Dizzy Gillespie And His Orchestra
Talking Verve:Dizzy Gillespie | Verve | 533846-2
Gene Krupa And His Orchestra
Mullenium | CBS | CK 65678
June Christy With The Pete Rugolo Orchestra
Something Cool(The Complete Mono & Stereo Versions) | Capitol | 534069-2
June Christy With The Shorty Rogers Orchestra
June Christy Big Band Special | Capitol | 498319-2
Terry Gibbs Big Band
Terry Gibbs Dream Band Vol.4:Main Stem | Contemporary | CCD 7656-2
Terry Gibbs Dream Band
Terry Gibbs Dream Band Vol.3:Flying Home | Contemporary | CCD 7654-2
Terry Gibbs Dream Band Vol.5:The Big Cat | Contemporary | CCD 7657-2
Terry Gibbs Dream Band Vol.6:One More Time | Contemporary | CCD 7658-2

Tristano,Lennie | (p,arrp-solo)
Lennie Tristano
Planet Jazz:Jazz Piano | RCA | 2169655-2
Lennie Tristano:The Copenhagen Concert | Storyville | 4960603
The New Tristano | Atlantic | 7567-80475-2
Requiem | Atlantic | 7567-80804-2
Lennie Tristano Quartet
Requiem | Atlantic | 7567-80804-2
Lennie Tristano Trio
The Story Of Jazz Piano | Laserlight | 24653
Requiem | Atlantic | 7567-80804-2
Lenny Tristano Quartet
Subconcious-Lee | Original Jazz Classics | OJCCD 186-2(P 7004)
Lenny Tristano Quintet
Subconcious-Lee | Original Jazz Classics | OJCCD 186-2(P 7004)
The Metronome All Stars
Planet Jazz:Dizzy Gillespie | Planet Jazz | 2152069-2

Triviatas | (1.Schwuler Männerchor Köln)
Kölner Saxophon Mafia With Triviatas(1.Schwuler Männerchor Köln)
Kölner Saxophon Mafia Proudly Presents | Jazz Haus Musik | JHM 0046 CD

Tröger,Kathrin | (v)
Uri Caine With The Concerto Köln
Concerto Köln | Winter&Winter | 910086-2

Trolle,Per | (perc)
Kim Kristensen
Pulse Of Time | dacapo | DCCD 9435

Tromans,Steve | (p)
John Mayer's Indio-Jazz Fusions
Ragatal | Nimbus Records | NI 5569

Trombonefire |
Trombonefire
Sliding Affairs | Laika Records | 35101462

Troncoso,Dave | (b)
Bobby Hutcherson Orchestra
Montara | Blue Note | 590956-2

Tröndle,Hartmut | (cello)
Stefanie Schlesiger And Her Group plus String Quartet
What Love Is | Enja | ENJ-9434 2

Tronzo,David | (bar-g,dobro,slide-g,waste-basket)
Leni Stern Group
Secrets | Enja | ENJ-5093 2
Michael Blake Group
Kingdom Of Champa | Intuition Records | INT 3189-2
Slow Poke
Redemption | Intuition Records | INT 3260-2

Tropea,John | (el-gg)
Billy Cobham Group
Spectrum | Atlantic | 7567-81428-2
Ron Carter Quintet With Strings
Pick 'Em/Super Strings | Milestone | MCD 47090-2
Ronnie Foster Group
Sweet Revival... | Blue Note | 581676-2

Trotman,Irving | (p)
Golden Gate Quartet
Americans Swinging In Paris:Golden Gate Quartet | EMI Records | 539659-2
From Spriritual To Swing Vol.2 | EMI Records | 780573-2
Spirituals To Swing 1955-69 | EMI Records | 791569-2

Trottenberg,Florian | (tb)
Jazz Orchester Rheinland-Pfalz
Last Season | Jazz Haus Musik | LJBB 9706

Trotter,Terry | (keyboardsp)

Ella Fitzgerald With Orchestra
Ella Abraca Jobim | Pablo | 2630201-2
Trottman,Lloyd | (b)
Al Sears & His Rock 'N' Rollers
Sear-iously | Bear Family Records | BCD 15668 AH
Al Sears And His Orchestra
Sear-iously | Bear Family Records | BCD 15668 AH
Bud Powell Trio
The Best Of Bud Powell On Verve | Verve | 523392-2
Duke Ellington Quartet
Great Times! | Original Jazz Classics | OJC20 108-2(RLP 475)
Duke Ellington-Billy Strayhorn Quintet
Great Times! | Original Jazz Classics | OJC20 108-2(RLP 475)
Henry Red Allen's All Stars
Planet Jazz:Coleman Hawkins | Planet Jazz | 2152055-2
Johnny Hodges And His Band
Verve Jazz Masters 35:Johnny Hodges | Verve | 521857-2
Johnny Hodges Orchestra
Highlights From The Duke Ellington Centennial Edition | RCA | 2663672-2
Lawrence Brown Quintet
Slide Trombone | Verve | 559930-2
Sister Rosetta Tharpe And Her Group
Gospel Train | Mercury | 841134-2
Sister Rosetta Tharpe And Her Group With The Harmonizing Four
Gospel Train | Mercury | 841134-2
Troudi,Mounir | (voc)
Erik Truffaz Quartet
Mantis | Blue Note | 535101-2
Troupe,Bobby | (announcements)
Warne Marsh Quintet
Jazz Of Two Cities | Fresh Sound Records | FSR-CD 342
Trovesi,Gianluigi | (alto-cl,b-cl,as,piccolo,sax,ss)
Gianlugi Trovesi Quartet With The WDR Big Band
Dedalo | Enja | ENJ-9419 2
Gianluigi Trovesi Nonet
Round About A Midsummer's Dream | Enja | ENJ-9384 2
Gianluigi Trovesi-Gianni Coscia
In Cerca Di Cibo | ECM | 1703(543034-2)
Italian Instabile Orchestra
Skies Of Europe | ECM | 1543
Michel Godard Ensemble
Castel Del Monte | Enja | ENJ-9362 2
Orchestre National De Jazz
Charmediterranéen | ECM | 1828(018493-2)
Willem Breuker Kollektief
La Banda/Banda And Jazz | Enja | ENJ-9326 2
Trovesi,Stefania | (v)
Gianluigi Trovesi Nonet
Round About A Midsummer's Dream | Enja | ENJ-9384 2
Trowers,Robert | (tb)
Dee Dee Bridgewater With Big Band
Dear Ella | Verve | 539102-2
Truan,Oliver | (keyboardsp)
World Quintet
World Quintet | TipToe | TIP-888843 2
Kol Simcha
Contemporary Klezmer | Laika Records | LK 93-048
World Quintet With The London Mozart Players
World Quintet | TipToe | TIP-888843 2
World Quintet With The London Mozart Players And Herbert Grönemeyer
World Quintet | TipToe | TIP-888843 2
Trübsbach,Florian | (cl,ss,asreeds)
Florian Trübsbach Quintet
Manson & Dixon | Jazz 4 Ever Records:Jazz Network | J4E 4759
Martin Auer Quintet
Martin Auer Quintett | Jazz 4 Ever Records:Jazz Network | J4E 4762
Munich Saxophon Family
Survival Song | JHM Records | JHM 3613
Nana Mouskouri With The Berlin Radio Big Band
Nana Swings | Mercury | 074394-2
Rainer Tempel Big Band
Melodies Of '98 | Jazz 4 Ever Records:Jazz Network | J4E 4744
Trueheart,John | (gbj)
Billie Holiday With Teddy Wilson And His Orchestra
Billie's Love Songs | Nimbus Records | NI 2000
Ella Fitzgerald And Her Famous Orchestra
The Radio Years 1940 | Jazz Unlimited | JUCD 2065
Ella Fitzgerald And Her Orchestra
Jazz Collection:Ella Fitzgerald | Laserlight | 24397
Louis Armstrong With Chick Webb's Orchestra
Best Of The Complete RCA Victor Recordings | RCA | 2663636-2
Louis Armstrong:A 100th Birthday Celebration | RCA | 2663694-2
Teddy Wilson And His All Stars
Jazz:The Essential Collection Vol.3 | IN+OUT Records | 78013-2
Truffaz,Erik | (tpfl-h)
Erik Truffaz Quartet
The Dawn | Blue Note | 493916-2
Bending New Corners | Blue Note | 522123-2
Mantis | Blue Note | 535101-2
Erik Truffaz Quartet Quintet
Mantis | Blue Note | 535101-2
Out Of A Dream | Blue Note | 855855-2
Truitt,Sonny | (p,tbbs)
Charlie Mariano Sextet
The Jazz Scene:San Francisco | Fantasy | FCD 24760-2
Miles Davis Septet
Miles Davis And Horns | Original Jazz Classics | OJC20 053-2(P 7025)
Trumbauer,Frank | (c-mel-sax,vocreeds)
Frank Trumbauer And His Orchestra
The Hollywood Session:The Capitol Jazzmen | Jazz Unlimited | JUCD 2044
Frankie Trumbauer And His Orchestra
Jazz:The Essential Collection Vol.2 | IN+OUT Records | 78012-2
Paul Whiteman And His Orchestra
Planet Jazz:Jack Teagarden | Planet Jazz | 2161236-2
Jazz:The Essential Collection Vol.3 | IN+OUT Records | 78013-2
The Three T's
Jazz:The Essential Collection Vol.3 | IN+OUT Records | 78013-2
Trumbauer,Frankie | (as,c-mel-saxvoc)
Frankie Trumbauer And His Orchestra
Jazz:The Essential Collection Vol.2 | IN+OUT Records | 78012-2
Paul Whiteman And His Orchestra
Planet Jazz:Jack Teagarden | Planet Jazz | 2161236-2
Planet Jazz:Jazz Trumpet | Planet Jazz | 2169654-2
Trumpet Summit |
The Trumpet Summit With The Oscar Peterson Big 4
The Trumpet Summit Meets The Oscar Peterson Big 4 | Original Jazz Classics | OJCCD 603-2
Trunk,Peter | (b,celloel-b)
Klaus Doldinger Quintet
Doldinger's Best | ACT | 9224-2
Klaus Doldinger Septet
Doldinger's Best | ACT | 9224-2
Klaus Doldinger-Peter Trunk
Doldinger's Best | ACT | 9224-2
Lucky Thompson Quartet
The Jazz Life! | Candid | CCD 79019
Paul Nero Sound
Doldinger's Best | ACT | 9224-2
Volker Kriegel Quintet
Spectrum | MPS | 9808699
Trussardi,Luigi | (b)
Dusko Goykovich Big Band
Balkan Connection | Enja | ENJ-9047 2
Phil Woods-Benny Carter Quintet
The Art Of Saxophone | Laserlight | 24652
Tryon,James | (v)
Yusef Lateef Orchestra
The Blue Yusef Lateef | Rhino | 8122-73717-2
Tsabropoulos,Vassilis | (p)
Arild Andersen Trio
The Triangle | ECM | 1752(0381212)
Kostas Konstantinou-Vassilis Tsabropoulos
Concentric Cycles | Nabel Records:Jazz Network | CD 4698
Vassilis Tsabropoulos Trio
Achirana | ECM | 1728(157462-2)
Tsangaris,Manos | (drperc)
Reiner Winterschladen-Manos Tsangaris
King Kong | Jazz Haus Musik | JHM 0056 CD
Tsiboe,Nana | (atupan-dr,brekete-dr,djembe,gonje)
Trevor Watts Moiré Music Drum Orchestra
A Wider Embrace | ECM | 1449
Tsilis,Gust William | (marimbavib)
Arthur Blythe Group
Hipmotism | Enja | ENJ-6088 2
Herb Robertson Quintet
'X'-cerpts:Live At Willisau | JMT Edition | 919013-2
Tsinman,Mikhail | (v)
Moscow Rachmaninov Trio
Groupe Lacroix:The Composer Group | Creative Works Records | CW CD 1030-2
Tubino,Marcio | (fl,ss,as,ts,perc,voice,caxixis)
Marcio Tubino Group
Festa Do Olho | Organic Music | ORGM 9723
Raiz De Pedra
Diario De Bordo | TipToe | TIP-888822 2
Raiz De Pedra feat. Egberto Gismonti
Diario De Bordo | TipToe | TIP-888822 2
Terra Brazil
Café Com Leite | art-mode-records | AMR 2101
Tuchacek,Alexander | (electronics,g,synthcomputer)
Sotto In Su
Südamerika Sept. 90 | Jazz Haus Musik | JHM 0051 CD
Vanitas | Poise | Poise 04
Tuck & Patti |
Tuck And Patti
Tears Of Joy | Windham Hill | 34 10111-2
Love Warriors | Windham Hill | 34 10116-2
Dream | Windham Hill | 34 10130-2
Tuck And Patti: |
A Gift Of Love | T&P Records | 9815810
Tuck,Deidre | (voc)
Les McCann Group
Another Beginning | Atlantic | 7567-80790-2
Tucker,Ben | (b,el-btambourine)
Art Pepper-Warne Marsh Quintet
The Way It Is | Original Jazz Classics | OJCCD 389-2
Bola Sete Quintet
Tour De Force:The Bola Sete Trios | Fantasy | FCD 24766-2
Eddie Lockjaw Davis Sextet feat. Paul Gonsalves
Planet Jazz:Jazz Saxophone | Planet Jazz | 2169653-2
Gerry Mulligan Quintet
Late Night Sax | CBS | 487798-2
Gil Evans Orchestra
The Individualism Of Gil Evans | Verve | 833804-2
Grant Green Quartet
Ballads | Blue Note | 537560-2
Grant Green Trio
Ballads | Blue Note | 537560-2
Green Street | Blue Note | 540032-2
Herbie Mann Group
The Best Of Herbie Mann | Atlantic | 7567-81369-2
Rhino Presents The Atlantic Jazz Gallery | Atlantic | 8122-71257-2
Herbie Mann Septet
Herbie Mann At The Village Gate | Atlantic | 7567-81350-2
James Moody Orchestra
The Blues And Other Colors | Original Jazz Classics | OJCCD 954-2(M 9023)
Jimmy Smith Quartet
Jimmy Smith-Talkin' Verve | Verve | 531563-2
Lou Donaldson Quintet
Blue Bossa | Blue Note | 795590-2
Gravy Train | Blue Note | 853357-2
Mose Allison Trio
The Word From Mose | Atlantic | 8122-72394-2
Pat Martino Quintet
Strings! | Original Jazz Classics | OJCCD 223-2(P 7547)
Pat Martino Septet
Strings! | Original Jazz Classics | OJCCD 223-2(P 7547)
Ray Crawford Sextet
Smooth Groove | Candid | CCD 79028
Warne Marsh Quintet
Jazz Of Two Cities | Fresh Sound Records | FSR-CD 342
Warne Marsh Quintet With Art Pepper
Jazz Of Two Cities | Fresh Sound Records | FSR-CD 342
Willis Jackson Sextet
At Large | Prestige | PCD 24243-2
Yusef Lateef Orchestra
The Centaur And The Phoenix | Original Jazz Classics | OJCCD 721-2(RLP 9337)
Tucker,Bobby | (cond,arrp)
Billie Holiday And Her All Stars
Verve Jazz Masters 12:Billie Holiday | Verve | 519825-2
The Billie Holiday Song Book | Verve | 823246-2
Billie Holiday With Bobby Tucker
Billie Holiday Story Vol.1:Jazz At The Philharmonic | Verve | 521642-2
The Complete Jazz At The Philharmonic On Verve 1944-1949 | Verve | 523893-2
Billie Holiday With The Bobby Tucker Quartet
Billie's Love Songs | Nimbus Records | NI 2000
Billie Holiday With The Tiny Grimes Quintet
Billie's Blues | Blue Note | 748786-2
Billy Eckstine And His Orchestra
Blue Velvet: Crooners, Swooners And Velvet Vocals | Blue Note | 521153-2
Billy Eckstine With Bobby Tucker And His Orchestra
The Antonio Carlos Jobim Songbook | Verve | 525472-2
Billy Eckstine Now Singing In 12 Great Movies | Verve | 589307-2
Tucker,Dion | (tb)
Eric Reed Orchestra
Happiness | Nagel-Heyer | CD 2010
Tucker,George | (b)
Booker Ervin Quartet
That's It | Candid | CCD 79014
Carmel Jones Quartet
Jay Hawk Talk | Original Jazz Classics | OJCCD 1938-2(P7401)
Carmel Jones Quintet
Jay Hawk Talk | Original Jazz Classics | OJCCD 1938-2(P7401)
Dexter Gordon Quintet
Doin' Allright | Blue Note | 784077-2
Dexter Gordon:Ballads | Blue Note | 796579-2
Jazz Profile:Dexter Gordon | Blue Note | 823514-2
Eric Dolphy Quartet
Eric Dolphy Birthday Celebration | Fantasy | FANCD 6085-2
Eric Dolphy Quintet
Eric Dolphy:The Complete Prestige Recordings | Prestige | 9 PRCD-4418-2
Eric Dolphy Birthday Celebration | Fantasy | FANCD 6085-2
Etta Jones And Her Band
Love Shout | Original Jazz Classics | OJCCD 941-2(P 7272)
Horace Parlan Quartet
Blue Bossa | Blue Note | 795590-2
Horace Parlan Quintet
The Best Of Blue Note Vol.2 | Blue Note | 797960-2
Jaki Byard Quartet
The Last From Lennie's | Prestige | PRCD 11029-2
Jimmy Witherspoon And His Band
Baby, Baby, Baby | Original Blues Classics | OBCCD 527-2(P 7290)
Jimmy Woods Sextet
Conflict | Original Jazz Classics | OJCCD 1954-2(S 7612)
Joe Zawinul Quartet
To You With Love | Fresh Sound Records | Strand SLS CD 1007
Joe Zawinul Trio
To You With Love | Fresh Sound Records | Strand SLS CD 1007
Lambert, Hendricks And Bavan
Planet Jazz:Male Jazz Vocalists | Planet Jazz | 2169657-2
Oliver Nelson Quintet
The Jazz Giants Play Sammy Cahn:It's Magic | Prestige | PCD 24226-2
Shirley Scott Quintet
Blue Seven | Original Jazz Classics | OJCCD 1050-2(P 7376)
Queen Of The Organ-Shirley Scott Memorial Album | Prestige | PRCD 11027-2
Shirley Scott Trio
Like Cozy | Prestige | PCD 24258-2
Sonny Red (Kyner) Quartet
Red,Blue & Green | Milestone | MCD 47086-2
Sonny Red (Kyner) Quintet
Red,Blue & Green | Milestone | MCD 47086-2
Willis Jackson Sextet
At Large | Prestige | PCD 24243-2
Nuther'n Like Thuther'n | Prestige | PRCD 24265-2
Tucker,Henry | (dr)
Helen Humes And Her All Stars
Lester Young:The Complete Aladdin Sessions | Blue Note | 832787-2
Lester Young And His Band
Lester Young:The Complete Aladdin Sessions | Blue Note | 832787-2
Tucker,Lee | (b)
The Modern Jazz Disciples
Disciples Blues | Prestige | PCD 24263-2
Tucker,Mickey | (el-p,keyboards,org,p,celeste,saw)
Jimmy Ponder Quartet
Jazzin' Vol.2: The Music Of Stevie Wonder | Fantasy | FANCD 6088-2
Louis Hayes Sextet
The Crawl | Candid | CCD 79045
Rahsaan Roland Kirk And His Orchestra
Blacknuss | Rhino | 8122-71408-2
Tucker,Patrick | (fr-h)
Yusef Lateef Ensemble
Nocturnes | Atlantic | 7567-81977-2
Tucker,Sid | (clbs)
Louis Armstrong And His Orchestra
Louis Armstrong:Swing That Music | Laserlight | 36056
Tull,Thomas | (tb)
Marcus Sukiennik Big Band
A Night In Tunisia Suite(7 Variationen über Dizzy Gillespie's 'A Night In Tunisia') | Jazz Haus Musik | ohne Nummer
Tulloch,Davey | (perc)
Deborah Henson-Conant Trio
Just For You | Laika Records | LK 95-063
Tulsi | (tamboura)
Alice Coltrane Sextet
Journey In Satchidananda | Impulse(MCA) | 951228-2
Tuncboyaci[Boyaciyan],Arto | (dr,perc,bakdav,hand-dr,voice,gongs)
Arthur Blythe Group
Hipmotism | Enja | ENJ-6088 2
Bob Stewart First Line Band
First Line | JMT Edition | 919014-2
Dino Saluzzi Group
Mojotoro | ECM | 1447
Ed Schuller & Band
The Eleventh Hour | Tutu Records | 888124-2*
Glen Moore Group
Nude Bass Ascending... | Intuition Records | INT 3192-2
Glen Moore-Arto Tuncboyaciyan
Northwest Passage | Intuition Records | INT 3191-2
Michael 'Patches' Stewart Group
Penetration | Hip Bop | HIBD 8018
Oregon
Northwest Passage | Intuition Records | INT 3191-2
Simon Nabatov, String Gang & Percussion
Inside Lookin' Out | Tutu Records | 888104-2*
Tunia,Raymond | (p)
Ella Fitzgerald With The JATP All Stars
Ella Fitzgerald-First Lady Of Song | Verve | 517898-2
JATP All Stars
JATP In Tokyo | Pablo | 2620104-2
Tunja F.M. | (rapvoc)
House Five
Frank Talk | Nabel Records:Jazz Network | CD 4674
Tuomarila,Alexi | (p)
Alexi Tuomarila Quartet
02 | Finladia Jazz | 0927-49148-2
Turbinton,Earl | (b-cl,ssas)
Joe Zawinul Group
Zawinul | Atlantic | 7567-81375-2
Turbo B. | (spoken words)
Balance
Elements | double moon | DMCHR 71033
Turczynski,Grzegorz | (tb)
European Jazz Youth Orchestra
Swinging Europe 3 | dacapo | DCCD 9461
Turk,John | (el-porg)
John Lee Hooker Group
Endless Boogie | MCA | MCD 10413
Turk,Mike | (harm)
Mike Turk With The Alkaline Jazz Trio
A Little Taste Of Cannonball | Organic Music | ORGM 9708
Turk,Tommy | (tb)
Charlie Parker And His Orchestra
Charlie Parker:The Best Of The Verve Years | Verve | 527815-2
Bird: The Complete Charlie Parker On Verve | Verve | 837141-2
Charlie Parker Septet
Charlie Parker | Verve | 539757-2
Ella Fitzgerald With The JATP All Stars
Ella Fitzgerald-First Lady Of Song | Verve | 517898-2
JATP All Stars
Verve Jazz Masters 28:Charlie Parker Plays Standards | Verve | 521854-2
The Complete Jazz At The Philharmonic On Verve 1944-1949 | Verve | 523893-2
Charlie Parker:The Best Of The Verve Years | Verve | 527815-2
Jazz At The Philharmonic:Best Of The 1940's Concerts | Verve | 557534-2
Talkin' Bird | Verve | 559859-2
Bird: The Complete Charlie Parker On Verve | Verve | 837141-2
Norman Granz' JATP: Carnegie Hall 1949 | Pablo | PACD 5311-2
Turkmani,Mahmoud | (goud)
Mahmoud Turkmani
Fayka | Enja | ENJ-9447 2
Nuqta | TipToe | TIP-888835 2
Mahmoud Turkmani Group
Zakira | Enja | ENJ-9475 2
Mahmoud Turkmani With The Ludus Guitar Quartet
Nuqta | TipToe | TIP-888835 2
Turmes,Jeff | (el-b)
Peter Malick Group feat. Norah Jones
New York City | Koch Records | 238678-2
Turner Jr.,Russell | (p)
Buddy Rich Big Band
The New One! | Pacific Jazz | 494507-2
Turner,Big Joe | (voc)
Big Joe Turner And His Orchestra
Planet Jazz:Male Jazz Vocalists | Planet Jazz | 2169657-2

Big Joe Turner And Pete Johnson With The Blues Band
Newport Jazz Festival 1958,July 3rd-6th Vol.3:Blues In The Night No.1 | Phontastic | NCD 8815
Big Joe Turner With Axel Zwingenberger
Let's Boogie Woogie All Night Long | Vagabond | VRCD 8.79012
Boogie Woogie Jubilee | Vagabond | VRCD 8.81010
Axel Zwingenberger And The Friends Of Boogie Woogie Vol.2 | Vagabond | VRCD 8.85005
Big Joe Turner With Pete Johnson
From Spiritual To Swing | Vanguard | VCD 169/71
Big Joe Turner With The Count Basie Orchestra
Flip Flop And Fly | Original Jazz Classics | OJCCD 1053-2(2310937)
Dizzy Gillespie's Trumpet Kings
The Trumpet Kings Meet Joe Turner | Original Jazz Classics | OJCCD 497-2
Joe Turner With Orchestra
Atlantic Jazz: Kansas City | Atlantic | 7567-81701-2
Super Black Blues Band
Super Black Blues Vol.II | RCA | 2663874-2

Turner,Brad | (ptp)
Francois Houle 5
Cryptology | Between The Lines | btl 012(Efa 10182-2)

Turner,Charles | (btuba)
Fats Waller And His Rhythm
Planet Jazz:Fats Waller | Planet Jazz | 2152058-2
Planet Jazz Sampler | Planet Jazz | 2152326-2
Planet Jazz:Male Jazz Vocalists | Planet Jazz | 2169657-2

Turner,Charlie | (tp)
Ella Fitzgerald With The Nelson Riddle Orchestra
Dream Dancing | Original Jazz Classics | OJCCD 1072-2(2310814)

Turner,Danny | (as,piccolo,fl,reeds,saxts)
Count Basie And His Orchestra
Fun Time | Pablo | 2310945-2
88 Basie Street | Original Jazz Classics | OJC 808(2310901)
Jazz Dance | Original Jazz Classics | OJCCD 1002-2(1210890)
Fancy Pants | Original Jazz Classics | OJCCD 1038-2(2310920)
I Told You So | Original Jazz Classics | OJCCD 824-2(2310767)
Digital III At Montreux | Original Jazz Classics | OJCCD 996-2(2308223)
The Jazz Giants Play Harry Warren:Lullaby Of Broadway | Prestige | PCD 24204-2
Count Basie Big Band
Montreux '77 | Original Jazz Classics | OJCCD 377-2
Farmers Market Barbecue | Original Jazz Classics | OJCCD 732-2(2310874)
Diane Schuur With The Count Basie Orchestra
The Best Of Diane Schuur | GRP | GRP 98882
Ella Fitzgerald With Count Basie And His Orchestra
Digital III At Montreux | Original Jazz Classics | OJCCD 996-2(2308223)
Ella Fitzgerald With The Count Basie Orchestra
Bluella:Ella Fitzgerald Sings The Blues | Pablo | 2310960-2
For The Love Of Ella Fitzgerald | Verve | 841765-2
Jack McDuff Orchestra
The Last Goodun' | Prestige | PRCD 24274-2
Jimmy McGriff Organ Blues Band
The Worm | Blue Note | 538699-2
Milt Jackson Orchestra
Sarah Vaughan Birthday Celebration | Fantasy | FANCD 6090-2
Milt Jackson With The Count Basie Orchestra
To Bags...With Love:Memorial Album | Pablo | 2310967-2
Milt Jackson Birthday Celebration | Fantasy | FANCD 6079-2
Milt Jackson + Count Basie + Big Band Vol.1 | Original Jazz Classics | OJCCD 740-2(2310822)
Milt Jackson + Count Basie + Big Band Vol.2 | Original Jazz Classics | OJCCD 741-2(2310823)
Pat Martino Sextet
El Hombre | Original Jazz Classics | OJCCD 195-2(P 7513)
Sarah Vaughan And The Count Basie Orchestra
Sarah Vaughan Birthday Celebration | Fantasy | FANCD 6090-2

Turner,Henry | (b)
Louis Jordan And His Tympany Five
Louis Jordan-Let The Good Times Roll: The Complete Decca Recordings 1938-1954 | Bear Family Records | BCD 15557 IH
Sidney Bechet And His Orchestra
Sidney Bechet:Summertime | Dreyfus Jazz Line | FDM 36712-2

Turner,Howard | (bs)
Itchy Fingers
Live | Enja | ENJ-6076 2

Turner,Jimmy | (dr)
Charles Earland Sextet
Jazzin' With The Soul Brothers | Fantasy | FANCD 6086-2
Charlie's Greatest Hits | Prestige | PCD 24250-2

Turner,Joe | (b,p,vocp-solo)
Cat Anderson And His All Stars
Americans Swinging In Paris:Cat Anderson | EMI Records | 539658-2
Joe Turner
The Giant Of Stride Piano In Switzerland | Jazz Connaisseur | JCCD 9106-2
Joe Turner And Friends
The Giant Of Stride Piano In Switzerland | Jazz Connaisseur | JCCD 9106-2
Joe Turner-Albert Nicholas Quartet
The Giant Of Stride Piano In Switzerland | Jazz Connaisseur | JCCD 9106-2
Joe Turner-Claude Dunson
The Giant Of Stride Piano In Switzerland | Jazz Connaisseur | JCCD 9106-2

Turner,Mark | (ssts)
Anke Helfrich Trio With Mark Turner
You'll See | double moon | CHRDM 71013
Chris Cheek Sextet
A Girl Named Joe | Fresh Sound Records | FSNT 032 CD
George Colligan Group
Unresolved | Fresh Sound Records | FSNT 054 CD
Jam Session
Jam Session Vol.4 | Steeplechase | SCCD 31527
Jam Session Vol.9 | Steeplechase | SCCD 31554
Joshua Redman Quartet feat. Mark Turner
Beyond | Warner | 9362-47465-2
Kurt Rosenwinkel Quartet
The Next Stop | Verve | 549162-2
Kurt Rosenwinkel Quintet
The Enemies Of Energy | Verve | 543042-2
Mark Turner Quartet
Ballad Session | Warner | 9362-47631-2
Dharma Days | Warner | 9362-47998-2
Mark Turner Quintet
Ballad Session | Warner | 9362-47631-2
Mark Turner Trio
Ballad Session | Warner | 9362-47631-2
Mark Turner-Chris Cheek Quintet
The Music Of Mercedes Rossy | Fresh Sound Records | FSNT 043 CD
Mark Zubeck Quartet
Horse With A Broken Leg | Fresh Sound Records | FSNT 078 CD
Perico Sambeat Group
Ademuz | Fresh Sound Records | FSNT 041 CD
Reid Anderson Quartet
Dirty Show Tunes | Fresh Sound Records | FSNT 030 CD
Abolish Bad Architecture | Fresh Sound Records | FSNT 062 CD

Turner,Milton | (dr)
David Fathead Newman Sextet
Atlantic Saxophones | Rhino | 8122-71256-2
Rhino Presents The Atlantic Jazz Gallery | Atlantic | 8122-71257-2
Fathead:Ray Charles Presents David Newman | Atlantic | 8122-73708-2
Hank Crawford Septet
More Soul | Atlantic | 8122-73709-2
Joe Gordon Quintet
Lookin' Good | Original Jazz Classics | OJCCD 1934-2(S 7597)
Sarah Vaughan And Her Band
Misty Blue:Sweet Sisters Swing Songs Of Sorrow And Sadness | Blue Note | 521151-2
Sarah Vaughan With The Gerald Wilson Orchestra
Ballads | Roulette | 537561-2

Turner,Sunny | (tp)
Buddy Guy Blues Band
Buddy Guy-The Complete Chess Studio Recordings | MCA | MCD 09337

Turner,Toby | (clas)
Earl Hines And His Orchestra
Jazz:The Essential Collection Vol.2 | IN+OUT Records | 78012-2

Turney,Norris | (as,cl,ts,sax,fl,as clreeds)
Carol Sloane With The Norris Turney Quartet
Something Cool | Choice | CHCD 71025
Duke Ellington And His Orchestra
New Orleans Suite | Rhino | 812273670-2
The Ellington Suites | Original Jazz Classics | OJC20 446-2(2310762)
The Afro-Eurasian Eclipse-A Suite In Eight Parts | Original Jazz Classics | OJCCD 645-2(F 9498)
Togo Brava Swuite | Storyville | STCD 8323
Duke Ellington Small Band
The Intimacy Of The Blues | Original Jazz Classics | OJCCD 624-2
Oscar Peterson With The Ernie Wilkins Orchestra
Verve Jazz Masters 16:Oscar Peterson | Verve | 516320-2
Roy Eldridge Septet
To Bags...With Love:Memorial Album | Pablo | 2310967-2
Roy Eldridge Sextet
Milt Jackson Birthday Celebration | Fantasy | FANCD 6079-2

Turnham,Floyd | (asbs)
Johnny Otis And His Orchestra
Verve Jazz Masters 43:Ben Webster | Verve | 525431-2

Turnland,George | (viola)
Dee Dee Bridgewater With Orchestra
Dear Ella | Verve | 539102-2

Turnovsky,Michael | (oboe)
Couch Ensemble
Winnetou | Jazz 'n' Arts Records | JNA 1503

Turnovsky,Regine | (v)

Turre,Steve | (b-tb,conch-shells,shells,tb,bells)
Andy Bey Group
Tuesdays In Chinatown | Minor Music | 801099
Bob Stewart First Line Band
First Line | JMT Edition | 919014-2
Christian McBride Group
Gettin' To It | Verve | 523989-2
Dizzy Gillespie And The United Nation Orchestra
7.Zelt-Musik-Festival:Jazz Events | Zounds | CD 2730001
Eddie Allen Sextet
Summer Days | Enja | ENJ-9388 2
Fred Wesley Group
New Friends | Minor Music | 801016
Jerry Gonzalez & Fort Apache Band
The River Is Deep | Enja | ENJ-4040 2
John Scofield Groups
Groove Elation | Blue Note | 832801-2
Lester Bowie's Brass Fantasy
I Only Have Eyes For You | ECM | 1296(825902-2)
Avant Pop | ECM | 1326
McCoy Tyner Big Band
The Best Of McCoy Tyner Big Band | Dreyfus Jazz Line | FDM 37012-2
Ray Barretto Orchestra
Portraits In Jazz And Clave | RCA | 2168452-2
Stefon Harris Group
Black Action Figure | Blue Note | 499546-2

Turrentine,Stanley | (tsarr)
Abbey Lincoln With The Max Roach Quintet
Abbey Is Blue | Original Jazz Classics | OJC20 069-2(RLP 1153)
Abbey Lincoln With The Max Roach Sextet
Abbey Is Blue | Original Jazz Classics | OJC20 069-2(RLP 1153)
Ahmad Jamal Quartet With Stanley Turrentine
Nature(The Essence Part III) | Atlantic | 3984-23105-2
Nature | Dreyfus Jazz Line | FDM 37018-2
Bernard Purdie's Soul To Jazz
Bernard Purdie's Soul To Jazz II | ACT | 9253-2
Bobby Lyle Group
The Journey | Atlantic | 7567-82138-2
Duke Pearson Orchestra
Blue N' Groovy | Blue Note | 780679-2
Herbie Hancock Septet
Herbie Hancock:The Complete Blue Note Sixties Sessions | Blue Note | 495569-2
Horace Parlan Quintet
The Best Of Blue Note Vol.2 | Blue Note | 797960-2
Horace Silver Quintet
Horace Silver Retrospective | Blue Note | 495576-2
Jimmy Smith Quartet
Prayer Meetin' | Blue Note | 576754-2
Back At The Chicken Shack | Blue Note | 746402-2
The Best Of Blue Note | Blue Note | 796110-2
Fourmost Return | Milestone | MCD 9311-2
Jimmy Smith Quintet
Prayer Meetin' | Blue Note | 576754-2
Kenny Burrell Quintet
Midnight Blue | Blue Note | 495335-2
The Best Of Blue Note | Blue Note | 796110-2
Max Roach Quintet
Clifford Brown-Max Roach:Alone Together-The Best Of The Mercury Years | Verve | 526373-2
Jazz In Paris:Max Roach-Parisian Sketches | EmArCy | 589963-2
Max Roach Sextet
Clifford Brown-Max Roach:Alone Together-The Best Of The Mercury Years | Verve | 526373-2
Oscar Brown Jr. And His Group
Live Every Minute | Minor Music | 801071
Roy Hargrove Quintet With Stanley Turrentine
Roy Hargrove Quintet With The Tenors Of Our Time | Verve | 523019-2
Shirley Scott Quartet
Blue Flames | Original Jazz Classics | OJCCD 328-2(P 7338)
Queen Of The Organ-Shirley Scott Memorial Album | Prestige | PRCD 11027-2
Stanley Turrentine And His Orchestra
The Lost Grooves | Blue Note | 831883-2
Pieces Of Dream | Original Jazz Classics | OJCCD 831-2(F 9465)
Stanley Turrentine Orchestra
Rough 'N' Tumble | Blue Note | 524552-2
The Spoiler | Blue Note | 853359-2
Stanley Turrentine Quartet
Blue Note Plays Gershwin | Blue Note | 520808-2
Never Let Me Go | Blue Note | 576750-2
Blue N' Groovy | Blue Note | 780679-2
The Roots Of Acid Jazz | Impulse(MCA) | IMP 12042
Stanley Turrentine Quintet
Hustlin' | Blue Note | 540036-2
Never Let Me Go | Blue Note | 576750-2
Stanley Turrentine With The Three Sounds
Blue Hour | Blue Note | 524586-2
Midnight Blue(The [Be]witching Hour) | Blue Note | 854365-2

Turrentine,Tommy | (tp)
Abbey Lincoln With The Max Roach Quintet
Abbey Is Blue | Original Jazz Classics | OJC20 069-2(RLP 1153)
Abbey Lincoln With The Max Roach Sextet
Abbey Is Blue | Original Jazz Classics | OJC20 069-2(RLP 1153)
Ahmed Abdullah Sextet
Jazz Sounds Of Africa | Prestige | PRCD 24279-2
Archie Shepp Orchestra
Mama Too Tight | Impulse(MCA) | 951248-2
Horace Parlan Quintet
The Best Of Blue Note Vol.2 | Blue Note | 797960-2
Jackie McLean Quintet
A Fickle Sonance | Blue Note | 524544-2
Lou Donaldson Quintet
The Natural Soul | Blue Note | 542307-2
Max Roach Quintet
Clifford Brown-Max Roach:Alone Together-The Best Of The Mercury Years | Verve | 526373-2
Jazz In Paris:Max Roach-Parisian Sketches | EmArCy | 589963-2
Max Roach Sextet
Clifford Brown-Max Roach:Alone Together-The Best Of The Mercury Years | Verve | 526373-2

Tuscher,Peter | (tpfl-h)
Al Porcino Big Band
Al Porcino Big Band Live! | Organic Music | ORGM 9717
Al Cohn Meets Al Porcino | Organic Music | ORGM 9730
Conexion Latina
Mambo 2000 | Enja | ENJ-7055 2
Roman Schwaller Nonet
The Original Tunes | JHM Records | JHM 3629
Thilo Kreitmeier & Group
Soul Call | Organic Music | ORGM 9711
Thilo Kreitmeier Quintet
Mo' Better Blues | Organic Music | ORGM 9706
Walter Lang Quintet
Tales Of 2 Cities | double moon | CHRDM 71016

Tuva Folk Ensemble |
Mikhail Alperin's Moscow Art Trio With The Tuva Folk & Russian Folk Ensemble
Prayer | JA & RO | JARO 4193-2

Tvaergard,Per | (p)
Leonardo Pedersen's Jazzkapel
The Golden Years Of Revival Jazz,Sampler | Storyville | 109 1001
The Golden Years Of Revival Jazz,Vol.11 | Storyville | STCD 5516

Twardzik,Dick | (p,celestetom-tom)
Lars Gullin And The Chet Baker Quartet
Lars Gullin 1955/56 Vol.1 | Dragon | DRCD 224

Tweedle,John | (b)
Terry Callier Duo
The New Folk Sound Of Terry Callier | Prestige | PRCD 11026-2

Twice A Week: |
Twice A Week & Steve Elson
Play Of Colours | Edition Collage | EC 511-2

Twillie,Carmen | (voc)
Bobby Lyle Group
The Journey | Atlantic | 7567-82138-2
Paulinho Da Costa Orchestra
Happy People | Original Jazz Classics | OJCCD 783-2(2312102)

Two Beat Stompers |
Two Beat Stompers
Deutsches Jazz Fesival 1954/1955 | Bear Family Records | BCD 15430

Tyler,Alvin 'Red' | (bsts)
Jack McDuff Sextet
The Soulful Drums | Prestige | PCD 24256-2

Tyner,McCoy | (dulcimer,fl,p,perc,koto,harpsichord)
Art Blakey Quartet
A Jazz Message | Impulse(MCA) | 547964-2
Blue Mitchell And His Orchestra
Blue Breaks Beats Vol.2 | Blue Note | 789907-2
Bobby Hutcherson Quintet
Blue N' Groovy | Blue Note | 780679-2
Freddie Hubbard Quintet
Open Sesame | Blue Note | 495341-2
Bossa Nova Bacchanal | Blue Note | 593875-2
Freddie Hubbard Sextet
Wayne Shorter:The Classic Blue Note Recordings | Blue Note | 540856-2
Grant Green Sextet
True Blue | Blue Note | 534032-2
Hank Mobley Quintet
Deep Blue-The United States Of Mind | Blue Note | 521152-2
Joe Henderson Quartet
The Blue Note Years-The Best Of Joe Henderson | Blue Note | 795627-2
Joe Henderson Quintet
Page One | Blue Note | 498795-2
The Blue Note Years-The Best Of Joe Henderson | Blue Note | 795627-2
John Coltrane And His Orchestra
Kulu Se Mama | Impulse(MCA) | 543412-2
Ascension | Impulse(MCA) | 543413-2
John Coltrane:Standards | Impulse(MCA) | 549914-2
Meditations | Impulse(MCA) | 951199-2
John Coltrane Group
Olé Coltrane | Atlantic | 7567-81349-2
Olé Coltrane | Rhino | 8122-73699-2
John Coltrane Quartet
Afro Blue Impressions | Pablo | 2PACD 2620101
Trane's Blues | Blue Note | 498240-2
Kulu Se Mama | Impulse(MCA) | 543412-2
Impressions | Impulse(MCA) | 543416-2
John Coltrane:Standards | Impulse(MCA) | 549914-2
Coltrane Spiritual | Impulse(MCA) | 589099-2
Ballads | Impulse(MCA) | 589548-2
Coltrane | Impulse(MCA) | 589567-2
A Love Supreme | Impulse(MCA) | 589596-2
A Love Supreme | Impulse(MCA) | 589945-2
Coltrane Jazz | Atlantic | 7567-81344-2
Coltrane Plays The Blues | Atlantic | 7567-81351-2
Coltrane's Sound | Atlantic | 7567-81358-2
The Best Of John Coltrane | Atlantic | 7567-81366-2
John Coltrane-Live Trane:The European Tours | Pablo | 7PACD 4433-2
Rhino Presents The Atlantic Jazz Gallery | Atlantic | 8122-71257-2
John Coltrane-The Heavyweight Champion:The Complete Atlantic Recordings | Atlantic | 8122-71984-2
My Favorite Things | Atlantic | 8122-75204-2
The Very Best Of John Coltrane | Rhino | 8122-79778-2
Coltrane Plays The Blues | Rhino | 8122-79966-2
The Gentle Side Of John Coltrane | Impulse(MCA) | 951107-2
Sun Ship | Impulse(MCA) | 951166-2
Live At Birdland | Impulse(MCA) | 951198-2
Crescent | Impulse(MCA) | 951200-2
The Coltrane Quartet Plays | Impulse(MCA) | 951214-2
Living Space | Impulse(MCA) | 951246-2
Live At The Village Vanguard:The Master Takes | Impulse(MCA) | 951251-2
John Coltrane:The Classic Quartet-Complete Impulse Studio Recordings | Impulse(MCA) | 951280-2
John Coltrane:The Complete 1961 Village Vanguard Recordings | Impulse(MCA) | 954322-2
The Other Village Vanguard Tapes | Impulse(MCA) | MCD 04137
Bye Bye Blackbird | Original Jazz Classics | OJC20 681-2(2308227)
The Paris Concert | Original Jazz Classics | OJC20 781-2(2308217)
John Coltrane Quartet With Brass
The Complete Africa/Brass Sessions | Impulse(MCA) | 952168-2
John Coltrane Quartet With Eric Dolphy
John Coltrane:The Complete 1961 Village Vanguard Recordings | Impulse(MCA) | 954322-2
John Coltrane Quartet With Johnny Hartman
The Gentle Side Of John Coltrane | Impulse(MCA) | 951107-2
John Coltrane Quintet
Impressions | Impulse(MCA) | 543416-2
John Coltrane:Standards | Impulse(MCA) | 549914-2
Live At The Village Vanguard:The Master Takes | Impulse(MCA) | 951251-2
Eric Dolphy Birthday Celebration | Fantasy | FANCD 6085-2
John Coltrane Quintet With Eric Dolphy
Coltrane Spiritual | Impulse(MCA) | 589099-2
John Coltrane-Live Trane:The European Tours | Pablo | 7PACD 4433-2

John Coltrane-The Heavyweight Champion:The Complete Atlantic Recordings | Atlantic | 8122-71984-2
John Coltrane:The Complete 1961 Village Vanguard Recordings | Impulse(MCA) | 954322-2
The Other Village Vanguard Tapes | Impulse(MCA) | MCD 04137
John Coltrane Septet With Eric Dolphy
John Coltrane:The Complete 1961 Village Vanguard Recordings | Impulse(MCA) | 954322-2
The Other Village Vanguard Tapes | Impulse(MCA) | MCD 04137
John Coltrane Sextet
Impressions | Impulse(MCA) | 543416-2
A Love Supreme | Impulse(MCA) | 589945-2
Live At The Village Vanguard:The Master Takes | Impulse(MCA) | 951251-2
John Coltrane:The Complete 1961 Village Vanguard Recordings | Impulse(MCA) | 954322-2
John Coltrane Sextet With Eric Dolphy
John Coltrane-The Heavyweight Champion:The Complete Atlantic Recordings | Atlantic | 8122-71984-2
John Coltrane-McCoy Tyner
Ballads | Impulse(MCA) | 589548-2
Johnny Hartman With The John Coltrane Quartet
John Coltrane:Standards | Impulse(MCA) | 549914-2
John Coltrane And Johnny Hartman | Impulse(MCA) | 951157-2
Julian Priester Sextet
Out Of This World | Milestone | MCD 47087-2
McCoy Tyner
Song For My Lady | Original Jazz Classics | OJCCD 313-2
Echoes Of A Friend | Original Jazz Classics | OJCCD 650-2(M 9055)
The Jazz Giants Play Rodgers & Hammerstein:My Favorite Things | Prestige | PCD 24223-2
McCoy Tyner Big Band
The Best Of McCoy Tyner Big Band | Dreyfus Jazz Line | FDM 37012-2
McCoy Tyner Group With Horns
Inner Voices | Original Jazz Classics | OJCCD 1039-2(M 9079)
McCoy Tyner Group With Horns And Voices
Inner Voices | Original Jazz Classics | OJCCD 1039-2(M 9079)
McCoy Tyner Group With Voices
Inner Voices | Original Jazz Classics | OJCCD 1039-2(M 9079)
McCoy Tyner Orchestra
Sama Layuca | Original Jazz Classics | OJCCD 1071-2(M 9056)
13th House | Original Jazz Classics | OJCCD 1089-2(M 9102)
McCoy Tyner Quartet
The Story Of Jazz Piano | Laserlight | 24653
The Real McCoy | Blue Note | 497807-2
Prelude And Sonata | Milestone | MCD 9244-2
Sahara | Original Jazz Classics | OJC20 311-2
Song For My Lady | Original Jazz Classics | OJCCD 313-2
McCoy Tyner Quintet
Asante | Blue Note | 493384-2
Live At Newport | Impulse(MCA) | 547980-2
Prelude And Sonata | Milestone | MCD 9244-2
McCoy Tyner Septet
Focal Point | Original Jazz Classics | OJCCD 1009-2(M 9072)
Song For My Lady | Original Jazz Classics | OJCCD 313-2
McCoy Tyner Sextet
Asante | Blue Note | 493384-2
Extensions | Blue Note | 837646-2
Focal Point | Original Jazz Classics | OJCCD 1009-2(M 9072)
McCoy Tyner Trio
Live At Newport | Impulse(MCA) | 547980-2
McCoy Tyner Plays John Coltrane | Impulse(MCA) | 589183-2
Chick Corea-Herbie Hancock-Keith Jarrett-McCoy Tyner | Atlantic | 7567-81402-2
McCoy Tyner Plays Ellington | Impulse(MCA) | 951216-2
Inception | Impulse(MCA) | 951220-2
Nights Of Ballads And Blues | Impulse(MCA) | 951221-2
Remembering John | Enja | ENJ-6080 2
Trident | Original Jazz Classics | OJC20 720-2(M 9063)
McCoy Tyner Trio + Latin Percussion
McCoy Tyner Plays Ellington | Impulse(MCA) | 951216-2
McCoy Tyner-Bobby Hutcherson Duo
Sama Layuca | Original Jazz Classics | OJCCD 1071-2(M 9056)
Michael Brecker Group
Tales From The Hudson | Impulse(MCA) | 951191-2
Milt Jackson Quartet
In A New Setting | Verve | 538620-2
Milt Jackson Quintet
In A New Setting | Verve | 538620-2
Stanley Turrentine And His Orchestra
The Lost Grooves | Blue Note | 831883-2
Stanley Turrentine Orchestra
Rough 'N' Tumble | Blue Note | 524552-2
The Spoiler | Blue Note | 853359-2
Stanley Turrentine Quartet
Blue N' Groovy | Blue Note | 780679-2
Stephane Grappelli-McCoy Tyner Duo
The Jazz Giants Play Rodgers & Hart:Blue Moon | Prestige | PCD 24205-2
Wayne Shorter Quartet
Juju | Blue Note | 499005-2
Wayne Shorter:The Classic Blue Note Recordings | Blue Note | 540856-2
Wayne Shorter Quintet
Wayne Shorter:The Classic Blue Note Recordings | Blue Note | 540856-2
Night Dreamer | Blue Note | 784173-2
Wayne Shorter Sextet
Wayne Shorter:The Classic Blue Note Recordings | Blue Note | 540856-2

Tyrell,Jimmy | (el-b)
King Curtis Band
King Curtis-Blow Man Blow | Bear Family Records | BCD 15670 CI

Tyson,June | (bells,voc,dancerv)
Sun Ra And His Astro-Infinity Arkestra
Space Is The Place | Impulse(MCA) | 951249-2
Sun Ra And His Intergalactic Research Arkestra
Black Myth/Out In Space | MPS | 557656-2

Uchitel,Dave | (viola)
Charlie Parker With Strings
Verve Jazz Masters 28:Charlie Parker Plays Standards | Verve | 521854-2
Charlie Parker With Strings:The Master Takes | Verve | 523984-2
Bird: The Complete Charlie Parker On Verve | Verve | 837141-2

UFB |
Jerry Granelli UFB
News From The Street | VeraBra Records | CDVBR 2146-2

Ugand,Jan | (sound-wiz)
Niels Landgren Funk Unit
Live In Stockholm | ACT | 9223-2

Uhl,Alex | (keyboards)
Rainer Tempel Band
Suite Ellington | Jazz 'n' Arts Records | JNA 0401

Uhlir,Frantisek | (b)
Dusko Goykovich Quintet With The NDR Radio-Philharmonie,Hannover
Balkan Blues | Enja | ENJ-9320 2

Uhrbrand,Peter | (fiddle)
ULG
Spring | Laika Records | 35101382

ULC |

Ulleberg,Odd | (fr-h)
Terje Rypdal Quintet
When Ever I Seem To Be Far Away | ECM | 1045

Ullmann Gebhard | (alto-fl,b-cl,ss,ts,b-fl,tape,fl,p)
Die Elefanten
Wasserwüste | Nabel Records:Jazz Network | CD 4634
Gebhard Ullmann Trio
Essencia | Between The Lines | btl 017(Efa 10187-2)
Suite Noire | Nabel Records:Jazz Network | CD 4649
Gebhard Ullmann-Andreas Willers
Suite Noire | Nabel Records:Jazz Network | CD 4649
Playful '93 | Nabel Records:Jazz Network | CD 4659
Ullmann-Wille-Haynes
Trad Corrosion | Nabel Records:Jazz Network | CD 4673
Ullmann-Willers-Schäuble-Lorenz
Out To Lunch | Nabel Records:Jazz Network | CD 4623

Ullmann,Gebhard | (flts)
Gebhard Ullmann Quartet
Per-Dee-Doo | Nabel Records:Jazz Network | CD 4640

Ullrich,Joachim | (arr,ld,b-cl,ts,cl,ss,voc,bass-sax)
Joachim Ullrich Orchestra
Faces Of The Duke | Jazz Haus Musik | JHM 0045 CD
Kölner Saxophon Mafia
Saxfiguren | Jazz Haus Musik | JHM 0036 CD
Mafia Years 1982-86 | Jazz Haus Musik | JHM 0058 CD
Place For Lovers | Jazz Haus Musik | JHM 0082 CD
Licence To Thrill | Jazz Haus Musik | JHM 0100 CD
Space Player | Jazz Haus Musik | JHM 0132 CD
Kölner Saxophon Mafia With Guests
Kölner Saxophon Mafia: 20 Jahre Saxuelle Befreiung | Jazz Haus Musik | JHM 0115 CD

Ulmer,James Blood | (b,el-g,voc,fl,gtalking)
Grant Calvin Weston Group
Dance Romance | IN+OUT Records | 7002-2
James Blood Ulmer Blues Experience
Live at The Bayerischer Hof | IN+OUT Records | 7018-2
James Blood Ulmer Group
Jazz Unlimited | IN+OUT Records | 7017-2
James Blood Ulmer Quartet
Revealing | IN+OUT Records | 7007-2
Jazz Unlimited | IN+OUT Records | 7017-2
Joe Henderson And His Orchestra
Joe Henderson:The Milestone Years | Milestone | 8MCD 4413-2
Joe Henderson Sextet
Multiple | Original Jazz Classics | OJCCD 763-2(M 9050)
John Patton Quartet
The Lost Grooves | Blue Note | 831883-2
Accent On The Blues | Blue Note | 853924-2
Karl Berger-James Blood Ulmer Duo
Conversations | IN+OUT Records | 77027-2

Ulrich,Dieter | (dr,buglewalkman)
Cadavre Exquis
Cadavre Exquis | Creative Works Records | CW CD 1014-1

Ulrich,Joachim | (b-cl,ts,arr,comp,ld,cl,reedssax)
Kölner Saxophon Mafia
Go Commercial... | Jazz Haus Musik | JHM 0065 CD
Kölner Saxophon Mafia With Arno Steffen
Kölner Saxophon Mafia Proudly Presents | Jazz Haus Musik | JHM 0046 CD
Kölner Saxophon Mafia With Bad Little Dynamos
Kölner Saxophon Mafia Proudly Presents | Jazz Haus Musik | JHM 0046 CD
Kölner Saxophon Mafia With Blasorchester Dicke Luft
Kölner Saxophon Mafia Proudly Presents | Jazz Haus Musik | JHM 0046 CD
Kölner Saxophon Mafia With Clarence Barlow
Kölner Saxophon Mafia Proudly Presents | Jazz Haus Musik | JHM 0046 CD
Kölner Saxophon Mafia With Dieter Wellershoff
Kölner Saxophon Mafia Proudly Presents | Jazz Haus Musik | JHM 0046 CD
Kölner Saxophon Mafia With Fleisch
Kölner Saxophon Mafia Proudly Presents | Jazz Haus Musik | JHM 0046 CD
Kölner Saxophon Mafia With Hans Süper
Kölner Saxophon Mafia Proudly Presents | Jazz Haus Musik | JHM 0046 CD
Kölner Saxophon Mafia With Ina Stachelhaus And Erik Schneider
Kölner Saxophon Mafia Proudly Presents | Jazz Haus Musik | JHM 0046 CD
Kölner Saxophon Mafia With Ingo Kümmel And Frank Köllges
Kölner Saxophon Mafia Proudly Presents | Jazz Haus Musik | JHM 0046 CD
Kölner Saxophon Mafia With Irene Lorenz
Kölner Saxophon Mafia Proudly Presents | Jazz Haus Musik | JHM 0046 CD
Kölner Saxophon Mafia With Jacki Liebezeit
Kölner Saxophon Mafia Proudly Presents | Jazz Haus Musik | JHM 0046 CD
Kölner Saxophon Mafia With Klaus Der Geiger
Kölner Saxophon Mafia Proudly Presents | Jazz Haus Musik | JHM 0046 CD
Kölner Saxophon Mafia With Kristina Würminghausen
Kölner Saxophon Mafia Proudly Presents | Jazz Haus Musik | JHM 0046 CD
Kölner Saxophon Mafia With Lydie Auvray
Kölner Saxophon Mafia Proudly Presents | Jazz Haus Musik | JHM 0046 CD
Kölner Saxophon Mafia With Nedim Hazar And Orhan Temur
Kölner Saxophon Mafia Proudly Presents | Jazz Haus Musik | JHM 0046 CD
Kölner Saxophon Mafia With Ramesh Shotham
Kölner Saxophon Mafia Proudly Presents | Jazz Haus Musik | JHM 0046 CD
Kölner Saxophon Mafia With Rick E. Loef
Kölner Saxophon Mafia Proudly Presents | Jazz Haus Musik | JHM 0046 CD
Kölner Saxophon Mafia With The Auryn Quartet
Kölner Saxophon Mafia Proudly Presents | Jazz Haus Musik | JHM 0046 CD
Kölner Saxophon Mafia With Triviatas(1.Schwuler Männerchor Köln)
Kölner Saxophon Mafia Proudly Presents | Jazz Haus Musik | JHM 0046 CD
Kölner Saxophon Mafia With V.Nick Nikitakis
Kölner Saxophon Mafia Proudly Presents | Jazz Haus Musik | JHM 0046 CD
Kölner Saxophon Mafia With Willie Gräff
Kölner Saxophon Mafia Proudly Presents | Jazz Haus Musik | JHM 0046 CD

Ulrich,Paul G. | (b)
Paul Kuhn Trio
Play It Again Paul | IN+OUT Records | 77040-2
Paul Kuhn Trio With Greetje Kauffeld
Play It Again Paul | IN+OUT Records | 77040-2
Paul Kuhn Trio With Greetje Kauffeld And Jean 'Toots' Thielemans
Play It Again Paul | IN+OUT Records | 77040-2
Paul Kuhn Trio With Jean 'Toots' Thielemans
Play It Again Paul | IN+OUT Records | 77040-2

Ulrich,Stephan | (dr,percvoc)
booMbooM meets Uli Beckerhoff
Resurection Lounge | Laika Records | 35101512

Ulrich,Thomas | (cello)
Jim Snidero Quartet With Strings
Strings | Milestone | MCD 9326-2

Ulrichi,Carlo | (percvoc)
Pili-Pili
Pili-Pili | JA & RO | JARO 4141-2
Hoomba-Hoomba | JA & RO | JARO 4192-2

Ulrik,Hans | (cl,sax,ssts)
Marilyn Mazur's Future Song
Small Labyrinths | ECM | 1559(533679-2)

Ulyate,Lloyd | (tb)
Billy Eckstine With The Billy May Orchestra
Once More With Feeling | Roulette | 581862-2
Buddy Bregman And His Orchestra
Swinging Kicks | Verve | 559514-2
Ella Fitzgerald With Frank De Vol And His Orchestra
Get Happy! | Verve | 523321-2
Ella Fitzgerald With The Buddy Bregman Orchestra
Ella Fitzgerald-First Lady Of Song | Verve | 517898-2
Love Songs:The Best Of The Song Books | Verve | 531762-2
Ella Fitzgerald Sings The Cole Porter Songbook | Verve | 537257-2
Ella Fitzgerald Sings The Rodgers And Hart Song Book | Verve | 537258-2
Ella Fitzgerald With The Frank DeVol Orchestra
Get Happy! | Verve | 523321-2
Ella Fitzgerald With The Marty Paich Orchestra
Get Happy! | Verve | 523321-2

Umansky,Mo | (bj)
Sandy Brown's Jazz Band
The Golden Years Of Revival Jazz,Sampler | Storyville | 109 1001
The Golden Years Of Revival Jazz,Vol.6 | Storyville | STCD 5511
The Golden Years Of Revival Jazz,Vol.8 | Storyville | STCD 5513
The Golden Years Of Revival Jazz,Vol.10 | Storyville | STCD 5515

Umgeher-Friesland,Silvia | (fujaravoc)
Das Obertontrio Und Toto Blanke
Energy Fields | ALISO Records | AL 1029
Toto Blanke-Rudolf Dasek With The Overtontrio
Meditation | ALISO Records | AL 1026

Umiliani,Piero | (pceleste)
Helen Merrill And Her Band
Planet Jazz:Female Jazz Vocalists | Planet Jazz | 2169656-2
Helen Merrill With The Piero Umilliani Group
Parole E Musica | RCA | 2174798-2

Umor,Skinsoh | (dr)
Al Jarreau With Band
High Crime | i.e. Music | 557848-2

Underwood,Ian | (as,ts,cond,flsynth)
Dave Grusin Group
Mountain Dance | GRP | GRP 95072

Underwood,Jerry | (ssts)
Carla Bley Big Band
The Carla Bley Big Band Goes To Church | Watt | 27(533682-2)
Gail Thompson Orchestra
Gail Thompson's Jazz Africa | Enja | ENJ-9053 2

Underwood,John | (viola)
Dee Dee Bridgewater With Orchestra
Dear Ella | Verve | 539102-2
Joe Temperley Quartet With Strings
Easy To Remember | Hep | CD 2083
Joe Temperley Quintet With Strings
Easy To Remember | Hep | CD 2083

Underwood,Tony | (tuba)
McCoy Tyner Big Band
The Best Of McCoy Tyner Big Band | Dreyfus Jazz Line | FDM 37012-2

Undy,Cameron | (b)
Mike Nock Quartet
Dark & Curious | VeraBra Records | CDVBR 2074-2

Ungaretti,Giuseppe | (lyrics)
Mona Larsen And The Danish Radio Big Band Plus Soloists
Michael Mantler:Cerco Un Paese Innocente | ECM | 1556

Unger,Walter | (v)
Bernd Konrad Jazz Group With Symphonie Orchestra
Wen Die Götter Lieben | Creative Works Records | CW CD 1010-1

Unit X |
Unit X
Rated X | Timescrapper | TSCR 9618

United Future Organization |
United Future Organizatio
United Future Organization | Talkin' Loud | 518166-2

United Jazz & Rock Ensemble |
Jon Hiseman With The United Jazz & Rock Ensemble And Babara Thompson's Paraphernalia
About Time Too! | VeraBra Records | CDVBR 2014-2

United Women's Orchestra,The |
The United Women's Orchestra
The Blue One | Jazz Haus Musik | JHM 0099 CD
United Women's Orchestra
Virgo Supercluster | Jazz Haus Musik | JHM 0123 CD

unkn. | (1 v,1 viola,1 cello,10 strings)
Anita O'Day With The Jimmy Giuffre Orchestra
Verve Jazz Masters 49:Anita O'Day | Verve | 527653-2
Arthur Young And Hatchett's Swingtette
Grapelli Story | Verve | 515807-2
Artie Shaw And His Orchestra
Planet JazzArtie Shaw | Planet Jazz | 2152057-2
Astrud Gilberto With Antonio Carlos Jobim And The Marty Paich Orchestra
The Antonio Carlos Jobim Songbook | Verve | 525472-2
Astrud Gilberto With The Walter Wanderley Quuitet
Verve Jazz Masters 9:Astrud Gilberto | Verve | 519824-2
Benny Waters & Jan Jankeje
Let's Talk About Jazz | G&J Records | GJ 2009 Maxi-CD
Billie Holiday With The JATP All Stars
Billie Holiday Story Vol.1:Jazz At The Philharmonic | Verve | 521642-2
The Complete Jazz At The Philharmonic On Verve 1944-1949 | Verve | 523893-2
Verve Jazz Masters 47:Billie Holiday Sings Standards | Verve | 527650-2
Billie Holiday With The Paul Whiteman Orchestra
Billie's Blues | Blue Note | 748786-2
Billie Holiday With The Ray Ellis Orchestra
Verve Jazz Masters 47:Billie Holiday Sings Standards | Verve | 527650-2
Billie Holiday With The Tiny Grimes Quintet
Billie's Blues | Blue Note | 748786-2
Billy Eckstine With The Billy May Orchestra
Once More With Feeling | Roulette | 581862-2
Brew Moore Quintet
The Brew Moore Quintet | Original Jazz Classics | OJCCD 100-2(F 3-222)
Buddy Guy Blues Band
Buddy Guy-The Complete Chess Studio Recordings | MCA | MCD 09337
Buddy Rich And His Orchestra
Big Swing Face | Pacific Jazz | 837989-2
Cal Tjader's Orchestra
Verve Jazz Masters 39:Cal Tjader | Verve | 521858-2
Talkin Verve/Roots Of Acid Jazz:Cal Tjader | Verve | 531562-2
Carmen McRae With Orchestra
Birds Of A Feather | Decca | 589515-2
Charlie Byrd Trio With Voices
Byrd Song | Original Jazz Classics | OJCCD 1092-2(RS 9481)
Charlie Christian All Stars
Charlie Christian-Jazz Immortal/Dizzy Gillespie 1944 | Original Jazz Classics | OJCCD 1932-2(ES 548)
Charlie Parker And His Orchestra
Bird: The Complete Charlie Parker On Verve | Verve | 837141-2
Charlie Parker With Orchestra & The Dave Lambert Singers
Verve Jazz Masters 28:Charlie Parker Plays Standards | Verve | 521854-2
Charlie Parker With Strings
Bird: The Complete Charlie Parker On Verve | Verve | 837141-2
Charlie Parker With The Joe Lipman Orchestra
Charlie Parker With Strings:The Master Takes | Verve | 523984-2
Charlie Parker Big Band | Verve | 559835-2
Chet Baker With String-Orchestra And Voices
Chet Baker With Fifty Italian Strings | Original Jazz Classics | OJC20 492-2(JLP 921)
Chico Hamilton Quintet With Strings
With Strings Attached/The Three Faces Of Chico | Warner | 9362-47874-2

INTERPRETENVERZEICHNIS

Clark Terry & Chico O Farril Orchestra
Spanish Rice | Verve | 9861050
Clifford Brown & The Neal Hefti Orchestra
Clifford Brown With Strings | Verve | 558078-2
Coleman Hawkins Sextet
Body And Soul Revisited | GRP | GRP 16272
Coleman Hawkins With Billy Byers And His Orchestra
Planet Jazz:Coleman Hawkins | Planet Jazz | 2152055-2
Creative Works Orchestra
Willisau And More Live | Creative Works Records | CW CD 1020-2
Dinah Washington And Her Band
After Hours With Miss D | Verve | 0760562
Verve Jazz Masters 40:Dinah Washington | Verve | 522055-2
Dizzy Gillespie Group
Verve Jazz Masters 10:Dizzy Gillespie | Verve | 516319-2
Don Senay With Orchestra And Strings
Charles Mingus-The Complete Debut Recordings | Debut | 12 DCD 4402-2
Dorothy Donegan Trio
The Many Faces Of Dorothy Donegan | Storyville | STCD 8362
Duke Ellington And His Kentucky Club Orchestra
Jazz:The Essential Collection Vol.2 | IN+OUT Records | 78012-2
Duke Ellington With Tommy Dorsey And His Orchestra
Highlights From The Duke Ellington Centennial Edition | RCA | 2663672-2
Ella Fitzgerald And Her All Stars
Ella Fitzgerald:Mr.Paganini | Dreyfus Jazz Line | FDM 36741-2
Ella Fitzgerald And Her Sextet
Ella Fitzgerald-First Lady Of Song | Verve | 517898-2
Ella Fitzgerald With Sy Oliver And His Orchestra
Ella Fitzgerald:The Decca Years 1949-1954 | Decca | 050668-2
Ella Fitzgerald With The Buddy Bregman Orchestra
The Best Of The Song Books:The Ballads | Verve | 521867-2
Love Songs:The Best Of The Song Books | Verve | 531762-2
Ella Fitzgerald Sings The Cole Porter Songbook | Verve | 537257-2
Ella Fitzgerald Sings The Rodgers And Hart Song Book | Verve | 537258-2
Eric Dolphy Quartet With The University Of Illinois Brass Ensemble
The Illinois Concert | Blue Note | 499826-2
Freddie Brocksieper Orchester
Shot Gun Boogie | Bear Family Records | BCD 16277 AH
Gene Ammons Quintet
Gentle Jug Vol.3 | Prestige | PCD 24249-2
George Benson Quartet
It's Uptown | CBS | 502469-2
Golden Gate Quartet
Americans Swinging In Paris:Golden Gate Quartet | EMI Records | 539659-2
Spirituals To Swing 1955-69 | EMI Records | 791569-2
Golden Gate Quartet With The Martial Solal Orchestra
From Spriritual To Swing Vol.2 | EMI Records | 780573-2
Harry James And His Orchestra
Trumpet Blues:The Best Of Harry James | Capitol | 521224-2
Herbie Mann-Tamiko Jones
The Best Of Herbie Mann | Atlantic | 7567-81369-2
Hugh Masekela Group
GRRR | Verve | 9860309
Irving Mills And His Hotsy Totsy Gang
Jazz:The Essential Collection Vol.3 | IN+OUT Records | 78013-2
Jack Dieval Trio
Jazz In Paris:Jack Diéval-Jazz Aux Champs Elysées | EmArCy | 018419-2
Jimmy McGriff Orchestra
Swingin' The Blues-Jumpin' The Blues | Laserlight | 24654
Jimmy Rushing With Oliver Nelson And His Orchestra
Every Day I Have The Blues | Impulse(MCA) | 547967-2
Jimmy Smith With The Claus Ogerman Orchestra
Any Number Can Win | Verve | 557447-2
Jimmy Smith With The Johnny Pate Orchestra
Jimmy Smith-Talkin' Verve | Verve | 531563-2
Jimmy Smith With The Oliver Nelson Orchestra
Jimmy Smith:Best Of The Verve Years | Verve | 527950-2
Jimmy Smith-Talkin' Verve | Verve | 531563-2
Joe Hill Louis Band
Joe Hill Louis: The Be-Bop Boy | Bear Family Records | BCD 15524 AH
Joe Williams And His Band
Blue Velvet: Crooners, Swooners And Velvet Vocals | Blue Note | 521153-2
Joe Williams With The Harry 'Sweets' Edison Sextet
Together/Have A Good Time | Roulette | 531790-2
John Hendricks WithThe Dave Lambert Singers
Sing A Song Of Basie | Verve | 543827-2
Johnny Smith Quartet
Moonlight In Vermont | Roulette | 596593-2
King Curtis Band
King Curtis-Blow Man Blow | Bear Family Records | BCD 15670 CI
Lawrence Brown With The Ralph Burns Orchestra
Slide Trombone | Verve | 559930-2
Lester Young Quintet
Jazz Gallery:Lester Young Vol.2(1946-59) | RCA | 2119541-2
Lionel Hampton And His Orchestra
Planet Jazz:Lionel Hampton | Planet Jazz | 2152059-2
Louis Armstrong And His Orchestra
Planet Jazz:Louis Armstrong | Planet Jazz | 2152052-2
Louis Armstrong:A 100th Birthday Celebration | RCA | 2663694-2
I Love Jazz | Verve | 543747-2
Jazz:The Essential Collection Vol.2 | IN+OUT Records | 78012-2
Louis Armstrong With Gordon Jenkins And His Orchestra And Choir
Satchmo In Style | Verve | 549594-2
Ambassador Louis Armstrong Vol.17:Moments To Remember(1952-1956) | Ambassador | CLA 1917
Louis Armstrong With Sy Oliver And His Orchestra
Louis And The Angels | Verve | 549592-2
Louis Armstrong With The Lyn Murray Chorus
Louis And The Good Book | Verve | 549593-2
Louis Jordan And His Tympany Five
Louis Jordan-Let The Good Times Roll: The Complete Decca Recordings 1938-1954 | Bear Family Records | BCD 15557 IH
Minton's Playhouse All Stars
Charlie Christian:Swing To Bop | Dreyfus Jazz Line | FDM 36715-2
Nat King Cole And His Trio With Strings
Nat King Cole:The Snader Telescriptions | Storyville | 4960103
Nat King Cole With Orchestra
Nat King Cole:Route 66 | Dreyfus Jazz Line | FDM 36716-2
Nina Simone And Orchestra
Planet Jazz:Nina Simone | Planet Jazz | 2165372-2
Nina Simone Quintet
Verve Jazz Masters Vol.58:Nina Simone Sings Nina | Verve | 529867-2
Oscar Peterson Quartet
Planet Music:Oscar Peterson | RCA | 2165365-2
Quincy Jones And His Orchestra
Big Band Bossa Nova | Verve | 557913-2
Rob Wasserman Duet
Duets | GRP | GRP 97122
Roger Wolfe Kahn And His Orchestra
Planet Jazz:Jack Teagarden | Planet Jazz | 2161236-2
Rosemary Clooney With The Buddy Cole Trio
Swing Around Rosie | Coral | 589485-2
Roy Eldridge And His Orchestra
The Complete Verve Roy Eldridge Studio Sessions | Verve | 9861278
Roy Eldridge And His Orchestra With Strings
The Complete Verve Roy Eldridge Studio Sessions | Verve | 9861278
Roy Eldridge With The Russell Garcia Orchestra
The Complete Verve Roy Eldridge Studio Sessions | Verve | 9861278
Sarah Vaughan And Her Band
Misty Blue:Sweet Sisters Swing Songs Of Sorrow And Sadness | Blue Note | 521151-2
Sarah Vaughan With The Jimmy Jones Quintet
Jazz Profile | Blue Note | 823517-2
Sarah Vaughan With The Joe Lippman Orchestra
Sarah Vaughan:Lover Man | Dreyfus Jazz Line | FDM 36739-2
Sonny Stitt Sextet
Milt Jackson Birthday Celebration | Fantasy | FANCD 6079-2
Stan Getz With Strings And Voices
Reflections | Verve | 523322-2
Stan Getz With The Claus Ogerman Orchestra
What The World Needs Now-Stan Getz Plays Bacharach And David | Verve | 557450-2
Stan Getz With The Eddie Sauter Orchestra
Verve Jazz Masters 8:Stan Getz | Verve | 519823-2
Ultimate Stan Getz selected by Joe Henderson | Verve | 557532-2
Stan Getz With The Richard Evans Orchestra
What The World Needs Now-Stan Getz Plays Bacharach And David | Verve | 557450-2
Stan Getz-Lionel Hampton Sextet
Hamp And Getz | Verve | 831672-2
Stephane Grappelli And His Musicians
Grapelli Story | Verve | 515807-2
Thad Jones And His Orchestra
Charles Mingus-The Complete Debut Recordings | Debut | 12 DCD 4402-2
Vince Guaraldi Trio
A Charlie Brown Christmas | Fantasy | FSA 8431-6
Vince Guaraldi-Bola Sete Quartet
Vince & Bola | Fantasy | FCD 24756-2
Wes Montgomery Quartet With The Claus Ogerman Orchestra
Willow Weep For Me | Verve | 589486-2
Wes Montgomery Sextet
Tequila | Verve | 547769-2
Willie Bobo Group
Juicy | Verve | 519857-2
Woody Herman And The Vanderbilt All Stars
Louis Armstrong-Jack Teagarden-Woody Herman:Midnights At V-Disc | Jazz Unlimited | JUCD 2048
Yusef Lateef Orchestra
The Centaur And The Phoenix | Original Jazz Classics | OJCCD 721-2(RLP 9337)
Yvonne Louis With The Orchestra Vola
Jazz In Paris:Django Reinhardt-Django Et Compagnie | EmArCy | 549241-2 PMS

unkn. Brazilian Musicians And Chorus |
Sarah Vaughan And Her Band
Sarah Vaughan Birthday Celebration | Fantasy | FANCD 6090-2

Unternaeher,Beat | (tb)
Peter A. Schmid Trio With Guests
Profound Sounds In An Empty Reservoir | Creative Works Records | CW CD 1033
Q4 Orchester Project
Yavapai | Creative Works Records | CW CD 1028-2

Uotila,Jukkis | (dr,keyboards,cowbell,cowbells)
SWR Big Band
Jazz In Concert | Hänssler Classics | CD 93.004
Toots Thielemans Quartet
Toots Thielemans:The Live Takes Vol.1 | IN+OUT Records | 77041-2

Upchurch,Phil | (b,b-g,el-b,el-g,gfeet-perc)
Albert King With The Willie Dixon Band
Windy City Blues | Stax | SCD 8612-2
Buddy Guy Blues Band
Buddy Guy-The Complete Chess Studio Recordings | MCA | MCD 09337
Diane Schuur With Orchestra And Strings
The Best Of Diane Schuur | GRP | GRP 98882
George Benson Group
Breezin' | Warner | 8122-76713-2
Howlin' Wolf London Session
Howlin' Wolf:The London Sessions | Chess | MCD 09297
Jimmy Smith All Stars
Jimmy Smith:Dot Com Blues | Blue Thumb | 543978-2
Stan Getz With The Richard Evans Orchestra
What The World Needs Now-Stan Getz Plays Bacharach And David | Verve | 557450-2

Upper Manhattan Jazz Society,The |
The Upper Manhattan Jazz Society
The Upper Manhattan Jazz Society | Enja | ENJ-4090 2

Uptown String Quartet,The |
Max Roach Double Quartet
To The Max! | Enja | ENJ-7021 22

Urbanator |
Urbanator
Urbanator II | Hip Bop | HIBD 8012
Hot Jazz Bisquits | Hip Bop | HIBD 8801

Urbaniak,Michal | (arr,lyricon,as,keyboards)
Just Friends
Nevertheless | IN+OUT Records | 7015-2
Jazz Unlimited | IN+OUT Records | 7017-2
Lenny White Group
Present Tense | Hip Bop | HIBD 8004
Hot Jazz Bisquits | Hip Bop | HIBD 8801
Miles Davis Group
Tutu | Warner | 7599-25490-2
Tom Browne Groups
Mo' Jamaica Funk | Hip Bop | HIBD 8002
Urbanator
Urbanator II | Hip Bop | HIBD 8012
Hot Jazz Bisquits | Hip Bop | HIBD 8801

Urcola,Diego | (tpfl-h)
Dee Dee Bridgewater With Big Band
Dear Ella | Verve | 539102-2
Freddie Bryant Group
Brazilian Rosewood | Fresh Sound Records | FSNT 035 CD

Urso,Phil | (as,ts,bsfl)
Chet Baker Big Band
The Best Of Chet Baker Plays | Pacific Jazz | 797161-2
Chet Baker Quintet
Chet Baker:The Most Important Jazz Album Of 1964/65 | Roulette | 581829-2
Chet Baker & Crew | Pacific Jazz | 582671-2
Chet Baker Sextet
Baby Breeze | Verve | 538328-2
Chet Baker & Crew | Pacific Jazz | 582671-2
The Best Of Chet Baker Plays | Pacific Jazz | 797161-2
Chet Baker-Art Pepper-Phil Urso Sextet
Picture Of Heath | Pacific Jazz | 494106-2
Elliot Lawrence And His Orchestra
Mullenium | CBS | CK 65678
Louis Armstrong With Sy Oliver And His Orchestra
Louis And The Angels | Verve | 549592-2
Oscar Pettiford Sextet
Charles Mingus-The Complete Debut Recordings | Debut | 12 DCD 4402-2

Urtreger,René | (arrp)
Bobby Jaspar Quintet
Jazz In Paris | EmArCy | 159941-2 PMS
Daniel Humair Soultet
Jazz In Paris | EmArCy | 548793-2
Hubert Fol Quartet
Jazz In Paris:Saxophones Á Saint-Germain Des Prés | EmArCy | 014060-2
Kenny Clarke Quintet
Jazz In Paris:Kenny Clarke Sextet Plays André Hodair | EmArCy | 834542-2 PMS
Les Double Six
Les Double Six | RCA | 2164314-2
Lionel Hampton All Stars
Jazz In Paris:Lionel Hampton And His French New Sound Vol.1 | EmArCy | 549405-2 PMS
Jazz In Paris:Lionel Hampton And His French New Sound Vol.2 | EmArCy | 549406-2 PMS
Miles Davis Quintet
Ascenseur Pour LÉchafaud | Fontana | 836305-2
Rene Thomas Quartet
Jazz In Paris:René Thomas-The Real Cat | EmArCy | 549400-2 PMS
Rene Thomas Quintet
Jazz In Paris:René Thomas-The Real Cat | EmArCy | 549400-2 PMS
Stan Getz Quintet
Stan Getz In Europe | Laserlight | 24657

v. Hadeln,Hajo | (dr)
Zona Sul
Pure Love | Nagel-Heyer | CD 3039

Vaché Sr.,Warren | (b)
The Vaché-Allred-Metz Family Jazz Band
Side By Side | Nagel-Heyer | CD 042

Vaché,Allan | (clts)
A Salute To Eddie Condon
A Salute To Eddie Condon | Nagel-Heyer | CD 004
One Two Three | Nagel-Heyer | CD 008
The First Sampler | Nagel-Heyer | NHR SP 5
Allan Vaché Big Four
Revisited! | Nagel-Heyer | CD 044
Allan Vaché Swingtet
Jazz Im Amerikahaus,Vol.3 | Nagel-Heyer | CD 013
Ellington For Lovers | Nagel-Heyer | NH 1009
The First Sampler | Nagel-Heyer | NHR SP 5
Allan Vaché-Antti Sarpila & 1 Sextet
Summit Meeting | Nagel-Heyer | CD 027
Allan Vaché-Antti Sarpila Quintet
Swing Is Here | Nagel-Heyer | CD 026
Blues Of Summer | Nagel-Heyer | NH 1011
The Second Sampler | Nagel-Heyer | NHR SP 6
Allan Vaché-Harry Allen Quintet
Allan And Allan | Nagel-Heyer | CD 074
Allan Vaché-Jim Galloway Sextet
Raisin' The Roof:Allan Vaché Meets Jim Galloway | Nagel-Heyer | CD 054
Allan Vaché's Florida Jazz Allstars
Allan Vaché's Floridy Jazz Allstars | Nagel-Heyer | CD 032
Byron Stripling And Friends
If I Could Be With You | Nagel-Heyer | NH 1010
Eddie Metz And His Gang
Tough Assignment:A Tribute To Dave Tough | Nagel-Heyer | CD 053
International Allstars
The International Allstars Play Benny Goodman:Vol.1 | Nagel-Heyer | CD 025
Mark Shane-Terry Blaine Group
With Thee I Swing! | Nagel-Heyer | CD 040
The International Allstars
The International Allstars Play Benny Goodman Vol.1 | Nagel-Heyer | CD 045
The Nagel-Heyer Allstars
Uptown Lowdown:A Jazz Salute To The Big Apple | Nagel-Heyer | CD 2004
The New York Allstars
Oh,Yeah! The New York Allstars Play More Music Of Louis Armstrong | Nagel-Heyer | CD 046
The Vaché-Allred-Metz Family Jazz Band
Side By Side | Nagel-Heyer | CD 042
Warren Vaché Quintet With Special Guest Allan Vaché
Jazz Im Amerikahaus,Vol.2 | Nagel-Heyer | CD 012
Warren Vaché-Allen Vaché Sextet
Mrs.Vaché's Boys | Nagel-Heyer | CD 050
Ellington For Lovers | Nagel-Heyer | NH 1009

Vaché,Warren | (co,voc,fl-htp)
Allan Vaché Swingtet
Jazz Im Amerikahaus,Vol.3 | Nagel-Heyer | CD 013
Ellington For Lovers | Nagel-Heyer | NH 1009
The First Sampler | Nagel-Heyer | NHR SP 5
Benny Goodman And His Orchestra
40th Anniversary Concert-Live At Carnegie Hall | London | 820349-2
Verve Jazz Masters 33:Benny Goodman | Verve | 844410-2
Benny Goodman Septet
Verve Jazz Masters 33:Benny Goodman | Verve | 844410-2
Benny Goodman Sextet
Verve Jazz Masters 33:Benny Goodman | Verve | 844410-2
Buck Clayton Swing Band
Swing's The Village | Nagel-Heyer | CD 5004
Blues Of Summer | Nagel-Heyer | NH 1011
Terrie Richard Alden And The Warren Vaché Quartet
Voice With Heart | Nagel-Heyer | CD 048
The Nagel-Heyer Allstars
Uptown Lowdown:A Jazz Salute To The Big Apple | Nagel-Heyer | CD 2004
The Vaché-Allred-Metz Family Jazz Band
Side By Side | Nagel-Heyer | CD 042
Warren Vaché And Bill Charlap
2Gether | Nagel-Heyer | CD 2011
Warren Vaché And The New York City All-Star Big Band
Swingtime! | Nagel-Heyer | CD 059
Warren Vaché Quartet
What Is There To Say? | Nagel-Heyer | CD 056
Warren Vaché Quintet
Warren Plays Warrey | Nagel-Heyer | CD 033
Blues Of Summer | Nagel-Heyer | NH 1011
The First Sampler | Nagel-Heyer | NHR SP 5
Warren Vaché Quintet With Special Guest Allan Vaché
Jazz Im Amerikahaus,Vol.2 | Nagel-Heyer | CD 012
Warren Vaché With Joe Puma
Blues Of Summer | Nagel-Heyer | NH 1011
Warren Vaché-Allen Vaché Sextet
Mrs.Vaché's Boys | Nagel-Heyer | CD 050
Ellington For Lovers | Nagel-Heyer | NH 1009

Vadala,Guillermo | (el-bvoice)
Dino Saluzzi Group
Mojotoro | ECM | 1447

Vadshold,Kaspar | (b)
The Orchestra
New Skies | dacapo | DCCD 9463

Vael Jr.,C. | (v)
Milt Jackson With Strings
To Bags...With Love:Memorial Album | Pablo | 2310967-2

Vaharandes,Emmanuel | (congas)
Johnny Otis And His Orchestra
Verve Jazz Masters 43:Ben Webster | Verve | 525431-2

Vai,Steve | (g)
Shankar/Caroline
The Epidemics | ECM | 1308

Vainio,Taito | (accordeon)
Edward Vesala Ensemble
Ode Of The Death Of Jazz | ECM | 1413(843196-2)
Edward Vesala Group
Lumi | ECM | 1339

Vaj,Marcy | (v)
Charlie Haden Quartet West With Strings
The Art Of The Song | Verve | 547403-2

Val,Vic | (ts)
Johnny Frigo Sextet
I Love John Frigo...He Swings | Mercury | 9861061

Valdejuli,Carl | (perc)
Arturo Sandoval And The Latin Train Band
Arturo Sandoval & The Latin Train | GRP | GRP 98202

Valdes,Alberto | (perc)
Cal Tjader's Orchestra
Verve Jazz Masters 39:Cal Tjader | Verve | 521858-2
Talkin Verve/Roots Of Acid Jazz:Cal Tjader | Verve | 531562-2

Valdés,Bebo | (p)

Bebo Valdés Trio
El Arte Del Sabor | Blue Note | 535193-2
Bebo Valdés Trio With Paquito D'Rivera
El Arte Del Sabor | Blue Note | 535193-2

Valdes,Chino | (conga,congasbongos)
Bobby Bryant Orchestra
Deep Blue-The United States Of Mind | Blue Note | 521152-2
Don Ellis Orchestra
Electric Bath | CBS | CK 65522

Valdes,Chucho | (parr)
Irakere
Yemayá | Blue Note | 498239-2
Roy Hargrove's Crisol
Habana | Verve | 537563-2

Valdés,Mayra Caridad | (voc)
Irakere
Yemayá | Blue Note | 498239-2

Valdez,Alberto | (perc)
Cal Tjader Group
Verve Jazz Masters Vol.60:The Collection | Verve | 529866-2
Cal Tjader Septet
Talkin Verve/Roots Of Acid Jazz:Cal Tjader | Verve | 531562-2

Valdez,Carlos 'Patato' | (bata,congas,bongos,guiro,perc,voc)
Bebo Valdés Trio
El Arte Del Sabor | Blue Note | 535193-2
Bebo Valdés Trio With Paquito D'Rivera
El Arte Del Sabor | Blue Note | 535193-2
Cal Tjader's Orchestra
Verve Jazz Masters 39:Cal Tjader | Verve | 521858-2
Talkin Verve/Roots Of Acid Jazz:Cal Tjader | Verve | 531562-2
Soul Burst | Verve | 557446-2
Charlie Rouse Orchestra
Bossa Nova Bacchanal | Blue Note | 593875-2
Blue Bossa | Blue Note | 795590-2
Grant Green Sextet
Blue Bossa | Blue Note | 795590-2
Herbie Mann Group
The Best Of Herbie Mann | Atlantic | 7567-81369-2
Herbie Mann Sextet
Verve Jazz Masters 56:Herbie Mann | Verve | 529901-2
Kenny Dorham Octet
Afro-Cuban | Blue Note | 0675619
Kenny Dorham Orchestra
Blue Bossa | Blue Note | 795590-2

Valdez,Gilbert | (fl)
Dizzy Gillespie Group
Verve Jazz Masters 10:Dizzy Gillespie | Verve | 516319-2
Dizzy Gillspie And His Latin American Rhythm
Afro | Verve | 517052-2

Valente,Caterina | (g,vocperc)
Caterina Valente With The Silvio Francesco Quartet
Deutsches Jazz Fesival 1954/1955 | Bear Family Records | BCD 15430
Caterina Valente-Catherine Michel
Girltalk | Nagel-Heyer | NH 1015
Kurt Edelhagen All Stars
Deutsches Jazz Fesival 1954/1955 | Bear Family Records | BCD 15430
Kurt Edelhagen All Stars Und Solisten
Deutsches Jazz Fesival 1954/1955 | Bear Family Records | BCD 15430
Lars Gullin And The Chet Baker Quartet
Lars Gullin 1955/56 Vol.1 | Dragon | DRCD 224
Quartet Der Kurt Edelhagen All Stars
Deutsches Jazz Fesival 1954/1955 | Bear Family Records | BCD 15430

Valente,Gary | (tb)
Carla Bley Band
Live! | Watt | 12(815730-2)
Heavy Heart | Watt | 14
Fleur Carnivore | Watt | 21
The Very Big Carla Bley Band | Watt | 23
Big Band Theory | Watt | 25(519966-2)
4X4 | Watt | 30(159547-2)
Carla Bley Big Band
The Carla Bley Big Band Goes To Church | Watt | 27(533682-2)
Charlie Haden Orchestra
The Ballad Of The Fallen | ECM | 1248(811546-2)
Ed Schuller & Band
The Eleventh Hour | Tutu Records | 888124-2*
Ed Schuller & The Eleventh Hour Band
Snake Dancing | Tutu Records | 888188-2*
Ed Schuller Group feat. Dewey Redman
The Force | Tutu Records | 888166-2*
Lester Bowie's Brass Fantasy
The Odyssey Of Funk & Popular Music | Dreyfus Jazz Line | FDM 37004-2
When The Spitit Returns | Dreyfus Jazz Line | FDM 37016-2
Orchestra Jazz Siciliana
Orchestra Jazz Siciliana Plays The Music Of Carla Bley | Watt | XtraWatt/4
The Carla Bley Band
Social Studies | Watt | 11(831831-2)
I Hate To Sing | Watt | 12,5

Valentine,Dave | (fl,bamboo-fl,bass-fl,pan-fl)
Lee Ritenour With Special Guests
Festival International De Jazz De Montreal | Spectra | 9811661

Valentine,Gerry | (tbarr)
Earl Hines And His Orchestra
Planet Jazz:Earl Hines | Planet Jazz | 2159973-2

Valentine,Jerry | (arr)
Prestige Blues-Swingers
Soul Street | Original Jazz Classics | OJCCD 987-2(NJ 8293)

Valentine,Rhea | (voice)
Steve Tibbetts Group
The Fall Of Us All | ECM | 1527(521144-2)

Valenzano,Nicola | (fl-h)
Banda Città Ruvo Di Puglia
La Banda/Banda And Jazz | Enja | ENJ-9326 2

Valizan,Louis | (tp)
Mongo Santamaria And His Band
Sabroso | Original Jazz Classics | OJCCD 281-2

Valk,Claudius | (fl,ss,tssax)
House Five
Frank Talk | Nabel Records:Jazz Network | CD 4674
Klaus König Orchestra
The Heart Project | Enja | ENJ-9338 2
Tim Sund Quartet
About Time | Laika Records | LK 93-043

Valle,Anamaria | (voc)
Marcos Valle With Orchestra
Samba '68 | Verve | 559516-2

Valle,Marcos | (gvoc)

Valle,Ramon | (p)
Ramon Valle Quintet
Ramon Valle Plays Ernesto Lecuona | ACT | 9404-2
Ramon Valle Trio
No Escape | ACT | 9424-2

Vallet,Philippe | (engl-hoboe)
Dave Liebman And The Lluis Vidal Trio With The Orquestra De Cambra Theatre Lliure
Dave Liebman And The Lluis Vidal Trio | Fresh Sound Records | FSNT 026 CD
Orquestra De Cambra Teatre Lliure
Orquestra De Cambra Teatre Lliure and Lluis Vidal Trio feat.Dave Liebman | Fresh Sound Records | FSNT 027 CD
Orquestra De Cambra Teatre Lliure feat. Dave Liebman
Orquestra De Cambra Teatre Lliure and Lluis Vidal Trio feat.Dave Liebman | Fresh Sound Records | FSNT 027 CD

Valli,Federica | (p)
La Gaia Scienza
Love Fugue-Robert Schumann | Winter&Winter | 910049-2

Valtinho | (perc)
Kenny Barron Group With Trio De Paz
Canta Brazil | EmArCy | 017993-2

Vamos,Roland | (v)
Gunther Schuller Ensemble
Beauty Is A Rare Thing:Ornette Coleman-The Complete Atlantic Recordings | Atlantic | 8122-71410-2

Van Baal,Koen | (pkeyboards)
Akili
Akili | M.A Music | NU 730-2

Van Beek,Romain | (g)
Dogs Don't Sing In The Rain
Bones For Breakfast | Edition Collage | EC 472-2
Vocal Moments | Take Twelve On CD | TT 008-2
Wind Moments | Take Twelve On CD | TT 009-2

Van Beest,Chris Van Voorst | (b)
Kalifactors
An Introduction To Kalifactors | Fresh Sound Records | FSNT 143 CD

Van Camp,Sus | (tb)
Django Reinhardt With Stan Brenders Et Son Grand Orchestre
Verve Jazz Masters 38:Django Reinhardt | Verve | 516931-2

Van Cleef,Marcel | (drperc)
Henning Wolter Trio
Two Faces | double moon | DMCD 1003-2
Henning Wolter Trio With Gerd Dudek
Two Faces | double moon | DMCD 1003-2
Henning Wolter Trio With Guests
Years Of A Trilogy | double moon | DMCHR 71021

Van Damme,Art | (accordeon)
Art Van Damme Group
State Of Art | MPS | 841413-2
Art Van Damme Quintet
Keep Going/Blue World | MPS | 529093-2
Singers Unlimited With The Art Van Damme Quintet
The Singers Unlimited:Magic Voices | MPS | 539130-2

Van De Geyn,Hein | (b,arrld)
Dee Dee Bridgewater With Her Quartet With Horace Silver
Love And Peace-A Tribute To Horace Silver | Verve | 527470-2
Dee Dee Bridgewater With Her Quintet
Love And Peace-A Tribute To Horace Silver | Verve | 527470-2
Dee Dee Bridgewater With Her Quintet With Jimmy Smith
Love And Peace-A Tribute To Horace Silver | Verve | 527470-2
Dee Dee Bridgewater With Her Trio
Keeping Tradition | Verve | 519607-2
Dee Dee Bridgewater In Montreux | Polydor | 847913-2
Philip Catherine Quartet
Blue Prince | Dreyfus Jazz Line | FDM 36614-2

Van De Wiele,Isabelle | (fr-h)
Lee Konitz With The Ed Partyka Jazz Orchestra
Dreams And Realities | Laika Records | 35101642

Van Den Brink,Bert | (pkeyboards)
Dee Dee Bridgewater With Her Trio
Dee Dee Bridgewater In Montreux | Polydor | 847913-2

Van Den Broeck,Rob | (p,el-p,synthp-solo)
Dudek-Van Den Broek-Haurand
Pulque | Konnex Records | KCD 5055
Crossing Level | Konnex Records | KCD 5077
European Jazz Ensemble
European Jazz Ensemble At The Philharmonic Cologne | M.A Music | A 800-2
20th Anniversary Tour | Konnex Records | KCD 5078
European Jazz Ensemble 25th Anniversary | Konnex Records | KCD 5100
European Jazz Ensemble & The Khan Family feat. Joachim Kühn
European Jazz Ensemble Meets The Khan Family | M.A Music | A 807-2
European Trumpet Summit
European Trumpet Summit | Konnex Records | KCD 5064
Rob Van Den Broeck
Ten Piano Players,Vol.1 | Green House Music | CD 1002
Rob Van Den Broeck-Wiro Mahieu
Departures | Green House Music | CD 1004
Stivin-Van Den Broeck-Haurand
Bordertalk | Konnex Records | KCD 5068
The Quartet
Crossing Level | Konnex Records | KCD 5077
The Quartet Live In Prague | P&J Music | P&J 101-1 CD
Wilton Gaynair Quintet
Alpharian | Konnex Records | KCD 5032

Van Den Broek,Rimis | (tp)
Brocksi-Quartett
Globetrotter | Bear Family Records | BCD 15912 AH

Van Den Plas,Jean |
Alfred 23 Harth Group
Sweet Paris | free flow music | ffm 0291

Van Den Plas,Nicole | (p)

Van Der Geld,Tom | (perc,vibmarimba)
Kenny Wheeler Sextet
Around 6 | ECM | 1156

Van Der Grinten,Maarten | (g)
The European Jazz Guitar Orchestra
The European Jazz Guitar Orchestra | Jardis Records | JRCD 9307

Van Der Hoeven,Frans | (b)
Jesse Van Ruller Trio
Trio | EmArCy | 017513-2
Martin Fredebeul Quartet
Search | Nabel Records:Jazz Network | CD 4652
Stochelo Rosenberg Group
Gypsy Swing | Verve | 527806-2
Stochelo Rosenberg Group With Strings
Gypsy Swing | Verve | 527806-2

Van Der Jeught,Jim | (g)
Django Reinhardt With Stan Brenders Et Son Grand Orchestre
Verve Jazz Masters 38:Django Reinhardt | Verve | 516931-2

Van Der Linde,Hedwig | (v)
Uri Caine With The Concerto Köln
Concerto Köln | Winter&Winter | 910086-2

Van Der Linden,Dick | (p)
The Swingcats
Face To Face:The Swingcats Live | Nagel-Heyer | CD 072

Van Der Schyff,Dylan | (drperc)
Francois Houle 5
Cryptology | Between The Lines | btl 012(Efa 10182-2)

Van Der Sys,Hans | (g,p,orgp-solo)
Freddie Brocksieper Und Seine Solisten
Freddie's Boogie Blues | Bear Family Records | BCD 16388 AH

Van Deven,Everett | (as)
Louis Armstrong With Sy Oliver And His Orchestra
Satchmo Serenaders | Verve | 543792-2

Van Diercks,Rene | (cello)
Toots Thielemans And His Orchestra
Verve Jazz Masters Vol.59:Toots Thielemans | Verve | 535271-2

Van Dijk,Louis | (pp-solo)
Laura Fygi Meets Michel Legrand
Watch What Happens | Mercury | 534598-2

Van Drakenstein,Henk Bosch | (b,bjcello)
Dutch Swing College Band
Digital Anniversary | Philips | 824585-2 PMS

Van Driessche,Andre | (fr-h)
Los Jovenes Flamencos With The WDR Big Band And Guests
Jazzpana | ACT | 9212-2

Van Duin,Sytze | (co)
Dutch Swing College Band
Digital Anniversary | Philips | 824585-2 PMS

Van Dyke,David | (ts)
Buddy Johnson And His Orchestra
Buddy And Ella Johnson 1953-1964 | Bear Family Records | BCD 15479 DH

Van Dyke,Earl | (org)
Fred Jackson Quartet
So Blue So Funky-Heroes Of The Hammond | Blue Note | 796563-2

Van Dyke,Marcia | (v)
Milt Jackson With Strings
To Bags...With Love:Memorial Album | Pablo | 2310967-2
Phil Woods Quartet With Orchestra & Strings
Round Trip | Verve | 559804-2

Van Endert,Philipp | (gg-synth)
Alex Gunia-Philipp Van Endert Group
Beauty Of Silence | Laika Records | 35101052
Lajos Dudas Quartet
Nightlight | double moon | DMCHR 71030
Lajos Dudas Quintet
Talk Of The Town | double moon | CHRDM 71012
Some Great Songs | double moon | DMCD 1005-2
Nightlight | double moon | DMCHR 71030
Lajos Dudas Sextet
Talk Of The Town | double moon | CHRDM 71012
Lajos Dudas Trio
Talk Of The Town | double moon | CHRDM 71012

Van Eps,Bobby | (p)
Louis Armstrong With Jimmy Dorsey And His Orchestra
Louis Armstrong:Swing That Music | Laserlight | 36056
Swing Legends:Louis Armstrong | Nimbus Records | NI 2012

Van Eps,George | (gg-solo)
Adrian Rollini And His Orchestra
Jazz:The Essential Collection Vol.3 | IN+OUT Records | 78013-2
Benny Goodman And His Orchestra
Planet Jazz:Benny Goodman | Planet Jazz | 2152054-2
Planet Jazz:Swing | Planet Jazz | 2169651-2

Van Eps,Johnny | (cl,saxts)
Jack Teagarden And His Orchestra
Jazz:The Essential Collection Vol.3 | IN+OUT Records | 78013-2
Tommy Dorsey And His Clambake Seven
Planet Jazz:Tommy Dorsey | Planet Jazz | 2159972-2
Planet Jazz:Swing | Planet Jazz | 2169651-2
Tommy Dorsey And His Orchestra
Planet Jazz:Tommy Dorsey | Planet Jazz | 2159972-2

Van Eyk,John | (keyboards)
Laura Fygi With Band
Bewitched | Verve | 514724-2

Van Helvoirt,George | (tp)
Coleman Hawkins Trio
Jazz:The Essential Collection Vol.3 | IN+OUT Records | 78013-2
Coleman Hawkins With The Ramblers
Jazz:The Essential Collection Vol.3 | IN+OUT Records | 78013-2

Van Herswingle,Jeff | (ts)
Django Reinhardt With Stan Brenders Et Son Grand Orchestre
Verve Jazz Masters 38:Django Reinhardt | Verve | 516931-2

Van Kaphengst,Christian | (bel-b)
Christof Sänger Trio
Chorinho | Laika Records | LK 93-033
Peter Fessler Quartet
Colours Of My Mind | Minor Music | 801063
Peter Fessler Quintet
Colours Of My Mind | Minor Music | 801063

Van Kemenade,Paul | (as)
Berlin Contemporary Jazz Orchestra
Berlin Contemporary Jazz Orchestra | ECM | 1409
Christoph Haberer Group
Pulsation | Jazz Haus Musik | JHM 0066 CD

Van Koten,Frank | (engl-hoboe)
The Rosenberg Trio With Orchestra
Noches Calientes | Verve | 557022-2

Van Kriedt,Dave | (ts)
Dave Brubeck Octet
The Dave Brubeck Octet | Original Jazz Classics | OJCCD 101-2(F 3239)
Dave Brubeck Quintet
Reunion | Original Jazz Classics | OJCCD 150-2
Paul Desmond Quintet
Desmond | Original Jazz Classics | OJCCD 712-2(F 3235/8082)

Van Lake,Turk | (g)
Benny Goodman And His Orchestra
The Legends Of Swing | Laserlight | 24659

Van Lier,Bart | (tbeuphonium)
Akili
Maasai Mara | M.A Music | A 802-2
Akili | M.A Music | NU 730-2
First Brass
First Brass | M.A Music | NU 158-3
Kenny Clarke-Francy Boland Big Band
Clark-Boland Big Band: TNP, October 29th, 1969 | Laserlight | 36129
The Rosenberg Trio With Orchestra
Noches Calientes | Verve | 557022-2
Toots Thielemans And His Orchestra
Verve Jazz Masters Vol.59:Toots Thielemans | Verve | 535271-2

Van Lier,Erik | (b-tb,tbtuba)
First Brass
First Brass | M.A Music | NU 158-3
Kenny Clarke-Francy Boland Big Band
Three Latin Adventures | MPS | 529095-2
More Smiles | MPS | 9814789
All Smiles | MPS | 9814790
Francy Boland-Fellini 712 | MPS | 9814805
Slide Hampton-Joe Haider Jazz Orchestra
Give Me A Double | JHM Records | JHM 3627

Van Loan,Joe | (voc)
The Ravens
Ultimate Ben Webster selected by James Carter | Verve | 557537-2

Van Nes,Wendy | (fl)
The Rosenberg Trio With Orchestra
Noches Calientes | Verve | 557022-2

Van Oosterhout,Hans | (drperc)
Philip Catherine Quartet
Blue Prince | Dreyfus Jazz Line | FDM 36614-2

Van Oven,Bob | (b)
Albert Nicholas With The Dutch Swing College Band
Albert Nicholas & The Dutch Swing College Band | Storyville | STCD 5522
Dutch Swing College Band
Swinging Studio Sessons | Philips | 824256-2 PMS
Dutch Swing College Band Live In 1960 | Philips | 838765-2
Albert Nicholas & The Dutch Swing College Band | Storyville | STCD 5522
Oscar Klein's Anniversary Band
Moonglow | Nagel-Heyer | CD 021
Ellington For Lovers | Nagel-Heyer | NH 1009
The Second Sampler | Nagel-Heyer | NHR SP 6
Rita Reys With The Dutch Swing College Band
The Very Best Of Dixieland Jazz | Verve | 535529-2

Van Rooyen,Ack | (fl-htp)
Eberhard Weber Group
The Colours Of Chloe | ECM | 1042
Horst Jankowski Orchestra With Voices
Jankowskeynotes | MPS | 9814806
Jon Hiseman With The United Jazz & Rock Ensemble And Babara Thompson's Paraphernalia
About Time Too! | VeraBra Records | CDVBR 2014-2
Kenny Clarke 8
Americans Swinging In Paris:Kenny Clarke | EMI Records | 539652-2
Klaus Weiss Orchestra
Live At The Domicile | ATM Records | ATM 3805-AH
Knut Kiesewetter With The Dieter Reith Orchestra
Reith On! | MPS | 557423-2
Miles Davis With Gil Evans Orchestra, The George Gruntz Concert Jazz Band And Guests
Miles & Quincy Live At Montreux | Warner | 9362-45221-2

Slide Hampton-Joe Haider Jazz Orchestra
Give Me A Double | JHM Records | JHM 3627
Stephan Dietz Quartet
Jazz Portraits | EGO | 95080

Van Ruller,Jesse | (g)
Fleurine With Band And Horn Section
Meant To Be! | EmArCy | 159085-2
Jesse Van Ruller Trio
Trio | EmArCy | 017513-2

Van Schaik,Joost | (dr)
Philip Catherine Quartet
Summer Night | Dreyfus Jazz Line | FDM 36637-2
Philip Catherine Trio
Summer Night | Dreyfus Jazz Line | FDM 36637-2

Van Schalk,Jan | (v)
Till Brönner Quartet & Deutsches Symphonieorchester Berlin
German Songs | Minor Music | 801057

Van Valkenburgh,Emily | (v)
Art Pepper Quintet With Strings
Art Pepper:The Complete Galaxy Recordings | Galaxy | 16GCD 1016-2
Winter Moon | Original Jazz Classics | OJC20 677-2(GXY 5140)
Herbie Hancock Group
Sunlight | CBS | 486570-2
Ron Carter With Strings
Pastels | Original Jazz Classics | OJCCD 665-2(M 9073)

Van Woudenberg,A. | (fr-h)
Toots Thielemans And His Orchestra
Verve Jazz Masters Vol.59:Toots Thielemans | Verve | 535271-2

Van Wouw,J. | (tb)

Vance,Dick | (tp,arrvoc)
Big Sid Catlett And His Orchestra
The Small Black Groups | Storyville | 4960523
Billie Holiday With Sy Oliver And His Orchestra
Billie's Love Songs | Nimbus Records | NI 2000
Ella Fitzgerald And Her Famous Orchestra
The Radio Years 1940 | Jazz Unlimited | JUCD 2065
Ella Fitzgerald And Her Orchestra
Jazz Collection:Ella Fitzgerald | Laserlight | 24397
Fletcher Henderson And His Orchestra
Jazz:The Essential Collection Vol.1 | IN+OUT Records | 78011-2
Jazz:The Essential Collection Vol.3 | IN+OUT Records | 78013-2

Vance,Richard T. | (tp)
Al Sears And His Orchestra
Sear-iously | Bear Family Records | BCD 15668 AH

Vandair,Maurice | (p)
Kenny Clarke 8
Americans Swinging In Paris:Kenny Clarke | EMI Records | 539652-2

Vandan,Thad | (dr)
Lu Watters' Jazz Band
Blues Over Bodega | Good Time Jazz | GTCD 12066-2

Vanden,Thad | (dr)
Turk Murphy And His Jazz Band
Atlantic Jazz: New Orleans | Atlantic | 7567-81700-2

Vander,Maurice | (el-p,org,pharpsichord)
Bireli Lagrene Quartet
Blue Eyes | Dreyfus Jazz Line | FDM 36591-2
Django Reinhardt And His Rhythm
Verve Jazz Masters 38:Django Reinhardt | Verve | 516931-2
Peche À La Mode-The Great Blue Star Sessions 1947/1953 | Verve | 835418-2
Django Reinhardt Quartet
Jazz In Paris:Django Reinhardt-Nuits De Saint-Germain-Des-Prés | EmArCy | 018427-2
Jazz In Paris:Django Reinhardt-Nuages | EmArCy | 018428-2
Django Reinhardt Sextet
Jazz In Paris:Django Reinhardt-Nuits De Saint-Germain-Des-Prés | EmArCy | 018427-2
Don Byas Quintet
Jazz In Paris:Don Byas-Laura | EmArCy | 013027-2
Elek Bacsik Quartet
Jazz In Paris:Elek Baczik | EmArCy | 542231-2
Henri Crolla Sextet
Jazz In Paris:Henri Crolla-Quand Refleuriront Les Lilas Blancs? | EmArCy | 018418-2
Jimmy Raney Quartet
Jimmy Raney Visits Paris Vol.2 | Vogue | 21434802
Jimmy Raney Quintet
Jimmy Raney Visits Paris Vol.2 | Vogue | 21434802
Joe Newman And His Band
Jazz In Paris:Joe Newman-Jazz At Midnight-Cootie Williams | EmArCy | 018446-2
Kenny Clarke 8
Americans Swinging In Paris:Kenny Clarke | EMI Records | 539652-2
Sarah Vaughan With The Quincy Jones Orchestra
Jazz In Paris:Sarah Vaughan-Vaughan And Violins | EmArCy | 065004-2
Stephane Grappelli Quartet
Grapelli Story | Verve | 515807-2
Jazz In Paris:Stephane Grappelli-Improvisations | EmArCy | 549242-2 PMS
Stephane Grappelli Sextet
Grapelli Story | Verve | 515807-2
Toots Thielemans Quintet
Verve Jazz Masters Vol.59:Toots Thielemans | Verve | 535271-2

Vanderbilt All Stars |
Woody Herman And The Vanderbilt All Stars
Louis Armstrong-Jack Teagarden-Woody Herman:Midnights At V-Disc | Jazz Unlimited | JUCD 2048

Vanderlek,Boris | (ts)
Christian Willisohn-Boris Vanderlek
Blues News | Blues Beacon | BLU-1019 2
Christian Willisohn-Boris Vanderlek-Ludwig Seuss
Blues News | Blues Beacon | BLU-1019 2

Vanderouderaa,Andre | (clts)
Coleman Hawkins Trio
Jazz:The Essential Collection Vol.3 | IN+OUT Records | 78013-2
Coleman Hawkins With The Ramblers
Jazz:The Essential Collection Vol.3 | IN+OUT Records | 78013-2

Vandever,Ed | (tp)
Coleman Hawkins And His Orchestra
Jazz:The Essential Collection Vol.3 | IN+OUT Records | 78013-2

Vandon,Thad | (dr)
Turk Murphy And His Jazz Band
The Very Best Of Dixieland Jazz | Verve | 535529-2

Vandroogenbroeck,Joel | (pfl)
Eje Thelin Quintet
At The German Jazz Festival 1964 | Dragon | DRCD 374

Vankenhove,Alain | (tpfl-h)
Orchestre National De Jazz
Charmediterranéen | ECM | 1828(018493-2)

Vann,Erwin | (ts)
Fabien Degryse Quintet
Medor Sadness | Edition Collage | EC 454-2

Vanoni,Ornella | (voc)
Paolo Fresu Quartet
Angel | RCA | 2155864-2

Van't Hof,Jasper | (church-org,el-p,keyboards,synth)
Archie Sheep-Jasper Van't Hof Duo
Mama Rose | Steeplechase | SCCD 31169
Daniel Guggenheim Group
Daniel Guggenheim Group feat. Jasper van't Hof | Laika Records | LK 990-018
David Friedman-Jasper Van't Hof
Birds Of A Feather | Traumton Records | 2428-2
Jasper Van't Hof
Pili-Pili | Warner | 2292-40458-2
Ten Piano Players,Vol.1 | Green House Music | CD 1002
Axioma | JA & RO | JARO 4250-2
Jasper Van't Hof Group
Blue Corner | ACT | 9228-2
Jasper Van't Hof-Charlie Mariano-Steve Swallow
Brutto Tempo | Intuition Records | INT 3309-2
Just Friends
Nevertheless | IN+OUT Records | 7015-2
Jazz Unlimited | IN+OUT Records | 7017-2
Philippe Caillat Special Project
Melodic Travel | Laika Records | LK 689-012
Pili-Pili
Jakko | JA & RO | JARO 4131-2
Be In Two Minds | JA & RO | JARO 4134-2
Pili-Pili Live 88 | JA & RO | JARO 4139-2
Pili-Pili | JA & RO | JARO 4141-2
Hotel Babo | JA & RO | JARO 4147-2
Stolen Moments | JA & RO | JARO 4159-2
Boogaloo | JA & RO | JARO 4174-2
Dance Jazz Live 1995 | JA & RO | JARO 4189-2
Hoomba-Hoomba | JA & RO | JARO 4192-2
Jazzy World | JA & RO | JARO 4200-2
Nomans Land | JA & RO | JARO 4209-2
Ballads Of Timbuktu | JA & RO | JARO 4240-2
Toto Blanke Group
Electric Circus' Best | ALISO Records | AL 1034
Uli Beckerhoff Trio
Camporondo | Nabel Records:Jazz Network | CD 4629

Vapirov,Anatoly | (b-cl,ts,double-sax,reedsss)
Fairy Tale Trio
Jazz Across The Border | Wergo | SM 1531-2

Vappie,Papa Don | (b,voc,bjg)
Wynton Marsalis Group
Standard Time Vol.6:Mr.Jelly Lord | CBS | CK 69872

Varady,György | (ts)
Mihaly Tabany Orchestra
Jubilee Edition | double moon | CHRDM 71020

Vardal,Vegar | (vharding-vele)
Mikhail Alperin-Vegar Vardal
Portrait | JA & RO | JARO 4227-2

Vardi,Emanuel | (vviola)
Lalo Schifrin And His Orchestra
Verve Jazz Masters 39:Cal Tjader | Verve | 521858-2
Louis Armstrong And His Friends
Planet Jazz:Louis Armstrong | Planet Jazz | 2152052-2
Planet Jazz Sampler | Planet Jazz | 2152326-2
Louis Armstrong And His Friends | Bluebird | 2663961-2
Nina Simone And Orchestra
Baltimore | Epic | 476906-2

Vardi,Emanuel 'Manny' | (vviola)
Bob James And His Orchestra
Jazzrock-Anthology Vol.3:Fusion | Zounds | CD 27100555
Earl Klugh Group With Strings
Late Night Guitar | Blue Note | 498573-2
Grover Washington Jr. Orchestra
Jazzrock-Anthology Vol.3:Fusion | Zounds | CD 27100555

Vargas,Joselin | (cajonhandclapping)
Los Jovenes Flamencos
Jazzpana | ACT | 9212-2
Los Jovenes Flamencos With The WDR Big Band And Guests
Jazzpana | ACT | 9212-2

Vargas,Shaun | (voice)
Gunter Hampel Next Generation
Next Generation | Birth | CD 043

various Friends | (handclaps)
The Brecker Brothers
Heavy Metal Be-Bop | RCA | 2119257-2

Varner,Tom | (fr-h)
Cadavre Exquis
Cadavre Exquis | Creative Works Records | CW CD 1014-1
Franz Koglmann Quintet
Make Believe | Between The Lines | btl 001(Efa 10171-2)
George Gruntz Concert Jazz Band '83
Theatre | ECM | 1265
Miles Davis With Gil Evans Orchestra, The George Gruntz Concert Jazz Band And Guests
Miles & Quincy Live At Montreux | Warner | 9362-45221-2
Neal Kirkwood Octet
Neal Kirkwood Octet | Timescrapper | TSCR 9612
Rabih Abou-Khalil Group
The Cactus Of Knowledge | Enja | ENJ-9401 2
Roman Schwaller Nonet
The Original Tunes | JHM Records | JHM 3629

Varro,Johnny | (p)
A Salute To Eddie Condon
A Salute To Eddie Condon | Nagel-Heyer | CD 004
One Two Three | Nagel-Heyer | CD 008
The First Sampler | Nagel-Heyer | NHR SP 5
Allan Vaché Swingtet
Jazz Im Amerikahaus,Vol.3 | Nagel-Heyer | CD 013
Ellington For Lovers | Nagel-Heyer | NH 1009
The First Sampler | Nagel-Heyer | NHR SP 5
Allan Vaché's Florida Jazz Allstars
Allan Vaché's Floridy Jazz Allstars | Nagel-Heyer | CD 032
Bill Allred-Roy Williams Quintet
Absolutely | Nagel-Heyer | CD 024
Ellington For Lovers | Nagel-Heyer | NH 1009
Blues Of Summer | Nagel-Heyer | NH 1011
The Second Sampler | Nagel-Heyer | NHR SP 6
Byron Stripling And Friends
If I Could Be With You | Nagel-Heyer | NH 1010
Eddie Condon All Stars
Jazz Festival Vol.1 | Storyville | 4960733
Eddie Metz And His Gang
Tough Assignment:A Tribute To Dave Tough | Nagel-Heyer | CD 053
George Masso Sextet
C'Est Magnifique! | Nagel-Heyer | CD 060
International Chicago-Jazz Orchestra
That's A Plenty | JHM Records | JHM 3621
Jeanie Lambe And The Danny Moss Quartet
Three Great Concerts:Live In Hamburg 1993-1995 | Nagel-Heyer | CD 019
Jeanie Lambe And The Danny Moss Septet
Three Great Concerts:Live In Hamburg 1993-1995 | Nagel-Heyer | CD 019
The New York Allstars
Oh,Yeah! The New York Allstars Play More Music Of Louis Armstrong | Nagel-Heyer | CD 046
Tom Saunders' 'Wild Bill Davison Band' & Guests
Exactly Like You | Nagel-Heyer | CD 023
The Second Sampler | Nagel-Heyer | NHR SP 6

Varsalona,Bart | (b-tbtb)
Charlie Parker And His Orchestra
The Cole Porter Songbook | Verve | 823250-2
Bird: The Complete Charlie Parker On Verve | Verve | 837141-2
Charlie Parker With Orchestra
Charlie Parker:The Best Of The Verve Years | Verve | 527815-2
Charlie Parker With Strings
Charlie Parker With Strings:The Master Takes | Verve | 523984-2
Charlie Parker With The Joe Lipman Orchestra
Verve Jazz Masters 28:Charlie Parker Plays Standards | Verve | 521854-2
Charlie Parker Big Band | Verve | 559835-2
Charlie Parker With The Neal Hefti Orchestra
Charlie Parker:The Best Of The Verve Years | Verve | 527815-2
Bird: The Complete Charlie Parker On Verve | Verve | 837141-2
Gil Evans And Ten
Gil Evans And Ten | Original Jazz Classics | OJC 346(P 7120)
The Jazz Giants Play Cole Porter:Night And Day | Prestige | PCD 24203-2
Gil Evans And Ten | Prestige | PRSA 7120-6
Stan Kenton And His Orchestra
Swing Vol.1 | Storyville | 4960343
One Night Stand | Choice | CHCD 71051
Woody Herman And His Orchestra
Woody Herman:Four Brother | Dreyfus Jazz Line | FDM 36722-2

Vasconcelos,Erasto | (handclaps,percvoice)
Jan Garbarek Group
Legend Of The Seven Dreams | ECM | 1381(837344-2)

Vasconcelos,Nana | (berimbau,voc,congas)
Arild Andersen Quartet
If You Look Far Enough | ECM | 1493(513902-2)
Arild Andersen Sextet
Sagn | ECM | 1435
Don Cherry Group
Multi Kulti | A&M Records | 395323-2
Don Cherry/Nana Vasconcelos/Collin Walcott
Codona | ECM | 1132(829371-2)
Codona 2 | ECM | 1177(833332-2)
Codona 3 | ECM | 1243
Egberto Gismonti
Danca Dàs Cabecas | ECM | 1089
Egberto Gismonti Group
Sol Do Meio Dia | ECM | 1116(829117-2)
Egberto Gismonti/Nana Vasconcelos
Duas Vozes | ECM | 1279
Freddy Studer Orchestra
Seven Songs | VeraBra Records | CDVBR 2056-2
Gato Barbieri Group
Planet Jazz:Gato Barbieri | RCA | 2165364-2
Gato Barbieri:The Best Of The Early Years | RCA | 2663523-2
Jan Garbarek Group
I Took Up The Runes | ECM | 1419(843850-2)
Jan Garbarek Trio
Eventyr | ECM | 1200
Nana Vasconcelos
Saudades | ECM | 1147
Nana Vasconcelos-Egberto Gismonti Duo And Strings
Saudades | ECM | 1147
Pat Metheny & Lyle Mays
As Falls Wichita, So Falls Wichita Falls | ECM | 1190(821416-2)
Pat Metheny Group
Offramp | ECM | 1216(817138-2)
Travels | ECM | 1252/53
Pat Metheny Group With Orchestra
Secret Story | Geffen Records | GED 24468
Pierre Favre Ensemble
Singing Drums | ECM | 1274

Vashi,Geeta | (taboura)
Lonnie Liston Smith & His Cosmic Echoes
Astral Travelling | RCA | 2663878-2

Vasquez,Frankie | (percvoc)
Marc Ribot Y Los Cubanos Postizos
Nuy Divertido(Very Entertaining) | Atlantic | 7567-83293-2

Vasquez,Papo | (tb,coroperc)
Ian Shaw With Band
Soho Stories | Milestone | MCD 9316-2
Jerry Gonzalez & Fort Apache Band
The River Is Deep | Enja | ENJ-4040 2

Vass,James 'Jimmy' | (fl,asss)
Charles Earland Septet
Charles Earland In Concert | Prestige | PRCD 24267-2

Vasseur,Benny | (tb)
Dizzy Gillespie Orchestra And The Operatic String Orchestra
Jazz In Paris:Dizzy Gillespie And His Operatic Strings Orchestra | EmArCy | 018420-2
Kenny Clarke 8
Americans Swinging In Paris:Kenny Clarke | EMI Records | 539652-2
Lucky Thompson With The Gerard Pochonet All-Stars
Planet Jazz:Jazz Saxophone | Planet Jazz | 2169653-2
Lucky Thompson's Modern Jazz Group Tentet
Jazz In Paris:Lucky Thompson-Modern Jazz Group | EmArCy | 159823-2 PMS
Sidney Bechet And His Orchestra
Jazz In Paris:Sidney Bechet Et Claude Luther | EmArCy | 159821-2 PMS

Vassilakis,Dimitrios | (ssts)
Dimitrios Vassilakis Daedalus Project
Labyrinth | Candid | CCD 79776

Vatcher,Michael | (dr,perccelesta)
John Zorn Group
Spy Vs. Spy-The Music Of Ornette Coleman | Nonesuch | 7559-60844-2

Vaughan,Sarah | (voc)
Dizzy Gillespie Sextet
Pleyel Jazz Concert 1953 | Vogue | 21409392
Milt Jackson Orchestra
Sarah Vaughan Birthday Celebration | Fantasy | FANCD 6090-2
Milt Jackson With The Count Basie Orchestra
Milt Jackson Birthday Celebration | Fantasy | FANCD 6079-2
Sarah Vaughan And Her Band
Songs Of The Beatles | Atlantic | 16037-2
Misty Blue:Sweet Sisters Swing Songs Of Sorrow And Sadness | Blue Note | 521151-2
Duke Ellington Song Book Two | Pablo | CD 2312116
Sarah Vaughan Birthday Celebration | Fantasy | FANCD 6090-2
Sarah Vaughan And Her Trio
Swingin' Easy | EmArCy | 514072-2
Verve Jazz Masters 42:Sarah Vaughan-The Jazz Sides | Verve | 526817-2
Verve Jazz Masters Vol.60:The Collection | Verve | 529866-2
4 By 4:Ella Fitzgerald/Sarah Vaughan/Billie Holiday/Dinah Washington | Verve | 559693-2
Sarah Vaughan And Joe Williams With The Count Basie Orchestra
Jazz Profile | Blue Note | 823517-2
Sarah Vaughan And The Count Basie Orchestra
Sarah Vaughan Birthday Celebration | Fantasy | FANCD 6090-2
Sarah Vaughan And The Thad Jones Orchestra
Verve Jazz Masters 42:Sarah Vaughan-The Jazz Sides | Verve | 526817-2
Sarah Vaughan Plus Two
Ballads | Roulette | 537561-2
Sarah Vaughan The The Joe Lippman Orchestra
Sarah Vaughan:Lover Man | Dreyfus Jazz Line | FDM 36739-2
Sarah Vaughan With Band
Linger Awhile | Pablo | 2312144-2
Sarah Vaughan With Barney Kessel And Joe Comfort
Jazz Profile | Blue Note | 823517-2
Sarah Vaughan With Dizzy Gillespie And His All Star Quintet
Sarah Vaughan:Lover Man | Dreyfus Jazz Line | FDM 36739-2
Sarah Vaughan With Dizzy Gillespie And His Orchestra
Planet Jazz:Female Jazz Vocalists | Planet Jazz | 2169656-2
Sarah Vaughan With Dizzy Gillespie And His Septet
Sarah Vaughan:Lover Man | Dreyfus Jazz Line | FDM 36739-2
Sarah Vaughan With Dori Caymmi
Sarah Vaughan Birthday Celebration | Fantasy | FANCD 6090-2
Sarah Vaughan With George Treadwell And His Allstars
Sarah Vaughan:Lover Man | Dreyfus Jazz Line | FDM 36739-2
Sarah Vaughan With Her Quartet
Verve Jazz Masters 42:Sarah Vaughan-The Jazz Sides | Verve | 526817-2
Jazz Profile | Blue Note | 823517-2
Sarah Vaughan With Joe Pass And Mike Wofford
Sarah Vaughan Birthday Celebration | Fantasy | FANCD 6090-2
Sarah Vaughan With John Kirby And His Orchestra
Sarah Vaughan Birthday Celebration | Fantasy | FANCD 6090-2
Sarah Vaughan:Lover Man | Dreyfus Jazz Line | FDM 36739-2
Sarah Vaughan With Mundell Lowe And George Duvivier
Ballads | Roulette | 537561-2

Jazz Profile | Blue Note | 823517-2
After Hours | Roulette | 855468-2
Sarah Vaughan With Orchestra
I Love Brazil | Pablo | 2312101-2
Sweet 'N' Sassy | Roulette | 531793-2
Ballads | Roulette | 537561-2
!Viva! Vaughan | Mercury | 549374-2
Sarah Vaughan Sings The Mancini Songbook | Verve | 558401-2
Sarah Vaughan Birthday Celebration | Fantasy | FANCD 6090-2
Sarah Vaughan With Small Group & Orchestra
Duke Ellington Song Book One | Pablo | CD 2312111
Sarah Vaughan With The Allstars
Sarah Vaughan:Lover Man | Dreyfus Jazz Line | FDM 36739-2
Sarah Vaughan With The Benny Carter Orchestra
Ballads | Roulette | 537561-2
Jazz Profile | Blue Note | 823517-2
Sarah Vaughan With The Billy May Orchestra
Jazz Profile | Blue Note | 823517-2
Sarah Vaughan With The Clifford Brown All Stars
Verve Jazz Masters 20:Introducing | Verve | 519853-2
Clifford Brown-Max Roach:Alone Together-The Best Of The Mercury Years | Verve | 526373-2
Sarah Vaughan | Verve | 543305-2
4 By 4:Ella Fitzgerald/Sarah Vaughan/Billie Holiday/Dinah Washington | Verve | 559693-2
Brownie-The Complete EmArCy Recordings Of Clifford Brown | EmArCy | 838306-2
Sarah Vaughan | EmArCy | 9860779
Sarah Vaughan With The Count Basie Band
Jazz Profile | Blue Note | 823517-2
Sarah Vaughan With The Don Costa Orchestra
Jazz Profile | Blue Note | 823517-2
Sarah Vaughan With The Frank Foster Orchestra
The Antonio Carlos Jobim Songbook | Verve | 525472-2
Sarah Vaughan With The Gerald Wilson Orchestra
Ballads | Roulette | 537561-2
Jazz Profile | Blue Note | 823517-2
Sarah Vaughan With The Hal Mooney Orchestra
Sarah Vaughan Sings Gershwin | Verve | 557567-2
4 By 4:Ella Fitzgerald/Sarah Vaughan/Billie Holiday/Dinah Washington | Verve | 559693-2
It's A Man's World | Mercury | 589487-2
Sarah Vaughan With The Hugo Winterhalter Orchestra
Sarah Vaughan:Lover Man | Dreyfus Jazz Line | FDM 36739-2
Sarah Vaughan With The Jimmy Jones Orchestra
Ballads | Roulette | 537561-2
Jazz Profile | Blue Note | 823517-2
Sarah Vaughan With The Jimmy Jones Quartet
Sarah Vaughan:Lover Man | Dreyfus Jazz Line | FDM 36739-2
Sarah Vaughan With The Jimmy Jones Quintet
Jazz Profile | Blue Note | 823517-2
Sarah Vaughan With The Jimmy Jones Trio
Linger Awhile | Pablo | 2312144-2
Sarah Vaughan | Verve | 543305-2
Sarah Vaughan Birthday Celebration | Fantasy | FANCD 6090-2
Sarah Vaughan With The Joe Lippman Orchestra
Sarah Vaughan:Lover Man | Dreyfus Jazz Line | FDM 36739-2
Sarah Vaughan With The Joe Pass Quartet
Linger Awhile | Pablo | 2312144-2
Joe Pass:Guitar Virtuoso | Pablo | 4 PACD 4423-2
Sarah Vaughan With The Lalo Schifrin Orchestra
Jazz Profile | Blue Note | 823517-2
Sarah Vaughan With The Marty Manning Orchestra
Jazz Profile | Blue Note | 823517-2
Sarah Vaughan With The Mike Wofford Trio
Sarah Vaughan Birthday Celebration | Fantasy | FANCD 6090-2
Sarah Vaughan With The Norman Leyden Orchestra
Sarah Vaughan:Lover Man | Dreyfus Jazz Line | FDM 36739-2
Sarah Vaughan With The Oscar Peterson Quartet
How Long Has This Been Going On? | Pablo | 2310821-2
Joe Pass:Guitar Virtuoso | Pablo | 4 PACD 4423-2
Sarah Vaughan Birthday Celebration | Fantasy | FANCD 6090-2
Sarah Vaughan With The Quincy Jones Orchestra
Jazz In Paris:Sarah Vaughan-Vaughan And Violins | EmArCy | 065004-2
Ballads | Roulette | 537561-2
4 By 4:Ella Fitzgerald/Sarah Vaughan/Billie Holiday/Dinah Washington | Verve | 559693-2
Jazz Profile | Blue Note | 823517-2
Sarah Vaughan With The Roland Hanna Quartet
Sarah Vaughan Birthday Celebration | Fantasy | FANCD 6090-2
Sarah Vaughan With The Teddy Wilson Quartet
Sarah Vaughan:Lover Man | Dreyfus Jazz Line | FDM 36739-2
Sarah Vaughan-Joe Pass
Sarah Vaughan Birthday Celebration | Fantasy | FANCD 6090-2
Sarah Vaughan-Ray Brown
Sarah Vaughan Birthday Celebration | Fantasy | FANCD 6090-2
Tony Scott And His Down Beat Club Sextet
Jazz:The Essential Collection Vol.3 | IN+OUT Records | 78013-2

Vavti,Mario | (tb)
Couch Ensemble
Winnetou | Jazz 'n' Arts Records | JNA 1503

V-Disc All Stars |
V-Disc All Star Jam Session
Louis Armstrong-Jack Teagarden-Woody Herman:Midnights At V-Disc | Jazz Unlimited | JUCD 2048
V-Disc All Stars
Jazz:The Essential Collection Vol.3 | IN+OUT Records | 78013-2

V-Disc Jumpers,The |
Bud Freeman And The V-Disc Jumpers
Muggsy Spanier And Bud Freeman:V-Discs 1944-45 | Jazz Unlimited | JUCD 2049
The V-Disc Jumpers
Muggsy Spanier And Bud Freeman:V-Discs 1944-45 | Jazz Unlimited | JUCD 2049

Veal Jr.,Charles | (v)
Chick Corea With String Quartet
Verve Jazz Masters 3:Chick Corea | Verve | 519820-2

Veal,Reginald | (btb)
A Band Of Friends
Wynton Marsalis Quartet With Strings | CBS | CK 68921
Eric Reed Trio
Pure Imagination | Impulse(MCA) | 951259-2
Greg Tardy Band
Serendipity | Impulse(MCA) | 951258-2
Mark Whitfield Quartet
The Marksman | Warner | 7599-26321-2
Wynton Marsalis Group
Standard Time Vol.4:Marsalis Plays Monk | CBS | CK 67503
Standard Time Vol.6:Mr.Jelly Lord | CBS | CK 69872

Veasley,Gerald | (b,vocel-b)
Bobby Lyle Group
The Journey | Atlantic | 7567-82138-2

Vecchi,Marco | (electronicssound-processing)
Evan Parker Electro-Acoustic Ensemble
Toward The Margins | ECM | 1612(453514-2)
Drawn Inward | ECM | 1693
Memory/Vision | ECM | 1852(0381172)

Veeck,Gerhard | (alto-cl,as,alto-fl,ss,bs,voc,fl)
Kölner Saxophon Mafia
Saxfiguren | Jazz Haus Musik | JHM 0036 CD
Mafia Years 1982-86 | Jazz Haus Musik | JHM 0058 CD
Go Commercial... | Jazz Haus Musik | JHM 0065 CD
Place For Lovers | Jazz Haus Musik | JHM 0082 CD
Licence To Thrill | Jazz Haus Musik | JHM 0100 CD
Kölner Saxophon Mafia With Arno Steffen
Kölner Saxophon Mafia Proudly Presents | Jazz Haus Musik | JHM 0046 CD
Kölner Saxophon Mafia With Bad Little Dynamos
Kölner Saxophon Mafia Proudly Presents | Jazz Haus Musik | JHM 0046 CD
Kölner Saxophon Mafia With Blasorchester Dicke Luft
Kölner Saxophon Mafia Proudly Presents | Jazz Haus Musik | JHM 0046 CD
Kölner Saxophon Mafia With Clarence Barlow
Kölner Saxophon Mafia Proudly Presents | Jazz Haus Musik | JHM 0046 CD
Kölner Saxophon Mafia With Dieter Wellershoff
Kölner Saxophon Mafia Proudly Presents | Jazz Haus Musik | JHM 0046 CD
Kölner Saxophon Mafia With Fleisch
Kölner Saxophon Mafia Proudly Presents | Jazz Haus Musik | JHM 0046 CD
Kölner Saxophon Mafia With Guests
Kölner Saxophon Mafia: 20 Jahre Saxuelle Befreiung | Jazz Haus Musik | JHM 0115 CD
Kölner Saxophon Mafia With Hans Süper
Kölner Saxophon Mafia Proudly Presents | Jazz Haus Musik | JHM 0046 CD
Kölner Saxophon Mafia With Ina Stachelhaus And Erik Schneider
Kölner Saxophon Mafia Proudly Presents | Jazz Haus Musik | JHM 0046 CD
Kölner Saxophon Mafia With Ingo Kümmel And Frank Köllges
Kölner Saxophon Mafia Proudly Presents | Jazz Haus Musik | JHM 0046 CD
Kölner Saxophon Mafia With Irene Lorenz
Kölner Saxophon Mafia Proudly Presents | Jazz Haus Musik | JHM 0046 CD
Kölner Saxophon Mafia With Jacki Liebezeit
Kölner Saxophon Mafia Proudly Presents | Jazz Haus Musik | JHM 0046 CD
Kölner Saxophon Mafia With Klaus Der Geiger
Kölner Saxophon Mafia Proudly Presents | Jazz Haus Musik | JHM 0046 CD
Kölner Saxophon Mafia With Kristina Würminghausen
Kölner Saxophon Mafia Proudly Presents | Jazz Haus Musik | JHM 0046 CD
Kölner Saxophon Mafia With Lydie Auvray
Kölner Saxophon Mafia Proudly Presents | Jazz Haus Musik | JHM 0046 CD
Kölner Saxophon Mafia With Nedim Hazar And Orhan Temur
Kölner Saxophon Mafia Proudly Presents | Jazz Haus Musik | JHM 0046 CD
Kölner Saxophon Mafia With Ramesh Shotham
Kölner Saxophon Mafia Proudly Presents | Jazz Haus Musik | JHM 0046 CD
Kölner Saxophon Mafia With Rick E. Loef
Kölner Saxophon Mafia Proudly Presents | Jazz Haus Musik | JHM 0046 CD
Kölner Saxophon Mafia With The Auryn Quartet
Kölner Saxophon Mafia Proudly Presents | Jazz Haus Musik | JHM 0046 CD
Kölner Saxophon Mafia With Triviatas(1.Schwuler Männerchor Köln)
Kölner Saxophon Mafia Proudly Presents | Jazz Haus Musik | JHM 0046 CD
Kölner Saxophon Mafia With V.Nick Nikitakis
Kölner Saxophon Mafia Proudly Presents | Jazz Haus Musik | JHM 0046 CD
Kölner Saxophon Mafia With Willie Gräff
Kölner Saxophon Mafia Proudly Presents | Jazz Haus Musik | JHM 0046 CD

Veera | (voice)
The Brecker Brothers
Return Of The Brecker Brothers | GRP | GRP 96842

Vees,Eugene | (g)
Django Reinhardt And The Quintet Du Hot Club De France
Jazz In Paris:Django Reinhardt-Django's Blues | EmArCy | 013545-2
Planet Jazz:Django Reinhardt | Planet Jazz | 2152071-2
Planet Jazz Sampler | Planet Jazz | 2152326-2
Peche Á La Mode-The Great Blue Star Sessions 1947/1953 | Verve | 835418-2
Django Reinhardt Quartet
Django Reinhardt:Echoes Of France | Dreyfus Jazz Line | FDM 36726-2
Quintet Du Hot Club De France
Jazz In Paris:Django Reinhardt-Swing From Paris | EmArCy | 159853-2 PMS
Grapelli Story | Verve | 515807-2
Verve Jazz Masters 38:Django Reinhardt | Verve | 516931-2
The Jazz Masters Vol.60:The Collection | Verve | 529866-2
Django/Django In Rome 1949-1050 | BGO Records | BGOCD 366
Django Reinhardt:Echoes Of France | Dreyfus Jazz Line | FDM 36726-2
Django Reinhardt:Souveniers | Dreyfus Jazz Line | FDM 36744-2

Vega,Carlos | (drperc)
Caldera
Jazzrock-Anthology Vol.3:Fusion | Zounds | CD 27100555

Veille,Jacques | (b-tbtb)
Pata Music Meets Arfi
News Of Roi Ubu | Pata Musik | PATA 10 CD

Vejvoda,Josef | (dr)
Benny Bailey Quartet With Strings
I Remember Love | Laika Records | 35101752

Velarde,Byardo | (perc,voc,timbales,cencerocongas)
Cal Tjader Quintet
Tjader Plays Mambo | Original Jazz Classics | OJCCD 274-2(F 3221)
The Jazz Giants Play Sammy Cahn:It's Magic | Prestige | PCD 24226-2
Cal Tjader Sextet
Cal Tjader's Latin Kick | Original Jazz Classics | OJCCD 642-2(F 8033)
Cal Tjader's Orchestra
Tjader Plays Mambo | Original Jazz Classics | OJCCD 274-2(F 3221)
Mongo Santamaria And His Band
Sabroso | Original Jazz Classics | OJCCD 281-2

Velarde.Benny | (timbales)
Vince Guaraldi Group
Charlie Brown's Holiday Hits | Fantasy | FCD 9682-2

Veldkamp,Erik | (tp)
Clark Terry With The Summit Jazz Orchestra
Clark | Edition Collage | EC 530-2

Veldmann,Eddy | (perc)
John Thomas & Lifeforce
3000 Worlds | Nabel Records:Jazz Network | CD 4604

Velez,Glen | (african-pods,buzz-sticks,frame-dr)
Javier Paxarino Group With Glen Velez
Temurá | ACT | 9227-2
Pat Metheny Group
Imaginary Day | Warner | 9362-46791-2
Rabih Abou-Khalil Group
Nafas | ECM | 1359(835781-2)
Bukra | Enja | ENJ-9372 2
Roots & Sprouts | Enja | ENJ-9373 2
Rabih Abou-Khalil Quintet
Between Dusk And Dawn | Enja | ENJ-9771 2
Rabih Abou-Khalil Septet
Between Dusk And Dawn | Enja | ENJ-9771 2

Velez,Wilfredo | (as,ssbs)
Jerry Gonzalez & Fort Apache Band
The River Is Deep | Enja | ENJ-4040 2

Venaas,Terje | (b)
Ketil Bjornstad Group
Early Years | EmArCy | 013271-2

Venegas,Victor | (b)
Cal Tjader Quartet
Black Hawk Nights | Fantasy | FCD 24755-2
Cal Tjader Quintet
Concerts In The Sun | Fantasy | FCD 9688-2
Cal Tjader Sextet
Black Hawk Nights | Fantasy | FCD 24755-2
Mongo Santamaria And His Band
Sabroso | Original Jazz Classics | OJCCD 281-2
Mongo At The Village Gate | Original Jazz Classics | OJCCD 490-2(RLP 9529)

Vennik,Dick | (fl,alto-fl,b-cl,ss,ts,reedssax)
Klaus Weiss Orchestra
Live At The Domicile | ATM Records | ATM 3805-AH

Ventura,Charlie | (as,ts,bs,ss,bass-saxvoc)
Anita O'Day With Gene Krupa And His Orchestra
Let Me Off Uptown:Anita O'Day With Gene Krupa | CBS | CK 65625
Charlie Ventura Quintet
High On An Open Mike | Fresh Sound Records | FSR-CD 314
Dizzy Gillespie And His Orchestra
Ultimate Dizzy Gillespie | Verve | 557535-2
Gene Krupa And His Orchestra
Mullenium | CBS | CK 65678
Gene Krupa Trio
The Complete Jazz At The Philharmonic On Verve 1944-1949 | Verve | 523893-2
Jazz At The Philharmonic:Best Of The 1940's Concerts | Verve | 557534-2
JATP All Stars
The Complete Jazz At The Philharmonic On Verve 1944-1949 | Verve | 523893-2
Sarah Vaughan With The Teddy Wilson Quartet
Sarah Vaughan:Lover Man | Dreyfus Jazz Line | FDM 36739-2
The Metronome All Stars
Planet Jazz:Dizzy Gillespie | Planet Jazz | 2152069-2

Venuti,Joe | (b,p,vld)
Eddie Lang-Joe Venuti And Their Allstars Orchestra
Jazz:The Essential Collection Vol.3 | IN+OUT Records | 78013-2
Frankie Trumbauer And His Orchestra
Jazz:The Essential Collection Vol.2 | IN+OUT Records | 78012-2
Hoagy Carmichael And His Orchestra
Planet Jazz:Bud Freeman | Planet Jazz | 2161240-2
Irving Mills And His Hotsy Totsy Gang
Jazz:The Essential Collection Vol.3 | IN+OUT Records | 78013-2
Roger Wolfe Kahn And His Orchestra
Planet Jazz:Jack Teagarden | Planet Jazz | 2161236-2

Venuti,Joe prob. | (v)
Irving Mills And His Hotsy Totsy Gang
Jazz:The Essential Collection Vol.3 | IN+OUT Records | 78013-2

Venuto,Joe | (percvib)
Stan Getz With The Eddie Sauter Orchestra
Stan Getz Plays The Music Of Mickey One | Verve | 531232-2

Veras,Nelson | (g)
Jean-Louis Matinier Quartet
Confluences | Enja | ENJ-9454 2

Verbruggen,Teun | (dr)
Alexi Tuomarila Quartet
02 | Finladia Jazz | 0927-49148-2

Verdejo,Tony | (bongos)
Conexion Latina
Calorcito | Enja | ENJ-4072 2

Verdier,Camille | (b-tb)
Raymond Fol Big Band
Jazz In Paris:Raymond Fol-Les 4 Saisons | EmArCy | 548791-2

Verdinelli,Sergio | (dr)
Hernan Merlo Quintet
Consin | Fresh Sound Records | FSNT 150 CD

Verdon,Roland | (dr)
Oscar Peterson Quartet
Planet Music:Oscar Peterson | RCA | 2165365-2
This Is Oscar Peterson | RCA | 2663990-2

Verdugo,Dale | (voc)
Horace Silver Quintet With Vocals
Horace Silver Retrospective | Blue Note | 495576-2

Vergés Sergi | (tbtuba)
Big Band Bellaterra
Don't Git Sassy | Fresh Sound Records | FSNT 048 CD
Orquestra De Cambra Teatre Lliure
Tributes To Duke Ellington | Fresh Sound Records | FSNT 084 CD

Vergés,Sergi | (tuba)
Dave Liebman And The Lluis Vidal Trio With The Orquestra De Cambra Theatre Lliure
Dave Liebman And The Lluis Vidal Trio | Fresh Sound Records | FSNT 026 CD
Orquestra De Cambra Teatre Lliure
Orquestra De Cambra Teatre Lliure and Lluis Vidal Trio feat.Dave Liebman | Fresh Sound Records | FSNT 027 CD
Orquestra De Cambra Teatre Lliure feat. Dave Liebman
Orquestra De Cambra Teatre Lliure and Lluis Vidal Trio feat.Dave Liebman | Fresh Sound Records | FSNT 027 CD

Verhovec,Michael | (drperc)
Gunter Hampel Next Generation
Next Generation | Birth | CD 043
Muriel Zoe Group
Red And Blue | ACT | 9416-2

Verlardi,Bernardo | (perc)
Cal Tjader's Modern Mambo Quintet(Sextet)
Mambo With Tjader | Original Jazz Classics | OJCCD 271-2(F 3202)

Verlardi,Edward | (bongo,congaperc)

Verly,Francois | (dr,perc,marimba,p,keyboards)
David Friedman Quartet
Other Worlds | Intuition Records | INT 3210-2
Nguyen Le Group
Tales From Viet-Nam | ACT | 9225-2

Vermeille,Francois | (p)
Django Reinhardt And The Quintet Du Hot Club De France
Planet Jazz:Django Reinhardt | Planet Jazz | 2152071-2

Vermeulen,Robert Jan | (p,org,ldp-solo)
Robert Jan Vermeulen
Ten Piano Players,Vol.1 | Green House Music | CD 1002

Vermie,Bart | (perc)
Pili-Pili
Hotel Babo | JA & RO | JARO 4147-2

Vernhes,Dominique | (clts)
Frank Wess Meets The Paris-Barcelona Swing Connection
Paris-Barcelona Connection | Fresh Sound Records | FSNT 002 CD

Vernon,George | (tb)
Coleman Hawkins With The Thore Ehrlings Orchestra
Coleman Hawkins At The Golden Circle | Dragon | DRCD 265

Verny,Cécile | (claves,shakervoc)
Cécile Verny Quartet
Métisse | double moon | CHRDM 71010
Kekeli | double moon | CHRDM 71028
Got A Ticket | double moon | DMCD 1002-2
Cécile Verny Quintet
Kekeli | double moon | CHRDM 71028

VerPlanck,Billy | (arr,condtb)
Sonny Stitt With Orchestra
Goin' Down Slow | Prestige | PRCD 24276-2

VerPlanck,Marlene | (voc)
Glenn Miller And His Orchestra
The Glenn Miller Orchestra In Digital Mood | GRP | GRP 95022

Verploegen,Angelo | (fl-htp)
Christian Willisohn New Band
Heart Broken Man | Blues Beacon | BLU-1026 2

Verrell,Ronnie | (dr)
André Holst With Chris Dean's European Swing Orchestra
That's Swing | Nagel-Heyer | CD 079

Versaci,Bill | (sax)
Sarah Vaughan With The Norman Leyden Orchestra
Sarah Vaughan:Lover Man | Dreyfus Jazz Line | FDM 36739-2

Verstraete,Charles | (tb)
Golden Gate Quartet With The Martial Solal Orchestra

INTERPRETENVERZEICHNIS

Americans Swinging In Paris:Golden Gate Quartet | EMI Records | 539659-2
From Spriritual To Swing Vol.2 | EMI Records | 780573-2
Michel De Villers Octet
Jazz In Paris:Saxophones Á Saint-Germain Des Prés | EmArCy | 014060-2
Raymond Fol Big Band
Jazz In Paris:Raymond Fol-Les 4 Saisons | EmArCy | 548791-2

Very Saxy |
Very Saxy
Very Saxy | Original Jazz Classics | OJCCD 458-2
The Prestige Legacy Vol.2:Battles Of Saxes | Prestige | PCD 24252-2

Vesala,Edward | (accordeon,perc,b,dr,angklung)
Edward Vesala Ensemble
Ode Of The Death Of Jazz | ECM | 1413(843196-2)
Edward Vesala Group
Nan Madol | ECM | 1077
Lumi | ECM | 1339
Edward Vesala Nordic Gallery
Sound & Fury | ECM | 1541
Edward Vesala Sound And Fury
Invisible Strom | ECM | 1461
Jan Garbarek Trio
Triptychon | ECM | 1029(847321-2)
Kenny Wheeler Sextet
Around 6 | ECM | 1156
Tomasz Stanko Quartet
Balladyna | ECM | 1071(519289-2)
Toto Blanke Group
Electric Circus' Best | ALISO Records | AL 1034

Vescovo,Al | (g)
Gene Harris And The Three Sounds
Deep Blue-The United States Of Mind | Blue Note | 521152-2
The Three Sounds
Blue Break Beats | Blue Note | 799106-2

Vesely,Ted | (tb)
Artie Shaw And His Orchestra
Planet JazzArtie Shaw | Planet Jazz | 2152057-2
Planet Jazz Sampler | Planet Jazz | 2152326-2
Planet Jazz:Swing | Planet Jazz | 2169651-2
Planet Jazz:Female Jazz Vocalists | Planet Jazz | 2169656-2
The Legends Of Swing | Laserlight | 24659
Benny Goodman And His Orchestra
Charlie Christian:Swing To Bop | Dreyfus Jazz Line | FDM 36715-2

Vespestad,Jarle | (dr)
Silje Nergard Group with Strings
Nightwatch | EmArCy | 9865648
Tord Gustavsen Trio
Changing Places | ECM | 1834(016397-2)

Vesta | (voc)
Christian McBride Group
A Family Affair | Verve | 557554-2

Vetterer,Werner | (gel-g)
HR Big Band
The American Songs Of Kurt Weill | hr music.de | hrmj 006-01 CD
Libertango:Homage An Astor Piazzolla | hr music.de | hrmj 014-02 CD
HR Big Band With Marjorie Barnes And Frits Landesbergen
Swinging Christmas | hr music.de | hrmj 012-02 CD
HR Big Band With Marjorie Barnes And Frits Landesbergen And Strings
Swinging Christmas | hr music.de | hrmj 012-02 CD

Viale,Jean-Louis | (drperc)
Bobby Jaspar Quintet
Jazz In Paris | EmArCy | 159941-2 PMS
Django Reinhardt And His Rhythm
Verve Jazz Masters 38:Django Reinhardt | Verve | 516931-2
Peche Á La Mode-The Great Blue Star Sessions 1947/1953 | Verve | 835418-2
Django Reinhardt Quartet
Jazz In Paris:Django Reinhardt-Nuages | EmArCy | 018428-2
Gigi Gryce-Clifford Brown Octet
Planet Jazz:Clifford Brown | Planet Jazz | 2161239-2
Gigi Gryce-Clifford Brown Sextet
Planet Jazz:Clifford Brown | Planet Jazz | 2161239-2
Hubert Fol Quartet
Jazz In Paris:Saxophones Á Saint-Germain Des Prés | EmArCy | 014060-2
Jimmy Raney Quartet
Jimmy Raney Visits Paris Vol.2 | Vogue | 21434802
Jimmy Raney Quintet
Jimmy Raney Visits Paris Vol.2 | Vogue | 21434802
Raymond Fol Big Band
Jazz In Paris:Raymond Fol-Les 4 Saisons | EmArCy | 548791-2
Rene Thomas Quartet
Jazz In Paris:René Thomas-The Real Cat | EmArCy | 549400-2 PMS
Rene Thomas Quintet
Jazz In Paris:René Thomas-The Real Cat | EmArCy | 549400-2 PMS
Stephane Grappelli Sextet
Grapelli Story | Verve | 515807-2
The Herdsmen
Nat Pierce-Dick Collins-Ralph Burns & The Herdsmen Play Paris | Fantasy | FCD 24759-2

Viale,Louis | (b)
Quintet Du Hot Club De France
Django Reinhardt:Echoes Of France | Dreyfus Jazz Line | FDM 36726-2
Django Reinhardt:Souveniers | Dreyfus Jazz Line | FDM 36744-2

Viapiano,Paul | (g)
Diane Schuur Quintet With B.B.King
The Best Of Diane Schuur | GRP | GRP 98882

VIBrations |
VIBrations
7.Zelt-Musik-Festival:Jazz Events | Zounds | CD 2730001

Vick,Harold | (as,ts,fl,saxss)
Big John Patton Quintet
So Blue So Funky-Heroes Of The Hammond | Blue Note | 796563-2
Grant Green Orchestra
Grant Green:Blue Breakbeat | Blue Note | 494705-2
Grant Green With Orchestra
The Final Comedown(Soundtrack) | Blue Note | 581678-2
Horace Silver Sextet
Horace Silver Retrospective | Blue Note | 495576-2
Deep Blue-The United States Of Mind | Blue Note | 521152-2
Horace Silver Sextet With Vocals
Horace Silver Retrospective | Blue Note | 495576-2
Jack McDuff Orchestra
The Last Goodun' | Prestige | PRCD 24274-2
Jack McDuff Quartet
Brother Jack Meets The Boss | Original Jazz Classics | OJCCD 326-2(P 7228)
The Last Goodun' | Prestige | PRCD 24274-2
Jack McDuff:The Prestige Years | Prestige | PRCD 24387-2
Jack McDuff Quartet With Gene Ammons
Brother Jack Meets The Boss | Original Jazz Classics | OJCCD 326-2(P 7228)
Jack McDuff Quintet
Jack McDuff:The Prestige Years | Prestige | PRCD 24387-2
Jack McDuff Trio
The Last Goodun' | Prestige | PRCD 24274-2
John Patton Quintet
Along Came John | Blue Note | 0675614
Along Came John | Blue Note | 831915-2
Les McCann Group
Another Beginning | Atlantic | 7567-80790-2

Vickers,Mike | (arr)
Ella Fitzgerald With Orchestra
Ella/Things Ain't What They Used To Be | Warner | 9362-47875-2

Victoria | (perc,congastambourine)
The Brecker Brothers
Heavy Metal Be-Bop | RCA | 2119257-2

Victory,Gene | (dr)
Chet Baker Quartet
Chet Baker In Milan | Original Jazz Classics | OJC20 370-2(JLP 18)
Chet Baker Sextet
Chet Baker In Milan | Original Jazz Classics | OJC20 370-2(JLP 18)

Vidacovich,Johnny | (dr,percp)
Ray Anderson Quintet
Blues Bred In The Bone | Enja | ENJ-5081 2

Vidal,Carlos | (bongos,congasperc)
Al Haig Sextet
Al Haig Trio And Sextets | Original Jazz Classics | OJCCD 1929-2(SPL 1118)
Charlie Parker And His Orchestra
Charlie Parker:The Best Of The Verve Years | Verve | 527815-2
Bird: The Complete Charlie Parker On Verve | Verve | 837141-2
Charlie Parker Septet
Charlie Parker | Verve | 539757-2
Jazz Crusaders
Chile Con Soul | Pacific Jazz | 590957-2

Vidal,Jacques | (b)
Florin Niculescu Quartet
Four Friends | Jardis Records | JRCD 9923

Vidal,Lluis | (p,arr,condp-solo)
Dave Liebman And The Lluis Vidal Trio
Dave Liebman And The Lluis Vidal Trio | Fresh Sound Records | FSNT 026 CD
Dave Liebman And The Lluis Vidal Trio With The Orquestra De Cambra Theatre Lliure
Dave Liebman And The Lluis Vidal Trio | Fresh Sound Records | FSNT 026 CD
Lluis Vidal
Lluis Vidal Piano Solo | Fresh Sound Records | FSNT 001 CD
Lluis Vidal Trio
Tren Nocturn | Fresh Sound Records | FSNT 003 CD
Milikituli | Fresh Sound Records | FSNT 009 CD
Orquestra De Cambra Teatre Lliure
Orquestra De Cambra Teatre Lliure and Lluis Vidal Trio feat.Dave Liebman | Fresh Sound Records | FSNT 027 CD
Porgy And Bess | Fresh Sound Records | FSNT 066 CD
Tributes To Duke Ellington | Fresh Sound Records | FSNT 084 CD
Orquestra De Cambra Teatre Lliure feat. Dave Liebman
Orquestra De Cambra Teatre Lliure and Lluis Vidal Trio feat.Dave Liebman | Fresh Sound Records | FSNT 027 CD

Vidusich,John | (v)
Johnny Hartman And His Orchestra
Unforgettable | Impulse(MCA) | IMP 11522

Viestra,Simone | (v)
Stochelo Rosenberg Group With Strings
Gypsy Swing | Verve | 527806-2

Vieti | (perc)
Omar Belmonte's Latin Lover
Vamos A Ver | EGO | 96170

Vig,Tommy | (drvib)
Lajos Dudas Quartet
Jubilee Edition | double moon | CHRDM 71020

Vignola,Frank | (g,bjel-g)
Frank Vignola Sextet
Off Broadway | Nagel-Heyer | CD 2006

Vignolo,Rémi | (bel-b)
Jacky Terrasson Trio
Smile | Blue Note | 542413-2
Richard Galliano Group
French Touch | Dreyfus Jazz Line | FDM 36596-2

Vijayan,Shalini | (v)
Paquito D'Rivera Group With The Absolute Ensemble
Habanera | Enja | ENJ-9395 2

Viklicky,Emil | (keyboardsp)
George Mraz Quartet
Morava | Milestone | MCD 9309-2

Vila,Daniel | (keyboardsvoc)
Omar Belmonte's Latin Lover
Vamos A Ver | EGO | 96170

Vilardi,Frank | (dr)
Bobby McFerrin Group
Bobby McFerrin | Elektra | 7559-60023-2

Villa,Trond | (viola)
Jon Balke w/Magnetic North Orchestra
Further | ECM | 1517

Villarini,Tommy | (tp,perccowbell)
Mongo Santamaria And His Band
Montreux Heat! | Pablo | PACD 5317-2
Mongo Santamaria Group With Dizzy Gillespie And Toots Thielemans
Montreux Heat! | Pablo | PACD 5317-2

Villariny,Tommy | (tpcow-bell)
Summertime-Digital At Montreux 1980 | Original Jazz Classics | OJCCD 626-2(2308229)

Ville,Christian | (drperc)
Louis Sclavis Quintet
Rouge | ECM | 1458

Villotte,Estelle | (viola)
Abdullah Ibrahim Trio And A String Orchestra
African Suite | TipToe | TIP-888832 2
String Orchestra
African Suite | TipToe | TIP-888832 2

Vinaccia,Paolo | (drperc)
Arild Andersen Quintet With The Cikada String Quartet
Hyperborean | ECM | 1631(537342-2)
Terje Rypdal Group
Skywards | ECM | 1608(533768-2)

Vinayakaram,T.H. | (ghatam,kanjeera,moorsing,nal,voc)
John McLaughlin Group
Remember Shakti | Verve | 559945-2
Shakti
Shakti With John McLaughlin | CBS | 467905-2

Vinayakram,Vikku | (ghatam)
Shankar Group
Nobody Told Me | ECM | 1397
Shankar Quartet
M.R.C.S. | ECM | 1403
Pancha Nadai Pallavi | ECM | 1407(841641-2)

Vince,Gerard | (v)
Harry James And His Orchestra
Trumpet Blues:The Best Of Harry James | Capitol | 521224-2

Vinceno,Éric | (b)
Hank Jones Meets Cheik-Tidiana Seck
Sarala | Verve | 528783-2

Vincent,Jennifer | (cello)
Abbey Lincoln And Her Trio With Guests
Over The Years | Verve | 549101-2

Vincente,Wilfredo | (congas)
Cal Tjader Group
Verve Jazz Masters 39:Cal Tjader | Verve | 521858-2
Cal Tjader Sextet
Talkin Verve/Roots Of Acid Jazz:Cal Tjader | Verve | 531562-2

Vinci,Gerry | (vconcertmaster)
Cal Tjader With The Clare Fischer Orchestra
Cal Tjader Plays Harold Arlen & West Side Story | Fantasy | FCD 24775-2
Dave Grusin Group
Migration | GRP | GRP 95922
Diane Schuur With Orchestra
Love Songs | GRP | GRP 97032
The Best Of Diane Schuur | GRP | GRP 98882
Ella Fitzgerald With The Billy May Orchestra
The Best Of The Song Books:The Ballads | Verve | 521867-2
Ella Fitzgerald Sings The Harold Arlen Song Book | Verve | 589108-2
Ella Fitzgerald With The Nelson Riddle Orchestra
The Best Of The Song Books:The Ballads | Verve | 521867-2
Love Songs:The Best Of The Song Books | Verve | 531762-2
Frank Sinatra With The Count Basie Orchestra
It Might As Well Be Spring | Reprise | 7599-27027-2
Hank Crawford Orchestra
Rhino Presents The Atlantic Jazz Gallery | Atlantic | 8122-71257-2
Mel Tormé With The Russell Garcia Orchestra
Swingin' On The Moon | Verve | 511385-2
Milt Jackson And His Orchestra
Reverence And Compassion | Reprise | 9362-45204-2
Milt Jackson With Strings
To Bags...With Love:Memorial Album | Pablo | 2310967-2
Phineas Newborn Jr. With Dennis Farnon And His Orchestra
While My Lady Sleeps | RCA | 2185157-2
Singers Unlimited With The Pat Williams Orchestra
The Singers Unlimited:Magic Voices | MPS | 539130-2

Vinding,Mads | (bel-b)
Bob Brookmeyer Quartet
Old Friends | Storyville | STCD 8292
Jesper Lundgaard & MadsVinding
Two Basses | Touché Music | TMcCD 020
The Danish Radio Jazz Orchestra
Nice Work | dacapo | DCCD 9446
Thomas Clausen Trio
She Touched Me | M.A Music | A 628-2
Thomas Clausen Trio With Gary Burton
Flowers And Trees | M.A Music | A 805-2
Café Noir | M.A Music | INTCD 004
ULG
Spring | Laika Records | 35101382

Vinjor,Nils-Einar | (g)
Silje Nergard Group with Strings
Nightwatch | EmArCy | 9865648

Vink,Martijn | (dr)
Jesse Van Ruller Trio
Trio | EmArCy | 017513-2

Vinnegar,Leroy | (b)
Benny Carter Quartet
The Jazz Giants Play Rodgers & Hart:Blue Moon | Prestige | PCD 24205-2
Benny Carter Quintet
Jazz Giant | Original Jazz Classics | OJC20 167-2(C 7555)
Benny Carter Sextet
Jazz Giant | Original Jazz Classics | OJC20 167-2(C 7555)
Chet Baker Quartet
The Best Of Chet Baker Plays | Pacific Jazz | 797161-2
Chet Baker Sextet
The Best Of Chet Baker Plays | Pacific Jazz | 797161-2
Gerry Mulligan-Ben Webster Quintet
Verve Jazz Masters 43:Ben Webster | Verve | 525431-2
The Complete Gerry Mulligan Meets Ben Webster Sessions | Verve | 539055-2
Ultimate Ben Webster selected by James Carter | Verve | 557537-2
Hampton Hawes Trio
The Sermon | Original Jazz Classics | OJCCD 1067-2(C 7653)
Jimmy Smith Quartet
Jimmy Smith-Talkin' Verve | Verve | 531563-2
Joe Albany Trio
Portrait Of A Legend | Fresh Sound Records | FSR-CD 317
Leroy Vinnegar Sextet
The Jazz Giants Play Harry Warren:Lullaby Of Broadway | Prestige | PCD 24204-2
Les McCann Group
Talkin' Verve:Les McCann | Verve | 557351-2
Les McCann Orchestra
Talkin' Verve:Les McCann | Verve | 557351-2
Les McCann Trio
Talkin' Verve:Les McCann | Verve | 557351-2
Les McCann-Eddie Harris Quintet
Rhino Presents The Atlantic Jazz Gallery | Atlantic | 8122-71257-2
Swiss Movement | Atlantic | 8122-72452-2
Lou Rawls With Les McCann Ltd.
Blue Velvet: Crooners, Swooners And Velvet Vocals | Blue Note | 521153-2
Stormy Monday | Blue Note | 791441-2
Serge Chaloff Quartet
Blue Serge | Capitol | 494505-2
Shelly Manne And His Friends
My Fair Lady | Original Jazz Classics | OJC 336(C 7527)
Shelly Manne And His Men
The Gambit | Original Jazz Classics | OJCCD 1007-2(C 7557)
More Swinging Sounds | Original Jazz Classics | OJCCD 320-2(C 7519)
Shelly Manne Trio
Li'l Abner | Original Jazz Classics | OJCCD 1087-2(S 7533)
Sonny Rollins & The Contemporary Leaders
Sonny Rollins & The Contemporary Leaders | Original Jazz Classics | OJCCD 340-2
Sonny Rollins And The Contemporary Leaders
Sonny Rollins-The Freelance Years:The Complete Riverside & Contemporary Recordings | Riverside | 5 RCD 4427-2
Sonny Stitt Quartet
Verve Jazz Masters 50:Sonny Sitt | Verve | 527651-2
Stan Getz Quartet
Stan Getz Highlights:The Best Of The Verve Years Vol.2 | Verve | 517330-2
Best Of The West Coast Sessions | Verve | 537084-2
Award Winner | Verve | 543320-2
Stan Getz And The 'Cool' Sounds | Verve | 547317-2
The Steamer | Verve | 547771-2
West Coast Jazz | Verve | 557549-2
Stan Getz Highlights | Verve | 847430-2
Stan Getz Quintet
Stan Getz Highlights:The Best Of The Verve Years Vol.2 | Verve | 517330-2
Verve Jazz Masters 8:Stan Getz | Verve | 519823-2
Best Of The West Coast Sessions | Verve | 537084-2
Ultimate Stan Getz selected by Joe Henderson | Verve | 557532-2
West Coast Jazz | Verve | 557549-2
Stan Getz Highlights | Verve | 847430-2
Stan Getz-Lionel Hampton Quintet
Stan Getz Highlights:The Best Of The Verve Years Vol.2 | Verve | 517330-2
Hamp And Getz | Verve | 831672-2
Stan Getz-Lionel Hampton Sextet
Hamp And Getz | Verve | 831672-2
The Jazz Crusaders
Kind Of Blue:Blue Note Celebrate The Music Of Miles Davis | Blue Note | 534255-2
Zoot Sims With The Joe Castro Trio
Live At Falcon Lair | Pablo | PACD 2310977-2

Vinson,Eddie 'Cleanhead' | (asvoc)
Count Basie And His Orchestra
Count Basie: Salle Pleyel, April 17th, 1972 | Laserlight | 36127
Count Basie And The Kansas City 7
Count Basie: Salle Pleyel, April 17th, 1972 | Laserlight | 36127
Eddie Cleanhead Vinson With Band
The Late Show-Recorded Live At Marla's Memory Lane Supper Club Vol.2 | Fantasy | FCD 9655-2
Eddie Cleanhead Vinson With The Cannonball Adderley Quintet
Cannonball Adderley Birthday Celebration | Fantasy | FANCD 6087-2
Eddie 'Cleanhead' Vinson With The Cannonball Adderley Quintet | Milestone | MCD 9324-2
Eddie Cleanhead Vinson With The Red Holloway Quartet
Blues In The Night-Volume One:The Early Show | Fantasy | FCD 9647-2
Etta James & Eddie Cleanhead Vinson With The Red Holloway Quartet
Blues In The Night-Volume One:The Early Show | Fantasy | FCD 9647-2
Etta James/Eddie 'Cleanhead' Vinson With Band
The Late Show-Recorded Live At Marla's Memory Lane Supper Club Vol.2 | Fantasy | FCD 9655-2

Kansas City 6
Count Basie:Kansas City 6 | Original Jazz Classics | OJC20 449-2(2310871)
Milt Jackson Septet
Milt Jackson Birthday Celebration | Fantasy | FANCD 6079-2
Sarah Vaughan And Her Band
Duke Ellington Song Book Two | Pablo | CD 2312116
Sarah Vaughan Birthday Celebration | Fantasy | FANCD 6090-2
Super Black Blues Band
Super Black Blues Vol.II | RCA | 2663874-2

Vinson,Millard 'Pete' | (drsynares)
Grover Washington Jr. Septet
Paradise | Elektra | 7559-60537-2

Vinson,Mose | (pvoc)
Mose Vinson Band
Joe Hill Louis: The Be-Bop Boy | Bear Family Records | BCD 15524 AH

Vinx | (perc)
Cassandra Wilson Group
Blue Light 'Til Dawn | Blue Note | 781357-2

Viola,Al | (g)
Ella Fitzgerald With The Marty Paich Orchestra
Ella Fitzgerald-First Lady Of Song | Verve | 517898-2
Whisper Not | Verve | 589947-2
For The Love Of Ella Fitzgerald | Verve | 841765-2
Pete Rugolo And His Orchestra
Thriller/Richard Diamon(Original Jazz Scores From 2 Classics TV Series) | Fresh Sound Records | FSCD 2015

Virgadamo,Pat | (tb)
Anita O'Day With Gene Krupa And His Orchestra
Let Me Off Uptown:Anita O'Day With Gene Krupa | CBS | CK 65625

Virji,Faez | (tb)
Carla Bley Band
The Very Big Carla Bley Band | Watt | 23

Visconte,Fréderic | (v)
Charlie Haden Quartet West With Strings
Now Is The Hour | Verve | 527827-2

Visentin,Caris | (engl-hoboe)
Dave Liebman Quintet
Homage To John Coltrane | Owl Records | 018357-2

Vital Information |
Vital Information
Ray Of Hope | VeraBra Records | CDVBR 2161-2
Where We Come From | Intuition Records | INT 3218-2
Live Around The World Where We Come From Tour '98-'99 | Intuition Records | INT 3296-2
Show 'Em Where You Live | Intuition Records | INT 3306-2

Vital,Raul | (voc)
Danilo Perez Group
Central Avenue | Impulse(MCA) | 951281-2

Vitale,Tony | (dr)
The Jimmy And Marion McPartland Sessions
Vic Lewis:The Golden Years | Candid | CCD 79754

Vitamine |
Stephan Meinberg VITAMINE
Horizontal | Jazz Haus Musik | JHM 0106 CD

Vitous,Miroslav | (b,el-b,el-p,synthp)
Bireli Lagrene Group
Bireli Lagrene 'Highlights' | Jazzpoint | JP 1027 CD
Bireli Lagrene | Jazzpoint | JP 1049 CD
Chick Corea Trio
Trio Music | ECM | 1232/33(159454-2)
Trio Music,Live In Europe | ECM | 1310(827769-2)
Chick Corea-Miroslav Vitous
Trio Music | ECM | 1232/33(159454-2)
Franco Ambrosetti Quintet
Light Breeze | Enja | ENJ-9331 2
Freddy Studer Orchestra
Seven Songs | VeraBra Records | CDVBR 2056-2
Herbie Mann Group
Memphis Underground | Atlantic | 7567-81364-2
Jack DeJohnette Quartet
The DeJohnette Complex | Original Jazz Classics | OJCCD 617-2
Jack DeJohnette Quintet
The DeJohnette Complex | Original Jazz Classics | OJCCD 617-2
Jack DeJohnette Sextet
The DeJohnette Complex | Original Jazz Classics | OJCCD 617-2
Jan Garbarek/Miroslav Vitous/Peter Erskine
Star | ECM | 1444(849649-2)
Joe Zawinul Group
Zawinul | Atlantic | 7567-81375-2
Larry Coryell-Miroslav Vitous
Dedicated To Bill Evans And Scott LaFaro | Jazzpoint | JP 1021 CD
Miroslav Vitous
Emergence | ECM | 1312
Miroslav Vitous Group
Journey's End | ECM | 1242(843171-2)
Universal Syncopations | ECM | 1863(038506-2)
Atlantic Jazz: Fusion | Atlantic | 7567-81711-2
Miroslav Vitous Quartet
First Meeting | ECM | 1145
Miroslav Vitous/Jan Garbarek
Atmos | ECM | 1475(513373-2)
Stan Getz Quartet
The Art Of Saxophone | Laserlight | 24652
Steve Kuhn Trio
Oceans In The Sky | Owl Records | 013428-2
Terje Rypdal Trio
To Be Continued | ECM | 1192
Terje Rypdal-Miroslav Vitous-Jack DeJohnette Trio
Terje Rypdal Miroslav Vitous Jack DeJohnette | ECM | 1125(825470-2)
Vic Juris-John Etheridge Quartet
Bohemia | Jazzpoint | JP 1023 CD
Wayne Shorter Sextet
Wayne Shorter:The Classic Blue Note Recordings | Blue Note | 540856-2
Weather Report
Sweetnighter | CBS | 485102-2
Weathe Report Live In Tokyo | CBS | 489208-2

Vizutti,Alan | (tpfl-h)
Woody Herman And The New Thundering Herd
Planet Jazz:Big Bands | Planet Jazz | 2169649-2
Woody Herman's Thundering Herd
Planet Jazz:Jazz Saxophone | Planet Jazz | 2169653-2

Vladimirova,Nadia | (voc)
Sergey Strarostin's Vocal Family
Journey | JA & RO | JARO 4226-2

Vlasek,Frank | (cello)
Charlie Byrd Orchestra
Latin Byrd | Milestone | MCD 47005-2

Vloeimans,Eric | (tp)
Henning Wolter Trio With Guests
Years Of A Trilogy | double moon | DMCHR 71021
Pili-Pili
Ballads Of Timbuktu | JA & RO | JARO 4240-2

Voctory,Gene | (dr)
Chet Baker With String-Orchestra And Voices
Chet Baker With Fifty Italian Strings | Original Jazz Classics | OJC20 492-2(JLP 921)

Vogel,Thomas | (tpfl-h)
Bill Ramsey With Orchestra
Gettin' Back To Swing | Bear Family Records | BCD 15813 AH
HR Big Band With Marjorie Barnes And Frits Landesbergen
Swinging Christmas | hr music.de | hrmj 012-02 CD
HR Big Band With Marjorie Barnes And Frits Landesbergen And Strings
Swinging Christmas | hr music.de | hrmj 012-02 CD
SWR Big Band
Jazz In Concert | Hänssler Classics | CD 93.004

Vogel,Tjitze Anne | (b)
Mark Alban Lotz/Tjitze Anne Vogel
Mostly Harmless... | Edition Collage | EC 470-2

Vogt,Dieter | (viola)
Till Brönner Quartet & Deutsches Symphonieorchester Berlin
German Songs | Minor Music | 801057

Vohwinkel,Gerhard | (tp)
Chris Barber's Jazz Band
The Golden Years Of Revival Jazz,Vol.2 | Storyville | STCD 5507
Papa Bue's New Orleans Band
The Golden Years Of Revival Jazz,Vol.4 | Storyville | STCD 5509
Papa Bue's Viking Jazzband
The Golden Years Of Revival Jazz,Vol.6 | Storyville | STCD 5511
The Golden Years Of Revival Jazz,Vol.8 | Storyville | STCD 5513

Voices | (eight)
Bobby Timmons Orchestra
Quartet And Orchestra | Milestone | MCD 47091-2
Donald Byrd Septet + Voices
A New Perspective | Blue Note | 499006-2

Voices Of The Modern Sound | (voc-group)
Babs Gonzales And His Band
Voilà | Fresh Sound Records | FSR CD 340

Vola,Louis | (accordeonb)
Andre Pasdoc With The Orchestra Vola
Jazz In Paris:Django Reinhardt-Django Et Compagnie | EmArCy | 549241-2 PMS
Django Reinhardt Quartet
Django/Django In Rome 1949-1050 | BGO Records | BGOCD 366
Michel Warlop Et Son Orchestre
Jazz In Paris:Django Reinhardt-Django Et Compagnie | EmArCy | 549241-2 PMS
Micheline Day Et Son Quatuor Swing
Jazz In Paris:Django Reinhardt-Django Et Compagnie | EmArCy | 549241-2 PMS
Quintet Du Hot Club De France
Jazz In Paris:Django Reinhardt-Swing From Paris | EmArCy | 159853-2 PMS
Grapelli Story | Verve | 515807-2
Verve Jazz Masters 38:Django Reinhardt | Verve | 516931-2
Verve Jazz Masters Vol.60:The Collection | Verve | 529866-2
Django/Django In Rome 1949-1050 | BGO Records | BGOCD 366
Django Reinhardt:Echoes Of France | Dreyfus Jazz Line | FDM 36726-2
Django Reinhardt:Souveniers | Dreyfus Jazz Line | FDM 36744-2
Willie Lewis And His Entertainers
Americans Swinging In Paris:Benny Carter | EMI Records | 539647-2
Yvonne Louis With The Orchestra Vola
Jazz In Paris:Django Reinhardt-Django Et Compagnie | EmArCy | 549241-2 PMS

Volkert,Mark | (v)
Ron Carter With Strings
Pastels | Original Jazz Classics | OJCCD 665-2(M 9073)

Voller,Bertil | (b-tb)
Toots Thielemans And His Orchestra
Verve Jazz Masters Vol.59:Toots Thielemans | Verve | 535271-2

Vollmer,Titus | (g)
Christian Willisohn Group
Live At Marians | ART BY HEART | ABH 2006 2
Christian Willisohn New Band
Heart Broken Man | Blues Beacon | BLU-1026 2
Martin Schmitt
Handful Of Blues | ESM Records | ESM 9303

Volpi,Dario | (g)
Palo Alto
Crash Test | Jazz 'n' Arts Records | JNA 1803

Von Alten,Brüning | (drokonkolo)
Lazaro Ros Ensemble
Ori Batá (Cuban Yoruba Music) | Enja | ENJ-9381 2

Von Der Nahmer,Martin | (viola)
Lisa Bassenge Trio With Guests
A Sight, A Song | Minor Music | 801100

Von Dobrzynsky,Stefan | (as,clsax)
Paul Nero Sound
Doldinger's Best | ACT | 9224-2

Von Dobrzynsky,Steffan | (as,ts,fl,clss)
Joe Pass With The NDR Big Band
Joe Pass In Hamburg | ACT | 9100-2

Von Essen,Eric | (b)
Alex Cline Group
The Lamp And The Star | ECM | 1372

Von Heijne,Claes | (p)
Rebecka Gordon Quartet
Yiddish'n Jazz | Touché Music | TMcCD 014

Von Kalnein,Heinrich | (reeds,saxEWI)
Heinrich Von Kalnein Group
New Directions | Nabel Records:Jazz Network | CD 4670

Von Kaphengst,Christian | (b)
Cafe Du Sport Jazzquartett
Cafe Du Sport Jazzquartett | Minor Music | 801096
Christoph Sänger Trio
Caprice | Laika Records | LK 94-057
Peter Fessler Quartet
Foot Prints | Minor Music | 801058
Tony Lakatos With The Martin Sasse Trio
Feel Alright | Edition Collage | EC 494-2

Von Kleewitz,Jack | (as)
Takabanda
La Leggenda Del Pescatore | Jazz 4 Ever Records:Jazz Network | J4E 4752
Ulla Oster Group
Beyond Janis | Jazz Haus Musik | JHM 0052 CD

Von Kleewitz,Jan | (as,clsax)
Jan Von Klewitz Quintet
Bonehenge Suite | Jazz Haus Musik | JHM 0078 CD
Norbert Scholly Quartet
Norbert Scholly Quartet | Jazz Haus Musik | JHM 0086 CD
Rudi Neuwirth Group
Sand | Traumton Records | 2413-2
Thärichens Tentett
Lady Moon | Minor Music | 801094
Yakou Tribe
Red & Blue Days | Traumton Records | 4474-2

Von Klenck,Franz | (ascl)
Die Deutsche All Star Band 1953
1.Deutsches Jazz Festival 1953 Frankfurt/Main | Bear Family Records | BCD 15611 AH
Helmut Zacharias mit dem Orchester Frank Folken
Ich Habe Rhythmus | Bear Family Records | BCD 15642 AH
Kurt Edelhagen All Stars
Deutsches Jazz Fesival 1954/1955 | Bear Family Records | BCD 15430
Kurt Edelhagen All Stars Und Solisten
Deutsches Jazz Fesival 1954/1955 | Bear Family Records | BCD 15430
Quartet Der Kurt Edelhagen All Stars
Deutsches Jazz Fesival 1954/1955 | Bear Family Records | BCD 15430
Stan Getz With The Kurt Edelhagen Orchestra
Stan Getz In Europe | Laserlight | 24657

Von Lenthe,Henriette | (tb)
The United Women's Orchestra
The Blue One | Jazz Haus Musik | JHM 0099 CD

Von Schlippenbach,Alexander | (ld,p,arr,cond,percp-solo)
Aki Takase-Alexander von Schlippenbach
Internationales Jazzfestival Münster | Tutu Records | 888110-2*
Berlin Contemporary Jazz Orchestra
Berlin Contemporary Jazz Orchestra | ECM | 1409
Gunter Hampel Quintet
Legendary: The 27th Of May 1997 | Birth | CD 045
Jazzensemble Des Hessischen Rundfunks
Atmosphering Conditions Permitting | ECM | 1549/50

Von Thiem[Vonthiem],Max | (dr,percprogramming)
Loft Line
Source | Laika Records | 35101122

Von Welck,Matthias | (bass-slit-dr,deep-,mallets)
Norbert Stein Pata Masters
Pata Maroc | Pata Musik | PATA 12(AMF 1063)
Graffiti | Pata Musik | PATA 9 CD
Norbert Stein Pata Masters meets Djaduk Ferianto Kua Etnika
Pata Java | Pata Musik | PATA 16 CD
Nornert Stein Pata Masters
Live In Australia | Pata Musik | PATA 15 CD
Pata Masters
Pata-Bahia | Pata Musik | PATA 11 CD
Pata Music Meets Arfi
News Of Roi Ubu | Pata Musik | PATA 10 CD

Voormann,Klaus | (bb-g)
Howlin' Wolf London Session
Howlin' Wolf:The London Sessions | Chess | MCD 09297
Paul Nero Sound
Doldinger's Best | ACT | 9224-2

Vorselen,Harry | (fr-h)
The Rosenberg Trio With Orchestra
Noches Calientes | Verve | 557022-2

Voss,Jochen | (asss)
Thomas Brendgens-Mönkemeyer & Jochen Voss
Jazz Guitar Highlights 1 | Jardis Records | JRCD 20141
Textures | Jardis Records | JRCD 9920

Voynow,Dick | (p)
The Wolverines
Jazz:The Essential Collection Vol.2 | IN+OUT Records | 78012-2

Vroomans,Hans | (el-p,grand-p,p,keyboardssynth)
Laura Fygi With Band
Bewitched | Verve | 514724-2
The Rosenberg Trio With Orchestra
Noches Calientes | Verve | 557022-2

Vu,Cuong | (tp,fl-hvoice)
Nils Wogram Octet
Odd And Awkward | Enja | ENJ-9416-2
Nils Wogram Sextet
Odd And Awkward | Enja | ENJ-9416-2

Vujin-Stein,Basa | (melodica,vocorg)
Norbert Stein Pata Orchester
Ritual Life | Pata Musik | PATA 5(JHM 50) CD

Wachsmann,Phil | (v,electronics,el-v,viola)
Evan Parker Electro-Acoustic Ensemble
Toward The Margins | ECM | 1612(453514-2)
Drawn Inward | ECM | 1693
Memory/Vision | ECM | 1852(0381172)
Philipp Wachsmann-Paul Lytton
Some Other Season | ECM | 1662

Wachter,Herbert | (drperc)
Uli Gutscher Quintet
Wind Moments | Take Twelve On CD | TT 009-2
Werner Lener Quartet
My Own | Satin Doll Productions | SDP 1013-1 CD
Personal Moments | Satin Doll Productions | SDP 1026-1 CD
Colours | Satin Doll Productions | SDP 1033-1 CD
Werner Lener Trio
My Own | Satin Doll Productions | SDP 1013-1 CD
Personal Moments | Satin Doll Productions | SDP 1026-1 CD
Colours | Satin Doll Productions | SDP 1033-1 CD

Wacker,Bob | (voc)
Louis Armstrong With The Hal Mooney Orchestra
Ambassador Louis Armstrong Vol.17:Moments To Remember(1952-1956) | Ambassador | CLA 1917

Wackerman,Chad | (dr,countoff,electronic-dr)
Allan Holdsworth Group
The Sixteen Man Of Tain | Cream Records | CR 610-2

Waddilove,Don | (tp)
Billie Holiday With The Paul Whiteman Orchestra
Billie's Blues | Blue Note | 748786-2

Wade,Eddie | (tp)
Paul Whiteman And His Orchestra
Planet Jazz:Jack Teagarden | Planet Jazz | 2161236-2
Jazz:The Essential Collection Vol.3 | IN+OUT Records | 78013-2

Wadenius,George | (el-g,vocg)
Joe Henderson And His Orchestra
Joe Henderson:The Milestone Years | Milestone | 8MCD 4413-2
Joe Henderson Sextet
Joe Henderson:The Milestone Years | Milestone | 8MCD 4413-2
Silje Nergard Group with Strings
Nightwatch | EmArCy | 9865648
Viktoria Tolstoy With The Esbjörn Svensson Trio
Viktoria Tolstoy:White Russian | Blue Note | 821220-2

Wadlow,Tommy | (p)
Gerard Presencer Group
Chasing Reality | ACT | 9422-2
Lisa Wahland And Her Trio
Marlene | Fine Music | FM 108-2

Wagenleiter,Klaus | (keyboards,background-vocp)
Bill Ramsey With Orchestra
Gettin' Back To Swing | Bear Family Records | BCD 15813 AH
Jan Jankeje Quintet
Zum Trotz | Jazzpoint | JP 1016 CD
Jan Jankeje Trio
A' Portrait Of Jan Jankeje | Jazzpoint | JP 1054 CD

Wagner,Babe | (tb)
Anita O'Day With Gene Krupa And His Orchestra
Let Me Off Uptown:Anita O'Day With Gene Krupa | CBS | CK 65625

Wagner,Christian | (ascl)
Bill Coleman Et Son Orchestre
Americans Swinging In Paris:Bill Coleman-The Elegance | EMI Records | 539662-2

Wagner,Claus | (drperc)
The Remedy
The Remedy | Jazz Haus Musik | JHM 0069 CD

Wagner,Rufus | (tb)
Frank Sinatra With The Count Basie Orchestra
Sinatra-Basie:An Historic Musical First | Reprise | 7599-27023-2

Wagner,Thilo | (p)
Antonio Petrocca Quartet
But Not For Me | Edition Musikat | EDM 047
Antonio Petrocca Trio
But Not For Me | Edition Musikat | EDM 047
Benny Waters Quartet
Swinging Again | Jazzpoint | JP 1037 CD
A' Portrait Of Jan Jankeje | Jazzpoint | JP 1054 CD
Davide Petrocca Quartet
Move | Edition Musikat | EDM 026
The New York Allstars
Hey Ba-Ba-Re-Bop!! The New York Allstars Play Lionel Hampton Vol.1 | Nagel-Heyer | CD 047
The New York Allstars Play Lionel Hampton,Vol.2: Stompin' At The Savoy | Nagel-Heyer | CD 077
Thilo Wagner Quintet
Just In Time | Satin Doll Productions | SDP 1011-1 CD
Thilo Wagner Trio
Wagner,Mörike.Beck,Finally. | Nagel-Heyer | CD 078
Just In Time | Satin Doll Productions | SDP 1011-1 CD
Wedeli Köhler Group
Swing & Folk | Jazzpoint | JP 1067 CD

Wagner,Wolfgang | (b)
Waltz For People Who Hate Waltzes
Noch Lauther | Bear Family Records | BCD 15942 AH
Wolfgang Lauth Quartet
Lauther | Bear Family Records | BCD 15717 AH
Noch Lauther | Bear Family Records | BCD 15942 AH
Wolfgang Lauth Septet
Noch Lauther | Bear Family Records | BCD 15942 AH

Wague,Ali | (pehl-fl)

Karim Ziad Groups
Ifrikya | ACT | 9282-2

Wagué,Aly | (africa-pleul-fl,vocfl)
Hank Jones Meets Cheik-Tidiana Seck
Sarala | Verve | 528783-2
Nguyen Le Group
Maghreb And Friends | ACT | 9261-2

Wahl,Andreas | (g,el-gfrettless-g)
Matthias Müller Quartet
Bhavam | Jazz Haus Musik | JHM 0126 CD

Wahl,Wolfgang | (clts)
Fisherman's Break
Fisherman's Break | Edition Collage | EC 450-2

Wahlandt,Lisa | (vocperc)
Gerwin Eisenhauer's The Gäff Gang feat. Lisa Wahland
Favorite Tunes | Edition Collage | EC 527-2
Lisa Wahland And Her Trio
Marlene | Fine Music | FM 108-2
Lisa Wahlandt & Mulo Francel And Their Fabulous Bossa Band
Bossa Nova Affair | Edition Collage | EC 534-2
Mind Games
Mind Games Plays The Music Of Stan Getz & Astrud Gilberto | Edition Collage | EC 515-2
Mind Games With Claudio Roditi
Live | Edition Collage | EC 501-2
Vocal Moments | Take Twelve On CD | TT 008-2

Wahmhoff,Susanne | (cello)
Uri Caine With The Concerto Köln
Concerto Köln | Winter&Winter | 910086-2

Wahnschaffe,Felix | (assax)
Association Urbanetique
Ass Bedient | Jazz 4 Ever Records:Jazz Network | J4E 4723
Berlin Contemporary Jazz Orchestra
Berlin Contemporary Jazz Orchestra | ECM | 1409
Brass Attack
Brecht Songs | Tutu Records | 888190-2*
Geoff Goodman Quintet
Naked Eye | Tutu Records | 888214-2*

Waidtlow,Claus | (reeds,ssts)
Jens Skou Olsen Group
September Veje | dacapo | DCCD 9451
The Danish Radio Jazz Orchestra
This Train:The Danish Radio Jazz Orchestra Plays The Music Of Ray Pitts | dacapo | DCCD 9428
The Orchestra
New Skies | dacapo | DCCD 9463

Wainapel,Harvey | (as,sax,ssts)
Lajos Dudas Quintet
Jubilee Edition | double moon | CHRDM 71020

Wainwright,Connie | (g)
Hot Lips Page Band
Planet Jazz:Jazz Trumpet | Planet Jazz | 2169654-2

Wainwright,Rob | (dr)
Conte Candoli-Carl Fontana Quintet
The Complete Phoenix Recordings Vol.1 | Woofy Productions | WPCD 121
The Complete Phoenix Recordings Vol.2 | Woofy Productions | WPCD 122
The Complete Phoenix Recordings Vol.3 | Woofy Productions | WPCD 123
The Complete Phoenix Recordings Vol.4 | Woofy Productions | WPCD 124
The Complete Phoenix Recordings Vol.5 | Woofy Productions | WPCD 125
The Complete Phoenix Recordings Vol.6 | Woofy Productions | WPCD 126

Waits,Freddie | (bass-dr,gongs,bass-marimba,dr,perc)
Andrew Hill Quintet
Grass Roots | Blue Note | 522672-2
Blue Bossa | Blue Note | 795590-2
Dick Griffin Septet
The Eighth Wonder & More | Konnex Records | KCD 5059
Duke Ellington Orchestra
Continuum | Fantasy | FCD 24765-2
Gary Bartz Quartet
Libra/Another Earth | Milestone | MCD 47077-2
Gary Bartz Sextet
Libra/Another Earth | Milestone | MCD 47077-2
Gene Harris And The Three Sounds
Deep Blue-The United States Of Mind | Blue Note | 521152-2
James Moody Orchestra
The Blues And Other Colors | Original Jazz Classics | OJCCD 954-2(M 9023)
Lee Morgan Orchestra
The Last Sessin | Blue Note | 493401-2
McCoy Tyner Sextet
Asante | Blue Note | 493384-2
Pharoah Sanders Orchestra
Karma | Impulse(MCA) | 951153-2
Toots Thielemans Quartet
Images | Choice | CHCD 71007

Waits,Nasheet | (drcowbell)
Antonio Hart Group
Here I Stand | Impulse(MCA) | 951208-2
Ama Tu Sonrisa | Enja | ENJ-9404 2
James Hurt Group
Dark Grooves-Mystcal Rhythms | Blue Note | 495104-2
Jason Moran Trio
The Bandwagon | Blue Note | 591893-2
Mark Turner Quartet
Dharma Days | Warner | 9362-47998-2
New Jazz Composers Octet
Walkin' the Line | Fresh Sound Records | FSNT 151 CD
The New Jazz Composers Octet
First Step Into Reality | Fresh Sound Records | FSNT 059 CD

Waits,Tom | (gvoc)
Dave Douglas Group
Witness | RCA | 2663763-2

Wakeman,Alan | (sax,ss,tsperc)
Mike Westbrook Band
Off Abbey Road | TipToe | TIP-888805 2
Mike Westbrook Brass Band
Glad Day:Settings Of William Blake | Enja | ENJ-9376 2
Mike Westbrook Orchestra
The Orchestra Of Smith's Academy | Enja | ENJ-9358 2

Wakenius,Ulf | (gel-g)
Niels-Henning Orsted-Pedersen Trio
Those Who Were | Verve | 533232-2
Niels-Henning Orsted-Pedersen Trio With Johnny Griffin
Those Who Were | Verve | 533232-2
Niels-Henning Orsted-Pedersen/Ulf Wakenius Duo
Those Who Were | Verve | 533232-2
Niels-Henning Orsted-Pedersen/Ulf Wakenius Duo With Lisa Nilsson
Those Who Were | Verve | 533232-2

Walcott,Collin | (bottle,tabla,cl,marimba,p,dr,congas)
Collin Walcott Group
Grazing Dreams | ECM | 1096
Collin Walcott Quartet
Cloud Dance | ECM | 1062(825469-2)
David Darling Group
Cycles | ECM | 1219
Don Cherry/Nana Vasconcelos/Collin Walcott
Codona | ECM | 1132(829371-2)
Codona 2 | ECM | 1177(833332-2)
Codona 3 | ECM | 1243
Egberto Gismonti Group
Sol Do Meio Dia | ECM | 1116(829117-2)
Miles Davis Group
On The Corner | CBS | CK 63980
Oregon
Oregon | ECM | 1258(811711-2)
Crossing | ECM | 1291(825323-2)
Ralph Towner
Trios/Solos | ECM | 1025(833328-2)
Steve Eliovson-Collin Walcott
Dawn Dance | ECM | 1198
Tony Scott Group
Tony Scott | Verve | 9861063
Tony Scott-Collin Walcott
Music For Yoga Meditation And Other Joys | Verve | 835371-2

Walden,Myron | (as)
Brian Blade Group
Fellowship | Blue Note | 859417-2
Dan Faulk Quartet
Spirit In The Night | Fresh Sound Records | FSNT 024 CD
New Jazz Composers Octet
Walkin' the Line | Fresh Sound Records | FSNT 151 CD
The New Jazz Composers Octet
First Step Into Reality | Fresh Sound Records | FSNT 059 CD

Walden,Narada Michael | (dr,rhythm-arrangements,handclapping)
Al Jarreau With Band
Heaven And Earth | i.e. Music | 557852-2
Chick Corea Quartet
My Spanish Heart | Polydor | 543303-3
Mahavishnu Orchestra
Apocalypse | CBS | 467092-2
Weather Report
Black Market | CBS | 468210-2

Waldman,Randy | (keyboardsp)
Diane Schuur Quintet With B.B.King
The Best Of Diane Schuur | GRP | GRP 98882

Waldner,H. | (tuba)
Vince Mendoza With The WDR Big Band And Guests
Sketches | ACT | 9215-2

Waldron,Mal | (el-p,p,p-solotalking)
Abbey Lincoln And Her Orchestra
Straight Ahead | Candid | CCD 79015
Billie Holiday And Her All Stars
The Billie Holiday Song Book | Verve | 823246-2
Billie Holiday With Buck Clayton And The Mal Waldron Trio
Billie Holiday Story Vol.1:Jazz At The Philharmonic | Verve | 521642-2
Billie Holiday With The Mal Waldron Trio
Billie Holiday Story Vol.1:Jazz At The Philharmonic | Verve | 521642-2
Billie Holiday With The Ray Ellis Orchestra
Lady In Satin | CBS | CK 65144
Charles Mingus And His Orchestra
Charles Mingus-Passion Of A Man:The Complete Atlantic Recordings 1956-1961 | Atlantic | 8122-72871-2
Charles Mingus Jazz Workshop
Charles Mingus-Passion Of A Man:The Complete Atlantic Recordings 1956-1961 | Atlantic | 8122-72871-2
Blues & Roots | Atlantic | 8122-75205-2
The Very Best Of Charles Mingus | Rhino | 8122-79988-2
Charles Mingus Quintet
Charles Mingus-The Complete Debut Recordings | Debut | 12 DCD 4402-2
Mingus At The Bohemia | Original Jazz Classics | OJC20 045-2
The Charles Mingus Quintet+Max Roach | Original Jazz Classics | OJC20 440-2(F 6009)
Eric Dolphy Quintet
Eric Dolphy At The Five Spot Vol.2 | Original Jazz Classics | OJC20 247-2(P 7294)
Eric Dolphy-Booker Little Quintet
Eric Dolphy Birthday Celebration | Fantasy | FANCD 6085-2
At The Five Spot,Vol.1 | Original Jazz Classics | OJC20 133-2
Eric Dolphy Memorial Album | Original Jazz Classics | OJCCD 353-2
Eric Dophy Quintet
Eric Dolphy:The Complete Prestige Recordings | Prestige | 9 PRCD-4418-2
Gene Ammons And His All Stars
John Coltrane-The Prestige Recordings | Prestige | 16 PCD 4405-2
Blue Gene | Original Jazz Classics | OJC20 192-2(P 7146)
Jammin' With Gene | Original Jazz Classics | OJCCD 211-2(P 7060)
The Big Sound | Original Jazz Classics | OJCCD 651-2(P 7132)
Groove Blues | Original Jazz Classics | OJCCD 723-2(PR 7201)
The Prestige Legacy Vol.2:Battles Of Saxes | Prestige | PCD 24252-2
Gene Ammons Quartet
The Mal Waldron Memorial Album:Soul Eyes | Prestige | PRCD 11024-2
A Stranger In Town | Prestige | PRCD 24266-2
Herbie Mann Sextet
Just Wailin' | Original Jazz Classics | OJCCD 900-2(NJ 8211)
Jackie McLean Quartet
4, 5 And 6 | Original Jazz Classics | OJC 056(P 7048)
A Long Drink Of The Blues | Original Jazz Classics | OJCCD 253-2(NJ 8253)
The Jazz Giants Play Jerome Kern:Yesterdays | Prestige | PCD 24202-2
Jackie McLean Quintet
4, 5 And 6 | Original Jazz Classics | OJC 056(P 7048)
Jackie McLean Sextet
4, 5 And 6 | Original Jazz Classics | OJC 056(P 7048)
Jeanne Lee-Mal Waldron
After Hours | Owl Records | 013426-2
Jim Pepper Flying Eagle
Live At New Morning,Paris | Tutu Records | 888194-2*
John Coltrane All Stars
Dakar | Original Jazz Classics | OJC20 393-2(P 7280)
John Coltrane Quintet
John Coltrane-The Prestige Recordings | Prestige | 16 PCD 4405-2
Coltrane | Original Jazz Classics | OJC20 020-2
The Mal Waldron Memorial Album:Soul Eyes | Prestige | PRCD 11024-2
John Coltrane Sextet
John Coltrane-The Prestige Recordings | Prestige | 16 PCD 4405-2
Coltrane | Original Jazz Classics | OJC20 020-2
The Prestige Legacy Vol.1:The High Priests | Prestige | PCD 24251-2
The Mal Waldron Memorial Album:Soul Eyes | Prestige | PRCD 11024-2
John Coltrane-Paul Quinichette Quintet
John Coltrane-The Prestige Recordings | Prestige | 16 PCD 4405-2
Cattin' | Original Jazz Classics | OJCCD 460-2
Kenny Dorham Septet
Cannonball Adderley Birthday Celebration | Fantasy | FANCD 6087-2
Mal Waldron
Moods | Enja | ENJ-3021 2
The Mal Waldron Memorial Album:Soul Eyes | Prestige | PRCD 11024-2
Mal Waldron & Jim Pepper
Art Of The Duo | Tutu Records | 888106-2*
Mal Waldron Quartet
Mal,Verve,Black & Blue | Tutu Records | 888170-2*
Mal Waldron Quartet feat. Jim Pepper
The Git-Go At Utopia,Volume Two | Tutu Records | 888148-2*
Mal Waldron Quartet feat.Jim Pepper
Mal, Dance And Soul | Tutu Records | 888102-2*
Quadrologue At Utopia Vol.1 | Tutu Records | 888118-2*
Mal Waldron Sextet
John Coltrane-The Prestige Recordings | Prestige | 16 PCD 4405-2
Eric Dolphy:The Complete Prestige Recordings | Prestige | 9 PRCD-4418-2
Moods | Enja | ENJ-3021 2
Eric Dolphy Birthday Celebration | Fantasy | FANCD 6085-2
The Quest | Original Jazz Classics | OJCCD 082-2(NJ 8269)
The Jazz Giants Play Jerome Kern:Yesterdays | Prestige | PCD 24202-2
The Mal Waldron Memorial Album:Soul Eyes | Prestige | PRCD 11024-2
Mal Waldron Trio
Free At Last | ECM | 1001
Mal, Dance And Soul | Tutu Records | 888102-2*
The Jazz Giants Play Rodgers & Hart:Blue Moon | Prestige | PCD 24205-2
Mal Waldron-Nicolas Simion
Art Of The Duo:The Big Rochade | Tutu Records | 888186-2*
Marty Cook Group feat. Jim Pepper
Red,White,Black & Blue | Tutu Records | 888174-2*
Max Roach All Stars
Candid Dolphy | Candid | CCD 79033
Max Roach Quartet
Speak, Brother, Speak | Original Jazz Classics | OJCCD 646-2(F 86007)
Max Roach Sextet With Choir
It's Time | Impulse(MCA) | 951185-2
Prestige All Stars
John Coltrane-The Prestige Recordings | Prestige | 16 PCD 4405-2
Wheelin' & Dealin' | Original Jazz Classics | OJCCD 672-2(P7131)
The Prestige Legacy Vol.1:The High Priests | Prestige | PCD 24251-2
The Prestige Legacy Vol.2:Battles Of Saxes | Prestige | PCD 24252-2
The Mal Waldron Memorial Album:Soul Eyes | Prestige | PRCD 11024-2
Prestige Jazz Quartet
The Mal Waldron Memorial Album:Soul Eyes | Prestige | PRCD 11024-2
Ray Draper Sextet
Tuba Sounds | Original Jazz Classics | OJCCD 1936-2(P 7096)
Ron Carter Quintet
Eric Dolphy:The Complete Prestige Recordings | Prestige | 9 PRCD-4418-2
Eric Dolphy Birthday Celebration | Fantasy | FANCD 6085-2
Where | Original Jazz Classics | OJCCD 432-2
Steve Lacy Quartet
Reflections-Steve Lacy Plays Thelonious Monk | Original Jazz Classics | OJCCD 063-2
The Mal Waldron Memorial Album:Soul Eyes | Prestige | PRCD 11024-2
The Prestige All Stars
Olio | Original Jazz Classics | OJCCD 1004-2(P 7084)
The Prestige Jazz Quartet
The Prestige Jazz Quartet | Original Jazz Classics | OJCCD 1937-2(P 7108)

Waldrop,Don | (b-tb,tuba,tbbar-h)
Bobby Bryant Orchestra
Deep Blue-The United States Of Mind | Blue Note | 521152-2
Joe Henderson And His Orchestra
Joe Henderson:The Milestone Years | Milestone | 8MCD 4413-2
Joe Henderson Group
Jazzin' Vol.2: The Music Of Stevie Wonder | Fantasy | FANCD 6088-2
Raul De Souza Orchestra
Cannonball Adderley Birthday Celebration | Fantasy | FANCD 6087-2
Singers Unlimited With The Pat Williams Orchestra
The Singers Unlimited:Magic Voices | MPS | 539130-2
Singers Unlimited With The Patrick Williams Orchestra
The Singers Unlimited:Magic Voices | MPS | 539130-2

Walicki,Olo | (b)
Zbigniew Namyslowski-Remy Filipovitch Quintet
Go! | Album | AS 66919 CD

Walkaway |
Walkaway With Urszula Dudziak
Saturation | IN+OUT Records | 77024-2

Walker,Aaron | (drperc)
Abbey Lincoln With Her Band
Who Used To Dance | Verve | 533559-2
Shirley Scott Quintet
A Wakin' Thing | Candid | CCD 79719

Walker,Archie | (keyboardsdr)
Brainstorm feat. Chico Freeman
The Mystical Dreamer | IN+OUT Records | 7006-2
Chico Freeman And Brainstorm
Jazz Unlimited | IN+OUT Records | 7017-2

Walker,Barbara | (voc)
The Sidewalks Of New York
Tin Pan Alley:The Sidewalks Of New York | Winter&Winter | 910038-2

Walker,Bill | (b)
Sarah Vaughan And Her Band
Duke Ellington Song Book Two | Pablo | CD 2312116
Sarah Vaughan Birthday Celebration | Fantasy | FANCD 6090-2

Walker,Chris | (el-b,keyboardsvoc)
Brainstorm feat. Chico Freeman
The Mystical Dreamer | IN+OUT Records | 7006-2
Chico Freeman And Brainstorm
Jazz Unlimited | IN+OUT Records | 7017-2
Michel Petrucciani Group
Michel Petrucciani:The Blue Note Years | Blue Note | 789916-2
Music | Blue Note | 792563-2

Walker,Clinton | (tuba)
King Oliver And His Orchestra
Jazz:The Essential Collection Vol.1 | IN+OUT Records | 78011-2

Walker,David T. | (g)
Bobbi Humphrey
Blue Break Beats | Blue Note | 799106-2
Bobbi Humphrey Group
Blue Breaks Beats Vol.2 | Blue Note | 789907-2
Dee Dee Bridgewater With Band
Dee Dee Bridgewater | Atlantic | 7567-80760-2
Diane Schuur With Orchestra
Blues For Schuur | GRP | GRP 98632
The Best Of Diane Schuur | GRP | GRP 98882
Donald Byrd & His Orchestra
Blue Breaks Beats Vol.2 | Blue Note | 789907-2
Donald Byrd Orchestra
Black Byrd | Blue Note | 784466-2
Ethiopian Knights | Blue Note | 854328-2
Gene Harris Group
Blue Breaks Beats Vol.2 | Blue Note | 789907-2
Herbie Hancock Group
Man-Child | CBS | 471235-2
Stanley Turrentine And His Orchestra
Pieces Of Dream | Original Jazz Classics | OJCCD 831-2(F 9465)

Walker,Earl | (dr)
Lionel Hampton And His Orchestra
Lionel Hampton:Flying Home | Dreyfus Jazz Line | FDM 36735-2
Lionel Hampton Quartet
Lionel Hampton:Flying Home | Dreyfus Jazz Line | FDM 36735-2

Walker,Gregory | (voc)
Herbie Hancock Group
Monster | CBS | 486571-2

Walker,Hugh | (dr)
Big John Patton Quartet
Got A Good Thing Goin' | Blue Note | 580731-2
George Braith Quartet
So Blue So Funky-Heroes Of The Hammond | Blue Note | 796563-2

Walker,James | (fl,alto-fl,piccolovoc)
Miles Davis-Marcus Miller Group
Siesta(Soundtrack) | Warner | 7599-25655-2

Walker,Jim | (fl,pan-flg)
Free Flight
Jazzrock-Anthology Vol.3:Fusion | Zounds | CD 27100555

Walker,Joe Louis | (g,slide-g,vocnational-steel-g)
James Cotton Group
Deep In The Blues | Verve | 529849-2
Joe Louis Walker
Deep In The Blues | Verve | 529849-2

Walker,Johnny | (bs,cl,reedstp)
Axel Zwingenberger With The Lionel Hampton Big Band
The Boogie Woogie Album | Vagabond | VRCD 8.88008

Walker,Mark | (dr,hand-dr,perc,prepared-kit)
Oregon
Northwest Passage | Intuition Records | INT 3191-2
Patricia Barber Group
Modern Cool | Blue Note | 521811-2
Patricia Barber Quartet
Café Blue | Blue Note | 521810-2
Ralph Towner-Mark Walker

Northwest Passage | Intuition Records | INT 3191-2
Walker,Melissa | (voc)
Melissa Walker And Her Band
I Saw The Sky | Enja | ENJ-9409 2
Walker,Mike | (g)
Roy Powell Quartet
North By Northwest | Nagel-Heyer | CD 2013
Walker,Ray | (g)
Ray Walker-John Pisano
Affinity | Jardis Records | JRCD 20032
Ray Walker-John Pisano Trio
Affinity | Jardis Records | JRCD 20032
Jazz Guitar Highlights 1 | Jardis Records | JRCD 20141
Walker,T-Bone | (g,pvoc)
JATP All Stars
J.A.T.P. In London 1969 | Pablo | 2CD 2620119
Welcome To Jazz At The Philharmonic | Fantasy | FANCD 6081-2
Super Black Blues Band
Super Black Blues Vol.II | RCA | 2663874-2
T-Bone Walker And His Band
Atlantic Jazz: Kansas City | Atlantic | 7567-81701-2
Wall,Dan | (org,psynth)
Dan Wall Quartet
Off The Wall | Enja | ENJ-9310 2
Dan Wall Trio
Off The Wall | Enja | ENJ-9310 2
John Abercrombie Sextet
Open Land | ECM | 1683(557652-2)
John Abercrombie Trio
While We're Young | ECM | 1489
Speak To The Devil | ECM | 1511
Tactics | ECM | 1623(533680-2)
Wall,Murray | (b)
Marty Grosz Quartet
Just For Fun! | Nagel-Heyer | CD 039
Warren Vaché And The New York City All-Star Big Band
Swingtime! | Nagel-Heyer | CD 059
Warren Vaché Quartet
What Is There To Say? | Nagel-Heyer | CD 056
Warren Vaché Quintet
Warren Plays Warrey | Nagel-Heyer | CD 033
Blues Of Summer | Nagel-Heyer | NH 1011
Warren Vaché With Joe Puma
Blues Of Summer | Nagel-Heyer | NH 1011
Wallace,Bennie | (ssts)
Bennie Wallace Quartet
Bennie Wallace Plays Monk | Enja | ENJ-3091 2
The Talk Of The Town | Enja | ENJ-7091 2
Bennie Wallace In Berlin | Enja | ENJ-9425 2
Bennie Wallace Trio
Bennie Wallace Plays Monk | Enja | ENJ-3091 2
Eric Watson Quartet
Full Metal Quartet | Owl Records | 159572-2
Wallace,Billy | (p)
Billy Mitchell Sextet
This Is Billy Mitchell | Smash | 065507-2
Max Roach Quintet
Clifford Brown-Max Roach:Alone Together-The Best Of The Mercury Years | Verve | 526373-2
Wallace,Cedric | (bdr)
Fats Waller And His Rhythm
Planet Jazz:Fats Waller | Planet Jazz | 2152058-2
Fats Waller-Cedric Wallace
Fats Waller:The Complete Associated Transcription Sessions 1935-1939 | Jazz Unlimited | JUCD 2076
Wallace,Matt | (as,tsvoc)
Maynard Ferguson And His Big Bop Nouveau Band
Maynard Ferguson '93-Footpath Café | Hot Shot Records | HSR 8312-2
Wallace,Simon | (p)
Nicki Leighton-Thomas Group
Forbidden Games | Candid | CCD 79778
Wallace,Sippie | (pvoc)
Sippie Wallace With Axel Zwingenberger
Sippie Wallace/Axel Zwingenberger And The Friends Of Boogie Woogie Vol.1 | Vagabond | VRCD 8.84002
An Evening With Sippie Wallace | Vagabond | VRCD 8.86006
Sippie Wallace With King Oliver And Hersal Thomas
Jazz:The Essential Collection Vol.1 | IN+OUT Records | 78011-2
Wallace,Wayne | (tb)
Pucho & His Latin Soul Brothers
Rip A Dip | Milestone | MCD 9247-2
Wallace,Wesley | (pvoc)
Wesley Wallace
Boogie Woogie | Laserlight | 24321
Wallander,Ulf | (ss,tsperc)
Beng Berger Band
Bitter Funeral Beer | ECM | 1179
Wallbank,A. | (b-cl)
Dee Dee Bridgewater With Orchestra
Dear Ella | Verve | 539102-2
Waller,Thomas 'Fats' | (org,voc,org-solo,p,celeste,bells)
A Jam Session At Victor
Planet Jazz:Fats Waller | Planet Jazz | 2152058-2
Planet Jazz:Jazz Greatest Hits | Planet Jazz | 2169648-2
Alberta Hunter
Planet Jazz:Female Jazz Vocalists | Planet Jazz | 2169656-2
Fats Waller
Planet Jazz:Fats Waller | Planet Jazz | 2152058-2
Fats Waller:The Complete Associated Transcription Sessions 1935-1939 | Jazz Unlimited | JUCD 2076
Fats Waller And His Buddies
Planet Jazz:Jack Teagarden | Planet Jazz | 2161236-2
Jazz:The Essential Collection Vol.3 | IN+OUT Records | 78013-2
Fats Waller And His Rhythm
Planet Jazz:Fats Waller | Planet Jazz | 2152058-2
Planet Jazz Sampler | Planet Jazz | 2152326-2
Planet Jazz:Male Jazz Vocalists | Planet Jazz | 2169657-2
Fats Waller:The Complete Associated Transcription Sessions 1935-1939 | Jazz Unlimited | JUCD 2076
Fats Waller Groups
100 Ans De Jazz:Fats Waller | RCA | 2177829-2
Fats Waller-Cedric Wallace
Fats Waller:The Complete Associated Transcription Sessions 1935-1939 | Jazz Unlimited | JUCD 2076
Fats Waller-Rudy Powell
Fats Waller:The Complete Associated Transcription Sessions 1935-1939 | Jazz Unlimited | JUCD 2076
Jack Teagarden And His Orchestra
Jazz:The Essential Collection Vol.3 | IN+OUT Records | 78013-2
Louisiana Sugar Babes
Planet Jazz:Jazz Trumpet | Planet Jazz | 2169654-2
McKinney's Cotton Pickers
Jazz:The Essential Collection Vol.3 | IN+OUT Records | 78013-2
Waller,Woody | (reeds)
Benny Moten's Kansas City Orchestra
Planet Jazz:Jimmy Rushing | RCA | 2165371-2
Wallez,Gus | (drtb)
Earl Hines Trio
Jazz In Paris:Earl Hines-Paris One Night Stand | EmArCy | 548207-2 PMS
Michel Legrand Trio
Jazz In Paris:Michel Legrand-Paris Jazz Piano | EmArCy | 548148-2 PMS
Swingle Singers
Jazz Sebastian Bach | Philips | 542552-2
Walli,Hasse | (gperc)
Piirpauke
Piirpauke-Global Servisi | JA & RO | JARO 4150-2
Wallin,Bengt-Arne | (tpfl-h)
Bengt-Arne Wallin Orchestra
The Birth+Rebirth Of Swedish Folk Jazz | ACT | 9254-2
Wallington,George | (pp-solo)
Terry Gibbs Septet
Early Stan | Original Jazz Classics | OJCCD 654-2(P 7255)
Zoot Sims-Al Cohn Sextet
The Brothers | Original Jazz Classics | OJCCD 008-2
Wallis,Bob | (tpvoc)
Bob Wallis Storyville Jazzmen
The Golden Years Of Revival Jazz,Vol.7 | Storyville | STCD 5512
Mr.Acker Bilk And His Paramount Jazz Band
The Golden Years Of Revival Jazz,Vol.2 | Storyville | STCD 5507
The Golden Years Of Revival Jazz,Vol.5 | Storyville | STCD 5510
The Golden Years Of Revival Jazz,Vol.6 | Storyville | STCD 5511
The Golden Years Of Revival Jazz,Vol.7 | Storyville | STCD 5512
The Golden Years Of Revival Jazz,Vol.9 | Storyville | STCD 5514
The Golden Years Of Revival Jazz,Vol.12 | Storyville | STCD 5517
The Golden Years Of Revival Jazz,Vol.13 | Storyville | STCD 5518
The Golden Years Of Revival Jazz,Vol.14 | Storyville | STCD 5519
The Golden Years Of Revibal Jazz,Vol.15 | Storyville | STCD 5520
Wallisch,Thomas | (gel-g)
Dominik Grimm-Thomas Wallisch Trio
A Brighter Day | Edition Collage | EC 510-2
Wallstädt,Niels | (tp)
Landes Jugend Jazz Orchester Hessen
Touch Of Lips | hr music.de | hrmj 004-01 CD
Wallumrod,Christian | (pharmonium)
Christian Wallumrod Ensemble
Sofienberg Variations | ECM | 1809(017067-2)
Christian Wallumrod Trio
No Birch | ECM | 1628(537344-2)
Trygve Seim-Oyvind Braekke-Per Oddvar Johansen Orchestra
The Source And Different Cikadas | ECM | 1764(014432-2)
Walp,Charlie | (tp)
Billy Eckstine And His Orchestra
Blue Velvet: Crooners, Swooners And Velvet Vocals | Blue Note | 521153-2
Cal Tjader's Orchestra
Tjader Plays Mambo | Original Jazz Classics | OJCCD 274-2(F 3221)
Woody Herman And His Orchestra
Woody Herman:Four Brother | Dreyfus Jazz Line | FDM 36722-2
Walrath,Jack | (tp,arr,fl-h,mouthpiece,voiceperc)
Bernard Purdie's Soul To Jazz
Bernard Purdie's Soul To Jazz II | ACT | 9253-2
Charles Mingus Orchestra
Three Or Four Shades Of Blues | Atlantic | 7567-81403-2
Cumbia & Jazz Fusion | Atlantic | 8122-71785-2
Charles Mingus Quintet
Changes One | Rhino | 8122-71403-2
Changes Two | Rhino | 8122-71404-2
Charles Mingus Sextet
Changes Two | Rhino | 8122-71404-2
Dannie Richmond Quintet
Three Or Four Shades Of Dannie Richmond Quintet | Tutu Records | 888120-2*
Miles Davis With Gil Evans Orchestra, The George Gruntz Concert Jazz Band And Guests
Miles & Quincy Live At Montreux | Warner | 9362-45221-2
Mingus Big Band 93
Nostalgia In Times Square | Dreyfus Jazz Line | FDM 36559-2
Neal Kirkwood Octet
Neal Kirkwood Octet | Timescrapper | TSCR 9612
Walsh,Danny | (as,tssax)
Lenny White Group
Present Tense | Hip Bop | HIBD 8004
Renderers Of Spirit | Hip Bop | HIBD 8014
Hot Jazz Bisquits | Hip Bop | HIBD 8801
Walsh,Ed | (synthsynth-programming)
Dave Grusin Group
Mountain Dance | GRP | GRP 95072
Walsh,Francine | (v)
Charlie Haden Quartet West With Strings
The Art Of The Song | Verve | 547403-2
Walter,Andreas | (b)
Jerry Granelli UFB
News From The Street | VeraBra Records | CDVBR 2146-2
Rinde Eckert Group
Story In,Story Out | Intuition Records | INT 3507-2
Walter,Hans | (b)
Helmut Zacharias mit seinem Orchester
Ich Habe Rhythmus | Bear Family Records | BCD 15642 AH
Walter,Peter | (keyboards,marimba,dr,perc,p)
Hugo Read Group
Songs Of A Wayfarer | Nabel Records:Jazz Network | CD 4653
Maria Joao Quintet
Conversa | Nabel Records:Jazz Network | CD 4628
Peter Herborn's Acute Insights
Peter Herborn's Acute Insights | JMT Edition | 919017-2
Walters,George | (tp)
June Christy With The Johnny Guarnieri Quintet
June Christy And The Johnny Guarnieri Quintet (1949) | Jazz Unlimited | JUCD 2084
Walters,Ted | (b,tubael-b)
Oriental Wind
Life Road | JA & RO | JARO 4113-2
Walters,Teddy | (el-gg)
Anita O'Day With Gene Krupa And His Orchestra
Let Me Off Uptown:Anita O'Day With Gene Krupa | CBS | CK 65625
Billie Holiday With Eddie Heywood And His Orchestra
Billie Holiday:The Complete Commodore Recordings | GRP | 543272-2
Cozy Cole All Stars
Ultimate Coleman Hawkins selected by Sonny Rollins | Verve | 557538-2
Jazz:The Essential Collection Vol.3 | IN+OUT Records | 78013-2
Waltkins,Doug | (b)
John Coltrane All Stars
Dakar | Original Jazz Classics | OJC20 393-2(P 7280)
Walton,Cedar | (keyboards,p,el-pp-solo)
Abbey Lincoln With The Max Roach Sextet
Abbey Is Blue | Original Jazz Classics | OJC20 069-2(RLP 1153)
Art Blakey And The Jazz Messengers
True Blue | Blue Note | 534032-2
Wayne Shorter:The Classic Blue Note Recordings | Blue Note | 540856-2
Caravan | Original Jazz Classics | OJC20 038-2
Ugetsu | Original Jazz Classics | OJC20 090-2(RLP 9464)
Art Farmer/Benny Golson Jazztet
The Jazztet At Birdhouse | Argo | 589762-2
Benny Golson Band
Benny Golson:Free | GRP | 951816-2
Blue Mitchell Quintet
Out Of The Blue | Original Jazz Classics | OJCCD 667-2(RLP 1131)
Cedar Walton Quartet
The Story Of Jazz Piano | Laserlight | 24653
First Set | Steeplechase | SCCD 31085
Third Set | Steeplechase | SCCD 31179
Cedar Walton Quintet
Soul Cycle | Original Jazz Classics | OJCCD 847-2(P 7693)
Cedar Walton Trio
God Bless Jug And Sonny | Prestige | PCD 11019-2
Left Bank Encores | Prestige | PRCD 11022-2
Clifford Jordan Quartet
Spellbound | Original Jazz Classics | OJCCD 766-2(RLP 9340)
Firm Roots | Steeplechase | SCCD 31033
Clifford Jordan Quintet
Mosaic | Milestone | MCD 47092-2
Dexter Gordon Quartet
Dexter Gordon Birthday Celebration | Fantasy | FANCD 6082-2
Tangerine | Original Jazz Classics | OJCCD 1041-2(P 10091)
Dexter Gordon Quintet
Dexter Gordon Birthday Celebration | Fantasy | FANCD 6082-2
Tangerine | Original Jazz Classics | OJCCD 1041-2(P 10091)
Generation | Original Jazz Classics | OJCCD 836-2(P 10069)
The Jazz Giants Play Miles Davis:Milestones | Prestige | PCD 24225-2
Donald Byrd Quintet
Slow Drag | Blue Note | 535560-2
Donald Byrd Sextet
Blue Breaks Beats Vol.2 | Blue Note | 789907-2
Blue Break Beats | Blue Note | 799106-2
Blackjack | Blue Note | 821286-2
Eddie Harris Group
Here Comes The Judge | CBS | 492533-2
Eddie Harris Quartet
The Best Of Eddie Harris | Atlantic | 7567-81370-2
Eddie Harris Quintet
The Best Of Eddie Harris | Atlantic | 7567-81370-2
Atlantic Saxophones | Rhino | 8122-71256-2
Eric Alexander Quartet
Man With A Horn | Milestone | MCD 9293-2
Eric Alexander Sextet
Man With A Horn | Milestone | MCD 9293-2
Essence All Stars
Hot Jazz Bisquits | Hip Bop | HIBD 8801
Frank Morgan Quartet
Easy Living | Original Jazz Classics | OJCCD 833-2(C 14013)
Freddie Hubbard Orchestra
The Body And The Soul | Impulse(MCA) | 951183-2
Freddie Hubbard Septet
The Body And The Soul | Impulse(MCA) | 951183-2
Freddie Hubbard Sextet
Hub Cap | Blue Note | 542302-2
Freddy Cole With Band
Le Grand Freddy:Freddy Cole Sings The Music Of Michel Legrand | Fantasy | FCD 9683-2
Freddy Cole With The Cedar Walton Trio
Love Makes The Changes | Fantasy | FCD 9681-2
Freddy Cole With The Cedar Walton Trio And Grover Washington Jr.
Love Makes The Changes | Fantasy | FCD 9681-2
Freddy Cole With The Eric Alexander Band
Love Makes The Changes | Fantasy | FCD 9681-2
Gene Ammons Quartet
God Bless Jug And Sonny | Prestige | PCD 11019-2
Gene Ammons-Sonny Stitt Quintet
God Bless Jug And Sonny | Prestige | PCD 11019-2
Left Bank Encores | Prestige | PRCD 11022-2
Houston Person Quintet
Trust In Me | Prestige | PCD 24264-2
Houston Person Sextet
Blue Odyssey | Original Jazz Classics | OJCCD 1045-2(P 7566)
Ian Shaw With Band
Soho Stories | Milestone | MCD 9316-2
Ian Shaw With The Cedar Walton Trio
In A New York Minute | Milestone | MCD 9297-2
Joe Henderson Septet
Mode For Joe | Blue Note | 591894-2
The Blue Note Years-The Best Of Joe Henderson | Blue Note | 795627-2
John Coltrane Quartet
John Coltrane-The Heavyweight Champion:The Complete Atlantic Recordings | Atlantic | 8122-71984-2
Giant Steps | Atlantic | 8122-75203-2
Lee Morgan Quintet
Sonic Boom | Blue Note | 590414-2
Caramba! | Blue Note | 853358-2
Lee Morgan Sextet
The Sixth Sense | Blue Note | 522467-2
Lucky Thompson Quartet
The Art Of Saxophone | Laserlight | 24652
Milt Jackson And His Colleagues
Bag's Bag | Original Jazz Classics | OJCCD 935-2(2310842)
Milt Jackson And His Orchestra
Reverence And Compassion | Reprise | 9362-45204-2
Milt Jackson Quartet
Milt Jackson Birthday Celebration | Fantasy | FANCD 6079-2
The Jazz Giants Play Harold Arlen:Blues In The Night | Prestige | PCD 24201-2
Milt Jackson Quintet
Milt Jackson At The Kosei Nenkin | Pablo | 2620103-2
Milt Jackson-Ray Brown Quartet
It Don't Mean A Thing If You Can't Tap Your Foot To It | Original Jazz Classics | OJCCD 601-2
Pat Martino Quintet
Strings! | Original Jazz Classics | OJCCD 223-2(P 7547)
Pat Martino Septet
Strings! | Original Jazz Classics | OJCCD 223-2(P 7547)
Ray Brown Trio
Something For Lester | Original Jazz Classics | OJCCD 412-2
Sonny Criss Quartet
The Beat Goes On! | Original Jazz Classics | OJCCD 1051-2(P 7558)
Sonny Red (Kyner) Quartet
Red,Blue & Green | Milestone | MCD 47086-2
Sonny Stitt Quartet
God Bless Jug And Sonny | Prestige | PCD 11019-2
Walton,Cedric | (b)
Freddie Hubbard Orchestra
The Body And The Soul | Impulse(MCA) | 951183-2
Walton,Greely | (cl,tsreeds)
Louis Armstrong And His Orchestra
Louis Armstrong:Swing That Music | Laserlight | 36056
Swing Legends:Louis Armstrong | Nimbus Records | NI 2012
Walton,Jon | (ts)
Artie Shaw And His Orchestra
Planet Jazz:Jazz Trumpet | Planet Jazz | 2169654-2
Peggy Lee With The Benny Goodman Orchestra
Peggy Lee & Benny Goodman:The Complete Recordings 1941-1947 | CBS | C2K 65686
Waltzer,Ben | (p)
Ben Waltzer Quintet
In Metropolitan Motion | Fresh Sound Records | FSNT 082 CD
Ben Waltzer Trio
For Good | Fresh Sound Records | FSNT 013 CD
Georgina Weinstein With Her Quartet
Come Rain Or Come Shine | Fresh Sound Records | FSNT 020 CD
Georgina Weinstein With Her Trio
Come Rain Or Come Shine | Fresh Sound Records | FSNT 020 CD
The Waltzer-McHenry Quartet
Jazz Is Where You Find It | Fresh Sound Records | FSNT 021 CD
Waltzer,Phil | (as)
Louis Armstrong And His Orchestra
Louis Armstrong:Swing That Music | Laserlight | 36056
Wamble,Doug | (gbj)
Cassandra Wilson Group
Traveling Miles | Blue Note | 854123-2
Lincoln Center Jazz Orchestra
Big Train | CBS | CK 69860
Wanderley,Walter | (orgp)
Astrud Gilberto With The Walter Wanderley Quartet
A Certain Smile A Certain Sadness | Verve | 557449-2
Astrud Gilberto With The Walter Wanderley Quintet
A Certain Smile A Certain Sadness | Verve | 557449-2
Astrud Gilberto With The Walter Wanderley Quintet
Verve Jazz Masters 9:Astrud Gilberto | Verve | 519824-2
Astrud Gilberto With The Walter Wanderley Trio
This Is Astrud Gilberto | Verve | 825064-2
Astrud Gilberto-Walter Wanderley

A Certain Smile A Certain Sadness | Verve | 557449-2

Wanderlust |
Wanderlust
Border Crossing | Laika Records | 35100812
Wanderlust + Guests
Full Bronte | Laika Records | 35101412

Wangenheim,Ulrich | (fl,asss)
Clark Terry With The Summit Jazz Orchestra
Clark | Edition Collage | EC 530-2
Mind Games With Claudio Roditi
Live | Edition Collage | EC 501-2
Vocal Moments | Take Twelve On CD | TT 008-2

Wantjc,Peter | (dr)
Old Merrytale Jazz Band
The Very Best Of Dixieland Jazz | Verve | 535529-2

Wanzo,Mel | (tb)
Big Joe Turner With The Count Basie Orchestra
Flip Flop And Fly | Original Jazz Classics | OJCCD 1053-2(2310937)
Count Basie And His Orchestra
Afrique | RCA | 2179618-2
Fun Time | Pablo | 2310945-2
Count Basie: Salle Pleyel, April 17th, 1972 | Laserlight | 36127
Jazz Dance | Original Jazz Classics | OJCCD 1002-2(1210890)
I Told You So | Original Jazz Classics | OJCCD 824-2(2310767)
Digital III At Montreux | Original Jazz Classics | OJCCD 996-2(2308223)
The Jazz Giants Play Harry Warren:Lullaby Of Broadway | Prestige | PCD 24204-2
Count Basie Big Band
Montreux '77 | Original Jazz Classics | OJCCD 377-2
Diane Schuur With The Count Basie Orchestra
The Best Of Diane Schuur | GRP | GRP 98882
Ella Fitzgerald With Count Basie And His Orchestra
Digital III At Montreux | Original Jazz Classics | OJCCD 996-2(2308223)
Ella Fitzgerald With The Count Basie Orchestra
Bluella:Ella Fitzgerald Sings The Blues | Pablo | 2310960-2
For The Love Of Ella Fitzgerald | Verve | 841765-2
Milt Jackson Orchestra
Sarah Vaughan Birthday Celebration | Fantasy | FANCD 6090-2
Milt Jackson With The Count Basie Orchestra
To Bags...With Love:Memorial Album | Pablo | 2310967-2
Milt Jackson Birthday Celebration | Fantasy | FANCD 6079-2
Milt Jackson + Count Basie + Big Band Vol.1 | Original Jazz Classics | OJCCD 740-2(2310822)
Milt Jackson + Count Basie + Big Band Vol.2 | Original Jazz Classics | OJCCD 741-2(2310823)

Ward,Carlos | (as,ts,fl,saxss)
Abdullah Ibrahim And Ekaya
Water From An Ancient Well | TipToe | TIP-888812 2
Carla Bley Band
Dinner Music | Watt | 6(825815-2)
Don Cherry Group
Multi Kulti | A&M Records | 395323-2
Ed Blackwell Project
Vol.1:What It Is? | Enja | ENJ-7089 2
Vol.2:What It Be Like? | Enja | ENJ-8054 2
Karl Berger-Carlos Ward Duo
Conversations | IN+OUT Records | 77027-2
Paul Motian Quintet
Tribute | ECM | 1048
The Carla Bley Band
Social Studies | Watt | 11(831831-2)

Ward,David 'The Cat' | (g,keyboards,dr,perc)
Marcus Miller Group
Tales | Dreyfus Jazz Line | FDM 36571-2
Live & More | Dreyfus Jazz Line | FDM 36585-2

Ward,Helen | (voc)
Benny Goodman And His Orchestra
Planet Jazz:Benny Goodman | Planet Jazz | 2152054-2
Planet Jazz:Swing | Planet Jazz | 2169651-2

Ward,Jackie | (voc)
Dee Dee Bridgewater With Band
Dee Dee Bridgewater | Atlantic | 7567-80760-2

Ward,John | (dr)
Joe Turner And Friends
The Giant Of Stride Piano In Switzerland | Jazz Connaisseur | JCCD 9106-2

Ward,Michael | (percts)
Maceo Parker Group
Southern Exposure | Minor Music | 801033

Wardoye | (peking,krincing,kendang,rebana)
Norbert Stein Pata Masters meets Djaduk Ferianto Kua Etnika
Pata Java | Pata Musik | PATA 16 CD

Ware,David S. | (fl,ts,foot,saxello,strich)
Beaver Harris & Davis S.Ware
African Drums | Owl Records | 018356-2
Cecil Taylor Unit
Dark To Themselves | Enja | ENJ-2084 2

Ware,Leon | (voc)
Quincy Jones And His Orchestra
Verve Jazz Masters Vol.59:Toots Thielemans | Verve | 535271-2

Ware,Leonard | (el-gg)
Kansas City Six
From Spiritual To Swing | Vanguard | VCD 169/71
Sidney Bechet And His Orchestra
Sidney Bechet:Summertime | Dreyfus Jazz Line | FDM 36712-2

Ware,Wilbur | (b)
Blue Mitchell Sextet
Blue Mitchell Big 6 | Original Jazz Classics | OJCCD 615-2(RLP 12-273)
Clifford Jordan Quintet
Mosaic | Milestone | MCD 47092-2
Coleman Hawkins Quartet
Monk's Music | Original Jazz Classics | OJC20 084-2
Gerry Mulligan-Thelonious Monk Quartet
Mulligan Meets Monk | Original Jazz Classics | OJC20 301-2(RLP 1106)
Grant Green Trio
Standards | Blue Note | 821284-2
Kenny Drew-Wilbur Ware
The Jazz Giants Play Harry Warren:Lullaby Of Broadway | Prestige | PCD 24204-2
Matthew Gee All-Stars
Jazz By Gee! | Original Jazz Classics | OJCCD 1884-2(RLP 221)
Sonny Clark All Stars
Dial S For Sonny | Blue Note | 0675621
Sonny Clark Trio
Dial S For Sonny | Blue Note | 0675621
Blue Note Plays Gershwin | Blue Note | 520808-2
Sonny Rollins Trio
A Night At The Village Vanguard | Blue Note | 499795-2
Ballads | Blue Note | 537562-2
The Blue Note Years-The Best Of Sonny Rollins | Blue Note | 793203-2
Sonny Rollins:The Blue Note Recordings | Blue Note | 821371-2
Jazz Profile:Sonny Rollins | Blue Note | 823516-2
Thelonious Monk Quartet
Thelonious Monk:85th Birthday Celebration | zyx records | FANCD 6076-2
Thelonious Monk With John Coltrane | Jazzland | JZSA 946-6
Thelonious Monk With John Coltrane | Original Jazz Classics | OJC20 039-2
Thelonious Himself | Original Jazz Classics | OJCCD 254-2
Thelonious Monk Septet
Thelonious Monk:85th Birthday Celebration | zyx records | FANCD 6076-2
Thelonious Monk With John Coltrane | Jazzland | JZSA 946-6
Thelonious Monk With John Coltrane | Original Jazz Classics | OJC20 039-2
Monk's Music | Original Jazz Classics | OJC20 084-2
Thelonious Monk Trio
Thelonious Monk:85th Birthday Celebration | zyx records | FANCD 6076-2

Thelonious Monk-Gerry Mulligan Quartet
Thelonious Monk:85th Birthday Celebration | zyx records | FANCD 6076-2
Tina Brooks Quintet
The Waiting Game | Blue Note | 540536-2

Warfield Jr.,Tim | (ss,tsvoice)
Christian McBride Group
A Family Affair | Verve | 557554-2
Nicholas Payton Quintet
Nick@Night | Verve | 547598-2
Payton's Place | Verve | 557327-2
Nicholas Payton Sextet
Gumbo Nouveau | Verve | 531199-2
Shirley Scott Quintet
A Wakin' Thing | Candid | CCD 79719

Waring,Rob | (vib)
Silje Nergard Group with Strings
Nightwatch | EmArCy | 9865648

Warland,Jean | (bel-b)
Kenny Clarke Quartet
Jazz In Paris:Kenny Clarke Sextet Plays André Hodair | EmArCy | 834542-2 PMS
Kenny Clarke Quintet
Jazz In Paris:Kenny Clarke Sextet Plays André Hodair | EmArCy | 834542-2 PMS
Kenny Clarke Sextet
Jazz In Paris:Kenny Clarke Sextet Plays André Hodair | EmArCy | 834542-2 PMS
Kenny Clarke-Francy Boland Big Band
Three Latin Adventures | MPS | 529095-2
Francy Boland-Fellini 712 | MPS | 9814805

Warleight,Ray | (as,fl,alto-fl,piccolo,ss,pan-pipe)
Kenny Wheeler Ensemble
Music For Large & Small Ensembles | ECM | 1415/16
Ronnie Scott And The Band
Live At Ronnie Scott's | CBS | 494439-2

Warlop,Michel | (ld,v,arrvoc)
Andre Pasdoc With The Orchestra Vola
Jazz In Paris:Django Reinhardt-Django Et Compagnie | EmArCy | 549241-2 PMS
Coleman Hawkins With Michel Warlop And His Orchestra
Django Reinhardt All Star Sessions | Capitol | 531577-2
Eddie South/Stephane Grappelli Quintet
Django/Django In Rome 1949-1050 | BGO Records | BGOCD 366
Michel Warlop Et Son Orchestre
Jazz In Paris:Django Reinhardt-Django Et Compagnie | EmArCy | 549241-2 PMS
Quintet Du Hot Club De France
Django/Django In Rome 1949-1050 | BGO Records | BGOCD 366
Yvonne Louis With The Orchestra Vola
Jazz In Paris:Django Reinhardt-Django Et Compagnie | EmArCy | 549241-2 PMS

Warnaar,Brad | (fr-h)
Singers Unlimited With Rob McConnell And The Boss Brass
The Singers Unlimited:Magic Voices | MPS | 539130-2
The Quincy Jones-Sammy Nestico Orchestra
Basie & Beyond | Warner | 9362-47792-2

Warner,Albert | (tb)
Eureka Brass Band
Atlantic Jazz: New Orleans | Atlantic | 7567-81700-2

Warner,Eddie | (ld)
Lionel Hampton And His Orchestra
Planet Jazz:Lionel Hampton | Planet Jazz | 2152059-2

Warner,Elmer | (g)
Louis Armstrong And His Orchestra
Best Of The Complete RCA Victor Recordings | RCA | 2663636-2
Louis Armstrong:A 100th Birthday Celebration | RCA | 2663694-2
Louis Armstrong:C'est Si Bon | Dreyfus Jazz Line | FDM 36730-2
Swing Legends:Louis Armstrong | Nimbus Records | NI 2012

Warner,Joseph | (b)
Joseph Warner Quartet
Mood Pieces | Jardis Records | JRCD 9921

Warner,Malcom-Jamal | (talkingb)
Terri Lyne Carrington Group
Jazz Is A Spirit | ACT | 9408-2

Warnes,Jennifer | (voc)
Rob Wasserman Duet
Duets | GRP | GRP 97122

Warren,Earl | (as,arr,voc,bs,cl,fl,ssreeds)
Billie Holiday And Her Orchestra
Billie's Love Songs | Nimbus Records | NI 2000
Count Basie And His Orchestra
Planet Jazz:Count Basie | Planet Jazz | 2152068-2
Jazz Collection:Count Basie | Laserlight | 24368
Jazz:The Essential Collection Vol.3 | IN+OUT Records | 78013-2
From Spiritual To Swing | Vanguard | VCD 169/71
Harry James And His Orchestra
The Legends Of Swing | Laserlight | 24659
Helen Humes With James P. Johnson And The Count Basie Orchestra
From Spiritual To Swing | Vanguard | VCD 169/71
Jimmy Rushing With Count Basie And His Orchestra
From Spiritual To Swing | Vanguard | VCD 169/71
Louis Jordan With The Nelson Riddle Orchestra
Louis Jordan-Let The Good Times Roll: The Complete Decca Recordings 1938-1954 | Bear Family Records | BCD 15557 IH
Milt Jackson Orchestra
Milt Jackson Birthday Celebration | Fantasy | FANCD 6079-2
Big Bags | Original Jazz Classics | OJCCD 366-2(RLP 9429)

Warren,Ed | (tp)
Don Ellis Orchestra
Electric Bath | CBS | CK 65522

Warren,Edward 'Butch' | (b)
Booker Ervin Quintet
Exultation! | Original Jazz Classics | OJCCD 835-2(P 7293)
Dexter Gordon Quartet
Go! | Blue Note | 498794-2
Dexter Gordon:Ballads | Blue Note | 796579-2
The Best Of Blue Note Vol.2 | Blue Note | 797960-2
Jazz Profile:Dexter Gordon | Blue Note | 823514-2
Midnight Blue(The [Be]witching Hour) | Blue Note | 854365-2
Don Wilkerson Quintet
Preach Brother! | Blue Note | 0677212
Blue N' Groovy | Blue Note | 780679-2
Donald Byrd Orchestra With Voices
True Blue | Blue Note | 534032-2
The Best Of Blue Note | Blue Note | 796110-2
Donald Byrd Quintet
Herbie Hancock:The Complete Blue Note Sixties Sessions | Blue Note | 495569-2
Free Form | Blue Note | 595961-2
Donald Byrd Septet + Voices
A New Perspective | Blue Note | 499006-2
Grant Green Quintet
Feelin' The Spirit | Blue Note | 746822-2
Hank Mobley Quintet
No Room For Squares | Blue Note | 524539-2
Herbie Hancock Quintet
Herbie Hancock:The Complete Blue Note Sixties Sessions | Blue Note | 495569-2
The Best Of Blue Note Vol.2 | Blue Note | 797960-2
Cantaloupe Island | Blue Note | 829331-2
Takin' Off | Blue Note | 837643-2
Jackie McLean Quartet
A Fickle Sonance | Blue Note | 524544-2
Jackie McLean Quintet
Herbie Hancock:The Complete Blue Note Sixties Sessions | Blue Note | 495569-2
Vertigo | Blue Note | 522669-2

A Fickle Sonance | Blue Note | 524544-2
Joe Henderson Quintet
Page One | Blue Note | 498795-2
The Blue Note Years-The Best Of Joe Henderson | Blue Note | 795627-2
Kenny Dorham Quintet
Una Mas | Blue Note | 521228-2
Thelonious Monk And His Orchestra
Greatest Hits | CBS | CK 65422
Thelonious Monk Quartet
Monk At Newport 1963 & 1965 | CBS | C2K 63905
Greatest Hits | CBS | CK 65422
Thelonious Monk Quartet With Pee Wee Russell
Monk At Newport 1963 & 1965 | CBS | C2K 63905

Warren,Goeff | (fl,keyboardsss)
Enver Ismailov & Geoff Warren
Art Of The Duo:Dancing Over The Moon | Tutu Records | 888168-2*
Ku-umba Frank Lacy & The Poker Bigband
Songs From The Musical 'Poker' | Tutu Records | 888150-2*

Warren,John | (cond,fl,asbs)
John Surman Orchestra
How Many Clouds Can You See? | Deram | 844882-2
John Surman-John Warren Group
The Brass Project | ECM | 1478

Warren,Leon | (g)
B.B.King And His Band
Live At San Quentin | MCA | MCD 06103

Warren,Mervyn | (voc)
Take 6
Goldmine | Reprise | 7599-25670-2
So Much To Say | Reprise | 7599-25892-2
He Is Christmas | Reprise | 7599-26665-2
Take 6 With The Yellow Jackets
He Is Christmas | Reprise | 7599-26665-2

Warren,Peter | (b,b-solocello)
Jack DeJohnette Quartet
Special Edition | ECM | 1152

Warren,Quentin | (g)
Jimmy Smith Quartet
Blue Note Plays Gershwin | Blue Note | 520808-2
Prayer Meetin' | Blue Note | 576754-2
Midnight Blue(The [Be]witching Hour) | Blue Note | 854365-2
Jimmy Smith Quintet
Prayer Meetin' | Blue Note | 576754-2
Rockin' the Boat | Blue Note | 576755-2
Jimmy Smith Trio
Jimmy Smith Trio: Salle Pleyel, May 28th, 1965 | Laserlight | 36135
Verve Jazz Masters 29:Jimmy Smith | Verve | 521855-2
Bucket! | Blue Note | 524550-2
Jimmy Smith:Best Of The Verve Years | Verve | 527950-2

Warrington,Tom | (bel-b)
Bill Perkins Quintet
Swing Spring | Candid | CCD 79752

Wartel,Henrik | (dr)
Lisa Ekdahl With The Peter Nordahl Trio
When Did You Leave Heaven | RCA | 2143175-2

Warwick,Carl | (tp)
Dizzy Gillespie And His Orchestra
Gillespiana And Carnegie Hall Concert | Verve | 519809-2
Verve Jazz Masters 20:Introducing | Verve | 519853-2
Dizzy Gillespie:Birks Works-The Verve Big Band Sessions | Verve | 527900-2
Talking Verve:Dizzy Gillespie | Verve | 533846-2
Ultimate Dizzy Gillespie | Verve | 557535-2
Dizzy Gillespie Orchestra
Verve Jazz Masters 10:Dizzy Gillespie | Verve | 516319-2
Woody Herman And His Orchestra
Woody Herman:Four Brother | Dreyfus Jazz Line | FDM 36722-2
Louis Armstrong-Jack Teagarden-Woody Herman:Midnights At V-Disc | Jazz Unlimited | JUCD 2048
Old Gold Rehearsals 1944 | Jazz Unlimited | JUCD 2079

Warwick,Jimmy | (tb)
Lionel Hampton Orchestra
The Big Bands Vol.1.The Snader Telescriptions | Storyville | 4960043

Wasama,Jukka | (dr)
Piirpauke
Piirpauke-Global Servisi | JA & RO | JARO 4150-2

Wasama,Oli Pekka | (b)

Wasdaris,Christian[Kristian] | (dr,perc,wave-drtablas)
Gebhard Ullmann-Andreas Willers
Playful '93 | Nabel Records:Jazz Network | CD 4659
Ute Kannenberg Quartet
Kannenberg On Purpose | Jazz Haus Musik | JHM 0109 CD
Ute Kannenberg Quartet With Guests
Kannenberg On Purpose | Jazz Haus Musik | JHM 0109 CD

Washington Jr.,Grover | (as,fl,ss,ts,bs,p,saxtin-whistle)
Bob James And His Orchestra
Jazzrock-Anthology Vol.3:Fusion | Zounds | CD 27100555
Boogaloo Joe Jones Quintet
Discovery:Grover Washington Jr.-The First Recordings | Prestige | PCD 11020-2
Boogaloo Joe Jones Sextet
Jazzin' With The Soul Brothers | Fantasy | FANCD 6086-2
Discovery:Grover Washington Jr.-The First Recordings | Prestige | PCD 11020-2
Charles Earland Sextet
Charlie's Greatest Hits | Prestige | PCD 24250-2
Freddy Cole With Band
Le Grand Freddy:Freddy Cole Sings The Music Of Michel Legrand | Fantasy | FCD 9683-2
Freddy Cole With The Cedar Walton Trio And Grover Washington Jr.
Love Makes The Changes | Fantasy | FCD 9681-2
Grover Washington Jr. Orchestra
Late Night Sax | CBS | 487798-2
Inside Moves | Elektra | 7559-60318-2
Jazzrock-Anthology Vol.3:Fusion | Zounds | CD 27100555
Grover Washington Jr. Septet
Paradise | Elektra | 7559-60537-2
Johnny 'Hammond' Smith Quintet
Discovery:Grover Washington Jr.-The First Recordings | Prestige | PCD 11020-2
Kenny Burrell-Grover Washington Quartet
Blue Note Plays Gershwin | Blue Note | 520808-2
Leon Spencer Sextet
Jazzin' With The Soul Brothers | Fantasy | FANCD 6086-2
Discovery:Grover Washington Jr.-The First Recordings | Prestige | PCD 11020-2

Washington Jr.,Jack | (as,bs,cl,tsreeds)
Benny Moten's Kansas City Orchestra
Planet Jazz:Ben Webster | RCA | 2165368-2
Planet Jazz:Jimmy Rushing | RCA | 2165371-2
Planet Jazz:Swing | Planet Jazz | 2169651-2
Jazz:The Essential Collection Vol.3 | IN+OUT Records | 78013-2
Billie Holiday And Her Orchestra
Billie's Love Songs | Nimbus Records | NI 2000
Count Basie And His Orchestra
Planet Jazz:Count Basie | Planet Jazz | 2152068-2
Planet Jazz Sampler | Planet Jazz | 2152326-2
Planet Jazz:Jimmy Rushing | RCA | 2165371-2
Planet Jazz:Jazz Greatest Hits | Planet Jazz | 2169648-2
Planet Jazz:Big Bands | Planet Jazz | 2169649-2
Jazz Collection:Count Basie | Laserlight | 24368
Jazz:The Essential Collection Vol.3 | IN+OUT Records | 78013-2
From Spiritual To Swing | Vanguard | VCD 169/71
Count Basie,His Instrumentals & Rhythm
Planet Jazz:Count Basie | Planet Jazz | 2152068-2
Harry James And His Orchestra
The Legends Of Swing | Laserlight | 24659

Helen Humes With James P. Johnson And The Count Basie Orchestra
From Spiritual To Swing | Vanguard | VCD 169/71
Jimmy Rushing With Count Basie And His Orchestra
From Spiritual To Swing | Vanguard | VCD 169/71

Washington,Albert | (cl,bs,tsreeds)
Louis Armstrong And His Orchestra
Satch Plays Fats(Complete) | CBS | CK 64927

Washington,Benny | (dr)
Earl Hines And His Orchestra
Jazz:The Essential Collection Vol.2 | IN+OUT Records | 78012-2

Washington,Booker | (co,drtp)
Benny Moten's Kansas City Orchestra
Planet Jazz:Jimmy Rushing | RCA | 2165371-2

Washington,Buck | (p)
Bessie Smith And Her Band
Jazz:The Essential Collection Vol.3 | IN+OUT Records | 78013-2

Washington,Darryl | (dr)
Charles Earland Septet
Charles Earland In Concert | Prestige | PRCD 24267-2
Richard 'Groove' Holmes Orchestra
Comin' On Home | Blue Note | 538701-2
Richard 'Groove' Holmes Sextet
Blue Break Beats | Blue Note | 799106-2

Washington,Dinah | (vibvoc)
All Star Live Jam Session
Brownie-The Complete EmArCy Recordings Of Clifford Brown | EmArCy | 838306-2
Clifford Brown All Stars With Dinah Washington
Verve Jazz Masters 40:Dinah Washington | Verve | 522055-2
Dinah Washington And Her Band
After Hours With Miss D | Verve | 0760562
Verve Jazz Masters 40:Dinah Washington | Verve | 522055-2
Dinah Washington And Her Orchestra
For Those In Love | EmArCy | 514073-2
Misty Blue:Sweet Sisters Swing Songs Of Sorrow And Sadness | Blue Note | 521151-2
Verve Jazz Masters 40:Dinah Washington | Verve | 522055-2
Dinah Washington And Her Sextet
Newport Jazz Festival 1958,July 3rd-6th Vol.4:Blues In The Night No.2 | Phontastic | NCD 8816
Dinah Washington With Orchestra
Mad About The Boy-The Best Of Dinah Washington | Mercury | 512214-2
Ballads | Roulette | 537559-2
Dinah Washington With The Belford Hendricks Orchestra
Verve Jazz Masters 20:Introducing | Verve | 519853-2
What A Diff'rence A Day Makes! | Verve | 543300-2
4 By 4:Ella Fitzgerald/Sarah Vaughan/Billie Holiday/Dinah Washington | Verve | 559693-2
Dinah Washington With The Eddie Chamblee Orchestra
Verve Jazz Masters 40:Dinah Washington | Verve | 522055-2
Dinah Sings Bessie Smith | Verve | 538635-2
Dinah Washington With The Jimmy Cobb Orchestra
Verve Jazz Masters 40:Dinah Washington | Verve | 522055-2
Ultimate Ben Webster selected by James Carter | Verve | 557537-2
Dinah Washington With The Newport All Stars
Dinah Sings Bessie Smith | Verve | 538635-2
Dinah Washington With The Quincy Jones Orchestra
Verve Jazz Masters 40:Dinah Washington | Verve | 522055-2
The Swingin' Miss 'D' | Verve | 558074-2
4 By 4:Ella Fitzgerald/Sarah Vaughan/Billie Holiday/Dinah Washington | Verve | 559693-2
Dinah Washington With The Terry Gibbs Band
Verve Jazz Masters 40:Dinah Washington | Verve | 522055-2
Dinah Washington With The Urbie Green Sextet
Newport Jazz Festival 1958,July 3rd-6th Vol.2:Mulligan The Main Man | Phontastic | NCD 8814
Lionel Hampton And His Septet
Lionel Hampton:Flying Home | Dreyfus Jazz Line | FDM 36735-2

Washington,Freddie | (bel-b)
Bobby Lyle Group
The Journey | Atlantic | 7567-82138-2
Herbie Hancock Group
Monster | CBS | 486571-2
Magic Window | CBS | 486572-2
The Meeting
Hot Jazz Bisquits | Hip Bop | HIBD 8801

Washington,George | (b,tbvoc)
Count Basie And His Orchestra
Planet Jazz:Count Basie | Planet Jazz | 2152068-2
Planet Jazz:Big Bands | Planet Jazz | 2169649-2
Johnny Otis And His Orchestra
Verve Jazz Masters 43:Ben Webster | Verve | 525431-2
Louis Armstrong And His Orchestra
Louis Armstrong:Swing That Music | Laserlight | 36056
Jazz:The Essential Collection Vol.2 | IN+OUT Records | 78012-2
Louis Armstrong:C'est Si Bon | Dreyfus Jazz Line | FDM 36730-2
Louis Armstrong-My Greatest Songs | MCA | MCD 18347
Swing Legends:Louis Armstrong | Nimbus Records | NI 2012
Spike Hughes And His Negro Orchestra
Jazz:The Essential Collection Vol.3 | IN+OUT Records | 78013-2

Washington,James | (org)
Albert King Blues Band
Wednesday Night In San Francisco | Stax | SCD 8556-2

Washington,Kenny | (dr)
Arturo Sandoval Quartet
I Remember Clifford | GRP | GRP 96682
Arturo Sandoval Quintet
I Remember Clifford | GRP | GRP 96682
Bill Charlap Trio
Stardust | Blue Note | 535985-2
Craig Bailey Band
A New Journey | Candid | CCD 79725
Eddie Lockjaw Davis-Johnny Griffin Quintet
Tough Tenors Back Again! | Storyville | STCD 8298
Flip Phillips Quintet
Swing Is The Thing | Verve | 543477-2
Flip Phillips Septet
Swing Is The Thing | Verve | 543477-2
Flip Phillips Sextet
Swing Is The Thing | Verve | 543477-2
Frank Wess With The Bill Charlap Trio
Stardust | Blue Note | 535985-2
Freddy Cole With Band
Le Grand Freddy:Freddy Cole Sings The Music Of Michel Legrand | Fantasy | FCD 9683-2
Freddy Cole With The Eric Alexander Band
Love Makes The Changes | Fantasy | FCD 9681-2
Hank Crawford Quartet
The World Of Hank Crawford | Milestone | MCD 9304-2
Hank Crawford Quintet
The World Of Hank Crawford | Milestone | MCD 9304-2
Hank Crawford Septet
The World Of Hank Crawford | Milestone | MCD 9304-2
Jim Hall With The Bill Charlap Trio
Stardust | Blue Note | 535985-2
Jimmy McGriff Sextet
Feelin' It | Milestone | MCD 9313-2
Johnny Griffin Quartet
Jazz Life Vol.1:From Village Vanguard | Storyville | 4960753
Joshua Redman Quartet
Joshua Redman | Warner | 9362-45242-2
Plas Johnson-Red Holloway Quintet
Keep That Groove Going! | Milestone | MCD 9319-2
Randy Sandke Quintet
Cliffhanger | Nagel-Heyer | CD 2037
Randy Sandke Sextet
Cliffhanger | Nagel-Heyer | CD 2037
Shirley Horn With The Bill Charlap Trio
Stardust | Blue Note | 535985-2
Tim Hagans-Marcus Printup Septet
Hub Songs | Blue Note | 859509-2
Tony Bennett With The Bill Charlap Trio
Stardust | Blue Note | 535985-2

Washington,Peter | (b)
Andy Bey Group
Tuesdays In Chinatown | Minor Music | 801099
Bennie Wallace Quartet
Bennie Wallace In Berlin | Enja | ENJ-9425 2
Bill Charlap Trio
Stardust | Blue Note | 535985-2
Byron Stripling Quintet
Byron,Get On Free | Nagel-Heyer | CD 2016
Byron Stripling Sextet
Striplingnow! | Nagel-Heyer | CD 2002
Dave Ellis Quartet
State Of Mind | Milestone | MCD 9328-2
Dave Ellis Quintet
State Of Mind | Milestone | MCD 9328-2
Eddie Henderson With The Mulgrew Miller Trio
Trumpet Legacy | Milestone | MCD 9286-2
Eric Alexander Quartet
The First Milestone | Milestone | MCD 9302-2
The Second Milestone | Milestone | MCD 9315-2
Eric Alexander Quintet
The First Milestone | Milestone | MCD 9302-2
The Second Milestone | Milestone | MCD 9315-2
Frank Wess With The Bill Charlap Trio
Stardust | Blue Note | 535985-2
Jim Hall With The Bill Charlap Trio
Stardust | Blue Note | 535985-2
Johnny King Quintet
Notes From The Underground | Enja | ENJ-9067 2
Lew Soloff With The Mulgrew Miller Trio
Trumpet Legacy | Milestone | MCD 9286-2
Nicholas Payton With The Mulgrew Miller Trio
Trumpet Legacy | Milestone | MCD 9286-2
Randy Sandke Quintet
Cliffhanger | Nagel-Heyer | CD 2037
Randy Sandke Sextet
Cliffhanger | Nagel-Heyer | CD 2037
Randy Sandke-Dick Hyman
The Re-Discovered Louis And Bix | Nagel-Heyer | CD 058
Shirley Horn With The Bill Charlap Trio
Stardust | Blue Note | 535985-2
The Dave Glasser/Clark Terry/Barry Harris Project
Uh! Oh! | Nagel-Heyer | CD 2003
Blues Of Summer | Nagel-Heyer | NH 1011
Tim Hagans-Marcus Printup Septet
Hub Songs | Blue Note | 859509-2
Tom Harrell With The Mulgrew Miller Trio
Trumpet Legacy | Milestone | MCD 9286-2
Tommy Flanagan Trio
Sunset And The Mockingbird-The Birthday Concert | Blue Note | 493155-2
Tony Bennett With The Bill Charlap Trio
Stardust | Blue Note | 535985-2

Washington,Reggie | (bel-b)
Steve Coleman And Five Elements
Curves Of Life | Novus | 2131693-2
Genesis & The Opening Of The Way | RCA | 2152934-2
The Sonic Language Of Myth | RCA | 2164123-2
Steve Coleman And Metrics
A Tale Of 3 Cities,The EP | Novus | 2124747-2
The Way Of The Cipher | Novus | 2131690-2
Steve Coleman And The Council Of Balance
Genesis & The Opening Of The Way | RCA | 2152934-2

Washington,Tyrone | (as,fl,ts,perc,congas,chimes,voc,cl)
Horace Silver Quintet
Horace Silver Retrospective | Blue Note | 495576-2

Wasilewski,Marcin | (p)
Thomas Stanko Quartet
Suspended Night | ECM | 1868(9811244)
Tomasz Stanko Quartet
Soul Of Things | ECM | 1788(016374-2)

Wasserman,Eddie | (bs,reedts)
Elliot Lawrence And His Orchestra
The Elliot Lawrence Big Band Swings Cohn & Kahn | Fantasy | FCD 24761-2
Stan Kenton And His Orchestra
Stan Kenton Portraits On Standards | Capitol | 531571-2

Wasserman,Rob | (bb-playback)
Rob Wasserman Duet
Duets | GRP | GRP 97122
Stephane Grappelli-David Grisman Group
Stephane Grappelli:Live In San Francisco | Storyville | 4960723

Watanabe,Butch | (tb)
Oscar Peterson Quartet
Paris Jazz Concert:Oscar Peterson | Laserlight | 36155

Watanabe,Sadao | (as,sopranino,flss)
Randy Brecker Group
Jazzrock-Anthology Vol.3:Fusion | Zounds | CD 27100555
Ron Carter Quartet
Carnaval | Original Jazz Classics | OJCCD 1070-2(GXY 5144)

Watanabe,Takahiro | (keyboard-b)
Toshinori Kondo & Ima
Red City Smoke | JA & RO | JARO 4173-2

Waterhouse,Lucy | (v)
Abdullah Ibrahim Trio And A String Orchestra
African Suite | TipToe | TIP-888832 2
String Orchestra
African Suite | TipToe | TIP-888832 2

Waterman,Steve | (tp)
Carla Bley Band
Big Band Theory | Watt | 25(519966-2)
Carla Bley Big Band
The Carla Bley Big Band Goes To Church | Watt | 27(533682-2)
John Surman-John Warren Group
The Brass Project | ECM | 1478
Nicki Leighton-Thomas Group
Forbidden Games | Candid | CCD 79778

Waters,Benny | (as,ts,arr,voc,cl,sssax)
Benny Waters & Jan Jankeje
Let's Talk About Jazz | G&J Records | GJ 2009 Maxi-CD
Benny Waters Quartet
Swinging Again | Jazzpoint | JP 1037 CD
A' Portrait Of Jan Jankeje | Jazzpoint | JP 1054 CD
Hurry On Down | Storyville | STCD 8264
Benny Waters Quintet
Benny Waters Plays Songs Of Love | Jazzpoint | JP 1039 CD
Benny Waters Sextet
A' Portrait Of Jan Jankeje | Jazzpoint | JP 1054 CD
Hot Lips Page Band
Planet Jazz:Jazz Trumpet | Planet Jazz | 2169654-2
Quartier Latin Jazz Band
Great Traditionalists | Jazzpoint | JP 1046 CD

Waters,Julia Tillman | (voc)
Bobby Lyle Group
The Journey | Atlantic | 7567-82138-2
Herbie Hancock Group
Magic Window | CBS | 486572-2

Waters,Luther | (voc)

Waters,Maxine Willard | (voc)
Bobby Lyle Group
The Journey | Atlantic | 7567-82138-2
Herbie Hancock Group
Magic Window | CBS | 486572-2

Waters,Monty | (as,vocss)
Ku-umba Frank Lacy & The Poker Bigband
Songs From The Musical 'Poker' | Tutu Records | 888150-2*
Marty Cook Group feat. Monty Waters
Borderlines | Tutu Records | 888122-2*
Monty Waters' Hot House
Live In Paris, Duc Des Lombards, Volume One | Tutu Records | 888140-2*
Monty Waters' Hot Rhythm Junction
Jazzoerty | Tutu Records | 888196-2*
Monty Waters Quartet
Monty Waters New York Calling Vol.2 | Tutu Records | 888182-2*

Waters,Oren | (voc)
Bobby Lyle Group
The Journey | Atlantic | 7567-82138-2
Herbie Hancock Group
Monster | CBS | 486571-2
Magic Window | CBS | 486572-2

Waters,Tony | (congas)
Joe Henderson Sextet
Joe Henderson:The Milestone Years | Milestone | 8MCD 4413-2

Wates,Matt | (as)
Itchy Fingers
Full English Breakfast | Enja | ENJ-7085 2
Jamie Cullum Group
Pointless Nostalgic | Candid | CCD 79782

Watkins,Derek | (tpfl-h)
Benny Goodman And His Orchestra
Verve Jazz Masters 33:Benny Goodman | Verve | 844410-2
First Brass
First Brass | M.A Music | NU 158-3
Kenny Clarke-Francy Boland Big Band
Clark-Boland Big Band: TNP, October 29th, 1969 | Laserlight | 36129
Kenny Wheeler Brass Ensemble
A Long Time Ago | ECM | 1691
Kenny Wheeler Ensemble
Muisc For Large & Small Ensembles | ECM | 1415/16

Watkins,Doug | (b,cello,percfinger-cymbals)
Art Blakey And The Jazz Messengers
Horace Silver Retrospective | Blue Note | 495576-2
At The Cafe Bohemia Vol.1 | Blue Note | 532148-2
At The Cafe Bohemia Vol.2 | Blue Note | 532149-2
The Jazz Messengers | CBS | CK 65265
Art Farmer Quartet
Plays The Arrangements And Compositions Of Gigi Gryce And Quincy Jones | Original Jazz Classics | OJCCD 054-2
Bobby Jaspar Quintet
Flute Flight | Original Jazz Classics | OJCCD 1084-2(P 2124)
Charles Mingus Quintet With Roland Kirk
Tonight At Noon | Atlantic | 7567-80793-2
Charles Mingus-Passion Of A Man:The Complete Atlantic Recordings 1956-1961 | Atlantic | 8122-72871-2
The Very Best Of Charles Mingus | Rhino | 8122-79988-2
Coleman Hawkins With The Red Garland Trio
Coleman Hawkins With The Red Garland Trio | Original Jazz Classics | OJCCD 418-2(SV 2001)
Donald Brown Quintet
Donald Byrd & Doug Watkins:The Tradition Sessions | Blue Note | 540528-2
Donald Byrd Quartet
Donald Byrd & Doug Watkins:The Tradition Sessions | Blue Note | 540528-2
Donald Byrd Quintet
Blue Bossa | Blue Note | 795590-2
Byrd In Paris Vol.1 | Polydor | 833394-2
Donald Byrd Sextet
Donald Byrd & Doug Watkins:The Tradition Sessions | Blue Note | 540528-2
Doug Watkins Sextet
Donald Byrd & Doug Watkins:The Tradition Sessions | Blue Note | 540528-2
Doug Watkins Trio
Donald Byrd & Doug Watkins:The Tradition Sessions | Blue Note | 540528-2
Gene Ammons And His All Stars
Blue Gene | Original Jazz Classics | OJC20 192-2(P 7146)
Jammin' With Gene | Original Jazz Classics | OJCCD 211-2(P 7060)
Gene Ammons Quartet
The Jazz Giants Play Rodgers & Hart:Blue Moon | Prestige | PCD 24205-2
Gene Ammons Quintet
Boss Tenor | Original Jazz Classics | OJC20 297-2(P-7180)
The Jazz Giants Play Jerome Kern:Yesterdays | Prestige | PCD 24202-2
The Jazz Giants Play Cole Porter:Night And Day | Prestige | PCD 24203-2
Gentle Jug Vol.3 | Prestige | PCD 24249-2
Hank Mobley Quintet
Hank Mobley | Blue Note | 0675622
The Art Of Saxophone | Laserlight | 24652
Horace Silver Quintet
Horace Silver Retrospective | Blue Note | 495576-2
Six Pieces Of Silver | Blue Note | 525648-2
The Best Of Blue Note Vol.2 | Blue Note | 797960-2
J.R. Monterose Quintet
Jaywalkin' | Fresh Sound Records | FSR-CD 320
Jackie McLean Quartet
4, 5 And 6 | Original Jazz Classics | OJC 056(P 7048)
The Jazz Giants Play Jerome Kern:Yesterdays | Prestige | PCD 24202-2
Jackie McLean Quintet
4, 5 And 6 | Original Jazz Classics | OJC 056(P 7048)
Jackie McLean Sextet
4, 5 And 6 | Original Jazz Classics | OJC 056(P 7048)
Joe Turner With Orchestra
Atlantic Jazz: Kansas City | Atlantic | 7567-81701-2
John Coltrane Sextet
The Mal Waldron Memorial Album:Soul Eyes | Prestige | PRCD 11024-2
Kenny Burrell Quintet
Kenny Burrell | Original Jazz Classics | OJCCD 019-2(P 7088)
Pepper Adams Quartet
10 To 4 At The 5-Spot | Original Jazz Classics | OJCCD 031-2(RLP 265)
Pepper Adams Quintet
10 To 4 At The 5-Spot | Original Jazz Classics | OJCCD 031-2(RLP 265)
Prestige All Stars
John Coltrane-The Prestige Recordings | Prestige | 16 PCD 4405-2
All Day Long | Original Jazz Classics | OJC20 456-2(P 7081)
The Cats | Original Jazz Classics | OJCCD 079-2(NJ 8217)
Wheelin' & Dealin' | Original Jazz Classics | OJCCD 672-2(P7131)
The Prestige Legacy Vol.2:Battles Of Saxes | Prestige | PCD 24252-2
Red Garland Trio
Stretching Out | Prestige | PRCD 24272-2
Sonny Rollins Quartet
True Blue | Blue Note | 534032-2
Ballads | Blue Note | 537562-2
Newk's Time | Blue Note | 576752-2
The Blue Note Years-The Best Of Sonny Rollins | Blue Note | 793203-2
Sonny Rollins:The Blue Note Recordings | Blue Note | 821371-2
Jazz Profile:Sonny Rollins | Blue Note | 823516-2
Saxophone Colossus | Original Jazz Classics | OJC20 291-2
The Prestige All Stars
Olio | Original Jazz Classics | OJCCD 1004-2(P 7084)
Tina Brooks Quintet
True Blue | Blue Note | 534032-2
Tommy Flanagan Trio
The Cats | Original Jazz Classics | OJCCD 079-2(NJ 8217)
Wilbur Harden Quintet

The Art Of Saxophone | Laserlight | 24652

Watkins,Earl | (dr)
Earl Hines Quartet
Another Monday Date | Prestige | PRCD 24043-2
Earl Hines-Muggsy Spanier All Stars
Earl Hines/Muggsy Spanier All Stars:The Chicago Dates | Storyville | STCD 6037

Watkins,Eddie | (el-b)
Herbie Hancock Group
Magic Window | CBS | 486572-2

Watkins,Joe | (drvoc)
George Lewis And His Band
Atlantic Jazz: New Orleans | Atlantic | 7567-81700-2
George Lewis And His New Orleans Ragtime Band
The Beverly Caverns Session | Good Time Jazz | GTCD 12058-2
George Lewis And His New Orleans Stompers
George Lewis And His New Orleans Stompers | Blue Note | 821261-2
George Lewis And His Original New Orleans Jazzmen
George Lewis In Stockholm,1959 | Dragon | DRCD 221

Watkins,Julius | (fr-h)
Benny Bailey Septet
Big Brass | Candid | CCD 79011
Blue Mitchell And His Orchestra
A Sure Thing | Original Jazz Classics | OJCCD 837-2
The Jazz Giants Play Jerome Kern:Yesterdays | Prestige | PCD 24202-2
Cal Massey Sextet
The Jazz Life! | Candid | CCD 79019
Blues To Coltrane | Candid | CCD 79029
Clark Terry Orchestra
Color Changes | Candid | CCD 79009
Curtis Fuller And Hampton Hawes With French Horns
Curtis Fuller And Hampton Hawes With French Horns | Original Jazz Classics | OJCCD 1942-2(NJ 8305)
Curtis Fuller And Teddy Charles With French Horns
Curtis Fuller And Hampton Hawes With French Horns | Original Jazz Classics | OJCCD 1942-2(NJ 8305)
Dizzy Gillespie And His Orchestra
Verve Jazz Masters 10:Dizzy Gillespie | Verve | 516319-2
Gillespiana And Carnegie Hall Concert | Verve | 519809-2
Talking Verve:Dizzy Gillespie | Verve | 533846-2
Freddie Hubbard Orchestra
The Body And The Soul | Impulse(MCA) | 951183-2
Gil Evans Orchestra
Verve Jazz Masters 23:Gil Evans | Verve | 521860-2
The Individualism Of Gil Evans | Verve | 833804-2
Blues In Orbit | Enja | ENJ-3069 2
John Coltrane And His Orchestra
John Coltrane:Standards | Impulse(MCA) | 549914-2
John Coltrane Quartet With Brass
The Complete Africa/Brass Sessions | Impulse(MCA) | 952168-2
Kenny Burrell With The Gil Evans Orchestra
Guitar Forms | Verve | 521403-2
Verve Jazz Masters 23:Gil Evans | Verve | 521860-2
Verve Jazz Masters 45:Kenny Burrell | Verve | 527652-2
Verve Jazz Masters Vol.60:The Collection | Verve | 529866-2
Les Spann Quintet
Gemini | Original Jazz Classics | OJCCD 1948-2(JLP 9355)
Miles Davis With Gil Evans & His Orchestra
Miles Davis At Carnegie Hall | CBS | CK 65027
This Is Jazz:Miles Davis Plays Ballads | CBS | CK 65038
Porgy And Bess | CBS | CK 65141
Quiet Nights | CBS | CK 65293
Milt Jackson Orchestra
Milt Jackson Birthday Celebration | Fantasy | FANCD 6079-2
Oscar Peterson With The Ernie Wilkins Orchestra
Verve Jazz Masters 16:Oscar Peterson | Verve | 516320-2
Oscar Pettiford Sextet
Charles Mingus-The Complete Debut Recordings | Debut | 12 DCD 4402-2
Pharoah Sanders Orchestra
Karma | Impulse(MCA) | 951153-2
The Roots Of Acid Jazz | Impulse(MCA) | IMP 12042
Quincy Jones And His Orchestra
The Quintessence | Impulse(MCA) | 951222-2
The Roots Of Acid Jazz | Impulse(MCA) | IMP 12042
Thad Jones-Mel Lewis Orchestra
The Groove Merchant/The Second Race | Laserlight | 24656
The Jazz Composer's Orchestra
Comminications | JCOA | 1001/2
Thelonious Monk Quintet
Thelonious Monk:The Complete Prestige Recordings | Prestige | 3 PRCD 4428-2
MONK | Original Jazz Classics | OJCCD 016-2
Thelonious Monk/Sonny Rollins | Original Jazz Classics | OJCCD 059-2
The Prestige Legacy Vol.1:The High Priests | Prestige | PCD 24251-2

Watkins,Mitch | (el-g,g,keyboardssynth)
Barbara Dennerlein Group
Take Off | Verve | 527664-2
Junkanoo | Verve | 537122-2
Outhipped | Verve | 547503-2
Barbara Dennerlein Quartet
Hot Stuff | Enja | ENJ-6050 2
Barbara Dennerlein Quintet
That's Me | Enja | ENJ-7043 2

Watkins,Tony | (voc)
Duke Ellington And His Orchestra
Highlights From The Duke Ellington Centennial Edition | RCA | 2663672-2
Togo Brava Swuite | Storyville | STCD 8323

Watley,Bobby | (org)
Funk Inc.
Jazzin' With The Soul Brothers | Fantasy | FANCD 6086-2

Watrous,Bill | (tbvoc)
Bill Watrous And His West Coast Friends
Art Pepper:The Hollywood All-Star Sessions | Galaxy | 5GCD 4431-2
Diane Schuur With Orchestra
The Best Of Diane Schuur | GRP | GRP 98882
Ella Fitzgerald With Orchestra
The Best Is Yet To Come | Original Jazz Classics | OJCCD 889-2(2312138)
Ella Fitzgerald With The Nelson Riddle Orchestra
Dream Dancing | Original Jazz Classics | OJCCD 1072-2(2310814)
Jackie Cain-Roy Kral Group
Full Circle | Fantasy | FCD 24768-2
Jimmy Witherspoon And His All Stars
Blues For Easy Livers | Original Blues Classics | OBCCD 585-2(PR 7475)
Kenny Burrell With The Don Sebesky Orchestra
Verve Jazz Masters 45:Kenny Burrell | Verve | 527652-2
Blues-The Common Ground | Verve | 589101-2
Sarah Vaughan With Orchestra
!Viva! Vaughan | Mercury | 549374-2
Shelly Manne And His Hollywood All Stars
Art Pepper:The Hollywood All-Star Sessions | Galaxy | 5GCD 4431-2
Singers Unlimited With Orchestra
The Singers Unlimited:Magic Voices | MPS | 539130-2
Singers Unlimited With The Patrick Williams Orchestra
The Singers Unlimited:Magic Voices | MPS | 539130-2
The Quincy Jones-Sammy Nestico Orchestra
Basie & Beyond | Warner | 9362-47792-2
Wes Montgomery With The Don Sebesky Orchestra
Verve Jazz Masters 14:Wes Montgomery | Verve | 519826-2
Wes Montgomery:The Verve Jazz Sides | Verve | 521690-2
Talkin' Jazz:Roots Of Acid Jazz | Verve | 529580-2
California Dreaming | Verve | 827842-2

Watson Sr.,John | (tb)
Count Basie And His Orchestra
Afrique | RCA | 2179618-2
Count Basie: Salle Pleyel, April 17th, 1972 | Laserlight | 36127

Watson,Alexandra | (voc)
Mike Westbrook Brass Band
Glad Day:Settings Of William Blake | Enja | ENJ-9376 2

Watson,Eric | (pp-solo)
Eric Watson Quartet
Full Metal Quartet | Owl Records | 159572-2

Watson,Julius | (tbvoc)
Buddy Johnson And His Orchestra
Buddy And Ella Johnson 1953-1964 | Bear Family Records | BCD 15479 DH

Watson,Leo | (b,voc,drtiple)
Benny Goodman And His Orchestra
Camel Caravan Broadcast 1939 Vol.1 | Phontastic | NCD 8817

Watson,Murray | (tp)
Albert King With The Willie Dixon Band
Windy City Blues | Stax | SCD 8612-2
Buddy Guy Blues Band
Buddy Guy-The Complete Chess Studio Recordings | MCA | MCD 09337

Watson,Robert 'Bobby' | (as,as-solo,fl,ss,tshammer)
Art Blakey And The Jazz Messengers
Night In Tunisia | Philips | 800064-2
Bobby Watson Quartet
Advance | Enja | ENJ-9075 2
Cornelius Claudio Kreusch Group
Scoop | ACT | 9255-2
Klaus Ignatzek Group
Live At Leverkusener Jazztage | Nabel Records:Jazz Network | CD 4630

Watson,Wah Wah | (b,voc,el-g,g,synthvoice bag)
Dizzy Gillespie With The Lalo Schifrin Orchestra
Free Ride | Original Jazz Classics | OJCCD 784-2(2310794)
Herbie Hancock Group
Sunlight | CBS | 486570-2
Monster | CBS | 486571-2
Magic Window | CBS | 486572-2
Herbie Hancock Septet
V.S.O.P. Herbie Hancock-Live At The City Center N.Y. | CBS | 486569-2

Watters,Lu | (cotp)
Lu Watters' Jazz Band
Blues Over Bodega | Good Time Jazz | GTCD 12066-2
Lu Watters' Yerba Buena Jazz Band
The Very Best Of Dixieland Jazz | Verve | 535529-2
Yerba Büena Jazz Band
Bunk & Lu | Good Time Jazz | GTCD 12024-2

Watts,Charlie | (dr,perccongas)
Howlin' Wolf London Session
Howlin' Wolf:The London Sessions | Chess | MCD 09297

Watts,Ernie | (as,ts,cl,fl,piccolo,reeds,ss,sax)
Albert King Blues Band
The Lost Session | Stax | SCD 8534-2
Arturo Sandoval Quintet
I Remember Clifford | GRP | GRP 96682
Bobby Bryant Orchestra
Deep Blue-The United States Of Mind | Blue Note | 521152-2
Bobby Hutcherson Orchestra
Montara | Blue Note | 590956-2
Buddy Rich And His Orchestra
Big Swing Face | Pacific Jazz | 837989-2
Buddy Rich Big Band
The New One! | Pacific Jazz | 494507-2
Charlie Haden And The Liberation Music Orchestra
The Montreal Tapes:Liberation Music Orchestra | Verve | 527469-2
Charlie Haden Quartet West
Haunted Heart | Verve | 513078-2
Always Say Goodbye | Verve | 521501-2
Now Is The Hour | Verve | 527827-2
Quartet West | Verve | 831673-2
In Angel City | Verve | 837031-2
Charlie Haden Quartet West With Strings
Now Is The Hour | Verve | 527827-2
The Art Of The Song | Verve | 547403-2
Charlie Haden Trio
Quartet West | Verve | 831673-2
Dizzy Gillespie With The Lalo Schifrin Orchestra
Free Ride | Original Jazz Classics | OJCCD 784-2(2310794)
Ella Fitzgerald With Orchestra
Ella/Things Ain't What They Used To Be | Warner | 9362-47875-2
Ernie Watts-Christof Sänger
Blue Topaz | Laika Records | 35101352
Flora Purim With Orchestra
Joe Henderson:The Milestone Years | Milestone | 8MCD 4413-2
Gene Harris Group
Blue Breaks Beats Vol.2 | Blue Note | 789907-2
GRP All-Star Big Band
GRP All-Star Big Band:Live! | GRP | GRP 97402
All Blues | GRP | GRP 98002
Herbie Hancock Group
Man-Child | CBS | 471235-2
Sunlight | CBS | 486570-2
J.J.Johnson Sextet
The J.J.Johnson Memorial Album | Prestige | PRCD 11025-2
Lee Ritenour Group
Rio | GRP | GRP 95242
Festival | GRP | GRP 95702
Stolen Moments | GRP | GRP 96152
Lee Ritenour With Special Guests
Festival International De Jazz De Montreal | Spectra | 9811661
The Meeting
Hot Jazz Bisquits | Hip Bop | HIBD 8801
The Quincy Jones-Sammy Nestico Orchestra
Basie & Beyond | Warner | 9362-47792-2
Willie Bobo Group
Jazzrock-Anthology Vol.3:Fusion | Zounds | CD 27100555

Watts,Gene | (tb)
Canadian Brass
Take The A Train | RCA | 2663455-2

Watts,Grady | (tp)
Louis Armstrong With The Casa Loma Orchestra
Louis Armstrong:Swing That Music | Laserlight | 36056

Watts,Jeff 'Tain' | (dr,percvoice)
Antonio Farao Trio
Black Inside | Enja | ENJ-9345 2
Barbara Dennerlein Group
Outhipped | Verve | 547503-2
Branford Marsalis Quartet
Crazy People Music | CBS | 466870-2
Reqiem | CBS | 69655-2
Branford Marsalis Trio
Trio Jeepy | CBS | 465134-2
Charles Mingus Orchestra
Tonight At Noon...Three Or Four Shades Of Love | Dreyfus Jazz Line | FDM 36633-2
Danilo Perez Group
Central Avenue | Impulse(MCA) | 951281-2
Danilo Perez Quartet
Panamonk | Impulse(MCA) | 951190-2
Danilo Perez Trio
Central Avenue | Impulse(MCA) | 951281-2
Lew Soloff Group
Rainbow Mountain | TipToe | TIP-888838 2
Michael Brecker Group
Time Is Of The Essence | Verve | 547844-2
Michael Brecker Quintet
Two Blocks From The Edge | Impulse(MCA) | 951261-2
Stanley Jordan Quartet
Live In New York | Blue Note | 497810-2
Wynton Marsalis Quintet
Wynton Marsalis | CBS | 468708-2
Wynton Marsalis Sextet
Hot House Flowers | CBS | 468710-2

Watts,Mamie | (voc)
Babs Gonzales And His Band
Voilà | Fresh Sound Records | FSR CD 340

Watts,Nathan | (b)
Paulinho Da Costa Orchestra
Happy People | Original Jazz Classics | OJCCD 783-2(2312102)

Watts,Reggie | (keyboards)
Wayne Horvitz Group
4+1 Ensemble | Intuition Records | INT 3224-2

Watts,Trevor | (as,perc,cl,sax,reedsss)
John Stevens Quartet
Re-Touch & Quartet | Konnex Records | KCD 5027
Katrina Krimsky-Trevor Watts
Stella Malu | ECM | 1199
Trevor Watts Moiré Music Drum Orchestra
A Wider Embrace | ECM | 1449

Wauschke,Bettina | (C-tuba)
European Tuba Quartet
Low And Behold | Jazz Haus Musik | JHM 0110 CD

Waverley,Mike | (b-tb)
Buddy Rich And His Orchestra
Swingin' New Big Band | Pacific Jazz | 835232-2

Wax,Hans | (g)
Clemens Maria Peters/Reinhold Bauer
Quadru Mana/Quadru Mania | Edition Collage | EC 464-2

Wayland,Hank | (b)
The Capitol Jazzmen
The Hollywood Session:The Capitol Jazzmen | Jazz Unlimited | JUCD 2044

Wayne,Chuck | (b,g,bjmangola)
Bud Powell Orchestra
Bebop | Pablo | PACD 2310978-2
Chuck Wayne Trio
Morning Mist | Original Jazz Classics | OJCCD 1097-2(P-7367)
Coleman Hawkins And His All Stars
Planet Jazz:Coleman Hawkins | Planet Jazz | 2152055-2
Planet Jazz:Bebop | RCA | 2169650-2
Jazz:The Essential Collection Vol.3 | IN+OUT Records | 78013-2
Dizzy Gillespie Sextet
Dizzy Gillespie:Night In Tunisia | Dreyfus Jazz Line | FDM 36734-2
George Shearing Quintet
Verve Jazz Masters 57:George Shearing | Verve | 529900-2
Jack Teagarden's Big Eight
Planet Jazz:Jack Teagarden | Planet Jazz | 2161236-2
Planet Jazz | Planet Jazz | 2169652-2
Jubilee All Stars
Jazz Gallery:Lester Young Vol.2(1946-59) | RCA | 2119541-2
Lester Young And His Band
Lester Young:The Complete Aladdin Sessions | Blue Note | 832787-2
Rolf Kühn Sextet
Rolf Kühn And His Sound Of Jazz | Fresh Sound Records | FSR-CD 326
Sarah Vaughan With The Allstars
Sarah Vaughan:Lover Man | Dreyfus Jazz Line | FDM 36739-2
Woody Herman And His Orchestra
The Legends Of Swing | Laserlight | 24659
Woody Herman:Four Brother | Dreyfus Jazz Line | FDM 36722-2

WDR Big Band |
Bernard Purdie's Soul To Jazz
Bernard Purdie's Soul To Jazz | ACT | 9242-2
Bob Brookmeyer Group With The WDR Big Band
Electricity | ACT | 9219-2
Eddie Harris Group With The WDR Big Band
Eddie Harris-The Last Concert | ACT | 9249-2
Gianlugi Trovesi Quartet With The WDR Big Band
Dedalo | Enja | ENJ-9419 2
Jens Winther And The WDR Big Band
The Escape | dacapo | DCCD 9437
Kevin Mahogany With The WDR Big Band And Guests
Pussy Cat Dues:The Music Of Charles Mingus | Enja | ENJ-9316 2
Vince Mendoza With The WDR Big Band And Guests
Sketches | ACT | 9215-2

WDR Big Band And Guests |
Los Jovenes Flamencos With The WDR Big Band And Guests
Jazzpana | ACT | 9212-2

WDR Radio Orchestra & Rememrerance Band |
Gunther Schuller With The WDR Radio Orchestra & Rememberance Band
Witchi Tia To, The Music Of Jim Pepper | Tutu Records | 888204-2*

We Three |
We Three
East Coasting | Organic Music | ORGM 9702
The Drivin' Beat | Organic Music | ORGM 9707
We Three With Roman Schwaller
East Coasting | Organic Music | ORGM 9702

Weakley,Steve | (g)
Funk Inc.
Jazzin' With The Soul Brothers | Fantasy | FANCD 6086-2

Weather Report |
Weather Report
Mr. Gone | CBS | 468208-2
Black Market | CBS | 468210-2
Night Passage | CBS | 468211-2
Sweetnighter | CBS | 485102-2
Weathe Report Live In Tokyo | CBS | 489208-2
Heavy Weather | CBS | CK 65108

Webb Jr.,Stan | (perc)
Paul Desmond Quartet With The Don Sebesby Orchestra
From The Hot Afternoon | Verve | 543487-2

Webb,Barry | (gvoc)
Tom Browne Groups
Mo' Jamaica Funk | Hip Bop | HIBD 8002

Webb,Champ | (reeds)
Ella Fitzgerald With The Nelson Riddle Orchestra
The Best Of The Song Books:The Ballads | Verve | 521867-2
Oh Lady Be Good:The Best Of The Gershwin Songbook | Verve | 529581-2
Love Songs:The Best Of The Song Books | Verve | 531762-2

Webb,Chick | (dr)
Ella Fitzgerald With The Chick Webb Orchestra
Jazz Collection:Ella Fitzgerald | Laserlight | 24397
Louis Armstrong With Chick Webb's Orchestra
Best Of The Complete RCA Victor Recordings | RCA | 2663636-2
Louis Armstrong:A 100th Birthday Celebration | RCA | 2663694-2
Mezz Mezzrow And His Orchestra
Planet Jazz:Bud Freeman | Planet Jazz | 2161240-2

Webb,Nick | (gsitar-g)
Acoustic Alchemy
Against The Grain | GRP | GRP 97832

Webb,Spider | (dr)
Hampton Hawes Orchestra
Northern Windows Plus | Prestige | PRCD 24278-2

Webb,Stanley | (as,bs,cl,fl,alto-fl,ts,oboe,piccolo)
Cab Calloway And His Orchestra
Planet Jazz:Cab Calloway | Planet Jazz | 2161237-2
Planet Jazz:Male Jazz Vocalists | Planet Jazz | 2169657-2
Cal Tjader With The Lalo Schifrin Orchestra
Talkin Verve/Roots Of Acid Jazz:Cal Tjader | Verve | 531562-2
Charlie Parker With Strings
Bird: The Complete Charlie Parker On Verve | Verve | 837141-2
Charlie Parker With The Joe Lipman Orchestra
Charlie Parker With Strings:The Master Takes | Verve | 523984-2
Charlie Parker Big Band | Verve | 559835-2

Dizzy Gillespie And His Orchestra
Ultimate Dizzy Gillespie | Verve | 557535-2
George Benson With The Don Sebesky Orchestra
Verve Jazz Masters 21:George Benson | Verve | 521861-2
Jimmy Smith With The Oliver Nelson Orchestra
Peter & The Wolf | Verve | 547264-2
Lalo Schifrin And His Orchestra
Verve Jazz Masters 39:Cal Tjader | Verve | 521858-2
Lena Horne With The Lennie Hayton Orchestra
Planet Jazz:Lena Horne | Planet Jazz | 2165373-2
Paul Desmond Quartet With The Don Sebesby Orchestra
From The Hot Afternoon | Verve | 543487-2
Paul Desmond With Strings
Planet Jazz:Paul Desmond | Planet Jazz | 2152061-2
Desmond Blue | RCA | 2663898-2
Quincy Jones And His Orchestra
Rahsaan/The Complete Mercury Recordings Of Roland Kirk | Mercury | 846630-2
Sarah Vaughan The The Joe Lippman Orchestra
Sarah Vaughan:Lover Man | Dreyfus Jazz Line | FDM 36739-2
Sarah Vaughan With The Hugo Winterhalter Orchestra
Sarah Vaughan:Lover Man | Dreyfus Jazz Line | FDM 36739-2
Wes Montgomery With The Don Sebesky Orchestra
Verve Jazz Masters 14:Wes Montgomery | Verve | 519826-2
Wes Montgomery:The Verve Jazz Sides | Verve | 521690-2
Talkin' Jazz:Roots Of Acid Jazz | Verve | 529580-2
California Dreaming | Verve | 827842-2

Webber,John | (b)
Eric Alexander Quartet
Summit Meeting | Milestone | MCD 9322-2
Eric Alexander Quintet
Summit Meeting | Milestone | MCD 9322-2
Horace Silver Quintet
Jazz Has... A Sense Of Humor | Verve | 050293-2
Jimmy Cobb's Mob
Cobb's Groove | Milestone | MCD 9334-2

Weber,Adrian | (tb)
Brigitte Dietrich-Joe Haider Jazz Orchestra
Consequences | JHM Records | JHM 3624

Weber,Eberhard | (b,b-g,el-b,perc,tarang,b-solo,cello)
Art Van Damme Group
State Of Art | MPS | 841413-2
Art Van Damme Quintet
Keep Going/Blue World | MPS | 529093-2
Baden Powell Quartet
Three Originals:Tristeza On Guitar/Poema On Guitar/Apaixonado | MPS | 519216-2
Baden Powell Trio
Three Originals:Tristeza On Guitar/Poema On Guitar/Apaixonado | MPS | 519216-2
Dieter Reith Quartet
Reith On! | MPS | 557423-2
Eberhard Weber
Orchestra | ECM | 1374
Pendulum | ECM | 1518(519707-2)
Eberhard Weber Colours
Little Movements | ECM | 1186
Eberhard Weber Group
The Colours Of Chloe | ECM | 1042
Fluid Rustle | ECM | 1137
Chorus | ECM | 1288(823844-2)
Endless Days | ECM | 1748(013420-2)
Eberhard Weber Orchestra
Orchestra | ECM | 1374
Eberhard Weber Quartet
Yellow Fields | ECM | 1066(843205-2)
Eberhard Weber Quintet
Later That Evening | ECM | 1231(829382-2)
Eberhard Weber With Orchestra
The Following Morning | ECM | 1084(829116-2)
Eberhard Weber/Colours
Silent Feet | ECM | 1107(835017-2)
Gary Burton Quartet With Eberhard Weber
Passengers | ECM | 1092(835016-2)
Gary Burton Quintet With Eberhard Weber
Ring | ECM | 1051
Jan Garbarek Group
Photo With Blue Skie, White Clouds, Wires, Windows And A Red Roof | ECM | 1135 (843168-2)
It's OK To Listen To The Gray Voice | ECM | 1294(825406-2)
Legend Of The Seven Dreams | ECM | 1381(837344-2)
I Took Up The Runes | ECM | 1419(843850-2)
Twelve Moons | ECM | 1500(519500-2)
Visible World | ECM | 1585(529086-2)
Rites | ECM | 1685/86(559006-2)
Jan Garbarek Quartet
Paths, Prints | ECM | 1223(829377-2)
Wayfarer | ECM | 1259(811968-2)
Jazzensemble Des Hessischen Rundfunks
Atmosphering Conditions Permitting | ECM | 1549/50
Jon Hiseman With The United Jazz & Rock Ensemble And Babara Thompson's Paraphernalia
About Time Too! | VeraBra Records | CDVBR 2014-2
Knut Kiesewetter With The Dieter Reith Orchestra
Reith On! | MPS | 557423-2
Monty Alexander Quartet
Three Originals:Love And Sunshine/Estade/Cobilimbo | MPS | 523526-2
Pat Metheny Quartet
Watercolors | ECM | 1097(827409-2)
Ralph Towner Quartet
Solstice | ECM | 1060(825458-2)
Sidney Smith & Eberhard Weber
Three Originals:Tristeza On Guitar/Poema On Guitar/Apaixonado | MPS | 519216-2
Singers Unlimited With The Art Van Damme Quintet
The Singers Unlimited:Magic Voices | MPS | 539130-2
Stephane Grappelli Quartet
Grapelli Story | Verve | 515807-2
Verve Jazz Masters 11:Stéphane Grappelli | Verve | 516758-2
The German Jazz Masters
Old Friends | ACT | 9278-2
The New Dave Pike Set & Grupo Baiafra De Bahia
Dave Pike Set:Masterpieces | MPS | 531848-2
Wolfgang Dauner Trio
Music Zounds | MPS | 9808190

Weber,Jon | (p-solo)
Jon Weber
Live In Concert:Jon Weber Flying Keys | Jazz Connaisseur | JCCD 9726-2

Weber,Michel | (cl,flts)
Miles Davis With Gil Evans Orchestra, The George Gruntz Concert Jazz Band And Guests
Miles & Quincy Live At Montreux | Warner | 9362-45221-2

Weber,Reto | (dr,perc,djembeghatam)
Albert Mangelsdorff Quartet
Shake,Shuttle And Blow | Enja | ENJ-9374 2
Albert Mangelsdorff-Reto Weber Percussion Orchestra
Live At Montreux | double moon | CHRDM 71009
Chico Freeman & Franco Ambrosetti Meet Reto Weber Percussion Orchestra
Face To Face | double moon | CHRDM 71018

Weber,Serge | (keyboards)
Uli Beckerhoff Group
Stay | Nabel Records:Jazz Network | CD 4636

Weber,Steffen 'Larose' | (ssts)
Schlosser/Weber/Böhm/Huber/Binder
L 14,16 | Jazz 4 Ever Records:Jazz Network | J4E 4760
Trio Larose
Debut | Jazz 'n' Arts Records | JNA 0802
Trio Larose With Toni Lakatos
Debut | Jazz 'n' Arts Records | JNA 0802

Weber,Tobias | (viola)
Marcio Tubino Group
Festa Do Olho | Organic Music | ORGM 9723

Weber,Ute | (cello)

Weber,Vince | (p,vocp-solo)
Axel Zwingenberger-Vince Weber
The Boogiemeisters | Vagabond | VRCD 8.99026
Vince Weber
The Boogiemeisters | Vagabond | VRCD 8.99026

Webster,Ben | (cl,ts,ptalking)
Art Tatum-Ben Webster Quartet
The Art Tatum Group Masterpieces Vol.8 | Pablo | 2405431-2
Art Tatum-The Complete Pablo Group Masterpieces | Pablo | 6 PACD 4401-2
The Tatum Group Masterpieces Vol.8 | Pablo | PACD20 431-2
The Jazz Giants Play Jerome Kern:Yesterdays | Prestige | PCD 24202-2
Barney Bigard And His Orchestra
Highlights From The Duke Ellington Centennial Edition | RCA | 2663672-2
Jazz:The Essential Collection Vol.3 | IN+OUT Records | 78013-2
Ben Webster All Stars
King Of The Tenors | Verve | 519806-2
Ben Webster And His Associates
Verve Jazz Masters 43:Ben Webster | Verve | 525431-2
Ultimate Ben Webster selected by James Carter | Verve | 557537-2
Ben Webster And Associates | Verve | 835254-2
Ben Webster And His Orchestra
Verve Jazz Masters 43:Ben Webster | Verve | 525431-2
Ben Webster Quartet
Soulville | Verve | 521449-2
Ultimate Ben Webster selected by James Carter | Verve | 557537-2
Jazz:The Essential Collection Vol.3 | IN+OUT Records | 78013-2
The Jazz Giants Play Duke Ellington:Caravan | Prestige | PCD 24227-2
My Man-Live At The Montmartre | Steeplechase | SCCD 31008
Ben Webster Quintet
Soulville | Verve | 521449-2
Jazz:The Essential Collection Vol.3 | IN+OUT Records | 78013-2
At The Renaissance | Original Jazz Classics | OJC 390(C 7646)
Ben Webster Septet
The Soul Of Ben Webster | Verve | 527475-2
Ben Webster Sextet
Verve Jazz Masters 43:Ben Webster | Verve | 525431-2
Verve Jazz Masters 52:Maynard Ferguson | Verve | 529905-2
Ben Webster With Orchestra And Strings
Verve Jazz Masters 43:Ben Webster | Verve | 525431-2
Music For Loving:Ben Webster With Strings | Verve | 527774-2
Ultimate Ben Webster selected by James Carter | Verve | 557537-2
Ben Webster With Strings
The Warm Moods-With Strings | Rhino | 8122-73721-2
Ben Webster With The Billy Strayhorn Trio
Music For Loving:Ben Webster With Strings | Verve | 527774-2
Ben Webster With The Kenny Drew Trio
The Art Of Saxophone | Laserlight | 24652
The Story Of Jazz Piano | Laserlight | 24653
Ben Webster With The Oscar Peterson Quartet
King Of The Tenors | Verve | 519806-2
Verve Jazz Masters 43:Ben Webster | Verve | 525431-2
Ultimate Ben Webster selected by James Carter | Verve | 557537-2
Ben Webster With The Oscar Peterson Trio
Ben Webster Meets Oscar Peterson | Verve | 521448-2
Verve Jazz Masters 43:Ben Webster | Verve | 525431-2
Ben Webster With The Teddy Wilson Trio
Verve Jazz Masters 43:Ben Webster | Verve | 525431-2
Music For Loving:Ben Webster With Strings | Verve | 527774-2
Ben Webster-André Previn
Swinging Kicks | Verve | 559514-2
Ben Webster-Stan Levey
Ultimate Ben Webster selected by James Carter | Verve | 557537-2
Benny Carter And His Chocolate Dandies
Planet Jazz:Ben Webster | RCA | 2165368-2
Jazz:The Essential Collection Vol.3 | IN+OUT Records | 78013-2
Benny Carter Sextet
Jazz Giant | Original Jazz Classics | OJC20 167-2(C 7555)
Benny Morton's All Stars
The Blue Note Swingtets | Blue Note | 495697-2
Jazz:The Essential Collection Vol.3 | IN+OUT Records | 78013-2
Benny Moten's Kansas City Orchestra
Planet Jazz:Ben Webster | RCA | 2165368-2
Planet Jazz:Swing | Planet Jazz | 2169651-2
Jazz:The Essential Collection Vol.3 | IN+OUT Records | 78013-2
Billie Holiday And Her All Stars
Verve Jazz Masters 12:Billie Holiday | Verve | 519825-2
Songs For Distingué Lovers | Verve | 539056-2
Billie Holiday And Her Band
Verve Jazz Masters 47:Billie Holiday Sings Standards | Verve | 527650-2
Billie Holiday With Teddy Wilson And His Orchestra
Billie's Love Songs | Nimbus Records | NI 2000
Buddy Bregman And His Orchestra
Swinging Kicks | Verve | 559514-2
Carmen McRae With Orchestra
Birds Of A Feather | Decca | 589515-2
Carmen McRae With The Ralph Burns Orchetra
Birds Of A Feather | Decca | 589515-2
Coleman Hawkins And Ben Webster With The Oscar Peterson Quartet
Coleman Hawkins Encounters Ben Webster | Verve | 521427-2
Verve Jazz Masters 43:Coleman Hawkins | Verve | 521856-2
Verve Jazz Masters 43:Ben Webster | Verve | 525431-2
Verve Jazz Masters Vol.60:The Collection | Verve | 529866-2
Ultimate Coleman Hawkins selected by Sonny Rollins | Verve | 557538-2
Coleman Hawkins And Confreres
Coleman Hawkins And Confreres | Verve | 835255-2 PMS
Cozy Cole All Stars
Jazz:The Essential Collection Vol.3 | IN+OUT Records | 78013-2
Dinah Washington With The Jimmy Cobb Orchestra
Verve Jazz Masters 40:Dinah Washington | Verve | 522055-2
Ultimate Ben Webster selected by James Carter | Verve | 557537-2
Duke Ellington And His Famous Orchestra
Duke Ellington:The Blanton-Webster Band | Bluebird | 21 13181-2
Planet Jazz:Duke Ellington | Planet Jazz | 2152053-2
Planet Jazz:Johnny Hodges | Planet Jazz | 2152065-2
Planet Jazz Sampler | Planet Jazz | 2152326-2
Planet Jazz:Ben Webster | RCA | 2165368-2
Planet Jazz:Big Bands | Planet Jazz | 2169649-2
Planet Jazz:Jazz Trumpet | Planet Jazz | 2169654-2
Planet Jazz:Female Jazz Vocalists | Planet Jazz | 2169656-2
Highlights From The Duke Ellington Centennial Edition | RCA | 2663672-2
Jazz:The Essential Collection Vol.2 | IN+OUT Records | 78012-2
Jazz:The Essential Collection Vol.3 | IN+OUT Records | 78013-2
Duke Ellington:Ko-Ko | Dreyfus Jazz Line | FDM 36717-2
Duke Ellington And His Orchestra
Highlights From The Duke Ellington Centennial Edition | RCA | 2663672-2
Carnegie Hall Concert January 1943 | Prestige | 2PCD 34004-2
Ella Fitzgerald And Duke Ellington:Cote D'Azure Concerts on Verve | Verve | 539033-2
Jazz:The Essential Collection Vol.2 | IN+OUT Records | 78012-2
Jazz:The Essential Collection Vol.3 | IN+OUT Records | 78013-2
The Duke At Fargo 1940 | Storyville | STCD 8316/17
At The Hurricane:Original 1943 Broadcasts | Storyville | STCD 8359
Ella Fitzgerald And Her All Stars
The Best Of The Song Books:The Ballads | Verve | 521867-2
Love Songs:The Best Of The Song Books | Verve | 531762-2
Ella Fitzgerald Sings The Duke Ellington Songbook | Verve | 559248-2
For The Love Of Ella Fitzgerald | Verve | 841765-2
Ella Fitzgerald And Her Quintet
Verve Jazz Masters 46:Ella Fitzgerald-The Jazz Sides | Verve | 527655-2
Ella Fitzgerald And Her Sextet
Ella Fitzgerald-First Lady Of Song | Verve | 517898-2
The Best Of The Song Books | Verve | 519804-2
Ella Fitzgerald With The Duke Ellington Orchestra
Ella Fitzgerald-First Lady Of Song | Verve | 517898-2
Ella & Duke At The Cote D'Azur | Verve | 539030-2
Ella Fitzgerald And Duke Ellington:Cote D'Azure Concerts on Verve | Verve | 539033-2
Ella Fitzgerald With The Frank DeVol Orchestra
Get Happy! | Verve | 523321-2
Ella Fitzgerald With The Oscar Peterson Quartet And Ben Webster
Verve Jazz Masters 43:Ben Webster | Verve | 525431-2
Fletcher Henderson And His Orchestra
Jazz:The Essential Collection Vol.1 | IN+OUT Records | 78011-2
Jazz:The Essential Collection Vol.3 | IN+OUT Records | 78013-2
Gerry Mulligan-Ben Webster Quintet
Verve Jazz Masters 43:Ben Webster | Verve | 525431-2
The Complete Gerry Mulligan Meets Ben Webster Sessions | Verve | 539055-2
Ultimate Ben Webster selected by James Carter | Verve | 557537-2
Harry Sweets Edison Sextet
The Soul Of Ben Webster | Verve | 527475-2
Jack Teagarden's Big Eight
Jazz:The Essential Collection Vol.3 | IN+OUT Records | 78013-2
James P.Johnson's Blue Note Jazzmen
Jazz:The Essential Collection Vol.3 | IN+OUT Records | 78013-2
The Blue Note Jazzmen | Blue Note | 821262-2
JATP All Stars
JATP In Tokyo | Pablo | 2620104-2
The Cole Porter Songbook | Verve | 823250-2
Joe Williams And Friends
At Newport '63 | RCA | 2663919-2
Joe Williams And His Band
Planet Jazz:Joe Williams | Planet Jazz | 2165370-2
Joe Williams With The Jimmy Jones Orchestra
Planet Jazz:Joe Williams | Planet Jazz | 2165370-2
Johnny Hodges And His Band
Verve Jazz Masters 35:Johnny Hodges | Verve | 521857-2
Johnny Hodges Orchestra
Side By Side | Verve | 521405-2
Verve Jazz Masters 43:Ben Webster | Verve | 525431-2
The Soul Of Ben Webster | Verve | 527475-2
Johnny Otis And His Orchestra
Verve Jazz Masters 43:Ben Webster | Verve | 525431-2
Lionel Hampton And His Orchestra
Planet Jazz:Coleman Hawkins | Planet Jazz | 2152055-2
Planet Jazz:Lionel Hampton | Planet Jazz | 2152059-2
Planet Jazz Sampler | Planet Jazz | 2152326-2
Planet Jazz:Ben Webster | RCA | 2165368-2
Planet Jazz:Jazz Saxophone | Planet Jazz | 2169653-2
Jazz:The Essential Collection Vol.3 | IN+OUT Records | 78013-2
Mundell Lowe And His All Stars
Planet Jazz:Ben Webster | RCA | 2165368-2
Norman Granz Jam Session
Verve Jazz Masters 26:Lionel Hampton with Oscar Peterson | Verve | 521853-2
Verve Jazz Masters 35:Johnny Hodges | Verve | 521857-2
Charlie Parker:The Best Of The Verve Years | Verve | 527815-2
Verve Jazz Masters Vol.60:The Collection | Verve | 529866-2
Talkin' Bird | Verve | 559859-2
Bird: The Complete Charlie Parker On Verve | Verve | 837141-2
Oliver Nelson And His Orchestra
More Blues And The Abstract Truth | Impulse(MCA) | 951212-2
Pete Johnson's Housewarmin'
Jazz:The Essential Collection Vol.3 | IN+OUT Records | 78013-2
Red Norvo Sextet
Planet Jazz:Ben Webster | RCA | 2165368-2
Rex Stewart And His Orchestra
Planet Jazz:Ben Webster | RCA | 2165368-2
Planet Jazz:Jazz Trumpet | Planet Jazz | 2169654-2
Jazz:The Essential Collection Vol.3 | IN+OUT Records | 78013-2
Richard 'Groove' Holmes Sextet
Somethin' Special | Pacific Jazz | 855452-2
Sidney Catlett Quartet
Jazz:The Essential Collection Vol.3 | IN+OUT Records | 78013-2
Teddy Wilson And His All Stars
Jazz:The Essential Collection Vol.3 | IN+OUT Records | 78013-2
Teddy Wilson And His Orchestra
Jazz:The Essential Collection Vol.3 | IN+OUT Records | 78013-2
The Ravens
Ultimate Ben Webster selected by James Carter | Verve | 557537-2
Tony Scott And His Down Beat Club Sextet
Jazz:The Essential Collection Vol.3 | IN+OUT Records | 78013-2
Willie Bryant And His Orchestra
Planet Jazz:Ben Webster | RCA | 2165368-2
Woody Herman And His Sextet
Songs For Hip Lovers | Verve | 559872-2
Woody Herman And The Vanderbilt All Stars
Louis Armstrong-Jack Teagarden-Woody Herman:Midnights At V-Disc | Jazz Unlimited | JUCD 2048

Webster,Freddie | (tp)
Billie Holiday With Eddie Heywood And His Orchestra
Billie Holiday:The Complete Commodore Recordings | GRP | 543272-2
Earl Hines And His Orchestra
Planet Jazz:Earl Hines | Planet Jazz | 2159973-2
Louis Jordan And His Tympany Five
Louis Jordan-Let The Good Times Roll: The Complete Decca Recordings 1938-1954 | Bear Family Records | BCD 15557 IH

Webster,Freddie or Kenneth Roane | (tp)

Webster,Paul | (cotp)
Ella Fitzgerald With Sy Oliver And His Orchestra
Ella Fitzgerald:Mr.Paganini | Dreyfus Jazz Line | FDM 36741-2
Ella Fitzgerald And Louis Armstrong With Sy Oliver And His Orchestra
Ella Fitzgerald:Mr.Paganini | Dreyfus Jazz Line | FDM 36741-2
Ella Fitzgerald With Sy Oliver And His Orchestra
Ella Fitzgerald:The Decca Years 1949-1954 | Decca | 050668-2
Louis Armstrong And Ella Fitzgerald With Sy Oliver's Orchestra
Louis Armstrong:C'est Si Bon | Dreyfus Jazz Line | FDM 36730-2
Louis Armstrong With Sy Oliver And His Orchestra
Satchmo Serenaders | Verve | 543792-2
Louis Armstrong:C'est Si Bon | Dreyfus Jazz Line | FDM 36730-2
Louis Armstrong-My Greatest Songs | MCA | MCD 18347

Wechsler,Moe | (p)
Billy Butterfield And His Modern Dixie Stompers
Soft Strut | Fresh Sound Records | FSR-CD 318
Chris Connor With Band
Chris Connor | Atlantic | 7567-80769-2

Weckl,Dave | (b,dr,brush-coverdub,brush-overdub)
Chick Corea Electric Band
The Chick Corea Electric Band | GRP | GRP 95352
Light Years | GRP | GRP 95462
Eye Of The Beholder | GRP | GRP 95642
Beneath The Mask | GRP | GRP 96492
Chick Corea Trio
Akoustic Band | GRP | GRP 95822
Dave Weckl Group
Master Plan | GRP | GRP 96192
Heads Up | GRP | GRP 96732
Hard-Wired | GRP | GRP 97602
GRP All-Star Big Band
GRP All-Star Big Band:Live! | GRP | GRP 97402
All Blues | GRP | GRP 98002
John Patitucci Group

Mistura Fina | GRP | GRP 98022
Randy Brecker Group
Jazzrock-Anthology Vol.3:Fusion | Zounds | CD 27100555

Weed,Buddy | (p)
Billie Holiday With The Paul Whiteman Orchestra
Billie's Blues | Blue Note | 748786-2
Bud Freeman And His Stars
Muggsy Spanier And Bud Freeman:V-Discs 1944-45 | Jazz Unlimited | JUCD 2049
Bud Freeman And The V-Disc Jumpers
Muggsy Spanier And Bud Freeman:V-Discs 1944-45 | Jazz Unlimited | JUCD 2049
Eight Squares And A Critic
Muggsy Spanier And Bud Freeman:V-Discs 1944-45 | Jazz Unlimited | JUCD 2049
The V-Disc Jumpers
Muggsy Spanier And Bud Freeman:V-Discs 1944-45 | Jazz Unlimited | JUCD 2049

Weeden,Paul | (gvoc)
Eddie Lockjaw Davis Quintet
The Jazz Giants Play Harry Warren:Lullaby Of Broadway | Prestige | PCD 24204-2
Gene Ammons-Sonny Stitt Quintet
Verve Jazz Masters 50:Sonny Sitt | Verve | 527651-2
Boss Tenors In Orbit!!! | Verve | 549371-2

Weeke,Stefan | (bperc)
Triocolor
Colours Of Ghana | ACT | 9285-2

Weeks,Jack | (tb)
Paul Desmond Quartet With The Bill Bates Singers
Desmond | Original Jazz Classics | OJCCD 712-2(F 3235/8082)

Wegele,Peter | (p)
Edith Steyer... Posterity Quintet
...On The Right Track | Jazz 4 Ever Records:Jazz Network | J4E 4745

Wegener,Sophie | (voc)
Zona Sul
Pure Love | Nagel-Heyer | CD 3039

Weglinski,Helmut | (v)
Helmut Weglinski Quintet
Deutsches Jazz Fesival 1954/1955 | Bear Family Records | BCD 15430

Wegner,Gerhard | (p)
Erwin Lehn Und Sein Südfunk-Tanzorchester
Deutsches Jazz Fesival 1954/1955 | Bear Family Records | BCD 15430

Wegscheider,Christian | (p)
Christian Wegscheider Trio
Live | Village | VILCD 1015-2

Wehr,Daniel | (dr)
Jazz Orchester Rheinland-Pfalz
Last Season | Jazz Haus Musik | LJBB 9706

Weichbrodt,Fritz | (tp)
Freddie Brocksieper Orchester
Shot Gun Boogie | Bear Family Records | BCD 16277 AH
Stan Getz With The Kurt Edelhagen Orchestra
Stan Getz In Europe | Laserlight | 24657

Weidenmüller,Johannes | (b)
Anke Helfrich Trio With Mark Turner
You'll See | double moon | CHRDM 71013
Jacques Schwarz-Bart/James Hurt Quartet
Immersion | Fresh Sound Records | FSNT 057 CD
Jam Session
Jam Session Vol.4 | Steeplechase | SCCD 31527

Weidinger,Tobias | (tpfl-h)
Al Porcino Big Band
Al Porcino Big Band Live! | Organic Music | ORGM 9717
Clark Terry With The Summit Jazz Orchestra
Clark | Edition Collage | EC 530-2
HR Big Band
Libertango:Homage An Astor Piazolla | hr music.de | hrmj 014-02 CD

Weidman,James | (keyboards,p,synthperc)
Cassandra Wilson Group
After The Beginning Again | JMT Edition | 514001-2

Weidner,Christian | (as,tsreeds)
Gunter Hampel Jazz Sextet
Gunter Hampel: The 8th Of Sept.1999 | Birth | CD 049
Gunter Hampel Next Generation
Next Generation | Birth | CD 043
Köln Concert Part 1 | Birth | CD 047
Köln Concert Part 2 | Birth | CD 048
Gunter Hampel-Christian Weider
Gunter Hampel: The 8th Of Sept.1999 | Birth | CD 049
Gunter Hampel-Christian Weider Duo
Solid Fun | Birth | CD 044

Weight,Alan | (tp)
Don Ellis Orchestra
Electric Bath | CBS | CK 65522

Weigt,Eckhard | (ts)
Eckhard Weigt Quartet
Standard Moods | Organic Music | ORGM 9718

Weil,Andreas | (tb)
Landes Jugend Jazz Orchester Hessen
Touch Of Lips | hr music.de | hrmj 004-01 CD

Wein,George | (p,ldvoc)
George Wein's Dixie Victors
The Magic Horn | RCA | 2113038-2
Planet Jazz | Planet Jazz | 2169652-2
The Chicago All Stars
Planet Jazz:Bud Freeman | Planet Jazz | 2161240-2

Weindorf,Hermann | (keyboardsvoc)
Klaus Doldinger's Passport
Man In The Mirror | Warner | 2292-40253-2
Running In Real Time | Warner | 2292-40633-2
Heavy Nights | Warner | 2292-42006-2
Earthborn | Atlantic | 2292-46477-2

Weinert,Martin | (bel-b)
Susan Weinert Band
Mysterious Stories | VeraBra Records | CDVBR 2111-2
The Bottom Line | VeraBra Records | CDVBR 2177-2
Point Of View | Intuition Records | INT 3272-2

Weinert,Susan | (g,el-gg-synth)
Mysterious Stories | VeraBra Records | CDVBR 2111-2
The Bottom Line | VeraBra Records | CDVBR 2177-2
Point Of View | Intuition Records | INT 3272-2

Weinhold,Tim | (bongos,bells,vaseperc)
Steve Tibbetts Group
Yr | ECM | 1355(835245-2)

Weinkopf,Gerald 'Gerry' | (flts)
Erwin Lehn Und Sein Südfunk-Tanzorchester
Deutsches Jazz Fesival 1954/1955 | Bear Family Records | BCD 15430
Wolfgang Lauth Septet
Noch Lauther | Bear Family Records | BCD 15942 AH

Weinstein,David | (electronics,keyboardsceleste)
John Zorn Group
Spillane | Nonesuch | 7559-79172-2

Weinstein,Georgina | (voc)
Big Band Bellaterra
Don't Git Sassy | Fresh Sound Records | FSNT 048 CD
Georgina Weinstein With Her Quartet
Come Rain Or Come Shine | Fresh Sound Records | FSNT 020 CD
Georgina Weinstein With Her Trio
Come Rain Or Come Shine | Fresh Sound Records | FSNT 020 CD

Weinstein,Jimmy | (dr)
Matt Renzi-Jimmy Weinstein Quartet
Matt Renzi-Jimmy Weinstein Quartet | Fresh Sound Records | FSNT 045 CD
Matt Renzi-Jimmy Weinstein-Masa Kamaguchi Trio
Lines And Ballads | Fresh Sound Records | FSNT 065 CD

Weinstein,Mark | (tb)
Cal Tjader's Orchestra
Talkin Verve/Roots Of Acid Jazz:Cal Tjader | Verve | 531562-2
Herbie Mann Group
The Best Of Herbie Mann | Atlantic | 7567-81369-2

Weinstein,Ruby | (tp)
Ben Pollack And His Park Central Orchestra
Planet Jazz:Jack Teagarden | Planet Jazz | 2161236-2
Jazz:The Essential Collection Vol.3 | IN+OUT Records | 78013-2

Weinstock,Leonore | (viola)
Earl Klugh Group With Strings
Late Night Guitar | Blue Note | 498573-2

Weir,Frank | (clas)
Arthur Young And Hatchett's Swingtette
Grapelli Story | Verve | 515807-2

Weisberg,Steve | (keyboardssynth)
Karen Mantler Group
My Cat Arnold | Watt | XtraWatt/3
Karen Mantler And Her Cat Arnold Get The Flu | Watt | XtraWatt/5

Weise,Steffen | (viola)
HR Big Band With Marjorie Barnes And Frits Landesbergen And Strings
Swinging Christmas | hr music.de | hrmj 012-02 CD

Weiser,Andreas | (perc,electronicsvoice)
Die Elefanten
Wasserwüste | Nabel Records:Jazz Network | CD 4634

Weisgaard,Ethan | (perc)
Jens Winther And The Danish Radio Jazz Orchestra
Angels | dacapo | DCCD 9442
Mona Larsen And The Danish Radio Big Band Plus Soloists
Michael Mantler:Cerco Un Paese Innocente | ECM | 1556
The Danish Radio Jazz Orchestra
This Train:The Danish Radio Jazz Orchestra Plays The Music Of Ray Pitts | dacapo | DCCD 9428
Nice Work | dacapo | DCCD 9446

Weisgard,Ethan | (perccongas)
Miles Davis With The Danish Radio Big Band
Aura | CBS | CK 63962
Stan Getz With The Danish Radio Big Band
Stan Getz In Europe | Laserlight | 24657
The Danish Radio Big Band
Aura | CBS | CK 63962

Weiss,Avram | (v)
Paul Desmond Quartet With The Don Sebesby Orchestra
From The Hot Afternoon | Verve | 543487-2

Weiss,Dan | (dr)
Sebastian Weiss Trio
Polaroid Memory | Fresh Sound Records | FSNT 085 CD

Weiss,David | (tpfl-h)
Bop City
Hot Jazz Bisquits | Hip Bop | HIBD 8801
New Jazz Composers Octet
Walkin' the Line | Fresh Sound Records | FSNT 151 CD
The New Jazz Composers Octet
First Step Into Reality | Fresh Sound Records | FSNT 059 CD
Tom Harrell Orchestra
Time's Mirror | RCA | 2663524-2

Weiss,Doug | (b)
Al Foster Quartet
Brandyn | Laika Records | 35100832
Phil Grenadier Quintet
Sweet Transients | Fresh Sound Records | FSNT 093 CD

Weiss,Häns'che | (gvoc)
Häns'che Weiss-Vali Mayer Duo
The Duo Live In Concert | MMM Records | CD 1296
Just Play | MMM Records | CD 1298
Just Play II | MMM Records | CD 1303

Weiss,Harald | (percvoice)
Harald Weiss
Trommelgeflüster | ECM | 1249

Weiss,Heinz | (p)
Brocksi-Quartett
Drums Boogie | Bear Family Records | BCD 15988 AH
Brocksi-Quintett
Drums Boogie | Bear Family Records | BCD 15988 AH
Freddie Brocksieper Orchester
Drums Boogie | Bear Family Records | BCD 15988 AH

Weiß,Kaki | (rh-g)
Traubeli Weiß Ensemble
Dreaming Of You | Edition Collage | EC 468-2

Weiss,Klaus | (dr)
Clifford Jordan Quintet
Clifford Jordan Meets Klaus Weiss | JHM Records | JHM 3617
HR Big Band
The American Songs Of Kurt Weill | hr music.de | hrmj 006-01 CD
Klaus Doldinger Quartet
Doldinger's Best | ACT | 9224-2
Klaus Weiss Orchestra
Live At The Domicile | ATM Records | ATM 3805-AH
Klaus Weiss Quintet
A Taste Of Jazz | ATM Records | ATM 3810-AH
Klaus Weiss Septet
All Night Through | ATM Records | ATM 3816 AH
Klaus Weiss Sextet
All Night Through | ATM Records | ATM 3816 AH

Weiss,Kurt | (tpfl-h)
Bob Sands Quintet
JumpSTART | Fresh Sound Records | FSNT 042 CD

Weiss,Martin | (g,vel-v)
Organ Jazztrio & Martin Weiss
Hommage | Edition Collage | EC 492-2

Weiss,Michael | (p)
Johnny Griffin-Steve Grossman Quintet
Johnny Griffin & Steve Grossman | Dreyfus Jazz Line | FDM 36615-2

Weiss,Otto | (org,pvib)
Buddy Tate With The Torsten Swingenberger Swintet
Tate Live | Nagel-Heyer | CD 080
Freddie Brocksieper Und Seine Solisten
Freddie's Boogie Blues | Bear Family Records | BCD 16388 AH
Jenny Evans And The Rudi Martini Quartet
At Lloyd's | ESM Records | ESM 9302

Weiss,Peter | (drperc)
Brecker-Engstfeld-Plümer-Weiss
ToGether | Nabel Records:Jazz Network | CD 4648
Changes
Jazz Portraits | EGO | 95080
Engstfeld-Plümer-Weiss
Drivin' | Nabel Records:Jazz Network | CD 4618
Hipsters In The Zone
Into The Afro-Latin Bag | Nabel Records:Jazz Network | CD 4663
Peter Weiss
Personal Choice | Nabel Records:Jazz Network | CD 4669
Peter Weiss Orchestra
Personal Choice | Nabel Records:Jazz Network | CD 4669
Peter Weiss Quartet
Personal Choice | Nabel Records:Jazz Network | CD 4669
Peter Weiss Sextet
Personal Choice | Nabel Records:Jazz Network | CD 4669
Peter Weiss-Claus Fischer
Personal Choice | Nabel Records:Jazz Network | CD 4669
Peter Weiss-Paul Imm
Personal Choice | Nabel Records:Jazz Network | CD 4669
Randy Brecker-Wolfgang Engstfeld Quartet
Mr. Max! | Nabel Records:Jazz Network | CD 4637
Wolfgang Engstfeld Quartet
Songs And Ballads | Nabel Records:Jazz Network | CD 4658

Weiss,Sam | (dr)
Louis Armstrong And His Orchestra
Louis Armstrong:Swing That Music | Laserlight | 36056
Tommy Dorsey And His Clambake Seven
Planet Jazz:Tommy Dorsey | Planet Jazz | 2159972-2
Planet Jazz:Swing | Planet Jazz | 2169651-2
Tommy Dorsey And His Orchestra
Planet Jazz:Tommy Dorsey | Planet Jazz | 2159972-2

Weiss,Sebastian | (p)
Sebastian Weiss Trio
Polaroid Memory | Fresh Sound Records | FSNT 085 CD

Weiss,Sid | (bg)
Artie Shaw And His Orchestra
Planet JazzArtie Shaw | Planet Jazz | 2152057-2
Planet Jazz Sampler | Planet Jazz | 2152326-2
Planet Jazz:Swing | Planet Jazz | 2169651-2
Planet Jazz:Female Jazz Vocalists | Planet Jazz | 2169656-2
The Legends Of Swing | Laserlight | 24659
Benny Goodman And His Orchestra
The Legends Of Swing | Laserlight | 24659
Duke Ellington And His Orchestra
Planet Jazz:Duke Ellington | Planet Jazz | 2152053-2
Peggy Lee With Benny Goodman And His Quintet
Peggy Lee & Benny Goodman:The Complete Recordings 1941-1947 | CBS | C2K 65686
Peggy Lee With Benny Goodman And His Sextet
Peggy Lee & Benny Goodman:The Complete Recordings 1941-1947 | CBS | C2K 65686
Peggy Lee With The Benny Goodman Orchestra
Peggy Lee & Benny Goodman:The Complete Recordings 1941-1947 | CBS | C2K 65686
Tommy Dorsey And His Orchestra
Planet Jazz:Frank Sinatra & Tommy Dorsey | Planet Jazz | 2152067-2
Planet Jazz Sampler | Planet Jazz | 2152326-2
Planet Jazz:Tommy Dorsey | Planet Jazz | 2159972-2
Planet Jazz:Big Bands | Planet Jazz | 2169649-2
Planet Jazz:Male Jazz Vocalists | Planet Jazz | 2169657-2
Frank Sinatra And The Tommy Dorsey Orchestra | RCA | 2668701-2
V-Disc All Star Jam Session
Louis Armstrong-Jack Teagarden-Woody Herman:Midnights At V-Disc | Jazz Unlimited | JUCD 2048

Weiß,Traubeli | (g)
Joe Bawelino Quartet
Happy Birthday Stéphane | Edition Collage | EC 458-2
Joe Bawelino Quartet & Martin Stegner
Happy Birthday Stéphane | Edition Collage | EC 458-2
Traubeli Weiß Ensemble
Dreaming Of You | Edition Collage | EC 468-2

Weiss,Walter | (ascl)
Brocksi-Quintett
Drums Boogie | Bear Family Records | BCD 15988 AH
Freddie Brocksieper Orchester
Drums Boogie | Bear Family Records | BCD 15988 AH

Weissbach,Bela | (tpfl-h)
Lajos Dudas Group
Jubilee Edition | double moon | CHRDM 71020

weitere Angaben lagen bei Redaktionsschluß nicht vor |
Monty Waters' Hot House
Live In Paris, Duc Des Lombards, Volume One | Tutu Records | 888140-2*

Wekenmann,Frank | (g,bjvoc)
Ralph Abelein Group
Mr. B's Time Machine | Satin Doll Productions | SDP 1042-1 CD

Welander,Jörgen | (tuba)
Matthias Stich Sevensenses
...mehrschichtig | Satin Doll Productions | SDP 1038-1 CD

Welch,Jimmy | (tpv-tb)
Tommy Dorsey And His Orchestra
Planet Jazz:Tommy Dorsey | Planet Jazz | 2159972-2
Planet Jazz:Big Bands | Planet Jazz | 2169649-2
Planet Jazz:Swing | Planet Jazz | 2169651-2

Welch,Jon | (tb)
Al Porcino Big Band
Al Cohn Meets Al Porcino | Organic Music | ORGM 9730
Joe Pass With The NDR Big Band And Radio Philharmonie Hannover
Joe Pass In Hamburg | ACT | 9100-2
Pee Wee Ellis & NDR Bigband
What You Like | Minor Music | 801064

Welcome To The Maze |
Welcome To The Maze
Welcome To The Maze:Puzzle | Nabel Records:Jazz Network | CD 4671

Well,Erich | (tb)
Helmut Zacharias mit dem Orchester Frank Folken
Ich Habe Rhythmus | Bear Family Records | BCD 15642 AH

Welle,Jochen | (drperc)
Wayne Bartlett With The Thomas Hufschmidt Group
Tokyo Blues | Laika Records | 35101212

Wellershoff,Dieter | (recitation)
Kölner Saxophon Mafia With Dieter Wellershoff
Kölner Saxophon Mafia Proudly Presents | Jazz Haus Musik | JHM 0046 CD

Wellman,Ricky | (dr)
Miles Davis Group
Miles Davis Live From His Last Concert In Avignon | Laserlight | 24327
Amandla | Warner | 7599-25873-2

Wells,Chris | (drperc)
Carla Bley Band
Fancy Chamber Music | Watt | 28(539937-2)
Jim Tomlinson Quartet
Brazilian Sketches | Candid | CCD 79769
Jim Tomlinson Quintet
Brazilian Sketches | Candid | CCD 79769

Wells,Dave | (bar-horn,b-tp,tbtp)
Mel Tormé With The Billy May Orchestra
Mel Tormé Goes South Of The Border With Billy May | Verve | 589517-2

Wells,Dicky | (tb,arrld)
Anita O'Day With The Russ Garcia Orchestra
Verve Jazz Masters 49:Anita O'Day | Verve | 527653-2
Bud Freeman All Stars
The Bud Freeman All-Star Sessions | Prestige | PRCD 24286-2
Count Basie And His Orchestra
Planet Jazz:Count Basie | Planet Jazz | 2152068-2
Planet Jazz Sampler | Planet Jazz | 2152326-2
Planet Jazz:Jimmy Rushing | RCA | 2165371-2
Jazz Collection:Count Basie | Laserlight | 24368
Jazz:The Essential Collection Vol.3 | IN+OUT Records | 78013-2
From Spiritual To Swing | Vanguard | VCD 169/71
Count Basie Octet
Planet Jazz:Count Basie | Planet Jazz | 2152068-2
Count Basie's Kansas City Seven
Jazz:The Essential Collection Vol.3 | IN+OUT Records | 78013-2
Dickie Wells-Buddy Tate Quintet
Every Day I Have The Blues | Impulse(MCA) | 547967-2
Dicky Wells And His Orchestra
Americans Swinging In Paris:Dicky Wells | EMI Records | 539664-2
Jazz:The Essential Collection Vol.3 | IN+OUT Records | 78013-2
Fletcher Henderson And His Orchestra
Jazz:The Essential Collection Vol.1 | IN+OUT Records | 78011-2
Jazz:The Essential Collection Vol.3 | IN+OUT Records | 78013-2
Frankie Laine With Buck Clayton And His Orchestra
Jazz Spectacular | CBS | CK 65507
Helen Humes With James P. Johnson And The Count Basie Orchestra
From Spiritual To Swing | Vanguard | VCD 169/71
Ida Cox With The James P. Johnson Septet
From Spiritual To Swing | Vanguard | VCD 169/71
Jimmy Rushing And His Orchestra
Every Day I Have The Blues | Impulse(MCA) | 547967-2
Jimmy Rushing With Count Basie And His Orchestra
From Spiritual To Swing | Vanguard | VCD 169/71
Jimmy Rushing With Oliver Nelson And His Orchestra
Every Day I Have The Blues | Impulse(MCA) | 547967-2
Kansas City Seven
Jazz:The Essential Collection Vol.3 | IN+OUT Records | 78013-2
Kansas City Six

Lester Young:Blue Lester | Dreyfus Jazz Line | FDM 36729-2
Nancy Harrow And The Buck Clayton All Stars
Wild Women Don't Have The Blues | Candid | CCD 79008
Spike Hughes And His Negro Orchestra
Jazz:The Essential Collection Vol.3 | IN+OUT Records | 78013-2

Wells,Fred | (el-g,gvoc)
Cold Sweat
Cold Sweat Plays J.B. | JMT Edition | 919025-2

Wells,Henry | (tbvoc)
Jimmy Lunceford And His Orchestra
Planet Jazz:Swing | Planet Jazz | 2169651-2

Wells,Junior | (harmvoc)
Buddy Guy Blues Band
Buddy Guy-The Complete Chess Studio Recordings | MCA | MCD 09337

Wells,Tim | (b)
Klaus König Orchestra
Times Of Devastation/Poco A Poco | Enja | ENJ-6014 22
Hommage A Douglas Adams | Enja | ENJ-6078 2
Paul Shigihara-Charlie Mariano Quartet
Tears Of Sound | Nabel Records:Jazz Network | CD 4616
Peter Herborn's Acute Insights
Peter Herborn's Acute Insights | JMT Edition | 919017-2

Wellstood,Dick | (p,talkingp-solo)
Dick Wellstood's Wallerites
Uptown And Lowdown | Prestige | PCD 24262-2
Dick Wellstood-Tommy Benford
Uptown And Lowdown | Prestige | PCD 24262-2
Nancy Harrow And The Buck Clayton All Stars
Wild Women Don't Have The Blues | Candid | CCD 79008
Odetta With The Buck Clayton Sextet
Odetta And The Blues | Original Blues Classics | OBCCD 509-2(RLP 9417)
Roy Eldridge And His Central Plaza Dixielanders
The Very Best Of Dixieland Jazz | Verve | 535529-2
The Complete Verve Roy Eldridge Studio Sessions | Verve | 9861278
Sidney Bechet With Bob Wilber's Wildcats
Sidney Bechet:Summertime | Dreyfus Jazz Line | FDM 36712-2

Welsch,Chauncey | (tb)
Cab Calloway And His Orchestra
Planet Jazz:Cab Calloway | Planet Jazz | 2161237-2
Planet Jazz:Male Jazz Vocalists | Planet Jazz | 2169657-2
Coleman Hawkins With Billy Byers And His Orchestra
The Hawk In Hi-Fi | RCA | 2663842-2
Coleman Hawkins With Many Albam And His Orchestra
Planet Jazz:Coleman Hawkins | Planet Jazz | 2152055-2
Elliot Lawrence And His Orchestra
The Elliot Lawrence Big Band Swings Cohn & Kahn | Fantasy | FCD 24761-2
Jimmy Smith With The Billy Byers Orchestra
Jimmy Smith:Best Of The Verve Years | Verve | 527950-2
Lena Horne With The Lennie Hayton Orchestra
Planet Jazz:Lena Horne | Planet Jazz | 2165373-2
Leon Thomas With Orchestra
Spirits Known And Unknown | RCA | 2663876-2
Singers Unlimited With The Pat Williams Orchestra
The Singers Unlimited:Magic Voices | MPS | 539130-2
Singers Unlimited With The Patrick Williams Orchestra
The Singers Unlimited:Magic Voices | MPS | 539130-2
Wes Montgomery Orchestra
Movin' Wes | Verve | 521433-2
Wes Montgomery With The Johnny Pate Orchestra
Verve Jazz Masters 14:Wes Montgomery | Verve | 519826-2
Wes Montgomery:The Verve Jazz Sides | Verve | 521690-2
Talkin' Jazz:Roots Of Acid Jazz | Verve | 529580-2

Welz,Joachim | (cl)
Till Brönner Quartet & Deutsches Symphonieorchester Berlin
German Songs | Minor Music | 801057

Wenclik,Anna | (v)
Bernd Konrad Jazz Group With Symphonie Orchestra
Wen Die Götter Lieben | Creative Works Records | CW CD 1010-1

Wendholt,Scott | (tpfl-h)
David Matthews & The Manhattan Jazz Orchestra
Back To Bach | Milestone | MCD 9312-2
Hey Duke! | Milestone | MCD 9320-2
Jam Session
Jam Session Vol.5 | Steeplechase | SCCD 31536

Wendlandt,Götz | (bg)
Horst Jankowski Orchestra With Voices
Jankowskeynotes | MPS | 9814806
Horst Jankowski Quartet
Jankowskinetik | MPS | 9808189

Wendt,Adam | (sax,ssts)
Urszula Dudziak And Band Walk Away
Magic Lady | IN+OUT Records | 7008-2
Walkaway With Urszula Dudziak
Saturation | IN+OUT Records | 77024-2

Wendt,George | (tp)
Artie Shaw And His Orchestra
Planet JazzArtie Shaw | Planet Jazz | 2152057-2
Planet Jazz:Big Bands | Planet Jazz | 2169649-2

Wendt,Tim | (tpfl-h)
Buddy Childers Big Band
It's What Happening Now! | Candid | CCD 79749

Wenig,Erhard | (ts)
Erhard Wenig Quartet
Deutsches Jazz Fesival 1954/1955 | Bear Family Records | BCD 15430
Hans Koller Nonet
Exclusiv | MPS | 9813440

Weniger,Peter | (as,ts,fl,ss,saxbs)
Jazz Baltica Ensemble
The Birth+Rebirth Of Swedish Folk Jazz | ACT | 9254-2
Klaus Weiss Quintet
A Taste Of Jazz | ATM Records | ATM 3810-AH
NDR Big Band
NDR Big Band-Bravissimo | ACT | 9232-2
SWR Big Band
Jazz In Concert | Hänssler Classics | CD 93.004

Wenk,Klaus | (voc)
Michael Riessler & Singer Pur with Vincent Courtois
Ahi Vita | ACT | 9417-2

Wennemar,Harald | (as)
Dogs Don't Sing In The Rain
Bones For Breakfast | Edition Collage | EC 472-2
Vocal Moments | Take Twelve On CD | TT 008-2
Wind Moments | Take Twelve On CD | TT 009-2

Wennermark,Eunice | (v)
Phineas Newborn Jr. With Dennis Farnon And His Orchestra
While My Lady Sleeps | RCA | 2185157-2

Wenzel,Hans | (g)
Horst Jankowski Orchestra With Voices
Jankowskeynotes | MPS | 9814806
Horst Jankowski Quartet
Jankowskinetik | MPS | 9808189

Wenzel,Helmut | (bs)
Harry Allen And Randy Sandke Meets The RIAS Big Band Berlin
The Music Of The Trumpet Kings | Nagel-Heyer | CD 037

Wenziker,Judith | (oboe)
Miles Davis With Gil Evans Orchestra, The George Gruntz Concert Jazz Band And Guests
Miles & Quincy Live At Montreux | Warner | 9362-45221-2

Werb,Rainer | (b)
Straight Talk
Pure | Jazz 4 Ever Records:Jazz Network | J4E 4719

Werner,Kenny | (keyboards,p,celeste,string-synth)
Dino Saluzzi Group
If | Enja | ENJ-9451 2
Ed Neumeister Quartet
Ed Neumeister Quartet/Quintet | Timescrapper | TSCR 9614
Joe Lovano Orchestra
Blue Note Plays Gershwin | Blue Note | 520808-2
Kenny Werner Trio
A Delicate Ballace | RCA | 2151694-2
Lee Konitz-Kenny Werner
Unleemited | Owl Records | 014727-2
Mack Goldsbury And The New York Connection
Songs I Love To Play | Timescrapper | TSCR 9615
Miriam Alter Quintet
Alter Ego | Intuition Records | INT 3258-2
Toots Thielemans Quartet
Toots Thielemans:The Live Takes Vol.1 | IN+OUT Records | 77041-2
Toots Thielemans-Kenny Werner Duo
Toots Thielemans & Kenny Werner | EmArCy | 014722-2

Werth,George | (tp)
Ella Fitzgerald With The Frank DeVol Orchestra
Get Happy! | Verve | 523321-2

Werther,Beto | (dr)
Big Allanbik
Batuque Y Blues | Blues Beacon | BLU-1031 2

Werther,Ricardo | (voc)

Wertico,Paul | (dr,cymbal,field-drperc)
Kurt Elling Group
This Time Its Love | Blue Note | 493543-2
Pat Metheny Group
First Circle | ECM | 1278(823342-2)
Imaginary Day | Warner | 9362-46791-2
We Live Here | Geffen Records | GED 24729
Quartet | Geffen Records | GED 24978

Wesley,Fred | (tb,keyboardsvoc)
Annette Lowman With Three Of A Kind, Fred Wesley And Rodney Jones
Brown Baby:A Tribute To Oscar Brown Jr. | Minor Music | 801061
Fred Wesley Group
New Friends | Minor Music | 801016
Swing & Be Funky | Minor Music | 801027
Amalgamation | Minor Music | 801045
Hans Theessink Group
Call Me | Minor Music | 801022
Maceo Parker Group
Roots Revisited | Minor Music | 801015
Mo' Roots | Minor Music | 801018
Southern Exposure | Minor Music | 801033
Maceo(Soundtrack) | Minor Music | 801046
Maceo Parker With The Rebirth Brass Band
Maceo(Soundtrack) | Minor Music | 801046
Milt Jackson Orchestra
Sarah Vaughan Birthday Celebration | Fantasy | FANCD 6090-2
Milt Jackson With The Count Basie Orchestra
To Bags...With Love:Memorial Album | Pablo | 2310967-2
Milt Jackson Birthday Celebration | Fantasy | FANCD 6079-2
Milt Jackson + Count Basie + Big Band Vol.1 | Original Jazz Classics | OJCCD 740-2(2310822)
Milt Jackson + Count Basie + Big Band Vol.2 | Original Jazz Classics | OJCCD 741-2(2310823)
Nils Landgren Funk Unit With Guests
5000 Miles | ACT | 9271-2
Pee Wee Ellis & NDR Bigband
What You Like | Minor Music | 801064
Pee Wee Ellis Quintet With Guests
A New Shift | Minor Music | 801060

Wess,Frank | (alto-fl,fl,ts,as,cl,arr,b-fl)
Benny Goodman And His Orchestra
40th Anniversary Concert-Live At Carnegie Hall | London | 820349-2
Verve Jazz Masters 33:Benny Goodman | Verve | 844410-2
Buck Clayton Swing Band
Swing's The Village | Nagel-Heyer | CD 5004
Blues Of Summer | Nagel-Heyer | NH 1011
Byron Stripling Quintet
Byron,Get On Free | Nagel-Heyer | CD 2016
Byron Stripling Sextet
Striplingnow! | Nagel-Heyer | CD 2002
Byron,Get On Free | Nagel-Heyer | CD 2016
Count Basie And His Orchestra
Jazz Gallery:Lester Young Vol.2(1946-59) | RCA | 2119541-2
Jazz Collection:Count Basie | Laserlight | 24368
The Legends Of Swing | Laserlight | 24659
Atomic Swing | Roulette | 497871-2
Verve Jazz Masters 2:Count Basie | Verve | 519819-2
Count Basie Swings-Joe Williams Sings | Verve | 519852-2
Verve Jazz Masters 20:Introducing | Verve | 519853-2
April In Paris | Verve | 521402-2
Breakfast Dance And Barbecue | Roulette | 531791-2
One O'Clock Jump | Verve | 559806-2
Chairman Of The Board | Roulette | 581664-2
The Complete Atomic Basie | Roulette | 828635-2
King Of Swing | Verve | 837433-2
Count Basie At Newport | Verve | 9861761
Count On The Coast Vol.1 | Phontastic | NCD 7555
Count On The Coast Vol.2 | Phontastic | NCD 7575
Count Basie And The Kansas City 7
Count Basie And The Kansas City 7 | Impulse(MCA) | 951202-2
Count Basie Sextet
Verve Jazz Masters 2:Count Basie | Verve | 519819-2
Duke Ellington And Count Basie With Their Orchestras
First Time! | CBS | CK 65571
Ella Fitzgerald And Joe Williams With The Count Basie Octet
For The Love Of Ella Fitzgerald | Verve | 841765-2
Ella Fitzgerald With The Count Basie Orchestra
Ella Fitzgerald-First Lady Of Song | Verve | 517898-2
Ella And Basie | Verve | 539059-2
Frank Sinatra With The Count Basie Orchestra
Sinatra-Basie:An Historic Musical First | Reprise | 7599-27023-2
It Might As Well Be Spring | Reprise | 7599-27027-2
Frank Vignola Sextet
Off Broadway | Nagel-Heyer | CD 2006
Frank Wess And His Orchestra
The Long Road | Prestige | PCD 24247-2
Frank Wess Meets The Paris-Barcelona Swing Connection
Paris-Barcelona Connection | Fresh Sound Records | FSNT 002 CD
Frank Wess Quintet
The Long Road | Prestige | PCD 24247-2
Frank Wess With The Bill Charlap Trio
Stardust | Blue Note | 535985-2
Gene Ammons Quintet
Gentle Jug Vol.3 | Prestige | PCD 24249-2
Harry Edison Sextet
Swing Summit | Candid | CCD 79050
Jimmy McGriff Orchestra
Swingin' The Blues-Jumpin' The Blues | Laserlight | 24654
Joe Newman And His Band
Jazz In Paris:Joe Newman-Jazz At Midnight-Cootie Williams | EmArCy | 018446-2
Joe Turner With Orchestra
Atlantic Jazz: Kansas City | Atlantic | 7567-81701-2
Johnny Hodges Orchestra
Verve Jazz Masters 35:Johnny Hodges | Verve | 521857-2
Les McCann Group
Another Beginning | Atlantic | 7567-80790-2
Prestige All Stars
John Coltrane-The Prestige Recordings | Prestige | 16 PCD 4405-2
Wheelin' & Dealin' | Original Jazz Classics | OJCCD 672-2(P7131)
Quincy Jones And His Orchestra
The Quintessence | Impulse(MCA) | 951222-2
The Roots Of Acid Jazz | Impulse(MCA) | IMP 12042
Red Holloway Quintet
Coast To Coast | Milestone | MCD 9335-2
Ron Carter Orchestra
Parade | Original Jazz Classics | OJCCD 1047-2(M 9088)
Sarah Vaughan And Her Band
Duke Ellington Song Book Two | Pablo | CD 2312116
Sarah Vaughan Birthday Celebration | Fantasy | FANCD 6090-2
Sarah Vaughan And Joe Williams With The Count Basie Orchestra
Jazz Profile | Blue Note | 823517-2
Sarah Vaughan And The Count Basie Orchestra
Ballads | Roulette | 537561-2
Sarah Vaughan And The Thad Jones Orchestra
Verve Jazz Masters 42:Sarah Vaughan-The Jazz Sides | Verve | 526817-2
Sarah Vaughan With Her Quartet
Verve Jazz Masters 42:Sarah Vaughan-The Jazz Sides | Verve | 526817-2
Sarah Vaughan With Small Group & Orchestra
Duke Ellington Song Book One | Pablo | CD 2312111
Sarah Vaughan With The Count Basie Band
Jazz Profile | Blue Note | 823517-2
Shirley Horn With Band
The Roots Of Acid Jazz | Impulse(MCA) | IMP 12042
Shirley Horn With Orchestra
Loads Of Love + Shirley Horn With Horns | Mercury | 843454-2
Thad Jones Quintet
Charles Mingus-The Complete Debut Recordings | Debut | 12 DCD 4402-2
The Dave Glasser/Clark Terry/Barry Harris Project
Uh! Oh! | Nagel-Heyer | CD 2003
Blues Of Summer | Nagel-Heyer | NH 1011
The Jazz Composer's Orchestra
Comminications | JCOA | 1001/2
The Prestige All Stars
Olio | Original Jazz Classics | OJCCD 1004-2(P 7084)
Zoot Sims With Orchestra
Passion Flower | Original Jazz Classics | OJCCD 939-2(2312120)

Wesseltoft,Jens Bugge | (keyboards,p,synth,perc,p-solo)
Arild Andersen Sextet
Sagn | ECM | 1435
Bugge Wesseltoft
It's Snowing On My Piano | ACT | 9260-2
Jan Garbarek Group
I Took Up The Runes | ECM | 1419(843850-2)
Rites | ECM | 1685/86(559006-2)
Jazz Baltica Ensemble
The Birth+Rebirth Of Swedish Folk Jazz | ACT | 9254-2
Sidsel Endresen Sextet
Exile | ECM | 1524(521721-2)
Sidsel Endresen-Bugge Wesseltoft
Nightsong | ACT | 9004-2

West,Alvy | (reeds)
Billie Holiday With The Paul Whiteman Orchestra
Billie's Blues | Blue Note | 748786-2

West,Bobby | (bel-b)
Ella Fitzgerald With Benny Carter's Magnificent Seven
30 By Ella | Capitol | 520090-2
Singers Unlimited With The Pat Williams Orchestra
The Singers Unlimited:Magic Voices | MPS | 539130-2

West,Danny Quebec | (as)
Thelonious Monk Sextet
Genius Of Modern Music,Vol.1 | Blue Note | 532138-2
Jazz Profile:Thelonious Monk | Blue Note | 823518-2

West,Harold 'Doc' | (dr)
Don Byas Quartet
Don Byas:Laura | Dreyfus Jazz Line | FDM 36714-2
Erroll Garner Trio
Erroll Garner:Trio | Dreyfus Jazz Line | FDM 36719-2
Lester Young Quartet
The Complete Jazz At The Philharmonic On Verve 1944-1949 | Verve | 523893-2
Sammy Price Septet
Jazz:The Essential Collection Vol.3 | IN+OUT Records | 78013-2
Una Mae Carlisle Quintet
Jazz:The Essential Collection Vol.3 | IN+OUT Records | 78013-2
Una Mae Carlisle Septet
Planet Jazz:Female Jazz Vocalists | Planet Jazz | 2169656-2

West,Harold 'Doc' prob. | (dr)
Woody Herman And The Vanderbilt All Stars
Louis Armstrong-Jack Teagarden-Woody Herman:Midnights At V-Disc | Jazz Unlimited | JUCD 2048

West,Paul | (b)
Dinah Washington And Her Sextet
Newport Jazz Festival 1958,July 3rd-6th Vol.4:Blues In The Night No.2 | Phontastic | NCD 8816
Dinah Washington With The Newport All Stars
Dinah Sings Bessie Smith | Verve | 538635-2
Dinah Washington With The Terry Gibbs Band
Verve Jazz Masters 40:Dinah Washington | Verve | 522055-2
Dinah Washington With The Urbie Green Sextet
Newport Jazz Festival 1958,July 3rd-6th Vol.2:Mulligan The Main Man | Phontastic | NCD 8814
Dizzy Gillespie And His Orchestra
Dizzy Gillespie:Birks Works-The Verve Big Band Sessions | Verve | 527900-2
Ultimate Dizzy Gillespie | Verve | 557535-2
Dizzy Gillespie Orchestra
Verve Jazz Masters 10:Dizzy Gillespie | Verve | 516319-2
Jimmy Ponder Quartet
Jazzin' Vol.2: The Music Of Stevie Wonder | Fantasy | FANCD 6088-2
Lisle Atkinson Quartet
Bass Contra Bass | Storyville | STCD 8270
Lisle Atkinson Quintet
Bass Contra Bass | Storyville | STCD 8270
Urbie Green Sextet
Newport Jazz Festival 1958,July 3rd-6th Vol.2:Mulligan The Main Man | Phontastic | NCD 8814

West,Tom | (p)
Peter Malick Group feat. Norah Jones
New York City | Koch Records | 238678-2

Westberg Andersen,Ellen | (voc)
Ketil Bjornstad Group
Early Years | EmArCy | 013271-2

Westberg,Ingemar | (p)
Lars Gullin Quartet
Lars Gullin 1951/52 Vol.5:First Walk | Dragon | DRCD 380
Lars Gullin Quintet
Lars Gullin 1951/52 Vol.5:First Walk | Dragon | DRCD 380

Westbrook,Chauncey 'Lord' | (g)
Buddy Johnson And His Orchestra
Buddy And Ella Johnson 1953-1964 | Bear Family Records | BCD 15479 DH
Charlie Rouse Orchestra
Bossa Nova Bacchanal | Blue Note | 593875-2
Blue Bossa | Blue Note | 795590-2

Westbrook,Kate | (bamboo-fl,piccolo,ten-horn,voice)
Mike Westbrook Band
Off Abbey Road | TipToe | TIP-888805 2
Mike Westbrook Brass Band
Glad Day:Settings Of William Blake | Enja | ENJ-9376 2
Mike Westbrook Orchestra
Bar Utopia-A Big Band Cabaret | Enja | ENJ-9333 2
The Orchestra Of Smith's Academy | Enja | ENJ-9358 2

Westbrook,Marsha | (viola)
Mahavishnu Orchestra
Apocalypse | CBS | 467092-2

Westbrook,Mike | (p,MD,tubavoice)
Mike Westbrook Band
Off Abbey Road | TipToe | TIP-888805 2
Mike Westbrook Brass Band
Glad Day:Settings Of William Blake | Enja | ENJ-9376 2

Mike Westbrook Orchestra
Bar Utopia-A Big Band Cabaret | Enja | ENJ-9333 2
The Orchestra Of Smith's Academy | Enja | ENJ-9358 2
Westendorp,André | (drco)
Albert Nicholas With The Dutch Swing College Band
Albert Nicholas & The Dutch Swing College Band | Storyville | STCD 5522
Dutch Swing College Band
Albert Nicholas & The Dutch Swing College Band | Storyville | STCD 5522
Westerheide,Reinhold | (g,marimba,percvib)
Ulli Bögershausen
Best Of Ulli Bögershausen | Laika Records | LK 93-045
Ulli Bögershausen-Reinhold Westerheide
Pictures | Laika Records | LK 35100932
Westling,Kjell | (b-clsopraninio)
Beng Berger Band
Bitter Funeral Beer | ECM | 1179
Weston,Cliff | (tpvoc)
Tommy Dorsey And His Orchestra
Planet Jazz:Tommy Dorsey | Planet Jazz | 2159972-2
Weston,Grant Calvin | (drvoc)
Grant Calvin Weston Group
Dance Romance | IN+OUT Records | 7002-2
James Blood Ulmer Group
Jazz Unlimited | IN+OUT Records | 7017-2
James Carter Group
Layin' In The Cut | Atlantic | 7567-83305-2
Lounge Lizards
Berlin 1991 Part 1 | Intuition Records | INT 2044-2
Live In Berlin 1991-Vol.2 | Intuition Records | INT 2055-2
Weston,Harvey | (bb-g)
The Alex Welsh Legacy Band
The Sound Of Alex Vol.1 | Nagel-Heyer | CD 070
Wrobel-Roberscheuten-Hopkins Jam Session
Jammin' At The IAJRC Convention Hamburg 1999 | Nagel-Heyer | CD 066
Weston,Paul | (arr,cl,condtalking)
Art Tatum Trio
Art Tatum:Complete Capitol Recordings | Capitol | 821325-2
Ella Fitzgerald With Paul Weston And His Orchestra
The Best Of The Song Books | Verve | 519804-2
Verve Jazz Masters 6:Ella Fitzgerald | Verve | 519822-2
Love Songs:The Best Of The Song Books | Verve | 531762-2
Ella Fitzgerald Sings The Irving Berlin Song Book | Verve | 543830-2
Ella Fitzgerald With The Paul Weston Orchestra
Ella Fitzgerald-First Lady Of Song | Verve | 517898-2
The Best Of The Song Books:The Ballads | Verve | 521867-2
Get Happy! | Verve | 523321-2
The Silver Collection: Ella Fitzgerald-The Songbooks | Verve | 823445-2 PMS
Peggy Lee With Benny Goodman And The Paul Weston Orchestra
Peggy Lee & Benny Goodman:The Complete Recordings 1941-1947 | CBS | C2K 65686
Ten Cats And A Mouse
The Hollywood Session:The Capitol Jazzmen | Jazz Unlimited | JUCD 2044
Tommy Dorsey And His Orchestra
Frank Sinatra And The Tommy Dorsey Orchestra | RCA | 2668701-2
Weston,Randy | (pp-solo)
Randy Weston
Randy Weston:Solo,Duo,Trio | Milestone | MCD 47085-2
Randy Weston African Rhythm
Khepera | Verve | 557821-2
Randy Weston African Rhythm Quintet and The Gnawa Master Musicians of Marocco
Spirit! The Power Of Music | Verve | 543256-2
Randy Weston Trio
Randy Weston:Solo,Duo,Trio | Milestone | MCD 47085-2
Randy Weston-Sam Gill
Randy Weston:Solo,Duo,Trio | Milestone | MCD 47085-2
Westray,Ronald | (tb)
Lincoln Center Jazz Orchestra
Big Train | CBS | CK 69860
Wycliffe Gordon Group
The Search | Nagel-Heyer | CD 2007
Westwood,Paul | (el-b)
Barbara Thompson Group
Shifting Sands | Intuition Records | INT 3174-2
Barbara Thompson's Paraphernalia
Lady Saxophone | VeraBra Records | CDVBR 2166-2
Wethington,Crawford | (as,bscl)
Carroll Dickerson's Savoyagers
Louis Armstrong:Fireworks | Dreyfus Jazz Line | FDM 36710-2
Louis Armstrong And His Orchestra
Satch Plays Fats(Complete) | CBS | CK 64927
Wetmore |
Anthony Ortega With The Robert Zieff Orchestra
Earth Dance | Fresh Sound Records | FSR-CD 325
Wetmore,Dick | (v)
Gerry Mulligan Sextet
The Gerry Mulligan Songbook | Pacific Jazz | 833575-2
Wettenhall,Simon | (tp)
Woody Allen And His New Orleans Jazz Band
Wild Man Blues | RCA | 2663353-2
Wettling,George | (dr)
A Jam Session At Victor
Planet Jazz:Fats Waller | Planet Jazz | 2152058-2
Planet Jazz:Jazz Greatest Hits | Planet Jazz | 2169648-2
Artie Shaw And His Orchestra
The Legends Of Swing | Laserlight | 24659
Bud Freeman And His Summa Cum Laude Orchestra
Planet Jazz:Jack Teagarden | Planet Jazz | 2161236-2
Planet Jazz:Bud Freeman | Planet Jazz | 2161240-2
Eddie Condon And His Boys
The Very Best Of Dixieland Jazz | Verve | 535529-2
Eddie Condon And His Orchestra
Jazz:The Essential Collection Vol.3 | IN+OUT Records | 78013-2
George Wettling's New Yorkers
Jazz:The Essential Collection Vol.3 | IN+OUT Records | 78013-2
Jimmy McPartland And His Dixielanders
Planet Jazz | Planet Jazz | 2169652-2
Louis Armstrong And His All Stars
Louis Armstrong:Wintergarden 1947/Blue Note 1948 | Storyville | STCD 8242
Muggsy Spanier And His V-Disc All Stars
Muggsy Spanier And Bud Freeman:V-Discs 1944-45 | Jazz Unlimited | JUCD 2049
The Chicago All Stars
Planet Jazz:Bud Freeman | Planet Jazz | 2161240-2
Wettling,George prob. | (dr)
Wettstein,Ruedi | (cl,asbs)
Brigitte Dietrich-Joe Haider Jazz Orchestra
Consequences | JHM Records | JHM 3624
Wetzel,Ray | (tpvoc)
Charlie Parker With Strings
Charlie Parker With Strings:The Master Takes | Verve | 523984-2
Charlie Parker With The Neal Hefti Orchestra
Charlie Parker:The Best Of The Verve Years | Verve | 527815-2
Bird: The Complete Charlie Parker On Verve | Verve | 837141-2
Stan Kenton And His Orchestra
Swing Vol.1 | Storyville | 4960343
One Night Stand | Choice | CHCD 71051
Woody Herman And His Orchestra
Woody Herman:Four Brother | Dreyfus Jazz Line | FDM 36722-2
Louis Armstrong-Jack Teagarden-Woody Herman:Midnights At V-Disc | Jazz Unlimited | JUCD 2048
Old Gold Rehearsals 1944 | Jazz Unlimited | JUCD 2079
Weyerer,Franz | (tpfl-h)
Al Porcino Big Band
Al Cohn Meets Al Porcino | Organic Music | ORGM 9730
Klaus Doldinger's Passport
Running In Real Time | Warner | 2292-40633-2
Thomas Faist Sextet
Gentle | Village | VILCD 1020-2
Whalum,Kirk | (sax,ssts)
Bobby Lyle Group
The Journey | Atlantic | 7567-82138-2
Kevin Mahogany With The Bob James Trio And Kirk Whalum
My Romance | Warner | 9362-47025-2
Kevin Mahogany With The Bob James Trio, Kirk Whalum And Strings
My Romance | Warner | 9362-47025-2
Larry Carlton Group
The Gift | GRP | GRP 98542
Marcus Miller Group
The Sun Don't Lie | Dreyfus Jazz Line | FDM 36560-2
The Quincy Jones-Sammy Nestico Orchestra
Basie & Beyond | Warner | 9362-47792-2
Wharton,Gib | (steel-g)
Cassandra Wilson Group
Blue Light 'Til Dawn | Blue Note | 781357-2
Wheat,David | (g)
Chet Baker Trio
Embraceable You | Pacific Jazz | 831676-2
Wheeler,Dave | (b-tb,tubatb)
Stan Kenton And His Orchestra
Adventures In Blues | Capitol | 520089-2
Adventures In Jazz | Capitol | 521222-2
Wheeler,De Priest | (tb)
Cab Calloway And His Orchestra
Planet Jazz:Cab Calloway | Planet Jazz | 2161237-2
Wheeler,Harold | (el-pkeyboards)
Bernard Purdie Group
Jazzin' With The Soul Brothers | Fantasy | FANCD 6086-2
Dee Dee Bridgewater With Band
Dee Dee Bridgewater | Atlantic | 7567-80760-2
Wheeler,Ian | (as,cl,harmonica,harm,saxss)
Chris Barber's Jazz And Blues Band
Chris Barber On The Road:A Jazz Documentary | Storyville | 4960683
Chris Barber:40 Years Jubilee Concert | Storyville | 4990013
Chris Barber's Jazzband & das Große Rundfunkorchester Berlin,DDR
Jazz Zounds: Chris Barber | Zounds | CD 2720007
Wheeler,James | (g)
Billy Boy Arnold Group
Eldorado Cadillac | Alligator Records | ALCD 4836
Wheeler,Kenny | (fl-h,co,tpocket-tp)
Azimuth
Azimuth '85 | ECM | 1298
How It Was Then...Never Again | ECM | 1538
Azimuth | ECM | 1546/48(523010-2)
Azimuth With Ralph Towner
Azimuth | ECM | 1546/48(523010-2)
Berlin Contemporary Jazz Orchestra
Berlin Contemporary Jazz Orchestra | ECM | 1409
Bill Frisell Quintet
Rambler | ECM | 1287
Dave Holland Quintet
Jumpin' In | ECM | 1269
Seeds Of Time | ECM | 1292
The Razor's Edge | ECM | 1353
George Adams Sextet
Soung Suggestions | ECM | 1141
John Abercrombie Sextet
Open Land | ECM | 1683(557652-2)
Jon Hiseman With The United Jazz & Rock Ensemble And Babara Thompson's Paraphernalia
About Time Too! | VeraBra Records | CDVBR 2014-2
Kenny Wheeler Brass Ensemble
A Long Time Ago | ECM | 1691
Kenny Wheeler Ensemble
Muisc For Large & Small Ensembles | ECM | 1415/16
Kenny Wheeler Quartet
Gnu High | ECM | 1069(825591-2)
Kenny Wheeler Quintet
Double, Double You | ECM | 1262(815675-2)
The Widow In The Window | ECM | 1417(843198-2)
Kenny Wheeler Sextet
Around 6 | ECM | 1156
Kenny Wheeler/Lee Konitz/Dave Holland/Bill Frisell
Angel Song | ECM | 1607(533098-2)
Klaus König Orchestra
Times Of Devastation/Poco A Poco | Enja | ENJ-6014 22
Hommage A Douglas Adams | Enja | ENJ-6078 2
Time Fragments:Seven Studies In Time And Motion | Enja | ENJ-8076 2
Lee Konitz-Kenny Wheeler Quartet
Live At Birdland Neuburg | double moon | CHRDM 71014
Leo Smith Group
Devine Love | ECM | 1143
Peter Herborn's Acute Insights
Peter Herborn's Acute Insights | JMT Edition | 919017-2
Pierre Favre Quintet
Window-Steps | ECM | 1584(529348-2)
Rabih Abou-Khalil Group
Blue Camel | Enja | ENJ-7053 2
The Sultan's Picnic | Enja | ENJ-8078 2
Rainer Brünninghaus Quartet
Freigeweht | ECM | 1187(847329-2)
Ralph Towner Quintet
Old Friends New Friends | ECM | 1153
Ronnie Scott And The Band
Live At Ronnie Scott's | CBS | 494439-2
Tony Oxley Quintet
The Baptist Traveller | CBS | 494438-2
Tony Oxley Sextet
4 Compositions For Sextet | CBS | 494437-2
Wolfgang Lackerschmid Sextet
One More Life | Bhakti Jazz | BR 29
When Granny Sleeps |
When Granny Sleeps
Welcome | dacapo | DCCD 9447
Whetsol,Arthur | (cotp)
Duke Ellington And His Cotton Club Orchestra
Planet Jazz:Duke Ellington | Planet Jazz | 2152053-2
Jazz:The Essential Collection Vol.2 | IN+OUT Records | 78012-2
Duke Ellington And His Famous Orchestra
Jazz:The Essential Collection Vol.2 | IN+OUT Records | 78012-2
Duke Ellington And His Orchestra
Highlights From The Duke Ellington Centennial Edition | RCA | 2663672-2
Jazz:The Essential Collection Vol.2 | IN+OUT Records | 78012-2
Jazz:The Essential Collection Vol.3 | IN+OUT Records | 78013-2
Whigham,Jiggs | (cond,tb,perctrombonium)
NDR Big Band With Guests
50 Years Of NDR Big Band:Bravissimo II | ACT | 9259-2
Whitaker,Rodney Thomas | (b)
Essence All Stars
Hot Jazz Bisquits | Hip Bop | HIBD 8801
Lincoln Center Jazz Orchestra
Big Train | CBS | CK 69860
Roy Hargrove Quartet
Family | Verve | 527630-2
Roy Hargrove Quintet
Roy Hargrove Quintet With The Tenors Of Our Time | Verve | 523019-2
Family | Verve | 527630-2
Roy Hargrove Quintet With Branford Marsalis
Roy Hargrove Quintet With The Tenors Of Our Time | Verve | 523019-2
Roy Hargrove Quintet With Joe Henderson
Roy Hargrove Quintet With The Tenors Of Our Time | Verve | 523019-2
Roy Hargrove Quintet With Johnny Griffin
Roy Hargrove Quintet With The Tenors Of Our Time | Verve | 523019-2
Roy Hargrove Quintet With Joshua Redman
Roy Hargrove Quintet With The Tenors Of Our Time | Verve | 523019-2
Roy Hargrove Quintet With Stanley Turrentine
Roy Hargrove Quintet With The Tenors Of Our Time | Verve | 523019-2
Roy Hargrove Sextet
Family | Verve | 527630-2
Teodross Avery Quartet
My Generation | Impulse(MCA) | 951181-2
Teodross Avery Quintet
My Generation | Impulse(MCA) | 951181-2
The Nagel-Heyer Allstars
Uptown Lowdown:A Jazz Salute To The Big Apple | Nagel-Heyer | CD 2004
Wycliffe Gordon Group
Slidin' Home | Nagel-Heyer | CD 2001
The Search | Nagel-Heyer | CD 2007
Ellington For Lovers | Nagel-Heyer | NH 1009
Blues Of Summer | Nagel-Heyer | NH 1011
Wycliffe Gordon Quintet
The Joyride | Nagel-Heyer | CD 2032
White,Andrew | (as,engl-h,el-b,oboe,ssts)
McCoy Tyner Quintet
Asante | Blue Note | 493384-2
McCoy Tyner Sextet
Asante | Blue Note | 493384-2
Weather Report
Sweetnighter | CBS | 485102-2
White,Barbara | (voc)
Archie Shepp Orchestra
The Cry Of My People | Impulse(MCA) | 9861488
White,Bobby | (dr)
Cal Tjader Quintet
Cal Tjader Plays Jazz | Original Jazz Classics | OJCCD 986-2(F 3-211)
Jimmy Raney Quartet
Jimmy Raney Visits Paris Vol.1 | Vogue | 21409352
The Three T's
Jazz:The Essential Collection Vol.3 | IN+OUT Records | 78013-2
White,Bukka | (gvoc)
Bukka White
Classic Blues | Zounds | CD 2700048
White,Chris | (b,arr,el-b,gvoc)
Dave Pike Quintet
Carnavals | Prestige | PCD 24248-2
Dave Pike Sextet
Carnavals | Prestige | PCD 24248-2
Dizzy Gillespie And His Orchestra
Talking Verve:Dizzy Gillespie | Verve | 533846-2
Ultimate Dizzy Gillespie | Verve | 557535-2
Dizzy Gillespie Quintet
Dizzie Gillespie: Salle Pleyel/Olympia | Laserlight | 36132
Verve Jazz Masters 10:Dizzy Gillespie | Verve | 516319-2
Talking Verve:Dizzy Gillespie | Verve | 533846-2
Ultimate Dizzy Gillespie | Verve | 557535-2
Something Old Something New | Verve | 558079-2
Dizzy Gillespie Septet
The Antonio Carlos Jobim Songbook | Verve | 525472-2
Dizzy Gillespie Sextet
Verve Jazz Masters 10:Dizzy Gillespie | Verve | 516319-2
Talking Verve:Dizzy Gillespie | Verve | 533846-2
Jambo Caribe | Verve | 557492-2
Ultimate Dizzy Gillespie | Verve | 557535-2
Nina Simone Quartet
Misty Blue:Sweet Sisters Swing Songs Of Sorrow And Sadness | Blue Note | 521151-2
Quincy Jones And His Orchestra
Big Band Bossa Nova | Verve | 557913-2
Rahsaan/The Complete Mercury Recordings Of Roland Kirk | Mercury | 846630-2
White,Daniel | (arr)
Dizzy Gillespie Orchestra And The Operatic String Orchestra
Jazz In Paris:Dizzy Gillespie And His Operatic Strings Orchestra | EmArCy | 018420-2
White,Dorothy | (voc)
Max Roach Sextet With The J.C.White Singers
Lift Every Voice And Sing | Atlantic | 7567-80798-2
White,Dr.Michael | (cl)
Wynton Marsalis Group
Standard Time Vol.6:Mr.Jelly Lord | CBS | CK 69872
White,Freddy | (bjg)
Fletcher Henderson And His Orchestra
Jazz:The Essential Collection Vol.1 | IN+OUT Records | 78011-2
White,Gil | (clts)
Sidney Bechet With Noble Sissle's Swingsters
Sidney Bechet:Summertime | Dreyfus Jazz Line | FDM 36712-2
White,Harold | (congas,drperc)
Junior Mance Quartet
That Lovin' Feelin' | Milestone | MCD 47097-2
White,Harry | (tbarr)
Cab Calloway And His Orchestra
Planet Jazz:Cab Calloway | Planet Jazz | 2161237-2
Hot Lips Page Band
Planet Jazz:Jazz Trumpet | Planet Jazz | 2169654-2
Louis Armstrong And His Orchestra
Louis Armstrong:Swing That Music | Laserlight | 36056
Swing Legends:Louis Armstrong | Nimbus Records | NI 2012
White,Hy | (el-gg)
Muggsy Spanier And His V-Disc All Stars
Muggsy Spanier And Bud Freeman:V-Discs 1944-45 | Jazz Unlimited | JUCD 2049
White,Jerry | (dr)
Buddy Childers Big Band
It's What Happening Now! | Candid | CCD 79749
White,Jim | (drtp)
Maynard Ferguson And His Big Bop Nouveau Band
Maynard Ferguson '93-Footpath Café | Hot Shot Records | HSR 8312-2
White,Judith | (voc)
Archie Shepp Orchestra
The Cry Of My People | Impulse(MCA) | 9861488
White,Lenny | (dr,music-stand,perc,congas,bongos)
Al Di Meola Group
Elegant Gypsy | CBS | 468213-2
Land Of The Midnight Sun | CBS | 468214-2
Anfrew Hill Nonet
Passing Ships | Blue Note | 593871-2
Dreyfus All Stars
Dreyfus Night In Paris | Dreyfus Jazz Line | FDM 36652-2
Essence All Stars
Afro Cubano Chant | Hip Bop | HIBD 8009
Hot Jazz Bisquits | Hip Bop | HIBD 8801
Freddie Hubbard Septet
This Is Jazz:Freddie Hubbard | CBS | CK 65041
Gato Barbieri Group
Planet Jazz:Gato Barbieri | RCA | 2165364-2
Gato Barbieri:The Best Of The Early Years | RCA | 2663523-2
Geri Allen And The Jazzpar 1996 Nonet
Some Aspects Of Water | Storyville | STCD 4212
Geri Allen Trio
Some Aspects Of Water | Storyville | STCD 4212
Geri Allen Trio With Johny Coles
Some Aspects Of Water | Storyville | STCD 4212
Ingrid Jensen Sextet
Vernal Fields | Enja | ENJ-9013 2
Joe Henderson Quintet
Joe Henderson:The Milestone Years | Milestone | 8MCD 4413-2
Joe Henderson Sextet

Joe Henderson:The Milestone Years | Milestone | 8MCD 4413-2
Lenny White Group
Present Tense | Hip Bop | HIBD 8004
Renderers Of Spirit | Hip Bop | HIBD 8014
Hot Jazz Bisquits | Hip Bop | HIBD 8801
Manhattan Project,The
Kind Of Blue:Blue Note Celebrate The Music Of Miles Davis | Blue Note | 534255-2
Wayne Shorter:The Classic Blue Note Recordings | Blue Note | 540856-2
Marcus Miller Group
The Sun Don't Lie | Dreyfus Jazz Line | FDM 36560-2
Tales | Dreyfus Jazz Line | FDM 36571-2
Live & More | Dreyfus Jazz Line | FDM 36585-2
Michael 'Patches' Stewart Group
Blue Patches | Hip Bop | HIBD 8016
Michel Petrucciani Group
Michel Petrucciani:The Blue Note Years | Blue Note | 789916-2
Music | Blue Note | 792563-2
Miles Davis Group
Bitches Brew | CBS | C2K 65774
Rachelle Ferrell With The Terrence Blanchard Quartet
First Instrumental | Blue Note | 827820-2
Rachelle Ferrell With The Wayne Shorter Sextet
First Instrumental | Blue Note | 827820-2
Return To Forever
Return To The 7th Galaxy-Return To Forever:The Anthology | Verve | 533108-2
Where Have I Known You Before | Polydor | 825206-2
Hymn Of The Seventh Galaxy | Polydor | 825336-2
Ron Carter Quartet
Stardust | somethin'else | 537813-2
Ron Carter Quintet
Stardust | somethin'else | 537813-2
Ron Carter Trio
Stardust | somethin'else | 537813-2
Urbanator
Hot Jazz Bisquits | Hip Bop | HIBD 8801

White,Leroy | (tp)
Earl Hines And His Orchestra
Planet Jazz:Earl Hines | Planet Jazz | 2159973-2

White,Lillias | (voc)
Lee Konitz-Wolfgang Lackerschmid Quintet
Chet Baker:The Legacy Vol.3:Why Shouldn't You Cry | Enja | ENJ-9337 2
Wolfgang Lackerschmid-Donald Johnston Group
New Singers-New Songs | Bhakti Jazz | BR 31

White,Maurice | (dr,vocvoc-samples)
Marcus Miller Group
The Sun Don't Lie | Dreyfus Jazz Line | FDM 36560-2
Weather Report
Mr. Gone | CBS | 468208-2

White,Michael | (dr,tp,v,percv-overdubbing)
Alice Coltrane Sextet
Joe Henderson:The Milestone Years | Milestone | 8MCD 4413-2
Marcus Miller Group
The Sun Don't Lie | Dreyfus Jazz Line | FDM 36560-2
McCoy Tyner Septet
Song For My Lady | Original Jazz Classics | OJCCD 313-2
Pharoah Sanders Orchestra
Message From Home | Verve | 529578-2
Thembi | Impulse(MCA) | 951253-2

White,Morris | (bjg)
Cab Calloway And His Orchestra
Planet Jazz:Cab Calloway | Planet Jazz | 2161237-2

White,Quentin 'Rocky' | (drperc)
Duke Ellington Orchestra
Continuum | Fantasy | FCD 24765-2

White,Richard | (oboe)
Charlie Byrd Group
Byrd In The Wind | Original Jazz Classics | OJCCD 1086(RS 9449)

White,Rocky | (dr)
Duke Ellington And His Orchestra
Highlights From The Duke Ellington Centennial Edition | RCA | 2663672-2

White,Sharaye | (voc)
Urbanator
Urbanator II | Hip Bop | HIBD 8012

White,Sonny | (p)
Benny Carter And His Chocolate Dandies
Planet Jazz:Ben Webster | RCA | 2165368-2
Jazz:The Essential Collection Vol.3 | IN+OUT Records | 78013-2
Billie Holiday And Her Quintet
Billie Holiday:The Complete Commodore Recordings | GRP | 543272-2
Billie Holiday With Frankie Newton And His Orchestra
Billie Holiday:The Complete Commodore Recordings | GRP | 543272-2
Billie's Love Songs | Nimbus Records | NI 2000
Sidney Bechet And His New Orleans Feetwarmers
Planet Jazz | Planet Jazz | 2169652-2
Sidney Bechet:Summertime | Dreyfus Jazz Line | FDM 36712-2
Wilbur DeParis And His New New Orleans Band
Atlantic Jazz: New Orleans | Atlantic | 7567-81700-2

Whitecage,Mark | (alto-cl,as,cymbal,fl,clss)
Gunter Hampel And His Galaxie Dream Band
Journey To The Song Within | Birth | 0017
Enfant Terrible | Birth | 0025
Live At The Berlin Jazzfestival 1978 | Birth | 0027
All Is Real | Birth | 0028
All The Things You Could Be If Charles Mingus Was Your Daddy | Birth | CD 031
Celestial Glory-Live At The Knitting Factory New York | Birth | CD 040
Gunter Hampel New York Orchestra
Fresh Heat-Live At Sweet Basil | Birth | CD 039
Jeanne Lee Group
Natural Affinities | Owl Records | 018352-2

Whitehead,Annie | (tbvoice)
Carla Bley Band
Big Band Theory | Watt | 25(519966-2)
Pili-Pili
Boogaloo | JA & RO | JARO 4174-2
Dance Jazz Live 1995 | JA & RO | JARO 4189-2
Nomans Land | JA & RO | JARO 4209-2

Whiteman,Paul | (ldv)
Billie Holiday With The Paul Whiteman Orchestra
Billie's Blues | Blue Note | 748786-2
Paul Whiteman And His Orchestra
Planet Jazz:Jack Teagarden | Planet Jazz | 2161236-2
Planet Jazz:Jazz Trumpet | Planet Jazz | 2169654-2
Jazz:The Essential Collection Vol.3 | IN+OUT Records | 78013-2

Whitfield,Mark | (el-g,gg-solo)
Courtney Pine Group
Modern Day Jazz Stories | Verve | 529028-2
Jimmy Smith Sextet
Angel Eyes-Ballads & Slow Jams | Verve | 527632-2
Mark Whitfield Group
Patrice | Warner | 7599-26659-2
Mark Whitfield Quartet
The Marksman | Warner | 7599-26321-2
Teodross Avery Quartet
My Generation | Impulse(MCA) | 951181-2

Whitfield,Scott | (tbvoc)
Rez Abbasi Group
Modern Memory | String Jazz | SJRCD 102

Whitford,Peter | (dr)
Vince Jones Group
For All Colours | Intuition Records | INT 3071-2

Whiting,Margaret | (voc)
Margaret Whiting With Russel Garcia And His Orchestra
Margaret Whiting Sings The Jerome Kern Song Book | Verve | 559553-2
Peggy Lee With Benny Goodman And The Paul Weston Orchestra
Peggy Lee & Benny Goodman:The Complete Recordings 1941-1947 | CBS | C2K 65686

Whiting,Trevor | (cl,asts)
Clare Teal And Her Band
Orsino's Songs | Candid | CCD 79783

Whitley,Chris | (g)
Cassandra Wilson Group
Blue Light 'Til Dawn | Blue Note | 781357-2

Whitley,Robert | (congas)
Abbey Lincoln And Her Orchestra
Straight Ahead | Candid | CCD 79015
Max Roach All Stars
Candid Dolphy | Candid | CCD 79033

Whitlock,Bob | (b,keyboards,synthp)
A Band Of Friends
The Best Of The Gerry Mulligan Quartet With Chet Baker | Pacific Jazz | 795481-2
Peggy Lee With Lou Levy's Orchestra
Pass Me By/Big Spender | Capitol | 535210-2
Stan Getz Quartet
Stan Getz And The 'Cool' Sounds | Verve | 547317-2
Stan Getz Plays | Verve | 833535-2
Stan Getz Highlights | Verve | 847430-2

Whitlock,Ellis | (tp)
Louis Armstrong And His Orchestra
Planet Jazz:Louis Armstrong | Planet Jazz | 2152052-2
Best Of The Complete RCA Victor Recordings | RCA | 2663636-2
Louis Armstrong:A 100th Birthday Celebration | RCA | 2663694-2
Jazz:The Essential Collection Vol.2 | IN+OUT Records | 78012-2

Whitlock,Elmer | (tp)
Planet Jazz:Louis Armstrong | Planet Jazz | 2152052-2
Best Of The Complete RCA Victor Recordings | RCA | 2663636-2
Louis Armstrong:A 100th Birthday Celebration | RCA | 2663694-2

Whitney,James | (tb)
Louis Armstrong:C'est Si Bon | Dreyfus Jazz Line | FDM 36730-2
Swing Legends:Louis Armstrong | Nimbus Records | NI 2012

Whitney-Barratt,Belinda | (v)
A Band Of Friends
Wynton Marsalis Quartet With Strings | CBS | CK 68921
Tom Harrell Group
Paradise | RCA | 2663738-2

Whittaker,Sebastian | (dr)
Ku-Umba Frank Lacy & His Quartet
Settegast Strut | Tutu Records | 888162-2*

Whitty,George | (keyboard-programming,keyboards)
Lenny White Group
Present Tense | Hip Bop | HIBD 8004
The Brecker Brothers
Return Of The Brecker Brothers | GRP | GRP 96842
Out Of The Loop | GRP | GRP 97842

Whyman,Peter | (as,cl,saxss)
Mike Westbrook Band
Off Abbey Road | TipToe | TIP-888805 2
Mike Westbrook Brass Band
Glad Day:Settings Of William Blake | Enja | ENJ-9376 2
Mike Westbrook Orchestra
Bar Utopia-A Big Band Cabaret | Enja | ENJ-9333 2
The Orchestra Of Smith's Academy | Enja | ENJ-9358 2
Steve Martland Band
The Orchestra Of Smith's Academy | Enja | ENJ-9358 2

Wiberny,Heiner | (as,reeds,saxss)
Bob Brookmeyer Group With The WDR Big Band
Electricity | ACT | 9219-2
Eddie Harris Group With The WDR Big Band
Eddie Harris-The Last Concert | ACT | 9249-2
Gianlugi Trovesi Quartet With The WDR Big Band
Dedalo | Enja | ENJ-9419 2
Jens Winther And The WDR Big Band
The Escape | dacapo | DCCD 9437
Kevin Mahogany With The WDR Big Band And Guests
Pussy Cat Dues:The Music Of Charles Mingus | Enja | ENJ-9316 2
Vince Mendoza With The WDR Big Band And Guests
Sketches | ACT | 9215-2

Wiberny,Karl Heinz | (as,fl,cl,ss,piccolosax)
Jazzensemble Des Hessischen Rundfunks
Atmosphering Conditions Permitting | ECM | 1549/50
Los Jovenes Flamencos With The WDR Big Band And Guests
Jazzpana | ACT | 9212-2

Wichert,Lutz | (ts)
Lutz Wichert Trio
Ambiguous | Edition Musikat | EDM 068

Wicht,Christian | (keyboards)
Marcus Miller Group
The Sun Don't Lie | Dreyfus Jazz Line | FDM 36560-2

Wickett,Alan 'Sticky' | (dr)
Chris Barber's Jazz And Blues Band
Chris Barber:40 Years Jubilee Concert | Storyville | 4990013

Wickman,Putte | (cl)
Putte Wickman And The Hal Galper trio
Time To Remember | Dragon | DRCD 378

Widelock,David | (g,el-g12-string-g)
Matthew Brubeck & David Widelock
Really! | Jazzpoint | JP 1030 CD

Widemann,Benoit | (p,el-psynth)
Aldo Romano Group
AlmaLatina | Owl Records | 018364-2

Widmark,Anders | (grand-p,pkeyboards)
Nils Landgren Group
Sentimental Journey | ACT | 9409-2

Widmer,Klaus | (ssts)
Horn Knox
The Song Is You | JHM Records | JHM 3625

Wiedmann,Martin | (g)
Horstmann-Wiedmann-Danek
Billy The Kid | Factory Outlet Records | FOR 2001-3 CD
Thomas Horstmann-Martin Wiedmann Group
Decade | Factory Outlet Records | WO 95001

Wiemes,Theo | (fr-h)
Joachim Kühn And The Radio Philharmonie Hannover NDR With Jazz Soloists
Europeana | ACT | 9220-2

Wiemeyer,Karl-Heinz | (fr-h)
Harald Banter Ensemble
Deutsches Jazz Fesival 1954/1955 | Bear Family Records | BCD 15430

Wienhold,Tim | (vase)
Steve Tibbetts Group
Bye Bye Safe Journey | ECM | 1270

Wienstroer,Konstantin | (b)
Konstantin Wienstroer-Veit Lange-Felix Elsner
Unfinished Business | Green House Music | CD 1005
Stephan-Max Wirth Quartet
Jazzchanson 20th Century Suite | double moon | DMCD 1008-2

Wienstroer,Markus | (g,bj,v,el-g,12-string-gtrumscheit)
Dirk Raulf Group
Theater I (Bühnenmusik) | Poise | Poise 07
Theater II(Bühnenmusik) | Poise | Poise 10
Frank Kirchner Group
Frank Kirchner | Laika Records | LK 93-036
Klaus König Orchestra
Reviews | Enja | ENJ-9061 2
The Heart Project | Enja | ENJ-9338 2

Wierbos,Wolter | (tb)
Albrecht Maurer Trio Works
Movietalks | Jazz Haus Musik | JHM 0119 CD
Carl Ludwig Hübsch Trio
Carl Ludwig Hübsch's Longrun Development Of The Universe | Jazz Haus Musik | JHM 0112 CD

Wiersich,Andreas | (g)
Florian Bührich Quintet
endlich Jazz...? | Jazz 4 Ever Records:Jazz Network | J4E 4764

Wieselman,Doug | (bs,cl,ss,as,ts,el-g,mand)
Bill Frisell Band
Before We Were Born | Nonesuch | 7559-60843-2

Wiesner,Dietmar | (fl,bass-flpiccolo)
Ensemble Modern
Ensemble Modern-Fred Frith:Traffic Continues | Winter&Winter | 910044-2

Wiesner,Klaus | (ts)
Marcus Klossek Imagination
As We Are | Jardis Records | JRCD 20134
Jazz Guitar Highlights 1 | Jardis Records | JRCD 20141

Wiester,Vaughn | (b-tbtb)
Woody Herman And His Orchestra
Jazzin' Vol.2: The Music Of Stevie Wonder | Fantasy | FANCD 6088-2
King Cobra | Original Jazz Classics | OJCCD 1068-2(F 9499)

Wiggins,Gerald 'Gerry' | (org,pp-solo)
Ben Webster Sextet
Verve Jazz Masters 43:Ben Webster | Verve | 525431-2
Verve Jazz Masters 52:Maynard Ferguson | Verve | 529905-2
Benny Carter And His Orchestra
Aspects | Capitol | 852677-2
Gus Mancuso Quartet
Gus Mancuso & Special Friends | Fantasy | FCD 24762-2
Joe Pass Quintet
Joe Pass:Guitar Virtuoso | Pablo | 4 PACD 4423-2
Kenny Clarke And His Orchestra
Americans Swinging In Paris:James Moody | EMI Records | 539653-2
Louis Armstrong With The Hal Mooney Orchestra
Ambassador Louis Armstrong Vol.17:Moments To Remember(1952-1956) | Ambassador | CLA 1917
Mel Brown Quintet
Chicken Fat | Impulse(MCA) | 9861047
Tal Farlow Quartet
Verve Jazz Masters 41:Tal Farlow | Verve | 527365-2

Wiggins,J. J. | (b)
Duke Ellington Orchestra
Continuum | Fantasy | FCD 24765-2

Wiggins,James 'Boodle It' | (harm,vocspeech)
Blind Leroy Garnett
Boogie Woogie | Laserlight | 24321

Wilanow String Quartet |
Adam Makowicz Trio With The Wilanow Quartet
7.Zelt-Musik-Festival:Jazz Events | Zounds | CD 2730001

Wilber,Bob | (as,cl,ssts)
Bob Wilber And Friends
What Swing Is All About | Nagel-Heyer | CD 035
Blues Of Summer | Nagel-Heyer | NH 1011
Bob Wilber's Bechet Legacy
The Hamburg Concert-Tribute To A Legend | Nagel-Heyer | CD 028
The Second Sampler | Nagel-Heyer | NHR SP 6
Bobby Hackett Sextet
Jazz Festival Vol.1 | Storyville | 4960733
Jazz Festival Vol.2 | Storyville | 4960743
Jimmy McPartland And His Dixielanders
Planet Jazz | Planet Jazz | 2169652-2
Ralph Sutton Quartet
Live At Sunnie's Rendezvous Vol.1 | Storyville | STCD 8280
Sidney Bechet With Bob Wilber's Wildcats
Sidney Bechet:Summertime | Dreyfus Jazz Line | FDM 36712-2
Summit Reunion
Jazz Im Amerikahaus,Vol.5 | Nagel-Heyer | CD 015
The First Sampler | Nagel-Heyer | NHR SP 5
The Six
The Very Best Of Dixieland Jazz | Verve | 535529-2

Wilborn,Dave | (bj,vocg)
Louis Armstrong And His Savoy Ballroom Five
Louis Armstrong:Fireworks | Dreyfus Jazz Line | FDM 36710-2
McKinney's Cotton Pickers
Jazz:The Essential Collection Vol.3 | IN+OUT Records | 78013-2

Wilburn,Vincent | (drsimmon's-dr)
Miles Davis Group
The Man With The Horn | CBS | 468701-2
Miles Davis With The Danish Radio Big Band
Aura | CBS | CK 63962
The Danish Radio Big Band
Aura | CBS | CK 63962

Wilcox,Eddie | (bs,p,arrceleste)
Jimmy Lunceford And His Orchestra
The Legends Of Swing | Laserlight | 24659

Wilcox,Edwin | (p)
Planet Jazz:Swing | Planet Jazz | 2169651-2

Wilcox,Larry | (ts)
John LaPorta Septet
Theme And Variations | Fantasy | FCD 24776-2

Wilczewski,Dave | (reedsts)
Nils Landgren First Unit And Guests
Nils Landgren-The First Unit | ACT | 9292-2

Wilde,Wilbur | (ts)
Vince Jones Group
For All Colours | Intuition Records | INT 3071-2

Wilder,Joe | (fl-htp)
Cab Calloway And His Orchestra
Planet Jazz:Cab Calloway | Planet Jazz | 2161237-2
Planet Jazz:Male Jazz Vocalists | Planet Jazz | 2169657-2
Coleman Hawkins Sextet
Body And Soul Revisited | GRP | GRP 16272
Count Basie And His Orchestra
King Of Swing | Verve | 837433-2
Dinah Washington With The Quincy Jones Orchestra
The Swingin' Miss 'D' | Verve | 558074-2
Dizzy Gillespie And His Orchestra
Verve Jazz Masters 10:Dizzy Gillespie | Verve | 516319-2
Gillespiana And Carnegie Hall Concert | Verve | 519809-2
Talking Verve:Dizzy Gillespie | Verve | 533846-2
Ella Fitzgerald With The Bill Doggett Orchestra
Ella Fitzgerald-First Lady Of Song | Verve | 517898-2
Rhythm Is My Business | Verve | 559513-2
George Russell And His Orchestra
Geogre Russell New York N.Y. | Impulse(MCA) | 951278-2
J.J.Johnson And His Orchestra
Planet Jazz:J.J.Johnson | Planet Jazz | 2159974-2
Jimmy Smith With The Billy Byers Orchestra
Jimmy Smith:Best Of The Verve Years | Verve | 527950-2
Jimmy Smith With The Oliver Nelson Orchestra
Verve Jazz Masters 29:Jimmy Smith | Verve | 521855-2
Jimmy Smith:Best Of The Verve Years | Verve | 527950-2
Lena Horne With The Lennie Hayton Orchestra
Planet Jazz:Lena Horne | Planet Jazz | 2165373-2
Les McCann Group
Another Beginning | Atlantic | 7567-80790-2
Louis Armstrong And His Orchestra
What A Wonderful World | MCA | MCD 01876
Mar Murphy With The Ernie Wilkins Orchestra
RAH | Original Jazz Classics | OJCCD 141-2(R 9395)
Oliver Nelson And His Orchestra
Verve Jazz Masters Vol.60:The Collection | Verve | 529866-2
Trigger Alpert's Absolutely All Star Seven
East Coast Sound | Original Jazz Classics | OJCCD 1012-2(JLP 11)

Wildi,Curt | (oboe)
Bernd Konrad Jazz Group With Symphonie Orchestra
Wen Die Götter Lieben | Creative Works Records | CW CD 1010-1

Wilen,Barney | (as,ss,tsbs)
Art Blakey And The Jazz Messengers

Les Liaisons Dangereuses(Original Soundtrack) | Fontana | 812017-2
Art Blakey And The Jazz Messengers With Barney Wilen And Bud Powell
Jazz In Paris:Paris Jam Session | EmArCy | 832692-2 PMS
Art Blakey-Barney Wilen Quartet
Les Liaisons Dangereuses(Original Soundtrack) | Fontana | 812017-2
Barney Wilen Quartet
Jazz In Paris:Barney Wilen-Jazz Sur Saine | EmArCy | 548317-2 PMS
Barney Wilen Quintet
Jazz In Paris:Barney Wilen-Jazz Sur Saine | EmArCy | 548317-2 PMS
Jazz In Paris:Jazz & Cinéma Vol.1 | EmArCy | 548318-2 PMS
Bud Powell Quartet
Parisian Thoroughfare | Pablo | CD 2310976-2
Bud Powell Quintet
The Story Of Jazz Piano | Laserlight | 24653
Parisian Thoroughfare | Pablo | CD 2310976-2
Bud Powell Paris Sessions | Pablo | PACD 2310972-2
Eje Thelin Group
Ejs Thelin 1966 With Barney Wilen | Dragon | DRCD 366
Eje Thelin Quartet
Ejs Thelin 1966 With Barney Wilen | Dragon | DRCD 366
Miles Davis Quintet
Ascenseur Pour LÉchafaud | Fontana | 836305-2

Wiles,Anthony | (perccga)
Pharoah Sanders Orchestra
Thembi | Impulse(MCA) | 951253-2
Deaf Dumb Blind | Impulse(MCA) | 951265-2

Wiley,Jackson | (cello)
Charles Mingus And His Orchestra
Charles Mingus-The Complete Debut Recordings | Debut | 12 DCD 4402-2
Don Senay With Orchestra And Strings
Charles Mingus-The Complete Debut Recordings | Debut | 12 DCD 4402-2
Jackie Paris With The Charles Mingus Quintet
Charles Mingus-The Complete Debut Recordings | Debut | 12 DCD 4402-2
Thad Jones And His Orchestra
Charles Mingus-The Complete Debut Recordings | Debut | 12 DCD 4402-2

Wiley,Lee | (voc)
Lee Wiley With The Dean Kincaide Dixieland Band
Planet Jazz:Female Jazz Vocalists | Planet Jazz | 2169656-2

Wilfert,Hanne | (tp)
Helmut Zacharias mit dem Orchester Frank Folken
Ich Habe Rhythmus | Bear Family Records | BCD 15642 AH
Kurt Edelhagen All Stars
Deutsches Jazz Fesival 1954/1955 | Bear Family Records | BCD 15430
Kurt Edelhagen All Stars Und Solisten
Deutsches Jazz Fesival 1954/1955 | Bear Family Records | BCD 15430
Quartet Der Kurt Edelhagen All Stars
Deutsches Jazz Fesival 1954/1955 | Bear Family Records | BCD 15430

Wilhelm,Andreas | (voc)
Jazzensemble Des Hessischen Rundfunks
Jazz Messe-Messe Für Unsere Zeit | hr music.de | hrmj 003-01 CD

Wilke,Rüdiger | (sax)
Salut!
Green & Orange | Edition Collage | EC 488-2

Wilkerson,Don | (bs,ts,tambourinesvoc)
Don Wilkerson Quartet
The Texas Twister | Original Jazz Classics | OJCCD 1950-2(RLP 1186)
Don Wilkerson Quintet
Preach Brother! | Blue Note | 0677212
Blue N' Groovy | Blue Note | 780679-2
The Texas Twister | Original Jazz Classics | OJCCD 1950-2(RLP 1186)

Wilkins,Dave | (g,tpvoc)
Stephane Grappelli Quintet
Grapelli Story | Verve | 515807-2

Wilkins,Ernie | (arr,ld,as,ts,bs,cond,drss)
Birdland Dream Band
Birdland Dream Band | RCA | 2663873-2
Cannonball Adderley And His Orchestra
Cannonball Adderley Birthday Celebration | Fantasy | FANCD 6087-2
Count Basie And His Orchestra
Jazz Gallery:Lester Young Vol.2(1946-59) | RCA | 2119541-2
Jazz Collection:Count Basie | Laserlight | 24368
Verve Jazz Masters 2:Count Basie | Verve | 519819-2
Chairman Of The Board | Roulette | 581664-2
King Of Swing | Verve | 837433-2
Dinah Washington With The Quincy Jones Orchestra
The Swingin' Miss 'D' | Verve | 558074-2
Dizzy Gillespie And His Orchestra
Verve Jazz Masters 20:Introducing | Verve | 519853-2
Dizzy Gillespie:Birks Works-The Verve Big Band Sessions | Verve | 527900-2
Ultimate Dizzy Gillespie | Verve | 557535-2
Dizzy Gillespie Orchestra
Verve Jazz Masters 10:Dizzy Gillespie | Verve | 516319-2
Joe Turner With Orchestra
Atlantic Jazz: Kansas City | Atlantic | 7567-81701-2
Joe Williams And His Band
Blue Velvet: Crooners, Swooners And Velvet Vocals | Blue Note | 521153-2
Joe Williams With The Harry 'Sweets' Edison Band
Together/Have A Good Time | Roulette | 531790-2
Joe Williams With The Harry 'Sweets' Edison Sextet
Together/Have A Good Time | Roulette | 531790-2
Mar Murphy With The Ernie Wilkins Orchestra
RAH | Original Jazz Classics | OJCCD 141-2(R 9395)
Maynard Ferguson And His Orchestra
Verve Jazz Masters 52:Maynard Ferguson | Verve | 529905-2
Milt Jackson Orchestra
Milt Jackson Birthday Celebration | Fantasy | FANCD 6079-2
Big Bags | Original Jazz Classics | OJCCD 366-2(RLP 9429)
Oscar Peterson With The Ernie Wilkins Orchestra
Verve Jazz Masters 16:Oscar Peterson | Verve | 516320-2
Philip Catherine/Niels-Henning Orsted-Pedersen With The Royal Copenhagen Chamber Orchestra
Spanish Nights | Enja | ENJ-7023 2
Sarah Vaughan With The Clifford Brown All Stars
Sarah Vaughan | EmArCy | 9860779
Sonny Rollins Orchestra
Sonny Rollins And The Big Brass | Verve | 557545-2

Wilkins,Jack | (g,el-g,pts)
Wolfgang Lackerschmid-Donald Johnston Group
New Singers-New Songs | Bhakti Jazz | BR 31

Wilkins,Jimmy | (tb)
Count Basie And His Orchestra
Jazz Gallery:Lester Young Vol.2(1946-59) | RCA | 2119541-2
Verve Jazz Masters 2:Count Basie | Verve | 519819-2

Wilkins,Joe Willie | (gvoc)
Mose Vinson Band
Joe Hill Louis: The Be-Bop Boy | Bear Family Records | BCD 15524 AH

Wilkins,Rick | (cl,ts,cond,arrsax)
Oscar Peterson With Orchestra
Oscar Peterson:The Composer | Pablo | 2310970-2
A Royal Wedding Suite | Original Jazz Classics | OJCCD 973-2(2312129)
Sarah Vaughan With The Clifford Brown All Stars
Verve Jazz Masters 20:Introducing | Verve | 519853-2
Clifford Brown-Max Roach:Alone Together-The Best Of The Mercury Years | Verve | 526373-2
Sarah Vaughan | Verve | 543305-2
4 By 4:Ella Fitzgerald/Sarah Vaughan/Billie Holiday/Dinah Washington | Verve | 559693-2
Brownie-The Complete EmArCy Recordings Of Clifford Brown | EmArCy | 838306-2
Sarah Vaughan | EmArCy | 9860779
Singers Unlimited With Rob McConnell And The Boss Brass
The Singers Unlimited:Magic Voices | MPS | 539130-2

Wilkinson,Mark 'Wilkie' | (dr)
Oscar Peterson Trio
Planet Music:Oscar Peterson | RCA | 2165365-2
This Is Oscar Peterson | RCA | 2663990-2

Wilkinson,Richard | (light-show)
Sun Ra And His Intergalactic Research Arkestra
Black Myth/Out In Space | MPS | 557656-2

Willach,Thilo | (fl,clts)
Jazz Orchester Rheinland-Pfalz
Like Life | Jazz Haus Musik | LJBB 9405

Willecke,Claas | (bsfl)
Thärichens Tentett
Lady Moon | Minor Music | 801094

Willemark,Lena | (fiddle,octave-fiddle,voc,wooden-fl)
Lena Willemark-Ale Möller Group
Nordan | ECM | 1536(523161-2)
Agram | ECM | 1610
Per Gudmundson-Ale Möller-Lene Willemark
Frifot | ECM | 1690(557653-2)

Willers,Andreas | (el-sitar,g,electronic-perc,el-g)
Andreas Willers
Can I Go Like This? | Jazz Haus Musik | JHM 0070 CD
Andreas Willers Group
Tin Drum Stories(inspired by the novel 'Die Blechtrommel' by Günter Grass) | Between The Lines | btl 009(Efa 10179-2)
Andreas Willers & Friends Play Jimi Hendrix:Experience | Nabel Records:Jazz Network | CD 4665
Andreas Willers Octet
The Ground Music | Enja | ENJ-9368 2
Blue Collar
Diary Of A Working Band | Jazz Haus Musik | JHM 0089 CD
dAs prOjekT
dAs prOjekT | Foolish Music | FM 211288
Dirk Raulf Group
Die Welt Ist Immer Wieder Schön | Poise | Poise 03
Gabriele Hasler-Elvira Plenar-Andreas Willers
Sonetburger-Nach Texten Von Oskar Pastior | Foolish Music | FM 211793
Gabriele Hasler-Hans Lüdemann-Andreas Willers plus Jörn Schipper
Familienglück | Foolish Music | FM 211097
Gebhard Ullmann Trio
Suite Noire | Nabel Records:Jazz Network | CD 4649
Gebhard Ullmann-Andreas Willers
Suite Noire | Nabel Records:Jazz Network | CD 4649
Playful '93 | Nabel Records:Jazz Network | CD 4659
Ullmann-Wille-Haynes
Trad Corrosion | Nabel Records:Jazz Network | CD 4673
Ullmann-Willers-Schäuble-Lorenz
Out To Lunch | Nabel Records:Jazz Network | CD 4623

Willette,Baby Face | (org)
Baby Face Willette Quartet
So Blue So Funky-Heroes Of The Hammond | Blue Note | 796563-2
Grant Green Trio
Grant's First Stand | Blue Note | 521959-2

Willia,Carolyn | (voc)
Dee Dee Bridgewater With Band
Dee Dee Bridgewater | Atlantic | 7567-80760-2

William,Tommy | (sb)
Stan Getz With The Gary McFarland Orchestra
Stan Getz Highlights:The Best Of The Verve Years Vol.2 | Verve | 517330-2
Verve Jazz Masters 53:Stan Getz-Bossa Nova | Verve | 529904-2
Big Band Bossa Nova | Verve | 825771-2 PMS

Williams Jr.,John | (bel-b)
Benny Waters Quintet
Benny Waters Plays Songs Of Love | Jazzpoint | JP 1039 CD
Louis Armstrong And His Friends
Planet Jazz:Louis Armstrong | Planet Jazz | 2152052-2
Planet Jazz Sampler | Planet Jazz | 2152326-2
Louis Armstrong And His Friends | Bluebird | 2663961-2

Williams,Al | (p)
Johnny Hodges Orchestra
Johnny Hodges At The Sportpalast, Berlin | Pablo | 2CD 2620102
The Jazz Giants Play Harry Warren:Lullaby Of Broadway | Prestige | PCD 24204-2
Vic Dickenson-Buck Clayton All Stars
Atlantic Jazz: Kansas City | Atlantic | 7567-81701-2

Williams,Albert | (p)
Joe Hill Louis
Joe Hill Louis: The Be-Bop Boy | Bear Family Records | BCD 15524 AH
Joe Hill Louis Band
Joe Hill Louis: The Be-Bop Boy | Bear Family Records | BCD 15524 AH
Walter Horton Band
Joe Hill Louis: The Be-Bop Boy | Bear Family Records | BCD 15524 AH

Williams,Albert prob. | (p)
Joe Hill Louis Band
Joe Hill Louis: The Be-Bop Boy | Bear Family Records | BCD 15524 AH

Williams,Alfred | (dr)
Jim Robinson's New Orleans Band
Atlantic Jazz: New Orleans | Atlantic | 7567-81700-2

Williams,Alyson | (voc)
Jean-Paul Bourelly Group
Jungle Cowboy | JMT Edition | 919009-2

Williams,Andrew | (tb)
New Jazz Composers Octet
Walkin' the Line | Fresh Sound Records | FSNT 151 CD
The New Jazz Composers Octet
First Step Into Reality | Fresh Sound Records | FSNT 059 CD

Williams,Big Joe | (9-string-g,voc,foot stomping,g)
Big Joe Williams
Classic Delta Blues | Original Blues Classics | OBCCD 545-2

Williams,Billy | (ts)
(Little)Jimmy Scott With The Lionel Hampton Orchestra
Everybody's Somebody's Fool | Decca | 050669-2
Lionel Hampton And His Orchestra
Lionel Hampton:Flying Home | Dreyfus Jazz Line | FDM 36735-2

Williams,Booker T. | (as,tsperc)
Cold Sweat
Cold Sweat Plays J.B. | JMT Edition | 919025-2

Williams,Bruce | (as,cowbelle-flat-cl)
Russel Gunn Group
Ethnomusicology Vol.1 | Atlantic | 7567-83165-2

Williams,Buddy | (dr,percel-dr)
Carla Bley Band
Fleur Carnivore | Watt | 21
Dizzy Gillespie And His Orchestra
Closer To The Source | Atlantic | 7567-80776-2
Grover Washington Jr. Orchestra
Inside Moves | Elektra | 7559-60318-2
Lee Ritenour Group
Rio | GRP | GRP 95242

Williams,Buster | (b,el-b,piccolo-b,voc,b-solosynth)
Abdullah Ibrahim Septet
No Fear, No Die(S'en Fout La Mort):Original Soundtrack | TipToe | TIP-888815 2
Alphonse Mouzon Group
Deep Blue-The United States Of Mind | Blue Note | 521152-2
Art Blakey And The Jazz Messengers
The Art Of Jazz | IN+OUT Records | 77028-2
Buster Williams Quintet
Something More | IN+OUT Records | 7004-2
Jazz Unlimited | IN+OUT Records | 7017-2
Charles McPherson Quartet
Jazzin' Vol.2: The Music Of Stevie Wonder | Fantasy | FANCD 6088-2
McPherson's Mood | Original Jazz Classics | OJCCD 1947-2(PR 7743)
Chet Baker Quintet
Peace | Enja | ENJ-4016 2
Chet Baker-Wolfgang Lackerschmid Quintet
Chet Baker:The Legacy Vol.3:Why Shouldn't You Cry | Enja | ENJ-9337 2
Dexter Gordon Quartet
Dexter Gordon Birthday Celebration | Fantasy | FANCD 6082-2
More Power | Original Jazz Classics | OJC20 815-2(P 7680)
Tangerine | Original Jazz Classics | OJCCD 1041-2(P 10091)
Tower Of Power | Original Jazz Classics | OJCCD 299-2(P 7623)
Dexter Gordon Quintet
Dexter Gordon Birthday Celebration | Fantasy | FANCD 6082-2
Tangerine | Original Jazz Classics | OJCCD 1041-2(P 10091)
Tower Of Power | Original Jazz Classics | OJCCD 299-2(P 7623)
Generation | Original Jazz Classics | OJCCD 836-2(P 10069)
The Jazz Giants Play Miles Davis:Milestones | Prestige | PCD 24225-2
Dexter Gordon-James Moody Quintet
More Power | Original Jazz Classics | OJC20 815-2(P 7680)
Dollar(Abdullah Ibrahim) Brand Group
African River | Enja | ENJ-6018 2
Eddie Henderson Orchestra
Blue Breaks Beats Vol.2 | Blue Note | 789907-2
Gene Ammons Quintet
Brother Jug! | Prestige | PR20 7792-2
Gene Ammons-Sonny Stitt Quintet
Gentle Jug Vol.3 | Prestige | PCD 24249-2
Herbie Hancock Group
Sextant | CBS | CK 64983
Herbie Hancock Orchestra
Herbie Hancock:The Complete Blue Note Sixties Sessions | Blue Note | 495569-2
The Prisoner | Blue Note | 525649-2
Herbie Hancock Sextet
V.S.O.P. Herbie Hancock-Live At The City Center N.Y. | CBS | 486569-2
Illinois Jacquet Quintet
The Blues That's Me! | Original Jazz Classics | OJCCD 614-2(P 7731)
Larry Coryell Quartet
Air Dancing | Jazzpoint | JP 1025 CD
McCoy Tyner Orchestra
Sama Layuca | Original Jazz Classics | OJCCD 1071-2(M 9056)
McCoy Tyner Quintet
Asante | Blue Note | 493384-2
Miles Davis Quintet
Miles Davis Quintet 1965-1968 | CBS | C6K 67398
Ron Carter Group
Peg Leg | Original Jazz Classics | OJCCD 621-2
Ron Carter Quartet
Pick 'Em/Super Strings | Milestone | MCD 47090-2
Roots
Saying Something | IN+OUT Records | 77031-2
For Diz & Bird | IN+OUT Records | 77039-2
Shirley Horn Quartet
You Won't Forget Me | Verve | 847482-2
Shirley Horn Trio
You Won't Forget Me | Verve | 847482-2
A Lazy Afternoon | Steeplechase | SCCD 31111
Shirley Horn Trio with Buck Hill
You Won't Forget Me | Verve | 847482-2
Stan Getz Quartet
Sony Jazz Collection:Stan Getz | CBS | 488623-2
The Upper Manhattan Jazz Society
The Upper Manhattan Jazz Society | Enja | ENJ-4090 2

Williams,Charles | (b)
Sarah Vaughan And Her Trio
Verve Jazz Masters 42:Sarah Vaughan-The Jazz Sides | Verve | 526817-2

Williams,Clarence | (arr,voc,bs,jug,ld,p,celeste,talking)
(Little)Jimmy Scott With The Lucky Thompson Orchestra
Everybody's Somebody's Fool | Decca | 050669-2
Clarence Williams' Blue Five
Jazz:The Essential Collection Vol.1 | IN+OUT Records | 78011-2

Williams,Claude | (g,vvoc)
Count Basie And His Orchestra
Jazz:The Essential Collection Vol.3 | IN+OUT Records | 78013-2

Williams,Cootie | (tp,percvoc)
Benny Goodman And His All Star Sextet
Charlie Christian:Swing To Bop | Dreyfus Jazz Line | FDM 36715-2
Benny Goodman And His Orchestra
Charlie Christian:Swing To Bop | Dreyfus Jazz Line | FDM 36715-2
Benny Goodman Band
Benny Goodman At Carnegie Hall 1938(Complete) | CBS | C2K 65143
Benny Goodman Septet feat.Count Basie
Charlie Christian:Swing To Bop | Dreyfus Jazz Line | FDM 36715-2
Cootie Williams Quintet
Jazz In Paris:Joe Newman-Jazz At Midnight-Cootie Williams | EmArCy | 018446-2
Duke Ellington And His Cotton Club Orchestra
Jazz:The Essential Collection Vol.2 | IN+OUT Records | 78012-2
Duke Ellington And His Famous Orchestra
Duke Ellington:The Blanton-Webster Band | Bluebird | 21 13181-2
Planet Jazz:Duke Ellington | Planet Jazz | 2152053-2
Planet Jazz:Johnny Hodges | Planet Jazz | 2152065-2
Planet Jazz Sampler | Planet Jazz | 2152326-2
Planet Jazz:Ben Webster | RCA | 2165368-2
Planet Jazz:Big Bands | Planet Jazz | 2169649-2
Planet Jazz:Jazz Trumpet | Planet Jazz | 2169654-2
Highlights From The Duke Ellington Centennial Edition | RCA | 2663672-2
Greatest Hits | CBS | 462959-2
Jazz:The Essential Collection Vol.2 | IN+OUT Records | 78012-2
Jazz:The Essential Collection Vol.3 | IN+OUT Records | 78013-2
Duke Ellington:Ko-Ko | Dreyfus Jazz Line | FDM 36717-2
Duke Ellington And His Orchestra
Planet Jazz:Johnny Hodges | Planet Jazz | 2152065-2
Duke Ellington's Far East Suite | RCA | 2174797-2
The Art Of Saxophone | Laserlight | 24652
Highlights From The Duke Ellington Centennial Edition | RCA | 2663672-2
The Popular Duke Ellington | RCA | 2663880-2
Duke Ellington: The Champs-Elysees Theater January 29-30th,1965 | Laserlight | 36131
Verve Jazz Masters 4:Duke Ellington | Verve | 516338-2
Verve Jazz Masters 20:Introducing | Verve | 519853-2
Ella & Duke At The Cote D'Azur | Verve | 539030-2
Ella Fitzgerald And Duke Ellington:Cote D'Azure Concerts on Verve | Verve | 539033-2
Soul Call | Verve | 539785-2
The Great Paris Concert | Atlantic | 7567-81303-2
Jazz:The Essential Collection Vol.2 | IN+OUT Records | 78012-2
Jazz:The Essential Collection Vol.3 | IN+OUT Records | 78013-2
New Orleans Suite | Rhino | 812273670-2
Afro-Bossa | Reprise | 9362-47876-2
Welcome To Jazz At The Philharmonic | Fantasy | FANCD 6081-2
The Ellington Suites | Original Jazz Classics | OJC20 446-2(2310762)
Latin America Suite | Original Jazz Classics | OJC20 469-2
The Afro-Eurasian Eclipse-A Suite In Eight Parts | Original Jazz Classics | OJCCD 645-2(F 9498)
Yale Concert | Original Jazz Classics | OJCCD 664-2
Jazz At The Philharmonis Berlin '65/Paris '67 | Pablo | PACD 5304-2
The Jazz Giants Play Duke Ellington:Caravan | Prestige | PCD 24227-2
Togo Brava Swuite | Storyville | STCD 8323
Duke Ellington Orchestra
Continuum | Fantasy | FCD 24765-2
Ella Fitzgerald With The Duke Ellington Orchestra
The Stockholm Concert 1966 | Pablo | 2308242-2
Ella Fitzgerald-First Lady Of Song | Verve | 517898-2
Verve Jazz Masters 46:Ella Fitzgerald-The Jazz Sides | Verve | 527655-2
Ella At Duke's Place | Verve | 529700-2

Ella & Duke At The Cote D'Azur | Verve | 539030-2
Ella Fitzgerald With The Duke Ellington Orchestra And Jimmy Jones Trio
Ella & Duke At The Cote D'Azur | Verve | 539030-2
Ella Fitzgerald And Duke Ellington:Cote D'Azure Concerts on Verve | Verve | 539033-2
Ella Fitzgerald With The Jimmy Jones Trio
Ella Fitzgerald And Duke Ellington:Cote D'Azure Concerts on Verve | Verve | 539033-2
Johnny Hodges Orchestra
Planet Jazz:Johnny Hodges | Planet Jazz | 2152065-2
Leonard Feather's Esquire All Stars
Jazz:The Essential Collection Vol.2 | IN+OUT Records | 78012-2
Oscar Peterson With The Duke Ellington Orchestra
Oscar Peterson Plays Duke Ellington | Pablo | 2310966-2
Peggy Lee With The Benny Goodman Orchestra
Peggy Lee & Benny Goodman:The Complete Recordings 1941-1947 | CBS | C2K 65686

Williams,Cootie prob. | (tpld)
Ella Fitzgerald With The Jimmy Jones Trio
Ella Fitzgerald And Duke Ellington:Cote D'Azure Concerts on Verve | Verve | 539033-2

Williams,Courtney | (tp)
Louis Jordan And His Tympany Five
Louis Jordan-Let The Good Times Roll: The Complete Decca Recordings 1938-1954 | Bear Family Records | BCD 15557 IH
Louis Jordan's Elks Rendez-Vous Band
Louis Jordan-Let The Good Times Roll: The Complete Decca Recordings 1938-1954 | Bear Family Records | BCD 15557 IH
Roger Sturgis With Lovie Jordan's Elks Rendez-Vous Band
Louis Jordan-Let The Good Times Roll: The Complete Decca Recordings 1938-1954 | Bear Family Records | BCD 15557 IH

Williams,Curtney | (tp)
Buddy Johnson And His Orchestra
Buddy And Ella Johnson 1953-1964 | Bear Family Records | BCD 15479 DH

Williams,David | (b,el-bg)
Abdullah Ibrahim And Ekaya
Water From An Ancient Well | TipToe | TIP-888812 2
Abdullah Ibrahim Sextet
Mindif | Enja | ENJ-5073 2
Art Pepper Quartet
Art Pepper:The Complete Galaxy Recordings | Galaxy | 16GCD 1016-2
Arthur's Blues | Original Jazz Classics | OJCCD 680-2
Roadgame | Original Jazz Classics | OJCCD 774-2(GXY 5142)
Art Pepper With The Duke Jordan Trio
Art Pepper With Duke Jordan In Copenhagen 1981 | Galaxy | 2GCD 8201-2
Freddy Cole With Band
Le Grand Freddy:Freddy Cole Sings The Music Of Michel Legrand | Fantasy | FCD 9683-2
Freddy Cole With The Eric Alexander Band
Love Makes The Changes | Fantasy | FCD 9681-2
Ian Shaw With The Cedar Walton Trio
In A New York Minute | Milestone | MCD 9297-2
Kenny Barron Quintet
Quickstep | Enja | ENJ-6084 2
Sonny Fortune Quartet
Monk's Mood | Konnex Records | KCD 5048

Williams,Debbie | (voc)
Landes Jugend Jazz Orchester Hessen
Touch Of Lips | hr music.de | hrmj 004-01 CD

Williams,Denice | (vocvoice)
Spyro Gyra & Guests
Love & Other Obsessions | GRP | GRP 98112
Weather Report
Mr. Gone | CBS | 468208-2

Williams,Devonia | (pld)
Johnny Otis And His Orchestra
Verve Jazz Masters 43:Ben Webster | Verve | 525431-2

Williams,Don | (drperc)
Jimmy McGriff Quartet
Feelin' It | Milestone | MCD 9313-2
Jimmy McGriff Septet
McGriff Avenue | Milestone | MCD 9325-2

Williams,Ed | (tp,fl-hvoice)
Lou Donaldson Orchestra
Blue Breaks Beats Vol.2 | Blue Note | 789907-2
Lou Donaldson Quintet
Blue Break Beats | Blue Note | 799106-2
Oscar Brown Jr. And His Group
Movin' On | Rhino | 8122-73678-2

Williams,Eddie | (as,b,tsvoc)
Al Grey And His Allstars
Snap Your Fingers | Verve | 9860307

Williams,Elmer | (as,ts,clbs)
Fletcher Henderson And His Orchestra
Jazz:The Essential Collection Vol.1 | IN+OUT Records | 78011-2
Jazz:The Essential Collection Vol.3 | IN+OUT Records | 78013-2
Louis Armstrong With Chick Webb's Orchestra
Best Of The Complete RCA Victor Recordings | RCA | 2663636-2
Louis Armstrong:A 100th Birthday Celebration | RCA | 2663694-2

Williams,Fleming | (voc)
Nat Adderley Group
Soul Of The Bible | Capitol | 358257-2

Williams,Francis | (tp)
Duke Ellington And His Orchestra
Planet Jazz:Duke Ellington | Planet Jazz | 2152053-2
The Legends Of Swing | Laserlight | 24659
Highlights From The Duke Ellington Centennial Edition | RCA | 2663672-2
Carnegie Hall Concert January 1946 | Prestige | 2PCD 24074-2
Carnegie Hall Concert December 1947 | Prestige | 2PCD 24075-2
Tito Puente Orchestra
Planet Jazz:Tito Puente | Planet Jazz | 2165369-2

Williams,Fred | (b,el-bdr)
Lester Bowie Group
The Great Pretender | ECM | 1209(829369-2)
Lester Bowie Quartet
The Great Pretender | ECM | 1209(829369-2)

Williams,Freddy | (cl,asts)
Billie Holiday With Sy Oliver And His Orchestra
Billie's Love Songs | Nimbus Records | NI 2000
Ella Fitzgerald With Sy Oliver And His Orchestra
Ella Fitzgerald:The Decca Years 1949-1954 | Decca | 050668-2
Louis Armstrong With Sy Oliver And His Orchestra
Satchmo Serenaders | Verve | 543792-2
Louis Armstrong-My Greatest Songs | MCA | MCD 18347

Williams,George | (arr,ld,cl,asdr)
Roy Eldridge And His Orchestra With Strings
The Complete Verve Roy Eldridge Studio Sessions | Verve | 9861278

Williams,Greg | (dr)
Grant Green Septet
Live At The Lighthouse | Blue Note | 493381-2

Williams,Gregory | (fr-h)
McCoy Tyner Orchestra
13th House | Original Jazz Classics | OJCCD 1089-2(M 9102)
The Quincy Jones-Sammy Nestico Orchestra
Basie & Beyond | Warner | 9362-47792-2

Williams,Harold Ivory | (keyboards,psitar)
Miles Davis Group
On The Corner | CBS | CK 63980

Williams,Ira Buddy | (dr)
Nat Adderley Septet
Don't Look Back | Steeplechase | SCCD 31059

Williams,J.C. | (sax)
Count Basie And His Orchestra
Count Basie: Salle Pleyel, April 17th, 1972 | Laserlight | 36127

Williams,Jabo | (p,vocp-solo)
Jabo Williams
Boogie Woogie | Laserlight | 24321

Williams,Jackie | (drtambourine)
Benny Waters Quintet
Benny Waters Plays Songs Of Love | Jazzpoint | JP 1039 CD
Jay McShann And His Orchestra
Atlantic Jazz: Kansas City | Atlantic | 7567-81701-2
Jay McShann Orchestra
The Last Of The Blue Devils | Atlantic | 7567-80791-2
Terrie Richard Alden And The Warren Vaché Quartet
Voice With Heart | Nagel-Heyer | CD 048
The Sidney Bechet Society
Jam Session Concert | Nagel-Heyer | CD 076

Williams,James | (g,p,org,p-solotb)
Art Blakey And The Jazz Messengers
Night In Tunisia | Philips | 800064-2
Dave Stryker Octet
Blue To The Bone III | Steeplechase | SCCD 31524
Jessica Williams
Ain't Misbehavin' | Candid | CCD 79763
Kevin Eubanks Trio
Live At Bradley's | Blue Note | 830133-2
Tom Harrell Quintet
Visions | Contemporary | CCD 14063-2
Sail Away | Original Jazz Classics | OJCCD 1095-2(C- 14054-2)
Tom Harrell Sextet
Visions | Contemporary | CCD 14063-2
Sail Away | Original Jazz Classics | OJCCD 1095-2(C- 14054-2)

Williams,Jeff | (congas,drperc)
Ari Ambrose Trio
United | Steeplechase | SCCD 31518
Bruce Cox Quartet With Guests
Stick To It | Minor Music | 801055
Dave Liebman Quintet
Jazz Portraits | EGO | 95080
Roberta Piket Trio
Speak,Memory | Fresh Sound Records | FSNT 088 CD

Williams,Jessica | (p,synth,whistles,p-solovoc)
Jessica Williams
Gratitude | Candid | CCD 79721
Jessica Williams Trio
Higher Standards | Candid | CCD 79736
Jazz In The Afternoon | Candid | CCD 79750

Williams,Joe | (b,bass-dr,bjvoc)
Arturo Sandoval And The Latin Train Band
Arturo Sandoval & The Latin Train | GRP | GRP 98202
Chuck Wayne Trio
Morning Mist | Original Jazz Classics | OJCCD 1097-2(P-7367)
Count Basie All Stars
The Legends Of Swing | Laserlight | 24659
Count Basie And His Orchestra
Verve Jazz Masters 2:Count Basie | Verve | 519819-2
Count Basie Swings-Joe Williams Sings | Verve | 519852-2
Breakfast Dance And Barbecue | Roulette | 531791-2
One O'Clock Jump | Verve | 559806-2
The Complete Atomic Basie | Roulette | 828635-2
Count Basie At Newport | Verve | 9861761
Count On The Coast Vol.1 | Phontastic | NCD 7555
Count On The Coast Vol.2 | Phontastic | NCD 7575
Count Basie And The Kansas City 7
Count Basie: Salle Pleyel, April 17th, 1972 | Laserlight | 36127
Diane Schuur And Her Band
The Best Of Diane Schuur | GRP | GRP 98882
Eddie Condon All Stars
Jazz Festival Vol.1 | Storyville | 4960733
Ella Fitzgerald And Joe Williams With The Count Basie Octet
For The Love Of Ella Fitzgerald | Verve | 841765-2
Joe Williams And Friends
Planet Jazz:Male Jazz Vocalists | Planet Jazz | 2169657-2
At Newport '63 | RCA | 2663919-2
Joe Williams And His Band
Planet Jazz:Joe Williams | Planet Jazz | 2165370-2
Blue Velvet: Crooners, Swooners And Velvet Vocals | Blue Note | 521153-2
Joe Williams With The Cannonball Adderley Sextet
Cannonball Adderley Birthday Celebration | Fantasy | FANCD 6087-2
Joe Williams With The Frank Hunter Orchestra
Planet Jazz:Joe Williams | Planet Jazz | 2165370-2
Joe Williams With The Harry 'Sweets' Edison Band
Together/Have A Good Time | Roulette | 531790-2
Joe Williams With The Harry 'Sweets' Edison Sextet
Together/Have A Good Time | Roulette | 531790-2
Joe Williams With The Jimmy Jones Orchestra
Planet Jazz:Joe Williams | Planet Jazz | 2165370-2
Joe Williams,With The Oliver Nelson Orchestra
Planet Jazz:Joe Williams | Planet Jazz | 2165370-2
Sarah Vaughan And Joe Williams With The Count Basie Orchestra
Jazz Profile | Blue Note | 823517-2

Williams,John | (arr,ld,as,bass-sax,bs,ts,b,b-cl,cl)
Big Joe Turner With The Count Basie Orchestra
Flip Flop And Fly | Original Jazz Classics | OJCCD 1053-2(2310937)
Cannonball Adderley And His Orchestra
Verve Jazz Masters 31:Cannonball Adderley | Verve | 522651-2
Cannonball Adderley Group
Julian 'Cannonball' Adderley | EmArCy | 830381-2
Count Basie And His Orchestra
88 Basie Street | Original Jazz Classics | OJC 808(2310901)
Diane Schuur With The Count Basie Orchestra
The Best Of Diane Schuur | GRP | GRP 98882
Horace Silver Quintet
Horace Silver Retrospective | Blue Note | 495576-2
Louis Armstrong And His Orchestra
Louis Armstrong:Swing That Music | Laserlight | 36056
Mel Tormé With Orchestra
Comin' Home Baby!/Sings Sunday In New York | Warner | 8122-75438-2
Phil Woods Quartet
Woodlore | Original Jazz Classics | OJCCD 052-2
Stan Getz Quintet
Stan Getz Highlights:The Best Of The Verve Years Vol.2 | Verve | 517330-2
Stan Getz And The 'Cool' Sounds | Verve | 547317-2

Williams,John B. | (b,el-b,vocbs)
Benny Carter Sextet
To Bags...With Love:Memorial Album | Pablo | 2310967-2
Milt Jackson Birthday Celebration | Fantasy | FANCD 6079-2
Billie Holiday And Her Quintet
Billie Holiday:The Complete Commodore Recordings | GRP | 543272-2
Billie Holiday With Frankie Newton And His Orchestra
Billie Holiday:The Complete Commodore Recordings | GRP | 543272-2
Billie's Love Songs | Nimbus Records | NI 2000
Billie Holiday With Teddy Wilson And His Orchestra
Billie's Love Songs | Nimbus Records | NI 2000
Billy Cobham Group
The Best Of Billy Cobham | Atlantic | 7567-81558-2
Bobby Hutcherson Quintet
Blue Breaks Beats Vol.2 | Blue Note | 789907-2
Coleman Hawkins All Star Octet
Planet Jazz:Coleman Hawkins | Planet Jazz | 2152055-2
Count Basie And His Orchestra
Afrique | RCA | 2179618-2
Count Basie Big Band
Farmers Market Barbecue | Original Jazz Classics | OJCCD 732-2(2310874)

Williams,Johnny | (b,voc,bs,dr,pharpsichord)
Count Basie And His Orchestra
Fancy Pants | Original Jazz Classics | OJCCD 1038-2(2310920)
Henry Mancini And His Orchestra
Combo! | RCA | 2147794-2
Sarah Vaughan And The Count Basie Orchestra
Sarah Vaughan Birthday Celebration | Fantasy | FANCD 6090-2
Stan Getz Quintet
Stan Getz Highlights | Verve | 847430-2

Williams,Kip | (keyboards,dr,rapvoc)
Tom Browne Groups
Mo' Jamaica Funk | Hip Bop | HIBD 8002

Williams,Larry | (as,dr,fl,sax,ts,keyboards,synth)
Al Jarreau With Band
Al Jarreau In London | i.e. Music | 557849-2
All Fly Home | Warner | 7599-27362-2
Diane Schuur With Orchestra
Blues For Schuur | GRP | GRP 98632
The Best Of Diane Schuur | GRP | GRP 98882
George Duke Group
Jazzrock-Anthology Vol.3:Fusion | Zounds | CD 27100555
Joe Sample Group
Ashes To Ashes | Warner | 7599-26318-2
Invitation | Warner | 9362-45209.2
Paulinho Da Costa Orchestra
Agora | Original Jazz Classics | OJCCD 630-2(2310785)

Williams,Lenny | (keyboardsstrings)
Chuck Brown And The Second Chapter Band
Timeless | Minor Music | 801068

Williams,Leroy | (drsteel-dr)
Barry Harris Trio
Magnificent! | Original Jazz Classics | OJCCD 1026-2(P 7733)
John Marshall Quintet
Dreamin' On The Hudson | Organic Music | ORGM 9713
John Patton Quartet
The Lost Grooves | Blue Note | 831883-2
Accent On The Blues | Blue Note | 853924-2
Lee Konitz Quartet
Lullaby Of Birdland | Candid | CCD 79709

Williams,Mars | (as,ts,bass-sax,bells,didgeridoo)
Hal Russell NRG Ensemble
The Finnish/Swiss Tour | ECM | 1455
The Hal Russell Story | ECM | 1498

Williams,Mary Lou | (arr,comp,pp-solo)
Benny Goodman And His Orchestra
40th Anniversary Concert-Live At Carnegie Hall | London | 820349-2
Verve Jazz Masters 33:Benny Goodman | Verve | 844410-2
Mary Lou Williams Quartet
The Story Of Jazz Piano | Laserlight | 24653
Mary Lou Williams Trio
Planet Jazz:Jazz Piano | RCA | 2169655-2
May Lou Williams Trio At Rick's Cafe Americain,Chicago,Ill. | Storyville | STCD 8285

Williams,Murray | (as,cl,reedssax)
Charlie Parker And His Orchestra
The Cole Porter Songbook | Verve | 823250-2
Bird: The Complete Charlie Parker On Verve | Verve | 837141-2
Charlie Parker With Orchestra
Charlie Parker:The Best Of The Verve Years | Verve | 527815-2
Charlie Parker With Strings
Charlie Parker With Strings:The Master Takes | Verve | 523984-2
Bird: The Complete Charlie Parker On Verve | Verve | 837141-2
Charlie Parker With The Joe Lipman Orchestra
Verve Jazz Masters 28:Charlie Parker Plays Standards | Verve | 521854-2
Charlie Parker With Strings:The Master Takes | Verve | 523984-2
Charlie Parker Big Band | Verve | 559835-2
Charlie Parker With The Neal Hefti Orchestra
Charlie Parker:The Best Of The Verve Years | Verve | 527815-2
Bird: The Complete Charlie Parker On Verve | Verve | 837141-2

Williams,Natalie | (voc)
European Jazz Youth Orchestra
Swinging Europe 3 | dacapo | DCCD 9461

Williams,Nelson | (tbtp)
Great Traditionalists In Europe
Great Traditionalists | Jazzpoint | JP 1046 CD
Quartier Latin Jazz Band
Great Traditionalists | Jazzpoint | JP 1046 CD

Williams,Norman | (b)
Lester Young And Earl Swope With The Bill Potts Trio
Lester Young In Washington,DC 1956:Vol.5 | Original Jazz Classics | OJCCD 993-2
Lester Young With The Bill Potts Trio
Lester Young In Washington,DC 1956:Vol.1 | Original Jazz Classics | OJCCD 782-2(2308219)
Lester Young In Washington,DC 1956:Vol.5 | Original Jazz Classics | OJCCD 993-2
The Jazz Giants Play Harry Warren:Lullaby Of Broadway | Prestige | PCD 24204-2

Williams,Patrick | (arr,condtp)
Singers Unlimited With The Pat Williams Orchestra
The Singers Unlimited:Magic Voices | MPS | 539130-2
Singers Unlimited With The Patrick Williams Orchestra
The Singers Unlimited:Magic Voices | MPS | 539130-2

Williams,Peter Seige | (pvoc)
Dieter Antritter And His Traveling Jazz Band
Great Traditionalists | Jazzpoint | JP 1046 CD

Williams,Quentin | (cello)
Barbara Thompson Group
Heavenly Bodies | VeraBra Records | CDVBR 2015-2

Williams,Ray | (voc)
Hans Theessink Group
Crazy Moon | Minor Music | 801052
Journey On | Minor Music | 801062

Williams,Richard | (tp)
Ahmed Abdul-Malik Orchestra
Jazz Sounds Of Africa | Prestige | PRCD 24279-2
Charles Mingus And His Orchestra
The Complete Town Hall Concert | Blue Note | 828353-2
Charles Mingus Group
Mingus Dynasty | CBS | CK 65513
Charles Mingus Orchestra
Charles Mingus:Pre-Bird(Mingus Revisited) | Verve | 538636-2
Mingus Mingus Mingus | Impulse(MCA) | 951170-2
The Black Saint And The Sinner Lady | Impulse(MCA) | 951174-2
Charles Mingus:The Complete 1959 Columbia Recordings | CBS | C3K 65145
Duke Ellington And His Orchestra
Afro-Bossa | Reprise | 9362-47876-2
Togo Brava Swuite | Storyville | STCD 8323
Eddie Lockjaw Davis And His Orchestra
Eric Dolphy:The Complete Prestige Recordings | Prestige | 9 PRCD-4418-2
Freddie Hubbard Orchestra
The Body And The Soul | Impulse(MCA) | 951183-2
Gil Evans Orchestra
Svengali | Rhino | 8122-73720-2
Jimmy McGriff Orchestra
Swingin' The Blues-Jumpin' The Blues | Laserlight | 24654
Jimmy Smith With The Oliver Nelson Orchestra
Verve Jazz Masters 29:Jimmy Smith | Verve | 521855-2
Jimmy Smith:Best Of The Verve Years | Verve | 527950-2
Jimmy Smith-Talkin' Verve | Verve | 531563-2
Peter & The Wolf | Verve | 547264-2
Max Roach Sextet With Choir
It's Time | Impulse(MCA) | 951185-2
Oliver Nelson Sextet
Eric Dolphy:The Complete Prestige Recordings | Prestige | 9 PRCD-4418-2
Eric Dolphy Birthday Celebration | Fantasy | FANCD 6085-2
Screamin' The Blues | Original Jazz Classics | OJC 080(NJ 8243)
The Prestige Legacy Vol.2:Battles Of Saxes | Prestige | PCD 24252-2

INTERPRETENVERZEICHNIS

Richard Williams Quintet
New Horn In Town | Candid | CCD 79003
Roland Kirk With The Benny Golson Orchestra
Rahsaan/The Complete Mercury Recordings Of Roland Kirk | Mercury | 846630-2
Sam Rivers Orchestra
Crystals | Impulse(MCA) | 589760-2
Thad Jones-Mel Lewis Orchestra
The Groove Merchant/The Second Race | Laserlight | 24656
Yusef Lateef Orchestra
The Centaur And The Phoenix | Original Jazz Classics | OJCCD 721-2(RLP 9337)
Yusef Lateef Quintet
Live at Pep's Vol.2 | Impulse(MCA) | 547961-2
The Roots Of Acid Jazz | Impulse(MCA) | IMP 12042

Williams,Richard 'Radu' | (b)
Ku-Umba Frank Lacy & His Quartet
Settegast Strut | Tutu Records | 888162-2*

Williams,Robin | (vvoc)
Barbara Thompson Group
Heavenly Bodies | VeraBra Records | CDVBR 2015-2
Bobby McFerrin Groups
Spontaneous Inventions | Blue Note | 746298-2

Williams,Rod | (psynth)
Craig Harris And Tailgater's Tales
Shelter | JMT Edition | 919008-2

Williams,Roy | (tbvoc)
Bill Allred-Roy Williams Quintet
Absolutely | Nagel-Heyer | CD 024
Ellington For Lovers | Nagel-Heyer | NH 1009
Blues Of Summer | Nagel-Heyer | NH 1011
The Second Sampler | Nagel-Heyer | NHR SP 6
Danny Moss-Roy Williams Quintet
Steamers! | Nagel-Heyer | CD 049
Ellington For Lovers | Nagel-Heyer | NH 1009
Great British Jazz Band
The Great British Jazz Band:Jubilee | Candid | CCD 79720
The Alex Welsh Legacy Band
The Sound Of Alex Vol.1 | Nagel-Heyer | CD 070
The European Jazz Ginats
Jazz Party | Nagel-Heyer | CD 009
The First Sampler | Nagel-Heyer | NHR SP 5
The Great British Jazz Band
A British Jazz Odyssey | Candid | CCD 79740
The New York Allstars
Hey Ba-Ba-Re-Bop!! The New York Allstars Play Lionel Hampton Vol.1 | Nagel-Heyer | CD 047
The New York Allstars Play Lionel Hampton,Vol.2: Stompin' At The Savoy | Nagel-Heyer | CD 077
Tom Saunders' 'Wild Bill Davison Band' & Guests
Exactly Like You | Nagel-Heyer | CD 023
The Second Sampler | Nagel-Heyer | NHR SP 6

Williams,Rudy | (as,bs,drts)
Charlie Christian All Stars
Charlie Christian-Jazz Immortal/Dizzy Gillespie 1944 | Original Jazz Classics | OJCCD 1932-2(ES 548)
Minton's Playhouse All Stars
Charlie Christian:Swing To Bop | Dreyfus Jazz Line | FDM 36715-2

Williams,Sandy | (tb)
Bunk Johnson-Sidney Bechet Sextet
Jazz:The Essential Collection Vol.1 | IN+OUT Records | 78011-2
Duke Ellington And His Orchestra
At The Hurricane:Original 1943 Broadcasts | Storyville | STCD 8359
Ella Fitzgerald And Her Famous Orchestra
The Radio Years 1940 | Jazz Unlimited | JUCD 2065
Ella Fitzgerald And Her Orchestra
Jazz Collection:Ella Fitzgerald | Laserlight | 24397
Ella Fitzgerald With The Chick Webb Orchestra
Jazz Collection:Ella Fitzgerald | Laserlight | 24397
Fletcher Henderson And His Orchestra
Jazz:The Essential Collection Vol.1 | IN+OUT Records | 78011-2
New Orleans Feetwarmers
Jazz:The Essential Collection Vol.1 | IN+OUT Records | 78011-2
Sidney Bechet And His New Orleans Feetwarmers
Sidney Bechet:Summertime | Dreyfus Jazz Line | FDM 36712-2

Williams,Sarah | (b-tb)
André Holst With Chris Dean's European Swing Orchestra
That's Swing | Nagel-Heyer | CD 079
Kenny Wheeler Brass Ensemble
A Long Time Ago | ECM | 1691

Williams,Scott | (voc)
Karen Mantler Group
Farewell | Watt | XtraWatt/8

Williams,Stephen E. 'Steve' | (drperc)
Carmen McRae With The Shirley Horn Trio
Planet Jazz:Female Jazz Vocalists | Planet Jazz | 2169656-2
The Collected Carmen McRae | RCA | 2668713-2
Shirley Horn Quartet
Light Out Of Darkness(A Tribute To Ray Charles) | Verve | 519703-2
The Main Ingredient | Verve | 529555-2
Loving You | Verve | 537022-2
Shirley Horn Quintet
Light Out Of Darkness(A Tribute To Ray Charles) | Verve | 519703-2
The Main Ingredient | Verve | 529555-2
Loving You | Verve | 537022-2
Shirley Horn Trio
Light Out Of Darkness(A Tribute To Ray Charles) | Verve | 519703-2
The Antonio Carlos Jobim Songbook | Verve | 525472-2
The Main Ingredient | Verve | 529555-2
You Won't Forget Me | Verve | 847482-2
Shirley Horn Trio with Branford Marsalis
You Won't Forget Me | Verve | 847482-2
Shirley Horn Trio with Miles Davis
You Won't Forget Me | Verve | 847482-2
Shirley Horn Trio with Toots Thielemans
You Won't Forget Me | Verve | 847482-2
Shirley Horn Trio with Wynton Marsalis
You Won't Forget Me | Verve | 847482-2
Shirley Horn With Strings
Here's To Life | Verve | 511879-2
Toots Thielemans With The Shirley Horn Trio
Verve Jazz Masters Vol.59:Toots Thielemans | Verve | 535271-2

Williams,Steve | (drharm)
Jimmy Smith Sextet
Jimmy Smith:Best Of The Verve Years | Verve | 527950-2
Root Down | Verve | 559805-2
Shirley Horn And Her Quartet
May The Music Never End | Verve | 076028-2
Shirley Horn And Her Trio
May The Music Never End | Verve | 076028-2

Williams,Tommy | (b)
Art Farmer/Benny Golson Jazztet
The Jazztet At Birdhouse | Argo | 589762-2
Benny Golson Band
Benny Golson:Free | GRP | 951816-2
Getz-Gilberto Quintet
Verve Jazz Masters 13:Antonio Carlos Jobim | Verve | 516409-2
Stan Getz Highlights:The Best Of The Verve Years Vol.2 | Verve | 517330-2
Verve Jazz Masters 20:Introducing | Verve | 519853-2
Getz/Gilberto | Polydor | 521414-2
A Life In Jazz:A Musical Biography | Verve | 535119-2
Kai Winding-J.J.Johnson Quintet
The Great Kai & J.J. | Impulse(MCA) | 951225-2
Stan Getz Group
Verve Jazz Masters 53:Stan Getz-Bossa Nova | Verve | 529904-2
Stan Getz Quintet
Verve Jazz Masters 53:Stan Getz-Bossa Nova | Verve | 529904-2
Stan Getz Quintet Feat. Astrud Gilberto
Verve Jazz Masters 8:Stan Getz | Verve | 519823-2
Getz/Gilberto | Verve | 589595-2 SACD
Stan Getz With The Gary McFarland Orchestra
Verve Jazz Masters 53:Stan Getz-Bossa Nova | Verve | 529904-2
Big Band Bossa Nova | Verve | 825771-2 PMS
Stan Getz Highlights | Verve | 847430-2
Stan Getz-Joao Gilberto Quintet
The Antonio Carlos Jobim Songbook | Verve | 525472-2
Stan Getz Highlights | Verve | 847430-2
Stan Getz-Luiz Bonfa Group
The Antonio Carlos Jobim Songbook | Verve | 525472-2
Stan Getz-Luiz Bonfa Orchestra
Verve Jazz Masters 13:Antonio Carlos Jobim | Verve | 516409-2
Jazz Samba Encore! | Verve | 823613-2

Williams,Tony | (dr,dr-machine,el-dr,maracas)
Andrew Hill Sextet
Point Of Departure | Blue Note | 499007-2
Blue Note All Stars
Town Hall Concert | Blue Note | 497811-2
Chet Baker-Wolfgang Lackerschmid Quintet
Chet Baker:The Legacy Vol.3:Why Shouldn't You Cry | Enja | ENJ-9337 2
Eric Dolphy Quintet
Out To Lunch | Blue Note | 498793-2
A Blue Conception | Blue Note | 534254-2
Gil Evans Orchestra
There Comes A Time | RCA | 2131392-2
Grachan Moncur III Quintet
A Blue Conception | Blue Note | 534254-2
Herbie Hancock Group
Sunlight | CBS | 486570-2
Herbie Hancock Quartet
Herbie Hancock:The Complete Blue Note Sixties Sessions | Blue Note | 495569-2
Empyrean Isles | Blue Note | 498796-2
Blue N' Groovy | Blue Note | 780679-2
Blue Break Beats | Blue Note | 799106-2
Cantaloupe Island | Blue Note | 829331-2
Herbie Hancock Quintet
V.S.O.P. Herbie Hancock-Live At The City Center N.Y. | CBS | 486569-2
Maiden Voyage | Blue Note | 495331-2
Herbie Hancock:The Complete Blue Note Sixties Sessions | Blue Note | 495569-2
The Best Of Blue Note | Blue Note | 796110-2
Cantaloupe Island | Blue Note | 829331-2
Herbie Hancock Septet
Herbie Hancock:The Complete Blue Note Sixties Sessions | Blue Note | 495569-2
My Point Of View | Blue Note | 521226-2
Cantaloupe Island | Blue Note | 829331-2
Herbie Hancock Sextet
Herbie Hancock:The Complete Blue Note Sixties Sessions | Blue Note | 495569-2
Jackie McLean Quintet
Herbie Hancock:The Complete Blue Note Sixties Sessions | Blue Note | 495569-2
Vertigo | Blue Note | 522669-2
Joe Henderson Quartet
Relaxin' At Camarillo | Original Jazz Classics | OJCCD 776-2(C 14006)
Kenny Dorham Quintet
Una Mas | Blue Note | 521228-2
Marcus Miller Group
The Sun Don't Lie | Dreyfus Jazz Line | FDM 36560-2
Michael Mantler Group
Movies | Watt | 7 (2313107)
Movies/More Movies | Watt | 7/10(543377-2)
Michel Petrucciani With The Graffiti String Quartet
Marvellous | Dreyfus Jazz Line | FDM 36564-2
Miles Davis Group
Circle In The Round | CBS | 467898-2
In A Silent Way | CBS | 86556-2
Miles Davis Quintet
Circle In The Round | CBS | 467898-2
The Complete Concert 1964:My Funny Valentine+Four & More | CBS | 471246-2
Highlights From The Plugged Nickel | CBS | 481434-2
Filles De Kilimanjaro | CBS | 86555-2
Miles Davis Quintet 1965-1968 | CBS | C6K 67398
Seven Steps To Heaven | CBS | CK 48827
This Is Jazz:Miles Davis Plays Ballads | CBS | CK 65038
Sorcerer | CBS | CK 65680
Nefertiti | CBS | CK 65681
Miles Smiles | CBS | CK 65682
Miles In The Sky | CBS | CK 65684
E.S.P. | CBS | CK65683
Miles Davis Sextet
Circle In The Round | CBS | 467898-2
Miles In The Sky | CBS | CK 65684
Miles Davis With Gil Evans & His Orchestra
Quiet Nights | CBS | CK 65293
Ron Carter Orchestra
Parade | Original Jazz Classics | OJCCD 1047-2(M 9088)
Ron Carter Quartet
Parade | Original Jazz Classics | OJCCD 1047-2(M 9088)
Carnaval | Original Jazz Classics | OJCCD 1070-2(GXY 5144)
Ron Carter Trio
Third Plane | Original Jazz Classics | OJCC20 754-2(M 9105)
Sam Rivers Quartet
A Blue Conception | Blue Note | 534254-2
Fuchsia Swing Song | Blue Note | 593874-2
Sonny Rollins Quartet
Easy Living | Original Jazz Classics | OJCCD 893-2
Sonny Rollins Quintet
Don't Stop The Carnival | Milestone | MCD 55005-2
No Problem | Original Jazz Classics | OJCCD 1014-2(M 9104)
Easy Living | Original Jazz Classics | OJCCD 893-2
Sonny Rollins Sextet
Jazzin' Vol.2: The Music Of Stevie Wonder | Fantasy | FANCD 6088-2
Don't Stop The Carnival | Milestone | MCD 55005-2
Easy Living | Original Jazz Classics | OJCCD 893-2
Stan Getz Quartet
Sony Jazz Collection:Stan Getz | CBS | 488623-2
Tony Williams Lifetime
Lifetime | Blue Note | 499004-2
Ego | Verve | 559512-2
Wayne Shorter Quartet
Sorcerer | CBS | CK 65680
Wayne Shorter Sextet
Wayne Shorter:The Classic Blue Note Recordings | Blue Note | 540856-2
Weather Report
Mr. Gone | CBS | 468208-2
Wynton Marsalis Quartet
Wynton Marsalis | CBS | 468708-2
Wynton Marsalis Quintet
Wynton Marsalis | CBS | 468708-2

Williams,Trevor | (v)
Dee Dee Bridgewater With Orchestra
Dear Ella | Verve | 539102-2

Williams,Victor | (perc)
John McLaughlin Group
The Heart Of Things | Verve | 539153-2
Live In Paris | Verve | 543536-2

Williams,Waddet | (tb)
Louis Armstrong And His Orchestra
Louis Armstrong:C'est Si Bon | Dreyfus Jazz Line | FDM 36730-2
Swing Legends:Louis Armstrong | Nimbus Records | NI 2012

Williams,Walter | (g,voctp)
(Little)Jimmy Scott With The Lionel Hampton Orchestra
Everybody's Somebody's Fool | Decca | 050669-2
Lionel Hampton And His Orchestra
Lionel Hampton's Paris All Stars | Vogue | 21511502
Lionel Hampton:Flying Home | Dreyfus Jazz Line | FDM 36735-2
Lionel Hampton Orchestra
The Big Bands Vol.1.The Snader Telescriptions | Storyville | 4960043

Williams,Willie | (cl,ts,dr,voc,g,sswbd)
Kevin Mahogany With Orchestra
Songs And Moments | Enja | ENJ-8072 2
Taylor's Wailers
Mr. A.T. | Enja | ENJ-7017 2
Willie Williams Trio
WW3 | Enja | ENJ-8060 2

Williams,Woody | (dr)
Russel Gunn Group
Ethnomusicology Vol.1 | Atlantic | 7567-83165-2

Williams-Miller,Birdia | (voc)
Hans Theessink Group
Crazy Moon | Minor Music | 801052

Williamson,Claude | (2 p with playback,p,celestep-solo)
Barney Kessel And His Orchestra
The Jazz Giants Play Rodgers & Hart:Blue Moon | Prestige | PCD 24205-2
Barney Kessel Quintet
Barney Kessel Plays Standards | Original Jazz Classics | OJCCD 238-2
Bud Shank And Trombones
Cool Fool | Fresh Sound Records | FSR CD 507
Bud Shank Quartet
Live At The Haig | Choice | CHCD 71030
Chet Baker And The Lighthouse All Stars
Witch Doctor | Original Jazz Classics | OJCCD 609-2
Ella Fitzgerald With The Marty Paich Orchestra
Get Happy! | Verve | 523321-2
Gerry Mulligan Quartet
The Art Of Saxophone | Laserlight | 24652
Gerry Mulligan-Johnny Hodges Quintet
Gerry Mulligan Meets Johnny Hodges | Verve | 065513-2
Verve Jazz Masters 35:Johnny Hodges | Verve | 521857-2
Howard Rumsey's Lighthouse All-Stars
Oboe/Flute | Original Jazz Classics | OJCCD 154-2(C 3520)
Howard Rumsey's Lighthouse All-Stars Vol.6 | Original Jazz Classics | OJCCD 386-2(C 3504)
June Christy With The Pete Rugolo Orchestra
Something Cool(The Complete Mono & Stereo Versions) | Capitol | 534069-2
Tal Farlow Quartet
Verve Jazz Masters 41:Tal Farlow | Verve | 527365-2

Williamson,Ernest | (b)
Sidney Bechet And His New Orleans Feetwarmers
Sidney Bechet:Summertime | Dreyfus Jazz Line | FDM 36712-2

Williamson,Paul | (bs,tsvoc)
Vince Jones Group
It All Ends Up In Tears | Intuition Records | INT 3069-2
For All Colours | Intuition Records | INT 3071-2
Tell Me A Secret | Intuition Records | INT 3072-2
Vince Jones Septet
On The Brink Of It | Intuition Records | INT 3068-2

Williamson,Robin | (g,harp,whistles,vocmand)
Robin Williamson
The Seed-At-Zero | ECM | 1732(543819-2)
Robin Williamson Group
Skirting The River Road | ECM | 1785(016372-2

Williamson,Sonny Boy [Rice Miller] | (g,vocharm)
Buddy Guy Blues Band
Buddy Guy-The Complete Chess Studio Recordings | MCA | MCD 09337
Roland Kirk Quartet With Sonny Boy Williamson
Talkin' Verve-Roots Of Acid Jazz:Roland Kirk | Verve | 533101-2
Sonny Boy Williamson Band
Classic Blues | Zounds | CD 2700048
Sonny Boy Williamson Group
The Blues | Storyville | 4960323

Williamson,Steve | (as,keyboards,ts,sax,percss)
Maceo Parker Group
Mo' Roots | Minor Music | 801018

Williamson,Stu | (tb,tpv-tb)
Astrud Gilberto With Antonio Carlos Jobim And The Marty Paich Orchestra
The Antonio Carlos Jobim Songbook | Verve | 525472-2
Astrud Gilberto With The Marty Paich Orchestra
Verve Jazz Masters 9:Astrud Gilberto | Verve | 519824-2
Benny Carter And His Orchestra
Aspects | Capitol | 852677-2
Bud Shank And Trombones
Cool Fool | Fresh Sound Records | FSR CD 507
Dizzy Gillespie And His Orchestra
Talking Verve:Dizzy Gillespie | Verve | 533846-2
Ella Fitzgerald With The Marty Paich Orchestra
Ella Fitzgerald-First Lady Of Song | Verve | 517898-2
Get Happy! | Verve | 523321-2
Whisper Not | Verve | 589947-2
Howard Rumsey's Lighthouse All-Stars
Howard Rumsey's Lighthouse All-Stars Vol.6 | Original Jazz Classics | OJCCD 386-2(C 3504)
Lennie Niehaus Quintet
Lennie Niehaus Vol.1:The Quintets | Original Jazz Classics | OJCCD 1933-2(C 3518)
Lennie Niehaus Sextet
Lennie Niehaus Vol.5:The Sextet | Original Jazz Classics | OJCCD 1944-2(C 3524)
Pete Rugolo And His Orchestra
Thriller/Richard Diamon(Original Jazz Scores From 2 Classics TV Series) | Fresh Sound Records | FSCD 2015
Shelly Manne And His Men
The Gambit | Original Jazz Classics | OJCCD 1007-2(C 7557)
More Swinging Sounds | Original Jazz Classics | OJCCD 320-2(C 7519)
Stan Kenton And His Orchestra
Stan Kenton Portraits On Standards | Capitol | 531571-2
Terry Gibbs Big Band
Terry Gibbs Dream Band Vol.4:Main Stem | Contemporary | CCD 7656-2
Terry Gibbs Dream Band
Terry Gibbs Dream Band Vol.2:The Sundown Sessions | Contemporary | CCD 7652-2
Terry Gibbs Dream Band Vol.3:Flying Home | Contemporary | CCD 7654-2
Terry Gibbs Dream Band Vol.5:The Big Cat | Contemporary | CCD 7657-2
Terry Gibbs Dream Band Vol.6:One More Time | Contemporary | CCD 7658-2
The Jazz Giants Play Jerome Kern:Yesterdays | Prestige | PCD 24202-2

Williamson[as 'Big Skol'],Sonny Boy [Rice Miller] | (harm)
Roland Kirk Quintet
Rahsaan/The Complete Mercury Recordings Of Roland Kirk | Mercury | 846630-2

Williard,Terry | (b)
Cal Tjader Quintet
Soul Bird | Verve | 549111-2

Willingham,Doris | (voc)
Nina Simone Quintet
Planet Jazz:Nina Simone | Planet Jazz | 2165372-2

Willis,Carolyn | (voc)
Quincy Jones And His Orchestra
Verve Jazz Masters Vol.59:Toots Thielemans | Verve | 535271-2

Stanley Turrentine And His Orchestra
Pieces Of Dream | Original Jazz Classics | OJCCD 831-2(F 9465)

Willis,Dave | (bssax)
Benny Goodman And His Orchestra
Verve Jazz Masters 33:Benny Goodman | Verve | 844410-2

Willis,Edgar | (b)
David Fathead Newman Sextet
Atlantic Saxophones | Rhino | 8122-71256-2
Rhino Presents The Atlantic Jazz Gallery | Atlantic | 8122-71257-2
Fathead:Ray Charles Presents David Newman | Atlantic | 8122-73708-2
Hank Crawford And His Orchestra
Atlantic Saxophones | Rhino | 8122-71256-2
Hank Crawford Septet
More Soul | Atlantic | 8122-73709-2
Ray Charles And His Orchestra
Ray Charles At Newport | Atlantic | 7567-80765-2
Sonny Stitt Quartet
Verve Jazz Masters 50:Sonny Sitt | Verve | 527651-2

Willis,Falk | (drperc)
Florian Trübsbach Quintet
Manson & Dixon | Jazz 4 Ever Records:Jazz Network | J4E 4759
Michael Lutzeier Quartet
Music 4 Food | Jazz 4 Ever Records:Jazz Network | J4E 4739
Peter O'Mara Quartet
Symmetry | Edition Collage | EC 484-2
Wind Moments | Take Twelve On CD | TT 009-2

Willis,Gary | (b)
Allan Holdsworth Group
None Too Soon | Cream Records | CR 400-2

Willis,Larry | (el-p,echoplex,ring-modulator,synth)
Alphonse Mouzon Group
Deep Blue-The United States Of Mind | Blue Note | 521152-2
Attila Zoller Quartet
When It's Time | Enja | ENJ-9031 2
Attila Zoller Quintet
When It's Time | Enja | ENJ-9031 2
Carla Bley Band
Night-Glo | Watt | 16
Carla Bley Sextet
Sextet | Watt | 17
Carmen McRae And Her Quartet
Carmen Sings Monk | RCA | 2663841-2
Freddy Cole With Band
A Circle Of Love | Fantasy | FCD 9674-2
Jackie McLean Quartet
Right Now | Blue Note | 595972-2
Jackie McLean Quintet
Jacknife | Blue Note | 540535-2
Jackie McLean Sextet
Jacknife | Blue Note | 540535-2
Jimmy Scott With Band
Over The Rainbow | Milestone | MCD 9314-2
Moon Glow | Milestone | MCD 9332-2
Joe Henderson And His Orchestra
Joe Henderson:The Milestone Years | Milestone | 8MCD 4413-2
Joe Henderson Quintet
Multiple | Original Jazz Classics | OJCCD 763-2(M 9050)
Joe Henderson Sextet
Multiple | Original Jazz Classics | OJCCD 763-2(M 9050)
Roy Hargrove Quintet
Family | Verve | 527630-2
Steve Swallow Group
Carla | Watt | XtraWatt/2

Willisohn,Christian | (g,p,vocaccordeon)
Christian Willisohn Group
Live At Marians | ART BY HEART | ABH 2006 2
Blues On The World | Blues Beacon | BLU-1025 2
Christian Willisohn New Band
Heart Broken Man | Blues Beacon | BLU-1026 2
Christian Willisohn-Boris Vanderlek
Blues News | Blues Beacon | BLU-1019 2
Christian Willisohn-Boris Vanderlek-Ludwig Seuss
Blues News | Blues Beacon | BLU-1019 2
Christian Willisohn-Lillian Boutté
Come Together | ART BY HEART | ABH 2002 2
Lillian Boutté And Her Group
You've Gotta Love Pops:Lillian Bouté Sings Louis Armstrong | ART BY HEART | ABH 2005 2

Willison,P. | (cello)
Dee Dee Bridgewater With Orchestra
Dear Ella | Verve | 539102-2

Wills,Edgar L. | (b)
Ray Charles Sextet With The Raylets
Newport Jazz Festival 1958,July 3rd-6th Vol.4:Blues In The Night No.2 | Phontastic | NCD 8816

Wilms,André | (voice)
Heiner Goebbels Group
Ou Bien Le Debarquement Desastreux | ECM | 1552

Wilson,Anthony | (g)
Diana Krall Group
The Girl In The Other Room | Verve | 9862246
Jacintha With Band And Strings
Lush Life | Groove Note | GRV 1011-2(Gold CD 2011)

Wilson,Arlandus | (voc)
Golden Gate Quartet
From Spiritual To Swing | Vanguard | VCD 169/71

Wilson,Carl | (borg)
Willis Jackson Quintet
Gravy | Prestige | PCD 24254-2
Soul Night Live! | Prestige | PRCD 24273-2
Willis Jackson Sextet
Gravy | Prestige | PCD 24254-2
Nuther'n Like Thuther'n | Prestige | PRCD 24265-2

Wilson,Cassandra | (dr-machine-programming,voc,g,p,perc)
Cassandra Wilson And Her Quintet
Point Of View | JMT Edition | 919004-2
Cassandra Wilson Group
After The Beginning Again | JMT Edition | 514001-2
Misty Blue:Sweet Sisters Swing Songs Of Sorrow And Sadness | Blue Note | 521151-2
Kind Of Blue:Blue Note Celebrate The Music Of Miles Davis | Blue Note | 534255-2
Blue Light 'Til Dawn | Blue Note | 781357-2
Traveling Miles | Blue Note | 854123-2
Midnight Blue(The [Be]witching Hour) | Blue Note | 854365-2
Cassandra Wilson With The Mulgrew Miller Trio
Blue Skies | JMT Edition | 919018-2
Courtney Pine Group
Modern Day Jazz Stories | Verve | 529028-2
Dave Holland Qartet
Dream Of The Elders | ECM | 1572(529084-2)
Steve Coleman And Five Elements
On The Edge Of Tomorrow | JMT Edition | 919005-2
Steve Coleman Group
Motherland Pulse | JMT Edition | 919001-2

Wilson,Chuck | (alto-fl,as,cl,fl,ss,piccolo,reeds)
Randy Sandke And The New York Allstars
The Re-Discovered Louis And Bix | Nagel-Heyer | CD 058
Randy Sandke-Dick Hyman
The Re-Discovered Louis And Bix | Nagel-Heyer | CD 058
Warren Vaché And The New York City All-Star Big Band
Swingtime! | Nagel-Heyer | CD 059

Wilson,Dennis | (tb)
Count Basie And His Orchestra
88 Basie Street | Original Jazz Classics | OJC 808(2310901)
Fancy Pants | Original Jazz Classics | OJCCD 1038-2(2310920)
Digital III At Montreux | Original Jazz Classics | OJCCD 996-2(2308223)
The Jazz Giants Play Harry Warren:Lullaby Of Broadway | Prestige | PCD 24204-2
Count Basie Big Band
Montreux '77 | Original Jazz Classics | OJCCD 377-2
Farmers Market Barbecue | Original Jazz Classics | OJCCD 732-2(2310874)
Diane Schuur With The Count Basie Orchestra
The Best Of Diane Schuur | GRP | GRP 98882
Ella Fitzgerald With Count Basie And His Orchestra
Digital III At Montreux | Original Jazz Classics | OJCCD 996-2(2308223)
Ella Fitzgerald With The Count Basie Orchestra
Bluella:Ella Fitzgerald Sings The Blues | Pablo | 2310960-2
For The Love Of Ella Fitzgerald | Verve | 841765-2
Milt Jackson Orchestra
Sarah Vaughan Birthday Celebration | Fantasy | FANCD 6090-2
Milt Jackson With The Count Basie Orchestra
To Bags...With Love:Memorial Album | Pablo | 2310967-2
Milt Jackson Birthday Celebration | Fantasy | FANCD 6079-2
Milt Jackson + Count Basie + Big Band Vol.1 | Original Jazz Classics | OJCCD 740-2(2310822)
Milt Jackson + Count Basie + Big Band Vol.2 | Original Jazz Classics | OJCCD 741-2(2310823)
Sarah Vaughan And The Count Basie Orchestra
Sarah Vaughan Birthday Celebration | Fantasy | FANCD 6090-2

Wilson,Edgar | (p)
Hannes Beckmann Quartet
Violin Tales | Tutu Records | 888202-2*

Wilson,Elizabeth | (v)
Milt Jackson And His Orchestra
Reverence And Compassion | Reprise | 9362-45204-2

Wilson,Garland | (celeste-solo,p,celestep-solo)
Dany Polo Trio
JazzIn Paris:Harlem Piano In Montmartre | EmArCy | 018447-2
Garland Wilson
JazzIn Paris:Harlem Piano In Montmartre | EmArCy | 018447-2

Wilson,Gerald | (arr,comp,ld,ptp)
Count Basie And His Orchestra
Planet Jazz:Count Basie | Planet Jazz | 2152068-2
Duke Ellington And His Orchestra
Anatomy Of A Murder | CBS | CK 65569
Gerald Wilson And His Orchestra
Deep Blue-The United States Of Mind | Blue Note | 521152-2
Blue Breaks Beats Vol.2 | Blue Note | 789907-2
Johnny Otis And His Orchestra
Verve Jazz Masters 43:Ben Webster | Verve | 525431-2
Leroy Vinnegar Sextet
The Jazz Giants Play Harry Warren:Lullaby Of Broadway | Prestige | PCD 24204-2
Sarah Vaughan And Her Band
Misty Blue:Sweet Sisters Swing Songs Of Sorrow And Sadness | Blue Note | 521151-2
Sarah Vaughan With The Benny Carter Orchestra
Ballads | Roulette | 537561-2
Sarah Vaughan With The Gerald Wilson Orchestra
Ballads | Roulette | 537561-2
Jazz Profile | Blue Note | 823517-2

Wilson,Jack | (arr,p,celeste,el-p,org,p-solotp)
Clark Terry Five
The Jazz Giants Play Duke Ellington:Caravan | Prestige | PCD 24227-2
Dinah Washington With The Eddie Chamblee Orchestra
Verve Jazz Masters 40:Dinah Washington | Verve | 522055-2
Dinah Sings Bessie Smith | Verve | 538635-2
Gerald Wilson And His Orchestra
Blue Breaks Beats Vol.2 | Blue Note | 789907-2
Jack Wilson Sextet
Blue N' Groovy | Blue Note | 780679-2
Lorez Alexandria With Orchestra
Misty Blue:Sweet Sisters Swing Songs Of Sorrow And Sadness | Blue Note | 521151-2
Deep Blue-The United States Of Mind | Blue Note | 521152-2

Wilson,Jim | (bongos)
Anita O'Day And Her Combo
Verve Jazz Masters 49:Anita O'Day | Verve | 527653-2

Wilson,Jimmy | (tb)
Benny Goodman And His Orchestra
Verve Jazz Masters 33:Benny Goodman | Verve | 844410-2

Wilson,Joe Lee | (fl,sax,percvoc)
Archie Shepp Orchestra
The Cry Of My People | Impulse(MCA) | 9861488

Wilson,Keve | (oboe)
Paquito D'Rivera Group With The Absolute Ensemble
Habanera | Enja | ENJ-9395 2

Wilson,Marty | (vib,xylophoneglockenspiel)
Coleman Hawkins With Billy Byers And His Orchestra
Planet Jazz:Coleman Hawkins | Planet Jazz | 2152055-2
The Hawk In Hi-Fi | RCA | 2663842-2

Wilson,Matt | (dr)
Lee Konitz With Strings
Strings For Holiday:A Tribute To Billie Holiday | Enja | ENJ-9304 2
Lee Konitz-Matt Wilson
Gone With The Wind | Steeplechase | SCCD 31528
Michael Blake Group
Drift | Intuition Records | INT 3212-2

Wilson,Nancy | (voc)
Nancy Wilson With George Shearing And His Quintet
The Swingin's Mutual | Capitol | 799190-2
Nancy Wilson With The Billy May Orchestra
Misty Blue:Sweet Sisters Swing Songs Of Sorrow And Sadness | Blue Note | 521151-2

Wilson,Ollie | (tbv-tb)
Artie Shaw And His Orchestra
Planet Jazz:Jazz Trumpet | Planet Jazz | 2169654-2
Woody Herman And His Orchestra
The Legends Of Swing | Laserlight | 24659
Woody Herman:Four Brother | Dreyfus Jazz Line | FDM 36722-2

Wilson,Orlandus | (voc)
Golden Gate Quartet
Americans Swinging In Paris:Golden Gate Quartet | EMI Records | 539659-2
From Spiritual To Swing Vol.2 | EMI Records | 780573-2
Spirituals To Swing 1955-69 | EMI Records | 791569-2
Golden Gate Quartet With The Martial Solal Orchestra
Americans Swinging In Paris:Golden Gate Quartet | EMI Records | 539659-2
From Spiritual To Swing Vol.2 | EMI Records | 780573-2

Wilson,Perry | (dr)
Cassandra Wilson Group
Traveling Miles | Blue Note | 854123-2
Sonny Rollins Quintet
This Is What I Do | Milestone | MCD 9310-2
Sonny Rollins Sextet
Global Warming | Milestone | MCD 9280-2

Wilson,Peter Niklas | (b)
Malcolm Goldstein-Peter Niklas Wilson
Goldstein-Wilson | true muze | TUMU CD 9801
Rajesh Metha
Reconfigurations | Between The Lines | btl 010(Efa 10180-2)

Wilson,Phil | (arrtb)
NDR Big Band With Guests
50 Years Of NDR Big Band:Bravissimo II | ACT | 9259-2
Woody Herman And His Orchestra
Verve Jazz Masters 54:Woody Herman | Verve | 529903-2
Woody Herman-1963 | Philips | 589490-2

Wilson,Phillip | (dr,perc,balafoncymbals)
Lester Bowie Group
The Great Pretender | ECM | 1209(829369-2)
Lester Bowie Quartet
The Great Pretender | ECM | 1209(829369-2)
Lester Bowie's Brass Fantasy
I Only Have Eyes For You | ECM | 1296(825902-2)
Avant Pop | ECM | 1326

Wilson,Quinn | (b,arrtuba)
Earl Hines And His Orchestra
Planet Jazz:Earl Hines | Planet Jazz | 2159973-2
The Legends Of Swing | Laserlight | 24659
Jazz:The Essential Collection Vol.2 | IN+OUT Records | 78012-2
Jelly Roll Morton's Red Hot Peppers
Planet Jazz:Jelly Roll Morton | Planet Jazz | 2152060-2
Jazz:The Essential Collection Vol.1 | IN+OUT Records | 78011-2

Wilson,Reuben | (org)
Reuben Wilson Quartet
Blue Breaks Beats Vol.2 | Blue Note | 789907-2
Reuben Wilson Sextet
The Lost Grooves | Blue Note | 831883-2

Wilson,Robert | (b)
Dinah Washington With The Eddie Chamblee Orchestra
Verve Jazz Masters 40:Dinah Washington | Verve | 522055-2
Dinah Sings Bessie Smith | Verve | 538635-2

Wilson,Roland | (bfender-b)
Donald Byrd Orchestra
Blue Break Beats | Blue Note | 799106-2

Wilson,Shadow | (dr)
Coleman Hawkins All Stars
Verve Jazz Masters 43:Coleman Hawkins | Verve | 521856-2
Coleman Hawkins Quartet
Body And Soul Revisited | GRP | GRP 16272
Count Basie And His Orchestra
Planet Jazz:Count Basie | Planet Jazz | 2152068-2
Jazz:The Essential Collection Vol.3 | IN+OUT Records | 78013-2
Erroll Garner Trio
Body & Soul | CBS | 467916-2
Esquire All-American Award Winners
Planet Jazz:Jazz Trumpet | Planet Jazz | 2169654-2
Gerry Mulligan-Thelonious Monk Quartet
Mulligan Meets Monk | Original Jazz Classics | OJC20 301-2(RLP 1106)
Jubilee All Stars
Jazz Gallery:Lester Young Vol.2(1946-59) | RCA | 2119541-2
Lester Young Quintet
The Art Of Saxophone | Laserlight | 24652
Jazz:The Essential Collection Vol.3 | IN+OUT Records | 78013-2
Lester Young:Blue Lester | Dreyfus Jazz Line | FDM 36729-2
Louis Jordan And His Tympany Five
Louis Jordan-Let The Good Times Roll: The Complete Decca Recordings 1938-1954 | Bear Family Records | BCD 15557 IH
Sonny Stitt And His Band
Kaleidoscope | Original Jazz Classics | OJCCD 060-2(P 7077)
Sonny Stitt Quintet
Kaleidoscope | Original Jazz Classics | OJCCD 060-2(P 7077)
Tadd Dameron And His Orchestra
Fontainebleau | Original Jazz Classics | OJCCD 055-2
Tadd Dameron Sextet
The Fabulous Fats Navarro Vol.1 | Blue Note | 0677207
Tadd Dameron-Fats Navarro Sextet
Fats Navarro:Nostalgia | Dreyfus Jazz Line | FDM 36736-2
Terry Gibbs Septet
Early Stan | Original Jazz Classics | OJCCD 654-2(P 7255)
Thelonious Monk Quartet
Wizard Of The Vibes | Blue Note | 532140-2
The Best Of Thelonious Monk:The Blue Note Years | Blue Note | 795636-2
Thelonious Monk:85th Birthday Celebration | zyx records | FANCD 6076-2
Thelonious Monk:Misterioso | Dreyfus Jazz Line | FDM 36743-2
Thelonious Monk With John Coltrane | Jazzland | JZSA 946-6
Thelonious Monk With John Coltrane | Original Jazz Classics | OJC20 039-2
Thelonious Himself | Original Jazz Classics | OJCCD 254-2
Thelonious Monk-Gerry Mulligan Quartet
Thelonious Monk:85th Birthday Celebration | zyx records | FANCD 6076-2

Wilson,Steve | (as,cl,fl,alto-fl,ssreeds)
Dave Holland Quintet
Point Of View | ECM | 1663(557020-2)
Ingrid Jensen Sextet
Vernal Fields | Enja | ENJ-9013 2
Johnny King Septet
The Meltdown | Enja | ENJ-9329 2
Kevin Mahogany With Orchestra
Songs And Moments | Enja | ENJ-8072 2
Michael Brecker Quindectet
Wide Angles | Verve | 076142-2
Michael 'Patches' Stewart Group
Blue Patches | Hip Bop | HIBD 8016
Michele Rosewoman And Quintessence
Guardians Of The Light | Enja | ENJ-9378 2
Michele Rosewoman Quintet
Harvest | Enja | ENJ-7069 2
Michele Rosewoman Sextet
Harvest | Enja | ENJ-7069 2

Wilson,Teddy | (pp-solo)
Ben Webster With Orchestra And Strings
Verve Jazz Masters 43:Ben Webster | Verve | 525431-2
Music For Loving:Ben Webster With Strings | Verve | 527774-2
Ben Webster With The Teddy Wilson Trio
Verve Jazz Masters 43:Ben Webster | Verve | 525431-2
Music For Loving:Ben Webster With Strings | Verve | 527774-2
Benny Goodman And His V-Disc All Star Band
The Legends Of Swing | Laserlight | 24659
Benny Goodman Quartet
Planet Jazz:Benny Goodman | Planet Jazz | 2152054-2
Jazz Collection:Benny Goodman | Laserlight | 24396
Together Again! | RCA | 2663881-2
Benny Goodman At Carnegie Hall 1938(Complete) | CBS | C2K 65143
Camel Caravan Broadcast 1939 Vol.1 | Phontastic | NCD 8817
Camel Caravan Broadcast 1939 Vol.2 | Phontastic | NCD 8818
More Camel Caravans | Phontastic | NCD 8841/2
More Camel Caravans | Phontastic | NCD 8843/4
More Camel Caravans | Phontastic | NCD 8845/6
Benny Goodman Trio
Planet Jazz:Benny Goodman | Planet Jazz | 2152054-2
Planet Jazz:Swing | Planet Jazz | 2169651-2
Planet Jazz:Jazz Piano | RCA | 2169655-2
Jazz Collection:Benny Goodman | Laserlight | 24396
Benny Goodman-The Complete Capitol Trios | Capitol | 521225-2
Benny Goodman At Carnegie Hall 1938(Complete) | CBS | C2K 65143
Camel Caravan Broadcast 1939 Vol.2 | Phontastic | NCD 8818
More Camel Caravans | Phontastic | NCD 8841/2
More Camel Caravans | Phontastic | NCD 8843/4
More Camel Caravans | Phontastic | NCD 8845/6
Billie Holiday With Teddy Wilson And His Orchestra
Billie's Love Songs | Nimbus Records | NI 2000
Coleman Hawkins' All-American Four
Verve Jazz Masters 43:Coleman Hawkins | Verve | 521856-2
Coleman Hawkins Quartet
Verve Jazz Masters 43:Coleman Hawkins | Verve | 521856-2
Ultimate Coleman Hawkins selected by Sonny Rollins | Verve | 557538-2
Coleman Hawkins Quintet
Verve Jazz Masters 43:Coleman Hawkins | Verve | 521856-2
Ultimate Coleman Hawkins selected by Sonny Rollins | Verve | 557538-2
Jazz:The Essential Collection Vol.3 | IN+OUT Records | 78013-2
Esquire All-American Award Winners
Planet Jazz:Jazz Trumpet | Planet Jazz | 2169654-2
JATP All Stars
J.A.T.P. In London 1969 | Pablo | 2CD 2620119
Welcome To Jazz At The Philharmonic | Fantasy | FANCD 6081-2
Lester Young Quartet

Verve Jazz Masters 30:Lester Young | Verve | 521859-2
Lester Young-Teddy Wilson Quartet
Jazz Gallery:Lester Young Vol.2(1946-59) | RCA | 2119541-2
Louis Armstrong And His Orchestra
Planet Jazz:Louis Armstrong | Planet Jazz | 2152052-2
Best Of The Complete RCA Victor Recordings | RCA | 2663636-2
Louis Armstrong:A 100th Birthday Celebration | RCA | 2663694-2
Jazz:The Essential Collection Vol.2 | IN+OUT Records | 78012-2
Sarah Vaughan With The Teddy Wilson Quartet
Sarah Vaughan:Lover Man | Dreyfus Jazz Line | FDM 36739-2
Teddy Wilson
The Keystone Transcriptions 1939-1940 | Storyville | STCD 8258
Teddy Wilson And His All Stars
Jazz:The Essential Collection Vol.3 | IN+OUT Records | 78013-2
Teddy Wilson And His Orchestra
Jazz:The Essential Collection Vol.3 | IN+OUT Records | 78013-2
Teddy Wilson Sextet
The Complete Associated Transcriptions,1944 | Storyville | STCD 8236
Teddy Wilson Trio
The Story Of Jazz Piano | Laserlight | 24653
J.A.T.P. In London 1969 | Pablo | 2CD 2620119
The Jazz Giants '56
Jazz Gallery:Lester Young Vol.2(1946-59) | RCA | 2119541-2
The Metronome All Stars
Jazz Gallery:Lester Young Vol.2(1946-59) | RCA | 2119541-2

Wilson,William Duke | (perc,congasbongos)
Monnette Sudler Sextet
Brighter Days For You | Steeplechase | SCCD 31087

Wilson,Willie | (tb)
Duke Pearson Sextet
Dedication! | Original Jazz Classics | OJCCD 1939-2(P 7729)

Wilson,Willsingh | (voice-perc)
Martin Koller's Third Movement
Right Now | Traumton Records | 4430-2

Wiltshire,Teacho | (p,arrld)
King Pleasure With Orchestra
Blue Velvet: Crooners, Swooners And Velvet Vocals | Blue Note | 521153-2

Wimberley,Bill | (tb)
Buddy Rich And His Orchestra
Big Swing Face | Pacific Jazz | 837989-2

Wimberley,Mike | (tb)
Ella Fitzgerald With Orchestra
Ella/Things Ain't What They Used To Be | Warner | 9362-47875-2

Wimberly,Michael | (cowbell,djembe,drperc)
Steve Coleman And Metrics
A Tale Of 3 Cities,The EP | Novus | 2124747-2

Wimbish,Doug | (el-belectronics)
Dhafer Youssef Group
Electric Sufi | Enja | ENJ-9412 2

Winch,Rainer | (drperc)
Jazz Indeed
Under Water | Traumton Records | 2415-2
Who The Moon Is | Traumton Records | 4427-2
Julia Hülsman Trio With Rebekka Bakken
Scattering Poems | ACT | 9405-2
Lisa Bassenge Trio With Guests
A Sight, A Song | Minor Music | 801100
Paul Brody's Tango Toy
Klezmer Stories | Laika Records | 35101222
Stephan Noel Lang Trio
Echoes | Nagel-Heyer | CD 2033
Yakou Tribe
Red & Blue Days | Traumton Records | 4474-2

Winchester,Daisy | (voc)
Louis Jordan And His Tympany Five
Louis Jordan-Let The Good Times Roll: The Complete Decca Recordings 1938-1954 | Bear Family Records | BCD 15557 IH

Winchester,Lem | (vib)
Etta Jones And Her Quartet
Something Nice | Original Jazz Classics | OJCCD 221-2(P 7194)
Etta Jones With The Oliver Nelson Quintet
Hollar! | Original Jazz Classics | OJCCD 1061(PR 7284)
Jack McDuff Quartet
Tough 'Duff | Original Jazz Classics | OJCCD 324-2(P 7185)
Jack McDuff:The Prestige Years | Prestige | PRCD 24387-2
Oliver Nelson Quintet
The Jazz Giants Play Sammy Cahn:It's Magic | Prestige | PCD 24226-2
Shirley Scott Quartet
Queen Of The Organ-Shirley Scott Memorial Album | Prestige | PRCD 11027-2

Wind,Martin | (b)
Gabriele Hasler Group
Gabriele Hasler's Rosensrücke | Foolish Music | FM 211096
Ulf Meyer & Martin Wind Group
Kinnings | Storyville | STCD 8374

Windfeld,Axel | (b-tb,tubatb)
Geri Allen And The Jazzpar 1996 Nonet
Some Aspects Of Water | Storyville | STCD 4212
Jens Winther And The Danish Radio Jazz Orchestra
Angels | dacapo | DCCD 9442
Miles Davis With The Danish Radio Big Band
Aura | CBS | CK 63962
Mona Larsen And The Danish Radio Big Band Plus Soloists
Michael Mantler:Cerco Un Paese Innocente | ECM | 1556
Stan Getz With The Danish Radio Big Band
Stan Getz In Europe | Laserlight | 24657
The Danish Radio Big Band
Aura | CBS | CK 63962
The Danish Radio Jazz Orchestra
This Train:The Danish Radio Jazz Orchestra Plays The Music Of Ray Pitts | dacapo | DCCD 9428
Nice Work | dacapo | DCCD 9446

Winding,Jai | (porg)
Diane Schuur With Orchestra
Blues For Schuur | GRP | GRP 98632
The Best Of Diane Schuur | GRP | GRP 98882

Winding,Kai | (tbv-tb)
(Little)Jimmy Scott With The Billy Taylor Orchestra
Everybody's Somebody's Fool | Decca | 050669-2
Astrud Gilberto With The Don Sebesky Orchestra
Verve Jazz Masters 9:Astrud Gilberto | Verve | 519824-2
Chubby Jackson Big Band
Gerry Mulligan Quartet feat.Chet Baker | Original Jazz Classics | OJCCD 711-2(F 8082/P 7641)
Ella Fitzgerald With The Bill Doggett Orchestra
Ella Fitzgerald-First Lady Of Song | Verve | 517898-2
Rhythm Is My Business | Verve | 559513-2
Four Trombones
Charles Mingus-The Complete Debut Recordings | Debut | 12 DCD 4402-2
The J.J.Johnson Memorial Album | Prestige | PRCD 11025-2
Frankie Laine With Buck Clayton And His Orchestra
Jazz Spectacular | CBS | CK 65507
J.J.Johnson-Kai Winding Quintet (Jay&Kai)
The J.J.Johnson Memorial Album | Prestige | PRCD 11025-2
Jimmy Smith With Orchestra
Jimmy Smith-Talkin' Verve | Verve | 531563-2
Jimmy Smith With The Claus Ogerman Orchestra
Verve Jazz Masters 29:Jimmy Smith | Verve | 521855-2
Any Number Can Win | Verve | 557447-2
Kai Winding-J.J.Johnson Quintet
The Great Kai & J.J. | Impulse(MCA) | 951225-2
Miles Davis And His Orchestra
The Complete Birth Of The Cool | Capitol | 494550-2
Birth Of The Cool | Capitol | 530117-2
Miles Davis:The Best Of The Capitol/Blue Note Years | Blue Note | 798287-2
Miles Davis:Milestones | Dreyfus Jazz Line | FDM 36731-2
Milt Jackson Septet
The Birdlanders Vol.1 | Original Jazz Classics | OJCCD 1930-2
Milt Jackson Sextet
The Birdlanders Vol.1 | Original Jazz Classics | OJCCD 1930-2
Modern Jazz Quartet And Orchestra
MJQ 40 | Atlantic | 7567-82330-2
Oscar Pettiford Sextet
The Birdlanders Vol.2 | Original Jazz Classics | OJCCD 1931-2
Quincy Jones Big Band
Rahsaan/The Complete Mercury Recordings Of Roland Kirk | Mercury | 846630-2
Sarah Vaughan And The Thad Jones Orchestra
Verve Jazz Masters 42:Sarah Vaughan-The Jazz Sides | Verve | 526817-2
Sarah Vaughan With Orchestra
!Viva! Vaughan | Mercury | 549374-2
Sarah Vaughan With The Hal Mooney Orchestra
It's A Man's World | Mercury | 589487-2
Stan Kenton And His Orchestra
Swing Vol.1 | Storyville | 4960343
Tadd Dameron Tentet
Jazz Profile:Dexter Gordon | Blue Note | 823514-2
The Metronome All Stars
Jazz Gallery:Lester Young Vol.2(1946-59) | RCA | 2119541-2
Planet Jazz:Dizzy Gillespie | Planet Jazz | 2152069-2
Zoot Sims-Al Cohn Sextet
The Brothers | Original Jazz Classics | OJCCD 008-2

Window,Gary | (as,b-clts)
Carla Bley Band
European Tour 1977 | Watt | 8
Musique Mecanique | Watt | 9
Michael Mantler Sextet
Movies/More Movies | Watt | 7/10(543377-2)

Winfield,John | (vocvoice)
Mike Westbrook Orchestra
Bar Utopia-A Big Band Cabaret | Enja | ENJ-9333 2

Wingold,Frank | (g,el-g,g-synthnoisetable)
Agog
Eat Time | Jazz Haus Musik | JHM 0072 CD
Jazz Orchester Rheinland-Pfalz
Like Life | Jazz Haus Musik | LJBB 9405
Last Season | Jazz Haus Musik | LJBB 9706

Winkler,? | (b)
Brocksi-Quartett
Globetrotter | Bear Family Records | BCD 15912 AH

Winkler,Sebastian | (cl,ts,ssas)
Ralph Schweizer Big Band
DAY Dream | Chaos | CACD 8177
Sax Mal Anders
Kontraste | Chaos | CACD 8185

Winkler,Willibald | (b)
Brocksi-Quartett
Globetrotter | Bear Family Records | BCD 15912 AH

Winn,R. | (fl)
Dee Dee Bridgewater With Orchestra
Dear Ella | Verve | 539102-2

Winner,Jerry | (as)
Tommy Dorsey And His Orchestra
Planet Jazz:Tommy Dorsey | Planet Jazz | 2159972-2

Winninghoff,Christian | (tpfl-h)
Bigband Der Musikschule Der Stadt Brühl Mit Gastsolisten
Pangäa | Indigo-Records | 1004 CD
Marcus Sukiennik Big Band
A Night In Tunisia Suite(7 Variationen über Dizzy Gillespie's 'A Night In Tunisia') | Jazz Haus Musik | ohne Nummer
Matthias Petzold Working Band
Elements | Indigo-Records | 1005 CD

Winogrand,Ethan | (dr)
Karen Mantler Group
My Cat Arnold | Watt | XtraWatt/3
Karen Mantler And Her Cat Arnold Get The Flu | Watt | XtraWatt/5

Winsberg,Louis | (g,el-gg-synth)
Dee Dee Bridgewater With Band
This Is New | Verve | 016884-2
Dee Dee Bridgewater Sings Kurt Weil | EmArCy | 9809601

Winsey,Stu | (b)
Bob Wallis Storyville Jazzmen
The Golden Years Of Revival Jazz,Vol.7 | Storyville | STCD 5512

Winslow,Ray | (tb)
Maynard Ferguson Orchestra With Chris Connor
Two's Company | Roulette | 837201-2

Winston Collymore Strings,The |
George Benson Orchestra
Talkin' Verve:George Benson | Verve | 553780-2

Winston,Albert | (bel-b)
George Benson Quartet + Guests
The George Benson Cookbook | CBS | 502470-2

Winston,George | (pp-solo)
George Winston
Linus & Lucy-The Music Of Vince Guaraldi | Windham Hill | 34 11187-2

Winstone,Norma | (vocvoice)
La Voce-Music For Voices,Trumpet And Bass | JA & RO | JARO 4208-2
Azimuth
Azimuth '85 | ECM | 1298
How It Was Then...Never Again | ECM | 1538
Azimuth | ECM | 1546/48(523010-2)
Azimuth With Ralph Towner
Azimuth | ECM | 1546/48(523010-2)
Eberhard Weber Group
Fluid Rustle | ECM | 1137
Kenny Wheeler Ensemble
Muisc For Large & Small Ensembles | ECM | 1415/16
Norma Winstone Trio
Somewhere Called Home | ECM | 1337

Winter,Claudio | (dr)
Terra Brazil
Café Com Leite | art-mode-records | AMR 2101

Winter,Herbert | (b)
Fred Bunge Star Band
Deutsches Jazz Fesival 1954/1955 | Bear Family Records | BCD 15430

Winter,Lois | (voc)
George Benson And His Orchestra
Giblet Gravy | Verve | 543754-2
Talkin' Verve:George Benson | Verve | 553780-2

Winter,Mette | (viola)
Michael Mantler Group
Songs And One Symphony | ECM | 1721

Winter,Paul | (v)
Ben Webster With Orchestra And Strings
Music For Loving:Ben Webster With Strings | Verve | 527774-2
Ultimate Ben Webster selected by James Carter | Verve | 557537-2
Wes Montgomery With The Jimmy Jones Orchestra
Wes Montgomery-The Complete Riverside Recordings | Riverside | 12 RCD 4408-2

Winter,Stefan | (pvoc)
Bigband Der Musikschule Der Stadt Brühl Mit Gastsolisten
Pangäa | Indigo-Records | 1004 CD

Winterhalter,Hugo | (arrld)
Sarah Vaughan With The Hugo Winterhalter Orchestra
Sarah Vaughan:Lover Man | Dreyfus Jazz Line | FDM 36739-2

Winterschladen,Reiner | (tp,fl-hkalimba)
Abdullah Ibrahim With The NDR Big Band
Ekapa Lodumo | TipToe | TIP-888840 2
Chromatic Alarm
Some Other Tapes | Fish Music | FM 009/10 CD
Ekkehard Jost & Chromatic Alarm
Von Zeit Zu Zeit | Fish Music | FM 005 CD
Wintertango | Fish Music | FM 008 CD
Ekkehard Jost Nonet
Out Of Jost's Songbook | Fish Music | FM 006 CD
Ekkehard Jost Quartet
Deep | Fish Music | FM 007 CD
Some Other Tapes | Fish Music | FM 009/10 CD
Ensemble Indigo
Reflection | Enja | ENJ-9417 2
European Jazz Ensemble & The Khan Family feat. Joachim Kühn
European Jazz Ensemble Meets The Khan Family | M.A Music | A 807-2
Giessen-Köln-Nonett
Some Other Tapes | Fish Music | FM 009/10 CD
Hans Lüdemann Rism 7
FutuRISM | Jazz Haus Musik | JHM 0092/93 CD
Hugo Read Group
Songs Of A Wayfarer | Nabel Records:Jazz Network | CD 4653
Joachim Ullrich Orchestra
Faces Of The Duke | Jazz Haus Musik | JHM 0045 CD
Klaus König Orchestra
Times Of Devastation/Poco A Poco | Enja | ENJ-6014 22
Hommage A Douglas Adams | Enja | ENJ-6078 2
Time Fragments:Seven Studies In Time And Motion | Enja | ENJ-8076 2
Reviews | Enja | ENJ-9061 2
Klaus König Orchestra & Guests
The Song Of Songs:Oratorio For Two Solo Voices,Choir And Orchestra | Enja | ENJ-7057 2
NDR Big Band
The Theatre Of Kurt Weil | ACT | 9234-2
Norbert Stein Pata Masters
Blue Slit | Pata Musik | PATA 8 CD
Norbert Stein Pata Orchester
Ritual Life | Pata Musik | PATA 5(JHM 50) CD
The Secret Act Of Painting | Pata Musik | PATA 7 CD
Oscar Brown Jr. with The NDR Big Band
Live Every Minute | Minor Music | 801071
Pata Masters
Pata-Bahia | Pata Musik | PATA 11 CD
Pee Wee Ellis & NDR Bigband
What You Like | Minor Music | 801064
Reiner Winterschladen-Manos Tsangaris
King Kong | Jazz Haus Musik | JHM 0056 CD
Transalpin Express Orchestra
Some Other Tapes | Fish Music | FM 009/10 CD
Ulla Oster Group
Beyond Janis | Jazz Haus Musik | JHM 0052 CD

Winterstein,Ziroli | (g)
Salut!
Green & Orange | Edition Collage | EC 488-2

Winther,Jens | (comp,ld,tpfl-h)
Carla Bley Band
Fleur Carnivore | Watt | 21
Dejan Terzic European Assembly
Coming Up | double moon | DMCHR 71034
Jens Winther And The Danish Radio Jazz Orchestra
Angels | dacapo | DCCD 9442
Jens Winther And The WDR Big Band
The Escape | dacapo | DCCD 9437
Miles Davis With The Danish Radio Big Band
Aura | CBS | CK 63962
SWR Big Band
Jazz In Concert | Hänssler Classics | CD 93.004
The Danish Radio Big Band
Aura | CBS | CK 63962
The Danish Radio Concert Orchestra
Symphonies Vol.2 | dacapo | DCCD 9441

Winther,Mette | (viola)
Michael Mantler Group With The Danish Radio Concert Orchestra Strings
The School Of Understanding(Sort-Of-An-Opera) | ECM | 1648/49(537963-2)
Michael Mantler Orchestra
Hide And Seek | ECM | 1738(549612-2)
Mona Larsen And The Danish Radio Big Band Plus Soloists
Michael Mantler:Cerco Un Paese Innocente | ECM | 1556

Wintsch,Michael | (p)
Michel Wintsch & Road Movie
Michel Wintsch & Road Movie featuring Gerry Hemingway | Between The Lines | btl 002(Efa 10172-2)

Winwood,Steve | (porg)
Howlin' Wolf London Session
Howlin' Wolf:The London Sessions | Chess | MCD 09297

Wirtel,Tom | (mellophone)
Stan Kenton And His Orchestra
Adventures In Blues | Capitol | 520089-2

Wirth,Rudolf | (cl)
Mihaly Tabany Orchestra
Jubilee Edition | double moon | CHRDM 71020

Wirth,Stephan-Max | (tsvoc)
Stephan-Max Wirth Quartet
Jazzchanson 20th Century Suite | double moon | DMCD 1008-2

Wise,Arnold | (dr)
Bill Evans Trio
The Complete Bill Evans On Verve | Verve | 527953-2
The Best Of Bill Evans Live | Verve | 533825-2
Ultimate Bill Evans selected by Herbie Hancock | Verve | 557536-2
Bill Evans At Town Hall | Verve | 831271-2
Bill Evans:The Secret Sessions | Milestone | 8MCD 4421-2
Helen Merrill With The Dick Katz Group
The Feeling Is Mutual | EmArCy | 558849-2

Wise,Buddy | (ts)
Gene Krupa And His Orchestra
Mullenium | CBS | CK 65678
Virgil Gonsalves Sextet
The Complete Nocturne Recordings:Jazz In Hollywood Series Vol.1 | Fresh Sound Records | NR 3CD-101

Wise,Hershel | (viola)
Milt Jackson And His Orchestra
Reverence And Compassion | Reprise | 9362-45204-2

Wise,Marcus | (perctabla)
Steve Tibbetts Group
Exploded View | ECM | 1335
Yr | ECM | 1355(835245-2)
Big Map Idea | ECM | 1380
The Fall Of Us All | ECM | 1527(521144-2)
Steve Tibbetts | ECM | 1814(017068-2)

Witham,Dave | (psynth)
John Patitucci Group
Sketchbook | GRP | GRP 96172

Witheim,Christine | (voc)
Jazzensemble Des Hessischen Rundfunks
Jazz Messe-Messe Für Unsere Zeit | hr music.de | hrmj 003-01 CD

Witherspoon,Jimmy | (tsvoc)
Jimmy Witherspoon And His All Stars
Blues For Easy Livers | Original Blues Classics | OBCCD 585-2(PR 7475)
Jimmy Witherspoon And His Band
Blue Velvet: Crooners, Swooners And Velvet Vocals | Blue Note | 521153-2
Baby, Baby, Baby | Original Blues Classics | OBCCD 527-2(P 7290)
Jimmy Witherspoon With Jay McShann And His Band
Planet Jazz:Male Jazz Vocalists | Planet Jazz | 2169657-2

Wito,Wietn | (el-bjew's-harp)
Alfred 23 Harth Group
Sweet Paris | free flow music | ffm 0291

Witte,Andy | (dr)
Tilman Jäger Tape 4
Abendlieder | Satin Doll Productions | SDP 1043-1 CD

Witte,Peter | (b,charango,ldel-b)
Art Van Damme Group

State Of Art | MPS | 841413-2
Bernd Konrad With Erwin Lehn und sein Südfunk Orchester Stuttgart
Wen Die Götter Lieben | Creative Works Records | CW CD 1010-1
Charly Antolini Orchestra
Drum Beat | MPS | 9808191
Dieter Reith Group
Reith On! | MPS | 557423-2
Dieter Reith Quintet
Reith On! | MPS | 557423-2
Dieter Reith Trio
Reith On! | MPS | 557423-2
Erwin Lehn Und Sein Südfunk-Tanzorchester
Deutsches Jazz Fesival 1954/1955 | Bear Family Records | BCD 15430

Witte,Willi | (dr)
Frank Kroll Quintet
Landscape | dml-records | CD 014
Patrick Bebelaar Quartet
Never Thought It Could Happen | dml-records | CD 007

Wittek,Fritz | (dr,perc,timbalesvoice)
Dirk Raulf Group
Theater I (Bühnenmusik) | Poise | Poise 07
Tome XX
The Red Snapper | Jazz Haus Musik | JHM 0047 CD
Third Degree | Jazz Haus Musik | JHM 0063 CD

Wittenberg,John | (v)
Jacintha With Band And Strings
Lush Life | Groove Note | GRV 1011-2(Gold CD 2011)

Wittich,Roland | (dr)
Dieter Reith Quartet
Reith On! | MPS | 557423-2
Wolfgang Dauner Trio
Music Zounds | MPS | 9808190

Wittington,Dick | (p)
Joe Gordon Quintet
Lookin' Good | Original Jazz Classics | OJCCD 1934-2(S 7597)

Wittström,Bengt | (b)
Lars Gullin Octet
Lars Gullin 1951/52 Vol.5:First Walk | Dragon | DRCD 380
Lars Gullin Quartet
Lars Gullin 1951/52 Vol.5:First Walk | Dragon | DRCD 380

Wittulski,Miriam | (cello)
Uri Caine With The Concerto Köln
Concerto Köln | Winter&Winter | 910086-2

Wittwer,Stephan | (el-g,synth,sequencer-programming,g)
Alfred 23 Harth Group
Sweet Paris | free flow music | ffm 0291
Christy Doran-Fredy Studer-Stephan Wittwer
Red Twist & Tuned Arrow | ECM | 1342
Freddy Studer Orchestra
Seven Songs | VeraBra Records | CDVBR 2056-2

Witzel,Reiner | (as,bs,fl,ss,ts,ts.didjeridoosax)
Christian Scheuber Quintet
Clara's Smile | double moon | DMCHR 71025
Hipsters In The Zone
Into The Afro-Latin Bag | Nabel Records:Jazz Network | CD 4663
Reiner Witzel Group
Passage To The Ear | Nabel Records:Jazz Network | CD 4668

Witzmann,Thomas | (dr,darabuka,midi-pads,perc)
Directors
Directors | Jazz Haus Musik | JHM 0040 CD

Wofford,Mike | (el-p,clavinet,grand-p-solo)
Diane Schuur With Orchestra And Strings
The Best Of Diane Schuur | GRP | GRP 98882
Ella Fitzgerald And Her All Stars
All That Jazz | Pablo | 2310938-2
Joe Pass Quartet
Joy Spring | Blue Note | 835222-2
Sarah Vaughan And Her Band
Duke Ellington Song Book Two | Pablo | CD 2312116
Sarah Vaughan Birthday Celebration | Fantasy | FANCD 6090-2
Sarah Vaughan With Band
Linger Awhile | Pablo | 2312144-2
Sarah Vaughan With Joe Pass And Mike Wofford
Sarah Vaughan Birthday Celebration | Fantasy | FANCD 6090-2
Sarah Vaughan With Orchestra
Sarah Vaughan Birthday Celebration | Fantasy | FANCD 6090-2
Sarah Vaughan With Small Group & Orchestra
Duke Ellington Song Book One | Pablo | CD 2312111
Sarah Vaughan With The Mike Wofford Trio
Sarah Vaughan Birthday Celebration | Fantasy | FANCD 6090-2
Shelly Manne Sextet
Alive In London | Original Jazz Classics | OJCCD 773-2(S 7629)
Zoot Sims Quintet
Quietly There-Zoot Sims Plays Johnny Mandel | Original Jazz Classics | OJCCD 787-2(2310903)

Wogram,Nils | (tb)
Gabriel Pérez Group
La Chipaca | Green House Music | CD 1011
Gunter Hampel Jazz Sextet
Gunter Hampel: The 8th Of Sept.1999 | Birth | CD 049
Gunter Hampel-Nils Wogram
Gunter Hampel: The 8th Of Sept.1999 | Birth | CD 049
Jazz Baltica Ensemble
The Birth+Rebirth Of Swedish Folk Jazz | ACT | 9254-2
Nils Wogram Octet
Odd And Awkward | Enja | ENJ-9416-2
Nils Wogram Quartet
Round Trip | Enja | ENJ-9307 2
Speed Life | Enja | ENJ-9346 2
Nils Wogram Sextet
Odd And Awkward | Enja | ENJ-9416-2
Simon Nabatov-Nils Wogram
Starting A Story | ACT | 9402-2

Wohletz,Joe | (perc)
Eddie Harris Group
The Best Of Eddie Harris | Atlantic | 7567-81370-2

Wohlleben,Johannes | (dr,bkeyboards)
Sax Mal Anders
Kontraste | Chaos | CACD 8185

Wolberts,Elke | (voc)
Jazzensemble Des Hessischen Rundfunks
Jazz Messe-Messe Für Unsere Zeit | hr music.de | hrmj 003-01 CD

Wolf,Hans | (as,flsax)
Art Van Damme Group
State Of Art | MPS | 841413-2

Wolf,John | (tb)
Gunter Hampel And His Galaxie Dream Band
Journey To The Song Within | Birth | 0017

Wolf,Lutz | (tp)
Brass Attack
Brecht Songs | Tutu Records | 888190-2*

Wolf,Robert | (g)
Lisa Wahlandt & Mulo Francel And Their Fabulous Bossa Band
Bossa Nova Affair | Edition Collage | EC 534-2

Wolfe,Benjamin Jonah 'Ben' | (b)
Diana Krall Group
When I Look In Your Eyes | Verve | 9513304
Diana Krall Group With Orchestra
When I Look In Your Eyes | Verve | 9513304
Eric Reed Quartet
Musicale | Impulse(MCA) | 951196-2
Eric Reed Trio
Musicale | Impulse(MCA) | 951196-2
Harry Connick Jr. Quartet
We Are In Love | CBS | 466736-2
Harry Connick Jr. Quartet With Branford Marsalis
We Are In Love | CBS | 466736-2
Wynton Marsalis Group
Standard Time Vol.4:Marsalis Plays Monk | CBS | CK 67503

Wolff,Mike | (el-p,keyboardsp)
Cannonball Adderley Group
Phenix | Fantasy | FCD 79004-2

Wollesen,Kenny | (broom,dr,perc,bug,samplesvoc)
Bill Frisell Band
Blues Dream | Nonesuch | 7559-79615-2
David Binney Group
Balance | ACT | 9411-2
Frank Carlberg Group
Variations On A Summer Day | Fresh Sound Records | FSNT 083 CD
Peter Herbert Group
B-A-C-H A Chromatic Universe | Between The Lines | btl 013(Efa 10183)
Slow Poke
Redemption | Intuition Records | INT 3260-2
Steve Cárdenas Trio
Shebang | Fresh Sound Records | FSNT 079 CD

Wollny,Michael | (p)
Clark Terry With The Summit Jazz Orchestra
Clark | Edition Collage | EC 530-2

Wölpl,Peter | (g,g-synthprogramming)
Wolfgang Schmid's Kick
No Filters | TipToe | TIP-888809 2

Wolter,Henning | (p)
Henning Wolter Trio
Two Faces | double moon | DMCD 1003-2
Henning Wolter Trio With Gerd Dudek
Two Faces | double moon | DMCD 1003-2
Henning Wolter Trio With Guests
Years Of A Trilogy | double moon | DMCHR 71021

Woltzenlogel,Celso | (fl)
Duo Fenix
Karai-Eté | IN+OUT Records | 7009-2

Wolverines,The |
The Wolverines
Jazz:The Essential Collection Vol.2 | IN+OUT Records | 78012-2

Wonder,Stevie | (harmsynth)
Dizzy Gillespie And His Orchestra
Closer To The Source | Atlantic | 7567-80776-2
Herbie Hancock Group
Man-Child | CBS | 471235-2

Wondra,Roland | (rh-g)
Joe Bawelino Quartet
Happy Birthday Stéphane | Edition Collage | EC 458-2
Joe Bawelino Quartet & Martin Stegner
Happy Birthday Stéphane | Edition Collage | EC 458-2

Wonsey,Athony | (p,celesteharpsichord)
Donald Harrison Quartet
Nouveau Swing | Impulse(MCA) | 951209-2
Eddie Allen Quintet
R 'N' B | Enja | ENJ-9033 2
Summer Days | Enja | ENJ-9388 2
Eddie Allen Sextet
Summer Days | Enja | ENJ-9388 2
Nicholas Payton Quartet
Gumbo Nouveau | Verve | 531199-2
Nicholas Payton Quintet
Nick@Night | Verve | 547598-2
Payton's Place | Verve | 557327-2
Nicholas Payton Sextet
Gumbo Nouveau | Verve | 531199-2
Payton's Place | Verve | 557327-2
Russell Malone Quartet
Look Who's Here | Verve | 543543-2

Wood,Andrew | (tp)
Buddy Johnson And His Orchestra
Buddy And Ella Johnson 1953-1964 | Bear Family Records | BCD 15479 DH

Wood,Bobby | (pel-p)
Herbie Mann Group
Memphis Underground | Atlantic | 7567-81364-2
The Best Of Herbie Mann | Atlantic | 7567-81369-2

Wood,Booty | (bar-horntb)
Count Basie And His Orchestra
88 Basie Street | Original Jazz Classics | OJC 808(2310901)
Fancy Pants | Original Jazz Classics | OJCCD 1038-2(2310920)
Digital III At Montreux | Original Jazz Classics | OJCCD 996-2(2308223)
Count Basie Big Band
Farmers Market Barbecue | Original Jazz Classics | OJCCD 732-2(2310874)
Duke Ellington And His Award Winners
Greatest Hits | CBS | 462959-2
Duke Ellington And His Orchestra
New Orleans Suite | Rhino | 812273670-2
The Ellington Suites | Original Jazz Classics | OJC20 446-2(2310762)
The Afro-Eurasian Eclipse-A Suite In Eight Parts | Original Jazz Classics | OJCCD 645-2(F 9498)
Togo Brava Swuite | Storyville | STCD 8323
Ella Fitzgerald With Count Basie And His Orchestra
Digital III At Montreux | Original Jazz Classics | OJCCD 996-2(2308223)
Ella Fitzgerald With The Count Basie Orchestra
Bluella:Ella Fitzgerald Sings The Blues | Pablo | 2310960-2
For The Love Of Ella Fitzgerald | Verve | 841765-2
Lionel Hampton And His Orchestra
Lionel Hampton:Flying Home | Dreyfus Jazz Line | FDM 36735-2
Sarah Vaughan And The Count Basie Orchestra
Sarah Vaughan Birthday Celebration | Fantasy | FANCD 6090-2

Wood,Brian | (tp)
Chas Burchell Quintet
Unsong Hero:The Undiscovered Genius Of Chas Burchell | IN+OUT Records | 7026-2
Chas Burchell Sextet
Unsong Hero:The Undiscovered Genius Of Chas Burchell | IN+OUT Records | 7026-2
Geoff Carter Quintet
Unsong Hero:The Undiscovered Genius Of Chas Burchell | IN+OUT Records | 7026-2
Lilly Thornton With The Benny Golson Sextet
Remembering Dinah-A Salute To Dinah Washington | Hot Shot Records | HSR 8313-2
Ronnie Scott With The Chas Burchell Quintet
Unsong Hero:The Undiscovered Genius Of Chas Burchell | IN+OUT Records | 7026-2
The Mike Hennessey Chastet
Shades Of Chas Burchell | IN+OUT Records | 7025-2

Wood,Chris | (bel-b)
John Scofield Quartet
A Go Go | Verve | 539979-2
Medeski Martin & Wood
Univisible | Blue Note | 535870-2

Wood,Dave | (b)
Cy Laurie Jazz Band
The Golden Years Of Revival Jazz,Sampler | Storyville | 109 1001
Cy Laurie's New Orleans Septet
The Golden Years Of Revival Jazz,Vol.6 | Storyville | STCD 5511

Wood,Gloria | (voc)
Paul Desmond Quartet With The Bill Bates Singers
Desmond | Original Jazz Classics | OJCCD 712-2(F 3235/8082)

Wood,Kent | (vib)
Chuck Brown And The Second Chapter Band
Timeless | Minor Music | 801068

Wood,Less | (cl)
Bob Wallis Storyville Jazzmen
The Golden Years Of Revival Jazz,Vol.7 | Storyville | STCD 5512

Wood,Linda | (harp)
Herbie Hancock Group
Sunlight | CBS | 486570-2

Wood,Vishnu Bill | (boud)
Alice Coltrane Quintet
Journey In Satchidananda | Impulse(MCA) | 951228-2

Woodard,Rickey | (as,ts,clss)
Rickey Woodard Quartet
California Cooking No.2 | Candid | CCD 79762
Warren Vaché And The New York City All-Star Big Band
Swingtime! | Nagel-Heyer | CD 059

Woodard,Will | (b)
Thomas Faist Jazzquartet
Visionary | JHM Records | JHM 3609

Woode,Jimmy | (b,vocp)
Annie Ross & PonyPoindexter With The Berlin All Stars
Annie Ross & Pony Poindexter with The Berlin All Stars | MPS | 9811257
Art Farmer Quintet
From Vienna With Art | MPS | 9811443
Bill Ramsey With The Paul Kuhn Trio
Caldonia And More... | Bear Family Records | BCD 16151 AH
Cat Anderson And His Orchestra
Americans Swinging In Paris:Cat Anderson | EMI Records | 539658-2
Charlie Parker Quintet
Charlie Parker At Storyville | Blue Note | 785108-2
Clark Terry And His Orchestra
Clark Terry And His Orchestra Feat. Paul Gonsalves | Storyville | STCD 8322
Clark Terry Quartet
Jazz Legends:Clark Terry-Duke Jordan | Storyville | 4960283
Duke Ellington And His Award Winners
Greatest Hits | CBS | 462959-2
Duke Ellington And His Orchestra
Jazz Collection:Duke Ellington | Laserlight | 24369
Greatest Hits | CBS | 462959-2
Verve Jazz Masters 4:Duke Ellington | Verve | 516338-2
Ellington '55 | Capitol | 520135-2
Great Swing Classics In Hi-Fi | Capitol | 521223-2
Ellington At Newport 1956(Complete) | CBS | CK 64932
Black Brown And Beige | CBS | CK 65566
Such Sweet Thunder | CBS | CK 65568
Anatomy Of A Murder | CBS | CK 65569
The Ellington Suites | Original Jazz Classics | OJC20 446-2(2310762)
Duke Ellington At The Alhambra | Pablo | PACD 5313-2
Duke Ellington Duo
The Ellington Suites | Original Jazz Classics | OJC20 446-2(2310762)
Ella Fitzgerald With The Duke Ellington Orchestra
Ella Fitzgerald-First Lady Of Song | Verve | 517898-2
The Best Of The Song Books | Verve | 519804-2
Verve Jazz Masters 6:Ella Fitzgerald | Verve | 519822-2
The Best Of The Song Books:The Ballads | Verve | 521867-2
Verve Jazz Masters 46:Ella Fitzgerald-The Jazz Sides | Verve | 527655-2
Love Songs:The Best Of The Song Books | Verve | 531762-2
Ella Fitzgerald Sings The Duke Ellington Songbook | Verve | 559248-2
For The Love Of Ella Fitzgerald | Verve | 841765-2
Fritz Pauer Trio
Live At The Berlin Jazz Galerie | MPS | 9811263
Great Traditionalists In Europe
Great Traditionalists | Jazzpoint | JP 1046 CD
Johnny Hodges And His Band
Verve Jazz Masters 35:Johnny Hodges | Verve | 521857-2
Johnny Hodges And The Ellington All-Stars Without Duke
Verve Jazz Masters 35:Johnny Hodges | Verve | 521857-2
Johnny Hodges And The Ellington Men
Verve Jazz Masters 35:Johnny Hodges | Verve | 521857-2
Johnny Hodges Orchestra
The Soul Of Ben Webster | Verve | 527475-2
Kenny Clarke-Francy Boland Big Band
Clark-Boland Big Band: TNP, October 29th, 1969 | Laserlight | 36129
Three Latin Adventures | MPS | 529095-2
More Smiles | MPS | 9814789
All Smiles | MPS | 9814790
Nat Pierce Quartet
My Pal Basie | Jazz Connaisseur | JCCD 8904-2
Nat Pierce Trio
My Pal Basie | Jazz Connaisseur | JCCD 8904-2
Raymond Fol Big Band
Jazz In Paris:Raymond Fol-Les 4 Saisons | EmArCy | 548791-2
Rosemary Clooney With The Duke Ellington Orchestra
Blue Rose | CBS | CK 65506

Woodford,David L. | (bs)
Etta James & The Roots Band
Burnin' Down he House | RCA | 3411633-2

Woodiel,Paul | (v)
Jim Snidero Quartet With Strings
Strings | Milestone | MCD 9326-2

Woodland,Nick | (g,mand,lap-steelvoc)
Nick Woodland And The Magnets
Big Heart | Blues Beacon | BLU-1013 2
Nick Woodland Quartet
Live Fireworks | Blues Beacon | BLU-1027 2

Woodlen,Bob | (tp)
Charlie Parker With Machito And His Orchestra
Charlie Parker:The Best Of The Verve Years | Verve | 527815-2
Talkin' Bird | Verve | 559859-2
Bird: The Complete Charlie Parker On Verve | Verve | 837141-2
Charlie Parker:April In Paris | Dreyfus Jazz Line | FDM 36737-2

Woodman,Britt | (bar-horntb)
Charles Mingus And His Orchestra
The Complete Town Hall Concert | Blue Note | 828353-2
Charles Mingus Orchestra
Mingus Mingus Mingus | Impulse(MCA) | 951170-2
Mingus | Candid | CCD 79021
Dizzy Gillespie And His Orchestra
Verve Jazz Masters 10:Dizzy Gillespie | Verve | 516319-2
Gillespiana And Carnegie Hall Concert | Verve | 519809-2
Talking Verve:Dizzy Gillespie | Verve | 533846-2
Ultimate Dizzy Gillespie | Verve | 557535-2
Duke Ellington And His Orchestra
Jazz Collection:Duke Ellington | Laserlight | 24369
The Legends Of Swing | Laserlight | 24659
100 Years Duke | Laserlight | 24906
Highlights From The Duke Ellington Centennial Edition | RCA | 2663672-2
Greatest Hits | CBS | 462959-2
The Big Bands Vol.1.The Snader Telescriptions | Storyville | 4960043
Verve Jazz Masters 4:Duke Ellington | Verve | 516338-2
Ellington '55 | Capitol | 520135-2
Great Swing Classics In Hi-Fi | Capitol | 521223-2
Ellington At Newport 1956(Complete) | CBS | CK 64932
Black Brown And Beige | CBS | CK 65566
Such Sweet Thunder | CBS | CK 65568
Anatomy Of A Murder | CBS | CK 65569
The Ellington Suites | Original Jazz Classics | OJC20 446-2(2310762)
Duke Ellington At The Alhambra | Pablo | PACD 5313-2
Ella Fitzgerald With Orchestra
Ella/Things Ain't What They Used To Be | Warner | 9362-47875-2
Ella Fitzgerald With The Bill Doggett Orchestra
Ella Fitzgerald-First Lady Of Song | Verve | 517898-2
Rhythm Is My Business | Verve | 559513-2
Ella Fitzgerald With The Duke Ellington Orchestra
Ella Fitzgerald-First Lady Of Song | Verve | 517898-2
The Best Of The Song Books | Verve | 519804-2
Verve Jazz Masters 6:Ella Fitzgerald | Verve | 519822-2
The Best Of The Song Books:The Ballads | Verve | 521867-2
Verve Jazz Masters 46:Ella Fitzgerald-The Jazz Sides | Verve | 527655-2
Love Songs:The Best Of The Song Books | Verve | 531762-2
Ella Fitzgerald Sings The Duke Ellington Songbook | Verve | 559248-2
For The Love Of Ella Fitzgerald | Verve | 841765-2

Hank Jones With Oliver Nelson's Orchestra
The Roots Of Acid Jazz | Impulse(MCA) | IMP 12042
James Moody Orchestra
The Blues And Other Colors | Original Jazz Classics | OJCCD 954-2(M 9023)
Jimmy Smith With The Oliver Nelson Orchestra
Verve Jazz Masters 29:Jimmy Smith | Verve | 521855-2
Jimmy Smith:Best Of The Verve Years | Verve | 527950-2
Jimmy Smith-Talkin' Verve | Verve | 531563-2
Peter & The Wolf | Verve | 547264-2
John Coltrane Quartet With Brass
The Complete Africa/Brass Sessions | Impulse(MCA) | 952168-2
Johnny Hodges And The Ellington Men
Verve Jazz Masters 35:Johnny Hodges | Verve | 521857-2
Junior Mance Trio & Orchestra
That Lovin' Feelin' | Milestone | MCD 47097-2
Lionel Hampton And His Orchestra
Planet Jazz:Big Bands | Planet Jazz | 2169649-2
Lionel Hampton:Flying Home | Dreyfus Jazz Line | FDM 36735-2
Miles Davis Quintet
Charles Mingus-The Complete Debut Recordings | Debut | 12 DCD 4402-2
Blue Moods | Original Jazz Classics | OJC20 043-2(DEB 120)
Oscar Peterson With The Ernie Wilkins Orchestra
Verve Jazz Masters 16:Oscar Peterson | Verve | 516320-2
Rosemary Clooney With The Duke Ellington Orchestra
Blue Rose | CBS | CK 65506
Sarah Vaughan With Orchestra
Sarah Vaughan Sings The Mancini Songbook | Verve | 558401-2
Zoot Sims With Orchestra
Passion Flower | Original Jazz Classics | OJCCD 939-2(2312120)

Woods,Chris | (as,fl,psax)

Clark Terry Quintet
Jazz Dance | Original Jazz Classics | OJCCD 1002-2(1210890)
Count Basie And His Orchestra
88 Basie Street | Original Jazz Classics | OJC 808(2310901)
Fancy Pants | Original Jazz Classics | OJCCD 1038-2(2310920)
Count Basie's Small Band
88 Basie Street | Original Jazz Classics | OJC 808(2310901)
Jimmy Forrest With The Oliver Nelson Orchestra
Soul Street | Original Jazz Classics | OJCCD 987-2(NJ 8293)

Woods,Jimmy | (asts)

Chico Hamilton Sextet
The Dealer | Impulse(MCA) | 547958-2
Jimmy Woods Sextet
Conflict | Original Jazz Classics | OJCCD 1954-2(S 7612)
Joe Gordon Quintet
Lookin' Good | Original Jazz Classics | OJCCD 1934-2(S 7597)

Woods,Phil | (as,arr,comp,el-p,perc,el-as,el-cl)

Anita O'Day With The Gary McFarland Orchestra
All The Sad Youn Men | Verve | 517065-2
Verve Jazz Masters 49:Anita O'Day | Verve | 527653-2
Benny Bailey Septet
Big Brass | Candid | CCD 79011
Benny Carter And His Orchestra
Further Definitions/Additions To Further Definotions | Impulse(MCA) | 951229-2
Benny Goodman And His Orchestra
The Legends Of Swing | Laserlight | 24659
Cannonball Adderley And His Orchestra
Ballads | Blue Note | 537563-2
Cannonball Adderley Quintet
Ballads | Blue Note | 537563-2
Cannonball Adderley With Sergio Mendes And The Bossa Rio Sextet
Ballads | Blue Note | 537563-2
Dizzy Gillespie And His Orchestra
Verve Jazz Masters 20:Introducing | Verve | 519853-2
Dizzy Gillespie:Birks Works-The Verve Big Band Sessions | Verve | 527900-2
Talking Verve:Dizzy Gillespie | Verve | 533846-2
Dizzy Gillespie Orchestra
Verve Jazz Masters 10:Dizzy Gillespie | Verve | 516319-2
Ella Fitzgerald With The Bill Doggett Orchestra
Ella Fitzgerald-First Lady Of Song | Verve | 517898-2
Rhythm Is My Business | Verve | 559513-2
Friedrich Gulda Septet
Friedrich Gulda At Birdland | RCA | 2112587-2
Gary Burton Sextet
Planet Jazz:Gary Burton | RCA | 2165367-2
Gary McFarland And His Orchestra
The Complete Bill Evans On Verve | Verve | 527953-2
George Russell And His Orchestra
Geogre Russell New York N.Y. | Impulse(MCA) | 951278-2
Gil Evans Orchestra
Verve Jazz Masters 23:Gil Evans | Verve | 521860-2
The Individualism Of Gil Evans | Verve | 833804-2
Hank Jones With Oliver Nelson's Orchestra
The Roots Of Acid Jazz | Impulse(MCA) | IMP 12042
Jimmy Rushing And His Orchestra
Five Feet Of Soul | Roulette | 581830-2
Jimmy Smith And Wes Montgomery With Orchestra
Jimmy & Wes-The Dynamic Duo | Verve | 521445-2
Jimmy Smith And Wes Montgomery With The Oliver Nelson Orchestra
Wes Montgomery:The Verve Jazz Sides | Verve | 521690-2
Jimmy Smith:Best Of The Verve Years | Verve | 527950-2
Talkin' Jazz:Roots Of Acid Jazz | Verve | 529580-2
Jimmy Smith With Orchestra
Jimmy Smith-Talkin' Verve | Verve | 531563-2
Jimmy Smith With The Claus Ogerman Orchestra
Verve Jazz Masters 29:Jimmy Smith | Verve | 521855-2
Any Number Can Win | Verve | 557447-2
Jimmy Smith With The Oliver Nelson Orchestra
Verve Jazz Masters 29:Jimmy Smith | Verve | 521855-2
Jimmy Smith:Best Of The Verve Years | Verve | 527950-2
Jimmy Smith-Talkin' Verve | Verve | 531563-2
Peter & The Wolf | Verve | 547264-2
Joe Williams With The Jimmy Jones Orchestra
Planet Jazz:Joe Williams | Planet Jazz | 2165370-2
Kenny Burrell Quartet
Verve Jazz Masters 45:Kenny Burrell | Verve | 527652-2
Kenny Clarke-Francy Boland Big Band
Three Latin Adventures | MPS | 529095-2
Modern Jazz Quartet And Orchestra
MJQ 40 | Atlantic | 7567-82330-2
Oliver Nelson And His Orchestra
Verve Jazz Masters Vol.60:The Collection | Verve | 529866-2
More Blues And The Abstract Truth | Impulse(MCA) | 951212-2
Oscar Peterson With Orchestra
With Respect To Nat | Verve | 557486-2
Phil Woods And His European Rhythm Machine
At The Montreux Jazz Festival | Verve | 065512-2
Americans Swinging In Paris:Phil Woods | EMI Records | 539654-2
Phil Woods Quartet
A Tribute To Charlie Parker Vol.2 | Storyville | 4960493
Woodlore | Original Jazz Classics | OJCCD 052-2
Phil Woods Quartet With Orchestra & Strings
Round Trip | Verve | 559804-2
Phil Woods-Benny Carter Quintet
The Art Of Saxophone | Laserlight | 24652
Prestige All Stars
The Prestige Legacy Vol.2:Battles Of Saxes | Prestige | PCD 24252-2
Quincy Jones And His Orchestra
Talkin' Verve-Roots Of Acid Jazz:Roland Kirk | Verve | 533101-2
Verve Jazz Masters Vol.59:Toots Thielemans | Verve | 535271-2
Big Band Bossa Nova | Verve | 557913-2
Rahsaan/The Complete Mercury Recordings Of Roland Kirk | Mercury | 846630-2
The Quintessence | Impulse(MCA) | 951222-2
The Roots Of Acid Jazz | Impulse(MCA) | IMP 12042
Quincy Jones Big Band
Rahsaan/The Complete Mercury Recordings Of Roland Kirk | Mercury | 846630-2
Sarah Vaughan And The Thad Jones Orchestra
Verve Jazz Masters 42:Sarah Vaughan-The Jazz Sides | Verve | 526817-2
Sarah Vaughan With The Hal Mooney Orchestra
It's A Man's World | Mercury | 589487-2
Sonny Rollins Orchestra
Alfie | Impulse(MCA) | 951224-2
Thelonious Monk And His Orchestra
Greatest Hits | CBS | CK 65422
Thelonious Monk:85th Birthday Celebration | zyx records | FANCD 6076-2
At Town Hall | Original Jazz Classics | OJCCD 135-2
Wes Montgomery With The Oliver Nelson Orchestra
Verve Jazz Masters 14:Wes Montgomery | Verve | 519826-2
Wes Montgomery:The Verve Jazz Sides | Verve | 521690-2
Talkin' Jazz:Roots Of Acid Jazz | Verve | 529580-2
Zoot Sims-Al Cohn-Phil Woods Sextet
Jazz Alive:A Night At The Half Note | Blue Note | 494105-2

Woodson,Terry | (tb)

Don Ellis Orchestra
Electric Bath | CBS | CK 65522

Woodward,Nate | (tp)

Gene Ammons Septet
A Stranger In Town | Prestige | PRCD 24266-2

Woodward,Ralph | (fr-h)

Eric Dolphy Quartet With The University Of Illinois Brass Ensemble
The Illinois Concert | Blue Note | 499826-2

Woodyard,Sam | (drperc)

Billy Strayhorn Orchestra
Johnny Hodges With Billy Strayhorn And The Orchestra | Verve | 557543-2
Buddy Rich Big Band
Backwoods Siseman/Pieces Of Dream | Laserlight | 24655
Cat Anderson And His All Stars
Americans Swinging In Paris:Cat Anderson | EMI Records | 539658-2
Cat Anderson And His Orchestra
Americans Swinging In Paris:Cat Anderson | EMI Records | 539658-2
Clark Terry And His Orchestra
Clark Terry And His Orchestra Feat. Paul Gonsalves | Storyville | STCD 8322
Duke Ellington And Count Basie With Their Orchestras
First Time! | CBS | CK 65571
Duke Ellington And His Orchestra
Jazz Collection:Duke Ellington | Laserlight | 24369
The Art Of Saxophone | Laserlight | 24652
Highlights From The Duke Ellington Centennial Edition | RCA | 2663672-2
The Popular Duke Ellington | RCA | 2663880-2
Duke Ellington: The Champs-Elysees Theater January 29-30th,1965 | Laserlight | 36131
Greatest Hits | CBS | 462959-2
Jazz Festival Vol.2 | Storyville | 4960743
Verve Jazz Masters 4:Duke Ellington | Verve | 516338-2
Verve Jazz Masters 20:Introducing | Verve | 519853-2
Ella & Duke At The Cote D'Azur | Verve | 539030-2
Ella Fitzgerald And Duke Ellington:Cote D'Azure Concerts on Verve | Verve | 539033-2
Soul Call | Verve | 539785-2
The Great Paris Concert | Atlantic | 7567-81303-2
Afro-Bossa | Reprise | 9362-47876-2
Ellington At Newport 1956(Complete) | CBS | CK 64932
Black Brown And Beige | CBS | CK 65566
Such Sweet Thunder | CBS | CK 65568
Duke Ellington And His Orchestra feat. Paul Gonsalves | Original Jazz Classics | OJCCD 623-2
Yale Concert | Original Jazz Classics | OJCCD 664-2
Jazz At The Philharmonis Berlin '65/Paris '67 | Pablo | PACD 5304-2
Duke Ellington At The Alhambra | Pablo | PACD 5313-2
The Jazz Giants Play Duke Ellington:Caravan | Prestige | PCD 24227-2
Duke Ellington-Coleman Hawkins Orchestra
Duke Ellington Meets Coleman Hawkins | Impulse(MCA) | 951162-2
Ella Fitzgerald With The Duke Ellington Orchestra
The Stockholm Concert 1966 | Pablo | 2308242-2
Ella Fitzgerald-First Lady Of Song | Verve | 517898-2
The Best Of The Song Books | Verve | 519804-2
Verve Jazz Masters 6:Ella Fitzgerald | Verve | 519822-2
The Best Of The Song Books:The Ballads | Verve | 521867-2
Verve Jazz Masters 46:Ella Fitzgerald-The Jazz Sides | Verve | 527655-2
Ella At Duke's Place | Verve | 529700-2
Love Songs:The Best Of The Song Books | Verve | 531762-2
Ella & Duke At The Cote D'Azur | Verve | 539030-2
Ella Fitzgerald And Duke Ellington:Cote D'Azure Concerts on Verve | Verve | 539033-2
Ella Fitzgerald Sings The Duke Ellington Songbook | Verve | 559248-2
For The Love Of Ella Fitzgerald | Verve | 841765-2
Gérard Badini Quartet
Jazz In Paris:Gérard Badini-The Swing Machine | EmArCy | 018417-2
John Coltrane-Duke Ellington Quartet
The Gentle Side Of John Coltrane | Impulse(MCA) | 951107-2
Duke Ellington & John Coltrane | Impulse(MCA) | 951166-2
Johnny Hodges And His Band
Verve Jazz Masters 35:Johnny Hodges | Verve | 521857-2
Johnny Hodges And The Ellington All-Stars Without Duke
Verve Jazz Masters 35:Johnny Hodges | Verve | 521857-2
Johnny Hodges And The Ellington Men
Verve Jazz Masters 35:Johnny Hodges | Verve | 521857-2
Johnny Hodges Orchestra
Johnny Hodges At The Sportpalast, Berlin | Pablo | 2CD 2620102
The Soul Of Ben Webster | Verve | 527475-2
The Jazz Giants Play Harry Warren:Lullaby Of Broadway | Prestige | PCD 24204-2
Johnny Hodges With Billy Strayhorn And The Duke Ellington Orchestra
Verve Jazz Masters 35:Johnny Hodges | Verve | 521857-2
Lionel Hampton All Stars
Jazz In Paris:Lionel Hampton-Ring Dem Bells | EmArCy | 159825-2 PMS
Rosemary Clooney With The Duke Ellington Orchestra
Blue Rose | CBS | CK 65506

Woon,Kim Sung | (kayagumkomungo)

Red Sun/SamulNori
Then Comes The White Tiger | ECM | 1499

Wooten,Billy | (vib)

Grant Green Sextet
Grant Green:Blue Breakbeat | Blue Note | 494705-2

Wooten,Mary | (cello)

Jim Snidero Quartet With Strings
Strings | Milestone | MCD 9326-2

Wooten,Red | (b)

Frank Sinatra With The Red Norvo Quintet(Sextet!)
Live In Australia,1959 | Blue Note | 837513-2
Frank Sinatra With The Red Norvo Quintet(Sextet!) & Orchestra
Live In Australia,1959 | Blue Note | 837513-2
Red Norvo And His Orchestra
Planet Jazz:Female Jazz Vocalists | Planet Jazz | 2169656-2
Red Norvo Sextet
Live In Australia,1959 | Blue Note | 837513-2

Wootn,Margaret R. | (v)

Herbie Hancock Group With String Quartet
Herbie Hancock The New Standards | Verve | 527715-2
Herbie Hancock Group With String Quartet,Woodwinds And Brass
Herbie Hancock The New Standards | Verve | 527715-2

Wordley,Mick | (g,perc,dobro,mando-gvoc)

Ronnie Taheny Group
Briefcase | Laika Records | 35101152

Workman,Miriam | (voc)

Leon Thomas With Orchestra
Spirits Known And Unknown | RCA | 2663876-2

Workman,Nioka | (cello)

Greg Osby Quartet With String Quartet
Symbols Of Light(A Solution) | Blue Note | 531395-2
Steve Coleman And The Council Of Balance
Genesis & The Opening Of The Way | RCA | 2152934-2

Workman,Reggie | (b,el-b,percwhistles)

Andrew Hill Sextet
Grass Roots | Blue Note | 522672-2
Archie Shepp Sextet
Four For Trane | Impulse(MCA) | 951218-2
Art Blakey And The Jazz Messengers
Caravan | Original Jazz Classics | OJC20 038-2
Ugetsu | Original Jazz Classics | OJC20 090-2(RLP 9464)
Booker Ervin-Dexter Gordon Quintet
Dexter Gordon Birthday Celebration | Fantasy | FANCD 6082-2
Cedar Walton Quintet
Soul Cycle | Original Jazz Classics | OJCCD 847-2(P 7693)
Charlie Rouse Quartet
Late Night Sax | CBS | 487798-2
Dave Pike Quartet
It's Time For Dave Pike | Original Jazz Classics | OJCCD 1951-2(RLP 9360)
Don Byron Quartet
Tuskegee Experiments | Nonesuch | 7559-79280-2
Don Byron-Reggie Workman
Tuskegee Experiments | Nonesuch | 7559-79280-2
Freddie Hubbard Orchestra
The Body And The Soul | Impulse(MCA) | 951183-2
Freddie Hubbard Quintet
Hub-Tones | Blue Note | 499008-2
Freddie Hubbard Septet
The Body And The Soul | Impulse(MCA) | 951183-2
Gary Bartz Quartet
Libra/Another Earth | Milestone | MCD 47077-2
Gary Bartz Sextet
Libra/Another Earth | Milestone | MCD 47077-2
Jean-Paul Bourelly Trance Atlantic
Boom Bop II | double moon | CHRDM 71023
John Coltrane And His Orchestra
John Coltrane:Standards | Impulse(MCA) | 549914-2
John Coltrane Group
Olé Coltrane | Atlantic | 7567-81349-2
Olé Coltrane | Rhino | 8122-73699-2
John Coltrane Quartet
John Coltrane:Standards | Impulse(MCA) | 549914-2
Live At The Village Vanguard:The Master Takes | Impulse(MCA) | 951251-2
John Coltrane:The Complete 1961 Village Vanguard Recordings | Impulse(MCA) | 954322-2
The Other Village Vanguard Tapes | Impulse(MCA) | MCD 04137
John Coltrane Quartet With Brass
The Complete Africa/Brass Sessions | Impulse(MCA) | 952168-2
John Coltrane Quartet With Eric Dolphy
John Coltrane:The Complete 1961 Village Vanguard Recordings | Impulse(MCA) | 954322-2
John Coltrane Quintet
Live At The Village Vanguard:The Master Takes | Impulse(MCA) | 951251-2
Eric Dolphy Birthday Celebration | Fantasy | FANCD 6085-2
John Coltrane Quintet With Eric Dolphy
Coltrane Spiritual | Impulse(MCA) | 589099-2
John Coltrane-Live Trane:The European Tours | Pablo | 7PACD 4433-2
John Coltrane-The Heavyweight Champion:The Complete Atlantic Recordings | Atlantic | 8122-71984-2
John Coltrane:The Complete 1961 Village Vanguard Recordings | Impulse(MCA) | 954322-2
The Other Village Vanguard Tapes | Impulse(MCA) | MCD 04137
John Coltrane Septet With Eric Dolphy
John Coltrane:The Complete 1961 Village Vanguard Recordings | Impulse(MCA) | 954322-2
The Other Village Vanguard Tapes | Impulse(MCA) | MCD 04137
John Coltrane Sextet
Impressions | Impulse(MCA) | 543416-2
Live At The Village Vanguard:The Master Takes | Impulse(MCA) | 951251-2
John Coltrane:The Complete 1961 Village Vanguard Recordings | Impulse(MCA) | 954322-2
John Coltrane Sextet With Eric Dolphy
John Coltrane-The Heavyweight Champion:The Complete Atlantic Recordings | Atlantic | 8122-71984-2
John Coltrane-Eric Dolphy Quartet
John Coltrane:The Complete 1961 Village Vanguard Recordings | Impulse(MCA) | 954322-2
The Other Village Vanguard Tapes | Impulse(MCA) | MCD 04137
Kenny Burrell-Grover Washington Quartet
Blue Note Plays Gershwin | Blue Note | 520808-2
Lee Morgan Orchestra
The Last Sessin | Blue Note | 493401-2
Lee Morgan Quintet
Caramba! | Blue Note | 853358-2
Lee Morgan Sextet
Taru | Blue Note | 522670-2
Search For The New Land | Blue Note | 591896-2
Pharoah Sanders Orchestra
Karma | Impulse(MCA) | 951153-2
The Roots Of Acid Jazz | Impulse(MCA) | IMP 12042
Richard Williams Quintet
New Horn In Town | Candid | CCD 79003
Roswell Rudd-Archie Shepp Group
Live In New York | EmArCy | 013482-2
The Jazz Composer's Orchestra
Comminications | JCOA | 1001/2
Wayne Shorter Quartet
Herbie Hancock:The Complete Blue Note Sixties Sessions | Blue Note | 495569-2
Juju | Blue Note | 499005-2
Kind Of Blue:Blue Note Celebrate The Music Of Miles Davis | Blue Note | 534255-2
Wayne Shorter:The Classic Blue Note Recordings | Blue Note | 540856-2
Adams Apple | Blue Note | 591901-2
Wayne Shorter Quintet
Wayne Shorter:The Classic Blue Note Recordings | Blue Note | 540856-2
Night Dreamer | Blue Note | 784173-2

World Quintet,The |

World Quintet
World Quintet | TipToe | TIP-888843 2
World Quintet With The London Mozart Players
World Quintet | TipToe | TIP-888843 2
World Quintet With The London Mozart Players And Herbert Grönemeyer
World Quintet | TipToe | TIP-888843 2

World Saxophone Quartet |

World Saxophone Quartet
Plays Duke Ellington | Nonesuch | 7559-79137-2
Dances And Ballads | Nonesuch | 7559-79164-2

World Trio |

World Trio
World Trio | VeraBra Records | CDVBR 2052-2

Worlitzsch,Volker | (vconcertmaster)

Joachim Kühn And The Radio Philharmonie Hannover NDR With Jazz Soloists

Europeana | ACT | 9220-2

Wormick,James | (tb)
(Little)Jimmy Scott With The Lionel Hampton Orchestra
Everybody's Somebody's Fool | Decca | 050669-2
Lionel Hampton And His Orchestra
Lionel Hampton:Flying Home | Dreyfus Jazz Line | FDM 36735-2

Worrall,Bill | (keyboardssynth)
Barbara Thompson's Paraphernalia
Barbara Thompson's Special Edition | VeraBra Records | CDVBR 2017-2

Worrell,Bernie | (electronic-keyboards,el-p,org,synth)
Pharoah Sanders Group
Save Our Children | Verve | 557297-2
Pharoah Sanders Orchestra
Message From Home | Verve | 529578-2

Worrell,Frank | (g)
Jess Stacy And His Orchestra
Planet Jazz:Jazz Piano | RCA | 2169655-2

Worrell,Lewis | (b)
Albert Ayler Quintet
Albert Ayler Live In Greenwich Village:The Complete Impulse Recordings | Impulse(MCA) | IMP 22732
Roswell Rudd Sextet
Mixed | Impulse(MCA) | IMP 12702

Wörsching,Heli | (b)
Freddie Brocksieper Und Seine Solisten
Freddie's Boogie Blues | Bear Family Records | BCD 16388 AH

Worth,Bobby | (dr)
Summit Reunion
Jazz Im Amerikahaus,Vol.5 | Nagel-Heyer | CD 015
The First Sampler | Nagel-Heyer | NHR SP 5
The Alex Welsh Legacy Band
The Sound Of Alex Vol.1 | Nagel-Heyer | CD 070
Wrobel-Roberscheuten-Hopkins Jam Session
Jammin' At The IAJRC Convention Hamburg 1999 | Nagel-Heyer | CD 066

Worthington,Tom | (b)
Vic Lewis West Coast All Stars
Vic Lewis Presenting A Celebration Of Contemporary West Coast Jazz | Candid | CCD 79711/12

Wöss,Martin | (pkeyboards)
Melanie Bong With Band
Fantasia | Jazz 4 Ever Records:Jazz Network | J4E 4755

Woznak,Uta | (v)
Till Brönner Quartet & Deutsches Symphonieorchester Berlin
German Songs | Minor Music | 801057

Wrase,Tina | (b-clss)
Association Urbanetique
Ass Bedient | Jazz 4 Ever Records:Jazz Network | J4E 4723

Wray,Ken | (tb,bass-tpv-tb)
Stan Getz With The Kurt Edelhagen Orchestra
Stan Getz In Europe | Laserlight | 24657

Wright,Arthur | (harmg)
Jimmy Witherspoon And His Band
Baby, Baby, Baby | Original Blues Classics | OBCCD 527-2(P 7290)
Mel Brown Quintet
Chicken Fat | Impulse(MCA) | 9861047

Wright,Bernard | (clavinet,el-p,org,synth,keyboards)
Lenny White Group
Present Tense | Hip Bop | HIBD 8004
Renderers Of Spirit | Hip Bop | HIBD 8014
Hot Jazz Bisquits | Hip Bop | HIBD 8801
Marcus Miller Group
Tales | Dreyfus Jazz Line | FDM 36571-2
Live & More | Dreyfus Jazz Line | FDM 36585-2
Stanley Jordan Quartet
Live In New York | Blue Note | 497810-2
Tom Browne Group
Hot Jazz Bisquits | Hip Bop | HIBD 8801
Tom Browne Groups
Mo' Jamaica Funk | Hip Bop | HIBD 8002

Wright,Charles 'Specs' | (dr,gongtympani)
Cannonball Adderley And His Orchestra
Verve Jazz Masters 31:Cannonball Adderley | Verve | 522651-2
Cannonball Adderley Quintet
Cannonball Adderley:Sophisticated Swing-The EmArCy Small Group Sessions | Verve | 528408-2
Coleman Hawkins With The Red Garland Trio
Coleman Hawkins With The Red Garland Trio | Original Jazz Classics | OJCCD 418-2(SV 2001)
Nat Adderley Quartet
Cannonball Adderley:Sophisticated Swing-The EmArCy Small Group Sessions | Verve | 528408-2
Ray Bryant Trio
Ray Bryant Trio | Original Jazz Classics | OJCCD 793-2(P 7098)
Red Garland Trio
Stretching Out | Prestige | PRCD 24272-2
Sonny Rollins Trio
Sonny Rollins And The Big Brass | Verve | 557545-2

Wright,Clyde | (voc)
Golden Gate Quartet
Americans Swinging In Paris:Golden Gate Quartet | EMI Records | 539659-2
From Spriritual To Swing Vol.2 | EMI Records | 780573-2
Spirituals To Swing 1955-69 | EMI Records | 791569-2
Golden Gate Quartet With The Martial Solal Orchestra
Americans Swinging In Paris:Golden Gate Quartet | EMI Records | 539659-2
From Spriritual To Swing Vol.2 | EMI Records | 780573-2

Wright,Eddie | (g)
Freddie Roach Quintet
Good Move | Blue Note | 524551-2
Freddie Roach Trio
Good Move | Blue Note | 524551-2

Wright,Edna | (voc)
Stanley Turrentine And His Orchestra
Pieces Of Dream | Original Jazz Classics | OJCCD 831-2(F 9465)

Wright,Edythe | (voc)
Tommy Dorsey And His Clambake Seven
Planet Jazz:Tommy Dorsey | Planet Jazz | 2159972-2
Planet Jazz:Bud Freeman | Planet Jazz | 2161240-2
Planet Jazz:Swing | Planet Jazz | 2169651-2
Tommy Dorsey And His Orchestra
Planet Jazz:Tommy Dorsey | Planet Jazz | 2159972-2

Wright,Elmon | (tp)
Dizzy Gillespie And His Orchestra
Dizzy Gillespie:Pleyel Jazz Concert 1948 + Max Roach Quintet 1949 | Vogue | 21409412
Planet Jazz:Dizzy Gillespie | Planet Jazz | 2152069-2
Planet Jazz:Bebop | RCA | 2169650-2
Planet Jazz:Male Jazz Vocalists | Planet Jazz | 2169657-2
Ella Fitzgerald With The Dizzy Gillespie Orchestra
Ella Fitzgerald:Mr.Paganini | Dreyfus Jazz Line | FDM 36741-2

Wright,Eugene 'Gene' | (b)
Cal Tjader Quartet
Our Blues | Fantasy | FCD 24771-2
Jazz At The Blackhawk | Original Jazz Classics | OJCCD 436-2(F 8096)
Cal Tjader Quintet
Cal Tjader Plays Jazz | Original Jazz Classics | OJCCD 986-2(F 3-211)
Dave Brubeck Quartet
The Great Concerts | CBS | 462403-2
Dave Brubeck's Greatest Hits | CBS | 465703-2
Time Out | CBS | CK 65122
Buried Treasures | CBS | CK 65777
Dave Brubeck Quartet With Orchestra
Brandenburg Gate:Revisited | CBS | CK 65725
Dave Brubeck Sextet
Bravo! Brubeck! | CBS | CK 65723

Freddie Roach Quartet
So Blue So Funky-Heroes Of The Hammond | Blue Note | 796563-2
Gus Mancuso Quartet
Gus Mancuso & Special Friends | Fantasy | FCD 24762-2
Gus Mancuso Quintet
Gus Mancuso & Special Friends | Fantasy | FCD 24762-2
Jerry Dodgion Quartet
The Jazz Scene:San Francisco | Fantasy | FCD 24760-2
Jimmy Rushing With The Dave Brubeck Quartet
Brubeck & Rushing | CBS | CK 65727
Paul Desmond Quartet
Planet Jazz:Paul Desmond | Planet Jazz | 2152061-2
Planet Jazz Sampler | Planet Jazz | 2152326-2
Bossa Antigua | RCA | 2174795-2
Easy Living | RCA | 2174796-2
Take Ten | RCA | 2179621-2
Paul Desmond-Gerry Mulligan Quartet
The Ballad Of Paul Desmond | RCA | 21429372
Sonny Stitt Quartet
Kaleidoscope | Original Jazz Classics | OJCCD 060-2(P 7077)
Vince Guaraldi Quartet
The Jazz Scene:San Francisco | Fantasy | FCD 24760-2

Wright,Herman | (b)
Al Grey And His Allstars
Snap Your Fingers | Verve | 9860307
Billy Mitchell Quintet
This Is Billy Mitchell | Smash | 065507-2
Billy Mitchell Sextet
This Is Billy Mitchell | Smash | 065507-2
Chet Baker Quintet
The Jazz Giants Play Rodgers & Hart:Blue Moon | Prestige | PCD 24205-2
Groovin' With The Chet Baker Quintet | Prestige | PR20 7460-2
Comin' On With The Chet Baker Quintet | Prestige | PR20 7478-2
Cool Burnin' With The Chet Baker Quintet | Prestige | PR20 7496-2
Boppin' With The Chet Baker Quintet | Prestige | PR20 7512-2
Smokin' With The Chet Baker Quintet | Prestige | PR20 7749-2
Terry Gibbs Octet
Jewis Melodies In Jazztime | Mercury | 589673-2
Yusef Lateef Quartet
The Golden Flute | Impulse(MCA) | 9681049
Into Something | Original Jazz Classics | OJCCD 700-2(NJ 8272)
Yusef Lateef Trio
Into Something | Original Jazz Classics | OJCCD 700-2(NJ 8272)

Wright,James | (ts)
Louis Jordan And His Tympany Five
Louis Jordan-Let The Good Times Roll: The Complete Decca Recordings 1938-1954 | Bear Family Records | BCD 15557 IH

Wright,Lammar | (cotp)
Cab Calloway And His Orchestra
Planet Jazz:Cab Calloway | Planet Jazz | 2161237-2
Dizzy Gillespie And His Orchestra
Dizzy Gillespie:Pleyel Jazz Concert 1948 + Max Roach Quintet 1949 | Vogue | 21409412
Planet Jazz:Dizzy Gillespie | Planet Jazz | 2152069-2
Planet Jazz:Bebop | RCA | 2169650-2
Lionel Hampton And His Orchestra
Lionel Hampton:Flying Home | Dreyfus Jazz Line | FDM 36735-2

Wright,Leo | (as,tambourine,vocfl)
Annie Ross & PonyPoindexter With The Berlin All Stars
Annie Ross & Pony Poindexter with The Berlin All Stars | MPS | 9811257
Antonio Carlos Jobim Group
The Antonio Carlos Jobim Songbook | Verve | 525472-2
Antonio Carlos Jobim With The Claus Ogerman Orchestra
Verve Jazz Masters 13:Antonio Carlos Jobim | Verve | 516409-2
The Composer Of 'Desafinado' Plays | Verve | 521431-2
Dave Pike Sextet
Carnavals | Prestige | PCD 24248-2
Dizzy Gillespie And His Orchestra
Verve Jazz Masters 10:Dizzy Gillespie | Verve | 516319-2
Gillespiana And Carnegie Hall Concert | Verve | 519809-2
Talking Verve:Dizzy Gillespie | Verve | 533846-2
Ultimate Dizzy Gillespie | Verve | 557535-2
Dizzy Gillespie Quintet
Dizzie Gillespie: Salle Pleyel/Olympia | Laserlight | 36132
An Electrifying Evening With The Dizzy Gillespie Quintet | Verve | 557544-2
Dizzy Gillespie Septet
The Antonio Carlos Jobim Songbook | Verve | 525472-2
Dizzy Gillespie Sextet
Dizzie Gillespie: Salle Pleyel/Olympia | Laserlight | 36132
Verve Jazz Masters 10:Dizzy Gillespie | Verve | 516319-2
Gloria Coleman Quartet
Soul Sisters | Impulse(MCA) | 8961048
Jack McDuff Quartet
Screamin' | Original Jazz Classics | OJCCD 875-2(P 7259)
Jack McDuff:The Prestige Years | Prestige | PRCD 24387-2
Jimmy Witherspoon And His Band
Baby, Baby, Baby | Original Blues Classics | OBCCD 527-2(P 7290)
Johnny Coles Sextet
True Blue | Blue Note | 534032-2
Knut Kiesewetter With The Dieter Reith Orchestra
Reith On! | MPS | 557423-2
Lalo Schifrin And His Orchestra
Tin Tin Deo | Fresh Sound Records | FSR-CD 319
Lalo Schifrin Sextet
Tin Tin Deo | Fresh Sound Records | FSR-CD 319
Richard Williams Quintet
New Horn In Town | Candid | CCD 79003

Wright,N. | (voc)
Sonny Rollins Group
What's New? | RCA | 2179626-2

Wright,Phillip | (p)
Abbey Lincoln With The Kenny Dorham Quintet
Abbey Is Blue | Original Jazz Classics | OJC20 069-2(RLP 1153)

Wright,Roscoe | (dr)
Bill Perkins Quartet
Swing Spring | Candid | CCD 79752

Wright,Ruth | (voc)
Sun Ra And His Astro-Infinity Arkestra
Space Is The Place | Impulse(MCA) | 951249-2

Wright,Wayne | (g)
Benny Goodman And His Orchestra
40th Anniversary Concert-Live At Carnegie Hall | London | 820349-2
Verve Jazz Masters 33:Benny Goodman | Verve | 844410-2
Buddy Rich Big Band
Backwoods Siseman/Pieces Of Dream | Laserlight | 24655

Wrightsman,Stan | (p)
Artie Shaw And His Orchestra
Planet JazzArtie Shaw | Planet Jazz | 2152057-2
Planet Jazz:Jazz Greatest Hits | Planet Jazz | 2169648-2
The Capitol Jazzmen
The Hollywood Session:The Capitol Jazzmen | Jazz Unlimited | JUCD 2044

WRO Orchestra Köln |
Louis Sclavis With The WRO Orchestra, Köln
Le Concerto Improvisé | Enja | ENJ-9397 2

Wrobel,Engelbert | (cl,as,arr,tsss)
Engelbert Wrobel-Chris Hopkins-Dan Barrett Sextet
Harlem 2000 | Nagel-Heyer | CD 082
Oscar Klein-Lino Patruno European Jazz Stars
Live at The San Marino Jazz Festival | Jazzpoint | JP 1052 CD
Oscar Klein's Anniversary Band
Moonglow | Nagel-Heyer | CD 021
Ellington For Lovers | Nagel-Heyer | NH 1009
The Second Sampler | Nagel-Heyer | NHR SP 6
Wrobel-Roberscheuten-Hopkins Jam Session
Jammin' At The IAJRC Convention Hamburg 1999 | Nagel-Heyer | CD 066

Wuchner,Jürgen | (bpiccolo-b)
Günther Klatt Quartet
Internationales Jazzfestival Münster | Tutu Records | 888110-2*
Jazzensemble Des Hessischen Rundfunks
Atmosphering Conditions Permitting | ECM | 1549/50
Uwe Oberg Quartet
Dedicated | Jazz 'n' Arts Records | JNA 1603

Wukits,Robin | (tp)
Jazzensemble Des Hessischen Rundfunks
Jazz Messe-Messe Für Unsere Zeit | hr music.de | hrmj 003-01 CD

Wülker,Nils | (tpfl-h)
Thärichens Tentett
Lady Moon | Minor Music | 801094

Wunsch,Frank | (pharpsichord)
Benny Bailey Quartet
I Thought About You | Laika Records | 35100762
Angel Eyes | Laika Records | 8695068
Benny Bailey Quartet With Wayne Bartlett
I Thought About You | Laika Records | 35100762
Lee Konitz-Frank Wunsch Quartet
S'Nice | Nabel Records:Jazz Network | CD 4641
Lee Konitz-Kenny Wheeler Quartet
Live At Birdland Neuburg | double moon | CHRDM 71014
Remy Filipovitch Quartet
All Night Long | Album | AS 11806

Wünschmann,Klaus Peter | (voc)
Jazzensemble Des Hessischen Rundfunks
Jazz Messe-Messe Für Unsere Zeit | hr music.de | hrmj 003-01 CD

Würminghausen,Kristina | (voice)
Kölner Saxophon Mafia With Kristina Würminghausen
Kölner Saxophon Mafia Proudly Presents | Jazz Haus Musik | JHM 0046 CD

Wurster,Emil | (as,saxts)
Albert Mangelsdorff With The NDR Big Band
NDR Big Band-Bravissimo | ACT | 9232-2
Chet Baker With The NDR-Bigband
NDR Big Band-Bravissimo | ACT | 9232-2
Heinz Sauer Quartet With The NDR Big Band
NDR Big Band-Bravissimo | ACT | 9232-2
Joe Pass With The NDR Big Band
Joe Pass In Hamburg | ACT | 9100-2
NDR Big Band-Bravissimo | ACT | 9232-2
Joe Pass With The NDR Big Band And Radio Philharmonie Hannover
Joe Pass In Hamburg | ACT | 9100-2
NDR Big Band
NDR Big Band-Bravissimo | ACT | 9232-2

Württemberger,Eva | (voc)
Werner Lener Trio
Colours | Satin Doll Productions | SDP 1033-1 CD

Wuster,E. | (reeds)
Chet Baker With The NDR-Bigband
My Favourite Songs: The Last Great Concert Vol.1 | Enja | ENJ-5097 2
The Last Concert Vol.I+II | Enja | ENJ-6074 22

Wuster,Emil | (as)
Johnny Griffin With The NDR Big Band
NDR Big Band-Bravissimo | ACT | 9232-2
NDR Big Band
NDR Big Band-Bravissimo | ACT | 9232-2

Wyand,Mark | (cl,ts,fl,reedsss)
Clark Terry With The Summit Jazz Orchestra
Clark | Edition Collage | EC 530-2
Nana Mouskouri With The Berlin Radio Big Band
Nana Swings | Mercury | 074394-2
Rainer Tempel Big Band
Melodies Of '98 | Jazz 4 Ever Records:Jazz Network | J4E 4744
Album 03 | Jazz 'n' Arts Records | JNA 1102
Rainer Tempel Quintet
Blick In Die Welt | Edition Musikat | EDM 038

Wyands,Richard | (el-p,pp-solo)
Charlie Mariano Quartet
The Jazz Scene:San Francisco | Fantasy | FCD 24760-2
Charlie Mariano Sextet
The Jazz Scene:San Francisco | Fantasy | FCD 24760-2
Eddie Lockjaw Davis And His Orchestra
Eric Dolphy:The Complete Prestige Recordings | Prestige | 9 PRCD-4418-2
Etta Jones And Her Quartet
Something Nice | Original Jazz Classics | OJCCD 221-2(P 7194)
Etta Jones With Her Trio
Something Nice | Original Jazz Classics | OJCCD 221-2(P 7194)
Etta Jones With The Oliver Nelson Quintet
Hollar! | Original Jazz Classics | OJCCD 1061(PR 7284)
Freddie Hubbard With Orchestra
This Is Jazz:Freddie Hubbard | CBS | CK 65041
Gene Ammons And His Orchestra
A Stranger In Town | Prestige | PRCD 24266-2
Gene Ammons Quartet
The Jazz Giants Play Rodgers & Hart:Blue Moon | Prestige | PCD 24205-2
Gene Ammons Quintet
The Jazz Giants Play Jerome Kern:Yesterdays | Prestige | PCD 24202-2
The Jazz Giants Play Cole Porter:Night And Day | Prestige | PCD 24203-2
Jimmy Cobb's Mob
Cobb's Groove | Milestone | MCD 9334-2
Kenny Burrel Quartet
'Round Midnight | Original Jazz Classics | OJCCD 990-2(F 9417)
Kenny Burrell Quartet
Stormy Monday Blues | Fantasy | FCD 24767-2
Kenny Burrell Sextet
Verve Jazz Masters 45:Kenny Burrell | Verve | 527652-2
Lisle Atkinson Quartet
Bass Contra Bass | Storyville | STCD 8270
Lisle Atkinson Quintet
Bass Contra Bass | Storyville | STCD 8270
Oliver Nelson Quintet
Eric Dolphy:The Complete Prestige Recordings | Prestige | 9 PRCD-4418-2
Eric Dolphy Birthday Celebration | Fantasy | FANCD 6085-2
Straight Ahead | Original Jazz Classics | OJCCD 099-2
Oliver Nelson Sextet
Eric Dolphy:The Complete Prestige Recordings | Prestige | 9 PRCD-4418-2
Eric Dolphy Birthday Celebration | Fantasy | FANCD 6085-2
Screamin' The Blues | Original Jazz Classics | OJC 080(NJ 8243)
The Prestige Legacy Vol.2:Battles Of Saxes | Prestige | PCD 24252-2
Richard Williams Quintet
New Horn In Town | Candid | CCD 79003
Richard Wyands
'Round Midnight | Original Jazz Classics | OJCCD 990-2(F 9417)
Richard Wyands Trio
Then Here And Now | Storyville | STCD 8269
Roland Kirk Quartet
Talkin' Verve-Roots Of Acid Jazz:Roland Kirk | Verve | 533101-2
Rahsaan/The Complete Mercury Recordings Of Roland Kirk | Mercury | 846630-2
Willis Jackson Quartet
At Large | Prestige | PCD 24243-2

Wyatt,Robert | (dr,perc,voicevoc)
Michael Mantler Group
Michael Mantler: No Answer/Silence | Watt | 2/5(543374-2)
The Hapless Child | Watt | 4
Silence | Watt | 5 (2313105)
Michael Mantler Group With The Danish Concert Radio Orchestra
Many Have No Speech | Watt | 19(835580-2)
Michael Mantler Group With The Danish Radio Concert Orchestra Strings

INTERPRETENVERZEICHNIS

The School Of Understanding(Sort-Of-An-Opera) | ECM | 1648/49(537963-2)
Michael Mantler Orchestra
Hide And Seek | ECM | 1738(549612-2)
Wyble,Jimmy | (g)
Frank Sinatra With The Red Norvo Quintet(Sextet!)
Live In Australia,1959 | Blue Note | 837513-2
Frank Sinatra With The Red Norvo Quintet(Sextet!) & Orchestra
Live In Australia,1959 | Blue Note | 837513-2
Red Norvo And His Orchestra
Planet Jazz:Female Jazz Vocalists | Planet Jazz | 2169656-2
Red Norvo Sextet
Live In Australia,1959 | Blue Note | 837513-2
Wydh,Roikey | (g)
Klaus Doldinger's Passport
Running In Real Time | Warner | 2292-40633-2
Wyman,Bill | (b-g,cowbellshakers)
Howlin' Wolf London Session
Howlin' Wolf:The London Sessions | Chess | MCD 09297
Wynn,Albert | (tb)
Fletcher Henderson And His Orchestra
Jazz:The Essential Collection Vol.3 | IN+OUT Records | 78013-2
Xiques,Eddie | (as,b-cl,bs,fl,sssax)
McCoy Tyner Group With Horns
Inner Voices | Original Jazz Classics | OJCCD 1039-2(M 9079)
McCoy Tyner Group With Horns And Voices
Inner Voices | Original Jazz Classics | OJCCD 1039-2(M 9079)
Xirgu,David | (dr)
Carme Canela With The Joan Monné Trio
Introducing Carme Canela | Fresh Sound Records | FSNT 014 CD
Dave Liebman And The Lluis Vidal Trio
Dave Liebman And The Lluis Vidal Trio | Fresh Sound Records | FSNT 026 CD
Dave Liebman And The Lluis Vidal Trio With The Orquestra De Cambra Theatre Lliure
Dave Liebman And The Lluis Vidal Trio | Fresh Sound Records | FSNT 026 CD
David Xirgu Quartet
Idolents | Fresh Sound Records | FSNT 077 CD
Gorka Benitez Quartet
Gorka Benitez Trio | Fresh Sound Records | FSNT 073 CD
Gorka Benitez Quintet
Gorka Benitez Trio | Fresh Sound Records | FSNT 073 CD
Gorka Benitez Trio
Gorka Benitez Trio | Fresh Sound Records | FSNT 073 CD
Joan Monné Trio
Mireia | Fresh Sound Records | FSNT 100 CD
Lluis Vidal Trio
Tren Nocturn | Fresh Sound Records | FSNT 003 CD
Milikituli | Fresh Sound Records | FSNT 009 CD
Orquestra De Cambra Teatre Lliure
Orquestra De Cambra Teatre Lliure and Lluis Vidal Trio feat.Dave Liebman | Fresh Sound Records | FSNT 027 CD
Porgy And Bess | Fresh Sound Records | FSNT 066 CD
Tributes To Duke Ellington | Fresh Sound Records | FSNT 084 CD
Orquestra De Cambra Teatre Lliure feat. Dave Liebman
Orquestra De Cambra Teatre Lliure and Lluis Vidal Trio feat.Dave Liebman | Fresh Sound Records | FSNT 027 CD
Pep O'Callaghan Grup
Tot Just | Fresh Sound Records | FSNT 017 CD
Yabe,Tadashi | (?)
United Future Organizatio
United Future Organization | Talkin' Loud | 518166-2
Yahel,Sam | (org)
Yaya 3
Yaya 3 | Loma | 936248277-2
Yahonikan,Leslie | (b-clbs)
Machito And His Orchestra
Afro-Cuban Jazz Moods | Original Jazz Classics | OJC20 447-2
Yahr,Barbara | (cond)
Abdullah Ibrahim Trio With The Munich Radio Symphony Orchestra
African Symphony | Enja | ENJ-9410 2
Yakou Tribe |
Yakou Tribe
Red & Blue Days | Traumton Records | 4474-2
Yale,Daniel | (viola)
Ron Carter With Strings
Pastels | Original Jazz Classics | OJCCD 665-2(M 9073)
Yamaha International Allstar Band,The |
The Yamaha International Allstar Band
Hapy Birthday Jazzwelle Plus | Nagel-Heyer | CD 005
The First Sampler | Nagel-Heyer | NHR SP 5
Yamaki,Hideo | (drperc)
Toshinori Kondo & Ima
Red City Smoke | JA & RO | JARO 4173-2
Toshinori Kondo & Ima plus Guests
Human Market | JA & RO | JARO 4146-2
Yamamoto,Hozan | (shakuhachi)
Tony Scott Trio
Music For Zen Meditation | Verve | 521444-2
Yamamoto,Yusuke | (perc)
Taylor Hawkins Group
Wake Up Call | Fresh Sound Records | FSCD 145 CD
Yampolsky,Viktor | (p)
Moscow Rachmaninov Trio
Groupe Lacroix:The Composer Group | Creative Works Records | CW CD 1030-2
Yanai,Naoki | (b)
Richard Elliot Sextet
City Speak | Blue Note | 832620-2
Yance,Ed | (g)
Anita O'Day With Gene Krupa And His Orchestra
Let Me Off Uptown:Anita O'Day With Gene Krupa | CBS | CK 65625
Yancey Estella 'Mama' | (voc)
Estella Mama Yancey With Axel Zwingenberger
Axel Zwingenberger And The Friends Of Boogie Woogie Vol.4: The Blues Of Mama Yancey | Vagabond | VRCD 8.88009
Yancey,Bill | (b)
Ella Fitzgerald And Her All Stars
Ella Fitzgerald-First Lady Of Song | Verve | 517898-2
Yaner,Milt | (as,cl,reeds,saxss)
Billie Holiday With Gordon Jenkins And His Orchestra
Billie's Love Songs | Nimbus Records | NI 2000
Ella Fitzgerald With Sy Oliver And His Orchestra
Ella Fitzgerald:Mr.Paganini | Dreyfus Jazz Line | FDM 36741-2
Ella Fitzgerald With Sy Oliver And His Orchestra
Ella Fitzgerald:The Decca Years 1949-1954 | Decca | 050668-2
Louis Armstrong And His Orchestra
Satchmo Serenaders | Verve | 543792-2
Louis Armstrong With Gordon Jenkins And His Orchestra And Choir
Satchmo In Style | Verve | 549594-2
Ambassador Louis Armstrong Vol.17:Moments To Remember(1952-1956) | Ambassador | CLA 1917
Louis Armstrong-My Greatest Songs | MCA | MCD 18347
Swing Legends:Louis Armstrong | Nimbus Records | NI 2012
Louis Armstrong With Sy Oliver And His Orchestra
Satchmo Serenaders | Verve | 543792-2
Louis Armstrong:C'est Si Bon | Dreyfus Jazz Line | FDM 36730-2
Louis Armstrong-My Greatest Songs | MCA | MCD 18347
Louis Armstrong With The Gordon Jenkins Orchestra
Ambassador Louis Armstrong Vol.17:Moments To Remember(1952-1956) | Ambassador | CLA 1917
Yanez,Felipe | (p)
Lalo Schifrin And His Orchestra
Tin Tin Deo | Fresh Sound Records | FSR-CD 319
Yankoulov,Stoyan | (perctupan)
Batoru
Tree Of Sounds | Nabel Records:Jazz Network | CD 4685
Dirk Strakhof & Batoru
Arabesque | Nabel Records:Jazz Network | CD 4696
Fairy Tale Trio
Jazz Across The Border | Wergo | SM 1531-2
Yannic | (dog-voices)
Jamenco
Conversations | Trick Music | TM 9202 CD
Yasuda,Fumio | (p-solo)
Fumio Yasuda
Schumann's Bar Music | Winter&Winter | 910081-2
Yates,Doug | (b-cl,clas)
Charles Mingus Orchestra
Tonight At Noon...Three Or Four Shades Of Love | Dreyfus Jazz Line | FDM 36633-2
Yates,Jojo | (bells,brekete-dr,cabasa,cowbells)
Trevor Watts Moiré Music Drum Orchestra
A Wider Embrace | ECM | 1449
Yaw,Bruce | (bb-g)
Everyman Band
Everyman Band | ECM | 1234
Without Warning | ECM | 1290
Yaw,Ralph | (arr)
Stan Kenton And His Orchestra
Stan Kenton-The Formative Years | Decca | 589489-2
Yé,Paco | (drperc)
Jon Hassell & Farafina
Flash Of The Spirit | Intuition Records | INT 3009-2
Ye,Sha | (v)
HR Big Band With Marjorie Barnes And Frits Landesbergen And Strings
Swinging Christmas | hr music.de | hrmj 012-02 CD
Yellin,Pete | (as,cl,fl,b-cl,reedsss)
Buddy Rich And His Orchestra
Swingin' New Big Band | Pacific Jazz | 835232-2
Buddy Rich Big Band
Backwoods Siseman/Pieces Of Dream | Laserlight | 24655
Joe Henderson Sextet
Joe Henderson:The Milestone Years | Milestone | 8MCD 4413-2
Pete Yellin Quartet
Pete Yellin's European Connection:Live! | Jazz 4 Ever Records:Jazz Network | J4E 4722
Yellowjackets |
Take 6 With The Yellow Jackets
He Is Christmas | Reprise | 7599-26665-2
Yellowjackets
Live Wires | GRP | GRP 96672
Run For Your Life | GRP | GRP 97542
Yeltes,Gerhard | (dr)
Pili-Pili
Hotel Babo | JA & RO | JARO 4147-2
Yerba Buena Jazz Band |
Bunk Johnson With The Yerba Buena Jazz Band
Bunk & Lu | Good Time Jazz | GTCD 12024-2
Yerba Buena Jazz Band
Bunk & Lu | Good Time Jazz | GTCD 12024-2
Yerke,Ken | (v)
Chick Corea With String Quartet
Verve Jazz Masters 3:Chick Corea | Verve | 519820-2
Yerno,Ana | (palmas)
Renaud Garcia-Fons Group
Oriental Bass | Enja | ENJ-9334 2
Yetman,Ahmed | (kanon)
Ahmed Abdul-Malik Orchestra
Planet Jazz:Lee Morgan | Planet Jazz | 2161238-2
Ylönen,Marko | (cello)
Edward Vesala Sound And Fury
Invisible Strom | ECM | 1461
Yocum,Clark | (gvoc)
Tommy Dorsey And His Orchestra
Planet Jazz:Frank Sinatra & Tommy Dorsey | Planet Jazz | 2152067-2
Planet Jazz Sampler | Planet Jazz | 2152326-2
Planet Jazz:Tommy Dorsey | Planet Jazz | 2159972-2
Planet Jazz:Big Bands | Planet Jazz | 2169649-2
Planet Jazz:Male Jazz Vocalists | Planet Jazz | 2169657-2
Frank Sinatra And The Tommy Dorsey Orchestra | RCA | 2668701-2
Yoder,Walt | (b)
Woody Herman And His Orchestra
The Legends Of Swing | Laserlight | 24659
Woody Herman:Four Brother | Dreyfus Jazz Line | FDM 36722-2
Yokum,Clark | (g)
Frank Sinatra With Orchestra
Planet Jazz:Frank Sinatra & Tommy Dorsey | Planet Jazz | 2152067-2
Tommy Dorsey And His Orchestra
Planet Jazz:Frank Sinatra & Tommy Dorsey | Planet Jazz | 2152067-2
Yong-Gu Zheng,Wang | (chin-zither)
Claudio Puntin Quartet
Mondo | Jazz Haus Musik | JHM 0134 CD
Yoon,Sun A | (voc)
Roman Bunka Group
Dein Kopf Ist Ein Schlafendes Auto | ATM Records | ATM 3818-AH
York,Pete | (dr,percvoc)
Passport And Guests
Doldinger Jubilee Concert | Atlantic | 2292-44175-2
Doldinger's Best | ACT | 9224-2
Yoshida,Sayumi | (voice)
Lee Konitz Quartet
Haiku | Nabel Records:Jazz Network | CD 4664
Youla,Fode | (bells,bote,djimbe,sico,voc,congoma)
Pili-Pili
Pili-Pili | JA & RO | JARO 4141-2
Hoomba-Hoomba | JA & RO | JARO 4192-2
Youle,Fode | (voc)
Jasper Van't Hof
Pili-Pili | Warner | 2292-40458-2
Young,Al | (bongos,timbales,engl-h,b-clts)
Chris Connor With Band
Chris Connor | Atlantic | 7567-80769-2
Young,Arthur | (novachordp)
Arthur Young And Hatchett's Swingtette
Grapelli Story | Verve | 515807-2
Young,Austin | (b,vvoc)
Bunk Johnson And His Superior Jazz Band
Authentic New Orleans Jazz | Good Time Jazz | GTCD 12048-2
Young,Dave | (as,b,sax,tp,bellsts)
Gene DiNovi Trio
Renaissance Of A Jazz Master | Candid | CCD 79708
Live At The Montreal Bistro | Candid | CCD 79726
Greg Clayton Trio
Live At Boomers | String Jazz | SJRCD 1013
Oscar Peterson Quartet
Time After Time | Pablo | 2310947-2
Jazz Dance | Original Jazz Classics | OJCCD 1002-2(1210890)
Oscar Peterson Quintet With Strings
Jazz Dance | Original Jazz Classics | OJCCD 1002-2(1210890)
Young,David | (cl,sax,reedsts)
Lionel Hampton And His Orchestra
Planet Jazz:Big Bands | Planet Jazz | 2169649-2
Young,Eldee | (b)
Ramsey Lewis Trio
Down To Earth | Verve | 538329-2
Young,Eugene \'Snooky\' | (fl-h)
Raul De Souza Orchestra
Cannonball Adderley Birthday Celebration | Fantasy | FANCD 6087-2
Young,Eugene Edward | (tp)
Count Basie And His Orchestra
The Legends Of Swing | Laserlight | 24659
Jimmy Rushing And His Orchestra
Five Feet Of Soul | Roulette | 581830-2
Jimmy Smith With The Claus Ogerman Orchestra
Any Number Can Win | Verve | 557447-2
Milt Jackson Orchestra
Milt Jackson Birthday Celebration | Fantasy | FANCD 6079-2
Big Bags | Original Jazz Classics | OJCCD 366-2(RLP 9429)
Sarah Vaughan And Joe Williams With The Count Basie Orchestra
Jazz Profile | Blue Note | 823517-2
Sarah Vaughan With The Count Basie Band
Jazz Profile | Blue Note | 823517-2
Young,Eugene 'Snooky' | (fl-h,tpvoc)
Cannonball Adderley And His Orchestra
Ballads | Blue Note | 537563-2
Charles Mingus And His Orchestra
The Complete Town Hall Concert | Blue Note | 828353-2
Clark Terry & Chico O Farril Orchestra
Spanish Rice | Verve | 9861050
Count Basie And His Orchestra
Planet Jazz:Count Basie | Planet Jazz | 2152068-2
Planet Jazz Sampler | Planet Jazz | 2152326-2
Planet Jazz:Jimmy Rushing | RCA | 2165371-2
Planet Jazz:Jazz Greatest Hits | Planet Jazz | 2169648-2
Planet Jazz:Big Bands | Planet Jazz | 2169649-2
Jazz Collection:Count Basie | Laserlight | 24368
Atomic Swing | Roulette | 497871-2
Verve Jazz Masters 2:Count Basie | Verve | 519819-2
Breakfast Dance And Barbecue | Roulette | 531791-2
Chairman Of The Board | Roulette | 581664-2
Jazz:The Essential Collection Vol.3 | IN+OUT Records | 78013-2
The Complete Atomic Basie | Roulette | 828635-2
Count On The Coast Vol.1 | Phontastic | NCD 7555
Count On The Coast Vol.2 | Phontastic | NCD 7575
Duke Ellington And Count Basie With Their Orchestras
First Time! | CBS | CK 65571
Eddie Harris Group
The Best Of Eddie Harris | Atlantic | 7567-81370-2
George Benson And His Orchestra
Giblet Gravy | Verve | 543754-2
Talkin' Verve:George Benson | Verve | 553780-2
George Benson Orchestra
Verve Jazz Masters 21:George Benson | Verve | 521861-2
Talkin' Verve:George Benson | Verve | 553780-2
Gil Evans Orchestra
Blues In Orbit | Enja | ENJ-3069 2
Grover Washington Jr. Orchestra
Jazzrock-Anthology Vol.3:Fusion | Zounds | CD 27100555
Hampton Hawes Orchestra
Northern Windows Plus | Prestige | PRCD 24278-2
Hank Jones With Oliver Nelson's Orchestra
The Roots Of Acid Jazz | Impulse(MCA) | IMP 12042
Helen Humes And Her All Stars
Lester Young:The Complete Aladdin Sessions | Blue Note | 832787-2
J.J.Johnson And His Orchestra
Planet Jazz:J.J.Johnson | Planet Jazz | 2159974-2
Jimmy Smith With Orchestra
Jimmy Smith-Talkin' Verve | Verve | 531563-2
Jimmy Smith With The Johnny Pate Orchestra
Jimmy Smith-Talkin' Verve | Verve | 531563-2
Jimmy Smith With The Lalo Schifrin Orchestra
Jimmy Smith:Best Of The Verve Years | Verve | 527950-2
Jimmy Smith-Talkin' Verve | Verve | 531563-2
The Cat | Verve | 539756-2
Jimmy Smith With The Oliver Nelson Orchestra
Verve Jazz Masters 29:Jimmy Smith | Verve | 521855-2
Jimmy Smith:Best Of The Verve Years | Verve | 527950-2
Jimmy Smith-Talkin' Verve | Verve | 531563-2
Peter & The Wolf | Verve | 547264-2
Joe Henderson And His Orchestra
Joe Henderson:The Milestone Years | Milestone | 8MCD 4413-2
Joe Henderson Group
Jazzin' Vol.2: The Music Of Stevie Wonder | Fantasy | FANCD 6088-2
Joe Williams,With The Oliver Nelson Orchestra
Planet Jazz:Joe Williams | Planet Jazz | 2165370-2
Johnny Hodges Orchestra
Verve Jazz Masters 35:Johnny Hodges | Verve | 521857-2
Kenny Burrell With The Don Sebesky Orchestra
Verve Jazz Masters 45:Kenny Burrell | Verve | 527652-2
Blues-The Common Ground | Verve | 589101-2
Lionel Hampton And His Orchestra
Planet Jazz:Big Bands | Planet Jazz | 2169649-2
Lionel Hampton:Flying Home | Dreyfus Jazz Line | FDM 36735-2
Modern Jazz Quartet & Guests
MJQ 40 | Atlantic | 7567-82330-2
Modern Jazz Quartet And Orchestra
MJQ 40 | Atlantic | 7567-82330-2
Oliver Nelson And His Orchestra
Verve Jazz Masters Vol.60:The Collection | Verve | 529866-2
Oscar Peterson With The Ernie Wilkins Orchestra
Verve Jazz Masters 16:Oscar Peterson | Verve | 516320-2
Quincy Jones And His Orchestra
Talkin' Verve-Roots Of Acid Jazz:Roland Kirk | Verve | 533101-2
Rahsaan/The Complete Mercury Recordings Of Roland Kirk | Mercury | 846630-2
The Quintessence | Impulse(MCA) | 951222-2
The Roots Of Acid Jazz | Impulse(MCA) | IMP 12042
Sarah Vaughan And The Count Basie Orchestra
Ballads | Roulette | 537561-2
Sarah Vaughan And The Thad Jones Orchestra
Verve Jazz Masters 42:Sarah Vaughan-The Jazz Sides | Verve | 526817-2
Thad Jones-Mel Lewis Orchestra
The Groove Merchant/The Second Race | Laserlight | 24656
Wes Montgomery Orchestra
Movin' Wes | Verve | 521433-2
Wes Montgomery With The Johnny Pate Orchestra
Verve Jazz Masters 14:Wes Montgomery | Verve | 519826-2
Wes Montgomery:The Verve Jazz Sides | Verve | 521690-2
Talkin' Jazz:Roots Of Acid Jazz | Verve | 529580-2
Yusef Lateef Ensemble
Atlantic Saxophones | Rhino | 8122-71256-2
Zoot Sims And His Orchestra
The Jazz Giants Play Duke Ellington:Caravan | Prestige | PCD 24227-2
Young,Gene | (tpfl-h)
Quincy Jones And His Orchestra
Verve Jazz Masters Vol.59:Toots Thielemans | Verve | 535271-2
Young,George | (as,cl,ss,ts,fl,piccolo,b-fl)
Benny Goodman And His Orchestra
40th Anniversary Concert-Live At Carnegie Hall | London | 820349-2
Verve Jazz Masters 33:Benny Goodman | Verve | 844410-2
Young,Graham | (tp)
Anita O'Day With Gene Krupa And His Orchestra
Let Me Off Uptown:Anita O'Day With Gene Krupa | CBS | CK 65625
Young,Horace Alexander | (fl,ss,aspiccolo)
Abdullah Ibrahim Septet
No Fear, No Die(S'en Fout La Mort):Original Soundtrack | TipToe | TIP-888815 2
Dollar(Abdullah Ibrahim) Brand Group
African River | Enja | ENJ-6018 2
Young,Jacob | (g)
Jacob Young Quintet
Evening Falls | ECM | 1876(9811780)
Young,Jeff | (keyboards,orgp)
John Stevens Quartet
Re-Touch & Quartet | Konnex Records | KCD 5027
Young,Larry | (el-p,org,synth,vocp)
Etta Jones And Her Band
Love Shout | Original Jazz Classics | OJCCD 941-2(P 7272)
Frant Green Quartet
Street Of Dreams | Blue Note | 821290-2
Grant Green Trio
Talkin' About | Blue Note | 521958-2

Jimmy Forrest Quartet
Forest Fire | Original Jazz Classics | OJCCD 199-2
Larry Young Quartet
Unity | Blue Note | 497808-2
So Blue So Funky-Heroes Of The Hammond | Blue Note | 796563-2
Miles Davis Group
Bitches Brew | CBS | C2K 65774
Tony Williams Lifetime
Ego | Verve | 559512-2

Young,Lee | (drvoc)
JATP All Stars
Jazz Gallery:Lester Young Vol.2(1946-59) | RCA | 2119541-2
The Complete Jazz At The Philharmonic On Verve 1944-1949 | Verve | 523893-2
Charlie Parker:The Best Of The Verve Years | Verve | 527815-2
Jazz At The Philharmonic:Best Of The 1940's Concerts | Verve | 557534-2
Bird: The Complete Charlie Parker On Verve | Verve | 837141-2
Lionel Hampton All Stars
Lionel Hampton:Flying Home | Dreyfus Jazz Line | FDM 36735-2
Nat King Cole Quartet
Penthouse Serenade | Capitol | 494504-2
Nat King Cole Quintet
After Midnight | Capitol | 520087-2
Nat King Cole Sextet
After Midnight | Capitol | 520087-2
The Hollywood Hucksters
The Hollywood Session:The Capitol Jazzmen | Jazz Unlimited | JUCD 2044

Young,Lester | (cl,tsvoc)
Benny Goodman Septet
Jazz:The Essential Collection Vol.3 | IN+OUT Records | 78013-2
Charlie Christian:Swing To Bop | Dreyfus Jazz Line | FDM 36715-2
Billie Holiday And Her Band
Billie's Love Songs | Nimbus Records | NI 2000
Billie Holiday And Her Orchestra
Jazz:The Essential Collection Vol.3 | IN+OUT Records | 78013-2
Billie's Love Songs | Nimbus Records | NI 2000
Billie Holiday With Eddie Heywood And His Orchestra
Billie's Love Songs | Nimbus Records | NI 2000
Billie Holiday With Teddy Wilson And His Orchestra
Billie's Love Songs | Nimbus Records | NI 2000
Billie Holiday With The JATP All Stars
Billie Holiday Story Vol.1:Jazz At The Philharmonic | Verve | 521642-2
The Complete Jazz At The Philharmonic On Verve 1944-1949 | Verve | 523893-2
Verve Jazz Masters 47:Billie Holiday Sings Standards | Verve | 527650-2
Jazz At The Philharmonic:Best Of The 1940's Concerts | Verve | 557534-2
Count Basie And His Orchestra
Jazz Gallery:Lester Young Vol.2(1946-59) | RCA | 2119541-2
Verve Jazz Masters 2:Count Basie | Verve | 519819-2
Jazz:The Essential Collection Vol.3 | IN+OUT Records | 78013-2
Count Basie At Newport | Verve | 9861761
From Spiritual To Swing | Vanguard | VCD 169/71
Count Basie Sextet
Jazz:The Essential Collection Vol.3 | IN+OUT Records | 78013-2
Count Basie's Kansas City Seven
Jazz:The Essential Collection Vol.3 | IN+OUT Records | 78013-2
Dicky Wells And His Orchestra
Jazz:The Essential Collection Vol.3 | IN+OUT Records | 78013-2
Ella Fitzgerald With The JATP All Stars
Ella Fitzgerald-First Lady Of Song | Verve | 517898-2
For The Love Of Ella Fitzgerald | Verve | 841765-2
Helen Humes And Her All Stars
Lester Young:The Complete Aladdin Sessions | Blue Note | 832787-2
Helen Humes With James P. Johnson And The Count Basie Orchestra
From Spiritual To Swing | Vanguard | VCD 169/71
Helen Humes With The Kansas City Five
From Spiritual To Swing | Vanguard | VCD 169/71
Jam Session
Jazz Gallery:Lester Young Vol.2(1946-59) | RCA | 2119541-2
Benny Goodman At Carnegie Hall 1938(Complete) | CBS | C2K 65143
JATP All Stars
Jazz Gallery:Lester Young Vol.2(1946-59) | RCA | 2119541-2
Verve Jazz Masters 28:Charlie Parker Plays Standards | Verve | 521854-2
The Complete Jazz At The Philharmonic On Verve 1944-1949 | Verve | 523893-2
Charlie Parker:The Best Of The Verve Years | Verve | 527815-2
Jazz At The Philharmonic:Best Of The 1940's Concerts | Verve | 557534-2
The Drum Battle:Gene Krupa And Buddy Rich At JATP | Verve | 559810-2
Talkin' Bird | Verve | 559859-2
Bird: The Complete Charlie Parker On Verve | Verve | 837141-2
Welcome To Jazz At The Philharmonic | Fantasy | FANCD 6081-2
Jazz At The Philharmonic-Frankfurt 1952 | Pablo | PACD 5305-2
Jimmy Rushing With Count Basie And His Orchestra
From Spiritual To Swing | Vanguard | VCD 169/71
Jones-Smith Incorporated
Jazz:The Essential Collection Vol.3 | IN+OUT Records | 78013-2
Jubilee All Stars
Jazz Gallery:Lester Young Vol.2(1946-59) | RCA | 2119541-2
Kansas City Five
Lester Young:Blue Lester | Dreyfus Jazz Line | FDM 36729-2
From Spiritual To Swing | Vanguard | VCD 169/71
Kansas City Seven
Jazz:The Essential Collection Vol.3 | IN+OUT Records | 78013-2
Kansas City Six
Jazz:The Essential Collection Vol.3 | IN+OUT Records | 78013-2
Charlie Christian:Swing To Bop | Dreyfus Jazz Line | FDM 36715-2
Lester Young:Blue Lester | Dreyfus Jazz Line | FDM 36729-2
From Spiritual To Swing | Vanguard | VCD 169/71
Lester Young And Earl Swope With The Bill Potts Trio
Lester Young In Washington,DC 1956:Vol.5 | Original Jazz Classics | OJCCD 993-2
Lester Young And His Band
Jazz Gallery:Lester Young Vol.2(1946-59) | RCA | 2119541-2
Jazz:The Essential Collection Vol.3 | IN+OUT Records | 78013-2
Lester Young:The Complete Aladdin Sessions | Blue Note | 832787-2
Lester Young:Blue Lester | Dreyfus Jazz Line | FDM 36729-2
Lester Young Quartet
Jazz Gallery:Lester Young Vol.2(1946-59) | RCA | 2119541-2
Verve Jazz Masters 30:Lester Young | Verve | 521859-2
The Complete Jazz At The Philharmonic On Verve 1944-1949 | Verve | 523893-2
Verve Jazz Masters Vol.60:The Collection | Verve | 529866-2
Jazz:The Essential Collection Vol.3 | IN+OUT Records | 78013-2
Lester Young:Blue Lester | Dreyfus Jazz Line | FDM 36729-2
Lester Young Quintet
Jazz Gallery:Lester Young Vol.2(1946-59) | RCA | 2119541-2
The Art Of Saxophone | Laserlight | 24652
The Complete Jazz At The Philharmonic On Verve 1944-1949 | Verve | 523893-2
Jazz:The Essential Collection Vol.3 | IN+OUT Records | 78013-2
Lester Young:Blue Lester | Dreyfus Jazz Line | FDM 36729-2
Lester Young Septet
Laughin' To Keep From Cryin' | Verve | 543301-2
Lester Young Trio
Verve Jazz Masters 30:Lester Young | Verve | 521859-2
Lester Young:Blue Lester | Dreyfus Jazz Line | FDM 36729-2
Lester Young With The Bill Potts Trio
Lester Young In Washington,DC 1956:Vol.1 | Original Jazz Classics | OJCCD 782-2(2308219)
Lester Young In Washington,DC 1956:Vol.5 | Original Jazz Classics | OJCCD 993-2
The Jazz Giants Play Harry Warren:Lullaby Of Broadway | Prestige | PCD 24204-2
Lester Young With The Oscar Peterson Quartet
Jazz Gallery:Lester Young Vol.2(1946-59) | RCA | 2119541-2
Lester Young With The Oscar Peterson Trio | Verve | 521451-2
Verve Jazz Masters 30:Lester Young | Verve | 521859-2
Lester Young-Harry Edison With The Oscar Peterson Quartet
Jazz Gallery:Lester Young Vol.2(1946-59) | RCA | 2119541-2
Lester Young-Nat Cole Trio
Lester Young:The Complete Aladdin Sessions | Blue Note | 832787-2
Midnight Blue(The [Be]witching Hour) | Blue Note | 854365-2
Lester Young:Blue Lester | Dreyfus Jazz Line | FDM 36729-2
Lester Young-Nat King Cole
Jazz:The Essential Collection Vol.3 | IN+OUT Records | 78013-2
Lester Young:Blue Lester | Dreyfus Jazz Line | FDM 36729-2
Lester Young-Roy Eldridge-Harry Edison Band
Jazz Gallery:Lester Young Vol.2(1946-59) | RCA | 2119541-2
Lester Young-Teddy Wilson Quartet
Jazz Gallery:Lester Young Vol.2(1946-59) | RCA | 2119541-2
Sammy Price Septet
Jazz:The Essential Collection Vol.3 | IN+OUT Records | 78013-2
Sarah Vaughan With Her Quartet
Jazz Profile | Blue Note | 823517-2
Teddy Wilson And His Orchestra
Jazz:The Essential Collection Vol.3 | IN+OUT Records | 78013-2
The Jazz Giants '56
Jazz Gallery:Lester Young Vol.2(1946-59) | RCA | 2119541-2
The Metronome All Stars
Jazz Gallery:Lester Young Vol.2(1946-59) | RCA | 2119541-2
Una Mae Carlisle Quintet
Jazz:The Essential Collection Vol.3 | IN+OUT Records | 78013-2
Una Mae Carlisle Septet
Planet Jazz:Female Jazz Vocalists | Planet Jazz | 2169656-2

Young,Michael Casey | (synth-programming)
Al Jarreau With Band
Al Jarreau In London | i.e. Music | 557849-2

Young,Mighty Joe | (gvoc)
Albert King With The Willie Dixon Band
Windy City Blues | Stax | SCD 8612-2
Billy Boy Arnold Group
Windy City Blues | Stax | SCD 8612-2

Young,Nadine | (voc)
Les Blue Stars
Jazz In Paris:Blossom Dearie-The Pianist/Les Blue Stars | EmArCy | 064784-2

Young,Reggie | (g)
Herbie Mann Group
Memphis Underground | Atlantic | 7567-81364-2
The Best Of Herbie Mann | Atlantic | 7567-81369-2

Young,Reginald | (tb)
Stan Getz With Orchestra
Apasionado | A&M Records | 395297-2
The Quincy Jones-Sammy Nestico Orchestra
Basie & Beyond | Warner | 9362-47792-2

Young,Richard | (percv)
John Mayer's Indio-Jazz Fusions
Ragatal | Nimbus Records | NI 5569
Ron Carter Quintet With Strings
Pick 'Em/Super Strings | Milestone | MCD 47090-2

Young,Sharon | (voc)
Al Jarreau With Band
Tenderness | i.e. Music | 557853-2

Young,Thomas | (voc)
Max Roach Chorus & Orchestra
To The Max! | Enja | ENJ-7021 22

Young,Trummy | (tbvoc)
Billie Holiday With Teddy Wilson And His Orchestra
Billie's Love Songs | Nimbus Records | NI 2000
Billie Holiday With The JATP All Stars
Billie Holiday Story Vol.1:Jazz At The Philharmonic | Verve | 521642-2
The Complete Jazz At The Philharmonic On Verve 1944-1949 | Verve | 523893-2
Billy May And His Orchestra With Members Of The Jimmy Lunceford Orchestra
Great Swing Classics In Hi-Fi | Capitol | 521223-2
Cozy Cole All Stars
Ultimate Coleman Hawkins selected by Sonny Rollins | Verve | 557538-2
Dizzy Gillespie All Stars
Dizzy Gillespie:Night In Tunisia | Dreyfus Jazz Line | FDM 36734-2
Ella Fitzgerald With Louis Armstrong And The All Stars
Ella Fitzgerald-First Lady Of Song | Verve | 517898-2
The Complete Ella Fitzgerald And Louis Armstrong On Verve | Verve | 537284-2
The Best Of Ella Fitzgerald And Louis Armstrong On Verve | Verve | 537909-2
JATP All Stars
The Complete Jazz At The Philharmonic On Verve 1944-1949 | Verve | 523893-2
Jazz At The Philharmonic:Best Of The 1940's Concerts | Verve | 557534-2
Jimmy Lunceford And His Orchestra
The Legends Of Swing | Laserlight | 24659
Louis Armstrong And Gary Crosby With Sonny Burke's Orchestra
Louis Armstrong-My Greatest Songs | MCA | MCD 18347
Louis Armstrong And His All Stars
Jazz Festival Vol.1 | Storyville | 4960733
Verve Jazz Masters 1:Louis Armstrong | Verve | 519818-2
I Love Jazz | Verve | 543747-2
Louis Armstrong:The Great Chicago Concert 1956 | CBS | C2K 65119
Louis Armstrong Plays W.C.Handy | CBS | CK 64925
Ambassador Satch | CBS | CK 64926
Satch Plays Fats(Complete) | CBS | CK 64927
Historic Barcelona Concerts At Windsor Palace 1955 | Fresh Sound Records | FSR-CD 3004
Louis Armstrong-My Greatest Songs | MCA | MCD 18347
Louis Armstrong And His All Stars With Benny Carter's Orchestra
Ambassador Louis Armstrong Vol.17:Moments To Remember(1952-1956) | Ambassador | CLA 1917
Louis Armstrong And His All Stars With Duke Ellington
Louis Armstrong-Duke Ellington:The Great Summit-Complete Session | Roulette | 524546-2
Louis Armstrong And His All Stars With Sonny Burke's Orchestra
Ambassador Louis Armstrong Vol.17:Moments To Remember(1952-1956) | Ambassador | CLA 1917
Louis Armstrong And His All Stars With The Sy Oliver Orchestra
Ambassador Louis Armstrong Vol.17:Moments To Remember(1952-1956) | Ambassador | CLA 1917
Louis Armstrong And His Orchestra
I Love Jazz | Verve | 543747-2
Satchmo Serenaders | Verve | 543792-2
Louis Armstrong With Benny Carter's Orchestra
Louis Armstrong-My Greatest Songs | MCA | MCD 18347
Louis Armstrong With Sy Oliver And His Orchestra
Satchmo Serenaders | Verve | 543792-2
Louis Armstrong With Sy Oliver's Choir And Orchestra
Jazz Collection:Louis Armstrong | Laserlight | 24366
Louis And The Good Book | Verve | 549593-2
Louis And The Good Book | Verve | 940130-0
Tiny Grimes Swingtet
The Blue Note Swingtets | Blue Note | 495697-2
Tony Scott And His Down Beat Club Sextet
Jazz:The Essential Collection Vol.3 | IN+OUT Records | 78013-2
V-Disc All Star Jam Session
Louis Armstrong-Jack Teagarden-Woody Herman:Midnights At V-Disc | Jazz Unlimited | JUCD 2048

Young,Victor | (ldv)
Jack Teagarden With Orchestra
Jazz:The Essential Collection Vol.3 | IN+OUT Records | 78013-2
Jerri Southern And The Victoe Young Orchestra
The Very Thought Of You:The Decca Years 1951-1957 | Decca | 050671-2

Young,Webster | (cotp)
Jackie McLean Sextet
A Long Drink Of The Blues | Original Jazz Classics | OJCCD 253-2(NJ 8253)
Prestige All Stars
John Coltrane-The Prestige Recordings | Prestige | 16 PCD 4405-2
The Mal Waldron Memorial Album:Soul Eyes | Prestige | PRCD 11024-2
Ray Draper Sextet
Tuba Sounds | Original Jazz Classics | OJCCD 1936-2(P 7096)

Young,David | (b)
Oscar Peterson Quartet
Oscar Peterson Live! | Pablo | 2310940-2
Oscar Peterson Plays Duke Ellington | Pablo | 2310966-2
Oscar Peterson:The Composer | Pablo | 2310970-2

Youssef,Dhafer | (oud,percvoc)
Dhafer Youssef Group
Electric Sufi | Enja | ENJ-9412 2
Paolo Fresu Quintet
Kind Of Porgy & Bess | RCA | 21951952
Paolo Fresu Sextet
Kind Of Porgy & Bess | RCA | 21951952

Ypma,Peter | (dr)
Dutch Swing College Band
Swinging Studio Sessons | Philips | 824256-2 PMS
Laura Fygi With Band
Bewitched | Verve | 514724-2

Yuize,Shinichi | (koto)
Tony Scott Trio
Music For Zen Meditation | Verve | 521444-2

Yukl,Joe | (tb)
Louis Armstrong With Jimmy Dorsey And His Orchestra
Louis Armstrong:Swing That Music | Laserlight | 36056
Swing Legends:Louis Armstrong | Nimbus Records | NI 2012

Yungo,Cun | (perc)
Buddy Childers With The Russ Garcia Strings
Artistry In Jazz | Candid | CCD 79735

Z,Rachel | (keyboards,p,synth,sequencing)
Susan Weinert Band
The Bottom Line | VeraBra Records | CDVBR 2177-2

Z.,Marq | (voc)
Scetches
Different Places | VeraBra Records | CDVBR 2102-2

Zacharias,Bernard | (tb)
Sidney Bechet All Stars
Planet Jazz:Sidney Bechet | Planet Jazz | 2152063-2
Planet Jazz Sampler | Planet Jazz | 2152326-2
Sidney Bechet With Claude Luter And His Orchestra
Planet Jazz:Sidney Bechet | Planet Jazz | 2152063-2
Sidney Bechet With Michel Attenoux And His Orchestra
Planet Jazz:Sidney Bechet | Planet Jazz | 2152063-2

Zacharias,Helmut | (g,org,v,dreffects)
Helmut Zacharias
Ich Habe Rhythmus | Bear Family Records | BCD 15642 AH
Helmut Zacharias & His Sax-Team
Ich Habe Rhythmus | Bear Family Records | BCD 15642 AH
Helmut Zacharias mit dem Orchester Frank Folken
Ich Habe Rhythmus | Bear Family Records | BCD 15642 AH
Helmut Zacharias mit Kleiner Tanz-Besetzung
Ich Habe Rhythmus | Bear Family Records | BCD 15642 AH
Helmut Zacharias mit seinem Orchester
Ich Habe Rhythmus | Bear Family Records | BCD 15642 AH
Helmut Zacharias mit seinen Verzauberten Geigen
Ich Habe Rhythmus | Bear Family Records | BCD 15642 AH
Helmut Zacharias mit seiner Swing-Besetzung
Ich Habe Rhythmus | Bear Family Records | BCD 15642 AH
Helmut Zacharias Quintet
Ich Habe Rhythmus | Bear Family Records | BCD 15642 AH
Helmut Zacharias Sextet
Ich Habe Rhythmus | Bear Family Records | BCD 15642 AH

Zack,George | (p)
Muggsy Spanier And His Ragtime Band
Planet Jazz | Planet Jazz | 2169652-2

Zadlo,Leszek | (fl,sax,ssts)
Wolfgang Lackerschmid Group
Mallet Connection | Bhakti Jazz | BR 33

Zagnit,Stuart | (voc)
The Sidewalks Of New York
Tin Pan Alley:The Sidewalks Of New York | Winter&Winter | 910038-2

Zahn,Tilman | (oboe)
Miles Davis With Gil Evans Orchestra, The George Gruntz Concert Jazz Band And Guests
Miles & Quincy Live At Montreux | Warner | 9362-45221-2

Zaiter,Halim | (percvoc)
Nguyen Le Group
Maghreb And Friends | ACT | 9261-2

Zaja,Markus | (clsax)
Thomas Horstmann-Markus Zaja
Somewhere | Factory Outlet Records | 400004-2

Zaletilo,Marat | (tb)
European Jazz Youth Orchestra
Swinging Europe 1 | dacapo | DCCD 9449
Swinging Europe 2 | dacapo | DCCD 9450

Zamagni,Tony | (org)
Billy Boy Arnold Group
Eldorado Cadillac | Alligator Records | ALCD 4836

Zampello,Giampietro | (harp)
Richard Galliano With Orchestra
Passatori | Dreyfus Jazz Line | FDM 36601-2

Zanchi,Attilo | (b,el-b,cello,g,voicesynth)
Paolo Fresu Quintet
Night On The City | Owl Records | 013425-2
Melos | RCA | 2178289-2

Zapha,Zaf | (el-bmystic-pipe)
Cornelius Claudio Kreusch Group
Scoop | ACT | 9255-2

Zapolski String Quartet |
Jim Hall Jazzpar Quartet +4
Jazzpar 98 | Storyville | STCD 4230
Jim Hall With The Zapolski Quartet
Jazzpar 98 | Storyville | STCD 4230
The Crossover Ensemble With The Zapolski Quartet
Helios Suite | dacapo | DCCD 9459

Zapolski,Alexander | (v)
Jim Hall Jazzpar Quartet +4
Jazzpar 98 | Storyville | STCD 4230
Jim Hall With The Zapolski Quartet
Jazzpar 98 | Storyville | STCD 4230
The Crossover Ensemble With The Zapolski Quartet
Helios Suite | dacapo | DCCD 9459

Zapp,Markus | (voc)
Michael Riessler & Singer Pur with Vincent Courtois
Ahi Vita | ACT | 9417-2

Zapponi,Caterina | (voc)
Kristian Jorgensen Quartet With Monty Alexander
Meeting Monty | Stunt Records | STUCD 01212

Zaratzian,Harry | (stringsviola)
Grant Green With Orchestra
The Final Comedown(Soundtrack) | Blue Note | 581678-2
Gunther Schuller Ensemble
Beauty Is A Rare Thing:Ornette Coleman-The Complete Atlantic Recordings | Atlantic | 8122-71410-2
Ron Carter Quintet With Strings
Pick 'Em/Super Strings | Milestone | MCD 47090-2

Zarchy,Reuben 'Zeke' | (tp)
Benny Goodman And His Orchestra
Planet Jazz:Benny Goodman | Planet Jazz | 2152054-2
Planet Jazz:Female Jazz Vocalists | Planet Jazz | 2169656-2
Bob Crosby And His Orchestra
Swing Legens:Bob Crosby | Nimbus Records | NI 2011
Glenn Miller And His Orchestra
Planet Jazz:Glenn Miller | Planet Jazz | 2152056-2
Louis Armstrong With The Hal Mooney Orchestra
Ambassador Louis Armstrong Vol.17:Moments To Remember(1952-1956) | Ambassador | CLA 1917
Tommy Dorsey And His Orchestra
Planet Jazz:Frank Sinatra & Tommy Dorsey | Planet Jazz | 2152067-2

Zari,Eda | (voc)
Eda Zari With The Mark Joggerst Trio
The Art Of Time | Laika Records | 35100902

Zari,Pookie | (synth)
Lenny White Group
Renderers Of Spirit | Hip Bop | HIBD 8014

Zaslav,Bernard | (viola)
Stan Getz With The Richard Evans Orchestra
What The World Needs Now-Stan Getz Plays Bacharach And David | Verve | 557450-2

Zaum,Reinhard | (b,tubavoc)
Old Merrytale Jazz Band
The Very Best Of Dixieland Jazz | Verve | 535529-2

Zavala,Jimmy Z. | (tsharm)
Etta James & The Roots Band
Burnin' Down he House | RCA | 3411633-2

Zavod,Allan | (el-p,grand-p,org,synth,clavinet)
Jean-Luc Ponty Quartet
Cosmic Messenger | Atlantic | 7567-81550-2
The Very Best Of Jean-Luc Ponty | Rhino | 8122-79862-2
Jean-Luc Ponty Quintet
Cosmic Messenger | Atlantic | 7567-81550-2
The Very Best Of Jean-Luc Ponty | Rhino | 8122-79862-2
Jean-Luc Ponty Sextet
Enigmatic Ocean | Atlantic | 19110-2
Cosmic Messenger | Atlantic | 7567-81550-2
The Very Best Of Jean-Luc Ponty | Rhino | 8122-79862-2

Zawadi,Kiane | (euphoniumtb)
Freddie Hubbard Sextet
Wayne Shorter:The Classic Blue Note Recordings | Blue Note | 540856-2
Les McCann Group
Another Beginning | Atlantic | 7567-80790-2

Zawadzki,Krystof | (drcymbals)
Urszula Dudziak And Band Walk Away
Magic Lady | IN+OUT Records | 7008-2
Walkaway With Urszula Dudziak
Saturation | IN+OUT Records | 77024-2

Zawinul,Joe | (b-tp,p,el-p,farfisa,org,synth,g)
Ben Webster Quartet
The Jazz Giants Play Duke Ellington:Caravan | Prestige | PCD 24227-2
Cannonball Adderley Quartet
Ballads | Blue Note | 537563-2
Cannonball Adderley Quintet
Julian Cannonball Adderlry: Salle Pleyel/Olympia | Laserlight | 36126
Jazz Workshop Revisited | Capitol | 529441-2
Ballads | Blue Note | 537563-2
The Best Of Cannonball Adderley:The Capitol Years | Capitol | 795482-2
Mercy Mercy Mercy | Capitol | 829915-2
Cannonball Adderley Sextet
Jazz Workshop Revisited | Capitol | 529441-2
Ballads | Blue Note | 537563-2
Cannonball Adderley Birthday Celebration | Fantasy | FANCD 6087-2
Dizzy's Business-Live In Concert | Milestone | MCD 47069-2
Cannonball Adderley In New York | Original Jazz Classics | OJC20 142-2(RLP 9404)
Nippon Soul | Original Jazz Classics | OJC20 435-2(RLP 9477)
Cannonball Adderley-Nat Adderley Sextet
The Best Of Cannonball Adderley:The Capitol Years | Capitol | 795482-2
Coleman Hawkins Quartet
Late Night Sax | CBS | 487798-2
Dinah Washington With The Belford Hendricks Orchestra
What A Diff'rence A Day Makes! | Verve | 543300-2
Eddie Cleanhead Vinson With The Cannonball Adderley Quintet
Cannonball Adderley Birthday Celebration | Fantasy | FANCD 6087-2
Eddie 'Cleanhead' Vinson With The Cannonball Adderley Quintet | Milestone | MCD 9324-2
Joe Zawinul
To You With Love | Fresh Sound Records | Strand SLS CD 1007
Joe Zawinul Group
Zawinul | Atlantic | 7567-81375-2
Joe Zawinul Quartet
To You With Love | Fresh Sound Records | Strand SLS CD 1007
Joe Zawinul Trio
To You With Love | Fresh Sound Records | Strand SLS CD 1007
Katia Labeque-Joe Zawinul
Little Girl Blue | Dreyfus Jazz Line | FDM 36186-2
Miles Davis Group
Circle In The Round | CBS | 467898-2
In A Silent Way | CBS | 86556-2
Live-Evil | CBS | C2K 65135
Bitches Brew | CBS | C2K 65774
Nat Adderley Quartet
Naturally! | Original Jazz Classics | OJCCD 1088-2(JLP 947)
Nat Adderley Quintet
Joe Henderson:The Milestone Years | Milestone | 8MCD 4413-2
Nat Adderley Sextet
Joe Henderson:The Milestone Years | Milestone | 8MCD 4413-2
Weather Report
Mr. Gone | CBS | 468208-2
Black Market | CBS | 468210-2
Night Passage | CBS | 468211-2
Sweetnighter | CBS | 485102-2
Weathe Report Live In Tokyo | CBS | 489208-2
Heavy Weather | CBS | CK 65108
Yusef Lateef Orchestra
The Centaur And The Phoenix | Original Jazz Classics | OJCCD 721-2(RLP 9337)

Zayde,Jack | (v)
Ben Webster With Orchestra And Strings
Verve Jazz Masters 43:Ben Webster | Verve | 525431-2
Music For Loving:Ben Webster With Strings | Verve | 527774-2

Zayde,Jack prob. | (v)
Charlie Parker With Strings
Bird: The Complete Charlie Parker On Verve | Verve | 837141-2
Charlie Parker With The Joe Lipman Orchestra
Charlie Parker With Strings:The Master Takes | Verve | 523984-2
Charlie Parker Big Band | Verve | 559835-2

Zayde,Sylvan prob. | (v)
Charlie Parker With Strings
Bird: The Complete Charlie Parker On Verve | Verve | 837141-2

Zegler,Manuel | (bassoon)
George Russell And His Orchestra
Bill Evans:Piano Player | CBS | CK 65361
The Modern Jazz Society
A Concert Of Contemporary Music | Verve | 559827-2

Zehnder,Philipp A. | (perc)
Peter A. Schmid Trio With Guests
Profound Sounds In An Empty Reservoir | Creative Works Records | CW CD 1033
Q4 Orchester Project
Lyon's Brood | Creative Works Records | CW CD 1018-3
Yavapai | Creative Works Records | CW CD 1028-2

Zehrt,Holger | (drperc)
Greenfish
Perfume Light... | TipToe | TIP-888831 2

Zeitlin,Denny | (pp-solo)
Denny Zeitlin-Charlie Haden Duo
Time Remembers One Time Once | ECM | 1239
Denny Zeitlin-David Friesen
Live At The Jazz Bakery | Intuition Records | INT 3257-2

Zelig,Tibor | (v)
Charlie Haden Quartet West With Strings
The Art Of The Song | Verve | 547403-2

Zenker,Martin | (b)
Al Porcino Big Band
Al Porcino Big Band Live! | Organic Music | ORGM 9717
Conte Candoli Quartet
Candoli Live | Nagel-Heyer | CD 2024

Zentner,Si | (ld,tbb-tb)
Billy May And His Orchestra
Billy May's Big Fat Brass/Bill's Bag | Capitol | 535206-2
Louis Armstrong And His All Stars With Benny Carter's Orchestra
Ambassador Louis Armstrong Vol.17:Moments To Remember(1952-1956) | Ambassador | CLA 1917
Louis Armstrong With Benny Carter's Orchestra
Louis Armstrong-My Greatest Songs | MCA | MCD 18347
Louis Armstrong With The Hal Mooney Orchestra
Ambassador Louis Armstrong Vol.17:Moments To Remember(1952-1956) | Ambassador | CLA 1917
Mel Tormé With The Billy May Orchestra
Mel Tormé Goes South Of The Border With Billy May | Verve | 589517-2

Zerlett,Helmut | (synth)
Freddy Studer Orchestra
Seven Songs | VeraBra Records | CDVBR 2056-2

Zeroual,Rachid | (kawalanei)
Norbert Stein Pata Masters
Pata Maroc | Pata Musik | PATA 12(AMF 1063)

Zetterlund,Monica | (voc)
Monica Zetterlund With The Bill Evans Trio
The Complete Bill Evans On Verve | Verve | 527953-2
Monica Zetterlund With The Zoot Sims Quartet
Planet Jazz:Female Jazz Vocalists | Planet Jazz | 2169656-2

Zhelannaya,Inna | (gvoc)
Farlanders
The Farlander | JA & RO | JARO 4222-2

Ziad,Karim | (bendir,gumbri,karkabous,tarija,voc)
Karim Ziad Groups
Ifrikya | ACT | 9282-2
Nguyen Le Group
Maghreb And Friends | ACT | 9261-2
Nguyen Le Trio With Guests
Bakida | ACT | 9275-2
Purple:Celebrating Jimi Hendrix | ACT | 9410-2
Renaud Garcia-Fons
Navigatore | Enja | ENJ-9418 2
Renaud Garcia-Fons Group
Navigatore | Enja | ENJ-9418 2

Zickerick,Ralf 'Zicke' | (tb)
Brass Attack
Brecht Songs | Tutu Records | 888190-2*

Zieburg,Martin | (perc)
Hipsters In The Zone
Into The Afro-Latin Bag | Nabel Records:Jazz Network | CD 4663

Zieff,Robert 'Bob' | (arrld)
Anthony Ortega With The Robert Zieff Orchestra
Earth Dance | Fresh Sound Records | FSR-CD 325

Ziegler Holm,Finn | (cond)
Stan Getz With The Danish Radio Big Band
Stan Getz In Europe | Laserlight | 24657

Ziegler,Gerhart | (dr)
Dieter Bihlmaier Selection
Mallet Connection | Bhakti Jazz | BR 33

Ziegler,Manny | (bassoon)
Modern Jazz Quartet & Guests
MJQ 40 | Atlantic | 7567-82330-2

Ziegler,Matthias | (flpiccolo-fl)
James Newton
7.Zelt-Musik-Festival:Jazz Events | Zounds | CD 2730001
Peter A. Schmid Trio With Guests
Profound Sounds In An Empty Reservoir | Creative Works Records | CW CD 1033

Ziegler,Pablo | (p)
Astor Piazzolla-Gary Burton Sextet
The New Tango | Warner | 2292-55069-2

Zielinski,David | (ts)
Billy Boy Arnold Group
Eldorado Cadillac | Alligator Records | ALCD 4836

Zielke,Rolf | (p,celestawhistling)
Ray Blue Quartet
Always With A Purpose | Ray Blue Music | JN 007(RMB 01)
Rolf Zielke Trio Feat. Mustafa Boztüy
Rolf Zielke Trio Feat. Mustafa Boztüy | Jazz 'n' Arts Records | JNA 0602

Zigmont,Jerry | (tb)
Woody Allen And His New Orleans Jazz Band
Wild Man Blues | RCA | 2663353-2

Zigmund,Eliot | (drperc)
Bill Evans Quintet
The Complete Fantasy Recordings | Fantasy | 9FCD 1012-2
Bill Evans Trio
You Must Believe In Spring | Rhino | 812273719-2
Bill Evans:The Secret Sessions | Milestone | 8MCD 4421-2
The Complete Fantasy Recordings | Fantasy | 9FCD 1012-2
I Will Say Goodbye | Original Jazz Classics | OJCCD 761-2(F 9593)
Bill Evans-Toots Thielemans Quintet
Affinity | Warner | 7599-27387-2
Gary Peacock Trio
Shift In The Wind | ECM | 1165
Michel Petrucciani Trio
Live At The Village Vanguard | Blue Note | 540382-2
Pianism | Blue Note | 746295-2
Michel Petrucciani:The Blue Note Years | Blue Note | 789916-2

Zilioli,Gianni | (marimba)
Gerry Mulligan With Astor Piazzolla And His Orchestra
Tango Nuevo | Atlantic | 2292-42145-2

Zillner,Robby | (tb)
Brocksieper-Jazz-Ensemble
Drums Boogie | Bear Family Records | BCD 15988 AH
Brocksieper-Solisten-Orchester
Globetrotter | Bear Family Records | BCD 15912 AH
Brocksieper-Special-Ensemble
Globetrotter | Bear Family Records | BCD 15912 AH

Zimbalista,Chen | (perc)
SheshBesh
SheshBesh | TipToe | TIP-888830 2

Zimitti,Bob | (dr)
Gato Barbieri Orchestra
Latino America | Impulse(MCA) | 952236-2

Zimmer,Tony | (ts)
Tommy Dorsey And His Orchestra
Planet Jazz:Frank Sinatra & Tommy Dorsey | Planet Jazz | 2152067-2

Zimmerle,Dieter | (narration)
Bernd Konrad With Erwin Lehn und sein Südfunk Orchester Stuttgart
Wen Die Götter Lieben | Creative Works Records | CW CD 1010-1

Zimmerman,Fred | (b)
Don Senay With Orchestra And Strings
Charles Mingus-The Complete Debut Recordings | Debut | 12 DCD 4402-2
Thad Jones And His Orchestra
Charles Mingus-The Complete Debut Recordings | Debut | 12 DCD 4402-2

Zimmermann,Jack | (tb)
Gene Krupa And His Orchestra
Mullenium | CBS | CK 65678

Zimmermann,Jurek | (b-clbs)
Rainer Tempel Big Band
Album 03 | Jazz 'n' Arts Records | JNA 1102

Zimmermann,Jürgen | (bs)
Clark Terry With The Summit Jazz Orchestra
Clark | Edition Collage | EC 530-2

Zimmermann,Stephan | (tpfl-h)
All That Jazz & Helena Paul
All That Jazz & Helena Paul | Satin Doll Productions | SDP 1031-1 CD
Jazzensemble Des Hessischen Rundfunks
Jazz Messe-Messe Für Unsere Zeit | hr music.de | hrmj 003-01 CD

Zimmermann,Utz | (b-tb)
Berlin Contemporary Jazz Orchestra
Berlin Contemporary Jazz Orchestra | ECM | 1409

Zingg,Drew | (g)
Marcus Miller Group
Live & More | Dreyfus Jazz Line | FDM 36585-2

Zino,Dave | (b)
Bill Lowe/Philippe Crettien Quintet
Sunday Train | Konnex Records | KCD 5051

Zippert,Shari | (v)
Milt Jackson And His Orchestra
Reverence And Compassion | Reprise | 9362-45204-2

Zir,Isadore | (vviola)
Charlie Parker With Strings
Charlie Parker:The Best Of The Verve Years | Verve | 527815-2
Bird: The Complete Charlie Parker On Verve | Verve | 837141-2
Charlie Parker:April In Paris | Dreyfus Jazz Line | FDM 36737-2
Charlie Parker With The Joe Lipman Orchestra
Verve Jazz Masters 28:Charlie Parker Plays Standards | Verve | 521854-2
Charlie Parker With Strings:The Master Takes | Verve | 523984-2
Charlie Parker Big Band | Verve | 559835-2
Coleman Hawkins With Billy Byers And His Orchestra
The Hawk In Hi-Fi | RCA | 2663842-2
Harry Carney And His Orchestra With Strings
Music For Loving:Ben Webster With Strings | Verve | 527774-2
Wes Montgomery With The Jimmy Jones Orchestra
Wes Montgomery-The Complete Riverside Recordings | Riverside | 12 RCD 4408-2
The Jazz Giants Play Rodgers & Hart:Blue Moon | Prestige | PCD 24205-2

Zirelli,Enzo | (dr)
Ron Ringwood's Crosscut Bluesband
Earth Tones | Organic Music | ORGM 9722

Zirilli,Enzo | (drperc)
Scenario
Jazz The Beatles | Organic Music | ORGM 9729

Zisman,Michael | (bandoneon)
Horn Knox
The Song Is You | JHM Records | JHM 3625

Zitano,Jimmy | (dr)
Donald Byrd Quartet
Donald Byrd & Doug Watkins:The Tradition Sessions | Blue Note | 540528-2
Doug Watkins Trio
Donald Byrd & Doug Watkins:The Tradition Sessions | Blue Note | 540528-2

Zito,Fred | (tb)
Elliot Lawrence And His Orchestra
The Elliot Lawrence Big Band Swings Cohn & Kahn | Fantasy | FCD 24761-2
King Curtis Band
King Curtis-Blow Man Blow | Bear Family Records | BCD 15670 CI

Zito,Jimmy | (tp)
June Christy With The Pete Rugolo Orchestra
Something Cool(The Complete Mono & Stereo Versions) | Capitol | 534069-2
Tommy Dorsey And His Orchestra
Planet Jazz:Frank Sinatra & Tommy Dorsey | Planet Jazz | 2152067-2
Planet Jazz:Tommy Dorsey | Planet Jazz | 2159972-2

Zito,Ronnie | (dr)
Glenn Miller And His Orchestra
The Glenn Miller Orchestra In Digital Mood | GRP | GRP 95022
Helen Merrill With Orchestra
Casa Forte | EmArCy | 558848-2

Zito,Torrie | (arr,cond,el-p,keyboardsp)
Helen Merrill-Torrie Zito Duo
Casa Forte | EmArCy | 558848-2

Zlotkin,Frederick | (cello)
A Band Of Friends
Wynton Marsalis Quartet With Strings | CBS | CK 68921

Znidaric,Mia | (voc)
Steve Klink Funk Unit
Places To Come From,Places To Go | Minor Music | 801098
Steve Klink Trio
Places To Come From,Places To Go | Minor Music | 801098
Steve Klink-Mia Znidaric
Feels Like Home | Minor Music | 801092

Zoe,Muriel | (vocg)
Muriel Zoe Group
Red And Blue | ACT | 9416-2

Zoepf,Joachim | (b-cl,bs,fl,kontra-b-cl)
Kölner Saxophon Mafia
Mafia Years 1982-86 | Jazz Haus Musik | JHM 0058 CD

Zollar,James | (tpfl-h)
Marty Ehrlich Group
The Long View | Enja | ENJ-9452 2
Tom Harrell Orchestra
Time's Mirror | RCA | 2663524-2

Zoller,Attila | (g,bg-solo)
Attila Zoller
Zoller-Koller-Solal | MPS | 8431072
Attila Zoller Quartet
When It's Time | Enja | ENJ-9031 2
Attila Zoller Quintet
When It's Time | Enja | ENJ-9031 2
Attila Zoller-Hans Koller
Zoller-Koller-Solal | MPS | 8431072
Attila Zoller-Lee Konitz
When It's Time | Enja | ENJ-9031 2
Attila Zoller-Martial Solal
Zoller-Koller-Solal | MPS | 8431072
Attila Zoller-Wolfgang Lackerschmid
Live Highlights '92 | Bhakti Jazz | BR 28
Cal Tjader's Orchestra
Verve Jazz Masters 39:Cal Tjader | Verve | 521858-2
Talkin Verve/Roots Of Acid Jazz:Cal Tjader | Verve | 531562-2
Soul Burst | Verve | 557446-2
Hans Koller Quartet
Exclusiv | MPS | 9813440
Jutta Hipp Quintet
Deutsches Jazz Fesival 1954/1955 | Bear Family Records | BCD 15430
Klaus Doldinger Quintet
Doldinger's Best | ACT | 9224-2
Lajos Dudas Quartet
Jubilee Edition | double moon | CHRDM 71020
Paul Nero Sound
Doldinger's Best | ACT | 9224-2
Tony Scott Group
Tony Scott | Verve | 9861063
Wolfgang Lackerschmid-Donald Johnston Group
New Singers-New Songs | Bhakti Jazz | BR 31
Zoller-Koller-Solal Trio
Zoller-Koller-Solal | MPS | 8431072

Zoller, Thomas | *(alto-fl,bs,synth,fl,b-clsax)*
  Al Porcino Big Band
            Al Cohn Meets Al Porcino | Organic Music | ORGM 9705
  Joe Pass With The NDR Big Band
            Joe Pass In Hamburg | ACT | 9100-2
  Munich Saxophon Family
            Balanced | Edition Collage | EC 487-2
            Survival Song | JHM Records | JHM 3613

Zona Zul |
  Zona Sul
            Pure Love | Nagel-Heyer | CD 3039

Zonce, George | *(tp)*
  Buddy Rich Big Band
            Keep The Customer Satisfied | EMI Records | 523999-2

Zor, Isadore | *(viola)*
  Charlie Parker Quartet With Strings
            The Cole Porter Songbook | Verve | 823250-2

Zordan, Giovanni | *(viola)*
  Uri Caine With The Concerto Köln
            Concerto Köln | Winter&Winter | 910086-2

Zorn, John | *(arr,ld,as,game-calls,voc,voice,cl)*
  Alfred 23 Harth-John Zorn
            Willisau And More Live | Creative Works Records | CW CD 1020-2
  Batman
            Naked City | Nonesuch | 7559-79238-2
  John Zorn Group
            Spy Vs. Spy-The Music Of Ornette Coleman | Nonesuch | 7559-60844-2
            Spillane | Nonesuch | 7559-79172-2
  John Zorn Group With The Kronos Quartet
            Spillane | Nonesuch | 7559-79172-2

Zubek, Mark | *(bdr)*
  Mark Zubeck Quartet
            Horse With A Broken Leg | Fresh Sound Records | FSNT 078 CD
  Mark Zubeck Quintet
            Horse With A Broken Leg | Fresh Sound Records | FSNT 078 CD
  Stéphane Mercier Group
            Flor De Luna | Fresh Sound Records | FSNT 097 CD

Zuckermann, Ariel | *(fl)*
  World Quintet
            World Quintet | TipToe | TIP-888843 2
  World Quintet With The London Mozart Players
            World Quintet | TipToe | TIP-888843 2
  World Quintet With The London Mozart Players And Herbert Grönemeyer
            World Quintet | TipToe | TIP-888843 2

Zufferey, Roger | *(as)*
  Benny Carter And His Orchestra
            The Art Of Saxophone | Laserlight | 24652

Zulaica, Al | *(p)*
  Cal Tjader Quintet
            Talkin Verve/Roots Of Acid Jazz:Cal Tjader | Verve | 531562-2

Zulfikarpasic, Bojan | *(el-pp)*
  Karim Ziad Groups
            Ifrikya | ACT | 9282-2
  Nguyen Le Group
            Maghreb And Friends | ACT | 9261-2
  Nguyen Le Trio With Guests
            Purple:Celebrating Jimi Hendrix | ACT | 9410-2

Zullo, Frank | *(tp)*
  Louis Armstrong With The Casa Loma Orchestra
            Louis Armstrong:Swing That Music | Laserlight | 36056

Zum Vohrde, Jan | *(fl,alto-fl,ss,asreeds)*
  Miles Davis With The Danish Radio Big Band
            Aura | CBS | CK 63962
  Mona Larsen And The Danish Radio Big Band Plus Soloists
            Michael Mantler:Cerco Un Paese Innocente | ECM | 1556
  The Danish Radio Big Band
            Aura | CBS | CK 63962
  The Danish Radio Jazz Orchestra
            This Train:The Danish Radio Jazz Orchestra Plays The Music Of Ray Pitts | dacapo | DCCD 9428

Zurke, Bob | *(p)*
  All Star Band
            Planet Jazz:Jack Teagarden | Planet Jazz | 2161236-2
  Bob Crosby And His Orchestra
            Swing Legens:Bob Crosby | Nimbus Records | NI 2011
  Bob Crosby's Bobcats
            Swing Legens:Bob Crosby | Nimbus Records | NI 2011

Zwahlen, Jean-Philippe | *(g)*
  Michel Wintsch & Road Movie
            Michel Wintsch & Road Movie featuring Gerry Hemingway | Between The Lines | btl 002(Efa 10172-2)

Zwartz, Jonathan | *(b)*
  Vince Jones Group
            Here's To The Miracles | Intuition Records | INT 3198-2

Zweig, Barry | *(g)*
  Buddy Rich And His Orchestra
            Swingin' New Big Band | Pacific Jazz | 835232-2

Zwerin, Mike | *(b-tptb)*
  Miles Davis And His Orchestra
            The Complete Birth Of The Cool | Capitol | 494550-2

Zwiauerm, Wolfgang | *(el-b)*
  Christy Doran's New Bag With Muthuswamy Balasubramoniam
            Black Box | double moon | CHRDM 71022

Zwingenberger, Axel | *(celeste,celeste-solo,p-solo)*
  Axel Zwingenberger
            Kansas City Boogie Jam | Vagabond | VRCD 8.00027
            Boogie Woogie Breakdown | Vagabond | VRCD 8.78013
  Sippie Wallace/Axel Zwingenberger And The Friends Of Boogie Woogie Vol.1 | Vagabond | VRCD 8.84002
  Axel Zwingenberger And The Friends Of Boogie Woogie Vol.2 | Vagabond | VRCD 8.85005
            Boogie Woogie Live | Vagabond | VRCD 8.85007
            An Evening With Sippie Wallace | Vagabond | VRCD 8.86006
  Axel Zwingenberger And The Friends Of Boogie Woogie Vol.4: The Blues Of Mama Yancey | Vagabond | VRCD 8.88009
            Boogie Woogie Classics | Vagabond | VRCD 8.92023
            The Boogiemeisters | Vagabond | VRCD 8.99026
  Axel Zwingenberger With Big Joe Duskin
            Kansas City Boogie Jam | Vagabond | VRCD 8.00027
  Axel Zwingenberger With Champion Jack Dupree & Torsten Zwingenberger
            Axel Zwingenberger & The Friends Of Boogie Woogie Vol.6 | Vagabond | VRLP 8.90016
  Axel Zwingenberger With Teddy Ibing
            Boogie Woogie Breakdown | Vagabond | VRCD 8.78013
  Axel Zwingenberger With The Lionel Hampton Big Band
            The Boogie Woogie Album | Vagabond | VRCD 8.88008
  Axel Zwingenberger With The Mojo Blues Band And Red Holloway
            Axel Zwingenberger And The Friends Of Boogie Woogie,Vol.8 | Vagabond | VRCD 8.93019
  Axel Zwingenberger-Jay McShann Quartet
            Kansas City Boogie Jam | Vagabond | VRCD 8.00027
  Axel Zwingenberger-Sam Price
            Kansas City Boogie Jam | Vagabond | VRCD 8.00027
  Axel Zwingenberger-Torsten Zwingenberger
            Boogie Woogie Bros. | Vagabond | VRCD 8.88015
  Axel Zwingenberger-Vince Weber
            The Boogiemeisters | Vagabond | VRCD 8.99026
  Big Joe Turner With Axel Zwingenberger
            Let's Boogie Woogie All Night Long | Vagabond | VRCD 8.79012
            Boogie Woogie Jubilee | Vagabond | VRCD 8.81010
            Axel Zwingenberger And The Friends Of Boogie Woogie Vol.2 | Vagabond | VRCD 8.85005
  Champion Jack Dupree Group
            Champ's Housewarming | Vagabond | VRCD 8.88014
  Champion Jack Dupree-Axel Zwingenberger Group
            Axel Zwingenberger And The Friends Of Boogie Woogie Vol.7: Champion Jack Dupree Sings Blues Classics | Vagabond | VRCD 8.92018
  Estella Mama Yancey With Axel Zwingenberger
            Axel Zwingenberger And The Friends Of Boogie Woogie Vol.4: The Blues Of Mama Yancey | Vagabond | VRCD 8.88009
  Joe Newman With Axel Zwingenberger
            Axel Zwingenberger And The Friends Of Boogie Woogie Vol.2 | Vagabond | VRCD 8.85005
  Lloyd Glenn-Axel Zwingenberger
            Axel Zwingenberger And The Friends Of Boogie Woogie Vol.2 | Vagabond | VRCD 8.85005
  Sippie Wallace With Axel Zwingenberger
            Sippie Wallace/Axel Zwingenberger And The Friends Of Boogie Woogie Vol.1 | Vagabond | VRCD 8.84002
            An Evening With Sippie Wallace | Vagabond | VRCD 8.86006

Zwingenberger, Torsten | *(drperc)*
  Axel Zwingenberger With Champion Jack Dupree & Torsten Zwingenberger
            Axel Zwingenberger & The Friends Of Boogie Woogie Vol.6 | Vagabond | VRLP 8.90016
  Axel Zwingenberger-Torsten Zwingenberger
            Boogie Woogie Bros. | Vagabond | VRCD 8.88015
  Big Joe Turner With Axel Zwingenberger
            Let's Boogie Woogie All Night Long | Vagabond | VRCD 8.79012
            Axel Zwingenberger And The Friends Of Boogie Woogie Vol.2 | Vagabond | VRCD 8.85005
  Buddy Tate With The Torsten Swingenberger Swintet
            Tate Live | Nagel-Heyer | CD 080
  Champion Jack Dupree Group
            Champ's Housewarming | Vagabond | VRCD 8.88014
  Joe Newman With Axel Zwingenberger
            Axel Zwingenberger And The Friends Of Boogie Woogie Vol.2 | Vagabond | VRCD 8.85005
  Lyambiko And Her Trio
            Out Of This Mood | Nagel-Heyer | CD 2021

Teil 3
Labelverzeichnis

LEGENDE: **Label | Vertrieb**
Bestell-Nummer | Plattentitel **(Neuerfassungen: *FETT + KURSIV*)**
Interpret | Gruppe
Lied-Titel
Aufnahmeort und -datum (soweit bekannt)
Interpret(en) | Instrument(e)
Besondere Anmerkungen (soweit bekannt)

A&M Records | Universal Music Germany

395297-2 | CD | Apasionado
Stan Getz With Orchestra
Apasionado | Coba | Waltz For Stan | Madrugada | Amorous Cat | Midnight Ride | Lonely Lady
A&M Studios,?, rec. details unknown
Getz,Stan (ts) | Smith Jr.,Noland (tp) | Baptist,Rick (tp) | Bohanon,George (tb) | Young,Reginald (tb) | Johnson,Tommy (tuba) | Green,William (sax) | Barron,Kenny (p) | Lang,Mike (el-p,synth) | Del Barrio,Eddie (synth,cond,arr) | Neves,Oscar Castro (el-g) | Johnson,Jimmy (b) | Pocaro,Jeff (dr) | Da Costa,Paulinho (perc)
Espanola
Getz,Stan (ts) | Smith Jr.,Noland (tp) | Baptist,Rick (tp) | Bohanon,George (tb) | Young,Reginald (tb) | Johnson,Tommy (tuba) | Green,William (sax) | Barron,Kenny (p) | Lang,Mike (el-p,synth) | Del Barrio,Eddie (synth,cond,arr) | Landau,Michael (el-g) | Neves,Oscar Castro (el-g) | Johnson,Jimmy (b) | Pocaro,Jeff (dr) | Da Costa,Paulinho (perc)

395323-2 | CD | Multi Kulti
Don Cherry
Trumpet | Flute | Melodica | Piano-Trumpet | Multikulti Soothsayer Player
NYC, rec. 20.1.1990
Cherry,Don (p,birchwood-fl,melodica,pocket-tp)
Don Cherry Group
Multikulti Soothsayer
Santa Monica,CA, rec. 23.2.1990
Cherry,Don (doussn'-gouni,pocket-tp,voice) | Serafine,Frank (synth) | Hamilton,Anthony (voice) | A Watts Prophet (voice)
Birdboy
Hollywood,CA, rec. 27.12.1988
Cherry,Don (pocket-tp,pods) | Sims,Mark Loudon (b) | Price,John L. (dr-programming) | Cherry,David (synth)
Dedicated To Thomas Mapfumo
NYC, rec. 20.11.1989
Cherry,Don (pocket-tp,voice) | Ward,Carlos (as) | Apfelbaum,Peter (ts,marimba,cowbell) | Stewart,Robert 'Bob' (tuba) | Berger,Karl (marimba) | Blackwell,Ed (dr) | Vasconcelos,Nana (perc) | Sertso,Ingrid (voc)
Pettiford Bridge
Cherry,Don (pocket-tp,voice) | Ward,Carlos (as) | Stewart,Robert 'Bob' (tuba) | Blackwell,Ed (dr)
Until The Rain Comes
Berkeley,CA, rec. 7.11.1989
Cherry,Don (pocket-tp,voice) | Hieroglyphics Ensemble,The | Ortiz,Bill (tp,voice) | Cressman,Jeff (tb,voice) | Jones,Tony (ts) | Jones,Jessica (ts) | Allmond,Peck (bs) | Apfelbaum,Peter (ts,p,org,synth,bells,gong) | Bernard,Will (g) | Franks,Stanley (g) | Freeman,Bo (b) | Jones,Josh (dr,perc,cowbell,timbales,voice) | Clairborne,Deszon X. (dr) | Huffman,'Buddha' Robert (congas,bell-tree,voice) | Ekeh,Frank (djun-djun,shekere) | Sertso,Ingrid (voc)
Divinity-Tree
Cherry,Don (pocket-tp,voice) | Hieroglyphics Ensemble,The | Ortiz,Bill (tp,voice) | Cressman,Jeff (tb,voice) | Harvey,James (tb) | Jones,Tony (ts) | Jones,Jessica (ts) | Allmond,Peck (bs) | Apfelbaum,Peter (ts,p,org,synth,bells,gong) | Bernard,Will (g) | Franks,Stanley (g) | Freeman,Bo (b) | Jones,Josh (dr,perc,cowbell,timbales,voice) | Clairborne,Deszon X. (dr) | Huffman,'Buddha' Robert (congas,bell-tree,voice) | Ekeh,Frank (djun-djun,shekere)
Rhumba Multikulti
Berkeley,CA, rec. 8.11.1989
Cherry,Don (hand-claps,pocket-tp,voc) | Apfelbaum,Peter (ts,p,hand-claps,palitos,voc) | Jones,Josh (clave,hand-claps,voice) | Clairborne,Deszon X. (dr) | Huffman,'Buddha' Robert (tumbadora,voice) | Berger,Karl (voc) | Sertso,Ingrid (voc) | Engelhart,Claudia (voc) | Ginsberg,Allen (voc) | Knight,Caren (voc)

9861062 | CD | Roger Kellaway Cello Quartet | EAN 602498610626
Roger Kellaway Cello Quartet With The A&M Symphony Orchestra
Saturnia | Sunrise | Morning Song | Esque | On Your Mark,Get Set-Blues | Invasion Of The Forest
Hollywood,CA, rec. ca.1972
Kellaway,Roger (p) | Lustgarten,Edgar 'Ed' (cello) | Domanico,Chuck (b) | Richards,Emil (perc) | A&M Symphony Orchestra
Jorjana (No.2)
Hollywood,CA, rec. ca 1972
Kellaway,Roger (p) | Pass,Joe (g) | Lustgarten,Edgar 'Ed' (cello) | Domanico,Chuck (b) | Richards,Emil (perc) | A&M Symphony Orchestra
Jorjana(No.8)
Hollywood,CA, rec. ca.1972
Kellaway,Roger (p) | Pass,Joe (g) | Neufeld,Erno (v,concertmaster) | Lustgarten,Edgar 'Ed' (cello) | Domanico,Chuck (b) | Richards,Emil (perc) | A&M Symphony Orchestra

ACT | Edel Contraire

9003-2 | CD | One For All
The Real Group
We're Five | The Venture Of Living | I Found The Key | Walking Down The Street | Hard To Say Goodbye | The Wonderful World Of Sports | I Sing,You Sing | Splanky | Three Poems: | A Word- | Simplicity- | The Lost Jewel- | Small Talk | One Summer | Swedish Hit Medley: | Hooked On A Feling- | Dancing Queen- | It Must Have Been Love- | The Sign- | Cotton Eyed Joe-
Stockholm,Sweden, rec. 1998
Real Group,The: | Jalkéus,Margareta (voc) | Nordström,Katarina (voc) | Edenroth,Anders (voc) | Karlsson,Peder (voc) | Jalkéus,Anders (voc)
The Real Group With Toots Thielemans
For My Lady | Vem Kan Segla Förutan Vind
Real Group,The: | Jalkéus,Margareta (voc) | Nordström,Katarina (voc) | Edenroth,Anders (voc) | Karlsson,Peder (voc) | Jalkéus,Anders (voc) | Thielemans,Jean 'Toots' (harm)

9004-2 | CD | Nightsong
Sidsel Endresen-Bugge Wesseltoft
Chain Of Fools | Full Moon-High Noon | I Think It's Going To Rain Today | Every Moment | A Brand New Song | Is Somewhere Out There | To Treat Love Lightly | The Lady Is A Tramp | Psalm | Nightsong
Oslo,N, rec. 1994
Endresen,Sidsel (voc) | Wesseltoft,Jens Bugge (synth,grand-p,thumb-p)

9005-2 | CD | Est-From Gagarin's Point Of View
Esbjörn Svensson Trio(E.S.T.)
The Return Of Mohammed | Definition Of A Dog | The Chapel | From Gagarin's Point Of View | Cornette | Southwest Loner | Dating | Dodge The Dodo | Subway | In The Face Of Day
Atlantis Studio,?, rec. May-November 1998
Svensson,Esbjörn (keyboards,perc,grand-p) | Berglund,Dan (b,perc) | Öström,Magnus (dr,perc,mohammed)

9007-2 | CD | Winter In Venice
Calling Home | Winter In Venice | At Saturday | Semblance(part 1-5) | Don't Cuddle That Crazy Cat | Dammed Black Blues | In The Fall Of Things | As The Crow Flies | The Second Page | Hercules Jonssons Lat
Little Big Room,?, rec. 6.-8.10.1997
Svensson,Esbjörn (keyboards) | Berglund,Dan (b) | Öström,Magnus (dr)

9009-2 | CD | Good Morning Susie Soho
Somewhere Else Before | Do The Jangle | Serenity | The Wraith | Last Letter From Lithuania | Good Morning Susie Soho | Providence | Pavane 'Thoughts Of A Septuagenarian' | Spam-Boo-Limbo | The Face Of Love | Reminiscence Of A Soul
Atlantis Studio,?, rec. March/April 2000
Svensson,Esbjörn (p) | Berglund,Dan (b) | Öström,Magnus (dr)

9010-2 | CD | EST Plays Monk
Criss Cross | Bemsha Swing | Rhythm-A-Ning | In Walked Bud | Little Rootie Tootie | Eronel | Evidence | Crepuscule With Nellie
Stockholm,Sweden, rec. 1996
Svensson,Esbjörn (p,perc) | Berglund,Dan (b) | Öström,Magnus (dr)
Esbjörn Svensson Trio(E.S.T) With Strings
I Mean You | Round About Midnight
Svensson,Esbjörn (p,perc) | Berglund,Dan (b) | Öström,Magnus (dr) | Forsberg,Uli (strings) | Jansson,Ulrika (strings) | Arnberg,Elisabeth (strings) | Edström,Ulrika (strings)

9011-2 | CD | Strange Place For Snow
Esbjörn Svensson Trio(E.S.T.)
Serenade For The Renegade | Strange Place For Snow | Behind The Yashmak | Bound For The Beauty Of The South | Years Of Yearning | When God Created The Coffebreak | Spunky Sprawl | Carcrash
Atlantis Studio,?, rec. April 2001
Svensson,Esbjörn (p,keyboards) | Berglund,Dan (b) | Öström,Magnus (dr,perc)
The Message
Roam Studio,?, rec. December 2001
Svensson,Esbjörn (p,keyboards) | Berglund,Dan (b) | Öström,Magnus (dr,perc)

9012-2 | CD | Seven Days Of Falling | EAN 614427901224
Ballad For The Unborn | Seven Days Of Falling | Mingle In The Mincing-Machine | Evening In Atlantis | Did They Ever Tell Cousteau? | Believe Beleft Below | Elevation Of Love | In My Garage | Why She Couldn't Come | O.D.R.I.P.
Diesel/Superstudio Gul.?, rec. 2003
Svensson,Esbjörn (p) | Berglund,Dan (b) | Öström,Magnus (dr)

9100-2 | CD | Joe Pass In Hamburg
Joe Pass With The NDR Big Band
Polka Dots And Moonbeams | Love For Sale | Fragments Of Blues | Summer Night | Waltz For Django | More Than You Know | Lullaby Of The Leaves | Soft Winds | Sister Sadie
Hamburg, rec. 23.-27.4.1990
Pass,Joe (g) | NDR Big Band | Axelsson,Lennart (tp) | Burkhardt,Ingolf (tp) | Habermann,Heinz (tp) | Moch,Manfred 'Mannie' (tp) | Elam,Larry (tp) | Puschka,Rolf (tp) | Ahlers,Wolfgang (tb) | Plato,Herman (tb) | Schön,Arnold (tb) | Christmann,Egon (b-tb) | Bleibel,Wolfgang (as) | Wurster,Emil (as) | Ende,Harald (ts) | Schmidt-Relenberg,Markus (ts) | Von Dobrzynsky,Steffan (ts) | Zoller,Thomas (bs) | Schlüter,Wolfgang (vib) | Norris,Walter (p) | Lindholm,Lucas (b) | Riel,Alex (dr)
Joe Pass With The NDR Big Band And Radio Philharmonie Hannover
On A Clear Day You Can See Forever | For Nina | Indian Summer | Sweet Bossa | I'll Know | Star Eyes
Hamburg, rec. 17.-21.2.1992
Pass,Joe (g) | NDR Big Band | Axelsson,Lennart (tp) | Burkhardt,Ingolf (tp) | Lanese,Bob (tp) | Moch,Manfred 'Mannie' (tp) | Gallardo,Joe (tb) | Welch,Jon (tb) | MacInnes,Charles (tb) | Schön,Arnold (tb) | Christmann,Egon (b-tb) | Geller,Herb (as) | Wurster,Emil (as) | Ende,Harald (ts) | Schwaller,Roman (ts) | Böther,Andreas (ts) | Johnson,Howard (bs) | Schlüter,Wolfgang (vib) | Grube,Harry (p) | Lindholm,Lucas (b) | Haffner,Wolfgang (dr) | Radio-Philharmonie Hannover | details not on the cover

9212-2 | CD | Jazzpana
Los Jovenes Flamencos
El Vito Cante
Live at The 'Philharmonie',Köln, rec. 9.7.1992
Los Jovenes Flamencos | Ramon[El Portugues] (voc) | Canizares,Juan Manuel (flamenco-g) | Pardo,Jorge (fl,ss,ts) | Benavent,Carlos (b-g,mandola) | Dantas,Rubém (cajon,handclapping,tinaja) | Vargas,Joselin (cajon,handclapping) | Paco[El Americano] (handclapping)
Los Jovenes Flamencos With The WDR Big Band And Guests
Tangos | Entre Tinieblas | Tanguillo | Soy Gitano | Buleria | Suite Fraternidad: | Generalife- | Albacin- | El Vito En Gran Tamano
Köln, rec. July 1992
Los Jovenes Flamencos | Ramon[El Portugues] (voc) | Canizares,Juan Manuel (flamenco-g) | Pardo,Jorge (fl,ss,ts) | Benavent,Carlos (b-g,mandola) | Dantas,Rubém (cajon,handclapping,tinaja) | Vargas,Joselin (cajon,handclapping) | Paco[El Americano] (handclapping) | WDR Big Band And Guests | Haderer,Andreas 'Andy' (tp,fl-h) | Bruynen,Rob (tp) | Osterloh,Klaus (tp,fl-h) | Kiefer,Rick (tp,fl-h) | Marshall,John (tp,fl-h) | Horler,David (tb) | Nuß,Ludwig (tb) | Laukamp,Bernt (tb) | Deuvall,Roy (b-tb) | Joy,Andrew (fr-h) | Jurkievicz,Rainer (fr-h) | Van Driessche,Andre (fr-h) | Nickel,Hans (tuba) | Wiberny,Karl Heinz (fl,cl,ss,as,piccolo) | Rosenstein,Harald (fl,cl,ss,as) | Peters,Oliver (cl,ss,ts) | Römer,Rolf (cl,ss,ts) | Brecker,Michael (ts) | Schorn,Steffen (b-cl,bs) | Di Meola,Al (el-g) | Khan,Steve (el-g) | Kasper,Michael M. (cello) | Lange,Rainer (cello) | Jung,Albert (cello) | Schmeisser,Uwe (cello) | Szperalski,Gerhard (cello) | Ilg,Dieter (b) | Erskine,Peter (dr) | Santiago,Freddie (perc) | Mendoza,Vince (cond,arr)

9214-2 | CD | The African American Epic Suite:Music For Quintet And Orchestra
Yusef Lateef With Eternal Wind And The 'Kölner Rundfunk Orchester'
The African-American Epic Suite: | The African As Non-American- | Transmutation- | Love For All- | Freedom-
Köln, rec. 25.10.-3.11.1993
Lateef,Yusef (fl,alto-fl,ts,algaita,bamboo-fl,moan-fl,shannie) | Eternal Wind | Moore,Charles (fl-h,conch-shells,dumbek,shofar) | Jones,Ralph (fl,b-cl,ss,ts,bamboo-fl,hichiriki) | Ramos,Federico 'Freddy' (g,el-g,gimbre) | Rudolph,Adam (perc,bells,cymbals,didjeridoo,gongs,hand-dr,tablas,talking-dr,udu-clay | Kölner Rundfunkorchester | details unknown

9215-2 | CD | Sketches
Vince Mendoza With The WDR Big Band And Guests
Pavane | Sketches(part 1-8)
Köln
November/December 1993
Mendoza,Vince (cond,arr) | WDR Big Band | Haderer,Andreas 'Andy' (tp) | Bruynen,Rob (tp) | Osterloh,Klaus (tp) | Kiefer,Rick (tp) | Marshall,John (tp) | Horler,David (tb) | Berg,Henning (tb) | Laukamp,Bernt (tb) | Deuvall,Roy (b-tb) | Kedves,G. (fr-h) | Rasch,L. (fr-h) | Putnam,M. (fr-h) | Waldner,H. (tuba) | Mariano,Charlie (as) | Liebman,Dave (ss) | Wiberny,Heiner (as) | Rosenstein,Harald (as) | Peters,Olivier (ts) | Römer,Rolf (ts) | Neufang,Jens (bs) | Le,Nguyen (g) | Chastenier,Frank (p) | Ilg,Dieter (b) | Erskine,Peter (dr)

9219-2 | CD | Electricity
Bob Brookmeyer Group With The WDR Big Band
Farewell, New York | Ugly Music | White Blues | Say Ah | No Song | The Crystal Palace
Köln, rec. March 1991
Brookmeyer,Bob (v-tb,arr) | WDR Big Band | Haderer,Andreas 'Andy' (tp) | Osterloh,Klaus (tp) | Kiefer,Rick (tp) | Horler,David (tb) | Laukamp,Bernt (tb) | Deuvall,Roy (tb) | Wiberny,Heiner (sax) | Peters,Olivier (sax) | Römer,Rolf (sax) | Peucker,Paul (sax) | Abercrombie,John (g) | Brüninghaus,Rainer (keyboards) | Chastenier,Frank (keyboards) | Ilg,Dieter (b) | Gottlieb,Dan 'Danny' (dr)

9220-2 | CD | Europeana
Joachim Kühn And The Radio Philharmonie Hannover NDR With Jazz Soloists
Jazzpony No.1: | Castles In Heaven | Black Is The Color Of My True Love's Hair | The Shepherd Of Breton | The Ingrian Rune Song | The Groom's Sister | Norwegian Psalm | Three Angels | Heaven Has Created | She Moved Through The Fair | Crebe De Chet | Midnight Sun | Danny Boy (Londonderry Air) | Otra Jazzpana
Hannover, rec. September-November 1994
Radio Philharmonie Hannover NDR | Worlitzsch,Volker (v,concertmaster) | Wiemes,Theo (fr-h) | Boyd,Douglas (oboe) | Stoll,Martin (oboe) | Stockhausen,Markus (fl-h,piccolo-tp) | Bates,Django (tenor-h) | Mangelsdorff,Albert (tb) | Doldinger,Klaus (ss) | Lauer,Christof (ts) | Galliano,Richard (accordeon) | Kühn,Joachim (p) | Jenny-Clark,Jean-Francois (b) | Christensen,Jon (dr) | Gibbs,Michael (arr,comp,ld)

9221-2 | CD | Million Waves
Nguyen Le Trio
Mille Vagues | Trilogy | Be Good | Mango Blues | Butterflies & Zebras | Little Wing | El Saola | Sledge | Moonshine | I Feel Good
Zerkall, rec. December 1994
Le,Nguyen (el-g,E-bow,g-synth) | Ilg,Dieter (b,mouth-jive) | Gottlieb,Dan 'Danny' (dr,perc)

9222-2 | CD | Sol Mestizo:Markus Stockhausen Plays The Music Of Enrique Diaz
Markus Stockhausen Orchestra
Creation | Ilumination | Lonconao | Reflexion | Canto Indio | Zampona | Divinidad | Adentro | In Your Mind | Queca | Desolacion | Asfalto | La Conquista | Yemaye | Reconciliacion | Emanacion | Takirari
Zerkall, rec. 13.-15.2.1995
Stockhausen,Markus (tp,fl-h) | Stockhausen,Simon (ss,keyboards) | Dominguez,Chano (p) | Catherine,Philip (g) | Schmidt,Jochen (el-b) | Diaz,Enrique (b,voc) | Alkier,Thomas (dr) | Mandingo,Filipe (perc,voc) | Lascarro,Juanita (voc) | Naumann,Alexandra (voc) | Miranda,Pia (voc)

9223-2 | CD | Livo In Stockholm
Niels Landgren Funk Unit
Traci | Sound Check | Impressions | Cheyenne | Simple Life | The Chicken | Ain't Nobody | So What | Mr.M | Red Horn | Yo-Yo
Live at Jazz & Blues Festival And Jazzclub Fasching,Stockholm, rec. 4.-6.7.1994
Landgren,Nils (tb,voc) | Parker,Maceo (as,voc) | Janson,Henrik (g) | Mejlvang,Jesper (keyboards,voc) | Danielsson,Lars (el-b) | Lindvall,Per (tp,dr,perc) | Price,Magnum Coltrane (rap,voc) | Ugand,Jan (sound-wiz)

9224-2 | CD | Doldinger's Best
Klaus Doldinger Quartet
Blues For George
Hamburg, rec. 25.1.1963
Doldinger,Klaus (ts) | Hoffmann,Ingfried (org) | Kandlberger,Helmut (b) | Weiss,Klaus (dr)
Minor Kick
Live at The Blue Note, Berlin, rec. 17.12.1963
Doldinger,Klaus (ts) | Hoffmann,Ingfried (org) | Kandlberger,Helmut (b) | Weiss,Klaus (dr)
Klaus Doldinger-Peter Trunk
Two Getting Together
Doldinger,Klaus (ts) | Trunk,Peter (b)
Klaus Doldinger Septet
Quartenwaltzer
Köln, rec. 17.3.1969
Doldinger,Klaus (ts) | Kriegel,Volker (g) | Hoffmann,Ingfried (p) | Trunk,Peter (b) | Kandlberger,Helmut (b) | See,Cees (dr) | Sadi,Fats (perc)
Klaus Doldinger Quintet
Fiesta | Viva Brazilia
Berlin, rec. 14.3.1965
Doldinger,Klaus (ss,ts) | Zoller,Attila (g) | Hoffmann,Ingfried (p) | Trunk,Peter (b) | See,Cees (dr)
Klaus Doldinger Quartet
Saragossa
München, rec. 19.8.1968
Doldinger,Klaus (ss) | Hoffmann,Ingfried (p) | Kandlberger,Helmut (b) | See,Cees (dr)
Raga Up And Down(Variations On An Indian Scale)
München, rec. 16.8.1969
Doldinger,Klaus (ts) | Hoffmann,Ingfried (p) | Kandlberger,Helmut (b) | See,Cees (dr)
NDR-Workshop
Waltz Of The Jive Cats
Live at The NDR Jazz Workshop, Recklinghausen, rec. 26.6.1964
NDR-Jazz-Workshop | Bailey,Benny (tp) | Byrd,Donald (tp) | Eardley,Jon (tp) | Renard,Johnny (tp) | Sulieman[Leonard Graham],Idrees (tp) | Mangelsdorff,Albert (tb) | Peck,Nat (tb) | Persson,Ake (tb) | Thelin,Eje (tb) | Doldinger,Klaus (ts) | Griffin,Johnny (ts) | Kühn,Rolf (cl,ts) | Scott,Johnny (fl,cl,as) | Shihab,Sahib (fl,bs) | Hoffmann,Ingfried (org) | Cavalli,Pierre (g) | Orsted-Pedersen,Niels-Henning (b) | Johansen,Egil (dr) | Koller,Hans (cond)
Klaus Doldinger Jubilee
I Feel Free
München, rec. June 1969
Doldinger,Klaus (ts) | Kübler,Olaf (ts) | Quick,Joe (g) | Jackson,Jimmy (org) | Maid,Lothar (b-g) | Pap,Wolfgang (dr)
Stormy Monday Blues(They Call It Stormy Monday)
Montreux,CH, rec. 10.7.1977
Mann,Herbie (fl) | Newman,David Fathead (ss) | Doldinger,Klaus (ts) | Tee,Richard (p) | Ray,Brian (g) | Berlin,Jeff (b) | Jordan,Steve (dr) | James,Etta (voc)
Passport And Guests
Compared To What
Live at Onkel Pö's Carnegie Hall, Hamburg, rec. 28.8.1975
Passport | Doldinger,Klaus (ts) | Griffin,Johnny (ts) | Catherine,Philip (g) | Guy,Buddy (g) | McCann,Les (el-p) | Schulze,Kristian (org) | Schmid,Wolfgang (b-g) | Cress,Curt (dr) | York,Pete (perc)
Paul Nero Sound
Guachi Guaro(Soul Sauce)
München, rec. April 1970

ACT | Edel Contraire Bielefelder Katalog 688 Jazz • Ausgabe 2004 ACT | Edel Contraire

Doldinger,Klaus (ts) | Goykovich,Dusko (tp) | Schneider Essleben,Florian (fl) | Kübler,Olaf (fl) | Schwab,Sigi (g) | Meid,Lothar (b) | Inzalaco,Tony (dr) | Champbell,Charles (perc) | Szenkar,Claudio (perc)
Comin' Home Baby
Berlin, rec. 14.3.1965
Doldinger,Klaus (ts) | Von Dobrzynsky,Stefan (as) | Shihab,Sahib (bs) | Zoller,Attila (g) | Hoffmann,Ingfried (org) | Trunk,Peter (b) | Voormann,Klaus (b-g) | Kemp,Gibson (dr)

9225-2 | CD | Tales From Viet-Nam
Nguyen Le Group
Spring Of Life
Gimmick Studios,Paris,France, rec. October/November 1995
Le,Nguyen (g,el-g,fretless-g,g-synth,programming) | Fresu,Paolo (tp,fl-h) | Hansen,Simon S. (fl,sax,african-fl,bass-fl) | Nhien[Pham],Hao (dan-bau,sao-fl,sapek-clappers,zither) | Benita,Michel (b) | Verly,Francois (marimba,p,keyboards,perc) | Thanh,Huong (voc)
The Wind Blew It Away | The Banyan Tree Song | Mangustao(part 1)
Le,Nguyen (g,el-g,fretless-g,g-synth,programming) | Fresu,Paolo (tp,fl-h) | Hansen,Simon S. (fl,sax,african-fl,bass-fl) | Nhien[Pham],Hao (dan-bau,sao-fl,sapek-clappers,zither) | Benita,Michel (b) | Verly,Francois (marimba,p,keyboards,perc) | Thanh,Huong (voc) | Allouche,Joel (dr)
The Black Horse
Le,Nguyen (g,el-g,fretless-g,g-synth,programming) | Fresu,Paolo (tp,fl-h) | Hansen,Simon S. (fl,sax,african-fl,bass-fl) | Nhien[Pham],Hao (dan-bau,sao-fl,sapek-clappers,zither) | Benita,Michel (b) | Verly,Francois (marimba,p,keyboards,perc) | Thanh,Huong (voc) | Allouche,Joel (dr) | Argüelles,Steve (dr,perc)
Trong Com(The Rice Drum) | Mangustao(part 2)
Le,Nguyen (g,el-g,fretless-g,g-synth,programming) | Fresu,Paolo (tp,fl-h) | Hansen,Simon S. (fl,sax,african-fl,bass-fl) | Nhien[Pham],Hao (dan-bau,sao-fl,sapek-clappers,zither) | Benita,Michel (b) | Verly,Francois (marimba,p,keyboards,perc) | Thanh,Huong (voc) | Argüelles,Steve (dr,perc)
Don't You Go Away My Friend
Le,Nguyen (g,el-g,fretless-g,g-synth,programming) | Fresu,Paolo (tp,fl-h) | An,Thai (moon-fl) | Hansen,Simon S. (fl,sax,african-fl,bass-fl) | Nhien[Pham],Hao (dan-bau,sao-fl,sapek-clappers,zither) | Benita,Michel (b) | Verly,Francois (marimba,p,keyboards,perc) | Thanh,Huong (voc) | Argüelles,Steve (dr,perc)
Hen Ho(Promise Of A Date) | Ting Ning
Le,Nguyen (g,el-g,fretless-g,g-synth,programming) | Fresu,Paolo (tp,fl-h) | Hansen,Simon S. (fl,sax,african-fl,bass-fl) | Nhien[Pham],Hao (dan-bau,sao-fl,sapek-clappers,zither) | Benita,Michel (b) | Verly,Francois (marimba,p,keyboards,perc) | Thanh,Huong (voc) | Gurtu,Trilok (dr,perc)

9226-2 | CD | Gotland
Nils Landgren-Tomasz Stanko
Gotland | Tjelvar | Olu | Guldrupe | Ainbusk | Vänge | Rank
Oskarskyrkan,Stockholm,Sweden, rec. details unknown
Landgren,Nils (tb) | Stanko,Tomasz (tp)
Nils Landgren-Tomasz Stanko With Anders Eljas And Claus Bantzer
Den Blomstertid Nu Kommer | Alskar Barnet Modernfamnen | Emil Kahl
Johanneskirche, Hamburg, rec. details unknown
Landgren,Nils (tb) | Stanko,Tomasz (tp) | Eljas,Anders (org) | Bantzer,Claus (org)

9227-2 | CD | Temurá
Javier Paxarino Group With Glen Velez
Conductus Mundi | Cortesanos | Preludio Y Danza | Canto Del Viento | Suspiro Del Moro | Rueda Del Juglar | Tierra Baja | Reyes Y Reinas | Temurá | Mater Aurea
Lanave Studio,?, rec. details unknown
Paxarino,Javier (fl,cl,ss,bass-fl,nay,shakuhachi,ti-tze) | Prittwitz,Andreas (cl,recorder) | Saiz,Suso (keyboards,hypnotics,ti-bow) | Laguillo (p,keyboards,voice) | Dominguez,Chano (p) | Ifrim,Christian (v,viola) | Martinez,Naldo (b) | Velez,Glen (bendir,bodharan,caxixis,mirzab,riq,shakers,tar) | Guerrero,Pablo (latin-lacution,voice) | Di Geraldo,Tino (g,b-g,cajon,darhuka) | De Mulder,J.Carlos (archlute,vihuela) | De SouzamRogerio (caxixis,chimes,surdo) | Estevan,Pedro (redoubling-dr) | Psonis,Dimitri (baglamá,santuri,tzuraz) | Iglesias,Alberto (sample,string-arr)

9228-2 | CD | Blue Corner
Jasper Van't Hof Group
Blue Bells(for Sam Francis) | Blau Klang(for Ernst W. Nay) | 'U'(for Francis Picabia) | Before Birth(for Joseph Beuys) | Blue Corner(for Bettina Blohm) | Two Brothers(for Gilbert + George) | Gog(for Emil Schumacher) | L'Epoque Bleue(for Ives Klein) | Another Night In Tunisia(for Georg Baselitz) | Icarus(for Henri Matisse) | Fate[Subo](for Konrad Klapheck) | Black Is The Color Of My True Love's Hair
details unknown, rec. details unknown
Van't Hof,Jasper (p,keyboards) | Malach,Bob (ts) | Krantz,Wayne (g) | Fiszman,Nicolas (b) | Allaert,Philippe (dr)

9232-2 | CD | NDR Big Band-Bravissimo
Johnny Griffin With The NDR Big Band
The Cat
NDR Hamburg, rec. 18.9.1992
Griffin,Johnny (ts) | NDR Big Band | Axelsson,Lennart (tp) | Burkhardt,Ingolf (tp) | Faber,Johannes (tp) | Moch,Manfred 'Mannie' (tp) | Gallardo,Joe (tb) | Plettendorf,Uli (tb) | Schön,Arnold (tb) | Christmann,Egon (b-tb) | Geller,Herb (as) | Wuster,Emil (as) | Schwaller,Roman (ts) | Coburger,Gabriel (ts) | Johnson,Howard (bs) | Schlüter,Wolfgang (vib,marimba) | Di Gioia,Roberto (p) | Diez,Stephan (g) | Lindholm,Lucas (b) | Tanggaard,Aage (dr) | Mühlbradt,Horst (arr) | Glawischnig,Dieter (cond)
NDR Big Band
Blue Monk
NDR Hamburg, rec. 1.3.1991
NDR Big Band | Axelsson,Lennart (tp) | Burkhardt,Ingolf (tp) | Faber,Johannes (tp) | Moch,Manfred 'Mannie' (tp) | Gallardo,Joe (tb) | Breuer,Hermann (tb) | Schön,Arnold (tb) | Christmann,Egon (b-tb) | Geller,Herb (as) | Büchner,Lutz (as) | Skidmore,Alan (ts) | Ende,Harald (ts) | Johnson,Howard (bs) | Schlüter,Wolfgang (vib) | Tracey,Stan (p,arr) | Diez,Stephan (g) | Lindholm,Lucas (b) | Gruvstedt,Lennart (dr) | Glawischnig,Dieter (cond)
Voodoo Chile
NDR Hamburg, rec. 23.4.1993
NDR Big Band | Axelsson,Lennart (tp) | Burkhardt,Ingolf (tp) | Faber,Johannes (tp) | Moch,Manfred 'Mannie' (tp) | Gallardo,Joe (tb) | Ahlers,Wolfgang (tb) | Grossmann,Manfred (tb) | Christmann,Egon (b-tb) | Geller,Herb (as) | Wurster,Emil (as) | Weniger,Peter (ts) | Schmidt-Relenberg,Tobias (ts) | Herzog,Edgar (bs) | Johnson,Howard (arr,tuba) | Schlüter,Wolfgang (vib,marimba) | Sendecki,Vladislaw (p) | Diez,Stephan (g) | Lindholm,Lucas (b) | Alkier,Thomas (dr) | Doctor,Marcio (perc) | Glawischnig,Dieter (cond)
Heinz Sauer Quartet With The NDR Big Band
Sagma
Live at The Fabrik,Hamburg, rec. 2.4.1989
Sauer,Heinz (ts) | Degen,Bob (p) | Lenz,Günter (b) | Stephenson,Ronnie (dr) | NDR Big Band | Niezgoda,Manfred (tp) | Moch,Manfred 'Mannie' (tp) | Habermann,Heinz (tp) | Kubatsch,Paul (tp) | Ahlers,Wolfgang (tb) | Grossmann,Manfred (tb) | Plato,Herman (tb) | Christmann,Egon (b-tb) | Geller,Herb (as) | Wurster,Emil (as) | Ment,Jochen (as) | Ende,Harald (ts) | Rönfeld,Werner (bs) | Schlüter,Wolfgang (vib,marimba) | Schultze,Heinz (g) | Freund,Joki (arr) | Glawischnig,Dieter (cond)
A Night In Tunisia
NDR Hamburg, rec. 24.6.1994
NDR Big Band | Axelsson,Lennart (tp) | Burkhardt,Ingolf (tp) | Faber,Johannes (tp) | Stötter,Claus (tp) | Gallardo,Joe (tb) | Danner,Michael (tb) | Christmann,Egon (tb) | Schmid,Lucas (b-tb) | Böther,Andreas (as) | Pfeiffer-Galilea,Stefan (as) | Lauer,Christof (ts) | Büchner,Lutz (ts) | Johnson,Howard (bs) | Schlüter,Wolfgang (vib) | Norris,Walter (p) | Diez,Stephan (g) | Lindholm,Lucas (b) | Haffner,Wolfgang (dr) | Doctor,Marcio (perc) | Mühlbradt,Horst (arr) | Glawischnig,Dieter (cond)
Take The 'A' Train
NDR Hamburg, rec. 28.3.1991
NDR Big Band | Axelsson,Lennart (tp) | Burkhardt,Ingolf (tp) | Faber,Johannes (tp) | Moch,Manfred 'Mannie' (tp) | Gallardo,Joe (tb) | Ahlers,Wolfgang (tb) | Grossmann,Manfred (tb) | Christmann,Egon (b-tb) | Büchner,Lutz (as) | Aspery,Ron (as) | Schwaller,Roman (ts) | Ende,Harald (ts) | Johnson,Howard (bs) | Gray,Steve (p,arr) | Diez,Stephan (g) | Lindholm,Lucas (b) | Tracey,Clark (dr) | Glawischnig,Dieter (cond)
Albert Mangelsdorff With The NDR Big Band
Supraconductivity | Mood Indigo
Live at The Fabrik,Hamburg, rec. 28.1.1993
Mangelsdorff,Albert (tb) | NDR Big Band | Axelsson,Lennart (tp) | Burkhardt,Ingolf (tp) | Faber,Johannes (tp) | Moch,Manfred 'Mannie' (tp) | Gallardo,Joe (tb) | Ahlers,Wolfgang (tb) | Grossmann,Manfred (tb) | Christmann,Egon (b-tb) | Wurster,Emil (as) | Büchner,Lutz (as) | Coburger,Gabriel (ts) | Lauer,Christof (ts) | Johnson,Howard (bs) | Schlüter,Wolfgang (vib,marimba) | Gessinger,Nils (p) | Diez,Stephan (g) | Lindholm,Lucas (b) | Haffner,Wolfgang (dr) | Freund,Joki (arr) | Hammerschmid,Hans (arr) | Glawischnig,Dieter (cond)
Joe Pass With The NDR Big Band
Sister Sadie
NDR Hamburg, rec. 27.11.1992
Pass,Joe (g) | NDR Big Band | Axelsson,Lennart (tp) | Burkhardt,Ingolf (tp) | Faber,Johannes (tp) | Moch,Manfred 'Mannie' (tp) | Gallardo,Joe (tb) | Schön,Arnold (tb) | Ahlers,Wolfgang (tb) | Christmann,Egon (b-tb) | Geller,Herb (as) | Wurster,Emil (as) | Schwaller,Roman (ts) | Curtis,Stuart (ts) | Johnson,Howard (bs) | Jasper,Lex (p,arr) | Lindholm,Lucas (b) | Stephenson,Ronnie (dr) | Glawischnig,Dieter (cond)
Chet Baker With The NDR-Bigband
Django
NDR Hamburg, rec. 28.4.1988
Baker,Chet (tp) | NDR Big Band | Axelsson,Lennart (tp) | Moch,Manfred 'Mannie' (tp) | Habermann,Heinz (tp) | Lanese,Bob (tp) | Ahlers,Wolfgang (tb) | Grossmann,Manfred (tb) | Plato,Herman (tb) | Christmann,Egon (b-tb) | Geller,Herb (as) | Böther,Andreas (as) | Ende,Harald (ts) | Wurster,Emil (ts) | Nagurski,Klaus (bs) | Schlüter,Wolfgang (vib,marimba) | Norris,Walter (p) | Schröder,John (g) | Lindholm,Lucas (b) | Tanggaard,Aage (dr) | Mühlbradt,Horst (arr) | Glawischnig,Dieter (cond)
NDR Big Band
Descent
NDR Hamburg, rec. 4.3.1993
NDR Big Band | Axelsson,Lennart (tp) | Burkhardt,Ingolf (tp) | Faber,Johannes (tp) | Maaß,Torsten (tp) | Gallardo,Joe (tb) | Ahlers,Wolfgang (tb) | Christmann,Egon (tb) | Schmid,Lucas (b-tb) | Wuster,Emil (as) | Pfeiffer-Galilea,Stefan (as) | Lauer,Christof (ts) | Böther,Andreas (ts) | Johnson,Howard (bs) | Schlüter,Wolfgang (vib,marimba) | Degen,Bob (p) | Schröder,John (g) | Lindholm,Lucas (b) | Dekker,Hans (dr) | Hübner,Ralf-R. (arr) | Glawischnig,Dieter (cond)

9234-2 | CD | The Theatre Of Kurt Weil
Mack The Knife(Moritat) | Dance Of The Tumblers | Alabama Song | Speak Low | Surabaya Johnny | Bilbao Song | Lost In The Stars | My Ship | Mack The Knife(Moritat,alt-take))
Live at The Rolf Liebermann Studio,?, rec. 10.3.2000
NDR Big Band | Axelsson,Lennart (tp) | Burkhardt,Ingolf (tp) | Stötter,Claus (tp) | Winterschladen,Reiner (tp) | Gallardo,Joe (tb) | Neudert,Jürgen (tb) | Lottermann,Stefan (tb) | Müller,Rainer (tb) | Felsch,Fiete (reeds) | Bolte,Peter (reeds) | Lauer,Christof (reeds) | Büchner,Lutz (reeds) | Argüelles,Julian (reeds) | Sendecki,Vladislaw (p) | Diez,Stephan (g) | Lindholm,Lucas (b) | Haffner,Wolfgang (dr) | Doctor,Marcio (perc) | Towns,Colin (cond,arr)

9235-2 | CD | Future Miles
Tim Hagans With Norrbotten Big Band
Fanfare For Miles | Kickass | Kinsey Report | Big Gig In Pajala | Miles Of The Blues | Concrete Hat | Future Cool | Boogaloo
Musikhögskolan I Pitea,Sweden, rec. 15.6.2000
Hagans,Tim (tp) | Strandberg,Bo (tp,fl-h) | Johansson,Dan (tp,fl-h) | Ekholm,Magnus (tp,fl-h) | Maunuvaara,Tapio (tp,fl-h) | Svanström,P-O (tb) | Puls,Magnus (tb) | Dahlgren,Peter (tb) | Hängsel,Björn (b-tb,tuba) | Broström,Hakan (fl,ss,as) | Hörlen,Johan (b-cl,as) | Garberg,Mats (fl,ts) | Ek,Bengt (cl,ts) | Moberg,Per (fl,bs) | Baciu,Ion (p) | Kinsey,Scott (keyboards,programming) | Jonsson,Fredrik (b) | Holgersson,Jones (dr)

9236-2 | CD | Korall
Geir Lysne Listening Ensemble
M.B. | Djambo | Theme For O.J. | P.T.1 | Korall
Oslo,N, rec. 6.-8.11.2001
Lysne,Geir (comp,cond) | Brohdal,Frank (tp,fl-h) | Haltli,Marius (tp,fl-h) | Myklebust,Ole Jorn (tp,fl-h) | Baur,Eckhard (tp,fl-h) | Sunde,Helge (tb) | Jaksjo,Christian (tb) | Gierde,Jorgen (tb) | Hovland,Ketil (b-tb) | Einarsen,Ketil V. (fl,piccolo) | Halle,Morton (fl,ss,as) | Graf,Klaus (fl,as) | Maile,Andreas 'Andi' (fl,ts) | Jensen,Fredrik O. (ts,bs) | Seland,Bernhard (b-cl,bs) | Oien,Jorn (keyboards) | Bratberg,Hallgrim (g) | Renvag,Jan Olav (b,el-b) | Aalefjaer,Knut (dr,perc) | Ekornes,Kenneth (dr,perc)
Ingen Vinner Frem Til Den Evige Ro
Lysne,Geir (comp,cond) | Brohdal,Frank (tp,fl-h) | Haltli,Marius (tp,fl-h) | Myklebust,Ole Jorn (tp,fl-h) | Baur,Eckhard (tp,fl-h) | Sunde,Helge (tb) | Jaksjo,Christian (tb) | Gierde,Jorgen (tb) | Hovland,Ketil (b-tb) | Einarsen,Ketil V. (fl,piccolo) | Halle,Morton (fl,ss,as) | Graf,Klaus (fl,as) | Maile,Andreas 'Andi' (fl,ts) | Jensen,Fredrik O. (ts,bs) | Seland,Bernhard (b-cl,bs) | Oien,Jorn (keyboards) | Bratberg,Hallgrim (g) | Renvag,Jan Olav (b,el-b) | Aalefjaer,Knut (dr,perc) | Ekornes,Kenneth (dr,perc) | Bratland,Sondre (voc)
-> Note: Charles McPherson & Sonny Rollins titles are only on the LP-version

9242-2 | CD | Bernard Purdie's Soul To Jazz
Bernard Purdie's Soul To Jazz
Moanin' | Supersition | Iko-Iko | Senor Blues | When A Man Loves A Woman | Freedom Jazz Dance | Sidewinder | Brother Where Are You | Wade In The Water | Work Song | Land Of 1000 Dancers | Moanin'(alt.take)
Köln, rec. 5.-15.3.1996
Purdie,Bernard 'Pretty' (dr) | Brecker,Randy (tp,fl-h) | Marshall,John (tp) | Brecker,Michael (sax) | Harris,Eddie (sax) | Landgren,Nils (tb) | Brown,Dean (g) | Chastenier,Frank (p,keyboards) | Goldstein,Gil (p,accordeon) | King,Dave (el-b) | WDR Big Band | Moss,Martin (voc) | Comerford,Jane (voc) | Pryce,Sharlie (voc) | details unknown

9243-2 | CD | Paint It Blue:A Tribute To Cannonball Adderley
Nils Landgren Funk Unit
Walk Tall | You Dig | Why Am I Treated So Bad | Another Nat | Inside Straight | Cannonball | Mercy, Mercy, Mercy | Mother Fonk | Primitivo | After The Party | Love All,Serve All | Julian
details unknown, rec. details unknown
Landgren,Nils (tp,tb) | Brecker,Randy (tp,fl-h) | Brönner,Till (tp) | Schorn,Steffen (b-cl) | Johansson,Per 'Ruskträsk' (sax) | Brecker,Michael (ts) | Janson,Henrik (g) | Svensson,Esbjörn (keyboards) | Price,Magnum Coltrane (synth,voc) | Danielsson,Lars (el-b) | Purdie,Bernard 'Pretty' (dr) | Moreira,Airto (perc) | Doctor,Marcio (perc)

9245-2 | CD | Nguyen Le:3 Trios
Nguyen Le Trio
Silk | Dance For The Comet | La Parfum | Blue Monkey
München, rec. 12.10.1996
Le,Nguyen (g,el-g,g-synth) | Johnson,Marc (b) | Erskine,Peter (dr)
Silver | Kinderhund | Woof | Straight No Chaser
Amiens,France, rec. 28.10.1996
Le,Nguyen (el-g,g-synth) | Ilg,Dieter (b) | Gottlieb,Dan 'Danny' (dr)
Sand | Foow | Idoma
Paris,France, rec. 18.11.1996
Le,Nguyen (el-g,E-bow,fretless-g,g-synth) | Garcia-Fons,Renaud (b) | Cinelu,Mino (dr,perc)

9249-2 | CD | Eddie Harris-The Last Concert
Eddie Harris Group With The WDR Big Band
Sidewinder | Moanin' | Wade In The Water | Freedom Jazz Dance | Work Song | When A Man Loves A Woman | Gimme Some Lovin'
Live in Concert,Köln, rec. 14.3.1996
Harris,Eddie (ts) | Landgren,Nils (tb) | Brown,Dean (g) | King,Dave (b) | Gregory,Haywood J. (voc) | WDR Big Band | Haderer,Andreas 'Andy' (tp) | Bruynen,Rob (tp) | Osterloh,Klaus (tp) | Baldauf,Rüdiger (tp) | Marshall,John (tp) | Horler,David (tb) | Berg,Henning (tb) | Laukamp,Bernt (tb) | Deuvall,Roy (tb) | Wiberny,Heiner (reeds) | Rosenstein,Harald (reeds) | Peters,Olivier (reeds) | Römer,Rolf (reeds) | Neufang,Jens (reeds) | Chastenier,Frank (p,org) | Goldsby,John (b)
You Stole My Heart(The Last Encore)
WDR Köln, rec. 15.3.1996
Harris,Eddie (ts,voc) | Goldstein,Gil (p)

9253-2 | CD | Bernard Purdie's Soul To Jazz II
Bernard Purdie's Soul To Jazz
Sometimes I Feel Like A Motherless Child
NYC, rec. 24.-26.1.1997
Purdie,Bernard 'Pretty' (dr) | Turrentine,Stanley (ts) | Dupree,Cornell (g) | Green,Benny (p) | Banks,Stanley (el-b) | Benny Diggs Singers
Nobody Knows The Trouble I've Seen
Purdie,Bernard 'Pretty' (dr) | Crawford,Hank (as) | Dupree,Cornell (g) | Mance,Junior[Julian C.] (p) | Banks,Stanley (el-b) | Benny Diggs Singers
New Orleans Strut | Jubilation
Purdie,Bernard 'Pretty' (dr) | Herring,Vincent (as) | Dupree,Cornell (g) | Mance,Junior[Julian C.] (p) | Naha,George (g) | Banks,Stanley (el-b) | DeJohnette,Jack (dr) | Morales,Pancho (congas)
Joshua
Purdie,Bernard 'Pretty' (dr) | Crawford,Hank (as) | Johnson,Howard (bs) | Dupree,Cornell (g) | Green,Benny (p) | Naha,George (g) | Banks,Stanley (el-b)
La Place Street
Purdie,Bernard 'Pretty' (dr) | Crawford,Hank (as) | Turrentine,Stanley (ts) | Dupree,Cornell (g) | Green,Benny (p) | Banks,Stanley (el-b) | Morales,Pancho (congas)
Mr.Magic
Purdie,Bernard 'Pretty' (dr) | Crawford,Hank (as) | Dupree,Cornell (g) | Green,Benny (p) | Naha,George (g) | Banks,Stanley (el-b) | Morales,Pancho (congas)
Theme From 'Shaft'
Purdie,Bernard 'Pretty' (dr) | Walrath,Jack (tp) | Herring,Vincent (as) | Johnson,Howard (bs) | Dupree,Cornell (g) | Green,Benny (p) | Naha,George (g) | Banks,Stanley (el-b) | Morales,Pancho (congas)
Amen
Purdie,Bernard 'Pretty' (dr) | Herring,Vincent (as) | Crawford,Hank (as) | Dupree,Cornell (g) | Mance,Junior[Julian C.] (p) | Naha,George (g) | Banks,Stanley (el-b) | Morales,Pancho (congas)

9254-2 | 2 CD | The Birth+Rebirth Of Swedish Folk Jazz
Bengt-Arne Wallin Orchestra
Vallat | The First Time In The World I Saw Your Eyes | THe Exquisite Crystal- | Neckan's Reel- | Oh You Beautiful Vermland | Pekkos-Per's Wedding March | Vallat(2)- | Rural Song From The District Of Karleby,Swedish Finland- | In Our Pasture- | Like A Star In The Clear Sky | In The Firmament- | The Maiden Went To The Spring- | The Gaerdeby Tune
Europa Film Studios,Sweden, rec. 5.& 18.6.1962
Wallin,Bengt-Arne (tp,fl-h) | Sulieman[Leonard Graham],Idrees (tp) | Nilsson,Erik (bs) | Eriksson,Sixter (tp) | Renliden,Weine (tp) | Henderson,Bob (tb) | Eriksson,Rune (tb) | Medberg,Gunnar (tb) | Holmquist,Olle (tb) | Hurtig,Uno (b-tuba) | Nyström,Karl (fr-h) | Domnerus,Arne (cl,as) | Falk,Rune (b-cl,bs) | Shihab,Sahib (fl,bs) | Blomquist,Rolf (fl,cl,ts) | Gillblad,Per Olof (engl-h,oboe) | Bäckman,Rolf (as) | Nerem,Bjarne (ts) | Sandström,Yngve (fl,alto-fl,piccolo) | Orsin,Bartil (v) | Saulesco,Mirecea (v) | Herjö,Axel (v) | Genetay,Claude (cello) | Stangberg,Anna (harp) | Jägerhult,Christer (vib,marimba,bongos,glockenspiel,triangle) | Gustafsson,Rune (g) | Riedel,Georg (b) | Johansson,Egil (dr) | Teimar,Margit (voc)
Jazz Baltica Ensemble
Down By The Old Well | Backwood Mating | O'Thy Beautiful | The Maid Is Pretty | Riverbank Air | The Cow And The Fiddle
Live at JazzBaltica Festival,Salzau, rec. 13.6.1997
Lindgren,Lars (tp) | Majewski,Robert (tp) | Stanko,Tomasz (tp) | Landgren,Nils (tb) | Wogram,Nils (tb) | Perko,Jukka (ss,as) | Labutis,Vytautas (ss,as,bs) | Weniger,Peter (fl,ss,ts) | Goldschmidt,Per (bs) | Schlüter,Wolfgang (vib) | Wesseltoft,Jens Bugge (p) | Danielsson,Lars (b) | Kjellberg,Anders (dr) | Diers,Lisbeth (perc)

9255-2 | CD | Scoop
Cornelius Claudio Kreusch Group
Niles
NYC/Paris,France, rec. December 1996-November 1997
Kreusch,Cornelius Claudio (p,muted-p) | Osby,Greg (as) | Zapha,Zaf (el-b) | Atef,Cyril (dr,perc,mystic-pipe)
Yarum
Kreusch,Cornelius Claudio (p) | Osby,Greg (as) | Zapha,Zaf (el-b) | Atef,Cyril (dr,perc) | Grimes,Thomas (poetry,rap)
Salif
Kreusch,Cornelius Claudio (p,kalimba,muted-p) | Kreusch,Johannes Tonio (g) | Zapha,Zaf (el-b) | Atef,Cyril (dr,perc,cuica,kakabobe) | Kaita,Salif (voc)
Scoop
Kreusch,Cornelius Claudio (p) | Grimes,Thomas (scoop-vib) | Genus,James (b) | Calhoun,Will (dr,perc,jungle-dr)
Imbao
Kreusch,Cornelius Claudio (p,melodica,muted-p) | Watson,Robert 'Bobby' (as) | Blake,Ron (ts) | Zapha,Zaf (el-b,mystic-pipe) | Atef,Cyril (dr,perc,berimbao,voc) | Carrington,Terri Lyne (voc) | Grimes,Thomas (voive)
Pulse
Kreusch,Cornelius Claudio (p,muted-p) | Osby,Greg (as) | Zapha,Zaf (el-b) | Atef,Cyril (dr,perc,hand-dr,zarb)
Faith
Kreusch,Cornelius Claudio (p,muted-p) | Watson,Robert 'Bobby' (as) | Kreusch,Johannes Tonio (g) | Zapha,Zaf (el-b) | Atef,Cyril (dr,perc) | Gainer,Camille (cymbal,snare-dr) | Grimes,Thomas (voive) | Kontomanon,Elisabeth (voc)
Feel
Kreusch,Cornelius Claudio (p) | Cox,Anthony (b) | Carrington,Terri Lyne (dr,perc)
Wocai
Kreusch,Cornelius Claudio (p) | Osby,Greg (as) | Zapha,Zaf (el-b) | Atef,Cyril (dr,perc,tambourine)
Flame
Kreusch,Cornelius Claudio (muted-p) | Kreusch,Johannes Tonio (african-vib,prepared-g) | Calhoun,Will (clay-dr) | Bona,Richard (voc)
Nomad
Kreusch,Cornelius Claudio (p) | Osby,Greg (as) | Zapha,Zaf (el-b) | Atef,Cyril (dr,perc)
Jafro
Kreusch,Cornelius Claudio (p) | Osby,Greg (as) | Watson,Robert 'Bobby' (as) | Horbar,Max (as) | Blake,Ron (ts) | Cox,Anthony (b) | Genus,James (el-b) | Zapha,Zaf (el-b) | Calhoun,Will (dr,perc,afro-beat,cymbals) | Atef,Cyril (dr,snare-dr) | Carrington,Terri Lyne (tom-tom) | Grimes,Thomas (poetry,rap)

9259-2 | CD | 50 Years Of NDR Big Band:Bravissimo II
NDR Big Band With Guests
Round About Midnight
NDR Hamburg, rec. 12.6.1973
Mikkelborg,Palle (tp,ld) | Schlüter,Wolfgang (vib) | Lindholm,Lucas (b) | Stephenson,Ronnie (dr) | Krog,Karin (voc) | Paich,Marty (arr) | NDR Big Band | details not on the cover

My Funny Valentine
NDR Hamburg, rec. 1.6.1977
Bailey,Benny (tp) | Geller,Herb (fl) | Kovacev,Lala (dr) | Garcia,Russell (cond,arr) | NDR Big Band | details not on the cover
Come Sunday
NDR Hamburg, rec. 10.9.1984
Stanko,Tomasz (tp) | Sauer,Heinz (ts) | Schlüter,Wolfgang (vib) | Norris,Walter (p) | Stephenson,Ronnie (dr) | Boland,Francy (arr) | Glawischnig,Dieter (cond) | NDR Big Band | details not on the cover
Blues For Alice
NDR Hamburg, rec. 10.12.1984
Bailey,Benny (tp) | Pauer,Fritz (p) | Marshall,John (dr) | Burghardt,Victor (arr) | Glawischnig,Dieter (cond) | NDR Big Band | details not on the cover
This Old Fairy-Tale
NDR Hamburg, rec. 27.1.1988
Dennerlein,Barbara (org) | Riel,Alex (dr) | Wilson,Phil (arr) | Whigham,Jiggs (cond) | NDR Big Band | details not on the cover
After You've Gone
NDR Hamburg, rec. 3.6.1989
Geller,Herb (as) | Schlüter,Wolfgang (vib) | Riel,Alex (dr) | Holman,Bill (arr) | Glawischnig,Dieter (cond) | NDR Big Band | details not on the cover
Carpet Ride
NDR Hamburg, rec. 22.1.1990
Krog,Karin (voc) | Surman,John (ss,arr) | Marshall,Joe (dr) | Gruntz,George (cond) | NDR Big Band | details not on the cover
Piano Groove
NDR Hamburg, rec. 31.5.1991
Catherine,Philip (g) | Schlüter,Wolfgang (vib) | Castellucci,Bruno (dr) | Reith,Dieter (arr) | Glawischnig,Dieter (cond) | NDR Big Band | details not on the cover
Love For Sale
NDR Hamburg, rec. 27.11.1992
Pass,Joe (g) | Jasper,Lex (p) | Lindholm,Lucas (b) | Stephenson,Ronnie (dr) | Geller,Herb (arr) | Whigham,Jiggs (cond) | NDR Big Band | details not on the cover
O Vos Omnis
NDR Hamburg, rec. 3.9.1993
Joao,Maria (voc) | Laginha,Mario (arr) | Glawischnig,Dieter (cond) | NDR Big Band | details not on the cover
Mosher
NDR Hamburg, rec. 24.11.1995
Burton,Gary (vib) | Lauer,Christof (ts) | Alkier,Thomas (dr) | Gibbs,Michael (cond,arr) | NDR Big Band | details not on the cover
Red Horn
NDR Hamburg, rec. 23.9.1997
Landgren,Nils (tb) | Diez,Stephan (g) | Sendecki,Vladislaw (p) | Lindholm,Lucas (b) | Brown,Gerry (dr) | Fahlström,Örjan (arr) | Glawischnig,Dieter (cond) | NDR Big Band | details not on the cover

9260-2 | CD | It's Snowing On My Piano
Bugge Wesseltoft
It's Snowing On My Piano | In Dulci Jubilo | Mitt Hjerte Alltid Vanker | Deiling Er Jorden | O Little Town Of Bethlehem | Du Gronne,Glitrende Tre | Det Kimer Na Til Julefest | What Child Is This(Greensleeves) | Kimer,I Klokker | Es Ist Ein Ros Entsprungen | Stille Nacht | Into Eternal Silence
Oslo,N, rec. 15./16.10.1997
Wesseltoft,Jens Bugge (p-solo)

9261-2 | CD | Maghreb And Friends
Nguyen Le Group
Ifrikyia | Constantine | Louanges | Yhadik Allah | Nora | FunkRai | L'Harka Li Jeya | Guinia | Nesraf
Yerres, France, rec. February/March 1998
Le,Nguyen (g,el-g,fretless-b,programming,viatnamese-zither) | Zulfikarpasic,Bojan (p) | Ziad,Karim (dr,perc,gumbri,voc) | Alibo,Michel (b) | Houariyat,B'net (perc,voc) | Bani,Zahra (perc,voc) | Haliba,Kadija (perc,voc) | Rhami,Malika (perc,voc) | Madrani,Saida (perc,voc) | Zaiter,Halim (perc,voc) | Fresu,Paolo (tp) | Nhien[Pham],Hao (vietnamese-fl) | Wagué,Aly (africa-pleul-fl,voc) | Debiossat,Alain (ss) | Di Battista,Stefano (ss,as) | Puschnig,Wolfgang (as) | Mami,Cheb (accordeon-synth) | Abdenour,Djemai (algerian-bj,mandola) | Ftati,Mejdoub (v) | Menni,Mohamed (perc,voc) | Avenel,Jean-Jacques (cora) | Sahmaoui,Aziz (voc) | Askeur,Mahdi (voc) | Thanh,Huong (voc) | Hervé,Gaelle (voc) | Hervé,Marielle (voc)

9265-2 | CD | Live In Montreux
Nils Landgren Funk Unit
Traci | Walk Tall | Professor Longhair | Mercy, Mercy, Mercy | Ain't Nobody | You Dig | Ack Värmeland Du Sköna | Compared To What | Gärdebylaten
Montreux,CH, rec. 17.7.1998
Landgren,Nils (tb,voc) | Johansson,Per 'Ruskträsk' (ss,as) | Svensson,Esbjörn (keyboards) | Janson,Henrik (g) | Price,Magnum Coltrane (b,voc) | Robertson,Jan (dr)

9266-2 | CD | Fragile Network
Christoph Lauer Quintet
Flying Carpets | Human Voice | Vernasio | Ferma L'Ali | Facing Interviews | Fais Attention P'tit Garcon | Ursus Maior | Open Noisy | Werther
Zerkall, rec. 23.-28.9.1998
Lauer,Christof (ss,ts) | Godard,Michel (serpent,tuba) | Ducret,Marc (g) | Cox,Anthony (b) | Jackson,Gene (dr)

9267-2 | CD | The Other World
Jan Erik Kongshaug Group
If I Should Lose You | The Other World | Airegin | Going West | July First | In Your Own Sweet Way | No Name Samba | Mina's Waltz | Like Someone In Love | When I Met You
Oslo,N, rec. 14./15.4.& 6.5.1998
Kongshaug,Jan Erik (g) | Herstad,Svein Olav (p) | Johnson,Harald (b) | Johansen,Per Oddvar (dr)

9268-2 | CD | Ballads
Nils Landgren Group
Don't Go To Strangers | Lament | There'll Never Be Another You | Here's That Rainy Day | Everything Happens To Me | They Say It's Wonderful | A Child Is Born | I Thought About You
Stockholm,Sweden, rec. March 1993
Landgren,Nils (tb) | Milder,Joakim (ts) | Stenson,Bobo (p) | Danielsson,Palle (b) | Kjellberg,Anders (dr)
Once Upon A Summertime | Killing Me Softly With His Song
Landgren,Nils (tb) | Milder,Joakim (ts) | Norberg,Johan (g) | Stenson,Bobo (p) | Danielsson,Palle (b) | Kjellberg,Anders (dr)
Nils Landgren With The Esbjörn Svensson Trio
You Stole My Heart
Stockholm,Sweden, rec. May 1998
Landgren,Nils (tb) | Svensson,Esbjörn (p) | Berglund,Dan (b) | Öström,Magnus (dr)

9271-2 | CD | 5000 Miles
Nils Landgren Funk Unit With Guests
Da Fonk | 5000 Miles | Six Beauties On A Rooftop | Sister Of Arequipa | In A Fonky Mood | Stop By | Roxane | Professor Longhair | Venus As A Boy | Nasty | Glen & Steve
Stockholm,Sweden, rec. March 1998-July 1999
Landgren,Nils (tb,voc) | Johansson,Per 'Ruskträsk' (as,wooden-fl) | Östlund,Robert (g,org) | Svensson,Esbjörn (el-p,keyboards,grand-p) | Price,Magnum Coltrane (el-b,voc) | Robertson,Janne (dr) | Janson,Henrik (g) | Norberg,Johan (sitar-g) | Berglund,Dan (b) | Sundquist,Ake (perc) | Öström,Magnus (perc) | Brönner,Till (tp) | Hargrove,Roy (tp,fl-h) | Hagans,Tim (tp) | Wesley,Fred (tb) | Alias,Don (perc) | Tolstoy,Viktoria (voc)

9273-2 | CD | Jens Thomas Plays Ennio Morricone
Jens Thomas
Overture To You Can't Keep A Good Cowboy Down | The Good The Bad And The Ugly | Cookey's Song | Deborah's Theme | The Battle Of Laatzen | Once Upon A Time In The West | Poverty | Here's To You
Oslo,N, rec. 26.7.1999
Thomas,Jens (p-solo)
Pioggia
Thomas,Jens (p) | Fresu,Paolo (tp,fl-h)
The Man With The Harmonica | Once Upon A Time In America | For Maestro Morricone
Thomas,Jens (p) | Fresu,Paolo (tp,fl-h) | Salis,Antonello (accordeon)

9274-2 | CD | Orange
Michael Riessler Group
W(Souvenirs D'Enfance) | 2 Dans Un Café | Wagon(1) | May Be | Wagon(2)- | Arabuno- | Wagon(3) | Atlas | Wagon(4) | Orange | Annonce- | Wagon(5)- | Itinéraires- | Verticalement- | Je | Je Me Souviens
Baden-Baden, rec. June-August 1999
Riessler,Michael (cl,b-cl,ss) | Matinier,Jean-Louis (accordeon) | Charial,Pierre (barrel-org) | Caron,Elise (voc)

9275-2 | CD | Bakida
Nguyen Le Trio
Bakida | Noche Y Luz | Feel Feliz
details unknown, rec. May-October 1999
Le,Nguyen (g) | Garcia-Fons,Renaud (b) | Di Geraldo,Tino (dr,perc)
Nguyen Le Trio With Guests
Encanto | Heaven
Le,Nguyen (g) | Benavent,Carlos (el-5-string-b) | Garcia-Fons,Renaud (b) | Di Geraldo,Tino (dr,perc)
Chinoir | Madal
Le,Nguyen (g) | Potter,Chris (ts) | Garcia-Fons,Renaud (b) | Di Geraldo,Tino (dr,perc)
Dding Dek
Le,Nguyen (g) | Erguner,Kudsi (ney) | Garcia-Fons,Renaud (b) | Di Geraldo,Tino (dr,perc) | Amar,Illya (marimba,tuned-gongs)
Lü
Le,Nguyen (g) | Fresu,Paolo (tp,fl-h) | Garcia-Fons,Renaud (b) | Di Geraldo,Tino (dr,perc) | Ziad,Karim (bendir,gumbri,karkabous,tarija,voc) | Nhien[Pham],Hao (meo-fl,sao-fl,voc)
Romanichel
Le,Nguyen (g) | Balke,Jon (p) | Garcia-Fons,Renaud (b) | Di Geraldo,Tino (dr,perc)

9276-2 | CD | Round About Bartok
Beirach-Hübner-Mraz
Around Scrijabin Prelude op.16 | Around Bartók Bagatelle No.4 | Around Stenkarasin | Around Bartók's World | Around Salcam De Vara | Around Porumbescu Balada | Around Dubrawuschka | Zal | Around Kodaly's World | Cossak's Farewell
Ludwigsburg, rec. December 1999
Beirach,Richard (p) | Hübner,Gregor (v) | Mraz,George 'Jiri' (b)

9278-2 | CD | Old Friends
The German Jazz Masters
Suggestion | Crosstalk | Und So Weiter,And So On | Es Sungen Drei Engel 2000 | Trans Tanz | Horizons | Song For Bam Bam | Elongate | Wendekreis Des Steinbocks | Yellow Cab | Changing Places | Old Friends Blues
Ludwigsburg, rec. 26.-28.6.2000
German Jazz Masters,The | Schoof,Manfred (tp,fl-h) | Mangelsdorff,Albert (tb) | Doldinger,Klaus (ss,ts) | Dauner,Wolfgang (p) | Weber,Eberhard (b) | Haffner,Wolfgang (dr)

9279-2 | CD | South
David Binney Group
Out Beyond Ideas | Moment In Memory | The Global Soul | Leaving The Sea | Traveler | New York Nature | Southplay | The Global Soul(reprise) | South
Brooklyn,NY, rec. 29./30.6.2000
Binney,David 'Dave' (ss,as,sampler) | Potter,Chris (ts) | Rogers,Adam (g) | Caine,Uri (p) | Colley,Scott (b) | Blade,Brian (dr)
Von Joshua | Tangles Outcome
Binney,David 'Dave' (ss,as,sampler) | Potter,Chris (ts) | Rogers,Adam (g) | Caine,Uri (p) | Colley,Scott (b) | Black,Jim (dr)

9281-2 | CD | Layers Of Light
Nils Landgren-Esbjörn Svensson
Song From The Valley | Calling The Goats | Kauk | Kristallen | Mattmar | Lakk | Höpsi | Calling The Cows | Lullaby | Simple Song | Layers Of Light | Lonely In The Lakeside | Norwegian Fox Trot | Nils Walksong | The Farewell
Oslo,N, rec. 2./3.12.1999
Landgren,Nils (tb) | Svensson,Esbjörn (p)

9282-2 | CD | Ifrikya
Karim Ziad Groups
Ait Oumrar | Ya Rijal | Awra | Lebnia | Alouhid | Sandiya | Amaliya | Gwarir | The Joker | Nesrafet
Studio Davout,?, rec. June/July 200
Ziad,Karim (dr,perc,gumbri,g,mandola,voc) | Aubel,David (fl) | Wague,Ali (pehl-fl) | Deblossat,Alain (ss,ts) | Mascart,Vincent (ts) | Miziallaoua,Khliff (g,voc) | Djemai,Abdenour (bj,mandola,voc) | Le,Nguyen (g) | Zulfikarpasic,Bojan (p) | Rykiel,Jean-Pilippe (synth) | Marthe,Linley (b) | Alibo,Michel (b) | Mestari,Hamid (outar,voc) | Merchane,Abdelkbir (voc) | Mohamed,Menni (perc,voc) | Hervé,Gaelle (voc) | Hervé,Marielle (voc)

9285-2 | CD | Colours Of Ghana
Triocolor
The Voice | Kalimba I | Drum Talking | African Magic | High Speed Spirit | Sakyi's Song | From The Wizard | Knowing Sowah | Shadows | Trip To Ghana | Kalimba II | You Know | At Ghanaba's Place | The Accrator I | By Now | The Accrator II | Epilog
Hannover, rec. 22.-24.5.2000
Tricolor | Thomas,Jens (p,perc,voice) | Weeke,Stefan (b,perc) | Lücker,Björn (dr,perc)

9286-2 | CD | Love Me Tender
Der Rote Bereich
Leba,Si? | Lizard | Love Me Tender | 50.000 KLeine Wichtigtuer | Simple | Ein Tag Im Leben Des Jungen L. | Short Romantic Schoolgirl Song | Chemischer Urlaub | Franken Global | Zambujeira Do Mar | Wer Kommt Mehr Vom Sozialamt? | Der Eine Zupft Den Anderen | Hüpfer | Berlin-Mitte
Hannover, rec. August 2000
Der Rote Bereich | Mahall,Rudi (b-cl) | Möbus,Frank (g) | Schröder,John (g,dr)

9289-2 | CD | ELB
Peter Erskine Trio
Zig Zag | Autumn Rose | Pong | Country Boy | Now Or Never | Sao Sen | Pirates | Meanville | Bee | Bass Desires | Free At Last
Oslo,N, rec. 30./31.10.2000
Erskine,Peter (dr) | Le,Nguyen (g) | Benita,Michel (b)

9292-2 | CD | Nils Landgren-The First Unit | EAN 614427929228
Nils Landgren First Unit And Guests
Tracy | Cheyenne | Eyes Of Love | Red Horn | Simple Life | Mr.M | Hold On | Baby Let Me Kiss You | Sound Check | Ouch!
Stockholm,Sweden, rec. 1992
Landgren,Nils (tb,keyboards,voc) | Mejlvang,Jesper (keyboards,el-p) | Jansson,Henrik (g,keyboards,voc) | Danielsson,Lars Danmark (b) | Lindvall,Per (dr) | Guest Unit: | Lindvall,Leif (tp) | Wilczewski,Dave (reeds) | Medin,Niklas (wurlitzer,org) | Ruff,Mitchael (el-p,org,voc) | Ruff,Nadia (voc) | Smith,Leslie (voc) | Fenger,Sos (voc) | Folkesson,Mija (voc) | Folkesson,Margaretha (voc) | Swedien,Bruce (snare) | Mr.Mad Dog (loops) | Löhr,Sweet Bernhard (loops)

9295-2 | CD | E.S.T. Live
Esbjörn Svensson Trio(E.S.T.)
Like Wash It Or Something
Uppsala, rec. 11.3.1995
Svensson,Esbjörn (p) | Berglund,Dan (b) | Öström,Magnus (dr)
The Rube Thing
Nyköping, rec. 14.3.1995
Svensson,Esbjörn (p) | Berglund,Dan (b) | Öström,Magnus (dr)
Happy Heads And Crazy Feds | What Did You Buy Today | Mr.& Mrs. Hankerchief
Jönköping, rec. 15.3.1995
Svensson,Esbjörn (p) | Berglund,Dan (b) | Öström,Magnus (dr)
Say Hello To Mr.D(To Mr.S) | Hymn Of The River Brown | Day After Day(Leaving)
Möindal, rec. 16.3.1995
Svensson,Esbjörn (p) | Berglund,Dan (b) | Öström,Magnus (dr)
Same As Before
Västeras, rec. 20.3.1995
Svensson,Esbjörn (p) | Berglund,Dan (b) | Öström,Magnus (dr)
Breadbasket
Arhus, rec. 15.7.1995
Svensson,Esbjörn (p) | Berglund,Dan (b) | Öström,Magnus (dr)

9296-2 | CD | Round About Federico Mompou
Richard Beirach Trio
Impressiones Intimas No.1 | Musica Callada No.6 | Fantasie On Musica Callada No.10 | Musica Callada No.10 | Bass Fantasie On Musica Callada No.1 | Musica Callada No.1 | Musica Callada No.27 | Around Musica Callada No.27 | Fantasie On Musica Callada No.19 | Around Musica Callada No.19 | Musica Callada No.19 | Musica Callada No.18 | Fantasie On Musica Callada No.18 | Musica Callada No.15 | Musica Callada No.22
Ludwigsburg, rec. May 2001
Beirach,Richard (p) | Hübner,Gregor (v) | Mraz,George 'Jiri' (b)

9297-2 | CD | Shadows In The Rain
Christof Lauer-Jens Thomas
Rosanne | Ecilop | Ballad For Sting | Synchronicity(I) | Moon Over Bourbon Street | No Matter What They Say | Every Breath You Take | Desert Rose | Synchronicity(II) | Roxanne(reprise)
Oslo,N, rec. 14.-17.6.2001
Lauer,Christof (ss,ts) | Thomas,Jens (p)
Shadows In The Rain
Lauer,Christof (ss,ts) | Thomas,Jens (p) | Endresen,Sidsel (voc)
Christof Lauer-Jens Thomas With The Cikada String Quartet
So Lonely | Russians | Tea In The Sahara | Every Little Thing
Lauer,Christof (ss,ts) | Thomas,Jens (p) | Cicada String Quartet | Hannisdal,Odd (v) | Hannisdal,Henrik (v) | Konstantynowicz,Marek (viola) | Cardas,Emery (cello) | Towns,Colin (arr)

9298-2 | CD | Swing Kings
Schlüter-Nabatov-Antolini
How High The Moon | What Is This Thing Called Love | Moonglow | China Boy | Just You Just Me | I'll Never Be The Same | Blues For Mike | More Than You Know | Oh! Lady Be Good | Dizzy Spells
Live at Birdland,Hamburg, rec. 12.9.1996
Schlüter,Wolfgang (vib) | Nabatov,Simon (p) | Antolini,Charly (dr)

9299-2 | CD | Fonk Da World
Nils Landgren Funk Unit
Riders On The Storm | Mo Stuff | Fonk Da World | Anytime,Anywhere | Rock It | Amtrak | Freedom Jazz Dance | Le Sunset | From Stockholm To Bejing | Calvados
Stockholm,Sweden, rec. June 2001
Landgren,Nils (tb,fl-h,voc) | Johansson,Per 'Ruskträsk' (as) | Nordenström,Jesper (el-p,org,synth) | Östlund,Robert (g,org,vib,synth) | Price,Magnum Coltrane (el-b,voc,rap,synth) | Gabrielsson,Niklas (dr,congas,voc) | Öström,Magnus (perc)
What's Up,What's Up | Booty Rock | New Morning
Landgren,Nils (tb,fl-h,voc) | Johansson,Per 'Ruskträsk' (as) | Svensson,Esbjörn (el-p) | Nordenström,Jesper (el-p,org,synth) | Östlund,Robert (g,org,vib,synth) | Price,Magnum Coltrane (el-b,voc,rap,synth) | Gabrielsson,Niklas (dr,congas,voc) | Öström,Magnus (perc)

9401-2 | CD | Three Stories,One End
Simon Nabatov Trio
Three Stories,One End | Emily | For Herbie | Epistrophy | Grooffa | I Wish I Knew | Giant Steps | St.Thomas | Wish I Were There
Köln, rec. 13./14.11.2000
Nabatov,Simon (p) | Gress,Drew (b) | Rainey,Tom (dr)

9402-2 | CD | Starting A Story
Simon Nabatov-Nils Wogram
Less Is Little | The Mistake | The Wheel Of Misfortune | Groofta | Integration | For Herbie | Keep Going | Starting A Story | Practise Makers Polfect | It It | East 117th Street
Köln, rec. 20.& 27.3.2000
Nabatov,Simon (p) | Wogram,Nils (tb)

9404-2 | CD | Ramon Valle Plays Ernesto Lecuona
Ramon Valle Quintet
Danza Le Los Nanigos | Malaguena | La Comparsa | Andalucia | Cordoba | Danza Negra | Gitanerias | La Conga De Medianoche | En Tres Por Cuatro | Y La Negra Ballada
Ludwigsburg, rec. 1.-3.9.2001
Valle,Ramon (p) | Puig,Carlos (tp) | Sambeat,Perico (ss,as) | Rodriguez,Omar (b) | Hernandez,Horacio 'El Negro' (dr)

9405-2 | CD | Scattering Poems | EAN 614470940522
Julia Hülsman Trio With Rebekka Bakken
Anyone | The Moon Is Hiding | The Wind Is A Lady | In Justspring | A Thousand Years
Berlin, rec. February 2001
Hülsmann,Julia (p) | Muellbauer,Marc (b) | Köbberling,Heinrich (dr) | Bakken,Rebekka (voc)
Same Girl | The City Sleeps | Love Is More Thicker Than Forget | Maggie And Milly And Molly And May | Tic Toc
Berlin, rec. May 2002
Hülsmann,Julia (p) | Muellbauer,Marc (b) | Winch,Rainer (dr) | Bakken,Rebekka (voc)

9406-2 | CD | Aurora Borealis-Nordic Lights
Geir Lysne Listening Ensemble
Aurora Borealis Suite: | Intro | Part I-III | Part IV(coda)
Live at 'Jazzfest',Berlin, rec. 11.1.2001
Lysne,Geir (comp,cond) | Brodahl,Frank (tp,fl-h) | Haltli,Marius (tp,fl-h) | Baur,Eckhard (tp,fl-h) | Myklebust,Ole Jorn (tp,fl-h) | Sunde,Helge (tb) | Jaksjo,Christian (tb) | Gjerde,Jorgen (tb) | Hovland,Ketil (b-tb) | Einarsen,Ketil V. (fl,piccolo) | Halle,Morton (ss,as) | Graf,Klaus (as) | Maile,Andreas 'Andi' (ts) | Jensen,Fredrik O. (ts) | Seland,Bernhard (bs) | Qien,Jorn (keyboards) | Bratberg,Hallgrim (g) | Renvag,Jan Olav (b,el-b,tuba) | Aalefjaer,Knut (dr,perc) | Ekornes,Kenneth (dr,perc)

9407-2 | CD | Risky Business
Der Rote Bereich
Mein Sportheim | Dream | Portugal | Da Da Dapp | Anderes Obst | Independent Swing | Hemdendienst Blues Minue One | Feijoada De Chocos | Wer Wird Wird Wirt | Ich Geh' Zur Polizei | Wo Ist Die 1 | Risky Business
Hamburg, rec. March 2002
Der Rote Bereich | Möbus,Frank (g) | Mahall,Rudi (b-cl) | Steidle,Oliver Bernd (dr)

9408-2 | CD | Jazz Is A Spirit
Terri Lyne Carrington Group
Jazz Is
Burbank,Los Angeles,CA, rec. February 2001
Carrington,Terri Lyne (dr) | Robinson,Danny (g) | Kurstin,Greg (keyboards) | Warner,Malcom-Jamal (talking,b) | Barguiarena,Ed (perc)
Little Jump
Carrington,Terri Lyne (dr) | Roney,Wallace (tp) | Thomas,Gary (ts) | Bollenback,Paul (g) | Hancock,Herbie (p) | Hurst III,Robert Leslie (b)
The Corner
Carrington,Terri Lyne (dr) | Buckingham,Katisse (ss) | Thomas,Gary (fl,ts) | Bollenback,Paul (g) | Kurstin,Greg (p,keyboards) | Jackson,Darryl 'Munyungo' (perc) | Hurst III,Robert Leslie (b)
Lost Star
Carrington,Terri Lyne (dr) | Thomas,Gary (ts) | Bollenback,Paul (g) | Kurstin,Greg (p) | Hurst III,Robert Leslie (b)
Samsara(for Wayne)
Carrington,Terri Lyne (dr) | Thomas,Gary (ts) | Eubanks,Kevin (g) | Hancock,Herbie (p) | Hurst III,Robert Leslie (b)
Journey Agent
Carrington,Terri Lyne (dr-solo)
Journey East From West
Carrington,Terri Lyne (dr) | Roney,Wallace (tp) | Eubanks,Kevin (g) | Kurstin,Greg (p,keyboards) | Hurst III,Robert Leslie (b) | Barguiarena,Ed (perc)

ACT | Edel Contraire Bielefelder Katalog 690 Jazz • Ausgabe 2004 ACT | Edel Contraire

Journey Of Now
Carrington,Terri Lyne (dr) | Roney,Wallace (tp) | Richman,Jeff (g) | Kurstin,Greg (p) | Hurst III,Robert Leslie (b) | Jackson,Darryl 'Munyungo' (perc)
Giggles
Carrington,Terri Lyne (dr) | Thomas,Gary (ts) | Bollenback,Paul (g) | Kurstin,Greg (p) | Hurst III,Robert Leslie (b)
Middle Way
Carrington,Terri Lyne (dr) | Blanchard,Terence (tp) | Thomas,Gary (ts) | Hancock,Herbie (p) | Hurst III,Robert Leslie (b)
Princess
Carrington,Terri Lyne (dr) | Thomas,Gary (ts) | Bollenback,Paul (g) | Hurst III,Robert Leslie (b)
Witch Hunt
Carrington,Terri Lyne (dr) | Thomas,Gary (ts) | Richman,Jeff (g) | Kurstin,Greg (keyboards) | Hurst III,Robert Leslie (b)
Mr.Joe Jones
Carrington,Terri Lyne (dr) | Papa Joe Jones Speaking To Terri Lyne in 1984
Jazz Is A Spirit
Carrington,Terri Lyne (dr,programming) | Roney,Wallace (tp) | Robinson,Danny (g) | Kurstin,Greg (keyboards) | Warner,Malcom-Jamal (talking,b) | Jackson,Darryl 'Munyungo' (perc) | Barguiarena,Ed (perc)

9409-2 | CD | Sentimental Journey
Nils Landgren Group
Speak Low | Ghost In This House | This Masquerade | Nature Boy | The Ballad Of All The Sad Young Men | My Foolish Heart | Should I Care | In A Sentimental Mood
Stockholm,Sweden, rec. 3.-7.6.2002
Landgren,Nils (tb,voc) | Widmark,Anders (grand-p) | Danielsson,Lars (b) | Haffner,Wolfgang (dr) | Flesh Quartet: | Lindgren,Jonas (v) | Högberg,Örjan (viola) | Hellden,Matthias (cello) | Öberg,Sebastian (cello)
Everything Must Change
Landgren,Nils (tb,voc) | Widmark,Anders (grand-p) | Danielsson,Lars (b) | Haffner,Wolfgang (dr) | Flesh Quartet: | Lindgren,Jonas (v) | Högberg,Örjan (viola) | Hellden,Matthias (cello) | Öberg,Sebastian (cello) | Olsson,Chrille (b)
Fragile
Landgren,Nils (tb,voc) | Widmark,Anders (grand-p) | Danielsson,Lars (b) | Haffner,Wolfgang (dr) | Flesh Quartet: | Lindgren,Jonas (v) | Högberg,Örjan (viola) | Hellden,Matthias (cello) | Öberg,Sebastian (cello) | Gustafsson,Rigmor (voc)
Be There For You
Landgren,Nils (tb,voc) | Widmark,Anders (grand-p) | Danielsson,Lars (b) | Haffner,Wolfgang (dr) | Flesh Quartet: | Lindgren,Jonas (v) | Högberg,Örjan (viola) | Hellden,Matthias (cello) | Öberg,Sebastian (cello) | Tolstoy,Viktoria (voc)
Sentimental Journey
Landgren,Nils (tb,voc) | Widmark,Anders (grand-p) | Danielsson,Lars (b) | Haffner,Wolfgang (dr) | Flesh Quartet: | Lindgren,Jonas (v) | Högberg,Örjan (viola) | Hellden,Matthias (cello) | Öberg,Sebastian (cello) | Hammar,Mimmi (tb) | Hammar,Karin (tb)
I Will Survive
Tutzing, rec. details unknown
Landgren,Nils (tb,voc) | Svensson,Esbjörn (el-p) | Östlund,Robert (g) | Price,Magnum Coltrane (b) | Robertson,Janne (dr)

9410-2 | CD | Purple:Celebrating Jimi Hendrix
Nguyen Le Trio With Guests
1983 A Merman I Should Turn To Be
Paris,France, rec. 16.-18.5.2002
Le,Nguyen (el-g,g-synth) | Zulfikarpasic,Bojan (p) | Alibo,Michel (el-b) | Carrington,Terri Lyne (dr,voc)
Manic Depression
Le,Nguyen (g) | Alibo,Michel (el-b) | Carrington,Terri Lyne (dr) | Khann,Aida (voc)
Are You Experienced?
Le,Nguyen (el-g,g-synth) | NdegéOcello,Me'Shell (el-b) | Carrington,Terri Lyne (dr) | Curschellas,Corina (voc)
Purple Haze | Burning Of The Midnight Lamp | South Saturn Delta | Up From The Skies
Le,Nguyen (g,el-g,g-synth) | Alibo,Michel (b) | Carrington,Terri Lyne (dr,voc)
If 6 Was 9
Le,Nguyen (g) | Alibo,Michel (el-b) | Zulfikarpasic,Bojan (el-p) | Carrington,Terri Lyne (dr) | Khann,Aida (voc)
Voodoo Child(Slight Return) | Third Stone From The Sun
Le,Nguyen (el-g,g-synth) | NdegéOcello,Me'Shell (el-b) | Carrington,Terri Lyne (dr) | Ziad,Karim (gumbri,perc) | Khann,Aida (voc)

9411-2 | CD | Balance
David Binney Group
Marvin Gaye | I'll Finally Answer | Midnight Sevilla | We Always Cried | Fidene
Brooklyn,NY, rec. July/August 2001
Binney,David 'Dave' (as) | Krantz,Wayne (g) | Caine,Uri (p,synth) | Lefebvre,Tim (b) | Black,Jim (dr) | Almond,Peck (brass) | Henri,Tanya (voc)
Balance
Binney,David 'Dave' (as) | Haffner,Jon (as) | McCaslin,Donny (ts) | Krantz,Wayne (g) | Caine,Uri (p,synth) | Lefebvre,Tim (b) | Black,Jim (dr) | Almond,Peck (brass) | Henri,Tanya (voc)
Arlmyn Trangent
Binney,David 'Dave' (as) | McCaslin,Donny (ts) | Krantz,Wayne (g) | Caine,Uri (p,synth) | Lefebvre,Tim (b) | Black,Jim (dr) | Almond,Peck (brass) | Henri,Tanya (voc)
Speedy's 9 Is 10
Binney,David 'Dave' (as) | McCaslin,Donny (ts) | Rogers,Adam (g) | Caine,Uri (p,synth) | Ephron,Fima (b) | Black,Jim (dr) | Almond,Peck (brass) | Henri,Tanya (voc)
Arlmyn Trangent Reliv
Binney,David 'Dave' (as) | Rogers,Adam (g) | Caine,Uri (p,synth) | Ephron,Fima (b) | Black,Jim (dr) | Almond,Peck (brass) | Henri,Tanya (voc)
Lurker
Binney,David 'Dave' (as) | McCaslin,Donny (ts) | Krantz,Wayne (g) | Caine,Uri (p,synth) | Black,Jim (dr) | Lefebvre,Tim (b) | Almond,Peck (brass) | Henri,Tanya (voc)
Rincon
Binney,David 'Dave' (ts) | McCaslin,Donny (ts) | Krantz,Wayne (g) | Caine,Uri (p,synth) | Black,Jim (dr) | Lefebvre,Tim (b) | Almond,Peck (brass) | Henri,Tanya (voc)
Perenne
Binney,David 'Dave' (synth) | Krantz,Wayne (g) | Caine,Uri (p,synth) | Black,Jim (dr) | Lefebvre,Tim (b) | Wollesen,Kenny (broom) | Almond,Peck (brass) | Henri,Tanya (voc)

9414-2 | CD | Live In Montreux
Soriba Kouyaté Quartet
Diarabi | Miriama | All Blues | Deli Guelema | Autumn Leaves | Afrilude | St.Louis-Dakar | Kaira | Bani
Live at The Montreux Jazz Festival, rec. 16.7.2000
Kouyaté,Soriba (kora) | Matthieu,Michel (tp) | Marthe,Linley (b) | Allouche,Joel (dr)

9416-2 | CD | Red And Blue
Muriel Zoe Group
Bye Bye Blackbird | You Go To My Head | Up Jumped Spring | Lovesong No.1 | My One And Only Love | Round About Midnight | Don't Explain | Willow Weep For Me | You Don't Know What Love Is | Second Time Around | Happiness Is A Thing Called Joe | I'm Afraid The Masquerade Is Over - (I'm Afraid) The Masquerade Is Over | All The Way | Autumn Leaves
Hamburg, rec. details unknown
Zoe,Muriel (voc,g) | Leuschner,Michael (tp) | Pogoda,Matthias (g,perc) | Huth,Johannes (b) | Verhovec,Michael (dr,perc)

9417-2 | CD | Ahi Vita | EAN 614427941725
Michael Riessler & Singer Pur with Vincent Courtois
O Dolorosa Gioia | Ahi Lingua, Ai Baci | Amor | Amor-Lamento Della Ninfa | Nasce La Pena Mia-Introduktion | Nasce La Pena Mia | Pleurez Mes Yeux(Riesler) | Pleurez Mes Yeux | Planxit | Cursum | Si Ch'io Vorrei Morire | Lugebat | Moro Lasso | Far Mi Deggio
Probstei St. Gerold,Austria, rec. 22.-27.4.2003
Riessler,Michael (cl,b-cl) | Courtois,Vincent (cello) | Singer Pur | Reinhard,Claudia (voc) | Wenk,Klaus (voc) | Zapp,Markus (voc) | Hirtreiter,Andreas (voc) | Heidloff,Guido (voc) | Schmidl,Marcus (voc)

9418-2 | CD | I Will Wait For You | EAN 614427941824
Rigmor Gustafsson With The Nils Landgren Quartet And The Fleshquartet
Empty Hearts | Is It A Crime | If You Go Away | Makin' Whoopee | Fire And Rain | It Never Entered My Mind | Fever | The Moon Is A Harsh Mistress | I Will Wait For You | It's Been Too Long | Black Coffee | The More I See You
Stockholm,Sweden, rec. January/April 2003
Gustafsson,Rigmor (voc) | Landgren,Nils (tb,voc) | Svensson,Staffan (tp) | Di Gioia,Roberto (p) | Danielsson,Lars (b) | Haffner,Wolfgang (dr) | Flesh Quartet (strings)

9420-2 | CD | Heaven
Christoph Lauer & Norwegian Brass
Eg Veit I Himmerik Ei Borg(Ich Weiß Im Himmelreich) | Maria Durch Einen Dornwald Ging | Overmade Fullt Av Nade | Die Nacht Ist Vorgedrungen | Kommet Ihr Hirten | Folkefreisar Til Oss Kom(Nun Komm,Der Heiden Heiland) | Joseph,Lieber Joseph Mein | Gelobt Seist Du,Jesu Christ | Mitt Hjerte Alltid Vanker | Wach,Nachtigal,Wach Auf | Es Ist Ein Ros Entsprungen | Stille Nacht Heilige Nacht
Valerengen Kirke,Oslo,N, rec. 29./30.5.2003
Lauer,Christof (ss,ts) | Norwegian Brass: | Brodahl,Frank (tp) | Haltli,Marius (tp) | Braekke,Oyvind (tb) | Brohdal,Rune (fr-h) | Haug,Lars Andreas (tuba) | Bratland,Sondre (voc) | Bakken,Rebekka (voc)

9421-2 | CD | Friendship | EAN 614427942128
Perico Sambeat Quartet
Orbis | Eterna | Miracel | Crazy She Calls Me | Actors | Iris
River Edge,NJ, rec. February 2003
Sambeat,Perico (ss,as) | Mehldau,Brad (p) | Street,Ben (b) | Ballard,Jeff (dr)
Mathilda
Sambeat,Perico (ss,as) | Mehldau,Brad (p) | Street,Ben (b) | Ballard,Jeff (dr) | Canela,Carme (voc)
Perico Sambeat Quintet
Bioy | Memoria De Un Sueno | Icaro
Sambeat,Perico (ss,as) | Rosenwinkel,Kurt (g) | Mehldau,Brad (p) | Street,Ben (b) | Ballard,Jeff (dr)

9422-2 | CD | Chasing Reality
Gerard Presencer Group
Chasing Reality: | Part One | Part Two | Part Three | Part Four | Part Five | Part Six
London,GB, rec. 2002
Presencer,Gerard (tp,fl-h) | Locke,Joe (vib) | Goldsmith,Adam (g) | Parricelli,John (g) | Keezer,Geoff (el-p,synth) | Wadlow,Tommy (p) | Brown,Jeremy (b,el-b) | Dagley,Chris (dr)
-> additional recordings: Cirta Rossbach(recitation), Uli Forster(el-p)

9424-2 | CD | No Escape | EAN 614427942425
Ramon Valle Trio
El Vigia | De Vuelta A Casa | Fourty Dregrees | Viva Coltrane | Andar Por Dentro | Ilegal | Alice Blues | Clouds | Kimbaran Pa Nico | Brindemos | Pesadilla
Ludwigsburg, rec. details unknown
Valle,Ramon (p) | Calvo,Omar Rodriguez (b) | Torriente,Liber (dr)

9427-2 | CD | Structure | EAN 614427942722
Terri Lyne Carrington Quartet
Mindful Intent | Black Halo | Ethiopia | The Invisible | Spiral | Facets Squared | Solance | Fire | Omega | Columbus,Ohio
Calabasas,CA, rec. November 2003
Carrington,Terri Lyne (dr,perc,voc) | Osby,Greg (as) | Rogers,Adam (g,el-g) | Haslip,Jimmy (b)

9428-2 | CD | Swedish Folk Modern
Nils Landgren-Esbjörn Svensson
Homlat | Vallat Fran Jämtland | Lapp Nils Polska | Free Esbjörn | Midsommarvaka From Svedish Rhapsody No.1(Hugo Alfven) | Hymn:Morgon Mellan Fjällen | Halling | The Winters Tale[Epilugue](Lars-Erik Larsen) | Vallat Fran Härjedalen | Gärdebylaten | Visa Fran Leksand | Vaggvisa | Free Nils
Stockholm,Sweden, rec. 9.-11.8.1997
Landgren,Nils (tb) | Svensson,Esbjörn (p)

9701-2 | CD | Shining On You
Viktoria Tolstoy Group & Strings
Upside Out | Equilibrium | Summer Calling | No Regrets | Waltz For The Lonely Ones | Some Day | Wonder Why | Foreverly
Stockholm,Sweden, rec. 3.6.& 29.9.2003
Tolstoy,Viktoria (voc) | Landgren,Nils (tb,voc) | Thielemans,Jean 'Toots' (harm) | Falk,Bror (p) | Danielsson,Lars (cello,b) | Holgersson,Jones (dr) | Stockholm Session Strings | Forsberg,Uli (concertmaster)
Shining On You | Wake Up Song | Things That Happen
Tolstoy,Viktoria (voc) | Landgren,Nils (tb,voc) | Falk,Bror (p) | Spering,Christian (b) | Haffner,Wolfgang (dr) | Stockholm Session Strings | Forsberg,Uli (concertmaster)
Love Is Real
Stockholm,Sweden, rec. 3.6.-29.9.2003
Tolstoy,Viktoria (voc) | Landgren,Nils (tb,voc) | Karlsson,Daniel (p) | Berglund,Dan (b) | Öström,Magnus (dr) | Stockholm Session Strings | Forsberg,Uli (concertmaster)

9702-2 | CD | Come Closer
Julia Hülsmann Trio With Anna Lauvergnac
Let's Burn Down The Cornfield | Cowboy | Mama Told Me Not To Come | I Think It's Going To Rain Today | Lonely At The Top | In Germany Before The War | Baltimore | You Can Leave Your Hat On | Sandman's Coming | Come Closer | Short People | Old Man On The Farm
Berlin, rec. August 2003
Hülsmann,Julia (p,fender-rhodes) | Muelbauer,Marc (b) | Köbberling,Heinrich (dr) | Lauvergnac,Anna (voc)

Album | Album Records

AS 11806 | LP | All Night Long
Remy Filipovitch Quartet
Good Message | Six Years | Mandalay Express | All Night Long | B.I.B. & Little Waltz | Flat Rate
Köln, rec. 16./19.& 21.8.1980
Filipovitch,Remy (ts) | Wunsch,Frank (p) | Klingelhöfer,Bodo (b) | Peters,Michael (dr)

AS 22927 | LP | All Day Long
Remy Filipovitch Trio
All Day Long | Cargo Area | Sunset Boulevard | California | The Booster | Room Upstairs | Tea For Three
Köln, rec. 26./27.8.1982
Filipovitch,Remy (ts) | Dylag,Roman (b) | Stephenson,Ronnie (dr,perc)

AS 331108 CD | CD | Open Your Eyes
Remy Filipovitch-Gediminas Laurinavicius
African Suite: | Ivory Coast- | Senegal- | Congo- | Sahara- | Meetings | Conversation | Sutartine | A Song | Three Mountains | Open Your Eyes | Sax Rap
Köln, rec. 2./3.11.1990
Filipovitch,Remy (ts,keyboards,chinese-gong) | Laurinavicius,Gediminas (synth,dr,perc,balafon)

AS 44677 CD | CD | Mysterious Traveler
Ron Marvin & Remy Filipovitch
Mysterious Traveler(part 1) | Dancing Dolphins | Diamonds In The Light | Deep Ocean | Unidentified Objects | African Dance | Mysterious Traveler(part 2)
Köln, rec. 1996/1997
Filipovitch,Remy (fl,alto-fl,cl,b-cl,ss,as,ts,bs,piccolo) | Marvin,Ron (keyboards,synth,electronic-perc)

AS 55417 CD | CD | Alone Together | EAN 4022685300028
Remy Filipovitch-Will Boulware
Prelude To A Kiss | I Love You | As Time Goes By | Alone Together | Someday My Prince Will Come | Played Twice | My One And Only Love
NYC, rec. 2000
Filipovitch,Remy (ts) | Boulware,Will (p)

AS 66919 CD | CD | Go! | EAN 4022685201226
Zbigniew Namyslowski-Remy Filipovitch Quintet
From The Bottom Drawer | From The Other Side | Go! | Listen To The Wind | Juzto Na 3 Juz Na 4 | From The Second Shelf | All That Dust | All Night Long | Jil
Warsaw, Poland, rec. 2003
Namyslowski,Zbigniew (ss,as) | Filipovitch,Remy (ts) | Herdzin,Krzysztof (p) | Walicki,Olo (b) | Grzyb,Grzegorz (dr)

ALISO Records | Aliso Records

AL 1019 | CD | Fools Paradise
Toto Blanke Group
Dali's Himmelfahrt | Locos De La Opera | Palomita | Mad House | Aquellas Cartas | El Fatha Morgana | Early Birds | Fool's Paradise | Hola, Gustavo(dedicated to G.Mahler)
Benhausen, rec. June/July 1989
Blanke,Toto (g,el-g,midi-g,voc) | Crisby,Elena (v,voc) | Schultz,Ekkart (prep-tapes,sampling) | Davidoff,Thomas (perc,dr-computer) | Montero,Raul (voc)

AL 1020 | CD | Che Bandoneon
René Marino Rivero
La Cumparsita | Recuerdo | Quejas De Bandoneon | Amurado | Introduction Y Danca(Nr.1) | Introduction Y Danca(Nr.2) | Adios Nonino | La Ultima Curda | Un Placer | Toccata And Fugue In D Minor(BWV 565) | Preludio Y Fuga In D-Major | Preludio Y Fuga In F-Major | Tres Tangos Nostalgicos Para Marianne Von Allmen: | De Berlin- | De Tübingen- | De Luzem-
Montevideo,Uruguay, rec. February 1990
Rivero,René Marino (bandoneon)

AL 1021 | CD | Talking Hands:Live
Jorge Cardoso
Brejeiro- | Missionerita- | Rasgido Doble- | Taquito Militar- | Preludio Y Danca
Live in St.Georgen/Kehl/Frankfurt, rec. 27.-29.9.1989
Cardoso,Jorge (g)
David Qualey
One Time Swing | Just A Moment | Parade Of The Wooden Soldiers | Joel's Song | Tilly's Two Step | Ride Of The Headless Horseman
Qualey,David (g)
Toto Blanke-Rudolf Dasek
Tres Pinas | Ciruja(to Paul Montero) | Palomita | Talking Hands
Blanke,Toto (g) | Dasek,Rudolf (g)

AL 1022 | CD | Two Much Guitar!
Impressions Of Cadiz | Cafe Fatal- | Ampurdan | Invention Nr.9- | All The Things You Are- | Family Portrait | Spinning | Little Banjo Man | Palomita(dedicated to Rose) | I'm A Sentimental Tango | Trio Infernal | Body And Soul
Gut Övelgönne & Standby Studio,?/Benhausen, rec. 10.-14.7.1991
Blanke,Toto (g,el-g,bj) | Dasek,Rudolf (g,el-g)

AL 1025 | CD | Che Guitarra
Juanjo Dominguez
Viejos Tiempos | Maxixe | Ramona | Mi Amigo Carlos | A Roberto Grela | Nunca Tuvo Novia | Alberti Y Chile | Sencillito Y De Alpargatas | Los Ejas De Mi Carreta | Noche Carioca | Nostalgias Santiagueras | Volvio Una Noche | Manhattan | Toro Y Miguel | Chopiniana
Paderborn, rec. 24./25.9.1992
Dominguez,Juanjo (g)

AL 1026 | CD | Meditation
Toto Blanke-Rudolf Dasek
Sunrise | Viva Dell' Amore | Ampurdan | Conversation | Rising Star(for Wilma) | Blue Spring | Cuckoo | Dominus, Vobistu? | Berberlied | Campanile | Kaffeepause
Live at Bartholomäuskapelle,Paderborn, rec. details unknown
Blanke,Toto (g,el-g,voc,whistling) | Dasek,Rudolf (g,el-g,voc,whistling)
Toto Blanke-Rudolf Dasek With The Overtontrio
Sphere | Siesta
Blanke,Toto (g,el-g,voc,whistling) | Dasek,Rudolf (g,el-g,voc,whistling) | Obertontrio,Das | Dabbert,Harald (voc) | Holthaus,Uschi (voc) | Umgeher-Friesland,Silvia (voc)

AL 1029 | CD | Energy Fields
Das Obertontrio Und Toto Blanke
Skydance | Phantasiereise | Violet | Strömung | Laranga | Chi Gong | Balance | Energy | Lichtbogen | Lemniscate | Vibrations
Live at Bartholomäuskapelle,Paderborn, rec. February & June 1994
Obertontrio,Das | Dabbert,Harald (fl,cl,didgeridoo,mouth-dr,shakuhachi,voc) | Holthaus,Uschi (voc,whistling) | Umgeher-Friesland,Silvia (fujara,voc) | Blanke,Toto (g,el-g)

AL 1030 | CD | Internationales Guitarren Festival '94
Juanjo Dominguez
Potpourri(A.Lauro) | Potpourri(Carlos Gardel) | Maxixe | Cuando Tu No Estas(When You Are Not There) | Adios Nonino
Paderborn, rec. 28./29.9.1994
Dominguez,Juanjo (g)
Pedro Javier Gonzales
Almandina | Buleria | La Intrigosa
Gonzales,Pedro Javier (g)
Christina Azuma
E De Lei | Parazula | Jongo
Azuma,Christina (g)
Ricardo Moyano
Sibel
Moyano,Ricardo (g)
Juan Falù
Niebla Del Riachuelo
Falù,Juan (g)
Ricardo Moyano-Juan Falù
La Vieja | De La Raiz A La Copa | Misionerita
Falù,Juan (g) | Moyano,Ricardo (g)
Vania Delmonaco
Capricio Arabe | Yesterday
Delmonace,Vania (g)

AL 1034 | CD | Electric Circus' Best
Toto Blanke Group
Mister Ed
Hamburg, rec. 1976
Blanke,Toto (g) | Lakatos,Tony (sax) | Goldberg,Stu (p) | Van't Hof,Jasper (keyboards) | Dömling,Norbert (el-b) | Vesala,Edward (dr,perc) | Gurtu,Trilok (dr,perc) | details unknown
Friends | Asiento | Billi
Sprenge, rec. 1979
Blanke,Toto (g) | Lakatos,Tony (sax) | Goldberg,Stu (p) | Van't Hof,Jasper (keyboards) | Dömling,Norbert (el-b) | Vesala,Edward (dr,perc) | Gurtu,Trilok (dr,perc) | details unknown
See You Tomorrow | Bella Donna | I'm A Sentimental Tango | Fools | Bavarian Square Dance | Bananas
Paderborn, rec. 1983
Blanke,Toto (g) | Lakatos,Tony (sax) | Goldberg,Stu (p) | Van't Hof,Jasper (keyboards) | Dömling,Norbert (el-b) | Vesala,Edward (dr,perc) | Gurtu,Trilok (dr,perc) | details unknown

AL 1035 | CD | Sur
Toto Blanke-Diego Jasca
Tomma Suki | La Negra | Alfonsina Y El Mar | Tapping In The Dark | El Pelado | Suite De Buenos Aires(part 1-5) | Why Not? | Dona Luchi | San Ignacio | El Bobo | Gürteltierblues | El Pelado(reprise)
Paderborn, rec. November 1996
Blanke,Toto (g,el-g) | Jasca,Diego (g,charango,metronome)

AL 1036 | CD | Troika
Viktoria Tabatchnikowa-Eugenij Belov
Girls Evening | Volkslieder: | Herzensring- | Mücken Im Wald- | Blue Sky- | Wolynka | Menuet | Sonate In E Moll: | Largo- | Allegro- | Largo- | Allegro- | Capriccio | Fuga | Tschastuschka | Kindersuite: | Die Uhr- | Singende Balalaika- | Kleiner Trommler- | Troika- | Menuet | Sonate 2. Satz | Pickaninny: | Waltz- | Blues- | Ragtime- | Bolero | Russisches Lied
Paderborn, rec. July 1999
Tabatchnikowa,Viktoria (p) | Belov,Eugenji (balalaika)

AL 1037 | CD | Mona Lisa
Toto Blanke-Rudolf Dasek
Mona Lisa | Monte Azul | Nuages | Renascimiento | Round About Midnight | San Ignacio | Cimicurri | Big Nick | Verano Sin Velo | La Paloma | Caminito | Tanz der Kraniche | La Comparsa
Paderborn, rec. 1999
Blanke,Toto (g) | Dasek,Rudolf (g)

AL 1038 | CD | Internationales Guitarren Festival '99
Carlos Mascardini
Donna Carmen | Camino De Las Tropas | A Los Tilingos
Live at Internationales Guitarrenfestival,Paderborn, rec. 1.10.1999
Moscardini,Carlos (g)
Trio De La Gorra
Balada Para Un Loco | Modinha | Pasilo Costaricense Pirre,Vals Venecolano Alp
Trio De La Gorra | Torge,Anna (mand) | Ernst,Peter (g) | Jascalevich,Diego (g,charango)
Europa String Choir
Marching Aunts | Improvisation No.2
Europa String Choir | Stevens,Cathy (viola) | Bruno,Alessandro (el-g) | Dziemanowsky,Udo (el-g) | Reuter,Markus (warr-touch-g)
Norbert Dömling
Seeheim Nightlife | Relationes
Live at Internationales Guitarrenfestival,Paderborn, rec. 2.10.1999
Dömling,Norbert (g)
Belov Duo
Russian Folksong No.1 | Russian Folksong No.2 | Russian Folksong No.3
Belov,Eugenji (balalaika) | Tabachnikowa,Viktoria (p)
Pepe Justicia-Amir Haddad Duo
Solo Agua | La Joaquina
Justicia,Pepe (g) | Haddad,Amir (g)

Alligator Records | Edel Contraire

ALCD 4836 | CD | Eldorado Cadillac
Billy Boy Arnold Group
Ain't I Got You | Sunday Morning Blues | Don't Stay Out All Night | Low-Down Thing Or Two | Been Gone Too Long | Mama's Bitter Sweet | Slick Chick | Sunny Road | Loving Mother For You
Chicago,Ill, rec. details unknown
Arnold,Billy Boy (harm,voc) | Margolin,Bob (g) | Wheeler,James (g) | Leyland,Carl 'Sonny' (p) | Hunt,Steve 'Slash' (b) | Cotton,Chuck (dr)
Too Many Old Flames
Arnold,Billy Boy (harm,voc) | Margolin,Bob (g) | Wheeler,James (g) | Leyland,Carl 'Sonny' (p) | Zamagni,Tony (org) | Hunt,Steve 'Slash' (b) | Cotton,Chuck (dr)
How Long Can This Go On? | Man Of Considerable Taste | It Should Have Been Me
Arnold,Billy Boy (harm,voc) | Zielinski,David (ts) | Margolin,Bob (g) | Wheeler,James (g) | Leyland,Carl 'Sonny' (p) | Hunt,Steve 'Slash' (b) | Cotton,Chuck (dr)

ALCD 4837 | CD | Betwen Midnight And Day
Corey Harris
Roots Woman | Pony Blues | Keep Your Lamp Trimmed And Burning | Early In The Morning | Feel Like Going Home | I'm A Rattlesnakin' Daddy | Between Midnight And Day | Bukka's Jitterbug Swing | Going To Brownsville | Write Me A Few Lines | She Moves Me | Bound To Miss Me | 61 Highway | Catfish Blues | I Ain't Gonna Be Worried No More | It Hurts Me Too
Springfield,VA, rec. 4.9.1994
Harris,Corey (g,voc)

Ambassador | Fenn Music

CLA 1917 | CD | Ambassador Louis Armstrong Vol.17:Moments To Remember(1952-1956)
Louis Armstrong With The Gordon Jenkins Orchestra
The Music Goes 'Round And 'Round
Los Angeles,CA, rec. 8.6.1952
Armstrong,Louis (tp,voc) | Orchestra | Jenkins,Gordon (ld) | details unknown
White Christmas | Winter Wonderland
NYC, rec. 22.9.1952
Armstrong,Louis (voc) | Berg,George (cl) | Penque,Romeo (cl) | McCracken,Bob (as) | Yaner,Milt (as) | Ferguson,Stitz (ts) | Napoleon,Marty (p) | Ryerson,Arthur 'Art' (g) | Shaw,Arvell (b) | Cole,William 'Cozy' (dr) | Strings | Chorus | Jenkins,Gordon (ld) | details unknown
Louis Armstrong With The Commanders
'Zat You,Zanta Claus? | Cool Yule | Someday You'll Be Sorry | The Gypsy | I Can't Afford To Miss This Dream
NYC, rec. 22.10.1953
Armstrong,Louis (tp,voc) | Butterfield,Billy (tp) | Ferretti,Andy (tp) | Poole,Carl (tp) | McGarity,Lou (tb) | Cutshall,Cutty (tb) | Giardina,Phil (tb) | Satterfield,Jack (tb) | Schertzer,Hymie (as,bs) | Klink,Al (ts) | Leighton,Bernie (p) | Mastren,Carmen (g) | Block,Sandy (b) | Grady,Eddie (dr) | Camarata,Toots (arr,ld)
Louis Armstrong With Gordon Jenkins And His Orchestra And Choir
Bye And Bye | Trees | Spooks | The Wiffenproof Song
NYC, rec. 13.4.1954
Armstrong,Louis (tp,voc) | Butterfield,Billy (tp) | Lawson,Yank (tp) | Griffin,Gordon (tp) | McGarity,Lou (tb) | Heather,Cliff (tb) | Yaner,Milt (cl) | Parshley,Tom (as) | Greenberg,Jack (as) | Richmond,Abraham (ts) | Berg,George (ts) | Leighton,Bernie (p) | Barnes,George (g) | Lesberg,Jack (b) | Jaeger,Harry (dr) | unkn. (10 strings) | Chorus | Jenkins,Gordon (cond,arr)
Louis Armstrong And Omer Simeon With The Sy Oliver Orchestra
Skokiaan(part 1&2)
NYC, rec. 13.8.1954
Armstrong,Louis (tp,voc) | Simeon,Omer (ss) | Shavers,Charlie (tp) | Jordan,Taft (tp) | Saloum,Abdul (tp) | Cobbs,Alfred (tb) | Crumley,Elmer (tb) | Selden,Paul F. (tb) | Bigard,Barney (cl) | Martin,David (p) | Barker,Danny (bj) | Shaw,Arvell (b) | Deems,Barrett (dr) | Oliver,Sy (cond,arr)
Louis Armstrong And His All Stars With Sonny Burke's Orchestra
Sincerely | Pledging My Love
Los Angeles,CA, rec. 18.1.1955
Armstrong,Louis (tp,voc) | Candoli,Pete (tp) | Young,Trummy (tb) | Bigard,Barney (cl) | Koch,Jos'Cook' (as) | Ruffell,Donald (ts) | Gentry,Chuck (bs) | Kyle,Billy (p) | Shaw,Arvell (b) | Deems,Barrett (dr) | Burke,Sonny (cond,arr)
Strutfin' With Some Barbecue
Armstrong,Louis (tp,voc) | Candoli,Pete (tp) | Young,Trummy (tb) | Bigard,Barney (cl) | Koch,Jos'Cook' (as) | Ruffell,Donald (ts) | Gentry,Chuck (bs) | Kyle,Billy (p) | Shaw,Arvell (b) | Deems,Barrett (dr) | Crosby,Gary (voc) | Burke,Sonny (cond,arr)
Ko Ko Mo(I Love You So)
Armstrong,Louis (tp,voc) | Candoli,Pete (tp) | Young,Trummy (tb) | Bigard,Barney (cl) | Koch,Jos'Cook' (as) | Ruffell,Donald (ts) | Gentry,Chuck (bs) | Kyle,Billy (p) | Shaw,Arvell (b) | Deems,Barrett (dr) | Crosby,Gary (voc) | Judd Conlin Rhythmaires,The (voc-group) | Burke,Sonny (cond,arr)
Louis Armstrong And His All Stars With Benny Carter's Orchestra
Only You | Christmas In New Orleans | Moments To Remember | Christmas Night In Harlem
Los Angeles,CA, rec. 8.8.1955
Armstrong,Louis (tp,voc) | Candoli,Pete (tp) | Klein,Manny (tp) | Mangano,Vito (tp) | Young,Trummy (tb) | Zentner,Si (tb) | Bigard,Barney (cl) | Herfurt,Arthur 'Skeets' (as) | Klee,Harry (as) | Russin,Irving 'Babe' (ts) | Ruffell,Donald (ts) | Kyle,Billy (p) | Shaw,Arvell (b) | Deems,Barrett (dr) | Carter,Benny (arr,ld)
Louis Armstrong With The Hal Mooney Orchestra
Rain Rain | I Never Saw A Better Day
Hollywood,CA, rec. 1.8.1958
Armstrong,Louis (tp,voc) | Klein,Manny (tp) | Zarchy,Reuben 'Zeke' (tp) | Beach,Frank (tp) | Zentner,Si (tb) | Kusby,Eddie (tb) | Roberts,George (tb) | Dumont,John (as) | Langinger,Ronald (as) | Russin,Irving 'Babe' (ts) | Ruffell,Donald (ts) | Gentry,Chuck (bs) | Wiggins,Gerald 'Gerry' (p) | Hendrickson,Al (g) | Comfort,Joe (b) | Cottler,Irv (dr) | Hamlin,Bob (voc) | Wacker,Bob (voc) | Lanham,Gene (voc) | Schrouder,Charles (voc) | Mooney,Hal (arr,ld)
Louis Armstrong And His All Stars With The Sy Oliver Orchestra
This Younger Generation | In Pursuit Of Happiness
NYC, rec. 14.12.1956
Armstrong,Louis (tp,voc) | Young,Trummy (tb) | Hall,Edmond (cl) | Dorsey,George (fl,as) | Jefferson,Hilton (as) | Thompson,Lucky (ts) | McRae,Dave (b-cl,bs) | Kyle,Billy (p) | Barksdale,Everett (g) | Gersh,Squire (b) | Deems,Barrett (dr) | Oliver,Sy (cond,arr)

Argo | Universal Music Germany

589762-2 | CD | The Jazztet At Birdhouse | EAN 731458976226
Art Farmer/Benny Golson Jazztet
Junction: | Farmer's Market | Darn That Dream | Shutterbug | Round About Midnight | November Afternoon
Live at The Birdhouse,Chicago,Ill, rec. 15.5.1961
Farmer,Art (tp) | Golson,Benny (ts) | McIntosh,Tom (tb) | Walton,Cedar (p) | Williams,Tommy (b) | Heath,Albert 'Tootie' (dr)

ART BY HEART | Art By Heart

ABH 2001 2 | CD | Skyliner
Helmut Nieberle-Helmut Kagerer
Skyliner | Django's Castle(Manoir De Mes Reves) | Taking A Chance On Love | Snow Waltz | Gone With The Wind | Just One Of Those Things | Poevis | Augustine | Monk Medley: | Reflections- | Bye-Ya- | Little Rootie Tootie- | Just You Just Me | Flecki's Walk | Moppin' The Bride | On Green Dolphin Street | Ain't Misbehavin' | Spring Is Here | It's Never Too Late For The Blues
München, rec. 1997
Kagerer,Helmut (g) | Nieberle,Helmut (g)

ABH 2002 2 | CD | Come Together
Christian Willisohn-Lillian Boutté
No One | Gee Baby Ain't I Good To You | Come Together | I Got It Bad And That Ain't Good | Thibodeaux Twister | I Wish I Could Be Free | Forty Four Blues | You've Got A Friend | Please Send Me Someone To Love | No Mission But You | Get Right Church | Laughing On The Outside(Crying On The Inside)
Willisohn,Christian (g,p,voc) | Boutté,Lillian (voc)

ABH 2003 2 | CD | Sophisticated
Bernd Lhotzky-Colin Dawson
Lush Life | Lover | Everything I Have Is Yours | Poor Butterfly | I've Grown Accustomed To Her Face | Pick Yourself Up | Sophisticated Lady | My Very Good Friend The Milkman | Just One Of Those Things | A Hundred Years From Today | My Romance | Love For Sale | Farewell Roker Park
Dawson,Colin (tp) | Lhotzky,Bernd (p)

ABH 2004 2 | CD | Mood Swings
David Paquette Trio
At Sundown | New Orleans | Nobody's Sweetheart | Soup Sandwich | You Can Depend On Me | My Buddy | Lahaina Cake Glide | Baby Won't You Please Come Home | It's The Talk Of The Town | In The Racket | St.James Infirmary | Nobody Got The Blues But Me | The Nearness Of You
München, rec. 1998
Paquette,David (p,voc) | Knauer,Rocky (b) | Hollander,Rick (dr)

ABH 2005 2 | CD | You've Gotta Love Pops:Lillian Bouté Sings Louis Armstrong
Lillian Boutté And Her Group
When It's Sleepy Time Down South | The Boy From New Orleans | C'Est Si Bon | Swing That Music | Black Benny | Old Man Mose | If We Never Meet Again | Someday You'll Be Sorry | Beale Street Blues | Mack The Knife(Moritat) | High Society Calypso | What A Wonderful World
München, rec. 1999
Boutté,Lillian (voc) | L'Etienne,Thomas (cl) | Ilett,Denny (g) | Gilliet,Michel (p) | Crowdy,Andy (b,perc) | Frost,Soren (dr)
I Thought I Heard Buddy Bolden Say | Farewell To Storyville
Boutté,Lillian (voc) | L'Etienne,Thomas (cl) | Ilett,Denny (g) | Willisohn,Christian (p) | Crowdy,Andy (b,perc) | Frost,Soren (dr)

ABH 2006 2 | 2 CD | Live At Marians
Christian Willisohn Group
Bring It On Home | Honky Tonk Blues | Basin Street | Black Fantasy | Little Red Rooster | Lestat's Lamento | Life | St.James Infirmary | 4 Meade | Josephine | Somebody Bigger | Rain | Lonely Avenue | Tin Pan Alley | Who Do You Love | After Hours | Alright | Hold On,I'm Waiting For You
Live at Marians Jazzroom,Bern,CH, rec. September 2000
Willisohn,Christian (p,voc) | Knauer,Rocky (b) | Hollander,Rick (dr) | Vollmer,Titus (g)

art-mode-records | Jazz Network

990014 | CD | Imagenes | EAN 4038662990014
Daniel Messina Band
Imagenes | Todos Los Reencuentros | Azul Azul Cielo | 500.000 Caricias Del Cielo | El Corazon De Mi Pueblo | Dos Palabras Necesarias
details unknown, rec. 28.2.1998
Messina,Daniel (dr,perc,voc) | Kroll,Frank (ss,as) | Demming,Hajo (g,el-g) | Müller,Klaus (p,keyboards) | Rotter,Thomas (b,el-b)
Todo Lo Que Queda Por Decir
Messina,Daniel (dr,perc,voc) | Kroll,Frank (ss,as) | Hann,Eberhard (pan-fl) | Demming,Hajo (g,el-g) | Müller,Klaus (p,keyboards) | Rotter,Thomas (b,el-b)
Asi Sin Pensar
Messina,Daniel (dr,perc,voc) | Reichert,Rolf (tp) | Sticker,Felix (tb) | Kroll,Frank (ss,as) | Demming,Hajo (g,el-g) | Müller,Klaus (p,keyboards) | Rotter,Thomas (b,el-b) | Romero,Martin (congas)

AMR 2101 | CD | Café Com Leite | EAN 4042064000738
Terra Brazil
Café Com Leite | Como O Chines E A Bicicleta | Partido Alto | Como Um Samba De Adeus | Quilombos | Haiti Arcoite Ou Nao | Vendaval | Fora Da Lei | Tudo Bem | Café Com Leite(part 2)
Augsburg, rec. December 1998-January 1999
Terra Brazil | Tubino,Marcio (fl,ss,as,ts) | Lackerschmid,Wolfgang (vib) | Lutter,Andy (p,keyboards) | Baika,Imre (b) | Winter,Claudio (dr) | De Sousa,Borel (perc) | Ferreira,Nice (voc)

AMR 21061 | CD | Prioridad A la Emoción | EAN 4042064000745
Quique Sinesi & Daniel Messina
Sin Tiempo Y Sin Distancia | Le Sed | Entre Tus Rios | Dos Soles | Cueca Del Árbol | Sonidos De Aquel Dia | Todos Los Reencuentros | Te Tango Entre Suenos
Augsburg, rec. 2001
Sinesi,Quinque (g) | Messina,Daniel (perc)
Quique Sinesi & Daniel Messina With Guests
Pa 'Delante Como Sea
Sinesi,Quinque (g) | Messina,Daniel (perc) | Stricker,Felix (tb)
Prioridad A La Emoción | Sol Naciente
Sinesi,Quinque (g) | Messina,Daniel (perc) | Lehel,Peter (ss,ts)
Dos De Tus Mascaras
Sinesi,Quinque (g) | Messina,Daniel (perc) | Lehel,Peter (ss,ts) | Battistessa,Gustavo (bandoneon)

Atlantic | Warner Classics & Jazz Germany

16037-2 | CD | Songs Of The Beatles
Sarah Vaughan And Her Band
Get Back | And I Love Her | Eleanor Rigby | Fool On The Hill | Blackbird | Something | Here, There And Everywhere | The Long And Winding Road | Yesterday | Hey Jude
Hollywood,CA, rec. details unknown
Vaughan,Sarah (voc) | Ritenour,Lee (g) | Parks,Dean (g) | Shelton,Louie (g) | Thielemans,Jean 'Toots' (harm) | Pocaro,Steve (synth) | Paich,David (keyboards,arr) | Paich,Marty (keyboards,arr) | Lang,Mike (keyboards) | Hungate,David (b) | Pocaro,Joe (dr,perc) | Hall,Bobbye Porter (perc) | Pocaro,Joe (perc) | Forman,Steve (perc) | Thedford,Billy (voc) | Morgan,Perry (voc) | Gilstrap,James (voc) | Strings | Sharp,Sidney 'Sid' (concertmaster)
Come Together | I Want You (She's So Heavy)
Vaughan,Sarah (voc) | Smith,John (ts) | Ritenour,Lee (g) | Parks,Dean (g) | Shelton,Louie (g) | Thielemans,Jean 'Toots' (harm) | Pocaro,Steve (synth) | Paich,David (keyboards,arr) | Paich,Marty (keyboards,arr) | Lang,Mike (keyboards) | Hungate,David (b) | Pocaro,Joe (dr,perc) | Hall,Bobbye Porter (perc) | Pocaro,Joe (perc) | Forman,Steve (perc) | Thedford,Billy (voc) | Morgan,Perry (voc) | Gilstrap,James (voc) | Strings | Sharp,Sidney 'Sid' (concertmaster)
You Never Give Me Your Money
Vaughan,Sarah (voc) | Ritenour,Lee (g) | Parks,Dean (g) | Shelton,Louie (g) | Thielemans,Jean 'Toots' (harm) | Pocaro,Steve (synth) | Paich,David (keyboards,arr) | Paich,Marty (keyboards,arr) | Lang,Mike (keyboards) | Magnusson,Bob (b) | Hungate,David (b) | Pocaro,Joe (dr,perc) | Hall,Bobbye Porter (perc) | Pocaro,Joe (perc) | Forman,Steve (perc) | Thedford,Billy (voc) | Morgan,Perry (voc) | Gilstrap,James (voc) | Strings | Sharp,Sidney 'Sid' (concertmaster)

19110-2 | CD | Enigmatic Ocean
Jean-Luc Ponty Sextet
Overture | The Trans-Love Express | Mirage | Enigmatic Ocean(part 1-4) | Nostalgic Lady | The Struggle Of The Turtle To The Sea(part 1-3)
rec. June/July 1977
Ponty,Jean-Luc (el-v,bells,grand-p,violectra) | Holdsworth,Allan (el-g) | Stuermer,Daryl (el-g) | Zavod,Allan (el-p,org,synth,clavinet,grand-p) | Armstrong,Ralphe (el-b) | Smith,Steve (dr,perc)

19333-2 | CD | Mystical Adventures
Jean-Luc Ponty Group
Mystical Adventures Suite(part 1-5) | Rhythms Of Hope | As | Final Truth(part 1-2)
Los Angeles,CA, rec. August/September 1981
Ponty,Jean-Luc (org,synth,v,el-v,vocoder,voice) | Glaser,Jamie (g) | Rhyne,Chris (p,el-p,synth) | Jackson,Randy (b) | Griffin,Rayford (dr)
Jig
Ponty,Jean-Luc (org,v) | Glaser,Jamie (g) | Rhyne,Chris (el-p,synth) | Jackson,Randy (b) | Griffin,Rayford (dr) | Da Costa,Paulinho (perc)

2292-42145-2 | CD | Tango Nuevo
Gerry Mulligan With Astor Piazzolla And His Orchestra
20 Years Ago | Close Your Eyes And Listen | Years Of Solitude | Deus Xango | 20 Years After | Aire De Buenos Aires | Reminiscence | Summit
Milano,Italy, rec. 24-26.9.&1-4.10.1974
Mulligan,Gerry (bs) | Piazzolla,Astor (arr,bandoneon) | Gatti,Angel Poncho (p,el-p,org) | Baldan,Alberto (marimba) | Zilioli,Gianni (marimba) | Dacco,Filippo (el-g) | Di Filippi,Bruno (el-g) | Michelangeli,Umberto Benedetti (v) | Riccio,Renato (viola) | Miori,Ennio (cello) | Prestipino,Giuseppe (el-b) | De Piscopo,Tullio (dr,perc)

2292-42148-2 | CD | Ataraxia
Passport
Ataraxia(part 1&2) | Sky Blue | Mandrake | Reng Ding Dang Dong | The Secret | Louisiana | Alegria
München-Grünwald, rec. details unknown
Passport | Doldinger,Klaus (fl,sax,keyboards) | Schaper,Hendrik (keyboards) | Louis,Roy (g) | Petereit,Dieter (el-b) | Ketzer,Willy (dr) | Louis,Elmer (perc) | Marchena,Guilhermo (perc,voc)

2292-42172-2 | CD | Handmade
Abracadabra | The Connexion | Yellow Dream | Proclamation | Hand Made | Puzzle | The Quiet Man
details unknown, rec. 1973
Passport | Doldinger,Klaus (ss,ts,el-p,synth,mellotron) | Roberts,Frank (p,org) | Schmid,Wolfgang (g,b-g) | Cress,Curt (dr)

2292-42178-2 | CD | Blue Tattoo
Klaus Doldinger's Passport
Riding On A Cloud | Radiation | Piece For Rock Orchestra | In A Melancholy Way
München-Grünwald, rec. details unknown
Passport | Doldinger,Klaus (sax,keyboards,synth,lyricon) | Mulligan,Kevin (g) | Schaper,Hendrik (el-p,synth) | Petereit,Dieter (b) | Crigger,Dave (dr)
Ragtag And Bobtail | Blue Tattoo | Rambling | Daybreak Delight
Passport | Doldinger,Klaus (sax,keyboards,synth,lyricon) | Mulligan,Kevin (g) | Petereit,Dieter (b) | Crigger,Dave (dr)

2292-44142-2 | CD | Uranus
Passport
Uranus | Schirokko | Hexensabbat | Nostalgia | Lemuria's Dance | Continuation | Madhouse Jam
details unknown, rec. 1970
Passport | Doldinger,Klaus (ss,ts,el-p,synth) | Kübler,Olaf (fl,ts) | Jackson,Jimmy (org) | Meid,Lothar (el-b) | Lindenberg,Udo (dr)

2292-44143-2 | CD | Second Passport
Mandragora | Nexus | Fairy Tale | Get Yourself A Second Passport | Registration O | Horizon Beyond | The Cat From Katmandu
details unknown, rec. 1972
Passport | Doldinger,Klaus (ss,ts,el-p,synth) | Mealing,John (el-p,org) | Schmid,Wolfgang (el-g,b-g) | Spring,Bryan (dr)

2292-44144-2 | CD | Looking Thru
Eternal Spiral | Looking Thru | Zwischenspiel | Rockport | Tarantula | Ready For Take Off | Eloquence | Things To Come
details unknown, rec. Oct.1973
Passport | Doldinger,Klaus (ss,ts,el-p,synth,mellotron) | Schultze,Kristian (el-p,org) | Schmid,Wolfgang (g,b) | Cress,Curt (dr,perc,el-perc)

2292-44145-2 | CD | Cross-Collateral
Homunculus | Cross-Collateral | Jadoo | Will O'The Wisp | Albatros Song | Damals
Tonstudio Dierks,?, rec. Nov.1974
Passport | Doldinger,Klaus (ss,ts,el-p,synth,mellotron) | Schultze,Kristian (el-p,org) | Schmid,Wolfgang (g,b) | Cress,Curt (dr,perc,el-perc)

2292-44146-2 | CD | Infinity Machine
Ju-Ju-Man | Morning Sun | Blue Aura | Infinity Machine | Ostinato | Contemplation
Tonstudio Dierks & Union Studio,?, rec. January 1976
Passport | Doldinger,Klaus (ss,ts,keyboards,synth,voice) | Schultze,Kristian (keyboards,synth) | Schmid,Wolfgang (g,el-b,harmonizer) | Cress,Curt (dr,perc)

2292-44147-2 | CD | Garden Of Eden
Big Bang | Dreamware | Cildren's Dance | Garden Of Eden: | Light I- | Snake-
München-Grünwald, rec. details unknown
Passport | Doldinger,Klaus (cl,ss,ts,keyboards) | Mulligan,Kevin (g,voc) | Schaper,Hendrik (keyboards) | Petereit,Dieter (el-b) | Ketzer,Willy (dr,perc)
Dawn-
Passport | Doldinger,Klaus (ts,keyboards,ss cl) | Mulligan,Kevin (g,voc) | Schaper,Hendrik (keyboards) | Petereit,Dieter (el-b) | Ketzer,Willy (dr,perc) | Ramthor,Horst (harp)
Light II- | Gates Of Paradise | Good Earth Smile
Passport | Doldinger,Klaus (cl,ss,ts,keyboards) | Mulligan,Kevin (g,voc) | Schaper,Hendrik (keyboards) | Petereit,Dieter (el-b) | Ketzer,Willy (dr,perc) | Bartney,Kathy (voc)

2292-44175-2 | CD | Doldinger Jubilee Concert
Passport And Guests
Hand Made
Düsseldorf, rec. 16.10.1973
Passport | Doldinger,Klaus (ts) | Griffin,Johnny (ts) | Kriegel,Volker (g) | Auger,Brian (org) | Schultze,Kristian (p,synth) | Schmid,Wolfgang (b) | Cress,Curt (dr) | York,Pete (perc)
Freedom Jazz Dance
Auger,Brian (org) | Schmid,Wolfgang (b) | Cress,Curt (dr) | York,Pete (dr,perc)
Schirokko
Passport | Doldinger,Klaus (ts) | Griffin,Johnny (ts) | Kriegel,Volker (g) | Schultze,Kristian (el-p) | Schmid,Wolfgang (b) | York,Pete (dr) | Cress,Curt (dr)
Rockport
Passport | Doldinger,Klaus (ts) | Griffin,Johnny (ts) | Kriegel,Volker (g) | Auger,Brian (org) | Korner,Alexis (g) | Schmid,Wolfgang (b) | Schultze,Kristian (el-p,mellotron) | York,Pete (dr) | Cress,Curt (dr)
Rock Me Baby
Passport | Doldinger,Klaus (ss) | Korner,Alexis (g,voc) | Kriegel,Volker (g) | Auger,Brian (p) | Schmid,Wolfgang (b) | Cress,Curt (perc) | York,Pete (dr)
Lemuria's Dance
Passport | Doldinger,Klaus (ts) | Griffin,Johnny (ts) | Kriegel,Volker (g) | Korner,Alexis (g) | Auger,Brian (org) | Schultze,Kristian (el-p) | Schmid,Wolfgang (b) | Cress,Curt (dr) | York,Pete (perc)

2292-46031-2 | CD | Iguacu
Passport
Bahia Do Sol | Aguamarinha | Praia Leme | Heavy Weight | Bird Of Paradise | Iguacu
München, rec. details unknown
Passport | Doldinger,Klaus (fl,ss,ts,synth) | Louis,Roy (g) | Schultze,Kristian (p,el-p,org) | Schmid,Wolfgang (b-g) | Cress,Curt (dr,berimbau)
Sambukada
Passport | Doldinger,Klaus (fl,ss,ts,synth) | Louis,Roy (g) | Schultze,Kristian (p,el-p,org) | Schmid,Wolfgang (b-g) | Cress,Curt (dr,berimbau) | Ribeiro,Clelio (berimbau) | Das Neves,Wilson (atapaques,pandeiro) | Pinheiro,Roberto Bastos (surdo) | Salazar,Marcello (perc)
Guna Guna
Passport | Doldinger,Klaus (fl,ss,ts,synth) | Louis,Roy (g) | Schultze,Kristian (p,el-p,org) | Schmid,Wolfgang (b-g) | Cress,Curt (dr,berimbau) | Santos,Pedro 'Sosongo' (perc,whistles) | Pinto,Noel Manuel (cuica) | Björklund,Mats (g)

2292-46477-2 | CD | Earthborn
Klaus Doldinger's Passport
Palm Tree Song | Ball The Jack | Bassic | Earthborn | Allemande | Leave Taking | Abakus | Night Delighter
München-Grünwald, rec. details unknown
Passport | Doldinger,Klaus (fl,sax,keyboards) | Mulligan,Kevin (g) | Weindorf,Hermann (keyboards,voc) | Petereit,Dieter (b) | Cress,Curt (dr,perc)
New Moon
Passport | Doldinger,Klaus (fl,sax,keyboards) | Mulligan,Kevin (g) | Björklund,Mats (g) | Weindorf,Hermann (keyboards,voc) | Petereit,Dieter (b) | Cress,Curt (dr,perc)

3984-23105-2 | CD | Nature(The Essence Part III)
Ahmad Jamal Quartet
If I Find You Again | Like Someone In Love | Chaperon | And We Were Lovers | Fantastic Vehicle | The End Of A Love Affair | Cabin In The Sky(medley): | Cabin In The Sky- | Poor Pierrot- | The Reprise-
Pernes Les Fontaines,France/NYC, rec. 23.-25.7.1997/2.1.1998
Jamal,Ahmad (p) | Cammack,James (b) | Muhammad,Idris[Leo Morris] (dr) | Molineaux,Othello (steel-dr)
Ahmad Jamal Quartet With Stanley Turrentine
Devil's In My Den
Jamal,Ahmad (p) | Turrentine,Stanley (ts) | Cammack,James (b) | Muhammad,Idris[Leo Morris] (dr) | Molineaux,Othello (steel-dr)
Ahmad Jamal-Othello Molineaux
If I Find You Again
Jamal,Ahmad (p) | Molineaux,Othello (steel-dr)

3984-26922-2 | CD | Back In New York:Blind Date
Klaus Doldinger Group
Friendship | Here To Be | September Song | Erinnerung
NYC, rec. 18.-20.11.1998
Doldinger,Klaus (ss,ts) | Hays,Kevin (p) | Coleman,Ira (b) | Lewis,Victor (dr)
What's New?
Doldinger,Klaus (ss,ts) | Harris,Stefon (vib) | Hays,Kevin (p) | Coleman,Ira (b) | Lewis,Victor (dr)
East River Drive
Doldinger,Klaus (ss,ts) | Harris,Stefon (vib) | Bernstein,Peter (g) | Hays,Kevin (p) | Coleman,Ira (b) | Lewis,Victor (dr)
Hasta Manana
Doldinger,Klaus (ss,ts) | Harris,Stefon (vib) | Hays,Kevin (p) | Coleman,Ira (b) | Lewis,Victor (dr) | Ernesto,Don (perc)
Blind Date
Doldinger,Klaus (ss,ts) | Bernstein,Peter (g) | Hays,Kevin (p) | Coleman,Ira (b) | Lewis,Victor (dr) | Ernesto,Don (perc)
Blue Circle | Stop And Go
Doldinger,Klaus (ss,ts) | Bernstein,Peter (g) | Hays,Kevin (p) | Coleman,Ira (b) | Lewis,Victor (dr)

7567-80475-2 | CD | The New Tristano
Lennie Tristano
Becoming | C Minor Complex | You Don't Know What Love Is | Deliberation | Scene And Variations: | Carol- | Tania- | Bud- | Love Lines | G Minor Complex
NYC, rec. July-August 1962
Tristano,Lennie (p-solo)

7567-80757-2 | CD | Bap-Tizum
Art Ensemble Of Chicago
Introduction by John Sinclair | N'Famoudou Boudougou | Immm | Unanka | Oouffnoon | Ohnedaruth | Odwalla
Live at The Ann Arbor Blues & Jazz Festival, rec. 9.9.1972
Art Ensemble Of Chicago | Bowie,Lester (tp,fl-h,perc,kelp-h,voc) | Mitchell,Roscoe (cl,ss,as,ts,bass-sax,perc,bells,gongs,voc) | Jarman,Joseph (alto-fl,ss,as,ts,bs,vib,perc,sopranino) | Favors,Malachi (b,el-b,gongs,log-dr,voc,whistles) | Moye,Famoudou Don (dr,perc,perc,bass-marimba,gongs,log-dr,voc,whistles)

7567-80760-2 | CD | Dee Dee Bridgewater
Dee Dee Bridgewater With Band
My Prayer(fast)
NYC, rec. details unknown
Bridgewater,Dee Dee (voc) | Morris,Cliff (g) | Friedman,Jerry (g) | Wheeler,Harold (keyboards) | Bushler,Herb (b) | Schwartzberg,Alan (dr) | November,Linda (voc) | Martell,Arleane (voc) | Cherry,Vivian (voc)
It Ain't Easy | Goin' Through The Motions | Every Man Wants Another Man's Woman | My Prayer(ballad)
Shefield,Alabama, rec. details unknown
Bridgewater,Dee Dee (voc) | Carr,Pete (g) | Johnson,Jimmy (g) | Beckett,Barry (keyboards) | Hood,David (b) | Hawkins,Roger (dr) | Groves,Lani (voc) | Guthrie,Gwen (voc) | Cherry,Vivian (voc)
My Lonely Room | He's Gone | You Saved Me
Los Angeles,CA, rec. details unknown
Bridgewater,Dee Dee (voc) | Ragin,Melvin (g) | Parker Jr.,Ray (g) | Parks,Dean (g) | Walker,David T. (g) | Hensley,Tom (keyboards) | Sample,Joe (keyboards) | Felder,Wilton (b) | Davis,Henry (b) | Greene,Ed (dr) | Coleman,Gary (perc) | Gilstrap,James (voc) | Johnson,August (voc) | Lehman,John (voc) | Willia,Carolyn (voc) | Ward,Jackie (voc) | McCall,Marti (voc) | Clayton,Merry (voc)

7567-80761-2 | CD | Truth Is Fallen
Dave Brubeck With The Erich Kunzel Orchestra
Prelude | Merciful Men Are Taken Away | Truth Is Fallen | Oh,That My Head Were Waters | Speak Out(duet)- | I Called And No One Answered- | Yea Truth Faileth | Truth(Planets Are Spinning) | Is The Lord's Hand Shortened? | Arise!
Cincinatti,OH, rec. ca.1973
Brubeck,Dave (p,oscillator) | Brubeck,Chris (tb,keyboards,voc) | Ruth,Peter (fl,harm,voc) | Cathcart,Jim (tp,org,voc) | Dudash,Stephan (g,v,voc) | Bonisteel,Peter (perc) | Brown,Chris (b,el-b,voc) | Mason,David (g,viola,voc) | Thompson,Lowell (bongos) | St.John Assambly | Franklin,Gordon (dir) | Cincinnati Symphony Orchestra,The | Kunzel,Erich (ld)

7567-80762-2 | CD | Alone At Last
Gary Burton
Moonchild- | In Your Quiet Place- | Green Mountains- | Arise Her Eyes- | The Sunset Bell | Hand Bags And Glad Rags | Hullo Bolinas | General Mojo's Well-Laid Plan | Chega De Saudade(No More Blues)
Live at The Monterey Jazz Festival,CA, rec. 19.6.1971
Burton,Gary (vib,p,el-p,org)

7567-80763-2 | CD | Paris Encounter
Gary Burton-Stephane Grappelli Quartet
Daphne | Blue In Green | Falling Grace | Here's That Rainy Day | Coquette | Sweet Rain | The Night Has A Thousand Eyes | Arpege | Eiderdown
Paris,France, rec. 4.11.1969
Burton,Gary (vib) | Grappelli,Stephane (v) | Swallow,Steve (el-b) | Goodwin,Bill (dr)

7567-80765-2 | CD | Ray Charles At Newport
Ray Charles And His Orchestra
The Right Time | In A Little Spanish Town | I Got A Woman | Blues Waltz | Hot Rod | Talkin' 'Bout You | Sherry | A Fool For You
Live at Newport,Rhode Island, rec. 5.7.1958
Charles,Ray (as,p,voc) | Harper,Lee (tp) | Belgrave,Marcus (tp) | Newman,David Fathead (ts) | Crawford,Bennie (bs) | Willis,Edgar (b) | Goldberg,Richie (dr) | Hendricks,Marjorie (voc) | Raylettes,The (voc)

7567-80767-2 | CD | This Is Our Music
Ornette Coleman Quartet
Blues Connotation | Kaleidoscope
rec. 19.7.1960
Coleman,Ornette (as) | Cherry,Don (pocket-tp) | Haden,Charlie (b) | Blackwell,Ed (dr)
Embraceable You | Humpty Dumpty
NYC, rec. 26.7.1960
Coleman,Ornette (as) | Cherry,Don (pocket-tp) | Haden,Charlie (b) | Blackwell,Ed (dr)
Beauty Is A Rare Thing | Poise | Folk Tale
NYC, rec. 2.8.1960
Coleman,Ornette (as) | Cherry,Don (pocket-tp) | Haden,Charlie (b) | Blackwell,Ed (dr)

7567-80769-2 | CD | Chris Connor
Chris Connor With The Ralph Burns Orchestra
My April Heart | For The Wind Was Green | He Was Too Good For Me | Something To Live For
NYC, rec. 19.1.1956
Connor,Chris (voc) | Burns,Ralph (cond,arr) | details unknown
Chris Connor With The John Lewis Quartet
Where Are You | I Get A Kick Out Of You | Every Time | Almost Like Being In Love
NYC, rec. 23.1.1956
Connor,Chris (voc) | Lewis,John (p) | Galbraith,Barry (g) | Pettiford,Oscar (b) | Kay,Connie (dr)
Chris Connor With Band
You Make Me Feel So Young | Anything Goes | Way Out There | Get Out Of Town
NYC, rec. 8.2.1956
Connor,Chris (voc) | Travis,Nick (tp) | Marowitz,Sam (as) | Beckenstein,Ray (as) | Young,Al (ts) | Sims,Zoot (ts) | Bank,Danny (bs) | Wechsler,Moe (p) | Galbraith,Barry (g) | Hinton,Milt (b) | Johnson,Osie (dr)

7567-80773-2 | CD | Sing Me Softly Of The Blues
Art Farmer Quartet
One For Majid
NYC, rec. 12.3.1965
Farmer,Art (fl-h) | Kuhn,Steve (p) | Swallow,Steve (b) | LaRoca,Pete (dr)
Ad Infinitum | Sing Me Softly Of The Blues | I Waited For You | Tears
NYC, rec. 16.3.1965
Farmer,Art (fl-h) | Kuhn,Steve (p) | Swallow,Steve (b) | LaRoca,Pete (dr)
Petite Belle
NYC, rec. 30.3.1965
Farmer,Art (fl-h) | Kuhn,Steve (p) | Swallow,Steve (b) | LaRoca,Pete (dr)

7567-80776-2 | CD | Closer To The Source
Dizzy Gillespie And His Orchestra
Could It Be You | It's Time For Love | Closer To The Source | You're No.1 In My Book | Iced Tea | Just Before Dawn | Textures
NYC, rec. 1984
Gillespie,Dizzy (tp) | Fortune,Sonny (as) | Marsalis,Branford (ts) | Bullock,Hiram (g) | Wonder,Stevie (synth,harm) | Kirkland,Kenny (p) | Eastmond,Barry (keyboards) | Raney,Thom (b) | Cintron,Tony (dr) | Williams,Buddy (dr) | Cinelu,Mino (perc) | Bracey,Marty (perc) | Rogers,Angel (voc)

7567-80777-2 | CD | Western Suite
Jimmy Giuffre 3
Western Suite: | Pony Express- | Apaches- | Saturday Night Dance- | Big Pow Wow- | Topsy | Blue Monk
NYC, rec. 3.12.1958
Giuffre,Jimmy (cl,ts,bs) | Brookmeyer,Bob (v-tb,p) | Hall,Jim (g)

7567-80783-2 | CD | El Juicio(The Judgement)
Keith Jarrett
Pardon My Rags
NYC, rec. 8.7.1971
Jarrett,Keith (p-solo)
Keith Jarrett Quartet
Pre-Judgement Armosphere
Jarrett,Keith (fl,ss,p) | Redman,Dewey (ts) | Haden,Charlie (b) | Motian,Paul (dr)
El Juicio(And Extensions Fabulosas)
Jarrett,Keith (fl,ss,p) | Redman,Dewey (ts) | Haden,Charlie (b) | Motian,Paul (dr)
Piece For Ornette(long version) | Gypsy Moth
NYC, rec. 15.7.1971
Jarrett,Keith (fl,ss,p) | Redman,Dewey (ts) | Haden,Charlie (b) | Motian,Paul (dr)
Piece For Ornette(short version) | Toll Road
NYC, rec. 16.7.1971
Jarrett,Keith (fl,ss,p) | Redman,Dewey (ts) | Haden,Charlie (b) | Motian,Paul (dr)

7567-80787-2 | CD | An Evening With Two Grand Pianos
John Lewis And Hank Jones
Stompin' At The Savoy | St.Louis Blues | Confirmation | Tears From The Children | Willow Weep For Me | Billie's Bounce | Odds Against Tomorrow | I'll Remember April
NYC, rec. 25./26.1.& 8./9.2.1979
Lewis,John (p) | Jones,Hank (p)

7567-80788-2 | CD | Charles Lloyd In Europe
Charles Lloyd Quartet
Tagore | Karma | Little Wahid's Day | Manhattan Carousel | European Fantasy | Hej Da!
Live at Aulaen Hall,Oslo,Norway, rec. 29.10.1966
Lloyd,Charles (ts) | Jarrett,Keith (p) | McBee,Cecil (b) | DeJohnette,Jack (dr)

7567-80790-2 | CD | Another Beginning
Les McCann Group
Maybe You'll Come Back | The Song Is Love
NYC/Los Angeles,CA, rec. details unknown
McCann,Les (p,el-p,synth,clavinet,voc) | Gaines,Roy (g) | Rainey,Chuck (el-b) | Humphrey,Paul (dr) | Clarke,Buck (perc) | Nadien,David (v) | Green,Emmanuel (v) | Gershman,Paul (v) | Clarke,Selwart (v) | Malin,Joe (v) | Raimondi,Matthew (v) | Allen,Sanford (v) | Lookofsky,Harry (v) | Ellen,Max (v) | Cykman,Harry (v) | Brown,Alfred (viola) | Barber,Julian (viola) | Moore,Kermit (cello) | Ricci,George (cello) | Bushler,Herb (b) | Loving,Tamiko (voc) | Moore,Laurence (voc)
When It's Over | Somebody's Been Lying 'Bout Me | Go On And Cry | My Soul Lies Deep | The Morning Song | Someday We'll Meet Again
McCann,Les (p,el-p,synth,clavinet,voc) | Kudykowski,Miroslaw (g) | Rowser,Jimmy (el-b) | Davis,Harold (dr) | Clarke,Buck (perc) | Moore,Danny (tp,fl-h) | Faddis,Jon (tp,fl-h) | Wilder,Joe (tp,fl-h) | Brown,Garnett (tb) | Zawadi,Kiane (tb) | Slapin,Bill (cl,sax) | Wess,Frank (sax) | Powell,Seldon (sax) | Vick,Harold (sax) | Stevens,Sally (voc) | McCall,Marti (voc) | Esty,Bob (voc) | Gilstrap,James (voc) | Bryant,Carmen (voc) | Gould,Vennette (voc) | Merrill-Smolen,Sandy (voc) | Collier,Kathy (voc) | Ames,Morgan (voc) | Houston,Cissy (voc) | Tuck,Deidre (voc) | Stafford,Rennelle (voc) | Holmes,Norma (voc)

7567-80791-2 | CD | The Last Of The Blue Devils
Jay McShann Orchestra
Confessin' The Blues | 'Taint Nobody's Bizness If I Do | Hootie Blues | Blue Devil Jump | My Chile | Jumpin' At The Woodside | Jot Biscuits | 'Fore Day Rider | Kansas City
NYC, rec. 29./30.6.1977
McShann,Jay (p,el-p,voc) | Newman,Joe (tp) | Quinichette,Paul (ts) | Tate,Buddy (ts) | Scofield,John (el-g) | Hinton,Milt (b) | Williams,Jackie (dr)
Jay McShann
Just For You
McShann,Jay (p-solo)

7567-80793-2 | CD | Tonight At Noon
Charles Mingus Jazz Workshop
Passions Of A Woman Loved | Tonight At Noon
NYC, rec. 12.3.1957
Mingus,Charles (b) | Knepper,Jimmy (tb) | Hadi [Curtis Porter],Shafti (as) | Legge,Wade (p) | Richmond,Dannie (dr)
Charles Mingus Quintet With Roland Kirk
Old Blues For Walt's Torin | Peggy's Blue Skylight | Invisible Lady
NYC, rec. 6.11.1961
Mingus,Charles (p,voc) | Kirk,Rahsaan Roland (fl,ts,manzello,siren,strich,voice) | Ervin,Booker (ts) | Knepper,Jimmy (tb) | Watkins,Doug (b) | Richmond,Dannie (dr)

7567-80794-2 | CD | The Modern Jazz Quartet At Music Inn With Sonny Rollins,Vol.2
Modern Jazz Quartet
Stardust- | I Can't Get Started- | Lover Man(Oh,Where Can You Be?)- | Yardbird Suite | Midsömmer | Festival Sketch
Live at Music Inn,Lenox,Mass., rec. 3.8.1958
MJQ (Modern Jazz Quartet) | Jackson,Milt (vib) | Lewis,John (p) | Heath,Percy (b) | Kay,Connie (dr)
Modern Jazz Quartet With Sonny Rollins
Bag's Groove | A Night In Tunisia
Live at Music Inn,Lenox,Mass., rec. 3.9.1958
MJQ (Modern Jazz Quartet) | Rollins,Sonny (ts) | Jackson,Milt (vib) | Lewis,John (p) | Heath,Percy (b) | Kay,Connie (dr)

7567-80798-2 | CD | Lift Every Voice And Sing
Max Roach Sextet With The J.C.White Singers
Sometimes I Feel Like A Motherless Child(for Marcus Garvey) | Garden Of Prayer(for My Mother And Father) | Troubled Waters(for Paul Robeson) | Let My People Go(for Patrice E.Lumuba) | Where You There When They Crucified My Lord(for Malcolm,Martin,Medgar And Many More) | Joshua(for Rev.Charles Koen And The People Of Cairo,Ill.
NYC, rec. 7./8.4.1971
Roach,Max (dr) | Bridgewater,Cecil (tp) | Harper,Billy (ts) | Cables,George (p) | Mathias,Eddie (el-b) | MacDonald,Ralph (perc) | J.C.White Singers | McClure,Ruby (voc) | White,Dorothy (voc)

7567-80804-2 | CD | Requiem
Lennie Tristano
Requiem
NYC, rec. 11.6.1955
Tristano,Lennie (p-solo)
Lennie Tristano Trio
Line Up | East Thirty-Second | Turkish Mambo
Tristano,Lennie (p) | Ind,Peter (b) | Morton,Jeff (dr)
Lennie Tristano Quartet
You Go To My Head | All The Things You Are | These Foolish Things Remind Me On You | If I Had You | I Don't Stand A Ghost Of A Chance With You
Tristano,Lennie (p) | Konitz,Lee (as) | Ramey,Gene (b) | Taylor,Arthur 'Art' (dr)
-> Bass & Drum were pre-recorded, parts of the Piano were dubbed later.

7567-81303-2 | 2 CD | The Great Paris Concert
Duke Ellington And His Orchestra
Kinda Dukish | Rockin' In Rhythm | On The Sunny Side Of The Street | The Star-Crossed Lovers | All Of Me | Theme From 'Asphalt Jungle' | Concerto For Cootie | Tutti For Cootie | Suite Thursday: | Misfit Blues- | Schwiphti- | Zweet Zurzday- | Lay-By- | Perdido | The Eight Veil | Rose Of The Rio Grande | Cop Out | Bula | Jam With Sam | Happy-Go-Lucky Local | Tone Paralell To Harlem | Black And Tan Fantasy | Creole Love Call | The Mooche | Pyramid | The Blues(from Black Brown And Beige) | Echoes Of Harlem
Live at The Olympia,Paris,France, rec. 1./2.& 23.2.1963
Ellington,Duke (p) | Williams,Cootie (tp) | Anderson,Cat (tp) | Burrowes,Roy (tp) | Nance,Ray (v,co) | Brown,Lawrence (tb) | Cooper,Frank 'Buster' (tb) | Connors,Chuck (tb) | Hodges,Johnny (as) | Procope,Russell (cl,as) | Hamilton,Jimmy (cl,ts) | Gonsalves,Paul (ts) | Carney,Harry (cl,bs) | Shepard,Ernie (b) | Woodyard,Sam (dr) | Grayson,Milt (voc)
Do Nothin' Till You Hear From Me | Things Ain't What They Used To Be | Satin Doll
Live, ?, rec. 1963
Ellington,Duke (p) | Williams,Cootie (tp) | Anderson,Cat (tp) | Burrowes,Roy (tp) | Nance,Ray (v,co) | Brown,Lawrence (tb) | Cooper,Frank 'Buster' (tb) | Connors,Chuck (tb) | Hodges,Johnny (as) | Procope,Russell (cl,as) | Hamilton,Jimmy (cl,ts) | Gonsalves,Paul (ts) | Carney,Harry (cl,bs) | Shepard,Ernie (b) | Woodyard,Sam (dr) | Grayson,Milt (voc)
Don't Get Around Much Anymore
details unknown, rec. ca 1963
Ellington,Duke (p) | Williams,Cootie (tp) | Anderson,Cat (tp) | Burrowes,Roy (tp) | Nance,Ray (v,co) | Brown,Lawrence (tb) | Cooper,Frank 'Buster' (tb) | Connors,Chuck (tb) | Hodges,Johnny (as) | Procope,Russell (cl,as) | Hamilton,Jimmy (cl,ts) | Gonsalves,Paul (ts) | Carney,Harry (cl,bs) | Shepard,Ernie (b) | Woodyard,Sam (dr)

7567-81304-2 | CD | Inner Space
Chick Corea Quintet
Straight Up And Down | Litha | Inner Space | Guijira
NYC, rec. 30.11./1.12.1966
Corea,Chick (p) | Shaw,Woody (tp) | Farrell,Joe (fl,ts) | Swallow,Steve (b) | Chambers,Joe (dr)
Chick Corea Quartet
Windows
NYC, rec. November 1968
Corea,Chick (p) | Laws,Hubert (fl) | Carter,Ron (b) | Tate,Grady (dr)
Chick Corea Trio
Trio For Flute Bassoon And Piano
Corea,Chick (p) | Porter,Karl (bassoon) | Laws,Hubert (fl)

7567-81332-2 | CD | Art Blakey's Jazz Messengers With Thelonious Monk
Art Blakey And The Jazz Messengers With Thelonious Monk
Blue Monk | I Mean You
NYC, rec. 14.5.1957
Monk,Thelonious (p) | Blakey,Art (dr) | Hardman,Bill (tp) | Griffin,Johnny (ts) | DeBrest,Jimmy 'Spanky' (b)

Rhythm-A-Ning | Purple Shades | Evidence | In Walked Bud
NYC, rec. 15.5.1957
Monk,Thelonious (p) | Blakey,Art (dr) | Hardman,Bill (tp) | Griffin,Johnny (ts) | DeBrest,Jimmy 'Spanky' (b)

7567-81341-2 | CD | Change Of The Century
Ornette Coleman Quartet
The Face Of The Bass | Bird Food | Una Muy Bonita | Change Of The Century
Hollywood,CA, rec. 8.10.1959
Coleman,Ornette (as) | Cherry,Don (pocket-tp) | Haden,Charlie (b) | Higgins,Billy (dr)
Ramblin' | Free | Forerunner
Hollywood,CA, rec. 9.10.1959
Coleman,Ornette (as) | Cherry,Don (pocket-tp) | Haden,Charlie (b) | Higgins,Billy (dr)

7567-81344-2 | CD | Coltrane Jazz
John Coltrane Quartet
Little Old Lady | I'll Wait And Pray | I'll Wait And Pray(alt.take)
NYC, rec. 24.11.1959
Coltrane,John (ts) | Kelly,Wynton (p) | Chambers,Paul (b) | Cobb,Jimmy (dr)
Harmonique | My Shining Hour | Fifth House | Like Sonny | Like Sonny(alt.take) | Some Other Blues
NYC, rec. 2.12.1959
Coltrane,John (ts) | Kelly,Wynton (p) | Chambers,Paul (b) | Cobb,Jimmy (dr)
Village Blues
NYC, rec. 21.10.1960
Coltrane,John (ts) | Tyner,McCoy (p) | Davis,Steve (b) | Jones,Elvin (dr)

7567-81349-2 | CD | Olé Coltrane
John Coltrane Group
Olé | Dahomey Dance | Aisha | To Her Ladyship
NYC, rec. 25.5.1961
Coltrane,John (ss,ts) | Hubbard,Freddie (tp) | Dolphy,Eric[as George Lane] (fl,as) | Tyner,McCoy (p) | Workman,Reggie (b) | Davis,Art (b) | Jones,Elvin (dr)

7567-81350-2 | CD | Herbie Mann At The Village Gate
Herbie Mann Sextet
Summertime | It Ain't Necessarily So
Live at The 'Village Gate',NYC, rec. 17.11.1961
Mann,Herbie (fl) | Hardy,Hagood (vib) | Abdul-Malik,Ahmed (b) | Collins,Rudy (dr) | Mantilla,Ray (perc) | Bey,Chief (perc)
Herbie Mann Septet
Comin' Home Baby
Mann,Herbie (fl) | Hardy,Hagood (vib) | Abdul-Malik,Ahmed (b) | Tucker,Ben (b) | Collins,Rudy (dr) | Mantilla,Ray (perc) | Bey,Chief (perc)

7567-81351-2 | CD | Coltrane Plays The Blues
John Coltrane Quartet
Blues To Elvin | Mr.Day | Mr.Syms | Mr.Knight | Untitled Blues(Original)
NYC, rec. 24.10.1960
Coltrane,John (ss,ts) | Tyner,McCoy (p) | Davis,Steve (b) | Jones,Elvin (dr)
John Coltrane Trio
Blues To Bechet | Blues To You
Coltrane,John (ss,ts) | Davis,Steve (b) | Jones,Elvin (dr)

7567-81358-2 | CD | Coltrane's Sound
Satelite
rec. 24.10.1960
Coltrane,John (ts) | Davis,Steve (b) | Jones,Elvin (dr)
John Coltrane Quartet
Central Park West | Body And Soul | Body And Soul(alt.take)
NYC, rec. 24.10.1960
Coltrane,John (ss,ts) | Tyner,McCoy (p) | Davis,Steve (b) | Jones,Elvin (dr)
Liberia | The Night Has A Thousand Eyes | Equinox | 26-2
NYC, rec. 26.10.1960
Coltrane,John (ss) | Tyner,McCoy (p) | Davis,Steve (b) | Jones,Elvin (dr)

7567-81364-2 | CD | Memphis Underground
Herbie Mann Group
Memphis Underground | New Orleans | Chain Of Fools | Battle Hymn Of The Republic
NYC, rec. 21.8.1968
Mann,Herbie (fl) | Ayers,Roy (vib,congas) | Emmons,Bobby (org) | Coryell,Larry (g) | Young,Reggie (g) | Sharrock,Sonny (g) | Wood,Bobby (p,el-p) | Cogbill,Tommy (el-b) | Leech,Mike (el-b) | Christman,Gene (dr)
Hold On I'm Coming
Mann,Herbie (fl) | Ayers,Roy (vib) | Emmons,Bobby (org) | Coryell,Larry (g) | Young,Reggie (g) | Sharrock,Sonny (g) | Wood,Bobby (p,el-p) | Vitous,Miroslav (el-b) | Christman,Gene (dr)

7567-81366-2 | CD | The Best Of John Coltrane
John Coltrane Quartet
Cousin Mary
NYC, rec. 4.5.1959
Coltrane,John (ts) | Flanagan,Tommy (p) | Chambers,Paul (b) | Taylor,Arthur 'Art' (dr)
Giant Steps
NYC, rec. 5.5.1959
Coltrane,John (ts) | Flanagan,Tommy (p) | Chambers,Paul (b) | Taylor,Arthur 'Art' (dr)
Naima
NYC, rec. 2.12.1959
Coltrane,John (ts) | Kelly,Wynton (p) | Chambers,Paul (b) | Cobb,Jimmy (dr)
My Favorite Things
NYC, rec. 21.10.1960
Coltrane,John (ss) | Tyner,McCoy (p) | Davis,Steve (b) | Jones,Elvin (dr)
Central Park West
NYC, rec. 24.10.1960
Coltrane,John (ss) | Tyner,McCoy (p) | Davis,Steve (b) | Jones,Elvin (dr)
Equinox
NYC, rec. 26.10.1960
Coltrane,John (ts) | Tyner,McCoy (p) | Davis,Steve (b) | Jones,Elvin (dr)

7567-81369-2 | CD | The Best Of Herbie Mann
Herbie Mann And His Orchestra
This Little Girl Of Mine
NYC, rec. 24.4.1961
Mann,Herbie (fl) | Palmieri,Charlie (p) | Gonzalez,Daniel (v) | Silva,Jose (v) | Andreu,Jose (v) | Garcia,Juan (b) | Totah,Nabil 'Knobby' (b) | Collins,Rudy (dr) | Mantilla,Ray (perc) | Barretto,Ray (perc)
Herbie Mann Group
Comin' Home Baby
Live at The 'Village Gate',NYC, rec. 17.11.1961
Mann,Herbie (fl) | Hardy,Hagood (vib) | Abdul-Malik,Ahmed (b) | Tucker,Ben (b) | Collins,Rudy (dr) | Bey,Chief (african-dr) | Mantilla,Ray (perc,congas)
Live at Newport,Rhode Island, rec. 3.7.1965
Mann,Herbie (fl) | Hitchcock,Jack (tb) | Weinstein,Mark (tb) | Pike,Dave (vib) | Corea,Chick (p) | Tucker,Ben (b) | Carr,Bruno (dr) | Valdez,Carlos 'Patato' (congas)
Herbie Mann And His Orchestra
Philly Dog
NYC, rec. 26.5.1966
Mann,Herbie (fl) | Newman,Joe (tp) | Markowitz,Irving 'Marky' (tp) | Jackson,Quentin (tb,b-tb) | Curtis,King (ts) | Adams,Pepper (bs) | Macey,Charlie (g) | Gorgoni,Al (g) | Macko,Joe (el-b) | Purdie,Bernard 'Pretty' (dr) | Smith,Warren (perc)
Herbie Mann-Tamiko Jones
A Man And A Woman
NYC, rec. 27.9.1966
Mann,Herbie (fl) | Jones,Tamiko (voc) | unkn. (rhythm section)
Herbie Mann Group
Memphis Underground
NYC, rec. 21.8.1968
Mann,Herbie (fl) | Ayers,Roy (vib,congas) | Emmons,Bobby (org) | Coryell,Larry (g) | Young,Reggie (g) | Sharrock,Sonny (g) | Wood,Bobby (p,el-p) | Cogbill,Tommy (el-b) | Leech,Mike (el-b) | Christman,Gene (dr)

7567-81370-2 | CD | The Best Of Eddie Harris
Eddie Harris Quartet
The Shadow Of Your Smile
NYC, rec. 9.8.1965
Harris,Eddie (ts) | Walton,Cedar (p) | Carter,Ron (b) | Higgins,Billy (dr)
Eddie Harris Quintet
Freedom Jazz Dance
NYC, rec. 30.8.1965
Harris,Eddie (ts) | Codrington,Ray (tp) | Walton,Cedar (p) | Carter,Ron (b) | Higgins,Billy (dr)
Eddie Harris Group
Shame Time
NYC, rec. 20.4.1967
Harris,Eddie (el-sax) | Lastie,Melvin (tp) | Newman,Joe (tp) | Curtis,King (ts) | Newman,David Fathead (ts) | Henry,Haywood (bs) | Christian,Jodie (p) | Jackson,Melvin (b) | Smith,Richard (dr)
Theme In Search Of A Movie
Harris,Eddie (el-sax) | Christian,Jodie (p) | Jackson,Melvin (b) | Smith,Richard (dr) | Strings | Mardin,Arif (arr)
Listen Here
Harris,Eddie (el-sax) | Christian,Jodie (p) | Jackson,Melvin (b) | Smith,Richard (dr) | Wohletz,Joe (perc) | Barretto,Ray (perc)
Live Right Now
NYC, rec. 14.3.1968
Harris,Eddie (el-sax) | Owens,Jimmy (tp) | Lastie,Melvin (tp) | Newman,Joe (tp) | McIntosh,Tom (tb) | Henry,Haywood (bs) | Christian,Jodie (p) | Rainey,Chuck (el-b) | Tate,Grady (dr)
1974 Blues
NYC, rec. 4.9.1968
Harris,Eddie (el-sax) | Young,Eugene 'Snooky' (tp) | Lastie,Melvin (tp) | Newman,Joe (tp) | Powell,Benny (b-tb) | Powell,Seldon (bs) | Christian,Jodie (p) | Jackson,Melvin (b) | Smith,Richard (dr)
Eddie Harris Quartet
Movin' On Out
Live at The 'Village Gate',NYC, rec. 19.4.1969
Harris,Eddie (el-sax) | Christian,Jodie (p) | Jackson,Melvin (b) | Hart,Billy (dr)
Eddie Harris Quintet
Boogie Woogie Bossa Nova
NYC, rec. 15.12.1969
Harris,Eddie (el-sax) | Christian,Jodie (el-p) | Spears,Louis (b) | Hart,Billy (dr) | Henry,Felix (perc)
Eddie Harris Group
A Child Is Born
NYC, rec. 25.7.1972
Harris,Eddie (el-sax) | Abrams,Muhal Richard (el-p) | Stewart,Mary Ann (voc) | Harrell,Vivian (voc) | Haywood,Marilyn (voc)
Is It In
NYC, rec. 16.12.1973
Harris,Eddie (keyboards,el-sax,voc) | Muldrow,Ronald (g,guitorgan) | Reid,Rufus (b) | James,William 'Billy' (dr,el-bongos)

7567-81374-2 | CD | Gary Burton & Keith Jarrett
Gary Burton-Keith Jarrett Quintet
Grow Your Own | Moonchild- | In Your Quiet Place- | Como En Vietnam | Fortune Smiles | The Raven Speaks
NYC, rec. 23.7.1970
Burton,Gary (vib) | Jarrett,Keith (ss,p,el-p) | Brown,Sam (g) | Swallow,Steve (b) | Goodwin,Bill (dr)

7567-81375-2 | CD | Zawinul
Joe Zawinul Group
Doctor Honoris Causa | In A Silent Way
NYC, rec. 6.8.1970
Zawinul,Joe (el-p) | Shaw,Woody (tp) | Davis,George (fl) | Turbinton,Earl (ss) | Hancock,Herbie (el-p) | Vitous,Miroslav (b) | Booker,Walter (b) | Hart,Billy (perc) | Lee,David (perc)
Arrival In New York
NYC, rec. 10.8.1970
Zawinul,Joe (el-p) | Owens,Jimmy (tp) | Hancock,Herbie (el-p) | Booker,Walter (b) | Chambers,Joe (dr) | Hart,Billy (perc) | Lee,David (perc) | DeJohnette,Jack (perc) | | Shaw,Woody (tp) | Laws,Hubert (fl) | Shorter,Wayne (ss)Vitous,Miroslav (b)
Double Image | His Last Journey
NYC, rec. 12.8.1970
Zawinul,Joe (el-p) | Owens,Jimmy (tp) | Hancock,Herbie (el-p) | Booker,Walter (b) | Chambers,Joe (dr) | Hart,Billy (dr) | Lee,David (dr) | DeJohnette,Jack (melodica)
-> Overdubbed in NYC, 28.10.1970:

7567-81382-2 | CD | The Last Set At Newport
Dave Brubeck Quartet With Gerry Mulligan
Introduction by Father Norman O'Connor | Blues For Newport | Take Five | Open The Gates(Out Of The Way Of The People)
Live at Newport,Rhode Island, rec. 3.7.1971
Brubeck,Dave (p) | Mulligan,Gerry (bs) | Six,Jack (b) | Dawson,Alan (dr)

7567-81390-2 | CD | We're All Together Again For The First Time
Dave Brubeck Quartet
Koto Song
Live at The Olympia,Paris,France, rec. 26.10.1972
Brubeck,Dave (p) | Desmond,Paul (as) | Six,Jack (b) | Dawson,Alan (dr)
Dave Brubeck Quartet With Gerry Mulligan
Rotterdam Blues
Live at De Doelen,Rotterdam,NL, rec. 28.10.1972
Brubeck,Dave (p) | Desmond,Paul (as) | Mulligan,Gerry (bs) | Six,Jack (b) | Dawson,Alan (dr)
Truth | Unfinished Woman | Take Five
Live at The 'Philharmonie',Berlin, rec. 4.11.1972
Brubeck,Dave (p) | Desmond,Paul (as) | Mulligan,Gerry (bs) | Six,Jack (b) | Dawson,Alan (dr)
Dave Brubeck
Sweet Georgia Brown
Live at De Doelen,Rotterdam,NL, rec. 28.10.1972
Brubeck,Dave (p-solo)

7567-81393-2 | CD | Blues On Bach
Modern Jazz Quartet
Regret | Blues In B Flat | Rise Up In The Morning | Blues In A Minor | Precious Joy | Blues In C Minor | Don't Stop This Train | Blues In H(B) | Tears From The Children
NYC, rec. 26./27.11.1973
MJQ (Modern Jazz Quartet) | Jackson,Milt (vib) | Lewis,John (p,harpsichord) | Heath,Percy (b) | Kay,Connie (dr,perc)

7567-81399-2 | CD | All The Things We Are
Dave Brubeck Trio
Jimmy Van Heusen Medley: | Deep In A Dream- | Like Someone In Love- | Here's That Rainy Day- | Polka Dots And Moonbeams- | It Could Happen To You-
NYC, rec. 17.7.1973
Brubeck,Dave (p) | Six,Jack (b) | Dawson,Alan (dr)
Dave Brubeck-Lee Konitz Duo
Don't Get Around Much Anymore
NYC, rec. 3.10.1974
Brubeck,Dave (p) | Konitz,Lee (as)
Dave Brubeck Quartet
Like Someone In Love
Brubeck,Dave (p) | Konitz,Lee (as) | Six,Jack (b) | Haynes,Roy (dr)
In Your Own Sweet Way
Brubeck,Dave (p) | Braxton,Anthony (as) | Six,Jack (b) | Haynes,Roy (dr)
Dave Brubeck Quintet
All The Things You Are
Brubeck,Dave (p) | Konitz,Lee (as) | Braxton,Anthony (as) | Six,Jack (b) | Haynes,Roy (dr)

7567-81402-2 | CD | Chick Corea-Herbie Hancock-Keith Jarrett-McCoy Tyner
Keith Jarrett Trio
Margot | Love No.1
NYC, rec. 21.12.1966
Jarrett,Keith (p) | Haden,Charlie (b) | Motian,Paul (dr)
Chick Corea Trio
Tones For Joan's Bones
NYC, rec. 30.11.1966
Corea,Chick (p) | Swallow,Steve (b) | Chambers,Joe (dr)
Chick Corea Quintet
This Is New
NYC, rec. 1.12.1966
Corea,Chick (p) | Shaw,Woody (tp) | Farrell,Joe (ts) | Swallow,Steve (b) | Chambers,Joe (dr)
McCoy Tyner Trio
Lazy Bird | In Your Own Sweet Way
NYC, rec. 24.10.1960
Tyner,McCoy (p) | Davis,Steve (b) | Jones,Elvin (dr)
Herbie Hancock Trio
Einbahnstrasse | Doom
NYC, rec. 7.10.1969
Hancock,Herbie (p) | Carter,Ron (b) | Cobham,Billy (dr)

7567-81403-2 | CD | Three Or Four Shades Of Blues
Charles Mingus Orchestra
Better Git It In Your Soul | Goodbye Pork Pie Hat | Noddin Ya Head Blues
NYC, rec. 9.3.1977
Mingus,Charles (b) | Walrath,Jack (tp) | Coleman,George (as,ts) | Ford,Ricky (ts) | Nellums,Bob (p) | Catherine,Philip (g) | Coryell,Larry (g) | Mraz,George 'Jiri' (b) | Richmond,Dannie (dr) | Jeffrey,Paul (arr)
Three Or Four Shades Of Blues
NYC, rec. 1977
Mingus,Charles (b) | Walrath,Jack (tp) | Coleman,George (as,ts) | Ford,Ricky (ts) | Nellums,Bob (p) | Rowles,Jimmy (p) | Scofield,John (g) | Coryell,Larry (g) | Richmond,Dannie (dr)
Nobody Knows
Mingus,Charles (b) | Walrath,Jack (tp) | Fortune,Sonny (as) | Ford,Ricky (ts) | Nellums,Bob (p) | Catherine,Philip (g) | Scofield,John (g) | Carter,Ron (b) | Richmond,Dannie (dr) | Jeffrey,Paul (arr)

7567-81428-2 | CD | Spectrum
Billy Cobham Group
Quadrant 4 | Searching For The Right Door | Taurian Matador | Stratus | To The Women In My Life | Snoopy's Search | Red Baron
NYC, rec. 14./15.5.1973
Cobham,Billy (dr,perc) | Bolin,Tommy (g) | Hammer,Jan (p,el-p,synth) | Sklair,Lee (el-b)
Spectrum
NYC, rec. 16.5.1973
Cobham,Billy (dr,perc) | Owens,Jimmy (tp,fl-h) | Farrell,Joe (fl,ss,as) | Hammer,Jan (el-p,synth) | Carter,Ron (b) | Barretto,Ray (congas)
Le Lis
Cobham,Billy (dr,perc) | Owens,Jimmy (tp,fl-h) | Farrell,Joe (fl,ss,as) | Tropea,John (g) | Hammer,Jan (el-p,synth) | Carter,Ron (b) | Barretto,Ray (congas)

7567-81455-2 | CD | Somewhere Before
Keith Jarrett Trio
My Back Pages | Pretty Ballad | Moving Soon | Somewhere Before | New Rag | A Moment For Tears | Pouts' Over(And The Day's Not Through) | Dedicated To You | Old Rag
Live at Shelly's Manne Hole,Los Angeles,CA, rec. 30./31.8.1968
Jarrett,Keith (p) | Haden,Charlie (b) | Motian,Paul (dr)

7567-81543-2 | CD | Aurora
Jean-Luc Ponty Quintet
Is Once Enough | Renaissance | Aurora(part 1) | Aurora(part 2) | Passenger Of The Dark | Lost Forest | Between You And Me | Waking Dream
Los Angeles,CA, rec. December 1975
Ponty,Jean-Luc (v,el-v,autoharp,violectra) | Stuermer,Daryl (g,el-g) | Rushen,Patrice (p,el-p,synth) | Fowler,Tom (b-g) | Flarrington,Norman (dr,perc)

7567-81550-2 | CD | Cosmic Messenger
Jean-Luc Ponty Sextet
Cosmic Messenger | The Art Of Happiness | Don't Let The World Pass You By | Puppet's Dance | Fake Paradise | Ethereal Mood
Hollywood,CA, rec. ca.1978
Ponty,Jean Luc (org,v,el-v) | Maunu,Peter (el-g) | Llevano,Joaquin (g,el-g) | Armstrong,Ralphe (el-b) | Zavod,Allan (el-p,org,synth) | Scheurell,Casey (dr,perc)
Jean-Luc Ponty Quintet
Egocentric Molecules
Ponty,Jean-Luc (el-v) | Lievano,Joaquin (el-g) | Maunu,Peter (g-synth) | Zavod,Allan (el-p,org,synth) | Armstrong,Ralphe (el-b)
Jean-Luc Ponty Quartet
I Only Feel Good With You
Ponty,Jean-Luc (org,synth,el-v,orchestron) | Zavod,Allan (el-p,grand-p) | Armstrong,Ralphe (el-b) | Scheurell,Casey (dr)

7567-81558-2 | CD | The Best Of Billy Cobham
Billy Cobham Group
Quadrant 4 | Snoopy's Search | Red Baron | Stratus
NYC, rec. 14./15.5.1973
Cobham,Billy (perc) | Bolin,Tommy (g) | Hammer,Jan (p,el-p,synth) | Sklair,Lee (el-b)
Spanish Moss- | The Pleasant Pheasant
NYC, rec. 1974
Cobham,Billy (perc) | Brecker,Randy (tp) | Brecker,Michael (reeds) | Brown,Garnett (tb) | Duke,George (keyboards) | Pastora,Lee (latin-perc) | Williams,John B. (b,el-b) | Abercrombie,John (g)
Moon Germs
Cobham,Billy (perc) | Brecker,Randy (tp,fl-h) | Ferris,Glenn (tb,b-tb) | Brecker,Michael (fl,ss,ts) | Abercrombie,John (g) | Dupree,Cornell (el-g) | Leviev,Milcho (keyboards) | Blake,Alex (el-b) | Earle,David (congas)
Solo | Panhalder
San Francisco,CA, rec. details unknown
Cobham,Billy (perc) | Brecker,Randy (tp) | Brecker,Michael (sax) | Scofield,John (g) | Ferris,Glenn (tb) | Leviev,Milcho (keyboards) | Blake,Alex (b)
Do What Cha Wanna
details unknown, rec. details unknown
Cobham,Billy (perc,voc) | Duke,George (keyboards,voc) | Johnson,Alphonso (el-b) | Scofield,John (el-g)

7567-81700-2 | CD | Atlantic Jazz: New Orleans
Paul Barbarin And His Band
Bourbon Street Parade | Eh-Las-Bas | Sing On
NYC, rec. January 1955
Barbarin,Paul (dr) | Brunious,John (tp) | Thomas,Bob (tb) | Humphrey,Willie (cl) | Santiago,Lester (p) | Barker,Danny (bj) | Hinton,Milt (b)
George Lewis And His Band
Burgundy Street Blues
New Orleans,Louisiana, rec. 7.7.1962
Lewis,George (cl) | Sayles,Emanuel (bj) | Pavageau,Alcide 'Slow Drag' (b) | Watkins,Joe (dr)
I'm A Salty Dog - (I'm A) Salty Dog
Lewis,George (cl) | Howard,Avery 'Kid' (tp) | Robinson,Jim (tb) | Sayles,Emanuel (bj) | Pavageau,Alcide 'Slow Drag' (b) | Watkins,Joe (dr)
Jim Robinson's New Orleans Band
My Bucket's Got A Hole In It
New Orleans,Louisiana, rec. 4.7.1962
Robinson,Jim (tb) | Cagnolatti,Ernie (tp) | Cottrell Jr.,Louis (cl) | Sayles,Emanuel (bj) | Pavageau,Alcide 'Slow Drag' (b) | Williams,Alfred (dr)
Wilbur DeParis And His New New Orleans Band
Cielito Lindo
Live at Symphony Hall,Boston, rec. 26.10.1956

DeParis,Wilbur (dr) | DeParis,Sidney (tp) | Simeon,Omer (cl) | White,Sonny (p) | Blair,Lee (bj) | Moten,Benny (b) | Kirk,Wilbert (dr)
Shreveport Stomp
NYC, rec. 11.9.1952
DeParis,Wilbur (dr) | DeParis,Sidney (tp) | Simeon,Omer (cl) | Kirkpatrick,Don (p) | Gibbs,Eddie (bj) | Jackson,Harold (b) | Moore,Fred[Freddie] (dr)

Turk Murphy And His Jazz Band
Maple Leaf Rag
San Francisco,CA, rec. 15.9.1971
Murphy,Turk (tb) | Oakley,Leon (co) | Howe,Phil (cl) | Maihack,Jim (tuba) | Clute,Pete (p) | Lunsford,Carl (bj) | Vanden,Thad (dr)

Eureka Brass Band
Joe Avery's Blues
New Orleans,Louisiana, rec. 2.7.1962
Eureka Brass Band,The | Humphrey,Percy (tp) | Cola,George 'Kid Sheik' (tp) | Bocage,Peter (tp) | Warner,Albert (tb) | Henry,Oscar (tb) | Humphrey,Willie (cl) | Paul,Emanuel (ts) | Tillman,Wilbert (sousaphone) | Frazier,Josiah 'Cie' (snare-dr) | Lewis,Robert 'Son' (bass-dr)

Punch Miller's Bunch & George Lewis
Nobody Knows The Way I Feel This Morning | Tiger Rag
New Orleans,Louisiana, rec. 6.7.1962
Miller,Ernest 'Punch' (tp) | Nelson,Louis (tb) | Lewis,George (cl) | Sayles,Emanuel (bj) | Joseph,Papa John (b) | Foster,Abbey (dr)

Joseph 'Dee Dee' Pierce And His Band
Shake It And Break It
New Orleans,Louisiana, rec. 3.7.1962
Pierce,Joseph 'Dee Dee' (tp) | Nelson,Louis (tb) | Lewis,George (cl) | Pierce,Billie (p) | Sayles,Emanuel (bj) | Joseph,Papa John (b) | Foster,Abbey (dr)

7567-81701-2 | CD | Atlantic Jazz: Kansas City
Joe Turner With Orchestra
Piney Brown Blues
NYC, rec. 6.3.1956
Turner,Big Joe (voc) | Newman,Joe (tp) | Brown,Lawrence (tb) | Brown,Pete (as) | Wess,Frank (ts) | Johnson,Pete (p) | Green,Freddie (g) | Page,Walter (b) | Leeman,Cliff (dr) | Wilkins,Ernie (arr)
You're Driving Me Crazy
NYC, rec. 7.3.1956
Turner,Big Joe (voc) | Nottingham,Jimmy (tp) | Brown,Lawrence (tb) | Brown,Pete (as) | Powell,Seldon (ts) | Johnson,Pete (p) | Green,Freddie (g) | Page,Walter (b) | Leeman,Cliff (dr) | Wilkins,Ernie (arr)
Until The Real Thing Comes Along
NYC, rec. 9.9.1959
Turner,Big Joe (voc) | Ricard,Paul (tp) | Dickenson,Vic (tb) | Richardson,Jerome (as) | Hawkins,Coleman (ts) | Jones,Jimmie (p) | Hall,Jim (g) | Watkins,Doug (b) | Persip,Charles (dr) | Wilkins,Ernie (arr)

Vic Dickenson-Buck Clayton All Stars
The Lamp Is Low | Undecided
NYC, rec. 28.10.1958
Clayton,Buck (tp) | Dickenson,Vic (tb) | Singer,Hal (ts) | Hall,Herb (cl) | Williams,Al (p) | Barker,Danny (g) | Ramey,Gene (b) | Foster,Marquis (dr)

Jay McShann And His Orchestra
Hootie Blues | Confessin' The Blues | Jumpin' At The Woodside
NYC, rec. June 1977
McShann,Jay (p,el-p,voc) | Newman,Joe (tp) | Quinichette,Paul (ts) | Tate,Buddy (ts) | Scofield,John (el-g) | Hinton,Milt (b) | Williams,Jackie (dr)

Buster Smith Orchestra
E-Flat Boogie
Fort Worth, Texas, rec. 17.6.1959
Smith,Buster (as) | Gillum,Charles (tp) | Smith,Clinton (tb) | Cadell,Eddie (ts) | Cooper,Leroy 'Hog' (bs) | Flowers,Herman (p) | Smith,Josea (b) | Cobbs,Robert (dr)
Buster's Tune
Smith,Buster (as) | Cooper,Leroy 'Hog' (bs) | Flowers,Herman (p) | Smith,Josea (b) | Cobbs,Robert (dr)

T-Bone Walker And His Band
Evenin'
Los Angeles,CA, rec. 27.12.1957
Walker,T-Bone (g,voc) | Johnson,Plas (ts) | Johnson,Ray (p) | Rankin,R.S. (g) | Kessel,Barney (g) | Comfort,Joe (b) | Palmer,Earl (dr)

7567-81711-2 | CD | Atlantic Jazz: Fusion
Miroslav Vitous Group
Freedom Jazz Dance
NYC, rec. 8.10.1969
Vitous,Miroslav (b) | Henderson,Joe (ts) | Hancock,Herbie (el-p) | McLaughlin,John (el-g) | DeJohnette,Jack (dr)

Les McCann Group
Beaux J.Poo Boo
NYC, rec. 4.5.1971
McCann,Les (p,el-p,synth) | Lateef,Yusef (fl,pneumatic-fl,temple-bells) | Spinozza,David (g,el-g) | Dupree,Cornell (el-g) | Christian,Jodie (el-p) | Salter,Bill (el-b) | Rowser,Jimmy (b) | Purdie,Bernard 'Pretty' (dr,perc) | Mouzon,Alphonse (dr,perc) | Dean,Donald (dr,perc) | Clark,William 'Buck' (perc,african-dr) | McDonald,Ralph (perc)

Billy Cobham Quartet
Quadrant 4
NYC, rec. May 1973
Cobham,Billy (dr,perc) | Hammer,Jan (p,el-p,synth) | Bolin,Tommy (el-g) | Sklair,Lee (el-b)

Larry Coryell-Alphonse Mouzon Quartet
Beneath The Earth
NYC, rec. February 1977
Coryell,Larry (el-g) | Mouzon,Alphonse (dr) | Catherine,Philip (g,el-g) | Lee,John (b)

Klaus Doldinger's Passport
Homunculus
München, rec. November 1974
Doldinger,Klaus (ss,ts,el-p,synth,mellotron) | Schultze,Kristian (el-p,org) | Schmid,Wolfgang (g,b-g) | Cress,Curt (dr,perc,el-perc)

Jean-Luc Ponty Group
Egocentric Molecules
Los Angeles,CA, rec. 1978
Ponty,Jean-Luc (el-v) | Lievano,Joaquin (el-g) | Maunu,Peter (g-synth) | Armstrong,Ralphe (el-b)

7567-81951-2 | 2 CD | Soul Brothers/Soul Meeting
Ray Charles-Milt Jackson Sextet
Soul Brothers | How Long Blues | Cosmic Rays | Blue Funk | 'Deed I Do | Bags Of Blues
NYC, rec. 12.9.1957
Jackson,Milt (vib,g,p) | Charles,Ray (as,p) | Mitchell,Billy (ts) | Best,Skeeter (g) | Pettiford,Oscar (b) | Kay,Connie (dr)

Ray Charles-Milt Jackson Quintet
Soul Meeting | Hallelujah I Love Her So | Blue Genius | Love On My Mind
NYC, rec. 10.4.1958
Jackson,Milt (vib,p) | Charles,Ray (as,p) | Burrell,Kenny (g) | Heath,Percy (b) | Taylor,Arthur 'Art' (dr)

Ray Charles-Milt Jackson Quartet
X-Ray Blues
Jackson,Milt (vib,p) | Charles,Ray (as,el-p) | Heath,Percy (b) | Taylor,Arthur 'Art' (dr)

7567-81977-2 | CD | Nocturnes
Yusef Lateef Ensemble
Warm Intensity | Estuary | Indefinite Expansion | Closed Space | Compassion Duration | Visible Particles | While On Earth | Elementary Substance | Soft Light | Life Property | Luminous Energy | Essential Element
Shutesbury,MA, rec. February 1989
Lateef,Yusef (fl,alto-fl,synth,grand-p,mirage-ensong) | Schick,Hugh (fl-h) | Tucker,Patrick (fr-h) | Salvo,Christopher (cl)

7567-82027-2 | CD | Jigsaw
Mike Stern Group
To Let You Know | Rhythm Or Reason | Kwirk
NYC, rec. February 1989
Stern,Mike (g) | Berg,Bob (ts) | Beard,Jim (keyboards,synth) | Andrews,Jeff (el-b) | Erskine,Les (dr)
Another Way Around
Stern,Mike (g) | Berg,Bob (ts) | Beard,Jim (keyboards,synth) | Andrews,Jeff (el-b) | Erskine,Peter (dr) | Badrena,Manolo (chekere)
Loose Ends | Jigsaw
Stern,Mike (g) | Berg,Bob (ts) | Beard,Jim (keyboards,synth) | Andrews,Jeff (el-b) | Chambers,Dennis (dr)
Chief
Stern,Mike (g) | Berg,Bob (ts) | Beard,Jim (keyboards,synth) | Brecker,Michael (synth) | Andrews,Jeff (el-b) | Chambers,Dennis (dr) | Badrena,Manolo (congas)

7567-8209-2 | CD | Pittsburgh
Ahmad Jamal Trio with Orchestra
Pittsburgh | Bellows | Mellowdrama | Foolish Ways | Divertimento | Cycles | Fly Away | Apple Avenue
rec. details unknown
Jamal,Ahmad (p) | Cammack,James (b) | Bowler,David (dr) | Orchestra & Strings | Evans,Richard (orchestrations) | details unknown

7567-82138-2 | CD | The Journey
Bobby Lyle Group
Viva Mandela- | The Journey-
Oceanway Studios,?, rec. details unknown
Lyle,Bobby (keyboards,dr-machine-programming) | Albright,Gerald (b) | Summers,Bill (perc) | Ndugu[Leon Chancler] (dr) | Waters,Maxine Willard (voc) | Waters,Julia Tillman (voc) | Waters,Oren (voc) | Twillie,Carmen (voc) | Gilstrap,James (voc) | Phinnessee,Darryl (voc) | Semeya,Kyphus (voc)
Sassy
Lyle,Bobby (keyboards) | Whalum,Kirk (ss) | Jackson,Paul (g) | Albright,Gerald (b) | Baker,Michael (dr) | Da Costa,Paulinho (perc)
Swing Jack
Lyle,Bobby (keyboards) | Whalum,Kirk (ts) | Jackson,Paul (g) | Patitucci,John (b) | Baker,Michael (dr)
Blues For Dexter
Lyle,Bobby (p) | Turrentine,Stanley (ts) | Simpkins,Andrew (b) | Baker,Michael (dr)
Struttin'
Lyle,Bobby (keyboards,string-arranging) | Fuller,Ray (g) | Washington,Freddie (b) | Spencer,Donnell (dr) | Da Costa,Paulinho (perc)
Reach Out For Love
Lyle,Bobby (keyboards) | Jackson,Paul (g) | Baker,Michael (dr-machine-programming) | Ndugu[Leon Chancler] (dr) | Ingram,Philip (voc) | Anderson,Maxine (voc) | Davis,Lynn (voc)
Love Eyes
Lyle,Bobby (keyboards,string-arranging) | Whalum,Kirk (ss) | Patitucci,John (b) | Baker,Michael (dr) | Da Costa,Paulinho (perc)
Othello
Lyle,Bobby (keyboards) | Flood,Kenny (ss) | Veasley,Gerald (b) | Kimpel,Larry (p) | Baker,Michael (dr)
Fly Away Spirit | It Never Entered My Mind
Lyle,Bobby (p-solo)

7567-82297-2 | CD | Odds Or Evens
Mike Stern Group
Keys | Seven Thirty | Walkie Talkie
NYC, rec. details unknown
Stern,Mike (g) | Berg,Bob (sax) | Beard,Jim (p,synth) | Goines,Lincoln (b) | Perowsky,Ben (dr) | Alias,Don (perc)
Common Ground
Stern,Mike (g) | Berg,Bob (sax) | Beard,Jim (p,synth) | Goines,Lincoln (b) | Chambers,Dennis (dr) | Alias,Don (perc)
D.C. | Odds Or Evens | If You Say So
Stern,Mike (g) | Berg,Bob (sax) | Beard,Jim (p,synth) | Jackson,Anthony (b) | Chambers,Dennis (dr) | Alias,Don (perc)

7567-82330-2 | 4 CD | MJQ 40
Modern Jazz Quartet
Vendome
NYC, rec. 22.12.1952
MJQ (Modern Jazz Quartet) | Jackson,Milt (vib) | Lewis,John (p) | Heath,Percy (b) | Clarke,Kenny (dr)
Delauney's Dilemma
NYC, rec. 25.6.1953
MJQ (Modern Jazz Quartet) | Jackson,Milt (vib) | Lewis,John (p) | Heath,Percy (b) | Clarke,Kenny (dr)
Milano
NYC, rec. 23.12.1954
MJQ (Modern Jazz Quartet) | Jackson,Milt (vib) | Lewis,John (p) | Heath,Percy (b) | Clarke,Kenny (dr)
La Ronde Suite
NYC, rec. 9.1.1955
MJQ (Modern Jazz Quartet) | Jackson,Milt (vib) | Lewis,John (p) | Heath,Percy (b) | Clarke,Kenny (dr)
Bluesology
NYC, rec. 14.2.1956
MJQ (Modern Jazz Quartet) | Jackson,Milt (vib) | Lewis,John (p) | Heath,Percy (b) | Kay,Connie (dr)

Modern Jazz Quartet feat.Jimmy Giuffre
A Fugue For Music Inn | Fun
Music Inn,Lenox,Mass., rec. 29.8.1956
MJQ (Modern Jazz Quartet) | Giuffre,Jimmy (cl) | Jackson,Milt (vib) | Lewis,John (p) | Heath,Percy (b) | Kay,Connie (dr)

Modern Jazz Quartet
The Golden Striker
NYC, rec. 4.4.1957
MJQ (Modern Jazz Quartet) | Jackson,Milt (vib) | Lewis,John (p) | Heath,Percy (b) | Kay,Connie (dr)
Festival Sketch
Music Inn,Lenox,Mass., rec. 3.8.1958
MJQ (Modern Jazz Quartet) | Jackson,Milt (vib) | Lewis,John (p) | Heath,Percy (b) | Kay,Connie (dr)

Modern Jazz Quartet With Sonny Rollins
Bag's Groove
Music Inn,Lenox,Mass., rec. 3.9.1958
MJQ (Modern Jazz Quartet) | Rollins,Sonny (ts) | Jackson,Milt (vib) | Lewis,John (p) | Heath,Percy (b) | Kay,Connie (dr)

Modern Jazz Quartet
Romaine
Music Inn,Lenox,Mass., rec. 5.8.1959
MJQ (Modern Jazz Quartet) | Jackson,Milt (vib) | Lewis,John (p) | Heath,Percy (b) | Kay,Connie (dr)
No Happiness For Slater | Odds Against Tomorrow
NYC, rec. 9.10.1959
MJQ (Modern Jazz Quartet) | Jackson,Milt (vib) | Lewis,John (p) | Heath,Percy (b) | Kay,Connie (dr)

Modern Jazz Quartet & Guests
Exposure
NYC, rec. 15.1.1960
MJQ (Modern Jazz Quartet) | Jackson,Milt (vib) | Lewis,John (p) | Heath,Percy (b) | Kay,Connie (dr) | Di Domenica,Bob (fl) | Ziegler,Manny (bassoon) | McColl,Bill (cl) | Ingraham,Paul (fr-h) | Tekula,Joe (cello) | Glauman,Betty (harp) | Schuller,Gunther (cond,arr)

Modern Jazz Quartet And Symphony Orchestra
England's Carol(God Rest Ye Merry Gentlemen)
Stuttgart, rec. 3.6.1960
MJQ (Modern Jazz Quartet) | Jackson,Milt (vib) | Lewis,John (p) | Heath,Percy (b) | Kay,Connie (dr) | Symphony Orchestra | details unknown | Schuller,Gunther (cond,arr)

Modern Jazz Quartet
I Remember Clifford | Round About Midnight
Stockholm,Sweden, rec. 11.& 13.4.1960
MJQ (Modern Jazz Quartet) | Jackson,Milt (vib) | Lewis,John (p) | Heath,Percy (b) | Kay,Connie (dr)
La Cantatrice
NYC, rec. 20.10.1960
MJQ (Modern Jazz Quartet) | Jackson,Milt (vib) | Lewis,John (p) | Heath,Percy (b) | Kay,Connie (dr) | Carroll,Diahann (voc)
New York 19 | Animal Dance
NYC, rec. 29.1.1962
MJQ (Modern Jazz Quartet) | Jackson,Milt (vib) | Lewis,John (p) | Heath,Percy (b) | Kay,Connie (dr)
Bachianas Brasileiras | Concorde
NYC, rec. 16.& 17.5.1963
MJQ (Modern Jazz Quartet) | Jackson,Milt (vib) | Lewis,John (p) | Heath,Percy (b) | Kay,Connie (dr)

Modern Jazz Quartet And Laurindo Almeida
Fugue In A Minor | Samba Da Una Nota So(One Note Samba)
NYC, rec. 21.7.1964
MJQ (Modern Jazz Quartet) | Almeida,Laurindo (g) | Jackson,Milt (vib) | Lewis,John (p) | Heath,Percy (b) | Kay,Connie (dr)

Modern Jazz Quartet And Orchestra
Ralph's New Blues | One Never Knows
NYC, rec. 27.5.& 25.6.1965
MJQ (Modern Jazz Quartet) | Jackson,Milt (vib) | Lewis,John (p) | Heath,Percy (b) | Kay,Connie (dr) | Terry,Clark (tp) | Royal,Ernie (tp) | Young,Eugene 'Snooky' (fl-h) | Glow,Bernie (tp) | Cleveland,Jimmy (tb) | Winding,Kai (tb) | Studd,Tony (tb) | Mariano,Charlie (as) | Woods,Phil (as) | Kamuca,Richie (ts) | Powell,Seldon (ts) | Kane,Wally (bs) | Collins,Howard (g)

Modern Jazz Quartet And The Swingle Singers
Alexander's Fugue
Paris,France, rec. 10.9.1966
MJQ (Modern Jazz Quartet) | Jackson,Milt (vib) | Lewis,John (p) | Heath,Percy (b) | Kay,Connie (dr) | Swingle Singers (voc-group) | Legrand,Christiane (voc) | Baucomont,Jeanette (voc) | Meunier,Claudine (voc) | Herald,Alice (voc) | Swingle,Ward (ld,voc) | Cussac,Jean (voc) | Germain,José (voc)

Modern Jazz Quartet
The Cylinder | Midsömmer | For Someone I Love | Winter Tale
Live at Kosei-Nenkin Hall,Tokyo,Japan, rec. 14.5.1966
MJQ (Modern Jazz Quartet) | Jackson,Milt (vib) | Lewis,John (p) | Heath,Percy (b) | Kay,Connie (dr)
Monterey Mist | Blues Milanese
Live at Carnegie Hall,NYC, rec. 27.4.1966
MJQ (Modern Jazz Quartet) | Jackson,Milt (vib) | Lewis,John (p) | Heath,Percy (b) | Kay,Connie (dr)
Novamo | Baseball
Live at The Lighthouse,Hermosa Beach,CA, rec. 16.& 17.3.1967
MJQ (Modern Jazz Quartet) | Jackson,Milt (vib) | Lewis,John (p) | Heath,Percy (b) | Kay,Connie (dr)

Modern Jazz Quartet & Guests
Blues In The Bergerie
NYC, rec. 24.5.1971
MJQ (Modern Jazz Quartet) | Jackson,Milt (vib) | Lewis,John (p) | Heath,Percy (b) | Kay,Connie (dr) | Young,Eugene 'Snooky' (tp) | Newman,Joe (tp) | Brown,Garnett (tb) | Buffington,Jimmy (fr-h) | Butterfield,Don (tuba)

Modern Jazz Quartet
Walkin' Stomp | The Trip | Trav'lin'
MJQ (Modern Jazz Quartet) | Jackson,Milt (vib) | Lewis,John (p) | Heath,Percy (b) | Kay,Connie (dr)

Paul Desmond And The Modern Jazz Quartet
Greensleeves
NYC, rec. 25.12.1971
Desmond,Paul (as) | MJQ (Modern Jazz Quartet) | Jackson,Milt (vib) | Lewis,John (p) | Heath,Percy (b) | Kay,Connie (dr)

Modern Jazz Quartet
Misty Roses
NYC, rec. 1.6.1972
MJQ (Modern Jazz Quartet) | Jackson,Milt (vib) | Lewis,John (p) | Heath,Percy (b) | Kay,Connie (dr)
Tears From The Children
NYC, rec. 26.11.1973
MJQ (Modern Jazz Quartet) | Jackson,Milt (vib) | Lewis,John (p) | Heath,Percy (b) | Kay,Connie (dr)

Modern Jazz Quartet And Symphony Orchestra
Jazz Ostinato | Adagio From Concierto De Aranjuez
NYC, rec. 5.11.1973
MJQ (Modern Jazz Quartet) | Jackson,Milt (vib) | Lewis,John (p) | Heath,Percy (b) | Kay,Connie (dr) | Symphony Orchestra | details unknown | Peress,Maurice (cond)

Modern Jazz Quartet
Skating In Central Park | The Jasmine Tree | The Legendary Profile | Django
Live at The 'Avery Fisher Hall',NYC, rec. 25.11.1974
MJQ (Modern Jazz Quartet) | Jackson,Milt (vib) | Lewis,John (p) | Heath,Percy (b) | Kay,Connie (dr)
That Slavic Smile | Sacha's March
NYC, rec. 6.3.1984
MJQ (Modern Jazz Quartet) | Jackson,Milt (vib) | Lewis,John (p) | Heath,Percy (b) | Kay,Connie (dr)
D And E
NYC, rec. 3.6.1985
MJQ (Modern Jazz Quartet) | Jackson,Milt (vib) | Lewis,John (p) | Heath,Percy (b) | Kay,Connie (dr)
For Ellington | Rockin' In Rhythm
NYC, rec. 1.& 3.2.1988
MJQ (Modern Jazz Quartet) | Jackson,Milt (vib) | Lewis,John (p) | Heath,Percy (b) | Kay,Connie (dr)

7567-82346-2 | CD | Pianomagic
Bobby Lyle Group
Pianomagic | Waltz For Debby | Love Song | So What | Eastern Lady | Blues All Day | The Very Thought Of You | You Stepped Out Of A Dream | Someday We'll All Be Free
Oceanway Studios,?, rec. details unknown
Lyle,Bobby (p-solo)
The Christmas Song | Finger Rap
Lyle,Bobby (p,keyboards)

7567-82419-2 | CD | Standards(And Other Songs)
Mike Stern Group
Like Someone In Love | Source | There Is No Greater Love | L Bird | Moment's Notice | Windows | Straight No Chaser | Peace | Jean Pierre
NYC, rec. details unknown
Stern,Mike (g) | Brecker,Randy (tp) | Berg,Bob (ts) | Goldstein,Gil (keyboards) | Anderson,Jay (b) | Foster,Al (dr)
Lost Time | Nardis
Stern,Mike (g) | Brecker,Randy (tp) | Berg,Bob (ts) | Goldstein,Gil (keyboards) | Perowsky,Ben (dr) | Grenadier,Larry (b)

7567-82742-2 | CD | The Real Quietstorm
James Carter Quartet
You Never Told Me That You Care | The Intimacy Of My Woman's Beautiful Eyes | Deep Throat Blues | A Ballad For A Doll
NYC, rec. 6./7.10.& 20.11.1994
Carter,James (b-cl,as,ts,bass-fl) | Taborn,Craig (p) | Holland,Dave (b) | Parker,Leon (dr)
1944 Stomp | The Stevedor's Serenade | Born To Be Blue
Carter,James (ss,ts) | Taborn,Craig (p) | Shahid,Jaribu (b) | Tabal,Tani (dr)

James Carter-Craig Tahorn
Round About Midnight
Carter,James (bs) | Taborn,Craig (p)

James Carter-Shahid Jaribu
Eventide
Carter,James (bs) | Shahid,Jaribu (b)

7567-82876-2 | CD | Earth Stories
Cyrus Chestnut Sextet
Cooldaddy's Perspective
NYC, rec. 28.11.1995
Chestnut,Cyrus (p) | Allen,Eddie E.J. (tp) | Hart,Antonio Maurice (as) | Carrington,Steven (ts) | Kirby,Steve (b) | Garnett,Alvester (dr)

Cyrus Chestnut Trio
Descisions,Descisions | Grandmama's Blues | My Song In The Night | Nutman's Invention No.1 | Blues From The East | Maria's Folly | East Of The Sun West Of The Moon | Gomez | Whoopi | In The Garden
NYC, rec. 29.30.11.995
Chestnut,Cyrus (p) | Kirby,Steve (b) | Garnett,Alvester (dr)

7567-82988-2 | CD | Conversin' With The Elders
James Carter Group
FreeReggaeHiBop | Atitled Valse
NYC, rec. 2.10.1995
Carter,James (ts) | Bowie,Lester (tp) | Taborn,Craig (p) | Shahid,Jaribu (b) | Tabal,Tani (dr)
Parker's Mood
NYC, rec. 5.2.1996
Carter,James (as) | Smith,Larry (as) | Taborn,Craig (p) | Shahid,Jaribu (b) | Tabal,Tani (dr)
Lester Leaps In | Centerpiece | Moten Swing
NYC, rec. 30.1.1996
Carter,James (ts) | Edison,Harry 'Sweets' (tp) | Taborn,Craig (p) | Shahid,Jaribu (b) | Tabal,Tani (dr)
Naima | Composition 400
NYC, rec. 5.2.1996
Carter,James (bs) | Bluiett,Hamiet (bs) | Taborn,Craig (p) | Shahid,Jaribu (b) | Tabal,Tani (dr)
Blue Creek
NYC, rec. 30.1.1996
Carter,James (b-cl) | Tate,Buddy (cl) | Taborn,Craig (p) | Shahid,Jaribu (b) | Tabal,Tani (dr)

7567-83036-2 | CD | Give And Take
Mike Stern Group
I Love You | Giant Steps
NYC, rec. 1997
Stern,Mike (g) | Patitucci,John (b) | DeJohnette,Jack (dr)
That's What You Think
Stern,Mike (g) | Sanborn,David (as) | Patitucci,John (b) | DeJohnette,Jack (dr)
Hook Up | One Liners | Jones Street
Stern,Mike (g) | Brecker,Michael (ts) | Patitucci,John (b) | DeJohnette,Jack (dr)
Lumpy | Rooms
Stern,Mike (g) | Goldstein,Gil (p) | Patitucci,John (b) | Alias,Don (perc)
Who Knows | Oleo
Stern,Mike (g) | Patitucci,John (b) | Alias,Don (perc)

7567-83116-2 | CD | The Proshetic Cubans
Marc Ribot Y Los Cubanos Postizos
Aurora En Pekin
Hoboken,NJ, rec. details unknown
Ribot,Marc (g) | Jones,Bradley (b) | Rodriguez,E.J. (perc) | Rodriguez,Robert J. (claves)
Aqui Como Alla
Ribot,Marc (g) | Medeski,John (org) | Jones,Bradley (b) | Rodriguez,E.J. (perc) | Rodriguez,Robert J. (dr,perc)
Como Se Goza En El Barrio
Ribot,Marc (g) | Coleman,Anthony (org) | Jones,Bradley (b) | Rodriguez,E.J. (perc) | Rodriguez,Robert J. (dr,perc)
Postizo
Ribot,Marc (g) | Medeski,John (org) | Jones,Bradley (b) | Rodriguez,E.J. (perc) | Rodriguez,Robert J. (dr,perc,voc) | Hunt-Ehrlich,Madeline (voc) | Ingram,Mattan (voc) | Ingram,Miles (voc)
No Me Llored Mas
Ribot,Marc (tp,g,voc) | Medeski,John (org,melotron) | Jones,Bradley (b) | Rodriguez,E.J. (perc,voc) | Rodriguez,Robert J. (dr,perc,voc)
Los Teenagers Bailan Changui
Ribot,Marc (g) | Coleman,Anthony (org) | Jones,Bradley (b) | Rodriguez,E.J. (perc)
Fiesta En El Solar
Ribot,Marc (g) | Jones,Bradley (b) | Rodriguez,E.J. (perc) | Rodriguez,Robert J. (dr,perc)
La Vida Es Un Sueno
Ribot,Marc (g,voc) | Medeski,John (org) | Jones,Bradley (b) | Rodriguez,E.J. (perc) | Rodriguez,Robert J. (dr,perc)
Esclavo Triste
Ribot,Marc (g) | Jones,Bradley (b) | Rodriguez,E.J. (perc) | Rodriguez,Robert J. (chekere)
Choserito Plena
Ribot,Marc (tp,g) | Ribot,Gregory (bs) | Rodriguez,E.J. (perc) | Rodriguez,Robert J. (dr,perc)

7567-83140-2 | CD | Cyrus Chestnut
Cyrus Chestnut Trio
Elegant Flower(for Jazz'min') | Mother's Blues | Great Is Thy Faithfulness | Strolling In Central Park
NYC, rec. 1998
Chestnut,Cyrus (p) | Carter,Ron (b) | Higgins,Billy (dr)
Cyrus Chestnut Trio With Anita Baker
Summertime | My Favorite Things
Chestnut,Cyrus (p,el-p) | Carter,Ron (b) | Nash,Lewis (dr) | Baker,Anita (voc)
Cyrus Chestnut Trio With James Carter
Miss Thing | The Journey
Chestnut,Cyrus (p) | Carter,James (as) | Carter,Ron (b) | Nash,Lewis (dr)
Cyrus Chestnut Trio With Joe Lovano
Any Way You Can
Chestnut,Cyrus (p) | Lovano,Joe (ts) | Carter,Ron (b) | Nash,Lewis (dr)
Cyrus Chestnut Trio With James Carter And Joe Lovano
Sharp
Chestnut,Cyrus (p) | Carter,James (as) | Lovano,Joe (ts) | Carter,Ron (b) | Nash,Lewis (dr)
Cyrus Chestnut
Nutman's Invention
Chestnut,Cyrus (p-solo)

7567-83150-2 | CD | Music Is My Life
Diane Schuur And Her Band
Invitation | Nardis
Los Angeles,CA, rec. 1999
Schuur,Diane (p,voc) | Hines,Roger (p) | Gibson,Dave (dr)
If You Could See Me Now
Schuur,Diane (voc) | Broadbent,Alan (p) | Hines,Roger (p) | Gibson,Dave (dr)
You'd Be So Nice To Come Home To | That Old Devil Called Love | Bewitched Bothered And Bewildered
Schuur,Diane (voc) | Tempo,Nino (ts) | Richards,Emil (vib) | Broadbent,Alan (p) | Berghofer,Chuck (b) | Marable,Lawrence (dr)
Keepin' Out Of Mischief Now
Schuur,Diane (voc) | Parks,Dean (g) | Broadbent,Alan (p) | Berghofer,Chuck (b) | Guerin,John (dr)
Good Morning Heartache
Schuur,Diane (voc) | Printup,Marcus (tp) | Napis,Ira (tb) | Tempo,Nino (ts) | Parks,Dean (g) | Broadbent,Alan (p) | Berghofer,Chuck (b) | Guerin,John (dr)
I Only Have Eyes For You
Schuur,Diane (voc) | Tempo,Nino (ts) | Parks,Dean (g) | Broadbent,Alan (p) | Berghofer,Chuck (b) | Guerin,John (dr)
Music Is My Life
Schuur,Diane (el-p,voc) | Tempo,Nino (ts) | Parks,Dean (g) | Berghofer,Chuck (b) | Guerin,John (dr)
Diane Schuur
Somewhere Over The Rainbow
Schuur,Diane (voc)

7567-83165-2 | CD | Ethnomusicology Vol.1
Russel Gunn Group
74 Miles Away(intro) | Shiva | DJ Apollo Interlude | Woody 1:On The New Ark | The Blackwiddow Blues | Folkz | Andre Heyward Interlude | Mr.Hurt
NYC, rec. 8.-10.7.1998
Gunn,Russell (tp,fl-h,perc,org-bass,tambourine,vox) | Heyward,Andre (tb) | Williams,Bruce (as,cowbell,e-flat-cl) | Tardy,Greg (fl,b-cl,ts) | Hurt,James (p,el-p,org) | Jordan,Rodney (b) | Williams,Woody (dr) | Bell,Khalil Kwame (perc) | DJ Apollo (turntables)
Doll
Gunn,Russell (tp,fl-h,perc,org-bass,tambourine,vox) | Heyward,Andre (tb) | Williams,Bruce (as,cowbell,e-flat-cl) | Tardy,Greg (fl,b-cl,ts) | Minucci,Chieli (g) | Hurt,James (p,el-p,org) | Jordan,Rodney (b) | Williams,Woody (dr) | Bell,Khalil Kwame (perc)

7567-83211-2 | CD | Evolution
John Lewis
Sweet Georgia Brown | September Song | Afternoon In Paris | Two Degrees East Three Degrees West | I'll Remember April | Django | Willow Weep For Me | Cherokee | For Ellington | Don't Blame Me | At The Horse Show
Tarrytown,NY, rec. 12.-15.1.1999
Lewis,John (p-solo)

7567-83219-2 | CD | Play
Mike Stern Group
Play | Small World
Seattle,WA, rec. December 1998
Stern,Mike (g) | Scofield,John (g) | Beard,Jim (keyboards) | Goines,Lincoln (b) | Perowsky,Ben (dr)
Outa Town
Stern,Mike (g) | Malach,Bob (ts) | Scofield,John (g) | Beard,Jim (keyboards) | Goines,Lincoln (b) | Perowsky,Ben (dr)
Tipatina's
Stern,Mike (g) | Malach,Bob (ts) | Beard,Jim (keyboards) | Goines,Lincoln (b) | Chambers,Dennis (dr)
All Heart
Stern,Mike (g) | Malach,Bob (ts) | Frisell,Bill (g) | Beard,Jim (keyboards) | Goines,Lincoln (b) | Perowsky,Ben (dr)
Frizz | Big Kids | Blue Tone
Stern,Mike (g) | Frisell,Bill (g) | Goines,Lincoln (b) | Perowsky,Ben (dr)
Link | Goin' Under
Stern,Mike (g) | Malach,Bob (ts) | Beard,Jim (keyboards) | Goines,Lincoln (b) | Chambers,Dennis (dr)

7567-83293-2 | CD | Nuy Divertido(Very Entertaining)
Marc Ribot Y Los Cubanos Postizos
Dame Un Cachito Pa'huele
NYC, rec. 1999
Ribot,Marc (g,voc) | Coleman,Anthony (keyboards) | Jones,Bradley (b) | Rodriguez,E.J. (congas,perc) | Rodriguez,Robert J. (dr,timbales,timpani,perc) | Nieve,Steve (org) | Balint,Eszter (voc)
Las Lomas De New Jersey
Ribot,Marc (g,voc) | Coleman,Anthony (keyboards) | Jones,Bradley (b) | Rodriguez,E.J. (congas,perc) | Rodriguez,Robert J. (dr,timbales,timpani,perc) | Vasquez,Frankie (perc,voc)
El Gaucho Rojo | El Divorcio | Jaguey
Ribot,Marc (g,voc) | Coleman,Anthony (keyboards) | Jones,Bradley (b) | Rodriguez,E.J. (congas,perc) | Rodriguez,Robert J. (dr,timbales,timpani,perc)
Obsesion
Ribot,Marc (g,voc) | Coleman,Anthony (keyboards) | Jones,Bradley (b) | Rodriguez,E.J. (congas,perc) | Rodriguez,Robert J. (dr,timbales,timpani,perc) | Rojas,Marcus (tuba) | Taub,Andy (keyboards)
Se Formo El Bochinche
Ribot,Marc (g,voc) | Coleman,Anthony (keyboards) | Jones,Bradley (b) | Rodriguez,E.J. (congas,perc) | Rodriguez,Robert J. (dr,timbales,timpani,perc) | Rojas,Marcus (tuba) | Taub,Andy (keyboards) | Balint,Eszter (voc) | Vasquez,Frankie (perc,voc)
Baile Baile Baile
Ribot,Marc (g,voc) | Coleman,Anthony (keyboards) | Jones,Bradley (b) | Rodriguez,E.J. (congas,perc) | Rodriguez,Robert J. (dr,timbales,timpani,perc) | Rojas,Marcus (tuba) | Taub,Andy (keyboards) | Balint,Eszter (voc) | Foster,JD (b)
No Puedo Prenar
Ribot,Marc (g,voc) | Coleman,Anthony (keyboards) | Jones,Bradley (b) | Rodriguez,E.J. (congas,perc) | Rodriguez,Robert J. (dr,timbales,timpani,perc) | Rojas,Marcus (tuba) | Taub,Andy (keyboards) | Osborne,Riley (org)
Carmela Dame La Llave
Ribot,Marc (g,voc) | Coleman,Anthony (keyboards) | Jones,Bradley (b) | Rodriguez,E.J. (congas,perc) | Rodriguez,Robert J. (dr,timbales,timpani,perc) | Rojas,Marcus (tuba) | Taub,Andy (keyboards) | Osborne,Riley (org) | Vasquez,Frankie (perc,voc)

7567-83304-2 | CD | Chasin' The Gypsy
James Carter Group
Nuages | La Dernière Bergére(The Last Shepherdess) | Manoir De Mes Reves(aka Django's Castle) | Artillerie Lourde(Heavy Artillery) | Chasin' The Gyssy | Oriental Shuffle | I'll Never Be The Same | Avalon | Imari's Lullaby
Carter,James (ss,f-mezzo-sax,ts,bass-sax) | Carter,Regina (v) | Berliner,Jay (g) | Lubambo,Romero (g) | Giordano,Charlie (accordeon) | Kirby,Steve (b) | Baron,Joey (dr) | Batista,Ciro (perc)

7567-83305-2 | CD | Layin' In The Cut
Layin' In The Cut | Motown Mash | Requiem For Hartford Ave. | Terminal 'B' | Drafadelic In Db | There's A Paddle | GP
Carter,James (as,ts) | Johnson,Jef Lee (el-g) | Ribot,Marc (el-g) | Tacuma,Jamaaladeen (el-b) | Weston,Grant Calvin (dr)

7567-83313-2 | CD | Eviolution II
John Lewis Quartet
The Festivale | That! Afternoon In Paris | Cain And Abel | Trieste | Django | Sammy
NYC, rec. 2000
Lewis,John (p) | Collins,Howard (g) | Johnson,Marc (b) | Nash,Lewis (dr)
One! Of Parker's Moods | December Remember | Come Rain Or Come Shine | What Is This Thing Called Love
Lewis,John (p) | Alden,Howard (g) | Mraz,George 'Jiri' (b) | Nash,Lewis (dr)

7567-90041-2 | CD | The Avant-Garde
John Coltrane-Don Cherry Quartet
Cherryco | The Blessing
NYC, rec. 28.6.1960
Cherry,Don (tp) | Coltrane,John (ss,ts) | Haden,Charlie (b) | Blackwell,Ed (dr)
Focus On Sanity | The Invisible | Bemsha Swing
NYC, rec. 8.7.1960
Cherry,Don (tp) | Coltrane,John (ss,ts) | Heath,Percy (b) | Blackwell,Ed (dr)

7567-90045-2 | CD | The Inflated Tear
Roland Kirk Quartet
The Black And Crazy Blues | Creole Love Call | The Inflated Tear
NYC, rec. 27.11.1967
Kirk,Rahsaan Roland (engl-h,fl,cl,ts,flexafone,manzello,stritch,whistle) | Burton,Ron (p) | Novosel,Steve (b) | Hopps,Jimmy (dr)
Fingers In The Wind | A Laugh For Rory | Many Blessings | A Handful Of Fives | Lovellevelliloqui
NYC, rec. 30.11.1967
Kirk,Rahsaan Roland (engl-h,fl,cl,ts,flexafone,manzello,stritch,whistle) | Burton,Ron (p) | Novosel,Steve (b) | Hopps,Jimmy (dr)
Roland Kirk Quintet
Fly By Night
Kirk,Rahsaan Roland (ts) | Griffith,Dick (tb) | Burton,Ron (p) | Novosel,Steve (b) | Hopps,Jimmy (dr)

7567-90140-2 | CD | Feeling + Finesse = Jazz
Stephane Grappelli Quintet
Django | Nuages | Alabamy Bound | You Better Go Now | Daphne | Le Tien | Minor Swing | Makin' Whoopee | How About You | Soft Winds
Paris,France, rec. 7.-9.3.1962
Grappelli,Stephane (v) | Cavalli,Pierre (el-g) | Petit,Leo (g) | Pedersen,Guy (b) | Humair,Daniel (dr)

7567-90141-2 | CD | Nirvana
Herbie Mann With The Bill Evans Trio
Nirvana | I Love You | Willow Weep For Me | Lover Man(Oh,Where Can You Be?)
NYC, rec. 8.12.1961
Mann,Herbie (fl) | Evans,Bill (p) | Israels,Chuck (b) | Motian,Paul (dr)
Gymnopedie | Cashmere
NYC, rec. 4.5.1962
Mann,Herbie (fl) | Evans,Bill (p) | Israels,Chuck (b) | Motian,Paul (dr)

7567-90532-2 | CD | Mingus At Antibes
Charles Mingus Quintet
Wednesday Night Prayer Meeting | Prayer For Passive Resistance | Folk Forms(No.1) | Better Git It In Your Soul
Jazz Festival Antibes,France, rec. 13.7.1960
Mingus,Charles (p,b) | Curson,Ted (tp) | Dolphy,Eric (b-cl,as) | Ervin,Booker (ts) | Richmond,Dannie (dr)
Charles Mingus Quartet
What Love
Mingus,Charles (p,b) | Curson,Ted (tp) | Dolphy,Eric (b-cl,as) | Richmond,Dannie (dr)
Charles Mingus Quintet With Bud Powell
I'll Remember April
Mingus,Charles (b) | Curson,Ted (tp) | Dolphy,Eric (as) | Ervin,Booker (ts) | Powell,Bud (p) | Richmond,Dannie (dr)

7567-90665-2 | CD | Lonely Woman
Modern Jazz Quartet
Trieste | Lonely Woman | Animal Dance | New York 19
NYC, rec. 24./25.& 29.1.1962
MJQ (Modern Jazz Quartet) | Jackson,Milt (vib) | Lewis,John (p) | Heath,Percy (b) | Kay,Connie (dr)
Belkis | Why Are You Blue | Fugato | Lamb Leopard
NYC, rec. 2.2.1962
MJQ (Modern Jazz Quartet) | Jackson,Milt (vib) | Lewis,John (p) | Heath,Percy (b) | Kay,Connie (dr)

7567-90981-2 | CD | The Jimmy Giuffre Three
Jimmy Giuffre 3
Gotta Dance | Two Kinds Of Blues | The Song Is You | Crazy She Calls Me | Voodoo | My All | That's The Way It Is | Crawdad Suite | The Train And The River
NYC, rec. 3./4.12.1956
Giuffre,Jimmy (cl,ts,bs) | Hall,Jim (g) | Pena,Ralph (b)

8122-71257-2 | CD | Rhino Presents The Atlantic Jazz Gallery
David Fathead Newman Sextet
Hard Times
NYC, rec. 5.11.1958
Newman,David Fathead (as) | Belgrave,Marcus (tp) | Charles,Ray (p) | Willis,Edgar (b) | Turner,Milton (dr) | Crawford,Hank (bs)
Les McCann-Eddie Harris Quintet
Compared To What
Live at The Montreux Jazz Festival, rec. 21.6.1969
Harris,Eddie (ts) | Bailey,Benny (tp) | McCann,Les (p) | Vinnegar,Leroy (b) | Dean,Donald (dr)
Hank Crawford Orchestra
Whispering Grass
Los Angeles,CA, rec. 16.2.1963
Crawford,Hank (as) | Cave,John (fr-h) | DeRosa,Vince (fr-h) | Maebe,Arthur (fr-h) | Hinshaw,William 'Bill' (fr-h) | Feldman,Victor (vib) | Hendrickson,Al (g) | Jolly,Pete (p) | Mondragon,Joe (b) | Lewis,Mel (dr) | Belnick,Arnold (v) | Getzoff,James (v) | Malarsky,Leonhard (v) | Marino,Amerigo (v) | Neufeld,Erno (v) | Raderman,Lou (v) | Shure,Paul (v) | Sosson,Marshall (v) | Vinci,Gerry (v) | Paich,Marty (arr,ld)
Modern Jazz Quartet
The Golden Striker
NYC, rec. 4.4.1957
MJQ (Modern Jazz Quartet) | Jackson,Milt (vib) | Lewis,John (p) | Heath,Percy (b) | Kay,Connie (dr)
Rahsaan Roland Kirk Quartet
The Inflated Tear
NYC, rec. 27.11.1967
Kirk,Rahsaan Roland (ts,flexafone,manzello,stritch) | Burton,Ron (p) | Novosel,Steve (b) | Hopps,Jimmy (dr)
Herbie Mann Group
Comin' Home Baby
Live at The 'Village Gate',NYC, rec. 17.11.1961
Mann,Herbie (fl) | Hardy,Hagood (vib) | Abdul-Malik,Ahmed (b) | Tucker,Ben (b) | Collins,Rudy (dr) | Bey,Chief (african-dr) | Mantilla,Ray (perc,congas)
Ornette Coleman Quartet
Ramblin'
NYC, rec. 9.10.1959
Coleman,Ornette (as) | Cherry,Don (pocket-tp) | Haden,Charlie (b) | Higgins,Billy (dr)
Mose Allison Trio
Your Mind Is On Vacation
NYC, rec. 15.3.1962
Allison,Mose (p,voc) | Farmer,Addison (b) | Johnson,Osie (dr)
John Coltrane Quartet
My Favorite Things
NYC, rec. 21.10.1960
Coltrane,John (ts) | Tyner,McCoy (p) | Davis,Steve (b) | Jones,Elvin (dr)
Ray Charles Trio
Sweet Sixteen Bars
NYC, rec. 20.11.1956
Charles,Ray (p) | Sheffield,Roosevelt (b) | Peeples,William (dr)
Yusef Lateef Orchestra
Nubian Lady
NYC, rec. 2.9.1971
Lateef,Yusef (fl) | Bryant,Ray (p) | Barron,Kenny (el-p) | Jones,Sam (b) | Cunningham,Bob (b) | Salter,Bill (el-b) | Heath,Albert 'Tootie' (dr) | Cammara,Ladzi (perc)
Charles Mingus Jazz Workshop
Wednesday Night Prayer Meeting
NYC, rec. 4.2.1959
Mingus,Charles (b) | Knepper,Jimmy (tb) | Dennis,Willie (tb) | McLean,Jackie (as) | Handy,John (as) | Ervin,Booker (ts) | Adams,Pepper (bs) | Parlan,Horace (p) | Richmond,Dannie (dr)

8122-71410-2 | 6 CD | Beauty Is A Rare Thing:Ornette Coleman-The Complete Atlantic Recordings
Ornette Coleman Quartet
Focus On Sanity | Chronology | Peace | Congeniality | Lonely Woman | Monk And The Nun | Just For You | Eventually
Hollywood,CA, rec. 22.5.1959
Coleman,Ornette (as) | Cherry,Don (co) | Haden,Charlie (b) | Higgins,Billy (dr)
Una Muy Bonita | Bird Food | Change Of The Century | Music Always | The Face Of The Bass
Hollywood,CA, rec. 8.10.1959
Coleman,Ornette (as) | Cherry,Don (pocket-tp) | Haden,Charlie (b) | Higgins,Billy (dr)
Forerunner | Free | The Circle With The Hole In The Middle | Ramblin'
Hollywood,CA, rec. 9.10.1959
Coleman,Ornette (as) | Cherry,Don (pocket-tp) | Haden,Charlie (b) | Higgins,Billy (dr)
Little Symphony | The Tribes Of New York | Kaleidoscope | Rise And Shine | Mr. And Mrs. People | Blues Connotation | I Heard It Over The Radio | P.S. Unless One Has(Blues Connotation No.2)
NYC, rec. 19.7.1960
Coleman,Ornette (as) | Cherry,Don (pocket-tp) | Haden,Charlie (b) | Blackwell,Ed (dr)
Brings Goodness | Joy Of A Toy | To Us | Humpty Dumpty | The Fifth Of Beethoven | Motive For Its Use | Moon Inhabitants | The Legend Of Bebop | Some Other | Embraceable You | All
NYC, rec. 26.7.1960
Coleman,Ornette (as) | Cherry,Don (pocket-tp) | Haden,Charlie (b) | Blackwell,Ed (dr)
Folk Tale | Poise | Beauty Is A Rare Thing
NYC, rec. 2.8.1960
Coleman,Ornette (as) | Cherry,Don (pocket-tp) | Haden,Charlie (b) | Blackwell,Ed (dr)
Ornette Coleman Double Quartet
Free Jazz | Free Jazz(alt.take)
NYC, rec. 21.12.1960
Coleman,Ornette (as) | Cherry,Don (pocket-tp) | Hubbard,Freddie (tp) | Dolphy,Eric (b-cl) | LaFaro,Scott (b) | Haden,Charlie (b) | Higgins,Billy (dr) | Blackwell,Ed (dr)
Ornette Coleman Quartet
Proof Readers | W.R.U. | Check Up | T. & T. | C. & D. | R.P.D.D. | The Alchemy Of Scott LaFaro
NYC, rec. 31.1.1961
Coleman,Ornette (as) | Cherry,Don (pocket-tp) | LaFaro,Scott (b) | Blackwell,Ed (dr)

Eos
NYC, rec. 22.3.1961
Coleman,Ornette (ts) | Cherry,Don (pocket-tp) | Garrison,Jimmy (b) | Blackwell,Ed (dr)
Enfant | Cross Breeding | Harlem's Manhattan | Mapa
NYC, rec. 27.3.1961
Coleman,Ornette (ts) | Cherry,Don (pocket-tp) | Garrison,Jimmy (b) | Blackwell,Ed (dr)
Gunther Schuller Ensemble
Abstraction
NYC, rec. 19.12.1960
Coleman,Ornette (as) | Hall,Jim (g) | Brehm,Alvin (b) | LaFaro,Scott (b) | Evans,Sticks (dr) | Contemporary String Quartet: | Libove,Charles (v) | Vamos,Roland (v) | Zaratzian,Harry (viola) | Tekula,Joe (cello) | Schuller,Gunther (cond,arr)
Variants On A Theme Of Thelonious Monk(Criss Cross): | Variant I- | Variant II- | Variant III- | Variant VI-
NYC, rec. 20.12.1960
Coleman,Ornette (as) | Dolphy,Eric (fl,b-cl,as) | Di Domenica,Bob (fl) | Costa,Eddie (vib) | Hall,Jim (g) | Evans,Bill (p) | Duvivier,George (b) | LaFaro,Scott (b) | Evans,Sticks (dr) | Contemporary String Quartet: | Libove,Charles (v) | Vamos,Roland (v) | Zaratzian,Harry (viola) | Tekula,Joe (cello) | Schuller,Gunther (cond,arr)

8122-71455-2 | CD | Ornette On Tenor
Ornette Coleman Quartet
Eos
NYC, rec. 22.3.1961
Coleman,Ornette (ts) | Cherry,Don (pocket-tp) | Garrison,Jimmy (b) | Blackwell,Ed (dr)
Cross Breeding | Mapa | Enfant | Ecars
NYC, rec. 27.3.1961
Coleman,Ornette (ts) | Cherry,Don (pocket-tp) | Garrison,Jimmy (b) | Blackwell,Ed (dr)

8122-71636-2 | CD | The Laws Of Jazz
Hubert Laws Quartet
Miss Thing | Black Eyed Peas And Rice | Bimbo Blue
NYC, rec. 2.4.1964
Laws,Hubert (fl) | Corea,Chick (p) | Davis,Richard (p) | Thomas,Bobby (dr)
All Soul | Bessie's Blues | And Don't You Forget It | Capers
NYC, rec. 22.4.1964
Laws,Hubert (fl) | Corea,Chick (p) | Davis,Richard (p) | Cobb,Jimmy (dr)

8122-71746-2 | CD | Forest Flower:Charles Lloyd At Monterey
Charles Lloyd Quartet
Forest Flower(Sunrise) | Forest Flower(Sunset) | Sorcery | Song For Her | East Of The Sun West Of The Moon
Live at The Monterey Jazz Festival,CA, rec. 18.9.1966
Lloyd,Charles (fl,ts) | Jarrett,Keith (p) | McBee,Cecil (b) | DeJohnette,Jack (dr)

8122-71785-2 | CD | Cumbia & Jazz Fusion
Charles Mingus Orchestra
Music For 'Todo Modo'
Rome,Italy, rec. 31.3.& 1.4.1976
Mingus,Charles (b) | Walrath,Jack (tp) | Piana,Dino (tb) | Maltoni,Quatro (as) | Del Bono,Anastasio (engl-h,oboe) | Laneri,Roberto (b-cl) | Sabatelli,Pasquale (bassoon) | Adams,George (alto-fl,ts) | Mixon,Danny (p,org) | Richmond,Dannie (dr)
Cumbia & Jazz Fusion
NYC, rec. 10.3.1977
Mingus,Charles (b,perc,voc) | Walrath,Jack (tp,perc) | Ford,Ricky (ts,perc) | Jeffrey,Paul (ts,oboe) | Smith,Mauricio (fl,ss,as,piccolo) | Anderson,Gary (b-cl,contra-b-cl) | Scholtes,Gene (bassoon) | Knepper,Jimmy (tb,b-tb) | Nellums,Bob (p) | Richmond,Dannie (dr) | Candido[Camero] (congas) | Gonzales,Daniel (congas) | Mantilla,Ray (congas) | Ramirez,Alfredo (congas) | Cunningham,Bradley (perc)

8122-71984-2 | 7 CD | John Coltrane-The Heavyweight Champion:The Complete Atlantic Recordings
John Coltrane-Milt Jackson Quintet
Stairway To The Stars | The Late Late Blues | Bag's & Trane | Three Little Words | The Night We Called It A Day | Bebop | Blues Legacy | Centerpiece
NYC, rec. 15.1.1959
Coltrane,John (ts) | Jackson,Milt (vib) | Jones,Hank (p) | Chambers,Paul (b) | Kay,Connie (dr)
John Coltrane Quartet
Giant Steps | Giant Steps(incomplete take 1) | Giant Steps(false start 1) | Giant Steps(incomplete take 2) | Giant Steps(incomplete take 3) | Giant Steps(alt.take) | Giant Steps(false start 2) | Giant Steps(incomplete take 4) | Naima | Naima(incomplete take 1) | Naima(incomplete take 2) | Naima(false start) | Naima(alt.take 1) | Naima(alt.take 2) | Like Sonny | Like Sonny(rehersal 1-false start) | Like Sonny(rehersal 2-incomplete take) | Like Sonny(false start 1) | Like Sonny(incomplete take 1) | Like Sonny(incomplete take 2) | Like Sonny(incomplete take 3) | Like Sonny(false start 2) | Like Sonny(alt.take) | Like Sonny(incomplete take 4)
NYC, rec. 26.3.1959
Coltrane,John (ts) | Walton,Cedar (p) | Chambers,Paul (b) | Humphries,Lex (dr)
Spiral | Countdown | Countdown(alt.take)
NYC, rec. 4.5.1959
Coltrane,John (ts) | Flanagan,Tommy (p) | Chambers,Paul (b) | Taylor,Arthur 'Art' (dr)
Syeeda's Song Flute | Syeeda's Song Flute(alt.take) | Mr.P.C. | Giant Steps | Giant Steps(incomplete take) | Giant Steps(alt.take) | Cousin Mary | Cousin Mary(alt.take)
NYC, rec. 5.5.1959
Coltrane,John (ts) | Flanagan,Tommy (p) | Chambers,Paul (b) | Taylor,Arthur 'Art' (dr)
I'll Wait And Pray | I'll Wait And Pray(alt.take) | Little Old Lady
NYC, rec. 24.11.1959
Coltrane,John (ts) | Kelly,Wynton (p) | Chambers,Paul (b) | Cobb,Jimmy (dr)
Like Sonny | Harmonique | My Shining Hour | Naima | Some Other Blues | Fifth House
NYC, rec. 2.12.1959
Coltrane,John (ts) | Kelly,Wynton (p) | Chambers,Paul (b) | Cobb,Jimmy (dr)
John Coltrane-Don Cherry Quartet
Cherryco | The Blessing
NYC, rec. 28.6.1960
Coltrane,John (ss,ts) | Cherry,Don (co) | Haden,Charlie (b) | Higgins,Billy (dr)
Focus On Sanity | The Invisible | Bemsha Swing
NYC, rec. 8.7.1960
Coltrane,John (ss,ts) | Cherry,Don (co) | Haden,Charlie (b) | Higgins,Billy (dr)
John Coltrane Quartet
Village Blues | Village Blues(alt.take) | My Favorite Things
NYC, rec. 21.10.1960
Coltrane,John (ss,ts) | Tyner,McCoy (p) | Davis,Steve (b) | Jones,Elvin (dr)
Central Park West | Mr.Syms | Untitled Original(Exotica) | Summertime | Body And Soul | Body And Soul(alt.take) | Mr.Knight | Blues To Elvin | Blues To Elvin(alt.take 1) | Blues To Elvin(alt.take 2) | Blues To Elvin(false start) | Mr.Day | Blues To You | Blues To You(alt.take 1) | Blues To You(alt.take 2) | Blues To Bechet | Satelite
NYC, rec. 24.10.1960
Coltrane,John (ss,ts) | Tyner,McCoy (p) | Davis,Steve (b) | Jones,Elvin (dr)
Every Time We Say Goodbye | 26-2 | But Not For Me | Liberia | The Night Has A Thousand Eyes | Equinox
NYC, rec. 26.10.1960
Coltrane,John (ss,ts) | Tyner,McCoy (p) | Davis,Steve (b) | Jones,Elvin (dr)
John Coltrane Sextet With Eric Dolphy
Olé | Dahomey Dance | Original Untitled Ballad(To Her Ladyship)
NYC, rec. 25.5.1961
Coltrane,John (ss,ts) | Hubbard,Freddie (tp) | Dolphy,Eric[as George Lane] (fl,as) | Tyner,McCoy (p) | Davis,Art (b) | Workman,Reggie (b) | Jones,Elvin (dr)
John Coltrane Quintet With Eric Dolphy
Aisha
Coltrane,John (ts) | Hubbard,Freddie (tp) | Dolphy,Eric[as George Lane] (as) | Tyner,McCoy (p) | Workman,Reggie (b) | Jones,Elvin (dr)

8122-72394-2 | CD | The Word From Mose
Mose Allison Trio
Don't Forget To Smile | I'm Not Talkin' | Days Like This | Wild Man | One Of These Days | New Parchman
NYC, rec. 10.3.1964
Allison,Mose (p,voc) | Tucker,Ben (b) | Lundberg,Ron (dr)
Your Red Wagon | Fool Killer | Rollin' Stone | Lost Mind | Look Here
NYC, rec. 12.3.1964
Allison,Mose (p,voc) | Tucker,Ben (b) | Lundberg,Ron (dr)

8122-72452-2 | CD | Swiss Movement
Les McCann-Eddie Harris Quintet
Compared To What | Cold Duck Time | Kathleen's Theme | You Got It In Your Soulness | The Generation Gap
Live at The Montreux Jazz Festival, rec. June 1969
Harris,Eddie (ts) | McCann,Les (p,voc) | Bailey,Benny (tp) | Vinnegar,Leroy (b) | Dean,Donald (dr)

8122-72871-2 | 6 CD | Charles Mingus-Passion Of A Man:The Complete Atlantic Recordings 1956-1961
Charles Mingus Jazz Workshop
Pithecanthropus Erectus | A Foggy Day(In London Town) | Profile Of Jackie | Love Chant
NYC, rec. 30.1.1956
Mingus,Charles (b) | McLean,Jackie (as) | Monterose,J.R. (ts) | Waldron,Mal (p) | Jones,Willie (dr)
Teddy Charles Quartet
Laura | When Your Lover Has Gone | Just One Of Those Things | Blue Greens
NYC, rec. 12.11.1956
Charles,Teddy (vib) | Overton,Hal (p) | Mingus,Charles (b) | Shaughnessy,Ed (dr)
Charles Mingus Quintet
The Clown
NYC, rec. 13.2.1957
Mingus,Charles (b) | Knepper,Jimmy (tb) | Hadi [Curtis Porter],Shafti (ts) | Legge,Wade (p) | Richmond,Dannie (dr) | Shepherd,Jean (narration)
Passions Of A Woman Loved | Blue Cee | Tonight At Noon | Re-Incarnation Of A Love Bird | Haitian Fight Song
NYC, rec. 12.3.1957
Mingus,Charles (b) | Knepper,Jimmy (tb) | Hadi [Curtis Porter],Shafti (as) | Legge,Wade (p) | Richmond,Dannie (dr)
Charles Mingus And His Orchestra
My Jelly Roll Soul | Tensions | Moanin' | Cryin' Blues | Wednesday Night Prayer Meeting | My Jelly Roll Soul(alt.take) | Tensions(alt.take) | Wednesday Night Prayer Meeting(alt.take)
NYC, rec. 4.2.1959
Mingus,Charles (b) | Knepper,Jimmy (tb) | Dennis,Willie (tb) | Handy,John (as) | McLean,Jackie (as) | Ervin,Booker (ts) | Adams,Pepper (bs) | Parlan,Horace (p) | Richmond,Dannie (dr)
E's Flat Ah's Flat Too | E's Flat Ah's Flat Too(alt.take)
Mingus,Charles (b) | Knepper,Jimmy (tb) | Dennis,Willie (tb) | Handy,John (as) | McLean,Jackie (as) | Ervin,Booker (ts) | Adams,Pepper (bs) | Waldron,Mal (p) | Richmond,Dannie (dr)
Charles Mingus Quintet
Prayer For Passive Resistance | Better Git It In Your Soul | Wednesday Night Prayer Meeting | Folk Forms(No.1) | What Love
Jazz Festival Antibes,France, rec. 13.7.1960
Mingus,Charles (p,b) | Curson,Ted (tp) | Dolphy,Eric (b-cl,as) | Ervin,Booker (ts) | Richmond,Dannie (dr)
Charles Mingus Quintet With Bud Powell
I'll Remember April
Mingus,Charles (b) | Curson,Ted (tp) | Dolphy,Eric (as) | Ervin,Booker (ts) | Powell,Bud (p) | Richmond,Dannie (dr)
Charles Mingus Quintet With Roland Kirk
Devil Woman | Ecclusiastics | Old Blues For Walt's Torin | Peggy's Blue Skylight | Hog Callin' Blues | Oh Lord Don't Let Them Drop That Atomic Bomb On Me | Passions Of A Man | Wham Bam Thank You Ma'Am | Invisible Lady | Eat That Chicken
NYC, rec. 6.11.1961
Mingus,Charles (p,voc) | Kirk,Rahsaan Roland (fl,ts,manzello,siren,strich,voice) | Ervin,Booker (ts) | Knepper,Jimmy (tb) | Watkins,Doug (b) | Richmond,Dannie (dr)
Charles Mingus
Interview(76:26) by Nesuhi Ertegun
NYC, rec. 1961
Mingus,Charles (talking)

8122-73708-2 | CD | Fathead:Ray Charles Presents David Newman | EAN 081227370824
David Fathead Newman Sextet
Hard Times | Weird Beard | Willow Weep For Me | Bill For Bennie | Sweet Eyes | Fathead | Mean To Me | Tin Tin Deo
NYC, rec. 5.11.1958
Newman,David Fathead (as,ts) | Belgrave,Marcus (tp) | Crawford,Bennie (bs) | Charles,Ray (p) | Willis,Edgar (b) | Turner,Milton (dr)

8122-73709-2 | CD | More Soul | EAN 081227370923
Hank Crawford Septet
Boo's Tune | Angel Eyes | Four Five Six | The Story | Dat Dere | Misty | Sister Sadie
NYC, rec. 7.10.1960
Crawford,Hank (as,p) | Guilbeau,Phil (tp) | Hunt,John (tp,fl-h) | Newman,David Fathead (ts) | Cooper,Leroy 'Hog' (bs) | Willis,Edgar (b) | Turner,Milton (dr)

8122-75203-2 | CD | Giant Steps
John Coltrane Quartet
Giant Steps | Naima
NYC, rec. 1.4.1959
Coltrane,John (ts) | Walton,Cedar (p) | Chambers,Paul (b) | Humphries,Lex (dr)
Countdown | Countdown(alt.take) | Spiral
NYC, rec. 4.5.1959
Coltrane,John (ts) | Flanagan,Tommy (p) | Chambers,Paul (b) | Taylor,Arthur 'Art' (dr)
Syeeda's Song Flute | Syeeda's Song Flute(alt.take) | Mr.P.C. | Giant Steps | Cousin Mary | Cousin Mary(alt.take)
NYC, rec. 5.5.1959
Coltrane,John (ts) | Flanagan,Tommy (p) | Chambers,Paul (b) | Taylor,Arthur 'Art' (dr)
Naima
NYC, rec. 2.12.1959
Coltrane,John (ts) | Kelly,Wynton (p) | Chambers,Paul (b) | Cobb,Jimmy (dr)

8122-75204-2 | CD | My Favorite Things
My Favorite Things
NYC, rec. 21.10.1960
Coltrane,John (ts) | Tyner,McCoy (p) | Davis,Steve (b) | Jones,Elvin (dr)
Summertime
Coltrane,John (ss) | Tyner,McCoy (p) | Davis,Steve (b) | Jones,Elvin (dr)
But Not For Me | Every Time We Say Goodbye
NYC, rec. 26.10.1960
Coltrane,John (ss,ts) | Tyner,McCoy (p) | Davis,Steve (b) | Jones,Elvin (dr)

8122-75205-2 | CD | Blues & Roots
Charles Mingus Jazz Workshop
E's Flat Ah's Flat Too | E's Flat Ah's Flat Too(alt.take)
NYC, rec. 4.2.1959
Mingus,Charles (b) | Knepper,Jimmy (tb) | Dennis,Willie (tb) | McLean,Jackie (as) | Handy,John (as) | Ervin,Booker (ts) | Adams,Pepper (bs) | Waldron,Mal (p) | Richmond,Dannie (dr)
My Jelly Roll Soul | My Jelly Roll Soul(alt.take) | Tensions | Tensions(alt.take) | Moanin' | Cryin' Blues | Wednesday Night Prayer Meeting | Wednesday Night Prayer Meeting(alt.take)
Mingus,Charles (b) | Knepper,Jimmy (tb) | Dennis,Willie (tb) | McLean,Jackie (as) | Handy,John (as) | Ervin,Booker (ts) | Adams,Pepper (bs) | Parlan,Horace (p) | Richmond,Dannie (dr)

8122-75207-2 | CD | The Inflated Tear
Roland Kirk Quartet
The Black And Crazy Blues | Creole Love Call | The Inflated Tear
NYC, rec. 27.11.1967
Kirk,Rahsaan Roland (engl-h,fl,cl,ts,flexafone,manzello,stritch,whistle) | Burton,Ron (p) | Novosel,Steve (b) | Hopps,Jimmy (dr)
Fingers In The Wind | A Laugh For Rory | Many Blessings | A Handful Of Fives | Lovellevelliloqui | I'm Glad There Is You
NYC, rec. 30.11.1967
Kirk,Rahsaan Roland (engl-h,fl,cl,ts,flexafone,manzello,stritch,whistle) | Burton,Ron (p) | Novosel,Steve (b) | Hopps,Jimmy (dr)
Roland Kirk Quintet
Fly By Night
Kirk,Rahsaan Roland (ts) | Griffith,Dick (tb) | Burton,Ron (p) | Novosel,Steve (b) | Hopps,Jimmy (dr)

8122-75208-2 | CD | Free Jazz
Ornette Coleman Double Quartet
Free Jazz | Free Jazz(alt.take)
NYC, rec. 21.12.1960
Coleman,Ornette (as) | Cherry,Don (pocket-tp) | Hubbard,Freddie (tp) | Dolphy,Eric (b-cl) | LaFaro,Scott (b) | Haden,Charlie (b) | Higgins,Billy (dr) | Blackwell,Ed (dr)

8122-75355-2 | CD | The Mourning Of A Star
Keith Jarrett Trio
Follow The Crooked Path(Through It Be Longer) | Interlude No.3 | Standing Outside | Everything That Lives Laments | Interlude No.1 | Trust | All I Want | Traces Of You | The Mourning Of A Star | Interlude No.2 | Sympathy
NYC, rec. 8.7.1971
Jarrett,Keith (ss,p,congas,recorder,steel-dr) | Haden,Charlie (b,steel-dr) | Motian,Paul (dr,congas,steel-dr)

8122-75356-2 | CD | Lee Konitz With Warne Marsh
Lee Konitz-Warne Marsh Quintet
Topsy | I Can't Get Started
NYC, rec. 14.6.1955
Konitz,Lee (as) | Marsh,Warne (ts) | Bauer,Billy (g) | Pettiford,Oscar (b) | Clarke,Kenny (dr)
Lee Konitz-Warne Marsh Sextet
There'll Never Be Another You | Donna Lee | Two Not One | Don't Squawk | Background Music
Konitz,Lee (as) | Marsh,Warne (ts) | Mosca,Sal (p) | Bauer,Billy (g) | Pettiford,Oscar (b) | Clarke,Kenny (dr)
Ronnie's Line
Konitz,Lee (as) | Marsh,Warne (ts) | Ball,Ronnie (p) | Bauer,Billy (g) | Pettiford,Oscar (b) | Clarke,Kenny (dr)

8122-75358-2 | CD | The Clown
Charles Mingus Jazz Workshop
The Clown
NYC, rec. 13.2.1957
Mingus,Charles (b) | Knepper,Jimmy (tb) | Hadi [Curtis Porter],Shafti (ts) | Legge,Wade (p) | Richmond,Dannie (dr) | Shepherd,Jean (narration)
Haitian Fight Song | Blue Cee | Re-Incarnation Of A Love Bird
NYC, rec. 12.3.1957
Mingus,Charles (b) | Knepper,Jimmy (tb) | Hadi [Curtis Porter],Shafti (as) | Legge,Wade (p) | Richmond,Dannie (dr)

ATM Records | ATM(Admission To Music)

ATM 3803-AH | CD | Privat
Mani Neumeir
Schall Und Rauch | Auf Alle Felle | Freibier Für Alle | Bacon | Over Heat | Into Gagaku | Mopsa Mopsa | Flieg Mein Herz | Feuer Und Flamme
Konstanz, rec. March 1992
Neumeier,Mani (dr,cymbals,gongs) | Gamclans,Tavil (steel-dr)
Mani Neumeier Group
Jungle Night | Antarktisch | Transmitter | I TouchYour Skin | Bayrischer Wald
Neumeier,Mani (dr,cymbals,gongs) | Gamclans,Tavil (steel-dr) | Greiner,Hubl (sampler)
My Master | Indian Morning
Neumeier,Mani (dr,cymbals,gamclans,gongs,steel-dr,tavil) | Pillhi,Parashiyama (tavil)
Over Heat
Neumeier,Mani (dr,cymbals,gamclans,gongs,steel-dr,tavil) | Pillhi,Parashiyama (tavil) | Fride,Jan (perc)
Das War 1999
Neumeier,Mani (dr,cymbals,gamclans,gongs,steel-dr,tavil) | Meinesses,Jim (perc)

ATM 3805-AH | CD | Live At The Domicile
Klaus Weiss Orchestra
Love Is Blue | I Just Want To Celebrate | Flowers | Spunkwater | Sail On | Little Big Horns | You're All I Need To Get By | Eleanor Rigby | Superstar | The Cage | Imagine | Get It On
Live at The 'Domicile', München, rec. 20.11.1971
Weiss,Klaus (dr) | Findley,Chuck (tp) | Van Rooyen,Ack (tp) | Mikkelborg,Palle (tp) | Lanese,Bob (tp) | Ross,Barry (tb) | Hampton,Slide (tb) | Orieux,Charles (tb) | Menza,Don (reeds) | Geller,Herb (reeds) | Povel,Ferdinand (reeds) | Vennik,Dick (reeds) | Kronberg,Günther (reeds) | Pauer,Fritz (p) | Catherine,Philip (g) | Lindholm,Lucas (b)

ATM 3809-AH | CD | Psychedelic Guitar
Ax Genrich Group
The Bording Hymn
Beindersheim/Ludwigshafen/Ritschweiler, rec. November 1992/May 1993/May 1994
Genrich,Ax (g) | Beyer,Raymund (synth) | Fadani,Mario (el-b) | Bender,Walter (dr)
Phenomena
Fabrik,Worms/Ritschweiler, rec. May 1993
Genrich,Ax (g,voice) | Dörsam,Matthias (sax) | Krug,Uli (el-b) | Ditzner,Erwin (dr) | Appleton,Pat (voice)
Helicopters
Fabrik,Worms, rec. May 1993
Genrich,Ax (g) | Krug,Uli (el-b) | Ditzner,Erwin (dr)
Marsyas
Fabrik,Worms/Ritschweiler, rec. May 1993
Genrich,Ax (g) | Dörsam,Matthias (b-cl) | Reffert,Hans (sitar-g) | Krug,Uli (el-b,sousaphone) | Ditzner,Erwin (dr)
South
Genrich,Ax (g) | Reffert,Hans (sitar-g) | Krug,Uli (el-b) | Appleton,Pat (voice)
Got Love
Fabrik,Worms, rec. May 1993
Genrich,Ax (g,voice) | Reffert,Hans (harp,lapsteel)
House Rent Stomp
Ludwigshafen, rec. May 1994
Genrich,Ax (bj)
Blow-Up
Ludwigshafen/Ritschweiler, rec. May /July 1994
Genrich,Ax (g) | Reffert,Hans (danelectro-g,melobar) | Schaab,Bruno (voice)
Source Of Light And Sound
Ludwigshafen/Ritschweiler, rec. May/July 1994
Genrich,Ax (g,el-g,bj) | Leroi,Laurent (accordeon) | Reffert,Hans (squareneck-dobro) | Fadani,Mario (b) | Bender,Walter (dr) | Levinson,Mira (voice)

ATM 3810-AH | CD | A Taste Of Jazz
Klaus Weiss Quintet

When You Said Goodbye | Namely You | Just Another Lullaby | Body And Soul |
West Coast Blues | What's New? | Who Cares
München, rec. 26.6.1988
Weiss,Klaus (dr) | Weniger,Peter (ss,ts) | Schröder,John (g) | Di Gioia,Roberto (p) | Stabenow,Thomas (b)
Yesterdays | I'm Old Fashioned | I'll Know | Save You Love For Me | Moon Ray
München, rec. 9.10.1988
Weiss,Klaus (dr) | Weniger,Peter (ss,ts) | Schröder,John (g) | Di Gioia,Roberto (p) | Stabenow,Thomas (b)

ATM 3813-AH | CD | Wave Cut
Ax Genrich Group
Come Back | Go! Lemgo | Fundador | The Rebel | Meat | Wave Cut
Bremen, rec. July 1995
Genrich,Ax (g,el-g,voice) | Fadani,Mario (b,el-b,voice) | Bender,Walter (dr,samples,special-effects,voice)

ATM 3815-AH | CD | Guru Guru/Uli Trepte
Guru Guru
Der LSD-Marsch | Bo Diddley
Live, ?, rec. 1972
Guru Guru | Neumeier,Mani (dr,voc) | Genrich,Ax (g) | Trepte,Uli (b,voc)
Uli Trepte Group
United Dish | Sitting In The Sun | White Line Fever | Ear-Mike Song
Conny's Studio,?, rec. July 1974
Trepte,Uli (b,voc) | Pape,Willi (fl,sax) | Bunka,Roman (g,voc) | Burchard,Christian (marimba,p,dr,perc) | Bohn,Carsten (dr,perc) | Rosy Rosy (voc)

ATM 3816 AH | CD | All Night Through
Klaus Weiss Sextet
Odje Ayne | The Git Go | All Night Through | The Bitches' Circle | M.T.
München, rec. 22.7.1974
Weiss,Klaus (dr) | Bridgewater,Cecil (tp) | Dodgion,Jerry (fl,ss,as) | Harper,Billy (ts) | Norris,Walter (p) | Mraz,George 'Jiri' (b)
Klaus Weiss Septet
Good View | Holunderkuchen
Weiss,Klaus (dr) | Bridgewater,Cecil (tp) | Dodgion,Jerry (fl,ss,as) | St.Peter,Frank (as) | Harper,Billy (ts) | Norris,Walter (p) | Mraz,George 'Jiri' (b)

ATM 3818-AH | CD | Dein Kopf Ist Ein Schlafendes Auto
Roman Bunka Group
Si Ga Ni Wa Ta | No More Jogging | Frag Mich Nicht... | The Heat | Glowin' | Heartbeat | On The Corner
Sunrise Studio,?,CH, rec. 21.-28.7.1980
Bunka,Roman (g,keyboard,oud,voc) | Hartwig,Gerald Luciano (b,sitar) | Setz,Freddy (p,dr) | Yoon,Sun A (voc) | Baba,Chili (voc)
What I Can Do You Can Do Too
Milbertshofener Zentrum,München, rec. 1980
Bunka,Roman (g,keyboard,oud,voc) | Hartwig,Gerald Luciano (b,sitar) | Setz,Freddy (p,dr)

ATM 3820-AH | CD | Real Time Music
Uli Trepte Group
Psylomobil | Crosswise Blues | Skrupptie Wupptie | Player's Digest | Contact Blues | Cyclologie | Riff Blues | Rotarumpo
Egloffstein, rec. 28.-30.11.1991
Trepte,Uli (b-g) | Hofmann,Edgar (fl,cl,sax) | Falk,Marika (perc,caxici,djembe,dombak,tarabuka)
Basic Basic | Reggae Blues | Footsie Wootsie | East 7th St.Blues | Close Hearing
Egloffstein, rec. January 1990
Trepte,Uli (b-g) | Hofmann,Edgar (fl,cl,sax) | Kohlman,Andy (perc)

ATM 3821-AH | CD | Monsters Of Drums-Live
Mani Neumeir-Peter Hollinger
Oszillato | Sunda | A So | Schlagoberst | Häckselmaschine | Frog Me | Wünsch Dir Was | Agung | Wellen Und Wolken | Lumumba | Zovirax | Bamboo | Taumel | Der Grüne Treibt | Der Verrückt Gewordene Schrotthaufen | St.Sticks
different Places, rec. 1994-1996
Neumeier,Mani (dr,perc) | Hollinger,Peter (dr,perc)

ATM 3823-AH | CD | Kickbit Information
Bitkicks
Psychedelic Review | Schnellbedienung | Hacksack-Serenade
Graue,D, rec. 22.2.1975
Bitkicks | Pape,Willi (fl,sax) | Richter,Otto (v) | Hegi,Fritz (el-p) | Trepte,Uli (b-g) | Bohn,Carsten (dr)

Bear Family Records | Bear Family Records GmbH

BCD 15430 | 8 CD | Deutsches Jazz Fesival 1954/1955
Two Beat Stompers
Jennie's Ball
Frankfurt/M, rec. 5.6.1954
Two Beat Stompers | Rehm,Werner (tp) | Simon,Dick (tb) | Dies,Werner (cl) | Theobald,Robert (p) | Schüttrumpf,Gerd (bj) | Reichel,Louis (sousaphon) | Lippmann,Horst (dr)
Hugo Strasser Combo
Flamingo
Frankfurt/M, rec. 6.6.1954
Strasser,Hugo (as) | Hipp,Jutta (p) | Kresse,Hans (b) | Sanner,Karl (dr)
Quartet Der Kurt Edelhagen All Stars
Just You Just Me
Schneebiegl,Rolf (tp) | Reinhardt,Helmut (bs) | Schultze,Werner (b) | Schmidt,Bobby (dr)
Is You Is Or Is You Ain't My Baby
Edelhagen,Kurt (ld) | Wilfert,Hanne (tp) | Schneebiegl,Rolf (tp) | Achhammer,Siegfried (tp) | Mitschele,Klaus (tp) | Hermannsdörfer,Heinz (tb) | Bredl,Otto (tb) | Hauck,Helmut (tb) | Betz,Werner (tb) | Von Klenck,Franz (as) | Reinhardt,Helmut (as) | Martin,Paul (ts) | Aderhold,Bubi (ts) | Feigl,Johnny (cl,bs) | Drexler,Werner (p) | Schultze,Werner (b) | Schmidt,Bobby (dr) | Valente,Caterina (voc)
Jazz Time Riff
Edelhagen,Kurt (ld) | Wilfert,Hanne (tp) | Schneebiegl,Rolf (tp) | Achhammer,Siegfried (tp) | Mitschele,Klaus (tp) | Hermannsdörfer,Heinz (tb) | Bredl,Otto (tb) | Hauck,Helmut (tb) | Betz,Werner (tb) | Von Klenck,Franz (as) | Reinhardt,Helmut (as) | Martin,Paul (ts) | Aderhold,Bubi (ts) | Feigl,Johnny (cl,bs) | Drexler,Werner (p) | Schultze,Werner (b) | Schmidt,Bobby (dr)
Hans Koller New Jazz Stars
Fine And Dandy
Frankfurt/M, rec. 5.6.1954
Koller,Hans (ts) | Mangelsdorff,Albert (tb) | Kovac,Roland (p) | Roeder,Shorty (b) | Sehring,Rudi (dr)
Jutta Hipp Quintet
I Never Knew
Frankfurt/M, rec. 6.6.1954
Hipp,Jutta (p) | Mangelsdorff,Emil (as) | Freund,Joki (ts) | Kresse,Hans (b) | Sanner,Karl (dr)
Fred Bunge Star Band
Creole Love Call
Frankfurt/M, rec. 5./6.6.1954
Bunge,Fred (tp) | Christmann,Egon (tb) | Hübner,Hans (cl,as) | Riedl,Franz Xaver (bs) | Klimm,Joe (p) | Winter,Herbert (b) | Paris,Teddy (dr)
Rolf Kühn All Stars
September Song
Frankfurt/M, rec. 5.6.1954
Kühn,Rolf (cl) | Kuhn,Paul (p) | Rediske,Johannes (g) | Last,Hans (b) | Paris,Teddy (dr)
Paul Kuhn Quartet
Paul's Festival Blues
Kuhn,Paul (p) | Hühns,Gerd (g) | Last,Hans (b) | Podehl,Hans (dr)
Johannes Rediske Quintet
Lullaby Of Birdland
Frankfurt/M, rec. 6.6.1954
Rediske,Johannes (g) | Noack,Lothar (cl,ts) | Spychalski,Alex (p) | Behrendt,Manfred (b) | Glaser,Joe (dr)
Heinz Schönberger Quintet
Klagita
Schönberger,Heinz (cl) | Becht,Erich (p) | Hühns,Gerd (g) | De Gruyter,George (b) | Podehl,Hans (dr)
Kurt Edelhagen All Stars Und Solisten
Festival Jump
Edelhagen,Kurt (ld) | Bohländer,Carlo (tp) | Wilfert,Hanne (tp) | Schneebiegl,Rolf (tp) | Achhammer,Siegfried (tp) | Mitschele,Klaus (tp) | Hermannsdörfer,Heinz (tb) | Bredl,Otto (tb) | Hauck,Helmut (tb) | Betz,Werner (tb) | Schönberger,Heinz (cl) | Mangelsdorff,Emil (as) | Von Klenck,Franz (as) | Reinhardt,Helmut (as) | Freund,Joki (ts) | Martin,Paul (ts) | Strasser,Hugo (bs) | Aderhold,Bubi (ts) | Feigl,Johnny (cl,bs) | Kuhn,Paul (p) | Hühns,Gerd (g) | Drexler,Werner (p) | Schultze,Werner (b) | Schmidt,Bobby (dr) | Valente,Caterina (voc)
Spree Cuty Stompers
Get Out Of Here | Just A Blues | That Da-Da Strain
Frankfurt/M, rec. 28.5.1955
Spree City Stompers | Geissler,Werner (tp) | Schneider,Hans Wolf 'Hawe' (tb) | Klein,Poldi (cl) | Schmidt,Eckart (p) | Laade,Wolfgang (b) | Keck,Thomas 'Leo' (dr)
Two Beat Stompers
Mississippi Mud | Got No Blues | Panama | Black Bottom Blues | I'm Confessin'(That I Love You) | The Music Goes 'Round And 'Round
Frankfurt/M, rec. 29.5.1955
Two Beat Stompers | Rehm,Werner (tp) | Simon,Dick (tb) | Dies,Werner (cl) | Theobald,Robert (p) | Schüttrumpf,Gerd (bj) | Lippmann,Horst (dr)
Delle Haensch Jump Combo
Manuscript Blues | Blue Moon | There's No One But You | Hey Good Lookin' | Flamingo
Frankfurt/M, rec. 28.5.1955
Haensch,Delle (as,bs) | Strasser,Hugo (cl,as) | Ogerman,Claus (p) | Schell,Harry (b) | Sanner,Karl (dr)
Kurt Edelhagen All Stars
Theme | There's No You | Big John's Special | You Go To My Head | Jazz 55 | Nancy And The Colonel | Light Stuff | Lover Man(Oh,Where Can You Be?) | Don't Blame Me | T-Time | Purple Hyazinth
Edelhagen,Kurt (ld) | Wilfert,Hanne (tp) | Schneebiegl,Rolf (tp) | Achhammer,Siegfried (tp) | Mitschele,Klaus (tp) | Hermannsdörfer,Heinz (tb) | Bredl,Otto (tb) | Hauck,Helmut (tb) | Betz,Werner (tb) | Von Klenck,Franz (cl,as) | Reinhardt,Helmut (as,bs) | Martin,Paul (ts) | Aderhold,Bubi (ts) | Feigl,Johnny (cl,bs) | Drexler,Werner (p) | Schultze,Werner (b) | Deutsch,Silo (dr)
My Funny Valentine | I Ain't Gonna Tell You
Edelhagen,Kurt (ld) | Wilfert,Hanne (tp) | Schneebiegl,Rolf (tp) | Achhammer,Siegfried (tp) | Mitschele,Klaus (tp) | Hermannsdörfer,Heinz (tb) | Bredl,Otto (tb) | Hauck,Helmut (tb) | Betz,Werner (tb) | Von Klenck,Franz (cl,as) | Reinhardt,Helmut (as,bs) | Martin,Paul (ts) | Aderhold,Bubi (ts) | Feigl,Johnny (cl,bs) | Drexler,Werner (p) | Schultze,Werner (b) | Deutsch,Silo (dr) | Valente,Caterina (voc)
Silvio Francesco Quartet
All The Things You Are
Frankfurt/M, rec. 28.-30.5.1955
Francesco,Silvio (cl) | Drexler,Werner (p) | Schultze,Werner (b) | Deutsch,Silo (dr)
Caterina Valente With The Silvio Francesco Quartet
Long Long Journey | Ain't Misbehavin'
Valente,Caterina (voc) | Francesco,Silvio (cl) | Drexler,Werner (p) | Schultze,Werner (b) | Deutsch,Silo (dr)
Glen Buschmann Quintet
Lagwood Walk | All Of Me | Farewell Blues
Frankfurt/M, rec. 29.5.1955
Buschmann,Rainer Glen (cl) | Mens,Klaus (p) | Buschmann,Pit (g) | Hohagen,Hans (b) | Koszorski,Siegfried (dr)
Wolfgang Sauer With The Glen Buschmann Quintet
St.Louis Blues | Blue Prelude | For You My Love
Sauer,Wolfgang (voc) | Buschmann,Rainer Glen (cl) | Mens,Klaus (p) | Buschmann,Pit (g) | Hohagen,Hans (b) | Koszorski,Siegfried (dr)
Heinz Schönberger Quintet
Just One Of Those Things | Shine | Embraceable You
Frankfurt/M, rec. 28.5.1955
Schönberger,Heinz (cl) | Becht,Erich (p) | Hühns,Gerd (g) | De Gruyter,George (b) | Podehl,Hans (dr)
Rolf Kühn And His Quintet
All The Things You Are | Too Marvelous For Words | Frankfurt Blues(Now's The Time)
Frankfurt/M, rec. 29.5.1955
Kühn,Rolf (cl) | Becker,Kurt (vib) | Hühns,Gerd (g) | Kuhn,Paul (p) | De Gruyter,George (b) | Sanner,Karl (dr)
Jutta Hipp Quintet
Hipp-Noses | The Song Is You | Indian Summer | A Cool Talk | These Foolish Things Remind Me On You | Gone With The Wind
Frankfurt/M, rec. 28.5.1955
Hipp,Jutta (p) | Freund,Joki (tb) | Zoller,Attila (g) | Pejakovic,Branko (b) | Sanner,Karl (dr)
Hans Koller New Jazz Stars
Jutta | Iris | When Your Lover Has Gone | Porsche
Frankfurt/M, rec. 30.5.1955
Koller,Hans (ts) | Sanner,Willie (bs) | Kovac,Roland (p) | Fischer,Johnny (b) | Sehring,Rudi (dr)
Helmut Brandt Combo
Just Squeeze Me(But Don't Tease Me) | Sum | The Breeze And I | I Can't Believe That You're In Love With Me
Brand,Helmut (bs) | Jackel,Conny (tp) | Ebert,Ludwig (p) | Gernhuber,Klaus (b) | Taubert,Hans-Dieter (dr)
Erhard Wenig Quartet
Out Of Nowhere | Tenor Jump | September Riff
Frankfurt/M, rec. 28./30.5.1955
Wenig,Erhard (ts) | Becht,Erich (p) | De Gruyter,George (b) | Sanner,Karl (dr)
Freddy Christman Quartet
Cynthia's In Love | As Long As There's Music | First Love | Passe
Frankfurt/M, rec. 30.5.1955
Christmann,Freddy (tp) | Auer,Pepsi (p) | Meyer,Alfred (b) | Cuntz,Uwe (dr)
Wolfgang Lauth Quartet
Thema In B | Tomorrow | Cool March | Cave Souvenir
Lauth,Wolfgang (p) | Pöhlert,Werner (g) | Kresse,Hans (b) | Hackbarth,Joe (dr)
Erwin Lehn Und Sein Südfunk-Tanzorchester
Jumpin' With Symphony Sid | Blues Intermezzo | Gerry Walks | Cool Street | Autumn Nocturne | Conference Mit Mosch | What Is This Thing Called Love | Blues For Tenorsaxophon | Lester Leaps In | E.V.G. | Flying Home
Frankfurt/M, rec. 29.5.1955
Lehn,Erwin (arr,ld) | Fischer,Horst (tp) | Ernszt,Georg (tp) | Bummerl,Franz (tp) | Schmitz-Schulz,Eberhard (tp) | Mosch,Ernst (tb) | Krause,Kurt (tb) | Lakatos,Ferenc (tb) | Becher,Rudi (tb) | Baumgart,Werner (as) | Tischendorf,Heinz (ss) | Weinkopf,Gerald 'Gerry' (ts) | Dautel,Fritz (ts) | Machwitz,Ernst (b-cl,as,bs) | Wegner,Gerhard (p) | Witte,Peter (b) | Mutschler,Hermann (dr)
Harald Banter Ensemble
Indikativ | Moon Over Miami | Autumn In New York | Tabu Jump | Polyphona | Nature Boy | Happy Days Are Here Again
Frankfurt/M, rec. 30.5.1955
Banter,Harald (ld) | Keuser,Josef 'Jupp' (tp) | Porz,Franz (tb) | Wiemeyer,Karl-Heinz (fr-h) | Schmitz,Bobby (cl,as) | Laufer,Heinrich (ts) | Aussem,Peter (bassoon) | Becker,Kurt (fl,vib) | Höttger,Heinz (p) | Klein,Ferdy (b) | Brock,Werner (dr) | Berlipp,Friedel (bongos)
Johnnes Rediske Quintet
Cloe | Out Of Nowhere | Boptical Illusion | Sweet Georgia Brown
Rediske,Johannes (g) | Noack,Lothar (cl,ts) | Spychalski,Alex (p) | Behrendt,Manfred (b) | Glaser,Joe (dr)
Paul Kuhn Quintet
Thou Swell | Dancing In The Dark | Delauney's Dilemma | Jumpin' At The Rosengarten
Frankfurt/M, rec. 29.5.1955
Kuhn,Paul (p) | Becker,Kurt (fl,vib) | Hühns,Gerd (g) | De Gruyter,George (b) | Podehl,Hans (dr)
Helmut Weglinski Quintet
Flip | I Don't Stand A Ghost Of A Chance With You | Crazy Rhythm
Frankfurt/M, rec. 30.5.1955
Weglinski,Helmut (v) | Mangelsdorff,Emil (cl,as) | Sachs,Klaus (p) | Fischer,Johnny (b) | Rösel,Heinz (dr)
New Jazz Group Hannover
To Dance Ot Not To Dance | I Only Have Eyes For You | Lover Man(Oh,Where Can You Be?) | Continuation
Frankfurt/M, rec. 28./30.5.1955
New Jazz Group Hannover | Rabe,Bernd (cl,as) | Mann,Gerd (vib,p) | Kitschenberg,Heinz (g) | Pommerenke,Eberhard (b,ld) | Perschke,Helmut (dr)

BCD 15479 DH | 4 CD | Buddy And Ella Johnson 1953-1964
Buddy Johnson And His Orchestra
That's How I Feel About You | Ecstasy | Hittin' On Me | Jit Jit
NYC, rec. 17.2.1953
Johnson,Buddy (p) | Henson,Purvis (ts) | Johnson,Ella (voc) | Lewis,Nolan (voc) | details unknown
I'm Just Your Fool | A-12 | I Never Had It So Good | Ain't Cha Got Me(Where You Want Me)
NYC, rec. ca.September 1953
Johnson,Buddy (p) | Henson,Purvis (ts) | Johnson,Ella (voc) | Lewis,Nolan (voc) | details unknown
Bring It Up, Van Dyke | My Old Man | One More Time | Let's Start All Over Again(Down On Bended Knee) | Shut Your Big Mouth(Girl) | Mush Mouth | Mush Mouth(alt.take)
Johnson,Buddy (p) | Harper,Rick (tp,voc) | Van Dyke,David (ts) | Henson,Purvis (ts) | Johnson,Ella (voc) | Lewis,Nolan (voc) | details unknown
Any Day Now | A Pretty Girl(A Cadillac And Some Money) | Ain't But One | There's No One Like You
NYC, rec. 19.3.1954
Johnson,Buddy (p) | Henson,Purvis (ts) | Johnson,Ella (voc) | Lewis,Nolan (voc) | Harper,Rick (voc) | details unknown
Thinking It Over | If You'd Say Yes | It Used To Hurt Me | We'll Do It
NYC, rec. 9.9.1954
Johnson,Buddy (p) | Henson,Purvis (ts) | Taylor,Sam 'The Man' (ts) | Johnson,Ella (voc) | details unknown
Bittersweet | Crazy 'Bout A Saxophone | Send Out For A Bucket Of Beer | Gotta Go Upside Your Head - (Gotta Go) Upside Your Head
NYC, rec. 15.12.1954
Johnson,Buddy (voc) | Henson,Purvis (ts) | Burdine,Johnny (ts) | Johnson,Ella (voc) | Lewis,Nolan (voc) | details unknown
Someday | Someday(alt.take) | Alright,Okay,You Win | If You Would Only Say You're Sorry | It's 'Bout To Break My Heart In Two
NYC, rec. 11.2.1955
Johnson,Buddy (p) | Williams,Curtney (tp) | Henson,Purvis (ts) | Taylor,Sam 'The Man' (ts) | Crump,William 'Bill' (bs) | Baker,Mickey (g) | Spann,Leon (b) | Simms,Emmanuel (dr) | Johnson,Ella (voc)
It's Obdacious | Save You Love For Me | So Good | Gone Walkin'
NYC, rec. 15.8.1955
Johnson,Buddy (voc) | Henson,Purvis (ts) | Johnson,Ella (voc) | Ryland,Floyd (voc) | Askey,Gil (voc) | details unknown
Doot Doot Dow | I Don't Want Nobody(To Have My Love But You) | You Got It Made | Bring It On Home
NYC, rec. 21.12.1955
Johnson,Buddy (p) | Askey,Gil (tp) | Orr,Raymond (tp) | Wood,Andrew (tp) | Nelson,Willis (tp) | Burke,Edward (tb) | Hampton,Slide (tb) | Rasheed[Howard Bowe],Haleem (tb) | Minerve,Geezil (as) | Small,Teddy (as) | Henson,Purvis (ts) | Lucas,Maxwell (bs) | Westbrook,Chauncey 'Lord' (g) | Spann,Leon (b) | Simms,Emmanuel (dr) | Johnson,Ella (voc) | Ryland,Floyd (voc) | Bee Jays,The (voc-group) | Henson,Purvis (voc) | Pulliam,Steve (voc) | Watson,Julius (voc)
Buddy's Boogie | Why Don't Cha Stop It | I'll Dearly Love You | Kool Kitty
NYC, rec. 28.3.1956
Johnson,Buddy (p) | Henson,Purvis (ts) | Johnson,Ella (voc) | Ryland,Floyd (voc) | details unknown
What A Day | Goodbye Baby Here I Go | That's What You Gotta Do | I Still Love You
NYC, rec. 5.6.1956
Johnson,Buddy (ld) | Robinson,Frank (tp) | Cooper,Frank 'Buster' (tb) | Simon,Maurice (ts) | Austin,Sil (ts) | Henry,Haywood (bs) | Stubbs,George (p) | Richardson,Wally (g) | Collier,Clarence (b) | Francis,David 'Panama' (dr) | Johnson,Ella (voc)
Oh Baby Don't You Know | You'd Better Believe Me | You're Everything My Heart Desires | Rock On | Rock On(alt.take)
NYC, rec. 3.1.1957
Johnson,Buddy (voc) | Henson,Purvis (ts) | Johnson,Ella (voc) | Ryland,Floyd (voc) | Bee Jays,The (voc-group) | Henson,Purvis (voc) | Pulliam,Steve (voc) | Watson,Julius (voc) | details unknown
Rockin' Time | They Don't Want Me To Rock No More | I've Surrendered | Slide's Mambo
NYC, rec. 24.6.1957
Johnson,Buddy (p) | Henson,Purvis (ts) | Johnson,Ella (voc) | Ryland,Floyd (voc) | details unknown
You're The One For Me | Don't Shout At Me, Daddy | No! I Ain't Gonna Let You Go | Don't Turn Your Back On Me
NYC, rec. 1.7.1957
Johnson,Buddy (ld) | Henson,Purvis (ts) | Johnson,Ella (voc) | details unknown
They All Say I'm The Biggest Fool | I Cry | Baby Don't You Cry | Goodbye Baby Here I Go | I Don't Care Who Knows | You'll Get Them Blues
NYC, rec. 4.11.1957
Johnson,Buddy (p) | Henson,Purvis (ts) | Johnson,Ella (voc) | Ryland,Floyd (voc) | details unknown
Stop Pretending | Please Mr. Johnson | Since I Fell For You | I Wonder Where Our Love Has Gone | Lil' Dog | Minglin'
NYC, rec. 6.11.1957
Johnson,Buddy (p,voc) | Henson,Purvis (ts) | Van Dyke,David (ts) | Johnson,Ella (voc) | Ryland,Floyd (voc) | details unknown
Far Cry | Lover Bird | No More | Untitled Instrumental
NYC, rec. 24.12.1957
Johnson,Buddy (p) | Henson,Purvis (ts) | Johnson,Ella (voc) | Ryland,Floyd (voc) | details unknown
Don't Fail Me Baby | Small Taste | Baby Hear My Humble Plea | Tuke Number One
NYC, rec. 19.12.1958
Johnson,Buddy (p) | Henson,Purvis (ts) | Johnson,Ella (voc) | Thomas,Lee (voc) | details unknown
Going To New York | Have Mercy On A Fool | Untitled Instrumental
NYC, rec. 28.4.1959
Johnson,Buddy (p) | Henson,Purvis (ts) | Johnson,Ella (voc) | details unknown
Real Fine Frame | Walk'Em | I'm Tired Of Crying Over You | You Better Change Your Way | Down Yonder
NYC, rec. 20.5.1959
Johnson,Buddy (p,voc) | Henson,Purvis (ts) | Johnson,Ella (voc) | Thomas,Lee (voc) | details unknown
Go Ahead And Rock | Get Down On The Road | Sliding Horns | Come Here Lovely Dovey
NYC, rec. 15.6.1959
Johnson,Buddy (p) | Henson,Purvis (ts) | Johnson,Ella (voc) | Thomas,Lee prob. (voc) | details unknown
Keeping My Love For You | Buddy's Rock | A Woman, A Lover, A Friend | I'll Be Glad
NYC, rec. 13.8.1959
Johnson,Buddy (p) | Henson,Purvis (ts) | Johnson,Ella (voc) | Thomas,Lee prob. (voc) | details unknown
Ha! Ha! Baby The Last Laugh's On You - (Ha! Ha! Baby) The Last Laugh's On You | Ever So Greatful | Good-Time Man
NYC, rec. 8.2.1961
Johnson,Buddy (p) | Henson,Purvis (ts) | Johnson,Ella (voc) | details unknown

Don't Be Messin' | Like You Do | I Gotta Talk To Somebody | Keep On Loving You
NYC, rec. 13.10.1964
Johnson,Buddy (ld) | Johnson,Ella (voc) | details unknown

BCD 15524 AH | CD | Joe Hill Louis: The Be-Bop Boy
Joe Hill Louis
She Treats Me Mean And Evil
Memphis,Tenn., rec. 31.3.1952
Louis,Joe Hill (g,voc) | Hall,Nolan (dr)
Dorothy Mae
Memphis,Tenn., rec. 18.7.1952
Louis,Joe Hill (g,voc) | Horton,Big Walter 'Shakey' (harm) | Kelly,Jack (p) | Nix,Willie (dr)
Walter Horton Band
Little Walter's Boogie(take 1) | Little Walter's Boogie(take 2) | West Winds Are Blowing(take 1)
Memphis,Tenn., rec. 15.9.1952
Horton,Big Walter 'Shakey' (harm,voc) | Louis,Joe Hill (g) | Kelly,Jack (p) | Nix,Willie (dr)
Joe Hill Louis
She Comes To See Me | Make My Love Stay Warm
Memphis,Tenn., rec. 17.11.1952
Louis,Joe Hill (g,harm,voc) | Williams,Albert (p) | Nix,Willie (dr)
Keep Your Arms Around Me | Sweetest Gal In Town | Got A New Woman | I'm A Poor Boy
Memphis,Tenn., rec. 8.12.1952
Louis,Joe Hill (g,harm,dr,voc) | Williams,Albert (p)
Walter Horton Band
In The Mood | We All Got To Go
Horton,Big Walter 'Shakey' (harm,voc) | Louis,Joe Hill (g,dr) | Williams,Albert (p)
Joe Hill Louis Band
We All Gotta Go Sometime(take 2) | We All Gotta Go Sometime(take 3)
Memphis,Tenn., rec. prob.29.12.1952 or early January 1953
Louis,Joe Hill (g,voc) | Williams,Albert prob. (p) | unkn. (dr)
Tiger Man
Memphis,Tenn., rec. Spring 1953
Louis,Joe Hill (g,voc) | unkn. (p,dr)
Hydrama Woman | Tiger Man | Shine Boy
Memphis,Tenn., rec. ca.May 1953
Louis,Joe Hill (g,voc) | Horton,Big Walter 'Shakey' (harm) | Williams,Albert (p) | unkn. (dr,perc,speech)
Walter Horton Band
Walter's Instrumental
Memphis,Tenn., rec. 28.5.1953
Horton,Big Walter 'Shakey' (harm) | Williams,Albert (p) | Hare,Pat (g) | Louis,Joe Hill (dr)
Mose Vinson Band
Worry You Off My Mind
Memphis,Tenn., rec. prob. Summer 1953
Vinson,Mose (p,voc) | Horton,Big Walter 'Shakey' (harm) | Wilkins,Joe Willie (g) | Coleman,Thomas 'Beale Street' (dr)
Reap What You Sow
Vinson,Mose (p,voc) | Wilkins,Joe Willie (g) | Coleman,Thomas 'Beale Street' (dr)
Mistreatin' Boogie
Vinson,Mose (p,voc) | Coleman,Thomas 'Beale Street' (dr)
44 Blues | My Love Has Gone
Memphis,Tenn., rec. 9.9.1953
Vinson,Mose (p,voc) | Louis,Joe Hill (g) | Banks,Kenneth (b) | Franklin,Israel (dr)
My Love Has Gone
Vinson,Mose (p,voc) | Louis,Joe Hill (hi-hat) | Banks,Kenneth (b) | Franklin,Israel (hand-clappings)
-> Joe Willie Wilkins is poss. Joe Hill Louis

BCD 15557 IH | 9 CD | Louis Jordan-Let The Good Times Roll: The Complete Decca Recordings 1938-1954
Roger Sturgis With Lovie Jordan's Elks Rendez-Vous Band
Toodle-Loo On Down | So Good | Away From You
NYC, rec. 20.12.1938
Sturgis,Roger (voc) | Jordan,Louis (cl,as,bs) | Williams,Courtney (tp) | Johnson,Lem (cl,ts) | Johnson,Clarence (p) | Drayton,Charlie (b) | Martin,Walter (dr)
Louis Jordan's Elks Rendez-Vous Band
Honey In The Bee Ball | Barnacle Bill The Sailor
Jordan,Louis (cl,as,bs,voc) | Williams,Courtney (tp) | Johnson,Lem (cl,ts) | Johnson,Clarence (p) | Drayton,Charlie (b) | Martin,Walter (dr)
Louis Jordan And His Tympany Five
Flat Face | Keep A-Knockin'(But You Can't Come In) | Sam Jones Done Snagged His Britches On | Swinging In A Cocoanut Tree | Doug The Jitterbug | At The Swing Cat's Ball
NYC, rec. 29.3.1938
Jordan,Louis (cl,as,bs,voc) | Williams,Courtney (tp) | Johnson,Lem (cl,ts) | Johnson,Clarence (p) | Drayton,Charlie (b) | Martin,Walter (dr)
Jake What A Snake | Honeysuckle Rose | 'Fore Day Blues | But I'll Be Back | You Ain't Nowhere | You're My Meat
NYC, rec. 14.10.1939
Jordan,Louis (cl,as,bs,voc) | Williams,Courtney (tp) | Simon,Stafford (fl,cl,ts) | Johnson,Clarence (p) | Drayton,Charlie (b) | Martin,Walter (dr)
June Tenth Jamboree | You Run Your Mouth,I'll Run My Business | Alabamy Bound | Hard Lovin' Blues
NYC, rec. 25.1.1940
Jordan,Louis (cl,as,bs) | Williams,Courtney (tp) | Simon,Stafford (ts) | Johnson,Clarence (p) | Drayton,Charlie (b) | Martin,Walter (dr) | Taylor,Yack (voc)
You Got To Go When The Wagon Comes | Lovie Joe | Somebody Done Hoodooed The Hoodoo Man | Bounce The Ball(Do Da Dittle Um Day) | Penthouse In The Basement | After School Swing Session(Swinging With Symphony Sid)
NYC, rec. 13.3.1940
Jordan,Louis (cl,as,bs,voc) | Williams,Courtney (tp) | Hollon,Kenneth (cl,ts) | Johnson,Clarence (p,taking) | Drayton,Charlie (b) | Martin,Walter (dr) | Robinson,Mabel (voc) | Winchester,Daisy (voc)
Oh Boy I'm In The Groove | Never Let Your Left Hand Know What Your Right Hand's Doin' | Don't Come Cryin' On My Shoulder | Waiting For The Robert E.Lee
NYC, rec. 29.4.1940
Jordan,Louis (cl,as,bs) | Williams,Courtney (tp) | Hollon,Kenneth (cl,ts) | Thomas,Arnold (p) | Drayton,Charlie (b) | Martin,Walter (dr)
A Chicken Ain't Nothin' But A Bird | Pompton Turnpike | Do You Call That A Buddy(Dirty Cat) | I Know You(I Know What You Wanna Do)
NYC, rec. 30.9.1940
Jordan,Louis (cl,as,bs) | Williams,Courtney (tp) | Hollon,Kenneth (cl,ts) | Thomas,Arnold (p) | Drayton,Charlie (b) | Martin,Walter (dr)
Pinetop's Boogie Woogie | The Two Little Squirrels(Nuts To You) | T-Bone Blues | Pan Pan
NYC, rec. 24.1.1941
Jordan,Louis (cl,as,bs,voc) | Webster,Freddie or Kenneth Roane (tp) | Simon,Stafford (cl,ts) | Thomas,Arnold (p) | Drayton,Charlie or Henry Turner (b) | Martin,Walter (dr)
Saint Vitus Dance | Saxa-Woogie | Brotherly Love | De Laff's On You | Boogie Woogie Came To Town | John, Stop Teasing Me
NYC, rec. 2.4.1941
Jordan,Louis (as,ts,voc) | Webster,Freddie (tp) | Simon,Stafford (cl,ts) | Thomas,Arnold (p) | Turner,Henry (b) | Martin,Walter (dr)
How 'Bout That | Teacher(How I Love My Teacher) | Mama Mama Blues(Rusty Dusty Blues) | Knock Me A Kiss
Chicago,Ill, rec. 15.11.1941
Jordan,Louis (as,ts,voc) | Roane,Eddie (tp) | Thomas,Arnold (p) | Bartley,Dallas (b) | Martin,Walter (dr)
The Green Grass Grows All Around | Mister Lovingood | Small Town Boy | I'm Gonna Move To The Outskirts Of Town
Chicago,Ill, rec. 22.11.1941
Jordan,Louis (as,ts,voc) | Roane,Eddie (tp) | Thomas,Arnold (p) | Bartley,Dallas (b) | Martin,Walter (dr)
What's The Use Of Getting Sober | The Chicks I Pick Are Slender Tender And Tall | I'm Gonna Leave You On The Outskirts Of Town | That'll Just 'Bout Knock Me Out | Dirty Snake | Somebody Done Changed The Lock On My Door | Five Guys Named Moe | It's A Low Down Dirty Shame | De Laff's On You
NYC, rec. 21.7.1942
Jordan,Louis (as,ts,voc) | Roane,Eddie (tp) | Thomas,Arnold (p) | Bartley,Dallas (b) | Martin,Walter (dr)
Ration Blues | Is You Is Or Is You Ain't My Baby | Deacon Jones | The Things I Want I Can't Get At Home
Los Angeles,CA, rec. 4.10.1943
Jordan,Louis (as,ts,voc) | Roane,Eddie (tp) | Thomas,Arnold (p) | Simpkins,Jesse (b) | Wilson,Shadow (dr)
How High Am I | I Like 'Em Fat Like That | The Truth Of The Matter | Hey! Now Let's Jive
NYC, rec. 1.3.1944
Jordan,Louis (as,voc) | Roane,Eddie (tp) | Thomas,Arnold (p) | Morgan,Albert 'Al' (b) | Wilson,Shadow (dr)
Mop Mop | G.I.Jive | You Can't Get That No More
NYC, rec. 15.3.1944
Jordan,Louis (as,voc) | Roane,Eddie (tp) | Thomas,Arnold (p) | Morgan,Albert 'Al' (b) | Jones,Wilmore 'Slick' (dr)
Louis' Oldsmobile Song | Your Socks Don't Match
Los Angeles,CA, rec. ca.July 1944
Jordan,Louis (as,voc) | Roane,Eddie (tp) | Thomas,Arnold (p) | Morgan,Albert 'Al' (b) | Jones,Wilmore 'Slick' (dr)
My Baby Said Yes(Yip, Yip De Hootie) | My Baby Said Yes(Yip, Yip De Hootie-alt.take) | Your Socks Don't Match
Los Angeles,CA, rec. 26.7.1944
Jordan,Louis (as,voc) | Roane,Eddie (tp) | Thomas,Arnold (p) | Morgan,Albert 'Al' (b) | Jones,Wilmore 'Slick' (dr) | Crosby,Bing (voc)
Buzz Me | They Raided The House | Caldonia Boogie | Somebody Done Changed The Lock On My Door
NYC, rec. 19.1.1945
Jordan,Louis (as,voc) | Sulieman[Leonard Graham],Idrees (tp) | Simon,Fred (ts) | Austin,William (p) | Morgan,Albert 'Al' (b) | Mitchell,Alex (dr)
How Long Must I Wait For You | Don't Worry 'Bout The Mule | Salt Pork West Virginia
NYC, rec. 16.7.1945
Jordan,Louis (as,voc) | Izenhall,Aaron (tp) | Jackson,Josh (ts) | Davis,Wild Bill (p) | Hogan,Carl (el-g) | Simpkins,Jesse (b) | Byrd,Eddie (dr)
No Baby Nobody But You | Paper Boy | Don't Worry 'Bout The Mule
NYC, rec. 18.7.1945
Jordan,Louis (as,voc) | Izenhall,Aaron (tp) | Jackson,Josh (ts) | Davis,Wild Bill (p) | Hogan,Carl (el-g) | Simpkins,Jesse (b) | Byrd,Eddie (dr)
Stone Cold Dead In The Market | Petootie Pie
NYC, rec. 8.10.1945
Jordan,Louis (as,voc) | Izenhall,Aaron (tp) | Jackson,Josh (ts) | Davis,Wild Bill (p) | Hogan,Carl (el-g) | Simpkins,Jesse (b) | Byrd,Eddie (dr) | Dial,Harry (maracas) | Lourie,Vic (claves) | Fitzgerald,Ella (voc)
Petootie Pie | Reconversion Blues
NYC, rec. 15.10.1945
Jordan,Louis (as,voc) | Izenhall,Aaron (tp) | Jackson,Josh (ts) | Davis,Wild Bill (p) | Hogan,Carl (el-g) | Simpkins,Jesse (b) | Byrd,Eddie (dr) | Fitzgerald,Ella (voc)
It's So Easy | Beware | Don't Let The Sun Catch You Cryin' | Choo Choo Ch' Boogie | Ain't That Just Like A Woman | That Chicks Too Young To Fry
NYC, rec. 23.1.1946
Jordan,Louis (as,voc) | Izenhall,Aaron (tp) | Jackson,Josh (ts) | Davis,Wild Bill (p) | Hogan,Carl (el-g) | Simpkins,Jesse (b) | Byrd,Eddie (dr)
No Sale | If It's Love You Want Baby, That's Me | Ain't Nobody Here But Us Chickens | Let The Good Times Roll
NYC, rec. 26.6.1946
Jordan,Louis (as,voc) | Izenhall,Aaron (tp) | Jackson,Josh (ts) | Davis,Wild Bill (p) | Hogan,Carl (el-g) | Simpkins,Jesse (b) | Byrd,Eddie (dr)
All For The Love Of Lil | Texas And Pacific | Jack You're Dead | Reet Petite And Gone | Sure, Had A Wonderful Time | I Know What You're Puttin' Down
NYC, rec. 10.10.1946
Jordan,Louis (as,voc) | Izenhall,Aaron (tp) | Wright,James (ts) | Davis,Wild Bill (p) | Hogan,Carl (el-g) | Simpkins,Jesse (b) | Morris[Chris Columbus],Joe (dr)
Open The Door Richard | Friendship
Los Angeles,CA, rec. 11.1.1947
Jordan,Louis (as,voc) | prob.personal: | Izenhall,Aaron (tp) | Wright,James (ts) | Davis,Wild Bill (p) | Hogan,Carl (el-g) | Simpkins,Jesse (b) | Morris[Chris Columbus],Joe (dr)
Open The Door Richard
Los Angeles,CA, rec. 23.1.1947
Jordan,Louis (as,voc) | prob.personal: | Izenhall,Aaron (tp) | Wright,James (ts) | Davis,Wild Bill (p) | Hogan,Carl (el-g) | Simpkins,Jesse (b) | Morris[Chris Columbus],Joe (dr)
Boogie Woogie Plate | Barnyard Boogie | Every Man To His Own Profession
NYC, rec. 23.4.1947
Jordan,Louis (as,voc) | Izenhall,Aaron (tp) | Johnson,Eddie (ts) | Davis,Wild Bill (p) | Hogan,Carl (el-g) | Bartley,Dallas (b) | Morris[Chris Columbus],Joe (dr)
Early In The Morning | Run Joe
Jordan,Louis (as,voc) | Izenhall,Aaron (tp) | Johnson,Eddie (ts) | Davis,Wild Bill (p) | Hogan,Carl (el-g) | Bartley,Dallas (b) | Morris[Chris Columbus],Joe (dr) | Calypso Boys,The (claves,maracas)
Look Out | Beans And Cornbread
NYC, rec. 4.6.1947
Jordan,Louis (as,voc) | Izenhall,Aaron (tp) | Johnson,Eddie (ts) | Davis,Wild Bill (p) | Hogan,Carl (el-g) | Bartley,Dallas (b) | Morris[Chris Columbus],Joe (dr)
Have You Got The Gumption | We Can't Agree | Chicky-Mo, Craney-Crow | Roamin' Blues
Los Angeles,CA, rec. 24.11.1947
Jordan,Louis (as,voc) | Izenhall,Aaron (tp) | Johnson,Eddie (ts) | Doggett,Bill (p) | Hogan,Carl (el-g) | Bartley,Dallas (b) | Morris[Chris Columbus],Joe (dr)
Inflation Blues | You're Much Too Fat(And That's That) | Chug Chug Boogie | There'll Be No Days Like That | Pattin' And Pokin'
Los Angeles,CA, rec. 1.12.1947
Jordan,Louis (as,voc) | Izenhall,Aaron (tp) | Johnson,Eddie (ts) | Doggett,Bill (p) | Hogan,Carl (el-g) | Bartley,Dallas (b) | Morris[Chris Columbus],Joe (dr)
You're On The Right Track, Baby | Don't Burn The Candle At Both Ends | Why D'You Do It | Swingin' With Daddy-O
Los Angeles,CA, rec. 8.12.1947
Jordan,Louis (as,voc) | Izenhall,Aaron (tp) | Johnson,Eddie (ts) | Davis,Wild Bill (p) | Hogan,Carl (el-g) | Bartley,Dallas (b) | Morris[Chris Columbus],Joe (dr) | Davis,Martha (voc)
Safe,Sane And Single | I Know What I've Got, Don't Know What I'm Getting | You Broke Your Promise
Los Angeles,CA, rec. 7.2.1949
Jordan,Louis (as,voc) | Izenhall,Aaron (tp) | Johnson,Eddie (ts) | Davis,Wild Bill (p) | Hogan,Carl (el-g) | Bartley,Dallas (b) | Morris[Chris Columbus],Joe (dr) | Davis,Martha (voc)
Push-Ka-Pee She Pie(The Saga Of Saga Boy) | Cole Slave | Beans And Cornbread
NYC, rec. 12.4.1949
Jordan,Louis (as,voc) | Izenhall,Aaron (tp) | Mitchell,Bob (tp) | Mitchell,Harold (tp) | Jackson,Josh (ts) | Doggett,Bill (p) | Jackson,James 'Ham' (el-g) | Hadnott,Billy (b) | Morris[Chris Columbus],Joe (dr) | unkn. (latin-perc,maracas)
Onion | Baby's Gonna Go, Bye Bye | Heed My Warning | Psycho-Loco
NYC, rec. 13.4.1949
Jordan,Louis (as,voc) | Izenhall,Aaron (tp) | Mitchell,Bob (tp) | Mitchell,Harold (tp) | Jackson,Josh (ts) | Doggett,Bill (p) | Jackson,James 'Ham' (el-g) | Hadnott,Billy (b) | Morris[Chris Columbus],Joe (dr)
Baby It's Cold Outside | Don't Cry Cry Baby | School Days
NYC, rec. 28.4.1949
Jordan,Louis (as,voc) | Izenhall,Aaron (tp) | Mitchell,Bob (tp) | Mitchell,Harold (tp) | Jackson,Josh (ts) | Doggett,Bill (p) | Jackson,James 'Ham' (el-g) | Hadnott,Billy (b) | Morris[Chris Columbus],Joe (dr) | Fitzgerald,Ella (voc)
Hungry Man | Love You 'Til You're Money's Gone Blues | Saturday Night Fish Fry(part 1) | Saturday Night Fish Fry(part 2)
NYC, rec. 9.8.1949
Jordan,Louis (as,voc) | Izenhall,Aaron (tp) | Mitchell,Bob (tp) | Mitchell,Harold (tp) | Jackson,Josh (ts) | Doggett,Bill (p) | Jackson,James 'Ham' (el-g) | Hadnott,Billy (b) | Morris[Chris Columbus],Joe (dr)
I Want A Roof Over My Head | Show Me How(You Milk The Cow) | Blue Light Boogie(part 1) | Blue Light Boogie(part 2)
Chicago,Ill, rec. 26.6.1950
Jordan,Louis (as,voc) | Izenhall,Aaron (tp) | Jackson,Josh (ts) | Doggett,Bill (p) | Jennings,Bill (g) | Bushnell,Bob (b) | Morris[Chris Columbus],Joe (dr)
'Tain't Nobody's Bizness But My Own
NYC, rec. 15.8.1950
Jordan,Louis (as,voc) | Izenhall,Aaron (tp) | Jackson,Josh (ts) | Doggett,Bill (p) | Jennings,Bill (g) | Bushnell,Bob (b) | Morris[Chris Columbus],Joe (dr)
I'll Never Be Free
Jordan,Louis (voc) | Fitzgerald,Ella (voc) | prob.personal: | Jones,Hank (p) | Collins,John (el-g) | Brown,Ray (b) | Smith,Charlie (congas)
You Dyed Your Hair Chartreuse - (You Dyed Your Hair) Chartreuse | It's A Great, Great Pleasure
NYC, rec. 18.8.1950
Jordan,Louis (as,voc) | Izenhall,Aaron (tp) | Jackson,Josh (ts) | Doggett,Bill (p) | Jennings,Bill (g) | Bushnell,Bob (b) | Morris[Chris Columbus],Joe (dr)
Tamburitza Boogie | Lemonade
Jordan,Louis (as,voc) | Izenhall,Aaron (tp) | Jackson,Josh (ts) | Doggett,Bill (p) | Jennings,Bill (g) | Bushnell,Bob (b) | Morris[Chris Columbus],Joe (dr) | unkn. (bells,latin-perc,maracas)
You Will Always Have A Friend
Jordan,Louis (as,voc) | Izenhall,Aaron (tp) | Jackson,Josh (ts) | Doggett,Bill (p) | Davis,Wild Bill (org) | Jennings,Bill (g) | Bushnell,Bob (b) | Morris[Chris Columbus],Joe (dr)
Louisville Lodge Meeting | Trouble Then Satisfaction | Crazy Baby
NYC, rec. 21.8.1950
Jordan,Louis (as,voc) | Izenhall,Aaron (tp) | Jackson,Josh (ts) | Doggett,Bill (p) | Jennings,Bill (g) | Bushnell,Bob (b) | Morris[Chris Columbus],Joe (dr)
Life Is So Peculiar | I'll Be Glad When You're Dead You Rascal You
NYC, rec. 23.8.1950
Jordan,Louis (as,voc) | Armstrong,Louis (tp,voc) | Izenhall,Aaron (tp) | Jackson,Josh (ts) | Doggett,Bill (p) | Jennings,Bill (g) | Bushnell,Bob (b) | Morris[Chris Columbus],Joe (dr)
Teardrops From My Eyes | If You've Got Some Place To Go
NYC, rec. 21.12.1950
Jordan,Louis (as,voc) | Izenhall,Aaron (tp) | Jackson,Josh (ts) | unkn. (bs) | Davis,Wild Bill (org) | Jennings,Bill (g) | Bushnell,Bob (b) | Morris[Chris Columbus],Joe (dr)
Weak-Minded Blues | Is My Pop In There? | I Can't Give You Anything But Love
NYC, rec. 1.3.1951
Jordan,Louis (as,voc) | Izenhall,Aaron (tp) | Jackson,Josh (ts) | unkn. (bs) | Davis,Wild Bill (org) | Jennings,Bill (g) | Bushnell,Bob (b) | Morris[Chris Columbus],Joe (dr)
If You So Smart, How Come You Ain't Rich | Trust In Me | Louisville Lodge Meeting | How Blue Can You Get | Happy Birthday Boogie
NYC, rec. 5.6.1951
Jordan,Louis (as,voc) | Izenhall,Aaron (tp) | Perry,Ermit V. (tp) | Mitchell,Bob (tp) | Comegys,Leon (tb) | Burgess,Bob 'Bobby' (tb) | Nelson,Oliver (as) | Jackson,Josh (ts) | Phillips,Reuben (ts) | Flax,Marty (bs) | Peterson,Jimmy (p) | Jennings,Bill (g) | Bushnell,Bob (b) | Morris[Chris Columbus],Joe (dr)
May Every Day Be Christmas | Please Don't Leave Me | Bone Dry | I Love That Kinda Carryin' On | Three Handed Woman | Fat Sam From Birmingham
NYC, rec. 13.6.1951
Jordan,Louis (as,voc) | prob.personal: | Izenhall,Aaron (tp) | Perry,Ermit V. (tp) | Mitchell,Bob (tp) | Comegys,Leon (tb) | Burgess,Bob 'Bobby' (tb) | Nelson,Oliver (as) | Jackson,Josh (ts) | Phillips,Reuben (ts) | Flax,Marty (bs) | Peterson,Jimmy (p) | Davis,Wild Bill (org,voc) | Jennings,Bill (g) | Bushnell,Bob (b) | Morris[Chris Columbus],Joe (dr)
Cook-A-Doodle-Doo | Garmoochie | There Must Be A Way
NYC, rec. 30.7.1951
Jordan,Louis (as,voc) | Izenhall,Aaron (tp) | Perry,Ermit V. (tp) | Mitchell,Bob (tp) | Comegys,Leon (tb) | Burgess,Bob 'Bobby' (tb) | Nelson,Oliver (as) | Jackson,Josh (ts) | Phillips,Reuben (ts) | Flax,Marty (bs) | Peterson,Jimmy (p) | Jennings,Bill (g) | Bushnell,Bob (b) | Morris[Chris Columbus],Joe (dr)
Come And Get It | Stop Makin' Music | Slow Down | Work, Baby, Work | Never Trust A Woman | All Of Me | There Goes My Heart | Lay Something On The Bar(Beside Your Below)
NYC, rec. 28.11.1951
Jordan,Louis (as,voc) | Izenhall,Aaron (tp) | Perry,Ermit V. (tp) | Mitchell,Bob (tp) | Johnson,Harold 'Money' (tp) | Cobbs,Alfred (tb) | Burgess,Bob 'Bobby' (tb) | Nelson,Oliver (as) | Jackson,Josh (ts) | Brown,Irving 'Skinny' (ts) | Moore,Numa 'Pee Wee' (bs) | Malachi,John (p) | Jennings,Bill (g) | Bushnell,Bob (b) | Morris[Chris Columbus],Joe (dr) | Ford,Valli (voc)
Gimme Gimme Blues | Junco Partner | Time Marches On | Azure-Te | Oil Well, Texas | There's Nothing Else That I Can Do
NYC, rec. 30.4.1952
Jordan,Louis (as,voc) | Mitchell,Bob (tp) | Peterson,Jimmy (p) | Payne,Bert (el-g) | Bushnell,Bob (b) | Rice,Charlie (dr)
Jordan For President | The Soon-A Baby
Washington,DC, rec. 8.5.1952
Jordan,Louis (as,voc) | Mitchell,Bob (tp) | Peterson,Jimmy (p) | Payne,Bert (el-g) | Bushnell,Bob (b) | Rice,Charlie (dr)
There's Nothing Else That I Can Do | The Soon-A Baby | You Didn't Want Me Baby | A Man's Best Friend Is A Bed
NYC, rec. 3.12.1953
Jordan,Louis (as,voc) | Mitchell,Bob (tp) | Peterson,Jimmy (p) | Payne,Bert (el-g) | Bushnell,Bob (b) | Rice,Charlie (dr)
Louis Jordan With The Nelson Riddle Orchestra
I Didn't Know What Time It Was | It's Better Wait For Love | Only Yesterday | Just Like A Butterfly
Los Angeles,CA, rec. 23.2.1952
Jordan,Louis (voc) | Orchestra | Riddle,Nelson (cond,arr) | details unknown
Hog Wash | House Party | Everything That's Made Of Wood | I Want You To Be My Baby | You Know It Too
NYC, rec. 28.5.1952
Jordan,Louis (as,voc) | Mitchell,Bob (tp) | Davis,Maxwell (ts) | Lane,Chester (p) | Payne,Bert (el-g) | Jay,Thurber 'Sam Guy' (el-b) | Kirkwood,Johnny (dr)
Locked Up | I Gotta Move | Nobody Knows You When You're Down And Out | If It's True | Wake Up Jacob | Lollypop | Perdido
NYC, rec. 4.1.1954
Jordan,Louis (as,voc) | Mitchell,Bob (tp) | Hastings,Lowell (ts) | Warren,Earl (bs) | Lane,Chester (p) | Payne,Bert (el-g) | Jay,Thurber 'Sam Guy' (el-b) | Kirkwood,Johnny (dr)

BCD 15611 AH | CD | 1.Deutsches Jazz Festival 1953 Frankfurt/Main
Die Deutsche All Star Band 1953
Festival Riff | It's The Talk Of The Town | The Man I Love | Basin Street Blues | How High The Moon | Oh! Lady Be Good | Perdido
Frankfurt/M, rec. 3.5.1953
Deutsche All Star Band 1953,Die | Bunge,Fred (tp) | Fuhlisch,Günter (tb) | Von Klenck,Franz (as) | Greger,Max (ts) | Kuhn,Paul (p) | Hühns,Gerd (g) | Last,Hans (b) | Paris,Teddy (dr)

BCD 15614 AH | CD | Why Don't You Take All Of Me
Inge Brandenburg mit Werner Müller und seinem Orchester
Sieben Tage, Sieben Nächte | Goody Goody | Bye Bye Benjamino | Das Gibt's Nur Einmal | Es Ist Doch Immer Wieder Schön | Mein Herz Schlägt Für Jacky(A-Tisket, A-Tasket) | Pennies From Heaven | Harry's Kleiner Ball-Salon | Don't Take Your Love From Me
Berlin, rec. May-November 1960
Brandenburg,Inge (voc) | Orchestra | Müller,Werner (ld)
Inge Brandenburg mit Kurt Edelhaben und seinem Orchester
Gauner Sind Sie Alle | Weil Ich Angst Hab' Vor Dir | Südlich Von Hawaii(Flaschenpost) | Um Mitternacht | Tiger Twist | Amateur D'Amour
Köln, rec. 16.4.& 11.11.1962
Brandenburg,Inge (voc) | Orchestra | Edelhagen,Kurt (ld)
Inge Brandenburg mit Hans Martin Majewski und seinem Orchester
Chrysanthemen Blues
Berlin, rec. August/November 1962
Brandenburg,Inge (voc) | Orchestra | Majewski,Hans-Martin (arr,ld)
Inge Brandenburg & Otto 'Fats' Ortwein und die King Beats
Hey Baby | Morgen Nehme Ich Dein Foto Von Der Wand | Ruh' Dich Mal Aus Bei Mir | Du Läßt Mich Nicht Los(I'll Never Be Free)
Walldorf, rec. 1965
Brandenburg,Inge (voc) | Ortwein,Otto 'Fats' (voc) | King Beats | details unknown
Inge Brandenburg
Ich Liebe Ihn | Ein Mann Ist Ein Mann
München, rec. 17.1.1967
Brandenburg,Inge (voc) | details unknown
Inge Brandenburg And Her All-Stars
Lover Man(Oh,Where Can You Be?) | There'll Never Be Another You
Berlin, rec. 10./11.11.1960
Brandenburg,Inge (voc) | Samp,Harry (tp) | Brand,Helmut (bs) | Cramer,Heinz (g) | Schemmler,Günter (p) | Mackowiak,Alex (b) | Niemeyer,Heinz (dr)
All Of Me
Brandenburg,Inge (voc) | Brand,Helmut (bs) | Feuerstein,Adi (vib) | Cramer,Heinz (g) | Schemmler,Günter (p) | Mackowiak,Alex (b) | Niemeyer,Heinz (dr)

BCD 15642 AH | CD | Ich Habe Rhythmus
Helmut Zacharias Quintet
Ich Küsse Ihre Hand Madame | Dark Eyes | Those Little White Lies | Swing '48
Hamburg, rec. 5.2.1949
Zacharias,Helmut (v) | Bohn,Rudi (p,org,harpsichord) | Schumann,Coco (g) | Dillmann,Klaus (b) | Grabert,Kurt (vib,dr)
Kosacken-Patrouille | The Man I Love | You Made Me Love You | Mob Mob
Hamburg
Zacharias,Helmut (v) | Bohn,Rudi (p,org,harpsichord) | Schumann,Coco (g) | Dillmann,Klaus (b) | Grabert,Kurt (vib,dr)
ca. mid March 1949
Zacharias,Helmut (v) | Bohn,Rudi (p,org,harpsichord) | Schumann,Coco (g) | Dillmann,Klaus (b) | Grabert,Kurt (vib,dr)
Helmut Zacharias Sextet
Embraceable You | What Is This Thing Called Love
Hamburg, rec. 27.3.1950
Zacharias,Helmut (v) | Kühn,Rolf (cl) | Bohn,Rudi (p) | Cramer,Heinz (g) | Greve,Carl (b) | Ahrens,Rolf (dr)
Helmut Zacharias mit dem Orchester Frank Folken
Presto(aus der Fantasie In Be-Bop) | How High The Moon
Hamburg, rec. 1.3.1951
Zacharias,Helmut (v) | Achhammer,Siegfried (tp) | Etzel,Hans (tp) | Wilfert,Hanne (tp) | Betz,Werner (tb) | Bredl,Otto (tb) | Dörfler,Hugo (tb) | Well,Erich (tb) | Von Klenck,Franz (as) | Biste,Paul (as) | Aderhold,Bubi (ts) | Martin,Paul (ts) | Feigl,Johnny (bs) | Kiessling,Heinz (p) | Helsing,E. (g) | Sydow,Joe (b) | Schmidt,Bobby (dr)
Helmut Zacharias
Tiger Rag
Hamburg, rec. April 1952
Zacharias,Helmut (g,org,v,dr,effects)
Helmut Zacharias & His Sax-Team
Blue Moon | C Jam Blues
Hamburg, rec. 30.5.1952
Zacharias,Helmut (v) | Kakerbeck,Franz (ss,as) | Miehm,Heinz (as) | Skokann,Fritz (ts) | Schneider,Heinrich (ts) | Overbeck,Pia (bs) | Surmann,Willi (bs) | Hausmann,Hermann (p) | Böttcher,Martin (g) | Last,Hans (b) | Enderlein,Siegfried (dr) | Schnittjer,Günther (voc)
Helmut Zacharias mit seiner Swing-Besetzung
Swing Party: | Sweet Sue Just You- | Tea For Two- | Blacksmith Blues- | Schwips Boogie
Hamburg, rec. 4.10.1952
Zacharias,Helmut (v) | details unknown
Helmut Zacharias mit Kleiner Tanz-Besetzung
Ich Habe Rhythmus(I Got Rhythm)
Hamburg, rec. 4.12.1952
Zacharias,Helmut (v) | Bohn,Rudi (p,harpsichord) | Cramer,Heinz (g) | Greve,Carl (b) | Enderlein,Siegfried (dr)
Mr.Callahan
Hamburg, rec. 9.3.1953
Zacharias,Helmut (v) | Bohn,Rudi (p,harpsichord) | Cramer,Heinz (g) | Greve,Carl (b) | Enderlein,Siegfried (dr)
Helmut Zacharias mit seinem Orchester
Carioca | Säbeltanz-Boogie
Hamburg, rec. 9.7.1953
Zacharias,Helmut (v) | Miehm,Heinz (as) | Kakerbeck,Franz (as) | Skokann,Fritz (ts) | Schneider,Heinrich (ts) | Surmann,Willi (bs) | Bohn,Rudi (p) | Böttcher,Martin (g) | Walter,Hans (b) | Enderlein,Siegfried (dr,perc) | Reschke,Viktor (dr,perc) | Glusgal,Ilja (dr,perc)
Helmut Zacharias mit seinen Verzauberten Geigen
Boogie Für Geige | Fiddler's Boogie
Hamburg, rec. 7.5.1954
Zacharias,Helmut (v) | details unknown
Blue Blues
Berlin, rec. 1.9.1954
Zacharias,Helmut (v) | details unknown
-> Multi-playback-recording

BCD 15668 AH | CD | Sear-iously
Big Al Sears And The Sparrows
125th Street, New York | Shake Hands | Tan Skin Lad | Brown Boy
NYC, rec. 19.12.1949
Sears,Al (ts) | Lee,Charles (ts) | Tinney,William (g,dr) | Tinney,Allen (p) | Palmer,Clarence (b)
Big Al Sears Band
Huffin' And Puffin' | Sear-iously | Mag's Alley | Fo-Yah | Fo-Yah(alt.take)
NYC, rec. 5.12.1952
Sears,Al (ts) | Baker,Harold 'Shorty' (tp) | Glenn,Tyree (tb) | Barefield,Eddie (sax) | Johnson,Budd (sax) | Acea,Johnny (p) | Benjamin,Joe (b) | Mahdi,Kalil (dr)
In The Good Old Summertime | Ivory Cliffs | Easy Ernie | Vo-Sa
NYC, rec. 2.3.1953
Sears,Al (ts,voc) | Collins,Lester 'Shad' (tp) | Robinson,Eli (tb) | Powell,Rudy (sax) | Johnson,Budd (sax) | Smalls,Cliff (p) | Benjamin,Joe (b) | Greer,William 'Sonny' (dr)
Al Sears & His Rock 'N' Rollers
Going Up Town | Tweedle Dee
NYC, rec. late 1954
Sears,Al (ts) | Henry,Haywood (bs) | Hayes,Ernest 'Ernie' (p) | Trottman,Lloyd (b) | Bailey,Dave (dr)
Al Sears And His Orchestra
Come And Dance With Me | Come A'Runnin' | Tom, Dick 'N' Harry | Tina's Canteen
NYC, rec. 22.4.1955
Sears,Al (as) | Jordan,Taft (tp) | Brown,Lawrence (tb) | Taylor,Sam 'The Man' (as) | Johnson,Budd (ts) | Hayes,Ernest 'Ernie' (p) | Baker,Mickey (g) | Hinton,Milt (b) | Marshall,Joe (dr) | Calhoun,Charles 'Jesse Stone' (voc) | Cooper,Herbert (voc)
Right Now, Right Now | Midnight Wail | Love Call | Rock And Roll Ball
NYC, rec. 10.1.1956
Sears,Al (ts) | Stone,Jesse (accordeon) | Kirk,Wilbert (harm) | Jackson,Milt (marimba) | Baker,Mickey (g) | Hayes,Ernest 'Ernie' (p) | Trottman,Lloyd (b) | Francis,Panama (dr)
Here's The Beat | Great Googa Mooga
NYC, rec. 13.7.1956
Sears,Al (ts) | Jordan,Taft (tp) | Vance,Richard T. (tp) | Brown,Lawrence (tb) | Chambers,Henderson (tb) | Taylor,Sam 'The Man' (sax) | Johnson,Budd (sax) | Henry,Haywood (sax) | Hayes,Ernest 'Ernie' (p) | Baker,Mickey (g) | Trottman,Lloyd (b) | Marshall,Joe (dr) | Calhoun,Charles 'Jesse Stone' (voc) | Cooper,Herbert (voc)

BCD 15670 CI | 3 CD | King Curtis-Blow Man Blow
King Curtis Band
Turn 'Em On(Mono) | Turn 'Em On(Stereo) | Beachparty
NYC, rec. 22.5.1962
Curtis,King (ts) | Butler,Billy (g) | Stubbs,George (p) | Hayes,Ernest 'Ernie' (org) | Richardson,Joe (g) | Lewis,Jimmy (b) | Lucas,Ray (dr)
Your Cheatin' Heart | Tennessee Waltz | High Noon | I'm Movin' On | Raunchy
NYC, rec. 5.6.1962
Curtis,King (ts,voc) | Johnson,Harold 'Money' (tp) | Jordan,Taft (tp) | Butler,Billy (g) | Lynch,Carl (g) | Massey,Charles (g) | Griffin,Paul (p,org) | Hayes,Ernest 'Ernie' (p,org) | Lewis,Jimmy (b) | Lucas,Ray (dr) | Chester,Gary (perc) | Glover,Leroy (ld)
Beautiful Brown Eyes | Wagon Wheels | Any Time | Home On The Range | Night Train To Memphis
Curtis,King (ts,voc) | Johnson,Harold 'Money' (tp) | Jordan,Taft (tp) | Butler,Billy (g) | Lynch,Carl (g) | Massey,Charles (g) | Griffin,Paul (p,org) | Hayes,Ernest 'Ernie' (p,org) | Lewis,Jimmy (b) | Lucas,Ray (dr) | Chester,Gary (perc) | Glover,Leroy (ld) | unkn. (female chourus)
Tumbling Tumbleweeds | Walking The Floor Over You
NYC, rec. 6.6.1962
Curtis,King (ts,voc) | Johnson,Harold 'Money' (tp) | Jordan,Taft (tp) | Butler,Billy (g) | Lynch,Carl (g) | Massey,Charles (g) | Griffin,Paul (p,org) | Hayes,Ernest 'Ernie' (p,org) | Lewis,Jimmy (b) | Lucas,Ray (dr) | Chester,Gary (perc) | Glover,Leroy (ld)
Slow Drag | New Dance | New Dance(alt.take)
NYC, rec. 23.8.1962
Curtis,King (ts) | unkn. (g,p,org,b,dr)
Frisky
NYC, rec. 25.10.1962
Butler,Billy (g) | Dupree,Cornell (el-g) | Stubbs,George (p) | Hayes,Ernest 'Ernie' (org) | Lewis,Jimmy (b) | Chester,Gary (dr) | Rodriguez,Willie (bongos)
Alexander's Ragtime Band | Amorosa(Bossa Nova) | Strollin' Home | Mess Around
Curtis,King (ts) | Butler,Billy (g) | Dupree,Cornell (el-g) | Stubbs,George (p) | Hayes,Ernest 'Ernie' (org) | Lewis,Jimmy (b) | Chester,Gary (dr) | Rodriguez,Willie (bongos)
Sykiyaki | Summer Dream
NYC, rec. 17.4.1963
Curtis,King (ts) | unkn. (vib,g,p,b,dr) | unkn. (strings)
Do The Monkey | Feel All Right
NYC, rec. 24.5.1963
Curtis,King (ts) | Zito,Fred (tb) | Houston,Tate (bs) | Dupree,Cornell (g) | Gale,Eric (g) | Stubbs,George (p) | Lewis,Jimmy (b) | Lucas,Ray (dr) | unkn. (background-voc)
Theme From 'Lillies Of The Field[Amen]'(part 1) | Theme From 'Lillies Of The Field[Amen]'(part 2)
Hollywood,CA, rec. 4.9.1963
Curtis,King (ss) | Kail,Jerome (tp) | Newman,Joe (tp) | Nottingham,Jimmy (tp) | Royal,Ernie (tp) | Cleveland,Jimmy (tb) | Jackson,Quentin (tb) | McIntosh,Tom (tb) | Studd,Tony (tb) | Beckenstein,Jay (sax) | Dorsey,George (as) | Penque,Romeo (sax) | Ashton,Bob (ts) | Barrow,George (ts) | Dupree,Cornell (g) | Griffin,Paul (p) | Lewis,Jimmy (b) | Lucas,Ray (dr)
More Soul | Soul Serenade
prob.NYC, rec. 1963
Curtis,King (as,ts) | details unknown
Honky Tonk | Watermelon Man | Memphis | Soul Twist | Night Train | Tequila | Wiggle Wobble | One Mint Julep | Can't Sit Down | Swinging Shepherd Blues | My Last Date | Hide Away | Harlem Nocturne
NYC, rec. 24.1.1964
Curtis,King (ts) | Butler,Billy (g) | Dupree,Cornell (g) | Stubbs,George (p) | Hayes,Ernest 'Ernie' (org) | Lewis,Jimmy (b) | Tyrell,Jimmy (el-b) | Lucas,Ray (dr)
Java
NYC, rec. 1964
Curtis,King (ts) | details unknown
Stranger On The Shore | Summer Dream | Melancholy Serenade
NYC, rec. 8.5.1964
Curtis,King (saxello) | Dupree,Cornell (g) | Stubbs,George (p) | Hayes,Ernest 'Ernie' (org) | Rainey,Chuck (b) | Lucas,Ray (dr)
Tanya | Hung Over | Hung Over(alt.take) | Soul Time[Chuck] | Soul Time[Chuck](alt.take)
NYC, rec. 16.10.1964
Curtis,King (ts) | Dupree,Cornell (g) | Stubbs,George (p) | unkn. (org) | Rainey,Chuck (b) | Lucas,Ray (dr)
Moon River | Girl From Ipanema(Garota De Ipanema) | Sister Sadie | Let It Be Me | Misty
NYC, rec. 17.10.1964
Curtis,King (ts) | Dupree,Cornell (g) | Stubbs,George (p) | unkn. (org) | Rainey,Chuck (b) | Lucas,Ray (dr)
Something You've Got | Something You've Got(overdub)
Curtis,King (ts,voc) | Dupree,Cornell (g) | Stubbs,George (p) | unkn. (org) | Rainey,Chuck (b) | Lucas,Ray (dr) | unkn. (voc-group)
Take These Chains From My Heart
Dupree,Cornell (g) | Stubbs,George (p) | unkn. (org) | Rainey,Chuck (b) | Lucas,Ray (dr)
Hung Over | Misty | Bill Bailey Won't You Please Come Home | Peter Gunn
NYC, rec. 19.10.1964
Curtis,King (ts) | Dupree,Cornell (g) | Stubbs,George (p) | unkn. (org) | Rainey,Chuck (b) | Lucas,Ray (dr)
Shake | Tennessee Waltz | Ain't That Good News | Twistin' The Night Away | Good Times
NYC, rec. 9.3.1965
Curtis,King (ts) | unkn. (tp,tb,bs) | Butler,Billy (g) | Dupree,Cornell (g) | Ott,Horace prob. (p) | Hayes,Ernest 'Ernie' (org) | Bushnell,Bob (b) | Lucas,Ray (dr,congas)
Send Me Some Lovin' | Bring It On Home | A Change Is Gonna Come | You Send Me
NYC, rec. 11.3.1965
Curtis,King (saxello) | Butler,Billy (g) | Dupree,Cornell (g) | Ott,Horace or Ernie Hayes (p) | Bushnell,Bob (b) | Lucas,Ray (dr) | unkn. (strings)
Cupid | Chain Gang | The Prance
NYC, rec. 12.3.1965
Curtis,King (ts,voc) | Butler,Billy (g) | Dupree,Cornell (g) | Ott,Horace or Ernie Hayes (p) | Bushnell,Bob (b) | Lucas,Ray (dr)
Having A Party
Curtis,King (ts,voc) | Butler,Billy (g) | Dupree,Cornell (g) | Ott,Horace or Ernie Hayes (p) | Bushnell,Bob (b) | Lucas,Ray (dr) | unkn. (brass)

BCD 15717 AH | CD | Lauther
Wolfgang Lauth Quartet
Cool Cave | I Only Have Eyes For You | Pastels | Lauthentic | Jeb | These Foolish Things Remind Me On You | Indian Summer | Goofy
Hamburg, rec. 14./15.5.1956
Lauth,Wolfgang (p) | Pöhlert,Werner (g) | Kresse,Hans (b) | Hackbarth,Joe (dr)
French Fries | Can't Help Lovin' Dat Man | Chicken Feet | Date On Wax
Frankfurt/M, rec. June 1956
Lauth,Wolfgang (p) | Pöhlert,Werner (g) | Kresse,Hans (b) | Hackbarth,Joe (dr)
Ich Nenne Alle Frauen Baby | Es Ist Nur Die Liebe | Durch Dich Wird Die Welt Erst Schön | Bei Dir War Es Immer So Schön
Hamburg, rec. 14.10.1957
Lauth,Wolfgang (p) | Hartschuh,Fritz (vib) | Wagner,Wolfgang (b) | Hackbarth,Joe (dr)
Warum Bist Du Fortgegangen
Hamburg, rec. 5.12.1958
Lauth,Wolfgang (p) | Hartschuh,Fritz (vib) | Wagner,Wolfgang (b) | Hackbarth,Joe (dr)
Johnnie Walker | Ich Werde Jede Nacht Von Ihnen Träumen | Kauf Dir Einen Bunten Luftballon | Lauther | Donald | Mein Herz Hat Heut' Premiere
Hamburg, rec. 6.12.1958
Lauth,Wolfgang (p) | Hartschuh,Fritz (vib) | Wagner,Wolfgang (b) | Hackbarth,Joe (dr)

BCD 15813 AH | CD | Gettin' Back To Swing
Bill Ramsey With Orchestra
Cheek To Cheek | I'm Beginning To See The Light | Without A Song | Night And Day | Blues In The Night | Gettin' Back To Swing | Satin Doll | The Lady Is A Tramp | Something Lingers | I've Got The World On A String | I'm Gonna Sit Right Down And Write Myself A Letter | I Get A Kick Out Of You | Misty | They Can't Take That Away From Me | Georgia On My Mind | Don't Get Around Much Anymore
Stuttgart, rec. 11.-21.4.1994
Ramsey,Bill (voc) | Vogel,Thomas (tp) | Rezanina,Lubomir (tp) | Farrent,Karl (tp) | Reindl,Rudolf (tp) | Hutter,Ernst (tb) | Nuß,Ludwig (tb) | Maus,Georg (b-tb) | Rabe,Bernd (as) | Kühn,Axel (as) | Kaufmann,Georg (ts) | Malle,Andreas (ts) | Heute,Rainer (bs) | Wagenleiter,Klaus (p) | Schöpper,Klaus-Peter (g) | Stabenow,Thomas (b) | Gebhardt,Jörg (dr) | Boiadjiev String-Ensemble | Boiadjiev,Nedeltcho (cond) | Reith,Dieter (ld)

BCD 15912 AH | CD | Globetrotter
Freddie Brocksieper Und Seine Solisten
Brocksi Foxtrot | So Ist Es
Berlin, rec. 14.10.1941
Brocksieper,Freddie (dr) | Leis,Detlev (ts) | Angeli,Primo (p)
Brocksi-Quartett
Die Trommel Und Ihr Rhythmus | Ich Wüsst' So Gern
Berlin, rec. 11.2.1942
Brocksieper,Freddie (dr) | Kleindin,Franz (ts) | Heantzschel,Georg (p) | Winkler,Willibald (b)
Rip-Tip-Tap | So Ist Es...(Det Var Det)
Berlin, rec. 5.3.1942
Brocksieper,Freddie (dr) | Lais,Detlev (ts) | Angeli,Primo (p) | Dobrzynski,Walter (b)
Ernst Und Heiter | Kosende Hände
Berlin, rec. 2.4.1942
Brocksieper,Freddie (dr) | Diaz,Fernando (tp) | Angeli,Primo (p) | Cavaion,Cesare (b)
Mir Ist's So Leicht(Letter Sagt Enn Gjort) | Leise Klingt's Über's Wasser(Bölgende Rytmer)
Berlin, rec. ca.20.5.1942
Brocksieper,Freddie (dr) | Van Den Broek,Rimis (tp) | Angeli,Primo (p) | Winkler,? (b)
Rampenlicht(I Rampelyset) | Habe Vertrau'n(Stol Pa Mig)
Berlin, rec. 5.8.1942
Brocksieper,Freddie (dr) | Henkel,Eugen (ts) | Schulze,Fritz (p) | Tittmann,Otto (b)
Mary's Traum(Mary's Dröm) | Peinlich(Desverre)
Berlin, rec. 28.9.1942
Brocksieper,Freddie (dr) | Breyere,Josse (tb) | Angeli,Primo (p) | Tittmann,Otto (b)
Improvisation(Improvisasjon) | Ewig Denke Ich An Dich(Jet Tenker Alltid Pa Deg)
Berlin, rec. 30.9.1942
Brocksieper,Freddie (dr) | Breyere,Josse (tb) | Angeli,Primo (p) | Tittmann,Otto (b)
Eccentric | Verrückte Beine
Berlin, rec. 27.1.1943
Brocksieper,Freddie (dr) | Impallomeni,Nino prob. (tp) | Angeli,Primo (p) | Tittmann,Otto (b)
Liebeslaunen(Milostne Nalady) | O,La La Madame!
Berlin, rec. 30.1.1943
Brocksieper,Freddie (dr) | Henkel,Eugen (ts) | Angeli,Primo (p) | Tittmann,Otto (b)
Sicherlich
Berlin, rec. 11.2.1943
Brocksieper,Freddie (dr) | prob.personal: | Impallomeni,Nino (tp) | Angeli,Primo (p) | Tittmann,Otto (b)
Brocksieper-Special-Ensemble
Barcarole
Brocksieper,Freddie (dr) | prob.personal: | Impallomeni,Nino (tp) | Marzaroli,Alfredo (tp) | Schmidt-Schulz,Eberhardt (tp) | Breyere,Josse (tb) | Zillner,Robby (tb) | Bossche,Henk (tb) | Johnson,Folke (tb) | Angeli,Primo (p) | Tevelian,Meg (g) | Tittmann,Otto (b) | Scheffers,Pi (arr)
Brocksi-Quartett
Ich Sing' Mir Eins | Silhuetten
Berlin, rec. 1.3.1943
Brocksieper,Freddie (dr) | Robert,Jean (ts) | Angeli,Primo (p) | Tittmann,Otto (b)
Brocksieper-Solisten-Orchester
Globetrotter | Melodie
Berlin, rec. 19.3.1943
Brocksieper,Freddie (dr) | prob.personal: | Impallomeni,Nino (tp) | Marzaroli,Alfredo (tp) | Schmidt-Schulz,Eberhardt (tp) | Breyere,Josse (tb) | Zillner,Robby (tb) | Bossche,Henk (tb) | Johnson,Folke (tb) | Angeli,Primo (p) | Tevelian,Meg (g) | Tittmann,Otto (b) | Scheffers,Pi (arr)

BCD 15942 AH | CD | Noch Lauther
Wolfgang Lauth Quartet
Schwetzinger Original | Round About Midnight
Baden-Baden, rec. Spring 1957
Lauth,Wolfgang (p) | Hartschuh,Fritz (vib) | Wagner,Wolfgang (b) | Hackbarth,Joe (dr)
Wolfgang Lauth Septet
Johnology | Dentology
Lauth,Wolfgang (p) | Mangelsdorff,Albert (tb) | Weinkopf,Gerald 'Gerry' (fl) | Freund,Joki (ts) | Pöhlert,Werner (g) | Wagner,Wolfgang (b) | Hackbarth,Joe (dr)
Wolfgang Lauth Quartet
Festival 57 | Malu | Sunday Picnic | Day By Day
Hamburg, rec. 14.10.1957
Lauth,Wolfgang (p) | Hartschuh,Fritz (vib) | Wagner,Wolfgang (b) | Hackbarth,Joe (dr)
Wolfgang Lauth Septet
Concerto In Jazz(part 1-3) | Tele-Funky | Trouble With Joe
Hamburg, rec. 19.5.1958
Lauth,Wolfgang (p) | Denu,Egon (tb) | Feuerstein,Adi (fl) | Steuernagel,Rudi (ts) | Pöhlert,Werner (g) | Wagner,Wolfgang (b) | Hackbarth,Joe (dr)
Wolfgang Lauth Quartet
Warum Bist Du Fortgegangen
Hamburg, rec. 5.12.1958
Lauth,Wolfgang (p) | Hartschuh,Fritz (vib) | Wagner,Wolfgang (b) | Hackbarth,Joe (dr)
Claude
Hamburg, rec. 6.12.1958
Lauth,Wolfgang (p) | Hartschuh,Fritz (vib) | Wagner,Wolfgang (b) | Hackbarth,Joe (dr)
Waltz For People Who Hate Waltzes
Blue Paintings
Heidelberg, rec. 3.6.1964
Lauth,Wolfgang (p) | Hartschuh,Fritz (vib) | Wagner,Wolfgang (b) | Seidelmann,Horst (dr)

BCD 15988 AH | CD | Drums Boogie
Brocksieper-Solisten-Orchester(Brocksi-Quartet)
Taktik | Harmonie
Berlin, rec. ca.April 1943
Brocksieper,Freddie (dr) | Impallomeni,Nino (tp) | Angeli,Primo (p) | Tittmann,Otto (b)
Brocksieper-Jazz-Ensemble
Cymbal-Promenade | Romanze | Kein Problem

Berlin, rec. 1.7.1943
Brocksieper,Freddie (dr) | prob.personal: | Impallomeni,Nino (tp) | Marzaroli,Alfredo (tp) | Schmidt-Schulz,Eberhardt (tp) | Breyere,Josse (tb) | Zillner,Robby (tb) | Bossche,Henk (tb) | Johnson,Folke (tb) | Angeli,Primo (p,cembalo) | Tevelian,Meg (g) | Tittmann,Otto (b) | Scheffers,Pi (arr)
Brocksi-Quintett
Swinging Tom Tom(incomplete) | Swinging Tom Tom(incomplete-2) | Kosende Hände(false-start) | Kosende Hände | Crazy Rhythm | Shoe Shine Boy
Stuttgart, rec. 17.4.1944
Brocksieper,Freddie (dr) | Impallomeni,Nino (tp) | Robert,Jean (cl,ts) | Fey,Martin (p) | Gursch,Max (g) | Tittmann,Otto (b)
Drums-Boogie(aka Drum Boogie) | Caravan | Cynthia's In Love | Take The 'A' Train | Sophisticated Lady
München, rec. ca.May 1947
Brocksieper,Freddie (dr) | Tabor,Charlie (tp) | Weiss,Walter (cl,as) | Weiss,Heinz (p) | Farkas,Mihaly (b)
Brocksi-Quartett
I Surrender Dear
Brocksieper,Freddie (dr) | Henkel,Eugen (ts) | Weiss,Heinz (p) | Farkas,Mihaly (b)
Brocksi-Quintett
Sing Sing Sing | Exactly Like You | Sweet Lorraine | Open The Door Richard | C Jam Blues
Brocksieper,Freddie (dr) | Tabor,Charlie (tp) | Henkel,Eugen (ts) | Weiss,Heinz (p) | Farkas,Mihaly (b)
Freddie Brocksieper Orchester
Give Me Five Minutes More | I Know That You Know
Brocksieper,Freddie (dr) | Tabor,Charlie (tp) | Schneider,Ubald (tp) | Richardson,Richard (tb) | Hahn,Sepp (tb) | Blauth,Johnny (tb) | Weiss,Walter (as) | Seitz,Joseph (ts) | Henkel,Eugen (ts) | Kleindin,Teddy (ts,arr) | Weiss,Heinz (p) | Farkas,Mihaly (b)
Brocksi-Quartett
Body And Soul | Hodge Podge
München, rec. 4.5.1948
Brocksieper,Freddie (dr) | Henkel,Eugen (ts) | Schmitz-Steinberg,Christian (p) | Farkas,Mihaly (b)
Brocksi-Sextett
Northwest Passage
Brocksieper,Freddie (dr) | Petz,Fritz (tp) | Strasser,Hugo (cl) | Henkel,Eugen (ts) | Schmitz-Steinberg,Christian (p) | Farkas,Mihaly (b)

BCD 16119 AH | CD | Re-Disc Bounce
Johannes Rediske Quintet
Little White Lies | Laura | Herbst-Serenade | How Deep Is The Ocean
Berlin, rec. 9.4.1953
Rediske,Johannes (g) | Noack,Lothar (cl,ts) | Spychalski,Alex (p) | Behrendt,Manfred (b) | Glaser,Joe (dr)
Once In A While | I'm Yours | Lover | Caravan
Berlin, rec. 28.8.1953
Rediske,Johannes (g) | Noack,Lothar (cl,ts) | Spychalski,Alex (p) | Behrendt,Manfred (b) | Glaser,Joe (dr)
Hot Toddy | Love For Sale
Berlin, rec. 29.1.1954
Rediske,Johannes (g) | Noack,Lothar (cl,ts) | Spychalski,Alex (p) | Behrendt,Manfred (b) | Glaser,Joe (dr)
Re-Disc Bounce
Berlin, rec. 12.11.1954
Rediske,Johannes (g) | Noack,Lothar (cl,ts) | Spychalski,Alex (p) | Behrendt,Manfred (b) | Glaser,Joe (dr)
So Wird's Nie Wieder Sein | Chrysanthemen Blues | Stephanie
Berlin, rec. 19.8.1955
Rediske,Johannes (g) | Noack,Lothar (cl,ts) | Spychalski,Alex (p) | Behrendt,Manfred (b) | Glaser,Joe (dr)
Reisefieber | Opus In Barock
Berlin, rec. 21.9.1955
Rediske,Johannes (g) | Noack,Lothar (cl,ts) | Spychalski,Alex (p) | Behrendt,Manfred (b) | Glaser,Joe (dr)
When The Quail Come Back To San Quentin
Berlin, rec. 3.2.1956
Rediske,Johannes (g) | Noack,Lothar (cl,ts) | Spychalski,Alex (p) | Behrendt,Manfred (b) | Glaser,Joe (dr)
Johannes Rediske Sextet
Struttin' With Some Barbecue | As Long As I Live
Rediske,Johannes (g) | Rückert,Peter (tp) | Noack,Lothar (cl,ts) | Spychalski,Alex (p) | Behrendt,Manfred (b) | Glaser,Joe (dr)
Interview mit Eberhard Kruppa- | Lullaby Of Birdland-
Berlin, rec. 28.2.1956
Rediske,Johannes (g) | Noack,Lothar (cl,ts) | Spychalski,Alex (p) | Behrendt,Manfred (b) | Glaser,Joe (dr)
Jockey-Bounce | Tom-Cat Mambo
Berlin, rec. 25.9.1956
Rediske,Johannes (g) | Noack,Lothar (cl,ts) | Spychalski,Alex (p) | Behrendt,Manfred (b) | Glaser,Joe (dr)

BCD 16151 AH | CD | Caldonia And More...
Bill Ramsey & His Trio
Caldonia | Outskirts Of Town | Goin' To Chicago | Frankie And Johnny | St.James Infirmary
Live in Sopot,Poland, rec. 15.7.1957
Ramsey,Bill (voc) | Big Bill (g,p) | King,Al (b) | Berk,Ata (dr)
Bill Ramsey
Caldonia | Big Fat Mama
Live at Kurhaus Scheveningen,NL, rec. 27.7.1957
Ramsey,Bill (p,voc)
Bill Ramsey With Eric Krans Dixieland Pipers And Guests
When The Saints Go Marching In
Ramsey,Bill (voc) | Coleman,Bill (tp) | Nicholas,Albert (cl) | Bryden,Beryl (voc) | Eric Krans Dixieland Pipers | details unknown
Bill Ramsey With The Paul Kuhn Trio
The Late Late Show | The More I See You | Where Or When | Worksong
Prag,CSFR, rec. 27.10.1966
Ramsey,Bill (voc) | Kuhn,Paul (p) | Woode,Jimmy (b) | Favre,Pierre (dr)
Bill Ramsey & Juraj Galan
Sunny | I'm Gonna Sit Right Down And Write Myself A Letter | Ellington Medley: | I'm Beginning To See The Light- | Sophisticated Lady- | Satin Doll- | Misty | Route 66 | Honeysuckle Rose | Ornithology- | How High The Moon- | Girl From Ipanema(Garota De Ipanema) | Pennies From Heaven- | I Can't Give You Anything But Love- | There'll Never Be Another You | Kansas City | The Shadow Of Your Smile
Live at The Unterhaus,Mainz, rec. 9.-11.5.1980
Ramsey,Bill (voc) | Galan,Juraj (g)

BCD 16172 AH | CD | Jumpin' At The Badewanne
Johannes Rediske Quintet
American Patrol | Poinciana | Undecided | Blue Skies
Berlin, rec. 13.3.1951
Rediske,Johannes (el-g) | Noack,Lothar (cl,ts) | Spychalski,Alex (p,accordeon) | Behrendt,Manfred (b) | Glaser,Joe (dr)
Don't Blame Me | Oh,Lady Be-Bop
Berlin, rec. 22.12.1951
Rediske,Johannes (el-g) | Noack,Lothar (cl) | Spychalski,Alex (p) | Behrendt,Manfred (b) | Glaser,Joe (dr) | Boom,Ricky (voc)
I'll Remember April | Pick Yourself Up | Jumpin' With Symphony Sid | Jumpin' At The Badewanne
Berlin, rec. 30.1.1952
Rediske,Johannes (el-g) | Noack,Lothar (cl) | Spychalski,Alex (p) | Behrendt,Manfred (b) | Glaser,Joe (dr)
Two Sleepy People | Flying Home(Homeward Bound) | Little Brown Jug
Berlin, rec. 31.10.1952
Rediske,Johannes (el-g) | Noack,Lothar (ts) | Spychalski,Alex (p) | Behrendt,Manfred (b) | Glaser,Joe (dr)
Leave Us Leap | A Night In Tunisia
Berlin, rec. 22.12.1952
Rediske,Johannes (el-g) | Noack,Lothar (cl) | Spychalski,Alex (p) | Behrendt,Manfred (b) | Glaser,Joe (dr)
Love For Sale | Caravan
Berlin, rec. 11.2.1954
Rediske,Johannes (el-g) | Noack,Lothar (ts) | Spychalski,Alex (p) | Behrendt,Manfred (b) | Glaser,Joe (dr,celeste)
The Man I Love(dedicated to The Box) | Re-Disc Bounce(im Trott) | Chloe | High Tide
Hamburg, rec. 21.9.1954
Rediske,Johannes (el-g) | Noack,Lothar (ts) | Spychalski,Alex (p) | Behrendt,Manfred (b) | Glaser,Joe (dr,celeste)
Re-Disc Boogie | Melodie In Es | Struttin' With Some Barbecue | Opus In Barock
Köln, rec. 26.6.1956
Rediske,Johannes (g) | Noack,Lothar (cl,ts) | Spychalski,Alex (p,harpsichord) | Behrendt,Manfred (b) | Niemeyer,Heinz (dr,bongos)

BCD 16277 AH | CD | Shot Gun Boogie
Freddie Brocksieper Orchester
The Man I Love | Idaho
München, rec. 4.5.1948
Brocksieper,Freddie (dr) | personal included: | Petz,Fritz (tp) | unkn. (tp) | unkn. (tb) | Strasser,Hugo (cl) | Henkel,Eugen (ts) | unkn. (3 reeds) | Schmitz-Steinberg,Christian (p) | Farkas,Mihaly (b) | Berson,Ingrid (voc)
Brocksi-Sextett
Smoke Gets In Your Eyes
München, rec. 15.5.1948
Brocksieper,Freddie (dr) | Petz,Fritz (tp) | Strasser,Hugo (cl) | Henkel,Eugen (ts) | Schmitz-Steinberg,Christian (p,arr) | Farkas,Mihaly (b)
Freddie Brocksieper Quintett
Buttons & Bows | How Do You Do
München, rec. 18.5.1949
Brocksieper,Freddie (dr) | Strasser,Hugo (cl) | Schneebiegl,Rolf (vib) | Scharfenberger,Werner (p,accordeon) | Farkas,Mihaly (b)
Freddie Brocksieper Star-Quintett
All Of Me | Muskrat Ramble | St.Louis Blues | Shine
Berlin, rec. 15.4.1950
Brocksieper,Freddie (dr) | Tabor,Charlie (tp) | Reinhardt,Helmut (cl,as) | Kuhn,Paul (p) | Farkas,Mihaly (b)
Freddie Brocksieper Und Seine Solisten
Exactly Like You | Hallo,Baby,Mademoiselle(Get Up On Those Stars) | Jeepers Creepers | Oui Sait?(Quizas) | Perdido | Cherokee
prob.Köln, rec. ca.1951
Brocksieper,Freddie (dr) | details unknown
Freddie Brocksieper Orchester
Mambo No.8 | Manhattan Mambo | Feuertanz(Ritual Fire Dance)
München, rec. 15.4.1952
Brocksieper,Freddie (dr,bongos) | Weichbrodt,Fritz (tp) | Haensch,Delle (cl,as) | Eberle,Heinz (ts) | Diernhammer,Carlos (p) | Farkas,Mihaly (b)
Bolero De Habana
Brocksieper,Freddie (dr,bongos) | Weichbrodt,Fritz (tp) | Haensch,Delle (as) | Koller,Hans (ts) | Eberle,Heinz (ts) | Diernhammer,Carlos (p) | Farkas,Mihaly (b)
Freddie Brocksieper Quartett
Shotgun Boogie | Crazy Rhythm(Schräger Rhythmus) | Mambo Jambo | Come Back To Sorento | Rhythmus Revue: | Dinah- | Honeysuckle Rose- | Blue Skies- | Rhythmus Revue: | Night And Day- | Begin The Beguine- | On The Sunny Side Of The Street-
Hamburg, rec. ca.May 1952
Brocksieper,Freddie (dr) | Koller,Hans (cl,ts) | Schemmler,Günter (p,accordeon) | Farkas,Mihaly (b)
Freddie Brocksieper Trio
Mambo Jambo
Brocksieper,Freddie (dr) | Schemmler,Günter (p) | Farkas,Mihaly (b)

BCD 16388 AH | CD | Freddie's Boogie Blues
Freddie Brocksieper And His Boys
Close Your Eyes | These Foolish Things Remind Me On You | Anything Can Happen | Bei Mir Bist Du Schön | Lullaby Of Birdland | Ain't Misbehavin' | Die Ganze Welt Ist Himmelblau | Sax Mambo | Carlito's Reise
München, rec. 7.11.1955
Brocksieper,Freddie (dr) | Brandenburg,Helmut (ts) | Diernhammer,Carlos (p,cembalo) | Farkas,Mihaly (b) | Forde,Cecily (voc)
Freddie's Boogie Blues
Brocksieper,Freddie (dr) | Tabor,Charlie (tp) | Raab,Walter (tp) | Richter,Gerc (tp) | Büttermann,Max (tb) | Mosch,Manfred (tb) | Hensch,Delle (as) | Strasser,Hugo (as) | Brandenburg,Helmut (ts) | Flierl,Rudi (cl,ts,bs) | Diernhammer,Carlos (p,cembalo) | Farkas,Mihaly (b) | Forde,Cecily (voc)
Freddie Brocksieper Four Stars
Rosetta | Temperatur | Swinging Mood | Softly As In A Morning Sunrise
Live at 'Studio 15',München, rec. 23.3.1957
Brocksieper,Freddie (dr) | Spannuth,Fred (cl,ts) | Diernhammer,Carlos (p) | Farkas,Mihaly (b)
Freddie Brocksieper Und Seine Solisten
Jalousie-Cha-Cha
München, rec. ca.1959
Brocksieper,Freddie (dr) | Spannuth,Fred (cl,ts) | Weiss,Otto (org) | Van Der Sys,Hans (g,p) | Farkas,Mihaly (b)
Begin The Beguine | Freddie's Melody | After Hours Rock | Caravan | Smoke Gets In Your Eyes | Frank's Melody | What Will I Do | Hot Canary | Playboy Rag
Uni-Reitschule,München, rec. 1959
Brocksieper,Freddie (dr) | Spannuth,Fred (cl,ts) | Tabor,Charlie (tp) | Neidlinger,Sepp (tb) | Weiss,Otto (vib,p,org) | Van Der Sys,Hans (g,p,org) | Wörsching,Heli (b)

Between The Lines | Efa-Medien GmbH

btl 001(Efa 10171-2) | CD | Make Believe
Franz Koglmann Quintet
Make Believe | Lotrecht In Die Tiefe | Rue Montmartre Trilogy: | L'Ecrevisse- | Interlude- | Rue Montmartre- | Eye,Ear,Nose | Der Vogel | Blut(Lullaby)
Frankfurt/M, rec. 24./25.11.1998
Koglmann,Franz (tp,fl-h) | Varner,Tom (fr-h) | Coe,Tony (cl,b-cl,ts) | Shepik,Brad (g) | Herbert,Peter (b)

btl 002(Efa 10172-2) | CD | Michel Wintsch & Road Movie featuring Gerry Hemingway
Michel Wintsch & Road Movie
Postludique | Night Train | Re-Pyrrect | Play Time | Italik(part 1) | Italik(part 2) | Hiver(part 1) | Hiver(part 2) | Natalia | Chords | Trash Road | Le Chien Du Héro
Live at Südbahnhof,Frankfurt/M, rec. 26.11.1998
Wintsch,Michael (p) | Schärli,Peter (tp) | Pedretti,Jean-Jacques (tb) | Baumann,Franziska (fl,voc) | Zwahlen,Jean-Philippe (g) | Saudan,Nathalie (v) | Beltraminelli,Daniela (v) | Schütz,Martin (cello) | Niggli,Lucas (dr) | Hemingway,Gerry (dr) | Kéraudren,Jean (sound)

btl 003(Efa 10173-2) | CD | Monitor
Michael Moore Trio
Riddled | Budnike | Five Bits | Misericordia | Gulls | Race In Space For Face | Focus | Bounding | Desinterresse En Deviatie,Opnieuw En Opnieuw | Monitor | Barium
Köln, rec. 22./23.2.1999
Moore,Michael (cl,b-cl,as) | Fuhler,Cor (p,org,keyolin) | Honsinger,Tristan (cello)

btl 004(Efa 10174-2) | CD | Duo En Noir
Enrico Rava-Ran Blake
Nature Boy | Vertigo- | Laura- | The Spiral Staircase | Shake The Cage | Certi Angoli | There's No You | Let's Stay Together | I Should Care | Tea For Two | There's A Small Hotel
Live at Südbahnhof,Frankfurt/M, rec. 23.9.1999
Rava,Enrico (tp,fl-h) | Blake,Ran (p)

btl 005(Efa 10175-2) | CD | Elelents Of Poetry
Oskar Aichinger Trio
Poemia Trois | Refugium | Elements Of Poetry 1 | Perdendosi | Elements Of Poetry 2 | Lugubre | Loose Calypso | Air | Andere | In Rillievo | Ridicolosamente | Concordanza
Wien,Austria, rec. 8.5.1999
Aichinger,Oskar (p) | Tang,Achim (b) | Skrepek,Paul (dr)

btl 006(Efa 10176-2) | CD | An Affair With Strauss
Monoblue Quartet
A Metropolitan Affair | Next To Nothing-A Non Affair | An Atypical Affair | Sauve Qui Peut(Vienne) | Dear Little Pipistrelle | Lover | Out Of Strauss | Good Night Vienna
Wien,Austria, rec. 27./28.6.1999
Monoblue Quartet | Koglmann,Franz (tp,fl-h) | Coe,Tony (cl,ts,voc) | Stangl,Burkhard (g) | Herbert,Peter (b)

btl 007(Efa 10177-2) | CD | British-American Blue
Tony Coe-Roger Kellaway
Carona Glass And Lady Maggie | Friend In The Mirror | The Caverns Of Volere | Conversations With Sparze | Dance Of The 3-Legged Elves | Off We Go Into The Wild Blue Yonder | Ballad For The Russian Princess | Monday's Child | Me And Tony | British-American Blue | The Burgundy Bruise
Wembley,GB, rec. 18.6.1978
Coe,Tony (cl) | Kellaway,Roger (p)

btl 008(Efa 10178-2) | CD | A Tree Frog Tonality
John Lindberg Ensemble
Thanksgiving Suite: | At Home- | Mellow T.- | Dreaming At...- | Four Fathers | Drifter | A Tree Frog Tonality | Good To Go | Little m And Big M
Graz, Austria, rec. 27./28.3.2000
Lindberg,John (b) | Smith,Leo[Wadada] (tp) | Ochs,Larry (ts,sopranino) | Cyrille,Andrew (dr)

btl 009(Efa 10179-2) | CD | Tin Drum Stories(inspired by the novel 'Die Blechtrommel' by Günter Grass)
Andreas Willers Group
Tin Drum Stories Part 1:Shelter | Tin Drum Stories Part 2:Glass | Tin Drum Stories Part 3:Ahead,Apart | Tin Drum Stories Part 4:Fortuna X | Piratenlied | Leinen Los! | The Bastard Period | Wasser, Brot, Schuhe | Reprise:Shelter | Behind The Fridge
Berlin, rec. 12./13.10.1999 & 6.7.2000
Willers,Andreas (g,el-g,bj,devices,ukelele,doorharp) | Nonnenmacher,Horst (b) | Griener,Michael (trap-set,dictaphone)

btl 010(Efa 10180-2) | CD | Reconfigurations
Rajesh Metha
Reconfigurations(part 1-3)
Berlin, rec. 22./23.6.2000
Metha-Metric Ensemble,The | Metha,Rajesh (tp,slide-tp,b-tp,extensions,hybrid-tp) | Kugan,Vlatko (cl,b-cl,ss,ts,melodica) | Kolkowski,Aleksander (stroh-v,viola) | Wilson,Peter Niklas (b) | Kaczynski,Ray (perc)

btl 011(Efa 10181-2) | CD | Opium
Franz Koglmann Quintet
Flops | Bowery 1 | Bowery 2 | Flaps
Wien,Austria, rec. 26.4.1973
Koglmann,Franz (tp,fl-h) | Lacy,Steve (ss) | Michlmayr,Toni (b) | Malli,Walter M. (perc) | Geier,Gerd (electronics)
Der Vogel- | Opium- | Carmilla
Paris,France, rec. 19.12.1975
Koglmann,Franz (fl-h) | Traindl,Josef (tb) | Lacy,Steve (ss) | Botelho,Cesarius Alvim (b) | Romano,Aldo (dr)
For Franz
Wien,Austria, rec. 6.8.1976
Koglmann,Franz (tp) | Dixon,Bill (tp) | Horenstein,Stephen (ts) | Silva,Alan (b) | Malli,Walter M. (cymbals)

btl 012(Efa 10182-2) | CD | Cryptology
Francois Houle 5
Le Corps Abstrait S'Abandonne À La Lumière
Vancouver,Canada, rec. 4./5.10.2000
Houle,Francois (comp) | Turner,Brad (p) | Lee,Peggy (cello) | Van Der Schyff,Dylan (perc)
Palinodia I | Prayer | Hive-Mind | Asymptote | Palinodia II | The Donkey's Tale | Keystream Mystery
Houle,Francois (cl,b-cl) | Turner,Brad (tp,p) | McDonald,Sheila (v) | Lee,Peggy (cello) | Van Der Schyff,Dylan (perc)

btl 013(Efa 10183) | CD | B-A-C-H A Chromatic Universe
Peter Herbert Group
Fuga | Stauber | B-A-C-H Bass | Stadtpfeifer | B-A-C-H Trumpet | Divi Blasli | B-A-C-H Piano | Hausmann | B-A-C-H Bass-Clarinet | Actus Tragicus | Heavy Snow
NYC, rec. 25./26.9.2000
Herbert,Peter (b) | Jensen,Ingrid (tp,fl-h) | Robinson,Carol (b-cl) | Copland,Marc (p) | Wollesen,Kenny (dr,perc,bug)

btl 015(Efa 10185-2) | CD | Luminous Cycles
James Emery Sextet
Luminous Cycles | One Red Thread | Beyond Words | En Rapport | Exit To Nowhere | Across The Water | Cardinal Points | Violet Into The Blue
Frankfurt/M, rec. 27./28.10.2000
Emery,James (g) | Ehrlich,Marty (fl,cl,ss,as) | Speed,Chris (cl,ts) | Gress,Drew (b) | Norton,Kevin (vib,marimba,tympani,bowed tam-tam) | Hemingway,Gerry (dr,glockenspiel)

btl 017(Efa 10186) | CD | Venus In Transit
Franz Koglmann Group
Venus In Transit: | Pardon,Ist Da Noch Frei?(I Wanne Be Loved By You) | Überstöhrung | Eigentlich Bin Ich Hautarzt | Ist Das Ansteckend? | Casta Diva | Danke,Frau Hofrat | Mit Dabei Sein | So Rühr' Ich Um Mit Meinem Säbel | Alois,Wir Entkommen Ihm Nicht | Voralberger Schuhgroßhändler(Some Like It Hot) | Toni,Du Dodl | Kreta | Wahlverwandtschaften: | LA,Case Study House | Urania,Wien | Maison À Bordeau
NYC, rec. 11./12.2.2001
Koglmann,Franz (tp) | Speed,Chris (cl,ts) | Rabinowitz,Michael (bassoon) | Fiuczynski,Dave (g) | Maneri,Mat (v) | Herbert,Peter (b) | Mettham,John (cocktail-dr,perc) |Derntl,Wolfram Igor (voc)

btl 017(Efa 10187-2) | CD | Essencia
Gebhard Ullmann Trio
Sombras E Nevoeiro- | A Luz Da Sombra- | Essencia Grave | Gospel | Haiku | O Profeta II | Pinoquio | Bella And Herr T. | Walking Poem No.2 | Planicies | Essencia Largo | Chinesisches Gedicht No.3 | Simple Melody
Berlin, rec. 22.-24.2.1999
Ullmann Gebhard (b-cl,ss,ts) | Thomas,Jens (p) | Bica,Carlos (b)

btl 020(Efa 10190-2) | CD | Fourth World
James Emery Quartet
Bellflower | Golden Horn | Fourth World | Worship | Splendido | La Scala | The Next Level | In A Secret Place | Hannah's Song
Paramus,NJ, rec. 15./16.5.2001
Emery,James (g) | Lovano,Joe (alto-cl,ss,as,ts,c-melody-sax,bells,perc) | Silvano,Judi (fl,voice) | Gress,Drew (b)

BGO Records | Edel Contraire

BGOCD 366 | CD | Django/Django In Rome 1949-1050
Django Reinhardt Quartet
Swing Guitars
Paris,France, rec. 15.10.1935
Reinhardt,Django (g) | Reinhardt,Joseph (g) | Ferret,Pierre (g) | Vola,Louis (b)
Quintet Du Hot Club De France
Charleston | You're Driving Me Crazy
Paris,France, rec. 21.4.1937
Quintet Du Hot Club De France | Grappelli,Stephane (v) | Reinhardt,Django (g) | Bianchi,Marcel (g) | Ferret,Pierre (g) | Vola,Louis (b)
Chicago | In A Sentimental Mood
Paris,France, rec. 26.4.1937
Quintet Du Hot Club De France | Grappelli,Stephane (v) | Reinhardt,Django (g) | Bianchi,Marcel (g) | Ferret,Pierre (g) | Vola,Louis (b)
I've Found A New Baby | Alabamy Bound
Paris/Berikon,CH, rec. 29.9.1937
Grappelli,Stephane (v) | Reinhardt,Django (g)
Eddie South/Stephane Grappelli Quintet

Oh! Lady Be Good
South,Eddie (v) | Grappelli,Stephane (v) | Warlop,Michel (v) | Reinhardt,Django (g) | Myers,Wilson Ernest (b)
Quintet Du Hot Club De France
Minor Swing | Viper's Dream
Paris,France, rec. 25.11.1937
Quintet Du Hot Club De France | Grappelli,Stephane (v) | Reinhardt,Django (g) | Reinhardt,Joseph (g) | Vees,Eugene (g) | Vola,Louis (b)
Swingin' With Django | Paramount Stomp
Paris,France, rec. 7.12.1937
Quintet Du Hot Club De France | Grappelli,Stephane (v) | Warlop,Michel (v) | Reinhardt,Django (g) | Reinhardt,Joseph (g) | Vees,Eugene (g) | Vola,Louis (b)
Django Reinhardt Trio
Bouncin' Around | St.Louis Blues
Paris,France, rec. 9.9.1937
Reinhardt,Django (g) | Gaste,Louis (g) | D'Hellemmes,Eugene (b)
Quintet Du Hot Club De France
Micro | Stormy Weather | Blue Skies | The Man I Love | The Peanut Vendor | It Might As Well Be Spring
Rome,Italy, rec. January/February 1949
Quintet Du Hot Club De France | Grappelli,Stephane (v) | Reinhardt,Django (g) | Safred,Gianni (p) | Pecori,Carlo (b) | De Carolis,Aurelio (dr)
Django Reinhardt Quintet
Micro | Danse Norvegienne | Dinette | Reverie | Place De Brouckere | Black Night | Boogie Woogie
Rome,Italy, rec. April/May 1950
Reinhardt,Django (g) | Ekyan,Andre (cl,as) | Schecroun,Ralph (p) | Masselier,Alf (b) | Paraboschi,Roger (dr)

Bhakti Jazz | Jazz Network

BR 28 | CD | Live Highlights '92
Attila Zoller-Wolfgang Lackerschmid
Jassfriends
München, rec. October 1991
Zoller,Attila (g) | Lackerschmid,Wolfgang (vib)
Hungarian Jazz Rhapsody
Wasserburg, rec. October 1991
Zoller,Attila (g) | Lackerschmid,Wolfgang (vib)
No Greater Lunch | In Your Own Sweet Way
Bremen, rec. March 1992
Zoller,Attila (g) | Lackerschmid,Wolfgang (vib)
When It's Time
Bremerhaven, rec. March 1992
Zoller,Attila (g) | Lackerschmid,Wolfgang (vib)
Meant To Be | Circle Waltz | Homage To O.P.
Paderborn, rec. March 1992
Zoller,Attila (g) | Lackerschmid,Wolfgang (vib)

BR 29 | CD | One More Life
Wolfgang Lackerschmid Sextet
Iris In The Rain
Live,at 'Jazztage' Leverkusen, rec. 10.10.1991
Lackerschmid,Wolfgang (vib) | Wheeler,Kenny (tp) | Lauer,Christof (ts) | Kühn,Joachim (p) | Danielsson,Palle (b) | Hart,Billy (dr)
Ray Pizzi Trio
Baiao Kathrin
München, rec. 22.10.1991
Pizzi,Ray (ss) | Lackerschmid,Wolfgang (vib,perc) | Stock,Christian (b)
Wolfgang Lackerschmid Quartet
One More Life | Bad Party | Schneeballschlacht | Ten-Sion
München, rec. 2.2.1992
Lackerschmid,Wolfgang (vib) | Leviev,Milcho (p) | Sieverts,Henning (b) | Elgart,Billy (dr)
No Greater Lunch
Karlsruhe, rec. 27.8.1992
Lackerschmid,Wolfgang (vib) | Johnston,Donald (p) | Knauer,Rocky (b) | Elgart,Billy (dr)

BR 31 | CD | New Singers-New Songs | EAN 4042064000899
Wolfgang Lackerschmid-Donald Johnston Group
Watch You Sleepin' | There's No Forgetting You
Brooklyn,NY, rec. August 1993
Lackerschmid,Wolfgang (vib,perc) | Feldman,Lawrence (fl,ss,ts) | Johnston,Donald (p) | McClure,Ron (b) | Hirshfield,Jeff (dr) | White,Lillias (voc)
Chet's Ballad
Lackerschmid,Wolfgang (vib,perc) | Feldman,Lawrence (fl,ss,as) | Johnston,Donald (p) | Konitz,Lee (as) | McClure,Ron (b) | Hirshfield,Jeff (dr) | White,Lillias (voc)
One More Life
Lackerschmid,Wolfgang (vib,perc) | Feldman,Lawrence (fl,ss,ts) | Johnston,Donald (p) | McClure,Ron (b) | Hirshfield,Jeff (dr) | Bey,Ronnell (voc)
I Don't Need Anymore | Looking At You
Lackerschmid,Wolfgang (vib,perc) | Feldman,Lawrence (fl,ss,ts) | Johnston,Donald (p) | Wilkins,Jack (g) | McClure,Ron (b) | Hirshfield,Jeff (dr) | Bey,Ronnell (voc)
Fly Away
Lackerschmid,Wolfgang (vib,perc) | Feldman,Lawrence (fl,ss,ts) | Johnston,Donald (p) | Wilkins,Jack (g) | McClure,Ron (b) | Hirshfield,Jeff (dr) | Carmello,Carolee (voc)
Welcome Back
Feldman,Lawrence (fl,ss,ts) | Lackerschmid,Wolfgang (vib,perc) | Johnston,Donald (p) | McClure,Ron (b) | Hirshfield,Jeff (dr) | Carmello,Carolee (voc)
When It's Time
Lackerschmid,Wolfgang (vib,perc) | Feldman,Lawrence (fl,ss,ts) | Zoller,Attila (g) | Johnston,Donald (p) | McClure,Ron (b) | Hirshfield,Jeff (dr) | Carmello,Carolee (voc)
Can't Make You Stay | August Morning | I Hear You
Lackerschmid,Wolfgang (vib,perc) | Feldman,Lawrence (fl,ss,ts) | Johnston,Donald (p) | McClure,Ron (b) | Hirshfield,Jeff (dr) | Ross,Holli (voc)

BR 33 | CD | Mallet Connection | EAN 4042064000912
Wolfgang Lackerschmid Group
Relaxin' Rain | Miss 'B' | Mystery Movie | Olenka | Balzwaltz
Stuttgart, rec. October 1977
Lackerschmid,Wolfgang (vib) | Joos,Herbert (tp,fl-h,alto-h) | Zadlo,Leszek (fl,sax) | Knauer,Rocky (b) | Stefanski,Janusz (dr)
Dieter Bihlmaier Selection
Kosmuus | Schmetterlinge(dedicated to Gerhard Ziegler)
Stuttgart, rec. 27.11.1976
Bihlmaier,Dieter (fl) | Lackerschmid,Wolfgang (vib) | Lauer,Wolfgang (b) | Ziegler,Gerhart (dr)

BR 43 | CD | You Are Here | EAN 4042064000936
Wolfgang Lackerschmid & Lynne Arriale Trio
There Is No Greater Love- | No Greater Lunch- | The Dove | Sarah's Bande | Calypso | Who T.F. Is Calling | Why Shouldn't You Cry | One More Life
Live at 'Alte Paketpost',Rottweil, rec. 19.11.1999
Lackerschmid,Wolfgang (vib) | Arriale,Lynne (p) | Sharfe,Mike (b) | Davis,Steve (dr)

Birth | Birth Records

0017 | LP | Journey To The Song Within
Gunter Hampel And His Galaxie Dream Band
Bolero (No.139-part 1) | Bolero (No.139-part 2) | Waltz For 11 Universes In A Corridor (No.57) | Spiral (No.125) | Waiting (No.161)
NYC, rec. 12.2.1974
Hampel,Gunter (b-cl,vib,p) | Robinson,Perry (cl) | Whitecage,Mark (fl,cl,as) | Praskin,Allan (fl,cl,as) | Keyserling,Thomas (fl,ts) | Cook,Marty (tb) | Wolf,John (tb) | Gregg,Jack (b) | Murray,Sunny (dr) | Lee,Jeanne (voice) | Kline,Jonathan (v)

0025 | LP | Enfant Terrible
Don't Fall Around Much Anymore(take 1) | Morning Bird Call | Touches | Yes Earth | Purple Skies | Metanois | Don't Fall Around Much Anymore(take 2)
rec. 23.9.1975
Hampel,Gunter (fl,b-cl,vib,p) | Braxton,Anthony (fl,cl,contra-b-cl,ss,as) | Robinson,Perry (cl) | Whitecage,Mark (fl,alto-cl,as) | Keyserling,Thomas (fl,ts) | Gregg,Jack (b) | Bues,Martin (dr) | Lee,Jeanne (voice)

0027 | LP | Live At The Berlin Jazzfestival 1978
Larry's Delight | That Came Down On Me | Your Ballad | Don't Fall Around Much Anymore
Live at Berliner Jazztage, rec. 5.11.1978
Hampel,Gunter (fl,b-cl,vib,arr) | Robinson,Perry (cl) | Whitecage,Mark (fl,as) | Bues,Martin (dr) | Lee,Jeanne (voice)

0028 | LP | All Is Real
While You Think Keep An Eye On Your Thoughts | Hope | All Is Real
rec. 18.11.1978
Hampel,Gunter (fl,b-cl,ts,vib) | Robinson,Perry (cl) | Whitecage,Mark (fl,alto-cl,as) | Keyserling,Thomas (fl,as) | Bues,Martin (dr,perc) | Lee,Jeanne (voice)

0038 | LP | Jubilation
CD 038 | CD | Jubilation
Gunter Hampel All Stars
Waiting | Little Bird | Waltz For Universes In A Corridor | Loughin' To Keep From Cryin' | Turbulence | Spielplatz
Ludwigsburg, rec. 8.11.1983
Hampel,Gunter (b-cl,bs,vib) | Schoof,Manfred (tp) | Mangelsdorff,Albert (tb) | Robinson,Perry (cl) | Brown,Marion (as) | Keyserling,Thomas (fl,alto-fl,as) | Phillips,Barre (b) | McCall,Steve (dr) | Lee,Jeanne (voice)

008 | LP | Familie
Gunter Hampel Group
Familie(part 1) | Familie(part 2)
rec. 1.4.1972
Hampel,Gunter (fl,b-cl,ss,vib) | Braxton,Anthony (fl,cl,contra-b-cl,as,sopranino-sax) | Lee,Jeanne (voice)

CD 001 | CD | The 8th Of July 1969
001 | 2 LP | The 8th Of July 1969
The 8th Of July 1969 | We Move(take 2) | We Move(take 3) | We Move(take 1) | Morning Song | Crepuscule
Nederhorst den Berg,Holland, rec. 8.7.1969
Hampel,Gunter (b-cl,vib,p) | Braxton,Anthony (contra-b-cl,ss,as) | Breuker,Willem (b-cl,ss,as,ts) | Gorter,Arjen (b,b-g) | McCall,Steve (dr) | Lee,Jeanne (voice)

CD 031 | CD | All The Things You Could Be If Charles Mingus Was Your Daddy
Gunter Hampel And His Galaxie Dream Band
While You Think Keep An Eye On Your Thoughts | All The Things You Could Be If Charles Mingus Was Your Daddy
Live at Zuckerfabrik,Stuttgart, rec. 18.11.1978
Hampel,Gunter (fl,b-cl,bs) | Robinson,Perry (cl) | Whitecage,Mark (fl,as) | Keyserling,Thomas (fl,as) | Bues,Martin (dr,perc) | Lee,Jeanne (voice)
All Is Real
Live at Goethe Institut,Göttingen, rec. 7.7.1980
Hampel,Gunter (fl,b-cl,bs) | Robinson,Perry (cl) | Whitecage,Mark (fl,as) | Keyserling,Thomas (fl,as) | Bues,Martin (dr,perc) | Lee,Jeanne (voice)

CD 037 | CD | Gemini
Marion Brown-Gunter Hampel Duo
Gemini | Horizon | Turbulence | Serenade For Marion Brown | Ask Me Now | New York Sunday Afternoon | Funky Get Down
Ludwigsburg, rec. 13.6.1983
Brown,Marion (as) | Hampel,Gunter (b-cl,vib)
Lights On A Satelite | Enlightenment | Spontaneous Simplicity | Information
Live at Dresden/Erfurt, rec. 17./18.6.1993
Brown,Marion (as) | Hampel,Gunter (b-cl,vib)

CD 039 | CD | Fresh Heat-Live At Sweet Basil
0039 | LP | Fresh Heat-Live At Sweet Basil
Gunter Hampel New York Orchestra
Sweet Basil | 211 E 11 Street | Lichtung(Clearing) | Hawkeye | Waiting
Live at Sweet Basil, NYC, rec. 4.2.1985
Hampel,Gunter (fl,bs,vib,arr,comp) | Haynes,Stephen (tp) | Provey,Vance R. (tp) | Fowlkes,Curtis (tb) | Stewart,Robert 'Bob' (tuba) | Robinson,Perry (cl) | Whitecage,Mark (fl,as) | Keyserling,Thomas (fl,as) | Hanlon,Bob (fl,ts) | Ennett,Lucky (ts) | Frisell,Bill (g) | Fujiwara,Kiyoto (b) | Smith,Marvin 'Smitty' (dr) | Lee,Jeanne (voice) | Jenkins,Arthur (voice)

CD 040 | CD | Celestial Glory-Live At The Knitting Factory New York
Gunter Hampel And His Galaxie Dream Band
By All Means | Are You Phoenix? | As If It Were A Bridge
Live at Knitting Factory,NYC, rec. 2.9.1991
Hampel,Gunter (b-cl,vib,lyrics) | Robinson,Perry (cl) | Whitecage,Mark (ss,as) | Keyserling,Thomas (fl,as) | Lee,Jeanne (voc)

CD 041 | CD | Dialog-Live At The Eldena Jazz Festival 1992
Gunter Hampel-Matthias Schubert Duo
Spielplatz | Her He's World | Bar Blues | After The Fact
Live at Eldena Jazz Festival, rec. 4.7.1992
Hampel,Gunter (b-cl,vib) | Schubert,Matthias (ts)

CD 042 | CD | Time Is Now-Live At The Eldena Jazz Festival 1992
Gunter Hampel Quartet
People | Time Is Now | Serenade For Marion Brown | That Came Down On Me | Song For My Father | Funky Get Down
Live at Eldena Jazz Festival, rec. 3.7.1992
Hampel,Gunter (fl,b-cl,vib,arr,voice) | Dietz,Mike (g) | Attig,Jürgen (b) | Köbberling,Heinrich (dr)

CD 043 | CD | Next Generation
Gunter Hampel Next Generation
You're In Charge | Iron Fist And Velvet Gloves | I Feel Your Vibes | Paradise Of The Have's And Hell Of The Have Not's | As If It Were A Bridge | Daddy's Rap | Perception | True Love | See What I Mean | Killing Time,Till Time Kills Me | I Like To See You More Around In My Life
Hannover, rec. 9.9.1995
Hampel,Gunter (b-cl,vib,lyrics) | Weidner,Christian (as,ts) | Dietz,Mike (g) | Busse,Christoph (keyboards) | Feger,Fritz (b) | Verhovec,Michael (dr) | Vargas,Shaun (voice) | Stüdemann,Barbara (voice) | Ruomi (rap,recitation) | Spax (rap) | One Soul (rap)

CD 044 | CD | Solid Fun
Gunter Hampel-Christian Weider Duo
Faces Around | More Power To You | Guch | Solid Fun | Relax | Culture Of One | Charlie Parker Place
Live at Auerbach Jazznight, rec. 9.9.1995
Hampel,Gunter (b-cl,vib) | Weidner,Christian (as,ts)
Love For Two
Live at L+L Festival,Göttingen, rec. 4.1.1996
Hampel,Gunter (b-cl,vib) | Weidner,Christian (as,ts)

CD 045 | CD | Legendary: The 27th Of May 1997
Gunter Hampel Quintet
Legendary | Spielplatz | All The Things You Could Be If Charles Mingus Was Your Daddy
Live at Stadtgarten,Köln, rec. 27.5.1997
Hampel,Gunter (fl,b-cl,vib) | Schoof,Manfred (tp,fl-h) | Von Schlippenbach,Alexander (p) | Gorter,Arjen (b) | Courbois,Pierre (dr)

CD 047 | CD | Köln Concert Part 1
Gunter Hampel Next Generation
You Ever Saw Birds Gather And Lift Off? | You Don't Want To Live? | Jazz Life | Think,Think,Think
Live at Music Triennale,Stadtgarten,Köln, rec. 28.5.1997
Hampel,Gunter (b-cl,vib) | Weidner,Christian (as) | Orth,Clemens (p) | Jaroslawski,Christian (b) | Juhnke,Gerrit (dr)

CD 048 | CD | Köln Concert Part 2
Paradiso | Bridges | Sun Down | Thinking Good,Thinking Bad
Hampel,Gunter (b-cl,vib) | Weidner,Christian (as) | Orth,Clemens (p) | Jaroslawski,Christian (b) | Juhnke,Gerrit (dr)

CD 049 | CD | Gunter Hampel: The 8th Of Sept.1999
Gunter Hampel Jazz Sextet
Who's Controlling Whom? | How Late Is It In Your Life? | Foreward To The Past | Preface(II) | Catering | Truth(II)
NYC, rec. 8.9.1999
Hampel,Gunter (vib) | Wogram,Nils (tb) | Weidner,Christian (as) | Orth,Clemens (p) | Roland,Larry (b) | Sadiq (dr)
Truth
Live at Knitting Factory,NYC, rec. 4.9.1999
Hampel,Gunter (vib) | Wogram,Nils (tb) | Weidner,Christian (as) | Orth,Clemens (p) | Roland,Larry (b) | Sadiq (dr)
Gunter Hampel-Nils Wogram
Preface
NYC, rec. 8.9.1999
Hampel,Gunter (vib) | Wogram,Nils (tb)
Gunter Hampel-Christian Welder
Preface To Truth
Hampel,Gunter (vib) | Weidner,Christian (as)

Blue Note | EMI Germany

0675597 | CD | Davis Cup | EAN 4988006755970
Walter Davis Quintet
Minor Mind | 'S Make It | Loodle-Lot | Millie's Delight | Rhumba Numba | Sweetness
Englewood Cliffs,NJ, rec. 2.8.1959
Davis Jr.,Walter (p) | Byrd,Donald (tp) | McLean,Jackie (as) | Jones,Sam (b) | Taylor,Arthur 'Art' (dr)

0675614 | CD | Along Came John | EAN 4988006756144
John Patton Quintet
The Silver Meter | Spiffy Diffy | Gee Gee | Along Came John | Pigfoot | I'll Never Be Free
Englewood Cliffs,NJ, rec. 5.4.1963
Patton,Big John (org) | Jackson,Fred (ts) | Vick,Harold (ts) | Green,Grant (g) | Dixon,Ben (dr)

0675619 | CD | Afro-Cuban
Kenny Dorham Octet
Afrodisia | Lotus Flower | Minor's Holiday | Basheer's Dream
NYC, rec. 29.3.1955
Dorham,Kenny (tp) | Johnson,J.J. (tb) | Mobley,Hank (ts) | Payne,Cecil (bs) | Silver,Horace (p) | Pettiford,Oscar (b) | Blakey,Art (dr) | Valdez,Carlos 'Patato' (congas)
K.D.'s Motion | The Villa | Venita's Dance
NYC, rec. 29.1.1955
Dorham,Kenny (tp) | Mobley,Hank (ts) | Payne,Cecil (bs) | Silver,Horace (p) | Heath,Percy (b) | Blakey,Art (dr)

0675621 | CD | Dial S For Sonny | EAN 4988006756212
Sonny Clark All Stars
Dial S For Sonny | Bootin' It | It Could Happen To You | Sonny's Mood | Shouting On A Riff
NYC, rec. 21.7.1957
Clark,Sonny (p) | Farmer,Art (tp) | Fuller,Curtis (tb) | Mobley,Hank (ts) | Ware,Wilbur (b) | Hayes,Louis (dr)
Sonny Clark Trio
Love Walked In
Clark,Sonny (p) | Ware,Wilbur (b) | Hayes,Louis (dr)

0675622 | CD | Hank Mobley
Hank Mobley Quintet
Funk In Deep Freeze | Wham And They're Off | Fin Dé L'Affaire | Startin' From Scratch | Stella-Wise | Base On Balls
NYC, rec. 9.3.1957
Mobley,Hank (ts) | Farmer,Art (tp) | Silver,Horace (p) | Watkins,Doug (b) | Blakey,Art (dr)

0675629 | CD | Bottoms Up | EAN 49880067562298
The Three Sounds
Soft Winds | Nothing Ever Changes For You My Love | Besame Mucho | Jenny Lou | I Could Write A Book | Love Walked In | Let's Love | It Could Happen To You
Hackensack,NJ, rec. 11.2.1959
Three Sounds,The | Harris,Gene (p) | Simpkins,Andrew (b) | Dowdy,Bill (dr)

0677179 | CD | Jutta Hipp At The Hickory House Vol.2 | EAN 4988006771796
Jutta Hipp Trio
Gone With The Wind | After Hours | The Squirrel | We'll Be Together Again | Horacio | I Married An Angel | Moonlight In Vermont | Star Eyes | If I Had You | My Heart Stood Still
Hickory House,NYC, rec. 5.4.1956
Hipp,Jutta (p) | Ind,Peter (b) | Thigpen,Ed (dr)

0677187 | CD | Movin' And Groovin' | EAN 4988006771871
Horace Parlan Trio
Bag's Groove | Stella By Starlight | There Is No Greater Love | On Green Dolphin Street | C Jam Blues | Up In Cynthia's Room | Lady Bird | It Could Happen To You
Englewood Cliffs,NJ, rec. 29.2.1960
Parlan,Horace (p) | Jones,Sam (b) | Harewood,Al (dr)

0677191 | CD | A Blowing Session | EAN 4988006771918
Johnny Griffin Septet
All The Things You Are | Ball Bearings | Smoke Stack | The Way You Look Tonight | Smoke Stack(alt.take)
Englewood Cliffs,NJ, rec. 8.4.1957
Griffin,Johnny (ts) | Morgan,Lee (tp) | Coltrane,John (ts) | Mobley,Hank (ts) | Kelly,Wynton (p) | Chambers,Paul (b) | Blakey,Art (dr)

0677207 | CD | The Fabulous Fats Navarro Vol.1 | EAN 4988006772976
Tadd Dameron Sextet
The Chase | The Chase(alt.master) | The Squirrel | The Squirrel(alt.master) | Our Delight | Our Delight(alt.master) | Dameronia | Dameronia(alt.master)
NYC, rec. 26.9.1947
Dameron,Tadd (p) | Navarro,Fats (tp) | Henry,Ernie (as) | Rouse,Charlie (ts) | Boyd,Nelson (b) | Wilson,Shadow (dr)
Bud Powell's Modernists
Wail(alt.master) | Bouncing With Bud(alt.master)
NYC, rec. 8.8.1949
Powell,Bud (p) | Navarro,Fats (tp) | Rollins,Sonny (ts) | Potter,Tommy (b) | Haynes,Roy (dr)
The McGhee-Navarro Boptet
Double Talk
NYC, rec. 11.10.1948
Navarro,Fats (tp) | McGhee,Howard (tp) | Henry,Ernie (as) | Jackson,Milt (vib,p) | Russell,Curly (b) | Clarke,Kenny (dr)

0677208 | CD | The Fabulous Fats Navarro Vol.2 | EAN 4988006772083
Tadd Dameron Septet
Lady Bird | Lady Bird(alt.master) | Jahbero | Jahbero(alt.master) | Symphonette | Symphonette(alt.master)
NYC, rec. 13.9.1948
Dameron,Tadd (p) | Navarro,Fats (tp) | Gray,Wardell (ts) | Eager,Allen (ts) | Russell,Curly (b) | Clarke,Kenny (dr) | Pozo,Chino (bongos)
The McGhee-Navarro Boptet
Double Talk(alt.master) | The Skunk(alt.master) | Boperation
NYC, rec. 11.10.1948
Navarro,Fats (tp) | McGhee,Howard (tp) | Henry,Ernie (as) | Jackson,Milt (vib,p) | Russell,Curly (b) | Clarke,Kenny (dr)
Bud Powell's Modernists
Bouncing With Bud(alt.master) | Dance Of The Infidels(alt.master)
NYC, rec. 8.8.1949
Powell,Bud (p) | Navarro,Fats (tp) | Rollins,Sonny (ts) | Potter,Tommy (b) | Haynes,Roy (dr)

0677212 | CD | Preach Brother! | EAN 4988006772120
Don Wilkerson Quintet
Jeanie-Weenie | Homesick Blues | Dem Tambourines | Camp Meeting | The Eldorado Shuffle | Pigeon Peas
NYC, rec. 18.6.1962
Wilkerson,Don (ts,voc) | Green,Grant (g) | Clark,Sonny (p) | Warren,Edward 'Butch' (b) | Higgins,Billy (dr,tambourines)

493072-2 | CD | Best Of Blakey 60
Art Blakey And The Jazz Messengers
Dat Dere | It's Only A Paper Moon
NYC, rec. 6.3.1960
Blakey,Art (dr) | Morgan,Lee (tp) | Shorter,Wayne (ts) | Timmons,Bobby (p) | Merritt,Jymie (b)
Giantis

Englewood Cliffs,NJ, rec. 7.8.1960
Blakey,Art (dr) | Morgan,Lee (tp) | Shorter,Wayne (ts) | Timmons,Bobby (p) | Merritt,Jymie (b)
A Night In Tunisia | So Tired
Englewood Cliffs,NJ, rec. 14.8.1960
Blakey,Art (dr) | Morgan,Lee (tp) | Shorter,Wayne (ts) | Timmons,Bobby (p) | Merritt,Jymie (b)
Ping Pong
NYC, rec. 18.2.1961
Blakey,Art (dr) | Morgan,Lee (tp) | Shorter,Wayne (ts) | Timmons,Bobby (p) | Merritt,Jymie (b)
Witchdoctor | Afrique | A Little Busy
NYC, rec. 14.3.1961
Blakey,Art (dr) | Morgan,Lee (tp) | Shorter,Wayne (ts) | Timmons,Bobby (p) | Merritt,Jymie (b)
Art Blakey
The Freedom Rider (Drum Solo)
NYC, rec. 27.5.1961
Blakey,Art (dr-solo)

493155-2 | CD | Sunset And The Mockingbird-The Birthday Concert
Tommy Flanagan Trio
Bird Song | With Malice Towards None | Let's | I Waited For You | Tin Tin Deo | Sunset And The Mocking Birds | The Balanced Scales- | The Cup Bearers- | Goodnight My Love
Live at The 'Village Vanguard',NYC, rec. 16.3.1997
Flanagan,Tommy (p) | Washington,Peter (b) | Nash,Lewis (dr)

493381-2 | CD | Live At The Lighthouse
Grant Green Septet
Introduction by Hank Stewart | Windjammer | Betcha By Golly Wow | Fancy Free | Flood In Franklyn Park | Jan Jan | Walk In The Night
Live at The Lighthouse,Hermosa Beach,CA, rec. 21.4.1972
Green,Grant (g) | Bartee,Claude (ss,ts) | Coleman,Gary (vib) | Laster,Shelton (org) | Felder,Wilton (el-b) | Williams,Greg (dr) | Hall,Bobbye Porter (congas)

493384-2 | CD | Asante | EAN 0724349338425
McCoy Tyner Sextet
Forbidden Land | Asian Lullaby | Hope
Englewood Cliffs,NJ, rec. 21.7.1970
Tyner,McCoy (p) | Laws,Hubert (fl,alto-fl) | Bartz,Gary (ss,as) | White,Andrew (oboe) | Lewis,Herbie (b) | Waits,Freddie (dr)
McCoy Tyner Quintet
Malika | Asante | Goin' Home | Fulfilment
Englewood Cliffs,NJ, rec. 10.9.1970
Tyner,McCoy (p) | White,Andrew (as) | Williams,Buster (b) | Hart,Billy (dr) | M'tume,James[Forman] (congas) | Songai (voc)

493401-2 | CD | The Last Sessin
Lee Morgan Orchestra
Capra Black | In What Direction Are You Headed | Angela | Croquet Ballet | Inner Passions-Out
Englewood Cliffs,NJ, rec. 17./18.9.1971
Morgan,Lee (tp,fl-h) | Humphrey,Bobbi (fl) | Harper,Billy (fl,ts) | Moncur III,Grachan (tb) | Mabern,Harold (p,el-p) | Merritt,Jymie (el-b) | Workman,Reggie (b,perc) | Waits,Freddie (dr,recorder)

493543-2 | CD | This Time Its Love
Kurt Elling Group
Too Young To Go Steady
Chicago,Ill, rec. December 1997-January 1998
Elling,Kurt (voc) | Johnson,Eddie (ts) | Hobgood,Laurence (p) | Amster,Rob (b) | Raynor,Michael 'Mike' (dr,perc)
I Feel So Smoochie
Elling,Kurt (voc) | Frigo,John (v) | Onderdonk,Dave (g) | Hobgood,Laurence (p) | Amster,Rob (b) | Raynor,Michael 'Mike' (dr,perc)
Where I Belong | A Time For Love
Elling,Kurt (voc) | Onderdonk,Dave (g) | Hobgood,Laurence (p) | Amster,Rob (b) | Wertico,Paul (dr)
Rosa Morena
Elling,Kurt (voc) | Onderdonk,Dave (g) | Amster,Rob (b) | Raynor,Michael 'Mike' (dr,perc)
My Foolish Heart | Freddie's Yen For Jen | My Love,Effendi | The Very Thought Of You | The Best Things Happen While You're Dancing
Elling,Kurt (voc) | Hobgood,Laurence (p) | Amster,Rob (b) | Raynor,Michael 'Mike' (dr,perc)
She's Funny That Way | Every Time We Say Goodbye
Elling,Kurt (voc) | Hobgood,Laurence (p)

493916-2 | CD | The Dawn
Erik Truffaz Quartet
Bukowsky-Chapter 1 | Yuri's Choice | The Dawn | Wet In Paris | Slim Pickings | Round-Trip | The Mask | Free Stylin'
Lausanne,CH, rec. 29.-31.12.1997
Truffaz,Erik (tp) | Muller,Patrick (p,el-p) | Giuliani,Marcello (b,el-b) | Erbetta,Marc (dr,perc) | Nya (voc)

494104-2 | CD | Nemmy Golson And The Philadelphians
Benny Golson Quintet
You're Not The Kind | Blues On My Mind | Stablemates | Thursday's Theme | Afternoon In Paris | Calgary
NYC, rec. 17.11.1958
Golson,Benny (ts) | Morgan,Lee (tp) | Bryant,Ray (p) | Heath,Percy (b) | Jones,Philly Joe (dr)
Blues March | I Remember Clifford | Moanin' | Stablemates(alt.take)
Paris,France, rec. 12.12.1958
Golson,Benny (ts) | Guerin,Roger (tp) | Timmons,Bobby (p) | Michelot,Pierre (b) | Garros,Christian (dr)

494105-2 | CD | Jazz Alive:A Night At The Half Note
Zoot Sims-Al Cohn Quintet
Lover Come Back To Me | It Had To Be You
Live at The Half Note Cafe,NYC, rec. 6.2.1959
Sims,Zoot (ts) | Cohn,Al (ts) | Allison,Mose (p) | Totah,Nabil 'Knobby' (b) | Motian,Paul (dr)
Zoot Sims-Al Cohn-Phil Woods Sextet
Wee Dot | After You've Gone
Live at The Half Note Cafe,NYC, rec. 7.2.1959
Woods,Phil (as) | Sims,Zoot (ts) | Cohn,Al (ts) | Allison,Mose (p) | Totah,Nabil 'Knobby' (b) | Motian,Paul (dr)

494107-2 | CD | Love For Sale
Cecil Taylor Trio
Get Out Of Town | I Love Paris | Love For Sale
NYC, rec. 15.4.1959
Taylor,Cecil (p) | Neidlinger,Buell (b) | Charles,Dennis (dr)
Cecil Taylor Quintet
Little Lees | Matie's Trophies(Motystrophe) | Carol- | Three Points-
Taylor,Cecil (p) | Curson,Ted (tp) | Barron,Bill (ts) | Neidlinger,Buell (b) | Charles,Dennis (dr)

494705-2 | CD | Grant Green:Blue Breakbeat
Grant Green Orchestra
Ain't It Funky Now | The Windjammer
NYC, rec. 30.1.1970
Green,Grant (g) | Mitchell,Blue (tp) | Bartee,Claude (ts) | Riggins,Emmanuel (org) | Lewis,Jimmy (b) | Muhammad,Idris[Leo Morris] (dr) | Candido[Camero] (congas) | Landrum,Richard 'Pablo' (bongos)
Grant Green Sextet
Ease Back
NYC, rec. 12.6.1970
Green,Grant (g) | Bartee,Claude (ts) | Bivens,William 'Yam' (vib) | Palmer,Clarence (el-p) | Lewis,Jimmy (el-b) | Muhammad,Idris[Leo Morris] (dr)
Sookie, Sookie
NYC, rec. 15.8.1970
Green,Grant (g) | Bartee,Claude (ts) | Bivens,William 'Yam' (vib) | Foster,Ronnie (org) | Muhammad,Idris[Leo Morris] (dr) | Armstrong,Joseph (congas)
Cantaloupe Woman
NYC, rec. 21.5.1971
Green,Grant (g) | Riggins,Emmanuel (el-p) | Wooten,Billy (vib) | Rainey,Chuck (el-b) | Muhammad,Idris[Leo Morris] (dr) | Armando,Ray (congas)
Grant Green Orchestra
The Final Comedown
NYC, rec. 13.12.1971
Green,Grant (g) | Stamm,Marvin (tp) | Markowitz,Irving 'Marky' (tp) | Vick,Harold (ss) | Bodner,Phil (reeds) | Tee,Richard (keyboards) | Dupree,Cornell (g) | Edwards,Gordon (b-g) | Tate,Grady (dr) | McDonald,Ralph (perc)

495104-2 | CD | Dark Grooves-Mystcal Rhythms
James Hurt Group
Waterfall
NYC, rec. 10.5.1997
Hurt,James (p,perc) | Hart,Antonio Maurice (as) | Burton,Abraham (as) | Schwartz-Bart,Jacques (ts) | Revis,Eric (b) | Hoenig,Ari (dr) | Kantumanou,Elizabeth (voc)
Pyramid
Hurt,James (p) | Hart,Antonio Maurice (as) | Revis,Eric (b) | Waits,Nasheet (dr)
Venus
Hurt,James (p) | Gunn,Russell (tp) | Eubanks,Robin (tb) | Irby,Sherman (as) | Tardy,Greg (ts) | Revis,Eric (b) | Murray,Dana (dr)
Eleven Dreams
NYC, rec. 1.2.1999
Hurt,James (p) | Moutin,Francois (b)
Faith | Orion's View | Neptune
Hurt,James (p) | Moutin,Francois (b) | Hoenig,Ari (dr)
The Tree Of Live | Mars | Jupiter | Sun Day | Dark Nines
Hurt,James (p) | Schwartz-Bart,Jacques (ts) | Moutin,Francois (b) | Hoenig,Ari (dr)

495324-2 | CD | Moanin'
Art Blakey And The Jazz Messengers
Warm-Up And Dialogue Between Lee And Rudy | Moanin' | Are You Real | Along Came Betty | The Drum Thunder (Miniature) Suite: | Drum Thunder- | Cry A Blue Tear- | Harlem's Disciples- | Blues March | Come Rain Or Come Shine | Moanin'(alt.take)
Hackensack,NJ, rec. 30.10.1958
Blakey,Art (dr) | Morgan,Lee (tp) | Golson,Benny (ts) | Timmons,Bobby (p) | Merritt,Jymie (b)

495327-2 | CD | Cool Struttin'
Sonny Clark Quintet
Cool Struttin' | Blue Minor | Sippin' At Bells | Deep Night | Royal Flush | Lover
Hackensack,NJ, rec. 5.1.1958
Clark,Sonny (p) | Farmer,Art (tp) | McLean,Jackie (as) | Chambers,Paul (b) | Jones,Philly Joe (dr)

495329-2 | CD | Somethin' Else | EAN 0724349532922
Cannonball Adderley Quintet
Autumn Leaves | Love For Sale | Somethin' Else | One For Daddy-O | Dancing In The Dark
NYC, rec. 9.3.1958
Adderley,Julian \'Cannonball\' (as) | Davis,Miles (tp) | Jones,Hank (p) | Jones,Sam (b) | Blakey,Art (dr)

495331-2 | CD | Maiden Voyage
Herbie Hancock Quintet
Maiden Voyage | The Eye Of The Hurricane | Little One | Survival Of The Fittest | Dolphin Dance
Englewood Cliffs,NJ, rec. 17.3.1965
Hancock,Herbie (p) | Hubbard,Freddie (tp) | Coleman,George (ts) | Carter,Ron (b) | Williams,Tony (dr)

495332-2 | CD | The Sidewinder
Lee Morgan Quintet
The Sidewinder | Totem Pole | Gary's Notebook | Boy What A Night | Hocus-Pocus | Totem Pole(alt.take)
Englewood Cliffs,NJ, rec. 21.12.1963
Morgan,Lee (tp) | Henderson,Joe (ts) | Harris,Barry (p) | Cranshaw,Bob (b) | Higgins,Billy (dr)

495335-2 | CD | Midnight Blue
Kenny Burrell Quintet
Chittlins Con Carne | Mule | Soul Lament | Midnight Blue | Wavy Gravy | Gee Baby Ain't I Good To You | Saturday Night Blues | Kenny's Sound | K Twist
Englewood Cliffs,NJ, rec. 21.4.1967
Burrell,Kenny (g) | Turrentine,Stanley (ts) | Holley,Major (b) | English,Bill (dr) | Barretto,Ray (congas)

495341-2 | CD | Open Sesame
Freddie Hubbard Quintet
Open Sesame | But Beautiful | Gypsy Blue | All Or Nothing At All | One Mint Julep | Hub's Nub | Open Sesame(alt.take) | Gypsy Blue(alt.take)
Englewood Cliffs,NJ, rec. 19.6.1960
Hubbard,Freddie (tp) | Brooks,Tina (ts) | Tyner,McCoy (p) | Jones,Sam (b) | Jarvis,Clifford (dr)

495342-2 | CD | Blowin' The Blues Away
Horace Silver Quintet
Blowin' The Blues Away | The Bagdad Blues
Englewood Cliffs,NJ, rec. 29.8.1959
Silver,Horace (p) | Mitchell,Blue (tp) | Cook,Junior (ts) | Taylor,Gene (b) | Hayes,Louis (dr)
Break City | Peace | Sister Sadie | How Did It Happen
Englewood Cliffs,NJ, rec. 30.8.1959
Silver,Horace (p) | Mitchell,Blue (tp) | Cook,Junior (ts) | Taylor,Gene (b) | Hayes,Louis (dr)
The St.Vitus Dance | Melancholy Mood
Englewood Cliffs,NJ, rec. 13.9.1959
Silver,Horace (p) | Mitchell,Blue (tp) | Cook,Junior (ts) | Taylor,Gene (b) | Hayes,Louis (dr)

495343-2 | CD | Soul Station
Hank Mobley Quartet
Remember | This I Dig Of You | Dig Dis | Split Feelin's | Soul Station | If I Should Lose You
Englewood Cliffs,NJ, rec. 7.2.1960
Mobley,Hank (ts) | Kelly,Wynton (p) | Chambers,Paul (b) | Blakey,Art (dr)

495447-2 | CD | Them Dirty Blues | EAN 72439544737
Cannonball Adderley Quintet
Del Sasser | Dat Dere | Soon | Dat Dere(alt.take)
NYC, rec. 1.2.1960
Adderley,Julian \'Cannonball\' (as) | Adderley,Nat (co) | Timmons,Bobby (p) | Jones,Sam (b) | Hayes,Louis (dr)
Work Song | Easy Living | Jeanine | Them Dirty Blues | Work Song(alt take)
Chicago,Ill, rec. 29.3.1960
Adderley,Julian \'Cannonball\' (as) | Adderley,Nat (co) | Harris,Barry (p) | Jones,Sam (b) | Hayes,Louis (dr)

495569-2 | 6 CD | Herbie Hancock:The Complete Blue Note Sixties Sessions
Donald Byrd Quintet
Three Wishes
Englewood Cliffs,NJ, rec. 11.12.1961
Byrd,Donald (tp) | Shorter,Wayne (ts) | Hancock,Herbie (p) | Warren,Edward 'Butch' (b) | Higgins,Billy (dr)
Herbie Hancock Quintet
Empty Pockets | Empty Pockets(alt.take) | Three Bags Full | Three Bags Full(alt.take) | Watermelon Man | Watermelon Man(alt.take) | The Maze | Driftin' | Alone And I
Englewood Cliffs,NJ, rec. 28.5.1962
Hancock,Herbie (p) | Hubbard,Freddie (tp,fl-h) | Gordon,Dexter (ts) | Warren,Edward 'Butch' (b) | Higgins,Billy (dr)
Jackie McLean Quintet
Yams
Englewood Cliffs,NJ, rec. 11.2.1963
McLean,Jackie (as) | Byrd,Donald (tp) | Hancock,Herbie (p) | Warren,Edward 'Butch' (b) | Williams,Tony (dr)
Herbie Hancock Quintet
A Tribute To Someone
Englewood Cliffs,NJ, rec. 19.3.1963
Hancock,Herbie (p) | Byrd,Donald (tp) | Mobley,Hank (ts) | Israels,Chuck (b) | Williams,Tony (dr)
Herbie Hancock Sextet
King Cobra | The Pleasure Is Mine
Hancock,Herbie (p) | Byrd,Donald (tp) | Moncur III,Grachan (tb) | Mobley,Hank (ts) | Israels,Chuck (b) | Williams,Tony (dr)
Herbie Hancock Septet
Blind Man, Blind Man | Blind Man, Blind Man(alt.take) | And What If I Don't
Hancock,Herbie (p) | Byrd,Donald (tp) | Moncur III,Grachan (tb) | Mobley,Hank (ts) | Green,Grant (g) | Israels,Chuck (b) | Williams,Tony (dr)
Herbie Hancock Quartet
Succotash | Triangle | Mimosa | Mimosa(alt.take) | A Jump Ahead | Jack Rabbit
Englewood Cliffs,NJ, rec. 30.8.1963
Hancock,Herbie (p) | Chambers,Paul (b) | Bobo,Willie (dr,timbales) | Martinez,Osvaldo 'Chihuahua' (congas,bongos)
Oliloqui Valley | One Finger Snap | Cantaloupe Island | The Egg | One Finger Snap(alt.take) | Oliloqui Valley(alt.take)
Englewood Cliffs,NJ, rec. 17.6.1964
Hancock,Herbie (p) | Hubbard,Freddie (co) | Carter,Ron (b) | Williams,Tony (dr)
Herbie Hancock Quintet
Maiden Voyage | The Eye Of The Hurricane | Dolphin Dance | Survival Of The Fittest | Little One
Englewood Cliffs,NJ, rec. 17.5.1965
Hancock,Herbie (p) | Hubbard,Freddie (tp) | Coleman,George (ts) | Carter,Ron (b) | Williams,Tony (dr)
Wayne Shorter Quartet
The Collector
Englewood Cliffs,NJ, rec. 24.2.1966
Shorter,Wayne (ts) | Hancock,Herbie (p) | Workman,Reggie (b) | Chambers,Joe (dr)
Bobby Hutcherson Quartet
Maiden Voyage
Englewood Cliffs,NJ, rec. 8.2.1966
Hutcherson,Bobby (vib) | Hancock,Herbie (p) | Cranshaw,Bob (b) | Chambers,Joe (dr)
Theme From Blow Up
Englewood Cliffs,NJ, rec. 21.7.1966
Hutcherson,Bobby (vib) | Hancock,Herbie (p) | Stinson,Albert (b) | Chambers,Joe (dr)
Herbie Hancock Sextet
Riot | Riot(alt.take 1) | Riot(alt.take 2) | Speak Like A Child
Englewood Cliffs,NJ, rec. 6.3.1968
Hancock,Herbie (p) | Jones,Thad (fl-h) | Phillips,Peter (b-tb) | Dodgion,Jerry (alto-fl) | Carter,Ron (b) | Roker,Granville 'Mickey' (dr)
Herbie Hancock Trio
First Trip
Hancock,Herbie (p) | Carter,Ron (b) | Roker,Granville 'Mickey' (dr)
Herbie Hancock Sextet
Goodbye To Childhood | Goodbye To Childhood(alt.take) | The Sorcerer
Englewood Cliffs,NJ, rec. 9.3.1968
Hancock,Herbie (p) | Jones,Thad (fl-h) | Phillips,Peter (b-tb) | Dodgion,Jerry (alto-fl) | Carter,Ron (b) | Roker,Granville 'Mickey' (dr)
Herbie Hancock Trio
Toys
Hancock,Herbie (p) | Carter,Ron (b) | Roker,Granville 'Mickey' (dr)
Herbie Hancock Orchestra
The Prisoner | The Prisoner(alt.take) | He Who Lives In Fear
Englewood Cliffs,NJ, rec. 18.4.1969
Hancock,Herbie (p,el-p) | Coles,Johnny (fl-h) | Brown,Garnett (tb) | Studd,Tony (b-tb) | Laws,Hubert (fl) | Richardson,Jerome (b-cl) | Henderson,Joe (alto-fl,ts) | Williams,Buster (b) | Heath,Albert 'Tootie' (dr)
I Have A Dream
Englewood Cliffs,NJ, rec. 21.4.1969
Hancock,Herbie (p) | Coles,Johnny (fl-h) | Brown,Garnett (tb) | Studd,Tony (b-tb) | Laws,Hubert (fl) | Richardson,Jerome (b-cl) | Henderson,Joe (alto-fl,ts) | Williams,Buster (b) | Heath,Albert 'Tootie' (dr)
Firewater | Firewater(alt.take) | Promise The Sun
Englewood Cliffs,NJ, rec. 23.4.1969
Hancock,Herbie (p) | Coles,Johnny (fl-h) | Brown,Garnett (tb) | Jeffers,Jack (b-tb) | Richardson,Jerome (fl) | Penque,Romeo (b-cl) | Henderson,Joe (alto-fl,ts) | Williams,Buster (b) | Heath,Albert 'Tootie' (dr)
Herbie Hancock Septet
Don't Even Go There
Englewood Cliffs,NJ, rec. 19.7.1966
Hancock,Herbie (p) | Lastie,Melvin (co) | Turrentine,Stanley (ts) | Gale,Eric (g) | Butler,Billy (g) | Cranshaw,Bob (b) | Purdie,Bernard 'Pretty' (dr)

495576-2 | 4 CD | Horace Silver Retrospective
Horace Silver Trio
Safari
NYC, rec. 9.10.1952
Silver,Horace (p) | Ramey,Gene (b) | Blakey,Art (dr)
Ecaroh
NYC, rec. 20.10.1952
Silver,Horace (p) | Russell,Curly (b) | Blakey,Art (dr)
Opus De Funk
NYC, rec. 23.11.1953
Silver,Horace (p) | Heath,Percy (b) | Blakey,Art (dr)
Art Blakey And The Jazz Messengers
Doodlin'
Hackensack,NJ, rec. 13.12.1954
Blakey,Art (dr) | Dorham,Kenny (tp) | Mobley,Hank (ts) | Silver,Horace (p) | Watkins,Doug (b)
The Preacher
Hackensack,NJ, rec. 6.2.1955
Blakey,Art (dr) | Dorham,Kenny (tp) | Mobley,Hank (ts) | Silver,Horace (p) | Watkins,Doug (b)
Horace Silver Quintet
Cool Eyes | Senor Blues
Hackensack,NJ, rec. 10.11.1956
Silver,Horace (p) | Byrd,Donald (tp) | Mobley,Hank (ts) | Watkins,Doug (b) | Hayes,Louis (dr)
Home Cookin' | Soulville
Hackensack,NJ, rec. 8.5.1957
Silver,Horace (p) | Farmer,Art (tp) | Mobley,Hank (ts) | Kotick,Teddy (b) | Hayes,Louis (dr)
The Outlaw
Hackensack,NJ, rec. 13.1.1958
Silver,Horace (p) | Farmer,Art (tp) | Jordan,Clifford (ts) | Kotick,Teddy (b) | Hayes,Louis (dr)
Bill Henderson With The Horace Silver Quintet
Senor Blues
Hackensack,NJ, rec. 15.6.1958
Silver,Horace (p) | Byrd,Donald (tp) | Cook,Junior (ts) | Taylor,Gene (b) | Hayes,Louis (dr) | Henderson,Bill (voc)
Horace Silver Quintet
Swinging The Samba | Cookin' At The Continental | Juicy Lucy
Hackensack,NJ, rec. 1.2.1959
Silver,Horace (p) | Mitchell,Blue (tp) | Cook,Junior (ts) | Taylor,Gene (b) | Hayes,Louis (dr)
Sister Sadie | Peace | Blowin' The Blues Away
Englewood Cliffs,NJ, rec. 29.8.1959
Silver,Horace (p) | Mitchell,Blue (tp) | Cook,Junior (ts) | Taylor,Gene (b) | Hayes,Louis (dr)
Strollin' | Nica's Dream
Englewood Cliffs,NJ, rec. 8.7.1960
Silver,Horace (p) | Mitchell,Blue (tp) | Cook,Junior (ts) | Taylor,Gene (b) | Brooks,Roy (dr)
Filthy McNasty
Live at The 'Village Gate',NYC, rec. 19.5.1961
Silver,Horace (p) | Mitchell,Blue (tp) | Cook,Junior (ts) | Taylor,Gene (b) | Brooks,Roy (dr)
The Tokyo Blues | Sayonara Blues
Englewood Cliffs,NJ, rec. 13.7.1961
Silver,Horace (p) | Mitchell,Blue (tp) | Cook,Junior (ts) | Taylor,Gene (b) | Harris,John 'Ironman' (dr)
Silver's Serenade

Englewood Cliffs,NJ, rec. 7./8.5.1963
Silver,Horace (p) | Mitchell,Blue (tp) | Cook,Junior (ts) | Taylor,Gene (b) | Brooks,Roy (dr)
Song For My Father | Que Pasa
Englewood Cliffs,NJ, rec. 26.10.1964
Silver,Horace (p) | Jones,Carmell (tp) | Henderson,Joe (ts) | Smith,Teddy (b) | Humphries,Roger (dr)
The Cape Verdean Blues
Englewood Cliffs,NJ, rec. 1.10.1965
Silver,Horace (p) | Shaw,Woody (tp) | Henderson,Joe (ts) | Cranshaw,Bob (b) | Humphries,Roger (dr)
Horace Silver Sextet
Nutville
Englewood Cliffs,NJ, rec. 22.10.1966
Silver,Horace (p) | Shaw,Woody (tp) | Johnson,J.J. (tb) | Henderson,Joe (ts) | Cranshaw,Bob (b) | Humphries,Roger (dr)
Horace Silver Quintet
The Jody Grind | Mexican Hip Dance
Englewood Cliffs,NJ, rec. 2.11.1966
Silver,Horace (p) | Shaw,Woody (tp) | Washington,Tyrone (ts) | Ridley,Larry (b) | Humphries,Roger (dr)
Serenade To A Soul Sister | Psychedelic Sally
Englewood Cliffs,NJ, rec. 23.2.1968
Silver,Horace (p) | Tolliver,Charles (tp) | Turrentine,Stanley (ts) | Cranshaw,Bob (b) | Roker,Granville 'Mickey' (dr)
It's Time
Englewood Cliffs,NJ, rec. 10.1.1969
Silver,Horace (p) | Brecker,Randy (tp) | Maupin,Bennie (ts) | Williams,John (b) | Cobham,Billy (dr)
The Happy Medium | Peace
Englewood Cliffs,NJ, rec. 8.4.1970
Silver,Horace (p,el-p) | Brecker,Randy (tp) | Coleman,George (ts) | Cranshaw,Bob (fender-b) | Roker,Granville 'Mickey' (dr) | Bey,Andy (voc)
Horace Silver Sextet
Old Mother Nature Calls
Englewood Cliffs,NJ, rec. 29.1.1971
Silver,Horace (p,el-p) | Bridgewater,Cecil (tp,fl-h) | Vick,Harold (ts) | Resnicoff,Richie (g) | Cranshaw,Bob (fender-b) | Roker,Granville 'Mickey' (dr) | Bey,Andy (voc)
Horace Silver-Gail Nelson
How Much Does Matter Really Matter
Englewood Cliffs,NJ, rec. 17.1.1972
Silver,Horace (el-p) | Nelson,Gail (voc)
Horace Silver Sextet With Vocals
All
Englewood Cliffs,NJ, rec. 14.2.1972
Silver,Horace (el-p,voc) | Bridgewater,Cecil (tp,fl-h) | Vick,Harold (ts) | Resnicoff,Richie (g) | Cranshaw,Bob (el-b) | Roker,Granville 'Mickey' (dr) | Bey,Andy (voc) | Nelson,Gail (voc)
Horace Silver Quartet
In Pursuit Of The 27th Man
Englewood Cliffs,NJ, rec. 6.10.1972
Silver,Horace (p) | Friedman,David (vib) | Cranshaw,Bob (el-b) | Roker,Granville 'Mickey' (dr)
Horace Silver Quintet
Gregory Is Here
Englewood Cliffs,NJ, rec. 10.11.1972
Silver,Horace (p) | Brecker,Randy (tp) | Brecker,Michael (ts) | Cranshaw,Bob (el-b) | Roker,Granville 'Mickey' (dr)
Horace Silver Quintet With Brass
Barbara | Adjustment
NYC, rec. 10.1.1975
Silver,Horace (p) | Harrell,Tom (tp) | Berg,Bob (ts) | Carter,Ron (b) | Foster,Al (dr) | Brashear,Oscar (tp) | Bryant,Bobby (tp,fr-h) | Rosolino,Frank (tb) | Spears,Maurice (b-tb) | DeRosa,Vince (fr-h) | Richardson,Jerome (cl,ss,as) | Collette,Buddy (fl,as) | Marcus,Wade (arr)
The Tranquilizer Suite Part 2:Slow Down | The Process Of Creation Suite Part 3:Assimilation
Los Angeles,CA, rec. 7.& 14.11.1975
Silver,Horace (p) | Harrell,Tom (tp) | Berg,Bob (ts) | Carter,Ron (b) | Foster,Al (dr) | Brown,Garnett (tb) | Richardson,Jerome (ss) | Collette,Buddy (fl,piccolo) | Jackson,Fred (fl,piccolo) | Morgan,Lanny (as) | Nimitz,Jack (bs) | Green,Bill (bass-sax)
Horace Silver Quintet With Vocals
All In Time
NYC, rec. 24.9.1976
Silver,Horace (p) | Harrell,Tom (tp,fl-h) | Berg,Bob (ts) | Carter,Ron (b) | Foster,Al (dr) | Mancini,Monica (voc) | Sommers,Avery (voc) | Copeland,Joyce (voc) | Page,Richard (voc) | Verdugo,Dale (voc) | Copeland,Alan (voc,dir)
Horace Silver Quintet
The Soul And Its Expression: | The Search For Direction- | Direction Discovered-
Englewood Cliffs,NJ, rec. 3.11.1978
Silver,Horace (p) | Harrell,Tom (fl-h) | Schneider,Larry (ts) | Carter,Ron (b) | Foster,Al (dr)
-> Note:The Vocal Ensemble was recorded on October 19.& 22. 1976 in Los Angeles,CA

495697-2 | CD | The Blue Note Swingtets
Tiny Grimes Swingtet
C Jam Blues | Tiny's Boogie Woogie
NYC, rec. 14.8.1946
Grimes,Tiny (g) | Young,Trummy (tb) | Hardee,John (ts) | Morris,Marlowe (p) | Butts,Jimmy (b) | Nicholson,Edward 'Eddie' (dr)
John Hardee Swingtet
Hardee's Partee | Idaho
NYC, rec. 28.2.1946
Hardee,John (ts) | Grimes,Tiny (g) | Benskin,Sammy (p) | Simmons,John (b) | Catlett,Big Sid (dr)
John Hardee Sextet
River Edge Rock
NYC, rec. 31.5.1946
Hardee,John (ts) | Bivens,William 'Yam' (vib) | Shirley,Jimmy (g) | Benskin,Sammy (p) | Ramey,Gene (b) | Catlett,Big Sid (dr)
Ike Quebec Quintet
Tiny's Exercise | Blue Harlem
NYC, rec. 18.7.1944
Quebec,Ike (ts) | Grimes,Tiny (g) | Ramirez,Roger 'Ram' (p) | Hinton,Milt (b) | Heard,J.C. (dr)
Sweethearts On Parade
NYC, rec. 10.4.1945
Quebec,Ike (ts) | Allen,Napoleon (g) | Rivera,Dave (p) | Hinton,Milt (b) | Heard,J.C. (dr)
Ike Quebec Swingtet
If I Had You
NYC, rec. 25.9.1944
Quebec,Ike (ts) | Jones,Jonah (tp) | Glenn,Tyree (tb) | Grimes,Tiny (g) | Ramirez,Roger 'Ram' (p) | Pettiford,Oscar (b) | Heard,J.C. (dr)
Ike Quebec Swing Seven
Topsy | I Surrender Dear
NYC, rec. 17.7.1945
Quebec,Ike (ts) | Clayton,Buck (tp) | Johnson,Keg (tb) | Grimes,Tiny (g) | Ramirez,Roger 'Ram' (p) | Moncur,Grachan (b) | Heard,J.C. (dr)
Basically Blue | Zig Billion
NYC, rec. 23.9.1946
Quebec,Ike (ts) | Collins,Lester 'Shad' (tp) | Johnson,Keg (tb) | Collins,John (g) | Ramirez,Roger 'Ram' (p) | Hinton,Milt (b) | Heard,J.C. (dr)
Benny Morton's All Stars
The Sheik Of Araby | Conversing In Blue
NYC, rec. 31.1.1945
Morton,Benny (tb) | Bigard,Barney (cl) | Webster,Ben (ts) | Benskin,Sammy (p) | Crosby,Israel (b) | Dougherty,Eddie (dr)
Jimmy Hamilton And The Duke's Men
Blues For Clarinet | Slapstick | Blues In My Music Room
NYC, rec. 21.11.1945
Hamilton,Jimmy (cl) | Nance,Ray (tp) | Chambers,Henderson (tb) | Hardwicke,Otto (cl,as) | Carney,Harry (cl,bs) | Jones,Jimmie (p) | Pettiford,Oscar (b) | Catlett,Big Sid (dr)

496685-2 | CD | Mirrors | EAN 072439668522
Joe Chambers Quintet
Tu-Way-Pock-E-Way | Mirrors | Caravanserai | Mariposa | Come Back To Me
NYC, rec. 7.7.1998
Chambers,Joe (dr) | Henderson,Eddie (tp) | Herring,Vincent (ss,ts) | Miller,Mulgrew (p) | Coleman,Ira (b)
Joe Chambers Quartet
Ruth
Chambers,Joe (dr) | Herring,Vincent (as) | Miller,Mulgrew (p) | Coleman,Ira (b)
Joe Chambers Trio
Lady In My Life
Chambers,Joe (vib,dr) | Miller,Mulgrew (p) | Coleman,Ira (b)
Ruthless
NYC, rec. 8.7.1998
Chambers,Joe (dr) | Miller,Mulgrew (p) | Coleman,Ira (b)
Joe Chambers
Circles
Chambers,Joe (vib,dr)

496860-2 | CD | Banned In New York | EAN 0724349686021
Greg Osby Quartet
13th Floor | Pent-Up House | I Didn't Know About You | Big Foot | Big Foot(excerpt) | 52nd Street Theme
Brooklyn,NY, rec. details unknown
Osby,Greg (as) | Moran,Jason (p) | Osada,Atushi[Az'shi] (b) | Green,Rodney (dr)

497807-2 | CD | The Real McCoy
McCoy Tyner Quartet
Passion Dance | Contemplation | Four By Five | Search For Peace | Blues On The Corner
Englewood Cliffs,NJ, rec. 21.4.1976
Tyner,McCoy (p) | Henderson,Joe (ts) | Carter,Ron (b) | Jones,Elvin (dr)

497808-2 | CD | Unity
Larry Young Quartet
Zoltan | Monk's Dream | If | The Montrane | Softly As In A Morning Sunrise | Beyond All Limits
NYC, rec. 10.11.1965
Young,Larry (org) | Shaw,Woody (tp) | Henderson,Joe (ts) | Jones,Elvin (dr)

497809-2 | CD | Sonny Rollins Vol.2
Sonny Rollins Quintet
Why Don't I | Wail March | You Stepped Out Of A Dream | Poor Butterfly
Hackensack,NJ, rec. 14.4.1957
Rollins,Sonny (ts) | Johnson,J.J. (tb) | Silver,Horace (p) | Chambers,Paul (b) | Blakey,Art (dr)
Sonny Rollins Sextet
Misterioso
Rollins,Sonny (ts) | Johnson,J.J. (tb) | Monk,Thelonious (p) | Silver,Horace (p) | Chambers,Paul (b) | Blakey,Art (dr)
Sonny Rollins Quartet
Reflections
Rollins,Sonny (ts) | Monk,Thelonious (p) | Chambers,Paul (b) | Blakey,Art (dr)

497810-2 | CD | Live In New York
Stanley Jordan
Flying Home | Willow Weep For Me | Over The Rainbow
Live at The Manhattan Center,NYC, rec. 21.3.1989
Jordan,Stanley (g-solo)
Stanley Jordan Quartet
Impressions | Autumn Leaves | For You | Cousin Mary
Jordan,Stanley (g) | Kirkland,Kenny (p) | Moffett,Charnett (b) | Watts,Jeff 'Tain' (dr)
Still Got The Blues | The Lady In My Life
Jordan,Stanley (g) | Wright,Bernard (keyboards) | Fine,Yossi (el-b) | Lewis,J.T. (dr)

497811-2 | CD | Town Hall Concert
Blue Note All Stars
Cantaloupe Island
Live at Town Hall,NYC, rec. 22.2.1985
Blue Note All Stars | Hubbard,Freddie (tp) | Henderson,Joe (ts) | Hancock,Herbie (p) | Carter,Ron (b) | Williams,Tony (dr)
Recorda-Me
Blue Note All Stars | Hubbard,Freddie (tp) | Henderson,Joe (ts) | Hutcherson,Bobby (vib) | Hancock,Herbie (p) | Carter,Ron (b) | Williams,Tony (dr)
Little B's Poem
Blue Note All Stars | Hutcherson,Bobby (vib) | Hancock,Herbie (p) | Carter,Ron (b) | Williams,Tony (dr)
Bouquet
Blue Note All Stars | Newton,James (fl) | Hutcherson,Bobby (vib) | Hancock,Herbie (p) | Carter,Ron (b)
Hat And Beard
Blue Note All Stars | Newton,James (fl) | Hutcherson,Bobby (vib) | Carter,Ron (b) | Williams,Tony (dr)

498222-2 | CD | Another Shade Of Blue
Lee Konitz Trio
Another Shade Of Blue | Everything Happens To Me | What's New? | Body And Soul | All Of Us
Live at The Bakery,Culver City,CA, rec. 21.12.1997
Konitz,Lee (as) | Mehldau,Brad (p) | Haden,Charlie (b)

498239-2 | CD | Yemayá
Irakere
Yemaya | Mister Bruce | Santa Amalia | La Explosion | San Francisco | Son Montuno | Chorrino
Havana,Cuba, rec. 1998
Irakere | Fernandez,Mario (tp) | Marquez,Basilo (tp) | Lopez,Cesar (as) | Thompson,Alfredo (ts) | Valdes,Chucho (p,arr) | Morales,Carlos Emilio (g) | Del Puerto,Carlos (b) | Pla,Enrique (trap-dr) | Miranda,Andrés (congas) | Meléndez,José Miguel (timbales) | Valdés,Mayra Caridad (voc)

498240-2 | CD | Trane's Blues
John Coltrane Quartet
Trane's Blues
Los Angeles,CA, rec. March 1956
Coltrane,John (ts) | Drew,Kenny (p) | Chambers,Paul (b) | Jones,Philly Joe (dr)
John Coltrane Sextet
Locomotion
Hackensack,NJ, rec. 1.9.1957
Coltrane,John (ts) | Morgan,Lee (tp) | Fuller,Curtis (tb) | Drew,Kenny (p) | Chambers,Paul (b) | Jones,Philly Joe (dr)
Sonny Clark Sextet
Sonny's Crib
Clark,Sonny (p) | Byrd,Donald (tp) | Fuller,Curtis (tb) | Coltrane,John (ts) | Chambers,Paul (b) | Taylor,Arthur 'Art' (dr)
Paul Chambers Sextet
Just For The Love
Hackensack,NJ, rec. 21.9.1957
Chambers,Paul (b) | Byrd,Donald (tp) | Coltrane,John (ts) | Burrell,Kenny (g) | Silver,Horace (p) | Jones,Philly Joe (dr)
John Coltrane Sextet
Blue Train
Hackensack,NJ, rec. 15.9.1957
Coltrane,John (ts) | Morgan,Lee (tp) | Fuller,Curtis (tb) | Drew,Kenny (p) | Chambers,Paul (b) | Jones,Philly Joe (dr)
John Coltrane Quartet
One And Four(aka Mr.Day)
Los Angeles,CA, rec. 6.9.1960
Coltrane,John (ts) | Tyner,McCoy (p) | Davis,Steve (b) | Jones,Elvin (dr)
Johnny Griffin Septet
Smoke Stack
Hackensack,NJ, rec. 6.4.1957
Griffin,Johnny (ts) | Morgan,Lee (tp) | Coltrane,John (ts) | Mobley,Hank (ts) | Kelly,Wynton (p) | Chambers,Paul (b) | Blakey,Art (dr)
Cecil Taylor Quintet
Shifting Down
NYC, rec. 13.10.1958
Taylor,Cecil (p) | Dorham,Kenny (tp) | Coltrane,John (ts) | Israels,Chuck (b) | Hayes,Louis (dr)

498573-2 | CD | Late Night Guitar
Earl Klugh
Smoke Gets In Your Eyes | Laura | Tenderly | Triste | Mirabellla
NYC, rec. 1970-1980
Klugh,Earl (g-solo)
Earl Klugh-Dr.Gibbs
Jamaica Farewell
Klugh,Earl (g) | Gibbs,Doc (perc)
Earl Klugh-Gloria Agostine
A Time For Love
Klugh,Earl (g) | Agostini,Gloria (harp)
Earl Klugh Group With Strings
Nice To Be Around(Nice To Have Around) | Like A Lover | Mona Lisa | Two For The Road | I'll Never Say Goodbye(The Promise)
Klugh,Earl (g) | Bodner,Phil (woodwinds) | Kane,Walter (woodwinds) | Friedman,David (vib,perc) | Nadien,David (v) | Finclair,Barry (v) | Libove,Charles (v) | Cykman,Harry (v) | Allen,Sanford (v) | Pintavalle,John (v) | Sortomme,Richard (v) | Kahn,Leo (v) | Morgenstern,Marvin (v) | Lumia,Guy (v) | Halprin,Diana (v) | Iandiorio,Regis (v) | Alsop,LaMar (viola) | Maximoff,Richard (viola) | Israel,Theodore (viola) | Vardi,Emanuel 'Manny' (viola) | Weinstock,Leonore (viola) | McCracken,Charles (cello) | Levy,Jesse (cello) | Lauridsen,Beverly (cello) | Abramowitz,Jonathan (cello) | Paer,Lewis (b) | Kulowitch,Jack (b) | Elfenbein,Jay (b) | Biondi,Gino (b) | Agostini,Gloria (harp)
Earl Klugh Group
Lisbon Antiqua
Klugh,Earl (g) | Gatchell,John (tp) | Shepley,Joe (tp) | Burtis,Sam (tb) | Tofani,David (ts) | Cuber,Ronnie (bs) | Ascher,Kenny (el-p) | Spinozza,David (g) | Miller,Marcus (el-b) | Madera Jr.,Jose (perc) | Collaza,Michael (perc)

498756-2 | CD | What It Is
Jacky Terrasson Group
Better World
NYC, rec. 16.11.1998
Terrasson,Jackie[Jacky] (p,el-p) | Bona,Richard (el-b) | Sawyer,Jaz (dr) | Cinelu,Mino (perc) | Laugart,Xiomara (voc)
Toot-Toot's | Money
Terrasson,Jackie[Jacky] (p,el-p) | Collins,Jay (fl) | Maret,Gregoire (harm) | Okegwo,Ugonna (b) | Sawyer,Jaz (dr) | Cinelu,Mino (perc,sound-effects)
What's Wrong With You
NYC, rec. 17.11.1998
Terrasson,Jackie[Jacky] (p) | Brecker,Michael (ts) | Okegwo,Ugonna (b) | Sawyer,Jaz (dr) | Cinelu,Mino (perc)
Baby Plum
Terrasson,Jackie[Jacky] (p,el-p) | Brecker,Michael (ts) | Bona,Richard (el-b) | Cinelu,Mino (perc)
Little Red Ribbon
NYC, rec. 18.11.1998
Terrasson,Jackie[Jacky] (p) | Okegwo,Ugonna (b) | Cinelu,Mino (dr)
Sam's Song
NYC, rec. 27.11.1998
Terrasson,Jackie[Jacky] (p) | Centalonza,Richard (fl) | Rogers,Adam (g) | Saunders,Fernando (el-b) | Cinelu,Mino (dr,perc)
Le Roi Brasil
Terrasson,Jackie[Jacky] (p) | Rogers,Adam (g) | Saunders,Fernando (el-b) | Cinelu,Mino (dr,perc)
Bolero
NYC, rec. 17.&27.11.1998
Terrasson,Jackie[Jacky] (p) | Centalonza,Richard (fl,oboe) | Okegwo,Ugonna (b) | Saunders,Fernando (el-b) | Cinelu,Mino (g,perc) | Sawyer,Jaz (dr)

498793-2 | CD | Out To Lunch
Eric Dolphy Quintet
Hat And Beard | Something Sweet Something Tender | Gazzelloni | Out To Lunch | Straight Up And Down
Englewood Cliffs,NJ, rec. 25.2.1964
Dolphy,Eric (fl,b-cl,as) | Hubbard,Freddie (tp) | Hutcherson,Bobby (vib) | Davis,Richard (b) | Williams,Tony (dr)

498794-2 | CD | Go!
Dexter Gordon Quartet
Cheese Cake | I Guess I'll Hang My Tears Out To Dry | Second Balcony Jump | Love For Sale | Where Are You | Three O'Clock In The Morning
Englewood Cliffs,NJ, rec. 27.8.1962
Gordon,Dexter (ts) | Clark,Sonny (p) | Warren,Edward 'Butch' (b) | Higgins,Billy (dr)

498795-2 | CD | Page One
Joe Henderson Quintet
Blue Bossa | La Mesha | Home Stretch | Recorda-Me | Jinrikisha | Out Of The Night
Englewood Cliffs,NJ, rec. 3.6.1963
Henderson,Joe (ts) | Dorham,Kenny (tp) | Tyner,McCoy (p) | Warren,Edward 'Butch' (b) | LaRoca,Pete (dr)

498796-2 | CD | Empyrean Isles | EAN 0724349879621
Herbie Hancock Quartet
One Finger Snap | Oliloqui Valley | Cantaloupe Island | The Egg | One Finger Snap(alt.take) | Oliloqui Valley(alt.take)
Englewood Cliffs,NJ, rec. 17.6.1964
Hancock,Herbie (p) | Hubbard,Freddie (co) | Carter,Ron (b) | Williams,Tony (dr)

499001-2 | CD | Speak No Evil | EAN 724349900127
Wayne Shorter Quintet
Witch Hunt | Fee-Fi-Fo-Fum | Dance Cadaverous | Speak No Evil | Infant Eyes | Wild Flower | Dance Cadaverous(alt.take)
Englewood Cliffs,NJ, rec. 24.12.1964
Shorter,Wayne (ts) | Hubbard,Freddie (tp) | Hancock,Herbie (p) | Carter,Ron (b) | Jones,Elvin (dr)

499002-2 | CD | Song For My Father | EAN 724349900226
Horace Silver Quintet
Calcutta Cutie | Lonely Woman | Sanctimonious Sam
Englewood Cliffs,NJ, rec. 31.10.1963
Silver,Horace (p) | Mitchell,Blue (tp) | Cook,Junior (ts) | Taylor,Gene (b) | Brooks,Roy (dr)
Horace Silver Trio
Que Pasa
Silver,Horace (p) | Taylor,Gene (b) | Brooks,Roy (dr)
Horace Silver Quintet
Sighin' And Cryin' | Silver Treads Among My Soul
Englewood Cliffs,NJ, rec. 28.1.1964
Silver,Horace (p) | Mitchell,Blue (tp) | Cook,Junior (ts) | Taylor,Gene (b) | Brooks,Roy (dr)
Song For My Father | The Natives Are Restless Tonight | Que Pasa | The Kicker
Englewood Cliffs,NJ, rec. 26.10.1964
Silver,Horace (p) | Jones,Carmell (tp) | Henderson,Joe (ts) | Smith,Teddy (b) | Humphries,Roger (dr)

499003-2 | CD | Idle Moments
Grant Green Sextet
Idle Moments | Nomad | Jean De Fleur(alt.take) | Django(alt.take)
Englewood Cliffs,NJ, rec. 4.11.1963
Green,Grant (g) | Henderson,Joe (ts) | Hutcherson,Bobby (vib) | Pearson,Duke (p) | Cranshaw,Bob (b) | Harewood,Al (dr)
Jean De Fleur | Django
Englewood Cliffs,NJ, rec. 15.11.1963
Green,Grant (g) | Henderson,Joe (ts) | Hutcherson,Bobby (vib) | Pearson,Duke (p) | Cranshaw,Bob (b) | Harewood,Al (dr)

499004-2 | CD | Lifetime
Tony Williams Lifetime
Piece Of One: | Red- | Green-
NYC, rec. 21./24.8.1964
Williams,Tony (dr) | Rivers,Sam (ts) | Davis,Richard (b) | Peacock,Gary (b)
Tomorrow Afternoon

Williams,Tony (dr) | Rivers,Sam (ts) | Peacock,Gary (b)
Memory
Williams,Tony (dr,maracas,triangle,tympani,wood-locks) | Hutcherson,Bobby (vib,marimba) | Hancock,Herbie (p)
Harbie Hancock/Ron Carter
Barb's Song To The Wizard
Hancock,Herbie (p) | Carter,Ron (b)

499005-2 | CD | Juju
Wayne Shorter Quartet
Juju | Deluge | House Of Jade | Mahjong | Yes Or No | Twelve More Bars To Go | Juju(alt.take) | House Of Jade(alt.take)
Englewood Cliffs,NJ, rec. 3.8.1964
Shorter,Wayne (ts) | Tyner,McCoy (p) | Workman,Reggie (b) | Jones,Elvin (dr)

499006-2 | CD | A New Perspective
Donald Byrd Septet + Voices
Elijah | Beast Of Burdon | Cristo Redentor | The Black Disciple | Chant
Englewood Cliffs,NJ, rec. 12.1.1963
Byrd,Donald (tp) | Mobley,Hank (ts) | Best,Donald (vib) | Burrell,Kenny (g) | Hancock,Herbie (p) | Warren,Edward 'Butch' (b) | Humphries,Lex (dr) | Voices | Perkinson,Coleridge (dir) | Pearson,Duke (arr)

499007-2 | CD | Point Of Departure
Andrew Hill Sextet
Refuge | New Monastory | Spectrum | Flight 19 | Dedication | New Monastory(alt.take) | Flight 19(alt.take) | Dedication(alt.take)
Englewood Cliffs,NJ, rec. 31.3.1964
Hill,Andrew (p) | Dorham,Kenny (tp) | Dolphy,Eric (fl,b-cl,as) | Henderson,Joe (ts) | Davis,Richard (b) | Williams,Tony (dr)

499008-2 | CD | Hub-Tones
Freddie Hubbard Quintet
You're My Everything | Prophet Jennings | Hub-Tones | Lament For Booker | For Spee's Sakes | You're My Everything(alt.take) | Hub-Tones(alt.take) | For Spee's Sakes(alt.take)
Hackensack,NJ, rec. 10.10.1962
Hubbard,Freddie (tp) | Spaulding,James (fl,as) | Hancock,Herbie (p) | Workman,Reggie (b) | Jarvis,Clifford (dr)

499125-2 | CD | Friendly Fire
Joe Lovano-Greg Osby Quintet
Geo J Lo | The Wild East | Serene | Broadway Blues | Monk's Mood | Idris | Truth Be Told | Silenos | Alexander The Great
NYC, rec. 15./16.12.1998
Lovano,Joe (fl,ss,ts) | Osby,Greg (ss,as) | Moran,Jason (p) | Brown,Cameron (b) | Muhammad,Idris[Leo Morris] (dr)

499187-2 | CD | Duo
Charlie Hunter-Leon Parker
Mean Streak | Belief | Do That Then | You Don't Know What Love Is | Recess | Don't Talk(Put Your Head On My Shoulder) | The Last Time | Dark Corner | The Spin Seekers | Calypso For Grampa
NYC, rec. details unknown
Hunter,Charlie (8-string-g) | Parker,Leon (dr,perc)

499241-2 | CD | Inner Voyage
Gonzalo Rubalcaba Trio
Yolanda Anas | Promenade | Sandyken | Here's That Rainy Day | Caravan | Joan | Joao
NYC, rec. 23.-25.11.1998
Rubalcaba,Gonzalo (p) | Chambers,Jeff (b) | Berroa,Ignacio (dr)
Gonzalo Rubalcaba Trio With Michael Brecker
The Hard One | Blues Lundvall
Rubalcaba,Gonzalo (p) | Brecker,Michael (sax) | Chambers,Jeff (b) | Berroa,Ignacio (dr)

499527-2 | CD | These Are Soulful Days
Benny Green Trio
Virgo | Bellarosa | Summer Nights | Punjab | These Are Soulful Days | Ernie's Tune | Hocus-Pocus | Come On Home
NYC, rec. 16./17.1.1999
Green,Benny (p) | Malone,Russell (g) | McBride,Christian (b)

499545-2 | CD | Romance With The Unseen
Don Byron Quartet
A Mural From Two Perspectives | Sad Twilight | Bernhard Goetz,James Ramseur And Me | I'll Follow The Sun | 'Lude | Homegoing | One Finger Snap | Basquiat | Perdido(Pegao) | Closer To Home
Bearsville,NY, rec. January 1999
Byron,Don (cl) | Frisell,Bill (g) | Gress,Drew (b) | DeJohnette,Jack (dr)

499546-2 | CD | Black Action Figure
Stefon Harris Group
Club Madness | Feline Blues | There Is No Greater Love | Of Things To Come | After The Day Is Done | Conversations At The Mess | Black Action Figure | Collage | You Stepped Out Of A Dream | Alovi | Bass Vibes | The Alchemist | Chorale | Faded Beauty | Musical Silence
NYC, rec. 14./15.2.1999
Harris,Stefon (vib) | Turre,Steve (tb) | Thomas,Gary (alto-fl,ts) | Osby,Greg (as) | Moran,Jason (p) | Mateen,Tarus (b) | Harland,Eric (dr)

499749-2 | CD | Live At Yoshi's
Pat Martino Trio
Oleo | All Blues | Mac Tough | Welcome To A Prayer | El Hombre | Recollection | Blue In Green | Catch
Live at Yoshi's Keystone Korner,Oakland,CA, rec. 15.-17.12.2000
Martino,Pat (g) | DeFrancesco,Joey (org) | Hart,Billy (dr)

499777-2 | 2 CD | Groovin' At Smalls' Paradise
Jimmy Smith Trio
Imagination | Walkin' | It's Only A Paper Moon | I Can't Give You Anything But Love | Back Home Again In Indiana | Body And Soul | The Champ | Lover Man(Oh,Where Can You Be?) | After Hours | My Funny Valentine | Slightly Monkish | Laura | Just Friends
Smalls' Paradise,NYC, rec. 15.11.1957
Smith,Jimmy (org) | McFadden,Eddie (g) | Bailey,Donald (dr)

499795-2 | 2 CD | A Night At The Village Vanguard
Sonny Rollins Trio
A Night In Tunisia
Live at The 'Village Vanguard',NYC, rec. 3.11.1957
Rollins,Sonny (ts) | Bailey,Don (b) | LaRoca,Pete (dr)
Softly As In A Morning Sunrise | Old Devil Moon | Striver's Row | Sonnymoon For Two | I Can't Get Started | I've Got You Under My Skin | A Night In Tunisia | Four | Woody'n You | What Is This Thing Called Love | Softly As In A Morning Sunrise(alt.take) | I'll Remember April | Get Happy | Get Happy(short version)
Rollins,Sonny (ts) | Ware,Wilbur (b) | Jones,Elvin (dr)

499826-2 | CD | The Illinois Concert
Eric Dolphy Quartet
Softly As In A Morning Sunrise | Something Sweet Something Tender | God Bless The Child | South Street Exit | Iron Man
Live at University Of Illinois,Champaign,Ill, rec. 10.3.1963
Dolphy,Eric (fl,b-cl,as) | Hancock,Herbie (p) | Khan,Eddie (b) | Moses,J.C. (dr)
Eric Dolphy
God Bless The Child
Dolphy,Eric (b-cl-solo)
Eric Dolphy Quartet With The University Of Illinois Brass Ensemble
Red Planet
Dolphy,Eric (fl,b-cl,as) | Hancock,Herbie (p) | Khan,Eddie (b) | Moses,J.C. (dr) | Bridgewater,Cecil (fr-h) | Woodward,Ralph (fr-h) | Holden,Carol (fr-h) | unkn. (3 fr-h) | unkn. (2 bar-h) | Johnson,Aaron (tuba)
Eric Dolphy Quartet With The University Of Illinois Big Band
G.W.
Dolphy,Eric (fl,b-cl,as) | Hancock,Herbie (p) | Khan,Eddie (b) | Moses,J.C. (dr) | Bridgewater,Cecil (tp) | Montz,Dick (tp) | Scafe,Bruce (tp) | Kennon,Joe (tp) | Popowycz,Roman (tp) | Franklin,Larry (tp) | Sporny,Dick (tb) | English,Jon (tb) | Barthelmy,Paul (tb) | Edmondson,Bob (tb) | Richmond,Kim (reeds) | Johnson,Vince (reeds) | Huffington,Bob (reeds) | Henson,Nick (reeds) | Scalise,Ron (reeds)

499871-2 | CD | Inner Circle | EAN 724349987128
Greg Osby Quintet
Entruption | Stride Logic | Diary If The Same Dream | Equalatogram | All Neon Like | Fragmatic Decoding | The Inner Circle Principle | Sons Of The Confidential | Self Portrait In Three Colors
Brooklyn,NY, rec. 22./23.4.1999
Osby,Greg (as) | Harris,Stefon (vib) | Moran,Jason (p) | Mateen,Tarus (b) | Harland,Eric (dr)

499997-2 | CD | Art & Soul
Renee Rosnes Trio
Blues Connotation | With A Little Help From My Friends | Good Bye | Romp | Little Spirit | Sanfona | Children's Song(No.3)
NYC, rec. 16.-18.2.1999
Rosnes,Renee (p) | Colley,Scott (b) | Drummond,Billy (dr)
Lazy Afternoon
Rosnes,Renee (p) | Colley,Scott (b) | Drummond,Billy (dr) | Reeves,Dianne (voc)
Renee Rosnes Quartet
Ancient Footprints
Rosnes,Renee (p) | Colley,Scott (b) | Drummond,Billy (dr) | Bona,Richard (djembe,shaker,udu) | Reeves,Dianne (voc)
Fleurette Africaine(African Flower)
Rosnes,Renee (p) | Colley,Scott (b) | Drummond,Billy (dr) | Bona,Richard (kalimba,rainstick)

520808-2 | CD | Blue Note Plays Gershwin
Stanley Turrentine Quartet
They Can't Take That Away From Me
Englewood Cliffs,NJ, rec. 18.1.1963
Turrentine,Stanley (ts) | Scott,Shirley (org) | Jones,Sam (b) | Johnston,Clarence (dr)
Jimmy Smith Quartet
Embraceable You
Englewood Cliffs,NJ, rec. 22.3.1960
Smith,Jimmy (org) | McLean,Jackie (as) | Warren,Quentin (g) | Bailey,Donald (dr)
Dexter Gordon Quartet
Our Love Is Here To Stay
Paris,France, rec. 23.5.1963
Gordon,Dexter (ts) | Powell,Bud (p) | Michelot,Pierre (b) | Clarke,Kenny (dr)
Benny Green Trio
Soon
NYC, rec. 4./5.3.1991
Green,Benny (p) | McBride,Christian (b) | Allen,Carl (dr)
Kenny Burrell-Grover Washington Quartet
Summertime
Live at Town Hall,NYC, rec. 22.2.1985
Burrell,Kenny (g) | Washington Jr.,Grover (ss) | Workman,Reggie (b) | Tate,Grady (dr)
Ike Quebec Quartet
I've Got A Crush On You
Englewood Cliffs,NJ, rec. 20.1.1962
Quebec,Ike (ts) | Clark,Sonny (p) | Hinton,Milt (b) | Blakey,Art (dr)
Sonny Clark Trio
Love Walked In
Hackensack,NJ, rec. 21.7.1957
Clark,Sonny (p) | Ware,Wilbur (b) | Hayes,Louis (dr)
Lou Donaldson Quintet
The Man I Love
Englewood Cliffs,NJ, rec. 28.2.1960
Donaldson,Lou (as) | Hardman,Bill (tp) | Parlan,Horace (p) | Jackson,Laymon (b) | Harewood,Al (dr)
Herbie Nichols Trio
Mine
Hackensack,NJ, rec. 19.4.1956
Nichols,Herbie (p) | Kotick,Teddy (b) | Roach,Max (dr)
Joe Lovano Orchestra
Someone To Watch Over Me
NYC, rec. 2./3.6.1996
Lovano,Joe (ts) | Oatts,Dick (reeds) | Nash,Ted (reeds) | Christensen,Thomas 'Tom' (reeds) | Werner,Kenny (p) | Friedlander,Erik (cello) | Mraz,George 'Jiri' (b) | Foster,Al (dr) | Silvano,Judi (voc) | Albam,Manny (arr)

521151-2 | CD | Misty Blue:Sweet Sisters Swing Songs Of Sorrow And Sadness
Holly Cole Trio
Calling You
Toronto,Canada, rec. June/July 1991
Cole,Holly (voc) | Davis,Art (b) | Piltch,Dave (b)
Dianne Reeves With Band
Softly As In A Morning Sunrise
Englewood Cliffs,NJ, rec. 27.4.1988
Reeves,Dianne (voc) | Osby,Greg (as) | Hutcherson,Bobby (vib) | Brown,Donald (p) | Moffett,Charnett (b) | Smith,Marvin 'Smitty' (dr) | Powell,Ron (perc)
Sheila Jordan-Steve Swallow
Dat Dere
Englewood Cliffs,NJ, rec. 19.9.1962
Jordan,Sheila (voc) | Swallow,Steve (b)
Cassandra Wilson Group
Tupelo Honey
NYC, rec. March 1993
Wilson,Cassandra (voc) | Ross,Brandon (g) | Plaxico,Lonnie (b) | Burnham,Charles (v,mandocello) | Johnson,Kevin (perc) | Carter,Lance (snare-dr)
Sarah Vaughan And Her Band
A Taste Of Honey
Los Angeles,CA, rec. June 1963
Vaughan,Sarah (voc) | Jones,Carmell (tp) | Edwards,Teddy (ts) | Freeman,Ernie (org) | unkn. (g) | unkn. (b) | Turner,Milton (dr) | Wilson,Gerald (arr)
Ella Fitzgerald With Orchestra
Misty Blue
Los Angeles,CA, rec. 21.12.1967
Fitzgerald,Ella (voc) | Feller,Sid (arr,ld) | details unknown
Billie Holiday With The Carl Drinkard Trio
All Of Me
Köln, rec. 5.1.1954
Holiday,Billie (voc) | Drinkard,Carl (p) | Mitchell,Red (b) | Leighton,Elaine (dr)
Peggy Lee With Orchestra
Fever
Los Angeles,CA, rec. 19.5.1958
Lee,Peggy (voc) | Marshall,Jack (arr,ld) | details unknown
Julie London With Orchestra
Fly Me To The Moon
Los Angeles,CA, rec. 1963
London,Julie (voc) | Freeman,Ernie (arr,ld) | details unknown
Lena Horne With The George Benson Quintet
It's All Right With Me
NYC, rec. May/June 1996
Horne,Lena (voc) | Benson,George (g) | Renzi,Mike (keybaords) | Forrester,Bobby (org) | Brown,Benjamin 'Ben' (b) | Tana,Akira (dr)
Betty Carter And The Harold Mabern Trio
My Favorite Things
NYC, rec. April 1964
Carter,Betty (voc) | Mabern,Harold (p) | Cranshaw,Bob (b) | McCurdy,Roy (dr)
Dinah Washington And Her Orchestra
Key To The Highway
NYC, rec. 28.11.1962
Washington,Dinah (voc) | Chamblee,Eddie (ts) | Butler,Billy (g) | Norman,Fred (arr,ld) | details unknown
Carmen McRae With The Dizzy Gillespie Quartet
Miss Otis Regrets
San Francisco,CA, rec. June 1976
McRae,Carmen (voc) | Gillespie,Dizzy (tp) | Otwell,Marshall (keyboards) | Bennett,Ed (b) | Baron,Joey (perc)
Dodo Greene With The Ike Quebec Quintet
Down By The Riverside
Englewood Cliffs,NJ, rec. 2.4.1962
Greene,Dodo (voc) | Quebec,Ike (ts) | Green,Grant (g) | Thompson,Sir Charles (org) | Hinton,Milt (b) | Harewood,Al (dr)
Lorez Alexandria With Orchestra
I Wish I Knew
Los Angeles,CA, rec. 10.8.1971
Alexandria,Lorez (voc) | Wilson,Jack (arr) | details unknown
Annie Ross With Her Quintet
I'm Just A Lucky So-And-So
Los Angeles,CA, rec. 1959
Ross,Annie (voc) | Perkins,Bill (ts) | Freeman,Russ (p) | Hall,Jim (g) | Budwig,Monty (b) | Lewis,Mel (dr)
Della Reese With The Sy Oliver Orchestra
Stormy Weather
NYC, rec. 24.9.1958
Reese,Della (voc) | Shavers,Charlie (tp) | Baker,Harold 'Shorty' (tp) | Berry,Emmett (tp) | Saracco,Frank (tb) | Byrne,Bobby (tb) | Hisson,Dick (tb) | Dorsey,George (reeds) | Press,Seymour (reeds) | Taylor,Sam 'The Man' (sax) | McRae,Dave (sax) | Martin,David (p) | Barnes,George (g) | Benjamin,Joe (b) | Donaldson,Bobby (dr) | Oliver,Sy (cond,arr)
Nancy Wilson With The Billy May Orchestra
Gee Baby Ain't I Good To You
Los Angeles,CA, rec. 26.1.1966
Wilson,Nancy (voc) | May,Billy (arr,ld) | details unknown
Jerri Southern And The Dick Hazard Quartet
I Get A Kick Out Of You
Live at The Crescendo Club,Los Angeles,CA, rec. 8.6.1959
Southern,Jeri (voc) | Hazard,Dick (p,arr) | Lustgarten,Edgar 'Ed' (cello) | Kitzmiller,John (b) | Capp,Frank (dr)
Nina Simone Quartet
Children Go Where I Send You
Live at The 'Village Gate',NYC, rec. 1961
Simone,Nina (p,voc) | Shackman,Al (g) | White,Chris (b) | Hamilton,Bobby (dr)

521152-2 | CD | Deep Blue-The United States Of Mind
Andrew Hill Orchestra
Illusions
Englewood Cliffs,NJ, rec. 1.8.1969
Hill,Andrew (p) | Maupin,Bennie (fl,ts) | Carter,Ron (b) | Roker,Granville 'Mickey' (dr) | Allen,Sanford (v) | Brown,Alfred (v) | Clarke,Selwart (v) | Moore,Kermit (cello)
Lonnie Smith Quintet
Psychedelic Pi
Englewood Cliffs,NJ, rec. 2.1.1970
Smith,Lonnie (org) | Hubbard,David (ts) | Cuber,Ronnie (bs) | McGhee,Larry (g) | Dukes,Joe (dr)
Bobby Hutcherson Orchestra
Inner City Blues
Los Angeles,CA, rec. 21.12.1971
Hutcherson,Bobby (vib) | Mitchell,Blue (tp) | Glenn,Tyree (tb) | McDonald,Clarence (keyboards) | Andrews,Reggie (keyboards) | Dupree,Cornell (g) | Adams,Arthur (g) | Rainey,Chuck (el-b) | Hooper,Nesbert 'Stix' (dr) | Errisson,King (congas,bongos)
Horace Silver Sextet
I Had A Little Talk
Englewood Cliffs,NJ, rec. 29.1.1971
Silver,Horace (el-p) | Bridgewater,Cecil (tp,fl-h) | Vick,Harold (ts) | Resnicoff,Richie (g) | Cranshaw,Bob (el-b) | Roker,Granville 'Mickey' (dr) | Bey,Andy (voc)
Gene Harris And The Three Sounds
Listen Here
NYC, rec. 30.6.1972
Harris,Gene (p) | Brown,Sam (g) | Dupree,Cornell (g) | Carter,Ron (b) | Waits,Freddie (dr) | Rodriguez,Johnny (congas) | Clay,Omar (perc)
Lee Morgan Sextet
Untitled Boogaloo
Englewood Cliffs,NJ, rec. 12.9.1969
Morgan,Lee (tp) | Priester,Julian (tb) | Coleman,George (ts) | Mabern,Harold (p) | Booker,Walter (b) | Roker,Granville 'Mickey' (dr)
Duke Pearson Sextet
Amanda
Englewood Cliffs,NJ, rec. 21.11.1964
Pearson,Duke (p) | Byrd,Donald (tp) | Spaulding,James (fl,as) | Henderson,Joe (ts) | Cranshaw,Bob (b) | Roker,Granville 'Mickey' (dr)
Marlena Shaw With Orchestra
Save The Children
NYC, rec. 11.8.1972
Shaw,Marlena (voc) | Marcus,Wade (cond,arr) | details unknown
Alphonse Mouzon Group
Sunflower
NYC, rec. December 1972
Mouzon,Alphonse (keyboards,dr,perc,voc) | Terry,Buddy (ss) | Fortune,Sonny (as) | Willis,Larry (p,el-p) | Williams,Buster (el-b)
Gene Harris And The Three Sounds
Book Of Slim
Los Angeles,CA, rec. 19./20.9.1968
Harris,Gene (p) | Horn,Jim (fl) | Estes,Alan (vib) | Vescovo,Al (g) | Simpkins,Andrew (b) | Burnett,Carl (dr) | Grayson,Miles (perc) | Ervin,Dee (perc) | Humphrey,Paul (perc) | Malarsky,Leonhard (v) | Kievman,Louis (viola) | Erlich,Jesser (strings) | Kurasch,William (v) | Felber,Henry (strings) | Steinberg,Albert (strings) | Higgins,Monk (arr,ld)
Lorez Alexandria With Orchestra
Until It's Time For Me To Go
Los Angeles,CA, rec. 15.9.1971
Alexandria,Lorez (voc) | Edwards,Teddy (ts) | Wilson,Jack (p,arr) | details unknown
Gerald Wilson And His Orchestra
Sunshine Of Your Love
Los Angeles,CA, rec. 3.9.1968
Ortega,Anthony (as) | Anthony,Mike (g) | Wilson,Gerald (arr,ld) | details unknown
Bobby Bryant Orchestra
I Wanna Testify
Los Angeles,CA, rec. 1969
Bryant,Bobby (tp) | Childers,Buddy (tp) | Hill,Fred 'Freddie' (tp) | Hubion,Paul (tp) | Bohanon,George (tb) | Ewing,John 'Steamline' (tb) | Tole,Bill (tb) | Duke,David (fr-h) | Waldrop,Don (tuba) | Riley,Herman (reeds) | Watts,Ernie (reeds) | Christlieb,Pete (reeds) | Bailey,Don (harm) | Moore,Melvin (v) | Sample,Joe (p) | Anthony,Mike (g) | Felder,Wilton (el-b) | Duke,John (b) | Lott,Carl (dr) | Valdes,Chino (conga) | Norris,Bob (conga)
Hank Mobley Quintet
Chain Reaction
Englewood Cliffs,NJ, rec. 17.6.1966
Mobley,Hank (p) | Morgan,Lee (tp) | Tyner,McCoy (p) | Cranshaw,Bob (b) | Higgins,Billy (dr)
Duke Pearson Orchestra
Christo Redentor
Englewood Cliffs,NJ, rec. 11.4.1969
Pearson,Duke (p,el-p,arr) | Gaffa,Al (g) | Cranshaw,Bob (b) | Roker,Granville 'Mickey' (dr) | Moreira,Airto (perc) | Bey,Andy (voc) | New York Group Singers' Big Band | Manno,Jack (cond,arr)

521153-2 | CD | Blue Velvet: Crooners, Swooners And Velvet Vocals
Mark Murphy And His Septet
Witchcraft
Murphy,Mark (voc) | Candoli,Conte (tp) | Candoli,Pete (tp) | Holman,Bill (bs,arr) | Bunker,Larry (vib) | Rowles,Jimmy (p) | Mondragon,Joe (b) | Lewis,Mel (dr)
Johnny Hartman With The Masahiko Kikuchi Trio
Nature Boy
Tokyo, Japan, rec. 1.12.1972
Hartman,Johnny (voc) | Kikuchi,Masabumi (p) | Suzuki,Yoshio (b) | Murakami,Hiroshi (dr)
King Pleasure With Orchestra
Jazz Jump
NYC, rec. 26.7.1962
Pleasure,King (voc) | Powell,Seldon (ts) | Wiltshire,Teacho (p,arr,ld) | details unknown
Horace Silver Quintet
The Show Has Begun
Silver,Horace (p) | Brecker,Randy (tp) | Coleman,George (ts) | Cranshaw,Bob (b) | Roker,Granville 'Mickey' (dr) | Bey,Andy (voc)
Louis Armstrong-Duke Ellington Group
I'm Just A Lucky So-And-So

NYC, rec. 4.4.1961
Armstrong,Louis (tp,voc) | Ellington,Duke (p) | Herbert,Mort (b) | Barcelona,Danny (dr)
Joe Williams And His Band
Summertime
NYC, rec. July 1961
Williams,Joe (voc) | Edison,Harry 'Sweets' (tp) | unkn. (sax) | unkn. (g) | Jones,Jimmy (p) | Benjamin,Joe (b) | Persip,Charles (dr) | Wilkins,Ernie (arr)
Billy Eckstine And His Orchestra
It Might As Well Be Spring
Live at The New Frontier Hotel,Las Vegas, rec. 20.8.1997
Eckstine,Billy (voc) | Walp,Charlie (tp) | Mainieri,Bucky (tb) | McLean,Charlie (reeds) | Balboa,Buddy (reeds) | Tucker,Bobby (p) | Grievey,Buddy (dr) | details unknown
Kurt Elling Group
My Love,Effendi
Chicago,Ill, rec. 8..12.1997
Elling,Kurt (voc) | Hobgood,Laurence (p) | Amster,Rob (b) | Raynor,Michael 'Mike' (dr,perc)
Babs Gonzales With The Jimmy Smith Trio
Round About Midnight
Hackensack,NJ, rec. 27.3.1956
Gonzales,Babs (voc) | Smith,Jimmy (org) | Schwartz,Thornel (g) | Bailey,Donald (dr)
Lou Rawls With Les McCann Ltd.
God Bless The Child
Los Angeles,CA, rec. 5.2.1962
Rawls,Lou (voc) | McCann,Les (p) | Vinnegar,Leroy (b) | Jefferson,Ron (dr)
Mel Tormé With The Jimmy Jones Orchestra
Midnight Swinger
Los Angeles,CA, rec. 3.6.1969
Tormé,Mel (voc) | Orchestra | Jones,Jimmy (cond,arr) | details unknown
Horace Silver Quintet
Senor Blues
Hackensack,NJ, rec. 15.6.1958
Silver,Horace (p) | Byrd,Donald (tp) | Cook,Junior (ts) | Taylor,Gene (b) | Hayes,Louis (dr) | Henderson,Bill (voc)
Leon Eason Group
I'm In The Mood For Love
Easson,Leon (voc) | details not on the cover
Bobby McFerrin Group
Drive My Car
McFerrin,Bobby (voice) | details not on the cover
Jimmy Witherspoon And His Band
Then The Lights Go Out
Witherspoon,Jimmy (voc) | details not on the cover
Mose Allison Trio
Top Forty
Allison,Mose (p,voc) | details not on the cover
Chet Baker Group
But Not For Me
Baker,Chet (tp,voc) | details not on the cover
Hoagy Carmichael And His Orchestra
Georgia On My Mind
Carmichael,Hoagy (voc) | details not on the cover

521226-2 | CD | My Point Of View
Herbie Hancock Septet
Blind Man, Blind Man | A Tribute To Someone | King Cobra | The Pleasure Is Mine | And What If I Don't | Blind Man, Blind Man(alt.take)
Englewood Cliffs,NJ, rec. 19.3.1963
Hancock,Herbie (p) | Byrd,Donald (tp) | Moncur III,Grachan (tb) | Mobley,Hank (ts) | Green,Grant (g) | Israels,Chuck (b) | Williams,Tony (dr)

521227-2 | CD | Time Waits
Bud Powell Trio
Buster Rides Again | Sub City | Time Waits | Marmalade | Monopoly | John's Abbey | Dry Soul | Sub City | John's Abbey(alt.take)
Englewood Cliffs,NJ, rec. 24.5.1958
Powell,Bud (p) | Jones,Sam (b) | Jones,Philly Joe (dr)

521228-2 | CD | Una Mas
Kenny Dorham Quintet
Una Mas(One More Time) | Straight Ahead | Sao Paolo | If Ever I Would Leave You
Englewood Cliffs,NJ, rec. 1.4.1963
Dorham,Kenny (tp) | Henderson,Joe (ts) | Hancock,Herbie (p) | Warren,Edward 'Butch' (b) | Williams,Tony (dr)

521229-2 | CD | The Rumproller
Lee Morgan Quintet
The Rumproller | Desert Moonlight | Eclipso | Edda | The Lady
Englewood Cliffs,NJ, rec. 21.4.1965
Morgan,Lee (tp) | Henderson,Joe (ts) | Mathews,Ronnie (p) | Sproles,Victor (b) | Higgins,Billy (dr)
Venus De Mildrew
Englewood Cliffs,NJ, rec. 9.4.1965
Morgan,Lee (tp) | Henderson,Joe (ts) | Mathews,Ronnie (p) | Sproles,Victor (b) | Higgins,Billy (dr)

521435-2 | CD | Six Views Of The Blues
Jimmy Smith Quartet
St.Louis Blues | Swingin' Shepherd Blues | Blues No.1
Hackensack,NJ, rec. 16.7.1958
Smith,Jimmy (org) | Payne,Cecil (bs) | Burrell,Kenny (g) | Blakey,Art (dr)
Blues No.2 | Blues No.3 | Blues No.4
Smith,Jimmy (org) | Payne,Cecil (bs) | Burrell,Kenny (g) | Bailey,Donald (dr)

521455-2 | CD | Drums Around The Corner
Art Blakey Percussion Ensemble
Moose The Mooche | Blakey's Blues | Lee's Tune | Let's Take 16 Bars | Drums In The Rain | Lover
Hackensack,NJ, rec. 2.11.1958
Blakey,Art (dr) | Morgan,Lee (tp) | Timmons,Bobby (p) | Merritt,Jymie (b) | Jones,Philly Joe (dr,tympani) | Haynes,Roy (dr) | Barretto,Ray (bongos)
Art Blakey-Paul Chambers
I've Got My Love To Keep Me Warm | What Is This Thing Called Love
Hackensack,NJ, rec. 29.3.1959
Blakey,Art (dr) | Chambers,Paul (b)

521810-2 | CD | Café Blue
Patricia Barber Quartet
What A Shame | Mourning Grace | The Thrill Is Gone | Romanesque | Yellow Car III | Wood Is A Pleasant Thing To Think About | The Inch Worm | Ode To Billy Joe | Too Rich For My Blood | A Taste Of Honey | Nardis | Manha De Carnaval(Morning Of The Carnival)
Chicago,Ill, rec. 28.6.-1.7.1994
Barber,Patricia (p,voc) | McLean,John (g) | Arnopol,Michael (b) | Walker,Mark (dr,perc)

521811-2 | CD | Modern Cool
Patricia Barber Group
Touch Of Trash | Winter | You And The Night And The Music | Constantinople | Light My Fire | Silent Partner | Company | Let It Rain | She's A Lady | Love,Put On Your Faces | Postmodern Blues | Let It Rain-Vamp
Chicago,Ill, rec. 6.1.-9.2.1998
Barber,Patricia (p,table-knifes on strings,voc) | Douglas,Dave (tp) | McLean,John (g) | Arnopol,Michael (b) | Walker,Mark (dr,perc,prepared-kit,tin can-o-phone) | Stitely,Jedd (udu) | Choral Thunder Vocal Choir

521956-2 | CD | Roots And Herbs
Art Blakey And The Jazz Messengers
Ping Pong(alt.take)
Englewood Cliffs,NJ, rec. 12.2.1961
Blakey,Art (dr) | Morgan,Lee (tp) | Shorter,Wayne (ts) | Timmons,Bobby (p) | Merritt,Jymie (b)
Ping Pong | Master Mind | Look At The Birdie | Master Mind
Englewood Cliffs,NJ, rec. 18.2.1961
Blakey,Art (dr) | Morgan,Lee (tp) | Shorter,Wayne (ts) | Timmons,Bobby (p) | Merritt,Jymie (b)
Roots And Herbs | United
Blakey,Art (dr) | Morgan,Lee (tp) | Shorter,Wayne (ts) | Davis Jr.,Walter (p) | Merritt,Jymie (b)
The Back Sliders | The Back Sliders(alt.take)
Englewood Cliffs,NJ, rec. 27.5.1961
Blakey,Art (dr) | Morgan,Lee (tp) | Shorter,Wayne (ts) | Timmons,Bobby (p) | Merritt,Jymie (b)

521957-2 | CD | The Witch Doctor
The Witch Doctor | Afrique | Those Who Sit And Wait | A Little Busy | Joelle | Lost And Found | The Witch Doctor(alt.take)
Englewood Cliffs,NJ, rec. 14.3.1961
Blakey,Art (dr) | Morgan,Lee (tp) | Shorter,Wayne (ts) | Timmons,Bobby (p) | Merritt,Jymie (b)

521958-2 | CD | Talkin' About
Grant Green Trio
Talkin' About J.C. | People | Luny Tune | You Don't Know What Love Is | I'm An Old Cowhand
Englewood Cliffs,NJ, rec. 11.12.1964
Green,Grant (g) | Young,Larry (org) | Jones,Elvin (dr)

521959-2 | CD | Grant's First Stand
Miss Ann's Tempo | Lullaby Of The Leaves | Blues For Willarene | Baby's Minor Lope | 'Tain't Nobody's Bizness If I Do | A Wee Bit O'Green
Englewood Cliffs,NJ, rec. 28.1.1961
Green,Grant (g) | Willette,Baby Face (org) | Dixon,Ben (dr)

522123-2 | CD | Bending New Corners
Erik Truffaz Quartet
Arroyo | More | Les Salades De L'Oncle Francois | Betty | Minaret | And
Lausanne,CH, rec. 3.-6.4.1999
Truffaz,Erik (tp) | Muller,Patrick (p,el-p) | Giuliani,Marcello (b,el-b) | Erbetta,Marc (dr,perc)
Sweet Mercy | Siegfried | Bending New Corners | Friendly Fire
Truffaz,Erik (tp) | Muller,Patrick (p,el-p) | Giuliani,Marcello (b,el-b) | Erbetta,Marc (dr,perc) | Nya (voc)

522211-2 | CD | Live In Chicago
Kurt Elling Group With Guests
Downtown | My Foolish Heart | Smoke Gets In Your Eyes | Oh My God | Night Dream | I Love You For Sentimental Reasons | Esperanto(Intro) | Esperanto | Don't Get Scared | Goin' To Chicago(Intro) | Goin' To Chicago | The Rent Party(Intro) | The Rent Party | Blue Chaser
Live at The Green Mill Jazz Club,Chicagi,Ill, rec. 14.-16.7.1999
Elling,Kurt (voc) | Hobgood,Laurence (p) | Amster,Rob (b) | Raynor,Michael 'Mike' (dr) | Freeman,Von (ts) | Johnson,Eddie (ts) | Petersen,Edward (ts) | El'Zabar,Kahlil (hand-dr) | Hendricks,Jon (voc)

522467-2 | CD | The Sixth Sense
Lee Morgan Sextet
The Sixth Sense | Short Count | Psychedelic | Afreeka | Anti Climax | The Cry Of My People
Englewood Cliffs,NJ, rec. 10.11.1967
Morgan,Lee (tp) | McLean,Jackie (as) | Mitchell,Frank (ts) | Walton,Cedar (p) | Sproles,Victor (b) | Higgins,Billy (dr)
Lee Morgan Quintet
Extemporaneous | Mickey's Tune | Leebop
Englewood Cliffs,NJ, rec. 13.9.1968
Morgan,Lee (tp) | Mitchell,Frank (ts) | Mabern,Harold (p) | Bass,Mickey (b) | Higgins,Billy (dr)

522665-2 | CD | Palo Congo
Sabu L. Martinez Group
El Cumbanchero | Billumba-Palo Congo | Choferito-Plena | Asabache | Simba | Aggo Elegua | Rhapsodia Del Maravilloso | Tribilin Cantore
NYC, rec. 27.4.1957
Martinez,Sabu (bongos,conga,voc) | Rodriguez,Arsenio (g,conga,voc) | Travieso,Raul 'Caesar' (conga,voc) | Travieso,Israel Moises 'Quinque' (conga) | Romero,Ray (conga) | Baro,Evaristo (b) | Capo,Willie (voc) | Baro,Sarah (voc)

522666-2 | CD | The African Beat
Art Blakey And The Afro Drum Ensemble
Prayer by Solomon G.Ilori | Ife L'ayo | Obirin African | Love, The Mystery Of | Ero Ti Nr'ojeje | Ayiko Ayiko | Tobi Ilu
Englewood Cliffs,NJ, rec. 24.1.1962
Blakey,Art (dr) | Latoof,Yusef (oboe) | Abdul-Malik,Ahmed (b) | Bey,Chief (african-dr) | Montego Joe (congas) | Masseaux,Garvin (perc) | Folami,James Ola (perc) | Crowder,Robert (perc) | Fuller,Curtis (perc) | Illori,Solomon (perc,voc)

522667-2 | CD | Cannonball's Bossa Nova
Cannonball Adderley With Sergio Mendes And The Bossa Rio Quartet
Clouds | Clouds(single-version) | Groovy Samba | Corcovado(Quiet Nights) | Corcovado(Quiet Nights-alt.take)
NYC, rec. 7.& 10.12.1962
Adderley,Julian \'Cannonball\' (as) | Mendes,Sergio (p) | Ferreira,Durval (g) | Bailly,Octavio (b) | Romao,Dom Um (dr)
Cannonball Adderley With Sergio Mendes And The Bossa Rio Sextet
O Amor En Paz(Once I Loved) | Minha Saudade | Joyce's Samba | Sambop | Batida Diferente
NYC, rec. 7./10.& 11.12.1962
Adderley,Julian \'Cannonball\' (as) | Mendes,Sergio (p) | Paulo,Pedro (tp) | Moura,Paulo (as) | Ferreira,Durval (g) | Bailly,Octavio (b) | Romao,Dom Um (dr)

522669-2 | CD | Vertigo
Jackie McLean Quintet
The Three Minors | Blues In A Riff | Blues For Jackie | Marilyn's Dilemma | Iddy Bitty | The Way I Feel
Englewood Cliffs,NJ, rec. 14.6.1962
McLean,Jackie (as) | Dorham,Kenny (tp) | Clark,Sonny (p) | Warren,Edward 'Butch' (b) | Higgins,Billy (dr)
Marney | Dusty Foot | Vertigo | Cheers | Yams
Englewood Cliffs,NJ, rec. 11.2.1963
McLean,Jackie (as) | Byrd,Donald (tp) | Hancock,Herbie (p) | Warren,Edward 'Butch' (b) | Williams,Tony (dr)

522670-2 | CD | Taru
Lee Morgan Sextet
Avotcja One | Haeschen | Dee Lawd | Get Yourself Together | Taru | What's Wrong With You | Durem
Englewood Cliffs,NJ, rec. 15.2.1968
Morgan,Lee (tp) | Maupin,Bennie (ts) | Benson,George (g) | Hicks,John (p) | Workman,Reggie (b) | Higgins,Billy (dr)

522672-2 | CD | Grass Roots
Andrew Hill Sextet
Venture Inward | Soul Special | Bayou Red | Love Nocturne
Englewood Cliffs,NJ, rec. April 1966
Hill,Andrew (p) | Shaw,Woody (tp) | Mitchell,Frank (ts) | Ponder,Jimmy (g) | Workman,Reggie (b) | Muhammad,Idris[Leo Morris] (dr)
Andrew Hill Quintet
Grass Roots | Venture Inward | Mira | Soul Special | Bayou Red
Englewood Cliffs,NJ, rec. 5.8.1968
Hill,Andrew (p) | Morgan,Lee (tp) | Ervin,Booker (ts) | Carter,Ron (b) | Waits,Freddie (dr)

522673-2 | CD | Complete Communion
Don Cherry Quartet
Complete Communion: | Complete Communion- | And Now- | Golden Heart- | Remembrance- | Elephantasy: | Elephantasy- | Our Feelings- | Bismillah- | Wind,Sand And Stars-
Englewood Cliffs,NJ, rec. 24.12.1965
Cherry,Don (co) | Barbieri,Gato (ts) | Grimes,Henry (b) | Blackwell,Ed (dr)

522674-2 | CD | My Conception
Sonny Clark Quintet
Minor Meeting | Eastern Incident | Little Sonny
Englewood Cliffs,NJ, rec. 8.12.1957
Clark,Sonny (p) | Jordan,Clifford (ts) | Burrell,Kenny (g) | Chambers,Paul (b) | LaRoca,Pete (dr)
Junka | Blues Blue | Minor Meeting | Royal Flush | Some Clark Bars | My Conception
Englewood Cliffs,NJ, rec. 29.3.1959
Clark,Sonny (p) | Byrd,Donald (tp) | Mobley,Hank (ts) | Chambers,Paul (b) | Blakey,Art (dr)

524539-2 | CD | No Room For Squares | EAN 724352453924
Hank Mobley Quintet
Up A Step | Old World, New Imports
NYC, rec. 7.3.1963
Mobley,Hank (ts) | Byrd,Donald (tp) | Hancock,Herbie (p) | Warren,Edward 'Butch' (b) | Jones,Philly Joe (dr)
Three Way Split | Carolyn | No Room For Squares | Me 'n You
NYC, rec. 2.10.1963
Mobley,Hank (ts) | Morgan,Lee (tp) | Hill,Andrew (p) | Ore,John (b) | Jones,Philly Joe (dr)

524540-2 | CD | The Turnaround | EAN 724352454020
Pat 'n Chat | Third Time Around | Hank's Waltz | The Turnaround | Straight Ahead | My Sin
Englewood Cliffs,NJ, rec. 5.2.1965
Mobley,Hank (ts) | Hubbard,Freddie (tp) | Harris,Barry (p) | Chambers,Paul (b) | Higgins,Billy (dr)

524542-2 | CD | House Party
Jimmy Smith All Stars
Just Friends
NYC, rec. 25.8.1957
Smith,Jimmy (org) | Morgan,Lee (tp) | Fuller,Curtis (tb) | Coleman,George (as) | McFadden,Eddie (g) | Bailey,Donald (dr)
Blues After All
Smith,Jimmy (org) | Morgan,Lee (tp) | Fuller,Curtis (tb) | Coleman,George (as) | Burrell,Kenny (g) | Bailey,Donald (dr)
Au Privave
NYC, rec. 25.2.1958
Smith,Jimmy (org) | Morgan,Lee (tp) | Donaldson,Lou (as) | Brooks,Tina (ts) | Burrell,Kenny (g) | Blakey,Art (dr)
Lover Man(Oh,Where Can You Be?)
Smith,Jimmy (org) | Donaldson,Lou (as) | McFadden,Eddie (g) | Bailey,Donald (dr)

524544-2 | CD | A Fickle Sonance | EAN 724352454426
Jackie McLean Quintet
Enitnerrut | Five Will Get You Ten | A Fickle Sonance | Lost | Sundu
Englewood Cliffs,NJ, rec. 26.10.1961
McLean,Jackie (as) | Turrentine,Tommy (tp) | Clark,Sonny (p) | Warren,Edward 'Butch' (b) | Higgins,Billy (dr)
Jackie McLean Quartet
Subdued
McLean,Jackie (as) | Clark,Sonny (p) | Warren,Edward 'Butch' (b) | Higgins,Billy (dr)

524546-2 | CD | Midnight Creeper | EAN 724352454921
Lou Donaldson Quintet
Midnight Creeper | Love Power | Elizabeth | Bag Of Jewels | Dapper Dan
Englewood Cliffs,NJ, rec. 15.3.1968
Donaldson,Lou (as) | Mitchell,Blue (tp) | Benson,George (g) | Smith,Lonnie (org) | Muhammad,Idris[Leo Morris] (dr)

524550-2 | CD | Bucket! | EAN 724352455027
Jimmy Smith Trio
Careless Love Blues | Sassy Mae | John Brown's Body | Come Rain Or Come Shine | Three For Four | Bucket | Just Squeeze Me(But Don't Tease Me)
Englewood Cliffs,NJ, rec. 1.2.1963
Smith,Jimmy (org) | Warren,Quentin (g) | Bailey,Donald (dr)

524551-2 | CD | Good Move | EAN 724352455126
Freddie Roach Trio
'Tain't What You Do (It's How You Do It) | It Ain't Necessarily So | Pastel | I.Q.Blues
Englewood Cliffs,NJ, rec. 29.11.1963
Roach,Freddie (org) | Wright,Eddie (g) | Johnston,Clarence (dr)
Freddie Roach Quintet
When Malindy Sings | Wine Wine Wine | On Our Way Up (Sister Candy) | Lots Of Lovely Love
Englewood Cliffs,NJ, rec. 9.12.1963
Roach,Freddie (org) | Mitchell,Blue (tp) | Mobley,Hank (ts) | Wright,Eddie (g) | Johnston,Clarence (dr)

524552-2 | CD | Rough 'N' Tumble | EAN 724352455225
Stanley Turrentine Orchestra
What Could I Do Without You | The Shake | Walk On By | And Satisfy | Baptismal | Feeling Good
Englewood Cliffs,NJ, rec. 1.7.1966
Turrentine,Stanley (ts) | Mitchell,Blue (tp) | Spaulding,James (as) | Adams,Pepper (bs) | Tyner,McCoy (p) | Green,Grant (g) | Cranshaw,Bob (b,el-b) | Roker,Granville 'Mickey' (dr)

524586-2 | 2 CD | Blue Hour
Stanley Turrentine With The Three Sounds
Where Or When | Blue Hour | There Is No Greater Love | Alone Together | Strike Up The Band
Englewood Cliffs,NJ, rec. 29.6.1960
Turrentine,Stanley (ts) | Three Sounds,The | Harris,Gene (p) | Simpkins,Andrew (b) | Dowdy,Bill (dr)
I Want A Little Girl | Gee Baby Ain't I Good To You | Blue Riff | Since I Fell For You | Willow Weep For Me | Blues In The Closet | Justin Time | Gee Baby Ain't I Good To You (alt.take)
Englewood Cliffs,NJ, rec. 16.12.1960
Turrentine,Stanley (ts) | Three Sounds,The | Harris,Gene (p) | Simpkins,Andrew (b) | Dowdy,Bill (dr)

525646-2 | CD | Whistle Stop | EAN 724352564620
Kenny Dorham Quintet
'Philly' Twist | Whistle Stop | Windmill | Sunset | Sunrise In Mexico | Dorham's Epitaph | Buffalo
Englewood Cliffs,NJ, rec. 15.1.1961
Dorham,Kenny (tp) | Mobley,Hank (ts) | Drew,Kenny (p) | Chambers,Paul (b) | Jones,Philly Joe (dr)

525647-2 | CD | Our Thing | EAN 724352564620
Joe Henderson Quintet
Teeter Totter | Pedro's Time | Our Thing | Back Road | Escapade
Englewood Cliffs,NJ, rec. 9.9.1963
Henderson,Joe (ts) | Dorham,Kenny (tp) | Hill,Andrew (p) | Khan,Eddie (b) | LaRoca,Pete (dr)

525648-2 | CD | Six Pieces Of Silver | EAN 724352564828
Horace Silver Quintet
Cool Eyes | Shirl | Camouflage | Enchantment | Senor Blues | Virgo | For Heaven's Sake
Hackensack,NJ, rec. 10.11.1956
Silver,Horace (p) | Byrd,Donald (tp) | Mobley,Hank (ts) | Watkins,Doug (b) | Hayes,Louis (dr)

525649-2 | CD | The Prisoner | EAN 724352564927
Herbie Hancock Orchestra
The Prisoner | He Who Lives In Fear
Englewood Cliffs,NJ, rec. 18.4.1969
Hancock,Herbie (p,el-p) | Coles,Johnny (fl-h) | Laws,Hubert (fl) | Richardson,Jerome (b-cl) | Studd,Tony (b-tb) | Henderson,Joe (alto-fl,ts) | Brown,Garnett (tb) | Williams,Buster (b) | Heath,Albert 'Tootie' (dr)
I Have A Dream
Englewood Cliffs,NJ, rec. 21.4.1969
Hancock,Herbie (p) | Coles,Johnny (fl-h) | Brown,Garnett (tb) | Studd,Tony (b-tb) | Laws,Hubert (fl) | Richardson,Jerome (b-cl) | Henderson,Joe (alto-fl,ts) | Williams,Buster (b) | Heath,Albert 'Tootie' (dr)
Firewater | Promise The Sun
Englewood Cliffs,NJ, rec. 23.4.1969
Hancock,Herbie (p,el-p) | Coles,Johnny (fl-h) | Jeffers,Jack (b-tb) | Laws,Hubert (fl) | Richardson,Jerome (b-cl) | Penque,Romeo (b-cl) | Studd,Tony (b-tb) | Henderson,Joe (alto-fl,ts) | Brown,Garnett (tb) | Williams,Buster (b) | Heath,Albert 'Tootie' (dr)

525650-2 | CD | Alive! | EAN 724352565023
Grant Green Sextet
Let The Music Take Your Mind | Sookie, Sookie
Live at The Cliché Lounge,Newark,NJ, rec. 15.8.1970
Green,Grant (g) | Bartee,Claude (ts) | Bivens,William 'Yam' (vib) | Foster,Ronnie (org) | Muhammad,Idris[Leo Morris] (dr) | Armstrong,Joseph (congas)

Time To Remember | Down Here On The Ground
Green,Grant (g) | Bartee,Claude (ts) | Bivens,William 'Yam' (vib) | Creque,Neal Earl (org) | Muhammad,Idris[Leo Morris] (dr) | Armstrong,Joseph (congas)

529747-2 | CD | The Mose Chronicles-Live In London,Vol.1 | EAN 724352974726
Mose Allison Trio
Excursion And Interlude | No Trouble Livin' | I Ain't Nothin' But The Blues | Everybody Cryin' Mercy | Meet Me At No Special Place | If You Only Knew | Middle Class White Boy | You Are My Sunshine | What's Your Movie? | How Much Truth | Ever Since The World Ended | You Call It Jogging | Trouble In Mind | I'm Not Talkin' | I Feel So Good | Since I Fell For You | Seventh Son | Hello There Universe | What Do You Do After You Ruin Your Life | Getting There | I Love The Life I Live | Finale
Live at The Pizza-Express,London, rec. 21.-23.1.2000
Allison,Mose (p,voc) | Babbington,Roy (b) | Taylor,Mark (dr)

529748-2 | CD | The Mose Chronicles-Live In London,Vol.2 | EAN 724352974825
Mose Allison Quartet
Just Like Livin' | I'm Just A Lucky So-And-So | Swingin' Machine | Tell Me Somethin' | Molecular Structure | One Of These Days | You'r Mind's On Vacation | Baby Please Don't Go | Fool's Paradise | City Home | Going To The City | Days Like This | Wild Man On The Loose | Do Nothin' Till You Hear From Me | Fool Killer | Don't Forget To Smile | You Can Count On Me
Live at The Pizza-Express,London, rec. 21./22.1.2000
Allison,Mose (p,voc) | Mullen,Jim (g) | Babbington,Roy (b) | Taylor,Mark (dr)

530499-2 | CD | Soul Manifesto
Rodney Jones Group
Soul Manifesto | Roll Call(Interlude) | One Turnip Green | Mobius 3 | Soul Eyes
NYC, rec. January 2001
Jones,Rodney (g) | Blythe,Arthur (as) | Smith,Lonnie (org) | Muhammad,Idris[Leo Morris] (dr)
Groove Bone(part 1) | Ain't No Sunshine | Groove Bone(part 2) | Final Call(interlude)
Jones,Rodney (g) | Parker,Maceo (as) | Smith,Lonnie (org) | Plaxico,Lonnie (b) | Muhammad,Idris[Leo Morris] (dr)
Soul Makossa | Wake Up Call(interlude)
Jones,Rodney (g) | Parker,Maceo (as) | Blythe,Arthur (as) | Smith,Lonnie (org) | Plaxico,Lonnie (b) | Muhammad,Idris[Leo Morris] (dr)

531113-2 | CD | Flirting With Twilight
Kurt Elling Group
Moonlight Serenade | Detour Ahead | You Don't Know What Love Is | Orange Blossom In Summertime | Not While I'm Around | Easy Living | Lil' Darlin' | I Get Along Without You Very Well- | Blame It On My Youth- | I'm Thru With Love | Say It | While You Are Mine | Je Tire Ma Révérence
Hollywood,CA, rec. 29.1.-1.2.2001
Elling,Kurt (voc) | Jenkins,Clay (tp) | Clayton,Jeff (as) | Sheppard,Bob (ss,ts) | Hobgood,Laurence (p) | Johnson,Marc (b) | Erskine,Peter (dr)

531172-2 | CD | Supernova
Gonzalo Rubalcaba Trio
Supernova(I) | Alma Via | La Voz Del Centro | Supernova(II) | Otra Mirada | The Hard One
NYC, rec. 2.-5.12.2000
Rubalcaba,Gonzalo (p,keyboards) | Henriquez,Carlos (b) | Berroa,Ignacio (dr)
Gonzalo Rubalcaba Quartet
El Cadete Constitucional | El Manicero
Rubalcaba,Gonzalo (p,keyboards) | Henriquez,Carlos (b) | Berroa,Ignacio (dr) | Quintero,Luis (timbales,guiro) | Quintero,Robert (congas)
Oren
Rubalcaba,Gonzalo (p,keyboards) | Henriquez,Carlos (b) | Berroa,Ignacio (dr,rainmaker) | Anderson,Jim (rainmaker)

531395-2 | CD | Symbols Of Light(A Solution)
Greg Osby Quartet With String Quartet
3 For Civility | Repay In Kind | M | The Keep | Golden Sunset | This Is Bliss | One Room | Northbound | Wild Is The Wind | Social Order | Minstrale Again
Brooklyn,NY, rec. 28./29.1.2001
Osby,Greg (ss,as) | Moran,Jason (p) | Colley,Scott (b) | Browden,Marlon (dr,perc) | Rice-Shaw,Marlene (v) | Howes,Christian 'Chris' (v) | Insell-Stack,Judith (viola) | Workman,Nioka (cello)

531868-2 | CD | Kindred
Stefon Harris-Jacky Terrasson Group
My Foolish Heart | Never Let Me Go
NYC, rec. 10./11.1.2001
Harris,Stefon (vib,marimba) | Terrasson,Jackie[Jacky] (p) | Muhammad,Idris[Leo Morris] (dr)
Tank's Tune | Summertime | Deja | Titi Boom | John's Abbey | Rat Race | Shané | Little Niles | Body And Soul
Harris,Stefon (vib,marimba) | Terrasson,Jackie[Jacky] (p) | Mateen,Tarus (b) | Gully,Terreon (dr)
What Is This Thing Called Love | Rat Entrance
Harris,Stefon (vib,marimba) | Terrasson,Jackie[Jacky] (p)

532136-2 | CD | The Amazing Bud Powell Vol.1
Bud Powell Quintet
Bouncing With Bud | Wail | Dance Of The Infidels | 52nd Street Theme | You Go To My Head | Ornithology | Bouncing With Bud(alt.take 1) | Bouncing With Bud(alt.take 2) | Wail(alt.take) | Dance Of The Infidels(alt.take) | Ornithology(alt.take)
NYC, rec. 8.8.1949
Powell,Bud (p) | Navarro,Fats (tp) | Rollins,Sonny (ts) | Potter,Tommy (b) | Haynes,Roy (dr)
Bud Powell Trio
Un Poco Loco | A Night In Tunisia | It Could Happen To You | Parisian Thoroughfare | Un Poco Loco(alt.take 1) | Un Poco Loco(alt.take 2) | A Night In Tunisia(alt.take) | It Could Happen To You(alt.take)
NYC, rec. 1.5.1951
Powell,Bud (p) | Russell,Curly (b) | Roach,Max (dr)

532137-2 | CD | The Amazing Bud Powell Vol.2
Autumn In New York | Reets And I | Sure Thing | Collard Greens And Black Eyed Peas | Polka Dots And Moonbeams | I Want To Be Happy | Audrey | Glass Enclosure | I've Got You Under My Skin | Autumn In New York(alt.take 1) | Autumn In New York(alt.take 2) | Reets And I(alt.take 1) | Reets And I(alt.take 2) | Sure Thing(alt.take) | Collard Greens And Black Eyed Peas(alt.take)
NYC, rec. 14.8.1953
Powell,Bud (p) | Duvivier,George (b) | Taylor,Arthur 'Art' (dr)

532138-2 | CD | Genius Of Modern Music,Vol.1
Thelonious Monk Sextet
Humph | Evonce | Suburban Eyes | Thelonious | Evonce(alt.take) | Suburban Eyes(alt.take)
NYC, rec. 15.10.1947
Monk,Thelonious (p) | Sulieman[Leonard Graham],Idrees (tp) | West,Danny Quebec (as) | Smith,Billy (ts) | Ramey,Gene (b) | Blakey,Art (dr)
Thelonious Monk Trio
Nice Work If You Can Get It | Ruby My Dear | Well You Needn't | April In Paris | Off Minor | Introspection | Nice Work If You Can Get It(alt.take) | Ruby My Dear(alt.take) | Well You Needn't(alt.take) | April In Paris(alt.take)
NYC, rec. 24.10.1947
Monk,Thelonious (p) | Ramey,Gene (b) | Blakey,Art (dr)
Thelonious Monk Quintet
In Walked Bud | Monk's Mood | Who Knows | Round About Midnight | Who Knows(alt.take)
NYC, rec. 21.11.1947
Monk,Thelonious (p) | Taitt,George (tp) | Shihab,Sahib (as) | Paige,Bob (b) | Blakey,Art (dr)

532139-2 | CD | Genius Of Modern Music,Vol.2 | EAN 724353213923
Four In One | Criss Cross | Eronel | Staight No Chaser | Ask Me Now | Willow Weep For Me | Nice Work If You Can Get It | Criss Cross(alt.take) | Ask Me Now(alt.take)
NYC, rec. 23.7.1951
Monk,Thelonious (p) | Shihab,Sahib (as) | Jackson,Milt (vib) | McKibbon,Al (b) | Blakey,Art (dr)
Thelonious Monk Sextet
Skippy | Hornin' In | Sixteen | Carolina Moon | Let's Cool One | I'll Follow You | Skippy(alt.take) | Hornin' In(alt.take) | Sixteen(alt.take)
NYC, rec. 30.5.1951
Monk,Thelonious (p) | Dorham,Kenny (tp) | Donaldson,Lou (as) | Thompson,Lucky (ts) | Boyd,Nelson (b) | Roach,Max (dr)

532140-2 | CD | Wizard Of The Vibes
Milt Jackson Quintet
Tahiti | Lillie | Bag's Groove | What's New? | Don't Get Around Much Anymore | On The Scene | Lillie(alt.take) | What's New?(alt.take) | Don't Get Around Much Anymore(alt.take)
NYC, rec. 7.4.1952
Jackson,Milt (vib) | Donaldson,Lou (as) | Lewis,John (p) | Heath,Percy (b) | Clarke,Kenny (dr)
Thelonious Monk Quartet
Evidence | Misterioso | Epistrophy | I Mean You | Misterioso(alt.take)
NYC, rec. 2.7.1948
Monk,Thelonious (p) | Jackson,Milt (vib) | Simmons,John (b) | Wilson,Shadow (dr)
All The Things You Are | I Should Care | I Should Care(alt.take)
Monk,Thelonious (p) | Jackson,Milt (vib) | Simmons,John (b) | Wilson,Shadow (dr) | Hagood,Kenny (voc)

532141-2 | CD | Clifford Brown Memorial Album
Lou Donaldson Quintet
Bellarosa | Carvin The Rock | Brownie Speaks | De-Dah | Cookin' | You Go To My Head | Carvin' The Rock(alt.take 1) | Cookin'(alt.take) | Carvin' The Bird(alt.take 2)
NYC, rec. 9.6.1953
Donaldson,Lou (as) | Brown,Clifford (tp) | Hope,Elmo (p) | Heath,Percy (b) | Jones,Philly Joe (dr)
Clifford Brown Sextet
Wail Bait | Hymn Of The Orient | Brownie Eyes | Cherokee | Easy Living | Minor Mood | Wail Bait(alt.take) | Cherokee(alt.take) | Hymn Of The Orient(alt.take)
NYC, rec. 28.8.1953
Brown,Clifford (tp) | Gryce,Gigi (fl,as) | Rouse,Charlie (ts) | Lewis,John (p) | Heath,Percy (b) | Blakey,Art (dr)

532143-2 | CD | The Eminent J.J.Johnson Vol.1
J.J.Johnson Sextet
Capri | Lover Man(Oh,Where Can You Be?) | Turnpike | Sketch(1) | It Could Happen To You | Get Happy | Capri(alt.take) | Turnpike(alt.take) | Get Happy(alt.take)
NYC, rec. 22.6.1953
Johnson,J.J. (tb) | Brown,Clifford (tp) | Heath,Jimmy (ts,bs) | Lewis,John (p) | Heath,Percy (b) | Clarke,Kenny (dr)

532144-2 | CD | The Eminent J.J.Johnson Vol.2
J.J.Johnson Quintet
Too Marvelous For Words | Jay | Old Devil Moon | It's You Or No One | Time After Time | Coffee Pot
Hackensack,NJ, rec. 24.9.1954
Johnson,J.J. (tb) | Kelly,Wynton (p) | Mingus,Charles (b) | Clarke,Kenny (dr) | Martinez,Sabu (congas)
Pennies From Heaven | Viscosity | You're Mine You | Daylie Double | Groovin' | Portrait Of Jenny | Pennies From Heaven(alt.take) | Viscosity(alt.take) | Daylie Double(alt.take)
Hackensack,NJ, rec. 6.6.1955
Johnson,J.J. (tb) | Mobley,Hank (ts) | Silver,Horace (p) | Chambers,Paul (b) | Clarke,Kenny (dr)

532146-2 | CD | A Night At Birdland Vol. 1
Art Blakey And The Jazz Messengers
Announcement by Pee Wee Marquette | Split Kick | Once In A While | Quicksilver | A Night In Tunisia | Mayreh | Wee Dot | Blues
Live at 'Birdland',NYC, rec. 21.2.1954
Blakey,Art (dr) | Brown,Clifford (tp) | Donaldson,Lou (as) | Silver,Horace (p) | Russell,Curly (b)

532147-2 | CD | A Night At Birdland Vol. 2
Wee Dot | If I Had You | Quicksilver(alt.take) | Now's The Time | Confirmation | The Way You Look Tonight | Lou's Blues
Blakey,Art (dr) | Brown,Clifford (tp) | Donaldson,Lou (as) | Silver,Horace (p) | Russell,Curly (b)

532148-2 | CD | At The Cafe Bohemia Vol.1
Announcement by Art Blakey | Soft Winds | The Theme | Minor's Holiday | Alone Together | Prince Albert | Lady Bird | What's New? | Deciphering The Message
Live at The Cafe Bohemia,Greenwich Village,NYC, rec. 23.11.1955
Blakey,Art (dr) | Dorham,Kenny (tp) | Mobley,Hank (ts) | Silver,Horace (p) | Watkins,Doug (b)

532149-2 | CD | At The Cafe Bohemia Vol.2
Announcement by Art Blakey | Sportin' Crowd | Like Someone In Love | Yesterdays | Avila And Tequila | I Waited For You | Just One Of Those Things | Hank's Symphony | Gone With The Wind
Blakey,Art (dr) | Dorham,Kenny (tp) | Mobley,Hank (ts) | Silver,Horace (p) | Watkins,Doug (b)

532610-2 | CD | Miles Davis Vol.1
Miles Davis All Stars
Dear Old Stockholm | Chance It | Donna | Woody'n You | Yesterdays | How Deep Is The Ocean | Chance It | Donna(alt.take) | Woody'n You(alt.take)
NYC, rec. 9.5.1952
Davis,Miles (tp) | Johnson,J.J. (tb) | McLean,Jackie (as) | Coggins,Gil (p) | Pettiford,Oscar (b) | Clarke,Kenny (dr)
Miles Davis Quartet
Take Off | Lazy Susan | The Leap | Well You Needn't | Weirdo | It Never Entered My Mind
Hackensack,NJ, rec. 6.3.1954
Davis,Miles (tp) | Silver,Horace (p) | Heath,Percy (b) | Blakey,Art (dr)

532611-2 | CD | Miles Davis Vol.2
Miles Davis All Stars
Kelo | Enigma | Ray's Idea | Tempus Fugit | C.T.A. | I Waited For You | Kelo(alt.take) | Enigma(alt.take) | Ray's Idea(alt.take) | Tempus Fugit(alt.take) | C.T.A.(alt.take)
NYC, rec. 20.4.1953
Davis,Miles (tp) | Johnson,J.J. (tb) | Heath,Jimmy (ts) | Coggins,Gil (p) | Heath,Percy (b) | Blakey,Art (dr)

533774-2 | CD | Sonny Clark
Sonny Clark Trio
Bebop | I Didn't Know What Time It Was | Two Bass Hit | Tadd's Delight | Softly As In A Morning Sunrise | I'll Remember April | I Didn't Know What Time It Was (alt.take) | Two Bass Hit (alt.take) | Tadd's Delight (alt.take)
Hackensack,NJ, rec. 13.11.1957
Clark,Sonny (p) | Chambers,Paul (b) | Jones,Philly Joe (dr)

533774-2 | CD | Sonny Clark Trio
I'll Remember April | Two Bass Hit | Softly As In A Morning Sunrise | I Didn't Know About You | Tadd's Delight | Bebop
NYC, rec. 13.11.1957
Clark,Sonny (p) | Chambers,Paul (b) | Jones,Philly Joe (dr)

533775-2 | 2 CD | The Complete Round About Midnight At The Cafe Bohemia
Kenny Dorham Sextet
K.D.'s Blues | Autumn In New York | Monaco | N.Y.Theme | K.D.'s Blues(alt.take) | Hills Edge | A Night In Tunisia | Who Cares | Royal Roost | Mexico City | Round About Midnight | Monaco(alt.take) | Who Cares(alt.take) | My Heart Stood Still | Riffin' | Mexico City(alt.take) | The Prophet
Live at The Cafe Bohemia,Greenwich Village,NYC, rec. 31.5.1956
Dorham,Kenny (tp) | Monterose,J.R. (ts) | Timmons,Bobby (p) | Burrell,Kenny (g) | Jones,Sam (b) | Edgehill,Arthur (dr)

534032-2 | CD | True Blue
Leo Parker Sextet
The Lion's Roar
Englewood Cliffs,NJ, rec. 20.10.1961
Parker,Leo (bs) | Burns,Dave (tp) | Swindell,Bill (ts) | Acea,Johnny (p) | Lucas,Al (b) | Hogan,Wilbert (dr)
Lee Morgan Quintet
Just One Of Those Things
Hackensack,NJ, rec. 29.9.1957
Morgan,Lee (tp) | Adams,Pepper (bs) | Timmons,Bobby (p) | Chambers,Paul (b) | Jones,Philly Joe (dr)
Art Blakey And The Jazz Messengers
Mosaic
Englewood Cliffs,NJ, rec. 2.10.1961
Blakey,Art (dr) | Hubbard,Freddie (tp) | Fuller,Curtis (tb) | Shorter,Wayne (ts) | Walton,Cedar (p) | Merritt,Jymie (b)
Hank Mobley Quintet
No Room For Squares
Englewood Cliffs,NJ, rec. 7.3.19963
Mobley,Hank (ts) | Morgan,Lee (tp) | Hill,Andrew (p) | Ore,John (b) | Jones,Philly Joe (dr)
Horace Silver Quintet
Sister Sadie
Englewood Cliffs,NJ, rec. 30.8.1959
Silver,Horace (p) | Mitchell,Blue (tp) | Cook,Junior (ts) | Taylor,Gene (b) | Hayes,Louis (dr)
Donald Byrd Orchestra With Voices
Black Desciples
Englewood Cliffs,NJ, rec. 12.1.1963
Byrd,Donald (tp) | Mobley,Hank (ts) | Best,Donald (vib) | Burrell,Kenny (g) | Hancock,Herbie (p) | Warren,Edward 'Butch' (b) | Humphries,Lex (dr) | Choir | Perkinson,Coleridge (dir) | Pearson,Duke (arr)
Grant Green Sextet
The Kicker
Englewood Cliffs,NJ, rec. 12.6.1964
Green,Grant (g) | Spaulding,James (as) | Henderson,Joe (ts) | Tyner,McCoy (p) | Cranshaw,Bob (b) | Jones,Elvin (dr)
Tina Brooks Quintet
Minor Move
Hackensack,NJ, rec. 16.3.1958
Brooks,Tina (ts) | Morgan,Lee (tp) | Clark,Sonny (p) | Watkins,Doug (b) | Blakey,Art (dr)
Dexter Gordon Quartet
Broadway
Paris,France, rec. 23.5.1963
Gordon,Dexter (ts) | Powell,Bud (p) | Michelot,Pierre (b) | Clarke,Kenny (dr)
Sonny Rollins Quartet
Tune Up
Hackensack,NJ, rec. 22.9.1957
Rollins,Sonny (ts) | Kelly,Wynton (p) | Watkins,Doug (b) | Jones,Philly Joe (dr)
Johnny Coles Sextet
Hobo Joe
Englewood Cliffs,NJ, rec. 18.7.1963
Coles,Johnny (tp) | Wright,Leo (fl,as) | Henderson,Joe (ts) | Pearson,Duke (p) | Cranshaw,Bob (b) | Perkins,Walter (dr)

534071-2 | CD | Takes Charge | EAN 724353407124
Cannonball Adderley Quartet
Serenata | If This Isn't Love | I Guess I'll Hang My Tears Out To Dry | I've Told Every Little Star | Barefoot Sunday Blues | Barefoot Sunday Blues(alt.take)
NYC, rec. 12.4.1959
Adderley,Julian \'Cannonball\' (as) | Kelly,Wynton (p) | Chambers,Paul (b) | Cobb,Jimmy (dr)
Poor Butterfly | I Remember You | I Remember You(alt.take)
NYC, rec. 12.5.1959
Adderley,Julian \'Cannonball\' (as) | Kelly,Wynton (p) | Heath,Percy (b) | Heath,Albert 'Tootie' (dr)

534254-2 | CD | A Blue Conception
Andrew Hill Quartet
The Griots
Englewood Cliffs,NJ, rec. 25.6.1964
Hill,Andrew (p) | Hutcherson,Bobby (vib) | Davis,Richard (b) | Chambers,Joe (dr)
Jackie McLean Quintet
Kahlil The Prophet
Englewood Cliffs,NJ, rec. 20.9.1963
McLean,Jackie (as) | Moncur III,Grachan (tb) | Hutcherson,Bobby (vib) | Ridley,Larry (b) | Haynes,Roy (dr)
Grachan Moncur III Quintet
Gnostic
Englewood Cliffs,NJ, rec. 6.7.1964
Moncur III,Grachan (tb) | Shorter,Wayne (ts) | Hancock,Herbie (p) | McBee,Cecil (b) | Williams,Tony (dr)
Bobby Hutcherson Sextet
Les Noirs Marchent
Englewood Cliffs,NJ, rec. 3.4.1965
Hutcherson,Bobby (vib,marimba) | Hubbard,Freddie (tp) | Rivers,Sam (fl,b-cl,ss,ts) | Hill,Andrew (p) | Davis,Richard (b) | Chambers,Joe (dr)
Jackie McLean Quintet
Plight
Englewood Cliffs,NJ, rec. 16.9.1964
McLean,Jackie (as) | Tolliver,Charles (tp) | Hutcherson,Bobby (vib) | McBee,Cecil (b) | Higgins,Billy (dr)
Sam Rivers Quartet
Fuchsia Swing Song
Englewood Cliffs,NJ, rec. 11.12.1964
Rivers,Sam (ts) | Byard,Jaki (p) | Carter,Ron (b) | Williams,Tony (dr)
Eric Dolphy Quintet
Straight Up And Down
Englewood Cliffs,NJ, rec. 25.2.1964
Dolphy,Eric (fl,b-cl,as) | Hubbard,Freddie (tp) | Hutcherson,Bobby (vib) | Davis,Richard (b) | Williams,Tony (dr)
Cecil Taylor Sextet
Conquistador
Englewood Cliffs,NJ, rec. 6.10.1966
Taylor,Cecil (p) | Dixon,Bill (tp) | Lyons,Jimmy (as) | Grimes,Henry (b) | Silva,Alan (b) | Cyrille,Andrew (dr)

534255-2 | CD | Kind Of Blue:Blue Note Celebrate The Music Of Miles Davis
Miles Davis Sextet
Tempus Fugit
NYC, rec. 20.4.1953
Davis,Miles (tp) | Johnson,J.J. (tb) | Heath,Jimmy (ts) | Coggins,Gil (p) | Heath,Percy (b) | Blakey,Art (dr)
The Jazz Crusaders
Milestones
Jazz Crusaders,The | Henderson,Wayne (tb) | Felder,Wilton (ts) | Sample,Joe (p) | Vinnegar,Leroy (b) | Hooper,Nesbert 'Stix' (dr)
Wayne Shorter Quartet
Footprints
Englewood Cliffs,NJ, rec. 24.2.1966
Shorter,Wayne (ts) | Hancock,Herbie (p) | Workman,Reggie (b) | Chambers,Joe (dr)
Miles Davis Quartet
Well You Needn't
Hackensack,NJ, rec. 6.3.1954
Davis,Miles (tp) | Silver,Horace (p) | Heath,Percy (b) | Blakey,Art (dr)
Cannonball Adderley Quintet
Autumn Leaves
Hackensack,NJ, rec. 9,3.1958
Adderley,Julian \'Cannonball\' (as) | Davis,Miles (tp) | Jones,Hank (p) | Jones,Sam (b) | Blakey,Art (dr)
Grant Green Quintet
Someday My Prince Will Come
Englewood Cliffs,NJ, rec. 23.12.1961
Green,Grant (g) | Quebec,Ike (ts) | Clark,Sonny (p) | Jones,Sam (b) | Hayes,Louis (dr)
Cassandra Wilson Group

Sky And Sea(Ceu E Mar)
Wilson,Cassandra (voc)
George Russell And The Living Time Orchestra
So What
Russell,George (arr,ld)
Manhattan Project,The
Nefertiti
Manhattan Project,The | Shorter,Wayne (ss,ts) | Petrucciani,Michel (p) | Goldstein,Gil (keyboards) | Levin,Pete (keyboards) | Clarke,Stanley (b,el-b) | White,Lenny (dr)

535101-2 | CD | Mantis
Erik Truffaz Quartet
The Point | La Mémoire Du Silence | Saisir | No Fear | Parlophone | Mantis | Yasmina | Mare Mosso | Tahun Bahu
Lausanne,CH, rec. March 2001
Truffaz,Erik (tp) | Codjia,Manu (g) | Benita,Michel (b) | Garcia,Philippe (dr,megaphone)
Magrouni
Truffaz,Erik (tp) | Codjia,Manu (g) | Benita,Michel (b) | Garcia,Philippe (dr) | Troudi,Mounir (voc)
Erik Truffaz Quartet Quintet
Nina Valeria
Truffaz,Erik (tp) | Codjia,Manu (g) | Brahem,Anouar (oud) | Benita,Michel (b) | Garcia,Philippe (dr)

535193-2 | CD | El Arte Del Sabor
Bebo Valdés Trio
Lamento Cubano | Son De La Loma | El Maranon | Bolero Potpourri: | Se Fue- | Quizas Quizas Quizas- | Aurora- | Negro De Sociedad | Buche Y Pluma 'Na Ma' | El Rloj De Pastora | Conga Potpourri: | Mirala Que Linda Viene- | Las Bolleras(Adios Mama)- | Los Dandy- | La Chambelona- | Una, Dos Y Tres- | Pare Cochero | Cumbanchero | Si Llego A Besarte | Guaracha Potpourri: | Virgen De Regla- | Ay Que Me Vango Cayendo- | Para Camagüey Se Va Panchita- | En Manzanillo Se Baila El Son- | A La Loma De Belen- | Se Acabo La Choricera- | Cabo De La Guardia- | Route 66 | Adios Panama- | Para Vigo Me Voy-
NYC, rec. 13.-16.3.2000
Valdés,Bebo (p) | Lopez,Israel 'Cachao' (b) | Valdez,Carlos 'Patato' (congas,perc)
Bebo Valdés Trio With Paquito D'Rivera
Priquitin Pin Pon | Ogguere | Romance En La Habana
Valdés,Bebo (p) | Lopez,Israel 'Cachao' (b) | Valdez,Carlos 'Patato' (congas,perc) | D'Rivera,Paquito (cl,as)

535518-2 | CD | At The Golden Circle Vol.One | EAN 724353551827
Ornette Coleman Trio
Announcement | Faces And Places | European Echoes | Dee Dee | Dawn | Faces And Places(alt.take) | European Echoes(alt.take) | Doughnuts
Live at The Golden Circle,Stockholm, rec. 3./4.12.1965
Coleman,Ornette (as) | Izenzon,David (b) | Moffett,Charles (dr)

535560-2 | CD | Slow Drag
Donald Byrd Quintet
Slow Drag | Secret Love | Book's Bossa | Jelly Roll | The Loner | My Ideal
Englewood Cliffs,NJ, rec. 12.5.1967
Byrd,Donald (tp) | Red (Kyner) | Walton,Cedar (p) | Booker,Walter (b) | Higgins,Billy (dr,voc)

535564-2 | CD | Am I Blue
Grant Green Quintet
Am I Blue | Take These Chains From My Heart | I Wanna Be Loved | Sweet Slumber | For All We Know
Englewood Cliffs,NJ, rec. 16.5.1963
Green,Grant (g) | Coles,Johnny (tp) | Henderson,Joe (ts) | Patton,Big John (org) | Dixon,Ben (dr)

535565-2 | 2 CD | Meet You At The Jazz Corner Of The World
Art Blakey And The Jazz Messengers
Announcement by Pee Wee Marquette | The Opener | What Know | The Theme | Announcement by Art Blakey | Round About Midnight | The Dreeze And I | Announcement by Pee Wee Marquette and Art Blakey | High Modes | Night Watch | The Things We Love | The Summit | The Theme
Live at 'Birdland',NYC, rec. 14.9.1960
Blakey,Art (dr) | Morgan,Lee (tp) | Shorter,Wayne (ts) | Timmons,Bobby (p) | Merritt,Jymie (b)

535585-2 | CD | The Amazing Bud Powell Vol.3:Bud!
Bud Powell Trio
Some Soul | Blue Pearl | Frantic Fancies | Bud On Bach | Keepin' In The Groove | Blue Pearl(alt.take)
Englewood Cliffs,NJ, rec. 8.3.1957
Powell,Bud (p) | Chambers,Paul (b) | Taylor,Arthur 'Art' (dr)
Bud Powell Quartet
Idaho | Don't Blame Me | Moose The Mooche
Powell,Bud (p) | Fuller,Curtis (tb) | Chambers,Paul (b) | Taylor,Arthur 'Art' (dr)

535586-2 | CD | Dialogue
Bobby Hutcherson Sextet
Catta | Idle While | Les Noirs Marchent | Dialogue | Ghetto Lights | Jasper
Englewood Cliffs,NJ, rec. 3.4.1965
Hutcherson,Bobby (vib,marimba) | Hubbard,Freddie (tp) | Rivers,Sam (fl,b-cl,ss,ts) | Hill,Andrew (p) | Davis,Richard (b) | Chambers,Joe (dr)

535587-2 | CD | Cool Blues
Jimmy Smith Quintet
Groovin' At Small's | Dark Eyes | Announcement by Babs Gonzales | A Night In Tunisia
Live at Small's Paradise,NYC, rec. 7.4.1958
Smith,Jimmy (org) | Donaldson,Lou (as) | Brooks,Tina (ts) | McFadden,Eddie (g) | Blakey,Art (dr)
Jimmy Smith Quartet
Cool Blues | What's New?
Smith,Jimmy (org) | Donaldson,Lou (as) | McFadden,Eddie (g) | Bailey,Donald (dr)
Jimmy Smith Trio
Small's Minor | Once In A While
Smith,Jimmy (org) | McFadden,Eddie (g) | Bailey,Donald (dr)

535870-2 | CD | Univisible | EAN 724353587024
Medeski Martin & Wood
Univisible | I Wanna Ride You | Your Name Is Snake Anthony | Pappy Check | Retirement Song | Ten Dollar High | Where Have You Been? | Reprise | Nocturnal Transmission | Smoke | First Time Long Time | The Edge Of The Night | Off The Table
Brooklyn,NY/Bearsville,NY/Magic Stop,NYC, rec. 2002
Medeski,John (p,el-p,org,clavinet,wurlitzer,keyboards,synth) | Wood,Chris (b,el-b) | Martin,Billy (dr,perc)

535985-2 | CD | Stardust | EAN 724353598525
Bill Charlap Trio
Jubilee | I Walk With Music | The Nearness Of You | One Morning In May | Georgia On My Mind | Skylark
NYC, rec. 6.-8.9.2001
Charlap,Bill (p) | Washington,Peter (b) | Washington,Kenny (dr)
Tony Bennett With The Bill Charlap Trio
I Get Along Without You Very Well
Bennett,Tony (voc) | Charlap,Bill (p) | Washington,Peter (b) | Washington,Kenny (dr)
Frank Wess With The Bill Charlap Trio
Rockin' Chair | Blue Orchids
Wess,Frank (ts) | Charlap,Bill (p) | Washington,Peter (b) | Washington,Kenny (dr)
Jim Hall With The Bill Charlap Trio
Two Sleepy People
Hall,Jim (g) | Charlap,Bill (p) | Washington,Peter (b) | Washington,Kenny (dr)
Shirley Horn With The Bill Charlap Trio
Stardust
Horn,Shirley (voc) | Charlap,Bill (p) | Washington,Peter (b) | Washington,Kenny (dr)

537560-2 | CD | Ballads | EAN 724353756024
Grant Green Quintet
My One And Only Love | Born To Be Blue
Englewood Cliffs,NJ, rec. 11.12.1961
Green,Grant (g) | Quebec,Ike (ts) | Clark,Sonny (p) | Jones,Sam (b) | Hayes,Louis (dr)
Grant Green Quartet
God Bless The Child
Englewood Cliffs,NJ, rec. 4.6.1961
Green,Grant (g) | Drew,Kenny (p) | Tucker,Ben (b) | Dixon,Ben (dr)
My Funny Valentine
Englewood Cliffs,NJ, rec. 1.8.1961
Green,Grant (g) | Lateef,Yusef (fl) | McDuff,Brother Jack (org) | Harewood,Al (dr)
Little Girl Blue
Englewood Cliffs,NJ, rec. 3.11.1962
Green,Grant (g) | Clark,Sonny (p) | Jones,Sam (b) | Hayes,Louis (dr)
Nancy(With The Laughing Face)
Englewood Cliffs,NJ, rec. 13.1.1962
Green,Grant (g) | Clark,Sonny (p) | Jones,Sam (b) | Blakey,Art (dr)
Grant Green Trio
Round About Midnight
Englewood Cliffs,NJ, rec. 1.4.1961
Green,Grant (g) | Tucker,Ben (b) | Bailey,Dave (dr)

537562-2 | CD | Ballads | EAN 724353756222
Sonny Rollins Trio
I Can't Get Started | Softly As In A Morning Sunrise
Live at The 'Village Vanguard',NYC, rec. 3.11.1957
Rollins,Sonny (ts) | Ware,Wilbur (b) | Jones,Elvin (dr)
Sonny Rollins Quintet
Poor Butterfly
Hackensack,NJ, rec. 14.4.1957
Rollins,Sonny (ts) | Johnson,J.J. (tb) | Silver,Horace (p) | Chambers,Paul (b) | Blakey,Art (dr)
Sonny Rollins Quartet feat.Thelonious Monk
Reflections
Rollins,Sonny (ts) | Monk,Thelonious (p) | Chambers,Paul (b) | Blakey,Art (dr)
Sonny Rollins Quartet
Namely You
Hackensack,NJ, rec. 22.9.1957
Rollins,Sonny (ts) | Kelly,Wynton (p) | Watkins,Doug (b) | Jones,Philly Joe (dr)
Sonny Rollins Quintet
How Are Things In Glocca Morra | Decision
Hackensack,NJ, rec. 16.12.1956
Rollins,Sonny (ts) | Byrd,Donald (tp) | Kelly,Wynton (p) | Ramey,Gene (b) | Roach,Max (dr)

537563-2 | CD | Ballads | EAN 724353756321
Cannonball Adderley Quartet
Dancing In The Dark
NYC, rec. 9.3.1958
Adderley,Julian \'Cannonball\' (as) | Jones,Hank (p) | Jones,Sam (b) | Blakey,Art (dr)
I Can't Get Started
NYC, rec. 23./24.8.1961
Adderley,Julian \'Cannonball\' (as) | Zawinul,Joe (p) | Jones,Sam (b) | Hayes,Louis (dr)
I Guess I'll Hang My Tears Out To Dry
NYC, rec. 12.4.1959
Adderley,Julian \'Cannonball\' (as) | Kelly,Wynton (p) | Chambers,Paul (b) | Cobb,Jimmy (dr)
Cannonball Adderley Sextet
Now I Have Everything
NYC, rec. 19.-21.10.1964
Adderley,Julian \'Cannonball\' (as) | Lloyd,Charles (fl) | Zawinul,Joe (p) | Jones,Sam (b) | Hayes,Louis (dr)
Cannonball Adderley Quartet
Easy Living
Chicago,Ill, rec. 29.3.1960
Adderley,Julian \'Cannonball\' (as) | Harris,Barry (p) | Jones,Sam (b) | Hayes,Louis (dr)
Cannonball Adderley And His Orchestra
I Worship You
NYC, rec. 26.4.1965
Adderley,Julian \'Cannonball\' (as) | Terry,Clark (tp) | Maxwell,Jimmy (tp) | Young,Eugene 'Snooky' (tp) | Nottingham,Jimmy (tp) | Dennis,Willie (tb) | Cleveland,Jimmy (tb) | Johnson,J.J. (tb) | Studd,Tony (tb) | Butterfield,Don (tuba) | Ashton,Bob (fl,b-cl) | Banks,Danny (fl,b-cl) | Johnson,Budd (fl,cl) | Woods,Phil (as) | Royal,Marshall (as) | Nelson,Oliver (arr)
Cannonball Adderley Quintet
Yvette
Los Angeles,CA, rec. March 1967
Adderley,Julian \'Cannonball\' (as) | Adderley,Nat (co) | Zawinul,Joe (p) | Gaskin,Victor (b) | McCurdy,Roy (dr) | Studd,Tony (tb) | Butterfield,Don (tuba) | Ashton,Bob (fl,b-cl) | Banks,Danny (fl,b-cl) | Johnson,Budd (fl,cl) | Woods,Phil (as) | Royal,Marshall (as) | Nelson,Oliver (arr)
Cannonball Adderley With Sergio Mendes And The Bossa Rio Sextet
O Amor En Paz(Once I Loved)
NYC, rec. 10.12.1962
Adderley,Julian \'Cannonball\' (as) | Paulo,Pedro (tp) | Moura,Paulo (as) | Mendes,Sergio (p) | Ferreira,Durval (g) | Bailly,Octavio (b) | Romao,Dom Um (dr) | McCurdy,Roy (dr) | Studd,Tony (tb) | Butterfield,Don (tuba) | Ashton,Bob (fl,b-cl) | Banks,Danny (fl,b-cl) | Johnson,Budd (fl,cl) | Woods,Phil (as) | Royal,Marshall (as) | Nelson,Oliver (arr)
Cannonball Adderley Sextet
The Song My Lady Sings
Live at Shelly's Manne Hole,Los Angeles,CA, rec. 31.7.-2.8.1964
Adderley,Julian \'Cannonball\' (as) | Adderley,Nat (co) | Lloyd,Charles (ts) | Zawinul,Joe (p) | Jones,Sam (b) | Hayes,Louis (dr)

538227-2 | CD | Money Jungle | EAN 724353822729
Ellington/Mingus/Roach Trio
Money Jungle | Fleurette Africaine(African Flower) | Very Special | Warm Valley | Rem Blues | A Little Max(Parfait) | Wig Wise | Switch Blade | Caravan | Backward Country Boy Blues | In My Solitude | A Little Max(Parfait)(alt.take) | In My Solitude(alt.take) | Switch Blade(alt.take) | Rem Blues(alt.take)
NYC, rec. 17.9.1962
Ellington,Duke (p) | Mingus,Charles (b) | Roach,Max (dr)

538228-2 | CD | Undercurrent | EAN 724353822828
Bill Evans-Jim Hall
I Hear A Rhapsody | Stairway To The Stars | I'm Getting Sentimental Over You
NYC, rec. 24.4.1962
Evans,Bill (p) | Hall,Jim (g)
My Funny Valentine | My Funny Valentine(alt.take) | Dream Gypsy | Romain | Romain(alt.take) | Skating In Central Park | Dam That Dream
NYC, rec. 14.5.1962
Evans,Bill (p) | Hall,Jim (g)

538329-2 | CD | 100 Hearts | EAN 724353832926
Michel Petrucciani
Turn Around | Three Forgotten Magic Words | Silence | St.Thomas | Medley: | Someday My Prince Will Come- | All The Things You Are- | A Child Is Born- | Very Early- | Pot Pourri Transitions- | 100 Hearts
NYC, rec. June 1983
Petrucciani,Michel (p-solo)

538697-2 | CD | Moon Rappin' | EAN 724353869724
Jack McDuff Quartet With Orchestra
Flat Backin' | Oblighetto | Moon Rappin' | Made In Sweden | Loose Foot
NYC, rec. 11.12.1969
McDuff,Brother Jack (org) | Phillips,Bill (fl,ts,bs) | Bird,Jerry (g) | Dukes,Joe (dr) | DuShon,Jean (voc) | Orchestra | details unknown

538699-2 | CD | The Worm | EAN 724353869922
Jimmy McGriff Organ Blues Band
The Worm | Keep Loose | Heavy Weight | Think | Look It Up | Girl Talk | Blue Juice | Take The 'A' Train
NYC, rec. 19.-22.8.1968
McGriff,Jimmy (org) | Mitchell,Blue (tp) | Turner,Danny (as) | Theus,Fats (ts) | Ashton,Bob (bs) | Schwartz,Thornel (g) | Bushnell,Bob (b) | Lewis,Mel or Grady Tate (dr)

538701-2 | CD | Comin' On Home | EAN 724353870126
Richard 'Groove' Holmes Orchestra
Groovin' For Mr.G | Mr.Clean | Down Home Funk | Don't Mess With Me Baby | Wave | This Here
NYC, rec. 19.5.1971
Holmes,Richard 'Groove' (org) | Hubbard,Gerald (g) | Irvine,Weldon (el-p) | Jemmott,Jerry (el-b) | Washington,Darryl (dr) | Armando,Ray (congas) | Davis,James (perc)
Theme From Love Story
Holmes,Richard 'Groove' (org) | Hubbard,Gerald (g) | Irvine,Weldon (el-p) | Rainey,Chuck (el-b) | Washington,Darryl (dr) | Armando,Ray (congas) | Davis,James (perc)

539838-2 | CD | Modernistic | EAN 724353983826
Jason Moran
You've Got To Be Modernistic | Body And Soul | Planet Rock | Planet Rock Postscript | Time Into Space Into Time | Gangsterism On Irons | Moran Tonk Circa 1936 | Passion | Gangsterism On A Lunchtable | Auf Einer Burg- | In A Fortress- | Gentle Shifts South
NYC, rec. 12.4.2002
Moran,Jason (p,mini-p)

540030-2) | CD | Roll Call | EAN 724354003028
Hank Mobley Quintet
Roll Call | My Groove Your Moove | Take Your Pick | A Baptist Beat | The More I See You | The Breakdown | A Baptist Beat
Englewood Cliffs,NJ, rec. 13.11.1960
Mobley,Hank (ts) | Hubbard,Freddie (tp) | Kelly,Wynton (p) | Chambers,Paul (b) | Blakey,Art (dr)

540032-2 | CD | Green Street | EAN 724354003226
Grant Green Trio
Green With Envy | Grant's Dimensions | Alone Together | Round About Midnight | No.1 Green Street | Green With Envy(alt.take) | Alone Together(alt.take)
Englewood Cliffs,NJ, rec. 1.4.1961
Green,Grant (g) | Tucker,Ben (b) | Bailey,Dave (dr)

540033-2 | CD | Capuchin Swing | EAN 724354003325
Jackie McLean Quintet
Francisco | Just For Now | Don't Blame Me | Condition Blue | Capuchin Swing | On The Lion
Englewood Cliffs,NJ, rec. 17.4.1960
McLean,Jackie (as) | Mitchell,Blue (tp) | Bishop Jr.,Walter (p) | Chambers,Paul (b) | Taylor,Arthur 'Art' (dr)

540034-2 | CD | Stylings Of Silver | EAN 724354003424
Horace Silver Quintet
Metamorphosis | No Smokin' | The Back Beat | Soulville | My One And Only Love | Home Comin'
Hackensack,NJ, rec. 8.5.1957
Silver,Horace (p) | Farmer,Art (tp) | Mobley,Hank (ts) | Kotick,Teddy (b) | Hayes,Louis (dr)

540036-2 | CD | Hustlin' | EAN 724354003622
Stanley Turrentine Quintet
Trouble | Love Letters | The Hustler | Ladyfingers | Something Happens To Me | Goin' Home
Englewood Cliffs,NJ, rec. 24.1.1964
Turrentine,Stanley (ts) | Scott,Shirley (org) | Burrell,Kenny (g) | Cranshaw,Bob (b) | Finch,Otis 'Candy' (dr)

540382-2 | CD | Live At The Village Vanguard | EAN 724354038228
Michel Petrucciani Trio
Nardis | Oleo | Le Bricoleur De Big Sur | To Erlinda | Say It Again And Again | Trouble | Three Forgotten Magic Words | Round About Midnight
Live at The 'Village Vanguard',NYC, rec. 16.3.1984
Petrucciani,Michel (p) | Danielsson,Palle (b) | Zigmund,Eliot (dr)

540528-2 | 2 CD | Donald Byrd & Doug Watkins:The Tradition Sessions | EAN 724354052828
Donald Brown Quintet
El Sino | Crazy Rhythm
Cambridge,Mass., rec. 2.12.1955
Byrd,Donald (tp) | Gordon,Joe (tp) | Silver,Horace (p) | Watkins,Doug (b) | Blakey,Art (dr)
Everything Happens To Me | Hank's Other Tune(aka The Late Show)
Byrd,Donald (tp) | Mobley,Hank (ts) | Silver,Horace (p) | Watkins,Doug (b) | Blakey,Art (dr)
Donald Byrd Sextet
Doug's Blues | Hank's Tune
Byrd,Donald (tp) | Gordon,Joe (tp) | Mobley,Hank (ts) | Silver,Horace (p) | Watkins,Doug (b) | Blakey,Art (dr)
Donald Byrd Quartet
Little Rock Getaway | Polka Dots And Moonbeams | If I Love Again | Stella By Starlight
Beacon Hill,Mass., rec. 2.5.1956
Byrd,Donald (tp) | Santisi,Ray (p) | Watkins,Doug (b) | Zitano,Jimmy (dr)
Doug Watkins Trio
People Will Say We're In Love | What's New?
Watkins,Doug (b) | Santisi,Ray (p) | Zitano,Jimmy (dr)
Doug Watkins Sextet
Return To Paradise | Phinupi | Phil T. McNasty's Blues | More Of The Same | Pannonica
NYC, rec. 8.12.1956
Watkins,Doug (b) | Byrd,Donald (tp) | Mobley,Hank (ts) | Burrell,Kenny (g) | Jordan,Duke (p) | Taylor,Arthur 'Art' (dr)

540532-2 | 2 CD | The Complete 'Is' Sessions | EAN 724354053221
Chick Corea Septet
It | The Brain | This | Song Of The Wind | Sundance | The Brain(alt.take) | This(alt.take) | Song Of The Wind(alt.take) | Sundance(alt.take) | Jamala | Converge | Is | Jamala(alt.take) | Converge(alt.take)
NYC, rec. 11.-13.5.1969
Corea,Chick (p,el-p) | Shaw,Woody (tp) | Laws,Hubert (fl,piccolo) | Maupin,Bennie (ts) | Holland,Dave (b) | DeJohnette,Jack (dr) | Arnold,Horacee (dr,perc)

540535-2 | CD | Jacknife | EAN 724354053528
Jackie McLean Quintet
On The Nile | Jacknife
Englewood Cliffs,NJ, rec. 24.9.1965
McLean,Jackie (as) | Tolliver,Charles (tp) | Willis,Larry (p) | Ridley,Larry (b) | DeJohnette,Jack (dr)
Climax | Blue Fable
McLean,Jackie (as) | Morgan,Lee (tp) | Willis,Larry (p) | Ridley,Larry (b) | DeJohnette,Jack (dr)
Jackie McLean Sextet
Soft Blue
Englewood Cliffs,NJ, rec. 24.8.1965
McLean,Jackie (as) | Tolliver,Charles (tp) | Morgan,Lee (tp) | Willis,Larry (p) | Ridley,Larry (b) | DeJohnette,Jack (dr)

540536-2 | CD | The Waiting Game | EAN 724354053627
Tina Brooks Quintet
Talkin' About | One For Myrtle | Dhyana | David The King | Stranger In Paradise | The Waiting Game
Englewood Cliffs,NJ, rec. 2.3.1961
Brooks,Tina (ts) | Coles,Johnny (tp) | Drew,Kenny (p) | Ware,Wilbur (b) | Jones,Philly Joe (dr)

540537-2 | CD | Redd's Blues | EAN 724354053726
Freddie Redd Sextet
Now | Cute Doot | Old Spice | Blues For Betsy | Somewhere | Love Lost
Englewood Cliffs,NJ, rec. 17.1.1961
Redd,Freddie (p) | Bailey,Benny (tp) | McLean,Jackie (as) | Brooks,Tina (ts) | Chambers,Paul (b) | Godfrey,John (dr)

540856-2 | 2 CD | Wayne Shorter:The Classic Blue Note Recordings | EAN 724354085628
Art Blakey And The Jazz Messengers
The Chess Players | Lester Left Town
Englewood Cliffs,NJ, rec. 6.3.1960
Blakey,Art (dr) | Morgan,Lee (tp) | Shorter,Wayne (ts) | Timmons,Bobby (p) | Merritt,Jymie (b)
Ping Pong | United

LABELVERZEICHNIS

Englewood Cliffs,NJ, rec. 18.2.1960
Blakey,Art (dr) | Morgan,Lee (tp) | Shorter,Wayne (ts) | Timmons,Bobby (p) | Merritt,Jymie (b)
Freddie Hubbard Sextet
Marie Antoinette
Englewood Cliffs,NJ, rec. 21.8.1961
Hubbard,Freddie (tp) | Shorter,Wayne (ts) | Zawadi,Kiane (euphonium) | Tyner,McCoy (p) | Davis,Art (b) | Jones,Elvin (dr)
Art Blakey And The Jazz Messengers
Children Of The Night
Englewood Cliffs,NJ, rec. 2.10.1961
Blakey,Art (dr) | Hubbard,Freddie (tp) | Fuller,Curtis (tb) | Shorter,Wayne (ts) | Walton,Cedar (p) | Merritt,Jymie (b)
Contemplation
Englewood Cliffs,NJ, rec. 28.11.1961
Blakey,Art (dr) | Hubbard,Freddie (tp) | Fuller,Curtis (tb) | Shorter,Wayne (ts) | Walton,Cedar (p) | Merritt,Jymie (b)
Wayne Shorter Quintet
Black Nile
Englewood Cliffs,NJ, rec. 29.4.1964
Fuller,Curtis (tb) | Morgan,Lee (tp) | Tyner,McCoy (p) | Workman,Reggie (b) | Jones,Elvin (dr) | Merritt,Jymie (b)
Wayne Shorter Quartet
Yes Or No
Englewood Cliffs,NJ, rec. 3.8.1964
Shorter,Wayne (ts) | Tyner,McCoy (p) | Workman,Reggie (b) | Jones,Elvin (dr)
Wayne Shorter Quintet
Speak No Evil | Infant Eyes | Witch Hunt
Englewood Cliffs,NJ, rec. 24.12.1964
Shorter,Wayne (ts) | Hubbard,Freddie (tp) | Hancock,Herbie (p) | Carter,Ron (b) | Jones,Elvin (dr)
Wayne Shorter Sextet
Angola
Englewood Cliffs,NJ, rec. 4.3.1965
Shorter,Wayne (ts) | Hubbard,Freddie (tp) | Spaulding,James (as) | Tyner,McCoy (p) | Carter,Ron (b) | Williams,Tony (dr)
Wayne Shorter Quartet
Etcetera
Englewood Cliffs,NJ, rec. 14.6.1965
Shorter,Wayne (ts) | Hancock,Herbie (p) | McBee,Cecil (b) | Chambers,Joe (dr)
Adam's Apple | Footprints
Englewood Cliffs,NJ, rec. 24.2.1925
Shorter,Wayne (ts) | Hancock,Herbie (p) | Workman,Reggie (b) | Chambers,Joe (dr)
Wayne Shorter Sextet
Tom Thumb
Englewood Cliffs,NJ, rec. 10.3.1967
Shorter,Wayne (ts) | Fuller,Curtis (tb) | Spaulding,James (as) | Hancock,Herbie (p) | Carter,Ron (b) | Chambers,Joe (dr)
Lee Morgan Sextet
Rio
Englewood Cliffs,NJ, rec. 14.7.1967
Morgan,Lee (tp) | Shorter,Wayne (ts) | Hutcherson,Bobby (vib) | Hancock,Herbie (p) | Carter,Ron (b) | Higgins,Billy (dr)
Wayne Shorter Sextet
Super Nova
NYC, rec. 29.8.1969
Shorter,Wayne (ss) | McLaughlin,John (g) | Sharrock,Sonny (g) | Corea,Chick (p) | Vitous,Miroslav (b) | DeJohnette,Jack (dr) | Higgins,Billy (dr)
Wayne Shorter Orchestra
Calm
NYC, rec. 26.8.1970
Shorter,Wayne (ts) | Friedman,David (vib) | Bertoncini,Gene (el-g) | Carter,Ron (b) | McBee,Cecil (b) | Hart,Billy (dr) | Mouzon,Alphonse (dr) | Cuome,Frank (perc)
Michel Petrucciani feat. Jim Hall and Wayne Shorter
Limbo
Live at The Montreux Jazz Festival, rec. 16.7.1986
Petrucciani,Michel (p) | Shorter,Wayne (ts) | Hall,Jim (g)
Manhattan Project,The
Nefertiti
NYC, rec. 16.12.1989
Manhattan Project,The | Shorter,Wayne (ts) | Petrucciani,Michel (p) | Goldstein,Gil (keyboards) | Levin,Pete (keyboards) | Clarke,Stanley (el-b) | White,Lenny (dr)

542081-2 | CD | Oh! | EAN 724354208126
Scolohofo
Oh! | Right About Now | The Winding Way | Bittersweet | Shorter Form | New Amsterdam | In Your Arms | The Dawn Of Time | Brandyn | Faces | Oh I See
NYC, rec. 30./31.7.2002
Lovano,Joe (ss,ts) | Scofield,John (g) | Holland,Dave (b) | Foster,Al (dr)

542302-2 | CD | Hub Cap | EAN 724354230226
Freddie Hubbard Sextet
Cry Me Not | Osie Mae | Hub Cup | Plexus | Earmon Jr. | Luana | Plexus(alt.take)
Englewood Cliffs,NJ, rec. 9.4.1961
Hubbard,Freddie (tp) | Priester,Julian (tb) | Heath,Jimmy (ts) | Walton,Cedar (p) | Ridley,Larry (b) | Jones,Philly Joe (dr)

542304-2 | CD | Finger Poppin' | EAN 724354230424
Horace Silver Quintet
Finger Poppin' | Come On Home | Cookin' At The Continental | Juicy Lucy | Swinging The Samba | Mellow D | You Happened My Way | Sweet Stuff
Hackensack,NJ, rec. 31.1.1959
Silver,Horace (p) | Mitchell,Blue (tp) | Cook,Junior (ts) | Taylor,Gene (b) | Hayes,Louis (dr)

542305-2 | CD | Byrd In Hand | EAN 724354230523
Donald Byrd Sextet
Here Am I | Witchcraft | Devil Whip | Bronze Dance | Clarion Call | The Injuns
Hackensack,NJ, rec. 31.5.1959
Byrd,Donald (tp) | Rouse,Charlie (ts) | Adams,Pepper (bs) | Davis Jr.,Walter (p) | Jones,Sam (b) | Taylor,Arthur 'Art' (dr)

542306-2 | CD | Blowing In From Chicago | EAN 724354230622
Cliff Jordan-John Gilmore Quintet
Status Quo | Bo-Till | Blue Lights | Billie's Bounce | Evil Eye | Everywhere | Let It Stand
Hackensack,NJ, rec. 3.3.1957
Jordan,Clifford (ts) | Gilmore,John (ts) | Silver,Horace (p) | Russell,Curly (b) | Blakey,Art (dr)

542307-2 | CD | The Natural Soul | EAN 724354230721
Lou Donaldson Quintet
Funky Mama | Love Walked In | Spaceman Twist | Sow Belly Blues | That's All | Nice 'N Greasy | Nice 'N Greasy | People Will Say We're In Love
Englewood Cliffs,NJ, rec. 9.5.1962
Donaldson,Lou (as) | Turrentine,Tommy (tp) | Green,Grant (g) | Patton,Big John (org) | Dixon,Ben (dr)

542413-2 | CD | Smile | EAN 724354241321
Jacky Terrasson Trio
Parisian Thoroughfare | Smile | The Dolphin | Nardis | Autumn Leaves | My Funny Valentine | 59 | Le Jardin D'Hiver | L'Education Sentimentale | L'Air De Rien
Pompignan,France, rec. 12.-21.6.2002
Terrasson,Jackie[Jacky] (p) | Smith,Sean (b) | Harland,Eric (dr)
Mo' Better Blues | Sous Le Ciel De Paris | Isn't She Lovely
Terrasson,Jackie[Jacky] (p) | Vignolo,Rémi (el-b) | Harland,Eric (dr)
-> Note: Einigen Titeln wurden Naturgeräuche unterlegt

557257-2 | CD | Into The Blue | EAN 724355725721
Jacky Terrasson-Emmanuel Pahud Quartet
Volière(Saint-Saens) | Pavane(Ravel) | Boléro(Ravel) | Après Un Reve(Fauré) | Printemps(Vivaldi) | Été(Vivaldi) | Automne(Vivaldi) | Hiver(Vivaldi) | Jimbo's Lullaby(Debussy) | Marche À La Turque(Mozart) | Pays Lointain(Schumann) | Moto Perpetuo(Paganini) | Vol Du Bourdon(Rimsky-Korsakov) | Véloce(Bolling)
Pompignan,France, rec. August 2001
Pahud,Emmanuel (fl) | Terrasson,Jackie[Jacky] (p,el-p,arr) | Smith,Sean (b) | Jackson,Ali 'Muhammed' (dr)

576749-2 | CD | Conquistador
Cecil Taylor Sextet
Conquistador | With (Exit) | With (Exit-alt.take)
Englewood Cliffs,NJ, rec. 6.10.1966
Taylor,Cecil (p) | Dixon,Bill (tp) | Lyons,Jimmy (as) | Grimes,Henry (b) | Silva,Alan (b) | Cyrille,Andrew (dr)

576750-2 | CD | Never Let Me Go
Stanley Turrentine Quartet
Never Let Me Go | They Can't Take That Away From Me
Englewood Cliffs,NJ, rec. 18.1.1963
Turrentine,Stanley (ts) | Scott,Shirley (org) | Jones,Sam (b) | Johnston,Clarence (dr)
Stanley Turrentine Quintet
Trouble | God Bless The Child | Sara's Dance | Without A Song | Major's Minor | You'll Never Get Away From Me
Englewood Cliffs,NJ, rec. 13.2.1963
Turrentine,Stanley (ts) | Scott,Shirley (org) | Holley,Major (b) | Harewood,Al (dr) | Barretto,Ray (congas,tambourine)

576752-2 | CD | Newk's Time
Sonny Rollins Quartet
Tune Up | Asiatic Race | Wonderful Wonderful | Blues For Philly Joe | Namely You
Hackensack,NJ, rec. 22.9.1957
Rollins,Sonny (ts) | Kelly,Wynton (p) | Watkins,Doug (b) | Jones,Philly Joe (dr)
Sonny Rollins/Philly Joe Jones
Surrey With The Fringe On Top
Rollins,Sonny (ts) | Jones,Philly Joe (dr)

576753-2 | CD | The Cape Verdean Blues
Horace Silver Quintet
The Cape Verdean Blues | The African Queen | Pretty Eyes
Englewood Cliffs,NJ, rec. 1.10.1965
Silver,Horace (p) | Shaw,Woody (tp) | Henderson,Joe (ts) | Cranshaw,Bob (b) | Humphries,Roger (dr)
Horace Silver Sextet
Nutville | Bonita | Mo' Joe
Englewood Cliffs,NJ, rec. 22.10.1965
Silver,Horace (p) | Shaw,Woody (tp) | Henderson,Joe (ts) | Cranshaw,Bob (b) | Humphries,Roger (dr) | Johnson,J.J. (tb)

576754-2 | CD | Prayer Meetin'
Jimmy Smith Quintet
Smith Walk | Lonesome Road
Englewood Cliffs,NJ, rec. 13.6.1960
Smith,Jimmy (org) | Turrentine,Stanley (ts) | Warren,Quentin (g) | Jones,Sam (b) | Bailey,Donald (dr)
Jimmy Smith Quartet
Stone Cold Dead In The Market | Picnickin' | Prayer Meetin' | I Almost Lost My Mind | When The Saints Go Marching In | Red Top
Englewood Cliffs,NJ, rec. 8.2.1963
Smith,Jimmy (org) | Turrentine,Stanley (ts) | Warren,Quentin (g) | Bailey,Donald (dr)

576755-2 | CD | Rockin' the Boat
Jimmy Smith Quintet
Mathilda,Mathilda | Pork Chops | When My Dreamboat Comes Home | Please Send Me Someone To Love | Just A Closer Walk With Thee | Can Heat | Trust In Me
Englewood Cliffs,NJ, rec. 7.2.1963
Smith,Jimmy (org) | Donaldson,Lou (as) | Warren,Quentin (g) | Bailey,Donald (dr) | Patton,Big John (tambourine)

580731-2 | CD | Got A Good Thing Goin' | EAN 724358073126
Big John Patton Quartet
The Yodel | Soul Woman | Ain't That Peculiar | The Shake | Amanda
Englewood Cliffs,NJ, rec. 29.4.1966
Patton,Big John (org) | Green,Grant (g) | Walker,Hugh (dr) | Landrum,Richard 'Pablo' (congas)

581676-2 | CD | Sweet Revival... | EAN 724358167627
Ronnie Foster Group
Sweet Revival | Lisa's Love | Back Stabbers | Me And Mrs.Jones | Alone Again(Naturally) | Where Is The Love | Some Neck | It's Just Gotta Be That Way | Superwoman(Where Were You When I Needed You) | Inot
NYC, rec. 14./15.12.1972
Foster,Ronnie (org) | Hayes,Ernest 'Ernie' (el-p) | Spinozza,David (el-g) | Tropea,John (el-g) | Orchestra | details unknown

581678-2 | CD | The Final Comedown(Soundtrack) | EAN 724358167825
Grant Green With Orchestra
Past,Present & Future | Fauntain Scene | Soul Food-African Shop | Slight Fear And Terror | Luanna's Theme
NYC, rec. 13.12.1971
Green,Grant (g) | Stamm,Marvin (tp,fl-h) | Markowitz,Irving 'Marky' (tp,fl-h) | Vick,Harold (as,ts) | Bodner,Phil (fl,as,oboe,piccolo) | Tee,Richard (p,org) | Dupree,Cornell (g) | Edwards,Gordon (b-g) | Tate,Grady (dr) | Devens,George (vib,tympany.timbales,perc) | Smith,Warren (marimba,tambourine) | McDonald,Ralph (congas,bongos) | Bianco,Gene (harp) | Barber,Julian (viola) | Zaratzian,Harry (viola) | McCracken,Charles (cello) | Barab,Seymour (cello) | Marcus,Wade (comp,cond)
Green,Grant (g) | Stamm,Marvin (tp,fl-h) | Markowitz,Irving 'Marky' (tp,fl-h) | Vick,Harold (as,ts) | Bodner,Phil (fl,as,oboe,piccolo) | Tee,Richard (p,org) | Dupree,Cornell (g) | Edwards,Gordon (b-g) | Tate,Grady (dr) | Devens,George (vib,tympany.timbales,perc) | Smith,Warren (marimba,tambourine) | McDonald,Ralph (congas,bongos) | Bianco,Gene (harp) | Barber,Julian (viola) | Zaratzian,Harry (viola) | McCracken,Charles (cello) | Barab,Seymour (cello) | Marcus,Wade (comp,cond)
The Final Comedown | Afro Party | Traveling To Get To Doc | One Second After Death
Green,Grant (g) | Stamm,Marvin (tp,fl-h) | Vick,Harold (as,ts) | Bodner,Phil (fl,as,oboe,piccolo) | Tee,Richard (p,org) | Dupree,Cornell (g) | Edwards,Gordon (b-g) | Tate,Grady (dr) | Devens,George (vib,tympany.timbales,perc) | Smith,Warren (marimba,tambourine) | McDonald,Ralph (congas,bongos) | Bianco,Gene (harp) | Barber,Julian (viola) | Zaratzian,Harry (viola) | McCracken,Charles (cello) | Barab,Seymour (cello) | Marcus,Wade (comp,cond)
Green,Grant (g) | Stamm,Marvin (tp,fl-h) | Vick,Harold (as,ts) | Bodner,Phil (fl,as,oboe,piccolo) | Tee,Richard (p,org) | Dupree,Cornell (g) | Edwards,Gordon (b-g) | Tate,Grady (dr) | Devens,George (vib,tympany.timbales,perc) | Smith,Warren (marimba,tambourine) | McDonald,Ralph (congas,bongos) | Bianco,Gene (harp) | Barber,Julian (viola) | Zaratzian,Harry (viola) | McCracken,Charles (cello) | Barab,Seymour (cello) | Marcus,Wade (comp,cond)
Father's Lament
NYC, rec. 14.12.1971
Green,Grant (g) | Stamm,Marvin (tp,fl-h) | Collins,Bert (tp,fl-h) | Vick,Harold (as,ts) | Penque,Romeo (fl,as) | Tee,Richard (p,org) | Dupree,Cornell (g) | Edwards,Gordon (b-g) | Purdie,Bernard 'Pretty' (dr) | Devens,George (vib,tympany.timbales,perc) | Smith,Warren (marimba,tambourine) | McDonald,Ralph (congas,bongos) | Bianco,Gene (harp) | Barber,Julian (viola) | Zaratzian,Harry (viola) | McCracken,Charles (cello) | Barab,Seymour (cello) | Marcus,Wade (comp,cond)
Green,Grant (g) | Stamm,Marvin (tp,fl-h) | Collins,Bert (tp,fl-h) | Vick,Harold (as,ts) | Penque,Romeo (fl,as) | Tee,Richard (p,org) | Dupree,Cornell (g) | Edwards,Gordon (b-g) | Purdie,Bernard 'Pretty' (dr) | Devens,George (vib,tympany.timbales,perc) | Smith,Warren (marimba,tambourine) | McDonald,Ralph (congas,bongos) | Bianco,Gene (harp) | Barber,Julian (viola) | Zaratzian,Harry (viola) | McCracken,Charles (cello) | Barab,Seymour (cello) | Marcus,Wade (comp,cond)
Battle Scene
Green,Grant (g) | Stamm,Marvin (tp,fl-h) | Collins,Bert (tp,fl-h) | Vick,Harold (as,ts) | Penque,Romeo (fl,as) | Tee,Richard (p,org) | Dupree,Cornell (g) | Edwards,Gordon (b-g) | Purdie,Bernard 'Pretty' (dr) | Devens,George (vib,tympany.timbales,perc) | Smith,Warren (marimba,tambourine) | McDonald,Ralph (congas,bongos) | Bianco,Gene (harp) | Barber,Julian (viola) | Zaratzian,Harry (viola) | Shulman,Alan (cello) | Barab,Seymour (cello) | Marcus,Wade (comp,cond)
Green,Grant (g) | Stamm,Marvin (tp,fl-h) | Collins,Bert (tp,fl-h) | Vick,Harold (as,ts) | Penque,Romeo (fl,as) | Tee,Richard (p,org) | Dupree,Cornell (g) | Edwards,Gordon (b-g) | Purdie,Bernard 'Pretty' (dr) | Devens,George (vib,tympany.timbales,perc) | Smith,Warren (marimba,tambourine) | McDonald,Ralph (congas,bongos) | Bianco,Gene (harp) | Barber,Julian (viola) | Zaratzian,Harry (viola) | Shulman,Alan (cello) | Barab,Seymour (cello) | Marcus,Wade (comp,cond)

584232-2 | CD | Martial Solal NY-1 | EAN 724358423228
Martial Solal Trio
NY-1 | What Is This Thing Called Love | Suspect Rhythm | Body And Soul | Zag-Zig | Softly As In A Morning Sunrise | Lombardy
Live at The 'Village Vanguard',NYC, rec. 21.-23.9.2001
Solal,Martial (p) | Moutin,Francois (b) | Stewart,Bill (dr)

590414-2 | CD | Sonic Boom | EAN 724359041421
Lee Morgan Quintet
Sonic Boom
Englewood Cliffs,NJ, rec. 14.4.1967
Morgan,Lee (tp) | Newman,David Fathead (ts) | Walton,Cedar (p) | Carter,Ron (b) | Higgins,Billy (dr)
Sneaky Pete | The Mercenary | Fathead | I'll Never Be The Same | Mumbo Jumbo
Englewood Cliffs,NJ, rec. 28.4.1967
Morgan,Lee (tp) | Newman,David Fathead (ts) | Walton,Cedar (p) | Carter,Ron (b) | Higgins,Billy (dr)
Lee Morgan Sextet
Stormy Weather | Mr.Johnson | Untitled Boogaloo
Englewood Cliffs,NJ, rec. 12.9.1969
Morgan,Lee (tp) | Priester,Julian (tb) | Coleman,George (ts) | Mabern,Harold (p) | Booker,Walter (b) | Roker,Granville 'Mickey' (dr)
Free Flow | Uncle Rough | Claw-Til-Da | Untitled Boogaloo
Englewood Cliffs,NJ, rec. 10.10.1969
Morgan,Lee (tp) | Priester,Julian (tb) | Coleman,George (ts) | Mabern,Harold (p) | Booker,Walter (b) | Roker,Granville 'Mickey' (dr)

590831-2 | CD | The Golden Striker | EAN 724359083124
Ron Carter Trio
The Golden Striker | On And On | N.Y.Slick | Concierto D'Aranjuez(Adagio) | Cedar Tree | A Quick Sketch | Parade | A Theme In 3-4 | Autumn Leaves
NYC, rec. 20.7.2002
Carter,Ron (b) | Miller,Mulgrew (p) | Malone,Russell (g)

590950-2 | CD | On This Day At The Vanguard | EAN 724359095028
Joe Lovano Nonet
At The Vanguard | Focus | After The Rain | Good Bait | Laura | On This Day(Just Like Any Other) | My Little Brown Book
Live at The 'Village Vanguard',NYC, rec. 29.9.2002
Lovano,Joe (ts) | Ries,Barry (tp) | Farrell,Larry (tb) | Slagle,Steve (as) | Garzone,George (ts) | Lalama,Ralph (ts) | Robinson,Scott (bs) | Hicks,John (p) | Irwin,Dennis (b) | Nash,Lewis (dr)

590956-2 | CD | Montara | EAN 724359095622
Bobby Hutcherson Orchestra
Carmel Rise
Los Angeles,CA, rec. 12.& 14.8.1975
Hutcherson,Bobby (vib,marimba) | Brashear,Oscar (tp) | Johnson,Plas (fl) | Watts,Ernie (ts) | Jackson,Fred (fl,ts) | Nash,Larry (el-p) | Budimir,Dennis (g) | Domanico,Chuck (b) | Mason,Harold (dr) | McDonald,Ralph (perc) | Matos,Bobby (perc) | Pantoja,Victor (perc) | Palomo,Johnny (perc)
Little Angel
Hutcherson,Bobby (vib,marimba) | Mitchell,Blue (tp) | Johnson,Plas (ss) | Watts,Ernie (fl,ts) | Nash,Larry (el-p) | Domanico,Chuck (b) | McDonald,Ralph (perc) | Matos,Bobby (perc) | Pantoja,Victor (perc) | Palomo,Johnny (perc)
Love Song
Hutcherson,Bobby (vib,marimba) | Mitchell,Blue (tp) | Johnson,Plas (ss) | Watts,Ernie (fl,ts) | Nash,Larry (el-p) | Domanico,Chuck (b) | Mason,Harold (dr) | McDonald,Ralph (perc) | Matos,Bobby (perc) | Pantoja,Victor (perc) | Palomo,Johnny (perc) | Bobo,Willie (mattets)
Montara | Se Acabo La Malanga - (Se Acabo) La Malanga | Yuyo | Oye Como Va
Hutcherson,Bobby (vib,marimba) | Mitchell,Blue (tp) | Brashear,Oscar (tp) | Watts,Ernie (fl,ts) | Cano,Eddie (p) | Troncoso,Dave (b) | Matos,Bobby (perc) | Pantoja,Victor (perc) | Palomo,Johnny (perc) | Calzado,Rudi (perc)

591721-2 | CD | Blue Train | EAN 724359172125
John Coltrane Sextet
Blue Train | Moment's Notice | Locomotion | I'm Old Fashioned | Lazy Bird | Blue Train(alt.take) | Lazy Bird(alt.take)
Hackensack,NJ, rec. 15.9.1957
Coltrane,John (ts) | Morgan,Lee (tp) | Fuller,Curtis (tb) | Drew,Kenny (p) | Chambers,Paul (b) | Jones,Philly Joe (dr)

591722-2 | CD | Our Man In Paris | EAN 724359172224
Dexter Gordon Quartet
Scrapple From The Apple | Willow Weep For Me | Broadway | Stairway To The Stars | A Night In Tunisia | Our Love Is Here To Stay | Like Someone In Love
Paris,France, rec. 23.5.1963
Gordon,Dexter (ts) | Powell,Bud (p) | Michelot,Pierre (b) | Clarke,Kenny (dr)

591723-2 | CD | Grantstand | EAN 724359172323
Grant Green Quartet
Grantstand | My Funny Valentine | Blues In Maude's Flat | Old Folks | Green's Greenery
Englewood Cliffs,NJ, rec. 1.8.1961
Green,Grant (g) | Lateef,Yusef (fl,ts) | McDuff,Brother Jack (org) | Harewood,Al (dr)

591724-2 | CD | Sonny Rollins:Vol.1 | EAN 724359172422
Sonny Rollins Quintet
Decision | Bluesnote | Plain Jane | Sonnysphere | How Are Things In Glocca Morra
Hackensack,NJ, rec. 16.12.1956
Rollins,Sonny (ts) | Byrd,Donald (tp) | Kelly,Wynton (p) | Ramey,Gene (b) | Roach,Max (dr)

591725-2 | CD | Horace Silver Trio And Spotlight On Drums:Art Blakey-Sabu | EAN 724359172521
Horace Silver Trio
Safari | Horoscope | Thou Swell
NYC, rec. 9.10.1952
Silver,Horace (p) | Ramey,Gene (b) | Blakey,Art (dr)
Ecaroh | Yeah | Prelude To A Kiss | Quicksilver | Knowledge Box
NYC, rec. 20.10.1952
Silver,Horace (p) | Russell,Curly (b) | Blakey,Art (dr)
How About You | I Remember You | Opus De Funk | Silverware | Day In Day Out | Buhaina
NYC, rec. 23.11.1953
Silver,Horace (p) | Heath,Percy (b) | Blakey,Art (dr)
Art Blakey-Sabu
Message From Kenia | Nothing But The Soul
Blakey,Art (dr) | Martinez,Sabu (conga)

591893-2 | CD | The Bandwagon | EAN 724359189321
Jason Moran Trio
Intro(ABR) | Another One | Intermezzo Op.118, No.2 | Ringing My Phone(Straight Outa Istanbul) | Out Front | Gentle Shifts South | Gangsterism On Stages | Body And Soul | Infospace | Planet Rock
Live at The 'Village Vanguard',NYC, rec. 29./30.11.2002
Moran,Jason (p) | Mateen,Tarus (b) | Waits,Nasheet (dr)

591894-2 | CD | Mode For Joe
Joe Henderson Septet
A Shade Of Jade | Mode For Joe | Black | Caribbean Firedance | Granted | Free Wheelin'
Englewood Cliffs,NJ, rec. 27.1.1966
Henderson,Joe (ts) | Morgan,Lee (tp) | Fuller,Curtis (tb) | Hutcherson,Bobby (vib,marimba) | Walton,Cedar (p) | Carter,Ron (b) | Chambers,Joe (dr)

591895-2 | CD | Let Freedom Ring
Jackie McLean Quartet
Melody For Melonae | I'll Keep Loving You | Rene | Omega
Englewood Cliffs,NJ, rec. 19.3.1962
McLean,Jackie (as) | Davis Jr.,Walter (p) | Lewis,Herbie (b) | Higgins,Billy (dr)

591896-2 | CD | Search For The New Land
Lee Morgan Sextet
Search For The New Land | The Joker | Mr.Kenyatta | Melancholy | Morgan The Pirate
Englewood Cliffs,NJ, rec. 15.2.1964
Morgan,Lee (tp) | Shorter,Wayne (ts) | Green,Grant (g) | Hancock,Herbie (p) | Workman,Reggie (b) | Higgins,Billy (dr)

591901-2 | CD | Adams Apple
Wayne Shorter Quartet
Adam's Apple | 502 Blues | El Gaucho | Footprints | Teru | Chief Crazy Horse
NYC, rec. 14.2.1966
Shorter,Wayne (ts) | Hancock,Herbie (p) | Workman,Reggie (b) | Chambers,Joe (dr)

592009-2 | CD | Think Tank | EAN 724359200927
Pat Martino Quintet
The Phineas Train | Think Tank | Dozen Down | Sun On My Hands | Africa | Quatessence | Befor You Ask | Earthings
NYC, rec. 8.-10.1.2003
Martino,Pat (g) | Lovano,Joe (ts) | Rubalcaba,Gonzalo (p) | McBride,Christian (b) | Nash,Lewis (dr)

593871-2 | CD | Passing Ships | EAN 724359387123
Anfrew Hill Nonet
Passing Ships | The Brown Queen | Cascade
Englewood Cliffs,NJ, rec. 7.11.1969
Hill,Andrew (p) | Shaw,Woody (tp) | Reece,Dizzy (tp) | Priester,Julian (tb) | Northern,Bob (fr-h) | Johnson,Howard (b-cl,tuba) | Farrell,Joe (fl,b-cl,ss,ts,engl-h) | Carter,Ron (b) | White,Lenny (dr)
Sideways | Plantation Bag | Noon Tide | Yesterday's Tomorrow
Englewood Cliffs,NJ, rec. 14.11.1969
Hill,Andrew (p) | Shaw,Woody (tp) | Reece,Dizzy (tp) | Priester,Julian (tb) | Northern,Bob (fr-h) | Johnson,Howard (b-cl,tuba) | Farrell,Joe (fl,b-cl,ss,ts,engl-h) | Carter,Ron (b) | White,Lenny (dr)

593872-2 | CD | The Flip | EAN 724359387222
Hank Mobley Sextet
The Flip | Feelin' Folsky | Snappin' Out | 18th Hole | Early Morning Stroll
Paris,France, rec. 12.7.1969
Mobley,Hank (ts) | Reece,Dizzy (tp) | Hampton,Slide (tb) | Benedetti,Vince (p) | Cullaz,Alby (b) | Jones,Philly Joe (dr)

593874-2 | CD | Fuchsia Swing Song | EAN 724359387420
Sam Rivers Quartet
Fuchsia Swing Song | Downstairs Blues Upstairs | Cyclic Episode | Luminous Monolith | Beatrice | Ellipsis
Englewood Cliffs,NJ, rec. 11.12.1964
Rivers,Sam (ts) | Byard,Jaki (p) | Carter,Ron (b) | Williams,Tony (dr)

593875-2 | CD | Bossa Nova Bacchanal | EAN 724359387529
Charlie Rouse Orchestra
Back To The Tropics | Aconteceu | Velhos Tempos | Samba De Orfeu | Un Dia | Meci Bon Dieu | In Martinique
Englewood Cliffs,NJ, rec. 11.11.1962
Rouse,Charlie (ts) | Burrell,Kenny (g) | Westbrook,Chauncey 'Lord' (g) | Gales,Larry (b) | Bobo,Willie (dr) | Valdez,Carlos 'Patato' (congas) | Masseaux,Garvin (chekere)
Freddie Hubbard Quintet
One For Five
Englewood Cliffs,NJ, rec. 22.1.1965
Hubbard,Freddie (tp) | Rouse,Charlie (ts) | Tyner,McCoy (p) | Cranshaw,Bob (b) | Higgins,Billy (dr)

595961-2 | CD | Free Form
Donald Byrd Quintet
Pentecostal Feeling | Night Flower | Nai Nai | Frenche Spice | Free Form
NYC, rec. 11.12.1961
Byrd,Donald (tp) | Adams,Pepper (bs) | Hancock,Herbie (p) | Warren,Edward 'Butch' (b) | Higgins,Billy (dr)

595972-2 | CD | Right Now
Jackie McLean Quartet
Eco | Poor Eric | Christel's Theme | Right Now | Right Now(alt.take)
Englewood Cliffs,NJ, rec. 29.1.1965
McLean,Jackie (as) | Willis,Larry (p) | Cranshaw,Bob (b) | Jarvis,Clifford (dr)

595974-2 | CD | Sweet Honey Bee
Duke Pearson Sextet
Sweet Honey Bee | Sudel | Big Bertha | Empathy | Ready Rudy
Englewood Cliffs,NJ, rec. 7.12.1966
Pearson,Duke (p) | Hubbard,Freddie (tp) | Spaulding,James (fl,as) | Henderson,Joe (ts) | Carter,Ron (b) | Roker,Granville 'Mickey' (dr)
Duke Pearson Quintet
Gaslight
Pearson,Duke (p) | Hubbard,Freddie (tp) | Henderson,Joe (ts) | Carter,Ron (b) | Roker,Granville 'Mickey' (dr)
Duke Pearson Quartet
After The Rain
Pearson,Duke (p) | Spaulding,James (fl) | Carter,Ron (b) | Roker,Granville 'Mickey' (dr)

746136-2 | CD | Speak Like A Child
Herbie Hancock Sextet
Riot | Speak Like A Child | First Trip | Toys | Goodbye To Childhood | The Sorcerer
rec. details unknown
Hancock,Herbie (p) | Jones,Thad (fl-h) | Dodgion,Jerry (alto-fl) | Phillips,Peter (b-tb) | Carter,Ron (b,dr)

746295-2 | CD | Pianism
Michel Petrucciani Trio
The Prayer | Our Tune | Face's Face | Night And Day | Here's That Rainy Day | Regina
NYC, rec. 20.12.1985
Petrucciani,Michel (p) | Danielsson,Palle (b) | Zigmund,Eliot (dr)

746298-2 | CD | Spontaneous Inventions
Bobby McFerrin Groups
Thinkin' About Your Body | Turtle Shoes | From Me To You | There Ya Go | Cara Mia | Another Night In Tunisia | Opportunity | Walkin' | I Hear Music | Beverly Hills Blues | Manana Iguana
rec. details unknown
McFerrin,Bobby (perc,voc) | Shorter,Wayne (ss,ts) | Hancock,Herbie (keyboards) | Hendricks,Jon (voc) | Williams,Robin (voc) | Manhattan Transfer,The (voc-group)

746402-2 | CD | Back At The Chicken Shack
Jimmy Smith Quartet
Back At The Chicken Shack | When I Grow Too Old To Dream | Minor Chant | Messy Bessie
rec. 25.4.1960
Smith,Jimmy (org) | Turrentine,Stanley (ts) | Burrell,Kenny (g) | Bailey,Donald (dr)

746427-2 | CD | Power Of Three-Live At Montreux
Michel Petrucciani feat. Jim Hall and Wayne Shorter
Limbo | Careful | Morning Blues | Waltz New | Beautiful Love | In A Sentimental Mood | Bimini
Jazz Festival Montreux,CH, rec. 14.7.1986
Petrucciani,Michel (p) | Shorter,Wayne (ss,ts) | Hall,Jim (g)

746822-2 | CD | Feelin' The Spirit | EAN 077774682220
Grant Green Quintet
Just A Closer Walk With Thee | Joshua Fit The Battle Of Jericho | Nobody Knows The Trouble I've Seen | Go Down Moses | Deep River | Sometimes I Feel Like A Motherless Child
Englewood Cliffs,NJ, rec. 21.12.1962
Green,Grant (g) | Hancock,Herbie (p) | Warren,Edward 'Butch' (b) | Higgins,Billy (dr) | Masseaux,Garvin (tambourine)

748679-2 | CD | Michel Plays Petrucciani
Michel Petrucciani Trio
She Did It Again | Sahara | 13th | Mr.K.J.
NYC, rec. 24.9.1987
Petrucciani,Michel (p) | Peacock,Gary (b) | Haynes,Roy (dr)
Michel Petrucciani Quartet
One For Us
Petrucciani,Michel (p) | Abercrombie,John (g) | Peacock,Gary (b) | Haynes,Roy (dr)
It's A Dance
NYC, rec. 9./10.12.1987
Petrucciani,Michel (p) | Abercrombie,John (g) | Gomez,Eddie (b) | Foster,Al (dr)
Brazilian Suite
Petrucciani,Michel (p) | Gomez,Eddie (b) | Foster,Al (dr) | Thornton,Steve (perc)
Michel Petrucciani Trio
One Night At Ken And Jessica's | La Champagne
Petrucciani,Michel (p) | Gomez,Eddie (b) | Foster,Al (dr)

748786-2 | CD | Billie's Blues
Billie Holiday With The Paul Whiteman Orchestra
Travelin' Light
Los Angeles,CA, rec. 12.6.1942
Holiday,Billie (voc) | Kelly,Monty (tp) | Neill,Larry (tp) | Waddilove,Don (tp) | Layton,Skip (tb) | McEachern,Murray (tb) | unkn. (tb) | West,Alvy (reeds) | D'Andre,Dan (reeds) | Hartman,Leonard 'Lennie' (reeds) | unkn. (reeds) | Weed,Buddy (p) | Pingitore,Mike (g) | Shapiro,Artie (b) | Rodriguez,Willie (dr) | Mundy,Jimmy (arr) | Whiteman,Paul (ld)
Billie Holiday With The Tiny Grimes Quintet
Blue Turning Grey Over You | Be Fair With Me Baby | Rocky Mountain Blues | Detour Ahead
NYC, rec. 29.4.1951
Holiday,Billie (voc) | Grimes,Tiny (g) | Henry,Haywood (ts,bs) | Tucker,Bobby (p) | unkn. (b,dr)
Billie Holiday With The Carl Drinkard Trio
Announcement by Leonard Feather | Blue Moon | All Of Me | My Man | Them There Eyes | I Cried For You(Now It's Your Turn To Cry Over Me) | What A Little Moonlight Can Do | I Cover The Waterfront
Köln, rec. 5.1.1954
Holiday,Billie (voc) | Drinkard,Carl (p) | Mitchell,Red (b) | Leighton,Elaine (dr)
Billie Holiday And Her All Stars
Billie's Blues | Lover Come Back To Me
Holiday,Billie (voc) | DeFranco,Buddy (cl) | Norvo,Red (vib) | Raney,Jimmy (g) | Clark,Sonny (p) | Booker,Beryl (p) | Mitchell,Red (b) | Leighton,Elaine (dr)

780251-2 | CD | Standards
Bireli Lagrene Trio
C'Est Si Bon | Softly As In A Morning Sunrise | Days Of Wine And Roses | Stella By Starlight | Smile | Autumn Leaves | Teach Me Tonight | Donna Lee | Body And Soul | How Insensitive(Insensatez)
Paris,France, rec. June 1992
Lagrene,Bireli (g) | Orsted-Pedersen,Niels-Henning (b) | Ceccarelli,André (dr)
Bireli Lagrene Quartet
Nuages
Lagrene,Bireli (g) | Orsted-Pedersen,Niels-Henning (b) | Di Piazza,Dominique (el-b) | Ceccarelli,André (dr)

780589-2 | CD | Michel Petrucciani Live
Michel Petrucciani Quintet
Black Magic | Miles Davis' Licks | Contradictions | Bite | Rachid | Looking Up | The You Note | Estate(Summer)
Live at The Arsenal,Metz,France, rec. November 1991
Petrucciani,Michel (p) | Holzman,Adam (keyboards) | Logan,Steve (b) | Jones,Victor (dr) | M'Boop,Abdou (perc)

780590-2 | CD | Promenade With Duke
Michel Petrucciani
Caravan | Lush Life | Take The 'A' Train | African Flower | In A Sentimental Mood | Hidden Joy | One Night In The Hotel | Satin Doll | C Jam Blues
NYC, rec. details unknown
Petrucciani,Michel (p-solo)

780679-2 | CD | Blue N' Groovy
Duke Pearson Orchestra
Chilli Peppers
NYC, rec. 13.9.1967
Pearson,Duke (p,arr) | Hubbard,Freddie (tp) | Brown,Garnett (tb) | Spaulding,James (as) | Dodgion,Jerry (alto-fl,as) | Turrentine,Stanley (ts) | Taylor,Gene (b) | Tate,Grady (dr)
Jack Wilson Sextet
On Children
NYC, rec. 22.9.1967
Wilson,Jack (p) | Morgan,Lee (tp) | Brown,Garnett (tb) | McLean,Jackie (as) | Cranshaw,Bob (b) | Higgins,Billy (dr)
Stanley Turrentine Quartet
Meatwave
NYC, rec. 8.7.1966
Turrentine,Stanley (ts) | Tyner,McCoy (p) | Cranshaw,Bob (b) | Roker,Granville 'Mickey' (dr)
Don Wilkerson Quintet
Dem Tambourines
NYC, rec. 18.6.1962
Wilkerson,Don (ts,voc) | Green,Grant (g) | Clark,Sonny (p) | Warren,Edward 'Butch' (b) | Higgins,Billy (dr,tambourines)
Lee Morgan Quintet
The Sidewinder
NYC, rec. 21.12.1963
Morgan,Lee (tp) | Henderson,Joe (ts) | Harris,Barry (p) | Cranshaw,Bob (b) | Higgins,Billy (dr)
Herbie Hancock Quartet
Cantaloupe Island
NYC, rec. 17.6.1964
Hancock,Herbie (p) | Hubbard,Freddie (fl-h,co) | Carter,Ron (b) | Williams,Tony (dr)
Art Blakey And The Jazz Messengers
Ping Pong
NYC, rec. 18.12.1961
Blakey,Art (dr) | Morgan,Lee (tp) | Shorter,Wayne (ts) | Timmons,Bobby (p) | Merritt,Jymie (b)
Tina Brooks Quintet
True Blue
NYC, rec. 25.6.1960
Brooks,Tina (ts) | Hubbard,Freddie (tp) | Jordan,Duke (p) | Jones,Sam (b) | Taylor,Arthur 'Art' (dr)
Donald Byrd Quintet
Jeannine
Live at The Half Note Cafe,NYC, rec. 11.11.1960
Byrd,Donald (tp) | Adams,Pepper (bs) | Pearson,Duke (p) | Jackson,Laymon (b) | Humphries,Lex (dr)
Bobby Hutcherson Quintet
8/4 Beat
NYC, rec. 14.7.1966
Hutcherson,Bobby (vib) | Henderson,Joe (ts) | Tyner,McCoy (p) | Lewis,Herbie (b) | Higgins,Billy (dr)
Wayne Shorter Sextet
Tom Thumb
NYC, rec. 10.3.1967
Shorter,Wayne (ts) | Fuller,Curtis (tb) | Spaulding,James (fl,as) | Hancock,Herbie (p) | Carter,Ron (b) | Chambers,Joe (dr)

781357-2 | CD | Blue Light 'Til Dawn
Cassandra Wilson Group
You Don't Know What Love Is
NYC, rec. details unknown
Wilson,Cassandra (voc) | Ross,Brandon (g) | Burnham,Charles (v)
Hellhound On My Trail
Wilson,Cassandra (voc) | Dara,Olu (tp) | Ross,Brandon (g)
Come On In My Kitchen
Wilson,Cassandra (voc) | Cedras,Tony (accordeon) | Ross,Brandon (g) | Davis,Kenneth 'Kenny' (b) | Carter,Lance (dr)
Tell Me You'll Wait For Me
Wilson,Cassandra (voc) | Davis,Kenneth 'Kenny' (b) | Johnson,Kevin (snare-dr)
Children Of The Night
Wilson,Cassandra (voc) | Ross,Brandon (g) | Vinx (perc) | Johnson,Kevin (perc) | Carter,Lance (perc)
Black Crow
Wilson,Cassandra (voc) | Byron,Don (cl) | Vinx (perc) | Johnson,Kevin (perc) | Carter,Lance (perc) | McClellan,Bill (perc) | Haynes,Jeff (perc) | Baptista,Cyro (perc)
Sankofa
Wilson,Cassandra (voices)
Estrellas | Redbone
Wilson,Cassandra (voc) | Wharton,Gib (steel-g) | Haynes,Jeff (perc) | Baptista,Cyro (perc)
Tupelo Honey
Wilson,Cassandra (voc) | Ross,Brandon (g) | Plaxico,Lonnie (b) | Burnham,Charles (v,mandocello) | Johnson,Kevin (perc) | Carter,Lance (snare-dr)
Blue Light 'Till Dawn
Wilson,Cassandra (voc) | Wharton,Gib (steel-g) | Burnham,Charles (v) | Davis,Kenneth 'Kenny' (b) | McClellan,Bill (dr) | Haynes,Jeff (perc) | Baptista,Cyro (perc)
I Can't Stand The Rain
Wilson,Cassandra (voc) | Whitley,Chris (g)

784049-2 | CD | A Night In Tunisia
Art Blakey And The Jazz Messengers
Yama | A Night In Tunisia | Sincerely Diana | Sincerely Diana(alt.take) | So Tired | Kozo's Waltz | When Your Lover Has Gone
NYC, rec. 14.8.1960
Blakey,Art (dr) | Morgan,Lee (tp) | Shorter,Wayne (ts) | Timmons,Bobby (p) | Merritt,Jymie (b)

784077-2 | CD | Doin' Allright
Dexter Gordon Quintet
I Was Doing Alright | You've Changed | For Regulars Only | Society Red | It's You Or No One
NYC, rec. 6.5.1961
Gordon,Dexter (ts) | Hubbard,Freddie (tp) | Parlan,Horace (p) | Tucker,George (b) | Harewood,Al (dr)

784080-2 | CD | Workout | EAN 077778408024
Hank Mobley Quintet
Smokin' | Uh Huh | The Best Things In Life Are Free | Workout | Greasin Easy
Englewood Cliffs,NJ, rec. 26.3.1961
Mobley,Hank (ts) | Kelly,Wynton (p) | Green,Grant (g) | Chambers,Paul (b) | Jones,Philly Joe (dr)
Hank Mobley Quartet
Three Coins In The Fountain
Mobley,Hank (ts) | Kelly,Wynton (p) | Chambers,Paul (b) | Jones,Philly Joe (dr)

784098-2 | CD | Blue And Sentimental | EAN 077778409823
Ike Quebec Quartet
Blue And Sentimental | Minor Impulse | Don't Take Your Love From Me | Blues For Charlie | Like | It's All Right With Me | That Old Black Magic
Englewood Cliffs,NJ, rec. 16.12.1961
Quebec,Ike (ts) | Green,Grant (g) | Chambers,Paul (b) | Jones,Philly Joe (dr)
Ike Quebec Quintet
Count Every Star
Englewood Cliffs,NJ, rec. 23.12.1961
Quebec,Ike (ts) | Green,Grant (g) | Clark,Sonny (p) | Chambers,Paul (b) | Jones,Philly Joe (dr)

784173-2 | CD | Night Dreamer | EAN 077778417323
Wayne Shorter Quintet
Night Dreamer | Oriental Folk Song | Virgo | Black Nile | Charcoal Blues | Armageddon
NYC, rec. 29.4.1964
Shorter,Wayne (ts) | Morgan,Lee (tp) | Tyner,McCoy (p) | Workman,Reggie (b) | Jones,Elvin (dr)

784271-2 | CD | Mr.Shing-A-Ling | EAN 077778427124
Lou Donaldson Quintet
Peepin' | The Kid | The Shadow Of Your Smile | The Humpback
Englewood Cliffs,NJ, rec. 27.10.1967
Donaldson,Lou (as) | Mitchell,Blue (tp) | Smith,Lonnie (org) | Ponder,Jimmy (g) | Muhammad,Idris[Leo Morris] (dr)
Lou Donaldson Quartet
Ode To Billy Joe
Donaldson,Lou (as) | Smith,Lonnie (org) | Ponder,Jimmy (g) | Muhammad,Idris[Leo Morris] (dr)

784466-2 | CD | Black Byrd | EAN 077778446620
Donald Byrd Orchestra
Flight Time | Mr.Thomas
Los Angeles,CA, rec. 3./4.4.1972
Byrd,Donald (tp,fl-h,el-tp,voc) | Mizell,Fonce (tp,voc) | Glenn,Roger (fl,sax) | Sample,Joe (p,el-p) | Perren,Fred (el-p,synth,voc) | Parks,Dean (g) | Felder,Wilton (el-b) | Mason,Harold (dr) | Hall,Bobbye Porter (perc) | Mizell,Larry (arr,voc)
Black Byrd | Love's So Far Away | Sky High | Slop Jar Blues | Where Are You Going
Byrd,Donald (tp,fl-h,el-tp,voc) | Mizell,Fonce (tp,voc) | Glenn,Roger (fl,sax) | Sample,Joe (p,el-p) | Perren,Fred (el-p,synth,voc) | Walker,David T. (g) | Rainey,Chuck (el-b) | Mason,Harold (dr) | Spruill,Stephanie (perc) | Mizell,Larry (arr,voc)

785108-2 | CD | Charlie Parker At Storyville
Charlie Parker Quartet
Moose The Mooche | I'll Walk Alone | Ornithology | Out Of Nowhere
Club Storyville,Boston, rec. 10.3.1953
Parker,Charlie (as) | Garland,Red (p) | Griggs,Bernie (b) | Haynes,Roy (dr)
Charlie Parker Quintet
Now's The Time | Don't Blame Me | Dancing On The Ceiling | Cool Blues | Groovin' High
Club Storyville,Boston, rec. 22.9.1953
Parker,Charlie (as) | Pomeroy,Herb (tp) | Thompson,Sir Charles (p) | Woode,Jimmy (b) | Clarke,Kenny (dr)

789907-2 | CD | Blue Breaks Beats Vol.2
Donald Byrd & His Orchestra
Street Lady
Los Angeles,CA, rec. 13.-15.6.1973
Byrd,Donald (tp,fl-h,voc) | Glenn,Roger (fl) | Mizell,Fonce (tp,clavinet) | Perrin,Fred (synth) | Walker,David T. (g) | Rainey,Chuck (b) | Peters,Jerry (p,el-p) | Mason,Harvey (dr) | Errisson,King (perc) | Spruill,Stephanie (perc)
Bobbi Humphrey Group
Jasper Country Man
Los Angeles,CA, rec. 7./8.6.1973
Humphrey,Bobbi (fl,voc) | Mizell,Fonce (tp,clavinet) | Perrin,Fred (synth) | Walker,David T. (g) | Rowin,John (g) | Rainey,Chuck (b) | Brown,Roy (el-b) | Peters,Jerry (p,el-p) | Mason,Harvey (dr) | Errisson,King (perc) | Spruill,Stephanie (perc)
Donald Byrd Sextet
Beale Street
NYC, rec. 1967
Byrd,Donald (tp) | Red (Kyner) | Mobley,Hank (ts) | Walton,Cedar (p) | Booker,Walter (b) | Higgins,Billy (dr)
Eddie Henderson Orchestra
Kumquat Kids
San Francisco,CA, rec. March/April 1964
Henderson,Eddie (tp,fl-h) | Priester,Julian (tb) | Maupin,Bennie (b-cl,ts) | Hutcherson,Bobby (marimba) | Duke,George (el-p,synth) | Johnson,Alphonso (el-b) | Williams,Buster (b) | Mason,Harold (dr) | Hart,Billy (dr)

Gene Harris Group
Higga Boom
Los Angeles,CA, rec. 1975
Harris,Gene (p,el-p) | Watts,Ernie (ts) | Muldrow,Sidney (fr-h) | Walker,David T. (g) | Rowe,John (g) | Peters,Jerry (p,el-p) | Rainey,Chuck (el-b) | Mason,Harold (dr) | Johnson,Ken (perc)
Reuben Wilson Quartet
Orange Peel
NYC, rec. 12.12.1969
Wilson,Reuben (org) | Manning,John (ts) | Sparks,Melvin (g) | Derrick,Tommy (dr)
Jimmy McGriff Orchestra
The Worm
details unknown, rec. details unknown
McGriff,Jimmy (org) | details unknown
Lou Donaldson Orchestra
The Caterpilar
NYC, rec. 16.7.1971
Donaldson,Lou (as) | Williams,Ed (tp) | Sparks,Melvin (g) | Spencer Jr.,Leon (org) | Jemmott,Jerry (el-b) | Muhammad,Idris[Leo Morris] (dr) | Armando,Ray (perc) | Brown,Mildred (voc) | Brown,Rosalyn (voc) | Thomas,Naomi (voc) | Briggs,Jimmy (voc-arr)
Grant Green Orchestra
Ain't It Funky Now
Englewood Cliffs,NJ, rec. 30.1.1970
Green,Grant (g) | Mitchell,Blue (tp) | Bartee,Claude (ts) | Riggins,Emmanuel (org) | Lewis,Jimmy (b) | Muhammad,Idris[Leo Morris] (dr) | Candido[Camero] (congas) | Landrum,Richard 'Pablo' (bongos)
Bobby Hutcherson Quintet
Ummh
Los Angeles,CA, rec. 15.7.1970
Hutcherson,Bobby (vib,marimba,perc) | Land,Harold (fl,ts) | Sample,Joe (p,el-p) | Williams,John B. (b,el-b) | Roker,Granville 'Mickey' (dr)
Blue Mitchell And His Orchestra
Good Humour Man
NYC, rec. 17.11.1967
Mitchell,Blue (tp) | Collins,Burt (tp) | Priester,Julian (tb) | Dodgion,Jerry (fl,as) | Cook,Junior (ts) | Adams,Pepper (bs) | Tyner,McCoy (p) | Taylor,Gene (b) | Foster,Al (dr)
Gerald Wilson And His Orchestra
Viva Tirado
Los Angeles,CA, rec. September 1962
Wilson,Gerald (tp,arr) | Jones,Carmell (tp) | Chaikin,Jules (tp) | Audino,Johnny (tp) | Hill,Fred 'Freddie' (tp) | Edmondson,Bob (tb) | Blackburn,Lou (tb) | Strong,Frank (tb) | Knight,Bobby (tb) | Shank,Bud (as) | Maini,Joe (as) | Edwards,Teddy (ts) | Land,Harold (ts) | Raffell,Don (bs) | Pass,Joe (g) | Wilson,Jack (p) | Bond,Jimmy (b) | Lewis,Mel (dr) | Duran,Modesto (congas)

789916-2 | CD | Michel Petrucciani:The Blue Note Years
Michel Petrucciani Group
Looking Up
Petrucciani,Michel (p,synth) | Holzman,Adam (synth) | Kondor,Robbie (synth) | Jackson,Anthony (el-b) | White,Lenny (dr) | Colon,Frank (perc)
Play Me
Petrucciani,Michel (p,synth) | Holzman,Adam (synth) | Kondor,Robbie (synth) | Walker,Chris (el-b) | White,Lenny (dr) | Colon,Frank (perc)
Lullababy
Petrucciani,Michel (p,synth) | Kondor,Robbie (synth) | Gomez,Eddie (b) | Jones,Victor (dr) | Colon,Frank (perc)
O Nana Oye
Petrucciani,Michel (p,voc) | Holzman,Adam (synth) | Kondor,Robbie (synth) | McKee,Andy (b) | Jones,Victor (dr) | Colon,Frank (perc) | Maria,Tania (voc)
September Song | Miles Davis' Licks | Home
Petrucciani,Michel (p,synth) | Holzman,Adam (synth,synth-programming) | Jackson,Anthony (b) | Hakim,Omar (dr) | Thornton,Steve (perc)
Michel Petrucciani Trio
La Champagne
Petrucciani,Michel (p) | Gomez,Eddie (b) | Foster,Al (dr)
Michel Petrucciani Quartet
Brasilian Suite
Petrucciani,Michel (p) | Gomez,Eddie (b) | Foster,Al (dr) | Thornton,Steve (perc)
Michel Petrucciani Trio
She Did It Again
Petrucciani,Michel (p) | Peacock,Gary (b) | Haynes,Roy (dr)
Our Tune
Petrucciani,Michel (p) | Danielsson,Palle (b) | Zigmund,Eliot (dr)
Michel Petrucciani feat. Jim Hall and Wayne Shorter
Bimini
Petrucciani,Michel (p) | Shorter,Wayne (ts) | Hall,Jim (g)

790264-2 | CD | I Remember
Dianne Reeves With Band
Softly As In A Morning Sunrise
Los Angeles,CA, rec. 27.4.1988
Reeves,Dianne (voc) | Osby,Greg (as) | Hutcherson,Bobby (vib) | Brown,Donald (p) | Moffett,Charnett (b) | Smith,Marvin 'Smitty' (dr) | Powell,Ron (perc)
Like A Lover
Reeves,Dianne (voc) | Eubanks,Kevin (g) | Powell,Ron (wind-chimes)
You Tought My Heart To Sing | For All We Know
Los Angeles,CA, rec. 28.4.1988
Reeves,Dianne (voc) | Miller,Mulgrew (p) | Moffett,Charnett (b) | Smith,Marvin 'Smitty' (dr)
How High The Moon
Los Angeles,CA, rec. 9.5.1988
Reeves,Dianne (voc) | Miller,Mulgrew (p) | Moffett,Charnett (b) | Carrington,Terri Lyne (dr) | Powell,Ron (perc)
Afro Blue
Englewood Cliffs,NJ, rec. 10.9.1990
Reeves,Dianne (voc) | Almario,Justo (sax) | Mims,Charles (p) | Severin,Chris (b) | Kilson,Billy (dr) | Summers,Bill (perc) | Conte,Luis (perc)
The Nearness Of You- | Misty- | I Remember Sky | Love For Sale
Englewood Cliffs,NJ, rec. 11.9.1990
Reeves,Dianne (voc) | Childs,Billy (p) | Severin,Chris (b) | Kilson,Billy (dr)

791441-2 | CD | Stormy Monday
Lou Rawls With Les McCann Ltd.
Stormy Monday Blues(They Call It Stormy Monday) | God Bless The Child | See See Rider | Willow Weep For Me | I'm Gonna Move To The Outskirts Of Town | In The Evening When The Sun Goes Down | 'Tain't Nobody's Bizness If I Do | Lost And Lookin' | I'd Rather Drink Muddy Water | Sweet Lover | Blues Is A Woman | A Little Les Of Lou's Blues | Stormy Monday Blues(They Call It Stormy Monday-alt.take)
Los Angeles,CA, rec. 5.& 12.2.1962
Rawls,Lou (voc) | McCann,Les (p) | Vinnegar,Leroy (b) | Jefferson,Ron (dr)

792563-2 | CD | Music
Michel Petrucciani Group
Looking Up | Memories Of Paris | My Bebop Tune | Brazilian Suite No.2 | Bite | Lullaby | O Nana Oye | Play Me
NYC, rec. 1989
Petrucciani,Michel (p,org,synth,voc) | Goldstein,Gil (accordeon) | Lubambo,Romero (g) | Holzman,Adam (synth) | Kondor,Robbie (synth) | McKee,Andy (b) | Gomez,Eddie (b) | Jackson,Anthony (el-b) | Walker,Chris (el-b) | White,Lenny (dr) | Jones,Victor (dr) | Maria,Tania (voc)

793203-2 | CD | The Blue Note Years-The Best Of Sonny Rollins
Sonny Rollins Quintet
Decision | How Are Things In Glocca Morra
Hackensack,NJ, rec. 16.12.1956
Rollins,Sonny (ts) | Byrd,Donald (tp) | Kelly,Wynton (p) | Ramey,Gene (b) | Roach,Max (dr)
Poor Butterfly | Why Don't I | Misterioso
Hackensack,NJ, rec. 14.4.1957
Rollins,Sonny (ts) | Johnson,J.J. (tb) | Silver,Horace (p) | Chambers,Paul (b) | Blakey,Art (dr)
Sonny Rollins Quartet
Tune Up
Hackensack,NJ, rec. 22.9.1957
Rollins,Sonny (ts) | Kelly,Wynton (p) | Watkins,Doug (b) | Jones,Philly Joe (dr)
Sonny Rollins Trio
Sonnymoon For Two | Softly As In A Morning Sunrise | Striver's Row
Live at The 'Village Vanguard',NYC, rec. 3.11.1957
Rollins,Sonny (ts) | Ware,Wilbur (b) | Jones,Elvin (dr)

795477-2 | CD | Play
Bobby McFerrin-Chick Corea
Spain | Even From Me | Autumn Leaves | Blues Connotation | Round About Midnight | Blue Bossa
Live at Wolftrap,Vienna,Virginia & Carnegie Hall,NYC, rec. 23.& 27.6.1990
McFerrin,Bobby (voice) | Corea,Chick (el-p)

795480-2 | CD | Playground
Michel Petrucciani Group
September Second | Home | P'tit Louis | Miles Davis' Licks | Brazilian Suite No.1 | Play School | Contradictions | Law Of Physics | Like That
NYC, rec. details unknown
Petrucciani,Michel (p,synth) | Holzman,Adam (synth,synth-programming) | Jackson,Anthony (b) | Hakim,Omar (dr) | Thornton,Steve (perc)
Rachid
Petrucciani,Michel (p,synth) | Holzman,Adam (synth,synth-programming) | Jackson,Anthony (b) | Romano,Aldo (dr) | Thornton,Steve (perc)
Piano Play The Man
Petrucciani,Michel (p,synth) | Holzman,Adam (synth,synth-programming) | Jackson,Anthony (b) | Thornton,Steve (perc)

795590-2 | CD | Blue Bossa
Horace Parlan Quartet
Congalegre
NYC, rec. 4.12.1960
Parlan,Horace (p) | Tucker,George (b) | Harewood,Al (dr) | Barretto,Ray (congas)
Charlie Rouse Orchestra
Back Down To The Tropics'
NYC, rec. 11.11.1962
Rouse,Charlie (ts) | Burrell,Kenny (g) | Westbrook,Chauncey 'Lord' (g) | Gales,Lawrence (b) | Bobo,Willie (dr) | Valdez,Carlos 'Patato' (congas) | Masseaux,Garvin (chekere)
Big John Patton Quartet
Latona
NYC, rec. 11.12.1965
Patton,Big John (org) | Hutcherson,Bobby (vib) | Green,Grant (g) | Fitch,Otis (dr)
Duke Pearson Orchestra
Sandalia Dela
NYC, rec. 5.5.1969
Pearson,Duke (keyboards) | Gaffa,Al (g) | Cranshaw,Bob (b) | Souze,Bebeto Jose (b) | Roker,Granville 'Mickey' (dr) | Moreira,Airto (perc) | Purim,Flora (voc) | Bey,Andy (voc)
Ike Quebec Quintet
Loie
Englewood Cliffs,NJ, rec. 5.10.1962
Quebec,Ike (ts) | Burrell,Kenny (g) | Marshall,Wendell (b) | Bobo,Willie (dr) | Masseaux,Garvin (chekere)
Cannonball Adderley With Sergio Mendes And The Bossa Rio Sextet
Sambop
NYC, rec. 10.12.1962
Adderley,Julian \'Cannonball\' (as) | Moura,Paulo (as) | Paulo,Pedro (tp) | Mendes,Sergio (p) | Perreiria,Durual (g) | Bielly Jr.,Octavio (b) | Romao,Dom Um (dr)
Kenny Dorham Orchestra
Afrodisia
NYC, rec. 29.3.1955
Dorham,Kenny (tp) | Johnson,J.J. (tb) | Mobley,Hank (ts) | Payne,Cecil (bs) | Silver,Horace (p) | Pettiford,Oscar (b) | Blakey,Art (dr) | Valdez,Carlos 'Patato' (congas)
Grant Green Sextet
Mambo Inn
NYC, rec. 26.4.1962
Green,Grant (g) | Acea,Johnny (p) | Marshall,Wendell (b) | Bobo,Willie (dr) | Valdez,Carlos 'Patato' (congas) | Masseaux,Garvin (chekere)
Horace Silver Quintet
The Cape Verdean Blues
NYC, rec. Oct.1965
Silver,Horace (p) | Shaw,Woody (tp) | Henderson,Joe (ts) | Cranshaw,Bob (b) | Humphries,Roger (dr)
Eliane Elias Trio
Waters Of March
NYC, rec. December 1989
Elias,Eliane (p) | Gomez,Eddie (b) | DeJohnette,Jack (dr)
Andrew Hill Quintet
Mira
Englewood Cliffs,NJ, rec. 5.8.1968
Hill,Andrew (p) | Morgan,Lee (tp) | Ervin,Booker (ts) | Carter,Ron (b) | Waits,Freddie (dr)
Hank Mobley Quintet
Recado Bossa Nova
Englewood Cliffs,NJ, rec. 18.6.1965
Mobley,Hank (ts) | Morgan,Lee (tp) | Mabern,Harold (p) | Ridley,Larry (b) | Higgins,Billy (dr)
Lou Donaldson Quintet
South Of The Border
Englewood Cliffs,NJ, rec. 27.4.1961
Donaldson,Lou (as) | Foster,Herman (p) | Tucker,Ben (b) | Bailey,Dave (dr) | Dorsey,Alec (congas)
Donald Byrd Quintet
Ghana
Englewood Cliffs,NJ, rec. 25.1.1960
Byrd,Donald (tp) | Mobley,Hank (ts) | Pearson,Duke (p) | Watkins,Doug (b) | Humphries,Lex (dr)

795627-2 | CD | The Blue Note Years-The Best Of Joe Henderson
Joe Henderson Quintet
Blue Bossa | Recorda-Me
Englewood Cliffs,NJ, rec. 3.6.1963
Henderson,Joe (ts) | Dorham,Kenny (tp) | Tyner,McCoy (p) | Warren,Edward 'Butch' (b) | LaRoca,Pete (dr)
Our Thing
Englewood Cliffs,NJ, rec. 9.9.1963
Henderson,Joe (ts) | Dorham,Kenny (tp) | Hill,Andrew (p) | Khan,Eddie (b) | LaRoca,Pete (dr)
Punjab | Serenity
Englewood Cliffs,NJ, rec. 10.4.1964
Henderson,Joe (ts) | Dorham,Kenny (tp) | Tyner,McCoy (p) | Davis,Richard (b) | Jones,Elvin (dr)
Joe Henderson Quartet
El Barrio
Englewood Cliffs,NJ, rec. 30.11.1964
Henderson,Joe (ts) | Tyner,McCoy (p) | Cranshaw,Bob (b) | Jones,Elvin (dr)
Joe Henderson Septet
Mode For Joe
Englewood Cliffs,NJ, rec. 27.1.1966
Henderson,Joe (ts) | Morgan,Lee (tp) | Fuller,Curtis (tb) | Hutcherson,Bobby (vib) | Walton,Cedar (p) | Carter,Ron (b) | Chambers,Joe (dr)
Joe Henderson Trio
Beatrice | Ask Me Now
Live at The 'Village Vanguard',NYC, rec. 14.-16.11.1985
Henderson,Joe (ts) | Carter,Ron (b) | Foster,Al (dr)

795636-2 | CD | The Best Of Thelonious Monk:The Blue Note Years
Thelonious Monk Quintet
Thelonious
NYC, rec. 15.10.1947
Monk,Thelonious (p) | Sulieman[Leonard Graham],Idrees (tp) | Quebec West,Danny (as) | Ramey,Gene (b) | Blakey,Art (dr)
Thelonious Monk Trio
Ruby My Dear | Well You Needn't | April In Paris
NYC, rec. 24.10.1947
Monk,Thelonious (p) | Ramey,Gene (b) | Blakey,Art (dr)
Thelonious Monk Quintet
Monk's Mood | In Walked Bud | Round About Midnight
NYC, rec. 21.11.1947
Monk,Thelonious (p) | Taitt,George (tp) | Shihab,Sahib (as) | Paige,Bob (b) | Blakey,Art (dr)
Thelonious Monk Quartet
Evidence | Misterioso | Epistrophy | I Mean You
NYC, rec. 2.7.1948
Monk,Thelonious (p) | Jackson,Milt (vib) | Simmons,John (b) | Wilson,Shadow (dr)
Thelonious Monk Quintet
Four In One | Criss Cross | Straight No Chaser | Ask Me Now
NYC, rec. 23.7.1951
Monk,Thelonious (p) | Shihab,Sahib (as) | Jackson,Milt (vib) | McKibbon,Al (b) | Blakey,Art (dr)

796110-2 | CD | The Best Of Blue Note
John Coltrane Sextet
Blue Train
Hackensack,NJ, rec. 15.9.1957
Coltrane,John (ts) | Morgan,Lee (tp) | Fuller,Curtis (tb) | Drew,Kenny (p) | Chambers,Paul (b) | Jones,Philly Joe (dr)
Herbie Hancock Quintet
Maiden Voyage
Englewood Cliffs,NJ, rec. 17.3.1965
Hancock,Herbie (p) | Hubbard,Freddie (tp) | Coleman,George (ts) | Carter,Ron (b) | Williams,Tony (dr)
Donald Byrd Orchestra With Voices
Cristo Redentor
Englewood Cliffs,NJ, rec. 12.1.1963
Byrd,Donald (tp) | Mobley,Hank (ts) | Best,Donald (vib) | Burrell,Kenny (g) | Hancock,Herbie (p) | Warren,Edward 'Butch' (b) | Humphries,Lex (dr) | Pearson,Duke (arr) | Coleridge Perkinson Choir,The | Perkinson,Coleridge (dir)
Art Blakey And The Jazz Messengers
Moanin'
Hackensack,NJ, rec. 30.10.1958
Blakey,Art (dr) | Morgan,Lee (tp) | Golson,Benny (ts) | Timmons,Bobby (p) | Merritt,Jymie (b)
Lou Donaldson Quintet
Blues Walk
Hackensack,NJ, rec. 28.7.1958
Donaldson,Lou (as) | Foster,Herman (p) | Morrison,Peck (b) | Bailey,Dave (dr) | Barretto,Ray (congas)
Horace Silver Quintet
Song For My Father
Englewood Cliffs,NJ, rec. 26.10.1964
Silver,Horace (p) | Jones,Carmell (tp) | Henderson,Joe (ts) | Smith,Teddy (b) | Humphries,Roger (dr)
Jimmy Smith Quartet
Back At The Chicken Shack
Englewood Cliffs,NJ, rec. 25.4.1960
Smith,Jimmy (org) | Turrentine,Stanley (ts) | Burrell,Kenny (g) | Bailey,Donald (dr)
Kenny Burrell Quintet
Chittlins Con Carne
Englewood Cliffs,NJ, rec. 8.1.1963
Burrell,Kenny (g) | Turrentine,Stanley (ts) | Holley,Major (b) | English,Bill (dr) | Barretto,Ray (congas)
Lee Morgan Quintet
The Sidewinder
Englewood Cliffs,NJ, rec. 21.12.1963
Morgan,Lee (tp) | Henderson,Joe (ts) | Harris,Barry (p) | Cranshaw,Bob (b) | Higgins,Billy (dr)

796563-2 | CD | So Blue So Funky-Heroes Of The Hammond
Fred Jackson Quartet
Hootin' 'N' Tootin'
Englewood Cliffs,NJ, rec. 5.2.1962
Jackson,Fred (ts) | Van Dyke,Earl (org) | Jones,Willie (g) | Hogan,Wilbert (dr)
George Braith Quartet
Boop Bop Bing Bash
Englewood Cliffs,NJ, rec. 16.12.1963
Braith,George (ss,ts,strich) | Gardner,Billy (org) | Green,Grant (g) | Walker,Hugh (dr)
Jack McDuff Group
Butter(For Yo' Popcorn)
Memphis,Tenn., rec. 10.6.1969
McDuff,Brother Jack (org) | Arnold,Jay (ts) | Freeman,Charlie (g) | Creason,Sammy (dr) | details unknown
Jimmy McGriff Trio
All About My Girl
NYC, rec. 1962
McGriff,Jimmy (org) | Dow,Morris (g) | Mills,Jackie (dr)
Big John Patton Quintet
The Silver Meter
Englewood Cliffs,NJ, rec. 5.4.1963
Patton,Big John (org) | Jackson,Fred (ts) | Vick,Harold (ts) | Green,Grant (g) | Dixon,Ben (dr)
Fat Judy
Englewood Cliffs,NJ, rec. 8.3.1965
Patton,Big John (org) | Mitchell,Blue (tp) | Vick,Harold (ts) | Green,Grant (g) | Dixon,Ben (dr)
Grant Green Orchestra
Ain't It Funky Now
Englewood Cliffs,NJ, rec. 30.1.1970
Green,Grant (g) | Mitchell,Blue (tp) | Bartee,Claude (ts) | Riggins,Emmanuel (org) | Lewis,Jimmy (b) | Muhammad,Idris[Leo Morris] (dr) | Candido[Camero] (congas) | Landrum,Richard 'Pablo' (bongos)
Lou Donaldson Sextet
Everything I Do Is Gonna Be Funky(From Now On)
Englewood Cliffs,NJ, rec. 9.1.1970
Donaldson,Lou (as) | Mitchell,Blue (tp) | Sparks,Melvin (g) | Smith,Lonnie (org) | Lewis,Jimmy (b) | Muhammad,Idris[Leo Morris] (dr)
Freddie Roach Quartet
Brown Sugar
Englewood Cliffs,NJ, rec. 19.3.1964
Roach,Freddie (org) | Henderson,Joe (ts) | Wright,Eugene 'Gene' (b) | Johnston,Clarence (dr)
Jimmy Smith Trio
I'm Movin' On
Englewood Cliffs,NJ, rec. 31.1.1963
Smith,Jimmy (org) | Green,Grant (g) | Bailey,Donald (dr)
Baby Face Willette Quartet
Face To Face
Englewood Cliffs,NJ, rec. 30.1.1961
Willette,Baby Face (org) | Jackson,Fred (ts) | Green,Grant (g) | Dixon,Ben (dr)
Larry Young Quartet
Plaza De Toros
Englewood Cliffs,NJ, rec. 12.11.1964
Young,Larry (org) | Rivers,Sam (ts) | Green,Grant (g) | Jones,Elvin (dr)

796579-2 | CD | Dexter Gordon:Ballads
Dexter Gordon Quintet
Darn That Dream
Paris,France, rec. 2.6.1964
Gordon,Dexter (ts) | Byrd,Donald (tp) | Drew,Kenny (p) | Orsted-Pedersen,Niels-Henning (b) | Taylor,Arthur 'Art' (dr)
Dexter Gordon Quartet
I Guess I'll Hang My Tears Out To Dry
Englewood Cliffs,NJ, rec. 27.8.1962
Gordon,Dexter (ts) | Clark,Sonny (p) | Warren,Edward 'Butch' (b) | Higgins,Billy (dr)

Don't Explain
Englewood Cliffs,NJ, rec. 29.8.1962
Gordon,Dexter (ts) | Clark,Sonny (p) | Warren,Edward 'Butch' (b) | Higgins,Billy (dr)
Dexter Gordon Quintet
I'm A Fool To Want You
Englewood Cliffs,NJ, rec. 27.5.1965
Gordon,Dexter (ts) | Hubbard,Freddie (tp) | Harris,Barry (p) | Cranshaw,Bob (b) | Higgins,Billy (dr)
Dexter Gordon Quartet
Ernie's Tune
Englewood Cliffs,NJ, rec. 9.5.1961
Gordon,Dexter (ts) | Drew,Kenny (p) | Chambers,Paul (b) | Jones,Philly Joe (dr)
Dexter Gordon Quintet
You've Changed
Englewood Cliffs,NJ, rec. 6.5.1961
Gordon,Dexter (ts) | Hubbard,Freddie (tp) | Parlan,Horace (p) | Tucker,George (b) | Harewood,Al (dr)
Dexter Gordon Quartet
Willow Weep For Me
Paris,France, rec. 23.5.1963
Gordon,Dexter (ts) | Powell,Bud (p) | Michelot,Pierre (b) | Clarke,Kenny (dr)
Body And Soul
Live at Keystone Korner,SF, rec. 16.9.1978
Gordon,Dexter (ts) | Cables,George (p) | Reid,Rufus (b) | Gladden,Eddie (dr)

797197-2 | CD | The Blessing
Gonzalo Rubalcaba Trio
Circuito | Sandino | Besame Mucho | Giant Steps | Sin Remedio, El Mar | Silver Hollow | The Blessing | Blue In Green | Sinpunto Y Contracopa | Mima
Toronto,Canada, rec. 12.-15.5.1991
Rubalcaba,Gonzalo (p) | Haden,Charlie (b) | DeJohnette,Jack (dr)

797960-2 | CD | The Best Of Blue Note Vol.2
Horace Silver Quintet
Senor Blues
Hackensack,NJ, rec. 10.11.1956
Silver,Horace (p) | Byrd,Donald (tp) | Mobley,Hank (ts) | Watkins,Doug (b) | Hayes,Louis (dr)
Sonny Rollins Quintet
Decision
Hackensack,NJ, rec. 16.12.1956
Rollins,Sonny (ts) | Byrd,Donald (tp) | Kelly,Wynton (p) | Ramey,Gene (b) | Roach,Max (dr)
Dexter Gordon Quartet
Three O'Clock In The Morning
Englewood Cliffs,NJ, rec. 27.8.1962
Gordon,Dexter (ts) | Clark,Sonny (p) | Warren,Edward 'Butch' (b) | Higgins,Billy (dr)
Art Blakey And The Jazz Messengers
Blues March
Hackensack,NJ, rec. 30.10.1958
Blakey,Art (dr) | Morgan,Lee (tp) | Golson,Benny (ts) | Timmons,Bobby (p) | Merritt,Jymie (b)
Horace Parlan Quintet
Wadin'
Englewood Cliffs,NJ, rec. 14.7.1960
Parlan,Horace (p) | Turrentine,Tommy (tp) | Turrentine,Stanley (ts) | Tucker,George (b) | Harewood,Al (dr)
Lee Morgan Quintet
The Rumproller
Englewood Cliffs,NJ, rec. 21.4.1965
Morgan,Lee (tp) | Henderson,Joe (ts) | Mathews,Ronnie (p) | Sproles,Victor (b) | Higgins,Billy (dr)
Cannonball Adderley Quintet
Somethin' Else
NYC, rec. 9.5.1958
Adderley,Julian \'Cannonball\' (as) | Davis,Miles (tp) | Jones,Hank (p) | Jones,Sam (b) | Blakey,Art (dr)
Herbie Hancock Quintet
Watermelon Man
Englewood Cliffs,NJ, rec. 28.5.1962
Hancock,Herbie (p) | Hubbard,Freddie (tp) | Gordon,Dexter (ts) | Warren,Edward 'Butch' (b) | Higgins,Billy (dr)

798287-2 | CD | Miles Davis:The Best Of The Capitol/Blue Note Years
Miles Davis And His Orchestra
Move | Godchild | Budo
NYC, rec. 21.1.1949
Davis,Miles (tp) | Winding,Kai (tb) | Collins,Junior (fr-h) | Barber,Bill (tuba) | Konitz,Lee (as) | Mulligan,Gerry (bs,arr) | Haig,Al (p) | Shulman,Joe (b) | Roach,Max (dr) | Lewis,John (arr)
Miles Davis Sextet
Dear Old Stockholm | Donna | Yesterdays
NYC, rec. 9.5.1952
Davis,Miles (tp) | Johnson,J.J. (tb) | McLean,Jackie (as) | Coggins,Gil (p) | Pettiford,Oscar (b) | Clarke,Kenny (dr)
Tempus Fugit | Enigma | C.T.A.
NYC, rec. 20.4.1953
Davis,Miles (tp) | Johnson,J.J. (tb) | Heath,Jimmy (ts) | Coggins,Gil (p) | Heath,Percy (b) | Blakey,Art (dr)
Miles Davis Quartet
Well You Needn't | It Never Entered My Mind | Weird-O
Hackensack,NJ, rec. 6.3.1954
Davis,Miles (tp) | Silver,Horace (p) | Heath,Percy (b) | Blakey,Art (dr)
Cannonball Adderley Quintet
Somethin' Else | Autumn Leaves
Hackensack,NJ, rec. 9.3.1958
Adderley,Julian \'Cannonball\' (as) | Davis,Miles (tp) | Jones,Hank (p) | Jones,Sam (b) | Blakey,Art (dr)

798636-2 | CD | From The Soul
Joe Lovano Quartet
Evolution | Portrait Of Jenny | Lines & Spaces | Body And Soul | Fort Worth | Central Park West | Work | Left Behind | His Dreams
NYC, rec. 28.12.1991
Lovano,Joe (ss,as,ts) | Petrucciani,Michel (p) | Holland,Dave (b) | Blackwell,Ed (dr)

799106-2 | CD | Blue Break Beats
Richard 'Groove' Holmes Sextet
Grooving With Mr.G.
NYC, rec. 19.5.1971
Holmes,Richard 'Groove' (org) | Hubbard,Gerald (g) | Irvine,Weldon (el-p) | Jemmott,Jerry (el-b) | Washington,Darryl (dr) | Armando,Ray (congas)
Grant Green Sextet
Sookie, Sookie
NYC, rec. 15.8.1970
Green,Grant (g) | Bartee,Claude (ts) | Bivens,William 'Yam' (vib) | Foster,Ronnie (org) | Muhammad,Idris[Leo Morris] (dr) | Armstrong,Joseph (congas)
Grant Green With Orchestra
The Final Comedown
NYC, rec. 13./14.12.1971
Green,Grant (g) | Orchestra | details unknown
Lou Donaldson Quintet
Who's Making Love | Turtle Walk
NYC, rec. 25.4.1967
Donaldson,Lou (as) | Williams,Ed (tp) | Sparks,Melvin (g) | Earland,Charles (org) | Muhammad,Idris[Leo Morris] (dr)
Donald Byrd Orchestra
Weasil
NYC, rec. 9.5.1969
Byrd,Donald (tp) | Priester,Julian (tb) | Tabackin,Lew (fl) | Foster,Frank (ts) | Ponder,Jimmy (g) | Pearson,Duke (el-p) | Wilson,Roland (fender-b) | Chambers,Joe (dr) | Richardson,John (perc) | Bettis,Nat (perc)
Donald Byrd Sextet
Blackjack
NYC, rec. 1.9.1967
Byrd,Donald (tp) | Red (Kyner) | Mobley,Hank (ts) | Walton,Cedar (p) | Booker,Walter (b) | Higgins,Billy (dr)
Eddie Henderson Orchestra
Kudu
San Francisco,CA, rec. details unknown
Henderson,Eddie (tp,fl-h) | Priester,Julian (tb) | Caliman,Hadley (fl,b-cl,ss) | Rushen,Patrice (el-p,synth,clavinet) | Jackson,Paul (b) | Hart,Billy (dr) | M'tume,James[Forman] (perc) | Clarke,Mike (perc) | Theus,Son Ship (perc)
Bobbi Humphrey
Harlem River Drive
Hollywood,CA, rec. 7./8.6.1973
Humphrey,Bobbi (fl,voc) | Peters,Jerry (p,el-p) | Rainey,Chuck (el-b) | Brown,Ron (el-b) | Mizell,Fonce (tp,clavinet) | Perren,Fred (synth) | Walker,David T. (g) | Mason,Harold (dr) | Errison,King (perc) | Spruill,Stephanie (perc)
Jimmy McGriff Band
Blue Juice
details unknown, rec. details unknown
McGriff,Jimmy (org) | details unknown
The Three Sounds
Your Love Is Too Much
details unknown, rec. July/August 1971
Three Sounds,The | Harris,Gene (p) | Vescovo,Al (g) | Robinson,Freddie (g) | Higgins,Monk (org,arr) | Hughes,Luther (el-b) | Burnett,Carl (dr) | Porter,Bobby (perc) | Humphrey,Paul (perc)
Herbie Hancock Quartet
Oliloqui Valley
NYC, rec. 17.6.1964
Hancock,Herbie (p) | Hubbard,Freddie (fl-h,co) | Carter,Ron (b) | Williams,Tony (dr)

799586-2 | CD | What We Do
John Scofield Quartet
Little Walk | Camp Out | Big Sky | Easy For You | Call 911 | Imaginary Time | Say The Word | Why Nogales? | What Thy Did
NYC, rec. May 1992
Scofield,John (g) | Lovano,Joe (sax) | Irwin,Dennis (b) | Stewart,Bill (dr)

821220-2 | CD | Viktoria Tolstoy:White Russian
Viktoria Tolstoy With The Esbjörn Svensson Trio
Solitary | Venus And Mars | My Garden | I Do Care | Holy Water | Wonderful Life | Invisible Changes | High-Heels | For Your Love | Casablanca | Spring
Stockholm,Sweden, rec. 1997
Tolstoy,Viktoria (voc) | Asplund,Peter (tp) | Landgren,Nils (tb) | Johansson,Per 'Ruskträsk' (as) | Öberg,Mats (harm) | Wadenius,George (el-g,voc) | Svensson,Esbjörn (vib,keyboards,glockenspiel) | Berglund,Dan (b) | Öström,Magnus (dr,perc,tablas) | Littwold,Micke (voc) | Strings | details unknown

821259-2 | CD | Runnin' Wild
Sidney Bechet's Blue Note Jazzmen
I Wish I Could Shimmy Like My Sister Kate | Tiger Rag | Tin Roof Blues | I Found A New Baby | Nobody Knows You When You're Down And Out | When The Saints Go Marching In
NYC, rec. 21.1.1949
Bechet,Sidney (cl) | Davison,Wild Bill (co) | Hodes,Art (p) | Page,Walter (b) | Moore,Fred[Freddie] (dr)
Basin Street Blues | Cakewalkin' Babies From Home | At The Jazz Band Ball | Joshua Fit The Battle Of Jericho | Fidgety Feet | Tailgate Ramble
NYC, rec. 23.3.1949
Bechet,Sidney (ss) | Davison,Wild Bill (co) | Diehl,Ray (tb) | Hodes,Art (p) | Page,Walter (b) | Jones,Wilmore 'Slick' (dr)
China Boy | Runnin' Wild | Runnin' Wild(alt.take) | I Ain't Gonna Give Nobody None Of My Jelly Roll(alt.take 1) | I Ain't Gonna Give Nobody None Of My Jelly Roll(alt.take 2) | Mandy Make Up Your Mind | Shim-Me-Sha-Wabble
NYC, rec. 19.4.1950
Bechet,Sidney (ss) | Davison,Wild Bill (co) | Archey,Jimmy (tb) | Sullivan,Joe (p) | Foster,George 'Pops' (b) | Jones,Wilmore 'Slick' (dr)

821261-2 | CD | George Lewis And His New Orleans Stompers
George Lewis And His New Orleans Stompers
When You Wore A Tulip | Gettysburg March(alt.take) | Walking With The King | Gettysburg March | Savoy Blues | Nobody Knows The Way I Feel This Morning | Bucket's Got A Hole In It
Hackensack,NJ, rec. 8.4.1955
Lewis,George (cl) | Howard,Avery 'Kid' (tp) | Robinson,Jim (tb) | Purnell,Alton (p) | Guesnon,George (bj) | Pavageau,Alcide 'Slow Drag' (b) | Watkins,Joe (dr,voc)
I Can't Escape From You | Mahogany Hall Stomp | Move The Body Over | Lord Lord Lord You've Sure Been Good To Me | Gettysburg March | High Society | See See Rider | Heebie Jeebies | When You Wore A Tulip
Hackensack,NJ, rec. 11.4.1955
Lewis,George (cl) | Howard,Avery 'Kid' (tp,voc) | Robinson,Jim (tb) | Purnell,Alton (p,voc) | Guesnon,George (bj) | Pavageau,Alcide 'Slow Drag' (b) | Watkins,Joe (dr,voc)

821262-2 | 2 CD | The Blue Note Jazzmen
Edmond Hall's Blue Note Jazzmen
High Society | High Society(take 1) | High Society(take 2) | Blues At Blue Note | Blues At Blue Note(alt.take) | Night Shift Blues | Night Shift Blues(alt.take) | Royal Garden Blues | Royal Garden Blues(alt.take) | Blue Note Boogie
NYC, rec. 29.11.1943
Hall,Edmond (cl) | DeParis,Sidney (tp) | Dickenson,Vic (tb) | Johnson,James P. (p) | Shirley,Jimmy (g) | Crosby,Israel (b) | Catlett,Big Sid (dr)
Sidney DeParis' Blue Note Jazzmen
Everybody Loves My Baby | Everybody Loves My Baby | Everybody Loves My Baby(alt.take) | Ballin' The Jack | Who's Sorry Now | Who's Sorry Now(alt.take) | The Call Of The Blues
NYC, rec. 4.3.1944
DeParis,Sidney (tp) | Dickenson,Vic (tb) | Hall,Edmond (cl) | Johnson,James P. (p) | Shirley,Jimmy (g) | Simmons,John (b) | Catlett,Big Sid (dr)
James P.Johnson's Blue Note Jazzmen
Blue Mizz | Blue Mizz(alt.take) | Victory Stride | Victory Stride(alt.take) | Joy Mentin' | After You've Gone
NYC, rec. 21.6.1944
Johnson,James P. (p) | DeParis,Sidney (tp) | Dickenson,Vic (tb) | Webster,Ben (ts) | Shirley,Jimmy (g) | Simmons,John (b) | Catlett,Big Sid (dr)
Tishomingo Blues | Tishomingo Blues(alt.take) | Walkin' The Dog | Walkin' The Dog(alt.take) | Easy Rider | At The Ball | At The Ball(alt.take)
NYC, rec. 26.10.1944
Johnson,James P. (p) | DeParis,Sidney (tp) | Dickenson,Vic (tb) | Hall,Edmond (cl) | Shirley,Jimmy (g) | Lucas,Al (b) | Trappier,Arthur (dr)

821282-2 | CD | Standards
Jimmy Smith Trio
Little Girl Blue
Hackensack,NJ, rec. 25.8.1957
Smith,Jimmy (org) | Burrell,Kenny (g) | Bailey,Donald (dr)
Bye Bye Blackbird | I'm Just A Lucky So-And-So | Ruby | September Song
Hackensack,NJ, rec. 15.7.1958
Smith,Jimmy (org) | Burrell,Kenny (g) | Bailey,Donald (dr)
I Didn't Know What Time It Was | Memories Of You | But Beautiful | Mood Indigo | While We're Young | It Might As Well Be Spring | The Last Dance
Hackensack,NJ, rec. 24.5.1959
Smith,Jimmy (org) | Burrell,Kenny (g) | Bailey,Donald (dr)

821283-2 | CD | Standards
Sonny Clark Trio
Gee Baby Ain't I Good To You | Ain't No Use | I Can't Give You Anything But Love | Black Velvet | I'm Just A Lucky So-And-So | The Breeze And I | Gee Baby Ain't I Good To You (alt.take)
Hackensack,NJ, rec. 16.11.1958
Clark,Sonny (p) | Merritt,Jymie (b) | Landers,Wes (dr)
Blues In The Night | Can't We Be Friends | Somebody Loves Me | All Of You | Dancing In The Dark | I Cover The Waterfront | Blues In The Night(alt.take)
Hackensack,NJ, rec. 7.12.1958
Clark,Sonny (p) | Chambers,Paul (b) | Landers,Wes (dr)

821284-2 | CD | Standards
Grant Green Trio
You Stepped Out Of A Dream | Love Walked In | If I Had You | I'll Remember April | You And The Night And The Music | All The Things You Are | I Remember You | If I Had You(alt.take)
Englewood Cliffs,NJ, rec. 29.8.1961
Green,Grant (g) | Ware,Wilbur (b) | Harewood,Al (dr)

821286-2 | CD | Blackjack | EAN 724382128625
Donald Byrd Sextet
Blackjack | West Of Pecos | Loki | Eldorado | Beale Street | Pentatonic
Englewood Cliffs,NJ, rec. 9.1.1967
Byrd,Donald (tp) | Red (Kyner) | Mobley,Hank (ts) | Walton,Cedar (p) | Booker,Walter (b) | Higgins,Billy (dr)

821287-2 | CD | Feedom Rider | EAN 724382128724
Art Blakey And The Jazz Messengers
Pisces | Blue Ching
NYC, rec. 12.2.1961
Blakey,Art (dr) | Morgan,Lee (tp) | Shorter,Wayne (ts) | Timmons,Bobby (p) | Merritt,Jymie (b)
Tell It Like It Is | El Toro | Pretty Larceny | Blue Lace | Uptight
NYC, rec. 27.5.1961
Blakey,Art (dr) | Morgan,Lee (tp) | Shorter,Wayne (ts) | Timmons,Bobby (p) | Merritt,Jymie (b)
Art Blakey
The Freedom Rider (Drum Solo)
Blakey,Art (dr-solo)

821288-2 | CD | Silver's Serenade
Horace Silver Quintet
Silver's Serenade | Let's Get To The Nitty Gritty | Sweet Sweetie Dee | The Dragon Lady | Nineteen Bars
rec. 11./12.4.1963
Silver,Horace (p) | Mitchell,Blue (tp) | Cook,Junior (ts) | Taylor,Gene (b) | Brooks,Roy (dr)

821289-2 | CD | Black Orchid | EAN 724382128922
The Three Sounds
Azule Scrape | For Dancers Only | Tadd's Delight | Nature Boy
Englewood Cliffs,NJ, rec. 4.2.1962
Three Sounds,The | Harris,Gene (p) | Simpkins,Andrew (b) | Dowdy,Bill (dr)
Secret Love | Oh Well,Oh Well | Black Orchid | A Foggy Day(In London Town) | For All We Know
Englewood Cliffs,NJ, rec. 7.3.1962
Three Sounds,The | Harris,Gene (p) | Simpkins,Andrew (b) | Dowdy,Bill (dr)
Saucer Eyes | Don't Go Don't Go | At Last
Englewood Cliffs,NJ, rec. 8.3.1962
Three Sounds,The | Harris,Gene (p) | Simpkins,Andrew (b) | Dowdy,Bill (dr)
You Dig It | Theme From M Suad | Back Home
Englewood Cliffs,NJ, rec. 27.6.1962
Three Sounds,The | Harris,Gene (p) | Simpkins,Andrew (b) | Dowdy,Bill (dr)

821290-2 | CD | Street Of Dreams | EAN 724382129028
Frant Green Quartet
Lazy Afternoon | I Wish You Love | Somewhere In The Night | Street Of Dreams
Englewood Cliffs,NJ, rec. 16.11.1964
Green,Grant (g) | Hutcherson,Bobby (vib) | Young,Larry (org) | Jones,Elvin (dr)

821371-2 | 5 CD | Sonny Rollins:The Blue Note Recordings | EAN 724382137122
Sonny Rollins Quintet
Decision | Bluesnote | How Are Things In Glocca Morra | Plain Jane | Sonnysphere
Hackensack,NJ, rec. 16.12.1956
Rollins,Sonny (ts) | Byrd,Donald (tp) | Kelly,Wynton (p) | Ramey,Gene (b) | Roach,Max (dr)
Why Don't I | Wail March | You Stepped Out Of A Dream | Poor Butterfly
NYC, rec. 14.4.1957
Rollins,Sonny (ts) | Johnson,J.J. (tb) | Silver,Horace (p) | Chambers,Paul (b) | Blakey,Art (dr)
Sonny Rollins Sextet
Misterioso
Rollins,Sonny (ts) | Johnson,J.J. (tb) | Monk,Thelonious (p) | Silver,Horace (p) | Chambers,Paul (b) | Blakey,Art (dr)
Sonny Rollins Quartet
Reflections
Rollins,Sonny (ts) | Monk,Thelonious (p) | Chambers,Paul (b) | Blakey,Art (dr)
Tune Up | Asiatic Raes | Wonderful Wonderful | Blues For Philly Joe | Namely You
NYC, rec. 22.9.1957
Rollins,Sonny (ts) | Kelly,Wynton (p) | Watkins,Doug (b) | Jones,Philly Joe (dr)
Sonny Rollins/Philly Joe Jones
The Surrey With The Fringe On Top
Rollins,Sonny (ts) | Jones,Philly Joe (dr)
Sonny Rollins Trio
A Night In Tunisia | I've Got You Under My Skin
Live at The 'Village Vanguard',NYC, rec. 3.11.1957
Rollins,Sonny (ts) | Bailey,Don (b) | LaRoca,Pete (dr)
A Night In Tunisia | Softly As In A Morning Sunrise | Four | Woody'n You | Old Devil Moon | What Is This Thing Called Love | Softly As In A Morning Sunrise(alt.take) | Sonnymoon For Two | I Can't Get Started | I'll Remember April | Get Happy | Striver's Row | All The Things You Are | Get Happy(short version)
Rollins,Sonny (ts) | Ware,Wilbur (b) | Jones,Elvin (dr)

823211-2 | CD | Gimeracs And Gewgaws
Mose Allison Quintet
MJA Jr. | Gimeracks And Gewgaws | Numbers On Paper | Cruise Control | St.Louis Blues | Mockingbird | The More You Get | Texanna | What Will It Be | So Tired | Somebody Gonna Have To Move | Fires Of Spring | What's With You | Old Man Blues
NYC, rec. 17./18.4.1997
Allison,Mose (p,voc) | Shim,Mark (ts) | Malone,Russell (g) | Harris,Ratzo (b) | Motian,Paul (dr)

823213-2 | CD | Standards
Lee Morgan Orchestra
This Is The Life | God Bless The Child | Blue Gardenia | A Lot Of Livin' To Do | Somewhere | If I Were A Carpenter | Blue Gardenia(alt.take)
Englewood Cliffs,NJ, rec. 13.1.1967
Morgan,Lee (tp) | Spaulding,James (fl,as) | Shorter,Wayne (ts) | Adams,Pepper (bs) | Hancock,Herbie (p) | Carter,Ron (b) | Roker,Granville 'Mickey' (dr)

823514-2 | CD | Jazz Profile:Dexter Gordon
Jesse Price And His Blues Band
Baby,Let's Be Friends
Los Angeles,CA, rec. 28.11.1947
Price,Jesse (voc) | Linn,Ray (tp) | Gordon,Dexter (ts) | Giuffre,Jimmy (ts) | Norvo,Red (p) | Kessel,Barney (g) | Callender,Red (b) | Mills,Jackie (dr)
Red Norvo Septet
Bop
Norvo,Red (vib) | Linn,Ray (tp) | Gordon,Dexter (ts) | Giuffre,Jimmy (ts) | Marmarosa,Dodo (p) | Kessel,Barney (g) | Callender,Red (b) | Mills,Jackie (dr)
Tadd Dameron Tentet
Sid's Delight
NYC, rec. 18.1.1949
Dameron,Tadd (p) | Navarro,Fats (tp) | Winding,Kai (tb) | Shihab,Sahib (as) | Gordon,Dexter (ts) | Payne,Cecil (bs) | Russell,Curly (b) | Clarke,Kenny (dr) | Iborra,Diego (bongos) | Bolado,Vidal (congas) | Pearl,Rae (voc)

Dexter Gordon Quintet
I Was Doing Alright
NYC, rec. 6.5.1961
Gordon,Dexter (ts) | Hubbard,Freddie (tp) | Parlan,Horace (p) | Tucker,George (b) | Harewood,Al (dr)
Dexter Gordon Quartet
Ernie's Tune
NYC, rec. 9.5.1961
Gordon,Dexter (ts) | Drew,Kenny (p) | Chambers,Paul (b) | Jones,Philly Joe (dr)
Second Balcony Jump | I Guess I'll Hang My Tears Out To Dry
NYC, rec. 27.8.1962
Gordon,Dexter (ts) | Clark,Sonny (p) | Warren,Edward 'Butch' (b) | Higgins,Billy (dr)
McSplivens
NYC, rec. 29.8.1962
Gordon,Dexter (ts) | Clark,Sonny (p) | Warren,Edward 'Butch' (b) | Higgins,Billy (dr)
Broadway
Paris,France, rec. 23.5.1963
Gordon,Dexter (ts) | Powell,Bud (p) | Michelot,Pierre (b) | Clarke,Kenny (dr)
Dexter Gordon Quintet
Heartaches
NYC, rec. 29.5.1965
Gordon,Dexter (ts) | Hutcherson,Bobby (vib) | Harris,Barry (p) | Cranshaw,Bob (b) | Higgins,Billy (dr)

823515-2 | CD | Jazz Profile:Miles Davis
Miles Davis Sextet
How Deep Is The Ocean
NYC, rec. 9.5.1952
Davis,Miles (tp) | Johnson,J.J. (tb) | McLean,Jackie (as) | Coggins,Gil (p) | Pettiford,Oscar (b) | Clarke,Kenny (dr)
Ray's Idea | Kelo
NYC, rec. 20.4.1953
Davis,Miles (tp) | Johnson,J.J. (tb) | Heath,Jimmy (ts) | Coggins,Gil (p) | Heath,Percy (b) | Blakey,Art (dr)
Miles Davis Quartet
Well You Needn't
Hackensack,NJ, rec. 6.3.1954
Davis,Miles (tp) | Silver,Horace (p) | Heath,Percy (b) | Blakey,Art (dr)
Cannonball Adderley Quintet
Love For Sale | Somethin' Else
Hackensack,NJ, rec. 9.3.1958
Adderley,Julian \'Cannonball\' (as) | Davis,Miles (tp) | Jones,Hank (p) | Jones,Sam (b) | Blakey,Art (dr)
Miles Davis And His Orchestra
Boplicity | Israel
NYC, rec. 22.4.1949
Davis,Miles (tp,arr) | Johnson,J.J. (tb) | Siegelstein,Sandy (fr-h) | Barber,Bill (tuba) | Konitz,Lee (as) | Mulligan,Gerry (bs,arr) | Lewis,John (p) | Boyd,Nelson (b) | Clarke,Kenny (dr) | Evans,Gil (arr) | Carisi,Johnny (arr)
Deception
NYC, rec. 13.3.1950
Davis,Miles (tp,arr) | Johnson,J.J. (tb) | Schuller,Gunther (fr-h) | Barber,Bill (tuba) | Konitz,Lee (as) | Mulligan,Gerry (bs) | Lewis,John (p) | McKibbon,Al (b) | Roach,Max (dr) | Carisi,Johnny (arr)
Miles Davis Sextet
Chance It | Dear Old Stockholm | Woody'n You
NYC, rec. 9.5.1952
Davis,Miles (tp) | Johnson,J.J. (tb) | McLean,Jackie (as) | Coggins,Gil (p) | Pettiford,Oscar (b) | Clarke,Kenny (dr)

823516-2 | CD | Jazz Profile:Sonny Rollins
Sonny Rollins Quintet
Plain Jane
Hackensack,NJ, rec. 16.12.1956
Rollins,Sonny (ts) | Byrd,Donald (tp) | Kelly,Wynton (p) | Ramey,Gene (b) | Roach,Max (dr)
You Stepped Out Of A Dream
Hackensack,NJ, rec. 14.4.1957
Rollins,Sonny (ts) | Johnson,J.J. (tb) | Silver,Horace (p) | Chambers,Paul (b) | Blakey,Art (dr)
Sonny Rollins Quartet
Reflections
Rollins,Sonny (ts) | Monk,Thelonious (p) | Chambers,Paul (b) | Blakey,Art (dr)
Sonny Rollins Trio
Sonnymoon For Two | Four | All The Things You Are
Live at The 'Village Vanguard',NYC, rec. 3.11.1957
Rollins,Sonny (ts) | Ware,Wilbur (b) | Jones,Elvin (dr)
Sonny Rollins Quartet
Blues For Philly Joe
Hackensack,NJ, rec. 22.9.1957
Rollins,Sonny (ts) | Kelly,Wynton (p) | Watkins,Doug (b) | Jones,Philly Joe (dr)

823517-2 | CD | Jazz Profile
Sarah Vaughan With Her Quartet
I Cried For You(Now It's Your Turn To Cry Over Me)
Live at Town Hall,NYC, rec. 8.11.1947
Vaughan,Sarah (voc) | Young,Lester (ts) | details unknown
Sarah Vaughan With The Count Basie Band
Perdido
Live at Carnegie Hall,NYC, rec. 25.9.1954
Vaughan,Sarah (voc) | prob.personal: | Basie,Count (p) | Jones,Thad (tp) | Cohn[Cohen],Sonny (tp) | Newman,Joe (tp) | Young,Eugene Edward (tp) | Coker,Henry (tb) | Grey,Al (tb) | Powell,Benny (tb) | Royal,Marshall (cl,as) | Wess,Frank (fl,ts) | Foster,Frank (ts) | Mitchell,Billy (ts) | Fowlkes,Charlie (bs) | Green,Freddie (g) | Jones,Eddie (b) | Payne,Sonny (dr)
Sarah Vaughan And Joe Williams With The Count Basie Orchestra
Teach Me Tonight
NYC, rec. 19.7.1960
Vaughan,Sarah (voc) | Williams,Joe (voc) | prob.personal: | Basie,Count (p) | Jones,Thad (tp) | Cohn[Cohen],Sonny (tp) | Newman,Joe (tp) | Young,Eugene Edward (tp) | Coker,Henry (tb) | Grey,Al (tb) | Powell,Benny (tb) | Royal,Marshall (cl,as) | Wess,Frank (fl,ts) | Foster,Frank (ts) | Mitchell,Billy (ts) | Fowlkes,Charlie (bs) | Green,Freddie (g) | Jones,Eddie (b) | Payne,Sonny (dr)
Sarah Vaughan With The Billy May Orchestra
Them There Eyes
Los Angeles,CA, rec. 8.10.1960
Vaughan,Sarah (voc) | May,Billy (arr,ld) | details unknown
Sarah Vaughan With The Jimmy Jones Quintet
When Your Lover Has Gone
NYC, rec. 31.10.1960
Vaughan,Sarah (voc) | Jones,Jimmie (p) | Edison,Harry 'Sweets' (tp) | unkn. (g,b,dr)
Sarah Vaughan With Mundell Lowe And George Duvivier
My Favorite Things
NYC, rec. 18.7.1961
Vaughan,Sarah (voc) | Lowe,Mundell (g) | Duvivier,George (b)
Sarah Vaughan With The Quincy Jones Orchestra
You're Mine You
NYC, rec. January/February 1962
Vaughan,Sarah (voc) | Jones,Quincy (arr,ld) | details unknown
Sarah Vaughan With The Marty Manning Orchestra
Once Upon A Summertime
NYC, rec. 5./8.3.1962
Vaughan,Sarah (voc) | Manning,Marty (arr,ld) | details unknown
Sarah Vaughan With The Don Costa Orchestra
Snowbound
NYC, rec. 23./25.7.1962
Vaughan,Sarah (voc) | Costa,Don (cond,arr) | details unknown
Sarah Vaughan With Barney Kessel And Joe Comfort
Key Largo
Los Angeles,CA, rec. 7.8.1962
Vaughan,Sarah (voc) | Kessel,Barney (g) | Comfort,Joe (b)
Sarah Vaughan With The Benny Carter Orchestra
Nobody Else But Me
Los Angeles,CA, rec. 8.8.1962
Vaughan,Sarah (voc) | Foster,Frank (ts) | Comfort,Joe (b) | Members of The Count Basie Band | Carter,Benny (arr,ld) | details unknown
Sarah Vaughan With The Marty Manning Orchestra
Star Eyes
NYC, rec. 27.2.1963
Vaughan,Sarah (voc) | Manning,Marty (arr,ld) | details unknown
Intermezzo
NYC, rec. 11.3.1963
Vaughan,Sarah (voc) | Manning,Marty (arr,ld) | details unknown
Sarah Vaughan With The Gerald Wilson Orchestra
Moanin'
Los Angeles,CA, rec. 31.5.1963
Vaughan,Sarah (voc) | Wilson,Gerald (tp,arr,ld) | details unknown
Sarah Vaughan With The Lalo Schifrin Orchestra
More Than You Know
Chicago,Ill, rec. June 1963
Vaughan,Sarah (voc) | Schifrin,Lalo (cond,arr) | details unknown
Sarah Vaughan With The Benny Carter Orchestra
Lonely Hours
Los Angeles,CA, rec. 13.-16.6.1963
Vaughan,Sarah (voc) | Carter,Benny (arr,ld) | details unknown
Sarah Vaughan With The Jimmy Jones Orchestra
Dreamy
NYC, rec. 19.4.1964
Vaughan,Sarah (voc) | Jones,Jimmy (cond,arr) | Edison,Harry 'Sweets' (tp) | Sanfino,Jerry (fl,ts) | Bright,Ronnell (p) | Soyer,Janet (harp) | Galbraith,Barry (g) | Davis,Richard (b) | Duvivier,George (b) | Brice,Percy (dr) | Strings | details unknown

823518-2 | CD | Jazz Profile:Thelonious Monk
Thelonious Monk Sextet
Humph
Hackensack,NJ, rec. 15.10.1947
Monk,Thelonious (p) | Sulieman[Leonard Graham],Idrees (tp) | West,Danny Quebec (as) | Smith,Billy (ts) | Ramey,Gene (b) | Blakey,Art (dr)
Thelonious Monk Trio
Ruby My Dear | Well You Needn't | April In Paris | Off Minor
NYC, rec. 24.10.1947
Monk,Thelonious (p) | Ramey,Gene (b) | Blakey,Art (dr)
Thelonious Monk Quintet
In Walked Bud | Monk's Mood | Round About Midnight
NYC, rec. 21.11.1947
Monk,Thelonious (p) | Taitt,George (tp) | Shihab,Sahib (as) | Paige,Bob (b) | Blakey,Art (dr)
Ask Me Now
NYC, rec. 23.7.1951
Monk,Thelonious (p) | McKibbon,Al (b) | Blakey,Art (dr)
Criss Cross | Straight No Chaser
Monk,Thelonious (p) | Shihab,Sahib (as) | Jackson,Milt (vib) | McKibbon,Al (b) | Blakey,Art (dr)
Thelonious Monk Sextet
Carolina Moon | Let's Cool One
NYC, rec. 30.5.1952
Monk,Thelonious (p) | Dorham,Kenny (tp) | Donaldson,Lou (as) | Thompson,Lucky (ts) | Boyd,Nelson (b) | Roach,Max (dr)
Thelonious Monk Quartet
Crepuscule With Nellie | Epistrophy
Live at The Five Spot Cafe,NYC, rec. 11.9.1958
Monk,Thelonious (p) | Coltrane,John (ts) | Abdul-Malik,Ahmed (b) | Haynes,Roy (dr)

827014-2 | CD | Tenor Legacy
Joe Lovano Sextet
Miss Etna | Love Is A Many-Splendored Thing | Blackwell's Message | Laura | Introspection | In The Land Of Ephesus | To Her Ladyship | Web Of Fire | Rounder's Mood | Bread And Wine
NYC, rec. 18.6.1993
Lovano,Joe (ts) | Redman,Joshua (ts) | Miller,Mulgrew (p) | McBride,Christian (b) | Nash,Lewis (dr) | Alias,Don (perc)

827327-2 | CD | Hand Jive
John Scofield Sextet
I'll Take Les | Dark Blue | Do Like Eddie | She's So Lucky | Checkered Past | 7th Floor | Golden Daze | Don't Shoot The Messenger | Whip The Mule | Out Of The City
NYC, rec. November 1993
Scofield,John (g) | Harris,Eddie (ts) | Goldings,Larry (p,org) | Irwin,Dennis (b) | Stewart,Bill (dr) | Alias,Don (perc)

827765-2 | CD | I Can See Your House From Here
John Scofield-Pat Metheny Quartet
I Can See Your House From Here | The Red One | No Matter What | Everybody's Party | Message To My Friend | No Way Jose | Say The Brother's Name | S.C.O. | Quiet Rising | One Way To Be | You Speak My Language
NYC, rec. December 1993
Scofield,John (g,el-g,steel-g) | Metheny,Pat (g,el-g,g-synth) | Swallow,Steve (b-g,el-b) | Stewart,Bill (dr)

827820-2 | CD | First Instrumental
Rachelle Ferrell With The Eddie Green Trio
You Send Me | You Don't Know What Love Is | Bye Bye Blackbird | Prayer Dance | My Funny Valentine | Don't Waste Your Time
different Places, rec. January/February 1990
Ferrell,Rachelle (voc) | Green,Eddie (p) | Brown,Tyrone (b) | Nally,Doug (dr)
Rachelle Ferrell With The Eddie Green Trio And Alex Foster
The Inch Worm
Ferrell,Rachelle (voc) | Foster,Alex (ss) | Green,Eddie (p) | Brown,Tyrone (b) | Nally,Doug (dr)
Rachelle Ferrell-Doug Nally
What Is This Thing Called Love
Ferrell,Rachelle (voc) | Nally,Doug (dr)
Rachelle Ferrell
Extensions
Ferrell,Rachelle (p,voc)
Rachelle Ferrell With The Terrence Blanchard Quartet
With Every Breath I Take
Ferrell,Rachelle (voc) | Blanchard,Terence (tp) | Goldstein,Gil (p) | Davis,Kenneth 'Kenny' (b) | White,Lenny (dr)
Rachelle Ferrell With The Wayne Shorter Sextet
Autumn Leaves
different Places, rec. 16.12.1989
Ferrell,Rachelle (voc) | Shorter,Wayne (ts) | Petrucciani,Michel (p) | Clarke,Stanley (b) | Goldstein,Gil (synth) | Levin,Pete (synth) | White,Lenny (dr)

828353-2 | CD | The Complete Town Hall Concert
Charles Mingus And His Orchestra
Freedom(part 1) | Freedom(part 2:aka Clark In The Dark) | Osmotin | Epitaph(part 1) | Peggy's Blue Skylight | Epitaph(part 2) | My Search | Portrait | Duke's Choice(aka Don't Come Back) | Please Don't Come Back From The Moon | In A Mellow Tone(aka Finale) | Epitaph(part 1alt.take)
Live at Town Hall,NYC, rec. 12.10.1962
Mingus,Charles (b) | Young,Eugene 'Snooky' (tp) | Royal,Ernie (tp) | Williams,Richard (tp) | Terry,Clark (tp) | Armour,Ed (tp) | Hillyer,Lonnie (tp) | Ericson,Rolf (tp) | Jackson,Quentin (tb) | Woodman,Britt (tb) | Cleveland,Jimmy (tb) | Dennis,Willie (tb) | Bert,Eddie (tb) | Faulise,Paul (b-tb) | Penque,Romeo (oboe) | Bank,Danny (b-cl) | Dolphy,Eric (as) | McPherson,Charles (as) | Mariano,Charlie (as) | Collette,Buddy (as) | Sims,Zoot (ts) | Berg,George (ts) | Richardson,Jerome (bs) | Adams,Pepper (bs) | Spann,Les (g) | Byard,Jaki (p) | Akiyoshi,Toshiko (p) | Hinton,Milt (b) | Richmond,Dannie (dr) | Smith,Warren (vib,perc) | Tate,Grady (perc) | Liston,Melba (arr) | Hammer,Bob (arr) | Roland,Gene (arr)

828879-2 | 2 CD | The State Of The Tenor Vol.1&2 | EAN 724382887928
Joe Henderson Trio
Beatrice | Friday The 13th | Happy Reunion | Loose Change | Ask Me Now | Isotope | Stella By Starlight | Boo Boo's Birthday | Cheryl | Y Ya La Quiero | Soulville | Portrait | The Bead Game | All The Things You Are
Live at The 'Village Vanguard',NYC, rec. 14.-16.11.1985
Henderson,Joe (ts) | Carter,Ron (b) | Foster,Al (dr)

829029-2 | 2 CD | Bemsha Swing | EAN 724382902928
Woody Shaw Quartet
Bemsha Swing | Nutty | Star Eyes | In A Capricornian Way | Theloniously Speaking
Live at Baker's Heyboard Lounge,Detroit, rec. 26.2.1996
Shaw,Woody (tp) | Allen,Geri (p) | Hurst III,Robert Leslie (b) | Brooks,Billy (dr)
Ginseng People | Well You Needn't | Eric | United
Live at Baker's Heyboard Lounge,Detroit, rec. 27.2.1996
Shaw,Woody (tp) | Allen,Geri (p) | Hurst III,Robert Leslie (b) | Brooks,Billy (dr)

829125-2 | 2 CD | Live At The Village Vanguard | EAN 724382912521
Joe Lovano Quartet
Fort Worth | Birds In Springtime Gone By | I Can't Get Started | Uprising | Sail Away | Blues Not To Lose | Song And Dance
Live at The 'Village Vanguard',NYC, rec. 12.3.1994
Lovano,Joe (ss,ts,c-mel-sax) | Harrell,Tom (tp,fl-h) | Cox,Anthony (b) | Hart,Billy (dr)
Lonnie's Lament | Reflections | Little Willie Leaps | This Is All I Ask | 26-2 | Duke Ellington's Sound Of Love | Sounds Of Joy
Live at The 'Village Vanguard',NYC, rec. 20.& 22.1.1965
Lovano,Joe (ts) | Miller,Mulgrew (p) | McBride,Christian (b) | Nash,Lewis (dr)

829331-2 | CD | Cantaloupe Island
Herbie Hancock Quartet
Cantaloupe Island
Englewood Cliffs,NJ, rec. 17.6.1964
Hancock,Herbie (p) | Hubbard,Freddie (co) | Carter,Ron (b) | Williams,Tony (dr)
Herbie Hancock Quintet
Watermelon Man | Driftin'
Englewood Cliffs,NJ, rec. 28.5.1962
Hancock,Herbie (p) | Hubbard,Freddie (tp) | Gordon,Dexter (ts) | Warren,Edward 'Butch' (b) | Higgins,Billy (dr)
Herbie Hancock Septet
Blind Man, Blind Man | And What If I Don't
Englewood Cliffs,NJ, rec. 19.3.1963
Hancock,Herbie (p) | Byrd,Donald (tp) | Moncur III,Grachan (tb) | Mobley,Hank (ts) | Green,Grant (g) | Israels,Chuck (b) | Williams,Tony (dr)
Herbie Hancock Quintet
Maiden Voyage
Englewood Cliffs,NJ, rec. 17.3.1965
Hancock,Herbie (p) | Hubbard,Freddie (tp) | Coleman,George (ts) | Carter,Ron (b) | Williams,Tony (dr)

829351-2 | CD | Jacky Terrasson
Jackie Terrasson Trio
I Love Paris | Just A Blues | My Funny Valentine | Homage A Lili Boulanger | Bye Bye Blackbird | He Goes On A Trip | I Fall In Love Too Easily | Time After Time | For Once In My Life | What A Difference A Day Made | Cumba's Dance
NYC, rec. June/August 1994
Terrasson,Jackie[Jacky] (p) | Okegwo,Ugonna (b) | Parker,Leon (dr)

830133-2 | CD | Live At Bradley's
Kevin Eubanks Trio
Speak Low | Sometimes I Feel Like A Motherless Child | June In January | In A Sentimental Mood | Altered Ego | Red Top | Mercy, Mercy, Mercy
Live at Bradley's Jazz Club,NYC, rec. 21.5.1994
Eubanks,Kevin (g) | Williams,James (p) | Hurst III,Robert Leslie (b)

830491-2 | CD | Imagine
Gonzalo Rubalcaba Quartet
Contagio | Woody'n You | Perfidia
Live at Wadsworth Hall,UCLA,Westwood,CA, rec. 24.6.1994
Rubalcaba,Gonzalo (p) | Melian,Reinaldo (tp) | Cabrera,Felipe (el-b) | Barreto,Julio (dr)
Gonzalo Rubalcaba Trio
First Song
Live at Lincoln Center's Alice Trully Hall,NYC, rec. 14.5.1993
Rubalcaba,Gonzalo (p) | Haden,Charlie (b) | DeJohnette,Jack (dr)
Gonzalo Rubalcaba
Imagine | Circuito(II)
Hollywood,CA, rec. 23.6.1994
Rubalcaba,Gonzalo (p-solo)
Mima
Live at Wadsworth Hall,UCLA,Westwood,CA, rec. 24.6.1994
Rubalcaba,Gonzalo (p-solo)

831883-2 | CD | The Lost Grooves
Reuben Wilson Sextet
Hold On I'm Coming
rec. 31.10.1969
Wilson,Reuben (org) | Morgan,Lee (tp) | Coleman,George (ts) | Green,Grant (g) | Muhammad,Idris[Leo Morris] (dr) | Sircus,Joe (congas)
Grant Green Sextet
It's Your Thing | Hey Western Union Man
rec. 15.8.1970
Green,Grant (g) | Bartee,Claude (ts) | Bivens,William 'Yam' (vib) | Foster,Ronnie (org) | Muhammad,Idris[Leo Morris] (dr) | Armstrong,Joseph (congas)
Lou Donaldson Quintet
The Scorpion(alt.take)
rec. 7.11.1970
Donaldson,Lou (as) | Ballard,Fred (tp) | Spencer Jr.,Leon (org) | Sparks,Melvin (g) | Muhammad,Idris[Leo Morris] (dr)
Brother Soul
rec. 6.11.1968
Donaldson,Lou (as) | Mitchell,Blue (tp) | Earland,Charles (org) | Ponder,Jimmy (g) | Muhammad,Idris[Leo Morris] (dr)
John Patton Quartet
Village Lee(alt.take)
rec. 15.8.1969
Patton,Big John (org) | Cabell,Marvin (ts) | Ulmer,James Blood (g) | Williams,Leroy (dr)
Stanley Turrentine And His Orchestra
Spooky
rec. 25.1.1968
Turrentine,Stanley (ts) | Stamm,Marvin (tp) | Collins,Burt (tp) | Brown,Garnett (tb) | Powell,Benny (tb) | Dodgion,Jerry (reeds) | Gibbons,Al (reeds) | Farrell,Joe (reeds) | Tyner,McCoy (p) | Barksdale,Everett (g) | Cranshaw,Bob (b) | Tate,Grady (dr)
Lonnie Smith Quintet
Dancin' In An Easy Groove
rec. 9.8.1969
Smith,Lonnie (org) | Jones,Rudy (ts) | Cuber,Ronnie (bs) | McGee,Larry (g) | Goshay,Sylvester (dr)
Stanley Turrentine And His Orchestra
You Want Me To Stop Loving You
rec. 28.7.1967
Turrentine,Stanley (ts) | Mitchell,Blue (tp) | Brown,Garnett (tb) | Spaulding,James (as) | Tyner,McCoy (p) | Cranshaw,Bob (el-b) | Lucas,Ray (dr) | Landrum,Richard 'Pablo' (perc) | Pearson,Duke (arr)

831915-2 | CD | Along Came John | EAN 724383191529
John Patton Quintet
The Silver Meter | Spiffy Diffy | Gee Gee | Along Came John | Pigfoot | I'll Never Be Free
Englewood Cliffs,NJ, rec. 5.4.1963
Patton,Big John (org) | Jackson,Fred (ts) | Vick,Harold (ts) | Green,Grant (g) | Dixon,Ben (dr)

832620-2 | CD | City Speak
Richard Elliot Sextet
City Speak | Walk The Walk | Unspoken Words | Amazon | I'll Make Love To You | Scotland | Sweet Surrender | Down Hill Run | When The Lights Go Out | All I Need | That's All She Wrote
Woodland Hills,CA, rec. 1996
Elliot,Richard (ts) | Smith,Richard (g) | Reinhardt,Ron (keyboards) | Yanai,Naoki (b) | Reinhardt,Dave (dr,perc) | Conte,Luis (perc)

832750-2 | CD | I'm Movin' On | EAN 724383275021
Jimmy Smith Trio
I'm Movin' On | Hotel Happiness | Cherry | 'Tain't No Use | Black Talk | What Kind Of Fool Am I | Organic Greenery | Day In Day Out
Englewood Cliffs,NJ, rec. 31.1.1963
Smith,Jimmy (org) | Green,Grant (g) | Bailey,Donald (dr)

832787-2 | 2 CD | Lester Young:The Complete Aladdin Sessions | EAN 724383278725
Lester Young-Nat Cole Trio
Back Home Again In Indiana | I Can't Get Started | Tea For Two | Body And Soul
Los Angeles,CA, rec. 15.7.1942
Young,Lester (ts) | Cole,Nat King (p) | Callender,Red (b)
Lester Young And His Band
D.B.Blues | Lester Blows Again | These Foolish Things Remind Me On You | Jumpin' At Mesners
Los Angeles,CA, rec. December 1945
Young,Lester (ts) | Dickenson,Vic (tb) | Marmarosa,Dodo (p) | Green,Freddie (g) | Callender,Red (b) | Tucker,Henry (dr)
It's Only A Paper Moon | After You've Gone | Lover Come Back To Me | Jammin' With Lester
Los Angeles,CA, rec. January 1946
Young,Lester (ts) | McGhee,Howard (tp) | Dickenson,Vic (tb) | Smith,Willie (as) | Jones,Wesley (p) | Counce,Curtis (b) | Otis,Johnny (dr)
New Lester Leaps In | You're Driving Me Crazy | She's Funny That Way | Lester's Be-Bop Boogie
Los Angeles,CA, rec. August 1946
Young,Lester (ts) | Albany,Joe (p) | Ashby,Irving (g) | Callender,Red (b) | Hamilton,Forrest 'Chico' (dr)
Sunday | S.M.Blues | No Eyes Blues | Jumpin' With Symphony Sid | Sax-O-Be-Bop | On The Sunny Side Of The Street
Chicago,Ill, rec. October 1946
Young,Lester (ts) | McConnell,Shorty (tp) | Hakim,Sadik[Argonne Thornton] (p) | Lacey,Fred (g) | Richardson,Rodney (b) | Marshall,Lyndell (dr)
Easy Does It | Easy Does It(alt.take) | Movin' With Lester | One O'Clock Jump | Jumpin' At The Woodside
Los Angeles,CA, rec. 18.2.1947
Young,Lester (ts) | McConnell,Shorty (tp) | Hakim,Sadik[Argonne Thornton] (p) | Lacey,Fred (g) | Briscoe,Ted (b) | Haynes,Roy (dr)
I'm Confessin'(That I Love You) | Lester Smooths It Out | Just Cooling
NYC, rec. 2.4.1947
Young,Lester (ts) | McConnell,Shorty (tp) | Hakim,Sadik[Argonne Thornton] (p) | Barakaat,Nasir (g) | Richardson,Rodney (b) | Marshall,Lyndell (dr)
Tea For Two | The Sheik Of Araby | East Of The Sun West Of The Moon | Something To Remember You By
NYC, rec. 29.12.1947
Young,Lester (ts) | DiNovi,Gene (p) | Wayne,Chuck (g) | Russell,Curly (b) | Kahn,Tiny (dr)
Helen Humes And Her All Stars
Riffin' With Helen | Please Let Me Forget | He Don't Love Me Anymore | Pleasing Man Blues | See See Rider | It's Better To Give Than To Receive
Los Angeles,CA, rec. 22.12.1945
Humes,Helen (voc) | Young,Eugene 'Snooky' (tp) | Smith,Willie (as) | Davis,Maxwell (ts) | Young,Lester (ts) | Bunn,Jimmy (p) | Barbour,Dave (g) | Rudd,Jimmy (b) | Tucker,Henry (dr)

832801-2 | CD | Groove Elation
John Scofield Groups
Lazy | Peculiar | Let The Cat Out | Kool | Old Soul | Groove Elation | Carlos | Soft Shoe | Let It Shine | Big Top
NYC, rec. 1995
Scofield,John (g,el-g) | Brecker,Randy (tp,fl-h) | Turre,Steve (tb) | Drewes,Billy (fl,ts) | Johnson,Howard (b-cl,bs,tuba) | Goldings,Larry (p,org) | Irwin,Dennis (b) | Muhammad,Idris[Leo Morris] (dr) | Alias,Don (perc)

833114-2 | CD | Trio Fascination
Joe Lovano Trio
New York Fascination | Sanctuary Park | Eternal Joy | I Don't Stand A Ghost Of A Chance With You | Studio Rivbea | Cymbalism | Impressionistic | Villa Paradiso | 4 On The Floor | Days Of Yore
NYC, rec. 16./17.9.1997
Lovano,Joe (alto-cl,ss,as,ts) | Holland,Dave (b) | Jones,Elvin (dr)

833571-2 | CD | The Best Of The Nat King Cole Trio:The Vocal Classics(1942-1946)
Nat King Cole Trio
All For You
Los Angeles,CA, rec. 11.10.1942
Cole,Nat King (p,voc) | Moore,Oscar (g) | Miller,Johnny (b)
Straighten Up And Fly Right | Gee Baby Ain't I Good To You | If You Can't Smile And Say Yes
Los Angeles,CA, rec. 30.11.1943
Cole,Nat King (p,voc) | Moore,Oscar (g) | Miller,Johnny (b)
Sweet Lorraine | Embraceable You | It's Only A Paper Moon
Los Angeles,CA, rec. 15.12.1943
Cole,Nat King (p,voc) | Moore,Oscar (g) | Miller,Johnny (b)
I Realize Now
Los Angeles,CA, rec. 6.3.1944
Cole,Nat King (p,voc) | Moore,Oscar (g) | Miller,Johnny (b)
I'm A Shy Guy
Los Angeles,CA, rec. 13.4.1945
Cole,Nat King (p,voc) | Moore,Oscar (g) | Miller,Johnny (b)
You're Nobody 'Til Somebody Loves You | What Can I Say After I Say I'm Sorry | I'm Thru With Love
NYC, rec. 15.5.1945
Cole,Nat King (p,voc) | Moore,Oscar (g) | Miller,Johnny (b)
Come To Baby Do | The Frim Fram Sauce
NYC, rec. 11.10.1945
Cole,Nat King (p,voc) | Moore,Oscar (g) | Miller,Johnny (b)
How Does It Feel
NYC, rec. 4.12.1945
Cole,Nat King (p,voc) | Moore,Oscar (g) | Miller,Johnny (b)
Get Your Kicks On Route 66
NYC, rec. 15.3.1946
Cole,Nat King (p,voc) | Moore,Oscar (g) | Miller,Johnny (b)
Baby Baby All The Time
NYC, rec. 17.4.1946
Cole,Nat King (p,voc) | Moore,Oscar (g) | Miller,Johnny (b)
But She's My Buddy's Chick | You Call It Madness But I Call It Love
NYC, rec. 1.5.1946
Cole,Nat King (p,voc) | Moore,Oscar (g) | Miller,Johnny (b)
The Best Man
NYC, rec. 19.8.1946
Cole,Nat King (p,voc) | Moore,Oscar (g) | Miller,Johnny (b)
I Love You For Sentimental Reasons
NYC, rec. 22.8.1946
Cole,Nat King (p,voc) | Moore,Oscar (g) | Miller,Johnny (b)
You're The Cream In My Coffee
NYC, rec. 18.12.1946
Cole,Nat King (p,voc) | Moore,Oscar (g) | Miller,Johnny (b)

835222-2 | CD | Joy Spring | EAN 724383522224
Joe Pass Quartet
Joy Spring | Some Time Ago | The Night Has A Thousand Eyes | Relaxin' At The Camarillo | There Is No Greater Love
rec. 6.2.1964
Pass,Joe (g) | Wofford,Mike (p) | Hughart,Jim (b) | Bailey,Colin (dr)

835228-2 | 3 CD | Live At The Lighthouse | EAN 724383522828
Lee Morgan Quintet
Introduction by Lee Morgan | Something Like This | 416 East 10th Street | The Sidewinder
Live at The Lighthouse,Hermosa Beach,CA, rec. 10.7.1970
Morgan,Lee (tp,fl-h) | Maupin,Bennie (fl,b-cl,ts) | Mabern,Harold (p) | Merritt,Jymie (b) | Roker,Granville 'Mickey' (dr)
Speedball
Morgan,Lee (tp,fl-h) | Maupin,Bennie (fl,b-cl,ts) | Mabern,Harold (p) | Merritt,Jymie (b) | DeJohnette,Jack (dr)
Aon | I Remember Britt | Nommo | Absolutions
Live at The Lighthouse,Hermosa Beach,CA, rec. 11.7.1970
Morgan,Lee (tp,fl-h) | Maupin,Bennie (fl,b-cl,ts) | Mabern,Harold (p) | Merritt,Jymie (b) | Roker,Granville 'Mickey' (dr)
Yunjanna | Neophilia | The Beehive | Peyote
Live at The Lighthouse,Hermosa Beach,CA, rec. 12.7.1970
Morgan,Lee (tp,fl-h) | Maupin,Bennie (fl,b-cl,ts) | Mabern,Harold (p) | Merritt,Jymie (b) | Roker,Granville 'Mickey' (dr)

836633-2 | CD | Ballads & Blues
Miles Davis And His Orchestra
Moon Dreams
NYC, rec. 9.3.1950
Davis,Miles (tp,arr) | Johnson,J.J. (tb) | Schuller,Gunther (fr-h) | Barber,Bill (tuba) | Konitz,Lee (as) | Mulligan,Gerry (bs,arr) | Lewis,John (p) | McKibbon,Al (b) | Roach,Max (dr) | Evans,Gil (arr)
Miles Davis Quartet
Yesterdays | How Deep Is The Ocean
NYC, rec. 9.5.1952
Davis,Miles (tp) | Coggins,Gil (p) | Pettiford,Oscar (b) | Clarke,Kenny (dr)
I Waited For You
NYC, rec. 20.4.1953
Davis,Miles (tp) | Coggins,Gil (p) | Heath,Percy (b) | Blakey,Art (dr)
Miles Davis Sextet
Enigma
rec. 20.4.1953
Davis,Miles (tp) | Johnson,J.J. (tb) | Heath,Jimmy (ts) | Coggins,Gil (p) | Heath,Percy (b) | Blakey,Art (dr)
Miles Davis Quartet
Weird-O | It Never Entered My Mind
Hackensack,NJ, rec. 6.3.1954
Davis,Miles (tp) | Silver,Horace (p) | Heath,Percy (b) | Blakey,Art (dr)
Cannonball Adderley Quintet
Autumn Leaves | One For Daddy-O
Hackensack,NJ, rec. 9.3.1958
Adderley,Julian \'Cannonball\' (as) | Davis,Miles (tp) | Jones,Hank (p) | Jones,Sam (b) | Blakey,Art (dr)

837101-2 | CD | Ready...Set...Shango!
Charlie Hunter Quartet
Ashby Man | Teabaggin' | Let's Get Medieval | The Shango Pt.III | Dersu | 911 | Shango...The Ballad | Thursday The 12th | Sutton
Marin Country,CA, rec. details unknown
Hunter,Charlie (8-string-g) | Spanier,Calder (as) | Ellis,David (ts) | Amendola,Scott (dr)

837513-2 | CD | Live In Australia,1959 | EAN 724383751327
Frank Sinatra With The Red Norvo Quintet(Sextet!)
I Could Have Danced All Night | Just One Of Those Things | I Get A Kick Out Of You | At Long Last Love | Willow Weep For Me | I've Got You Under My Skin | Moonlight In Vermont | The Lady Is A Tramp | Sinatra Speaks | Angel Eyes | Come Fly With Me | All The Way | Dancing In The Dark | One For My Baby(And One More For The Road)
West Melburne Stadium,Australia, rec. 1.4.1959
Sinatra,Frank (voc) | Norvo,Red (vib) | Dodgion,Jerry (fl,as) | Miller,Bill (p) | Wyble,Jimmy (g) | Wooten,Red (b) | Markham,John (dr)
Red Norvo Sextet
Perdido | Between The Devil And The Deep Blue Sea
West Melburne Stadium,Australia, rec. 31.3.1959
Norvo,Red (vib) | Dodgion,Jerry (fl,as) | Miller,Bill (p) | Wyble,Jimmy (g) | Wooten,Red (b) | Markham,John (dr)
Frank Sinatra With The Red Norvo Quintet(Sextet!) & Orchestra
All Of Me | On The Road To Mandalay | Night And Day
West Melburne Stadium,Australia, rec. 31.3./1.4.1959
Sinatra,Frank (voc) | Norvo,Red (vib) | Dodgion,Jerry (fl,as) | Miller,Bill (p) | Wyble,Jimmy (g) | Wooten,Red (b) | Markham,John (dr) | Orchestra | details unknown

837570-2 | CD | Reach
Jackie Terrasson Trio
I Should Care | The Rat Race | Baby Plum | I Love You For Sentimental Reasons | Reach- | Smoke Gets In Your Eyes- | Reach- | Happy Man | First Affair | Just One Of Those Things | All My Life
details unknown, rec. details unknown
Terrasson,Jackie[Jacky] (p) | Okegwo,Ugonna (b) | Parker,Leon (dr)

837643-2 | CD | Takin' Off | EAN 724383764327
Herbie Hancock Quintet
Watermelon Man | Watermelon Man(alt.take) | Three Bags Full | Three Bags Full(alt.take) | Empty Pockets | Empty Pockets(alt.take) | The Maze | Driftin' | Alone And I
Englewood Cliffs,NJ, rec. 28.5.1962
Hancock,Herbie (p) | Hubbard,Freddie (tp) | Gordon,Dexter (ts) | Warren,Edward 'Butch' (b) | Higgins,Billy (dr)

837646-2 | CD | Extensions | EAN 724383764624
McCoy Tyner Sextet
Message From The Nile | The Wanderer | Survival Blues | His Blessing
rec. 9.2.1970
Tyner,McCoy (p) | Bartz,Gary (as) | Shorter,Wayne (ss,ts) | Coltrane,Alice (harp) | Carter,Ron (b) | Jones,Elvin (dr)

837717-2 | CD | Antiguo | EAN 724383771721
Gonzalo Rubalcaba & Cuban Quartet
Opening | Circuito(III) | Ellioko(Yoruba Word Foe 'Two' | Desierto | Intermitencia | Coral Negro | Circuito(IV) | Oddi Lobbe | Eshun Agwe(Yoruba Word For 'Party') | Homenaje | Closing
different Places, rec. 1997
Rubalcaba,Gonzalo (p,keyboards,perc) | Melian,Reynaldo (tp) | Crego,Jose M. (tb) | Filu,Roman (as) | Thompson,Alfredo (ts) | Cabrera,Felipe (b) | Barreto,Julio (dr) | Hidalgo,Manenquito Giovanni (perc) | Aldama,Carlos (perc) | Martinez,Alexander (perc) | Aldama,Michael (perc) | Hernandez,Maridalia (voc) | Ros,Lazaro (voc)

853355-2 | CD | The Tokyo Blues
Horace Silver Quintet
Sayonara Blues | The Tokyo Blues
Englewood Cliffs,NJ, rec. 13.7.1962
Silver,Horace (p) | Mitchell,Blue (tp) | Cook,Junior (ts) | Taylor,Gene (b) | Harris Jr.,John (dr)
Too Much Sake | Cherry Blossom | Ah! So
Englewood Cliffs,NJ, rec. 14.7.1962
Silver,Horace (p) | Mitchell,Blue (tp) | Cook,Junior (ts) | Taylor,Gene (b) | Harris Jr.,John (dr)

853357-2 | CD | Gravy Train
Lou Donaldson Quintet
Gravy Train | South Of The Border | Polka Dots And Moonbeams | Avalon | Candy | Twist Time | Glory Of Love | Gravy Train(alt.take) | Glory Of Love(alt.take)
Englewood Cliffs,NJ, rec. 27.4.1961
Donaldson,Lou (as) | Foster,Herman (p) | Tucker,Ben (b) | Bailey,Dave (dr) | Dorsey,Alec (congas)

853358-2 | CD | Caramba!
Lee Morgan Quintet
Caramba | Suicide City | Cunning Lee | Soulita | Helen's Ritual | A Baby's Smile
Englewood Cliffs,NJ, rec. 3.5.1968
Morgan,Lee (tp) | Maupin,Bennie (ts) | Walton,Cedar (p) | Workman,Reggie (b) | Higgins,Billy (dr)

853359-2 | CD | The Spoiler
Stanley Turrentine Orchestra
The Magilla | When The Sun Comes Out | La Fiesta | Sunny | Maybe September | You're Gonna Hear From Me | Lonesome Lover
Englewood Cliffs,NJ, rec. 22.9.1966
Turrentine,Stanley (ts) | Mitchell,Blue (tp) | Priester,Julian (tb) | Spaulding,James (fl,as) | Adams,Pepper (bs) | Tyner,McCoy (p) | Cranshaw,Bob (b,el-b) | Roker,Granville 'Mickey' (dr) | Rivera,Joseph (shakers,tambourine) | Pearson,Duke (arr)

853360-2 | CD | Home Cookin'
Jimmy Smith Trio
Since I Fell For You
Hackensack,NJ, rec. 15.7.1958
Smith,Jimmy (org) | Burrell,Kenny (g) | Bailey,Donald (dr)
Motorin' Along | Motorin' Along(alt.take) | Since I Fell For You-(alt.take)
Hackensack,NJ, rec. 17.7.1958
Smith,Jimmy (org) | Burrell,Kenny (g) | Bailey,Donald (dr)
I Got A Woman
Hackensack,NJ, rec. 24.5.1959
Smith,Jimmy (org) | Burrell,Kenny (g) | Bailey,Donald (dr)
Sugar Hill | Groanin'
Hackensack,NJ, rec. 16.6.1959
Smith,Jimmy (org) | Burrell,Kenny (g) | Bailey,Donald (dr)
Jimmy Smith Quartet
See See Rider | Messin' Around | Gracie | Come On Baby | Apostrophe
Smith,Jimmy (org) | France,Percy (ts) | Burrell,Kenny (g) | Bailey,Donald (dr)

853422-2 | CD | My Corner Of The Sky
Caecilie Norby With Band
The Look Of Love
NYC/Copenhagen,DK, rec. details unknown
Norby,Caecilie (voc) | Robinson,Scott (fl) | Kikoski,David 'Dave' (p) | Danielsson,Palle (b) | Carrington,Terri Lyne (dr,perc)
Snow
Norby,Caecilie (voc) | Brecker,Michael (ts) | Kikoski,David 'Dave' (p) | Danielsson,Palle (b) | Carrington,Terri Lyne (dr)
Spinning Wheel
Norby,Caecilie (voc) | Brecker,Michael (ts) | Calderazzo,Joey (p) | Kikoski,David 'Dave' (org) | Danielsson,Lars (b) | Carrington,Terri Lyne (dr,perc) | Norby,Louise (voc)
The Right Of Love | African Fairytale | A Song For You
Norby,Caecilie (voc) | Kikoski,David 'Dave' (p) | Danielsson,Palle (b) | Carrington,Terri Lyne (dr)
Set Them Free
Norby,Caecilie (voc) | Jansson,Lars (p,org) | Ginman,Lennart V. (b) | Riel,Alex (dr) | Andersen,Jacob (perc)
Suppertime
Norby,Caecilie (voc) | Jansson,Lars (p) | Ginman,Lennart V. (b) | Riel,Alex (dr)
What Do You See In Her
Norby,Caecilie (voc) | Jansson,Lars (p) | Danielsson,Lars (b) | Boudreaux,Jeff (dr)
Life On Mars
Norby,Caecilie (voc) | Brecker,Randy (fl-h) | Danielsson,Lars (b) | Carrington,Terri Lyne (dr)
Just One Of Those Things | Calling You
Norby,Caecilie (voc) | Calderazzo,Joey (p) | Danielsson,Lars (b) | Carrington,Terri Lyne (dr)

853428-0 | CD | Blue Train(The Ultimate Blue Train)
John Coltrane Sextet
Blue Train | Moment's Notice | Locomotion | I'm Old Fashioned | Lazy Bird | Blue Train(alt.take) | Lazy Bird(alt.take) | CD-ROM Track
Hackensack,NJ, rec. 15.9.1957
Coltrane,John (ts) | Morgan,Lee (tp) | Fuller,Curtis (tb) | Drew,Kenny (p) | Chambers,Paul (b) | Jones,Philly Joe (dr)

853924-2 | CD | Accent On The Blues | EAN 724385392429
John Patton Quartet
Buddy Boy | 2 J | Sweet Pea
Englewood Cliffs,NJ, rec. 9.6.1969
Patton,Big John (org) | Cabell,Marvin (ss,ts) | Coleman,George (ts) | Williams,Leroy (dr)
Lite Hit | Freedom Jazz Dance | Captain Nasty | Don't Let Me Lose This Dream | Rakin' And Scrapin' | Village Lee | Lite Hit)alt.take)
Englewood Cliffs,NJ, rec. 15.8.1969
Patton,Big John (org) | Cabell,Marvin (fl,saxello,ts) | Ulmer,James Blood (el-g) | Williams,Leroy (dr)

854123-2 | CD | Traveling Miles
Cassandra Wilson Group
Run The VooDoo Down | VooDoo Reprise
NYC, rec. December 1997
Wilson,Cassandra (voc) | Dara,Olu (co) | Sewell,Marvin (el-g) | Breit,Kevin (el-g) | Lewis,Eric (p) | Holland,Dave (b) | Baylor,Marcus (dr) | Haynes,Jeff (perc) | Kidjo,Angelique (voc)
Traveling Miles
Wilson,Cassandra (voc) | Coleman,Steve (as) | Sewell,Marvin (g) | Wamble,Doug (g) | Plaxico,Lonnie (b) | Wilson,Perry (dr) | Cinelu,Mino (perc)
Right Here Right Now
Wilson,Cassandra (voc) | Sewell,Marvin (g) | Wamble,Doug (g) | Smith,Cecilia (marimba) | Plaxico,Lonnie (b) | Wilson,Perry (dr) | Haynes,Jeff (perc)
Resurrection Blues(Tutu)
Wilson,Cassandra (voc) | Sewell,Marvin (g) | Wamble,Doug (g) | Smith,Cecilia (marimba) | Plaxico,Lonnie (b) | Wilson,Perry (dr)
Time After Time
Wilson,Cassandra (voc) | Sewell,Marvin (g) | Breit,Kevin (el-g,bozouki) | Plaxico,Lonnie (b) | Haynes,Jeff (perc)
When The Sun Goes Down
Wilson,Cassandra (g,voc) | Henry,Vince (harm) | Sewell,Marvin (g,el-g) | Plaxico,Lonnie (b) | Haynes,Jeff (perc)
Seven Steps
Wilson,Cassandra (voc) | Harris,Stefon (vib) | Lewis,Eric (p) | Carter,Regina (v) | Plaxico,Lonnie (b) | Baylor,Marcus (dr,perc)
Someday My Prince Will Come
Wilson,Cassandra (voc) | Sewell,Marvin (g) | Breit,Kevin (el-mand) | Carter,Regina (v) | Plaxico,Lonnie (b) | Baylor,Marcus (dr) | Haynes,Jeff (perc)
Never Broken(ESP)
Wilson,Cassandra (voc) | Sewell,Marvin (g) | Breit,Kevin (mandocello,resophonic-g) | Harris,Stefon (vib) | Carter,Regina (v) | Plaxico,Lonnie (b) | Haynes,Jeff (perc)
Sky And Sea(Blue In Green)
Wilson,Cassandra (voc) | Metheny,Pat (g) | Breit,Kevin (g,mand) | Lewis,Eric (p) | Holland,Dave (b) | Haynes,Jeff (perc)
Piper
Wilson,Cassandra (g,voc) | Sewell,Marvin (g,bozouki)

854325-2 | CD | Good Gracious | EAN 724385432521
Lou Donaldson Quartet
The Holy Ghost | Good Gracious | Caracas | Cherry | Bad John | Don't Worry 'Bout Me
Englewood Cliffs,NJ, rec. 24.1.1963
Donaldson,Lou (as) | Green,Grant (g) | Patton,Big John (org) | Dixon,Ben (dr)

854326-2 | CD | Places And Spaces | EAN 724385432620
Donald Byrd Orchestra
Change(Makes You Want To Hustle) | Wind Parade | Dominoes | Places And Spaces | You And Music | Night Whistler | Just My Imagination
Hollywood,CA, rec. August/September 1975
Byrd,Donald (tp,fl-h,voc) | Brown,Raymond (tp) | Bohanon,George (tb) | Glenn Jr.,Tyree (ts) | Mizell,Fonce (tp,clavinet,voc) | Mizell,Fonce (tp,clavinet) | Scarborough,Skip (el-p,synth) | McMullen,Craig (g) | Rowin,John (g) | Rainey,Chuck (el-b) | Mason,Harold (dr) | Correa,Mayuto (congas,perc) | Errison,King (congas) | Carter,James (whistling) | Haith,Kay (voc) | Mizell,Larry (p,arr,voc)

854327-2 | CD | Down With It | EAN 724385432729
Blue Mitchell Quintet
Samba De Stacy | Hi-Heel Sneakers | Alone, Alone and Alone | Perception | March On Selma | One Shirt
Englewood Cliffs,NJ, rec. 14.7.1965
Mitchell,Blue (tp) | Cook,Junior (ts) | Corea,Chick (p) | Taylor,Gene (b) | Foster,Al (dr)

854328-2 | CD | Ethiopian Knights
Donald Byrd Orchestra
The Emperor | Jamie
Los Angeles,CA, rec. 25.8.1971
Byrd,Donald (tp) | Green,Thurman (tb) | Land,Harold (ts) | Hutcherson,Bobby (vib) | Peake,Don (g) | Poree,Greg (g) | Sample,Joe (org) | Henderson,William 'Bill' (p,el-p) | Felder,Wilton (el-b) | Greene,Ed (dr) | Hall,Bobbye Porter (congas,tambourine)
The Little Rasti
Los Angeles,CA, rec. 26.8.1971
Byrd,Donald (tp) | Green,Thurman (tb) | Land,Harold (ts) | Hutcherson,Bobby

(vib) | Peake,Don (g) | Walker,David T. (g) | Sample,Joe (org) | Henderson,William 'Bill' (p,el-p) | Felder,Wilton (el-b) | Greene,Ed (dr) | Hall,Bobbye Porter (congas,tambourine)

854365-2 | CD | Midnight Blue(The [Be]witching Hour)
Ike Quebec Quartet
Ill Wind
Quebec,Ike (ts) | Thompson,Sir Charles (org) | Hinton,Milt (b) | Heard,J.C. (dr)
Jimmy Smith Quartet
Please Send Me Someone To Love
Smith,Jimmy (org) | Donaldson,Lou (as) | Warren,Quentin (g) | Bailey,Donald (dr)
Lawrence Marable Quartet feat. James Clay
Lover Man(Oh,Where Can You Be?)
Marable,Lawrence (dr) | Clay,James (ts) | Clark,Sonny (p) | Bond,Jimmy (b)
Johnny Hartman With The Terumasa Hino Quartet
The Nearness Of You
Hartman,Johnny (voc) | Hino,Terumasa (tp) | Masuda,Mikio (p) | Ikeda,Yoshio (b) | Hino,Motohiko (dr)
Bud Shank With The Len Mercer Strings
Smoke Gets In Your Eyes
Shank,Bud (as) | Strings | Mercer,Len (arr,ld) | details unknown
Coleman Hawkins With The Glenn Osser Orchestra
Autumn Leaves
Hawkins,Coleman (ts) | Strings | Osser,Glenn (arr,ld) | details unknown
Nat King Cole And George Shearing With Orchestra
Fly Me To The Moon
Cole,Nat King (voc) | Shearing,George (p) | Strings | details unknown
Duke Pearson Sextet
After The Rain
Pearson,Duke (p) | Hubbard,Freddie (tp) | Spaulding,James (fl,as) | Henderson,Joe (ts) | Carter,Ron (b) | Roker,Granville 'Mickey' (dr)
Bill Perkins-Richie Kamuca Quintet
Sweet And Lovely
Perkins,Bill (fl,b-cl,ts) | Kamuca,Richie (ts) | Hawes,Hampton (p) | Mitchell,Red (b) | Lewis,Mel (dr)
Cassandra Wilson Group
You Don't Know What Love Is
Wilson,Cassandra (voc) | Ross,Brandon (g) | Burnham,Charles (v)
Grant Green Quartet
Nancy(With The Laughing Face)
Green,Grant (g) | Clark,Sonny (p) | Jones,Sam (b) | Blakey,Art (dr)
Dexter Gordon Quartet
Until The Real Thing Comes Along
Gordon,Dexter (ts) | Clark,Sonny (p) | Warren,Edward 'Butch' (b) | Higgins,Billy (dr)
Stanley Turrentine With The Three Sounds
Willow Weep For Me
Turrentine,Stanley (ts) | Three Sounds,The | Harris,Gene (p) | Simpkins,Andrew (b) | Dowdy,Bill (dr)
Lester Young-Nat Cole Trio
I Can't Get Started
Young,Lester (ts) | Cole,Nat King (p) | Callender,Red (b)

855855-2 | CD | Out Of A Dream
Erik Truffaz Quartet Quintet
Downtown | Out Of A Dream | Beaute Bleue | Wet In Paris | Porta Camollia | Indigo | Saisir | Elegie | Samara | Up Town | Betty
Montpellier, France, rec. February 1996
Truffaz,Erik (tp) | Bugnon,Cyrille (ts) | Muller,Patrick (p) | Giuliani,Marcello (b) | Erbetta,Marc (dr)

856092-2 | CD | Flying Colors
Joe Lovano-Gonzalo Rubalcaba
Flying Colors | How Deep Is The Ocean | Boss Town | Bird Food | Spontaneous Color | Phantasm | Ugly Beauty | Hot House | Gloria's Step | Mr.Hyde | I Love Music | Along Came Betty
Celio Systems,?, rec. 11.1.1997
Lovano,Joe (alto-cl,ss,ts,dr,gongs) | Rubalcaba,Gonzalo (p)

857184-2 | 2 CD | Blue Lights Vol.1&2 | EAN 724385718427
Kenny Burrell Septet
Yes Baby
rec. 15.5.1958
Burrell,Kenny (g) | Smith,Louis (tp) | Cook,Junior (ts) | Brooks,Tina (ts) | Jordan,Duke (p) | Jones,Sam (b) | Blakey,Art (dr)
Scotch Blues | Caravan
Burrell,Kenny (g) | Smith,Louis (tp) | Cook,Junior (ts) | Brooks,Tina (ts) | Timmons,Bobby (p) | Jones,Sam (b) | Blakey,Art (dr)
Kenny Burrell Quartet
Autumn In New York
Burrell,Kenny (g) | Timmons,Bobby (p) | Jones,Sam (b) | Blakey,Art (dr)
Kenny Burrell Septet
The Man I Love | Phinupi
Burrell,Kenny (g) | Smith,Louis (tp) | Cook,Junior (ts) | Brooks,Tina (ts) | Jordan,Duke (p) | Jones,Sam (b) | Blakey,Art (dr)
Rock Salt | Chuckin'
Burrell,Kenny (g) | Cook,Junior (ts) | Brooks,Tina (ts) | Timmons,Bobby (p) | Jones,Sam (b) | Blakey,Art (dr)

857191-2 | 2 CD | A New Sound A New Star:Jimmy Smith At The Organ | EAN 724385719127
Jimmy Smith Trio
You Get 'Cha | Oh! Lady Be Good | The Preacher | But Not For Me | The Way You Look Tonight | The High And The Mighty | Tenderly | Joy | Midnight Sun
Hackensack,NJ, rec. 18.2.1956
Smith,Jimmy (org) | Schwartz,Thornel (g) | Perry,Bazeley (dr)
Turquoise | Moonlight In Vermont | Ready And Able | Deep Purple | Gone With The Wind | The Champ | Bayou | Bubbis
Hackensack,NJ, rec. 27.3.1956
Smith,Jimmy (org) | Schwartz,Thornel (g) | Bailey,Donald (dr)
Willow Weep For Me | Jamey | My Funny Valentine | Autumn Leaves | Fiddlin t | Lover Come Back To Me | Well You Needn't | I Cover The Waterfront | I Can't Give You Anything But Love | Judo Mambo | Slightly Monkish
Hackensack,NJ, rec. 18.6.1956
Smith,Jimmy (org) | Schwartz,Thornel (g) | Bailey,Donald (dr)

857456-2 | CD | And I Thought About You | EAN 724385745621
Johnny Hartman And The Rudy Traylor Orchestra
Mam'selle | To Each His Own | Sunday | Alone | Long Ago And Far Away | I Should Care | Little Girl Blue | But Beautiful | After You've Gone | There's A Lull In My Life | How Long Has This Been Going On | I Thought About You
NYC, rec. ca.1958
Hartman,Johnny (voc) | Traylor,Rudy (cond) | Brass & Strings | details unknown

859352-2 | 3 CD | Herbie Nichols:The Complete Blue Note Recordings | EAN 724385935220
Herbie Nichols Trio
The Third World | The Third World(alt.take) | Step Tempest | Dance Line | Blue Chopsticks | Double Exposure | Double Exposure(alt.take) | Cro-Magnon Nights | Cro-Magnon Nights(alt.take)
Hackensack,NJ, rec. 6.5.1955
Nichols,Herbie (p) | McKibbon,Al (b) | Blakey,Art (dr)
It Didn't Happen | Amoeba's Dance | Brass Rings | Brass Rings(alt.take) | 2300 Skiddoo | 2300 Skiddoo(alt.take) | Shuffle Montgomery | It Didn't Happen(alt.take) | Crisp Day | Shuffle Montgomery(alt.take)
Hackensack,NJ, rec. 13.6.1955
Nichols,Herbie (p) | McKibbon,Al (b) | Blakey,Art (dr)
The Gig | Applejackin' | Hangover Triangle | Lady Sings The Blues | Chit Chattin' | House Party Starting | The Gig(alt.take)
Hackensack,NJ, rec. 1.8.1955
Nichols,Herbie (p) | McKibbon,Al (b) | Roach,Max (dr)
Furthermore | Furthermore(alt.take 1) | 117th Street | 117th Street(alt.take) | Sunday Stroll | Nick At T's | Furthermore(alt.take 2) | Terpsichore | 'Orse At Safari | Applejackin' | Applejackin'(alt.take)
Hackensack,NJ, rec. 7.8.1955
Nichols,Herbie (p) | McKibbon,Al (b) | Roach,Max (dr)
Wild Flower | Mine | Mine(alt.take) | Trio | Trio(alt.take) | The Spinning Song | The Spinning Song(alt.take) | Riff Primitif | Riff Primitif(alt.take) | Query | Query(alt.take)
Hackensack,NJ, rec. 19.4.1956
Nichols,Herbie (p) | Kotick,Teddy (b) | Roach,Max (dr)

859417-2 | CD | Fellowship
Brian Blade Group
The Undertow | Folklore | In Spite Of Everything | Lifeline | If You See Lurah | Loving Without Asking
Oxnard,CA, rec. 1997
Blade,Brian (dr) | Walden,Myron (as) | Butler,Melvin (ss,ts) | Cowherd,Jon (p,wurlitzer) | Parker,Jeff (g,el-g) | Easley,Dave (pedal-steel-g) | Thomas,Christopher (b)
Red River Revel | Mohave
Blade,Brian (dr) | Walden,Myron (as) | Butler,Melvin (ss,ts) | Cowherd,Jon (p,wurlitzer) | Parker,Jeff (el-g) | Lanois,Daniel (mando-g,white-mustang) | Easley,Dave (pedal-steel-g) | Thomas,Christopher (b)

859509-2 | CD | Hub Songs
Tim Hagans-Marcus Printup Septet
Backlash | Happy Times | Hub Cup | Lament For Booker | On The Que-Tee | Crisis | Byrdlike | Thermo | Up Jumped Spring | Life Flight
NYC, rec. 1./2.8.1997
Hagans,Tim (tp) | Printup,Marcus (tp) | Herring,Vincent (as) | Jackson,Javon (ts) | Green,Benny (p) | Washington,Peter (b) | Washington,Kenny (dr)

859651-2 | CD | Alive
Jacky Terrasson Trio
Things Ain't What They Used To Be | Cumba's Dance | Sister Cheryl | Simple Things | Nature Boy | Love For Sale | Fog Taking Over Noe Valley | The Theme | There's No Disappointment In Heaven
Live at The Iridium Jazz Club,NYC, rec. 14.6.1997
Terrasson,Jackie[Jacky] (p) | Okegwo,Ugonna (b) | Parker,Leon (dr)

Blue Thumb | Universal Music Germany

543978-2 | CD | Jimmy Smith:Dot Com Blues
Jimmy Smith All Stars
Only In It For The Money
Los Angeles,CA, rec. February-June 2000
Smith,Jimmy (org) | Leonard,Darrell (tp,fl-h,arr) | Brashear,Oscar (tp,fl-h) | Drayton,Leslie (tp,fl-h) | Bohanon,George (tb) | Spears,Maurice (b-tb) | Riley,Herman (ts) | SublettJoe (ts) | Dr.John[MacRebenack] (p,voc) | Porter,John (g) | McBride,Reggie (b-g) | Mason,Harvey (dr) | Castro,Lenny (perc)
I Just Want To Make Love To You
Smith,Jimmy (org) | Leonard,Darrell (tp,fl-h,arr) | Brashear,Oscar (tp,fl-h) | Drayton,Leslie (tp,fl-h) | Bohanon,George (tb) | Spears,Maurice (b-tb) | Riley,Herman (ts) | SublettJoe (ts) | Upchurch,Phil (g) | Dr.John[MacRebenack] (el-p) | Porter,John (b-g) | McBride,Reggie (b-g) | Mason,Harvey (dr) | Castro,Lenny (perc) | James,Etta (voc) | Atkinson,Sweet Pea (voc) | Bowens,Harry (voc)
Over And Over
Smith,Jimmy (org) | Leonard,Darrell (tp,fl-h,arr) | Brashear,Oscar (tp,fl-h) | Drayton,Leslie (tp,fl-h) | Bohanon,George (tb) | Spears,Maurice (b-tb) | SublettJoe (ts) | Upchurch,Phil (g) | Cleary,Jon (el-p) | McBride,Reggie (b-g) | Mason,Harvey (dr) | Castro,Lenny (perc) | Keb' Mo' (g,voc) | Atkinson,Sweet Pea (voc) | Bowens,Harry (voc)
Mr.Johnson
Smith,Jimmy (org) | Leonard,Darrell (fl-h) | Riley,Herman (ts) | SublettJoe (ts) | Upchurch,Phil (g) | Porter,John (g) | Dr.John[MacRebenack] (p) | McBride,Reggie (b-g) | Mason,Harvey (dr) | Castro,Lenny (perc)
Three O'Clock Blues
Smith,Jimmy (org) | Hubbard,Neil (g) | Porter,John (g) | Stainton,Chris (p) | Palladino,Pino (el-b) | Newark,Andy (dr) | King,B.B. (g,voc)
8 Counts For Rita
Smith,Jimmy (org) | Malone,Russell (g) | McBride,Reggie (b-g) | Mason,Harvey (dr) | Castro,Lenny (perc)
Strut
Smith,Jimmy (org) | Mahal,Taj (g,voc) | Malone,Russell (g) | McBride,Reggie (b-g) | Mason,Harvey (dr) | Castro,Lenny (perc)
C.C.Rider | Dot Com Blues | Tuition Blues
Smith,Jimmy (org) | Malone,Russell (g) | McBride,Reggie (b-g) | Mason,Harvey (dr)
Mood Indigo
Smith,Jimmy (org) | Malone,Russell (g) | Clayton,John (b) | Mason,Harvey (dr)

BTR 70042 | CD | Handful Of Blues
Robben Ford & The Blue Line
Rugged Road
Los Angeles,CA, rec. details unknown
Ford,Robben (g,voc) | Beck,Roscoe (b,background-voc) | Brechtlein,Tommy (dr,background-voc)
When I Leave Here
Los Angeles,CA/NYC, rec. details unknown
Ford,Robben (g,voc) | Butler,Henry (p) | Beck,Roscoe (b,background-voc) | Brechtlein,Tommy (dr,background-voc)
The Miller's Son | Running Out On Me
Ford,Robben (g,voc) | Ford,Mark (harm) | Beck,Roscoe (b,background-voc) | Brechtlein,Tommy (dr,background-voc)
Chevrolet
Ford,Robben (g,voc) | Ford,Mark (harm) | Kortchmar,Danny (g) | Beck,Roscoe (b,background-voc) | Brechtlein,Tommy (dr,background-voc)
I Just Want To Make Love To You
Ford,Robben (g,voc) | Butler,Henry (p) | Ford,Mark (harm) | Kortchmar,Danny (g) | Beck,Roscoe (b,background-voc) | Brechtlein,Tommy (dr,background-voc)
Tired Of Talkin'
Ford,Robben (g,voc) | Kortchmar,Danny (g) | Beck,Roscoe (b,background-voc) | Brechtlein,Tommy (dr,background-voc)
Top Of The Hill | Good Thing
Ford,Robben (g,voc) | Ferrante,Russell (el-p) | Beck,Roscoe (b,background-voc) | Brechtlein,Tommy (dr,background-voc)
Don't Let Me Be Misunderstood
Ford,Robben (g,voc) | Peterson,Ricky (org) | Ferrante,Russell (el-p) | Beck,Roscoe (b,background-voc) | Brechtlein,Tommy (dr,background-voc)
Think Twice | Strong Will To Live
Ford,Robben (g,voc) | Peterson,Ricky (org) | Beck,Roscoe (b,background-voc) | Brechtlein,Tommy (dr,background-voc)

Bluebird | BMG-Ariola Classics GmbH

21 13181-2 | 3 CD | Duke Ellington:The Blanton-Webster Band
Duke Ellington And His Famous Orchestra
You You Darlin' | Jack The Bear | Ko-Ko | Morning Glory | So Far So Good
Chicago,Ill, rec. 6.3.1940
Ellington,Duke (p) | Stewart,Rex (co) | Williams,Cootie (tp) | Jones,Wallace (tp) | Nanton,Joe 'Tricky Sam' (tb) | Tizol,Juan (tb) | Brown,Lawrence (tb) | Bigard,Barney (cl,ts) | Hodges,Johnny (ss,as) | Hardwicke,Otto (as,bass-s) | Webster,Ben (ts) | Carney,Harry (cl,as,bs) | Guy,Fred (g) | Blanton,Jimmy (b) | Greer,William 'Sonny' (dr) | Anderson,Ivie (voc) | Jeffries,Herb (voc)
Conga Brava | Concerto For Cootie | Me And You
Chicago,Ill, rec. 15.3.1940
Ellington,Duke (p) | Stewart,Rex (co) | Williams,Cootie (tp) | Jones,Wallace (tp) | Nanton,Joe 'Tricky Sam' (tb) | Tizol,Juan (tb) | Brown,Lawrence (tb) | Bigard,Barney (cl,ts) | Hodges,Johnny (ss,as) | Hardwicke,Otto (as,bass-s) | Webster,Ben (ts) | Carney,Harry (cl,as,bs) | Guy,Fred (g) | Blanton,Jimmy (b) | Greer,William 'Sonny' (dr) | Anderson,Ivie (voc)
Cotton Tail | Never No Lament
Hollywood,CA, rec. 4.5.1940
Ellington,Duke (p,arr) | Jones,Wallace (tp) | Williams,Cootie (tp) | Stewart,Rex (co) | Nanton,Joe 'Tricky Sam' (tb) | Brown,Lawrence (tb) | Tizol,Juan (v-tb) | Bigard,Barney (cl) | Hodges,Johnny (cl,ss,as) | Hardwicke,Otto (as,bass-s) | Webster,Ben (ts) | Carney,Harry (cl,as,bs) | Guy,Fred (g) | Blanton,Jimmy (b) | Greer,William 'Sonny' (dr)
Dusk | Bojangles | Portrait Of Bert Williams | Blue Goose
Chicago,Ill, rec. 28.5.1940
Ellington,Duke (p,arr) | Jones,Wallace (tp) | Williams,Cootie (tp) | Stewart,Rex (co) | Nanton,Joe 'Tricky Sam' (tb) | Brown,Lawrence (tb) | Tizol,Juan (v-tb) | Bigard,Barney (cl) | Hodges,Johnny (cl,ss,as) | Hardwicke,Otto (as,bass-s) | Webster,Ben (ts) | Carney,Harry (cl,as,bs) | Guy,Fred (g) | Blanton,Jimmy (b) | Greer,William 'Sonny' (dr)
Harlem Air Shaft | At A Dixie Roadside Diner | All Too Soon | Rumpus In Richmond
NYC, rec. 22.7.1940
Ellington,Duke (p,arr) | Jones,Wallace (tp) | Williams,Cootie (tp) | Stewart,Rex (co) | Nanton,Joe 'Tricky Sam' (tb) | Brown,Lawrence (tb) | Tizol,Juan (v-tb) | Bigard,Barney (cl) | Hodges,Johnny (cl,ss,as) | Hardwicke,Otto (as,bass-s) | Webster,Ben (ts) | Carney,Harry (cl,as,bs) | Guy,Fred (g) | Blanton,Jimmy (b) | Greer,William 'Sonny' (dr)
My Greatest Mistake | Sepia Panorama
NYC, rec. 24.7.1940
Ellington,Duke (p,arr) | Jones,Wallace (tp) | Williams,Cootie (tp) | Stewart,Rex (co) | Nanton,Joe 'Tricky Sam' (tb) | Brown,Lawrence (tb) | Tizol,Juan (v-tb) | Bigard,Barney (cl) | Hodges,Johnny (cl,ss,as) | Hardwicke,Otto (as,bass-s) | Webster,Ben (ts) | Carney,Harry (cl,as,bs) | Guy,Fred (g) | Blanton,Jimmy (b) | Greer,William 'Sonny' (dr)
There Shall Be No Night | In A Mellow Tone | Five O'Clock Whistle
Chicago,Ill, rec. 5.9.1940
Ellington,Duke (p,arr) | Jones,Wallace (tp) | Williams,Cootie (tp) | Stewart,Rex (co) | Nanton,Joe 'Tricky Sam' (tb) | Brown,Lawrence (tb) | Tizol,Juan (v-tb) | Bigard,Barney (cl) | Hodges,Johnny (cl,ss,as) | Hardwicke,Otto (as,bass-s) | Webster,Ben (ts) | Carney,Harry (cl,as,bs) | Guy,Fred (g) | Blanton,Jimmy (b) | Greer,William 'Sonny' (dr)
Warm Valley | The Flaming Sword
Chicago,Ill, rec. 17.10.1940
Ellington,Duke (p,arr) | Jones,Wallace (tp) | Williams,Cootie (tp) | Stewart,Rex (co) | Nanton,Joe 'Tricky Sam' (tb) | Brown,Lawrence (tb) | Tizol,Juan (v-tb) | Bigard,Barney (cl) | Hodges,Johnny (cl,ss,as) | Hardwicke,Otto (as,bass-s) | Webster,Ben (ts) | Carney,Harry (cl,as,bs) | Guy,Fred (g) | Blanton,Jimmy (b) | Greer,William 'Sonny' (dr)
Across The Track Blues | Chloe (Song Of The Swamp) | Never Felt This Way Before
Chicago,Ill, rec. 28.10.1940
Ellington,Duke (p,arr) | Jones,Wallace (tp) | Williams,Cootie (tp) | Stewart,Rex (co) | Nanton,Joe 'Tricky Sam' (tb) | Brown,Lawrence (tb) | Tizol,Juan (v-tb) | Bigard,Barney (cl) | Hodges,Johnny (cl,ss,as) | Hardwicke,Otto (as,bass-s) | Webster,Ben (ts) | Carney,Harry (cl,as,bs) | Guy,Fred (g) | Blanton,Jimmy (b) | Greer,William 'Sonny' (dr) | Jeffries,Herb (voc)
The Sidewalks Of New York | The Girl In My Dreams Tries To Look Like You
Chicago,Ill, rec. 28.12.1940
Ellington,Duke (p,arr) | Jones,Wallace (tp) | Williams,Cootie (tp) | Stewart,Rex (co) | Nanton,Joe 'Tricky Sam' (tb) | Brown,Lawrence (tb) | Tizol,Juan (v-tb) | Bigard,Barney (cl) | Hodges,Johnny (cl,ss,as) | Hardwicke,Otto (as,bass-s) | Webster,Ben (ts) | Carney,Harry (cl,as,bs) | Guy,Fred (g) | Blanton,Jimmy (b) | Greer,William 'Sonny' (dr) | Jeffries,Herb (voc)
Flamingo
Ellington,Duke (arr,ld) | Jones,Wallace (tp) | Williams,Cootie (tp) | Stewart,Rex (co) | Nanton,Joe 'Tricky Sam' (tb) | Brown,Lawrence (tb) | Tizol,Juan (v-tb) | Bigard,Barney (cl) | Hodges,Johnny (cl,ss,as) | Hardwicke,Otto (as,bass-s) | Webster,Ben (ts) | Carney,Harry (cl,as,bs) | Strayhorn,Billy (p) | Guy,Fred (g) | Blanton,Jimmy (b) | Greer,William 'Sonny' (dr) | Jeffries,Herb (voc)
After All
Hollywood,CA, rec. 15.2.1941
Ellington,Duke (arr,ld) | Jones,Wallace (tp) | Williams,Cootie (tp) | Stewart,Rex (co) | Nanton,Joe 'Tricky Sam' (tb) | Brown,Lawrence (tb) | Tizol,Juan (v-tb) | Bigard,Barney (cl) | Hodges,Johnny (cl,ss,as) | Hardwicke,Otto (as,bass-s) | Webster,Ben (ts) | Carney,Harry (cl,as,bs) | Strayhorn,Billy (p) | Guy,Fred (g) | Blanton,Jimmy (b) | Greer,William 'Sonny' (dr) | Jeffries,Herb (voc)
Take The 'A' Train | Jumpin' Punkins | John Hardy's Wife | Blue Serge
Ellington,Duke (p,arr) | Jones,Wallace (tp) | Williams,Cootie (tp) | Stewart,Rex (co) | Nanton,Joe 'Tricky Sam' (tb) | Brown,Lawrence (tb) | Tizol,Juan (v-tb) | Bigard,Barney (cl) | Hodges,Johnny (cl,ss,as) | Hardwicke,Otto (as,bass-s) | Webster,Ben (ts) | Carney,Harry (cl,as,bs) | Guy,Fred (g) | Blanton,Jimmy (b) | Greer,William 'Sonny' (dr)
Bakiff | Are You Sticking | Just A-Sittin' And A-Rockin' | The Giddybug Gallop
Hollywood,CA, rec. 5.6.1941
Ellington,Duke (p,arr) | Jones,Wallace (tp) | Nance,Ray (tp) | Stewart,Rex (co) | Nanton,Joe 'Tricky Sam' (tb) | Brown,Lawrence (tb) | Tizol,Juan (v-tb) | Bigard,Barney (cl) | Hodges,Johnny (cl,ss,as) | Hardwicke,Otto (as,bass-s) | Webster,Ben (ts) | Carney,Harry (cl,as,bs) | Guy,Fred (g) | Blanton,Jimmy (b) | Greer,William 'Sonny' (dr)
Chocolate Shake | I Got It Bad And That Ain't Good
Hollywood,CA, rec. 26.6.1941
Ellington,Duke (p,arr) | Jones,Wallace (tp) | Nance,Ray (tp) | Stewart,Rex (co) | Nanton,Joe 'Tricky Sam' (tb) | Brown,Lawrence (tb) | Tizol,Juan (v-tb) | Bigard,Barney (cl) | Hodges,Johnny (cl,ss,as) | Hardwicke,Otto (as,bass-s) | Webster,Ben (ts) | Carney,Harry (cl,as,bs) | Guy,Fred (g) | Blanton,Jimmy (b) | Greer,William 'Sonny' (dr) | Anderson,Ivie (voc)
Clementine | Brown-Skinned Gal In The Calico Gown | Jump For Joy | Moon Over Cuba
Hollywood,CA, rec. 2.7.1941
Ellington,Duke (p,arr) | Jones,Wallace (tp) | Nance,Ray (tp) | Stewart,Rex (co) | Nanton,Joe 'Tricky Sam' (tb) | Brown,Lawrence (tb) | Tizol,Juan (v-tb) | Bigard,Barney (cl) | Hodges,Johnny (cl,ss,as) | Hardwicke,Otto (as,bass-s) | Webster,Ben (ts) | Carney,Harry (cl,as,bs) | Guy,Fred (g) | Blanton,Jimmy (b) | Greer,William 'Sonny' (dr) | Jeffries,Herb (voc)
Five O'Clock Drag | Bli-Blip
Hollywood,CA, rec. 26.9.1941
Ellington,Duke (p,arr) | Jones,Wallace (tp) | Nance,Ray (tp,voc) | Stewart,Rex (co) | Nanton,Joe 'Tricky Sam' (tb) | Brown,Lawrence (tb) | Tizol,Juan (v-tb) | Bigard,Barney (cl) | Hodges,Johnny (cl,ss,as) | Hardwicke,Otto (as,bass-s) | Webster,Ben (ts) | Carney,Harry (cl,as,bs) | Guy,Fred (g) | Blanton,Jimmy (b) | Greer,William 'Sonny' (dr)
Rocks In My Bed
Ellington,Duke (ld) | Jones,Wallace (tp) | Nance,Ray (tp) | Stewart,Rex (co) | Nanton,Joe 'Tricky Sam' (tb) | Brown,Lawrence (tb) | Tizol,Juan (v-tb) | Bigard,Barney (cl) | Hodges,Johnny (cl,ss,as) | Hardwicke,Otto (as,bass-s) | Webster,Ben (ts) | Carney,Harry (cl,as,bs) | Strayhorn,Billy (p) | Guy,Fred (g) | Blanton,Jimmy (b) | Greer,William 'Sonny' (dr) | Anderson,Ivie (voc)
Chelsea Bridge | Raincheck | What Good Would It Do?
Hollywood,CA, rec. 2.12.1941
Ellington,Duke (ld) | Jones,Wallace (tp) | Nance,Ray (tp) | Stewart,Rex (co) | Nanton,Joe 'Tricky Sam' (tb) | Brown,Lawrence (tb) | Tizol,Juan (v-tb) | Bigard,Barney (cl) | Hodges,Johnny (cl,ss,as) | Hardwicke,Otto (as,bass-s) | Webster,Ben (ts) | Carney,Harry (cl,as,bs) | Strayhorn,Billy (p) | Guy,Fred (g) | Raglin,Alvin 'Junior' (b) | Greer,William 'Sonny' (dr) | Jeffries,Herb (voc)
I Don't Know What Kind Of Blues I Got
Ellington,Duke (p) | Jones,Wallace (tp) | Nance,Ray (tp) | Stewart,Rex (co) | Nanton,Joe 'Tricky Sam' (tb) | Brown,Lawrence (tb) | Tizol,Juan (v-tb) | Bigard,Barney (cl) | Hodges,Johnny (cl,ss,as) | Hardwicke,Otto (as,bass-s) | Webster,Ben (ts) | Carney,Harry (cl,as,bs) | Guy,Fred (g) | Raglin,Alvin 'Junior' (b) | Greer,William 'Sonny' (dr) | Jeffries,Herb (voc)
Perdido | C Jam Blues | Moon Mist
Chicago,Ill, rec. 21.1.1942
Ellington,Duke (p,arr) | Jones,Wallace (tp) | Nance,Ray (tp) | Stewart,Rex (co) | Nanton,Joe 'Tricky Sam' (tb) | Brown,Lawrence (tb) | Tizol,Juan

(v-tb) | Bigard,Barney (cl) | Hodges,Johnny (cl,ss,as) | Hardwicke,Otto (as,bass-s) | Webster,Ben (ts) | Carney,Harry (cl,as,bs) | Guy,Fred (g) | Blanton,Jimmy (b) | Greer,William 'Sonny' (dr)
What Am I Here For | I Don't Mind | Someone
NYC, rec. 26.2.1942
Ellington,Duke (p,arr) | Jones,Wallace (tp) | Nance,Ray (tp) | Stewart,Rex (co) | Nanton,Joe 'Tricky Sam' (tb) | Brown,Lawrence (tb) | Tizol,Juan (v-tb) | Bigard,Barney (cl) | Hodges,Johnny (cl,ss,as) | Hardwicke,Otto (as,bass-s) | Webster,Ben (ts) | Carney,Harry (cl,as,bs) | Guy,Fred (g) | Blanton,Jimmy (b) | Greer,William 'Sonny' (dr) | Anderson,Ivie (voc)
My Little Brown Book | Johnny Comes Lately
Hollywood,CA, rec. 26.6.1942
Ellington,Duke (ld) | Jones,Wallace (tp) | Nance,Ray (tp) | Stewart,Rex (co) | Nanton,Joe 'Tricky Sam' (tb) | Brown,Lawrence (tb) | Tizol,Juan (v-tb) | Bigard,Barney (cl) | Hodges,Johnny (cl,ss,as) | Hardwicke,Otto (as,bass-s) | Webster,Ben (ts) | Carney,Harry (cl,as,bs) | Strayhorn,Billy (p,arr) | Guy,Fred (g) | Blanton,Jimmy (b) | Greer,William 'Sonny' (dr)
Main Stem
Ellington,Duke (p,arr) | Jones,Wallace (tp) | Nance,Ray (tp) | Stewart,Rex (co) | Nanton,Joe 'Tricky Sam' (tb) | Brown,Lawrence (tb) | Tizol,Juan (v-tb) | Bigard,Barney (cl) | Hodges,Johnny (cl,ss,as) | Hardwicke,Otto (as,bass-s) | Webster,Ben (ts) | Carney,Harry (cl,as,bs) | Guy,Fred (g) | Blanton,Jimmy (b) | Greer,William 'Sonny' (dr)
Hayfoot Strawfoot | Sentimental Lady | Sherman Shuffle
Chicago,Ill, rec. 28.7.1942
Ellington,Duke (p,arr) | Jones,Wallace (tp) | Nance,Ray (tp) | Stewart,Rex (co) | Nanton,Joe 'Tricky Sam' (tb) | Brown,Lawrence (tb) | Tizol,Juan (v-tb) | Bigard,Barney (cl) | Hodges,Johnny (cl,ss,as) | Hardwicke,Otto (as,bass-s) | Webster,Ben (ts) | Carney,Harry (cl,as,bs) | Guy,Fred (g) | Blanton,Jimmy (b) | Greer,William 'Sonny' (dr) | Anderson,Ivie (voc)
A Slip Of The Lip(Can Sink A Ship)
Chicago,Ill, rec. 28.7.1972
Ellington,Duke (ld) | Jones,Wallace (tp) | Nance,Ray (tp,voc) | Stewart,Rex (co) | Nanton,Joe 'Tricky Sam' (tb) | Brown,Lawrence (tb) | Tizol,Juan (v-tb) | Bigard,Barney (cl) | Hodges,Johnny (cl,ss,as) | Hardwicke,Otto (as,bass-s) | Webster,Ben (ts) | Carney,Harry (cl,as,bs) | Strayhorn,Billy (p) | Guy,Fred (g) | Blanton,Jimmy (b) | Greer,William 'Sonny' (dr)

2663957-2 | CD | Djangology | EAN 090266395729
Quintet Du Hot Club De France
I Saw Stars | After You've Gone | Heavy Artillery(Artillery Lourde) | Beyond The Sea(La Mer) | Minor Swing | Menilmontant | Brick Top | Swing Guitars | All The Things You Are | Daphne | It's Only A Paper Moon | Improvisation On Pathétique(Andante) | The World Is Waiting For The Sunrise | Djangology | Ou Es-Tu Mon Amour | Marie | I Surrender Dear | Hallelujah | Swing '42 | I'll Never Be The Same | Honeysuckle Rose | Lover Man(Oh,Where Can You Be?) | I Got Rhythm
Rome,Italy, rec. January/February 1949
Quintet Du Hot Club De France | Grappelli,Stephane (v) | Reinhardt,Django (g) | Safred,Gianni (p) | Pecori,Carlo (b) | De Carolis,Aurelio (dr)

2663961-2 | CD | Louis Armstrong And His Friends | EAN 090266396122
Louis Armstrong And His Friends
What A Wonderful World | Mood Indigo | My One And Only Love | Here Is My Heart For Christmas
NYC, rec. 26.5.1970
Armstrong,Louis (voc) | Spaulding,James (fl) | Owens,Frank (p) | Brown,Sam (g) | Burrell,Kenny (g) | Davis,Richard (b) | Duvivier,George (b) | Williams Jr.,John (el-b) | Purdie,Bernard 'Pretty' (dr) | Black,Arnold (v) | Clarke,Selwart (v) | Collymore,Winston (v) | Gersham,Paul (v) | Green,Manny (v) | Lookofsky,Harry (v) | Orloff,Gene (v) | Malin,Joe (v) | Pollikoff,Max (v) | Barber,Julian (viola) | Brown,Alfred (viola) | Schwartz,David (viola) | Vardi,Emanuel (viola) | McCracken,Charles (cello) | Moore,Kermit (cello) | Ricci,George (cello) | Schulman,Allan (cello)
The Creator Has A Master Plan(Peace) | Everybody's Talkin'(Echoes) | His Father Wore Long Hair | The Creator Has A Master Plan(Peace alt.take 1) | The Creator Has A Master Plan(Peace alt.take 2)
NYC, rec. 27.5.1970
Armstrong,Louis (voc) | Spaulding,James (fl) | Owens,Frank (p) | Brown,Sam (g) | Burrell,Kenny (g) | Davis,Richard (b) | Duvivier,George (b) | Williams Jr.,John (el-b) | Purdie,Bernard 'Pretty' (dr) | Black,Arnold (v) | Clarke,Selwart (v) | Collymore,Winston (v) | Gersham,Paul (v) | Green,Manny (v) | Lookofsky,Harry (v) | Raimondi,Matthew (v) | Malin,Joe (v) | Pollikoff,Max (v) | Barber,Julian (viola) | Brown,Alfred (viola) | Schwartz,David (viola) | Vardi,Emanuel (viola) | McCracken,Charles (cello) | Moore,Kermit (cello) | Ricci,George (cello) | Schulman,Allan (cello) | Golden,Gene (congas) | Thomas,Leon (voc)
Boy From New Orleans | Give Peace A Chance | This Black Cat Has Nine Lives | We Shall Overcome
NYC, rec. 29.5.1970
Armstrong,Louis (voc) | Jones,Thad (tp) | Owens,Jimmy (tp) | Royal,Ernie (tp) | Stamm,Marvin (tp,fl-h) | Brown,Garnett (tb) | Campbell,William (tb) | Grey,Al (tb) | Jackson,Quentin (tb) | Ashton,Bob (reeds) | Beckonstein,Ray (sax) | Bank,Danny (reeds) | Dodgion,Jerry (sax) | Harper,Billy (sax) | Owens,Frank (p) | Brown,Sam (g) | Burrell,Kenny (g) | Rainey,Chuck (el-b) | Purdie,Bernard 'Pretty' (dr) | Golden,Gene (congas) | Hall,Carl (voc) | Bell,Janice (voc) | Govan,Ila (voc) | Ledbetter,Matthew (voc) | Thomas,Tasha (voc)

2664008-2 | CD | Dave Douglas Freak In | EAN 090266400829
Dave Douglas Group
Hot Club Of 13th Street
Brooklyn,NY, rec. July-September 2002
Douglas,Dave (tp,keyboards,voc) | Ribot,Marc (el-g) | Saft,Jamie (keyboards,loops,progamming) | Jones,Bradley (b,ampeg-baby-b) | Baron,Joey (dr) | Mori,Ikue (electronic-perc)
Freak In
Douglas,Dave (tp,keyboards,voc) | Blake,Seamus (sax) | Ribot,Marc (el-g) | Saft,Jamie (keyboards,loops,progamming) | Jones,Bradley (b,ampeg-baby-b) | Baron,Joey (dr) | Mori,Ikue (electronic-perc) | Kale,Karsh (dr,tabla)
Black Rock Park | Eastern Parkway | Maya
Douglas,Dave (tp,keyboards,voc) | Blake,Seamus (sax) | Ribot,Marc (el-g) | Saft,Jamie (keyboards,loops,progamming) | Jones,Bradley (b,ampeg-baby-b) | Baron,Joey (dr) | Mori,Ikue (electronic-perc)
Culver City Park
Douglas,Dave (tp,keyboards,voc) | Speed,Chris (cl,sax) | Lubambo,Romero (g) | Ribot,Marc (el-g) | Saft,Jamie (keyboards,loops,progamming) | Jones,Bradley (b,ampeg-baby-b) | Baron,Joey (dr) | Mori,Ikue (electronic-perc)
November | The Great Schism | Wild Blue
Douglas,Dave (tp,keyboards,voc) | Speed,Chris (cl,sax) | Ribot,Marc (el-g) | Saft,Jamie (keyboards,loops,progamming) | Jones,Bradley (b,ampeg-baby-b) | Baron,Joey (dr) | Mori,Ikue (electronic-perc)
Porto Allegro | Traveler There Is No Road
Douglas,Dave (tp,keyboards,voc) | Speed,Chris (cl,sax) | Ribot,Marc (el-g) | Taborn,Craig (el-p) | Saft,Jamie (keyboards,loops,progamming) | Jones,Bradley (b,ampeg-baby-b) | Baron,Joey (dr) | Sarin,Michael (dr) | Mori,Ikue (electronic-perc)

ND 82001 | CD | Chet Baker-The Italian Sessions
Chet Baker Sextet
Well You Needn't | These Foolish Things Remind Me On You | Barbados | Star Eyes | Somewhere Over The Rainbow | Pent-Up House | Ballata In Forma Di Blues | Blues In The Closet
Rome,Italy, rec. 5.1.1962
Baker,Chet (tp) | Jaspar,Bobby (fl,ts) | Thomas,Rene (g) | Tommasi,Amedeo (p) | Quersin,Benoit (b) | Humair,Daniel (dr)

Blues Beacon | Enja Eigenvertrieb

BLU-1013 2 | CD | Big Heart
Nick Woodland And The Magnets
Outskirts Of Town | Precious Time | Wayfaring Stranger | Just A Little Bit | Cross My Heart | Quiet Kinda Guy | Teacher Teacher | Waiting On You- | Help Me- | I Got A Mind To Give Up Living | Gospel Train
details unknown, rec. details unknown
Woodland,Nick (g,mand,lap-steel,voc) | Ingram,Willy Ray (ts) | Esser,Georg (b,lap-steel,voc) | Seuss,Ludwig (p,org,accordeon) | Klopfenstein,Jim (b) | Fries,Fats (dr) | Ferstl,Henrik (dr) | Sireens (voc)

BLU-1019 2 | CD | Blues News
Christian Willisohn-Boris Vanderlek
After Hours | Willow Weep For Me | Georgia On My Mind | Heart-Broken Man
Live at 'Birdland',Neuburg/Donau, rec. 12.9.1993
Willisohn,Christian (p,voc) | Vanderlek,Boris (ts)
Christian Willisohn-Boris Vanderlek-Ludwig Seuss
Money | I'm Gonna Move To The Outskirts Of Town | Doodlin' | Nobody Knows You When You're Down And Out | Bring It On Home
Willisohn,Christian (p,voc) | Vanderlek,Boris (ts) | Seuss,Ludwig (org)

BLU-1025 2 | CD | Blues On The World
Christian Willisohn Group
Little Angel | Diddlin' | Tin Pan Alley | See See Rider | Sykesism | Let Them Talk | How Long
München, rec. April 1995
Willisohn,Christian (p,voc) | Knauer,Rocky (b,voc) | Hollander,Rick (dr,voc)
Mystery Train
Willisohn,Christian (p,voc) | Heggen,Henry (harm) | Knauer,Rocky (b,voc) | Hollander,Rick (dr,voc)
Blues On The World
Willisohn,Christian (p,voc) | Knauer,Rocky (b,voc) | Hollander,Rick (dr,voc) | Boutté,Lillian (voc)
I'd Rather Go Blind | Baby What You Want Me To Do
Willisohn,Christian (p,voc) | Lopez,Manuel (g) | Knauer,Rocky (b,voc) | Hollander,Rick (dr,voc) | Boutté,Lillian (voc)

BLU-1026 2 | CD | Heart Broken Man
Christian Willisohn New Band
A Girl Like You | Heart-Broken Man | Congo Square | Raven | The Man In Your Life
München, rec. details unknown
Willisohn,Christian (g,p,voc) | Holstein,Stephan (cl,sax) | Seuss,Ludwig (org,accordeon) | Vollmer,Titus (g) | Knauer,Rocky (b,voc) | Hollander,Rick (dr,voc)
New York City
Willisohn,Christian (p,voc) | Breuer,Hermann (tb) | Holstein,Stephan (cl,sax) | Seuss,Ludwig (org,accordeon) | Vollmer,Titus (g) | Knauer,Rocky (b,voc) | Hollander,Rick (dr,voc)
Un-Autentic Blues | Funeral
Willisohn,Christian (p,voc) | Breuer,Hermann (tb) | Holstein,Stephan (cl,sax) | Seuss,Ludwig (org,accordeon) | Vollmer,Titus (g) | Knauer,Rocky (b,voc) | Hollander,Rick (dr,voc) | Auchtor,Carmen (voc) | Hawkins,Eva (voc)
On The Bayou
Willisohn,Christian (p,accordeon,voc) | Holstein,Stephan (cl,sax) | Seuss,Ludwig (org,accordeon) | Vollmer,Titus (g) | Knauer,Rocky (b,voc) | Hollander,Rick (dr,voc) | Matzkeit,Bodo (perc) | Auchtor,Carmen (voc) | Hawkins,Eva (voc)
Little Voodoo Baby
Willisohn,Christian (p,voc) | Holstein,Stephan (cl,sax) | Seuss,Ludwig (org,accordeon) | Vollmer,Titus (g) | Knauer,Rocky (b,voc) | Hollander,Rick (dr,voc) | Matzkeit,Bodo (perc)
Macho Man | Drown In My Own Tears
Willisohn,Christian (p,voc) | Verploegen,Angelo (tp) | Delfos,Rolf (as) | Middlehoff,Barend (ts) | Holstein,Stephan (cl,sax) | Seuss,Ludwig (org,accordeon) | Vollmer,Titus (g) | Knauer,Rocky (b,voc) | Hollander,Rick (dr,voc)

BLU-1027 2 | CD | Live Fireworks
Nick Woodland Quartet
Rock'n Roll Man | Train(23 Stops) | Worried Life Blues | Freight Train | The Race Is On | I Love Another Woman | Cross My Heart | My Babe | Got A Mind To Give Up Living | Hip Shake | Double Trouble
München, rec. 9./10.7.1996
Woodland,Nick (g,voc) | Seuss,Ludwig (keyboards) | Esser,Georg (b,voc) | Fries,Fats (dr)

BLU-1030 2 | CD | Tried & True
Marty Hall Band
My Babe | Ecoman | Easy Rhythm | Stranger In My Hometown | Honest I Do | The Hardest Time | I'll Provide The Thrills | Moondance In Tajikistan | No Respect | Trouble In Mind | Rock Me | You Gotta Go
Lahr, rec. March 1997
Hall,Marty (g,el-g,12-string-g,voc) | Hilliam,David (dobro) | Coulter,Butch (harm) | Kopf,Tobias (b) | Blanchet,Alain 'T-Blanc' (perc)

BLU-1031 2 | CD | Batuque Y Blues
Big Allanbik
Gully Low Blues | My Babe | I Just Want To Make Love To You | Let It Loose | Jessica | Fare | Let The Good Times Roll | Blues For Douglaston | Seventh Son | Evil | Stormy Monday Blues(They Call It Stormy Monday)
NYC, rec. 1996
Big Allanbik | Werther,Ricardo (voc) | Gilson,Big (g,el-g) | Stander,Bob (g) | Ghreen,Alan (p,org) | Perrotta,Ugo (b) | Werther,Beto (dr) | 'Siri',Ricardo (perc) | Michel,John (voc) | Cavill,Chris (voc)

BLU-1033 2 | CD | Who's Been Talkin'?s
Marty Hall Band
Can't Judge A Book By Its Cover | Can't Let It Go | Misbehavin' | I've Got Dreams To Remember | One Of A Kind
Lahr, rec. February/March 1998
Hall,Marty (g,el-g,12-string-g,voc) | Coulter,Butch (harm) | Smith,Nigel Portman (p,b) | Kempf,Vladi (dr,perc)
Tick Tock
Hall,Marty (g,el-g,12-string-g,voc) | Coulter,Butch (harm) | Smith,Nigel Portman (p,b) | Kempf,Vladi (dr,perc) | Selby,Sidney 'Guitar Crusher' (voc)
Who's Been Talkin'?
Hall,Marty (g,el-g,12-string-g,voc) | Coulter,Butch (harm) | Holliday,Simon (p) | Smith,Nigel Portman (b) | Kempf,Vladi (dr,perc) | Selby,Sidney 'Guitar Crusher' (voc) | Kandri,Driss (perc,darabuka)
Matching Pair
Hall,Marty (g,el-g,12-string-g,voc) | Coulter,Butch (harm) | Holliday,Simon (p) | Smith,Nigel Portman (b) | Kempf,Vladi (dr,perc)
That's Why I Love You Like I Do
Hall,Marty (g,el-g,12-string-g,voc) | Coulter,Butch (harm) | Löwenthal,André (el-g) | Holliday,Simon (p) | Smith,Nigel Portman (b) | Kempf,Vladi (dr,perc)
Words Of Wisdom
Hall,Marty (g,el-g,12-string-g,voc) | Coulter,Butch (harm) | Löwenthal,André (el-g) | Smith,Nigel Portman (p,b) | Kempf,Vladi (dr,perc)

BLU-1034 2 | CD | Sharper Than A Tack
Al Jones Blues Band
Baby What You Want Me To Do | Wild Woman | Born Under A Bad Sign | I Can't Quit You Baby | West Side Stroll | I Got The Blues | Shadow OnThe Floor | I Feel Good | Don't Change Your Mind
Memmingen, rec. details unknown
Jones,Al (g,voc) | Kreitmeier,Thilo (reeds,arr) | Hollstein,David (g) | Schmid,Peter (b) | Pöhnl,Oscar (dr)
We All Wanna Boogie
Jones,Al (g,voc) | Kreitmeier,Thilo (reeds,arr) | Hummel,Markus (org) | Hollstein,David (g) | Schmid,Peter (b) | Pöhnl,Oscar (dr)
Sharper Than A Tack
Jones,Al (g,voc) | Kreitmeier,Thilo (reeds,arr) | Fliegauf,Johannes 'Hans' (harm) | Hummel,Markus (org) | Hollstein,David (g) | Schmid,Peter (b) | Pöhnl,Oscar (dr)
Five Long Years
Jones,Al (g,voc) | Kreitmeier,Thilo (reeds,arr) | Fliegauf,Johannes 'Hans' (harm) | Hollstein,David (g) | Schmid,Peter (b) | Pöhnl,Oscar (dr)

Blues Beacon | Soulfood

BLU-1017 2 | CD | The Gospel Book
Lillian Boutté And Her Group & The Soulful Heavenly Stars
Joshua Fit The Battle Of Jericho | Search Me Lord | God Is Real | Come On Children Let's Sing | He Touched Me | Journey To The Sky | I Asked The Lord | Strange Things Happening Every Day | I Said I Wasn't Gonna Tell Nobody | If We Never Needed The Lord Before
New Orleans,Louisiana, rec. 3.-16.2.1993
Boutté,Lillian (voc) | L'Etienne,Thomas (cl,ts) | Frank,Edward (p) | Bemiss,Albert (org) | Lambert,Lloyd (b) | Frost,Soren (dr) | Soulful Heavenly Stars,The | Johnson,Alvin 'Big Al' (voc) | Austin,Henry (voc) | Grove,Henry (voc) | Chaney,Marvin (voc)
Lillian Boutté And Her Group
I'm On My Way | If We Never Needed The Lord Before
Boutté,Lillian (voc) | L'Etienne,Thomas (cl,ts) | Frank,Edward (p) | Bemiss,Albert (org) | Lambert,Lloyd (b) | Frost,Soren (dr) | Sha'Ron (voc)

Candid | Fenn Music

CCD 79001 | CD | Otis Spann Is The Blues
Otis Spann/Robert Lockwood Jr.
The Hard Way | Take A Little Walk With Me | Little Boy Blue | Country Boy | Beat-Up Team | My Daily Wish | I Got Rambling On My Mind | Worried Life Blues
NYC, rec. 23.8.1960
Spann,Otis (p,voc) | Lockwood Jr.,Robert (g,voc)
Otis Spann
Otis In The Dark | Great Northern Stomp
Spann,Otis (p-solo)

CCD 79002 | CD | We Insist: Freedom Now Suite
Max Roach Group
Driva Man
rec. 31.8.& 6.9.1960
Roach,Max (dr) | Little,Booker (tp) | Priester,Julian (tb) | Hawkins,Coleman (ts) | Benton,Walter (ts) | Schenk,James (b) | Lincoln,Abbey (voc)
Freedom Day
Roach,Max (dr) | Little,Booker (tp) | Priester,Julian (tb) | Benton,Walter (ts) | Schenk,James (b) | Lincoln,Abbey (voc)
Max Roach-Abbey Lincoln
Triptych: | Prayer- | Protest- | Peace-
Roach,Max (dr) | Lincoln,Abbey (voc)
Max Roach Group
All Africa | Tears For Johannesburg
Roach,Max (dr) | Little,Booker (tp) | Priester,Julian (tb) | Benton,Walter (ts) | Schenk,James (b) | Olatunji,Babatunde (congas) | Mantilla,Ray (perc) | Du Vall,Tomas (perc) | Lincoln,Abbey (voc)

CCD 79003 | CD | New Horn In Town
Richard Williams Quintet
I Can Dream Can't I | I Remember Clifford | Ferris Wheel | Raucous Notes | Blues In Quandary | Over The Rainbow | Renita's Bounce
rec. 27.9.1960
Williams,Richard (tp) | Wright,Leo (fl,as) | Wyands,Richard (p) | Workman,Reggie (b) | Thomas,Bobby (dr)

CCD 79005 | CD | Charles Mingus Presents Charles Mingus
Charles Mingus Quartet
Folk Forms(No.1) | Original Faubus Fables | What Love | All The Things You Could Be By Now If Sigmund Freud's Wife Was Your Mother
rec. 20.10.1960
Mingus,Charles (b) | Curson,Ted (tp) | Dolphy,Eric (b-cl,as) | Richmond,Dannie (dr)

CCD 79006 | CD | The World Of Cecil Taylor
Cecil Taylor Trio
This Nearly Was Mine | Port Of Call | E.B.
rec. 12./13.10.1960
Taylor,Cecil (p) | Neidlinger,Buell (b) | Charles,Dennis (dr)
Cecil Taylor Quartet
Air | Lazy Afternoon
Taylor,Cecil (p) | Shepp,Archie (ts) | Neidlinger,Buell (b) | Charles,Dennis (dr)

CCD 79008 | CD | Wild Women Don't Have The Blues
Nancy Harrow And The Buck Clayton All Stars
Take Me Back Baby | All Too Soon | Can't We Be Friends | On The Sunny Side Of The Street | Wild Women Don't Have The Blues | I've Got The World On A String | I Don't Know What Kind Of Blues I've Got | Blues For Yesterday
rec. 2./3.11.1960
Harrow,Nancy (voc) | Clayton,Buck (tp) | Wells,Dicky (tb) | Gwaltney,Tommy (cl,as) | Tate,Buddy (ts) | Bank,Danny (bs) | Burrell,Kenny (g) | Wellstood,Dick (p) | Hinton,Milt (b) | Jackson,Oliver (dr)

CCD 79009 | CD | Color Changes
Clark Terry Orchestra
Blue Waltz | Brother Terry | Flutin' And Fluglin' | No Problem | La Rive Gauche | Chat Qui Peche(A Cat That Fishes)
rec. 19.11.1960
Terry,Clark (tp,fl-h) | Knepper,Jimmy (tb) | Watkins,Julius (fr-h) | Lateef,Yusef (engl-h,fl,ts,oboe) | Powell,Seldon (ts) | Flanagan,Tommy (p) | Benjamin,Joe (b) | Shaughnessy,Ed (dr)
Nahstye Blues
Terry,Clark (tp,fl-h) | Knepper,Jimmy (tb) | Watkins,Julius (fr-h) | Lateef,Yusef (engl-h,fl,ts,oboe) | Powell,Seldon (ts) | Johnson,Buddy (p) | Benjamin,Joe (b) | Shaughnessy,Ed (dr)

CCD 79011 | CD | Big Brass
Benny Bailey Septet
Hard Sock Dance | Alison | Tipsy | Please Say Yes | A Kiss To Build A Dream On | Maud's Mood
rec. 25.11.1960
Bailey,Benny (tp) | Watkins,Julius (fr-h) | Woods,Phil (b-cl,as) | Spann,Les (fl,g) | Flanagan,Tommy (p) | Catlett,Buddy (b) | Taylor,Arthur 'Art' (dr)

CCD 79012 | CD | Toshiko Mariano Quartet
Toshiko Mariano Quartet
When You Meet Her | Little T | Toshiko's Elegy | Deep River | Long Yellow Road
rec. 5.12.1960
Akiyoshi,Toshiko (p) | Mariano,Charlie (as) | Cherico,Gene (b) | Marshall,Eddie (dr)

CCD 79014 | CD | That's It
Booker Ervin Quartet
Mojo | Uranus | Poinciana | Speak Low | Booker's Blues | Boo
rec. 6.1.1961
Ervin,Booker (ts) | Parlan,Horace (p) | Tucker,George (b) | Harewood,Al (dr)

CCD 79015 | CD | Straight Ahead
Abbey Lincoln And Her Orchestra
Straight Ahead | When Malindy Sings | In The Red(A Xmas Carol) | Blue Monk | Left Alone | Retribution
rec. 22.2.1961
Lincoln,Abbey (voc) | Little,Booker (tp) | Priester,Julian (tb) | Dolphy,Eric (fl,b-cl,as) | Hawkins,Coleman (ts) | Benton,Walter (ts) | Waldron,Mal (p) | Davis,Art (b) | Roach,Max (dr)
African Lady
Lincoln,Abbey (voc) | Little,Booker (tp) | Priester,Julian (tb) | Dolphy,Eric (fl,b-cl,as) | Hawkins,Coleman (ts) | Benton,Walter (ts) | Waldron,Mal (p) | Davis,Art (b) | Roach,Max (dr) | Sanders,Roger (congas) | Whitley,Robert (congas)

CCD 79017 | CD | New York City R&B
Cecil Taylor/Buell Neidlinger Trio
O.P. | Cindy's Main Mood
NYC, rec. 9./10.1.1961
Taylor,Cecil (p) | Neidlinger,Buell (b) | Higgins,Billy (dr,tympani)
Cecil Taylor/Buell Neidlinger Quartet
Cell Walk For Celeste

Taylor,Cecil (p) | Neidlinger,Buell (b) | Shepp,Archie (ts) | Charles,Dennis (dr)

Cecil Taylor/Buell Neidlinger Orchestra
Things Ain't What They Used To Be
Taylor,Cecil (p) | Neidlinger,Buell (b) | Terry,Clark (tp) | Rudd,Roswell (tb) | Lacy,Steve (ss) | Shepp,Archie (ts) | Davis,Charles (bs) | Higgins,Billy (dr)

CCD 79018 | CD | Blues For Smoke
Jaki Byard
Excerpts From European Episode: | Journey | Hollis Stomp- | Milan To Lyon- | Aluminum Baby | Tribute To The Ticklers | Spanish Tinge(No.1) | Flight Of The Fly | Blues For Smoke | Intro To Byard's Favorite Medleys | Diane's Melody | II-V-I
rec. 1960
Byard,Jaki (p-solo)

CCD 79019 | CD | The Jazz Life!
Charles Mingus Group
R & R
NYC, rec. 11.11.1960
Mingus,Charles (b) | Eldridge,Roy (tp) | Knepper,Jimmy (tb) | Dolphy,Eric (as) | Flanagan,Tommy (p) | Jones,Jo (dr)
Lightnin' Hopkins
Black Cat
NYC, rec. 15.11.1960
Hopkins,Sam Lightnin' (g,voc)
Cal Massey Sextet
Father And Son
NYC, rec. 13.1.1961
Massey,Cal (tp) | Watkins,Julius (fr-h) | Brodie,Hugh (ts) | Bown,Patti (p) | Garrison,Jimmy (b) | Hogan,Granville T. (dr)
Lucky Thompson Quartet
Lord,Lord Am I Ever Gonna Know
NYC, rec. ca.1960
Thompson,Lucky (ts) | Solal,Martial (p) | Trunk,Peter (b) | Clarke,Kenny (dr)
Charles Mingus Group
Vassarlean
NYC, rec. 11.11.1960
Mingus,Charles (b) | Hillyer,Lonnie (tp) | Curson,Ted (tp) | Dolphy,Eric (b-cl) | McPherson,Charles (as) | Ervin,Booker (ts) | Bunick,Floris Nico (p) | Richmond,Dannie (dr)
Max Roach Septet
Oh Yeah,Oh Yeah
NYC, rec. 1.11.1960
Roach,Max (dr) | Dorham,Kenny (tp) | Bailey,Benny (tp) | Priester,Julian (tb) | Benton,Walter (ts) | Payne,Cecil (bs) | Morrison,John 'Peck' (b)

CCD 79021 | CD | Mingus
Charles Mingus Orchestra
MDM
rec. 20.10.1960
Mingus,Charles (b) | Curson,Ted (tp) | Hillyer,Lonnie (tp) | Knepper,Jimmy (tb) | Woodman,Britt (tb) | Dolphy,Eric (b-cl,as) | McPherson,Charles (as) | Ervin,Booker (ts) | Bunick,Floris Nico (p) | Richmond,Dannie (dr)
Lock 'Em Up
rec. 11.11.1960
Mingus,Charles (b) | Curson,Ted (tp) | Hillyer,Lonnie (tp) | Dolphy,Eric (as) | McPherson,Charles (as) | Ervin,Booker (ts) | Bley,Paul (p) | Richmond,Dannie (dr)
Charles Mingus Quartet
Stormy Weather
rec. 20.10.1960
Mingus,Charles (b) | Curson,Ted (tp) | Dolphy,Eric (as) | Richmond,Dannie (dr)

CCD 79022 | CD | Newport Rebels-Jazz Artists Guild
Jazz Artists Guild
Mysterious Blues
NYC, rec. 11.11.1960
Jazz Artists Guild | Eldridge,Roy (tp) | Knepper,Jimmy (tb) | Dolphy,Eric (as) | Flanagan,Tommy (p) | Mingus,Charles (b) | Jones,Jo (dr)
Wrap Your Troubles In Dreams | Me And You
Jazz Artists Guild | Eldridge,Roy (tp) | Flanagan,Tommy (p) | Mingus,Charles (b) | Jones,Jo (dr)
Cliff Walk
NYC, rec. 1.11.1960
Jazz Artists Guild | Little,Booker (tp) | Priester,Julian (tb) | Benton,Walter (ts) | Morrison,Peck (b) | Roach,Max (dr) | Jones,Jo (dr)
'Tain't Nobody's Bizness If I Do
Jazz Artists Guild | Bailey,Benny (tp) | Dorham,Kenny (tp) | Dolphy,Eric (as) | Morrison,Peck (b) | Jones,Jo (dr) | Lincoln,Abbey (voc)

CCD 79024 | CD | Memphis Slim USA
Memphis Slim
Born With The Blues | Just Let Me Be | Red Haired Boogie | Blue And Disgusted | New Key To The Highway | I'd Take Her To Chicago | Harlem Bound | El Capitan | I Just Landed In Your Town | John Henry | I Believe I'll Settle Down | Bad Luck And Troubles | Late Afternoon Blues | Memphis Slim U.S.A.
NYC, rec. 16.1.1961
Memphis Slim[Peter Chatman] (p,voc) | Gillum,William 'Bill Jazz' (harm,voc) | Stidham,Arbee (g,voc)

CCD 79025 | CD | Walking The Blues
Otis Spann
It Must Have Been The Devil | Otis Blues | Going Down Slow | Half Ain't Been Told | Monkey Woman | This Is The Blues | Evil Ways | Come Day Go Day | Walking The Blues | Bad Condition | My Home Is In The Delta
NYC, rec. 23.8.1960
Spann,Otis (p,voc) | Lockwood Jr.,Robert (g,voc) | Oden,James[St.Louis Jimmy] (voc)

CCD 79027 | CD | Out Front
Booker Little Sextet
We Speak | Quiet Please | A New Day
rec. 17.3.1961
Little,Booker (tp) | Priester,Julian (tb) | Dolphy,Eric (fl,b-cl,as) | Friedman,Don (p) | Davis,Art (b) | Roach,Max (dr)
Strength And Sanity | Moods In Free Time | Man Of Words | Hazy Hues
rec. 4.4.1961
Little,Booker (tp) | Priester,Julian (tb) | Dolphy,Eric (fl,b-cl,as) | Friedman,Don (p) | Carter,Ron (b) | Roach,Max (dr)

CCD 79028 | CD | Smooth Groove
Ray Crawford Sextet
The Compendium Suite | Miss April | Impossible | I Know Prez | Smooth Groove
NYC, rec. Feb.1961
Crawford,Ray (g) | Coles,Johnny (tp) | Payne,Cecil (bs) | Mance,Junior[Julian C.] (p) | Tucker,Ben (b) | Dunlop,Frankie (dr)

CCD 79029 | CD | Blues To Coltrane
Cal Massey Sextet
Blues To Coltrane | What's Wrong | Bakai | These Are Soulful Days | Father And Son
NYC, rec. 13.1.1961
Massey,Cal (tp) | Watkins,Julius (fr-h) | Brodie,Hugh (ts) | Bown,Patti (p) | Garrison,Jimmy (b) | Hogan,Granville T. (dr)

CCD 79030 | CD | Plays Pal Joey
Chamber Jazz Sextet
Zip | I Could Write A Book | There's A Small Hotel | My Funny Valentine | The Lady Is A Tramp | Bewitched Bothered And Bewildered | That Terrific Rainbow | I Didn't Know What Time It Was
Hollywood,CA, rec. 3.6.1958
Chamber Jazz Sextet | Hart,Dent (tp,b) | Leal,Frank (as) | Briseno,Modesto (cl,ts,bs) | Ferguson,Allyn (fr-h,p,arr) | Dutton,Fred (b,bassoon) | Reynolds,Tom (dr) | Holman,Bill (arr)

CCD 79032 | CD | Out Of Nowhere
Don Ellis Trio
Sweet And Lovely | My Funny Valentine | I Love You(take 2) | I'll Remember April | Just One Of Those Things(take 8) | You Stepped Out Of A Dream | All The Things You Are(take 5) | Out Of Nowhere | Just One Of Those Things(take 5) | I Love You(take 1)
NYC, rec. 21.4.1961
Ellis,Don (tp) | Bley,Paul (p) | Swallow,Steve (b)

CCD 79033 | CD | Candid Dolphy
Charles Mingus Group
Re-Incarnation Of A Love Bird | Stormy Weather(take 1)
NYC, rec. 20.10.1960
Mingus,Charles (b) | Curson,Ted (tp) | Hillyer,Lonnie (tp) | Dolphy,Eric (fl,b-cl,as) | McPherson,Charles (as) | Bunick,Floris Nico (p) | Richmond,Dannie (dr)
Abbey Lincoln And Her All Stars(Newport Rebels)
'Tain't Nobody's Bizness If I Do(take 3)
NYC, rec. 1.11.1960
Lincoln,Abbey (voc) | Bailey,Benny (tp) | Dolphy,Eric (b-cl) | Dorham,Kenny (p) | Morrison,Peck (b) | Jones,Jo (dr)
Newport Rebels
Body And Soul(take 2)
NYC, rec. 11.11.1960
Newport Rebels | Eldridge,Roy (tp) | Knepper,Jimmy (tb) | Dolphy,Eric (as) | Flanagan,Tommy (p) | Mingus,Charles (b) | Jones,Jo (dr)
Max Roach All Stars
African Lady(take 4)
NYC, rec. 2.2.1961
Roach,Max (dr) | Little,Booker (tp) | Priester,Julian (tb) | Dolphy,Eric (piccolo) | Hawkins,Coleman (ts) | Benton,Walter (ts) | Waldron,Mal (p) | Davis,Art (b) | Sanders,Roger (congas) | Whitley,Robert (congas) | Lincoln,Abbey (voc)
Booker Little Sextet
Quiet Please(take 1)
NYC, rec. 17.3.1961
Little,Booker (tp) | Priester,Julian (tb) | Dolphy,Eric (fl,as) | Friedman,Don (p) | Davis,Art (b) | Roach,Max (dr,tympani)
Moods In Free Time(take 5) | Hazy Hues(take 5)
NYC, rec. 4.4.1961
Little,Booker (tp) | Priester,Julian (tb) | Dolphy,Eric (fl,as) | Friedman,Don (p) | Carter,Ron (b) | Roach,Max (dr,tympani)

CCD 79036 | CD | Manhattan Blues
Ricky Ford Quartet
In Walked Bud | Misty | Ode To Crispus Attucks | Portrait Of Mingus | Bob Nouveau | My Little Strayhorn | Manhattan Blues | Land Preserved | Half Nelson
NYC, rec. 4.3.1989
Ford,Ricky (ts) | Byard,Jaki (p) | Hinton,Milt (b) | Riley,Ben (dr)

CCD 79040 | CD | Dreamers
Erica Lindsay Quintet
First Movement | Walking Together | Dreamer | At The Last Moment | Gratitude
NYC, rec. 3.-5.3.1989
Lindsay,Erica (ts) | Johnson,Howard (fl-h,bs,penny-whistle,tuba) | Tanksley,Francesca (p) | Cox,Anthony (b) | Baker,Newman (dr)
Erica Lindsay Sextet
Day Dream
Lindsay,Erica (ts) | Eubanks,Robin (tb) | Johnson,Howard (fl-h,bs,penny-whistle,tuba) | Tanksley,Francesca (p) | Cox,Anthony (b) | Baker,Newman (dr)

CCD 79041 | CD | Blue Head
David Fathead Newman Quintet Plus Clifford Jordan
Strike Up The Band | Blue Head | Willow Weep For Me | Blues For David | What's New? | Eye Witness Blues
Live at Riverside Park Arts Festival,NYC, rec. 3.9.1989
Newman,David Fathead (fl,as,ts) | Jordan,Clifford (ss,ts) | Dunbar,Ted (g) | Montgomery,Buddy (p) | Coolman,Todd (b) | Smith,Marvin 'Smitty' (dr)

CCD 79042 | CD | Mysterious Blues
Charles Mingus Group
Mysterious Blues | Body And Soul
NYC, rec. 11.11.1960
Mingus,Charles (b) | Eldridge,Roy (tp) | Knepper,Jimmy (tb) | Dolphy,Eric (as) | Flanagan,Tommy (p) | Jones,Jo (dr)
Wrap Your Troubles In Dreams | Me And You Blues
Mingus,Charles (b) | Eldridge,Roy (tp) | Flanagan,Tommy (p) | Jones,Jo (dr)
Vassarlean
NYC, rec. 20.10.1960
Mingus,Charles (b) | Curson,Ted (tp) | Hillyer,Lonnie (tp) | Dolphy,Eric (fl,b-cl,as) | McPherson,Charles (as) | Ervin,Booker (ts) | Bunick,Floris Nico (p) | Richmond,Dannie (dr)
Re-Incarnation Of A Love Bird
Mingus,Charles (b) | Curson,Ted (tp) | Hillyer,Lonnie (tp) | Dolphy,Eric (fl,b-cl,as) | McPherson,Charles (as) | Bunick,Floris Nico (p) | Richmond,Dannie (dr)
Danny Richmond
Melody From The Drums
Richmond,Dannie (dr-solo)

CCD 79044 | CD | Rhythm-A-Ning
Kenny Barron-John Hicks Quartet
Sunshower | Naima's Love Song | Blue Monk | After The Morning | Ghost Of Yesterday | Rhythm-A-Ning
Live at Riverside Park Arts Festival,NYC, rec. 3.9.1989
Barron,Kenny (p) | Hicks,John (p) | Booker,Walter (b) | Cobb,Jimmy (dr)

CCD 79045 | CD | The Crawl
Louis Hayes Sextet
Escape Velocity | The Crawl | Yesterdays | Run Before The Sun | Autumn In New York | Blues In Five Dimensions | Bushman Song
Live at New Birdland,NYC, rec. 14.10.1989
Hayes,Louis (dr) | Tolliver,Charles (tp) | Bartz,Gary (as) | Stubblefield,John (ss,ts) | Tucker,Mickey (p) | Houston,Clint (b)

CCD 79046 | CD | Cecil Taylor: Air
Cecil Taylor Quartet
Air(take 9) | Air(take 21) | Air(take 24) | Port Of Call(take 3)
NYC, rec. 13.10.1960
Taylor,Cecil (p) | Shepp,Archie (ts) | Neidlinger,Buell (b) | Charles,Dennis (dr)
Number One(take 1) | Number One(take 2)
NYC, rec. 12.10.1960
Taylor,Cecil (p) | Shepp,Archie (ts) | Neidlinger,Buell (b) | Murray,Sunny (dr)

CCD 79049 | CD | West 42nd Street
Gary Bartz Quintet
Introduction by Mark Morganelli | West 42nd Street | Speak Low | It's Easy To Remember | Cousins | The Night Has A Thousand Eyes
Live at New Birdland,NYC, rec. 31.3.1990
Bartz,Gary (ss,as) | Roditi,Claudio (tp,fl-h) | Hicks,John (p) | Drummond,Ray (b) | Foster,Al (dr)

CCD 79050 | CD | Swing Summit
Harry Edison Sextet
Centerpiece | 'S Wonderful | Out Of Nowhere | Bag's Groove | Just Friends | Blue Creek | Idaho
Live at New Birdland,NYC, rec. 27./28.4.1990
Edison,Harry 'Sweets' (tp) | Tate,Buddy (cl,ts) | Wess,Frank (fl,ts) | Lawson,Hugh (p) | Drummond,Ray (b) | Durham,Bobby (dr)

CCD 79053 | CD | Ebony Rhapsody
Ricky Ford Quartet
Introduction by Mark Morganelli | Ebony Rhapsody | Mon Amour | Independence Blues | Mirror Man | In A Sentimental Mood | Setting Sun Blues | Broadway | Red,Crack And Blue
Live at 'Birdland',NYC, rec. 2.6.1990
Ford,Ricky (ts) | Byard,Jaki (p) | Hinton,Milt (b) | Riley,Ben (dr)

CCD 79054 | CD | Speak Low
Mark Morganelli And The Jazz Forum All Stars
Speak Low | Dreams | Blues For Ian | When I Fall In Love | Summertime | Opus 1,5 | Lamb Kurma | A Child Is Born | The Jolly Jumper
Live at 'Birdland',NYC, rec. 13.6.1990
Morganelli,Mark (tp,fl-h) | Barron,Kenny (p) | Carter,Ron (b) | Cobb,Jimmy (dr)

CCD 79703 | CD | Brazilian Sunset
Mongo Santamaria And His Band
Bonita | Costa Del Oro | Summertime | Gumbo Man | Brazilian Sunset | When Love Begins | Being Here With You | Soca Me Nice | Dawn's Light | Breaking It In | Watermelon Man | Sofrito
Live at 'Birdland',NYC, rec. 9./10.10.1992
Santamaria,Mongo (perc) | Allen,Eddie E.J. (tp,fl-h) | Crozier,Jimmy (fl,as,bs) | Rivers,Craig (fl,ts) | Gonzalez,Ricardo (p) | Edgehill,Guillermo (b) | Almendra,John Andreu (dr,timbales) | Rodriguez,Eddie (perc)

CCD 79705 | CD | Skylark
Shirley Scott Trio
Skylark | I Still Want You- | You Are My Heart's Delight- | All The Things You Are | Alone Together | Peace | McGhee And Me | The Party's Over- | Theme-
Live at 'Birdland',NYC, rec. 22./23.11.1991
Scott,Shirley (p) | Harper,Arthur (b) | Roker,Granville 'Mickey' (dr)

CCD 79707 | CD | New Gold!
Bud Shank Sextet
Port Townsend | Alternate Root | Let Me Tell You Why | Straight No Chaser | Perkolater | Grizzly | Finger Therapy(For Sherman) | Linda | Killer Joe | Funcused Blues | Little Rootie Tootie
North Hollywood,CA, rec. 6./7.12.1993
Shank,Bud (as) | Candoli,Conte (tp) | Perkins,Bill (ss,ts) | Nimitz,Jack (bs) | Clayton,John (b) | Ferguson,Sherman (dr)

CCD 79708 | CD | Renaissance Of A Jazz Master
Gene DiNovi Trio
A Cockeyed Optimist | Springsville | Till The Clouds Roll By | Right As The Rain | Bill | It Never Entered My Mind | Budding Memories | Elegy | My Old Flame | Have A Heart | Speak Low
Toronto,Canada, rec. 31.3.1993
DiNovi,Gene (p) | Young,Dave (b) | Clarke,Terry (dr)

CCD 79709 | CD | Lullaby Of Birdland
Lee Konitz Quartet
Lullaby Of Birdland | This Is Always | Anthropology | Ask Me Now | East Of The Sun West Of The Moon | Cherokee | Round About Midnight | The Song Is You
Live at 'Birdland',NYC, rec. 6./7.9.1991
Konitz,Lee (ss,as) | Harris,Barry (p) | Hill,Calvin (b) | Williams,Leroy (dr)

CCD 79710 | CD | The Candid Jazz Masters:For Miles
Candid Jazz Masters
Milestones | All Blues | Nardis | My Funny Valentine | Walkin' | So What | If I Where A Bell | Milestrane
Live at 'Birdland',NYC, rec. 29./30.11.1991
Candid Jazz Masters,The | Roditi,Claudio (tp,fl-h) | Harrison,Donald (as) | Ford,Ricky (ts) | Barron,Kenny (p) | Gales,Larry (b) | Chambers,Joe (dr)

CCD 79711/12 | 2 CD | Vic Lewis Presenting A Celebration Of Contemporary West Coast Jazz
Vic Lewis West Coast All Stars
On The Bayou | Enigma | A Backward Glance | Blue Daniel | No More | U.M.M.G.(Upper Manhattan Medical Group)
Woodland Hills,CA, rec. 9.4.1993
Lewis,Vic (ld) | Martin,Andy (tb) | Shelton,Don (fl,cl,as,piccolo) | Perkins,Bill (fl,cl,as) | Cooper,Bob (fl,cl,ts) | Efford,Bob (cl,ts,bs,oboe) | Nimitz,Jack (b-cl,bs) | Strazzeri,Frank (p) | Worthington,Tom (b) | Leatherbarrow,Bob (dr)
Summer Wishes,Winter Dreams
Lewis,Vic (ld) | Martin,Andy (tb) | Shelton,Don (fl,cl,as,piccolo) | Perkins,Bill (fl,cl,as) | Cooper,Bob (fl,cl,ts) | Efford,Bob (cl,ts,bs,oboe) | Nimitz,Jack (b-cl,bs) | Strazzeri,Frank (p) | Worthington,Tom (b) | Leatherbarrow,Bob (dr) | Raney,Sue (voc)
It's Not Going That Way | Look A-Here Andy
Lewis,Vic (ld) | Martin,Andy (tb) | Shelton,Don (fl,cl,as,piccolo) | Perkins,Bill (fl,cl,as) | Cooper,Bob (fl,cl,ts) | Efford,Bob (cl,ts,bs,oboe) | Nimitz,Jack (b-cl,bs) | Strazzeri,Frank (p) | Leitham,John (b) | Leatherbarrow,Bob (dr)
Lydia's Crush
Lewis,Vic (ld) | Martin,Andy (tb) | Shelton,Don (fl,cl,as,piccolo) | Perkins,Bill (fl,cl,as) | Cooper,Bob (fl,cl,ts) | Efford,Bob (cl,ts,bs,oboe) | Nimitz,Jack (b-cl,bs) | Jacob,Christian (p) | Worthington,Tom (b) | Leatherbarrow,Bob (dr)
Funqui's Blues
Lewis,Vic (ld) | Martin,Andy (tb) | Shelton,Don (fl,cl,as,piccolo) | Perkins,Bill (fl,cl,as) | Cooper,Bob (fl,cl,ts) | Efford,Bob (cl,ts,bs,oboe) | Nimitz,Jack (b-cl,bs) | Fischer,Clare (p) | Worthington,Tom (b) | Leatherbarrow,Bob (dr)
Silky
Lewis,Vic (ld) | Martin,Andy (tb) | Shelton,Don (fl,cl,as,piccolo) | Perkins,Bill (fl,cl,as) | Cooper,Bob (fl,cl,ts) | Efford,Bob (cl,ts,bs,oboe) | Nimitz,Jack (b-cl,bs) | Florence,Bob (p) | Worthington,Tom (b) | Leatherbarrow,Bob (dr)
Bear Bones | Sure Thing | Stock And After Shock | Summer Serenade | Kelo | Shiny Stockings
North Hollywood,CA, rec. 25.2.1994
Lewis,Vic (ld) | Huffstetter,Steven (tp,fl-h) | Martin,Andy (tb) | Lopez,Charlie (tb) | Eyles,Alex (tb) | McCheskie,Bob (tb) | Perkins,Bill (fl,ss,as,ts,bs) | Strazzeri,Frank (p) | Leitham,John (b) | Kreibich,Paul (dr)
Bebop Love Song | Waltz For Coop | Lavender Dreams | We'll Be Together Again
Lewis,Vic (ld) | Huffstetter,Steven (tp,fl-h) | Martin,Andy (tb) | Lopez,Charlie (tb) | Eyles,Alex (tb) | McCheskie,Bob (tb) | Perkins,Bill (fl,ss,as,ts,bs) | Strazzeri,Frank (p) | Worthington,Tom (b) | Kreibich,Paul (dr)

CCD 79715 | CD | Dr. Jeckyll & Mr. Hyde
Greg Abate Quintet
Fast Lane Rhythm | From The Heart | C.C.A. | Dr.Jeckyll & Mr.Hyde | Chan's House Of Jazz | My Friend From Rio | I'll Remember Murph | Tommy Hawk | Parallel | For Tony | Vera's Song | Bebop Baby
Live at Chan's,Providence,R.I., rec. 18./19.11.1994
Abate,Greg (fl,ss,as,ts,bs) | Cole,Richie (as) | Neville,Chris (p) | Delnero,Paul (b) | Cabral,Artie (dr)

CCD 79717 | CD | Keepin' Out Of Mischief Now
Art Hodes
Tennessee Waltz | When You Lover Has Gone | I'm Gonna Sit Right Down And Write Myself A Letter | Saturday Night Function | I'm A Salty Dog - (I'm A) Salty Dog | Makin' Whoopee | Four Or Five Times | Love For Sale | See See Rider | You Don't Know What It Means To Miss New Orleans- | Dear Old Southland- | Struttin' With Some Barbecue | Basin Street Blues | Keepin' Out Of Mischief Now | Just A Closer Walk With Thee | The Preacher
London,GB, rec. 3./4.11.1988
Hodes,Art (p-solo)

CCD 79719 | CD | A Wakin' Thing
Shirley Scott Quintet
Carnival | D.T.Blues | A Walkin' Thing | When A Man Loves A Woman | What Makes Harold Sing? | Shades Of Bu | How Am I To Know? | Remember
Englewood Cliffs,NJ, rec. 17.11.1992
Scott,Shirley (org) | Stafford,Terell (tp) | Warfield Jr.,Tim (ts) | Harper,Arthur (b) | Walker,Aaron (dr)

CCD 79720 | CD | The Great British Jazz Band:Jubilee
Great British Jazz Band
Jubilee | Jazz Me Blues | Original Dixieland One Step | Washboard Blues | Prelude To A Kiss | Idaho | Imagination | This Is The End Of... A Beautiful Friendship - (This Is The End Of...) A Beautiful Friendship | Petite Fleur | Someday Sweetheart | Apex Blues | All I Do Is Dream Of You | Chelsea Bridge | Tiger Rag
Mottingham,GB, rec. 6./7.4.1994
Great British Jazz Band,The | Fairweather,Didby (tp) | Cotton,Mike (tp) | Williams,Roy (tb) | Strange,Pete (tb) | Shepherd,Dave (cl) | Barnes,John (cl,ts,bs) | Lemon,Brian (p) | Douglas,Jim (g) | Skeat,Len (b) | Ganley,Allan (dr)

CCD 79721 | CD | Gratitude
Jessica Williams
The Sheikh | I Cover The Waterfront | Mr.Syms | Justice | Serenata | Round About Midnight | Like Sonny | Nice Work If You Can Get It | Last Trane
Portland,Oregon, rec. 10./21.6.1995
Williams,Jessica (p-solo)

CCD 79724 | CD | Swinging For The Count
The Basie Alumni
Red Bank Shuffle | The Snapper | Jive At Five | Swinging For The Count | Blue And Sentimental | Kansas City Kitty | Slow Boat | Jumpin' At The Woodside
NYC, rec. 12.6.1992
Basie Alumni,The | Edison,Harry 'Sweets' (tp) | Terry,Clark (tp,fl-h) | Powell,Seldon (ts) | Pizzarelli,Bucky (g) | Hanna,Sir Roland (p) | Hinton,Milt (b) | Durham,Bobby (dr)
Basie Like
Basie Alumni,The | Edison,Harry 'Sweets' (tp) | Terry,Clark (tp,fl-h) | Morganelli,Mark (tp) | Powell,Seldon (ts) | Pizzarelli,Bucky (g) | Hanna,Sir Roland (p) | Hinton,Milt (b) | Durham,Bobby (dr)

CCD 79725 | CD | A New Journey
Craig Bailey Band
C.B. No.1 | No Hip Hop
NYC, rec. 7./8.3.1995
Bailey,Craig (fl,as) | Gardner,Derrick (tp,fl-h) | Georges,Dupor (tb) | Lewis,Eric (p) | Lemon,Eric (b) | Washington,Kenny (dr)
What Would I Do Without You
Bailey,Craig (fl,as) | Gardner,Derrick (tp,fl-h) | Georges,Dupor (tb) | Hartog,Jim (bs) | Payne,Enos (p) | Lemon,Eric (b) | Washington,Kenny (dr)
Laura
Bailey,Craig (fl,as) | Stafford,Terell (tp) | Feldman,Mark (v) | Childs,Billy (p) | Lemon,Eric (b) | Washington,Kenny (dr) | Haynes,Jeff (perc)
Bells
Bailey,Craig (fl,as) | Stafford,Terell (tp) | Childs,Billy (p) | Lemon,Eric (b) | Washington,Kenny (dr)
Soul Flower
Bailey,Craig (fl,as) | Stafford,Terell (tp,fl-h) | Gardner,Derrick (tp,fl-h) | Childs,Billy (p) | Lemon,Eric (b) | Washington,Kenny (dr)
Cherokee
Bailey,Craig (fl,as) | Rickman,Patrick (tp) | Lemon,Eric (b) | Cox,Bruce (dr)
Clasanova
Bailey,Craig (fl,as) | Lewis,Eric (p) | Lemon,Eric (b) | Washington,Kenny (dr)
Lil' Darlin'
Bailey,Craig (fl,as) | Caldwell,George (p) | Lemon,Eric (b) | Washington,Kenny (dr)
Love Dreams
Bailey,Craig (fl,as) | Feldman,Mark (v) | Childs,Billy (p) | Lemon,Eric (b) | Washington,Kenny (dr)
A New Journey
Bailey,Craig (fl,as) | Payne,Enos (p) | Lemon,Eric (b) | Washington,Kenny (dr)

CCD 79726 | CD | Live At The Montreal Bistro
Gene DiNovi Trio
Introduction by Ted O'Reilly | T.N.T. | Happy Harvest | The Things We Did Last Summer- | Indian Summer- | Terry's Little Tune | Nieves | A Tune For Mac | A.B.'s Blues | It Happened In Monterey | You Better Go Now | Coffee Time | Tiny's Blues
Live at The Montreal Bistro,Toronto,Canada, rec. 20.-22.10.1993
DiNovi,Gene (p) | Young,Dave (b) | Clarke,Terry (dr)

CCD 79728 | CD | A Jazz Portrait Of Frank Sinatra
David Newton
My Kind Of Town(Chicago Is) | I've Got The World On A String | I Fall In Love Too Easily | Witchcraft | The Lady Is A Tramp | This Is All I Ask | It's Nice To Go Trav'ling | Violets For Your Furs | All Or Nothing At All | You Make Me Feel So Young | All The Way | Twelfth Of The Twelfth | Only The Lonely | Saturday Night Is The Loneliest Night Of The Week | In The Wee Small Hours Of The Morning
London,GB, rec. 3./4.8.1995
Newton,David (p-solo)

CCD 79734 | CD | Wild As Springtime
Lee Konitz-Harold Danko Duo
Ezz-thetic | Hairy Canary | She's As Wild As Springtime | It's You | Prelude No.20 | Spinning Waltz | Silly Samba | Hi-Beck | Ko | Hairy Canary(alt.take) | Ezz-thetic(alt.take)
Glasgow,Scotland, rec. 29./30.3.1984
Konitz,Lee (as) | Danko,Harold (p)

CCD 79735 | CD | Artistry In Jazz
Buddy Childers With The Russ Garcia Strings
Come Home Again | The Shadow Of Your Smile | Stardust | You Are Too Beautiful | Body And Soul | Round About Midnight | My Diane | Lush Life | Stars Fell On Alabama | Sophisticated Lady | Angel Eyes | Din Di(Jin Je)
Hollywood,CA, rec. 31.8.1993
Childers,Buddy (fl-h) | Russ Garcia Strings | Graham,Marilyn (concertmaster) | Garcia,Russell (vib,cond,arr) | O'Bourke,Brian (p) | Leitham,John (b) | Field,Gregg (dr) | Yungo,Cun (perc)

CCD 79736 | CD | Higher Standards
Jessica Williams Trio
Get Out Of Town | When You Lover Has Gone | Mack The Knife(Moritat) | A Night In Tunisia | Don't Take Your Love From Me | East Of The Sun West Of The Moon | Solitude | Midnight Sun | My Heart Belongs To Daddy
Portland,Oregon, rec. 19./20.11.1996
Williams,Jessica (p) | Captein,Dave (b) | Brown,Mel (dr)

CCD 79737 | CD | Close Your Eyes
Stacey Kent And Her Quintet
More Than You Know | Dream Dancing | Close Your Eyes | There's A Lull In My Life | It's De-Lovely | There's No You | I'm Old Fashioned | You Go To My Head | Little White Lies | Sleep Warm | Day In Day Out
Curtis Schwartz Studios,Sussex,GB, rec. 18./19.11.1996
Kent,Stacey (voc) | Tomlinson,Jim (ts) | Oxley,Colin (g) | Newton,David (p) | De Jong Cleyndert,Andrew (b) | Brown,Steve (dr)

CCD 79739 | CD | Me And You!
Vic Lewis West Coast All Stars
Bl-You-Uuz | You And The Night And The Music | Me And You | You're My Thrill | You And Me | My Ideal | Between You And Me And The Gatepost | Somebody Loves Me
Burbank,Los Angeles,CA, rec. 26.3.1997
Lewis,Vic (ld) | Saunders,Carl (tp) | Stout,Ron (tp) | Martin,Andy (tb) | Perkins,Bill (ss,ts,bs) | Herman,Ray (ts) | Jacob,Christian (p) | Clayton,John (b) | Hamilton,Jeff (dr)

CCD 79740 | CD | A British Jazz Odyssey
The Great British Jazz Band
Riff Up Them Stairs | K.C.Blues | The Very Thought Of You | Sizzle | The Badger | Duke's Joke | A Nightingale Sang In Berkeley Square | Jump | Serenade For A Whealty Widow | Blues For Welshie | We Fell Out Of Love | Go Ghana | The Gypsy | Limehouse Blues
Greenford,Middlesex,GB, rec. 13./14.3.1996
Great British Jazz Band,The | Fairweather,Didby (tp) | Cotton,Mike (tp) | Williams,Roy (tb) | Strange,Pete (tb) | Barnes,John (cl,ts,bs,voc) | Shepherd,Dave (cl) | Douglas,Jim (g) | Litton,Martin (p) | Skeat,Len (b) | Ganley,Allan (dr)

CCD 79741 | CD | As Time Goes By...
Ruby Braff Trio
Shoe Shine Boy | Lonely Moments | This Is All I Ask | Love Me Or Leave Me | Liza | As Long As I Live | Jeepers Creepers | My Shining Hour | Sugar | As Time Goes By | You're Sensational- | I Love You Samantha- | True Love- | Basin Street Blues | Linger Awhile
Live at University College School,Hampstead,London,GB, rec. 16.5.1991
Braff,Ruby (co) | Alden,Howard (g) | Tate,Frank (b)

CCD 79742 | CD | DNA
David Newton Quartet
DNA | Julia | High Wire | Where Is The One | Feet On The Ground | Gardens Of Dreams | Ablution | The Scribe | We'll Be Together Again
Curtis Schwartz Studios,Sussex,GB, rec. 20./21.11.1996
Newton,David (p) | Dixon,Iain (ss,ts) | Miles,Matt (b) | Brown,Steve (dr)

CCD 79749 | CD | It's What Happening Now!
Buddy Childers Big Band
Killer Joe | Polka Dots And Moonbeams | Time On My Hands | Someone To Watch Over Me | Dearly Beloved | Come Home Again | The Boy From Ipanema | Star Eyes | Out Of Nowhere | Bernie's Tune | Goodbye Old Friend | The 'Bone' Zone
Los Angeles,CA, rec. ca.1996
prob.personal: | Childers,Buddy (tp,fl-h) | King,Ron (tp,fl-h) | Stout,Ron (tp,fl-h) | Wendt,Tim (tp,fl-h) | Halopoff,Gary (tp,fl-h) | Kaye,Jeff (tp,fl-h) | Schwartz,Brian (tp,fl-h) | Trigg,Dave (tp,fl-h) | Bergeron,Deborah (tp,fl-h) | Martin,Andy (tb) | Hamilton,Dick (tb) | Greene,Thurman (tb) | Morillas,Charlie (tb) | Alcroft,Randy (tb) | Redmond,Jack (tb) | Shroyer,Kenny (b-tb) | Byers,Bryant (b-tb) | Reed,Ray (sax) | Patterson,Ann (sax) | Garrett,Glenn (sax) | Harper,George (sax) | Orena,Charles (sax) | Stevens,John (sax) | Owens,Charles (sax) | Murphy,Paul (g) | MacDonald,Doug (g) | O,Rourke,Brian (p) | Henry,Trey (b) | Newmark,Harvey (b) | Razze,Ralph (dr) | White,Jerry (dr) | Sutton,Tierney (voc)

CCD 79750 | CD | Jazz In The Afternoon
Jessica Williams Trio
Green Chimneys | I Remember Dexter | Light Blue | Straight No Chaser | Swanee | I'm Confessin'(That I Love You) | Basic Blue | Evidence | Dirty Dog Blues
Live at Chemekata College,Oregon, rec. 8.2.1998
Williams,Jessica (p) | Captein,Dave (b) | Brown,Mel (dr)

CCD 79751 | CD | The Tender Trap
Stacey Kent And Her Quintet
The Tender Trap | I Didn't Know About You | Comes Love | In The Still Of The Night | Fools Rush In | East Of The Sun West Of The Moon | Zing! Went The Strings Of My Heart | They Say It's Wonderful | Don't Be That Way | They All Laughed | In The Wee Small Hours Of The Morning | It's A Wonderful World
Ardingly,West Sussex,GB, rec. 1./2.2.1998
Kent,Stacey (voc) | Tomlinson,Jim (ts) | Oxley,Colin (g) | Newton,David (p) | Green,Dave (b) | Hamilton,Jeff (dr)

CCD 79752 | CD | Swing Spring
Bill Perkins Quintet
I Hear Ya Talkin' | Sea Swirls | For Jo Ann | Swing Spr | Procession Of The Bulls | Love Walked In | Fer Now | Barbados | Summer Night | Lotus Blossom | Nica's Tempo
Van Nuys,CA, rec. 28./29.5.1996
Perkins,Bill (alto-fl,ss,ts) | Jenkins,Clay (tp) | Strazzeri,Frank (p) | Warrington,Tom (b) | Berg,Bill (dr)
Bill Perkins Quartet
Bebop Love Song
Kihei Maui,Hawaii, rec. 8.6.1996
Perkins,Bill (ts) | Cuomo,Brian (p) | Johnson,Marc (b) | Wright,Roscoe (dr)

CCD 79754 | CD | Vic Lewis:The Golden Years
Vic Lewis Jam Session
I Found A New Baby | I Never Knew | It's The Talk Of The Town | Tri-Colour Blues
London,GB, rec. 12.3.1945
Lewis,Vic (g) | Best,John (tp) | Hawkins,Derek (cl,as) | Chamberlain,Ronnie (ss,as) | Grappelli,Stephane (p,v) | Bromley,Tom (b) | Krahmer,Carlo (dr)
Yellow Dog Blues
AEF Broadcast,London,GB, rec. 12.3.1945
Lewis,Vic (g) | Baker,Kenny (tp) | Best,John (tp) | Mouncey,Arthur (tp) | Busby,Laddie (tb) | Phillips,Woolf (tb) | Takvorian,Tak (tb) | LaPolla,Ralph (cl) | Hawkins,Derek (cl,as) | Chamberlain,Ronnie (ss,as) | Franks,Aubrey (ts) | Donahue,Sam (ts) | Colucci,Michael 'Rocky' (p) | Caton,Lauderic (g) | Nussbaumn,Joe (b) | Krahmer,Carlo (dr)
Rosetta | Down The Old Mill Stream | Johnny's Blues | Mean To Me
London,GB, rec. 15.3.1945
Lewis,Vic (g) | Best,John (tp) | Busby,Laddie (tb) | Chamberlain,Ronnie (ss,as) | Franks,Aubrey (ts) | Moore,Gerry (p) | Howard,Bert (b) | Krahmer,Carlo (dr)
The Jimmy And Marion McPartland Sessions
The World Is Waiting For The Sunrise | Max Blues | I've Found A New Baby | Rose Room | Sweet Lorraine
London,GB, rec. 6.1.1946
McPartland,Jimmy (co) | Magnusson,Clarence (cl) | Chamberlain,Ronnie (ss,as) | Skidmore,Jimmy (ts) | Lewis,Vic (g) | McPartland,Marian (p) | Bachelder,Ken (b) | Nardy,Joe (dr) | Scott,Gracie (voc)
Jazz Me Blues
London,GB, rec. 6.1.1945
McPartland,Jimmy (co) | Magnusson,Clarence (cl) | Chamberlain,Ronnie (ss,as) | Skidmore,Jimmy (ts) | Lewis,Vic (g) | Schwartz,Jerry (p) | Quest,John (b) | Vitale,Tony (dr)
I Got Rhythm
London,GB, rec. 6.1.1946
McPartland,Marian (p) | Schwartz,Jerry (p) | Quest,John (b) | Vitale,Tony (dr)
Vic Lewis And His Band
I Ain't Got Nobody | Stooge Blues | Shine On Harvest Moon | Angry
London,GB, rec. 30.6.1938
Lewis,Vic (g) | Hutchinson,Leslie (tp) | Chisholm,George (tb) | King,Bertie (cl,ts) | Shearing,George (p) | Muslin,Joe (b) | Krahmer,Carlo (dr,vib)

CCD 79757 | CD | Her Point Of View
Olga Konkova Trio
Adam's Checking In | Her Point Of View | Egberto | Sophisticated Lady | Blackbird | The Little Prince
Oslo,N, rec. 7./8.8.1998
Konkova,Olga (p) | Mathisen,Per (b) | Nussbaum,Adam (dr)
Olga Konkova
Limited | Round About Midnight | Summertime | On Green Dolphin Street | Someday My Prince Will Come
Al Kulturhus,Oslo,N, rec. 12./13.5.1997
Konkova,Olga (p-solo)

CCD 79758 | CD | Only Trust Your Heart
Jim Tomlinson Quintet
Makin' Brownies | Only The Lonely | Only Trust Your Heart | Vienne Blues | El Cajon | Blue Comers
Ardingly,West Sussex,GB, rec. 28./29.10.1998
Tomlinson,Jim (ts) | Oxley,Colin (g) | Pearce,John (p) | Thorpe,Simon (b) | Brown,Steve (dr)
Glad To Be Unhappy | If You Ever Come To Me
Ardingly,West Sussex,GB, rec. 28./29.8.1998
Tomlinson,Jim (ts) | Oxley,Colin (g) | Pearce,John (p) | Thorpe,Simon (b) | Brown,Steve (dr) | Kent,Stacey (voc)
Jim Tomlinson Sextet
Just A Child | What Will I Tell My Heart
Ardingly,West Sussex,GB, rec. 28./29.10.1998
Tomlinson,Jim (ts) | Barker,Guy (tp) | Oxley,Colin (g) | Pearce,John (p) | Thorpe,Simon (b) | Brown,Steve (dr)
I'm Just A Lucky So-And-So
Tomlinson,Jim (ts) | Barker,Guy (tp) | Oxley,Colin (g) | Pearce,John (p) | Thorpe,Simon (b) | Brown,Steve (dr) | Kent,Stacey (voc)

CCD 79761 | CD | Just Buddy's | EAN 708857976126
Buddy Childers Big Band
Nica's Dream | Looking Up Old Friends | What The Hell | Crimp Cut
Chicago,Ill, rec. 12.& 19.11.1983/31.1.& 7.2.1984
Childers,Buddy (tp,fl-h) | Barber,Danny (tp) | Thompson,Mark (tp) | Murphy,Nipper (tp) | Davis,Art (tp) | Bleige,Scott (tb) | Kordus,Tom (tb) | Lustrea,Bob (tb) | Blane,John (tb) | Samborski,Bob (tb) | Smith,Mike (as) | Ballin,Peter (sax) | Brandom,Dave (sax) | Kolber,Ron (bs) | Dimusio,Jerry (sax) | Schiff,Bobby (p) | Roberts,Steve (g) | Gray,Larry (b) | Spencer,Joel (dr)
Off Broadway | Arriving Soon
Childers,Buddy (tp,fl-h) | Barber,Danny (tp) | Thompson,Mark (tp) | Davis,Art (tp) | Fleming,Peter (tp) | Kime,Warren (tp) | Bleige,Scott (tb) | Kordus,Tom (tb) | Lustrea,Bob (tb) | Blane,John (tb) | Samborski,Bob (tb) | Smith,Mike (as) | Ballin,Peter (sax) | Brandom,Dave (sax) | Kolber,Ron (bs) | Dimusio,Jerry (sax) | Schiff,Bobby (p) | Roberts,Steve (g) | Gray,Larry (b) | Spencer,Joel (dr)
The Underdog Has Arisen
Childers,Buddy (tp,fl-h) | Barber,Danny (tp) | Murphy,Nipper (tp) | Davis,Art (tp) | Fleming,Peter (tp) | Kime,Warren (tp) | Bleige,Scott (tb) | Kordus,Tom (tb) | Lustrea,Bob (tb) | Blane,John (tb) | Bentall,Dave (tb) | Samborski,Bob (tb) | Smith,Mike (as) | Negus,John (sax) | Brandom,Dave (sax) | Kolber,Ron (bs) | Dimusio,Jerry (sax) | Ripp,Brian (sax) | Schiff,Bobby (p) | Roberts,Steve (g) | Lanphier,Bill (b) | Spencer,Joel (dr)
Just Buddy's
Childers,Buddy (tp,fl-h) | Barber,Danny (tp) | Murphy,Nipper (tp) | Davis,Art (tp) | Kime,Warren (tp) | Bleige,Scott (tb) | Lustrea,Bob (tb) | Blane,John (tb) | Bentall,Dave (tb) | Samborski,Bob (tb) | Smith,Mike (as) | Negus,John (sax) | Brandom,Dave (sax) | Kolber,Ron (bs) | Dimusio,Jerry (sax) | Schiff,Bobby (p) | Roberts,Steve (g) | Lanphier,Bill (b) | Spencer,Joel (dr)
Pretty
Childers,Buddy (tp,fl-h) | Barber,Danny (tp) | Murphy,Nipper (tp) | Davis,Art (tp) | Bleige,Scott (tb) | Lustrea,Bob (tb) | Blane,John (tb) | Bentall,Dave (tb) | Samborski,Bob (tb) | Smith,Mike (as) | Negus,John (sax) | Ballin,Peter (sax) | Brandom,Dave (sax) | Dimusio,Jerry (sax) | Ripp,Brian (sax) | Schiff,Bobby (p) | Roberts,Steve (g) | Lanphier,Bill (b) | Spencer,Joel (dr)
Try A Little Tenderness
Childers,Buddy (tp,fl-h) | Barber,Danny (tp) | Thompson,Mark (tp) | Davis,Art (tp) | Fleming,Peter (tp) | Bleige,Scott (tb) | Kordus,Tom (tb) | Lustrea,Bob (tb) | Blane,John (tb) | Samborski,Bob (tb) | Smith,Mike (as) | Ballin,Peter (sax) | Brandom,Dave (sax) | Kolber,Ron (bs) | Dimusio,Jerry (sax) | Schiff,Bobby (p) | Roberts,Steve (g) | Gray,Larry (b) | Spencer,Joel (dr)

CCD 79762 | CD | California Cooking No.2 | EAN 708857976225
Rickey Woodard Quartet
Blue Top | Flamingo | Lover Man(Oh,Where Can You Be?) | Speak Low | But Not For Me | You Go To My Head | Water Jug | Mambo Inn | Bloomdido
North Hollywood,CA, rec. 7./8.2.2001
Woodard,Rickey (as,ts) | Grissett,Danny (p) | Littleton,Jeff (b) | King,Gerryck (dr)

CCD 79763 | CD | Ain't Misbehavin' | EAN 708857976324
Jessica Williams
El Salvador | Alone Together | The Eulipians | Paul's Pal | Too Young To Go Steady | Black Diamond | Don't Blame Me | Joyful Sorrow | Ain't Misbehavin' | After The Rain
Live at The Holywell Music Room,Oxford,GB, rec. 10.3.1996
Williams,James (p-solo)

CCD 79764 | CD | Let Yourself Go-Celebrating Fred Astaire
Stacey Kent And Her Quintet
Let Yourself Go | They Can't Take That Away From Me | I Won't Dance | Isn't This A Lovely Day | They All Laughed | He Loves And She Loves | Shall We Dance? | One For My Baby(And One More For The Road) | 'S Wonderful | A Fine Romance | I Guess I'll Have To Change My Plans | I'm Putting All My Eggs In One Basket | By Myself
Ardingly,West Sussex,GB, rec. 26./27.7.1999
Kent,Stacey (voc) | Tomlinson,Jim (cl,as,ts) | Oxley,Colin (g) | Newton,David (p) | Thorpe,Simon (b) | Brown,Steve (dr)

CCD 79766 | CD | Northern Crossing | EAN 708857976621
Olga Konkova-Per Mathisen Quartet
Fifth Corner | Encounter | Independent Blues | East By Northwest | On The Move | Olga's Dream | Watch Out | Homage | Northern Crossing
River Edge,NJ, rec. 11.-13.9.1997
Konkova,Olga (p) | Mathisen,Ole (ss,ts) | Mathisen.Per (b) | Mayer,JoJo (dr)

CCD 79768 | CD | Kind Of New | EAN 708857976829
Donald Harrison Sextet
So What | All Blues
NYC, rec. 21./22.11.2001
Harrison,Donald (as) | Scott,Christian (tp,fl-h) | Jackson,Javon (ts) | Barron,Kenny (p) | Archer,Vincente (b) | Allen,Carl (dr)
Kind Of New | Blue In Green | Freddie Freeloader | It Is | Flamenco Sketches | What's Next?
Harrison,Donald (as) | Scott,Christian (tp,fl-h) | Jackson,Javon (ts) | Reed,Eric (p) | Archer,Vincente (b) | Allen,Carl (dr)

CCD 79769 | CD | Brazilian Sketches | EAN 708857976928
Jim Tomlinson Quintet
Dreamer | So Nice
Ardingly,West Sussex,GB, rec. 13./14.4.2001
Tomlinson,Jim (ts) | Oxley,Colin (g) | Pearce,John (p) | Thorpe,Simon (b) | Wells,Chris (dr,perc) | Kent,Stacey (voc)
So Danco Samba(I Only Dance The Samba) | Once I Loved | No More Blues
Tomlinson,Jim (ts) | Oxley,Colin (g) | Pearce,John (p) | Thorpe,Simon (b) | Wells,Chris (dr,perc)
Caminhos Cruzados
Tomlinson,Jim (ts) | Oxley,Colin (g) | Newton,David (p) | Thorpe,Simon (b) | Wells,Chris (dr,perc)
I Concentrate On You | The Gentle Rain (Chuva Delicada)
Tomlinson,Jim (ts) | Oxley,Colin (g) | Newton,David (p) | Thorpe,Simon (b) | Wells,Chris (dr,perc) | Kent,Stacey (voc)
Jim Tomlinson Quartet
Ligia | Portrait In Black And White | She's A Carioca
Tomlinson,Jim (ts) | Oxley,Colin (g) | Thorpe,Simon (b) | Wells,Chris (dr,perc)

CCD 79770 | CD | The Hymn | EAN 708857977024
Clark Terry Quintet
The Hymn | My Romance | Ow! | On The Sunny Side Of The Street | Is It True What They Say About Dixie | Mood Indigo | On The Trail(From The Grand Canyon Suite) | Blues For Rebecca | Rhythm Ride
Live at 'Birdland',NYC, rec. 25./26.6.1993
Terry,Clark (tp,fl-h,voc) | Davis,Jesse (as) | Friedman,Don (p) | McLaurine,Marcus (b) | Cuenca,Sylvia (dr)

CCD 79775 | CD | Dreamsville | EAN 708857977529
Stacey Kent With The Jim Tomlison Quintet
I've Got A Crush On You | When Your Lover Has Gone | Isn't It A Pity | You Are There | Under A Blanket Of Blue | Dreamsville | Polka Dots And Moonbeams | Hushabye Mountain | Little Girl Blue | You're Looking | Violets For Your Furs | Thanks For The Memory
Ardingly,West Sussex,GB, rec. 19.-21.6.2000
Kent,Stacey (voc) | Tomlinson,Jim (fl,cl,ts) | Oxley,Colin (g) | Newton,David (p) | Thorpe,Simon (b) | Kviberg,Jasper (dr)

CCD 79776 | CD | Labyrinth | EAN 708857977628
Dimitrios Vassilakis Daedalus Project
Daedalus | Epitaph | Ariadne's Thread | Pasiphae's Dance | Oracle Of The Wise One | Icarus In Flight | Labyrinth | Theseus And Minotauros | Blue In Green
NYC, rec. 25.9.2000
Vassilakis,Dimitrios (ss,ts) | Peterson,Ralph (tp,dr) | Liebman,Dave (ss,ts) | Sheppard,Andy (ss,ts) | Saridakis,Emmanuel (p.org) | Contrafouris,George (p) | Johnson,Marc (b) | Haddad,Jamey (dr,perc) | Spassov,Theodossij (kaval)

CCD 79778 | CD | Forbidden Games | EAN 708857977826
Nicki Leighton-Thomas Group
Forbidden Games
Snake Ranch Studios,?, rec. details unknown
Leighton-Thomas,Nicki (voc) | O'Higgins,Dave (ts) | Bell,Clive (shakuhachi) | Wallace,Simon (p) | Hutton,Mick (b) | Dodds,Roy (dr) | Hammond,Gary (perc)

Scars
Leighton-Thomas,Nicki (voc) | Wallace,Simon (p) | Schaefer,Frank (cello) | Hutton,Mick (b) | Dodds,Roy (dr) | Hammond,Gary (perc)
Living In Overdrive
Leighton-Thomas,Nicki (voc) | Palmer,Dave (tb) | Stacey,Paul (g) | Wallace,Simon (p) | Hutton,Mick (b) | Dodds,Roy (dr) | Hammond,Gary (perc) | Shaw,Ian (voc)
Music Reaches Places
Leighton-Thomas,Nicki (voc) | Wallace,Simon (p)
Waiter The Check
Leighton-Thomas,Nicki (voc) | Ramsden,Mark (as) | Fox,Max (dulcimer) | Wallace,Simon (p) | Hutton,Mick (b) | Dodds,Roy (dr) | Hammond,Gary (perc)
Only Why No More
Leighton-Thomas,Nicki (voc) | O'Higgins,Dave (ts) | Bell,Clive (shakuhachi) | Wallace,Simon (p) | Hutton,Mick (b) | Dodds,Roy (dr)
Every Now And Then
Leighton-Thomas,Nicki (voc) | Hutton,Mick (b)
I'm Not Taking Any Chances
Leighton-Thomas,Nicki (voc) | Foley,Ken (g) | Levy,Rob (b)
Tomorrow Never Came
Leighton-Thomas,Nicki (voc) | Wallace,Simon (p) | Levy,Rob (b) | Dodds,Roy (dr)
In A New York Minute | Nick's Dilemma
Leighton-Thomas,Nicki (voc) | Waterman,Steve (tp) | O'Higgins,Dave (ts) | Wallace,Simon (p) | Hutton,Mick (b) | Dodds,Roy (dr) | Hammond,Gary (perc)
Love's Eyes
Leighton-Thomas,Nicki (voc) | Stacey,Paul (g) | Schaefer,Frank (cello)
Down
Leighton-Thomas,Nicki (voc) | Waterman,Steve (tp) | Wallace,Simon (p) | Hutton,Mick (b) | Dodds,Roy (dr) | Hammond,Gary (perc)

CCD 79782 | CD | Pointless Nostalgic | EAN 708857978229
Jamie Cullum Group
You And The Night And The Music
London,GB, rec. 2002
Cullum,Jamie (p,voc) | Shaw,Martin (tp) | Gascoyne,Geoff (b) | De Krom,Sebastiaan (dr)
I Can't Get Started
Cullum,Jamie (p,voc) | Wates,Matt (as) | Gascoyne,Geoff (b) | De Krom,Sebastiaan (dr)
Devil May Care
Cullum,Jamie (p,voc) | Shaw,Martin (tp) | Gladdish,Martin (tb) | Wates,Matt (as) | Castle,Ben (ts) | O'Higgins,Dave (ts) | Gascoyne,Geoff (b) | De Krom,Sebastiaan (dr)
Too Close For Comfort | Lookin' Good | In The Wee Small Hours Of The Morning
Cullum,Jamie (p,voc) | Shaw,Martin (tp) | Gladdish,Martin (tb) | Wates,Matt (as) | Castle,Ben (ts) | Gascoyne,Geoff (b) | De Krom,Sebastiaan (dr)
You're Nobody 'Til Somebody Loves You | Pointless Nostalgic | It Ain't Necessarily So | High And Dry | I Want To Be A Popstar
Cullum,Jamie (p,voc) | Gascoyne,Geoff (b) | De Krom,Sebastiaan (dr)
Well You Needn't
Cullum,Jamie (p,voc) | Castle,Ben (ts) | Gascoyne,Geoff (b) | De Krom,Sebastiaan (dr)
A Time For Love
Cullum,Jamie (p,voc) | O'Higgins,Dave (ts)

CCD 79783 | CD | Orsino's Songs | EAN 708857978328
Clare Teal And Her Band
Blues In The Night | I Only Have Eyes For You | I Loves You Porgy | You Make Me Feel So Young | Mountain Greenery
Blah Street Studios,?, rec. 25.-30.3.2002
Teal,Clare (voc) | Whiting,Trevor (cl,as,ts) | Solberg,Nils (g) | Litton,Martin (p) | Day,John (b) | Brown,Rod (dr,perc)
Life Plans
Teal,Clare (voc) | Smith,Malcom (tb) | Whiting,Trevor (cl,as,ts) | Solberg,Nils (g) | Litton,Martin (p) | Day,John (b) | Brown,Rod (dr,perc)
California Dreaming | The Way You Look Tonight
Teal,Clare (voc) | Barnes,Alan (cl,as) | Solberg,Nils (g) | Litton,Martin (p) | Day,John (b) | Brown,Rod (dr,perc)
In The Still Of The Night | Ready For Love To Begin
Teal,Clare (voc) | Solberg,Nils (g) | Litton,Martin (p) | Day,John (b) | Brown,Rod (dr,perc)
Let's Not Take A Raincheck
Teal,Clare (voc) | Solberg,Nils (g) | Litton,Martin (p) | Day,John (b) | Brown,Rod (dr,perc) | Shaw,Ian (voc)
Who Bought The Car?
Teal,Clare (voc) | Solberg,Nils (g) | Litton,Martin (p) | Day,John (b) | Brown,Rod (dr,perc) | Hannan,Nick (voc) | Chambers,Dan (voc) | Trace,Ella (voc)

CCD 79786 | CD | In Love Again | EAN 708857978625
Stacy Kent With The Jim Tomlinson Quintet
Shall We Dance? | Bewitched Bothered And Bewildered | My Heart Stood Still | It Never Entered My Mind | I Wish I Were In Love Again | Thou Swell | It Might As Well Be Spring | Nobody's Heart | I'm Gonna Wash That Man Right Outa My Hair | This Can't Be Love | Easy To Remember | Manhattan | Bali Ha'i
Ardingly,West Sussex,GB, rec. 3./4.7.& 7.9.2001
Kent,Stacey (voc) | Tomlinson,Jim (fl,ts) | Oxley,Colin (g) | Newton,David (p) | Thorpe,Simon (b) | Kviberg,Jasper (dr)

CCD 79797 | CD | The Boy Next Door | EAN 708857979721
The Best Is | The Boy Next Door | The Trolley Song | Say It Isn't So | Too Darn Hot | Makin' Whoopee | What The World Needs Now Is Love | You've Got A Friend | I Got It Bad And That Ain't Good | Ooh-Shoo-Be-Doo-Bee | People Will Say We're In Love | 'Tis Autumn | All I Do Is Dream Of You | I Get Along Without You Very Well | You're The Top | Bookends
Ardingly,West Sussex,GB, rec. 18.-22.2.2003
Kent,Stacey (voc) | Tomlinson,Jim (sax,voc) | Oxley,Colin (g) | Newton,David (p,keyboards,voc) | Chamberlain,Dave (b) | Home,Matt (dr) | Schwartz,Curtis (voc)

Capitol | EMI Germany

358257-2 | 2 CD | Soul Of The Bible | EAN 724358257229
Nat Adderley Group
In The Beginning | Yield | Obeah | Fun In The Church | The Eternal Walk | Krukma | Gone | Behold | Psalm 24 | Make Your Own Temple | Taj | Psalm 54 | Amani | Space Spiritual
Hollywood,CA, rec. 1972
Adderley,Nat (co) | Adderley,Julian \'Cannonball\' (as) | Adderley Jr.,Nat (p,el-p) | Duke,George (p,el-p) | Booker,Walter (b) | McCurdy,Roy (dr) | Moreira,Airto (perc) | Mayuto (perc) | Octavio (perc) | Ericson,King (perc) | Williams,Fleming (voc) | James,Olga (voc) | Spruill,Stephanie (voc) | Charma,Arthur (voc)

494504-2 | CD | Penthouse Serenade
Nat King Cole Trio
Too Young | Unforgettable
NYC, rec. 2.1.1952
Cole,Nat King (p,voc) | Collins,John (g) | Harris,Charles (b)
Nat King Cole Quartet
Walking My Baby Back Home | Too Marvelous For Words | That's My Girl | It's Only A Paper Moon
Cole,Nat King (p,voc) | Collins,John (g) | Harris,Charles (b) | Costanzo,Jack (congas,bongos)
Penthouse Serenade | Somebody Loves Me | Laura | Polka Dots And Moonbeams | If I Should Lose You | Rose Room
Los Angeles,CA, rec. 18.7.1952
Cole,Nat King (p) | Collins,John (g) | Harris,Charles (b) | Shawker,Norris 'Bunny' (dr)
Nat King Cole Quintet
Once In A Blue Moon | Down By The Old Mill Stream
Cole,Nat King (p) | Collins,John (g) | Harris,Charles (b) | Shawker,Norris 'Bunny' (dr) | Costanzo,Jack (congas,bongos)
Nat King Cole Quartet
Rose Room | I Surrender Dear | It Could Happen To You | Don't Blame Me | Little Girl | I Surrender Dear(alt.take)
Los Angeles,CA, rec. 14.7.1955
Cole,Nat King (p) | Collins,John (g) | Harris,Charles (b) | Young,Lee (dr)

494505-2 | CD | Blue Serge
Serge Chaloff Quartet
A Handful Of Stars | The Goof And I | Thanks For The Memory | I've Got The World On A String | Susie's Blues
Los Angeles,CA, rec. 14.3.1956
Chaloff,Serge (bs) | Clark,Sonny (p) | Vinnegar,Leroy (b) | Jones,Philly Joe (dr)
All The Things You Are | Stairway To The Stars | How About You
Los Angeles,CA, rec. 16.3.1956
Chaloff,Serge (bs) | Clark,Sonny (p) | Vinnegar,Leroy (b) | Jones,Philly Joe (dr)

494550-2 | CD | The Complete Birth Of The Cool
Miles Davis And His Orchestra
Move | Jeru | Godchild | Budo
NYC, rec. 21.1.1949
Davis,Miles (tp) | Winding,Kai (tb) | Collins,Junior (fr-h) | Barber,Bill (tuba) | Konitz,Lee (as) | Mulligan,Gerry (bs,arr) | Haig,Al (p) | Shulman,Joe (b) | Roach,Max (dr) | Lewis,John (arr)
Venus De Milo | Rouge | Boplicity | Israel
NYC, rec. 22.4.1949
Davis,Miles (tp,arr) | Johnson,J.J. (tb) | Siegelstein,Sandy (fr-h) | Barber,Bill (tuba) | Konitz,Lee (as) | Mulligan,Gerry (bs,arr) | Lewis,John (p) | Boyd,Nelson (b) | Clarke,Kenny (dr) | Evans,Gil (arr) | Carisi,Johnny (arr)
Deception | Rocker | Moon Dreams
NYC, rec. 9.3.1950
Davis,Miles (tp,arr) | Johnson,J.J. (tb) | Schuller,Gunther (fr-h) | Barber,Bill (tuba) | Konitz,Lee (as) | Mulligan,Gerry (bs,arr) | Lewis,John (p) | McKibbon,Al (b) | Roach,Max (dr) | Evans,Gil (arr)
Darn That Dream
Davis,Miles (tp) | Johnson,J.J. (tb) | Schuller,Gunther (fr-h) | Barber,Bill (tuba) | Konitz,Lee (as) | Mulligan,Gerry (bs) | Lewis,John (p) | McKibbon,Al (b) | Roach,Max (dr) | Evans,Gil (arr) | Hagood,Kenny (voc)
Birth Of The Cool(Theme) | Announcement by 'Symphony Sid Torin' | Move | Why Do I Love You | Godchild | Introduction by 'Symphony Sid Torin' | S'il Vous Plait | Moon Dreams | Budo
Live at The Royal Roost,NYC, rec. 4.9.1948
Davis,Miles (tp) | Zwerin,Mike (tb) | Collins,Junior (fr-h) | Barber,Bill (tuba) | Konitz,Lee (as) | Mulligan,Gerry (bs) | Lewis,John (p) | McKibbon,Al (b) | Roach,Max (dr) | Evans,Gil (arr) | Hagood,Kenny (voc)
Darn That Dream | Move | Moon Dreams | Budo
Live at The Royal Roost,NYC, rec. 18.9.1948
Davis,Miles (tp) | Zwerin,Mike (tb) | Collins,Junior (fr-h) | Barber,Bill (tuba) | Konitz,Lee (as) | Mulligan,Gerry (bs) | Lewis,John (p) | McKibbon,Al (b) | Roach,Max (dr) | Evans,Gil (arr) | Hagood,Kenny (voc)

495447-2 | CD | Them Dirty Blues
Cannonball Adderley Quintet
Work Song | Jeannie | Easy Living | Them Dirty Blues
Chicago,Ill, rec. 29.3.1960
Adderley,Julian \'Cannonball\' (as) | Adderley,Nat (co) | Harris,Barry (p) | Jones,Sam (b) | Hayes,Louis (dr)
Dat Dere | Del Sasser | Soon | Work Song(alt take) | Dat Dere(alt.take)
NYC, rec. 1.2.1960
Adderley,Julian \'Cannonball\' (as) | Adderley,Nat (co) | Timmons,Bobby (p) | Jones,Sam (b) | Hayes,Louis (dr)

498319-2 | CD | June Christy Big Band Special
June Christy With The Shorty Rogers Orchestra
Is You Is Or Is You Ain't My Baby | A Night In Tunisia | It Don't Mean A Thing If It Ain't Got That Swing
Los Angeles,CA, rec. 25.10.1962
Christy,June (voc) | Candoli,Conte (tp) | Katzman,Lee (tp) | Porcino,Al (tp) | Triscari,Ray (tp) | Friley,Vernon (tb) | Halliburton,John (tb) | McCreary,Lou (tb) | Shroyer,Kenny (b-tb) | Maini,Joe (as) | Kennedy,Charlie (as) | Cooper,Bob (ts) | Perkins,Bill (ts) | Nimitz,Jack (bs) | Rowles,Jimmy (p) | Mondragon,Joe (b) | Lewis,Mel (dr)
Stompin' At The Savoy | Good Bye | Time Was(Duerme)
Los Angeles,CA, rec. 5.11.1952
Christy,June (voc) | Candoli,Conte (tp) | Katzman,Lee (tp) | Porcino,Al (tp) | Triscari,Ray (tp) | Friley,Vernon (tb) | Rosolino,Frank (tb) | McCreary,Lou (tb) | Shroyer,Kenny (b-tb) | Maini,Joe (as) | Shank,Bud (as) | Cooper,Bob (ts) | Perkins,Bill (ts) | Nimitz,Jack (bs) | Rowles,Jimmy (p) | Mondragon,Joe (b) | Lewis,Mel (dr)
You Came A Long Way From St. Louis | Swingin' On Nothin' | Prelude To A Kiss | Skyliner | Frenesi | Until(The Mole)
Los Angeles,CA, rec. 19.11.1963
Christy,June (voc) | Candoli,Conte (tp) | Katzman,Lee (tp) | Porcino,Al (tp) | Triscari,Ray (tp) | Nash,Dick (tb) | Halliburton,John (tb) | McCreary,Lou (tb) | Shroyer,Kenny (b-tb) | Maini,Joe (as) | Shank,Bud (as) | Cooper,Bob (ts) | Perkins,Bill (ts) | Nimitz,Jack (bs) | Rowles,Jimmy (p) | Mondragon,Joe (b) | Lewis,Mel (dr)

520086-2 | CD | Cannonball Adderley And The Poll Winners
Cannonball Adderley And The Poll Winners
The Chant | Lolita | Azule Serape
San Francisco,CA, rec. 21.5.1960
Adderley,Julian \'Cannonball\' (as) | Montgomery,Wes (g) | Feldman,Victor (vib,p) | Brown,Ray (b) | Hayes,Louis (dr)
Au Privave | Yours Is My Heart Alone | Never Will I Marry | Au Privave(alt.take)
Los Angeles,CA, rec. 5.6.1960
Adderley,Julian \'Cannonball\' (as) | Montgomery,Wes (g) | Feldman,Victor (vib,p) | Brown,Ray (b) | Hayes,Louis (dr)

520087-2 | CD | After Midnight
Nat King Cole Quintet
Sweet Lorraine | It's Only A Paper Moon | Get Your Kicks On Route 66 | You Can Depend On Me | Candy
Los Angeles,CA, rec. 15.8.1956
Cole,Nat King (p,voc) | Edison,Harry 'Sweets' (tp) | Collins,John (g) | Harris,Charles (b) | Young,Lee (dr)
Just You Just Me | You're Looking At Me | Don't Let It Go To Your Head | I Was A Little Too Lonely | You're Laughing At Me(alt.take)
Los Angeles,CA, rec. 14.9.1956
Cole,Nat King (p,voc) | Smith,Willie (as) | Collins,John (g) | Harris,Charles (b) | Young,Lee (dr)
Nat King Cole Sextet
Caravan | Lonely One
Los Angeles,CA, rec. 21.9.1956
Cole,Nat King (p,voc) | Tizol,Juan (v-tb) | Collins,John (g) | Harris,Charles (b) | Young,Lee (dr) | Costanzo,Jack (congas,bongos)
Nat King Cole Quintet
Blame It On My Youth | What Is There To Say
Cole,Nat King (p,voc) | Tizol,Juan (v-tb) | Collins,John (g) | Harris,Charles (b) | Young,Lee (dr)
Sometimes I'm Happy | I Know That You Know | When I Grow Too Old To Dream | Two Loves Have I
Los Angeles,CA, rec. 24.9.1956
Cole,Nat King (p,voc) | Smith,Stuff (v) | Collins,John (g) | Harris,Charles (b) | Young,Lee (dr)

520088-2 | CD | Blues Cross Country
Peggy Lee With The Quincy Jones Orchestra
Kansas City Blues | I Lost My Sugar In Salt Lake City
Los Angeles,CA, rec. 14.4.1961
Lee,Peggy (voc) | Jones,Quincy (arr,ld) | Fowler,Bob (tp) | Gozzo,Conrad (tp) | Porcino,Al (tp) | Sheldon,Jack (tp) | Friley,Vernon (tb) | McGreery,Lewis (tb) | Rosolino,Frank (tb) | Knight,Bobby (b-tb) | Carter,Benny (as) | Collette,Buddy (as) | Green,Bill (ts) | Perkins,Bill (ts) | Nimitz,Jack (bs) | Strazzeri,Frank (p) | Budimir,Dennis (g) | Bennett,Max (b) | Levey,Stan (dr) | Pozo,Chino (congas,bongos)
Going To Chicago Blues | Boston Beans | The Grain Belt Blues | Basin Street Blues
Los Angeles,CA, rec. 15.4.1961
Lee,Peggy (voc) | Jones,Quincy (arr,ld) | Fowler,Bob (tp) | Gozzo,Conrad (tp) | Porcino,Al (tp) | Sheldon,Jack (tp) | Friley,Vernon (tb) | McGreery,Lewis (tb) | Rosolino,Frank (tb) | Roberts,George (tb) | Carter,Benny (as) | Green,Bill (as) | Johnson,Plas (ts) | Perkins,Bill (ts) | Nimitz,Jack (bs) | Rowles,Jimmy (p) | Roberts,Howard (g) | Budimir,Dennis (g) | Bennett,Max (b) | Levey,Stan (dr) | Pozo,Chino (congas,bongos)
New York City Blues | Fisherman's Wharff | San Francisco Blues
Los Angeles,CA, rec. 17.4.1961
Lee,Peggy (voc) | Jones,Quincy (arr,ld) | Fowler,Bob (tp) | Gozzo,Conrad (tp) | Porcino,Al (tp) | Sheldon,Jack (tp) | Friley,Vernon (tb) | McGreery,Lewis (tb) | Rosolino,Frank (tb) | Knight,Bobby (b-tb) | Carter,Benny (as,arr) | Green,Bill (as) | Gordon,Justin (ts) | Perkins,Bill (ts) | Nimitz,Jack (bs) | Rowles,Jimmy (p) | Strazzeri,Frank (p) | Budimir,Dennis (g) | Bennett,Max (b) | Levey,Stan (dr) | Pozo,Chino (congas,bongos)
St.Louis Blues | The Train Blues
Los Angeles,CA, rec. 19.4.1961
Lee,Peggy (voc) | Jones,Quincy (arr,ld) | Fowler,Bob (tp) | Graves,Joe (tp) | Triscari,Joe (tp) | Candoli,Pete (tp) | Sheldon,Jack (tp) | McGreery,Lewis (tb) | Rosolino,Frank (tb) | Shepard,Tom (tb) | Knight,Bobby (b-tb) | Carter,Benny (as) | Green,Bill (as) | Collette,Buddy (ts) | Perkins,Bill (ts) | Nimitz,Jack (bs) | Rowles,Jimmy (p) | Budimir,Dennis (g) | Bennett,Max (b) | Levey,Stan (dr) | Guerrero,Frank 'Chico' (perc)
Los Angeles Blues | Hey Look Me Over
Los Angeles,CA, rec. 19.5.1961
Lee,Peggy (voc) | Jones,Quincy (arr,ld) | Fowler,Bob (tp) | Porcino,Al (tp) | Candoli,Pete (tp) | Triscari,Joe (tp) | McGreery,Lewis (tb) | Nash,Dick (tb) | Bohanon,Hoyt (tb) | Knight,Bobby (b-tb) | Carter,Benny (as) | Green,Bill (as) | Johnson,Plas (ts) | Perkins,Bill (ts) | Nimitz,Jack (bs) | Rowles,Jimmy (p) | Budimir,Dennis (g) | Bennett,Max (b) | Levey,Stan (dr)
The Shining Sea
Los Angeles,CA, rec. 21.5.1966
Lee,Peggy (voc) | Jones,Quincy (arr,ld) | Lott,Sinclair (fr-h) | Henshaw,Bill (fr-h) | Bouck,Aubrey (fr-h) | Sigismonti,Henry (fr-h) | Klee,Harry (reeds) | Cooper,Bob (reeds) | Shank,Bud (reeds) | Nimitz,Jack (reeds) | Budimir,Dennis (g) | Pisano,John (g) | Bain,Bob (g) | Thielemans,Jean 'Toots' (g) | Levy,Lou (p) | Kane,Artie (org) | Bennett,Max (b) | Palmer,Earl (dr) | Bunker,Larry (perc) | Richards,Emil (perc) | Strings

520089-2 | CD | Adventures In Blues
Stan Kenton And His Orchestra
Ten Bars Ago | Lady Luck
Los Angeles,CA, rec. 21.9.1960
Kenton,Stan (p) | Brisbois,Wilbur 'Bud' (tp) | Smith,Dalton (tp) | Noto,Sam (tp) | Rolfe,Bob (tp) | Huffstetter,Steven (tp) | Hyde,Dick (tb) | Sikora,Ray (tb) | Amlotte,Jim (tb) | Knight,Bobby (tb) | Pollan,Albert (tuba) | Roland,Gene (mellophone) | Carver,Dwight (mellophone) | Burnett,Joe (mellophone) | Horan,Bill (mellophone) | Wirtel,Tom (mellophone) | Baltazar,Gabe (as) | Donahue,Sam (ts) | Renzi,Paul (ts) | Holladay,Marvin (bs) | Dunstan,Wayne (bs,bass-sax) | Chivily,Pete (b) | Anton,Artie (dr)
Night At The Gold Nugget
Los Angeles,CA, rec. 7.7.1961
Kenton,Stan (p) | Brisbois,Wilbur 'Bud' (tp) | Behrendt,Bob (tp) | Rolfe,Bob (tp) | Smith,Dalton (tp) | Stamm,Marvin (tp) | Spurlock,Jack (tb) | Fitzpatrick,Bob (tb) | Parker,Bud (tb) | Carver,Dwight (mellophone) | LaMotte,Keith (mellophone) | Saunders,Carl (mellophone) | Roland,Gene (mellophone) | Baltazar,Gabe (as) | Renzi,Paul (ts) | Donahue,Sam (ts) | Holladay,Marvin (bs) | Dunstan,Wayne (bass-sax) | Mitchell,Red (b) | Lestock[McKenzie],Jerry (dr)
Reuben's Blues | Blue Ghost | Exit Stage Left
Los Angeles,CA, rec. 7.12.1961
Kenton,Stan (p) | Baltazar,Norman (tp) | Behrendt,Bob (tp) | Rolfe,Bob (tp) | Smith,Dalton (tp) | Stamm,Marvin (tp) | Barton,Dee (tb) | Fitzpatrick,Bob (tb) | Parker,Bud (tb) | Amlotte,Jim (b-tb) | Wheeler,Dave (b-tb,tuba) | Carver,Dwight (mellophone) | LaMotte,Keith (mellophone) | Saunders,Carl (mellophone) | Starling,Ray (mellophon) | Roland,Gene (ss,mellophone) | Baltazar,Gabe (as) | Arnold,Buddy (ts) | Renzi,Matt (ts) | Beutler,Allan (bs) | Kaye,Joel (bs,bass-sax) | Senatore,Pat (b) | Lestock[McKenzie],Jerry (dr)
Fitz
Los Angeles,CA, rec. 12.12.1961
Kenton,Stan (p) | Baltazar,Norman (tp) | Behrendt,Bob (tp) | Rolfe,Bob (tp) | Smith,Dalton (tp) | Stamm,Marvin (tp) | Barton,Dee (tb) | Fitzpatrick,Bob (tb) | Parker,Bud (tb) | Amlotte,Jim (b-tb) | Wheeler,Dave (b-tb,tuba) | Roland,Gene (ss,mellophone) | Carver,Dwight (mellophone) | LaMotte,Keith (mellophone) | Saunders,Carl (mellophone) | Starling,Ray (mellophon) | Baltazar,Gabe (as) | Renzi,Paul (ts) | Arnold,Buddy (ts) | Donahue,Sam (ts) | Beutler,Allan (bs) | Kaye,Joel (bs,bass-sax) | Senatore,Pat (b) | Lestock[McKenzie],Jerry (dr)
Dragonwyck | Night At The Gold Nugget(alt.take) | The Blues Story
Los Angeles,CA, rec. 13.12.1961
Kenton,Stan (p) | Baltazar,Norman (tp) | Behrendt,Bob (tp) | Rolfe,Bob (tp) | Smith,Dalton (tp) | Stamm,Marvin (tp) | Barton,Dee (tb) | Fitzpatrick,Bob (tb) | Parker,Bud (tb) | Amlotte,Jim (b-tb) | Wheeler,Dave (b-tb,tuba) | Roland,Gene (ss,mellophone) | Carver,Dwight (mellophone) | LaMotte,Keith (mellophone) | Saunders,Carl (mellophone) | Starling,Ray (mellophon) | Baltazar,Gabe (as) | Arnold,Buddy (ts) | Renzi,Matt (ts) | Beutler,Allan (bs) | Kaye,Joel (bs,bass-sax) | Senatore,Pat (b) | Lestock[McKenzie],Jerry (dr)
Formula | Aphrodesia
Los Angeles,CA, rec. 14.12.1961
Kenton,Stan (p) | Smith,Dalton (tp) | Stamm,Marvin (tp) | Behrendt,Bob (tp) | Rolfe,Bob (tp) | Baltazar,Norman (tp) | Fitzpatrick,Bob (tb) | Barton,Dee (tb) | Parker,Bud (tb) | Amlotte,Jim (b-tb) | Wheeler,Dave (b-tb,tuba) | Roland,Gene (ss,mellophone) | Starling,Ray (mellophon) | Carver,Dwight (mellophone) | LaMotte,Keith (mellophone) | Saunders,Carl (mellophone) | Roland,Gene (mellophone) | Baltazar,Gabe (as) | Arnold,Buddy (ts) | Renzi,Paul (ts) | Kaye,Joel (bs,bass-sax) | Beutler,Allan (bs) | Senatore,Pat (b) | Lestock[McKenzie],Jerry (dr)

520090-2 | CD | 30 By Ella
Ella Fitzgerald With Benny Carter's Magnificent Seven
Medley: | On Green Dolphin Street- | How Am I To Know?- | Just Friends- | I Cried For You(Now It's Your Turn To Cry Over Me)- | Seems Like Old Times- | You Stepped Out Of A Dream- | Medley: | No Regrets- | I've Got A Feeling You're Fooling- | Don't Blame Me- | Deep Purple- | Rain- | You're Sweetheart-
Los Angeles,CA, rec. 28.5.1968
Fitzgerald,Ella (voc) | Carter,Benny (as,arr) | Edison,Harry 'Sweets' (tp) | Auld,Georgie (ts) | Jones,Jimmy (p) | Collins,John (g) | West,Bobby (b) | Francis,Panama (dr)
Medley: | My Mother's Eyes- | Try A Little Tenderness- | I Got It Bad And That Ain't Good- | Everything I Have Is Yours- | I Never Knew- | Goodnight My Love- | Medley: | If I Gave My Heart To You- | Once In A While- | Ebb Tide- | The Lamp Is Low- | Where Are You- | Thinking Of You-
Los Angeles,CA, rec. 29.5.1968
Fitzgerald,Ella (voc) | Carter,Benny (as,arr) | Edison,Harry 'Sweets' (tp) | Auld,Georgie (ts) | Jones,Jimmy (p) | Collins,John (g) | West,Bobby (b) | Bellson,Louie (dr)
Medley: | Four Or Five Times- | Maybe- | Taking A Chance On Love- | Elmer's Tune- | At Sundown- | It's A Wonderful World- | Medley: | Candy- | All I Do Is Dream Of You- | Spring Is Here- | 720 In The Books- | It Happened In Monterey- | What Can I Say After I Say I'm Sorry- | Hawaiian War Chant

Los Angeles,CA, rec. 3.6.1968
Fitzgerald,Ella (voc) | Carter,Benny (as,arr) | Edison,Harry 'Sweets' (tp) | Auld,Georgie (ts) | Jones,Jimmy (p) | Collins,John (g) | West,Bobby (b) | Bellson,Louie (dr)

520135-2 | CD | Ellington '55
Duke Ellington And His Orchestra
Flying Home
NYC, rec. 21.12.1953
Ellington,Duke (p) | Terry,Clark (tp) | Anderson,Cat (tp) | Cook,Willie (tp) | Nance,Ray (tp,v,voc) | Jackson,Quentin (tb) | Woodman,Britt (tb) | Cobbs,Alfred (tb) | Procope,Russell (cl,as) | Henderson,Rick (as) | Gonsalves,Paul (ts) | Hamilton,Jimmy (cl,ts) | Carney,Harry (b-cl,bs) | Marshall,Wendell (b) | Black,Dave (dr)
Stompin' At The Savoy
Chicago,Ill, rec. 28.12.1953
Ellington,Duke (p) | Terry,Clark (tp) | Anderson,Cat (tp) | Cook,Willie (tp) | Nance,Ray (tp,v,voc) | Jackson,Quentin (tb) | Woodman,Britt (tb) | Jean,George (tb) | Procope,Russell (cl,as) | Henderson,Rick (as) | Gonsalves,Paul (ts) | Hamilton,Jimmy (cl,ts) | Carney,Harry (b-cl,bs) | Marshall,Wendell (b) | Black,Dave (dr)
Black And Tan Fantasy
Chicago,Ill, rec. 29.12.1953
Ellington,Duke (p) | Terry,Clark (tp) | Anderson,Cat (tp) | Cook,Willie (tp) | Nance,Ray (tp,v,voc) | Jackson,Quentin (tb) | Woodman,Britt (tb) | Jean,George (tb) | Procope,Russell (cl,as) | Henderson,Rick (as) | Gonsalves,Paul (ts) | Hamilton,Jimmy (cl,ts) | Carney,Harry (b-cl,bs) | Strayhorn,Billy (celeste) | Marshall,Wendell (b) | Black,Dave (dr)
In The Mood
Chicago,Ill, rec. 1.1.1954
Ellington,Duke (p) | Terry,Clark (tp) | Anderson,Cat (tp) | Cook,Willie (tp) | Nance,Ray (tp,v,voc) | Jackson,Quentin (tb) | Woodman,Britt (tb) | Jean,George (tb) | Procope,Russell (cl,as) | Henderson,Rick (as) | Gonsalves,Paul (ts) | Hamilton,Jimmy (cl,ts) | Carney,Harry (b-cl,bs) | Marshall,Wendell (b) | Black,Dave (dr)
One O'Clock Jump
Chicago,Ill, rec. 2.1.19954
Ellington,Duke (p) | Terry,Clark (tp) | Anderson,Cat (tp) | Cook,Willie (tp) | Nance,Ray (tp,v,voc) | Jackson,Quentin (tb) | Woodman,Britt (tb) | Jean,George (tb) | Procope,Russell (cl,as) | Henderson,Rick (as) | Gonsalves,Paul (ts) | Hamilton,Jimmy (cl,ts) | Carney,Harry (b-cl,bs) | Marshall,Wendell (b) | Black,Dave (dr)
Rockin' In Rhythm | Happy-Go-Lucky Local
Chicago,Ill, rec. 17.1.1954
Ellington,Duke (p) | Terry,Clark (tp) | Anderson,Cat (tp) | Cook,Willie (tp) | Nance,Ray (tp) | Jackson,Quentin (tb) | Woodman,Britt (tb) | Jean,George (tb) | Procope,Russell (cl,as) | Henderson,Rick (as) | Gonsalves,Paul (ts) | Hamilton,Jimmy (cl,ts) | Carney,Harry (b-cl,bs) | Marshall,Wendell (b) | Black,Dave (dr)
It Don't Mean A Thing If It Ain't Got That Swing
NYC, rec. 17.6.1954
Ellington,Duke (p) | Terry,Clark (tp) | Anderson,Cat (tp) | Cook,Willie (tp) | Nance,Ray (tp,voc) | Jackson,Quentin (tb) | Woodman,Britt (tb) | Sanders,John (tb) | Procope,Russell (cl,as) | Henderson,Rick (as) | Gonsalves,Paul (ts) | Hamilton,Jimmy (cl,ts) | Carney,Harry (b-cl,bs) | Marshall,Wendell (b) | Black,Dave (dr)
Body And Soul
Chicago,Ill, rec. 18.5.1955
Ellington,Duke (p) | Terry,Clark (tp) | Anderson,Cat (tp) | Cook,Willie (tp) | Nance,Ray (tp,voc) | Jackson,Quentin (tb) | Woodman,Britt (tb) | Sanders,John (tb) | Procope,Russell (cl,as) | Henderson,Rick (as) | Gonsalves,Paul (ts) | Hamilton,Jimmy (cl,ts) | Carney,Harry (b-cl,bs) | Woode,Jimmy (b) | Black,Dave (dr)

521222-2 | CD | Adventures In Jazz
Stan Kenton And His Orchestra
It Might As Well Be Spring
Los Angeles,CA, rec. 5.7.1961
Kenton,Stan (p) | Brisbois,Wilbur 'Bud' (tp) | Behrendt,Bob (tp) | Rolfe,Bob (tp) | Smith,Dalton (tp) | Stamm,Marvin (tp) | Spurlock,Jack (tb) | Fitzpatrick,Bob (tb) | Parker,Bud (tb) | Carver,Dwight (mellophone) | LaMotte,Keith (mellophone) | Saunders,Carl (mellophone) | Roland,Gene (mellophone) | Baltazar,Gabe (as) | Renzi,Paul (ts) | Donahue,Sam (ts) | Holladay,Marvin (bs) | Dunstan,Wayne (bass-sax) | Mitchell,Red (b) | Lestock[McKenzie],Jerry (dr)
Waltz Of The Prophets(alt.take) | Body And Soul(alt.take)
NYC, rec. 26.9.1961
Kenton,Stan (p) | Baltazar,Norman (tp) | Behrendt,Bob (tp) | Rolfe,Bob (tp) | Smith,Dalton (tp) | Stamm,Marvin (tp) | Barton,Dee (tb) | Fitzpatrick,Bob (tb) | Parker,Bud (tb) | Amlotte,Jim (b-tb) | Wheeler,Dave (b-tb,tuba) | Carver,Dwight (mellophone) | LaMotte,Keith (mellophone) | Saunders,Carl (mellophone) | Starling,Ray (mellophon) | Baltazar,Gabe (as) | Renzi,Matt (ts) | Donahue,Sam (ts) | Holladay,Marvin (bs) | Beutler,Allan (bs,bass-sax) | Senatore,Pat (b) | Lestock[McKenzie],Jerry (dr)
Stairway To The Stars
Los Angeles,CA, rec. 11.12.1961
Kenton,Stan (p) | Baltazar,Norman (tp) | Behrendt,Bob (tp) | Rolfe,Bob (tp) | Smith,Dalton (tp) | Stamm,Marvin (tp) | Barton,Dee (tb) | Fitzpatrick,Bob (tb) | Parker,Bud (tb) | Amlotte,Jim (b-tb) | Wheeler,Dave (b-tb,tuba) | Carver,Dwight (mellophone) | LaMotte,Keith (mellophone) | Saunders,Carl (mellophone) | Starling,Ray (mellophon) | Baltazar,Gabe (as) | Arnold,Buddy (ts) | Renzi,Matt (ts) | Beutler,Allan (bs) | Kaye,Joel (bs,bass-sax) | Senatore,Pat (b) | Lestock[McKenzie],Jerry (dr)
Limehouse Blues | Malaguena | Waltz Of The Prophets | Body And Soul
Los Angeles,CA, rec. 12.12.1961
Kenton,Stan (p) | Baltazar,Norman (tp) | Behrendt,Bob (tp) | Rolfe,Bob (tp) | Smith,Dalton (tp) | Stamm,Marvin (tp) | Barton,Dee (tb) | Fitzpatrick,Bob (tb) | Parker,Bud (tb) | Amlotte,Jim (b-tb) | Wheeler,Dave (b-tb,tuba) | Carver,Dwight (mellophone) | LaMotte,Keith (mellophone) | Saunders,Carl (mellophone) | Starling,Ray (mellophon) | Baltazar,Gabe (as) | Renzi,Paul (ts) | Arnold,Buddy (ts) | Donahue,Sam (ts) | Beutler,Allan (bs) | Kaye,Joel (bs,bass-sax) | Senatore,Pat (b) | Lestock[McKenzie],Jerry (dr)
Turtle Talk | Misty
Los Angeles,CA, rec. 14.12.1961
Kenton,Stan (p) | Baltazar,Norman (tp) | Behrendt,Bob (tp) | Rolfe,Bob (tp) | Smith,Dalton (tp) | Stamm,Marvin (tp) | Barton,Dee (tb) | Fitzpatrick,Bob (tb) | Parker,Bud (tb) | Amlotte,Jim (b-tb) | Wheeler,Dave (b-tb,tuba) | Carver,Dwight (mellophone) | LaMotte,Keith (mellophone) | Saunders,Carl (mellophone) | Starling,Ray (mellophon) | Baltazar,Gabe (as) | Arnold,Buddy (ts) | Renzi,Matt (ts) | Beutler,Allan (bs) | Kaye,Joel (bs,bass-sax) | Senatore,Pat (b) | Lestock[McKenzie],Jerry (dr)

521223-2 | CD | Great Swing Classics In Hi-Fi
Benny Goodman And His Orchestra
Jumpin' At The Woodside
NYC, rec. 9.11.1954
Goodman,Benny (cl) | Braff,Ruby (tp) | Griffin,Chris (tp) | Poole,Carl (tp) | Privin,Bernie (tp) | Bradley,Will (tb) | Brown,Vernon (tb) | Cutshall,Cutty (tb) | Schertzer,Hymie (as) | Ricci,Paul (as) | Richman,Abe 'Boomie' (ts) | Klink,Al (ts) | Schlinger,Sol (bs) | Powell,Mel (p) | Jordan,Steve (g) | Duvivier,George (b) | Donaldson,Robert (dr)
Somebody Stole My Gal
Hollywood,CA, rec. 24.9.1954
Goodman,Benny (cl) | Braff,Ruby (tp) | Griffin,Chris (tp) | Poole,Carl (tp) | Privin,Bernie (tp) | Bradley,Will (tb) | Brown,Vernon (tb) | Cutshall,Cutty (tb) | Schertzer,Hymie (as) | Ricci,Paul (as) | Richman,Abe 'Boomie' (ts) | Klink,Al (ts) | Schlinger,Sol (bs) | Powell,Mel (p) | Jordan,Steve (g) | Duvivier,George (b) | Donaldson,Robert (dr)
Duke Ellington And His Orchestra
Harlem Air Shaft
Chicago,Ill, rec. 17.5.1955
Ellington,Duke (p) | Terry,Clark (tp) | Anderson,Cat (tp) | Cook,Willie (tp) | Nance,Ray (tp,voc) | Jackson,Quentin (tb) | Woodman,Britt (tb) | Sanders,John (tb) | Procope,Russell (cl,as) | Henderson,Rick (as) | Gonsalves,Paul (ts) | Hamilton,Jimmy (cl,ts) | Carney,Harry (b-cl,bs) | Woode,Jimmy (b) | Black,Dave (dr)
Stan Kenton And His Orchestra
Intermission Riff | The Peanut Vendor
Hollywood,CA, rec. 12.2.1956
Kenton,Stan (p) | prob.personal: | Candoli,Pete (tp) | Leddy,Ed (tp) | Ferguson,Maynard (tp) | Noto,Sam (tp) | Paladino,Don (tp) | Tanno,Vinnie (tp) | Fitzpatrick,Bob (tb) | Bernhart,Milton 'Milt' (tb) | Fontana,Carl (tb) | Kelly,Don (tb) | Larsen,Kent (tb) | Herfurt,Arthur 'Skeets' (as) | Niehaus,Lennie (as) | Nimitz,Jack (ts) | Musso,Vido (ts) | Perkins,Bill (ts) | Sinatra,Spencer (bs) | Blaze,Ralph (g) | Bagley,Don (b) | Lewis,Mel (dr) | Guerrero,Joe 'Chico' (timbales)
Harry James And His Orchestra
I'm Beginning To See The Light
Hollywood,CA, rec. 20.7.1955
James,Harry (tp) | personal included: | Smith,Willie (as) | Reuss,Allan (g) | Forrest,Helen (voc) | details not on the cover
Crazy Rhythm
Hollywood,CA, rec. 20.1.1956
James,Harry (tp) | personal included: | Corcoran,Corky (ts) | details not on the cover
Glen Gray And His Orchestra
Just An Old Manuscript | Come And Get It
Hollywood,CA, rec. 21.6.1956
Gray,Glen (ld) | personal included: | Sherock,Shorty (tp) | Russin,Irving 'Babe' (ts) | Sherman,Ray (p) | details not on the cover
Les Brown And His Orchestra
A Good Man Is Hard To Find | I've Got My Love To Keep Me Warm
Hollywood,CA, rec. May 1958
Brown,Les (arr,ld) | personal included: | Stone,Butch (voc) | details not on the cover
Billy May And His Orchestra With Members Of The Jimmy Lunceford Orchestra
Annie Laurie | Margie
Hollywood,CA, rec. May 1957
May,Billy (arr,ld) | personal included: | Thomas,Joe (tp) | Mitchell,Ollie (tp) | Young,Trummy (tb,voc) | Smith,Willie (as) | Hendrickson,Al (g) | Stoller,Alvin (dr) | details not on the cover
Woody Herman And His Orchestra
Sleep
Hollywood,CA, rec. 24.9.1954
Herman,Woody (cl) | personal included: | Perkins,Bill (ts) | Nimitz,Jack (bs) | Pierce,Nat (p) | details not on the cover

521224-2 | CD | Trumpet Blues:The Best Of Harry James
Harry James And His Orchestra
Trumpet Blues | Cherry | Music Makers | I'm Beginning To See The Light | Two O'Clock Jump | Jam Session | Sleepy Lagoon | I've Heard That Song Before | You Made Me Love You | It's Been A Long Long Time | Ciribiribin
Hollywood,CA, rec. 18.-21.7.1955
James,Harry (tp) | Gozzo,Conrad (tp) | Buono,Nick (tp) | McDonald,Everett (tp) | Osborne,Ralph (tp) | Tizol,Juan (tb) | Bohannon,Hoyt (tb) | Main,Roy (tb) | McCreary,Lou (tb) | Smith,Willie (as) | Lorden,Herb (sax) | Massingill,Bill (sax) | Chartrand,Pat (sax) | Poland,Bob (bs) | Parker,Doug (p) | Reuss,Allan (g) | Stone,Bob (b) | Mills,Jackie (dr) | Estes,Gene (vib,dr) | Forest,Helen (voc) | unkn. (9 strings)
Strictly Instrumental
Hollywood,CA, rec. 20.1.1956
James,Harry (tp) | Gozzo,Conrad (tp) | Buono,Nick (tp) | DePew,Art (tp) | Mangano,Mickey (tp) | Tizol,Juan (v-tb) | Roberts,George (tb) | Nash,Dick (tb) | Smith,Willie (as) | Lorden,Herb (cl,as) | Massingill,Bill (ts) | Corcoran,Corky (ts) | Suthers,Tom (bs) | Kinnamon,Larry (p) | Timbrell,Tiny (g) | Comfort,Joe (b) | Combine,Buddy (dr) | Russell,Mischa (v) | Lube,Dan (v) | Sasson,Marshall (v) | Shore,Paul (v) | Dieterle,Kurt (v) | Vince,Gerard (v) | Robyn,Paul (viola) | Sterkin,David (viola) | Bernard,Cy (cello)
Blues On Account
Hollywood,CA, rec. 2.5.1957
James,Harry (tp) | Rolfe,Bob (tp) | DePew,Art (tp) | Buono,Nick (tp) | Paladino,Don (tp) | Mangano,Mickey (tp) | Edmondson,Bob (tb) | Sims,Ray (tb) | Robinson,Robert (tb) | Smith,Willie (as) | Lorden,Herb (cl,as) | Corcoran,Corky (ts) | Polifroni,Francis (ts) | Small,Ernie (bs) | Kinnamon,Larry (p) | Reuss,Allan (g) | Phillips,Russ (b) | Rich[as 'Buddy Poor'],Buddy (dr)
Barn 12
Hollywood,CA, rec. 4.5.1957
James,Harry (tp) | Rolfe,Bob (tp) | Linn,Ray (tp) | Buono,Nick (tp) | Paladino,Don (tp) | Mangano,Mickey (tp) | Edmondson,Bob (tb) | Harper,Herbie (tb) | Robinson,Robert (tb) | Smith,Willie (as) | Lorden,Herb (cl,as) | Corcoran,Corky (ts) | Polifroni,Francis (ts) | Small,Ernie (bs) | Kinnamon,Larry (p) | Reuss,Allan (g) | Phillips,Russ (b) | Rich[as 'Buddy Poor'],Buddy (dr)
Moten Swing | Willow Weep For Me
Hollywood,CA, rec. 1.7.1958
James,Harry (tp) | Rolfe,Bob (tp) | Mitchell,Ollie (tp) | Buono,Nick (tp) | Edmondson,Bob (tb) | Sims,Ray (tb) | Tack,Ernie (tb) | Smith,Willie (as) | Lorden,Herb (cl,as) | Small,Ernie (ts) | Firmatura,Sam (ts) | Poland,Bob (bs) | Perciful,Jack (p) | Budimir,Dennis (g) | Phillips,Russ (b) | Mills,Jackie (dr)

521225-2 | CD | Benny Goodman-The Complete Capitol Trios
Benny Goodman Trio
Blue And Broken Hearted | After Hours | All I Do Is Dream Of You | I'll Never Be The Same | Bye Bye Pretty Baby | Shoe Shine Boy
NYC, rec. 7.11.1947
Goodman,Benny (cl) | Wilson,Teddy (p) | Crawford,James 'Jimmy' (dr)
At Sundown | When You're Smiling | All I Do Is Dream Of You(II) | Stompin' At The Savoy
NYC, rec. 17.11.1947
Goodman,Benny (cl) | Wilson,Teddy (p) | Crawford,James 'Jimmy' (dr)
Mean To Me | Puttin' On The Ritz | I Never Knew | Up A Lazy River
Los Angeles,CA, rec. 16.4.1947
Goodman,Benny (cl) | Rowles,Jimmy (p) | Romersa,Tom 'Tommy' (dr)
There'll Be Some Changes Made | Everything I've Got Belongs To You | But Not For Me | Margie
NYC, rec. 28.1.1954
Goodman,Benny (cl) | Powell,Mel (p) | Grady,Eddie (dr)
Rose Room | What Can I Say After I Say I'm Sorry
NYC, rec. 16.11.1954
Goodman,Benny (cl) | Powell,Mel (p) | Donaldson,Bobby (dr)

521859-2 | CD | Live At The Circle Room
Nat King Cole Trio
Oh But I Do | I'm Thru With Love | C Jam Blues | My Sugar Is So Refined
Live at The Circle Room,Hotel LaSalle,Milwaykee,Wis., rec. 21.9.1946
Cole,Nat King (p,voc) | Moore,Oscar (g,voc) | Miller,Johnny (b,voc)
I'm In The Mood For Love | I Found A New Baby | I Don't Know Why(I Just Do) | If You Can't Smile And Say Yes
Live at The Circle Room,Hotel LaSalle,Milwaykee,Wis., rec. 22.9.1946
Cole,Nat King (p,voc) | Moore,Oscar (g) | Miller,Johnny (b)
It's Only A Paper Moon | One O'Clock Jump | Everyone Is Saying Hello Again
Live at The Circle Room,Hotel LaSalle,Milwaykee,Wis., rec. 23.9.1946
Cole,Nat King (p,voc) | Moore,Oscar (g) | Miller,Johnny (b)
Opening Theme | Sweet Georgia Brown | Sweet Lorraine | Oh But I Do | My Sugar Is So Refined | Closing Theme
Live at The Circle Room,Hotel LaSalle,Milwaykee,Wis., rec. 25.9.1946
Cole,Nat King (p,voc) | Moore,Oscar (g,voc) | Miller,Johnny (b,voc)

529441-2 | CD | Jazz Workshop Revisited | EAN 724352944125
Cannonball Adderley Sextet
Introduction by Cannonball Adderley | The Jive Samba | Lillie
Live at The Jazz Workshop,San Francisco,CA, rec. 21.9.1962
Adderley,Julian \'Cannonball\' (as) | Adderley,Nat (co) | Lateef,Yusef (fl,ts,oboe) | Zawinul,Joe (p) | Jones,Sam (b) | Hayes,Louis (dr)
Cannonball Adderley Quintet
Unit 7 | Jessica's Birthday | Primitivo | Marney | Mellow Buno | Time To Go Now...Really by Cannonball Adderley
Adderley,Julian \'Cannonball\' (as) | Adderley,Nat (co) | Zawinul,Joe (p) | Jones,Sam (b) | Hayes,Louis (dr)

530117-2 | CD | Birth Of The Cool | EAN 724353011727
Miles Davis And His Orchestra
Move | Jeru | Godchild | Budo
NYC, rec. 21.1.1949
Davis,Miles (tp) | Winding,Kai (tb) | Collins,Junior (fr-h) | Barber,Bill (tuba) | Konitz,Lee (as) | Mulligan,Gerry (bs,arr) | Haig,Al (p) | Shulman,Joe (b) | Roach,Max (dr) | Lewis,John (arr)
Venus De Milo | Rouge | Boplicity | Israel
NYC, rec. 22.4.1949
Davis,Miles (tp,arr) | Johnson,J.J. (tb) | Siegelstein,Sandy (fr-h) | Barber,Bill (tuba) | Konitz,Lee (as) | Mulligan,Gerry (bs,arr) | Lewis,John (p) | Boyd,Nelson (b) | Clarke,Kenny (dr) | Evans,Gil (arr) | Carisi,Johnny (arr)
Deception | Rocker | Moon Dreams
NYC, rec. 9.3.1950
Davis,Miles (tp,arr) | Johnson,J.J. (tb) | Schuller,Gunther (fr-h) | Barber,Bill (tuba) | Konitz,Lee (as) | Mulligan,Gerry (bs,arr) | Lewis,John (p) | McKibbon,Al (b) | Roach,Max (dr) | Evans,Gil (arr)
Darn That Dream
Davis,Miles (tp) | Johnson,J.J. (tb) | Schuller,Gunther (fr-h) | Barber,Bill (tuba) | Konitz,Lee (as) | Mulligan,Gerry (bs) | Lewis,John (p) | McKibbon,Al (b) | Roach,Max (dr) | Evans,Gil (arr) | Hagood,Kenny (voc)

531571-2 | CD | Stan Kenton Portraits On Standards
Stan Kenton And His Orchestra
Street Of Dreams
Los Angeles,CA, rec. 20.9.1951
Kenton,Stan (p) | Howell,John (tp) | Ferguson,Maynard (tp) | Candoli,Conte (tp) | Williamson,Stu (tp) | Coppola,John (tp) | Fitzpatrick,Bob (tb) | Betts,Harry (tb) | Russo,William 'Bill' (tb) | Kenney,Dick (tb) | Roberts,George (b-tb) | Fletcher,Stan (tuba) | Shank,Bud (as) | Pepper,Art (as) | Cooper,Bob (ts) | Caldarell,Bart (ts) | Gioga,Bob (bs) | Blaze,Ralph (g) | Bagley,Don (b) | Manne,Shelly (dr)
Baia
Chicago,Ill, rec. 8.4.1953
Kenton,Stan (p) | Childers,Buddy (tp) | Royal,Ernie (tp) | Candoli,Conte (tp) | Dennis,Don (tp) | Smith,Don (tp) | Burgess,Bob 'Bobby' (tb) | Rosolino,Frank (tb) | Shepard,Tom (tb) | Moon,Keith (tb) | Roberts,George (tb) | Dean,Vinnie (as) | Konitz,Lee (as) | Holman,Bill (ts) | Kamuca,Richie (ts) | Levy,Hank (bs) | Salvador,Sal (g) | Roberts,Glen (b) | Levey,Stan (dr) | Connor,Chris (voc)
You And The Night And The Music | My Reverie | I've Got You Under My Skin | Autumn In New York | April In Paris | How High The Moon | Crazy Rhythm | I Got It Bad And That Ain't Good
Chicago,Ill, rec. 8.7.1953
Kenton,Stan (p) | Childers,Buddy (tp) | Royal,Ernie (tp) | Candoli,Conte (tp) | Dennis,Don (tp) | Smith,Don (tp) | Burgess,Bob 'Bobby' (tb) | Rosolino,Frank (tb) | Shepard,Tom (tb) | Moon,Keith (tb) | Roberts,George (tb) | Carone,Don (as) | Konitz,Lee (as) | Sims,Zoot (ts) | Wasserman,Eddie (ts) | Ferina,Tony (bs) | Salvador,Sal (g) | Bagley,Don (b) | Levey,Stan (dr)
Don't Take Your Love From Me | More Love Than Your Love | Alone Too Long | The Lady In Red
Los Angeles,CA, rec. 31.3.1954
Kenton,Stan (p) | Childers,Buddy (tp) | Ferguson,Maynard (tp) | Williamson,Stu (tp) | Candoli,Pete (tp) | Paladino,Don (tp) | Bernhart,Milton 'Milt' (tb) | Fitzpatrick,Bob (tb) | Betts,Harry (tb) | Halliburton,John (tb) | Roberts,George (b-tb) | Fletcher,Stan (tuba) | Shank,Bud (as) | Klee,Harry (as) | Cooper,Bob (ts) | Holman,Bill (ts) | Gordon,Bob (bs) | Almeida,Laurindo (g) | Bagley,Don (b) | Levey,Stan (dr)
Under A Blanket Of Blue
Los Angeles,CA, rec. 6.5.1954
Kenton,Stan (p) | Candoli,Pete (tp) | Ferguson,Maynard (tp) | Williamson,Stu (tp) | Fagerquist,Don (tp) | Paladino,Don (tp) | Bernhart,Milton 'Milt' (tb) | Harper,Herbie (tb) | Howard,Joe (tb) | Halliburton,John (tb) | Roberts,George (b-tb) | Fletcher,Stan (tuba) | Shank,Bud (as) | Lang,Ronnie (as) | Cooper,Bob (ts) | Holman,Bill (ts) | Gordon,Bob (bs) | Gibbons,Joe (g) | Bagley,Don (b) | Levey,Stan (dr)

531572-2 | CD | At The Lighthouse
Cannonball Adderley Quintet
Sack O'Woe | Big 'P' | Blue Daniel | Azule Serape | Exodus | What Is This Thing Called Love | Our Delight
Live at The Lighthouse,Hermosa Beach,CA, rec. 16.10.1960
Adderley,Julian \'Cannonball\' (as) | Adderley,Nat (co) | Feldman,Victor (p) | Jones,Sam (b) | Hayes,Louis (dr)

531574-2 | CD | The Shearing Piano
George Shearing
Stella By Starlight | On The Street Where You Live | It Might As Well Be Spring | If | Sight No More | So Would I | Tenderly
Los Angeles,CA, rec. 10.12.1956
Shearing,George (p-solo)
Guilty | For Every Man There's A Woman | My Funny Valentine | Can't We Be Friends | It Never Entered My Mind | Memories Of You | Don't Explain | Homesick That's All | Reverie
Los Angeles,CA, rec. 12.12.1956
Shearing,George (p-solo)
Friendly Persuation | High On The Windy Hill | A Tune For Humming | In The Still Of The Night
Los Angeles,CA, rec. 23.6.1957
Shearing,George (p-solo)

531577-2 | CD | Django Reinhardt All Star Sessions
Coleman Hawkins With Michel Warlop And His Orchestra
Blue Moon | Avalon | What A Difference A Day Made | Stardust
Paris,France, rec. 2.3.1935
Hawkins,Coleman (ts) | Warlop,Michel (ld) | Briggs,Arthur (tp) | Chiboust,Noel (tp) | Allier,Pierre (tp) | Paquinet,Guy (tb) | Ekyan,Andre (as) | Lisee,Charles (as) | Combelle,Alix (ts) | Reinhardt,Django (g) | Grappelli,Stephane (p) | D'Hellemmes,Eugene (b) | Chaillou,Maurice (dr)
Coleman Hawkins And His All Star Jam Band
Honeysuckle Rose | Crazy Rhythm | Out Of Nowhere
Paris,France, rec. 28.4.1937
Hawkins,Coleman (ts) | Carter,Benny (as) | Ekyan,Andre (as) | Reinhardt,Django (g) | Grappelli,Stephane (p) | D'Hellemmes,Eugene (b) | Benford,Tommy (dr)
Benny Carter And His Orchestra
I'm Coming Virginia | Farewell Blues | Blue Light Blues
Paris,France, rec. 7.3.1938
Carter,Benny (tp,as) | Allen,Fletcher (as) | King,Bertie (cl,ts) | Combelle,Alix (ts) | Reinhardt,Django (g) | De Souza,Yorke (p) | Harrison,Len (b) | Montmarche,Robert (dr)
Rex Stewart And His Feetwarmers
Montmartre(Django's Jump) | Low Cotton | Finesse | I Know That You Know | Solid Old Man
Paris,France, rec. 5.4.1939
Stewart,Rex (co) | Bigard,Barney (cl,dr) | Reinhardt,Django (g) | Taylor,Billy (b)

534069-2 | CD | Something Cool(The Complete Mono & Stereo Versions) | EAN 724353406929
June Christy With The Pete Rugolo Orchestra
Something Cool
Los Angeles,CA, rec. 14.8.1953
Christy,June (voc) | Ferguson,Maynard (tp) | Gozzo,Conrad (tp) | Rogers,Shorty (tp) | Zito,Jimmy (tp) | Bernhart,Milton 'Milt' (tb) | Harper,Herbie (tb) | Pederson,Pullman 'Tommy' (tb) | Roberts,George (tb) | Bivona,Gus (as) | Shank,Bud (as) | Cooper,Bob (ts) | Nash,Ted (ts) |

LABELVERZEICHNIS

Gentry,Chuck (bs) | Clarkson,Geoff (p) | Kessel,Barney (g) | Mondragon,Joe (b) | Carlson,Frank (dr) | Rugolo,Pete (cond,arr)

Midnight Sun
Los Angeles,CA, rec. 27.12.1953
Christy,June (voc) | Gozzo,Conrad (tp) | Beach,Frank (tp) | Linn,Ray (tp) | Triscari,Ray (tp) | Rasey,Uan (tp) | Bernhart,Milton 'Milt' (tb) | Pederson,Pullman 'Tommy' (tb) | DiMaio,Nick (tb) | Noel,Dick (tb) | Reynolds,Dick (tb) | Herfurt,Arthur 'Skeets' (as) | Schwartz,Wilbur (as) | Fallensby,Fred (ts) | Nash,Ted (ts) | Gentry,Chuck (bs) | Smith,Paul (p) | Rizzi,Tony (g) | Mondragon,Joe (b) | Stoller,Alvin (dr) | Rugolo,Pete (cond,arr)

It Could Happen To You | Lonely House | I Should Care
Los Angeles,CA, rec. 18.1.1954
Christy,June (voc) | Ferguson,Maynard (tp) | Gozzo,Conrad (tp) | Rogers,Shorty (tp) | Bernhart,Milton 'Milt' (tb) | Betts,Harry (tb) | Pederson,Pullman 'Tommy' (tb) | Klee,Harry (as) | Shank,Bud (as) | Cooper,Bob (ts) | Nash,Ted (ts) | Rotella,John (bs) | Freeman,Russ (p) | Roberts,Howard (g) | Mondragon,Joe (b) | Manne,Shelly (dr) | Rugolo,Pete (cond,arr)

I'll Take Romance | A Stranger Called The Blues
Los Angeles,CA, rec. 19.1.1954
Christy,June (voc) | Ferguson,Maynard (tp) | Gozzo,Conrad (tp) | Rogers,Shorty (tp) | Bernhart,Milton 'Milt' (tb) | Betts,Harry (tb) | Pederson,Pullman 'Tommy' (tb) | Klee,Harry (as) | Shank,Bud (as) | Cooper,Bob (ts) | Nash,Ted (ts) | Gentry,Chuck (as) | Freeman,Russ (p) | Roberts,Howard (g) | Mondragon,Joe (b) | Manne,Shelly (dr) | Rugolo,Pete (cond,arr)

Softly As In A Morning Sunrise
Los Angeles,CA, rec. 29.5.1954
Christy,June (voc) | Candoli,Conte (tp) | Gozzo,Conrad (tp) | Rogers,Shorty (tp) | Bernhart,Milton 'Milt' (tb) | Fitzpatrick,Bob (tb) | Harper,Herbie (tb) | Shank,Bud (as) | Cooper,Bob (ts) | Giuffre,Jimmy (ts) | Gordon,Bob (bs) | Williamson,Claude (p) | Roberts,Howard (g) | Mondragon,Joe (b) | Manne,Shelly (dr) | Rugolo,Pete (cond,arr)

This Time The Dream's On Me | The Night We Called It A Day | I'm Thrilled
Los Angeles,CA, rec. 10.5.1955
Christy,June (voc) | Candoli,Conte (tp) | Childers,Buddy (tp) | Gozzo,Conrad (tp) | Rogers,Shorty (tp) | Zito,Jimmy (tp) | Bernhart,Milton 'Milt' (tb) | Betts,Harry (tb) | Halliburton,John (tb) | Harper,Herbie (tb) | Roberts,George (tb) | Klee,Harry (as) | Shank,Bud (as) | Holman,Bill (ts) | Montrose,Jack (ts) | Giuffre,Jimmy (bs) | Rugolo,Pete (p,arr,cond) | Almeida,Laurindo (g) | Mondragon,Joe (b) | Manne,Shelly (dr)

Softly As In A Morning Sunrise | Midnight Sun | Something Cool
Los Angeles,CA, rec. 26.4.1960
Christy,June (voc) | Candoli,Conte (tp) | Gozzo,Conrad (tp) | Mitchell,Ollie (tp) | Beach,Frank (tp) | Bernhart,Milton 'Milt' (tb) | Betts,Harry (tb) | Rosolino,Frank (tb) | Roberts,George (b-tb) | Klee,Harry (as) | Shank,Bud (as) | Horn,Paul (as) | Cooper,Bob (ts) | Gentry,Chuck (bs) | Castro,Joe (p) | Marshall,Jack (g) | Mondragon,Joe (b) | Bunker,Larry (dr) | Rugolo,Pete (cond,arr)

It Could Happen To You | I'll Take Romance | A Stranger Called The Blues | I'm Thrilled
Los Angeles,CA, rec. 27.4.1960
Christy,June (voc) | Candoli,Conte (tp) | Gozzo,Conrad (tp) | Beach,Frank (tp) | Bernhart,Milton 'Milt' (tb) | Rosolino,Frank (tb) | Roberts,George (b-tb) | DeRosa,Vince (fr-h) | Stephens,Phil (tuba) | Collette,Buddy (fl,as) | Shank,Bud (as) | Horn,Paul (as) | Cooper,Bob (ts) | Gentry,Chuck (bs) | Castro,Joe (p) | Marshall,Jack (g) | Mondragon,Joe (b) | Bunker,Larry (dr) | Rugolo,Pete (cond,arr)

I Should Care | This Time The Dream's On Me | Lonely House | The Night We Called It A Day
Los Angeles,CA, rec. 28.4.2960
Christy,June (voc) | Candoli,Conte (tp) | Beach,Frank (tp) | Gozzo,Conrad (tp) | Bernhart,Milton 'Milt' (tb) | Rosolino,Frank (tb) | Roberts,George (b-tb) | DeRosa,Vince (fr-h) | Stephens,Phil (tuba) | Klee,Harry (as) | Shank,Bud (as) | Horn,Paul (as) | Cooper,Bob (ts) | Gentry,Chuck (bs) | Castro,Joe (p) | Marshall,Jack (g) | Mondragon,Joe (b) | Bunker,Larry (dr) | Rugolo,Pete (cond,arr)

535206-2 | CD | Billy May's Big Fat Brass/Bill's Bag
Billy May And His Orchestra
Brassmen's Holiday | Autumn Leaves | Love Is The Thing | Ping Pong | Moonlight Becomes You | Pawn Ticket | Solving The Riddle | Invitation | The Continental | Return Of The Zombie | On A Little Street In Singapore | Joom Jooms
Los Angeles,CA, rec. 1958
May,Billy (arr,ld) | Gozzo,Conrad (tp) | Beach,Frank (tp) | Best,John (tp) | Rasey,Uan (tp) | Candoli,Pete (tp) | Klein,Manny (tp) | Zentner,Si (tb) | Pederson,Pullman 'Tommy' (tb) | Kusby,Eddie (tb) | Roberts,George (b-tb) | DeRosa,Vince (fr-h) | Cave,Jack (fr-h) | Decker,James 'Jimmy' (fr-h) | Perissi,Richard 'Dick' (fr-h) | Franz,Art (fr-h) | Callender,Red (tuba) | Karella,Clarance (tuba) | Mills,Verley (harp) | Smith,Paul (p) | Hendrickson,Al (g) | Mondragon,Joe (b) | Penner,Ralph (b) | Stoller,Alvin (dr)

Children Of The Night | Uh! Oh!(Nutty Squirrels) | The Preacher | Playboy's Theme | The Late Late Show | Dat Dere | Filet Of Soul | Whisper Not | Miles Behind | Moanin' | My Little Suede Shoes | Shiny Stockings
Los Angeles,CA, rec. 1963
May,Billy (arr,ld) | Horn,Paul (reeds) | Orchestra | details unknown

535208-2 | CD | About The Blues/London By Night
Julie London With Russ Garcia And His Orchestra
Basin Street Blues | I Gotta Right To Sing The Blues | A Nightingale Sang In Berkeley Square | Get Set For The Blues | Invitation To The Blues | Bye Bye Blues | Meaning Of The Blues | About Three The Blues | Sunday Blues | The Blues Is All I Ever Had | Blues In The Night | Bouquet Of Blues
details unknown, rec. details unknown
London,Julie (voc) | Garcia,Russell (cond,arr) | details unknown
Julie London With Pete King And His Orchestra
Well Sir | That's For Me | Mad About The Boy | In The Middle Of A Kiss | Just The Way I Am | My Man's Gone Now | Something I Dreamed Last Night | Pousse Cafe | Nobody's Heart | The Exciting Life | That Old Feeling | Cloudy Morning
London,Julie (voc) | King,Pete (arr,cond) | details unknown

535209-2 | CD | This Is June Christy/June Christy Recalls Those Kenton Days
June Christy With Orchestra
My Heart Belongs To Daddy | Whee Baby | You Took Advantage Of Me | Get Happy | Look Out Up There | Great Scot | Kicks | Why Do You Have To Go Home | Bei Mir Bist Du Schön | Until The Real Thing Comes Along | I'll Remember April | I Never Want To Look Into Those Eyes | Just A-Sittin' And A-Rockin' | A Hundred Years From Today | The Lonesome Road | She's Funny That Way | It's A Pitty To Say Goodnight | Willow Weep For Me | Easy Street | Across The Alley From The Alamo | Come Rain Or Come Shine | How High The Moon
different Places, rec. 1956-1959
Christy,June (voc) | Orchestra | details not on the cover

535210-2 | CD | Pass Me By/Big Spender
Peggy Lee With Orchestra
Pass Me By | That's What It Takes
Los Angeles,CA, rec. 9.12.1964
Lee,Peggy (voc) | Big Band | Grusin,Dave (ld) | Rogers,Shorty (arr,ld) | details unknown
Peggy Lee With Lou Levy's Orchestra
A Hard Day's Night | Dear Heart | Bewitched Bothered And Bewildered | Snakin' Up On You | I Wanna Be Around | My Love,Forgive Me | Quiet Nights Of Quiet Stars(Corcovado) | Love | You Always Hurt The One You Love
Los Angeles,CA, rec. 1965
Lee,Peggy (voc) | personal included: | Levy,Lou (p) | Bain,Bob (g) | Pisano,John (g) | Pittman,Bill (g) | Budimir,Dennis (g) | Whitlock,Bob (b) | Guerin,John (dr) | Aquabella,Francisco (congas,bongos) | details unknown
Peggy Lee With The Bill Holman Orchestra
It's A Wonderful World | Let's Fall In Love | Come Back To Me | Big Spender
Los Angeles,CA, rec. 27.10.1965
Lee,Peggy (voc) | Holman,Bill (arr,ld) | details unknown
I Must Know | I'll Only Miss Him When I Think Of Him | Gotta Travel On | Watch What Happens
Los Angeles,CA, rec. 29.10.1965
Lee,Peggy (voc) | Holman,Bill (arr,ld) | details unknown
Peggy Lee With Orchestra
You Don't Know | You've Got Possibilities
Los Angeles,CA, rec. 1.2.1966
Lee,Peggy (voc) | details unknown
Alright,Okay,You Win
Los Angeles,CA, rec. 1967
Lee,Peggy (voc) | details unknown

535211-2 | CD | Home Of Happy Feet/Swing! Staged For Sound!
Van Alexander Orchestra
Let's Get Together | Chant Of The Weed | East St.Louis Toodle-Oo | Ride Red Ride
Los Angeles,CA, rec. 1959
Alexander,Van (ld) | Gozzo,Conrad (tp) | Klein,Manny (tp) | Rasey,Uan (tp) | Sherock,Shorty (tp) | Howard,Joe (tb) | Kusby,Eddie (tb) | Pederson,Pullman 'Tommy' (tb) | Shroyer,Kenny (tb) | Horn,Paul (reeds) | Jacobs,Jules (reeds) | Johnson,Plas (reeds) | Most,Abe (reeds) | Stone,Butch (reeds) | Kessel,Barney (g) | Smith,Paul (p) | Comfort,Joe (b) | Cottler,Irv (dr)
Until The Real Thing Comes Along | Uptown Rhapsody | I Would Do Anything For You | A-Tisket A-Tasket
Alexander,Van (ld) | Gozzo,Conrad (tp) | Klein,Manny (tp) | Sherock,Shorty (tp) | Howard,Joe (tb) | Bernhart,Milton 'Milt' (tb) | Gentry,Chuck (reeds) | Johnson,Plas (reeds) | Most,Abe (reeds) | Lang,Ronnie (reeds) | Kessel,Barney (g) | Sherman,Ray (p) | Mondragon,Joe (b) | Manne,Shelly (dr)
Stompin' At The Savoy | Undecided | Organ Grinder's Swing | Christopher Columbus
Alexander,Van (ld) | Klein,Manny (tp) | Sherock,Shorty (tp) | Bernhart,Milton 'Milt' (tb) | Gentry,Chuck (reeds) | Johnson,Plas (reeds) | Most,Abe (reeds) | Lang,Ronnie (reeds) | Kessel,Barney (g) | Clarkson,Geoff (p) | Mondragon,Joe (b) | Manne,Shelly (dr)
Get Me To The Church On Time | I Won't Dance | Way Down Yonder In New Orleans | In A Mellow Tone | Stealin' Apples | Tappin' On The Trapps | Ol' Man River | Lulu's Back In Town | High Noon | Say It Isn't So | Blues In Twos | Strike Up The Band
Los Angeles,CA, rec. 1961
Alexander,Van (ld) | personal included: | Graves,Joe (tp) | Sherock,Shorty (tp) | Bernhart,Milton 'Milt' (tb) | Kenney,Dick (tb) | Clark,Mahlon (reeds) | Rosa,Eddie (reeds) | Jacob,Julie (reeds) | Gordon,Justin (reeds) | Johnson,Plas (reeds) | Russin,Irving 'Babe' (reeds) | Rose,Henri (p) | Stevenson,Bobby (p) | Manne,Shelly (dr) | Stoller,Alvin (dr) | Guerrero,Frank 'Chico' (perc) | Holland,Milt (perc) | Cottler,Irv (perc) | Navarra,Jack (perc) | details unknown

538225-2 | CD | Basie Meets Bond | EAN 724353822521
Count Basie And His Orchestra
007 | The Golden Horn | Girl Trouble | Kingston Calypso | Goldfinger | Thunderball | From Russia With Love | Dr. No's Fantasy | Underneath The Mango Tree | The James Bond Theme | Dr. No's Fantasy(alt.take)
NYC, rec. December 1965
Basie,Count (p) | Aarons,Albert 'Al' (tp) | Cohn[Cohen],Sonny (tp) | Davenport,Wallace (tp) | Guilbeau,Phil (tp) | Chambers,Henderson (tb) | Grey,Al (tb) | Mitchell,Grover (tb) | Hughes,Bill (b-tb) | Royal,Marshall (as) | Plater,Bobby (fl,as) | Dixon,Eric (fl,ts) | Davis,Eddie 'Lockjaw' (ts) | Fowlkes,Charlie (b-cl,bs) | Green,Freddie (g) | Keenan,Norman (b) | Payne,Sonny (dr)

542308-2 | CD | Beauty And The Beat | EAN 724354230820
Peggy Lee With George Shearing
Do I Love You | I Lost My Sugar In Salt Lake City | If Dreams Come True | All Too Soon | Blue Prelude | You Came A Long Way From St. Louis | Always True To You In My Fashion | There'll Be Other Spring | Get Out Of Town
Live at The Americana Hotel,Miami,Florida, rec. 29.5.1959
Lee,Peggy (voc) | Shearing,George (p) | Richards,Emil (vib) | Thielemans,Jean 'Toots' (g) | Pruitt,Carl (b) | Brice,Percy (dr) | Peraza,Armando (congas)
George Shearing And His Quintet
Isn't It Romantic | Satin Doll | Mambo In Miami
Shearing,George (p) | Richards,Emil (vib) | Thielemans,Jean 'Toots' (g) | Pruitt,Carl (b) | Brice,Percy (dr) | Peraza,Armando (congas)
Peggy Lee With The George Shearing Trio
Nobody's Heat Belongs To Me | Don't Ever Leave Me
Lee,Peggy (voc) | Shearing,George (p) | Pruitt,Carl (b) | Brice,Percy (dr)

590955-2 | CD | Latin Fever:The Wild Rhythms Of Jack Costanza | EAN 724359095523
Jack Costanzo Group
Sax Con Ritmo | Peanut Vendor | Bajo Numero Uno | Taboo | Malaguena | Latin Fever | Cumbanchero | Hornacopia | La Paloma | Oye Negra | Mama Yo Quiero | Drum-A-Mania
Los Angeles,CA, rec. 1958
Costanza,Jack (bongos) | Lopez,Paul (tp) | Alcaraz,Angie (fl) | Corre,Jay (ts) | Cano,Eddie (p) | Reyes,Tony (b) | Aparicio,Eddie (dr) | Rivera,Ray (dr)

597072-2 | LP | Things Are Swingin'
Peggy Lee With Jack Marshall's Music
It's A Wonderful World | Things Are Swingin' | Alright,Okay,You Win | Ridin' High | It's Been A Long Long Time | Lullaby In Rhythm | Alone Together | I'm Beginning To See The Light | It's A Good Good Night | You're Getting To Be A Habit With Me | You're Mine You | Life Is For Livin'
Los Angeles,CA, rec. 1958/1959
Lee,Peggy (voc) | Marshall,Jack (ld) | details unknown

795482-2 | CD | The Best Of Cannonball Adderley:The Capitol Years
Cannonball Adderley-Nat Adderley Sextet
The Work Song
Live in Belgium, rec. 5.8.1962
Adderley,Julian \'Cannonball\' (as) | Adderley,Nat (co) | Lateef,Yusef (ts) | Zawinul,Joe (p) | Jones,Sam (b) | Hayes,Louis (dr)
The Jive Samba
Live at The Jazz Workshop,San Francisco,CA, rec. 22.9.1962
Adderley,Julian \'Cannonball\' (as) | Adderley,Nat (co) | Lateef,Yusef (fl) | Zawinul,Joe (p) | Jones,Sam (b) | Hayes,Louis (dr)
Fiddler On The Roof
NYC, rec. 19.10.1964
Adderley,Julian \'Cannonball\' (as) | Adderley,Nat (co) | Lloyd,Charles (ts) | Zawinul,Joe (p) | Jones,Sam (b) | Hayes,Louis (dr)
Cannonball Adderley Quintet
Mercy, Mercy, Mercy
Los Angeles,CA, rec. 20.10.1966
Adderley,Julian \'Cannonball\' (as) | Adderley,Nat (co) | Zawinul,Joe (el-p) | Gaskin,Victor (b) | McCurdy,Roy (dr)
Why Am I Treated So Bad
Los Angeles,CA, rec. 6.3.1967
Adderley,Julian \'Cannonball\' (as) | Adderley,Nat (co) | Zawinul,Joe (el-p) | Gaskin,Victor (b) | McCurdy,Roy (dr)
Walk Tall
Los Angeles,CA, rec. 12.6.1967
Adderley,Julian \'Cannonball\' (as) | Adderley,Nat (co) | Zawinul,Joe (el-p) | Gaskin,Victor (b) | McCurdy,Roy (dr)
74 Miles Away
Los Angeles,CA, rec. 24.6.1967
Adderley,Julian \'Cannonball\' (as) | Adderley,Nat (co) | Zawinul,Joe (el-p) | Gaskin,Victor (b) | McCurdy,Roy (dr)
Country Preacher
Live in Chicago,Ill, rec. October 1969
Adderley,Julian \'Cannonball\' (as) | Adderley,Nat (co) | Zawinul,Joe (el-p) | Booker,Walter (b) | McCurdy,Roy (dr)

798288-2 | CD | The Instrumental Classics
Nat King Cole Trio
The Man I Love | Body And Soul | Prelude In C Sharp Minor | What Is This Thing Called Love
Los Angeles,CA, rec. 17.1.1944
Cole,Nat King (p) | Moore,Oscar (g) | Miller,Johnny (b)
Easy Listening Blues
Los Angeles,CA, rec. 6.3.1944
Cole,Nat King (p) | Moore,Oscar (g) | Miller,Johnny (b)
Sweet Georgia Brown
Los Angeles,CA, rec. 23.5.1945
Cole,Nat King (p) | Moore,Oscar (g) | Miller,Johnny (b)
This Way Out
NYC, rec. 18.10.1945
Cole,Nat King (p) | Moore,Oscar (g) | Miller,Johnny (b)
Jumpin' At Capitol
Los Angeles,CA, rec. 30.11.1945
Cole,Nat King (p) | Moore,Oscar (g) | Miller,Johnny (b)
Smoke Gets In Your Eyes
NYC, rec. 30.10.1946
Cole,Nat King (p) | Moore,Oscar (g) | Miller,Johnny (b)
Honeysuckle Rose
Los Angeles,CA, rec. 2.7.1947
Cole,Nat King (p) | Moore,Oscar (g) | Miller,Johnny (b)
Rhumba Azul
Los Angeles,CA, rec. 6.8.1947
Cole,Nat King (p) | Moore,Oscar (g) | Miller,Johnny (b)
Moonlight In Vermont | How High The Moon
Los Angeles,CA, rec. 13.8.1947
Cole,Nat King (p) | Moore,Oscar (g) | Miller,Johnny (b)
I'll Never Be The Same | These Foolish Things Remind Me On You
Los Angeles,CA, rec. 20.8.1947
Cole,Nat King (p) | Moore,Oscar (g) | Miller,Johnny (b)
Nat King Cole Quartet
Laugh! Cool Clown
NYC, rec. 22.3.1949
Cole,Nat King (p) | Ashby,Irving (g) | Comfort,Joe (b) | Costanzo,Jack (bongos)
Nat King Cole Quartet With The Pete Rugolo Orchestra
Peaches
NYC, rec. 30.3.1949
Cole,Nat King (p) | Ashby,Irving (g) | Comfort,Joe (b) | Costanzo,Jack (bongos) | Rugolo,Pete (cond,arr) | details unknown

799190-2 | CD | The Swingin's Mutual
Nancy Wilson With George Shearing And His Quintet
The Things We Did Last Summer | All Night Long | Born To Be Blue | My Gentleman Friend | I Remember Clifford
NYC, rec. 29.6.1960
Wilson,Nancy (voc) | Shearing,George (p) | Chaisson,Warren (vib) | Garcia,Dick (g) | Pena,Ralph (b) | Fournier,Vernell (dr) | Peraza,Armando (perc)
On Green Dolphin Street | Let's Live Again | Whisper Not
NYC, rec. 5.7.1960
Wilson,Nancy (voc) | Shearing,George (p) | Chaisson,Warren (vib) | Garcia,Dick (g) | Pena,Ralph (b) | Fournier,Vernell (dr) | Peraza,Armando (perc)
The Nearness Of You | Evansville | Don't Call Me I'll Call You | Inspiration
NYC, rec. 6.7.1960
Wilson,Nancy (voc) | Shearing,George (p) | Chaisson,Warren (vib) | Garcia,Dick (g) | Pena,Ralph (b) | Fournier,Vernell (dr) | Peraza,Armando (perc)
George Shearing And His Quintet
You Are There | Wait 'Till You See Her | Blue Lou | Oh Look At Me Now | Lullaby Of Birdland
NYC, rec. 7.1.1961
Shearing,George (p) | Chaisson,Warren (vib) | Garcia,Dick (g) | Pena,Ralph (b) | Fournier,Vernell (dr) | Peraza,Armando (perc)

821325-2 | 2 CD | Art Tatum:Complete Capitol Recordings | EAN 724382132523
Art Tatum
Willow Weep For Me | I Cover The Waterfront | Aunt Hagar's Blues | Nice Work If You Can Get It | Someone To Watch Over Me | Dardanella
Los Angeles,CA, rec. 13.7.1949
Tatum,Art (p-solo)
Time On My Hands | Sweet Lorraine | Somebody Loves Me | Don't Blame Me
Los Angeles,CA, rec. 25.7.1949
Tatum,Art (p-solo)
My Heart Stood Still | You Took Advantage Of Me | I Gotta Right To Sing The Blues | How High The Moon | Goin' Home | Makin' Whoopee | Blue Skies | It's The Talk Of The Town | Dancing In The Dark | Tenderly
Los Angeles,CA, rec. 29.9.1949
Tatum,Art (p-solo)
Art Tatum Trio
September Song | Melody In F,Opus 3 No.1 | Tea For Two | Out Of Nowhere | Just One Of Those Things | Back Home Again In Indiana | Would You Just Like To Take A Walk | Lover
NYC, rec. 20.12.1952
Tatum,Art (p) | Barksdale,Everett (g) | Stewart,Slam (b)
Interview with Art Tatum and Paul Weston
Tatum,Art (talking) | Weston,Paul (talking)

829915-2 | CD | Mercy Mercy Mercy
Cannonball Adderley Quintet
Fun | Games | Mercy, Mercy, Mercy | Sticks | Hippodelphia | Sack O'Woe
Live at 'The Club,Los Angels,CA, rec. 20.10.1966
Adderley,Julian \'Cannonball\' (as) | Adderley,Nat (co) | Zawinul,Joe (p,el-p) | Gaskin,Victor (b) | McCurdy,Roy (dr)

852677-2 | CD | Aspects | EAN 724385267727
Benny Carter And His Orchestra
June In January | February Fiesta | I'll Remember April | On Morning In May | August Moon | September Song | February Fiesta(alt.take) | August Moon(alt.take)
Los Angeles,CA, rec. late summer 1958
Carter,Benny (as) | Gozzo,Conrad (tp) | Sherock,Shorty (tp) | Candoli,Pete (tp) | Rasey,Uan (tp) | Pederson,Pullman 'Tommy' (tb) | Harper,Herbie (tb) | Roberts,George (tb) | Collette,Buddy (reeds) | Gordon,Justin (reeds) | Gentry,Chuck (reeds) | Bunker,Larry (vib,bongos) | Ross,Arnold (p) | Gibbons,Bobby (g) | Comfort,Joe (b) | Manne,Shelly (dr)
March Wind | June Is Busting Out All Over | Sleigh Ride In July | Something For October | Swingin' In November | Roses In December | June Is Busting Out All Over(alt.take) | Swingin' In November(alt.take)
Carter,Benny (as) | Porcino,Al (tp) | Williamson,Stu (tb) | Triscari,Joe (tp) | Gordon,Joe (tp) | Pederson,Pullman 'Tommy' (tb) | Rosolino,Frank (tb) | Bown,Russ (tb) | Collette,Buddy (reeds) | Green,Bill (reeds) | Grant,Jewell (reeds) | Johnson,Plas (reeds) | Wiggins,Gerald 'Gerry' (p) | Kessel,Barney (g) | Comfort,Joe (b) | Manne,Shelly (dr)

855455-2 | CD | The Song Is June | EAN 724385545528
June Christy With The Pete Rugolo Orchestra
Nobody's Heart | Night Time Was My Mother | Saturday's Children
Los Angeles,CA, rec. 24.7.1958
Christy,June (voc) | Orchestra | Rugolo,Pete (cond,arr) | details unknown
The One I Love Belongs To Somebody Else | My Shining Hour | I Wished On The Moon | As Long As I Live
Los Angeles,CA, rec. 11.8.1958
Christy,June (voc) | Orchestra | Rugolo,Pete (cond,arr) | details unknown
Spring Can Really Hang You Up The Most | I Remember You | The Song Is You
Los Angeles,CA, rec. 15.8.1958

Christy,June (voc) | Orchestra | Rugolo,Pete (cond,arr) | details unknown

You Wear Love So Well | The Bad And The Beautiful | Who Cares About April | Out Of The Shadow | Somewhere If Not In Heaven

Los Angeles,CA, rec. 8.8.1960

Christy,June (voc) | Orchestra | Rugolo,Pete (cond,arr) | details unknown

Remind Me | Out Of This World | Off Beat | You Say You Care | A Sleeping Bee

Los Angeles,CA, rec. 19.8.1960

Christy,June (voc) | Orchestra | Rugolo,Pete (cond,arr) | details unknown

Caprice | Fenn Music

CAP 21440 | CD | Contra Post

Palle Danielsson Quartet

Contra Post | Tiramisu | Indecisione | Penta | Out Of Habit | 7 Notes,7 Days,7 Planets | Not Yet | Blue Lilacs

Oslo,N, rec. 30.5.-1.6.1994

Danielsson,Palle (b) | Milder,Joakim (sax) | Marcotulli,Rita (p) | Kjellberg,Anders (dr)

Palle Danielsson Quintet

Monk's Mood | Luna

Palle Danielsson's Home,Kolsäter, rec. 29.4.& 29.6.1994

Danielsson,Palle (b) | Milder,Joakim (sax) | Klinghagen,Göran (g) | Marcotulli,Rita (p) | Kjellberg,Anders (dr)

CBS | Sony Music

460883-2 | CD | If This Bass Could Only Talk

Stanley Clarke-Gregory Himes

If This Bass Could Only Talk | Basically Taps

Los Angeles,CA, rec. 1988

Clarke,Stanley (b) | Hines,Gregory (tap-dancing)

Stanley Clarke-John Robinson

I Want To Play For Ya

Clarke,Stanley (synth,b,el-b) | Robinson,John (dr)

Stanley Clarke Group

Goodbye Pork Pie Hat(dedicated to Jaco Pastorius & Gil Evans)

Los Altos Hill,CA, rec. 1988

Clarke,Stanley (b,el-b) | Shorter,Wayne (ss) | Arkin,Edward (synth) | Brown,Gerry (dr)

Stories To Tell

Los Angeles,CA, rec. 1988

Clarke,Stanley (synth,b,el-b) | Holdsworth,Allan (el-g) | Copeland,Stewart (dr)

Workin' Man | Tradition

Clarke,Stanley (el-b) | Hunt,Steve (synth) | Earl,Jimmy (low-b) | Brown,Gerry (dr)

Funny How Time Flies(When You're Having Fun)

Clarke,Stanley (b-g,el-b) | Hubbard,Freddie (tp) | Taylor,Vance (p) | Miller,Byron (b-synth) | Ndugu[Leon Chancler] (dr) | Da Costa,Paulinho (perc)

Come Take My Hand

Clarke,Stanley (synth,el-b) | Howard,George (ss) | Duke,George (p) | Robinson,John (dr)

461099-2 | CD | Ballads

Miles Davis Quintet

Bye Bye Blackbird

Live at The Black Hawk,San Francisco,CA, rec. 21.4.1961

Davis,Miles (tp) | Mobley,Hank (ts) | Kelly,Wynton (p) | Chambers,Paul (b) | Cobb,Jimmy (dr)

Miles Davis With Orchestra

Corcovado(Quiet Nights)

NYC, rec. 27.7.1962

Davis,Miles (tp) | Lacy,Steve (ss) | details unknown,Orchestra

Miles Davis With Gil Evans & His Orchestra

Once Upon A Summertime | Song No.2

NYC, rec. 6.11.1962

Davis,Miles (tp) | Evans,Gil (cond,arr) | Royal,Ernie (tp) | Buffington,Jimmy (fr-h) | Barrows,John (fr-h) | Rehak,Frank (tb) | Putnam,Janet (harp) | Cobb,Jimmy (dr) | Jones,Elvin (perc) | details unknown

Miles Davis Quintet

I Fall In Love Too Easily | Baby Won't You Please Come Home | Basin Street Blues

NYC, rec. 16.4.1963

Davis,Miles (tp) | Coleman,George (ts) | Feldman,Victor (p) | Carter,Ron (b) | Butler,Frank (dr)

462403-2 | CD | The Great Concerts

Dave Brubeck Quartet

Pennies From Heaven | For All We Know | Blue Rondo A La Turk | Take Five

Live at Carnegie Hall,NYC, rec. 21.2.1963

Brubeck,Dave (p) | Desmond,Paul (as) | Wright,Eugene 'Gene' (b) | Morello,Joe (dr)

Take The 'A' Train | The Real Ambassador

Concertgebouw,Amsterdam, rec. 3.12.1962

Brubeck,Dave (p) | Desmond,Paul (as) | Wright,Eugene 'Gene' (b) | Morello,Joe (dr)

Wonderful Copenhagen | Like Someone In Love | Tangerine

Copenhagen,Denmark, rec. 5.3.1958

Brubeck,Dave (p) | Desmond,Paul (as) | Wright,Eugene 'Gene' (b) | Morello,Joe (dr)

462959-2 | CD | Greatest Hits

Duke Ellington And His Orchestra

Take The 'A' Train | Sophisticated Lady | I Got It Bad And That Ain't Good | Skin Deep

Live at Newport,Rhode Island, rec. 7.7.1956

Ellington,Duke (p) | Cook,Willie (tp) | Nance,Ray (tp) | Terry,Clark (tp) | Anderson,Cat (tp) | Sanders,John (tb) | Jackson,Quentin (tb) | Woodman,Britt (tb) | Procope,Russell (as) | Hodges,Johnny (as) | Gonsalves,Paul (ts) | Hamilton,Jimmy (cl,ts) | Carney,Harry (bs) | Woode,Jimmy (b) | Woodyard,Sam (dr)

Mood Indigo

NYC, rec. 9.9.1957

Ellington,Duke (p) | Cook,Willie (tp) | Nance,Ray (tp) | Terry,Clark (tp) | Anderson,Cat (tp) | Baker,Harold 'Shorty' (tp) | Sanders,John (tb) | Woodman,Britt (tb) | Jackson,Quentin (tb) | Procope,Russell (as) | Hodges,Johnny (as) | Hamilton,Jimmy (cl,ts) | Gonsalves,Paul (ts) | Carney,Harry (bs) | Woode,Jimmy (b) | Woodyard,Sam (dr)

Prelude To A Kiss

rec. 1.10.1957

Ellington,Duke (p) | Cook,Willie (tp) | Nance,Ray (tp) | Terry,Clark (tp) | Anderson,Cat (tp) | Baker,Harold 'Shorty' (tp) | Sanders,John (tb) | Woodman,Britt (tb) | Jackson,Quentin (tb) | Procope,Russell (as) | Hodges,Johnny (as) | Hamilton,Jimmy (cl,ts) | Gonsalves,Paul (ts) | Carney,Harry (bs) | Woode,Jimmy (b) | Woodyard,Sam (dr)

In My Solitude

rec. 14.10.1957

Ellington,Duke (p) | Cook,Willie (tp) | Nance,Ray (tp) | Terry,Clark (tp) | Anderson,Cat (tp) | Baker,Harold 'Shorty' (tp) | Sanders,John (tb) | Woodman,Britt (tb) | Jackson,Quentin (tb) | Procope,Russell (as) | Hodges,Johnny (as) | Hamilton,Jimmy (cl,ts) | Gonsalves,Paul (ts) | Carney,Harry (bs) | Woode,Jimmy (b) | Woodyard,Sam (dr)

Satin Doll

NYC, rec. 31.3.1958

Ellington,Duke (p) | Ford,Andrew (tp) | Terry,Clark (tp) | Anderson,Cat (tp) | Baker,Harold 'Shorty' (tp) | Sanders,John (tb) | Woodman,Britt (tb) | Jackson,Quentin (tb) | Procope,Russell (as) | Hodges,Johnny (as) | Hamilton,Jimmy (cl,ts) | Gonsalves,Paul (ts) | Carney,Harry (bs) | Woode,Jimmy (b) | Woodyard,Sam (dr)

Perdido | The Mooche

Chicago,Ill, rec. 10.8.1952

Ellington,Duke (p) | Cook,Willie (tp) | Nance,Ray (tp) | Terry,Clark (tp) | Anderson,Cat (tp) | Tizol,Juan (tb) | Jackson,Quentin (tb) | Woodman,Britt (tb) | Procope,Russell (as) | Jefferson,Hilton (as) | Hamilton,Jimmy (cl,ts) | Gonsalves,Paul (ts) | Carney,Harry (bs) | Marshall,Wendell (b) | Bellson,Louie (dr)

Duke Ellington And His Award Winners

C Jam Blues

NYC, rec. 2.12.1959

Ellington,Duke (p) | Nance,Ray (tp,v) | Wood,Booty (tb) | Gee,Matthew (tb) | Procope,Russell (cl,as) | Hodges,Johnny (as) | Hamilton,Jimmy (cl,ts) | Gonsalves,Paul (ts) | Carney,Harry (bs) | Woode,Jimmy (b) | Johnson,James (dr)

Duke Ellington And His Famous Orchestra

Caravan

NYC, rec. 14.5.1937

Ellington,Duke (p) | Williams,Cootie (tp) | Stewart,Rex (tp) | Jones,Wallace (tp) | Nanton,Joe 'Tricky Sam' (tb) | Tizol,Juan (tb) | Brown,Lawrence (tb) | Bigard,Barney (cl,ts) | Hodges,Johnny (as) | Hardwicke,Otto (as) | Carney,Harry (bs) | Guy,Fred (g) | Taylor,Billy (b) | Alvis,Hayes (b) | Greer,William 'Sonny' (dr)

465134-2 | CD | Trio Jeepy

Branford Marsalis Trio

Housed From Edward | The Nearness Of You | Three Little Words | Makin' Whoopee | U.M.M.G.(Upper Manhattan Medical Group) | Gut Bucket Steepy | Makin' Whoopee(reprise)

NYC, rec. 3./4.1.1988

Marsalis,Branford (sax) | Hinton,Milt (b) | Watts,Jeff 'Tain' (dr)

Doxy | Peace | Random Abstract(Tain's Rampage)

Marsalis,Branford (sax) | Felix,Delbert (b) | Watts,Jeff 'Tain' (dr)

465703-2 | CD | Dave Brubeck's Greatest Hits

Dave Brubeck Quartet

Take Five | It's A Raggy Waltz | Unsquare Dance | The Duke | Mister Broadway | I'm In A Dancing Mood | Trolley Song | Camptown Races | In Your Own Sweet Way | Blue Rondo A La Turk

rec. details unknown

Brubeck,Dave (p) | Desmond,Paul (as) | Morello,Joe (dr) | Wright,Eugene 'Gene' (b)

466736-2 | CD | We Are In Love

Harry Connick Jr. Quartet

We Are In Love | Only 'Cause I Don't Have You | Recipe For Love | Drifting | Forever, For Now | Heavenly | Just A Boy | I've Got A Great Idea | It's All Right With Me | Burried In Blue

North Hollywood,CA/NYC, rec. March-May 1990

Connick Jr.,Harry (p,voc) | Malone,Russell (g) | Wolfe,Benjamin Jonah 'Ben' (b) | Powell,Shannon (dr)

Harry Connick Jr. Quartet With Branford Marsalis

A Nightingale Sang In Berkeley Square | I'll Dream Of You Again

Connick Jr.,Harry (p,voc) | Marsalis,Branford (ss,ts) | Malone,Russell (g) | Wolfe,Benjamin Jonah 'Ben' (b) | Powell,Shannon (dr)

466870-2 | CD | Crazy People Music

Branford Marsalis Quartet

Spartacus | The Dark Knight | Wolverine | Mr.Steepee | Rose Petals | Random Abstract(Diddle-It) | The Ballad Of Chet Kincaid(Hikky-Burr)

NYC, rec. 1990

Marsalis,Branford (ss,ts) | Kirkland,Kenny (p) | Hurst III,Robert Leslie (b) | Watts,Jeff 'Tain' (dr)

467087-2 | 2 CD | Pangaea

Miles Davis Group

Zimbabwe(part 1&2) | Gondwana(part 1&2)

rec. 1.2.1975

Davis,Miles (tp,org) | Fortune,Sonny (fl,ss,as) | Henderson,Michael (el-b) | Cosey,Pete (g,synth,perc) | Lucas,Reggie (g) | Foster,Al (dr) | M'tume,James[Forman] (perc,congas,rythm-box,water-dr)

467092-2 | CD | Apocalypse

Mahavishnu Orchestra

Power Of Love | Vision Is A Naked Sword | Smile Of The Beyond | Wings Og Karma | Hymn To Him

rec. March 1974

Mahavishnu Orchestra | McLaughlin,John (g,voc) | Ponty,Jean-Luc (el-v) | Moran,Gayle (keyboards,voc) | Thomas,Michael Tilson (p,cond) | Westbrook,Marsha (viola) | Shive,Carol (v,voc) | Hirschi,Philip (cello,voc) | Armstrong,Ralphe (b,b-g,voc) | Walden,Narada Michael (dr) | Gibbs,Michael (arr) | London Symphony Orchestra,The

467897-2 | 2 CD | Agharta

Miles Davis Group

Prelude(part 1&2) | Interlude | Theme From Jack Johnson | Maiysha

rec. 1.2.1975

Davis,Miles (tp,org) | Fortune,Sonny (fl,ss,as) | Lucas,Reggie (g) | Henderson,Michael (el-b) | Cosey,Pete (g,synth,perc) | Foster,Al (dr) | M'tume,James[Forman] (perc,congas,rythm-box,water-dr)

467898-2 | 2 CD | Circle In The Round

Miles Davis Quintet

Two Bass Hit

rec. 27.10.1955

Davis,Miles (tp) | Coltrane,John (ts) | Garland,Red (p) | Chambers,Paul (b) | Jones,Philly Joe (dr)

Miles Davis Sextet

Love For Sale

rec. 26.5.1958

Davis,Miles (tp) | Adderley,Julian \'Cannonball\' (as) | Coltrane,John (ts) | Evans,Bill (p) | Chambers,Paul (b) | Cobb,Jimmy (dr)

Miles Davis Quintet

Blues No.2

rec. 21.3.1961

Davis,Miles (tp) | Mobley,Hank (ts) | Kelly,Wynton (p) | Chambers,Paul (b) | Jones,Philly Joe (dr)

Miles Davis Sextet

Circle In The Round

rec. 4.12.1967

Davis,Miles (tp,bells,chimes) | Shorter,Wayne (ts) | Beck,Joe (g) | Hancock,Herbie (celeste) | Carter,Ron (b) | Williams,Tony (dr)

Miles Davis Quintet

Teo's Bag

rec. 16.1.1968

Davis,Miles (tp) | Shorter,Wayne (ts) | Hancock,Herbie (p) | Carter,Ron (b) | Williams,Tony (dr)

Side Car I

rec. 13.2.1968

Davis,Miles (tp) | Shorter,Wayne (ts) | Hancock,Herbie (p) | Carter,Ron (b) | Williams,Tony (dr)

Miles Davis Sextet

Side Car II

Davis,Miles (tp) | Shorter,Wayne (ts) | Benson,George (g) | Hancock,Herbie (p) | Carter,Ron (b) | Williams,Tony (dr)

Sanctuary

rec. 15.2.1968

Davis,Miles (tp) | Shorter,Wayne (ts) | Benson,George (g) | Hancock,Herbie (p) | Carter,Ron (b), | Williams,Tony (dr)

Miles Davis Group

Splash

rec. 25.11.1968

Davis,Miles (tp) | Shorter,Wayne (ts) | Hancock,Herbie (el-p) | Corea,Chick (el-p) | Zawinul,Joe (p) | Holland,Dave (b) | Williams,Tony (dr)

Guinnevere

rec. 27.1.1970

Davis,Miles (tp) | Maupin,Bennie (b-cl) | Shorter,Wayne (ss,ts) | Corea,Chick (keyboards) | Zawinul,Joe (keyboards) | Holland,Dave (b) | Brooks,Harvey (el-b) | DeJohnette,Jack (dr) | Cobham,Billy (dr) | Moreira,Airto (perc) | Balakrishna,Khalil (sitar)

Miles Davis Quintet

Two Bass Hit

NYC, rec. 27.10.1955

Davis,Miles (tp) | Coltrane,John (ts) | Garland,Red (p) | Chambers,Paul (b) | Jones,Philly Joe (dr)

Miles Davis Sextet

Love For Sale

NYC, rec. 26.5.1958

Davis,Miles (tp) | Adderley,Julian \'Cannonball\' (as) | Coltrane,John (ts) | Evans,Bill (p) | Chambers,Paul (b) | Cobb,Jimmy (dr)

Miles Davis Quintet

Blues No.2

NYC, rec. 21.3.1961

Davis,Miles (tp) | Mobley,Hank (ts) | Kelly,Wynton (p) | Chambers,Paul (b) | Jones,Philly Joe (dr)

Miles Davis Sextet

Circle In The Round

NYC, rec. 4.12.1967

Davis,Miles (tp,bells,chimes) | Shorter,Wayne (ts) | Hancock,Herbie (celeste) | Beck,Joe (el-g) | Carter,Ron (b) | Williams,Tony (dr)

Miles Davis Quintet

Teo's Bag

NYC, rec. 16.1.1968

Davis,Miles (tp) | Shorter,Wayne (ts) | Hancock,Herbie (p) | Carter,Ron (b) | Williams,Tony (dr)

Car 1

rec. 13.2.1968

Davis,Miles (tp) | Shorter,Wayne (ts) | Hancock,Herbie (p) | Carter,Ron (b) | Williams,Tony (dr)

Miles Davis Sextet

Car 2

NYC, rec. 13.2.1968

Davis,Miles (tp) | Shorter,Wayne (ts) | Hancock,Herbie (p) | Benson,George (el-g) | Carter,Ron (b) | Williams,Tony (dr)

Miles Davis Group

Splash

NYC, rec. 25.11.1968

Davis,Miles (tp) | Shorter,Wayne (ts) | Hancock,Herbie (el-p) | Corea,Chick (el-p) | Zawinul,Joe (p) | Holland,Dave (b) | Williams,Tony (dr)

Miles Davis Sextet

Sanctuary

NYC, rec. 15.2.1968

Davis,Miles (tp) | Shorter,Wayne (ts) | Hancock,Herbie (p) | Benson,George (el-g) | Carter,Ron (b) | Williams,Tony (dr)

Miles Davis Group

Guinnevere

NYC, rec. 27.1.1970

Davis,Miles (tp) | Shorter,Wayne (ss,ts) | Maupin,Bennie (b-cl) | Corea,Chick (keyboards) | Zawinul,Joe (keyboards) | Holland,Dave (b) | Brooks,Harvey (el-b) | DeJohnette,Jack (dr) | Cobham,Billy (dr) | Moreira,Airto (perc) | Balakrishna,Khalil (sitar)

467904-2 | CD | Visions Of The Emerald Beyond

Mahavishnu Orchestra

Eternity's Breath(part 1) | Eternity's Breath(part 2) | Lila's Dance | Can't Stand Your Funk | Pastoral | Faith | Be Happy | Earth Ship | Pegasus | Opus 1 | On The Way Home To Earth

rec. 1975

Mahavishnu Orchestra | McLaughlin,John (g) | details unknown

467905-2 | CD | Shakti With John McLaughlin

Shakti

Joy | Lotus Feet | What Need Have I For This...

rec. 5.7.1975

Shakti | McLaughlin,John (g) | Shankar (v) | Raghavan,R. (mridangam) | Vinayakaram,T.H. (ghatam,mridangam) | Hussain,Zakir (tabla)

467916-2 | CD | Body & Soul

Erroll Garner Trio

The Way You Look Tonight | Body And Soul | Back Home Again In Indiana | Honeysuckle Rose | I'm In The Mood For Love | I Can't Get Started | Play Piano Play | Undecided

NYC, rec. 11.1.1951

Garner,Erroll (p) | Simmons,John (b) | Wilson,Shadow (dr)

You're Blasé | Sophisticated Lady | Ain't She Sweet | I Didn't Know | Fine And Dandy | Robbin's Nest | Please Don't Talk About Me When I'm Gone | It's The Talk Of The Town

Hollywood,CA, rec. 2.7.1951

Garner,Erroll (p) | Simmons,John (b) | Wilson,Shadow (dr)

You're Driving Me Crazy | Ja-Da | Summertime | I Never Knew

NYC, rec. 3.1.1952

Garner,Erroll (p) | Simmons,John (b) | Wilson,Shadow (dr)

468208-2 | CD | Mr. Gone

Weather Report

River People | The Elders

details unknown, rec. details unknown

Weather Report | Shorter,Wayne (ss,ts) | Zawinul,Joe (keyboards,synth) | Pastorius,Jaco (b,dr,tympani,voice)

Mr.Gone | Punk Jazz

Weather Report | Shorter,Wayne (ss,ts) | Zawinul,Joe (keyboards,synth) | Pastorius,Jaco (el-b) | Williams,Tony (dr)

Pinocchio

Weather Report | Shorter,Wayne (ss,ts) | Zawinul,Joe (keyboards,synth) | Pastorius,Jaco (el-b) | Erskine,Peter (dr)

Young And Fine

Weather Report | Shorter,Wayne (ts) | Zawinul,Joe (keyboards,high hat,melodica,voice) | Erskine,Peter (high hat) | Pastorius,Jaco (el-b) | Gadd,Steve (dr)

The Pursuit Of The Woman With The Feathered Hat

Weather Report | Shorter,Wayne (ss,voc) | Zawinul,Joe (keyboards,bells,kalimbas,thumbeki-dr,voc) | Pastorius,Jaco (b,dr,voc) | Erskine,Peter (dr,voc) | Badrena,Manolo (voice) | Lucien,Jon (voc)

And Then

Weather Report | Shorter,Wayne (as,ts) | Zawinul,Joe (keyboards) | Pastorius,Jaco (el-b) | Gadd,Steve (dr) | Williams,Denice (voice) | White,Maurice (voc)

468210-2 | CD | Black Market

Gibraltar | Elegant People | Three Clowns | Herandnu

Hollywood,CA, rec. 1976

Weather Report | Shorter,Wayne (ss,ts,lyricon) | Zawinul,Joe (el-p,synth) | Johnson,Alphonso (el-b) | Pastorius,Jaco (el-b) | Thompson,Chester (dr) | Acuna,Alejandro Neciosup (perc,congas)

Barbary Coast

Weather Report | Shorter,Wayne (ss,ts,lyricon) | Zawinul,Joe (el-p,synth) | Alias,Don (perc,congas) | Pastorius,Jaco (el-b) | Thompson,Chester (dr) | Acuna,Alejandro Neciosup (perc,congas)

Cannonball

Weather Report | Shorter,Wayne (ss,ts,lyricon) | Zawinul,Joe (el-p,synth) | Walden,Narada Michael (dr) | Pastorius,Jaco (el-b) | Thompson,Chester (dr) | Acuna,Alejandro Neciosup (perc,congas)

Black Market

Weather Report | Shorter,Wayne (ss,ts,lyricon) | Zawinul,Joe (el-p,synth) | Walden,Narada Michael (dr) | Pastorius,Jaco (el-b) | Thompson,Chester (dr) | Acuna,Alejandro Neciosup (perc,congas) | Johnson,Alphonso (el-b) | Alias,Don (perc,congas)

468211-2 | CD | Night Passage

Night Passage | Dream Clock | Port Of Entry | Forlon | Rockin' In Rhythm | Fast City | Three Views Of A Secret | Madagascar

Los Angeles,CA, rec. 1980

Weather Report | Shorter,Wayne (sax) | Zawinul,Joe (keyboards) | Pastorius,Jaco (el-b) | Erskine,Peter (dr,perc) | Thomas Jr.,Robert (hand-dr)

468213-2 | CD | Elegant Gypsy

Al Di Meola Group

Flight Over Rio

rec. 1976

Di Meola,Al (el-g) | Hammer,Jan (el-p,synth) | Jackson,Anthony (b-g) | Gadd,Steve (dr) | Lewis,Mingo (org,synth,perc,congas)

Midnight Tango

Di Meola,Al (g,el-g,synth,perc) | Jackson,Anthony (b-g) | Miles,Barry (p,el-p) | White,Lenny (dr) | Lewis,Mingo (congas)

Mediterranean Sundance

Di Meola,Al (g) | De Lucia,Paco (g) | White,Lenny (timbales) | Lewis,Mingo (congas,shakers)

Race With Devil On Spanish Highway

Di Meola,Al (el-g,timbales) | Miles,Barry (p,el-p,synth) | Jackson,Anthony (b-g) | White,Lenny (dr) | Lewis,Mingo (congas)

Al Di Meola

Lady Of Rome Sister Of Brazil

Di Meola,Al (g-solo)

Al Di Meola Group

LABELVERZEICHNIS

Elegant Gypsy Suite
Di Meola,Al (g,p,synth,perc,el-g maracas,12-string-g) | Hammer,Jan (el-p,synth) | Jackson,Anthony (b-g) | Gadd,Steve (dr) | Lewis,Mingo (congas,cowbell,timbales)

468214-2 | CD | Land Of The Midnight Sun
The Wizard
NYC, rec. 1976
Di Meola,Al (g,12-string-g) | Lewis,Mingo (keyboards,perc) | Jackson,Anthony (b-g) | Gadd,Steve (dr)
Land Of The Midnight Sun
Di Meola,Al (el-g) | Miles,Barry (el-p,synth) | Jackson,Anthony (b-g) | White,Lenny (dr) | Lewis,Mingo (perc)
Joe Pass
Sarabande From Violin Sonata In B Minor
Di Meola,Al (g-solo)
Al Di Meola Group
Love Theme From Pictures Of The Sea
San Francisco,CA, rec. 1976
Di Meola,Al (g,el-g,synth,chimes,12-string-g,voc) | Clarke,Stanley (el-b,voc) | Lewis,Mingo (perc) | Buyukas,Patty (voc)
Suite-Golden Dawn: | Morning Fire- | Calmer Of Tempest- | From Ocean To The Clouds-
NYC, rec. 1976
Di Meola,Al (el-g) | Miles,Barry (el-p,synth) | Pastorius,Jaco (el-b) | Mouzon,Alphonse (dr) | Lewis,Mingo (perc)
Al Di Meola-Chick Corea
Short Tales Of The Black Forest
Di Meola,Al (g,gong) | Corea,Chick (marimba,p)

468215-2 | CD | Casino
Al Di Meola Group
Egyptian Dance
rec. details unknown
Di Meola,Al (el-g) | Miles,Barry (p,el-p,synth) | Jackson,Anthony (b-g) | Gadd,Steve (dr)
Hal Di Meola Group
Chasin' The Voodoo | Dark Eye Tango | Senor Mouse
Di Meola,Al (el-g) | Miles,Barry (marimba,p,el-p,org) | Jackson,Anthony (b-g) | Gadd,Steve (dr) | Lewis,Mingo (perc,bongo,conga)
Casino
Di Meola,Al (el-g) | Miles,Barry (marimba,p,el-p,org) | Jackson,Anthony (b-g) | Gadd,Steve (dr) | Lewis,Mingo (perc,bongo,conga) | Colon,Eddie (roto-toms,timbales)
Fantasia Suite For Two Guitars: | Viva La Danzarina- | Guitars Of The Exotic Isle- | Rhapsody Italia- | Bravoto Fantasia-
Di Meola,Al (g,mand,castanets,foot stomps,hand-claps,muted c& bongos)

468701-2 | CD | The Man With The Horn
Miles Davis Group
Fat Time
NYC, rec. 1980
Davis,Miles (tp) | Evans,Bill (ss) | Finnerty,Barry (el-g) | Miller,Marcus (el-b) | Foster,Al (dr) | Figueroa,Sammy (perc)
Back Seat Betty | Aida | Ursula
Davis,Miles (tp) | Evans,Bill (ss) | Stern,Mike (el-g) | Miller,Marcus (el-b) | Foster,Al (dr) | Figueroa,Sammy (perc)
The Man With The Horn
Davis,Miles (tp) | Evans,Bill (ss) | Irving III,Robert (p,el-p) | Hall,Randy (g,synth,celeste,voc) | Crews,Felton (el-b) | Wilburn,Vincent (dr)
Shout
Davis,Miles (tp) | Irving III,Robert (p,el-p) | Finnerty,Barry (el-g) | Hall,Randy (g,synth,celeste,voc) | Crews,Felton (el-b) | Wilburn,Vincent (dr) | Figueroa,Sammy (perc)

468702-2 | CD | Decoy
Decoy | Code M.D. | That's Right
Live at Montreal/Canada, rec. details unknown
Davis,Miles (tp,synth) | Marsalis,Branford (ss) | Scofield,John (g) | Jones,Darryl (el-b) | Irving III,Robert (synth,el-dr) | Foster,Al (dr) | Cinelu,Mino (perc)
What Is This? | That's What Happened
Davis,Miles (tp,synth) | Evans,Bill (ss) | Scofield,John (g) | Jones,Darryl (el-b) | Irving III,Robert (synth,el-dr) | Foster,Al (dr) | Cinelu,Mino (perc)
Freaky Deaky
Davis,Miles (synth) | Jones,Darryl (el-b) | Foster,Al (dr) | Cinelu,Mino (perc)
Robot 415
Davis,Miles (tp,synth) | Irving III,Robert (synth,b-synth,el-dr) | Cinelu,Mino (perc)

468708-2 | CD | Wynton Marsalis
Wynton Marsalis Quintet
Father Time | I'll Be There When The Time Is Right
NYC, rec. details unknown
Marsalis,Wynton (tp) | Marsalis,Branford (ts) | Kirkland,Kenny (p) | Seay,Clarence (b) | Watts,Jeff 'Tain' (dr)
Twilight
Marsalis,Wynton (tp) | Marsalis,Branford (ts) | Kirkland,Kenny (p) | Fambrough,Charles (b) | Watts,Jeff 'Tain' (dr)
R.J. | Sister Cheryl
Tokyo, Japan, rec. details unknown
Marsalis,Wynton (tp) | Marsalis,Branford (ts) | Hancock,Herbie (p) | Carter,Ron (b) | Williams,Tony (dr)
Wynton Marsalis Quartet
Who Can I Turn To
Marsalis,Wynton (tp) | Hancock,Herbie (p) | Carter,Ron (b) | Williams,Tony (dr)
Hesitation
Marsalis,Wynton (tp) | Marsalis,Branford (ts) | Carter,Ron (b) | Williams,Tony (dr)

468710-2 | CD | Hot House Flowers
Wynton Marsalis Sextet
Stardust | Lazy Afternoon | For All We Know | When You Wish Upon A Star | Django | Melancholia | Hot House Flowers | I'm Confessin'(That I Love You)
NYC, rec. 30./31.5.1984
Marsalis,Wynton (tp) | Jordan,Kent (alto-fl) | Marsalis,Branford (ss,ts) | Kirkland,Kenny (p) | Carter,Ron (b) | Watts,Jeff 'Tain' (dr)

469402-2 | CD | We Want Miles
Miles Davis Group
Jean Pierre(short) | Back Seat Betty | Fast Track | Jean Pierre | My Man's Gone Now | Kix
Boston/New York City, rec. 27.6./5.7.& 4.10.1981
Davis,Miles (tp,keyboards) | Evans,Bill (ss) | Stern,Mike (g) | Miller,Marcus (el-b) | Foster,Al (dr) | Cinelu,Mino (perc)

471003-2 | CD | A Tribute To Jack Johnson
Right Off | Yesternow
rec. details unknown
Davis,Miles (tp) | details unknown

471235-2 | CD | Man-Child
Herbie Hancock Group
Hang Up Your Hangups | Sun Touch | The Traitor | Bubbles | Steppin' In It | Heatbeat
Hancock,Herbie (p,el-p,synth,clavinet) | Brisbois,Wilbur 'Bud' (tp) | DaVersa,Jay (tp) | Brown,Garnett (tb) | Hyde,Dick (bass-tb,tuba) | Watts,Ernie (fl,reeds) | Horn,Jim (fl,reeds) | Shorter,Wayne (ss) | Maupin,Bennie (alto-fl,b-cl,ss,ts,bass-fl,saxello) | McKnight,Blackbird (g) | Walker,David T. (g) | Jackson,Paul (b) | Johnson,Louis (b) | Davis,Henry (b) | Clark,Mike (dr) | Mason,Harvey (dr) | Gadson,James (dr) | Wonder,Stevie (harm) | Summers,Bill (perc)

471246-2 | 2 CD | The Complete Concert 1964:My Funny Valentine+Four & More
Miles Davis Quintet
Introduction by Mort Fega | My Funny Valentine | All Of You | Go-Go(Theme And Re-Introduction) | Stella By Starlight | All Blues | I Thought About You | So What | Walkin' | Joshua | Go-Go(Theme And Announcement) | Four | Seven Steps To Heaven | There Is No Greater Love | Go-Go(Theme And Announcement)
Live at Lincoln Center's Philharmonic Hall, rec. 12.2.1964
Davis,Miles (tp) | Coleman,George (ts) | Hancock,Herbie (p) | Carter,Ron (b) | Williams,Tony (dr)

480410-2 | CD | Kind Of Blue
Blue In Green
NYC, rec. 2.3.1959
Davis,Miles (tp) | Coltrane,John (ts) | Kelly,Wynton (p) | Chambers,Paul (b) | Cobb,Jimmy (dr)
Miles Davis Sextet
Freddie Freeloader
Davis,Miles (tp) | Coltrane,John (ts) | Kelly,Wynton (p) | Chambers,Paul (b) | Cobb,Jimmy (dr) | Adderley,Julian \'Cannonball\' (as)
So What | Flamenco Sketches | All Blues
NYC, rec. 22.4.1959
Davis,Miles (tp) | Coltrane,John (ts) | Evans,Bill (p) | Chambers,Paul (b) | Cobb,Jimmy (dr) | Adderley,Julian \'Cannonball\' (as)

481434-2 | CD | Highlights From The Plugged Nickel
Miles Davis Quintet
Round About Midnight
Live at The Plugged Nickel,Chicago,Ill, rec. 22.12.1965
Davis,Miles (tp) | Shorter,Wayne (ts) | Hancock,Herbie (p) | Carter,Ron (b) | Williams,Tony (dr)
Milestones | Yesterdays | So What | Stella By Starlight | Walkin'
Live at The Plugged Nickel,Chicago,Ill, rec. 23.12.1965
Davis,Miles (tp) | Shorter,Wayne (ts) | Hancock,Herbie (p) | Carter,Ron (b) | Williams,Tony (dr)

485102-2 | CD | Sweetnighter
Weather Report
Boogie Woogie Waltz | Manolete | Adios | 125th Street Congress | Will | Non-Stop Home
rec. details unknown
Weather Report | Zawinul,Joe (p,el-p,synth) | Shorter,Wayne (ss) | White,Andrew (engl-h,el-b) | Vitous,Miroslav (b) | Gravatt,Eric (dr) | Romao,Dom Um (perc) | Murugar (perc) | Dwellingham,Hershel (dr)

486569-2 | 2 CD | V.S.O.P. Herbie Hancock-Live At The City Center N.Y.
Herbie Hancock
Piano Introduction
Live at Lincoln Center's Philharmonic Hall, rec. 29.6.1976
Hancock,Herbie (p-solo)
Herbie Hancock Quintet
Maiden Voyage | Nefertiti | Introduction Of Players | Eye Of The Hurricane
Hancock,Herbie (p) | Hubbard,Freddie (tp) | Shorter,Wayne (ss,ts) | Carter,Ron (b) | Williams,Tony (dr)
Herbie Hancock Sextet
Toys | Introduction | You'll Know When You Get There
Hancock,Herbie (p,el-p,clavichord) | Henderson,Eddie (tp,fl-h) | Maupin,Bennie (alto-fl) | Priester,Julian (tb) | Williams,Buster (b) | Hart,Billy (dr)
Herbie Hancock Septet
Hang Up Your Hangups | Spider
Hancock,Herbie (el-p,synth) | Maupin,Bennie (ss,ts,lyrichord) | Watson,Wah Wah (g,synth) | Parker,Ray (g) | Jackson,Paul (el-b) | Levi,James (dr) | Nash,Kenneth (perc)

486570-2 | CD | Sunlight
Herbie Hancock Group
I Thought It Was You
San Francisco,CA, rec. 1977
Hancock,Herbie (keyboards,synth) | Watson,Wah Wah (g) | Parker,Ray (g) | Miller,Byron (b) | Ndugu[Leon Chancler] (dr) | Rekow,Raul (congas) | Shew,Bobby (tp,fl-h) | Bryant Sr.,Robert O. (tp) | Brown,Garnett (tb) | Spears,Maurice (tb,b-tb) | Jackson Jr.,Fred (reeds) | Watts,Ernie (reeds) | Riddles,David Willard (reeds) | Nimitz,Jack (reeds) | Rubin,Nathan (v) | Granger,Lawrence (v) | Van Valkenburgh,Emily (v) | Malan,Roy (viola) | Adams,Terry (cello) | Wood,Linda (harp)
Come Running To Me
Hancock,Herbie (keyboards,synth) | Jackson,Paul (el-b) | Levi,James (dr) | Summers,Bill (perc) | Duru,Baba (tabla) | Rekow,Raul (congas) | Shew,Bobby (tp,fl-h) | Bryant Sr.,Robert O. (tp) | Brown,Garnett (tb) | Spears,Maurice (tb,b-tb) | Jackson Jr.,Fred (reeds) | Watts,Ernie (reeds) | Riddles,David Willard (reeds) | Nimitz,Jack (reeds) | Rubin,Nathan (v) | Granger,Lawrence (v) | Van Valkenburgh,Emily (v) | Malan,Roy (viola) | Adams,Terry (cello) | Wood,Linda (harp)
Sunlight
Los Angeles,CA, rec. 1977
Hancock,Herbie (keyboards,synth) | Maupin,Bennie (ss) | Parker,Ray (g) | Jackson,Paul (el-b) | Levi,James (dr) | Summers,Bill (perc) | Shew,Bobby (tp,fl-h) | Bryant Sr.,Robert O. (tp) | Brown,Garnett (tb) | Spears,Maurice (tb,b-tb) | Jackson Jr.,Fred (reeds) | Watts,Ernie (reeds) | Riddles,David Willard (reeds) | Nimitz,Jack (reeds) | Rubin,Nathan (v) | Granger,Lawrence (v) | Van Valkenburgh,Emily (v) | Malan,Roy (viola) | Adams,Terry (cello) | Wood,Linda (harp)
No Means Yes
Hancock,Herbie (keyboards,synth) | Jackson,Paul (el-b) | Mason,Harvey (dr) | Summers,Bill (perc) | Rekow,Raul (congas)
Good Question
Hancock,Herbie (keyboards,synth) | Gleeson,Pat (synth) | Pastorius,Jaco (el-b) | Williams,Tony (dr) | Summers,Bill (perc) | Rekow,Raul (congas)

486571-2 | CD | Monster
Saturday Night | Stars In Your Eyes | Go For It | Don't Hold It In | Making Love | It All Comes Round
San Francisco,CA, rec. 1980
Hancock,Herbie (p,keyboards,synth) | Watson,Wah Wah (el-g) | Parker,Ray (el-g) | Hansen,Randy (g) | Santana,Carlos (el-g) | Washington,Freddie (el-b) | Mouzon,Alphonse (keyboards,dr) | Escovedo,Sheila (perc) | Waters,Oren (voc) | Champlin,Bill (voc) | Walker,Gregory (voc) | Christopher,Gavin (voc) | details unknown

486572-2 | CD | Magic Window
Magic Number
San Francisco,CA, rec. 1981
Hancock,Herbie (keyboards,synth) | Parker,Ray (el-g) | Washington,Freddie (el-b) | Robinson,John (dr) | Escovedo,Pete (perc) | Escovedo,Sheila (perc) | Escovedo,Juan (perc) | Tracy,Jeanie (voc) | Sylvester (voc)
Tonight's The Night
Hancock,Herbie (keyboards,synth,el-b) | Brecker,Michael (ts) | Parker,Ray (el-g,dr) | Randle,Vicki (voc) | Spencer,Ngoh (voc) | Dickerson,Dede (voc)
Everybody's Broke
Hancock,Herbie (keyboards,synth,voc) | Johnson,George (g) | Johnson,Louis (el-b) | Robinson,John (dr) | Christopher,Gavin (voc) | Randle,Vicki (voc) | Spencer,Ngoh (voc) | Dickerson,Dede (voc) | Bottom,Davis (voc) | Cohen,Jeffrey (voc)
Help Yourself
Hancock,Herbie (keyboards,synth) | Brecker,Michael (ts) | McKay,Al (g) | Watkins,Eddie (el-b) | Gadson,James (dr) | Christopher,Gavin (brass-arr,voc) | Randle,Vicki (voc) | Spencer,Ngoh (voc) | Dickerson,Dede (voc)
Satisfied With Love
Los Angeles,CA, rec. 1981
Hancock,Herbie (keyboards,synth) | Watson,Wah Wah (g) | Washington,Freddie (el-b) | Mouzon,Alphonse (dr) | Christopher,Gavin (voc) | Waters,Maxine Willard (voc) | Waters,Julia Tillman (voc) | Waters,Luther (voc) | Waters,Oren (voc)
The Twiligth Clone
San Francisco,CA, rec. 1981
Hancock,Herbie (keyboards,synth,dr-machine) | Belew,Adrian (el-g) | Johnson,George (g) | Johnson,Louis (el-b) | Da Costa,Paulinho (dr)

487445-2 | CD | Glenn Miller Serenade
Glenn Miller Orchestra
In The Mood | Elmer's Tune | Blue Velvet | Chattanooga Choo Choo | Pennsylvania Six Five Thousand | Serenade In Blue | Carribean Clipper | Little Brown Jug | At Last | Sun Valley Jump | Moonlight Cocktail | Everybody Loves My Baby | Canadian Sunset
details unknown, rec. details unknown
Hackett,Bobby (tp) | McKinley,Ray (dr,ld) | DeFranco,Buddy (ld) | details not on the cover

487798-2 | CD | Late Night Sax
Paul Desmond Orchestra
Take Ten
NYC, rec. November/December 1973
Desmond,Paul (as) | Bertoncini,Gene (g) | Szabo,Gabor (g) | James,Bob (p,el-p) | Ricci,George (cello) | Carter,Ron (b) | DeJohnette,Jack (dr) | MacDonald,Ralph (perc) | Sebesky,Don (cond,arr)
Gerry Mulligan Quintet
Blue Boy
NYC, rec. 30.6.1962
Mulligan,Gerry (bs) | Flanagan,Tommy (p) | Tucker,Ben (b) | Bailey,Dave (dr) | Dorsey,Alec (congas)
Bob Brookmeyer Sextet
Misty
NYC, rec. 27.5.1964
Brookmeyer,Bob (v-tb) | Getz,Stan (ts) | Burton,Gary (vib) | Hancock,Herbie (p) | Carter,Ron (b) | Jones,Elvin (dr)
Grover Washington Jr. Orchestra
Stella By Starlight
details unknown, rec. details unknown
Washington Jr.,Grover (sax) | Butman,Igor (sax) | details unknown
Charlie Rouse Quartet
Rouse's Point
details unknown, rec. 1990
Rouse,Charlie (ts) | Mahones,Gildo (p) | Workman,Reggie (b) | Taylor,Arthur 'Art' (dr)
Coleman Hawkins Quartet
These Foolish Things Remind Me On You
details unknown, rec. 1963
Hawkins,Coleman (ts) | Zawinul,Joe (p) | Marshall,Wendell (b) | Haynes,Roy (dr)
Illinois Jacquet With The Joey DeFrancesco Quartet
But Not For Me
details unknown, rec. 1990
Jacquet,Illinois (ts) | DeFrancesco,Joey (org) | details not on the cover
Buddy Tate With The Marlow Morris Quintet
I Loves You Porgy
NYC, rec. 8.2.1962
Tate,Buddy (ts) | Morris,Marlowe (org) | Clayton,Buck (tp) | Hall,Edmond (cl) | Jones,Jo (dr) | Barretto,Ray (bongos)

488623-2 | CD | Sony Jazz Collection:Stan Getz
Bob Brookmeyer Quintet
Who Cares | Misty
NYC, rec. 27.5.1964
Brookmeyer,Bob (v-tb) | Getz,Stan (ts) | Burton,Gary (vib) | Hancock,Herbie (p) | Carter,Ron (b) | Jones,Elvin (dr)
Stan Getz Quartet
La Fiesta | Captain Marvel
NYC, rec. 3.3.1972
Getz,Stan (ts) | Corea,Chick (p,el-p) | Clarke,Stanley (b) | Williams,Tony (dr)
Stan Getz-Joao Gilberto Orchestra
Aguas De Marco(Waters Of March) | Ligia
NYC, rec. 21.3.1975
Getz,Stan (ts,multiplay) | Gilberto,Joao (g,perc,voc) | Dailey,Albert (p) | Neves,Oscar Castro (g) | Houston,Clint (b) | Swallow,Steve (b-g) | Hart,Bill (dr) | Tate,Grady (dr) | Moreira,Airto (perc) | Bassini,Rubens (perc) | Armando,Ray (perc) | Carr,Sonny (perc) | De Hollanda,Heloise Buarque (voc)
Stan Getz Quartet
Lester Left Town
NYC, rec. October 1975
Getz,Stan (ts) | Rowles,Jimmy (p) | Williams,Buster (b) | Jones,Elvin (dr)
Stan Getz-Jimmy Rowles
The Peacocks
Getz,Stan (ts) | Rowles,Jimmy (p)
Stan Getz Quintet
Blue Serge
Montreux,CH, rec. 13.9.1977
Getz,Stan (ts) | LaVerne,Andy (p) | Richmond,Mike (b) | Hart,Bill (dr) | Toro,Efrain (perc)

489208-2 | 2 CD | Weathe Report Live In Tokyo
Weather Report
Medley: | Vertical Invader- | Seventh Arrow- | T.H.- | Doctor Honoris Causa- | Surucucu- | Lost- | Early Minor- | Directions- | Orange Lady | Medley: | Eurydice- | The Moors- | Tears- | Umbrellas-
Live at Shibuya Philharmonic Hall,Tokyo,Japan, rec. 13.1.1972
Weather Report | Shorter,Wayne (ss,ts) | Zawinul,Joe (p,el-p) | Vitous,Miroslav (b,el-b) | Gravatt,Eric (dr) | Romao,Dom Um (perc)

492533-2 | CD | Here Comes The Judge
Eddie Harris Group
People
NYC, rec. 22.9.1964
Harris,Eddie (ts) | Walton,Cedar (p) | Burrell,Kenny (g) | Cranshaw,Bob (b) | Brooks,Billy (dr)
East End Blues | Deep In A Dream | Goldfinger | What's New? | Rice Pudding | Ineffable | That's Tough
NYC, rec. 1964/1965
Harris,Eddie (ts) | details unknown

493006-2 | 2 CD | Robert Johnson-King Of The Delta Blues
Robert Johnson
Kind Hearted Woman | Kind Hearted Woman(alt.take) | I Believe I Dust My Broom | Sweet Home Chicago | Rambling On My Mind | Rambling On My Mind(alt.take) | When You Got A Good Friend | When You Got A Good Friend(alt.take) | Come On In My Kitchen | Come On In My Kitchen(alt.take) | Terraplane Blues | Phonograph Blues | Phonograph Blues(alt.take)
San Antonio,Texas, rec. 23.11.1936
Johnson,Robert (g,voc)
32-20 Blues
San Antonio,Texas, rec. 26.11.1936
Johnson,Robert (g,voc)
They're Red Hot | Dead Shrimp Blues | Cross Road Blues | Cross Road Blues(alt.take) | Walking Blues | Last Fair Deal Gone Down | Preaching Blues[Up Jumped The Devil] | If I Had Possession Over Judgement Day
San Antonio,Texas, rec. 27.11.1936
Johnson,Robert (g,voc)
Stones In My Passway | I'm A Steady Rollin' Man | From Four Till Late
Dallas,TX, rec. 19.6.1937
Johnson,Robert (g,voc)
Hellhound On My Trail | Little Queen Of Spades | Little Queen Of Spades(alt.take) | Malted Milk | Drunken Hearted Man | Drunken Hearted Man(alt.take) | Me And The Devil Blues | Me And The Devil Blues(alt.take) | Stop Breakin' Down Blues | Stop Breakin' Down Blues(alt.take) | Traveling Riverside Blues | Honeymoon Blues | Love In Vain | Love In Vain(alt.take) | Milk Cow's Calf Blues | Milk Cow's Calf Blues(alt.take)
Dallas,TX, rec. 20.6.1937
Johnson,Robert (g,voc)

494434-2 | CD | The Day Will Come
Howard Riley Trio
Sphere | Sad Was The Song | Winter | Dawn Vision | Funeral Song | Playtime | Eclipse | Deeper | Games | Score | High | The Day Will Come
London,GB, rec. 1.3.& 17.4.1970
Riley,Howard (p) | Guy,Barry (b) | Jackson,Alan (dr)

494437-2 | CD | 4 Compositions For Sextet
Tony Oxley Sextet
Satunalia | Scintilla | Amass | Megaera
London,GB, rec. ca.1970
Oxley,Tony (dr) | Wheeler,Kenny (tp,fl-h) | Rutherford,Paul (tb) | Parker,Evan (sax) | Bailey,Derek (g) | Clyne,Jeff (b)

494438-2 | CD | The Baptist Traveller
Tony Oxley Quintet
Crossing- | 2.Arrival- | Stone Garden | Preparation
London,GB, rec. 3.1.1969
Oxley,Tony (dr) | Wheeler,Kenny (tp,fl-h) | Parker,Evan (ts) | Bailey,Derek (g) | Clyne,Jeff (b)

494439-2 | CD | Live At Ronnie Scott's
Ronnie Scott And The Band
Recorda-Me | King Pete | Second Question | Marmasita | Too Late Too Late | Lord Of The Reedy River | Macumba
Live at Ronnie Scott's,London,GB, rec. 25./26.10.1968
Scott,Ronnie (ts) | Wheeler,Kenny (tp,fl-h) | Payne,Chris (tb) | Warleight,Ray (fl,as) | Surman,John (ss,bs) | Beck,Gordon (p,org) | Mathewson,Ron (b,b-g) | Clare,Kenny (dr) | Oxley,Tony (dr)

502469-2 | CD | It's Uptown
George Benson Quartet
Clockwise
NYC, rec. 10.1.1966
Benson,George (g) | Cuber,Ronnie (bs) | Smith,Lonnie (org) | Lucas,Ray (dr) | unkn. (2 perc)
Clockwise | Jaguar | Willow Weep For Me | A Foggy Day(In London Town) | Bullfight | Myna Bird Blues | J.H. Bossa Nova
NYC, rec. 2.9.1966
Benson,George (g) | Cuber,Ronnie (bs) | Smith,Lonnie (org) | Lovelace,Jimmy (dr)
Summertime | Ain't That Peculiar | Eternally(short version)
NYC, rec. 15.3.1966
Benson,George (g) | Cuber,Ronnie (bs) | Smith,Lonnie (org) | Lucas,Ray (dr)
Hello Birdie | Stormy Weather | Eternally
Benson,George (g,voc) | Cuber,Ronnie (bs) | Smith,Lonnie (org) | Lovelace,Jimmy (dr)
George Benson Quintet
Sideman | Minor Chant
NYC, rec. 22.5.1967
Benson,George (g,voc) | Mitchell,Blue (tp) | Cuber,Ronnie (bs) | Smith,Lonnie (org) | Persip,Charles (dr)

502470-2 | CD | The George Benson Cookbook
George Benson Quartet + Guests
Benny's Back | Bossa Rocka | All Of Me | Ready And Able | Jumpin' With Symphony Sid | Let Them Talk
NYC, rec. 1.8.1966
Benson,George (g,voc) | Green,Bennie (tb) | Hall,Al (tb) | Cuber,Ronnie (bs) | Smith,Lonnie (org) | Winston,Albert (el-b) | Kaye,Billy (dr) | Seed,Lenny (congas)
George Benson Quartet
The Borgia Stick | Slow Scene
NYC, rec. 6.9.1966
Benson,George (g) | Cuber,Ronnie (bs) | Smith,Lonnie (org) | Lovelace,Jimmy (dr)
George Benson Quartet + Guests
The Cooker | Big Fat Lady | Benson's Rider
NYC, rec. 1.10.1966
Benson,George (g) | Cuber,Ronnie (bs) | Smith,Lonnie (org) | Winston,Albert (el-b) | Booker,Marion (dr)
Return Of The Prodigal Son
Benson,George (g) | Curtis,King (ts) | Cuber,Ronnie (bs) | Smith,Lonnie (org) | Winston,Albert (el-b) | Booker,Marion (dr)
The Man From Toledo | Goodnight
NYC, rec. 22.11.1966
Benson,George (g) | Mitchell,Blue (tp) | Curtis,King (el-ts) | Cuber,Ronnie (bs) | Smith,Lonnie (org) | Winston,Albert (el-b) | Booker,Marion (dr)

510666-2 | CD | These Are The Vistas | EAN 5099751066620
The Bad Plus
Big Eater | Keep The Bugs Off Your Glass And The Bears Off Your Ass | Smells Like Teen Spirit | Everywhere You Turn | 1972 Bronze Medalist | Guilty | Boo Wah | Flim | Heart Of Glass | Silence Is The Question | What Love Is This
Wiltshire,GB, rec. 30.9.-5.10.2002
The Bad Plus: | Iverson,Ethan (p) | Anderson,Reid (b) | King,Dave (b)

510886-2 | CD | Friednship | EAN 5099751088622
Clark Terry-Max Roach Quartet
Statements | Let's Cool One(Come With Me) | Brushes And Brass | Simple Waltz | I Remember Clifford | Lil' Max | But Beautiful | The Profit | When I Fall In Love | For Dancers Only | Makin' Whoopee | To Basie With Love | The Nearness Of You
NYC, rec. 10.3.2002
Terry,Clark (tp,fl-h) | Roach,Max (dr) | Friedman,Don (p) | McLaurine,Marcus (b)

69655-2 | CD | Reqiem
Branford Marsalis Quartet
Doctone | Trieste | A Thousand Autumns | Lykief | Bullworth | Elysium | Cassandra | 16th St. Baptist Church
Tarrytown,NY, rec. 17.-20.8.1998
Marsalis,Branford (sax) | Kirkland,Kenny (p) | Revis,Eric (b) | Watts,Jeff 'Tain' (dr)

86555-2 | CD | Filles De Kilimanjaro
Miles Davis Quintet
Filles De Kilimanjaro
NYC, rec. 19.6.1968
Davis,Miles (tp) | Shorter,Wayne (ts) | Hancock,Herbie (p) | Carter,Ron (b) | Williams,Tony (dr)
Petit Machins(Little Stuff) | Tout De Suite
Davis,Miles (tp) | Shorter,Wayne (ts) | Hancock,Herbie (el-p) | Carter,Ron (el-b) | Williams,Tony (dr)
Mademoiselle Mabry | Frelon Brun (Brown Hornet)
NYC, rec. 24.9.1968
Davis,Miles (tp) | Shorter,Wayne (ts) | Hancock,Herbie (p) | Holland,Dave (b) | Williams,Tony (dr)

86556-2 | CD | In A Silent Way
Miles Davis Group
Shhh- | Peaceful- | In A Silent Way- | It's About Time-
NYC, rec. 18.2.1969
Davis,Miles (tp) | Shorter,Wayne (ts) | Hancock,Herbie (el-p) | Corea,Chick (el-p) | Zawinul,Joe (el-p,org) | McLaughlin,John (g) | Holland,Dave (b) | Williams,Tony (dr)

C2K 63905 | 2 CD | Monk At Newport 1963 & 1965 | EAN 5099706390527
Thelonious Monk Quartet
Criss Cross | Light Blue | Epistrophy
Live at Newport,Rhode Island, rec. 3.7.1963
Monk,Thelonious (p) | Rouse,Charlie (ts) | Warren,Edward 'Butch' (b) | Dunlop,Frankie (dr)
Thelonious Monk Quartet With Pee Wee Russell
Nutty | Blue Monk
Monk,Thelonious (p) | Russell,Pee Wee (cl) | Rouse,Charlie (ts) | Warren,Edward 'Butch' (b) | Dunlop,Frankie (dr)
Thelonious Monk Quartet
Off Minor | Ruby My Dear | Hackensack | Epistrophy
Live at Newport,Rhode Island, rec. 4.7.1965
Monk,Thelonious (p) | Rouse,Charlie (ts) | Gales,Larry (b) | Riley,Ben (dr)

C2K 65119 | 2 CD | Louis Armstrong:The Great Chicago Concert 1956
Louis Armstrong And His All Stars
Flee As A Bird | Oh Didn't He Ramble- | Memphis Blues- | Frankie And Johnny- | Tiger Rag- | Do You Know What It Means To Miss New Orleans | Basin Street Blues | Black And Blue | West End Blues | On The Sunny Side Of The Street | Struttin' With Some Barbecue | When It's Sleepy Time Down South | Manhattan- | When It's Sleepy Time Down South- | Back Home Again In Indiana | The Gypsy | The Faithfull Husar | Rockin' Chair | Bucket's Got A Hole In It | Perdido | Clarinet Marmalade | Mack The Knife(Moritat) | Tenderly- | You'll Never Walk Alone- | Stompin' At The Savoy | Margie | Big Mama's Back In Town | That's My Desire | Ko Ko Mo(I Love You So) | When The Saints Go Marching In | The Star Spangled Banner
Live at Medina Temple,Chicago,Ill, rec. 1.6.1956
Armstrong,Louis (tp,voc) | Young,Trummy (tb,voc) | Hall,Edmond (cl,voc) | Kyle,Billy (p) | Deems,Barrett (dr) | Middleton,Velma (voc)

C2K 65135 | 2 CD | Live-Evil
Miles Davis Group
Sivad | What I Say | Funky Tonk | Inamorata And Narration
Live at The Cellar Door,Washington,DC, rec. 19.12.1970
Davis,Miles (tp) | Bartz,Gary (as) | Jarrett,Keith (p,el-p) | McLaughlin,John (g) | Henderson,Michael (el-b) | DeJohnette,Jack (dr) | Moreira,Airto (perc)
Medley: | Gemini- | Double Image-
NYC, rec. 6.2.1970
Davis,Miles (tp) | Shorter,Wayne (ss,ts) | McLaughlin,John (g) | Zawinul,Joe (keyboards) | Corea,Chick (keyboards) | Holland,Dave (b) | Cobham,Billy (dr) | Moreira,Airto (perc) | Balakrishna,Khalil (sitar)
Nem Um Talvez | Selim
NYC, rec. 3.6.1970
Davis,Miles (tp) | Grossman,Steve (sax) | Hancock,Herbie (keyboards) | Jarrett,Keith (keyboard) | Corea,Chick (keyboards) | Carter,Ron (b) | DeJohnette,Jack (dr) | Moreira,Airto (perc) | Pascoal,Hermeto (voc)
Little Church
NYC, rec. 4.6.1970
Davis,Miles (tp) | Grossman,Steve (sax) | Jarrett,Keith (keyboard) | Corea,Chick (keyboards) | Hancock,Herbie (keyboards) | McLaughlin,John (g) | Pascoal,Hermeto (el-p,whistling) | Holland,Dave (b) | DeJohnette,Jack (dr) | Moreira,Airto (perc)

C2K 65137 | 2 CD | Dark Magus
Moja(part 1) | Moja(part 2) | Wili(part 1) | Wili(part 2) | Tatu(part 1) | Tatu(part 2) | Nne(part 1) | Nne(part 2)
Live at Carnegie Hall,NYC, rec. 30.3.1974
Davis,Miles (tp,org) | Liebman,Dave (sax) | Lawrence,Azar (sax) | Cosey,Pete (g) | Lucas,Reggie (g) | Gaumont,Dominique (g) | Henderson,Michael (el-b) | Foster,Alan (voc) | M'tume,James[Forman] (perc)

C2K 65138 | 2 CD | Black Beauty-Miles Davis At Filmore West
Miles Davis Sextet
Black Beauty(part 1-4): | Directions- | Miles Runs The Voodoo Down- | Sanctuary- | It's About That Time- | Bitches Brew- | Masqualero- | Spanish Key- | The Theme-
Live at Filmore West,San Francisco,CA, rec. 10.4.1970
Davis,Miles (tp) | Grossman,Steve (ss) | Corea,Chick (el-p) | Holland,Dave (el-b) | DeJohnette,Jack (dr) | Moreira,Airto (perc)
Miles Davis Quintet
Willie Nelson- | I Fall In Love Too Easily-
Davis,Miles (tp) | Corea,Chick (el-p) | Holland,Dave (el-b) | DeJohnette,Jack (dr) | Moreira,Airto (perc)

C2K 65139 | 2 CD | Live At The Fillmore East
Miles Davis Group
Directions | Bitches Brew | The Mask | It's About That Time | Bitches Brew- | The Theme-
Live at Filmore East,NYC, rec. 17.6.1970
Davis,Miles (tp) | Grossman,Steve (ss) | Corea,Chick (el-p) | Jarrett,Keith (org) | Holland,Dave (b,el-b) | DeJohnette,Jack (dr) | Moreira,Airto (perc)
Directions | The Mask | It's About Time
Live at Filmore East,NYC, rec. 18.6.1970
Davis,Miles (tp) | Grossman,Steve (ss) | Corea,Chick (el-p) | Jarrett,Keith (org) | Holland,Dave (b,el-b) | DeJohnette,Jack (dr) | Moreira,Airto (perc)
It's About That Time | I Fall In Love Too Easily | Sanctuary | Bitches Brew- | The Theme-
Live at Filmore East,NYC, rec. 19.6.1970
Davis,Miles (tp) | Grossman,Steve (ss) | Corea,Chick (el-p) | Jarrett,Keith (org) | Holland,Dave (b,el-b) | DeJohnette,Jack (dr) | Moreira,Airto (perc)
It's About That Time | I Fall In Love Too Easily | Sanctuary | Bitches Brew | Willie Nelson- | The Theme-
Live at Filmore East,NYC, rec. 20.6.1970
Davis,Miles (tp) | Grossman,Steve (ss) | Corea,Chick (el-p) | Jarrett,Keith (org) | Holland,Dave (b,el-b) | DeJohnette,Jack (dr) | Moreira,Airto (perc)

C2K 65140 | 2 CD | In Concert
Foot Foolers-In Concert Part 1&2: | Rated X- | Honky Tonk- | Theme From Jack Johnson- | Black Satin- | Theme- | Slickaphonics-In Concert Part 3&4: | Ife- | Right Off- | Theme-
Live at Philharmonic Hall,NYC, rec. 29.9.1972
Davis,Miles (tp) | Garnett,Carlos Alfredo (sax) | Lucas,Cedric (g) | Balakrishna,Khalil (el-sitar) | Lawson,Cedric (keyboards) | Henderson,Michael (el-b) | Foster,Al (dr) | Roy,Badal (tablas) | M'tume,James[Forman] (perc)

C2K 65143 | 2 CD | Benny Goodman At Carnegie Hall 1938(Complete)
Benny Goodman And His Orchestra
Don't Be That Way | Sometimes I'm Happy | One O'Clock Jump | Shine | Life Goes To A Party | Blue Skies | Blue Room | Swingtime In The Rockies | Sing Sing Sing | If Dreams Come True | Big John's Special
Live at Carnegie Hall,NYC, rec. 16.1.1938
Goodman,Benny (cl) | Elman,Ziggy (tp) | Griffin,Chris (tp) | James,Harry (tp) | Ballard,Red (tb) | Brown,Vernon (tb) | Schertzer,Hymie (as) | Koenig,George (as) | Rollini,Arthur (as,ts) | Russin,Irving 'Babe' (ts) | Stacy,Jess (p) | Reuss,Allan (g) | Goodman,Harry (b) | Krupa,Gene (dr)
Loch Lomond | Bei Mir Bist Du Schön
Goodman,Benny (cl,voc) | Elman,Ziggy (tp) | Griffin,Chris (tp) | James,Harry (tp) | Ballard,Red (tb) | Brown,Vernon (tb) | Schertzer,Hymie (as) | Koenig,George (as) | Rollini,Arthur (as,ts) | Russin,Irving 'Babe' (ts) | Stacy,Jess (p) | Reuss,Allan (g) | Goodman,Harry (b) | Krupa,Gene (dr) | Tilton,Martha (voc)
Benny Goodman Quartet
Avalon | The Man I Love | I Got Rhythm | Stompin' At The Savoy | Dizzy Spells
Goodman,Benny (cl) | Hampton,Lionel (vib) | Wilson,Teddy (p) | Krupa,Gene (dr)
Benny Goodman Trio
Body And Soul | China Boy
Goodman,Benny (cl) | Wilson,Teddy (p) | Krupa,Gene (dr)
Benny Goodman Dixieland Quintet
Sensation Rag
Goodman,Benny (cl) | Hackett,Bobby prob. (co) | Brown,Vernon (tb) | Stacy,Jess (p) | Krupa,Gene (dr)
Benny Goodman Combo
When My Baby Smiles At Me
Goodman,Benny (cl) | Hackett,Bobby prob. (co) | Brown,Vernon prob (tb) | Stacy,Jess (p) | Reuss,Allan (g) | Goodman,Harry (b) | Krupa,Gene (dr)
Benny Goodman Band
I'm Coming Virginia
Goodman,Benny (cl) | Hackett,Bobby (co) | Ballard,Red (tb) | Brown,Vernon (tb) | Schertzer,Hymie (as) | Koenig,George (as) | Rollini,Arthur (ts) | Russin,Irving 'Babe' (ts) | Stacy,Jess (p) | Reuss,Allan (g) | Goodman,Harry (b) | Krupa,Gene (dr)
Blue Reverie
Goodman,Benny (cl) | Williams,Cootie (tp) | Brown,Vernon (tb) | Hodges,Johnny (ss) | Carney,Harry (bs) | Stacy,Jess (p) | Reuss,Allan (g) | Goodman,Harry (b) | Krupa,Gene (dr)
Jam Session
Honeysuckle Rose
Jam Session | Goodman,Benny (cl) | Clayton,Buck (tp) | James,Harry (tp) | Elman,Ziggy (tp) | Griffin,Chris (tp) | Brown,Vernon (tb) | Ballard,Red (tb) | Hodges,Johnny (as) | Schertzer,Hymie (as) | Koenig,George (as) | Rollini,Arthur (ts) | Russin,Irving 'Babe' (ts) | Young,Lester (ts) | Carney,Harry (bs) | Stacy,Jess (p) | Reuss,Allan (g) | Goodman,Harry (b) | Krupa,Gene (dr)
Benny Goodman
Introducing the Tunes(3:30)
NYC, rec. 1950
Goodman,Benny (talking)
-> Plus Applause, Setting Ups & Tuning Ups between the titels.

C2K 65189 | 2 CD | Live At The Jazz Workshop-Complete
Thelonious Monk Quartet
Don't Blame Me | Ba-Lue Bolivar Ba-Lues-Are | Well You Needn't | Evidence- | Rhythm-A-Ning- | Epistrophy(theme) | Hackensack | Bright Mississippi | Evidence | Epistrophy | Round About Midnight | I'm Getting Sentimental Over You | Just You Just Me | Epistrophy(alt.take) | Blue Monk | Well You Needn't(alt.take) | Bright Mississippi(alt.take) | Bemsha Swing | Round About Midnight(alt.take) | Nutty | Straight No Chaser | Thelonious | Hackensack | Misterioso | Ba-Lue Bolivar Ba-Lues-Are | Epistrophy(theme)
Live at The Jazz Workshop,San Francisco,CA, rec. 3./4.11.1964
Monk,Thelonious (p) | Rouse,Charlie (ts) | Gales,Larry (b) | Riley,Ben (dr)
Thelonious Monk
Memories Of You
Monk,Thelonious (p-solo)

C2K 65288 | 2 CD | Live At The It Club:Complete
Thelonious Monk Quartet
Blue Monk | Well You Needn't | Round About Midnight | Rhythm-A-Ning | Blues Five Spot | Bemsha Swing | Evidence | Nutty | Epistrophy(theme) | Straight No Chaser | Teo | I'm Getting Sentimental Over You | Misterioso | Gallop's Gallop | Ba-Lue Bolivar Ba-Lues-Are | Bright Mississippi | Just You Just Me | All The Things You Are | Epistrophy(theme)
Live at The 'It Club',Los Angeles,CA, rec. 31.10./1.11.1964
Monk,Thelonious (p) | Rouse,Charlie (ts) | Gales,Larry (b) | Riley,Ben (dr)

C2K 65495 | 2 CD | Monk Alone:The Complete Columbia Solo Studio Recordings
Thelonious Monk
Body And Soul
NYC, rec. 31.10.1962
Monk,Thelonious (p-solo)
Body And Soul | Body And Soul(alt.take)
NYC, rec. 1.11.1962
Monk,Thelonious (p-solo)
Just A Gigolo
NYC, rec. 2.11.1962
Monk,Thelonious (p-solo)
Don't Blame Me
NYC, rec. 28.2.1962
Monk,Thelonious (p-solo)
NYC, rec. 27.2.1963
Monk,Thelonious (p-solo)
Nice Work If You Can Get It
NYC, rec. 29.1.1964
Monk,Thelonious (p-solo)
Memories Of You
NYC, rec. 9.3.1964
Monk,Thelonious (p-solo)
I Love You Sweetheart Of All My Dreams | I Love You Sweetheart Of All My Dreams(alt.take)
NYC, rec. 6.10.1964
Monk,Thelonious (p-solo)
I Surrender Dear | Sweet And Lovely | Everything Happens To Me | I Should Care | North Of The Sunset | Sweet And Lovely(alt.take) | Everything Happens To Me(alt.take 1) | Everything Happens To Me(alt.take 2)
Los Angeles,CA, rec. 31.10.1964
Monk,Thelonious (p-solo)
These Foolish Things Remind Me On You | I Hadn't Anyone 'Till Now | I Hadn't Anyone 'Till You(alt.take) | Dinah | Dinah(alt.take) | I'm Confessin'(That I Love You) | I'm Confessin'(That I Love You)(alt.take) | Monk's Point
Los Angeles,CA, rec. 2.11.1964
Monk,Thelonious (p-solo)
Ask Me Now | Ask Me Now(alt.take) | Everything Happens To Me
NYC, rec. 23.2.1965
Monk,Thelonious (p-solo)
Ruby My Dear | Ruby My Dear(alt.take) | Introspection | Introspection(alt.take) | Darn That Dream
NYC, rec. 2.3.1965
Monk,Thelonious (p-solo)
This Is My Story,This Is My Song
NYC, rec. 14.11.1966
Monk,Thelonious (p-solo)
Between The Devil And The Deep Blue Sea
NYC, rec. 10.1.1967
Monk,Thelonious (p-solo)
Round About Midnight
Los Angeles,CA, rec. 19.11.1968
Monk,Thelonious (p-solo)

C2K 65686 | 2 CD | Peggy Lee & Benny Goodman:The Complete Recordings 1941-1947
Peggy Lee With The Benny Goodman Orchestra
Elmer's Tune | I See A Million People | My Old Flame
Chicago,Ill, rec. 15./20.8.1941
Lee,Peggy (voc) | Goodman,Benny (cl) | Butterfield,Billy (tp) | Williams,Cootie (tp) | Maxwell,Jimmy (tp) | Davis,Al (tp) | McGarity,Lou (tb) | Cutshall,Cutty (tb) | Martin,Skippy (as) | Neagley,Clint (as) | Musso,Vido (ts) | Berg,George (ts) | Gentry,Charles (bs) | Powell,Mel (p,arr) | Morgan,Tom (g) | Simmons,John (b) | Catlett,Big Sid (dr)
That's The Way It Goes | Let's Do It(Let's Fall In Love)
NYC, rec. 25.9.1941
Lee,Peggy (voc) | Goodman,Benny (cl) | Butterfield,Billy (tp) | Williams,Cootie (tp) | Maxwell,Jimmy (tp) | Davis,Al (tp) | McGarity,Lou (tb) | Cutshall,Cutty (tb) | Martin,Skippy (as) | Neagley,Clint (as) | Musso,Vido (ts) | Berg,George (ts) | Gentry,Charles (bs) | Powell,Mel (p,arr) | Morgan,Tom (g) | Stuhlmaker,Mort (b)
I Got It Bad And That Ain't Good | My Old Flame
NYC, rec. 2.10.1941
Lee,Peggy (voc) | Goodman,Benny (cl) | Butterfield,Billy (tp) | Williams,Cootie (tp) | Maxwell,Jimmy (tp) | Davis,Al (tp) | McGarity,Lou (tb) | Cutshall,Cutty (tb) | Martin,Skippy (as) | Neagley,Clint (as) | Musso,Vido (ts) | Berg,George (ts) | Gentry,Charles (bs) | Powell,Mel (p,arr) | Morgan,Tom (g) | Stuhlmaker,Mort (b) | Catlett,Big Sid (dr)
How Deep Is The Ocean | Shady Lady Bird
NYC, rec. 8.10.1941
Lee,Peggy (voc) | Goodman,Benny (cl) | Butterfield,Billy (tp) | Williams,Cootie (tp) | Maxwell,Jimmy (tp) | Davis,Al (tp) | McGarity,Lou (tb) | Cutshall,Cutty (tb) | Martin,Skippy (as) | Neagley,Clint (as) | Musso,Vido (ts) | Berg,George (ts) | Gentry,Charles (bs) | Powell,Mel (p,arr) | Morgan,Tom (g) | Weiss,Sid (b) | Collier,Ralph (dr)
Let's Do It
NYC, rec. 21.10.1941
Lee,Peggy (voc) | Goodman,Benny (cl) | Butterfield,Billy (tp) | Williams,Cootie (tp) | Maxwell,Jimmy (tp) | Davis,Al (tp) | McGarity,Lou (tb) | Cutshall,Cutty (tb) | Schwartz,Julie (as) | Neagley,Clint (as) | Musso,Vido (ts) | Berg,George (ts) | Gentry,Charles (bs) | Powell,Mel (p,arr) | Morgan,Tom (g) | Weiss,Sid (b) | Collier,Ralph (dr)
Somebody Else Is Taking My Place | Somebody Noboday Loves | How Long Has That Train Been Gone | That Did It,Marie
NYC, rec. 13.11.1941
Lee,Peggy (voc) | Goodman,Benny (cl) | Butterfield,Billy (tp) | Williams,Cootie (tp) | Maxwell,Jimmy (tp) | Davis,Al (tp) | McGarity,Lou (tb) | Cutshall,Cutty (tb) | Schwartz,Julie (as) | Neagley,Clint (as) | Musso,Vido (ts) | Berg,George (ts) | Gentry,Charles (bs) | Powell,Mel (p,arr) | Morgan,Tom (g) | Weiss,Sid (b) | Collier,Ralph (dr)
Winter Weather | Everything I Love
NYC, rec. 27.11.1941
Lee,Peggy (voc) | Goodman,Benny (cl) | Ferrante,Joe (tp) | Maxwell,Jimmy (tp) | Davis,Al (tp) | McGarity,Lou (tb) | Cutshall,Cutty (tb) | Kane,Sol (as) | Neagley,Clint (as) | Musso,Vido (ts) | Berg,George (ts) | Gentry,Charles (bs) | Powell,Mel (p) | Morgan,Tom (g) | Weiss,Sid (b) | Collier,Ralph (dr) | London,Art (voc)

Not Mine | Not A Care In The World
NYC, rec. 10.12.1941
Lee,Peggy (voc) | Goodman,Benny (cl) | Privin,Bernie (tp) | Maxwell,Jimmy (tp) | Davis,Al (tp) | McGarity,Lou (tb) | Cutshall,Cutty (tb) | Kane,Sol (as) | Neagley,Clint (as) | Musso,Vido (ts) | Berg,George (ts) | Gentry,Charles (bs) | Powell,Mel (p,arr) | Morgan,Tom (g) | Weiss,Sid (b) | Collier,Ralph (dr)

Peggy Lee With Benny Goodman And His Sextet
Blues In The Night | Where Or When | On The Sunny Side Of The Street | NYC
rec. 24.12.1941
Lee,Peggy (voc) | Goodman,Benny (cl) | McGarity,Lou (tb) | Cutshall,Cutty (tb) | Powell,Mel (p,arr) | Morgan,Tom (g) | Weiss,Sid (b) | Collier,Ralph (dr)

Peggy Lee With The Benny Goodman Orchestra
The Lamp OfMemory(Incertidumbre) | If You Build A Better Moustrap | When The Roses Bloom Again
NYC, rec. 15.1.1942
Lee,Peggy (voc) | Goodman,Benny (cl) | Privin,Bernie (tp) | Maxwell,Jimmy (tp) | Davis,Al (tp) | McGarity,Lou (tb) | Cutshall,Cutty (tb) | Kane,Sol (as) | Neagley,Clint (as) | Musso,Vido (ts) | Berg,George (ts) | Gentry,Charles (bs) | Powell,Mel (p,arr) | Morgan,Tom (g) | Weiss,Sid (b) | Collier,Ralph (dr)

My Little Cousin
NYC, rec. 5.2.1942
Lee,Peggy (voc) | Goodman,Benny (cl) | Privin,Bernie (tp) | Maxwell,Jimmy (tp) | Davis,Al (tp) | McGarity,Lou (tb) | Cutshall,Cutty (tb) | Kane,Sol (as) | Neagley,Clint (as) | Musso,Vido (ts) | Berg,George (ts) | Ralston,Art (bs) | Powell,Mel (p,arr) | Morgan,Tom (g) | Weiss,Sid (b) | Collier,Ralph (dr)

Peggy Lee With Benny Goodman And His Quintet
The Way You Look Tonight
NYC, rec. 10.3.1942
Lee,Peggy (voc) | Goodman,Benny (cl) | McGarity,Lou (tb) | Powell,Mel (p,arr) | Morgan,Tom (g) | Weiss,Sid (b) | Collier,Ralph (dr)

Peggy Lee With The Benny Goodman Orchestra
I Threw A Kiss In The Ocean | We'll Meet Again | Full Moon(Noche De Luna) | There Won't Be A Shortage Of Love
NYC, rec. 12.3.1942
Lee,Peggy (voc) | Goodman,Benny (cl) | Privin,Bernie (tp) | Maxwell,Jimmy (tp) | Napton,John (tp) | McGarity,Lou (tb) | Cutshall,Cutty (tb) | Kane,Sol (as) | Shiffman,Bud (as) | Musso,Vido (ts) | Berg,George (ts) | Ralston,Art (bs) | Powell,Mel (p,arr) | Morgan,Tom (g) | Weiss,Sid (b) | Collier,Ralph (dr)

You're Easy To Dance With | All I Need Is You
NYC, rec. 14.5.1942
Lee,Peggy (voc) | Goodman,Benny (cl) | Privin,Bernie (tp) | Maxwell,Jimmy (tp) | Napton,John (tp) | McGarity,Lou (tb) | Castaldo,Charlie (tb) | Kane,Sol (as) | Shiffman,Bud (as) | Musso,Vido (ts) | Berg,George (ts) | Ralston,Art (bs) | Powell,Mel (p,arr) | Morgan,Tom (g) | Weiss,Sid (b) | Stoller,Alvin (dr)

Why Don't You Do Right | Let's Say A Prayer
NYC, rec. 27./30.7.1942
Lee,Peggy (voc) | Goodman,Benny (cl) | Faso,Tony (tp) | Maxwell,Jimmy (tp) | Stearns,Lawrence (tp) | McGarity,Lou (tb) | Castaldo,Charlie (tb) | Schertzer,Hymie (as) | Neagley,Clint (as) | Walton,Jon (ts) | Sims,Zoot (ts) | Poland,Bob (bs) | Powell,Mel (p,arr) | Barbour,Dave (g) | Hill,Cliff (b) | Davies,Howard (dr)

Peggy Lee With Benny Goodman And The Paul Weston Orchestra
The Freedom Train
Hollywood,CA, rec. 12.9.1947
Lee,Peggy (voc) | Goodman,Benny (cl) | Whiting,Margaret (voc) | Mercer,Johnny (voc) | Pied Piepers,The (voc) | Orchestra | Weston,Paul (cond,arr) | details unknown

Peggy Lee With The Benny Goodman Orchestra
Keep Me In Mind | For Every Man There's A Woman
Hollywood,CA, rec. 2.12.1947
Lee,Peggy (voc) | Goodman,Benny (cl) | Best,John (tp) | Kusby,Eddie (tb) | Lott,Sinclair (fr-h) | Kievman,Louis (viola) | McLarand,Paul (as) | Dumont,Jack (as) | Meyers,Bumps (ts) | Gentry,Chuck (bs) | Norvo,Red (vib) | Powell,Mel (p,arr) | Hendrickson,Al (g) | Shapiro,Artie (b) | Romersa,Tom 'Tommy' (dr)

C2K 65774 | 2 CD | Bitches Brew

Miles Davis Group
Sanctuary
NYC, rec. 19.8.1969
Davis,Miles (tp) | Shorter,Wayne (ss) | Corea,Chick (el-p) | Holland,Dave (b) | DeJohnette,Jack (dr) | Riley,Jim (perc)

Bitches Brew
Davis,Miles (el-tp) | Shorter,Wayne (ss) | Maupin,Bennie (b-cl) | Zawinul,Joe (el-p) | Brooks,Harvey (el-b) | McLaughlin,John (el-g) | White,Lenny (dr) | Alias,Charles (dr)

Spanish Key
NYC, rec. 20.8.1969
Davis,Miles (el-tp) | Shorter,Wayne (ss) | Maupin,Bennie (b-cl) | Zawinul,Joe (el-p) | Young,Larry (el-p) | Brooks,Harvey (el-b) | McLaughlin,John (el-g) | White,Lenny (dr) | Alias,Charles (dr)

Miles Runs The Voodoo Down
Davis,Miles (tp) | Shorter,Wayne (ss) | Maupin,Bennie (b-cl) | Young,Larry (el-p) | Brooks,Harvey (el-b) | McLaughlin,John (el-g) | White,Lenny (dr) | Alias,Charles (dr)

Pharoah's Dance
NYC, rec. 21.8.1969
Davis,Miles (tp) | Shorter,Wayne (ss) | Maupin,Bennie (b-cl) | Young,Larry (el-p) | Zawinul,Joe (el-p) | Brooks,Harvey (el-b) | McLaughlin,John (el-g) | White,Lenny (dr) | Alias,Charles (dr)

John McLaughlin
Maupin,Bennie (b-cl) | Young,Larry (el-p) | Zawinul,Joe (el-p) | Brooks,Harvey (el-b) | McLaughlin,John (el-g) | White,Lenny (dr) | Alias,Charles (dr)

Feio
NYC, rec. 28.1.1970
Davis,Miles (tp) | Shorter,Wayne (ss) | Maupin,Bennie (b-cl) | Corea,Chick (el-p) | Zawinul,Joe (el-p) | McLaughlin,John (el-g) | Holland,Dave (b) | Cobham,Billy (dr) | DeJohnette,Jack (dr) | Moreira,Airto (perc)

C2K 65900 | 2 CD | Expectations

Keith Jarrett Group
The Magician In You | Take Me Back
NYC, rec. 5.4.1972
Jarrett,Keith (ss,p,tambourine) | Brown,Sam (g) | Haden,Charlie (b) | Motian,Paul (dr) | Moreira,Airto (congas)

Keith Jarrett Group With Brass
Nomads
Jarrett,Keith (p,org,tambourine) | Brown,Sam (g) | Haden,Charlie (b) | Motian,Paul (dr) | Moreira,Airto (congas) | Brass Section

Keith Jarrett With Strings
Vision
NYC, rec. 6.4.1972
Jarrett,Keith (p) | String Section

Keith Jarrett Group With Strings
Expectations
Jarrett,Keith (p) | Haden,Charlie (b) | Motian,Paul (dr) | String Section
There's A Road (God's River)
Jarrett,Keith (p) | Brown,Sam (g) | Motian,Paul (dr) | String Section

Keith Jarrett Group
Bring Back The Time When (If)
Jarrett,Keith (ss,p,tambourine) | Redman,Dewey (ts) | Haden,Charlie (b) | Motian,Paul (dr) | Moreira,Airto (perc)

Keith Jarrett Group With Brass
Common Mama
Jarrett,Keith (ss,p,tambourine) | Redman,Dewey (ts) | Haden,Charlie (b) | Motian,Paul (dr) | Moreira,Airto (perc) | Brass Section

Keith Jarrett Group
Roussillon
NYC, rec. 27.4.1972
Jarrett,Keith (ss,p) | Redman,Dewey (ts,cowbell) | Haden,Charlie (b) | Motian,Paul (dr)

The Circular Letter (For J.K.) | Sundance
Jarrett,Keith (ss,p) | Redman,Dewey (ts) | Brown,Sam (g) | Haden,Charlie (b) | Motian,Paul (dr) | Moreira,Airto (perc)

C3K 65145 | 3 CD | Charles Mingus:The Complete 1959 Columbia Recordings

Charles Mingus Septet
Better Git It In Your Soul | Better Git It In Your Soul(alt.take) | Fables Of Faubus | Pussy Cat Dues | Jelly Roll | Jelly Roll(alt.take) | Pedal Point Blues | GG Train | Girls Of My Dreams
NYC, rec. 5.5.1959
Mingus,Charles (b) | Knepper,Jimmy (tb) | Handy,John (cl,as) | Hadi [Curtis Porter],Shafti (as,ts) | Ervin,Booker (ts) | Parlan,Horace (p) | Richmond,Dannie (dr)

Bird Calls | Bird Calls(alt.take)
Mingus,Charles (b) | Handy,John (as) | Hadi [Curtis Porter],Shafti (as,ts) | Ervin,Booker (ts) | Parlan,Horace (p) | Richmond,Dannie (dr)
Open Letter To Duke | Boogie Stomp Shuffle | Self-Portrait In 3 Colors
NYC, rec. 12.5.1959
Mingus,Charles (b) | Dennis,Willie (tb) | Handy,John (as) | Hadi [Curtis Porter],Shafti (as) | Ervin,Booker (ts) | Parlan,Horace (p) | Richmond,Dannie (dr)

Goodbye Pork Pie Hat
Mingus,Charles (b) | Handy,John (as) | Hadi [Curtis Porter],Shafti (as) | Ervin,Booker (ts) | Parlan,Horace (p) | Richmond,Dannie (dr)

Charles Mingus Orchestra
Gunslinging Bird | Song With Orange | Song With Orange(alt.take) | Diana | Diana(alt.take) | Far Wells Mill Valley
NYC, rec. 1.11.1959
Mingus,Charles (b) | Williams,Richard (tp) | Knepper,Jimmy (tb) | Handy,John (as) | Ervin,Booker (ts) | Golson,Benny (ts) | Richardson,Jerome (bs) | Charles,Teddy (vib) | Hanna,Sir Roland (p) | Richmond,Dannie (dr)

Strollin'
Mingus,Charles (b) | Williams,Richard (tp) | Knepper,Jimmy (tb) | Handy,John (as) | Ervin,Booker (ts) | Golson,Benny (ts) | Richardson,Jerome (bs) | Charles,Teddy (vib) | Bunick,Floris Nico (p) | Richmond,Dannie (dr) | Gordon,Honey[Honi] (voc)
New Now Know How | New Now Know How(alt.take)
Mingus,Charles (b) | Williams,Richard (tp) | Knepper,Jimmy (tb) | Handy,John (as) | Ervin,Booker (ts) | Golson,Benny (ts) | Richardson,Jerome (bs) | Bunick,Floris Nico (p) | Richmond,Dannie (dr) | Gordon,Honey[Honi] (voc)
Things Ain't What They Used To Be | Mood Indigo | Slop
NYC, rec. 13.11.1959
Mingus,Charles (b) | Ellis,Don (tp) | Knepper,Jimmy (tb) | Handy,John (as) | Ervin,Booker (ts) | Hanna,Sir Roland (p) | Richmond,Dannie (dr)
Put Me In That Dungeon
Mingus,Charles (b) | Ellis,Don (tp) | Knepper,Jimmy (tb) | Handy,John (as) | Ervin,Booker (ts) | Hanna,Sir Roland (p) | Brown,Maurice (cello) | Barab,Seymour (cello) | Richmond,Dannie (dr)

C4K 87106 | CD | Miles Davis In Person-Friday Night At The Blackhawk,San Francisco,Vol.1 | EAN 5099708710620

Miles Davis Quintet
Oleo | No Blues | If I Were A Bell | If I Were A Bell(alt.take) | Fran-Dance | On Green Dolphin Street | On Green Dolphin Street(alt.take) | The Theme | The Theme(alt.take) | Round About Midnight | Well You Needn't | Autumn Leaves | Two Bass Hit | Neo | Neo(alt.take) | I Thought About You | I Thought About You(alt.take) | Walkin' | Walkin'(alt.take) | Walkin' | Bye Bye Blackbird | All Of You | No Blues | No Blues(alt.take) | So What | Bye Bye(Theme) | Love I've Found You | Love I've Found You(alt.take) | Someday My Prince Will Come | Softly As In A Morning Sunrise
Live at The Black Hawk,San Francisco,CA, rec. 21./22.4.1961
Davis,Miles (tp) | Mobley,Hank (ts) | Kelly,Wynton (p) | Chambers,Paul (b) | Cobb,Jimmy (dr)

C6K 67398 | 6 CD | Miles Davis Quintet 1965-1968

E.S.P. | R.J.
Los Angeles,CA, rec. 20.1.1965
Davis,Miles (tp) | Shorter,Wayne (ts) | Hancock,Herbie (p) | Carter,Ron (b) | Williams,Tony (dr)

Eighty-One | Little One
Los Angeles,CA, rec. 21.1.1965
Davis,Miles (tp) | Shorter,Wayne (ts) | Hancock,Herbie (p) | Carter,Ron (b) | Williams,Tony (dr)

Irish | Agitation | Mood
Los Angeles,CA, rec. 22.1.1965
Davis,Miles (tp) | Shorter,Wayne (ts) | Hancock,Herbie (p) | Carter,Ron (b) | Williams,Tony (dr)

Circle | Orbits | Dolores | Freedom Jazz Dance
NYC, rec. 24.10.1966
Davis,Miles (tp) | Shorter,Wayne (ts) | Hancock,Herbie (p) | Carter,Ron (b) | Williams,Tony (dr)

Gingerbread Boy | Footprints
NYC, rec. 25.10.1966
Davis,Miles (tp) | Shorter,Wayne (ts) | Hancock,Herbie (p) | Carter,Ron (b) | Williams,Tony (dr)

Limbo
Hollywood,CA, rec. 9.5.1966
Davis,Miles (tp) | Shorter,Wayne (ts) | Hancock,Herbie (p) | Williams,Buster (b) | Williams,Tony (dr)

Limbo | Vonetta
NYC, rec. 16.5.1967
Davis,Miles (tp) | Shorter,Wayne (ts) | Hancock,Herbie (p) | Carter,Ron (b) | Williams,Tony (dr)

Masqualero | Masqualero(alt.take) | The Sorcerer
NYC, rec. 17.5.1967
Davis,Miles (tp) | Shorter,Wayne (ts) | Hancock,Herbie (p) | Carter,Ron (b) | Williams,Tony (dr)

Prince Of Darkness
NYC, rec. 24.5.1967
Davis,Miles (tp) | Shorter,Wayne (ts) | Hancock,Herbie (p) | Carter,Ron (b) | Williams,Tony (dr)

Pee Wee
Shorter,Wayne (ts) | Hancock,Herbie (p) | Carter,Ron (b) | Williams,Tony (dr)

Water Babies | Nefertiti
NYC, rec. 7.6.1967
Davis,Miles (tp) | Shorter,Wayne (ss,ts) | Hancock,Herbie (p) | Carter,Ron (b) | Williams,Tony (dr)

Capricorn | Madness(rehersal)
NYC, rec. 13.6.1967
Davis,Miles (tp) | Shorter,Wayne (ss,ts) | Hancock,Herbie (p) | Carter,Ron (b) | Williams,Tony (dr)

Hand Jive | Hand Jive(alt.take 1) | Hand Jive(alt.take 2)
NYC, rec. 22.6.1967
Davis,Miles (tp) | Shorter,Wayne (ts) | Hancock,Herbie (p) | Carter,Ron (b) | Williams,Tony (dr)

Madness | Madness(alt.take) | Sweet Pea
NYC, rec. 23.6.1967
Davis,Miles (tp) | Shorter,Wayne (ts) | Hancock,Herbie (p) | Carter,Ron (b) | Williams,Tony (dr)

Fall | Pinocchio | Pinocchio(alt.take) | Riot
NYC, rec. 19.7.1967
Davis,Miles (tp) | Shorter,Wayne (ts) | Hancock,Herbie (p) | Carter,Ron (b) | Williams,Tony (dr)

Thisness(rehersal)
NYC, rec. May/July 1967
Davis,Miles (tp) | Shorter,Wayne (ts) | Hancock,Herbie (p) | Carter,Ron (b) | Williams,Tony (dr)

Circle In The Round
NYC, rec. 4.12.1967
Davis,Miles (tp,chimes) | Shorter,Wayne (ts) | Beck,Joe (g) | Hancock,Herbie (celeste) | Carter,Ron (b) | Williams,Tony (dr)
Water On The Pond
NYC, rec. 28.12.1967
Davis,Miles (tp,chimes) | Shorter,Wayne (ts) | Beck,Joe (g) | Hancock,Herbie (el-p,el-harpsichord) | Carter,Ron (b) | Williams,Tony (dr)

Fun
NYC, rec. 12.1.1968
Davis,Miles (tp,chimes) | Shorter,Wayne (ts) | Pizzarelli,Bucky (g) | Hancock,Herbie (el-harpsichord) | Carter,Ron (b) | Williams,Tony (dr)
Teo's Bag | Teo's Bag(alt.take)
NYC, rec. 16.1.1968
Davis,Miles (tp) | Shorter,Wayne (ts) | Hancock,Herbie (p) | Carter,Ron (b) | Williams,Tony (dr)

Paraphernalia
Davis,Miles (tp) | Shorter,Wayne (ts) | Benson,George (g) | Hancock,Herbie (p) | Carter,Ron (b) | Williams,Tony (dr)
I Have A Dream(rehersal) | Speak Like A Child(rehersal)
NYC, rec. 25.1.1968
Davis,Miles (tp) | Shorter,Wayne (ts) | Benson,George or Joe Beck (g) | Hancock,Herbie (p) | Carter,Ron (b) | Williams,Tony (dr)

Slide Car(incomplete)
NYC, rec. 13.2.1968
Davis,Miles (tp) | Shorter,Wayne (ts) | Beck,Joe (g) | Hancock,Herbie (p) | Carter,Ron (b) | Williams,Tony (dr)

Slide Car
NYC, rec. 15.2.1968
Davis,Miles (tp) | Shorter,Wayne (ts) | Hancock,Herbie (p) | Carter,Ron (b) | Williams,Tony (dr)

Slide Car | Sanctuary
Davis,Miles (tp) | Shorter,Wayne (ts) | Benson,George (g) | Hancock,Herbie (p) | Carter,Ron (b) | Williams,Tony (dr)

Country Son | Country Son(alt.take)
NYC, rec. 15.5.1968
Davis,Miles (tp) | Shorter,Wayne (ts) | Hancock,Herbie (p) | Carter,Ron (b) | Williams,Tony (dr)

Black Comedy | Black Comedy(alt.take)
NYC, rec. 16.5.1968
Davis,Miles (tp) | Shorter,Wayne (ts) | Hancock,Herbie (p) | Carter,Ron (b) | Williams,Tony (dr)

Stuff
NYC, rec. 17.5.1968
Davis,Miles (tp) | Shorter,Wayne (ts) | Hancock,Herbie (el-p) | Carter,Ron (el-b) | Williams,Tony (dr)

Tout De Suite(incomplete)
NYC, rec. 21.5.1968
Davis,Miles (tp) | Shorter,Wayne (ts) | Hancock,Herbie (el-p) | Carter,Ron (el-b) | Williams,Tony (dr)

Petits Machines
NYC, rec. 19.6.1968
Davis,Miles (tp) | Shorter,Wayne (ts) | Hancock,Herbie (el-p) | Carter,Ron (el-b) | Williams,Tony (dr)

Tout De Suite | Tout De Suite(alt.take)
NYC, rec. 20.6.1968
Davis,Miles (tp) | Shorter,Wayne (ts) | Hancock,Herbie (el-p) | Carter,Ron (el-b) | Williams,Tony (dr)

Filles De Kilimanjaro
NYC, rec. 21.6.1968
Davis,Miles (tp) | Shorter,Wayne (ts) | Hancock,Herbie (el-p) | Carter,Ron (el-b) | Williams,Tony (dr)

CK 32766 | CD | Between Nothingness & Eternity

The Mahavishnu Orchestra
Trilogy: | The Sunlit Path- | La Mere De La Mer- | Tomorrow's Story Not The Same- | Sister Andrea | Dream
Live at Central Park,NYC, rec. August 1973
Mahavishnu Orchestra | McLaughlin,John (g) | Goodman,Jerry (v) | Hammer,Jan (p,synth) | Laird,Rick (b) | Cobham,Billy (dr)

CK 48827 | CD | Seven Steps To Heaven

Miles Davis Quintet
I Fall In Love Too Easily | Baby Won't You Please Come Home
Los Angeles,CA, rec. 16.4.1963
Davis,Miles (tp) | Coleman,George (ts) | Feldman,Victor (p) | Carter,Ron (b) | Butler,Frank (dr)
Seven Steps To Heaven | So Near So Far | Joshua
NYC, rec. 14.5.1963
Davis,Miles (tp) | Coleman,George (ts) | Hancock,Herbie (p) | Carter,Ron (b) | Williams,Tony (dr)

CK 61468 | CD | Jazz:Ted Hot And Cool

Dave Brubeck Quartet
Lover | Little Girl Blue | Fare Thee Well, Annabelle | Sometimes I'm Happy | The Duke | Back Home Again In Indiana | Love Walked In | Taking A Chance On Love | Closing Time Blues
Live at Basin Street,NYC, rec. 12.10.1954/23.7.& 9.8.1955
Brubeck,Dave (p) | Desmond,Paul (as) | Bates,Bob (b) | Dodge,Joe (dr)

CK 63536 | CD | Monk's Dream | EAN 5099706353621

Thelonious Monk Quartet
Bye-Ya | Blue Bolivar Blues | Blue Bolivar Blues(alt.take)
NYC, rec. 31.10.1962
Monk,Thelonious (p) | Rouse,Charlie (ts) | Ore,John (b) | Dunlop,Frankie (dr)

Bright Mississippi | Bright Mississippi(alt.take)
NYC, rec. 1.11.1962
Monk,Thelonious (p) | Rouse,Charlie (ts) | Ore,John (b) | Dunlop,Frankie (dr)

Monk's Dream | Monk's Dream(alt.take)
NYC, rec. 2.11.1925
Monk,Thelonious (p) | Rouse,Charlie (ts) | Ore,John (b) | Dunlop,Frankie (dr)

Sweet And Lovely | Blues Five Spot
NYC, rec. 6.11.1962
Monk,Thelonious (p) | Rouse,Charlie (ts) | Ore,John (b) | Dunlop,Frankie (dr)

Thelonious Monk
Body And Soul | Body And Soul(alt.take) | Just A Gigolo
NYC, rec. 1./2.11.1962
Monk,Thelonious (p-solo)

CK 63962 | CD | Aura

Miles Davis With The Danish Radio Big Band
Intro | White | Red | Green | Blue | Electric Red
Copenhagen,Denmark, rec. 31.1.985
Davis,Miles (tp) | Danish Radio Big Band,The | Mikkelborg,Palle (tp,fl-h,cond,arr) | Rosenfeld,Benny (tp,fl-h) | Bolvig,Palle (tp,fl-h) | Sulieman[Leonard Graham],Idrees (tp,fl-h) | Winther,Jens (tp,fl-h) | Knudsen,Perry (tp,fl-h) | Nilsson,Vincent (tb) | Larsen,Ture (tb) | Jensen,Ole Kurt (tb) | Engel,Jens (b-tb) | Windfeld,Axel (b-tb,tuba) | Zum Vohrde,Jan (fl,ss,as) | Thilo,Jesper (fl,ss,ts) | Carsten,Per (fl,as) | Jaedig,Bent (fl,ss,ts) | Karskov,Uffe (fl,alto-fl,cl,ts) | Madsen,Flemming (fl,cl,b-cl,bs) | Eje,Niels (oboe) | Tornquist,Lillian (harp) | Hansen,Ole Kock (keyboards) | Clausen,Thomas (keyboards) | Knudsen,Kenneth (keyboards) | Roupe,Bjarne (g) | Orsted-Pedersen,Niels-Henning (b) | Stief,Bo (el-b) | Gruvstedt,Lennart (dr) | Weisgard,Ethan (perc) | Mazur,Marilyn (perc) | Wilburn,Vincent (simmon's-dr) | Hess-Taysen,Eva (voice)

Orange | Violet
Copenhagen,Denmark, rec. 31.1.1985
Davis,Miles (tp) | Danish Radio Big Band,The | Mikkelborg,Palle (tp,fl-h,cond,arr) | Rosenfeld,Benny (tp,fl-h) | Bolvig,Palle (tp,fl-h) | Sulieman[Leonard Graham],Idrees (tp,fl-h) | Winther,Jens (tp,fl-h) | Knudsen,Perry (tp,fl-h) | Nilsson,Vincent (tb) | Larsen,Ture (tb) | Jensen,Ole Kurt (tb) | Engel,Jens (b-tb) | Windfeld,Axel (b-tb,tuba) | Zum Vohrde,Jan (fl,ss,as) | Thilo,Jesper (fl,ss,ts) | Carsten,Per (fl,as) | Jaedig,Bent (fl,ss,ts) | Karskov,Uffe (fl,alto-fl,cl,ts) | Madsen,Flemming (fl,cl,b-cl,bs) | Eje,Niels (oboe) | Tornquist,Lillian (harp) | Hansen,Ole Kock (keyboards) | Clausen,Thomas (keyboards) | Knudsen,Kenneth (keyboards) | Roupe,Bjarne (g) | McLaughlin,John (g) | Orsted-Pedersen,Niels-Henning (b) | Stief,Bo (el-b) | Gruvstedt,Lennart (dr) | Weisgard,Ethan (perc) | Mazur,Marilyn (perc) | Wilburn,Vincent (simmon's-dr) | Hess-Taysen,Eva (voice)

The Danish Radio Big Band
Yellow | Indigo
Danish Radio Big Band,The | Mikkelborg,Palle (tp,fl-h,cond,arr) | Rosenfeld,Benny (tp,fl-h) | Bolvig,Palle (tp,fl-h) | Sulieman[Leonard

Graham],Idrees (tp,fl-h) | Winther,Jens (tp,fl-h) | Knudsen,Perry (tp,fl-h) | Nilsson,Vincent (tb) | Larsen,Ture (tb) | Jensen,Ole Kurt (tb) | Engel,Jens (b-tb) | Windfeld,Axel (b-tb,tuba) | Zum Vohrde,Jan (fl,ss,as) | Thilo,Jesper (fl,ss,ts) | Carsten,Per (fl,as) | Jaedig,Bent (fl,ss,ts) | Karskov,Uffe (fl,alto-fl,cl,ts) | Madsen,Flemming (fl,cl,b-cl,bs) | Eje,Niels (oboe) | Tornquist,Lillian (harp) | Hansen,Ole Kock (keyboards) | Clausen,Thomas (keyboards) | Knudsen,Kenneth (keyboards) | Roupe,Bjarne (g) | Orsted-Pedersen,Niels-Henning (b) | Stief,Bo (el-b) | Gruvstedt,Lennart (dr) | Weisgard,Ethan (perc) | Mazur,Marilyn (perc) | Wilburn,Vincent (simmon's-dr) | Hess-Taysen,Eva (voice)

CK 63980 | CD | On The Corner
Miles Davis Group
On The Corner | New York Girl | Thinkin' One Thing And Doin' Another | Vote For Miles
NYC, rec. 1.6.1972
Davis,Miles (tp) | Liebman,Dave (ss) | Macero,Teo (sax) | Corea,Chick (keyboards) | Hancock,Herbie (keyboards) | Williams,Harold Ivory (keyboards) | McLaughlin,John (g) | Henderson,Michael (el-b) | Walcott,Collin (el-sitar) | Roy,Badal (tablas) | Hart,Billy (dr) | Alias,Don (dr) | DeJohnette,Jack (dr)
One And One | Helen Butte | Mr.Freedom X
NYC, rec. 6.6.1972
Davis,Miles (tp) | Garnett,Carlos Alfredo (ss,ts) | Hancock,Herbie (keyboards) | Williams,Harold Ivory (keyboards) | Kreamen,David (g) | Henderson,Michael (el-b) | Walcott,Collin (el-sitar) | Roy,Badal (tablas) | Hart,Billy (dr) | DeJohnette,Jack (dr) | M'tume,James[Forman] (perc)
Black Satin
NYC, rec. 7.7.1972
Davis,Miles (tp) | Lawson,Cedric (org) | Lucas,Reggie (g) | Henderson,Michael (el-b) | Balakrishna,Khalil (el-sitar) | Roy,Badal (tablas) | Foster,Al (dr) | M'tume,James[Forman] (perc)

CK 64925 | CD | Louis Armstrong Plays W.C.Handy
Louis Armstrong And His All Stars
Loveless Love | Loveless Love(rehersal sequence) | Aunt Hagar's Blues | Beale Street Blues | Ole Miss | Hesitation Blues | Hesitation Blues(rehersal sequence)
Chicago,Ill, rec. 12.7.1954
Armstrong,Louis (tp,voc) | Young,Trummy (tb) | Bigard,Barney (cl) | Kyle,Billy (p) | Shaw,Arvell (b) | Deems,Barrett (dr) | Middleton,Velma (voc)
St.Louis Blues | Memphis Blues | Atlanta Blues | Monologue by Louis Armstrong | Long Gone | Long Gone(rehersal sequence)
Chicago,Ill, rec. 13.7.1954
Armstrong,Louis (tp,voc) | Young,Trummy (tb) | Bigard,Barney (cl) | Kyle,Billy (p) | Shaw,Arvell (b) | Deems,Barrett (dr) | Middleton,Velma (voc)
Yellow Dog Blues | Chantez Les Bas
Chicago,Ill, rec. 14.7.1954
Armstrong,Louis (tp,voc) | Young,Trummy (tb) | Bigard,Barney (cl) | Kyle,Billy (p) | Shaw,Arvell (b) | Deems,Barrett (dr)
Alligator Story | Interview(2:44) with W.C.Handy by George Avakian
Chicago,Ill, rec. 12.-14.7.1954
Armstrong,Louis (talking) | Handy,W.C. (talking) | Avakian,George (interviewer)

CK 64926 | CD | Ambassador Satch
Tin Roof Blues | Undecided | Dardanella
Live at Amsterdam, rec. 29.10.1955
Armstrong,Louis (tp) | Young,Trummy (tb) | Hall,Edmond (cl) | Kyle,Billy (p) | Shaw,Arvell (b) | Deems,Barrett (dr)
The Faithfull Husar | All Of Me | 12th Street Rag | West End Blues | Tiger Rag | Clarinet Marmalade | Someday You'll Be Sorry
Live at Milano,Italy, rec. 20./21.12.1955
Armstrong,Louis (tp,voc) | Young,Trummy (tb) | Hall,Edmond (cl) | Kyle,Billy (p) | Shaw,Arvell (b) | Deems,Barrett (dr)
Royal Garden Blues | Muskrat Ramble | When The Red Red Robin Comes Bob Bob Bobbin' Along
Los Angeles,CA, rec. 24.1.1956
Armstrong,Louis (tp) | Young,Trummy (tb) | Hall,Edmond (cl) | Kyle,Billy (p) | Shaw,Arvell (b) | Deems,Barrett (dr)

CK 64927 | CD | Satch Plays Fats(Complete)
I've Got A Feeling I'm Falling | Honeysuckle Rose | Ain't Misbehavin' | Black And Blue | Black And Blue(alt.take) | I've Got A Feeling I'm Falling(alt.take)
NYC, rec. 26.4.1955
Armstrong,Louis (tp,voc) | Young,Trummy (tb) | Bigard,Barney (cl) | Kyle,Billy (p) | Shaw,Arvell (b) | Deems,Barrett (dr) | Middleton,Velma (voc)
Blue Turning Grey Over Me | I'm Crazy 'Bout My Baby | All That Meat And No Potatoes | Blue Turning Grey Over You(alt.take) | I'm Crazy 'Bout My Baby(alt.take)
NYC, rec. 27.4.1955
Armstrong,Louis (tp,voc) | Young,Trummy (tb) | Bigard,Barney (cl) | Kyle,Billy (p) | Shaw,Arvell (b) | Deems,Barrett (dr) | Middleton,Velma (voc)
Squeeze Me | Keepin' Out Of Mischief Now
NYC, rec. 3.5.1955
Armstrong,Louis (tp,voc) | Young,Trummy (tb) | Bigard,Barney (cl) | Kyle,Billy (p) | Shaw,Arvell (b) | Deems,Barrett (dr) | Middleton,Velma (voc)
Louis Armstrong And His Hot Five
Squeeze Me
Chicago,Ill, rec. 29.6.1928
Armstrong,Louis (tp,voc) | Robinson,Fred (tb) | Strong,Jimmy (cl) | Hines,Earl 'Fatha' (p) | Carr,Mancy (bj,voc) | Singleton,Zutty (dr)
Louis Armstrong And His Orchestra
Black And Blue | Sweet Savannah Sue | That Rhythm Man
NYC, rec. 22.7.1929
Armstrong,Louis (tp,voc) | Hobson,Homer (tp) | Robinson,Fred (tb) | Strong,Jimmy (cl,ts) | Wethington,Crawford (as) | Curry,Bert (as) | Dickerson,Carroll (v) | Anderson,Gene (p) | Carr,Mancy (bj) | Briggs,Pete (tuba) | Singleton,Zutty (dr)
Ain't Misbehavin'
NYC, rec. 19.7.1929
Armstrong,Louis (tp,voc) | Hobson,Homer (tp) | Robinson,Fred (tb) | Strong,Jimmy (cl,ts) | Wethington,Crawford (as) | Curry,Bert (as) | Dickerson,Carroll (v) | Anderson,Gene (p) | Carr,Mancy (bj) | Briggs,Pete (tuba) | Singleton,Zutty (dr)
Blue Turning Grey Over Me
NYC, rec. 1.2.1930
Armstrong,Louis (tp,voc) | Johnson,Otis (tp) | Allen,Henry Red (tp) | Higginbotham,J.C. (tb) | Blue,William Thornton (cl,as) | Holmes,Charlie (cl,ss,as) | Hill,Teddy (ts) | Russell,Luis (p,arr) | Johnson,Will (g) | Foster,George 'Pops' (b) | Barbarin,Paul (dr)
Keepin' Out Of Mischief Now
Chicago,Ill, rec. 11.3.1932
Armstrong,Louis (tp,voc) | Randolph,Zilmer (tp) | Jackson,Preston (tb) | Boone,Lester (cl,as) | James,George (cl,ss,as) | Washington,Albert (cl,ts) | Alexander,Charlie (p) | McKendrick,Mike (g,bj) | Lindsey,Johny (b) | Hall,Tubby (dr)

CK 64932 | 2 CD | Ellington At Newport 1956(Complete)
Duke Ellington And His Orchestra
Star Spangled Banner | Black And Tan Fantasy | Tea For Two
Live at Newport,Rhode Island, rec. 7.7.1956
Ellington,Duke (p) | Cook,Willie (tp) | Anderson,Cat (tp) | Woodman,Britt (tb) | Jackson,Quentin (tb) | Sanders,John (v-tb) | Hodges,Johnny (as) | Procope,Russell (cl,as) | Gonsalves,Paul (ts) | Carney,Harry (bs) | Lucas,Al (b) | Woodyard,Sam (dr)
Take The 'A' Train | Newport Festival Suite: | Festival Junction- | Blues To Be There- | Newport Up- | Sophisticated Lady | Day In Day Out | Diminuendo And Crescendo In Blue | I Got It Bad And That Ain't Good | Jeep's Blues | Tulip Or Turnip | Skin Deep | Mood Indigo
Live at Newport,Rhode Island, rec. 7./8.7.1956
Ellington,Duke (p) | Anderson,Cat (tp) | Cook,Willie (tp) | Terry,Clark (tp) | Nance,Ray (tp,voc) | Jackson,Quentin (tb) | Woodman,Britt (tb) | Sanders,John (v-tb) | Hamilton,Jimmy (cl) | Procope,Russell (cl,as) | Hodges,Johnny (as) | Gonsalves,Paul (ts) | Carney,Harry (bs) | Woode,Jimmy (b) | Woodyard,Sam (dr) | Grissom,Jimmy (voc)
I Got It Bad And That Ain't Good | Newport Festival Suite: | Festival Junction- | Blues To Be There- | Newport Up- | Tuning Up- | Festival Junction(rehersal)- | Jeep's Blues
Newport(Studio), rec. 9.7.1956
Ellington,Duke (p) | Anderson,Cat (tp) | Cook,Willie (tp) | Terry,Clark (tp) | Nance,Ray (tp) | Jackson,Quentin (tb) | Woodman,Britt (tb) | Sanders,John (v-tb) | Hamilton,Jimmy (cl) | Procope,Russell (cl,as) | Hodges,Johnny (as) | Gonsalves,Paul (ts) | Carney,Harry (bs) | Woode,Jimmy (b) | Woodyard,Sam (dr)

CK 64935 | CD | Kind Of Blue
Miles Davis Sextet
Freddie Freeloader
NYC, rec. 2.3.1959
Davis,Miles (tp) | Adderley,Julian \'Cannonball\' (as) | Coltrane,John (ts) | Kelly,Wynton (p) | Chambers,Paul (b) | Cobb,Jimmy (dr)
So What
Davis,Miles (tp) | Adderley,Julian \'Cannonball\' (as) | Coltrane,John (ts) | Evans,Bill (p) | Chambers,Paul (b) | Cobb,Jimmy (dr)
Miles Davis Quintet
Blue In Green
Davis,Miles (tp) | Coltrane,John (ts) | Evans,Bill (p) | Chambers,Paul (b) | Cobb,Jimmy (dr)
Miles Davis Sextet
Flamenco Sketches | Flamenco Sketches(alt.take) | All Blues
NYC, rec. 22.4.1959
Davis,Miles (tp) | Adderley,Julian \'Cannonball\' (as) | Coltrane,John (ts) | Evans,Bill (p) | Chambers,Paul (b) | Cobb,Jimmy (dr)

CK 64983 | CD | Sextant
Herbie Hancock Group
Rain Dance | Hidden Shadows | Hornets
San Francisco,CA, rec. 1973
Hancock,Herbie (p,el-p,perc,clavinet,melotron) | Henderson,Eddie (tp,fl-h) | Priester,Julian (tb,b-tb,bells) | Maupin,Bennie (b-cl,ss,perc,piccolo) | Williams,Buster (b,el-b) | Hart,Billy (dr)

CK 64984 | CD | Thrust
Spank-A-Lee | Butterfly | Actual Prof | Palm Grease
San Francisco,CA, rec. August 1974
Hancock,Herbie (p,el-p,synth,clavinet) | Maupin,Bennie (alto-fl,b-cl,ss,ts,saxello) | Jackson,Paul (el-b) | Clark,Mike (dr) | Summers,Bill (perc)

CK 65027 | 2 CD | Miles Davis At Carnegie Hall
Miles Davis Quintet
So What | No Blues | Oleo | Teo | I Thought About You
Live at Carnegie Hall,NYC, rec. 19.5.1961
Davis,Miles (tp) | Mobley,Hank (ts) | Kelly,Wynton (p) | Chambers,Paul (b) | Cobb,Jimmy (dr)
Miles Davis With Gil Evans & His Orchestra
Spring Is Here
Davis,Miles (tp) | Royal,Ernie (tp) | Glow,Bernie (tp) | Coles,Johnny (tp) | Mucci,Louis (tp) | Knepper,Jimmy (tb) | Hixon,Richard 'Dick' (tb) | Rehak,Frank (tb) | Watkins,Julius (fr-h) | Ingraham,Paul (fr-h) | Swisshelm,Robert (fr-h) | Barber,Bill (tuba) | Penque,Romeo (reeds) | Richardson,Jerome (reeds) | Caine,Eddie (reeds) | Tricarico,Bob (reeds) | Bank,Danny (reeds) | Putnam,Janet (harp) | Kelly,Wynton (p) | Chambers,Paul (b) | Cobb,Jimmy (dr) | Rosengarden,Bobby (perc) | Evans,Gil (cond,arr)
Someday My Prince Will Come | The Meaning Of The Blues- | Lament- | New Rhumba | Walkin' | Concierto D'Aranjuez
Davis,Miles (tp) | Royal,Ernie (tp) | Glow,Bernie (tp) | Coles,Johnny (tp) | Mucci,Louis (tp) | Knepper,Jimmy (tb) | Hixon,Richard 'Dick' (tb) | Rehak,Frank (tb) | Watkins,Julius (fr-h) | Ingraham,Paul (fr-h) | Swisshelm,Robert (fr-h) | Barber,Bill (tuba) | Penque,Romeo (reeds) | Richardson,Jerome (reeds) | Caine,Eddie (reeds) | Tricarico,Bob (reeds) | Bank,Danny (reeds) | Putnam,Janet (harp) | Chambers,Paul (b) | Cobb,Jimmy (dr) | Rosengarden,Bobby (perc) | Evans,Gil (cond,arr)

CK 65038 | CD | This Is Jazz:Miles Davis Plays Ballads
Miles Davis Quintet
Circle | Mood
NYC, rec. 26.10.1966
Davis,Miles (tp) | Shorter,Wayne (ts) | Hancock,Herbie (p) | Carter,Ron (b) | Williams,Tony (dr)
Old Folks
NYC, rec. 20.3.1961
Davis,Miles (tp) | Mobley,Hank (ts) | Kelly,Wynton (p) | Chambers,Paul (b) | Cobb,Jimmy (dr)
Dear Old Stockholm
NYC, rec. 5.6.1956
Davis,Miles (tp) | Coltrane,John (ts) | Garland,Red (p) | Chambers,Paul (b) | Jones,Philly Joe (dr)
Miles Davis Sextet
Flamenco Sketches
NYC, rec. 22.4.1959
Davis,Miles (tp) | Adderley,Julian \'Cannonball\' (as) | Coltrane,John (ts) | Evans,Bill (p) | Chambers,Paul (b) | Cobb,Jimmy (dr)
Miles Davis With Gil Evans & His Orchestra
My Ship
NYC, rec. 10./27.5.1957
Davis,Miles (fl-h) | Glow,Bernie (tp) | Royal,Ernie (tp) | Jordan,Taft (tp) | Mucci,Louis (tp) | Carisi,Johnny (tp) | Cleveland,Jimmy (tb) | Bennett,Joe (tb) | Mitchell,Tom (b-tb) | Ruff,Willie (fr-h) | Miranda,Tony (fr-h) | Barber,Bill (tuba) | Konitz,Lee (as) | Caine,Eddie (fl,cl) | Penque,Romeo (fl,cl,b-cl,oboe) | Cooper,Sid (fl,cl,b-cl,oboe) | Bank,Danny (b-cl) | Chambers,Paul (b) | Taylor,Arthur 'Art' (dr) | Evans,Gil (cond,arr)
I Loves You Porgy
NYC, rec. 18.8.1958
Davis,Miles (tp,fl-h) | Evans,Gil (cond,arr) | Coles,Johnny (tp) | Glow,Bernie (tp) | Royal,Ernie (tp) | Mucci,Louis (tp) | Bennett,Joe (tb) | Rehak,Frank (tb) | Cleveland,Jimmy (tb) | Hixon,Richard 'Dick' (b-tb) | Ruff,Willie (fr-h) | Watkins,Julius (fr-h) | Schuller,Gunther (fr-h) | Barber,Bill (tuba) | Adderley,Julian \'Cannonball\' (as) | Richardson,Jerome (reeds) | Penque,Romeo (fl) | Bank,Danny (b-cl) | Chambers,Paul (b) | Cobb,Jimmy (dr)
Miles Davis Quartet
Basin Street Blues
Hollywood,CA, rec. 16.4.1963
Davis,Miles (tp) | Feldman,Victor (p) | Carter,Ron (b) | Butler,Frank (dr)
Miles Davis Group
Time After Time
NYC, rec. 1984
Davis,Miles (tp) | Irving III,Robert (synth) | Scofield,John (el-g) | Jones,Darryl (el-b) | Foster,Al (dr) | Thornton,Steve (perc)

CK 65041 | CD | This Is Jazz:Freddie Hubbard
Freddie Hubbard Septet
Red Clay
Englewood Cliffs,NJ, rec. 27.1.1970
Hubbard,Freddie (tp) | Henderson,Joe (ts) | Hancock,Herbie (el-p) | Carter,Ron (b) | Bushnell,Bob (el-b) | White,Lenny (dr) | Shaughnessy,Ed (perc)
Freddie Hubbard Quintet
Spirits Of Trane
Englewood Cliffs,NJ, rec. October 1973
Hubbard,Freddie (tp) | Cook,Junior (ts) | Cables,George (el-p) | Carter,Ron (b) | Penland,Ralph (dr)
Freddie Hubbard With Orchestra
Sky Dive | In A Mist
Englewood Cliffs,NJ, rec. 4./5.10.1972
Hubbard,Freddie (tp) | Rubin,Alan (tp,fl-h) | Stamm,Marvin (tp,fl-h) | Andre,Wayne (tb) | Brown,Garnett (tb) | Faulise,Paul (b-tb) | Price,Tony (tuba) | Bodner,Phil (fl,alto-fl,b-cl,bass-fl,piccolo) | Kane,Walter (b-cl,piccolo) | Penque,Romeo (engl-h,fl,alto-fl,cl,oboe) | Laws,Hubert (fl,alto-fl) | Jarrett,Keith (el-p) | Benson,George (g) | Carter,Ron (b) | Cobham,Billy (dr) | Barretto,Ray (perc) | Moreira,Airto (perc) | Sebesky,Don (arr)
First Light
Englewood Cliffs,NJ, rec. 16.9.1971
Hubbard,Freddie (tp) | Alonge,Ray (fr-h) | Buffington,Jimmy (fr-h) | Kane,Walter (fl,bassoon) | Penque,Romeo (engl-h,fl,cl,oboe) | Laws,Hubert (fl) | Marge,George (fl,cl) | Taylor,Jane (bassoon) | Kraus,Phil (vib) | Ross,Margaret (harp) | Benson,George (g) | Wyands,Richard (el-p) | Carter,Ron (b) | DeJohnette,Jack (dr) | Nadien,David (v) | Gershman,Paul (v) | Green,Emmanuel (v) | Kohon,Harold (v) | Malin,Joe (v) | Orloff,Gene (v) | Raimondi,Matthew (v) | Samaroff,Tosha (v) | Spice,Irving (v) | Sebesky,Don (arr)
Freddie Hubbard Trio
Here's That Rainy Day
Englewood Cliffs,NJ, rec. 16.11.1970
Hubbard,Freddie (fl-h) | Benson,George (g) | Carter,Ron (b)

CK 65108 | CD | Heavy Weather
Weather Report
A Remark You Made | Havona
Hollywood,CA, rec. 1976
Weather Report | Zawinul,Joe (p,el-p,synth) | Shorter,Wayne (ss,ts) | Pastorius,Jaco (el-b) | Acuna,Alejandro Neciosup (dr)
Teen Town
Weather Report | Zawinul,Joe (p,el-p,synth) | Shorter,Wayne (ss,ts) | Pastorius,Jaco (el-b) | Badrena,Manolo (congas)
Birdland | Harlequin | Palladium | The Juggler
Weather Report | Zawinul,Joe (g,p,el-p,synth,melodica,table,voc) | Shorter,Wayne (ss,ts) | Pastorius,Jaco (el-b) | Acuna,Alejandro Neciosup (dr,congas,tom-tom) | Badrena,Manolo (congas,tambourine,voc)
Rumba Mama
rec. 1976
Weather Report | Badrena,Manolo (congas,timbales,voc) | Acuna,Alejandro Neciosup (congas,tom-tom)

CK 65121 | CD | Miles Ahead
Miles Davis + 19
The Maids Of Cadiz | The Duke
NYC, rec. 6.5.1957
Davis,Miles (tp) | Evans,Gil (cond,arr) | Glow,Bernie (tp) | Royal,Ernie (tp) | Mucci,Louis (tp) | Jordan,Taft (tp) | Carisi,Johnny (tp) | Rehak,Frank (tb) | Cleveland,Jimmy (tb) | Bennett,Joe (tb) | Mitchell,Tom (b-tb) | Ruff,Willie (fr-h) | Miranda,Tony (fr-h) | Buffington,Jimmy (fr-h) | Barber,Bill (tuba) | Konitz,Lee (as) | Bank,Danny (b-cl) | Penque,Romeo (fl,cl) | Cooper,Sid (fl,cl) | Caine,Eddie (fl,cl) | Chambers,Paul (b) | Taylor,Arthur 'Art' (dr)
My Ship | Miles Ahead
NYC, rec. 10.5.1957
Davis,Miles (tp) | Evans,Gil (cond,arr) | Glow,Bernie (tp) | Royal,Ernie (tp) | Mucci,Louis (tp) | Jordan,Taft (tp) | Carisi,Johnny (tp) | Rehak,Frank (tb) | Cleveland,Jimmy (tb) | Bennett,Joe (tb) | Mitchell,Tom (b-tb) | Ruff,Willie (fr-h) | Miranda,Tony (fr-h) | Buffington,Jimmy (fr-h) | Barber,Bill (tuba) | Konitz,Lee (as) | Bank,Danny (b-cl) | Penque,Romeo (fl,cl) | Cooper,Sid (fl,cl) | Caine,Eddie (fl,cl) | Chambers,Paul (b) | Taylor,Arthur 'Art' (dr)
Springsville | New Rhumba | The Meaning Of The Blues- | Lament-
NYC, rec. 23.5.1957
Davis,Miles (tp) | Evans,Gil (cond,arr) | Glow,Bernie (tp) | Royal,Ernie (tp) | Mucci,Louis (tp) | Jordan,Taft (tp) | Carisi,Johnny (tp) | Rehak,Frank (tb) | Cleveland,Jimmy (tb) | Bennett,Joe (tb) | Mitchell,Tom (b-tb) | Ruff,Willie (fr-h) | Miranda,Tony (fr-h) | Buffington,Jimmy (fr-h) | Barber,Bill (tuba) | Konitz,Lee (as) | Bank,Danny (b-cl) | Penque,Romeo (fl,cl) | Cooper,Sid (fl,cl) | Caine,Eddie (fl,cl) | Chambers,Paul (b) | Taylor,Arthur 'Art' (dr)
Blues For Pablo | I Don't Wanna Be Kissed
NYC, rec. 27.5.1957
Davis,Miles (tp) | Evans,Gil (cond,arr) | Glow,Bernie (tp) | Royal,Ernie (tp) | Mucci,Louis (tp) | Jordan,Taft (tp) | Carisi,Johnny (tp) | Rehak,Frank (tb) | Cleveland,Jimmy (tb) | Bennett,Joe (tb) | Mitchell,Tom (b-tb) | Ruff,Willie (fr-h) | Miranda,Tony (fr-h) | Buffington,Jimmy (fr-h) | Barber,Bill (tuba) | Konitz,Lee (as) | Bank,Danny (b-cl) | Penque,Romeo (fl,cl) | Cooper,Sid (fl,cl) | Caine,Eddie (fl,cl) | Chambers,Paul (b) | Taylor,Arthur 'Art' (dr)

CK 65122 | CD | Time Out
Dave Brubeck Quartet
Kathy's Waltz | Three To Get Ready And Four To Go | Everybody's Jumpin'
NYC, rec. 25.6.1959
Brubeck,Dave (p) | Desmond,Paul (as) | Wright,Eugene 'Gene' (b) | Morello,Joe (dr)
Take Five | Strange Meadow Lark
NYC, rec. 1.7.1959
Brubeck,Dave (p) | Desmond,Paul (as) | Wright,Eugene 'Gene' (b) | Morello,Joe (dr)
Blue Rondo A La Turk | Pick Up Sticks
NYC, rec. 18.8.1959
Brubeck,Dave (p) | Desmond,Paul (as) | Wright,Eugene 'Gene' (b) | Morello,Joe (dr)

CK 65123 | CD | Head Hunters
Herbie Hancock Group
Chameleon | Watermelon Man | Sly | Vein Melter
San Francisco,CA, rec. Fall 1973
Hancock,Herbie (el-p,synth,clavinet,pipes) | Maupin,Bennie (fl,b-cl,ss,ts,saxello) | Jackson,Paul (el-b,marimbula) | Mason,Harvey (dr) | Summers,Bill (perc,congas,balafon)

CK 65141 | CD | Porgy And Bess
Miles Davis With Gil Evans & His Orchestra
My Man's Gone Now | Gone Gone Gone | Gone | Gone(alt.take)
NYC, rec. 22.7.1958
Davis,Miles (tp,fl-h) | Evans,Gil (cond,arr) | Coles,Johnny (tp) | Glow,Bernie (tp) | Royal,Ernie (tp) | Mucci,Louis (tp) | Bennett,Joe (tb) | Rehak,Frank (tb) | Cleveland,Jimmy (tb) | Hixon,Richard 'Dick' (b-tb) | Ruff,Willie (fr-h) | Watkins,Julius (fr-h) | Schuller,Gunther (fr-h) | Barber,Bill (tuba) | Adderley,Julian \'Cannonball\' (as) | Bodner,Phil (fl) | Penque,Romeo (fl) | Bank,Danny (b-cl) | Chambers,Paul (b) | Jones,Philly Joe (dr)
Here Comes De Honey Man | Bess You Is My Woman Now | It Ain't Necessarily So | Fisherman Strawberry And Devil Crab
NYC, rec. 29.7.1958
Davis,Miles (tp,fl-h) | Evans,Gil (cond,arr) | Coles,Johnny (tp) | Glow,Bernie (tp) | Royal,Ernie (tp) | Mucci,Louis (tp) | Bennett,Joe (tb) | Rehak,Frank (tb) | Cleveland,Jimmy (tb) | Hixon,Richard 'Dick' (b-tb) | Ruff,Willie (fr-h) | Watkins,Julius (fr-h) | Schuller,Gunther (fr-h) | Barber,Bill (tuba) | Adderley,Julian \'Cannonball\' (as) | Bodner,Phil (fl) | Penque,Romeo (fl) | Bank,Danny (b-cl) | Chambers,Paul (b) | Cobb,Jimmy (dr)
Prayer | Bess Oh Where's My Bess | Buzzard Song
NYC, rec. 4.8.1958
Davis,Miles (tp,fl-h) | Evans,Gil (cond,arr) | Coles,Johnny (tp) | Glow,Bernie (tp) | Royal,Ernie (tp) | Mucci,Louis (tp) | Bennett,Joe (tb) | Rehak,Frank (tb) | Cleveland,Jimmy (tb) | Hixon,Richard 'Dick' (b-tb) | Ruff,Willie (fr-h) | Watkins,Julius (fr-h) | Schuller,Gunther (fr-h) | Barber,Bill (tuba) | Adderley,Julian \'Cannonball\' (as) | Richardson,Jerome (reeds) | Penque,Romeo (fl) | Bank,Danny (b-cl) | Chambers,Paul (b) | Cobb,Jimmy (dr)
Summertime | There's A Boat Dat's Leavin' Soon For New York | I Loves You Porgy | I Loves You Porgy(alt.take)
NYC, rec. 14.8.1958
Davis,Miles (tp,fl-h) | Evans,Gil (cond,arr) | Coles,Johnny (tp) | Glow,Bernie (tp) | Royal,Ernie (tp) | Mucci,Louis (tp) | Bennett,Joe (tb) | Rehak,Frank (tb) | Cleveland,Jimmy (tb) | Hixon,Richard 'Dick' (b-tb) | Ruff,Willie (fr-h) | Watkins,Julius (fr-h) | Schuller,Gunther (fr-h) | Barber,Bill (tuba) | Adderley,Julian \'Cannonball\' (as) | Richardson,Jerome (reeds) | Penque,Romeo (fl) | Bank,Danny (b-cl) | Chambers,Paul (b) | Cobb,Jimmy (dr)

CK 65142 | CD | Sketches Of Spain
Concierto D'Aranjuez | Concierto D'Aranjuez(part 1) | Concierto D'Aranjuez(part 2)

NYC, rec. 20.11.1959
Davis,Miles (fl-h) | Evans,Gil (arr) | Glow,Bernie (tp) | Royal,Ernie (tp) | Jordan,Taft (tp) | Mucci,Louis (tp) | Hixon,Richard (tb) | Rehak,Frank (tb) | Barrows,John (fr-h) | Buffington,Jimmy (fr-h) | Chapin,Earl (fr-h) | Glickman,Loren (bassoon) | McAllister,Jay (tuba) | Caine,Eddie (fl) | Block,Al (fl,piccolo) | Bank,Danny (alto-fl,b-cl) | Feldman,Harold (b-cl,oboe) | Putnam,Janet (harp) | Chambers,Paul (b) | Cobb,Jimmy (dr) | Jones,Elvin (perc)

The Pan Piper
NYC, rec. 10.3.1960
Davis,Miles (tp) | Evans,Gil (arr) | Glow,Bernie (tp) | Royal,Ernie (tp) | Coles,Johnny (tp) | Hixon,Richard (tb) | Rehak,Frank (tb) | Singer,Joe (fr-h) | Miranda,Tony (fr-h) | Buffington,Jimmy (fr-h) | Knitzer,Jack (bassoon) | Barber,John (tuba) | Feldman,Harold (fl) | Caine,Eddie (fl) | Block,Al (fl,piccolo) | Bank,Danny (alto-fl,b-cl) | Penque,Romeo (oboe) | Putnam,Janet (harp) | Chambers,Paul (b) | Cobb,Jimmy (dr) | Jones,Elvin (perc)

Solea | Saeta | Will O'The Wisp | Song Of Our Country
NYC, rec. 11.3.1960
Davis,Miles (tp) | Evans,Gil (arr) | Glow,Bernie (tp) | Royal,Ernie (tp) | Coles,Johnny (tp) | Mucci,Louis (tp) | Hixon,Richard (tb) | Rehak,Frank (tb) | Singer,Joe (fr-h) | Miranda,Tony (fr-h) | Buffington,Jimmy (fr-h) | Knitzer,Jack (bassoon) | Barber,John (tuba) | Feldman,Harold (fl) | Caine,Eddie (fl) | Block,Al (fl,piccolo) | Bank,Danny (alto-fl,b-cl) | Penque,Romeo (oboe) | Putnam,Janet (harp) | Chambers,Paul (b) | Cobb,Jimmy (dr) | Jones,Elvin (perc)

CK 65144 | CD | Lady In Satin
Billie Holiday With The Ray Ellis Orchestra
You Don't Know What Love Is | I'll Be Around | For Heaven's Sake
NYC, rec. 18.2.1958
Holiday,Billie (voc) | Davis,Mel (tp) | Green,Urbie (tb) | Green,Jack (tb) | Mitchell,Tom (b-tb) | Powell,Eddie (reeds) | Penque,Romeo (reeds) | Parshley,Tom (reeds) | Bodner,Phil (reeds) | Rosengarden,Bobby (xylophone) | Waldron,Mal (p) | Galbraith,Barry (g) | Hinton,Milt (b) | Johnson,Osie (dr) | Ockner,George (v) | Lomask,Milt (v) | Green,Emmanuel (v) | Katzman,Harry (v) | Sarcer,David (v) | Rand,Sam (v) | Kruczek,Leo (v) | Meinikoff,Harry (v) | Hoffman,Harry (v) | Newman,Dave (v) | Brecher,Sid (viola) | Dickler,Richard (viola) | Soyer,David (cello) | Brown,Maurice (cello) | Putnam,Janet (harp) | Ellis,Ray (cond,arr)

But Beautiful | For All We Know | It's Easy To Remember | I'm A Fool To Want You | I'm A Fool To Want You(alt.take 1) | I'm A Fool To Want You(alt.take 2)
NYC, rec. 19.2.1958
Holiday,Billie (voc) | Davis,Mel (tp) | Green,Urbie (tb) | Green,Jack (tb) | Mitchell,Tom (b-tb) | Powell,Eddie (reeds) | Penque,Romeo (reeds) | Parshley,Tom (reeds) | Bodner,Phil (reeds) | Rosengarden,Bobby (xylophone) | Waldron,Mal (p) | Galbraith,Barry (g) | Hinton,Milt (b) | Johnson,Osie (dr) | Ockner,George (v) | Lomask,Milt (v) | Green,Emmanuel (v) | Katzman,Harry (v) | Sarcer,David (v) | Rand,Sam (v) | Kruczek,Leo (v) | Meinikoff,Harry (v) | Hoffman,Harry (v) | Newman,Dave (v) | Brecher,Sid (viola) | Dickler,Richard (viola) | Soyer,David (cello) | Brown,Maurice (cello) | Putnam,Janet (harp) | Ellis,Ray (cond,arr)

The End Of A Love Affair(Mono) | The End Of A Love Affair(Stereo) | The End Of A Love Affair(The Audio Story) | Glad To Be Unhappy | You've Changed | I Get Along Without You Very Well | Violets For Your Furs
NYC, rec. 20.2.1958
Holiday,Billie (voc) | Davis,Mel (tp) | Green,Urbie (tb) | Johnson,J.J. (tb) | Mitchell,Tom (b-tb) | Powell,Eddie (reeds) | Penque,Romeo (reeds) | Parshley,Tom (reeds) | Bodner,Phil (reeds) | Spinney,Bradley (xylophone) | Waldron,Mal (p) | Galbraith,Barry (g) | Hinton,Milt (b) | Lamond,Don (dr) | Ockner,George (v) | Berger,Eugene (v) | Cahn,Max (v) | Giglio,Felix (v) | Katzman,Harry (v) | Sarcer,David (v) | Rand,Sam (v) | Kruczek,Leo (v) | Hoffman,Harry (v) | Newman,Dave (v) | Brecher,Sid (viola) | Dickler,Richard (viola) | Soyer,David (cello) | Brown,Maurice (cello) | Putnam,Janet (harp) | Ellis,Ray (cond,arr)

CK 65186 | CD | A Tribute To Cannonball
Don Byas-Bud Powell Quartet
Just One Of Those Things | Jackie My Little Cat | Cherokee | I Remember Clifford | Jackie My Little Cat(alt.take) | Cherokee(alt.take)
Paris,France, rec. 15.12.1961
Byas,Don (ts) | Powell,Bud (p) | Michelot,Pierre (b) | Clarke,Kenny (dr)
Don Byas-Bud Powell Quintet
Good Bait | Jeannine | All The Things You Are | Myth
Byas,Don (ts) | Sulieman[Leonard Graham],Idrees (tp) | Powell,Bud (p) | Michelot,Pierre (b) | Clarke,Kenny (dr)

CK 65265 | CD | The Jazz Messengers
Art Blakey And The Jazz Messengers
Infra-Rae | Nica's Dream | It's You Or No One | Ecaroh | Carol's Interlude | The End Of A Love Affair | Hank's Symphony | Ill Wind | Weird-O
NYC, rec. 6.4.1956
Blakey,Art (dr) | Byrd,Donald (tp) | Mobley,Hank (ts) | Silver,Horace (p) | Watkins,Doug (b)
Late Show | Decicifering The Message | Carol's Interlude(alt.take)
NYC, rec. 4.5.1956
Blakey,Art (dr) | Byrd,Donald (tp) | Mobley,Hank (ts) | Silver,Horace (p) | Watkins,Doug (b)

CK 65293 | CD | Quiet Nights
Miles Davis With Gil Evans & His Orchestra
Corcovado(Quiet Nights) | Aos Pes Da Cruz
rec. 27.7.1962
Davis,Miles (tp) | Evans,Gil (cond,arr) | Royal,Ernie (tp) | Coles,Johnny (tp) | Glow,Bernie (tp) | Mucci,Louis (tp) | Knepper,Jimmy (tb) | Hixon,Richard 'Dick' (tb) | Rehak,Frank (tb) | Watkins,Julius (fr-h) | Ingraham,Paul (fr-h) | Swisshelm,Robert (fr-h) | Barber,Bill (tuba) | Lacy,Steve (ss) | Penque,Romeo (reeds) | Richardson,Jerome (reeds) | Caine,Eddie (reeds) | Bank,Bob (reeds) | Putnam,Janet (harp) | Chambers,Paul (b) | Cobb,Jimmy (dr) | Rosengarden,Bobby (perc)
Song No.1 | Wait 'Till You See Her
rec. 13.8.1962
Davis,Miles (tp) | Evans,Gil (cond,arr) | Royal,Ernie (tp) | Coles,Johnny (tp) | Glow,Bernie (tp) | Mucci,Louis (tp) | Knepper,Jimmy (tb) | Hixon,Richard 'Dick' (tb) | Rehak,Frank (tb) | Watkins,Julius (fr-h) | Ingraham,Paul (fr-h) | Swisshelm,Robert (fr-h) | Barber,Bill (tuba) | Lacy,Steve (ss) | Penque,Romeo (reeds) | Richardson,Jerome (reeds) | Caine,Eddie (reeds) | Bank,Bob (reeds) | Putnam,Janet (harp) | Chambers,Paul (b) | Cobb,Jimmy (dr) | Rosengarden,Bobby (perc)
Once Upon A Summertime | Song No.2
rec. 6.11.1962
Davis,Miles (tp) | Evans,Gil (cond,arr) | Royal,Ernie (tp) | Coles,Johnny (tp) | Glow,Bernie (tp) | Mucci,Louis (tp) | Knepper,Jimmy (tb) | Hixon,Richard 'Dick' (tb) | Rehak,Frank (tb) | Watkins,Julius (fr-h) | Buffington,Jimmy (fr-h) | Barrows,John (fr-h) | Barber,Bill (tuba) | Lacy,Steve (ss) | Penque,Romeo (reeds) | Richardson,Jerome (reeds) | Caine,Eddie (reeds) | Tricarico,Bob (reeds) | Bank,Danny (reeds) | Putnam,Janet (harp) | Chambers,Paul (b) | Cobb,Jimmy (dr) | Jones,Elvin (perc)
The Time Of The Barracudas
Hollywood,CA, rec. 10.10.1963
Davis,Miles (tp) | Evans,Gil (cond,arr) | Leith,Dick (b-tb) | Perissi,Richard 'Dick' (fr-h) | Hinshaw,William 'Bill' (fr-h) | Maebe,Arthur (fr-h) | Horn,Paul (fl,alto-fl,ts) | Cipriano,Gene (alto-fl,ts,oboe) | Dutton,Fred (bassoon) | Call,Marjorie (harp) | Hancock,Herbie (p) | Carter,Ron (b) | Williams,Tony (dr)

CK 65361 | CD | Bill Evans:Piano Player
George Russell And His Orchestra
All About Rosie(3rd Section-alt.take)
NYC, rec. 10.6.1957
Russell,George (arr,ld) | Farmer,Art (tp) | Mucci,Louis (tp) | Knepper,Jimmy (tb) | Buffington,Jimmy (fr-h) | Di Domenica,Bob (fl) | LaPorta,John (as) | McKusick,Hal (ts) | Zegler,Manuel (bassoon) | Charles,Teddy (vib) | Ross,Margaret (harp) | Evans,Bill (p) | Galbraith,Barry (g) | Benjamin,Joe (b) | Summers,Ted (dr)
Miles Davis Quartet
My Funny Valentine
Live at The Plaza Hotel,NYC, rec. 9.9.1958
Davis,Miles (tp) | Evans,Bill (p) | Chambers,Paul (b) | Jones,Philly Joe (dr)
Dave Pike Quartet
Vierd Blues | Besame Mucho
NYC, rec. 6.& 8.2.1962
Pike,Dave (vib) | Evans,Bill (p) | Lewis,Herbie (b) | Perkins,Walter (dr)
Bill Evans-Eddie Gomez Duo
Morning Glory
NYC, rec. 23.11.1970
Evans,Bill (p,el-p) | Gomez,Eddie (b,el-b)
Django | Waltz For Debby | T.T.T.(Twelve Tone Tune) | Comrade Conrad | Gone With The Wind
NYC, rec. 24.11.1970
Evans,Bill (p,el-p) | Gomez,Eddie (b)
Bill Evans Trio
Fun Ride
NYC, rec. 17.5.1971
Evans,Bill (p) | Gomez,Eddie (b) | Morell,Marty (dr)

CK 65422 | CD | Greatest Hits
Thelonious Monk Quartet
Crepuscule With Nellie
NYC, rec. 29.3.1963
Monk,Thelonious (p) | Rouse,Charlie (ts) | Ore,John (b) | Dunlop,Frankie (dr)
Misterioso
Live at Philharmonic Hall,NYC, rec. 30.12.1963
Monk,Thelonious (p) | Rouse,Charlie (ts) | Warren,Edward 'Butch' (b) | Dunlop,Frankie (dr)
Blue Monk
Live at The 'It Club',Los Angeles,CA, rec. 31.10.1964
Monk,Thelonious (p) | Rouse,Charlie (ts) | Gales,Larry (b) | Riley,Ben (dr)
Bemsha Swing
San Francisco,CA, rec. 4.11.1964
Monk,Thelonious (p) | Rouse,Charlie (ts) | Gales,Larry (b) | Riley,Ben (dr)
Well You Needn't
Live at Brandeis University,Waldham, rec. 27.2.1965
Monk,Thelonious (p) | Rouse,Charlie (ts) | Gales,Larry (b) | Riley,Ben (dr)
Straight No Chaser
Hollywood,CA, rec. 19.11.1968
Monk,Thelonious (p) | Rouse,Charlie (ts) | Gales,Larry (b) | Riley,Ben (dr)
Thelonious Monk
Ruby My Dear
NYC, rec. 2.3.1965
Monk,Thelonious (p-solo)
Round About Midnight
Hollywood,CA, rec. 19.11.1968
Monk,Thelonious (p-solo)
Thelonious Monk And His Orchestra
Epistrophy
NYC, rec. 30.12.1963
Monk,Thelonious (p) | Jones,Thad (tp) | Travis,Nick (tp) | Bert,Eddie (tb) | Lacy,Steve (ss) | Woods,Phil (as) | Rouse,Charlie (ts) | Allen,Gene (sax) | Warren,Edward 'Butch' (b) | Dunlop,Frankie (dr)

CK 65446 | CD | Free Fall
Jimmy Giuffre Three
Propulsion | Present Notion | Future Plans | Past Mistakes | Time Will Tell | Let's See
NYC, rec. 9.7.1962
Giuffre,Jimmy (cl) | Bley,Paul (p) | Swallow,Steve (b)
Threewe | Man Alone | Spasmodic | The Five Ways | Motion Suspended
NYC, rec. 10.10.1962
Giuffre,Jimmy (cl) | Bley,Paul (p) | Swallow,Steve (b)
Ornothoids | Dichotomy | Yggdrasill | Divided Man | Primordial Call
NYC, rec. 1.11.1962
Giuffre,Jimmy (cl) | Bley,Paul (p) | Swallow,Steve (b)

CK 65506 | CD | Blue Rose
Rosemary Clooney With The Duke Ellington Orchestra
Hey Baby | Me And You | Sophisticated Lady | Passion Flower | I Let A Song Go Out Of My Heart | It Don't Mean A Thing If It Ain't Got That Swing | Grievin' | Blue Rose | I'm Checking Out Goodbye | I Got It Bad And That Ain't Good | Mood Indigo | If You Were In My Place (What Would You Do) | Just A-Sittin' And A-Rockin'
Chicago,Ill, rec. Spring,1956
Clooney,Rosemary (voc) | Ellington,Duke (p,arr) | Cook,Willie (tp) | Nance,Ray (tp) | Terry,Clark (tp) | Anderson,Cat (tp) | Jackson,Gordon (tb) | Woodman,Britt (tb) | Sanders,John (tb) | Hodges,Johnny (as) | Procope,Russell (cl,as) | Hamilton,Jimmy (cl,ts) | Gonsalves,Paul (ts) | Carney,Harry (bs) | Woode,Jimmy (b) | Woodyard,Sam (dr)

CK 65507 | CD | Jazz Spectacular
Frankie Laine With Buck Clayton And His Orchestra
S' Posin' | Stars Fell On Alabama | My Old Flame | You Can Depend On Me | That Old Feeling | Baby Baby All The Time | You'd Be So Nice To Come Home To
NYC, rec. 9.1.1956
Laine,Frankie (voc) | Clayton,Buck (tp) | Copeland,Ray (tp) | Johnson,J.J. (tb) | Winding,Kai (tb) | Green,Urbie (tb) | Jefferson,Hilton (as) | Johnson,Budd (ts) | Nicholas,George 'Big Nick' (ts) | McRae,Dave (bs) | Thompson,Sir Charles (p) | Best,Cliff (g) | Hinton,Milt (b) | Jones,Jo (dr)
Roses Of Picardy
Laine,Frankie (voc) | Clayton,Buck (tp) | Copeland,Ray (tp) | Johnson,J.J. (tb) | Winding,Kai (tb) | Green,Urbie (tb) | Brown,Lawrence (tb) | Jefferson,Hilton (as) | Johnson,Budd (ts) | Nicholas,George 'Big Nick' (ts) | McRae,Dave (bs) | Thompson,Sir Charles (p) | Best,Cliff (g) | Hinton,Milt (b) | Jones,Jo (dr)
If You Were Mine
Laine,Frankie (voc) | Clayton,Buck (tp) | Copeland,Ray (tp) | Johnson,J.J. (tb) | Winding,Kai (tb) | Wells,Dicky (tb) | Jefferson,Hilton (as) | Johnson,Budd (ts) | Nicholas,George 'Big Nick' (ts) | McRae,Dave (bs) | Thompson,Sir Charles (p) | Best,Cliff (g) | Hinton,Milt (b) | Jones,Jo (dr)
Taking A Chance On Love
Laine,Frankie (voc) | Clayton,Buck (tp) | Copeland,Ray (tp) | Johnson,J.J. (tb) | Winding,Kai (tb) | Wells,Dicky (tb) | Jefferson,Hilton (as) | Johnson,Budd (ts) | Nicholas,George 'Big Nick' (ts) | McRae,Dave (bs) | Thompson,Sir Charles (p) | Best,Cliff (g) | Hinton,Milt (b) | Donaldson,Bobby (dr)
Until The Real Thing Comes Along
Laine,Frankie (voc) | Clayton,Buck (tp) | Copeland,Ray (tp) | Johnson,J.J. (tb) | Winding,Kai (tb) | Wells,Dicky (tb) | Jefferson,Hilton (as) | Johnson,Budd (ts) | Sears,Al (ts) | McRae,Dave (bs) | Thompson,Sir Charles (p) | Best,Cliff (g) | Hinton,Milt (b) | Donaldson,Bobby (dr)

CK 65512 | CD | Mingus Ah Um
Charles Mingus Group
Better Git It In Your Soul | Fables Of Faubus | Jelly Roll | Pedal Point Blues
NYC, rec. 5.5.1959
Mingus,Charles (p,b) | Knepper,Jimmy (tb) | Handy,John (cl,as) | Hadi [Curtis Porter],Shafti (as) | Ervin,Booker (ts) | Parlan,Horace (p) | Richmond,Dannie (dr)
Bird Calls
Mingus,Charles (b) | Handy,John (cl,as) | Hadi [Curtis Porter],Shafti (as) | Ervin,Booker (ts) | Parlan,Horace (p) | Richmond,Dannie (dr)
Pussy Cat Dues
Mingus,Charles (b) | Knepper,Jimmy (tb) | Handy,John (cl,as) | Ervin,Booker (ts) | Parlan,Horace (p) | Richmond,Dannie (dr)
Open Letter To Duke | Boogie Stomp Shuffle | Self-Portrait In 3 Colors | GG Train | Girl Of My Dreams
NYC, rec. 12.5.1959
Mingus,Charles (b) | Dennis,Willie (tb) | Handy,John (cl,as) | Hadi [Curtis Porter],Shafti (as) | Ervin,Booker (ts) | Parlan,Horace (p) | Richmond,Dannie (dr)
Goodbye Pork Pie Hat
Mingus,Charles (b) | Handy,John (cl,as) | Ervin,Booker (ts) | Parlan,Horace (p) | Richmond,Dannie (dr)

CK 65513 | CD | Mingus Dynasty
Dina | Song With Orange | Gunslinging Bird | Far Wells Mill Valley
NYC, rec. 1.11.1959
Mingus,Charles (b) | Williams,Richard (tp) | Knepper,Jimmy (tb) | Handy,John (as) | Ervin,Booker (ts) | Golson,Benny (ts) | Richardson,Jerome (bs) | Charles,Teddy (vib) | Hanna,Sir Roland (p) | Richmond,Dannie (dr)
New Now Know How
Mingus,Charles (b) | Knepper,Jimmy (tb) | Handy,John (as) | Ervin,Booker (ts) | Bunick,Floris Nico (p) | Richmond,Dannie (dr)
Strollin'
Mingus,Charles (b) | Williams,Richard (tp) | Knepper,Jimmy (tb) | Handy,John (as) | Ervin,Booker (ts) | Golson,Benny (ts) | Richardson,Jerome (bs) | Bunick,Floris Nico (p) | Richmond,Dannie (dr) | Gordon,Honey[Honi] (voc)
Things Ain't What They Used To Be
NYC, rec. 13.11.1959
Mingus,Charles (b) | Ellis,Don (tp) | Knepper,Jimmy (tb) | Handy,John (as) | Ervin,Booker (ts) | Hanna,Sir Roland (p) | Richmond,Dannie (dr)
Slop | Put Me In That Dungeon
Mingus,Charles (b) | Ellis,Don (tp) | Knepper,Jimmy (tb) | Handy,John (as) | Ervin,Booker (ts) | Hanna,Sir Roland (p) | Brown,Maurice (cello) | Barab,Seymour (cello) | Richmond,Dannie (dr)

CK 65522 | CD | Electric Bath
Don Ellis Orchestra
Indian Lady | Alone | Open Beauty | Indian Lady(single-version)
Hollywood,CA, rec. 19.9.1967
Ellis,Don (tp) | Stuart,Glenn (tp) | Weight,Alan (tp) | Warren,Ed (tp) | Harmon,Bob (tp) | Myers,Ronald (tb) | Sanchez,David (tb) | Woodson,Terry (tb) | Leon,Ruben (fl,ss,as) | Roccisano,Joe (fl,ss,as) | Shulman,Ira (fl,cl,ts,piccolo) | Starr,Ron (fl,cl,ts) | Magruder,John (fl,b-cl,bs) | Lang,Mike (p,el-p,clavinet) | Neapolitan,Ray (b,sitar) | De La Rosa,Frank (b) | Parlato,Dave (b) | Bohanon,Steve (dr) | Valdes,Chino (congas,bongos) | Stevens,Mark (vib,perc,timbales) | Estes,Alan (perc)
Turkish Bath | New Horizons | Turkish Bath(single-version)
Hollywood,CA, rec. 20.9.1967
Ellis,Don (tp) | Stuart,Glenn (tp) | Weight,Alan (tp) | Warren,Ed (tp) | Harmon,Bob (tp) | Myers,Ronald (tb) | Sanchez,David (tb) | Woodson,Terry (tb) | Leon,Ruben (fl,ss,as) | Roccisano,Joe (fl,ss,as) | Shulman,Ira (fl,cl,ts,piccolo) | Starr,Ron (fl,cl,ts) | Magruder,John (fl,b-cl,bs) | Lang,Mike (p,el-p,clavinet) | Neapolitan,Ray (b,sitar) | De La Rosa,Frank (b) | Parlato,Dave (b) | Bohanon,Steve (dr) | Valdes,Chino (congas,bongos) | Stevens,Mark (vib,perc,timbales) | Estes,Alan (perc)

CK 65523 | CD | The Inner Mounting Flame
Mahavishnu Orchestra
Meetings In The Spirit | Dawn | The Noonward Race | A Lotus On Irish Streams | Vital Transformation | The Dance Of Maya | You Know You Know | Awakening
NYC, rec. 14.8.1971
Mahavishnu Orchestra | McLaughlin,John (el-g) | Goodman,Jerry (v,el-v) | Hammer,Jan (p,el-p) | Laird,Rick (b,el-b) | Cobham,Billy (dr)

CK 65566 | CD | Black Brown And Beige
Duke Ellington And His Orchestra
Track 360(Trains That Pass In The Night) | Black Brown And Beige: Part 1(alt.take) | Part 2(alt.take) | Light(alt.take)
Los Angeles,CA, rec. 4.2.1958
Ellington,Duke (p) | Anderson,Cat (tp) | Baker,Harold 'Shorty' (tp) | Terry,Clark (tp) | Nance,Ray (tp,v) | Jackson,Quentin (tb) | Sanders,John (v-tb) | Woodman,Britt (tb) | Hamilton,Jimmy (cl) | Procope,Russell (cl,as) | Graham,Bill (as) | Gonsalves,Paul (ts) | Carney,Harry (bs) | Woode,Jimmy (b) | Woodyard,Sam (dr)
Black Brown And Beige: | Part 1 | Part 2
Los Angeles,CA, rec. 5.2.1958
Ellington,Duke (p) | Anderson,Cat (tp) | Baker,Harold 'Shorty' (tp) | Terry,Clark (tp) | Nance,Ray (tp,v) | Jackson,Quentin (tb) | Sanders,John (v-tb) | Woodman,Britt (tb) | Hamilton,Jimmy (cl) | Procope,Russell (cl,as) | Graham,Bill (as) | Gonsalves,Paul (ts) | Carney,Harry (bs) | Woode,Jimmy (b) | Woodyard,Sam (dr)
Black Brown And Beige: | Come Sunday | Come Sunday (alt.take) | 23rd Psalm | 23rd Psalm(alt.take)
Los Angeles,CA, rec. 11.2.1958
Ellington,Duke (p) | Anderson,Cat (tp) | Baker,Harold 'Shorty' (tp) | Terry,Clark (tp) | Nance,Ray (tp,v) | Jackson,Quentin (tb) | Sanders,John (v-tb) | Woodman,Britt (tb) | Hamilton,Jimmy (cl) | Procope,Russell (cl,as) | Graham,Bill (as) | Gonsalves,Paul (ts) | Carney,Harry (bs) | Woode,Jimmy (b) | Woodyard,Sam (dr) | Jackson,Mahalia (voc)
Black Brown And Beige: | Light | Come Sunday(a capella) | Come Sunday (alt.take) | Blues In Orbit(aka Tender)
Los Angeles,CA, rec. 12.2.1958
Ellington,Duke (p) | Anderson,Cat (tp) | Baker,Harold 'Shorty' (tp) | Terry,Clark (tp) | Nance,Ray (tp,v) | Jackson,Quentin (tb) | Sanders,John (v-tb) | Woodman,Britt (tb) | Hamilton,Jimmy (cl) | Procope,Russell (cl,as) | Graham,Bill (as) | Gonsalves,Paul (ts) | Carney,Harry (bs) | Woode,Jimmy (b) | Woodyard,Sam (dr) | Jackson,Mahalia (voc)

CK 65568 | CD | Such Sweet Thunder
In A Flat Minor(rehersal) | In A Flat Minor | Half The Fun | Half The Fun(alt.take) | Suburban Beauty | Suburban Beauty(alt.take)
NYC, rec. 7.8.1956
Ellington,Duke (p) | Cook,Willie (tp) | Anderson,Cat (tp) | Terry,Clark (tp) | Nance,Ray (tp) | Woodman,Britt (tb) | Jackson,Quentin (tb) | Sanders,John (tb) | Hodges,Johnny (as) | Procope,Russell (cl,as) | Hamilton,Jimmy (cl,ts) | Gonsalves,Paul (ts) | Carney,Harry (bs) | Woode,Jimmy (b) | Woodyard,Sam (dr)
Cafe Au Lait(Lucky) | Cafe Au Lait(Lucky-outtakes) | Pretty Girl
NYC, rec. 6.12.1956
Ellington,Duke (p) | Cook,Willie (tp) | Anderson,Cat (tp) | Terry,Clark (tp) | Nance,Ray (tp) | Woodman,Britt (tb) | Jackson,Quentin (tb) | Sanders,John (tb) | Hodges,Johnny (as) | Procope,Russell (cl,as) | Hamilton,Jimmy (cl,ts) | Gonsalves,Paul (ts) | Carney,Harry (bs) | Woode,Jimmy (b) | Woodyard,Sam (dr)
Sonet For Caesar | Sonet In Search Of Amour | Sonnet For Sister Kate
NYC, rec. 15.4.1957
Ellington,Duke (p) | Cook,Willie (tp) | Anderson,Cat (tp) | Terry,Clark (tp) | Nance,Ray (tp) | Woodman,Britt (tb) | Jackson,Quentin (tb) | Sanders,John (tb) | Hodges,Johnny (as) | Procope,Russell (cl,as) | Hamilton,Jimmy (cl,ts) | Gonsalves,Paul (ts) | Carney,Harry (bs) | Woode,Jimmy (b) | Woodyard,Sam (dr)
Up And Down,Up And Down(Puck) | Such Sweet Thunder(Cleo) | Lady Mac(Lady Macbeth)
NYC, rec. 24.4.1957
Ellington,Duke (p) | Cook,Willie (tp) | Anderson,Cat (tp) | Terry,Clark (tp) | Nance,Ray (tp) | Woodman,Britt (tb) | Jackson,Quentin (tb) | Sanders,John (tb) | Hodges,Johnny (as) | Procope,Russell (cl,as) | Hamilton,Jimmy (cl,ts) | Gonsalves,Paul (ts) | Carney,Harry (bs) | Woode,Jimmy (b) | Woodyard,Sam (dr)
Sonnet To Hank Cinq | The Telecasters | Madness In Great Ones(Hamlet) | The Star-Crossed Lovers | The Star-Crossed Lovers(stereo-LP-master) | Circle Of Fourth | Circle Of Fourth(stereo-LP-master)
NYC, rec. 3.5.1957
Ellington,Duke (p) | Cook,Willie (tp) | Anderson,Cat (tp) | Terry,Clark (tp) | Nance,Ray (tp) | Woodman,Britt (tb) | Jackson,Quentin (tb) |

Sanders,John (tb) | Hodges,Johnny (as) | Procope,Russell (cl,as) | Hamilton,Jimmy (cl,ts) | Gonsalves,Paul (ts) | Carney,Harry (bs) | Woode,Jimmy (b) | Woodyard,Sam (dr)

CK 65569 | CD | Anatomy Of A Murder

Anatomy Of A Murder | Flirtbird | Flirtbird(II) | Almost Cried | Happy Anatomy | Hero To Zero | Way Early Subtone | Sunwept Sunday | Main Title Of Anatomy Of A Murder | Upper And Outest | Anatomy Of A Murder(Sountrack): | Low Key Lightly | Happy Anatomy | Grace Valse | Midnight Indigo | Happy Anatomy(II) | More Blues

Los Angeles,CA, rec. 29.5.& 1.-2.6.1959

Ellington,Duke (p,celeste) | Nance,Ray (tp) | Terry,Clark (tp) | Anderson,Cat (tp) | Baker,Harold 'Shorty' (tp) | Wilson,Gerald (tp) | Woodman,Britt (tb) | Jackson,Quentin (tb) | Sanders,John (tb) | Hodges,Johnny (as) | Procope,Russell (cl,as) | Hamilton,Jimmy (cl,ts) | Gonsalves,Paul (ts) | Carney,Harry (bs) | Strayhorn,Billy (p,celeste) | Woode,Jimmy (b) | Johnson,Jimmy (dr)

CK 65571 | CD | First Time!

Duke Ellington And Count Basie With Their Orchestras

Corner Pocket(aka Until I Met You) | To You | Segue In C

NYC, rec. 6.7.1961

Ellington,Duke (p,ld) | Basie,Count (p,ld) | Cook,Willie (tp) | Mullens,Eddie (tp) | Anderson,Cat (tp) | Ford,Fats (tp) | Jones,Thad (tp) | Cohn[Cohen],Sonny (tp) | Young,Eugene 'Snooky' (tp) | Johnson,Lennie (tp) | Nance,Ray (tp,v) | Brown,Lawrence (tb) | Tizol,Juan (tb) | Blackburn,Lou (tb) | Coker,Henry (tb) | Jackson,Quentin (tb) | Powell,Benny (tb,b-tb) | Hamilton,Jimmy (cl,ts) | Royal,Marshall (cl,as) | Procope,Russell (cl,as) | Hodges,Johnny (as) | Wess,Frank (fl,as,ts) | Gonsalves,Paul (ts) | Foster,Frank (ts) | Johnson,Budd (ts) | Carney,Harry (bs) | Fowlkes,Charlie (bs) | Green,Freddie (g) | Jones,Eddie (b) | Payne,Sonny (dr)

Wild Man(aka Wild Man Moore) | Wild Man(aka Wild Man Moore-alt.take)

Ellington,Duke (p,ld) | Basie,Count (p,ld) | Cook,Willie (tp) | Mullens,Eddie (tp) | Anderson,Cat (tp) | Ford,Fats (tp) | Jones,Thad (tp) | Cohn[Cohen],Sonny (tp) | Young,Eugene 'Snooky' (tp) | Johnson,Lennie (tp) | Nance,Ray (tp,v) | Brown,Lawrence (tb) | Tizol,Juan (tb) | Blackburn,Lou (tb) | Coker,Henry (tb) | Jackson,Quentin (tb) | Powell,Benny (tb,b-tb) | Hamilton,Jimmy (cl,ts) | Royal,Marshall (cl,as) | Procope,Russell (cl,as) | Hodges,Johnny (as) | Wess,Frank (fl,as,ts) | Gonsalves,Paul (ts) | Foster,Frank (ts) | Johnson,Budd (ts) | Carney,Harry (bs) | Fowlkes,Charlie (bs) | Green,Freddie (g) | Bell,Aaron (b) | Woodyard,Sam (dr)

Battle Royal | Battle Royal(rehersal take)

Ellington,Duke (p,ld) | Basie,Count (p,ld) | Cook,Willie (tp) | Mullens,Eddie (tp) | Anderson,Cat (tp) | Ford,Fats (tp) | Jones,Thad (tp) | Cohn[Cohen],Sonny (tp) | Young,Eugene 'Snooky' (tp) | Johnson,Lennie (tp) | Nance,Ray (tp,v) | Brown,Lawrence (tb) | Tizol,Juan (tb) | Blackburn,Lou (tb) | Coker,Henry (tb) | Jackson,Quentin (tb) | Powell,Benny (tb,b-tb) | Hamilton,Jimmy (cl,ts) | Royal,Marshall (cl,as) | Procope,Russell (cl,as) | Hodges,Johnny (as) | Wess,Frank (fl,as,ts) | Gonsalves,Paul (ts) | Foster,Frank (ts) | Johnson,Budd (ts) | Carney,Harry (bs) | Fowlkes,Charlie (bs) | Green,Freddie (g) | Bell,Aaron (b) | Woodyard,Sam (dr) | Payne,Sonny (dr)

Take The 'A' Train(rehersal take)

Ellington,Duke (p,ld) | Cook,Willie (tp) | Mullens,Eddie (tp) | Anderson,Cat (tp) | Ford,Fats (tp) | Jones,Thad (tp) | Cohn[Cohen],Sonny (tp) | Young,Eugene 'Snooky' (tp) | Johnson,Lennie (tp) | Nance,Ray (tp,v) | Brown,Lawrence (tb) | Tizol,Juan (tb) | Blackburn,Lou (tb) | Coker,Henry (tb) | Jackson,Quentin (tb) | Powell,Benny (tb,b-tb) | Hamilton,Jimmy (cl,ts) | Royal,Marshall (cl,as) | Procope,Russell (cl,as) | Hodges,Johnny (as) | Wess,Frank (fl,as,ts) | Gonsalves,Paul (ts) | Foster,Frank (ts) | Johnson,Budd (ts) | Carney,Harry (bs) | Fowlkes,Charlie (bs) | Strayhorn,Billy (p) | Green,Freddie (g) | Bell,Aaron (b) | Woodyard,Sam (dr)

Take The 'A' Train

NYC, rec. 7.7.1961

Ellington,Duke (p,ld) | Cook,Willie (tp) | Mullens,Eddie (tp) | Anderson,Cat (tp) | Ford,Fats (tp) | Jones,Thad (tp) | Cohn[Cohen],Sonny (tp) | Young,Eugene 'Snooky' (tp) | Johnson,Lennie (tp) | Nance,Ray (tp,v) | Brown,Lawrence (tb) | Tizol,Juan (tb) | Blackburn,Lou (tb) | Coker,Henry (tb) | Jackson,Quentin (tb) | Powell,Benny (tb,b-tb) | Hamilton,Jimmy (cl,ts) | Royal,Marshall (cl,as) | Procope,Russell (cl,as) | Hodges,Johnny (as) | Wess,Frank (fl,as,ts) | Gonsalves,Paul (ts) | Foster,Frank (ts) | Johnson,Budd (ts) | Carney,Harry (bs) | Fowlkes,Charlie (bs) | Strayhorn,Billy (p) | Green,Freddie (g) | Bell,Aaron (b) | Woodyard,Sam (dr)

B.D.B. | B.D.B.(alt.take) | Jumpin' At The Woodside | Jumpin' At The Woodside(alt.take) | One More Once | Blues In Hoss' Flat(Blues In Frankie's Flat)

NYC, rec. 7.6.1961

Ellington,Duke (p,ld) | Basie,Count (p,ld) | Cook,Willie (tp) | Mullens,Eddie (tp) | Anderson,Cat (tp) | Ford,Fats (tp) | Jones,Thad (tp) | Cohn[Cohen],Sonny (tp) | Young,Eugene 'Snooky' (tp) | Johnson,Lennie (tp) | Nance,Ray (tp,v) | Brown,Lawrence (tb) | Tizol,Juan (tb) | Blackburn,Lou (tb) | Coker,Henry (tb) | Jackson,Quentin (tb) | Powell,Benny (tb,b-tb) | Hamilton,Jimmy (cl,ts) | Royal,Marshall (cl,as) | Procope,Russell (cl,as) | Hodges,Johnny (as) | Wess,Frank (fl,as,ts) | Gonsalves,Paul (ts) | Foster,Frank (ts) | Johnson,Budd (ts) | Carney,Harry (bs) | Fowlkes,Charlie (bs) | Green,Freddie (g) | Jones,Eddie (b) | Payne,Sonny (dr)

CK 65625 | CD | Let Me Off Uptown:Anita O'Day With Gene Krupa

Anita O'Day With Gene Krupa And His Orchestra

Georgia On My Mind

NYC, rec. 12.3.1941

O'Day,Anita (voc) | Krupa,Gene (dr) | Eldridge,Roy (tp) | Young,Graham (tp) | Halten,Torg (tp) | Sherock,Shorty (tp) | Murphy,Norman (tp) | Wagner,Babe (tb) | Kelliher,Jay (tb) | Virgadamo,Pat (tb) | Ruffo,Mascagni 'Musky' (as) | Neagley,Clint (as) | Musiker,Sam (ts) | Bates,Walter (ts) | Kitsis,Bob (p) | Biondi,Ray (g) | Bastien,Biddy (b)

Just A Little Bit North Of South Carolina | Slow Down

NYC, rec. 19.3.1941

O'Day,Anita (voc) | Krupa,Gene (dr) | Eldridge,Roy (tp) | Young,Graham (tp) | Halten,Torg (tp) | Sherock,Shorty (tp) | Murphy,Norman (tp) | Wagner,Babe (tb) | Kelliher,Jay (tb) | Virgadamo,Pat (tb) | Ruffo,Mascagni 'Musky' (as) | Neagley,Clint (as) | Musiker,Sam (ts) | Bates,Walter (ts) | Kitsis,Bob (p) | Biondi,Ray (g) | Bastien,Biddy (b)

Green Eyes | Let Me Off Uptown

NYC, rec. 8.5.1941

O'Day,Anita (voc) | Krupa,Gene (dr) | Eldridge,Roy (tp,voc) | Young,Graham (tp) | Halten,Torg (tp) | Murphy,Norman (tp) | Wagner,Babe (tb) | Kelliher,Jay (tb) | Grassi,John (tb) | Ruffo,Mascagni 'Musky' (as) | Neagley,Clint (as) | Bates,Walter (ts) | Kitsis,Bob (p) | Biondi,Ray (g) | Bastien,Biddy (b)

Kick It!

NYC, rec. 5.6.1941

O'Day,Anita (voc) | Krupa,Gene (dr) | Eldridge,Roy (tp,voc) | Young,Graham (tp) | Halten,Torg (tp) | Murphy,Norman (tp) | Wagner,Babe (tb) | Kelliher,Jay (tb) | Grassi,John (tb) | Ruffo,Mascagni 'Musky' (as) | Neagley,Clint (as) | Bates,Walter (ts) | Kitsis,Bob (p) | Biondi,Ray (g) | Bastien,Biddy (b)

Stop The Red Light's On

Chicago,Ill, rec. 18.8.1941

O'Day,Anita (voc) | Krupa,Gene (dr) | Eldridge,Roy (tp,voc) | Young,Graham (tp) | Halten,Torg (tp) | Murphy,Norman (tp) | Wagner,Babe (tb) | Kelliher,Jay (tb) | Virgadamo,Pat (tb) | Ruffo,Mascagni 'Musky' (as) | Listengard,Sam (as) | Musiker,Sam (ts) | Migliori,Jimmy (ts) | Bates,Walter (ts) | Raskin,Milt (p) | Biondi,Ray (g) | Mihelich,Ed (b)

Watch The Birdie

Chicago,Ill, rec. 20.8.1941

O'Day,Anita (voc) | Krupa,Gene (dr) | Eldridge,Roy (tp) | Young,Graham (tp) | Halten,Torg (tp) | Murphy,Norman (tp) | Wagner,Babe (tb) | Kelliher,Jay (tb) | Grassi,John (tb) | Ruffo,Mascagni 'Musky' (as) | Neagley,Clint (as) | Musiker,Sam (cl,as) | Bates,Walter (ts) | Migliori,Jimmy (as) | Raskin,Milt (p) | Biondi,Ray (g) | Mihelich,Ed (b) | Bastien,Biddy (b)

Bolero At The Savoy

NYC, rec. 25.10.1941

O'Day,Anita (voc) | Krupa,Gene (dr) | Eldridge,Roy (tp) | Young,Graham (tp) | Beck,Al (tp) | Murphy,Norman (tp) | Wagner,Babe (tb) | Kelliher,Jay (tb) | Grassi,John (tb) | Ruffo,Mascagni 'Musky' (as) | Neagley,Clint (as) | Musiker,Sam (cl,as) | Bates,Walter (ts) | Migliori,Jimmy (as) | Raskin,Milt (p) | Biondi,Ray (g) | Mihelich,Ed (b) | Bastien,Biddy (b)

Skylark | Thanks For The Boogie Ride

Chicago,Ill, rec. 25.11.1941

O'Day,Anita (voc) | Krupa,Gene (dr) | Eldridge,Roy (tp,voc) | Young,Graham (tp) | Beck,Al (tp) | Sherock,Shorty (tp) | Murphy,Norman (tp) | Wagner,Babe (tb) | Kelliher,Jay (tb) | Virgadamo,Pat (tb) | Ruffo,Mascagni 'Musky' (as) | Listengard,Sam (as) | Musiker,Sam (ts) | Bates,Walter (ts) | Migliori,Jimmy (as) | Raskin,Milt (p) | Biondi,Ray (g) | Bastien,Biddy (b)

Harlem On Parade

NYC, rec. 23.1.1942

O'Day,Anita (voc) | Krupa,Gene (dr) | Eldridge,Roy (tp) | Beck,Al (tp) | Mangano,Mickey (tp) | Murphy,Norman (tp) | Wagner,Babe (tb) | Kelliher,Jay (tb) | Grassi,John (tb) | Feeman,Ben (sax) | Brassfield,Don (sax) | Kittig,Rex (sax) | Musiker,Sam (cl,ts) | Migliori,Jimmy (as) | Raskin,Milt (p) | Biondi,Ray (g) | Mihelich,Ed (b)

Massachusetts

NYC, rec. 13.7.1942

O'Day,Anita (voc) | Krupa,Gene (dr) | Eldridge,Roy (tp) | Beck,Al (tp) | Mangano,Mickey (tp) | Murphy,Norman (tp) | Wagner,Babe (tb) | Pederson,Pullman 'Tommy' (tb) | Phillips,Greg (tb) | Feeman,Ben (sax) | Brassfield,Don (sax) | Kittig,Rex (sax) | Musiker,Sam (cl,ts) | Migliori,Jimmy (as) | Raskin,Milt (p) | Walters,Teddy (g) | Mihelich,Ed (b)

That's What You Think

NYC, rec. 26.2.1942

O'Day,Anita (voc) | Krupa,Gene (dr) | Eldridge,Roy (tp) | Mangano,Mickey (tp) | Beck,Al (tp) | Murphy,Norman (tp) | Wagner,Babe (tb) | Kelliher,Jay (tb) | Grassi,John (tb) | Feeman,Ben (sax) | Brassfield,Don (sax) | Kittig,Rex (sax) | Musiker,Sam (cl,ts) | Migliori,Jimmy (as) | Springer,Joe (p) | Biondi,Ray (g) | Mihelich,Ed (b)

Barrel House Bessie From Basin Street

Chicago,Ill, rec. 2.4.1942

O'Day,Anita (voc) | Krupa,Gene (dr) | Eldridge,Roy (tp,voc) | Mangano,Mickey (tp) | Beck,Al (tp) | Murphy,Norman (tp) | Wagner,Babe (tb) | Kelliher,Jay (tb) | Grassi,John (tb) | Feeman,Ben (sax) | Brassfield,Don (sax) | Kittig,Rex (sax) | Musiker,Sam (cl,ts) | Migliori,Jimmy (as) | Springer,Joe (p) | Biondi,Ray (g) | Mihelich,Ed (b)

Opus One | Boogie Blues

NYC, rec. 21.8.1945

O'Day,Anita (voc) | Krupa,Gene (dr) | Russo,Tony (tp) | Fagerquist,Don (tp) | Triscari,Joe (tp) | Hughes,Vince (tp) | Cox,Leon (tb) | Pederson,Pullman 'Tommy' (tb) | Cully,Billy (tb) | Tei,Adrian (sax) | Olson,Stewart (sax) | Ventura,Charlie (ts) | Bothwell,Johnny (as) | Kennedy,Charlie (sax) | Napoleon,Teddy (p) | Yance,Ed (g) | Lang,Irving (b) | Dale,Joe (tp)

Tea For Two

NYC, rec. 23./24.10.1945

O'Day,Anita (voc) | Krupa,Gene (dr) | Russo,Tony (tp) | Fagerquist,Don (tp) | Triscari,Joe (tp) | Hughes,Vince (tp) | Cox,Leon (tb) | Pederson,Pullman 'Tommy' (tb) | Cully,Billy (tb) | Tei,Adrian (sax) | Olson,Stewart (sax) | Ventura,Charlie (ts) | Bothwell,Johnny (as) | Kennedy,Charlie (sax) | Napoleon,Teddy (p) | Yance,Ed (g) | Lang,Irving (b) | Dale,Joe (tp)

CK 65678 | CD | Mullenium

Gene Krupa And His Orchestra

How High The Moon

NYC, rec. 27.5.1946

Krupa,Gene (dr) | Triscari,Joe (tp) | Triscari,Ray (tp) | Anelli,Tony (tp) | Rodney,Red (tp) | Covington,Warren (tb) | Elmer,Ziggy (tb) | Taylor,Dick (tb) | Seaman,Ben (tb) | Terrill,Harry (as) | Kennedy,Charlie (as) | Ventura,Charlie (ts) | Wise,Buddy (ts) | Schwartz,Jack (bs) | Napoleon,Teddy (p) | Triscari,Mike (g) | Munoz,Bob (b) | Mulligan,Gerry (cond,arr)

Disc Jockey Jump | Disc Jockey Jump(alt.take)

NYC, rec. 22.1.1947

Krupa,Gene (dr) | Triscari,Ray (tp) | Porcino,Al (tp) | Badgley,Ed (tp) | Fagerquist,Don (tp) | Hervey,Clay (tb) | Taylor,Dick (tb) | Mazaneo,Emil (tb) | Zimmermann,Jack (tb) | Terrill,Harry (as) | Kennedy,Charlie (as) | Wise,Buddy (ts) | Melnick,Mitchell (ts) | Schwartz,Jack (bs) | Neal,Buddy (p) | Lesher,Bob (g) | Strahl,Bob (b) | Mulligan,Gerry (cond,arr)

Elliot Lawrence And His Orchestra

Evelation

NYC, rec. 13.4.1949

Dee,Johnny (tp) | Techner,Joe (tp) | Padget,Jimmy (tp) | Danzizen,Bill (tp) | Forrest,Vince (tb) | Berger,Sy (tb) | Harris,Chuck (tb) | Soldo,Joe (as) | Giamo,Louis (as) | Urso,Phil (ts) | Rondinelli,Bruno (ts) | Bredwell,Merle (bs) | Karsh,Bob (p) | O'Neil,Tom (b) | Mann,Howie (dr) | Mulligan,Gerry (arr) | Lawrence,Elliott (ld)

Between The Devil And The Deep Blue Sea

NYC, rec. 10.10.1949

Dee,Johnny (tp) | Techner,Joe (tp) | Padget,Jimmy (tp) | Danzizen,Bill (tp) | Berger,Sy (tb) | Hunter,Frank (tb) | Hessler,Gene (tb) | Soldo,Joe (as) | Mulligan,Gerry (as,bs,arr) | Urso,Phil (ts) | Rondinelli,Bruno (ts) | Bredwell,Merle (bs) | Lawrence,Elliott (p,ld) | O'Neil,Tom (b) | Mann,Howie (dr)

Gerry Mulligan And His Orchestra

Thruway | Mullenium | Thruway(alt.take)

NYC, rec. 19.4.1957

Mulligan,Gerry (bs,p) | Sunkel,Phil (tp) | Lloyd,Jerry (tp) | Joseph,Don (tp) | Ferrara,Don (tp) | Brookmeyer,Bob (v-tb) | Rehak,Frank (tb) | Dahl,Jimmy (tb) | McKusick,Hal (as) | Konitz,Lee (as) | Sims,Zoot (ts) | Rouse,Charlie (ts) | Allen,Gene (bs) | Benjamin,Joe (b) | Bailey,Dave (dr)

Motel | All The Things You Are | Motel(alt.take)

NYC, rec. 20.4.1957

Mulligan,Gerry (bs,p) | Sunkel,Phil (tp) | Lloyd,Jerry (tp) | Joseph,Don (tp) | Ferrara,Don (tp) | Brookmeyer,Bob (v-tb) | Rehak,Frank (tb) | Dahl,Jimmy (tb) | McKusick,Hal (as) | Konitz,Lee (as) | Sims,Zoot (ts) | Rouse,Charlie (ts) | Allen,Gene (bs) | Benjamin,Joe (b) | Bailey,Dave (dr)

CK 65680 | CD | Sorcerer

Miles Davis Sextet

Nothing Like You

NYC, rec. 21.8.1962

Davis,Miles (tp) | Rehak,Frank (tb) | Shorter,Wayne (ts) | Dorough,Bob (p,voc) | Chambers,Paul (b) | Cobb,Jimmy (dr) | Bobo,Willie (congas)

Miles Davis Quintet

Limbo | Limbo(alt.take) | Vonetta

NYC, rec. 16.5.1967

Davis,Miles (tp) | Shorter,Wayne (ts) | Hancock,Herbie (p) | Carter,Ron (b) | Williams,Tony (dr)

Masqualero | Masqualero(alt.take) | The Sorcerer

NYC, rec. 17.5.1967

Davis,Miles (tp) | Shorter,Wayne (ts) | Hancock,Herbie (p) | Carter,Ron (b) | Williams,Tony (dr)

Prince Of Darkness

NYC, rec. 24.4.1967

Davis,Miles (tp) | Shorter,Wayne (ts) | Hancock,Herbie (p) | Carter,Ron (b) | Williams,Tony (dr)

Wayne Shorter Quartet

Pee Wee

NYC, rec. 24.5.1967

Shorter,Wayne (ts) | Hancock,Herbie (p) | Carter,Ron (b) | Williams,Tony (dr)

CK 65681 | CD | Nefertiti

Miles Davis Quintet

Nefertiti

NYC, rec. 7.6.1967

Davis,Miles (tp) | Shorter,Wayne (ts) | Hancock,Herbie (p) | Carter,Ron (b) | Williams,Tony (dr)

Madness | Madness(alt.take) | Hand Jive | Hand Jive(alt.take 1) | Hand Jive(alt.take 2)

NYC, rec. 22.6.1967

Davis,Miles (tp) | Shorter,Wayne (ts) | Hancock,Herbie (p) | Carter,Ron (b) | Williams,Tony (dr)

Fall | Pinocchio | Pinocchio(alt.take) | Riot

NYC, rec. 19.7.1967

Davis,Miles (tp) | Shorter,Wayne (ts) | Hancock,Herbie (p) | Carter,Ron (b) | Williams,Tony (dr)

CK 65682 | CD | Miles Smiles

Circle | Orbits | Dolores | Freedom Jazz Dance

NYC, rec. 24.10.1966

Davis,Miles (tp) | Shorter,Wayne (ts) | Hancock,Herbie (p) | Carter,Ron (b) | Williams,Tony (dr)

Gingerbread Boy | Footprints

NYC, rec. 25.10.1966

Davis,Miles (tp) | Shorter,Wayne (ts) | Hancock,Herbie (p) | Carter,Ron (b) | Williams,Tony (dr)

CK 65684 | CD | Miles In The Sky

Country Son | Country Son(alt.take)

NYC, rec. 15.5.1968

Davis,Miles (tp) | Shorter,Wayne (ts) | Hancock,Herbie (p) | Carter,Ron (b) | Williams,Tony (dr)

Black Comedy | Black Comedy(alt.take)

NYC, rec. 16.5.1968

Davis,Miles (tp) | Shorter,Wayne (ts) | Hancock,Herbie (p) | Carter,Ron (b) | Williams,Tony (dr)

Stuff

NYC, rec. 17.5.1968

Davis,Miles (tp) | Shorter,Wayne (ts) | Hancock,Herbie (p) | Carter,Ron (b) | Williams,Tony (dr)

Miles Davis Sextet

Paraphernalia

NYC, rec. 16.1.1968

Davis,Miles (tp) | Shorter,Wayne (ts) | Benson,George (g) | Hancock,Herbie (p) | Carter,Ron (b) | Williams,Tony (dr)

CK 65723 | CD | Bravo! Brubeck!

Dave Brubeck Sextet

Introduction | Cielito Lindo | La Paloma Azul | Sobre Las Olas(Over The Waves) | Besame Mucho | Nostalgia De Mexico | Poinciana | Alla En El Rancho Grande | Frenesi | Estrellita | La Bamba

Live in Mexico City, rec. 12.-14.5.1967

Brubeck,Darius (p) | Desmond,Paul (as) | Wright,Eugene 'Gene' (b) | Morello,Joe (dr) | Agüeros,Salvador 'Rabito' (congas,bongos) | Correa,Benjamin 'Chamin' (g)

CK 65724 | CD | Brubeck Time

Dave Brubeck Quartet

Audrey | Jeepers Creepers | A Fine Romance

Live at Basin Street,NYC, rec. 12.10.1954

Brubeck,Dave (p) | Desmond,Paul (as) | Bates,Bob (b) | Dodge,Joe (dr)

Stompin' For Mili | Brother Can You Spare A Dime

NYC, rec. 13.10.1954

Brubeck,Dave (p) | Desmond,Paul (as) | Bates,Bob (b) | Dodge,Joe (dr)

Pennies From Heaven | Why Do I Love You

NYC, rec. 14.10.1954

Brubeck,Dave (p) | Desmond,Paul (as) | Bates,Bob (b) | Dodge,Joe (dr)

Keepin' Out Of Mischief Now

NYC, rec. 10.11.1954

Brubeck,Dave (p) | Desmond,Paul (as) | Bates,Bob (b) | Dodge,Joe (dr)

CK 65725 | CD | Brandenburg Gate:Revisited

Dave Brubeck Quartet With Orchestra

Summer Song | G Flat Theme

NYC, rec. 21.8.1961

Brubeck,Dave (p) | Desmond,Paul (as) | Wright,Eugene 'Gene' (b) | Morello,Joe (dr) | Orchestra & Strings | Brubeck,Howard (ld)

Brandenburg Gate | In Your Own Sweet Way | Kathy's Waltz

NYC, rec. 22.8.1961

Brubeck,Dave (p) | Desmond,Paul (as) | Wright,Eugene 'Gene' (b) | Morello,Joe (dr) | Orchestra & Strings | Brubeck,Howard (ld)

CK 65727 | CD | Brubeck & Rushing

Jimmy Rushing With The Dave Brubeck Quartet

There'll Be Some Changes Made | Am I Blue | Blues In The Dark | Shine On Harvest Moon

NYC, rec. 29.1.1960

Rushing,Jimmy (voc) | Brubeck,Dave (p) | Desmond,Paul (as) | Wright,Eugene 'Gene' (b) | Morello,Joe (dr)

My Melancholy Baby | You Can Depend On Me

NYC, rec. 16.2.1960

Rushing,Jimmy (voc) | Brubeck,Dave (p) | Desmond,Paul (as) | Wright,Eugene 'Gene' (b) | Morello,Joe (dr)

I Never Knew(I Could Love Anybody Like I'm Loving You) | Ain't Misbehavin' | Evenin' | All By Myself | River Stay Away From My Door

NYC, rec. 4.8.1960

Rushing,Jimmy (voc) | Brubeck,Dave (p) | Desmond,Paul (as) | Wright,Eugene 'Gene' (b) | Morello,Joe (dr)

CK 65777 | CD | Buried Treasures

Dave Brubeck Quartet

Introduction | Mr.Broadway | Koto Song | Sweet Georgia Brown | Forty Days | You Go To My Head | Take Five | St.Louis Blues

Mexico City, rec. 12.-14.5.1967

Brubeck,Dave (p) | Desmond,Paul (as) | Wright,Eugene 'Gene' (b) | Morello,Joe (dr)

CK 65919 | CD | Someday My Prince Will Come

Miles Davis Quintet

Pfrancing | Drag-Dog

NYC, rec. 7.3.1961

Davis,Miles (tp) | Mobley,Hank (ts) | Kelly,Wynton (p) | Chambers,Paul (b) | Cobb,Jimmy (dr)

Old Folks

NYC, rec. 20.3.1961

Davis,Miles (tp) | Mobley,Hank (ts) | Kelly,Wynton (p) | Chambers,Paul (b) | Cobb,Jimmy (dr)

Miles Davis Sextet

Someday My Prince Will Come | Someday My Prince Will Come(alt.take) | Blues No.2

Davis,Miles (tp) | Mobley,Hank (ts) | Coltrane,John (ts) | Kelly,Wynton (p) | Chambers,Paul (b) | Cobb,Jimmy (dr)

Miles Davis Quartet

I Thought About You

NYC, rec. 21.3.1961

Davis,Miles (tp) | Kelly,Wynton (p) | Chambers,Paul (b) | Cobb,Jimmy (dr)

Miles Davis Quintet

Teo

Davis,Miles (tp) | Coltrane,John (ts) | Kelly,Wynton (p) | Chambers,Paul (b) | Cobb,Jimmy (dr)

CK 67503 | CD | Standard Time Vol.4:Marsalis Plays Monk

Wynton Marsalis Group

Thelonious | Worry Later

NYC, rec. 17./18.9.1993
Marsalis,Wynton (tp) | Gordon,Wycliffe (tb) | Anderson,Wessell 'Wes' (as) | Goines,Victor (ts) | Blandings Jr.,Walter (ts) | Reed,Eric (p) | Wolfe,Benjamin Jonah 'Ben' (b) | Veal,Reginald (b) | Riley,Herlin (dr)
Evidence | We See | Monk's Mood | Four In One | In Walked Bud | Hackensack | Let's Cool One | Brilliant Corners | Brake's Sake | Ugly Beauty | Green Chimneys
NYC, rec. 3./4.10.1994
Marsalis,Wynton (tp) | Gordon,Wycliffe (tb) | Anderson,Wessell 'Wes' (as) | Goines,Victor (ts) | Blandings Jr.,Walter (ts) | Reed,Eric (p) | Wolfe,Benjamin Jonah 'Ben' (b) | Veal,Reginald (b) | Riley,Herlin (dr)

CK 68921 | CD | Wynton Marsalis Quartet With Strings
A Band Of Friends
The Party's Over | You're Blasé | After You've Gone | Glad To Be Unhappy | It Never Entered My Mind | Baby Won't You Please Come Home | I Guess I'll Hang My Tears Out To Dry | I Got Lost In Her Arms | Ballad Of The Sad Young Men | Spring Will Be A Little Late This Year | My Man's Gone Now | The Midnight Blues
NYC, rec. 15.-18.9.1997
Marsalis,Wynton (tp) | Reed,Eric (p) | Veal,Reginald (b) | Nash,Lewis (dr) | Peabody,Paul (concertmaster) | Appleman,Abe (v) | Chassau,Robert (v) | Chorberg,Israel (v) | Bennion Feeney ,Krista (v) | Figuer,Narcisco (v) | Finclair,Barry (v) | Garvey,Winterton (v) | Gordon,Kenneth (v) | Henrickson,Richard (v) | Inderio,Regis (v) | Ingraham,Jeanne (v) | Leathers,Ann (v) | McAlhany,Nancy (v) | Oakland,Ron (v) | Ornstein,Susan (v) | Park,Sandra (v) | Pintavalle,John (v) | Raimondi,Matthew (v) | Seaton,Laura (v) | Sortomme,Richard (v) | Steinberg,Lisa (v) | Stoner,Martin (v) | Tecco,Donna (v) | Whitney-Barratt,Belinda (v) | Alsop,LaMar (viola) | Davis,Lenny (viola) | Dryfus,Karen (viola) | Ewing, Mary Helen (viola) | Landon,Carol (viola) | Pray,Sue (viola) | Roach,Maxine (viola) | Locker,Richard (cello) | Friedlander,Erik (cello) | Moye,Eugene (cello) | Ruede,Clay (cello) | Schuman,Mark (cello) | Zlotkin,Frederick (cello) | Beal,John (b) | Glazener,Lawrence (b) | Harris,Paul (b) | Freedman,Robert (cond,arr) | Charlap,Emile (contractor)

CK 69860 | CD | Big Train
Lincoln Center Jazz Orchestra
All Aboard | Observation Car | Union Pacific Big Boy | Smokestack Shuffle | Northbound-Southbound | Dining Car | Night Train | Engine | Bullet Train | Sleeper Car | Station Car | The Caboose
NYC, rec. 20.12.1998
Lincoln Center Jazz Orchestra,The | Black,Seneca (tp) | Kisor,Ryan (tp) | Printup,Marcus (tp) | Marsalis,Wynton (tp,ld) | Mullins,Riley (tp) | Goodman,Wayne (tb) | Westray,Ronald (tb) | Gordon,Wycliffe (tb,tuba) | Anderson,Wessell 'Wes' (cl,as,sopranino) | Nash,Ted (fl,cl,b-cl,ss,as,piccolo) | Blandings Jr.,Walter (cl,ss,as,ts) | Goines,Victor (cl,b-cl,ss,as,ts) | Temperley,Joe (b-cl,ss,bs) | Barron,Farid (p) | Wamble,Doug (g,bj) | Whitaker,Rodney Thomas (b) | Riley,Herlin (dr) | Guerrero,Rolando (perc)

CK 69872 | CD | Standard Time Vol.6:Mr.Jelly Lord
Wynton Marsalis Group
New Orleans Stomp | King Porter Stomp | The Pearls | Deep Creek | Sidewalk Blues | Jungle Blues | Big Lip Blues | Dead Man Blues | Smokehouse Blues | Courthouse Bump | Black Bottom Stomp
NYC, rec. 12./13.1.1999
Marsalis,Wynton (tp) | Barbarin,Lucien (tb) | White,Dr.Michael (cl) | Anderson,Wessell 'Wes' (as) | Goines,Victor (cl,ss,ts) | Lewis,Eric (p) | Vappie,Papa Don (g,bj) | Veal,Reginald (b) | Riley,Herlin (dr)
Red Hot Pepper
Marsalis,Wynton (tp) | Barbarin,Lucien (tb) | Gordon,Wycliffe (tp,tb,tuba) | White,Dr.Michael (cl) | Anderson,Wessell 'Wes' (as) | Goines,Victor (cl,ss,ts) | Lewis,Eric (p) | Vappie,Papa Don (g,bj) | Veal,Reginald (b) | Riley,Herlin (dr)
Mamamita
Marsalis,Wynton (tp) | Barbarin,Lucien (tb) | White,Dr.Michael (cl) | Anderson,Wessell 'Wes' (as) | Goines,Victor (cl,ss,ts) | Perez,Danilo (p) | Vappie,Papa Don (g,bj) | Veal,Reginald (b) | Riley,Herlin (dr)
Billy Goat Stomp
Marsalis,Wynton (tp) | Barbarin,Lucien (tb) | White,Dr.Michael (cl) | Anderson,Wessell 'Wes' (as) | Goines,Victor (cl,ss,ts) | Connick Jr.,Harry (p) | Vappie,Papa Don (g,bj) | Veal,Reginald (b) | Riley,Herlin (dr)
Tom Cat Blues
Marsalis,Wynton (tp) | Barbarin,Lucien (tb) | White,Dr.Michael (cl) | Anderson,Wessell 'Wes' (as) | Goines,Victor (cl,ss,ts) | Reed,Eric (p) | Vappie,Papa Don (g,bj) | Veal,Reginald (b) | Riley,Herlin (dr)

CK 86564 | CD | MONK. | EAN 5099708656423
Thelonious Monk Quartet
Theo
NYC, rec. 9.3.1964
Monk,Thelonious (p) | Rouse,Charlie (ts) | Gales,Larry (b) | Riley,Ben (dr)
Liza(All The Clouds'll Roll Away) | Medley: | Just You Just Me- | Liza(All The Clouds'll Roll Away)-
NYC, rec. 6.10.1964
Monk,Thelonious (p) | Rouse,Charlie (ts) | Gales,Larry (b) | Riley,Ben (dr)
Children's Song(That Old Man)
NYC, rec. 7.10.1964
Monk,Thelonious (p) | Rouse,Charlie (ts) | Gales,Larry (b) | Riley,Ben (dr)
April In Paris | Just You Just Me | Pannonia | April In Paris(alt.take) | Pannonica(alt.take)
NYC, rec. 8.10.1964
Monk,Thelonious (p) | Rouse,Charlie (ts) | Gales,Larry (b) | Riley,Ben (dr)
Thelonious Monk
I Love You Sweetheart Of All My Dreams
NYC, rec. 6.10.1964
Monk,Thelonious (p-solo)

CK65683 | CD | E.S.P.
Miles Davis Quintet
E.S.P. | R.J.
Los Angeles,CA, rec. 20.1.1965
Davis,Miles (tp) | Shorter,Wayne (ts) | Hancock,Herbie (p) | Carter,Ron (b) | Williams,Tony (dr)
Eighty-One | Little One
Los Angeles,CA, rec. 21.1.1965
Davis,Miles (tp) | Shorter,Wayne (ts) | Hancock,Herbie (p) | Carter,Ron (b) | Williams,Tony (dr)
Agitation | Iris | Mood
Los Angeles,CA, rec. 22.1.1965
Davis,Miles (tp) | Shorter,Wayne (ts) | Hancock,Herbie (p) | Carter,Ron (b) | Williams,Tony (dr)

COLCD 62130 | CD | Stille Nacht
COL40 62130 | MC | Stille Nacht
Mahalia Jackson With Choir And Orchestra
Sweet Little Jesus Boy | A Star Stood Still | Hark! The Herald Angels Sing | Christmas Comes To Us All Once Year | Joy To The World | O Come All Ye Faithful | O Little Town Of Bethlehem | What Can I Give | Go Tell It On The Mountain | Silent Night Holy Night
rec. details unknown
Jackson,Mahalia (voc) | details unknown

Chaos | Jazz Network

CACD 8177 | CD | DAY Dream | EAN 4012116817737
Ralph Schweizer Big Band
Harlem Speaks | Black And Tan Fantasy | Don't Get Around Much Anymore | Cotton Tail | Imagine My Frustration | Queen's Suite: | Sunset And The Mocking Birds- | Lightning Bugs And Frogs- | Le Sucrier Velours- | Northern Lights- | The Single Petal Of A Rose- | Apes And Peacocks- | Things Ain't What They Used To Be
Ludwigsburg, rec. 26.-28.3.2002
Schweizer,Ralph (cl,b-cl,ld) | Irmler,Markus (tp) | Huy,Volker (tp) | Haas,Matthias (tp) | Haas,Stefan (tp) | Reinhard,Benno (tb) | Erb,Matthias (tb) | Heimes,Martina (tb) | Rumig,Dirk (cl,as,ts) | Dahner,Manuel (as,ts) | Pfisterer,Nicolai (as,ts) | Winkler,Sebastian (cl,ts) | Gareis,Benedikt (cl,bs) | Hartmann,Alexander (p) | Beck,Horst (b) | Disch,Wolfgang (dr) | Metzger,Nicole (voc)
Day Dream
Schweizer,Ralph (cl,b-cl,ld) | Burkhardt,Ingolf (tp) | Irmler,Markus (tp) | Huy,Volker (tp) | Haas,Matthias (tp) | Haas,Stefan (tp) | Reinhard,Benno (tb) | Erb,Matthias (tb) | Heimes,Martina (tb) | Rumig,Dirk (cl,as,ts) | Dahner,Manuel (as,ts) | Pfisterer,Nicolai (as,ts) | Winkler,Sebastian (cl,ts) | Gareis,Benedikt (cl,bs) | Hartmann,Alexander (p) | Beck,Horst (b) | Disch,Wolfgang (dr)

CACD 8185 | CD | Kontraste | EAN 4012116818536
Sax Mal Anders
Introduction Et Variations Sur Une Ronde Populaire | Songs For Tony I | Bordell 1900 | Café 1930 | Sensitivity(part 1-3) | Carmen | Segment | One Chance At Life | Quark | When I'm 64
Ludwigsburg, rec. May 2002
Sax Mal Anders | Winkler,Sebastian (ss,as,ts) | Dahner,Manuel (as) | Pfisterer,Nicolai (ts) | Gareis,Benedikt (bs)
Free At Last
Sax Mal Anders | Winkler,Sebastian (ss,as,ts) | Dahner,Manuel (as) | Pfisterer,Nicolai (ts) | Gareis,Benedikt (bs) | Hartmann,Alexander (fl-h\1) | Disch,Wolfgang (perc)
Ulla In Africa | Black Bottom Stomp
Sax Mal Anders | Winkler,Sebastian (ss,as,ts) | Dahner,Manuel (as) | Pfisterer,Nicolai (ts) | Gareis,Benedikt (bs) | Disch,Wolfgang (perc)
Boogie Stop Shuffle
Sax Mal Anders | Winkler,Sebastian (ss,as,ts) | Dahner,Manuel (as) | Pfisterer,Nicolai (ts) | Gareis,Benedikt (bs) | Rumig,Dirk (ss) | Disch,Wolfgang (perc)
Segment
Sax Mal Anders | Winkler,Sebastian (ss,as,ts) | Dahner,Manuel (as) | Pfisterer,Nicolai (ts) | Gareis,Benedikt (bs) | Wohlleben,Johannes (dr,b)

CACD 8186 | CD | Don't Walk Outside Thos Area | EAN 4012116818635
Schlaier-Hirt Duo
Cat I See | Don't Walk Outside This Area | G/Soxx | Labyrinth
Ludwigsburg, rec. 30.5.2001
Hirt,Thomas (fl,ss,ts) | Schlaier,Manne (g,polysub-b)
Panta Rhei | Juicy | World Of Ideas | Nowhere | Pressure | Daddy Longlegs | Mungo Park
Ludwigsburg, rec. 11.9.2002
Hirt,Thomas (fl,ss,ts) | Schlaier,Manne (g,polysub-b)

Chess | Universal Music Germany

076139-2 | CD | Involvement | EAN 044007613924
John Klemmer Quartet
Will 'N' Jug | You Don't Know What Love Is | Stand In The Sun | Passion Food
Chicago,Ill, rec. June 1967
Klemmer,John (ts) | Thomas,Sam (g) | Jackson,Melvin (b) | Campbell,Wilbur (dr)
My Blues | How Deep Is The Ocean | Later With Them Woes
Klemmer,John (ts) | Christian,Jodie (p) | Jackson,Melvin (b) | Campbell,Wilbur (dr)

940910-2 | CD | At The Pershing-But Not For Me
Ahmad Jamal Trio
But Not For Me | The Surrey With The Fringe On Top | Moonlight In Vermont | Put Another Nickel In Music! Music! Music! - (Put Another Nickel In) Music! Music! Music! | There Is No Greater Love | Poinciana | Woody'n You | What's New?
Live at The Pershing Lounge,Chicago,Ill, rec. 16./17.1.1958
Jamal,Ahmad (p) | Crosby,Israel (b) | Fournier,Vernell (dr)

MCD 09199 | CD | John Lee Hooker Plays And Sings The Blues
John Lee Hooker
The Journey | I Don't Want Your Money | Hey Baby | Mad Man Blues | Bluebird | Worried Life Blues | Apologize | Lonely Boy Blues | Please Don't Go | Dreamin' Blues | Hey Boogie
Detroit, rec. 1951/1952
Hooker,John Lee (g,voc)
Just Me And My Telefone
Hooker,John Lee (g,voc) | Kirkland,Eddie (b-g)

MCD 09258 | CD | House Of The Blues
Walkin' The Boogie | Love Blues | Union Station Blues | It's My Own Fault | Leave My Wife Alone | Rambling By Myself | Sugar Mama Blues | Down At The Landing | Louise | Ground Hog Blues | High Priced Woman | Women And Money
different Places, rec. 1951-1954
Hooker,John Lee (g,voc) | personal included: | Kirkland,Eddie (g) | Thurman,Bob (p) | details unknown

MCD 09297 | CD | Howlin' Wolf:The London Sessions
Howlin' Wolf London Session
Rockin' Daddy | I Ain't Superstitious | Sittin' On The Top Of The World | Worried About My Baby | What A Woman | Poor Boy | Built For Comfort | Who's Been Talkin'? | The Red Rooster(Rehearsal) | The Red Rooster | Do The Do | Highway | Wang Dang Doodle
London,GB, rec. 1972
Howlin' Wolf[Chester Burnett] (g,harm,voc) | Clapton,Eric (g) | Winwood,Steve (p,org) | Stewart,Ian (p) | Simon,John (p) | Leake,Lafayette (p) | Sumlin,Hubert (g) | Carp,Jeffrey M. (harm) | Wyman,Bill (b-g,cowbell,shakers) | Upchurch,Phil (b) | Voormann,Klaus (b) | Watts,Charlie (dr,perc,congas) | Richie (dr) | Miller,Joe (horns) | Sandke,Jordan (tp,co) | Lansing,Dennis (horns)

Choice | Fenn Music

CHCD 71001 | CD | Night Dance | EAN 708857100125
Jimmy Giuffre Trio
Night Dance | Phoenix | Feast Dance | Moonlight | The Waiting | Dervish | The Bird | Mosquito Dance | The Chanting | The Butterfly | Flute Song | Eternal Chant
Sea Cliff,NY, rec. 16.11.1971
Giuffre,Jimmy (fl,cl,ts) | Tokunaga,Kiyoshi (b) | Kaye,Randy (dr)

CHCD 71006 | CD | Getting Sentimental
Zoot Sims Quartet
Fred | Restless | Caravan | Dream Dancing | Getting Sentimental Over You | I'm Getting Sentimental Over You(alt.take) | The Very Thought Of You | Love Me
Sea Cliff,NY, rec. 20.4.1974
Sims,Zoot (ss,ts) | Rowles,Jimmy (p) | Cranshaw,Bob (b) | Roker,Granville 'Mickey' (dr)

CHCD 71007 | CD | Images
Toots Thielemans Quartet
Days Of Wine And Roses | I Never Told You | Dr.Pretty | Airegin | Images | Day Dream | Giant Steps | Snooze | Stella By Starlight | Revol
Sea Cliff,NY, rec. 16.9.1974
Thielemans,Jean 'Toots' (harm) | Brackeen,JoAnne (p) | McBee,Cecil (b) | Waits,Freddie (dr)

CHCD 71011 | CD | The Train And The River
Jimmy Giuffre Trio
Tree People | Elephant | Tibetan Sun | The Train And The River | The Tide Is In | River Chant | Om | The Listening | Celebration
Sea Cliff,NY, rec. 25.4.1975
Giuffre,Jimmy (fl,cl,ts,b-fl) | Tokunaga,Kiyoshi (b) | Kaye,Randy (perc)

CHCD 71012 | CD | Where Is Love?
Irene Kral With Alan Broadbent
I Like You You're Nice | When I Look In Your Eyes | A Time For Love- | Small World- | Love Come On Stealthy Fingers | Never Let Me Go | Spring Can Really Hang You Up The Most | Lucky To Be Me- | Some Other Time- | Where Is Love | Don't Look Back
Los Angeles,CA, rec. December 1974
Kral,Irene (voc) | Broadbent,Alan (p)

CHCD 71017 | CD | Lush Life | EAN 708857101726
Buddy DeFranco Quartet
The Dreaded Lergy | Lush Life | Waterbed | Sunnyside Beach | Uncle Horsley
Writhes Again | Here's That Rainy Day
St. Agathe,Quebec,Canada, rec. Janury & May 1977
DeFranco,Buddy (cl) | Fleming,George (accordeon) | Donato,Michel (b) | Magadini,Pete (dr)

CHCD 71019 | CD | Tenorlee
Lee Konitz Trio
Skylark | You Are Too Beautiful | Autumn Nocturne | Tangerine
Sea Cliff,NY, rec. 7.1.1977
Konitz,Lee (ts) | Rowles,Jimmy (p) | Moore,Michael (b)
I Remember You | Thanks For The Memory | Handful Of Stars | Oh! Lady Be Good-
Sea Cliff,NY, rec. 24.7.1977
Konitz,Lee (ts) | Rowles,Jimmy (p) | Moore,Michael (b)
The Gypsy | 'Tis Autumn
Sea Cliff,NY, rec. 23.3.1978
Konitz,Lee (ts) | Rowles,Jimmy (p) | Moore,Michael (b)
Lee Konitz
Tenorlee-
Konitz,Lee (ts-solo)

CHCD 71025 | CD | Something Cool | EAN 708857102525
Carol Sloane With The Norris Turney Quartet
Cotton Tail
Sea Cliff,NY, rec. 30.11.1978
Sloane,Carol (voc) | Turney,Norris (fl,as) | Aronov,Ben (p) | Mraz,George 'Jiri' (b) | LaBarbera,Joe (dr)
Something Cool | Jackie | Baby Don't You Quit Now | Can't We Be Friends | You're A Bad Influence On Me | Some Other Spring | Tomorrow Mountain
Sea Cliff,NY, rec. 6.12.1978
Sloane,Carol (voc) | Turney,Norris (fl,as) | Aronov,Ben (p) | Mraz,George 'Jiri' (b) | LaBarbera,Joe (dr)

CHCD 71030 | CD | Live At The Haig | EAN 708857103027
Bud Shank Quartet
I Heard You | Lover Man(Oh,Where Can You Be?) | Ambassador Blues | How About You | Out Of This World | Miles Sign-Off
Live at The Haig,LA, rec. January 1956
Shank,Bud (fl,as) | Williamson,Claude (p) | Prell,Don | Flores,Chuck (dr)

CHCD 71051 | CD | One Night Stand | EAN 708857105120
Stan Kenton And His Orchestra
Artistry In Rhythm(Opening Theme) | Jambo | Autumn Leaves | Southern Scandal | Yesterdays | Viva Prado | Walkin' By The River | Lullaby In Rhythm | I'll Remember April | Love For Sale | Painted Rhythm | Laura | Blues In Riff | Eager Beaver | I Only Have Eyes For You | Collaboration | Intermission Riff | 'Round Robin | Artistry In Rhythm(Closing Theme)
Live at The Hollywood Palladium,Hollywood,CA, rec. March 1951
Kenton,Stan (p) | Wetzel,Ray (tp) | Ferguson,Maynard (tp) | Howell,John (tp) | Rogers,Shorty (tp) | Alvarez,Chico (tp) | Bernhart,Milton 'Milt' (tb) | Betts,Harry (tb) | Fitzpatrick,Bob (tb) | Kenny,Dick (tb) | Varsalona,Bart (b-tb) | Shank,Bud (as) | Pepper,Art (as) | Cooper,Bob (ts) | Calderell,Bart (ts) | Bagley,Don (b) | Manne,Shelly (dr) | Johnson,Jay (voc)

Contemporary | ZYX Music GmbH

9CCD-4417-2 | 9 CD | Art Pepper:The Complete Village Vanguard Sessions
Art Pepper Quartet
Spoken Introduction | Blues For Heard | Scrapple From The Apple | But Beautiful | My Friend John | Cherokee | Blues For Heard(alt.take) | For Freddie | Valse Triste | Live At The Vanguard | Caravan | Blues For Heard(alt.take-2) | Over The Rainbow | The Trip | Blues For Les | A Night In Tunisia
Live at The 'Village Vanguard',NYC, rec. 28.7.1977
Pepper,Art (as) | Cables,George (p) | Mraz,George 'Jiri' (b) | Jones,Elvin (dr)
Spoken Introduction | No Limit | Valse Triste | My Friend John | You Go To My Head | Cherokee | Blues For Heard | Blues For Heard(alt.take) | Anthropology | These Foolish Things Remind Me On You | For Freddie | Blues For Heard(alt.take-2) | Las Cuevas De Mario | Stella By Starlight | Good Bye | Vanguard Max | Blues For Heard(alt.take-3)
Live at The 'Village Vanguard',NYC, rec. 29.7.1977
Pepper,Art (as,ts) | Cables,George (p) | Mraz,George 'Jiri' (b) | Jones,Elvin (dr)
Vanguard Max | Las Cuevas De Mario | Good Bye | For Freddie | Blues For Heard | My Friend John | More For Less | Cherokee | Blues For Heard(alt.take) | For Freddie(alt.take) | More For Less(alt.take) | Caravan | Labyrinth | My Friend John(alt.take)
Live at The 'Village Vanguard',NYC, rec. 30.7.1977
Pepper,Art (as,ts) | Cables,George (p) | Mraz,George 'Jiri' (b) | Jones,Elvin (dr)
-> Note: Between most of the titles are spoken introductions by Art Pepper!

CCD 14059-2 | CD | Form
Tom Harrell Quintet
Vista | Brazilian Song | Scene | January Sring | Rhythm Form | For Heaven's Sake
NYC, rec. 8./9.4.1990
Harrell,Tom (tp,fl-h) | Lovano,Joe (ts) | Perez,Danilo (p) | Haden,Charlie (b) | Motian,Paul (dr)

CCD 14063-2 | CD | Visions
April Mist
NYC, rec. 22.3.1989
Harrell,Tom (fl-h) | Lovano,Joe (ts) | Williams,James (p) | Drummond,Ray (b) | Nussbaum,Adam (dr)
Tom Harrell Sextet
Visions Of Gaudi
NYC, rec. 23.3.1989
Harrell,Tom (fl-h) | Liebman,Dave (ss) | Abercrombie,John (g-synth) | Williams,James (p) | Drummond,Ray (b) | Nussbaum,Adam (dr)
Tom Harrell Quintet
Suspended View
NYC, rec. 27.1.1988
Harrell,Tom (fl-h) | Berg,Bob (ss) | Doky,Niels Lan (p) | Drummond,Ray (b) | Hart,Billy (dr)
Autumn Picture
NYC, rec. 8./9.4.1990
Harrell,Tom (fl-h) | Lovano,Joe (ss) | Perez,Danilo (p) | Haden,Charlie (b) | Motian,Paul (dr)
Tom Harrell Sextet
I Didn't Know
Harrell,Tom (fl-h) | Pyle,Cheryl (fl) | Lovano,Joe (ss) | Perez,Danilo (p) | Haden,Charlie (b) | Motian,Paul (dr)
George Robert-Tom Harrell Quintet
Opaling | Because I Love You | Everything I Love
Lausanne,CH, rec. 18./19.4.1987
Harrell,Tom (fl-h) | Robert,George (as) | Moroni,Dado (p) | Johnson,Reggie (b) | Goodwin,Bill (dr)

CCD 14086-2 | CD | San Francisco Samba
Art Pepper Quartet
Blue Bossa | Art Meets Mr. Beautiful | Here's That Rainy Day | Samba Mom Mom
Live at Keystone Korner,SF, rec. 6.& 8.8.1977
Pepper,Art (as) | Cables,George (p) | Formanek,Michael (b) | Marshall,Eddie (dr)

CCD 14090-2 | CD | One On One
Russ Freeman-Shelly Manne
I'm Getting Sentimental Over You | How About That | I'm Old Fashioned | On Green Dolphin Street | Take The 'A' Train | Prime Time | Loose As A Goose | Lullaby Of The Leaves | Blue Monk | One On One | Name That Tune | Blue Monk(alt.take) | Loose As A Goose(alt.take) | On Green Dolphin Street(alt.take) | Lullaby Of The Leaves(alt.take)
Hollywood,CA, rec. 14.6.1982
Freeman,Russ (p) | Manne,Shelly (dr)

CCD 7652-2 | CD | Terry Gibbs Dream Band Vol.2:The Sundown Sessions

Terry Gibbs Dream Band
The Song Is You | Moonglow | The Fat Man | It Could Happen To You | Back Bay Shuffle | Dancing In The Dark | Blue Lou | Softly As In A Morning Sunrise | No Heat | My Reverie | The Claw
Live at Sundown,Hollywood,CA, rec. November 1959
Gibbs,Terry (vib) | Audino,Johnny (tp) | Candoli,Conte (tp) | Higgins,Frank (tp) | Williamson,Stu (tp) | Burgess,Bob 'Bobby' (tb) | Fryley,Vern (tb) | Smiley,Bill (tb) | Maini,Joe (as) | Kennedy,Charlie (as) | Perkins,Bill (ts) | Flory,Med (ts,arr) | Schwartz,Jack (bs) | Levy,Lou (p) | Clark,Buddy (b) | Lewis,Mel (dr) | Holman,Bill (arr) | Cohn,Al (arr) | Albam,Manny (arr) | Niehaus,Lennie (arr) | Paich,Marty (arr)

CCD 7654-2 | CD | Terry Gibbs Dream Band Vol.3:Flying Home
Midnight Sun | Evil Eyes | I'm Getting Sentimental Over You | Flying Home | Moten Swing
Seville,Hollywood,CA, rec. 17.-19.3.1959
Gibbs,Terry (vib) | Porcino,Al (tp) | Triscari,Ray (tp) | Candoli,Conte (tp) | Williamson,Stu (tp) | Enevoldsen,Bob (tb) | Friley,Vernon (tb) | Cadena,Joe (tb) | Maini,Joe (as) | Kennedy,Charlie (as) | Holman,Bill (ts) | Flory,Med (ts) | Schwartz,Jack (bs) | Jolly,Pete (p) | Bennett,Max (b) | Lewis,Mel (dr)
Airegin | Just Plain Meyer | It Might As Well Be Swing
Live at Sundown,Hollywood,CA, rec. Nov.1959
Gibbs,Terry (vib) | Audino,Johnny (tp) | Huggins,Frank (tp) | Candoli,Conte (tp) | Williamson,Stu (tp) | Burgess,Bob 'Bobby' (tb) | Friley,Vernon (tb) | Smiley,Bill (tb) | Maini,Joe (as) | Kennedy,Charlie (as) | Perkins,Bill (ts) | Flory,Med (ts) | Schwartz,Jack (bs) | Levy,Lou (p) | Clark,Buddy (b) | Lewis,Mel (dr)
Avalon
Gibbs,Terry (vib) | Porcino,Al (tp) | Triscari,Ray (tp) | Huggins,Frank (tp) | Candoli,Conte (tp) | Williamson,Stu (tp) | Enevoldsen,Bob (tb) | Friley,Vernon (tb) | Rosolino,Frank (tb) | Maini,Joe (as) | Kennedy,Charlie (as) | Perkins,Bill (ts) | Kamuca,Richie (ts) | Nimitz,Jack (bs) | Moran,Pat (p) | Clark,Buddy (b) | Lewis,Mel (dr)
Bright Eyes
Gibbs,Terry (vib) | Audino,Johnny (tp) | Huggins,Frank (tp) | Candoli,Conte (tp) | Williamson,Stu (tp) | Burgess,Bob 'Bobby' (tb) | Friley,Vernon (tb) | Smiley,Bill (tb) | Maini,Joe (as) | Kennedy,Charlie (as) | Perkins,Bill (ts) | Flory,Med (ts) | Schwartz,Jack (bs) | Aronov,Ben (p) | Clark,Buddy (b) | Lewis,Mel (dr)
Wonderful You
Gibbs,Terry (vib) | Audino,Johnny (tp) | Candoli,Conte (tp) | Williamson,Stu (tp) | Katzman,Lee (tp) | Burgess,Bob 'Bobby' (tb) | Friley,Vernon (tb) | Smiley,Bill (tb) | Maini,Joe (as) | Kennedy,Charlie (as) | Perkins,Bill (ts) | Flory,Med (ts) | Schwartz,Jack (bs) | Levy,Lou (p) | Clark,Buddy (b) | Lewis,Mel (dr)

CCD 7656-2 | CD | Terry Gibbs Dream Band Vol.4:Main Stem
Terry Gibbs Big Band
Day In Day Out | Summit Blues | Limerick Waltz | You Don't Know What Love Is | Sweet Georgia Brown | Nose Cone | Too Close For Comfort | Main Stem | Ja-Da | T.And S.
Live at The Summit Club,Los Angeles,CA, rec. January 1961
Gibbs,Terry (vib) | Porcino,Al (tp) | Triscari,Ray (tp) | Candoli,Conte (tp) | Williamson,Stu (tp) | Huggins,Frank (tp) | Rosolino,Frank (tb) | Friley,Vernon (tb) | Edmondson,Bob (tb) | Maini,Joe (as) | Kennedy,Charlie (as) | Kamuca,Richie (ts) | Perkins,Bill (ts) | Nimitz,Jack (bs) | Moran,Pat (p) | Clark,Buddy (b) | Lewis,Mel (dr)

CCD 7657-2 | CD | Terry Gibbs Dream Band Vol.5:The Big Cat
Terry Gibbs Dream Band
Tico Tico | Big Bad Bob | The Big Cat | Soft Eyes | Billie's Bounce | Pretty Blue Eyes | I'll Take Romance | Do You Wanna Jump Children | Nature Boy | Jump The Blues Away | Sleep
Gibbs,Terry (vib) | Porcino,Al (tp) | Triscari,Ray (tp) | Candoli,Conte (tp) | Williamson,Stu (tp) | Huggins,Frank (tp) | Rosolino,Frank (tb) | Friley,Vernon (tb) | Edmondson,Bob (tb) | Maini,Joe (as) | Kennedy,Charlie (as) | Kamuca,Richie (ts) | Perkins,Bill (ts) | Nimitz,Jack (bs) | Moran,Pat (p) | Clark,Buddy (b) | Lewis,Mel (dr)

CCD 7658-2 | CD | Terry Gibbs Dream Band Vol.6:One More Time | EAN 025218765824
The Fuzz | Opus One | Smoke Gets In Your Eyes | Prelude To A Kiss | Just Plain Meyer | Jumpin' At The Woodside
Live at The Seville,Hollywood, rec. March 1959
Porcino,Al (tp) | Triscari,Ray (tp) | Candoli,Conte (tp) | Williamson,Stu (tp) | Enevoldsen,Bob (tb) | Friley,Vernon (tb) | Cadena,Joe (tb) | Kennedy,Charlie (as) | Maini,Joe (as,ts) | Holman,Bill (ts) | Flory,Med (ts) | Schwartz,Jack (bs) | Gibbs,Terry (vib,ld) | Jolly,Pete (p) | Bennett,Max (b) | Lewis,Mel (dr)
Flying Home | I Remember You | The Fat Man | The Subtle Sermon
Live at Sundown,Hollywood,CA, rec. November 1959
Audino,Johnny (tp) | Candoli,Conte (tp) | Katzman,Lee (tp) | Williamson,Stu (tp) | Burgess,Bob 'Bobby' (tb) | Fryley,Vern (tb) | Smiley,Bill (tb) | Maini Joe (as) | Kennedy,Charlie (as) | Perkins,Bill (ts) | Flory,Med (ts,arr) | Schwartz,Jack (bs) | Gibbs,Terry (vib,ld) | Levy,Lou (p) | Clark,Buddy (b) | Lewis,Mel (dr)
Slittin' Sam(The Shaychet Man) | Sometimes I'm Happy | Moonlight In Vermont | Lover Come Back To Me
Audino,Johnny (tp) | Candoli,Conte (tp) | Katzman,Lee (tp) | Williamson,Stu (tp) | Burgess,Bob 'Bobby' (tb) | Fryley,Vern (tb) | Smiley,Bill (tb) | Maini,Joe (as) | Kennedy,Charlie (as) | Perkins,Bill (ts) | Flory,Med (ts,arr) | Schwartz,Jack (bs) | Gibbs,Terry (vib,ld) | Aronov,Ben (p) | Clark,Buddy (b) | Lewis,Mel (dr)

CCD 9005-2 | CD | Latinsville | EAN 090204922772
Victor Feldman Orchestra
Poinciana | Spain | Cuban Love Song | Woody'n You
Los Angeles,CA, rec. 3.3.1959
Feldman,Victor (vib) | Candoli,Conte (tp) | Rosolino,Frank (tb) | Benton,Walter (ts) | Guaraldi,Vince (p) | LaFaro,Scott (b) | Levey,Stan (dr) | Bobo,Willie (timbales) | Santamaria,Mongo (congas) | Peraza,Armando (bongos)
The Gypsy | In A Little Spanish Town
Feldman,Victor (vib) | Candoli,Conte (tp) | Benton,Walter (ts) | Guaraldi,Vince (p) | LaFaro,Scott (b) | Bobo,Willie (timbales) | Santamaria,Mongo (congas) | Peraza,Armando (bongos)
South Of The Border | Flying Down To Rio | Lady Of Spain
Los Angeles,CA, rec. 20.3.1959
Feldman,Victor (vib) | Candoli,Conte (tp) | Benton,Walter (ts) | Guaraldi,Vince (p) | McKibbon,Al (b) | Bobo,Willie (timbales) | Santamaria,Mongo (congas) | Peraza,Armando (bongos)
She's A Latin From Manhattan | Cuban Pete | Fiesta
Los Angeles,CA, rec. 4.5.1959
Feldman,Victor (vib) | Thomas,Andy (p) | Reyes,Tony (b) | Guerrero,Frank 'Chico' (timbales) | Rivera,Ramon (congas)
Poinciana | Pancho
Los Angeles,CA, rec. 8.12.1958
Feldman,Victor (vib) | Rosolino,Frank (tb) | Benton,Walter (ts) | LaFaro,Scott (b) | Martinis,Nick (dr)
The Breeze And I | Bullues Bullose | Lady Of Spain
Los Angeles,CA, rec. 9.12.1958
Feldman,Victor (p,vib) | Rosolino,Frank (tb) | Benton,Walter (ts) | LaFaro,Scott (b) | Martinis,Nick (dr)

CSA 7568-6 | SACD | Art Pepper + Eleven | EAN 025218731164
Art Pepper Plus Eleven
Opus De Funk | Round About Midnight | Walkin' Shoes | Airegin
Los Angeles,CA, rec. 14.3.1959
Pepper,Art (cl,as,ts) | Candoli,Pete (tp) | Sheldon,Jack (tp) | Nash,Dick (tb) | Enevoldsen,Bob (v-tb,ts) | DeRosa,Vince (fr-h) | Geller,Herb (as) | Perkins,Bill (ts) | Flory,Med (bs) | Freeman,Russ (p) | Mondragon,Joe (b) | Lewis,Mel (dr) | Paich,Marty (cond,arr)
Groovin' High | Shaw 'Nuff | Donna Lee | Donna Lee(alt.take) | Anthropology
Los Angeles,CA, rec. 28.3.1959
Pepper,Art (cl,as,ts) | Porcino,Al (tp) | Sheldon,Jack (tp) | Nash,Dick (tb) | Enevoldsen,Bob (v-tb,ts) | DeRosa,Vince (fr-h) | Shank,Bud (as) | Perkins,Bill (ts) | Flory,Med (bs) | Freeman,Russ (p) | Mondragon,Joe (b) | Paich,Marty (cond,arr) | Lewis,Mel (dr)
Move | Four Brothers | Bernie's Tune | Walkin' | Walkin'(alt.take 1) | Walkin'(alt.take 2)
Los Angeles,CA, rec. 12.5.1959
Pepper,Art (cl,as,ts) | Porcino,Al (tp) | Sheldon,Jack (tp) | Nash,Dick (tb) | Enevoldsen,Bob (v-tb,ts) | DeRosa,Vince (fr-h) | Kennedy,Charlie (as,ts) | Kamuca,Richie (ts) | Flory,Med (bs) | Freeman,Russ (p) | Mondragon,Joe (b) | Lewis,Mel (dr) | Paich,Marty (cond,arr)

Coral | Universal Music Germany

589485-2 | CD | Swing Around Rosie | EAN 731458948520
Rosemary Clooney With The Buddy Cole Trio
'Deed I Do | You Took Advantage Of Me | Blue Moon | Sing You | A Touch Of The Blues | Goody Goody | Too Close For Comfort | Do Nothin' Till You Hear From Me | Moonlight Mississippi | I Wish I Were In Love Again | Sunday In Savannah | This Can't Be Love
details unknown, rec. 1958/1959
Clooney,Rosemary (voc) | Cole,Buddy (p) | unkn. (b,dr)

Cream Records | Fenn Music

CR 400-2 | CD | None Too Soon
Allan Holdsworth Group
Countdown | Nuages | How Deep Is The Ocean | Isotope | None Too Soon(part 1) | Interlude | None Too Soon(part 2) | Norwegian Wood | Very Early | San Marcos | Inner Urge
At The Brewery,?, rec. 1996
Holdsworth,Allan (g,synthaxe) | Beck,Gordon (digital-p) | Willis,Gary (b) | Covington,Kirk (dr)

CR 610-2 | CD | The Sixteen Man Of Tain
The Sixteen Men Of Tain | Abow And Below | The Drums Were Yellow | Eidolon | Abow And Below(reprise)
San Diego,CA, rec. details unknown
Holdsworth,Allan (g,synthaxe) | Carpenter,Dave (b) | Novak,Gary (dr)
0274 | Texas
Holdsworth,Allan (g,synthaxe) | Fowler,Walt (tp) | Carpenter,Dave (b,el-b) | Novak,Gary (dr)
Downside Up
Holdsworth,Allan (g,synthaxe) | Carpenter,Dave (b) | Novak,Gary (dr) | Wackerman,Chad (dr)

JMS 18733-2 | CD | The Name Of A Woman | EAN 3383001873321
Zone I | Proto-Cosmos | White Line | Atavachron | Zone II | Pud Wud | House Of Mirrors | Non-Brewed Condiment | Zone III
details unknown, rec. details unknown
Holdsworth,Allan (g,bar-g) | Hunt,Steve (keyboards) | Johnson,Jimmy (el-b) | Husband,Gary (dr)

Creative Works Records | Creative Works

CW CD 1010-1 | CD | Wen Die Götter Lieben
Bernd Konrad Jazz Group With Symphonie Orchestra
Marilyn(Requiem For An Actress)
Live at The Konzil,Konstanz, rec. 15.10.1986
Konrad,Bernd (cl,as) | Schwarz,Paul (p,synth) | Heidepriem,Thomas (el-b) | D'Agostino,Roberto (dr) | Försch,Ferdinand (perc) | Newton,Lauren (narration,voice) | Ackermann,Gottfried (v) | Fischer,Franz-Peter (v) | Staicov,Constantin (v) | Ormanlidis,Nikos (v) | Horvath,Csaba (v) | Kryvenko-Fandel,Olga (v) | Rose,Hans-Joachim (v) | Szabo,Gabor (v) | Schwarz,Terry (v) | Wenclik,Anna (v) | Radochay,Karin (v) | Sulic,Lujo (v) | Beldeanu,Michael (v) | Irmer,Alfred (v) | Schneider,Helmut (v) | Rüben,Bruno (v) | Schober,Andreas (v) | Unger,Walter (v) | Mohr,Hans-Jürgen (viola) | Billert-Kucharski,Renate (viola) | Müller,Gotthart (viola) | Reimann,Bruno (viola) | Rutz,Brigitta (viola) | Schwartz,Christine (viola) | Polgar,Zsolt (cello) | Radle,Alois (cello) | Pozar,Vlado (cello) | Merck,Rüdiger (cello) | Rothe,Gert (cello) | Gabor,Robert (b) | Darvas,Julius (b) | Graf,Heinz-Peter (b) | Creutzburg,Ekkehard (fl) | Fandel,Leo (fl) | Fischer,Vera (fl) | Patt,Ralf-Peter (oboe) | Wildi,Curt (oboe) | Ahrens,Kai (cl) | Dohnke,Heinz (cl) | Greiner,Paul (cl) | Banse,Hans (bassoon) | Felkay,Laszlo (bassoon)
Bernd Konrad With Erwin Lehn und sein Südfunk Orchester Stuttgart
The Whale(A Green Piece For Blue People)
Stuttgart, rec. 15.5.1983
Konrad,Bernd (ss,bs) | Rezanina,Lubomir (tp) | Faber,Johannes (tp) | Rader,Don (tp) | Reindl,Rudolf (tp,fl-h) | Burgess,Bob 'Bobby' (tb) | Gallardo,Joe (tb) | Pendzialek,Alfred (tb) | Krause,Kurt (tb) | Rabe,Bernd (cl,as) | Dautel,Fritz (fl,as) | Freund,Joki (ss,ts) | Hoffbauer,Manfred (fl,ts) | Machwitz,Ernst (cl,bs) | Kirchgässner,Helmut (p) | Reiter,Joerg (p) | Schöpfer,Klaus (g) | Witte,Peter (el-b) | Gebhard,Jörg (dr) | Santiago,Freddie (perc) | Försch,Ferdinand (perc) | Zimmerle,Dieter (narration)

CW CD 1011-1 | CD | Basse Partout
Klaus Koch
Chameleon,Madrepore And A Wind Rose | C'est Le Son Qui La (Remini) Scene | Talking Strings In Silver Grey | Breakfast Am Vierwaldstädter See Oder Vollmundiger Gesang Nach Einer Vollmondnacht | Another Ambience | Restons En La! | Il Est Grand Temps (Perdu?) | Franz-Branntwein(dedicated to F.K., a dear friend in Vienna) | Hot Couscous,Cool Night And A Dog Barking | Monk's Food & Feet | Lacis Ou C'Est Dans Le Lac!
Frankfurt/M, rec. 27.-29.1.1987
Koch,Klaus (b-solo)

CW CD 1013-1 | CD | Entupadas
Corina Curschellas-John Wolf Brennan
Entupadas-Berliner Version(Encounters) | La Spuda(The Slope) | Hommage Boris Vian | Ballade Vom Weib Und Dem Soldaten | La Malaura(The Tempest) | Nineteeneightyfour | Get Your Kicks On Route 66 | Ils Vagants-Senza Patria(Homeless)
Bern,CH, rec. 26.11.1985
Curschellas,Corina (fl,accordeon,dr,dulcimer,kalimba,siren,voice,zither) | Brennan,John Wolf (p,synth,invisible-strings)
Waldsterben(Dying Of The Forest) | AIDS | Bizarre Roundabout | Steel | Nordsee-Mordsee(The Unanswered Call) | Don't Hurt A Woman-It's A Boomerang
Live at Kleintheater,Luzern,CH, rec. 31.3.1988
Curschellas,Corina (fl,p,accordeon,dr,dulcimer,kalimba,siren,voice,zither) | Brennan,John Wolf (p,synth,invisible-strings)

CW CD 1014-1 | CD | Cadavre Exquis
Cadavre Exquis
A March Is An Introduction | Kinderlieder Nach A.Wölfli | Wucherung II | La Belle Et La Bete | Kännsch Hönng? | Ballade | The Soundville Syndrome(part 1-3)
Luzern,CH, rec. October 1987
Cadavre Exquis | Gordon-Lenox,Ian (tp,fl-h) | Dahinden,Roland (tb) | Taylor,Dave (b-tb) | Varner,Tom (fr-h) | Blöchlinger,Urs (ss,as,bass-sax) | Su,Nat (as) | Schlumpf,Martin (b-cl,ss) | Baumann,Christoph (p) | Hämmerli,Urs 'Hämi' (b) | Ulrich,Dieter (dr)

CW CD 1017-1 | CD | The Beauty Of Fractals
John Wolf Brennan
Lower East Side Story | Nantucket | Be Flat | Zooming On A Corner On The Mandelbrot Set | La Mort C'est La Vie(Hommage á Jean Tinguely) | Do U See The Way? | Parto | Kiss The Night,Huntin' Santa Claus | Kerava | Goofy's Waltz | Eleven-One | Circle Of Coherence
Ludwigsburg, rec. 16.12.1988
Brennan,John Wolf (p-solo)
Bifurcation | Nantucket Took It
Live at Kleintheater,Luzern,CH, rec. 9.12.1988
Brennan,John Wolf (p-solo)
Lower East Side Story
NYC, rec. 16.8.1988
Brennan,John Wolf (p-solo)

CW CD 1018-3 | CD | Lyon's Brood
Q4 Orchester Project
El-Qahira | Hundtage | Lyon's Brood
Basel,CH, rec. 25./26.11.1989
Q4 Orchester Project | Grau,Jürg U. (tp) | Böhringer,Peter (tp) | Anliker,Hans (tb) | Lüdi,Werner (as) | Gräminger,Kurt (as) | Poffet,Joseph (b-cl,as) | Baumgartner,Heiri (as,bs) | Schmid,Peter (b-cl,ss,bs) | Rissi,Mathias (as,ts,ld) | Stauss,Markus (ts,bs) | Mazzola,Guerino (p) | Broger,Werner (b) | Hirt,Tomi (b) | Schaffner,Dani (dr,perc) | Gutmann,Pit (dr,perc) | Zehnder,Philipp A. (perc)

CW CD 1019-1 | CD | The Bird Who Makes The Cloud Sing As He Drums It-Live At The Montreux Jazz Festival
Lüdi-Öcal
Lisa Mona Overdrive | Flow Motian | Collision Cruise | The Wind Whales If Ishmael | Fragments Of A Hologram Rose
Jazz Festival Montreux,CH, rec. 16.7.1989
Lüdi,Werner (as) | Öcal,Burhan (bells,darbuka,dawul,gongs,kettle-dr)

CW CD 1020-2 | CD | Willisau And More Live
Creative Works Orchestra
Dance,You Monster,To My Soft Song!
Live at Willisau,CH, rec. September 1990
Creative Works Orchestra | Schärli,Peter (tp) | Lindvall,Lars (tp) | Cooper,Lindsay (bassoon) | Koltermann,Eckard (ss,bs) | Puschnig,Wolfgang (ss,as) | Konrad,Bernd (as,bs) | Brennan,John Wolf (p,ld) | Goodman,Steve (v) | Gattiker,David (cello) | Patumi,Daniele (b) | Argüelles,Steve (dr) | Oecal,Burhan (perc) | Curschellas,Corina (voc)
T.N.T.(Twelth Night Tango)
Creative Works Orchestra | Schärli,Peter (tp) | Lindvall,Lars (tp) | Konrad,Bernd (ss) | Cooper,Lindsay (bassoon) | Koltermann,Eckard (b-cl) | Puschnig,Wolfgang (as) | Brennan,John Wolf (p,ld) | Goodman,Steve (v) | Gattiker,David (cello) | Patumi,Daniele (b) | Argüelles,Steve (dr) | Oecal,Burhan (perc) | Curschellas,Corina (voc) | unkn. (wistle-solo-introduction)
Werner Lüdi-Burhan Öcal
Grand Bazar
Luzern,CH, rec. January 1988
Lüdi,Werner (as) | Öcal,Burhan (bells,darbuka,dawul,gongs,kettle-dr,tanbur)
Fragments Of A Hologram Rose
Montreux,CH, rec. July 1989
Lüdi,Werner (as) | Öcal,Burhan (bells,darbuka,dawul,gongs,kettle-dr,tanbur)
Peter Schärli Quintet With Glenn Ferris
Tira Tira
Zürich,CH, rec. 1.& 13.4.1988
Schärli,Peter (tp) | Ferris,Glenn (tb) | Philipp,Roland (ts) | Nicolai,Giancarlo (g) | Dürst,Thomas (b) | Käppeli,Marco (dr)
John Wolf Brennan
Be Flat
Live at The Kleintheater,Lucerne,CH, rec. December 1988
Brennan,John Wolf (p-solo)
Klaus Koch
Breakfast Am Vierwaldstädter See Oder Vollmundiger Gesang Nach Einer Vollmondnacht
Frankfurt/M, rec. 27.-29.1.1987
Koch,Klaus (b-solo)
Trio KoKoKo
Good Night(dedicated to Seamus Heaney) | Lied Des 20. Novembers
Luzern,CH, rec. 26./27.11.1985
Trio KoKoKo | Koglmann,Franz (tp,fl-h) | Koltermann,Eckard (b-cl,bs) | Koch,Klaus (b)
Corina Curschellas-John Wolf Brennan
La Malaura(The Tempest)
Bern,CH, rec. 16.11.1985
Curschellas,Corina (dulcimer,voice) | Brennan,John Wolf (p)
Alfred 23 Harth-John Zorn
Atom-Sex-Kino
FTF-Studio, rec. June 1986
Harth,Alfred 23 (ts) | Zorn,John (as)
John Wolf Brennan
Xednindex
Ludwigsburg, rec. 12./13.4.1990
Brennan,John Wolf (p,cymbals,midi-p,prepared-p,sound-objects,symbols,tom-tom)

CW CD 1021-2 | CD | Irisations
Epsilon | Alpha | Ypsilon
Live at The Kleintheater,Lucerne,CH, rec. 9.4.1990
Brennan,John Wolf (p,cymbals,prepared-p,sound-objects,symbols,tom-tom)
ADDR | Lambda | Phi | Tau(2) | Xi | Delta | Chi | Omikron | Sigma | Theta | Tau(3) | Omega | Psi | Catastrophe | Xednindex
Ludwigsburg, rec. 12./13.4.1990
Brennan,John Wolf (p,cymbals,midi-p,prepared-p,sound-objects,symbols,tom-tom)

CW CD 1022-2 | CD | Mute Songs & Drumscapes
Georg Hofmann-Lucas Niggli Duo
Jazz+ Afrika - (Jazz+) Afrika | Yaaba | Upper Bakossi | Ivory Dance | Udu Udu | Song For B. | Metal Winds | 5 For Elvin | Halfway Bakossi
Winterthur,CH, rec. August 1992
Hofmann,Georg (dr,perc) | Niggli,Lucas (dr,perc)

CW CD 1023-2 | CD | Grimson Flames
Motus Quartett
Some Skunk Funk | Peaches En Regalia | Goodbye Pork Pie Hat | Meditations | Caravan | Karminrote Flammen(Streichquartett Nr.2, 1991): | Mit Erhobenem Zeigefinger, Ein Grauer Flanellzwerg- | Die Himmel Brennen- | Der 3.Weltkrieg Von Der Tribüne Aus Gesehen- | Sprich Ein Zauberwort- | Es Muß Doch Irgend Einen Ausweg Geben- | Weit Zurück, Auf Einer Enlosen Landstraße...- | Eines Tages...- | Epilog:Der Freudenspender Kommt-
Schloß Weinberg/Kefermarkt, rec. 29.11.-3.12.1992
Motus Quartett: | Theissing,Tscho (v,voc) | Radanovics,Michael (v,voc) | Bayer,Franz (viola,voc) | Dallinger,Michael (cello,voc) | Lewis,Joanna (voc)
I'll Be Your Baby Tonight
Live at Orchesterhaus,Salzburg, rec. 10.12.1992
Motus Quartett: | Theissing,Tscho (v,voc) | Radanovics,Michael (v,voc) | Bayer,Franz (viola,voc) | Dallinger,Michael (cello,voc)

CW CD 1024-2 | CD | ATonALL
ATonALL
Serigraphien I-III | Miniaturen I&II | Bird's Eye | Nebbiolo | Horizonte | Lower East Side | Timbuktu | Miniaturen III
Zürich,CH, rec. 16.-18.3.1993
ATonALL | Schmid,Peter A. (b-cl,ss,as,bamboo-fl) | Girod,Roger (p,klangflügel) | Gutmann,Pit (dr,klangobjecte)
Regenwald | Metazoen
ATonALL | Schmid,Peter A. (b-cl) | Girod,Roger (p) | Gutmann,Pit (dr,klangobjecte) | Spühler,Martin (klangsäulen)
Geysir
ATonALL | Schmid,Peter A. (bs) | Girod,Roger (klangobjecte) | Gutmann,Pit (klangschalen) | Spühler,Martin (klangschalen)

CW CD 1025-2 | CD | Text, Context, Co-Text & Co-Co-Text
John Wolf Brennan
Traces Of Origin | Mesolithic Tomtomfool | If You Can't Know If You Mustn't Ask,Why Look? | A.L.P.Traum(a deconstruction) | Cagey | L.Eave's Dropping On Higgledy Piggledy | What We Know We Think About | Song Of The Moon(Shadows & Traffic Lights) | Sience Friction | Bloo(m)himwhom | Figs(a de-deconstruction:piano duet) | Relationshipping With Controlled Probalities | What We Think We Know - ...What We Think We Know | Strollin' Down Memory Lane | Some Other Time | Index | Figs(the poem:recited by Macdara Woods))
Live at The Theater Tuchlaude,Aarau,CH, rec. 26.1.1994
Brennan,John Wolf (p,prepared-p)

CW CD 1026-2 | CD | René Wohlhauser Werkauswahl 1978-1993
A Band Of Friends
Ci-Ic für Flöte uns Viola | Duometric für Flöte und Bassklarinette | Orgelstück für Orgel | Klarinettentrio Metamusil für drei B-Klarinettes | Drei Stücke für Klavier | Adagio Assai für Streichquartet | Atemlinie für

LABELVERZEICHNIS

Horn und Tamtam | Lumière(s) für Orgel | Souvenirs De L'Occitanie für A-Klarinette | Schlagzeugtrio für drei Schlagzeuger | In Statu Mutandi für Orchester
different Places, rec. different Dates
-> die Aufnahmen dieser CD gehören in den Bereich 'Neue Musik'!

CW CD 1027-2 | CD | Windschief
Roger Girod-Peter A.Schmid
Fax I-III | Steppenwolf | Sunset II-V | Soundscapes X-XII | Holzwurm II | Caravan | Ornaments | Fax IV-VI | Jam & Ham | Tim Booked Two | Tales From Blackwood Forest | Calisto | Windschief
Zürich,CH, rec. 18./19.11.1995
Girod,Roger (p) | Schmid,Peter A. (b-cl,ss,as,bamboo-fl)

CW CD 1028-2 | CD | Yavapai
Q4 Orchester Project
Havasupai | Tohono O'Otam | Yavapai
Wetzikon,CH, rec. 17.12.1995
Q4 Orchester Project | Schenker,Daniel 'Dani' (tp) | Böhringer,Peter (tp,mellophone) | Anliker,Hans (tb) | Unternaeher,Beat (tb) | Rissi,Mathias (as,ld) | Gräminger,Kurt (as) | Blaser,Beat (bs) | Stauss,Markus (ss,bass-sax) | Mazzola,Guerino (p) | Hirt,Tomi (b) | Geisser,Heinz (dr) | Zehnder,Philipp A. (perc)

CW CD 1029-2 | CD | Fuego
Rissi-Mazzola-Geisser
Fue | Ninja | Browser | Blue Monk | Pagago | Anasazi | Cora | Arcosanti | Alla | Go
Wetzikon,CH, rec. 13.12.1995
Rissi,Mathias (as,ts) | Mazzola,Guerino (p) | Geisser,Heinz (dr)

CW CD 1030-2 | CD | Groupe Lacroix:The Composer Group
Moscow Rachmaninov Trio
Empreintes(Jean-Luc Darbellay) | Tombal(Marianne Schroeder) | Novalis 24(Christian Henking) | Rhap.s.odie(John Wolf Brennan) | Touch[e]!(Michael Schneider) | Berceuse(Michael Baumgartner) | Variation On A Thme By Schubert(Edison Denissov)
Moskau,USSR, rec. 8./9.12.1996
Moscow Rachmaninov Trio | Tsinman,Mikhail (v) | Savinova,Natalia (cello) | Yampolsky,Viktor (p)

CW CD 1032-2 | CD | The Well-Prepared Clavier/Das Wohlpräparierte Klavier
John Wolf Brennan
Prelude(Isle Of View) | Assonance | Russian Doors No.1(Pushkin) | Resonance | To György K.(Ur Tag) | Russian Doors No.2(Moscow:Container Lid) | Seven Studies For Prepared Piano: | Agitato(medium)- | Con Fuoco(fast)- | Sotto Voce(interpunctuated)- | Veloce(very fast)- | Misterioso(slow)- | Scivolando(stretto)- | Risoluto(an imaginary thriller)- | To Henry C.(O Well) | Russian Doors No.3(Mos Cowboys & Shriking Hinges) | Mile End | Bow Road | Russian Doors No.4(St.Petersburg A Walk On The Riverside) | Rump-L-Rumba(7-4 For 5 Hands) | Smithy Street,Stepney(Clavinova) | Aldgate East(mend the gap under ground) | Russian Doors No.5(Dubna:Steps In A Staircase | Postlude(for two light and an invisdible reft hand[s])
Weggis,CH, rec. 29./30.4.1997
Brennan,John Wolf (p,prepared-p)
John Wolf Brennan-Marianne Schroeder
R2D2
Live at Composer's Union House,Moscow, rec. 27.5.1995
Brennan,John Wolf (p) | Schroeder,Marianne (p)
John Wolf Brennan
Sience Friction II(Elephant And Castle) | All The Strings You Are | To John C.(Age) | C3PO(Variations On Sergej Kuryokhin's 'The Situation Of The Asian Protelariat In America') | The Last Waltz(Sergej Kuryokhin) | Be Flat(QEH Live Version)
Live at Queen Elizabeth Hall,London, rec. 16.5.1997
Brennan,John Wolf (p)

CW CD 1033 | CD | Profound Sounds In An Empty Reservoir
Peter A. Schmid Trio With Guests
Ditscheriduddel | Oropendula | Steppenwind | Derwisch | Five Cat Cuts | Blasblues | Marimbula | Bazar | Akzente
Zürich,CH, rec. June & September 1999
Schmid,Peter A. (b-cl,ss,as,alto-fl,bamboo-fl) | Grau,Jürg U. (tp,truempi,perc) | Zehnder,Philipp A. (perc)
Zara's Song
Grau,Jürg U. (tp) | Dobler,Thomas (vib) | Peier,Marius (perc)
Hormony
Schmid,Peter A. (b-cl) | Böhringer,Peter (tp) | Unternaeher,Beat (tb) | Peris,Charles (b-fl)
Ich Bin Da...
Unternaeher,Beat (tb) | Zehnder,Philipp A. (perc)
Wortlaut - (Wort)laut
Rüdisüli,Robi (blowing-stuff) | Zehnder,Philipp A. (perc)
Flöten - (F)löten
Schmid,Peter A. (b-shakuhachi) | Ziegler,Matthias (piccolo-fl)

CW CD 1034 | CD | Duets,Dialogues & Duels
Peter A. Schmid Duos
Alpine Dialogue: | Beleba | Gamsi | Murmeltanz | Dackelwackel | Adlerflug | Sieben Wachteln | Geiereier
Zürich,CH, rec. 14./15.11.1999
Schmid,Peter A. (b-cl,contra-b-cl) | Schiltknecht,Roland (swiss-hammered-dulcimer,bass-dulcimer)
Buschwerk: | Rapid Rabbit | Bitte-meeh! | BallAde | The Marabou | Abi-gaah! | The One And Lonely Bass Clarinet Blues
Schmid,Peter A. (b-cl) | Burger,Dominik (vib,dr)
Zendances: | Trialogue | Zendances 4 Too(I,II,II,IV,VI,VII)
Schmid,Peter A. (b-cl) | Gutmann,Pit (marimba,klangobjecte)

CW CD 1036 | CD | September Duos
Evan Parker-Peter A.Schmid
Lichen | Flies & Mosquitos | Ants | Mushrooms | Bugs | Worms
Zürich,CH, rec. 9.9.2000
Parker,Evan (ss,ts) | Schmid,Peter A. (cl,b-cl,contra-b-cl)

CW CD 1037-2 | CD | Flügel
John Wolf Brennan
Anyway...Was There Ever Nothing? | You Can't Be Sirius! | Kissing Joy(As It Flies) | Monk In Cage | Thrillr | Meditation On Two Medieval Songs: | Ach Bitt'rer Winter | Es Geht Eine Dunkle Wolke Herein | Kyoto
Luzern,CH, rec. 28.11.1998
Brennan,John Wolf (p-solo)
O Pen,To Be | Trompe L'Oreille | String Theory | Pump & Circumstance | Para.ph(r)ase | Robotalk | Pumpkinet(h)ics | Tailgate | Air(cut) | Index-E Pi? Lo Go,Lipe!-?S...Is Pony S?
Winterthur,CH, rec. 13.1.2002
Brennan,John Wolf (p-solo)

CW CD 1038/39 | 2 CD | September Winds
Anliker-Parker-Schmid-Senn-Solothurnmann
Spar Sam! | Hallo Heino | Winds | Insects(part 1) | Solopark | Blackwood | Anlipark | Blown Chairs | Sagssolo | Insects(part 2) | Red Points | Tar Á Got | Almost One Hour
Zürich,CH, rec. 20.11.& 11.12.2000
Anliker,Hans (tb) | Parker,Evan (ss,ts) | Schmid,Peter A. (cl,b-cl,contra-b-cl,ss,wooden-fl) | Senn,Reto (cl,b-cl,taragot) | Solothurnmann,Jürg (ss,as)

CW CD 1041 | CD | Schmilz
Schmilz
Rampid Rabbit | Serendipity I | Barasco | Mars And Milky Way | Serendipity II-VI | Serendipity II-VI | Floating Away | Jamabiko | Biffhei-No! | Serendipity VIII | Mara Pooh | Serendipity IX-XIII | Nihil | Melting Point
Winterthur,CH, rec. 21./22.10.2001
Kramis,Herbert (b) | Schmid,Peter A. (cl,b-cl,contra-b-cl) | Pilz,Michel (b-cl) | Schmilz | Burger,Dominik (dr)

MIWI 1014-2 | CD | Drei Seelen/Three Souls
Peter Schärli Quintet With Glenn Ferris
Tira Tira | Il'e 'Ak'e | Drei Seelen-Three Souls | I Remember Wolfred | Magic Walk | Wenn's Im Sommer Ins Kino Schneit
Zürich,CH, rec. 11.& 13.4.1988
Schärli,Peter (tp,fl-h,half-tp) | Ferris,Glenn (tb) | Philipp,Roland (ts) | Nicolai,Giancarlo (g) | Dürst,Thomas (b) | Käppeli,Marco (dr)

CTI | Sony Music

EPC 450554-2 | CD | Carnegie Hall Concert Vol. 1/2
Chet Baker-Gerry Mulligan Group
Line For Lyons | Song For An Unfinished Woman | My Funny Valentine | Song For Strayhorn | It's Sandy At The Beach | Bernie's Tune | K-4 Pacific | There'll Never Be Another You
rec. 24.11.1974
Baker,Chet (tp) | Mulligan,Gerry (bs) | Byrne,Ed (tb) | Samuels,Dave (vib,perc) | James,Bob (p,el-p) | Scofield,John (g) | Carter,Ron (b) | Mason,Harvey (dr)

ZK 65131 | CD | Sunflower
Milt Jackson And His Orchestra
For Someone I Love | What Are You Doing The Rest Of Your Life | People Makes The World Go Round | Sunflower | S.K.J.
Englewood Cliffs,NJ, rec. 12./13.12.1972
Jackson,Milt (vib) | Hubbard,Freddie (tp,fl-h) | Bodner,Phil (engl-h,fl,alto-fl,piccolo) | Marge,George (engl-h,alto-fl,cl,b-cl) | Penque,Romeo (engl-h,alto-fl,oboe) | Berliner,Jay (g) | Hancock,Herbie (p) | Carter,Ron (b) | Cobham,Billy (dr) | MacDonald,Ralph (perc) | Ross,Margaret (harp) | Ellen,Max (v) | Gershman,Paul (v) | Green,Emmanuel (v) | Libove,Charles (v) | Malin,Joe (v) | Nadien,David (v) | Orloff,Gene (v) | Rosoff,Elliot (v) | Spice,Irving (v) | McCracken,Charles (cello) | Ricci,George (cello) | Shulman,Alan (cello)

ZK 65133 | CD | Skylark
Paul Desmond Orchestra
Take Ten | Romance De Amor | Was A Sunny Day | Music For A While | Skylark | Indian Summer | Skylark(alt.take) | Indian Summer(alt.take)
Englewood Cliffs,NJ, rec. 27./28.11.& 4.12.1973
Desmond,Paul (as) | Bertoncini,Gene (g) | Szabo,Gabor (g) | James,Bob (p,el-p) | Ricci,George (cello) | Carter,Ron (b) | DeJohnette,Jack (dr) | MacDonald,Ralph (perc) | Sebesky,Don (cond,arr)

dacapo | Naxos Deutschland

8.224085 CD | CD | Gert Sorensen Plays Poul Ruders
Gert Sorensen
Regime | Alarm | Cha Cha Cha | Towards The Precipice
Copenhagen,Denmark, rec. 1998
Sorensen,Gert (keyboards,perc,sound-design)
Fingerprint(I) | Fingerprint(II) | Fingerprint(III)
Sorensen,Gert (keyboards,perc,sound-design) | Mikkelborg,Palle (keyboards) | Ruders,Paul (keyboards)

DCCD 9428 | CD | This Train:The Danish Radio Jazz Orchestra Plays The Music Of Ray Pitts
The Danish Radio Jazz Orchestra
Liberty City | After All This Years | Brighter Daze | Uffe's Solo | At Our House | Deelirium | That Special Feeling | Havets Herrer(Master Of the Sea) | Atlantic Avenue | Bird Day
Copenhagen,Denmark, rec. 14.-25.10.1991
Danish Radio Jazz Orchestra | Rosenfeld,Benny (tp) | Bolvig,Palle (tp) | Bolberg Pedersen,Henik (tp,fl-h) | Togeby,Lars (tp) | Knudsen,Perry (tp) | Nilsson,Vincent (tb) | Hansen,Steen (tb) | Larsen,Ture (tb) | Gerhardt,Niels (tb) | Lundberg,Jan Olov (tb) | Windfeld,Axel (tb) | Zum Vohrde,Jan (reeds) | Hove,Michael (reeds) | Waidtlow,Claus (reeds) | Markussen,Uffe (reeds) | Franck,Tomas (reeds) | Madsen,Flemming (reeds) | Bentzon,Nikolaj (p) | Pitts,Ray (keyboards,cond) | Lindvall,Anders 'Chico' (g) | Roupe,Bjarne (g) | Ovesen,Thomas (b) | Johansen,Jonas (dr) | Weisgaard,Ethan (perc) | Dandanell,Lise (voc)

DCCD 9429 | CD | Fit As A Fiddle
Svend Asmussen Quartet
A Night In Tunisia
Växjö,Sweden, rec. 27.3.1996
Asmussen,Svend (v) | Fischer,Jacob (g) | Lundgaard,Jesper (b) | Tanggaard,Aage (dr)
Runnin' Wild | Bye Bye Blackbird | Take Off Blues | I Loves You Porgy | Wrap It Up | Groove Merchant | Latino
Linköping,Sweden, rec. 30.3.1996
Asmussen,Svend (v) | Fischer,Jacob (g) | Lundgaard,Jesper (b) | Tanggaard,Aage (dr)
Columbine Polka Mazurka | The Mooche | Prelude To A Kiss
Copenhagen,Denmark, rec. 20.9.1996
Asmussen,Svend (v) | Fischer,Jacob (g) | Lundgaard,Jesper (b) | Tanggaard,Aage (dr)

DCCD 9430 | CD | Shape To Twelve
Copenhagen Art Ensemble
Shape To Twelve | Naked | Funeral Procession | Song For Tomas
Copenhagen,Denmark, rec. 10./11.2.1997
Copenhagen Art Ensemble | Riis,Jesper (tp,fl-h) | Godtholdt (tp,fl-h) | Tranberg,Kasper (tp,fl-h) | Larsen,Ture (tb) | Löhrer,Klaus (b-tb,tuba) | Fuglsang,Peter (cl,alto-cl,as) | Anker,Lotte (ss,ts) | Agergaard,Thomas (fl,ts) | Fridell,Pelle (b-cl,bs) | Clausen,Thomas (p,el-p) | Davidsen,Nils (b) | Mogensen,Anders (dr)
Direction Switch | Descension
Copenhagen Art Ensemble | Riis,Jesper (tp,fl-h) | Godtholdt (tp,fl-h) | Tranberg,Kasper (tp,fl-h) | Larsen,Ture (tb) | Löhrer,Klaus (b-tb,tuba) | Fuglsang,Peter (cl,alto-cl,as) | Anker,Lotte (ss,ts) | Agergaard,Thomas (fl,ts) | Fridell,Pelle (b-cl,bs) | Clausen,Thomas (p,el-p) | Davidsen,Nils (b) | Mogensen,Anders (dr) | Mazur,Marilyn (perc)
Icebird Song
Copenhagen Art Ensemble | Riis,Jesper (tp,fl-h) | Godtholdt (tp,fl-h) | Tranberg,Kasper (tp,fl-h) | Larsen,Ture (tb) | Löhrer,Klaus (b-tb,tuba) | Fuglsang,Peter (cl,alto-cl,as) | Anker,Lotte (ss,ts) | Agergaard,Thomas (fl,ts) | Fridell,Pelle (b-cl,bs) | Clausen,Thomas (p,el-p) | Davidsen,Nils (b) | Mogensen,Anders (dr) | Mazur,Marilyn (perc) | Larsen,Mona (voc)
More Streetprayers
Copenhagen Art Ensemble | Riis,Jesper (tp,fl-h) | Godtholdt (tp,fl-h) | Tranberg,Kasper (tp,fl-h) | Larsen,Ture (tb) | Löhrer,Klaus (b-tb,tuba) | Fuglsang,Peter (cl,alto-cl,as) | Anker,Lotte (ss,ts) | Agergaard,Thomas (fl,ts) | Fridell,Pelle (b-cl,bs) | Clausen,Thomas (p,el-p) | Davidsen,Nils (b) | Mogensen,Anders (dr) | Mazur,Marilyn (perc) | Hoeg,T.S. (recitation)

DCCD 9433 | CD | Music For Eyes
Kenneth Knudsen-Christian Skeel
Music For Eyes: | Amberish- | Interlude With Spasms- | Citrus To Ceder- | Oakmoss- | As You Wish- | Toy Shop At Night | The Melancholy Speed Skater's Dream
Copenhagen,Denmark, rec. March/July 1997
Knudsen,Kenneth (keyboards,synth) | Skeel,Christian (computer,samples)

DCCD 9434 | CD | The River:Image Of Time And Life
The Crossover Ensemble
Small Drops Of Happiness | The River:Image Of Time And Life: | Echoes- | Visions- | Presence Always Presence- | Blossom | Mahogni | Ballad In C Minor
Copenhagen,Denmark, rec. May/June 1997
Crossover Ensemble,The | Riis,Jesper (tp,fl-h) | Agerskov,Flemming (tp,fl-h) | Hyhne,Mads (tb) | Jönsson,Cennet (reeds) | Gustafsson,Thoams (reeds) | Gade,Per (g) | Davidsen,Jakob (p,keyboards) | Davidsen,Nils (b) | Mogensen,Anders (dr)

DCCD 9435 | CD | Pulse Of Time
Kim Kristensen
Pulse Of Time | Last Breath | No Belonging | Naked In The Jungle- | Cosmic Biotope-
Kimilydlab, rec. 1997/1998
Kristensen,Kim (fl,keyboards,electronic-perc,grand-p)
Noise Of The World
Kristensen,Kim (fl,keyboards,electronic-perc,grand-p) | Lomhoft,Aviaja (voc,voice-samples)
First Breath | Salmon Flight | Northern Tribes
Kristensen,Kim (fl,keyboards,electronic-perc,grand-p) | Lokke,Birgit (perc)
Tegn | The Death Of A Dreamer
Kristensen,Kim (fl,keyboards,electronic-perc,grand-p) | Trolle,Per (perc)
Cadenza
Kristensen,Kim (fl,keyboards,electronic-perc,grand-p) | Snajer,Ernesto (g)

DCCD 9436 | CD | Wondering
Simon Spang-Hanssen & Maneklar
Omvendt | Medium Rare | Dreamworld | Maneklar | Le Nez Du Sphinx | Soir Bon
Copenhagen,Denmark, rec. 25./26.8.1998
Spang-Hansen,Simon (ss,as) | Bitran,Mariane (fl,alto-fl) | Danstrup,Peter (b,b-synth) | Theill,Ole (tablas) | Andersen,Jacob (perc)
Charbon | Wondering
Spang-Hansen,Simon (ss,as) | Bitran,Mariane (fl,alto-fl) | Danstrup,Peter (b,b-synth) | Theill,Ole (tablas) | Andersen,Jacob (perc) | Nordsoe,Klaus (congas)
Brain Forest | Space On Earth
Spang-Hansen,Simon (ss,as) | Bitran,Mariane (fl,alto-fl) | Danstrup,Peter (b,b-synth) | Theill,Ole (tablas) | Andersen,Jacob (perc) | Mazur,Marilyn (dr,udo)

DCCD 9437 | CD | The Escape
Jens Winther And The WDR Big Band
The Escape | Sience Fiction
Köln, rec. 24.1.1994
Winther,Jens (tp) | WDR Big Band | Haderer,Andreas 'Andy' (tp) | Bruynen,Rob (tp) | Osterloh,Klaus (tp) | Kiefer,Rick (tp) | Marshall,John (tp) | Horler,David (tb) | Berg,Henning (tb) | Laukamp,Bernt (tb) | Partyka,Edward (tb) | Deuvall,Roy (tb) | Wiberny,Heiner (reeds) | Rosenstein,Harald (reeds) | Peters,Olivier (reeds) | Römer,Rolf (reeds) | Neufang,Jens (reeds) | Chastenier,Frank (p) | Shigihara,Paul (g) | Goldsby,John (b) | Nussbaum,Adam (dr) | Peil,Roland (perc)
Child Of Nature | Den Gra Dame(The Grey Lady) | Labyrinths
Live at Stadtgarten,Köln, rec. 4.2.1994
Winther,Jens (tp) | WDR Big Band | Haderer,Andreas 'Andy' (tp) | Bruynen,Rob (tp) | Osterloh,Klaus (tp) | Kiefer,Rick (tp) | Marshall,John (tp) | Horler,David (tb) | Berg,Henning (tb) | Laukamp,Bernt (tb) | Partyka,Edward (tb) | Deuvall,Röy (tb) | Wiberny,Heiner (reeds) | Rosenstein,Harald (reeds) | Peters,Olivier (reeds) | Römer,Rolf (reeds) | Neufang,Jens (reeds) | Chastenier,Frank (p) | Shigihara,Paul (g) | Goldsby,John (b) | Nussbaum,Adam (dr) | Peil,Roland (perc)

DCCD 9440 | CD | Giraf
Pierre Dorge's New Jungle Orchestra
Stranger Than Jim | Lullaby For Tchicai | Lilli Goes To Town | Song For The Swan | Giraffe | Abe Teyata | Baton- | Lonely Woman- De Fructa Oris | Hawkm Meets Sun Ra | Baby Gorilla Walk | To You S.A. | Something ELSE
Copenhagen,Denmark, rec. November/December 1998
De Fructa Oris | Dorge,Pierre (g,voc) | Tranberg,Kasper (co) | Agerholm,Kenneth (tb,voc) | Hyhne,Mads (tb,voc) | Mygind,Jacob (ss,as) | Carlsen,Morten (ts,taragot) | Tchicai,John (ss,ts,voc) | Succi,Achille (b-cl) | Becker,Irene (p,keyboards,voc) | Ehde,John (cello) | Rasmussen,Hugo (b) | Clausen,Bent (vib,dr) | Solomon,Ayi (perc) | Cronholm,Josefine (voc)

DCCD 9441 | CD | Symphonies Vol.2
The Danish Radio Concert Orchestra
Concerto For Solo Trumpet, Percussion And Orchestra
Copenhagen,Denmark, rec. details unknown
Winther,Jens (tp) | Danish Radio Concert Orchestra | Firman,David (cond) | details unknown
Concert For Marimba, Harp And Strings
Savery,Uffe (marimba) | Tomquist,Lillian (harp) | Danish Radio Concert Orchestra | Friis,Morton (cond) | details unknown
Tide
Harris,Niels (ts) | Dansgaard,Trine (voc) | Danish Radio Concert Orchestra | Firman,David (cond) | details unknown

DCCD 9442 | CD | Angels
Jens Winther And The Danish Radio Jazz Orchestra
Angels(part 1-5)
Copenhagen,Denmark, rec. November 1998
Danish Radio Jazz Orchestra | Lindgren,Lars (tp) | Rosenfeld,Benny (tp) | Riis,Jesper (tp) | Bolberg Pedersen,Herik (tp) | Fryland,Thomas (tp) | Nilsson,Vincent (tb) | Hansen,Steen (tb) | Jensen,Peter (tb) | Löhrer,Klaus (tb,b-tb) | Windfeld,Axel (tb,b-tb) | Hove,Michael (reeds) | Schultz,Nicolai (reeds) | Markussen,Uffe (reeds) | Franck,Tomas (reeds) | Madsen,Flemming (reeds) | Bentzon,Nikolaj (p,keyboards) | Lindvall,Anders 'Chico' (g,perc) | Oyeesen,Thomas (b,el-b) | Johansen,Jonas (dr) | Weisgaard,Ethan (perc) | Winther,Jens (comp,ld)

DCCD 9443 | CD | Chinese Compass
Chinese Compass
Va,Crudele! | Mistero | Tutte Le Bocche Belle | Plante Ris | Tutta Comprendo,O Misera | Obscure | Duesoprani | Feather Dance | Sospiro E Gemo | Oh,Qual Traspare Orribile | Blue Flower | Perfido | Recitativo | Ballroom | Gelo,E Poi Sento | Wu Chou | Voi,Che Sapete | Ma Risparmia Un Innocente! | Overture En Re
Copenhagen,Denmark, rec. 31.8./1.9.1998
Chinese Compass | Schou,Jens (cl) | Kaltoft,Erik (p) | Ehde,John (cello) | Jun,Yu (gu-zeng) | Hansen,Frans (perc) | Mai-Mai,Djina (voc) | Mei,Shi Hong (voc) | Simonsen,Annette L. (voc) | Humphries,Charles (voc) | Dorge,Pierre (comp)

DCCD 9444 | CD | Moonstone Journey
Ok Nok...Kongo
Moonstone Journey | Fidding The Path | The Frog And The Snake | A Chaos With Some Kind Of Order | Spirals Of Ruby | Climbing The Mountain | Hypothesis | At The Lotus Lake | Holy Coordinator | Monk Me
Copenhagen,Denmark, rec. details unknown
Ok Nok...Kongo | Tranberg,Kasper (co) | Hyhne,Mads (tb) | Tchicai,John (ss,ts) | Fuglsang,Peter (cl,as) | Agergaard,Thomas (fl,ss,ts) | Knudsen,Niklas (g) | Davidsen,Nils (b) | Andersen,Martin (dr)

DCCD 9445 | CD | Face To Face
Flemming Agerskov Quintet
Hannya Plain | Aftenland | No Purpose | Stray Geese | We Just Want To Dance Our Steps | Remembrance | The Pleasure Of Everyday Activity | Face To Face | Tre Fortaellinger | In A While There Will Be...
Oslo,N, rec. January 1999
Agerskov,Flemming (tp) | Argüelles,Julian (fl,sax) | Nordenström,Jesper (p) | Andersson,Hansd (b) | France,Martin (dr)

DCCD 9446 | CD | Nice Work
The Danish Radio Jazz Orchestra
Pete's Feet | And Rhythm - ...And Rhythm | Moksha | Rough Night | Reflection | Nice Work If You Can Get It
Copenhagen,Denmark, rec. 8.-16.10.1998
Danish Radio Jazz Orchestra | Lindgren,Lars (tp) | Rosenfeld,Benny (tp) | Riis,Jesper (tp) | Pedersen,Henrik Bolberg (tp) | Fryland,Thomas (tp) | Nilsson,Vincent (tb) | Hansen,Steen (tb) | Jensen,Peter (tb) | Löhrer,Klaus (tb) | Windfeld,Axel (tb,b-tb) | Hove,Michael (reeds) | Schultz,Nicolai (reeds) | Markussen,Uffe (reeds) | Franck,Tomas (reeds) | Madsen,Flemming (reeds) | Bentzon,Nikolaj (p) | Lindvall,Anders 'Chico' (g) | Ovesen,Thomas (b) | Johansen,Jonas (dr) | Weisgaard,Ethan (perc) | McNeely,Jim (p,cond)
Syretha's Gift
Danish Radio Jazz Orchestra | Lindgren,Lars (tp) | Rosenfeld,Benny (tp) | Riis,Jesper (tp) | Pedersen,Henrik Bolberg (tp) | Fryland,Thomas (tp) | Nilsson,Vincent (tb) | Hansen,Steen (tb) | Jensen,Peter (tb) | Löhrer,Klaus (tb) | Windfeld,Axel (tb,b-tb) | Hove,Michael (reeds) | Schultz,Nicolai (reeds) | Gaardmand,Anders (reeds) | Franck,Tomas (reeds) | Madsen,Flemming (reeds) | Bentzon,Nikolaj (p) | Lindvall,Anders 'Chico' (g) | Vinding,Mads (b) | Johansen,Jonas (dr) | Weisgaard,Ethan (perc) | McNeely,Jim (cond)

DCCD 9447 | CD | Welcome
When Granny Sleeps
Spiril | Slapstick Slope | It Matters,JR. | Welcome | Aluminum(7,57%) | Tytte | Alphabet Call | The Dark Side Of Country Music | Little Man | Consequences | Short Notice | Traditional New Orleans Piece- | Apollo Tropical

Copenhagen,Denmark, rec. December 1997 & May 1999
When Granny Sleeps | Tranberg,Kasper (co) | Knudsen,Niklas (g) | Davidsen,Nils (b) | Mogensen,Anders (dr,perc)

DCCD 9448 | CD | Identified
Simon Cato Spang-Hansen Quartet
A Night In Copenhagen | Jazzhousing | Valse Du Vendredi | Et Si? | Open Sky Blue | Red Dwarf | Alone With A Lovely Girl | Evening Sky | Earth Blues
Copenhagen,Denmark, rec. 14.1.1999
Spang-Hansen,Simon (as) | Clausen,Thomas (p) | Lundgaard,Jesper (b) | Hart,Billy (dr)

DCCD 9449 | CD | Swinging Europe 1
European Jazz Youth Orchestra
Wulongcha | Random Brande | Paradoxy
Live at Concert Hall,Aarhus,Denmark, rec. 2.7.1998
European Jazz Youth Orchestra | Bruinsma,Ray (tp) | Klammer,Sven (tp) | Jevic,Marko Djord (tp) | Fishwick,Stephen (tp) | Baron,Moran (tb) | Rissanen,Antti (tb) | Zaletilo,Marat (tb) | Ronan,Karl (b-tb) | Dubuis,Lucien (as) | Poprawski,Lukasz (as) | Sööt,Raul (ts) | Guerrini,Mirko (ts) | Mockunas,Liudas (bs) | Garcia,Albert Sanz (p) | Pais,Afonso (g) | Mayerl,Andy (b) | Isenmann,Luc (dr) | Ekdahl,Per (perc,comp,ld) | Roggen,Live Maria (perc,voc) | Dorge,Pierre (comp,ld) | Moseholm,Erik (artistic director)
Wooden Fantasy
Live at Fasching,Stockholm, rec. 6.7.1998
European Jazz Youth Orchestra | Bruinsma,Ray (tp) | Klammer,Sven (tp) | Jevic,Marko Djord (tp) | Fishwick,Stephen (tp) | Baron,Moran (tb) | Rissanen,Antti (tb) | Zaletilo,Marat (tb) | Ronan,Karl (b-tb) | Dubuis,Lucien (as) | Poprawski,Lukasz (as) | Sööt,Raul (ts) | Guerrini,Mirko (ts) | Mockunas,Liudas (bs) | Garcia,Albert Sanz (p) | Pais,Afonso (g) | Mayerl,Andy (b) | Isenmann,Luc (dr) | Ekdahl,Per (perc,comp,ld) | Roggen,Live Maria (perc,voc) | Dorge,Pierre (comp,ld) | Moseholm,Erik (artistic director)
Forbidden Romance
Live at Kalkscheune,Berlin, rec. 17.7.1998
European Jazz Youth Orchestra | Bruinsma,Ray (tp) | Klammer,Sven (tp) | Jevic,Marko Djord (tp) | Fishwick,Stephen (tp) | Baron,Moran (tb) | Rissanen,Antti (tb) | Zaletilo,Marat (tb) | Ronan,Karl (b-tb) | Dubuis,Lucien (as) | Poprawski,Lukasz (as) | Sööt,Raul (ts) | Guerrini,Mirko (ts) | Mockunas,Liudas (bs) | Garcia,Albert Sanz (p) | Pais,Afonso (g) | Mayerl,Andy (b) | Isenmann,Luc (dr) | Ekdahl,Per (perc,comp,ld) | Roggen,Live Maria (perc,voc) | Dorge,Pierre (comp,ld) | Moseholm,Erik (artistic director)

DCCD 9450 | CD | Swinging Europe 2
To Be Or Not To Bop | Night | Sulkyhoola | Dream Of The Day | Ambra | Dimma
Live at Fasching,Stockholm, rec. 6.7.1998
European Jazz Youth Orchestra | Bruinsma,Ray (tp) | Klammer,Sven (tp) | Jevic,Marko Djord (tp) | Fishwick,Stephen (tp) | Baron,Moran (tb) | Rissanen,Antti (tb) | Zaletilo,Marat (tb) | Ronan,Karl (b-tb) | Dubuis,Lucien (as) | Poprawski,Lukasz (as) | Sööt,Raul (ts) | Guerrini,Mirko (ts) | Mockunas,Liudas (bs) | Garcia,Albert Sanz (p) | Pais,Afonso (g) | Mayerl,Andy (b) | Isenmann,Luc (dr) | Ekdahl,Per (perc,comp,ld) | Roggen,Live Maria (perc,voc) | Dorge,Pierre (comp,ld) | Moseholm,Erik (artistic director)
Amen
Live at Kalkscheune,Berlin, rec. 17.7.1998
European Jazz Youth Orchestra | Bruinsma,Ray (tp) | Klammer,Sven (tp) | Jevic,Marko Djord (tp) | Fishwick,Stephen (tp) | Baron,Moran (tb) | Rissanen,Antti (tb) | Zaletilo,Marat (tb) | Ronan,Karl (b-tb) | Dubuis,Lucien (as) | Poprawski,Lukasz (as) | Sööt,Raul (ts) | Guerrini,Mirko (ts) | Mockunas,Liudas (bs) | Garcia,Albert Sanz (p) | Pais,Afonso (g) | Mayerl,Andy (b) | Isenmann,Luc (dr) | Ekdahl,Per (perc,comp,ld) | Roggen,Live Maria (perc,voc) | Dorge,Pierre (comp,ld) | Moseholm,Erik (artistic director)

DCCD 9451 | CD | September Veje
Jens Skou Olsen Group
September Veje(Sptember Roads) | Winter | Himmelgrunden(Star Field) | Lyse Dage(Bright Days) | Storby Blues(Big City Blues) | Henad Aften(Towards Evening) | Drommevise(Dream Song) | Karrusel(Roundabout) | Jeg Vil Ga Tur Langs Maelkevejen
Copenhagen,Denmark, rec. 24.-26.3.1999
Olsen,Jens Skov (b) | Waldtlow,Claus (ss,ts) | Norbo,Soren (p) | Juul,Lars (dr)

DCCD 9452 | CD | Angels' Share
Copenhagen Art Ensemble
A Fantasic Story | Seven Secrets | Chorale | Twisted Song | Echoes Of A Memory | Three Faces Of Intimate Game | Angels' Share | Jumps
Copenhagen,Denmark, rec. Spring 1999
Copenhagen Art Ensemble | Riis,Jesper (tp) | Sveidahl,Jesper (tp) | Tranberg,Kasper (co) | Riis,Jacob (tb) | Löhrer,Klaus (b-tb,tuba) | Fuglsang,Peter (cl,alto-cl,as) | Anker,Lotte (ss,ts) | Agergaard,Thomas (fl,alto-fl,ts) | Fridell,Pelle (fl,b-cl,bs) | Clausen,Thomas (p,mini-moog) | Davidsen,Nils (b) | Mogensen,Anders (dr) | Larsen,Ture (cond)

DCCD 9454 | CD | Jordsange
Marilyn Mazur With Ars Nova And The Copenhagen Art Ensemble
Jordsang(Earth Song) | Det Virkelige Ord(The True Word) | Min Verden(My World) | De Som Blaeser Ud...(He Who Blows Out...) | Ja Ja Ja(Yes Yes Yes) | Gaderne(My Mystery) | Uromkvaed(Primal Chorus) | Gal(Go!) | Se Efter(Look) | Evigheden(Eternety)
Sun Studio,Denmark, rec. September 1998
Mazur,Marilyn (dr,perc) | Aarset,Eivind (g) | Lumholt,Aviaja (voc) | Copenhagen Art Ensemble | Ringkjobing,Bjorn (tp) | Tranberg,Kasper (co) | Agerskov,Flemming (tp) | Larsen,Ture (tb) | Löhrer,Klaus (tb) | Fuglsang,Peter (cl,as) | Anker,Lotte (ss,as) | Agergaard,Thomas (fl-h,ts) | Gaardmand,Anders (fl,b-cl,bs) | Clausen,Thomas (p,keyboards) | Davidsen,Nils (b) | Mogensen,Anders (DW-dr,cymbals) | Ars Nova | Pedersen,Helle Charlotte (voc) | Schröder,Else Torp (voc) | Gaardsdal,Tine (voc) | Kidon,Klaudio (voc) | Fischer,Nina (voc) | Brink Christensen,Ellen Marie (voc) | Hanke,Maria (voc) | Eythorstdotir,Sigga (voc) | Haugland,Stefan (voc) | Nandfred,Kim Glies (voc) | Gad,Bo (voc) | Hansen,Ivan (voc) | Flor,Kristian (voc) | Hansen,Claus K. (voc) | Klorby,Thoams (voc)

DCCD 9457 | CD | Push
Takuan
24 Nanno | Wyoming Bill Kelso | Whirling | Water Ballet | Zul | Okam | Bona Fide | Fire! Fire? FIRE!!! | Spring Surprise | The Beginning
Soundscape Studio,?, rec. details unknown
Takuan | Agerskov,Flemming (tp,fl-h,voc-effects) | Davidson,Jakob (keyboards,samples) | Juul,Lars (dr,perc)

DCCD 9458 | CD | Lys Pa Himlen
Christina Nielsen-Carsten Dahl Duo
Pigen In Rodt | Drommen | Jeg Har En Angst | Lys Pa Himlen | Christina's Sang | Bla | Jeg Ved En Dejlig Rose | Haven | Sol | Til Er Jeg Glad
Sun Studio,Denmark, rec. 29./30.1.2000
Nielsen,Christina (ss) | Dahl,Carsten (p)

DCCD 9459 | CD | Helios Suite
The Crossover Ensemble With The Zapolski Quartet
Helios Suite: | Nat(Night) | Gry(Dawn) | Formiddag(Morning) | Middag(Noon) | Eftermiddag(Afternoon) | Aften(Evening) | Ny Nat(New Night) | Manenat(Moon Night) | Crackington Haven And Ginger Crackers | Til Sjaellands Morke Skove(To The Dark Forest Of Zealand) | Fortryllede Dage(Bewitched Days)
Copenhagen,Denmark, rec. February 2000
Crossover Ensemble,The | Agerskov,Flemming (tp,fl-h) | Lund,Flemming (fl,alto-fl,bass-fl,piccolo) | Jönsson,Cennet (b-cl,ss) | Fuglsang,Peter (cl,as) | Düring,Peter (vib,perc) | Davidsen,Jakob (p,cond) | Andersson,Hansd (b) | Danemo,Peter (dr) | Zapolski String Quartet | Zapolski,Alexander (v) | Soelberg,Jacob (v) | Reinhold-Bundgaard,Kathrine (viola) | Louro,Vanja (cello)

DCCD 9460 | CD | Poetic Justice
Lotte Anker-Marilyn Crispell-Marilyn Mazur
Poetic Justice | Last Escape | Cyclic Sight Song | Drum Ffarment | Battlefield | Stop-Sound | Maloma | Japanese Gong Piece | Lat Scream | A Ghost Called M | Salute
Copenhagen,Denmark, rec. 22./23.8.2000
Anker,Lotte (ss,ts) | Crispell,Marilyn (p) | Mazur,Marilyn (dr,perc)
November | Song For Thomas | Shell
Anker,Lotte (ss,ts) | Crispell,Marilyn (p) | Mazur,Marilyn (dr,perc) | Cronholm,Josefine (voc)

DCCD 9461 | CD | Swinging Europe 3
European Jazz Youth Orchestra
1.4.E:M | Butterfly's Debut | Frozen Footsteps | A Walk In The Centerpoint | Brazilian Waves | Like A Secret
Slovak Radio,Bratislava, rec. 24.7.2000
European Jazz Youth Orchestra | Kjuus,Birgit (tp) | Smith,Dave (tp) | Besson,Airelle (tp) | Guassora,Mei Berit (tp) | Bamert,Bernhard (tb) | Turczynski,Grzegorz (tb) | Skerlecz,Gabor | Blume,Steffen (tb) | Lackner,Marko (ss,as) | Innanen,Mikko (ss,as) | Suchomel,Miroslav (ts) | Riedler,Ilse (ts) | Trcek,Blaz (bs) | Bardaro,Pasquale (vib) | Duppler,Lars (p) | Estades,Roberto Danobeitia (g) | Gudmundsson,Gulli (b) | Taeger,Vincent (dr) | Williams,Natalie (voc) | Albin,Helge (cond)

DCCD 9462 | CD | Via
Per Carsten Quintet
Dance With Me | Barroom Room Serenade | Expanding | Nymanebla(Interlude) | Tropican Sunday | Magic Man | Invinisible Turtle | Cosmic Turtle | At The End Of The Day | Lady Lover | Blue Orchid
Easy Sound Studio,?, rec. June & September 1996
Carsten,Per (fl,as) | Gade,Per (g) | Emborg,Jorgen (p,keyboards) | Mosgaard,Ole Skipper (b) | Johansen,Jonas (dr)

DCCD 9463 | CD | New Skies
The Orchestra
New Skies | Shorter Voyage | Christmas Quarrels
Copenhagen,Denmark, rec. 6./7.11.2000
Orchestra,The | Gustafsson,Christer (tp) | Lundgren,Marten (tp) | Jorgensen,Hendrik (tp) | Guassora,Mei Berit (tp) | Pedersen,Nikolai Begelund (tb) | Riis,Jacob (tb) | Gerhardt,Niels (tb) | Löhrer,Klaus (tb) | Fuglsang,Peter (reeds) | Waidtlow,Claus (reeds) | Moller,Lars (reeds) | Nielsen,Christina (reeds) | Kristensen,Niels Jakob 'Filt' (reeds) | Pedersen,Henrik Gunde (p) | Gade,Per (g) | Vadshold,Kaspar (b) | Lund,Morten (dr)
Borderline | Uneac(Suite) | Tranquilo
Orchestra,The | Gustafsson,Christer (tp) | Lundgren,Marten (tp) | Jorgensen,Hendrik (tp) | Guassora,Mei Berit (tp) | Pedersen,Nikolai Begelund (tb) | Riis,Jacob (tb) | Gerhardt,Niels (tb) | Löhrer,Klaus (tb) | Fuglsang,Peter (reeds) | Waidtlow,Claus (reeds) | Moller,Lars (reeds) | Nielsen,Christina (reeds) | Kristensen,Niels Jakob 'Filt' (reeds) | Pedersen,Henrik Gunde (p) | Gade,Per (g) | Vadshold,Kaspar (b) | Lund,Morten (dr) | Olesen,Rune Harder (perc)

Debut | ZYX Music GmbH

12 DCD 4402-2 | 12 CD | Charles Mingus-The Complete Debut Recordings
Spaulding Givens
Yesterdays
Los Angeles,CA, rec. April 1951
Givens[Nadi Qamar],Spaulding (p-solo)
Spaulding Givens/Charles Mingus
What Is This Thing Called Love | Darn That Dream | Body And Soul | Blue Moon | Blue Tide | Darn That Dream(alt.take) | Jeepers Creepers(take 1) | Jeepers Creepers(take 2)
Givens[Nadi Qamar],Spaulding (p) | Mingus,Charles (b)
Jackie Paris With The Charles Mingus Quintet
Portrait(take 1) | Portrait(take 2)
NYC, rec. 12.4.1952
Paris,Jackie (voc) | Mingus,Charles (b) | Konitz,Lee (as) | Pinkerton,Phyllis (p) | Koutzen,George (cello) | Levitt,Al (dr)
Bob Benton With The Charles Mingus Quintet
I've Lost My Love(take 1) | I've Lost My Love(take 2)
Benton,Bob (voc) | Mingus,Charles (b) | Konitz,Lee (as) | Pinkerton,Phyllis (p) | Koutzen,George (cello) | Levitt,Al (dr)
Charles Mingus Quintet
Extrasensory Perceptions | Extrasensory Perceptions(alt.take)
Mingus,Charles (b) | Konitz,Lee (as) | Pinkerton,Phyllis (p) | Koutzen,George (cello) | Levitt,Al (dr)
Jackie Paris With The Charles Mingus Quintet
Make Believe | Paris In Blue | Montage
NYC, rec. 16.9.1952
Paris,Jackie (voc) | Mingus,Charles (b) | Brook,Paige (fl,as) | Mehegan,John (p) | Wiley,Jackson (cello) | Roach,Max (dr)
Spaulding Givens Trio
Day Dream(take 1) | Day Dream(take 2) | Theme From 'Rhapsody In Blue'(take 1) | Theme From 'Rhapsody In Blue'(take 2) | Jet(take 1) | Jet(take 2)
NYC, rec. 14.4.1953
Givens[Nadi Qamar],Spaulding (p) | Mingus,Charles (b) | Roach,Max (dr)
Hank Jones Trio
You Go To My Head-
NYC, rec. 29.4.1953
Jones,Hank (p) | Mingus,Charles (b) | Roach,Max (dr)
Hank Jones Trio With The Gordons's
Can You Blame Me | You And Me | Bebopper | Cupid
Jones,Hank (p) | Mingus,Charles (b) | Roach,Max (dr) | Gordon,Honey[Honi] (voc) | Gordon,Richard (voc) | Gordon,George (voc) | Gordon Sr.,George (voc)
Max Roach
Drum Conversation
Massey Hall,Toronto, rec. 15.5.1953
Roach,Max (dr-solo)
Bud Powell Trio
I've Got You Under My Skin | Embraceable You | Sure Thing | Cherokee | Hallelujah | Lullaby Of Birdland
Powell,Bud (p) | Mingus,Charles (b) | Roach,Max (dr)
Quintet Of The Year
Perdido | Salt Peanuts | All The Things You Are | 52nd Street Theme | Wee | Hot House | A Night In Tunisia
Quintet Of The Year | Gillespie,Dizzy (tp) | Parker,Charlie (as) | Powell,Bud (p) | Mingus,Charles (b) | Roach,Max (dr)
Billy Taylor Trio
Bass-Ically Speaking | Bass-Ically Speaking(alt.take 1) | Bass-Ically Speaking(alt.take 2) | Bass-Ically Speaking(alt.take 3) | Untitled Blues
NYC, rec. Summer 1953
Taylor,Billy (p) | Mingus,Charles (b) | Roach,Max or Art Taylor (dr)
Four Trombones
Wee Dot(Blues For Some Bones) | Stardust | Move | I'll Remember April | Now's The Time | Trombosphere | Ow! | Chazzanova | Yesterdays | Kai's Day
Live at Putnam Central Club,Brookly,NY, rec. 18.9.1953
Four Trombones | Johnson,J.J. (tb) | Winding,Kai (tb) | Green,Bennie (tb) | Dennis,Willie (tb) | Lewis,John (p) | Mingus,Charles (b) | Taylor,Arthur 'Art' (dr)
Charles Mingus And His Orchestra
Pink Topsy | Miss Bliss | Pink Topsy(alt.take)
NYC, rec. 28.10.1953
Royal,Ernie (tp) | Dennis,Willie (tb) | Caine,Eddie (fl,as) | Macero,Teo (cl,ts) | Bank,Danny prob (bs) | Lewis,John (p) | Wiley,Jackson (cello) | Mingus,Charles (b) | Clarke,Kenny (dr) | Givens[Nadi Qamar],Spaulding (arr)
Blue Tide | Eclipse | Eclipse(alt.take)
Royal,Ernie (tp) | Dennis,Willie (tb) | Caine,Eddie (fl,as) | Macero,Teo (cl,ts) | Bank,Danny prob (bs) | Lewis,John (p) | Wiley,Jackson (cello) | Mingus,Charles (b) | Clarke,Kenny (dr) | Thurlow,Janet (voc) | Givens[Nadi Qamar],Spaulding (arr)
Paul Bley Trio
Opus 1 | Opus 1(alt.take) | Walkin' | Like Someone In Love | I Can't Get Started | Split Kick | This Time The Dream's On Me | Zootcase | Santa Claus Is Coming To Town
NYC, rec. 30.11.1953
Bley,Paul (p) | Mingus,Charles (b) | Blakey,Art (dr)
Oscar Pettiford Sextet
The Pendulum At Falcon's Lair | Jack The Fieldstalker | Stockholm Sweetnin' | Low And Behold
NYC, rec. 29.12.1953
Pettiford,Oscar (cello) | Watkins,Julius (fr-h) | Urso,Phil (ts) | Bishop Jr.,Walter (p) | Mingus,Charles (b) | Brice,Percy (dr)
Thad Jones Quintet
Bitty Ditty | Chazzanova | I'll Remember April | Elusive | Sombre Intrusion | You Don't Know What Love Is
Hackensack,NJ, rec. 11.8.1954
Jones,Thad (tp) | Wess,Frank (fl,ts) | Jones,Hank (p) | Mingus,Charles (b) | Clarke,Kenny (dr)
Hazel Scott Trio
Like Someone In Love | Peace Of Mind | Lament | The Jeep Is Jumpin' | Git Up From There | A Foggy Day(In London Town) | Mountain Greenery | Git Up From There(alt.take) | Lament(alt.take)
Hackensack,NJ, rec. 21.1.1955
Scott,Hazel (p) | Mingus,Charles (b) | Roach,Max (dr)
Thad Jones Quartet
One More | I Can't Get Started | More Of The Same | Get Out Of Town | One More(alt.take)
Hackensack,NJ, rec. 10.3.1955
Jones,Thad (tp) | Dennis,John (p) | Mingus,Charles (b) | Roach,Max (dr)
John Dennis Trio
Ensenada | Machajo | Cherokee | Seven Moons | Seven Moons(alt.take) | All The Things You Are(take 1) | All The Things You Are(take 2) | Cherokee(alt.take)
Hackensack,NJ, rec. prob.10.3.1955
Dennis,John (p) | Mingus,Charles (b) | Roach,Max (dr)
Miles Davis Quintet
Nature Boy | Alone Together | There Is No You | Easy Living
Hackensack,NJ, rec. 9.7.1955
Davis,Miles (tp) | Woodman,Britt (tb) | Charles,Teddy (vib) | Mingus,Charles (b) | Jones,Elvin (dr)
Don Senay With Orchestra And Strings
The Edge Of Love | Makin' Whoopee | Fanny
NYC, rec. 18.9.1955
Senay,Don (voc) | Jones,Thad (tp) | Mucci,Louis (tp) | LaPorta,John (woodwinds) | Baker,Julius (woodwinds) | Taylor,Billy (p) | Wiley,Jackson (cello) | Hinton,Milt (b) | Zimmerman,Fred (b) | Mingus,Charles prob. (b) | Morello,Joe (dr) | unkn. (perc,strings,brass,harp) | Levister,Alonzo (arr)
Thad Jones And His Orchestra
Portrait
NYC, rec. prob.26.9.1955
Jones,Thad (tp,overdubbing) | Mucci,Louis (tp) | LaPorta,John (woodwinds) | Baker,Julius (woodwinds) | Taylor,Billy (p) | Wiley,Jackson (cello) | Hinton,Milt (b) | Zimmerman,Fred (b) | Mingus,Charles prob. (b) | Morello,Joe (dr) | unkn. (perc,strings,brass,harp) | Levister,Alonzo (arr)
Charles Mingus Quintet
Jump Monk | Serenade In Blue | The Work Song | Septemberly | All The Things You C | Love Chant | A Foggy Day(In London Town) | Haitian Fight Song | Lady Bird | Jump Monk(alt.take) | All The Things You C(alt.take) | A Foggy Day(In London Town-alt.take) | Haitian Fight Song(alt.take) | Love Chant(alt.take) | Lady Bird(alt.take) | What Is This Thing Called Love
Live at The Cafe Bohemia,Greenwich Village,NYC, rec. 23.12.1955
Mingus,Charles (b) | Bert,Eddie (tb) | Barrow,George (ts) | Waldron,Mal (p) | Jones,Willie (dr)
I'll Remember April | I'll Remember April(alt.take) | Drums | Drums(alt.take 1) | Drums(alt.take 2) | Percussion Discussion
Mingus,Charles (b) | Bert,Eddie (tb) | Barrow,George (ts) | Waldron,Mal (p) | Roach,Max (dr)
Jimmy Knepper Quintet
Latterday Saint | Cunningbird | The Jumpin' Blues | The Masher | Latterday Saint(alt.take 1) | Latterday Saint(alt.take 2) | Latterday Saint(alt.take 3) | The Masher(alt.take)
NYC, rec. 10.6.1957
Knepper,Jimmy (tb) | Maini,Joe (as) | Triglia,Bill (p) | Mingus,Charles (b) | Richmond,Dannie (dr)
Charles Mingus Workshop
Untitled Original Blues(take 1) | Stella By Starlight(take 4) | Stella By Starlight(take 5) | Untitled Original Composition(take 3) | Untitled Original Composition(take 5) | Autumn In New York(take 1) | Autumn In New York(take 2) | Long Ago And Far Away(take 2) | Long Ago And Far Away(take 4) | Long Ago And Far Away(take 5) | Untitled Original Blues(take 2)
NYC, rec. prob. September 1957
Shaw,Clarence (tp) | Hadi [Curtis Porter],Shafti (ts) | Adams,Pepper (bs) | Kelly,Wynton or Wade Legge (p) | Mingus,Charles or Henry Grimes (b) | Richmond,Dannie (dr)
Joldi(take 4) | Joldi(take 5)
Shaw,Clarence (tp) | Hadi [Curtis Porter],Shafti (ts) | Adams,Pepper (bs) | Kelly,Wynton or Wade Legge (p) | Grimes,Henry (b) | Richmond,Dannie (dr)
Untitled Percussion Composition
NYC, rec. 1957 or 1958
Hadi [Curtis Porter],Shafti prob. (fl) | Richmond,Dannie (dr) | Mingus,Charles (p,perc,voice) | Knepper,Jimmy (perc) | Shaw,Clarence (perc) | Parlan,Horace prob. (perc) | Newborn Jr.,Phineas (perc)
-> Note: Charles Mingus recorded a new bass part in summer 1953

DSA 124-6 | SACD | The Quintet-Jazz At Massey Hall |
EAN 025218731263
Quintet Of The Year
Perdido | Salt Peanuts | All The Things You Are | 52nd Street Theme | Wee(Allen's Alley) | Hot House | A Night In Tunisia
Live at Massey Hall,Toronto, rec. 15.5.1953
Quintet Of The Year | Gillespie,Dizzy (tp) | Parker[as 'Charlie Chan'],Charlie (as) | Powell,Bud (p) | Mingus,Charles (b) | Roach,Max (dr)

Decca | Universal Music Germany

050668-2 | CD | Ella Fitzgerald:The Decca Years 1949-1954 |
EAN 011105066822
Ella Fitzgerald With Sy Oliver And His Orchestra
In The Evening When The Sun Goes Down | Basin Street Blues
NYC, rec. 20.9.1949
Fitzgerald,Ella (voc) | prob.personal: | Privin,Bernie (tp) | Chambers,Henderson (tb) | Kyle,Billy (p) | Oliver,Sy (cond,arr) | details unknown
Solid As A Rock | I've Got The World On A String
NYC, rec. 6.3.1950
Fitzgerald,Ella (voc) | Oliver,Sy (cond,arr) | Privin,Bernie (tp) | Faso,Tony (tp) | Webster,Paul (tp) | Chambers,Henderson (tb) | Yaner,Milt (as) | Cooper,Sid (as) | Jerome,Jerry (ts) | Klink,Al (ts) | Jones,Hank (p) | Barksdale,Everett (g) | Brown,Ray (b) | Crawford,Jimmy (dr) | unkn. (voc-group)
Dream A Little Dream Of Me | Can Anyone Explain
NYC, rec. 15.8.1950
Fitzgerald,Ella (voc) | Oliver,Sy (cond,arr) | Armstrong,Louis (tp,voc) | Webster,Paul (tp) | D'Amico,Hank (cl) | Ludwig,Frank (ts) | Jones,Hank (p) | Barksdale,Everett (g) | Brown,Ray (b) | Crawford,Jimmy (dr)
Because Of Rain
NYC, rec. 27.3.1951
Fitzgerald,Ella (voc) | Oliver,Sy (cond,arr) | Privin,Bernie (tp) | Faso,Tony (tp) | Webster,Paul (tp) | Bullman,Morton (tb) | Baker,Art (as) | Dorsey,George (as) | Holcombe,Bill (ts) | Klink,Al (ts) | Jones,Hank (p) | Barksdale,Everett (g) | Block,Sandy (b) | Crawford,Jimmy (dr)
I Don't Want To Take A Chance | There Never Was A Baby Like My Baby | Give A Little, Get A Little

NYC, rec. 18.7.1951
Fitzgerald,Ella (voc) | Oliver,Sy (cond,arr) | Privin,Bernie (tp) | Jordan,Taft (tp) | Poole,Carl (tp) | Chambers,Henderson (tb) | Saccaro,Frank (tb) | Schertzer,Hymie (as) | Yaner,Milt (as) | Williams,Freddy (ts) | Klink,Al (ts) | Blake,Stewart (bs) | Jones,Hank (p) | Barksdale,Everett (g) | Block,Sandy (b) | Blowers,Johnny (dr)
A Guy Is A Guy | Goody Goody
NYC, rec. 25.2.1952
Fitzgerald,Ella (voc) | Jordan,Taft (tp) | Privin,Bernie (tp) | Nottingham,Jimmy (tp) | Bullman,Morton (tb) | Grey,Al (tb) | Yaner,Milt (as) | Cooper,Sid (as) | Jacobs,Dick (ts) | Taylor,Sam 'The Man' (ts) | McRae,Dave (bs) | Jones,Hank (p) | Barksdale,Everett (g) | Block,Sandy (b) | Crawford,Jimmy (dr)
You'll Have To Swing It(Mr.Paganini part 1+2) | Early Autumn | Angel Eyes
NYC, rec. 26.6.1952
Fitzgerald,Ella (voc) | Jordan,Taft (tp) | Privin,Bernie (tp) | Nottingham,Jimmy (tp) | Byrne,Bobby (tb) | Bullman,Morton (tb) | Grey,Al (tb) | Yaner,Milt (as) | Cooper,Sid (as) | Jacobs,Dick (ts) | Taylor,Sam 'The Man' (ts) | McRae,Dave (bs) | Jones,Hank (p) | Barksdale,Everett (g) | Block,Sandy (b) | Crawford,Jimmy (dr)
Preview
Fitzgerald,Ella (voc) | Taylor,Sam 'The Man' (ts) | Jones,Hank (p) | Barksdale,Everett (g) | Block,Sandy (b) | Crawford,Jimmy (dr)
Careless | Blue Lou
NYC, rec. 13.2.1953
Fitzgerald,Ella (voc) | Jordan,Taft (tp) | Shavers,Charlie (tp) | Nottingham,Jimmy (tp) | Chambers,Henderson (tb) | Saracco,Frank (tb) | Baker,Art (as) | Dorsey,George (as) | Taylor,Sam 'The Man' (ts) | Taitt,Mel (ts) | Albam,Manny (bs) | Jones,Hank (p) | Barksdale,Everett (g) | Duvivier,George (b) | Crawford,Jimmy (dr)
Melancholy Me
NYC, rec. 23.12.1953
Fitzgerald,Ella (voc) | Jordan,Taft (tp) | Shavers,Charlie (tp) | Nottingham,Jimmy (tp) | Satterfield,Jack (tb) | Saracco,Frank (tb) | Holcombe,Bill (as) | Dorsey,George (as) | Taylor,Sam 'The Man' (ts) | McRae,Dave (bs) | Martin,David (p) | Barksdale,Everett (g) | Block,Sandy (b) | Crawford,Jimmy (dr)
Lullaby Of Birdland
NYC, rec. 4.6.1954
Fitzgerald,Ella (voc) | prob.personal: | Taylor,Sam 'The Man' (ts) | Jones,Hank (p) | Doggett,Bill (org) | Barksdale,Everett (g) | Block,Sandy (b) | Crawford,Jimmy (dr) | unkn. (voc-group)

050669-2 | CD | Everybody's Somebody's Fool | EAN 011105066921
(Little)Jimmy Scott With The Lionel Hampton Orchestra
I've Been A Fool(Thinking You Cared)
NYC, rec. 5.1.1950
Scott,Jimmy[Little] (voc) | Bailey,Benny (tp) | Mullens,Eddie (tp) | Garrette,Duke (tp) | Shepherd,Leo (tp) | Williams,Walter (tp) | Grey,Al (tb) | Powell,Benny (tb) | Wormick,James (tb) | Lee,Paul[Higaki] (tb) | Richardson,Jerome (fl,as) | Plater,Bobby (as) | Board,Johnny (ts) | Williams,Billy (ts) | Lowe,Curtis (ts) | Shaw,Lonnie (bs) | Hampton,Lionel (vib) | Duke,Douglas (p,org) | Montgomery,Wes (g) | Johnson,Roy (b) | Bartee,Ellis (dr)
Everybody's Somebody's Fool | I Wish I Knew | Please Give Me A Chance
NYC, rec. 25./26.1.1950
Scott,Jimmy[Little] (voc) | Bailey,Benny (tp) | Mullens,Eddie (tp) | Garrette,Duke (tp) | Shepherd,Leo (tp) | Williams,Walter (tp) | Grey,Al (tb) | Powell,Benny (tb) | Wormick,James (tb) | Lee,Paul[Higaki] (tb) | Richardson,Jerome (fl,as) | Plater,Bobby (as) | Board,Johnny (ts) | Williams,Billy (ts) | Lowe,Curtis (ts) | Shaw,Lonnie (bs) | Hampton,Lionel (vib) | Duke,Douglas (p,org) | Montgomery,Wes (g) | Johnson,Roy (b) | Bartee,Ellis (dr)
(Little)Jimmy Scott With Orchestra
Wheel Of Fortune | Come What May | They Say You Cry
NYC, rec. 10.1.1952
Scott,Jimmy[Little] (voc) | details unknown
(Little)Jimmy Scott With The Billy Taylor Orchestra
When You Surrender | Alone With A Memory | Do You Mind(If I Hang Around)? | Something From A Fool
NYC, rec. 5.3.1952
Scott,Jimmy[Little] (voc) | Baker,Harold 'Shorty' (tp) | Jordan,Taft (tp) | Glenn,Tyree (tb) | Winding,Kai (tb) | Sanfino,Jerry (as) | Jerome,Jerry (as) | Getz,Stan (ts) | Berg,George (ts) | Bank,Danny (bs) | Taylor,Billy (p) | Simmons,John (b) | Hunt,John (dr)
(Little)Jimmy Scott With The Lucky Thompson Orchestra
Why Was I Born | The Bluest Blues | You Never Miss The Water Till The Well Runs Dry | Solitude
NYC, rec. 1.8.1952
Scott,Jimmy[Little] (voc) | Askey,Gil (tp) | Saunders,John (tb) | Alexander,Kirkby (as) | Thompson,Lucky (ts) | Williams,Clarence (bs) | Swanston,Ed (p) | Morrison,Peck (b) | Lovelle,Herbie (dr)

050670-2 | CD | Crazy Rhythm:His Debut Recordings | EAN 011105067027
Mark Murphy With The Ralph Burns Orchestra
Give It Back To The Indians | You Mustn't Kick It Around | Fascinating Rhythm | Limehouse Blues
NYC, rec. 26.6.1956
Murphy,Mark (voc) | Orchestra | Burns,Ralph (cond,arr) | details unknown
I Guess I'll Hang My Tears Out To Dry | A Nightingale Sang In Berkeley Square | If I Could Be With You One Hour Tonight
NYC, rec. 9.8.1956
Murphy,Mark (voc) | Orchestra | Burns,Ralph (cond,arr) | details unknown
Exactly Like You
NYC, rec. 13.8.1956
Murphy,Mark (voc) | Orchestra | Burns,Ralph (cond,arr) | details unknown
I Got Rhythm | Takin' A Chance On Love | 'Tain't No Sin
NYC, rec. 23.4.1957
Murphy,Mark (voc) | Orchestra | Burns,Ralph (cond,arr) | details unknown
Ridin' High | Crazy Rhythm | Elmer's Tune | The Lady In Red
NYC, rec. 3.5.1957
Murphy,Mark (voc) | Orchestra | Burns,Ralph (cond,arr) | details unknown
Little Jazz Bird | Robbin's Nest | Pick Yourself Up | Lullaby In Rhythm
NYC, rec. 22.5.1957
Murphy,Mark (voc) | Small Band | Burns,Ralph (cond,arr) | details unknown
Let Yourself Go
NYC, rec. 15.8.1957
Murphy,Mark (voc) | Orchestra | Burns,Ralph (cond,arr) | details unknown

050671-2 | CD | The Very Thought Of You:The Decca Years 1951-1957 | EAN 011105067126
Jerri Southern And The Toots Camarata Orchestra
You Better Go Now
Hollywood,CA, rec. 9.10.1951
Southern,Jeri (voc) | Orchestra | Camarata,Toots (arr,ld) | details unknown
He Was Too Good To Me | I Remember You | Smoke Gets In Your Eyes
Hollywood,CA, rec. 28.6.1956
Southern,Jeri (voc) | Orchestra | Camarata,Toots (arr,ld) | details unknown
My Ship | Someone To Watch Over Me
Hollywood,CA, rec. 6.7.1956
Southern,Jeri (voc) | Orchestra | Camarata,Toots (arr,ld) | details unknown
Jerri Southern And The Dave Barbour Trio
The Very Thought Of You
Hollywood,CA, rec. 16.2.1954
Southern,Jeri (voc) | Barbour,Dave (g) | details unknown
All In Fun | Every Time We Say Goodbye
Hollywood,CA, rec. 2.3.1954
Southern,Jeri (voc) | Barbour,Dave (g) | details unknown
You're Nearer | Nobody's Heart
Hollywood,CA, rec. 26.11.1957
Southern,Jeri (voc) | Barbour,Dave (g) | details unknown
Jerri Southern Quartet
It's De-Lovely | I Hadn't Anyone 'Till Now | I Don't Know Where To Turn
Hollywood,CA, rec. 4.-10.3.1955
Southern,Jeri (p,voc) | Roland,E.J. (g) | Hills,Clifford (b) | Morales,Lloyd (dr,perc)
Jerri Southern And The Ralph Burns Orchestra
If I Had You | No Moon At All
Hollywood,CA, rec. 20.11.1956
Southern,Jeri (voc) | Orchestra | Burns,Ralph (cond,arr) | details unknown
Jerri Southern And The Norman Leyden Orchestra
Dancing On The Ceiling
Hollywood,CA, rec. 16.9.1952
Southern,Jeri (voc) | Orchestra | Leyden,Norm (cond,arr) | details unknown
Jerri Southern And The Victoe Young Orchestra
When I Fall In Love
Hollywood,CA, rec. 3.4.1952
Southern,Jeri (p,voc) | Orchestra | Young,Victor (ld) | details unknown
Jerri Southern And The Sonny Burke Orchestra
Remind Me
Hollywood,CA, rec. 5.5.1954
Southern,Jeri (voc) | Orchestra | Burke,Sonny (cond,arr) | details unknown
Jerri Southern And The Frank Meriweather Orchestra
An Occasional Man
Hollywood,CA, rec. 27.7.1955
Southern,Jeri (voc) | Orchestra | Meriweather,Frank (cond,arr) | details unknown
Jerri Southern And The Gus Levene Orchestra
Close As Pages In A Book
Hollywood,CA, rec. 25.7.1957
Southern,Jeri (voc) | Orchestra | Levene,Gus (cond) | details unknown

157561-2 | CD | Play Bach No.1
Jacques Loussier Trio
Prelude No.1 In C Major(BWV 846) | Fugue No.1 In C Major(BWV 846) | Prelude No.2 In C Minor(BWV 847) | Fugue No.2 In C Minor(BWV 847) | Toccata And Fugue In D Minor(BWV 565) | Prelude No.8 In E Flat Minor(BWV 853) | Prelude No.5 In D Major(BWV 850) | Fugue No.5 In D Major(BWV 850)
Paris,France, rec. 1959
Loussier,Jacques (p) | Garros,Christian (dr) | Michelot,Pierre (b)

157562-2 | CD | Play Bach No.2
Partita No.1 In B Flat Major(BWV 825): | Allemande | Courante | Sarabande | Menuet 1 | Menuet 2 | Gigue | Choral Jesus Bleibet Meine Freude(BWV 147) | Prelude No.6 In D Minor(BWV 851) | Aria In D Major(BWV 1068) | Prelude No.16 In G Minor(BWV 861) | Fugue No.1 In G Minor(BWV 861) | Prelude No.21 In B Flat Major(BWV 866)
Paris,France, rec. 1960
Loussier,Jacques (p) | Michelot,Pierre (b) | Garros,Christian (dr)

157892-2 | CD | Play Bach No.3
Italien Concerto In F Major(BWV 971): | Allegro | Andante | Presto | Two Part Invention No.1 In C Major(BWV 772) | Two Part Invention No.13 In A Minor(BWV 784) | Two Part Invention No.8 In F Major(BWV 779) | Two Part Invention No.14 In B Flat Major(BWV 785) | Two Part Invention No.15 In B Minor(BWV 796) | Fantasia In C Minor(BWV 906)
Paris,France, rec. 1961
Loussier,Jacques (p) | Michelot,Pierre (b) | Garros,Christian (dr)

157893-2 | CD | Play Bach No.4
Sinfonia. Cantata No.29 'Wir Danken Dir Gott wir Danken Dir'(BWV 29) | Choral 'Erbarm Dich Mein O Herre Gott'(BWV 721) | Choral No.16 'Christ Unser Herr Zum Jordan Kam'(BWV 684) | Fantasia And Fugue In G Minor(BWV 542) | Choral No.1 'Wachet Auf Ruft Uns Die Stimme'(BWV 645)
Paris,France, rec. 1963
Loussier,Jacques (p,org) | Michelot,Pierre (b) | Garros,Christian (dr,perc)

159194-2 | CD | Play Bach No.5
Toccata In C Major(BWV 564): | Toccata- | Adagio- | Fugue- | Sicilienne In G Minor(BWV 1031) | Choral Nr.1(BWV 645) | Passacaglia In C Minor(BWV 582)
Paris,France, rec. 1965
Loussier,Jacques (p) | Michelot,Pierre (b) | Garros,Christian (dr,perc)

159203-2 | 2 CD | Play Bach Aux Champs-Élyssées
Prelude No.1 In C Major(BWV 846) | Italien Concerto In F Major(BWV 971): | Allegro- | Andante- | Finale-Presto- | Partita No.1 In B Flat Major(BWV 825): | Prelude- | Allemande- | Courante- | Sarabande- | Minuetto I- | Minuetto II- | Gigue- | Choral Jesus Bleibet Meine Freude(BWV 147) | Toccata And Fugue In D Minor(BWV 565) | Two Part Invention No.8 In F Major(BWV 779) | Prelude No.2 In C Minor(BWV 847) | Prelude No.12 In F Minor(BWV 881) | Harpsichord Concerto No.1 In D Minor(BWV 1052): | Allegro- | Adagio- | Allegro- | Aria From Orchester Suite No.3 In D Major(BWV 1068) | Choral Nr.1 Wachet Auf Ruft Uns Die Stimme(BWV 645) | Sinfonia(BWV 29)
Live at The Theatre Des Champs-Elysees,Paris,France, rec. 29.4.1965
Loussier,Jacques (p) | Michelot,Pierre (b) | Garros,Christian (dr,perc)

589489-2 | CD | Stan Kenton-The Formative Years | EAN 731458948926
Stan Kenton And His Orchestra
Taboo | Adios | This Love Of Mine | The Nango
Hollywood,CA, rec. 11.9.1941
Alvarez,Chico (tp) | Beach,Frank (tp) | Collier,Earl (tp) | Cole,Dick (tb) | Forbes,Harry (tb) | Ordean,Jack (as) | Romersa,Ted (as) | Dorris,Red (cl,ts,voc) | Bridwell,Hollis (cl,ts) | Gioga,Bob (b-cl,bs) | Kenton,Stan (p,arr) | Costi,Al (g) | Rumsey,Howard (b) | George,Marvin (dr) | Yaw,Ralph (arr)
Gambler's Blues(St.James Infirmary) | Lamento Gitano | Concerto For Doghouse | El Choclo
NYC, rec. 13.2.1942
Alvarez,Chico (tp) | Beach,Frank (tp) | Collier,Earl (tp) | Cole,Dick (tb) | Forbes,Harry (tb) | Aaron,Lorin (tb) | Ordean,Jack (as) | Lahey,Bill (cl,as) | Dorris,Red (cl,ts,voc) | Romersa,Ted (cl,ts) | Gioga,Bob (b-cl,bs) | Kenton,Stan (p,arr) | Costi,Al (g) | Rumsey,Howard (b) | George,Marvin (dr) | Rizzo,Joe (arr)
Reed Rapture
Ordean,Jack (as) | Lahey,Bill (cl,as) | Dorris,Red (ts) | Romersa,Ted (cl,ts) | Gioga,Bob (b-cl,bs) | Kenton,Stan (p,arr) | Costi,Al (g) | Rumsey,Howard (b) | George,Marvin (dr)

589515-2 | CD | Birds Of A Feather | EAN 731458951520
Carmen McRae With The Ralph Burns Orchestra
Mr.Meadowlark | Skylark | Bye Bye Blackbird | Flamingo | A Nightingale Sang In Berkeley Square | When The Swallows Come Back To Capistrano
NYC, rec. 4.8.1958
McRae,Carmen (voc) | Markowitz,Irving 'Marky' (tp) | Kelin,Fred (fr-h) | Corrado,Donald (fr-h) | Berg,Dick (fr-h) | Miranda,Tony (fr-h) | Webster,Ben (ts) | Abney,Don (p) | Lowe,Mundell (g) | Bell,Aaron (b) | Sommer,Ted (dr) | Burns,Ralph (cond,arr)
Carmen McRae With Orchestra
The Eagle And Me | When The Red Red Robin Comes Bob Bob Bobbin' Along
NYC, rec. 6.8.1958
McRae,Carmen (voc) | Markowitz,Irving 'Marky' (tp) | Webster,Ben (ts) | Cohn,Al (ts) | Abney,Don (p) | Lowe,Mundell (g) | Bell,Aaron (b) | Stabulas,Nick (dr)
His Eye Is On The Sparrow
McRae,Carmen (voc) | Markowitz,Irving 'Marky' (tp) | Webster,Ben (ts) | Cohn,Al (ts) | Abney,Don (p) | Lowe,Mundell (g) | Bell,Aaron (b) | Stabulas,Nick (dr) | Charles,Ray (voc) | unkn. (4 voices)
Bob White(Whatcha Gonna Swing Tonight) | Baltimore Oriole | Chicken Today,Feathers Tomorrow
NYC, rec. 8.8.1958
McRae,Carmen (voc) | Markowitz,Irving 'Marky' (tp) | Webster,Ben (ts) | Cohn,Al (ts) | Abney,Don (p) | Galbraith,Barry (g) | Bell,Aaron (b) | Lamond,Don (dr)

Deram | Universal Music Germany

844882-2 | CD | How Many Clouds Can You See?
John Surman Orchestra
Galata Bridge
London,GB, rec. 20.3.1969
Surman,John (bs) | Beckett,Harry (tp,fl-h) | Griffiths,Malcolm (tb) | Osborne,Mike (as) | Skidmore,Alan (ts) | Taylor,John (p) | Miller,Harry (b) | Jackson,Alan (dr)
Premonition
London,GB, rec. 20.-24.3.1969
Surman,John (bs) | Beckett,Harry (tp,fl-h) | Holdsworth,Dave (tp) | Griffiths,Malcolm (tb) | Pyne,Chris (tb) | Osborne,Mike (as) | Skidmore,Alan (ts) | Warren,John (fl,bs) | Smith,George (tuba) | Taylor,John (p) | Phillips,Barre (b) | Oxley,Tony (dr)
John Surman Quartet
Event | Gathering- | Ritual- | Circle Dance- | How Many Clouds Can You See
Surman,John (b-cl,ss,bs) | Taylor,John (p) | Phillips,Barre (b) | Oxley,Tony (dr)

dml-records | Fenn Music

CD 007 | CD | Never Thought It Could Happen | EAN 4011550200075
Patrick Bebelaar Quartet
Roblinga | Glipse | A La Prima Vera Corta Que Tuvimos | Never Thought It Could Happen | Die Sweet Dé Snove(-18,-19) | Lenny | My Late Coming Out | Saarländer Mädel
Ludwigsburg, rec. 6.-8.10.1997
Bebelaar,Patrick (p) | Kroll,Frank (cl,sax) | Mumm,Henrik (cello,b) | Witte,Willi (dr)

CD 011 | CD | But Where's The Moon? | EAN 4011550200112
Sputnik 27
The Princess Coming Home | This Way | Don't Stop | Gleiten Auf Dem Eis | Nobody At Home | No Snow Here | But Where's te Moon? | The Honky-Tonk Cowboy | Dance Of The One's Beyond- | Lost Souls- | Dance Of The One's Beyond(2)- | Flight For The Exit- | Searching In Heavy Weather
Stuttgart, rec. 3./4.12.2001
Sputnik 27 | Joos,Herbert (tp,fl-h) | Kroll,Frank (b-cl,sax) | Amros,Jo (g) | Lange,Uwe (cello,b) | Settelmeyer,Bernd (dr,perc)

CD 012 | CD | Elegie | EAN 4011550200129
Schwarz-Hübner Duo
Concertino Cappricioso | Elegie I: | Prolog | Epilog | Philips Hymn | Elegie II: | Leggiero Up | Elegie | Uptime Down | Elegie III: | Sounds Of The Way | 26 Bars | Elegie IV: | Chinatown | Careful
details unknown, rec. 16.1.2001 & 14.1.2002
Schwarz,Paul (p) | Hübner,Gregor (v)

CD 013 | CD | Per Anno | EAN 4011550200136
Kelm 3
Koengskreis | Evans | Katzenmusik I | Elis | X | Nii Voi Naa | Katzenmusik II | Walzer Nr.4 | Pace | Intro <143 | 12x12=143 | Popsong
Karlsruhe, rec. 30.5.2002
Kolm 3 | Rössle,Ekkehard (sax) | Kischkat,Boris (g) | Randalu,Kritjan (p)

CD 014 | CD | Landscape | EAN 4011550200143
Frank Kroll Quintet
Landscape I Heavy Weather | Landscape II Rain | Landscape III Silence And Storm | Landscape IV Ice And Sun | Ludi Garden | Blue Desert | Talk Together | Peace For Kabul | Arrak | Schachriars Dream | In Your Arms
Ludwigsburg, rec. 29.3.-1.4.2002
Kroll,Heribert (ss) | Bebelaar,Patrick (p) | Mumm,Henrik (b,el-b) | Witte,Willi (dr) | Ludin,Hakim (perc)

CD 015 | CD | You Never Lose An Island | EAN 4011550200150
Patrick Bebelaar Quartet
You Never Lose An Island: | Leaving- | Arriving- | Morning Light- | Drowning- | Keep Holding- | Will We Meet Again | Tango | Maienlied | Pos Pregatz Mi
Leonberg, rec. 11.6.2002
Bebelaar,Patrick (p) | Joos,Herbert (tp,fl-h,co) | Kroll,Frank (cl,b-cl,ss) | Godard,Michel (serpent,tuba)

CD 016 | CD | Wanderlust | EAN 4011550200167
Jo Ambros Group
Seven Seas | Melanga Raikiki | Mikesh | Abba | Komite | Republic Of... | Black And Tan Fantasy | Republic Of..(II) | Spirals Of Ruby | Kapazunder | Watermelon In Easterhay
Stuttgart, rec. 11.& 13.1.2003
Ambros,Jo (g,el-g) | Bruetsch,Florian (vib,marimba,perc) | Schulze,Nicolas (accordeon) | Klein,Matthias (b,el-b) | Dapper,Frank (dr,congas) | Settelmeyer,Bernd (dr,marimba)
Qued
Ambros,Jo (g,el-g) | Feucht,Jochen (cl) | Bruetsch,Florian (vib,marimba,perc) | Schulze,Nicolas (accordeon) | Klein,Matthias (b,el-b) | Dapper,Frank (dr,congas) | Settelmeyer,Bernd (dr,marimba)
Lark
Ambros,Jo (g,el-g) | Feucht,Jochen (basset-h) | Bruetsch,Florian (vib,marimba,perc) | Schulze,Nicolas (accordeon) | Klein,Matthias (b,el-b) | Dapper,Frank (dr,congas) | Settelmeyer,Bernd (dr,marimba) | Speth,Micha (viola) | Schimer,Jonathan (cello) | Timofejev,Kirill (cello)

CD 017 | CD | Point Of View | EAN 4011550200174
Patrick Bebelaar Group
Point Of View(part 1-3 | Raga
Stuttgart, rec. 7.9.2003
Bebelaar,Patrick (p) | Godard,Michel (serpent,tuba) | Kroll,Frank (sax) | Maharaj,Pandit Vikash (sarod) | Maharaj,Pandit Prakash (tabla) | Maharaj,Vikash (tambourine)

Dot | Universal Music

589761-2 | CD | Slim Gaillard Rides Again | EAN 731458976127
Slim Gaillard Group
Oh! Lady Be Good | I Don't Stand A Ghost Of A Chance With You | How High The Moon | Slim's Cee | One Minute Of Flamenco For Three Minutes | Chicken Rhythm | I Love You | Tall And Slim | My Blue Heaven | Thunderbird | Walkin' And Cookin' Blues | Sukiyaki Cha Cha | Don't Blame Me
NYC, rec. November 1958
Gaillard,Slim (g,p,voc) | details unknown

double moon | sunny moon Musikvertrieb

CHRDM 71007 | CD | Art De Fakt-Ray Federman:Surfiction Jazz No.2
Art De Fakt
Words Out Of A Bad Dream | Van Gogh Admist The Flowers | Morning Rain | The Potato That Became Tomato | El Eventones | Before Us | Duel Of Jester And The Tyrant | Fear | H. D. 2 | History Of The Balloon | Avenue(Footprints)
details unknown, rec. details unknown
Art De Fakt | Schäfer,Brigitta (sax) | Singer,Ludger (tp,tb,p,keyboards,voc) | Elsässer,Urban (g,voc) | Proske,Markus (b) | Lieven,Thomas (dr)

CHRDM 71009 | CD | Live At Montreux
Albert Mangelsdorff-Reto Weber Percussion Orchestra
The First Step | On The Road Again | Looking Back | Remember | Togetherness | Bone Blue | Landscapes
Live at The Montreux Jazz Festival, rec. 11.7.1994
Mangelsdorff,Albert (tb) | Weber,Reto (perc) | Nketia,Nana Twum (perc) | Chemirani,Keyvan (zarb)

CHRDM 71010 | CD | Métisse
Cécile Verny Quartet
What If | A Cradle Song | Métisse | Running After Dreams | What Without The Beauty Within? | Lines In The Sky | Tout Passe | Badobe Ya | All Is Gone | Il Est Trop Tarde | I've Got You Under My Skin

Sandhausen, rec. 13.-16.5.1999
Verny,Cécile (shaker,voc) | Erchinger,Andreas (p,synth) | Heizler,Bernd (b) | Daneck,Matthias (xyl,dr,perc)

CHRDM 71011 | CD | Live At Birdland Neuburg
Enrico Rava With The Michael Flügel Quartet
Diva | My Funny Valentine | You Don't Know What Love Is | Secrets | East Broadway Run Down | Certi Angoli Secreti
Live at 'Birdland',Neuburg/Donau, rec. 23.10.1999
Rava,Enrico (tp) | Flügel,Michael (p) | Lauber,Frank (as) | Fuhr,Dietmar (b) | Terzic,Dejan (dr)

CHRDM 71012 | CD | Talk Of The Town
Lajos Dudas Quintet
A Foggy Day(In London Town) | Pirouette | Urban Blues
Köln, rec. November 1999
Dudas,Lajos (cl) | Berger,Karl (vib) | Van Endert,Philipp (g) | Jones,Leonard (b) | Billker,Kurt (dr)
Lajos Dudas Sextet
Where's That Summer | Let's Call The Whole Thing Off
Dudas,Lajos (cl) | Berger,Karl (vib) | Van Endert,Philipp (g) | Jones,Leonard (b) | Billker,Kurt (dr) | Büttner,Jochen (perc)
Lajos Dudas Quintet
In Your Own Sweet Way
Dudas,Lajos (cl) | Van Endert,Philipp (g) | Jones,Leonard (b) | Billker,Kurt (dr) | Büttner,Jochen (perc)
Lajos Dudas Trio
Children At Play | Gloomy Sunday | Valse Hot
Dudas,Lajos (cl) | Van Endert,Philipp (g) | Büttner,Jochen (perc)

CHRDM 71013 | CD | You'll See
Anke Helfrich Trio With Mark Turner
Upper Westside | Pannonica | You'll See | Alone Together | Song For Larry | Start Up! | Take Care | September In The Rain | When I Fall In Love
NYC, rec. January 1999
Helfrich,Anke (p) | Turner,Mark (ts) | Weidenmüller,Johannes (b) | Rückert,Jochen (dr)

CHRDM 71014 | CD | Live At Birdland Neuburg
Lee Konitz-Kenny Wheeler Quartet
Lennies | Where Do We Go From Here | Kind Folk | Thingin | Sternenblume | On Mo | Olden Times | Aldebaran | Play Fiddle Play | Kary's Trance
Live at 'Birdland',Neuburg/Donau, rec. November 1999
Wheeler,Kenny (tp,fl-h) | Konitz,Lee (as) | Wunsch,Frank (p) | Plümer,Gunnar (b)

CHRDM 71015 | CD | Echoes Of Blue
Marion Brown & Jazz Cussion
Mirante Do Vale | Naima | Little Sunflower | You Don't Know What Love Is | Prelude To A Kiss | Polka Dots And Moonbeams | Once I Loved
Göttingen, rec. 2000
Brown,Marion (as) | Möhring,Michel (g,berimbau,balafon,perc) | Krug,Peter (b) | Nawothnig,Bernd (dr) | Kropp,Wolfgang (perc,congas)
Echoes Of Blue
Brown,Marion (as) | Möhring,Michel (g) | Krug,Peter (b)
Stella By Starlight
Möhring,Michel (g) | Krug,Peter (b) | Nawothnig,Bernd (dr)

CHRDM 71016 | CD | Tales Of 2 Cities
Walter Lang Quintet
Far Away Clouds | Hear What I Mean | Prelude To Club Vinyl | Club Vinyl | A Day At The Races | Rue De Lafayette | Minesan's Dream | Jubilation | Something Else | Swimming In The Mist
Thorstadl,Obing, rec. 28.9.1999
Lang,Walter (p) | Tuscher,Peter (tp) | Rössle,Ekkehard (ss,ts) | Höfler,Karoline (b) | Hollander,Rick (dr)

CHRDM 71017 | CD | Joana's Dance
Johannes Mössinger-Wolfgang Lackerschmid
Again And Again | Memories | Shoe It Yourself | Ugly Beauty | Suite 4-2-5: | Aleppo | Desert View | Joana's Dance,Epilog | Stundenwalzer | Canadian Domino | Nimm Zwei | Volta Trais
Augsburg, rec. 21.-23.6.2000
Lackerschmid,Wolfgang (vib) | Mössinger,Johannes (p)

CHRDM 71018 | CD | Face To Face
Chico Freeman & Franco Ambrosetti Meet Reto Weber Percussion Orchestra
Monsieur Sel | For Your Ears Only | Tripti | Face To Face | Danke Bestens
Live at 'Jazzfest',Berlin, rec. November 1999
Ambrosetti,Franco (tp,fl-h) | Freeman,Chico (ss,ts) | Weber,Reto (dr,perc) | Balasubramoniam,Musthwamy (mridangam) | Chemirani,Djamchid (zarb) | Addy,Mustapha Tettey (african-perc)

CHRDM 71019 | CD | An Encounter With Higher Forces
Muneer B.Fennell & The Rhythm String Band
Anti Ego Groove | Big Inside | Bourelly's Brush Stroke | Papalongi | Japanese Flute & Raindrops | It Don't Mean A Thing If It Ain't Got That Swing | Running After This & That | Bourelly Broad Stroke | And Peace Is A Lonely Quest Together | Gently Rocking The Boat | On Mediterian Waves | Inscenes | And Other | Mysteries Unfolding
Live At The 'Vorderhaus',Freiburg, rec. 13.-16.11.2000
Fennell,Munner Bernhard (cello,perc,balafon,voc) | Adams,Dwight (tp,fl-h) | Tenda,Toru (alto-fl,piccolo,japanese-fl,bass-fl) | Bourelly,Jean-Paul (el-g) | Blake,John (v) | Betsch,John (dr)

CHRDM 71020 | CD | Jubilee Edition
Mihaly Tabany Orchestra
Night And Day- | Sonny Boy-
Budapest, rec. 1962
Dudas,Lajos (as) | Wirth,Rudolf (cl) | Bergendy,Istvan (as) | Varady,György (ts) | Bergendy,Peter (ts) | Tabany,Mihaly (accordin,ld) | Tihany,Peter (p) | Kovacev,Branislav (dr) | Pege,Aladar (b) | Kovac,Gyola (dr)
Lajos Dudas Group
Blues
Köln, rec. 1968
Dudas,Lajos (ss) | Weissbach,Bela (tp) | details unknown
Lajos Dudas Quintet
Csardas Macabre
details unknown, rec. details unknown
Dudas,Lajos (as) | Bünting,Erhard (g) | Herting,Michael (el-p,synth) | Haurand,Ali (b) | Szudy,Janos (dr,perc)
Lamentation
Dudas,Lajos (ss) | Szudy,Janos (dr,perc)
Lajos Dudas Trio
Deep Purple | Mistral
Dudas,Lajos (cl) | Stoykov,Teodossi (b) | Bilker,Kurt (dr)
Lajos Dudas Quartet
Benny
Dudas,Lajos (cl) | Vig,Tommy (vib) | Stoykov,Teodossi (b) | Szudy,Janos (dr)
The Gambler
Köln, rec. details unknown
Dudas,Lajos (cl) | Zoller,Attila (g) | Thompson,Bert (b) | Bilker,Kurt (dr)
Surfriding
Dudas,Lajos (cl) | Hartmann,Ernst G. (keyboards) | Stoykov,Teodossi (b) | Köszegi,Imre (dr)
Lajos Dudas Quintet
Pacific Coast Highway
Dudas,Lajos (cl) | Blanke,Toto (g) | Hartmann,Ernst G. (keyboards) | Stoykov,Teodossi (b) | Köszegi,Imre (dr)
Lajos Dudas Quartet
Back To L.A.
Dudas,Lajos (cl) | Blanke,Toto (g) | Hartmann,Ernst G. (b-synth) | Köszegi,Imre (dr)
Lajos Dudas Quintet
Change Of Time
Baden-Baden, rec. details unknown
Dudas,Lajos (cl) | Sparla,Hans (tb) | Wainapel,Harvey (as) | Rek,Vitold (b) | Tarasov,Vladimir (dr)
Radio Jazzgroup Frankfurt
Blueduette
Frankfurt/M, rec. details unknown
Radio Jazzgroup Frankfurt | Mangelsdorff,Albert (tb) | Dudas,Lajos (cl) |
Ponzol,Peter (as) | Sauer,Heinz (ts) | Lauer,Christof (ts) | Freund,Joki (ts) | Becker,Markus (p) | Lenz,Günter (b) | Hübner,Ralf-R. (dr)

CHRDM 71022 | CD | Black Box
Christy Doran's New Bag With Muthuswamy Balasubramoniam
Sugarpie | Written In Your Face | Caviar | Structured Clay | Black Box | Pantrova
Zürich,CH, rec. 10.-23.11.2000
Doran,Christy (el-g) | Zwiauerm,Wolfgang (el-b) | Kuratli,Fabian (dr,perc) | Balasubramoniam,Musthwamy (mridangam) | Amstad,Bruno (voc)

CHRDM 71023 | CD | Boom Bop II
Jean-Paul Bourelly Trance Atlantic
The Spirit Wheel
NYC, rec. 1997-2001
Bourelly,Jean-Paul (g,sonic-treatments) | Dara,Olu (co) | Bowie,Joseph (tb) | Henry,Vince (as,ts) | Threadgill,Henry (fl,as) | Bourelly,Carl (synth,programming) | Talamacus,Big Royal (filtered-boom-b) | Chambers,Dennis (dr)
Cool Papa N'Diaye
Bourelly,Jean-Paul (g,sonic-treatments) | Dara,Olu (co) | Bowie,Joseph (tb) | Henry,Vince (as,ts) | Threadgill,Henry (fl,as) | Bourelly,Carl (synth,programming) | Talamacus,Big Royal (filtered-boom-b) | Chambers,Dennis (dr) | Diop,Abdourahmane (voc)
Fatima
Bourelly,Jean-Paul (g,sonic-treatments) | Dara,Olu (co) | Bourelly,Carl (synth,programming) | Workman,Reggie (b) | Calhoun,Will (dr,korg-wave-dr) | Diop,Abdourahmane (voc)
Blowin' Omni
NYC, rec. 1997-201
Bourelly,Jean-Paul (g,sonic-treatments) | Dara,Olu (co) | Bowie,Joseph (tb) | Threadgill,Henry (fl,as) | Bourelly,Carl (synth,programming) | Talamacus,Big Royal (filtered-boom-b) | Calhoun,Will (dr,korg-wave-dr) | Diop,Abdourahmane (voc)
Pluto Launge
NYC, rec. 1997-2001
Bourelly,Jean-Paul (g,sonic-treatments) | Dara,Olu (co) | Bowie,Joseph (tb) | Henry,Vince (as,ts) | Threadgill,Henry (fl,as) | Bourelly,Carl (synth,programming) | Workman,Reggie (b) | Chambers,Dennis (dr)
Thiemo De Conakry
Bourelly,Jean-Paul (g,sonic-treatments) | Dara,Olu (co) | Bowie,Joseph (tb) | Henry,Vince (as,ts) | Threadgill,Henry (fl,as) | Bourelly,Carl (synth,programming) | Talamacus,Big Royal (filtered-boom-b) | Chambers,Dennis (dr) | Calhoun,Will (dr,korg-wave-dr) | Diop,Abdourahmane (voc)
The Scent Of The Healer
Bourelly,Jean-Paul (g,sonic-treatments) | Dara,Olu (co) | Bowie,Joseph (tb) | Henry,Vince (as,ts) | Threadgill,Henry (fl,as) | Bourelly,Carl (synth,programming) | Talamacus,Big Royal (filtered-boom-b) | Chambers,Dennis (dr) | Diop,Abdourahmane (voc)
Harmofuncalodia
Bourelly,Carl (synth,programming) | Talamacus,Big Royal (filtered-boom-b) | Chambers,Dennis (dr)
Trance Atlantic
Bourelly,Jean-Paul (g,sonic-treatments) | Bourelly,Carl (synth,programming) | Gibbs,Melvin (el-b) | Calhoun,Will (dr,korg-wave-dr) | Diop,Abdourahmane (voc)
Myth And Diffusion | Awakening
Bourelly,Carl (synth,programming)
Traffic
Bourelly,Jean-Paul (g,sonic-treatments) | Henry,Vince (as,ts) | Bourelly,Carl (synth,programming) | Talamacus,Big Royal (filtered-boom-b) | Chambers,Dennis (dr)
Freedom Delta
Bourelly,Jean-Paul (g,sonic-treatments) | Bourelly,Carl (synth,programming) | Calhoun,Will (dr,korg-wave-dr)

CHRDM 71024 | CD | Live At Birdland Neuburg
Full Moon Trio
Daily Rose | Sarah's Bande | Lovethings | Monsieur Hulot | Springbirds | There's No Greater Lunch | Chil-Lee
Live at 'Birdland',Neuburg/Donau, rec. December 2000
Full Moon Trio | Lackerschmid,Wolfgang (vib) | Lang,Walter (p) | Holstein,Stephan (cl,as)

CHRDM 71026 | CD | Twilight
Russ Spiegel Group
Jeannine
Mannheim, rec. 16./17.10.2000
Spiegel,Russ (el-g) | Meyers,Christian (tp) | Jacobson,Allen (tb) | James,Derrick (as) | Menendez,Alberto (ts) | Dewinkel,Torsten (g) | Reiter,Joerg (p) | Stabenow,Thomas (b) | Merk,Sebastian (dr) | Plasencia,Omar (perc)
Twilight
Spiegel,Russ (g) | Meyers,Christian (fl-h) | James,Derrick (as) | Seefelder,Jürgen (ts) | Reiter,Joerg (p) | Stabenow,Thomas (b) | Merk,Sebastian (dr)
Giant Steps
Spiegel,Russ (el-g) | Meyers,Christian (tp) | Jacobson,Allen (tb) | James,Derrick (as) | Seefelder,Jürgen (ts) | Reiter,Joerg (p) | Stabenow,Thomas (b) | Merk,Sebastian (dr)
Number One
Spiegel,Russ (el-g) | Meyers,Christian (tp) | James,Derrick (as) | Seefelder,Jürgen (ts) | Reiter,Joerg (p) | Stabenow,Thomas (b) | Merk,Sebastian (dr)
Fourth Floor
Spiegel,Russ (el-g) | Seefelder,Jürgen (ts) | Reiter,Joerg (p) | Stabenow,Thomas (b) | Merk,Sebastian (dr)
Brother Grimm
Spiegel,Russ (el-g) | Reiter,Joerg (p) | Stabenow,Thomas (b) | Merk,Sebastian (dr)
The Night Has A Thousand Eyes
Spiegel,Russ (el-g) | Menendez,Alberto (ts) | Stabenow,Thomas (b) | Merk,Sebastian (dr)
Do Nothin' Till You Hear From Me
Spiegel,Russ (el-g) | Dennerlein,Barbara (org) | Merk,Sebastian (dr)
Peaceful
Spiegel,Russ (g) | Reiter,Joerg (p)

CHRDM 71028 | CD | Kekeli
Cécile Verny Quartet
Kekeli | Drums Call For The Dance | A Gainsbourg | It Could Have Been A Lovely Night | Harvest | Move | Arlequin | The Nearness Of You
Stuttgart, rec. 29.10.-1.11.2001
Verny,Cécile (shaker,voc) | Erchinger,Andreas (p,el-p) | Heizler,Bernd (b) | Krill,Torsten (dr)
Cécile Verny Quintet
Silently Invisibly
Verny,Cécile (shaker,voc) | Rössle,Ekkehard (ss) | Erchinger,Andreas (p,el-p) | Heizler,Bernd (b) | Krill,Torsten (dr)
On Another's Sorrow
Verny,Cécile (shaker,voc) | Kuruc,Frank (g) | Erchinger,Andreas (p,el-p) | Heizler,Bernd (b) | Krill,Torsten (dr)

DMCD 1001-2 | CD | Zeitwärts:Reime Vor Pisin
Peter Kleindienst Group
M IV | Reime Vor Pisin | Zap Zap Zap(für Mutter) | Overdrive | Move(für Ina) | GitMa | Kreise I | Mingus | M V | Kurz Vor Zein | Going Alone | M VI | Searching For The A.M.(contains portions of Reincarnation Of A Lovebird)
Freiburg,Brg., rec. 13.& 17.6.1997
Kleindienst,Peter (g) | Stich,Matthias (b-cl,as,sopranino) | Schweizer,Mike (ss,ts,sopranino) | Döling,Florian (b,el-b) | Dierstein,Christian (marimba,perc) | Lang,Evelyn (voc)

DMCD 1002-2 | CD | Got A Ticket
Cécile Verny Quartet
Sleeping Bee | Hometown Blues | Devil May Care | Listen To The Rainbow | Je Ne Veux Pas Mentir | Got A Ticket | Mina's Song | An Ocean Goes To Sea(or voce e maluco) | Hideaway | African Flower
Staufen im Breisgau, rec. 6.-9.10.1997
Verny,Cécile (claves,shaker,voc) | Erchinger,Andreas (p,synth) | Heitzler,Bernd (b) | Daneck,Matthias (dr)

DMCD 1003-2 | CD | Two Faces
Henning Wolter Trio
Waiting For Angel Eyes | African Child | Bitter Sweet Waltz | Hibble And Hydes | Mystery Trip | Bretagne | Memories Of Tomorrow | Angel Eyes
Monster,NL, rec. 11./12.5.1998
Wolter,Henning (p) | Matheeuwsen,Lucien (b) | Van Cleef,Marcel (dr)
Henning Wolter Trio With Gerd Dudek
My Little Sad Lucie | Two Faces | Terschelling | Just One Hour
Dudek,Gerd (sax) | Wolter,Henning (p) | Matheeuwsen,Lucien (b) | Van Cleef,Marcel (dr)

DMCD 1004-2 | CD | Spring In Versailles
Johannes Mössinger
Warrior | Monk's Mood | Lush Life | Feuertanz | Spring In Versailles(part 1) | Spring In Versailles(part 2) | Traumbilder | Voice Of A Lion | Little Niles | Interludium | Date In The Morning | Wandlungen | Giant Steps | Memories
Schallstadt, rec. February-April 1998
Mössinger,Johannes (p-solo)

DMCD 1005-2 | CD | Some Great Songs
Lajos Dudas Quintet
This Masquerade | I Remember Clifford | All The Things You Are | Days Of Wine And Roses | Caravan | West Coast | Mouse | A Thousand Dreams | Don't Forgett Fatty | How High The Moon | Zugabe
Live at AtM Studio,Köln, rec. September 1998
Dudas,Lajos (cl) | Van Endert,Philipp (g) | Jones,Leonard (b) | Billker,Kurt (dr) | Büttner,Jochen (perc)

DMCD 1006-2 | CD | Neurotransmitter
Achim Jaroschek-Peter Brötzmann
Brain Change | Vagus | Mirror Act
Krefeld, rec. details unknown
Brötzmann,Peter (sax) | Jaroschek,Achim (grand-p)

DMCD 1008-2 | CD | Jazzchanson 20th Century Suite
Stephan-Max Wirth Quartet
Koffer In Berlin | Non,Je Ne Regrette Rien- | Mehir 1- | Honey,Wenn Du Geburtstag Hast | Duch Feelings- | Mehir 2- | Sans Chant | Mehir 3- | Seidenduft- | Lola | Vivre Avec Toi | Ne Me Quitte Pas
Köln, rec. 4./6.9.1998
Wirth,Stephan-Max (ts,voc) | Speight,Martin (p) | Wienstroer,Konstantin (b) | Hillmann,Christoph (dr)
Parole,Parole
Wirth,Stephan-Max (ts,voc) | Speight,Martin (p) | Wienstroer,Konstantin (b) | Hillmann,Christoph (dr) | Chabrier,Mlle.E. (?)

DMCHR 71021 | CD | Years Of A Trilogy
Henning Wolter Trio With Guests
7x2 New Orleans | Lucien's Sweet Suite | Via Ronco | Normandie | Lonely Voyager | The Voyager Returns | Karen's Call | Everything Reminds Me On You | Peja | Septology
Monster,NL, rec. 13./14.11.2000
Wolter,Henning (p) | Vloeimans,Eric (tp) | Dudek,Gerd (ss) | Matheeuwsen,Lucien (b) | Van Cleef,Marcel (dr,perc)

DMCHR 71025 | CD | Clara's Smile | EAN 608917102529
Christian Scheuber Quartet
Ckara's Smile | I Hear A Rhapsody | When Will I Loose My Memory | Questions Without Answer | Think Of One
Köln, rec. November 2000
Scheuber,Christian (dr) | Bollenback,Paul (g) | Kondakov,Andrei (p) | Genus,James (b)
Christian Scheuber Quintet
On The Road | Joyeses Farces
Scheuber,Christian (dr) | Witzel,Reiner (as) | Bollenback,Paul (g) | Kondakov,Andrei (p) | Genus,James (b)
Don't Let Me Go | Song For Claudia
Scheuber,Christian (dr) | Ker-Ourio,Oliver (harm) | Bollenback,Paul (g) | Kondakov,Andrei (p) | Genus,James (b)

DMCHR 71030 | CD | Nightlight | EAN 608917103021
Lajos Dudas Quartet
Bouree(BWV 966) | Sunday Afternoon | The Lady Is A Tramp | I'll Remember April | Bagpiper
details unknown, rec. January 2002
Dudas,Lajos (cl) | Van Endert,Philipp (g) | Gjakonovski,Martin (b) | Billker,Kurt (dr)
Lajos Dudas Quintet
All Of Me | Folk Song | Journey To Recife | Like Sonny | Filthy McNasty
Dudas,Lajos (cl) | Dudek,Gerd (fl,ss) | Van Endert,Philipp (g) | Gjakonovski,Martin (b) | Billker,Kurt (dr)

DMCHR 71032 | CD | Monk's Corner | EAN 608917103229
Johannes Mössinger New York Trio
Bemsha Swing | I Mean You | Well You Needn't | Monk's Dream | Back Up | Monk's Mood | Criss Cross | Tango Du Soleil
Augsburg, rec. October 2001
Mössinger,Johannes (p) | Klaiber,German (b) | Latham,Karl (dr)
Johannes Mössinger New York Trio with Joe Lovano
Quirilunga
NYC, rec. May 2002
Mössinger,Johannes (p) | Lovano,Joe (sax) | Klaiber,German (b) | Latham,Karl (dr)
Brilliant Corners | Twilight
Mössinger,Johannes (p) | Lovano,Joe (sax) | Driscoll,Kermit (b) | Latham,Karl (dr)

DMCHR 71033 | CD | Elements | EAN 608917103328
Balance
Third Rail | Elements | Rainfall | Q | Trance Angle | Yellow Umbrella | Feather One's Nest
Köln, rec. details unknown
Balance | Sprenger,Raphael (tp) | Koch,Michael (keyboards,el-p) | Schäfers,Michael (b) | Bürger,Michael 'Bamy' (dr) | DJ Kaspar (turntables,perc)
Cote D'Azur
Balance | Sprenger,Raphael (tp) | Koch,Michael (keyboards,el-p) | Schäfers,Michael (b) | Bürger,Michael 'Bamy' (dr) | DJ Kaspar (turntables,perc) | Turbo B. (spoken words)

DMCHR 71034 | CD | Coming Up | EAN 608917103427
Dejan Terzic European Assembly
Soft Aberration | Tectonic | Ardor | Well,Add Black | Virgo | Steal Your Licks
Ludwigsburg, rec. 5.3.2001
Terzic,Dejan (dr) | Winther,Jens (tp) | Lakatos,Tony (sax) | Farao,Antonio (p) | Gjakonovski,Martin (b)
Coming Up | Position Konkret | New Start | Summer 86
Ludwigsburg, rec. 27.5.2001
Terzic,Dejan (dr) | Winther,Jens (tp) | Lakatos,Tony (sax) | Farao,Antonio (p) | Gjakonovski,Martin (b)

Dragon | Fenn Music

DRCD 221 | CD | George Lewis In Stockholm,1959
George Lewis And His Original New Orleans Jazzmen
Should I | Royal Garden Blues | Burgundy Street Blues | Red Wing | Lord Lord Lord You've Sure Been Good To Me | Tin Roof Blues | Runnin' Wild | Milneberg Joys | Tishomingo Blues | Nobody Knows The Way I Feel This Morning | Mahogany Hall Stomp | Over The Waves
Live at Concert Hall,Stockholm,Sweden, rec. 10.2.1959
Lewis,George (cl) | Howard,Avery 'Kid' (tp,voc) | Robinson,Jim (tb) | Robichaux,Joe (p) | Pavageau,Alcide 'Slow Drag' (b) | Watkins,Joe (dr,voc)

DRCD 224 | CD | Lars Gullin 1955/56 Vol.1
Lars Gullin Quartet
Danny's Dream
Live at Concert Hall,Stockholm,Sweden, rec. 25.4.1955
Gullin,Lars (bs) | Berg,Rolf (g) | Riedel,Georg (b) | Bosse,Stoor (dr)
Lars Gullin Quintet
Igloo | Last Meet Jeff
Gullin,Lars (p) | Billberg,Rolf (ts) | Berg,Rolf (g) | Riedel,Georg (b) | Bosse,Stoor (dr)
Lars Gullin And The Chet Baker Quartet
Cool Blues | Brash | Lover Man(Oh,Where Can You Be?)

Stuttgart, rec. 15.10.1955
Baker,Chet (tp) | Gullin,Lars (bs) | Twardzik,Dick (p) | Bond,Jimmy (b) | Littman,Peter (dr)
I'll Remember April
Baker,Chet (tp) | Gullin,Lars (bs) | Twardzik,Dick (p) | Bond,Jimmy (b) | Littman,Peter (dr) | Valente,Caterina (voc)
Lars Gullin Quartet
All Of Me | Like Someone In Love | Jeepers Creepers | You Go To My Head
Sundbyberg,Sweden, rec. 24.4.1956
Gullin,Lars (bs) | Öfwerman,Rune (p) | Carlsson,Bengt (b) | Dahlander,Nils-Bertil (dr)
Lars Gullin Octet
Fedja | Ma | Perntz
Stockholm,Sweden, rec. 31.5.1956
Gullin,Lars (bs) | Olsson,Gordon (tb) | Domnerus,Arne (cl,as) | Nerem,Bjarne (ts) | Jansson,Lennart (bs) | Svensson,Gunnar (p) | Riedel,Georg (b) | Johansen,Egil (dr)

DRCD 228 | CD | Live In Stockholm
Miles Davis Quintet
If I Were A Bell | All Of You | Walkin' | All Blues | The Theme | No Blues | On Green Dolphin Street
Konserthuset,Stockholm, rec. 13.10.1960
Davis,Miles (tp) | Stitt,Sonny (as,ts) | Kelly,Wynton (p) | Chambers,Paul (b) | Cobb,Jimmy (dr)

DRCD 229 | CD | St.Thomas:Sonny Rollins In Stockhom 1959
Sonny Rollins Trio
St.Thomas
Live at Nalen,Sweden, rec. 2.3.1959
Rollins,Sonny (ts) | Grimes,Henry (b) | LaRoca,Pete (dr)
There'll Never Be Another You | Stay As Sweet As You Are | I've Told Every Little Star | How High The Moon | Oleo | Paul's Pal
Live at The Swedish Radio,Stockholm, rec. 4.3.1959
Rollins,Sonny (ts) | Grimes,Henry (b) | LaRoca,Pete (dr)
It Don't Mean A Thing If It Ain't Got That Swing | Paul's Pal | Love Letters
Live at Södra Teatern,Stockholm, rec. 4.3.1959
Rollins,Sonny (ts) | Grimes,Henry (b) | Harris,Joe (dr)
Sonny Rollins
Interview
Stockholm,Sweden, rec. 4.3.1959
Rollins,Sonny (talking)

DRCD 234 | CD | Lars Gullin 1953,Vol.2:Moden Sounds
Lars Gullin With The Wade Legge Trio
All The Things You Are | The Squirrel
Stockholm,Sweden, rec. 3.2.1953
Gullin,Lars (bs) | Legge,Wade (p) | Hackney,Lou (b) | Jones,Al (dr)
Rita Reys With The Lars Gullin Quartet
'Deed I Do | Over The Rainbow | Lullaby In Rhythm | He's Funny That Way
Stockholm,Sweden, rec. 2.3.1953
Reys,Rita (voc) | Gullin,Lars (as,bs) | Svensson,Gunnar (p) | Brehm,Simon (b) | Ilcken,Wessel (dr)
Lars Gullin Quartet
You Go To My Head | The Things We Did Last Summer | Ablution | Ladyfingers
Stockholm,Sweden, rec. 11.3.1953
Gullin,Lars (bs) | Lindblom,Putte (p) | Akerberg,Yngve (b) | Noren,Jack (dr)
Lars Gullin Quintet
The Front | The Boy Next Door | North Express | Hershey Bar
Stockholm,Sweden, rec. 31.3.1953
Gullin,Lars (as,bs) | Renliden,Weine (tp) | Lindblom,Putte (p) | Riedel,Georg (b) | Noren,Jack (dr)
Lars Gullin Quartet
That Old Black Magic | They Didn't Believe Me
Stockholm,Sweden, rec. 16.4.1953
Gullin,Lars (bs) | Lindblom,Putte (p) | Riedel,Georg (b) | Stoor,Bosse (dr)
Kettil Ohlsson Quintet
Night And Day | Chloe
Stockholm,Sweden, rec. 8.7.1953
Ohlsson,Kettil (bs) | Gullin,Lars (as) | Lindblom,Putte (p) | Pettersson,Lars (b) | Stoor,Bosse (dr)
Lars Gullin American All Stars
Dedicated To Lee | Dedicated To Lee(alt.take) | Late Date
Stockholm,Sweden, rec. 25.8.1953
Gullin,Lars (bs) | Candoli,Conte (tp) | Rosolino,Frank (tb) | Konitz,Lee (as) | Sims,Zoot (ts) | Bagley,Don (b) | Levey,Stan (dr)
Lars Gullin With The Bob Laine Trio
Love Me Or Leave Me
Stockholm,Sweden, rec. 21.10.1953
Gullin,Lars (bs) | Laine,Bob (p) | Brehm,Simon (b) | Noren,Jack (dr)
Jack Noren Quartet
Yvette | You Go To My Head
Helsinki, Finland, rec. 1.12.1953
Noren,Jack (dr) | Gullin,Lars (bs) | Olsson,Mats (p) | Suojärvi,Tauno (b)

DRCD 265 | CD | Coleman Hawkins At The Golden Circle
Coleman Hawkins With The Göran Lindberg Trio
Introduction | Oh! Lady Be Good | If I Had You | Bean And The Boys | Ow! | All The Things You Are | It's The Talk Of The Town
Live at The Golden Circle,Stockholm, rec. 29.1.&1.2.1963
Hawkins,Coleman (ts) | Lindberg,Göran (p) | Lindgren,Kurt (b) | Carlsson,Rune (dr)
Coleman Hawkins With The Adrian Acea Trio
Body And Soul
Live at Stockholm Concert Hall,Sweden, rec. 2.10.1954
Hawkins,Coleman (ts) | Acea,Adrian (p) | Lucas,Al (b) | Johnson,Osie (dr)
Coleman Hawkins With The Thore Ehrlings Orchestra
Body And Soul | The Man I Love
Live at Stockholm Concert Hall,Sweden, rec. 23.1.1950
Hawkins,Coleman (ts) | prob.personal: | Törner,Gösta (tp) | Johansson,Arnold (tp) | Linder,John (tp) | Vernon,George (tb) | Domnerus,Arne (as) | Gabrielsson,Stig (as) | Arnold,Harry (ts) | Blomquist,Curt (bs) | Holm,Stig (p) | Tellemar,Hasse (b) | Frylmark,Bertil (dr)

DRCD 366 | CD | Ejs Thelin 1966 With Barney Wilen | EAN 7391953003662
Eje Thelin Group
Pam Kan | To A Moment Of Truth | Doj-Doj | Forever
Stockholm,Sweden, rec. March 1966
Thelin,Eje (tb) | Wilen,Barney (ts) | Sjösten,Lars (p) | Lundborg,Erik (b) | Carlsson,Rune (dr) | (unkn. 3 tb,fl, b-cl)
Eje Thelin Quartet
Doj-Doj | To A Moment Of Truth | It Could Happen To You | Ack Värmeland Du Sköna | Fast
Live at Dans In,Gröna Lund,Stockholm,Sweden, rec. 18.7.1966
Thelin,Eje (tb) | Wilen,Barney (ss,ts) | Danielsson,Palle (b) | Carlsson,Rune (dr)

DRCD 374 | CD | At The German Jazz Festival 1964 | EAN 7391953003747
Eje Thelin Quintet
The Opener | It Ain't Necessarily So | Filmballad | I'm Old Fashioned | Gasoline My Beloved | Marquese De Villamagna | What Is This Thing Called Love
Live at The Deutsches Jazz Fesival Frankfurt/M., rec. 9.5.1964
Thelin,Eje (tb) | Andersson,Ulf (ts) | Vandroogenbroeck,Joel (p,fl) | Dylag,Roman (b) | Carlsson,Rune (dr)

DRCD 378 | CD | Time To Remember | EAN 7391953003785
Putte Wickman And The Hal Galper trio
I'll Remember April | A Dear One | But Not For Me | After The Storm | Up With The Lark | I Thought About You | Miss Oidipus | A Dear One(alt.take)
Stockholm,Sweden, rec. 19.11.1986
Wickman,Putte (cl) | Galper,Hal (p) | Gilmore,Steve (b) | Goodwin,Bill (dr)

DRCD 380 | CD | Lars Gullin 1951/52 Vol.5:First Walk | EAN 7391953003808
Lars Gullin Quartet
That's It | Gull In A Gulch | All Yours | Deep Purple
Stockholm,Sweden, rec. 21.2.1951
Gullin,Lars (bs) | Hallberg,Bengt (p) | Almsted,Gunnar (b) | Noren,Jack (dr)
Lars Gullin Octet
Danny-O | Laura | All God's Children | Blue Lou
Stockholm,Sweden, rec. 21.4.1951
Gullin,Lars (bs) | Ericson,Rolf (tp) | Persson,Ake (tb) | Sundevall,Leppe (tenor-h) | Bergström,Jonas (as) | Olsson,Mat | Wittström,Bengt (b) | Dahlander,Nils-Bertil (dr)
Lars Gullin Quartet
Dancing In The Dark | Alone
Stockholm,Sweden, rec. September 1951
Gullin,Lars (bs) | Svensson,Gunnar (p) | Akerberg,Yngve (b) | Noren,Jack (dr)
The Continental | I Got It Bad And That Ain't Good | Dancing In The Dark | Alone
Stockholm,Sweden, rec. 9.10.1951
Gullin,Lars (bs) | Svensson,Gunnar (p) | Akerberg,Yngve (b) | Noren,Jack (dr)
All The Things You Are | Mean To Me
Stockholm,Sweden, rec. 1.11.1952
Gullin,Lars (bs) | Westberg,Ingemar (p) | Wittström,Bengt (b) | Burman,Anders 'Andrew' (dr)
Lars Gullin Quintet
Dorica | I'll Remember April
Stockholm,Sweden, rec. 19.1.1952
Gullin,Lars (bs) | Svensson,Gunnar (p) | Akerberg,Yngve (b) | Noren,Jack (dr)
Lars Gullin Sextet
Who Sleeps
Gullin,Lars (bs) | Björkman,Ake (fr-h) | Blomquist,Rolf (ts) | Svensson,Gunnar (p) | Akerberg,Yngve (b) | Noren,Jack (dr)
First Walk
Gullin,Lars (bs) | Persson,Ake (tb) | Björkman,Ake (fr-h) | Svensson,Gunnar (p) | Akerberg,Yngve (b) | Noren,Jack (dr)
Lars Gullin Quartet
Long Ago And Far Away
Stockholm,Sweden, rec. 15.5.1952
Gullin,Lars (bs) | Renliden,Weine (tp) | Svensson,Gunnar (p) | Akerberg,Yngve (b) | Noren,Jack (dr)
Lars Gullin Septet
Liza | Top Hat
Gullin,Lars (bs) | Renliden,Weine (tp) | Björkman,Ake (fr-h) | Lindgren,Carl-Eric (ts) | Svensson,Gunnar (p) | Akerberg,Yngve (b) | Noren,Jack (dr)
Lars Gullin Quintet
Toll Bridge
Gullin,Lars (bs) | Renliden,Weine (tp) | Westberg,Ingemar (p) | Akerberg,Yngve (b) | Noren,Jack (dr)
Lars Gullin Quartet
Smart Aleck | Sov Du Lilla Vide Ung
Stockholm,Sweden, rec. 2.10.1952
Gullin,Lars (bs) | Svensson,Gunnar (p) | Akerberg,Yngve (b) | Noren,Jack (dr)

Dreyfus Jazz Line | Soulfood

FDM 36186-2 | CD | Little Girl Blue
Katia Labeque
Little Girl Blue
Labeque,Katia (p-solo)
Katia Labeque-Chick Corea
We Will Meet Again | Turn Out The Stars
Labeque,Katia (p) | Corea,Chick (p)
Katia Labeque-Herbie Hancock
My Funny Valentine
Labeque,Katia (p) | Hancock,Herbie (p)
Katia Labeque-Marielle Labeque
On Fire
Labeque,Katia (p) | Labeque,Marielle (p)
Katia Labeque-Gonzalo Rubalcaba
Besame Mucho | Prologo Comienzo | Quizas Quizas Quizas
Labeque,Katia (p) | Rubalcaba,Gonzalo (p)
Katia Labeque-Joe Zawinul
Volcano For Hire
Labeque,Katia (p) | Zawinul,Joe (p)
Katia Labeque-Joey DeFrancesco
Summertime
Labeque,Katia (p) | DeFrancesco,Joey (p)
Katia Labeque-Michel Camilo
La Comparsa
Labeque,Katia (p) | Camilo,Michel (p)

FDM 36505-2 | CD | Duo
Charlie Haden/Christian Escoudé
Django | Bolero | Manoir De Mes Reves | Gitane | Nuages | Dinette | Improvisation
Paris,France, rec. 22.9.1978
Escoudé,Christian (g) | Haden,Charlie (b)

FDM 36511-9 | CD | Chet Baker & The Boto Brasilian Quartet
Chet Baker & The Boto Brasilian Quartet
Salsamba | Balsa | Forget Full | Inaia | Seila | Balao | Julinho | Novos Tempos
Paris,France, rec. 21.-23.7.1980
Baker,Chet (tp) | Boto,José (dr,perc) | Galliano,Richard (accordeon) | Pentoja Leite,Riqué (el-p) | Peyratoux,Michel (b-g)

FDM 36513-9 | CD | Spleen
Richard Galliano Quartet
Sexy Dream | Honey Finger | Every Time You're Near | Tea For Toots | For Lolo | Spleen
Paris,France, rec. June 1985
Galliano,Richard (tb,p,el-p,synth,accordeon,accordina) | Stibon,Franck (p,synth,voc) | Jafet,Jean-Marc (b-g) | Augusto,Luiz (dr,per)
Richard Galliano Quintet
Ballade Pour Marion
Galliano,Richard (tb,p,el-p,synth,accordeon,accordina) | Giausserand,Eric (fl-h) | Stibon,Franck (p,voc) | Jafet,Jean-Marc (b-g) | Augusto,Luiz (dr,per)
M.F.
Galliano,Richard (el-p,synth,accordeon,accordina) | Leloup,Denis (tb) | Stibon,Franck (p) | Jafet,Jean-Marc (b-g) | Augusto,Luiz (dr,per)

FDM 36514-2 | CD | Panamanhattan
Ron Carter-Richard Galliano Duo
Summer In Central Park | Spleen | Doom | Allée Des Brouillards | A Small Ballad | Portrait Of Jenny | Ballade Pour Marion | Little Waltz | Des Voiliers
Paris,France, rec. 23.7.1990
Galliano,Richard (accordeon,accordina) | Carter,Ron (b)

FDM 36558-9 | CD | Chet Baker In Bologna
Chet Baker Trio
Conception | My Foolish Heart | Tune Up | My Funny Valentine | But Not For Me | Down
Live at Teatro Delle Celebrazione,Bologna, rec. 20.4.1985
Baker,Chet (tp) | Catherine,Philip (g) | Rassinfosse,Jean-Louis (b)

FDM 36559-2 | CD | Nostalgia In Times Square
Mingus Big Band 93
Nostalgia In Time Square | Moanin' | Self-Portrait In 3 Colors | Don't Be Afraid,The Clown's Afraid,Too | Duke Ellington's Sound Of Love | Weird Nightmare | Open Letter To Duke | Invisible Lady | Ecclusiastics
NYC, rec. 1./2.3.1993
Mingus Big Band 93 | Brecker,Randy (tp) | Kisor,Ryan (tp) | Soloff,Lew (tp) | Walrath,Jack (tp) | Kase,Christopher (tp) | Baron,Art (tb) | Burtis,Sam (tb) | Lacy,Ku-umba Frank (tb) | Taylor,Dave (b-tb,tuba) | Foster,Alex (as) | Slagle,Steve (as) | Potter,Chris (as,ts) | Stubblefield,John (ts) | Handy,Craig (ts) | Cuber,Ronnie (bs) | Rosenberg,Roger (bs) | Drew Jr.,Kenny (p) | Formanek,Michael (b) | McKee,Andy (b) | Smith,Marvin 'Smitty' (dr) | Jones,Victor (dr) | Mantilla,Ray (congas)
Mingus Fingers
Mingus Big Band 93 | Brecker,Randy (tp) | Kisor,Ryan (tp) | Soloff,Lew (tp) | Walrath,Jack (tp) | Kase,Christopher (tp) | Baron,Art (tb) | Burtis,Sam (tb) | Lacy,Ku-umba Frank (tb) | Taylor,Dave (b-tb,tuba) | Foster,Alex (as) | Slagle,Steve (as) | Potter,Chris (as,ts) | Stubblefield,John (ts) | Handy,Craig (ts) | Cuber,Ronnie (bs) | Rosenberg,Roger (bs) | Locke,Joe (vib) | Drew Jr.,Kenny (p) | Formanek,Michael (b) | McKee,Andy (b) | Smith,Marvin 'Smitty' (dr) | Jones,Victor (dr) | Mantilla,Ray (congas)

FDM 36560-2 | CD | The Sun Don't Lie
Marcus Miller Group
Panther
Miller,Marcus (b-cl,g,keyboards,b-g,dr-programming) | Brown,Dean (g) | Bell,Poogie (dr) | White,Lenny (perc) | Miles,Jason (sound-programming)
Steveland
Miller,Marcus (b-cl,g,keyboards,b-g,dr-programming) | Sanborn,David (as) | Shorter,Wayne (ts) | Butler,Jonathan (g) | White,Lenny (dr) | Alias,Don (perc) | Da Costa,Paulinho (perc) | Miles,Jason (sound-programming)
Rampage
Miller,Marcus (g,keyboards,b-g,dr-programming) | Davis,Miles (tp) | Marquez,Sal (tp) | Reid,Vernon (g) | Calhoun,Will (dr) | Miles,Jason (sound-programming)
The Sun Don't Lie
Miller,Marcus (keyboards,b-g) | Sample,Joe (p) | White,Michael (dr) | Narell,Andy (steel-dr) | Da Costa,Paulinho (perc) | Persing,Eric (sound-programming)
Scoop
Miller,Marcus (b-cl,keyboards,perc,b-g,dr-programming) | Garrett,Kenny (as) | Jackson,Paul (g) | White,Maurice (voc-samples)
Mr.Pastorius
Miller,Marcus (b-g)
Funny(All She Needs Is Love)
Miller,Marcus (b-cl,g,keyboards,b-g,voc) | Stewart,Michael (tp) | Harp,Everett (ss) | Brown,Dean (g) | Bell,Poogie (dr) | Thornton,Steve (perc) | Persing,Eric (sound-programming) | Miles,Jason (sound-programming)
Moons
Miller,Marcus (b-cl,keyboards,perc,b-g,dr-programming)
Teen Town
Miller,Marcus (b-cl,b-g) | Bullock,Hiram (g) | Saisse,Phillippe (keyboards) | Ferrone,Steve (dr,perc) | Hakim,Omar (dr,perc) | Alias,Don (congas) | Narell,Andy (steel-dr) | Da Costa,Paulinho (perc)
Juju
Miller,Marcus (g,keyboards,b-g,perc-programming) | Harp,Everett (as) | Whalum,Kirk (ts) | Wight,Christian (keyboards) | Bell,Poogie (dr) | White,Michael (dr) | Persing,Eric (sound-programming) | Saisse,Phillippe (sound-programming) | Miller,Jonathan 'Juici' (voice) | Miller,Julian 'Juju' (voice)
The King Is Gone(for Miles)
Miller,Marcus (b-cl,keyboards,b-g) | Shorter,Wayne (ss,ts) | Williams,Tony (dr) | Persing,Eric (sound-programming)
-> Recorded at different places

FDM 36562-9 | CD | Viaggio
Richard Galliano Quartet
Waltz For Nicky | Java Indigo | Viaggio | Billie-Doo | Tango Pour Claude | Christopher's Bossa | Coloriage | Romance | Little Muse | La Liberte Est Un Fleur
Paris,France, rec. 21.-23.6.1993
Galliano,Richard (p,accordeon,accordina) | Lagrene,Bireli (g,el-g) | Michelot,Pierre (b) | Bellonzi,Charles (dr)

FDM 36564-2 | CD | Marvellous
Michel Petrucciani With The Graffiti String Quartet
Manhattan | Charlie Brown | Even Mice Dance | Why | Hidden Joy | Shooting Stars | You Are My Waltz | Dumb Breaks | 92's Last | Besame Mucho
Paris,France, rec. ca.1994
Petrucciani,Michel (p) | Holland,Dave (b) | Williams,Tony (dr) | Graffiti String Quartet | Pagliarin,Vincent (v) | Krassik,Nicolas (v) | Lemarchand,Pierre (viola) | Courtois,Vincent (cello)

FDM 36570-2 | 2 CD | Au Theatre Des Champ-Elysees(Paris Concert)
Michel Petrucciani
Medley Of My Favorite Songs | Night Sun In Blois | Radio Dial- | These Foolish Things Remind Me On You- | I Mean You- | Round About Midnight- | Even Mice Dance- | Caravan- | Love Letter | Besame Mucho
Live at The Theatre Des Champs-Elysees,Paris,France, rec. 14.11.1994
Petrucciani,Michel (p-solo)

FDM 36571-2 | CD | Tales
Marcus Miller Group
Tales
Miller,Marcus (synth,b-g,dr-programming,sound-programming) | Stewart,Michael (tp) | Garrett,Kenny (as) | Wright,Bernard (clavinet) | Bell,Poogie (dr) | Ward,David 'The Cat' (sound-programming) | Pointer Sisters,The (voc-samples)
Tales(reprise)
Miller,Marcus (synth,b-g,dr-programming,sound-programming) | Stewart,Michael (tp) | Garrett,Kenny (as) | Wright,Bernard (clavinet) | Bell,Poogie (dr) | Ward,David 'The Cat' (sound-programming) | Pointer Sisters,The (voc-samples) | Sample,Joe (rap)
Eric
Miller,Marcus (g,org,synth,b-g,dr-programming,sound-programming,wurlitzer-p) | Garrett,Kenny (as) | Bullock,Hiram (g) | Wright,Bernard (org) | Bell,Poogie (dr) | White,Lenny (dr) | Ward,David 'The Cat' (sound-programming) | Gale,Eric (voice-recording)
True Geminis
Miller,Marcus (b-cl,g,b-g,dr-programming,sound-programming) | Stewart,Michael (tp) | Garrett,Kenny (as) | Redman,Joshua (ts) | Miles,Jason (sound-programming) | Davis,Miles (voice-recording)
Rush Over
Miller,Marcus (b-cl,keyboards,b-g,sound-programming) | Bell,Poogie (dr) | NdegéOcello,Me'Shell (synth,voc)
Running Through My Dreams(Interlude)
Miller,Marcus (keyboards,african-fl,b-g,dr-programming,sound-programming) | Ward,David 'The Cat' (sound-programming)
Ethiopia
Miller,Marcus (b-cl,synth,b-g,dr-programming) | Stewart,Michael (tp) | Garrett,Kenny (as) | Wright,Bernard (marimba,synth) | Bell,Poogie (dr) | Johnson,Bashiri (perc-samples)
Strange Fruit
Miller,Marcus (b-cl,synth,sound-programming) | Ward,David 'The Cat' (sound-programming)
Visions
Miller,Marcus (b-cl,keyboards,b-g,dr-programming,sound-programming) | Stewart,Michael (tp) | Garrett,Kenny (as) | Bell,Poogie (dr) | Ward,David 'The Cat' (sound-programming)
Brazilian Rhyme
Miller,Marcus (keyboards,b-g,sound-programming) | Stewart,Michael (tp) | Garrett,Kenny (as) | Wright,Bernard (synth) | Bell,Poogie (dr) | Hathaway,Lalah (voc) | Ward,David 'The Cat' (sound-programming)
For Evermore
Miller,Marcus (keyboards,b-g,dr-programming,sound-programming,voice-recording) | Stewart,Michael (tp) | Bell,Poogie (dr) | Ward,David 'The Cat' (sound-programming)
Infatuation
Miller,Marcus (keyboards,b-g,dr-programming,sound-programming,voc-samples) | Garrett,Kenny (as) | Wright,Bernard (el-p) | Hathaway,Lalah (voc) | Ward,David 'The Cat' (sound-programming)
Come Together
Miller,Marcus (g,b-g,dr-programming,voc-samples) | Stewart,Michael (tp) |

Garrett,Kenny (as) | Brown,Dean (g) | Wright,Bernard (synth) | Bell,Poogie (dr) | Ward,David 'The Cat' (sound-programming) | Miller,Jonathan 'Juici' (voice) | Miller,Julian 'Juju' (voice)
-> Recorded at different places

FDM 36572-9 | CD | Laurita
Richard Galliano Group
Libertango | La Javanaise | Blue | Mr.Clifton | Marutcha
Paris,France, rec. November 1994
Galliano,Richard (accordeon) | Danielsson,Palle (b) | Baron,Joey (dr)
Giselle | Laurita
Galliano,Richard (accordeon) | Thielemans,Jean 'Toots' (harm) | Danielsson,Palle (b) | Baron,Joey (dr)
Leo, Estante Num Instante
Galliano,Richard (accordeon) | Portal,Michel (b-cl) | Danielsson,Palle (b) | Baron,Joey (dr)
Decisione
Galliano,Richard (accordeon) | Lockwood,Didier (v) | Danielsson,Palle (b) | Baron,Joey (dr)
Milonga Del Angel
Galliano,Richard (accordeon) | Portal,Michel (b-cl) | Lockwood,Didier (v) | Danielsson,Palle (b)

FDM 36574-2 | CD | My Favorite Django
Bireli Lagrene Quartet
Daphne | Moppin' The Bride | Babik | Melodie Au Crepuscule | Place De Brouckere | Nuages | Blues For Ike | Nuits De St.Germain-Des-Pres | Claire De Lune | Troublant Bolero | Solo
NYC, rec. January 1995
Lagrene,Bireli (g,el-g) | Koono (p,synth) | Jackson,Anthony (b) | Chambers,Dennis (dr)

FDM 36580-2 | CD | Flamingo
Stephane Grappelli-Michel Petrucciani Quartet
These Foolish Things Remind Me On You | Little Peace In C For U | Flamingo | Sweet Georgia Brown | I Can't Get Started | I Got Rhythm | I Love New York In June | Misty | I Remember April | Lover Man(Oh,Where Can You Be?) | There'll Never Be Another You | Valse Du Passe
Paris,France, rec. 15.-17.6.1995
Grappelli,Stephane (v) | Petrucciani,Michel (p) | Mraz,George 'Jiri' (b) | Haynes,Roy (dr)

FDM 36581-2 | CD | New York Tango
Richard Galliano Quartet
Vuelvo Al Sur | Soleil | New York Tango | Ten Years Ago | Fou Rire | Sertao | A L'Encre Rouge | Blue Day | Perle | To Django | Three Views Of A Secret
NYC, rec. 11.-13.6.1996
Galliano,Richard (accordeon,accordina) | Lagrene,Bireli (g) | Mraz,George 'Jiri' (b) | Foster,Al (dr)

FDM 36585-2 | CD | Live & More
Marcus Miller Group
Intro | Panther | Tutu | Funny | Strange Fruit | Summertime | Maputo | People Makes The World Go Round | Sophie | Jazz In The House
different Places, rec. July-October 1996
Miller,Marcus (b-cl,ss,g,keyboards,el-b,voc,vocoder) | Stewart,Michael (tp,fl-h) | Garrett,Kenny (ss,as) | Harp,Everett (ts) | Ryam,Roger (ts) | Bullock,Hiram (g) | Brown,Dean (g) | Zingg,Drew (g) | Wright,Bernard (keyboards,b-programming) | Delhomme,Dave (g,keyboards) | Ward,David 'The Cat' (g,keyboards,dr,perc,sound-programming) | Bell,Poogie (dr) | White,Lenny (dr) | Hathaway,Lalah (voc)

FDM 36589-2 | CD | Blow Up
Galliano-Portal
Mozambique | Libertango | Taraf | Little Tango | Oblivion | Chorinho Pra Ele | Ten Years Ago | Viaggio | Leo, Estante Num Instante | Blow-Up
Paris,France, rec. 18./19.5.1996
Galliano,Richard (p,accordeon) | Portal,Michel (cl,b-cl,bandoneon,jazzophone)

FDM 36590-2 | CD | Both Worlds
Michel Petrucciani Sextet
35 Seconds Of Music And More | Brazilian Like | Training | Colors | Petite Louise | Chloé Meets Gershwin | Chimes | Guadeloupe | On Top Of The Roof
NYC, rec. 1997
Petrucciani,Michel (p) | Boltro,Flavio (tp) | Brookmeyer,Bob (v-tb) | Di Battista,Stefano (ss,as) | Jackson,Anthony (b) | Gadd,Steve (dr)

FDM 36591-2 | CD | Blue Eyes | EAN 3460503659124
Bireli Lagrene Quartet
A Foggy Day(In London Town) | Witchcraft | The Lady Is A Tramp | I've Got A Crush On You | My Kind Of Town | I've Got You Under My Skin | It's All Right With Me | You Make Me Feel So Young | Come Fly With Me | Here's That Rainy Day | Luck Be A Lady | April In Paris | Autumn In New York
Paris,France, rec. 9./10.6.1997
Lagrene,Bireli (el-g,voc) | Vander,Maurice (p) | Doky,Christian Minh (b) | Ceccarelli,André (dr)

FDM 36596-2 | CD | French Touch
Richard Galliano Group
A French Touch | Caruso | Augusta | L'Envers Du Décor | Tacot Blues
Paris,France, rec. 8.-10.5.1998
Galliano,Richard (accordeon) | Jenny-Clark,Jean-Francois (b) | Humair,Daniel (dr)
Sanguine
Galliano,Richard (accordeon) | Jenny-Clark,Jean-Francois (b)
Passarinho
Galliano,Richard (accordeon) | Humair,Daniel (dr)
J.F.
Galliano,Richard (accordeon) | Portal,Michel (ss) | Jenny-Clark,Jean-Francois (b) | Humair,Daniel (dr)
Bebé | Sanfona
Paris,France, rec. 8.6.1998
Galliano,Richard (accordeon,accordina) | Ecay,Jean-Marie (g) | Vignolo,Rémi (b) | Ceccarelli,André (dr)
Heavy Tango | You Must Believe In Spring
Galliano,Richard (accordeon,accordina) | Vignolo,Rémi (b) | Ceccarelli,André (dr)

FDM 36597-2 | CD | Live In Germany
Michel Petrucciani
Looking Up | Besame Mucho | Rachid | Chloé Meets Gershwin | Home | Brazilian Like | Little Piece In C For U | Romantic But Not Blue | Trilogy In Blois(Morning Sun,Noon Sun And Night Sun In Blois) | Caravan | She Did It Again- | Take The 'A' Train- | She Did It Again-
Live at Alte Oper,Frankfurt/M., rec. 27.2.1997
Petrucciani,Michel (p-solo)

FDM 36599-2 | CD | Guitar Groove
Philip Catherine Quartet
Merci Afrique | Sunset Shuffle | Guitar Groove | Good Morning Bill | Hello George | To My Sister | Chinese Lamp | Stardust | Here And Now | Nuances | Simply | For Wayne And Joe | Blue Bells
NYC, rec. 23.-25.5.1998
Catherine,Philip (g) | Beard,Jim (keyboards) | Johnson,Alphonso (el-b) | Holmes,Rodney (dr)

FDM 36601-2 | CD | Passatori
Richard Galliano With Orchestra
Opale Concerto In Three Movements(for Accordeon And Orchestra) | Oblivion | San Peyre | La Valse A Margaux | Melodicelli | Habanerando | Concerto In Three Movements(for Bandoneon,Harp,Piano And Orchestra)
London,GB, rec. 25.2.1999
Galliano,Richard (accordeon) | Zampello,Gianpietro (harp) | Conte,Cinzia (p) | Bollani,Stefano (perc) | Tortelli,Morgan M. (perc) | Farelli,Jonathan (perc) | I Solisti Dell'Orchestra Della Toscana | details unknown

FDM 36602-2 | CD | Steve Grossman Quartet
Steve Grossman Quartet
Ebb Tide | Inner Circle | Song For My Mother | Parisian Welcome | You Go To My Head | Body And Soul | Why Don't I | Don't Blame Me | Theme For Ernie | In A Sentimental Mood
Paris,France, rec. 23.-25.1.1998
Grossman,Steve (sax) | Petrucciani,Michel (p) | McKee,Andy (b) | Farnsworth,Joe (dr)

FDM 36604-2 | CD | Duet
Sylvain Luc-Biréli Lagrène
Time After Time | Douce Ambiance | Estate(Summer) | Made In France | La Ballade Irlandaise | Isn't She Lovely | Road Song | Zurezat | Stompin' At The Savoy | Les Amoureux Des Bancs Publics | Blackbird | Syracuse | Looking Up
Pompignan,France, rec. 3.-5.6.1999
Luc,Sylvain (g) | Lagrene,Bireli (g)

FDM 36605-2 | CD | Trio In Tokyo | EAN 3460503660595
Michel Petrucciani Trio
Training | September Second | Home | Little Peace In C For U | Love Letters | Cantabile | Colors | So What
Live at The Blue Note,Tokyo,Japan, rec. November 1997
Petrucciani,Michel (p) | Jackson,Anthony (b) | Gadd,Steve (dr)

FDM 36611-2 | CD | Tribute To Stépane Grappelli
Didier Lockwood Trio
Les Valseuses | I Got Rhythm | Nuages | Barbizon Blues | All The Things You Are | My One And Only Love | The Kid | Someday My Prince Will Come | Minor Swing | Misty | Paint Up House | Tears | In A Sentimental Mood | Beautiful Love
Paris,France, rec. 1999
Lockwood,Didier (v) | Lagrene,Bireli (g) | Orsted-Pedersen,Niels-Henning (b)

FDM 36612-2 | CD | SUD
Sylvain Luc-André Ceccarelli-Jean Marc Jafet
A Night In Tunisia | Bella Vista | Jade Et Melody | Mojo | Overture | Ameskeri | Roots 6406 | This Guy's In Love With You | Chez Laurette | Requiem | Little Man You've Had A Busy Day | There'll Never Be Another You | Moon River
Antibes,France, rec. 18.-20.8.1999
Luc,Sylvain (g) | Jafet,Jean-Marc (b) | Ceccarelli,André (dr)

FDM 36614-2 | CD | Blue Prince
Philip Catherine Quartet
Coffee Groove | Global Warming | With A Song In My Heart | The Creeper | The Postman | More Bells | Memories Of You | Kwa Heri | Blue Prince | Arthur Rainbow | Magic Box | Sweet Lorraine
Paris,France, rec. 13.-15.6.2000
Catherine,Philip (g) | Joris,Bert (tp,fl-h) | Van De Geyn,Hein (b) | Van Oosterhout,Hans (dr)

FDM 36615-2 | CD | Johnny Griffin & Steve Grossman
Johnny Griffin-Steve Grossman Quintet
Take The 'D' Train | Waltswing | Don't Say Goodbye(Just Leave) | Nica's Tompo | Power Station | Little Pugie | You've Never Been There | This Time The Dream's On Me | Taurus People
Paris,France, rec. 28.-30.5.2000
Griffin,Johnny (ts) | Grossman,Steve (ts) | Weiss,Michael (p) | Michelot,Pierre (b) | Queen,Alvin (dr)

FDM 36616-2 | CD | Gallianissimo! The Best Of Richard Galliano
Richard Galliano Quartet
New York Tango | Fou Rire
Galliano,Richard (accordeon) | Lagrene,Bireli (g) | Mraz,George 'Jiri' (b) | Foster,Al (dr)
Laurita | Giselle
Galliano,Richard (accordeon) | Thielemans,Jean 'Toots' (harm) | Danielsson,Palle (b) | Baron,Joey (dr)
Richard Galliano Trio
La Javanaise
Galliano,Richard (accordeon) | Danielsson,Palle (b) | Baron,Joey (dr)
Richard Galliano Quartet
Waltz For Nicky | Viaggio | Tango Pour Claude
Galliano,Richard (accordeon) | Lagrene,Bireli (g,el-g) | Michelot,Pierre (b) | Bellonzi,Charles (dr)
Richard Galliano Group I Solisti Dell'Orchestra Della Toscana
Invierno Porteno | La Valse A Margaux | Oblivion
Galliano,Richard (accordeon) | Bollani,Stefano (p) | Tacchi,Andrea (v) | Solisti Dell'Orchestra Della Toscana
Richard Galliano Quartet
J.F.
Galliano,Richard (accordeon) | Portal,Michel (sax) | Jenny-Clark,Jean-Francois (b) | Humair,Daniel (dr)
Richard Galliano Trio
Caruso
Galliano,Richard (accordeon) | Jenny-Clark,Jean-Francois (b) | Humair,Daniel (dr)
Richard Galliano Quartet
Spleen
Galliano,Richard (accordeon) | Stibon,Franck (p) | Jafet,Jean-Marc (b-g) | Augusto,Luiz (dr)
Richard Galliano-Michel Portal
Leo, Estante Num Instante
Galliano,Richard (accordeon) | Portal,Michel (cl)

FDM 36617-2 | CD | Conversations | EAN 3460503661721
Michel And Tony Petrucciani
Summertime | Sometime Ago | All The Things You Are | My Funny Valentine | Nuages | Nardis | Michels Tune | Someday My Prince Will Come | Billie's Bounce | Satin Doll
Live at The Maison De La Dance,Lyon,France, rec. 10.11.1992
Petrucciani,Michel (p) | Petrucciani,Tony (g)

FDM 36625-2 | CD | Birds Of A Feather:A Tribute To Charlie Parker | EAN 3460503662520
Roy Haynes Quintet
Diverse(Segment) | Ah-Leu-Cha | April In Paris | Moose The Mooche | Now's The Time | Rocker | Barbados | Yardbird Suite | The Gypsy | My Heart Belongs To Daddy | What Is This Thing Called Love
NYC, rec. 26./27.3.2001
Haynes,Roy (dr) | Hargrove,Roy (tp) | Garrett,Kenny (as) | Kikoski,David 'Dave' (p) | Holland,Dave (b)

FDM 36629-2 | CD | Ahmad Jamal Á L'Olympia | EAN 3460503662926
Ahmad Jamal Quartet
The Night Has A Thousand Eyes | How Deep Is The Ocean | Autumn Leaves | My Foolish Heart | Appreciation | Aftermath
Live at The Olympia,Paris,France, rec. 6.11.2000
Jamal,Ahmad (p) | Coleman,George (ts) | Cammack,James (b) | Muhammad,Idris[Leo Morris] (dr)

FDM 36630-2 | CD | Welcome Home | EAN 3460503663022
Jean-Michel Pilc Trio
So What | I Got It Bad And That Ain't Good | Stella By Starlight | Autumn In Newfane | Colchiques Dans Les Prés | In My Solitude | Cousin Mary | Giant Steps | Tenderly | Welcome Home | Serial Mother Blues | Scarborough Fair | Rhythm-A-Ning | Beginning
Paris,France, rec. 28.-30.9.2001
Pilc,Jean-Michel (p) | Moutin,Francois (b) | Hoenig,Ari (dr)

FDM 36631-2 | CD | The Electric Bill | EAN 3460503663121
Bill Carrothers Quartet
Wrong Wrong Wrong | Rebellion | Voice Of The People | Evolution | The Castaways | Aftermath | A Kindred Spirit | Mojo Clinton | Sing
Minneapolis,USA, rec. 25../26.3.2001
Carrothers,Bill (el-p) | Lewis,Mike (ss,ts) | Anderson,Reid (b,el-b) | King,Dave (dr)

FDM 36633-2 | CD | Tonight At Noon...Three Or Four Shades Of Love | EAN 3460503663329
Charles Mingus Orchestra
Tonight At Noon | Invisible Lady
NYC, rec. 3.11.2001
Charles Mingus Orchestra | Sipiagin,Alex (tp) | Herwig,Conrad (tb) | Routch,Bob (fr-h) | Yates,Doug (b-cl) | Rabinowitz,Michael (bassoon) | Blake,Seamus (ss) | Foster,Alex (as) | Kikoski,David 'Dave' (p) | Rogers,Adam (g) | Kozlov,Boris (b) | Watts,Jeff 'Tain' (dr) | Costello,Elvis (voc)
Noon Night | Eclipse
Charles Mingus Orchestra | Sipiagin,Alex (tp) | Herwig,Conrad (tb) | Routch,Bob (fr-h) | Yates,Doug (b-cl) | Rabinowitz,Michael (bassoon) | Blake,Seamus (ss) | Robinson,Scott (fl) | Kikoski,David 'Dave' (p) | Rogers,Adam (g) | Kozlov,Boris (b) | Watts,Jeff 'Tain' (dr)
Mingus Big Band
Love Is A Dangerous Necessity | Passions Of A Woman Loved | Sweet Sucker Dance | Devil Woman | Love's Fury | The Black Saint And The Sinner Lady
NYC, rec. 7.12.2001
Mingus Big Band | Rampton,Kenny (tp) | Gardner,Earl (tp) | Brecker,Randy (tp) | Pelt,Jeremy (tp) | Sipiagin,Alex (tp) | Herwig,Conrad (tb) | Lacy,Ku-umba Frank (tb,voc) | McIntyre,Earl (tb) | Taylor,Dave (b-tb,tuba) | Foster,Alex (fl,cl,ss,as) | Herring,Vincent (ss,as) | Shaw,Jaleel (as) | Blake,Seamus (ts) | Handy,Craig (ts) | Escoffery,Wayne (ts) | Stubblefield,John (ts) | Cuber,Ronnie (bs) | Kikoski,David 'Dave' (p) | Kozlov,Boris (b) | McKee,Andy (b) | Blake,Johnathan (dr,tambourine)

FDM 36637-2 | CD | Summer Night | EAN 3460503663725
Philip Catherine Trio
Summer Night | Birth Of Janet | Laura | If I Should Lose You | Round About Midnight | Gilles Et Mirona
Paris,France, rec. 29.-31.5.2002
Catherine,Philip (g) | Aerts,Philippe (b) | Van Schaik,Joost (dr)
Philip Catherine Quartet
Tiger Groove | Letter From My Mother | Francis' Delight | Janet | Time After Time | All Through The Day | Le Jardin De Madi
Catherine,Philip (g) | Joris,Bert (tp,fl-h) | Aerts,Philippe (b) | Van Schaik,Joost (dr)

FDM 36642-2 | CD | Piazzolla Forever | EAN 3460503664227
Richard Galliano Septet
Otono Porteno | Invierno Porteno | Sur:Regresso Al Amor(South:Regression To Love) | Concerto Pour Bandoneon Et Orchestre Aconcagua:Final | Milonga Del Angel | Michelangelo | Improvisation Sur Le Theme Libertango | Laura Et Astor | Escualo | Presentation Du Septet | Verano Porteno | Primavera Porteno
Live at Willisau,CH, rec. 29.8.2002
Galliano,Richard (accordeon,bandoneon) | Phillips-Varjabédian (v) | Schmit,Lyonal (v) | Apap,Jean Marc (viola) | Pidoux,Raphael (cello) | Logerot,Stephane (b) | Sellin,Hervé (p)

FDM 36644-2 | CD | In Search Of Momentum (1-10) | EAN 3460503664425
Ahmad Jamal Trio
In Search Of... | Should I | Excerpts From I'll Take The 20 | Island Fever | I've Never Been In Love Before | Where Are You | Where Are You Now? | You Can See | Perfidia | I'll Always Be With You
Millbrook,NY, rec. 22.-28.8.2002
Jamal,Ahmad (p) | Cammack,James (b) | Muhammad,Idris[Leo Morris] (dr)

FDM 36649-2 | CD | Cardinal Points | EAN 3460503664920
Jean-Michel Pilc Quartet
Fred's Walk
NYC, rec. 17./18.12.2002
Pilc,Jean-Michel (p) | Genus,James (b,el-b) | Hoenig,Ari (dr) | M'boup,Abdou (perc)
Jean-Michel Pilc Quintet
South | East | Cardinal Points
Pilc,Jean-Michel (p,melodica,perc) | Newsome,Sam (ss) | Genus,James (b,el-b) | Hoenig,Ari (dr) | M'boup,Abdou (perc)
Jean-Michel Pilc Quartet
West | North | Aris's Mode | Mood Indigo
Pilc,Jean-Michel (p) | Newsome,Sam (ss) | Genus,James (b,el-b) | Hoenig,Ari (dr)
Jean-Michel Pilc Trio
Trio Sonata (part 1-4)
Pilc,Jean-Michel (p) | Moutin,Francois (b) | Hoenig,Ari (dr)

FDM 36650-2 | CD | Solo Ambre | EAN 3460503665026
Sylvain Luc
A Child Is Born | Gentil Coquelicot | Bakean(Paisiblement) | Omenaldi(Hommage) | Oréade | Opposite World | Berceuse Basque | All Blues | Ambre | Folklore Imaginaire(Miss Moustique) | The Shadow Of Your Smile | Warm Color
Antibes,France, rec. 4.-6.12.2002
Luc,Sylvain (g-solo)

FDM 36652-2 | CD | Dreyfus Night In Paris | EAN 3460503665224
Dreyfus All Stars
Tutu | The King Is Gone(for Miles) | Looking Up
Live at Palais Des Sports,Paris,France, rec. 7.7.1994
Dreyfus All Stars | Garrett,Kenny (sax) | Lagrene,Bireli (el-g) | Petrucciani,Michel (p) | Miller,Marcus (el-b) | White,Lenny (dr)

FDM 36661-2 | CD | Concerts | EAN 3460503666122
Michel Portal-Richard Galliano
Tango Pour Claude | Indifference | Mozambique
Live at The Acrimboldi Theater,Milano,Italy, rec. 5.5.2003
Portal,Michel (cl,b-cl,ss,jazzophone,bandoneon) | Galliano,Richard (accordeon)
Taraf | Giselle | Little Tango | Oblivion | Chorinho Para Ele | Ivan Ivanovitch Kossiakof | Viaggio | Libertango
Live at The Middelheim Jazzfestival,Antwerp,Belgium, rec. 19.8.2001
Portal,Michel (cl,b-cl,ss,jazzophone,bandoneon) | Galliano,Richard (accordeon)
Face To Face | J.F. | Beija-Flor
Live at NDR Studio,Hamburg, rec. 29.10.1998
Portal,Michel (cl,b-cl,ss,jazzophone,bandoneon) | Galliano,Richard (accordeon)

FDM 36663-2 | CD | Fountain Of Youth | EAN 3460503666320
Roy Haynes Quartet
Greensleeves | Trinkle Tinkle | Summer Night | Ask Me Now | Butch And Butch | Inner Trust | Green Chimneys | Remember | Question And Answer
Live at 'Birdland',NYC, rec. 4./5.12.2002
Haynes,Roy (dr) | Strickland,Marcus (b-cl,ss,ts) | Bejerano,Martin (p) | Sullivan,John (b)

FDM 36710-2 | CD | Louis Armstrong:Fireworks | EAN 3460503671027
Louis Armstrong And His Hot Five
A Monday Date | Skip The Gutter | Fireworks
Chicago,Ill, rec. 27.6.1928
Armstrong,Louis (tp,voc) | Robinson,Fred (tb) | Strong,Jimmy (cl,ts) | Hines,Earl 'Fatha' (p,voc) | Cara,Mancy (bj,voc) | Singleton,Zutty (dr)
West End Blues | Don't Jive Me | Sugarfoot Strut
Chicago,Ill, rec. 28.6.1928
Armstrong,Louis (tp,voc) | Robinson,Fred (tb) | Strong,Jimmy (cl,ts) | Hines,Earl 'Fatha' (p,voc) | Cara,Mancy (bj,voc) | Singleton,Zutty (dr)
Two Deuces | Squeeze Me
Chicago,Ill, rec. 29.6.1928
Armstrong,Louis (tp,voc) | Robinson,Fred (tb) | Strong,Jimmy (cl) | Hines,Earl 'Fatha' (p) | Carr,Mancy (bj,voc) | Singleton,Zutty (dr)
Louis Armstrong And His Orchestra
Kneedrops
Chicago,Ill, rec. 5.7.1928
Armstrong,Louis (tp,voc) | Robinson,Fred (tb) | Strong,Jimmy (cl) | Hines,Earl 'Fatha' (p) | Carr,Mancy (bj,voc) | Singleton,Zutty (dr)
Carroll Dickerson's Savoyagers
Symphonic Raps | Savoyager's Stomp
Dickerson,Carroll (v,cond) | Armstrong,Louis (tp) | Hobson,Homer (tp) | Robinson,Fred (tb) | Curry,Bert (as) | Wethington,Crawford (as) | Strong,Jimmy (cl,ts) | Hines,Earl 'Fatha' (p) | Carr,Mancy (bj) | Briggs,Pete (tuba) | Singleton,Zutty (dr)
Louis Armstrong And His Orchestra
Basin Street Blues | No(No,Papa,No)
Chicago,Ill, rec. 4.12.1928
Armstrong,Louis (tp) | Robinson,Fred (tb) | Strong,Jimmy (cl,ts) | Hines,Earl 'Fatha' (p) | Carr,Mancy (bj) | Singleton,Zutty (dr)
Louis Armstrong-Earl Hines
Weather Bird Rag
Chicago,Ill, rec. 5.12.1928
Armstrong,Louis (tp) | Hines,Earl 'Fatha' (p)
Louis Armstrong And His Savoy Ballroom Five
Beau Koo Jack | No One Else But You | Save It Pretty Mama
Armstrong,Louis (tp,voc) | Robinson,Fred (tb) | Redman,Don (cl,as,arr) | Strong,Jimmy (cl,ts) | Hines,Earl 'Fatha' (p) | Wilborn,Dave (bj) | Singleton,Zutty (dr)

LABELVERZEICHNIS

Muggles | St.James Infirmary | Hear Me Talkin' To Ya | Tight Like This
Chicago,Ill, rec. 12.12.1928
Armstrong,Louis (tp,voc) | Robinson,Fred (tb) | Redman,Don (as,voc) | Strong,Jimmy (cl,ts) | Hines,Earl 'Fatha' (p,voc) | Carr,Mancy (bj) | Singleton,Zutty (dr)

FDM 36712-2 | CD | Sidney Bechet:Summertime | EAN 3460503671225

Sidney Bechet With Noble Sissle's Swingsters
When The Sun Sets Down South(Southern Sunset)
NYC, rec. 10.2.1938
Bechet,Sidney (ss) | Brereton,Clarence (tp) | White,Gil (cl,ts) | Brooks,Harry (p) | Miller,Jimmy (g) | Jones,Jimmy (b) | Kirk,Wilbert (dr)

Sidney Bechet And His Orchestra
Jungle Drums
NYC, rec. 6.11.1938
Bechet,Sidney (ss) | Caceres,Ernie (bs) | Bowman,Dave (p) | Ware,Leonard (g) | Turner,Henry (b) | Singleton,Zutty (dr)

Sidney Bechet And His New Orleans Feetwarmers
Indian Summer
NYC, rec. 5.2.1940
Bechet,Sidney (ss) | White,Sonny (p) | Howard,Charlie (g) | Myers,Wilson Ernest (b) | Clarke,Kenny (dr)
Shake It And Break It
NYC, rec. 4.6.1940
Bechet,Sidney (cl,ss) | DeParis,Sidney (tp) | Williams,Sandy (tb) | Jackson,Cliff (p) | Addison,Bernard (g) | Braud,Wellman (b) | Catlett,Big Sid (dr)

Sidney Bechet And The Chamber Music Society Of Lower Basin Street
St.Louis Blues
NYC, rec. 28.7.1940
Bechet,Sidney (ss) | Levine,Henry 'Hot Lips' (tp) | Epstein,Jack (tb) | Evans,Alfie (cl) | Adler,Rudolph (ts) | Janarro,Mario (p) | Collucci,Tonny (g) | Patent,Harry (b) | Levine,Nat (dr)

Sidney Bechet And His New Orleans Feetwarmers
Stompy Jones | Blues In Thirds
NYC, rec. 6.9.1940
Bechet,Sidney (ss) | Stewart,Rex (co) | Hines,Earl 'Fatha' (p) | Lindsey,Johny (b) | Dodds,Warren 'Baby' (dr)

Sidney Bechet And The Chamber Music Society Of Lower Basin Street
Muskrat Ramble
NYC, rec. 11.11.1940
Bechet,Sidney (ss) | Levine,Henry 'Hot Lips' (tp) | Epstein,Jack (tb) | Evans,Alfie (cl) | Adler,Rudolph (ts) | Janarro,Mario (p) | Collucci,Tonny (g) | Patent,Harry (b) | Levine,Nat (dr)

Sidney Bechet And His New Orleans Feetwarmers
Georgia Cabin
NYC, rec. 13.9.1941
Bechet,Sidney (cl,ss) | Shavers,Charlie (tp) | Smith,Willie 'The Lion' (p) | Barksdale,Everett (g) | Braud,Wellman (b) | Johnson,Manzie (dr)
Blues In The Air
NYC, rec. 14.10.1941
Bechet,Sidney (ss) | Goodwin,Henry (tp,laughing) | Dickenson,Vic (tb,voc) | Donaldson,Don (p) | Williamson,Ernest (b) | Johnson,Manzie (dr)
What Is This Thing Called Love | Rose Room | 12th Street Rag
NYC, rec. 24.10.1941
Bechet,Sidney (ss) | Shavers,Charlie (tp) | Smith,Willie 'The Lion' (p) | Barksdale,Everett (g) | Braud,Wellman (b) | Catlett,Big Sid (dr)

Sidney Bechet's Blue Note Jazzmen
High Society
NYC, rec. 29.1.1945
Bechet,Sidney (cl,ss) | Kaminsky,Max (tp) | Lugg,George (tb) | Hodes,Art (p) | Foster,George 'Pops' (b) | Moore,Fred[Freddie] (dr)

This Is Jazz All Stars
Summertime
NYC, rec. 24.3.1947
Bechet,Sidney (ss) | Hodes,Art (p) | Barker,Danny (g) | Foster,George 'Pops' (b) | Dodds,Warren 'Baby' (dr)

Sidney Bechet With Bob Wilber's Wildcats
Kansas City Man Blues
NYC, rec. 14.7.1947
Bechet,Sidney (cl,ss) | Wilber,Bob (cl) | Glasel,John (co) | Mielke,Bob (tb) | Wellstood,Dick (p) | Traeger,Charles (b) | Strong,Dennis (dr)

Sidney Bechet With Claude Luter And His Orchestra
Les Oignons | Bechet's Creole Blues
Paris,France, rec. 14.10.1949
Bechet,Sidney (ss) | Luter,Claude (cl) | Dervaux,Pierre (tp) | Jospin,Mowgli (tb) | Azzi,Christian (p) | Philippe,Claude (bj) | Bianchini,Roland (b) | Galepides,Francois 'Moustache' (dr)

Sidney Bechet And His All Stars
American Rhythm | Mon Homme(My Man)
Paris,France, rec. 20.10.1949
Bechet,Sidney (ss) | Lewis,Charles (p) | Michelot,Pierre (b) | Clarke,Kenny (dr)

Sidney Bechet And His Feetwarmers
After You've Gone | Margie
Paris,France, rec. 5.11.1949
Bechet,Sidney (ss) | Bernard,Eddie (p) | Michelot,Pierre (b) | Clarke,Kenny (dr)

FDM 36714-2 | CD | Don Byas:Laura | EAN 3460503671423

Hot Lips Page And His Orchestra
These Foolish Things Remind Me On You
NYC, rec. 29.9.1944
Page,Oran 'Hot Lips' (tp) | Bostic,Earl (as) | Hammond,B.G. (as) | Byas,Don (ts) | Hart,Clyde (p) | Lucas,Al (b) | Parker,Jack 'The Bear' (dr)

Don Byas/Slam Stewart
I Got Rhythm
Live at Town Hall,NYC, rec. 9.6.1945
Byas,Don (ts) | Stewart,Slam (b)

Don Byas All Star Quintet
Out Of Nowhere | Deep Purple
NYC, rec. 27.6.1945
Byas,Don (ts) | Clayton,Buck (tp) | Guarnieri,Johnny (p) | Safranski,Eddie (b) | Best,Denzil (dr)

Don Byas Quartet
Stardust
NYC, rec. 6.9.1945
Byas,Don (ts) | Guarnieri,Johnny (p) | Stewart,Slam (b) | Heard,J.C. (dr)

Don Byas All Stars
Blue And Sentimental | My Melancholy Baby
NYC, rec. 3.10.1945
Byas,Don (ts) | Guarnieri,Johnny (p) | Safranski,Eddie (b) | Heard,J.C. (dr)

Don Byas Quartet
Wrap Your Troubles In Dreams
NYC, rec. 1.11.1945
Byas,Don (ts) | Garner,Erroll (p) | Stewart,Slam (b) | West,Harold 'Doc' (dr)
Cherokee | Old Folks | September In The Rain
NYC, rec. 17.5.1946
Byas,Don (ts) | Brannon,Teddy (p) | Skeete,Frank (b) | Radcliffe,Fred (dr)
September Song
NYC, rec. 21.8.1946
Byas,Don (ts) | Gold,Sanford (p) | Gaskin,Leonard (b) | Roach,Max (dr)
Body And Soul
Paris,France, rec. 6.1.1947
Byas,Don (ts) | Taylor,Billy (p) | Bouchety,Jean (b) | Oliver,Buford (dr)

Tyree Glenn
I Surrender Dear
Paris,France, rec. 13.1.1947
Taylor,Billy (p) | Tilche,Jean-Jacques (g) | Glenn,Tyree (tb) | Holland,Peanuts (tp) | Rostaing,Hubert (as) | Byas,Don (ts) | Bouchety,Jean (b) | Oliver,Buford (dr)

Don Byas Ree-Boppers
Walking Around | Laura
Paris,France, rec. 27.1.1947
Byas,Don (ts) | Holland,Peanuts (tp) | Tilche,Jean-Jacques (g) | Taylor,Billy (p) | Bouchety,Jean (b) | Oliver,Buford (dr)

Don Byas And His Orchestra
These Foolish Things Remind Me On You | Stormy Weather
Paris,France, rec. 12.6.1947
Byas,Don (ts) | Dieval,Jack (p) | Tilche,Jean-Jacques (g) | Simoens,Lucien (b) | Molinetti,Armand (dr)

Bill Coleman And His Orchestra
Lover Man(Oh,Where Can You Be?)
Paris,France, rec. 5.1.1949
Coleman,Bill (tp) | Byas,Don (ts) | Peiffer,Bernard (p) | Bouchety,Jean (b) | Paraboschi,Roger (dr)

Don Byas Quartet
Yesterdays
Byas,Don (ts) | Peiffer,Bernard (p) | Bouchety,Jean (b) | Paraboschi,Roger (dr)

FDM 36715-2 | CD | Charlie Christian:Swing To Bop | EAN 3460503671522

Benny Goodman Sextet
Flying Home
NYC, rec. 2.10.1939
Goodman,Benny (cl) | Hampton,Lionel (vib) | Henderson,Fletcher (p) | Christian,Charlie (g) | Bernstein,Artie (b) | Fatool,Nick (dr)
Seven Come Eleven
NYC, rec. 22.11.1939
Goodman,Benny (cl) | Hampton,Lionel (vib) | Henderson,Fletcher (p) | Christian,Charlie (g) | Bernstein,Artie (b) | Fatool,Nick (dr)

Benny Goodman And His Orchestra
Honeysuckle Rose
Goodman,Benny (cl) | Elman,Ziggy (tp) | Maxwell,Jimmy (tp) | Martel,Johnny (tp) | Ballard,Red (tb) | Brown,Vernon (tb) | Vesely,Ted (tb) | Mondello,Toots (as) | Estes,Buff (as) | Bassey,Bus (ts) | Jerome,Jerry (ts) | Henderson,Fletcher (p) | Christian,Charlie (g) | Bernstein,Artie (b) | Fatool,Nick (dr)

Kansas City Six
Pagin' The Devil | Good Mornin' Blues
Live at Carnegie Hall,NYC, rec. 24.12.1939
Kansas City Six,The | Clayton,Buck (tp) | Young,Lester (ts) | Christian,Charlie (g) | Green,Freddie (g) | Page,Walter (b) | Jones,Jo (dr)

Benny Goodman Septet
Ad Lib Blues
NYC, rec. 28.10.1940
Goodman,Benny (cl) | Clayton,Buck (tp) | Young,Lester (ts) | Christian,Charlie (g) | Basie,Count (p) | Green,Freddie (g) | Page,Walter (b) | Jones,Jo (dr)

Benny Goodman Septet feat.Count Basie
Benny's Bugle
NYC, rec. 7.11.1940
Goodman,Benny (cl) | Williams,Cootie (tp) | Auld,Georgie (ts) | Christian,Charlie (g) | Basie,Count (p) | Bernstein,Artie (b) | Jaeger,Harry (dr)
I Found A New Baby
NYC, rec. 15.1.1941
Goodman,Benny (cl) | Williams,Cootie (tp) | Auld,Georgie (ts) | Christian,Charlie (g) | Basie,Count (p) | Bernstein,Artie (b) | Jones,Jo (dr)

Benny Goodman And His Orchestra
Solo Flight
NYC, rec. 4.3.1941
Goodman,Benny (cl) | Maxwell,Jimmy (tp) | Williams,Cootie (tp) | Fila,Alex (tp) | Goodman,Irving (tp) | McGarity,Lou (tb) | Cutshall,Cutty (tb) | Bivona,Gus (as) | Martin,Lloyd 'Skippy' (as) | Auld,Georgie (ts) | Mondello,Pete (ts) | Snyder,Bob (bs) | Guarnieri,Johnny (p) | Christian,Charlie (g) | Bernstein,Artie (b) | Tough,Dave (dr) | Harding,Buster (arr)

Benny Goodman And His All Star Sextet
Good Enough To Keep(aka Airmail Special)
NYC, rec. 13.3.1941
Goodman,Benny (cl) | Williams,Cootie (tp) | Auld,Georgie (ts) | Guarnieri,Johnny (p) | Christian,Charlie (g) | Bernstein,Artie (b) | Tough,Dave (dr)

Minton's Playhouse All Stars
Swing To Bop | Stompin' At The Savoy
Live at Minton's Play House,NYC, rec. 12.5.1941
Minton's Playhouse All Stars | Guy,Joe (tp) | Christian,Charlie (g) | Kersey,Kenny (p) | Fenton,Nick (b) | Clarke,Kenny (dr)
Up On Teddy's Hill
Live at Minton's Play House,NYC, rec. May 1941
Minton's Playhouse All Stars | Guy,Joe (tp) | Gillespie,Dizzy (tp) | Byas,Don (ts) | Christian,Charlie (g) | unkn. (p,b,dr)
Guy's Got To Go | Lips Flips(On With Charlie Christian)
Minton's Playhouse All Stars | Guy,Joe (tp) | Page,Oran 'Hot Lips' (tp) | Coulson,Victor (tp) | Williams,Rudy (as) | Byas,Don (ts) | Scott,Kermit (ts) | Christian,Charlie (g) | Ebenezer,Paul (b) | Miller,T.prob. (dr)

FDM 36716-2 | CD | Nat King Cole:Route 66 | EAN 3460503671621

Nat King Cole Trio
Straighten Up And Fly Right | Gee Baby Ain't I Good To You
Los Angeles,CA, rec. 30.11.1943
Cole,Nat King (p,voc) | Moore,Oscar (g) | Miller,Johnny (b)
Sweet Lorraine
Los Angeles,CA, rec. 15.12.1943
Cole,Nat King (p,voc) | Moore,Oscar (g) | Miller,Johnny (b)
Frim Fram Sauce
Los Angeles,CA, rec. 11.10.1945
Cole,Nat King (p,voc) | Moore,Oscar (g) | Miller,Johnny (b)
Get Your Kicks On Route 66
Los Angeles,CA, rec. 15.3.1946
Cole,Nat King (p,voc) | Moore,Oscar (g) | Miller,Johnny (b)
Could Ja | Baby Baby All The Time
Los Angeles,CA, rec. 17.4.1946
Cole,Nat King (p,voc) | Moore,Oscar (g) | Miller,Johnny (b)

Nat King Cole With Orchestra
The Christmas Song
Los Altos Hill,CA, rec. 19.8.1946
Cole,Nat King (p,voc) | Moore,Oscar (g) | Miller,Johnny (b) | Parker,Jack 'The Bear' (dr) | Strings | unkn. (harp) | Grean,Charlie (arr) | details unknown

Nat King Cole Trio
That's What
Los Angeles,CA, rec. 13.6.1947
Cole,Nat King (p,voc) | Moore,Oscar (g) | Miller,Johnny (b)
When I Take My Sugar To Tea | Makin' Whoopee | Too Marvelous For Words
Los Angeles,CA, rec. 6.-8.8.1947
Cole,Nat King (p,voc) | Moore,Oscar (g) | Miller,Johnny (b)
Ke Mo Ki Mo(The Magic Song)
Los Angeles,CA, rec. 15.8.1947
Cole,Nat King (p,voc) | Cole,Buddy prob. (celeste) | Moore,Oscar (g) | Miller,Johnny (b)

Nat King Cole Trio With Frank DeVol's Orchestra
Nature Boy
Los Angeles,CA, rec. 22.8.1947
Cole,Nat King (p,voc) | Moore,Oscar (g) | Miller,Johnny (b) | DeVol,Frank (cond,arr) | details unknown

Nat King Cole Trio
Love Nest | Dream A Little Dream Of Me
Los Angeles,CA, rec. 28.10.1947
Cole,Nat King (p,voc) | Ashby,Irving (g) | Miller,Johnny (b)
Little Girl
Los Angeles,CA, rec. 3.11.1947
Cole,Nat King (p,voc) | Ashby,Irving (g) | Miller,Johnny (b)
Lulubelle
Los Angeles,CA, rec. 20.12.1947
Cole,Nat King (p,voc) | Ashby,Irving (g) | Miller,Johnny (b)
'Tis Autumn
Los Altos Hill,CA, rec. 29.3.1949
Cole,Nat King (p,voc) | Ashby,Irving (g) | Miller,Johnny (b)

Nat King Cole And His Trio
Yes Sir That's My Baby
Los Angeles,CA, rec. 29.3.1949
Cole,Nat King (p,voc) | Ashby,Irving (g) | Miller,Johnny (b) | Costanzo,Jack (congas,bongos)

FDM 36717-2 | CD | Duke Ellington:Ko-Ko | EAN 3460503671720

Duke Ellington And His Famous Orchestra
Jack The Bear | Ko-Ko | Morning Glory
Chicago,Ill, rec. 6.3.1940
Ellington,Duke (p) | Stewart,Rex (co) | Williams,Cootie (tp) | Jones,Wallace (tp) | Nanton,Joe 'Tricky Sam' (tb) | Tizol,Juan (tb) | Brown,Lawrence (tb) | Bigard,Barney (cl,ts) | Hodges,Johnny (ss,as) | Hardwicke,Otto (as,bass-s) | Webster,Ben (ts) | Carney,Harry (cl,as,bs) | Guy,Fred (g) | Blanton,Jimmy (b) | Greer,William 'Sonny' (dr) | Strayhorn,Billy (arr)
Conga Brava | Concerto For Cootie
Chicago,Ill, rec. 15.3.1940
Ellington,Duke (p) | Stewart,Rex (co) | Williams,Cootie (tp) | Jones,Wallace (tp) | Nanton,Joe 'Tricky Sam' (tb) | Tizol,Juan (tb) | Brown,Lawrence (tb) | Bigard,Barney (cl,ts) | Hodges,Johnny (ss,as) | Hardwicke,Otto (as,bass-s) | Webster,Ben (ts) | Carney,Harry (cl,as,bs) | Guy,Fred (g) | Blanton,Jimmy (b) | Greer,William 'Sonny' (dr)
Cotton Tail | Never No Lament
Chicago,Ill, rec. 4.5.1940
Ellington,Duke (p) | Stewart,Rex (co) | Williams,Cootie (tp) | Jones,Wallace (tp) | Nanton,Joe 'Tricky Sam' (tb) | Tizol,Juan (tb) | Brown,Lawrence (tb) | Bigard,Barney (cl,ts) | Hodges,Johnny (ss,as) | Hardwicke,Otto (as,bass-s) | Webster,Ben (ts) | Carney,Harry (cl,as,bs) | Guy,Fred (g) | Blanton,Jimmy (b) | Greer,William 'Sonny' (dr)
Dusk | Bojangles | A Portrait Of Bert Williams
Chicago,Ill, rec. 28.5.1940
Ellington,Duke (p,arr) | Jones,Wallace (tp) | Williams,Cootie (tp) | Stewart,Rex (co) | Nanton,Joe 'Tricky Sam' (tb) | Brown,Lawrence (tb) | Tizol,Juan (v-tb) | Bigard,Barney (cl) | Hodges,Johnny (cl,ss,as) | Hardwicke,Otto (as,bass-s) | Webster,Ben (ts) | Carney,Harry (cl,as,bs) | Guy,Fred (g) | Blanton,Jimmy (b) | Greer,William 'Sonny' (dr)
Harlem Air Shaft | All Too Soon | Rumpus In Richmond
NYC, rec. 22.7.1940
Ellington,Duke (p,arr) | Jones,Wallace (tp) | Williams,Cootie (tp) | Stewart,Rex (co) | Nanton,Joe 'Tricky Sam' (tb) | Brown,Lawrence (tb) | Tizol,Juan (v-tb) | Bigard,Barney (cl) | Hodges,Johnny (cl,ss,as) | Hardwicke,Otto (as,bass-s) | Webster,Ben (ts) | Carney,Harry (cl,as,bs) | Guy,Fred (g) | Blanton,Jimmy (b) | Greer,William 'Sonny' (dr)
Sepia Panorama
NYC, rec. 24.7.1940
Ellington,Duke (p,arr) | Jones,Wallace (tp) | Williams,Cootie (tp) | Stewart,Rex (co) | Nanton,Joe 'Tricky Sam' (tb) | Brown,Lawrence (tb) | Tizol,Juan (v-tb) | Bigard,Barney (cl) | Hodges,Johnny (cl,ss,as) | Hardwicke,Otto (as,bass-s) | Webster,Ben (ts) | Carney,Harry (cl,as,bs) | Guy,Fred (g) | Blanton,Jimmy (b) | Greer,William 'Sonny' (dr)
In A Mellow Tone | Warm Valley
Chicago,Ill, rec. 5.9.1940
Ellington,Duke (p,arr) | Jones,Wallace (tp) | Williams,Cootie (tp) | Stewart,Rex (co) | Nanton,Joe 'Tricky Sam' (tb) | Brown,Lawrence (tb) | Tizol,Juan (v-tb) | Bigard,Barney (cl) | Hodges,Johnny (cl,ss,as) | Hardwicke,Otto (as,bass-s) | Webster,Ben (ts) | Carney,Harry (cl,as,bs) | Guy,Fred (g) | Blanton,Jimmy (b) | Greer,William 'Sonny' (dr)
Across The Track Blues | Chloe (Song Of The Swamp)
Chicago,Ill, rec. 28.10.1940
Ellington,Duke (p,arr) | Jones,Wallace (tp) | Williams,Cootie (tp) | Stewart,Rex (co) | Nanton,Joe 'Tricky Sam' (tb) | Brown,Lawrence (tb) | Tizol,Juan (v-tb) | Bigard,Barney (cl) | Hodges,Johnny (cl,ss,as) | Hardwicke,Otto (as,bass-s) | Webster,Ben (ts) | Carney,Harry (cl,as,bs) | Guy,Fred (g) | Blanton,Jimmy (b) | Greer,William 'Sonny' (dr)

Duke Ellington/Jimmy Blanton
Pitter Panther Patter
Chicago,Ill, rec. 1.10.1940
Ellington,Duke (p) | Blanton,Jimmy (b)

FDM 36719-2 | CD | Erroll Garner:Trio | EAN 3460503671928

Erroll Garner Trio
Back Home Again In Indiana
NYC, rec. 25.9.1945
Garner,Erroll (p) | Levy,John (b) | De Hart,George (dr)
Memories Of You | Don't Blame Me
Hollywood,CA, rec. 14.7.1946
Garner,Erroll (p) | Callender,Red (b) | Singer,Lou (dr)
Trio
Hollywood,CA, rec. 19.2.1947
Garner,Erroll (p) | Callender,Red (b) | West,Harold 'Doc' (dr)

Erroll Garner
Erroll's Bounce
Hollywood,CA, rec. 22.4.1947
Garner,Erroll (p-solo)

Erroll Garner Quartet
Lover
Pasadena,CA, rec. 29.4.1947
Garner,Erroll (p) | Ashby,Irving (g) | Callender,Red (b) | Mills,Jackie (dr)

Erroll Garner
Love For Sale | Loose Nut
Hollywood,CA, rec. 10.6.1947
Garner,Erroll (p-solo)

Erroll Garner Trio
Stompin' At The Savoy
Los Angeles,CA, rec. 2.2.1949
Garner,Erroll (p) | Simmons,John (b) | Stoller,Alvin (dr)
Penthouse Serenade | I Cover The Waterfront | I Don't Stand A Ghost Of A Chance With You | Undecided | Over The Rainbow
Los Angeles,CA, rec. 29.3.1949
Garner,Erroll (p) | Simmons,John (b) | Stoller,Alvin (dr)
This Can't Be Love | Moonglow | The Man I Love
Los Angeles,CA, rec. 20.6.1949
Garner,Erroll (p) | Simmons,John (b) | Stoller,Alvin (dr)
On The Sunny Side Of The Street
Los Angeles,CA, rec. August 1949
Garner,Erroll (p) | Simmons,John (b) | Stoller,Alvin (dr)

FDM 36722-2 | CD | Woody Herman:Four Brother | EAN 3460503672222

Woody Herman And His Orchestra
Laura | Apple Honey
NYC, rec. 19.2.1945
Herman,Woody (cl,as) | Berman,Sonny (tp) | Candoli,Pete (tp) | Frankhauser,Chuck (tp) | Warwick,Carl (tp) | Wetzel,Ray (tp) | Harris,Bill (tb) | Kiefer,Ed (tb) | Pfeffner,Ralph (tb) | Marowitz,Sam (as) | LaPorta,John (as) | Mondello,Pete (ts) | Phillips,Flip (ts) | DeSair,Skippy (bs) | Burns,Ralph (p,arr) | Bauer,Billy (g) | Hyams,Marjorie (vib) | Jackson,Chubby (b) | Tough,Dave (dr)
Goosey Gander
NYC, rec. 1.3.1945
Herman,Woody (cl,as) | Berman,Sonny (tp) | Candoli,Pete (tp) | Frankhauser,Chuck (tp) | Warwick,Carl (tp) | Wetzel,Ray (tp) | Harris,Bill (tb) | Kiefer,Ed (tb) | Pfeffner,Ralph (tb) | Marowitz,Sam (as) | LaPorta,John (as) | Mondello,Pete (ts) | Phillips,Flip (ts) | DeSair,Skippy (bs) | Burns,Ralph (p,arr) | Bauer,Billy (g) | Hyams,Marjorie (vib) | Jackson,Chubby (b) | Tough,Dave (dr)
The Good Earth | Bijou(Rhumba A La Jazz)
NYC, rec. 20.8.1945
Herman,Woody (cl,as) | Berman,Sonny (tp) | Hefti,Neal (tp) | Candoli,Pete (tp) | Candoli,Conte (tp) | Linn,Ray (tp) | Pfeffner,Ralph (tb) | Kiefer,Ed (tb) | Harris,Bill (tb) | Marowitz,Sam (as) | LaPorta,John (as) | Mondello,Pete (ts) | Phillips,Flip (ts) | DeSair,Skippy (bs) | Aless,Tony (p) | Bauer,Billy (g) | Jackson,Chubby (b) | Tough,Dave (dr)
Your Father's Moustache
NYC, rec. 5.9.1945
Herman,Woody (cl,as) | Berman,Sonny (tp) | Hefti,Neal (tp) | Candoli,Pete (tp) | Candoli,Conte (tp) | Linn,Ray (tp) | Lewis,Irving (tp) | Pfeffner,Ralph (tb) | Kiefer,Ed (tb) | Harris,Bill (tb) | Marowitz,Sam (as) | LaPorta,John (as) | Mondello,Pete (ts) | Phillips,Flip (ts) | DeSair,Skippy (bs) | Norvo,Red (vib) | Aless,Tony (p) | Bauer,Billy (g) | Jackson,Chubby (b) | Rich,Buddy (dr)
Summer Sequence(part 1-3)
Hollywood,CA, rec. 17.9.1946
Herman,Woody (cl,as) | Berman,Sonny (tp) | Candoli,Pete (tp) | Gozzo,Conrad

(tp) | Lewis,Cappy (tp) | Rogers,Shorty (tp) | Pfeffner,Ralph (tb) | Kiefer,Ed (tb) | Harris,Bill (tb) | Marowitz,Sam (as) | LaPorta,John (as) | Folus,Mickey (ts) | Phillips,Flip (ts) | Rubinowitch,Sam (bs) | Norvo,Red (vib) | Rowles,Jimmy (p) | Wayne,Chuck (g) | Mondragon,Joe (b) | Lamond,Don (dr)

Lady McGowans Dream(pert 1 2)
Hollywood,CA, rec. 18.9.1946
Herman,Woody (cl,as) | Berman,Sonny (tp) | Candoli,Pete (tp) | Gozzo,Conrad (tp) | Lewis,Cappy (tp) | Rogers,Shorty (tp) | Pfeffner,Ralph (tb) | Kiefer,Ed (tb) | Harris,Bill (tb) | Marowitz,Sam (as) | LaPorta,John (as) | Folus,Mickey (ts) | Phillips,Flip (ts) | Rubinowitch,Sam (bs) | Norvo,Red (vib) | Rowles,Jimmy (p) | Wayne,Chuck (g) | Mondragon,Joe (b) | Lamond,Don (dr)

Woodshopper's Ball
Chicago,Ill, rec. 10.12.1946
Herman,Woody (cl,as) | Porcino,Al (tp) | Peck,Bob (tp) | Gozzo,Conrad (tp) | Lewis,Cappy (tp) | Peterson,Chuck (tp) | Pfeffner,Ralph (tb) | Kiefer,Ed (tb) | Harris,Bill (tb) | Marowitz,Sam (as) | LaPorta,John (as) | Folus,Mickey (ts) | Phillips,Flip (ts) | Rubinowitch,Sam (bs) | Rowles,Jimmy (p) | Wayne,Chuck (g) | Mondragon,Joe (b) | Lamond,Don (dr) | Hefti,Neal (arr)

Keen And Peachy
Hollywood,CA, rec. 22.12.1927
Herman,Woody (cl,as) | Fishelson,Stan (tp) | Markowitz,Irving 'Marky' (tp) | Glow,Bernie (tp) | Royal,Ernie (tp) | Swift,Bob (tb) | Swope,Earl (tb) | Wilson,Ollie (tb) | Marowitz,Sam (as) | Stewart,Herbie (ts) | Sims,Zoot (ts) | Getz,Stan (ts) | Chaloff,Serge (bs) | Otis,Fred (p) | Sargent,Gene (g) | Yoder,Walt (b) | Lamond,Don (dr)

The Goof And I
Hollywood,CA, rec. 24.12.1947
Herman,Woody (cl,as) | Fishelson,Stan (tp) | Markowitz,Irving 'Marky' (tp) | Glow,Bernie (tp) | Royal,Ernie (tp) | Swift,Bob (tb) | Swope,Earl (tb) | Wilson,Ollie (tb) | Marowitz,Sam (as) | Stewart,Herbie (ts) | Sims,Zoot (ts) | Getz,Stan (ts) | Chaloff,Serge (bs) | Otis,Fred (p) | Sargent,Gene (g) | Yoder,Walt (b) | Lamond,Don (dr)

Four Brothers
Hollywood,CA, rec. 27.12.1947
Herman,Woody (cl,as) | Fishelson,Stan (tp) | Markowitz,Irving 'Marky' (tp) | Glow,Bernie (tp) | Royal,Ernie (tp) | Swift,Bob (tb) | Swope,Earl (tb) | Wilson,Ollie (tb) | Marowitz,Sam (as) | Stewart,Herbie (ts) | Sims,Zoot (ts) | Getz,Stan (ts) | Chaloff,Serge (bs) | Otis,Fred (p) | Sargent,Gene (g) | Yoder,Walt (b) | Lamond,Don (dr)

Early Autumn
Hollywood,CA, rec. 30.12.1948
Herman,Woody (cl,as) | Fishelson,Stan (tp) | Glow,Bernie (tp) | Rodney,Red (tp) | Royal,Ernie (tp) | Rogers,Shorty (tp) | Harris,Bill (tb) | Swope,Earl (tb) | Wilson,Ollie (tb) | Swift,Bob (b-tb) | Marowitz,Sam (as) | Cohn,Al (ts) | Sims,Zoot (ts) | Getz,Stan (ts) | Chaloff,Serge (bs) | Gibbs,Terry (vib) | Levy,Lou (p) | Jackson,Chubby (b) | Lamond,Don (dr)

More Moon
NYC, rec. 26.5.1949
Herman,Woody (cl) | Fishelson,Stan (tp) | Porcino,Al (tp) | Royal,Ernie (tp) | Rogers,Shorty (tp) | Walp,Charlie (tp) | Harris,Bill (tb) | Swope,Earl (tb) | Wilson,Ollie (tb) | Varsalona,Bart (tb) | Marowitz,Sam (as) | Ammons,Gene (ts) | Savitt,Buddy (ts) | Giuffre,Jimmy (ts) | Chaloff,Serge (bs) | Gibbs,Terry (vib) | Levy,Lou (p) | Pettiford,Oscar (b) | Manne,Shelly (dr)

Not Really The Blues
Hollywood,CA, rec. 14.7.1949
Herman,Woody (cl) | Fishelson,Stan (tp) | Porcino,Al (tp) | Walp,Charlie (tp) | Royal,Ernie (tp) | Rogers,Shorty (tp) | Harris,Bill (tb) | Swope,Earl (tb) | Wilson,Ollie (tb) | Varsalona,Bart (b-tb) | Marowitz,Sam (as) | Ammons,Gene (ts) | Savitt,Buddy (ts) | Giuffre,Jimmy (ts) | Chaloff,Serge (bs) | Gibbs,Terry (vib) | Levy,Lou (p) | Pettiford,Oscar (b) | Manne,Shelly (dr)

Rhapsody In Wood
Hollywood,CA, rec. 20.7.1949
Herman,Woody (cl) | Fishelson,Stan (tp) | Porcino,Al (tp) | Walp,Charlie (tp) | Royal,Ernie (tp) | Rogers,Shorty (tp) | Harris,Bill (tb) | Swope,Earl (tb) | Wilson,Ollie (tb) | Varsalona,Bart (b-tb) | Marowitz,Sam (as) | Ammons,Gene (ts) | Savitt,Buddy (ts) | Giuffre,Jimmy (ts) | Chaloff,Serge (bs) | Gibbs,Terry (vib) | Levy,Lou (p) | Mondragon,Joe (b) | Manne,Shelly (dr)

<u>FDM 36724-2 | CD | Charlie Parker:Now's The Time | EAN 3460503672420</u>

Charlie Parker's Beboppers
Now's The Time | Billie's Bounce
NYC, rec. 26.11.1945
Parker,Charlie (as) | Davis,Miles (tp) | Gillespie,Dizzy (p) | Russell,Curly (b) | Roach,Max (dr)

Charlie Parker Septet
A Night In Tunisia | Ornithology | Moose The Mooche | The Famous Alto Break
Los Angeles,CA, rec. 28.3.1946
Parker,Charlie (as) | Davis,Miles (tp) | Thompson,Lucky (ts) | Marmarosa,Dodo (p) | Garrison,Arvin (g) | McMillan,Vic (b) | Porter,Roy (dr)

Charlie Parker's New Stars
Relaxin' At The Camarillo
Los Angeles,CA, rec. 26.2.1947
Parker,Charlie (as) | McGhee,Howard (tp) | Gray,Wardell (ts) | Marmarosa,Dodo (p) | Kessel,Barney (g) | Callender,Red (b) | Lamond,Don (dr)

Charlie Parker Quintet
Chasin' The Bird | Donna Lee
NYC, rec. 8.5.1947
Parker,Charlie (as) | Davis,Miles (tp) | Powell,Bud (p) | Potter,Tommy (b) | Roach,Max (dr)

Dizzy Gillespie Quintet
Confirmation | Ko-Ko
Live at Carnegie Hall,NYC, rec. 29.9.1947
Gillespie,Dizzy (tp) | Parker,Charlie (as) | Lewis,John (p) | McKibbon,Al (b) | Harris,Joe (dr)

Charlie Parker Quintet
Bird Of Paradise | Embraceable You
NYC, rec. 28.10.1947
Parker,Charlie (as) | Davis,Miles (tp) | Jordan,Duke (p) | Potter,Tommy (b) | Roach,Max (dr)

Scrapple From The Apple | Out Of Nowhere | Don't Blame Me
NYC, rec. 4.11.1947
Parker,Charlie (as) | Davis,Miles (tp) | Jordan,Duke (p) | Potter,Tommy (b) | Roach,Max (dr)

Bluebird | Another Hair-Do
Detroit, rec. 21.12.1941
Parker,Charlie (as) | Davis,Miles (tp) | Jordan,Duke (p) | Potter,Tommy (b) | Roach,Max (dr)

Charlie Parker All Stars
Parker's Mood | Ah-Leu-Cha
NYC, rec. 18.9.1948
Parker,Charlie (as) | Lewis,John (p) | Russell,Curly (b) | Roach,Max (dr)

Marmaduke | Steeplechase | Merry-Go-Round
NYC, rec. 24.9.1948
Parker,Charlie (as) | Davis,Miles (tp) | Lewis,John (p) | Russell,Curly (b) | Roach,Max (dr)

<u>FDM 36725-2 | CD | Bud Powell:Bouncing With Bud | EAN 3460503672529</u>

Bud Powell Trio
I'll Remember April | Everything Happens To Me | Back Home Again In Indiana | I Should Care | Nice Work If You Can Get It | Off Minor | Bud's Bubble | Somebody Loves Me
NYC, rec. 10.1.1947
Powell,Bud (p) | Russell,Curly (b) | Roach,Max (dr)

Tempus Fugit | Celia | Cherokee
NYC, rec. January/February 1949
Powell,Bud (p) | Brown,Ray (b) | Roach,Max (dr)

Strictly Confidential | I'll Keep Loving You | All God's Chillun Got Rhythm
NYC, rec. Spring 1949
Powell,Bud (p) | Brown,Ray (b) | Roach,Max (dr)

You Go To My Head | Ornithology
NYC, rec. 8.8.1949
Powell,Bud (p) | Potter,Tommy (b) | Haynes,Roy (dr)

Bud Powell Quintet
Bouncing With Bud | Wail | Dance Of The Infidels | 52nd Street Theme
Powell,Bud (p) | Navarro,Fats (tp) | Rollins,Sonny (ts) | Potter,Tommy (b) | Haynes,Roy (dr)

<u>FDM 36726-2 | CD | Django Reinhardt:Echoes Of France | EAN 3460503672628</u>

Quintet Du Hot Club De France
Limehouse Blues | Oriental Shuffle | Are You In The Mood
Paris,France, rec. 4.5.1936
Quintet Du Hot Club De France | Grappelli,Stephane (v) | Reinhardt,Django (g) | Reinhardt,Joseph (g) | Ferret,Pierre (g) | Simoens,Lucien (b)

Sweet Chorus
Paris,France, rec. 15.10.1936
Quintet Du Hot Club De France | Grappelli,Stephane (v) | Reinhardt,Django (g) | Reinhardt,Joseph (g) | Ferret,Pierre (g) | Vola,Louis (b)

Tears | In A Sentimental Mood
Paris,France, rec. 21.4.1937
Quintet Du Hot Club De France | Grappelli,Stephane (v) | Reinhardt,Django (g) | Bianchi,Marcel (g) | Ferret,Pierre (g) | Viale,Louis (b)

Django Reinhardt Trio
Bouncing Around | St.Louis Blues
Paris,France, rec. 9.9.1937
Reinhardt,Django (g) | Gaste,Louis (g) | D'Hellemmes,Eugene (b)

Eddie South/Stephane Grappelli Quintet
Daphne
Paris,France, rec. 29.9.1937
South,Eddie (v) | Grappelli,Stephane (v) | Reinhardt,Django (g) | Chaput,Roger (g) | Myers,Wilson Ernest (b)

Quintet Du Hot Club De France
Minor Swing | Viper's Dream
Paris,France, rec. 25.11.1937
Quintet Du Hot Club De France | Grappelli,Stephane (v) | Reinhardt,Django (g) | Reinhardt,Joseph (g) | Vees,Eugene (g) | Vola,Louis (b)

Sweet Sue Just You | Nuages
Paris,France, rec. 13.12.1940
Reinhardt,Django (g) | Rostaing,Hubert (ts) | Combelle,Alix (cl,chimes) | Reinhardt,Joseph (g) | Rovira,Tony (b) | Fouad,Pierre (dr)

Django Reinhardt Quartet
Blues Clair
Paris,France, rec. 26.2.1943
Reinhardt,Django (g) | Vees,Eugene (g) | Storne,Jean (b) | Leonard,Gaston (dr)

Quintet Du Hot Club De France
Django's Tiger | Echoes Of France(La Marseillaise)
London,GB, rec. 31.1.1946
Reinhardt,Django (g) | Grappelli,Stephane (v) | Llewellyn,Jack (g) | Hodgkiss,Allan (g) | Goode,Coleridge (b)

Si Tu Savais
Paris,France, rec. 14.11.1947
Quintet Du Hot Club De France | Reinhardt,Django (g) | Grappelli,Stephane (v) | Reinhardt,Joseph (g) | Vees,Eugene (g) | Ermelin,Fred (b)

Ol' Man River
Paris,France, rec. 21.11.1947
Quintet Du Hot Club De France | Reinhardt,Django (g) | Grappelli,Stephane (v) | Reinhardt,Joseph (g) | Vees,Eugene (g) | Ermelin,Fred (b)

<u>FDM 36727-2 | CD | Art Tatum:Over The Rainbow | EAN 3460503672727</u>

Art Tatum
Moonglow | Somebody Loves Me
NYC, rec. 22.8.1934
Tatum,Art (p-solo)

Get Happy
Los Angeles,CA, rec. 22.2.1940
Tatum,Art (p-solo)

Begin The Beguine
Los Angeles,CA, rec. 11.4.1940
Tatum,Art (p-solo)

Tea For Two
Los Angeles,CA, rec. 2.5.1940
Tatum,Art (p-solo)

If I Had You
Los Angeles,CA, rec. 9.5.1940
Tatum,Art (p-solo)

Art Tatum Trio
I Would Do Anything For You | I Got Rhythm | Honeysuckle Rose | Dark Eyes
NYC, rec. 5.1.1944
Tatum,Art (p) | Grimes,Tiny (g) | Stewart,Slam (b)

Art Tatum
In A Sentimental Mood | Tenderly | Over The Rainbow | She's Funny That Way
Los Angeles,CA, rec. 1948
Tatum,Art (p-solo)

Someone To Watch Over Me | Nice Work If You Can Get It | Willow Weep For Me | Somebody Loves Me
Los Angeles,CA, rec. 25.7.1949
Tatum,Art (p-solo)

Dancing In The Dark | Blue Skies | You Took Advantage Of Me | It's The Talk Of The Town
Los Angeles,CA, rec. 29.9.1949
Tatum,Art (p-solo)

<u>FDM 36729-2 | CD | Lester Young:Blue Lester | EAN 3460503672925</u>

Lester Young-Nat Cole Trio
Back Home Again In Indiana | I Can't Get Started | Body And Soul
Los Angeles,CA, rec. 15.7.1942
Young,Lester (ts) | Cole,Nat King (p) | Callender,Red (b)

Lester Young Quartet
Just You Just Me | I Never Knew
NYC, rec. 1.5.1944
Young,Lester (ts) | Guarnieri,Johnny (p) | Stewart,Slam (b) | Catlett,Big Sid (dr)

Kansas City Five
Lester Leaps Again
NYC, rec. 22.3.1944
Kansas City Five,The | Young,Lester (ts) | Basie,Count[as 'Prince Charming'] (p) | Green,Freddie (g) | Richardson,Rodney (b) | Jones,Jo (dr)

Kansas City Six
I Got Rhythm
NYC, rec. 28.3.1944
Kansas City Six,The | Young,Lester (ts) | Coleman,Bill (tp) | Wells,Dicky (tb) | Bushkin,Joe (p) | Simmons,John (b) | Jones,Jo (dr)

Lester Young Quintet
Jump Lester J | I Don't Stand A Ghost Of A Chance With You | Blue Lester
NYC, rec. 1.5.1944
Young,Lester (ts) | Basie,Count (p) | Green,Freddie (g) | Richardson,Rodney (b) | Wilson,Shadow (dr)

Lester Young And His Band
These Foolish Things Remind Me On You
Los Angeles,CA, rec. December 1945
Young,Lester (ts) | Marmarosa,Dodo (p) | Green,Freddie (g) | Callender,Red (b) | Green,Henry (dr)

Lester Young Trio
The Man I Love | Back To The Land | I Want To Be Happy
Los Angeles,CA, rec. March/April 1946
Young,Lester (ts) | Cole,Nat King (p) | Rich,Buddy (dr)

Lester Young-Nat King Cole
Peg O' My Heart
Young,Lester (ts) | Cole,Nat King (p)

Lester Young And His Band
She's Funny That Way
Los Angeles,CA, rec. August 1946
Young,Lester (ts) | Albany,Joe (p) | Ashby,Irving (g) | Callender,Red (b) | Hamilton,Forrest 'Chico' (dr)

I'm Confessin'(That I Love You)
NYC, rec. 2.4.1947
Young,Lester (ts) | McConnell,Shorty (tp) | Hakim,Sadik[Argonne Thornton] (p) | Barakaat,Nasir (g) | Richardson,Rodney (b) | Marshall,Lyndell (dr)

Lester Young Quartet
Polka Dots And Moonbeams | Too Marvelous For Words
NYC, rec. 17.9.1949
Young,Lester (ts) | Jones,Hank (p) | Brown,Ray (b) | Rich,Buddy (dr)

<u>**FDM 36730-2 | CD | Louis Armstrong:C'est Si Bon | EAN 3460503673021**</u>

Louis Armstrong And His Orchestra
Perdido Street Blues
NYC, rec. 27.5.1940
Armstrong,Louis (tp,voc) | Jones,Claude (tb) | Bechet,Sidney (cl,as) | Russell,Luis (p) | Addison,Bernard (g) | Braud,Wellman (b) | Singleton,Zutty (dr)

When It's Sleepy Time Down South
Chicago,Ill, rec. 16.11.1941
Armstrong,Louis (tp,voc) | Hemphill,Shelton (tp) | Prince,Gene (tp) | Galbraith,Frank (tp) | Washington,George (tb) | Chambers,Henderson (tb) | Greene,Norman (tb) | Cole,Rupert (as) | Frye,Carl (as) | Garland,Joe (cl,ts) | Robinson,Prince (cl,ts) | Russell,Luis (p,arr) | Lucie,Lawrence (g) | Alvis,Hayes (b) | Catlett,Big Sid (dr)

I Wonder
NYC, rec. 14.1.1945
Armstrong,Louis (tp,voc) | Butterfield,Billy (tp) | Stoneburn,Sid (as) | Rubin,Jules (cl,as) | Stegmeyer,Bill (cl,ts) | Rollini,Arthur (cl,ts) | Ricci,Paul (b-cl,bs) | Bowman,Dave (p) | Kress,Carl (g) | Haggart,Bob (b) | Blowers,Johnny (dr)

Leonard Feather's Esquire All-Americans
Long Long Journey
NYC, rec. 10.1.1946
Esquire All-Americans,Leonard Feather's | Armstrong,Louis (tp,voc) | Shavers,Charlie (tp) | Hamilton,Jimmy (cl) | Hodges,Johnny (as) | Byas,Don (ts) | Strayhorn,Billy (p) | Ellington,Duke (p) | Palmieri,Remo (g) | Jackson,Chubby (b) | Greer,William 'Sonny' (dr)

Louis Armstrong And Ella Fitzgerald With Bob Hagger's Orchestra
You Won't Be Satisfied Until You Break My Heart
NYC, rec. 18.1.1946
Armstrong,Louis (tp,voc) | Fitzgerald,Ella (voc) | Butterfield,Billy (tp) | Stegmeyer,Bill (cl,as) | Koenig,George (as) | Greenberg,Jack (ts) | Drellinger,Art (ts) | Chatz,Milton (bs) | Bushkin,Joe (p) | Perri,Danny (g) | Alpert,Trigger (b) | Cole,William 'Cozy' (dr) | Haggart,Bob (cond,arr)

Louis Armstrong And His Orchestra
Back O'Town Blues
NYC, rec. 27.4.1946
Armstrong,Louis (tp,voc) | Mullens,Eddie (tp) | Jordan,Ludwig (tp) | Ford,Andrew (tp) | Scott,William (tp) | Moore,Russel 'Big Chief' (tb) | Martin,Adam (tb) | Powe,Norman (tb) | Cobbs,Alfred (tb) | Hill,Don (as) | Gordon,Amos (as) | Garland,Joe (ts) | Sparrow,John (ts) | Thompson,Ernest (cl,bs) | Swanston,Ed (p) | Warner,Elmer (g) | Shaw,Arvell (b) | Ballard,Butch (dr) | Middleton,Velma (voc)

Louis Armstrong And His Hot Seven
Blues For Yesterday
Los Angeles,CA, rec. 6.9.1946
Armstrong,Louis (tp,voc) | Dickenson,Vic (tb) | Bigard,Barney (cl) | Feather,Leonard (p) | Reuss,Allan (g) | Callender,Red (b) | Singleton,Zutty (dr)

Louis Armstrong And His Dixieland Seven
Do You Know What It Means To Miss New Orleans | Where The Blues Were Born In New Orleans
Los Angeles,CA, rec. 17.10.1946
Armstrong,Louis (tp,voc) | Ory,Edward 'Kid' (tb) | Bigard,Barney (cl) | Beal,Charlie (p) | Scott,Bud (g) | Callender,Red (b) | Hall,Minor 'Ram' (dr)

Louis Armstrong And His Orchestra
The Blues Are Brewin'
Armstrong,Louis (tp,voc) | Butler,Robert (tp) | Gray,Louis (tp) | Ford,Fats (tp) | Mullens,Eddie (tp) | Moore,Russel 'Big Chief' (tb) | Williams,Waddet (tb) | Allen,Nat (tb) | Whitney,James (tb) | Hill,Don (as) | Gordon,Amos (as) | Garland,Joe (ts) | Sparrow,John (ts) | Thompson,Ernest (bs) | Mason,Earl (p) | Warner,Elmer (g) | Shaw,Arvell (b) | McConney,Edmond (dr)

Rockin' Chair | Jack-Armstrong Blues
Live at Town Hall,NYC, rec. 10.6.1947
Armstrong,Louis (tp,voc) | Hackett,Bobby (tp) | Teagarden,Jack (tb,voc) | Hucko,Peanuts (cl) | Caceres,Ernie (sax) | Guarnieri,Johnny (p) | Casey,Al (g) | Hall,Al (b) | Cole,William 'Cozy' (dr)

Louis Armstrong And His All Stars
Lovely Weather We're Having
Chicago,Ill, rec. 16.10.1947
Armstrong,Louis (tp,voc) | Teagarden,Jack (tb,voc) | Bigard,Barney (cl) | Cary,Dick (p) | Shaw,Arvell (b) | Catlett,Big Sid (dr)

Louis Armstrong And Billie Holiday With Sy Oliver's Orchestra
You Can't Lose A Broken Heart
NYC, rec. 30.9.1949
Armstrong,Louis (tp,voc) | Holiday,Billie (voc) | Privin,Bernie (tp) | Cooper,Sid (as) | Mince,Johnny (as) | Drellinger,Art (ts) | Nizza,Pat (ts,bs) | Kyle,Billy (p) | Barksdale,Everett (g) | Benjamin,Joe (b) | Crawford,James (dr) | Oliver,Sy (cond,arr)

Louis Armstrong And His All Stars
That's For Me | New Orleans Function: | Flee As A Bird- | Oh Didn't He Ramble-
NYC, rec. 26.4.1950
Armstrong,Louis (tp,narration) | Teagarden,Jack (tb) | Bigard,Barney (cl) | Hines,Earl 'Fatha' (p) | Shaw,Arvell (b) | Cole,William 'Cozy' (dr)

Louis Armstrong With Sy Oliver And His Orchestra
C'Est Si Bon | La Vie En Rose
NYC, rec. 26.6.1950
Armstrong,Louis (tp,voc) | Solomon,Melvin (tp) | Privin,Bernie (tp) | Webster,Paul (tp) | Bullman,Morton (tb) | Schertzer,Hymie (as) | Yaner,Milt (as) | Drellinger,Art (ts) | Holcombe,Bill (ts) | Hines,Earl 'Fatha' (p) | Barksdale,Everett (g) | Duvivier,George (b) | Blowers,Johnny (dr) | Oliver,Sy (cond,arr)

Louis Armstrong And Ella Fitzgerald With Sy Oliver's Orchestra
Dream A Little Dream Of Me
Armstrong,Louis (tp,voc) | Fitzgerald,Ella (voc) | Webster,Paul (tp) | D'Amico,Hank (cl) | Ludwig,Frank (ts) | Jones,Hank (p) | Barksdale,Everett (g) | Brown,Ray (b) | Blowers,Johnny (dr) | Oliver,Sy (cond,arr)

Louis Armstrong With Louis Jordan And His Tympany Five
I'll Be Glad When You're Dead You Rascal You
NYC, rec. 23.8.1950
Armstrong,Louis (tp,voc) | Jordan,Lewis (as,voc) | Izenhall,Aaron (tp) | Jackson,Josh (ts) | Doggett,Bill (p) | Jennings,Bill (g) | Bushnell,Bob (b) | Morris,Joe (dr)

<u>FDM 36731-2 | CD | Miles Davis:Milestones | EAN 3460503673120</u>

Miles Davis All Stars
Milestones | Little Willie Leaps | Half Nelson | Sippin' At Bells
NYC, rec. 14.8.1947
Davis,Miles (tp) | Parker,Charlie (ts) | Lewis,John (p) | Boyd,Nelson (b) | Roach,Max (dr)

Miles Davis And His Orchestra
Jeru | Godchild | Move
NYC, rec. 21.1.1949
Davis,Miles (tp) | Winding,Kai (tb) | Collins,Junior (fr-h) | Barber,Bill (tuba) | Konitz,Lee (as) | Mulligan,Gerry (bs,arr) | Haig,Al (p) | Shulman,Joe (b) | Roach,Max (dr)

Venus De Milo | Boplicity
NYC, rec. 22.4.1949
Davis,Miles (tp,arr) | Johnson,J.J. (tb) | Siegelstein,Sandy (fr-h) | Barber,Bill (tuba) | Konitz,Lee (as) | Mulligan,Gerry (bs,arr) | Lewis,John (p,arr) | Boyd,Nelson (b) | Clarke,Kenny (dr)

Miles Davis/Tadd Dameron Quintet
Rifftide | Good Bait | Don't Blame Me
Paris,France, rec. 8.5.1949
Davis,Miles (tp) | Dameron,Tadd (p,arr) | Moody,James (ts) | Spieler,Barney (b) | Clarke,Kenny (dr)
Miles Davis Sextet
Ray's Idea | Woody'n You
NYC, rec. 18.2.1950
Davis,Miles (tp) | Johnson,J.J. (tb) | Getz,Stan (ts) | Dameron,Tadd (p) | Ramey,Gene (b) | Blakey,Art (dr)
Miles Davis And His Orchestra
Moon Dreams
NYC, rec. 9.3.1950
Davis,Miles (tp) | Johnson,J.J. (tb) | Schuller,Gunther (fr-h) | Barber,Bill (tuba) | Konitz,Lee (as) | Mulligan,Gerry (bs,arr) | Lewis,John (p) | McKibbon,Al (b) | Roach,Max (dr)

FDM 36733-2 | CD | Stan Getz:Imagination | EAN 3460503673328
Stan Getz Five Brothers Bop Tenor Sax Stars
Five Brothers | Battle Of The Saxes
NYC, rec. 8.4.1949
Getz,Stan (ts) | Cohn,Al (ts) | Eager,Allen (ts) | Moore,Brew (ts) | Sims,Zoot (ts) | Bishop Jr.,Walter (p) | Ramey,Gene (b) | Perry,Charlie (dr)
Stan Getz Quartet
Long Island Sound | Indian Summer
NYC, rec. 21.6.1949
Getz,Stan (ts) | Haig,Al (p) | Ramey,Gene (b) | Levey,Stan (dr)
I've Got You Under My Skin | Too Marvelous For Words | There's A Small Hotel | What's New?
NYC, rec. 6.1.1950
Getz,Stan (ts) | Haig,Al (p) | Potter,Tommy (b) | Haynes,Roy (dr)
My Old Flame | You Stepped Out Of A Dream
NYC, rec. 14.4.1950
Getz,Stan (ts) | Aless,Tony (p) | Heath,Percy (b) | Lamond,Don (dr)
On The Alamo | You Go To My Head | Gone With The Wind | Hershey Bar | Yesterdays | Sweetie Pie
NYC, rec. 17.5.1950
Getz,Stan (ts) | Haig,Al (p) | Potter,Tommy (b) | Haynes,Roy (dr)
Out Of Nowhere | Imagination | 'S Wonderful | Tootsie Roll | Strike Up The Band
NYC, rec. 10.12.1950
Getz,Stan (ts) | Silver,Horace (p) | Calloway,Joe (b) | Bolden,Walter (dr)

FDM 36734-2 | CD | Dizzy Gillespie:Night In Tunisia | EAN 3460503673427
Dizzy Gillespie All Stars
I Can't Get Started | Good Bait
NYC, rec. 9.1.1945
Gillespie,Dizzy (tp) | Young,Trummy (tb) | Byas,Don (ts) | Hart,Clyde (p) | Pettiford,Oscar (b) | Manne,Shelly (dr)
Dizzy Gillespie Sextet
Blue 'N' Boogie
NYC, rec. 9.2.1945
Gillespie,Dizzy (tp) | Gordon,Dexter (ts) | Papareli,Frank (p) | Wayne,Chuck (g) | Shipinsky,Murray (b) | Kluger,Irv (dr)
All The Things You Are
NYC, rec. 28.2.1945
Gillespie,Dizzy (tp) | Parker,Charlie (as) | Hart,Clyde (p) | Palmieri,Remo (g) | Stewart,Slam (b) | Cole,William 'Cozy' (dr)
Dizzy Gillespie All Stars
Hot House | Salt Peanuts | Shaw 'Nuff
NYC, rec. 11.5.1945
Gillespie,Dizzy (tp) | Parker,Charlie (as) | Haig,Al (p) | Russell,Curly (b) | Catlett,Big Sid (dr)
Tempo Jazzmen
Dynamo A | Confirmation | Round About Midnight
NYC, rec. 6.2.1946
Tempo Jazzmen | Gillespie,Dizzy (tp) | Thompson,Lucky (ts) | Jackson,Milt (vib) | Haig,Al (p) | Brown,Ray (b) | Levey,Stan (dr)
Dizzy Gillespie And His Orchestra
A Night In Tunisia | Ol' Man Rebop | 52nd Street Theme
NYC, rec. 22.2.1946
Gillespie,Dizzy (tp) | Byas,Don (ts) | Jackson,Milt (vib) | Haig,Al (p) | De Arango,Bill (g) | Brown,Ray (b) | Heard,J.C. (dr)
Anthropology
Gillespie,Dizzy (tp) | Jackson,Milt (vib) | Haig,Al (p) | De Arango,Bill (g) | Brown,Ray (b) | Heard,J.C. (dr)
Dizzy Gillespie Sextet
Oop-Bop-Sh-Bam | That's Earl Brother
NYC, rec. 15.5.1946
Gillespie,Dizzy (tp,voc) | Stitt,Sonny (as) | Jackson,Milt (vib) | Haig,Al (p) | Brown,Ray (b) | Clarke,Kenny (dr) | Fuller,Gil (voc)
Dizzy Gillespie Quintet
Groovin' High | Dizzy Atmosphere
Live at Carnegie Hall,NYC, rec. 29.9.1947
Gillespie,Dizzy (tp) | Parker,Charlie (as) | Lewis,John (p) | McKibbon,Al (b) | Harris,Joe (dr)

FDM 36735-2 | CD | Lionel Hampton:Flying Home | EAN 3460503673526
Lionel Hampton And His Orchestra
Blue Because Of You
NYC, rec. 12.10.1939
Hampton,Lionel (vib) | Cole,Nat King (p) | Moore,Oscar (g) | Prince,Wesley (b) | Spieldock,Al (dr)
Central Avenue Breakdown
Hollywood,CA, rec. 10.5.1940
Hampton,Lionel (p) | Cole,Nat King (p) | Moore,Oscar (g) | Prince,Wesley (b) | Spieldock,Al (dr)
Flying Home
NYC, rec. 16.5.1942
Hampton,Lionel (vib) | Royal,Ernie (tp) | George,Karl (tp) | Newman,Joe (tp) | Beckett,Fred (tb) | Craven,Luther 'Sonny' (tb) | Sloane,Carol (voc) | Royal,Marshall (as) | Perry,Ray (as) | Gordon,Dexter (ts) | Jacquet,Illinois (ts) | McVea,Jack (bs) | Buckner,Milt (p) | Ashby,Irving (g) | Alley,Vernon (b) | Jenkins,George (dr)
Loose Wig
NYC, rec. 2.3.1944
Hampton,Lionel (vib) | Anderson,Cat (tp) | Wright,Lammar (tp) | McCoy,Roy (tp) | Morris,Joe (tp) | Hayse,Alvin (tb) | Wood,Booty (tb) | Beckett,Fred (tb) | Bostic,Earl (as) | Evans,Gus (as) | Sears,Al (ts) | Cobb,Arnett (ts) | Fowlkes,Charlie (bs) | Buckner,Milt (p) | Miller,Eric (g) | King,Vernon (b) | Radcliffe,Fred (dr)
Million Dollar Smile
Los Angeles,CA, rec. 16.10.1944
Hampton,Lionel (vib) | Young,Eugene 'Snooky' (tp) | Culley,Wendell (tp) | Morris,Joe (tp) | Page,Dave (tp) | Wright,Lammar (tp) | Porter,Vernon (tb) | Beckett,Fred (tb) | Penn,Andrew (tb) | Craven,Luther 'Sonny' (tb) | Durham,Allen (tb) | Dorsey,George (as) | Evans,Gus (as) | Cobb,Arnett (ts) | Simon,Fred (ts) | Fowlkes,Charlie (bs) | Buckner,Milt (p) | Mackel,Billy (g) | Harris,Charles (b) | Sinclair,Ted (b) | Radcliffe,Fred (dr)
Beulah's Boogie
NYC, rec. 21.5.1945
Hampton,Lionel (p) | Culley,Wendell (tp) | Morris,Joe (tp) | Wright,Lammar (tp) | Page,Dave (tp) | Killian,Al (tp) | Morris,John (tb) | Hamid,Abdul (tb) | Hayse,Alvin (tb) | Penn,Andrew (tb) | Fields,Herbie (as) | Evans,Gus (as) | Peters,Jay (ts) | Cobb,Arnett (ts) | Fowlkes,Charlie (bs) | Beckenbridge,Dardanelle (p) | Mackel,Billy (g) | Harris,Charles (b) | Siclair,Ted (b) | Jenkins,George (dr)
Lionel Hampton And His Septet
Blow Top Blues
Hampton,Lionel (vib) | Culley,Wendell (tp) | Fields,Herbie (as) | Cobb,Arnett (ts) | Mehegan,John (p) | Mackel,Billy (g) | Harris,Charles (b) | Jones,George (dr) | Washington,Dinah (voc)
Lionel Hampton And His Orchestra
Rockin' In Rhythm
NYC, rec. 29.1.1946
Hampton,Lionel (vib,dr) | Morris,Joe (tp) | Culley,Wendell (tp) | Page,Dave (tp) | Nottingham,Jimmy (tp) | Wright,Lammar (tp) | Wormick,James (tb) | Wood,Booty (tb) | Penn,Andrew (tb) | Hayse,Alvin (tb) | Plater,Bobby (as) | Kynard,Ben (as) | Cobb,Arnett (ts) | Griffin,Johnny (ts) | Fowlkes,Charlie (bs) | Buckner,Milt (p,arr) | Mackel,Billy (g) | Harris,Charles (b) | Sinclair,Ted (b) | Jenkins,George (dr)
Air Mail Special
NYC, rec. 31.1.1946
Hampton,Lionel (vib,dr) | Morris,Joe (tp) | Culley,Wendell (tp) | Page,Dave (tp) | Nottingham,Jimmy (tp) | Wright,Lammar (tp) | Wormick,James (tb) | Wood,Booty (tb) | Penn,Andrew (tb) | Hayse,Alvin (tb) | Plater,Bobby (as) | Kynard,Ben (as) | Cobb,Arnett (ts) | Griffin,Johnny (ts) | Fowlkes,Charlie (bs) | Buckner,Milt (p,arr) | Mackel,Billy (g) | Harris,Charles (b) | Sinclair,Ted (b) | Jenkins,George (dr)
Lionel Hampton All Stars
Stardust
Live at Pasadena Civic Auditorium,CA, rec. 4.8.1947
Hampton,Lionel (vib) | Shavers,Charlie (tp) | Smith,Willie (as) | Corcoran,Corky (ts) | Todd,Tommy (p) | Kessel,Barney (g) | Stewart,Slam (b) | Young,Lee (dr)
Lionel Hampton And His Orchestra
Midnight Sun | Muchacho Azul
Los Angeles,CA, rec. 10.11.1947
Hampton,Lionel (vib) | Culley,Wendell (tp) | Garrette,Duke (tp) | Buckner,Teddy (tp) | Sheppard,Leo (tp) | Robinson,James (tb) | Penn,Andrew (tb) | Wormick,James (tb) | Woodman,Britt (tb) | Kelso,Jack (cl,as) | Plater,Bobby (as) | Kynard,Ben (as) | Lane,Morris (ts) | Sparrow,John (ts) | Fowlkes,Charlie (bs) | Buckner,Milt (p,arr) | Mackel,Billy (g) | Comfort,Joe (b) | Mingus,Charles (b) | Walker,Earl (dr) | Burke,Sonny (arr) | Doggett,Bill (arr)
Lionel Hampton Quartet
Moonglow
NYC, rec. 26.4.1949
Hampton,Lionel (vib) | Montgomery,Wes (g) | Johnson,Roy (b) | Walker,Earl (dr)
Lionel Hampton And His Orchestra
The Hucklebuck
NYC, rec. 10.5.1949
Hampton,Lionel (vib) | Mullens,Eddie (tp) | Culley,Wendell (tp) | Sheppard,Leo (tp) | Williams,Walter (tp) | Bailey,Benny (tp) | Bass,Lester (tb) | Grey,Al (tb) | Outcalt,Al 'Chippy' (tb) | Wormick,James (tb) | Plater,Bobby (as) | Board,Johnny (as) | Morris,Gene (ts) | Sparrow,John (ts) | Williams,Billy (ts) | Kynard,Ben (bs) | Gaddison,Frances (p) | Montgomery,Wes (g) | Johnson,Roy (b) | Walker,Earl (dr) | Carter,Betty (voc)
Hamp's Gumbo | Sad Feeling
NYC, rec. 25.1.1950
Hampton,Lionel (vib) | Mullens,Eddie (tp) | Sheppard,Leo (tp) | Williams,Walter (tp) | Bailey,Benny (tp) | Garrette,Duke (tp) | Grey,Al (tb) | Wormick,James (tb) | Powell,Benny (tb) | Higaki,Paul (tb) | Plater,Bobby (as,arr) | Richardson,Jerome (as) | Board,Johnny (ts) | Lowe,Curtis (ts) | Williams,Billy (ts) | Shaw,Lonnie (bs) | Duke,Douglas (p) | Montgomery,Wes (g) | Johnson,Roy (b) | Bartee,Ellis (dr) | Parker,Sonny (voc)

FDM 36736-2 | CD | Fats Navarro:Nostalgia | EAN 3460503673625
Kenny Clarke And His 52nd Street Boys
52nd Street Theme | Rue Chaptal | Oop-Bop-Sh-Bam
NYC, rec. 5.9.1946
Clarke,Kenny (dr) | Navarro,Fats (tp) | Dorham,Kenny (tp) | Stitt,Sonny (as) | Abrams,Ray (ts) | De Verteuil,Eddie (bs) | Powell,Bud (p) | Collins,John (g) | Hall,Al (b) | Fuller,Gil (arr)
Fats Navarro Quintet
Goin' To Mintons | Fat Girl | Ice Freezes Red | Eb Pob
NYC, rec. January 1947
Navarro,Fats (tp) | Parker,Leo (bs) | Dameron,Tadd (p,arr) | Ramey,Gene (b) | Best,Denzil (dr)
Tadd Dameron-Fats Navarro Sextet
The Squirrel | Our Delight | Dameronia
NYC, rec. 26.9.1947
Navarro,Fats (tp) | Henry,Ernie (as) | Rouse,Charlie (ts) | Dameron,Tadd (p,arr) | Boyd,Nelson (b) | Wilson,Shadow (dr)
Tadd Dameron-Fats Navarro Quintet
The Tadd Walk
NYC, rec. 28.10.1947
Navarro,Fats (tp) | Henry,Ernie (as) | Dameron,Tadd (p,arr) | Russell,Curly (b) | Clarke,Kenny (dr)
Fats Navarro Quintet
Nostalgia | Be Bop Romp | Barry's Bop | Fats Blows | The Chase
NYC, rec. 5.12.1947
Navarro,Fats (tp) | Rouse,Charlie (ts) | Dameron,Tadd (p,arr) | Boyd,Nelson (b) | Blakey,Art (dr)
Dexter Gordon Quintet
Dextrose
NYC, rec. 22.12.1947
Gordon,Dexter (ts) | Navarro,Fats (tp) | Dameron,Tadd (p) | Boyd,Nelson (b) | Mardigan,Art (dr)
Tadd Dameron Septet
Lady Bird
NYC, rec. 13.9.1948
Dameron,Tadd (p) | Navarro,Fats (tp) | Gray,Wardell (ts) | Eager,Allen (ts) | Russell,Curly (b) | Clarke,Kenny (dr) | Pozo,Chino (bongos)
Don Lanphere Quintet
Infatuation | Stop | Wailing Wall
NYC, rec. 20.9.1949
Lanphere,Don (ts) | Navarro,Fats (tp) | Haig,Al (p) | Potter,Tommy (b) | Roach,Max (dr)

FDM 36737-2 | CD | Charlie Parker:April In Paris | EAN 3460503673724
Charlie Parker With Machito And His Orchestra
Okiedoke
NYC, rec. January 1949
Parker,Charlie (as) | Machito (Raul Grillo) | Bauza,Mario (tp) | Davilla,Frank 'Paquito' (tp) | Woodlen,Bob (tp) | Johnson,Gene (as) | Skerritt,Fred (as) | Madera,Jose (ts) | Johnakins,Leslie (bs) | Fernandez,Rene (p) | Rodriguez,Roberto (b) | Mangual,Jose (bongos) | Miranda,Luis (dr,congas) | Nieto,Ubaldo (timbales)
Charlie Parker With Strings
April In Paris | Everything Happens To Me | Just Friends | Summertime | If I Should Lose You | I Didn't Know What Time It Was
NYC, rec. 30.10.1949
Parker,Charlie (as) | Miller,Mitch (engl-horn,oboe) | Gimpel,Bronislaw (v) | Hollander,Max (v) | Lamask,Milton (v) | Brieff,Frank (viola) | Miller,Frank (cello) | Rosen,Meyer (harp) | Freeman,Stan (p) | Brown,Ray (b) | Rich,Buddy (dr) | Carroll,Jimmy (arr,dir)
Charlie Parker Quartet
Star Eyes | I'm In The Mood For Love
NYC, rec. March/April 1950
Parker,Charlie (as) | Jones,Hank (p) | Brown,Ray (b) | Rich,Buddy (dr)
Charlie Parker And His Orchestra
My Melancholy Baby
NYC, rec. 6.6.1950
Parker,Charlie (as) | Gillespie,Dizzy (tp) | Monk,Thelonious (p) | Russell,Curly (b) | Rich,Buddy (dr)
Charlie Parker With Strings
Laura | Out Of Nowhere | East Of The Sun West Of The Moon | I'll Remember April | Easy To Love | Dancing In The Dark | I'm In The Mood For Love | They Can't Take That Away From Me
NYC, rec. Summer 1950
Parker,Charlie (as) | Singer,Joe (fr-h) | Brown,Eddie (oboe) | Caplan,Sam (v) | Kay,Howard (v) | Melnikoff,Harry (v) | Rand,Sam (v) | Smirnoff,Kelly (v) | Zir,Isadore (viola) | Brown,Maurice (cello) | Mills,Verley (harp) | Leighton,Bernie (p) | Brown,Ray (b) | Rich,Buddy (dr) | Lippman,Joe (cond,arr)

FDM 36738-2 | CD | Oscar Peterson:Get Happy | EAN 3460503673823
Oscar Peterson-Ray Brown Duo
Carnegie Blues | I Only Have Eyes For You
Live at Carnegie Hall,NYC, rec. 18.8.1949
Peterson,Oscar (p) | Brown,Ray (b)
Three O'Clock In The Morning | Tenderly | Debut | Lover Come Back To Me | Oscar's Blues | They Didn't Believe Me | All The Things You Are | Where Or When
NYC, rec. March 1950
Peterson,Oscar (p) | Brown,Ray (b)
Oscar Peterson-Major Holley Duo
Exactly Like You | Little White Lies | Nameless | Two Sleepy People | In The Middle Of A Kiss | Get Happy | Jumpin' With Symphony Sid | Robbin's Nest
NYC, rec. May 1950
Peterson,Oscar (p) | Holley,Major (b)
Oscar Peterson-Ray Brown Duo
Salute To Gamer
NYC, rec. August 1950
Peterson,Oscar (p) | Brown,Ray (b)

FDM 36739-2 | CD | Sarah Vaughan:Lover Man | EAN 3460503673922
Sarah Vaughan With The Teddy Wilson Quartet
September Song
NYC, rec. 19.11.1944
Vaughan,Sarah (voc) | Wilson,Teddy (p) | Ventura,Charlie (ts) | Palmieri,Remo (g) | Taylor,Billy (b)
Sarah Vaughan With The Allstars
Interlude(A Night In Tunisia) | East Of The Sun West Of The Moon | No Smoke Blues | Singing Off
NYC, rec. 31.12.1944
Vaughan,Sarah (voc) | Gillespie,Dizzy (tp) | Sachs,Aaron (cl) | Auld,Georgie (ts) | Feather,Leonard (p) | Wayne,Chuck (g) | Lesberg,Jack (b) | Feld,Morey (dr)
Sarah Vaughan With Dizzy Gillespie And His All Star Quintet
Lover Man(Oh,Where Can You Be?)
NYC, rec. 11.5.1945
Vaughan,Sarah (voc) | Gillespie,Dizzy (tp) | Parker,Charlie (as) | Haig,Al (p) | Russell,Curly (b) | Catlett,Big Sid (dr)
Sarah Vaughan With Dizzy Gillespie And His Septet
Mean To Me | What More Can A Woman Do
NYC, rec. 25.5.1945
Vaughan,Sarah (voc) | Gillespie,Dizzy (tp) | Parker,Charlie (as) | Phillips,Flip (ts) | Jaffe,Nat (p) | De Arango,Bill (g) | Russell,Curly (b) | Roach,Max (dr)
I'd Rather Have A Memory Than A Dream
Vaughan,Sarah (voc) | Gillespie,Dizzy (tp) | Parker,Charlie (as) | Phillips,Flip (ts) | Dameron,Tadd (p) | De Arango,Bill (g) | Russell,Curly (b) | Roach,Max (dr)
Sarah Vaughan With John Kirby And His Orchestra
I'm Scared | You Go To My Head
NYC, rec. 9.1.1946
Vaughan,Sarah (voc) | Kirby,John (b) | Brereton,Clarence (tp) | Bailey,Buster (cl) | Procope,Russell (as) | Kyle,Billy (p) | Beason,Bill (dr)
Sarah Vaughan With The Jimmy Jones Quartet
What A Difference A Day Made
NYC, rec. 29.12.1947
Vaughan,Sarah (voc) | Jones,Jimmy (p) | Collins,John (g) | McKibbon,Al (b) | Clarke,Kenny (dr)
Sarah Vaughan With The Joe Lippman Orchestra
Black Coffee
NYC, rec. 20.1.1949
Vaughan,Sarah (voc) | Griffin,Gordon (tp) | Maxwell,Jimmy (tp) | Solomon,Melvin (tp) | Morrow,Buddy (tb) | D'Agostino,John (tb) | Kaufman,Bernard (as) | Terrill,Harry (as) | Ross,Hank (ts) | Feldman,Harold (ts) | Tannenbaum,Wolfe (bs) | Rowland,Bill (p) | Haggart,Bob (b) | Shawker,Norris 'Bunny' (dr) | unkn. (harp) | unkn. (7 strings)
Sarah Vaughan With The Hugo Winterhalter Orchestra
I Cried For You(Now It's Your Turn To Cry Over Me)
NYC, rec. 28.9.1949
Vaughan,Sarah (voc) | Ferretti,Andy (tp) | Butterfield,Billy (tp) | Maxwell,Jimmy (tp) | Bradley,Will (tb) | D'Agostino,John (tb) | Pritchard,Bill (tb) | Cooper,Sid (as) | Webb,Stanley (as) | Ross,Hank (ts) | Feldman,Harold (ts) | Kaufman,Bernard (bs) | Jones,Jimmie (p) | Mottola,Tony (g) | Haggart,Bob (b) | Snyder,Terry (dr) | Winterhalter,Hugo (arr,ld)
Sarah Vaughan The The Joe Lippman Orchestra
Summertime
NYC, rec. 21.12.1949
Vaughan,Sarah (voc) | Butterfield,Billy (tp) | Jordan,Taft (tp) | Bradley,Will (tb) | Mondello,Toots (as) | Schertzer,Hymie (as) | Drellinger,Art (ts) | Kelly,George (ts) | Webb,Stanley (bs) | Jones,Jimmy (p) | Caiola,Al (g) | Safranski,Eddie (b) | Cole,William 'Cozy' (dr)
Sarah Vaughan With George Treadwell And His Allstars
Ain't Misbehavin'
NYC, rec. 18.5.1950
Vaughan,Sarah (voc) | Davis,Miles (tp) | Green,Bennie (tb) | Scott,Tony (cl) | Johnson,Budd (ts) | Jones,Jimmy (p) | Green,Freddie (g) | Taylor,Billy (b) | Heard,J.C. (dr)
Can't Get Out Of This Mood
Vaughan,Sarah (voc) | Green,Bennie (tb) | Scott,Tony (cl) | Johnson,Budd (ts) | Jones,Jimmy (p) | Green,Freddie (g) | Taylor,Billy (b) | Heard,J.C. (dr)
It Might As Well Be Spring
Vaughan,Sarah (voc) | Davis,Miles (tp) | Scott,Tony (cl) | Jones,Jimmy (p) | Taylor,Billy (b) | Heard,J.C. (dr)
Come Rain Or Come Shine | Nice Work If You Can Get It
NYC, rec. 19.5.1950
Vaughan,Sarah (voc) | Davis,Miles (tp) | Green,Bennie (tb) | Scott,Tony (cl) | Johnson,Budd (ts) | Jones,Jimmy (p) | Lowe,Mundell (g) | Taylor,Billy (b) | Heard,J.C. (dr)
Sarah Vaughan With The Norman Leyden Orchestra
Perdido
NYC, rec. 5.9.1950
Vaughan,Sarah (voc) | Solomon,Melvin (tp) | Griffith,Gus (tp) | Maxwell,Jimmy (tp) | Morrow,Buddy (tb) | Satterfield,Jack (tb) | Versaci,Bill (sax) | Fulton,John (sax) | Abato,Jimmy (sax) | Banzer,Russ (sax) | Odriche,Jimmy (sax) | Freeman,Stan (p) | Lowe,Mundell (g) | Carroll,Frank (b) | Snyder,Terry (dr)

FDM 36740-2 | CD | Nat King Cole:For Sentimental Reasons | EAN 3460503674028
Nat King Cole Trio
If You Can't Smile And Say Yes
Los Angeles,CA, rec. 30.11.1943
Cole,Nat King (p,voc) | Moore,Oscar (g) | Miller,Johnny (b)
It's Only A Paper Moon
Los Angeles,CA, rec. 15.12.1943
Cole,Nat King (p,voc) | Moore,Oscar (g) | Miller,Johnny (b)
I'm An Errand Boy For Rhythm
NYC, rec. 18.10.1945
Cole,Nat King (p,voc) | Moore,Oscar (g) | Miller,Johnny (b)
Don't Blame Me
Los Angeles,CA, rec. 19.5.1945
Cole,Nat King (p,voc) | Moore,Oscar (g) | Miller,Johnny (b)
I'm In The Mood For Love
Los Angeles,CA, rec. 15.3.1946
Cole,Nat King (p,voc) | Moore,Oscar (g) | Miller,Johnny (b)
What Can I Say After I Say I'm Sorry
Los Angeles,CA, rec. 11.4.1946
Cole,Nat King (p,voc) | Moore,Oscar (g) | Miller,Johnny (b)
On The Sunny Side Of The Street
Los Angeles,CA, rec. 18.4.1946
Cole,Nat King (p,voc) | Moore,Oscar (g) | Miller,Johnny (b)
I Love You For Sentimental Reasons
NYC, rec. 22.8.1946
Cole,Nat King (p,voc) | Moore,Oscar (g) | Miller,Johnny (b)
You're The Cream In My Coffee
NYC, rec. 18.12.1946
Cole,Nat King (p,voc) | Moore,Oscar (g) | Miller,Johnny (b)
This Is My Night To Dream
NYC, rec. 7.8.1947

Cole,Nat King (p,voc) | Moore,Oscar (g) | Miller,Johnny (b)
I'll String Along With You
Los Angeles,CA, rec. 8.8.1947
Cole,Nat King (p,voc) | Moore,Oscar (g) | Miller,Johnny (b)
Cole Capers | If I Had You
NYC, rec. 6.11.1947
Cole,Nat King (p,voc) | Ashby,Irving (g) | Miller,Johnny (b)
I've Got A Way With Women
Los Angeles,CA, rec. 24.11.1947
Cole,Nat King (p,voc) | Ashby,Irving (g) | Miller,Johnny (b)
Nat King Cole Trio With Strings
Portrait Of Jenny
NYC, rec. 14.1.1949
Cole,Nat King (p,voc) | Ashby,Irving (g) | Comfort,Joe (b) | Strings | Hall,Carlyle (arr)
Nat King Cole Quartet
Bop Kick
NYC, rec. 22.3.1949
Cole,Nat King (p,voc) | Ashby,Irving (g) | Comfort,Joe (b) | Costanzo,Jack (congas,bongos)
I Used To Love You
NYC, rec. 29.3.1949
Cole,Nat King (p,voc) | Ashby,Irving (g) | Comfort,Joe (b) | Costanzo,Jack (congas,bongos)
'Deed I Do
NYC, rec. 9.3.1950
Cole,Nat King (p,voc) | Ashby,Irving (g) | Comfort,Joe (b) | Costanzo,Jack (congas,bongos)
Nat King Cole Quartet With The Stan Kenton Orchestra
Orange Coloured Sky
Los Angeles,CA, rec. 16.8.1950
Cole,Nat King (p,voc) | Ashby,Irving (g) | Comfort,Joe (b) | Costanzo,Jack (congas,bongos) | Ferguson,Maynard (tp) | Salko, | Childers,Buddy (tp) | Alvarez,Chico (tp) | Rogers,Shorty (tp) | Bernhart,Milton 'Milt' (tb) | Betts,Harry (tb) | Fitzpatrick,Bob (tb) | Halliburton,John (tb) | Harper,Herbie (tb) | Shank,Bud (as) | Pepper,Art (as) | Cooper,Bob (ts) | Calderal,Bert (ts) | Gloga,Bob (bs) | Kenton,Stan (ld) | Rugolo,Pete (arr)
Nat King Cole Trio With Pete Rugolo's Orchestra
That's My Girl
Los Angeles,CA, rec. 1.2.1951
Cole,Nat King (p) | Ashby,Irving (g) | Comfort,Joe (b) | Costanzo,Jack (bongos) | Orchestra | Rugolo,Pete (cond,arr) | details unknown
Nat King Cole With The Billy May Orchestra
Walking My Baby Back Home
Los Angeles,CA, rec. 4.9.1951
Cole,Nat King (p) | Klein,Manny (tp) | Gozzo,Conrad (tp) | Linn,Ray (tp) | Best,John (tp) | Kusby,Eddie (tb) | Pederson,Pullman 'Tommy' (tb) | McEachern,Murray (tb) | Priddy,Jimmy (tb) | Herfurt,Arthur 'Skeets' (as) | Schwartz,Willie (as) | Nash,Ted (ts) | Falensby,Fred (ts) | Gentry,Chuck (bs) | Rowles,Jimmy (p) | Kessel,Barney (g) | Stephens,Phil (b) | Stoller,Alvin (dr) | May,Billy (arr,ld)

FDM 36741-2 | CD | Ella Fitzgerald:Mr.Paganini | EAN 3460503674127
Ella Fitzgerald With The Dizzy Gillespie Orchestra
Almost Like Being In Love | Lover Man(Oh,Where Can You Be?) | How High The Moon
Live at Carnegie Hall,NYC, rec. 29.12.1947
Fitzgerald,Ella (voc) | Gillespie,Dizzy (tp) | Burns,Dave (tp) | Wright,Elmon (tp) | Orr,Raymond (tp) | McKay,Matthew (tp) | Baird,Taswell (tb) | Shepherd,William 'Bill' (tb) | Johnson,Howard (as) | Brown,John (as) | Moody,James (ts) | Nicholas,George 'Big Nick' (ts) | Gayles,Joe (ts) | Payne,Cecil (as) | Lewis,John (p) | McKibbon,Al (b) | Clarke,Kenny (dr) | Pozo,Chano (congas)
Ella Fitzgerald With The Hank Jones Trio
There's A Small Hotel
Live at The Royal Roost,NYC, rec. 27.11.1948
Fitzgerald,Ella (voc) | Jones,Hank (p) | Brown,Ray (b) | Smith,Charlie (dr) | Shepherd,William 'Bill' (tb) | Johnson,Howard (as) | Brown,John (as) | Moody,James (ts) | Nicholas,George 'Big Nick' (ts) | Gayles,Joe (ts) | Payne,Cecil (as) | Lewis,John (p) | McKibbon,Al (b) | Clarke,Kenny (dr) | Pozo,Chano (congas)
Ool-Ya-Koo
Live at The Royal Roost,NYC, rec. 4.12.1948
Fitzgerald,Ella (voc) | Jones,Hank (p) | Brown,Ray (b) | Smith,Charlie (dr)
Mr.Paganini
Live at The Royal Roost,NYC, rec. 15.4.1949
Fitzgerald,Ella (voc) | Jones,Hank (p) | Brown,Ray (b) | Smith,Charlie (dr)
Robbin's Nest | Thou Swell
Live at The Royal Roost,NYC, rec. 23.4.1949
Fitzgerald,Ella (voc) | Jones,Hank (p) | Brown,Ray (b) | Smith,Charlie (dr)
Ella Fitzgerald And Her All Stars
Flying Home
Fitzgerald,Ella (voc) | McGhee,Howard (tp) | Phillips,Flip (ts) | Moore,Brew (ts) | unkn. (tb) | Jones,Hank (p) | Brown,Ray (b) | Smith,Charlie (dr) | Members of Machito's Rhythm Section)
Ella Fitzgerald With The Hank Jones Trio
In A Mellow Tone
Live at The Royal Roost,NYC, rec. 30.4.1949
Fitzgerald,Ella (voc) | Jones,Hank (p) | Brown,Ray (b) | Smith,Charlie (dr)
Ella Fitzgerald With Sy Oliver And His Orchestra
I've Got The World On A String
NYC, rec. 6.3.1950
Fitzgerald,Ella (voc) | Privin,Bernie (tp) | Faso,Tony (tp) | Webster,Paul (tp) | Chambers,Henderson (tb) | Yaner,Milt (cl,as) | Cooper,Sid (as) | Jerome,Jerry (ts) | Klink,Al (ts) | Jones,Hank (p) | Barksdale,Everett (g) | Brown,Ray (b) | Crawford,James 'Jimmy' (dr) | Oliver,Sy (cond,arr)
Ella Fitzgerald With Louis Jordan And His Tympany Five
Ain't Nobody's Business But My Own
NYC, rec. 15.8.1950
Fitzgerald,Ella (voc) | Jordan,Louis (as,voc) | Izenhall,Aaron (tp) | Jackson,Josh (ts) | Doggett,Bill (p) | Jennings,Bill (g) | Bushnell,Bob (b) | Morris[Chris Columbus],Joe (dr)
Ella Fitzgerald And Louis Armstrong With Sy Oliver And His Orchestra
Can Anyone Explain
NYC, rec. 25.8.1950
Fitzgerald,Ella (voc) | Armstrong,Louis (tp,voc) | Webster,Paul (tp) | D'Amico,Hank (cl) | Ludwig,Frank (ts) | Jones,Hank (p) | Barksdale,Everett (g) | Brown,Ray (b) | Crawford,James 'Jimmy' (dr) | Oliver,Sy (cond,arr)
Ella Fitzgerald With Ellis Larkins
Someone To Watch Over Me | But Not For Me | How Long Has This Been Going On
NYC, rec. 11.9.1950
Fitzgerald,Ella (voc) | Larkins,Ellis (p)
Ella Fitzgerald With The Hank Jones Quartet
Love You Madly
NYC, rec. 24.5.1951
Fitzgerald,Ella (voc) | Jones,Hank (p) | Barksdale,Everett (g) | Block,Sandy (b) | Crawford,James 'Jimmy' (dr)
Ella Fitzgerald With Bill Doggett's Orchestra
Smooth Sailing
NYC, rec. 26.6.1951
Fitzgerald,Ella (voc) | Doggett,Bill (org) | Jones,Hank (p) | Barksdale,Everett (g) | Fishkin,Arnold (b) | Blowers,Johnny (dr) | Ray Charles Singers
Ella Fitzgerald And Louis Armstrong With Dave Barbour And His Orchestra
Who Walks In When I Walk Out | Would You Like To Take A Walk | Necessary Evil | Oops!
Los Angeles,CA, rec. 23.11.1951
Fitzgerald,Ella (voc) | Armstrong,Louis (p,voc) | Neill,Larry (tp) | Howard,Frank (tb) | Dumont,Jack (as) | Gentry,Chuck (as) | Beau,Heinie (cl,as,ts) | Barbour,Dave (g,ld) | Jones,Hank (p) | Brown,Ray (b) | Stoller,Alvin (dr)

FDM 36743-2 | CD | Thelonious Monk:Misterioso | EAN 3460503674325
Thelonious Monk Sextet
Thelonious
NYC, rec. 15.10.1947
Monk,Thelonious (p) | Sulieman[Leonard Graham],Idrees (tp) | Quebec West,Danny (as) | Smith,Billy (ts) | Ramey,Gene (b) | Blakey,Art (dr)
Thelonious Monk Trio
Well You Needn't | April In Paris | Nice Work If You Can Get It | Ruby My Dear | Introspection
NYC, rec. 24.10.1947
Monk,Thelonious (p) | Ramey,Gene (b) | Blakey,Art (dr)
Thelonious Monk Quintet
In Walked Bud | Round About Midnight
NYC, rec. 17.11.1947
Monk,Thelonious (p) | Taitt,George (tp) | Shihab,Sahib (as) | Paige,Bob (b) | Blakey,Art (dr)
Thelonious Monk Quartet
Evidence | Misterioso | Epistrophy | I Mean You
NYC, rec. 2.7.1948
Monk,Thelonious (p) | Jackson,Milt (vib) | Simmons,John (b) | Wilson,Shadow (dr)
Charlie Parker-Dizzy Gillespie Quintet
Mohawk | Bloomdido
NYC, rec. 6.6.1950
Gillespie,Dizzy (tp) | Parker,Charlie (as) | Monk,Thelonious (p) | Russell,Curly (b) | Rich,Buddy (dr)
Thelonious Monk Quintet
Straight No Chaser | Four In One | Criss Cross | Eronel
NYC, rec. 23.7.1951
Jackson,Milt (vib) | Shihab,Sahib (as) | Monk,Thelonious (p) | McKibbon,Al (b) | Blakey,Art (dr)
Thelonious Monk Quartet
Willow Weep For Me
Jackson,Milt (vib) | Monk,Thelonious (p) | McKibbon,Al (b) | Blakey,Art (dr)
Thelonious Monk Trio
Ask Me Now
Monk,Thelonious (p) | McKibbon,Al (b) | Blakey,Art (dr)

FDM 36744-2 | CD | Django Reinhardt:Souveniers | EAN 3460503674424
Quintet Du Hot Club De France
Djangology
Paris,France, rec. 2.9.1935
Quintet Du Hot Club De France | Grappelli,Stephane (v) | Reinhardt,Django (g) | Reinhardt,Joseph (g) | Ferret,Pierre (g) | Vola,Louis (b)
Body And Soul | When Day Is Done
Paris,France, rec. 22.4.1937
Quintet Du Hot Club De France | Grappelli,Stephane (v) | Reinhardt,Django (g) | Bianchi,Marcel (g) | Ferret,Pierre (g) | Viale,Louis (b)
Liebestraum
Paris,France, rec. 26.4.1937
Quintet Du Hot Club De France | Grappelli,Stephane (v) | Reinhardt,Django (g) | Bianchi,Marcel (g) | Ferret,Pierre (g) | Viale,Louis (b)
Django Reinhardt
Tea For Two
Paris,France, rec. 27.12.1937
Reinhardt,Django (g-solo)
Quintet Du Hot Club De France
Souvenirs | My Sweet
London,GB, rec. 31.1.1938
Quintet Du Hot Club De France | Grappelli,Stephane (v) | Reinhardt,Django (g) | Chaput,Roger (g) | Vees,Eugene (g) | Vola,Louis (b)
Swing '39
Paris,France, rec. 21.3.1939
Quintet Du Hot Club De France | Reinhardt,Django (g) | Grappelli,Stephane (v) | Reinhardt,Joseph (g) | Ferret,Pierre (g) | Soudieux,Emmanuel (b)
Django Reinhardt Trio
I'll See You In My Dreams
Paris,France, rec. 30.6.1939
Reinhardt,Django (g) | Ferret,Etienne (g) | Soudieux,Emmanuel (b)
Quintet Du Hot Club De France
Embraceable You | Coquette
London,GB, rec. 31.1.1946
Reinhardt,Django (g) | Grappelli,Stephane (v) | Llewellyn,Jack (g) | Hodgkiss,Allan (g) | Goode,Coleridge (b)
Belleville | Melodie Au Crepuscule
London,GB, rec. 1.2.1946
Reinhardt,Django (g) | Grappelli,Stephane (v) | Llewellyn,Jack (g) | Hodgkiss,Allan (g) | Goode,Coleridge (b)
Django Reinhardt With Duke Ellington And His Orchestra
Ride Red Ride | A Blues Riff
Chicago,Ill, rec. 10.11.1946
Reinhardt,Django (g) | Ellington,Duke (p) | Hemphill,Shelton (tp) | Jordan,Taft (tp) | Anderson,Cat (tp) | Baker,Harold 'Shorty' (tp) | Nance,Ray (tp) | Brown,Lawrence (tb) | Jones,Claude (tb) | DeParis,Wilbur (tb) | Procope,Russell (as) | Hodges,Johnny (as) | Hamilton,Jimmy (cl,ts) | Sears,Al (ts) | Carney,Harry (bs) | Guy,Fred (g) | Pettiford,Oscar (b) | Greer,William 'Sonny' (dr)
Quintet Du Hot Club De France
Just One Of Those Things
Brussels,Belgium, rec. 21.5.1947
Quintet Du Hot Club De France | Rostaing,Hubert (cl) | Reinhardt,Django (g) | Vees,Eugene (g) | Reinhardt,Joseph (g) | Soudieux,Emmanuel (b) | Fouad,Pierre (dr)
Danse Norvegienne
Paris,France, rec. 6.7.1947
Quintet Du Hot Club De France | Rostaing,Hubert (cl) | Reinhardt,Django (g) | Reinhardt,Joseph (g) | Czabancyk,Ladislas (b) | Jourdan,Andre (dr)
Swing '41
Radio Broadcast, Paris,France, rec. 29.8.1947
Quintet Du Hot Club De France | Meunier,Maurice (cl) | Reinhardt,Django (g) | Vees,Eugene (g) | Soudieux,Emmanuel (b) | Jourdan,Andre (dr)
Topsy
Paris,France, rec. 4.10.1947
Quintet Du Hot Club De France | Rostaing,Hubert (cl) | Reinhardt,Django (g) | Reinhardt,Joseph (g) | Soudieux,Emmanuel (b) | Jourdan,Andre (dr)
Fantastic | Festival 48
Paris,France, rec. 10.3.1948
Quintet Du Hot Club De France | Reinhardt,Django (g) | Grappelli,Stephane (v) | Reinhardt,Joseph (g) | Ferret,Challin (g) | Soudieux,Emmanuel (b)
Django Reinhardt And His Quintet
Vamp
Paris,France, rec. 11.5.1951
Reinhardt,Django (g) | Hullin,Bernard (tp) | Fol,Hubert (as) | Fol,Raimond (p) | Michelot,Pierre (b) | Lemarchand,Pierre (dr)

FDM 37003-2 | CD | Coming Home Jamaica | EAN 3460503700321
Art Ensemble Of Chicago
Grape Escape | Odwalla Theme | Jamaica Farewell | Mama Wants You | Villa Tiamo | Malachi(The Messenger) | Lotta Colada
Bonham Springs,Ocho Rios,Jamaica, rec. 27.12.1995
Art Ensemble Of Chicago | Bowie,Lester (tp,fl-h,bass-dr) | Mitchell,Roscoe (fl,cl,ss,as,ts,bs,perc,bamboo-fl,bamboo-sax,piccolo,sopranino) | Favors,Malachi (b,perc) | Moye,Famoudou Don (dr,perc,congas,bongos)
Strawberry Mango
Art Ensemble Of Chicago | Bowie,Lester (tp,fl-h,bass-dr) | Mitchell,Roscoe (fl,cl,ss,as,ts,bs,perc,bamboo-fl,bamboo-sax,piccolo,sopranino) | Favors,Malachi (b,perc) | Moye,Famoudou Don (dr,perc,congas,bongos) | Bowie,Bahnamous Lee (keyboards)

FDM 37004-2 | CD | The Odysse Of Funk & Popular Music | EAN 3460503700420
Lester Bowie's Brass Fantasy
The Birth Of The Blues | Two Become One | Don't Cry For Me Argentina | Beautiful People | In The Still Of The Night | Nessun Dorma(Turandot) | If You Don't Know Me By Now
Brooklyn,NY, rec. 27.-30.9.& 1.10.1997
Bowie,Lester (tp) | Gollehon,Joseph 'Mac' (tp) | Best,Ravi (tp) | Brazel,Gerald (tp) | Bonilla,Luis (tb) | Roseman,Joshua 'Josh' (tb) | Valente,Gary (tb) | Chancey,Vincent (fr-h) | Stewart,Robert 'Bob' (tuba) | Johnson,Vinnie (dr) | See Yuen,Victor (perc)
Notorious Thugs
Bowie,Lester (tp) | Gollehon,Joseph 'Mac' (tp) | Best,Ravi (tp) | Brazel,Gerald (tp) | Bonilla,Luis (tb) | Roseman,Joshua 'Josh' (tb) | Valente,Gary (tb) | Chancey,Vincent (fr-h) | Stewart,Robert 'Bob' (tuba) | Johnson,Vinnie (dr) | See Yuen,Victor (perc) | Bowman,Dean (voc)
Next
Bowie,Lester (tp) | Gollehon,Joseph 'Mac' (tp) | Best,Ravi (tp) | Brazel,Gerald (tp) | Bonilla,Luis (tb) | Roseman,Joshua 'Josh' (tb) | Valente,Gary (tb) | Bowie,Joseph (tb,voc) | Chancey,Vincent (fr-h) | Stewart,Robert 'Bob' (tuba) | Johnson,Vinnie (dr) | See Yuen,Victor (perc)

FDM 37006-2 | CD | Stephane Grappelli 1992 Live | EAN 3460503700628
Stephane Grappelli Quartet
Minor Swing | Galerie Des Princes | Ballade | Tears | Blues For Django | And Stephane | Stella By Starlight | Sweet Chorus | Oh! Lady Be Good | Someone To Watch Over Me
Live in Colombes,France, rec. 27./28.3.1992
Grappelli,Stephane (v) | Catherine,Philip (g,el-g) | Fosset,Marc (g,el-g) | Orsted-Pedersen,Niels-Henning (b)

FDM 37007-2 | CD | The Essence Part 1 | EAN 3460503700727
Ahmad Jamal Quartet
Flight | Toulouse | Lover Man(Oh,Where Can You Be?) | Catalina | Street Of Dreams | Bahia
Paris,France, rec. 30./31.10.1994
Jamal,Ahmad (p) | Cammack,James (b) | Muhammad,Idris[Leo Morris] (dr) | Badrena,Manolo (perc)
Ahmad Jamal Quintet
The Essence | Autumn Leaves
Jamal,Ahmad (p) | Coleman,George (ts) | Nasser,Jamil[George Joyner] (b) | Muhammad,Idris[Leo Morris] (dr) | Badrena,Manolo (perc)

FDM 37008-2 | CD | Big Byrd | EAN 3460503700826
Ahmad Jamal Trio
Lament | There's A Lull In My Life
La Plaine Saint-Denis,France, rec. 30./31.10.1994
Jamal,Ahmad (p) | Cammack,James (b) | Muhammad,Idris[Leo Morris] (dr)
Ahmad Jamal Quartet
Jamie My Boy | I Love You
Jamal,Ahmad (p) | Cammack,James (b) | Muhammad,Idris[Leo Morris] (dr) | Badrena,Manolo (perc)
Ahmad Jamal Quintet
Manhattan Reflections
NYC, rec. 6./7.2.1995
Jamal,Ahmad (p) | Kennedy,Joe (v) | Nasser,Jamil[George Joyner] (b) | Muhammad,Idris[Leo Morris] (dr) | Badrena,Manolo (perc)
Big Byrd
Jamal,Ahmad (p) | Byrd,Donald (tp) | Nasser,Jamil[George Joyner] (b) | Muhammad,Idris[Leo Morris] (dr) | Badrena,Manolo (perc)

FDM 37012-2 | CD | The Best Of McCoy Tyner Big Band | EAN 3460503701229
McCoy Tyner Big Band
Passion Dance | Let It Go | High Priest | Fly With The Wind
NYC, rec. 19./20.11.1991
Tyner,McCoy (p) | Adilifu,Kamau (tp) | Gardner,Earl (tp) | Jones,Virgil (tp) | Turre,Steve (tb) | Lacy,Ku-umba Frank (tb) | Clark,John (fr-h) | Johnson,Howard (tuba) | Harris,Douglas (fl,ss) | Ford,Joe (as) | Stubblefield,John (ts) | Cook,Junior (ts) | Sharpe,Avery (b) | Scott,Aaron (dr) | Gonzalez,Jerry (perc) | Belden,Bob (ld)
Angel Eyes
Tyner,McCoy (p) | Adilifu,Kamau (tp) | Gardner,Earl (tp) | Jones,Virgil (tp) | Turre,Steve (tb) | Lacy,Ku-umba Frank (tb) | Clark,John (fr-h) | Johnson,Howard (tuba) | Harris,Douglas (fl,ss) | Ford,Joe (as) | Stubblefield,John (ts) | Cook,Junior (ts) | Sharpe,Avery (b) | Scott,Aaron (dr) | Gonzalez,Jerry (perc) | Hampton,Slide (arr,ld)
Peresina | Blues On The Corner
NYC, rec. 24.-26.5.1993
Tyner,McCoy (p) | Gardner,Earl (tp) | Jones,Virgil (tp) | Henderson,Eddie (tp) | Turre,Steve (tb) | Lacy,Ku-umba Frank (tb) | Clark,John (fr-h,hornette) | Underwood,Tony (tuba) | Harris,Douglas (fl,as) | Ford,Joe (as) | Harper,Billy (ts) | Stubblefield,John (ts) | Sharpe,Avery (b) | Scott,Aaron (dr) | Gonzalez,Jerry (perc)

FDM 37015-2 | CD | Tribute To Charlie Parker Vol.2 | EAN 3460503701526
Don Sickler Orchestra
Shaw 'Nuff | Billie's Bounce | Relaxin' At The Camarillo | Don't Blame Me | Scrapple From The Apple | Dewey Square | Big Foot
Live at Theatre De Boulogne-Billancourt,France, rec. 7.6.1989
Sickler,Don (tp,arr) | McLean,Jackie (as) | Griffin,Johnny (ts) | Payne,Cecil (bs) | Jordan,Duke (p) | Carter,Ron (b) | Haynes,Roy (dr)

FDM 37016-2 | CD | When The Spitit Returns | EAN 3460503701625
Lester Bowie's Brass Fantasy
Player Hater | Waterfall | Count On Me | Solitude | Biggie's Ride | One Love | Unchained Melody | Naakkurat Na | Save The Best For Last | When The Spirit Returns
NYC, rec. 27.9.-4.10.1997
Bowie,Lester (tp) | Best,Ravi (tp) | Brazel,Gerald (tp) | Gollehon,Joseph 'Mac' (tp) | Bonilla,Luis (tb) | Roseman,Joshua 'Josh' (tb) | Valente,Gary (tb) | Chancey,Vincent (fr-h) | Stewart,Robert 'Bob' (tuba) | Johnson,Vinnie (dr) | See Yuen,Victor (perc) | Bowman,Dean (voc)

FDM 37018-2 | CD | Nature | EAN 3460503701823
Ahmad Jamal Quartet
If I Find You Again | Like Someone In Love | Chaperon | And We Were Lovers | Fantastic Vehicle | The End Of A Love Affair | Cabin In The Sky(medley): | Cabin In The Sky- | Poor Pierrot- | The Reprise-
Pernes Les Fontaines,France/NYC, rec. 23.-25.7.1997/2.1.1998
Jamal,Ahmad (p) | Cammack,James (b) | Muhammad,Idris[Leo Morris] (dr) | Molineaux,Othello (steel-dr)
Ahmad Jamal Quartet With Stanley Turrentine
Devil's In My Den
Pernes Les Fontaines,France, rec. 23.-25.7.1997
Jamal,Ahmad (p) | Turrentine,Stanley (ts) | Cammack,James (b) | Muhammad,Idris[Leo Morris] (dr) | Molineaux,Othello (steel-dr)

FDM 37019-2 | CD | Live In Paris 1992 | EAN 3460503701922
Ahmad Jamal Trio
The Tube | Alone Together- | Laura- | Wild Is The Wind- | Caravan | Easy Living | Acorn | Appreciation | Look For The Silver Lining | The Aftermath
Live at La Salle de Spectacles de Colombes,France, rec. 3./4.4.1992
Jamal,Ahmad (p) | Cammack,James (b-g) | Bowler,David (dr)
Dreamy
Jamal,Ahmad (p) | Coolman,Todd (b) | Lane,Gordon (dr)

FDM 37020-2 | CD | Live In Paris 1996 | EAN 3460503702028
Ahmad Jamal Septet
Bellows | Patches | Autumn Leaves | Devil's In My Den | There's A Lull In My Life
Live at Salle Pleyel,Paris,France, rec. 26.10.1996
Jamal,Ahmad (p) | Coleman,George (ts) | Kennedy,Joe (v) | Keys,Calvin (g) | Chambers,Jeff (b) | Israel,Yoron (dr) | Badrena,Manolo (perc)

East-West | Warner Classics & Jazz Germany

4509-92004-2 | CD | Jazz Meets The Symphony
Lalo Schifrin Trio With The London Philharmonic

Battle Hymn Of The Republic | Echoes Of Duke Ellington | Bach To The Blues | Brush Strokes | I Can't Get Started | Brazilian Impressions | Blues In The Basement | The Fox | As Time Goes By | Dizzy Gillespie Fireworks
London,GB, rec. November 1992
Schifrin,Lalo (p,cond,arr) | Brown,Ray (b) | Tate,Grady (dr) | London Philharmonia Orchestra,The

9031-77125-2 | CD | Two The Max
James Morrison-Ray Brown Quartet
Max | Honeysuckle Rose | Moten Swing | Seven Steps To Heaven | Ain't That Nothin' | My Beautiful | Freddie Freeloader | Our Waltz | Nice 'N' Easy | Imagination
Hollywood,CA, rec. 22./23.12.1991
Morrison,James (tp,fl-h,tb) | Brown,Ray (b) | Green,Benny (p) | Hamilton,Jeff (dr)

ECM | ECM Export

1001 | CD | Free At Last
1001 | LP | Free At Last
Mal Waldron Trio
Rat Now | Balladina | 1-3-234 | Rock My Soul | Willow Weep For Me | Boo
rec. 24.11.1969
Waldron,Mal (p) | Eckinger,Isla (b) | Becton,Clarence (dr)

1003 | CD | Paul Bley With Gary Peacock
Paul Bley Trio
Blues | Getting Started | When Will The Blues Leave | Long Ago And Far Away | Moor
rec. details unknown
Bley,Paul (p) | Peacock,Gary (b) | Motian,Paul (dr)
Gary | Big Foot | Albert's Love Theme
Bley,Paul (p) | Peacock,Gary (b) | Elgart,Billy (dr)

1004 | CD | Afternoon Of A Georgia Faun
Marion Brown Orchestra
Afternoon Of A Georgia Faun
NYC, rec. 10.8.1970
Brown,Marion (as,perc,zomari) | Braxton,Anthony (fl,cl,contra-b-cl,ss,as) | Maupin,Bennie (fl,b-cl,ts,perc,acorn,bells) | Corea,Chick (p,perc,bells,gong) | Palmore,Gale (p,perc,voice) | Gregg,Jack (b,perc) | Cyrille,Andrew (dr,perc) | Lee,Jeanne (perc,voc)
Djinji's Corner
Brown,Marion (as,perc,zomari) | Braxton,Anthony (fl,cl,contra-b-cl,ss,as) | Maupin,Bennie (fl,b-cl,ts,perc,acorn,bells) | Corea,Chick (p,perc,bells,gong) | Palmore,Gale (p,perc,voice) | Gregg,Jack (b,perc) | Cyrille,Andrew (dr,perc) | Curtis,Larry (perc) | Green,William (perc,topo'lin) | Malone,Billy (african-dr)

1009 | CD | A.R.C.
1009 | LP | A.R.C.
Chick Corea Trio
Nefertiti | Ballad For Tillie | A.R.C. | Vadana | Thanatos | Games
rec. 11.-13.1.1971
Corea,Chick (p) | Holland,Dave (b) | Altschul,Barry (dr)

1023 | CD | Open, To Love
1023 | LP | Open, To Love
Paul Bley
Closer | Ida Lupino | Started | Open To Love | Harlem | Seven | Nothing Ever Was, Anyway
rec. 11.9.1972
Bley,Paul (p-solo)

1030 | CD | The New Quartet
Gary Burton Quartet
Open Your Eyes, You Can Fly | Choral | Tying Up Loose Ends | Brownout | Olhos De Gato | Mallet Man | Four Or Less | Nonsequence
rec. 5./6.3.1973
Burton,Gary (vib) | Goodrick,Mick (g) | Laboriel,Abe (b) | Blazer,Harry (dr)

1031 | CD | What Comes After
Terje Rypdal Quintet
Bend It | Yearning | Icing What Comes After | Sejours | Back Of J.
rec. 7./8.8.1973
Rypdal,Terje (fl,g) | Larsen,Erik Niord (oboe) | Phillips,Barre (b) | Hovensjo,Sveinung (el-b) | Christensen,Jon (org,perc)

1045 | CD | When Ever I Seem To Be Far Away
1045 | LP | When Ever I Seem To Be Far Away
Silverbird Is Heading For The Sun | The Hunt
rec. 1974
Rypdal,Terje (g) | Ulleberg,Odd (fr-h) | Knutsen,Pete (el-p,mellotron) | Hovensjo,Sveinung (b) | Christensen,Jon (dr)
Terje Rypdal With Strings
Whenever I Seem To Be Far Away
Rypdal,Terje (g) | Hedrich,Christian (viola) | Geiger,Helmut (v) | Südfunk Symphony Orchestra,Members of the

1051 | CD | Ring
Gary Burton Quintet With Eberhard Weber
Mevlevia | Unfinished Sympathy | Tunnel For Love | Intrude | Silent Spring | The Colours Of Chloe
rec. 23./24.7.1974
Burton,Gary (vib) | Goodrick,Mick (g) | Metheny,Pat (el-g) | Swallow,Steve (el-b) | Weber,Eberhard (b) | Moses,Bobby (dr,perc)

1057 | CD | Theme To The Gaurdian
1057 | LP | Theme To The Gaurdian
Bill Connors
Theme To The Gaurdian | Child's Eyes | Song For A Crow | Sad Hero | Sea Song | Frantic Desire | Folk Song | My Favorite Fantasy | The Highest Mountain
rec. Nov.1974
Connors,Bill (g-solo)

1067/8 | CD | Odyssey
Terje Rypdal Group
Darkness Falls | Midnite | Adagio | Better Off With You | Over Birkerot | Farewell | Ballade | Rolling Stone
rec. August 1975
Rypdal,Terje (ss,g,string ensemble) | Sunde,Torbjorn (tb) | Blix,Brynjulf (fender-b) | Christiansen,Svein (dr)

1072 | CD | Dreams So Real
Gary Burton Quintet
Dreams So Real | Ictus- | Syndrome- | Jesus Maria | Vox Humana | Doctor | Intermission Music
rec. December 1975
Burton,Gary (vib) | Goodrick,Mick (g) | Metheny,Pat (g,el-12 string-g) | Swallow,Steve (el-b) | Moses,Bobby (dr)

1076 | CD | Mountainscapes
1076 | LP | Mountainscapes
Barre Phillips Group
Mountainscape I | Mountainscape II | Mountainscape III | Mountainscape IV | Mountainscape V | Mountainscape VI | Mountainscape VII
rec. March 1976
Phillips,Barre (b) | Surman,John (b-cl,ss,bs,synth) | Feichtner,Dieter (synth) | Martin,Stu (synth,dr)
Barre Phillips Quintet
Mountainscape VIII
Phillips,Barre (b) | Surman,John (b-cl,ss,bs,synth) | Feichtner,Dieter (synth) | Martin,Stu (synth,dr) | Abercrombie,John (g)

1077 | CD | Nan Madol
Edward Vesala Group
Nan Madol
rec. 25./26.4.1974
Vesala,Edward (fl,dr,perc) | Backlund,Kaj (tp) | Aaltonen,Juhani (ss) | Kukko,Sakari (fl) | Poutanen,Juhani (v) | Hauta-aho,Teppo (b)
The Way Of...
Vesala,Edward (dr) | Backlund,Kaj (tp) | Aaltonen,Juhani (ts,piccolo) | Leistola,Elisabeth (harp) | Poutanen,Juhani (v) | Hauta-aho,Teppo (b)
Areous Vlor Ta
Vesala,Edward (dr) | Backlund,Kaj (tp) | Stan,Mircea (tb) | Paakkunainen,Seppo 'Paroni' (ss) | Lahti,Pentti (ss) | Mariano,Charlie (ss,nagaswaram) | Aaltonen,Juhani (ts) | Poutanen,Juhani (v) | Hauta-aho,Teppo (b)
The Wind
Vesala,Edward (fl,dr,perc) | Paakkunainen,Seppo 'Paroni' (fl) | Aaltonen,Juhani (fl,bells,voice) | Lahti,Pentti (b-cl) | Hauta-aho,Teppo (b,voice) | Poutanen,Juhani (bells,voice)
Love For Living
Vesala,Edward (harp) | Aaltonen,Juhani (ss)
Call From The Sea
Vesala,Edward (perc-solo)

1079 | CD | Pictures
Jack DeJohnette
Picture 1 | Picture 2 | Picture 6
Oslo,N, rec. February 1976
DeJohnette,Jack (p,org,dr)
Jack DeJohnette-John Abercrombie Duo
Picture 3 | Picture 4 | Picture 5
DeJohnette,Jack (p,org,dr) | Abercrombie,John (g,el-g)

1096 | CD | Grazing Dreams
1096 | LP | Grazing Dreams
Collin Walcott Group
Song Of The Morrow | Gold Sun | The Swarm | Mountain Morning | Jewel Ornament | Grazing Dreams | Samba Tala | Moon Lake
rec. Feb.1977
Walcott,Collin (sitar,tabla) | Cherry,Don (tp,doussn'gouni,wood-fl) | Abercrombie,John (g,el-g,el-mand) | Danielsson,Palle (b) | Romao,Dom Um (perc,berimbau,chica,tambourin)

1111 | CD | Times Square
Gary Burton Quartet
Semblance | Coral | Careful | Peau Douce | Midnight | Radio | True Or False | Como En Vietnam
rec. Jan.1978
Burton,Gary (vib) | Okoshi,Tiger (tp) | Swallow,Steve (b-g) | Haynes,Roy (dr)

1117 | CD | Characters
John Abercrombie
Parable | Memoir | Telegram | Backward Glance | Ghost Dance | Paramour | Afterthoughts | Evensong
rec. Nov.1977
Abercrombie,John (el-g,el-mand)

1122 | CD | Enrico Rava Quartet
Enrico Rava Quartet
Lavori Casalinghi | The Fearless Five | Tramps | Round About Midnight | Blackmail
Ludwigsburg, rec. March 1978
Rava,Enrico (tp) | Rudd,Roswell (tb) | Jenny-Clark,Jean-Francois (b) | Romano,Aldo (dr)

1128 | CD | New Directions
Jack DeJohnette Quartet
Bayou Fever | Where Or Wayne | Dream Stalker | One Handed Woman | Silver Hollow
rec. June 1978
DeJohnette,Jack (p,dr) | Bowie,Lester (tp) | Abercrombie,John (g,mand) | Gomez,Eddie (b)

1137 | CD | Fluid Rustle
Eberhard Weber Group
Quiet Departures | Fluid Rustle | A Pale Smile | Visible Thoughts
rec. Jan.1979
Weber,Eberhard (b,tarang) | Burton,Gary (vib,marimba) | Frisell,Bill (g,balalaika) | Herman,Bonnie (voc) | Winstone,Norma (voc)

1138 | CD | Le Voyage
Paul Motian Trio
Folk Song For Rosie | Abacus | Cabala | Drum Mucis | The Sunflower | Le Voyage
Ludwigsburg, rec. March 1979
Motian,Paul (dr,perc) | Jenny-Clark,Jean-Francois (b) | Brackeen,Charles (ss,ts)

1139 | CD | In Pas(s)ing
Mick Goodrick Quartet
Feebles Fables And Ferns | In The Tavern Of Ruin | Summer Band Camp | Pedalpusher | In Passing
rec. Nov.1978
Goodrick,Mick (g) | Surman,John (b-cl,ss,bs) | Gomez,Eddie (b) | DeJohnette,Jack (dr)

1141 | CD | Soung Suggestions
George Adams Sextet
Baba | Imani's Dance | Stay Informed | Got Somethin' Good For You | A Spire
rec. May 1979
Adams,George (ts,voc) | Wheeler,Kenny (tp,fl-h) | Sauer,Heinz (ts) | Beirach,Richard (p) | Holland,Dave (p) | DeJohnette,Jack (dr)

1149 | CD | Journal Violone II
Barre Phillips Trio
Journal Violone II(part 5:to Aquirax Aida) | Journal Violone II(part 6) | Journal Violone II(part 1-4)
Ludwigsburg, rec. June 1979
Phillips,Barre (b) | Surman,John (b-cl,ss,bs,synth) | Kemanis,Aina (voice)

1152 | CD | Special Edition
1152 | LP | Special Edition
Jack DeJohnette Quartet
One For Eric | Zoot Suite | Central Park West | India | Journey To The Twin Planet
rec. March 1979
DeJohnette,Jack (p,dr,melodica) | Murray,David (b-cl,ts) | Blythe,Arthur (as) | Warren,Peter (cello,b)

1153 | CD | Old Friends New Friends
Ralph Towner Quintet
New Moon | Yesterday And Long Ago | Celeste | Special Delivery | Kupala | Beneath An Evening Sky
rec. July 1979
Towner,Ralph (fr-h,g,p,12-string-g) | Wheeler,Kenny (tp,fl-h) | Darling,David (cello) | Gomez,Eddie (b) | DiPasqua,Michael (dr,perc)

1154 | LP | Old And New Dreams
1154 | CD | Old And New Dreams
Old And New Dreams
Lonely Woman | Togo | Guinea | Open Or Close | Orbit of LA-BA | Song For The Whales
rec. August 1979
Old And New Dreams | Cherry,Don (tp,p) | Redman,Dewey (ts,musette) | Haden,Charlie (b) | Blackwell,Ed (dr)

1156 | CD | Around 6
Kenny Wheeler Sextet
Mai We Go Round | Solo One | May Ride | Follow Down | Riverrun | Lost Woltz
Ludwigsburg, rec. August 1979
Wheeler,Kenny (tp,fl-h) | Thelin,Eje (tb) | Parker,Evan (ss,ts) | Van Der Geld,Tom (vib) | Jenny-Clark,Jean-Francois (b) | Vesala,Edward (dr)

1157 | CD | In Europe
Jack DeJohnette New Directions
Salsa For Eddie G. | Where Or Wayne | Bayou Fever | Multo Spilliagio
rec. June 1979
DeJohnette,Jack (dr) | Bowie,Lester (tp) | Abercrombie,John (g,mand-g) | Gomez,Eddie (b)

1158 | CD | Swimming With A Hole In My Body
Bill Connors
Feet First | Wade | Sing And Swim | Frog Stroke | Surrender To The Water | Survive | With Strings Attached | Breath
rec. August 1979
Connors,Bill (g-solo)

1165 | CD | Shift In The Wind
Gary Peacock Trio
So Green | Fractions | Last First | Shift In The Wind | Centers | Caverns Beneath The Zoth | Valentine
rec. Feb.1980
Peacock,Gary (b) | Lande,Art (p) | Zigmund,Eliot (dr)

1174 | CD | Sacred Hymns Of G.I.Gurdjieff
1174 | LP | Sacred Hymns Of G.I.Gurdjieff
Keith Jarrett
Reading Of Sacred Books | Prayer And Despair | Religious Ceremony | Hymn | Orthodox Hymn From Asia Minor | Hymn For Good Friday
rec. March 1980
Jarrett,Keith (p-solo)

1175 | CD | The Celestial Hawk
Keith Jarrett With The Syracuse Symphony
First Movement | Second Movement | Third Movement
Jarrett,Keith (p) | Syracuse Symphony | Keene,Christopher (cond)

1179 | CD | Bitter Funeral Beer
Beng Berger Band
Bitter Funeral Beer | Chetu | Dorafo | Funeral Dance(Dar Kpee)
Stockholm,Sweden, rec. January 1981
Berger,Bengt (lo-birifor-funeral-xyl) | Cherry,Don (pocket-tp) | Adolfsson,Tommy (tp) | Gartz,Tomas Mera (ts,v,dr) | Wallander,Ulf (ss,ts) | Westling,Kjell (b-cl,sopraninio) | Bothen,Christer (b-cl,ts) | Adolfsson,Jürgen (ss,as,sopranino) | Bengtsson,Tord (el-g,v) | Hellden,Matthias (cello) | Krantz,Sigge (el-g,b,b-g) | Livstrand,Anita (bells,rattle,voice) | Skoglund,Bosse (dr)
Blekete | Tongsi
Berger,Bengt (axatse,master-dr) | Adolfsson,Tommy (sogo) | Gartz,Tomas Mera (kidi) | Bothen,Christer (bells) | Hellden,Matthias (dondos) | Krantz,Sigge (kagan) | Livstrand,Anita (axatse,sogo) | Skoglund,Bosse (kagan)

1186 | LP | Little Movements
1186 | CD | Little Movements
Eberhard Weber Colours
The Last Stage Of A Journey | Bali | A Dark Spell | Little Movements | 'No Trees?' He Said
Ludwigsburg, rec. July 1980
Weber,Eberhard (b) | Mariano,Charlie (fl,ss) | Brüninghaus,Rainer (p,synth) | Marshall,Joe (dr,perc)

1192 | CD | To Be Continued
Terje Rypdal Trio
Maya | Mountain In The Clouds | Morning Lake | To Be Continued | This Morning | Topplue Votter & Skjerf | Uncomposed Appendix
Oslo,N, rec. Jan.1981
Rypdal,Terje (fl,g) | Vitous,Miroslav (p,b,el-b) | DeJohnette,Jack (dr,voice)

1198 | CD | Dawn Dance
1198 | LP | Dawn Dance
Steve Eliovson-Collin Walcott
Venice | Earth End | Awakening | Song For The Masters | Wanderer | Dawn Dance | Slow Jazz | Africa | Memories | Eternity
rec. Jan.1981
Eliovson,Steve (g) | Walcott,Collin (perc)

1199 | CD | Stella Malu
1199 | LP | Stella Malu
Katrina Krimsky-Trevor Watts
Mial | Stella Malu | Duogeny | Rhythm Circle | Crystal Morning | Song For Hans | Moonbeams | Villa In Brazil | Mial | Stella Malu | Duogeny | Rhythm Circle | Crystal Morning | Song For Hans | Moonbeams | Villa In Brazil
rec. March 1981
Krimsky,Katrina (p) | Watts,Trevor (ss,as)

1205 | CD | Playing
Old And New Dreams
Happy House | Mopti | New Dream | Rushour | Broken Shadows | Playing
rec. June 1980
Old And New Dreams | Cherry,Don (tp,p) | Redman,Dewey (ts,musette) | Haden,Charlie (b) | Blackwell,Ed (dr)

1208 | CD | Skylight
Art Lande Trio
Skylight | Dance Of The Silver Skeezix | Duck In A Colorful Blanket(For Here) | Chillum | Moist Windows | Lawn Party | Ente(To Go) | Willow
Ludwigsburg, rec. May 1981
Lande,Art (p,perc) | McCandless,Paul (engl-h,b-cl,ss,oboe,wood-fl) | Samuels,Dave (vib,marimba,perc)

1211/12 | 2 CD | Urban Bushmen
Art Ensemble Of Chicago
Promenade: Cote Bamako(I) | Bush Magic | Urban Magic: | March- | Warm Night Blues Stroll- | Down The Walkway- | RM Express- | Sun Precondition Two | Theme For Sco: | Soweto Messenger- | Bushman Triumphant- | Entering The City- | Announcement Of Victory- | New York Is Full Of Lonely People | Ancestral Meditation | Uncle | Peter And Judith | Promenade: Cote Bamako(II) | Odwalla | Theme
rec. 4./5.5.1980
Art Ensemble Of Chicago | Bowie,Lester (tp,bass-dr,long-horn,voice) | Jarman,Joseph (fl,cl,ss,as,ts,bs,vib,dr,perc,bassoon,bass-s,celeste,siren) | Mitchell,Roscoe (fl,cl,ss,as,bs,bamboo-fl,bass-s,bwhistles,conga,gongs,pans,piccolo,voice) | Favors,Malachi (b,perc,bass-pan-dr,el-b,melodica,voc) | Moye,Famoudou Don (dr,perc,congas,balafon,chekere,cymbales,gongs,tympany)

1214 | CD | Axum
James Newton
Feelings | Axum | Susenyos And Werzelyna | The Neser | The Dabtara | Malak 'Uqabe | Solomon Chief Of Wise Men | Addis Ababa | Choir
rec. 1981
Newton,James (fl)

1218 | CD | Northern Song
1218 | LP | Northern Song
Steve Tibbetts Duo
The Big Wind | Form | Walking | Aerial View | Nine Doors | Breathing Space
rec. 26.-28.10.1981
Tibbetts,Steve (g,kalimba,12-string-g,tape-loops) | Anderson,Marc (perc,congas,bongos)

1219 | CD | Cycles
David Darling Group
Cycle Song | Cycle One: Namaste | Fly | Ode | Cycle Two: Trio | Cycle Three: Quintet And Coda | Jessica's Sunwheel
Oslo,N, rec. Nov.1981
Darling,David (cello,8-string-el-cello) | Garbarek,Jan (ss,ts) | Castro-Neves,Oscar (g) | Walcott,Collin (perc,sitar,tabla) | Kuhn,Steve (p) | Andersen,Arild (b)

1220 | CD | Ondas
Mike Nock Trio
Forgotten Love | Ondas | Visionary | Land Of The Long White Cloud | Doors
rec. Nov.1981
Nock,Mike (p) | Gomez,Eddie (b) | Christensen,Jon (dr)

1222 | CD | Psalm
Paul Motian Band
Psalm | White Magic | Boomerang | Fantasm | Mandeville | Second Hand | Etude | Yahllah
Ludwigsburg, rec. December 1981
Motian,Paul (dr) | Lovano,Joe (ts) | Drewes,Billy (as,ts) | Frisell,Bill (g) | Schuller,Ed (b)

1230 | CD | El Corazon
1230 | LP | El Corazon
Don Cherry/Ed Blackwell
Mutron | Bemsha Swing | Solidarity | Arabian Nightingale(Dedicated to Om Kaltsom) | Roland Alphonso | Makondi | Street Dancing | Short Stuff | El Corazon | Rhythm For Runner | Near-in | Voice Of The Silence
rec. Feb.1982
Cherry,Don (p,org,doussn'gouni,melodica,pocket-tp) | Blackwell,Ed (dr,cowbell,wood-dr)

1238 | CD | Life Cycle
David Holland

Life Cycle: | Inception- | Discovery- | Longing- | Search- | Resolution- | Sonnet | Rune | Troubador Tale | Grapevine | Morning Song | Chanson Pour La Nuit
rec. Nov.1982
Holland,Dave (cello-solo)

1239 | CD | Time Remembers One Time Once
Denny Zeitlin-Charlie Haden Duo
Chairman Mao | Bird Food | As Long As There's Music | Time Remembers One Time Once | Love For Sale | Ellen David | Satelite- | How High The Moon- | The Dolphin
Live at Keystone Korner,SF, rec. July 1981
Zeitlin,Denny (p) | Haden,Charlie (b)

1243 | CD | Codona 3
1243 | LP | Codona 3
Don Cherry/Nana Vasconcelos/Collin Walcott
Goshakabuchi | Hey Da Ba Doom | Travel By Night | Lullaby | Trayra Boia | Clicky Clacky | Inner Organs
rec. September 1982
Codona | Walcott,Collin (dulcimer,sanza,sitar,tablas,voice) | Cherry,Don (tp,org,doussn'gouni,voice) | Vasconcelos,Nana (perc,berimbau,voice)

1245 | CD | Scenes
Michael Galasso
Scene 1-9
Ludwigsburg, rec. October 1982
Galasso,Michael (v-solo)

1249 | CD | Trommelgeflüster
Harald Weiss
Trommelgeflüster(part 1&2)
Ludwigsburg, rec. September 1982
Weiss,Harald (perc,voice)

1256 | CD | Jyothi
Charlie Mariano & The Karnataka College Of Percussion
Voice Solo | Vandanam | Varshini | Saptarshi | Kartik | Bhajan
Ludwigsburg, rec. February 1983
Mariano,Charlie (fl,ss) | Karnataka College of Percussion,The | Ramamani,R.A. (tamboura,voc) | Mani,T.A.S. (mridamgam) | Rajagopal,R.A. (ghantam,konakkol,morsing) | Shashikumar,T.N. (kanjira,konakkol)

1263 | CD | Eos
Terje Rypdal-David Darling Duo
Laser | Eos | Bedtime Story | Light Years | Melody | Mirage | Adagietto
Oslo,N, rec. May 1983
Rypdal,Terje (casio mt-30,electronic-g) | Darling,David (cello,8-string-el-cello)

1265 | CD | Theatre
George Gruntz Concert Jazz Band '83
El Chancho | In The Tradition Of Switzerland | No One Can Explain It | The Holy Grail Of Jazz And Joy
Ludwigsburg, rec. July 1983
Gruntz,George (keyboards) | Pusey,Bill (tp,fl-h) | Belgrave,Marcus (tp,fl-h) | Harrell,Tom (tp,fl-h) | Mikkelborg,Palle (tp,fl-h) | Bargeron,Dave (tb,euphonium) | Priester,Julian (tb) | Taylor,Dave (b-tb) | Gordon,Peter (fr-h) | Varner,Tom (fr-h) | Johnson,Howard (b-cl,bs,tuba) | Petrowsky,Ernst-Ludwig (cl,ss,as) | Mariano,Charlie (fl,ss,as) | Paakkunainen,Seppo 'Paroni' (fl,ts) | Saluzzi,Dino (bandoneon) | Egan,Mark (b) | Moses,Bobby (dr) | Jordan,Sheila (voc)

1269 | CD | Jumpin' In
Dave Holland Quintet
Jumpin' In | First Snow | The Dragon And The Samurai | New-One | Sunrise | Shadow Dance | You I Love
Ludwigsburg, rec. October 1983
Holland,Dave (cello,b) | Wheeler,Kenny (tp,fl-h,co,pocket-tp) | Priester,Julian (tb) | Coleman,Steve (fl,as) | Ellington,Steve (dr)

1270 | LP | Bye Bye Safe Journey
1270 | CD | Bye Bye Safe Journey
Steve Tibbetts Group
Test | Climbing | Running | Night Again | My Last Chance | Vision | Any Minute | Mission | Burning Up | Going Somewhere
St.Paul, Minnesota, rec. 1983
Tibbetts,Steve (g,kalimba,tapes) | Hughes,Bob (b) | Anderson,Marc (perc,congas,steel-dr) | Cochrane,Steve (tablas) | Wienhold,Tim (vase)

1273 | CD | The Third Decade
1273 | LP | The Third Decade
Art Ensemble Of Chicago
Prayer For Jimbo Kwesi | Funky AECO | Walking In The Moonlight | The Bell Piece | Zero | Third Decade
Ludwigsburg, rec. June 1984
Art Ensemble Of Chicago | Bowie,Lester (tp,fl-h,bass-dr,cymbal-rack) | Jarman,Joseph (fl,cl,b-cl,ss,as,ts,bs,synth,congas,bass-pan-dr,bell-rack,bike-horns,con | Mitchell,Roscoe (fl,cl,ss,as,ts,bass-sax,bongos,bells,bike-horns,conga,dinner-chimes,gl | Favors,Malachi (b,perc,balafon,bass-pan-dr,cans,cymbals,el-b,melodica) | Moye,Famoudou Don (congas,bongos,balafon,bass-pan-dr,bendir,bike-horns,blocks,chekere

1274 | CD | Singing Drums
Pierre Favre Ensemble
Rain Forest | Carnaval Of The Four | Metal Birds | Edge Of The Wing | Prism | Frog Songs | Beyond The Blue
Mohren,Willisau, rec. 27./28.5.1984
Favre,Pierre (dr,crotales,cymbals,gongs) | Motian,Paul (dr,calebasses,crotales,gongs,rodbrushes) | Studer,Freddy (dr,cymbals,gongs,log-dr) | Vasconcelos,Nana (congas,bells,berimbau,shakers,tympani,voice,water-pot)

1279 | CD | Duas Vozes
1279 | LP | Duas Vozes
Egberto Gismonti/Nana Vasconcelos
Aquarela Do Brazil | Rio De Janeiro | Tomarapeba | Dancando | Fogueira | Bianca | Don Quixote | O Dia A Noite
Oslo,N, rec. June 1984
Gismonti,Egberto (fl,g,p,dilruba,voive) | Vasconcelos,Nana (perc,berimbau,voice)

1280 | CD | Album Album
Jack DeJohnette's Special Edition
Ahmad The Terrible | Monk's Mood | Festival | New Orleans Strut | Third World Anthem | Zoot Suite
NYC, rec. June 1984
DeJohnette,Jack (keyboards,dr) | Purcell,John (ss,as) | Murray,David (ts) | Johnson,Howard (bs,tuba) | Reid,Rufus (b,el-b)

1282 | CD | Voyage
1282 | LP | Voyage
Chick Corea-Steve Kujala
Mallorca | Diversions | Star Island | Free Fall | Hong Kong
Ludwigsburg, rec. July 1984
Corea,Chick (p) | Kujala,Steve (fl)

1283 | CD | It Should've Happened A Long Time Ago
Paul Motian Trio
It Should've Happened A Long Time Ago | Fiasco | Conception Vessel | Introduction | India | In The Year Of The Dragon | Two Women From Padua
Motian,Paul (dr,perc) | Lovano,Joe (ts) | Frisell,Bill (g,synth)

1284 | CD | Best Laid Plans
David Torn/Geoffrey Gordon
Before The Bitter Wind | Best Laid Plans | The Hum Of Its Parts | Removable Tongue | In The Fifth Direction | Two-Face Flash | Angle Of Incidents
Oslo,N, rec. July 1984
Torn,David (g) | Gordon,Geoffrey (perc)

1287 | CD | Rambler
Bill Frisell Quintet
Tone | Music I Heard | Rambler | When I Go | Resitor | Strange Meeting | Wizard Of Odds
NYC, rec. August 1984
Frisell,Bill (g,g-synth) | Wheeler,Kenny (tp,fl-h,co) | Stewart,Robert 'Bob' (tuba) | Harris,Jerome (b-g) | Motian,Paul (dr)

1290 | CD | Without Warning
Everyman Band
Patterns Which Connect | Talking With Myself | Multibluetonic Blues | Celebration(7) | Trick Of The Wool | Huh What He Say | Al Ur
rec. December 1984
Everyman Band | Torn,David (g) | Fogel,Marty (ss,ts) | Yaw,Bruce (b-g) | Suchovsky,Michael (dr)

1292 | CD | Seeds Of Time
1292 | LP | Seeds Of Time
Dave Holland Quintet
Uhren | Homecoming | Perspicuity | Celebration | World Protection Blues | Gridlock | Walk-A-Way | The Good Doctor | Double Vision
Ludwigsburg, rec. Nov.1984
Holland,Dave (b) | Wheeler,Kenny (tp,fl-h,co,pocket-tp) | Priester,Julian (tb) | Coleman,Steve (fl,ss,as) | Smith,Marvin 'Smitty' (dr,perc)

1293 | CD | Real Life Hits
1293 | LP | Real Life Hits
Gary Burton Quartet
Syndrome | The Beatles | Fleurette Africaine(African Flower) | Ladies In Mercedes | Real Life Hits | I Need You Here | Ivanushka Durachok
Burton,Gary (vib) | Ozone,Makoto (p) | Swallow,Steve (b-g) | Hyman,Mike (dr)

1297 | CD | Septet
1297 | LP | Septet
Chick Corea With String Quartet,Flute And French Horn
Septet(5 Movements) | The Temple Of Isfahan
Los Angeles,CA, rec. October 1984
Corea,Chick (p) | Kujala,Steve (fl) | Gordon,Peter (fr-h) | Kavafian,Ida (v) | Arm,Theodore (v) | Tenenbom,Steven (viola) | Sherry,Fred (cello)

1298 | CD | Azimuth '85
Azimuth
Adios Iony | Dream- | Lost Song- | Who Are You | Breathtaking | Potion(1) | February Daze | Til Bakeblikk | Potion(2)
Oslo,N, rec. March 1985
Azimuth | Wheeler,Kenny (tp,fl-h) | Taylor,John (p,org) | Winstone,Norma (voc)

1303 | CD | Chaser
1303 | LP | Chaser
Terje Rypdal Trio
Ambiguity | Once Upon A Time | Geysir | A Closer Look | Ornen | Chaser | Transition | Imagi(Theme)
Oslo,N, rec. May 1985
Rypdal,Terje (el-g,keyboards) | Kjellemyr,Bjorn (b,el-b) | Kleive,Audun (dr,perc)

1306 | CD | Slide Show
1306 | LP | Slide Show
Ralph Towner-Gary Burton
Maelstrom | Vessel | Around The Bend | Blue In Green | Beneath An Evening Sky | The Donkey Jamboree | Continental Breakfast | Charlotte's Tangle | Innocenti
Ludwigsburg, rec. May 1985
Towner,Ralph (g,12-string-g) | Burton,Gary (vib,marimba)

1307 | CD | Erendira
1307 | LP | Erendira
First House
A Day Away | Innocent Erendira | The Journeyers To The East | Bracondale | Grammenos | Stranger Than Paradise | Bridge Call | Doubt | Further Away
Oslo,N, rec. July 1985
First House | Stubbs,Ken (ss,as) | Bates,Django (p) | Hutton,Mick (b) | France,Martin (dr,perc)

1308 | CD | The Epidemics
1308 | LP | The Epidemics
Shankar/Caroline,
Never Take No For An Answer | What Would I Do Without You | Situations | You Don't Love Me Anymore | You Can Be Anything | No Cure | Don't I Know You | Give An Inch | Full Moon
rec. 1985
Shankar (synth,dr-machine,10-string-double-v,voc) | Caroline (synth,tamboura,voc) | Vai,Steve (g) | Kaufman,Gilbert (synth) | Jones,Percy (b)

1312 | CD | Emergence
1312 | LP | Emergence
Miroslav Vitous
Epilogue | Transformation | Atlantis Suite: | Emergence Of The Spirit- | Matter And Spirit- | The Choice- | Destruction Into Energy- | Wheels Of Fortune(When Face Gets Pale) | Regards To Gershwin's Honeyman | Alice In Wonderland | Morning Lake Forever | Variations On Spanish Themes
Ludwigsburg, rec. September 1985
Vitous,Miroslav (b)

1319 | CD | Bande A Part
1319 | LP | Bande A Part
Masqualero
3 For 5 | Natt | Sort Of | Vanilje | Bali | Tutte | No Soap | Nyl
Oslo,N, rec. August/December 1985
Masqualero | Molvaer,Nils Petter (tp) | Brunborg,Tore (ss,ts) | Balke,Jon (p,el-p,synth) | Andersen,Arild (b,el-b) | Christensen,Jon (dr,perc)

1320 | LP | Fragments
1320 | CD | Fragments
Paul Bley Quartet
Memories | Monica Jane | Line Down | Seven | Closer | Once Around The Park | Hand Dance | For The Love Of Sarah | Nothing Ever Was, Anyway
Oslo,N, rec. Jan.1986
Bley,Paul (p) | Surman,John (b-cl,ss,bs) | Frisell,Bill (g) | Motian,Paul (dr)

1326 | CD | Avant Pop
1326 | LP | Avant Pop
Lester Bowie's Brass Fantasy
The Emperor | Saving All My Love For You | B Funk | Blueberry Hill | Crazy | Macho(Dedicated To Machito) | No Shit | Oh What A Night
Ludwigsburg, rec. March 1986
Bowie,Lester (tp) | Davis,Stanton (tp) | Thompson,Malachi (tp) | Siddik,Rasul (tp) | Turre,Steve (tb) | Lacy,Ku-umba Frank (tb) | Chancey,Vincent (fr-h) | Stewart,Robert 'Bob' (tuba) | Wilson,Phillip (dr)

1327 | LP | Power Spot
Jon Hassell Group
Power Spot
Ontario, rec. Oct.1983/Dec.1984
Hassell,Jon (tp) | Deane,J.A. (alto-fl,perc,electronic-perc) | Rykiel,Jean-Pilippe (electronic-keyboards) | Brook,Michael (g,electonics) | Horowitz,Richard (electronic-keyboards)
Passege D.E. | Miracle Steps
Hassell,Jon (tp) | Deane,J.A. (alto-fl,perc,electronic-perc) | Rykiel,Jean-Pilippe (electronic-keyboards) | Brook,Michael (g,electonics) | Horowitz,Richard (electronic-keyboards) | Richard Armin (strings,raad electro-acoustic) | Paul Armin (strings,raad electro-acoustic)
Solaire | Wing Melodies | Solaire | Wing Melodies
Hassell,Jon (tp) | Deane,J.A. (alto-fl,perc,electronic-perc) | Rykiel,Jean-Pilippe (electronic-keyboards) | Brook,Michael (g,electonics) | Horowitz,Richard (electronic-keyboards) | Eno,Brian (el-b)
Air
Hassell,Jon (tp) | Deane,J.A. (alto-fl,perc,electronic-perc) | Frasconi,Miguel (fl) | Rykiel,Jean-Pilippe (electronic-keyboards)
The Elephant And The Orchid
Hassell,Jon (tp) | Deane,J.A. (alto-fl,perc,electronic-perc) | Rykiel,Jean-Pilippe (electronic-keyboards) | Brook,Michael (g,electonics)

1329 | CD | Whiz Kids
Gary Burton Quintet
The Last Clown | Yellow Fever | Soulful Bill | La Divetta | Cool Train | The Loop
Ludwigsburg, rec. June 1986
Burton,Gary (vib) | Smith,Tommy (sax) | Ozone,Makoto (p) | Swallow,Steve (el-b) | Richards,Martin (dr)

1335 | CD | Exploded View
1335 | LP | Exploded View
Steve Tibbetts Group
Name Everything | Another Year | A Clear Day And No Memories | Your Cat | Forget | Drawing Down The Moon | The X Festival | Metal Summer | Assembly Field
St.Paul, Minnesota, rec. 1985-1986
Tibbetts,Steve (g,kalimba,tapes) | Hughes,Bob (b) | Anderson,Marc (perc,congas,berimbau,steel-dr) | Wise,Marcus (tabla) | Schmidt,Claudia (voice) | Henry,Bruce (voice) | Reimer,Jan (voice)

1337 | CD | Somewhere Called Home
Norma Winstone Trio
Cafe | Somewhere Called Home | Sea Lady | Some Time Ago | Prologue | Celeste | Hi Lili Hi Lo | Out Of This World | Tea For Two
Oslo,N, rec. July 1986
Winstone,Norma (voc) | Coe,Tony (cl,ts) | Taylor,John (p)

1338 | CD | We Begin
Mark Isham-Art Lande
The Melancholy Of Departure | Ceremony In Starlight | We Begin | Lord Ananea | Surface And Symbol | Sweet Circle | Fanfare
Oslo,N, rec. Jan.1987
Isham,Mark (tp,fl-h,synth,perc,piccolo-tp) | Lande,Art (p,synth,perc)

1339 | CD | Lumi
1339 | LP | Lumi
Edward Vesala Group
The Wind | Frozen Melody | Calypso Bulbosa | Third Moon | Lumi | Camel Walk | Fingo | Early Messenger | Together
Helsinki, Finland, rec. June 1986
Vesala,Edward (dr,perc) | Heikkinen,Esko (tp,piccolo-tp) | Bildo,Tom (tb,tuba) | Lahti,Pentti (fl,as,bs) | Tapio,Jorma (fl,cl,b-cl,as) | Rinne,Tapani (cl,b-cl,ss,ts) | Heinilä,Kari (fl,ss,ts) | Björkenheim,Raoul (g) | Vainio,Taito (accordeon) | Haarla,Iro (p,harp) | Häkä (b)

1342 | CD | Red Twist & Tuned Arrow
1342 | LP | Red Twist & Tuned Arrow
Christy Doran-Fredy Studer-Stephan Wittwer
Canon Canon | 1374 | Quasar | Belluard | Backtalk | Messing | D.T.E.T.
Luzern,CH, rec. Nov.1986
Doran,Christy (g,el-g) | Wittwer,Stephan (el-g,synth,sequencer-programming) | Studer,Freddy (dr,perc)

1343 | CD | Volver
1343 | LP | Volver
Enrico Rava-Dino Saluzzi Quintet
Le But Du Souffle | Minguito | Luna-Volver | Tiempos De Ausencias | Ballantine For Valentine | Visions
Ludwigsburg, rec. Oct.1986
Saluzzi,Dino (bandoneon) | Rava,Enrico (tp) | Pepl,Harry (g) | Di Castri,Furio (b) | Ditmas,Bruce (dr)

1352 | LP | Guamba
1352 | CD | Guamba
Gary Peacock Quartet
Guamba | Requiem | Celina | Thyme Time | Lila | Introending | Gardenia
Oslo,N, rec. March 1987
Peacock,Gary (b) | Mikkelborg,Palle (tp,fl-h) | Garbarek,Jan (ss,ts) | Erskine,Peter (dr,dr-computer)

1353 | CD | The Razor's Edge
1353 | LP | The Razor's Edge
Dave Holland Quintet
Brother Ty | Vedana | The Razor's Edge | Blues For C.M. | Vortex | 5 Four Six | Wights Waits For Weights | Figit Time
Ludwigsburg, rec. Feb.1987
Holland,Dave (b) | Wheeler,Kenny (tp,fl-h,co) | Eubanks,Robin (tb) | Coleman,Steve (as) | Smith,Marvin 'Smitty' (dr)

1354 | CD | Ecotopia
1354 | LP | Ecotopia
Oregon
Twice Around The Sun | Innocente | WBAI | Zephyr | Ecotopia | Leather Cats | ReDial | Song Of The Morrow
Ludwigsburg, rec. March 1987
Oregon | Towner,Ralph (g,p,synth,dr-machine,12-string-g) | McCandless,Paul (engl-h,ss,synth,oboe) | Moore,Glen (b) | Gurtu,Trilok (perc,tabla)

1356 | CD | Cracked Mirrors
Harry Pepl/Herbert Joos/Jon Christensen
Wolkenbilder(1) | Reflections In A Cracked Mirror | Schikaneder Delight | Die Alte Mär Und Das Mann | More Far Out Than East | Wolkenbilder(2) | Purple Light | Tintenfisch Inki
rec. Feb.1987
Joos,Herbert (fl-h) | Pepl,Harry (g,p,g-synth) | Christensen,Jon (dr)

1357 | CD | Accélération
1357 | LP | Accélération
Hans Koch/Martin Schütz/Marco Käppeli
Shy Csardas | Im Delirium | Midori | Loisaida | Glas(s)no(s)t | Tatzelwurm | Nitrams Rock | Acceleration Controlee | GG-U-GG-U-RR-U-GG
Ludwigsburg, rec. June 1987
Koch,Hans (cl,b-cl,ss,ts) | Schütz,Martin (cello,b) | Käppeli,Marco (dr)

1358 | LP | Twilight Fields
1358 | CD | Twilight Fields
1358 | MC | Twilight Fields
Stephan Micus
Twilight Fields(part 1-5)
Ludwigsburg, rec. Nov.1987
Micus,Stephan (hammered-dulcimer,nay,shakuhachi,water-tuned-flowerpots)

1367 | CD | Aero
1367 | LP | Aero
Masqualero
Aero | Science | Venice | Printer | Balet | Return | Bee Gee
Oslo,N, rec. November 1987
Masqualero | Molvaer,Nils Petter (tp) | Brunborg,Tore (ss,ts) | Alnaes,Frode (g) | Andersen,Arild (b) | Christensen,Jon (dr)

1371 | CD | Cosi Lontano...Quasi Dentro
1371 | LP | Cosi Lontano...Quasi Dentro
Markus Stockhausen Quartet
So Far | Forward | Late | Across Bridges | In Parallel | Breaking | Through | Almost Inside
Oslo,N, rec. March 1988
Stockhausen,Markus (tp,fl-h,synth) | Ottaviucci,Fabrizio (p) | Peacock,Gary (b) | Babel,Zoro (dr)

1372 | CD | The Lamp And The Star
1372 | LP | The Lamp And The Star
Alex Cline Group
A Blue Robe In The Distance | Eminence | Emerald Light | Altar Stone | Accepting The Chalice
Los Angeles,CA, rec. September 1987
Cline,Alex (perc,voice) | Peet,Wayne (p,org) | Gauthier,Jeff (v,viola,voice) | Roberts,Hank (cello,voice) | Von Essen,Eric (b) | Rawcliffe,Susan (didjerdu) | Kemanis,Aina (voice) | Cline,Nels (voice)

1373 | CD | Triplicate
1373 | LP | Triplicate
Dave Holland Trio
Games | Quiet Fire | Take The Coltrane | Rivers Run | Four Winds | Triple Dance | Blue | African Lullaby | Segment
NYC, rec. March 1988
Holland,Dave (b) | Coleman,Steve (as) | DeJohnette,Jack (dr)

1374 | LP | Orchestra

Eberhard Weber Orchestra
Seven Movements
Ludwigsburg, rec. May & Aug.1988
Weber,Eberhard (b,perc) | Joos,Herbert (fl-h) | Jillich,Anton (fl-h) | Czelusta,Wolfgang (tb) | Richter,Andreas (tb) | Rapp,Winfried (b-tb) | Diebetsberger,Rudolf (fr-h) | Hauschild,Thomas (fr-h) | Stagl,Franz (tuba)
Too Early To Leave
Weber,Eberhard (b) | Joos,Herbert (fl-h) | Jillich,Anton (fl-h) | Rapp,Winfried (b-tb) | Diebetsberger,Rudolf (fr-h) | Hauschild,Thomas (fr-h) | Stagl,Franz (tuba)
Eberhard Weber
Broken Silence | Before Dawn | Just A Moment | Air | Ready Out There | A Daydream | Trio | Epilogue
Weber,Eberhard (b)
On A Summer's Evening
Weber,Eberhard (keyboards,b)

1380 | CD | Big Map Idea
Steve Tibbetts Group
Black Mountain Side | Black Year | Big Idea | Wish | Station | Start | Mile 234 | 100 Moons | 3 Letters(part 1-3)
St.Paul, Minnesota/Boudhanath
1987-1988
Tibbetts,Steve (g,dobro,kalimba,pianolin,tapes) | Anderson,Marc (perc,congas,berimbau,steel-dr) | Wise,Marcus (tabla) | Kinney,Michelle (cello)

1388 | CD | City Of Eyes
Ralph Towner Quintet
Jamaica Stopover | Cascades | Les Douzilles | City Of Eyes | Sipping The Past | Far Cry | Janet | Sustained Release | Tundra | Blue Gown
Oslo,N, rec. November 1988
Towner,Ralph (g,synth,co,12-string-g) | Stockhausen,Markus (tp,fl-h,piccolo-tp) | McCandless,Paul (engl-h,oboe) | Peacock,Gary (b) | Granelli,Jerry (dr,electronic-dr)

1389 | CD | Undisonus
Terje Rypdal(comp)
Undisonus Op.23 for Violin And Orchestra
St.Peter's Church,Morden,London, rec. September 1987
Tonnesen,Terje (v) | Royal Philharmonic Orchestra, London
Ineo Op.29 for Choir And Chamber Orchestra
Oslo,N, rec. November 1987
Grex Vocalis | Hogest,Carl (ld) | Rainbow Orchestra,The | Eggen,Christian (cond)

1393 | CD | Cantilena
1393 | LP | Cantilena
First House
Cantilena | Underfelt | Dimple | Sweet William | Low-Down(Toytown) | Hollyhocks | Madeleine After Prayer | Shining Brightly | Jay-Tee | Pablo
Oslo,N, rec. March 1989
First House | Stubbs,Ken (as) | Bates,Django (p,tenor-h) | Hutton,Mick (b) | France,Martin (dr)

1394 | CD | ...And She Answered
1394 | LP | ...And She Answered
AM 4
Streets And Rivers | And She Answered: When You Return To Me, I Will Open Quick The Cage Door, I Will Let The Red Bird Flee | Lonely Woman | Mi-La | Bhagavad | Over The Rainbow | Far Horizon | The Sadness Of Yuki | Oh! | One T'une
Oslo,N, rec. April 1989
AM 4 | Puschnig,Wolfgang (alto-fl,as,hojak,shakuhachi) | Scherer,Uli (p,keyboards,prepared-p) | Sharrock,Linda (voc)

1396 | CD | Wave Over Sorrow
1396 | LP | Wave Over Sorrow
Mikhail Alperin/Arkady Shilkloper
Song | Poem | Wave Over Sorrow | Toccata | Unisons | Introduction And Dance In 7-4 | Short Story | Prelude In B Minor | Miniature | Epilogue
Oslo,N, rec. July 1989
Alperin,Mikhail 'Misha' (p,melodica,voice) | Shilkloper,Arkady (fl-h,fr-h,jagdhorn,voice)

1397 | CD | Nobody Told Me
1397 | LP | Nobody Told Me
Shankar Group
Chittham Irangaayo | Chodhanai Thanthu | Nadru Dri Dhom-Tilana
Los Angeles,CA, rec. 1989
Shankar (double-v,voc) | Lakshminarayana,V. (v,double-v,voc) | Hussain,Zakir (tabla) | Vinayakram,Vikku (ghatam) | Rao,Ganam (voc) | Caroline (voc)

1403 | CD | M.R.C.S.
1403 | MC | M.R.C.S.
1403 | LP | M.R.C.S.
Shankar Quartet
Adagio | March | All I Care | Reasons | Back Again | Al's Hallucinations | Sally | White Buffalo | Ocean Waves
Ludwigsburg/Oslo,N, rec. 1989
Shankar (double-v) | Christensen,Jon (dr) | Vinayakram,Vikku (ghatam) | Hussain,Zakir (tabla)

1404 | CD | Aparis
1404 | LP | Aparis
Aparis
Aparis | Poseidon | Carnaval | High Tide | Rejoice | Peach
Oslo,N, rec. August 1989
Aparis | Stockhausen,Markus (tp,fl-h) | Stockhausen,Simon (sax,synth) | Thönes,Jo (dr,electronic-dr)

1409 | CD | Berlin Contemporary Jazz Orchestra
1409 | LP | Berlin Contemporary Jazz Orchestra
Berlin Contemporary Jazz Orchestra
Ana | Salz | Reef And Kneebus
Berlin, rec. May 1989
Berlin Contemporary Jazz Orchestra | Bailey,Benny (tp) | Heberer,Thomas (tp) | Lowther,Quentin (tp) | Wheeler,Kenny (tp,fl-h) | Berg,Henning (tb) | Breuer,Hermann (tb) | Katzenbeier,Hubert (tb) | Zimmermann,Utz (b-tb) | Van Kemenade,Paul (as) | Wahnschaffe,Felix (as) | Dudek,Gerd (fl,cl,ss,ts) | Gauchel,Walter (ts) | Petrowsky,Ernst-Ludwig (bs) | Breuker,Willem (b-cl,bs) | Takase,Aki (p) | Mengelberg,Misha (p) | Lenz,Günter (b) | Thigpen,Ed (dr) | Von Schlippenbach,Alexander (ld)

1411 | CD | Animato
1411 | LP | Animato
John Abercrombie Trio
Right Now | Single Moon | Agitato | First Light | Last Light | For Hope Of Hope | Bright Reign | Ollie Mention
Oslo,N, rec. October 1989
Abercrombie,John (g,g-synth) | Mendoza,Vince (synth) | Christensen,Jon (dr,perc)

1415/16 | 2 CD | Muisc For Large & Small Ensembles
1415/16 | 2 LP | Muisc For Large & Small Ensembles
Kenny Wheeler Ensemble
Opening- | For H.- | For Jan | For P.A. | Know Where You Are | Consolation | Freddy C | Closing | Sophie | Sea Lady | Gentle Piece | Trio | Duet 1 | Duet 2 | Duet 3 | Trio 2 | By Myself
London,GB, rec. January 1990
Wheeler,Kenny (tp,fl-h) | Watkins,Derek (tp) | Lowther,Henry (tp) | Downey,Alan (tp) | Hamer,Ian (tp) | Horler,David (tb) | Pyne,Chris (tb) | Rutherford,Paul (tb) | Fraser,Hugh (tb) | Warleight,Ray (as) | Lamont,Duncan (sax) | Parker,Evan (sax) | Argüelles,Julian (sax) | Sulzman,Stan (fl,ts) | Abercrombie,John (g) | Taylor,John (p) | Holland,Dave (b) | Erskine,Peter (dr) | Winstone,Norma (voc)

1428 | CD | Infancia
1428 | MC | Infancia
1428 | LP | Infancia
Egberto Gismonti Group
Ensaio De Escola De Samba(Danca Dos Escravos) | 7 Anéis | Meninas | Infancia | A Fala Da Paixao | Recife & O Amor Que Move O Sol E Outras Estrelas | Danca(No.1) | Danca(No.2)
Oslo,N, rec. November 1990
Gismonti,Egberto (g,p) | Carneiro,Zeca (g,synth) | Assumpacao,Zeca (b) | Morelenbaum,Jacques (cello)

1435 | CD | Sagn
Arild Andersen Sextet
Sagn | Gardsjenta | Eisemo | Toll | Draum | Laurdagskveld | Tjovane | Sorgmild | Svarm | Gamlestev | Reven | Nystev | Lussi | Rysen | Belare | Sagn(II)
Oslo,N, rec. August 1990
Andersen,Arild (b) | Hofseth,Bendik (ss,ts) | Alnaes,Frode (g) | Wesseltoft,Jens Bugge (keyboards) | Vasconcelos,Nana (perc,voc) | Berg,Kirsten Braten (voc)

1436 | CD | Musik Für Zwei Kontrabässe, Elektrische Gitarre & Schlagzeug
1436 | LP | Musik Für Zwei Kontrabässe, Elektrische Gitarre & Schlagzeug
Doran/Studer/Burri/Magnenat
Siren | Chemistries(I) | Chemistries(II) | Collage | Ma Perché | 'Seen A Man About A Dog | SCD | Ü 7
Luzern,CH, rec. May 1990
Doran,Christy (el-g) | Magnenat,Olivier (b) | Burri,Bobby (b) | Studer,Freddy (dr,perc)

1445 | LP | Nonsentration
1445 | CD | Nonsentration
Jon Balke w/Oslo 13
Stealing Space(I&II) | Stop | Blic | Contructing Stop | The Laws Of Freedom | Disappear Here | Nord | Circling The Square | The Art Of Being
Oslo,N, rec. September 1990
Balke,Jon (keyboards) | Jorgensen,Per (tp) | Molvaer,Nils Petter (tp) | Sunde,Torbjorn (tb) | Halle,Morton (as) | Brunborg,Tore (ts) | Frang,Arne (ts) | Kleive,Audun (dr) | Christensen,Jon (dr,perc) | Sletten,Finn (perc) | N'Doye,Miki (perc)

1446 | CD | Solitudes
1446 | MC | Solitudes
Tamia/Pierre Favre
Chant D'Exil | Drame | Clair-Obscur | Pluies | Allegria | Erba Luce | Sables | Solitudes
Oslo,N, rec. April 1991
Tamia (voice) | Favre,Pierre (dr)

1449 | CD | A Wider Embrace
Trevor Watts Moiré Music Drum Orchestra
Egugu | Medley: | Ahoom Mbram- | Tetegramatan- | Free Flow- | Tetegramatan(reprise)- | Opening Gambit | Otublohu | Bomsu | Hunter's Song:Ibrumankuman | The Rocky Road To Dublin | Brekete Takai | Southern Memories | We Are
London,GB, rec. April 1993
Watts,Trevor (ss,as) | Tsiboe,Nana (atupan-dr,brekete-dr,djembe,gonje,odukro-gya-dr,twanga,voc,wea-fl) | Patato,Nee-Daku (congas,bells,berimbau,brekete-dr,cabasa,odukro-gya-dr,tamale-dr,voc) | Yates,Jojo (bells,brekete-dr,cabasa,cowbells,gyamadudu-dr,mbira,odukro-gya-dr,t | Appiah,Nana (brekete-dr,cabasa,cowbell,odukro-gya-dr,shakers,voc,wea-fl) | Mensah,Paapa J. (kit-dr,shakers,voc,wea-fl) | McKenzie,Colin (b-g)

1451 | CD | Aquarian Rain
1451 | LP | Aquarian Rain
Barre Phillips
Ebb | Water Shed
Oslo,N, rec. May 1991
Phillips,Barre (b-solo)
Barre Phillips Group
Bridging | Ripples Edge | Eddie's Blues
Phillips,Barre (b) | Joule,Alain (perc)
The Flow | Between I And E | Early Tide | Aquarian Rain
Phillips,Barre (b) | Joule,Alain (perc) | Estager,Jean-Francois (perc) | Giroudon,James (perc)
Alain Joule
Promenade De Memoire
Joule,Alain (perc)

1455 | CD | The Finnish/Swiss Tour
1455 | LP | The Finnish/Swiss Tour
Hal Russell NRG Ensemble
Monica's Having A Baby | Aila- | 35 Basic- | Temporarily | Raining Violets | For MC | Dance Of The Spider People | Ten Letters Of Love | Hal The Weenie | Linda's Rock Vamp | Mars Theme
Jazz Festival Zürich,CH/Tampere Jazz Happening,Finland, rec. November 1990
Russell,Hal (tp,ss,ts,vib,dr) | Williams,Mars (ss,ts,didgeridoo) | Sandstrom,Brian (tp,g,b) | Kessler,Kent (b,b-g,didgeridoo) | Hunt,Steve (vib,dr,didgeridoo)

1458 | CD | Rouge
1458 | MC | Rouge
1458 | LP | Rouge
Louis Sclavis Quintet
One | Nacht | Kali La Nuit | Reflet | Reeves | Les Bouteilles | Moment Donné | Face Nord | Rouge- | Pourquoi Une Valse- | Yes Love
Oslo,N, rec. September 1991
Sclavis,Louis (cl,b-cl,ss) | Pifarely,Dominique (v) | Raulin,Francois (p,synth) | Chevillon,Bruno (b) | Ville,Christian (dr)

1461 | CD | Invisible Strom
Edward Vesala Sound And Fury
Sheets And Shrouds | Somnamblues | Sarastus | The Haze Of The Frost
Helsinki, Finland, rec. May/June 1991
Vesala,Edward (dr,perc) | Riikonen,Matti (tp) | Tapio,Jorma (b-cl,as,perc,flb-fl) | Kannisto,Jouni (fl,ts) | Päivinnen,Pepa (fl,alto-fl,ss,ts,bs) | Sumen,Jimi (g) | Haarla,Iro (p,keyboards,harp)
Murmuring Morning | Shadows On The Frontier | In The Gate Of Another Gate | The Wedding Of All Essential Parts | The Invisible Storm
Vesala,Edward (dr,perc) | Riikonen,Matti (tp) | Tapio,Jorma (b-cl,as,perc,flb-fl) | Kannisto,Jouni (fl,ts) | Päivinnen,Pepa (fl,alto-fl,ss,ts,bs) | Sumen,Jimi (g) | Haarla,Iro (p,keyboards,harp) | Ylönen,Marko (cello)
Gordion's Flashes
Vesala,Edward (dr,perc) | Riikonen,Matti (tp) | Tapio,Jorma (b-cl,as,perc,flb-fl) | Kannisto,Jouni (fl,ts) | Päivinnen,Pepa (fl,alto-fl,ss,ts,bs) | Sumen,Jimi (g) | Haarla,Iro (p,keyboards,harp) | Nauseef,Mark (bongos)
Caccaroo Boohoo
Vesala,Edward (dr,perc) | Riikonen,Matti (tp) | Tapio,Jorma (b-cl,as,perc,flb-fl) | Kannisto,Jouni (fl,ts) | Päivinnen,Pepa (fl,alto-fl,ss,ts,bs) | Sumen,Jimi (g) | Haarla,Iro (p,keyboards,harp) | Sarmato,Pekka (b)

1466 | CD | Volition
1466 | LP | Volition
Krakatau
Brujo | Volition | Naiads | Bullroarer | Changgo | Little Big Horn | Dalens Ande
Oslo,N, rec. December 1991
Krakatau | Takamäki,Jone (ts,krakaphone,toppophone,whirlpipe) | Björkenheim,Raoul (g,shekere) | Krokfors,Uffe (b) | Forsman,Alf (dr)

1474 | CD | Q.E.D.
Terje Rypdal With The Borealis Ensemble
Q.E.D.(Quod erat demonstrandum) | Largo
Oslo,N, rec. August/December 1991
Rypdal,Terje (el-g) | Borealis Ensemble | Rosning,Lasse (piccolo-tp) | Martinsen,Jan Olav (fr-h) | Aarset,Vidar (fr-h) | Oestby,Inger-Johanne (fl) | Pedersen,Leif Arne (cl) | Hannisdal,Per (bassoon) | Joergensen,Kjell Arne (v) | Siegel,Eileen (v) | Sandbakken,Are (viola) | Rissanen,Marja-Liisa (viola) | Ravnam,Kari (cello) | Solum,Bjorn (cello) | Kjellemyr,Bjorn (b) | Eggen,Christian (cond)

1478 | CD | The Brass Project
John Surman-John Warren Group
The Returning Exile | Coastline | The New One Two(part 1) | The New One Two(part 2) | Spacial Motive | Wider Vision | Silent Lake | Mellstock Quire | Tantrum Clangley | All For A Shadow
London,GB, rec. April 1992
Surman,John (cl,alto-cl,ss,bs,p) | Warren,John (cond) | Lowther,Henry (tp) | Waterman,Steve (tp) | Brooks,Stuart (tp) | Griffiths,Malcolm (tb) | Pyne,Chris (tb) | Stewart,David (b-tb) | Edwards,Richard (b-tb) | Laurence,Chris (b) | Marshall,Joe (dr,perc)

1480 | CD | Shadow/Landscape With Argonauts
Heiner Goebbels Group
Shadow/Landscapes With Argonauts-With Words by Edgar Allen Poe and Heiner Müller
Boston,MA/Stoughton,MA, rec. February/September/October 1990
Goebbels,Heiner (keyboards,accordeon,programming) | Govetas,Christos (cl,chumbush,gardon) | Lussier,René (g) | Hayward,Charles (dr,hand-perc,tipan) | Deihim,Sussan (voc) | 100 Voices on the streets of Boston

1484 | CD | Hal's Bells
Hal Russell
Buddhi | Millard Mottker | Portrait Of Benny | Strangest Kiss | Susanna | Carolina Moon | Kenny G | I Need You Now | For Free | Moon Of Manakoora
Oslo,N, rec. May 1992
Russell,Hal (tp,ss,ts,vib,dr,perc,congas,bass-marimba,bells,gongs,musette,voice)

1485 | CD | Folly Seeing All This
Michael Mantler Quintet With The Balanescu Quartet
Folly Seeing All This | News | What Is The Word
London,GB, rec. June 1992
Mantler,Michael (tp) | Puschnig,Wolfgang (alto-fl) | Fenn,Rick (g) | Mantler,Karen (p,voice) | Adams,Dave (vib,chimes) | Balanescu Quartet: | Balanescu,Alexander (v) | Connors,Clare (v) | Hawkes,Bill (viola) | Fenton,Jane (cello) | Bruce,Jack (voice) | Beckett,Samuel (words)

1488 | CD | In The Evenings Out There
Paul Bley Quartet
Afterthoughts | Portrait Of Silence | Soft Touch | Speak Easy | Interface | Alignment | Fair Share | Article Four | Married Alive | Spe-cu-lay-ting | Tomorrow Today | Note Police
Oslo,N, rec. September 1991
Bley,Paul (p) | Surman,John (b-cl,bs) | Peacock,Gary (b) | Oxley,Tony (dr)

1489 | CD | While We're Young
John Abercrombie Trio
Rain Forest | Stormz | Dear Rain | Mirrors | Carol's Carol | Scomotion | A Matter Of Time | Dolorosa
NYC, rec. June 1992
Abercrombie,John (g,el-g) | Wall,Dan (org) | Nussbaum,Adam (dr)

1498 | CD | The Hal Russell Story
Hal Russell NRG Ensemble
Hall Russell Story,The | Part One-Family Jam: | Intro & Fanfare- | Toy Parade- | Trumpet March- | Riverside Jump- | Part Two-Scholar And Fan: | Krupa- | You're Blasé- | Dark Rapture- | World Class- | Part Three-Hit The Road,Hal: | Wood Chips- | Ny Little Grass Shack- | O&B- | Part Four-Fast Company: | Mor M- | Gloomy Sunday- | Hair Male- | Bossa G- | Mildred- | Dope Music- | Part Five-The Birth Of The Free: | 2x2- | Ayler Songs- | Part Six-NRG Rising: | Rehcabnettul- | Steve's Freedom Principle- | Encores: | Lady In The Lake- | Oh Well-
Winterthur,CH, rec. July 1992
Russell,Hal (tp,ss,ts,xyl,dr,perc,gong,narration) | Williams,Mars (as,ts,bass-sax,bells,didgeridoo,narration,sounds,toy-horns,wood-fl) | Sandstrom,Brian (tp,el-g,b,perc,toy-horns) | Kessler,Kent (tb,b) | Hunt,Steve (vib,dr,perc,tympani)

1499 | CD | Then Comes The White Tiger
Red Sun/SamulNori
Nanjang(The Meeting Place) | Peaceful Question | Kil-Kun-Ak | Hear Them Say | Piri | Soo Yang Kol(The Valley Of Weeping Willows) | Flute Sanjo | Komungo | Full House(part 1) | Full House(part 2) | Far Away- | Ariang-
Seoul,Korea, rec. May 1993
Red Sun | Puschnig,Wolfgang (alto-fl,as) | Innacone,Rick (el-g) | Tacuma,Jamaaladeen (b-g) | Sharrock,Linda (voc) | SamulNori | Soo,Kim Duk (changgo,ching,hojok,piri) | Soo,Lee Kwang (ching,k'kwaengwari,voice) | Seok,Kang Min (buk,ching) | Tae,Kim Woon (bara,buk,ching) | Woon,Kim Sung (kayagum,komungo)

1507 | CD | Kulture Jazz
Wadada Leo Smith
Don't You Remember? | Kulture Of Jazz | Song Of The Humanity(Kanto Pri Homaro) | Fire-Sticks,Chrysanthemums And Moonlight(for Harumi) | Seven Rings Of Light In The Hola Trinity | Louis Armstrong Counter-Pointing | Albert Ayler In A Spiritual Light | The Kemet Omega Reigns(for Billie Holiday) | Love Supreme(for John Coltrane) | Mississippi Delta Sunrise(for Bobbie) | Mother: Sarah Brown-Smith-Wallace | The Healer's Voyage On The Sacred River(for Ayl Kwel Armah) | Uprising(for Jessie And Yvonne)
Winterthur,CH, rec. October 1992
Smith,Leo[Wadada] (tp,fl-h,harm,perc,bamboo-fl,koto,mbira,voc)

1511 | CD | Speak To The Devil
John Abercrombie Trio
Angel Food | Now And Again | Mahat | Chorale | Farewell | BT-U | Early To Bed | Dreamland | Hell's Gate
Oslo,N, rec. July 1993
Abercrombie,John (g,el-g) | Wall,Dan (org) | Nussbaum,Adam (dr)

1517 | CD | Further
Jon Balke w/Magnetic North Orchestra
Departure | Step One | Horizontal Song | Flying Thing | Shaded Place | Taraf | Moving Carpet | Eastern Forest | Changing Song | Wooden Voices | Arrival
Oslo,N, rec. June 1993
Balke,Jon (p,keyboards) | Magnetic North Orchestra | Antonsen,Jens Petter (tp) | Jorgensen,Per (tp,voc) | Halle,Morton (as) | Brunborg,Tore (ss,ts) | Okland,Gertrud (v) | Villa,Trond (viola) | Franke-Blom,Jonas (cello) | Jormin,Anders (b) | Kleive,Audun (dr) | Mazur,Marilyn (perc)

1526 | CD | Acoustic Quartet
Louis Sclavis Quartet
Sensible | Bafouée | Abrupto | Elke | Hop! | Seconde | Beata | Rhinoceros
Oslo,N, rec. September 1993
Sclavis,Louis (cl,b-cl) | Pifarely,Dominique (v) | Ducret,Marc (g,12-string-g) | Chevillon,Bruno (b)

1529 | CD | Matinale
Krakatau
Matinale | Unseen Sea Scene | Jai-Ping | Rural | For Bernard Moore | Sarajevo | Suhka | Raging Thirst
Winterthur,CH, rec. November 1993
Krakatau | Takamäki,Jone (ss,as,ts,bass-sax,bell,krakaphone,reed-fl,wooden-fl) | Björkenheim,Raoul (g,bass-recorder,gong) | Krokfors,Uffe (b,perc) | Kätkä,Ippe (dr,perc,gongs)

1532 | CD | Time Being
Peter Erskine Trio
Terraces | For The Time Being | If Only I Had Known | Evansong | Page 172 | Liten Visa Till Karin | Bulgaria | Ambleside | Phase One | Palle's Headache | Pieds-en-l'air
Oslo,N, rec. November 1993
Erskine,Peter (dr) | Taylor,John (p) | Danielsson,Palle (b)

1534 | CD | Stranger Than Fiction
John Surman Quartet
Cantile With Response | A Distant Spring | Tess | Promising Horizons | Across The Bridge | Moonshine Dancer | Running Sands | Triptych: | Hidden Orchid- | Synapsis- | Paratactic Paths-
Oslo,N, rec. December 1993
Surman,John (alto-cl,b-cl,ss,bs) | Taylor,John (p) | Laurence,Chris (b) | Marshall,John (dr)

1537 | CD | Time Will Tell
Paul Bley/Evan Parker/Barre Phillips
Poetic Justice | Time Will Tell | Above The Three Line | Sprung | No Questions | Marsh Tides | Burlesque
Oslo,N, rec. January 1994
Bley,Paul (p) | Parker,Evan (ss,ts) | Phillips,Barre (b)
Paul Bley/Barre Phillips
You Will,Oscar,You Will
Bley,Paul (p) | Phillips,Barre (b)
Paul Bley/Evan Parker
Clawback
Bley,Paul (p) | Parker,Evan (ss,ts)
Evan Parker/Barre Phillips
Vine Laces | Instance
Parker,Evan (ss,ts) | Phillips,Barre (b)

1538 | CD | How It Was Then...Never Again
Azimuth
How It Was Then | Looking On | Whirlpool | Full Circle | How Deep Is The Ocean | Stango | Mindiatyr | Wintersweet
Oslo,N, rec. April 1994
Azimuth | Wheeler,Kenny (tp,fl-h) | Taylor,John (p) | Winstone,Norma (voice)

1541 | CD | Sound & Fury
Edward Vesala Nordic Gallery
Bird In The High Room | Fulflandia | The Quay Of Meditative Future | Hadenas | Unexpected Guests | Bluego | Lavender Lass Blossom | Streaming Below The Time | One-Two-Three Or Four-Five-Six | A Significant Look Of Birch Grove | On The Shady Side Of Forty | Flavor Lust
Korkeakoski,Finland, rec. 1993/1994
Vesala,Edward (b,dr,perc,angklung,tamboura) | Riikonen,Matti (tp) | Rinne,Tapani (cl) | Tapio,Jorma (alto-fl,alto-cl,b-cl,as) | Päivinnen,Pepa (fl,alto-fl,ss,ts,bs,bass-sax,piccolo) | Kannisto,Jouni (fl,ts) | Ikkelä,Petri (accordeon) | Haarla,Iro (p,keyboards,accordeon,harp,koto) | Sumen,Jimi (g) | Linsted,Kari (cello) | Sarmanto,Pekka (b)

1543 | CD | Skies Of Europe
Italian Instabile Orchestra
Il Maestro Muratore: | Il Maestro Muratore- | Squilli Di Morte- | Corbu- | Meru Lo Snob- | L'Arte Mistica Del Vasaio- | Il Maestro Muratore(reprise)- | Skies Of Europe: | Du Du Duchamp- | Quand Duchamp Joue Du Marteau- | Il Suono Giallo- | Marlene E Gli Ospiti Misterioso- | Satin Satie- | Masse D'Urto(a Michelangelo Antonioni)- | Fellini Song-
Live at F.L.O.G. Auditiorium,Florence,Italia, rec. May 1994
Italian Instabile Orchestra | Minafra,Pino (tp,megaphone) | Mandarini,Alberto (tp) | Mazzon,Guido (tp) | Schiaffini,Giancarlo (tb,tuba) | Rossi,Lauro (tb) | Tramontana,Sebi (tb) | Mayes,Martin (fr-h) | Schiano,Mario (ss,as) | Colombo,Eugenio (fl,ss,as) | Trovesi,Gianluigi (cl,alto-cl,b-cl,as) | Dato,Carlo Actis (b-cl,ts,bs) | Cavallanti,Daniele (ts,bs) | Geremia,Renato (v) | Damiani,Paolo (cello) | Gaslini,Giorgio (p,anvil) | Tommaso,Bruno (b) | Tononi,Tiziano (dr,perc) | Mazzone,Vincenzo (dr,perc,tympani)

1549/50 | 2 CD | Atmosphering Conditions Permitting
Jazzensemble Des Hessischen Rundfunks
Bagpipe Song
Frankfurt/M, rec. 9.12.1967
Jazzensemble Des Hessischen Rundfunk | Mangelsdorff,Albert (tb) | Scott,Tony (cl) | Krautgartner,Karel (cl) | Mangelsdorff,Emil (as) | Freund,Joki (ts) | Sauer,Heinz (ts) | Kronberg,Günther (bs) | Lenz,Günter (b) | Hübner,Ralf-R. (dr)
Incantation For An Alto Player
Frankfurt/M, rec. 2.6.1973
Jazzensemble Des Hessischen Rundfunk | Mangelsdorff,Albert (tb) | Mangelsdorff,Emil (fl) | Kronberg,Günther (as) | Freund,Joki (ts) | Sauer,Heinz (ts) | Kriegel,Volker (g) | Brüninghaus,Rainer (el-p) | Weber,Eberhard (b) | Hübner,Ralf-R. (dr)
Walzer Für Sabinchen
Frankfurt/M, rec. 28.12.1973
Jazzensemble Des Hessischen Rundfunk | Christmann,Günter (tb) | Kowald,Peter (tuba) | Wiberny,Karl Heinz (fl) | Jörgensmann,Theo (cl) | Carl,Rüdiger (cl) | Von Schlippenbach,Alexander (p) | Kott,Alois (b) | Lovens,Paul (dr) | Schönenberg,Detlef (dr)
Nachwort
Frankfurt/M, rec. 23.3.1974
Jazzensemble Des Hessischen Rundfunk | Mangelsdorff,Emil (as-playback) | Freund,Joki (ss,ts-playback) | Sauer,Heinz (ts,bs-playback) | Kronberg,Günther (bs-playback) | Wuchner,Jürgen (b) | Hübner,Ralf-R. (dr)
Accelerated Service
Frankfurt/M, rec. 7.5.1977
Jazzensemble Des Hessischen Rundfunk | Mangelsdorff,Emil (as) | Freund,Joki (ts) | Kronberg,Günther (bs) | Brüninghaus,Rainer (p) | Petereit,Dieter (b) | Giger,Peter (dr)
Concierto De Charagojazz
Frankfurt/M, rec. 2.5.1978
Sauer,Heinz (ts) | Torres,Jaime (charango) | Pereyra,Norberto (g)
Oben
Frankfurt/M, rec. 5.12.1978
Liefland,Wilhelm (narration) | Degen,Bob (p) | Niebergall,Buschi (b)
Schattenlehre
Liefland,Wilhelm (narration) | Pilz,Michel (b-cl) | Hübner,Ralf-R. (dr)
Blues, Eternal Turn On
Frankfurt/M, rec. 20.9.1980
Jazzensemble Des Hessischen Rundfunk | Mangelsdorff,Albert (tb) | Sauer,Heinz (ts) | Degen,Bob (p) | Lenz,Günter (b) | Hübner,Ralf-R. (dr)
Niemandsland
Frankfurt/M, rec. 20.6.1981
Jazzensemble Des Hessischen Rundfunk | Mangelsdorff,Emil (fl) | Freund,Joki (ss) | Lauer,Christof (ts) | Frisell,Bill (g) | Reiter,Joerg (p) | Lenz,Günter (b) | Weber,Eberhard (b) | Hübner,Ralf-R. (dr)
Von Der Gewöhnlichen Traurigkeit
Frankfurt/M, rec. 1.10.1981
Jazzensemble Des Hessischen Rundfunk | Mangelsdorff,Albert (tb) | Mangelsdorff,Emil (fl) | Freund,Joki (ts) | Sauer,Heinz (ts) | Pirchner,Werner (vib) | Degen,Bob (p) | Roidinger,Adelhard (b) | Weber,Eberhard (b) | Hübner,Ralf-R. (dr)
Krötenbalz
Frankfurt/M, rec. 8.12.1981
Lovens,Paul (dr,perc,cymbals)
Auf In Den Wald
Frankfurt/M, rec. 22.1.1982
Jazzensemble Des Hessischen Rundfunk | Beckerhoff,Uli (tp) | Mangelsdorff,Emil (as) | Freund,Joki (as) | Sauer,Heinz (as) | Lauer,Christof (ts) | Degen,Bob (p) | Lenz,Günter (b) | Hübner,Ralf-R. (dr)
The Truth Is Unavailable
Frankfurt/M, rec. 5.3.1982
Jazzensemble Des Hessischen Rundfunk | Mangelsdorff,Albert (tb) | Mangelsdorff,Emil (fl) | Freund,Joki (ts) | Sauer,Heinz (ts) | Lauer,Christof (ts) | Becker,Markus (p) | Lenz,Günter (b) | Hübner,Ralf-R. (dr)
Stomp Blasé
Frankfurt/M, rec. 3.11.1982
Jazzensemble Des Hessischen Rundfunk | Freund,Joki (ss) | Mangelsdorff,Emil (as) | Sauer,Heinz (ts) | Degen,Bob (p) | Lenz,Günter (b) | Hübner,Ralf-R. (dr)
Darauf Der Schnee Danach
Frankfurt/M, rec. 23.2.1983
Jazzensemble Des Hessischen Rundfunk | Freund,Joki (ss) | Mangelsdorff,Emil (as) | Sauer,Heinz (ts) | Lauer,Christof (ts) | Degen,Bob (p) | Linke,Rainer (b) | Hübner,Ralf-R. (dr)
Repepetititive
Frankfurt/M, rec. 30.3.1983
Jazzensemble Des Hessischen Rundfunk | Mangelsdorff,Albert (tb) | Freund,Joki (ts) | Sauer,Heinz (ts) | Lauer,Christof (ts) | Brüninghaus,Rainer (el-p,synth) | Heidepriem,Thomas (b) | Hübner,Ralf-R. (dr)
Käuze Und Käuzchen
Frankfurt/M, rec. 14.7.1984
Jazzensemble Des Hessischen Rundfunk | Shterev,Simeon (fl) | Mangelsdorff,Albert (tb) | Freund,Joki (ss) | Sauer,Heinz (ts) | Degen,Bob (p) | Lenz,Günter (b) | Hübner,Ralf-R. (dr)
Noldes Himmel
Frankfurt/M, rec. 10.10.1985
Jazzensemble Des Hessischen Rundfunk | Mangelsdorff,Albert (tb) | Mangelsdorff,Emil (fl) | Freund,Joki (ss) | Konitz,Lee (as) | Sauer,Heinz (ts) | Lauer,Christof (ts) | Becker,Markus (synth) | Heidepriem,Thomas (b) | Hübner,Ralf-R. (dr)
Für Den Vater
Frankfurt/M, rec. 21.7.1987
Jazzensemble Des Hessischen Rundfunk | Ponzol,Peter (ss) | Freund,Joki (ss) | Sauer,Heinz (ss) | Lauer,Christof (ss,ts) | Becker,Markus (p,synth) | Lenz,Günter (b) | Hübner,Ralf-R. (synth,dr)
Merge Song
Frankfurt/M, rec. 19.3.1988
Jazzensemble Des Hessischen Rundfunk | Sauer,Heinz (ss,synth) | Mangelsdorff,Emil (as) | Freund,Joki (ts) | Degen,Bob (p) | Lenz,Günter (b) | Hübner,Ralf-R. (dr)
Out Of June
Frankfurt/M, rec. 4.6.1988
Jazzensemble Des Hessischen Rundfunk | Mangelsdorff,Emil (fl) | Freund,Joki (ss) | Sauer,Heinz (as,synth,dr-computer) | Lüdemann,Hans (p) | Lenz,Günter (b)
Herbstschleife
Frankfurt/M, rec. 22.10.1988
Jazzensemble Des Hessischen Rundfunk | Freund,Joki (ss) | Sauer,Heinz (as,sequencer) | Lauer,Christof (ts) | Becker,Markus (p) | Heidepriem,Thomas (b) | Hübner,Ralf-R. (dr)
Reverse
Frankfurt/M, rec. 29.4.1989
Jazzensemble Des Hessischen Rundfunk | Mangelsdorff,Emil (ss) | Freund,Joki (ss) | Sauer,Heinz (as) | Degen,Bob (p) | Lenz,Günter (b) | Hübner,Ralf-R. (dr)
Der Fahle Zwerg Auf Dem Kahlen Berg
Frankfurt/M, rec. 27.9.1989
Jazzensemble Des Hessischen Rundfunk | Mangelsdorff,Albert (tb) | Mangelsdorff,Emil (fl) | Freund,Joki (ss) | Sauer,Heinz (as,synth) | Lauer,Christof (ts) | Degen,Bob (p) | Schmolck,Stefan (b) | Hübner,Ralf-R. (dr)
Fin 89...Oder Was Der Mensch So Braucht
Frankfurt/M, rec. 28.12.1989
Jazzensemble Des Hessischen Rundfunk | Mangelsdorff,Emil (fl) | Freund,Joki (ss) | Sauer,Heinz (ts,synth) | Schröder,John (g) | Degen,Bob (p) | Lenz,Günter (b) | Hübner,Ralf-R. (dr)
Manipulation
Frankfurt/M, rec. 5.2.1992
Jazzensemble Des Hessischen Rundfunk | Mangelsdorff,Albert (tb) | Freund,Joki (ss) | Mangelsdorff,Emil (as) | Sauer,Heinz (ts) | Lauer,Christof (ts) | Leviev,Milcho (p) | Lenz,Günter (b) | Hübner,Ralf-R. (dr) | Spassov,Theodossij (kaval)
Kauf Dir Einen Bunten Luftballon
Frankfurt/M, rec. 26.4.1992
Heberer,Thomas (tp) | Takase,Aki (p,celeste)
Bloody Nose
Frankfurt/M, rec. 4.12.1992
Jazzensemble Des Hessischen Rundfunk | Lottermann,Stefan (tb) | Freund,Joki (ss) | Mangelsdorff,Emil (as) | Lauer,Christof (ts) | Degen,Bob (p) | Lenz,Günter (b) | Hübner,Ralf-R. (dr)
Winterballade
Frankfurt/M, rec. 7.1.1993
Jazzensemble Des Hessischen Rundfunk | Mangelsdorff,Albert (tb) | Mangelsdorff,Emil (ss) | Freund,Joki (ss) | Sauer,Heinz (ts,synth) | Lauer,Christof (ts) | Degen,Bob (p) | Lenz,Günter (b) | Hübner,Ralf-R. (dr)
Fährmann Charon
Frankfurt/M, rec. 19.5.1993
Jazzensemble Des Hessischen Rundfunk | Mangelsdorff,Albert (tb) | Mangelsdorff,Emil (ss) | Freund,Joki (ss) | Sauer,Heinz (as) | Becker,Markus (p) | Lenz,Günter (b) | Hübner,Ralf-R. (synth,dr)

1552 | CD | Ou Bien Le Debarquement Desastreux
Heiner Goebbels Group
Ou Bien Le Débarquement Désastreux(part 1-31)
Paris,France, rec. June 1994
Goebbels,Heiner (programming,sampling) | Robert,Ives (tb) | Meyer,Alexandre (el-g,daxophone,table-g) | Garcia,Xavier (keyboards,programming,sampling) | Djebate,Boubakar (kora,voc) | Sissoko,Moussa (djembe) | Djebate,Sira (voc) | Wilms,André (voice)

1553 | CD | Nordic Quartet
Nordic Quartet
Traces | Unwritten Letter | Offshore Piper | Gone To The Dogs | Double Tripper | Ved Sorevatn | Watching Shadows | The Illusion | Wild Bird
Oslo,N, rec. August 1994
Nordic Quartet | Surman,John (b-cl,ss,as,bs) | Rypdal,Terje (g) | Storaas,Vigleik (p) | Krog,Karin (voc)

1556 | CD | Michael Mantler:Cerco Un Paese Innocente
Mona Larsen And The Danish Radio Big Band Plus Soloists
Cerco Un Paese Innocente(part 1-4): | Introduzione- | Girovago- | Intermezzo(1)- | Eterno- | Intermezzo(2)- | Perché?- | Sempre Notte- | Inizio(1)- | Solitudine- | Lontano- | Inizio(2)- | L'illuminata Rugiada- | Proverbi(Uno)- | Intermezzo(3)- | Destino- | Rilucere Inveduto- | Un'Altra Notte- | Se Una Tua Mano- | Intermezzo(4)- | Vanità- | Quando Un Giorno- | Le Ansie- | E Senza Fiato- | Intermezzo(5)- | Non Gridate Più- | Tutto Ho Perduto-
Copenhagen,Denmark, rec. January 1994
Larsen,Mona (voc) | Mantler,Michael (tp,comp) | Roupe,Bjarne (g) | Kristensen,Kim (p) | Sorensen,Marianne (v) | Winther,Mette (viola) | Lychou,Gunnar (viola) | Sorensen,Helle (cello) | Danish Radio Big Band,The | Hansen,Ole Kock (ld) | Kohlin,Jan (tp,fl-h) | Rosenfeld,Benny (tp,fl-h) | Bolvig,Palle (tp,fl-h) | Pedersen,Henrik Bolberg (tp,fl-h) | Togeby,Lars (tp,fl-h) | Nilsson,Vincent (tb) | Hansen,Steen (tb) | Ipsen,Kjeld (tb) | Bellincampi,Giordano (b-tb) | Windfeld,Axel (b-tb,tuba) | Zum Vohrde,Jan (fl,alto-fl,ss) | Hove,Michael (fl,cl,ss) | Markussen,Uffe (fl,cl,b-cl) | Rockwell,Bob (cl,ss) | Madsen,Flemming (fl,cl,b-cl) | Bentzon,Nikolaj (synth) | Ovesen,Thomas (b) | Johansen,Jonas (dr) | Weisgaard,Ethan (perc) | Ungaretti,Giuseppe (lyrics)

1557 | CD | All My Relations
Charles Lloyd Quartet
Piercing The Veil | Little Peace | Thelonious Theonlyus | Cape To Cairo Suite(Hommage to Mandela) | Evanstide, Where Lotus Bloom | All My Relations | Hymne To The Mother | Milarepa
Oslo,N, rec. July 1994
Lloyd,Charles (fl,ts,chinese-oboe) | Stenson,Bobo (p) | Jormin,Anders (b) | Hart,Billy (dr)

1582 | CD | ZigZag
Egberto Gismonti Trio
Mestico & Caboclo | Orixás | Carta De Amor | Um Anjo | Forrobodó
Oslo,N, rec. April 1995
Gismonti,Egberto (p,14-string-g,10-string-g) | Carneiro,Nando (g-synth) | Assumpacao,Zeca (b)

1594 | CD | As It Is
Peter Erskine Trio
Glebe Ascending | The Lady In The Lake | Episode | Woodcocks | Esperanca | Touch Her Soft Lips And Part | Au Contraire | For Ruth | Romeo & Juliet
Oslo,N, rec. September 1995
Erskine,Peter (dr) | Taylor,John (p) | Danielsson,Palle (b)

1596 | CD | North Story
Misha Alperin Quintet
Morning | Psalm No.1 | Ironical Evening | Alone | Afternoon | Psalm No.2 | North Story | Etude | Kristi-Blodsdaper(Fucsia)
Alperin,Mikhail 'Misha' (p) | Shilkloper,Arkady (fl-h,fr-h) | Brunborg,Tore (ts) | Gewelt,Terje (b) | Christensen,Jon (dr)

1597 | CD | Three Men Walking
Joe Maneri-Joe Morris-Mat Maneri
Calling | What's New? | Bird's In The Belfry | If Not Now | Let Me Tell You | Through A Glas Darkly | Three Men Walking | Deep Paths | Diutumal | Fevered | Gestalt | To Anne's Eyes | Arc And Point | For Josef Schmid
Winterthur,CH, rec. October/November 1995
Maneri,Joe (cl,as,ts,p) | Maneri,Mat (el-6-string-v) | Morris,Joe (el-g)

1610 | CD | Agram
Lena Willemark-Ale Möller Group
Syster Glas | Agram | Sasom Fagelen | Fastän | Björnen | Samsingen | Per Andsu Lietjin | Josef Fran Arimatea | Lager Och Jon | Blamari | Slängpolskor | Elvedansen | Simonpolskan
Oslo,N, rec. 30.3.-3.4.1996
Willemark,Lena (viola,fiddle,voc) | Möller,Ale (mand,folk-harp,hammered-dulcimer,lute,natural-fl,shawm,wooden-tp) | Knutsson,Jones (ss,bs,perc) | Edén,Mats (drone-fiddle) | Danielsson,Palle (b) | Johansson,Tina (perc)

1622 | CD | Circa
Michael Cain-Ralph Alessi-Peter Epstein
Siegfried And Roy | Social Drones | Ped Cruc | Miss M | Circa | Egg | Top O'The Dunes | And Their White Tigers | Red Rock Rain | The Suchness Of Dory Philpott | Marche
Oslo,N, rec. August 1996
Cain,Michael 'Mike' (p) | Alessi,Ralph (tp,fl-h) | Epstein,Peter (ss,ts)

1639 | CD | Proverbs And Songs
John Surman-John Taylor With Chorus
Prelude | The Sons | The Kings | Wisdom | Job | No Twilight | Pride | The Proverbs | Abraham Arise!
Salisbury Cathedral,GB, rec. 1.6.1996
Surman,John (b-cl,ss,bs) | Taylor,John (org) | Salisbury Festival Chorus | Moody,Howard (cond)

1647 | CD | Poros
Dominique Pifarély-Francois Couturier
Trois Images | Poros | Labyrintus | La Nuit Ravie | Retours | Warm Canto | Vertigo | Images 4,2,3 | Galactic Landscape
Festeburg Kirche,Frankfurt/M., rec. April 1997
Pifarely,Dominique (v) | Couturier,Francois (p)

1660 | CD | Milvus
Mats Eden-Jonas Simonson With The Cikada String Quartet
Haväng | Polska Efter Ärtbergs Kalle Karlström | Stegen Pa Taket-Polska Efter Per Larsson | Variation I | Septemberljus | Den Lyckliga(Beate Virgine) | Nordafjalls-Efter Torleiv Björgum | Vardag | Variation II | Bäckahästen | Sjöraets Polska-Efter Olof Schyman | Spillet | String Quartet No.1
Oslo,N, rec. September 1997
Edén,Mats (v,viola,drone-fiddle) | Simonson,Jonas (fl,alto-fl) | Cikada String Quartet | Hannisdal,Odd (v) | Hannisdal,Henrik (v) | Konstantynowicz,Marek (viola) | Hannisdal,Morten (cello)

1662 | CD | Some Other Season
Philipp Wachsmann-Paul Lytton
The Re(de)fining Of Methods And Means | Shuffle | Leonardo's Spoon | Choisya | Shell | The Lightning Fields(Field 1-5) | Nu Shu | Riser | The Peacock's Tail | Whispering Chambers | A La Table | The Claw And Spur | Glide | From The Chalk Cliffs | Some Othe Season
Winterthur,CH, rec. October 1997
Wachsmann,Phil (v,viola,electronics) | Lytton,Paul (perc,electronics)

1678 | CD | Tales Of Rohnlief
Maneri/Phillips/Maneri
Rohnlief | A Long Way From Home | Sunned | When The Ship Went Down | The Aftermath | Bonewith | Flaull Clon Sleare | Hold The Tiger | Canzone Di Peppe | The Field | Nelgat | Elma My Dear | Third Hand | Pilvetslednah
Winterthur,CH, rec. June 1998
Maneri,Joe (cl,as,ts,p,voice) | Maneri,Mat (bar-v,el-6-string-v) | Phillips,Barre (b)

1691 | CD | A Long Time Ago
Kenny Wheeler Brass Ensemble
The Long Time Ago Suite | One Plus Three(version 1) | Ballad For A Dead Child | Eight Plus Three- | Alice My Dear- | Going For Baroque | Gnu Suite | One Plus Three(version 2)
Kingston-Upon-Thames,GB, rec. September 1997 & January 1998
Wheeler,Kenny (fl-h) | Watkins,Derek (tp) | Barclay,John (tp) | Lowther,Henry (tp) | Hamer,Ian (tp) | Beachill,Pete (tb) | Nightingale,Mark (tb) | Williams,Sarah (b-tb) | Stewart,Dave (b-tb) | Taylor,John (p) | Parricelli,John (g) | Faulkner,Tony (cond)

1693 | CD | Drawn Inward
Evan Parker Electro-Acoustic Ensemble
The Crooner(for Johnny Hartman) | Serpent In Sky | Travel In The Homeland | Spouting Bowl | Collect Calls | Aka Lotan | Reanascreena | At Home In The Universe(for Stuart Kauffman) | Writing On Ice | Phloy In The Frame | DrawnInward
Kingston-Upon-Thames,GB, rec. December 1998
Parker,Evan (ss,ts,khène) | Wachsmann,Phil (v,viola,electronics) | Guy,Barry (b) | Lytton,Paul (perc,electronics) | Casserley,Lawrence (electronics,sound-processing) | Prati,Walter (electronics,sound processing) | Vecchi,Marco (electronics,sound-processing)

1719 | CD | Trinity
Mat Maneri
Pure Mode | Almost Pretty | Trinity | Sun Ship | Blue Deco | Veiled | Iron Man | Lattice | November 1st | Lady Day's Lament
Kingston Upon Thames,Surrey,GB, rec. July 1999
Maneri,Mat (v,viola)

1721 | CD | Songs And One Symphony
Michael Mantler Group
Opening- | So Far- | For Ever- | Interlude- | Nothing More- | Darker Than Light- | How Long Are Our Nights | Mark,Nothing Appears- | Everything Seems- | The Breath Exchanged- | Speechless-
Copenhagen,Denmark, rec. 11.10.1993
Mantler,Michael (tp) | Roupe,Bjarne (g) | Kristensen,Kim (p) | Sorensen,Marianne (v) | Winter,Mette (viola) | Lychou,Gunnar (viola) | Sorensen,Helle (cello) | Larsen,Mona (voc)
Radio Symphony Orchestra Frankfurt
One Symphony(part 1-4)
Frankfurt/M, rec. 13./14.11.1998
Radio Symphony Orchestra Frankfurt/M. | Rundel,Peter (cond) | Mantler,Michael (comp)

ECM | Universal Music Germany(alle LP's nur direkt über ECM-Export)

1014(811979-2) | CD | Piano Improvisations-Vol.1
1014 | LP | Piano Improvisations-Vol.1
Chick Corea
Noon Song | Song For Sally | Ballad For Anna | Song Of The Wind | 'Sometimes Ago | Where Are You Now? | A Suite In 8 Pictures
rec. 21./22.4.1971
Corea,Chick (p-solo)

1015(839305-2) | CD | Sart
Jan Garbarek Quintet
Sart | Fountaine Of Tears(part 1&2) | Song Of Space | Close Enough For Jazz | Irr | Lontano
rec. 14./15.4.1971
Garbarek,Jan (fl,ts,b-sax) | Stenson,Bobo (p,el-p) | Rypdal,Terje (g) | Andersen,Arild (b) | Christensen,Jon (dr)

1016(527645-2) | CD | Terje Rypdal
Terje Rypdal Sextet
Keep It Like That-Tight | Rainbow | Lontano II
Oslo,N, rec. 12./13.8.1971
Rypdal,Terje (fl,g,voice) | Fint,Eckehard (engl-h,oboe) | Garbarek,Jan (fl,cl,ts) | Stenson,Bobo (el-p) | Andersen,Arild (b,el-b) | Christensen,Jon (dr,perc) | Rypdal,Inger Lise (voc)
Fantasy

Rypdal,Terje (fl,g,voice) | Fint,Eckehard (engl-h,oboe) | Garbarek,Jan (fl,cl,ts) | Halversen,Tom (el-p) | Andersen,Arild (b,el-b) | Christensen,Jon (dr,perc) | Rypdal,Inger Lise (voc)
Taugh Enough
Rypdal,Terje (fl,g,voice) | Fint,Eckehard (engl-h,oboe) | Garbarek,Jan (fl,cl,ts) | Stenson,Bobo (el-p) | Andresen,Bjornar (b,el-b) | Christensen,Jon (dr,perc)

1017(827132-2) | CD | Facing You
1017 | LP | Facing You
Keith Jarrett
In Front | Ritooria | Lalene | My Lady | Landscape For Future Earth | Starbright | Vapallia | Semblance
rec. 10.11.1971
Jarrett,Keith (p-solo)

1018/19(843163-2) | 2 CD | Paris Concert
Circle
Nefertiti | Song For A Newborn | Duet | Lookout Farm | 73 Degrees Kalvin(Variation-3) | Toy Room | There Is No Greater Love
rec. 21.2.1971
Circle | Corea,Chick (p) | Braxton,Anthony (reeds,perc) | Holland,Dave (cello,b) | Altschul,Barry (dr,perc)

1020(829190-2) | CD | Piano Improvisations-Vol.2
1020 | LP | Piano Improvisations-Vol.2
Chick Corea
After Noon Song | Song For Lee Lee | Song For Thad | Trinkle Tinkle | Masqualero | Preparation(1) | Preparation(2) | Departure From Planet Earth | A New Place:Arrival-Scenery-Imps Walk-Rest
rec. 21./22.4.1971
Corea,Chick (p-solo)

1021(513776-2) | CD | Ruta + Daitya
Keith Jarrett - Jack DeJohnette
Overture-Communion | Ruta + Daitya | All We Got | Sounds Of Peru-Submergence-Awakening | Algeria | You Know You Know | Pastel Morning
Los Angeles,CA, rec. May 1971
Jarrett,Keith (fl,p,el-p,org) | DeJohnette,Jack (dr,perc)

1022(811978-2) | CD | Return To Forever
1022 | LP | Return To Forever
Chick Corea Quartet
Return To Forever | Crystal Silence | What Game Shall We Play Today | Sometime Ago-La Fiesta
rec. 2./3.2.1973
Corea,Chick (el-p) | Farrell,Joe (fl,ss) | Clarke,Stanley (b,el-b) | Moreira,Airto (dr,perc) | Purim,Flora (voc)

1024(831331-2) | CD | Crystal Silence
1024 | LP | Crystal Silence
Chick Corea/Gary Burton
Senor Mouse | Arise,Her Eyes | I'm Your Pal | Dessert Air | Crystal Silence | Falling Grace | Feelings And Things | Children's Song | What Game Shall We Play Today
rec. 6.11.1972
Corea,Chick (p) | Burton,Gary (vib)

1025(833328-2) | CD | Trios/Solos
Ralph Towner
Winter Light | 1x12 | Suite 3x12 | Reach Me, Friend
rec. 27./28.11.1972
Towner,Ralph (g,p)
Re:Person I Knew
Towner,Ralph | Moore,Glen (b)
Noctuary | Raven's Wood
Towner,Ralph (g,p) | Moore,Glen (b) | McCandless,Paul (oboe)
Brujo
Towner,Ralph (g,p) | Moore,Glen (b) | Walcott,Collin (tabla)
A Belt Of Asteroids
Towner,Ralph (g,p) | Walcott,Collin (tabla) | McCandless,Paul (oboe)

1027(829373-2) | CD | Conference Of The Birds
David Holland Quartet
Four Winds | Q&A | Conference Of The Birds | Interception | Now Here(Nowhere) | See Saw
rec. 30.11.1972
Holland,Dave (b) | Rivers,Sam (fl,reeds) | Braxton,Anthony (fl,reeds) | Altschul,Barry (marimba,perc)

1028(519279-2) | CD | Conception Vessel
Paul Motian Trio
Georgian Bay | Rebica
NYC, rec. 25./26.11.1972
Motian,Paul (perc) | Brown,Sam (g) | Haden,Charlie (b)
Paul Motian-Keith Jarrett
Conception Vessel | American Indian:Song Of Sitting Bull
Motian,Paul (perc) | Jarrett,Keith (p)
Paul Motian Quartet
Inspiration From A Vietnamese Lullaby
Motian,Paul (perc) | Friend,Becky (fl) | Jenkins,Leroy (v) | Haden,Charlie (b)
Paul Motian
Ch'l Energy
Motian,Paul (perc-solo)

1029(847321-2) | CD | Triptychon
Jan Garbarek Trio
Rim | Selje | J.E.V. | Sang | Triptykon | Etu Hei! | Bruremarsj
Oslo,N, rec. 8.11.1972
Garbarek,Jan (fl,ss,ts,bs) | Andersen,Arild (b) | Vesala,Edward (perc)

1032(829157-2) | CD | Diary
1032 | LP | Diary
Ralph Towner
Dark Spirit | Entry In A Diary | Images Unseen | Icarus | Mon Enfant | Ogden Road | Erg | The Silence Of A Candle
rec. 4./4.4.1973
Towner,Ralph (g,p,gongs,12-string-g)

1033/4 | 2 LP | In The Light
Keith Jarrett With Strings
Metamorphosis
rec. 1973
Freivogel,Willi (fl) | Jarrett,Keith (comp.) | Südfunk Symphony Orchestra,String Section of the
Keith Jarrett With The American Brass Quintet
Fughata For Harpsichord
Jarrett,Keith (p) | American Brass Quintet
Keith Jarrett With String Quartet
A Pagan Hymn | String Quartet
Jarrett,Keith (p) | Sonnleitner,Fritz (v) | Klein,Günter (v) | Meinecke,Siegfried (viola) | Kiskalt,Fritz (cello)
Ralph Towner With Strings
Short Piece For Guitar And Strings
Towner,Ralph (g) | Jarrett,Keith (cond.) | Südfunk Symphony Orchestra,String Section of the
Crystal Moment
Jarrett,Keith (comp.)
Keith Jarrett With Strings
In The Cave In The Light
Jarrett,Keith (p,perc,cond.,gong) | Südfunk Symphony Orchestra,String Section of the

1035/7(827747-2) | 2 CD | Solo-Concerts(Bremen-Lausanne)
Keith Jarrett
Bremen(part 1) | Bremen(part 2a) | Bremen(part 2b)
rec. 12.7.1973
Jarrett,Keith (p-solo)
Lausanne(part 1a) | Lausanne(part 1b) | Lausanne(part 2a) | Lausanne(part 2b)
rec. 20.3.1973
Jarrett,Keith (p-solo)

1038(829383-2) | CD | Red Lanta
Art Lande-Jan Garbarek
Quintennaissance | Velvet | Waltz For A | Awakening-Midweek | Verdulac | Miss Fortune | Medley: Open Return-Cancion Del Momento | Meanwhile | Cherifen Dream Of Renate
rec. 19./20.11.1973
Garbarek,Jan (fl,ss,bass-s) | Lande,Art (p)

1041(833330-2) | CD | Witchi-Tai-To
1041 | LP | Witchi-Tai-To
Jan Garbarek-Bobo Stenson Quartet
A.I.R | Kuka | Hasta Siempre | Witchi-Tai-To | Desireless
rec. 27./28.11.1973
Garbarek,Jan (ss,ts) | Stenson,Bobo (p) | Danielsson,Palle (b) | Christensen,Jon (dr)

1042 | LP | The Colours Of Chloe
Eberhard Weber Group
More Colours | An Evening With Vincent Van Ritz | No Motion Picture
rec. December 1973
Weber,Eberhard (cello,b,ocarine) | Brüninghaus,Rainer (p,synth) | Van Rooyen,Ack (fl-h) | Giger,Hans-Peter (dr,perc) | Südfunk Symphony Orchestra Stuttgart | Chorus | Colours Of Chloe,The
The Colours Of Chloe
Weber,Eberhard (cello,b,ocarine) | Brüninghaus,Rainer (p,synth) | Van Rooyen,Ack (fl-h) | Giger,Hans-Peter (dr) | Hübner,Ralf-R. (dr)

1047(829114-2) | CD | Timeless
1047 | LP | Timeless
John Abercrombie Trio
Lungs | Love Song | Ralph's Piano Waltz | Red And Orange | Remembering | Timeless
rec. June 1974
Abercrombie,John (g) | Hammer,Jan (p,org,synth) | DeJohnette,Jack (dr)

1048 | LP | Tribute
Paul Motian Quintet
Victoria | Tuesday Ends Saturday | War Orphans | Sod House | Song For Che
rec. May 1974
Motian,Paul (dr,perc) | Ward,Carlos (as) | Brown,Sam (g,el-g) | Metzke,Paul (el-g) | Haden,Charlie (b)

1049(839307-2) | CD | Luminessence
1049 | LP | Luminessence
Keith Jarreett/Jan Garbarek With Strings
Numinor | Wind Sons | Luminessence
rec. July 1974
Garbarek,Jan (ss,ts) | Jarrett,Keith (comp.) | Südfunk Symphony Orchestra,String Section of the

1050(829115-2) | CD | Belonging
1050 | LP | Belonging
1050 | MC | Belonging
Keith Jarrett Quartet
Spiral Dance | Blossom | Long As You Know | You're Living Yours | Belonging | The Windup | Solistice
rec. 24./25.4.1974
Jarrett,Keith (p) | Garbarek,Jan (ss,ts) | Danielsson,Palle (b) | Christensen,Jon (dr)

1055(835586-2) | CD | Hotel Hello
Gary Burton-Steve Swallow
Chelsea Bells (For Hern) | Hotel Overture + Vamp | Inside In | Domino Biscuit | Vashkar | Sweet Henry | Impromptu | Sweeping Up
Fayville,Mass., rec. 13./14.5.1974
Burton,Gary (vib,marimba,org) | Swallow,Steve (p,el-b)

1056(835014-2) | CD | Matchbook
Ralph Towner-Gary Burton
Drifting Petals | Some Other Time | Brotherhood | Icarus | Song For A Friend | Matchbook | 1 x 6 | Aurora | Goodbye Pork Pie Hat
rec. 26./27.7.1974
Burton,Gary (vib) | Towner,Ralph (g)

1060(825458-2) | CD | Solstice
1060 | LP | Solstice
Ralph Towner Quartet
Oceanus | Visitation | Drifting Petals | Nimbus | Winter Solstice | Piscean Dance | Red And Black | Sand
rec. December 1974
Towner,Ralph (p,q,12-string-g) | Garbarek,Jan (fl,ss,ts) | Weber,Eberhard (cello,b) | Christensen,Jon (dr,perc)

1061(829192-2) | CD | Gateway
1061 | LP | Gateway
John Abercrombie Trio
Back-Woods Song | Waiting | May Dance | Unshielded Desire | Jamala | Sorcery I
rec. March 1975
Abercrombie,John (g) | Holland,Dave (b) | DeJohnette,Jack (dr)

1062(825469-2) | CD | Cloud Dance
1062 | LP | Cloud Dance
Collin Walcott Quartet
Margueritte | Prancing | Night Glider | Scimitar | Vadana | Eastern Song | Padma | Cloud Dance
Walcott,Collin (sitar,tablas) | Abercrombie,John (g) | Holland,Dave (b) | DeJohnette,Jack (dr)

1063(847322-2) | CD | The Pilgrim And The Stars
1063 | LP | The Pilgrim And The Stars
Enrico Rava Quartet
The Pilgrim And The Stars | Parks | Bella | Pesce Naufrago | Surprise Hotel | By The Sea | Blancasnow
rec. June 1975
Rava,Enrico (tp) | Abercrombie,John (g) | Danielsson,Palle (b) | Christensen,Jon (dr)

1064/65(810067-2) | CD | The Köln Concert
1064/65 | 2 MC | The Köln Concert
1064/65 | 2 LP | The Köln Concert
Keith Jarrett
Köln, January 24, 1975(part 1) | Köln, January 24, 1975(part 2)
Köln, rec. 24.1.1975
Jarrett,Keith (p-solo)

1066(843205-2) | CD | Yellow Fields
1066 | LP | Yellow Fields
Eberhard Weber Quartet
Touch | Sand-Glass | Yellow Fields | Left Lane
rec. September 1975
Weber,Eberhard (b) | Mariano,Charlie (ss,nagaswaram,shenai) | Brüninghaus,Rainer (p,el-p) | Christensen,Jon (dr)

1069(825591-2) | CD | Gnu High
1069 | LP | Gnu High
Kenny Wheeler Quartet
Heyoke | Smatter | Gnu Suite
rec. June 1975
Wheeler,Kenny (fl-h) | Jarrett,Keith (p) | Holland,Dave (b) | DeJohnette,Jack (dr)

1070(825592-2) | CD | Arbour Zena
1070 | LP | Arbour Zena
Keith Jarrett Trio With Strings
Runes | Solara March | Mirrors
rec. Oct.1975
Jarrett,Keith (p) | Garbarek,Jan (ss,ts) | Haden,Charlie (b) | Members of Radio Symphony Orchestra Stuttgart (strings) | Gutesha,Mladen (cond)

1071(519289-2) | CD | Balladyna
Tomasz Stanko Quartet
First Song | Tale | Num | Duet | Balladyna | Last Song | Nenaliina
rec. December 1975
Stanko,Tomasz (tp) | Szukalski,Tomasz (ss,ts) | Holland,Dave (b) | Vesala,Edward (dr)

1073(827133-2) | CD | Bright Size Life
1073 | LP | Bright Size Life
Pat Metheny Trio
Bright Size Life | Sirabhorn | Unity Village | Missouri Uncompromised | Midwestern Nights Dream | Unquity Road | Omaha Celebration | Round Trip- | Broadway Blues-
Metheny,Pat (g,el-12 string-g) | Pastorius,Jaco (el-b) | Moses,Bobby (dr)

1075(829193-2) | CD | Dansere
1075 | LP | Dansere
Jan Garbarek-Bobo Stenson Quartet
Dansere | Svevende | Bris | Skrik & Hyl | Lokk(Etter Thorvald Tronsgard) | Till Vennene
rec. Nov.1975
Garbarek,Jan (ss,ts) | Stenson,Bobo (p) | Danielsson,Palle (b) | Christensen,Jon (dr)

1078 | CD | The Plot
Enrico Rava Quartet
Tribe | On The Red Side Of The Street | Amici | Dr.Ra And Mr.Va | Foto Di Famiglia | The Plot
Oslo,N, rec. August 1976
Rava,Enrico (tp) | Abercrombie,John (g,el-g) | Danielsson,Palle (b) | Christensen,Jon (dr)

1080 | CD | Sargasso Sea
John Abercrombie-Ralph Towner Duo
Fable | Avenue | Sargasso Sea | Over And Gone | Elbow Room | Staircase | Romantic Descension | Parasol
rec. May 1976
Abercrombie,John (g,el-g) | Towner,Ralph (g,p,12-string-g)

1081 | CD | Rubisa Patrol
Art Lande Quartet
Celestial Guests | Many Chinas | Jaimi's Birthday Song | Romany | Bulgarian Folk Tune | Corinthian Melodies | For Nancy | A Monk In A Simple Room
Oslo,N, rec. May 1976
Lande,Art (p) | Isham,Mark (tp,fl-h,ss) | Douglas,Bill (fl,b,bamboo-fl) | Cronkhite,Glenn (dr,perc)

1084(829116-2) | CD | The Following Morning
1084 | LP | The Following Morning
Eberhard Weber With Orchestra
T.On A White Horse | Moana I | The Following Morning | Moana II
rec. details unknown
Weber,Eberhard (b) | Brüninghaus,Rainer (p) | Members of the Philharmonic Orchestra Oslo (fr-h,celli,oboe)

1085(827131-2) | CD | The Survivor's Suite
1085 | LP | The Survivor's Suite
Keith Jarrett Quartet
The Survivors' Suite: Beginning | The Survivors' Suite: Conclusion
rec. April 1976
Jarrett,Keith (ss,p,b-recorder,celeste,osi-dr) | Redman,Dewey (ts,perc) | Haden,Charlie (b) | Motian,Paul (dr,perc)

1086/7 | 2 LP | Hymns/Spheres
Keith Jarrett
Hymn Of Remembrance | Spheres-1st Movement | Spheres-2nd Movement | Spheres-3rd Movement | Spheres-4th Movement | Spheres-5th Movement | Spheres-6th Movement | Spheres-7th Movement | Spheres-8th Movement | Spheres-9th Movement | Hymn Of Release
rec. September 1976
Jarrett,Keith (church-org-solo)

1089 | LP | Danca Das Cabecas
1089(827750-2) | CD | Danca Das Cabecas
1089 | MC | Danca Das Cabecas
Egberto Gismonti
Quarto Mundo(No.1) | Danca Das Cabecas | Aguas Luminosas | Celebracao De Nupcias | Porta Encantada | Quarto Mundo(No.2) | Tango | Bambuzal | Fe Cega Faca Amolada | Danca Solitaria
rec. Nov.1976
Gismonti,Egberto (p,8-string-g,voice,wood-fl) | Vasconcelos,Nana (perc,berimbau,corpo,voice)

1090/91 | 2 LP | Staircase
1090/91(827337-2) | 2 CD | Staircase
Keith Jarrett
Staircase | Hourglases | Sundial | Sand
rec. May 1976
Jarrett,Keith (p-solo)

1092(835016-2) | CD | Passengers
1092 | LP | Passengers
Gary Burton Quartet With Eberhard Weber
Sea Journey | Nacada | The Whopper | B&G (Midwestern Nights Dream) | Yellow Fields | Claude And Betty
rec. Nov.1976
Burton,Gary (vib) | Weber,Eberhard (b) | Metheny,Pat (el-g) | Swallow,Steve (b-g) | Gottlieb,Dan 'Danny' (dr)

1093(827408-2) | CD | Dis
1093 | LP | Dis
Jan Garbarek-Ralph Towner
Krusning | Yr
rec. December 1976
Garbarek,Jan (ss,ts,wood-fl) | Towner,Ralph (g,12-string-g)
Jan Garbarek-Ralph Towner Group
Vandrere | Viddene | Dis
Garbarek,Jan (ss,ts,wood-fl) | Towner,Ralph (g,12-string-g) | North Sea Wind (windharp)
Skygger
Garbarek,Jan (ss,ts,wood-fl) | Towner,Ralph (g,12-string-g) | Norske Messingsekstett,Den (brass)

1097(827409-2) | CD | Watercolors
1097 | LP | Watercolors
Pat Metheny Quartet
Watercolors | Icefire | Oasis | Lakes | River Quay | Suite: | Floriday Greeting Song- | Legend Of The Fountain- | Sea Song
rec. Feb.1977
Metheny,Pat (g,12-string-g,15-string-harp-g) | Mays,Lyle (p) | Weber,Eberhard (b) | Gottlieb,Dan 'Danny' (dr)

1100(843028-2) | 6 CD | Sun Bear Concerts
Keith Jarrett
Kyoto(part 1&2)
rec. 5.11.1976
Jarrett,Keith (p-solo)
Osaka(part 1&2)
rec. 8.11.1976
Jarrett,Keith (p-solo)
Nagoya(part 1&2)
rec. 12.11.1976
Jarrett,Keith (p-solo)
Tokyo(part 1&2)
rec. 14.11.1976
Jarrett,Keith (p-solo)
Sapporo(part 1&2)
rec. 18.11.1976
Jarrett,Keith (p-solo)

1101(827418-2) | CD | Tales Of Another
1101 | LP | Tales Of Another
Gary Peacock Trio
Vignette | Tone Field | Major Major | Trilogy(1) | Trilogy(2) | Trilogy(3)
rec. Feb.1977
Peacock,Gary (b) | Jarrett,Keith (p) | DeJohnette,Jack (dr)

1105(847323-2) | CD | Gateway 2
1105 | LP | Gateway 2
John Abercrombie Trio
Opening | Reminiscence | Sing Song | Nexux | Blue
Oslo,N, rec. July 1977
Abercrombie,John (g,el-g,el-mand) | Holland,Dave (b) | DeJohnette,Jack (p,dr)

1107(835017-2) | CD | Silent Feet
1107 | LP | Silent Feet
Eberhard Weber/Colours
Seriously Deep | Silent Feet | Eyes That Can See In The Dark
rec. Nov.1977
Weber,Eberhard (b) | Mariano,Charlie (fl,ss) | Brüninghaus,Rainer (p,synth) | Marshall,Joe (dr)

1109(529087-2) | CD | Emerald Tears
Dave Holland

Spheres | Emerald Tears | Combination | B-40 M23-6K RS-4-W | Under Redwoods | Solar | Flurries | Hooveling
Oslo,N, rec. August 1977
Holland,Dave (b-solo)

1110(827419-2) | CD | Waves
Terje Rypdal Quartet
Per Ulv | Karussell | Stenskoven | Waves | The Dain Curse | Charisma
rec. September 1977
Rypdal,Terje (el-g,synth) | Mikkelborg,Palle (tp,fl-h,synth,ringmodulator) | Hovensjo,Sveinung (el-b) | Christensen,Jon (dr,perc)

1114(825593-2) | CD | Pat Metheny Group
1114 | LP | Pat Metheny Group
Pat Metheny Group
San Lorenzo | Phase Dance | Jaco | April Wind | April Joy | Lone Jack
rec. Jan.1978
Metheny,Pat (g) | Mays,Lyle (p,synth,autoharp) | Egan,Mark (b) | Gottlieb,Dan 'Danny' (dr)

1115(821406-2) | CD | My Song
1115 | MC | My Song
1115 | LP | My Song
Keith Jarrett Quartet
Questar | My Song | Tabarka | Country | Mandala | The Journey Home
rec. Nov.1977
Jarrett,Keith (p) | Garbarek,Jan (ss,ts) | Danielsson,Palle (b) | Christensen,Jon (dr)

1116(829117-2) | CD | Sol Do Meio Dia
1116 | LP | Sol Do Meio Dia
Egberto Gismonti Group
Palacio De Pinturas | Raga | Kalimba | Coracao | Cafe | Sapain | Danca Solitaria(No.2) | Baiao Malandro
Gismonti,Egberto (g,p,kalimba,voice,wood-fl) | Garbarek,Jan (ss) | Towner,Ralph (g,bottle) | Walcott,Collin (bottle,tabla) | Vasconcelos,Nana (perc,berimbau,bottle,corpo,tama,voice)

1118(829195-2) | CD | Places
1118 | LP | Places
Jan Garbarek Quartet
Reflections | Entering | Going Places | Passing
rec. December 1977
Garbarek,Jan (ss,ts) | Connors,Bill (g) | Taylor,John (p,org) | DeJohnette,Jack (dr)

1119 | CD | December Poems
Gary Peacock-Jan Garbarek
Winterlude | December Greenwings
Oslo,N, rec. December 1977
Peacock,Gary (b) | Garbarek,Jan (ss,ts)
Gary Peacock
Snow Dance | A Northern Tale | Flower Crystals | Celebrations
Peacock,Gary (b-solo)

1120(847324-2) | CD | Of Mist And Melting
Bill Connors Quartet
Melting | Not Forgetting | Face In The Water | Aubade | Cafe Vue | Unending
Connors,Bill (g) | Garbarek,Jan (ss,ts) | Peacock,Gary (b) | DeJohnette,Jack (dr)

1121(847325-2) | CD | Batik
Ralph Towner Trio
Waterwheel | Shades Of Sutton Hoo | Trellis | Batik | Green Room
rec. Jan.1978
Towner,Ralph (g,p,12-string-g) | Gomez,Eddie (b) | DeJohnette,Jack (dr)

1125(825470-2) | CD | Terje Rypdal Miroslav Vitous Jack DeJohnette
Terje Rypdal-Miroslav Vitous-Jack DeJohnette Trio
Sunrise | Den Forste Sne | Will | Believer | Flight | Seasons
rec. June 1978
Rypdal,Terje (g,org,synth) | Vitous,Miroslav (el-p,b) | DeJohnette,Jack (dr)

1126 | CD | Nice Guys
1126 | LP | Nice Guys
Art Ensemble Of Chicago
Ja | Nice Guys | Folkus | 597-59 | Cyp | Dreaming Of The Master
rec. May 1978
Art Ensemble Of Chicago | Bowie,Lester (tp,bass-dr,celeste) | Jarman,Joseph (fl,cl,ss,as,ts,vib,perc,gongs,sopranino,voc) | Mitchell,Roscoe (fl,cl,ss,as,ts,gongs,oboe,piccolo) | Favors,Malachi (b,perc,melodica) | Moye,Famoudou Don (marimba,dr,congas,bells,chimes,sun-perc,tympani,whistles,woodblocks)

1131(825471-2) | CD | New Chautauqua
1131 | LP | New Chautauqua
Pat Metheny
New Chautauqua | Country Poem | Long-Ago Child | Fallen Star | Hermitage | Sueno Con Mexico | Daybreak
rec. August 1978
Metheny,Pat (g,el-g,el-b,15-string-harp-g)

1132(829371-2) | CD | Codona
1132 | LP | Codona
Don Cherry/Nana Vasconcelos/Collin Walcott
Like That Of Sky | Codona | Colemanwonder: | Race Face- | Sortie- | Sir Duke
rec. September 1978
Walcott,Collin (dulcimer,sanza,sitar,tabla,voice) | Cherry,Don (tp,fl,doussn'gouni,voice) | Vasconcelos,Nana (perc,berimbau,cuica,voice)

1135 (843168-2) | CD | Photo With Blue Skie, White Clouds, Wires, Windows And A Red Roof
Jan Garbarek Group
Blue Sky | White Cloud | Windows | Red Roof | Wires | The Picture
Oslo,N, rec. December 1978
Garbarek,Jan (ss,ts) | Connors,Bill (g,el-g) | Taylor,John (p) | Weber,Eberhard (b) | Christensen,Jon (dr)

1136 | LP | Solo
1136(827135-2) | CD | Solo
Egberto Gismonti
Selva Amazonica | Pau Rolov(dedicated to Nana Vasconcelos) | And Zero | Frevo | Salvador | Ciranda Nordestina
rec. Nov.1978
Gismonti,Egberto (g,p,cooking-bells,surdo,voice)

1140(829941-2) | CD | Duet
Gary Burton-Chick Corea
Duet Suite | Children's Song(No.15) | Children's Song(No.2) | Children's Song(No.5) | Children's Song(No.6) | Radio | Song To Gayle | Never | La Fiesta
rec. 23.-25.10.1978
Burton,Gary (vib) | Corea,Chick (p)

1143 | CD | Devine Love
Leo Smith Group
Devine Love
Ludwigsburg, rec. September 1978
Smith,Leo[Wadada] (tp,fl,perc,gongs,steel-o-phone) | Andrews,Dwight (alto-fl,b-cl) | Naughton,Bobby (vib,marimba,bells)
Spirituals: The Language Of Love
Smith,Leo[Wadada] (tp,fl-h,perc,gongs,steel-o-phone) | Andrews,Dwight (alto-fl,b-cl) | Naughton,Bobby (vib,marimba,bells) | Haden,Charlie (b)
Tastalun
Smith,Leo[Wadada] (tp,fl-h,perc,gongs,stee-o-phone) | Andrews,Dwight (alto-fl,b-cl) | Naughton,Bobby (vib,marimba,bells) | Bowie,Lester (tp) | Wheeler,Kenny (tp)

1144 | CD | Descendre
1144 | LP | Descendre
Terje Rypdal Trio
Avskjed | Circles | Descendre | Innseiling | Men Of Mystery | Speil
rec. March 1979
Rypdal,Terje (fl,g,keyboards) | Mikkelborg,Palle (tp,fl-h,keyboards) | Christensen,Jon (dr,perc)

1145 | CD | First Meeting
Miroslav Vitous Quartet
Silver Lake | Beautiful Place To | Trees | Recycle | First Meeting | Concerto In Three Parts | You Make Me So Happy
Oslo,N, rec. May 1979
Vitous,Miroslav (b) | Surman,John (b-cl,ss) | Kirkland,Kenny (p) | Christensen,Jon (dr)

1147 | LP | Saudades
1147(829380-2) | CD | Saudades
Nana Vasconcelos
O Berimbau | Vozes(Saudades) | Ondas(Na Ohlos De Petronila) | Dado
rec. March 1979
Vasconcelos,Nana (perc,berimbau,gongs,voice)
Nana Vasconcelos-Egberto Gismonti Duo And Strings
Cego Aderaldo
Vasconcelos,Nana (perc,berimbau) | Gismonti,Egberto (g) | Radio Symphony Orchestra | Gutesha,Mladen (cond)

1148(825472-2) | CD | Upon Reflection
1148 | LP | Upon Reflection
John Surman
Edges Of Illusion | Filigree | Caithness To Kerry | Beyond The Shadow | Prelude And Rustic Dance | The Lamplighter | Following Behind | Constellation
rec. May 1979
Surman,John (b-cl,ss,bs,synth)

1150(825476-2) | CD | Eyes Of The Heart
Keith Jarrett Quartet
Eyes Of The Heart(part 1&2)
rec. May 1976
Jarrett,Keith (ss,p,osi-dr,tambourine) | Redman,Dewey (ts,maracas,tambourine) | Haden,Charlie (b) | Motian,Paul (dr,perc)
Keith Jarrett
Encore(a-b-c)
Jarrett,Keith (p-solo)

1151(823474-2) | CD | Magico
1151 | LP | Magico
Charlie Haden Trio
Bailarina | Magico | Silence | Spor | Palhaco
rec. June 1979
Haden,Charlie (b) | Garbarek,Jan (sax) | Gismonti,Egberto (g,p)

1155(827134-2) | CD | American Garage
1155 | MC | American Garage
1155 | LP | American Garage
Pat Metheny Group
Cross The Heartland | Ballad | The Search | American Garage | Golden Arches
rec. July 1979
Metheny,Pat (g) | Mays,Lyle (p,synth,autoharp) | Egan,Mark (b) | Gottlieb,Dan 'Danny' (dr)

1160(513424-2) | CD | Home
Steve Swallow Group
Some Echoes | She Was Young | Nowhere One | Colors | Home | In The Fall | You Didn't Think | Ice Cream | Echo | Midnight
NYC, rec. September 1979
Swallow,Steve (b) | Liebman,Dave (sax) | Kuhn,Steve (p) | Mays,Lyle (synth) | Moses,Bobby (dr) | Jordan,Sheila (voc)

1167(829197-2) | CD | Full Force
1167 | LP | Full Force
Art Ensemble Of Chicago
Magg Zelma | Care Free | Charlie M | Old Time Southside Street Dance | Full Force
rec. Jan.1980
Art Ensemble Of Chicago | Bowie,Lester (tp) | Jarman,Joseph (fl,alto-fl,cl,ss,as,ts,bs,vib,perc,bassoon,bass-s,sopranino) | Mitchell,Roscoe (fl,cl,ss,as,ts,bs,perc,bass-s,congan,glockenspiel,gongs,piccolo) | Favors,Malachi (b,perc,melodica,voc) | Moye,Famoudou Don (dr,sun-perc)

1169(839304-2) | CD | Aftenland
Jan Garbarek-Kjell Johnsen Duo
Aftenland | Syn | Linje | Bue | Enigma | Kilden | Spill | Iskirken | Tegn
rec. December 1979
Garbarek,Jan (ss,ts,wood-fl) | Johnsen,Kjell (pipe-org)

1170(827705-2) | CD | Folk Songs
1170 | LP | Folk Songs
Charlie Haden Trio
Folk Song | Bodas De Prata | Cego Aderaldo | Veien | Equilibrista | For Turiya
rec. Nov.1979
Haden,Charlie (b) | Garbarek,Jan (ss,ts) | Gismonti,Egberto (g,p)

1171/72(829119-2) | 2 CD | Nude Ants
1171/72 (2641171) | 2 LP | Nude Ants
Keith Jarrett Quartet
Chant Of The Soil | Processional | Oasis | New Dance | Sunshine Song | Chant Of The Soil | Innocence | Processional | Oasis | New Dance | Sunshine Song
rec. May 1979
Jarrett,Keith (p,perc,timbales) | Garbarek,Jan (ss,ts) | Danielsson,Palle (b) | Christensen,Jon (dr,perc)

1173(827268-2) | CD | Solo Concert
1173 | LP | Solo Concert
Ralph Towner
Spirit Lake | Ralph's Piano Waltz | Train Of Thought | Zoetrope | Nardis | Chelsea Courtyard | Timeless
rec. Oct.1979
Towner,Ralph (g,12-string-g)

1177(833332-2) | CD | Codona 2
1177 | LP | Codona 2
Don Cherry/Nana Vasconcelos/Collin Walcott
Que Faser | Godumaduma | Malinye | Drip-Dry | Walking On Eggs | Again And Again,Again
rec. May 1980
Codona | Cherry,Don (tp,doussn'gouni,melodica,voice) | Walcott,Collin (sanza,sitar,tabla,timpani,voice) | Vasconcelos,Nana (perc,talking-dr,voice)

1180/81 (843169-2) | 2 CD | 80/81
Pat Metheny Quartet
Two Folk Songs | Everyday I Have The Blues
rec. 26.-29.5.1980
Metheny,Pat (g) | Brecker,Michael (ts) | Haden,Charlie (b) | DeJohnette,Jack (dr)
80 | 81
Metheny,Pat (g) | Redman,Dewey (ts) | Haden,Charlie (b) | DeJohnette,Jack (dr)
Pat Metheny Quintet
The Bat | Open | Pretty Scattered | Turn Around | Goin' Ahead
Metheny,Pat (g) | Brecker,Michael (ts) | Redman,Dewey (ts) | Haden,Charlie (b) | DeJohnette,Jack (dr)

1182/83 | 2 LP | In Concert, Zürich, October 28, 1979
1182/83(821415-2) | CD | In Concert, Zürich, October 28, 1979
Chick Corea-Gary Burton
Senor Mouse | Bud Powell | Crystal Silence | Tweak | I'm Your Pal- | Hullo Bolinas- | Love Castle | Falling Grace | Mirror Mirror | Song To Gayle | Endless Trouble Endless Pleasure
rec. 28.10.1979
Corea,Chick (p) | Burton,Gary (vib)

1187(847329-2) | CD | Freigeweht
1187 | LP | Freigeweht
Rainer Brünninghaus Quartet
Stufen | Spielraum | Radspuren | Die Flüsse Hinauf | Täuschung Der Luft | Freigeweht
Oslo,N, rec. August 1980
Brüninghaus,Rainer (p,synth) | Wheeler,Kenny (fl-h) | Hoff,Brynjar (engl-h,oboe) | Christensen,Jon (dr)

1190(821416-2) | CD | As Falls Wichita, So Falls Wichita Falls
1190 | LP | As Falls Wichita, So Falls Wichita Falls
Pat Metheny & Lyle Mays
As Falls Wichita,So Fall Wichita Falls | Ozark | September Fifteenth (Dedicated To Bill Evans) | It's For You | Estupenda Graca
rec. September 1980
Metheny,Pat (g,el-g,b) | Mays,Lyle (p,org,synth,autoharp) | Vasconcelos,Nana (dr,perc,berimbau,voc)

1193(829160-2) | CD | The Amazing Adventures Of Simon Simon
1193 | LP | The Amazing Adventures Of Simon Simon
John Surman-Jack DeJohnette
Nestor's Saga (The Tale Of The Ancient) | The Buccaneers | Kentish Hunting (Lady Margaret's Air) | The Pilgrim's Way (To The Seventeen Walls) | Within' The Hall Of Neptune | Phoenix And The Fire | Fide Et Amore (By Faith And Love) | Merry Pranks (The Jester's Song) | A Fitting Epitaph
rec. Jan.1981
Surman,John (b-cl,ss,bs,synth) | DeJohnette,Jack (el-p,dr,congas)

1194 | LP | First Avenue
First Avenue
Band One | Band Two | Band Three | Band Four | Band Five | Band Six | Band Seven | Band Eight
rec. Nov. 1980
First Avenue | Goodhew,Denney (fl,b-cl,as) | Jensen,Eric (cello) | Knapp,James (tp,fl-h,waterphone)

1195 | LP | Who's To Know
1195(827269-2) | CD | Who's To Know
Shankar
Ragam-Tanam-Pallavi | Ananda Nadamadum Tillai Sankara
Shankar (double-v,tamboura) | Sivaraman,Umayalpuram K. (Mridagam) | Hussain,Zakir (tabla) | Lakshminarayana,V. (cond tala keeping)

1200 | LP | Eventyr
1200(829384-2) | CD | Eventyr
Jan Garbarek Trio
Soria Maria | Lillekort | Eventyr | Weaving A Garland | Once Upon A Time | The Companion | Snipp Snapp Snute | East Of The Sun West Of The Moon
rec. December 1980
Garbarek,Jan (fl,ss,ts) | Abercrombie,John (g,mand,12-string-g) | Vasconcelos,Nana (perc,berimbau,talking-dr,voice)

1201/02(825473-2) | 2 CD | Invocations/The Moth And The Flame
Keith Jarrett
Invocations: | First (Solo Voice)- | Second (Mirages, Realities)- | Third (Power, Resolve)- | Forth (Shock, Scatter)- | Fifth (Recognition)- | Sixth (Celebration)- | Seventh (Solo Voice)-
rec. Oct.1980
Jarrett,Keith (as,pipe-org)
The Moth And The Flame: | Part 1-5
rec. Nov.1979
Jarrett,Keith (p-solo)

1203/04(829391-2) | CD | Sanfona
Egberto Gismonti & Academia De Dancas
Maracatu | 10 Anos | Frevo | Loro | Em Familia- | Sanfona- | Danca Dos Pes- | Eterna-
rec. Nov. 1980
Gismonti,Egberto (p,indian-org,10-string-g,voice) | Senise,Mauro (fl,ss,as) | Assumpacao,Zeca (b) | Nene (dr,perc)
Egberto Gismonti
De Repente | Vale Do Eco | Cavaquinho | 12 De Fevereio | Carta De Amor
rec. April 1981
Gismonti,Egberto (g,indian-org,10-string-g,voice)

1209(829369-2) | CD | The Great Pretender
1209 | LP | The Great Pretender
Lester Bowie Quartet
Howdy Doody Time | When The Doom (Moon) Comes Over The Mountain | Rios Negroes | Rose Drop | Oh How The Ghost Sings
rec. June 1981
Bowie,Lester (tp) | Smith,Donald (p,org) | Williams,Fred (b,el-b) | Wilson,Phillip (dr)
Lester Bowie Group
The Great Pretender
Bowie,Lester (tp) | Smith,Donald (p,org) | Williams,Fred (b,el-b) | Wilson,Phillip (dr) | Bluiett,Hamiet (bs) | Bass,Fontella (voc) | Peaston,David (voc)

1210(517768-2) | CD | Voice From The Past-Paradigm
1210 | LP | Voice From The Past-Paradigm
Gary Peacock Quartet
Voice From The Past | Legends | Moor | Allegory | Paradigm | Ode For Tomten
rec. August 1981
Peacock,Gary (b) | Stanko,Tomasz (tp) | Garbarek,Jan (ss,ts) | DeJohnette,Jack (dr)

1216(817138-2) | CD | Offramp
1216 | MC | Offramp
1216 | LP | Offramp
Pat Metheny Group
Barcarole | Are You Going With Me | Au Lait | Eighteen | Offramp | James | The Bat(part II)
rec. Oct.1981
Metheny,Pat (g,synth) | Mays,Lyle (p,org,synth) | Rodby,Steve (b,el-b) | Gottlieb,Dan 'Danny' (dr) | Vasconcelos,Nana (perc,berimbau,voice)

1217 | LP | Lask
Ulrich P. Lask Group
Drain Brain | Tattooed Lady | Kidnapped | Should We Geanie | Unknown Realms(Shirli Sees) | Poor Child | Too Much - Not Enough
rec. Nov.1981
Lask,Ulrich P. (as,synth) | Nicols,Maggie (voice) | Bauschulte,Meinolf (dr)

1223(829377-2) | CD | Paths, Prints
1223 | LP | Paths, Prints
Jan Garbarek Quartet
The Path | Footprints | Kite Dance | To B.E. (t '80) | The Move | ARC | Considerung The Snail | Still
rec. December 1981
Garbarek,Jan (ss,ts,perc,wooden-fl) | Frisell,Bill (g) | Weber,Eberhard (b) | Christensen,Jon (dr,perc)

1225 | LP | The Struggle Continues
Dewey Redman Quartet
Thren | Love Is | Turn It Over Baby | Joie De Vivre | Combinations | Dewey Square
rec. Jan.1982
Redman,Dewey (ts) | Eubanks,Charles (p) | Helias,Mark (b) | Blackwell,Ed (dr)

1227(827286-2) | CD | Concerts(Bregenz)
1227 | LP | Concerts(Bregenz)
Keith Jarrett
Bregenz,May 28, 1981(part 1 + 2) | Untitled | Heartland
rec. 28.5.1981
Jarrett,Keith (p-solo)

1227/9 | 3 LP | Concerts(Bregenz/München)
Bregenz(part 1) | Bregenz(part 2) | Untitled | Heartland
Jarrett,Keith (p-solo)
München(part 1) | München(part 2) | München(part 3) | München(part 4) | Mon Coer Est Rouge | Heartland-2
rec. 2.6.1981
Jarrett,Keith (p-solo)

1231(829382-2) | CD | Later That Evening
1231 | LP | Later That Evening
Eberhard Weber Quintet
Maurizius | Death In The Carwash | Often In The Open | Later In The Evening
rec. March 1982
Weber,Eberhard (b) | McCandless,Paul (engl-h,b-cl,ss,oboe) | Frisell,Bill (g) | Mays,Lyle (p) | DiPasqua,Michael (dr,perc)

1232/33(159454-2) | 2 CD | Trio Music
Chick Corea Trio
Trio Improvisations(1-5) | Rhythm-A-Ning | Round About Midnight | Eronel | Think Of One | Little Rootie Tootie | Reflections | Hackensack
Los Angeles,CA, rec. November 1981
Corea,Chick (p) | Vitous,Miroslav (b) | Haynes,Roy (dr)
Chick Corea-Miroslav Vitous
Duet Improvisations(1&2)
Corea,Chick (p) | Vitous,Miroslav (b)
Chick Corea
Slippery When Wet
Corea,Chick (p-solo)

1234 | LP | Everyman Band
Everyman Band
Morals In The Mud | Japan Smiles | Lonely Streets | On The Spot | The Mummy Club | Nuclear Suite | Fatt Blatt
rec. March 1982
Everyman Band | Fogel,Marty (sax) | Tom,David (g) | Yaw,Bruce (b) | Suchovsky,Michael (dr)

1241(837019-2) | CD | In Line
Bill Frisell
Throughout | Two Arms | Smile On You | In Line
rec. August 1982
Frisell,Bill (g,el-g)
Bill Frisell-Arild Andersen
Start | Shorts | The Beach | Three | Godson Song
rec. details unknown
Frisell,Bill (g,el-g) | Andersen,Arild (b)

1242(843171-2) | CD | Journey's End
Miroslav Vitous Group
U Dunaje U Prespurka | Tess | Carry On No.1 | Paragraph Jay | Only One | Windfall
rec. July 1982
Vitous,Miroslav (b) | Surman,John (b-cl,ss,bs) | Taylor,John (p) | Christensen,Jon (dr)

1244 | LP | Inflation Blues
Jack DeJohnette's Special Edition
Starburst | Ebony | The Islands | Inflation Blues | Slow Down
NYC, rec. September 1982
DeJohnette,Jack (p,dr,clavinet,voc) | Carroll,Baikida (tp) | Purcell,John (alto-fl,cl,alto-cl,b-cl,as,bs,piccolo) | Freeman,Chico (b-cl,ss,ts) | Reid,Rufus (b)

1248(811546-2) | CD | The Ballad Of The Fallen
1248 | LP | The Ballad Of The Fallen
Charlie Haden Orchestra
Els Segadors(The Reapers) | The Ballad Of The Fallen | If You Want To Write Me | Grandola Vila Morena | Introduction To People | The People United Will Never Be Defeated | Silence | Too Late | La Pasionaria | La Santa Espina
Ludwigsburg, rec. November 1982
Haden,Charlie (b) | Cherry,Don (pocket-tp) | Mantler,Michael (tp) | Valente,Gary (tb) | Freeman,Sharon (fr-h) | Jeffers,Jack (tuba) | Pepper,Jim (fl,ss,ts) | Redman,Dewey (ts) | Slagle,Steve (fl,cl,ss,as) | Goodrick,Mick (g) | Bley,Carla (p,glockenspiel) | Motian,Paul (dr,perc)

1250(829162-2) | CD | Blue Sun
Ralph Towner
Blue Sun | The Prince And The Sage | C.T.Kangaroo | Mevlana Etude | Wedding Of The Streams | Shadow Fountain | Rumours Of Rain
Oslo,N, rec. December 1982
Towner,Ralph (fr-h,g,p,synth,perc,co,12-string-g)

1251(821407-2) | CD | Kultrum
1251 | LP | Kultrum
Dino Saluzzi
Kultrum Pampa | Gabriel Kondor | Agua De Paz | Pajaros Y Ceibos | Ritmo Arauca: | Canto A La Lluvia- | Pajaros Choiques- | Huaino- | El Rio Y El Abuelo | Pasos Que Quedan | Por El Sol Y Por La Lluvia
Ludwigsburg, rec. November 1982
Saluzzi,Dino (fl,perc,bandoneon,voice)

1252/53 | 2 LP | Travels
1252/53(810622-2) | 2 CD | Travels
Pat Metheny Group
Are You Going With Me | The Fields The Sky | Good Bye | Phase Dance | Straight On Red | Farmer's Trust | Extradition | Goin' Ahead | As Falls Wichita So Fall Wichita Falls | Travels | Song For Bilbao | San Lorenzo
Dallas/Philadelphia/, rec. July-November 1982
Metheny,Pat (g,g-synth) | Mays,Lyle (p,org,synth,autoharp,synclavier) | Rodby,Steve (b,b-synth,el-b) | Gottlieb,Dan 'Danny' (dr) | Vasconcelos,Nana (perc,berimbau,voice)

1254(810621-2) | CD | Such Winters Of Memory
John Surman Trio
Saturday Night | Sunday Morning | My Friend | Seaside Postcard 1951 | On The Wing Again | Expressions | Mother Of Light | Persepolis
Oslo,N, rec. December 1982
Surman,John (b-cl,ss,bs,p,synth,recorder,voice) | Krog,Karin (ring-modulator,tamboura,voice) | Favre,Pierre (dr)

1255(811966-2) | CD | Standarts Vol.1
1255 | MC | Standarts Vol.1
1255 | LP | Standarts Vol.1
Keith Jarrett Trio
Meaning Of The Blues | All The Things You Are | It Never Entered My Mind | I'm Afraid The Masquerade Is Over - (I'm Afraid) The Masquerade Is Over | God Bless The Child
NYC, rec. January 1983
Jarrett,Keith (p) | Peacock,Gary (b) | DeJohnette,Jack (dr)

1258(811711-2) | CD | Oregon
1258 | LP | Oregon
Oregon
Rapids | Beacon | Taos | Beside A Brook | Arianne | There Was No Moon That Night | Skyline | Impending Bloom
Ludwigsburg, rec. February 1983
Oregon | Towner,Ralph (g,p,synth,12-string-g) | McCandless,Paul (engl-h,b-cl,ss,musette,oboe,tin-fl) | Moore,Glen (p,viola,b) | Walcott,Collin (perc,bass-dr,sitar,tongue-dr,voice)

1259(811968-2) | CD | Wayfarer
1259 | LP | Wayfarer
Jan Garbarek Quartet
Gesture | Wayfarer | Gentle | Pendulum | Spor | Sing Song
Oslo,N, rec. March 1983
Garbarek,Jan (ss,ts) | Frisell,Bill (g) | Weber,Eberhard (b) | DiPasqua,Michael (dr,perc)

1261(811969-2) | CD | Vision
1261 | LP | Vision
Shankar Trio
All For You | Vision | Astral Projection | Psychic Elephant | The Message
Oslo,N, rec. April 1983
Shankar (perc,10-string-double-v) | Garbarek,Jan (ss,ts,bass-sax,perc) | Mikkelborg,Palle (tp,fl-h)

1262(815675-2) | CD | Double, Double You
Kenny Wheeler Quintet
Foxy Trot | Ma Bel | W.W. | Three For D'reen- | Blue For Lou- | Mark Time-
NYC, rec. May 1983
Wheeler,Kenny (tp,fl-h) | Brecker,Michael (ts) | Taylor,John (p) | Holland,Dave (b) | DeJohnette,Jack (dr)

1264 | LP | This Earth!
Alfred Harth Quintet
Female Is The Sun | Relation To Light Colour And Feeling | Studying Walk A Landscape | Body & Mention | Energy: Blood | Air | Three Acts Of Recognition | Come Oekotopia | Waves Of Beeing | Transformate Transcend Tones And Images
Ludwigsburg, rec. May 1983
Harth,Alfred 23 (b-cl,ss,as,ts) | Bley,Paul (p) | Phillips,Barre (b) | Gurtu,Trilok (perc) | Nicols,Maggie (voice)

1266(815679-2) | CD | Continuum
Rainer Brünninghaus Trio
Strahlenspur | Stille | Continuum | Raga Rag | Schattenfrei | Innerfern
Oslo,N, rec. September 1983
Stockhausen,Markus (tp,fl,piccolo-tp) | Brünninghaus,Rainer (p,synth) | Studer,Freddy (dr)

1267(815680-2) | CD | Children's Songs
1267 | LP | Children's Songs
Chick Corea
Children's Songs(No.1-20)
Ludwigsburg, rec. July 1983
Corea,Chick (p-solo)

1271(817795-2) | CD | Rejoicing
Pat Metheny Trio
Lonely Woman | Tears Inside | Humpty Dumpty | Blues For Pat | Rejoicing | Story From A Stranger | The Calling | Waiting For An Answer
NYC, rec. 29./30.11.1983
Metheny,Pat (g) | Haden,Charlie (b) | Higgins,Billy (dr)

1272(823212-2) | CD | Night
1272 | LP | Night
John Abercrombie Quartet
Ethereggae | Night | 3 East | Look Around | Believe You Me | Four In One
NYC, rec. April 1984
Abercrombie,John (g) | Brecker,Michael (ts) | Hammer,Jan (keyboards) | DeJohnette,Jack (dr)

1276(817436-2) | CD | Changes
1276 | LP | Changes
Keith Jarrett Trio
Flying Part(1&2) | Prism
NYC, rec. January 1983
Jarrett,Keith (p) | Peacock,Gary (b) | DeJohnette,Jack (dr)

1278(823342-2) | CD | First Circle
1278 | LP | First Circle
Pat Metheny Group
Forward March | Yolanda You Learn | The First Circle | If I Could | Tell It All | End Of The Game | Mas Alla(Beyond) | Praise
NYC, rec. 15.-19.2.1984
Metheny,Pat (g,g-synth,sitar,synclavier) | Mays,Lyle (tp,p,org,synth,agogo-bells) | Rodby,Steve (b,b-dr,b-g) | Aznar,Pedro (g,perc,glockenspiel,voice,whistle) | Wertico,Paul (dr,cymbal,field-dr)

1286(823795-2) | CD | Song For Everyone
1286 | LP | Song For Everyone
Shankar/Garbarek/Hussain/Gurtu
Paper Nut | I Know | Watching You | Conversation | Song For Everyone | Let's Go Home | Rest In Peace
Oslo,N, rec. September 1984
Garbarek,Jan (ss,ts) | Hussain,Zakir (congas,table) | Gurtu,Trilok (perc)

1288(823844-2) | CD | Chorus
1288 | LP | Chorus
Eberhard Weber Group
Chorus(part 1 & 2)
Ludwigsburg, rec. September 1984
Weber,Eberhard (synth,b) | Garbarek,Jan (ss,ts) | Hoffbauer,Manfred (fl,cl) | Künstner,Martin (engl-h,oboe) | Hübner,Ralf-R. (dr)

1289(825015-2) | CD | Standards Vol.2
1289 | LP | Standards Vol.2
Keith Jarrett Trio
So Tender | Moon And Sand | In Love In Vain | Never Let Me Go | If I Should Lose You | I Fall In Love Too Easily
NYC, rec. Jan.1983
Jarrett,Keith (p) | Peacock,Gary (b) | DeJohnette,Jack (dr)

1291(825323-2) | CD | Crossing
Oregon
Queen Of Sidney | Pepe Linque | Alpenbride | Travel By Day | Kronach Waltz | The Glide | Amaryllis | Looking-Glass Man | Crossing
Ludwigsburg, rec. Oct.1984
Oregon | McCandless,Paul (engl-h,b-cl,ss,oboe) | Towner,Ralph (g,p,synth,co,12-string-g) | Moore,Glen (fl,p,b) | Walcott,Collin (perc,b-dr,sitar,snare-dr,tabla)

1294(825406-2) | CD | It's OK To Listen To The Gray Voice
1294 | LP | It's OK To Listen To The Gray Voice
Jan Garbarek Group
White Noise Of Forgetfulness | The Crossing Place | One Day In March I Go Down To The Sea And Listen | Mission: To Be Where I Am | It's OK To Phone Island That Is A Mirage | It's OK To Listen To The Gray Voice | I'm The Knife-Thrower's Partner
Oslo,N, rec. December 1984
Garbarek,Jan (ss,ts) | Tom,David (g,g-synth) | Weber,Eberhard (b) | DiPasqua,Michael (dr,perc)

1295(825407-2) | CD | Withholding Pattern
1295 | LP | Withholding Pattern
John Surman
Doxology | Changes Of Season | All Cat's Whiskers And Bee's Knees | Holding Pattern 1 | Skating On Thin Ice | The Snooper | Wild Cat Blues | Holding Pattern 2
Surman,John (b-cl,ss,bs,synth)

1296(825902-2) | CD | I Only Have Eyes For You
1296 | LP | I Only Have Eyes For You
Lester Bowie's Brass Fantasy
I Only Have Eyes For You | Think | Lament | Coming Back, Jamaica | Nonet | When The Spirit Returns
Brooklyn,NY, rec. February 1985
Bowie,Lester (tp) | Davis,Stanton (tp,fl-h) | Thompson,Malachi (tp) | Purse,Bruce (tp) | Harris,Craig (tb) | Turre,Steve (tb) | Chancey,Vincent (fr-h) | Stewart,Robert 'Bob' (tuba) | Wilson,Phillip (dr)

1299(827743-2) | CD | Bass Desires
1299 | LP | Bass Desires
Marc Johnson Quartet
Samurai Hee-Haw | Resolution | Black Is The Color Of My True Love's Hair | Bass Desires | A Wishing Doll | Mojo Highway | Thanks Again
NYC, rec. May 1985
Johnson,Marc (b) | Frisell,Bill (g,g-synth) | Scofield,John (g) | Erskine,Peter (dr)

1302(827463-2) | CD | Spheres
Keith Jarrett
Spheres-1st Movement | Spheres-3rd Movement | Spheres-7th Movement | Spheres-9th Movement
Ottobeuren, rec. September 1976
Jarrett,Keith (church-org-solo)

1309(827768-2) | CD | Once Upon A Time-Far Away In The South
1309 | LP | Once Upon A Time-Far Away In The South
Dino Saluzzi Quartet
Jose Valeria Matias | And The Father Said...(Intermediate) | The Revelation(Ritual) | Silence | And He Loved His Brother Till The End - ...And He Loved His Brother Till The End | Far Away The South | We Are The Children
Ludwigsburg, rec. July 1985
Saluzzi,Dino (bandoneon) | Mikkelborg,Palle (tp,fl-h) | Haden,Charlie (b) | Favre,Pierre (perc)

1310(827769-2) | CD | Trio Music,Live In Europe
1310 | LP | Trio Music,Live In Europe
Chick Corea Trio
The Loop | I Hear A Rhapsody | Summer Night | Night And Day | Prelude No.2 | Mock Up | Hittin' It | Mirovisions
Willisau,CH/Reutlingen, rec. September 1984
Corea,Chick (p) | Vitous,Miroslav (b) | Haynes,Roy (dr)

1311(827770-2) | CD | Current Event
1311 | LP | Current Event
John Abercrombie Trio
Clint | Alice In Wonderland | Ralph's Piano Waltz | Lisa | Hippityville | Killing Time | Still
Oslo,N, rec. September 1985
Abercrombie,John (g,g-synth) | Johnson,Marc (b) | Erskine,Peter (dr)

1317(827827-2) | CD | Standards Live
1317 | LP | Standards Live
Keith Jarrett Trio
Stella By Starlight | The Wrong Blues | Falling In Love With Love | Too Young To Go Steady | The Way You Look Tonight | The Old Country
Palais Des Congres,, rec. 2.7.1982
Jarrett,Keith (p) | Peacock,Gary (b) | DeJohnette,Jack (dr)

1318(829279-2) | CD | Ocean
1318 | MC | Ocean
1318 | LP | Ocean
Stephan Micus
Ocean(part 1-4)
Ludwigsburg, rec. Jan.1986
Micus,Stephan (dulcimer,nay,shakuhachi,sho,zither)

1321(833494-2) | CD | Getting There
1321 | LP | Getting There
John Abercrombie Quartet
Sidekicks | Upon A Time | Getting There | Remember Hymn | Thalia | Furs On Ice | Chance | Labour Day
NYC, rec. April 1987
Abercrombie,John (g,el-g,g-synth) | Brecker,Michael (ts) | Johnson,Marc (b) | Erskine,Peter (dr)

1322(831108-2) | CD | Cloud About Mercury
1322 | LP | Cloud About Mercury
David Torn Quartet
Suyafhu Skin...Snapping The Hollow Reed | The Mercury Grid | 3 Minutes Of Pure Entertainment | Previous Man | Network Of Sparks(The Delicate Code) | Egg Learns To Walk...Suyafhu Seal
London,GB, rec. March 1986
Torn,David (g,el-g) | Isham,Mark (tp,fl-h,synth,piccolo-tp) | Levin,Tony (chapman-stick,synth-b) | Bruford,Bill (perc,simmons-dr,synth-dr)

1324(831394-2) | CD | All Those Born With Wings
1324 | LP | All Those Born With Wings
Jan Garbarek
1st Piece | 2nd Piece | 3rd Piece | 4th Piece | 5th Piece | 6th Piece
Oslo,N, rec. August 1986
Garbarek,Jan (reeds,synth,perc)

1333/34(829467-2) | 2 CD | Spirits
1333/34 | 2 LP | Spirits
Keith Jarrett
Spirits(No.1-26)
New Jersey,NJ, rec. July 1985
Jarrett,Keith (ss,g,p,b-recorder,cowbell,folk-fl,glockenspiel,naz,pakistani-fl,recorder,

1344/45(831396-2) | CD | Book Of Ways
1344/45 | 2 LP | Book Of Ways
Book Of Ways(part One: 1-10) | Book Of Ways(part Two: 1-9)
Ludwigsburg, rec. July 1986
Jarrett,Keith (clavichord-solo)

1346(831516-2) | CD | Blue
1346 | LP | Blue
Terje Rypdal And The Chasers
The Curse | Compet Gar | I Disremember Quite Well | Og Hva Synes Vi Om Det | Last Nite | Blue | Tanga | Om Bare
Oslo,N, rec. Nov.1986
Rypdal,Terje (el-g,keyboards) | Kjellemyr,Bjorn (b,el-b) | Kleive,Audun (dr,perc)

1349 | LP | Making Music
1349(831544-2) | CD | Making Music
Zakir Hussain Group
Making Music | Zakir | Water Girl | Toni | Anisa | Sunjog | You And Me | Sabah
Oslo,N, rec. December 1986
Hussain,Zakir (perc,tabla,voice) | Chaurasia,Hariprasad (fl) | Garbarek,Jan (ss,ts) | McLaughlin,John (g)

1350(833495-2) | CD | Lookout For Hope
1350 | LP | Lookout For Hope
The Bill Frisell Band
Lookout For Hope | Little Brother Bobby | Hangdog | Remedios The Beauty | Lonesome | Melody For Jack | Hackensack | Little Bigger | The Animal Race | Alien Prints(For D.Sharpe)
NYC, rec. March 1987
Frisell,Bill (g,el-g,bj) | Roberts,Hank (cello,voice) | Driscoll,Kermit (b) | Baron,Joey (dr)

1351(833038-2) | CD | Second Sight
1351 | LP | Second Sight
Marc Johnson's Bass Desires
Crossing The Corpus Callosum | Small Hands | Sweet Soul | Twister | Thrill Seekers | Prayer Beads | 1951 | Hymn For Her
Oslo,N, rec. March 1987
Johnson,Marc (b) | Frisell,Bill (g) | Scofield,John (g) | Erskine,Peter (dr)

1355(835245-2) | CD | Yr
Steve Tibbetts Group
Ur | Here Comes The Sphexes | Ten Years | One Day
St.Paul, Minnesota, rec. 1980
Tibbetts,Steve (g,keyboards,mand,dobro,kalimbas,sitar) | Hughes,Robert (b) | Anderson,Marc (dr,congas,agogo-bell,bells,bell-tree,clave,cowbell,glockenspiel,maraca | Cochrane,Steve (tablas) | Weinhold,Tim (bongos,bells,vase)
Three Primates | You And It | The Alien Lounge | 10 YR Dance
Tibbetts,Steve (g,keyboards,mand,dobro,kalimbas,sitar) | Hughes,Robert (b) | Anderson,Marc (dr,congas,agogo-bell,bells,bell-tree,clave,cowbell,glockenspiel,maraca | Wise,Marcus (tabla) | Weinhold,Tim (bongos,bells,vase)

1359(835781-2) | CD | Nafas
1359 | LP | Nafas
Rabih Abou-Khalil Group
Awakening | Window | Gaval Dance | The Return(I) | The Return(II) | Incantation | Waiting | Amal Hayati | Nafas | Nandi
Oslo,N, rec. February 1988
Abou-Khalil,Rabih (oud) | Kusur,Selim (nay,voice) | Velez,Glen (frame-dr) | Sarkissian,Setrak (daraboukka)

1360/61(835008-2) | 2 CD | Still Live
1360/61 | 2 LP | Still Live
Keith Jarrett Trio
My Funny Valentine | Autumn Leaves | When I Fall In Love | The Song Is You | Come Rain Or Come Shine | Late Lament | You And The Night And The Music | Extension | Someday My Prince Will Come | I Remember Clifford
Philharmonie,München, rec. 13.7.1986
Jarrett,Keith (p) | Peacock,Gary (b) | DeJohnette,Jack (dr)

1365(835250-2) | CD | The Paul Bley Quartet
Paul Bley Quartet
Interplay | Heat | After Dark | One In Four | Triste
rec. details unknown
Bley,Paul (p) | Surman,John (reeds) | Frisell,Bill (g) | Motian,Paul (dr)

1366 | LP | Private City
1366(835780-2) | CD | Private City
John Surman
Portrait Of A Romantic | On Hubbard's Hill | Not Love Perhaps | Levitation | Undernote | The Wanderer | Roundelay | The Wizzard Song
Oslo,N, rec. December 1987
Surman,John (b-cl,ss,bs,synth,recorders)

1369(837110-2) | CD | Der Mann Im Fahrstuhl
1369 | LP | Der Mann Im Fahrstuhl
Heiner Goebbels/Heiner Müller
Der Mann Im Fahrstuhl(Text Heiner Müller)
Berlin/NYC, rec. March 1988
Goebbels,Heiner (p,synth,programming) | Cherry,Don (tp,doussn'gouni,voice) | Lewis,George (tb) | Rothenberg,Ned (b-cl,sax) | Lindsay,Arto (g,voc) | Frith,Fred (g,b) | Hayward,Charles (dr,metal) | Stötzner,Ernst (voice) | Müller,Heiner (author)

1375(837186-2) | CD | Andina
1375 | LP | Andina
Dino Saluzzi
Dance | Winter | Transmutation | Remoteness | Tango Of Oblivion | Choral | Waltz For Verena | Andina | Memories
Oslo,N, rec. May 1988
Saluzzi,Dino (fl,bandoneon)

1379(837342-2) | CD | Dark Intervals
1379 | LP | Dark Intervals
Keith Jarrett
Opening | Hymn | Americana | Entrance | Parallels | Fire Dance | Ritual Prayer | Recitative
Suntory Hall, Tokyo,Japan, rec. 11.4.1987
Jarrett,Keith (p-solo)

1381(837344-2) | CD | Legend Of The Seven Dreams
Jan Garbarek Group
He Comes From The North | Brother Wind | Voy Cantando
Oslo,N, rec. July 1988
Garbarek,Jan (ss,ts) | Brüninghaus,Rainer (keyboards) | Vasconcelos,Erasto (perc,voice)
Tongue Of Secrets | Send Word
Garbarek,Jan (fl,ss) | Weber,Eberhard (b) | Brüninghaus,Rainer (keyboards) | Vasconcelos,Erasto (perc)
Aichuri, The Song Man | It's Name Is Secret Road | Mirror Stone(I) | Mirror Stone(II)
Garbarek,Jan (ss,ts,perc)

1382(837361-2) | CD | Personal Mountains
1382 | MC | Personal Mountains
1382 | LP | Personal Mountains
Keith Jarrett Quartet
Personal Mountains | Prism | Oasis | Innocence | Late Night Willie
Tokyo, Japan, rec. April 1979
Jarrett,Keith (p,perc) | Garbarek,Jan (ss,ts) | Danielsson,Palle (b) | Christensen,Jon (dr)

1383(837749-2) | CD | The Singles Collection
1383 | MC | The Singles Collection
1383 | LP | The Singles Collection
Terje Rypdal Quartet
There Is A Hot Lady In My Bedroom And I Need A Drink | Sprott | Mystery Man | The Last Hero | Strange Behaviour | U.'N.I. | Coyote | Somehow, Somewhere | Steady | Crooner Song
Oslo,N, rec. August 1988
Rypdal,Terje (g) | Dangerfield,Allen (keyboards,synclavier) | Kjellemyr,Bjorn (b) | Kleive,Audun (dr)

1384(837750-2) | CD | The Muisc Of Stones
Stephan Micus
The Music Of The Stones(part 4) | The Music Of The Stones(part 5)
Kathedral,Ulm, rec. 1988
Micus,Stephan (resonating-stones,shakuhachi,stone-chimes,tin-whistle,voice)
The Music Of The Stones(part 1)
Micus,Stephan (resonating-stones,shakuhachi,stone-chimes,tin-whistle,voice) | Daucher,Elmar (resonating-stones)
The Music Of The Stones(part 2)
Micus,Stephan (resonating-stones,shakuhachi,stone-chimes,tin-whistle,voice) | Federer,Günther (resonating-stones)
The Music Of The Stones(part 3)
Micus,Stephan (resonating-stones,shakuhachi,stone-chimes,tin-whistle,voice) | Micus,Nobuko (resonating-stones)
The Music Of The Stones(part 6)
Micus,Stephan (resonating-stones,shakuhachi,stone-chimes,tin-whistle,voice) | Micus,Nobuko (resonating-stones) | Daucher,Elmar (resonating-stones) | Federer,Günther (resonating-stones)

1387(837753-2) | CD | Danca Dos Escravos
1387 | LP | Danca Dos Escravos
Egberto Gismonti
2 Violones(Vermelho) | Lundu(Azul) | Trenzinho Do Caipira(Verde) | Alegrinho(Amarelo) | Danca Dos Escravos(Preto) | Salvador(Branco) | Memoria A Fado(Marrom)
Oslo,N, rec. November 1988
Gismonti,Egberto (g)

1390(837756-2) | CD | John Abercrombie/Marc Johnson/Peter Erskine
1390 | LP | John Abercrombie/Marc Johnson/Peter Erskine
John Abercrombie-Marc Johnson-Peter Erskine
Furs On Ice | Stella By Starlight | Alice In Wonderland | Beautiful Love | Innerplay | Light Beam | Drum Solo | Four In One | Samurai Hee-Haw | Haunted Heart
Live at The Nightstage,Boston,MA, rec. 21.4.1988
Abercrombie,John (el-g,g-synth) | Johnson,Marc (b) | Erskine,Peter (dr)

1392(839618-2) | CD | Changeless
1392 | MC | Changeless
1392 | LP | Changeless
Keith Jarrett Trio
Dancing | Endless | Lifeline | Exstacy
Lexington/Denver/Dallas/Houston, rec. 9./11./12.& 14.10.1987
Jarrett,Keith (p) | Peacock,Gary (b) | DeJohnette,Jack (dr)

1398 | LP | Fish Out Of Water
1398(841088-2) | CD | Fish Out Of Water
1398 | MC | Fish Out Of Water
Charles Lloyd Quartet
Fish Out Of Water | Haghia Sophia | The Dirge | Bharati | Eyes Of Love | Mirror | Tellaro
Oslo,N, rec. July 1989
Lloyd,Charles (fl,ts) | Stenson,Bobo (p) | Danielsson,Palle (b) | Christensen,Jon (dr)

1401(839173-2) | CD | Paris Concert
1401 | MC | Paris Concert
1401 | LP | Paris Concert
Keith Jarrett
October 17, 1988 | The Wind | Blues
Live at Salle Pleyel,Paris,France, rec. 17.10.1988
Jarrett,Keith (p-solo)

1402(839293-2) | CD | Rosensfole-Medieval Songs From Norway
1402 | MC | Rosensfole-Medieval Songs From Norway
1402 | LP | Rosensfole-Medieval Songs From Norway
Agnes Buen Garnas-Jan Garbarek
Innferd | Rosensfole | Margjit Og Targjei Risvollo | Maalfri Mi Fruve | Venelite | Stolt Oli | Signe Lita | Lillebroer Og Storebroer | Grisilla | Utfred
Oslo,N, rec. Autumn 1988
Gernas,Agnes Buen (voice) | Garbarek,Jan (ss,ts,synth,perc)

1407(841641-2) | CD | Pancha Nadai Pallavi
1407 | LP | Pancha Nadai Pallavi
Shankar Quartet
Ragam-Tanam-Pallavi | Ragam Sankarabharanam | Ragam-Tanam-Pallavi | Talam Mahalakshimi Tala 9,5 Brats | Pacha Nadai Pallavi
Oslo,N, rec. July 1989
Shankar (double-v,voc) | Hussain,Zakir (tabla) | Vinayakram,Vikku (ghatam) | Caroline (sruthi,talam)

1408(841776-2) | CD | So I Write
1408 | MC | So I Write
1408 | LP | So I Write
Sidsel Endresen Quartet
So I Write | This Is The Movie | Dreamland | Words | Mirror Image | Spring | Truth | Horses In Rain
Oslo,N, rec. June 1990
Endresen,Sidsel (voc) | Molvaer,Nils Petter (tp,fl-h,perc) | Bates,Django (p) | Christensen,Jon (dr)

1410(841778-2) | CD | Extensions
1410 | LP | Extensions
Dave Holland Qartet
Nemesis | Processional | Black Hole | The Oracle | 101 Fahrenheit(Slow Meltdown) | Color Of Mind
NYC, rec. September 1989
Holland,Dave (b) | Coleman,Steve (as) | Eubanks,Kevin (g) | Smith,Marvin 'Smitty' (dr)

1413(843196-2) | CD | Ode Of The Death Of Jazz
1413 | LP | Ode Of The Death Of Jazz
Edward Vesala Ensemble
Sylvan Swizzle | Infinite Express | Time To Think | Winds Of Sahara | Watching For The Signal | A Glimmer Of Sepal | Mop Mop | What? Where? Hum Hum
Helsinki, Finland, rec. April/May 1989
Vesala,Edward (dr) | Riikonen,Matti (tp) | Tapio,Jorma (fl,b-cl,as) | Kannisto,Jouni (fl,ts) | Päivinen,Pepa (fl,cl,b-cl,ss,ts,bs) | Ferchen,Tim (marimba,tubular-bells) | Vainio,Taito (accordeon) | Haarla,Iro (p,keyboards,harp) | Sumen,Jimi (g) | Krokfors,Uffe (b)

1417(843198-2) | CD | The Widow In The Window
1417 | LP | The Widow In The Window
Kenny Wheeler Quintet
Aspire | Ma Belle Hélène | The Widow In The Window | Ana | Hotel Le Hot | Now,And Now Again
Oslo,N, rec. February 1990
Wheeler,Kenny (tp,fl-h) | Abercrombie,John (g) | Taylor,John (p) | Holland,Dave (b) | Erskine,Peter (dr)

1418(843849-2) | CD | Road To Saint Ives
1418 | MC | Road To Saint Ives
1418 | LP | Road To Saint Ives
John Surman
Polperro | Tintagel | Trethevy Quoit | Rame Head | Mevagissey | Lostwithiel | Perranporth | Bodmin Moor | Kelly Bray | Piperspool | Marazion | Bedruthan Steps
Oslo,N, rec. April 1990
Surman,John (b-cl,ss,bs,keyboards,perc)

1419(843850-2) | CD | I Took Up The Runes
1419 | MC | I Took Up The Runes
1419 | LP | I Took Up The Runes
Jan Garbarek Group
Gula Gula | Molde Canticle(part 1-5) | His Eyes Were Suns | I Took Up The Runes | Bueno Hora, Buenos Vientos | Rahkki Sruvvis
Oslo,N, rec. August 1990
Garbarek,Jan (ss,ts) | Brüninghaus,Rainer (p) | Weber,Eberhard (b) | Katché,Manu (dr) | Vasconcelos,Nana (perc) | Wesseltoft,Jens Bugge (synth) | Gaup,Ingor Antte Ailu (voice)

1420/21 | 2 LP | Tribute
1420/21(847135-2) | 2 CD | Tribute
1420/21 | 2 MC | Tribute
Keith Jarrett Trio
Lover Man(Oh,Where Can You Be?) | I Hear A Rhapsody | Little Girl Blue | Solar | Sun Prayer | Just In Time | Smoke Gets In Your Eyes | All Of You | Ballad Of The Sad Young Men | All The Things You Are | It's Easy To Remember | U Dance
Live at The 'Philharmonie',Köln, rec. 15.10.1989
Jarrett,Keith (p) | Peacock,Gary (b) | DeJohnette,Jack (dr)

1426(847940-2) | CD | Alpstein
Paul Giger Trio
Zäuerli | Karma Shadub | Alpsegen | Zäuerli(II) | Zäuerli(III) | Chuereihe | Chlauseschuppel
Oslo,N, rec. 1990-1991
Giger,Paul (v) | Garbarek,Jan (ts) | Favre,Pierre (perc)
Trogener Chiblitäbe
Trogen,CH, rec. 1990
Giger,Paul (v) | Garbarek,Jan (ts) | Favre,Pierre (perc) | Silvesterchlauseschuppel | Schellenschötter

1427(847272-2) | CD | Darkness And Light
1427 | MC | Darkness And Light
1427 | LP | Darkness And Light
Stephan Micus
Darkness And Light(part 1-3)
München, rec. January/February 1990
Micus,Stephan (g,balinese-gong,ballast-strings,dilruba,ki un ki,kortholt,sho,suling,tin-whistle)

1432(847540-2) | CD | Barzakh
1432 | MC | Barzakh
1432 | LP | Barzakh
Anouar Brahem Trio
Raf Raf | Barzakh | Sadir | Ronda | Hou | Sarandib | Souga | Parfum De Gitane | Bou Naouara | Kerkenah | La Nuit Des Yeux | Le Belvédère Assiége | Oaf
Oslo,N, rec. September 1990
Brahem,Anouar (oud) | Selmi,Bechir (v) | Hosni,Lassad (perc)

1437(847939-2) | CD | Re-Enter
1437 | LP | Re-Enter
Masqualero
Re-Enter | Lil' Lisa | Heiemo Gardsjenta | Gaia | Little Song | There Is No Jungle In Baltimore | Find Aother Animal | Skykkevis Og Delt
Oslo,N, rec. December 1990
Masqualero | Molvaer,Nils Petter (tp) | Brunborg,Tore (ss,ts) | Andersen,Arild (b) | Christensen,Jon (dr,perc)

1438/39(849644-2) | 2 CD | Jimmy Giuffre 3, 1961
Jimmy Giuffre 3
Jesus Maria | Emphasis | In The Mornings Out There | Scootin' About | Cry Want | Brief Hesitation | Venture | Afternoon | Trudgin'
NYC, rec. 3.3.1961
Giuffre,Jimmy (cl) | Bley,Paul (p) | Swallow,Steve (b)
Ictus | Carla | Sonic | Whirrrr | That's True That's True | Good Bye | Flight | The Gamut | Me Too | Temporarily | Herb & Ictus
NYC, rec. 4.8.1981
Giuffre,Jimmy (cl) | Bley,Paul (p) | Swallow,Steve (b)

1440(849650-2) | CD | The Cure
1440 | MC | The Cure
Keith Jarrett Trio
Bemsha Swing | Old Folks | Woody'n You | Blame It On My Youth | Golden Earrings | Body And Soul | The Cure | Things Ain't What They Used To Be
Live at Town Hall,NYC, rec. 21.4.1990
Jarrett,Keith (p) | Peacock,Gary (b) | DeJohnette,Jack (dr)

1442(511263-2) | CD | Ragas And Sagas
Jan Garbarek With Ustad Fateh Ali Khan & Musicians From Pakistan
Raga I | Raga II | Raga III | Raga IV
Oslo,N, rec. May 1990
Garbarek,Jan (ss,ts) | Ali Khan,Ustad Fateh (voice) | Hussain,Ustad Shaukat (tabla) | Ali Khan,Ustad Nazim (sarangi) | Thathaal,Deepika (voice)
Saga
Garbarek,Jan (ss,ts) | Ali Khan,Ustad Fateh (voice) | Hussain,Ustad Shaukat (tabla) | Ali Khan,Ustad Nazim (sarangi) | Thathaal,Deepika (voice) | Katché,Manu (dr)

1444(849649-2) | CD | Star
1444 | MC | Star
1444 | LP | Star
Jan Garbarek/Miroslav Vitous/Peter Erskine
Star | Jumper | Lamenting | Anthem | Roses For You | Clouds In The Mountain | Snowman | The Music Of The People
Oslo,N, rec. January 1991
Garbarek,Jan (ss,ts) | Vitous,Miroslav (b) | Erskine,Peter (dr)

1447 | LP | Mojotoro
1447(511952-2) | CD | Mojotoro
Dino Saluzzi Group
Mojotoro | Tango A Mi Padre(Nocturno-Elegia) | Mundos(Exposicion-Desarrollo-Cadensia-Imitacion-Marcha-Recapitulacion) | Lustrin | Viemes Santo(Introduccion-Part a-Part b) | Milonga(La Punalado) | El Camino(Introduccion-Imitacion)
Buenos Aires, rec. May 1991
Saluzzi,Dino (perc,bandoneon,voice) | Saluzzi,Felix 'Cuchara' (cl,ss,ts) | Saluzzi,Celso (perc,bandoneon,voice) | Alonso,Armando (g,voice) | Vadala,Guillermo (el-b,voice) | Saluzzi,José Maria (dr,pec,voice) | Tuncboyaci[Boyaciyan].Arto (perc,voice)

1448(521727-2) | CD | Dona Nostra
Don Cherry Group
In Memoriam | Fort Cherry | Arrows | Mbizo | Race Face | Prayer | What Reason Could I Give | Vienna | Ahayu-Da
Oslo,N, rec. March 1993
Cherry,Don (tp) | Aberg,Lennart (alto-fl,ss,ts) | Stenson,Bobo (p) | Jormin,Anders (b) | Kjellberg,Anders (dr) | Temiz,Okay (perc)

1457(511959-2) | CD | Conte De L'Incroyable Amour
1457 | MC | Conte De L'Incroyable Amour
Anouar Brahem Quartet
Etincelles | Le Chien Sur Les Genoux De La Devineresse | L'Oiseau De Bois | Lumiere Du Silence | Conte De L'Incroyable Amour | Peshrev Hidjaz Homayoun | Diversion | Nayzak | Bettements | En Souvenir D'Iram | Epilogue
Oslo,N, rec. October 1991
Brahem,Anouar (oud) | Erköse,Barbaros (cl) | Erguner,Kudsi (ney) | Hosni,Lassad (bendir,darbouka)

1462(511980-2) | CD | Open Letter
1462 | LP | Open Letter
Ralph Towner-Peter Erskine
The Sigh | Whistful Thinking | Adrift | Infection | Alar | Short'n Stout | Waltz For Debby | I Fall In Love Too Easily | Magic Pouch | Magnolia Island | Nightfall
Oslo,N, rec. July 1991 & February 1992
Towner,Ralph (g,synth,12-string-g) | Erskine,Peter (dr)

1463(511981-2) | CD | Adventure Playground
John Surman Quartet
Only Yesterday | Pigfoot | Quadraphonic Question | Twice Said Once | Just For Now | As If We Knew | Twisted Roots | Duet For One | Seven
Oslo,N, rec. September 1991
Surman,John (b-cl,ss,bs) | Bley,Paul (p) | Peacock,Gary (b) | Oxley,Tony (dr)

1464(511982-2) | CD | Cello
David Darling
Darkwood(1) | No Place Nowhere | Fables | Darkwood(2) | Lament | Two Or Three Things | Indiana Indian | Totem | Psalm | Choral | The Bell | In November | Darkwood(3)
Oslo,N, rec. November 1991 & January 1992
Darling,David (cello,8-string-el-cello)

1465(511999-2) | CD | Notes From Big Sur
1465 | LP | Notes From Big Sur
Charles Lloyd Quartet
Requiem | Sister | Pilgrimage To The Mountain-Part 1:Persevere | Sam Song | Takur | Monk In Paris | When Miss Jessye Sings | Pilgrimage To The Mountain-Part 2:Surrender
Oslo,N, rec. November 1991
Lloyd,Charles (ts) | Stenson,Bobo (p) | Jormin,Anders (b) | Peterson,Ralph (dr)

1467(513074-2) | CD | Bye Bye Blackbird
1467 | MC | Bye Bye Blackbird
Keith Jarrett Trio
Bye Bye Blackbird | You Won't Forget Me | Butch And Butch | Summer Night | For Miles | Straight No Chaser | I Thought About You | Blackbird,Bye Bye
NYC, rec. 12.10.1991
Jarrett,Keith (p) | Peacock,Gary (b) | DeJohnette,Jack (dr)

1475(513373-2) | CD | Atmos
Miroslav Vitous/Jan Garbarek
Pegasos | Goddess | Forthcoming | Atmos | Time Out(part 1) | Direvision | Time Out(part 2) | Helikon | Hippukrene
Oslo,N, rec. 1992
Garbarek,Jan (ss,ts) | Vitous,Miroslav (b)

1481(513437-2) | CD | Vienna Concert
1481(513437-4) | MC | Vienna Concert
Keith Jarrett
Vienna(part 1) | Vienna(part 2)
Live at 'Staatsoper' Wien,Austria, rec. 13.7.1991
Jarrett,Keith (p-solo)

1486(513780-2) | CD | To The Evening Child
1486 | MC | To The Evening Child
Stephan Micus
Nomad Song | Yuko's Eyes | Young Moon | To The Evening Child | Morgenstern | Equinox | Desert Poem
MCM Studio,?, rec. January/February 1992
Micus,Stephan (dilruba,kortholt,nay,sinding,steel-dr,suling)

1490(521350-2) | CD | Oracle
Gary Peacock-Ralph Towner
Gaya | Flutter Step | Empty Carrousel | Hat And Cane | Inside Inside | St. Helens | Oracle | Burly Hello | Tramonto
Oslo,N, rec. May 1993
Towner,Ralph (g,12-string-g) | Peacock,Gary (b)

1493(513902-2) | CD | If You Look Far Enough
Arild Andersen Quartet
If You Look | Svev | For All We Know | Backé | The Voice | The Woman | The Place | The Drink | Main Man | The Song I Used To Play | Far Enough | Jonah
Oslo,N, rec. Spring 1988/July 1991/February 1992
Andersen,Arild (b) | Towner,Ralph (g) | Vasconcelos,Nana (perc) | Kleive,Audun (snare-dr)

1496(517717-2) | CD | Despite The Fire Fighters' Efforts...
Aparis
Sunrise | Waverterms | Welcome | Fire | Green Piece | Orange | Hannibal
Oslo,N, rec. July 1992
Aparis | Stockhausen,Markus (tp,fl-h) | Stockman,Eberhard (ss,keyboards) | Thönes,Jo (dr,electronic-dr)

1497(517353-2) | CD | You Never Know
Peter Erskine Trio
New Old Age | Clapperclowe | On The Lake | Amber Waves | She Never Has A Window | Evans Above | Pure & Simple | Heart Game | Everything I Love
Erskine,Peter (dr) | Taylor,John (p) | Danielsson,Palle (b)

1500(519500-2) | CD | Twelve Moons
Jan Garbarek Group
Twelve Moons: | Winter-Summer(part 1)- | Summer-Winter(part 2)-
Oslo,N, rec. September 1992
Garbarek,Jan (ss,synth) | Katché,Manu (dr) | Mazur,Marilyn (perc)
Psalm
Garbarek,Jan (ss) | Weber,Eberhard (b) | Mazur,Marilyn (perc) | Garnas,Agnes Buen (voc)
Brother Wind March | The Tall Tears Trees | Witchi-Tai-To
Garbarek,Jan (ss,ts) | Brüninghaus,Rainer (p,synth) | Weber,Eberhard (b) | Katché,Manu (dr)
There Were Swallows... | Gautes-Margjit | Huhai
Garbarek,Jan (ss) | Brüninghaus,Rainer (p) | Weber,Eberhard (b) | Katché,Manu (dr) | Mazur,Marilyn (perc)
Arietta
Garbarek,Jan (ss) | Brüninghaus,Rainer (p) | Weber,Eberhard (b) | Mazur,Marilyn (perc)
Darvanan
Garbarek,Jan (ts) | Boine,Mari (voc)

1502(519073-2) | CD | November
John Abercrombie Quartet
The Cat's Back | J.S. | Right Brain Patrol | Prelude | November | Rise And Fall | John's Waltz | Ogeda | Tuesday Afternoon | To Be | Come Rain Or Come Shine | Big Music
Oslo,N, rec. November 1992
Abercrombie,John (g) | Surman,John (b-cl,ss,bs) | Johnson,Marc (b) | Erskine,Peter (dr)

1503(519076-2) | CD | Water Stories
Ketil Bjornstad Group
Part One:Blue Ice(The Glacier): | Glacial Reconstruction | Levels And Degrees | Surface Movements | The View(I) | Between Memory And Presentiment
Oslo,N, rec. January 1993
Bjornstad,Ketil (p) | Rypdal,Terje (g) | Kjellemyr,Bjorn (b) | Christensen,Jon (dr)
Part Two:Approaching The Sea: | Ten Thousand Years Later | Waterfall | Flotation And Surroundings | Riverscape | Approaching The Sea | The View(II) | History
Bjornstad,Ketil (p) | Rypdal,Terje (g) | Kjellemyr,Bjorn (b) | Hillestad,Per (dr)

1509(519706-2) | CD | Musica De Sobrevivencia
Egberto Gismonti Group
Carmen | Bianca | Lundu(No.2) | Forro | Alegrinho(No.2) | Natura, Festa Do Interior
Oslo,N, rec. April 1993
Gismonti,Egberto (fl,g,p) | Carneiro,Nando (g,synth,caxixi) | Morelenbaum,Jacques (cello,bottle) | Assumpacao,Zeca (b,rainwood)

1515(519075-2) | CD | Madar
1515 | MC | Madar
Jan Garbarek Trio
Sull Lull | Madar | Sabika | Bahia | Ramy | Jaw | Joron | Qaws | Epilogue
Oslo,N, rec. August 1992
Garbarek,Jan (ss,ts) | Brahem,Anouar (oud) | Hussain,Ustad Shaukat (tabla)

1516(523160-2) | CD | Reflections
Bobo Stenson Trio
The Enlightener | My Man's Gone Now | Dörrmattan | Q | Reflections In D | 12 Tones Old | Mindiatyr
Oslo,N, rec. May 1993
Stenson,Bobo (p) | Jormin,Anders (b) | Christensen,Jon (dr)

1518(519707-2) | CD | Pendulum
Eberhard Weber
Bird Out Of Cage | Notes After An Evening | Delirium | Children's Song(No.1) | Street Scenes | Silent For A While | Pendulum | Unfinished Self-Portrait | Closing Scene
München, rec. Spring 1993
Weber,Eberhard (b-solo)

1519(523750-2) | CD | Dark Wood
David Darling
Darkwood(4) | Dawn- | In Motion- | Journey- | Darkwood(5) | Light- | Earth- | Passage- | Darkwood(6) | Beginning- | Up Side Down- | Searching- | Medieval Dance- | Darkwood(7) | The Picture | Returning- | New Morning-
Oslo,N, rec. July 1993
Darling,David (cello)

1522(517719-2) | CD | The Call
Charles Lloyd Quartet
Nocturne | Song | Dwija | Glimpse | Imke | Amarma | Figure In Blue, Memories Of Duke | The Blessing | Brother On The Rooftop
Lloyd,Charles (ts) | Stenson,Bobo (p) | Jormin,Anders (b) | Hart,Billy (dr)

1524(521721-2) | CD | Exile
Sidsel Endresen Sextet
Here The Moon | Quest | Stages(I,II,III) | Hunger | Theme(I) | Waiting Train | The Dreaming | Dust | Variations(III) | Theme(II) | Exile:
Oslo,N, rec. August 1993
Endresen,Sidsel (voc) | Molvaer,Nils Petter (tp) | Bates,Django (p,tenor-h) | Wesseltoft,Jens Bugge (keyboards) | Darling,David (cello) | Christensen,Jon (dr,perc)

1527(521144-2) | CD | The Fall Of Us All
Steve Tibbetts Group
Dzogchen Punks | Full Moon Dogs | Nyemma | Formless | Roam And Spy | Hellbound Train | All For Nothing | Fade Away | Drinking Lesson | Burnt Offering | Travel Alone
St.Paul, Minnesota/Boudhanath, rec. details unknown
Tibbetts,Steve (g,perc,discs) | Olson,Mike (synth) | Anton,Jim (b) | Anderson,Eric (b) | Anderson,Marc (perc,congas,steel-dr) | Wise,Marcus (tabla) | Schmidt,Claudia (voice) | Valentine,Rhea (voice)

1528(523749-2) | CD | A Biography Of The Rev. Absolom Dawe
John Surman
First Light | Countless Journeys | A Monastic Calling | Druid's Circle | 'Twas But Piety | Three Aspects | The Long Narrow Road | Wayfarer | The Far Corners | An Image
Oslo,N, rec. October 1994
Surman,John (alto-cl,b-cl,ss,bs,keyboards)

1531(517720-2) | CD | At The Deer Head Inn
1531 | MC | At The Deer Head Inn
Keith Jarrett Trio
Solar | Basin Street Blues | Chandra | You Don't Know What Love Is | You And The Night And The Music | Bye Bye Blackbird | It's Easy To Remember
Live at The Deer Head Inn,Allentown,PA, rec. 16.9.1992
Jarrett,Keith (p) | Peacock,Gary (b) | Motian,Paul (dr)

1536(523161-2) | CD | Nordan
Lena Willemark-Ale Möller Group
Trilo | Kom Helga Ande | Gullharpan | Manneling | Polska Efter Rolings Per | Homlat | Sven I Rosengard | S:t Göran Och Draken | Tacker Herranom- | Mats Hansu Polskan- | Knut Hauling | Polska Efter Jones Olle | Svanegångare- | Sven Svanehvit | Jemsken | Batman- | Turklaten- | Vallsvit | Drömspar-Efterspel
Oslo,N, rec. December 1993
Willemark,Lena (fiddle,voc) | Möller,Ale (mand,accordeon,cows-horn,folk-harp,hammered-dulcimer,natural-fl,shawm) | Edén,Mats (drone-fiddle,kantele) | Gudmundson,Per (fiddle,swedish-bagpipes) | Knutsson,Jones (sax,perc) | Danielsson,Palle (b) | Johansson,Tina (perc) | Tollin,Björn (perc)

1542(521717-2) | CD | Standards In Norway
1542 | MC | Standards In Norway
Keith Jarrett Trio
All Of You | Little Girl Blue | Just In Time | Old Folks | Love Is A Many-Splendored Thing | Dedicated To You | I Hear A Rhapsody | How About You
Live at The Konserthus,Oslo, rec. 7.10.1989
Jarrett,Keith (p) | Peacock,Gary (b) | DeJohnette,Jack (dr)

1544(523986-2) | CD | Matka Joanna
Thomasz Stanko Quartet
Monastery In The Dark | Green Sky | Maldoror's War Song | Tales For A Girl,12 | Matka Joanna From The Angels | Cain's Brand | Nun Seh's Mood | Celina | Two Preludes For Tales | Klostergeist
Oslo,N, rec. May 1994
Stanko,Tomasz (tp) | Stenson,Bobo (p) | Jormin,Anders (b) | Oxley,Tony (dr)

1545(521718-2) | CD | The Sea
Ketil Bjornstad Group
The Sea(part 1-12)
Oslo,N, rec. September 1994
Bjornstad,Ketil (p) | Rypdal,Terje (g) | Darling,David (cello) | Christensen,Jon (dr)

1546/48(523010-2) | 3 CD | Azimuth
Azimuth
Siren Song | O | Azimuth | The Tunnel | Greek Triangle | Jacob
Oslo,N, rec. March 1977
Azimuth | Wheeler,Kenny (tp,fl-h) | Taylor,John (p,synth) | Winstone,Norma (voc)
Eulogy | Silver | Mayday | Jero | Prelude | See
Oslo,N, rec. June 1978
Azimuth | Wheeler,Kenny (tp,fl-h) | Taylor,John (p,org,synth) | Winstone,Norma (voc)
Azimuth With Ralph Towner
The Longest Day | Autumn | Arrivee | Touching Points: | From The Window- | Windfall- | The Rabbit- | Charcoal Traces- | Depart | The Longest Day(Reprise)
Oslo,N, rec. December 1979
Azimuth | Wheeler,Kenny (tp,fl-h) | Taylor,John (p,org) | Towner,Ralph (g,12-string-g) | Winstone,Norma (voc)

1551(523292-2) | CD | Athos-A Journey To The Holy Mountain
Stephan Micus
On The Way | The First Night | The First Day | The Second Night | The Second Day | The Third Night | The Third Day | On The Way Back
MCM Studio,?, rec. November 1993-February 1994
Micus,Stephan (nay,satar,shakuhachi,suling,voices in playback,zither)

1554(523987-2) | CD | If Mountains Could Sing
Terje Rypdal Group
The Return Of Per Ulv | It's In The Air | Foran Peisen | One For The Roadrunner | Genie | Lonesome Guitar
Oslo,N, rec. January/June 1994
Rypdal,Terje (el-g) | Kjellemyr,Bjorn (b,el-b) | Kleive,Audun (dr)
But On The Other Hand | If Mountains Could Sing | Private Eye | Dancing Without Reindeers | Blue Angel
Rypdal,Terje (el-g) | Tonnesen,Terje (v) | Tomter,Lars Anders (viola) | Birkeland,Oystein (cello) | Eggen,Christian (cond)

1558(531024-2) | CD | Dancing With Nature Spirits
Jack DeJohnette Trio
Dancing With Nature Spirits | Anatolia | Healing Song For Mother Earth | Emanations | Time Warps
West Hurley,NY, rec. May 1995
DeJohnette,Jack (dr,perc) | Gorn,Steve (cl,ss,bansuri-fl) | Cain,Michael 'Mike' (p,keyboards)

1559(533679-2) | CD | Small Labyrinths
Marilyn Mazur's Future Song
A World Of Gates | Drum Tunnel | The Electric Cave | The Dreamcatcher | Visions In The Wood | Back To Dreamfog Mountain | Creature Talk | See There | Valley Of Fragments | Enchanted Place | Castle Of Air | The Holey
Copenhagen,Denmark, rec. August 1994
Mazur,Marilyn (perc) | Molvaer,Nils Petter (tp) | Ulrik,Hans (sax) | Aarset,Eivind (g) | Plenar,Elvira (p,keyboards) | Hovman,Klavs (b) | Kleive,Audun (dr) | Kemanis,Aina (voice)

1560(537798-2) | CD | Khmer
Nils Petter Molvaer Group
Khmer | Tien | Access- | Song Of Sands(I)- | On Stream | Platonic Years | Phum | Song Of Sands(II) | Exit
Oslo,N, rec. 1996-1997
Molvaer,Nils Petter (tp,g,perc,b-g,samples) | Aarset,Eivind (g,talk-box,treatments) | Molster,Morten (g) | Ludvigsen,Roger (g,perc,dulcimer) | Arnesen,Rune (dr) | Holand,Ulf W.O. (samples) | Skar,Reidar (sound treatment)

1561(527093-2) | CD | Khomsa
Anouar Brahem Group
Comme Un Départ | L'Infini Un Vent De Sable | Regard De Mounette | Sur L'Infini Bleu | Claquent Les Voiles | Vague | E La Nave Va | Ain Ghazel | Seule | Nouvelle Vague | En Robe D'Olivier | Des Rayons Et Des Ombres | Un Setier D'Alliance | Comme Une Absence
Oslo,N, rec. September 1994
Brahem,Anouar (oud) | Larché,Jean-Marc (ss) | Galliano,Richard (accordeon) | Selmi,Bechir (v) | Couturier,Francois (p,synth) | Danielsson,Palle (b) | Christensen,Jon (dr)

1562(527637-2) | CD | Gateway
John Abercrombie Trio
Homecoming | Waltz New | Modern Times | Calypso Falto | Short Cut | How's Never | In Your Arms | 7th D | Oneness
NYC, rec. December 1994
Abercrombie,John (g) | Holland,Dave (b) | DeJohnette,Jack (p,dr)

1563(529347-2) | CD | Lost And Found
Ralph Towner Quartet
Harbinger | Trill Ride | Elan Vital | Summers End | Col Legno | Soft Landing | Flying Cows | Mon Enfant | A Breath Away | Scrimshaw | Midnight Blue...Red Shift | Moonless | Sco Cone | Tattler | Taxi's Waiting
Oslo,N, rec. May 1995
Towner,Ralph (g,12-string-g) | Goodhew,Denney (b-cl,ss,bs,sopranino) | Johnson,Marc (b) | Christensen,Jon (dr)

1567(559964-2) | CD | Double Concerto/5th Symphony
Terje Rypdal With The Riga Festival Orchestra
Double Concerto For Two Electric Guitars And Symphony Orchestra | 5th Symphony
Riga/Nyhagen, rec. June/August 1998
Rypdal,Terje (el-g) | Le Tekro,Ronni (el-g) | Riga Festival Orchestra | Sne,Normunds (cond)

1572(529084-2) | CD | Dream Of The Elders
Dave Holland Qartet
The Winding Way | Lazy Snake | Claressence | Equality | Ebb & Flo | Dream Of The Elders | Second Thoughts | Equality(II)
NYC, rec. März 1995
Holland,Dave (b) | Person,Eric (ss,as) | Nelson,Steve (vib) | Jackson,Gene (dr) | Wilson,Cassandra (voc)

1573(529035-2) | CD | Remembering Tomorrow
Steve Kuhn Trio
The Rain Forest | Oceans In The Sky | Lullababy | Trance | Life's Backward Glance | All The Rest Is The Same | Emmanuel | Remembering Tomorrow | The Feeling Within | Bittersweet Passages | Silver
Oslo,N, rec. March 1995
Kuhn,Steve (p) | Finck,David (b) | Baron,Joey (dr)

1574(529346-2) | CD | In The Moment
Gateway
In The Moment | The Enchanted Forest | Cinucen | Shrubberies | Soft
NYC, rec. December 1994
Gateway | Abercrombie,John (g) | Holland,Dave (b) | DeJohnette,Jack (p,dr,perc)

1575/80(527638-2) | 6 CD | Keith Jarrett At The Blue Note-The Complete Recordings
Keith Jarrett Trio
In Your Own Sweet Way | How Long Has That Train Been Gone | While We're Young | Partners | No Lonely Nights | Now's The Time | Lament | I'm Old Fashioned | Everything Happens To Me | If I Were A Bell | In The Wee Small Hours Of The Morning | Oleo | Alone Together | Skylark | Things Ain't What They Used To Be
Live at The 'Blue Note',NYC, rec. 3.6.1994
Jarrett,Keith (p) | Peacock,Gary (b) | DeJohnette,Jack (dr)
Autumn Leaves | Days Of Wine And Roses | Bop-Be | You Don't Know What Love Is- | Muezzin- | When I Fall In Love | How Deep Is The Ocean | Close Your Eyes | Imagination | I'll Close My Eyes | I Fall In Love Too Easily- | The Fire Within- | Things Ain't What They Used To Be
Live at The 'Blue Note',NYC, rec. 4.6.1994
Jarrett,Keith (p) | Peacock,Gary (b) | DeJohnette,Jack (dr)
On Green Dolphin Street | My Romance | Don't Ever Leave Me | You'd Be So Nice To Come Home To | La Valse Bleue | No Lonely Nights | Straight No Chaser | Time After Time | For Heaven's Sake | Partners | Desert Sun | How About You
Live at The 'Blue Note',NYC, rec. 5.6.1994
Jarrett,Keith (p) | Peacock,Gary (b) | DeJohnette,Jack (dr)

1584(529348-2) | CD | Window-Steps
Pierre Favre Quintet
Snow | Cold Nose | Lea | Girimella | En Passant | Aguilar | Passage
Oslo,N, rec. June 1995
Favre,Pierre (dr) | Wheeler,Kenny (tp,fl-h) | Ottaviano,Roberto (ss) | Darling,David (cello) | Swallow,Steve (b-g)

1585(529086-2) | CD | Visible World
Jan Garbarek Group
Red Wind | The Creek | The Survivor | The Healing Smoke | Visible World(chiaro) | Desolate Mountains(I) | Desolate Mountains(II) | Visible World(scuro) | Giulietta | Desolate Mountains(III) | Pygmy Lullaby | The Quest | The Scythe
Garbarek,Jan (ss,ts,perc,keybords,meraaker-cl) | Brüninghaus,Rainer (p,synth) | Weber,Eberhard (b) | Mazur,Marilyn (dr,perc) | Katché,Manu (dr)
The Arrow
Garbarek,Jan (ss,ts,perc,keybords) | Brüninghaus,Rainer (p,synth) | Weber,Eberhard (b) | Mazur,Marilyn (dr,perc) | Katché,Manu (dr) | Gurtu,Trilok (tabla)
Evening Land
Garbarek,Jan (ss,ts,perc,keybords) | Brüninghaus,Rainer (p,synth) | Weber,Eberhard (b) | Mazur,Marilyn (dr,perc) | Katché,Manu (dr) | Boine,Mari (voc)

1586(533681-2) | CD | Meeting Point
Egberto Gismonti With The Lithuanian State Symphony Orchestra
Strawa No Sertao-Zabumba | Strawa No Sertao-Maxixe | Musica Para Cordas | Frevo | A Pedrinha Cai | Eterna | Musica De Sobrevivencia
Vilnius,Litauen, rec. June 1995
Gismonti,Egberto (p) | Lithuanian State Symphony Orchestra | Rinkevicius,Gintaras (cond)

1588(533128-2) | CD | Les Violences De Rameau
Louis Sclavis Sextet
Le Diable Et Son Train | De Ce Trait Enchante | Venez Punir Son Injustice | Charmes | La Torture D'Alphise | Usage De Faux | Reponses A Gavotte | Charmes(II) | Pour Vous...Ces Quelques Fleurs | Ismenor | Post-Mesotonique
Pernes Les Fontaines,France, rec. September 1995 & January 1996
Sclavis,Louis (cl,b-cl,ss) | Robert,Yves (tb) | Pifarely,Dominique (v,el-v) | Raulin,Francois (p,keyboards) | Chevillon,Bruno (b) | Lassus,Francis (dr)

1593(531170-2) | CD | The River
Ketil Bjornstad-David Darling
The River(I-XII)
Oslo,N, rec. June 1996
Bjornstad,Ketil (p) | Darling,David (cello)

1602(531623-2) | CD | A Closer View
Ralph Towner-Gary Peacock
Opalesque | Viewpoint | Mingusiana | Creeper | Infrared | From Branch To Branch | Postcard To Salta | Toledo | Amber Captive | Moor | Beppo | A Closer View
Oslo,N, rec. December 1995
Towner,Ralph (g,12-string-g) | Peacock,Gary (b)

1603(531693-2) | CD | Leosia
Tomasz Stanko Quartet
Morning Heavy Song | Die Weisheit Von Le Comte Lautréamont | A Farewell To Maria | Brace | Trinity | Forlorn Walk | Hungry Howl | No Bass Trio | Leosia
Oslo,N, rec. January 1996
Stanko,Tomasz (tp) | Stenson,Bobo (p) | Jormin,Anders (b) | Oxley,Tony (dr)

1604(539723-2) | CD | War Orphans
Bobo Stenson Trio
Oleo De Mujer Con Sombrero | Natt | All My Life | Eleventh Of January | War Orphans | Sediment | Bengali Blue | Melancholia
Oslo,N, rec. May 1997
Stenson,Bobo (p) | Jormin,Anders (b) | Christensen,Jon (dr)

1607(533098-2) | CD | Angel Song
Kenny Wheeler/Lee Konitz/Dave Holland/Bill Frisell
Nicolette | Present Past | Kind Folk | Unti | Angel Song
Onmo
Nonetheless | Past Present(2) | Kind Of Gentle
NYC, rec. February 1996
Wheeler,Kenny (tp,fl-h) | Konitz,Lee (as) | Holland,Dave (b) | Frisell,Bill (el-g)

1608(533768-2) | CD | Skywards
Terje Rypdal Group
Skywards | Into The Wilderness | It's Not Over Until The Fat Lady Sings! | The Pleasure Is Mine,I'm Sure | Out Of This World(Sinfonietta) | Shining | Remember To Remember
Oslo,N, rec. February 1996
Rypdal,Terje (el-g) | Mikkelborg,Palle (tp) | Tonnesen,Terje (v) | Darling,David (cello) | Eggen,Christian (p,keyboards) | Christensen,Jon (dr) | Vinaccia,Paolo (dr,perc)

1609(157899-2) | CD | St.Gerold
Paul Bley/Evan Parker/Barre Phillips
Sankt Gerold Variations 1-12
Live at The Monastery of Sankt Gerold, rec. April 1996
Parker,Evan (ss,ts) | Bley,Paul (p) | Phillips,Barre (b)

1611(537023-2) | CD | Ana
Ralph Towner
The Reluctant Bride | Tale Of Saverio | Joyful Departure | Green And Golden | I Knew It Was You | Les Douzilles | Veldt(Seven Pieces For Twelve Strings) | Between The Clouds | Child On The Porch | Carib Crib(1) | Slavic Mood | Carib Crib(2) | Toru | Sage Brush Rider
Oslo,N, rec. March 1996
Towner,Ralph (g,12-string-g)

1612(453514-2) | CD | Toward The Margins
Evan Parker Electro-Acoustic Ensemble
Toward The Margins | Turbulent Mirror | Field And Figure | The Regenerative Landscape(for AMM) | Cain Of Chance | Trahütten | Shadow Without An Object | Epanados | Born Cross-Eyed(Remembering Fuller) | Philipp's Pavilion | The Hundred Books(for Idries Shah) | Contradance
Surrey,GB, rec. May 1996
Parker,Evan (ss) | Guy,Barry (b) | Lytton,Paul (perc,electronics) | Wachsmann,Phil (v,viola,electronics,sound-processing) | Prati,Walter (electronics,sound processing) | Vecchi,Marco (electronics,sound-processing)

1616(533316-2) | CD | Cité De La Musique
Dino Saluzzi Trio
Cité De La Musique | Introduccion Y Milonga Del Ausente | El Rio Y El Abuelo | Zurdo | Romance | Winter | How My Heart Sings | Gorrion | Coral Para Mi Pequeno Y Lejano Pueblo
Oslo,N, rec. June 1996
Saluzzi,Dino (bandoneon) | Johnson,Marc (b) | Saluzzi,José Maria (g)

1617(537048-2) | CD | In Full Cry
Joe Maneri Quartet
Coarser And Finer | Tenderly | Outside The Dance Hall | A Kind Of Birth | The Seed And All | Pulling The Boat In | Nobody Knows | In Full Cry | Shaw Was A Good Man,Peewee | Lift | Motherless Child | Prelude To A Kiss
Winterthur,CH, rec. June 1996
Maneri,Joe (cl,as,ts,p) | Maneri,Mat (el-6-string-v) | Lockwood,John (b) | Peterson,Randy (dr,perc)

1623(533680-2) | CD | Tactics
John Abercrombie Trio
Sweet Sixteen | Last Waltz | Bo Diddy | You And The Night And The Music | Chumbida | Dear Rain | Mr.Magoo | Long Ago And Far Away
Live at Visiones Jazz & Supper Club,NYC, rec. 13.-15.7.1996
Abercrombie,John (g,el-g) | Wall,Dan (org) | Nussbaum,Adam (dr)

1626/27(537222-2) | 2 CD | Nothing Ever Was,Anyway.Music Of Annette Peacock
Marilyn Crispell Trio
Nothing Ever Was, Anyway(Version 1) | Butterflies That I Feel Inside Me | Open To Love | Cartoon | Albert's Love Theme | Touching | Both | You've Left Me | Miracles | Ending | Blood | Nothing Ever Was, Anyway(Version 2)
NYC, rec. September 1996
Crispell,Marilyn (p) | Peacock,Gary (b) | Motian,Paul (dr)
Dreams(If Time Weren't)
Crispell,Marilyn (p) | Peacock,Gary (b) | Motian,Paul (dr) | Peacock,Annette (voice)

1628(537344-2) | CD | No Birch
Christian Wallumrod Trio
She Passes The House Of Her Grandmother | The Birch(1) | Royal Garden | Somewhere East | Traveling: | Far East- | Slow Brook- | I Lost My Heart In Moscow- | The Birch(2) | Ballimaran | Watering | Before Church | The Birch(3) | Two Waltzing,One Square And Then | Fooling Around | The Gardener | The Birch(4)

Oslo,N, rec. November 1996
Wallumrod,Christian (p) | Henriksen,Arve (tp) | Kjos Sorensen,Hans-Kristian (perc)

1631(537342-2) | CD | Hyperborean
Arild Andersen Quintet With The Cikada String Quartet
Patch Of Light(I) | Hyperborean | Patch Of Light(II) | Duke Vinaccia | Infinite Distance | Vanishing Waltz | The Island | Invisible Sideman | Rambler | Dragon Dance | Stillness | Too Late For A Picture
Oslo,N, rec. December 1996
Andersen,Arild (b) | Brunborg,Tore (ss,ts) | Hofseth,Bendik (ts) | Knudsen,Kenneth (keyboards) | Vinaccia,Paolo (dr,perc) | Cikada String Quartet | Hannisdal,Odd (v) | Hannisdal,Henrik (v) | Konstantynowicz,Marek (viola) | Hannisdal,Morten (cello)

1632(537162-2) | CD | The Garden Of Mirrors
Stephan Micus
Earth | Passing Cloud | Violeta | Flowers In Chaos | In The High Valleys | Gates Of Fire | Mad Bird | Night Circles | Words Of Truth
MCM Studio,?, rec. 1995-1996
Micus,Stephan (bolombatto,nay,shakuhachi,sinding,steel-dr,suling,tin-whistle)

1633(537341-2) | CD | The Sea II
Ketil Bjornstad Group
Laila | Outward Bound | Brand | The Mother | Song For A Planet | Consequences | Agnes | Mime | December | South
Oslo,N, rec. December 1996
Bjornstad,Ketil (p) | Rypdal,Terje (g) | Darling,David (cello) | Christensen,Jon (dr)

1635(537345-2) | CD | Canto
Charles Lloyd Quartet
Tales Of Rumi | How Can I Tell You | Desolation Sound | Canto | Nachiketa's Lament | M | Durga Durga
Lloyd,Charles (ts,tibetan-oboe) | Stenson,Bobo (p) | Jormin,Anders (b) | Hart,Billy (dr)

1636(537551-2) | CD | Litania
Tomasz Stanko Sextet
Svantetic | Sleep Save And Warm(Version 1) | Night-Time,Daytime Requiem | Ballada | Litania | Repetition | Ballad For Bernt
Oslo,N, rec. February 1997
Stanko,Tomasz (tp) | Milder,Joakim (ss,ts) | Rosengren,Bernt (ts) | Stenson,Bobo (p) | Danielsson,Palle (b) | Christensen,Jon (dr)
Tomasz Stanko Septet
The Witch | Sleep Save And Warm(Version 3)
Stanko,Tomasz (tp) | Milder,Joakim (ss,ts) | Rosengren,Bernt (ts) | Rypdal,Terje (el-g) | Stenson,Bobo (p) | Danielsson,Palle (b) | Christensen,Jon (dr)
Tomasz Stanko-Terje Rypdal
Sleep Save And Warm(Version 2)
Stanko,Tomasz (tp) | Rypdal,Terje (el-g)

1637(537343-2) | CD | Oneness
Jack DeJohnette Quartet
Welcome Blessing | Free Above Sea | Priestesses Of The Mist | Jack In | From The Heart | C.M.A.
NYC, rec. January 1997
DeJohnette,Jack (dr,perc) | Harris,Jerome (el-g,b-g) | Cain,Michael 'Mike' (p) | Alias,Don (perc)

1640(537268-2) | CD | La Scala
Keith Jarrett
La Scala(part 1) | La Scala(part 2) | Over The Rainbow
Live at Teatro alla Scala,Milano,Italy, rec. 13.2.1995
Jarrett,Keith (p-solo)

1641(539888-2) | CD | Thimar
Anouar Brahem Trio
Badhra | Kashf | Houdouth | Talwin | Waqt | Uns | Al Hizam Al Dhahbi | Ourb | Mazad | Kernow | Hulmu Rabia
Oslo,N, rec. 13.-15.3.1997
Brahem,Anouar (oud) | Surman,John (b-cl,ss) | Holland,Dave (b)

1648/49(537963-2) | 2 CD | The School Of Understanding(Sort-Of-An-Opera)
Michael Mantler Group With The Danish Radio Concert Orchestra Strings
Prelude | Introduction | First Lesson | News | Love Begins | War | Pause | Understanding | Health And Poverty | Love Continues | Platitudes | Intolerance | Love Ends | What's Left To Say | What Is The Word(by Samuel Beckett)
Copenhagen,Denmark, rec. August-December 1996
Mantler,Michael (tp,comp) | Jannotta,Roger (fl,cl,b-cl,oboe) | Noordhoek,Tineke (vib,marimba) | Kristensen,Kim (p,synth) | Roupe,Bjarne (g) | Sorensen,Marianne (v) | Brandt,Mette (v) | Winther,Mette (viola) | Sorensen,Helle (cello) | Preston,Don (synth,voc) | Bruce,Jack (voc) | Jorgensen,Per (voc) | Larsen,Mona (voc) | Hyldgaard,Susi (voc) | Mantler,Karen (voc) | Greaves,John (voc) | Wyatt,Robert (voc) | Danish Radio Concert Orchestra Strings,The | Bellincampi,Giordano (cond)

1651(539725-2) | CD | Nine To Get Ready
Roscoe Mitchell And The Note Factory
Leola | Dream And Response | For Lester B | Jamaican Farewell | Hop Hip Bip Bir Rip | Nine To Get Ready | Bessie Harris | Fallen Heroe | Move Toward The Light | Big Red Peaches
NYC, rec. May 1997
Mitchell,Roscoe (ss,as,ts) | Ragin,Hugh (tp) | Lewis,George (tb) | Shipp,Matthew (p) | Taborn,Craig (p) | Shahid,Jaribu (b,voc) | Parker,William (b) | Tabbal,Tani (dr,gembe,voice) | Cleaver,Gerald (dr)

1657(539726-2) | CD | Juni
Peter Erskine Trio
Prelude No.2 | Windfall | For Jan | The Ant & The Elk | Siri | Fable | Twelve | Namasti
Oslo,N, rec. Juni 1997
Erskine,Peter (dr) | Taylor,John (p) | Danielsson,Palle (b)

1661(557365-2) | CD | Blessed
Joe Maneri-Mat Maneri
At The Gate | There Are No Doors | Sixty-One Joys | From Loosened Soil | Five Fantasies | Never Said A Mumblin' Word | Is Nothing Near? | Body And Soul | Race You Home | Gardenias For Gerdenis | Outside The Whole Thing | Blessed
Winterthur,CH, rec. October 1997
Maneri,Joe (cl,as,ts,p) | Maneri,Mat (v,bar-v,el-5-string-viola,el-6-string-v)

1663(557020-2) | CD | Point Of View
Dave Holland Quintet
The Balance | Mr.B | BedouinTrail | Metamorphos | Ario | Herbaceous | The Benevolent One | Serenade
NYC, rec. 25./26.9.1997
Holland,Dave (b) | Eubanks,Robin (tb) | Wilson,Steve (ss,as) | Nelson,Steve (vib,marimba) | Kilson,Billy (dr)

1664(557650-2) | CD | First Impression
Misha Alperin Group With John Surman
Overture | First Impression | Second Impression | Twilight Hour | City Dance | Movement | Third Impression | Fourth Impression | Fifth Impression
Oslo,N, rec. December 1997
Alperin,Mikhail 'Misha' (p) | Shilkloper,Arkady (fl-h,fr-h) | Surman,John (ss,bs) | Gewelt,Terje (b) | Christensen,Jon (dr) | Sorensen,Hans-Kristian Kjos (marimba,perc)

1666(539955-2) | CD | Tokyo '96
Keith Jarrett Trio
It Could Happen To You | Never Let Me Go | Billie's Bounce | Summer Night | I'll Remember April | Mona Lisa | Autumn Leaves | Last Night When We Were Young | Caribbean Sky | John's Abbey | My Funny Valentine | Song
Live at Orchard Hall,Tokyo,Japan, rec. 30.3.1996
Jarrett,Keith (p) | Peacock,Gary (b) | DeJohnette,Jack (dr)

1670(559447-2) | CD | Not Two, Not One
Paul Bley Trio
Not Zero:In Three Parts | Entelechy | Now | Fig Foot | Vocal Tracked | Intente | Noosphere | Set Up Set | Dialogue Amour | Don't You Know | Not Zero:In One Part
NYC, rec. January 1998
Bley,Paul (p) | Peacock,Gary (b) | Motian,Paul (dr)

1674(559445-2) | CD | Voice In The Night
Charles Lloyd Quartet
Voice In The Night | God Give Me Strength | Dorotea's Studie | Requiem | Pocket Full Of Blues:- | Island Blues- | Little Sister's Dance- | Shade Tree- | Mud Island- | Homage | Forest Flower(Sunrise) | Forest Flower(Sunset) | A Flower Is A Lovesome Thing
NYC, rec. May 1998
Lloyd,Charles (ts) | Abercrombie,John (g) | Holland,Dave (b) | Higgins,Billy (dr)

1675(547949-2) | CD | The Melody At Night,With You
Keith Jarrett
I Loves You Porgy | I Got It Bad And That Ain't Good | Don't Ever Leave Me | Someone To Watch Over Me | My Wild Irish Rose | Blame It On My Youth | Meditation | Something To Remember You By | Be My Love | Shenandoah | I'm Through With You
Cavelight Studio,?, rec. 1998/1999
Jarrett,Keith (p-solo)

1680(547336-2) | CD | From The Green Hill
Tomasz Stanko Sextet
Domino | Litania | Stone Ridge | Y Despues De Todo - ...Y Despues De Todo | Litania(2) | Quintet's Time | Pantronic | The Lark In The Dark | Love Theme From Farewell To Maria | From The Green Hill - ...From The Green Hill | Buschka | Roberto Zucco | Domino's Intro | Argentyna
Oslo,N, rec. August 1998
Stanko,Tomasz (tp) | Surman,John (b-cl,bs) | Saluzzi,Dino (bandoneon) | Makarski,Michelle (v) | Jormin,Anders (b) | Christensen,Jon (dr)

1683(557652-2) | CD | Open Land
John Abercrombie Sextet
Just In Tune | Open Land | Spring Song | Gimme Five | Speak Easy | Little Booker | Free Piece Suit(e) | Remember When | That's For Sure
NYC, rec. September 1998
Abercrombie,John (g) | Wheeler,Kenny (tp,fl-h) | Lovano,Joe (ts) | Feldman,Mark (v) | Wall,Dan (org) | Nussbaum,Adam (dr)

1684(543159-2) | CD | Epigraphs
Ketil Bjornstad-David Darling
Epigraph No.1 | Upland | Wakening | Epigraph No.1(Var.1) | Pavane | Fantasia | Epigraph No.1(Var.2) | The Guest | After Celan | Song For TKJD | Silent Dream | The Lake | Gothic | Epigraph No.1(Var.3) | Le Jour S'endort | Factus Est Repente
Oslo,N, rec. September 1998
Bjornstad,Ketil (p) | Darling,David (cello)

1685/86(559006-2) | 2 CD | Rites
Jan Garbarek Group
Rites | Where The Rivers Meet | Vast Plain,Clouds | So Mild The Wind,So Meek The Water | Song,Tread Lightly | It's OK To Listen To The Gray Voice | Her Wild Ways | It's High Time | One Ying For Every Yang | Pan | We Are The Stars | The Moon Over Mtatsminda | Malinye | The White Clown | Evenly They Danced | Last Rite
Oslo,N, rec. March 1998
Garbarek,Jan (ss,ts,synth,perc,samples) | Brüninghaus,Rainer (p,keyboards) | Weber,Eberhard (b) | Mazur,Marilyn (dr,perc) | Wesseltoft,Jens Bugge (synth,accordeon,electronics) | Kakhidze,Jansug (cond,voc) | Tbilisi Symphony Orchestra | Boys From The Choir Solvguttene | Grythe,Torstein (cond)

1690(557653-2) | CD | Frifot
Per Gudmundson-Ale Möller-Lene Willemark
Abba Fader | Stjäman | Tjugmyren | Kolarpolskan | I Hela Naturen- | Mjukfoten- | Förgäves | Kära Sol- | Sjungar Lars-Polska- | Hemvändaren | Fafänglighet | Silder- | Bingsjö Stora Langdans- | Drömsken | Skur Leja | Metaren | Roligs Per-Latar | Om Stenen- | Snygg Olle- | Morgonlat
Oslo,N, rec. September 1998
Gudmundson,Per (fiddle,octave-fiddle,swedish-bagpipes,voc) | Möller,Ale (mand,folk-harp,hammered-dulcimer,natural-fl,shawm,voc) | Willemark,Lena (fiddle,octave-fiddle,voc,wooden-fl)

1698(547950-2) | CD | Prime Directive
Dave Holland Quintet
Looking Up | Make Believe | A Searching Spirit | High Wire | Jugglers Parade | Candlelight Vigil | Wonders Never Cease | Down Time
NYC, rec. 10.-12.12.1998
Holland,Dave (b) | Eubanks,Robin (tb,cowbell) | Potter,Chris (ss,as,ts) | Nelson,Steve (vib,marimba) | Kilson,Billy (dr)

1702(543033-2) | CD | Coruscating
John Surman With String Quartet
At Dusk | Dark Corners | Stone Flower | Moonless Midnight | Winding Passages | An Illusive Shadow | Christal Walls | For The Moment
London,GB, rec. January 1999
Surman,John (b-cl,contra-b-cl,ss,bs) | Laurence,Chris (b) | Manning,Rita (v) | Pascoe,Keith (v) | Hawkes,Bill (viola) | Cooper,Nick (cello)

1703(543034-2) | CD | In Cerca Di Cibo
Gianluigi Trovesi-Gianni Coscia
In Cerca Di Cibo | Geppetto | Villanella | Il Postino | Minor Dance | Pinocchio:In Groppa Al Tonno | Django | Le Giostre Di Piazza Savona | Lucignolo | Tre Bimbi Di Campagna | Celebre Mazurka Alterata | Fata Turchina | El Choclo
Zürich,CH, rec. February 1999
Trovesi,Gianluigi (cl) | Coscia,Gianni (accordeon)

1704(543035-2) | CD | Karta
Markus Stockhausen Quartet
Sezopen | Flower Of Now | Wood And Naphta | Sway | Auma | Legacy | Invocation | Wild Cat | Emanation | Choral | Lighthouse
Oslo,N, rec. December 1999
Stockhausen,Markus (tp,fl-h) | Rypdal,Terje (el-g) | Andersen,Arild (b) | Heral,Patrice (dr,perc,live-electronics)

1705(159927-2) | CD | L'Affrontement Des Prétendants
Louis Sclavis Quartet
Distances | Contre Contre | Hors Les Murs | Possibles | Hommage À Lounès Matoub | Le Temps D'Après | Maputo Introduction | Maputo | Le Mémoire Des Mains
Pernes Les Fontaines,France, rec. September 1999
Sclavis,Louis (cl,b-cl,ss) | Cappola,John (tp) | Courtois,Vincent (cello) | Chevillon,Bruno (b) | Merville,Francois (dr)

1718(159494-2) | CD | Astrakan Café
Anouar Brahem Trio
Aube Rouge À Grozny | Astrakan Café(1) | The Mozdok's Train | Blue Jewels | Nihawend Lunga | Ashkabad | Halfaoine | Parfum De Gitane | Khotan | Karakoum | Astara | Dar Es Salam | Hijaz Pechref | Astrakan Café(2)
Monastery of St.Gerold,Austria, rec. June 1999
Brahem,Anouar (oud) | Erköse,Barbaros (cl) | Hosni,Lassad (bendir,darbouka)

1722(543365-2) | CD | Solid Ether
Nils Petter Molvaer Group
Dead Indeed | Vilderness 1 | Kakonita | Merciful 1 | Ligotage | Trip | Vilderness 2 | Tragamar | Solid Ether | Merciful 2
Oslo,N, rec. 1999
Molvaer,Nils Petter (tp,p,synth,perc,samples,sounds) | Aarset,Eivind (g,electronics) | Erlien,Audun (b,electronics) | Lindvall,Per (dr) | Arnesen,Rune (dr) | Skar,Reidar (sound treatment) | DJ Strangefruit (beats,samples,ambience) | Endresen,Sidsel (voc)

1724/25(543813-2) | 2 CD | Whisper Not
Keith Jarrett Trio
Bouncing With Bud | Whisper Not | Groovin' High | Chelsea Bridge | Wrap Your Troubles In Dreams | Round About Midnight | Sandu | What Is This Thing Called Love | Conception | Prelude To A Kiss | Hallucinations | All My Tomorrows | Poinciana | When I Fall In Love
Live at Palais De Congrès,Paris,France, rec. 5.7.1999
Jarrett,Keith (p) | Peacock,Gary (b) | DeJohnette,Jack (dr)

1728(157462-2) | CD | Achirana
Vassilis Tsabropoulos Trio
Achirana | Diamond Cut Diamond | Valley | Mystic | The Spell | She's Gone | Fable | Song For Phyllis | Monologue
Oslo,N, rec. October 1999
Tsabropoulos,Vassilis (p) | Andersen,Arild (b) | Marshall,John (dr)

1732(543819-2) | CD | The Seed-At-Zero
Robin Williamson
The World | The Seed-At-Zero | Skull And Nettlework | Holy Spring | To God In God's Absence | Lament Of The Old Man | In My Craft Or Sullen Art | Verses At Balwearie Tower | Can Y Gwynt | By Weary Well | The Bells Of Rhymney | On No Work Of Words | The Barley | Hold Hard,These Ancient Minutes In The Cuckoo's Month | Cold Day Of February | Poem On His Birthday | For Mr.Thomas
Cardiff,GB, rec. March 2000
Williamson,Robin (g,mand,harp,voc)

1733(159496-2) | CD | An Acrobat's Heart
Annette Peacock With The Cikada String Quartet
Mia's Proof | Tho | Weightless | Over | As Long As Now | U Slide | B 4 U Said | The Heart Keeps | Ways It Isnt | Unspoken | Safe | Free The Memory | Ever 2 B Gotten | Camille | Lost A t Last
Oslo,N, rec. January & April 2000
Peacock,Annette (p,voc) | Cikada String Quartet | Hannisdal,Henrik (v) | Hannisdal,Odd (v) | Konstantynowicz,Marek (viola) | Hannisdal,Morten (cello)

1734(549043-2) | CD | The Water Is Wide
Charles Lloyd Quintet
Georgia | The Water Is Wide | Black Butterfly | Ballade And Allegro | Figure In Blue | Lotus Blossom | The Monk And The Mermaid | Song For Her | Lady Day | Heaven | There Is A Balm In Gilead | Prayer
Los Angeles,CA, rec. December 1999
Lloyd,Charles (ts) | Abercrombie,John (g) | Mehldau,Brad (p) | Grenadier,Larry (b) | Higgins,Billy (dr)

1738(549612-2) | CD | Hide And Seek
Michael Mantler Orchestra
Unsaid(1) | What Did You Say? | Unsaid(2) | It's All Just Words | If You Have Nothing To Say | Unsaid(3) | What Do You See? | Absolutely Nothing | Unsaid(4) | What Can We Do? | Unsaid(5) | It All Has To End Sometime | Unsaid(6) | I Don't Deny It | I'm Glad You're Glad | Do You Think We'll Ever Find It? | It Makes No Difference To Me
Copenhagen,Denmark, rec. September 2000
Wyatt,Robert (voice) | Hyldgaard,Susi (accordeon,voice) | Mantler,Michael (tp,ld) | Nilsson,Vincent (tb) | Cholewa,Martin (fr-h) | Jannotta,Roger (fl,cl,oboe) | Roupe,Bjarne (g) | Noordhoek,Tineke (vib,marimba) | Salo,Per (p) | Sorensen,Marianne (v) | Winther,Mette (viola) | Sorensen,Helle (cello)

1740/41(543611-2) | 2 CD | Serenity
Bobo Stenson Trio
T. | West Print | North Print | East Print | South Print | Polska Of Despair(I) | Golden Rain | Swee Pea | Simple & Sweet | Der Pflaumenbaum | El Mayor | Fader V(Father World) | More Cymbals | Extra Low | Die Nachtigall | Rimbaud Gedichte | Polska Of Despair(II) | Serenity | Tonus
HageGärden Music Center,Brunskog,Sweden, rec. April 1999
Stenson,Bobo (p) | Jormin,Anders (b) | Christensen,Jon (dr)

1742(013400-2) | CD | Amaryllis
Marilyn Crispell-Gary Peacock-Paul Motian
Voice From The Past | Amaryllis | Requiem | Conception Vessel- | Circle Dance- | Voices | December Greenwings | Silence | M.E. | Rounds | Avatar | Morpion | Prayer
NYC, rec. February 2000
Crispell,Marilyn (p) | Peacock,Gary (b) | Motian,Paul (dr)

1743(543814-2) | CD | Anthem | EAN 731454381420
Ralph Towner
Solitary Woman | Anthem | Haunted | The Lutemaker | Simone | Gloria's Step | Four Comets | Raffish | Very Late | The Prowler | Three Comments | Goodbye Pork Pie Hat
Oslo,N, rec. February 2000
Towner,Ralph (g,12-string-g)

1744(159521-2) | CD | Different Rivers
Trygve Seim Group
Sorrows
Oslo,N, rec. 1998-1999
Seim,Trygve (ts) | Henriksen,Arve (tp,voc) | Tafjord,Hild Sofie (fr-h) | Gald,David (tuba) | Carstensen,Stian (accordeon) | Lund,Havard (b-cl)
Ulrikas Dans
Seim,Trygve (ts) | Henriksen,Arve (tp) | Braekke,Oyvind (tb) | Tafjord,Hild Sofie (fr-h) | Gald,David (tuba) | Lund,Havard (b-cl) | Jansen,Nils (bass-sax) | Lund,Bernt Simen (cello) | Johansen,Per Oddvar (dr)
Intangible Waltz
Seim,Trygve (ts) | Henriksen,Arve (tp) | Tafjord,Hild Sofie (fr-h) | Gald,David (tuba) | Carstensen,Stian (accordeon) | Lund,Havard (b-cl) | Lund,Bernt Simen (cello) | Johansen,Per Oddvar (dr)
Different Rivers
Seim,Trygve (ss) | Henriksen,Arve (tp) | Gald,David (tuba) | Lund,Havard (cl) | Jansen,Nils (bass-sax) | Hannisdal,Morten (cello) | Johansen,Per Oddvar (dr)
Bhavana | For Edward | Between
Seim,Trygve (ss,ts) | Henriksen,Arve (tp,trumpophone)
he Aftermanth- | African Sunrise-
Seim,Trygve (ts) | Henriksen,Arve (tp) | Tafjord,Hild Sofie (fr-h) | Gald,David (tuba) | Carstensen,Stian (accordeon) | Lund,Havard (b-cl) | Jansen,Nils (contra-b-cl) | Lund,Bernt Simen (cello) | Johansen,Per Oddvar (dr) | Nilssen-Love,Paal (dr)
Search Silence
Seim,Trygve (ss) | Henriksen,Arve (tp) | Tafjord,Hild Sofie (fr-h) | Gald,David (tuba) | Lund,Havard (b-cl) | Jansen,Nils (sopranino) | Lund,Bernt Simen (cello)
Breathe
Seim,Trygve (ts) | Henriksen,Arve (tp) | Tafjord,Hild Sofie (fr-h) | Lund,Havard (b-cl) | Jansen,Nils (bass-sax) | Lund,Bernt Simen (cello) | Endresen,Sidsel (recitation)

1746(543813-2) | CD | In Montreal
Charlie Haden-Egberto Gismonti
Salvador | Maracatu | First Song | Palhaco | Silence | Em Familia | Loro | Frevo | Don Quixote
Live at The International Jazz Festival,Montreal,Canada, rec. 6.7.1989
Haden,Charlie (b) | Gismonti,Egberto (g,p)

1748(013420-2) | CD | Endless Days
Eberhard Weber Group
Concerto For Bass | French Diary | Solo For Bass | Nuit Blanthe | A Walk In The Garrigue | Concerto For Piano | Endless Days | The Last Stage Of A Long Journey
Oslo,N, rec. April 2000
Weber,Eberhard (b) | McCandless,Paul (engl-h,b-cl,oboe,ts) | Brüninghaus,Rainer (p,keyboards) | DiPasqua,Michael (dr,perc)

1749(158570-2) | CD | Ýlir
Claudio Puntin/Gerdur Gunnarsdóttir
Ýlir | Huldofólk I,II | Einbúinn | Engin Lát Ödrum Frekt | Skerpla | Peysireid | Vorbankar | Hvert Östrutt Spor | Sofdu Unga Ástin Min | Huldofólk III | L'Ultimo Abbraccio | Kwaedid Um Fuglana | Leysing | Epilogue
Bremen, rec. 1997-1999
Puntin,Claudio (cl,b-cl) | Gunnarsdóttir,Gerdur (v,voc)

1751(159924-2) | CD | Rosslyn | EAN 601215992427
John Taylor Trio
The Bowl Song | How Deep Is The Ocean | Between Moons | Rosslyn | Ma Bel | Tramontò | Field Day
Oslo,N, rec. April 2002
Taylor,John (p) | Johnson,Marc (b) | Baron,Joey (dr)

1752(0381212) | CD | The Triangle | EAN 044003812123
Arild Andersen Trio
Straight | Pavane | Saturday | Choral | Simple Thoughts | Prism | Lines | European Triangle | Cinderella Song
Oslo,N, rec. January 2003
Andersen,Arild (b) | Tsabropoulos,Vassilis (p) | Marshall,John (dr)

1757(159739-2) | CD | Desert Poems

ECM | Universal Music Germany(alle LP's nur direkt über ECM-Export) Bielefelder Katalog 750 Jazz • Ausgabe 2004 ECM | Universal Music Germany(alle LP's nur direkt über ECM-Export)

Stephan Micus
The Horses Of Nizami | Adela | Night | Mikail's Dream | First Snow | Thirteen Eagles | Contessa Entellina | Shen Khar Venakhi | For Yuko
MCM Studio,?, rec. 1997-2000
Micus,Stephan (different instruments,voc in multi-playback)

1758(014004-2) | CD | Not For Nothin'
Dave Holland Quintet
Global Citizen | For All You Are | Lost And Found | Shifting Sands | Billows Of Rhythm | What Goes Around Comes Around | Go Fly A Kite | Not For Nothin' | Cosmosis
NYC, rec. 21.-23.9.2000
Holland,Dave (b) | Eubanks,Robin (tb,cowbell) | Potter,Chris (ss,as,ts) | Nelson,Steve (vib,marimba) | Kilson,Billy (dr)

1760(9812050) | CD | Easy Living | EAN 602498120507
Enrico Rava Quintet
Cromosoni | Drops | Sand | Easy Living | Agir Dalbughi | Blancasnow | Traveling Night | Hornette And The Drum Thing | Rain
Undine, Italy, rec. June 2003
Rava,Enrico (tp) | Petrella,Gianluca (tb) | Bollani,Stefano (p) | Bonaccorso,Rosario (b) | Gatto,Roberto (dr)

1762(013998-2) | CD | Xieyi
Anders Jormin
Giv Meg Ej Glans | I Denna Ljuva Sommartid | Gracias A La Vida | Idas Sommarvisa | Decimas | Och Kanske Är Det Natt | Tenk | Sonett Till Cornelis | Scents | Fragancia | War Orphans
Kungälv,Sweden, rec. 2.10.2000
Jormin,Anders (b-solo)
Anders Jormin With Brass Quartet
Choral(1) | Xieyi | Sul Tasto | Romance-Distance | Q | Choral(2)
Jormin,Anders (b) | Rydquist,Robin (tp,fl-h) | Petersen,Krister (fr-h) | Carlsson,Lars-Göran (tb) | Rydh,Niclas (b-tb)

1764(014432-2) | CD | The Source And Different Cikadas | EAN 044001443220
Trygve Seim-Oyvind Braekke-Per Oddvar Johansen Orchestra
Organismus Vitalis | Mmball | Funebre | Deluxe | Bhavana | Saltpastil | Flipper | Plukk | Obecni Dum | Suppressions | Number Eleven | Fort-Jazz | Sen Kjellertango | Uten Forbindelse | Tutti Free
Oslo,N, rec. November 2000
Braekke,Oyvind (tb) | Seim,Trygve (ss,ts) | Johansen,Per Oddvar (dr) | Henriksen,Arve (tp) | Haltli,Frode (b-tb,accordeon) | Wallumrod,Christian (p) | Hannisdal,Odd (v) | Hannisdal,Henrik (v) | Konstantynowicz,Marek (viola) | Hannisdal,Morten (cello) | Guttormsen,Finn (b)

1766(013999-2) | CD | April
Susanne Abbuehl Group
Yes Is A Pleasant Country | Ida Lupino | Closer | All I Need | A.I.R.(All India Radio) | Seven,Somewhere I Have Never Travelled,Gladly Beyond | Skies May Be Blue | Round About Midnight | Maggie And Milly And Molly And May | Since Feeling Is First | Mane Na
Abbuehl,Susanne (voice) | May,Christof (cl,b-cl) | Brederode,Wolfert (p,harmonium,melodia) | Rohrer,Samuel (dr,perc)

1768(549610-2) | CD | At Home
Misha Alperin
At Home | Emptiness(dedicated to Olivier Messian) | Nostalgia | Seconds | Nightfall | Hailing | Light | Game | Shadows | 10th Of February(dedicated to Efim Alperin) | The Wind | Njeto
Misha Alperin's Home), rec. February 1998
Alperin,Mikhail 'Misha' (p-solo)

1769(014431-2) | CD | Night After Night | EAN 044001443121
Misha Alperin Trio
Tuesday | Tango | Adagio | Second Game | Dark Drops | Night | Heavy Hour | Far Far...
Live at Vossa Jazz Festival,Norway, rec. 4.4.1998
Alperin,Mikhail 'Misha' (p,claviola) | Lechner,Anja (cello) | Kjos Sorensen,Hans-Kristian (marimba,perc,voice)

1770(014001-2) | CD | Cat 'N' Mouse
John Abercrombie Quartet
A Nice Idea | Convolution | String Thing | Soundtrack | Third Stream Samba | On The Loose | Stop And Go | Show Of Hands
NYC, rec. December 2000
Abercrombie,John (g) | Feldman,Mark (v) | Johnson,Marc (b) | Baron,Joey (dr)

1777(014002-2) | CD | What Goes Around | EAN 044001400223
Dave Holland Big Band
Triple Dance | Blues For C.M. | The Razor's Edge | What Goes Around Comes Around | Upswing | First Snow | Shadow Dance
NYC, rec. January 2001
Holland,Dave (b) | Gardner,Earl (tp,fl-h) | Sipiagin,Alex (tp,fl-h) | Eubanks,Duane (tp,fl-h) | Eubanks,Robin (tb) | Hayward,Andre (tb) | Roseman,Joshua 'Josh' (tb) | Hart,Antonio Maurice (as) | Gross,Mark (as) | Potter,Chris (ts) | Smulyan,Gary (bs) | Nelson,Steve (vib) | Kilson,Billy (dr)

1780(014005-2) | CD | Inside Out
Keith Jarrett Trio
From The Body | Inside Out | 341 Free Fade | Riot | When I Fall In Love
Live at Royal Festival Hall,London,GB, rec. 26.& 28.7.2000
Jarrett,Keith (p) | Peacock,Gary (b) | DeJohnette,Jack (dr)

1784(014000-2) | CD | Hyperion With Higgins
Charles Lloyd Quintet
Dancing Waters,Big Sur To Bahia | Bharati | Secret Life Of The Forbidden City | Miss Jessye | Hyperion With Higgins | Darkness On The Delta Suite | Dervish On The Glory B | The Caravan Moves On
Los Angeles,CA, rec. December 1999
Lloyd,Charles (ts,taragota) | Abercrombie,John (g) | Mehldau,Brad (p) | Grenadier,Larry (b) | Higgins,Billy (dr,perc)

1785(016372-2 | CD | Skirting The River Road | EAN 044001637223
Robin Williamson Group
The Morning Watch- | A Song Of Joy- | Here To Burn | The Four Points Are Thus Beheld | Infant Joy | Dalliance Of Eagles | Abstinence Sows Sand | The Journey | The Terrible Doubt- | The Price Of Experience- | West From California's Shores | Shepherd's Tune | The Map With No North | The Spider | The Fly | Crossing Brooklyn Ferry | The World Of Light
Kingston-Upon-Thames,GB, rec. March/April 2001
Williamson,Robin (g,harp,whistles,voc) | Dunmall,Paul (cl,ss,ts,border-pipes,ocarina,moxeno) | Möller,Ale (vib,mand,lute,clarino,drone-fl,bamboo-fl,hammered-dulcimer,natural-fl | Maneri,Mat (v,viola) | Hutton,Mick (b)

1787(016375-2) | CD | In Touch | EAN 044001637520
Yves Robert Trio
In Touch | Let's Lay Down | La Tendresse | In Touch(variation I) | L'Air D'y Toucher | Basculement Du Désir | L'Attente Reste | In Touch(variation II)
Paris,France, rec. March 2001
Robert,Yves (tb) | Courtois,Vincent (cello) | Atef,Cyril (dr)

1788(016374-2) | CD | Soul Of Things | EAN 044001637421
Tomasz Stanko Quartet
Soul Of Things(part I-XIII)
Oslo,N, rec. August 2001
Stanko,Tomasz (tp) | Wasilewski,Marcin (p) | Kurkiewicz,Slawomir (b) | Miskiewicz,Michal (dr)

1792(016373-2) | CD | Le Pas Du Chat Noir | EAN 044001637322
Anouar Brahem Trio
Le Pas Du Chat Noir | De Tout Ton Coeur | Laila Au Pays Du Carrousel | Pique Nique À Nagpur | C'est Ailleurs | Toi Qui Sait | L'arbre Qui Voit | Un Point Bleu | Les Ailes Du Bourak | Rue De Départ | Laila Au Pays Du Carrousel(variations) | Déjà La Nuit
Zürich,CH, rec. July 2001
Brahem,Anouar (oud) | Couturier,Francois (p) | Matinier,Jean-Louis (accordeon)

1796(016376-2) | CD | Invisible Nature
John Surman-Jack DeJohnette
Mysterium | Rising Tide | Outback Spirits | Underground Movement | Ganges Groove | Fair Trade | Song For World Forgiveness
Tampere Jazz Happening & Jazzfest Berlin, rec. November 2000
Surman,John (b-cl,ss,bs,synth) | DeJohnette,Jack (dr,el-perc,p)

1800/01(018766-2) | 2 CD | Always Let Me Go | EAN 044001878626
Keith Jarrett Trio
Hearts In Space | The River | Tributaries | Paradox | Waves | Facing East | Tsunami | Relay
Live at Orchard Hall Bunka Kaikan,Tokyo,Japan, rec. April 2001
Jarrett,Keith (p) | Peacock,Gary (b) | DeJohnette,Jack (dr)

1802(017065-2) | CD | Printed In Germany | EAN 044001706523
John Surman-Jack DeJohnette With The London Brass
Preamble | Groundwork | Sea Change | Back And Forth | Fire | Debased Line | In The Shadow | Free And Equal | Epilogue
Live at Queen Elizabeth Hall,London, rec. June 2001
Surman,John (b-cl,ss,bs) | DeJohnette,Jack (p,dr) | London Brass | Crowley,Andrew (tp) | Archibald,Paul (tp) | Barclay,John (tp) | McAneney,Anne (tp,fl-h) | Jenkins,Dan (tb) | Edwards,Richard (tb) | Purser,David (tb,euphonium) | Stewart,David (b-tb) | Bissill,Richard (fr-h) | Slade,Owen (tuba)

1804(159453-2) | CD | Towards The Wind | EAN 601215945324
Stephan Micus
Towards The Wind: | Before Sunrise | Morning Breeze | Flying Horses | Padre | Birds At Dawn | Virgin De La Nieve | Eastern Princess | Crossing Dark Rivers
MCM Studio,?, rec. 1999-2001
Micus,Stephan (different instruments in multi-playback)

1805(589524-2) | CD | Dans La Nuit | EAN 731458952428
Louis Sclavis Group
Dia Dia(1) | Le Travail | Dans La Nuit(1) | Fete Foraine | Retour De Noce | Mauvais Reve | Amour Et Beauté | L'Accident(part 1) | L'Accident(part 2) | Le Moroir | Dans La Nuit(2) | La Fuite | La Peur Du Noir | Les 2 Visages | Dia Dia(2) | Dans La Nuit(3)
La Buissonne,France, rec. October 2000
Sclavis,Louis (cl,b-cl) | Matinier,Jean-Louis (accordeon) | Pifarely,Dominique (v) | Courtois,Vincent (cello) | Merville,Francois (perc,marimba)

1808(017066-2) | CD | Tribute To Lester | EAN 044001706622
Art Ensemble Of Chicago
Sangaredi | Suite For Lester | Zero-Alternate Line | Tutankhamun(Tutanchamon) | As Clear As The Sun | He Speaks To Me Often In Dreams
Chicago,Ill, rec. September 2001
Art Ensemble Of Chicago | Mitchell,Roscoe (fl,whistle,sopranino,ss,as,ts,bass-sax,perc) | Favors,Malachi (b,bells,whistles,gongs) | Moye,Famoudou Don (dr,congas,bongos,bell,whistles,gongs,chimes,counsel-dr)

1809(017067-2) | CD | Sofienberg Variations | EAN 044001706721
Christian Wallumrod Ensemble
Sofienberg Variations: | Memor | Edith | Alas Alert | Small Picture No.1 | Psalm | Liturgia | Small Picture No.2 | Small Picture No.3 | Small Picture No.3,5 | Edith Variation | Memor Variation | Losing Temple
Sofienberg Kirke,Oslo,N, rec. October 2001
Wallumrod,Christian (p,harmonium) | Henriksen,Arve (tp) | Okland,Nils (v,fiddle) | Johansen,Per Oddvar (dr)
Sarabande Nouvelle | Sarabande Nouvelle Variation 1 | Sarabande Nouvelle Variation 2
Wallumrod,Christian (p,harmonium) | Henriksen,Arve (tp) | Seim,Trygve (ts) | Okland,Nils (v,fiddle) | Johansen,Per Oddvar (dr)

1814(017068-2) | CD | Steve Tibbetts | EAN 044001706820
Steve Tibbetts Group
Lupra | Red Temple | Black Temple | Burning Temple | Glass Everywhere | Lochana | Chandoha | Koshala
St.Paul, Minnesota, rec. details unknown
Tibbetts,Steve (g,perc) | Anton,Jim (b) | Anderson,Marc (perc) | Wise,Marcus (perc)

1815(0675222) | CD | Promises Kept | EAN 044006752228
Steve Kuhn With Strings
Lullaby | Life's Backward Glance | Trance | Morning Dew | Promises Kept | Adagio | Celtig Princess | Nostalgia | Oceans In The Sky | Pastorale
NYC, rec. June/September 2000
Kuhn,Steve (p) | Finck,David (b) | Bennion Feeney ,Krista (v) | Lim-Dutton,Elizabeth (v) | Sortomme,Richard (v) | Kawahara,Karl (v) | Finclair,Barry (v) | Kim,Helen (v) | Shaw,Robert (v) | Pool,Carol (v) | Nicolau,Anca (v) | Pray,Sue (viola) | Lionti,Vince (viola) | Ritscher,Karen (viola) | Cummings,Stephanie (cello) | Locker,Richard (cello) | Gordon,Joshua 'Josh' (cello) | Franzetti,Carlos (cond)

1816(017069-2) | CD | Responsorium | EAN 044001706929
Dino Saluzzi Trio
A Mi Hermano Celso | Monica | Responso Por La Muerte De Cruz | Dele...,Don!! | Reprise:Los Hijos De Fierro | La Pequena Historia De...! | Cuchara | Vienen Del Sur Los Recuerdos | Pamoeana 'Mapu'
Oslo,N, rec. November 2001
Saluzzi,Dino (bandoneon) | Saluzzi,José Maria (g) | Danielsson,Palle (b)

1818(017070-2) | CD | Lux Aeterna | EAN 044001707025
Terje Rypdal Quartet With The Bergen Chamber Ensemble
Lux Aeterna: | 1th Movement:Luminous Galaxy | 2nd Movement:Fjelldapen | 3rd Movement:Escalator | 4th Movement:Toccata | 5th Movement:Lux Aeterna
Live at The Molde Jazz Festival, rec. 19.7.2000
Rypdal,Terje (g) | Mikkelborg,Palle (tp) | Gundersen,Ashild (ss) | Kleive,Iver (org) | Bergen Chamber Ensemble | Tellnes,Thorsten (p) | Batnes,Elise (v,ld) | Folleso,Annar (v) | Blo,Harald (v) | Flolo,Jon (v) | Sollesnes,Ellisiv (v) | Stangenes,Geir Atle (v) | Holtlien,Gunnvo (v) | Svanes,Elisabeth (v) | Selle,Elna Foleide (v) | Hagen,Hans Gunnar (viola) | Rensvik,Anders (viola) | Solberg,Nils Olaf (viola) | Erdal,Bodil (cello) | Kleiveland,Gunn Berit (cello) | Kieszek,Adam (b) | Kolve,Ivar (perc) | Bredesen-Vestby,Ellen (perc) | Seim,Kjell (cond)

1822(017278-2) | CD | Kyanos | EAN 044001727825
Jon Balke w/Magnetic North Orchestra
Phanai | Zygotos | Mutatio | Ganglion | Katabolic | In Vitro | Plica | Nano | Karyon | Kyanos | Apsis
Oslo,N, rec. November 2001
Balke,Jon (p,keyboards) | Jorgensen,Per (tp,voc) | Henriksen,Arve (tp) | Halle,Morton (fl,sax) | Henryson,Svante (cello) | Jormin,Anders (b) | Kleive,Audun (dr,perc)

1828(018493-2) | CD | Charmediterranéen | EAN 044001849329
Orchestre National De Jazz
Sequenze Orfiche | Prologo:L'Orfeo | Sequenza Prima | Sequenza Seconda | Sequenza Terza | Sequenza Quartra | Epilogo | Estramadura(part 1-3) | Montbéliard Trio | Artefact(part 1-2) | Argentiera | Charmediterranéen | Argentiera(2)
Montbéliard,France, rec. 15./16.10.2001
Orchestre National De Jazz | Vankenhove,Alain (tp,fl-h) | Collignon,Médéric (pocket-co,fl-h,voice) | Petrella,Gianluca (tb) | Jeanneau,Francois (fl,ss,ld) | Trovesi,Gianluigi (cl,as) | De Pourquery,Thomas (ss,as,ts) | Larché,Jean-Marc (ss,bs) | Havet,Didier (sousaphone) | Brahem,Anouar (oud) | Benoit,Olivier (g) | Huby,Régis (v) | Damiani,Paolo (cello,ld) | Rogers,Paul (b) | Marguet,Christophe (dr)

1832/33(018783-2) | 2 CD | Lift Every Voice | EAN 044001878329
Charles Lloyd Quintet
Hymn To The Mother | Amazing Grace | East Virginia,West Memphis | What's Going On | Angel Oak | Te Amaré | Rabo De Nube(Tail Of The Tornado) | Go Down Moses | Prayer,The Crossing | Hafez,Shattered Heart
Los Angeles,CA, rec. January/February 2002
Lloyd,Charles (fl,ts,taragota) | Abercrombie,John (g) | Allen,Geri (p) | Johnson,Marc (b) | Hart,Billy (dr)
You Are So Beautiful | I'm Afraid | Blood Count | Beyond Darkness | Wayfaring Stranger | Deep River | Lift Every Voice And Sing
Lloyd,Charles (fl,ts,taragota) | Abercrombie,John (g) | Allen,Geri (p) | Grenadier,Larry (b) | Hart,Billy (dr)
Charles Lloyd Sextet
Nocturne
Lloyd,Charles (fl,ts,taragota) | Abercrombie,John (g) | Allen,Geri (p) | Johnson,Marc (b) | Grenadier,Larry (b) | Hart,Billy (dr)

1834(016397-2) | CD | Changing Places | EAN 044001639722
Tord Gustavsen Trio
Deep As Love | Graceful Touch | IGN | Melted Matter | At A Glance | Song Of Yearning | Turning Point | Interlude | Where Breathing Starts | Going Places | Your Eyes | Graceful Touch(Variation)
Oslo,N, rec. December 2001/June 2002
Gustavsen,Tord (p) | Johnson,Harald (b) | Vespestad,Jarle (dr)
Tord Gustavsen
Song Of The Yearning
Gustavsen,Tord (p-solo)

1836(066069-2) | CD | Vindonissa | EAN 044006606927
Paul Giger Trio
Vindonissa(intro) | Oogoogajoo | Introitus | Lava Colls | Kyrie | Fractal Joy | Chorale | Afterlife Calypso | Gloria Et Tarantella | An Ear On Buddha's Belly | Vindonissa
details unknown, rec. 1995-2000
Giger,Paul (v,v-d'amore,viola-d'amore,foot-bells) | Dick,Robert (fl,glissandi-fl,bass-fl,contra-bass-fl) | Takeishi,Satoshi (perc)

1838/39(157628-2) | 2 CD | Abaton | EAN 601215762822
Sylvie Courvoisier Group
Ianicum | Orodruin | Poco A Poco | Abaton | Nineteen Improvisations
Oslo,N, rec. September 2002
Courvoisier,Sylvie (p) | Feldman,Mark (v) | Friedlander,Erik (cello)

1840(066627-2) | CD | The Rain | EAN 044006662725
Kayhan Kalhor Trio
Fire | Dawn | Eternity
Live at Radio DRS,Bern, rec. 28.5.2001
Kalhor,Kayhan (kamancheh) | Khan,Shujaat Husain (sitar,voc) | Das,Sandeep (tabla)

1846(0381182) | CD | Class Trip | EAN 044003811829
John Abercrombie Quartet
Dansir | Risky Business | Decending Grace | Illinoise | Catwalk | Excuse My Shoes | Swirls | Jack And Betty | Class Trip | Soldier's Song | Epilogue
NYC, rec. February 2003
Abercrombie,John (g) | Feldman,Mark (v) | Johnson,Marc (b) | Baron,Joey (dr)

1847(0381192) | CD | Story Teller | EAN 044003811928
Marilyn Crispell Trio
Wild Rose | Flight Of The Blue Jay | The Storyteller | Alone | Harmonic Line | Cosmology | Limbo | The Sunflower | So Far So Near
Crispell,Marilyn (p) | Helias,Mark (b) | Motian,Paul (dr)

1852(0381172) | CD | Memory/Vision | EAN 044003811720
Evan Parker Electro-Acoustic Ensemble
Memory-Vision(Staring Into The Time Cone)
Oslo,N, rec. October 2002
Parker,Evan (ss,tapes,samples) | Wachsmann,Phil (v,electronics) | Fernandez,Agusti (p,prep-p) | Guy,Barry (b) | Lytton,Paul (perc,electronics) | Casserley,Lawrence (signal-processing-instruments) | Ryan,Joel (computer,sound-processing) | Prati,Walter (electronics,sound processing) | Vecchi,Marco (electronics,sound-processing)

1857(038504-2) | CD | Napoli's Walls | EAN 044003850422
Louis Sclavis Group
Colleur De Nuit | Napoli's Wall | Mercé | Kennedy In Napoli | Divinazione Moderna I | Divinazione Moderna II | Guetteur D'Inapercu | Les Apparences | Porta Segreta | Il Disegno Smangiato D'Un Uomo
Pernes Les Fontaines,France, rec. December 2002
Sclavis,Louis (cl,b-cl,ss,bs) | Collignon,Médéric (pocket-tp,horn,electronics,perc,voice) | Courtois,Vincent (cello,electronics) | Poulsen,Hasse (g)

1863(038506-2) | CD | Universal Syncopations | EAN 044003850620
Miroslav Vitous Group
Bamboo Forest | Univoyage | Tramp Blues | Faith Run | Sun Flower | Miro Bop | Beethoven | Medium | Brazil Waves
Oslo,N, rec. March 2003
Vitous,Miroslav (b) | Garbarek,Jan (ss,ts) | McLaughlin,John (g) | Corea,Chick (p) | DeJohnette,Jack (dr)

1864/65(038505-2) | 2 CD | Extended Play | EAN 044003850521
Dave Holland Quintet
The Balance | High Wire | Jugglers Parade | Make Believe | Free For All | Claressence | Prime Directive | BedouinTrail | Metamorphos
Live at 'Birdland',NYC, rec. 21.-24.11.2001
Holland,Dave (b) | Eubanks,Robin (tb,cowbell) | Potter,Chris (ss,as,ts) | Nelson,Steve (vib,marimba) | Kilson,Billy (dr)

1868(9811244) | CD | Suspended Night | EAN 602498112441
Thomas Stanko Quartet
Song For Sarah | Suspendet Variations(I-X)
Oslo,N, rec. July 2003
Stanko,Tomasz (tp) | Wasilewski,Marcin (p) | Kurkiewicz,Slawomir (b) | Miskiewicz,Michal (dr)

1876(9811780) | CD | Evening Falls | EAN 602498117804
Jacob Young Quintet
Blue | Evening Air | Minor Peace | Looking For Jon | Sky | Presence Of Descant | Formerly | The Promise | Falling
Oslo,N, rec. December 2002
Young,Jacob (g) | Eick,Mathias (tp) | Johansen,Vidar (b-cl) | Eilertsen,Mats (b) | Christensen,Jon (dr)

1878/79(9811796) | 2 CD | Which Way Is East | EAN 602498117965
Charles Lloyd-Billy Higgins
What Is Man | Divans | Salaam | All This Is That | Desire | Devotion | Light Of Love | Surrender
Montecito,CA, rec. January 2001
Lloyd,Charles (fl,alto-fl,bass-fl,as,ts,tibetan-oboe,taragota,p,perc,voice) | Higgins,Billy (g,dr,guimbri,syrian-one-dtring,hand-dr,wood-box,perc,voice)

804 SP | CD | Koan
Stephan Micus
Koan(part 1-5)
rec. 1977
Micus,Stephan (g,angklung,bells,bodhran,gender,kyeezee,rabab,sarangi,Shakuhachi,v

Edition Collage | Georg Löffler Musikverlag

EC 441-2 | CD | Talking To A Goblin
Cornelius Claudio Kreusch
Cantus | Stella Backstage | Taiga | Prelude Para Riccarda | One Way In Harlem | Somewhere Over The Rainbow- | Song For Lila-
Oslo,N, rec. October 1990
Kreusch,Cornelius Claudio (p-solo)
Piece For Paul Bley
Kreusch,Cornelius Claudio (p,melodica)

EC 443-2 | CD | Fire
Chris Jarrett
Broken Stone | Blue Nights- | White Nights- | 3 Folk Songs | Rondo 21 | Down South | Dance(from 2 dances) | Fire | Paprika Lady | Transitions
Old School,Hesseln, rec. April 1991
Jarrett,Chris (p)
2 Scenes From '...Liebt Mich Nicht'(for two pianos)
Jarrett,Chris (p-overdubbing)

EC 450-2 | CD | Fisherman's Break
Fisherman's Break
Tashunka Witko | Traum | We Are The Two Only Ones | Wogen | Oriental Spices | Sweet Blue | Fisherman's Dance | Béla | Schwirbel
München, rec. 7.-9.5.1991
Fisherman's Break | Wahl,Wolfgang (cl,ts) | Klentze,Thorsten (g,el-g) | Todd,Gary (b) | Keul,Michael (dr)

EC 452-2 | CD | Say Yes!
Florian Poser Group
Say Yes | Bagdad By Bus | Waltz No.5 | Count It | Malambo | Waiting | Just A Tune | Let's Groove | Count It(short cut)
Monster,NL, rec. 30./31.10.1989

Poser,Florian (vib,marimba) | Anders,Jörn (tp) | Kucan,Vlatko (ss,ts) | Braune,Buggy (p) | Biller,Thomas (b) | Köbberling,Heinrich (dr)
O Amor En Paz(Once I Loved)
Monster,NL, rec. 23.12.1991
Poser,Florian (vib) | Anders,Jörn (tp) | Kucan,Vlatko (ts) | Braune,Buggy (p) | Biller,Thomas (b) | Köbberling,Heinrich (dr)

EC 453-2 | CD | Wes Trane
Helmut Kagerer/Helmut Nieberle
Battle Of Twins | Waltz For AZ | I Wonder Who's In Love With Me | Little Island | Valse À Clignancourt | Sweet Emma- | Jubilation- | Take The Wess Trane | Meant To Be | Mayreh | Hands And Feet | Pintoso- | Querido Luis- | Song For A Mellow Fellow | Eps Vom Schorsch | Tenthousand Only | Joana | Riffs'n Changes | Cute | Safari | Goody Goody
Nürnberg, rec. 13./14.5.1992
Kagerer,Helmut (g) | Nieberle,Helmut (g)

EC 454-2 | CD | Medor Sadness
Fabien Degryse Quintet
Tohama | Nineties | Three Children In The Garden | Medor Sadness | June Spleen | Now | Pauvre Terre | Autumn's Reverie
Beaumont,Belgium, rec. 13.-15.1.1992
Degryse,Fabien (g) | Vann,Erwin (ts) | Legnini,Eric (p) | Rassinfosse,Jean-Louis (b) | Engels,John (dr)

EC 458-2 | CD | Happy Birthday Stéphane
Joe Bawelino Quartet
Studio 1 | Schuga Souni | Moonlight In Vermont | Lola Swing | Happy Birthday Stéphane | Polka Dots And Moonbeams | I'll Close My Eyes | Tenderly | There'll Never Be Another You | Mona | Valse De Weiß | Out Of Nowhere
München, rec. 1993
Bawelino,Joe (g) | Weiß,Traubeli (g) | Wondra,Roland (rh-g) | Opp,Joachim (b)
Night And Day | All Of Me
Bawelino,Joe (g) | Weiß,Traubeli (g) | Wondra,Roland (rh-g) | Opp,Joachim (b) | Sampson,Beate (voc)
Joe Bawelino Quartet & Martin Stegner
Days Of Wine And Roses
Bawelino,Joe (g) | Weiß,Traubeli (g) | Wondra,Roland (rh-g) | Stegner,Martin (v,viola) | Opp,Joachim (b) | Sampson,Beate (voc)
Round About Midnight
Bawelino,Joe (g) | Weiß,Traubeli (g) | Wondra,Roland (rh-g) | Stegner,Martin (v,viola) | Opp,Joachim (b)

EC 460-2 | CD | Glad To See You
Colin Dunwoodie Quartet
Think It Over | Afro Blue | Tact | Fours Bars Shorter | Once Again | Lonnie's Lament | Just A Piece Of Cake | Glad To See You | Bop Or Not To Be
Burgsinn, rec. 4./5.8.1993
Dunwoodie,Colin (fl,ss,as,ts) | Seitz,Ernst (p) | Brenner,Udo (b) | Bozem,Günter (dr,perc)

EC 461-2 | CD | Smile
Maximilian Geller Quartet feat. Melanie Bong
How Insensitive(Insensatez) | You've Changed | I've Never Been In Love Before | Beautiful Love | You Turned The Tables On Me | If You Never Came To Me | Reflexion | Smile | The Very Thought Of You | I'll Never Smile Again | East Of The Sun West Of The Moon | Please Don't Talk About Me When I'm Gone | Spring Will Be A Little Late This Year
München, rec. 4.6.1993
Geller,Maximilian (sax) | Mihilic,Peter (p) | Mariella,Fracesco (b) | Lesczak,Vito (dr) | Bong,Melanie (voc)

EC 463-2 | CD | Tell Her It's All Right
Pino Distaso/Roberto Gotta/Beto Cutillo
Children Games | Tramps Road | Il Fiume | Hostel Psychiatrique
Milano,Italy, rec. March 1992
Gotta,Roberto (tp,fl,sax,perc,sounds) | Distaso,Pino (g) | Cuttillo,Norberto (dr,perc,berimbao)
Ubik | L'Apolide | Meduse | Choro Porteno | Men Hunters | Erwartung
Live in Milano, rec. February 1993
Gotta,Roberto (tp,fl,sax,perc,sounds) | Distaso,Pino (g) | Cuttillo,Norberto (dr,perc,berimbao)

EC 464-2 | CD | Quadru Mana/Quadru Mania
Clemens Maria Peters/Reinhold Bauer
Trenzinho Do Caipira | Lilian | Tanguito | Petite Valse | Benedikt | Camino Inka | Farruca | El Corazon De La Tierra
Straubing, rec. July 1993
Peters,Clemens Maria (fl,g,hungarian-zither,mandoloncello,voc) | Bauer,Reinhold (perc,voc)
Brasilero | Florestal
Peters,Clemens Maria (fl,g,hungarian-zither,mandoloncello,voc) | Bauer,Reinhold (perc,voc) | Grande,Jürgen (b)
Caminando Al Mar(für Bobolina)
Peters,Clemens Maria (fl,g,hungarian-zither,mandoloncello,voc) | Bauer,Reinhold (perc,voc) | Wax,Hans (g) | Grande,Jürgen (b)
Zeilen Der Zärtlichkeit
Peters,Clemens Maria (fl,g,hungarian-zither,mandoloncello,voc) | Bauer,Reinhold (perc,voc) | Wax,Hans (g)

EC 465-2 | CD | Music For Two Pianos
Cornelius Claudio Kreusch/Hans Poppel
Music For Two Pianos(part 1-17)
Concert Hall,Musikhochschule,München, rec. 28.8.1992
Kreusch,Cornelius Claudio (p) | Poppel,Hans (p)

EC 468-2 | CD | Dreaming Of You
EC 468-4 | MC | Dreaming Of You
Traubeli Weiß Ensemble
Swing For Mangala | Laica | Samba Night | How About You | Polka Dots And Moonbeams | All The Things You Are | Estate(Summer) | Cherokee | For Us | Red Label | On A Clear Day You Can See Forever | Amoureux | Magic | Valse De Weiß(II) | Cindy | Dreaming Of You
Simbach/Inn, rec. January 1994
Weiß,Traubeli (g) | Bawelino,Joe (g) | Weiß,Kaki (rh-g) | Lengenfeld,Hans (b)

EC 470-2 | CD | Mostly Harmless...
Mark Alban Lotz/Tjitze Anne Vogel
Free Interlude
Wasserturm,Berlin, rec. 9.2.1992
Lotz,Mark Alban (fl,alto-fl,b-fl,piccolo) | Vogel,Tjitze Anne (b)
Beauty Is A Rare Thing | Portrait Of The Artist As A Small Furry Creature From Betelgeuze IV
Utrecht,NL, rec. 26.10.1992
Lotz,Mark Alban (fl,alto-fl,b-fl,piccolo) | Vogel,Tjitze Anne (b)
Weird Walsje No.1 | Open Spaces | Piccoloco | F.M.G.(Franz Mark gewidmet) | Quasimodo | Wights Waits For Weights | Congenialilty
Concerthall Streekmuziesschool,Alpen a/d Rijn,NL, rec. 8./9.10.1003
Lotz,Mark Alban (fl,alto-fl,b-fl,piccolo) | Vogel,Tjitze Anne (b)
Aeroflotz | Gancini Horo | Sophisticated Lady
Utrecht,NL, rec. 7.11.1993
Lotz,Mark Alban (fl,alto-fl,b-fl,piccolo) | Vogel,Tjitze Anne (b)
So(u)loflotz
Utrecht,NL, rec. 20.12.1993
Lotz,Mark Alban (fl,alto-fl,b-fl,piccolo) | Vogel,Tjitze Anne (b)

EC 472-2 | CD | Bones For Breakfast
Dogs Don't Sing In The Rain
Back To You | 16:55 | Georgia On My Mind | Out Of A Bandbox | Did You Expect That...? | Tinka's Dreams | Bones For Breakfast | U Always Know | See What's Going On | What's Up,Dogs?
Köln, rec. 27.-31.12.1993
Dogs Don't Sing In The Rain | Wennemar,Harald (as) | Van Beek,Romain (g) | Pütz,Mark (synth,grand-p) | Jaegers,Marcus (b) | Cox,Luuk (dr,perc) | Janssen,Digna (voc)
U Always Know(blue remix)
Dogs Don't Sing In The Rain | Huynen,Marc (tp) | Wennemar,Harald (as) | Van Beek,Romain (g) | Pütz,Mark (synth,grand-p) | Jaegers,Marcus (b) | Cox,Luuk (dr,perc) | Janssen,Digna (voc)

EC 482-2 | CD | Pretty Fonky
Mind Games
Los Uncoolos | On Bleeker Street | Can You See The Dancing Gnomes? | Channel Surfer | Murder On Heaven Seven | Mind Spaces | El Uncoolito
München, rec. December 1993
Mind Games | Binder,Andreas 'Andi' (fr-h) | Sterzer,Philipp (fl) | Franzl,Andy Mulo (ss,ts) | Despot,Dalio (p,keyboards) | Lowka,Didi 'D.D.' (b) | Schmitz,Csaba (dr) | Rupcic,Hrvoje (perc) | Hupfauer,Pidi (voc)
Mind Games With Philip Catherine
Caravan | Is Everybody Sees I'm Oldfashioned | Pretty Fonky | Trip To Your Town
Mind Games | Binder,Andreas 'Andi' (fr-h) | Sterzer,Philipp (fl) | Franzl,Andy Mulo (ss,ts) | Catherine,Philip (g) | Despot,Dalio (p,keyboards) | Lowka,Didi 'D.D.' (b) | Schmitz,Csaba (dr) | Rupcic,Hrvoje (perc) | Hupfauer,Pidi (voc)

EC 484-2 | CD | Symmetry
Peter O'Mara Quartet
Fifth Dimesion | The Gift | Catalyst | Seven Up | Chances | Symmetry | Steppin' Out | Expressions | Blues Dues
Brooklyn,NY, rec. 24.-26.5.1994
O'Mara,Peter (g,el-g) | Mintzer,Bob (ss,ts) | Johnson,Marc (b) | Willis,Falk (dr)

EC 485-2 | CD | Caminos
Bajazzo
Fast Lane | Telares | Louizalaan | Santiago | Clouds | Caminos | Sin Pensar | Epilogue | Samba Now!
Burgsinn, rec. August 1993-February 1994
Bajazzo | Breitkreuz,Falk (sax) | Heckel,Jürgen (g,el-g,arr,cavaquinto) | Andrees,Juwe (p,keyboards) | Kubach,Gerhard (b,el-b) | Michailow,Peter (dr) | Marquez,Jose Miguel (perc) | Gioia,Topo (perc)

EC 487-2 | CD | Balanced
Munich Saxophon Family
Road To Gopala | Auf Spurensuche | Profile Of Jackie | Abenteuer Unter Wasser | Balanced-Im Gleichgewicht | Played Twice | Fortsetzung Folgt Now | Latin Quartet No.4 | Transition Inzwischen
München, rec. 10./12./13.11.& 10.12.1993
Munich Saxophone Family | Zoller,Thomas (bs,synth) | Schwaller,Roman (ts) | Seefelder,Jürgen (ts) | Tate,Evan (ss,as)
Federleicht-Kinderleicht
Munich Saxophone Family | Zoller,Thomas (alto-fl) | Schwaller,Roman (cl) | Seefelder,Jürgen (fl,ss) | Tate,Evan (fl,ss)
Minor Journey
Munich Saxophone Family | Zoller,Thomas (bs,synth) | Schwaller,Roman (ts) | Seefelder,Jürgen (ts) | Tate,Evan (ss,as) | Ruhland,Martin (gongs,tam-tam)
Chant
Munich Saxophone Family | Zoller,Thomas (bs) | Schwaller,Roman (ts) | Seefelder,Jürgen (ts) | Tate,Evan (ss,as) | Schneider Heermann (tampura)

EC 488-2 | CD | Green & Orange
Salut!
Minor Swing | Farina | Blues For Wes | Break It Down | Walking The Blues | Valse À Häns'che | Sjerze Djewuschki | I Can Only Let You Feel It... | Valse À Hojok | Sweet Georgia Brown
details unknown, rec. details unknown
Salut! | Wilke,Rüdiger (sax) | Heitbaum,Gerold (g,b) | Winterstein,Ziroli (g) | Glöder,Reinhard (b)
Nuages | Meditation | I'll Remember April | Moonglow
Salut! | Wilke,Rüdiger (sax) | Heitbaum,Gerold (g) | Winterstein,Ziroli (g) | Glöder,Reinhard (b) | Sachs,Helen (voc)

EC 489-2 | CD | Say No More
Gerd Baumann-Alessandro Ricciarelli Quartet
Undicesima Strada(The Crossing Of Water) | Untitled(per Carletto) | Grotta(for Martin) | Braceful | Delphine | Rashim | Jessica | Any Day Now | Until We Sleep(Lullaby)
München, rec. October 1995
Baumann,Gerd (g,el-g,mand,balalaika,fretless-g) | Ricciarelli,Alessandro (g,el-g) | Abrams,Marc (b) | Di Renzo,Davide (dr,perc)

EC 490-2 | CD | Live In Tübingen
Chris Jarrett
Protzeduren | Wanderings | Dance Dreams | Musica Satirica | Ballade | Moon Music
Live at The Sudhaus Tübingen, rec. 13.1.1995
Jarrett,Chris (p-solo)

EC 491-2 | CD | A Contrast Music
Radtke/Bauer/Basmann
Long Nite | Central Guitar | Luriecal | Shankar | Jungle- | Song- | Nightshade Rounds | Meeting Of The Spirits | Pas De Nuit- | Tituber- | A-B-C | Pas De Nuit
Augsburg, rec. August 1995
Radtke,Carsten (g,el-g) | Bauer,Andreas (b) | Basmann,Günther (dr,perc,vibraphonette)
From Uganda
Radtke,Carsten (marimba) | Bauer,Andreas (marimba) | Basmann,Günther (marimba)

EC 492-2 | CD | Hommage
Organ Jazztrio & Martin Weiss
Blues For Steph & Stuff | Rendezvous | Vette | Vouz Et Moi | Lentement Mademoiselle | Artillerie Lourde | Nuits De St.Germain-Des-Pres | Troublant Bolero | Un Mercredi En Juillet | Double Scotch | Nuages
Hannover, rec. 14./15.12.1995
Organ Jazztrio | Bätzel,Matthias (org) | Seidel,Jörg (g) | Bätzel,Alexander (dr) | Weiss,Martin (v,el-v)

EC 494-2 | CD | Feel Alright
Tony Lakatos With The Martin Sasse Trio
Decision | Tune In Three | Fast Food | Twelve Bars But Not Blues | Mr.K. | Feel Allright | Between The Lines | Spring Is Here | Misty
Monster,NL, rec. details unknown
Lakatos,Tony (ss,ts) | Sasse,Martin (p) | Von Kaphengst,Christian (b) | Kutschke,Jürgen (dr)

EC 495-2 | CD | Mellow Acid
Peter Möltgen Quartet
Sugar | Groovin' High | Freedom Jazz Dance | Mr.J.L.M. | A Prayer 4 The Blind | Lover Man(Oh,Where Can You Be?) | St.Thomas | Angel | Nostalgia | Mellow Acid
München, rec. 27.7.-2.8.1995
Möltgen,Peter (fl,piccolo) | Reiter,Adrian (g) | Christ,Peter (org) | Buchacher,Willy (dr)

EC 496-2 | CD | Maximilian Geller Goes Bossa
Maximilian Geller Group
Brigas, Nunca Mais(No More Quarrels) | Vivo Sohando | So Many Stars | Fotografia | Antes Que Seja Tarde | Wild Is The Wind | Chovendo Na Roseira(Double Rainbow) | Ponteio | Watercolor Dream | Retrato En Branco E Prieto | O Morro Nao Tem Vez(One I Loved) | Manha De Carnaval(Morning Of The Carnival) | Poinciana
München, rec. 6./7.2.1996
Geller,Maximilian (fl,as) | Kaupp,Gil (fl-h) | Correa,Fernando (g) | Mihilic,Peter (p) | Teepe,Joris (b) | Lesczak,Vito (dr) | Bong,Melanie (voc) | Tobocman,Susan (voc) | Sciubba,Sabina (voc)

EC 497-2 | CD | Lee Konitz With Oliver Strauch Group & Peter Decker
Lee Konitz With The Oliver Strauch Group & Peter Decker
Yardbird Suite | Lover Man(Oh,Where Can You Be?) | Thing'In | Nightlee Vienna | If You Could See Me Now | Subconscious-Lee | A Little Doctor | Friend Lee | Dim The Light
Klangstudio Leyh,Sandhausen, rec. 20./21.11.1995
Konitz,Lee (as) | Decker,Peter (ts) | Strauch,Oliver (dr) | Schwickerath,Dany (g) | Schädlich,Johannes (b)

EC 499-2 | CD | Thinking Of You
Johannes Herrlich Quintet
Matches In Bermuda | I Hear Music | Final Inspiration | Lament | Bewitched Bothered And Bewildered | Little Bossa | Thinkin' Of You | Polka Dots And Moonbeams | Streching Out
München, rec. 25./26.3.1966
Herrlich,Johannes (tb) | Seizer,Jason (ss,ts) | Lang,Walter (p) | Thys,Nicolas 'Nic' (b) | Hollander,Rick (dr)

EC 500-2 | CD | Winds
Florian Poser
Next Please! | Rainy Day | Funky Marimba | Winds | Lazy Train | Thinkin' Of You | The Musical Clock | Autumn Mood | The Fool On The Hill | Spain | Hello G.
Intersound Tonstudio,?, rec. June 1996
Poser,Florian (vib,xyl,marimba,g,el-p,synth,perc,cymbald,el-b,glockenspiel,grand-p,rh

EC 501-2 | CD | Live
Mind Games With Claudio Roditi
Lost Song | As Everybody Sees I'm Oldfashioned | La Vida Del Senor Lorenzo | Quiet Adventure
Live at The Bayerischer Hof Club,München, rec. 16.4.1996
Mind Games | Roditi,Claudio (tp,fl-h) | Binder,Andreas 'Andi' (fr-h) | Franzl,Andy Mulo (cl,ss,ts) | Wangenheim,Ulrich (fl,as) | Pusch,Bastian (p,keyboards) | Lowka,Didi 'D.D.' (b) | Schmitz,Csaba (dr) | Maass,Stephan (perc) | Wahlandt,Lisa (voc)
Los Uncoolos | Love For Sale | Chicago | Hasta Pronto | Nostalgia | Ata | Moondance | Corcovado(Quiet Nights)
Live at The A-Train Jazzclub,Berlin, rec. 20.4.1996
Mind Games | Roditi,Claudio (tp,fl-h) | Binder,Andreas 'Andi' (fr-h) | Franzl,Andy Mulo (cl,ss,ts) | Wangenheim,Ulrich (fl,as) | Pusch,Bastian (p,keyboards) | Lowka,Didi 'D.D.' (b) | Schmitz,Csaba (dr) | Maass,Stephan (perc) | Wahlandt,Lisa (voc)

EC 503-2 | CD | Imaginary Directions
Eugen Apostolidis Quartet
Destination | Circle | Minor Billy | My Socks | Don't Ask Me | Sula's Dream | Body And Soul | Trial | Speak Low | Groove Positive
Nürnberg, rec. 13./14.3.1995
Apostolidis,Eugen (b) | Sim,Mike (sax) | Farao,Antonio (p) | Calderazzo,Gene (dr)

EC 505-2 | CD | Maimilian Geller Goes Bossa Encore
Maximilian Geller Group
A Felicidade(Happiness)
München, rec. August 1996
Geller,Maximilian (as) | Correa,Fernando (g) | Mihilic,Peter (p,el-p) | Teepe,Joris (b) | Lesczak,Vito (dr)
Maximilian Geller Quartet feat. Melanie Bong
Meditacao(Meditation) | Bolinha De Papel | Caminhos Cruzados | Luiza
Geller,Maximilian (as) | Correa,Fernando (g) | Mihilic,Peter (p,el-p) | Teepe,Joris (b) | Lesczak,Vito (dr) | Bong,Melanie (voc)
Maximilian Geller Quartet feat. Susan Tobocman
Only Trust You Heart | Estate(Summer) | Once I Loved
Geller,Maximilian (as) | Correa,Fernando (g) | Mihilic,Peter (p,el-p) | Teepe,Joris (b) | Lesczak,Vito (dr) | Tobocman,Susan (voc)
Maximilian Geller Quartet feat. Sabina Sciubba
Madolena | Estrada Do Sol | Berimbau | Aruanda
Geller,Maximilian (as) | Correa,Fernando (g) | Mihilic,Peter (p,el-p) | Teepe,Joris (b) | Lesczak,Vito (dr) | Sciubba,Sabina (voc)

EC 506-2 | CD | Vienna's Heardt
Thomas Reimer Trio
Tritone Samba | A Thursday In October | Lester Left Town | Step By Step | Waltz Hollandaise | St.Pepper | Take The Eartrain | Giant Steps | Bee Tango-Waltz | She's Leaving Home | No Name | Vienna's Heardt
München, rec. October 1996
Reimer,Thomas (g) | Bockius,Peter (b) | Pöschl,Sunk (dr)

EC 507-2 | CD | Cookin' Good
Jörg Krückel-Brad Leali Quartet
I Still Do | Squabble | Love Letters | B's Dilemma | When A Sinner Kissed An Angel | Astoria Blues | Ric's Hum | Dumas | Porto Allegro
NYC, rec. 22.8.1997
Leali,Brad (sax) | Krückel,Jörg (p) | Teepe,Joris (b) | Leszak,Vito (dr)

EC 508-2 | CD | Midnight Sun
William Galison-Mulo Franzl Group
Chiaroscuro | Don't Watch The Girls | The Midnight Sun Will Never Set | Never Never Land | Lucita | For Pauline | Yeti | I've Grown Accustomed To Your Face | Too Soon | Joy Spring | I'm Calling You
München, rec. January 1997
Galison,William (harm) | Franzl,Andy Mulo (b-cl,ss,ts) | Binder,Andreas 'Andi' (fr-h) | Doepke,Christian (p,keyboards) | Lowka,Didi 'D.D.' (b,udu-dr) | Eppinger,Stephan (dr)

EC 509-2 | CD | Colours And Standards
Thomas Karl Fuchs Trio
Rhapsody In Blue- | The Man I Love- | 'S Wonderful | There Is No Greater Love | Stella By Starlight | Lullaby Of Birdland | Someday My Prince Will Come | On Green Dolphin Street | Caravan | Body And Soul | Blues For Joe | Run And See | Black Orpheus | Pepper Con Salsa | Colours
details unknown, rec. 6.7.1997
Fuchs,Thomas Karl (grand-p) | Schmalzried,Dieter (b) | Glöckler,Ted (dr)

EC 510-2 | CD | A Brighter Day
Dominik Grimm-Thomas Wallisch Trio
I'm Afraid The Masquerade Is Over - (I'm Afraid) The Masquerade Is Over | Lush Life | Your Song | Part Of Life | Old Devil Moon | My One And Only Love | Summertime Is Over | The Good Life- | There'll Never Be Another You- | I've Heard It All Before | Stockholm Sweetnin' | New York State Of Mind | Who Cares
Studio Brunner,?,Austria, rec. December 1997
Grimm,Dominik (voc) | Wallisch,Thomas (g,el-g) | Gfrerrer,Stefan (b) | Tozzi,Wolfgang (dr)

EC 511-2 | CD | Play Of Colours
Twice A Week & Steve Elson
Dark Rooms | Shaky Shuffler | Toy | Salamander | Play Of Colours | Call Me Bop | Road Runner | Locomonktion | Multiply | To Carry Beans | Blues 2
Studio Stäfa,CH, rec. 27./28.10.1997
Elson,Steve (ss,ts) | Twice A Week: | Koch,Mark (p) | Schläppi,Daniel (b) | Fischer,Peter (dr)

EC 512-2 | CD | Rendezvous
Evelyn Huber-Mulo Franzl
Susanata | Nostalgia | Nature Boy | Rendezvous | Für Mich Soll's Rote Rosen Regnen | Aquatintes-Coloured Water | Valse Lento | Kauf Dir Einen Bunten Luftballon | Little Sunflower | Flambee Montalbanaise | Fata Morgana | Ich Bin Von Kopf Bis Fuß Auf Liebe Eingestellt
München, rec. May 1998
Huber,Evelyn (harp) | Franzl,Andy Mulo (cl,alto-cl,b-cl,ss,ts)

EC 513-2 | CD | Don't Change Your Hair For Me
Sören Fischer Quartet
Tres Tequilas | One For Kirk | Rio-Kyoto-Blues | It's You Or No One | Moonwaltz | My Ship | 3 Views Of Secret | Snow In March
Hannover, rec. 1998
Fischer,Sören (tb,voc) | Prins,Jeanfrancois (el-g) | Hughes,Max (el-b) | Baroudi,Nadja (dr)

EC 514-2 | CD | Le Canzoni Italiana
Alex De Santis Jazz Quartet
Volare | Caruso | T'Ho Volute Bene | O Sole Mio | Sapore Di Sale | Regginella | Malafemmena
Live at The Unterfahrt/Höfbräukeller,München, rec. 10.4.& 22.5.1998
De Santis,Alessandro 'Alex' (ts) | Roberts,Davide (p) | Schießl,Rudi (b) | Elwenspoek,Thomas (dr)

EC 515-2 | CD | Mind Games Plays The Music Of Stan Getz & Astrud Gilberto
Mind Games
Agua De Beber(Water To Drink) | So Danco Samba(I Only Dance The Samba) | Telephone Song | No One Like You(for Ursula) | Corcovado(Quiet Nights) | Orfeo Negro | O Pato(The Duck) | Paixao | Dindi | Voce E Eu(You And I) | Bim Bom | E Luxo So | How Insensitive(Insensatez) | Girl From Ipanema(Garota De Ipanema) | Agua De Beber(Water To Drink-reprise)
München, rec. January 1999
Mind Games | Francel,Mulo (ts) | Mensing,Knud (g) | Lowka,Didi 'D.D.' (b) | Schmitz,Csaba (dr) | Kainar,Robert (perc) | Wahlandt,Lisa (voc)

EC 516-2 | CD | Gypsy Feeling
Jermaine Landsberger Trio

Flair | Nuits De St.Germain-Des-Pres | Michels Tune | Bossalero | Spontaneous Samba | Swing For Oscar | Good Morning Heartache
Regensburg, rec. January 1999
Landsberger,Jermaine (p) | Apostolidis,Eugen (b) | Gmelin,Matthias (dr)
Jermaine Landsberger Trio With Bireli Lagrene
Gypsy Feeling | Cool Blue | Valse Manouche
Landsberger,Jermaine (p) | Lagrene,Bireli (g) | Apostolidis,Eugen (b) | Gmelin,Matthias (dr)

EC 517-2 | CD | European Faces
Matthias Bröde Quartet
Si Peu De Temps | Ich Weiß,Es Wird Einmal Ein Wunder Gescheh'n | Twelve | Ich Bin Von Kopf Bis Fuß Auf Liebe Eingestellt | September Ballad
Köln, rec. 4./5.12.1998
Bröde,Matthias (p,harm) | Eidens,Christoph (vib,marimba) | Heinze,Volker (b) | Astor,Felix (dr)
Matthias Bröde Quintet
European Faces | Pipo's Walk | Up And Down | Ja Ja Ja | She Loves To Dance
Bröde,Matthias (p,harm) | Engstfeld,Wolfgang (ts) | Eidens,Christoph (vib,marimba) | Heinze,Volker (b) | Astor,Felix (dr)

EC 518-2 | CD | The Exhibition
Ulli Jünemann-Morton Ginnerup European Jazz Project
Bedalia | Calvin's Song(One For Mum) | Mr. G's Stepping Shoes | Das Step | Ballad For A.(Little Rose) | Never Again | Tango Al Dente | Olives In The Ashtray
Monster,NL, rec. November 1998
Jünemann,Uli (ss,as) | Ginnerup,Morten (p) | Kappe,Christian (tp,fl-h) | Sohier,Martijn (tb) | Loh,Jens (b) | Grau,Thorsten (dr) | Droste,Silvia (voc)

EC 519-2 | CD | Harlequin Galaxy
Bajazzo
Dixieland | Gimme Five | Half-Bopp Waltz | Harlequin Galaxy | Kalimba Theme | Y2K | Far Away
Burgsinn, rec. 1998
Bajazzo | Breitkreuz,Falk (fl,sax) | Greve,Volker (vib) | Heckel,Jürgen (g,el-g,cavaquino,kalimba,keyboards) | Kubach,Gerhard (b) | Michailow,Peter (dr) | Gioia,Topo (perc) | Joch,Micha (perc)
California
Bajazzo | Breitkreuz,Falk (fl,sax) | Schlott,Volker (as) | Greve,Volker (vib) | Heckel,Jürgen (g,el-g,cavaquino,kalimba,keyboards) | Kubach,Gerhard (b) | Hughes,Max (el-b) | Michailow,Peter (dr) | Gioia,Topo (perc) | Joch,Micha (perc)
3438 | Timekeeper
Bajazzo | Breitkreuz,Falk (fl,sax) | Greve,Volker (vib) | Heckel,Jürgen (g,el-g,cavaquino,kalimba,keyboards) | Kubach,Gerhard (b) | Hughes,Max (el-b) | Michailow,Peter (dr) | Gioia,Topo (perc) | Joch,Micha (perc)

EC 520-2 | CD | A Tribute To B.A.C.H.
Rolf Römer-Bill Dobbins Quartet
Presto | Gigue Aus Der Partita Nr.3 A-Moll | Präludium Nr.12 f-moll | Suite Für Violincello Nr.1 G-Dur | Air On The G String | Opus On B.A.C.H. | Pennies In D(for J.S.B.) | Andante
Köln, rec. 10.-12.8.1999
Römer,Rolf (ss,ts) | Dobbins,Bill (p) | Goldsby,John (b) | Schröteler,Daniel 'Danny' (dr,perc)

EC 521-2 | CD | In The Park
Norbert Emminger Quintet
In The Park | Brasov In The Clouds | Brazil At Union Sqare | Roxi Music | Ma Cheuse | Waltz For A Princess | Round 'Bout Five | Madame | Better Git It In Your Soul
Fürth, rec. 6.5.1999
Emminger,Norbert (bs) | Hahn,Jürgen (tp,fl-h) | Flügel,Michael (p) | Schieferdecker,Markus (b) | Terzic,Dejan (dr)

EC 524-2 | CD | Samba In June
Jermaine Landsberger Trio & Gina
In A Sentimental Mood | Come Fly With Me | Fotografia | That's All | A Felicidade(Happiness) | Teach Me Tonight | It's A Samba
München, rec. 26./27.6.2000
Landsberger,Jermaine (p,keyboards) | Petrocca,Davide (b,el-b) | Gmelin,Matthias (dr) | Gina (voc)
Jermaine Landsberger Trio With Helmut Kagerer & Gina
Corcovado(Quiet Nights) | Brigas, Nunca Mais(No More Quarrels) | Samba In June | Watch What Happens
Landsberger,Jermaine (p,keyboards) | Kagerer,Helmut (g) | Petrocca,Davide (b,el-b) | Gmelin,Matthias (dr) | Gina (voc)

EC 525-2 | CD | Ma Vie En Rose
Corinne Chatel Quintet
L'Effet Que Tu Me Fais | Boplicity | Naima | Wave | How High The Moon | La Vie En Rose | Celtic Song | Les Feuilles Mortes
Live at The Unterfahrt,München, rec. 10.2.2000
Chatel,Corinne (voc) | Sigg,Stefan (tp) | Roberts,Davide (p) | Richter,Jürgen (b) | Elwenspoek,Thomas (dr)

EC 526-2 | CD | 4 In One
Andreas Schnerman Quartet
Rudy My Beer | First Love | Total Eclipse | Little Poolie | Quick Zap | Multichronik | Circle Nightmare | Munchquell | No More Lonely Nights
Hannover, rec. May 2000
Schnermann,Andreas (p) | Bergmann,Matthias (tp,fl-h) | Berns,Pepe (b) | Perko,Matt (dr)

EC 527-2 | CD | Favorite Tunes
Gerwin Eisenhauer's The Gäff Gang feat. Lisa Wahland
50 Ways To Leave Your Lover | Dat Dere | Dindi
Amberg, rec. March 2000
Eisenhauer,Gerwin (dr) | Nagel,Norbert (fl,cl,ss) | Eisenhauer,Rüdiger (g,tres) | Barnikel,Johannes 'Jo' (p) | Diener,Christian (b) | Böck,Charly (perc) | Wahlandt,Lisa (voc)
The Monster And The Flower | Guataca City | Vera Cruz | Footprints | Dom De Illudir | La Charanga
Eisenhauer,Gerwin (dr) | Nagel,Norbert (fl,cl,ss) | Eisenhauer,Rüdiger (g,tres) | Preißinger,Matthias (p) | Diener,Christian (b) | Böck,Charly (perc) | Wahlandt,Lisa (voc)

EC 530-2 | CD | Clark
Clark Terry With The Summit Jazz Orchestra
Walkin' Tiptoe | Clark: | Autumn Leaves- | When I Fall In Love- | Spaceman- | Two Sides | I Want A Little Girl | Miles' Mode | Just Friends | Mumbles
Monster,NL, rec. 29./30.4.2000
Terry,Clark (tp,fl-h,voc) | Weidinger,Tobias (tp,fl-h) | Schlosser,Axel (tp,fl-h) | Klammer,Sven (tp,fl-h) | Auer,Martin (tp,fl-h) | Goetz,Mathias (tb) | Arens,Lars (tb) | Ostermeier,Martin (tb) | Lihocky,Markus (ss,as) | Wangenheim,Ulrich (fl,ss,as) | Wyand,Mark (cl,ts) | Siegmeth,Hugo (ts) | Zimmermann,Jürgen (bs) | Wollny,Michael (p) | Busch,Hanno (g) | Schieferdecker,Markus (b) | Höchstädter,Jean-Paul (dr)
Lady Sophie
Terry,Clark (tp) | Weidinger,Tobias (tp,fl-h) | Schlosser,Axel (tp,fl-h) | Veldkamp,Erik (tp) | Auer,Martin (tp,fl-h) | Goetz,Mathias (tb) | Arens,Lars (tb) | Ostermeier,Martin (tb) | Lihocky,Markus (ss,as) | Wangenheim,Ulrich (fl,ss,as) | Wyand,Mark (cl,ts) | Siegmeth,Hugo (ts) | Zimmermann,Jürgen (bs) | Wollny,Michael (p) | Busch,Hanno (g) | Schieferdecker,Markus (b) | Höchstädter,Jean-Paul (dr)

EC 531-2 | CD | Cole Porter-Live!
Manfred Junker Quartet
From This Moment On
Live at Jazzclub 'Armer Konrad',Weinstadt, rec. 1.-4.3.2001
Junker,Manfred (g) | Suhner,Reto (ss,as,ts) | Merk,Heiner (b) | Deufel,Martin (dr)
I Love Paris | After You | You'd Be So Nice To Come Home To | Love For Sale | Get Out Of Town
Live at Jazzclub 'Altes E-Werk',Öhringen, rec. 1.-4.3.2001
Junker,Manfred (g) | Suhner,Reto (ss,as,ts) | Merk,Heiner (b) | Deufel,Martin (dr)
All Of You
Live at Jazzclub 'Cave 61',Heilbronn, rec. 1.-4.3.2001
Junker,Manfred (g) | Suhner,Reto (ss,as,ts) | Merk,Heiner (b) | Deufel,Martin (dr)
Dream Dancing | I Get A Kick Out Of You
Live at 'Café Wintergarten' Ulm, rec. 1.-4.3.2001
Junker,Manfred (g) | Suhner,Reto (ss,as,ts) | Merk,Heiner (b) | Deufel,Martin (dr)
Manfred Junker
So In Love
details unknown, rec. 17.4.2001
Junker,Manfred (g-solo)

EC 532-2 | CD | I Feel So Smoochie: A Tribute To Nat King Cole
Jörg Seidel Group
I Feel So Smoochie | Sweet Lorraine | You Don't Learn That In School | I'm Thru With Love | The Trouble With Me Is You | Straighten Up And Fly Right | Nature Boy | Walkin' My Baby Back Home | 'Deed I Do | The Boulevard Of Broken Dreams | Yes Sir That's My Baby | Dream A Little Dream Of Me | Mona Lisa
Abensberg, rec. 6.7.2001
Seidel,Jörg (g) | Harper,Lee (fl-h) | Polzer,Peter (p) | Gfrerrer,Stefan (b)

EC 533-2 | CD | Live At The Jazzclub Unterfahrt
Hugo Siegmeth Quintet
One Day With You | Kaul | Siga,Siga | Oscar | Zigeuner
Live at The Unterfahrt,München, rec. 5.10.2000
Siegmeth,Hugo (ts) | Shew,Bobby (tp,fl-h) | Jost,Tizian (p) | Scharf,Harry (b) | Probst,Martin (dr)

EC 534-2 | CD | Bossa Nova Affair | EAN 4014063153425
Lisa Wahlandt & Mulo Francel And Their Fabulous Bossa Band
Little Boat | As Everybody Sees I'm Oldfashioned | Voce E Linda | Berimbau | Only Trust You Heart | Soiree Mignonne | Un Home Et Une Femme | Recado Bossa Nova | Greensleeves | Tu Es A Flor | Senhor Gor
details unknown, rec. 2002
Wahlandt,Lisa (voc) | Francel,Mulo (sax) | Stamm,Ruppert (vib,bow-vibes) | Hinterseher,Andreas (accordeon) | Wolf,Robert (g) | Lang,Walter (p) | Lowka,Didi 'D.D.' (b) | Kainar,Robert (dr,perc) | De Sousa,Borel (berimbau,perc)
O Meu Amor | The Shadow Of Your Smile
Wahlandt,Lisa (voc) | Francel,Mulo (sax) | Stamm,Ruppert (vib,bow-vibes) | Hinterseher,Andreas (accordeon) | Eisenhauer,Rüdiger (g) | Lang,Walter (p) | Diener,Christian (b) | Eisenhauer,Gerwin (dr,perc) | De Sousa,Borel (berimbau,perc)

EC 535-2 | CD | Welcome To My Backyard | EAN 4014063153524
Andreas Schnerman Quartet
The Night You Looked Two Ways | Spanish Harlem | Wurundjeri The Majestic | The English Man And The Girl | Inner Child | Backyard Blues
Köln, rec. April 2002
Schnermann,Andreas (p) | Bergman,Matthias (tp,fl-h) | Berns,Pepe (b) | Perko,Matt (dr,perc)
Andreas Schnerman Quintet
My Secret Friends
Schnermann,Andreas (p) | Bergman,Matthias (tp,fl-h) | Brückner,Kai (g) | Berns,Pepe (b) | Perko,Matt (dr,perc)
Andreas Schnerman Sextet
Backyard Suite
Schnermann,Andreas (p) | Bergman,Matthias (tp,fl-h) | Schoen,Jonas (fl,sax) | Brückner,Kai (g) | Berns,Pepe (b) | Perko,Matt (dr,perc)
Flyfisher
Schnermann,Andreas (p) | Bergman,Matthias (tp,fl-h) | Muche,Matthias (tb) | Schoen,Jonas (fl,sax) | Berns,Pepe (b) | Perko,Matt (dr,perc)

Edition Musikat | Jazz Network

EDM 002 | CD | Insieme | EAN 4022228200013
Lorenzo Petrocca Quartet Feat. Bruno De Filippi
Lean Years | Stella By Starlight | Botta E Risposta | A Weaver Of Dreams | Do You Have A Name | Estate(Summer) | Message From Milan | When I'm Alone | Latin For Luca | Excuse Me | Love Is A Splendored Thing
details unknown, rec. 1995
Petrocca,Lorenzo (g) | DeFilippi,Bruno (harm) | Scheu,Joachim (p) | Petrocca,Davide (el-b) | Fischer,Armin (dr)

EDM 018 | CD | Stop It | EAN 4022228818003
Lozenzo Petrocca Quartet
Almost Like Being In Love | Will You Still Be Mine | Stop It | I Can't Get Started | Opus De Don | Spider Man | Anema E Core | Night Train
Remshalden, rec. 8.& 10.2.1998
Petrocca,Lorenzo (g) | Linke,Jörg (ts) | Marsico,Alberto (org) | Fischer,Armin (dr)

EDM 023 | CD | Limits No Limits | EAN 4022228823007
Frank Kuruc Band
Addis | Ciano Marco | Jaco Past | Used To Have A Yellow Jacket | Blues For Khan | Last Exit To Brooklyn | Cool Hopper | Abricotine | Äwwi Metall
details unknown, rec. 1996
Kuruc,Frank (g) | Stötter,Claus (tp,fl-h) | Möck,Uli 'Ull' (p,keyboards) | Schröder,Eberhard (b) | Kersting,Michael (dr,perc)

EDM 026 | CD | Move | EAN 4022228826008
Davide Petrocca Quartet
Move | Like Someone In Love | A Nightingale Sang In Berkeley Square | Speak Italian | Blue Train | In A Sentimental Mood | Tricotism | Blue Monk | Lac Lamand | Taking A Chance On Love
details unknown, rec. 1999
Petrocca,Davide (b) | Petrocca,Lorenzo (g) | Wagner,Thilo (p) | Drew,Martin (dr)

EDM 034 | CD | Stuttgarter Gitarren Trio Vol.2 | EAN 4022228834003
Stuttgarter Gitarren Trio
Broadway | Sweep | I've Found A New Baby | Square Dance | I Still Do | Tea For Two | Days Of Wine And Roses | Con Alma | Guinea Fowl
Stuttgarter Gitarren Trio | Petrocca,Lorenzo (g) | Fischer,Dieter (g) | Kuruc,Frank (g) | Klaiber,German (b) | Krill,Torsten (dr)

EDM 038 | CD | Blick In Die Welt
Rainer Tempel Quintet
Paris | Kenny's Pennies | The Ordinary Fortune | Ohne Worte | Conan | Fragment | Der Atlas | Blick In Die Welt
Stuttgart, rec. Summer 1999
Tempel,Rainer (p) | Schlosser,Axel (tp,fl-h,co) | Wyand,Mark (ss,ts) | Bodenseh,Markus (b) | Gandela,Andreas (dr)

EDM 038 | CD | Sun Dance | EAN 4022228838001
Digital Masters Feat. Bryan Steele
Sundance(part 1-11)
Stuttgart/NYC, rec. 1999
Schneider-Hollek,Matthias (electronics) | Krämer,Oliver (electronics) | Steele,Bryan (sax)

EDM 047 | CD | But Not For Me | EAN 4022228847003
Antonio Petrocca Trio
Oh Tannenbaum | Move | But Not For Me | Drew | Nicole | Long Ago And Far Away | Someday My Prince Will Come
details unknown, rec. 2000
Petrocca,Antonio (dr) | Wagner,Thilo (p) | Petrocca,Davide (b)
Antonio Petrocca Quartet
Topsy | Lover Man(Oh,Where Can You Be?) | Gentle Rain
Petrocca,Antonio (dr) | Studnitzky,Sebastian (tp,fl-h) | Wagner,Thilo (p) | Petrocca,Davide (b)

EDM 053 | CD | Cello Tango
Eckart Runge-Jacques Ammon
El Choclo | El Dia Que Me Quieras | A Fuego Lento | Tango Alemán | Jalousie | Imagen | Libertango | La Félure | Novitango | Milonga Del Angel | La Muerte Del Angel | La Resureccion Del Angel
Stuttgart, rec. details unknown
Runge,Eckart (cello) | Ammon,Jacques (p) | Hensel,Lothar (bandoneon) | Nagler,Christof (voc)

EDM 056 | CD | Short Stories For Piano
Chris Jarrett
Punic Dance | Four Legends: | Ave Crux | Tremolo | Legend In C Minor | Rhythmic Battle | Return To Ulster(Variations On A Scottish Theme) | Six Preludes: | Adrift | Loom | Douz | Tuba | Cats | Glühwi | Meditatio Carthage | Onward
details unknown, rec. 2001
Jarrett,Chris (p-solo)

EDM 061 | CD | Pedestrian Tales | EAN 4022228861009
Gilbert Paeffgen Trio
Ijri | Pedestrian Tales | Descending Motion | Love Calculator | Lu | Crosspoints | Cous Cous | Gregor Is My Friend | Morgen | Schweigsam | Throw It Away
Zürich,CH, rec. 22./23.1.2001
Paeffgen,Gilbert (dr,dulcimer) | Moret,Patrice (b) | Pfammatter,Hans Peter (p)

EDM 062 | CD | Italy
Franco & Lorenzo Petrocca
Sao Cristovao | Italy | Bellamonte | Meditarranean Bossa | Estate(Summer) | Fotografia
details unknown, rec. details unknown
Petrocca,Franco (g) | Petrocca,Lorenzo (g) | Lima,Alyrio (perc)
O Sole Mio
Petrocca,Franco (g) | Petrocca,Lorenzo (g)
Nostalgia | Caruso
Petrocca,Franco (g)
Standard Medley
Petrocca,Lorenzo (g)

EDM 064 | CD | 9Q | EAN 4022228864000
Müller-Svoboda-Dähn-Kniel
Q1 | Q2 | Q3 | Q4 | Q5 | Q6 | Q7 | Q8 | Q9
Tübingen, rec. 2001
Svoboda,Michael 'Mike' (tb,sousaphone) | Müller,Helmut J. (ss,ts) | Dähn,Fried (el-cello) | Kniel,Manfred (dr)

EDM 067 | CD | Chris Jarrett Trio Plays New World Music | EAN 4022228867001
Chris Jarrett Trio
Al Hadba(The Hunchback Lady) | Punic Dance | Samai Shadd Araban | Tunisian Journey | Cancion Sefardi | Meditation Carthage
Stuttgart, rec. 4.& 6.4.2002
Jarrett,Chris (p) | Hassan,Karim Othman (oud) | Ertek,Shakir (dr,perc)

EDM 068 | CD | Ambiguous | EAN 4022228868008
Lutz Wichert Trio
Zootphone Dance | Despedida Sincopada | You Know You Never Know | La Curda | Loose But Cues | Message Du Dylph | Ambiguous | Twice Is Nice
Stuttgart, rec. 17./18.5.2002
Wichert,Lutz (ts) | Morsey,Alexander (b) | Michler,Robert (dr)

EDM 069 | CD | Ten Strings For Bill Evans | EAN 4022228869005
Carlos Denia-Uli Glaszmann
Turn Out The Stars | Very Early | Re:Person I Knew | Show-Type Tune | Time Remembered | Comrade Conrad | Interplay
details unknown, rec. 2002
Denia,Carlos (g) | Glaszmann,Uli (b)

EDM 071 | CD | Sirkle
Wieland Kleinbub
Sabiza | Sirkle | Where I Live | The Way To The Vestibule | Hard Working Man Blues | Kinderspiel | Vorgestern | Blue Life | Agathon | Dreaming Of Abroad | Bach And Me | Potpüree | Im Lichthaus
Kleinbub,Wieland (p-solo)

EDM 072 | CD | Kamafra Live | EAN 4022228872005
Kamafra
Mambo Influenciado | Ecotopia | Wait And Smile | Made In New York | Chevere | Vatapá | Encore
Live at Stadthalle,Korntal, rec. 2002
Kamafra | Asaf,Ofer (sax) | Müller,Klaus (p) | Petrocca,Franco (b) | Schmidt,Markus (dr) | Carneiro,Edmundo (perc)

EGO | Ego Records GmbH

93020 | CD | Falling Lovers
Litschie Hrdlicka Group
Falling Loves
München, rec. 1993
Hrdlicka,Litschie (b) | Lakatos,Tony (ts) | Bickl,Gerhard 'Zwei' (p) | Eppinger,Stephan (dr,perc)
Thinking About The Future And The Past
Hrdlicka,Litschie (b) | Lakatos,Tony (ss) | Hess,Bernd (g) | Bickl,Gerhard 'Zwei' (keyboards) | Eppinger,Stephan (dr)
Time To Change
Hrdlicka,Litschie (b) | Hess,Bernd (g) | Bickl,Gerhard 'Zwei' (keyboards) | Eppinger,Stephan (dr)
Nobody's Name | Ginger & Jack
Hrdlicka,Litschie (b) | Keller,Rich (fl,midi-wind-controller) | Bickl,Gerhard 'Zwei' (keyboards) | Eppinger,Stephan (dr)
The Touch
Hrdlicka,Litschie (b) | Bickl,Gerhard 'Zwei' (keyboards,grand-p) | Eppinger,Stephan (dr)
Blues For All The Monsters
Hrdlicka,Litschie (b) | Keller,Rick (ts) | Eppinger,Stephan (dr)
Dancing In The Sky
Hrdlicka,Litschie (b) | Baumann,Franz D. (fl-h) | Braun,Thomas (fr-h) | Keller,Rick (fl) | Derlath,Dorothea (fl) | Bickl,Gerhard 'Zwei' (p) | Eppinger,Stephan (dr) | Belmonte,Omar (perc)

95080 | CD | Jazz Portraits
Benny Bailey Quintet
Little 'B'
Ludwigsburg, rec. December 1976
Bailey,Benny (tp,fl-h) | Povel,Ferdinand (ts) | Haider,Joe (p) | Eckinger,Isla (b) | Clarke,Kenny (dr)
Fritz Pauer Trio
For La Rives
Ludwigsburg, rec. November 1977
Pauer,Fritz (p) | Eckinger,Isla (b) | Brooks,Billy (dr)
Stephan Dietz Quartet
Amber Sounds
details unknown, rec. 8.3.1978
Diez,Stephan (g) | Van Rooyen,Ack (fl-h) | Todd,Gary (b) | Canedy,Todd (dr)
Joe Haider Trio
Capricorn
details unknown, rec. October 1971
Haider,Joe (p) | Eckinger,Isla (b) | Favre,Pierre (dr)
Dave Liebman Quintet
Thoughts Of Loss
Ludwigsburg, rec. February 1976
Liebman,Dave (ss,ts) | Isham,Mark (tp,fl-h) | Formanek,Michael (b) | Barsimento,Mike (dr) | Williams,Jeff (dr)
Horace Parlan Quartet
Billie's Bossa
details unknown, rec. March 1980
Parlan,Horace (p) | Gaynair,Wilton (ss,ts) | Eckinger,Isla (b) | Brooks,Billy (dr)
Sigi Busch-Alexander Sputh Duo
Lydian Waltz
details unknown, rec. April 1980
Busch,Sigi (b) | Sputh,Alexander (g)
Dusko Goykovich-Joe Haider Quintet
Summit
Innsbruck, rec. May 1980
Goykovich,Dusko (tp) | Haider,Joe (p) | Schwaller,Roman (ts) | Eckinger,Isla (b) | Queen,Alvin (dr)
Austria Drei
Lonely Frog
details unknown, rec. July 1979
Austria Drei | Pirchner,Werner (vib,marimba) | Pepl,Harry (g) | Roidinger,Adelhard (b) | Canedy,Todd (dr)
Changes
Blues Open
details unknown, rec. December 1980
Changes | Beckerhoff,Uli (tp) | Engstfeld,Wolfgang (ss,ts) | Kröger,Ed (p) | Beier,Detlev (b) | Weiss,Peter (dr)
Litschie Hrdlicka Group
Nobody's Name
München, rec. 1993
Hrdlicka,Litschie (b) | Keller,Rich (fl,midi-wind-controller) | Bickl,Gerhard 'Zwei' (keyboards) | Eppinger,Stephan (dr)

95100 | CD | Staubfrei
Max Neissendorfer Trio
Ich Bin Von Kopf Bis Fuß Auf Liebe Eingestellt | Staubfrei | Präludium Nr.1 | Bei Mir Bist Du Schön | Lichter Der Venus | Ich Weiß Nicht Was Soll Es Bedeuten | Jetzt Oder Nie | Dein Ist Mein Ganzes Herz | Ich Brech' Die Herzen Der Stolzesten Frau'n | Nebenan | Caprifischer | Wir Machen Musik | Unsa Oide Kath Mecht A No
Kempten, rec. 1995
Neissendorfer,Max (p) | Poffet,Michael (b) | Elias,David (dr)

96170 | CD | Vamos A Ver
Omar Belmonte's Latin Lover
Vamos A Ver | Mejor Me Pongo A Bailar
Belmote,Omar (dr,perc,voc) | Vila,Daniel (keyboards,voc) | Leis,Daniel (g,voc) | Giuliano,Gustavo (b) | Contanzaro,Agostino (dr) | Enriquez,Hugo (perc,voc) | Medina,Roberto (perc) | Silzer,Werner (perc) | Hoisl-Rausch,Sabine (perc) | Vieti (perc) | Del Cioppo,Jorge (voc)

Einstein Music | ZYX Music GmbH

EM 01081 | CD | Love Again | EAN 4025745010813
Tok Tok Tok
Winterwonderland | Eleanor Rigby | Wade In The Water | Bebeep
Hamburg, rec. June 2000
Tok Tok Tok | Klein,Morton (ts) | Fiedler,Frank (b) | Akinro,Tokunbo (voc)
Don't Let The Sun | Have A Talk With God
Tok Tok Tok | Klein,Morton (ts) | Staringer,Richie (fender-rhodes) | Fiedler,Frank (b) | Akinro,Tokunbo (voc)
Look Of Love | Satisfaction | Love Again | Walk On The Wild Side | O Tannenbaum | Waters Of March
Tok Tok Tok | Klein,Morton (ts) | Casimir,Olaf (b) | Akinro,Tokunbo (voc)

EM 21103 | CD | It Took So Long | EAN 4025745211036
It Took So Long | The Weight | Like Music From The Skies | Secret Of The Night | Nothing Stays The Same | I Cannot Sleep | A Day In The Life | Something Restless | Spooky | Can You Keep It? | When You're Far Away
Hamburg, rec. 2003
Tok Tok Tok | Akinro,Tokunbo (voc) | Klein,Morton (ts,g,mouth-dr) | Staringer,Richie (fender-rhodes) | Fiedler,Frank (b)

EM 91051 | CD | 50 Ways To Leave Your Lover | EAN 4025745910519
Day Tripper | I'll Never Fall In Love Again | Straighten Up And Fly Right | I Wish | Her Majesty
Hamburg, rec. 1999
Tok Tok Tok | Klein,Morton (ts) | Fiedler,Frank (b) | Akinro,Tokunbo (voc)
Hallelujah
Tok Tok Tok | Klein,Morton (ts) | Staringer,Richie (fender-rhodes) | Fiedler,Frank (b) | Akinro,Tokunbo (voc)
Sometimes I Feel Like A Motherless Child | Boogie Woogie Bossa Nova
Tok Tok Tok | Klein,Morton (ts) | Staringer,Richie (fender-rhodes) | Casimir,Olaf (b) | Akinro,Tokunbo (voc)
Monkey See Monkey Do | Alone Again(Naturally) | 50 Ways To Leave Your Lover | Crime Of Crimes | The Jack
Tok Tok Tok | Klein,Morton (ts) | Casimir,Olaf (b) | Akinro,Tokunbo (voc)

Elektra | Warner Classics & Jazz Germany

7559-60023-2 | CD | Bobby McFerrin
Bobby McFerrin Group
Dance With Me
San Francisco,CA, rec. 1982
McFerrin,Bobby (voc) | Feldman,Victor (p,el-p) | Maunu,Peter (g) | Klein,Larry (b) | Guerin,John (dr) | Nash,Kenneth (perc)
Feline
Brooklyn,NY, rec. 1982
McFerrin,Bobby (voc) | Erquiaga,Steve (g) | Karsh,Ken (g) | Feldman,Stu (b) | Preston,James (dr)
You've Really Got A Hold On Me
San Francisco,CA, rec. 1982
McFerrin,Bobby (voc) | Snow,Phoebe (voc) | Maunu,Peter (g) | Caro,Joe (g) | Siegler,John (b) | Vilardi,Frank (dr)
All Feets Can Dance
NYC, rec. 1982
McFerrin,Bobby (voc) | Bennett,H.B. (dr)
Moondance | Peace | Chicken
Los Angeles,CA, rec. 1982
McFerrin,Bobby (voc) | Feldman,Victor (p) | Klein,Larry (b) | Guerin,John (dr)
Sightless Bird
San Francisco,CA, rec. 1982
McFerrin,Bobby (el-p,voc) | Maunu,Peter (g) | Erquiaga,Steve (g) | Jackson,Randy (b) | Preston,James (dr)
Jubilee
Los Angeles,CA, rec. 1982
McFerrin,Bobby (voc) | Feldman,Victor (p,el-p) | Klein,Larry (b) | Guerin,John (dr) | Background Vocals
Halucinations
NYC, rec. 1982
McFerrin,Bobby (voc)

7559-60168-2 | CD | Steps Ahead
Steps Ahead
Pools | Islands | Loxodrome | Both Sides Of The Coin | Skyward Bound | Northern Cross | Trio(An Improvisation)
NYC, rec. ca.1983
Steps Ahead | Brecker,Michael (ts) | Mainieri,Mike (vib,marimba,synth) | Elias,Eliane (p) | Gomez,Eddie (b) | Erskine,Peter (dr)

7559-60318-2 | CD | Inside Moves
Grover Washington Jr. Orchestra
Inside Moves
NYC, rec. June 1984
Washington Jr.,Grover (ss,as,bs) | Gale,Eric (g) | Tee,Richard (el-p) | Miller,Marcus (synth,el-b) | Gadd,Steve (dr) | MacDonald,Ralph (perc,congas,computer-dr) | Lucien,Jon (voc)
Dawn Song | Secret Sounds
Washington Jr.,Grover (ss,as,bs) | Gale,Eric (g) | Tee,Richard (el-p) | Miller,Marcus (synth,el-b) | Williams,Buddy (dr) | MacDonald,Ralph (perc,congas,computer-dr) | Lucien,Jon (voc)
Sassy Stew
Washington Jr.,Grover (ss,as,bs) | Gale,Eric (g) | Tee,Richard (el-p) | Miller,Marcus (synth,el-b) | Williams,Buddy (dr) | MacDonald,Ralph (perc,congas,computer-dr) | MacDonald,Anthony (perc) | Lucien,Jon (voc)
Jet Stream | When I Look At You
Washington Jr.,Grover (ss,as,bs) | Gale,Eric (g) | Tee,Richard (el-p) | Miller,Marcus (synth,el-b) | Williams,Buddy (dr) | MacDonald,Ralph (perc,congas,computer-dr) | MacDonald,Anthony (perc) | Lucien,Jon (voc) | Groves,Lani (voc) | Lewis,Yvonne (voc) | Stewart,Maeretha (voc)
Watching You Watching Me
Washington Jr.,Grover (ss,as,bs) | Gale,Eric (g) | Tee,Richard (el-p) | Jackson,Anthony (el-b) | Williams,Buddy (dr) | MacDonald,Ralph (perc,congas,computer-dr) | Lucien,Jon (voc) | Harris,Hilda (voc) | Lewis,Yvonne (voc) | Eaton,William (voc) | Floyd,Frank (voc) | Saunders,Zack (voc) | McCullough,Yolanda (voc) | Brown,Alfred (v,cond) | Nadien,David (strings) | Abramowitz,Jonathan (cello) | Moore,Kermit (strings) | Israel,Theodore (viola) | Barber,Julian (viola) | Eley,Lewis (strings) | Allen,Sanford (v) | Garvey,Winterton (strings) | Gersham,Paul (v) | Romondi,Matthew (strings) | Lookofsky,Harry (v,vola) | Morgenstern,Marvin (strings) | Ellen,Max (v)

7559-60351-2 | CD | Modern Times
Steps Ahead
Safari | Oops! | Self Portrait | Modern Times
NYC, rec. Jan./Feb.1984
Steps Ahead | Brecker,Michael (ss,ts) | Mainieri,Mike (vib,marimba,synth) | Bernhardt,Warren (keyboards) | Gomez,Eddie (b) | Erskine,Peter (dr,perc)
Old Town
Steps Ahead | Brecker,Michael (ss,ts) | Mainieri,Mike (vib,marimba,synth) | Bernhardt,Warren (keyboards) | Peyton,Craig (synth) | Gomez,Eddie (b) | Erskine,Peter (dr,perc) | Levin,Tony (chapman-stick)
Radio-Active
Steps Ahead | Brecker,Michael (ss,ts) | Mainieri,Mike (vib,marimba) | Bernhardt,Warren (keyboards) | Peyton,Craig (synth) | Gomez,Eddie (b) | Erskine,Peter (dr,perc)
Now You Know
Steps Ahead | Brecker,Michael (ss,ts) | Mainieri,Mike (vib,marimba) | Bernhardt,Warren (keyboards) | Loeb,Chuck (g) | Gomez,Eddie (b) | Erskine,Peter (dr,perc)

7559-60366-2 | CD | The Voice
Bobby McFerrin
I Feel Good | Blackbird | Donna Lee- | Big Top- | We're In The Money- | T.J.
Live in Köln/Mannheim, rec. 17.& 19.3.1984
McFerrin,Bobby (voice)
Take The 'A' Train | The Jump | El Brujo | In My Own Walkman | Music Box I'm Alone
Live,Hamburg/Stuttgart, rec. 21.& 26.3.1984
McFerrin,Bobby (voice)

7559-60537-2 | CD | Paradise
Grover Washington Jr. Septet
Paradise | Icey | The Answer In Your Eyes | Asia's Theme | Shana | Tell Me About It Now | Feel It Comin'
Philadelphia,PA, rec. details unknown
Washington Jr.,Grover (fl,ss,ts,bs,p) | Blake Jr.,John E. (v) | Simmons,James 'Sid' (p,el-p) | Steacker,Richard Lee (g,el-g) | Brown,Tyrone (b,el-b) | Vinson,Millard 'Pete' (dr,synares) | Gibbs,Leonard (perc,congas,tambourine,triangle)

EmArCy | Universal Music Germany

013027-2 | CD | Jazz In Paris:Don Byas-Laura
Don Byas Quintet
Summertime | Flamingo | Stardust | Ol' Man River | A Pretty Girl Is Like A Melody
Paris,France, rec. 4.7.1950
Byas,Don (ts) | Tilche,Jean-Jacques (g) | Simmons,Art (p) | Grasset,Roger (b) | Marty,Claude (dr)
Night And Day | Easy To Love | Where Or When | The Man I Love | Georgia On My Mind | Over The Rainbow
Paris,France, rec. 19.4.1951
Byas,Don (ts) | Sasson,Jean-Pierre (g) | Vander,Maurice (p) | Medvedkjo,Georges 'Popov' (b) | Bennett,Benny (dr)
Don Byas Quartet
Laura | Somebody Loves Me | Old Folks At Home | Riviera Blues(Blues A La Don) | Smoke Gets In Your Eyes | I Cover The Waterfront
Paris,France, rec. 10.4.1952
Byas,Don (ts) | Simmons,Art (p) | Benjamin,Joe (b) | Clark,Bill (dr)

013028-2 | CD | Jazz In Paris:Oscar Peterson-Stephane Grappelli Quartet Vol.1
Oscar Peterson-Stephane Grappelli Quartet
Them There Eyes | Flamingo | Makin' Whoopee | Looking At You | Walkin' My Baby Back Home | My One And Only Love | Thou Swell
Paris,France, rec. 22./23.2.1973
Grappelli,Stephane (v) | Peterson,Oscar (p) | Orsted-Pedersen,Niels-Henning (b) | Clarke,Kenny (dr)

013029-2 | CD | Jazz In Paris:Oscar Peterson-Stephane Grappelli Quartet Vol.2
I Won't Dance | The Folks Who Live On The Hill | Autumn Leaves | My Heart Stood Still | Blues For Musidisc | If I Had You
Grappelli,Stephane (v) | Peterson,Oscar (p) | Orsted-Pedersen,Niels-Henning (b) | Clarke,Kenny (dr)

013030-2 | CD | Jazz In Paris:Louis Armstrong:The Best Live Concer Vol.1
Louis Armstrong And His All Stars
When It's Sleepy Time Down South | Back Home Again In Indiana | Tiger Rag | When I Grow Too Old To Dream | Perdido | Hello Dolly | On The Alamo | A Kiss To Build A Dream On | Lover Come Back To Me | Can't Help Lovin' Dat Man | Mop Mop | Blueberry Hill
Live at The Palais Du Sport,Paris,France, rec. 4.6.1965
Armstrong,Louis (tp,voc) | Glenn,Tyree (tb) | Shu,Eddie (cl) | Kyle,Billy (p) | Catlett,Buddy (b) | Barcelona,Danny (dr) | Brown,Jewel (voc)

013031-2 | CD | Jazz In Paris:Louis Armstrong-The Best Live Concert Vol.2
Muskrat Ramble | Volare | Cocktails For Two | Stompin' At The Savoy | It's Easy To Remember | Teach Me Tonight | I Left My Heart In San Francisco | My Man | Bill Bailey Won't You Please Come Home | When The Saints Go Marching In | Hello Dolly
Armstrong,Louis (tp,voc) | Glenn,Tyree (tb) | Shu,Eddie (cl) | Kyle,Billy (p) | Catlett,Buddy (b) | Barcelona,Danny (dr) | Brown,Jewel (voc)

013043-2 | CD | Jazz In Paris:Chet Baker-Broken Wing
Chet Baker Quartet
Broken Wing | Black Eyes | Oh! You Crazy Moon | How Deep Is The Ocean | Blue Gilles | Black Eyes(alt.take) | How Deep Is The Ocean(alt.take)
Paris,France, rec. 28..12.1978
Baker,Chet (tp) | Markovitz,Phil (p) | Jenny-Clark,Jean-Francois (b) | Brillinger,Jeff (dr)

013271-2 | CD | Early Years
Ketil Bjornstad Group
Blamann(Blue Moon)
Oslo,N, rec. 1970's
Bjornstad,Ketil (p,keyboards) | Riisnaes,Knut (sax) | Eberson,Jon (g) | Andersen,Arild (b) | Thowsen,Pal (dr)
Drommen Om Havet(Ocean Dream)
Bjornstad,Ketil (p,keyboards) | Riisnaes,Knut (sax) | Andersen,Arild (b) | Thowsen,Pal (dr)
Berget Det Bla(Blue Mountain)
Bjornstad,Ketil (p,keyboards) | Eberson,Jon (g) | Andersen,Arild (b) | Thowsen,Pal (dr)
Sommernat Ved Fjorden(Summer Night By The Fjord)
Bjornstad,Ketil (p,keyboards) | Ekomess,Oyvind (cello) | Westberg Andersen,Ellen (voc)
Gjesten(The Visitor) | Selena
Bjornstad,Ketil (p,keyboards) | Knutsen,Pete (g) | Alterhaug,Bjorn (b) | Thowsen,Pal (dr)
Finnes Du Noensteds Ikveld(Are You There,Somewhere,Tonight)
Bjornstad,Ketil (p,keyboards) | Riisnaes,Knut (sax) | Andersen,Arild (b) | Thowsen,Pal (dr)
Apne Havner(Open Harbours)
Bjornstad,Ketil (p,keyboards) | Riisnaes,Knut (sax) | Andersen,Arild (b) | Thowsen,Pal (dr) | Larsen,Sverre (wind-harp)
Tidevann(Tide)
Bjornstad,Ketil (p,keyboards) | Eberson,Jon (g) | Riisnaes,Knut (sax) | Venaas,Terje (b) | Thowsen,Pal (dr)
Avskjet Pa Forskudd(Farewell In Advance)
Bjornstad,Ketil (p,keyboards) | Thowsen,Pal (dr)
Dager Pa Skajaeret(Days By The Shore)
Bjornstad,Ketil (p,keyboards) | Riisnaes,Knut (sax) | Eberson,Jon (g) | Knutsen,Pete (g) | Venaas,Terje (b) | Thowsen,Pal (dr)
Dedication
Bjornstad,Ketil (p,keyboards) | Andersen,Arild (b) | Christensen,Jon (dr)
Naermere(Closer) | Klovnen Synger(The Clown Wings)
Bjornstad,Ketil (p,keyboards) | Eberson,Jon (g) | Andersen,Arild (b) | Christensen,Jon (dr)

013482-2 | CD | Live In New York | EAN 044001348228
Roswell Rudd-Archie Shepp Group
Keep Your Heart Right | Acute Motelitis | Steam | Pazuzu | We Are The Blues | Ujama | Bamako | Slide By Slide | Deja Vu | Hope No.2
Live at The Jazz Standerd,NYC, rec. 23./24.9.2000
Rudd,Roswell (tb) | Shepp,Archie (ts,p,voc) | Moncur III,Grachan (tb) | Workman,Reggie (b) | Cyrille,Andrew (dr) | Baraka,Amiri (recitation)

013545-2 | CD | Jazz In Paris:Django Reinhardt-Django's Blues | EAN 044001354526
Django Reinhardt And The Quintet Du Hot Club De France
September Song | Brazil | I'll Never Smile Again(take 1) | I'll Never Smile Again(take 2) | New York City | Django's Blues | Love's Mood | I Love You
Paris,France, rec. 18.7.1947
Reinhardt,Django (g) | Rostaing,Hubert (cl) | Vees,Eugene (g) | Soudieux,Emmanuel (b) | Jourdan,Andre (dr)
Topsy | Moppin' The Bride(Micro) | Insensiblement | Mano | Blues Primitif | Gypsy With A Song(take 1) | Gypsy With A Song(take 2)
Paris,France, rec. 14.10.1947
Reinhardt,Django (g) | Rostaing,Hubert (cl) | Reinhardt,Joseph (g) | Soudieux,Emmanuel (b) | Jourdan,Andre (dr)

013610-2 | CD | Palationo Chap.3 | EAN 044001361029
Palatino
Tempete A Florence | Sud-Quest Jump | Sapore Di Si Minore | La Sevigliana | Soleil A Genes | Into Somewhere | City Boy | Drum Storm | Aeroidea | Mormorio | Arte Povera | Holy | In My Dream | Juke | In A Misty Night
Pernes Les Fontaines,France, rec. 1.-4.10.2000
Palatino | Fresu,Paolo (tp) | Ferris,Glenn (tb) | Benita,Michel (b) | Romano,Aldo (dr)

013622-2 | CD | Grace | EAN 044001362224
Ketil Bjornstad Group
No Man Is An Island | Lover's Infinteness | The Bait | White | The Anniversary | Love's Growth | Song | Love's Usury | Naked | Grace | The Indifferent | Mystery | The Canonization | Take A Flat Map... | No Man Is An Island(Finale)
Live at the Vossajazz Festival,Voss,Norway, rec. 14.4.2000
Bjornstad,Ketil (p) | Hofseth,Bendik (sax,voc) | Aarset,Eivind (g) | Andersen,Arild (b) | Drecker,Anneli (voc) | Bang,Jan (live-sampling) | Gurtu,Trilok (perc)

014060-2 | CD | Jazz In Paris:Saxophones À Saint-Germain Des Prés | EAN 044001406027
Hubert Fol Quartet
A Fine Romance | They Can't Take That Away From Me | You Go To My Head
Paris,France, rec. 18.1.1956
Fol,Hubert (as) | Urtreger,René (p) | Ingrand,Jean-Marie (b) | Viale,Jean-Louis (dr)
Michel De Villers Octet
Cat On The Stairs | These Foolish Things Remind Me On You | I Only Have Eyes For You | Penitas De Amor
Paris,France, rec. 1954
De Villers,Michel (bs) | Verstraete,Charles (tb) | Fol,Hubert (as) | Meunier,Maurice (ts) | Daly,Geo (vib) | Persiany,Andre (p,arr) | Bret,Alix (b) | Planchenault,Bernard (dr)
Sonny Criss Quartet
Mighty Low | Don't Blame Me | Black Coffee | We'll Be Together Again
Paris,France, rec. 10.10.1962
Criss,Sonny (as) | Renaud,Henri (p) | Gaudry,Michel (b) | Combelle,Philippe (dr)
Sonny Criss Quintet
Early And Later(part 1) | Early And Later(part 2) | Blues Pour Flirter No.2
Paris,France, rec. April 1963
Criss,Sonny (as) | Thomas,Rene (g) | Arvanitas,Georges (p,org) | Michelot,Pierre (b) | Combelle,Philippe (dr)

014103-2 | CD | Puschnig-Scherer | EAN 044001410321
Wolfgang Puschnig-Uli Scherer
Hommage | India | In A Sentimental Mood | No.12 | The Sadness Of Yuki | Du Red'st Allweil Vom Scheiden | Traces Of Taegum | Georgia On My Mind | Echoes Of The Deep | Traces Of The East | Naima | Stara Baska
Wien,Austria, rec. 7./8.4.1999
Puschnig,Wolfgang (fl,as,hojak) | Scherer,Uli (p)

014378-2 PMS | CD | Jazz In Paris:Chet Baker Quartet Plays Standards
Chet Baker Quartet
Summertime | You Go To My Head | Tenderly | Lover Man(Oh,Where Can You Be?) | There's A Small Hotel | Autumn In New York | These Foolish Things Remind Me On You | I'll Remember April
Paris,France, rec. 24.10.1955
Baker,Chet (tp) | Goustin,Gerard (p) | Bond,Jimmy (b) | Dahlander,Nils-Bertil (dr)

014722-2 | CD | Toots Thielemans & Kenny Werner | EAN 044001472220
Toots Thielemans-Kenny Werner Duo
Dolphin Dance | The Dolphin | All The Way- | My Way- | Tender Is The Night | You Must Believe In Spring- | Windmills Of Your Mind- | I Will Wait For You- | Smile | Inspiration | Windows | Time Remembered- | Very Early- | Autumn Leaves | When You Wish Upon A Star- | Someday My Prince Will Come- | What A Wonderful World
Biblo Kalmthout, rec. 13.-15.6.2001
Thielemans,Jean 'Toots' (harm) | Werner,Kenny (p,keyboards,string-synth)

016671-2 | CD | Universal Time | EAN 044001667121
Joachim Kühn Group
Still In Thalys | The Night | Concorde | Monroe
Brooklyn,NY, rec. 31.5./1.6.2001
Kühn,Joachim (p) | Colley,Scott (b) | Hernandez,Horacio 'El Negro' (dr)
Thoughts About My Mother
Kühn,Joachim (as) | Potter,Chris (ts) | Colley,Scott (b) | Hernandez,Horacio 'El Negro' (dr)
Begegnungen(Meetings) | August In Paris | Phrasen | The Freedom In There | Three Ways In One | Round Trip
Brooklyn,NY, rec. 3./4.1.2001
Kühn,Joachim (p,as) | Potter,Chris (ts) | Portal,Michel (b-cl,as) | Colley,Scott (b) | Hernandez,Horacio 'El Negro' (dr)

017265-2 | CD | New Life | EAN 044001726521
Ketil Bjornstad
Blue Man | The Night | Song For The Sun | By The Fjord | Ophelia's Arrival | The Token | Sara | Late Summer | Turning Around | Days In Paris | When Sleep Brings Us Apart | New Life
Oslo,N, rec. 6.12.1997
Bjornstad,Ketil (p-solo)

017267-2 | CD | The Bach Variations | EAN 044001726729
Prelude In C Sharp Minor(BWV 849) | Fugue In C Sharp Minor(BWV 849) | Variation 1-23
Bjornstad,Ketil (p-solo)

017513-2 | CD | Trio | EAN 044001751325
Jesse Van Ruller Trio
High-Higher-Her | Everything Happens To Me | Sno' Peas | Take The Cake | Have A Heart | Trick Of The Light | Blame It On My Youth | Con Alma | Without A Song | My One And Only Love | Way Out
Fendal Studio,?, rec. November 2001
Van Ruller,Jesse (g) | Van Der Hoeven,Frans (b) | Vink,Martijn (dr)

017993-2 | CD | Canta Brazil | EAN 044001799327
Kenny Barron Group With Trio De Paz
Zumbi | Clouds | Paraty | Until Then | Bachiao | Thoughts And Dreams | Dona Maria
NYC, rec. 13./14.2.2002
Barron,Kenny (p) | Drummond,Anne (fl) | Trio De Paz | Lubambo,Romero (g) | Matta,Nilson (b) | Fonseca,Duduca (dr) | Valtinho (perc)
This One
Barron,Kenny (p) | Drummond,Anne (fl) | Trio De Paz | Lubambo,Romero (g) | Matta,Nilson (b) | Fonseca,Duduca (dr) | Valtinho (perc) | Adnet,Maucha (voc)

018417-2 | CD | Jazz In Paris:Gérard Badini-The Swing Machine | EAN 044001841729
Gérard Badini Quartet
It Don't Mean A Thing If It Ain't Got That Swing | Let's Do It | Sam Woodyard Is Back In Town | Cute | Asphodèle | Stop Look And Listen
Paris,France, rec. 30.5.1975
Badini,Gerard (ts) | Fol,Raimond (p,celeste) | Gaudry,Michel (b) | Woodyard,Sam (dr)

018418-2 | CD | Jazz In Paris:Henri Crolla-Quand Refleuriront Les Lilas Blancs? | EAN 044001841828

Henri Crolla Quartet
Quand Refleuriront Las Lilas Blancs? | Je Cherche Après Titine | Have You Met Miss Jones | La Romance De Maitre Pathelin | Ay,Ay,Ay | I Only Have Eyes For You
Paris,France, rec. November 1955
Crolla,Henri (g) | Solal,Martial as Lalos Bing (p) | Soudieux,Emmanuel (b) | David,Jacques (dr)
Henri Crolla Sextet
Love For Sale | September Song | Out Of Nowhere | Sweet Georgia Brown | Solitude | Yardbird Suite | Tenderly
Paris,France, rec. June 1955
Crolla,Henri (g) | Meunier,Maurice (cl,ts) | Hausser,Michel (vib) | Vander,Maurice (p) | Soudieux,Emmanuel (b) | David,Jacques (dr)

018419-2 | CD | Jazz In Paris:Jack Diéval-Jazz Aux Champs Elysées | EAN 044001841927
Jack Dieval And The J.A.C.E. All-Stars
Idicatif | Introduction | Jumpin' At The Woodside | Solitude | Do Not Disturb | The Man I Love | In A Mellow Tone | Rif Hi-Fi | The Nearness Of You | Blues For Polydor | Outro | Indicatif(2)
Live at The Theatre Pigalle,Paris,France, rec. 24.7.1957
Dieval,Jack (p) | Lafitte,Guy (ts) | De Villers,Michel (bs) | Distel,Sacha (g) | Rovere,Paul (b) | Garros,Christian (dr)
Jack Dieval Trio
Learnin' The Blues | Tenderly | Pour Penser À Toi | Donne Ta Main Et Viens
Paris,France, rec. 26.3.1956
Dieval,Jack (p) | unkn. (b,dr)

018420-2 | CD | Jazz In Paris:Dizzy Gillespie And His Operatic Strings Orchestra | EAN 044001842023
Dizzy Gillespie Quartet And The Operatic String Orchestra
Stormy Weather | The Very Thought Of You | Jalousie | I've Got You Under My Skin | Fine And Dandy | Pennies From Heaven
Live at The Theatre Des Champs-Elysees,Paris,France, rec. 22.2.1953
Gillespie,Dizzy (tp) | Legge,Wade (p) | Hackney,Lou (b) | Jones,Al (dr) | Operatic String Orchestra,The | details unknown
Dizzy Gillespie Orchestra And The Operatic String Orchestra
Night And Day | My Old Flame | I Waited For You | Sweet And Lovely | The Man I Love | I Don't Stand A Ghost Of A Chance With You | Night And Day | My Old Flame | Sweet And Lovely(alt.take 2) | Sweet And Lovely(alt.take 1)
Live at The Theatre Des Champs-Elysees,Paris,France, rec. 6.4.1952
Gillespie,Dizzy (tp) | Gosset,Andre (tb) | Vasseur,Benny (tb) | Destanges,Guy (tb) | Gillot,Albert (cl) | Bigerille,Rene (fl) | Ross,Arnold (p) | Tilche,Jean-Jacques (g) | Benjamin,Joe (b) | Clark,Bill (dr) | Boyer,Joe (arr) | White,Daniel (arr) | Operatic String Orchestra,The | details unknown

018421-1 | CD | Jazz In Paris:Stephane Grappelli-Django | EAN 044001842122
Stephane Grappelli Quartet
You Better Go Now | Like Someone In Love | Daphne
Paris,France, rec. 7.3.1962
Grappelli,Stephane (v) | Cavalli,Pierre (g) | Pedersen,Guy (b) | Humair,Daniel (dr)
Django | Nuages | Alabamy Bound | Le Tien | Minor Swing | Soft Winds | Pent-Up House | How About You | Makin' Whoopee
Paris,France, rec. 9.3.1962
Grappelli,Stephane (v) | Cavalli,Pierre (g) | Pedersen,Guy (b) | Humair,Daniel (dr)

018423-2 | CD | Jazz In Paris:Bobby Jaspar-Jeux De Quartes | EAN 044001842320
Bobby Jaspar Quintet
Cliff Cliff | Phenil Isopropil Amin | Misterioso | Lullaby Of The Leaves | Waiting For Irene | Chasing The Bird | Speak Low | Jeux De Quartes | Jeux De Quartes(alt.take)
Paris,France, rec. 19.12.1958
Jaspar,Bobby (fl) | Hausser,Michel (vib) | Rovere,Paul (b) | Clarke,Kenny (dr) | Canto,Umberto (perc)
There'll Never Be Another You | Le Jamf | Doxology(Memory Of Dick)
Paris,France, rec. 20.12.1958
Jaspar,Bobby (fl) | Sadi,Fats (vib) | Merritt,Jymie (b) | Clarke,Kenny (dr) | Canto,Umberto (perc)

018425-2 | CD | Jazz In Paris:The Bernard Peiffer Trio Plays Standards | EAN 044001842528
Bernard Peiffer Trio
Memory Of A Dream | Prelude To A Kiss | What More Can A Woman Do | Collard Greens And Black Eyed Peas
Paris,France, rec. 12.12.1954
Peiffer,Bernard (p) | Ingrand,Jean-Marie (b) | Paraboschi,Roger (dr)
Cheek To Cheek | You Are My Seetheart | Lullaby Of Birdland
Paris,France, rec. 13.12.1954
Paraboschi,Roger (dr) | Ingrand,Jean-Marie (b) | Peiffer,Bernard (p)
Someone To Watch Over Me | Willow Weep For Me | Deep Purple | Good For Nothin'(But Love)
Paris,France, rec. 15.12.1954
Paraboschi,Roger (dr) | Ingrand,Jean-Marie (b) | Peiffer,Bernard (p)
If I Had You | Polka Dots And Moonbeams | Just You Just Me
Paris,France, rec. 16.12.1954
Paraboschi,Roger (dr) | Ingrand,Jean-Marie (b) | Peiffer,Bernard (p)
I Surrender Dear | Sweetie Pie | Ain't Misbehavin'
Paris,France, rec. 17.12.1954
Paraboschi,Roger (dr) | Ingrand,Jean-Marie (b) | Peiffer,Bernard (p)

018426-2 | CD | Jazz In Paris:Sammy Price And Doc Cheatham Play Gershwin | EAN 044001842627
Sammy Price
I Can't Give You Anything But Love | Can't Help Lovin' Dat Man | Keepin' Out Of Mischief Now | Rosetta | Someone To Watch Over Me | Baby Won't You Please Come Home | Blues In My Heart | St.Louis Blues | Tata's Blues | Tea For Two | Cinema's Boogie | Willow Weep For Me | Pinetop's Boogie Woogie | Valetta | On The Sunny Side Of The Street | Adieu
Paris,France, rec. 9.4.1926
Price,Sammy (p-solo)
Doc Cheatham And Sammy Price
Oh! Lady Be Good | The Man I Love | I Got Rhythm | Summertime | Somebody Loves Me | Embraceable You | 'S Wonderful | Rhapsody In Blue
Paris,France, rec. October 1958
Cheatham,Doc (tp) | Price,Sammy (p)

018427-2 | CD | Jazz In Paris:Django Reinhardt-Nuits De Saint-Germain-Des-Prés | EAN 044001842726
Django Reinhardt Quintet
Vamp
Paris,France, rec. 11.5.1951
Reinhardt,Django (g) | Fol,Hubert (as) | Fol,Raimond (p) | Michelot,Pierre (b) | Lemarchand,Pierre (dr)
Django Reinhardt Sextet
Double Whiskey | Dream Of You | Impromptu
Reinhardt,Django (g) | Hullin,Bernard (tp) | Fol,Hubert (as) | Fol,Raimond (p) | Michelot,Pierre (b) | Lemarchand,Pierre (dr)
Keep Cool | Fleche D'Or | Troublant Bolero | Nuits De St.Germain-Des-Pres
Paris,France, rec. 30.1.1952
Reinhardt,Django (g) | Guerin,Roger (tp) | Fol,Hubert (cl) | Fol,Raimond (p) | Michelot,Pierre (b) | Lemarchand,Pierre (dr)
Crazy Rhythm | Fine And Dandy
Paris,France, rec. 30.1.1953
Reinhardt,Django (g) | Guerin,Roger (tp) | Fol,Hubert (cl) | Vander,Maurice (p) | Michelot,Pierre (b) | Lemarchand,Pierre (dr)
Django Reinhardt Quartet
Anouman | D.R. Blu
Reinhardt,Django (g) | Vander,Maurice (p) | Michelot,Pierre (b) | Lemarchand,Pierre (dr)

018428-2 | CD | Jazz In Paris:Django Reinhardt-Nuages | EAN 044001842825
Blues For Ike | September Song | Night And Day | Insensiblement | Manoir De Mes Reves | Nuages | Brazil | Confessin'
Paris,France, rec. 10.3.1953
Reinhardt,Django (g) | Vander,Maurice (p) | Michelot,Pierre (b) | Viale,Jean-Louis (dr)
Django Reinhardt Quintet
Le Soir | Chez Moi | I Cover The Waterfront | Deccaphonie
Paris,France, rec. 8.4.1953
Reinhardt,Django (g) | Sadi,Fats (vib) | Solal,Martial (p) | Michelot,Pierre (b) | Lemarchand,Pierre (dr)

018446-2 | CD | Jazz In Paris:Joe Newman-Jazz At Midnight-Cootie Williams | EAN 044001844621
Joe Newman And His Band
Blues On The Champ-Elysées | A Girl Named Rigmor | Lover Man(Oh,Where Can You Be?)
Paris,France, rec. 8.10.1956
Newman,Joe (tp) | Cocker,Henry (tb) | Wess,Frank (ts) | Graham,Bill (bs) | Vander,Maurice (p) | Jones,Eddie (b) | Payne,Sonny (dr)
Cootie Williams Quintet
Night Train | Mood Indigo | Lil' Darlin' | Easy Swing | Three O'Clock In The Morning
Live at The Olympia,Paris,France, rec. 3.11.1959
Williams,Cootie (tp) | Clark,George (ts) | Jarvis,Arnold (org) | Dale,Larry (g,voc) | Jesnkins,Lester (dr) | Newman,Joe (tp)

018447-2 | CD | JazzIn Paris:Harlem Piano In Montmartre | EAN 044001844720
Garland Wilson
Blues En Si Bémol | Get Up Bessie | Mood Indigo | China Boy | Minnie The Moocher's Wedding Day | Rhapsody In Love
Paris,France, rec. November 1924
Kinney Nina Mae (voc) | Wilson,Garland (p) | Wilson,Garland (p-solo)
Herman Chittison
Honeysuckle Rose | Bugle Call Rag | You'll Be My Lover | Stormy Weather | St.Louis Blues | Red Jill Rag | Nagasaki | Tres
Paris,France, rec. May-July 1934
Chittinson,Herman (p-solo)
Heat Wave | Miss Otis Regrets
Day,Arita (voc) | Chittinson,Herman (p)
Dany Polo Trio
You Made Me Love You | Montmartre Ioan
Paris,France, rec. 30.1.1939
Polo,Danny (cl) | Wilson,Garland (p) | Mengo,Jerry (dr)
Charlie Lewis Trio
Coquette | Long Ago And Far Away | Some Of These Days | April In Paris
Paris,France, rec. 21.4.1941
Lewis,Charles (p) | Soudieux,Emmanuel (b) | Mengo,Jerry (dr)

064784-2 | CD | Jazz In Paris:Blossom Dearie-The Pianist/Les Blue Stars | EAN 044006478425
Blossom Dearie Trio
The Continental | The Boy Next Door | They Can't Take That Away From Me | Moonlight Saving Time | The Surrey With The Fringe On Top | April In Paris | Blue Moon | Down The Depths Of The 90th Floor
Paris,France, rec. 1955
Dearie,Blossom (p) | Garst,Herman (b) | Planchenault,Bernard (dr)
Les Blue Stars
La Legende Du Pays Des Oiseaux(Lullaby Of Birdland) | Lettre A Virginie | Toute Ma Joie(That's My Girl) | Embrasse-Moi Bien
Paris,France, rec. November 1954
Les Blue Stars | Dearie,Blossom (voc) | Legrand,Christiane (voc) | De Waleyne,Janine (voc) | Young,Nadine (voc) | Sadi,Fats (voc,vib) | Chevallier,Christian (voc) | Guerin,Roger (voc,tp) | Mercadier,Jean (voc) | Legrand,Michel (p,arr) | Orchestra | details unknown

065004-2 | CD | Jazz In Paris:Sarah Vaughan-Vaughan And Violins | EAN 044006500423
Sarah Vaughan With The Quincy Jones Orchestra
Please Be Kind | The Midnight Sun Will Never Set | Live For Love | Misty
Paris,France, rec. 7.7.1958
Vaughan,Sarah (voc) | Jones,Quincy (arr,ld) | Hrasko,Marcel (as) | Sims,Zoot (ts) | Boucaya,William (bs) | Hrasko,Joe (bs) | Hausser,Michel (vib) | Bright,Ronnell (p) | Cullaz,Pierre (g) | Davis,Richard (b) | Clarke,Kenny (dr) | Strings
I'm Lost | Love Me | That's All
Paris,France, rec. 8.7.1958
Vaughan,Sarah (voc) | Jones,Quincy (arr,ld) | Hrasko,Marcel (as) | Sims,Zoot (ts) | Boucaya,William (bs) | Hrasko,Joe (bs) | Hausser,Michel (vib) | Bright,Ronnell (p) | Cullaz,Pierre (g) | Davis,Richard (b) | Clarke,Kenny (dr) | Strings
Day By Day | Gone With The Wind | I'll Close My Eyes | The Thrill Is Gone
Paris,France, rec. 12.7.1958
Vaughan,Sarah (voc) | Jones,Quincy (arr,ld) | Bright,Ronnell (p) | Vander,Maurice (p) | Davis,Richard (b) | Paraboschi,Roger (dr) | Fields,Kansas (dr) | Strings

159085-2 | CD | Meant To Be!
Fleurine With Band And Horn Section
Lazy And Satisfied | My Souldance With You | Favorite Love Affair | Velejar | Meant To Be! | My Hearts Escapade | I've Got Just About Everything | When I Think Of One | Escolher | It's All In The Mind | Better Call Me Now | One Dream Come | High In The Sky
Englewood Cliffs,NJ, rec. 1./2.10.1995
Fleurine (voc) | Harrell,Tom (fl-h) | Moore,Ralph (ts) | Van Ruller,Jesse (g) | Rosnes,Renee (p) | McBride,Christian (b) | Drummond,Billy (dr) | Horn Section: | Sickler,Don (fl-h) | Porcelli,Bobby (fl,as) | details unknown

159734-2 PMS | CD | Jazz In Paris:Dizzy Gillespie-The Giant
Dizzy Gillespie Quintet
Stella By Starlight | I Waited For You | Girl Of My Dreams | Serenity
Paris,France, rec. 13.4.1973
Gillespie,Dizzy (tp) | Drew,Kenny (p) | Orsted-Pedersen,Niels-Henning (b) | Clarke,Kenny (dr) | Canto,Humberto (tumbas)
Fiesta Mojo
Gillespie,Dizzy (tp) | Griffin,Johnny (ts) | Drew,Kenny (p) | Orsted-Pedersen,Niels-Henning (b) | Clarke,Kenny (dr) | Canto,Humberto (tumbas)

159821-2 PMS | CD | Jazz In Paris:Sidney Bechet Et Claude Luther
Sidney Bechet And His Orchestra
Honeysuckle Rose | High Society | On The Sunny Side Of The Street | I Can't Believe That You're In Love With Me
Paris,France, rec. 16.5.1949
Bechet,Sidney (ss) | Bayol,Gerard (tp) | Vasseur,Benny (tb) | Bernard,Eddie (p) | Sasson,Jean-Pierre (g) | De Fatto,Guy (b) | Jourdan,Andre (dr)
Sidney Bechet And His Feetwarmers
Wrap Your Troubles In Dreams | It Had To Be You | Baby Won't You Please Come Home | Please Don't Talk About Me When I'm Gone | Ooh! Boogie! | After You've Gone | I'm Going Way Down Home | Margie
Paris,France, rec. 3.11.949
Bechet,Sidney (ss) | Bernard,Eddie (p) | Michelot,Pierre (b) | Clarke,Kenny (dr)
Claude Luter Et Ses L'Orientais
Gatemouth | South African Blues | Snake Rag | Weary Way Blues | Sweet Lovin' Man | Panama
Paris,France, rec. 23.6.1948
Luter,Claude (cl) | Merlin,Pierre (tp) | Rabanit,Claude (tp) | Jospin,Mowgli (tb) | Azzi,Christian (p) | Philippe,Claude (bj) | Bianchini,Roland (b) | Pacout,Michel (dr)

159823-2 PMS | CD | Jazz In Paris:Lucky Thompson-Modern Jazz Group
Lucky Thompson's Modern Jazz Group Tentet
Souscription | Influence | Marcel Le Fourreur | Meet Quincy Jones | G And B
Paris,France, rec. 5.& 7.3.1956
Thompson,Lucky (ts) | Gerard,Fred (tp) | Guerin,Roger (tp) | Vasseur,Benny (tb) | Hameline,Teddy (as) | Chautemps,Jean-Louis (ts) | Boucaya,William (bs) | Renaud,Henri (p) | Quersin,Benoit (b) | Paraboschi,Roger (dr)
Lucky Thompson's Modern Jazz Group Quartet
The Man I Love | There's No You | Tight Squeeze | Gone With The Wind
Paris,France, rec. 7.3.1956
Thompson,Lucky (ts) | Renaud,Henri (p) | Quersin,Benoit (b) | Garros,Christian (dr)

159825-2 PMS | CD | Jazz In Paris:Lionel Hampton-Ring Dem Bells
Lionel Hampton All Stars
Ring Dem Bells | Psychedelic Sally | Hamp's Thing
Paris,France, rec. 25.5.1976
Hampton,Lionel (vib,voc) | Gousset,Claude (tb) | Attenoux,Michel (as) | Badini,Gerard (ts) | Fol,Raimond (p) | Mackel,Billy (g) | Gaudry,Michel (b) | Woodyard,Sam (dr)
Seven Come Eleven
Hampton,Lionel (vib) | Attenoux,Michel (as) | Doriz,Danny (vib) | Fol,Raimond (p) | Mackel,Billy (g) | Gaudry,Michel (b) | Woodyard,Sam (dr)
On The Sunny Side Of The Street | Blue Lou | Vibraphone Blues
Paris,France, rec. 26.5.1976
Hampton,Lionel (vib,voc) | Attenoux,Michel (as) | Mullins,Reynolds (p,org) | Mackel,Billy (g) | Gaudry,Michel (b) | Woodyard,Sam (dr)

159852-2 PMS | CD | Jazz In Paris:Guy Lafitte-Blue And Sentimental
Guy Lafitte Sextet
Blue And Sentimental | She's Funny That Way | If I Had You | Get Happy | Stardust | I've Got The World On A String | Where Or When | Krum Elbow Blues
Paris,France, rec. 1954
Lafitte,Guy (ts) | Daly,Geo (vib) | Bonal,Jean (g) | Fol,Raimond (p) | Bret,Alix (b) | Planchenault,Bernard (dr)
Guy Lafitte-Peanuts Holland And Their Orchestra
Boogie Blues
Lafitte,Guy (ts) | Holland,Peanuts (tp) | Daly,Geo (vib) | Pelletier,Jean-Claude (p) | Blareau,Charlie (b) | Reilles,André 'Mac Kac' (dr)

159853-2 PMS | CD | Jazz In Paris:Django Reinhardt-Swing From Paris
Quintet Du Hot Club De France
St.Louis Blues | Limehouse Blues | I Got Rhythm
Paris,France, rec. 30.9.1935
Quintet Du Hot Club De France | Grappelli,Stephane (v) | Reinhardt,Django (g) | Reinhardt,Joseph (g) | Ferret,Pierre (g) | Vola,Louis (b)
Stephane Grappelli And His Hot Four
I've Found A New Baby | It Was So Beautiful | China Boy | Moonglow | It Don't Mean A Thing If It Ain't Got That Swing
Paris,France, rec. 21.10.1935
Grappelli,Stephane (v) | Reinhardt,Django (g) | Reinhardt,Joseph (g) | Ferret,Pierre (g) | Rovira,Tony (b)
Quintet Du Hot Club De France
Billets Doux | Swing From Paris | Them There Eyes | Three Little Words | Appel Direct
Paris,France, rec. 14.6.1938
Quintet Du Hot Club De France | Grappelli,Stephane (v) | Reinhardt,Django (g) | Reinhardt,Joseph (g) | Vees,Eugene (g) | Grasset,Roger (b)
Hungaria(take 1) | Hungaria(take 2)
Paris,France, rec. 21.3.1939
Quintet Du Hot Club De France | Grappelli,Stephane (v) | Reinhardt,Django (g) | Reinhardt,Joseph (g) | Ferret,Pierre (g) | Soudieux,Emmanuel (b)

159854-2 PMS | CD | Jazz In Paris:Django Reinhardt-Swing 39
Jeepers Creepers(take 1) | Jeepers Creepers(take 2) | Japanese Sandman | I Wonder Where My Baby Is Tonight(take 1) | I Wonder Where My Baby Is Tonight(take 2)
Quintet Du Hot Club De France | Grappelli,Stephane (v) | Reinhardt,Django (g) | Reinhardt,Joseph (g) | Ferret,Pierre (g) | Soudieux,Emmanuel (b)
Tea For Two(take 1) | Tea For Two(take 2) | My Melancholy Baby(take 1) | Time On My Hands | Twelfth Year(take 1) | Twelfth Year(take 2) | My Melancholy Baby(take 2)
Paris,France, rec. 23.3.1939
Quintet Du Hot Club De France | Grappelli,Stephane (v) | Reinhardt,Django (g) | Reinhardt,Joseph (g) | Ferret,Pierre (g) | Soudieux,Emmanuel (b)
Japanese Sandman | Tea For Two | I Wonder Where My Baby Is Tonight | Hungaria
Paris,France, rec. 17.5.1939
Quintet Du Hot Club De France | Grappelli,Stephane (v) | Reinhardt,Django (g) | Reinhardt,Joseph (g) | Ferret,Pierre (g) | Soudieux,Emmanuel (b)

159941-2 PMS | CD | Jazz In Paris
Bobby Jaspar Quintet
Bag's Groove | Memory Of Dick | Milestones | Minor Drop | I'll Remember April | You Stepped Out Of A Dream | I Can't Get Started | A Night In Tunisia
Paris,France, rec. 27. 29.12.1955
Jaspar,Bobby (fl,ts) | Distel,Sacha (g) | Urtreger,René (p) | Quersin,Benoit (b) | Viale,Jean-Louis (dr)

510134-2 | 2 CD | People Time
Stan Getz-Kenny Barron
East Of The Sun West Of The Moon | Night And Day | I'm Okay | Like Someone In Love | Stablemates | I Remember Clifford | Gone With The Wind | First Song(For Ruth) | There Is No Greater Love | The Surrey With The Fringe On Top | People Time | Softly As In A Morning Sunrise | Hush-A-Bye | Soul Eyes
Live at The 'Jazzhus' Montmartre,Copenhagen, rec. 3.-6.3.1991
Getz,Stan (ts) | Barron,Kenny (p)

514072-2 | CD | Swingin' Easy
Sarah Vaughan And Her Trio
Shulie A Bop | Lover Man(Oh,Where Can You Be?) | Polka Dots And Moonbeams | Prelude To A Kiss | You Hit The Spot | If I Knew Then(What I Know Now) | Body And Soul | They Can't Take That Away From Me
NYC, rec. 2.4.1954
Vaughan,Sarah (voc) | Malachi,John (p) | Benjamin,Joe (b) | Haynes,Roy (dr)
I Cried For You(Now It's Your Turn To Cry Over Me) | All Of Me | Words Can't Describe | Pennies From Heaven | Linger Awhile
NYC, rec. 14.2.1957
Vaughan,Sarah (voc) | Jones,Jimmie (p) | Davis,Richard (b) | Haynes,Roy (dr)

514073-2 | CD | For Those In Love
Dinah Washington And Her Orchestra
I Get A Kick Out Of You | Blue Gardenia | Easy Living | You Don't Know What Love Is | This Can't Be Love | My Old Flame | I Could Write A Book | Make The Man Love Me | Ask A Woman Who Knows | If I Had You
NYC, rec. 15.-17.3.1955
Washington,Dinah (voc) | Terry,Clark (tp) | Cleveland,Jimmy (tb) | Quinichette,Paul (ts) | Payne,Cecil (bs) | Kelly,Wynton (p) | Galbraith,Barry (g) | Betts,Keter (b) | Cobb,Jimmy (dr) | Jones,Quincy (arr)

538184-2 | CD | Free Form
Joe Harriott Quintet
Formation | Coda | Abstract Blues | Impression- | Parallel | Straight Lines | Calypso | Tempo
London,GB, rec. 1960
Harriott,Joe (as) | Keane,Shake (tp) | Smythe,Pat (p) | Goode,Coleridge (b) | Seamen,Phil (dr)

542231-2 | CD | Jazz In Paris:Elek Baczik
Elek Bacsik Trio
Conception | Work Song | Over The Rainbow | Three To Got Ready | The Midnight Sun Will Never Set | So What | Goodbye | Room 608
Paris,France, rec. 1963
Bacsik,Elek (g) | Pedersen,Guy (b) | Humair,Daniel (dr)
Elek Bacsik Quartet
Loin Du Brésil
Bacsik,Elek (g) | Pedersen,Guy (b) | Humair,Daniel (dr) | Riestra,Pepito (perc)

Tenderly | La Saison Des Pluies | Gemini
Bacsik,Elek (g) | Vander,Maurice (org) | Pedersen,Guy (b) | Humair,Daniel (dr)

542320-2 | CD | The Diminished Augmented System
Joachim Kühn
Harmonic Bearing | Rhythmic Inclinations | Formal Schematics | Come As It Goes | Subsequent Influence | The View(From The House) | Deep Low | Range | Portrait Of My Mother | Thought Of JF | Sex Is For Woman | Pointe Dancing | Researching Has No Limits | Foodstamps On The Moon | Sarabande(from Partita 2) | Ciacona(from Partita 2) | Allemande(from Partita 2)
Hamburg/Schloss Elman, rec. 25.6.& 17.7.1999
Kühn,Joachim (p-solo)

548148-2 PMS | CD | Jazz In Paris:Michel Legrand-Paris Jazz Piano
Michel Legrand Trio
Sous Le Ponts De Paris | Paris In The Spring | April In Paris | Sous Le Ciel De Paris | Paris Canaille | Paris Je T'Aime | I Love Paris | The Last Time I Saw Paris | Moulin Rouge | La Vie En Rose
Paris,France, rec. 1959
Legrand,Michel (p) | Pedersen,Guy (b) | Wallez,Gus (dr)

548150-2 PMS | CD | Jazz In Paris:Jean-Luc Ponty-Jazz Long Playing
Jean-Luc Ponty Quartet
Une Nuit Au Violon | Spanish Castle | Snigglin' The Blues | I Want To Talk About You
Paris,France, rec. June/July 1964
Ponty,Jean-Luc (v) | Louiss,Eddie (org) | Rovere,Gilbert 'Bibi' (b) | Humair,Daniel (dr)
Jean-Luc Ponty Quintet
Modo Azul | Au Privave
Ponty,Jean-Luc (v) | Portal,Michel (fl) | Louiss,Eddie (org) | Rovere,Gilbert 'Bibi' (b) | Humair,Daniel (dr)
Jean-Luc Ponty Quartet
Postlude In C | Manoir De Mes Reves | YTNOP Blues | A Night In Tunisia | Satin Doll
Ponty,Jean-Luc (v) | Louiss,Eddie (org) | Pedersen,Guy (b) | Humair,Daniel (dr)

548151-2 PMS | CD | Jazz In Paris:Claude Bolling Plays Original Piano Greats
Claude Bolling
The Preacher | In A Sentimental Mood | Honeysuckle Rose- | Ain't Misbehavin'- | Alligator Crawl | Viper's Drag | Round About Midnight | King Porter Stomp | Echoes Of Spring | Morning Air
Paris,France, rec. 1972
Bolling,Claude (p-solo)

548207-2 PMS | CD | Jazz In Paris:Earl Hines-Paris One Night Stand
Earl Hines Trio
Love Is Just Around The Corner | You're Getting To Be A Habit With Me | Hallelujah | I Got It Bad And That Ain't Good | Royal Garden Blues | Save It Pretty Mama | If I Could Be With You One Hour Tonight | Walkin' My Baby Back Home | Moonlight In Vermont | Makin' Whoopee | Muskrat Ramble | Am I Waisting My Time | 'S Wonderful | Perdido | Nice Work If You Can Get It | Muskrat Ramble(alt.take)
Paris,France, rec. 15./16.11.1957
Hines,Earl 'Fatha' (p) | Pedersen,Guy (b) | Wallez,Gus (dr)

548317-2 PMS | CD | Jazz In Paris:Barney Wilen-Jazz Sur Saine
Barney Wilen Quartet
Vamp | Menilmontant | John's Groove | B.B.B. Bag's Barney Blues | Swingin' Parisian Rhythm(Jazz Sur Saine) | J'ai Ta Main | Nuages | La Route Enchantée | Que Reste-T-Il De Nos Amours | Minor Swing
Paris,France, rec. 13./14.2.1958
Wilen,Barney (ts) | Jackson,Milt (vib) | Heath,Percy (b) | Clarke,Kenny (dr)
Barney Wilen Quintet
Swing '39 | Epistrophy
Wilen,Barney (ts) | Jackson,Milt (vib) | Heath,Percy (b) | Clarke,Kenny (dr) | M'Bow,Gana (perc)

548318-2 PMS | CD | Jazz In Paris:Jazz & Cinéma Vol.1
Un Temois Dans La Ville | Temoin Dans La Ville | La Pendaison | Melodie Pour Les Radio-Taxis | Pousuite Et Metro | Ambiance Pourpre | Premeditation Das L'Appartement | La Vie N'est Qu'une Lutte | Complainte Du Chauffeur | Sur L'Antelle | S.O.S. Radio-Taxis | Final Au Jardin D'Acclimation
Paris,France, rec. April 1959
Wilen,Barney (ss,ts) | Dorham,Kenny (tp) | Jordan,Duke (p) | Rovere,Paul (b) | Clarke,Kenny (dr)
Alain Goraguer Orchestra
J'rai Cracher Sur Vos Tombes | Blues De Memphis(1) | Generique | Theme D'Amour | Theme De Liz | Blues De Memphis(2) | Surprise-Partie Au Bord De L'Eau
Paris,France, rec. 1959
personal included: | Guerin,Roger (tp) | Guiot,Raymond (fl) | Grenu,Georges (ts) | Hauser,Michel (vib) | Goraguer,Patrick (p,comp,arr,ld) | Garden,Claude (harm) | Michelot,Pierre (b) | Garros,Christian (dr)

548790-2 | CD | Jazz In Paris | EAN 731454879026
Lou Bennett Trio
Peter's Waltz | Repetition | Meeting
Paris,France, rec. January 1966
Bennett,Lou (org) | Thomas,Rene (g) | Clarke,Kenny (dr)
Lou Bennett Trio With The Paris Jazz All Stars
Pentacostal Feeling | Echoes | That Preachin' Man
Paris,France, rec. March 1966
Bennett,Lou (org) | Thomas,Rene (g) | Clarke,Kenny (dr) | Paris Jazz All Stars,The | Byrd,Donald (tp,arr) | details unknown
Lou Bennett Trio
Easy Living
Bennett,Lou (org) | Thomas,Rene (g) | Clarke,Kenny (dr)

548791-2 | CD | Jazz In Paris:Raymond Fol-Les 4 Saisons | EAN 731454879125
Raymond Fol Big Band
Concerto No.1:Le Printemps | Allegro- | Largo- | Allegro- | Concerto No.2: L'Été | Allegro Non Molto- | Adagio- | Presto- | Concerto No.3:L'Automne | Allegro- | Adagio Molto- | Allegro- | Concerto No.4 | Allegro Non Molto- | Largo- | Allegro-
Paris,France, rec. 9.& 15.7.1965
Fol,Raimond (p,celeste,comp,ld) | Thomas,Maurice (tp) | Gerard,Fred (tp) | Guerin,Roger (tp) | Julien,Ivan (tp) | Poli,Michel (tp) | Katarzynski,Raymond (tb) | Verstraete,Charles (tb) | Guizien,Christian (tb) | Verdier,Camille (b-tb) | Dumont,Pierre (fr-h) | Guy,Raymond (fl) | Plockyn,Michel (fl) | Fournier,Denis (cl,as) | Nourredine,Jacques (b-cl,as) | Griffin,Johnny (ts) | Chanson,Dominique (ts) | Grenu,Georges (cl,ts) | Chautemps,Jean-Louis (bs) | Sadi,Fats (vib,bongos) | Cullaz,Pierre (g) | Woode,Jimmy (b) | Taylor,Arthur 'Art' (dr) | Viale,Jean-Louis (perc) | Lalue,Georges (perc) | Cavallaro,Armand (perc)

548792-2 | CD | Jazz In Paris:Le Jazz Groupe De Paris Joue André Hodeir | EAN 731454879224
Andre Hodeir And His Jazz Group De Paris
On A Scale | Parisian Thoroughfare | Bicinum | Evanescence
Paris,France, rec. 26.6.1956
Hodeir,Andre (cond,arr) | Liesse,Jean (tp) | Guerin,Roger (tp) | Peck,Nat (tb) | Algedon,Jean (as) | Grenu,Georges (ts) | Sadi,Fats (vib) | Migiani,Armand (p) | Michelot,Pierre (b) | Garros,Christian (dr)
Jordu | Tension Detente
Paris,France, rec. 27.6.1956
Hodeir,Andre (cond,arr) | Liesse,Jean (tp) | Guerin,Roger (tp) | Peck,Nat (tb) | Algedon,Jean (as) | Grenu,Georges (ts) | Sadi,Fats (vib) | Migiani,Armand (p) | Michelot,Pierre (b) | Garros,Christian (dr)
Paradoxe I | Criss Cross
Hodeir,Andre (cond,arr) | Liesse,Jean (tp) | Guerin,Roger (tp) | Grenu,Georges (ts) | Sadi,Fats (vib) | Migiani,Armand (p) | Michelot,Pierre (b) | Garros,Christian (dr)
Triads | Milano
Paris,France, rec. 2.7.1956
Hodeir,Andre (cond,arr) | Liesse,Jean (tp) | Guerin,Roger (tp) | Peck,Nat (tb) | Algedon,Jean (as) | Grenu,Georges (ts) | Sadi,Fats (vib) | Migiani,Armand (p) | Michelot,Pierre (b) | Garros,Christian (dr)

548793-2 | CD | Jazz In Paris | EAN 731454879323
Alain Goraguer Orchestra
Les Loups Dans La Bergerie: | Generique | Fuite Du Rouquin | Le Loups Dans La Bergerie | Cha Cha Cha Du Luop | Les Loups Dans La Bergerie(fin)
Paris,France, rec. 28.10.1959
Guerin,Roger (tp) | Guiot,Raymond (fl) | Grenu,Georges (as) | Boucaya,William (bs) | Goraguer,Alain (p,arr,ld) | Michelot,Pierre (b) | Garros,Christian (dr)
Le Jazz Group De Paris
Rhythm And Blues No.1 | Spiritual | Danse | Le Desert | Blues
Paris,France, rec. 1959
Le Jazz Group De Paris | Guerin,Roger (tp) | Gossez,Pierre (as) | Legrand,Christiane (voc) | Hodeir,Andre (comp) | details unknown
Daniel Humair Soultet
The Connection: | Theme For Sister Salvation | Overdose | Wigglin' | Music Forever | One Mint Julep
Paris,France, rec. 29.5.1961
Humair,Daniel (dr) | Grey,Sonny (tp) | Fuentes,Luis (tb,arr) | Chautemps,Jean-Louis (ts) | Louiss,Eddie (p) | Pedersen,Guy (b) | Urtreger,René (arr)

549099-2 | CD | Live at Bradley's
Kenny Barron Trio
Everybody Loves My Baby | Solar | Blue Moon | Altered Ego | Canadian Sunset
Live at Bradley's Jazz Club,NYC, rec. 3./4.4.1996
Barron,Kenny (p) | Drummond,Ray (b) | Riley,Ben (dr)

549231-2 PMS | CD | Jazz In Paris:Sonny Criss-Mr.Blues Pour Flirter
Sonny Criss Quintet
Don't Get Around Much Anymore | This Can't Be Love | Early And Later(part 1) | Early And Later(part 2) | Once In A While | St.Louis Blues | Day Dream | On Green Dolphin Street | God Bless The Child
Paris,France, rec. 1963
Criss,Sonny (as) | Thomas,Rene (g) | Arvanitas,Georges (p) | Michelot,Pierre (b) | Combelle,Philippe (dr)

549241-2 PMS | CD | Jazz In Paris:Django Reinhardt-Django Et Compagnie
Michel Warlop Et Son Orchestre
Cloud Castles | Magic Strings | Crazy Strings | Novel Pets | Budding Dancers
Paris,France, rec. 17.2.1936
Warlop,Michel (v) | Renard,Alex (tp) | Cizeron,Maurice (fl,as) | Combelle,Alix (ts) | Reinhardt,Django (g) | Stern,Emile (p) | Reinhardt,Joseph (g) | Vola,Louis (b)
Nitta Rette Et Son Trio Hot
Point Roses | Un Instand D'Infini | Mon Coer Reste De Toi
Paris,France, rec. 2./6.9.1935
Rette,Nitta (voc) | Grappelli,Stephane (v) | Reinhardt,Django (g) | Stern,Emile (p)
Andre Pasdoc With The Orchestra Vola
Pourquoi,Pourquoi? | Vivre Pour Toi
Paris,France, rec. 13.10.1935
Pasdoc,André (voc) | Vola,Louis (accordeon) | Grappelli,Stephane (v) | Warlop,Michel (v) | Reinhardt,Joseph (g)
Yvonne Louis With The Orchestra Vola
Mirages(Chasing Shadows)
Louis,Yvonne (voc) | Grappelli,Stephane (v) | Warlop,Michel (v) | Reinhardt,Django (g) | Reinhardt,Joseph (g)
Au Grand Large
Paris,France, rec. 12.3.1936
Louis,Yvonne (voc) | unkn. (cl) | Grappelli,Stephane (v) | Schmidt,Sylvio prob. (v) | Warlop,Michel (v) | Emer,Michel (p) | Vola,Louis (accordeon) | Reinhardt,Django (g) | unkn. (perc)
Micheline Day Et Son Quatuor Swing
Y A Du Soleil Dans La Boutique | Cheri,Est-Ce Que Tu M'Aimes?
Paris,France, rec. 26.10.1937
Day,Micheline (voc) | Grappelli,Stephane (v) | Emer,Michel or Emil Stern (p) | Vola,Louis (b) | Reinhardt,Django or Henri Schaap (g)
Wal-Berg Et Son Jazz Francais
Horizons Nouveaux | Love Again
Paris,France, rec. 12.3.1935
Allier,Pierre (tp) | Renard,Alex (tp) | D'Hellemmes,Eugene (tb) | Ekyan,Andre (as) | Combelle,Alix (ts) | Lamory,Andre (as) | Chaput,Roger (g) | Allier,Roger (b) | Chaillou,Maurice (dr)

549242-2 PMS | CD | Jazz In Paris:Stephane Grappelli-Improvisations
Stephane Grappelli Quartet
The Lady Is A Tramp | Fascinating Rhythm | Dans La Vie | Cheek To Cheek | A Nightingale Sang In Berkeley Square | Taking A Chance On Love | 'S Wonderful | Someone To Watch Over Me | If I Had You | Body And Soul | I Want To Be Happy | She's Funny That Way | Time After Time | Just One Of Those Things | I'll Be Around(Slow En Ré Majeur) | Taking A Chance On Love(alt.take) | Someone To Watch Over Me(alt.take)
Paris,France, rec. 1956
Grappelli,Stephane (v) | Vander,Maurice (p) | Michelot,Pierre (b) | Reilles,Jean-Baptiste 'Mac Kac' (dr)

549287-2 PMS | CD | Jazz In Paris:Rhoda Scott + Kenny Clarke
Rhoda Scott-Kenny Clarke
Bitter Street | Satin Doll | It's Impossible | Speak Low | Now's The Time | Out Of Nowhere | What Are You Doing The Rest Of Your Life | Toe Jam | On Green Dolphin Street
Paris,France, rec. 10./11.5.1977
Scott,Rhoda (org) | Clarke,Kenny (dr)

549400-2 PMS | CD | Jazz In Paris:René Thomas-The Real Cat
Rene Thomas Quartet
How About You | Relaxin' At The Grand Balcon | Lover Man(Oh,Where Can You Be?) | The Continental | There'll Never Be Another You
Paris,France, rec. 17.4.1954
Thomas,Rene (g) | Urtreger,René (p) | Ingrand,Jean-Marie or Benoit Quersin (b) | Viale,Jean-Louis (dr)
Rene Thomas Quintet
L'Imbécile | All The Things You Are | If I Had You
Thomas,Rene (g) | Ross,André (ts) | Urtreger,René (p) | Ingrand,Jean-Marie or Benoit Quersin (b) | Viale,Jean-Louis (dr)
Shine | My Old Flame | Goodnight,Wherever You Are | Easy To Love | The Real Cat | Someone To Watch Over Me | Get Happy | A Night In Tunisia
Paris,France, rec. 22.3.1956
Thomas,Rene (g) | Monville,Serge 'Bib' (ts) | Ronchaud,Roland (p) | Quersin,Benoit (b) | Bourguignon,José (dr)

549401-2 PMS | CD | Jazz In Paris:Bill Coleman-From Boogie To Funk
Bill Coleman Septet
From Boogie To Funk(part 1) | From Boogie To Funk(part 2) | Bill,Budd And Butter | Afromotive In Blue | Colemanology | Have Blues Will Play'Em
Paris,France, rec. 21./22.1.1960
Coleman,Bill (tp) | Jackson,Quentin (tb) | Johnson,Budd (ts) | Spann,Les (g) | Bown,Patti (p) | Catlett,Buddy (b) | Harris,Joe (dr)

549403-2 PMS | CD | Jazz In Paris:Toots Thielemans-Blues Pour Flirter
Toots Thielemans Quartet
Winter In Madrid | Willow Weep For Me | Satin Doll | Bag's Groove | We'll Be Together Again | Hot Toddy | Try A Little Tenderness | Talk To Me | Le Trottoir | Honeysuckle Rose | Flirt
Paris,France, rec. 3./4.1.1961
Thielemans,Jean 'Toots' (g) | Arvanitas,Georges (p) | Lobligeois,Roland (b) | Combelle,Philippe (dr)

549405-2 PMS | CD | Jazz In Paris:Lionel Hampton And His French New Sound Vol.1
Lionel Hampton All Stars
Voice Of The North | Crazy Rhythm | Zebu
Schola Cantorum,Paris, rec. 19.3.1955
Hampton,Lionel (vib) | Adderley,Nat (tp) | Bailey,Benny (tp) | Hulin,Bernard (tp) | Amram,David (fr-h) | Meunier,Maurice (cl,ts) | Boucaya,William (bs) | Urtreger,René (p) | Pedersen,Guy (b) | Reilles,Jean-Baptiste 'Mac Kac' (dr) | Chevallier,Christian (arr)
A La French
Hampton,Lionel (vib) | Distel,Sacha (g) | Urtreger,René (p) | Pedersen,Guy (b) | Reilles,Jean-Baptiste 'Mac Kac' (dr)

549406-2 PMS | CD | Jazz In Paris:Lionel Hampton And His French New Sound Vol.2
I Cover The Waterfront
Hampton,Lionel (vib) | Hulin,Bernard (tp) | Meunier,Maurice (cl,ts) | Urtreger,René (p) | Pedersen,Guy (b) | Reilles,Jean-Baptiste 'Mac Kac' (dr) | Chevallier,Christian (arr)
Red Ribbon
Hampton,Lionel (vib) | Adderley,Nat (tp) | Bailey,Benny (tp) | Hulin,Bernard (tp) | Amram,David (fr-h) | Meunier,Maurice (cl,ts) | Boucaya,William (bs) | Urtreger,René (p) | Pedersen,Guy (b) | Reilles,Jean-Baptiste 'Mac Kac' (dr) | Chevallier,Christian (arr)
All The Things You Are | Night And Day
Hampton,Lionel (vib) | Distel,Sacha (g) | Urtreger,René (p) | Pedersen,Guy (b) | Reilles,Jean-Baptiste 'Mac Kac' (dr)

549812-2 | CD | Jazz In Paris:René Thomas-Meeting Mister Thomas | EAN 731454981224
Rene Thomas Quartet
If You Were The Only Girl In The World | Wonderful Wonderful
Paris,France, rec. 22.3.1963
Thomas,Rene (g) | Bennett,Lou (org) | Rovere,Gilbert 'Bibi' (b) | Bellonzi,Charles (dr)
West Coast Blues
Thomas,Rene (g) | Bennett,Lou (org) | Quersin,Benoit (b) | Bellonzi,Charles (dr)
Rene Thomas Quintet
Hannie's Dream | Dr.Jackle
Thomas,Rene (g) | Pelzer,Jacques (fl,as) | Bennett,Lou (org) | Quersin,Benoit (b) | Bellonzi,Charles (dr)
Meeting
Thomas,Rene (g) | Pelzer,Jacques (as) | Bennett,Lou (org) | Rovere,Gilbert 'Bibi' (b) | Bellonzi,Charles (dr)

549879-2 PMS | CD | Jazz In Paris:Rhoda Scott-Live At The Olympia
Rhoda Scott Trio
Bluesette | Hymne A L'Amour | Equinox | Wade In The Water | People | Lil' Darlin' | Ain't No Use | Ca Va Mieux | Thank You(For Let Me Be Myself) | I Hear Music
Live at The Olympia,Paris,France, rec. 11.10.1971
Scott,Rhoda (org,voc) | Thomas,Joe (fl,ts) | Kranenburg,Cornelius 'Cees' (dr)

558683-2 | CD | At Ronnie Scott's:Blossom Time
Blossom Dearie Trio
On Broadway | When The World Was Young | When In Rome | The Shadow Of Your Smile | Everything I've Got Belongs To You | Once Upon A Summertime | I'm Hip | Mad About The Boy | The Shape Of Things | Satin Doll
Live at Ronnie Scott's,London,GB, rec. March 1966
Dearie,Blossom (p,voc) | Clyne,Jeff (b) | Butts,Johnny (dr)

558690-2 | CD | Tripple Entente
Kühn/Humair/Jenny-Clark
Ornette | Enna | La Galinette | Salinas | Missing A Page | The Tonica | Sunny Sunday | Early In The Morning | Croquis | Call Money | More Tuna
Paris,France, rec. 5.-8.12.1997
Kühn,Joachim (p) | Jenny-Clark,Jean-Francois (b) | Humair,Daniel (dr)

558848-2 | CD | Casa Forte
Helen Merrill With Orchestra
Natural Sounds | So Many Stars | Like A Lover | How Insensitive(Insensatez)
NYC, rec. 11.4./14.& 27.5.1980
Merrill,Helen (voc) | Pizzarelli,Bucky (g) | Mraz,George 'Jiri' (b) | Tate,Grady (dr) | Bassini,Rubens (perc) | Nadien,David (v) | Eley,Lewis (v) | Finclair,Barry (v) | Tarak,Gerald (v) | Morgenstern,Marvin (v) | Mullen,Jan (v) | Libove,Charles (v) | Geist,Judy (viola) | Alsop,LaMar (viola) | McCracken,Charles (cello) | Agostini,Gloria (harp)
Casa Forte | Too Marvelous For Words
Merrill,Helen (voc) | Green,Urbie (tb) | Buffington,Jimmy (fr-h) | Gordon,Peter (fr-h) | Clark,John (fr-h) | Pizzarelli,Bucky (g) | Centeno,Francisco (el-b) | Kroon,Steve (perc) | Romao,Dom Um (dr,perc)
Vera Cruz
Merrill,Helen (voc) | Green,Urbie (tb) | Buffington,Jimmy (fr-h) | Gordon,Peter (fr-h) | Clark,John (fr-h) | Nistico,Sal (ts) | Zito,Torrie (p) | Pizzarelli,Bucky (g) | Centeno,Francisco (el-b) | Kroon,Steve (perc) | Romao,Dom Um (dr,perc)
Antonio's Song | Close Enough For Love
Merrill,Helen (voc) | Zito,Torrie (p) | Beck,Joe (g) | McCracken,Charles (cello) | Mraz,George 'Jiri' (b) | Zito,Ronnie (dr)
Helen Merrill-Torrie Zito Duo
Wave
Merrill,Helen (voc) | Zito,Torrie (p)

558849-2 | CD | The Feeling Is Mutual
Helen Merrill With The Dick Katz Group
It Don't Mean A Thing If It Ain't Got That Swing | Don't Explain | What Is This Thing Called Love | Day Dream
NYC, rec. 1965
Merrill,Helen (voc) | Jones,Thad (co) | Hall,Jim (g) | Katz,Dick (p) | Carter,Ron (b) | LaRoca,Pete (dr)
Baltimore Oriole | My Discontent
Merrill,Helen (voc) | Jones,Thad (co) | Hall,Jim (g) | Katz,Dick (p) | Carter,Ron (b) | Wise,Arnold (dr)
You're My Thrill
Merrill,Helen (voc) | Katz,Dick (p) | Carter,Ron (b)
Helen Merrill-Dick Katz Duo
Here's That Rainy Day
Merrill,Helen (voc) | Katz,Dick (p)
Helen Merrill-Jim Hall Duo
Deep In A Dream
Merrill,Helen (voc) | Hall,Jim (g)

558850-2 | CD | Chasin' The Bird(Gershwin)
Helen Merrill With The Pepper Adams Quintet
It Ain't Necessarily So | Embraceable You | I Can't Be Bothered Now | Summertime | I Got Rhythm | I Loves You Porgy | Someone To Watch Over Me
NYC, rec. 7.& 9.3.1979
Merrill,Helen (voc) | Adams,Pepper (bs) | Puma,Joe (g) | Katz,Dick (p) | Reid,Rufus (b) | Lewis,Mel (dr)
Isn't It A Pity
Merrill,Helen (voc) | Adams,Pepper (bs) | Puma,Joe (g) | Katz,Dick (p) | McClure,Ron (b) | Lewis,Mel (dr)

558851-2 | CD | A Shade Of Difference
Helen Merrill With The Dick Katz Group
Spring Can Really Hang You Up The Most | Lover Come Back To Me | Never Will I Marry | A Lady Must Live
NYC, rec. July 1968
Merrill,Helen (voc) | Katz,Dick (p,arr) | Jones,Thad (fl-h,co) | Laws,Hubert (fl) | Hall,Jim (g) | Carter,Ron (b) | Jones,Elvin (dr)
I Want A Little Boy | I Should Care
Merrill,Helen (voc) | Katz,Dick (p,arr) | Hall,Jim (g) | Carter,Ron (b) | Jones,Elvin (dr)
While We're Young
Merrill,Helen (voc) | Hall,Jim (g) | Carter,Ron (b) | Jones,Elvin (dr)
Where Do You Go
Merrill,Helen (voc) | Hall,Jim (g) | Carter,Ron (b)
Helen Merrill-Don Carter Duo
My Funny Valentine
Merrill,Helen (voc) | Carter,Ron (b)
Helen Merrill With Richard Davis & Gary Bartz
Lonely Woman
Merrill,Helen (voc) | Bartz,Gary (as) | Davis,Richard (b)

586755-2 | CD | Stan Getz Cafe Montmartre | EAN 731458675525
Stan Getz Quartet
I Thought About You | I Can't Get Started | Falling In Love | Blood Count
Live at 'Cafe Montmartre',Copenhagen, rec. 6.7.1987
Getz,Stan (ts) | Barron,Kenny (p) | Reid,Rufus (b) | Lewis,Victor (dr)

Stan Getz-Kenny Barron
People Time | Soul Eyes | I'm Okay | I Remember Clifford | First Song(For Ruth)
Live at 'Cafe Montmartre',Copenhagen, rec. 3.-6.3.1991
Getz,Stan (ts) | Barron,Kenny (p)

589963-2 | CD | Jazz In Paris:Max Roach-Parisian Sketches | EAN 731458996323
Max Roach Quintet
Parisian Sketches: | The Tower- | The Champs- | The Caves- | The Left Bank- | The Arch- | Petit Déjeuner | Un Nouveau Complet
Paris,France, rec. 1.3.1960
Roach,Max (dr) | Turrentine,Tommy (tp) | Priester,Julian (tb) | Turrentine,Stanley (ts) | Boswell,Bobby (b)
Nica | Liberté
Paris,France, rec. 2.3.1960
Boswell,Bobby (b) | Turrentine,Stanley (ts) | Priester,Julian (tb) | Turrentine,Tommy (tp) | Roach,Max (dr)

814646-2 | CD | Study In Brown
Clifford Brown-Max Roach Quintet
Gerkin' For Perkin | Take The 'A' Train | Lands End | Swingin'
NYC, rec. 23.2.1955
Brown,Clifford (tp) | Land,Harold (ts) | Powell,Richie (p) | Morrow,George (b) | Roach,Max (dr)
George's Dilemma | If I Love Again
NYC, rec. 24.2.1955
Brown,Clifford (tp) | Land,Harold (ts) | Powell,Richie (p) | Morrow,George (b) | Roach,Max (dr)
Cherokee | Jacqui | Sandu
NYC, rec. 25.2.1955
Brown,Clifford (tp) | Land,Harold (ts) | Powell,Richie (p) | Morrow,George (b) | Roach,Max (dr)

830381-2 | CD | Julian 'Cannonball' Adderley | EAN 042283038127
Cannonball Adderley Group
The Song Is You | Cynthia's In Love | Hurricane Connie | Purple Shades
NYC, rec. 21.7.1955
Adderley,Julian \'Cannonball\' (as) | Adderley,Nat (co) | Cleveland,Jimmy (tb) | Richardson,Jerome (fl,ts) | Payne,Cecil (bs) | Williams,John (p) | Chambers,Paul (b) | Clarke,Kenny (dr) | Jones,Quincy (arr)
Cannonball | Nat's Everglade | You'd Be So Nice To Come Home To
NYC, rec. 29.7.1955
Adderley,Julian \'Cannonball\' (as) | Adderley,Nat (co) | Johnson,J.J. (tb) | Richardson,Jerome (fl,ts,bs) | Payne,Cecil (bs) | Williams,John (p) | Chambers,Paul (b) | Clarke,Kenny (dr)
Willows | Fallen Feathers | Rose Room
NYC, rec. 5.8.1955
Adderley,Julian \'Cannonball\' (as) | Adderley,Nat (co) | Johnson,J.J. (tb) | Richardson,Jerome (fl,ts,bs) | Payne,Cecil (bs) | Williams,John (p) | Chambers,Paul (b) | Roach,Max (dr)

832659-2 PMS | CD | Jazz In Paris:Art Blakey-1958-Paris Olympia
Art Blakey And The Jazz Messengers
Just By Myself | I Remember Clifford | Are You Real
Live at The Olympia,Paris,France, rec. 22.11.1958
Blakey,Art (dr) | Morgan,Lee (tp) | Golson,Benny (ts) | Timmons,Bobby (p) | Merritt,Jymie (b)
Moanin' | Justice | Blues March | Whisper Not
Live at The Olympia,Paris,France, rec. 17.12.1958
Blakey,Art (dr) | Morgan,Lee (tp) | Golson,Benny (ts) | Timmons,Bobby (p) | Merritt,Jymie (b)

832692-2 PMS | CD | Jazz In Paris:Paris Jam Session
The Midgets | A Night In Tunisia
Live at The Theatre Des Champs-Elysees,Paris,France, rec. 18.12.1959
Blakey,Art (dr) | Morgan,Lee (tp) | Shorter,Wayne (ts) | Davis Jr.,Walter (p) | Merritt,Jymie (b)
Art Blakey And The Jazz Messengers With Barney Wilen And Bud Powell
Dance Of The Infidels | Bouncing With Bud
Blakey,Art (dr) | Morgan,Lee (tp) | Wilen,Barney (as) | Shorter,Wayne (ts) | Powell,Bud (p) | Merritt,Jymie (b)

834542-2 PMS | CD | Jazz In Paris:Kenny Clarke Sextet Plays André Hodair
Kenny Clarke Quintet
On A Riff
Paris,France, rec. 26.10.1956
Clarke,Kenny (dr) | Byers,Billy (tb) | Migiani,Armand (bs) | Solal,Martial (p) | Michelot,Pierre (b) | Hodeir,Andre (arr)
Round About Midnight | When Lights Are Low
Clarke,Kenny (dr) | Guerin,Roger (tp) | Peck,Nat (tb) | Urtreger,René (p) | Michelot,Pierre (b) | Hodeir,Andre (arr)
Kenny Clarke Sextet
Oblique | Jeru | Eronel | Tahiti
Paris,France, rec. 21.11.1956
Clarke,Kenny (dr) | Byers,Billy (tb) | Rostaing,Hubert (as) | Migiani,Armand (bs) | Solal,Martial (p) | Warland,Jean (b) | Hodeir,Andre (arr)
Kenny Clarke Quintet
Bemsha Swing | Blue Serge | Swing Spring | Cadenze
Paris,France, rec. 30.11.1956
Clarke,Kenny (dr) | Byers,Billy (tb) | Migiani,Armand (bs) | Solal,Martial (p) | Warland,Jean (b) | Hodeir,Andre (arr)
Kenny Clarke Quartet
The Squirrel
Clarke,Kenny (dr) | Byers,Billy (tb) | Solal,Martial (p) | Warland,Jean (b) | Hodeir,Andre (arr)

838306-2 | 10 CD | Brownie-The Complete EmArCy Recordings Of Clifford Brown
Clifford Brown-Max Roach Quintet
Delilah | Darn That Dream | Parisian Thoroughfare
Los Angeles,CA, rec. 2.8.1954
Brown,Clifford (tp) | Land,Harold (ts) | Powell,Richie (p) | Morrow,George (b) | Roach,Max (dr)
Jordu | Sweet Clifford | Sweet Clifford(Clifford's Fantasy) | I Don't Stand A Ghost Of A Chance With You | I Don't Stand A Ghost Of A Chance With You(alt.take)
Los Angeles,CA, rec. 3.8.1954
Brown,Clifford (tp) | Land,Harold (ts) | Powell,Richie (p) | Morrow,George (b) | Roach,Max (dr)
Stompin' At The Savoy | I Get A Kick Out Of You | I Get A Kick Out Of You(alt.take) | I'll String Along With You
Los Angeles,CA, rec. 5.8.1954
Brown,Clifford (tp) | Land,Harold (ts) | Powell,Richie (p) | Morrow,George (b) | Roach,Max (dr)
Joy Spring | Joyspring(alt.take) | Mildama | Mildama(alt.take 1) | Mildama(alt.take 2) | Mildama(alt.take 3) | Mildama(alt.take 4) | Mildama(alt.take 5) | Mildama(alt.take 6) | These Foolish Things Remind Me On You | Daahoud | Daahoud(alt.take)
Los Angeles,CA, rec. 6.8.1954
Brown,Clifford (tp) | Land,Harold (ts) | Powell,Richie (p) | Morrow,George (b) | Roach,Max (dr)
Clifford Brown All Stars
Corona | Corona(alt.take 1) | Corona(alt.take 2) | You Go To My Head | Caravan | Caravan(The Boss Man) | Autumn In New York
Los Angeles,CA, rec. 11.8.1954
Brown,Clifford (tp) | Geller,Herb (as) | Maini,Joe (as) | Benton,Walter (ts) | Drew,Kenny (p) | Counce,Curtis (b) | Roach,Max (dr)
All Star Live Jam Session
Introduction by Bob Shad | What Is This Thing Called Love | I've Got You Under My Skin | No More | Move | Darn That Dream | You Go To My Head | My Funny Valentine- | Don't Worry 'Bout Me- | Bess You Is My Woman Now- | It Might As Well Be Spring- | Lover Come Back To Me | Alone Together- | Summertime- | Come Rain Or Come Shine- | Crazy He Calls Me | There Is No Greater Love | I'll Remember April
Los Angeles,CA, rec. 14.8.1954
All Star Live Jam Session | Brown,Clifford (tp) | Terry,Clark (tp) | Ferguson,Maynard (tp) | Geller,Herb (as) | Land,Harold (ts) | Powell,Richie (p) | Mance,Junior[Julian C.] (p) | Betts,Keter (b) | Morrow,George (b) | Roach,Max (dr) | Washington,Dinah (voc)

Sarah Vaughan With The Clifford Brown All Stars
September Song | Lullaby Of Birdland | Lullaby Of Birdland(alt.take) | I'm Glad There Is You | You're Not The Kind
NYC, rec. 16.12.1954
Vaughan,Sarah (voc) | Brown,Clifford (tp) | Mann,Herbie (fl) | Quinichette,Paul (ts) | Jones,Jimmy (p) | Benjamin,Joe (b) | Haynes,Roy (dr) | Wilkins,Rick (cond,arr)
Jim | He's My Guy | April In Paris | It's Crazy | Embraceable You
NYC, rec. 18.12.1954
Vaughan,Sarah (voc) | Brown,Clifford (tp) | Mann,Herbie (fl) | Quinichette,Paul (ts) | Jones,Jimmy (p) | Benjamin,Joe (b) | Haynes,Roy (dr) | Wilkins,Rick (cond,arr)
Helen Merrill With The Quincy Jones Orchestra
Don't Explain | Born To Be Blue | You'd Be So Nice To Come Home To | 'S Wonderful
NYC, rec. 22.12.1954
Merrill,Helen (voc) | Brown,Clifford (tp) | Bank,Danny (fl,bs) | Jones,Jimmy (p) | Galbraith,Barry (g) | Hinton,Milt (b) | Johnson,Osie (dr) | Jones,Quincy (arr,ld)
Yesterdays | Falling In Love With Love | What's New?
NYC, rec. 24.12.1954
Merrill,Helen (voc) | Brown,Clifford (tp) | Bank,Danny (fl,bs) | Jones,Jimmy (p) | Galbraith,Barry (g) | Pettiford,Oscar (b) | Donaldson,Bobby (dr) | Jones,Quincy (arr,ld)
Clifford Brown With Strings
Portrait Of Jenny | Yesterdays | Where Or When | Can't Help Lovin' Dat Man | Smoke Gets In Your Eyes | Laura | Memories Of You | Embraceable You | Blue Moon | Willow Weep For Me | Stardust
NYC, rec. 18.-20.1.1955
Brown,Clifford (tp) | Powell,Richie (p) | Galbraith,Barry (g) | Morrow,George (b) | Roach,Max (dr) | Strings | Hefti,Neal (cond,arr) | details unknown
Clifford Brown-Max Roach Quintet
Gerkin' For Perkin | Take The 'A' Train | Lands End | Lands End(alt.take) | Swingin'
NYC, rec. 23.2.1955
Brown,Clifford (tp) | Land,Harold (ts) | Powell,Richie (p) | Morrow,George (b) | Roach,Max (dr)
George's Dilemma | If I Love Again | The Blues Walk | The Blues Walk(alt.take)
NYC, rec. 24.2.1955
Brown,Clifford (tp) | Land,Harold (ts) | Powell,Richie (p) | Morrow,George (b) | Roach,Max (dr)
What Am I Here For | Cherokee | Jacqui | Sandu
NYC, rec. 25.2.1955
Brown,Clifford (tp) | Land,Harold (ts) | Powell,Richie (p) | Morrow,George (b) | Roach,Max (dr)
Gertrude's Bounce | Step Lightly(Junior's Arrival) | Powell's Prances
NYC, rec. 4.1.1956
Brown,Clifford (tp) | Rollins,Sonny (ts) | Powell,Richie (p) | Morrow,George (b) | Roach,Max (dr)
I'll Remember April | I'll Remember April(alt.take 1) | I'll Remember April(alt.take 2) | Time | Love Is A Many-Splendored Thing | Love Is A Many-Splendored Thing(alt.take 1) | Love Is A Many-Splendored Thing(alt.take 2)
NYC, rec. 16.2.1956
Brown,Clifford (tp) | Rollins,Sonny (ts) | Powell,Richie (p) | Morrow,George (b) | Roach,Max (dr)
The Scene Is Clean | Flossie Lou | Flossie Lou(alt.take 1) | Flossie Lou(alt.take 2) | Flossie Lou(alt.take 3) | What Is This Thing Called Love | What Is This Thing Called Love(alt.take)
Brown,Clifford (tp) | Rollins,Sonny (ts) | Powell,Richie (p) | Morrow,George (b) | Roach,Max (dr) | Dameron,Tadd (arr)

838769-2 | CD | Anniversary !
Stan Getz Quartet
El Cahon | I Can't Get Started | Stella By Starlight | Stan's Blues | I Thought About You | What Is This Thing Called Love | Blood Count
Live at The 'Jazzhus' Montmartre',Copenhagen, rec. 6.7.1987
Getz,Stan (ts) | Barron,Kenny (p) | Reid,Rufus (b) | Lewis,Victor (dr)

838770-2 | CD | Serenity
838770-4 | MC | Serenity
On Green Dolphin Street | Voyage | Falling In Love | I Remember You | I Love You
Getz,Stan (ts) | Barron,Kenny (p) | Reid,Rufus (b) | Lewis,Victor (dr)

838771-2 | CD | Billy Highstreet Samba
Stan Getz Sextet
Hospitality Creek | Anytime Tomorrow | Be There Then | Billy Highstreet Samba | The Dirge | Page Two | Body And Soul | Tuesday Next
Paris,France, rec. 4.11.1981
Getz,Stan (ss,ts) | Loeb,Chuck (g) | Forman,Mitchel (p) | Egan,Mark (b) | Lewis,Victor (dr) | Thomas Jr.,Robert (perc)

9809601 | DVD | Dee Dee Bridgewater Sings Kurt Weil | EAN 602498096017
Dee Dee Bridgewater With Band
Intro | I'm A Stranger Here Myself | Youkali | This Is New | Here I'll Stay | The Saga Of Jenny | Lost In The Stars | Interlude | Bilbao | Alabama Song | Extras:Photo Gallery & Biography
Live at The Northsea Festival, rec. July 2002
Bridgewater,Dee Dee (voc) | Folmer,Nicolas (tp) | Abraham,Phil (tb) | Scannapieco,Daniele (fl,as) | Winsberg,Louis (g) | Eliez,Thierry (p,org) | Coleman,Ira (b) | Ceccarelli,André (dr) | Garay,Minino (perc)

9811568 | CD | Tribute To Django Reinhardt | EAN 602498115688
9811569 | DVD | Tribute To Django Reinhardt | EAN 602498115695
The Rosenberg Trio
Intro | Swing '42 | Rose Room | Belleville | Chicago | Ol' Man River | Oriental Shuffle | Viper's Dream | Nuages | Daphne | Artillerie Lourde | Festival 48 | Flamingo | Rhythme Futur | Minor Swing | China Boy | Les Yeux Noirs | It Don't Mean A Thing If It Ain't Got That Swing
Live In Samois, rec. 2003
Rosenberg,Stochelo (g) | Rosenberg,Nou'che (g) | Rosenberg,Nonnie (b)

9814976 | CD | For You,For Me For Evermore | EAN 602498149768
Frank Castenier Group
The Way You Look Tonight | Someday My Prince Will Come | Alone Again(Naturally)
Berlin, rec. 2003
Chastenier,Frank (p) | Goldsby,John (b) | Dekker,Hans (dr) | Strings | Deutsches Filmorchester Babelsberg
Mensch | I'll Never Smile Again | For You
Chastenier,Frank (p) | Brönner,Till (tp,fl-h) | Goldsby,John (b) | Dekker,Hans (dr) | Strings | Deutsches Filmorchester Babelsberg
Bei Dir War Es Immer So Schön | Berlin, Dein Gesicht Hat Sommersprossen
Chastenier,Frank (p) | Lefebvre,Tim (b) | Dekker,Hans (dr) | Strings | Deutsches Filmorchester Babelsberg

9860779 | SACD | Sarah Vaughan | EAN 602498607794
Sarah Vaughan With The Clifford Brown All Stars
Lullaby Of Birdland | You're Not The Kind | I'm Glad There Is You | September Song | Lullaby Of Birdland(alt.take)
NYC, rec. 16.12.1954
Vaughan,Sarah (voc) | Brown,Clifford (tp) | Mann,Herbie (fl) | Quinichette,Paul (ts) | Jones,Jimmy (p) | Benjamin,Joe (b) | Haynes,Roy (dr) | Wilkins,Ernie (cond,arr)
April In Paris | He's My Guy | Jim | It's Crazy
NYC, rec. 18.12.1954
Vaughan,Sarah (voc) | Brown,Clifford (tp) | Mann,Herbie (fl) | Quinichette,Paul (ts) | Jones,Jimmy (p) | Benjamin,Joe (b) | Haynes,Roy (dr) | Wilkins,Ernie (arr,ld)
Embraceable You
Vaughan,Sarah (voc) | Jones,Jimmy (p) | Benjamin,Joe (b) | Haynes,Roy (dr) | Wilkins,Rick (cond,arr)

9865648 | CD | Nightwatch | EAN 602498656488
Silje Nergard Group with Strings
How Am I Supposed To See The Stars | One I Held A Moon | Dance Me Love | You Send Me Flowers | I Don't Want To See You Cry | In A Sentence | Take A Long Walk | This Is Not America | Be Gone | Borrowing Moons | Unbreakable Heart | On And On
Oslo,N, rec. February 2003
Nergaard,Silje (voc) | Gustavsen,Tord (p,fender-rhodes) | Johnson,Harald (b) | Vespestad,Jarle (dr) | Asplund,Peter (tp,fl-h) | Hendricksen,Arve (tp) | Brunborg,Tore (sax) | Lindgren,Magnus (fl,sax) | Bratberg,Hallgrim (g) | Wadenius,George (g,voc) | Waring,Rob (vib) | Lund,Tom (g,voc) | Vinjor,Nils-Einar (g) | Strings

9865777 | CD | Seafarer's Song | EAN 602498657775
Ketil Bjornstad Group
Seafarer's Song | He Struggled To The Surface | Dying To Get To Europe | Orion | Tidal Waves | How Sweet The Moonlight Sleeps Upon This Bank | Navigatore | Ung Forelsket Kvinne | The Beach | Her Voice | Dreaming Of The North | I Had Been Hungry All The Years | The Exile's Line | When Police Came They Also Hit Me | Refugees At The Rich Man's Gate | I Many Times Thought Peace Had Come | The Night Is Darking Round Me
Live at Harstad Kulturhus,N, rec. 21.6.2003
Bjornstad,Ketil (p,keyboards) | Molvaer,Nils Petter (tp) | Aarset,Eivind (g) | Henryson,Svante (cello) | Kjellemyr,Bjorn (b) | Lindvall,Per (dr) | Asbjornsen,Kristin (voc)

EMI Records | EMI Germany

523999-2 | LP | Keep The Customer Satisfied | EAN 724352399925
Buddy Rich Big Band
Keep The Customer Satisfied | Long Days Journey | Midnight Cowboy Medley: | Midnight Cowboy- | He Quit Me- | Everybody's Talkin'- | Tears And Joys- | Celebration | Groovin' Hard | The Juicer Is Wild | Winning The West
Tropicana Hotel,Las Vegas, rec. Feb.1970
Rich,Buddy (dr) | Giorgiani,Joe (tp) | Madrid,John (tp) | Price,Mike (tp) | Zonce,George (tp) | Stepton,Rick (tb) | Lada,Tony (tb) | Fisher,Larry (b-tb) | Cole,Richie (fl,as) | Mosher,Jimmy (fl,as) | LaBarbera,Pat (fl,ss,ts) | Englert,Don (fl,ts) | Suchoski,Bob (bs) | McClain,Meridith (p) | Laird,Rick (el-b) | Holman,Bill (arr) | Menza,Don (arr) | Piestrup,Don (arr) | Neuman,Roger (arr) | Sample,Joe (arr)

539646-2 | CD | Americans Swinging In Paris:Zoot Sims | EAN 724353964627
Zoot Sims Quintet
Captain Jetter | Nuzzolese Blues | Everything I Love | On The Alamo | Evening In Paris | My Old Flame | Little John Special
Paris,France, rec. 16.3.1956
Sims,Zoot (ts) | Eardley,Jon (tp) | Renaud,Henri (p) | Quersin,Benoit (b) | Saudrais,Charles (dr)

539647-2 | CD | Americans Swinging In Paris:Benny Carter | EAN 724353964726
Willie Lewis And His Entertainers
I've Got A Feeling You're Fooling | Stay Out Of Love | All Of Me | Stardust | Just A Mood
Paris,France, rec. 17.1.1936
Lewis,Willie (as,voc) | Martin,Bobby (tp) | Renard,Alex (tp) | Carter,Benny (tp,as,arr) | Johnson,George (as) | Hayman,Joe (ts) | Kiehn,Charles 'Coco' (ts) | Chittison,Herman (p,celeste) | Mitchell,John (g) | Vola,Louis (b) | Fields,Ted (dr) | Cole,June (voc) | Oliver,Sy (arr)
Coleman Hawkins And His All Star Jam Band
Honeysuckle Rose | Crazy Rhythm | Out Of Nowhere | Sweet Georgia Brown
Paris,France, rec. 28.4.1937
Hawkins,Coleman (ts) | Carter,Benny (tp,as,arr) | Ekyan,Andre (as) | Combelle,Alix (cl,ts) | Reinhardt,Django (g) | Grappelli,Stephane (p) | D'Hellemmes,Eugene (b) | Benford,Tommy (dr)
Benny Carter And His Orchestra
I'm Coming Virginia | Farewell Blues | Blue Light Blues
Paris,France, rec. 7.3.1938
Carter,Benny (tp,as) | Allen,Fletcher (as) | King,Bertie (cl,ts) | Combelle,Alix (ts) | De Souza,Yorke (p) | Reinhardt,Django (g) | Harrison,Len (b) | Montmarche,Robert (dr) | Hawkins,Coleman (ts) | Carter,Benny (tp,as,arr) | Ekyan,Andre (as) | Combelle,Alix (cl,ts) | Grappelli,Stephane (p) | D'Hellemmes,Eugene (b) | Benford,Tommy (dr)

539648-2 | CD | Americans Swinging In Paris:Slide Hampton | EAN 724353964825
Slide Hampton Quartet
In Case Of Emergency | Last Minute Blues | Chop Suey | Lament | Impossible Waltz
Paris,France, rec. 6.1.1969
Hampton,Slide (tb) | Kühn,Joachim (p) | Orsted-Pedersen,Niels-Henning (b) | Jones,Philly Joe (dr)

539649-2 | CD | Americans Swinging In Paris:Lionel Hampton | EAN 724353964924
Lionel Hampton Quintet
La Piege
Paris,France, rec. 3.5.1956
Hampton,Lionel (vib) | Bolling,Claude (p) | Mackel,Billy (g) | Rovere,Paul (b) | Hamner,Curley (dr)
Lionel Hampton Trio
What's New? | What's New?(alt.take)
Hampton,Lionel (vib) | Rovere,Paul (b) | Hamner,Curley (dr)
Lionel Hampton Sextet
Panama | Blues For Lorraine | Genevieve | Jazz Stars News | Sweethearts On Parade | Hamp Swings The Bells(Ring Dem Bells) | Honeysuckle Rose | Body And Soul | Jam For Brigitte
Hampton,Lionel (vib,p,voc) | Lafitte,Guy (ts) | Bolling,Claude (p) | Mackel,Billy (g) | Rovere,Paul (b) | Hamner,Curley (dr)

539650-2 | CD | Americans Swinging In Paris:Sammy Price | EAN 724353965020
Emmett Berry-Sammy Price Orchestra
Swingin' The Berrys | I'm Wondering | Boogie Woogie A La Parisienne | Sammy Plays The Blues For Mezz
Paris,France, rec. 6.1.1956
Berry,Emmett (tp) | Price,Sammy (p) | Lafitte,Guy (ts) | Foster,George 'Pops' (b) | Moore,Fred[Freddie] (dr) | Mezzrow,Milton Mezz (supervision)
Twelve O'Clock Blues | Sad Blues
Paris,France, rec. 22.2.1956
Berry,Emmett (tp) | Price,Sammy (p) | Lafitte,Guy (ts) | Foster,George 'Pops' (b) | Moore,Fred[Freddie] (dr)
Sammy Price Trio
Usis Blues | Hot Club Boogie | Love For Sale
Paris,France, rec. 14.5.1956
Price,Sammy (p) | Michelot,Pierre (b) | Reilles,Jean-Baptiste 'Mac Kac' (dr)
Sammy Price Quintet
The Sheik Of Araby | Avalon | Goodbye Paris | Mister New Orleans Blues
Price,Sammy (p) | Berry,Emmett (tp) | Saury,Maxim (cl) | Michelot,Pierre (b) | Reilles,Jean-Baptiste 'Mac Kac' (dr)
Sammy Price
Jelly Roll Junior Blues | D'Accord Mon Pote Boogie
Paris,France, rec. 22.2.1956
Price,Sammy (p-solo)

539651-2 | CD | Americans Swinging In Paris:Lucky Thompson | EAN 724353965129
Lucky Thompson Trio
Thin Ice | Thin Ice(alt.take)
Paris,France, rec. 21.2.1956
Thompson,Lucky (ts,arr) | Quersin,Benoit (b) | Pochonet,Gerard 'Dave' (dr)
Lucky Thompson Quartet
Sophisticated Lady(Medley part 1)- | Takin' Care O'Business | Takin' Care O'Business(alt.take)
Thompson,Lucky (ts,arr) | Renaud,Henri (p) | Quersin,Benoit (b) | Pochonet,Gerard 'Dave' (dr)

Lucky Thompson Quintet
These Foolish Things Remind Me On You(Medley part 2)- | A Minor Delight | One Cool Night | One Cool Night(alt.take)
Paris,France, rec. 22.2.1956
Berry,Emmett (tp) | Thompson,Lucky (ts,arr) | Renaud,Henri (p) | Quersin,Benoit (b) | Pochonet,Gerard 'Dave' (dr)
Jean Pierre Sasson Quartet
You Are My Dream | Lucky Strikes | My Love Supreme
Paris,France, rec. 27.3.1956
Sasson,Jean-Pierre (g) | Thompson,Lucky (ts,arr) | Rovere,Paul (b) | Pochonet,Gerard 'Dave' (dr)
Lucky Thompson Quintet
Passing Time | Why Weep | To A Mornin' Sunrise
Paris,France, rec. 5.4.1956
Thompson,Lucky (ts) | Lafitte,Guy (ts) | Solal,Martial (p) | Quersin,Benoit (b) | Paraboschi,Roger (dr)
Lucky Thompson Quartet
Nothin' But The Soul
Thompson,Lucky (ts) | Solal,Martial (p) | Quersin,Benoit (b) | Paraboschi,Roger (dr)
Lucky Thompson And His Orchestra
You Move You Lose | Velvet Rain | One Last Goodbye
Paris,France, rec. 20.4.1956
Thompson,Lucky (ts) | Solal,Martial (p) | Quersin,Benoit (b) | Garros,Christian (dr)

539652-2 | CD | Americans Swinging In Paris:Kenny Clarke |
EAN 724353965228
Hubert Fol And His Be-Bop Minstrels
This Fol-Ish Thing | These Foolish Strings | These Foolish Things Remind Me On You | Out Of Nowhere
Paris,France, rec. 3.3.1950
Fol,Hubert (as) | Fol,Raimond (p) | Michelot,Pierre (b) | Clarke,Kenny (dr)
Kenny Clarke 8
Jean-Paul
Paris,France, rec. 24.6.1957
Clarke,Kenny (dr) | Liesse,Jean (tp) | Peck,Nat (tb) | Scott,Tony (cl,ts) | Fol,Hubert (as) | Aldegon,Jean (as) | Migiani,Armand (bs) | Fol,Raimond (p) | Michelot,Pierre (b) | Chevallier,Christian (arr)
Fantasy For Bass | Love Me Or Leave Me | Fun For | Jackie My Little Cat
Paris,France, rec. 23.9.1957
Clarke,Kenny (dr) | Hullin,Bernard (tp) | Van Rooyen,Ack (tp) | Peck,Nat (tb) | Byers,Billy (tb) | Fol,Hubert (as) | Thompson,Lucky (ts) | Gossez,Pierre (ts) | Migiani,Armand (bs) | Vandair,Maurice (p) | Michelot,Pierre (b,arr)
Kenny Clarke Quartet
Stompin' At The Savoy | Now's The Time | Four | The Squirrel
Paris,France, rec. 26.9.1957
Clarke,Kenny (dr) | Thompson,Lucky (ts) | Solal,Martial (p) | Michelot,Pierre (b,arr)
Kenny Clarke 8
Black Knight
Paris,France, rec. 10.10.1957
Clarke,Kenny (dr) | Van Rooyen,Ack (tp) | Peck,Nat (tb) | Fol,Hubert (as) | Aldegon,Jean (as) | Gossez,Pierre (ts) | Migiani,Armand (bs) | Vander,Maurice (p) | Michelot,Pierre (b) | Chevallier,Christian (arr)
Gold Fish | Dream Time
Paris,France, rec. 11.3.1958
Clarke,Kenny (dr) | Guerin,Roger (tp) | Vasseur,Benny (tb) | Fol,Hubert (as,ts.arr) | Nicholas,Mickey (as) | Gossez,Pierre (ts) | Grenu,Georges (ts) | Migiani,Armand (bs) | Vander,Maurice (p) | Michelot,Pierre (b) | Chevallier,Christian (arr)

539653-2 | CD | Americans Swinging In Paris:James Moody |
EAN 724353965327
Ernie Royal And The Duke Knights
Perdido(part 1&2)
Paris,France, rec. 13.4.1950
Royal,Ernie (tp) | Kelly,Ted (tb) | Procope,Russell (as) | Moody,James (ts) | Fol,Hubert (bs) | Aspar,Henri (bs) | Michelot,Pierre (b) | Fol,Raimond (p) | Clarke,Kenny (dr)
Jack Dieval And His Quartet
Lou Easy | No! | Ouch! | Cherokee
Paris,France, rec. 26.5.1950
Dieval,Jack (p) | Peck,Nat (tb) | Moody,James (ts,arr) | Soudieux,Emmanuel (b) | Clarke,Kenny (dr)
Kenny Clarke And His Orchestra
I'll Get You Let | Be Good Girl
Paris,France, rec. 7.6.1950
Clarke,Kenny (dr,arr) | Peck,Nat (tb) | Moody,James (ts,arr) | Fol,Hubert (as) | Wiggins,Gerald 'Gerry' (p) | Michelot,Pierre (b)
James Moody Boptet
Real Cool | Voila | Delooney | In The Anna(Indiana)
Paris,France, rec. 3.7.1950
Moody,James (ts,arr) | Peck,Nat (tb) | Allen,Red (as) | Fol,Hubert (as) | Pallier,Claude (bs) | Fol,Raimond (p,celeste) | Banks,Alvin 'Buddy' (b) | Bennett,Benny (dr)
James Moody Quartet
Neath(take 1) | Neath(take 2) | I Can't Get Started | Riffin' And Raffin' | St.Louis Blues | In A Rush | Embraceable You
Paris,France, rec. 9.10.1950
Moody,James (ts,arr) | Schecroun,Ralph (p) | Michelot,Pierre (b) | Clarke,Kenny (dr)

539654-2 | CD | Americans Swinging In Paris:Phil Woods |
EAN 724353965426
Phil Woods And His European Rhythm Machine
Stolen Moments | And When You Are Young(dedicated to Bob Kennedy) | Alive And Well | Doxy | Freedom Jazz Dance
Paris,France, rec. 14./15.11.1968
Woods,Phil (as) | Gruntz,George (p) | Texier,Henri (b) | Humair,Daniel (dr)

539655-2 | CD | Americans Swinging In Paris:Don Byas |
EAN 724353965525
Don Byas Quartet
Gloria
Paris,France, rec. 18.10.1946
Byas,Don (ts) | Taylor,Billy (p) | Sturgis,Ted (b) | Oliver,Buford (dr)
Don Byas And His Orchestra
The Mohawk Special
Byas,Don (ts) | Holland,Peanuts (tp) | Glenn,Tyree (tb) | Rostaing,Hubert (as) | Taylor,Billy (p) | Sturgis,Ted (b) | Oliver,Buford (dr)
Tyree Glenn And His Orchestra
Working Eyes
Paris,France, rec. 4.12.1946
Glenn,Tyree (tb) | Byas,Don (ts) | Holland,Peanuts (tp) | Taylor,Billy (p) | Sturgis,Ted (b) | Oliver,Buford (dr)
Peanuts Holland And His Orchestra
Peanut Butter Blues
Holland,Peanuts (tp,voc) | Glenn,Tyree (tb) | Byas,Don (ts) | Taylor,Billy (p) | Sturgis,Ted (b) | Oliver,Buford (dr)
Don Byas Quartet
I'm Beginning To See The Light | Rosetta | Ain't Misbehavin' | Body And Soul | Blue And Sentimental
Byas,Don (ts) | Taylor,Billy (p) | Bouchety,Jean (b) | Oliver,Buford (dr)
Yesterdays
Paris,France, rec. 5.1.1949
Byas,Don (ts) | Peiffer,Bernard (p) | Bouchety,Jean (b) | Paraboschi,Roger (dr)
Bill Coleman Quintet
What Is This Thing Called Love | Lover Man(Oh,Where Can You Be?)
Coleman,Bill (tp) | Byas,Don (ts) | Peiffer,Bernard (p) | Bouchety,Jean (b) | Paraboschi,Roger (dr)

539658-2 | CD | Americans Swinging In Paris:Cat Anderson |
EAN 724353965822
Cat Anderson And His All Stars
A 'Chat' With Cat | Don't Get Around Much Anymore | Muskrat Ramble | C Jam Blues
Paris,France, rec. 20.3.1964
Anderson,Cat (tp) | Cooper,Frank 'Buster' (tb) | Procope,Russell (cl,as) | Gonsalves,Paul (ts) | Turner,Joe (p) | Lobligeois,Roland (b) | Woodyard,Sam (dr)
A Gathering In A Clearing | Confessin' | For Jammers Only
Anderson,Cat (tp) | Cooper,Frank 'Buster' (tb) | Procope,Russell (cl,as) | Gonsalves,Paul (ts) | Bolling,Claude (p,arr) | Lobligeois,Roland (b) | Woodyard,Sam (dr)
Cat Anderson And His Orchestra
Concerto For Cootie | Black And Tan Fantasy | Blues For Laurence | Ain't Misbehavin' | You're The Cream In My Coffee
Paris,France, rec. 30.10.1958
Anderson,Cat (tp) | Jackson,Quentin (tb) | Procope,Russell (cl) | Arvanitas,Georges (p) | Woode,Jimmy (b) | Woodyard,Sam (dr)

539659-2 | CD | Americans Swinging In Paris:Golden Gate Quartet |
EAN 724353965921
Golden Gate Quartet
Shadrack | Swing Low Sweet Cadillac | Joshua Fit The Battle Of Jericho
Paris,France, rec. 16.11.1955
Golden Gate Quartet,The (voc) | Wilson,Orlandus (voc) | Riddick,Clyde (voc) | Wright,Clyde (voc) | Ginyard,Julius Caleb (voc) | Trotman,Irving (p) | Rovere,Paul (b) | Seamen,Phil (dr)
Down By The Riverside
Paris,France, rec. 9.4.1958
Golden Gate Quartet,The (voc) | Wilson,Orlandus (voc) | Riddick,Clyde (voc) | Wright,Clyde (voc) | Ginyard,Julius Caleb (voc) | Cullaz,Pierre (g) | Michelot,Pierre (b) | Garros,Christian (dr)
Golden Gate Quartet With The Martial Solal Orchestra
My Heart Is An Open Book
Paris,France, rec. 22.11.1959
Golden Gate Quartet,The (voc) | Wilson,Orlandus (voc) | Riddick,Clyde (voc) | Wright,Clyde (voc) | Ginyard,Julius Caleb (voc) | Gossez,Pierre (as) | Chautemps,Jean-Louis (bs) | Hauser,Michel (vib) | Solal,Martial (p) | Rovere,Paul (b) | Humair,Daniel (dr)
Mister Blue | Primrose Lane
Golden Gate Quartet: | Wilson,Orlandus (voc) | Riddick,Clyde (voc) | Wright,Clyde (voc) | Ginyard,Julius Caleb (voc) | Verstraete,Charles (tb) | Gossez,Pierre (as) | Chautemps,Jean-Louis (ts) | Solal,Martial (p,arr) | Hauser,Michel (vib) | Rovere,Paul (b) | Humair,Daniel (dr)
Oh! Why?(Mon Amour Oublié)
Paris,France, rec. 18.2.1960
Golden Gate Quartet: | Wilson,Orlandus (voc) | Riddick,Clyde (voc) | Wright,Clyde (voc) | Ginyard,Julius Caleb (voc) | Boucaya,William (bs) | Solal,Martial (p,arr) | Hauser,Michel (vib) | Rovere,Paul (b) | Humair,Daniel (dr)
Golden Gate Quartet
White Christmas
Paris,France, rec. 20.10.1960
Golden Gate Quartet,The (voc) | Wilson,Orlandus (voc) | Riddick,Clyde (voc) | Wright,Clyde (voc) | Ginyard,Julius Caleb (voc) | Burgess,Glenn (p) | unkn. (b,dr)
Ballin' The Jack
Paris,France, rec. 21.10.1960
Golden Gate Quartet,The (voc) | Wilson,Orlandus (voc) | Riddick,Clyde (voc) | Wright,Clyde (voc) | Ginyard,Julius Caleb (voc) | Lafitte,Guy (ts) | Burgess,Glenn (p) | Michelot,Pierre (b) | unkn. (dr)
Alexander's Ragtime Band
Paris,France, rec. 25.10.1960
Golden Gate Quartet,The (voc) | Wilson,Orlandus (voc) | Riddick,Clyde (voc) | Wright,Clyde (voc) | Ginyard,Julius Caleb (voc) | Lafitte,Guy (ts) | Burgess,Glenn (p) | Michelot,Pierre (b) | unkn. (dr)
Memories Of You
Paris,France, rec. 7.11.1960
Golden Gate Quartet,The (voc) | Wilson,Orlandus (voc) | Riddick,Clyde (voc) | Wright,Clyde (voc) | Ginyard,Julius Caleb (voc) | Lafitte,Guy (ts) | Burgess,Glenn (p) | Michelot,Pierre (b) | unkn. (dr)
Deep River
Paris,France, rec. 29.11.1960
Golden Gate Quartet,The (voc) | Wilson,Orlandus (voc) | Riddick,Clyde (voc) | Wright,Clyde (voc) | Ginyard,Julius Caleb (voc) | Burgess,Glenn (p) | unkn. (vib,g,b,dr)
Over There
Paris,France, rec. 7.9.1964
Golden Gate Quartet,The (voc) | Wilson,Orlandus (voc) | Riddick,Clyde (voc) | Wright,Clyde (voc) | Ginyard,Julius Caleb (voc) | unkn. (g,p,b,dr)
Glory Hallelujah
Paris,France, rec. 8.9.1964
unkn. (org) | Golden Gate Quartet,The (voc) | Wilson,Orlandus (voc) | Riddick,Clyde (voc) | Wright,Clyde (voc) | Ginyard,Julius Caleb (voc)
Basin Street Blues | The Birth Of The Blues | On The Sunny Side Of The Street
Paris,France, rec. 14.11.1964
Golden Gate Quartet,The (voc) | Wilson,Orlandus (voc) | Riddick,Clyde (voc) | Wright,Clyde (voc) | Ginyard,Julius Caleb (voc) | Orchestra | details unknown
Oh Happy Day
Paris,France, rec. 30.7.1969
Golden Gate Quartet,The (voc) | Wilson,Orlandus (voc) | Riddick,Clyde (voc) | Wright,Clyde (voc) | Ginyard,Julius Caleb (voc)

539660-2 | CD | Americans Swinging In Paris:Mezz Mezzrow |
EAN 724353966027
Milton Mezz Mezzrow Sextet
Minor With A Bridge(part I slow) | Minor With A Bridge(part I fast) | Minor With A Bridge(part II slow) | Minor With A Bridge(part II fast)
Live at The Schola Cantorum,Paris,France, rec. 20.5.1955
Mezzrow,Milton Mezz (cl) | Holland,Peanuts (tp) | Longnon,Guy (tp) | Sealey,Milton (p) | De Haas,Eddie (b) | Fields,Kansas (dr)
Milton Mezz Mezzrow-Maxim Saury Quintet
Rosetta | All Of Me | Someday Sweetheart | Wailin' With Saury | Sweet Sue Just You
Live at The Schola Cantorum,Paris,France, rec. 5.7.1955
Mezzrow,Milton Mezz (cl) | Saury,Maxim (cl) | Sealey,Milton (p) | De Haas,Eddie (b) | Fields,Kansas (dr)

539661-2 | CD | Americans Swinging In Paris:Earl Hines |
EAN 724353966126
Earl Hines
I Surrender Dear | I Cover The Waterfront | Second Balcony Jump | A Pretty Girl Is Like A Melody | I Can't Give You Anything But Love | Blue Because Of You | Somebody Loves Me | Sixty-Five Faubourg | On The Sunny Side Of The Street | Sweet Sue Just You | Rose Room | Rose Room(alt.take-1) | Rose Room(alt.take-2)
Paris,France, rec. 27.5.1965
Hines,Earl 'Fatha' (p-solo,voc)

539662-2 | CD | Americans Swinging In Paris:Bill Coleman-The Elegance |
EAN 724353966225
Alix Combelle Et Son Orchestre
Exactly Like You | Alexander's Ragtime Band | Hangover Blues
Paris,France, rec. 4.9.1937
Combelle,Alix (cl,ts) | Coleman,Bill (tp,voc) | Martin,David (p) | Chaput,Roger (g) | Myers,Wilson Ernest (b) | Mengo,Jerry (dr)
Bill Coleman Et Son Orchestre
Back Home Again In Indiana | Rose Room | Bill Street Blues | After You've Gone | The Merry-Go-Round Broke Down
Paris,France, rec. 12.11.1937
Coleman,Bill (tp,voc) | Grappelli,Stephane (p,v) | Reinhardt,Joseph (g) | Myers,Wilson Ernest (b) | Fields,Ted (dr)
I Ain't Got Nobody | Baby Won't You Please Come Home | Baby Won't You Please Come Home(alt.take) | Big Boy Blues | Swing Guitars
Paris,France, rec. 19.11.1937
Coleman,Bill (tp,voc) | Wagner,Christian (cl,as) | Goodie,Frank 'Big Boy' (cl,ts) | Stern,Emile (p) | Reinhardt,Django (g) | Simoens,Lucien (b) | Mengo,Jerry (dr)
Bill Coleman-Django Reinhardt Duo
Bill Coleman Blues
Paris,France, rec. 19.11.1930
Coleman,Bill (tp) | Reinhardt,Django (g)
Eddie Brunner And His Orchestra
In A Little Spanish Town | I Double Dare You | Bagatelle | Montmartre Blues | Margie
Paris,France, rec. 13.6.1938
Brunner,Eddie (cl,ts) | Coleman,Bill (tp) | Combelle,Alix (ts) | Chiboust,Noel (ts) | Chittison,Herman (p) | Aleman,Oscar (g) | Grasset,Roger (b) | Benford,Tommy (dr)
Bill Coleman Quintet
Way Down Yonder In New Orleans | I Wish I Could Shimmy Like My Sister Kate
Paris,France, rec. 28.9.1938
Coleman,Bill (tp) | Courance,Edgar (cl,ts) | Mitchell,John (g) | Myers,Wilson Ernest (b,voc) | Benford,Tommy (dr)

539663-2 | CD | Americans Swinging In Paris:Bill Coleman |
EAN 724353966324
Bill Coleman Sextet
Satin Doll | On Green Dolphin Street | Do You Know What It Means To Miss New Orleans | 'S Wonderful
Live at The Caveau de La Huchette,Paris,France, rec. 21./22.3.1979
Coleman,Bill (fl-h,voc) | Buhrer,Rolf (tb) | Doriz,Danny (vib) | Authier,Patrice (p) | Tischitz,Henri (b) | Denis,Michel (dr)

539664-2 | CD | Americans Swinging In Paris:Dicky Wells |
EAN 724353966423
Dicky Wells And His Orchestra
Bugle Call Rag | Between The Devil And The Deep Blue Sea | I Got Rhythm
Paris,France, rec. 7.7.1937
Wells,Dicky (tb,arr) | Dillard,Bill (tp) | Collins,Lester 'Shad' (tp) | Coleman,Bill (tp) | Reinhardt,Django (g) | Fullbright,Richard (b) | Beason,Bill (dr) | Eldridge,Roy (arr)
Sweet Sue Just You | Hangin' Around Boudon | Japanese Sandman
Wells,Dicky (tb) | Coleman,Bill (tp,voc) | Reinhardt,Django (g) | Fullbright,Richard (b) | Beason,Bill (dr)
I've Found A New Baby | Dinah
Paris,France, rec. 12.7.1937
Wells,Dicky (tb) | Dillard,Bill (tp) | Collins,Lester 'Shad' (tp) | Johnson,Howard (as) | Allen,Sam (p) | Chaput,Roger (g) | Beason,Bill (dr)
Nobody's Blues But My Own
Wells,Dicky (tb) | Collins,Lester 'Shad' (tp) | Johnson,Howard (as) | Allen,Sam (p) | Chaput,Roger (g) | Beason,Bill (dr)
Hot Club Blues
Wells,Dicky (tb) | Dillard,Bill (tp) | Johnson,Howard (as) | Allen,Sam (p) | Chaput,Roger (g) | Beason,Bill (dr)
Oh! Lady Be Good | Dicky Wells Blues
Wells,Dicky (tb) | Allen,Sam (p) | Chaput,Roger (g) | Beason,Bill (dr)

539665-2 | CD | Americans Swinging In Paris:Wild Bill Davis |
EAN 724353966522
Wild Bill Davis Group
Gone With The Wind
Live at The Caveau de La Huchette,Paris,France, rec. May 1977
Davis,Wild Bill (org) | Guerault,Stephane (ts) | Doriz,Danny (vib) | Martin,Maurice (dr)
Back Home Again In Indiana | Jumpin' With Symphony Sid
Davis,Wild Bill (org) | Guerault,Stephane (ts) | Doriz,Danny (vib) | Clarke,Kenny (dr)
Strike Up The Band | Lullaby Of Birdland | Wild Bill Blues At The Huchette
Davis,Wild Bill (org) | Guerault,Stephane (ts) | Doriz,Danny (vib) | Pochonet,Gerard 'Dave' (dr)
Body And Soul | Lil' Darlin'
Davis,Wild Bill (org) | Doriz,Danny (vib) | Pochonet,Gerard 'Dave' (dr)

539666-2 | CD | Americans Swinging In Paris:Memphis Slim |
EAN 724353966621
Memphis Slim Trio
Pinetop's Boogie Woogie | Blues For Jimmy Yancey | Drums Boogie Woogie | New Three And One Boogie | Huchette Blues | All By Myself | Boogie For Chuck Berry | I'm Lost Without | Bye Bye Blues | Celestial Boogie | Huchette Boogie Woogie | Boogie And Drums
Live at The Caveau de La Huchette,Paris,France, rec. 29.8.1984
Memphis Slim[Peter Chatman] (p,voc) | Amouroux,Jean-Paul (o,org,celeste) | Denis,Michel (dr)

539667-2 | CD | Americans Swinging In Paris:Art Ensemble Of Chicago |
EAN 724353966720
Art Ensemble Of Chicago
People In Sorrow(part 1&2)
Paris,France, rec. 7.7.1969
Art Ensemble Of Chicago | Bowie,Lester (tp,fl-h) | Mitchell,Roscoe (fl,ss,as,perc) | Jarman,Joseph (fl,ss,as,perc) | Favors,Malachi (b)
Theme De Yoyo | Theme De Celine | Variations Sur Un Theme De Monteverdi(part 1-3) | Theme De L'Amour Universel | Proverbes(part 1-3)
Paris,France, rec. 22.7.1970
Art Ensemble Of Chicago | Bowie,Lester (tp,fl-h,perc) | Mitchell,Roscoe (fl,ss,as,perc) | Jarman,Joseph (fl,ss,as,perc) | Favors,Malachi (b,perc) | Moye,Famoudou Don (dr,perc) | Bass,Fontella (p,voc)

780573-2 | CD | From Sprititual To Swing Vol.2
Golden Gate Quartet
Didn't Rain | I Just Telephon Upstairs | I Pitched My Tend | Invisible Hands | You Never Walk Alone
Paris,France, rec. 16.11.1955
Golden Gate Quartet: | Wilson,Orlandus (voc) | Riddick,Clyde (voc) | Wright,Clyde (voc) | Ginyard,Julius Caleb (voc) | Trotman,Irving (p)
Steel Away
Paris,France, rec. 8.4.1958
Golden Gate Quartet: | Wilson,Orlandus (voc) | Riddick,Clyde (voc) | Wright,Clyde (voc) | Ginyard,Julius Caleb (voc) | Burgess,Glenn (p)
Sometimes I Feel Like A Motherless Child
Paris,France, rec. 9.4.1958
Golden Gate Quartet: | Wilson,Orlandus (voc) | Riddick,Clyde (voc) | Wright,Clyde (voc) | Ginyard,Julius Caleb (voc) | Burgess,Glenn (org) | Cullaz,Pierre (g) | Michelot,Pierre (b) | Garros,Christian (dr)
Golden Gate Quartet With The Martial Solal Orchestra
My Heart Is A n Open Book
Paris,France, rec. 22.12.1959
Golden Gate Quartet: | Wilson,Orlandus (voc) | Riddick,Clyde (voc) | Wright,Clyde (voc) | Ginyard,Julius Caleb (voc) | Gossez,Pierre (as) | Chautemps,Jean-Louis (ts) | Solal,Martial (p,arr) | Hauser,Michel (vib) | Rovere,Paul (b) | Humair,Daniel (dr)
Primrose lane | Mister Blue
Golden Gate Quartet: | Wilson,Orlandus (voc) | Riddick,Clyde (voc) | Wright,Clyde (voc) | Ginyard,Julius Caleb (voc) | Verstraete,Charles (tb) | Gossez,Pierre (as) | Chautemps,Jean-Louis (ts) | Solal,Martial (p,arr) | Hauser,Michel (vib) | Rovere,Paul (b) | Humair,Daniel (dr)
Oh! Why?(Mon Amour Oublié)
Paris,France, rec. 18.2.1960
Golden Gate Quartet: | Wilson,Orlandus (voc) | Riddick,Clyde (voc) | Wright,Clyde (voc) | Ginyard,Julius Caleb (voc) | Verstraete,Charles (tb) | Boucaya,William (bs) | Solal,Martial (p,arr) | Hauser,Michel (vib) | Rovere,Paul (b) | Humair,Daniel (dr)
Get On Board
Paris,France, rec. 28.3.1960
Golden Gate Quartet: | Wilson,Orlandus (voc) | Riddick,Clyde (voc) | Wright,Clyde (voc) | Ginyard,Julius Caleb (voc) | Burgess,Glenn (p,celeste) | Sim,Pierre prob. (b) | unkn. (dr)
Goodbye Mister Froggie | Alabamy Bound
Paris,France, rec. 29.4.1960
Golden Gate Quartet: | Wilson,Orlandus (voc) | Riddick,Clyde (voc) | Wright,Clyde (voc) | Ginyard,Julius Caleb (voc) | Burgess,Glenn (p,celeste) | Sim,Pierre prob. (b) | unkn. (dr)
Roll Jordan Roll | Good News
Paris,France, rec. 20.5.1960
Golden Gate Quartet: | Wilson,Orlandus (voc) | Riddick,Clyde (voc) | Wright,Clyde (voc) | Ginyard,Julius Caleb (voc) | Burgess,Glenn (p,celeste) | Sim,Pierre prob. (b) | unkn. (dr)
Ezekiel Saw 'De Wheel

Paris,France, rec. 21.6.1960
Golden Gate Quartet: | Wilson,Orlandus (voc) | Riddick,Clyde (voc) | Wright,Clyde (voc) | Ginyard,Julius Caleb (voc) | Burgess,Glenn (p,celeste) | Sim,Pierre prob. (b) | unkn. (dr)
Rudolph The Red Nosed Reindeer
Paris,France, rec. 20.10.1960
Golden Gate Quartet: | Wilson,Orlandus (voc) | Riddick,Clyde (voc) | Wright,Clyde (voc) | Ginyard,Julius Caleb (voc) | Hauser,Michel (vib) | Burgess,Glenn (p,celeste) | Cullaz,Pierre (g) | Sim,Pierre prob. (b) | unkn. (dr)
Poor Little Jesus
Paris,France, rec. 21.10.1960
Golden Gate Quartet: | Wilson,Orlandus (voc) | Riddick,Clyde (voc) | Wright,Clyde (voc) | Ginyard,Julius Caleb (voc) | Lafitte,Guy (ts) | Hauser,Michel (vib) | Burgess,Glenn (p,celeste) | Cullaz,Pierre (g) | Sim,Pierre (b) | Bellonzi,Charles (dr)
Waillie-Waillie
Paris,France, rec. 25.10.1960
Golden Gate Quartet: | Wilson,Orlandus (voc) | Riddick,Clyde (voc) | Wright,Clyde (voc) | Ginyard,Julius Caleb (voc) | Lafitte,Guy (ts) | Hauser,Michel (vib) | Burgess,Glenn (p,celeste) | Cullaz,Pierre (g) | Sim,Pierre (b) | Bellonzi,Charles (dr)
The King Of Kings | For The Rest Of My Life
Paris,France, rec. 7.11.1960
Golden Gate Quartet: | Wilson,Orlandus (voc) | Riddick,Clyde (voc) | Wright,Clyde (voc) | Ginyard,Julius Caleb (voc) | Lafitte,Guy (ts) | Hauser,Michel (vib) | Burgess,Glenn (p,celeste) | Cullaz,Pierre (g) | Sim,Pierre (b) | Bellonzi,Charles (dr)
Golden Slippers | The World Outside(Warsow Concerto)
Paris,France, rec. 10.11.1960
Golden Gate Quartet: | Wilson,Orlandus (voc) | Riddick,Clyde (voc) | Wright,Clyde (voc) | Ginyard,Julius Caleb (voc) | Lafitte,Guy (ts) | Hauser,Michel (vib) | Burgess,Glenn (p,celeste) | Cullaz,Pierre (g) | Sim,Pierre (b) | Bellonzi,Charles (dr)
There Is No Greater Love
Paris,France, rec. 21.11.1960
Golden Gate Quartet: | Wilson,Orlandus (voc) | Riddick,Clyde (voc) | Wright,Clyde (voc) | Ginyard,Julius Caleb (voc) | unkn. (ts) | Hauser,Michel (vib) | Burgess,Glenn (p,celeste) | Cullaz,Pierre (g) | Sim,Pierre (b) | Bellonzi,Charles (dr)
Me And Brother Bill
Paris,France, rec. 29.11.1960
Golden Gate Quartet: | Wilson,Orlandus (voc) | Riddick,Clyde (voc) | Wright,Clyde (voc) | Ginyard,Julius Caleb (voc) | Burgess,Glenn (p,celeste) | Cullaz,Pierre (g) | Sim,Pierre (b) | Bellonzi,Charles (dr)

791569-2 | CD | Spirituals To Swing 1955-69
Golden Gate Quartet
Shadrack | Swing Low Sweet Chariot | Joshua Fit The Battle Of Jericho
Paris,France, rec. 16.11.1955
Golden Gate Quartet,The (voc) | Wilson,Orlandus (voc) | Riddick,Clyde (voc) | Wright,Clyde (voc) | Ginyard,Julius Caleb (voc) | Trotman,Irving (p) | Rovere,Paul (b) | Seamen,Phil (dr)
Nobody Knows The Trouble I've Seen
Berlin, rec. 5.7.1957
Golden Gate Quartet,The (voc) | Wilson,Orlandus (voc) | Riddick,Clyde (voc) | Wright,Clyde (voc) | Ginyard,Julius Caleb (voc) | Trotman,Irving (p)
Elijah | Down By The Riverside | 'Round The Bay Of Mexico
Paris,France, rec. 8./9.4.1958
Golden Gate Quartet,The (voc) | Wilson,Orlandus (voc) | Riddick,Clyde (voc) | Wright,Clyde (voc) | Ginyard,Julius Caleb (voc) | Burgess,Glenn (p) | Cullaz,Pierre (g) | Sim,Pierre (b) | Garros,Christian (dr)
Casey Jones
Paris,France, rec. 29.4.1960
Golden Gate Quartet,The (voc) | Wilson,Orlandus (voc) | Riddick,Clyde (voc) | Wright,Clyde (voc) | Ginyard,Julius Caleb (voc) | Burgess,Glenn (p)
White Christmas
Paris,France, rec. 20.10.1960
Golden Gate Quartet,The (voc) | Wilson,Orlandus (voc) | Riddick,Clyde (voc) | Wright,Clyde (voc) | Ginyard,Julius Caleb (voc) | Burgess,Glenn (p) | unkn. (b,dr)
Ballin' The Jack | Alexander's Ragtime Band | Memories Of You | When The Saints Go Marching In | Margie
Paris,France, rec. 21./25.10.& 7./21.11.1960
Golden Gate Quartet,The (voc) | Wilson,Orlandus (voc) | Riddick,Clyde (voc) | Wright,Clyde (voc) | Ginyard,Julius Caleb (voc) | Lafitte,Guy (ts) | Burgess,Glenn (p) | Michelot,Pierre (b) | unkn. (dr)
St.Louis Blues | Deep River
Paris,France, rec. 29.11.1960
Golden Gate Quartet,The (voc) | Wilson,Orlandus (voc) | Riddick,Clyde (voc) | Wright,Clyde (voc) | Ginyard,Julius Caleb (voc) | Burgess,Glenn (p) | unkn. (vib,g,b,dr)
Rock My Soul | Same Train | Over There | Glory, Hallelujah
Paris,France, rec. 7./8.9.1964
Golden Gate Quartet,The (voc) | Wilson,Orlandus (voc) | Riddick,Clyde (voc) | Wright,Clyde (voc) | Ginyard,Julius Caleb (voc)
Basin Street Blues | The Birth Of The Blues | On The Sunny Side Of The Street | Sweet Georgia Brown
Paris,France, rec. 14.11.1965
Golden Gate Quartet,The (voc) | Wilson,Orlandus (voc) | Riddick,Clyde (voc) | Wright,Clyde (voc) | Ginyard,Julius Caleb (voc)
Oh Happy Day
Paris,France, rec. 30.7.1969
Golden Gate Quartet,The (voc) | Wilson,Orlandus (voc) | Riddick,Clyde (voc) | Wright,Clyde (voc) | Ginyard,Julius Caleb (voc)

859622-2 | 3 CD | Stan Getz-The Complete Roost Sessions |
EAN 724385962226
Stan Getz Quartet
On The Alamo | On The Alamo(alt.take) | Gone With The Wind | Yesterdays | Sweetie Pie | You Go To My Head | Hershey Bar
NYC, rec. 17.5.1950
Getz,Stan (ts) | Haig,Al (p) | Potter,Tommy (b) | Haynes,Roy (dr)
Tootsie Roll | Strike Up The Band | Imagination | Imagination(alt.take) | For Stompers Only | Navy Blues | Out Of Nowhere | 'S Wonderful
NYC, rec. 10.12.1950
Getz,Stan (ts) | Silver,Horace (p) | Calloway,Joe (b) | Bolden,Walter (dr)
Penny | Split Kick | Split Kick(alt.take) | It Might As Well Be Spring | It Might As Well Be Spring(alt.take) | The Best Thing For You
NYC, rec. 1.3.1951
Getz,Stan (ts) | Silver,Horace (p) | Calloway,Joe (b) | Bolden,Walter (dr)
Stan Getz Quintet
Melody Express | Yvette | Potter's Luck | The Song Is You | Wildwood
NYC, rec. 15.8.1951
Getz,Stan (ts) | Raney,Jimmy (g) | Silver,Horace (p) | Gaskin,Leonard (b) | Haynes,Roy (dr)
Johnny Smith-Stan Getz Quintet
Where Or When | Tabu | Moonlight In Vermont | Jaguar
NYC, rec. 11.3.1952
Getz,Stan (ts) | Smith,Johnny (g) | Gold,Sanford (p) | Safranski,Eddie (b) | Lamond,Don (dr)
Sometimes I'm Happy | Stars Fell On Alabama | Nice Work If You Can Get It | Tenderly
NYC, rec. 9.11.1952
Getz,Stan (ts) | Smith,Johnny (g) | Gold,Sanford (p) | Safranski,Eddie (b) | Lamond,Don (dr)
Stan Getz Quintet
Lullaby Of Birdland | Autumn Leaves | Autumn Leaves(alt.take) | Fools Rush In | Fools Rush In(alt.take) | These Foolish Things Remind Me On You
NYC, rec. 19.12.1952
Getz,Stan (ts) | Raney,Jimmy (g) | Jordan,Duke (p) | Crow,Bill (b) | Isola,Frank (dr)
You're Driving Me Crazy | Lover Come Back To Me | Ain't Nobody's Bizness If I Do
Live at Club Storyville,Boston, rec. 29.10.1951
Getz,Stan (ts) | Harding,Buster (p) | Fields,John (b) | Foster,Marquis (dr) | Holiday,Billie (voc)
Signal | Budo | Budo(alt.take) | The Song Is You | Parker 51 | Mosquito Knees | Thou Swell | Yesterdays | Jumpin' With Symphony Sid | Pennies From Heaven | Move | Rubberneck | Hershey Bar | Signal(alt.take) | Everything Happens To Me | Wildwood
Live at The Storyville Club,Boston,MA, rec. 28.10.1951
Getz,Stan (ts) | Raney,Jimmy (g) | Haig,Al (p) | Kotick,Teddy (b) | Kahn,Tiny (dr)

Enja | Enja Eigenvertrieb

ENJ-2040 2 | CD | Songs For Love
Tete Montoliu
Rainy Day | Django | Two Catalan Songs | Gentofte 4349 | Apartment 512 | Autumn In New York | Ballad For Line | Little Camila
München, rec. 25.9.1971
Montoliu,Tete (p-solo)

ENJ-2044 2 | CD | Drifting
Walter Norris-George Mraz Duo
Nota Cambiata | Thumbs Up | Spring Can Really Hang You Up The Most | Space Maker | Drifting | A Child Is Born | Rose Waltz | Falling In Love With Love
rec. 18.8.1974
Norris,Walter (p) | Mraz,George 'Jiri' (b)
Maple Leaf Rag
Norris,Walter (p-solo)

ENJ-3069 2 | CD | Blues In Orbit
Gil Evans Orchestra
General Assembly | Proclamation | Love In The Open | Spaced | Variations On The Misery | So Long
rec. 1969
Evans,Gil (p,el-p) | Young,Eugene 'Snooky' (tp) | Lawrence,Mike (tp) | Cleveland,Jimmy (tb) | Knepper,Jimmy (tb) | Watkins,Julius (fr-h) | Johnson,Howard (tuba) | Laws,Hubert (fl) | Harper,Billy (ts) | Beck,Joe (g) | Bianco,Gene (harp) | Bushler,Herb (b) | Jones,Elvin (dr) | Evans,Suzan 'Sue' (perc)
Thoroughbred | Blues In Orbit
rec. 1971
Evans,Gil (p,el-p) | Royal,Ernie (tp) | Coles,Johnny (tp) | Brown,Garnett (tb) | Cleveland,Jimmy (tb) | Watkins,Julius (fr-h) | Alonge,Ray (fr-h) | Marge,George (fl,ss) | Harper,Billy (fl,ts) | Johnson,Howard (bs,tuba) | Beck,Joe (g) | Bushler,Herb (b) | Mouzon,Alphonse (dr) | McDonald,Donald (perc)

ENJ-4014 2 | CD | Confirmation
Tommy Flanagan Trio
Maybe September | Confirmation | Cup Bearers | 50-21
rec. 4.2.1977
Flanagan,Tommy (p) | Mraz,George 'Jiri' (b) | Jones,Elvin (dr)
Tommy Flanagan/George Mraz
How High The Moon | It Never Entered My Mind
rec. 15.11.1978
Flanagan,Tommy (p) | Mraz,George 'Jiri' (b)

ENJ-4040 2 | CD | The River Is Deep
Jerry Gonzalez & Fort Apache Band
Introduction by Jerry Gonzalez | Elegua | Bebop | Rio Esta Hondo | Guiro Apache | Parisian Thoroughfare | Wawina Era Wo
Live at Berlin, rec. 5.11.1982
Gonzalez,Jerry (tp,fl-h,bells,conga,voc) | Turre,Steve (tb,b-tb) | Vasquez,Papo (tb) | Velez,Wilfredo (as) | Miranda,Edgardo (g,quarto) | Dalto,Jorge (p) | Gonzalez,Andy (b,voc) | Berrios,Steve (dr,bata,chekkere,voc) | Golden,Gene (bata,checkere,congas,bells) | Hernandez,Hector 'Flaco' (congas,bata,chekere) | Marrero,Nicky (perc,guataca,timbales) | Rodriguez,Frankie (claves,conga,voc)

ENJ-4052 2 | CD | Thelonica
Tommy Flanagan Trio
Off Minor | Pannonica | North Of The Sunset | Thelonious | Reflections | Ugly Beauty
NYC, rec. 3o.11./1.12.1982
Flanagan,Tommy (p) | Mraz,George 'Jiri' (b) | Taylor,Arthur 'Art' (dr)
Tommy Flanagan
Thelonica(1) | Thelonica(2)
Flanagan,Tommy (p-solo)

ENJ-4072 2 | CD | Calorcito
Conexion Latina
Calorcito | Como El Viento | Como Volver A Tenerte | Despacito | Bomba Puertoriquene | Acumulando Puntos | Tirate | Latin Groove | Asi Es La Vida | Cantado La Melodia | Latin Connection
Ludwigsburg, rec. 30.1.-5.2.1984
Conexion Latina | Garcia,Luis (cond) | Bailey,Benny (tp) | Rader,Don (tp) | Coassin,Bob (tp) | Gallardo,Joe (tb) | Fuesers,Rudi (tb) | Monge,Luis (p) | Cruz,Hectir (el-b) | Granados,Cesar (timbales) | Rodriguez,Jose 'Papo' (congas) | Verdejo,Tony (bongos) | Hernandez,Wilfredo (perc) | Rodriguez,Irwin 'Wito' (voc)

ENJ-4088 2 | CD | In Concert
Art Farmer/Slide Hampton Quintet
Half Nelson | Barbados | Darn That Dream | I'll Remember April
NYC, rec. July 1984
Farmer,Art (tp) | Hampton,Slide (tb) | McNeely,Jim (p) | McClure,Ron (b) | Nussbaum,Adam (dr)

ENJ-4090 2 | CD | The Upper Manhattan Jazz Society
The Upper Manhattan Jazz Society
Lil' Sherry | Naima's Love Song | Mr.McGee | Spelunke | After The Morning
NYC, rec. Nov.1981
Upper Manhattan Jazz Society,The | Rouse,Charlie (ts,ld) | Bailey,Benny (tp) | Dailey,Albert (p) | Williams,Buster (b) | Copeland,Keith (dr)

ENJ-5011 2 | CD | Clark Terry-Red Mitchell
Clark Terry-Red Mitchell Duo
Big'n And The Bear | Shiny Stockings | I Got It Bad And That Ain't Good | C Jam Blues | Moten Swing | It Don't Mean A Thing If It Ain't Got That Swing | Swinging The Blues | Hey Mr. Mumbles,What Did You Say? | Thanks For Everything | It Don't Mean A Thing If It Ain't Got That Swing(alt.take)
Stockholm,Sweden, rec. February 1986
Terry,Clark (tp,fl-h,voice) | Mitchell,Red (p,b,voc)

ENJ-5071 2 | CD | Live At Fat Tuesdays
Kenny Barron Quintet
There Is No Greater Love | Misterioso | Lunacy | Sand Dune | 518
Fat Tuesday's,NYC, rec. 15./16.1.1988
Barron,Kenny (p) | Henderson,Eddie (tp) | Stubblefield,John (ts) | McBee,Cecil (b) | Lewis,Victor (dr)

ENJ-5081 2 | CD | Blues Bred In The Bone
Ray Anderson Quintet
Blues Bred In The Bone | 53rd And Greenwood | Mona Lisa | Datune | A Flower Is A Lovesome Thing | Hemlines | I Don't Want To Set The World On Fire
NYC, rec. 27./28.3.1988
Anderson,Ray (tb) | Scofield,John (g) | Davis,Anthony (p) | Dresser,Mark (b) | Vidacovich,Johnny (dr)

ENJ-5093 2 | CD | Secrets
Leni Stern Group
Ground Hog | Maybe | Amethyst | Secrets | Who Loves You | Silver Fox | Point Falling | For Now
NYC, rec. 24.-26.9.1988
Stern,Leni (g) | Berg,Bob (ts) | Krantz,Wayne (g) | Tronzo,David (slide-g) | Goines,Lincoln (el-b) | Swartz,Harvie (b) | Chambers,Dennis (dr) | Alias,Don (perc)

ENJ-6014 22 | 2 CD | Times Of Devastation/Poco A Poco
Klaus König Orchestra
Times Of Devestation | The Double Rainbow Over Heeper Street | Statements | Valse Triste | The Darker Side | That Time | Pandemonium | Epilogue
Stadtgarten,Köln, rec. 19.6.1989
Koenig,Klaus (comp,ld) | Wheeler,Kenny (tp,fl-h) | Winterschladen,Reiner (tp,fl-h) | Anderson,Ray (tb) | Collings,Bruce (tb) | Struck,Frank (fr-h) | Godard,Michel (tuba) | Ehrlich,Marty (cl,b-cl,as) | Gratkowski,Frank (fl,b-cl,ss,as) | Schubert,Matthias (ts,oboe) | Cordovani,Renato (b-cl) | Nabatov,Simon (p) | Wells,Tim (b) | Betsch,John (dr)
Bodyguard From Scotland Yard | Feel The Pain | Niet Pivo Niet Blues | Some Kind Of Destruction | Poco A Poco | Cries For South Africa | For Lacy
Köln, rec. 28./29.6.1989
König,Klaus (ts) | Winterschladen,Reiner (tp) | Pilz,Michel (b-cl) | Schubert,Matthias (ts,oboe) | Gratkowski,Frank (fl,ss,as) | Wells,Tim (b) | Köllges,Frank (dr)

ENJ-6034 2 | CD | Closer To The Light
Leni Stern Group
Nobody's Something
NYC, rec. 27.11.-1.12.1989
Stern,Leni (g) | Sanborn,David (as) | Krantz,Wayne (g) | Socolow,Paul (el-b) | Danzinger,Zachary (dr) | Alias,Don (perc)
Sand Box | Red Stripe
Stern,Leni (g) | Krantz,Wayne (g) | Socolow,Paul (el-b) | Danzinger,Zachary (dr) | Alias,Don (perc)
All Or Nothing
Stern,Leni (g) | Sanborn,David (as) | Goines,Lincoln (el-b) | Chambers,Dennis (dr)
Phoenix
Stern,Leni (g) | Krantz,Wayne (g) | Goines,Lincoln (el-b) | Chambers,Dennis (dr) | Alias,Don (perc)
Tbilissi
Stern,Leni (g) | Krantz,Wayne (g) | Socolow,Paul (el-b) | Danzinger,Zachary (dr)
Closer To The Light
Stern,Leni (g) | Krantz,Wayne (g)
All Or Nothing | Show Me
Stern,Leni (g) | Krantz,Wayne (g) | Goines,Lincoln (el-b) | Chambers,Dennis (dr)

ENJ-6072 2 | CD | Blues 'N Dues Et Cetera
George Gruntz Concert Jazz Band
Q-Base
NYC, rec. 4./5.& 29.1.1991
Gruntz,George (p) | Stamm,Marvin (tp) | Millikan,Robert 'Bob' (tp) | Brecker,Randy (tp) | Mossman,Michel Philip (tp) | Clark,John (fr-h) | Peel,Jerry (fr-h) | Bargeron,Dave (euphonium) | Pugh,Jim (euphonium) | Johnson,Howard (tuba) | Hunter,Chris (as) | Mintzer,Bob (ts) | Malach,Bob (ts) | Bergonzi,Jerry (ts) | Scofield,John (g) | Richmond,Mike (b) | Nussbaum,Adam (dr) | D.J.A.D. (scratch)
Blues 'N' Dues Et Cetera | Two Friends
Gruntz,George (p) | Stamm,Marvin (tp) | Millikan,Robert 'Bob' (tp) | Brecker,Randy (tp) | Mossman,Michel Philip (tp) | Clark,John (fr-h) | Peel,Jerry (fr-h) | Bargeron,Dave (euphonium) | Pugh,Jim (euphonium) | Johnson,Howard (tuba) | Hunter,Chris (as) | Mintzer,Bob (ts) | Malach,Bob (ts) | Bergonzi,Jerry (ts) | Richmond,Mike (b) | Nussbaum,Adam (dr)
Forest Cathedral
Gruntz,George (p) | Stamm,Marvin (fl-h) | Ambrosetti,Franco (fl-h) | Clark,John (fr-h) | Peel,Jerry (fr-h) | Bargeron,Dave (euphonium) | Pugh,Jim (euphonium) | Johnson,Howard (tuba) | Scofield,John (g) | Richmond,Mike (b) | Nussbaum,Adam (dr)
Sentimental Over Mental Food- | In A Sentimental Mood- | Giuseppi
Gruntz,George (p) | Stamm,Marvin (fl-h) | Clark,John (fr-h) | Peel,Jerry (fr-h) | Bargeron,Dave (euphonium) | Pugh,Jim (euphonium) | Johnson,Howard (tuba) | Richmond,Mike (b) | Nussbaum,Adam (dr)
Datune
Gruntz,George (p) | Stamm,Marvin (tp) | Faddis,Jon (tp) | D'Earth,John (tp) | Roney,Wallace (tp) | Anderson,Ray (tb) | Baron,Art (tb) | Taylor,Dave (tb) | Bargeron,Dave (tb) | Hunter,Chris (as) | Mann,Dave (as) | Malach,Bob (ts) | Foster,Alex (ts) | Rosenberg,Roger (bs) | Richmond,Mike (b) | Nussbaum,Adam (dr)
Rap For Nap
Gruntz,George (p) | Stamm,Marvin (tp) | Faddis,Jon (tp) | D'Earth,John (tp) | Roney,Wallace (tp) | Anderson,Ray (tb,rap-voc) | Baron,Art (tb) | Taylor,Dave (tb) | Bargeron,Dave (tb) | Hunter,Chris (as) | Mann,Dave (as) | Malach,Bob (ts) | Foster,Alex (ts) | Rosenberg,Roger (bs) | Richmond,Mike (b) | Nussbaum,Adam (dr) | D.J.A.D. (scratch) | Desire (rap-voc)
General Cluster
NYC, rec. 4./5.&.29.1.1991
Gruntz,George (p) | Stamm,Marvin (tp) | Faddis,Jon (tp) | D'Earth,John (tp) | Roney,Wallace (tp) | Anderson,Ray (tb,rap-voc) | Baron,Art (tb,bass-recorder,conch-chell) | Taylor,Dave (tb,voice) | Bargeron,Dave (tb,euphonium) | Pugh,Jim (euphonium) | Clark,John (fr-h) | Peel,Jerry (fr-h) | Johnson,Howard (tuba) | Hunter,Chris (as) | Mann,Dave (as) | Malach,Bob (ts) | Foster,Alex (ts) | Rosenberg,Roger (bs) | Richmond,Mike (b) | Nussbaum,Adam (dr)

ENJ-6076 2 | CD | Live
Itchy Fingers
The Headmasters Daughter | Storm | Invitation | The Devil's Pulpit | Building
Vilshofen, rec. 17.6.1989
Itchy Fingers | Mower,Mike (fl,ts) | Graham,John (ss,as,ts) | Hitchcock,Nigel (as) | Turner,Howard (bs)
Seven Pounds Fifty | Dakhut | Woe
Freiburg,Brg., rec. 20.6.1989
Itchy Fingers | Mower,Mike (fl,ts) | Graham,John (ss,as,ts) | Hitchcock,Nigel (as) | Turner,Howard (bs)
Ford Fiasco | It's Lovely Once You're In
Lyon, France, rec. 23.6.1989
Itchy Fingers | Mower,Mike (fl,ts) | Graham,John (ss,as,ts) | Hitchcock,Nigel (as) | Turner,Howard (bs)
Yuppieville Rodeo
Hull,GB, rec. 11.4.1988
Itchy Fingers | Mower,Mike (fl,ts) | Graham,John (ss,as,ts) | Hitchcock,Nigel (as) | Turner,Howard (bs)

ENJ-6078 2 | CD | Hommage A Douglas Adams
Klaus König Orchestra
Introducing Arthur Dent(Overture) | Prostetnic Vogon Jeltz | Marvin's Song | Deep Thought | The Babel Fish | The Pan Galactic Gargle Blaster(or Beeblebrox' Blues) | The Earth | The Restaurant At The End Of The Universe(including Trillian's Dance)
Live at The 'Philharmonie',Berlin, rec. 7./8.3.1991
Koenig,Klaus (comp,ld) | Wheeler,Kenny (tp) | Winterschladen,Reiner (tp) | Bauer,Conrad (tb) | Grabosch,Horst (fr-h) | Massot,Michel (tuba) | Sclavis,Louis (cl) | Bloom,Jane Ira (ss) | Gratkowski,Frank (fl,as) | Schubert,Matthias (ts,oboe) | Kaiser,Wollie (bs) | Nabatov,Simon (p) | Wells,Tim (b) | Manderscheid,Dieter (b) | Betsch,John (dr) | Rainey,Tom (dr)

ENJ-6080 2 | CD | Remembering John
McCoy Tyner Trio
India | Giant Steps | In Walked Bud | Like Someone In Love | One And Four | Up 'Gainst The Wall | Good Morning Heartache | Pursuance | The Wise One
NYC, rec. 27./28.2.1991
Tyner,McCoy (p) | Sharpe,Avery (b) | Scott,Aaron (dr)

ENJ-6084 2 | CD | Quickstep
Kenny Barron Quintet
Once Upon A Time | I Wanted To Say | Until Then | Hindsight | Here And There | Big Girls | Quick Step
Englewood Cliffs,NJ, rec. 18.2.1991
Barron,Kenny (p) | Henderson,Eddie (tp) | Stubblefield,John (ts) | Williams,David (b) | Lewis,Victor (dr)

ENJ-6088 2 | CD | Hipmotism
Arthur Blythe Group
Dear Dessa | Dance Benita Dance | Cousin Sidney | Shadows | Hipmotism | Miss Eugie | Matter Of Fact | Bush Baby | My Son Ra

Brooklyn,NY, rec. 15.-17.3.1991
Blythe,Arthur (as) | Bluiett,Hamiet (bs) | Stewart,Robert 'Bob' (tuba) | Tsilis,Gust William (vib,marimba) | Bell,Kelvyn (g) | Moye,Famoudou Don (dr) | Tuncboyaci[Boyaciyan],Arto (perc,voice)

ENJ-7003 2 | CD | Mythology
Daniel Schnyder Quintet With String Quartet
Hudi The Witch | Mantes | Eternal Ascension To A Topless Mountain | Barbara | Fully Mechanized Peaks | Carnival | Eugenia The Bride | Mars | Cat Dance | Heroes
NYC, rec. 24.-27.4.1991
Schnyder,Daniel (fl,ss,ts) | Soloff,Lew (tp,electronic-tp,piccolo-tp) | Mossman,Michel Philip (tp,fl-h,tb) | Formanek,Michael (b) | Hirshfield,Jeff (dr) | Feldman,Mark (v) | Rowell,Mary (v) | Martin,Lois (viola) | Friedlander,Erik (cello)

ENJ-7005 2 | CD | Children Of Ibeji
Ivo Perlman Group
Mina Do Sante | Little Rocks Of Aruanda
NYC, rec. 22.5./9.& 10.7.1991
Perlman,Ivo (ts) | Hopkins,Fred (b) | Cyrille,Andrew (dr) | Franco,Guilherme (perc) | Colon,Frank (perc) | Purim,Flora (voc)
Tom's Diner
Perlman,Ivo (ts) | Hopkins,Fred (b) | Cyrille,Andrew (dr) | Franco,Guilherme (perc,el-berimbao) | Colon,Frank (perc)
O Morro Nao Tem Vez(One I Loved)
Perlman,Ivo (ts) | Pullen,Don (p) | Hopkins,Fred (b) | Cyrille,Andrew (dr) | Franco,Guilherme (perc) | Colon,Frank (perc)
Chant For Oshum
Perlman,Ivo (ts) | Pullen,Don (p) | Hopkins,Fred (b) | Cyrille,Andrew (dr) | Franco,Guilherme (perc,voc) | Colon,Frank (perc,voc) | Badrena,Manolo (perc,voc) | Thiam,Mor (perc,voc)
Oh! Que Noite Tao Bonita
Perlman,Ivo (ts) | Hopkins,Fred (b) | Cyrille,Andrew (dr)
Chant For Oshala
Perlman,Ivo (ts) | Hopkins,Fred (b) | Franco,Guilherme (dr)
Cantor
Perlman,Ivo (ts) | Ross,Brandon (g) | DeMoraes Azenha,Ana Luisa (voc)
Chant For Logum
Perlman,Ivo (ts) | Bley,Paul (p)
Chant For Ibeji
Perlman,Ivo (ts-solo)

ENJ-7009 2 | CD | In Europe
Elvin Jones Jazz Machine
Ray | Doll Of The Bride | Island Birdie
Jazz An Der Donau Festival,Vilshofen, rec. 23.6.1991
Jones,Elvin (dr) | Fortune,Sonny (fl,ts) | Coltrane,Ravi (ss,ts) | Pickens,Willie (p) | Jackson,Charles 'Chip' (b)

ENJ-7017 2 | CD | Mr. A.T.
Taylor's Wailers
Mr.A.T. | Hi Fly | Soul Eyes | Bullet Train | It Doesn't Matter | Ahmad's Blues | Gingerbread Boy | Mr.A.T.(alt.take)
Englewood Cliffs,NJ, rec. 9.12.1991
Taylor,Arthur 'Art' (dr) | Burton,Abraham (as) | Williams,Willie (ts) | Cary,Marc Anthony (p) | Mitchell,Tyler (b)

ENJ-7021 22 | 2 CD | To The Max!
Max Roach Chorus & Orchestra
Ghost Dance(part 1) | Ghost Dance(part 2)
NYC, rec. 15.6.1991
Roach,Max (dr) | Cables,George (p) | John Motley Singers,The | Baskerville,Priscilla (voc) | Jackson,Florence (voc) | Jackson,Karen (voc) | Jacobsen,Lucille J. (voc) | Rodgers,Sarah Ann (voc) | Balfour,Robbin L. (voc) | Taub,Brenda Lee (voc) | Pickens,Christopher (voc) | Shelton,Abraham (voc) | Young,Thomas (voc) | Gainer,James (voc) | Greg,Jones (voc) | Lawrence,T. Ray (voc) | Motley,John (ld,voc) | Bey,Ronnell (voc)
Max Roach Quartet
The Profit | Tears
NYC, rec. 25.6.1991
Roach,Max (dr) | Bridgewater,Cecil (tp) | Pope,Odean (ts) | Brown,Tyrone (b)
Tricotism
Buffalo,NY, rec. 30.11.1990
Roach,Max (dr) | Bridgewater,Cecil (tp) | Pope,Odean (ts) | Brown,Tyrone (b)
Mwalimu
Northampton,Mass., rec. 29.4.1991
Roach,Max (dr) | Bridgewater,Cecil (tp) | Pope,Odean (ts) | Brown,Tyrone (b)
Max Roach Double Quartet
A Little Booker
NYC, rec. 25.6.1991
Roach,Max (dr) | Bridgewater,Cecil (tp) | Pope,Odean (ts) | Brown,Tyrone (b) | Uptown String Quartet,The | Monroe,Diane (v) | Terry,Lesa (v) | Roach,Maxine (viola) | Folson,Eileen M. (cello)
M'Boom
Ghost Dance(part 3) | Street Dance | A Quiet Place
NYC, rec. 24.6.1991
M'Boom | Roach,Max (dr) | Brooks,Roy (dr,perc) | Chambers,Joe (dr,perc) | Clay,Omar (dr,perc) | Fountain,Eli (perc) | King,Fred (concert-bells) | Mantilla,Ray (perc) | Mora,Francisco (perc) | Smith,Warren (dr,perc)
Max Roach
Self Portrait | Drums Unlimited
Paris,France, rec. 15.9.1990
Roach,Max (dr-solo)

ENJ-7025 2 | CD | Topsy
Freddie Hubbard Quartet
Topsy | As Time Goes By | Black Orpheus | All Of You | Golden Earrings | Lamento
NYC, rec. 10./11.12.1989
Hubbard,Freddie (tp) | Green,Benny (p) | Reid,Rufus (b) | Allen,Carl (dr)
Freddie Hubbard Quintet
Caravan | Cherokee | Love Me Or Leave Me
Hubbard,Freddie (tp) | Garrett,Kenny (as) | Green,Benny (p) | Reid,Rufus (b) | Allen,Carl (dr)

ENJ-7027 2 | CD | The Old Country
Nat Adderley Quintet
The Old Country | Bohemia After Dark | Jeannine | Almost Always | Love For Sale | One For Daddy-O | Stella By Starlight | The Chant | Nippon Soul
NYC, rec. 5./6.12.1990
Adderley,Nat (co) | Herring,Vincent (as) | Bargad,Rob (p) | Genus,James (b) | Drummond,Billy (dr)

ENJ-7051 2 | CD | Youngblood
Elvin Jones Quintet
Not Yet | Have You Seen Elveen? | Lady Luck | The Bisquit Man | Strange | Young Blood
Englewood Cliffs,NJ, rec. 20./21.4.1992
Jones,Elvin (dr) | Payton,Nicholas (tp) | Jackson,Javon (ts) | Redman,Joshua (ts) | Mraz,George 'Jiri' (b)
Elvin Jones Trio
Angel Eyes | Body And Soul
Jones,Elvin (dr) | Redman,Joshua (ts) | Mraz,George 'Jiri' (b)
Elvin Jones-George Mraz
My Romance
Jones,Elvin (dr) | Mraz,George 'Jiri' (b)
Elvin Jones
Ding-A-Ling-A-Ling
Jones,Elvin (dr)

ENJ-7055 2 | CD | Mambo 2000
Conexion Latina
Mambo 2000 | Caribe-Cha | Mai Gel | Bubba And The Whale | Euro Salsa | Setembro | No Te Imaginas | Naima | Penar
Live at The 'Loft', Munich, rec. 9./10.7.1992
Conexion Latina | Bailey,Benny (tp) | Laughlin,Richard (tp) | Reichstaller,Claus (tp) | Tuscher,Peter (tp) | Fuesers,Rudi (tb,ld) | Lievano,Edilberto (tb) | Stern,Bobby (ts) | Aliva,José (p) | Lopez,Leslie (b) | Marrero,Nicky (timbales) | Tofft,Claus 'Vikingo' (congas) | Moreno,Daniel (perc,bongos) | Plaza,Javier (coro,voc) | Martinez,Anthony (coro,voc) | Herrador,Roberto (coro) | Perez,Tomas (perc,coro)

ENJ-7057 2 | CD | The Song Of Songs:Oratorio For Two Solo Voices,Choir And Orchestra
Klaus König Orchestra & Guests
The Day Of Bliss And Joy | Spirits And Goddesses | May He Smother Me With Kisses | Sixty Queens | Dark,But Lovely | The Dance Of The Double Camp | The Veil | Set Me As A Seal
Köln, rec. 22./23.11.1992
Clayton,Jay (voc) | Minton,Phil (voc) | Montreal Jubilation Gospel Choir | Robertson,Herb (tp,fl-h) | Winterschladen,Reiner (tp) | Huke,Jörg (tb) | Collings,Bruce (tb) | Godard,Michel (tuba) | Newton,James (fl) | Gratkowski,Frank (fl,b-cl,ss,as) | Moore,Michael (cl,as) | Schubert,Matthias (ts,oboe) | Kaiser,Wollie (b-cl,bass-sax) | Ducret,Marc (g) | Nabatov,Simon (p) | Dresser,Mark (b) | Rainey,Tom (dr) | Koenig,Klaus (comp,ld)

ENJ-7061 2 | CD | As Time Goes By
Chris Connor With The Hank Jones Trio
Falling In Love With Love | As Time Goes By | September In The Rain | Gone With The Wind | Everything I've Got | Long Ago And Far Away | A Lovely Way To Spend An Evening | A Foggy Day(In London Town) | Strike Up The Band | Good Bye
NYC, rec. 30.3.-2.4.1991
Connor,Chris (voc) | Jones,Hank (p) | Mraz,George 'Jiri' (b) | Copeland,Keith (dr)

ENJ-7065 2 | CD | Live At The Blue Note
Franco Ambrosetti Quintet
Introduction | Blues 'N' Dues Et Cetera | Just Friends | Body And Soul | Phantoms | Voyage
Live at The 'Blue Note',NYC, rec. 13.7.1992
Ambrosetti,Franco (fl-h) | Blake,Seamus (ts) | Barron,Kenny (p) | Coleman,Ira (b) | Lewis,Victor (dr)

ENJ-7069 2 | CD | Harvest
Michele Rosewoman Quintet
From Tear To Here | Patrick's Mood | Miracle | Occasion To Rise | Blood Count | Path To The Shore | K.T.
Mamaroneck,NY, rec. 21.-23.9.1992
Rosewoman,Michele (p) | Wilson,Steve (ss,as) | Thomas,Gary (fl,ts) | Davis,Kenneth 'Kenny' (b,el-b) | Jackson,Gene (dr)
Michele Rosewoman Sextet
The Egun(Egg-Oon) And The Harvest | Warriors(Guerreros)
Rosewoman,Michele (p,clave,voc) | Wilson,Steve (ss,as) | Thomas,Gary (fl,ts) | Davis,Kenneth 'Kenny' (b,el-b) | Jackson,Gene (dr) | Bobè,Eddie (congas,cajon,palitos,quinto,voc)

ENJ-7085 2 | CD | Full English Breakfast
Itchy Fingers
The Easter Islander | The Dome | A Night In Tunisia
London,GB, rec. October 1992
Itchy Fingers | Long,Pete (cl,as) | Wates,Matt (as) | O'Higgins,Dave (ts) | Mower,Mike (fl,cl,ts,bs)
Full English Breakfast | Academicians | Svea Rike | This Time's Hard | The Crillon Controller | You're Financially Disturbed
Itchy Fingers | Panayi,Andy (ss,as,ts) | Wates,Matt (as) | O'Higgins,Dave (ts) | Mower,Mike (fl,cl,ts,bs)

ENJ-7089 2 | CD | Vol.1:What It Is?
Ed Blackwell Project
Introduction | 'Nette | Pettiford Bridge | Beau Regard | Thumbs Up | Mallet Song | Rosa Takes A Stand(for Rosa Parks) | Applause
Live at Yoshi's Night Club,Oakland,CA, rec. 8.8.1992
Blackwell,Ed (dr) | Haynes,Graham (co) | Ward,Carlos (as) | Helias,Mark (b)

ENJ-7091 2 | CD | The Talk Of The Town
Bennie Wallace Quartet
The Best Things In Life Are Free | It's The Talk Of The Town | Thangs | I Concentrate On You | The Picayune | It Has Happened To Me | If I Lose | Blues Velvet
Hollywood,CA, rec. January 1993
Wallace,Bennie (ts) | Hahn,Jerry (g) | Huntington,Bill (b) | Queen,Alvin (dr)

ENJ-7095 2 | CD | Going Home
Elvin Jones Jazz Machine
The Shell Game | Going Home | Cross Purpose | You've Changed | Truth | East Of The Sun West Of The Moon | In 3-4 Thee | April 8th
Englewood Cliffs,NJ, rec. 15./16.10.1992
Jones,Elvin (dr) | Payton,Nicholas (tp) | Jordan,Kent (fl,piccolo) | Coltrane,Ravi (ss,ts) | Jackson,Javon (ts) | Pickens,Willie (p) | Jones,Bradley (b)

ENJ-7099 2 | CD | Long To Be Loose
Wayne Krantz Trio
These Instrumental Pieces Were | Not Consciously Written About | Specific People,Places,Things Or Ideas | Although One Began | From A Little Croaking Sound | A Friend's DAT Machine Makes | What They Were Written About | Is Something I Don't Understand Yet | But I Know It When I See It | And Hopefully,So Will You
NYC, rec. March 1993
Krantz,Wayne (g) | Goines,Lincoln (b) | Danzinger,Zachary (dr)

ENJ-8036 2 | CD | Morning Song
John Stubblefield Quartet
Blues For The Moment | King Of Harts | So What | Morning Song | Blue Moon | A Night In Lisbon | The Shaw Of Newark | In A Sentimental Mood | Slick Stud & Sweet Thang | Here And There | Here's One
Brooklyn,NY, rec. May 1993
Stubblefield,John (ss,ts) | Cables,George (p) | Houston,Clint (b) | Lewis,Victor (dr)

ENJ-8038 2 | CD | Barefoot
Greetje Bijma Trio
Barefoot | Bosnia | Painter At Work | As I Drive By | Glazed Frost | Lonely Walk | Katsijma | Sing With Strings - ... Sing With Strings | Duck Pond | Guess Where It's Coming From | Vortex
Monster,NL, rec. 9./10.7.1993
Bijma,Greetje (voice) | Crispell,Marilyn (p) | Dresser,Mark (b)

ENJ-8046 2 | CD | Retroflection
Arthur Blythe Quartet
Jana's Delight | J.B.Blues | Peacemaker | Light Blue | Lenox Avenue Breakdown | Faceless Woman | Break Tune
Live at The 'Village Vanguard',NYC, rec. 25./26.6.1993
Blythe,Arthur (as) | Hicks,John (p) | McBee,Cecil (b) | Battle,Bobby (dr)

ENJ-8054 2 | CD | Vol.2:What It Be Like?
Ed Blackwell Project
Nebula | Grandma's Shoes | Pentahouve | First Love(for Thelonious Monk) | Lito(part 1) | Lito(part 3)
Live at Yoshi's Night Club,Oakland,CA, rec. 8.8.1992
Blackwell,Ed (dr) | Haynes,Graham (co) | Ward,Carlos (fl,as) | Helias,Mark (b)
Lito(part 2)
Blackwell,Ed (dr) | Cherry,Don (tp) | Haynes,Graham (co) | Ward,Carlos (fl,as) | Helias,Mark (b)

ENJ-8060 2 | CD | WW3
Willie Williams Trio
Out For A Walk | Frozen Sun | The Third Time Is A Charm | Takin' It With Me | La Mesha | Dr.Jackle | You Can It If You Try | WW3: | Armageddon- | The Choice Is Yours- | Babylon Falls- | One Thousand Years Of Peace
Brooklyn,NY, rec. 28.9.1993
Williams,Willie (ss,ts) | Colley,Scott (b) | Summey Jr.,Harold (dr)

ENJ-8068 2 | CD | Nucleus
Daniel Schnyder Quintet
Angry Blackbird | Soleil Noir | The Mystified Churchgoer | Scherzo | Retrogradus Ex Machina | Teiresias | Triplex | No Opera | DoReMi | Collector's Choice
Brooklyn,NY, rec. 25./26.1.1994
Schnyder,Daniel (fl,ts) | Mossman,Michel Philip (tp,fl-h,tb,piccolo-tp) | Drew Jr.,Kenny (p) | Formanek,Michael (b) | Smith,Marvin 'Smitty' (dr)

ENJ-8070 2 | CD | Don't Mow Your Lawn
Ray Anderson Alligatory Band
Don't Mow Your Lawn | Diddleybop | Damaged But Good | Alligator Pecadillo | What 'cha Gonna Do With That | Airwaves | Blow Your Own Horn | Disguise The Limit
Brooklyn,NY, rec. 23.-25.3.1994
Anderson,Ray (tb,voc) | Soloff,Lew (tp) | Harris,Jerome (g,voc) | Jones,Gregory (b-g,voc) | Campbell,Tommy (dr) | Colon,Frank (perc)

ENJ-8072 2 | CD | Songs And Moments
Kevin Mahogany With Orchestra
The Coaster | The City Lights | Night Flight | Caravan | Red Top | Jim's Ballad | Take The 'A' Train | When I Fall In Love
Brooklyn,NY, rec. 29./30.3.1994
Mahogany,Kevin (voc) | Mossman,Michel Philip (tp) | Eubanks,Robin (tb) | Wilson,Steve (cl,as) | Williams,Willie (cl,ts) | Brenner,Phil (alto-fl,ss) | Smulyan,Gary (b-cl,bs) | Hicks,John (p) | Drummond,Ray (b) | Smith,Marvin 'Smitty' (dr)
Next Time You See Me | My Foolish Heart
Mahogany,Kevin (voc) | Mossman,Michel Philip (tp) | Eubanks,Robin (tb) | Blythe,Arthur (as) | Wilson,Steve (cl,as) | Williams,Willie (cl,ts) | Brenner,Phil (alto-fl,ss) | Smulyan,Gary (b-cl,bs) | Hicks,John (p) | Drummond,Ray (b) | Smith,Marvin 'Smitty' (dr)
West Coast Blues
Mahogany,Kevin (voc) | Mossman,Michel Philip (tp) | Eubanks,Robin (tb) | Wilson,Steve (cl,as) | Williams,Willie (cl,ts) | Brenner,Phil (alto-fl,ss) | Smulyan,Gary (b-cl,bs) | Eubanks,Kevin (g) | Hicks,John (p) | Drummond,Ray (b) | Smith,Marvin 'Smitty' (dr)
Songs And Moments
Mahogany,Kevin (voc) | Mossman,Michel Philip (tp) | Eubanks,Robin (tb) | Wilson,Steve (cl,as) | Williams,Willie (cl,ts) | Brenner,Phil (alto-fl,ss) | Smulyan,Gary (b-cl,bs) | Eubanks,Kevin (g) | Hicks,John (p) | Drummond,Ray (b) | Smith,Marvin 'Smitty' (dr) | Pollakusky,Jennifer (voc) | Marcantonio,Lara (voc) | Fenelly,Kate (voc) | Sullivan,Kate (ld)

ENJ-8074 2 | CD | Closest To The Sun
Abraham Burton Quartet
Minor March | Laura | E=MC | Romancing You | So Gracefully | Corrida De Toros | Left Alone | Closest To The Sun | So Gracefully(radio version)
Brooklyn,NY, rec. 11./12.3.1994
Burton,Abraham (as) | Cary,Marc Anthony (p) | Johnson,Billy (b) | McPherson,Eric (dr)

ENJ-8076 2 | CD | Time Fragments:Seven Studies In Time And Motion
Klaus König Orchestra
Waltzin' Over T'Yours | Once Upon A Time | Call That Going,Call That On | Mean Wile | Does Time Go By? | Later That Night That Knight Laid Her | Fine Nelly In Fin Alley
Stadtgarten,Köln, rec. 19.-21.5.1994
Koenig,Klaus (comp,ld) | Winterschladen,Reiner (tp) | Wheeler,Kenny (tp,fl-h) | Huke,Jörg (tb) | Godard,Michel (tuba) | Dick,Robert (fl,piccolo) | Gratkowski,Frank (fl,ss,as) | Kaiser,Wollie (b-cl,ss) | Schubert,Matthias (ts,oboe) | Bauer,Stefan (marimba) | Feldman,Mark (v) | Dresser,Mark (b) | Hemingway,Gerry (dr)

ENJ-9003 2 | CD | Momentum Mobile
Michael Riessler And The Ensemble 13
Anekdoten | La Rage | Ein Ittlige Sprak Hat Ir Eigen Art | Luigi | Marathon | Ba Binga | Marsch Der Ketzer | Ost-West | Old Orleans,New Orleans | Song Mecanique
Live at 'Donaueschinger Musiktage', rec. 16.10.1993
Riessler,Michael (cl,b-cl,as) | Levy,Howard (harm) | Charial,Pierre (barrel-org) | Garcia-Fons,Renaud (b) | Ameen,Robert 'Robbie' (dr) | Ensemble 13 | Finkler,Markus (tp) | Maertens,Falk (tp) | Strunkeit,Sven (tb) | Favre,Yves (tb) | Soldner,Tobias (bass-tuba) | Lehmann,Willy (v) | Lehmann,Martin (v) | Souchy,Jean-Eric (viola) | Eychmüller,Susanne (cello)

ENJ-9011 2 | CD | Green Dolphy Suite
Double Trio(Trio De Clarinettes&Arcado)
Green Dolphy Suite | Cold Water Music | Clic | Bosnia | Suite Domestique
Ludwigsburg, rec. 15.9.1994
Double Trio (Trio De Clarinettes&Arcado) | Sclavis,Louis (cl,b-cl) | Angster,Armand (cl,b-cl) | Di Donato,Jacques (cl,b-cl) | Feldman,Mark (v) | Reijseger,Ernst (cello) | Dresser,Mark (b)

ENJ-9013 2 | CD | Vernal Fields
Ingrid Jensen Sextet
Marsh Blues | Skookum Spook | Vernal Fields | Every Time We Say Goodbye | I Love You | The Mingus That I Knew | Stuck In The Dark | Christiane | By Myself
NYC, rec. 11./12.10.1994
Jensen,Ingrid (tp,fl-h) | Wilson,Steve (ss,as) | Garzone,George (ts) | Barth,Bruce (p) | Grenadier,Larry (b) | White,Lenny (dr)

ENJ-9017 2 | CD | Signature
Ferenc Snétberger Quartet
Toni's Carnival II | Passages | Obsession | Tangoa Free | Poems For My People | Surprise | Variations On Nuages
Cessalto(TV),Italy, rec. 7.-13.11.1994
Snétberger,Ferenc (g) | Friedman,David (vib) | Gjakonovski,Martin (b) | Levacic,Kruno (dr)

ENJ-9025 2 | CD | New York Child
Marty Ehrlich Quintet
New York Child | Generosity | Georgia Blue | Tell Me This | Elvin's Exit | Prelude | Time And The Wild Words | Untitled | Turn Again
NYC, rec. 24./25.2.1995
Ehrlich,Marty (cl,b-cl,ss,as) | Strickland,Stan (ts) | Cain,Michael 'Mike' (p) | Formanek,Michael (b) | Stewart,Bill (dr)

ENJ-9031 2 | CD | When It's Time
Attila Zoller Quintet
Joy For Joy | Lu And Shu
Englewood Cliffs,NJ, rec. 12./13.12.1994
Zoller,Attila (g) | Konitz,Lee (as) | Willis,Larry (p) | Debriano,Santi Wilson (b) | Israel,Yoron (dr)
Attila Zoller Quartet
When It's Time | Mean To Be
Zoller,Attila (g) | Konitz,Lee (as) | Debriano,Santi Wilson (b) | Israel,Yoron (dr)
After The Morning | Homage To O.P. | Voyage
Zoller,Attila (g) | Willis,Larry (p) | Debriano,Santi Wilson (b) | Israel,Yoron (dr)
Attila Zoller-Lee Konitz
The Song Is You
Zoller,Attila (g) | Konitz,Lee (as)

ENJ-9033 2 | CD | R 'N' B
Eddie Allen Quintet
Frick & Frack | As Quiet As It Kept | Clairvoyant | Almost You | Schism | The Seduction | The Quest
Brooklyn,NY, rec. 18./19.1.1995
Allen,Eddie E.J. (tp) | Harrison,Donald (as) | Wonsey,Athony (p) | McBride,Christian (b) | Smith,Marvin 'Smitty' (dr)

ENJ-9035 2 | CD | Point In Time
Fred Hersch Trio
You Don't Know What Love Is | As Long As There's Music | The Peacocks | Cat's Paws
Brooklyn,NY, rec. 20./21.& 24.3.1995
Hersch,Fred (p) | Gress,Drew (b) | Rainey,Tom (dr)
Fred Hersch Quartet
Infant Eyes
Hersch,Fred (p) | Perry,Richard 'Rich' (ts) | Gress,Drew (b) | Rainey,Tom (dr)
Too Soon
Hersch,Fred (p) | Douglas,Dave (tp) | Gress,Drew (b) | Rainey,Tom (dr)
Fred Hersch Quintet
Point Of Time | Spring Is Here | Evidence | Drew's Blues
Hersch,Fred (p) | Douglas,Dave (tp) | Perry,Richard 'Rich' (ts) | Gress,Drew (b) | Rainey,Tom (dr)

ENJ-9037 2 | CD | The Magician

Abraham Burton Quartet
I Can't Get Started | Little Melonae | An Addition To The Family | It's To You | Mari's Soul | Gnossienne(No.1) | The Magician
NYC, rec. 17./18.3.1995
Burton,Abraham (as) | Cary,Marc Anthony (p) | Johnson,Bill (b) | McPherson,Eric (dr)

ENJ-9047 2 | CD | Balkan Connection
Dusko Goykovich Big Band
Doboy | You're My Everything | The Bopper | Manhattan Mood | Balkan Blue | You Don't Know What Love Is | A Handful O'Soul | Why Not You | Nights Of Skopje | Nella
München, rec. 9./10.5.1995
Goykovich,Dusko (tp,fl-h) | Bendzko,Thomas (tp) | Kaupp,Gil (tp) | Howard,Tom (tp) | Rivera,Joe (tp) | Budziat,Eberhard (tb) | Plettendorf,Uli (tb) | Köhler,Michael (tb) | Müller,Rainer (tb) | Peuker,Peter (as) | Bouterwerk,Thomas (as) | Basso,Gianni (ts) | Lakatos,Tony (ts) | Lutzeier,Michael (bs) | Michelich,Peter (p) | Trussardi,Luigi (b) | Divjak,Ratko (dr)

ENJ-9049 2 | CD | Loopin' The Cool
Mark Helias Group
Munchkins | Loop The Cool | One Time Only | Sector 51 | Seventh Siga | Pentahouve | Thumbs Up | Hung Over Easy | El Baz | Pacific Rim
Brooklyn,NY, rec. 14./15.12.1994
Helias,Mark (b) | Eskelin,Ellery (ts) | Carter,Regina (v) | Rainey,Tom (dr,perc) | Bangoura,Epizo (perc,djembe)

ENJ-9051 2 | CD | Calling Card
Arthur Blythe Quartet
As Of Yet | Blue Blues | Naima's Love Song | Hip Dripper | Odessa | Elaborations | Jitterbug Waltz | Break Tune
Live at The 'Village Vanguard',NYC, rec. 26.6.1993
Blythe,Arthur (as) | Hicks,John (p) | McBee,Cecil (b) | Battle,Bobby (dr)

ENJ-9053 2 | CD | Gail Thompson's Jazz Africa
Gail Thompson Orchestra
Long Time Ago | Burkina Faso | Kamara River | Expedition | Stressless | Finale
Mercator Halle,Duisburg, rec. 18.5.1995
Thompson,Gail (fl) | Deppa,Claude (tp,fl-h) | Beckett,Harry (tp,fl-h) | Hartley,Patrick (tb) | Parlett,Mike (fl,as) | Underwood,Jerry (ss,ts) | Harris,Tom (fl,ss,ts) | Africa,Mervyn (p,synth) | McKay,Jim (synth) | Ranku,Lucky (el-g) | Castronari,Mario (b,el-b) | Alleyne,Cheryl (dr) | Legwabe,Joe Ditsebe (perc)

ENJ-9055 2 | CD | Heads And Tales
Ray Anderson Alligatory Band
The Four Reasons: | Hunting And Gathering | Heads And Tales | Matters Of The Heart | Unsong Songs | Cheek To Cheek | Tapajack | Tough Guy | Road Song | Drink And Blather
Brooklyn,NY, rec. 17.-19.5.1995
Anderson,Ray (tb,voc) | Soloff,Lew (tp) | Harris,Jerome (g) | Jones,Gregory (b-g) | Colon,Frank (perc,berimbau)

ENJ-9061 2 | CD | Reviews
Klaus König Orchestra
Sniffing Attitudes | Harry Laughs | Who's That Guy? | Mission To Stars | Multiple Choice | A Matter Of Taste | Tuba Boons | Harry Laughs Still | Black Polo-Necks | Avantgarde Noise Pollution | Who Would Have Thought That | The Day After
Köln, rec. 18.-20.9.& 7.10.1995
Koenig,Klaus (comp,ld) | Winterschladen,Reiner (tp) | D'Earth,John (tp,fl-h) | Anderson,Ray (tb) | Huke,Jörg (tb) | Massot,Michel (tuba) | Puntin,Claudio (cl) | Gratkowski,Frank (fl,piccolo-fl,as) | Schubert,Matthias (ts) | Kaiser,Wollie (contra-b-cl,ss,ts,bass-sax) | Feldman,Mark (v) | Wienstroer,Markus (g,bj,v) | Manderscheid,Dieter (b) | Hemingway,Gerry (dr) | Bobs,The: | Scott,Janie Bob (voc) | Stull,Matthew Bob (voc) | Finetti,Joe Bob (voc) | Greene,Richard Bob (voc) | Moss,David (narrator)

ENJ-9065 2 | CD | La Conexión
Conexion Latina
Llegué A La Cima | Maravilla De Son | La Clave | La Conexión | Yo Quiero También | Palmira | Ritmo Internacional | Atacando | Fiesta De Despedida
Live at 'Schlachthof' München, rec. 17.10.1995
Conexion Latina | Rivera,Joe (tp) | Büchel,Richard (tp) | Reichstaller,Claus (tp) | Fuesers,Rudi (tb,ld) | Rothchild,David (tb) | Avila,José (p) | Lopez,Leslie (b) | Marrero,Nicky (timbales) | Tofft,Claus 'Vikingo' (congas) | Rosalies,Edward (bongo) | Martinez,Anthony (coro,voc) | Plaza,Javier (coro,voc) | Martinez,Yma America (coro) | Diaz,Luis Chico (coro)

ENJ-9067 2 | CD | Notes From The Underground
Johnny King Quintet
Gnosis | Notes From The Underground | Soliloquy | Cafeine | Mean To Me | Blow-Up | The Common Law | Las Ramblas
Brooklyn,NY, rec. 28./29.9.1995
King,Jonny (p) | Redman,Joshua (ss,ts) | Nelson,Steve (vib) | Washington,Peter (b) | Drummond,Billy (dr)

ENJ-9071 2 | CD | Loose Wires
Michel Godard-Miroslav Tadic-Mark Nauseef
Chanson Pour Lise | Stara Pesma | Monster | It's Still Quite Dark,But There Are Some Signs Of Light | Bakija | Les Enfants Qui S'Aiment | Emilio | Spiritual | The Locust Have Returned...And They Are Bigger Than Ever!!! | Down Home Where The Blowfish Roam | The Immaculate Conception
Zerkall, rec. June 1995
Godard,Michel (serpent,tuba) | Tadic,Miroslav (g) | Nauseef,Mark (perc)

ENJ-9075 2 | CD | Advance
Bobby Watson Quartet
But Not For Me | Karita | Round About Midnight | You're Lucky To Me | E.T.A.
NYC, rec. July 1984
Watson,Robert 'Bobby' (as) | McNeely,Jim (p) | Coolman,Todd (b) | Nussbaum,Adam (dr)

ENJ-9302 2 | CD | Tanatula
Daniel Schnyder Group
With The Devil In The Backseat | Water | Samiel | Angst
details unknown, rec. 1994-1996
Schnyder,Daniel (ss,ts) | Mossman,Michel Philip (tp,fl-h) | Pugh,Jim (tb) | Taylor,Dave (b-tb) | Clark,John (fr-h) | Laws,Hubert (fl,alto-fl,piccolo) | Formanek,Michael (b)
Cool Sweets | Dolphy's Dance | Homunculus
Schnyder,Daniel (ss,ts) | Mossman,Michel Philip (tp,fl-h) | Pugh,Jim (tb) | Taylor,Dave (b-tb) | Clark,John (fr-h) | Chapin,Thomas[Tom] (fl) | McKee,Andy (b)
Tarantula | El Cigaro
Schnyder,Daniel (ss,ts) | Mossman,Michel Philip (tp,fl-h) | Pugh,Jim (tb) | Taylor,Dave (b-tb) | Clark,John (fr-h) | Chapin,Thomas[Tom] (fl) | McKee,Andy (b) | Sanabria,Bobby (perc,congas)
Daniel Schnyder With String Quartet
Cairo | Cairo Cadenza | Mister M | Wedding Song | No Smoking
Schnyder,Daniel (ss,ts) | Rutkauskas,Alejandro (v) | Taubitz,Adam (v) | Hasegawa,Akiko or Juerg Daehler (viola) | Pezzotti,Daniel (cello)
Daniel Schnyder With The NDR Radio Philharmonie Hannover
Short Life | Memories
Schnyder,Daniel (ss,ts) | NDR Radio-Philharmonie Hannover | Gruntz,George (ld) | details unknown

ENJ-9304 2 | CD | Strings For Holiday:A Tribute To Billie Holiday
Lee Konitz With Strings
The Man I Love | You've Changed | God Bless The Child | But Beautiful | I Cried For You(Now It's Your Turn To Cry Over Me) | Lover Man(Oh,Where Can You Be?) | All Of Me | Good Morning Heartache | For Heaven's Sake | Easy Living | These Foolish Things Remind Me On You | For All We Know
NYC, rec. 18./19.3.1996
Konitz,Lee (as) | Feldman,Mark (v) | Cummings,Genovia (v) | Jaffe,Jill (viola) | Lawrence,Ronald 'Ron' (viola) | Friedlander,Erik (cello) | Pezzotti,Daniel (cello) | Formanek,Michael (b) | Wilson,Matt (dr)

ENJ-9307 2 | CD | Round Trip
Nils Wogram Quartet
Chopska | Round Trip | Diary Suite(part 1-3) | Ballade | Fratzen,I Love The Smell Of Garbage | Rock I
Ludwigsburg, rec. 9./10.10.& 4.12.1995
Wogram,Nils (tb) | Nabatov,Simon (p) | Fuhr,Dietmar (b) | Rückert,Jochen (dr)

ENJ-9309 2 | CD | A Morning In Paris
Sathima Bea Benjamin Group
I Got It Bad And That Ain't Good | Solitude
Paris,France, rec. 23.2.1963
Benjamin,Sathima Bea (voc) | Ellington,Duke (p) | Asmussen,Svend (v) | Gertze,Johnny (b) | Ntshoko,Makaya (dr)
Your Love Has Faded | Lover Man(Oh,Where Can You Be?)
Benjamin,Sathima Bea (voc) | Strayhorn,Billy (p) | Asmussen,Svend (v) | Gertze,Johnny (b) | Ntshoko,Makaya (dr)
Darn That Dream | I Could Write A Book | I Should Care | Spring Will Be A Little Late This Year | The Man I Love | I'm Glad There Is You | Soon | A Nightingale Sang In Berkeley Square
Benjamin,Sathima Bea (voc) | Brand,Dollar[Abdullah Ibrahim] (p) | Asmussen,Svend (v) | Gertze,Johnny (b) | Ntshoko,Makaya (dr)

ENJ-9310 2 | CD | Off The Wall
Dan Wall Trio
13 Steps | Black Ice | The Electric Ballroom | Carol's Bridge | Zakatak
NYC, rec. 23./24.7.1996
Wall,Dan (org) | Ratzer,Karl (g) | Nussbaum,Adam (dr)
Dan Wall Quartet
The End Of A Love Affair
Wall,Dan (org) | Ratzer,Karl (g) | Larue,Lester (g) | Nussbaum,Adam (dr)
I Didn't Know What Time It Was | Waltz For John | Off The Wall
Wall,Dan (org) | Jensen,Ingrid (tp,fl-h) | Ratzer,Karl (g) | Nussbaum,Adam (dr)

ENJ-9311 2 | CD | Eeeyyess!
Victor Lewis Sextet
Eeeyyess! | Vulnerability | Un-Til | Buttercups | Alter Ego | No More Misunderstanding | Stamina | Here's To...You Baby | Shakehandre
Brooklyn,NY, rec. 21./22.7.1996
Lewis,Victor (dr,voice) | Stafford,Terell (tp,fl-h) | Blake,Seamus (ss,ts) | Scott,Stephen (p) | Howard,Ed (b) | Alias,Don (perc)

ENJ-9312 2 | CD | Standing On A Whale...
James Emery Quartet
New Water | In A Secret Place | Cobalt Blue | Strings Of Thread | Texas Koto Blues | Crepuscule With Nellie | Standing On A Whale | Fishing For Minnows | ARC,Into Distant Night | Black Diamond And Pink Whispers | Epicenter | Poetry In Stillness
Brooklyn,NY, rec. 10./11.9.& 16.10.1996
Emery,James (g,soprano-g) | Ehrlich,Marty (fl,cl,as) | Formanek,Michael (b) | Hemingway,Gerry (vib,marimba,dr)

ENJ-9313 2 | CD | Here On Earth
Ingrid Jensen Quintet
Shiva's Dance | Woodcarvings | Here On Earth | Time Remembered | You Do Something To Me | The Time Of The Barracudas | Ninety-One | Consolation | Fallin' | Avila And Tequila
Brooklyn,NY, rec. 19./20.9.1996
Jensen,Ingrid (tp,fl-h) | Bartz,Gary (ss,as) | Colligan,George (p) | Burno,Dwayne (b) | Stewart,Bill (dr) | Seifers,Jill (voc)

ENJ-9316 2 | CD | Pussy Cat Dues:The Music Of Charles Mingus
Kevin Mahogany With The WDR Big Band And Guests
Eclipse | Pussy Cat Dues | Portrait | Re-Incarnation Of A Love Bird | Mingus Medley | Boogie Stop Shuffle- | Jelly Roll- | Goodbye Pork Pie Hat- | Better Git It In Your Soul- | Tonight At Noon
Köln, rec. 3.2.1995
Mahogany,Kevin (voc) | Knepper,Jimmy (tb) | McPherson,Charles (as) | Mackrel,Dennis (dr) | WDR Big Band | Haderer,Andreas 'Andy' (tp) | Bruynen,Rob (tp) | Osterloh,Klaus (tp) | Kiefer,Rick (tp) | Marshall,John (tp) | Horler,David (tb) | Maus,Georg (tb) | Laukamp,Bernt (tb) | Feil,Peter (tb) | Wiberny,Heiner (as) | Rosenstein,Harald (as) | Peters,Olivier (ts) | Römer,Rolf (ts) | Neufang,Jens (bs) | Chastenier,Frank (p) | Lulic,Milan (g) | Goldsby,John (b) | Dobbins,Bill (cond)

ENJ-9322 2 | CD | Bassdrumbone(Hence The Reason)
Mark Helias/Gerry Hemingway/Ray Anderson
Hence The Real Reason | For Don C. | Fictionary | Sambali | Moto Proto | Speak Again Brother | The Disappearing Afternoon | Lips Apart | When Zweeble Walked By
Bimhuis,Amsterdam,Holland, rec. 9.3.1996
Anderson,Ray (tb) | Helias,Mark (b) | Hemingway,Gerry (dr)

ENJ-9323 2 | CD | Ocre
Sylvie Courvoisier Group
Gugging | Anecdote 1 | La Goualante De L'Idiot | Anecdote 2 | Machines-A-Sons | Ensorcelirradiant | Triton Et Demi | Anecdote 3 | Curio In Trivia(in memory of Hugo Pratt) | Anecdote 4 | Terre D'Agala | Viable | Paradiso Perduto | Tabular | Gnou-Gnou Valse
Zerkall, rec. August 1996
Courvoisier,Sylvie (p,prepared-p) | Godard,Michel (serpent,tuba) | Charial,Pierre (barrel-org) | Overwater,Tony (b) | Nauseef,Mark (perc)

ENJ-9324-2 | CD | Dangerous Rip
Bobby Previte's Latin For Travelers
Surf Medley
NYC, rec. 22.1.1997
Previte,Robert 'Bobby' (dr) | Ducret,Marc (el-g) | Harris,Jerome (el-g,el-b,voice) | Cutler,Stewart (el-g) | Saft,Jamie (el-p,org,el-b,mini-moog)
Heart On My Sleeve | Clear The Bridge | You Tell Me | Bobby's New Mood | Open Jaw
NYC, rec. 25.5.1998
Previte,Robert 'Bobby' (dr) | Harris,Jerome (el-g,el-b,voice) | Cutler,Stewart (el-g) | Saft,Jamie (el-p,org,el-b,mini-moog)

ENJ-9327 2 | CD | Jazz Standard On Mars
Robert Dick Group With The Soldier String Quartet
India | Water Babies | Three Wishes
Mamaroneck,NY, rec. 5.9.1995 & 18.2.1995
Dick,Robert (fl) | Carter,Regina (v) | Soldier,Dave (v,metal-v) | Bona,Richard (el-b) | Argüelles,Steve (dr) | Naranjo,Valerie (perc)
Sometimes Perpetually
NYC, rec. 5.9.1995 & 18.2.1996
Dick,Robert (piccolo) | Carter,Regina (v) | Bona,Richard (el-b) | Argüelles,Steve (dr) | Naranjo,Valerie (perc)
Gazzelloni | Machine Gun | Something Sweet Something Tender
Mamaroneck,NY, rec. 5.9.1995 & 18.2.1995
Dick,Robert (fl,b-fl,contra-b-fl) | Soldier String Quartet,The | Carter,Regina (v) | Soldier,Dave (bj,v) | Insell-Stack,Judith (viola) | Buckholz,Dawn (cello) | Dresser,Mark (b) | Driscoll,Kermit (el-b) | Perowsky,Ben (dr)

ENJ-9329 2 | CD | The Meltdown
Johnny King Septet
The Meltdown | After Six | The Third Rail | Quiet As It's Kept | So Sorry Please | Jacqueline's Chimes | Lady Macbeth | The Wellspring | Cochbamba | For Tomorrow | Blues For Andrew Hill
Brooklyn,NY, rec. 11./12.3.1997
King,Jonny (p) | Davis,Steve (tb) | Wilson,Steve (ss,as) | Sanchez,David (ts) | Grenadier,Larry (b) | Drummond,Billy (dr) | Cardona,Milton (perc,congas)

ENJ-9331 2 | CD | Light Breeze
Franco Ambrosetti Quintet
Versace | Silli's Nest | Deborah | Culture And Sensivity | Contempo Latinsky | Elegia | My Foolish Heart | Virtuosismo | One For The Kids | Percussion Dreams | Giant Steps | Silli In The Sky
NYC, rec. 11./12.4.1997
Ambrosetti,Franco (fl-h) | Abercrombie,John (g,el-g) | Farao,Antonio (p) | Vitous,Miroslav (b) | Drummond,Billy (dr)

ENJ-9332 2 | CD | Catability
Bob Degen Trio
Courage | My Old Flame | Sophie | Worth A Week's Anguish | Catability | MC | Ode To Sammy Davis Jr. | Colleen | Fading Day | Round Trip | Parting
Brooklyn,NY, rec. 29./30.4.1997
Degen,Bob (p) | Formanek,Michael (b) | Stewart,Bill (dr)

ENJ-9333 2 | CD | Bar Utopia-A Big Band Cabaret
Mike Westbrook Orchestra
Overture | Nowhere | Utopia Blues | Honest Love | Dialogue | Utopia Ballad | The Happy Jazz Singer | Bar Utopia
London,GB, rec. 13./14.10.1996
Westbrook,Mike (p) | Langley,Noel (tp) | Bush,Andy (tp) | Edmonds,Paul (tp,fl-h) | McMillan,James (tp,fl-h) | Lane,Adrian (tb) | Bassey,Mark (tb) | Holloway,Tracey (tb) | Grappy,Andy (tuba) | Whyman,Peter (cl,ss,as) | Biscoe,Chris (as) | Bitelli,Dave (cl,as,ts) | Caldwell,Chris (bs) | Street,Karen (ts,accordeon) | Kerr,Anthony (vib) | Adler,Stanley (cello) | Berry,Steve (b,el-b) | Fairclough,Peter (dr) | Westbrook,Kate (voc) | Winfield,John (voc)

ENJ-9338 2 | CD | The Heart Project
Klaus König Orchestra
You Bet | Men At Work | Does Money Matter | Reality Check | The Sweet Smell Of Success | Buy One, Get None Free | Turn The Tables | Good To Know
Köln, rec. 1.-3.12.1997
Koenig,Klaus (tb) | Stötter,Claus (tp,fl-h) | Gratkowski,Frank (cl,b-cl,as) | Valk,Claudius (fl,ss,ts) | Neumann,Werner (g,el-g) | Wienstroer,Markus (g,el-g) | Manderscheid,Dieter (b) | Alkier,Thomas (dr)

ENJ-9339 2 | CD | Jadu(Jazz Africa Down Under)
Jazz Africa All Nations Big Band
Stopover Sidney | Dumela Azania | Surfers' Paradise | Coolangata | Cairns For Courtney | Mandela
London,GB, rec. 6.2.1999
Jazz Africa All Nations Big Band | Graham,Colin (tp) | Collins,Michael (tp) | Hartley,Patrick (tb) | Revell,Adrian (fl,ss,as) | Coates,Michael (fl,ts) | Elliot,Louise (fl,ts) | Africa,Mervyn (p) | Neil,Brian (g) | Castronari,Mario (b) | Randle,Sean (dr) | Legwabe,Joe Ditsebe (perc) | Farrenden,Sean (didgeridoo)

ENJ-9340 2 | CD | Funkorific
Ray Anderson Lapis Lazuli Band
Pheromonical | Runnin' Round | Mirror Mirror | Damaged But Good | Hammond Eggs | Monkey Talk | I'm Not A Spy | Funkorific | Willie & Muddy
NYC, rec. 18.-22.1.1998
Anderson,Ray (tb,voc) | Myers,Amina Claudine (p,org,voc) | Harris,Jerome (g) | Plaxico,Lonnie (b) | Campbell,Tommy (dr)

ENJ-9341 2 | CD | Relativity
Marty Ehrlich-Peter Erskine-Michael Formanek
Incident At Harpham Flat | Eloi Lament | Lucky Life | The Pivot | Holy Waters | 'Round The Four Corners | Jiggle The Handle | Relativo | Taglioni | I'n A Child's Eyes
NYC, rec. 23./24.2.1998
Ehrlich,Marty (fl,cl,as,ts) | Formanek,Michael (b) | Erskine,Peter (dr)

ENJ-9343 2 | CD | In The Grass
Marc Ducret-Bobby Previt
Fifty Is A Hundred,A Hundred Ia A Thousand... | Familles | Handy | Very Handy | Tight Lipstick | Du Du Du | Walking In The Dust | Very Handy Indeed | And The Rest Are What They Are - ...And The Rest Are What They Are | Qui Parle?
Wien,Austria, rec. 11.9.1996
Ducret,Marc (el-g,bar-el-g,fretless-el-g) | Previte,Robert 'Bobby' (p,keyboards,dr,CAT-controller)

ENJ-9344 2 | CD | Spectral Domains
James Emery Septet
Red Spaces In A Blue Field(part 1) | Red Spaces In A Blue Field(part 2) | Far Wells Mill Valley | Cosmology | Chromosphere | Standing On A Whale Fishing For Minnows | Kathelin Gray | Sound Action Seven | Strings Of Thread
Brooklyn,NY, rec. 17./18.9.1997
Emery,James (g) | Ehrlich,Marty (fl,ss,as) | Speed,Chris (cl,ts) | Feldman,Mark (v) | Formanek,Michael (b) | Hemingway,Gerry (dr) | Norton,Kevin (vib,marimba,perc,gongs,tympani)
James Emery Quartet
Trinkle Tinkle
Emery,James (g) | Speed,Chris (ts) | Hemingway,Gerry (dr) | Norton,Kevin (marimba)

ENJ-9347 2 | CD | Vision Quest
Stephen Scott Trio
Cheek To Cheek | Vision Quest | Interlude(1) | Virgo | Round About Midnight | Live And Learn | Interlude(3)
Brooklyn,NY, rec. 4.3.1998
Scott,Stephen (p,keyboards) | Carter,Ron (b) | Lewis,Victor (dr)
Stephen Scott Quartet
Like A Child At PLay | Where Is The Love | Abstract Realities | Interlude(3) | Yum | A Work In Process | Da'At
Scott,Stephen (p,keyboards) | Carter,Ron (b) | Lewis,Victor (dr) | Kroon,Steve (perc)

ENJ-9348 2 | CD | My Man In Sidney
Bobby Previte's Latin For Travelers
Albuquerque Bar Band | My Man In Sidney | London Duty Free | Bear Right At Burma | Deep Dish Chicago(Blues for Scooter) | Love Cry New York
Live,at The 'Basement Club',Sidney,Australia, rec. 20.-23.1.1997
Previte,Robert 'Bobby' (dr,voice) | Harris,Jerome (el-g,el-b,voice) | Ducret,Marc (el-g) | Saft,Jamie (el-p,org,mini-moog)

ENJ-9351 2 | CD | Three Guys
Lee Konitz Trio
It's You | Come Rain Or Come Shine | Thingin | Luiza | From Time To Time | Ladie's Waders | Johnny Broken Wing | Eiderdown | A Minor Blues In F
Zürich,CH, rec. 4./5.5.1998
Konitz,Lee (as) | Swallow,Steve (el-b) | Motian,Paul (dr)

ENJ-9352 2 | CD | Bright Nights
Johannes Enders Quintet
Thanksgiving | Bright Nights | Brooklyn Blue | Egon | 400 Years Ago Tomorrow | Butterfly | So Near So Far
München, rec. 23.11.1997
Enders,Johannes (ss,ts) | Jensen,Ingrid (tp,fl-h) | Colligan,George (p) | Burno,Dwayne (b) | Curtis,Howard (dr)

ENJ-9353 2 | CD | Higher Grounds
Ingrid Jensen Quintet
Seventh Avenue | Juriki | Higher Grounds | Litha | Longing | Touch Her Soft Lips And Part | I Fall In Love Too Easily | Dear John | Land Of Me
Brooklyn,NY, rec. 28./29.4.1998
Jensen,Ingrid (tp,fl-h) | Thomas,Gary (fl,ts) | Kikoski,David 'Dave' (p,el-p) | Howard,Ed (b) | Lewis,Victor (dr)

ENJ-9358 2 | CD | The Orchestra Of Smith's Academy
Mike Westbrook Orchestra
Checking In At Hotel Le Prieure | I.D.M.A.T.(It Don't Mean A Thing) | Measure For Measure | So We'll Go No More A'Roving | Blighters | Viennese Waltz
Outside In Festival,Crawley,GB, rec. 7.9.1992
Westbrook,Mike (p,MD) | Russell,Graham (tp) | Brooks,Stuart (tp) | Langley,Noel (tp) | McMillan,James (tp) | Nieman,Paul (tb) | Lane,Adrian (tb) | Holloway,Tracey (tb,euphonium) | Grappy,Andy (tuba) | Biscoe,Chris (sax) | Barnes,Alan (sax) | Whyman,Peter (sax) | Bitelli,Dave (sax) | Wakeman,Alan (sax) | Caldwell,Chris (sax) | Kerr,Anthony (vib) | Saberton,Pete (p,synth) | Pifarely,Dominique (v) | Schaefer,Frank (cello) | Berry,Steve (b) | Fairclough,Peter (dr) | Westbrook,Kate (voc)
Steve Martland Band
Blues For Terenzi
Cheltenham Festival,GB, rec. 3.7.1995
Butler,Lee (tp) | Kearsey,Mike (tb) | Whyman,Peter (sax) | Hamilton,Steve (sax) | Caldwell,Chris (sax) | Maple,Tim (g) | Farrer,Pvt R (marimba) | Maric,Davis (p) | Boyden,Phil (v) | Moore,Malcolm (b-g) | Pearson,Simon (dr) | Martland,Steve (cond)

ENJ-9359 2 | CD | La Phare

Enja | Enja Eigenvertrieb Bielefelder Katalog 761 Jazz • Ausgabe 2004 Enja | Enja Eigenvertrieb

Louis Sclavis & The Bernard Struber Jazztet
Le Retour D'Ottomar | Le Phare | Derniere Regard | Procession | Manoir | Kampala | Les Marches
Pernes Les Fontaines,France, rec. September 1997
Sclavis,Louis (cl,b-cl,ss) | Struber,Bernard (g) | Capozzo,Jean-Luc (tp,fl-h) | Eglin,Jean-Claude (tb) | Thuillier,Francois (tuba) | Glod,Roby (ss,as) | Halbeisen,Raymond (fl,cl,as) | Tempo,Denis (cl,as) | Aubry,Philippe (ts) | Moussay,Benjamin (p) | Lirola,Jeremy (b) | Echampard,Eric (dr) | Chaarani,Abdellatif (perc)

ENJ-9368 2 | CD | The Ground Music
Andreas Willers Octet
Tell Me Wry | Schlaf Du Mein Erquicker | Cycles | On Both Sides Of The Fence | Subversive Resurrektionen | X | Articulate Tumbling(Slight Return) | The Music Grinder(A German Sax Waltz) | Flying Circus
Ludwigsburg, rec. 7./8.12.1998
Willers,Andreas (g,el-g) | Shilkloper,Arkady (fl-h,fr-h) | Huke,Jörg (tb) | Puntin,Claudio (cl,b-cl) | Schubert,Matthias (ts) | Pifarely,Dominique (v) | Ilg,Dieter (b) | Rainey,Tom (dr)

ENJ-9369 2 | CD | Words Within Music
Daniel Schnyder Group
Il Pastor Fido | Matthäus Passion Suite(Johann Sebastian Bach): | Der Heiland Fällt Vor Seinem Vater Nieder- | Gerne Will Ich Mich Bequemen- | Sie Schrieen:Lass Ihn Kreuzigen- | Ach Golgatha,Unsel'ges Golgatha- | Mache Dich,Mein Herze,Rein- | Pilatus Sprach Zu Ihnen:Da Habt Ihr Die Hüter- | Wir Setzen Uns In Tränen Nieder- | Trio For Soprano Saxophone,Bass Trombone And Piano | Gershwin-Wagner Triptychon | Beep-Hop(Duo For Soprano Saxophone And Bass Trombone) | Memoires | Winter | Teiresias
Brooklyn,NY, rec. 21./22.11.1998
Schnyder,Daniel (fl,ss,ts) | Taylor,Dave (b-tb) | Drew Jr.,Kenny (p)

ENJ-9370 2 | CD | Speaking In Togues
David Murray Group
How I Got Over | Nobody Knows The Trouble I've Seen | Jimane's Creation | Missionary | Don't Know What I Would Do | Amazing Grace | Blessed Assurance | Just A Closer Walk With Thee
Paris,France, rec. 5.12.1997
Murray,David (b-cl,ts) | Ragin,Hugh (tp) | Franks,Stanley (g) | Nelson,Jimane (p,org,synth) | Jenkins,Clarence 'Pookie' (el-b) | Merritt,Renzell (dr) | Flemming,Leopoldo F. (perc)

ENJ-9376 2 | 2 CD | Glad Day:Settings Of William Blake
Mike Westbrook Brass Band
Glad Day | London Song | Lullaby | Holy Thursday | A Poison Tree | Long Johns Brown And Little Mary Bell | The Human Abstract
London,GB, rec. 13.-15.11.1997
Westbrook,Mike (p,voice) | Westbrook,Kate (piccolo,ten-horn,voc) | Whyman,Peter (ss,as) | Wakeman,Alan (ss,ts,perc) | Biscoe,Chris (ss,as,bs) | Berry,Steve (b) | Barry,Dave (dr,perc)
Let The Slave Incorporating The Prince Of Experience | The Tiger And The Lamb | The Fields | I See Thy Form
Westbrook,Mike (p,voice) | Westbrook,Kate (piccolo,ten-horn,voc) | Whyman,Peter (ss,as) | Wakeman,Alan (ss,ts,perc) | Biscoe,Chris (ss,as,bs) | Berry,Steve (b) | Barry,Dave (dr,perc) | Senior Girls Choir Of Blackheath Conservatoire Of Music And The Arts | Atterburry Thomas,Rosa (voc) | Baulch,Sarah (voc) | Beccham,Chloe (voc) | Biggs,Caroline (voc) | Blake,Joanna (voc) | Brady,Francesca (voc) | Dove,Rebecca (voc) | Faulks,Lucy (voc) | Ferran,Francesca (voc) | Grant,Laura (voc) | Hughes,Tara (voc) | Jumaily,Rania (voc) | Kelly,Jemina (voc) | Kinder,Rhiannon (voc) | Leal,Beatrice (voc) | Martin,Juliana (voc) | McLean,Sarah (voc) | Mountaine,Andrea (voc) | Okapel,Rachel (voc) | O'Shea-Ramdeholl,Jacinta (voc) | Palmer,Chloe (voc) | Parsons,Karina (voc) | Pye,Livia (voc) | Ranger-Snell,Laura (voc) | Raynsford,Helen (voc) | Stevens,Felicity (voc) | Thomas,Tamara (voc) | Watson,Alexandra (voc)
Song Of Spring
Westbrook,Mike (p,voice) | Westbrook,Kate (piccolo,ten-horn,voc) | Whyman,Peter (ss,as) | Wakeman,Alan (ss,ts,perc) | Biscoe,Chris (ss,as,bs) | Hill,Alan (g) | Godding,Brian (g) | Potter,Roger (g) | Hirsh,Paul (g) | Berry,Steve (b) | Barry,Dave (dr,perc) | Senior Girls Choir Of Blackheath Conservatoire Of Music And The Arts | Atterburry Thomas,Rosa (voc) | Baulch,Sarah (voc) | Beccham,Chloe (voc) | Biggs,Caroline (voc) | Blake,Joanna (voc) | Brady,Francesca (voc) | Dove,Rebecca (voc) | Faulks,Lucy (voc) | Ferran,Francesca (voc) | Grant,Laura (voc) | Hughes,Tara (voc) | Jumaily,Rania (voc) | Kelly,Jemina (voc) | Kinder,Rhiannon (voc) | Leal,Beatrice (voc) | Martin,Juliana (voc) | McLean,Sarah (voc) | Mountaine,Andrea (voc) | Okapel,Rachel (voc) | O'Shea-Ramdeholl,Jacinta (voc) | Palmer,Chloe (voc) | Parsons,Karina (voc) | Pye,Livia (voc) | Ranger-Snell,Laura (voc) | Raynsford,Helen (voc) | Stevens,Felicity (voc) | Thomas,Tamara (voc) | Watson,Alexandra (voc)

ENJ-9378 2 | CD | Guardians Of The Light
Michele Rosewoman And Quintessence
The Trill Of Real Love | Weird Nightmare | West Africa Blue | Where It Comes From | Free To Be | Fuzz Junk | Ask Me Now | Akomado(for Babaluaye) | Vamp For Ochum
details unknown, rec. March 1999
Rosewoman,Michele (p,gankogui,voc) | Wilson,Steve (ss,as) | Handy,Craig (ts) | Davis,Kenneth 'Kenny' (b,el-b) | Jackson,Gene (dr)

ENJ-9380 2 | CD | Translucide
Vincent Courtois Quartet
Ligne Droite | Translucide | Lettre À Louis | Que Reste-T-Il De Nos Yorks? | Cadence Du Milieu | La Fille Et L'Affiche | Vol D'Elephant(part 1) | Vol D'Elephant(part 2) | Soft Disortions | L'Ombre Sout Le Lit | Le Petit Cheval | Blanc Sur Blanc
details unknown, rec. July 1999
Courtois,Vincent (cello) | Robert,Yves (tb) | Godard,Michel (serpent,tuba) | Akchoté,Noel (g)

ENJ-9381 2 | CD | Ori Batá (Cuban Yoruba Music)
Lazaro Ros Ensemble
Elegba | Oggun | Ochosi | Babalu Ayé | Aggayu | Chango | Obatala | Yemaya
details unknown, rec. 1998-1999
Ros,Lazaro (voc) | Duran,Hilario (p,keyboards) | Gonzalez,Andy (b) | Bolanos,Angel Pedro (iya) | Guerra,Julio (itolele) | Von Alten,Brüning (okonkolo) | Diaz,Candito Zayas (voc)

ENJ-9383 2 | CD | Y2K
Sylvie Courvoisier Group
Y2K | Too Suite | Abra | La Valse Des Fromages Blancs | La Cigale Ivre S'Envoie El L'Air | Mutant | Sarajevo | Crasse-Tignasse | Machines-A-Sons | Fluxus
details unknown, rec. March 1999
Courvoisier,Sylvie (p,prepared-p) | Charial,Pierre (barrel-org) | Godard,Michel (serpent,tuba)

ENJ-9385 2 | CD | Book Of Tells
Mark Feldman Quartet
Windsor Quartet
NYC, rec. 20.8.1999
Feldman,Mark (v) | Hammann,Joyce (v) | Martin,Lois (viola) | Friedlander,Erik (cello)
Kit Suite: | Kit- | Les Tenebrides- | Murmur- | Xanas | Book Of Tells | Real Joe
Winterthur,CH, rec. 23.5.1998
Feldman,Mark (v) | Cummings,Genovia (v) | Hammann,Joyce (viola) | Friedlander,Erik (cello)

ENJ-9388 2 | CD | Summer Days
Eddie Allen Quintet
Eye Of The Hurricane | You Say | Always | Inner Glimpse | Mystic Dreams | Later
Brooklyn,NY, rec. 26./27.7.1999
Allen,Eddie E.J. (tp) | Faulk,Dan (ss,ts) | Wonsey,Athony (p) | Goods,Richie (b) | Blackman,Cindy (dr)
Eddie Allen Sextet
You Were Never Lovelier | Summer Days | Stablemates | The Crusade
Allen,Eddie E.J. (tp) | Turre,Steve (tb) | Faulk,Dan (ss,ts) | Wonsey,Athony (p) | Goods,Richie (b) | Blackman,Cindy (dr)

ENJ-9389 2 | CD | Time Immemorial
Dave Liebman
Before | Then | Now | After
Zerkall, rec. May-November 1997
Liebman,Dave (fl,as,ss,ts,bs,dido)

ENJ-9390 2 | CD | Quiet Fire
Johannes Enders Quintet
Day Number One | Prayer | Norwegian Wood | Subliminal | Timothy | Quiet Fire | Waltz For Susann
Augsburg, rec. 20./21.4.1999
Enders,Johannes (ts) | Herring,Vincent (ss,as) | Di Gioia,Roberto (p) | Abrams,Marc (b) | Hollander,Rick (dr)

ENJ-9396 2 | CD | Song
Marty Ehrlich Quartet
Waltz | The Price Of The Ticket(after James Baldwin) | Day Of The Dark Bright Light | I Pity The Door Immigrant | Fauve | The Falling Rains Of Life
NYC, rec. 18.10.1999
Ehrlich,Marty (b-cl,ss,as) | Caine,Uri (p) | Formanek,Michael (b) | Drummond,Billy (dr)
Marty Ehrlich Quintet
Blue Boye's Blues
Ehrlich,Marty (b-cl,ss,as) | Anderson,Ray (tb) | Caine,Uri (p) | Formanek,Michael (b) | Drummond,Billy (dr)

ENJ-9397 2 | CD | Le Concerto Improvisé
Louis Sclavis With The WRO Orchestra, Köln
Le Concerto Improvisé(part 1-8)
Köln, rec. November 1999-April 2000
Sclavis,Louis (cl,b-cl) | WRO Orchestra Köln | details not on the cover

ENJ-9398 2 | CD | Invention Is You
Antoine Hervé Quintet
Long Hair Woman | Soul As A Dance | La Fille Bleue | Sharing | Silence Comes In Waves | Serenity | La Boite A Musique | Something About Wolfgang | Salsita | Chango Chango
Live at Duc Des Lombardes,Paris, rec. November 1997
Hervé,Antoine (p) | Stockhausen,Markus (tp,fl-h) | Moutin,Francois (b) | Moutin,Louis (dr) | Franck,Arnaud (perc)

ENJ-9402 2 | CD | Mambo Nights
Conexion Latina
Mambo Nights | Hace Rato | Flotando En El Aire | Felicidad | Lotus Blossom | Zapata | Mambo A La Mintzer | Fiesta De Soneros | Alna's Connexus
München, rec. November 1999 & January 2000
Conexion Latina | Bendzko,Thomas (tp) | Reichstaller,Claus (tp) | Kaupp,Gil (tp) | Goykovich,Dusko (tp,fl-h) | Shew,Bobby (tp) | Mears,Adrian (tb) | Perez,Cesar (tb) | Schwatlo,Peter (tb) | Häfner,Lutz (to,bs) | Millimer,Jesse (p) | Perez,Tomas (ld,b,coro) | Rengifo Sr.,Felipe (congas,shekere,cumaco) | Ramirez,Pablo (bongos,cow-bell) | Rengifo Jr.,Felipe (timbales,campana de cumaco) | Plaza,Javier (maracas,guira de parranda,coro,voc) | Naranjo,Albertolaures,claves,director) | Fajarro,Osvaldo (voc,coro) | America,Yma (voc,coro)

ENJ-9404 2 | CD | Ama Tu Sonrisa
Antonio Hart Group
For Amadou | Ama Tu Sonrisa | Distant Cousins | Wayne's Lament | Forward Motion | Have You Met Miss Jones | Somewhere | Peace,Love And Light | Grover Washington Jr. | El Professor
details unknown, rec. details unknown
Hart,Antonio Maurice (fl,ss,as) | Terry,Yosvanny (ts) | Nelson,Steve (vib) | Hays,Kevin (p) | Goods,Richie (b) | Gainer,Camille (dr) | Waits,Nasheet (dr) | Thoms,Renato (perc) | Morales,Rolando (perc) | Kwame-Bell,Khalil (perc) | Helm,Lenora (voc) | Acuna,Claudia (voc)

ENJ-9407 2 | CD | The Satchmo Legacy
Benny Bailey Quintet
Someday You'll Be Sorry | Ain't Misbehavin' | West End Blues | After You've Gone | Basin Street Blues | Pennies From Heaven | Do You Know What It Means To Miss New Orleans | Home(When The Shadows Fall) | A Kiss To Build A Dream On
Englewood Cliffs,NJ, rec. 16./17.11.1999
Bailey,Benny (tp,voc) | Pizzarelli,Bucky (g) | Bunch,John (p) | Leonhart,Jay (b) | Tate,Grady (dr)

ENJ-9411 2 | CD | The Fitting Room
Vincent Courtois Trio
Celine(part 1-3) | Oranges Améres | Homére S'Arrange | Miroirs | The Fitting Room | Par Les Gouffres | Tom | Les Il/ | Vitrines
Les Lilas,France, rec. December 2000
Courtois,Vincent (cello) | Ducret,Marc (el-g,12-string-g) | Pifarely,Dominique (v)

ENJ-9413 2 | CD | New School
Mark Helias' Open Loose
Molecule | Startle | Dominoes | Mapa | Gentle Ben | Pick And Roll | Question Time(Knitting Our Quitting-part 5)
NYC, rec. 21.9.2000
Helias,Mark (b) | Malaby,Tony (ts) | Rainey,Tom (dr)

ENJ-9417 2 | CD | Reflection
Ensemble Indigo
Warm Canto | Reflexe: | Allegro Apassionato- | Adagio Sostenuto- | Allegro Assai- | Valinor | Musical Toys: | Mechanical Accordeon- | The Trumpeter In The Forest- | A Bear Playing Double Bass And The Black Woman- | April Day- | Song Of The Fisherman- | The Magic Smith- | Mweya | West-Östlicher Divan
Loft,Köln, rec. 14.-17.9.2000
Ensemble Indigo | Winterschladen,Reiner (tp) | Haushalter,Heike (v) | Stalz,Petra (v) | Malek,Monika (viola) | Hangen,Gesa (cello) | Kott,Alois (b)

Enja | Soulfood

ENJ-2070 2 | CD | The Children Of Africa
Dollar Brand Trio
Banyana-The Children Of Africa | Asr | Ishmael | The Honey-Bird | The Dream | Yukio-Khalifa
rec. 27.1.1976
Brand,Dollar[Abdullah Ibrahim] (ss,p,voc) | McBee,Cecil (b) | Brooks,Roy (dr)

ENJ-2084 2 | CD | Dark To Themselves
Cecil Taylor Unit
Streams | Chorus Of Seed
Jazz Festival,Ljubljaba,YU, rec. 18.6.1976
Taylor,Cecil (p) | Malik,Raphe (tp) | Ware,David S. (ts) | Lyons,Jimmy (as) | Edwards,Marc (dr)
Streams and Chorus Of Seed(complete performance)
Taylor,Cecil (p) | Malik,Raphe (tp) | Ware,David S. (ts) | Lyons,Jimmy (as) | Edwards,Marc (dr)

ENJ-3021 2 | CD | Moods
Mal Waldron Sextet
Minoat | A Case Of Plus 4's | Sieg Haille
rec. 7.5.1978
Waldron,Mal (p) | Hino,Terumasa (co) | Breuer,Hermann (tb) | Lacy,Steve (ss) | Brown,Cameron (b) | Ntshoko,Makaya (dr)
Mal Waldron
Aniexty | Lonely | Happiness | I Thought About You
Ludwigsburg
Waldron,Mal (p) | Hino,Terumasa (co) | Breuer,Hermann (tb) | Lacy,Steve (ss) | Brown,Cameron (b) | Ntshoko,Makaya (dr)
Soul Eyes | Thoughtful | Duquility
Ludwigsburg, rec. 8.5.1978
Waldron,Mal (p-solo)

ENJ-3039 2 | CD | Africa Tears And Laugher
Dollar Brand Quartet
Tsakve | The Perfumed Forest Wet With Rain | Ishmael | Did You Hear That Sound | Liberation Dance (When Tarzan Meets The African Freedom Figh | Imam
rec. 11.3.1979
Brand,Dollar[Abdullah Ibrahim] (ss,p,voc) | Qadr,Talib (ss,as,voc) | Brown,Greg (b) | Betsch,John (dr)

ENJ-3047 2 | CD | Echoes From Africa
Dollar Brand-Johnny Dyani Duo
Namhanje(Today) | Lakutshonilanga(When The Sun Sets) | Saud(Dedicated To McCoy Tyner) | Ziki(Remembrance Of Allah)
rec. 7.9.1979
Brand,Dollar[Abdullah Ibrahim] (p,voc) | Dyani,Johnny (b,voc)

ENJ-3091 2 | CD | Bennie Wallace Plays Monk
Bennie Wallace Trio
Skippy | Round About Midnight | Straight No Chaser | Prelude | Variations On A Theme (Trinkle Tinkle)
NYC, rec. 4./5.3.1981
Wallace,Bennie (ts) | Gomez,Eddie (b) | Richmond,Dannie (dr)
Bennie Wallace Quartet
Ask Me Now | Evidence | Ugly Beauty
Wallace,Bennie (ts) | Knepper,Jimmy (tb) | Gomez,Eddie (b) | Richmond,Dannie (dr)

ENJ-4016 2 | CD | Peace
Chet Baker Quintet
Syzygies | Peace | Lament For Thelonious | The Song Is You | Shadows | For Now
rec. 23.2.1982
Baker,Chet (tp) | Friedman,David (vib,marimba) | Williams,Buster (b) | Chambers,Joe (dr)

ENJ-4030 2 | CD | African Dawn
Dollar Brand
Blues For A Hip King | A Flower Is A Lovesome Thing | African Dawn | African Piano | For Monk | Round About Midnight | Blue Monk | For Coltrane
rec. 7.6.1982
Brand,Dollar[Abdullah Ibrahim] (p-solo)

ENJ-5005 2 | CD | Strollin'
Chet Baker Trio
Strollin' | Love For Sale | Leaving | But Not For Me
rec. July 1985
Baker,Chet (tp,voc) | Catherine,Philip (g) | Rassinfosse,Jean-Louis (b)

ENJ-5013 2 | CD | What If
Kenny Barron Trio
Close To You Alone
Englewood Cliffs,NJ, rec. 17.2.1986
Barron,Kenny (p) | McBee,Cecil (b) | Lewis,Victor (dr)
Kenny Barron Quintet
Phantoms | Voyage | What If | Lullaby
Barron,Kenny (p) | Roney,Wallace (tp) | Stubblefield,John (ts) | McBee,Cecil (b) | Lewis,Victor (dr)
Kenny Barron-Victor Lewis
Dexterity
Barron,Kenny (p) | Lewis,Victor (dr)
Kenny Barron
Trinkle Tinkle
Barron,Kenny (p-solo)

ENJ-5037 2 | CD | It Just So Happens
Ray Anderson Sextet
Once In A While | It Just So Happens | Ross The Boss | Elegy For Joe Scott | La Vie En Rose | Raven's Jolly Jump-Up | Fatelet | Fishin' With Gramps
rec. details unknown
Anderson,Ray (tb) | Davis,Stanton (tp) | Robinson,Perry (cl) | Stewart,Robert 'Bob' (tuba) | Dresser,Mark (b) | Burrage,Ronnie (dr)

ENJ-5073 2 | CD | Mindif
Abdullah Ibrahim Sextet
Earth Bird | African Market | Mindif | Pule(Rain) | Protee | Star Dance | Thema For Monk
Englewood Cliffs,NJ, rec. 7./8.3.1988
Brand,Dollar[Abdullah Ibrahim] (fl,p,voc) | Powell,Benny (tb) | Ford,Ricky (ss,ts) | Handy,Craig (fl,ts) | Williams,David (b) | Higgins,Billy (dr,gambray)

ENJ-5097 2 | CD | My Favourite Songs: The Last Great Concert Vol.1
Chet Baker With The NDR-Bigband
All Blues | Well You Needn't | Django
Funkhaus,Hannover, rec. 29.4.1988
Baker,Chet (tp,voc) | NDR Big Band | Axelsson,Lennart (tp) | Habermann,Heinz (tp) | Lanese,Bob (tp) | Moch,Manfred 'Mannie' (tp) | Ahlers,Wolfgang (tb) | Plato,Herman (tb) | Grossmann,Manfred (tb) | Christmann,Egon (tb) | Geller,Herb (fl,as) | Böther,Andreas (sax) | Wuster,E. (reeds) | Ende,Harald (sax) | Nagurski,K. (reeds) | Schlüter,Wolfgang (vib) | Norris,Walter (p) | Schröder,John (g) | Lindholm,Lucas (b) | Tanggaard,Aage (dr) | Glawischnig,Dieter (cond)
Chet Baker With The Radio Orchestra Hannover(NDR)
My Funny Valentine | Summertime | I Fall In Love Too Easily
Baker,Chet (tp,voc) | Hannover,Radio Orchestra (NDR) | Norris,Walter (p) | Schröder,John (g) | French-Horns | Strings,Woodwinds | Glawischnig,Dieter (cond)
Chet Baker Quintet
In Your Own Sweet Way
Baker,Chet (tp) | Norris,Walter (p) | Schröder,John (g) | Lindholm,Lucas (b) | Tanggaard,Aage (dr)

ENJ-6018 2 | CD | African River
Dollar(Abdullah Ibrahim) Brand Group
Toi-Toi | African River | Joan-Capetown Flower | Chisa | Sweet Samba | Duke 88 | The Wedding | The Mountain Of Night
Englewood Cliffs,NJ, rec. 1.6.1989
Brand,Dollar[Abdullah Ibrahim] (p) | Eubanks,Robin (tb) | Stubblefield,John (fl,ts) | Young,Horace Alexander (ss,as,piccolo) | Johnson,Howard (bs,tuba) | Williams,Buster (b) | Adams,Brian (dr)

ENJ-6020 2 | CD | Straight From The Heart-The Last Concert Vol.2
Chet Baker Quintet/NDR Big Band/Radio Orchestra Hannover
Look For The Silver Lining | I Get Along With You Very Well | Conception | There's A Small Hotel | Sippin' At Bells | Tenderly | My Funny Valentine
Funkhaus,Hannover, rec. 28.4.1988
Baker,Chet (tp,voc) | Geller,Herb (as) | Norris,Walter (p) | Schröder,John (g) | Lindholm,Lucas (b) | Tanggaard,Aage (dr) | NDR Big Band | Radio Orchester Hannover

ENJ-6048 2 | CD | Signals
Wayne Krantz
One Of Two
NYC, rec. May/June 1990
Krantz,Wayne (g)
Wayne Krantz Quartet
Faith In The Process | Don't Tell Me | Signals
Krantz,Wayne (g) | Beard,Jim (keyboards) | Jackson,Anthony (contra-b-g) | Chambers,Dennis (dr)
Wayne Krantz Duo
Alliance | Sossity,You're A Woman
Krantz,Wayne (g) | Alias,Don (perc)
As Is
Krantz,Wayne (g) | Stern,Leni (g)
For Susan
Krantz,Wayne (g) | Bullock,Hiram (b,dr-program)

ENJ-6050 2 | CD | Hot Stuff
Barbara Dennerlein Quartet
Hot Stuff | Wow! | Top Secret | Birthday Blues | Polar Lights | Killer Joe | My Invitation | Seven Steps To Heaven | Toscanian Sunset
Ludwigsburg, rec. 6.-8.6.1990
Dennerlein,Barbara (org,synth) | Sheppard,Andy (ts) | Watkins,Mitch (g) | Mondesir,Mark (dr)

ENJ-6068 2 | CD | There Was A Time-Echo Of Harlem
Eddie Harris Quartet
Love Letters | Historia De Un Amor | Autumn In New York | Photographs Of You | The Song Is You | Harlem Nocturne | There Was A Time-Echo Of Harlem | Lover Come Back To Me
NYC, rec. 9.5.1990
Harris,Eddie (ts) | Barron,Kenny (p) | McBee,Cecil (b) | Riley,Ben (dr)

ENJ-6074 22 | 2 CD | The Last Concert Vol.I+II
Chet Baker With The NDR-Bigband
All Blues | Well You Needn't | Django
Funkhaus,Hannover, rec. 29.4.1988

LABELVERZEICHNIS

Baker,Chet (tp,voc) | NDR Big Band | Axelsson,Lennart (tp) | Habermann,Heinz (tp) | Lanese,Bob (tp) | Moch,Manfred 'Mannie' (tp) | Ahlers,Wolfgang (tb) | Plato,Herman (tb) | Grossmann,Manfred (tb) | Christmann,Egon (tb) | Geller,Herb (fl,as) | Böther,Andreas (sax) | Wuster,E. (reeds) | Ende,Harald (sax) | Nagurski,K. (reeds) | Schlüter,Wolfgang (vib) | Norris,Walter (p) | Schröder,John (g) | Lindholm,Lucas (b) | Tanggaard,Aage (dr) | Glawischnig,Dieter (cond)

Chet Baker With The Radio Orchestra Hannover(NDR)
My Funny Valentine | Summertime | I Fall In Love Too Easily
Baker,Chet (tp,voc) | Hannover,Radio Orchestra (NDR) | Norris,Walter (p) | Schröder,John (g) | French-Horns | Strings,Woodwinds | Glawischnig,Dieter (cond)

Chet Baker Quintet
In Your Own Sweet Way
Baker,Chet (tp) | Norris,Walter (p) | Schröder,John (g) | Lindholm,Lucas (b) | Tanggaard,Aage (dr)

Chet Baker Quintet/NDR Big Band/Radio Orchestra Hannover
Look For The Silver Lining | I Get Along With You Very Well | Conception | There's A Small Hotel | Sippin' At Bells | Tenderly | My Funny Valentine
Funkhaus,Hannover, rec. 28.4.1988
Baker,Chet (tp,voc) | Geller,Herb (as) | Norris,Walter (p) | Schröder,John (g) | Lindholm,Lucas (b) | Tanggaard,Aage (dr) | NDR Big Band | Radio Orchester Hannover

ENJ-6090 2 | CD | Al-Jadida
Rabih Abou-Khalil Group
Catania | Nashwa | An Evening With Jerry | When The Lights Go Out | Storyteller | Ornette Never Sleeps | Nadim | Wishing Well
Ludwigsburg, rec. 8.-10.10.1990
Abou-Khalil,Rabih (oud) | Fortune,Sonny (as) | Moore,Glen (b) | Shotham,Ramesh (perc,south-indian-dr) | Khaiat,Nabil (perc,frame-dr)

ENJ-7011 2 | CD | Desert Flowers
Abdullah Ibrahim
The Praise Song | Just Arrived | Ancient Cape | Desert Air | Come Sunday | District Six | Sweet Devotion | Edie | For John Coltrane | Tsidi | Mizu-Water
Englewood Cliffs,NJ, rec. 18.12.1991
Brand,Dollar[Abdullah Ibrahim] (p,synth,voc)

ENJ-7023 2 | CD | Spanish Nights
Philip Catherine/Niels-Henning Orsted-Pedersen With The Royal Copenhagen Chamber Orchestra
Spanish Nights | Aranjuez | Django | My Favorite Things | Leaving | Esmeralda | Armando's Rhumba | Black Orpheus | Little Anna | Que Pasa | Rene Thomas
Copenhagen,Denmark, rec. 11.-13.5.1989
Catherine,Philip (g) | Orsted-Pedersen,Niels-Henning (b) | Royal Copenhagen Chamber Orchestra,The | Drew,Kenny (arr) | Wilkins,Ernie (arr) | Hansen,Ole Kock (arr)

ENJ-7043 2 | CD | That's Me
Barbara Dennerlein Quintet
Grandfather's Funk | Dancing Shoes | That's Me | Three Hearts | Monkology | Love Affair-The Ballad | Love Affair-Forever And Never | One For Miss D. | Downtown N.Y.
Ludwigsburg, rec. 3./4.9.& 10.3.1992
Dennerlein,Barbara (org,synth) | Anderson,Ray (tb) | Berg,Bob (ts) | Watkins,Mitch (g) | Chambers,Dennis (dr)

ENJ-7053 2 | CD | Blue Camel
Rabih Abou-Khalil Group
Sahara | Tsarka | Ziriab | Blue Camel | On Time | A Night In The Mountains | Rabou-Abou-Kabou | Beirut
Köln, rec. 19.-21.5.1992
Abou-Khalil,Rabih (oud) | Wheeler,Kenny (tp,fl-h) | Mariano,Charlie (as) | Swallow,Steve (b-g) | Shotham,Ramesh (perc,south-indian-dr) | Khaiat,Nabil (frame-dr) | Cardona,Milton (congas)

ENJ-7083 2 | CD | Tarab
Bushman In The Desert | After Dinner | Awakening | Haneen Wa Hanaan | Lost Centuries | In Search Of The Well | Orange Fields | A Tooth Lost | Arabian Waltz
Köln, rec. 28.2.& 1.3.1992
Abou-Khalil,Rabih (oud,voice) | Kusur,Selim (nay) | Moore,Glen (b) | Khaiat,Nabil (perc,frame-dr) | Shotham,Ramesh (perc,south-indian-dr)

ENJ-8044 2 | CD | Soul Connection
Dusko Goykovich Quartet
Ballad For Miles | I'll Close My Eyes | NYC | Blues Valse
Brooklyn,NY, rec. 28./29.6.1993
Goykovich,Dusko (tp,fl-h) | Flanagan,Tommy (p) | Gomez,Eddie (b) | Roker,Granville 'Mickey' (dr)

Dusko Goykovich Quintet
Soul Connection | Inga | Blues Time | Adriatica | Teamwork Song
Goykovich,Dusko (tp,fl-h) | Heath,Jimmy (ts) | Flanagan,Tommy (p) | Gomez,Eddie (b) | Roker,Granville 'Mickey' (dr)

ENJ-8078 2 | CD | The Sultan's Picnic
8078-1(Audiophile) | LP | The Sultan's Picnic
Rabih Abou-Khalil Group
Sunrise In Montreal | In My Solitude | Dog River | Moments | Lamentation | Nocturne Au Villaret | The Happy Sheik | Snake Soup
Köln, rec. 13.-16.3.1994
Abou-Khalil,Rabih (bass-oud,oud) | Wheeler,Kenny (tp,fl-h) | Mariano,Charlie (as) | Levy,Howard (harm) | Godard,Michel (serpent,tuba) | Swallow,Steve (el-b) | Nauseef,Mark (dr) | Cardona,Milton (congas) | Khaiat,Nabil (frame-dr)

ENJ-9021 2 | CD | Chet Baker-The Legacy Vol.1
Chet Baker With The NDR-Bigband
Here's That Rainy Day | How Deep Is The Ocean | Mister B | In Your Own Sweet Way | All Of You | Dolphin Dance | Look For The Silver Lining | Django | All Blues
Auditorium Maximum,Universität,Hamburg, rec. 14.11.1987
Baker,Chet (tp) | NDR Big Band | Axelsson,Lennart (tp) | Habermann,Heinz (tp) | Moch,Manfred 'Mannie' (tp) | Kubatsch,Paul (tp) | Ahlers,Wolfgang (tb) | Plato,Herman (tb) | Grossmann,Manfred (tb) | Christmann,Egon (tb) | Geller,Herb (as) | Ment,Jochen (as) | Sulzman,Stan (ts) | Ende,Harald (ts) | Rönfeld,Werner (bs) | Norris,Walter (p) | Schröder,John (g) | Lindholm,Lucas (b) | Riel,Alex (dr)

ENJ-9043 2 | CD | 2 Drinks Minimum
Wayne Krantz Trio
Whippersnapper | Dove Gloria | Shirts Off | Dream Called Love | AFKaP | Isabelle | Alliance- | Secrets- | Lynxpaw
Live at The 55 Bar,NYC, rec. February-April 1995
Krantz,Wayne (g) | Goines,Lincoln (el-b) | Danzinger,Zachary (dr)

ENJ-9057 2 | CD | Alboreá
Renaud Garcia-Fons Quartet
Al Camarón | Alboreá | Natgo | Secret Zambra | Eosine | Gus's Smile | Amadu | Sacre Coeur | Rue De Buci | Fort Apache | Tropea
Montreuil,France, rec. 12.-16.6.1995
Garcia-Fons,Renaud (5-string-b) | Matinier,Jean-Louis (accordeon) | Torchinsky,Yves (b) | Mahieux,Jacques (dr)

ENJ-9059 2 | CD | Arabian Waltz
Rabih Abou-Khalil Group
Arabian Waltz | Dream Of A Dying City | Ornette Never Sleeps | Georgina | No Visa | The Pain After
Baden-Baden/Zerkall, rec. 22.-26.9.& 18.-23.12.1995
Abou-Khalil,Rabih (oud) | Godard,Michel (serpent,tuba) | Khaiat,Nabil (frame-dr) | Balanescu Quartet: Balanescu,Alexander (v) | Connors,Clare (v) | Martin,Paul (viola) | Cunliffe,David (cello)

ENJ-9077 2 | CD | Chet Baker-The Legacy Vol.2:I Remember You
Chet Baker Quartet
But Not For Me | Broken Wing | Nardis | You Go To My Head | Just Friends
Live at 'Cafe Montmartre',Copenhagen, rec. 28.2.1985
Baker,Chet (tp,p,voc) | Raney,Doug (g) | Lundgaard,Jesper (b) | Tanggaard,Aage (dr)

ENJ-9314 2 | CD | Légendes
Renaud Garcia-Fons
Funambule | Aube | Sesame | Inanga | Moreno | Like Someone In Love | Procession | Fille Des Sables | La Guitare A King Kong | Legendes | Elle | Mi Saeta
St.Omen/Montreuil,France, rec. December 1992
Garcia-Fons,Renaud (b-solo)

ENJ-9317 2 | CD | Shiny Stockings
Jenny Evans And Her Quintet
Shiny Stockings | Good Old Days | Softly As In A Morning Sunrise | That's What Zoot Said | You Go To My Head | In A Mellow Tone | Caravan | Willow Weep For Me | Alright,Okay,You Win | Honeysuckle Rose | The Song Of Autmn | April In Paris | All Of Me
München, rec. October 1996
Evans,Jenny (voc) | Goykovich,Dusko (tp,fl-h) | Basso,Gianni (ts) | Gazarov,David (p) | Pejakovic,Branko (b) | Martini,Rudi (dr)

ENJ-9320 2 | CD | Balkan Blues
Dusko Goykovich Quintet
Simona | Yardbird Suite | Medium Rare | Adriatica | You've Changed | Miss Bo | Nights Of Skopje | Snapshot | You'd Be So Nice
Skopje,Macedonia, rec. 29./30.10.1994
Goykovich,Dusko (tp,fl-h) | Basso,Gianni (ts) | Michelich,Peter (p) | Gjakonovski,Martin (b) | Levacic,Kruno (dr)

Dusko Goykovich Quintet With The NDR Radio-Philharmonie,Hannover
Balkan Blues(A Jazz Suite by Dusko Goykovich) | Balkan Dance | Bosna Calling | Pannonia | East Of Montenegro | Macedonia | Shumadya | Haze On The Danube | Ohrid | Finale
Live at Raschplatz Pavillon,Hannover, rec. 14.11.1992
Goykovich,Dusko (tp,fl-h) | Rokovic,Bora (p) | Uhlir,Frantisek (b) | Castellucci,Bruno (dr) | Schlüter,Wolfgang (perc) | Radio-Philharmonie Hannover | Mikkelborg,Palle (arr,ld)

ENJ-9326 2 | 2 CD | La Banda/Banda And Jazz
Banda Città Ruvo Di Puglia
Toreador(Carmen) | La Gitana(Il Trovatore) | La Donna E Mobile & Quaretteo(Rigoletto) | Deh,Non Volerli Vittime E Finale(Norma) | A Me,Fanciulla(La Traviata) | Nessun Dorma(Turandot) | E Lucevan Le Stelle(Tosca) | Largo Al Factotum(Il Barbiere Di Siviglia)
Live at 'Donaueschinger Musiktage', rec. 19.10.1996
Banda Città Ruvo Di Puglia | Dell'Erba,Pasquale (tp) | Palmitessa,Luciano (tp) | Lozuppone,Leonatdo (fl-h) | Bucci,Vincenzo (fl-h) | Luzio,Giuseppe (fl-h) | Barile,Salvatore (fl-h) | Valenzano,Nicola (fl-h) | Mercadante,Bartolo (tb) | Rubini,Vicenco (tb) | D'Ambra,Annibale (fr-h) | Fracchiolla,Antonio (fr-h) | Lovino,Simone (fr-h) | Bisceglie,Nino (tuba) | Ditano,Giuseppe (tuba) | Di Muro,Pasquale (tuba) | Parente,Giuseppe (tuba) | Mastropirro,Vincenzo (fl) | Di Puppo,Franco (fl) | Milella,Pietro (oboe) | De Michele,Giuseppe (e-flat-cl) | Ciliberti,Giambattista (cl) | Di Cintio,Vito (cl) | Cattedra,Leonardo (cl) | Carabellese,Nunzio (cl) | Lentini,Giuseppe (cl) | Di Puppo,Vincenzo (cl) | Di Rella,Rocco (cl) | Angione,Gianluigi (cl) | Puntillo,Nicola (b-cl) | Pisani,Nicola (ss) | Debenedetto,Paolo (as) | Galasso,Franco (ts) | De Caro,Lorenzo (bs) | Mazzone,Vincenzo (perc) | Ivan,Mancinello (perc) | Salvatoriello,Simone (perc)

Willem Breuker Kollektief
Una Serenata | Tra La Folla,Mora,Mormora | This Is An Empty Bottle Of Wine | Sacra Romana Rota
Breuker,Willem (b-cl,sax) | Minafra,Pino (tp,megaphone) | Trovesi,Gianluigi (cl,b-cl,sax) | Matinier,Jean-Louis (accordeon) | Godard,Michel (serpent,tuba) | Galeazzi,Lucilla (voc) | Tommaso,Bruno (arr,ld) | Members of The Banda Città Ruvo Di Puglia

ENJ-9330 2 | CD | Odd Times
Rabih Abou-Khalil Group
The Sphinx And I | Dr. Gieler's Presccription | Elephant Hips | Q-Tips | Son Of Ben Hur | The Happy Sheik | One Of Those Days | Rabou-Abou-Kabou
Live at Stadtgarten,Köln, rec. 11.-13.5.1997
Abou-Khalil,Rabih (oud) | Levy,Howard (harm) | Godard,Michel (serpent,tuba) | Nauseef,Mark (dr) | Khaiat,Nabil (frame-dr)

ENJ-9334 2 | CD | Oriental Bass
Renaud Garcia-Fons Group
Oriental Bass | San Juan | Goodjinns | Oryssa | Ghazali | Jullundur | Hommage A Ostad | Bajo Andaluz | Jam Buleria | Djani
Montreuil,France, rec. August 1997
Garcia-Fons,Renaud (perc,palmas,5-string-b) | Favre,Yves (tb) | Hayward,Chris (fl) | Sansalone,Bruno (cl) | Matinier,Jean-Louis (accordeon) | Antonini,Claire (lute,theorbe) | Pradal,Vicente (flamenco-g,palmas) | Khalfa,Rabah (bendir,tar,tarabouka) | Roger,Jean-Francois (marimba,perc,tables) | Schlamminger,Sam (daf) | Yerno,Ana (palmas)

ENJ-9337 2 | CD | Chet Baker:The Legacy Vol.3:Why Shouldn't You Cry
Chet Baker-Wolfgang Lackerschmid Duo
You Don't Know What Love Is | Five Years Ago | Dessert
Stuttgart, rec. 8./9.1.1979
Baker,Chet (tp) | Lackerschmid,Wolfgang (vib,gongs)

Chet Baker-Wolfgang Lackerschmid Quintet
Rue Gregoire Du Tour | Balzwaltz | Toku-Do
Stuttgart, rec. November 1979
Baker,Chet (tp,voc) | Lackerschmid,Wolfgang (vib) | Coryell,Larry (g) | Williams,Buster (b) | Williams,Tony (dr)

Chet Baker-Wolfgang Lackerschmid Trio
Why Shouldn't You Cry
Bischofsmais, rec. 26.-28.8.1987
Baker,Chet (tp) | Lackerschmid,Wolfgang (vib) | Lenz,Günter (b)
Waltz For Berlin
Baker,Chet (tp) | Lackerschmid,Wolfgang (vib) | Stilo,Nicola (fl)

Lee Konitz-Wolfgang Lackerschmid Quintet
Chet's Ballad(Why Shouldn't You Cry)
Brooklyn,NY, rec. August 1993
Konitz,Lee (as) | Lackerschmid,Wolfgang (vib) | Johnston,Donald (p) | McClure,Ron (b) | Hirshfield,Jeff (dr) | White,Lillias (voc)

ENJ-9345 2 | CD | Black Inside
Antonio Farao Trio
Memories | Black Inside | Latin Dance | Just In Time | Basel | Sweet | Brother Kenny | Chaotic Romance | Dumb Show | My One And Only Love
Brooklyn,NY, rec. 23./24.4.1998
Farao,Antonio (p) | Coleman,Ira (b) | Watts,Jeff 'Tain' (dr)

ENJ-9346 2 | CD | Speed Life
Nils Wogram Quartet
Morphing | Hotel Blues | King Of Trash | Circle | Newsed | Alien's Earworm | The Beauty Of Meat | Annoying Neighbour | Speed Life
Ludwigsburg, rec. 2./3.12.1997
Wogram,Nils (tb) | Nabatov,Simon (p) | Thys,Nicolas 'Nic' (b) | Rückert,Jochen (dr)

ENJ-9360 2 | CD | Yara
Rabih Abou-Khalil Group
Requiem | Imminent Journey | A Gracious Man | On A Bus | Grateful Parting | The Passage Of Life | Through The Window | Lithe Dream | Puppet Master | Bint El Bahr | The End Of Faith | The Knowledge Of A Child
Zerkall, rec. 4.-6.6.1998
Abou-Khalil,Rabih (oud) | Pifarely,Dominique (v) | Courtois,Vincent (cello) | Khaiat,Nabil (frame-dr)

ENJ-9362 2 | CD | Castel Del Monte
Michel Godard Ensemble
Ciacona | La Muntagnella | Serpent D'Or | C'era Una Strega,C'era Una Fata | Canto Della Sibilla | Huit | Preghiera | Un | Ah! Vita Bella | Crisbell | Le Vent Respire | Magnificat | Una Serenata | Cathedrale Sans Nom | Murmures | Voi Che Amate
details unknown, rec. September 1998
Godard,Michel (serpent,tuba) | Minafra,Pino (tp,fl-h) | Trovesi,Gianluigi (cl,b-cl,as) | Matinier,Jean-Louis (accordeon) | Garcia-Fons,Renaud (b) | Favre,Pierre (dr,perc) | Galeazzi,Lucilla (voc) | Bsiri,Linda (voc)

ENJ-9363 2 | CD | Girl Talk
Jenny Evans And Band
Too Close For Comfort | I Wanna Be Near To You | Miss Otis Regrets | Love For Sale | Girl Talk | Autumn Leaves | Jenny's Place | Song For My Father | There'll Never Be Another You | Mr.Bojangles | Dat Dere | St.Thomas | 'S Wonderful
Live at The Allotria,München, rec. 20.4.1993
Evans,Jenny (voc) | Bickl,Gerhard 'Zwei' (p) | Gnettner,Kartsten (b) | Eppinger,Stephan (dr)

ENJ-9364 2 | CD | Fuera
Renaud Garcia-Fons & Jean-Louis Matinier
Derniere Route | Sanlucar | Amischa | Le Byzantin | Bari | Mer Blanche | Born To Play | Lueurs Perdues | Upepidde | Munecas Aminadas | Perpetua | Khormiloi | Ruvo(for Pablo,Solea & Gabriel)
Zerkall, rec. December 1998-March 1999
Garcia-Fons,Renaud (5-string-b) | Matinier,Jean-Louis (accordeon,accordina)

ENJ-9366 2 | CD | Where Home Is
Ray Anderson Pocket Brass Band
Bimwa Swing | The Alligatory Abagua | The Mooche | I Mean You | Where Home Is | Peace In Our Time | The Pineapple Rag
Englewood Cliffs,NJ, rec. 3./4.11.1998
Anderson,Ray (tb) | Soloff,Lew (tp) | Perrine,Matt (sousaphone) | Previte,Robert 'Bobby' (dr)

ENJ-9372 2 | CD | Bukra
Rabih Abou-Khalil Group
Fortune Seeker | Bukra | Kibbe | Remember... The Desert | Nayla | Time
Köln, rec. May 1988
Abou-Khalil,Rabih (oud) | Fortune,Sonny (as) | Moore,Glen (b) | Velez,Glen (perc,frame-dr,overtone-singing) | Shotham,Ramesh (perc,south-indian-dr)

ENJ-9373 2 | CD | Roots & Sprouts
Remembering Machghara | Walking On Air | Nida | Revelation | Wordless | Sweet Rain | Outlook | Caravan | Dreams Of A Dying City
Köln, rec. 23.-25.11.1990
Abou-Khalil,Rabih (oud) | Kusur,Selim (nay) | El-Achek,Yassin (v) | Moore,Glen (b) | Velez,Glen (frame-dr) | Al-Sous,Mohammad (darabuka)

ENJ-9374 2 | CD | Shake,Shuttle And Blow
Albert Mangelsdorff Quartet
Do You Like Pastrami? | Bolghatty Dreams | Shake,Shuttle And Blow | Barrel Without Bottom | Up And Push | Tri-Van Drumming | Saxobonia | 01/799
Zürich,CH, rec. 3./4.1.1999
Mangelsdorff,Albert (tb) | Spoerri,Bruno (ss,as,syntophone) | Doran,Christy (el-g) | Weber,Reto (dr,perc,djembe,ghatam)

ENJ-9384 2 | CD | Round About A Midsummer's Dream
Gianluigi Trovesi Nonet
L'Infanta Arcibizzarra | Crisbell | C'era Una Strega,C'era Una Fata | Puck | Orobop | Fragment From Concerto In G Minor For Violin And Strings Op.8 N.2(Summer) | Villanella | Oberon | Animali In Marcia | Adagietto Bergomasco | Puppet Theatre | Bottom | Canzonetta
Live at Tollhaus,Karlsruhe & Studio Baden-Baden, rec. 5.-8.7.1999
Trovesi,Gianluigi (piccolo-cl,b-cl,as) | Manzolini,Paolo (g) | Matinier,Jean-Louis (accordeon) | Garcia-Fons,Renaud (b) | Maras,Fulvio (dr,perc) | Rizzo,Carlo (tambourello,voice) | Montanari,Stefano (v) | Trovesi,Stefania (v) | Ballanti,Paolo (cello)

ENJ-9387 2 | CD | For My People
Ferenc Snétberger
Landscapes | Fantazia | Vals Criollo- | Vals Gitano-
details unknown, rec. May/September 1999
Snétberger,Ferenc (g-solo)

Ferenc Snétberger-Markus Stockhausen
Hajnal | Gond Nelkül | Alkony
Snétberger,Ferenc (g) | Stockhausen,Markus (tp,fl-h)

Ferenc Snétberger With The Franz Liszt Chamber Orchestra
Hallgató | Emlékek | Tánk
Snétberger,Ferenc (g) | Franz Liszt Chamber Orchestra | details unknown

ENJ-9392 2 | CD | Cherry
Josh Roseman Unit
Don't Be Cruel | If I Fell | Kashmir | Land Of Make Believe | Daddy Gonna Tell You No Lie | Extra Virgin | Just To Keep You Satisfied | Love In Outer Space | Trousertrout | Frank Mills Jr. | Smells Like Teen Spirit | Daddy Redux
Studio 900,?, rec. 3./4.1.1998
Roseman,Joshua 'Josh' (tb) | Bowie,Lester (tp) | Shulman,Matt (tp) | Rodrigues,Jay (reeds) | Jensen,Dave (ts) | Stewart,Robert 'Bob' (tuba) | Fiuczynski,Dave (g) | Monder,Ben (g) | Medeski,John (keyboards) | Colley,Scott (b) | Baron,Joey (dr) | Hoenig,Ari (dr) | Rodriguez,E.J. (perc)

ENJ-9395 2 | CD | Habanera
Paquito D'Rivera Group With The Absolute Ensemble
Habanera | Birk's Works | Variations On I Got Rhythm And Cuban Overture | Moon Dance(1) | Caravan | Vals Venezolano | Moon Dance(2) | Lecuonerias
NYC, rec. September 1999
D'Rivera,Paquito (cl,as) | Taylor,Dave (b-tb) | Drew Jr.,Kenny (p) | Formanek,Michael (b) | Penn,Clarence (dr) | Cinelu,Mino (perc) | Absolute Ensemble | Porter,Charles (tp) | Ballou,Dave (tp) | Seltzer,Mike (tb) | Evans,Greg (fr-h) | Chermiset,Valerie (fl,piccolo) | Wilson,Keve (oboe) | Floyd,Derek (oboe,engl-h) | Lando,Vadim (cl) | Suzuki,Michiyo (b-cl) | Kuusskmann,Martin (bassoon) | Herskowitz,Matt (p) | Rozenblatt,David (perc) | Rieppi,Pablo (perc) | Gellev,Vesselin (v) | Vijayan,Shalini (v) | Terlitzky,Olga (viola) | Kim,Ann (cello) | Fieldes,Mat (b) | Järvi,Kristjan (cond)
Afro | Alborada Y Son
D'Rivera,Paquito (cl,as) | Taylor,Dave (b-tb) | Drew Jr.,Kenny (p) | Formanek,Michael (b) | Penn,Clarence (dr) | Cinelu,Mino (perc) | Absolute Ensemble | Porter,Charles (tp) | Seltzer,Mike (tb) | Evans,Greg (fr-h) | Ellsworth,Ann (fr-h) | Chermiset,Valerie (fl,piccolo) | Wilson,Keve (oboe) | Floyd,Derek (oboe,engl-h) | Lando,Vadim (cl) | Suzuki,Michiyo (b-cl) | Kuusskmann,Martin (bassoon) | Herskowitz,Matt (p) | Rozenblatt,David (perc) | Rieppi,Pablo (perc) | Gellev,Vesselin (v) | Vijayan,Shalini (v) | Terlitzky,Olga (viola) | Kim,Ann (cello) | Fieldes,Mat (b) | Järvi,Kristjan (cond)
Wapango
D'Rivera,Paquito (cl,as) | Taylor,Dave (b-tb) | Drew Jr.,Kenny (p) | Formanek,Michael (b) | Penn,Clarence (dr) | Cinelu,Mino (perc) | Absolute Ensemble | Porter,Charles (tp) | Ballou,Dave (tp) | Seltzer,Mike (tb) | Evans,Greg (fr-h) | Ellsworth,Ann (fr-h) | Chermiset,Valerie (fl,piccolo) | Wilson,Keve (oboe) | Floyd,Derek (oboe,engl-h) | Lando,Vadim (cl) | Suzuki,Michiyo (b-cl) | Kuusskmann,Martin (bassoon) | Herskowitz,Matt (p) | Rozenblatt,David (perc) | Rieppi,Pablo (perc) | Gellev,Vesselin (v) | Vijayan,Shalini (v) | Terlitzky,Olga (viola) | Kim,Ann (cello) | Fieldes,Mat (b) | Järvi,Kristjan (cond)
Three Preludes: | Allegro Ben Ritmato E Decisco | Andante Con Moto A Poco Rubato | Allegro Ben Ritmato E Decisco(2)
D'Rivera,Paquito (cl,as) | Taylor,Dave (b-tb) | Drew Jr.,Kenny (p) | Formanek,Michael (b) | Penn,Clarence (dr) | Cinelu,Mino (perc) | Absolute Ensemble | Porter,Charles (tp) | Ballou,Dave (tp) | Seltzer,Mike (tb) | Evans,Greg (fr-h) | Chermiset,Valerie (fl,piccolo) | Wilson,Keve (oboe) | Floyd,Derek (oboe,engl-h) | Lando,Vadim (cl) | Suzuki,Michiyo (b-cl) | Kuusskmann,Martin (bassoon) | Herskowitz,Matt (p) | Rozenblatt,David (perc) | Rieppi,Pablo (perc) | Gellev,Vesselin (v) | Vijayan,Shalini (v) | Terlitzky,Olga (viola) | Kim,Ann (cello) | Fieldes,Mat (b) | Järvi,Kristjan (cond)

ENJ-9399 2 | CD | Thorn
Antonio Farao Trio
Time Back | Preludio | Caravan | B.E. | Malinconie
NYC, rec. 19./20.4.2000
Farao,Antonio (p) | Gress,Drew (b) | DeJohnette,Jack (dr)

Antonio Farao Quartet
Thorn | Epoché | Arabesco | Tandem
Farao,Antonio (p) | Potter,Chris (ss,ts) | Gress,Drew (b) | DeJohnette,Jack (dr)

ENJ-9401 2 | CD | The Cactus Of Knowledge
Rabih Abou-Khalil Group
The Lewinsky March | Business As Usual | Fraises Et Creme Fraiche | Got To Go Home | Oum Said | Maltese Chicken Farm | Ma Muse M'amuse | Pont Neuf
Köln, rec. 22.-30.7.2000
Abou-Khalil,Rabih (oud) | Allen,Eddie E.J. (tp) | Ballou,Dave (tp) | Varner,Tom (fr-h) | Bargeron,Dave (euphonium) | Godard,Michel (tuba) | Mirabassi,Gabriele (cl) | Hart,Antonio Maurice (as) | Eskelin,Ellery (ts) | Courtois,Vincent (cello) | Cagwin,Jarrod (dr) | Khaiat,Nabil (frame-dr)

ENJ-9408 2 | CD | In My Dreams
Dusko Goykovich Quartet
In My Dreams | St.Germain Des Pres | Sequoia Song | Introduction | Skylark | One Morning In May | All About Love | Little Theo | I Miss You So
Monster,NL, rec. 29.9.2000
Goykovich,Dusko (fl-h) | Degen,Bob (p) | Eckinger,Isla (b) | Cagwin,Jarrod (dr)

ENJ-9409 2 | CD | I Saw The Sky
Melissa Walker And Her Band
I Saw The Sky | Let's Take An Old Fashioned Walk | I'm In Love
Brooklyn,NY, rec. 28.-30.11.2000
Walker,Melissa (voc) | Mitchell,Shedrick (p) | Kitagawa,Kiyoshi (b) | Penn,Clarence (dr)
Some Other Time
Walker,Melissa (voc) | Mitchell,Shedrick (p) | Kitagawa,Kiyoshi (b) | Penn,Clarence (dr) | Gellev,Vesselin (v) | Bock,Deborah (v) | Terlitzky,Olga (viola) | Kim,Ann (cello)
Return To Me
Walker,Melissa (voc) | Ozone,Makoto (p) | Kitagawa,Kiyoshi (b) | Penn,Clarence (dr) | Gellev,Vesselin (v) | Bock,Deborah (v) | Terlitzky,Olga (viola) | Kim,Ann (cello)
My Shining Hour
Walker,Melissa (voc) | Ozone,Makoto (p) | Kitagawa,Kiyoshi (b) | Penn,Clarence (dr)
Nothing Ever Changes My Love For You | I Get Along Without You Very Well | The Face I Love
Walker,Melissa (voc) | Harris,Stefon (vib,marimba) | Mitchell,Shedrick (p) | Kitagawa,Kiyoshi (b) | Penn,Clarence (dr)
I'm Old Fashioned | Twilight Song
Walker,Melissa (voc) | Barron,Kenny (p) | Kitagawa,Kiyoshi (b) | Penn,Clarence (dr)

ENJ-9410 2 | CD | African Symphony
Abdullah Ibrahim Trio With The Munich Radio Symphony Orchestra
African Symphony: | Damara Blue | Mountain In The Night | The Call | Blanton | Ishmael | Barakaat | Tintinyana | The Wedding | Mindif | African Marketplace
München, rec. 26.-28.1.1998
Brand,Dollar[Abdullah Ibrahim] (p) | McLaurine,Marcus (b) | Gray,George (dr) | Schnyder,Daniel (arr) | Munich Radio Symphony Orchestra | Yahr,Barbara (cond)
Absolute Ensemble
Ritus
Brooklyn,NY, rec. 13.2.2001
Absolute Ensemble | Almond,Frank (v) | Gellev,Vesselin (v) | Nielson,Elizabeth (v) | Lee,Pauline (v) | Bechtold,Lynn (v) | Martin,Lois (viola) | Terlitzky,Olga (viola) | Kim,Ann (cello) | Lallemand,Ariane (cello) | Fieldes,Mat (b)

ENJ-9412 2 | CD | Electric Sufi
Dhafer Youssef Group
Mandakini | Yabay | Electric Sufi | Oil On Water | La Prière De L'Absent | Man Of Wool | La Nuit Sacrée | Nouba | Farha | Nafha | Al-Hallaj | Surbj | Langue Muette
Brooklyn,NY, rec. November/December 2000
Youssef,Dhafer (oud,perc,voc) | Stockhausen,Markus (tp,fl-h) | Muthspiel,Wolfgang (g) | Ram,Deepak (bansuri) | Ilg,Dieter (b) | Wimbish,Doug (el-b,electronics) | Cinelu,Mino (dr,perc) | Calhoun,Will (dr,loops) | Packe,Rodericke (sounds)

ENJ-9416-2 | 2 CD | Odd And Awkward
Nils Wogram Sextet
Children's Hunt | Mayamalaragaula | Tea Time(part 1) | Tea Time(part 2) | Spring(part 1) | Spring(part 2) | Ganamurti
SWR Studios?, rec. June 2000
Wogram,Nils (tb) | Vu,Cuong (tp) | Speed,Chris (cl,ts) | Chisholm,Hayden (cl,as) | Schorn,Steffen (alto-fl,b-cl,contra-b-cl,bs) | Rückert,Jochen (dr)
Nils Wogram Octet
The Search(part 1) | The Search(part 2) | New Neighbour | Peace Above | Piano Interlude | Constant Travel | Muffin | Floating | Odd And Awkward
Wogram,Nils (tb) | Vu,Cuong (tp) | Speed,Chris (cl,ts) | Chisholm,Hayden (cl,as) | Schorn,Steffen (alto-fl,b-cl,contra-b-cl,bs) | Nabatov,Simon (p) | Sieverts,Henning (b) | Rückert,Jochen (dr)

ENJ-9418 2 | CD | Navigatore
Renaud Garcia-Fons Group
Navigatore | Wadi Rum(introducing) | Bolbol | Tavakkol
Studio Cargo,?, rec. March/June 2001
Garcia-Fons,Renaud (5-string-b,perc,hand-clapping) | Malet,Laurent (fl-h) | Favre,Yves (tb) | Hayward,Chris (fl) | Erguner,Kudsi (ney) | Sansalone,Bruno (cl,b-cl) | Hamon,Pierre (bagpipes,recorder) | Matinier,Jean-Louis (accordeon) | Ruiz,Antonio 'Kiko' (flamenco-g) | Tortiller,Frank (marimba,timbales,gongs) | Khalfa,Dahmane (carcabas,saguetes,tbel,derbouka,bendir) | Khalfa,Rabah (bendir,carcabas,derbouka) | Shams El Dine,Adel (riq) | Caillat,Bruno (tablas,daf) | Trasante,Jorge 'Negrito' (dr,congas,perc) | Antonini,Claire (lute,cistre,tambur,saz) | Gungor,Hakan (kanoun) | Ziad,Karim (gumbri) | Couvert,Francoise (v) | Couvert,Philippe (v) | Pichon,Frank (v)
Fui Piedra | Sahari | Alto Pais | Ultimo Fandango | Vagabundo | Mohabbat
Garcia-Fons,Renaud (5-string-b,perc,hand-clapping) | Malet,Laurent (fl-h) | Favre,Yves (tb) | Hayward,Chris (fl) | Erguner,Kudsi (ney) | Sansalone,Bruno (cl,b-cl) | Hamon,Pierre (bagpipes,recorder) | Matinier,Jean-Louis (accordeon) | Ruiz,Antonio 'Kiko' (flamenco-g) | Tortiller,Frank (marimba,timbales,gongs) | Khalfa,Dahmane (carcabas,saguetes,tbel,derbouka,bendir) | Khalfa,Rabah (bendir,carcabas,derbouka) | Shams El Dine,Adel (riq) | Caillat,Bruno (tablas,daf) | Heral,Patrice (dr,snare-dr,tambourin) | Antonini,Claire (lute,cistre,tambur,saz) | Gungor,Hakan (kanoun) | Ziad,Karim (gumbri) | Couvert,Francoise (v) | Couvert,Philippe (v) | Pichon,Frank (v)
Renaud Garcia-Fons
Wadi Rum | Alto Pais | Monajat(Le Temps Ne Revient Pas) | Chokr
Garcia-Fons,Renaud (5-string-b,perc,hand-clapping) | Malet,Laurent (fl-h) | Favre,Yves (tb) | Hayward,Chris (fl) | Erguner,Kudsi (ney) | Sansalone,Bruno (cl,b-cl) | Hamon,Pierre (bagpipes,recorder) | Matinier,Jean-Louis (accordeon) | Ruiz,Antonio 'Kiko' (flamenco-g) | Tortiller,Frank (marimba,timbales,gongs) | Khalfa,Dahmane (carcabas,saguetes,tbel,derbouka,bendir) | Khalfa,Rabah (bendir,carcabas,derbouka) | Shams El Dine,Adel (riq) | Caillat,Bruno (tablas,daf) | Heral,Patrice (dr,snare-dr,tambourin) | Antonini,Claire (lute,cistre,tambur,saz) | Gungor,Hakan (kanoun) | Ziad,Karim (gumbri) | Couvert,Francoise (v) | Couvert,Philippe (v) | Pichon,Frank (v)

ENJ-9419 2 | CD | Dedalo | EAN 063757941927
Gianluigi Trovesi Quartet With The WDR Big Band
Harcab | Herbop(fragment) | Herbob | Dance For A King(fragment 1) | Now I Can | Dance For The King(fragment 2) | From G To G | Scotch | Dance For The East No.2 | Dance For The King(fragment 3)
WDR Köln, rec. 28.-30.5.2001
Trovesi,Gianluigi (alto-cl,b-cl,as) | Stockhausen,Markus (tp,fl-h) | Rainey,Tom (dr) | Maras,Fulvio (perc) | WDR Big Band | Haderer,Andreas 'Andy' (tp) | Bruynen,Rob (tp) | Osterloh,Klaus (tp) | Marshall,John (tp) | Kiefer,Rick (tp) | Horler,David (tb) | Nuß,Ludwig (tb) | Laukamp,Bernt (tb) | Schmid,Lucas (b-tb,tuba) | Wiberny,Heiner (ss,as) | Rosenstein,Harald (ss,as) | Peters,Oliver (fl,ts) | Römer,Rolf (b-cl,ts) | Neufang,Jens (bs) | Shigihara,Paul (g) | Chastenier,Frank (p) | Goldsby,John (b)
Dedalo | Hercab(live version)
Live at The Moers New Jazz Festival, rec. 1.6.2001
Trovesi,Gianluigi (alto-cl,b-cl,as) | Stockhausen,Markus (tp,fl-h) | Rainey,Tom (dr) | Maras,Fulvio (perc) | WDR Big Band | Haderer,Andreas 'Andy' (tp) | Bruynen,Rob (tp) | Osterloh,Klaus (tp) | Marshall,John (tp) | Kiefer,Rick (tp) | Horler,David (tb) | Nuß,Ludwig (tb) | Laukamp,Bernt (tb) | Schmid,Lucas (b-tb,tuba) | Wiberny,Heiner (ss,as) | Rosenstein,Harald (ss,as) | Peters,Oliver (fl,ts) | Römer,Rolf (b-cl,ts) | Neufang,Jens (bs) | Shigihara,Paul (g) | Chastenier,Frank (p) | Goldsby,John (b)

ENJ-9421 2 | CD | A Latin Shade Of Blue | EAN 063757942122
Joe Gallardo's Latino Blue
Bluesiando | Salseando | East L.A. | Surf Walk | To Love Is To Love You | Just A Moment | Volando | Suenos
Hamburg, rec. 2000
Gallardo,Joe (tb,p) | Burkhardt,Ingolf (tp,fl-h) | Büchner,Lutz (fl,ss,ts) | Calvo,Omar Rodriguez (b,el-b) | Lichus,Heinz (dr) | Calquin,Mauricio (bongos,congas,perc) | Altmann,Thomas (bongos,timbales,perc)
Bahia
Gallardo,Joe (tb,p) | Burkhardt,Ingolf (tp,fl-h) | Büchner,Lutz (fl,ss,ts) | Delle,Frank (ts) | Calvo,Omar Rodriguez (b,el-b) | Lichus,Heinz (dr) | Calquin,Mauricio (bongos,congas,perc) | Altmann,Thomas (bongos,timbales,perc)
Wake Up
Gallardo,Joe (tb,p) | Burkhardt,Ingolf (tp,fl-h) | Landgren,Nils (tb) | Büchner,Lutz (fl,ss,ts) | Calvo,Omar Rodriguez (b,el-b) | Lichus,Heinz (dr) | Calquin,Mauricio (bongos,congas,perc) | Altmann,Thomas (bongos,timbales,perc)

ENJ-9422 2 | CD | My Marilyn
David Klein Quintet
Kiss | My Heart Belongs To Daddy | Incurably Romantic | You'd Be Surprised | Let's Make Love | She Acts Like A Woman Should | Specialisation | Diamonds Are A Girl's Best Friend | Some Like It Hot | I'm Through With You
Winterthur,CH, rec. details unknown
Klein,David (sax) | Miller,Mulgrew (p) | Coleman,Ira (b) | Pellitteri,Marcello (dr) | Klein,Miriam (voc) | Otis,Jon (perc)

ENJ-9423 2 | CD | Deep In A Dream | EAN 063757942320
Charlie Mariano Quartet
You Better Go Now | Dew Drops | Spring Is Here | I'm A Fool To Want You | I Only Miss Her When I Think Of Her | The Touch Of Your Lips | Etosha | Close Enough For Love | Yours Is My Heart Alone | Deep In A Dream
Monster,NL, rec. 2./3.11.2001
Mariano,Charlie (as) | Degen,Bob (p) | Eckinger,Isla (b) | Cagwin,Jarrod (dr)

ENJ-9425 2 | CD | Bennie Wallace In Berlin
Bennie Wallace Quartet
It Ain't Necessarily So | I Loves You Porgy | It Has Happened To Me | It's Only A Paper Moon | Someone To Watch Over Me | Thangs | At Lulu White's
Live at Berliner Jazztage, rec. 6.11.1999
Wallace,Bennie (ts) | Cables,George (p) | Washington,Peter (b) | Riley,Herlin (dr)

ENJ-9430 2 | CD | Next Stories | EAN 063757943020
Antonio Farao Trio
Creole | Sweet | I Could Have Done More | What Is This Thing Called Love
Ludwigsburg, rec. 30./31.10.2001
Farao,Antonio (p) | Howard,Ed (b) | Jackson,Gene (dr)
Antonio Farao Quartet
I'm Waiting | Theme For Bond | Next Stories | Few Days | Sabrina And Joseph
Farao,Antonio (p) | Howard,Ed (b) | Jackson,Gene (dr) | Marquez,Pibo (perc)

ENJ-9431 2 | CD | Castel Del Monte II | EAN 063757943129
Michel Godard Ensemble
Psalmodia Serpent | Stupor Mundi | Magnificat | Cantiga De Santa Maria | Acqua,Aria,Fioco,Terra | The Front Door | Penthés(il)ée | Introduction | Psalmodia Calixtinus | Tintinnabullum | Tourne Ton Esprit
Castel Del Monte,Ruvo Di Puglia,Italy, rec. 18.-21.4.2001
Godard,Michel (serpent,tuba) | Mirabassi,Gabriele (cl) | Courtois,Vincent (cello) | Petit,Marie Ange (perc) | Bsiri,Linda (voc)
Kyrie
Godard,Michel (serpent) | Mirabassi,Gabriele (cl) | Courtois,Vincent (cello) | Petit,Marie Ange (perc) | Bsiri,Linda (voc) | Ensemble Calixtinus | La Zazzera,Massimo (recorder) | Nesta,Nicola (lute,voice) | Quarta,Alexandro (voice) | D'Abbico,Dario (voice) | Giovine,Cossimo (voice) | Regina,Francesco (voice) | Magarelli,Gaetano (voice) | De Gennaro,Gianni (ld)
Princess Song | Pietre Di Luca | Puer Apuliae | Il Manto Porpora
Godard,Michel (serpent) | Mirabassi,Gabriele (cl) | Courtois,Vincent (cello) | Petit,Marie Ange (perc) | Bsiri,Linda (voc) | Ensemble Calixtinus | La Zazzera,Massimi (recorder) | Nesta,Nicola (lute,voice) | De Gennaro,Gianni (viella,voice,ld) | Quarta,Alexandro (voice) | D'Abbico,Dario (voice) | Giovine,Cossimo (voice) | Regina,Francesco (voice) | Magarelli,Gaetano (voice)
-> This titeles are wrong dated as 4.10.1937

ENJ-9432 2 | CD | Balance | EAN 063757943228
Ferenc Snétberger
Autumn Leaves | Fantasia Alla Tango | Obsession | My One And Only Love | Song To The East | Invention | Gipsy | One More String | Kunst Der Fuge(Contrapunctus)
Live at The 'Philharmonie',Berlin, rec. 12.10.2001
Snétberger,Ferenc (g-solo)

ENJ-9434 2 | CD | What Love Is | EAN 063757943426
Stefanie Schlesinger And Her Group
Why Shouldn't You Cry | I Wish | Baiao Kathrin | Luz Do Sol | Cry Me A River | Watch You Sleepin' | Sing Me Softly Of The Blues | Estate(Summer) | You Don't Know What Love Is | Send In The Clowns
Augsburg, rec. details unknown
Schlesinger,Stefanie (voc) | Lackerschmid,Wolfgang (vib,marimba) | Tagliani,Pedro (g) | Degen,Bob (p) | Eckinger,Isla (b) | Cagwin,Jarrod (dr)
Stefanie Schlesiger And Her Group plus String Quartet
Laudate
Schlesinger,Stefanie (voc) | Lackerschmid,Wolfgang (vib,marimba) | Tagliani,Pedro (g) | Degen,Bob (p) | Eckinger,Isla (b) | Cagwin,Jarrod (dr) | Augsburg String Quartet | Christian,Harry (v) | Hornung,Ludwig (v) | Schmalhofer,Ludwig (viola) | Tröndle,Hartmut (cello)

ENJ-9440 2 | CD | Il Sospiro | EAN 063757944027
Rabih Abou-Khalil
La Seduction: | Qawarma- | Charao Et Tout- | Arouss Labneh- | My Favorite Feet | Serenade To A Mule | Jardin De Chine | Ghantous | La Ladra Di Cuori | Yakhbeir John | Bofinger | An Oyster In Paris | The Birthday Gift | Afterthought
Zerkall, rec. details unknown
Abou-Khalil,Rabih (oud)

ENJ-9441 2 | CD | Latakia Blend | EAN 063757944126
Gabriele Mirabassi Trio
Girotondo | Gorizia | Latakia Blend | Passacaille | Isfahan | Non Ci Resta Che...Chorar! | Segura Ele | Burley E Perique | Michelone | Les Vieux Alemands | Hotel Danubio
Pernes Les Fontaines,France, rec. 1.-3.2.2002
Mirabassi,Gabriele (cl) | Biondini,Luciano (acc) | Godard,Michel (tuba)

ENJ-9447 2 | CD | Fayka | EAN 063757944720
Mahmoud Turkmani
Fayka | Soudfa
Traunwalchen, rec. June 2001
Turkmani,Mahmoud (g,oud)
Mazééj,Wahdi Trikni | Yara | Zikra
Turkmani,Mahmoud (g,oud) | Guy,Barry (b)
Mouwasha Lamma Bada | Hkékét Jidde | Shukran Paco De Lucia
Turkmani,Mahmoud (g,oud) | Chemirani,Keyvan (perc)

ENJ-9448 2 | CD | All The Way
Karl Ratzer Quintet
Nature Boy | South Of Greenwich Village | Kollerland | Who Can I Turn To | Candombre | Don't Make A Fool Of Me | Saturn Returning
details unknown, rec. details unknown
Ratzer,Karl (g,voc) | Kent,Oliver (p,el-p) | Knapp,Herfried (b) | Dudli,Joris (dr) | Mateus,Ricardo (perc)

ENJ-9451 2 | CD | If | EAN 063757945123
Dino Saluzzi Group
Waking Up | Home | If | I Think On It | It's All There | Children Play | An Intrigant Melody | Moving Somewhere | You Should Stay | Where You Belong
NYC, rec. 20./21.6.2001
Saluzzi,Dino (bandoneon) | Ruocco,John (cl) | Werner,Kenny (p) | Cohen,Greg (b) | Baron,Joey (dr) | Alter,Myriam (comp)

ENJ-9452 2 | CD | The Long View | EAN 063757945222
Marty Ehrlich Group
The Long View: | Movement I
NYC, rec. 19./20.4.2002
Ehrlich,Marty (as,ts) | Allen,Eddie E.J. (tp) | Zollar,James (tp) | Gayton,Clark (tb) | Clark,John (fr-h) | Rojas,Marcus (tuba) | Furnace,Sam (as) | Rothenberg,Ned (as) | De Bellis,Robert (ts) | Parran,J.D. (ts) | Laster,Andy (bs) | Dresser,Mark (b) | Sarin,Michael (dr) | Helias,Mark (cond)
Movement II
Ehrlich,Marty (ss) | Feldman,Mark (v) | Farris,Ralph (viola) | Friedlander,Erik (cello) | Helias,Mark (b) | Bobè,Eddie (bongos,cowbell) | Previte,Robert 'Bobby' (dr,tambourine)
Movement III
Ehrlich,Marty (cl,ss,as) | Allen,Eddie E.J. (tp) | Zollar,James (tp) | Gayton,Clark (tb) | Clark,John (fr-h) | Rojas,Marcus (tuba) | Furnace,Sam (fl,as) | Rothenberg,Ned (b-cl,as) | De Bellis,Robert (cl,ts) | Parran,J.D. (contra-b-cl) | Laster,Andy (cl,bs) | Helias,Mark (cond)
Movemenet IV
Ehrlich,Marty (fl,as) | Horvitz,Wayne (p) | Dresser,Mark (b) | Previte,Robert 'Bobby' (dr)
Movement V
Ehrlich,Marty (as,muted-as,ts) | Anderson,Ray (tb) | Feldman,Mark (v) | Friedlander,Erik (cello) | Horvitz,Wayne (p) | Helias,Mark (b) | AkLaff,Pheeroan (dr)
Movement VI
Ehrlich,Marty (as) | Allen,Eddie E.J. (tp) | Zollar,James (tp) | Gayton,Clark (tb) | Clark,John (fr-h) | Rojas,Marcus (tuba) | Furnace,Sam (as) | Rothenberg,Ned (b-cl,as) | De Bellis,Robert (ss,ts) | Parran,J.D. (conra-b-cl,ts) | Laster,Andy (bs) | Dresser,Mark (b) | AkLaff,Pheeroan (dr) | Helias,Mark (cond)
Postlude
Ehrlich,Marty (b-cl,ts) | Horvitz,Wayne (p)

ENJ-9453 2 | CD | Chet Baker-The Legacy Vol.4:Oh You Crazy Moon | EAN 063757945321
Chet Baker Quartet
The Touch Of Your Lips | Beautiful Black Eyes | Oh! You Crazy Moon | Love For Sale | Once Upon A Summertime | My Funny Valentine
Kulturzentrum,Ludwigsburg, rec. 9.12.1978
Baker,Chet (tp,fl-h) | Markovitz,Phil (p) | Lee,Scott (b) | Brillinger,Jeff (dr)

ENJ-9454 2 | CD | Confluences | EAN 063757945420
Jean-Louis Matinier Quartet
Soleil Rouge | Rio D'Oro | Seven Steppes | Plainitude | Jardins D'Enfance | Sambadynos | Unité-Multiple | Confluences | Mistytorway
details unknown, rec. details unknown
Matinier,Jean-Louis (accordeon) | Rangell,Bobby (fl) | Veras,Nelson (g) | Garcia-Fons,Renaud (b)

ENJ-9458 2 | CD | Look What They've Done To My Song | EAN 063757945826
Carlos Bica & Azul
Waiting For Tom | Password | Chao | Look What They've Done To My Song(What have They Done To My Song,Ma) | Episodio:A Flor Da Pele | New World | The Navigator | Clara Linda | Bela | Herancas | Durme
Hamburg, rec. October/November 2002
Bica,Carlos (b) | Möbus,Frank (el-g) | Black,Jim (dr,perc)

ENJ-9460 2 | CD | Colossus Of Sound
NDR Radio Philharmonic Orchestra
Violin Concerto(3 movements) | Symphony No.4 | Trumpet Concerto(3 movements) | African Fanfare
details unknown, rec. details unknown
NDR Radio Philharmonic Orchestra | Järvi,Kristjan (cond) | Rabus,Kathrin (v) | Friedrich,Reihold (tp,fl-h) | Schnyder,Daniel (comp)

ENJ-9464 2 | CD | Entremundo | EAN 063757946427
Renaud Garcia-Fons Group
Sueno Vivo | Cristobal | Entremundo | Mahoor | Dias(Solea) | Entre Continentes(Buleria) | Mursiya | Rosaria | Doust | Sareban
Montreuil,France, rec. details unknown
Garcia-Fons,Renaud (5-string-b,perc,tanbour,voice) | Slovinsky,Philippe (tp) | Tournier,Henri (fl,bansuri) | Hoist,Allen (ts) | Ruiz,Antonio 'Kiko' (flamenco-g) | Antonini,Claire (lute,cistre,tar) | Sylvestre,Gaston (cymbal) | Sanchez-Gonzalez,Angel (palmascajon,jaleo,pandeiro) | Caillat,Bruno (tablas,daf,kanjeera)
Renaud Garcia-Fons
Aqa Jan
Garcia-Fons,Renaud (5-string-b-solo)

ENJ-9466 2 | CD | Dry Humping The American Dream
Gutbucket
Snarling Wrath Of Angry Gods | Dry Humping The American Dream | Lift Cover,Pull Cord | O.J. Bin Laden | The Polka Of Doom | War On Drugs | Should've Gone Before You Left | Dance Of The Demented Pigeon | Another World Is Possible | Liberation
NYC, rec. May 2002
Gutbucket | Thompson,Ken (as) | Citerman,Ty (g) | Rockwin,Eric (b) | Chuffo,Paul (dr)

ENJ-9467 2 | CD | Nuages | EAN 063757946724
Jenny Evans And Her Quintet
Mad About The Boys | Remember Me | Nuages | Our Revels Now Are Ended | Within' You,Without You | Flow My Tears | I'm Alone After All | The Feeling Of You | Veris Leta Facies | No Love Without Tears | What Joy
München, rec. July & September 2003
Evans,Jenny (voc) | Francel,Mulo (b-cl,ss,ts,mand) | Lang,Walter (p) | Lachotta,Chris (b) | Martini,Rudi (dr) | Kainar,Robert (perc)

ENJ-9468 2 | CD | Joyosa
Markus Stockhausen Quartet
Gio | Basswave | Madhawi | Gommé | Joyosa | Mona | Freund | Our Father | Jasmin | The Waltz
details unknown, rec. details unknown
Stockhausen,Markus (tp,fl-h) | Snétberger,Ferenc (g) | Andersen,Arild (b) | Heral,Patrice (dr)

ENJ-9472 2 | CD | Uwa I
Boi Akih
Mariaaa | Pamamurolo | Potu Loto Potu | Imi | Unde Atoluwe Naiowe | Manu Pombo | Leamata | Maritiine | Jhana
Boi Akih | Akihary,Monica (voc) | Brouwer,Niels (g) | Reijseger,Ernst (cello) | Bhattacharya,Sandip (tablas,balafon,frame-dr)

ENJ-9473 2 | CD | Samba Do Mar
Dusko Goykovich Quartet
Samba Do Mar | Jim's Ballad | Chega De Saudare | Insensatez(How Insensitive) | Bachianas Brazileiras(No.5) | The Fish | Quo Vadis | Love And Deception | Danca Comigo | Sunset
Goykovich,Dusko (tp,fl-h) | Snétberger,Ferenc (g) | Gjakonovski,Martin (b) | Cagwin,Jarrod (dr)

ENJ-9475 2 | CD | Zakira | EAN 063757947523
Mahmoud Turkmani Group
Mouwasha Arjii Ya Alfa Layla | Mouwasha Aytatouhou Ma Sala | Mouwasha

Zanalil Mahboub | Mouwasha Imlalil Aqdaha | Mouwasha Nozuhatoul Arwah | Taqassoum | Bulerias
Cairo,Egypt, rec. 7./8.12.2003
Turkmani,Mahmoud (g,oud) | El Badri,Hani (ney) | Owaida,Khaled (v) | El Sayed,Nehad (oud) | Hamdy,Ahmad (cello) | Osman,Ahmad (b) | Abou Higazi,Khaled (doff) | Sattar,Saber Ardel (qanoun) | Mostafa,Amr (req) | Metawee,Rehab (voc)

ENJ-9771 2 | CD | Between Dusk And Dawn
Rabih Abou-Khalil Quintet
Dusk | Bat Dance | Nightfall | Ugo In Love | Chess With Mal | Dawn | And Finally...The Oasis
Ludwigsburg, rec. 1986
Abou-Khalil,Rabih (fl,oud) | Mariano,Charlie (ss,as) | Moore,Glen (b) | Velez,Glen (perc,bodharan,darabukka,frame-dr) | Shotham,Ramesh (perc,dholak,ghatam,kanjira,mouth-harp,tavil)
Rabih Abou-Khalil Septet
The Thing That Came Out Of The Swamp
Abou-Khalil,Rabih (fl) | Mariano,Charlie (as) | Burchard,Christian (marimba) | Armann,Michael (p) | Moore,Glen (b) | Velez,Glen (perc,bodharan,darabukka,frame-dr,voc) | Shotham,Ramesh (perc,dholak,ghatam,kanjira,mouth-harp,tavil)

Epic | Sony Music

476906-2 | CD | Baltimore
Nina Simone And Orchestra
Everything Must Change | My Father | Music For Lovers | That's All I Want From You | Balm In The Gilead
Brussels,Belgium, rec. January 1978
Simone,Nina (p,voc) | Gale,Eric (g) | King,Gary (b) | Ellen,Max (v) | Finclair,Barry (v) | Glickman,Harry (v) | Libove,Charles (v) | Lookofsky,Harry (v) | Morgenstern,Marvin (v) | Nadien,David (v) | Sorkin,Herbert (v) | Sortomme,Richard (v) | Alsop,LaMar (viola) | Brown,Alfred (viola) | Vardi,Emanuel (viola) | Abramowitz,Jonathan (cello) | McCracken,Charles (cello) | Shulman,Alan (cello) | Beal,John (b) | Israels,Charles (b) | Mensch,Homer (b) | Armstead,Joshie (voc) | McDuffie,Debbie (voc) | Robinson,Albertine (voc) | Stewart,Maeretha (voc) | Floyd,Babi (voc) | Floyd,Frank (voc) | Grayson,Milt (voc) | Simpson,Ray (voc) | Madison,Jimmy (dr) | Marrero,Nicky (perc)
Forget
Simone,Nina (p,voc) | Matthews,David (p) | Gale,Eric (g) | King,Gary (b) | Ellen,Max (v) | Finclair,Barry (v) | Glickman,Harry (v) | Libove,Charles (v) | Lookofsky,Harry (v) | Morgenstern,Marvin (v) | Nadien,David (v) | Sorkin,Herbert (v) | Sortomme,Richard (v) | Aslop,LaMar (viola) | Brown,Alfred (viola) | Vardi,Emanuel (viola) | Abramowitz,Jonathan (cello) | McCracken,Charles (cello) | Shulman,Alan (cello) | Beal,John (b) | Israels,Charles (b) | Mensch,Homer (b) | Armstead,Joshie (voc) | McDuffie,Debbie (voc) | Robinson,Albertine (voc) | Stewart,Maeretha (voc) | Floyd,Babi (voc) | Floyd,Frank (voc) | Grayson,Milt (voc) | Simpson,Ray (voc) | Madison,Jimmy (dr) | Marrero,Nicky (perc)
The Family
Simone,Nina (p,voc) | Matthews,David (p) | Friedman,Jerry (g) | King,Gary (b) | Ellen,Max (v) | Finclair,Barry (v) | Glickman,Harry (v) | Libove,Charles (v) | Lookofsky,Harry (v) | Morgenstern,Marvin (v) | Nadien,David (v) | Sorkin,Herbert (v) | Sortomme,Richard (v) | Alsop,LaMar (viola) | Brown,Alfred (viola) | Vardi,Emanuel (viola) | Abramowitz,Jonathan (cello) | McCracken,Charles (cello) | Shulman,Alan (cello) | Beal,John (b) | Israels,Charles (b) | Mensch,Homer (b) | Armstead,Joshie (voc) | McDuffie,Debbie (voc) | Robinson,Albertine (voc) | Stewart,Maeretha (voc) | Floyd,Babi (voc) | Floyd,Frank (voc) | Grayson,Milt (voc) | Simpson,Ray (voc) | Madison,Jimmy (dr) | Marrero,Nicky (perc)
Rich Girl
Simone,Nina (p,voc) | Friedman,Jerry (g) | Lee,Will (b) | Ellen,Max (v) | Finclair,Barry (v) | Glickman,Harry (v) | Libove,Charles (v) | Lookofsky,Harry (v) | Morgenstern,Marvin (v) | Nadien,David (v) | Sorkin,Herbert (v) | Sortomme,Richard (v) | Alsop,LaMar (viola) | Brown,Alfred (viola) | Vardi,Emanuel (viola) | Abramowitz,Jonathan (cello) | McCracken,Charles (cello) | Shulman,Alan (cello) | Beal,John (b) | Israels,Charles (b) | Mensch,Homer (b) | Armstead,Joshie (voc) | McDuffie,Debbie (voc) | Robinson,Albertine (voc) | Stewart,Maeretha (voc) | Floyd,Babi (voc) | Floyd,Frank (voc) | Grayson,Milt (voc) | Simpson,Ray (voc) | Neumark,Andy (dr) | Marrero,Nicky (perc)
Baltimore | If You Pray Right
Simone,Nina (p,voc) | Schackman,Al (p,tambourine) | Gale,Eric (g) | King,Gary (b) | Ellen,Max (v) | Finclair,Barry (v) | Glickman,Harry (v) | Libove,Charles (v) | Lookofsky,Harry (v) | Morgenstern,Marvin (v) | Sorkin,Herbert (v) | Sortomme,Richard (v) | Alsop,LaMar (viola) | Brown,Alfred (viola) | Vardi,Emanuel (viola) | Abramowitz,Jonathan (cello) | McCracken,Charles (cello) | Shulman,Alan (cello) | Beal,John (b) | Israels,Charles (b) | Mensch,Homer (b) | Armstead,Joshie (voc) | McDuffie,Debbie (voc) | Robinson,Albertine (voc) | Stewart,Maeretha (voc) | Floyd,Babi (voc) | Floyd,Frank (voc) | Grayson,Milt (voc) | Simpson,Ray (voc) | Madison,Jimmy (dr) | Marrero,Nicky (perc)

489772-2 | CD | Pike's Peak
Dave Pike Quartet
Why Not? | In A Sentimental Mood | Vierd Blues | Besame Mucho | Wild Is The Wind
NYC, rec. 6.& 8.2.1962
Pike,Dave (vib) | Evans,Bill (p) | Lewis,Herbie (b) | Perkins,Walter (dr)

ESM Records | Edition Soundmaster Musikproduktion

ESM 9301 | CD | Live At The Allotria
Jenny Evans And Band
Too Close For Comfort | I Wanna Be Near To You | Miss Otis Regrets | Love For Sale | Girl Talk | Autumn Leaves | Jenny's Place | Song For My Father | There'll Never Be Another You | Mr.Bojangles | Dat Dere | St.Thomas | 'S Wonderful
Live at The Allotria,München, rec. 20.4.1993
Evans,Jenny (voc) | Bickl,Gerhard 'Zwei' (p) | Gnettner,Kartsten (b) | Eppinger,Stephan (dr)

ESM 9302 | CD | At Lloyd's
Jenny Evans And The Rudi Martini Quartet
Don't Get Around Much Anymore | How High The Moon | Stormy Weather | Lullaby Of Birdland | The Lady Is A Tramp | I've Got You Under My Skin | The Shadow Of Your Smile | Take The 'A' Train | Night And Day | Sweet Georgia Brown | Summertime | I Got Rhythm | Get Your Kicks On Route 66
Live at 'Da Capo',Stuttgart, rec. May 1993
Evans,Jenny (voc) | Martini,Rudi (dr) | Friedrich,Gerry (cl,ts) | Weiss,Otto (p) | Pejakovic,Branko (b)

ESM 9303 | CD | Handful Of Blues
Martin Schmitt
The Cat | Let's Go Get Stoned | 324 Blues | Experience | All I Wanna Ever Do | Come Rain Or Come Shine | Lonely Hours | Doodlin' | Too Fat To Boogie | She's Not The One For Me
Bürgerhaus,Gräfelfing, rec. 28./29.7.1993
Schmitt,Martin (p,voc)
Big Legged Woman
Schmitt,Martin (p,voc) | Matzkeit,Bodo (wbd)
Keep Your Hands Off Her | Ain't Nobody's Business
Schmitt,Martin (p,voc) | Vollmer,Titus (g)

ESM 9305 | CD | Shiny Stockings | EAN 063757931720
Jenny Evans And Her Quintet
Shiny Stockings | Good Old Days | Softly As In A Morning Sunrise | That's What Zoot Said | You Go To My Head | In A Mellow Tone | Caravan | Willow Weep For Me | Alright,Okay,You Win | Honeysuckle Rose | The Song Of Autumn | April In Paris | All Of Me
München, rec. October 1996
Evans,Jenny (voc) | Goykovich,Dusko (tp,fl-h) | Basso,Gianni (ts) | Gazarov,David (p) | Pejakovic,Branko (b) | Martini,Rudi (dr)

ESM 9306 | CD | Girl Talk | EAN 063757936329
Jenny Evans And Band
Too Close For Comfort | Girl Talk | Love For Sale | Miss Otis Regrets | Song For My Father | There'll Never Be Another You | Autumn Leaves | Dat Dere | Jenny's Place | St.Thomas | Mr.Bojangles | I Wanna Be Near To You | 'S Wonderful
Live at The Allotria,München, rec. 20.4.1993
Evans,Jenny (voc) | Bickl,Gerhard 'Zwei' (p) | Gnettner,Kartsten (b) | Eppinger,Stephan (dr)

ESM 9307 | CD | Gonna Go Fishin' | EAN 063757940326
Jenny Evans And Her Quintet
I'm Gonna Go Fishin' | Hope | Love Is The Answer | The Man I Love | Stolen Moments | Für Eine Nacht Voller Seligkeit | In A Natural Way | Still She | Black Coffee | I'm Gonna Live 'Till I Die | Angel Eyes
Live at The Unterfahrt,München, rec. 15./16.3.2000
Evans,Jenny (voc) | O'Mara,Peter (g) | Lang,Walter (p) | Heller,Ingmar (b) | May,Guido (dr) | Darouiche,Biboul Ferkouzad (perc)

ESM 9308 | CD | Nuages | EAN 063757946724
Mad About The Boy | Remember Me | Nuages | Our Revels Now Are Ended | Within' You,Without You | Flow My Tears | I'm Alone After All | The Feeling Of You | Veris Leta Facies | No Love Without Tears | What Joy
München, rec. July & September 2003
Evans,Jenny (voc) | Francel,Mulo (b-cl,ss,ts,mand) | Lang,Walter (p) | Lachotta,Chris (b) | Martini,Rudi (dr) | Kainar,Robert (perc)

Factory Outlet Records | Jazz Network

400004-2 | CD | Somewhere
Thomas Horstmann-Markus Zaja
Doppel | Bicinium 1 | Bicinium 2 | Chateau Bellevue | Saxtett | Somewhere | Arbeit | Tiptap | Choral | F
details unknown, rec. details unknown
Horstmann,Thomas (g,synth) | Zaja,Markus (cl,sax)

FOR 2001-3 CD | CD | Billy The Kid | EAN 4042064000783
Horstmann-Wiedmann-Daneck
Billy The Kid | Pablo's Story | One Look,One Touch | Dave's Tune | Waiting For Maria | You Knew | S/Catch | Flying | Homeward Bound | Folksong
Tübingen, rec. 1.-3.3.2001
Horstmann,Thomas (g,fretless-g,synth) | Wiedmann,Martin (g) | Daneck,Matthias (dr,perc)

FOR 2002-1 CD | CD | Some Other Time | EAN 4042064001490
The Atlantic Jazz Trio
A Short One | To Be Or To U.B. | Children's Song | Diabolus | Goodbye Pork Pie Hat | PlumbThe Bayou | Sometimes Ago | Keep Me In Mind | From Anywhere To Somewhere | Some Other Time
The Office,?, rec. June 2001
Atlantic Jazz Trio | Horstmann,Thomas (g,el-g) | Hagberg,Garry (g) | Schönfeld,Peter (b,b-g,fretless-b)

FOR 2501-1 CD | CD | First Meeting | EAN 4042064000059
The Atlantic String Trio
My Romance | Alone Together | Recorda-Me | Interlude:Not All Blues | Nardis | Self Portrait In Three Colors | Footprints | Interlude:Blue | Blue In Green | Things Ain't What They Used To Be | Peace | Interlude:Green | Stolen Moments | Song For A Friend | Getting Even With Autumn Leaves | Diabolus(A Fragment)
The Office,?, rec. September 2000
Atlantic String Trio,The | Hagberg,Garry (g) | Horstmann,Thomas (g) | Schönfeld,Peter (b)

WO 95001 | CD | Decade
Thomas Horstmann-Martin Wiedmann Group
Carissima
Tübingen, rec. 27.-29.1.1995
Horstmann,Thomas (g) | Wiedmann,Martin (g)
Walking | The Free,Chained | The Left Side Of The Moon Is Blue | Blues For Klaus | Innocenti | Pacific Breeze | Lost And Found | Don't Call On Me
Horstmann,Thomas (g,synth) | Wiedmann,Martin (g) | Killinger,Johannes (b) | Daneck,Matthias (dr,perc)
Losing You
Horstmann,Thomas (g,synth) | Wiedmann,Martin (g) | Stötter,Claus (fl-h) | Killinger,Johannes (b) | Daneck,Matthias (dr,perc)

Fantasy | ZYX Music GmbH

9FCD 1012-2 | 9 CD | The Complete Fantasy Recordings
Bill Evans Trio
Morning Glory | Up With The Lark | Yesterday I Heard The Rain | My Romance | When Autumn Comes | T.T.T.(Twelve Tone Tune) | Hullo Bolinas | Gloria's Step | On Green Dolphin Street
Live at Yubin Chokin Hall,Tokyo,Japan
Evans,Bill (p) | Gomez,Eddie (b) | Morell,Marty (dr)
Up With The Lark | Quiet Now | Gloria's Step | It Amazes Me
Live at Shelly's Manne Hole,Los Angeles,CA, rec. November 1973
Evans,Bill (p) | Gomez,Eddie (b) | Morell,Marty (dr)
Bill Evans
When In Rome
Evans,Bill (p-solo)
Bill Evans Trio
Since We Met | Midnight Mood | See Saw | Elsa | Sareen Jurer | Time Remembered | Turn Out The Stars | But Beautiful | Re:Person I Knew | Sugar Plum | Alfie | T.T.T. | Dolphin Dance-(Excerpts) | Very Early-(Excerpts) | 34 Skidoo | Emily | All The Things You Are
Live at The 'Village Vanguard',NYC, rec. 11./12.1.1974
Evans,Bill (p) | Gomez,Eddie (b) | Morell,Marty (dr)
Bill Evans-Eddie Gomez Duo
Invitation | Blue Serge | Show-Type Tune | The Nature Of Things | Are You All The Things | A Face Without A Name | Falling Grace | Hi Lili Hi Lo
Berkeley,CA, rec. 7.-10.11.1974
Evans,Bill (p,el-p) | Gomez,Eddie (b)
Gone With The Wind | Saudade Do Brazil
Hollywood,CA, rec. 7./8.11.1974
Evans,Bill (p,el-p) | Gomez,Eddie (b)
Tony Bennett-Bill Evans
My Foolish Heart | The Touch Of Your Lips | Some Other Time | When In Rome | We'll Be Together Again | Young And Foolish | Waltz For Debby | But Beautiful | Days Of Wine And Roses
Berkeley,CA, rec. 10.-13.6.1975
Bennett,Tony (voc) | Evans,Bill (p)
Bill Evans-Eddie Gomez Duo
Elsa | Milano | Venutian Rhythm Dance | Django | But Beautiful | Minha(All Mine) | Driftin' | I Love You | Summer Of '42(The Summer Knows) | In A Sentimental Mood
Live at The Montreux Jazz Festival, rec. 20.7.1975
Evans,Bill (p,el-p) | Gomez,Eddie (b)
Bill Evans
The Touch Of Your Lips | In Your Own Sweet Way | Make Someone Happy | What Kind Of Fool Am I | People
Berkeley,CA, rec. 16.-18.12.1975
Evans,Bill (p-solo)
All Of You | Since We Met | But Not For Me- | Isn't It Romantic- | The Opener
Hollywood,CA, rec. 16.-18.12.1975
Evans,Bill (p-solo)
Bill Evans Quintet
Sweet Dulcinea | Martina | Second Time Around | A Child Is Born | Bass Face | Nobody Else But Me
Berkeley,CA, rec. 27.-30.5.1976
Evans,Bill (p) | Land,Harold (ts) | Burrell,Kenny (g) | Brown,Ray (b) | Jones,Philly Joe (dr)
Bill Evans Trio
Sugar Plum | Time Remembered | 34 Skidoo | T.T.T. | Turn Out The Stars | Someday My Prince Will Come | Minha(All Mine) | All Of You | Waltz For Debby
Live in Paris,France, rec. 5.11.1976
Evans,Bill (p) | Gomez,Eddie (b) | Zigmund,Eliot (dr)
Bill Evans Quintet
Eiderdown | Every Time We Say Goodbye | Speak Low | Pensativa | When I Fall In Love | Night And Day
Berkeley,CA, rec. 28.2.& 1.-3.3.1977
Evans,Bill (p) | Konitz,Lee (as) | Marsh,Warne (ts) | Gomez,Eddie (b) | Zigmund,Eliot (dr)
Bill Evans Trio
Nobody Else But Me | Orson's Theme
Berkeley,CA, rec. May 1977
Evans,Bill (p) | Gomez,Eddie (b) | Zigmund,Eliot (dr)
I Will Say Goodbye | Dolphin Dance | Seascape | Peau Douce | I Will Say Goodbye(alt.take) | The Opener | Quiet Light | A House Is Not A Home
Berkeley,CA, rec. 11.-13.5.1979
Evans,Bill (p) | Gomez,Eddie (b) | Zigmund,Eliot (dr)
Bill Evans
Kaleidoscope(theme) | Waltz For Debby | All Of You | In Your Own Sweet Way | The Touch Of Your Lips | Reflections In D | I Love You | Days Of Wine And Roses | This Is All I Ask | While We're Young
Baldwin Piano Show Room,NYC, rec. 6.11.1978
Evans,Bill (p,talking) | McPartland,Marian (interviewer)
-> Marian McPartland's Piano Jazz Interwiew for National Public Radio

FANCD 6079-2 | 3 CD | Milt Jackson Birthday Celebration | EAN 090204946891
Modern Jazz Quartet
All The Things You Are
NYC, rec. 22.12.1952
MJQ (Modern Jazz Quartet) | Jackson,Milt (vib) | Lewis,John (p) | Heath,Percy (b) | Clarke,Kenny (dr)
Delauney's Dilemma
NYC, rec. 25.6.1953
MJQ (Modern Jazz Quartet) | Jackson,Milt (vib) | Lewis,John (p) | Heath,Percy (b) | Clarke,Kenny (dr)
Sonny Rollins With The Modern Jazz Quartet
The Stopper
NYC, rec. 7.10.1953
Rollins,Sonny (ts) | MJQ (Modern Jazz Quartet) | Jackson,Milt (vib) | Lewis,John (p) | Heath,Percy (b) | Clarke,Kenny (dr)
Miles Davis All Stars
Bag's Groove(take 2)
Hackensack,NJ, rec. 24.12.1954
Davis,Miles (tp) | Jackson,Milt (vib) | Monk,Thelonious (p) | Heath,Percy (b) | Clarke,Kenny (dr)
Modern Jazz Quartet
Django
Hackensack,NJ, rec. 23.12.1954
MJQ (Modern Jazz Quartet) | Jackson,Milt (vib) | Lewis,John (p) | Heath,Percy (b) | Clarke,Kenny (dr)
Ralph's New Blues | Softly As In A Morning Sunrise
Hackensack,NJ, rec. 2.7.1955
MJQ (Modern Jazz Quartet) | Jackson,Milt (vib) | Lewis,John (p) | Heath,Percy (b) | Kay,Connie (dr)
The Cylinder | The Martyr
Live at The Montreux Jazz Festival, rec. 25.7.1982
MJQ (Modern Jazz Quartet) | Jackson,Milt (vib) | Lewis,John (p) | Heath,Percy (b) | Kay,Connie (dr)
Topsy | Nature Boy
NYC, rec. 3./4.6.1985
MJQ (Modern Jazz Quartet) | Jackson,Milt (vib) | Lewis,John (p) | Heath,Percy (b) | Kay,Connie (dr)
Echoes
NYC, rec. 6.3.1984
MJQ (Modern Jazz Quartet) | Jackson,Milt (vib) | Lewis,John (p) | Heath,Percy (b) | Kay,Connie (dr)
Coleman Hawkins All Star Octet
Bean And The Boys
NYC, rec. December 1946
Hawkins,Coleman (ts) | Navarro,Fats (tp) | Johnson,J.J. (tb) | Kilbert,Porter (as) | Jackson,Milt (vib) | Jones,Hank (p) | Russell,Curly (b) | Roach,Max (dr)
Milt Jackson Quintet
Slits
Detroit, rec. April 1948
Jackson,Milt (vib) | Lewis,John (p) | Jackson,Alvin 'Al' (b) | Clarke,Kenny (dr) | Pozo,Chano (congas)
Sonny Stitt Sextet
Bebop Blues
Detroit, rec. April/June 1948
Stitt,Sonny (as) | Jacquet,Russell (tp) | Jackson,Milt (vib) | Thompson,Sir Charles (p) | unkn. (b) | unkn. (dr)
Dizzy Gillespie All Stars
She's Gone Again
NYC, rec. 16.9.1950
Gillespie,Dizzy (tp) | Heath,Jimmy (as) | Oliver,Jimmy (ts) | Jackson,Milt (p) | Heath,Percy (b) | Harris,Joe (dr)
Milt Jackson Trio
Lullaby Of The Leaves
NYC, rec. 7.3.1954
Jackson,Milt (p) | Heath,Percy (b) | Smith,Charlie (dr)
Milt Jackson Quintet
Opus De Funk
Hackensack,NJ, rec. 16.6.1954
Jackson,Milt (vib) | Boozier,Henry (tp) | Silver,Horace (p) | Heath,Percy (b) | Clarke,Kenny (dr)
Milt Jackson Quartet
I Should Care
Hackensack,NJ, rec. 20.3.1955
Jackson,Milt (vib) | Silver,Horace (p) | Heath,Percy (b) | Kay,Connie (dr)
Miles Davis-Milt Jackson Quintet
Bitty Ditty
Hackensack,NJ, rec. 5.8.1955
Davis,Miles (tp) | Jackson,Milt (vib) | Bryant,Ray (p) | Heath,Percy (b) | Taylor,Arthur 'Art' (dr)
Milt Jackson Quartet
Wonder Why
Hackensack,NJ, rec. 20.5.1955
Jackson,Milt (vib) | Silver,Horace (p) | Heath,Percy (b) | Kay,Connie (dr)
Cannonball Adderley-Milt Jackson Quintet
Blues Oriental | Things Are Getting Better
NYC, rec. 28.10.1958
Adderley,Julian \'Cannonball\' (as) | Jackson,Milt (vib) | Kelly,Wynton (p) | Heath,Percy (b) | Blakey,Art (dr)
Milt Jackson-Wes Montgomery Quintet
Stairway To The Stars
NYC, rec. 18.12.1961
Jackson,Milt (vib) | Montgomery,Wes (g) | Kelly,Wynton (p) | Jones,Sam (b) | Jones,Philly Joe (dr)
S.K.J.
NYC, rec. 19.12.1961
Jackson,Milt (vib) | Montgomery,Wes (g) | Kelly,Wynton (p) | Jones,Sam (b) | Jones,Philly Joe (dr)
Milt Jackson Orchestra
Namesake
NYC, rec. 5.7.1962
Jackson,Milt (vib) | Terry,Clark (tp,fl-h) | Royal,Ernie (tp) | Young,Eugene Edward (tp) | McIntosh,Tom (tb) | Liston,Melba (tb) | Ruff,Willie (fr-h) | Warren,Earl (as) | Moody,James (fl,as) | Heath,Jimmy (ts) | Richardson,Jerome (fl,ts) | Houston,Tate (bs) | Jones,Hank (p) | Carter,Ron (b) | Kay,Connie (dr) | Dameron,Tadd (arr) | Wilkins,Ernie (arr)
Milt Jackson Quartet
Time After Time
Live at The 'Village Gate',NYC, rec. December 1963
Jackson,Milt (vib) | Jones,Hank (p) | Cranshaw,Bob (b) | Heath,Albert 'Tootie' (dr)
Milt Jackson Sextet
Poom-A-Loom

NYC, rec. 11.11.1962
Jackson,Milt (vib) | Dorham,Kenny (tp) | Jones,Virgil (tp) | Flanagan,Tommy (p) | Carter,Ron (b) | Kay,Connie (dr)

Milt Jackson Orchestra
Extraordinary Blues
NYC, rec. 18.3.1963
Jackson,Milt (vib) | Terry,Clark (tp) | Burns,Dave (tp) | Young,Eugene Edward (tp) | Jones,Thad (tp) | Jackson,Quentin (tb) | Cleveland,Jimmy (tb) | Rains,John (tb) | Holley,Major (tuba) | Watkins,Julius (fr-h) | Northern,Bob (fr-h) | Alonge,Ray (fr-h) | Jones,Hank (p) | Davis,Richard (b) | Persip,Charles (dr) | Liston,Melba (arr)

Roy Eldridge Sextet
Recado Bossa Nova
NYC, rec. 16.1.1976
Eldridge,Roy (tp) | Turney,Norris (fl) | Jackson,Milt (vib) | Simmons,Norman (p) | Sturgis,Ted (b) | Locke,Eddie (dr)

The Big Three
Come Sunday
Los Angeles,CA, rec. 25.8.1975
Big Three,The | Jackson,Milt (vib) | Pass,Joe (g) | Brown,Ray (b)

Benny Carter Sextet
Easy Money
NYC, rec. 11.2.1976
Carter,Benny (as) | Jackson,Milt (vib) | Pass,Joe (g) | Flanagan,Tommy (p) | Williams,John B. (b) | Hanna,Jake (dr)

Milt Jackson With The Count Basie Orchestra
Lena And Lenny
Hollywood,CA, rec. 18.1.1978
Jackson,Milt (vib) | Basie,Count (p) | Reed,Waymon (tp) | Biviano,Lyn (tp) | Cohn[Cohen],Sonny (tp) | Minger,Pete (tp) | Hughes,Bill (tb) | Wanzo,Mel (tb) | Wesley,Fred (tb) | Wilson,Dennis (tb) | Turner,Danny (as) | Plater,Bobby (as) | Dixon,Eric (ts) | Hing,Kenny (ts) | Fowlkes,Charlie (bs) | Green,Freddie (g) | Clayton Jr.,John (b) | Miles,Butch (dr) | Vaughan,Sarah (voc)

Count Basie Kansas City 5
Jive At Five
Burbank,Los Angeles,CA, rec. 26.1.1977
Jackson,Milt (vib) | Basie,Count (p) | Pass,Joe (g) | Heard,John (b) | Bellson,Louie (dr)

Milt Jackson-Ray Brown Jam
Beautiful Friendship
Montreux,CH, rec. 13.7.1977
Terry,Clark (tp) | Davis,Eddie 'Lockjaw' (ts) | Jackson,Milt (vib) | Alexander,Monty (p) | Brown,Ray (b) | Smith,Jimmie (dr)

Quadrant
Take The 'A' Train
Hollywood,CA, rec. 21.1.1980
Quadrant | Jackson,Milt (vib) | Pass,Joe (g) | Brown,Ray (b) | Roker,Granville 'Mickey' (dr)

Milt Jackson Quartet
Impressions
Live at Ronnie Scott's,London,GB, rec. 23./24.4.1982
Jackson,Milt (vib) | Alexander,Monty (p) | Brown,Ray (b) | Roker,Granville 'Mickey' (dr)
In Walked Bud
Live at Ronnie Scott's,London,GB, rec. 28.4.1982
Jackson,Milt (vib) | Alexander,Monty (p) | Brown,Ray (b) | Roker,Granville 'Mickey' (dr)

Milt Jackson Septet
Blues In My Heart
Venice,CA, rec. 14.4.1980
Jackson,Milt (vib) | Edison,Harry 'Sweets' (tp) | Vinson,Eddie 'Cleanhead' (as) | Davis,Eddie 'Lockjaw' (ts) | Hillery,Art (p) | Brown,Ray (b) | Marable,Lawrence (dr)

Milt Jackson-Oscar Peterson
A Time For Love | Just You Just Me
NYC, rec. 30.11.1981
Jackson,Milt (vib) | Peterson,Oscar (p)

Milt Jackson
Lullaby Of The Leaves
NYC, rec. 17.5.1985
Jackson,Milt (vib-solo)

Milt Jackson Quartet
Midnight Waltz
NYC, rec. July 1984
Jackson,Milt (vib) | Walton,Cedar (p) | Brown,Ray (b) | Roker,Granville 'Mickey' (dr)

FANCD 6081-2 | 2 CD | Welcome To Jazz At The Philharmonic |
EAN 090204947782

JATP All Stars
Introduction by Norman Granz | How High The Moon | Drew's Blues
Live at Frankfurt/M., rec. 20.11.1952
JATP All Stars | Eldridge,Roy (tp) | Young,Lester (ts) | Phillips,Flip (ts) | Jones,Hank (p) | Brown,Ray (b) | Roach,Max (dr)
Little David
Live at Stockholm,Sweden, rec. 2.2.1955
JATP All Stars | Eldridge,Roy (tp) | Gillespie,Dizzy (tp) | Harris,Bill (tb) | Phillips,Flip (ts) | Peterson,Oscar (p) | Brown,Ray (b) | Bellson,Louie (dr)
Now's The Time
NYC/Hollywood/Oakland, rec. June/July 1967
JATP All Stars | Terry,Clark (tp) | Carter,Benny (as) | Sims,Zoot (ts) | Gonsalves,Paul (ts) | Peterson,Oscar (p) | Jones,Sam (b) | Durham,Bobby (dr)

Duke Ellington And His Orchestra
Very Tenor
NYC/Hollywood/Oakland, rec. July 1967
Ellington,Duke (p) | Anderson,Cat (tp) | Ellington,Mercer (tp) | Jones,Herbie (tp) | Williams,Cootie (tp) | Cooper,George 'Buster' (tb) | Connors,Chuck (tb) | Procope,Russell (cl,as) | Hodges,Johnny (as) | Carney,Harry (bs) | Lamb,John (b) | Jones,Rufus (dr)

JATP All Stars
Ow!
Live at London,GB, rec. March 1969
JATP All Stars | Gillespie,Dizzy (tp) | Terry,Clark (tp) | Sims,Zoot (ts) | Moody,James (fl,ts) | Wilson,Teddy (p) | Cranshaw,Bob (b) | Bellson,Louie (dr)
Stormy Monday Blues(They Call It Stormy Monday)
JATP All Stars | Gillespie,Dizzy (tp) | Terry,Clark (tp) | Sims,Zoot (ts) | Moody,James (fl,ts) | Walker,T-Bone (g) | Wilson,Teddy (p) | Cranshaw,Bob (b) | Bellson,Louie (dr)
Blue Lou
JATP All Stars | Carter,Benny (as) | Hawkins,Coleman (ts) | Wilson,Teddy (p) | Cranshaw,Bob (b) | Bellson,Louie (dr)
In A Mellow Tone | Ballad Medley: | Makin' Whoopee- | If I Had You- | She's Funny That Way- | Blue And Sentimental- | I Surrender Dear-
Live at Santa Monica Civic Auditorium,CA, rec. 2.6.1972
JATP All Stars | Eldridge,Roy (tp) | Edison,Harry 'Sweets' (tp) | Grey,Al (tb) | Getz,Stan (ts) | Davis,Eddie 'Lockjaw' (ts) | Basie,Count (p) | Green,Freddie (g) | Brown,Ray (b) | Thigpen,Ed (dr)
C Jam Blues
JATP All Stars | Fitzgerald,Ella (voc) | Eldridge,Roy (tp) | Edison,Harry 'Sweets' (tp) | Grey,Al (tb) | Getz,Stan (ts) | Davis,Eddie 'Lockjaw' (ts) | Basie,Count (p) | Green,Freddie (g) | Brown,Ray (b) | Thigpen,Ed (dr)
Sunday | Flying Home
Live at The Tokyo Yoyogi National Stadium,Japan, rec. 1983
Blues
JATP All Stars | Pass,Joe (g) | Peterson,Oscar (p) | Orsted-Pedersen,Niels-Henning (b) | Drew,Martin (dr)

FANCD 6082-2 | 3 CD | Dexter Gordon Birthday Celebration |
EAN 090204922369

Wardell Gray's Los Angeles All Stars
Move
Liveat The Hula Hut Club,Los Angeles,CA, rec. 22.8.1950
Gray,Wardell (ts) | Terry,Clark (tp) | Criss,Sonny (as) | Gordon,Dexter (ts) | Bunn,Jimmy (p) | Hadnott,Billy (b) | Thompson,Chuck (dr)

Dexter Gordon Quartet
Jodi
Los Angeles,CA, rec. 13.10.1960
Gordon,Dexter (ts) | Coker,Dolo (p) | Greene,Charles 'Flip' (b) | Marable,Lawrence (dr)

Booker Ervin-Dexter Gordon Quintet
Settin' The Pace
München, rec. 27.101965
Ervin,Booker (ts) | Gordon,Dexter (ts) | Byard,Jaki (p) | Workman,Reggie (b) | Dawson,Alan (dr)

Dexter Gordon Quartet
Those Were The | Boston Bernie | Meditation
NYC, rec. 4.4.1969
Gordon,Dexter (ts) | Harris,Barry (p) | Williams,Buster (b) | Heath,Albert 'Tootie' (dr)
Misty | Broadway
Live at The Famous Ballroom,Baltimore,MD, rec. 4.5.1969
Gordon,Dexter (ts) | Timmons,Bobby (p) | Gaskin,Victor (b) | Brice,Percy (dr)

Eddie Jefferson And His Band
Dexter Digs In
NYC, rec. 12.8.1969
Jefferson,Eddie (voc) | Hardman,Bill (tp) | McPherson,Charles (as) | Harris,Barry (p) | Taylor,Gene (b,el-b) | English,Bill (dr)

Dexter Gordon Quartet
Body And Soul | The Christmas Song
NYC, rec. 7.7.1970
Gordon,Dexter (ts) | Flanagan,Tommy (p) | Ridley,Larry (b) | Dawson,Alan (dr)
Fried Bananas | Sophisticated Lady
Live at The Montreux Jazz Festival, rec. 18.6.1970
Gordon,Dexter (ts) | Mance,Junior[Julian C.] (p) | Rivera,Martin (b) | Jackson,Oliver (dr)

Gene Ammons-Dexter Gordon Quintet
The Chase
Live at The North Park Hotel,Chicago,Ill, rec. 26.7.1970
Ammons,Gene (ts) | Gordon,Dexter (ts) | Christian,Jodie (p) | Reid,Rufus (b) | Campbell,Wilbur (dr)

Dexter Gordon Quartet
Star Eyes | If You Could See Me Now | The Jumpin' Blues(alt.take)
Englewood Cliffs,NJ, rec. 27.8.1970
Gordon,Dexter (ts) | Kelly,Wynton (p) | Jones,Sam (b) | Brooks,Roy (dr)

Dexter Gordon Quintet
The Group
Englewood Cliffs,NJ, rec. 22.6.1972
Gordon,Dexter (ts) | Hubbard,Freddie (tp) | Walton,Cedar (p) | Williams,Buster (b) | Higgins,Billy (dr)

Dexter Gordon Quartet
Days Of Wine And Roses
Gordon,Dexter (ts) | Walton,Cedar (p) | Williams,Buster (b) | Higgins,Billy (dr)

Dexter Gordon Quintet
Airegin | The First Time Ever I Saw Your Face | Tangerine
Englewood Cliffs,NJ, rec. 28.6.1972
Gordon,Dexter (ts) | Jones,Thad (tp,fl-h) | Jones,Hank (p) | Clarke,Stanley (b) | Hayes,Louis (dr)

Dexter Gordon Quartet
Some Other Spring
Live at The Montreal Jazz Festival, rec. 7.7.1973
Gordon,Dexter (ts) | Hawes,Hampton (el-p) | Cranshaw,Bob (el-b) | Clarke,Kenny (dr)

Gene Ammons And His All Stars
'Treux Bleu
Live at The Montreux Jazz Festival, rec. 7.7.1973
Ammons,Gene (ts) | Adderley,Nat (co) | Adderley,Julian \'Cannonball\' (as) | Gordon,Dexter (ts) | Hawes,Hampton (el-p) | Cranshaw,Bob (el-b) | Clarke,Kenny (dr) | Nash,Kenneth (congas)

Dexter Gordon Quartet
Polka Dots And Moonbeams
Berkeley,CA, rec. 29.11.-1.12.1977
Gordon,Dexter (ts,spoken lyrics) | Cables,George (p) | Carter,Ron (b) | Jones,Philly Joe (dr)

FANCD 6085-2 | 3 CD | Eric Dolphy Birthday Celebration |
EAN 090204922703

Eric Dolphy Quintet
G.W. | On Green Dolphin Street
Englewood Cliffs,NJ, rec. 1.4.1960
Dolphy,Eric (b-cl,as) | Hubbard,Freddie (tp) | Byard,Jaki (p) | Tucker,George (b) | Haynes,Roy (dr)

Eric Dolphy Quartet
April Fool
Dolphy,Eric (fl) | Byard,Jaki (p) | Tucker,George (b) | Haynes,Roy (dr)

Oliver Nelson Sextet
The Drive
Englewood Cliffs,NJ, rec. 27.5.1960
Nelson,Oliver (as,ts) | Williams,Richard (tp) | Dolphy,Eric (as) | Wyands,Richard (p) | Duvivier,George (b) | Haynes,Roy (dr)

Ken McIntyre Quintet feat.Eric Dolphy
Lautir
Englewood Cliffs,NJ, rec. 28.6.1960
McIntyre,Ken (as) | Dolphy,Eric (fl) | Bishop Jr.,Walter (p) | Jones,Sam (b) | Taylor,Arthur 'Art' (dr)

Eric Dolphy Quartet
Eclipse | Feather
Englewood Cliffs,NJ, rec. 16.8.1960
Dolphy,Eric (fl,cl,b-cl,as) | Carter,Ron (cello) | Duvivier,George (b) | Haynes,Roy (dr)

The Latin Jazz Quintet Plus Guest: Eric Dolphy
Sunday Go Meelin'
Englewood Cliffs,NJ, rec. 19.8.1960
Latin Jazz Quintet,The | Dolphy,Eric (fl) | Simons,Charles (vib) | Casey,Gene (p) | Ellington,Bill (b) | Amalbert,Juan (conga) | Ramos,Manny (dr,timbales)

Eric Dolphy Quartet
Left Alone
Englewood Cliffs,NJ, rec. 21.12.1960
Dolphy,Eric (fl) | Byard,Jaki (p) | Carter,Ron (b) | Haynes,Roy (dr)

Booker Little Quintet
Serene
Little,Booker (tp) | Dolphy,Eric (b-cl) | Byard,Jaki (p) | Carter,Ron (b) | Haynes,Roy (dr)

Eric Dolphy
Tenderly
Dolphy,Eric (as-solo)

Oliver Nelson Quintet
Images | Ralph's New Blues
Englewood Cliffs,NJ, rec. 1.3.1961
Nelson,Oliver (cl,as) | Dolphy,Eric (b-cl) | Wyands,Richard (p) | Duvivier,George (b) | Haynes,Roy (dr)

George Russell Sextet
Honesty | Round About Midnight
NYC, rec. 8.5.1961
Russell,George (p) | Ellis,Don (tp) | Baker,Dave (tb) | Dolphy,Eric (as) | Swallow,Steve (b) | Hunt,Joe (dr)

Ron Carter Quintet
Rally
Englewood Cliffs,NJ, rec. 20.6.1961
Carter,Ron (cello) | Dolphy,Eric (b-cl) | Waldron,Mal (p) | Duvivier,George (b) | Persip,Charles (dr)

Mal Waldron Sextet
Warm Canto | Status Seeking
Englewood Cliffs,NJ, rec. 27.6.1961
Waldron,Mal (p) | Dolphy,Eric (cl,as) | Ervin,Booker (ts) | Carter,Ron (cello) | Benjamin,Joe (b) | Persip,Charles (dr)

Eric Dolphy-Booker Little Quintet
The Prophet | Aggression | Booker's Waltz
Live at The Five Spot Cafe,NYC, rec. 16.7.1961
Dolphy,Eric (b-cl,as) | Little,Booker (tp) | Waldron,Mal (p) | Davis,Richard (b) | Blackwell,Ed (dr)

Eric Dolphy Quartet
Les
Live at The Berlingske Has,Copenhagen, rec. 6.9.1961
Dolphy,Eric (as) | Axen,Bent (p) | Moseholm,Erik (b) | Elniff,Jorn (dr)
Woody'n You
Live at The Studenterforeningen Foredragssal,Copenhagen,Denmark, rec. 8.9.1961
Dolphy,Eric (as) | Axen,Bent (p) | Moseholm,Erik (b) | Elniff,Jorn (dr)

Eric Dolphy
God Bless The Child
Dolphy,Eric (b-cl-solo)

John Coltrane Quintet
My Favorite Things
Live in Hamburg, rec. 25.11.1961
Coltrane,John (ss) | Dolphy,Eric (fl) | Tyner,McCoy (p) | Workman,Reggie (b) | Jones,Elvin (dr)

Charles Mingus Sextet
So Long Eric
Live at Town Hall,NYC, rec. 4.4.1964
Mingus,Charles (b) | Coles,Johnny (tp) | Dolphy,Eric (as) | Jordan,Clifford (ts) | Byard,Jaki (p) | Richmond,Dannie (dr)

FANCD 6086-2 | CD | Jazzin' With The Soul Brothers |
EAN 090204922840
FANCD 6086-1(LP) | 2 LP | Jazzin' With The Soul Brothers |
EAN 090204922857

Pucho & His Latin Soul Brothers
Sex Machine | Trouble Man
details unknown, rec. 1995
Pucho (timbales) | Pazant,Al (tp) | Bivins,Willie (vib) | Spruill,John (p,org) | Horne,Marvin (g) | Colon,Ernesto (dr) | Killian,Lawrence (congas) | James,Ricky \'Bongo\' (bongos) | Berrios,Steve (bells,clave)

Funk Inc.
Give Me Your Love | Runnin' Away
Englewood Cliffs,NJ, rec. 1972
Funk Inc. | Barr,Gene (ts) | Weakley,Steve (g) | Watley,Bobby (org) | Mumford,Jimmy (dr) | Hunt,Cecil (congas)

Charles Earland Sextet
Sing A Simple Song | You Cought Me Smilin' - (You Cought Me) Smilin'
Englewood Cliffs,NJ, rec. 1969
Earland,Charles (org) | Jones,Virgil (tp) | Pruden,Layton (tb) | Heath,Jimmy (ts) | Parker,Maynard (g) | Turner,Jimmy (dr)

Idris Muhammad Group
Super Bad
Englewood Cliffs,NJ, rec. 1970
Muhammad,Idris[Leo Morris] (dr) | Jones,Virgil (tp) | Thomas,Clarence (ts) | Sparks,Melvin (g) | Mabern,Harold (el-p) | Lewis,Jimmy (b) | Allende,Angel (perc) | Caldwell,Buddy (congas)

Melvin Sparks Quintet
Thank You-Fallettinme Be Mice Elf Agin
Sparks,Melvin (g) | Jones,Virgil (tp) | Manning,John (ts) | Spencer Jr.,Leon (org) | Muhammad,Idris[Leo Morris] (dr)

Leon Spencer Sextet
Mercy Mercy Me
Englewood Cliffs,NJ, rec. 1971
Spencer Jr.,Leon (org) | Jones,Virgil (tp) | Washington Jr.,Grover (ts) | Sparks,Melvin (g) | Muhammad,Idris[Leo Morris] (dr) | Caldwell,Buddy (congas)

Houston Person Sextet
Yester-Me, Yester-You, Yesterday
Person,Houston (ts) | Green,Grant (g) | Phillips,Sonny (el-p) | Lewis,Jimmy (b) | Muhammad,Idris[Leo Morris] (dr) | Caldwell,Buddy (congas)

Boogaloo Joe Jones Sextet
Ain't No Sunshine
Jones,Boogaloo Joe (g) | Washington Jr.,Grover (ts) | Cornell,Butch (org) | Lewis,Jimmy (b) | Purdie,Bernard 'Pretty' (dr) | Caldwell,Buddy (congas)

Rusty Bryant Quintet
If You Really Love Me
Bryant,Rusty (ts) | Ponder,Jimmy (g) | Mason,Bill (org) | Muhammad,Idris[Leo Morris] (dr) | Caldwell,Buddy (congas)

Hank Crawford-Jimmy McGriff Quartet
What's Going On
details unknown, rec. 1998
Crawford,Hank (as) | McGriff,Jimmy (org) | Dupree,Cornell (g) | Purdie,Bernard 'Pretty' (dr)

Bernard Purdie Group
Cold Sweat
Englewood Cliffs,NJ, rec. 1971
Purdie,Bernard 'Pretty' (dr) | Larkin,Tippy (tp) | Brown,Charlie (ts) | Daniels,Warren (ts) | Nichols,Billy (g) | Dunbar,Ted (g) | Wheeler,Harold (el-p) | Edwards,Gordon (b) | Pride,Norman (congas)

FANCD 6087-2 | 3 CD | Cannonball Adderley Birthday Celebration |
EAN 090204922970

Cannonball Adderley Quintet
A Foggy Day(In London Town)
Live at Newport,Rhode Island, rec. 5.7.1957
Adderley,Julian \'Cannonball\' (as) | Adderley,Nat (tp) | Mance,Junior[Julian C.] (p) | Jones,Sam (b) | Cobb,Jimmy (dr)
Nardis
NYC, rec. 1.7.1958
Adderley,Julian \'Cannonball\' (as) | Mitchell,Blue (tp) | Evans,Bill (p) | Jones,Sam (b) | Jones,Philly Joe (dr)

Cannonball Adderley-Milt Jackson Quintet
Just One Of Those Things | Serves Me Right
NYC, rec. 28.10.1958
Adderley,Julian \'Cannonball\' (as) | Jackson,Milt (vib) | Kelly,Wynton (p) | Heath,Percy (b) | Blakey,Art (dr)

Cannonball Adderley Quartet
Alabama Concerto(Benson Brooks, 1st movement): | The Henry John Story- | Green Green Rocky Road- | Job's Red Wagon-
NYC, rec. 25./31.8.1958
Adderley,Julian \'Cannonball\' (as) | Farmer,Art (tp) | Galbraith,Barry (g) | Hinton,Milt (b)

Kenny Dorham Septet
Spring Cannon
NYC, rec. 20.1.1959
Dorham,Kenny (tp) | Amram,David (fr-h) | Adderley,Julian \'Cannonball\' (as) | Payne,Cecil (bs) | Waldron,Mal (p) | Chambers,Paul (b) | Jones,Philly Joe (dr)

Philly Joe Jones Big Band
Stablemates
NYC, rec. 11.5.1959
Jones,Philly Joe (dr) | Mitchell,Blue (tp) | Morgan,Lee (tp) | Fuller,Curtis (tb) | Adderley,Julian \'Cannonball\' (as) | Golson,Benny (ts) | Shihab,Sahib (bs) | Kelly,Wynton (p) | Jones,Sam (b)

Cannonball Adderley Quintet
This Here | Hi Fly
Live at The Jazz Workshop,San Francisco,CA, rec. 20.10.1959
Adderley,Julian \'Cannonball\' (as) | Adderley,Nat (co) | Timmons,Bobby (p) | Jones,Sam (b) | Hayes,Louis (dr)

Nat Adderley And The Big Sax Section
You Leave Me Breathless
NYC, rec. 9.8.1960
Adderley,Nat (co) | Adderley,Julian \'Cannonball\' (as) | Lateef,Yusef (fl,ts) | Heath,Jimmy (ts) | Rouse,Charlie (ts) | Houston,Tate (bs) | Hall,Jim (g) | Jones,Sam (b) | Cobb,Jimmy (dr)

Cannonball Adderley Quintet
Work Song | Jeannine
Paris,France, rec. 1960
Adderley,Julian \'Cannonball\' (as) | Adderley,Nat (co) | Feldman,Victor (p) | Jones,Sam (b) | Hayes,Louis (dr)
One For Daddy-O | Azule Serape | The Chant
Live in ?,Europe, rec. November 1960
Adderley,Julian \'Cannonball\' (as) | Adderley,Nat (co) | Feldman,Victor (p) | Jones,Sam (b) | Hayes,Louis (dr)

Jimmy Heath Orchestra
On Green Dolphin Street
NYC, rec. 24.6.1960
Heath,Jimmy (ts) | Terry,Clark (tp) | Adderley,Nat (co) | McIntosh,Tom (tb) | Berg,Dick (fr-h) | Adderley,Julian \'Cannonball\' (as) | Patrick,Pat (bs) | Flanagan,Tommy (p) | Heath,Percy (b) | Heath,Albert 'Tootie' (dr)

Sam Jones Plus 10

Blues On Down
NYC, rec. 26.1.1961
Jones,Sam (b) | Adderley,Nat (co) | Mitchell,Blue (tp) | Liston,Melba (tb) | Adderley,Julian \'Cannonball\' (as) | Heath,Jimmy (ts) | Houston,Tate (bs) | Feldman,Victor (p,arr) | Spann,Les (g) | Hayes,Louis (dr)

Cannonball Adderley Quartet
Toy
NYC, rec. 21.2.1961
Adderley,Julian \'Cannonball\' (as) | Evans,Bill (p) | Heath,Percy (b) | Kay,Connie (dr)
Nancy(With The Laughing Face)
NYC, rec. 27.1.1961
Adderley,Julian \'Cannonball\' (as) | Evans,Bill (p) | Heath,Percy (b) | Kay,Connie (dr)
Waltz For Debby
NYC, rec. 13.3.1961
Adderley,Julian \'Cannonball\' (as) | Evans,Bill (p) | Heath,Percy (b) | Kay,Connie (dr)

Cannonball Adderley And His Orchestra
African Waltz
NYC, rec. 26.2.1961
Adderley,Julian \'Cannonball\' (as) | Adderley,Nat (co) | Terry,Clark (tp) | Royal,Ernie (tp) | Newman,Joe (tp) | Sparrow,Arnett (tb) | Matthews,George (tb) | Cleveland,Jimmy (tb) | Faulise,Paul (tb) | Matthews,George (fl,as) | Richardson,Jerome (fl,ts) | Nelson,Oliver (fl,ts) | Clark,Arthur (bs) | Butterfield,Don (tuba) | Kelly,Wynton (p) | Jones,Sam (b) | Hayes,Louis (dr) | Olatunji,Babatunde (congas) | Persip,Charles (bongos) | Wilkins,Ernie (arr)

Cannonball Adderley Quintet Plus
New Delhi
NYC, rec. 11.5.1961
Adderley,Julian \'Cannonball\' (as) | Adderley,Nat (co) | Feldman,Victor (vib) | Kelly,Wynton (p) | Jones,Sam (b) | Hayes,Louis (dr)

Eddie Cleanhead Vinson With The Cannonball Adderley Quintet
Hold It
Chicago,Ill, rec. 19.9.1961
Vinson,Eddie 'Cleanhead' (as,voc) | Adderley,Julian \'Cannonball\' (as) | Adderley,Nat (co) | Zawinul,Joe (p) | Jones,Sam (b) | Hayes,Louis (dr)

Cannonball Adderley Sextet
Introduction by Cannonball Adderley | Gemini
Live at The 'Village Vanguard',NYC, rec. 12.& 14.1.1962
Adderley,Julian \'Cannonball\' (as) | Adderley,Nat (co) | Lateef,Yusef (fl,ts,oboe) | Zawinul,Joe (p) | Jones,Sam (b) | Hayes,Louis (dr)
Never Say Yes
Live at The Jazz Workshop,San Francisco,CA, rec. 21.9.1962
Adderley,Julian \'Cannonball\' (as) | Adderley,Nat (co) | Zawinul,Joe (p) | Jones,Sam (b) | Hayes,Louis (dr)

Nat Adderley Sextet
Sister Wilson
New Orleans,Louisiana, rec. 9.5.1962
Adderley,Nat (co) | Adderley,Julian \'Cannonball\' (as) | Perrilliat,Nat (ts) | Marsalis,Ellis (p) | Jones,Sam (b) | Black,James (dr)

Cannonball Adderley Sextet
Jive Samba | Easy To Love | Tengo Tango
Live at Sankei Hall,Tokyo,Japan, rec. 14./15.7.1963
Adderley,Julian \'Cannonball\' (as) | Adderley,Nat (co) | Lateef,Yusef (fl) | Zawinul,Joe (p) | Jones,Sam (b) | Hayes,Louis (dr)
Inside Straight
Berkeley,CA, rec. 4.6.1973
Adderley,Julian \'Cannonball\' (as) | Adderley,Nat (co) | Galper,Hal (el-p) | Booker,Walter (b) | McCurdy,Roy (dr) | Ericson,King (perc)

Joe Williams With The Cannonball Adderley Sextet
Who She Do
Berkeley,CA, rec. 7.8.1973
Williams,Joe (voc) | Adderley,Julian \'Cannonball\' (as) | Duke,George (p) | Booker,Walter (b) | Kaye,Carol (el-b) | McCurdy,Roy (dr) | Ericson,King (congas)

Cannonball Adderley Duo
The King And I(part 1 from Suite Cannon)
details unknown, rec. ca.1974
Adderley,Julian \'Cannonball\' (as) | Ericson,King prob. (congas)
Oh Bess Where's My Bess
Adderley,Julian \'Cannonball\' (ss) | Jones,Jimmy (p)

Raul De Souza Orchestra
Canto De Ossanha
Berkeley,CA, rec. October 1974
De Souza,Raoul (tb) | Young,Eugene \'Snooky\' (fl-h) | Brashear,Oscar (fl-h) | Bohanon,George (tb,bar-h) | Waldrop,Don (tb,bar-h) | Richardson,Jerome (reeds) | Adderley,Julian \'Cannonball\' (ss) | Shihab,Sahib (reeds) | Davis,Richard (b) | DeJohnette,Jack (dr) | Nash,Kenneth (perc) | Moreira,Airto (perc) | Johnson,J.J. (arr)

Cannonball Adderley Sextet
Sack O'Woe | Walk Tall- | Mercy, Mercy, Mercy-
Berkeley,CA, rec. March/April 1975
Adderley,Julian \'Cannonball\' (as) | Adderley,Nat (co) | Duke,George (keyboards,synth) | Jones,Sam (b) | Hayes,Louis (dr) | Moreira,Airto (perc)

FANCD 6088-2 | CD | Jazzin' Vol.2: The Music Of Stevie Wonder | EAN 090204923236
FANCD 6088-1(LP) | 2 LP | Jazzin' Vol.2: The Music Of Stevie Wonder | EAN 090204923243

Freddie Cole
Isn't She Lovely
details unknown, rec. 1994
Cole,Freddy (voc) | Stripling,Byron (tp) | Eubanks,Robin (tb) | Hart,Antonio Maurice (as) | Jackson,Javon (ts) | Chestnut,Cyrus (p) | Hubbard,Tom (b) | Israel,Yoron (dr)

Woody Herman And His Orchestra
Don't Worry 'Bout A Thing
details unknown, rec. 1975
Herman,Woody (cl,ss,as) | Stahl,Dave (tp) | Hatt,Nelson (tp) | Powers,Buddy (tp) | Dotson,Dennis (tp) | Byrne,Billy (tp,fl-h) | Pugh,Jim (tb) | Kirkland,Dale (tb) | Wiester,Vaughn (b-tb) | Tiberi,Frank (fl,ts) | Anderson,Gary (fl,ts) | Herbert,Greg (fl,ts) | Oslawski,John (bs) | LaVerne,Andy (el-p) | Paley,Ron (b) | Brillinger,Jeff (dr) | Nash,Kenneth (perc)

Ron Holloway-Paul Bollenback
You And I
details unknown, rec. 1996
Holloway,Ron (ts) | Bollenback,Paul (g)

Ella Fitzgerald With The Tommy Flanagan Trio
You Are The Sunshine Of My Life
Live at The Montreux Jazz Festival, rec. 1977
Fitzgerald,Ella (voc) | Flanagan,Tommy (p) | Betts,Keter (b) | Durham,Bobby (dr)

Jimmy Ponder Quartet
Superstition
NYC, rec. 1983
Ponder,Jimmy (g) | Tucker,Mickey (p) | West,Paul (b) | Jones,Victor (dr)

Joe Pass Sextet
I Can't Help It
NYC, rec. 1985
Pass,Joe (g) | Grusin,Don (el-p) | Pisano,John (g) | Laboriel,Abe (b) | Mason,Harvey (dr) | Da Costa,Paulinho (perc)

David Fathead Newman Septet
I Am Singing
Englewood Cliffs,NJ, rec. 1977
Newman,David Fathead (as) | Cables,George (el-p) | Ruiz,Hilton (el-p) | Davis,George (g) | Ritenour,Lee (g) | Bascomb,Wilbur (b) | Muhammad,Idris[Leo Morris] (dr)

Mongo Santamaria And His Orchestra
You've Got It Bad Girl
details unknown, rec. 1995
Santamaria,Mongo (congas) | Allen,Eddie E.J. (tp) | Martin,Mel (fl) | Byam,Roger Gordon (ts) | De Bellis,Robert (fl,as,bs) | Hernandez,Oscar (keyboards) | Benitez,John (b) | Ameen,Robert 'Robbie' (dr) | Bauzo,Louis (perc) | Askew,Greg (chekere) | Almendra,John Andreu (perc,timbales) | Berrios,Steve (checkere,perc)

Luis Gasca Group
Visions
details unknown, rec. 1975
Gasca,Luis (tp) | Rosolino,Frank (tb) | Draper,Ray (tuba) | Menza,Don (sax) | Rushen,Patrice (keyboards) | Mason,Harold (dr)

Gary Bartz Ntu Troop
Black Maybe
Englewood Cliffs,NJ, rec. 1972
Bartz,Gary (as) | Bey,Andy (el-p,voc) | James,Stafford (b) | King,Howard (dr)

Joe Henderson Group
My Cherie Amour
NYC, rec. 1975
Henderson,Joe (ts) | Brashear,Oscar (tp,fl-h) | Young,Eugene 'Snooky' (tp,fl-h) | Bohanon,George (tb) | Waldrop,Don (b-tb,tuba) | Caliman,Hadley (fl,ts) | Duke,George (el-p,synth,clavinet) | Carter,Ron (el-b) | Mason,Harold (dr) | Summers,Bill (perc)

Art Pepper-George Cables Duo
Isn't She Lovely
NYC, rec. 1982
Pepper,Art (cl,as) | Cables,George (p)

Charles McPherson Quartet
My Cherie Amour
Englewood Cliffs,NJ, rec. 1969
McPherson,Charles (as) | Harris,Barry (p) | Williams,Buster (b) | Brooks,Roy (dr)

Sonny Rollins Sextet
Isn't She Lovely
NYC, rec. 1977
Rollins,Sonny (ts) | Duke,George (p,mini-moog) | Johnson,Charles Icarus (g) | Miller,Byron (b) | Williams,Tony (dr) | Summers,Bill (congas)

FANCD 6090-2 | 3 CD | Sarah Vaughan Birthday Celebration | EAN 090204923540

Sarah Vaughan With John Kirby And His Orchestra
You Go To My Head | I'm Scared | I Could Make You Love Me | It Might As Well Be Spring
NYC, rec. 9.1.1946
Vaughan,Sarah (voc) | Brereton,Clarence (tp) | Bailey,Buster (cl) | Procope,Russell (as) | Kyle,Billy (p) | Kirby,John (b,ld) | Beason,Bill (dr)

Sarah Vaughan With The Jimmy Jones Trio
If This Isn't Love | I'm Afraid The Masquerade Is Over - (I'm Afraid) The Masquerade Is Over | All Of Me | Black Coffee | Poor Butterfly | Linger Awhile | Time- | Tenderly-
Live at Newport,Rhode Island, rec. 7.7.1957
Vaughan,Sarah (voc) | Jones,Jimmy (p) | Davis,Richard (b) | Haynes,Roy (dr)

Sarah Vaughan With Orchestra
Someone To Light Up My Life | Triste | Roses And
Rio De Janeiro,Brazil, rec. 31.10.& 3.-7.11.1977
Vaughan,Sarah (voc) | Caymmi,Danilo (fl,voc) | Jobim,Paulo (fl) | Delmiro,Helio (g) | Einhorn,Mauricio (harm) | Angelo,Nelson (el-g) | Frederico,Edson (p,arr) | Jobim,Tom (el-p) | Bertrami,Jose Roberto (el-p) | Barroso,Sergio (b) | Betrami,Claudio (b) | Novelli (el-b) | Das Neves,Wilson (dr) | Batera,Chico (perc) | Ariovaldo (perc) | Nascimento,Milton (g,voc)

Sarah Vaughan With Dori Caymmi
Like A Lover(Cantador)
Vaughan,Sarah (voc) | Caymmi,Dori (g,voc)

Sarah Vaughan With The Oscar Peterson Quartet
How Long Has This Been Going On | Teach Me Tonight(alt.take) | I've Got The World On A String | When Your Lover Has Gone | Easy Living
Hollywood,CA, rec. 25.4.1978
Vaughan,Sarah (voc) | Peterson,Oscar (p) | Pass,Joe (g) | Brown,Ray (b) | Bellson,Louie (dr)

Sarah Vaughan-Ray Brown
Body And Soul
Vaughan,Sarah (voc) | Brown,Ray (b)

Sarah Vaughan-Joe Pass
My Old Flame
Vaughan,Sarah (voc) | Pass,Joe (g)

Sarah Vaughan With Orchestra
I Let A Song Go Out Of My Heart(alt.take) | In A Mellow Tone
NYC, rec. 12./13.9.1979
Vaughan,Sarah (voc) | Foster,Frank (ts) | Pizzarelli,Bucky (g) | Wofford,Mike (p) | Simpkins,Andrew (b) | Tate,Grady (dr) | Orchestra | Byers,Billy (arr) | details unknown
In A Sentimental Mood | Black Butterfly | It Don't Mean A Thing If It Ain't Got That Swing
Vaughan,Sarah (voc) | Pizzarelli,Bucky (g) | Wofford,Mike (p) | Simpkins,Andrew (b) | Tate,Grady (dr) | Orchestra | Byers,Billy (arr) | details unknown

Sarah Vaughan With The Mike Wofford Trio
Chelsea Bridge
Vaughan,Sarah (voc) | Wofford,Mike (p) | Simpkins,Andrew (b) | McCurdy,Roy (dr)

Sarah Vaughan With Joe Pass And Mike Wofford
I Ain't Got Nothin' But The Blues | Everything But You
Vaughan,Sarah (voc) | Pass,Joe (g) | Wofford,Mike (p)

Sarah Vaughan And Her Band
Day Dream
Hollywood,CA, rec. 16.8.1979
Vaughan,Sarah (voc) | Reed,Waymon (tp) | Sims,Zoot (ts) | Pass,Joe (g) | Rowles,Jimmy (p) | Simpkins,Andrew (b) | Tate,Grady (dr)
What Am I Here For
Vaughan,Sarah (voc) | Reed,Waymon (tp) | Rowles,Jimmy (p) | Simpkins,Andrew (b) | Tate,Grady (dr)
I Didn't Know About You
Hollywood,CA, rec. 15./16.8.1979
Vaughan,Sarah (voc) | Rowles,Jimmy (p) | Simpkins,Andrew (b) | Tate,Grady (dr)
Rocks In My Bed
NYC, rec. 12./13.9.1979
Vaughan,Sarah (voc) | Vinson,Eddie 'Cleanhead' (as,voc) | Glenn,Lloyd (p) | Crayton,Pee Wee (g) | Walker,Bill (b) | Randell,Charles (dr)
I Got It Bad And That Ain't Good
Vaughan,Sarah (voc) | Reed,Waymon (tp) | Pizzarelli,Bucky (g) | Wofford,Mike (p) | Simpkins,Andrew (b) | Tate,Grady (dr)
Sophisticated Lady
Hollywood,CA, rec. 15./16.8.1979
Vaughan,Sarah (voc) | Wess,Frank (ts) | Pass,Joe (g) | Rowles,Jimmy (p) | Simpkins,Andrew (b) | Tate,Grady (dr)

Milt Jackson Orchestra
Lena And Lenny
Hollywood,CA, rec. 18.1.1978
Jackson,Milt (vib) | Basie,Count (p) | Reed,Waymon (tp) | Biviano,Lyn (tp) | Cohn[Cohen],Sonny (tp) | Minger,Pete (tp) | Hughes,Bill (tb) | Wanzo,Mel (tb) | Wesley,Fred (tb) | Wilson,Dennis (tb) | Turner,Danny (as) | Plater,Bobby (as) | Dixon,Eric (ts) | Hing,Kenny (ts) | Fowlkes,Charlie (bs) | Green,Freddie (g) | Clayton Jr.,John (b) | Miles,Butch (dr) | Vaughan,Sarah (voc)

Sarah Vaughan And The Count Basie Orchestra
All The Things You Are | I Gotta Right To Sing The Blues | Just Friends | If You Could See Me Now | Send In The Clowns | From This Moment On
Hollywood,CA, rec. 16./18.2.&16.5.1981
Vaughan,Sarah (voc) | Basie,Count (p) | Cohn[Cohen],Sonny (tp) | Szabo,Frank (tp) | Cook,Willie (tp) | Summers,Bob (tp) | Carley,Dale (tp) | Hughes,Bill (tb) | Wilson,Dennis (tb) | Wood,Booty (tb) | Mitchell,Grover (tb) | Turner,Danny (as) | Plater,Bobby (as) | Dixon,Eric (ts) | Hing,Kenny (ts) | Williams,Johnny (bs) | Green,Freddie (g) | Simpkins,Andrew (b) | Jones,Harold (dr) | Nestico,Sam (arr) | Ferguson,Audrey (arr)

Sarah Vaughan And Her Band
Bonita | Dreamer | The Smiling Hour
Rio De Janeiro,Brazil, rec. 1.-5.10.1979
Vaughan,Sarah (voc) | Delmiro,Helio (g,el-g) | Simpkins,Andrew (b) | Tate,Grady (dr) | Das Neves,Wilson (perc) | unkn. Brazilian Musicians And Chorus
Dindi | Gentle Rain
Vaughan,Sarah (voc) | Delmiro,Helio (g,el-g) | Simpkins,Andrew (b)

Sarah Vaughan With The Roland Hanna Quartet
The Island | Autumn Leaves | In Love In Vain | You Are Too Beautiful | I Didn't Know What Time It Was | That's All
Hollywood,CA, rec. 1./2.3.1962
Vaughan,Sarah (voc) | Hanna,Sir Roland (p) | Pass,Joe (g) | Simpkins,Andrew (b) | Jones,Harold (dr)

FCD 24755-2 | CD | Black Hawk Nights

Cal Tjader Sextet
Stompin' At The Savoy | I Hadn't Anyone 'Till You | Bill B. | Blue And Sentimental | I Love Paris | A Night In Tunisia
Live at The Black Hawk,San Francisco,CA, rec. December 1958
Tjader,Cal (vib) | Silva,Jose 'Chombo' (ts) | Guaraldi,Vince (p) | McKibbon,Al (b) | Bobo,Willie (dr) | Santamaria,Mongo (congas)
Mambo Terrifico
Live at The Black Hawk,San Francisco,CA, rec. 1959
Tjader,Cal (vib) | Lozano,Rolando (fl) | Hewitt,Lonnie (p) | Venegas,Victor (b) | Bobo,Willie (dr,timbales) | Santamaria,Mongo (congas)

Cal Tjader Quartet
Autumn Leaves | My Romance | Theme From The Bad And The Beautiful | You Stepped Out Of A Dream | Raccoons Strait
Tjader,Cal (vib) | Hewitt,Lonnie (p) | Venegas,Victor (b) | Bobo,Willie (dr,timbales)

FCD 24756-2 | CD | Vince & Bola

Vince Guaraldi-Bola Sete Quartet
Casaba | Mambossa | Star Song | Moon Rays | Days Of Wine And Roses
Los Altos Hill,CA, rec. 1963
Sete,Bola (g) | Guaraldi,Vince (p) | unkn. (b,dr)
El Matador | I'm A Loser | Nobody Else | More (Theme From Mondo Cane) | O Morro Nao Tem(Somewhere In The Hills) | Black Orpheus Suite | People
Los Angeles,CA, rec. 1966
Sete,Bola (g) | Guaraldi,Vince (p) | Marshall,Fred (b) | Granelli,Jerry (dr)

FCD 24758-2 | CD | The Red Rodney Quintets

Red Rodney Quintet
Taking A Chance On Love | Dig This | Red Is Blue | Clap Hands Here Comes Charlie | On Mike | The Song Is You | You And The Night And The Music | Laura | Hail To Dale | Jeffie | I Love The Rhythm In A Riff | Swingin' With Daddy-O
Chicago,Ill, rec. 8.& 27.6.1955
Rodney,Red (tp,voc) | Sullivan,Ira (tp,as,ts) | Simmons,Norman (p) | Sproles,Victor (b) | Haynes,Roy (dr)
Red Wig | The Baron | Smoke Gets In Your Eyes | Coogan's Bluff | This Time The Dream's On Me | If You Are But A Dream | Mark
NYC, rec. 27.9.1951
Rodney,Red (tp) | Ford,Jimmy (as,voc) | Raphael,Phil (p) | Leshin,Phil (b) | Brown,Phil (dr)

FCD 24759-2 | CD | Nat Pierce-Dick Collins-Ralph Burns & The Herdsmen Play Paris

The Herdsmen
Pot Luck | So What Could Be New | Palm Cafe | Just 40 Bars
Paris,France, rec. 23.4.1954
Herdsmen,The | Collins,Dick (tp) | Touff,Cy (bass-tp) | Perkins,Bill (ts) | Hafer,John 'Dick' (ts) | Renaud,Henri (p) | Kelly,Red (b) | Viale,Jean-Louis (dr)
Embarkation | Wet Back In The Left Bank
Paris,France, rec. 5.5.1954
Herdsmen,The | Touff,Cy (bass-tp) | Coker,Jerry (ts) | Burns,Ralph (p) | Gourley,Jimmy (g) | Ingrand,Jean-Marie (b) | Flores,Chuck (dr)
Gypsy | Thanks For You
Herdsmen,The | Touff,Cy (bass-tp) | Burns,Ralph (p) | Ingrand,Jean-Marie (b) | Flores,Chuck (dr)

Nat Pierce/Dick Collins Nonet
Drop The Other Shoe | I'll Never Be The Same | Honey Babe | Easy Living | Keepin' Out Of Mischief Now | Some Of These Days | Blue Lester | The King
Live at Marines' Memorial Auditorium,San Francisco,CA, rec. 27.1.1954
Pierce,Nat (p) | Collins,Dick (tp) | Howell,John (tp) | Touff,Cy (bass-tp) | Coker,Jerry (cl,ts) | Hafer,John 'Dick' (cl,as,ts) | Nimitz,Jack (bs) | Kelly,Red (b) | Gustafsson,Gus (dr)

FCD 24760-2 | CD | The Jazz Scene:San Francisco

Vince Guaraldi Quartet
Calling Dr.Funk | Between 8th And 9th Mission Street
San Francisco,CA, rec. August 1955
Guaraldi,Vince (p) | Dodgion,Jerry (as) | Wright,Eugene 'Gene' (b) | Markham,John (dr)

Ron Crotty Trio
Ginza | The Night We Called It A Day | I'm Afraid The Masquerade Is Over - (I'm Afraid) The Masquerade Is Over
Crotty,Ron (b) | Guaraldi,Vince (p) | Duran,Eddie (g)

Jerry Dodgion Quartet
Miss Jackie's Dish | The Groove
Dodgion,Jerry (as) | Clark,Sonny (p) | Wright,Eugene 'Gene' (b) | Marable,Lawrence (dr)

Charlie Mariano Sextet
My Friend Ethyl | After Coffee | Trouble Is A Man | Let's Get Away From It All | The Thrill Is Gone | The Nymph
San Francisco,CA, rec. March 1953
Mariano,Charlie (as,ts,bs) | Collins,Dick (tp) | Truitt,Sonny (tb,bs) | Wyands,Richard (p) | Alley,Vernon (b) | McDonald,Joe (dr)

Charlie Mariano Quartet
Come Rain Or Come Shine
Mariano,Charlie (as) | Wyands,Richard (p) | Alley,Vernon (b) | McDonald,Joe (dr)

FCD 24761-2 | CD | The Elliot Lawrence Big Band Swings Cohn & Kahn

Elliot Lawrence And His Orchestra
T.N.T. | The Blue Room | My Heart Stood Still | Jeepers Creepers
NYC, rec. 30.1.1956
Lawrence,Elliott (p,arr,ld) | Travis,Nick (tp) | Glow,Bernie (tp) | DeRisi,Al (tp) | Fishelson,Stan (tp) | Bert,Eddie (tb) | Green,Urbie (tb) | Selden,Paul F. (tb) | Miranda,Tony (fr-h) | Marowitz,Sam (as) | McKusick,Hal (as) | Cohn,Al (ts) | Sims,Zoot (ts) | Wasserman,Eddie (ts) | O'Kane,Charles (bs) | Jones,Buddy (b) | Gubin,Sol (dr)
Who Fard That Shot
NYC, rec. 31.1.1956
Lawrence,Elliott (p,arr,ld) | Travis,Nick (tp) | Glow,Bernie (tp) | DeRisi,Al (tp) | Fishelson,Stan (tp) | Royal,Ernie (tp) | Bert,Eddie (tb) | Green,Urbie (tb) | Selden,Paul F. (tb) | Miranda,Tony (fr-h) | Marowitz,Sam (as) | McKusick,Hal (as) | Cohn,Al (ts) | Sims,Zoot (ts) | Wasserman,Eddie (ts) | O'Kane,Charles (bs) | Jones,Buddy (b) | Gubin,Sol (dr)
El's Bells | Blues Alley | Good Wood | Maybe | Moten Swing | Walkin' My Baby Back Home | Alone Together | Between The Devil And The Deep Blue Sea | Hand Made | Ponce | Snapped Cap | Tenderly
Steel Pier,NJ, rec. 16.-21.6.1956
Lawrence,Elliott (p,arr,ld) | Travis,Nick (tp) | Glow,Bernie (tp) | DeRisi,Al (tp) | Fishelson,Stan (tp) | Bert,Eddie (tb) | Zito,Fred (tb) | Selden,Paul F. (tb) | Marowitz,Sam (as) | McKusick,Hal (as) | Cohn,Al (ts) | Wasserman,Eddie (ts) | O'Kane,Charles (bs) | Saunders,Russ (b) | Gubin,Sol (dr)
Hackin' Around
NYC, rec. 9.1.1957
Lawrence,Elliott (p,arr,ld) | Travis,Nick (tp) | Glow,Bernie (tp) | DeRisi,Al (tp) | Fishelson,Stan (tp) | Bert,Eddie (tb) | Zito,Fred (tb) | Welsch,Chauncey (tb) | Marowitz,Sam (as) | McKusick,Hal (as) | Cohn,Al (ts) | Wasserman,Eddie (ts) | O'Kane,Charles (bs) | Jones,Buddy (b) | Gubin,Sol (dr) | Mandell,Johnny (arr)

Music For Swinging Dancers | The Ivy Walk
Lawrence,Elliott (p,arr,ld) | Travis,Nick (tp) | Glow,Bernie (tp) | DeRisi,Al (tp) | Fishelson,Stan (tp) | Stratton,Don (tp) | Bert,Eddie (tb) | Zito,Fred (tb) | Welsch,Chauncey (tb) | Marowitz,Sam (as) | McKusick,Hal (as) | Cohn,Al (ts) | Wasserman,Eddie (ts) | O'Kane,Charles (bs) | Jones,Buddy (b) | Gubin,Sol (dr) | Mandell,Johnny (arr)
Cupcake | Mood Midnight
NYC, rec. 11.1.1957
Lawrence,Elliott (p,arr,ld) | Travis,Nick (tp) | DeRisi,Al (tp) | Fishelson,Stan (tp) | Stratton,Don (tp) | Bert,Eddie (tb) | Green,Urbie (tb) | Welsch,Chauncey (tb) | Marowitz,Sam (as) | McKusick,Hal (as) | Cohn,Al (ts) | Wasserman,Eddie (ts) | Socolow,Frank (ts) | O'Kane,Charles (bs) | Saunders,Russ (b) | Gubin,Sol (dr)
Nightfall | Jazz Lullaby
NYC, rec. 17.9.1957
Lawrence,Elliott (p,arr,ld) | Travis,Nick (tp) | DeRisi,Al (tp) | Fishelson,Stan (tp) | Stratton,Don (tp) | Bert,Eddie (tb) | Byers,Billy (tb) | Dahl,Jimmy (tb) | Miranda,Tony (fr-h) | Pfeiffer,Fred (engl-h) | Marowitz,Sam (as) | Quill,Gene (as) | Cohn,Al (ts) | Socolow,Frank (ts) | O'Kane,Charles (bs) | Saunders,Russ (b) | Gubin,Sol (dr)

__FCD 24762-2 | CD | Gus Mancuso & Special Friends__
Gus Mancuso Quartet
I'm Glad There Is You | The Ruble And The Yen | Goody Goody
Hollywood,CA, rec. June 1956
Mancuso,Gus (bar-horn) | Wiggins,Gerald 'Gerry' (p) | Wright,Eugene 'Gene' (b) | Douglas,Bill (dr)
Ev'ry Time | By The Way | How Do You Like Your Eggs In The Morning? | Every Time We Say Goodbye
San Francisco,CA, rec. November 1956
Mancuso,Gus (bar-horn) | Duran,Eddie (g) | Wright,Eugene 'Gene' (b) | Tjader,Cal (dr)
Gus Mancuso Quintet
Brother Aintz | And Baby Makes Three | A Hatful Of Dandruff
Mancuso,Gus (bar-horn) | Kamuca,Richie (ts) | Guaraldi,Vince (p) | Wright,Eugene 'Gene' (b) | Tjader,Cal (dr)
Love Is A Simple Thing | Monotonous | Scratch My Back | O-Fayces | The Boston Beguine | Guess Who I Saw Today | Love Is Never Out Of Season | I'm In Love With Miss Logan
San Francisco,CA, rec. 22.4.1958
Mancuso,Gus (bar-horn) | Romano,Joe (ts) | Jolly,Pete (p) | Mitchell,Red (b) | Greve,Buddy (dr)

__FCD 24763-2 | CD | The Sandole Brothers__
Sandole Brothers
Wings Over Persia | Magic Carpet | Drums | Arabu
NYC, rec. July 1955
Sandole,Dennis (g,arr) | Farmer,Art (tp) | Russo,Sonny (tb) | LaPorta,John (as) | Macero,Teo (ts) | Barrow,George (bs) | Del Governatore,Al (p) | Hinton,Milt (b) | DeRosa,Clem (dr) | Sandole,Adolphe (arr)
Perhaps One Touch Of | Grenadine | The Tamaret | The Boys From Istanbul | Way Down | Pieces Of Eight
NYC, rec. 1955
Sandole,Dennis (g,arr) | Farmer,Art (tp) | Russo,Sonny (tb) | LaPorta,John (as) | Macero,Teo (ts) | Barrow,George (bs) | Del Governatore,Al (p) | Marshall,Wendell (b) | DeRosa,Clem (dr) | Sandole,Adolphe (arr)
John LaPorta Trio
Darn That Dream | Wrap Your Troubles In Dreams | Dirge For Dorsey | Between The Devil And The Deep Blue Sea
NYC, rec. 24.9.1956
LaPorta,John (cl) | Keller,Jack (p) | DeRosa,Clem (dr)

__FCD 24765-2 | CD | Continuum__
Duke Ellington Orchestra
Drop Me Off In Harlem | Blue Serge | Wave
NYC, rec. 16./17.7.1974
Ellington,Mercer (cond) | Williams,Cootie (tp) | Bolden,James 'Buddy' (tp) | Johnson,Money (tp) | Hall,Barry Lee (tp) | Connors,Chuck (tb) | Prudente,Vince (tb) | Baron,Art (tb) | Minerve,Harold (as) | Spaulding,James (as) | Simon,Maurice (ts) | Ashby,Harold (ts) | Carney,Harry (bs) | Mayers,Lloyd (p) | Ridley,Larry (b) | White,Quentin 'Rocky' (dr)
Happy-Go-Lucky Local
NYC, rec. 12.5.1975
Ellington,Mercer (cond) | Williams,Cootie (tp) | Bolden,James 'Buddy' (tp) | Singleton,Willie (tp) | Hall,Barry Lee (tp) | Connors,Chuck (tb) | Prudente,Vince (tb) | Baron,Art (tb) | Minerve,Harold (as) | Simon,Maurice (as) | Ford,Ricky (ts) | Easley,Bill (cl,ts) | Marion,Percy (bs) | Mayers,Lloyd (p) | Ellington II,Edward (g) | Wiggins,J. J. (b) | White,Quentin 'Rocky' (dr)
Jump For Joy | Black And Tan Fantasy | Warm Valley | All Too Soon | Rock Skippin' At The Blue Note | Jeep's Blues | Ko-Ko | Carney | Conga Brava | Blem | Harlem Air Shaft
Chicago,Ill, rec. 6.-7.1.1975
Ellington,Mercer (cond) | Williams,Cootie (tp) | Bolden,James 'Buddy' (tp) | Johnson,Money (tp) | Hall,Barry Lee (tp) | Ladner,Calvin (tp) | Connors,Chuck (tb) | Prudente,Vince (tb) | Baron,Art (tb) | Minerve,Harold (as) | Simon,Maurice (as) | Ashby,Harold (ts) | Ford,Ricky (ts) | Gerasimov,Anatole (ts) | Temperley,Joe (bs) | Mayers,Lloyd (p) | Ellington II,Edward (g) | Wiggins,J. J. (b) | Waits,Freddie (dr)

__FCD 24766-2 | CD | Tour De Force:The Bola Sete Trios__
Bola Sete Quintet
Up The Creek | My Different World | Dilemma | Sweet Thing | If You Return | Samba Do Perroquet | Manha De Carnaval(Morning Of The Carnival) | Brazilian Bossa Galore | You're The Reason | Wagging Along | Ash Wednesday | Without You
NYC, rec. 22.-26.10.1962
Sete,Bola (g) | Tucker,Ben (b) | Bailey,Dave (dr) | Paula,J.D. (perc) | Costa,Carmen (perc)
Bola Sete Trio
Baccara | Moon River | Mambeando | Sky And Sea(Ceu E Mar) | Asturias | Samba De Orfeu | Sad Note(Nota Triste) | Tour De Force | Night Of My Love(A Noite Do Meu Bem) | Bourée
San Francisco,CA, rec. 18.6.1963
Sete,Bola (g) | Schrieber,Fred (b) | Rae,John (dr)

__FCD 24767-2 | CD | Stormy Monday Blues__
Kenny Burrell
Why Did I Choose You
Berkeley,CA, rec. 18.-20.6.1974
Burrell,Kenny (g-solo)
Kenny Burrell Quartet
Stormy Monday Blues(They Call It Stormy Monday) | I'm Afraid The Masquerade Is Over - (I'm Afraid) The Masquerade Is Over
Burrell,Kenny (g) | Wyands,Richard (p) | Heard,John (b) | Goldberg,Richie (dr)
Azure-Te(Paris Blues) | One For My Baby(And One More For The Road) | I Got It Bad And That Ain't Good
Burrell,Kenny (g) | Wyands,Richard (p) | Heard,John (b) | McBrowne,Lennie (dr)
Kenny Burrell Quintet
Three Thousand Miles Back Home | Kim-Den-Strut | Habiba | Quiet Lady
Berkeley,CA, rec. 29./30.1.1975
Burrell,Kenny (g) | Richardson,Jerome (ss,ts) | Lightsey,Kirk (p,el-p) | Gilbert,Stanley (b,el-b) | Marshall,Eddie (dr)

__FCD 24768-2 | CD | Full Circle__
Jackie Cain/Roy Kral Quartet
Humphrey Bogart | Play It Again Sam | As Time Goes By | Bogie | Key Largo | Moanin' Low | Am I Blue | That Fat Man | How Little We Know | Peter Lorre | Hong Kong Blues | Too Marvelous For Words
San Francisco,CA, rec. 14./15.2.1986
Cain,Jackie (voc) | Kral,Roy (p,voc) | McCain,Seward (b) | Moore,Curt (dr)
Jackie Cain-Roy Kral Group
Cherokee | To Jackie And Roy | Line For Lyons
Hollywood,CA, rec. 31.5.-2.6.1988
Cain,Jackie (voc) | Kral,Roy (p,voc) | Candoli,Conte (tp,fl-h) | Watrous,Bill (tb) | Cooper,Bob (ts) | Budwig,Monty (b) | Hamilton,Jeff (dr)
Sleigh Ride In July | Never In A Single Year | Full Circle
Cain,Jackie (voc) | Kral,Roy (p,voc) | Candoli,Conte (tp,fl-h) | Watrous,Bill (tb) | Cooper,Bob (ts) | Perkins,Bill (bs) | Budwig,Monty (b) | Hamilton,Jeff (dr)

__FCD 24771-2 | CD | Our Blues | EAN 025218247122__
Cal Tjader Quartet
S.S.Groove | Goodbye | Moment In Madrid | Love For Sale | Then I'll Be Tired Of You | Theme For Duke
Sacramento City College,CA., rec. 15.2.1960
Tjader,Cal (vib) | Hewitt,Lonnie (p) | Coleman,Eddie (b) | Bobo,Willie (dr)
Cal Tjader Quintet
Cuban Fantasy
Tjader,Cal (vib) | Hewitt,Lonnie (p) | Coleman,Eddie (b) | Bobo,Willie (dr,timbales) | Santamaria,Mongo (congas)
Cal Tjader Quartet
Summertime- | Bess You Is My Woman Now- | Strawberry Woman- | Line For Lyons
San Francisco,CA, rec. 10.4.1957
Tjader,Cal (vib) | Guaraldi,Vince (p) | Wright,Eugene 'Gene' (b) | Torres,Al (dr)
And Baby Makes Three
San Francisco,CA, rec. 11.4.1957
Tjader,Cal (vib) | Guaraldi,Vince (p) | Wright,Eugene 'Gene' (b) | Torres,Al (dr)
Our Blues | When Lights Are Low | That's All | Lover Man(Oh,Where Can You Be?)- | Willow Weep For Me- | Round About Midnight-
San Francisco,CA, rec. 15.4.1957
Tjader,Cal (vib) | Guaraldi,Vince (p) | Wright,Eugene 'Gene' (b) | Torres,Al (dr)

__FCD 24775-2 | CD | Cal Tjader Plays Harold Arlen & West Side Story | EAN 025218247528__
Between The Devil And The Deep Blue Sea | Ill Wind(You're Blowin' Me No Good) | When The Sun Comes Out | Happiness Is A Thing Called Joe | I Got A Right To Sing The Blues | Come Rain Or Come Shine
Los Angeles,CA, rec. 1.6.1960
Tjader,Cal (vib) | Motsinger,Buddy (p) | McKibbon,Al (b) | Bobo,Willie (dr)
Over The Rainbow | Out Of This World | Last Night When We Were Young | The Man That Got Away | Blues In The Night
Los Angeles,CA, rec. 2.6.1960
Tjader,Cal (vib) | Motsinger,Buddy (p) | Mitchell,Red (b) | Rae,John (dr)
Cal Tjader With The Clare Fischer Orchestra
Prologue- | The Jet Song- | Something's Coming | Maria Interlude | Maria | Tonight | America | Cool | One Hand One Heart | I Feel Pretty- | Somewhere-
Los Angeles,CA, rec. 18.10.1960
Tjader,Cal (vib) | Roberts,George (b-tb) | DeRosa,Vince (fr-h) | Decker,James 'Jimmy' (fr-h) | Perissi,Richard 'Dick' (fr-h) | Callender,Red (tuba) | Horn,Paul (fl) | Fischer,Clare (p,celeste,arr,ld) | Mitchell,Red (b) | Holland,Milt (dr) | Manne,Shelly (dr) | Vinci,Gerry (v) | Sosson,Marshall (v) | Clebanoff,Herman (v) | Marino,Amerigo (v) | Malarsky,Leonhard (v) | Barene,Robert (v) | Pepper,Jack (v) | Sugar,Henry (v) | Dinkin,Alvin (v) | Majewski,Virginia (viola) | Gottlieb,Victor (cello) | Gotthoffer,Catherine (harp)

__FCD 24776-2 | CD | Theme And Variations | EAN 090204932405__
John LaPorta Octet
Concertina For Clarinet | Nightly Vigil | Perdido | Triplets,You Say | Small Blue Opus | Little Fantasy | Absente | Washday | En Rapport | Lou's Tune | Fermé La Porta
NYC, rec. 4./5.6.1956
LaPorta,John (cl,as) | Mucci,Louis (tp) | Russo,Sonny (tb) | Barrow,George (bs) | Schlinger,Sol (bs) | Cirillo,Wally (p) | Marshall,Wendell (b) | DeRosa,Clem (dr)
John LaPorta Septet
Theme:Blues Chorale | 1st Variation:Basso Profundo | 2nd Variation:Jazz Canon | 3rd Variation:Tribute To Bird | 4th Variation:Images | 5th Variation:Jazz Fugue | 6th Variation:From The Cool School | 7th Variation:Changing Times | 8th Variation:Two Brothers | 9th Variation:Lucidity | 10th Variation:Forward Motion | 11th Variation:Nuage | 12th Variation:Two For One(Finale) | Theme
NYC, rec. December 1957-January 1958
LaPorta,John (cl,as) | Mucci,Louis (tp) | Russo,Sonny (tb) | Wilcox,Larry (ts) | Cirillo,Wally (p) | Marshall,Wendell (b) | DeRosa,Clem (dr)

__FCD 24777-2 | CD | Cuban Fantasy__
Cal Tjader Sextet
Cuban Fantasy | Tu Crees Que | Silenciosa
Live at The Great American Muisc Hall,San Francisco,CA, rec. 17.6.1977
Tjader,Cal (vib,timbales,perc) | Fischer,Clare (el-p) | Redfield,Bob (el-g) | Fisher,Rob (b) | Riso,Pete (dr) | Sanchez,Poncho (congas,perc)
Guarabe | Tamanco No Samba(Samba Blim) | Descarga Cachao | Manuel Deeghit | Guachi Guaro(Soul Sauce)
Live at The Great American Muisc Hall,San Francisco,CA, rec. 18.6.1977
Tjader,Cal (vib,timbales,perc) | Fischer,Clare (el-p) | Redfield,Bob (el-g) | Fisher,Rob (b) | Riso,Pete (dr) | Sanchez,Poncho (congas,perc)

__FCD 60-013 | CD | The Dave Brubeck Quartet feat. Paul Desmond In Concert__
Dave Brubeck Quartet
Perdido | These Foolish Things Remind Me On You | Stardust | The Way You Look Tonight
Live at Oberlin College, rec. 2.3.1953
Brubeck,Dave (p) | Desmond,Paul (as) | Crotty,Ron (b) | Davis,Lloyd (dr)
I'll Never Smile Again | I Remember You | For All We Know | All The Things You Are | Lullaby In Rhythm
Live at The College Of Pacific,Stockton,CA, rec. 14.12.1953
Brubeck,Dave (p) | Desmond,Paul (as) | Crotty,Ron (b) | Dodge,Joe (dr)

__FCD 79004-2 | CD | Phenix__
Cannonball Adderley Group
High Fly | The Work Song | Sack O'Woe | Jive Samba | This Here | The Sidewalks Of New York
Berkeley,CA, rec. February-April 1975
Adderley,Julian 'Cannonball' (ss,as) | Adderley,Nat (co) | Duke,George | Jones,Sam (b) | Hayes,Louis (dr) | Moreira,Airto (perc) | Strings
Hamba Nami | 74 Miles Away | Walk Tall-
Adderley,Julian 'Cannonball' (ss,as) | Adderley,Nat (co) | Wolff,Mike (keyboards) | Booker,Walter (b,el-b) | McCurdy,Roy (dr) | Moreira,Airto (perc)
Domination | Country Preacher | Mercy, Mercy, Mercy-
Adderley,Julian 'Cannonball' (ss,as) | Adderley,Nat (co) | Wolff,Mike (keyboards) | Duke,George (synth) | Booker,Walter (b,el-b) | McCurdy,Roy (dr) | Moreira,Airto (perc)
Stars Fell On Alabama
Adderley,Julian \'Cannonball\' (as) | Wolff,Mike (p)

__FCD 9647-2 | CD | Blues In The Night-Volume One:The Early Show__
Etta James With The Red Holloway Quartet
Something's Got A Hold On Me | At Last- | Trust In Me- | Sunday Kind Of Love- | I Just Want To Make Love To You | Misty
Marla's M.L.Supper Club,LA, rec. 30./31.5.1986
James,Etta (voc) | Holloway,Red (as,ts,bs) | Otis,Shuggie (g) | Reid,Richard (b,b-g) | Humphrey,Paul (dr)
Etta James With The Red Holloway Quintet
Lover Man(Oh,Where Can You Be?)
James,Etta (voc) | Holloway,Red (as,ts,bs) | Otis,Shuggie (g) | McDuff,Brother Jack (org) | Reid,Richard (b,b-g) | Humphrey,Paul (dr)
Eddie Cleanhead Vinson With The Red Holloway Quartet
Kidney Stew | Railroad Porter Blues
Vinson,Eddie 'Cleanhead' (as,voc) | Holloway,Red (as,ts,bs) | Otis,Shuggie (g) | Reid,Richard (b,b-g) | Humphrey,Paul (dr)
Etta James & Eddie Cleanhead Vinson With The Red Holloway Quartet
Please Send Me Someone To Love
James,Etta (voc) | Vinson,Eddie 'Cleanhead' (as,voc) | Holloway,Red (as,ts,bs) | Otis,Shuggie (g) | Reid,Richard (b,b-g) | Humphrey,Paul (dr)

__FCD 9655-2 | CD | The Late Show-Recorded Live At Marla's Memory Lane Supper Club Vol.2__
Eddie Cleanhead Vinson With Band
Old Maid Boogie | Home Boy
Los Angeles,CA, rec. 30./31.5.1986
Vinson,Eddie 'Cleanhead' (as,voc) | Holloway,Red (as,ts,bs,ld) | Otis,Shuggie (g) | Reid,Richard (b,el-b) | Humphrey,Paul (dr)
Etta James/Eddie 'Cleanhead' Vinson With Band
Teach Me Tonight | He's Got The Whole World In His Hands
James,Etta (voc) | Vinson,Eddie 'Cleanhead' (as,voc) | Holloway,Red (as,ts,bs,ld) | Otis,Shuggie (g) | McDuff,Brother Jack (org) | Reid,Richard (b,el-b) | Humphrey,Paul (dr)
Etta James With Band
Baby What You Want Me To Do | I'd Rather Go Blind | Only Women Bleed | Sweet Little Angel
James,Etta (voc) | Holloway,Red (as,ts,bs,ld) | Otis,Shuggie (g) | McDuff,Brother Jack (org) | Reid,Richard (b,el-b) | Humphrey,Paul (dr)

__FCD 9663-2 | CD | Fine And Mellow__
Ruth Brown With Orchestra
Fine And Mellow | I Ain't Got Nothin' But The Blues | Salty Papa Blues
Hollywood,CA, rec. 1./2.4.1991
Brown,Ruth (voc) | Berry,Bill (co) | Cooper,Frank 'Buster' (tb) | Clayton,Jeff (as) | Riley,Herman (ts) | Nimitz,Jack (bs) | Jones,Rodney (g) | Owens,Frank (p,ld) | Forrester,Bobby (org) | McKibbon,Al (b) | Ferguson,Sherman (dr)
A World I Never Made | I'll Drown In My Own Tears | I'll Be Satisfied
Brown,Ruth (voc) | Berry,Bill (co) | Clayton,Jeff (as) | Riley,Herman (ts) | Jones,Rodney (g) | Owens,Frank (p,ld) | Forrester,Bobby (org) | McKibbon,Al (b) | Ferguson,Sherman (dr)
Knock Me A Kiss | It's Just A Matter Of Time | Don't Get Around Much Anymore | Nothing Takes The Place Of You
NYC, rec. 13.8.1991
Brown,Ruth (voc) | Jones,Virgil (tp) | Easley,Bill (as) | Goines,Victor (ts) | Jones,Rodney (g) | Owens,Frank (p,ld) | Forrester,Bobby (org) | Cranshaw,Bob (b,el-b) | Tana,Akira (dr)

__FCD 9674-2 | CD | A Circle Of Love__
Freddy Cole With Band
Manha De Carnaval(Morning Of The Carnival)
NYC, rec. 26./27.9.1993
Cole,Freddy (voc) | Byrd,Jerry (g) | Willis,Larry (p) | Hubbard,Tom (b) | Berrios,Steve (dr)
A Circle Of Love
Cole,Freddy (voc) | Braden,Don (ss) | Byrd,Jerry (g) | Willis,Larry (p) | Hubbard,Tom (b) | Berrios,Steve (dr)
Angel Eyes | All Too Soon
Cole,Freddy (voc) | Moore,Danny (tp) | Byrd,Jerry (g) | Willis,Larry (p) | Hubbard,Tom (b) | Berrios,Steve (dr)
Temptation
Cole,Freddy (voc) | Ford,Joe (ss) | Byrd,Jerry (g) | Willis,Larry (p) | Hubbard,Tom (b) | Berrios,Steve (dr)
September Morning
Cole,Freddy (voc) | Willis,Larry (p) | Hubbard,Tom (b) | Berrios,Steve (dr)
Never Let Me Go
Cole,Freddy (voc) | Willis,Larry (p)
How Little We Know | I Wonder Who My Daddy Is
Cole,Freddy (p,voc) | Hubbard,Tom (b) | Berrios,Steve (dr)
You're Nice To Be Around
NYC, rec. 5.12.1995
Cole,Freddy (voc) | Martin,Mel (fl) | Locke,Joe (vib) | Chestnut,Cyrus (p) | Mraz,George 'Jiri' (b) | Berrios,Steve (dr)
They Didn't Believe Me | If I Had You
Cole,Freddy (voc) | Chestnut,Cyrus (p) | Mraz,George 'Jiri' (b) | Berrios,Steve (dr)

__FCD 9675-2 | CD | To The End Of The Earth__
To The Ends Of The Earth | I Didn't Mean To Love You
NYC, rec. 6./7.1.1997
Cole,Freddy (voc) | Locke,Joe (vib) | Chestnut,Cyrus (p) | Mraz,George 'Jiri' (b) | Berrios,Steve (dr,perc)
Candy | Should've Been
Cole,Freddy (voc) | Ford,Joe (ss) | Locke,Joe (vib) | Chestnut,Cyrus (p) | Mraz,George 'Jiri' (b) | Berrios,Steve (dr,perc)
I'll Buy You A Star | You Don't Have To Say You're Sorry | Love Walked In
Cole,Freddy (voc) | Chestnut,Cyrus (p) | Mraz,George 'Jiri' (b) | Berrios,Steve (dr,perc)
In The Still Of The Night
Cole,Freddy (voc) | Perowsky,Frank (cl) | Martin,Mel (fl) | Kerr,William (fl,as) | Rosenburg,Roger (b-cl) | Scott,Jeff (fr-h) | Locke,Joe (vib) | Chestnut,Cyrus (p) | Hubbard,Tom (b) | Israel,Yoron (dr) | Berrios,Steve (perc)
Two For The Road- | Close Enough For Love-
Cole,Freddy (voc) | Stripling,Byron (tp) | Eubanks,Robin (tb) | Martin,Mel (b-cl) | Hart,Antonio Maurice (as) | Jackson,Javon (ts) | Locke,Joe (vib) | Chestnut,Cyrus (p) | Hubbard,Tom (b) | Israel,Yoron (dr)
One At A Time | NYC
rec. 6./7.1.1997
Cole,Freddy (voc) | Chestnut,Cyrus (p) | Hubbard,Tom (b) | Israel,Yoron (dr)
For All We Know
NYC, rec. 6./7.1.1997
Cole,Freddy (voc) | Locke,Joe (vib) | Chestnut,Cyrus (p) | Hubbard,Tom (b) | Israel,Yoron (dr)
Once You've Been In Love
NYC, rec. 6./7.1.1999
Cole,Freddy (voc) | Locke,Joe (vib)
I'll Be Seeing You
NYC, rec. 6./7.1.1997
Cole,Freddy (p,voc) | Ford,Joe (ss)

__FCD 9681-2 | CD | Love Makes The Changes__
Freddy Cole With The Cedar Walton Trio And Grover Washington Jr.
Love Makes The Change | The Right To Love
NYC, rec. 6./7.1.1999
Cole,Freddy (voc) | Washington Jr.,Grover (ss,ts) | Walton,Cedar (p) | Mraz,George 'Jiri' (b) | Riley,Ben (dr)
Freddy Cole With The Cedar Walton Trio
On My Way To You | Wonder Why | A Sinner Kissed An Angel | Do You Know Why
Cole,Freddy (voc) | Walton,Cedar (p) | Mraz,George 'Jiri' (b) | Riley,Ben (dr)
Freddy Cole With The Eric Alexander Band
Alone With My Thoughts Of You
Cole,Freddy (voc) | Alexander,Eric (ts) | Walton,Cedar (p) | Mraz,George 'Jiri' (b) | Riley,Ben (dr)
Brother Where Are You
Cole,Freddy (voc) | Alexander,Eric (ts) | Bullock,Hiram (g) | Walton,Cedar (p) | Lee,Will (b) | Williams,David (g) | Washington,Kenny (dr)
Just The Way You Are
Cole,Freddy (voc) | Alexander,Eric (ts) | Bullock,Hiram (g) | Walton,Cedar (p) | Williams,David (g) | Washington,Kenny (dr)
Like A Quiet Storm
Cole,Freddy (p,voc) | Alexander,Eric (ts) | Bullock,Hiram (g) | Williams,David (g) | Washington,Kenny (dr)

__FCD 9682-2 | CD | Charlie Brown's Holiday Hits__
Vince Guaraldi Group
Joe Cool
Los Angeles,CA, rec. details unknown
Guaraldi,Vince (p) | Harrell,Tom (tp) | McCain,Seward (b) | Cronkhite,Glenn (dr)

Surfin' Snoopy
Guaraldi,Vince (p) | Copolla,John (tp) | Snow,Frank (tp) | Duran,Eddie (g) | Firth,Pat (b) | Charlton,Lee (dr)
Heartburn Waltz
Guaraldi,Vince (p) | Gray,John (g) | Budwig,Monty (b) | Pompeo,John (dr)
Track Meet | Camptown Races
Guaraldi,Vince (p) | Duran,Eddie (g) | Marshall,Fred (b) | Granelli,Jerry (dr) | Fitch,Bill (congas) | Velarde.Benny (timbales)
Oh,Good Grief(vocal)
Guaraldi,Vince (p) | Children's Chorus
Charlie Brown Theme | Schroeder | Linus And Lucy | Christmas Time Is Here(vocal) | Christmas Time Is Here
Guaraldi,Vince (p) | Marshall,Fred (b) | Granelli,Jerry (dr) | Children's Chorus
Charlie's Blues | Thanksgiving Theme
Guaraldi,Vince (p) | Harrell,Tom (tp) | Bennett,Chuck (tb) | McCain,Seward (b) | Clark,Mike (dr)
Great Pumpkin Waltz
Los Altos Hill,CA, rec. details unknown
Guaraldi,Vince (p) | Klein,Emanuel (tp) | Gray,John (g) | Budwig,Monty (b) | Bailey,Colin (dr)

FCD 9683-2 | CD | Le Grand Freddy:Freddy Cole Sings The Music Of Michel Legrand
Freddy Cole With Band
You Must Believe In Spring
NYC, rec. 8.12.1994
Cole,Freddy (voc) | Washington Jr.,Grover (ss) | Chestnut,Cyrus (p) | Mraz,George 'Jiri' (b) | Israel,Yoron (dr) | Allen,Sanford (v) | Terry,Lesa (v) | Folson,Eileen M. (cello) | Brown,Alfred (viola) | McIntosh,Tom (arr)
Once You've Been In Love
NYC, rec. 7.1.1997
Cole,Freddy (voc) | Locke,Joe (vib)
On My Way To You
NYC, rec. 6.1.1998
Cole,Freddy (voc) | Walton,Cedar (p) | Williams,David (b) | Washington,Kenny (dr)
Love Makes The Change
NYC, rec. 7.1.1998
Cole,Freddy (voc) | Washington Jr.,Grover (ts) | Walton,Cedar (p) | Mraz,George 'Jiri' (b) | Riley,Ben (dr)
I Will Wait For You
NYC, rec. 14.2.1999
Cole,Freddy (voc) | Soloff,Lew (tp) | Marini,Lou (ts) | Locke,Joe (vib) | Renzi,Mike (p) | Mraz,George 'Jiri' (b) | Tate,Grady (dr)
How Do You Keep The Music Playing
Cole,Freddy (voc) | Marini,Lou (alto-fl) | Locke,Joe (vib) | Renzi,Mike (p) | Mraz,George 'Jiri' (b) | Tate,Grady (dr)
I Will Say Goodbye
Cole,Freddy (voc) | Renzi,Mike (p) | Mraz,George 'Jiri' (b) | Tate,Grady (dr)
Once Upon A Summertime
Cole,Freddy (voc) | Soloff,Lew (tp) | Renzi,Mike (p) | Mraz,George 'Jiri' (b) | Tate,Grady (dr)
The Windmills Of You Mind
Cole,Freddy (voc) | Marini,Lou (alto-fl) | Renzi,Mike (p) | Mraz,George 'Jiri' (b) | Tate,Grady (dr)
Make The World Your Own
Cole,Freddy (voc) | Locke,Joe (vib) | Renzi,Mike (p) | Mraz,George 'Jiri' (b) | Tate,Grady (dr)

FCD 9688-2 | CD | Concerts In The Sun | EAN 090204932764
Cal Tjader Quintet
Walkin' With Wally | My Romance | Sigmund Stern Groove | Day In Day Out | Love For Sale | Goodbye
Live at Santa Monica Civic Auditorium,CA, rec. 27.5.1960
Tjader,Cal (vib) | Hewitt,Lonnie (p) | Coleman,Eddie (b) | Bobo,Willie (dr) | Santamaria,Mongo (congas,bongos)
Walkin' With Wally | My Romance | Sigmund Stern Groove | Day In Day Out | Love For Sale | Goodbye | Raccoons Strait | Cubano Chant | Afro Blue | Tumbao
Live at Civic Auditorium,Santa Monica,CA, rec. 27.5.1960
Tjader,Cal (vib) | Hewitt,Lonnie (p) | Venegas,Victor (b) | Bobo,Willie (dr) | Santamaria,Mongo (congas,bongos)
Live at Waikiki Shell,Honolulu,Hawaii, rec. 7.10.1960
Tjader,Cal (vib) | Hewitt,Lonnie (p) | Venegas,Victor (b) | Bobo,Willie (dr) | Santamaria,Mongo (congas,bongos)
Raccoons Strait | Cubano Chant | Afro Blue | Tumbao
Live at The Waikiki Shell,Honolulu,Hawaii, rec. 7.10.1960
Tjader,Cal (vib) | Hewitt,Lonnie (p) | Venegas,Victor (b) | Bobo,Willie (dr) | Santamaria,Mongo (congas,bongos)

FSA 8431-6 | SACD | A Charlie Brown Christmas | EAN 025218730327
Vince Guaraldi Trio
O Tannenbaum | What Child Is This(Greensleeves) | My Little Drum(Little Drummer Boy) | Linus And Lucy | Christmas Time Is Here | Christmas Time Is Here(vocal) | Skating | Hark! The Herald Angels Sing | Christmas Is Coming | Für Elise | The Christmas Song | Greensleeves
Berkeley,CA, rec. 1964
Guaraldi,Vince (p) | Budwig, Monty or Fred Marshall (b) | Bailey,Colin or Jerry Grannelly (dr) | unkn. (voices)

Fine Music | Georg Löffler Musikverlag

FM 108-2 | CD | Marlene | EAN 4014063410825
Lisa Wahland And Her Trio
Wenn Der Sommer Wieder Einzieht(intro) | Ich Bin Von Kopf Bis Fuß Auf Liebe Eingestellt | Mein Mann Ist Verhindert | Paff, Der Zauberdrachen | Ach, Frl. Annie Wohnt Schon Lang Nicht Hier | Wenn Ich Mir Was | Sei Lieb Zu Mir | I Love Paris | Muss I Denn Zum Städtele Hinaus | Sag Mir Wo Die Blumen Sind | Wenn Der Sommer Wieder Einzieht | Gehst Du Mit Mir Die Strassen Entlang | Ich Bin Von Kopf Bis Fuß Auf Liebe Eingestellt(alt.take)
Unkn.Place and Live at Erdinger Jazztage, rec. ? and 11.11.2002
Wahlandt,Lisa (voc,perc) | Lang,Walter (el-p,claviola,arr) | Diener,Christian (b,el-b) | Eisenhauer,Gerwin (dr,perc,electronics,g,lapsteel-g,arr) | Wadlow,Tommy (p)
-> additional recordings: Cirta Rossbach(recitation), Uli Forster(el-p)

Finladia Jazz | Warner Classics & Jazz Germany

0927-49148-2 | CD | 02 | EAN 809274914828
Alexi Tuomarila Quartet
Tribu | Shades Of Gray | Noadi | Sacrament | Goodbye Little Godfather | Solar | Esperanto | For Example
Pernes Les Fontaines,France, rec. 24.-27.7.2002
Tuomarila,Alexi (p) | Kummert,Nicolas (sax) | Devisscher,Christophe (b) | Verbruggen,Teun (dr)
Bone-Yard Jive
Tuomarila,Alexi (p) | Kummert,Nicolas (sax) | Devisscher,Christophe (b) | Verbruggen,Teun (dr) | Edelmann,Samuli (voc)

Fish Music | Jazz Haus Musik

FM 004 CD | CD | Weimarer Balladen
Ekkehard Jost Ensemble
Komm Auf Die Schaukel,Luise | Auf Den Straßen Zu Singen | Johnny,Wenn Du Geburtstag Hast | Heymann's Alea | Tritt Mir Bloß Nicht Auf Die Schuh | Bei Dir War Es Immer So Schön | Das Gaslied-| Oh Lord Don't Let Them Drop That Atomic Bomb On Me- | Eine Nacht In Monte Carlo | So Oder So Ist Das Leben- | Out Of Weimar-
Live In Giessen, rec. 29.11.1991
Jost,Ekkehard (bs,contrab-cl) | Hellhund,Herbert (tp,fl-h) | Landeck,Detlef (tb) | Orth,Uli (ss,as) | Pfleiderer,Martin (ts) | Kaiser,Wollie (contra-b-cl,ss,ts,bass-sax) | Stein,Gerd (g) | Becker,Manfred (accordeon) | Glawischnig,Dieter (p) | Manderscheid,Dieter (b) | Bonica,Joe (dr) | Nicklaus,Friederike (voc)

FM 005 CD | CD | Von Zeit Zu Zeit
Ekkehard Jost & Chromatic Alarm
Am Sausenden Webstuhl Der Zeit | Ode(an einen Rittmeister der Tonkunst) | Kleine Serenade Für HeHe | Von Teit Zu Zeit | Gingo Biloba | Nordlicht | O.C. | Über Meiner Mütze Nur Die Sterne | Alles In Ordnung | Haste Gesagt | Divertimento Per Cinque
Giessen, rec. 9.-11.4.1993
Jost,Ekkehard (bs,accordeon,contrab-cl,zube-tube) | Winterschladen,Reiner (tp) | Landeck,Detlef (tb) | Manderscheid,Dieter (b) | Bonica,Joe (dr,perc)

FM 006 CD | CD | Out Of Jost's Songbook
Ekkehard Jost Nonet
Rapidité(Départ) | Ich Weiß Auch Nicht,Was Los Ist | Rapidité(Arrivée) | Palestrinas Reise Nach Cadiz | Stieselkick & Dat Walzerle | Mobibobi- | Donald Mu- | Omega Jive- | Rue De Lappe | Oh Hangelstein- | Segeln In Der Wetterau-
Live at Stadtgarten,Köln, rec. 11.6.1994
Jost,Ekkehard (bs,bass-sax,contrab-cl) | Winterschladen,Reiner (tp) | Landeck,Detlef (tb) | Gratkowski,Frank (ss,as) | Kaiser,Wollie (contra-b-cl,ss,ts,bass-sax) | Becker,Manfred (accordeon) | Glawischnig,Dieter (p) | Manderscheid,Dieter (b) | Bonica,Joe (dr,perc)

FM 007 CD | CD | Deep
Ekkehard Jost Quartet
Vallat For Four | Le Lapin | Es Geht Eine Dunkle Wolke Herein | Ist Ein Bauer In' Brunnen Gefall'n | Deep | Ich Hab' Des Nachts Geträumet | Murphy | Lotta Libera | Ich Bin Ein Freier Bauernknecht
Live at Universität,Giessen, rec. 23.1.1997
Jost,Ekkehard (bs,contrab-cl) | Winterschladen,Reiner (tp) | Oberleitner,Ewald (b) | Oxley,Tony (dr)

FM 008 CD | CD | Wintertango
Ekkehard Jost & Chromatic Alarm
Sound Piece 2(Green) | Canto Intervale | Wintertango | Gemischtes Wetter
Universität Giessen, rec. 30.10.1997
Jost,Ekkehard (bs,accordeon,contrab-cl,zither) | Winterschladen,Reiner (tp) | Landeck,Detlef (tb) | Manderscheid,Dieter (b) | Bonica,Joe (dr)
Der Streichholzhändler | Tempi Passati | Backspace
Kunststadion Klein-Sassen, rec. 31.10.1997
Jost,Ekkehard (bs,accordeon,contrab-cl,zither) | Winterschladen,Reiner (tp) | Landeck,Detlef (tb) | Manderscheid,Dieter (b) | Bonica,Joe (dr)
Zatopek | Sound Piece 1(Yellow) | No Calypso Tonight | Sound Piece3(Blue)
Waggonhale Marburg, rec. 1.11.1997
Jost,Ekkehard (bs,accordeon,contrab-cl,zither) | Winterschladen,Reiner (tp) | Landeck,Detlef (tb) | Manderscheid,Dieter (b) | Bonica,Joe (dr)

FM 009/10 CD | 2 CD | Some Other Tapes
Sommer-Jost DuOh!
Il Passo Pesante
Giessen, rec. 2.11.1987
Jost,Ekkehard (b-cl) | Sommer,Günter 'Baby' (perc)
Amman Boutz
Die Ungelösten Fragen Der Sippe Valdez
Live at The Jazz Festival Leipzig, rec. 1.10.1989
Amman Boutz | Hellhund,Herbert (tp) | Jost,Ekkehard (bs) | Manderscheid,Dieter (b) | Bonica,Joe (dr)
Balance
Quasi
Giessen, rec. 25.5.1989
Balance | Jost,Ekkehard (b-cl) | Pape,Winfried (cello) | Geisselbrecht,Peter (p)
Ekkehard Jost Trio
Das Grüne Pferd | Deep Steelze Kick
Giessen, rec. 17.8.1990
Jost,Ekkehard (contra-b-cl,bs) | Manderscheid,Dieter (b) | Sommer,Günter 'Baby' (perc)
Transalpin Express Orchestra
Nun Ruhen Alle Wälder
Giessen, rec. 5.6.1993
Transalpin Express Orchestra | Winterschladen,Reiner (tp) | Landeck,Detlef (tb) | Tramontana,Sebi (tb) | Colombo,Eugenio (as) | Kaiser,Wollie (ts) | Jost,Ekkehard (bs) | Glawischnig,Dieter (p) | Manderscheid,Dieter (b) | Bonica,Joe (dr)
Giessen-Köln-Nonett
La Santa Espina
Giessen, rec. 10.6.1994
Giessen-Köln-Nonet | Winterschladen,Reiner (tp) | Landeck,Detlef (tb) | Colombo,Eugenio (as) | Gratkowski,Frank (as) | Kaiser,Wollie (ts) | Jost,Ekkehard (bs) | Becker,Freddie (accordeon) | Glawischnig,Dieter (p) | Manderscheid,Dieter (b) | Bonica,Joe (dr)
Architektur
Giessen, rec. 27.1.1995
Giessen-Köln-Nonet | Winterschladen,Reiner (tp) | Landeck,Detlef (tb) | Colombo,Eugenio (as) | Gratkowski,Frank (fl) | Kaiser,Wollie (ts) | Jost,Ekkehard (bs) | Becker,Freddie (accordeon) | Glawischnig,Dieter (p) | Manderscheid,Dieter (b) | Bonica,Joe (rain-stick) | Nicklaus,Friederike (voc)
Über Meiner Mütze Nur Die Sterne & The End
Giessen, rec. 10.6.1994
Giessen-Köln-Nonet | Winterschladen,Reiner (tp) | Landeck,Detlef (tb) | Colombo,Eugenio (as) | Gratkowski,Frank (fl) | Kaiser,Wollie (ts) | Jost,Ekkehard (bs) | Becker,Freddie (accordeon) | Glawischnig,Dieter (p) | Manderscheid,Dieter (b) | Bonica,Joe (rain-stick)
Spiegelmensch
Live at Jazzclub Oase,Siegen, rec. 18.1.1995
Giessen-Köln-Nonet | Winterschladen,Reiner (tp) | Landeck,Detlef (tb) | Colombo,Eugenio (as) | Gratkowski,Frank (as) | Kaiser,Wollie (bass-sax) | Jost,Ekkehard (bass-sax) | Becker,Freddie (accordeon) | Glawischnig,Dieter (p) | Manderscheid,Dieter (b) | Bonica,Joe (dr)
Ekkehard Jost-Vinko Globokar
Dos À Dos
Darmstadt, rec. 7.4.1993
Globokar,Vinko (tb) | Jost,Ekkehard (bs)
Ekkehard Jost Quartet
Voyage Noir
Darmstadt, rec. 2.4.1996
Jost,Ekkehard (contra-b-cl) | Globokar,Vinko (tb,electronics) | Kaiser,Wollie (b-cl) | Francois,Jean-Charles (perc)
Ekkehard Jost Trio
Lover Man(dedicated to Mario Schiano)
Giessen, rec. 10.9.1996
Jost,Ekkehard (bs) | Rohde,Kai (b) | Bonica,Joe (dr)
Composizione '92
Teatro Colosseo,Roma, rec. 13.10.1992
Jost,Ekkehard (bs) | Geremia,Renato (ts,p) | Orselli,Mauro (perc)
Transalpin Express Orchestra
Bella Ciao
Giessen, rec. 15.6.1996
Transalpin Express Orchestra | Winterschladen,Reiner (tp) | Landeck,Detlef (tb) | Lottermann,Stefan (tb) | Tremontana,Sebi (tb) | Colombo,Eugenio (ss,as) | Gratkowski,Frank (as) | Kaiser,Wollie (ts) | Jost,Ekkehard (bs) | Becker,Freddie (p) | Manderscheid,Dieter (b) | Bonica,Joe (dr)
Ekkehard Jost Quintet
Zahara De Los Atunes
Giessen, rec. 11.12.1997
Jost,Ekkehard (contra-b-cl,sopranino) | Tremontana,Sebi (tb) | Pape,Winfried (cello) | Manderscheid,Dieter (b) | Michelmann,Joachim (perc)
Ekkehard Jost Quartet
Der Laufende Hase
Live at Jazzclub Katakombe,Hagen, rec. 16.4.1994
Jost,Ekkehard (bs) | Kuchenbuch,Ludolf (ts) | Manderscheid,Dieter (b) | Bonica,Joe (dr)
Chromatic Alarm
Divertimento Per Cinque
Saarbrücken, rec. 10.9.1993
Chromatic Alarm | Winterschladen,Reiner (tp) | Landeck,Detlef (tb) | Jost,Ekkehard (bs) | Manderscheid,Dieter (b) | Bonica,Joe (dr)
Ekkehard Jost Quintet
Ich Bin Ein Freier Bauernknecht | Lonely Langgöns
Giessen, rec. 5.11.1997
Jost,Ekkehard (bs) | Kaiser,Wollie (ts) | Picker,Kai (g) | Manderscheid,Dieter (b) | Bonica,Joe (dr)
Ekkehard Jost Quartet
Cafe Aristoxenos
Giessen, rec. 8.6.1995
Jost,Ekkehard (bs) | Brötzmann,Peter (ts) | Manderscheid,Dieter (b) | Bonica,Joe (dr)
Schnecke Turtur
Giessen, rec. 23.1.1997
Jost,Ekkehard (bs) | Winterschladen,Reiner (tp) | Oberleitner,Ewald (b) | Oxley,Tony (perc)

Fontana | Universal Music Germany

812017-2 | CD | Les Liaisons Dangereuses(Original Soundtrack)
Art Blakey And The Jazz Messengers
No Problem | Valmontana | Miguel's Party | Prelude In Blue(Chez Miguel) | No Problem(take 2) | Weehawken Mad Pad | Valmontana(take 2)
Paris,France, rec. 28./29.7.1959
Blakey,Art (dr) | Morgan,Lee (tp) | Wilen,Barney (ts) | Timmons,Bobby (p) | Merritt,Jymie (b)
Art Blakey-Barney Wilen Quartet
Prelude In Blue(A L'Esquinade)
Blakey,Art (dr) | Wilen,Barney (ss) | Timmons,Bobby (p) | Merritt,Jymie (b)
Art Blakey And The Afrocuban Boys
No Hay Problema | No Hay Problema(take 2)
Blakey,Art (dr) | Timmons,Bobby (p) | Merritt,Jymie (b) | Rodriguez,Johnny (bongos) | Lopez,Tommy (congas) | Rodriguez,Willie (congas)

836305-2 | CD | Ascenseur Pour LÉchafaud
Miles Davis Quintet
Nuit Sur Les Champs-Elysees(4 takes) | Assassinat(3 takes) | Motel | Final(3 takes) | Ascenseur | Le Petit Bal(2 takes) | Sequence Voiture(2 takes) | Generique | L'Assassinat De Carala | Sur L'Autoroute | Julien Dans L'Ascenseur | Florence Sur Les Champs-Elysees | Diner Au Motel | Evasion De Julien | Visite Du Vigile | Au Bar Du Petit Bac | Chez Le Photographie Du Motel
Paris,France, rec. 4./5.12.1957
Davis,Miles (tp) | Wilen,Barney (ts) | Urtreger,René (p) | Michelot,Pierre (b) | Clarke,Kenny (dr)

Foolish Music | Jazz Haus Musik

FM 111186 | LP | God Is A She
FM 211186 | CD | God Is A She
Gabriele Hasler & Foolish Heart
Rebirth | Lila Lullaby | Sunday | You Are So Strong | Steinway And Daughter | Water | God Is A She | Creatoxygenology
Ludwigsburg, rec. September 1986
Hasler,Gabriele (voc) | Degen,Bob (p) | Bründl,Manfred (b) | Schipper,Jörn (dr)

FM 211003 | CD | Love Songs
Gabriele Hasler-Roger Hanschel Duo
Can He Excuse My Wrongs | Dear,If You Change | Change | Who Ever Thinks Or Hope Of Love | Restless | Go,Crystal Tears | Love | My Thoughts Are Wing'd With Hopes | Hopes | Wrongs | Come Again,Sweet Love Doth Now Invite | Tears | Go
St.Nikolai,Lüneburg, rec. 4.-6.5.2003
Hasler,Gabriele (voice) | Hanschel,Roger (as)

FM 211096 | CD | Gabriele Hasler's Rosenstücke
Gabriele Hasler Group
Rosenchor | Rosenrot | Notiz I | Schönes Kind(für Lena-Marie) | Notiz II | Ein Knabe Ist Ein... | Dialog On Lamm | Notiz III | Rosenstück | Leb In Meinem Gamichts | Der 13.Wunsch(Dornröschens Taufe) | Eine Reprise Ist Eine...
WDR Köln, rec. June 1996
Hasler,Gabriele (voice) | Heberer,Thomas (tp) | Huke,Jörg (tb) | Kaiser,Wollie (b-cl,contra-b-cl,ss,ts) | Müller-Hornbach,Susanne (cello) | Wind,Martin (b) | Schipper,Jörn (dr,glockenspiel)

FM 211097 | CD | Familienglück
Gabriele Hasler-Hans Lüdemann-Andreas Willers plus Jörn Schipper
Seinesgleichen: | Strophe I | Kel Enkle O Pender | Strophe II | Eng Leise Nische | Strophe III | Palma Latex Tuteflum | Strophe IV
Odenthal/Köln/Treis, rec. April/Mai 1996 & Juni 1997
Hasler,Gabriele (voc) | Willers,Andreas (g) | Lüdemann,Hans (p) | Schipper,Jörn (dr)

FM 211288 | CD | dAs prOjekT
FM 111288 | LP | dAs prOjekT
dAs prOjekT
Time's A Rhythm | Fly Off | Green Glasses | D.Day For Eric | Trilogie: | Ägypten | Kairo | Led Connossence | Musenkuss | Berlin Babes
Ludwigsburg, rec. August 1988
dAs ptOjekT | Hasler,Gabriele (voice) | Read,Hugo (ss,as) | Willers,Andreas (g) | Heideprlem,Thomas (b) | Schipper,Jörn (dr)

FM 211389 | CD | Listening To Löbering
FM 111389 | LP | Listening To Löbering
Gabriele Hasler Group
Song Hollandaise | Listening To Löbering | Out Of My Mind | Two Spanish Flies | Seven Signs | Ark | Frockles | Lazy Afternoon | Nicaragua | Thank You!!! | Out Of My Mind(2)
Bremen, rec. 28.2.1989
Hasler,Gabriele (voice) | Bründl,Manfred (b) | Schipper,Jörn (dr)

FM 211490 | CD | Gabriele Hasler's Personal Notebook
Page 1 | Explanation For The Not So Successful Life Of Sheep | Esperango | Note(I) | Working Week | Note(II) | Entranced | Note(III) | Well Make It | Grün | Note(IV) | Greenhouse Wife | Tango Reprise
Ludwigsburg, rec. January 1991
Hasler,Gabriele (voc) | Lindvall,Lars (tp,fl-h) | Muthspiel,Christian (tb) | Kaiser,Wollie (b-cl,contra-b-cl,bass-sax) | Schipper,Jörn (dr)

FM 211591 | CD | House In The Country
Cool Blue
The Travelling Suite: | Slow Motion | South Of The Sun | Maitre Baboma | Nicaragua | The Town And Country Suite: | Time's A Rhythm | Over The Hills | House In The Country | The Cool Suite: | The Dance | Being In The Frontline | Basic Structures
Bremen, rec. January 1991
Cool Blue | Marstatt,German (tp,fl-h,bar-horn) | Seidemann,Johannes (fl,alto-fl,cl,ss,as,ts,bs) | Henze,Andreas (b) | Schipper,Jörn (dr,perc,euphonium)
Out Of My Mind
Cool Blue | Marstatt,German (tp,fl-h,bar-horn) | Seidemann,Johannes (fl,alto-fl,cl,ss,as,ts,bs) | Henze,Andreas (b) | Schipper,Jörn (dr,perc) | Hasler,Gabriele (voc)

FM 211793 | CD | Sonetburger-Nach Texten Von Oskar Pastior
Gabriele Hasler-Elvira Plenar-Andreas Willers
Melisme | Womisch Kloi Tomisch | Triftig O Du Triftig | Liminipse | Sonetburger | Pisa Luna | Der Bug Hat Zwei Fübe | Familia Faluta Forte | Knabe Mit Dem Bildnusch | Blunduffel Hendelechs | Lieder Ohne Sorte | Yntest | Lied Der Seemaid
Frankfurt/M, rec. January 1993
Hasler,Gabriele (voice) | Willers,Andreas (g) | Plenar,Elvira (p)

FM 211893 | CD | Spider's Lovesong
Gabriele Hasler-Georg Ruby
Back On Earth | Hotel Dead End | Wordless(I) | Dancing On The Ceiling | Beams | Dialogue(I) | My One And Only Love | Paradox | Dialogue(II) | The New Ark | Wordless(II) | Spider's Lovesong | Bricks
Karlsruhe, rec. March 1993
Hasler,Gabriele (voice) | Ruby,Georg (p,voice)

FM 211993 | CD | Solitude
Blue Room Ensemble
Drop Me Off In Harlem | Creole Love Call

Jazzhaus Köln, rec. April 1993
Blue Room Ensemble | Marstatt,German (tp) | Lottermann,Stefan (tb) | Kaiser,Wollie (b-cl) | Manderscheid,Dieter (cello,b) | Schipper,Jörn (dr,tuba)
Chelsea Bridge | Rabazzo Moderne | Things Ain't What They Used To Be | Caravan- | Minor Circles- | In The Tradition | Strange Inspirations | Come Sunday
Blue Room Ensemble | Marstatt,German (tp,alto-h,co) | Lottermann,Stefan (tb) | Kaiser,Wollie (b-cl,ss,ts) | Manderscheid,Dieter (cello,b) | Schipper,Jörn (dr) | Hasler,Gabriele (voc)
I Think A Lot Of How To Be Smart
Blue Room Ensemble | Lottermann,Stefan (tb) | Kaiser,Wollie (b-cl) | Manderscheid,Dieter (cello) | Schipper,Jörn (dr) | Hasler,Gabriele (voc)
In My Solitude
Manderscheid,Dieter (b) | Hasler,Gabriele (voc)
Desert Places
Marstatt,German (alto-h) | Lottermann,Stefan (tb) | Schipper,Jörn (euphonium)
Increasing Silence
Schipper,Jörn (dr,euphonium)

free flow music | free flow music production

ffm 0191 | CD | I Was Just...
Elvira Plenar Trio
Hi Hat | Clairvoyance II | Chaos' Order | For Samuel B. | Filigree Snippety | Homunculus | Pavane | Beautiful Fractals
Frankfurt/M, rec. 17./18.1.1991
Plenar,Elvira (p) | Kowald,Peter (b) | Betsch,John (dr)

ffm 0291 | CD | Sweet Paris
Alfred 23 Harth Group
Sweet Paris: | Pyramides | Stille Bars- | La Chapelle- | Unberührbarkeit & Vergewaltigung | Oberkampf | Stalingrad | Parrhesia | Des Fetes | Champ-De-Mars | Crimée Rome | Mairie Des Lilas | De St.Cloud- | Cafe Montmartre- | Dauphine | Melancholy Blues- | Invalides- | Sweet & Bitter Little Death
different Places, rec. 1965-1987
Harth,Alfred 23 (saxes) | Rudolph,Lars (tp,g,keyboards,voc) | Wittwer,Stephan (g,electronics) | Wito,Wieth (el-b) | Van Den Plas,Nicole (p) | Van Den Plas,Jean | Kowald,Peter (b) | Lovens,Paul (dr,perc) | Anders,Christoph (el-g,org,synth,perc,sounds,voice) | Schmitt,Uwe (dr) | Beresford,Steve (p,voc) | Richard,Ferdinand (b-g) | Szameitat,Winfried | Otto,Bernd K. (g) | Pauli,Rebecca (narration) | Pehlke,Wolf (writer:letters from Paris) | Bauer,Peter (dr-programming)
-> Note:Das Programm dieser CD ist eine O-Ton-Collage der Stadt Paris.

ffm 0392 | CD | Ballade Noire
Herbert Joos Trio
Ballade Noire | Ballad Medley: | The Shadow Of Your Smile- | When I Fall In Love- | Every Time We Say Goodbye- | Janine | Janine(alt.take) | Heavy Chicken | Heavy Chicken(alt.take) | Amely
Ludwigsburg, rec. 26.12.1991
Joos,Herbert (fl-h,co) | Schwarz,Paul (p) | Koinzer,Joe (perc)

ffm 0493 | CD | POPending EYE
Alfred 23 Harth QuasarQuartet
1st2nd3rd&4th | BukzokWestWostokSude
Live at 'Hindemith-Saal',Alte Oper,Frankfurt/M., rec. 5.12.1992
Harth,Alfred 23 (b-cl,ts) | Nabatov,Simon (p) | Rek,Vitold (b) | Tarasov,Vladimir (dr,perc)

ffm 0594 | CD | Lost Ends:Live at Alte Oper Frankfurt
Heinz Sauer Quintet
Long Note | Prologue From Outside | Floating Circles | Don't Explain | A Tail Of A B-Tune | Vom Himmel Hoch... | Tangent A | Orbital Excursion | Ocean Drive Talk | Come Sunday | Laughing At Dinosaurs | Ich Bin Kein Held,Das Ist Nicht Mein Job(to whom it may concern) | Tangent B | Ruby My Dear | Lost Ends | Long Note(reprise)
Live at 'Hindemith-Saal',Alte Oper,Frankfurt/M., rec. 30.1.1993
Sauer,Heinz (sax,synth) | Lottermann,Stefan (tb) | Becker,Markus (p) | Schmolck,Stefan (b) | Argüelles,Steve (dr)

ffm 0695 | CD | Exchange
Heinz Sauer Trio
Kieser's Exchange | The Narrator | Sequence | Der Wahn Im Grund | ABC | Küss' Die Hand,Madame | Sui Me | D.B.Exchange | Deep River | I'm Grätenwald
Frankfurt/M, rec. May 1995
Sauer,Heinz (sax,synth) | Degen,Bob (p) | Schmolck,Stefan (b,sound-processing)

ffm 0796 | CD | Mondspinner
Ralph R.Hübner-Christoph Lauer
Sechskant | Schausteller | Graugänse Ins Exil | Abschied Im Dezember | Geh' Dahin-Weiß Nicht Wohin
Frankfurt/M, rec. April 1995
Lauer,Christof (ts) | Hübner,Ralf-R. (synth,dr,computer-programming)
Ralph R.Hübner-Christoph Lauer Quartet
Hitzeplanscher | Schummer | Märchenstunde | Die Phasen Der Nacht | Trüblich? | Mondspinner
Lauer,Christof (ts) | Hübner,Ralf-R. (synth,dr,computer-programming) | Sendecki,Vladislaw (p,synth) | Rek,Vitold (b)
Jaycee
Live at The 25. Deutsches Jazz Festival,Frankfurt/M., rec. details unknown
Lauer,Christof (ts) | Hübner,Ralf-R. (synth,dr) | Sendecki,Vladislaw (p,synth) | Rek,Vitold (b)

ffm 0897 | CD | Sandcastle
Bob Degen
At Long Last First | Pier 14 | Etosha | Crape Myrtle | Sandcastle | Secluded Branch | The Other Side Of Five | Faithful
Festeburg Kirche,Frankfurt/M., rec. 23.9.1997
Degen,Bob (p-solo)

ffm 0998 | CD | Exchange 2
Heinz Sauer 4tet
I Let A Song Go Out Of My Heart | Welcome To What You Think You Hear | Roses Are Black | Evidence | Don't Explain | Meadow Bells | Amuse Gueule | Lush Life | Roses Are Black(fast version) | No More Princess | Accelerated Service | Naima | Trouble With Mutation | I Let A Song Go Out Of My Heart(alt.take) | Damals Vor Jahren
Frankfurt/M, rec. 18./19.5.& 28./29.8.1998
Sauer,Heinz (ss,as,ts) | Degen,Bob (p) | Schmolck,Stefan (b,sound-processing) | Ritter,Bertram (dr)

Fresh Sound Records | Fenn Music

FSCD 1031 | 2 CD | Live at The Left Bank Jazz Society,Baltimore,1967 | EAN 8427328610315
Wynton Kelly Trio With Hank Mobley
On A Clear Day You Can See Forever | Hackensack | On Green Dolphin Street | Milestones | If You Can See Me Now | Speak Low
Live at The Famous Ballroom,Baltimore.MD, rec. 12.11.1967
Mobley,Hank (ts) | Kelly,Wynton (p) | McBee,Cecil (b) | Cobb,Jimmy (dr)

FSCD 1032 | 2 CD | Live at The Left Bank Jazz Society,Baltimore,1968 | EAN 8427328610322
Wynton Kelly-George Coleman Quartet
Announcement | Unit 7 | Surrey With The Fringe On Top | On The Trail(From The Grand Canyon Suite) | Mr.P.C. | On A Clear Day You Can See Forever | Here's That Rainy Day | Theme
Live at The Left Bank Jazz Society,Baltimore, rec. 22.9.1968
Coleman,George (ts) | Kelly,Wynton (p) | McClure,Ron (b) | Cobb,Jimmy (dr)

FSCD 145 CD | CD | Wake Up Call | EAN 8427328421454
Taylor Hawkins Group
You Have Everything You Need | Equal Being | Dream With You | Hecuba | Nomads | Parking Lots | Please Be Quiet,Please | Wake Up Call | Ooga Booga | Précipice | Live Free Or Die | Last Poem
Tedesco Studios,?, rec. 2000
Haskins,Taylo | Rathbun,Andrew (reeds) | Monder,Ben (g) | Klein,Guillermo (p) | Street,Ben (b) | Bellantese,Regina (v) | Hirshfield,Jeff (dr) | Yamamoto,Yusuke (perc) | Smith,Aubrey (voc)

FSCD 2015 | CD | Thriller/Richard Diamon(Original Jazz Scores From 2 Classics TV Series) | EAN 8427328620154
Pete Rugolo And His Orchestra
Theme From Thriller | Voodoo Man | Twisted Image | Finger Of Fear | The Man In The Middle
The Guilty Men, rec. 23.2.1961
Rugolo,Pete (cond,arr) | Beach,Frank (tp) | Fagerquist,Don (tp) | Mitchell,Ollie (tp) | Rasey,Uan (tp) | Bernhart,Milton 'Milt' (tb) | Roberts,George (tb) | Rosolino,Frank (tb) | Nash,Dick (tb) | Decker,James 'Jimmy' (fr-h) | DeRosa,Vince (fr-h) | Perissi,Richard 'Dick' (fr-h) | Callender,Red (tuba) | Shank,Bud (fl,piccolo-fl,as) | Klee,Harry (fl,as,piccolo) | Cipriano,Gene (fl,piccolo-fl,ts) | Cooper,Bob (b-cl,ts) | Lang,Ronnie (fl,piccolo-fl,bs) | Rowles,Jimmy (p) | Cockerly,Jack (org) | Bain,Bob (g) | Mondragon,Joe (b) | Stoller,Alvin (dr) | Bunker,Larry (vib,xyl,marimba,perc) | Holland,Milt (vib,perc) | Singer,Lou (perc)
The Hungry Glass | Girl With A Secret | The Purple Room | Rose's Last Summer | Child's Play | Finger Of Fear
Los Angeles,CA, rec. 24.2.1961
Rugolo,Pete (cond,arr) | Bernhart,Milton 'Milt' (tb) | Roberts,George (tb) | DeRosa,Vince (fr-h) | Perissi,Richard 'Dick' (fr-h) | Callender,Red (tuba) | Lang,Ronnie (fl) | Herzberg,Norman (bassoon) | Giovaninni,Caesar (p) | Cockerly,Jack (org) | Bain,Bob (g) | Mondragon,Joe (b) | Mitchell,Red (b) | Stoller,Alvin (dr) | Singer,Lou (perc) | Flynn,Frank (perc) | Clebanoff,Herman (v) | Kaminsky,Anatol (v) | Freed,Sam (v) | Neufeld,Erno (v) | Raderman,Lou (v) | Kaproff,Armand (v) | Murray,Alex (v) | Limonick,Marvin (v) | Neumann,Irma (v) | Gill,Ben (v) | Russo,Ambrose (v) | Herbert,Mort (v) | Klass,Lou (v) | Miller,William (v) | Pepper,Jack (v) | Trebacz,Leon (v) | Lustgarten,Edgar 'Ed' (cello) | Kramer,Raphael (cello) | Kaproff,Armand (cello) | Slatkin,Eleanor (cello) | DiTullio,Justin (cello) | Manahan,Marie (cello) | Saxon,Joseph (cello) | Schneier,Harold (cello)
Diamonds On The Move | I'm Always Chasing Butterflies | The Teaser | Does Mama Know You're Out?
Hollywood,CA, rec. 9.4.1959
Rugolo,Pete (cond,arr) | Linn,Ray (tp) | Childers,Buddy (tp) | Salko,Jim (tp) | Mangano,Vito (tp) | Rosolino,Frank (tb) | Howard,Joe (tb) | Roberts,George (tb) | Sherry,Claude (fr-h) | Horn,Paul (fl,piccolo-fl,as) | Shank,Bud (fl,piccolo-fl,as) | Collette,Buddy (fl,cl,ts) | Cooper,Bob (b-cl,ts) | Issenhuth,Dale (bs) | Rowles,Jimmy (p) | Viola,Al (g) | Lustgarten,Edgar 'Ed' (cello) | Stephens,Phil (b) | Bundock,Rowland 'Rolly' (b) | Kluger,Irv (dr) | Bunker,Larry (vib,perc)
Richard Diamond Theme | Fancy Meeting Karen | Teen Age Rock | Richard Diamond's Blues
Hollywood,CA, rec. 10.3.1959
Rugolo,Pete (cond,arr) | Candoli,Pete (tp) | Triscari,Joe (tp) | Williamson,Stu (tp) | Mitchell,Ollie (tp) | Bernhart,Milton 'Milt' (tb) | Fitzpatrick,Francis (tb) | Rosolino,Frank (tb) | Roberts,George (tb) | Horn,Paul (fl,piccolo-fl,as) | Shank,Bud (fl,piccolo-fl,as) | Cooper,Bob (b-cl,ts) | Gentry,Chuck (bs) | Rowles,Jimmy (p) | Viola,Al (g) | Lustgarten,Edgar 'Ed' (cello) | Mitchell,Red (b) | Manne,Shelly (dr) | Mattinson,Edward (vib,perc)
Who's Sam? | All Star | Ye Olde Curiosity Shape | The Sleeve Job
Hollywood,CA, rec. 31.3.1959
Rugolo,Pete (cond,arr) | Candoli,Pete (tp) | Triscari,Joe (tp) | Childers,Buddy (tp) | Fagerquist,Don (tp) | Bernhart,Milton 'Milt' (tb) | Rosolino,Frank (tb) | Roberts,George (tb) | DeRosa,Vince (fr-h) | Horn,Paul (fl,piccolo-fl,as) | Shank,Bud (fl,piccolo-fl,as) | Cooper,Bob (b-cl,ts) | Issenhuth,Dale (bs) | Rowles,Jimmy (p) | Viola,Al (g) | Lustgarten,Edgar 'Ed' (cello) | Mitchell,Red (b) | Stephens,Phil (b) | Manne,Shelly (dr) | Bunker,Larry (vib,xyl,perc)

FSNT 001 CD | CD | Lluis Vidal Piano Solo
Lluis Vidal
En Joan Petit | Bolero | Divertiment | No Ni No | El Agarejo | Primavera 1986 | Ocre
Barcelona,Spain, rec. 16./17.12.1991
Vidal,Lluis (p-solo)

FSNT 002 CD | CD | Paris-Barcelona Connection
Frank Wess Meets The Paris-Barcelona Swing Connection
Hi, Mr.Wess | Bluesin' In Cadaques | Shiny Stockings | In A Sentimental Mood | Tickle Toe | Close Your Eyes | The Midgets | Natacha's Blues | Always | Ellington Ballad Medley: | Prelude To A Kiss- | Star Crossed Lovers- | Shufflin'
Paris/Berikon,CH, rec. 20./21.5.1992
Paris-Barcelona Swing Connection | Artero,Patrick (tp,fl-h) | Berthenet,Gilles (tp) | Lhiver,Thierry (tb) | Wess,Frank (fl,ts) | Chagne,Philippe (as,ts,bs) | Vernhes,Dominique (cl,ts) | Bordas,Oriol (as,vib,ld) | Duchemin,Philippe (p) | Fossati,Ramon (g,el-g) | Rebillard,Jean-Pierre (b) | Roger,Stephane (dr)

FSNT 003 CD | CD | Tren Nocturn
Lluis Vidal Trio
El Escatime | El Agarejo | Ocre | Blau De Nit | Canco De No Fer Res | Suite De Nadal: | El Petit Bailet- | El Dimoni Escuat- | El Rabada-
Barcelona,Spain, rec. 18./19.12.1991
Vidal,Lluis (p) | Gaspar,Jordi (b) | Xirgu,David (dr)

FSNT 004 CD | CD | Es La Historia De Un Amor
Eladio Reinon Quintet
La Cita | Like Someone In Love
Barcelona,Spain, rec. 9./10.11.1992
Reinon,Eladio (ts) | Simon,Matthew L. (tp) | Bover,Albert (p) | Rossy,Mario (b) | Muhammad,Idris[Leo Morris] (dr)
Infant Eyes
Reinon,Eladio (ts) | Bover,Albert (p) | Rossy,Mario (b) | Muhammad,Idris[Leo Morris] (dr)
Mr.Henderson
Reinon,Eladio (ts) | Leavitt,Sean (g) | Bover,Albert (p) | Rossy,Mario (b) | Muhammad,Idris[Leo Morris] (dr)
Stablemates | En-Mocion
Reinon,Eladio (ts) | Simon,Matthew L. (tp) | Montoliu,Tete (p) | Rossy,Mario (b) | Muhammad,Idris[Leo Morris] (dr)
Body And Soul
Reinon,Eladio (ts) | Montoliu,Tete (p) | Rossy,Mario (b) | Muhammad,Idris[Leo Morris] (dr)
Historia De Amor (Love Story)
Reinon,Eladio (ts) | Montoliu,Tete (p) | Rossy,Mario (b) | Muhammad,Idris[Leo Morris] (dr) | Bejar,Quino (pailas) | Gomez,Pere (congas) | Mercader,Nan (bongos)

FSNT 005 CD | CD | Shell Blues
Mitchell-Terraza Group
Why Don't | Boo Boo's Back In Town | Funk In Deep Freeze | Shell Blues | The Cat
Barcelona,Spain, rec. 26./27.11.1992
Mitchell,David (g) | Leff,Jim (tb) | Lalama,Ralph (ts) | Terraza,Ignasi (p) | Fernandez,Nono (b) | Bombardo,Pau (dr)
I Thought About You
Lalama,Ralph (ts) | Terraza,Ignasi (p) | Fernandez,Nono (b) | Bombardo,Pau (dr)
Anna | Silvering
Leff,Jim (tb) | Lalama,Ralph (ts) | Terraza,Ignasi (p) | Fernandez,Nono (b) | Bombardo,Pau (dr)

FSNT 006 CD | CD | Dr.Jeckyl
José Luis Gámez Quartet
Will You Still Be Mine | Impressions | Duke Ellington's Sound Of Love
Barcelona,Spain, rec. 20.1.1993
Gámez,José Luis (g) | Bover,Albert (p) | Rossy,Mario (b) | Rossy,Jorge 'Jordi' (dr)
Gotta Dance
Gámez,José Luis (g) | Sambeat,Perico (as) | Rossy,Mario (b) | Rossy,Jorge 'Jordi' (dr)
José Luis Gámez Quintet
R.B. | Klact-Oveedseds-Tene | Guybrush Reggae N'Blues | Parisian Thoroughfare | Salvese Quien Pueda
Gámez,José Luis (g) | Sambeat,Perico (ss,as) | Bover,Albert (p) | Rossy,Mario (b) | Rossy,Jorge 'Jordi' (dr)

FSNT 007 CD | CD | When I Fall In Love
Mehldau & Rossy Trio
Anthropology | A La Loss | When I Fall In Love | Countdown | Convalescent | I Fall In Love Too Easily | I Didn't Know What Time It Was
Barcelona,Spain, rec. 9./10.10.1993
Mehldau,Brad (p) | Rossy,Mario (b) | Rossy,Jorge 'Jordi' (dr)

FSNT 008 CD | CD | Regards From Norma Desmond
Vinny Golia Quintet
Teribee,Three Palm Slammy | The Cry(for Booker Little) | 3 Things For The Practitioner- | Sent A Message- | Professor Mackel's Famous Ride- | It's Played Slowly-
Los Angeles,CA, rec. 15.10.1986
Golia,Vinny (bs) | Fuma,John (tp) | Peet,Wayne (p) | Filano,Ken (b) | Cline,Alex (dr)

FSNT 009 CD | CD | Milikituli
Lluis Vidal Trio
Milikituli | Havanera | La Meva Enamorada | D'Ara Endavant | Ball De Capvespre | Verd Mari | Els Miquelets D'Espanya | I Can't See The Beautiful Codillo
Barcelona,Spain, rec. 5./6.12.1994
Vidal,Lluis (p) | Gaspar,Jordi (b) | Xirgu,David (dr)

FSNT 011 CD | CD | Rosebud
Manel Camp & Matthew Simon Acustic Jazz Quintet
Desassossec | Pas A Pas | Un Negre Amb Un Saxo | Rosebud | Envottats De Boira | M x M
Barcelona,Spain, rec. 9.-11.10.1995
Simon,Matthew L. (tp,fl-h) | Camp,Manel (p) | Figuerola,Xavier (ss,ts) | Fumero,Horacio (b) | Mercader,Nan (perc)
Un Perfil A L'Horitzó
Simon,Matthew L. (tp) | Camp,Manel (p)

FSNT 012 CD | CD | Amaia
Victor De Diego Group
Vamonos | No Dispareu Contra El Baixista | Dlidi Clidi | Amaia | Fast Dance | Tres Para S.
Barcelona,Spain, rec. 13./14.5.1996
De Diego,Victor (ts) | Palet,Benet (tp) | Bover,Albert (p) | Ferrer,Raimon 'Rai' (b) | Caviglia,Aldo (dr)
Love Is A Many-Splendored Thing | En Condicions | In A Sentimental Mood- | My One And Only Love- | Blues In The Closet
De Diego,Victor (ts) | Bondell,Jordi (g) | Ferrer,Raimon 'Rai' (b) | Caviglia,Aldo (dr)
Take The Coltrane
De Diego,Victor (ts) | Ferrer,Raimon 'Rai' (b) | Caviglia,Aldo (dr)
It's Easy To Remember
De Diego,Victor (ts) | Bover,Albert (p)

FSNT 013 CD | CD | For Good
Ben Waltzer Trio
Ian's Move | Rain | Bright Mississippi | Two People | For Good | Skylark | Home Away From Home | Sketch | Secret Love
NYC, rec. 30.4.& 18.6.1996
Waltzer,Ben (p) | Anderson,Reid (b) | Rossy,Jorge 'Jordi' (dr)

FSNT 014 CD | CD | Introducing Carme Canela
Carme Canela With The Joan Monné Trio
Speak Low | I Didn't Know What Time It Was | Estels Foscos En Un Cel Tan Clar | Vera Cruz | Es Mold Tard | You Don't Know What Love Is | Isn't It A Pity | Afro Blue | Walking On The Moon | Ribbon In The Sky | Madalena
Barcelona,Spain, rec. 24./25.6.1996
Canela,Carme (voc) | Monné,Joan (p) | Ferrer,Raimon 'Rai' (b) | Xirgu,David (dr)

FSNT 015 CD | CD | San
Joaquin Chacón Group
November Song | Manuel
Madrid, Spain, rec. October 1995
Chacón,Joaquin (g,12-string-g,el-g) | Markussen,Uffe (ts) | Dominguez,Chano (p) | Ibanez,Carlos (b) | Barroso,Juan M. (dr)
Lamento
Chacón,Joaquin (g,el-g) | Pardo,Jorge (ss) | Dominguez,Chano (p) | Ibanez,Carlos (b) | Barroso,Juan M. (dr)
Otono | Gris | Momentos Dificiles
Chacón,Joaquin (g) | Markussen,Uffe (b-cl,ts) | Perez,Alejandro (ss,ts) | Salvador,Inaki (p) | Ibanez,Carlos (b) | Barroso,Juan M. (dr)
Segundo Plano | Ultima Hora
Chacón,Joaquin (g) | Markussen,Uffe (ts) | Salvador,Inaki (p) | Ibanez,Carlos (b) | Barroso,Juan M. (dr)
Politicos | Otro Comienzo
Chacón,Joaquin (g,el-g) | Markussen,Uffe (b-cl,ts) | Ibanez,Carlos (b) | Barroso,Juan M. (dr)
Old Folks
Chacón,Joaquin (g) | Ibanez,Carlos (b) | Barroso,Juan M. (dr)
Dueto
Chacón,Joaquin (g) | Salvador,Inaki (p)

FSNT 016 CD | CD | East Coast Love Affair
Kurt Rosenwinkel Trio
East Coast Love Affair | All Or Nothing At All | Turn Out The Stars | Pannonia | Lazy Bird | Round About Midnight | Little White Lies | B Blues
Live at Smalls Jazz Club,NYC, rec. 10.& 24.7.1996
Rosenwinkel,Kurt (g) | Cohen,Avishai (b) | Rossy,Jorge 'Jordi' (dr)

FSNT 017 CD | CD | Tot Just
Pep O'Callaghan Grup
Vaccio | Shades | Reggae Boats | Sleep Tight
Barcelona,Spain, rec. 17./18.9.1996
O'Callaghan,Pep (g,el-g) | Andueza,Mikel (ss,as) | Monné,Joan (p) | Ferrer,Raimon 'Rai' (b) | Xirgu,David (dr)
El Pla De La Calma
O'Callaghan,Pep (g,el-g) | Monné,Joan (p) | Ferrer,Raimon 'Rai' (b) | Xirgu,David (dr)
Tot Just
O'Callaghan,Pep (g,el-g) | Andueza,Mikel (as) | De Diego,Victor (ts) | Monné,Joan (p) | Ferrer,Raimon 'Rai' (b) | Xirgu,David (dr)
Els Vells Temps
O'Callaghan,Pep (g,el-g) | Monné,Joan (p) | 'Cucurel.La',Josep (fretless-b) | Xirgu,David (dr)

FSNT 018 CD | CD | Triangles
Elisabet Raspall Quintet
Cada 2x3 | Sorra I Escuma | Soham | Distàncies | Togo | El Cel Puja | Els Angles Triangles | Secret | N'hi Ha Un Altre
Barcelona,Spain, rec. 2./3.7.1996
Raspall,Elisabet (p) | Palet,Benet (tp) | Cheek,Chris (ss,ts) | 'Cucurel.La',Josep (el-b) | Miralta,Marc (dr)

FSNT 019 CD | CD | Monkiana:A Tribute To Thelonious Monk
David Mengual Quartet
Boo Boo's Birthday | Bye-Ya | Brilliant Corners | In Walked Bud | Ruby My Dear | Straight No Chaser | Bemsha Swing | Mi Querido Monk...
Barcelona,Spain, rec. 11.& 21.10.1996
Mengual,David (b) | Hogue,Norman (tb,voc) | De Diego,Victor (ts) | Krause,Jo (dr)
Trinkle Tinkle | Ask Me Now
Mengual,David (b) | De Diego,Victor (ts) | Robles,Ion (ts) | Krause,Jo (dr)
David Mengual Quintet
Monk's Mood
Mengual,David (b) | Hogue,Norman (tb) | Robles,Ion (ts) | De Diego,Victor (ts) | Krause,Jo (dr)

FSNT 020 CD | CD | Come Rain Or Come Shine
Georgina Weinstein With Her Trio
It Don't Mean A Thing If It Ain't Got That Swing
Barcelona,Spain, rec. 22./23.9.1996
Weinstein,Georgina (voc) | Waltzer,Ben (p) | Mengual,David (b) | Rossy,Jorge 'Jordi' (dr)
Georgina Weinstein With Her Quartet
Come Rain Or Come Shine | You Go To My Head | Skylark | You Stepped Out Of A Dream | It Could Happen To You | Lover Man(Oh,Where Can You Be?) | My One And Only Love

LABELVERZEICHNIS

Weinstein,Georgina (voc) | Cheek,Chris (ts) | Waltzer,Ben (p) | Mengual,David (b) | Rossy,Jorge 'Jordi' (dr)
What Is This Thing Called Love | I'm A Fool To Want You
Weinstein,Georgina (voc) | Reinon,Eladio (ts) | Waltzer,Ben (p) | Mengual,David (b) | Rossy,Jorge 'Jordi' (dr)

FSNT 021 CD | CD | Jazz Is Where You Find It
The Waltzer-McHenry Quartet
Time On My Hands | Suddenly It's Spring | Eix | Two Degrees East Three Degrees West | Greenwich | The Touch Of Your Lips | The Thick Plottens | Quasimodo | As Long As There's Music
Live at The Pipa Club,Barcelona,Spain, rec. 13./14.3.1997
McHenry,Bill (ts) | Waltzer,Ben (p) | Cuadrado,Alexis (b) | Krause,Jo (dr)

FSNT 022 CD | CD | I Wish I Knew
Chris Cheek Quartet
I Wish I Knew | At Long Last Love | Skylark | Stairway To The Stars | I'll Be Seing You | Garden Floor | Time Remembered | I Don't Want To Set The World On Fire | What'll I Do
Brooklyn,NY, rec. October 1996 & January 1997
Cheek,Chris (ts) | Rosenwinkel,Kurt (g) | Higgins,Chris (b) | Rossy,Jorge 'Jordi' (dr)

FSNT 023 CD | CD | Alguimia 'U'
Alguimia
Mason Changes | De Moment Una Samba | Noctum | Faustus | La Broma | Wayne | Birds And Flies | Alta Fidelitat | La Rateta Que Escombrava L'Escaleta | Jazz Total 1
Live at 'Jamboree',Barcelona,Spain, rec. 1.-3.5.1997
Alguimia | Garcia,Guim (as) | Monné,Joan (p) | Cuadrado,Alexis (b) | Gomez,David (dr)
Blues Foll
Alguimia | Garcia,Guim (as) | Benitez,Gorka (ts) | Monné,Joan (p) | Cuadrado,Alexis (b) | Gomez,David (dr)

FSNT 024 CD | CD | Spirit In The Night
Dan Faulk Trio
The Night Has A Thousand Eyes | Peace Waltz | Our Love Is Here To Stay | Black Orpheus | Those Dirty Blues | Spirits In The Night
New Jersey,NJ, rec. 29.10.1996
Faulk,Dan (ss,ts) | Martin,Joe (b) | Rossy,Jorge 'Jordi' (dr)
Dan Faulk Quartet
The Heath Blues | Angel Eyes | Stop 'N' Go | Three Cheers For Paul Chambers | But Beautiful
Faulk,Dan (ss,ts) | Walden,Myron (as) | Martin,Joe (b) | Rossy,Jorge 'Jordi' (dr)

FSNT 025 CD | CD | Duo
Albert Bover-Horacio Fumero
Au Privave | Infant Eyes | Alone Together | Inception | You Go To My Head | Bluebird | Darn That Dream | You Don't Know What Love Is | Anthropology
Live at 'La Vella',Andorra, rec. September 1995
Bover,Albert (p) | Fumero,Horacio (b)

FSNT 026 CD | CD | Dave Liebman And The Lluis Vidal Trio
Dave Liebman And The Lluis Vidal Trio
Stella By Starlight | Ocre | The Panderer | Primavera 1986 | Gnid | Verd Mari
Live at The Theatre Lliure,Barcelona, rec. 7.10.1995
Liebman,Dave (ss) | Vidal,Lluis (p) | Gaspar,Jordi (b) | Xirgu,David (dr)
Dave Liebman And The Lluis Vidal Trio With The Orquestra De Cambra Theatre Lliure
Estate(Summer) | The Gravel And The Bird
Liebman,Dave (ss) | Vidal,Lluis (p) | Gaspar,Jordi (b) | Xirgu,David (dr) | Simon,Matthew L. (tp) | Casero,Ricardo (tb) | Thompson,David (fr-h) | Vergés,Sergi (tuba) | Cortadellas,Jaume (fl,bass-fl,piccolo) | Vallet,Philippe (engl-h,oboe) | Figuerola,Xavier (cl,b-cl,ts) | Cardo,Ramon (ss,as)

FSNT 027 CD | CD | Orquestra De Cambra Teatre Lliure and Lluis Vidal Trio feat.Dave Liebman
Orquestra De Cambra Teatre Lliure
Milikituli | El Agarejo | Suite Portugalia: | Vai-Te Embora,O Papao- | O Milho Verde- | Papagaio Louro- | Ball De Capvespre
Live at Teatre Lliure,Barcelona,Spain, rec. 5.-8.10.1995
Orquestra De Cambra Teatre Lliure | Simon,Matthew L. (tp) | Casero,Ricardo (tb) | Thompson,David (fr-h) | Vergés,Sergi (tuba) | Cortadellas,Jaume (fl,bass-fl,piccolo) | Vallet,Philippe (engl-h,oboe) | Figuerola,Xavier (cl,b-cl,ts) | Cardo,Ramon (ss,as) | Vidal,Lluis (p,cond) | Gaspar,Jordi (b) | Xirgu,David (dr)
Orquestra De Cambra Teatre Lliure feat. Dave Liebman
Havanera | El Gegant I El Cargol: | El Gegant Del Pi- | Cargo Treu Banya- | El Escatime
Orquestra De Cambra Teatre Lliure | Simon,Matthew L. (tp) | Casero,Ricardo (tb) | Thompson,David (fr-h) | Vergés,Sergi (tuba) | Cortadellas,Jaume (fl,bass-fl,piccolo) | Vallet,Philippe (engl-h,oboe) | Liebman,Dave (ss) | Figuerola,Xavier (cl,b-cl,ts) | Cardo,Ramon (ss,as) | Vidal,Lluis (p,cond) | Gaspar,Jordi (b) | Xirgu,David (dr)

FSNT 028 CD | CD | Colores
José Luis Gámez Trio
Gigante
Barcelona,Spain, rec. 15./16.2.1997
Gámez,José Luis (g) | Gaspar,Jordi (b) | Krause,Jo (dr)
José Luis Gámez Quartet
Tema Y Gancho | Mensajero | A Newton | Cornette
Gámez,José Luis (g) | Capellas,Xavier 'Xavi' (org,keyboards) | Gaspar,Jordi (b) | Krause,Jo (dr)
Otra De Piratas | Multimedia Bonus Track
Gámez,José Luis (g) | Sambeat,Perico (as) | Gaspar,Jordi (b) | Krause,Jo (dr)
José Luis Gámez Quintet
Pyzzle | Olor De Lavanda | Moonlight Serenade | Perico-Lo
Gámez,José Luis (g) | Sambeat,Perico (as) | Capellas,Xavier 'Xavi' (org,keyboards) | Gaspar,Jordi (b) | Krause,Jo (dr)

FSNT 030 CD | CD | Dirty Show Tunes
Reid Anderson Quartet
Dirty Showtunes | Kafka | Not Sentimental | Leaping Greenly Spirits | Imagination Is Important | Character Study | Magic Squares | Think Of Mingus | I Want You So Bad
Brooklyn,NY, rec. 14./15.5.1997
Anderson,Reid (b) | Turner,Mark (ts) | Iverson,Ethan (p) | Rossy,Jorge 'Jordi' (dr)

FSNT 031 CD | CD | New York-Barcelona Crossing Vol.1
Brad Mehldau With The Rossy Trio
Wonderful | Spring Can Really Hang You Up The Most | Old Folks | Sushi | Bodi | Comencar De Novo | Just One Of Those Things | No Blues- | Spoken Announcement by Perico Sambeat
Live at 'Jamboree',Barcelona,Spain
Mehldau,Brad (p) | Sambeat,Perico (as) | Rossy,Mario (b) | Rossy,Jorge 'Jordi' (dr)

FSNT 032 CD | CD | A Girl Named Joe
Chris Cheek Sextet
Slide | September | Arctic Barbecue | Lowered | Late Green | Plant Dance | A Girl Named Joe | Then | Siege | Water Mile
New Jersey,NJ, rec. 19.5.1997
Cheek,Chris (ts) | Turner,Mark (ts) | Monder,Ben (g) | Johnson,Marc (b) | Rossy,Jorge 'Jordi' (dr) | Rieser,Dan (dr)

FSNT 033 CD | CD | Rest Stop
Bill McHenry Quartet
Afterthought | Hebuwuba | Silly | Blues-| Duo I(Pull Over) | No Idea | The Sky Bird That Flies Away | 9-12 | Duo II(Rest Stop)
Paramus,NJ, rec. 21.& 29.9.1997
McHenry,Bill (ts) | Monder,Ben (g) | Higgins,Chris (b) | Rieser,Dan (dr)

FSNT 034 CD | CD | Insomnio
Joan Abril Quartet
Feliz | S'Allota Si,Si | Algebra | Colores | Charlie | Exodo | The Secret
Barcelona,Spain, rec. 11./12.11.1997
Abril,Joan (g) | Diaz,Joan (p) | Galvez,Curro (b) | Reina,Jesus (dr)
Joan Abril Quintet
Gerson & Julia | Insomnio
Abril,Joan (g) | Bondell,Jordi (g) | Diaz,Joan (p) | Galvez,Curro (b) | Reina,Jesus (dr)
You And The Night And The Music
Abril,Joan (g) | Diaz,Joan (p) | Galvez,Curro (b) | Mengual,David (b) | Reina,Jesus (dr)

FSNT 035 CD | CD | Brazilian Rosewood
Freddie Bryant Group
Brazilian Rosewood | Meditation For Christie | Remember | Patchwork In D | Lullaby For The Newborn | Serenade | Niahnie's Dance | Altos E Baixos | Light Green | Late Fall
New Jersey,NJ, rec. 11./12.12.1997
Bryant,Freddie (g,el-g) | Urcola,Diego (tp) | Cheek,Chris (ss,ts) | Simon,Eduardo (p) | Cohen,Avishai (b) | Rossy,Jorge 'Jordi' (dr) | Gilad (perc)

FSNT 036 CD | CD | BCN
Mikel Andueza Quintet
Caos | Pragmático | Amores Que Matan | Lo Pass | Doble Nacionalidad | Cuenta,Cuenta | Estella By Starlight | Drop
Barcelona,Spain, rec. 1.12.1997
Andueza,Mikel (ss,as) | Palet,Benet (tp) | Diaz,Joan (p) | Ferrer,Raimon 'Rai' (b) | Gómez,David (dr,perc)

FSNT 037 CD | CD | New York-Barcelona Crossing Vol.2
Brad Mehldau With The Rossy Trio
I've Told Every Little Star | Un Poco Loco | Easy To Remember | Played Twice | Dat Dere | Cousin Mary | No Blues
Live at The 'Jamboree',Barcelona, rec. 10.5.1993
Sambeat,Perico (as) | Mehldau,Brad (p) | Rossy,Mario (b) | Rossy,Jorge 'Jordi' (dr)

FSNT 038 CD | CD | The J.Way
Nat Su Quartet
The J. Way | Without A Song | All Or Nothing At All | Su City | Epiphany | Hubris | Isfahan | Karry's Trance | My Little Brown Book | Blues For Yard | U.M.M.G.(Upper Manhattan Medical Group)
Barcelona,Spain, rec. 5.11.1997
Su,Nat (as) | Kanan,Michael 'Mike' (p) | Martin,Joe (b) | Rossy,Jorge 'Jordi' (dr)

FSNT 039 CD | CD | Núcleo
José Luis Gutiérrez Trio
Bicéfalo | Quechua | Piel De Toro | Ancha Es Castilla | Aromas | TT (A Tete Montoliu) | Sabe Más El Diablo Por Viejo,Que No For Diablo | Al Mal Tiempo Buena Cara
Madrid, Spain, rec. December 1997
Gutiérrez,José Luis (ss,ts) | Martinez,Baldo (b) | Khalsa,Nirankar (dr,perc)

FSNT 040 CD | CD | Wysiwyg
Javier Feierstein Quartet
Et Pourquois Pas | Lo Que Todos Sabemos | With A Heart In My Song | From Now On | No Olvides | Wysiwyg | Two People In Boston | Blessed Wind | 4x3 | El Otro | Shelley's Eyes
Barcelona,Spain, rec. 20./21.3.1998
Feierstein,Javier (g) | Robles,Ion (ts) | Qálvez,Curro (b,el-b) | Gómez,David (dr,perc)

FSNT 041 CD | CD | Ademuz
Perico Sambeat Group
A Free K | Ademuz | Tu Rostro Oculto | Expedicion | La Noche De Lemuria | Porta Do Ferro | Barri De La Coma
Valencia,Spain, rec. August & November 1995
Sambeat,Perico (fl,as,keyboards) | Leonhart,Michael 'Mike' (tp) | Turner,Mark (ts) | Rosenwinkel,Kurt (g) | Mehldau,Brad (p,keyboards) | Martin,Joe (b) | Rossy,Jorge 'Jordi' (dr) | McGill,Guillermo (perc) | Canada,Enric (perc) | Morente,Enrique (voc)

FSNT 042 CD | CD | JumpSTART
Bob Sands Quartet
Slow Boat To China | Scablemates | You Don't Know What Love Is
Madrid, Spain, rec. 31.3./1.4.1997
Sands,Bobby (ts) | Rover,Albert (p) | Barretto,Carlos (b) | Soirat,Felipe (dr)
Bob Sands Quintet
Teseract | Jumpstart | Conversaciones En La Plate
Sands,Bobby (ts) | Sambeat,Perico (as) | Rover,Albert (p) | Barretto,Carlos (b) | Soirat,Felipe (dr)
Tren A Palencia | Fjord March
Sands,Bobby (ts) | Weiss,Kurt (tp,fl-h) | Rover,Albert (p) | Barretto,Carlos (b) | Soirat,Felipe (dr)

FSNT 043 CD | CD | The Music Of Mercedes Rossy
Mark Turner-Chris Cheek Quintet
Some Like To Love More Than One | Amidst A Yesterday's Presence | Lost Ocean | The Other Side Of Time | 1991 | Water Stones | 6 D'Octubre | Gone But Not Forgotten | The Newcomer
Live at 'Luz de Gas',Barcelona,Spain, rec. 15.11.1996
Turner,Mark (ts) | Cheek,Chris (ss,ts) | Colligan,George (p) | Rossy,Mario (b) | Rossy,Jorge 'Jordi' (dr)

FSNT 044 CD | CD | O Si No Que?
Ramón Diaz Group
Rraam | Temprano | Funky Eaeco | Cantos Canarios- | Arroro- | Cannis- | O Si No Que? | Mistery Song | Pateiros | Wednesday Night Prayer Meeting- | Better Git It In Your Soul- | Cancion Turca
Barcelona,Spain, rec. 15./16.5.1998
Diaz,Ramón (dr,perc) | Andueza,Mikel (ss,as) | De Diego,Victor (fl,ss,ts) | Galvez,Curro (b,el-b,cl)

FSNT 045 CD | CD | Matt Renzi-Jimmy Weinstein Quartet
Matt Renzi-Jimmy Weinstein Quartet
Intro- | Cape Verdean Song- | Along Came Betty | The Noodle Song | Her Melancholy Piano | Wolf Stump | Work | Nooks And Crannies | Tears Inside | Go-Getter
Brooklyn,NY, rec. 6.5.1998
Renzi,Matt (ts) | Weinstein,Jimmy (dr) | Monder,Ben (g) | Higgins,Chris (b)
Smile
Jimmy Weinsteins's Living Room, rec. 4.5.1998
Renzi,Matt (ts) | Weinstein,Jimmy (dr) | Monder,Ben (g) | Higgins,Chris (b)

FSNT 046 CD | CD | Contruction Zone(Originals)
Ethan Iverson Trio
What The Kraken Knows | Jorge's Bolero | New Chimes Blues | Mystique | Hullabaloo | 3-D Montevideo | In Memoriam | The Inevitable Wall
New Jersey,NJ, rec. 4./5.4.1998
Iverson,Ethan (p) | Anderson,Reid (b) | Rossy,Jorge 'Jordi' (dr)

FSNT 047 CD | CD | Decontruction Zone(Originals)
I'm Getting Sentimental Over You | The Song Is You | This Nearly Was Mine | All Of Me | I'll Remember April | Smoke Gets In Your Eyes | Have You Met Miss Jones
Iverson,Ethan (p) | Anderson,Reid (b) | Rossy,Jorge 'Jordi' (dr)

FSNT 048 CD | CD | Don't Git Sassy
Big Band Bellaterra
Don't Get Sassy | Shiny Stockings | Manteca | Take The 'A' Train | Polka Dots And Moonbeams | Ruby My Dear | Off Minor | Evidence
Live at Nova Jazz Cava de Terrassa,Spain, rec. 28.12.1997
Big Band Bellaterra | Pastor,David (tp) | Simon,Matthew L. (tp) | Hernandez,Denis 'El Huevo' (tp) | Palet,Benet (tp) | Arrom,Juanjo (tb) | DuBuclet,John (tb) | Martin,Carlos (tb) | Vergés Sergi (tb) | Figuerola,Xavier (as) | Andueza,Mikel (as) | Reinon,Eladio (ts,ld) | De Diego,Victor (ts) | Robles,Ion (ts) | Chamorro,Joan (bs) | Capellas,Xavier 'Xavi' (p) | Sabatés,Riqui (g) | Rossy,Mario (b) | Rossy,Jorge 'Jordi' (dr) | Weinstein,Georgina (voc)
How High The Moon | Almost Like Being In Love | La Cita
Big Band Bellaterra | Pastor,David (tp) | Simon,Matthew L. (tp) | Hernandez,Denis 'El Huevo' (tp) | Cuadrada,Ramon (tp) | Arrom,Juanjo (tb) | DuBuclet,John (tb) | Martin,Carlos (tb) | Vergés Sergi (tb) | Figuerola,Xavier (as) | Andueza,Mikel (as) | Reinon,Eladio (ts,ld) | De Diego,Victor (ts) | Robles,Ion (ts) | Chamorro,Joan (bs) | Capellas,Xavier 'Xavi' (p) | Sabatés,Riqui (g) | Rossy,Mario (b) | Rossy,Jorge 'Jordi' (dr) | Weinstein,Georgina (voc)

FSNT 049 CD | CD | Alguimia:Standards
Alguimia
Bewitched Bothered And Bewildered | They Say It's Wonderful | Straight Street | Retrato En Branco E Prieto | Old Devil Moon | My Ideal | Informia | Red Cross
Barcelona,Spain, rec. 20./22.7.1998
Alguimia | Garcia,Guim (as) | Monné,Joan (p) | Cuadrado,Alexis (b) | Gomez,David (dr)

FSNT 050 CD | CD | Alguimia Dos
Serial Blues | Alegria | This Is For David | Dos | TNT | Unknown Title | Txatxatxell | CCS | The Clownster
Alguimia | Garcia,Guim (as) | Monné,Joan (p) | Cuadrado,Alexis (b) | Gomez,David (dr)

FSNT 051 CD | CD | Time
Joaquin Chacón-Uffe Markussen European Quintet
Apunte | Very Early | I Fall In Love Too Easily | Quicksilver | Think Of One | Ozone | Time | Dancing Cats | Monk's Mood | Wonderful Wonderful
Copenhagen,Denmark, rec. 17.12.1997
Markussen,Uffe (b-cl,ts) | Chacón,Joaquin (g,el-g) | Besiakov,Ben (p,celeste) | Ovesen,Thomas (b) | Rifbjerk,Frands (dr)

FSNT 052 CD | CD | Original Moments
Moments Quartet
Dies De Nens I Nenes | G.T.B. | Sweet Bossa | Un Toc De Groc | Brisas | Globus
Girona,Spain, rec. 7.-9.8.1998
Moments Quartet | Juanco,Javier (g) | Escuadra,Lluis (p) | Pujol,Toni (b) | Martinez,Cesar (dr)
Islero
Moments Quartet | Lorenz,Marta (fl) | Juanco,Javier (g) | Escuadra,Lluis (p) | Pujol,Toni (b) | Martinez,Cesar (dr)
Caraculiambro
Moments Quartet | Carrascosa,Alfons (as) | Juanco,Javier (g) | Escuadra,Lluis (p) | Pujol,Toni (b) | Martinez,Cesar (dr)

FSNT 053 CD | CD | Buen Rollo
Grant Stewart Quartet
It's All Right With Me | Pannonica | Cyclops | Dizzy Moods | Manhattan | O.D. | Scotch Thing | Something To Live For
Barcelona,Spain, rec. 2./3.6.1998
Stewart,Grant (ts) | Miano,Fabio (p) | Higgins,Chris (b) | Miralta,Marc (dr)

FSNT 054 CD | CD | Unresolved
George Colligan Group
Danger Zone
Paramus,NJ, rec. details unknown
Colligan,George (org) | Gordon,Jon (as) | Turner,Mark (ts) | Curtis,Howard (dr)
Year's End
Colligan,George (p-solo)
Why Does It Happen To Me Every Time?
Colligan,George (org) | Turner,Mark (ts) | Rosenwinkel,Kurt (g) | Curtis,Howard (dr)
Modeidi's Modalities
Colligan,George (dr) | Turner,Mark (ts) | Rosenwinkel,Kurt (g) | Gress,Drew (b)
Gray Days
Colligan,George (ensoniq ASR) | Gordon,Jon (ss) | Turner,Mark (ts) | Gress,Drew (b) | Curtis,Howard (dr)
Train To St.Gallen | Nebulosity | Evil Ambition | Unresolved | The Very Last Waltz
Colligan,George (p,org,tp,ensoniq ASR) | Turner,Mark (ts) | Gress,Drew (b) | Curtis,Howard (dr)

FSNT 055 CD | CD | Convergence
Michael Kanan Trio
Cross Currents | A Family Song | Victory Ball | I Don't Stand A Ghost Of A Chance With You | Leave Me | Subconscious-Lee | Stardust | Ablution | You Do Something To Me
Brooklyn,NY, rec. 15./16.1.1999
Kanan,Michael 'Mike' (p) | Street,Ben (b) | Pleasant,Tim (dr)

FSNT 056 CD | CD | Graphic
Bill McHenry Quartet
Not What It Seems | Art- | Omi- | Blocks And Dots | Casi Te Amo | Old Tune | C Major Tune | Eleven Eleven
Paramus,NJ, rec. 26.9.1998
McHenry,Bill (ts) | Monder,Ben (g) | Anderson,Reid (b) | Cleaver,Gerald (dr)

FSNT 057 CD | CD | Immersion
Jacques Schwarz-Bart/James Hurt Quartet
The Price To Pay | Slow Down Baby | A Kick In The Bone | Lament | Invitation | Impressions | Blue In Green | The Price I Thought I'd Pay
NYC, rec. 24.2.1999
Schwarz-Bart,Jacques (ts) | Hurt,James (p) | Weidenmüller,Johannes (b) | Hoenig,Ari (dr)

FSNT 058 CD | CD | Lila
Elisabet Raspall Grup
Qui S'ha Begut La Lluna? | Vals 7 | Ocult | Vale La Pena | Va En Serio | Canco Neta | Mots Muts | Els Teus Ulls Són Transparents | Experiment | Nonom | Elipso | Comiat
Barcelona,Spain, rec. 26.-28.10.1998
Raspall,Elisabet (p) | Palet,Benet (tp) | Miralta,Cesc (ss,ts) | Higgins,Chris (b) | Miralta,Marc (dr,tablas)

FSNT 059 CD | CD | First Step Into Reality
The New Jazz Composers Octet
First Step Into Reality | Tribute To The Elders | I'm A Comin' On Home | Untitled In Ab Minor | Liberation
RPM Studio,?, rec. 28.3.1997
New Jazz Composers Octet,The | Weiss,David (tp) | Williams,Andrew (tb) | Walden,Myron (as) | Tardy,Greg (ts) | Farnsworth,James (bs) | Davis,Xavier (p) | Burno,Dwayne (b) | Waits,Nasheet (dr)
I'll Always Love You | D Minor Mint | When The Spirit Hits
RPM Studio,?, rec. 3.5.1998
New Jazz Composers Octet,The | Weiss,David (tp) | Williams,Andrew (tb) | Walden,Myron (as) | Greene,Jimmy (ts) | Riekenberg,Dave (bs) | Davis,Xavier (p) | Burno,Dwayne (b) | Waits,Nasheet (dr)

FSNT 060 CD | CD | The Dreamer
Amos Hoffman Quartet
Doobie Time | The Flip | Three | Memories | The Dreamer | Francine | Blues Time | Bookie & Ofi | Another Dream
Paramus,NJ, rec. 2.2.1999
Hoffmand,Amos (g) | Eubanks,Duane (tp) | Cohen,Avishai (b) | Rossy,Jorge 'Jordi' (dr)

FSNT 061 CD | CD | States
Andrew Adair Group
My Old Kentucky Home(Prologue) | I Left My Heart In San Francisco | My Old Kentucky Home,Good Night | Back Home Again In Indiana | My Old Kentucky Home(Epilogue)
Brooklyn,NY, rec. 25.-27.5.1999
Adair,Andrew (p) | Ginsburg,Josh (b) | Edwards,Donald (dr)
Moonlight In Vermont | Stars Fell On Alabama | Carolina In The Morning | Meet Me In St.Louis,Louis | When It's Sleepy Time Down South
Brooklyn,NY, rec. 25.-27.5.1999
Adair,Andrew (p,voc) | Jekabson,Erik (tp) | DiRubbo,Mike (as) | Ellis,John (ts) | Ginsburg,Josh (b) | Edwards,Donald (dr)

FSNT 062 CD | CD | Abolish Bad Architecture
Reid Anderson Quartet
Todas Las Cosas Se Van | Miro | Shimmering | Abolish Bad Architecture | Every Day Is Beautiful | Mystery Girl | Granada | Hommage:Mahler
Paramus,NJ, rec. 18./19.5.1999
Anderson,Reid (b) | Turner,Mark (ts) | Iverson,Ethan (p) | Ballard,Jeff (dr)

FSNT 063 CD | CD | Stranger Things Have Happened
Seamus Blake Quartet
Perk | Happenstance | Token Cello | Extranjero | G.S.S. | Taurus People | Of Ours
Brooklyn,NY, rec. 10./11.3.1999
Blake,Seamus (ss,ts) | Rosenwinkel,Kurt (g) | Grenadier,Larry (b) | Rossy,Jorge 'Jordi' (dr)

Seamus Blake Quintet
Northern Light
Blake,Seamus (ss,ts) | Rosenwinkel,Kurt (g) | Harris,Jesse (g) | Grenadier,Larry (b) | Rossy,Jorge 'Jordi' (dr)

FSNT 064 CD | CD | The Minor Passions
Ethan Iverson Trio
Other Roses | Body And Soul | Blues For The Groundskeeper | Milestones | The Minor Passions | Where Or When | Neon | Lullaby
Live at The Greenwich House Music School,NYC, rec. 28./29.5.1999
Iverson,Ethan (p) | Anderson,Reid (b) | Hart,Bill (dr)

FSNT 065 CD | CD | Lines And Ballads
Matt Renzi-Jimmy Weinstein-Masa Kamaguchi Trio
New Line | Eronel | My Love | Ah-Leu-Cha | Turn Out The Stars | Dear Max | East Of The Sun West Of The Moon | Ballad Of The Sad Young Men | Barbados
Brooklyn,NY, rec. 28.6.1999
Renzi,Matt (ts) | Kamaguchi,Masa (b) | Weinstein,Jimmy (dr)

FSNT 066 CD | CD | Porgy And Bess
Orquestra De Cambra Teatre Lliure
Jasbo Brown Blues | My Man's Gone Now | Summertime | Bess You Is My Woman Now | I Loves You Porgy | Here Comes De Honey Man | Buzzard Song | I Got Plenty O'Nuttin' | Gone Gone Gone | There's A Boat Dat's Leavin' Soon For New York
Live at Teatre Lliure,Barcelona,Spain, rec. 10.-12.11.1998
Orquestra De Cambra Teatre Lliure | Bosch,Miguel Angel (tp,fl-h) | Martin,Carlos (tb) | Renteria,Jorge (fr-h) | Picot,Pasqual (tuba) | Cortadellas,Jaume (fl,bass-fl,piccolo) | Figuerola,Xavier (ss,as) | Cardo,Ramon (ss,as) | Benitez,Gorka (fl,ss,ts) | Vidal,Lluis (p,cond) | Amargós,Joan Albert (p,keyboards,cond) | Fumero,Horacio (b) | Xirgu,David (dr) | Canela,Carme (voc)

FSNT 067 CD | CD | Eternal Balance
Charles Owens Quartet
No Resolution | In The Still Of The Night | I Got It Bad And That Ain't Good | Yesterdays | Virginia's Song | Eternal Balance | April In Paris
NYC, rec. 18.5.1999
Owens,Charles (ts) | Lindner,Jason (p) | Avital,Omer (b) | Freedman,Daniel (dr)

FSNT 068 CD | CD | Gäel Horellou Versus David Sauzay
Gäel Horellou-David Sauzay Quintet
Evidence | 12-99 | Ask Me Now | To Hank Mobley | Weed | Kyser Sozée | Everything Happens To Me | Versus
Barcelona,Spain, rec. 10.5.1999
Horellou,Gäel (as) | Sauzay,David (ts) | Courthaliac,Laurent (p) | Mengual,David (b) | Garcia,Philippe (dr)

FSNT 069 CD | CD | Port O'Clock
Pep O'Callaghan Grup
The Crane's Dance | Noray Rai | Out Coming Voices | Dando Vueltas | Treck 'N' Dorough | Vell Pelegri
Barcelona,Spain, rec. 29./30.4.1999
O'Callaghan,Pep (g,el-g) | Monné,Joan (p) | Ferrer,Raimon 'Rai' (b) | Miralta,Marc (dr)
Nicolas El Valiente
O'Callaghan,Pep (g,el-g) | Delgado,Publio (g) | Monné,Joan (p) | Ferrer,Raimon 'Rai' (b) | Miralta,Marc (dr)
Port O'Clock | Help,Support!!
O'Callaghan,Pep (g,el-g) | Robles,Ion (ts) | Monné,Joan (p) | Ferrer,Raimon 'Rai' (b) | Miralta,Marc (dr)

FSNT 070 CD | CD | Trilingual
OAM Trio
The Loneliest Marc | Bismillah | 26-2 | Sea Shantey | Woody'n You | Never Let Me Go | Cheryl | Devil Head
Paramus,NJ, rec. 21./22.5.1999
OAM Trio | Goldberg,Aaron (p) | Avital,Omer (b) | Miralta,Marc (dr)

FSNT 071 CD | CD | Desire
George Colligan Quartet
Battle Cry | Darkness Rising | Ancestra Wisdom | Desire | Last November | Colors Of Love | Open | Epilogue | Upper Manhattan Medical Group 'U.M.M.G.'
Barcelona,Spain, rec. 1./2.2.1999
Colligan,George (p,tp) | Sambeat,Perico (fl,ss,as) | Rossy,Mario (b) | Miralta,Marc (dr)

FSNT 072 CD | CD | The Waiting
Jill Seifers And Her Quartet
I've Never Been Blue Before | The Waiting | Paris Blues | Solitude | Shallow Dreamers | Gentle Rain | Four | Eclipse | May This Be Love | And So It Goes
Paramus,NJ, rec. 7.3.1999
Seifers,Jill (voc) | Rosenwinkel,Kurt (g) | Kanan,Michael 'Mike' (p) | Martin,Joe (b) | Rossy,Jorge 'Jordi' (dr)

FSNT 073 CD | CD | Gorka Benitez Trio
Gorka Benitez Trio
Super Zortzi | Blue Note Singes Again | Sual | Loisaida | En Que Toni Chabeli?
Barcelona,Spain, rec. 1.10.& 28./29.12.1998
Benitez,Gorka (ts) | Ferrer,Raimon 'Rai' (b) | Xirgu,David (dr)
Gorka Benitez Quartet
Para Petra | Trakeando
Benitez,Gorka (ts) | Monder,Ben (g) | Ferrer,Raimon 'Rai' (b) | Xirgu,David (dr)
Gorka Benitez Quintet
De Romeria
Benitez,Gorka (ts) | Monder,Ben (g) | Pérez,Daniel 'Dani' (g) | Ferrer,Raimon 'Rai' (b) | Xirgu,David (dr)

FSNT 074 CD | CD | Lay-Up
Chris Lightcap Quartet
Lay-Up | I Heard It Over The Radio | Port-Au-Prince | Guinbre | All Choked Up | Las Tijeras | Sad Morning | Philly's Blount
Paramus,NJ, rec. 13./14.9.1999
Lightcap,Chris (b) | Malaby,Tony (ts) | McHenry,Bill (ts) | Cleaver,Gerald (dr)

FSNT 075 CD | CD | Suspicions
Tom Beckham Quartet
Village Children | No Agenda | Little Booboo | Ascent | Snoop | Suspicions | Sweet Tooth | Ground Control | Kansas Tale
NYC, rec. 22./23.6.1999
Beckham,Tom (vib) | Cheek,Chris (ss,ts) | Anderson,Reid (b) | Schuller,George (dr)

FSNT 076 CD | CD | Jade
Andrew Rathbun Group
Music Based On A Poem By Cathy Song | Jade(part I-VI)
Paramus,NJ, rec. June 1998
Rathbun,Andrew (reeds) | Haskins,Taylor (tp) | Komer,Chris (fr-h) | Richman,Helen (fl) | Stetch,John (p) | Street,Ben (b) | Schuller,George (dr) | Souza,Luciana (voc)

FSNT 077 CD | CD | Idolents
David Xirgu Quartet
Txitxiriko | En Vista Del Éxito | Txi-Khan | Gavotte | Dr.Moriarty,Suposo | Orlando Di Lata | La Casa Sin Luz | Mrs.PC | Fellini Buscando A Benet | Old Folks | Life On Mars
Barcelona,Spain, rec. 2./3.2.2000
Xirgu,David (dr) | Benitez,Gorka (ts) | Pérez,Daniel 'Dani' (g) | Ferrer,Raimon 'Rai' (b)

FSNT 078 CD | CD | Horse With A Broken Leg
Mark Zubeck Quintet
Yes Yes | Horse With A Broken Leg | No No | Low Down | Manic Depression
NYC, rec. 17./18.11.1999
Zubek,Mark (b) | Thomas,Philippe (tp) | Cheek,Chris (ts) | Blake,Seamus (ts) | Sardjoi,Chander (dr)
Mark Zubeck Quartet
Petite Rosalie | 2513
Zubek,Mark (b) | Thomas,Philippe (tp) | Turner,Mark (ts) | Sardjoi,Chander (dr)

FSNT 079 CD | CD | Shebang
Steve Cárdenas Trio
Across The Way | Lucky Number | Del Cenote | Shebang | Safer Than Heaven | Tai Chi Chai Tea | Mr.Mule | Sacre Coeur | Make It So | Para Ti
NYC, rec. 1./2.9.1999
Cardenas,Steve (g) | Grenadier,Larry (b) | Wollesen,Kenny (dr)

FSNT 080 CD | CD | When Least Expected
Daniel Flors Group
And So It Goes | Three On A Row | Quatretonic
Valencia,Spain, rec. details unknown
Flors,Daniel (g) | Navalon,Santi (p) | Rossy,Mario (b) | Garcera,Juanjo (dr)
Duckaddiction
Flors,Daniel (g) | Bosch,Miguel Angel (tp) | Martin,Carlos (tb) | Cardo,Ramon (as) | Santandreu,Jesus (ts) | Navalon,Santi (p) | Rossy,Mario (b) | Garcera,Juanjo (dr)
Who But Mariah
Flors,Daniel (g) | Leon,Pierre (cl) | Navalon,Santi (p) | Rossy,Mario (b) | Garcera,Juanjo (dr)
Groove Therapy
Flors,Daniel (g) | Bosch,Miguel Angel (tp) | Pastor,David (tp) | Piqueras,Pasqual (tp) | Martin,Carlos (tb) | Belenguer,Toni (tb) | Casany,David M. (fl) | Leon,Pierre (cl) | Cardo,Ramon (as) | Granell,José Luis (as) | Santandreu,Jesus (ts) | Marcian,Vicente (ts) | Bianco,Francisco (bs) | Navalon,Santi (p) | Rossy,Mario (b) | Garcera,Juanjo (dr)
Autobio
Flors,Daniel (g) | Bosch,Miguel Angel (tp) | Martin,Carlos (tb) | Santandreu,Jesus (ts) | Navalon,Santi (p) | Rossy,Mario (b) | Garcera,Juanjo (dr)
Relocco's Blues
Flors,Daniel (g) | Cardo,Ramon (ss,as) | Santandreu,Jesus (ts) | Bianco,Francisco (bs) | Navalon,Santi (p) | Rossy,Mario (b) | Garcera,Juanjo (dr)
Waiting For Siro
Flors,Daniel (g-solo)

FSNT 081 CD | CD | A New Beginning
Alex Norris Quintet
New Beginning | Ontology | Night Bus | Good Addiction | Ugly Beauty | Delta | Sympathy | Blues For The Guardian Angels
NYC, rec. 15./16.8.1999
Norris,Alex (tp,fl-h) | Tardy,Greg (ts) | Colligan,George (p) | Burno,Dwayne (b) | Strasser,Joe (dr)
You Go To My Head | Ze Kol Ma Sheyesh
Norris,Alex (tp,fl-h) | Tardy,Greg (ts) | Colligan,George (p) | Burno,Dwayne (b) | Strasser,Joe (dr) | Acuna,Claudia (voc)

FSNT 082 CD | CD | In Metropolitan Motion
Ben Waltzer Quintet
El Abadonado | Crooked Timber | La Ville Tentaculaire | Par(nas)se | Rumination,Prenzlauerberg | Kira Da Anshi(I) | Arbella | Bass Line | The Blonde Bedouin | Rumination,Oranienburg Str. | Kira Da Anshi(II) | Sooky-Sooky Now | Prelude No.4 | Layla's Dream | Port Royal | Rumination,Dasein Blues
Paramus,NJ, rec. 24.12.1999
Waltzer,Ben (p) | McHenry,Bill (ts) | Lightcap,Chris (b) | Cleaver,Gerald (dr) | Ali,Mohammed Neseehu (talking-dr,djimbe)

FSNT 083 CD | CD | Variations On A Summer Day
Frank Carlberg Group
Introduction | Say Of The Gulls | A Music | The Rocks Of The Cliffs | Star Over Monhegan | Shaken And Shaken | Forever Young | One Sparrow | An Exercise | Night And Day(This Cloudy World) | To Change Nature | Everywhere | Round And Round
Brooklyn,NY, rec. 13./14.1.1999
Carlberg,Frank (p) | Hasselbring,Curtis (tb) | Speed,Chris (cl,ts) | D'Angelo,Andrew (b-cl,as) | Cheek,Chris (ts) | Street,Ben (b) | Wollesen,Kenny (dr) | Correa,Christine (voc)

FSNT 084 CD | CD | Tributes To Duke Ellington
Orquestra De Cambra Teatre Lliure
The Duke(Clare Fischer) | Duke Ellington's Sound Of Love | Open Letter To Duke | He Loved Him Madly | Portrait Of The Duke | One For Duke | The Duke(Dave Brubeck) | Thoughts About Duke | Sir Duke
Barcelona,Spain, rec. 29./30.11.1999
Orquestra De Cambra Teatre Lliure | Simon,Matthew L. (tp,fl-h) | Vergés Sergi (tb,tuba) | Figuerola,Xavier (cl,sax) | Bardagi,Pere (v) | Pérez,Daniel 'Dani' (g) | Vidal,Lluis (p,arr,cond) | Cuadrado,Alexis (b) | Xirgu,David (dr)

FSNT 085 CD | CD | Polaroid Memory
Sebastian Weiss Trio
Across The Water | Shifting Views | Polaroid Memory | Picture Of Kerstin | Tioga | Blues For A Bave Drummer | In The Fading Light | Nonsense Conversation | Change Of Pace | Things To Come
Paramus,NJ, rec. November 1999
Weiss,Sebastian (p) | Bowen III,Bob (b) | Weiss,Dan (dr)

FSNT 086 CD | CD | Vine
Chris Cheek Quintet
So It Seems | The Wing Key | Vine | Ice Fall | Granada | Reno | What's Left | Not A Samba
Avatar Studios,?, rec. 20./21.12.1999
Cheek,Chris (ss,ts) | Rosenwinkel,Kurt (g) | Mehldau,Brad (p,el-p) | Penman,Matt (b) | Rossy,Jorge 'Jordi' (dr)

FSNT 087 CD | CD | Sun Sol
Seamus Blake-Marc Miralta Trio
Go | Circle K | Boston In 3-4 | Now And Here | Pure Imagination | Mr. Omaha | 70's Child | Sunsol
Paramus,NJ, rec. 2./3.8.1999
Blake,Seamus (ts) | Cohen,Avishai (b) | Miralta,Marc (dr)

FSNT 088 CD | CD | Speak,Memory
Roberta Piket Trio
Too Sensible | A Time For Love | Gone | Up Up And Away | Lost In The Stars | When The Sun Comes Out | Hands | Speak,Memory | The Man That Got Away
Brooklyn,NY, rec. 25.2.2000
Piket,Roberta (p) | Kamaguchi,Masa (b) | Williams,Jeff (dr)

FSNT 089 CD | CD | Rumbo Dorte
José Luis Gámez Quintet
Rumbo Norte | Aire Puro | Limbo | Expressions | Desde Dentro | Flipo | Devlus | With A Song In My Heart | Four Steps | I'll See You In My Dreams
Barcelona,Spain, rec. 30.3.2000
Gámez,José Luis (g) | Sambeat,Perico (ss,as) | Sassetti,Bernardo (p) | Ferrer,Raimon 'Rai' (b) | Rossy,Jorge 'Jordi' (dr)

FSNT 090 CD | CD | Where Eagles Fly
Bruce Barth Quartet
Identity Crisis | San Francisco Holiday | Secret Name | Autumn Leaves | El Gavilan- | Where Eagles Fly- | For Mercedes | Transparency | 3 More Minors | You've Changed
Barcelona,Spain, rec. 9.11.1998
Barth,Bruce (p) | Newsome,Sam (ss) | O'Leary,Pat (b) | Cruz,Adam (dr)

FSNT 092 CD | CD | Eric
Joan Abril Quintet
Perry Mason | Riera Blanca | Un Gato Deprimido | Eric | Lo De Siempre | Algebra
Barcelona,Spain, rec. 16./17.5.2000
Abril,Joan (g) | Miralta,Cesc (ts) | Monné,Joan (p) | Galvez,Curro (b) | Reina,Jesus (dr)
Joan Abril Sextet
Ilúsiao
Abril,Joan (g) | Miralta,Cesc (ts) | Monné,Joan (p) | Galvez,Curro (b) | Reina,Jesus (dr) | Nunes,William (perc)

FSNT 093 CD | CD | Sweet Transients
Phil Grenadier Quintet
Sweet Transients | Alone Together | Portrait In Black And White | Emma | Ma Belle Hélène | Cali Mist | Lonely Woman | Nefertiti
Brooklyn,NY, rec. 12./13.6.2000
Grenadier,Phil (tp) | Blake,Seamus (ts,windchimes) | Iverson,Ethan (p,dr) | Grenadier,Larry (b) | Stewart,Bill (dr,p)
Derelict
Grenadier,Phil (tp) | Blake,Seamus (ts) | Iverson,Ethan (p) | Weiss,Doug (b) | Stewart,Bill (dr)

FSNT 094 CD | CD | José Luis Gámez Quattro
José Luis Gámez Quartet
Old Style | Bonito Tema | Morenito | Cinco Minutos Sin Ti | Sin Limite | Beia Flor | An Affair Ro Remember | What'll I Do | Lazy Bird
Barcelona,Spain, rec. 31.3.2000
Gámez,José Luis (g) | Sanz,Albert (p) | Mengual,David (b) | Krause,Jo (dr)

FSNT 097 CD | CD | Flor De Luna
Stéphane Mercier Group
Night Meandering | WGZFM | Half Moon | Flor De Luna | She Sells Sea Shells | Avenue A | Samsara | Fool Moon
NYC, rec. May 2000
Mercier,Stéphane (fl,as) | Thomas,Philippe (tp) | Butler,Melvin (ts) | Gromaire,Thomas (g) | Bourgeyx,Vincent (p,el-p,org) | Zubek,Mark (b) | Beckett,Darren (dr) | Thoms,Renato (perc)

FSNT 098 CD | CD | Sol De Nit
Cesc Miralta Quartet
El Nou Mil-Lenni | Sol De Nit | El Bosc De Les Fades | Roc Blanc | Boira Al Montensy | Ossa Nova | Universal | 23 Xiprers | Rosa Del Desert
Barcelona,Spain
Miralta,Cesc (ts) | Sanz,Albert (p) | Higgins,Chris (b) | Miralta,Marc (dr)

FSNT 099 CD | CD | True Stories
Andrew Rathbun Group
Vignette I | True Stories(part 1-3) | Vignette II | Another Aspect | Cards | Bluejays | Majority | She Who Chose(The Lies That That Daylight Told Us) | Vignette III
Paramus,NJ, rec. August 2000
Rathbun,Andrew (reeds) | Haskins,Taylor (tp) | Colligan,George (p,el-p,tp) | Herbert,John (b) | Hirshfield,Jeff (dr) | Souza,Luciana (voc)

FSNT 100 CD | CD | Mireia
Joan Monné Trio
Suite: | Son Song- | Mireia- | Mariona,Maria,Mare- | 1934 | Maria | Ugrix | De Mica En Mica | For Brad | Lluna | All The Things You Are
Barcelona,Spain, rec. 17./18.6.2000
Monné,Joan (p) | Ferrer,Raimon 'Rai' (b) | Xirgu,David (dr)

FSNT 107 CD | CD | The Bad Plus | EAN 8427328421072
The Bad Plus
Knowing Me Knowing | Blue Moon | 1972 Bronze Medalist | The Breakout | Smells Like Teen Spirit | Labyrinth | Scurry | Love Is The Answer
Minneapolis,USA, rec. 28.12.2000
The Bad Plus: | Iverson,Ethan (p) | Anderson,Reid (b) | King,David (dr)

FSNT 143 CD | CD | An Introduction To Kalifactors | EAN 8427328421430
Kalifactors
Wher Am I | Kalifactors | Bu's Beat | The Magician | The Rhumba | Un Ultimo Esfuerzo | A.M.
Massachusetts, rec. 2001
Kalifactors | Stillman,Robert (ts) | Sanz,Albert (p) | Van Beest,Chris Van Voorst (b) | Scott,Kendrick (dr)

FSNT 144 CD | CD | Buenos Aires-Barcelona Connections | EAN 8427328421447
Dani Perez Quartet
Pio Rhythm | Nata | Senales | El Regalo | Mal Menor | 10 Estrella
Buenos Aires, rec. details unknown
Pérez,Daniel 'Dani' (g) | Dominguez,Rodrigo (ss,ts) | Delgado,Guillermo (b) | Steimberg,Mariano (dr)

FSNT 147 CD | CD | The Gentleman Is A Dope | EAN 8427328421478
Michael Kanan Trio
Tautology | Adorée | Ghost Of Yesterday | Unbelieveable | The Gentleman Is A Dope | I Don't Know How To Turn | Red On Maroon | Thelonious
details unknown, rec. details unknown
Kanan,Michael 'Mike' (p) | Street,Ben (b) | Pleasant,Tim (dr)

FSNT 149 CD | CD | Carretera Austal | EAN 8427328421492
Cesc Miralta Quartet
Venecia | D.O. Priorat | Sandernes | Abril | Carretera Austral | Stata El Sol De Ponenet | Ulls Verds | No Beguis Mai Got | Carrer 8,5
Barcelona,Spain, rec. 2002
Miralta,Cesc (ss,ts) | Sanz,Albert (p) | Higgins,Chris (b) | Miralta,Marc (dr)

FSNT 150 CD | CD | Consin | EAN 8427328421508
Hernan Merlo Quintet
En El Mismo Lada | Dos Marias | Taracira | El Pendulo | A La Cabeza | Consin
Buenos Aires, rec. December 2001
Melo,Hernon (b) | Lastra,Carlos (ss,as) | Dominguez,Rodrigo (cl,as) | Jodos,Ernesto (p) | Verdinelli,Sergio (dr)

FSNT 151 CD | CD | Walkin' the Line | EAN 8427328421515
New Jazz Composers Octet
Deadweight | A Little Twist | Walkin' The Line | Abdullah's Demeanor | Inner Space | The Dove | The
details unknown, rec. details unknown
New Jazz Composers Octet,The | Weiss,David (tp) | Davis,Steve (tb) | Williams,Andrew (tb) | Walden,Myron (as) | Greene,Jimmy (ss,ts) | Handy,Craig (ss,as,ts) | Karlic,Chris (bs) | Davis,Xavier (p) | Burno,Dwayne (b) | Waits,Nasheet (dr)

FSNT 161 CD | CD | The Trumpet Player | EAN 8427328421614
Avishai Cohen Trio
The Fast | The Trumpet Player | Dear Lord | Shablool
NYC, rec. 25.11.2001
Cohen,Avishai (tp) | Sullivan,Joe (p) | Ballard,Jeff (dr)
Avishai Cohen Quartet
Olympus | Idaho | Giggin'
Cohen,Avishai (tp) | Frahm,Joel (ts) | Sullivan,Joe (p) | Ballard,Jeff (dr)

FSR CD 338 | CD | Sounds From Rikers Island | EAN 8427328603386
Elmo Hope Ensemble
One For Joe | Ecstasy | Three Silver Quarters | A Night In Tunisia | Trippin' | Kevin | Monique
NYC, rec. 19.8.1963
Hope,Elmo (p) | Jackson,Lawrence (tp) | Douglas,Freddie (ss,as) | Gilmore,John (ts) | Boykins,Ronnie (b) | Jones,Philly Joe (dr)
It Shouldn't Happen To A Dream
Hope,Elmo (p) | Jackson,Lawrence (tp) | Douglas,Freddie (ss,as) | Gilmore,John (ts) | Boykins,Ronnie (b) | Jones,Philly Joe (dr) | Coleman,Earl (voc)
Groovin' High
Hope,Elmo (p) | Jackson,Lawrence (tp) | Douglas,Freddie (ss,as) | Gilmore,John (ts) | Boykins,Ronnie (b) | Jones,Philly Joe (dr) | Daniels,Marcelle (voc)

FSR CD 340 | CD | Voilà | EAN 8427328603409
Babs Gonzales And His Band
Le Continental | Me Spelled M-E Me | Them Jive New Yorkers | Lullaby Of The Doomed | The Preacher | A Nite In Tunisia | Movin' And Groovin'
NYC, rec. 16.7.1958
Gonzales,Babs (voc) | Spann,Les (fl) | Rouse,Charlie (b-cl) | Griffin,Johnny (ts) | Crawford,Ray (g) | Parlan,Horace (p) | Morrison,Peck (b) | Haynes,Roy (dr) | Voices Of The Modern Sound (voc-group) | Bailey,Joe (voc) | Lewis,Curtis (voc) | Freeman,Lee (voc) | Watts,Mamie (voc) | Liston,Melba (arr)
You've Changed | Beginning Of The End | Lonely One | Babs Mood For Love
NYC, rec. ca.1958
Gonzales,Babs (voc) | prob.personal: | Nance,Ray (v) | Jones,Hank (p) | Hinton,Milt (b) | Haynes,Roy (dr)
Cool Cookin'
Live at Insane Ayslum Cabaret,NYC, rec. ca.1958
Gonzales,Babs (voc) | prob.personal: | Terry,Clark (tp) | Griffin,Johnny (ts) | Jones,Hank (p) | Catlett,Buddy (b) | Haynes,Roy (dr)

FSR CD 345 | CD | The Complete Unedited 'Sweets At The Haig' 1953 Recordings | EAN 8427328603454
Harry Edison Quartet
September In The Rain | 'S Wonderful | Just You Just Me | Back Home Again In Indiana | Pennies From Heaven | These Foolish Things Remind Me On You | Tea For Two
Live at The Haig,LA, rec. 1.7.1953
Edison,Harry 'Sweets' (tp) | Ross,Arnold (p) | Comfort,Joe (b) | Stoller,Alvin (dr)

FSR CD 507 | CD | Cool Fool | EAN 8427328605076
Bud Shank And Trombones
Baby's Birthday Party | You Don't Know What Love Is | Sing Something Simple | Mobile
Hollywood,CA, rec. 3.4.1954
Shank,Bud (as) | Enevoldsen,Bob (v-tb) | Ferguson,Maynard (v-tb) | Williamson,Stu (v-tb) | Williamson,Claude (p) | Mondragon,Joe (b) | Manne,Shelly (dr) | Cooper,Bob (arr)
Wailing Vessel | Valve Head | Cool Fool | Little Girl Blue | Wailing Vessel(alt.take)
Hollywood,CA, rec. 22.6.1954
Shank,Bud (as) | Enevoldsen,Bob (v-tb) | Ferguson,Maynard (v-tb) | Williamson,Stu (v-tb) | Williamson,Claude (p) | Mondragon,Joe (b) | Manne,Shelly (dr) | Cooper,Bob (arr)
Low Life | Rustic Hop | With The Wind And The Rain In Your Hair | Low Life(alt.take)
Hollywood,CA, rec. 7.1.1955
Shank,Bud (as) | Brookmeyer,Bob (v-tb,arr) | Williamson,Claude (p) | Clark,Buddy (b) | Bunker,Larry (dr) | String Quartet | Mandell,Johnny (arr)
When Your Lover Has Gone | Out Of This World | There's A Small Hotel | You Are Too Beautiful
Hollywood,CA, rec. 29.5.1955
Shank,Bud (as) | Brookmeyer,Bob (v-tb) | Williamson,Claude (p) | Clark,Buddy (b) | Bunker,Larry (dr) | String Quartet | Garcia,Russell (arr)

FSR-CD 3004 | 2 CD | Historic Barcelona Concerts At Windsor Palace 1955
Louis Armstrong And His All Stars
When It's Sleepy Time Down South(Opening Theme) | Back Home Again In Indiana | Basin Street Blues | Tin Roof Blues | Bucket's Got A Hole In It | All The Things You Are | Dardanella | The Gypsy | On The Sunny Side Of The Street | How High The Moon | Undecided | Velma's Blues | Ko Ko Mo(I Love You So) | Mop Mop | When It's Sleepy Time Down South(Finale) | When It's Sleepy Time Down South(Opening Theme) | When The Saints Go Marching In | Black And Blue | Ole Miss | All Of Me | St.Louis Blues | Struttin' With Some Barbecue | Some Day | Perdido | Sweet Georgia Brown | Margie | That's My Desire | C'Est Si Bon | La Vie En Rose | Royal Garden Blues | When It's Sleepy Time Down South(Finale)
Live at The Winsor Palace,Barcelona,Spain, rec. 23.12.1955
Armstrong,Louis (tp,voc) | Young,Trummy (tb,voc) | Hall,Edmond (cl) | Kyle,Billy (p) | Shaw,Arvell (b) | Deems,Barrett (dr) | Middleton,Velma (voc)

FSR-CD 312 | CD | My Old Flame | EAN 8427328603126
Lou Levy Trio
I've Never Been In Love Before | The Trolley Song- | If You Could See Me Now | My Old Flame | Old Devil Moon | Gentle Rain | A Gal In C | Love Walked In
Hollywood,CA, rec. November 1978
Levy,Lou (p) | Atwood,Fred (b) | Dentz,John (dr)

FSR-CD 313 | CD | Just You & He & Me | EAN 8427328603133
Arnold Ross Trio
N S A | Just You & He & Me | Reliable Source | Then Or Now | Hugo
Hollywood,CA, rec. 30.10.1975
Ross,Arnold (p) | Babasin,Harry (b) | Harte,Roy (dr)
Bubbles,Bangles And Beans | Might Be
Hollywood,CA, rec. 8.6.1976
Ross,Arnold (p) | Babasin,Harry (b) | Harte,Roy (dr)
Look For The Silver Lining | The Love Nest | We Always Knew | Girl
Hollywood,CA, rec. 19.10.1976
Ross,Arnold (p) | Babasin,Harry (b) | Harte,Roy (dr)

FSR-CD 314 | CD | High On An Open Mike | EAN 8427328603140
Charlie Ventura Quintet
High On An Open Mike(Intro) | Charlie's Ant | Cry Me A River | Love And The Weather | Euphoria | Parlay 2 | Jazz Roost | Sleep Till Noon | East Of Suez | Bernie's Tune | Bernie's Tune(Ad Lib)
NYC, rec. 13.9.1956
Ventura,Charlie (ts,bs) | Bean,Billy (g) | Hildinger,Dave (p) | Davis,Richard (b) | Alexander,Mousie (dr)
Runnin' Wild | Honeysuckle Rose | When The Saints Go Marching In | It's Only A Paper Moon | Sweet Sue Just You | Dark Eyes | Bill Bailey Won't You Please Come Home | Stardust | Sweet Lorraine | Shine On Harvest Moon | Exactly Like You | I've Got You Under My Skin
NYC, rec. 18./19.7.1956
Ventura,Charlie (ts,bs) | Bean,Billy (g) | McKenna,Dave (p) | Davis,Richard (b) | Alexander,Mousie (dr)

FSR-CD 317 | CD | Portrair Of A Legend | EAN 8427328603171
Joe Albany Trio
Barbados | Bluebird | Little Suede Shoes | There Is No Greater Love | Au Privave | Lush Life | A.B.Blues | Old Friends | Woody'n You
Burbank,Los Angeles,CA, rec. 15./16.3.1966
Albany,Joe (p) | Vinnegar,Leroy (b) | Capp,Frank (dr)

FSR-CD 318 | CD | Soft Strut | EAN 8427328603164
Billy Butterfield And His Modern Dixie Stompers
Ti-Pi-Tin | Soft Strut | Says My Heart | I've Got The World On A String | I'm A Old Cowhand | All Right Be That Way | I Would Do Anything For You | He's A Devil In His Own Home Town | Somewhere Along The Way
NYC, rec. 1956
Butterfield,Billy (tp) | McGarity,Lou (tb) | McKusick,Hal (cl) | Richman,Abe 'Boomie' (b-cl,ts) | Wechsler,Moe (p) | Hinton,Milt (b) | Lamond,Don (dr)

FSR-CD 318 | CD | Sonny Criss Quartet Feat. Wynton Kelly | EAN 8427328603188
Sonny Criss Quartet
Sweet Lorraine | You Don't Know What Love Is | I Got It Bad And That Ain't Good
Chicago,Ill, rec. January 1959
Criss,Sonny (as) | Kelly,Wynton (p) | Cranshaw,Bob (b) | Perkins,Walter (dr)
Sonny Criss Quintet
Softly As In A Morning Sunrise | Butt's Delight | Sylvia | Back Home Again In Indiana
Criss,Sonny (as) | Hansen,Ole (tb) | Kelly,Wynton (p) | Cranshaw,Bob (b) | Perkins,Walter (dr)

FSR-CD 319 | CD | Tin Tin Deo | EAN 8427328603195
Lalo Schifrin And His Orchestra
Tin Tin Deo | Pega Joso | Mambo Jazz Opus No.7 | Kush | Harlem Nocturne
NYC, rec. 1962
Schifrin,Lalo (cond,arr) | Terry,Clark (tp) | Clevelanders,The | Wright,Leo (fl,as) | Powell,Seldon (fl,ts) | Richardson,Jerome (bs) | Yanez,Felipe (p) | Schifano,Frank (b) | Collins,Rudy (dr) | Mena,Antonio 'Chocolate' Diaz (perc) | Avila,Miguel (perc) | Allende,Victor (perc)
Lalo Schifrin Sextet
Cubano Be | Kush | An Evening In Sao Paulo | The Snake's Dance | Sphyros | Mount Olive | Desafinado | Rhythm-A-Ning
Schifrin,Lalo (p,arr) | Wright,Leo (fl,as) | Raney,Jimmy (g) | Davis,Art (b) | Collins,Rudy (dr) | Rodriguez,Willie (timbales)

FSR-CD 320 | CD | Jaywalkin' | EAN 8427328603201
J.R. Monterose Quintet
Jaywalkin' | Spice | Bradley's Beans | Suger Hips | Brainwasher | My Old Flame
NYC, rec. 25.2.& 9.3.1955
Monterose,J.R. (ts) | Sunkel,Phil (tp) | Legge,Wade (p) | Watkins,Doug (b) | Bradley,Bill (dr)
J.R. Monterose Sextet
Moods For Mitch | Manhattan | Plutocrat At The Automat | Have You Met Miss Jones | Man On The Couch | There's A Small Hotel | Love Walked In | Darn That Dream | Slightly Oliver
NYC, rec. June 1955
Monterose,J.R. (ts) | Charles,Teddy (vib) | Puma,Joe (g) | Sharon,Ralph (p) | Mingus,Charles (b) | Clarke,Kenny (dr)
It Don't Mean A Thing If It Ain't Got That Swing | A Fine Romance | Mynah Lament | That Goldblatt Magic
NYC, rec. November 1956
Monterose,J.R. (ts) | Costa,Eddie (vib) | Puma,Joe (g) | Sharon,Ralph (p) | Hinton,Milt (b) | Clarke,Kenny (dr)

FSR-CD 321 | CD | Little Big Horn | EAN 8427328603218
Ruby Braff And His Big City Six
Only A Blues | I'll Never Be The Same | In The Shade Of The Old Apple Tree | Deep River | I'm Shooting | Between The Devil And The Deep Blue Sea | The Lonesome Road | 'Deed I Do | Flakey | Love Me Or Leave Me
NYC, rec. 25.4.1955

FSR-CD 324 | CD | Chubby Takes Over | EAN 8427328603249
Chubby Jackson And His All Star Big Band
Loch Lomond | When The Saints Go Marching In | Oh Look At Me Now | Tradition | A Ballad For Jai | Mount Everest
NYC, rec. 25.-28.7.& 1.8.1958
Jackson,Chubby (b,ld) | Glow,Bernie (tp) | Markowitz,Irving 'Marky' (tp) | Royal,Ernie (tp) | Stewart,Al (tp) | Travis,Nick (tp) | Brookmeyer,Bob (v-tb,arr) | Dahl,Jimmy (tb) | Elton,Bill (tb) | Mitchell,Tom (tb) | Marowitz,Sam (as) | Most,Sam (fl,cl,as) | Cohn,Al (ts,arr) | Mondello,Pete (ts) | Bank,Danny (bs) | Napoleon,Marty (p) | Lamond,Don (dr)
It's De-Lovely | Alexander's Ragtime Band | Yes Indeed | Cover The Earth With Your Loveliness | Woodshed | Hail Hail The Herd's All Here
Jackson,Chubby (b,ld) | Ferrante,Joe (tp) | Markowitz,Irving 'Marky' (tp) | Royal,Ernie (tp) | Stewart,Al (tp) | Travis,Nick (tp) | Brookmeyer,Bob (v-tb,arr) | Dahl,Jimmy (tb) | Elton,Bill (tb) | Hixon,Richard 'Dick' (tb) | Marowitz,Sam (as) | Most,Sam (fl,cl,as) | Cohn,Al (ts,arr) | Mondello,Pete (ts) | Bank,Danny (bs) | Napoleon,Marty (p) | Lamond,Don (dr)

FSR-CD 325 | CD | Earth Dance | EAN 8427328603256
Anthony Ortega With String Orchestra
Smoke Gets In Your Eyes | Where Or When
NYC, rec. 20.6.1957
Ortega,Anthony (as) | Strings | Jacobs,Dick (arr,ld) | details unknown
Anthony Ortega With The Nat Pierce Orchestra
Just One Of Those Things | Bat Man's Blues | These Foolish Things Remind Me On You | Tune For Mona | No Fi
NYC, rec. November 1956
Ortega,Anthony (fl,cl,as,ts) | Starling,Ray (tp,mellophone) | Cleveland,Jimmy (tb) | Hafer,John 'Dick' (ts) | Cameron,Jay (bs) | Timmons,Bobby (p,celeste) | May,Earl (b) | Thigpen,Ed (dr) | Pierce,Nat (arr,ld)
Anthony Ortega With The Robert Zieff Orchestra
Four To Four | I Can't Get Started | Cinderella's Curfew | I Don't Stand A Ghost Of A Chance With You | Patting
Ortega,Anthony (fl,cl,as) | Farmer,Art (tp) | Buffington,Jimmy (fr-h) | Hafer,John 'Dick' (b-cl) | Tricarico,Bob (bassoon) | Wetmore | Abdul-Malik,Ahmed (b) | Zieff,Robert 'Bob' (arr,ld)

FSR-CD 326 | CD | Rolf Kühn And His Sound Of Jazz | EAN 8427328603263
Rolf Kühn Sextet
Istambul | South Of The Border | Atlanta,GA | Chicago
NYC, rec. 1960
Kühn,Rolf (cl) | Sheldon,Jack (tp) | Wayne,Chuck (g) | Bunch,John (p) | Grimes,Henry (b) | Mosca,Ray (dr)
Rolf Kühn Quintet
Lady Of Spain | A Touch Of Berlin
Kühn,Rolf (cl) | Hall,Jim (g) | Bunch,John (p) | Grimes,Henry (b) | Mosca,Ray (dr)
Caravan
Kühn,Rolf (cl) | Hall,Jim (g) | Bunch,John (p) | Duvivier,George (b) | Lamond,Don (dr)
Rolf Kühn Quartet
Waltzing Mathilda | Canadian Sunset | Manhattan
Kühn,Rolf (cl) | Bunch,John (p,org) | Duvivier,George (b) | Lamond,Don (dr)

FSR-CD 342 | 2 CD | Jazz Of Two Cities | EAN 8427328603423
Warne Marsh Quintet
Smog Eyes | Ear Conditioning | Lover Man(Oh,Where Can You Be?) | Quintessence
Hollywood,CA, rec. 3.10.1956
Marsh,Warne (ts) | Brown,Ted (ts) | Ball,Ronnie (p) | Tucker,Ben (b) | Morton,Jeff (dr)
Jazz Of Two Cities | Dixie's Dilemma | These Are The Things I Love | I Never Knew | Jazz Of Two Cities(alt.take) | I Never Knew(alt.take)
Hollywood,CA, rec. 11.10.1956
Marsh,Warne (ts) | Brown,Ted (ts) | Ball,Ronnie (p) | Tucker,Ben (b) | Morton,Jeff (dr)
Ben Blew | Time's Up | Earful | Blackjack
Hollywood,CA, rec. 24.10.1956
Marsh,Warne (ts) | Brown,Ted (ts) | Ball,Ronnie (p) | Tucker,Ben (b) | Morton,Jeff (dr)
Warne Marsh Quintet With Art Pepper
Aretha | Long Gone | Once We Were Young | Foolin' Myself | Avalon | Slow Boat To China | Crazy She Calls Me | Broadway | Arrival
Hollywood,CA, rec. 21.12.1956
Marsh,Warne (ts) | Pepper,Art (as) | Brown,Ted (ts) | Ball,Ronnie (p) | Tucker,Ben (b) | Morton,Jeff (dr)
Warne Marsh Quintet
Au Privave | Ad Libido | Warne Marsh(talking with Bobby Troupe) | These Are The Things I Love | Background Music | Bop Goes The Leesel
Live at 'Stars Of Jazz TV',Hollywood,CA, rec. 11.3.1957
Marsh,Warne (ts) | Brown,Ted (ts) | Ball,Ronnie (p) | Tucker,Ben (b) | Morton,Jeff (dr) | Troupe,Bobby (announcements)

NR 3CD-101 | 3 CD | The Complete Nocturne Recordings:Jazz In Hollywood Series Vol.1
Bud Shank Quintet
Casa De Luz | Lotus Bud | Left Bank | Shank's Pranks | Jasmine | Just A Few
Hollywood,CA, rec. 25.3.1954
Shank,Bud (fl,as) | Rogers,Shorty (fl-h) | Rowles,Jimmy (p) | Babasin,Harry (b) | Harte,Roy (dr)
Harry Babasin Quintet
La Rosita | Skylark | Tangerine | When You Wish Upon A Star | The Girl Friend | Easy To Remember | Babo-Ling
Hollywood,CA, rec. 18.4.1954
Babasin,Harry (cello,b) | Enevoldsen,Bob (v-tb,b) | Bunker,Larry (vib) | Rowles,Jimmy (p) | Harte,Roy (dr)
Bob Enevoldsen Quintet
Fast Buck | My Old Flame | Lulu's Back In Town | Bob White(Whatcha Gonna Swing Tonight) | Where Did The Gentleman Go | Snootie Little Cutie
Hollywood,CA, rec. 14.7.1954
Enevoldsen,Bob (v-tb,ts) | Paich,Marty (p) | Roberts,Howard (g) | Babasin,Harry (b) | Heath,Don (dr)
Bob Enevoldsen Sextet
Danca Do Brasil
Hollywood,CA, rec. 18.7.1954
Enevoldsen,Bob (v-tb,ts) | Paich,Marty (p) | Roberts,Howard (g) | Babasin,Harry (b) | Heath,Don (dr) | Harte,Roy (bongos)
Herbie Harper Quintet
Jeepers Leapers | Dinah | Five Brothers | Herbstone | Summertime | Jive At Five | Jeepers Leapers | Dinah | Five Brothers | Herbstone | Summertime | Jive At Five
Hollywood,CA, rec. 27.2.1954
Harper,Herbie (tb) | Gordon,Bob (bs) | Rowles,Jimmy (p) | Babasin,Harry (b) | Harte,Roy (dr)
The New York City Ghost | Sanguine | Now Playing | The Happy Clown
Hollywood,CA, rec. 16.9.1954
Harper,Herbie (tb) | Shank,Bud (ts,bs) | Paich,Marty (p) | Babasin,Harry (b) | Harte,Roy (dr)
Herbie Harper Quartet
Patty | Julie Is Her Name | 6-4 Mambo | Bananera | Indian Summer
Hollywood,CA, rec. 27.9.1954
Harper,Herbie (tb) | Hendrickson,Al (g) | Babasin,Harry (b) | Harte,Roy (dr)
Virgil Gonsalves Sextet
Bounce | Out Of Nowhere | Too Marvelous For Words | It Might As Well Be Spring | Yesterdays | Love Me Or Leave Me
Hollywood,CA, rec. 29.9.1954
Gonsalves,Virgil (bs) | Enevoldsen,Bob (bs) | Wise,Buddy (ts) | Levy,Lou (p) | Babasin,Harry (b) | Bunker,Larry (dr)
Lou Levy Trio
The Gentleman Is A Dope | Serenade In Blue | Woody'n You | Tres Palabras(Without You) | All The Things You Are | Tiny's Other Blues | Like Someone In Love | Bloo Denim
Hollywood,CA, rec. 29.8.1954
Levy,Lou (p) | Babasin,Harry (b) | Bunker,Larry (dr)
Jimmy Rowles Trio
Let's Fall In Love | All The Things You Are | The Day You Came Along | So Far So Good | I Wouldn't Change You For The World- | You Are Too Beautiful- | Serenade In Blue | Let's Fall In Love(alt.take) | Remember Me- | There Goes My Heart- | Oh! Lady Be Good | Chloe | Topsy
Hollywood,CA, rec. 13.12.1954
Rowles,Jimmy (p) | Mitchell,Red (b) | Mardigan,Art (dr)
-> Note: This 3-CD-Box incl. the 10'-LP's of Nocturne NLP-1/2/3/6/7/8/10 & 12)

Strand SLS CD 1007 | CD | To You With Love
Joe Zawinul Trio
It Might As Well Be Spring | Sweet And Lovely
NYC, rec. September 1959
Zawinul,Joe (p) | Tucker,George (b) | Dunlop,Frankie (dr)
Joe Zawinul Quartet
I Should Care | Easy Living | Please Send Me Someone To Love | Love For Sale | Squeeze Me | My One And Only Love | I'm Afraid The Masquerade Is Over - (I'm Afraid) The Masquerade Is Over
Zawinul,Joe (p) | Tucker,George (b) | Dunlop,Frankie (dr) | Barretto,Ray (congas)
Joe Zawinul
Greensleeves
Zawinul,Joe (p-solo)

G&J Records | Jazzpoint

GJ 2001 | CD | Gipsy Fascination | EAN 722746720126
Karol Adam Ensemble
Die Lerche | Zigeuner Romanze (e-moll) | Pfeifender Berg | Moldau | Sophisticated Lady | Monti Chardas | Zigeuner Tanz | Over The Rainbow | Ungarische Lieder | Säbel | Fascination | Granada | Ungarisches Potpourri
Stuttgart, rec. 2.6.1991
Adam,Karol (v) | Holub,Roman (cl) | Godla,Dezider (viola) | Holub,Robert (cimbal) | Bunda,Vojtech (b)

GJ 2009 Maxi-CD | CD | Let's Talk About Jazz
Benny Waters & Jan Jankeje
Let's Talk About Jazz | When The Saints Go Marching In | Let's Talk About Jazz(instrumental version) | When The Saints Go Marching In(instrumental version)
Stuttgart, rec. November 1996
Waters,Benny (as,voc) | Jankeje,Jan (b) | Lawrence,Andy (tp) | Katz,Alexander (tb) | Graf,Klaus (ts) | Polziehn,Olaf (p) | unkn. (synth,background-vocals,dr-computer) | Ritz,Ellen (voc)

Galaxy | ZYX Music GmbH

16GCD 1016-2 | 16 CD | Art Pepper:The Complete Galaxy Recordings
Art Pepper Quartet
Over The Rainbow | Miss Who | Lover Come Back To Me | Patricia | These Foolish Things Remind Me On You | Chris's Blues | Over The Rainbow | Yardbird Suite | I Love You | Pepper Pot | These Foolish Things Remind Me On You(alt.take) | Over The Rainbow(alt.take)
Berkeley,CA, rec. 1./2.12.1978
Pepper,Art (as) | Cowell,Stanley (p) | McBee,Cecil (b) | Haynes,Roy (dr)
Art Pepper Quintet
Mambo Koyama
Pepper,Art (as) | Cowell,Stanley (p) | McBee,Cecil (b) | Haynes,Roy (dr) | Nash,Kenneth (perc,conga)
Art Pepper Quartet
A Night In Tunisia | A Night In Tunisia(alt.take) | Straight No Chaser | Straight No Chaser(alt.take) | My Friend John | Yesterdays | Diane
NYC, rec. 23.2.1979
Pepper,Art (as) | Jones,Hank (p) | Carter,Ron (b) | Foster,Al (dr)
Art Pepper-Ron Carter Duo
Duo Blues
Pepper,Art (as) | Carter,Ron (b)
Art Pepper
Lover Man(Oh,Where Can You Be?) | Body And Soul | You Go To My Head
Burbank,Los Angeles,CA, rec. 25./26.5.1979
Pepper,Art (as-solo)
Art Pepper Trio
Anthropology | In A Mellow Tone
Pepper,Art (cl) | Dumas,Tony (b) | Higgins,Billy (dr)
Art Pepper Quartet
Blues For Blanche | Blues For Blanche(alt.take) | Blues For Blanche(alt.take-2) | Landscape | Stardust | Stardust(alt.take) | Donna Lee | Donna Lee(alt.take) | So In Love | Tin Tin Deo | My Friend John | My Friend John(alt.take)
Pepper,Art (as) | Cables,George (p) | Haden,Charlie (b) | Higgins,Billy (dr)
True Blue | Avalon | The Trip | Landscape | Sometime | Mambo De La Pinta | Red Car | Over The Rainbow | Mambo Koyama | Straight Life | Besame Mucho
Live at Shiba Yubin Chokin Hall,Tokyo,Japan, rec. 16.7.1979
Pepper,Art (cl,as) | Cables,George (p) | Dumas,Tony (b) | Higgins,Billy (dr)
True Blues | Avalon | The Shadow Of Your Smile | Landscape | Sometime | Mambo De La Pinta | Red Car | Over The Rainbow | Mambo Koyama | Straight Life | Besame Mucho
Live at Shiba Yubin Chokin Hall,Tokyo,Japan, rec. 23.7.1979
Pepper,Art (cl,as) | Cables,George (p) | Dumas,Tony (b) | Higgins,Billy (dr)
Art Pepper
But Beautiful | When You're Smiling
NYC, rec. 21.8.1979
Pepper,Art (as-solo)
Art Pepper Quartet
Surf Ride | Nature Boy | Straight Life | September Song | Long Ago And Far Away | Nature Boy(alt.take)
Berkeley,CA, rec. 21.9.1979
Pepper,Art (as) | Flanagan,Tommy (p) | Mitchell,Red (b) | Higgins,Billy (dr)
Art Pepper Quintet
Make A List Make A Wish
Pepper,Art (as) | Flanagan,Tommy (p) | Mitchell,Red (b) | Higgins,Billy (dr) | Nash,Kenneth (cowbell,reco-reco)
Art Pepper Quintet With Strings
Our Song | Our Song(alt.take) | Here's That Rainy Day | Here's That Rainy Day(alt.take) | That's Love | Winter Moon | Winter Moon(alt.take) | When The Sun Comes Out | When The Sun Comes Out(alt.take) | Blues In The Night | The Prisoner | The Prisoner(alt.take) | Ol' Man River
Berkeley,CA, rec. 3./4.9.1980
Pepper,Art (cl,as) | Cowell,Stanley (p) | Roberts,Howard (g) | McBee,Cecil (b) | Burnett,Carl (dr) | Rubin,Nathan (v,concertmaster) | Tenney,John (v) | Mazmanian,Greg (v) | Anderson,Patrice (v) | Foster,Clifton (v) | Smiley,Dan (v) | Desilva,Audrey (v) | Gibson,Elizabeth (v) | Gehl,Stephen (v) | Van Valkenburgh,Emily (v) | Meredith,Mary Ann (cello) | Adams,Terry (cello) | Holman,Bill (arr) | Bond,Jimmy (arr)
Art Pepper Quartet
Close To You Alone | There'll Never Be Another You | There'll Never Be Another You(alt.take) | Melolev | Melolev(alt.take) | Goodbye Again | Goodbye Again(alt.take)

Berkeley,CA, rec. 5.9.1980
Pepper,Art (cl,as) | Cowell,Stanley (p) | McBee,Cecil (b) | Burnett,Carl (dr)
Art Pepper Quintet
Mr.Big Falls His J.G. Hand
Pepper,Art (cl,as) | Roberts,Howard (g) | Cowell,Stanley (p) | McBee,Cecil (b) | Burnett,Carl (dr)
Art Pepper Quartet
Brazil
Pepper,Art (cl,as) | Roberts,Howard (g) | McBee,Cecil (b) | Burnett,Carl (dr)
Donna Lee | What's New? | Landscape | Valse Triste | Thank You Blues
Live at The Maiden Voyage,LA, rec. 13.8.1981
Pepper,Art (cl,as) | Cables,George (p) | Williams,David (b) | Burnett,Carl (dr)
For Freddie | Mambo Koyama | Road Waltz | Landscape | But Beautiful
Live at The Maiden Voyage,LA, rec. 14.8.1981
Pepper,Art (cl,as) | Cables,George (p) | Williams,David (b) | Burnett,Carl (dr)
Everything Happens To Me | Roadgame | Mambo Koyama | Allen's Alley | Road Waltz | Samba Mom Mom | Arthur's Blues | When You're Smiling | For Freddie | Roadgame
Live at The Maiden Voyage,LA, rec. 15.8.1981
Pepper,Art (as) | Cables,George (p) | Williams,David (b) | Burnett,Carl (dr)
Art Pepper-George Cables Duo
But Beautiful
Pepper,Art (as) | Cables,George (p)
Over The Rainbow | Over The Rainbow(alt.take) | Tete-A-Tete | Darn That Dream | Body And Soul | Body And Soul(alt.take) | The Way You Look Tonight | Round About Midnight | A Night In Tunisia | Samba Mom Mom | Last Thing Blues
Berkeley,CA, rec. 13./14.4.1982
Pepper,Art (as) | Cables,George (p)
Goin' Home | Samba Mom Mom | In A Mellow Tone | Don't Let The Sun Catch You Cryin' | Don't Let The Sun Catch You Cryin'(alt.take) | Don't Let The Sun Catch You Cryin'(alt.take-2) | Isn't She Lovely | Billie's Bounce | Lover Man(Oh,Where Can You Be?) | The Sweetest Sounds | You Go To My Head | You Go To My Head(alt.take) | Stardust | Darn That Dream
Berkeley,CA, rec. 11.5.1982
Pepper,Art (cl,as) | Cables,George (p)

2GCD 8201-2 | 2 CD | Art Pepper With Duke Jordan In Copenhagen 1981
Art Pepper With The Duke Jordan Trio
Blues Montmartre | What Is This Thing Called Love | Over The Rainbow | Caravan | Rhythm-A-Ning | You Go To My Head | Besame Mucho | Cherokee | Radio Blues | Good Bait | All The Things You Are
Live at 'Cafe Montmartre',Copenhagen, rec. 3.7.1981
Pepper,Art (cl,as) | Jordan,Duke (p) | Williams,David (b) | Burnett,Carl (dr)

5GCD 4431-2 | 5 CD | Art Pepper:The Hollywood All-Star Sessions
Bill Watrous And His West Coast Friends
Just Friends | Begin The Beguine | For Art's Sake | Funny Blues | Angel Eyes | P-Town | Funny Blues(alt.take) | Angel Eyes(alt.take)
Hollywood,CA, rec. 26./27.3.1979
Watrous,Bill (tb) | Pepper,Art (as) | Freeman,Russ (p) | Magnusson,Bob (b) | Burnett,Carl (dr)
Jack Sheldon And His West Coast Friends
Angel Wings | Softly As In A Morning Sunrise | You'd Be So Nice To Come Home To | Jack's Blues | Broadway | Historia De Un Amor | Minority | You'd Be So Nice To Come Home To(alt.take) | Broadway(alt.take)
Hollywood,CA, rec. 21./22.2.1980
Sheldon,Jack (tp) | Pepper,Art (as) | Leviev,Milcho (p) | Dumas,Tony (b) | Burnett,Carl (dr)
Pete Jolly And His West Coast Friends
Strike Up The Band | You Go To My Head | I Surrender Dear | Y.I.Blues | Night And Day | Everything Happens To Me | Out Of Nowhere | Y.I.Blues(alt.take)
Hollywood,CA, rec. 26./27.2.1980
Jolly,Pete (p) | Pepper,Art (as) | Magnusson,Bob (b) | McCurdy,Roy (dr)
Sonny Stitt And His West Coast Friends
Scrapple From The Apple | Wee | Bernie's Tune | How High The Moon | Walkin' | Groovin' High | Groovin' High(alttake)
Hollywood,CA, rec. 28./29.7.1980
Stitt,Sonny (as) | Pepper,Art (as) | Levy,Lou (p) | Domanico,Chuck (b) | Burnett,Carl (dr)
Atlas Blues | Lester Leaps In | My Funny Valentine | Imagination
Hollywood,CA, rec. 30./31.7.1980
Stitt,Sonny (as,ts) | Pepper,Art (as,ts) | Freeman,Russ (p) | Heard,John (b) | Burnett,Carl (dr)
Shelly Manne And His Hollywood All Stars
Just Friends | These Foolish Things Remind Me On You | Hollywood Jam Blues | Love Come Back To Me | Limehouse Blues | I'm Getting Sentimental Over You | I'm Getting Sentimental Over You(alt.take)
Hollywood,CA, rec. 4.8.1981
Manne,Shelly (dr) | Watrous,Bill (tb) | Pepper,Art (as) | Cooper,Bob (ts) | Jolly,Pete (p) | Budwig,Monty (b)
Lee Konitz And His West Coast Friends
'S Wonderful | Whims Of Chambers | A Minor Blues In F | High Jingo | The Shadow Of Your Smile | Anniversary Song | Cherokee | 'S Wonderful(alt.take) | Whims Of Chambers(alt.take)
Hollywood,CA, rec. 18./19.1.1982
Konitz,Lee (as) | Pepper,Art (cl,as) | Lang,Mike (p) | Magnusson,Bob (b) | Dentz,John (dr)

GCD 4202-2 | CD | Renascene
Art Pepper Quartet
Good Bait | What Laurie Likes | Here's That Rainy Day | Straight Life
Live at The Bach Dancing and Dynamite Society,Half Moon Bay,CA, rec. 28.9.1975
Pepper,Art (as) | Kelly,Ed (p) | Jenkins,Kenny (b) | Bilhorn,Brad (dr)

Geffen Records | Universal Music Germany

GED 24096 | CD | Song X
Pat Metheny/Ornette Coleman Group
Song X | Mob Job | Endangered Species | Video Games | Kathelin Gray | Trigonomerty | Song X Duo | Long Time No See
Live at Power Station,NYC, rec. 12.-14.12.1985
Coleman,Ornette (as,v) | Metheny,Pat (g,g-synth) | Haden,Charlie (b) | DeJohnette,Jack (dr) | Coleman,Denardo (dr,perc)

GED 24245 | CD | Letter From Home
GEC 24245 | MC | Letter From Home
GEF 24245 | LP | Letter From Home
Pat Metheny Group
Have You Heard | Every Summer Night | Better Days Ahead | Spring Ain't Here | 45-8 | 5-5-7 | Beat 70 | Dream Of Return | Are We There Yet | Vidala | Slip Away | Letter From Home
NYC, rec. Spring 1989
Metheny,Pat (g,el-g,g-synth,12-string-g,synclavier,tiple) | Anzar,Pedro (ts,vib,marimba,g,perc,charango,melodica,pan-pipe,voice) | Mays,Lyle (tp,p,org,accordeon,keyborads,synclavier) | Rodby,Steve (b,el-b) | Marcal,Armando (perc)

GED 24468 | CD | Secret Story
Pat Metheny Group With Orchestra
Abow The Treetops | Facing West | Cathedral In A Suitcase | Finding And Believing | The Longest Summer | Sunlight | Rain River | Always And Forever | See The World | As A Flower Blossom(I Am Running To You) | Antonia | The Truth Will Always Be | Tell Her You Saw Me | Not To Be Forgotten(Our Final Hour)
NYC, rec. 1991/92
Metheny,Pat (g,el-g,p,keyboards,el-b) | Mays,Lyle (p) | Lee,Will (el-b) | Vasconcelos,Nana (perc) | London Orchestra,The | Lubbock,Jeremy (cond)

GED 24601 | CD | The Road To You
Pat Metheny Group
Have You Heard | First Circle | The Road To You | Half Life Of Absolution | Last Train Home | Better Days Ahead | Naked Moon | Beat 70 | Letter From Home | Third Wind | Solo From 'More Travels'
details unknown, rec. details unknown
Metheny,Pat (g,el-g,g-synth,12-string-g,synclavier,tiple) | Anzar,Pedro (ts,vib,marimba,g,perc,charango,melodica,pan-pipe,voice) | Mays,Lyle (tp,p,org,accordeon,keyborads,synclavier) | Rodby,Steve (b,el-b) | Marcal,Armando (perc)

GED 24626 | CD | Zero Tolerance For Silence
Pat Metheny
Zero Tolerance For Silence(part 1-5)
NYC, rec. 16.12.1992
Metheny,Pat (g,el-g)

GED 24729 | CD | We Live Here
Pat Metheny Group
Here To Stay | And Then I Knew | The Girls Next Door | To The End Of The Of The World | We Live Here | Episode D'Azur | Something To Remind You | Red Sky | Stranger In Town
NYC, rec. 1994
Metheny,Pat (g,el-g,g-synth) | Ledford,Mark (tp,fl-h,voc,whistling) | Mays,Lyle (p,keyboards) | Rodby,Steve (b,el-b) | Wertico,Paul (dr) | Conte,Luis (perc) | Blamires,David (voc) | Merendino,Sammy (dr-programming) | Samuels,Dave (cymbal-rolls)

GED 24978 | CD | Quartet
Introduction | When We Were Free | Montevideo | Take Me There | Seven Days | Oceania | Dismantling Utopia | Double Blind | Second Thought | Mojave | Badland | Glacier | Language Of Time | Sometimes I See | As I Am
NYC, rec. May 1996
Metheny,Pat (g,el-g,e-bows,fretless-g,g-synth,slide,soprano-g,12-string-g,42-string-p | Mays,Lyle (p,el-p,autoharps,clavinet,harmonium,non-tuned-spinet-p) | Rodby,Steve (b,piccolo-b) | Wertico,Paul (dr,perc)
-> The limited audiophile edition of this CD is a 24 karat gold compact disc, No. GEFD 25118

GGG-Verlag:GGG Verlag und Mailorder | gggverlaggggverlagundmailorder

CD 01.03 | CD | Jazz Fresh
Jazz Fresh
Lift It | Double Mail | Jungle Of My Life
Magdeburg, rec. 2003
Jazz Fresh | Ratai,Jörg (g) | Käpernick,Guido (b) | Eggert,Gören (dr,perc)
Body And Soul | Killing Me Softly With His Song | Hicup
Jazz Fresh | Ratai,Jörg (g) | Käpernick,Guido (b) | Eggert,Gören (dr,perc) | Pannier,Tanja (voc)
Sunset
Jazz Fresh | Busch,Gregor (sax) | Ratai,Jörg (g) | Käpernick,Guido (b) | Eggert,Gören (dr,perc)
3 And 3
Jazz Fresh | Busch,Andreas (tp) | Hensel,Markus (tb) | Busch,Gregor (sax) | Ratai,Jörg (g) | Käpernick,Guido (b) | Eggert,Gören (dr,perc) | Failla,Jonathan (voc)
The Thrill Is Gone
Jazz Fresh | Busch,Andreas (tp) | Hensel,Markus (tb) | Busch,Gregor (sax) | Hensel,Ronald (org) | Ratai,Jörg (g) | Käpernick,Guido (b) | Eggert,Gören (dr,perc)
G.T.B.
Jazz Fresh | Busch,Andreas (tp) | Hensel,Markus (tb) | Busch,Gregor (sax) | Ratai,Jörg (g) | Käpernick,Guido (b,keyboards) | Eggert,Gören (dr,perc)

GNP Crescendo | ZYX Music GmbH

GNPD 56 | CD | Gene Norman Presents The Original Gerry Mulligan Tentet And Quartet
Gerry Mulligan Tentette
Westwood Walk | A Ballad | Walking Shoes | Rocker
Los Angeles,CA, rec. 29.1.1953
Mulligan,Gerry (bs) | Baker,Chet (tp) | Candoli,Pete (tp) | Enevoldsen,Bob (v-tb) | Graas,John (fr-h) | Siegel,Ray (tuba) | Shank,Bud (as) | Davidson,Don (bs) | Mondragon,Joe (b) | Hamilton,Forrest 'Chico' (dr)
Taking A Chance On Love | Flash | Simbah | Ontet
Los Angeles,CA, rec. 31.1.1953
Mulligan,Gerry (bs) | Baker,Chet (tp) | Candoli,Pete (tp) | Enevoldsen,Bob (v-tb) | Graas,John (fr-h) | Siegel,Ray (tuba) | Shank,Bud (as) | Davidson,Don (bs) | Mondragon,Joe (b) | Bunker,Larry (dr)
Gerry Mulligan Quartet
Varsity Drag | Speak Low | Half Nelson | Lady Bird | Love Me Or Leave Me | Swing House
Los Angeles,CA, rec. 7.5.1953
Mulligan,Gerry (bs) | Baker,Chet (tp) | Smith,Carson (b) | Bunker,Larry (dr)

Good Time Jazz | ZYX Music GmbH

FCD 60-008 | CD | Dixieland Favorites
Firehouse Five Plus Two
Bill Bailey Won't You Please Come Home
Los Angeles,CA, rec. 4.11.1958
Firehouse Five Plus Two | Alguire,Danny (tp) | Kimball,Ward (tb) | Probert,George (cl,ss) | Thomas,Frank (p) | Roberts,Dick (bj) | Kinch,Don (tuba) | Forrest,Eddie (dr)
When The Saints Go Marching In
Los Angeles,CA, rec. 11.5.1959
Firehouse Five Plus Two | Alguire,Danny (tp) | Kimball,Ward (tb) | Probert,George (cl,ss) | Thomas,Frank (p) | Roberts,Dick (bj) | Kinch,Don (tuba) | Forrest,Eddie (dr)
Come Back Sweet Papa
Los Angeles,CA, rec. 29.9.1959
Firehouse Five Plus Two | Alguire,Danny (co) | Kimball,Ward (tb) | Probert,George (cl,ss) | Thomas,Frank (p) | Roberts,Dick (bj) | Kinch,Don (b,tuba) | Forrest,Eddie (dr)
Jazz Me Blues | Working Man Blues
Los Angeles,CA, rec. 4.11.1959
Firehouse Five Plus Two | Alguire,Danny (co) | Kimball,Ward (tb) | Probert,George (cl,ss) | Thomas,Frank (p) | Roberts,Dick (bj) | Kinch,Don (b,tuba) | Forrest,Eddie (dr)
I Wish I Could Shimmy Like My Sister Kate
Los Angeles,CA, rec. 11.5.1959
Firehouse Five Plus Two | Alguire,Danny (co) | Kimball,Ward (tb) | Probert,George (cl,ss) | Thomas,Frank (p) | Roberts,Dick (bj) | Kinch,Don (b,tuba) | Forrest,Eddie (dr)
Muskrat Ramble | Canal Street Blues | Royal Garden Blues | That's A Plenty
Los Angeles,CA, rec. 14.3.1960
Firehouse Five Plus Two | Alguire,Danny (co) | Kimball,Ward (tb) | Probert,George (cl,ss) | Thomas,Frank (p) | Roberts,Dick (bj) | Kinch,Don (b,tuba) | Forrest,Eddie (dr)
Fidgety Feet | Storyville Blues | D.Jazz
Los Angeles,CA, rec. 21.3.1960
Firehouse Five Plus Two | Alguire,Danny (co) | Kimball,Ward (tb) | Probert,George (cl,ss) | Thomas,Frank (p) | Roberts,Dick (bj) | Kinch,Don (b,tuba) | Forrest,Eddie (dr)
A Hot Time In The Old Town | Firehouse Stomp
Los Angeles,CA, rec. 20./26.4.18.5.& 1.6.1964
Firehouse Five Plus Two | Alguire,Danny (co) | Kimball,Ward (tb) | Probert,George (cl,ss) | Thomas,Frank (p) | Kinch,Don (b,tuba) | Roberts,Dick (bj) | Forrest,Eddie (dr)
Yellow Dog Blues
Los Angeles,CA, rec. 6.-8.10.1969
Firehouse Five Plus Two | Alguire,Danny (co) | Kinch,Don (tp) | Kimball,Ward (tb) | Probert,George (ss) | Eckland,K.O. (p) | Newman,Bill (bj) | Bruns,George (tuba) | Forrest,Eddie (dr)

GTCD 10038-2 | CD | Crashes A Party
Mama Inez | Button Up Your Overcoat
Los Angeles,CA, rec. 29.9.1958
Firehouse Five Plus Two | Alguire,Danny (co) | Kimball,Ward (tb) | Probert,George (cl;ss) | Thomas,Frank (p) | Roberts,Dick (bj) | Kinch,Don (b,tuba) | Forrest,Eddie (dr)
Bill Bailey Won't You Please Come Home
Los Angeles,CA, rec. 4.11.1958
Firehouse Five Plus Two | Alguire,Danny (co) | Kimball,Ward (tb) | Probert,George (cl,ss) | Thomas,Frank (p) | Roberts,Dick (bj) | Kinch,Don (b,tuba) | Forrest,Eddie (dr)
Heart Of My Heart | You Are My Sunshine | I Want A Girl Just Like The Girl That Married Dear Old Dad
Los Angeles,CA, rec. 20.4.1959
Firehouse Five Plus Two | Alguire,Danny (co) | Kimball,Ward (tb) | Probert,George (cl;ss) | Thomas,Frank (p) | Roberts,Dick (bj) | Kinch,Don (b,tuba) | Forrest,Eddie (dr)
At The Jazz Band Ball | When The Saints Go Marching In
Los Angeles,CA, rec. 11.5.1959
Firehouse Five Plus Two | Alguire,Danny (co) | Kimball,Ward (tb) | Probert,George (cl,ss) | Thomas,Frank (p) | Roberts,Dick (bj) | Kinch,Don (b,tuba) | Forrest,Eddie (dr)
Let's Have A Party | At The Fireman's Ball | Ballin' The Jack | Nobody's Sweetheart
Los Angeles,CA, rec. 10.11.1959
Firehouse Five Plus Two | Alguire,Danny (co) | Kimball,Ward (tb) | Probert,George (cl,ss) | Thomas,Frank (p) | Roberts,Dick (bj) | Kinch,Don (b,tuba) | Forrest,Eddie (dr)

GTCD 10046-2 | CD | Free 'N' Easy
Don Ewell
Muskrat Ramble | Rumpus Rag | Parlor Social | Wild Man Blues
Baltimore,MD, rec. 1947
Ewell,Don (p-solo)
Ain't Misbehavin' | Lulu's Back In Town | Just You Just Me | Chicago Breakdown | All The Wrongs You've Done To Me
San Francisco,CA, rec. 21.22.6.1957
Ewell,Don (p-solo)
Don Ewell Trio
Blue Turning Grey Over Me
San Francisco,CA, rec. 21./22.6.1957
Ewell,Don (p) | Foster,George 'Pops' (b) | Hall,Minor 'Ram' (dr)
Don Ewell Quartet
Wolverine Blues | If I Could Be With You One Hour Tonight | Blues My Naughty Sweetie Gives To Me | Delmar Rag | What's The Use
Ewell,Don (p) | Howard,Darnell (cl) | Foster,George 'Pops' (b) | Hall,Minor 'Ram' (dr)

GTCD 10052-2 | CD | Goes To A Fire
Firehouse Five Plus Two
Fire | Keep The Home Fires Burning | Flaming Mamie | Hot Lips | Smokey Mokes | The Midnight Fire Alarm | Fireman Save My Child | Smokey The Bear | Hot Time In The Old Town Tonight | I Don't Want To Set The World On Fire | Oh Sister Ain't That Hot | Firehouse Stomp
Los Angeles,CA, rec. 20./26.4/18.5.& 1.6.1964
Firehouse Five Plus Two | Alguire,Danny (co) | Kimball,Ward (tb) | Probert,George (cl,ss) | Thomas,Frank (p) | Kinch,Don (b,tuba) | Roberts,Dick (bj) | Forrest,Eddie (dr)

GTCD 10065-2 | CD | Hooray For Bix!
Marty Grosz And His Honoris Causa Jazz Band
Changes | Cryin' All Day | Lonely Melody | I'm Gonna Meet My Sweety Now | Sorry | The Love Nest | Clementine | Wa-Da-Da | For No Reason At All In C
Yellow Springs,OH, rec. December 1957
Grosz,Marty (g,voc) | Halen,Carl (co) | Budd,Harry (tb) | Chace,Frank (cl,bs) | Skiver,Bob (cl,ts) | Soper,Tut (p) | Neilson,Chuck (b) | Boggs,Peter (dr)
My Pet | Oh, Miss Hannah | Because My Baby Don't Mean May Be Now
Grosz,Marty (g,voc) | Halen,Carl (co) | Santos,Turk (co,g) | Budd,Harry (tb) | Chace,Frank (cl,bs) | Skiver,Bob (cl,ts) | Soper,Tut (p) | Neilson,Chuck (b) | Boggs,Peter (dr)

GTCD 12018-2 | CD | Goes South
Firehouse Five Plus Two
Tuck Me To Sleep | Basin Street Blues | Georgia Camp Meeting
Los Angeles,CA, rec. 23.1.1954
Firehouse Five Plus Two | Alguire,Danny (co) | Kimball,Ward (tb) | Probert,George (cl,ss) | Thomas,Frank (p) | Roberts,Dick (bj) | Penner,Ed (b,tuba) | Mountjoy,Monte (dr)
Alabama Jubilee | I'm Gonna Charleston | Original Dixieland One Step
Los Angeles,CA, rec. 30.3.1954
Firehouse Five Plus Two | Alguire,Danny (co) | Kimball,Ward (tb) | Probert,George (cl,ss) | Thomas,Frank (p) | Goff,Harper (bj) | Penner,Ed (b,tuba) | Mountjoy,Monte (dr)
Swanee River | Birmingham Papa | Milneberg Joys | Tishomingo Blues
Los Angeles,CA, rec. 11.10.1956
Firehouse Five Plus Two | Alguire,Danny (co) | Kimball,Ward (tb) | Probert,George (cl,ss) | Thomas,Frank (p) | Roberts,Dick (bj) | Penner,Ed (b,tuba) | McDonald,Jim (dr)

GTCD 12024-2 | CD | Bunk & Lu
Yerba Buena Jazz Band
At A Georgia Camp Meeting | Irish Black Bottom | Original Jelly Roll Blues | Smoky Mokes | Maple Leaf Rag | Memphis Blues | Black And White Rag | Muskrat Ramble
San Francisco,CA, rec. 19.12.1941
Yerba Buena Jazz Band | Watters,Lu (co) | Scobey,Bob (co) | Murphy,Turk (tb) | Horne,Ellis (cl) | Rose,Wally (p) | Hayes,Clancy (bj) | Bennett,Russ (bj) | Lammi,Dick (tuba) | Dart,Bill (dr)
Bunk Johnson With The Yerba Buena Jazz Band
Careless Love Blues | 2:19 Blues | The Girls Go Crazy About The Way I Walk | When I Move To The Sky | Ace In The Hole | Ory's Creole Trombone | Nobody's Fault But Mine | Down By The Riverside
San Francisco,CA, rec. Spring 1944
Johnson,Bunk (tp,voc) | Yerba Buena Jazz Band | Murphy,Turk (tb) | Horne,Ellis (cl) | Bales,Burt (p) | Patton,Pat (bj) | Girsback,Squire (b) | Hayes,Clancy (dr,voc) | Peavey,Sister Lottie (voc)

GTCD 12045-2 | CD | This Kid's The Greatest!
Kid Ory's Creole Jazz Band
South Rampart Street Parade | The Girls Go Crazy About The Way I Walk | St.James Infirmary | Bill Bailey Won't You Please Come Home
Los Angeles,CA, rec. 17.7.1953
Ory,Edward 'Kid' (tb) | Buckner,Teddy (tp) | Brown,Pud (cl) | Glenn,Lloyd (p) | Davidson,Julian (g) | Garland,Ed (b) | Hall,Minor 'Ram' (dr)
Milneberg Joys | My Bucket's Got A Hole In It | Creole Love Call | Aunt Hagar's Blues
Los Angeles,CA, rec. 1.12.1953
Ory,Edward 'Kid' (tb) | Buckner,Teddy (tp) | McCracken,Bob (cl) | Ewell,Don (p) | Davidson,Julian (g) | Corb,Morty (b) | Hall,Minor 'Ram' (dr)
How Came You Do Me Like You Do | Four Or Five Times | Ballin' The Jack
Los Angeles,CA, rec. 1./2.12.1954
Ory,Edward 'Kid' (tb) | Alcorn,Alvin (tp) | Probert,George (cl) | Ewell,Don (p) | Kessel,Barney (g) | Garland,Ed (b) | Hall,Minor 'Ram' (dr)
Creole Song
Los Angeles,CA, rec. 18.6.1956
Ory,Edward 'Kid' (tb) | Alcorn,Alvin (tp) | Gomez,Phil (cl) | Haywood,Cedric (p) | Davidson,Julian (g) | Braud,Wellman (b) | Hall,Minor 'Ram' (dr)

GTCD 12048-2 | CD | Authentic New Orleans Jazz
Bunk Johnson And His Superior Jazz Band
Panama | Down By The Riverside | Storyville Blues | Ballin' The Jack | Make Me A Pallet On The Floor | Weary Blues | Moose March | Bunk's Blues | Yes, Lord I'm Crippled
New Orleans,Louisiana, rec. 11.6.1942
Johnson,Bunk (tp) | Robinson,Jim (tb) | Lewis,George (cl) | Decou,Walter (p) | Marrero,Lawrence (bj) | Young,Austin (b) | Rogers,Ernest (dr)

Bunk Johnson
Bunk Johnson Talking Records(9:29)
Johnson,Bunk (talking)

GTCD 12058-2 | CD | The Beverly Caverns Session
George Lewis And His New Orleans Ragtime Band
Down By The Riverside | Dallas Blues | Four Or Five Times | We Shall Walk Through The Streets Of The City | Tin Roof Blues | Lord Lord Lord You've Sure Been Good To Me | Just A Closer Walk With Thee | Bugle Boy March | Burgundy Street Blues | Darling Nelly Gray | Washington And Lee Swing | When The Saints Go Marching In
Live at The Beverly Caverns,Hollywood,CA, rec. 26./27.5.1953
Lewis,George (cl) | Howard,Avery 'Kid' (tp,voc) | Robinson,Jim (tb) | Purnell,Alton (p) | Marrero,Lawrence (bj) | Pavageau,Alcide 'Slow Drag' (b) | Watkins,Joe (dr,voc)

GTCD 12063-2 | CD | Meet Me Where They Play The Blues
Jack Teagarden And His Band
Original Dixieland One Step | Eccentric | Bad Actin' Woman | High Society
NYC, rec. 12./13.11.1954
Teagarden,Jack (tb,voc) | McPartland,Jimmy (tp) | Hall,Edmond (cl) | Cary,Dick (p) | Page,Walter (b) | Jones,Jo (dr)
Riverboat Shuffle | Mis'ry And The Blues | Milneberg Joys | King Porter Stomp
Teagarden,Jack (tb,voc) | Greenleaf,Fred (tp) | Davern,Kenny (cl) | Teagarden,Norma (p) | Malone,Kasper 'Kass' (b) | Bauduc,Ray (dr)
Blue Funk | Davenport Blues | Meet Me Where They Play The Blues | Music To Love By
Teagarden,Jack (tb,voc) | Cary,Dick (tp) | Hall,Edmond (cl) | Feather,Leonard (p) | Kress,Carl (g) | Page,Walter (b) | Bauduc,Ray (dr)

GTCD 12066-2 | CD | Blues Over Bodega
Lu Watters' Jazz Band
San Andreas Fault | See See Rider | The Villain | Some Of These Days | Blues Over Bodega | Willie The Weeper | Pork And Beans | San Francisco Bay Blues | Emperor Norton's Hunch
San Francisco,CA, rec. 1963
Watters,Lu (tp) | Mielke,Bob (tb) | Helm,Bob (cl) | Rose,Wally (p) | Ballou,Monte (bj) | Short,Bob (b,tuba) | Vandan,Thad (dr) | Dane,Barbara (voc)

Green House Music | sunny moon Musikvertrieb

CD 1001 | CD | Floating Pictures
René Pretschner
After All | Floating Pictures Sonata No.1[part 1-3](dedicated to Regina Donner)
Wuppertal, rec. 1995
Pretschner,René (p-solo)
René Pretschner Trio
Deep In The Water | On My Own
Pretschner,René (p) | Foltynowicz,Jens (b) | Schönburg,Kai (dr)
René Pretschner Quartet
Joey & Jerry | The Summer '95 | Kaspar Hauser
Pretschner,René (p) | Boelens,Miguel (as) | Foltynowicz,Jens (b) | Schönburg,Kai (dr)
In The Jazzclub
Pretschner,René (p) | Jacobi,Frank (ts) | Foltynowicz,Jens (b) | Schönburg,Kai (dr)

CD 1002 | CD | Ten Piano Players,Vol.1
John Taylor
Quatorze
Wuppertal, rec. March 1995
Taylor,John (p-solo)
Mike Del Pedro
Waltz Three
Del Pedro,Mike (p-solo)
Robert Jan Vermeulen
Central Station
Vermeulen,Robert Jan (p-solo)
Aki Takase
Yao And Mama's Dance
Takase,Aki (p-solo)
René Pretschner
After All
Pretschner,René (p-solo)
Rob Van Den Broeck
Freefair
Van Den Broeck,Rob (p-solo)
Melo Mafali
The White Lady And The Black Tarot
Mafali,Melo (p-solo)
Jasper Van't Hof
The Quiet American
Van't Hof,Jasper (p-solo)
Christian Doepke
Abschiedslied
Doepke,Christian (p-solo)
Simon Nabatov
Ligibul
Nabatov,Simon (p-solo)

CD 1003(Maxi) | CD | Naranja
Jazz Bomberos
Up And At It | Naranja | Schmalz On The Bottom | Red Baron
Wuppertal, rec. March 1996
Jazz Bomberos | Gärtner,Chancy (sax) | Janssen,Jens (g) | Pretschner,René (el-p,org) | Krebs,Klaus (el-b) | Meyer,Friedemann (dr,perc)

CD 1004 | CD | Departures
Rob Van Den Broeck-Wiro Mahieu
Departures | Marathon Man | Little One | Roundtrip | Song For Eddie | Monk's Mood | Freefair | Slowmotion | The Very Thought | Metal Beauty | Sailing | Interaction | Epilogue
Wuppertal, rec. October 1996
Van Den Broeck,Rob (p) | Mahieu,Wiro (b)

CD 1005 | CD | Unfinished Business
Konstantin Wienstroer-Veit Lange-Felix Elsner
Renard & Les Déserteurs
Wuppertal, rec. October 1995
Lange,Veit (b-cl,ts) | Elsner,Felix (p,keyboards) | Wienstroer,Konstantin (b)
Triggerfinger Suite: | Rain- | Triggerfingers- | Low Pressure Liquid Colorado- | Triggerfingers(2)- | Left Hand(Fovea Sanguinis) | The Basilisk | 2nd Order Kinetic | Brief And Die Pharisäer
Wuppertal, rec. November 1996
Lange,Veit (b-cl,ts) | Elsner,Felix (p,keyboards) | Wienstroer,Konstantin (b)
Pyjama- | Table Talk-
Lange,Veit (b-cl,ts) | Elsner,Felix (p,keyboards) | Wienstroer,Konstantin (b) | Engelhardt,Raimund (pakawaj,tablas)

CD 1006 | CD | The Piano Duo:El Latino
René Pretschner & Melo Mafali
La Ciudad Habana | Besame Mucho | En El Final De La Noche | La Morte Douce | Deep In The Water | Sing The Song | Mutazione | Inferno | Over The Rainbow
Wuppertal, rec. 19.-22.5.1997
Pretschner,René (p) | Mafali,Melo (p)

CD 1008 | CD | The Shimmering Colours Of The Stained Glass
Hubert Nuss Trio
The Shimmering Colours Of The Stained Glass(I) | Awakening | Remembering The Start Of A Never Ending Story | Stomp | The Shimmering Colours Of The Stained Glass(II) | More Than You Ever Know | A Tender Farewell To A Spanish Woman | Song For A Real Friend | I Have A Love- | The Lion Queen- | Anxiety-The Colonal Of Mortal Life | Llonio's Song
Topaz Audio Studio,?, rec. 26./27.5.1997
Nuß,Hubert (p) | Goldsby,John (b) | Riley,John (dr)

CD 1011 | CD | La Chipaca
Gabriel Pérez Group
Viva Los Novios | Con Plastillina Verde | Verve Y Agua | Que Dios Te Lo Deba | La Viejita Clotilde | Tierra Tibia | Tres De Azucar | Grillitos | La Chipaca
Bonn, rec. 1997
Pérez,Gabriel (fl,cl,sax,keyboards) | Hesse,Oliver (tp,fl-h) | Wogram,Nils (tb) | Leicht,Oliver (cl,b-cl) | Sinese,Quinque (g,charango,spanish-7-string-g) | Friedrich,Jürgen (p) | Heinze,Volker (b) | Doctor,Marcio (perc)

CD 1013 | CD | Story Of A Jazz Piano Vol.1
René Pretschner
When I Fall In Love | Days Of Wine And Roses | Stella By Starlight | Body And Soul | Our Spanish Love Song | So Tender | Farmer's Trust | Michelle | Lush Life
Wuppertal, rec. May-July 2000
Pretschner,René (p-solo)
Things Ain't What They Used To Be
Pretschner,René (p) | Eller,Harald 'Haro' (b)

Groove Note | Fenn Music

GN 1005(180gr-Pressung) | LP | What A Wonderful World
GRV 1005-2 | CD | What A Wonderful World
Jay McShann Quintet
Piney Brown Blues | Cherry Red | Just For Fun | Gee Baby Ain't I Good To You | Crazy Legs And Friday Strut | Rain Is Such A Lonesome Sound | Land Of Dreams | Lonely Boy Blues | Hot Biscuits | Blue Monday | What A Wonderful World
Kansas City,MO, rec. 3./4.5.1999
McShann,Jay (p,voc) | Alaadeen,Ahmad (ts) | Kenner,Sonny (g) | Spaits,Gerald (b) | Strait,Todd (dr)

GRV 1005-2 | CD | What A Wonderful World
McShann,Jay (p,voc) | Alaadeen,Ahmad (ts) | Kenner,Sonny (g) | Spaits,Gerald (b) | Strait,Todd (dr)

GRV 1011-2(Gold CD 2011) | CD | Lush Life | EAN 660318101129
Jacintha With Band And Strings
Black Coffee | Lush Life | Smile
Hollywood,CA, rec. 24./25.8.2001
Jacintha (voc) | Cunliffe,Bill (p,arr) | Oles,Darek (b) | LaBarbera,Joe (dr) | Kent,Peter (v) | Hughes,Norman (v) | Wittenberg,John (v) | Kronstadt,Gina (v) | Stein,Eddie (v) | Chatman,Susan (v) | Frazier,Virginia (viola) | Mayer,Marium (viola) | Koven,Renita (viola) | Stein,Rudi (cello) | Baldwin,Peggy (cello) | Shulman,Amy (harp)
Boulevard Of Broken Dreams
Jacintha (voc) | Marocco,Frank (accordeon) | Wilson,Anthony (g) | Cunliffe,Bill (p,arr) | Oles,Darek (b) | LaBarbera,Joe (dr) | Kent,Peter (v) | Hughes,Norman (v) | Wittenberg,John (v) | Kronstadt,Gina (v) | Stein,Eddie (v) | Chatman,Susan (v) | Frazier,Virginia (viola) | Mayer,Marium (viola) | Koven,Renita (viola) | Stein,Rudi (cello) | Baldwin,Peggy (cello) | Shulman,Amy (harp)
Manha De Carnaval(Morning Of The Carnival)
Jacintha (voc) | Wilson,Anthony (g) | Cunliffe,Bill (p,arr) | Oles,Darek (b) | LaBarbera,Joe (dr) | Kent,Peter (v) | Hughes,Norman (v) | Wittenberg,John (v) | Kronstadt,Gina (v) | Stein,Eddie (v) | Chatman,Susan (v) | Frazier,Virginia (viola) | Mayer,Marium (viola) | Koven,Renita (viola) | Stein,Rudi (cello) | Baldwin,Peggy (cello) | Shulman,Amy (harp)
The Shadow Of Your Smile | September Song
Jacintha (voc) | Matheny,Dmitri (fl-h) | Wilson,Anthony (g) | Cunliffe,Bill (p,arr) | Oles,Darek (b) | LaBarbera,Joe (dr) | Kent,Peter (v) | Hughes,Norman (v) | Wittenberg,John (v) | Kronstadt,Gina (v) | Stein,Eddie (v) | Chatman,Susan (v) | Frazier,Virginia (viola) | Mayer,Marium (viola) | Koven,Renita (viola) | Stein,Rudi (cello) | Baldwin,Peggy (cello) | Shulman,Amy (harp)
Summertime | When The World Was Young | Harlem Nocturne
Jacintha (voc) | Matheny,Dmitri (fl-h) | Cunliffe,Bill (p,arr) | Oles,Darek (b) | LaBarbera,Joe (dr) | Kent,Peter (v) | Hughes,Norman (v) | Wittenberg,John (v) | Kronstadt,Gina (v) | Stein,Eddie (v) | Chatman,Susan (v) | Frazier,Virginia (viola) | Mayer,Marium (viola) | Koven,Renita (viola) | Stein,Rudi (cello) | Baldwin,Peggy (cello) | Shulman,Amy (harp)

GRP | Universal Music Germany

543272-2 | CD | Billie Holiday:The Complete Commodore Recordings
Billie Holiday With Frankie Newton And His Orchestra
Strange Fruit | Fine And Mellow | I Gotta Right To Sing The Blues
NYC, rec. 20.4.1939
Holiday,Billie (voc) | Newton,Frankie (tp) | Smith,Tab (as) | Hollon,Kenneth (ts) | Payne,Stanley (ts) | White,Sonny (p) | McLin,Jimmy (g) | Williams,John B. (b) | Dougherty,Eddie (dr)
Billie Holiday And Her Quintet
Yesterdays
rec. 20.4.1939
Holiday,Billie (voc) | Hollon,Kenneth (ts) | White,Sonny (p) | McLin,Jimmy (g) | Williams,John B. (b) | Dougherty,Eddie (dr)
Billie Holiday With Eddie Heywood And His Orchestra
How Am I To Know? | My Old Flame | I'll Get By(As Long As I Have You) | I Cover The Waterfront
NYC, rec. 25.3.1944
Holiday,Billie (voc) | Heywood,Eddie (p) | Cheatham,Doc (tp) | Dickenson,Vic (tb) | Davis,Lem (as) | Walters,Teddy (el-g) | Simmons,John (b) | Catlett,Big Sid (dr)
I'll Be Seeing You | I'm Yours | Embraceable You | As Time Goes By
NYC, rec. 1.4.1944
Holiday,Billie (voc) | Heywood,Eddie (p) | Cheatham,Doc (tp) | Dickenson,Vic (tb) | Davis,Lem (as) | Simmons,John (b) | Catlett,Big Sid (dr)
Billie's Blues | On The Sunny Side Of The Street
NYC, rec. 8.4.1944
Holiday,Billie (voc) | Heywood,Eddie (p) | Webster,Freddie (tp) | Dickenson,Vic (tb) | Davis,Lem (as) | Walters,Teddy (el-g) | Simmons,John (b) | Catlett,Big Sid (dr)
He's Funny That Way | Lover Come Back To Me
Holiday,Billie (voc) | Heywood,Eddie (p) | Simmons,John (b) | Catlett,Big Sid (dr)

951816-2 | CD | Benny Golson:Free
Benny Golson Band
You're My Thrill | My Heart Belongs To Daddy | The Best Thing For You | Impromptune | Little Karin
NYC, rec. 13.12.1960
Golson,Benny (ts) | Walton,Cedar (p) | Williams,Tommy (b) | Heath,Albert 'Tootie' (dr)

951827-2 | CD | Al And Zoot
Al Cohn Quintet feat. Zoot Sims
It's A Wonderful World | Brandy And Beer | Two Funky People | Chasin' The Blues | Halley's Comet | You're A Lucky Guy | The Wailing Boat | Just You Just Me
NYC, rec. 27.3.1957
Cohn,Al (ts) | Sims,Zoot (cl,ts) | Allison,Mose (p) | Kotick,Teddy (b) | Stabulas,Nick (dr)

GRP 16272 | CD | Body And Soul Revisited
Coleman Hawkins All Star Octet
It's No Sin - (It's No) Sin | And So To Sleep Again
NYC, rec. 19.10.1951
Hawkins,Coleman (ts) | Harris,Benny (tp) | Sulieman[Leonard Graham],Idrees (tp) | Ghee,Matthew (tb) | Payne,Cecil (bs) | Jordan,Duke (p) | Henry,Conrad (b) | Taylor,Arthur 'Art' (dr)
Coleman Hawkins Quintet
Carioca
NYC, rec. 31.1.1952
Hawkins,Coleman (ts) | Gold,Sanford (p) | Casimenti,Al (g) | Alpert,Trigger (b) | Shawker,Norris 'Bunny' (dr)
Coleman Hawkins Quintet With Strings
Spellbound | Lost In A Fog
Hawkins,Coleman (ts) | Gold,Sanford (p) | Casimenti,Al (g) | Alpert,Trigger (b) | Shawker,Norris 'Bunny' (dr) | Strings | details unknown
Coleman Hawkins Sextet
Midnight Sun
NYC, rec. 26.2.1952
Hawkins,Coleman (ts) | Wilder,Joe (tp) | Doggett,Bill (p,org) | Makia,Sam (hawaiian-g) | Mendelsohn,Danny (cello) | Alpert,Trigger (b) | Crawford,James 'Jimmy' (dr)
If I Could Be With You One Hour Tonight | I Can't Get Started
NYC, rec. 30.7.1952
Hawkins,Coleman (ts) | Barnes,George (g) | unkn. (vib,p,b,dr)
Coleman Hawkins With Paul Neilson's Orchestra
Ruby | Song From Moulin Rouge
NYC, rec. 27.4.1953
Hawkins,Coleman (ts) | Orchestra | Hefti,Neal (cond) | details unknown
Cozy Cole's Big Seven
My Blue Heaven | Honeysuckle Rose | Organ Grinder's Swing | Perdido | Sweethearts On Parade
NYC, rec. mid 1950s
Cole,William 'Cozy' (dr) | Stewart,Rex (co) | Glenn,Tyree (tb) | Hawkins,Coleman (ts) | Hopkins,Claude (p) | Bauer,Billy (g) | Shaw,Arvell (b)
Coleman Hawkins
Foolin' Around
Live at Pythian Temple,NYC, rec. 7.11.1955
Hawkins,Coleman (ts-solo)
Coleman Hawkins Quartet
The Man I Love | Time On My Hands
Hawkins,Coleman (ts) | Jones,Hank (p) | Marshall,Wendell (b) | Wilson,Shadow (dr)
Tony Scott And The All Stars
Body And Soul
NYC, rec. 13.10.1958
Scott,Tony (cl) | Hawkins,Coleman (ts) | Flanagan,Tommy (p) | Ramey,Gene (b) | Bolden,Walter (dr)
Ornithology | Unlisted Blues
Scott,Tony (cl) | Knepper,Jimmy (tb) | Hawkins,Coleman (ts) | Flanagan,Tommy (p) | Ramey,Gene (b) | Bolden,Walter (dr)

GRP 16362 | CD | Pure Ella
Ella Fitzgerald With Ellis Larkins
Looking For A Boy | My One And Only | How Long Has This Been Going On | I've Got A Crush On You
NYC, rec. 11.9.1950
Fitzgerald,Ella (voc) | Larkins,Ellis (p)
But Not For Me | Soon | Someone To Watch Over Me | Maybe
NYC, rec. 12.9.1950
Fitzgerald,Ella (voc) | Larkins,Ellis (p)
I'm Glad There Is You | Baby, What Else Can I Do? | What Is There To Say | Makin' Whoopee | Until The Real Thing Comes Along | People Will Say We're In Love
NYC, rec. 29.3.1954
Fitzgerald,Ella (voc) | Larkins,Ellis (p)
Please Be Kind | Imagination | My Heart Belongs To Daddy | You Leave Me Breathless | Nice Work If You Can Get It | Stardust
NYC, rec. 20.3.1954
Fitzgerald,Ella (voc) | Larkins,Ellis (p)

GRP 20062 | CD | In Tribute
Diane Schuur Trio
Black Coffee | Sophisticated Lady
Capitol & Pacifique Studios,?, rec. details unknown
Schuur,Diane (p,voc) | Domanico,Chuck (b) | LaBarbera,Joe (dr)
Diane Schuur With Orchestra
Them There Eyes | God Bless The Child | Sweet Georgia Brown | How High The Moon | Love For Sale | The Best Is Yet To Come
Schuur,Diane (voc) | personal included: | Menza,Don (ts) | Budimir,Dennis (g) | Broadbent,Alan (p) | Clayton,John (b) | Hamilton,Jeff (dr) | Brass | details not on the cover
Diane Schuur Trio With Orchestra And Strings
The Man I Love | I Guess I'll Hang My Tears Out To Dry | Round About Midnight | Body And Soul | Every Time We Say Goodbye
Schuur,Diane (voc) | personal included: | Menza,Don (ts) | Budimir,Dennis (g) | Broadbent,Alan (p) | Clayton,John (b) | Hamilton,Jeff (dr) | Brass | Strings | details not on the cover

GRP 95022 | CD | The Glenn Miller Orchestra In Digital Mood
Glenn Miller And His Orchestra
In The Mood | Chattanooga Choo Choo | American Patrol | A String Of Pearls | Little Brown Jug | Kalamazoo | Tuxedo Junction | St.Louis Blues March | Pennsylvania Six Five Thousand | Moonlight Serenade
NYC, rec. ca.1983
O'Brien,Larry (cond) | Stamm,Marvin (tp) | Markowitz,Irving 'Marky' (tp) | Maxwell,Jimmy (tp) | Frosk,John (tp) | Russo,Sonny (tb) | Andre,Wayne (tb) | Masso,George (tb) | Faulise,Paul (tb) | Levinsky,Walt (cl,sax) | Bodner,Phil (reeds) | Slapin,Bill (reeds) | Lewis,Morty (reeds) | Schlinger,Sol (reeds) | Leighton,Bernie (p) | Grusin,Dave (p) | Pizzarelli,Bucky (g) | Leonhart,Jay (b) | Zito,Ronnie (dr) | La Rosa,Julius (voc) | Tormé,Mel (voc) | VerPlanck,Marlene (voc) | Nelson,Marty (voc)

GRP 95072 | CD | Mountain Dance
Dave Grusin Group
Rag Bag | Rondo | Mountain Dance | Captain Caribe | Either Way
NYC, rec. details unknown
Grusin,Dave (p,el-p,synth) | Mironov,Jeff (el-g) | Walsh,Ed (synth) | Underwood,Ian (synth) | Miller,Marcus (el-b) | Mason,Harvey (dr) | Bassini,Rubens (perc)
Friends And Strangers | City Lights
Grusin,Dave (p,el-p,synth) | Walsh,Ed (synth) | Underwood,Ian (synth) | Miller,Marcus (el-b) | Mason,Harvey (dr) | Bassini,Rubens (perc)
Dave Grusin
Thanksong
Grusin,Dave (p-solo)

GRP 95242 | CD | Rio
Lee Ritenour Group
Rainbow | Simplicidad
Rio De Janeiro,Brazil/Santa Barbara,CA/NYC, rec. details unknown
Ritenour,Lee (g) | Grusin,Don (keyboards) | Neves,Oscar Castro (g) | Maia,Luizao (b) | Braga,Paulinho (dr) | Batera,Chico (perc) | Da Silva,Jose (perc) | Pinheiro,Roberto Bastos (perc) | Marcal,Armando (perc)
San Juan Sunset | Rio Funk | A Little Bit Of This And A Little Bit Of That
Ritenour,Lee (g) | Grusin,Dave (keyboards) | Mironov,Jeff (g) | Miller,Marcus (b) | Williams,Buddy (dr) | Bassini,Rubens (perc)
It Happens Everyday | Ipanema Sol
Ritenour,Lee (g) | Watts,Ernie (fl,ss) | Grusin,Don (keyboards) | Laboriel,Abe (b) | Acuna,Alejandro Neciosup (dr) | Forman,Steve (perc)

GRP 95352 | CD | The Chick Corea Elektric Band
Chick Corea Electric Band
Rumble
Los Angeles,CA, rec. details unknown
Corea,Chick (keyboards,synth) | Weckl,Dave (dr,perc)
Sidewalk
Corea,Chick (keyboards,synth) | Rios,Carlos (el-g) | Weckl,Dave (dr,perc)
Cool Weasel Boogie | Elektric City
Corea,Chick (keyboards,synth) | Rios,Carlos (el-g) | Patitucci,John (b,el-b) | Weckl,Dave (dr,perc)
Got A Match? | No Zone | India Town | All Love
Corea,Chick (keyboards,synth) | Patitucci,John (b,el-b) | Weckl,Dave (dr,perc)
City Gate | King Cockroach | Silver Temple
Corea,Chick (keyboards,synth) | Henderson,Scott (g) | Patitucci,John (b,el-b) | Weckl,Dave (dr,perc)

GRP 95462 | CD | Light Years
Light Years | Second Sight | Flamingo | Prism | Time Track | Starlight | Your Eyes | The Dragon | View From The Outside
NYC, rec. details unknown
Corea,Chick (keyboards,synth) | Marienthal,Eric (sax) | Gambale,Frank (g) | Patitucci,John (b,el-b) | Weckl,Dave (dr)

GRP 95642 | CD | Eye Of The Beholder
Home Universe | Forgotten Past | Passage | Beauty | Cascade(part 1+2) | Tance Dance | Eye Of The Beholder

rec. details unknown
Corea,Chick (p,synth) | Marienthal,Eric (sax) | Gambale,Frank (el-g) | Patitucci,John (el-b) | Weckl,Dave (dr)
Eternal Child
Corea,Chick (p,synth) | Marienthal,Eric (sax) | Gambale,Frank (el-g) | Novello,John (synth) | Patitucci,John (el-b) | Weckl,Dave (dr)

GRP 95702 | CD | Festival
Lee Ritenour Group
Night Rhythms | Latin Lovers | Humana | Rio Sol | Odile Odila | Linda | New York-Brazil | The Inner Look
Ritenour,Lee (g,g-synth) | Watts,Ernie (as,ts) | James,Bob (keyboards) | Grusin,Dave (keyboards) | Miller,Marcus (el-b) | Jackson,Anthony (b-g) | Hakim,Omar (dr) | Da Costa,Paulinho (perc) | Brown,Carlinhos (perc) | Leporace,Gracinha (voc)

GRP 95822 | CD | Akoustic Band
Chick Corea Trio
Bessie's Blues | My One And Only Love | So In Love | Sophisticated Lady | Autumn Leaves | Someday My Prince Will Come | Morning Sprite | T.B.C.(Terminal Baggage Claim) | Circles | Spain
NYC, rec. details unknown
Corea,Chick (p) | Patitucci,John (b) | Weckl,Dave (dr)

GRP 95882 | CD | Tourist In Paradise
The Rippingtons
Tourist In Paradise | Jupiter's Child | Aruba | One Summer Night In Brazil | Earthbound | Let's Stay Together | One Ocean Way | Destiny | The Princess
North Hollywood,CA, rec. details unknown
Rippingtons,The | Fields,Brandon (ss,as) | Freeman,Russ (g,el-g,keyboards,synth,arr,g-synth) | Mullins,Rob (keyboards) | Bailey,Steve (b-g) | Morales,Tony (dr,perc,cymbals,hi-hat) | Reid,Steve (perc,programming) | Anderson,Carl (voc)

GRP 95922 | CD | Migration
Dave Grusin Group
Punta Del Soul | T.K.O.
Los Angeles,CA, rec. details unknown
Grusin,Dave (keyboards) | Marsalis,Branford (ss,ts) | Miller,Marcus (b) | Hakim,Omar (dr) | Fisher,Michael (perc)
Dancing In The Township
Grusin,Dave (keyboards) | Masekela,Hugh (fl-h) | Marsalis,Branford (ts) | Miller,Marcus (b) | Hakim,Omar (dr) | Fisher,Michael (perc)
Polina
Grusin,Dave (keyboards) | Masekela,Hugh (fl-h) | Miller,Marcus (b) | Hakim,Omar (dr)
Southwest Passage | First-Time Love | Western Woman
Grusin,Dave (keyboards) | Laboriel,Abe (b) | Mason,Harvey (dr) | Fisher,Michael (perc)
Old Bones | In The Middle Of The Night
Grusin,Dave (keyboards) | Rios,Carlos (g) | Laboriel,Abe (b) | Mason,Harvey (dr) | Fisher,Michael (perc)
Suite From The Milagro Beanfield War: | Lupita- | Coyote Angel- | Pistolero- | Milagro- | Fiesta-
Grusin,Dave (keyboards) | Laboriel,Abe (b) | Mason,Harvey (dr) | Fisher,Michael (perc) | Strings | Vinci,Gerry (v,concertmaster)

GRP 96152 | CD | Stolen Moments
Lee Ritenour Group
Uptown | Stolen Moments | 24th Street Blues | Blue In Green | Sometime Ago
Hollywood,CA, rec. details unknown
Ritenour,Lee (el-g) | Watts,Ernie (ts) | Broadbent,Alan (p) | Patitucci,John (b) | Mason,Harvey (dr)
Waltz For Carmen | St.Bart's
Ritenour,Lee (el-g) | Watts,Ernie (ts) | Holder,Mitch (g) | Broadbent,Alan (p,el-p) | Patitucci,John (b) | Mason,Harvey (dr)
Haunted Heart
Ritenour,Lee (el-g) | Broadbent,Alan (p) | Patitucci,John (b) | Mason,Harvey (dr)

GRP 96172 | CD | Sketchbook
John Patitucci
Backwoods
Los Angeles,CA, rec. details unknown
Patitucci,John (b-solo)
John Patitucci Group
Joab | Junk Man
Patitucci,John (el-b) | Beasley,John (p,synth,dr-programming) | Acuna,Alejandro Neciosup (perc)
Two Worlds
Patitucci,John (b) | Brecker,Michael (ts) | Witham,Dave (synth) | Beasley,John (synth) | Acuna,Alejandro Neciosup (perc)
Spaceship
Patitucci,John (el-b) | Brecker,Michael (ts) | Witham,Dave (synth) | Beasley,John (p) | Colaiuta,Vinnie (dr)
Scophile | They Heard It Twice
Patitucci,John (b) | Scofield,John (el-g) | Beasley,John (synth) | Colaiuta,Vinnie (dr)
If You Don't Mind
Patitucci,John (b) | Crosse,Jon (ss) | Witham,Dave (p) | Beasley,John (synth) | Colaiuta,Vinnie (dr)
From A Rainy Night
Patitucci,John (b) | Crosse,Jon (ss) | Witham,Dave (p) | Beasley,John (synth) | Acuna,Alejandro Neciosup (dr,perc)
Greatest Gift
Patitucci,John (b) | Witham,Dave (p) | Silveira,Ricardo (g) | Colaiuta,Vinnie (dr) | Da Costa,Paulinho (perc) | Caymmi,Dori (voc)
'Trane
Patitucci,John (b) | Brecker,Michael (ts) | Carrington,Terri Lyne (dr)
Through The Clouds
Patitucci,John (b) | Miller,Judy (synth) | Erskine,Peter (dr)

GRP 96192 | CD | Master Plan
Dave Weckl Group
Tower Of Inspiration
Weckl,Dave (dr) | Hey,Jerry (tp) | Reichenbach,Bill (tb) | Oliver,Jay (org,keyboards,g-programming,sound-effects,synth-horns,synth-progra | Kennedy,Tom (b)
Here And There | In Common
Weckl,Dave (dr,brush-overdub,timbales) | Marienthal,Eric (ss,as) | Mayer,Peter (g) | Oliver,Jay (keyboards) | Jackson,Anthony (b)
Festival De Ritmo
Weckl,Dave (dr) | Hey,Jerry (tp) | Reichenbach,Bill (tb) | Marienthal,Eric (as) | Oliver,Jay (keyboards,synth-horns) | Jackson,Anthony (b)
Garden Wall
Weckl,Dave (dr,perc-programming) | Brecker,Michael (ts) | Corea,Chick (synth) | Oliver,Jay (keyboards,programming) | Jackson,Anthony (b)
Master Plan
Weckl,Dave (dr) | Corea,Chick (p) | Oliver,Jay (synth) | Jackson,Anthony (b) | Gadd,Steve (dr)
Island Magic
Weckl,Dave (dr,perc-programming,timbales) | Corea,Chick (synth) | Oliver,Jay (keyboards,synth,programming) | Jackson,Anthony (b)
Auratune
Weckl,Dave (dr) | Alspach,Scott (tp) | Oliver,Jay (keyboards,synth,programming) | Mayer,Peter (voc)
Softly As In A Morning Sunrise
Weckl,Dave (dr) | Kennedy,Ray (p) | Kennedy,Tom (b)

GRP 96222 | CD | Now You See It...(Now You Don't)
Michael Brecker Group
Ode To The Doo Da Day
NYC, rec. details unknown
Brecker,Michael (ts,synth) | Herington,Joe (g) | Beard,Jim (keyboards,synth) | Alias,Don (perc)
Never Alone | Quiet City
Brecker,Michael (ts) | Beard,Jim (keyboards,synth) | Bailey,Victor (el-b) | Hakim,Omar (perc) | Alias,Don (perc)
The Meaning Of The Blues
Brecker,Michael (ts) | Calderazzo,Joey (p) | Anderson,Jay (b) | Nussbaum,Adam (dr)
Peepnyv
rec. details unknown
Brecker,Michael (ts,synth) | Calderazzo,Joey (p) | Beard,Jim (keyboards) | Herington,Joe (g) | Anderson,Jay (b) | Bailey,Victor (el-b) | Nussbaum,Adam (dr) | Miller,Judd (synth-progamming)
Escher Sketch
NYC, rec. details unknown
Brecker,Michael (ts,keyboards,synth) | Beard,Jim (synth) | Herington,Joe (g) | Anderson,Jay (b) | Bailey,Victor (el-b) | Nussbaum,Adam (dr) | Miller,Judd (synth-progamming) | Miles,Jason (synth-programming) | Bralower,Jimmy (dr-programming)
Dogs In The Wine Shopnyc
rec. details unknown
Brecker,Michael (ts,keyboards,synth) | Calderazzo,Joey (p) | Beard,Jim (synth) | Bailey,Victor (el-b) | Alias,Don (perc) | Cardona,Milton (perc) | Berrios,Steve (perc) | Miller,Judd (synth-progamming)

GRP 96492 | CD | Beneath The Mask
Chick Corea Electric Band
Beneath The Mask | Little Things That Count | One Of Us Is Over | A Wave Groove | Lifescape | Jammin E. Cricket | Charged Particles | Free Step | 99 Flavors | Illusions
Los Angeles,CA, rec. details unknown
Corea,Chick (keyboards,synth) | Marienthal,Eric (ss,as) | Gambale,Frank (el-g,g-synth) | Patitucci,John (el-b) | Weckl,Dave (dr,perc,electronic-dr)

GRP 96672 | CD | Live Wires
Yellowjackets
Homecoming | Bright Lights | Freedomland | Downtown | Claire's Song | The Spin | Wildlife
Live at The Roxy,Los Angeles,CA, rec. 15./16.11.1991
Yellowjackets | Mintzer,Bob (b-cl,sax,synth) | Ferrante,Russell (keyboards) | Haslip,Jimmy (b) | Kenney,William (dr)
Revelation
Yellowjackets | Mintzer,Bob (b-cl,sax,synth) | Ferrante,Russell (keyboards) | Haslip,Jimmy (b) | Kenney,William (dr) | Take 6 (voc-group)
Geraldine
Yellowjackets | Mintzer,Bob (b-cl,sax,synth) | Ferrante,Russell (keyboards) | Haslip,Jimmy (b) | Kenney,William (dr) | Croes,Steve (synclavier) | Da Costa,Paulinho (perc) | Mendoza,Vince (string-arrangements)
The Dream
Yellowjackets | Mintzer,Bob (b-cl,sax,synth) | Ferrante,Russell (keyboards) | Haslip,Jimmy (b) | Kenney,William (dr) | Franks,Michael (voc) | Russell,Brenda (background-voc) | Scott,Marilyn (background-voc)

GRP 96682 | CD | I Remember Clifford
Arturo Sandoval Quartet
I Left This Space For You
NYC, rec. details unknown
Sandoval,Arturo (tp,fl-h) | Kirkland,Kenny (p) | Moffett,Charnett (b) | Washington,Kenny (dr)
Arturo Sandoval Quintet
I Remember Clifford
Sandoval,Arturo (tp,fl-h) | Kirkland,Kenny (p) | Gomez,Felix (keyboards) | Moffett,Charnett (b) | Washington,Kenny (dr)
Joy Spring
Sandoval,Arturo (tp,fl-h) | Calle,Ed (ts) | Kirkland,Kenny (p) | Moffett,Charnett (b) | Washington,Kenny (dr)
Daahoud | Cherokee | Sandu | Jordu | Caravan
Sandoval,Arturo (tp,fl-h) | Watts,Ernie (ts) | Kirkland,Kenny (p) | Moffett,Charnett (b) | Washington,Kenny (dr)
Parisian Thoroughfare | The Blues Walk | I Get A Kick Out Of You
Sandoval,Arturo (tp,fl-h) | Sanchez,David (ts) | Kirkland,Kenny (p) | Moffett,Charnett (b) | Washington,Kenny (dr)

GRP 96732 | CD | Heads Up
Dave Weckl Group
7th Ave. South
Chatsworth,CA, rec. details unknown
Weckl,Dave (dr) | Brecker,Randy (tp) | Marienthal,Eric (ss) | Oliver,Jay (keyboards,synth-programming) | Earl,Jimmy (b)
Taboo
Weckl,Dave (dr) | Marienthal,Eric (as) | Oliver,Jay (keyboards,synth-programming) | Patitucci,John (b) | Earl,Jimmy (b)
Heads Up
Weckl,Dave (b,dr) | Marienthal,Eric (ss) | Oliver,Jay (p,keyboards,synth-programming)
Tomatillo
Weckl,Dave (dr,timbalitos) | Earl,Jimmy (b) | Oliver,Jay (keyboards,synth-programming)
Tee Funk
Weckl,Dave (dr) | Marienthal,Eric (as) | Earl,Jimmy (b) | Oliver,Jay (keyboards,synth-programming)
Peripheral Vision
Weckl,Dave (dr) | Beal,Jeff (tp) | Tavaglione,Steve (ts) | Earl,Jimmy (fretless-b) | Oliver,Jay (keyboards,synth-programming)
Against The Wall
Weckl,Dave (dr,synth-programming) | Tavaglione,Steve (ts) | Novak,Gary (keyboards,b) | Oliver,Jay (keyboards,synth-programming)
Full Moon
Weckl,Dave (dr,synth-programming) | Tavaglione,Steve (ts) | Patitucci,John (keyboards,b) | Oliver,Jay (keyboards,synth-programming)
Trigger Happy
Weckl,Dave (dr,electronics)

GRP 96842 | CD | Return Of The Brecker Brothers
The Brecker Brothers
Song For Barry
details unknown, rec. details unknown
Brecker,Randy (tp,fl-h) | Brecker,Michael (ts,keyboards,synth) | Stern,Mike (g) | Whitty,George (keyboards) | Sabal-Lecco,Armand (b,piccolo-b,voc) | Risenhoover,Max (synth,perc-programming)
King Of The Lobby
Brecker,Randy (tp,fl-h) | Brecker,Michael (ts,keyboards,synth) | Sanborn,David (as) | Brown,Dean (g) | Stern,Mike (g) | Whitty,George (keyboards) | Risenhoover,Max (synth,perc-programming) | Veera (voice)
Big Idea
Brecker,Randy (tp) | Brecker,Michael (ts) | Maz (keyboards,dr-programming) | Whitty,George (keyboards) | Risenhoover,Max (synth,perc-programming) | Veera (voice)
Above & Below
Brecker,Randy (tp) | Brecker,Michael (ts) | Stern,Mike (g) | Whitty,George (keyboards) | Genus,James (b) | Chambers,Dennis (dr) | Johnson,Bashiri (perc)
That's All There Is To It
Brecker,Randy (tp,voc) | Brecker,Michael (ts) | Brown,Dean (g) | Whitty,George (keyboards) | Sabal-Lecco,Armand (b) | Chambers,Dennis (dr) | Lee,Will (background-voc) | Pollack,Malcolm (background-voc)
Wakaria(What's Up?)
Brecker,Randy (tp,fl-h) | Brecker,Michael (ss,ts,synth) | Whitty,George (keyboards) | Sabal-Lecco,Armand (b,dr,perc,piccolo-b,voc) | Chambers,Dennis (dr) | Risenhoover,Max (cymbal,snare-programming)
On The Backside
Brecker,Randy (tp) | Brecker,Michael (ts) | Whitty,George (p,programming) | Maz (keyboards,dr-programming) | Kilgore,Robby (p,bass-synth) | Genus,James (b)
Sozinho(Alone)
Brecker,Randy (tp) | Brecker,Michael (ts) | Stern,Mike (g) | Whitty,George (keyboards) | Genus,James (b,el-b) | Chambers,Dennis (dr) | Alias,Don (perc) | Risenhoover,Max (cymbal)
Spherical
Brecker,Randy (tp) | Brecker,Michael (ts,keyboards,synth-programming) | Stern,Mike (g) | Whitty,George (keyboards,synth-programming) | Lee,Will (b) | Chambers,Dennis (dr) | Alias,Don (perc)
Good Gracious
Brecker,Randy (tp) | Brecker,Michael (ts) | Stern,Mike (g) | Whitty,George (keyboards) | Genus,James (b) | Chambers,Dennis (dr)
Roppongi
Brecker,Randy (tp) | Brecker,Michael (ts,synth) | Stern,Mike (g) | Brown,Dean (g) | Whitty,George (keyboards,synth-programming) | Genus,James (b) | Chambers,Dennis (dr) | Alias,Don (perc)

GRP 97032 | CD | Love Songs
Diane Schuur With Orchestra
When I Fall In Love | Speak Low | I Thought About You | Prelude To A Kiss | Our Love Is Here To Stay | Voce Vai Ver(You'll See) | September In The Rain | The More I See You | Crazy | My One And Only Love | Here's That Rainy Day
Woodland Hills,CA, rec. details unknown
Schuur,Diane (voc) | Sheldon,Jack (tp) | Scott,Tom (sax) | Christlieb,Pete (ts) | Thielemans,Jean 'Toots' (harm) | Pisano,John (g) | Gale,Eric (g) | Caymmi,Dori (g) | Vinci,Gerry (v,concertmaster) | Kellaway,Roger (p) | Ranier,Tom (p) | Domanico,Chuck (b) | Berghofer,Chuck (b) | Kennedy,William (dr) | Humphries,Ralph (dr) | Brass | Strings

GRP 97122 | CD | Duets
Rob Wasserman Duet
Stardust
Hollywood,CA, rec. details unknown
Wasserman,Rob (b) | Neville,Aaron (voc) | unkn. (background-voc)
The Moon Is Made Of Gold | Autumn Leaves
Wasserman,Rob (b) | Jones,Rickie Lee (g,voc)
Brothers
Wasserman,Rob (b) | McFerrin,Bobby (voice)
Duet
Wasserman,Rob (b-playback)
One For My Baby(And One More For The Road)
Wasserman,Rob (b) | Reed,Lou (g,voc)
Ballad Of The Runaway Horse
Wasserman,Rob (b) | Warnes,Jennifer (voc)
Gone With The Wind-
Wasserman,Rob (b) | Hicks,Dan (voc)
Angel Eyes
Wasserman,Rob (b) | Bentyne,Cheryl (voc)
Over The Rainbow
Wasserman,Rob (b) | Grappelli,Stephane (v)

GRP 97402 | CD | GRP All-Star Big Band:Live!
GRP All-Star Big Band
Oleo | My Man's Gone Now | Manteca | Blues For Howard | Blue Train | 'S Wonderful | Sister Sadie | Introduction by Dave Grusin
Live at Kan-i-Hoken Hall,Tokyo,Japan, rec. 31.1.1993
GRP All Stars | Sandoval,Arturo (tp,fl-h) | Brecker,Randy (tp,fl-h) | Findley,Chuck (tp,fl-h) | Stripling,Byron (tp,fl-h) | Bohanon,George (tb) | Bent,Phillip (fl) | Daniels,Eddie (cl) | Marienthal,Eric (ss,as) | Rangell,Nelson (fl,ss,as) | Watts,Ernie (ss,ts) | Mintzer,Bob (b-cl,ss,ts) | Scott,Tom (as,ts,bs,ld) | Burton,Gary (vib) | Grusin,Dave (p) | Patitucci,John (b) | Weckl,Dave (dr)
Sing Sing Sing | Cherokee
GRP All Stars | Sandoval,Arturo (tp,fl-h) | Brecker,Randy (tp,fl-h) | Findley,Chuck (tp,fl-h) | Stripling,Byron (tp,fl-h) | Bohanon,George (tb) | Bent,Phillip (fl) | Daniels,Eddie (cl) | Marienthal,Eric (ss,as) | Rangell,Nelson (fl,ss,as) | Watts,Ernie (ss,ts) | Mintzer,Bob (b-cl,ss,ts) | Scott,Tom (as,ts,bs,ld) | Burton,Gary (vib) | Ferrante,Russell (p) | Patitucci,John (b) | Weckl,Dave (dr)

GRP 97542 | CD | Run For Your Life
Yellowjackets
Jacket Town | Even Song | Runferyerlife | The Red Sea | Muhammed | City Of Lights | Sage | Ancestors | Wisdom
Los Angeles,CA, rec. details unknown
Yellowjackets | Mintzer,Bob (b-cl,ss,ts,synth) | Ford,Robben (g) | Ferrante,Russell (keyboards) | Croes,Steve (synclavier) | Miller,Judd (synth-progamming) | Haslip,Jimmy (b) | Kennedy,William (dr)

GRP 97602 | CD | Hard-Wired
Dave Weckl Group
Hard-Wired
Weckl,Dave (dr) | Tavaglione,Steve (as) | Oliver,Jay (synth) | Jackson,Anthony (b-g)
Afrique
Weckl,Dave (dr,perc,programming) | Alspach,Scott (tp) | Oliver,Jay (synth) | Jackson,Anthony (b-g)
Dis' Place This
Alspach,Scott (tp,fl-h) | Tavaglione,Steve (ts) | Oliver,Jay (keyboards) | Jackson,Anthony (b-g)
In Flight | Tribute
Weckl,Dave (dr) | Tavaglione,Steve (ts) | Oliver,Jay (p,keyboards,synth) | Patitucci,John (b,b-g,fretless-b)
Crazy Horse
Weckl,Dave (dr) | Alspach,Scott (tp) | Tavaglione,Steve (as) | Oliver,Jay (synth) | Genus,James (b-g)
Just An Illusion | Where's Tom
Weckl,Dave (dr,perc,programming) | Tavaglione,Steve (ts,synth) | Oliver,Jay (keyboards) | Genus,James (b-g)
In The Pocket
Weckl,Dave (dr,programming) | Alspach,Scott (tp) | Tavaglione,Steve (as) | Oliver,Jay (org,keyboards,synth,programming)

GRP 97732 | CD | Expressions
Chick Corea
Lush Life | This Nearly Was Mine | It Could Happen To You | My Ship | I Didn't Know What Time It Was | Monk's Mood | Oblivion | Pannonica | Someone To Watch Over Me | Armando's Rhumba | Blues For Art | Stella By Starlight | Anna | I Want To Be Happy | Smile
Corea,Chick (p-solo)

GRP 97832 | CD | Against The Grain
Acoustic Alchemy
Against The Grain
London,GB, rec. 1994
Acoustic Alchemy | Webb,Nick (g) | Carmichael,Greg (g) | Parsons,John (dobro) | Brüninghaus,Rainer (p) | McArthur,Iain (programming)
Lazeez
Acoustic Alchemy | Webb,Nick (g) | Carmichael,Greg (g) | Parsons,John (el-g) | Brüninghaus,Rainer (p) | Harriman,Paul (b) | Smaak,Bert (dr) | Jardim,Luis (perc)
A Different Kind Of Freedom
Acoustic Alchemy | Todd,Phil (fl,ss,ts) | Webb,Nick (g) | Carmichael,Greg (g) | Parsons,John (el-g) | Brüninghaus,Rainer (keyboards) | Harriman,Paul (b) | Smaak,Bert (dr)
Lady Lynda
Acoustic Alchemy | Todd,Phil (fl,ss,ts) | Webb,Nick (g) | Carmichael,Greg (g) | Brüninghaus,Rainer (p,keyboards) | Disley,Terry (keyboards) | Harriman,Paul (b) | Smaak,Bert (dr) | Jardim,Luis (perc)
Road Dogs
Acoustic Alchemy | Webb,Nick (g) | Carmichael,Greg (g) | Douglas,Jerry (dobro) | Harriman,Paul (b) | Smaak,Bert (dr)
Shoot The Loop
Acoustic Alchemy | Webb,Nick (g) | Carmichael,Greg (g) | Parsons,John (g,el-g) | McArthur,Iain (programming)
Across The Golden Gate
Acoustic Alchemy | Webb,Nick (g) | Carmichael,Greg (g) | Douglas,Jerry (dobro) | Herting,Mike (keyboards) | Harriman,Paul (b) | Smaak,Bert (dr) | Jardim,Luis (perc)
Papillon
Acoustic Alchemy | Webb,Nick (g) | Carmichael,Greg (g) | Todd,Phil (ss) | Brüninghaus,Rainer (p,keyboards) | Harriman,Paul (b) | Smaak,Bert (dr) | Jardim,Luis (perc)
Silent Partner
Acoustic Alchemy | Webb,Nick (g) | Carmichael,Greg (g) | Disley,Terry (keyboards) | Harriman,Paul (b) | Jardim,Luis (perc)
Nouveau Tango
Acoustic Alchemy | Webb,Nick (g) | Carmichael,Greg (g) | Parsons,John (el-g) | Brüninghaus,Rainer (keyboards) | Harriman,Paul (b) | Smaak,Bert (dr) | Jardim,Luis (perc)

GRP 97842 | CD | Out Of The Loop
The Brecker Brothers
Slang | Harpoon | The Nightwalker | And Then She Wept
NYC, rec. details unknown
Brecker,Randy (tp) | Brecker,Michael (ts,synth) | Whitty,George (keyboards,hammond-b) | Brown,Dean (g) | Genus,James (b) | Jordan,Steve (dr) | Thornton,Steve (perc)
Scrunch
Brecker,Randy (tp) | Brecker,Michael (ts) | Brown,Dean (g) | Genus,James (b) | Kilgare,Robbie (keyboard-rhythm-programming) | Kessler,Maz (keyboard-rhythm-programming)
When It Was
Brecker,Randy (tp) | Brecker,Michael (ts) | Brown,Dean (g) | Kilgare,Robbie (g,keyboards) | Kessler,Maz (g,keyboards)
Evocations
Brecker,Randy (tp) | Brecker,Michael (ts) | Whitty,George (p) | Brown,Dean (g) | Genus,James (b) | Saltzman,Larry (g) | Pelton,Slawn (dr) | Thornton,Steve (perc) | Botti,Chris (keyboard-b-dr-programming) | Snitzer,Andy (keyboard-b-dr-programming)
African Skies
Brecker,Randy (tp) | Brecker,Michael (ss,ts,synth) | Whitty,George (keyboards,perc-programming) | Brown,Dean (g) | Sabal-Lecco,Armand (b,piccolo-b,voc) | Holmes,Rodney (dr) | Thornton,Steve (perc)
Secret Heart
Brecker,Randy (tp) | Brecker,Michael (ss,ts,synth) | Whitty,George (keyboards,perc-programming) | Elias,Eliane (keyboards,voc) | Brown,Dean (g) | Genus,James (b) | Holmes,Rodney (dr) | Thornton,Steve (perc) | Whitty,George (keyboard-programming) | Ledford,Mark (voc)

GRP 98002 | CD | All Blues
GRP All-Star Big Band
Cookin' At The Continental | Goodbye Pork Pie Hat | Some Other Blues
Los Angeles,CA, rec. 8./9.1.1994
GRP All-Star Big Band | Sandoval,Arturo (tp,fl-h) | Brecker,Randy (tp,fl-h) | Findley,Chuck (tp,fl-h) | Bohanon,George (tb) | Marienthal,Eric (ss,as) | Rangell,Nelson (fl,ss,as) | Watts,Ernie (ss,ts) | Mintzer,Bob (ss,ts,bs) | Scott,Tom (ss,ts,bs) | Ferrante,Russell (p) | Patitucci,John (b) | Weckl,Dave (dr)
Stormy Monday Blues(They Call It Stormy Monday)
GRP All-Star Big Band | Sandoval,Arturo (tp,fl-h) | Brecker,Randy (tp,fl-h) | Findley,Chuck (tp,fl-h) | Bohanon,George (tb) | Marienthal,Eric (ss,as) | Rangell,Nelson (fl,ss,as) | Watts,Ernie (ss,ts) | Mintzer,Bob (ss,ts,bs) | Scott,Tom (ss,ts,bs) | King,B.B. (g,voc) | Lewis,Ramsey (p) | Ferrante,Russell (org) | Patitucci,John (el-b) | Weckl,Dave (dr)
Aunt Hagar's Blues | Senor Blues
GRP All-Star Big Band | Sandoval,Arturo (tp,fl-h) | Brecker,Randy (tp,fl-h) | Findley,Chuck (tp,fl-h) | Bohanon,George (tb) | Marienthal,Eric (ss,as) | Rangell,Nelson (fl,ss,as) | Watts,Ernie (ss,ts) | Mintzer,Bob (ss,ts,bs) | Scott,Tom (ss,ts,bs) | Lewis,Ramsey (p) | Patitucci,John (b) | Weckl,Dave (dr)
Birk's Works | All Blues
GRP All-Star Big Band | Sandoval,Arturo (tp,fl-h) | Brecker,Randy (tp,fl-h) | Findley,Chuck (tp,fl-h) | Bohanon,George (tb) | Marienthal,Eric (ss,as) | Rangell,Nelson (fl,ss,as) | Watts,Ernie (ss,ts) | Mintzer,Bob (ss,ts,bs) | Scott,Tom (ss,ts,bs) | Grusin,Dave (p) | Patitucci,John (b) | Weckl,Dave (dr)
Blue Miles | Ba-Lue Bolivar Ba-Lues-Are- | Mysterioso-
GRP All-Star Big Band | Sandoval,Arturo (tp,fl-h) | Brecker,Randy (tp,fl-h) | Findley,Chuck (tp,fl-h) | Bohanon,George (tb) | Marienthal,Eric (ss,as) | Rangell,Nelson (fl,ss,as) | Watts,Ernie (ss,ts) | Mintzer,Bob (ss,ts,bs) | Scott,Tom (ss,ts,bs) | Corea,Chick (p) | Patitucci,John (b) | Weckl,Dave (dr)

GRP 98022 | CD | Mistura Fina
John Patitucci Group
Mistura Fina
Los Angeles,CA, rec. June/August 1994
Patitucci,John (6-string-b) | Tavaglione,Steve (ts) | Beasley,John (p,synth) | Acuna,Alejandro Neciosup (perc) | Shapiro,Michael (dr,perc) | Brandolino,Cathy (voc) | Pardini,Lou (voc) | Lettau,Kevyn (voc) | Mayo,Scott (voc) | Cantos,Bill (voc) | Jorge,Kleber (voc)
Puccini
Patitucci,John (6-string-b) | Tavaglione,Steve (EWI) | Goldblatt,David (p,synth) | Sabal-Lecco,Armand (b,piccolo-b,voc) | Weckl,Dave (dr) | Acuna,Alejandro Neciosup (perc) | Brandolino,Cathy (voc)
Bata Balaio | Agua Mae Agua | Varadero
Patitucci,John (b,6-string-b) | Bosco,Joao (g,voc) | Acuna,Alejandro Neciosup (perc)
Samba Novo
Los Angeles,CA, rec. June/Augsut 1994
Patitucci,John (6-string-b) | Caymmi,Dori (g,voc) | Beasley,John (p,synth) | Shapiro,Michael (dr) | Acuna,Alejandro Neciosup (perc)
Barra Da Tijuca
Los Angeles,CA, rec. June/August 1994
Patitucci,John (b) | Beasley,John (p) | Shapiro,Michael (dr) | Acuna,Alejandro Neciosup (perc) | Lettau,Kevyn (voc)
Assim Nao Da
Patitucci,John (6-string-b) | Kleber,Jorge (g,voc) | Beasley,John (p,synth) | Shapiro,Michael (dr) | Acuna,Alejandro Neciosup (perc)
The Four Lovers
Patitucci,John (6-string-b) | Beasley,John (p,synth) | Erskine,Peter (dr) | Acuna,Alejandro Neciosup (perc) | Lins,Ivan (voc) | Brandolino,Cathy (voc)
Soul Song
Patitucci,John (b,6-string-b) | Tavaglione,Steve (ss) | Beasley,John (p) | Erskine,Peter (dr) | Acuna,Alejandro Neciosup (perc) | Lins,Ivan (voc)
Joys And Sorrows
Patitucci,John (6-string-b) | Tavaglione,Steve (ss) | Beasley,John (p,synth) | Acuna,Alejandro Neciosup (perc)
Samba School | Long Story
Patitucci,John (b,6-string-b)

GRP 98112 | CD | Love & Other Obsessions
Spyro Gyra & Guests
Lost And Found | Ariana | Serengeti | Fine Time To Explain | Third Street | Group Therapy | Horizon's Edge | Let's Say Goodbye | On Liberty Road(For South Africa) | Rockin' A Heart Place | Baby Dreams | Open Season
NYC, rec. details unknown
Spyro Gyra | Beckenstein,Jay (sax) | Fernandez,Julio (g) | Schuman,Tom (keyboards) | Ambush,Scott (b) | Rosenblatt,Joel (dr) | Samuels,Dave (vib,marimba,synth,marching-dr) | Ferrante,Russell (keyboards) | Johnson,Bashiri (perc) | Merendino,Sammy (dr-programming) | Skinner,Steve (dr-programming) | Henderson,Barringtn (voc) | Williams,Denice (voc) | Cliff,Billy (voc) | Hutchinson,Wondress (voc) | Thomas,Vaneese (voc) | Pompa,Anthony Michael (voc) | Jillis,Jana (voc) | Fluitt,Keith (voc) | No Sweat Horns: Danielian,Barry (tp,fl-h) | Andos,Randy (tb,b-tb) | Kreitzer,Scott (fl,alto-fl,b-cl,sax)

GRP 98202 | CD | Arturo Sandoval & The Latin Train
Arturo Sandoval And The Latin Train Band
Bebop | La Guarapachanga | A La P.P. | Waheera | I Can't Get Started | Marte Belona | Royal Poinciana | The Latin Train | Candela(Yo Si Como Candela)- | Quimbombo- | Drume Negrita | Orula | I Can't Get Started(instrumental)
Miami,Florida, rec. 6.-11.1.1995
Sandoval,Arturo (tp,fl-h,p,perc) | Teboe,Dana (tb) | Anderson,Kenny (sax) | Calle,Ed (fl,alto-fl,ts) | Ruiz,Otmaro (p) | Toledo,Rene L. (g) | Enos,Dave (b) | Serfaty,Aaron (dr) | Castrillo,Manuel 'Egui' (perc) | Enriquez,Luis (perc,voc) | Bonilla,Edwin (perc) | Valdejuli,Carl (perc) | Williams,Joe (voc) | Cruz,Celia (voc) | D'Leon,Oscar (voc) | Rojas,Vicente (voc) | Pifferer,Laura (voc) | Quinones,Cheito (voc)

GRP 98212 | CD | Patti Austin:The Ultimate Collection
Patti Austin And Her Band
Hold Me | Ability To Swing | Givin' In To Love | We Fell In Love Anyway | The Heat Of Heat | Through The Test Of Time | You Who Brought Me Love | The Girl Who Used To Be Me | Love Is Gonna Getcha | Soldier Boy | I'll Keep Your Dreams Alive | Reach
different Places, rec. details unknown
Austin,Patti (voc) | Francis,Cleve (voc) | Mathis,Johnny (voc) | Benson,George (g,voc) | details not on the cover
-> Some titles are never released before!

GRP 98312 | CD | The Best Of David Benoit 1987-1995
David Benoit Group
Drive Time | Every Step Of The Way | Cast Your Fate To The Wind | Searching For June | M.W.A.(Musicians With Attitude) | Linus And Lucy | Kei's Song | The Key To You | Freedom At Midnight | Still Standing | Wailea | Letter To Evan | Urban Daydreams | Mediterranean Nights
different Places, rec. 1987-1995
Benoit,David (p,el-p,synth,electronics)
-> (Different groups

GRP 98542 | CD | The Gift
Larry Carlton Group
Ridin' The Treasure | Things We Said Today | Goin' Nowhere | The Gift | Shop 'Till You Drop | Pammie Dear | Osaka Cool | My Old Town | Morning Dove | Buddy
Nashville,TN, rec. details unknown
Carlton,Larry (g) | Whalum,Kirk (sax) | Rollings,Matt (keyboards) | Jackson,Rick (keyboards) | Kimpel,Larry (b) | Bissonette,Gregg (dr) | Fisher,Michael (perc)
Things We Said Today
Carlton,Larry (g) | Jackson,Rick (keyboards) | Davis,Melvin (b) | Richards,Land (dr) | Da Costa,Paulinho (perc) | Carlton,Michele Pillar (voc)
Pammie Dear
Carlton,Larry (g) | Jackson,Rick (keyboards) | Emmons,Buddy (steel-g)

GRP 98632 | CD | Blues For Schuur
Diane Schuur With Orchestra
I'm Not Ashamed To Sing The Blues | When Did You Leave Heaven | Stormy Monday Blues(They Call It Stormy Monday) | These Blues | Moonlight And Shadows | Allright Okay You Win | Who Will The Next Fool Be | Save You Love For Me | Someone To Love | Toodle-Loo On Down | You've Got To Hurt Before You Heal | I Want To Go Home
Hollywood,CA, rec. 1997
Schuur,Diane (voc) | Adams,Greg (tp) | Findley,Chuck (tp) | Lane,Nick (tb) | Finders,Matt (tb) | Herbig,Gary (sax) | Bamont,Johnnie (sax) | Williams,Larry (sax) | Walker,David T. (g) | Winding,Jai (p,org) | Davis,Melvin (b) | Mason,Harvey (dr)

GRP 98652 | CD | Two For The Road:The Music Of Henry Mancini
Dave Grusin Orchestra
Moment To Moment | Two For The Road | Days Of Wine And Roses
NYC, rec. 1996
Grusin,Dave (p) | Grant,Gary (tp) | Martin,Andy (tb) | Higgins,Dan (sax) | Scott,Tom (sax) | Marienthal,Eric (sax) | Patitucci,John (b) | Mason,Harvey (dr) | Orchestra | Strings | details unknown
Dreamsville
Grusin,Dave (p) | Grant,Gary (tp) | Martin,Andy (tb) | Higgins,Dan (sax) | Scott,Tom (sax) | Marienthal,Eric (sax) | Malone,Russell (g) | Patitucci,John (b) | Mason,Harvey (dr) | Krall,Diana (voc) | Orchestra | Strings | details unknown
Soldier In The Rain
Grusin,Dave (p) | Grant,Gary (tp) | Martin,Andy (tb) | Higgins,Dan (sax) | Scott,Tom (sax) | Marienthal,Eric (sax) | Patitucci,John (b) | Mason,Harvey (dr) | Krall,Diana (voc) | Orchestra | Strings | details unknown
Peter Gunn
Grusin,Dave (p) | Grant,Gary (tp) | Martin,Andy (tb) | Higgins,Dan (sax) | Scott,Tom (sax) | Marienthal,Eric (sax) | Malone,Russell (g) | Patitucci,John (b) | Mason,Harvey (dr) | Jerry Hey And The Hot Band | details unknown
Baby Elephant Walk
Grusin,Dave (p) | Grant,Gary (tp) | Martin,Andy (tb) | Higgins,Dan (sax) | Scott,Tom (sax) | Marienthal,Eric (sax) | Ollestad,Tollak (harm) | Patitucci,John (b) | Mason,Harvey (dr) | Jerry Hey And The Hot Band | details unknown
Whistling Away The Dark
Grusin,Dave (p) | Grant,Gary (tp) | Martin,Andy (tb) | Higgins,Dan (sax) | Scott,Tom (sax) | Marienthal,Eric (sax) | Ollestad,Tollak (harm) | Patitucci,John (b) | Mason,Harvey (dr) | Da Costa,Paulinho (perc)
Hatari | Mr.Lucky
Grusin,Dave (p) | Grant,Gary (tp) | Martin,Andy (tb) | Higgins,Dan (sax) | Scott,Tom (sax) | Marienthal,Eric (sax) | Patitucci,John (b) | Mason,Harvey (dr) | Da Costa,Paulinho (perc)

GRP 98822 | CD | Alive In L.A.
Lee Ritenour Sextet
A Little Bumpin' | Night Rhythms | Boss City | San Juan Sunset | Uptown | Waltz For Carmen | Wes Bound | Pacific Nights | Radio Funk | 4 On 6
Live at The Ash Grove,Santa Monica,CA, rec. 23.-25.1.1997
Ritenour,Lee (g,el-g) | Evans,Bill (fl,ss,ts) | Pasqua,Alan (p,el-p,org) | Finch,Barnaby (keyboards) | Davis,Melvin (b) | Emory,Sonny (dr)

GRP 98882 | CD | The Best Of Diane Schuur
Diane Schuur With Orchestra
Allright Okay You Win | Stormy Monday Blues(They Call It Stormy Monday)
Schuur,Diane (voc) | Adams,Greg (tp) | Findley,Chuck (tp) | Lane,Nick (tb) | Finders,Matt (tb) | Herbig,Gary (sax) | Bamont,Johnnie (sax) | Williams,Larry (sax) | Walker,David T. (g) | Winding,Jai (p,org) | Davis,Melvin (b) | Mason,Harvey (dr)
Diane Schuur Quintet With B.B.King
Try A Little Tenderness | At Last
Schuur,Diane (voc) | King,B.B. (g,voc) | Viapiano,Paul (g) | Waldman,Randy (p) | Berghofer,Chuck (b) | Colaiuta,Vinnie (dr)
Diane Schuur With Orchestra
Them There Eyes | Round About Midnight
Schuur,Diane (voc) | personal included: | Menza,Don (ts) | Budimir,Dennis (g) | Broadbent,Alan (p) | Clayton,John (b) | Hamilton,Jeff (dr) | Brass | Broadbent,Alan (arr) | details not on the cover
Diane Schuur With Orchestra And Strings
Sunday Kind Of Love | Blue Gardenia
Schuur,Diane (voc) | personal included: | Sheldon,Jack (tp) | Bergeron,Wayne (tp) | Martin,Andy (tb) | Todd,Richard (fr-h) | Johnson,John T. (tuba) | Christlieb,Pete (sax) | Foster,Gary (sax) | Upchurch,Phil (g) | Wofford,Mike (p) | Patitucci,John (b) | Guerin,John (dr) | Drori,Assa (v,concertmaster) | Strings | details not on the cover
Diane Schuur With Orchestra
Speak Low
Schuur,Diane (voc) | Sheldon,Jack (tp) | Scott,Tom (sax) | Christlieb,Pete (ts) | Thielemans,Jean 'Toots' (harm) | Pisano,John (g) | Gale,Eric (g) | Caymmi,Dori (g) | Vinci,Gerry (v,concertmaster) | Kellaway,Roger (p) | Ranier,Tom (p) | Domanico,Chuck (b) | Berghofer,Chuck (b) | Kennedy,William (dr) | Humphries,Ralph (dr) | Brass | Strings | details not on the cover
Diane Schuur And Her Band
'Deed I Do
Schuur,Diane (voc) | Szabo,Frank (tp) | Smith,Nolan (tp) | Huffstetter,Steven (fl-h) | Brashear,Oscar (tp) | Loper,Charles (tb) | Brown,Garnett (tb) | Hyde,Dick (tb) | Spears,Maurice (tb) | Jackson,Fred (sax) | Fields,Ernie (sax) | Peskin,Joel C. (sax) | Nimitz,Jack (sax) | Garvin,Tom (p) | Geissman,Grant (g) | Hughart,Jim (b) | Jones,Harold (dr) | Williams,Joe (voc) | Holman,Bill (arr)
Diane Schuur With Orchestra
A Time For Love
Schuur,Diane (voc) | Findley,Chuck (tp) | Hey,Jerry (tp) | Grant,Gary (tp) | Luening,Warren (tp) | Loper,Charles (tb) | Reichenbach,Bill (tb) | Watrous,Bill (tb) | Johnson,Tommy (tb,tuba) | Perkins,Bill (sax) | Scott,Tom (sax) | Christlieb,Pete (sax) | Herbig,Gary (sax) | Nimitz,Jack (sax) | Getz,Stan (ts) | Kerber,Randy (keyboards) | Lang,Mike (keyboards) | Grusin,Dave (keyboards) | Ritenour,Lee (g) | Domanico,Chuck (b) | Berghofer,Chuck (b) | Neidlinger,Buell (b) | Schaeffer,Steve (dr) | Fisher,Michael (perc) | Bunker,Larry (perc) | Strings
Diane Schuur With The Dave Grusin Orchestra
New York State Of Mind
Schuur,Diane (voc) | Grusin,Dave (p,el-p,synth,perc) | Getz,Stan (ts) | Grusin,Don (synth) | Roberts,Howard (el-g) | Dean,Don (el-b) | Lucas,Moyes (dr) | Strings
Diane Schuur With The Count Basie Orchestra
Deedles' Blues
Schuur,Diane (voc) | Ojeda,Bob (tp) | Stripling,Byron (tp) | Cohn[Cohen],Sonny (tp) | Mustafa,Melton (tp) | Banks,Clarence (tb) | Hughes,Bill (tb) | Wanzo,Mel (tb) | Wilson,Dennis (tb) | House,Danny (as) | Turner,Danny (as) | Foster,Frank (ts,ld) | Hing,Kenny (ts) | Dixon,Eric (ts) | Williams,John (bs) | Carson,Donald T. (p) | Green,Freddie (g) | Seaton,Lynn (b) | Mackrel,Dennis (dr)

Hänssler Classics | Naxos Deutschland

CD 93.004 | CD | Jazz In Concert | EAN 4010276010951
SWR Big Band
The Fourth Way | Child Of Nature | Lifetime | Alien Cult | The Hierophant | Science Fiction
SWR Studios?, rec. 1995
SWR Big Band | Winther,Jens (tp) | Vogel,Thomas (tp) | Rezanina,Lubomir (tp) | Baldauf,Rüdiger (tp) | Farrent,Karl (tp) | Reindl,Rudolf (tp) | Hutter,Ernst (tb) | Nuß,Ludwig (tb) | Cumming,Ian (tb) | Budziat,Eberhard (tb) | Maus,Georg (tb) | Rabe,Bernd (as) | Kühn,Axel (as) | Weniger,Peter (ts) | Maile,Andreas 'Andi' (ts) | Heute,Rainer (bs) | Schrack,Martin (p) | Schöpfer,Klaus (g) | Stabenow,Thomas (b) | Uotila,Jukkis (dr) | Gebhardt,Jörg (perc)

Hep | Fenn Music

CD 2066 | CD | Herb Geller Plays The Al Cohn Songbook | EAN 603366206620
Herb Geller Quartet
Mr.George | Danielle | Mr.Music | Halley's Comet | Pensive | The Fluegelbird | High On You | You 'N' Me | Woody's Lament | El Cajon | The Underdog | Tasty Pudding | 'Tain't No Use | Infinity
Hollywood,CA, rec. 11./12.7.1994
Geller,Herb (ss,as) | Ranier,Tom (cl,b-cl,ts,p) | Leitham,John (b) | Kreibich,Paul (dr) | Price,Ruth (voc)

CD 2078 | CD | Hollywood Portraits | EAN 603366207825
Herb Geller-Brian Kellock
Carole Lombard | Marlene Dietrich | Rita Hayworth | Ginger Rogers | Audrey Hepburn | Claudette Colbert | Joan Crawford | Mae West | Judy Garland | Bette Davis | Judy Holliday | Gloria Swanson | Gracy Kelly | Elinor Powell | Marilyn Monroe | Ingrid Bergman | Betty Grable | Vivien Leigh | Greta Garbo | Lana Turner
London,GB, rec. 5.10.1999
Geller,Herb (ss,as) | Kellock,Brian (p)

CD 2083 | CD | Easy To Remember | EAN 603366208327
Joe Temperley Quartet
That Old Feeling | I Let A Song Go Out Of My Heart | Someone To Watch Over Me
London,GB, rec. 10.4.2001
Temperley,Joe (ss,bs) | Pearce,John (p) | Cleyndert,Andrew (b) | Brown,Steve (dr)
Joe Temperley Quintet
Just Friends | Things Ain't What They Used To Be
Temperley,Joe (ss,bs) | Coe,Tony (ss) | Pearce,John (p) | Cleyndert,Andrew (b) | Brown,Steve (dr)
Joe Temperley Quartet
East Of The Sun West Of The Moon | Torpedo
London,GB, rec. 11.4.2001
Temperley,Joe (ss,bs) | Pearce,John (p) | Cleyndert,Andrew (b) | Brown,Steve (dr)
Joe Temperley Quartet With Strings
The Very Thought Of You | Easy To Remember | Ask Me Now
London,GB, rec. 10.4.2001
Temperley,Joe (ss,bs) | Pearce,John (p) | Cleyndert,Andrew (b) | Brown,Steve (dr) | Francis,John (v) | Laing,Andy (v) | Underwood,John (viola) | Bruce-Mitford,Myrtle (cello)
Joe Temperley Quintet With Strings
Warm Valley | How Little We Know
Temperley,Joe (ss,bs) | Griffith,Frank (cl,arr) | Pearce,John (p) | Cleyndert,Andrew (b) | Brown,Steve (dr) | Francis,John (v) | Laing,Andy (v) | Underwood,John (viola) | Bruce-Mitford,Myrtle (cello)
Joe Temperley
Hielan' Laddie
London,GB, rec. 11.4.2001
Temperley,Joe (bs-solo)

CD 2084 | CD | To Benny & Johnny | EAN 603366208426
Herb Geller Quartet
Key Largo | Warm Valley | Morning Glory | Johnny Comes Lately | Souvenir | Only Trust Your Heart | Dancers In Love | Isfahan | Lonely Woman | When Lights Are Low | Ballad For Very Tired And Very Sad Lotus Eaters | Summer Serenade
Hollywood,CA, rec. 16./17.6.2001
Geller,Herb (ss,as) | O'Brien,Hod (p) | Berghofer,Chuck (b) | Kreibich,Paul (dr)
Herb Geller-Hod O'Brien
I Didn't Know About You
Geller,Herb (as) | O'Brien,Hod (p)
Herb Geller-Chuck Berghofer
Twelve By Two For Squatty Boo
Geller,Herb (as) | Berghofer,Chuck (b)

Hip Bop | Edel Contraire

HIBD 8002 | CD | Mo' Jamaica Funk
Tom Browne Groups
Jam Fo' Real | Too Hot | The Work Song | Give Me The Night | Everybody Loves The Sunshine | Milestones | Ghetto Horn | That's What Friends Are For | Culture Shock(Let's Dance)
different Places, rec. details unknown
Browne,Tom (tp,fl-h,keyboards,dr-programming,voc,vocoder) | Najee (ts) | Orehucla,Roberto (vib) | Steadman,Jim (g,voc) | Pfiffner,John (g) | G.,Bobby (g) | Webb,Barry (g,voc) | Wright,Bernard (keyboards) | Battle,Turner (keyboards) | Urbaniak,Michal (as,keyboards,dr-programming) | Williams,Kip (keyboards,dr,rap,voc) | Miller,Marcus (el-b) | Earl,Jimmy (el-b) | Brown,John V. (b) | King,Al (perc) | Keller,Rich (dr-programming) | Bourne[Notorious] (rap) | Robinson,Silivea (voc) | Stewart,Shannon (scratsh) | Rhue,Phanalphie (voc) | Murrell,Christopher 'Chris' (voc) | O'Neil,Buffy (voc) | Duell,Shela (voc) | Miller,Leah (rap)
-> different groups

HIBD 8004 | CD | Present Tense
Lenny White Group
Thick
White,Lenny (dr,sound-programming) | Brecker,Michael (sax) | Wright,Bernard (keyboards) | Miller,Marcus (b)
East St.Louis
White,Lenny (dr,sound-programming) | Stewart,Michael (tp,fl-h) | Roney,Antoine (ts) | Wright,Bernard (p) | Fambrough,Charles (b) | Muckhead (rap)
Who Do You Love
White,Lenny (dr,sound-programming) | Brown,Dean (g) | Wright,Bernard (keyboards) | Miller,Marcus (b) | Urbaniak,Michal (v) | Khan,Chaka (voc) | Ledford,Mark (voc)
Door No.3
White,Lenny (dr,sound-programming) | Garrett,Kenny (as) | Brown,Dean (g) | Corea,Chick (p,synth) | Wright,Bernard (el-p,org,synth) | Bailey,Victor (b)

Hip Bop | Edel Contraire Bielefelder Katalog 777 Jazz • Ausgabe 2004 Hip Bop | Edel Contraire

Sweet Tooth
White,Lenny (dr,sound-programming) | Scofield,John (g) | Corea,Chick (p,el-p) | Dryden,Jon (synth) | Bailey,Victor (b)
Wolfbane
White,Lenny (dr,sound-programming) | Garrett,Kenny (ss) | Scofield,John (g) | Brown,Dean (g) | Purrone,Tony (g) | Corea,Chick (el-p,org) | Wright,Bernard (keyboards) | Bailey,Victor (b)
Tea In The Sahara
White,Lenny (keyboards,dr,perc,sound-programming) | Brown,Dean (g) | Corea,Chick (p) | Goldstein,Gil (synth) | Bailey,Victor (b) | Richards,Nicki (voc)
Dark
White,Lenny (keyboards,dr,sound-programming) | Margitza,Rick (ts) | Purrone,Tony (g) | Clarke,Stanley (tenor-b)
And Then You'll Know
White,Lenny (dr) | Brecker,Michael (ts) | Miller,Mulgrew (p) | Wright,Bernard (p) | Levin,Pete (synth,sound-programming) | Genus,James (b)
By Any Means Necessary
White,Lenny (keyboards,dr,sound-programming) | Walsh,Danny (ts) | Wright,Bernard (p) | McClain,Jean (voc) | Ledford,Mark (voc) | Sybill (voc) | Charvoni (voc) | McKay,Stephanie (voc)
Two Weeks In Another Town
White,Lenny (keyboards,dr,perc,sound-programming) | Brecker,Michael (ts) | Levin,Pete (synth,sound-programming) | Whitty,George (synth) | Miller,Marcus (b)
The Shadow Of Lo
White,Lenny (dr,sound-programming) | Walsh,Danny (as) | Brown,Dean (g) | Holzman,Adam (synth,sound-programming) | Genus,James (b)
Caprice
White,Lenny (dr,sound-programming) | Scofield,John (g) | Corea,Chick (p,el-p) | Goldstein,Gil (synth) | Bailey,Victor (b)
-> Recorded at different places

HIBD 8009 | CD | Afro Cubano Chant
Essence All Stars
Cubano Chant | Tanya | Suave | Mui Tarde Amor | Los Dos Lorettas | Nica's Dream | Casablanca
Stamford,CT, rec. September 1995
Essence All Stars | Barbieri,Gato (ts) | Mainieri,Mike (vib) | James,Bob (p) | Gonzalez,Andy (b) | White,Lenny (dr,timbales) | Berrios,Steve (perc)

HIBD 8011 | CD | Another Shade Of Browne
Tom Browne Quintet
Bluesanova | 'Philly' Twist | A Sleepy Lagoon | Povo | Bee Tee's Minor Plea | In A Sentimental Mood | Eighty-One
NYC, rec. April 1996
Browne,Tom (tp,fl-h) | Jackson,Javon (ts) | Goldings,Larry (p) | Carter,Ron (b) | Muhammad,Idris[Leo Morris] (dr)

HIBD 8012 | CD | Urbanator II
Urbanator
Urbanate The Area 2 | Basia | New Yorker | Magic | Urbal Tea | Moody's Mood For Love | Anytime,Anywhere | Mantra | All Blues | Hi Ho Silver | Polak
details unknown, rec. details unknown
Urbanator | Dryden,Jon (keyboards) | Urbaniak,Michal (ss,ts,keyboards,el-v,lyricon,voc) | MacDowell,Al (keyboards,b,piccolo-b) | Holmes,Rodney (dr) | Browne,Tom (tp,fl-h) | Igarashi,Issel (tp) | Hamilton,Ed (g) | Miller,Denzil (keyboards) | Snare,Tod (dr) | Solid (rap) | Six (rap) | White,Sharaye (voc) | Johnson,Mark (programming)

HIBD 8014 | CD | Renderers Of Spirit
Lenny White Group
Whew! What A Dream
NYC, rec. details unknown
White,Lenny (keyboards,dr,sound-programming) | Walsh,Danny (as) | Brown,Dean (g) | Jenkins,Dechown (g) | Blackman,Donald (el-p,org) | Wright,Bernard (synth) | Bailey,Victor (b)
Ho-Cake
White,Lenny (org,keyboards,dr,sound-programming) | Walsh,Danny (sax) | Evans,Vincent Leroy (keyboards) | Duke,George (synth) | Howes,Christian 'Chris' (v) | Brooks,Jerry (b) | Clarke,Stanley (b) | Foley (b)
Walk On By
White,Lenny (dr,music-stand) | Ledford,Mark (tp) | Walsh,Danny (as) | Maupin,Bennie (ts) | Evans,Vincent Leroy (p,keyboards) | Blackman,Donald (synth) | Brooks,Jerry (b) | Foley (b) | Northington,Audrey (voc) | Lesley,Kim (voc) | Machaum (voc) | McClain,Jean (voc)
Pick Pocket
White,Lenny (dr,sound-programming) | Walsh,Danny (sax) | Jenkins,Dechown (g) | Wright,Bernard (synth) | Blackman,Donald (synth) | Dryden,Jon (synth) | Bailey,Victor (b)
Savant
White,Lenny (dr,sound-programming) | Walsh,Danny (sax) | Brown,Dean (g) | Jenkins,Dechown (g) | Rushen,Patrice (p,keyboards) | Dryden,Jon (synth) | Jones,Darryl (b)
Sailing
White,Lenny (dr,sound-programming) | Allen,Geri (p) | Levin,Pete (keyboards,sound-programming) | Zan,Pookie (synth) | Bailey,Victor (b) | Richards,Nicki (voc)
The Abyss
White,Lenny (dr,sound-programming) | Brecker,Michael (sax) | Rushen,Patrice (p) | Dryden,Jon (keyboards,synth) | Bailey,Victor (b)
Swing Time
White,Lenny (keyboards,dr,sound-programming) | Stewart,Michael (tp) | Maupin,Bennie (ss) | Jackson,Javon (ts) | Wright,Bernard (p) | Rushen,Patrice (synth) | Levin,Pete (synth,sound-programming) | Bailey,Victor (b)
Beggin'
White,Lenny (keyboards,dr,sound-programming) | Ledford,Mark (g,voc) | Wright,Bernard (synth) | Foley (b) | Camel,William (b) | Johnson,Elyse (voc) | Lesley,Kim (voc)
Countdown
White,Lenny (keyboards,dr,sound-programming) | Stewart,Michael (tp) | Maupin,Bennie (b-cl) | Evans,Vincent Leroy (p,keyboards,synth) | Foley (b) | Brooks,Jerry (b) | Irvine,Weldon (words)
Dr.Jackle-Africa Talks To You
White,Lenny (dr) | Brecker,Randy (tp) | Maupin,Bennie (ts) | Walsh,Danny (as) | Evans,Vincent Leroy (p,el-p) | Blackman,Donald (synth) | Foley (b) | Brooks,Jerry (b)

HIBD 8016 | CD | Blue Patches
Michael 'Patches' Stewart Group
In Your Own Sweet Way | Stella By Starlight | Caruso | My Foolish Heart | I Waited For You | Alone Together
Van Nuys,CA, rec. details unknown
Stewart,Michael (tp,fl-h) | Bery,Shelly (p) | Rosen,Adrian (b) | Leatherbarrow,Bob (dr)
Pfrancing | One For Daddy-O
Stewart,Michael (tp,fl-h) | Albright,Gerald (sax) | Bery,Shelly (p) | Rosen,Adrian (b) | Leatherbarrow,Bob (dr)
Fly Me To The Moon
NYC, rec. details unknown
Stewart,Michael (tp,fl-h) | Wilson,Steve (as) | Terrasson,Jackie[Jacky] (p) | Evans,Vincent Leroy (keyboards) | Fambrough,Charles (b) | White,Lenny (dr) | Tornquist,Rebecka (voc)

HIBD 8018 | CD | Penetration
Sass | Some Will Dream | Fields Of Gold | Pénétration(El Nino) | Diana | My Funny Valentine | Patmos | Sarah | Pavane | Cat 'N Mouse
NYC/Brooklyn,NY, rec. details unknown
Stewart,Michael (tp,fl-h) | Garrett,Kenny (as) | Heick,Aaron (engl-h,fl,as,oboe) | Evans,Bill (ss,ts) | Miller,Marcus (b-cl,b-g) | Galison,William (harm) | Herington,Joe (g) | Bullock,Hiram (g) | Rogers,Adam (el-g) | Beard,Jim (keyboards) | Genus,James (b) | Saturnino (b) | Danzinger,Zachary (loop-dr) | Tuncboyaci[Boyaciyan],Arto (perc) | Jarreau,Al (voice) | Hey,Henry (sample-programming)

HIBD 8801 | CD | Hot Jazz Bisquits
Lenny White Group
Who Do You Love
White,Lenny (dr,sound-programming) | Brown,Dean (g) | Wright,Bernard (keyboards) | Miller,Marcus (b) | Urbaniak,Michal (v) | Khan,Chaka (voc) | Ledford,Mark (voc)
Urbanator
Hot Jazz Biscuits
Urbanator | Urbaniak,Michal (sax,v) | Browne,Tom (tp) | Dryden,Jon (keyboards) | MacDowell,Al (b) | White,Lenny (dr,perc) | Solid (rap)
Tom Browne Quintet
Bluesanova
Browne,Tom (tp,fl-h) | Jackson,Javon (ts) | Goldings,Larry (p) | Carter,Ron (b) | Muhammad,Idris[Leo Morris] (dr)
Essence All Stars
Luny Tune
Essence All Stars | Garrett,Kenny (as) | Purrone,Tony (g) | DeFrancesco,Joey (org) | White,Lenny (dr)
Bop City
Funk In Deep Freeze
Bop City | McMurray,David (as,ts) | Smooth,C.L. (voc) | Fiuczynski,Dave (g) | Burno,Dwayne (b) | Kilson,Billy (dr) | Weiss,David (tp) | Dryden,Jon (p)
Tom Browne Group
Jam Fo' Real
Browne,Tom (tp,keyboards,voc) | G.,Bobby (g) | Wright,Bernard (keyboards) | Miller,Marcus (el-b) | Keller,Rich (dr-programming)
Essence All Stars
Up Jumped Spring
Essence All Stars | Henderson,Eddie (tp) | Jackson,Javon (ts) | Walton,Cedar (p) | Carter,Ron (b) | White,Lenny (dr)
The Meeting
Late One Night
The Meeting | Watts,Ernie (ss,as,ts) | Rushen,Patrice (keyboards,perc) | Washington,Freddie (b) | Ndugu[Leon Chancler] (dr,perc)
Essence All Stars
Dr.Jackle
Marsalis,Branford (ss) | Johnson,Lamont (p) | Whitaker,Rodney Thomas (b) | Muhammad,Idris[Leo Morris] (dr)
Cubano Chant
Essence All Stars | Barbieri,Gato (ts) | Mainieri,Mike (vib) | James,Bob (p) | Gonzalez,Andy (b) | White,Lenny (dr,timbales) | Berrios,Steve (perc)
Urbanator
Magic
Urbanator | Dryden,Jon (keyboards) | Urbaniak,Michal (ss,ts,keyboards,el-v,lyricon,voc) | MacDowell,Al (keyboards,b,piccolo-b) | Holmes,Rodney (dr)
Lenny White Group
Savant
White,Lenny (dr,sound-programming) | Walsh,Danny (sax) | Brown,Dean (g) | Jenkins,Dechown (g) | Rushen,Patrice (p,keyboards) | Dryden,Jon (synth) | Jones,Darryl (b)
Essence All Stars
Bass Blues
Essence All Stars | Handy,Craig (as) | Walton,Cedar (p) | Carter,Ron (b) | White,Lenny (dr) | Burrell,Kenny (g)
Freedom Jazz Dance
Essence All Stars | Browne,Tom (tp) | Maupin,Bennie (ts) | Childs,Billy (p) | Carter,Ron (b) | White,Lenny (dr)

Hot Shot Records | IN+OUT records

HSR 8312-2 | CD | Maynard Ferguson '93-Footpath Café
Maynard Ferguson And His Big Bop Nouveau Band
Get It To Go | Footpath Café | Brazil | That's My Desire | Cruisin' For A Bluesin' | Poison Ya' Blues | Breake The Ice | Hit And Run
Live at 'Hanita Jazz Club', Heist-op-den-Berg, Belgium, rec. July 1992
Ferguson,Maynard (tp,fl-h) | Ingram,Roger (tp) | Owens,Jon (tp) | Thompson,Brian (tp) | Luciani,Dante (tb) | Kricker,John (b-tb) | Scaglione,Nunzio (as) | McNeil,Chip (ss,ts) | Wallace,Matt (as,ts) | Kostur,Glenn (bs) | Bickel,Doug (p,keyboards) | Marks,Dennis (b,b-g) | White,Jim (dr)

HSR 8313-2 | CD | Remembering Dinah-A Salute To Dinah Washington
Jan Harrington With The Arthur Blythe Quartet
I Tought About You
Sandhausen, rec. 16.2.1993
Harrington,Jan (voc) | Blythe,Arthur (as) | Hennessey,Mike (p) | Bockius,Peter (b) | Bockius,Frank (dr)
Jan Harrington With The Mike Hennesey Trio
Makin' Whoopee
Sandhausen, rec. 9.9.1994
Harrington,Jan (voc) | Hennessey,Mike (p) | Betts,Keter (b) | Cobb,Jimmy (dr)
Nat Adderley Quintet
Just Friends | Centerpiece | Salty Papa Blues
Erding, rec. 12.11.1994
Adderley,Nat (co) | Mitchell,Billy (ts) | Hennessey,Mike (p) | Betts,Keter (b) | Cobb,Jimmy (dr)
If I Had You
Chemnitz, rec. 14.11.1994
Adderley,Nat (co) | Mitchell,Billy (ts) | Hennessey,Mike (p) | Betts,Keter (b) | Cobb,Jimmy (dr)
Jan Harrington With The Nat Adderley Quintet
Evil Gal Blues | Willow Weep For Me | Bye Bye Blues- | Rue Chaptal-
Harrington,Jan (voc) | Adderley,Nat (co,voc) | Mitchell,Billy (ts) | Hennessey,Mike (p) | Betts,Keter (b) | Cobb,Jimmy (dr)
Keter Betts
Olé
Betts,Keter (b-solo)
Lilly Thornton With The Mike Hennesey Trio
Teach Me Tonight
Sandhausen, rec. 1.10.1995
Thornton,Lilly (voc) | Hennessey,Mike (p) | Simmons,Alan (b) | Merritt,Al (dr)
Lilly Thornton With The Benny Golson Quartet
All Of Me
Thornton,Lilly (voc) | Golson,Benny (ts) | Hennessey,Mike (p) | Simmons,Alan (b) | Merritt,Al (dr)
Lilly Thornton With The Benny Golson Sextet
Sometimes I'm Happy
Thornton,Lilly (voc) | Wood,Brian (tp) | Golson,Benny (ts) | Carter,Geoff (ts) | Hennessey,Mike (p) | Simmons,Alan (b) | Merritt,Al (dr)
Lilly Thornton With The Mike Hennesey Trio
What A Difference A Day Made | Love Walked In | For All We Know
Sandhausen, rec. 11.3.1996
Thornton,Lilly (voc) | Hennessey,Mike (p) | Düringer,Roland (b) | Jenne,Meinhard (dr)

hr music.de | HR Media Lizenz

hrmj 001-01 CD | CD | The Three Sopranos
The Three Sopranos With The HR Big Band
Seeing Salinas Again | Stride Rite | Groovin' High | Too Trite | We'll Always Be Together
Frankfurt/M, rec. 26.-28.11.1998
DeFranco,Buddy (cl) | Kühn,Rolf (cl) | Daniels,Eddie (cl) | HR Big Band | Lanzerath,Paul (tp) | Auer,Martin (tp) | Malempre,Alex (tp) | Meyers,Christian (tp) | Molgaard,Torolf (tb) | Feil,Peter (tb) | Bollman,Günter (tb) | Honetschläger,Manfred (b-tb) | Petersen,Harry (as) | Sauerborn,Hans Dieter (as) | Leicht,Oliver (ts) | Lakatos,Tony (ts) | Oslawski,John (bs) | Crona,Claes (p) | Beier,Detlev (b,el-b) | Rückert,Jochen (dr)
Falling In Love With You | Why Was I Born | Just Friends | Lover Man(Oh,Where Can You Be?) | Scrapple From The Apple | To The Point
DeFranco,Buddy (cl) | Kühn,Rolf (cl) | Daniels,Eddie (cl) | HR Big Band | Lanzerath,Paul (tp) | Auer,Martin (tp) | Malempre,Alex (tp) | Meyers,Christian (tp) | Molgaard,Torolf (tb) | Feil,Peter (tb) | Bollman,Günter (tb) | Honetschläger,Manfred (b-tb) | Petersen,Harry (as) | Sauerborn,Hans Dieter (as) | Heute,Rainer (ts) | Lakatos,Tony (ts) | Oslawski,John (bs) | Crona,Claes (p) | Beier,Detlev (b,el-b) | Rückert,Jochen (dr)

hrmj 003-01 CD | CD | Jazz Messe-Messe Für Unsere Zeit
Jazzensemble Des Hessischen Rundfunks
Veni Creator Spiritus | Kyrie | Gloria | Agnus Dei | Dona Nobis Pacem
Frankfurt/M, rec. 1.-3.10.2000
Jazzensemble Des Hessischen Rundfunk | Wukits,Robin (tp) | Zimmermann,Stephan (tp) | Fenchel,Reiner (tp) | Kowalsky,Alexander (tb) | Friedrich,Hartmut (tb) | Scharf,Hans Kaspar (tb) | Krause,Ralf (tb) | MacDonald,John (fr-h) | Seidemann,Johannes (sax) | Reiter,Peter (p) | Schädlich,Johannes (b) | Astor,Felix (dr) | Born,Michael (perc) | Hessische Chorensemble | Bieler,Barbara (voc) | Eckert,Elke (voc) | Graeser,Stetanie (voc) | Greiner,Angelika (voc) | Heinrichs,Johanna (voc) | Herbstleb,Vaness (voc) | Höfer,Monika (voc) | Kreuzer,Marion (voc) | Lehrbach,Irmgard (voc) | Mahr,Monika (voc) | Paschke,Stefani (voc) | Preisser,Comelia (voc) | Rach,Corinna (voc) | Sander-Laun,Ira (voc) | Schlunck,Anke (voc) | Brüssau,Brigitte (voc) | Clemens,Gabriele (voc) | Danish,Silvia (voc) | Feig,Gabi (voc) | Jeschke,Gisela (voc) | Lehrian,Barbara (voc) | Metzger,Gitta (voc) | Pfatt,Beate (voc) | Scharf,Monika (voc) | Witheim,Christine (voc) | Wolberts,Elke (voc) | Brüssau,Reinhard (voc) | Höffken,Manfred (voc) | Karg,Björn (voc) | Maruhn,Armand (voc) | Reschauer,Werner (voc) | Salzwedel,Martin (voc) | Appel,Dirk (voc) | Bender,Helmut (voc) | Busch,Johannes (voc) | Kügler,Joachim (voc) | Martini,Karl (voc) | Wilhelm,Andreas (voc) | Peter,Klaus (voc) | Wünschmann,Klaus Peter (voc)
Sanctus- | Benedictus-
Jazzensemble Des Hessischen Rundfunk | Wukits,Robin (tp) | Zimmermann,Stephan (tp) | Fenchel,Reiner (tp) | Kowalsky,Alexander (tb) | Friedrich,Hartmut (tb) | Scharf,Hans Kaspar (tb) | Krause,Ralf (tb) | MacDonald,John (fr-h) | Seidemann,Johannes (sax) | Reiter,Peter (p) | Heidepriem,Thomas (b) | Astor,Felix (dr) | Born,Michael (perc) | Hessische Chorensemble | Bieler,Barbara (voc) | Eckert,Elke (voc) | Graeser,Stetanie (voc) | Greiner,Angelika (voc) | Heinrichs,Johanna (voc) | Herbstleb,Vaness (voc) | Höfer,Monika (voc) | Kreuzer,Marion (voc) | Lehrbach,Irmgard (voc) | Mahr,Monika (voc) | Paschke,Stefani (voc) | Preisser,Comelia (voc) | Rach,Corinna (voc) | Sander-Laun,Ira (voc) | Schlunck,Anke (voc) | Brüssau,Brigitte (voc) | Clemens,Gabriele (voc) | Danish,Silvia (voc) | Feig,Gabi (voc) | Jeschke,Gisela (voc) | Lehrian,Barbara (voc) | Metzger,Gitta (voc) | Pfatt,Beate (voc) | Scharf,Monika (voc) | Witheim,Christine (voc) | Wolberts,Elke (voc) | Brüssau,Reinhard (voc) | Höffken,Manfred (voc) | Karg,Björn (voc) | Maruhn,Armand (voc) | Reschauer,Werner (voc) | Salzwedel,Martin (voc) | Appel,Dirk (voc) | Bender,Helmut (voc) | Busch,Johannes (voc) | Kügler,Joachim (voc) | Martini,Karl (voc) | Wilhelm,Andreas (voc) | Peter,Klaus (voc) | Wünschmann,Klaus Peter (voc)
Credo
Jazzensemble Des Hessischen Rundfunk | Wukits,Robin (tp) | Zimmermann,Stephan (tp) | Fenchel,Reiner (tp) | Krause,Uwe (tp) | Kowalsky,Alexander (tb) | Friedrich,Hartmut (tb) | Scharf,Hans Kaspar (tb) | Krause,Ralf (tb) | MacDonald,John (fr-h) | Seidemann,Johannes (sax) | Reiter,Peter (p) | Schädlich,Johannes (b) | Astor,Felix (dr) | Born,Michael (perc) | Hessische Chorensemble | Bieler,Barbara (voc) | Eckert,Elke (voc) | Graeser,Stetanie (voc) | Greiner,Angelika (voc) | Heinrichs,Johanna (voc) | Herbstleb,Vaness (voc) | Höfer,Monika (voc) | Kreuzer,Marion (voc) | Lehrbach,Irmgard (voc) | Mahr,Monika (voc) | Paschke,Stefani (voc) | Preisser,Cornelia (voc) | Rach,Corinna (voc) | Sander-Laun,Ira (voc) | Schlunck,Anke (voc) | Brüssau,Brigitte (voc) | Clemens,Gabriele (voc) | Danish,Silvia (voc) | Feig,Gabi (voc) | Jeschke,Gisela (voc) | Lehrian,Barbara (voc) | Metzger,Gitta (voc) | Pfatt,Beate (voc) | Scharf,Monika (voc) | Witheim,Christine (voc) | Wolberts,Elke (voc) | Brüssau,Reinhard (voc) | Höffken,Manfred (voc) | Karg,Björn (voc) | Maruhn,Armand (voc) | Reschauer,Werner (voc) | Salzwedel,Martin (voc) | Appel,Dirk (voc) | Bender,Helmut (voc) | Busch,Johannes (voc) | Kügler,Joachim (voc) | Martini,Karl (voc) | Wilhelm,Andreas (voc) | Peter,Klaus (voc) | Wünschmann,Klaus Peter (voc)
Erzählung
Jazzensemble Des Hessischen Rundfunk | Wukits,Robin (tp) | Zimmermann,Stephan (tp) | Fenchel,Reiner (tp) | Krause,Uwe (tp) | Marstatt,German (tp) | Kowalsky,Alexander (tb) | Friedrich,Hartmut (tb) | Scharf,Hans Kaspar (tb) | Krause,Ralf (tb) | MacDonald,John (fr-h) | Seidemann,Johannes (sax) | Reiter,Peter (p) | Schädlich,Johannes (b) | Astor,Felix (dr) | Born,Michael (perc) | Hessische Chorensemble | Bieler,Barbara (voc) | Eckert,Elke (voc) | Graeser,Stetanie (voc) | Greiner,Angelika (voc) | Heinrichs,Johanna (voc) | Herbstleb,Vaness (voc) | Höfer,Monika (voc) | Kreuzer,Marion (voc) | Lehrbach,Irmgard (voc) | Mahr,Monika (voc) | Paschke,Stefani (voc) | Preisser,Cornelia (voc) | Rach,Corinna (voc) | Sander-Laun,Ira (voc) | Schlunck,Anke (voc) | Brüssau,Brigitte (voc) | Clemens,Gabriele (voc) | Danish,Silvia (voc) | Feig,Gabi (voc) | Jeschke,Gisela (voc) | Lehrian,Barbara (voc) | Metzger,Gitta (voc) | Pfatt,Beate (voc) | Scharf,Monika (voc) | Witheim,Christine (voc) | Wolberts,Elke (voc) | Brüssau,Reinhard (voc) | Höffken,Manfred (voc) | Karg,Björn (voc) | Maruhn,Armand (voc) | Reschauer,Werner (voc) | Salzwedel,Martin (voc) | Appel,Dirk (voc) | Bender,Helmut (voc) | Busch,Johannes (voc) | Kügler,Joachim (voc) | Martini,Karl (voc) | Wilhelm,Andreas (voc) | Peter,Klaus (voc) | Wünschmann,Klaus Peter (voc)

hrmj 004-01 CD | CD | Touch Of Lips
Landes Jugend Jazz Orchester Hessen
Isi's Choice | Touch Of Your Lips | Goin' Wess
Frankfurt/M, rec. 8.-13.1.2001
Landes Jugend Jazz Orchester Hessen | Bogaart,Robert (tp) | Lokken,Herwin (tp) | Szurmant,Jan (tp) | Wallstädt,Niels (tp) | Käthner,Ulrich (tb) | Götz,Johannes (tb) | Weil,Andreas (tb) | Schappert,Axel (tb) | Engel,Benjamin (as) | Roth,Yvonne (as) | Gürtler,John (ts) | Tischbirek,Alexander (ts) | Salamon,Udo (bs) | Born,Michael (vib) | Bernhardt,Jens (p) | Koslowski,Jan (g) | Repka,Johannes (g) | Manns,Andreas (b) | Merk,Sebastian (dr)
Blue Variations
Landes Jugend Jazz Orchester Hessen | Mangelsdorff,Albert (tb) | Bogaart,Robert (tp) | Lokken,Herwin (tp) | Szurmant,Jan (tp) | Wallstädt,Niels (tp) | Käthner,Ulrich (tb) | Götz,Johannes (tb) | Weil,Andreas (tb) | Schappert,Axel (tb) | Engel,Benjamin (as) | Roth,Yvonne (as) | Gürtler,John (ts) | Tischbirek,Alexander (ts) | Salamon,Udo (bs) | Born,Michael (vib) | Bernhardt,Jens (p) | Koslowski,Jan (g) | Repka,Johannes (g) | Manns,Andreas (b) | Merk,Sebastian (dr)
Lovers | Old Cape Cod
Landes Jugend Jazz Orchester Hessen | Bogaart,Robert (tp) | Lokken,Herwin (tp) | Szurmant,Jan (tp) | Wallstädt,Niels (tp) | Käthner,Ulrich (tb) | Götz,Johannes (tb) | Weil,Andreas (tb) | Schappert,Axel (tb) | Engel,Benjamin (as) | Roth,Yvonne (as) | Gürtler,John (ts) | Tischbirek,Alexander (ts) | Salamon,Udo (bs) | Born,Michael (vib) | Bernhardt,Jens (p) | Koslowski,Jan (g) | Repka,Johannes (g) | Manns,Andreas (b) | Merk,Sebastian (dr) | Alley Scatz: | Henry,Pamela (voc) | Meyer,Barbara Leah (voc) | Williams,Debbie (voc)
The Flea
Frankfurt/M, rec. 6.-13.1.2001
Landes Jugend Jazz Orchester Hessen | Bogaart,Robert (tp) | Lokken,Herwin (tp) | Szurmant,Jan (tp) | Wallstädt,Niels (tp) | Käthner,Ulrich (tb) | Götz,Johannes (tb) | Weil,Andreas (tb) | Schappert,Axel (tb) | Engel,Benjamin (as) | Fröhlich,Holger (as) | Gürtler,John (ts) | Tischbirek,Alexander (ts) | Salamon,Udo (bs) | Born,Michael (vib) |

LABELVERZEICHNIS

Bernhardt,Jens (p) | Koslowski,Jan (g) | Repka,Johannes (g) | Manns,Andreas (b) | Merk,Sebastian (dr) | Groen,Elwyn L. (rap)
I'm Gonna Sit Right Down And Write Myself A Letter | The Swinger | In The Jungle | The Session
Landes Jugend Jazz Orchester Hessen | Bogaart,Robert (tp) | Lokken,Herwin (tp) | Szurmant,Jan (tp) | Wallstädt,Niels (tp) | Käthner,Ulrich (tb) | Götz,Johannes (tb) | Weil,Andreas (tb) | Schappert,Axel (tb) | Engel,Benjamin (as) | Fröhlich,Holger (as) | Gürtler,John (ts) | Tischbirek,Alexander (ts) | Salamon,Udo (bs) | Born,Michael (vib) | Bernhardt,Jens (p) | Koslowski,Jan (g) | Repka,Johannes (g) | Manns,Andreas (b) | Merk,Sebastian (dr) | Bell,Madeleine (voc)
Dance,You Monster,To My Soft Song! | Tell Your Story | Chunky | My Lament
Landes Jugend Jazz Orchester Hessen | Bogaart,Robert (tp) | Lokken,Herwin (tp) | Szurmant,Jan (tp) | Wallstädt,Niels (tp) | Käthner,Ulrich (tb) | Götz,Johannes (tb) | Weil,Andreas (tb) | Schappert,Axel (tb) | Engel,Benjamin (as) | Fröhlich,Holger (as) | Gürtler,John (ts) | Tischbirek,Alexander (ts) | Salamon,Udo (bs) | Born,Michael (vib) | Bernhardt,Jens (p) | Koslowski,Jan (g) | Repka,Johannes (g) | Manns,Andreas (b) | Merk,Sebastian (dr)

hrmj 006-01 CD | CD | The American Songs Of Kurt Weill
HR Big Band
Moon-Faced,Star-Eyed
Frankfurt/M, rec. August-November 2000
HR Big Band | Lanzerath,Paul (tp) | Malempre,Alex (tp) | Auer,Martin (tp) | Hesse,Ralph (tp) | Molgaard,Torolf (tb) | Feil,Peter (tb) | Bollmann,Günter (tb) | Honetschläger,Manfred (b-tb) | Sauerborn,Hans Dieter (as) | Petersen,Harry (as) | De Oliveira,Wilson (ts) | Lakatos,Tony (ts) | Herzog,Edgar (bs) | Grimm,Jürgen (p) | Vetterer,Werner (g) | Heidepriem,Thomas (b) | Bings,Herbert (dr) | Droste,Silvia (voc) | Cascaro,Jeff (voc)
September Song
HR Big Band | Lanzerath,Paul (tp) | Malempre,Alex (tp) | Auer,Martin (tp) | Hesse,Ralph (tp) | Molgaard,Torolf (tb) | Feil,Peter (tb) | Bollmann,Günter (tb) | Honetschläger,Manfred (b-tb) | Sauerborn,Hans Dieter (as) | Petersen,Harry (as) | De Oliveira,Wilson (ts) | Lakatos,Tony (ts) | Bartelt,Marcus (bs) | Reiter,Peter (p) | Vetterer,Werner (g) | Heidepriem,Thomas (b) | Weiss,Klaus (dr)
Lost In The Stars | A Rhyme For Angela | My Week
HR Big Band | Lanzerath,Paul (tp) | Malempre,Alex (tp) | Auer,Martin (tp) | Hesse,Ralph (tp) | Molgaard,Torolf (tb) | Feil,Peter (tb) | Bollmann,Günter (tb) | Honetschläger,Manfred (b-tb) | Sauerborn,Hans Dieter (as) | Petersen,Harry (as) | De Oliveira,Wilson (ts) | Bachmann,Thomas (ts) | Bartelt,Marcus (bs) | Reiter,Peter (p) | Vetterer,Werner (g) | Heidepriem,Thomas (b) | Bings,Herbert (dr) | Droste,Silvia (voc) | Cascaro,Jeff (voc)
This Is New | Sing Me Not A Ballad | Green-Up Time | There's Nowhere To Go But Up | Mr.Right | Girl Of The Moment | Lonely House | The River Is So Blue | Here I'll Stay
HR Big Band | Lanzerath,Paul (tp) | Malempre,Alex (tp) | Auer,Martin (tp) | Hesse,Ralph (tp) | Molgaard,Torolf (tb) | Feil,Peter (tb) | Bollmann,Günter (tb) | Honetschläger,Manfred (b-tb) | Sauerborn,Hans Dieter (as) | Petersen,Harry (as) | De Oliveira,Wilson (ts) | Lakatos,Tony (ts) | Bartelt,Marcus (bs) | Reiter,Peter (p,el-p) | Vetterer,Werner (g) | Heidepriem,Thomas (b) | Bings,Herbert (dr) | Droste,Silvia (voc) | Cascaro,Jeff (voc)

hrmj 012-02 CD | CD | Swinging Christmas | EAN 4035714100124
HR Big Band With Marjorie Barnes And Frits Landesbergen
Jingle Bells | The Christmas Song | Greensleeves | Let It Snow, Let It Snow, Let It Snow | Winter Wonderland | Little Drummer Boy | Es Ist Ein Ros Entsprungen | What Are You Doing New Year's Eve? | Silent Night
Hessischer Rundfunk,Frankfurt/M., rec. 12.-25.6.2002
HR Big Band | Keller,Jörg Achim (cond) | Lanzerath,Paul (tp) | Auer,Martin (tp,fl-h) | Vogel,Thomas (tp) | Hesse,Ralph (tp) | Malempre,Alex (tp) | Maaß,Torsten (tp) | Molgaard,Torolf (tb) | Feil,Peter (tb) | Bollmann,Günter (tb) | Honetschläger,Manfred (b-tb) | Petersen,Harry (fl,as) | Sauerborn,Hans Dieter (as) | De Oliveira,Wilson (fl,ts) | Lakatos,Tony (ts) | Heute,Rainer (bs) | Landesbergen,Frits (vib) | Reiter,Peter (p,el-p) | Vetterer,Werner (g) | Heidepriem,Thomas (b,el-b) | Heller,Ingmar (b,el-b) | Bings,Herbert (dr) | Roggenbuck,Burkhard (perc) | Barnes,Marjorie (voc)
HR Big Band With Marjorie Barnes And Frits Landesbergen And Strings
Rudolph The Red Nosed Reindeer | All I Want For Christmas | Santa Claus Is Coming To Town | White Christmas | Have Yourself A Merry Little Christmas
HR Big Band | Keller,Jörg Achim (cond) | Lanzerath,Paul (tp) | Auer,Martin (tp,fl-h) | Vogel,Thomas (tp) | Malempre,Alex (tp) | Molgaard,Torolf (tb) | Feil,Peter (tb) | Bollmann,Günter (tb) | Honetschläger,Manfred (b-tb) | Petersen,Harry (fl,as) | Sauerborn,Hans Dieter (as) | De Oliveira,Wilson (fl,ts) | Lakatos,Tony (ts) | Heute,Rainer (bs) | Landesbergen,Frits (vib) | Reiter,Peter (p,el-p) | Vetterer,Werner (g) | Heidepriem,Thomas (b,el-b) | Heller,Ingmar (b,el-b) | Bings,Herbert (dr) | Roggenbuck,Burkhard (perc) | Barnes,Marjorie (voc) | Streichergruppe des Radio-Sinfonie-Orchesters Frankfurt | Hendal,Karin (v) | Ilg,Cornelia (v) | Ionescu,Sorin (v) | Mäding-Lemmerich,Ulrike (v) | Metzendorf,Sonja (v) | Miesen,Gerhard (v) | Mokatsian,Hovhannes (v) | Schwamm,Klaus (v) | Ye,Sha (v) | Albert,Ingrid (viola) | Hüllemann-Watson,Kerstin (viola) | Weise,Steffen (viola) | Ilg,Arnold (cello) | Looser,Barbara (cello)

hrmj 014-02 CD | CD | Libertango:Homage An Astor Piazolla | EAN 4035714100148
HR Big Band
Michelangelo | La Camorra
Hessischer Rundfunk,Frankfurt/M., rec. 14.-18.8.2001
HR Big Band | Keller,Jörg Achim (cond) | Lanzerath,Paul (tp,fl-h) | Auer,Martin (tp,fl-h) | Baldauf,Rüdiger (tp,fl-h) | Engels,Jorg (tp) | Molgaard,Torolf (tb) | Feil,Peter (tb) | Bollmann,Günter (tb,euphonium) | Honetschläger,Manfred (b-tb,tuba) | Petersen,Harry (fl,piccolo,cl,ss,as) | Sauerborn,Hans Dieter (fl,alto-fl,cl,ss,as) | De Oliveira,Wilson (fl,alto-fl,cl,ss,ts) | Lakatos,Tony (fl,ss,ts) | Heute,Rainer (b-cl,bs) | Reiter,Peter (p) | Vetterer,Werner (g,el-g) | Heidepriem,Thomas (b,el-b) | Haffner,Wolfgang (dr) | Haus,Matthias (perc)
Milonga Del Angel | Tres Minutos Con La Realidad | Resurrection Del Angel | Mumuki | Libertango
HR Big Band | Keller,Jörg Achim (cond) | Lanzerath,Paul (tp,fl-h) | Auer,Martin (tp,fl-h) | Malempre,Alex (tp,fl-h) | Grünewald,Dieter (tp,fl-h) | Molgaard,Torolf (tb) | Feil,Peter (tb) | Bollmann,Günter (tb,euphonium) | Hartmann,Achim (b-tb,tuba) | Petersen,Harry (fl,piccolo,cl,ss,as) | Sauerborn,Hans Dieter (fl,alto-fl,cl,ss,as) | Leicht,Oliver (fl,cl,alto-cl,ss,as) | Lakatos,Tony (fl,ss,ts) | Heute,Rainer (b-cl,bs) | Reiter,Peter (p) | Vetterer,Werner (g,el-g) | Heidepriem,Thomas (b,el-b) | Bings,Herbert (dr) | Haus,Matthias (perc)
Zum
HR Big Band | Keller,Jörg Achim (cond) | Weidinger,Tobias (tp,fl-h) | Auer,Martin (tp,fl-h) | Malempre,Alex (tp,fl-h) | Grünewald,Dieter (tp,fl-h) | Molgaard,Torolf (tb) | Feil,Peter (tb) | Bollmann,Günter (tb,euphonium) | Hartmann,Achim (b-tb,tuba) | Petersen,Harry (fl,piccolo,cl,ss,as) | Sauerborn,Hans Dieter (fl,alto-fl,cl,ss,as) | Leicht,Oliver (fl,cl,alto-cl,ss,as) | Lakatos,Tony (fl,ss,ts) | Heute,Rainer (b-cl,bs) | Reiter,Peter (p) | Vetterer,Werner (g,el-g) | Heidepriem,Thomas (b,el-b) | Bings,Herbert (dr) | Haus,Matthias (perc)

hrmn 018-03 CD | CD | Elliott Sharp:Racing Hearts/Tessalation Row/Calling | EAN 4035714100186
Radio Symphony Orchestra Frankfurt
Racing Heart(version 1998)
Hessischer Rundfunk,Frankfurt/M., rec. 13.11.1998
Radio Symphony Orchestra Frankfurt/M. | Rundel,Peter (cond)
Calling(2001)
Hessischer Rundfunk,Frankfurt/M., rec. 3.7.2002
Radio Symphony Orchestra Frankfurt/M. | Rundel,Peter (cond)
Ensemble Modern
Tessalation Row
Hessischer Rundfunk,Frankfurt/M., rec. 9.4.1999
Ensemble Modern | De Roo,Kasper (cond)

i.e. Music | Universal Music Germany

557847-2 | CD | Jarreau
Al Jarreau With Band
Mornin' | Boogie Down | I Will Be Here For You(Nitakungodea Milele) | Save Me | Step By Step | Black And Blues | Trouble In Paradise | Not Like This | Love Is Waiting
Studio City,CA, rec. 1983
Jarreau,Al (voice) | Hey,Jerry (tp,horns-arr) | Findley,Chuck (tp) | Grant,Gary (tp) | Reichenbach,Bill (tb) | Loper,Charles (tb) | Canning,Tom (p,el-p,synth) | Graydon,Jay (g) | Laboriel,Abe (b) | Gadd,Steve (dr)

557848-2 | CD | High Crime
Raging Waters | Imagination | Murphy's Law | Tell Me | After All | High Crime | Let's Pretend | Sticky Wicket | Love Speaks Louder Than Words | Fallin'
Sherman Oaks,CA, rec. ca.1984
Jarreau,Al (voice) | personal included: | Hey,Jerry (fl-h) | Grant,Gary (fl-h) | Jackson,Paul (g) | Graydon,Jay (g,synth,arr) | Tomlin,Bo (p) | Foster,David (p,synth) | Buchanan,Robbie (synth) | East,Nathan (b) | Beats,Bob (b) | Umor,Skinsoh (dr) | McSticks,Chip (dr) | Background Vocals | details unknown

557849-2 | CD | Al Jarreau In London
Racing Waters | Black And Blues | I Will Be Here For You(Nitakungodea Milele) | Let's Pretend | High Crime | Roof Garden | Teach Me Tonight | We're In This Love Together
Live at 'Wembley Arena',London,GB, rec. November 1984
Jarreau,Al (voice) | Stewart,Michael (tp,fl-h) | Hey,Jerry (tp) | Paulo,Michael, (fl,sax) | Johnson,Charles Icarus (g,voc) | Lyle,Bobby (keyboards,ld,voc) | Studer,Jim (keyboards,voc) | Williams,Larry (synth) | East,Nathan (b,voc) | Buchanan,Robbie (synth,b) | Lawson,Ricky (dr) | Gassama,Malando (perc) | Page,Richard (voc) | George,Steve (voc) | Young,Michael Casey (synth-programming)

557850-2 | CD | L Is For Lover
Tell Me(What I Got To Do) | L Is For Lover | Says | Pleasure | Across The Midnight Sky | We Got Telepathy - (We Got) Telepathy | Give Me A Little More Lovin' | No Ordinary Romance | Real Tight
NYC, rec. details unknown
Jarreau,Al (voice) | Sasse,Philippe (keyboards) | Bralower,Jimmy (dr,perc) | Rodgers,Nile (g,keyboards) | Bullock,Hiram (g) | Scherer,Peter (keyboards) | Gollehon,Joseph 'Mac' (tp) | Arron,Robert (reeds) | Gibbs,Doc (perc) | Background Vocals

557851-2 | CD | Heart's Horizon
All Or Nothing At All | So Good | All Of My Love | Pleasure Of Pain | Yo' Jeans | Way To Your Heart | One Way | Hi | I Must Have Been A Fool | More Love | Killer Love | Heart's Horizon
Jarreau,Al (voice) | Band | Background Vocals

557852-2 | CD | Heaven And Earth
What You Do To Me | It's Not Hard To Love You | Blue Angel | Heaven And Earth | Superfine Love | Whenever I Hear Your Name | Love Of My Life | If I Break | Blue In Green(Tapestry): | The Dedication(part 1)- | The Dance(part 2)-
details unknown, rec. details unknown
Jarreau,Al (voice) | Walden,Narada Michael (dr,rhythm-arrangements) | Hey,Jerry (tp) | McCandless,Paul (oboe) | Higgins,Dan (sax) | Biancaniello,Louis (keyboards,synth,programming) | Background Vocals

557853-2 | CD | Tenderness
Mas Que Nada | Try A Little Tenderness | My Favorite Things | Your Song | She's Leaving Home | Summertime | Save Your Love For Me | You Don't See Me | Wait For The Magic | Dinosaur | Go Away Little Girl
Los Angeles,CA, rec. 1993
Jarreau,Al (voice) | Stewart,Michael (tp) | Sanborn,David (as) | Garrett,Kenny (as) | Brecker,Michael (ts) | Gale,Eric (g) | Jackson,Paul (g) | Sample,Joe (p,el-p) | Larsen,Neil (org) | Saisse,Phillippe (synth) | Miles,Jason (synth) | Miller,Marcus (keyboards,b-g) | Gadd,Steve (dr) | Da Costa,Paulinho (perc) | Johnson,Bashiri (perc) | Alias,Don (perc) | Battle,Kathleen (voc) | Campbell,Stacy (voc) | Ramsey,Jeffry (voc) | Young,Sharon (voc)

Impulse(MCA) | Universal Music Germany

543412-2 | CD | Kulu Se Mama
John Coltrane Quartet
Welcome
Englewood Cliffs,NJ, rec. 10.6.1965
Coltrane,John (ts) | Tyner,McCoy (p) | Garrison,Jimmy (b) | Jones,Elvin (dr)
Dusk-Dawn | Dusk-Dawn(alt.take)
Englewood Cliffs,NJ, rec. 16.6.1965
Coltrane,John (ss,ts) | Tyner,McCoy (p) | Garrison,Jimmy (b) | Jones,Elvin (dr)
Vigil
Coltrane,John (ts) | Jones,Elvin (dr)
John Coltrane And His Orchestra
Kulu Se Mama | Selflessness
Los Angeles,CA, rec. 14.10.1965
Coltrane,John (ts) | Sanders,Pharoah (ts) | Tyner,McCoy (p) | Garrison,Jimmy (b) | Garrett,Donald Rafael (b-cl,b) | Jones,Elvin (dr) | Butler,Frank (dr,perc) | Lewis,Juno (perc,voc)

543413-2 | CD | Ascension
Ascension(edition I) | Ascension(edition II)
Englewood Cliffs,NJ, rec. 28.6.1965
Coltrane,John (ts) | Hubbard,Freddie (tp) | Johnson,Dewey (tp) | Brown,Marion (as) | Tchicai,John (as) | Sanders,Pharoah (ts) | Shepp,Archie (ts) | Tyner,McCoy (p) | Davis,Art (b) | Garrison,Jimmy (b) | Jones,Elvin (dr)

543415-2 | CD | Interstellar Space
John Coltrane-Rashied Ali Duo
Mars | Leo | Venus | Jupiter | Jupiter(Variation) | Saturn
NYC, rec. 22.2.1967
Coltrane,John (ts,bells) | Ali,Rashied (dr,perc)

543416-2 | CD | Impressions
John Coltrane Sextet
India
Live at The 'Village Vanguard',NYC, rec. 2./3..11.1961
Coltrane,John (ss) | Dolphy,Eric (b-cl) | Tyner,McCoy (p) | Workman,Reggie (b) | Garrison,Jimmy (b) | Jones,Elvin (dr)
John Coltrane Quartet
Impressions
Live at The 'Village Vanguard',NYC, rec. 5.11.1961
Coltrane,John (ts) | Tyner,McCoy (p) | Garrison,Jimmy (b) | Jones,Elvin (dr)
Up 'Gainst The Wall
NYC, rec. 18.9.1962
Coltrane,John (ts) | Tyner,McCoy (p) | Garrison,Jimmy (b) | Jones,Elvin (dr)
John Coltrane Quintet
After The Rain | Dear Old Stockholm
NYC, rec. 29.4.1963
Coltrane,John (ts) | Tyner,McCoy (p) | Garrison,Jimmy (b) | Haynes,Roy (dr)

547958-2 | CD | The Dealer
Chico Hamilton Quartet
The Dealer | A Trip | Thoughts | Jim-Jeannie
NYC, rec. 9.9.1966
Hamilton,Forrest 'Chico' (dr) | Lawrence,Arnie (as) | Coryell,Larry (g) | Davis,Richard (b)
Chico Hamilton Quintet
Baby You Know | Larry Of Arabia
Hamilton,Forrest 'Chico' (dr) | Lawrence,Arnie (as) | Coryell,Larry (g) | Davis,Richard (b) | Hayes,Ernest 'Ernie' (org)
For Mods Only
Hamilton,Forrest 'Chico' (dr) | Lawrence,Arnie (as) | Coryell,Larry (g) | Davis,Richard (b) | Shepp,Archie (p)
Chico Hamilton
Big Noise From Winnetka
Englewood Cliffs,NJ, rec. 15.3.1965
Hamilton,Forrest 'Chico' (dr) | Bobo,Willie (cowbell)
Chico Hamilton Sextet
Chic Chic Chico
Hamilton,Forrest 'Chico' (dr) | Lloyd,Charles (fl) | Woods,Jimmy (ts) | Szabo,Gabor (g) | Stinson,Albert (b,voc) | Bobo,Willie (maracas)
Chico Hamilton Quintet
The Second Time Around | El Toro
Englewood Cliffs,NJ, rec. 18.9.1962
Hamilton,Forrest 'Chico' (dr) | Bohanon,George (tb,perc,maracas) | Lloyd,Charles (fl,ts) | Szabo,Gabor (g) | Stinson,Albert (b)

547959-2 | CD | Heavy Sounds
Elvin Jones-Richard Davis Quartet
Raunchy Rita | M.E. | Elvin's Guitar Blues | Here's That Rainy Day
NYC, rec. 20.6.1967
Jones,Elvin (g,dr) | Davis,Richard (b) | Foster,Frank (ts) | Greene,Billy (p)
Elvin Jones-Richard Davis Duo
Summertime
NYC, rec. 19.6.1967
Jones,Elvin (dr) | Davis,Richard (b)
Elvin Jones-Richard Davis Trio
Shiny Stockings
NYC, rec. 20.6.1967
Jones,Elvin (dr) | Davis,Richard (b) | Foster,Frank (ts)

547961-2 | CD | Live at Pep's Vol.2
Yusef Lateef Quintet
Brother John | P-Bouk | Nu-Bouk | Yusef's Mood | I Remember Clifford | Listen To The Wind | Delilah | The Magnolia Triangle(alt.take)
Live at Pep's Lounge,Philadelphia, rec. 29.6.1964
Lateef,Yusef (fl,ts,argol,bamboo-fl,oboe,shenai) | Williams,Richard (tp) | Nock,Mike (p) | Farrow,Ernie (b) | Black,James (dr)
Yusef Lateef Quartet
I Loved
Lateef,Yusef (ts) | Nock,Mike (p) | Farrow,Ernie (b) | Black,James (dr)

547964-2 | CD | A Jazz Message
Art Blakey Quartet
Cafe | Just Knock On My Door | Summertime | Blues Back | Sunday | The Song Is You
Englewood Cliffs,NJ, rec. 16.7.1963
Blakey,Art (dr) | Stitt,Sonny (as,ts) | Tyner,McCoy (p) | Davis,Art (b)

547966-2 | CD | Fort Yawuh
Keith Jarrett Quintet
If The Misfits (Wear It) - (If The) Misfits (Wear It) | Forth Yawuh | De Drums | Still Life Still Live | Road Travelled,Road Veiled
Live at The 'Village Vanguard',NYC, rec. 24.2.1973
Jarrett,Keith (ss,p,tambourine) | Redman,Dewey (ts,maracas,musette) | Haden,Charlie (b) | Motian,Paul (dr) | Johnson,Danny (perc)

547967-2 | CD | Every Day I Have The Blues
Jimmy Rushing With Oliver Nelson And His Orchestra
Baby Don't You Tell On Me | Berkeley Campus Blues | Blues In The Dark | Everyday I Have The Blues | Keep The Faith Baby | I Left My Baby | You Can't Run Around | Undecided Blues
NYC, rec. 9.2.1967
Rushing,Jimmy (voc) | Nelson,Oliver (arr,ld) | Terry,Clark (tp) | Wells,Dicky (tb) | Ashton,Bob (ts) | Jones,Hank (p,org) | unkn. (g) | Duvivier,George (b) | Tate,Grady (dr)
Evil Blues
NYC, rec. 10.2.1967
Rushing,Jimmy (voc) | Nelson,Oliver (arr,ld) | Terry,Clark (tp) | Wells,Dicky (tb) | Ashton,Bob (ts) | Burrell,Kenny (g) | Jones,Hank (p) | Scott,Shirley (org) | Duvivier,George (b) | Tate,Grady (dr)
Jimmy Rushing And His Orchestra
Sent For You Yesterday And Here You Come Today | Sony Boy Blues | Bad Loser | Tell Me I'm Not Too Late | Crying Blues | Take Me Back Baby
NYC, rec. 1968
Rushing,Jimmy (voc) | Wells,Dicky (tb) | Tate,Buddy (ts) | Frishberg,Dave (p) | Richardson,Wally (g) | McCracken,Hugh (g) | Bushnell,Bob (el-b) | Marshall,Joe (dr)
Dickie Wells-Buddy Tate Quintet
We Remember Pres
Wells,Dicky (tb) | Tate,Buddy (ts) | Frishberg,Dave (p) | Bushnell,Bob (el-b) | Marshall,Joe (dr)

547980-2 | CD | Live At Newport
McCoy Tyner Quintet
Newport Romp | My Funny Valentine | Woody'n You
Live at Newport,Rhode Island, rec. 5.7.1963
Tyner,McCoy (p) | Terry,Clark (tp) | Mariano,Charlie (as) | Cranshaw,Bob (b) | Roker,Granville 'Mickey' (dr)
McCoy Tyner Trio
All Of You | Monk's Blues
Tyner,McCoy (p) | Cranshaw,Bob (b) | Roker,Granville 'Mickey' (dr)

549914-2 | CD | John Coltrane:Standards
John Coltrane And His Orchestra
Greensleeves
Englewood Cliffs,NJ, rec. 23.5.1961
Coltrane,John (ss) | Hubbard,Freddie (tp) | Little,Booker (tp) | Greenlee,Charles (euphonium) | Priester,Julian (euphonium) | Watkins,Julius (fr-h) | Corrado,Donald (fr-h) | Northern,Bob (fr-h) | Swisshelm,Robert (fr-h) | Buffington,Jimmy (fr-h) | Barber,Bill (tuba) | Bushell,Garvin (piccolo,reeds) | Dolphy,Eric (fl,b-cl,as,cond) | Patrick,Pat (bs) | Tyner,McCoy (p) | Workman,Reggie (b) | Jones,Elvin (dr)
John Coltrane Quartet
Softly As In A Morning Sunrise
Live at The 'Village Vanguard',NYC, rec. 2.11.1961
Coltrane,John (ss) | Tyner,McCoy (p) | Workman,Reggie (b) | Jones,Elvin (dr)
The Inch Worm | Out Of This World
Englewood Cliffs,NJ, rec. 11.4.1962
Coltrane,John (ss) | Tyner,McCoy (p) | Garrison,Jimmy (b) | Jones,Elvin (dr)
All Or Nothing At All | What's New?
Englewood Cliffs,NJ, rec. 13.11.1962
Coltrane,John (ts) | Tyner,McCoy (p) | Garrison,Jimmy (b) | Jones,Elvin (dr)
Johnny Hartman With The John Coltrane Quartet
Lush Life | Autumn Serenade
Englewood Cliffs,NJ, rec. 7.3.1963
Hartman,Johnny (voc) | Coltrane,John (ts) | Tyner,McCoy (p) | Garrison,Jimmy (b) | Jones,Elvin (dr)
John Coltrane Quartet
I Want To Talk About You
Live at 'Birdland',NYC, rec. 8.10.1963
Coltrane,John (ts) | Tyner,McCoy (p) | Garrison,Jimmy (b) | Jones,Elvin (dr)
John Coltrane Quintet
Feelin' Good
Englewood Cliffs,NJ, rec. 18.2.1965
Coltrane,John (ts) | Tyner,McCoy (p) | Garrison,Jimmy (b) | Davis,Art (b) | Jones,Elvin (dr)

589099-2 | CD | Coltrane Spiritual | EAN 731458909927
John Coltrane Quintet With Eric Dolphy
Spiritual
Live at The 'Village Vanguard',NYC, rec. 3.11.1961
Coltrane,John (ss,ts) | Dolphy,Eric (b-cl) | Tyner,McCoy (p) | Workman,Reggie (b) | Jones,Elvin (dr)
John Coltrane Quartet
Tunji
Englewood Cliffs,NJ, rec. 29.6.1962
Coltrane,John (ts) | Tyner,McCoy (p) | Garrison,Jimmy (b) | Jones,Elvin (dr)

Wise One
Englewood Cliffs,NJ, rec. 27.4.1964
Coltrane,John (ts) | Tyner,McCoy (p) | Garrison,Jimmy (b) | Jones,Elvin (dr)
A Love Supreme(part 1:Acknowledgement)
Englewood Cliffs,NJ, rec. 9.12.1964
Coltrane,John (ts) | Tyner,McCoy (p) | Garrison,Jimmy (b) | Jones,Elvin (dr)
Song Of Praise
Englewood Cliffs,NJ, rec. 17.5.1965
Coltrane,John (ts) | Tyner,McCoy (p) | Garrison,Jimmy (b) | Jones,Elvin (dr)
Dear Lord
Englewood Cliffs,NJ, rec. 26.5.1965
Coltrane,John (ts) | Tyner,McCoy (p) | Garrison,Jimmy (b) | Haynes,Roy (dr)
Welcome
Englewood Cliffs,NJ, rec. 10.6.1965
Coltrane,John (ts) | Tyner,McCoy (p) | Garrison,Jimmy (b) | Jones,Elvin (dr)
Ogunde
Englewood Cliffs,NJ, rec. 7.3.1967
Coltrane,John (ts) | Coltrane,Alice (p) | Garrison,Jimmy (b) | Ali,Rashied (dr)

589120-2 | CD | The Olatunji Concert:The Last Live Recording
John Coltrane Group
Introduction by Billy Taylor | Ogunde | My Favorite Things
Live at The Olatunji Center Of African Culture,NYC, rec. 23.4.1967
Coltrane,John (ss,ts) | Sanders,Pharoah (ts) | Coltrane,Alice (p) | Garrison,Jimmy (b) | Ali,Rashied (dr) | DeWitt,Algie (bata-dr) | Santos,Jumma prob. (perc)

589183-2 | CD | McCoy Tyner Plays John Coltrane
McCoy Tyner Trio
Naima | Moment's Notice | Crescent | After The Rain | Afro Blue | I Want To Talk About You | Mr.Day
Live at The 'Village Vanguard',NYC, rec. 23.9.1997
Tyner,McCoy (p) | Mraz,George 'Jiri' (b) | Foster,Al (dr)

589548-2 | 2 CD | Ballads | EAN 731458954828
John Coltrane Quartet
It's Easy To Remember | Easy To Remember(alt.take 1) | Easy To Remember(alt.take 2) | Easy To Remember(alt.take 3) | Easy To Remember(alt.take 4) | Easy To Remember(alt.take 5) | Easy To Remember(alt.take 6) | Greensleeves | Greensleeves(alt.take 1) | Greensleeves(alt.take 2) | Greensleeves(alt.take 3) | Greensleeves(45-rpm take) | Easy To remember(alt.take 2)
Englewood Cliffs,NJ, rec. 21.12.1961
Coltrane,John (ts) | Tyner,McCoy (p) | Garrison,Jimmy (b) | Jones,Elvin (dr)
Nancy(With The Laughing Face) | What's New?
Englewood Cliffs,NJ, rec. 18.9.1962
Coltrane,John (ts) | Tyner,McCoy (p) | Garrison,Jimmy (b) | Jones,Elvin (dr)
Say It Over And Over Again | You Don't Know What Love Is | Too Young To Go Steady | All Or Nothing At All | I Wish I Knew | All Or Nothing At All(alt.take)
Englewood Cliffs,NJ, rec. 13.11.1962
Coltrane,John (ts) | Tyner,McCoy (p) | Garrison,Jimmy (b) | Jones,Elvin (dr)
John Coltrane-McCoy Tyner
They Say It's Wonderful
Coltrane,John (ts) | Tyner,McCoy (p)

589567-2 | 2 CD | Coltrane | EAN 731458956723
John Coltrane Quartet
The Inch Worm | Big Nick
Englewood Cliffs,NJ, rec. 11.4.1962
Coltrane,John (ss,ts) | Tyner,McCoy (p) | Garrison,Jimmy (b) | Jones,Elvin (dr)
Out Of This World | Soul Eyes
Englewood Cliffs,NJ, rec. 19.6.1962
Coltrane,John (ts) | Tyner,McCoy (p) | Garrison,Jimmy (b) | Jones,Elvin (dr)
Miles' Mode | Miles Mode(alt.take) | Not Yet | Tunji | Tunji(alt.take 1) | Tunji(alt.take 2) | Tunji(alt.take 3) | Impressions | Impressions(alt.take)
Englewood Cliffs,NJ, rec. 20.6.1962
Coltrane,John (ts) | Tyner,McCoy (p) | Garrison,Jimmy (b) | Jones,Elvin (dr)
Tunji
Englewood Cliffs,NJ, rec. 29.6.1962
Coltrane,John (ts) | Tyner,McCoy (p) | Garrison,Jimmy (b) | Jones,Elvin (dr)
John Coltrane Trio
Up 'Gainst The Wall
Englewood Cliffs,NJ, rec. 18.9.1962
Coltrane,John (ts) | Garrison,Jimmy (b) | Jones,Elvin (dr)

589596-2 | SACD | A Love Supreme | EAN 731458959625
John Coltrane Quartet
A Love Supreme(Suite): | Acknowledgement | Resulution | Pursuance | Psalm
Englewood Cliffs,NJ, rec. 9.12.1964
Coltrane,John (ts) | Tyner,McCoy (p) | Garrison,Jimmy (b) | Jones,Elvin (dr)

589760-2 | CD | Crystals | EAN 731458976028
Sam Rivers Orchestra
Exultation | Tranquility | Postlude | Bursts | Orb | Earth Song
NYC, rec. 1974
Rivers,Sam (fl,ss,ts,arr) | Daniel,Ted (tp) | Williams,Richard (tp) | Acey,Sinclair (tp) | Stephens,Charles (tb) | Greenlee,Charles (tb) | Dailey,Joe (tb,tuba) | Ferguson,Joe (fl,ss,as,ts) | Jeffrey,Paul (fl,oboe,bassoon,bassett-h,cl,ts) | Alexander,Roland (fl,ss,ts,p) | Kelly,Fred (fl,piccolo,ss,bs) | Marker,Gregory (b,el-b) | Smith,Warren (dr,perc) | Smith,Harold (dr,perc)

589945-2 | 2 CD | A Love Supreme | EAN 731458994527
John Coltrane Quartet
Acknowledgement- | Resolution- | Persuance- | Psalm- | Resolution(alt.take)- | Resolution(alt.take,breakdown)-
Englewood Cliffs,NJ, rec. 9.12.1964
Coltrane,John (ts,voc) | Tyner,McCoy (p) | Garrison,Jimmy (b) | Jones,Elvin (dr)
John Coltrane Sextet
Acknowledgement | Acknowledgement(alt,take)
Englewood Cliffs,NJ, rec. 10.12.1964
Coltrane,John (ts) | Shepp,Archie (ts) | Tyner,McCoy (p) | Davis,Art (b) | Garrison,Jimmy (b) | Jones,Elvin (dr)
John Coltrane Quartet
Introduction by André Francis | A Love Supreme: | Acknowledgement- | Resolution- | Pursuance- | Psalm-
Live at Festival Mondial Du Jazz,Antibes,France, rec. 26.7.1965
Coltrane,John (ts,voc) | Tyner,McCoy (p) | Garrison,Jimmy (b) | Jones,Elvin (dr)

755742-2 | CD | Ask Me Now! | EAN 602475574224
Pee Wee Russell Quartet
Turnaround | How About Me | Ask Me Now | Some Other Blues | I'd Climb The Highest Mountain | Licorice Stick | Prelude To A Kiss | Baby You Can Count On Me | Hackensack | Angel Eyes | Calypso Walk
NYC, rec. 9./10.4.1963
Russell,Pee Wee (cl) | Brown,Marshall (v-tb,bass-tp) | George,Russell (b) | Bedford,Ronnie (dr)

8961048 | CD | Soul Sisters | EAN 602498610480
Gloria Coleman Quartet
Quee Baby | Sadie Green | Hey Sonny Red | Melba's Minor | Funky Bob | My Ladies Waltz
Englewood Cliffs,NJ, rec. 31.5.1963
Coleman,Gloria (org) | Wright,Leo (as) | Green,Grant (g) | Roberts,Pola (dr)

950113-2 | CD | Michael Brecker
Michael Brecker Group
Sea Glass | Syzgy | Choices | Nothing Personal | The Cost Of Living | Original Rays | My One And Only Love
NYC, rec. 1987
Brecker,Michael (ts,EWI) | Metheny,Pat (g) | Kirkland,Kenny (keyboards) | Haden,Charlie (b) | DeJohnette,Jack (dr)

950114-2 | CD | Don't Try This At Home
Itsbynne Reel
NYC, rec. 1988
Brecker,Michael (ts,EWI) | Stern,Mike (g) | O'Connor,Mark (v) | Grolnick,Don (p) | Haden,Charlie (b) | Andrews,Jeff (el-b) | DeJohnette,Jack (dr)
Taking To Myself
Brecker,Michael (ts) | Stern,Mike (g) | Grolnick,Don (p) | Andrews,Jeff (el-b) | Erskine,Peter (dr) | Beard,Jim (synth)
The Gentleman & Hizcaine
Brecker,Michael (ts) | Hancock,Herbie (p) | Haden,Charlie (b) | DeJohnette,Jack (dr)
Chime This
Brecker,Michael (ts) | Stern,Mike (g) | Grolnick,Don (p) | Haden,Charlie (b) | Nussbaum,Adam (dr)
Suspone
Brecker,Michael (ts,EWI) | Stern,Mike (g) | Calderazzo,Joey (p) | Andrews,Jeff (el-b) | Nussbaum,Adam (dr)
Everything Happens When You're Gone
Brecker,Michael (ts) | Calderazzo,Joey (p) | Haden,Charlie (b) | Nussbaum,Adam (dr)
Don't Try This At Home
Brecker,Michael (ts,EWI) | Stern,Mike (g) | Hancock,Herbie (p) | Haden,Charlie (b) | DeJohnette,Jack (dr) | Miller,Judd (synth-progamming)

951107-2 | 2 CD | The Gentle Side Of John Coltrane
John Coltrane Quartet
Soul Eyes
NYC, rec. 19.6.1962
Coltrane,John (ss,ts) | Tyner,McCoy (p) | Garrison,Jimmy (b) | Jones,Elvin (dr)
What's New? | Nancy(With The Laughing Face)
NYC, rec. 18.9.1962
Coltrane,John (ss,ts) | Tyner,McCoy (p) | Garrison,Jimmy (b) | Jones,Elvin (dr)
Alabama
NYC, rec. 18.11.1963
Coltrane,John (ss,ts) | Tyner,McCoy (p) | Garrison,Jimmy (b) | Jones,Elvin (dr)
I Want To Talk About You
Live at 'Birdland',NYC, rec. 8.10.1963
Coltrane,John (ss,ts) | Tyner,McCoy (p) | Garrison,Jimmy (b) | Jones,Elvin (dr)
Dear Lord
NYC, rec. 26.5.1965
Coltrane,John (ss,ts) | Tyner,McCoy (p) | Garrison,Jimmy (b) | Jones,Elvin (dr)
Welcome
NYC, rec. 28.6.1965
Coltrane,John (ss,ts) | Tyner,McCoy (p) | Garrison,Jimmy (b) | Jones,Elvin (dr)
Wise One
NYC, rec. 27.4.1964
Coltrane,John (ss,ts) | Tyner,McCoy (p) | Garrison,Jimmy (b) | Jones,Elvin (dr)
John Coltrane Quartet With Johnny Hartman
Lush Life | My One And Only Love
NYC, rec. 7.3.1963
Coltrane,John (sax) | Coltrane,John (ss,ts) | Tyner,McCoy (p) | Garrison,Jimmy (b) | Jones,Elvin (dr) | Hartman,Johnny (voc)
John Coltrane-Duke Ellington Quartet
My Little Brown Book
NYC, rec. 26.9.1962
Coltrane,John (ss,ts) | Ellington,Duke (p) | Bell,Aaron (b) | Woodyard,Sam (dr)
In A Sentimental Mood
rec. 26.9.1962
Coltrane,John (ss,ts) | Ellington,Duke (p) | Bell,Aaron (b) | Jones,Elvin (dr)
John Coltrane Quartet
After The Rain
NYC, rec. 29.4.1963
Coltrane,John (ts) | Tyner,McCoy (p) | Garrison,Jimmy (b) | Haynes,Roy (dr)

951153-2 | CD | Karma
Pharoah Sanders Orchestra
The Creator Has A Master Plan
NYC, rec. 14.2.1969
Sanders,Pharoah (ts) | Spaulding,James (fl) | Watkins,Julius (fr-h) | Smith,Lonnie Liston (p) | Davis,Richard (b) | Workman,Reggie (b) | Bettis,Nat (perc) | Thomas,Leon (perc,voc) | Hart,Billy (dr)
Colours
NYC, rec. 19.2.1969
Sanders,Pharoah (ts) | Watkins,Julius (fr-h) | Smith,Lonnie Liston (p) | Workman,Reggie (b) | Carter,Ron (b) | Waits,Freddie (dr) | Bettis,Nat (perc) | Thomas,Leon (perc,voc)

951154-2 | CD | Blues And The Abstract Truth
Oliver Nelson And His Orchestra
Stolen Moments | Hoe Down | Cascades | Yearnin' | Butch And Butch
NYC, rec. 23.2.1961
Nelson,Oliver (as,ts,arr) | Hubbard,Freddie (tp) | Hubbard,Eric (fl,as) | Barrow,George (bs) | Evans,Bill (p) | Chambers,Paul (b) | Haynes,Roy (dr)
Teenie's Blues
Nelson,Oliver (as,ts) | Dolphy,Eric (as) | Evans,Bill (p) | Chambers,Paul (b) | Haynes,Roy (dr)

951157-2 | CD | John Coltrane And Johnny Hartman
Johnny Hartman With The John Coltrane Quartet
They Say It's Wonderful | Dedicated To You | My One And Only Love | Lush Life | You Are Too Beautiful | Autumn Serenade
NYC, rec. 7.3.1963
Hartman,Johnny (voc) | Coltrane,John (ts) | Tyner,McCoy (p) | Garrison,Jimmy (b) | Jones,Elvin (dr)

951158-2 | CD | Fire Music
Archie Shepp Sextet
Hambone | Los Olvidados | Prelude To A Kiss | Girl From Ipanema(Garota De Ipanema)
NYC, rec. 16.2.1965
Shepp,Archie (ts) | Curson,Ted (tp) | Orange,Joseph (tb) | Brown,Marion (as) | Johnson,Reggie (b) | Chambers,Joe (dr)
Archie Shepp Trio
Malcolm Malcolm-Semper Malcolm
NYC, rec. 9.3.1965
Shepp,Archie (ts) | Izenzon,David (b) | Moses,J.C. (dr)

951161-2 | CD | East Broadway Run Down
Sonny Rollins Trio
Blessing In Disguise | We Kiss In The Shadow
NYC, rec. 9.5.1966
Rollins,Sonny (ts) | Garrison,Jimmy (b) | Jones,Elvin (dr)
Sonny Rollins Quartet
East Broadway Run Down
Rollins,Sonny (ts) | Hubbard,Freddie (tp) | Garrison,Jimmy (b) | Jones,Elvin (dr)

951162-2 | CD | Duke Ellington Meets Coleman Hawkins
Duke Ellington-Coleman Hawkins Orchestra
You Dirty Dog | Ray Charles' Place | Mood Indigo | The Jeep Is Jumpin' | Self Portrait(Of The Bean) | Limbo Jazz | Wanderlust | In My Solitude
Englewood Cliffs,NJ, rec. 18.8.1962
Hawkins,Coleman (ts) | Ellington,Duke (p) | Nance,Ray (tp,v) | Brown,Lawrence (tb) | Hodges,Johnny (as) | Carney,Harry (bs) | Bell,Aaron (b) | Woodyard,Sam (dr)
The Recitic
Hawkins,Coleman (ts) | Ellington,Duke (p) | Nance,Ray (tp,v) | Bell,Aaron (b) | Woodyard,Sam (dr)

951164-2 | CD | All For You-A Dedication To The Nat King Cole Trio
Diana Krall Trio
I'm An Errand Girl For Rhythm | Gee Baby Ain't I Good To You | You Call It Madness But I Call It Love | Frim Fram Sauce | Baby Baby All The Time | Hit That Jive Jack | You're Looking At Me | I'm Thru With Love | 'Deed I Do | A Blossom Fell | When I Grow Too Old To Dream
NYC, rec. 3.-8.10.1995
Krall,Diana (p,voc) | Malone,Russell (g) | Keller,Paul (b)
Diana Krall Quartet
Boulevard Of Broken Dreams
Krall,Diana (p,voc) | Malone,Russell (g) | Keller,Paul (b) | Kroon,Steve (perc)
If I Had You
Krall,Diana (voc) | Green,Benny (p) | Malone,Russell (g) | Keller,Paul (b)

951166-2 | CD | Duke Ellington & John Coltrane
John Coltrane-Duke Ellington Quartet
Stevie | My Little Brown Book | The Feeling Of Jazz
NYC, rec. 26.9.1962
Coltrane,John (ss,ts) | Ellington,Duke (p) | Bell,Aaron (b) | Woodyard,Sam (dr)
In A Sentimental Mood
Coltrane,John (ss,ts) | Ellington,Duke (p) | Bell,Aaron (b) | Jones,Elvin (dr)
Angelica | Big | Big Nick | Take The Coltrane
Coltrane,John (ss,ts) | Ellington,Duke (p) | Garrison,Jimmy (b) | Jones,Elvin (dr)

951166-2 | CD | Sun Ship
John Coltrane Quartet
Sun Ship | Dearly Beloved | Amen | Attaining | Ascent
NYC, rec. 26.8.1965
Coltrane,John (ts) | Tyner,McCoy (p) | Garrison,Jimmy (b) | Jones,Elvin (dr)

951169-2 | CD | Stellar Regions
Seraphic Light | Sun Star | Stellar Regions | Iris | Offering | Configuration | Jimmy's Mode | Tranesonic | Stellar Regions(alt.take) | Sun Star(alt.take) | Tranesonic(alt.take)
Englewood Cliffs,NJ, rec. 15.2.1967
Coltrane,John (ts) | Coltrane,Alice (p) | Garrison,Jimmy (b) | Ali,Rashied (dr)

951170-2 | CD | Mingus Mingus Mingus
Charles Mingus Orchestra
Celia | Better Git It In Your Soul
rec. 20.1.1963
Mingus,Charles (b) | Ericson,Rolf (tp) | Williams,Richard (tp) | Jackson,Quentin (tb) | Butterfield,Don (tuba) | Richardson,Jerome (fl,as,bs) | Hafer,John 'Dick' (fl,ts) | Mariano,Charlie (as) | Byard,Jaki (p) | Berliner,Jay (g) | Richmond,Dannie (dr)
IX Love | Theme For Lester Young | II B.S. | Mood Indigo
rec. 20.9.1963
Mingus,Charles (b) | Preston,Eddie (tp) | Williams,Richard (tp) | Woodman,Britt (tb) | Butterfield,Don (tuba) | Dolphy,Eric (fl,b-cl,as) | Richardson,Jerome (fl,as,bs) | Hafer,John 'Dick' (fl,ts) | Ervin,Booker (ts) | Byard,Jaki (p) | Richmond,Dannie (dr)

951173-2 | CD | Duke Ellington Live At The Whitney
Duke Ellington
Opening Remarks | Medley: | Black And Tan Fantasy- | Prelude To A Kiss- | Do Nothin' Till You Hear From Me- | Caravan- | Meditation | A Mural From Two Perspectives | Sophisticated Lady- | In My Solitude- | New World A-Coming | Flamingo | Le Sucrier Velours
Live at The Whitney Museum of American Art,NYC, rec. 10.4.1972
Ellington,Duke (p-solo)
Duke Ellington Trio
Amour, Amour | Soul Soothing Beach | Lotus Blossom | The Night Shepherd | C Jam Blues | Mood Indigo | I'm Beginning To See The Light | Dancers In Love | Kixx | Satin Doll
Ellington,Duke (p) | Benjamin,Joe (b) | Jones,Rufus (dr)

951174-2 | CD | The Black Saint And The Sinner Lady
Charles Mingus Orchestra
Solo Dancer | Duet Solo Dancers | Group Dancers | Trio And Group Dancers | Single Solo And Group Dance | Group And Solo Dance
NYC, rec. 20.1.1963
Mingus,Charles (b) | Williams,Richard (tp) | Ericson,Rolf (tp) | Jackson,Quentin (tb) | Butterfield,Don (tuba) | Richardson,Jerome (fl,ss,bs) | Mariano,Charlie (as) | Hafer,John 'Dick' (ts) | Byard,Jaki (p) | Berliner,Jay (g) | Richmond,Dannie (dr)

951175-2 | CD | Impulse!Art Blakey!Jazz Messengers!
Art Blakey And The Jazz Messengers
I Hear A Rhapsody | Circus | Alamode | Gee Baby Ain't I Good To You | Invitation | You Don't Know What Love Is
NYC, rec. 13./14.6.1961
Blakey,Art (dr) | Morgan,Lee (tp) | Fuller,Curtis (tb) | Shorter,Wayne (ts) | Timmons,Bobby (p) | Merritt,Jymie (b)

951178-2 | CD | Swing Low, Sweet Cadillac
Dizzy Gillespie Quintet
Swing Low Sweet Cadillac | Mas que nada (Pow, Pow, Pow) | Bye | Something In Your Smile | Kush
Memory Lane,Los Angeles,CA, rec. 25./26.5.1967
Gillespie,Dizzy (tp) | Moody,James (fl,as,ts) | Longo,Michael (p) | Schifano,Frank (el-b) | Finch,Otis 'Candy' (dr)

951180-2 | CD | Out Of The Afternoon
Roy Haynes Quartet
Fly Me To The Moon | Raoul | Snap Crackle | If I Should Lose You
Englewood Cliffs,NJ, rec. 16.5.1962
Haynes,Roy (dr) | Kirk,Rahsaan Roland (ts,manzello,nose-fl,stritch) | Flanagan,Tommy (p) | Grimes,Henry (b)
Moon Ray | Long Wharf | Some Other Spring
Englewood Cliffs,NJ, rec. 23.5.1962
Haynes,Roy (dr) | Kirk,Rahsaan Roland (ts,manzello,nose-fl,stritch) | Flanagan,Tommy (p) | Grimes,Henry (b)

951181-2 | CD | My Generation
Teodross Avery Quartet
Mode For My Father | Theme For Malcolm | Sphere
NYC, rec. 10.-12.10.1995
Avery,Teodross (ss,ts) | Scofield,John (g) | Whitaker,Rodney Thomas (b) | Hutchinson,Gregory (dr)
Lover Man(Oh,Where Can You Be?) | It's About That Time
Avery,Teodross (ss,ts) | Whitfield,Mark (g) | Whitaker,Rodney Thomas (b) | Hutchinson,Gregory (dr)
My Generation
Avery,Teodross (ss,ts) | Whitfield,Mark (g) | Whitaker,Rodney Thomas (b) | Hutchinson,Gregory (dr) | Black Thought of 'The Roots' (rap)
Mr.Wonsey
Avery,Teodross (ss,ts) | Bernstein,Peter (g) | Whitaker,Rodney Thomas (b) | Hutchinson,Gregory (dr)
Addis Ababa | Salomé(Sal-Owe-May) | Anytime Anyplace
Avery,Teodross (ss,ts) | Craig,Charles (p) | Whitaker,Rodney Thomas (b) | Hutchinson,Gregory (dr)
Teodross Avery Quintet
To The East
Avery,Teodross (ss,ts) | Craig,Charles (p) | Whitaker,Rodney Thomas (b) | Hutchinson,Gregory (dr) | Daniels,Andrew (perc)

951183-2 | CD | The Body And The Soul
Freddie Hubbard Orchestra
Skylark | I Got It Bad And That Ain't Good | Chocolate Shake
NYC, rec. 8.3.1963
Hubbard,Freddie (tp) | Armour,Ed (tp) | Williams,Richard (tp) | Liston,Melba (tb) | Fuller,Curtis (tb) | Northern,Bob (fr-h) | Watkins,Julius (fr-h) | Dolphy,Eric (as) | Richardson,Jerome (bs) | Walton,Cedric (b) | Workman,Reggie (b) | Jones,Philly Joe (dr) | Cykman,Harry (v) | Stonzek,Morris (v) | Eidus,Arnold (v) | Shapiro,Sol (v) | McCracken,Charles (v) | Katzman,Harry (v) | Lookofsky,Harry (v) | Orloff,Gene (v) | Held,Julius (v) | Poliakin,Raoul (v) | Shorter,Wayne (arr)
Carnival | Thermo | Aries
NYC, rec. 11.3.1963
Hubbard,Freddie (tp) | DeRisi,Al (tp) | Terry,Clark (tp) | Royal,Ernie (tp)

| Liston,Melba (tb) | Fuller,Curtis (tb) | Dolphy,Eric (as) | Powell,Seldon (ts) | Richardson,Jerome (bs) | Davis,Charles (bs) | Powell,Robert (tu) | Walton,Cedar (p) | Workman,Reggie (b) | Jones,Philly Joe (dr) | Northern,Bob (fr-h) | Shorter,Wayne (arr)

Freddie Hubbard Septet
Body And Soul | Dedicated To You | Clarence's Place
NYC, rec. 2.5.1963
Hubbard,Freddie (tp) | Fuller,Curtis (tb) | Dolphy,Eric (fl,as) | Shorter,Wayne (ts) | Walton,Cedar (p) | Workman,Reggie (b) | Hayes,Louis (dr)

951184-2 | CD | Today And Now
Coleman Hawkins Quartet
Go Lil' Liza | Quintessence | Don't Love Me | Love Dong From Apache | Put On Your Old Grey Bonnet | Swingin' Scotch | Don't Sit Under The Apple Tree
Englewood Cliffs,NJ, rec. 9.9.1962
Hawkins,Coleman (ts) | Flanagan,Tommy (p) | Holley,Major (b) | Locke,Eddie (dr)

951185-2 | CD | It's Time
Max Roach Sextet With Choir
It's Time | Another Valley | Sunday Afternoon | Living Room | The Profit | Lonesome Lover
NYC, rec. 1961/1962
Roach,Max (dr) | Williams,Richard (tp) | Priester,Julian (tb) | Jordan,Clifford (ts) | Waldron,Mal (p) | Davis,Art (b) | Lincoln,Abbey (voc) | Choir | Perkinson,Coleridge (dir)

951186-2 | CD | Out Of The Cool
Gil Evans Orchestra
La Nevada
NYC, rec. 18.11.1960
Evans,Gil (p,arr) | Coles,Johnny (tp) | Sunkel,Phil (tp) | Knepper,Jimmy (tb) | Johnson,Keg (tb) | Studd,Tony (b-tb) | Barber,Bill (tuba) | Beckenstein,Ray (fl,as,piccolo) | Johnson,Budd (ss,ts) | Tricarico,Bob (fl,bassoon) | Crawford,Ray (g) | Carter,Ron (b) | Jones,Elvin (dr) | Persip,Charles (dr)
Bilbao Song | Sister Sadie
NYC, rec. 30.11.1960
Evans,Gil (p,arr) | Coles,Johnny (tp) | Sunkel,Phil (tp) | Knepper,Jimmy (tb) | Johnson,Keg (tb) | Studd,Tony (b-tb) | Barber,Bill (tuba) | Beckenstein,Ray (fl,as,piccolo) | Johnson,Budd (ss,ts) | Tricarico,Bob (fl,bassoon) | Crawford,Ray (g) | Carter,Ron (b) | Jones,Elvin (dr) | Persip,Charles (dr)
Sunken Treasure
NYC, rec. 10.12.1960
Evans,Gil (p,arr) | Coles,Johnny (tp) | Sunkel,Phil (tp) | Knepper,Jimmy (tb) | Johnson,Keg (tb) | Studd,Tony (b-tb) | Barber,Bill (tuba) | Caine,Eddie (fl,as,piccolo) | Johnson,Budd (ss,ts) | Tricarico,Bob (fl,bassoon) | Crawford,Ray (g) | Carter,Ron (b) | Jones,Elvin (dr) | Persip,Charles (dr)
Stratusphunk | Where Flamingos Fly
NYC, rec. 15.12.1960
Evans,Gil (p,arr) | Coles,Johnny (tp) | Sunkel,Phil (tp) | Knepper,Jimmy (tb) | Johnson,Keg (tb) | Studd,Tony (b-tb) | Barber,Bill (tuba) | Caine,Eddie (fl,as,piccolo) | Johnson,Budd (ss,ts) | Tricarico,Bob (fl,bassoon) | Crawford,Ray (g) | Carter,Ron (b) | Jones,Elvin (dr) | Persip,Charles (dr)

951188-2 | CD | Liberation Music Orchestra
Charlie Haden's Liberation Music Orchestra
Song Of The United Front | We Shall Overcome
NYC, rec. 27.-29.4.1969
Haden,Charlie (b) | Mantler,Michael (tp) | Rudd,Roswell (tb) | Northern,Bob (fr-h,perc,whistle) | Johnson,Howard (tuba) | Robinson,Perry (cl) | Barbieri,Gato (cl,ts) | Redman,Dewey (as,ts) | Bley,Carla (p,org,tambourine) | Motian,Paul (dr,perc)
Circus '68 '69
Haden,Charlie (b) | Mantler,Michael (tp) | Rudd,Roswell (tb) | Northern,Bob (fr-h,perc,whistle) | Johnson,Howard (tuba) | Robinson,Perry (cl) | Barbieri,Gato (cl,ts) | Redman,Dewey (as,ts) | Bley,Carla (p,org,tambourine) | Motian,Paul (dr,perc) | Cyrille,Andrew (perc)
The Introduction | The Ending Of The First Side | War Orphans | The Interlude(Drinking Music)
Haden,Charlie (b) | Mantler,Michael (tp) | Rudd,Roswell (tb) | Northern,Bob (fr-h,perc,whistle) | Johnson,Howard (tuba) | Robinson,Perry (cl) | Barbieri,Gato (as,ts) | Redman,Dewey (as,ts) | Brown,Sam (g,tanganyikan-g,thumb-p) | Bley,Carla (p,org,tambourine) | Motian,Paul (dr,perc)
El Quinto Regimiento(The First Regiment) | Los Cuatro Generales(The Four Generales) | Viva La Quince Brigada(Long Live The Fifteenth Brigade) | Song For Che
Haden,Charlie (b) | Cherry,Don (co,indian-fl) | Mantler,Michael (tp) | Rudd,Roswell (tb) | Northern,Bob (fr-h,perc,whistle) | Johnson,Howard (tuba) | Robinson,Perry (cl) | Barbieri,Gato (cl,ts) | Redman,Dewey (as,ts) | Brown,Sam (g,tanganyikan-g,thumb-p) | Bley,Carla (p,org,tambourine) | Motian,Paul (dr,perc)

951190-2 | CD | Panamonk
Danilo Perez Quartet
Panamonk | Think Of One | Hot Bean Strut | Reflections
NYC, rec. 3./4.1.1996
Perez,Danilo (p) | Cohen,Avishai (b) | Watts,Jeff 'Tain' (dr)
Bright Mississippi | Mercedes Mood | Everything Happens To Me | Evidence- | Four In One-
Perez,Danilo (p) | Cohen,Avishai (b) | Carrington,Terri Lyne (dr)
September In Rio
Perez,Danilo (p) | Cohen,Avishai (b) | Carrington,Terri Lyne (dr) | Roman,Olga (voc)

Danilo Perez
Round About Midnight | Monk's Mood | Monk's Mood(reprise)
Perez,Danilo (p-solo)

951191-2 | CD | Tales From The Hudson
Michael Brecker Group
Slings And Arrows | Midnight Voyage | Beau Rivage | Introduction To Naked Soul | Naked Soul | Willie T. | Cabin Fever
NYC, rec. 1995
Brecker,Michael (ts) | Metheny,Pat (g) | Calderazzo,Joey (p) | Holland,Dave (b) | DeJohnette,Jack (dr)
Song For Bilbao | African Skies
Brecker,Michael (ts) | Metheny,Pat (g,g-synth) | Tyner,McCoy (p) | Holland,Dave (b) | DeJohnette,Jack (dr) | Alias,Don (perc)

951196-2 | CD | Musicale
Eric Reed Trio
Longhair's Rhumba | Frog's Legs | Scandal(I) | A Love Divine | Shug | No Sadness No Pain
NYC, rec. 10.3.1966
Reed,Eric (p) | Wolfe,Benjamin Jonah 'Ben' (b) | Hutchinson,Gregory (dr)

Eric Reed Quartet
Baby Sis
NYC, rec. 10.3.1996
Reed,Eric (p) | Gordon,Wycliffe (tb) | Wolfe,Benjamin Jonah 'Ben' (b) | Hutchinson,Gregory (dr)
Upper Wess Side
NYC, rec. 19.4.1996
Reed,Eric (p) | Anderson,Wessell 'Wes' (as) | Carter,Ron (b) | Riggins,Karriem (dr)

Eric Reed Quintet
Black,As In Buhaina | Cosa Nostra(Our Thing) | Scandal(II) | Pete And Repete | Scandal(III) | Blues To Come)
Reed,Eric (p) | Payton,Nicholas (tp) | Anderson,Wessell 'Wes' (as) | Carter,Ron (b) | Riggins,Karriem (dr)

951198-2 | CD | Live At Birdland
John Coltrane Quartet
Villa
Englewood Cliffs,NJ, rec. 6.3.1963
Coltrane,John (ss) | Tyner,McCoy (p) | Garrison,Jimmy (b) | Jones,Elvin (dr)
Afro Blue | I Want To Talk About You | The Promise
Live at 'Birdland',NYC, rec. 8.10.1963
Coltrane,John (ss,ts) | Tyner,McCoy (p) | Garrison,Jimmy (b) | Jones,Elvin (dr)
Alabama | Your Lady
Englewood Cliffs,NJ, rec. 18.11.1963
Coltrane,John (ss,ts) | Tyner,McCoy (p) | Garrison,Jimmy (b) | Jones,Elvin (dr)

951199-2 | CD | Meditations
John Coltrane And His Orchestra
The Father And The Son And The Holy Ghost | Compassion | Love | Consequence | Serenity
Englewood Cliffs,NJ, rec. 23.11.1965
Coltrane,John (ss,ts) | Sanders,Pharoah (ts) | Tyner,McCoy (p) | Garrison,Jimmy (b) | Jones,Elvin (dr) | Ali,Rashied (dr)

951200-2 | CD | Crescent
John Coltrane Quartet
Wise One | Lonnie's Lament | The Drum Thing
Englewood Cliffs,NJ, rec. 27.4.1964
Coltrane,John (ts) | Tyner,McCoy (p) | Garrison,Jimmy (b) | Jones,Elvin (dr)
Crescent | Bessie's Blues
Englewood Cliffs,NJ, rec. 1.6.1964
Coltrane,John (ts) | Tyner,McCoy (p) | Garrison,Jimmy (b) | Jones,Elvin (dr)

951201-2 | CD | Ptah The El Daoud
Alice Coltrane Quintet
Ptah, The El Daoud | Turiya And Ramakrishna | Blue Nile | Mantra
NYC, rec. 26.1.1970
Coltrane,Alice (p,harp) | Sanders,Pharoah (alto-fl,ts,bells) | Henderson,Joe (alto-fl,ts) | Carter,Ron (b) | Riley,Ben (dr)

951202-2 | CD | Count Basie And The Kansas City 7
Count Basie And The Kansas City 7
Secrets | Senator Whitehead | What 'cha Talkin' | Trey Of Hearts
NYC, rec. 21.3.1962
Basie,Count (p) | Jones,Thad (tp) | Wess,Frank (fl) | Dixon,Eric (fl) | Green,Freddie (g) | Jones,Eddie (b) | Payne,Sonny (dr)
Oh! Lady Be Good | I Want A Little Girl | Shoe Shine Boy | Count't Place | Tally-Ho Mr.Basie
NYC, rec. 22.3.1962
Basie,Count (p,org) | Jones,Thad (tp) | Foster,Frank (ts) | Dixon,Eric (fl,ts) | Green,Freddie (g) | Jones,Eddie (b) | Payne,Sonny (dr)

951208-2 | CD | Here I Stand
Antonio Hart Group
The Community | Millenium
NYC, rec. 1997
Hart,Antonio Maurice (as) | Hurt,James (p) | Benitez,John (b) | Waits,Nasheet (dr)
True Friends
Hart,Antonio Maurice (ss) | Eubanks,Robin (tb) | Gross,Mark (fl,as) | Diallo,Amadou (ts) | Hurt,James (p) | Benitez,John (b) | Waits,Nasheet (dr) | Saturino,Pernell (perc)
Flamingo
Hart,Antonio Maurice (as) | Scott,Shirley (org) | Waits,Nasheet (dr)
Like My Own
Hart,Antonio Maurice (as) | Scott,Shirley (org) | Ormond,John (b) | Waits,Nasheet (dr)
Brother Nasheet | Riots...The Voice Of The Unheard
Hart,Antonio Maurice (ss) | Rickman,Patrick (tp) | Eubanks,Robin (tb) | Gross,Mark (fl,as) | Diallo,Amadou (ts) | Hurt,James (p) | Benitez,John (b) | Waits,Nasheet (dr)
Ven Devorame Otra Vez
Hart,Antonio Maurice (as) | Rickman,Patrick (tp) | Eubanks,Robin (tb) | Diallo,Amadou (ts) | Branford,Jay (bs) | Hurt,James (p) | Benitez,John (b) | Saturino,Pernell (perc)
The Words Don't Fit In My Mouth
Hart,Antonio Maurice (as) | Eubanks,Robin (tb) | Hurt,James (p) | Ormond,John (b) | Moore,Jessica Care (voc)

951209-2 | CD | Nouveau Swing
Donald Harrison Quartet
Nouveau Swing | Come Back Jack | Eighty-One | Sincerely Yours | Setembro | One Of A Kind | Christopher Jr.
NYC, rec. 11.-13.8.1996
Harrison,Donald (as) | Wonsey,Athony (p) | McBride,Christian (b) | Allen,Carl (dr)
Bob Marley | Little Flowers | New Hope | Dance Hall
Harrison,Donald (as) | Wonsey,Athony (p) | Rodgers,Rueben (b) | Parson,Dion (dr)
South Side People | Duck's Groove
Harrison,Donald (as) | Wonsey,Athony (p) | Rodgers,Rueben (b) | Allen,Carl (dr)

Donald Harrison
Amazing Grace
Harrison,Donald (as-solo)

951212-2 | CD | More Blues And The Abstract Truth
Oliver Nelson And His Orchestra
Midnight Blue | Blues For Mr.Broadway
Englewood Cliffs,NJ, rec. 10.11.1964
Nelson,Oliver (arr,ld) | Jones,Thad (tp) | Woods,Phil (as) | Webster,Ben (ts) | Bodner,Phil (engl-h,ts) | Adams,Pepper (bs) | Kellaway,Roger (p) | Davis,Richard (b) | Tate,Grady (dr)
One For Bob | Going To Chicago Blues | One For Phil
Nelson,Oliver (arr,ld) | Jones,Thad (tp) | Woods,Phil (as) | Bodner,Phil (engl-h,ts) | Adams,Pepper (bs) | Kellaway,Roger (p) | Davis,Richard (b) | Tate,Grady (dr)
Blues And The Abstract Truth | The Critic's Choice
Englewood Cliffs,NJ, rec. 11.11.1964
Nelson,Oliver (arr,ld) | Jones,Thad (tp) | Moore,Danny (tp) | Woods,Phil (as) | Bodner,Phil (engl-h,ts) | Adams,Pepper (bs) | Kellaway,Roger (p) | Davis,Richard (b) | Tate,Grady (dr)
Blues O'Mighty | Theme From Mr.Broadway | Night Lights
Nelson,Oliver (arr,ld) | Jones,Thad (tp) | Woods,Phil (as) | Bodner,Phil (engl-h,ts) | Adams,Pepper (bs) | Kellaway,Roger (p) | Davis,Richard (b) | Tate,Grady (dr)

951213-2 | CD | Live At The Village Vanguard Again
John Coltrane Quintet
Naima | Introduction To 'My Favorite Things' | My Favorite Things
Live at The 'Village Vanguard',NYC, rec. 28.5.1966
Coltrane,John (b-cl,ss,ts) | Sanders,Pharoah (fl,ts) | Coltrane,Alice (p) | Garrison,Jimmy (b) | Ali,Rashied (dr) | Rahim,Emmanuel (perc)

951214-2 | CD | The Coltrane Quartet Plays
John Coltrane Quartet
Nature Boy(first version)
Englewood Cliffs,NJ, rec. 17.2.1965
Coltrane,John (ts) | Tyner,McCoy (p) | Davis,Art (b) | Jones,Elvin (dr)
Nature Boy | Feelin' Good
Live at The 'Village Gate',NYC, rec. 18.2.1965
Coltrane,John (ts) | Tyner,McCoy (p) | Davis,Art (b) | Jones,Elvin (dr)
Chim Chim Cheree | Brazilia | Song Of Praise
Live at The 'Village Gate',NYC, rec. 17.5.1965
Coltrane,John (ss,ts) | Tyner,McCoy (p) | Garrison,Jimmy (b) | Jones,Elvin (dr)
Nature Boy
Live at The 'Village Gate',NYC, rec. 28.5.1965
Coltrane,John (ts) | Tyner,McCoy (p) | Garrison,Jimmy (b) | Jones,Elvin (dr)

951216-2 | CD | McCoy Tyner Plays Ellington
McCoy Tyner Trio
It Don't Mean A Thing If It Ain't Got That Swing | I Got It Bad And That Ain't Good
Englewood Cliffs,NJ, rec. 2.12.1964
Tyner,McCoy (p) | Garrison,Jimmy (b) | Jones,Elvin (dr)
In My Solitude | Mr.Gentle And Mr.Cool | Gypsy With A Song | Gypsy With A Song(alt.take)
Englewood Cliffs,NJ, rec. 7.12.1964
Tyner,McCoy (p) | Garrison,Jimmy (b) | Jones,Elvin (dr)

McCoy Tyner Trio + Latin Percussion
Duke's Place(C Jam Blues) | Caravan | Searchin' | Satin Doll
Englewood Cliffs,NJ, rec. 8.12.1964
Tyner,McCoy (p) | Garrison,Jimmy (b) | Jones,Elvin (dr) | Rodriguez,Willie (perc) | Pacheco,Johnny (perc)

951217-2 | CD | Mingus Plays Piano
Charles Mingus
Myself When I Am Real | I Can't Get Started | Body And Soul | Roland Kirk's Message | Memories Of You | She's Just Miss Popular Hybrid | Orange Was The Colour Of Her Dress Then Blue Silk | Meditations For Moses | Old Portrait | I'm Getting Sentimental Over You | Compositional Theme Story:Anthems And Folklore
NYC, rec. 30.7.1963
Mingus,Charles (p-solo)

951218-2 | CD | Four For Trane
Archie Shepp Sextet
Syeeda's Song Flute | Mr.Syms | Cousin Mary | Naima | Rufus
Englewood Cliffs,NJ, rec. 10.8.1964
Shepp,Archie (ts) | Shorter,Alan (tp) | Rudd,Roswell (tb) | Tchicai,John (as) | Workman,Reggie (b) | Moffett,Charles (dr)

951219-2 | CD | Black Unity
Pharoah Sanders Group
Black Unity
NYC, rec. 24.11.1971
Sanders,Pharoah (ss,ts,balafon) | Peterson,Hanibal Marvin (tp) | Garnett,Carlos Alfredo (fl,ts) | Bonner,Joe (p) | McBee,Cecil (b) | Clarke,Stanley (b) | Connors,Norman (dr) | Hart,Billy (dr) | Killian,Lawrence (congas,balafon,talking-dr)

951220-2 | CD | Inception
McCoy Tyner Trio
Inception | Sunset | Effendi
Englewood Cliffs,NJ, rec. 10.1.1962
Tyner,McCoy (p) | Davis,Art (b) | Jones,Elvin (dr)
There Is No Greater Love | Blues For Gwen | Speak Low
Englewood Cliffs,NJ, rec. 11.1.1962
Tyner,McCoy (p) | Davis,Art (b) | Jones,Elvin (dr)

951221-2 | CD | Nights Of Ballads And Blues
Satin Doll | We'll Be Together Again | Round About Midnight | For Heaven's Sake | Star Eyes | Blue Monk | Groove Waltz | Days Of Wine And Roses
Englewood Cliffs,NJ, rec. 4.3.1963
Tyner,McCoy (p) | Davis,Steve (b) | Humphries,Lex (dr)

951222-2 | CD | The Quintessence
Quincy Jones And His Orchestra
The Twitch | For Lena And Lennie
NYC, rec. 29.11.1961
Jones,Quincy (arr) | Kail,Jerry (tp) | Reasinger,Clyde (tp) | Terry,Clark (tp) | Newman,Joe (tp) | Byers,Billy (tb) | Liston,Melba (tb) | Faulise,Paul (tb) | Woods,Phil (reeds) | Dixon,Eric (sax) | Richardson,Jerome (sax) | Scott,Bobby (p) | Catlett,George (b) | Martin,Stu (dr) | Watkins,Julius (fr-h)
Hard Sock Dance | Little Karen | Robot Portrait
NYC, rec. 18.12.1961
Jones,Quincy (arr) | Jones,Thad (tp) | DeRisi,Al (tp) | Hubbard,Freddie (tp) | Young,Eugene 'Snooky' (tp) | Levitt,Rod (tb) | Liston,Melba (tb) | Faulise,Paul (tb) | Byers,Billy (tb) | Woods,Phil (reeds) | Richardson,Jerome (sax) | Dixon,Eric (sax) | Wess,Frank (reeds) | Nelson,Oliver (sax) | Bown,Patti (p) | Hinton,Milt (b) | English,Bill (dr) | Watkins,Julius (fr-h)
Invitation | Straight No Chaser | Quintessence
NYC, rec. 22.12.1961
Jones,Quincy (arr) | Young,Eugene 'Snooky' (tp) | Jones,Thad (tp) | Newman,Joe (tp) | Royal,Ernie (tp) | Liston,Melba (tb) | Fuller,Curtis (tb) | Faulise,Paul (tb) | Mitchell,Tom (tb) | Byers,Billy (tb) | Woods,Phil (reeds) | Nelson,Oliver (sax) | Richardson,Jerome (sax) | Bown,Patti (p) | Hinton,Milt (b) | Johnson,James (dr) | Watkins,Julius (fr-h) | Chapin,Earl (fr-h) | Alonge,Ray (fr-h) | Buffington,Jimmy (fr-h) | Phillips,Harvey (tuba) | Agostini,Gloria (harp)

951223-2 | CD | Sonny Rollins On Impulse
Sonny Rollins Quartet
On Green Dolphin Street | Everything Happens To Me | Hold 'Em Joe | Blue Room | Three Little Words
Englewood Cliffs,NJ, rec. 8.7.1965
Rollins,Sonny (ts) | Bryant,Ray (p) | Booker,Walter (b) | Roker,Granville 'Mickey' (dr)

951224-2 | CD | Alfie
Sonny Rollins Orchestra
Street Runner With Child | Alfie's Theme Differently
Englewood Cliffs,NJ, rec. 26.1.1966
Rollins,Sonny (ts) | Johnson,J.J. (tb) | Woods,Phil (as) | Ashton,Bob (ts) | Bank,Danny (bs) | Kellaway,Roger (p) | Burrell,Kenny (g) | Booker,Walter (b) | Dunlop,Frankie (dr) | Nelson,Oliver (arr,ld)
Alfie's Theme | He's Younger Than You Are | Transition Theme For Minor Blues Or Little Malcolm Loves His Dad | On Impulse
Rollins,Sonny (ts) | Cleveland,Jimmy (tb) | Woods,Phil (as) | Ashton,Bob (ts) | Bank,Danny (bs) | Kellaway,Roger (p) | Burrell,Kenny (g) | Booker,Walter (b) | Dunlop,Frankie (dr) | Nelson,Oliver (arr,ld)

951225-2 | CD | The Great Kai & J.J.
Kai Winding-J.J.Johnson Quintet
This Could Be The Start Of Something | I Concentrate On You | Blue Monk | Side By Side
Englewood Cliffs,NJ, rec. 2.11.1960
Winding,Kai (tb) | Johnson,J.J. (tb) | Evans,Bill (p) | Chambers,Paul (b) | Haynes,Roy (dr)
Alone Together | Theme From 'Picnic' | Georgia On My Mind | Just For A Thrill
Englewood Cliffs,NJ, rec. 4.11.1960
Winding,Kai (tb) | Johnson,J.J. (tb) | Evans,Bill (p) | Williams,Tommy (b) | Taylor,Arthur 'Art' (dr)
Judy | Trixie | Going, Going, Gong!
Englewood Cliffs,NJ, rec. 9.11.1960
Winding,Kai (tb) | Johnson,J.J. (tb) | Evans,Bill (p) | Williams,Tommy (b) | Taylor,Arthur 'Art' (dr)

951227-2 | CD | Desafinado
Coleman Hawkins Sextet
I'm Looking Over A Four Leaf Clover | Samba Para Bean | I Remember You | Samba Da Una Nota So(One Note Samba)
Englewood Cliffs,NJ, rec. 12.9.1962
Hawkins,Coleman (ts) | Galbraith,Barry (g) | Collins,Howard (g) | Holley,Major (b) | Locke,Eddie (dr,perc) | Flanagan,Tommy (claves) | Rodriguez,Willie (perc)

Coleman Hawkins Septet
Desafinado | O Pato(The Duck) | Un Abraco No Bonfa | Stumpy Bossa Nova
Englewood Cliffs,NJ, rec. 17.9.1962
Hawkins,Coleman (ts) | Galbraith,Barry (g) | Collins,Howard (g) | Holley,Major (b) | Locke,Eddie (dr,perc) | Flanagan,Tommy (claves) | Rodriguez,Willie (perc)

951228-2 | CD | Journey In Satchidananda
Alice Coltrane Quintet
Isis And Osiris
NYC, rec. 4.7.1970
Coltrane,Alice (harp) | Sanders,Pharoah (ss,perc) | Wood,Vishnu Bill (oud) | Haden,Charlie (b) | Ali,Rashied (dr)

Alice Coltrane Sextet
Journey In Satchidananda | Shiva-Loka | Stopover Bombay | Something About John Coltrane
NYC, rec. 8.11.1970
Coltrane,Alice (p,harp) | Sanders,Pharoah (ss,perc) | Tulsi (tamboura) | McBee,Cecil (b) | Ali,Rashied (dr) | Shabazz,Majid (bells,tamboura)

951229-2 | CD | Further Definitions/Additions To Further Definotions
Benny Carter And His Orchestra
Honeysuckle Rose | The Midnight Sun Will Never Set | Crazy Rhythm | Cherry
NYC, rec. 13.11.961
Carter,Benny (as) | Woods,Phil (as) | Hawkins,Coleman (ts) | Rouse,Charlie (ts) | Katz,Dick (p) | Collins,John (g) | Garrison,Jimmy (b) | Jones,Jo (dr)

Blue Star | Cotton Tail | Body And Soul | Doozy
NYC, rec. 15.11.1961
Carter,Benny (as) | Woods,Phil (as) | Hawkins,Coleman (ts) | Rouse,Charlie (ts) | Katz,Dick (p) | Collins,John (g) | Garrison,Jimmy (b) | Jones,Jo (dr)
If Dreams Come True | Fantastic,That's You | Come On Back | Prohibido
Los Angeles,CA, rec. 2.3.1966
Carter,Benny (as) | Shank,Bud (as) | Collette,Buddy (ts) | Edwards,Teddy (ts) | Hood,Bill (bs) | Abney,Don (p) | Kessel,Barney (g) | Brown,Ray (b) | Stoller,Alvin (dr)
Doozy | We Were In Love | Titmouse | Rock Bottom
Los Angeles,CA, rec. 4.3.1966
Carter,Benny (as) | Shank,Bud (as) | Perkins,Bill (ts) | Edwards,Teddy (ts) | Hood,Bill (bs) | Abney,Don (p) | Lowe,Mundell (g) | McKibbon,Al (b) | Stoller,Alvin (dr)

951234-2 | CD | Love Scenes
Diana Krall Trio
All Or Nothing At All | Peel Me A Grape | I Don't Know Enough About You | I Miss You So | They Can't Take That Away From Me | Lost Mind | I Don't Stand A Ghost Of A Chance With You | You're Getting To Be A Habit With Me | Gentle Rain | How Deep Is The Ocean | My Love Is | Garden In The Rain | That Old Feeling
NYC, rec. 1997
Krall,Diana (p,voc) | Malone,Russell (g) | McBride,Christian (b)

951238-2 | CD | A Prescription For The Blues
Horace Silver Quintet
A Prescription For The Blues | Whenever Lester Plays The Blues | You Gotta Shake That Thing | Yodel Lady Blues | Brother John And Brother Gene | Free At Last | Walk On | Sunrise In Malibu | Doctor Jazz
NYC, rec. 29./30.5.1997
Silver,Horace (p) | Brecker,Randy (tp) | Brecker,Michael (ts) | Carter,Ron (b) | Hayes,Louis (dr)

951246-2 | CD | Living Space
John Coltrane Quartet
Untitled 90314 | Untitled 90320
Englewood Cliffs,NJ, rec. 10.6.1965
Coltrane,John (ss,ts) | Tyner,McCoy (p) | Garrison,Jimmy (b) | Jones,Elvin (dr)
Living Space | Dusk-Dawn | The Last Blues
Englewood Cliffs,NJ, rec. 16.6.1965
Coltrane,John (ss,ts) | Tyner,McCoy (p) | Garrison,Jimmy (b) | Jones,Elvin (dr)

951247-2 | CD | Jewels Of Thought
Pharoah Sanders Orchestra
Hum-Allah-Hum-Allah-Hum-Allah
NYC, rec. 20.10.1969
Sanders,Pharoah (ts,perc) | Smith,Lonnie Liston (p,perc) | McBee,Cecil (b) | Haynes,Roy (dr,perc) | Muhammad,Idris[Leo Morris] (dr,perc) | Haynes,Roy (dr) | Thomas,Leon (perc,voc)
Sun In Aquarius
Sanders,Pharoah (ts,perc) | Smith,Lonnie Liston (p,perc) | McBee,Cecil (b) | Davis,Richard (b,perc) | Haynes,Roy (dr,perc) | Muhammad,Idris[Leo Morris] (dr,perc) | Haynes,Roy (dr) | Thomas,Leon (perc,voc)

951248-2 | CD | Mama Too Tight
Archie Shepp Orchestra
A Portrait Of Robert Thompson(As A Young Man) | Prelude To A Kiss- | The Break Strain-King Cotton- | Dem Basses- | Mama Too Tight | Theme For Ernie | Basheer
Englewood Cliffs,NJ, rec. 19.8.1966
Shepp,Archie (ts) | Turrentine,Tommy (tp) | Robinson,Perry (cl) | Rudd,Roswell (tb) | Moncur III,Grachan (tb) | Johnson,Howard (tuba) | Haden,Charlie (b) | Harris,Beaver (dr)

951249-2 | CD | Space Is The Place
Sun Ra And His Astro-Infinity Arkestra
Space Is The Place | Images | Discipline | Sea Of Sounds | Rocket Number Nine
Chicago,Ill, rec. 19./20.10.1972
Sun Ra (p,org) | Ebah,Akh Tal (tp,fl-h) | Hadi,Kwame (tp) | Omoe,Elo (fl,b-cl) | Allen,Marshall (fl,as) | Davis,Danny (fl,as) | Gilmore,John (ts,voc) | Thompson,Danny (fl,bs,voc) | Patrick,Pat (bs,el-b,voc) | Humphries,Lex (dr) | Morgan,Stanley 'Atakatun' (perc) | Branch,Russell 'Odun' (perc) | Tyson,June (voc) | Wright,Ruth (voc) | Banks,Cheryl (voc) | Holton,Judith (voc)

951251-2 | CD | Live At The Village Vanguard:The Master Takes
John Coltrane Quartet
Softly As In A Morning Sunrise
Live at The 'Village Vanguard',NYC, rec. 2.11.1961
Coltrane,John (ss,ts) | Tyner,McCoy (p) | Workman,Reggie (b) | Jones,Elvin (dr)
John Coltrane Trio
Chasin' The Trane
Coltrane,John (ts) | Garrison,Jimmy (b) | Jones,Elvin (dr)
John Coltrane Quintet
Spiritual
Live at The 'Village Vanguard',NYC, rec. 3.11.1961
Coltrane,John (ss) | Dolphy,Eric (b-cl) | Tyner,McCoy (p) | Workman,Reggie (b) | Jones,Elvin (dr)
John Coltrane Sextet
India
Coltrane,John (ss) | Dolphy,Eric (b-cl) | Tyner,McCoy (p) | Workman,Reggie (b) | Garrison,Jimmy (b) | Jones,Elvin (dr)

951253-2 | CD | Thembi
Pharoah Sanders Orchestra
Astral Traveling | Red Black And Green
NYC, rec. 25.11.1970
Sanders,Pharoah (ss,ts,perc,bells) | White,Michael (v,perc) | Smith,Lonnie Liston (p,el-p,perc,claves) | McBee,Cecil (b,perc,finger-cymbals) | Jarvis,Clifford (dr,perc,bells,maracas)
Thembi
Sanders,Pharoah (ss,ts,perc,bells) | White,Michael (v,perc) | Smith,Lonnie Liston (p,el-p,perc,claves) | McBee,Cecil (b,perc,finger-cymbals) | Jarvis,Clifford (dr,perc,bells,maracas) | Jordan,James (ring-cimbals)
Morning Prayer | Bailophone Dance
NYC, rec. 12.1.1971
Sanders,Pharoah (alto-fl,ts,bailophone,brass-bell,cow-horn,fifes,koto,maracas) | Smith,Lonnie Liston (p,bailophone,ring-cymbals,shouts) | McBee,Cecil (b,bird-effects) | Haynes,Roy (dr) | Bey,Chief (perc) | Shabazz,Majid (perc) | Wiles,Anthony (perc) | Bettis,Nat (perc)
Cecil McBee
Love
NYC, rec. 25.11.1970
McBee,Cecil (b-solo)

951258-2 | CD | Serendipity
Greg Tardy Band
Prisoner Of Love
NYC, rec. 13./14.9.1997
Tardy,Greg (ts) | Miller,Mulgrew (p) | Harland,Eric (dr)
Ask Me Now
Tardy,Greg (ts) | Veal,Reginald (b) | Harland,Eric (dr)
Forgiveness | Whenever,Whenever,Whenever
Tardy,Greg (ts) | Miller,Mulgrew (p) | Veal,Reginald (b) | Harland,Eric (dr)
Talking With Tom
Tardy,Greg (ts) | Harrell,Tom (tp) | Miller,Mulgrew (p) | Veal,Reginald (b) | Harland,Eric (dr)
The Fractar Question
Tardy,Greg (ts) | Harrell,Tom (tp) | Goldberg,Aaron (p) | Veal,Reginald (b) | Harland,Eric (dr)
JL's Wish | Serendipity
Tardy,Greg (ts) | Goldberg,Aaron (p) | Veal,Reginald (b) | Harland,Eric (dr)
Blues To Professor Pickens | Ah-Ite
Tardy,Greg (ts) | Gunn,Russell (tp) | Miller,Mulgrew (p) | Veal,Reginald (b) | Harland,Eric (dr)

951259-2 | CD | Pure Imagination
Eric Reed Trio
Overture | Maria | Hello Young Lovers | Pure Imagination | 42nd Street | Send In The Clowns | My Man's Gone Now- | Gone Gone Gone- | Nice Work If You Can Get It | You'll Never Walk Alone | I Got Rhythm | Finale(Last Trip)
North Hollywood,CA, rec. 28./29.7.1997
Reed,Eric (p) | Veal,Reginald (b) | Hutchinson,Gregory (dr)
Don't Cry For Me Argentina
Reed,Eric (p) | Rogers,Reuben (b) | Allen,Carl (dr)

951261-2 | CD | Two Blocks From The Edge
Michael Brecker Quintet
Madame Toulouse | Two Blocks From The Edge | Bye George | El Nino | Cat's Cradle | The Impaler | How Long 'Til The Sun | Delta City Blues | Skylark
NYC, rec. 1998
Brecker,Michael (ts) | Calderazzo,Joey (p) | Genus,James (b) | Watts,Jeff 'Tain' (dr) | Alias,Don (perc)

951265-2 | CD | Deaf Dumb Blind
Pharoah Sanders Orchestra
Let Us Go Into The House Of The Lord | Summun,Bukmun,Umyun
NYC, rec. 1.7.1970
Sanders,Pharoah (ss,perc,bells,thumb-p,whistle,wood-fl) | Shaw,Woody (tp,maracas,yodeling) | Bartz,Gary (as,perc,bells,shakers) | Smith,Lonnie Liston (p,perc,cowbell,thumb-p) | McBee,Cecil (b) | Jarvis,Clifford (dr) | Bettis,Nat (xyl,perc,yodeling) | Wiles,Anthony (perc,cga)

951267-2 | CD | A Monastic Trio
Alice Coltrane Quartet
Lord Help Me To Be | The Sun | Ohnedaruth
Coltrane Studios,Dix Hills,NY, rec. 29.1.1968
Coltrane,Alice (p) | Sanders,Pharoah (fl,b-cl,ts) | Garrison,Jimmy (b) | Riley,Ben (dr) | Coltrane John (voice)
Alice Coltrane Trio
Gospel Trane | I Want To See You | Lovely Sky Boat | Oceanic Beloved | Atomic Peace
Coltrane Studios,Dix Hills,NY, rec. 6.6.1968
Coltrane,Alice (p,harp) | Garrison,Jimmy (b) | Ali,Rashied (dr) | Coltrane John (voice)
Alice Coltrane
Altruvista
Englewood Cliffs,NJ, rec. 7.3.1967
Coltrane,Alice (p-solo)

951272-2 | CD | The Way Ahead
Archie Shepp Sextet
Damn If I Know (The Stroller) | Sophisticated Lady
NYC, rec. 29.1.1968
Shepp,Archie (ts) | Owens,Jimmy (tp) | Moncur III,Grachan (tb) | Davis Jr.,Walter (p) | Carter,Ron (b) | Harris,Beaver (dr)
Frankenstein | Fiesta
Shepp,Archie (ts) | Owens,Jimmy (tp) | Moncur III,Grachan (tb) | Davis Jr.,Walter (p) | Carter,Ron (b) | Haynes,Roy (dr)
Archie Shepp Septet
New Africa | Bakai
NYC, rec. 26.2.1969
Shepp,Archie (ts) | Owens,Jimmy (tp) | Moncur III,Grachan (tb) | Davis,Charles (bs) | Burrell,Dave (p) | Booker,Walter (b) | Harris,Beaver (dr)

951278-2 | CD | Geogre Russell New York N.Y.
George Russell And His Orchestra
Manhattan
NYC, rec. 12.9.1958
Farmer,Art (tp) | Severinsen,Doc (tp) | Royal,Ernie (tp) | Brookmeyer,Bob (tb) | Rehak,Frank (tb) | Mitchell,Tom (tb) | McKusick,Hal (as) | Coltrane,John (ts) | Schlinger,Sol (bs) | Evans,Bill (p) | Galbraith,Barry (g) | Hinton,Milt (b) | Persip,Charles (dr) | Hendricks,Jon (narrator) | Russell,George (arr,ld)
A Helluva Town | Manhattan-Rico
NYC, rec. 24.11.1958
Farmer,Art (tp) | Wilder,Joe (tp) | Royal,Ernie (tp) | Brookmeyer,Bob (tb) | Cleveland,Jimmy (tb) | Mitchell,Tom (tb) | McKusick,Hal (as) | Woods,Phil (as) | Cohn,Al (ts) | Allen,Gene (bs) | Evans,Bill (p) | Galbraith,Barry (g) | Duvivier,George (b) | Roach,Max (dr) | Hendricks,Jon (narrator) | Russell,George (arr,ld)
Big City Blues | East Side Medley: | Autumn In New York- | How About You-
NYC, rec. 25.3.1959
Farmer,Art (tp) | Wilder,Joe (tp) | Ferrante,Joe (tp) | Brookmeyer,Bob (tb) | Rehak,Frank (tb) | Mitchell,Tom (tb) | McKusick,Hal (fl,cl,as) | Woods,Phil (fl,cl,as) | Golson,Benny (ts) | Schlinger,Sol (bs) | Evans,Bill (p) | Galbraith,Barry (g) | Hinton,Milt (b) | Persip,Charles (dr) | Hendricks,Jon (narrator) | Russell,George (arr,ld)

951280-2 | 8 CD | John Coltrane:The Classic Quartet-Complete Impulse Studio Recordings
John Coltrane Quartet
Greensleeves | It's Easy To Remember
Englewood Cliffs,NJ, rec. 21.12.1961
Coltrane,John (ss,ts) | Tyner,McCoy (p) | Garrison,Jimmy (b) | Jones,Elvin (dr)
The Inch Worm | Big Nick
Englewood Cliffs,NJ, rec. 11.4.1962
Coltrane,John (ss) | Tyner,McCoy (p) | Garrison,Jimmy (b) | Jones,Elvin (dr)
Out Of This World | Soul Eyes
Englewood Cliffs,NJ, rec. 19.6.1962
Coltrane,John (ts) | Tyner,McCoy (p) | Garrison,Jimmy (b) | Jones,Elvin (dr)
Miles' Mode
Englewood Cliffs,NJ, rec. 20.6.1962
Coltrane,John (ts) | Tyner,McCoy (p) | Garrison,Jimmy (b) | Jones,Elvin (dr)
Tunji
Englewood Cliffs,NJ, rec. 29.6.1962
Coltrane,John (ts) | Tyner,McCoy (p) | Garrison,Jimmy (b) | Jones,Elvin (dr)
Nancy(With The Laughing Face) | What's New? | Up 'Gainst The Wall
Englewood Cliffs,NJ, rec. 18.9.1962
Coltrane,John (ts) | Tyner,McCoy (p) | Garrison,Jimmy (b) | Jones,Elvin (dr)
Too Young To Go Steady | All Or Nothing At All | I Wish I Knew | You Don't Know What Love Is | Say It Over And Over Again
Englewood Cliffs,NJ, rec. 13.11.1962
Coltrane,John (ts) | Tyner,McCoy (p) | Garrison,Jimmy (b) | Jones,Elvin (dr)
Vilia
Englewood Cliffs,NJ, rec. 6.3.1963
Coltrane,John (ss) | Tyner,McCoy (p) | Garrison,Jimmy (b) | Jones,Elvin (dr)
After The Rain | Dear Old Stockholm
Englewood Cliffs,NJ, rec. 29.4.1963
Coltrane,John (ts) | Tyner,McCoy (p) | Garrison,Jimmy (b) | Haynes,Roy (dr)
Your Lady | Alabama
Englewood Cliffs,NJ, rec. 18.11.1963
Coltrane,John (ss,ts) | Tyner,McCoy (p) | Garrison,Jimmy (b) | Jones,Elvin (dr)
Crescent(first version) | Lonnie's Lament | Wise One | Bessie's Blues(first version-incomplete) | Song Of Praise(first version)
Englewood Cliffs,NJ, rec. 27.3.1964
Coltrane,John (ts) | Tyner,McCoy (p) | Garrison,Jimmy (b) | Jones,Elvin (dr)
John Coltrane Trio
The Drum Thing
Englewood Cliffs,NJ, rec. 27.4.1964
Coltrane,John (ts) | Garrison,Jimmy (b) | Jones,Elvin (dr)
John Coltrane Quartet
Crescent | Bessie's Blues
Englewood Cliffs,NJ, rec. 1.6.1964
Coltrane,John (ts) | Tyner,McCoy (p) | Garrison,Jimmy (b) | Jones,Elvin (dr)
A Love Supreme: | Acknowledgement- | Resolution- | Resolution(alt.take)- | Pursuance- | Psalm-
Englewood Cliffs,NJ, rec. 9.12.1964
Coltrane,John (ts) | Tyner,McCoy (p) | Garrison,Jimmy (b) | Jones,Elvin (dr)
Nature Boy(first version)
Englewood Cliffs,NJ, rec. 17.2.1965
Coltrane,John (ts) | Tyner,McCoy (p) | Davis,Art (b) | Jones,Elvin (dr)
Nature Boy | Feelin' Good | Feelin' Good(alt.take)
Englewood Cliffs,NJ, rec. 18.2.1965
Coltrane,John (ts) | Tyner,McCoy (p) | Garrison,Jimmy (b) | Davis,Art (b) | Jones,Elvin (dr)
Chim Chim Cheree | Brazilia | Song Of Praise
Englewood Cliffs,NJ, rec. 17.5.1965
Coltrane,John (ss,ts) | Tyner,McCoy (p) | Garrison,Jimmy (b) | Jones,Elvin (dr)
After The Crescent | Dear Lord(breakdowns and alt.take) | Dear Lord | One Down, One Up
Englewood Cliffs,NJ, rec. 26.5.1965
Coltrane,John (ts) | Tyner,McCoy (p) | Garrison,Jimmy (b) | Haynes,Roy (dr)
Welcome | Untitled 90314 | Transition | Suite(5 parts)
Englewood Cliffs,NJ, rec. 10.6.1965
Coltrane,John (ss,ts) | Tyner,McCoy (p) | Garrison,Jimmy (b) | Jones,Elvin (dr)
John Coltrane Trio
The Last Blues
Coltrane,John (ss,ts) | Garrison,Jimmy (b) | Jones,Elvin (dr)
John Coltrane Quartet
Living Space(breakdown and alt.take) | Living Space | Dusk-Dawn | Untitled 90320
Englewood Cliffs,NJ, rec. 16.6.1965
Coltrane,John (ts) | Tyner,McCoy (p) | Garrison,Jimmy (b) | Jones,Elvin (dr)
John Coltrane-Elvin Jones
Vigil
Coltrane,John (ts) | Jones,Elvin (dr)
John Coltrane Quartet
Dearly Beloved | Attaining | Sun Ship | Ascent | Amen
Englewood Cliffs,NJ, rec. 26.8.1965
Coltrane,John (ts) | Tyner,McCoy (p) | Garrison,Jimmy (b) | Jones,Elvin (dr)
Meditations(Suite): | Love- | Compassion- | Joy- | Consequences- | Serenity-
Englewood Cliffs,NJ, rec. 2.9.1965
Coltrane,John (ts) | Tyner,McCoy (p) | Garrison,Jimmy (b) | Jones,Elvin (dr)
Joy
San Francisco,CA, rec. 22.9.1965
Coltrane,John (ts) | Tyner,McCoy (p) | Garrison,Jimmy (b) | Jones,Elvin (dr)

951281-2 | CD | Central Avenue
Danilo Perez Trio
Blues For The Saints | Lush Life
NYC, rec. 7.-9.4.1998
Perez,Danilo (p) | Patitucci,John (b) | Ballard,Jeff (dr)
Cosa Linda
NYC, rec. 7.-9-4-1998
Perez,Danilo (p) | Benitez,John (b) | Ballard,Jeff (dr)
Rhythm In Blue Suite: | Playground- | Sideways- | Love In 5-
NYC, rec. 7.-9.4.1998
Perez,Danilo (p) | Patitucci,John (b) | Watts,Jeff 'Tain' (dr)
Danilo Perez Group
Impromptu(Conversations)
Perez,Danilo (p) | Patitucci,John (b) | Watts,Jeff 'Tain' (dr) | Spiegel,Ray (tablas) | Saturnino,Pernell (congas,guiro) | Souza,Luciana (voc)
Impressions
Perez,Danilo (p) | Benitez,John (b) | Watts,Jeff 'Tain' (dr) | Saturnino,Pernell (congas,clave,okonkolo,shekere) | Souza,Luciana (voc)
Panama Blues
Perez,Danilo (p) | Patitucci,John (b) | Watts,Jeff 'Tain' (dr) | Diaz,Miguel (itotele,iya,okonkolo) | Baez,Aquiles (cuatro) | Vital,Raul (voc)
Danilo Perez
Smoke Gets In Your Eyes
Perez,Danilo (p-solo)

951282-2 | CD | Sweet Georgia Peach
Russell Malone Quartet
To Benny Golson | Strange Little Smile- | With You I'm Born Again- | Sweet Georgia Peach | Mean What You Say | Song For Darius | Bright Mississippi | Someone's Rocking My Dreamboat | For Toddlers Only | Swing Low Sweet Chariot | Yesterdays
NYC, rec. 17.-19.2.1998
Malone,Russell (g) | Barron,Kenny (p) | Carter,Ron (b) | Nash,Lewis (dr)
Russell Malone Quintet
Mugshot | Rise
Malone,Russell (g) | Barron,Kenny (p) | Carter,Ron (b) | Nash,Lewis (dr) | Kroon,Steve (perc)

951283-2 | CD | Free To Be
Donald Harrison Quartet
Free To Be | Softly As In A Morning Sunrise | Feelin' Jazzy,Baby
NYC, rec. 18.-20.8.1998
Harrison,Donald (as) | Adair,Andrew (p) | Rogers,Reuben (b) | Lamkin,John (dr)
Cissy Strut
Harrison,Donald (as) | Adair,Andrew (p) | Archer,Vincente (b) | Lamkin,John (dr)
Blue Rose | Duck's Step
NYC, rec. 18.-20.8.1988
Harrison,Donald (as) | Miller,Mulgrew (p) | McBride,Christian (b) | Allen,Carl (dr)
Donald Harrison Quintet
Again Never
NYC, rec. 18.-20.8.1998
Harrison,Donald (as) | Lynch,Brian (tp) | Miller,Mulgrew (p) | McBride,Christian (b) | Allen,Carl (dr)
Indian Blues
Harrison,Donald (as) | Avery,Teodross (ts) | Miller,Mulgrew (p) | McBride,Christian (b) | Allen,Carl (dr)
Donald Harrison Sextet
Mr.Cool Breeze | Smooth Sailing | Nouveau Swing(reprise)
Harrison,Donald (ss,as,voc) | Jones,Rodney (g) | Adair,Andrew (p) | Rogers,Reuben (b) | Lamkin,John (dr) | Claussell,Jose (perc)
Slowvisor
NYC, rec. 18.-20.9.1998
Harrison,Donald (as) | Lynch,Brian (tp) | Palmieri,Eddie (p) | McBride,Christian (b) | Allen,Carl (bass-dr) | Claussell,Jose (perc)

952168-2 | 2 CD | The Complete Africa/Brass Sessions
John Coltrane Quartet With Brass
Greensleeves | Greensleeves(alt.take) | Song Of The Underground Railroad | The Damned Don't Cry
Englewood Cliffs,NJ, rec. 23.5.1961
Coltrane,John (ss,ts) | Tyner,McCoy (p) | Workman,Reggie (b) | Jones,Elvin (dr) | Little,Booker (tp) | Hubbard,Freddie (tp) | Priester,Julian (euphonium) | Greenlee,Charles (euphonium) | Watkins,Julius (fr-h) | Corrado,Donald (fr-h) | Northern,Bob (fr-h) | Buffington,Jimmy (fr-h) | Swisshelm,Robert (fr-h) | Barber,Bill (tuba) | Dolphy,Eric (fl,b-cl,as) | Bushell,Garvin (reeds) | Patrick,Pat (bs)
Africa(1.version)
Coltrane,John (ts) | Tyner,McCoy (p) | Workman,Reggie (b) | Jones,Elvin (dr) | Little,Booker (tp) | Hubbard,Freddie (tp) | Priester,Julian (euphonium) | Greenlee,Charles (euphonium) | Watkins,Julius (fr-h) | Corrado,Donald (fr-h) | Northern,Bob (fr-h) | Buffington,Jimmy (fr-h) |

Swisshelm,Robert (fr-h) | Barber,Bill (tuba) | Dolphy,Eric (fl,b-cl,as,arr) | Bushell,Garvin (reeds) | Patrick,Pat (bs) | Chambers,Paul (b)
Africa | Africa(alt.take)
Englewood Cliffs,NJ, rec. 7.6.1961
Coltrane,John (ts) | Tyner,McCoy (p) | Workman,Reggie (b) | Jones,Elvin (dr) | Little,Booker (tp) | Woodman,Britt (tb) | Bowman,Carl (euphonium) | Watkins,Julius (fr-h) | Corrado,Donald (fr-h) | Northern,Bob (fr-h) | Swisshelm,Robert (fr-h) | Barber,Bill (tuba) | Dolphy,Eric (fl,b-cl,as,arr) | Patrick,Pat (bs) | Davis,Art (b)
Blues Minor
Coltrane,John (ts) | Tyner,McCoy (p) | Workman,Reggie (b) | Jones,Elvin (dr) | Little,Booker (tp) | Woodman,Britt (tb) | Bowman,Carl (euphonium) | Watkins,Julius (fr-h) | Corrado,Donald (fr-h) | Northern,Bob (fr-h) | Swisshelm,Robert (fr-h) | Barber,Bill (tuba) | Dolphy,Eric (fl,b-cl,as) | Patrick,Pat (bs)

952236-2 | 2 CD | Latino America
Gato Barbieri Orchestra
Encuentros | La China Leonica Arreo La Correntinada Trajo Entre La Muchachada La Flor De La Juvuntud
Buenos Aires, rec. 17.4.1973
Barbieri,Gato (ts) | Mercado,Raul (quena) | Monges,Amadeo (indian harp) | Palacios,Quelo (g) | Lew,Ricardo (el-g) | Fumero,Isoca (charango) | Cevasco,Adalberto (el-b) | Lapuble,Pocho (dr) | Cura,Domingo (bombo indian) | Pantoja,Antonio (perc) | Roizner,El Zurdo (perc) | Padin,Jorge (perc)
India | Juana Azurduy
Buenos Aires, rec. 18.4.1973
Barbieri,Gato (ts) | Mercado,Raul (quena) | Monges,Amadeo (indian harp) | Palacios,Quelo (g) | Cevasco,Adalberto (el-b) | Cura,Domingo (bombo indian) | Pantoja,Antonio (perc) | Roizner,El Zurdo (perc)
Nunca Mas
Buenos Aires, rec. 24.4.1973
Barbieri,Gato (ts) | Bellingieri,Osvaldo (p) | Saluzzi,Dino (bandoneon) | Cevasco,Adalberto (el-b)
Latino Amarica | To Be Continued
Rio De Janeiro,Brazil, rec. 28.4.1973
Barbieri,Gato (ts,voice) | Delmiro,Helio (g) | De Azevado,Daudeth (cavaco) | Novelli (el-b) | Paulinho,Paulo (dr)
La China Leonica Arreo La Correntinada Trajo Entre La Muchachada La Flor De La Juvuntud | Nunca Mas(alt.take)
Los Angeles,CA, rec. 15.10.1973
Barbieri,Gato (ts,voice) | Mercado,Raul (quena) | Monges,Amadeo (indian harp) | Palacios,Quelo (g) | Lew,Ricardo (el-g) | Cevasco,Adalberto (el-b) | Cura,Domingo (bombo indian) | Pantoja,Antonio (perc) | Roizner,El Zurdo (perc)
Latino Amarica
Los Angeles,CA, rec. 16.10.1973
Barbieri,Gato (ts) | Mercado,Raul (quena) | Monges,Amadeo (indian harp) | Palacios,Quelo (g) | Lew,Ricardo (el-g) | Cevasco,Adalberto (el-b) | Cura,Domingo (bombo indian) | Pantoja,Antonio (perc) | Roizner,El Zurdo (perc)
Para Nosotros
Los Angeles,CA, rec. 17.10.1973
Barbieri,Gato (ts,voice) | Mercado,Raul (quena) | Monges,Amadeo (indian harp) | Palacios,Quelo (g) | Lew,Ricardo (el-g) | Cevasco,Adalberto (el-b) | Cura,Domingo (bombo indian) | Pantoja,Antonio (perc) | Roizner,El Zurdo (perc)
Maté
Los Angeles,CA, rec. 18.10.1978
Barbieri,Gato (ts,voice) | Mercado,Raul (quena) | Monges,Amadeo (indian harp) | Palacios,Quelo (g) | Lew,Ricardo (el-g) | Cevasco,Adalberto (el-b) | Cura,Domingo (bombo indian) | Pantoja,Antonio (perc) | Roizner,El Zurdo (perc)
Gato Gato
Los Angeles,CA, rec. 4.2.1974
Barbieri,Gato (fl,ts) | Ritenour,Lee (el-g) | Pisano,John (g) | Hughart,Jim (b) | Zimitti,Bob (dr) | Correa,Mayuto (perc)
Encontros | Marissea
Rio De Janeiro/Los Angeles,CA, rec. 28.4.1973/4.2.1974
Barbieri,Gato (ts) | Delmiro,Helio (g) | De Azevado,Daudeth (cavaco) | Novelli (el-b) | Paulinho,Paulo (dr) | Hughart,Jim (b) | Correa,Mayuto (congas,triangle)

954322-2 | 4 CD | John Coltrane:The Complete 1961 Village Vanguard Recordings
John Coltrane Sextet
India
Live at The 'Village Vanguard',NYC, rec. 1.11.1961
Coltrane,John (ts) | Dolphy,Eric (b-cl) | Tyner,McCoy (p) | Garrison,Jimmy (b) | Workman,Reggie (b) | Abdul-Malik,Ahmed (oud) | Jones,Elvin (dr)
John Coltrane-Eric Dolphy Quartet
Chasin' The Trane | Brazilia
Coltrane,John (ts) | Dolphy,Eric (as) | Workman,Reggie (b) | Jones,Elvin (dr)
John Coltrane Quartet With Eric Dolphy
Spiritual | Miles' Mode | Naima
Coltrane,John (ts) | Dolphy,Eric (as) | Tyner,McCoy (p) | Workman,Reggie (b) | Jones,Elvin (dr)
Impressions
Coltrane,John (ts) | Dolphy,Eric (as) | Tyner,McCoy (p) | Garrison,Jimmy (b) | Jones,Elvin (dr)
John Coltrane-Eric Dolphy Quartet
Chasin' The Trane
Live at The 'Village Vanguard',NYC, rec. 2.11.1961
Coltrane,John (ts) | Dolphy,Eric (as) | Workman,Reggie (b) | Haynes,Roy (dr)
John Coltrane Septet With Eric Dolphy
India
Coltrane,John (ss) | Dolphy,Eric (b-cl) | Bushell,Garvin (oboe) | Tyner,McCoy (p) | Abdul-Malik,Ahmed (oud) | Garrison,Jimmy (b) | Workman,Reggie (b) | Jones,Elvin (dr)
John Coltrane Quintet With Eric Dolphy
Spiritual
Coltrane,John (ss,ts) | Dolphy,Eric (b-cl) | Bushell,Garvin (contra-bassoon) | Tyner,McCoy (p) | Workman,Reggie (b) | Jones,Elvin (dr)
John Coltrane Quartet
Softly As In A Morning Sunrise | Greensleeves
Coltrane,John (ss) | Tyner,McCoy (p) | Workman,Reggie (b) | Jones,Elvin (dr)
John Coltrane Trio
Chasin' The Trane
Coltrane,John (ts) | Garrison,Jimmy (b) | Jones,Elvin (dr)
John Coltrane Quartet With Eric Dolphy
Impressions
Coltrane,John (ts) | Dolphy,Eric (as) | Tyner,McCoy (p) | Garrison,Jimmy (b) | Jones,Elvin (dr)
Spiritual | Naima
Live at The 'Village Vanguard',NYC, rec. 3.11.1961
Coltrane,John (ss,ts) | Dolphy,Eric (b-cl) | Tyner,McCoy (p) | Workman,Reggie (b) | Jones,Elvin (dr)
John Coltrane Quintet With Eric Dolphy
India | Miles' Mode
Coltrane,John (ss,ts) | Dolphy,Eric (b-cl,as) | Tyner,McCoy (p) | Workman,Reggie (b) | Garrison,Jimmy (b) | Jones,Elvin (dr)
John Coltrane Quartet
Impressions
Coltrane,John (ts) | Tyner,McCoy (p) | Garrison,Jimmy (b) | Jones,Elvin (dr)
Greensleeves
Coltrane,John (ss) | Tyner,McCoy (p) | Workman,Reggie (b) | Jones,Elvin (dr)
John Coltrane Septet With Eric Dolphy
India
Live at The Villa,Paris,France, rec. 5.11.1961
Coltrane,John (ss) | Dolphy,Eric (b-cl) | Bushell,Garvin (oboe) | Tyner,McCoy (p) | Abdul-Malik,Ahmed (oud) | Workman,Reggie (b) | Garrison,Jimmy (b) | Jones,Elvin (dr)
John Coltrane Quintet With Eric Dolphy
Spiritual
Live at The 'Village Vanguard',NYC, rec. 5.11.1961
Coltrane,John (ss,ts) | Dolphy,Eric (b-cl) | Bushell,Garvin (contra-bassoon) | Tyner,McCoy (p) | Workman,Reggie (b) | Jones,Elvin (dr)

9681049 | CD | The Golden Flute | EAN 602498610497
Yusef Lateef Quartet
Road Runner | Straighten Up And Fly Right | Oasis | I Don't Stand A Ghost Of A Chance With You | Exactly Like You | The Golden Flute | Rosetta | Head Hunters | The Smart Set
NYC, rec. 15./16.6.1966
Lateef,Yusef (fl,ts,oboe) | Lawson,Hugh (p) | Wright,Herman (b) | Brooks,Roy (dr)

9861047 | CD | Chicken Fat | EAN 602498610473
Mel Brown Quintet
Chicken Fat | Home James | Sad But True | I'm Goin' To Jackson
Los Angeles,CA, rec. 31.5.1967
Brown,Mel (g) | Wiggins,Gerald 'Gerry' (org) | Ellis,Herb (g) | Brown,Ron (b) | Humphrey,Paul (dr)
Mel Brown Quartet
Greasy Spoon
Brown,Mel (g) | Ellis,Herb (g) | Brown,Ron (b) | Humphrey,Paul (dr)
Mel Brown Quintet
Shanty | Slalom | Anacrusis | Hobo Flats
Los Angeles,CA, rec. 1.6.1967
Brown,Mel (g) | Wright,Arthur (harm,g) | Wiggins,Gerald 'Gerry' (org) | Brown,Ron (b) | Humphrey,Paul (dr)

9861488 | CD | The Cry Of My People | EAN 602498614884
Archie Shepp Orchestra
Rest Enough(Song To Mother)
NYC, rec. 25.-27.9.1972
Mabern,Harold (p) | Dupree,Cornell (g) | Carter,Ron (el-b) | Purdie,Bernard 'Pretty' (dr) | Defense,Nene (tambourine) | Blue,Peggie (voc) | White,Judith (voc) | Stephens,Mary (voc) | White,Barbara (voc) | Lane,Mildred (voc) | Franklin,Andre (voc)
Prayer
Shepp,Archie (ss) | McGhee,Charles (tp) | Greenlee,Charles (tb) | Stephens,Charles (tb) | Mabern,Harold (p) | Jenkins,Leroy (v) | Slessinger,Lois (v) | Dixon,Gayle (v) | Blake,John (v) | Mellon,Ester (cello) | Dixon,Pat (cello) | Garrison,Jimmy (b) | Carter,Ron (el-b) | Purdie,Bernard 'Pretty' (dr) | Defense,Nene (perc) | Blue,Peggie (voc) | White,Judith (voc) | Stephens,Mary (voc) | White,Barbara (voc) | Lane,Mildred (voc) | Franklin,Andre (voc) | Franceschini,Romulus (cond) | Massey,Cal (arr)
All God's Children Got A Home In The Universe
Shepp,Archie (ts) | McGhee,Charles (tp) | Greenlee,Charles (tb) | Stephens,Charles (tb) | Mabern,Harold (p) | Dupree,Cornell (g) | Carter,Ron (el-b) | Harris,Beaver (dr) | Defense,Nene (tambourine) | Blue,Peggie (voc) | White,Judith (voc) | Stephens,Mary (voc) | White,Barbara (voc) | Lane,Mildred (voc) | Franklin,Andre (voc)
The Lady
Shepp,Archie (ss,ts) | McGhee,Charles (tp) | Greenlee,Charles (tb) | Stephens,Charles (tb) | Mabern,Harold (p) | Jenkins,Leroy (v) | Little,Jerry (v) | Da Costa,Noel (v) | Dixon,Gayle (v) | Mellon,Ester (cello) | Dixon,Pat (cello) | Garrison,Jimmy (b) | Harris,Beaver (dr) | Defense,Nene (perc) | Wilson,Joe Lee (voc) | Franceschini,Romulus (cond) | Massey,Cal (arr)
The Cry Of My People
Shepp,Archie (ts) | McGhee,Charles (tp) | Greenlee,Charles (tb) | Stephens,Charles (tb) | Mabern,Harold (p) | Slessinger,Lois (v) | Jenkins,Leroy (v) | Blake,John (v) | Dixon,Gayle (v) | Mellon,Ester (cello) | Dixon,Pat (cello) | Garrison,Jimmy (b) | Carter,Ron (el-b) | Harris,Beaver (dr) | Defense,Nene (perc) | Blue,Peggie (voc) | White,Judith (voc) | Stephens,Mary (voc) | White,Barbara (voc) | Lane,Mildred (voc) | Franklin,Andre (voc) | Franceschini,Romulus (cond) | Massey,Cal (arr)
African Drum Suite(part 1)
Greenlee,Charles (tb) | Burrell,Dave (p) | Garrison,Jimmy (b) | Wilson,Joe Lee (voc)
African Drum Suite(part 2)
Shepp,Archie (ss) | McGhee,Charles (tp) | Greenlee,Charles (tb) | Burrell,Dave (p,arr,cond) | Jenkins,Leroy (v) | Da Costa,Noel (v) | Little,Jerry (v) | Dixon,Gayle (v) | Mellon,Ester (cello) | Dixon,Pat (cello) | Garrison,Jimmy (b) | Harris,Beaver (dr) | Defense,Nene (bongos,congas) | Quaye,Terry (tambourine,congas,voc) | Franco,Guilherme (perc,berimbau) | Wilson,Joe Lee (voc) | Blue,Peggie (voc) | White,Judith (voc) | Stephens,Mary (voc) | White,Barbara (voc) | Lane,Mildred (voc) | Franklin,Andre (voc)
Come Sunday
Shepp,Archie (ts) | McGhee,Charles (tp) | Stephens,Charles (tb) | Mabern,Harold (p) | Jenkins,Leroy (v) | Da Costa,Noel (v) | Little,Jerry (v) | Dixon,Gayle (v) | Mellon,Ester (cello) | Dixon,Pat (cello) | Garrison,Jimmy (b) | Harris,Beaver (dr) | Defense,Nene (perc) | Wilson,Joe Lee (voc) | Blue,Peggie (voc) | White,Judith (voc) | Stephens,Mary (voc) | White,Barbara (voc) | Lane,Mildred (voc) | Franklin,Andre (voc) | Greenlee,Charles (arr,cond)

IMP 11522 | CD | Unforgettable
Johnny Hartman And His Orchestra
Almost Like Being In Love | Once In A While | Isn't It Romantic | Our Love Is Here To Stay
Los Angeles,CA, rec. 15.2.1966
Hartman,Johnny (voc) | Chaikin,Jules (tp) | Hill,Fred 'Freddie' (tp) | Moore,Melvin (tp) | Brisbois,Wilbur 'Bud' (tp) | Porcino,Al (tp) | Barone,Mike (tb) | Ewing,John 'Steamline' (tb) | Robertson,Lester (tb) | Tack,Ernie (b-tb) | Land,Harold (ts) | Edwards,Teddy (ts) | Amy,Curtis (ts) | Nimitz,Jack (bs) | Melvoin,Mike (p) | Ellis,Herb (g) | Bond,Jimmy (b) | Levey,Stan (dr)
The More I See You | What Do I Owe Here | Bidin' My Time | Down In The Depths
Los Angeles,CA, rec. 17.2.1966
Hartman,Johnny (voc) | Chaikin,Jules (tp) | Hill,Fred 'Freddie' (tp) | Moore,Melvin (tp) | Brisbois,Wilbur 'Bud' (tp) | Porcino,Al (tp) | Barone,Mike (tb) | Ewing,John 'Steamline' (tb) | Robertson,Lester (tb) | Tack,Ernie (b-tb) | Land,Harold (ts) | Edwards,Teddy (ts) | Amy,Curtis (ts) | Nimitz,Jack (bs) | Melvoin,Mike (p) | Gray,John (g) | Brown,Ray (b) | Levey,Stan (dr)
Fools Rush In | The Very Thought Of You | Unforgettable | Ain't Misbehavin'
Los Angeles,CA, rec. 18.2.1966
Hartman,Johnny (voc) | Melvoin,Mike (p) | Gray,John (g) | Brown,Ray (b) | Levey,Stan (dr) | Gill,Vinny (v) | Nuttycomb,Wilbert (v) | Reisler,Jerome (v) | Vidusich,John (v) | Marks,Betty (v) | Malarsky,Leonhard (v) | Poole,George (v) | Terwilliger,Robert (v) | Boghossian,Sam (viola) | Rinkin,Alvin (viola) | Ditullio,Joseph (cello) | Sargeant,Emmet (cello)
Today I Love Ev'rybody | 'T'Ain't No Need | For The Want Of A Kiss | Girl Talk | That Old Black Magic
Los Angeles,CA, rec. 28.9.1966
Hartman,Johnny (voc) | Mitchell,Ollie (tp) | Porcino,Al (tp) | Candoli,Conte (tp) | Byers,Billy (tb) | Barone,Mike (tb) | Baltazar,Gabe (as) | Green,Bill (ts) | Johnson,Plas (ts) | Hood,Bill (bs) | Melvoin,Mike (p) | Ellis,Herb (g) | Roberts,Howard (g) | Mondragon,Joe (b) | Manne,Shelly (dr) | Lockert,James (perc)

IMP 12042 | CD | The Roots Of Acid Jazz
Dizzy Gillespie Quintet
Swing Low Sweet Cadillac
rec. 1967
Gillespie,Dizzy (tp) | Moody,James (fl,as,ts) | Longo,Michael (p) | Schifano,Frank (el-b) | Finch,Otis 'Candy' (dr)
Chico Hamilton Quintet
For Mods Only
rec. 1966
Hamilton,Forrest 'Chico' (dr) | Lawrence,Arnie (as) | Coryell,Larry (g) | Shepp,Archie (p) | Davis,Richard (b)
Quincy Jones And His Orchestra
Hard Sock Dance
rec. 1961
Jones,Quincy (arr) | Jones,Thad (tp) | DeRisi,Al (tp) | Hubbard,Freddie (tp) | Young,Eugene 'Snooky' (tp) | Levitt,Rod (tb) | Liston,Melba (tb) | Faulise,Paul (tb) | Byers,Billy (tb) | Woods,Phil (reeds) | Richardson,Jerome (sax) | Dixon,Eric (sax) | Wess,Frank (reeds) | Nelson,Oliver (sax) | Bown,Patti (p) | Hinton,Milt (b) | English,Bill (dr) | Watkins,Julius (fr-h)
Oliver Nelson And His Orchestra
Stolen Moments
Nelson,Oliver (as,ts) | Hubbard,Freddie (tp) | Dolphy,Eric (fl,as) | Barrow,George (bs) | Evans,Bill (p) | Chambers,Paul (b) | Haynes,Roy (dr)
Shirley Horn With Band
Big City
rec. 1967
Horn,Shirley (p,voc) | Newman,Joe (tp) | Wess,Frank (fl,as) | Richardson,Jerome (fl) | Burrell,Kenny (g) | Hawkins,Marshall (b) | Sweetney,Bernard (dr) | Pate,Johnny (arr)
Gabor Szabo Quintet
The Beat Goes On
Szabo,Gabor (g) | Stewart,Jimmy (g) | Kabok,Louis (b) | Morell,Marty (dr) | Gordon,Hal (perc)
Sonny Rollins Quartet
Hold 'Em Joe
rec. 1965
Rollins,Sonny (ts) | Bryant,Ray (p) | Booker,Walter (b) | Roker,Granville 'Mickey' (dr)
Hank Jones With Oliver Nelson's Orchestra
Winchester Cathedral
rec. 1966
Jones,Hank (el-harpsichord) | Nelson,Oliver (arr,ld) | Royal,Ernie (tp) | Young,Eugene 'Snooky' (tp) | Newman,Joe (tp) | Terry,Clark (tp,voice) | Johnson,J.J. (tb) | Cleveland,Jimmy (tb) | Mitchell,Tom (tb) | Woodman,Britt (tb) | Ashton,Bob (reeds) | Dodgion,Jerry (reeds) | Woods,Phil (reeds) | Richardson,Jerome (reeds) | Bank,Danny (reeds) | Duvivier,George (b) | Tate,Grady (dr)
Stanley Turrentine Quartet
Ciao Ciao
Turrentine,Stanley (ts) | Scott,Shirley (org) | Carter,Ron (b) | Simpkins,Mack (dr)
Gato Barbieri Orchestra
La Podrida
rec. 1974
Barbieri,Gato (ts) | Rubin,Alan (tp,fl-h) | Morrow,Buddy (tb) | Ralph,Alan (b-tb) | Alonge,Ray (fr-h) | Buffington,Jimmy (fr-h) | Johnson,Howard (fl-h,b-cl,tuba) | Powell,Seldon (fl,alto-fl,as,bs,piccolo) | Martinez,Eddie (p,el-p) | Davis,George (g,el-g) | Metzke,Paul (el-g) | Carter,Ron (b) | Tate,Grady (dr) | Armando,Ray (perc) | Mangual,Luis (perc) | Mantilla,Ray (perc) | Portinho,Thelmo Martins Porto (perc)
Keith Jarrett Quintet
Southern Smiles
rec. 1975
Jarrett,Keith (p,perc) | Redman,Dewey (ts,maracas,tambourine) | Haden,Charlie (b) | Motian,Paul (dr,perc) | Franco,Guilherme (perc)
Pharoah Sanders Orchestra
The Creator Has A Master Plan(edited version)
rec. 1969
Sanders,Pharoah (ts) | Spaulding,James (fl) | Watkins,Julius (fr-h) | Smith,Lonnie Liston (p) | Davis,Richard (b) | Workman,Reggie (b) | Bettis,Nat (perc) | Thomas,Leon (perc,voc) | Hart,Billy (dr)
Coleman Hawkins Quartet
Go Lil' Liza
rec. 1962
Hawkins,Coleman (ts) | Flanagan,Tommy (p) | Holley,Major (b) | Locke,Eddie (dr)
Yusef Lateef Quintet
Slippin' And Slidin'
rec. 1964
Lateef,Yusef (fl) | Williams,Richard (tp) | Nock,Mike (p) | Farrow,Ernie (b) | Black,James (dr)

IMP 12112 | CD | The Sorcerer
Gabor Szabo Quintet
The Beat Goes On | O Barquinho(Little Boat) | Lou-ise | What Is This Thing Called Love | Space | Stronger Than Us | Mizrab | Comin' Back | Los Matodoros | People | Corcovado(Quiet Nights)
Live at The Jazz Workshop,Boston,MA, rec. 14./15.4.1967
Szabo,Gabor (g) | Stewart,Jimmy (g) | Kabok,Louis (b) | Morell,Marty (dr) | Gordon,Hal (perc)

IMP 12262 | CD | The Awakening
Ahmad Jamal Trio
The Awakening | I Love Music | Dolphin Dance | Stolen Moments | Patterns | You're My Everything | Wave
NYC, rec. 2./3.2.1970
Jamal,Ahmad (p) | Nasser,Jamil[George Joyner] (b) | Gant,Frank (dr)

IMP 12702 | CD | Mixed
Cecil Taylor Unit
Bulbs | Pots
NYC, rec. 10.10.1961
Taylor,Cecil (p) | Shepp,Archie (ts) | Lyons,Jimmy (as) | Grimes,Henry (b) | Murray,Sunny (dr)
Mixed
Taylor,Cecil (p) | Curson,Ted (tp) | Rudd,Roswell (tb) | Shepp,Archie (ts) | Lyons,Jimmy (as) | Grimes,Henry (b) | Murray,Sunny (dr)
Roswell Rudd Sextet
Everywhere | Yankee No-How | Respects | Satan's Dance
NYC, rec. 8.7.1966
Rudd,Roswell (tb) | Logan,Giuseppi (fl,b-cl) | Kenyatta,Robin (as) | Haden,Charlie (b) | Worrell,Lewis (b) | Harris,Beaver (dr)

IMP 22732 | 2 CD | Albert Ayler Live In Greenwich Village:The Complete Impulse Recordings
Albert Ayler Quintet
Holy Ghost
Live at The 'Village Gate',NYC, rec. 28.3.1965
Ayler,Albert (ts) | Ayler,Donald (tp) | Freedman,Joel (cello) | Worrell,Lewis (b) | Murray,Sunny (dr)
Albert Ayler Sextet
Truth Is Marching In | Our Prayer | Spirits Rejoice
Live at The 'Village Vanguard',NYC, rec. 18.12.1966
Ayler,Albert (ts) | Ayler,Donald (tp) | Sampson,Michael (v) | Folwell,Bill (b) | Grimes,Henry (b) | Harris,Beaver (dr)
Albert Ayler Duo
Angels
Ayler,Albert (ts) | Cobbs,Call prob. (p)
Albert Ayler Group
For John Coltrane
Live at The Village Theatre,NYC, rec. 26.2.1967
Ayler,Albert (as) | Sampson,Michael (v) | Freedman,Joel (cello) | Folwell,Bill (b) | Silva,Alan (b)
Changes Has Come | Light In Darkness | Heavenly Home | Spiritual Rebirth | Infinite Spirit | Omega Is The Alpha
Ayler,Albert (ts) | Ayler,Donald (tp) | Sampson,Michael (v) | Freedman,Joel (cello) | Folwell,Bill (b) | Silva,Alan (b) | Harris,Beaver (dr)
Universal Thoughts
Ayler,Albert (ts) | Ayler,Donald (tp) | Steele,George (tb) | Sampson,Michael (v) | Freedman,Joel (cello) | Folwell,Bill (b) | Silva,Alan (b) | Harris,Beaver (dr)

MCD 04137 | 2 CD | The Other Village Vanguard Tapes
John Coltrane-Eric Dolphy Quartet
Chasin' The Trane
Live at The 'Village Vanguard',NYC, rec. 2.-5.11.1961
Coltrane,John (ss,ts) | Dolphy,Eric (b-cl,as) | Workman,Reggie (b) | Jones,Elvin (dr)
John Coltrane Quintet With Eric Dolphy
Spiritual
Coltrane,John (ss,ts) | Dolphy,Eric (b-cl,as) | Tyner,McCoy (p) | Workman,Reggie (b) | Jones,Elvin (dr)

Untitled Original
Coltrane,John (ss,ts) | Dolphy,Eric (b-cl,as) | Tyner,McCoy (p) | Garrison,Jimmy (b) | Jones,Elvin (dr)
Spiritual
Coltrane,John (ss,ts) | Dolphy,Eric (b-cl,as) | Tyner,McCoy (p) | Workman,Reggie (b) | Jones,Elvin (dr) | Bushell,Garvin (contra-bassoon,oboe)
John Coltrane Septet With Eric Dolphy
India
Coltrane,John (ss,ts) | Dolphy,Eric (b-cl,as) | Tyner,McCoy (p) | Workman,Reggie (b) | Jones,Elvin (dr) | Bushell,Garvin (contra-bassoon,oboe) | Garrison,Jimmy (b) | Abdul-Malik,Ahmed (oud)
John Coltrane Quartet
Greensleeves
Coltrane,John (ss) | Tyner,McCoy (p) | Workman,Reggie (b) | Jones,Elvin (dr)

MCD 10648 | CD | Byablue
Keith Jarrett
Byablue
Burbank,Los Angeles,CA, rec. 1976
Jarrett,Keith (p-solo)
Keith Jarrett Trio
Rainbow
Jarrett,Keith (p) | Haden,Charlie (b) | Motian,Paul (dr)
Fantasm
Jarrett,Keith (p) | Redman,Dewey (ts) | Haden,Charlie (b)
Keith Jarrett Quartet
Byablue | Konya | Trieste | Yahllah
Jarrett,Keith (ss,p) | Redman,Dewey (ts,musette) | Haden,Charlie (b) | Motian,Paul (dr,perc)

IN+OUT Records | IN+OUT Records GmbH

001-2 | CD | The Colours Of Life
Airto Moreira/Flora Purim
Berimbau Do Sul | Anatelio | Treme Terra
Santa Barbara,CA, rec. 1980
Moreira,Airto (dr,perc) | Purim,Flora (voc)
Espiritual Rain Forest | Partido Alto | Bingo | Escape | Misterioso
Freiburg,Brg., rec. Nov.1987
Moreira,Airto (dr,perc) | Purim,Flora (voc)

7002-2 | CD | Dance Romance
Grant Calvin Weston Group
Chocolate Rock | I Can Tell | Planetarian Citizen | Preview | Dance Romance | House Blues
Ludwigsburg, rec. details unknown
Weston,Grant Calvin (dr,voc) | Dixon,Fostina (sax) | Ulmer,James Blood (g) | Tacuma,Jamaaladeen (keyboards,el-b,voc)

7003-2 | CD | In My Own Sweet Way
Woody Shaw Quartet
The Oregon Grinder | In Your Own Sweet Way | The Dragon | Just A Ballad For Woody | Sippin' At Bells | Estate(Summer) | Joshua C.
Bazillus Club,Zürich, rec. 7.2.1987
Shaw,Woody (tp) | Henke,Fred (p) | Swainson,Neil (b) | Deutsch,Alex (dr)

7004-2 | CD | Something More
7004-1 | LP | Something More
Buster Williams Quintet
Air Dancing | Christina | Fortune Dance | Something More | Decepticon | Sophisticated Lady | I Didn't Know What Time It Was
Englewood Cliffs,NJ, rec. 8./9.3.1989
Williams,Buster (b,piccolo-b) | Ohno,Shunzo (tp) | Shorter,Wayne (ss,ts) | Hancock,Herbie (p,keyboards) | Foster,Al (dr)

7006-2 | CD | The Mystical Dreamer
Brainstorm feat. Chico Freeman
Footprints | Did I Say Anything,Prelude | On The Nile | Sojourn | The Mystical Dreamer | Reach Out I'll Be There - (Reach Out) I'll Be There | Did I Say Anything
New Morning,Paris,France, rec. 18.5.1989
Brainstorm | Freeman,Chico (sax,keyboards,pitchrider) | Brown,Delmar (keyboards,voc) | Walker,Chris (keyboards,el-b,voc) | Walker,Archie (keyboards,dr) | Hedman,Norman (perc)

7007-2 | CD | Revealing
James Blood Ulmer Quartet
Revealing | Raw Groove | Overtime | Love Nest
NYC, rec. 1977
Ulmer,James Blood (el-g) | Adams,George (b-cl,ts) | McBee,Cecil (b) | Hammond,Doug (dr,perc)

7008-2 | CD | Magic Lady
Urszula Dudziak And Band Walk Away
Samba Ulla | Po Tamtej Stronie Gory | She Wants To Be Free | Wake Up Call | Papaya | Theme From The Motion Picture Rosemary's Baby | Sorrow Is Not Forever | No Else Thank You | Tico Tico
Live at Riviera-Remont Club,Warsaw, Poland, rec. 25.4.1989
Dudziak,Urszula (voc) | Wendt,Adam (ss,ts) | Maseli,Bernard (vib) | Jakubek,Zbigniew (keyboards) | Jastrzebski,Pawel Maciwoda (el-b) | Zawadzki,Krystof (dr)

7009-2 | CD | Karai-Eté
Duo Fenix
Catu
details unknown, rec. details unknown
Duo Fenix | Senise,Mauro (sax) | Fischer,Delia (p) | Assumpcao,Nico (b) | Bala,Carlos (dr) | Duarte,Cassio (perc) | De Cuica,Zeca (cuica) | Dauelsberg,Claudio (teclados)
Spain
Duo Fenix | Dauelsberg,Claudio (p) | Fischer,Delia (p) | Assumpcao,Nico (b) | Bala,Carlos (dr) | Duarte,Cassio (perc) | Claumir (tambourine) | Gordinho (surdo,tambourine) | Suzano,Marcos (cuica)
Via Appia
Duo Fenix | Lagrene,Bireli (g) | Dauelsberg,Claudio (p,teclados) | Mariano,Toquarto (g) | Souza,Fernado (b) | Kujack,Götz (dr) | Duarte,Cassio (perc) | Claumir (tambourine) | Gordinho (tambourine) | Jaguaraci (tambourine)
Baiao De Dois
Duo Fenix | Franco,Renato (sax) | Fischer,Delia (p) | Dauelsberg,Claudio (p) | Assumpcao,Nico (b) | Bala,Carlos (dr) | Duarte,Cassio (perc)
Raoni
Duo Fenix | Woltzenlogel,Celso (fl) | Senise,Mauro (fl) | Fischer,Delia (p) | Dauelsberg,Claudio (p) | Fialho,Tavinho (b) | Suzano,Marcos (block,caxixi,moringa,pandeiro)
Senor Mouse
Duo Fenix | Fischer,Delia (p) | Dauelsberg,Claudio (p)
Infancia
Duo Fenix | Dauelsberg,Claudio (p) | Carvalho,Alexandro (v) | Assumpcao,Nico (b) | Moreira,Jurim (dr)

7010-2 | CD | Sweet Explosion
Chico Freeman And Brainstorm
Peaceful Heart | Exotic Places | Afro Tang | My Heart | Pacifica(I,II & III) | On The Nile
Live at Ronnie Scott's,London,GB, rec. April 1990
Brainstorm | Freeman,Chico (ss,ts,synth) | Brown,Delmar (p,keyboards,voc) | Blake,Alex (b,el-b) | Campbell,Tommy (dr) | Hedman,Norman (perc)
Read The Signs
Brainstorm | Freeman,Chico (ss,ts,synth,voc) | Brown,Delmar (p,keyboards) | Blake,Alex (b,el-b) | Campbell,Tommy (dr) | Hedman,Norman (perc) | Leyh,W. (voc)

7011-2 | CD | Voicings
7011-1 | LP | Voicings
Lucas Heidepriem Quartet
Voicings | When Elephants Fall In Love | Never Did It | Giovanni | Down In Copenhagen | Stella By Starlight | Jazz Oder Später | For Albert
Freiburg,Brg., rec. details unknown
Heidepriem,Lucas (tb) | Möck,Uli 'Ull' (p,keyboards) | Höfler,Karoline (b) | Hug,Martin (dr)

7012-2 | CD | We Remember Cannon
7012-1 | LP | We Remember Cannon
Nat Adderley Quintet
I'll Remember April | Unit 7 | Talkin' About You, Cannon | The Work Song | Soul Eyes | Stella By Starlight | Autumn Leaves
Live at The Moonwalker,Aarburg,CH, rec. 18.11.1989
Adderley,Nat (co) | Herring,Vincent (as) | Resnick,Art (p) | Booker,Walter (b) | Cobb,Jimmy (dr)

7014-2 | CD | Out Of The Rim
Hans Koller Groups
In Memoriam Of Stan Getz | Out Of The Rim(1) | Kanon | Out Of The Rim(2) | Out Of The Rim(3) | Out Of The Rim(4) | Out Of The Rim(5) | Kalligrafil Dance | Lush Life | Amely | Out Of The Rim(6) | Out Of The Rim(7)
details unknown, rec. March/May & June 1991
Koller,Hans (ss,ts,sopranino) | Puschnig,Wolfgang (as) | Fuss,Martin (ts) | Dickbauer,Klaus (ts,bs) | Konrad,Bernd (as,bass-sax)
Warne Marsh(In Memoriam)
Luxembourg, rec. 1984
Koller,Hans (ts) | Marsh,Warne (ts)

7015-2 | CD | Nevertheless
7015-1 | LP | Nevertheless
Just Friends
Poobly | Some People | Sorrow Is Not Forever | In Your Eyes | Liliana | Baker's Daughter | Mute | Funky Waltz | Jazz Friends
details unknown, rec. details unknown
Just Friends | Malach,Bob (sax) | Urbaniak,Michal (el-v) | Van't Hof,Jasper (p) | Stief,Bo (b) | Mouzon,Alphonse (dr)

7016-2 | CD | Salutes The Saxophone
7016-1 | LP | Salutes The Saxophone
Roots
Cotton Tail | Parker's Mood | Impressions | You Don't Know What Love Is | The Panther | Body And Soul | St.Thomas | Red Top | Lester Leaps In
Roots | Blythe,Arthur (sax) | Freeman,Chico (sax) | Rivers,Sam (sax) | Davis,Nathan (sax) | Pullen,Don (p) | Debriano,Santi Wilson (b) | Campbell,Tommy (dr)

7016-3 | LP | Salutes The Saxophones: Tributes To Gene Ammons, Eric Dolphy, Coleman Hawkins And Charlie Parker
Parker's Mood | You Don't Know What Love Is | Body And Soul | Red Top
Roots | Blythe,Arthur (sax) | Freeman,Chico (sax) | Rivers,Sam (sax) | Davis,Nathan (sax) | Pullen,Don (p) | Debriano,Santi Wilson (b) | Campbell,Tommy (dr)

7017-2 | CD | Jazz Unlimited
Nat Adderley Quintet
The Work Song
Adderley,Nat (co) | Herring,Vincent (as) | Resnick,Art (p) | Booker,Walter (b) | Cobb,Jimmy (dr)
Airto Moreira/Flora Purim Group
Bingo
Moreira,Airto (perc) | Purim,Flora (voc) | Meek,Gary (sax) | Silva,Marcos (keyboards) | Harrison,Bob (b) | Shapiro,Michael (dr,perc,voc)
Woody Shaw Quartet
Sippin' At Bells
Shaw,Woody (tp) | Henke,Fred (p) | Swainson,Neil (b) | Deutsch,Alex (dr)
Lucas Heidepriem
For Albert
Heidepriem,Lucas (tb-solo)
Buster Williams Quintet
Something More
Williams,Buster (b) | Ohno,Shunzo (tp) | Shorter,Wayne (sax) | Hancock,Herbie (p,keyboards) | Foster,Al (dr)
Just Friends
In Your Eyes
Just Friends | Malach,Bob (sax) | Urbaniak,Michal (el-v) | Van't Hof,Jasper (p) | Stief,Bo (b) | Mouzon,Alphonse (dr)
Chico Freeman And Brainstorm
Reach Out I'll Be There - (Reach Out) I'll Be There
Freeman,Chico (sax) | Brainstorm | Brown,Delmar (keyboards,voc) | Hedman,Norman (perc) | Walker,Chris (keyboards,el-b,voc) | Walker,Archie (keyboards,dr)
Overtime
Freeman,Chico (sax) | Brainstorm | Brown,Delmar (keyboards) | Hedman,Norman (perc) | Blake,Alex (b) | Campbell,Tommy (dr)
James Blood Ulmer Group
House Blues
Ulmer,James Blood (b) | Tacuma,Jamaaladeen (b) | Weston,Grant Calvin (dr)
Roots
Lester Leaps In
Roots | Blythe,Arthur (sax) | Freeman,Chico (sax) | Rivers,Sam (sax) | Davis,Nathan (sax) | Pullen,Don (p) | Debriano,Santi Wilson (b) | Campbell,Tommy (dr)
Warne Marsh/Hans Koller
Warne Marsh(In Memoriam)
Marsh,Warne (ts) | Koller,Hans (sax)
James Blood Ulmer Quartet
Overtime
Ulmer,James Blood (b) | Adams,George (sax) | McBee,Cecil (b) | Hammond,Doug (dr)
Urszula Dudziak
Po Tamtej Stronie Gory
Dudziak,Urszula (voc-solo)

7018-2 | CD | Live at The Bayerischer Hof
7018-1 | LP | Live at The Bayerischer Hof
James Blood Ulmer Blues Experience
Burning Up | Church | Crying | Let Me Take You Home | Boss Lady | Street Bride | Timeless | Make It Right
Live at The Bayerischer Hof Club,München, rec. 25.4.1994
Ulmer,James Blood (el-g,voc) | Ali,Amin (el-b) | Dayle,Aubrey (dr)

7019-2 | CD | The Fire This Time
7019-1(Audiophile Pressing) | LP | The Fire This Time
Lester Bowie's Brass Fantasy
Night Time Is The Right Time | For Louis | Journey Towards Freedom | Remember The Time | Strange Fruit | Siesta For The Fiesta | Night Life | Black Or White | Three For The Festival | The Great Pretender
Live at The Moonwalker,Aarburg,CH, rec. 1.5.1992
Bowie,Lester (tp) | Allen,Eddie E.J. (tp) | Brazel,Gerald (tp) | Barrero,Tony (tp) | Lacy,Ku-umba Frank (tb) | Bonilla,Luis (tb) | Chancey,Vincent (fr-h) | Stewart,Robert 'Bob' (tuba) | Johnson,Vinnie (dr) | Moye,Famoudou Don (perc)

7020-1 | LP | Welcome Mr. Chancey
7020-2 | CD | Welcome Mr. Chancey
Vincent Chancey Quartet
The Man Say Something | The Spell | A Night To Remember | A Day In Ocho Rios | Barefoot Bahian Girl | Chazz
Brooklyn,NY, rec. June 1989
Chancey,Vincent (fr-h) | Gilmore,David (g) | Harris,Kevin Bruce (el-b) | Burrage,Ronnie (dr)

7021-2 | CD | Stablemates
Roots
Stolen Moments | Linden Boulevard | Requiem For A Rabbit | I Remember Eric Dolphy | Stablemates | Ah, George, We Hardly Knew Ya' | Walkin'
Heidelberg, rec. 14./15.2.1992
Roots | Blythe,Arthur (ss,as) | Davis,Nathan (ss,as,ts) | Freeman,Chico (ss,as,ts) | Rivers,Sam (ss,ts) | Pullen,Don (p,org) | Debriano,Santi Wilson (b) | Muhammad,Idris[Leo Morris] (dr)
Night Train
Heidelberg, rec. 14./15.12.1992
Roots | Blythe,Arthur (ss,as) | Davis,Nathan (ss,as,ts) | Freeman,Chico (ss,as,ts) | Rivers,Sam (ss,ts) | Nieberle,Helmut (g) | Pullen,Don (p,org) | Debriano,Santi Wilson (b) | Muhammad,Idris[Leo Morris] (dr)
The Party's Over
Heidelberg, rec. 14./15.2.1992
Roots | Blythe,Arthur (ss,as) | Davis,Nathan (ss,as,ts) | Freeman,Chico (ss,as,ts) | Rivers,Sam (ss,ts) | Kagerer,Helmut (g) | Pullen,Don (p,org) | Debriano,Santi Wilson (b) | Muhammad,Idris[Leo Morris] (dr)

7022-2 | CD | Threshold
Chico Freeman And Brainstorm
Mist | Blues For Miles | Chejudo
Heidelberg, rec. 27./28.10.1992
Freeman,Chico (sax) | Brainstorm | Lee,Jack (g) | Evans,Vincent Leroy (p,keyboards) | Dyson,Dave (b) | Jackson,Gene (dr) | Hedman,Norman (perc)
Chant | The Awakening
Freeman,Chico (sax) | Brainstorm | Lee,Jack (g) | Evans,Vincent Leroy (p,keyboards) | Dyson,Dave (b) | Jackson,Gene (dr) | Hedman,Norman (perc) | Khumalo,Thulise (voc)
Subway
Freeman,Chico (sax) | Brainstorm | Lee,Jack (g) | Evans,Vincent Leroy (p,keyboards) | Dyson,Dave (b) | Jackson,Gene (dr) | Hedman,Norman (perc) | Dyer,Ada (voc) | Re,Andrea (voc) | Jackson,Rita (voc) | Harris,Rodney (rap)
Trespasser
Freeman,Chico (sax) | Brainstorm | Lee,Jack (g) | Evans,Vincent Leroy (p,keyboards) | Dyson,Dave (b) | Jackson,Gene (dr) | Hedman,Norman (perc) | Dudziak,Urszula (voc) | Harris,Rodney (rap)
Duet | Lena's Lullaby | Oleo
Freeman,Chico (sax) | Brainstorm | Lee,Jack (g) | Evans,Vincent Leroy (p,keyboards) | Dyson,Dave (b) | Jackson,Gene (dr) | Hedman,Norman (perc) | Dudziak,Urszula (voc)

7025-2 | CD | Shades Of Chas Burchell
7025-1(Audiophile Pressing) | LP | Shades Of Chas Burchell
The Mike Hennessey Chastet
Shades | High On You | Blues On My Mind | Days Of Wine And Roses | Dreamstepper | Dig It | Gaby | Just Friends | Soft Shoe | Hanging Loose | Westwood Walk | Fair Weather | You've Changed
Sandhausen, rec. 3./4.10.1993
Hennessey,Mike (p) | Wood,Brian (tp) | Carter,Geoff (cl,ts) | Simmons,Alan (b) | Merritt,Al (dr)

7026-2 | CD | Unsong Hero:The Undiscovered Genius Of Chas Burchell
Chas Burchell Quintet
Juicy Lucy | Bobblin' | Gone Into It
London,GB, rec. 1962
Burchell,Chas (ts) | Wood,Brian (tp) | Hennessey,Mike (p) | Simmons,Alan (b) | Scott,Mike (dr)
Chas Burchell Trio/Quartet
Have You Met Miss Jones
Thistleworth Tennis Club,Osterley,Middlesex,GB, rec. ca.1977
Burchell,Chas (ts) | Eppy,Bernard (p) | Adams,Alec (dr) | Simmons,Alan (b-overdubbed)
Chas Burchell Sextet
It's You Or No One- | Shades- | Marsh Bars | Which Way?
Town House Club,London,GB, rec. 15.1.1980
Burchell,Chas (ts) | Wood,Brian (tp) | Hirschman,Bob (tb) | Hennessey,Mike (p) | Simmons,Alan (b) | Merritt,Al (dr)
Clark Terry Quintet
Just Squeeze Me(But Don't Tease Me) | Blue Monk
Pengethley Manor Hotel,Herfordshire,GB, rec. 20.5.1982
Terry,Clark (tp,fl-h,voc) | Burchell,Chas (ts) | Hennessey,Mike (p) | Simmons,Alan (b) | Merritt,Al (dr)
Chas Burchell Quartet
Tickle Toe | Comeback
Mike Hennessey's Home,West Hampstaed,GB, rec. 1984
Burchell,Chas (ts) | Hennessey,Mike (p) | Simmons,Alan (b) | Merritt,Al (dr)
Chas Burchell Quintet
Sometimes
Thistleworth Tennis Club,Osterley,Middlesex,GB, rec. 1984 or 1985
Burchell,Chas (ts) | Wood,Brian (tp) | Hennessey,Mike (p) | Simmons,Alan (b) | Merritt,Al (dr)
Ronnie Scott With The Chas Burchell Quintet
Sonnymoon For Two
Rest Hotel,Kenton,Middlesex,GB, rec. 28.5.1985
Scott,Ronnie (ts) | Burchell,Chas (ts) | Wood,Brian (tp) | Hennessey,Mike (p) | Simmons,Alan (b) | Merritt,Al (dr)
Geoff Carter Quintet
Solea
London,GB, rec. October 1993
Carter,Geoff (ts) | Wood,Brian (tp) | Ross,Matt (p) | Simmons,Alan (b) | Merritt,Al (dr)

77024-2 | CD | Saturation
7024-1 | LP | Saturation
Walkaway With Urszula Dudziak
Saturation | Many Kochanas | For You | Bobok | Softly | Sheet | She's Like A Sexmachine | Joy Is Better | Sambula
Krakow,Poland, rec. 11.5.1993
Walkaway | Wendt,Adam (ss,ts) | Jakubek,Zbigniew (keyboards) | Maseli,Marek (synth) | Blaszczyk,Marek (el-b) | Zawadzki,Krystof (dr,cymbals) | Noya,Nippy (perc) | Dudziak,Urszula (voc)

77027-2 | CD | Conversations
7027-1 | LP | Conversations
Karl Berger-Carlos Ward Duo
At Last | Out There Alone
New Jersey,NJ, rec. 11.-14.3.1994
Berger,Karl (vib,p) | Ward,Carlos (fl,as)
Karl Berger-Dave Holland Duo
Presently | Still
Berger,Karl (vib,p) | Holland,Dave (b)
Karl Berger-Marc Feldman Duo
Lover Man(Oh,Where Can You Be?) | Another
Berger,Karl (vib,p) | Feldman,Mark (v)
Karl Berger-Ray Anderson Duo
Bemsha Swing | St.Thomas
Berger,Karl (vib,p) | Anderson,Ray (tb)
Karl Berger-Ingrid Sertso Duo
Why Is It That It's Not | Freedom, Getting There
Berger,Karl (vib,p) | Sertso,Ingrid (voc)
Karl Berger-James Blood Ulmer Duo
North | South
Berger,Karl (vib,p) | Ulmer,James Blood (el-g)

77028-2 | CD | The Art Of Jazz
7028-1 | LP | The Art Of Jazz
Art Blakey And The Jazz Messengers
Two Of A Kind | Moanin' | Along Came Betty | Lester Left Town | Mr.Blakey | Blues March | Drum Duo(Art Blakey & Roy Haynes) | Buhaina's Valediction
Live,at 'Jazztage' Leverkusen, rec. 9.10.1989
Blakey,Art (dr) | Blanchard,Terence (tp) | Hubbard,Freddie (tp) | Lynch,Brian (tp) | Fuller,Curtis (tb) | Lacy,Ku-umba Frank (tb) | McLean,Jackie (as) | Golson,Benny (ts) | Shorter,Wayne (ts) | Jackson,Javon (ts) | Davis Jr.,Walter (p) | Keezer,Geoff (p) | Williams,Buster (b) | Haynes,Roy (dr) | Hendricks,Michelle (voc)
Art Blakey
Interview(12:49) with Art Blakey by Mike Hennessey
Nice,France, rec. 14.7.1976
Blakey,Art (talking)
-> Different combinations!

77030-2 | CD | Cris De Balaines
7030-1 | LP | Cris De Balaines
Francis Coletta Trio + One
Invention | E-Flat Blues | La Boheme | Misty Cat | Corrida | Roberto | Onion Field | Bravo | Circus | Cris De Balaines | Three Views Of A Secret | Drum Meets Bum | Samba
Klangstudio Leyh,Sandhausen, rec. February 1996
Coletta,Francis (g) | Mayer,Capo (b) | Lübke,Peter (dr) | Civilotti,Anibal (perc)

77031-2 | CD | Saying Something
7031-1(Audiophile Pressing) | LP | Saying Something
Roots

Lester Left Town | Night Dreamer | Heaven Dance | Ballads For Trane: | It's Easy To Remember- | Soul Eyes- | You Leave Me Breathless- | In A Sentimental Mood- | How Deep Is The Ocean- | Samba For Now | Toku-Do | Lester Leaps In
Live at Muddy's Club,Weinheim, rec. 14.6.1995
Roots | Blythe,Arthur (as) | Davis,Nathan (ss,ts) | Freeman,Chico (ts) | Golson,Benny (ts) | Lightsey,Kirk (p) | Williams,Buster (b) | Thigpen,Ed (dr)

77035-2 | CD | Der Erste Bericht
Carl Ludwig Hübsch
M1 | Lacaille 8760 | M2 | M3 | Kashmir | Wolf 424 | M4 | Prokyon | Ross 780 | Groombridge 34 | M5 | M6
Köln, rec. 1996/1979
Hübsch,Carl Ludwig 'Lu' (tuba)

77039-2 | CD | For Diz & Bird
Roots
Blue 'N' Boogie | Yardbird Suite | Bebop | Moose The Mooche
Sandhausen, rec. July 1996
Roots | Roditi,Claudio (tp) | Blythe,Arthur (as) | Davis,Nathan (ss,ts) | Freeman,Chico (ss,ts) | Golson,Benny (ts,ld) | Lightsey,Kirk (p) | Williams,Buster (b) | Thigpen,Ed (dr)
Stolen Moments | Toku-Do | To Hear A Teardrop In The Rain | Lester Leaps In
Live at The Cheltenham Jazz Festival,GB, rec. 14.4.1996
Roots | Blythe,Arthur (as) | Davis,Nathan (ss,ts) | Freeman,Chico (ss,ts) | Golson,Benny (ts,ld) | Lightsey,Kirk (p) | Williams,Buster (b) | Thigpen,Ed (dr)

77040-2 | CD | Play It Again Paul
Paul Kuhn Trio
More | Sugar Daddy | A Child Is Born | Anthropology | Don't Get Around Much Anymore | Prelude To A Kiss
Sandhausen, rec. 6./7.7.2000
Kuhn,Paul (p) | Ulrich,Paul G. (b) | Ketzer,Willy (dr)
'Deed I Do | A Foggy Day(In London Town) | The Nearness Of You
Kuhn,Paul (p,voc) | Ulrich,Paul G. (b) | Ketzer,Willy (dr)
Paul Kuhn Trio With Greetje Kauffeld
Falling In Love With Love | Tenderly | They Can't Take That Away From Me
Kuhn,Paul (p) | Ulrich,Paul G. (b) | Ketzer,Willy (dr) | Kauffeld,Greetje (voc)
Paul Kuhn Trio With Jean 'Toots' Thielemans
The Nearness Of You(harm-solo) | Just Friends | Polka Dots And Moonbeams
Kuhn,Paul (p) | Ulrich,Paul G. (b) | Ketzer,Willy (dr) | Thielemans,Jean 'Toots' (harm)
Paul Kuhn Trio With Greetje Kauffeld And Jean 'Toots' Thielemans
You Make Me Feel So Young
Kuhn,Paul (p,voc) | Ulrich,Paul G. (b) | Ketzer,Willy (dr) | Thielemans,Jean 'Toots' (harm) | Kauffeld,Greetje (voc)

77041-2 | CD | Toots Thielemans:The Live Takes Vol.1
Toots Thielemans Quartet
I Do It For Your Love | Three Views Of A Secret
Live at The Forum,Liege,Belgium, rec. March 1994
Thielemans,Jean 'Toots' (harm) | Herr,Michel (p,keyboards) | Hatzigeorgiou,Michel (b) | Castellucci,Bruno (dr)
That Misty Red Beast
Live at De Plote,Ternat,Belgium, rec. April 1994
Thielemans,Jean 'Toots' (harm) | Werner,Kenny (keyboards) | Anderson,Jay (b) | Nussbaum,Adam (dr)
Body And Soul | All The Way
Live at Biblo,Kalmhout,Belgium, rec. February 1995
Thielemans,Jean 'Toots' (harm) | Werner,Kenny (keyboards) | Anderson,Jay (b) | Nussbaum,Adam (dr)
Toots Thielemans-Michel Herr
Stardust
Live at DeSingel,Antwerp,Belgium, rec. February 1995
Thielemans,Jean 'Toots' (harm) | Herr,Michel (p)
Toots Thielemans Quartet
Comecar De Novo | Hard To Say Goodbye
Live at 'Birdland',NYC, rec. November 1997
Thielemans,Jean 'Toots' (harm) | Werner,Kenny (keyboards) | Drummond,Ray (b) | Uotila,Jukkis (dr)
I Loves You Porgy- | Summertime-
Live at The Palais Des Congres,Brussels,Belgium, rec. October 1998
Thielemans,Jean 'Toots' (harm) | Loriers,Natalie (p) | La Rocca,Sal (b) | Castellucci,Bruno (dr)

77045-2 | CD | The Art Of Three | EAN 798747704526
Billy Cobham Trio
Stella By Starlight | Autumn Leaves | New Waltz | Bouncing With Bud | Round About Midnight | And Then Again | I Thought About You | Someday My Prince Will Come
Live at Odense,Denmark & Oslo,Norway, rec. January 2001
Cobham,Billy (dr) | Barron,Kenny (p) | Carter,Ron (b)

77047-2 | CD | Swinging Piano Classics
Eugen Cicero-Decebal Badila
Christina's Song | Sonata In C-Major | Fantasy & Prelude | Misty- | Tea For Two- | Ah! Vous Dirais-Je,Maman | Fantasy In D-Minor | Sunny | Autumn Leaves | Badinerie | Rumanian Folk Song | Heidschi Bumbeidschi
Live at Kursaal,Überlingen, rec. 13.12.1996
Cicero,Eugen (p) | Badila,Decebal (b)

77059-2 | CD | Arise
Lynne Arriale Trio
Frevo | American Woman | Arise | Lean On Me | Esperanza | Change The World | The Fallen | Upswing | Kum Ba Ya
NYC, rec. 2003
Arriale,Lynne (p) | Anderson,Jay (b) | Davis,Steve (dr)

77061-2 | CD | Love Stories
Joachim Kühn-Rolf Kühn
Misty | Like Someone In Love | In Your Own Sweet Way | Angel Eyes | What Is This Thing Called Love | I Love You | Easy Living | The Man I Love | Peace | Free Love
details unknown, rec. details unknown
Kühn,Rolf (cl) | Kühn,Joachim (p)

77063-2 | CD | Art Of Five
Billy Cobham Group
Lzatso | Good For The Soul | Jacquelyne | Carmouflage | Time Lapse Photos | Infinite Heart | My Brother | Change Parners
Cobham,Billy (dr) | Barker,Guy (tp) | Reed,Eric (p) | Joseph,Julian (p) | Harrison,Donald (as) | Le Flemming,Orlando (b) | Hurst III,Robert Leslie (b)

78011-2 | 5 CD | Jazz:The Essential Collection Vol.1
King Oliver's Creole Jazz Band
Canal Street Blues | Mandy Lee Blues | Snake Rag
Richmond, Indiana, rec. 5.4.1923
Oliver,Joseph 'King' (co) | Armstrong,Louis (co) | Dutrey,Honore (tb) | Dodds,Johnny (cl) | Armstrong [Hardin],Lil (p) | Johnson,Bill (bj) | Dodds,Warren 'Baby' (dr)
Weather Bird Rag | Dippermouth Blues | Froggie Moore
Richmond, Indiana, rec. 6.4.1923
Oliver,Joseph 'King' (co) | Armstrong,Louis (co) | Dutrey,Honore (tb) | Dodds,Johnny (cl) | Armstrong [Hardin],Lil (p) | Johnson,Bill (bj,voc) | Dodds,Warren 'Baby' (dr)
Sweet Lovin' Man
Chicago,Ill, rec. 22.6.1923
Oliver,Joseph 'King' (co) | Armstrong,Louis (co) | Dutrey,Honore (tb) | Dodds,Johnny (cl) | Armstrong [Hardin],Lil (p) | Scott,Bud (bj,voc) | Dodds,Warren 'Baby' (dr)
Dippermouth Blues | Jazzin' Babies Blues
Chicago,Ill, rec. 23.6.1923
Oliver,Joseph 'King' (co) | Armstrong,Louis (co) | Dutrey,Honore (tb) | Dodds,Johnny (cl) | Armstrong [Hardin],Lil (p) | Scott,Bud (bj,voc) | Dodds,Warren 'Baby' (dr)
Alligator Hop
Richmond, Indiana, rec. 5.10.1923
Oliver,Joseph 'King' (co) | Armstrong,Louis (co) | Dutrey,Honore (tb) | Dodds,Johnny (cl) | Evans,Paul 'Stump' (c-mel-sax) | Armstrong [Hardin],Lil (p) | St.Cyr,Johnny (bj) | Dodds,Warren 'Baby' (dr)
King Oliver's Jazz Band
Chattanooga Stomp
Chicago,Ill, rec. 15.10.1923
Oliver,Joseph 'King' (co) | Armstrong,Louis (co) | Atkins,Ed (tb) | Noone,Jimmie (cl) | Armstrong [Hardin],Lil (p) | St.Cyr,Johnny (bj) | Dodds,Warren 'Baby' (dr)
London Cafe Blues(A New Orleans Stomp)
Chicago,Ill, rec. 16.10.1923
Oliver,Joseph 'King' (co) | Armstrong,Louis (co) | Atkins,Ed (tb) | Bailey,Buster (cl) | Armstrong [Hardin],Lil (p) | St.Cyr,Johnny (bj) | Dodds,Warren 'Baby' (dr)
Buddy's Habits | Tears
Chicago,Ill, rec. 25.10.1923
Oliver,Joseph 'King' (co) | Armstrong,Louis (co,slide-whistle) | Dutrey,Honore (tb) | Dodds,Johnny (cl) | Jackson,Charlie (bass-s) | St.Cyr,Johnny (bj) | Armstrong [Hardin],Lil (p) | Dodds,Warren 'Baby' (dr)
Riverside Blues | Sweet Baby Doll | Working Man Blues | Mabel's Dream
Chicago,Ill, rec. 26.10.1923
Oliver,Joseph 'King' (co) | Armstrong,Louis (co) | Dutrey,Honore (tb) | Dodds,Johnny (cl) | Jackson,Charlie (bass-s) | Armstrong [Hardin],Lil (p) | St.Cyr,Johnny (bj) | Dodds,Warren 'Baby' (dr)
The Southern Stomps
Chicago,Ill, rec. 24.12.1923
Oliver,Joseph 'King' (co) | Armstrong,Louis (co) | Dutrey,Honore (tb) | Dodds,Johnny (cl) | Jackson,Charlie (bass-s) | Armstrong [Hardin],Lil (p) | Dodds,Warren 'Baby' (dr)
Sippie Wallace With King Oliver And Hersal Thomas
Morning Dove Blues
Chicago,Ill, rec. 24.2.1925
Wallace,Sippie (voc) | Oliver,Joseph 'King' (co) | Thomas,Hersal (p)
King Oliver's Jazz Band
Too Bad
Chicago,Ill, rec. 11.3.1926
Oliver,Joseph 'King' (co) | Shoffner,Bob (tp) | Ory,Edward 'Kid' (tb) | Nicholas,Albert (cl,ss,as) | Paige,Billy (cl,ss,as) | Bigard,Barney (ss,ts) | Russell,Luis (p) | Scott,Bud (bj) | Cobb,Bert (tuba) | Barbarin,Paul (dr)
King Oliver And His Dixie Syncopators
Wa-Wa-Wa
Chicago,Ill, rec. 29.5.1926
Oliver,Joseph 'King' (co) | Shoffner,Bob (tp) | Ory,Edward 'Kid' (tb) | Nicholas,Albert (cl,as) | Paige,Billy (cl,as) | Bigard,Barney (cl,ts) | Russell,Luis (p) | Scott,Bud (bj,voc) | Cobb,Bert (tuba) | Barbarin,Paul (dr)
Snag It
Chicago,Ill, rec. 17.9.1926
Oliver,Joseph 'King' (co) | Shoffner,Bob (tp) | Ory,Edward 'Kid' (tb) | Evans,Paul 'Stump' (ss,as) | Howard,Darnell (cl,as) | Bigard,Barney (cl,ts) | Russell,Luis (p) | Scott,Bud (bj) | Cobb,Bert (tuba) | Barbarin,Paul (dr)
Blind Willie Dunn's Gin Bottle Four
Jet Black Blues
Chicago,Ill, rec. 30.4.1929
Blind Willie Dunn's Gin Bottle Four | Oliver,Joseph 'King' (co) | Shoffner,Bob (tp) | Johnson,J.C. prob. (p) | Lang,Eddie (g) | Johnson,Lonnie (g) | Carmichael,Hoagy (perc,voc)
King Oliver And His Orchestra
Sweet Like This | Too Late
NYC, rec. 8.10.1929
Oliver,Joseph 'King' (tp) | Nelson,Davidson C.'Dave' (tp) | Archey,Jimmy (tb) | Holmes,Bobby (cl,as) | Jefferson,Hilton or Glyn Pacque (as) | Frazier,Charles prob. (ts) | Frye,Don (p) | Taylor,Arthur or Walter Jones (bj) | Walker,Clinton (tuba) | Jones,Edmond (dr) | Rodgers,George (cond)
Jelly Roll Morton
King Porter Stomp
Chicago,Ill, rec. 20.4.1926
Morton,Jelly Roll (p-solo)
Jelly Roll Morton's Red Hot Peppers
Black Bottom Stomp | Smokehouse Blues | The Chant
Chicago,Ill, rec. 15.9.1926
Morton,Jelly Roll (p) | Mitchell,George (co) | Ory,Edward 'Kid' (tb) | Simeon,Omer (cl) | St.Cyr,Johnny (bj) | Lindsey,Johny (b) | Hilaire,Andrew (dr)
Sidewalk Blues | Dead Man Blues
Chicago,Ill, rec. 21.9.1926
Morton,Jelly Roll (p,voc) | Mitchell,George (co) | Ory,Edward 'Kid' (tb) | Simeon,Omer (cl) | Bigard,Barney (cl) | Howard,Darnell (cl) | St.Cyr,Johnny (bj) | Lindsey,Johny (b) | Hilaire,Andrew (dr) | Bloom,Marty (effects)
Steamboat Stomp
Morton,Jelly Roll (p) | Mitchell,George (co) | Ory,Edward 'Kid' (tb) | Simeon,Omer (cl) | St.Cyr,Johnny (bj) | Lindsey,Johny (b) | Hilaire,Andrew (dr) | Bloom,Marty (effects)
Grandpa's Spells | Original Jelly Roll Blues | Doctor Jazz | Cannon Ball Blues
Chicago,Ill, rec. 16.12.1926
Morton,Jelly Roll (p,voc) | Mitchell,George (co) | Ory,Edward 'Kid' (tb) | Simeon,Omer (cl,b-cl) | St.Cyr,Johnny (g) | Lindsey,Johny (b) | Hilaire,Andrew (dr)
Wild Man Blues | Jungle Blues
Chicago,Ill, rec. 4.6.1927
Morton,Jelly Roll (p,voc) | Mitchell,George (co) | Reeves,Gerald (tb) | Dodds,Johnny (cl) | Evans,Paul 'Stump' (as) | Scott,Bud (g) | Wilson,Quinn (tuba) | Dodds,Warren 'Baby' (dr)
Beale Street Blues | The Pearls
Chicago,Ill, rec. 10.6.1927
Morton,Jelly Roll (p) | Mitchell,George (co) | Reeves,Gerald (tb) | Dodds,Johnny (cl) | Evans,Paul 'Stump' (as) | Scott,Bud (g) | Wilson,Quinn (tuba) | Dodds,Warren 'Baby' (dr)
Jelly Roll Morton Trio
Wolverine Blues | Mr.Jelly Lord
Morton,Jelly Roll (p) | Dodds,Johnny (cl) | Dodds,Warren 'Baby' (traps)
Jelly Roll Morton's Red Hot Peppers
Georgia Swing | Kansas City Stomps | Shoe Shiner's Drag
NYC, rec. 11.6.1928
Morton,Jelly Roll (p) | Pinkett,Ward (tp) | Fields,Geechie (tb) | Simeon,Omer (cl) | Blair,Lee (bj) | Benford,Bill (tuba) | Benford,Tommy (dr)
Jelly Roll Morton And His Orchestra
Deep Creek
NYC, rec. 6.12.1928
Morton,Jelly Roll (p) | Anderson,Edward (tp) | Swayzee,Edwin (tp) | Kato,William G. (tb) | Procope,Russell (cl,as) | Barnes,Paul (ss) | Garland,Joe (ts) | Blair,Lee (g) | Moore,Bass (tuba) | Johnson,Manzie (dr)
Jelly Roll Morton
Pep | Seattle Hunch
Camden,NJ, rec. 8.7.1929
Morton,Jelly Roll (p-solo)
Bessie Smith And Her Band
Sing Sing Prison Blues
NYC, rec. 6.12.1924
Smith,Bessie (voc) | Bailey,Buster (cl) | Redman,Don (cl) | Longshaw,Fred (p)
Dying Gambler's Blues
NYC, rec. 13.12.1924
Smith,Bessie (voc) | Green,Charlie (tb) | Longshaw,Fred (p)
Bessie Smith With Louis Armstrong And Fred Longshaw
St.Louis Blues | Reckless Blues | Sobbin' Hearted Blues | Cold In Hand Blues | You've Been A Good Old Wagon(Daddy But You Done Broke Down)
NYC, rec. 14.1.1925
Smith,Bessie (voc) | Armstrong,Louis (co) | Longshaw,Fred (p,harmonium)
Henderson's Hot Six
Cakewalkin' Babies From Home
NYC, rec. 5.5.1925
Smith,Bessie (voc) | Henderson,Fletcher (p) | Smith,Joe (co) | Green,Charlie (tb) | Hawkins,Coleman (ts) | Dixon,Charlie (bj) | Escudero,Ralph (tuba)
Bessie Smith And Her Band
Soft Pedal Blues
NYC, rec. 14.5.1925
Smith,Bessie (voc) | Green,Charlie (tb) | Henderson,Fletcher (p)
Nashville Woman's Blues
NYC, rec. 26.5.1925
Smith,Bessie (voc) | Armstrong,Louis (co) | Green,Charlie (tb) | Henderson,Fletcher (p)
Muddy Water(A Mississippi Moan)
NYC, rec. 2.3.1927
Smith,Bessie (voc) | Smith,Joe (co) | Harrison,Jimmy (tb) | Bailey,Buster (cl) | Hawkins,Coleman (cl) | Henderson,Fletcher (p) | Dixon,Charlie (bj)
Bessie Smith With Her Blue Boys
Trombone Cholly | Send Me To The 'Lectric Chair | Them's Graveyard Words
NYC, rec. 3.3.1927
Smith,Bessie (voc) | Smith,Joe (co) | Harrison,Jimmy (tb) | Henderson,Fletcher (p)
Bessie Smith With James P. Johnson
Sweet Mistreater | Lock And Key
NYC, rec. 1.4.1927
Smith,Bessie (voc) | Johnson,James P. (p)
Bessie Smith And Her Band
Mean Old Bed Bug Blues | A Good Man Is Hard To Find
NYC, rec. 27.9.1927
Smith,Bessie (voc) | Grainger,Porter (p) | Conaway,Lincoln (g)
Homeless Blues
NYC, rec. 28.9.1927
Smith,Bessie (voc) | Elliott,Ernest (as) | Grainger,Porter (p)
Dyin' By The Hour | Foolish Man Blues
NYC, rec. 27.10.1927
Smith,Bessie (voc) | Ladnier,Tommy (tp) | Henderson,Fletcher (p) | Cole,June (tuba)
Thinking Blues | Pick Pocket Blues
NYC, rec. 9.2.1928
Smith,Bessie (voc) | Dean,Demas (tp) | Green,Charlie (tb) | Longshaw,Fred (p)
Clarence Williams' Blue Five
Wild Cat Blues | Kansas City Moan
NYC, rec. 30.7.1923
Williams,Clarence (p) | Morris,Thomas (co) | Mayfield,John (tb) | Bechet,Sidney (cl,ss) | Christian,Buddy (bj)
Texas Moaner Blues
NYC, rec. 17.10.1924
Williams,Clarence (p) | Armstrong,Louis (co) | Irvis,Charlie (tb) | Bechet,Sidney (cl,ss) | Christian,Buddy (bj)
Cakewalkin' Babies From Home
NYC, rec. 8.1.1925
Williams,Clarence (p) | Armstrong,Louis (co) | Irvis,Charlie (tb) | Bechet,Sidney (cl,ss) | Christian,Buddy (bj) | Taylor,Eva (voc)
New Orleans Feetwarmers
Maple Leaf Rag
NYC, rec. 15.9.1932
New Orleans Feetwarmers,The | Ladnier,Tommy (tp) | Nixon,Teddy (tb) | Bechet,Sidney (cl,ss) | Duncan,Hank (p) | Myers,Wilson Ernest (b) | Morand,Morris (dr)
Tommy Ladnier And His Orchestra
Really The Blues
NYC, rec. 28.11.1932
Ladnier,Tommy (tp) | Bechet,Sidney (cl,ss) | Mezzrow,Milton Mezz (cl,ts) | Jackson,Cliff (p) | James,Elmer (b) | Johnson,Manzie (dr)
Bechet-Spanier Big Four
Up A Lazy River | China Boy
NYC, rec. 28.3.1940
Spanier,Francis 'Muggsy' (co) | Bechet,Sidney (cl,ss) | Mastren,Carmen (g) | Braud,Wellman (b)
New Orleans Feetwarmers
Shake It And Break It | Old Man Blues | Wild Man Blues | Nobody Knows The Way I Feel This Morning
NYC, rec. 4.6.1940
New Orleans Feetwarmers,The | DeParis,Sidney (tp) | Williams,Sandy (tb) | Bechet,Sidney (ss) | Jackson,Cliff (p) | Addison,Bernard (g) | Braud,Wellman (b) | Catlett,Big Sid (dr)
Sidney Bechet Trio
Blues In Thirds
Chicago,Ill, rec. 6.9.1940
Bechet,Sidney (cl) | Hines,Earl 'Fatha' (p) | Dodds,Warren 'Baby' (dr)
New Orleans Feetwarmers
Coal Black Shine | Egyptain Fantasy | Slippin' And Slidin'
NYC, rec. 8.1.1941
New Orleans Feetwarmers,The | Allen,Henry Red (tp) | Higginbotham,J.C. (tb) | Bechet,Sidney (cl) | Tolliver,James (p) | Braud,Wellman (b) | Heard,J.C. (dr)
Sidney Bechet's Blue Note Jazzmen
Blue Horizon
NYC, rec. 20.12.1944
Bechet,Sidney (cl,ss) | DeParis,Sidney (tp) | Dickenson,Vic (tb) | Hodes,Art (p) | Foster,George 'Pops' (b) | Johnson,Manzie (dr)
Bunk Johnson-Sidney Bechet Sextet
Milneberg Joys | Lord, Let Me In The Lifeboat | Days Beyond Recall | Up In Sidney's Flat
NYC, rec. 10.3.1945
Johnson,Bunk (tp) | Bechet,Sidney (cl) | Williams,Sandy (tb) | Jackson,Cliff (p) | Foster,George 'Pops' (b) | Johnson,Manzie (dr)
Fletcher Henderson And His Orchestra
Go Long Mule
NYC, rec. 7.10.1924
Henderson,Fletcher (p) | Scott,Howard (tp) | Chambers,Elmer (tp) | Armstrong,Louis (tp) | Green,Charlie (tb) | Bailey,Buster (cl,ss,as) | Redman,Don (cl,as) | Hawkins,Coleman (cl,ts) | Dixon,Charlie (bj) | Escudero,Bob (tuba) | Marshall,Kaiser (dr)
Shanghai Shuffle
NYC, rec. 10.10.1924
Henderson,Fletcher (p) | Scott,Howard (tp) | Chambers,Elmer (tp) | Armstrong,Louis (tp) | Green,Charlie (tb) | Bailey,Buster (cl,ss,as) | Redman,Don (cl,as) | Hawkins,Coleman (cl,ts) | Dixon,Charlie (bj) | Escudero,Bob (tuba) | Marshall,Kaiser (dr)
Copenhagen
NYC, rec. 30.10.1924
Henderson,Fletcher (p) | Scott,Howard (tp) | Chambers,Elmer (tp) | Armstrong,Louis (tp) | Green,Charlie (tb) | Bailey,Buster (cl,ss,as) | Redman,Don (cl,as) | Hawkins,Coleman (cl,ts) | Dixon,Charlie (bj) | Escudero,Bob (tuba) | Marshall,Kaiser (dr)
The Lousiana Stompers
Hop Off
NYC, rec. September/October 1927
Louisiana Stompers,The | Henderson,Fletcher (p) | Smith,Russell prob. (tp) | Smith,Joe (co) | Morton,Benny prob. (tb) | Bailey,Buster (cl,as) | Pasquall,Jerome (as) | Hawkins,Coleman (bass-sax) | Dixon,Charlie (bj)
Fletcher Henderson And His Orchestra
Keep A Song In Your Soul
NYC, rec. 2.12.1930
Henderson,Fletcher (p) | Smith,Russell (tp) | Stark,Bobby (tp) | Stewart,Rex (co) | Harrison,Jimmy (tb) | Jones,Claude (tb) | Carter,Benny (cl,as) | Boone,Harvey (as) | Hawkins,Coleman (ts) | Holiday,Clarence (g,bj) | Kirby,John (b,tuba) | Johnson,Walter (dr)
Sugarfoot Stomp | Hot And Anxious
NYC, rec. 19.3.1931
Henderson,Fletcher (p) | Smith,Russell (tp) | Stewart,Rex (tp) | Stark,Bobby (tp) | Jones,Claude (tb) | Morton,Benny (tb) | Boone,Harvey (as) | Procope,Russell (cl,as) | Hawkins,Coleman (cl,ts,bs) | Holiday,Clarence (g,bj) | Kirby,John (tuba) | Johnson,Walter (dr)

Honeysuckle Rose | New King Porter Stomp
NYC, rec. 9..12.1932
Henderson,Fletcher (p) | Smith,Russell (tp) | Stark,Bobby (tp) | Stewart,Rex (co) | Higginbotham,J.C. (tb) | Procope,Russell (cl,as) | Jefferson,Hilton (as) | Hawkins,Coleman (ts) | White,Freddy (bj) | Kirby,John (tuba) | Johnson,Walter (dr)

Queer Notions
NYC, rec. 18.8.1933
Henderson,Fletcher (p) | Smith,Russell (tp) | Stark,Bobby (tp) | Allen,Henry Red (tp) | Wells,Dicky (tb) | Williams,Sandy (tb) | Procope,Russell (cl,as) | Jefferson,Hilton (as) | Hawkins,Coleman (cl,ts) | Addison,Bernard (g) | Kirby,John (b) | Johnson,Walter (dr)

It's The Talk Of The Town
NYC, rec. 22.9.1933
Smith,Russell (tp) | Stark,Bobby (tp) | Allen,Henry Red (tp) | Wells,Dicky (tb) | Jones,Claude (tb) | Procope,Russell (cl,as) | Jefferson,Hilton (as) | Hawkins,Coleman (cl,ts) | Henderson,Horace (p) | Addison,Bernard (g) | Kirby,John (b) | Johnson,Walter (dr) | Henderson,Fletcher (ld)

I'm Rhythm Crazy Now | I've Got To Sing A Torch Song
NYC, rec. 3.10.1033
Smith,Russell (tp) | Stark,Bobby (tp) | Allen,Henry Red (tp) | Wells,Dicky (tb) | Jones,Claude (tb) | Procope,Russell (cl,as) | Jefferson,Hilton (as) | Hawkins,Coleman (cl,ts) | Henderson,Horace (p) | Addison,Bernard (g) | Kirby,John (b) | Johnson,Walter (dr) | Henderson,Fletcher (ld)

Down South Camp Meeting | Wrappin' It Up
NYC, rec. 12.9.1934
Smith,Russell (tp) | Randolph,Irving 'Mouse' (tp) | Allen,Henry Red (tp) | Jones,Claude (tb) | Johnson,Keg (tb) | Bailey,Buster (cl,ts) | Procope,Russell (cl,as) | Jefferson,Hilton (cl,as) | Webster,Ben (ts) | Henderson,Horace (p) | Lucie,Lawrence (g) | James,Elmer (b) | Johnson,Walter (dr) | Henderson,Fletcher (ld)

Christopher Columbus | Stealin' Apples
Chicago,Ill, rec. 27.3.1936
Smith,Russell (tp) | Vance,Dick (tp) | Thomas,Joe (tp) | Eldridge,Roy (tp) | Arbello,Fernando (tb) | Cuffee,Ed (tb) | Bailey,Buster (cl,as) | Carey,Scoops (as) | Williams,Elmer (cl,ts) | Berry,Leon 'Chu' (ts) | Henderson,Horace (p) | Lessey,Bob (g) | Kirby,John (b) | Catlett,Big Sid (dr) | Henderson,Fletcher (ld)

Jangled Nerves
Chicago,Ill, rec. 9.4.1936
Henderson,Fletcher (p,arr) | Vance,Dick (tp) | Thomas,Joe (tp) | Eldridge,Roy (tp) | Cuffee,Ed (tb) | Arbello,Fernando (tb) | Bailey,Buster (cl,as) | Simeon,Omer (cl,as) | Williams,Elmer (ts,bs) | Berry,Leon 'Chu' (ts) | Henderson,Horace (p,arr) | Lessey,Bob (g) | Crosby,Israel (b) | Catlett,Big Sid (dr)

78012-2 | 5 CD | Jazz:The Essential Collection Vol.2

Louis Armstrong And His Hot Five
Comet Chop Suey
Chicago,Ill, rec. 26.2.1926
Armstrong,Louis (tp,voc) | Ory,Edward 'Kid' (tb) | Dodds,Johnny (cl) | Armstrong [Hardin],Lil (p) | St.Cyr,Johnny (bj)

Lil's Hot Shots
Drop That Sack
Chicago,Ill, rec. 28.5.1926
Lil's Hot Shots | Armstrong [Hardin],Lil (p) | Armstrong,Louis (co,voc) | Ory,Edward 'Kid' (tb) | Dodds,Johnny (cl) | St.Cyr,Johnny (bj)

Louis Armstrong And His Hot Seven
Willie The Weeper | Wild Man Blues
Chicago,Ill, rec. 7.5.1927
Armstrong,Louis (tp) | Thomas,John (tb) | Dodds,Johnny (cl) | Armstrong [Hardin],Lil (p) | St.Cyr,Johnny (bj) | Briggs,Pete (tuba) | Dodds,Warren 'Baby' (dr)

Alligator Crawl | Potato Head Blues
Chicago,Ill, rec. 10.5.1927
Armstrong,Louis (tp) | Thomas,John (tb) | Dodds,Johnny (cl) | Armstrong [Hardin],Lil (p) | St.Cyr,Johnny (bj) | Briggs,Pete (tuba) | Dodds,Warren 'Baby' (dr)

Louis Armstrong And His Hot Five
Skip The Gutter
Chicago,Ill, rec. 27.6.1928
Armstrong,Louis (tp) | Robinson,Fred (tb) | Strong,Jimmy (cl) | Hines,Earl 'Fatha' (p) | Cara,Mancy (bj) | Singleton,Zutty (dr)

West End Blues
Chicago,Ill, rec. 28.6.1928
Armstrong,Louis (co,voc) | Robinson,Fred (tb) | Strong,Jimmy (cl) | Hines,Earl 'Fatha' (p) | Carr,Mancy (bj) | Singleton,Zutty (dr)

Two Deuces
Chicago,Ill, rec. 29.6.1928
Armstrong,Louis (tp) | Robinson,Fred (tb) | Strong,Jimmy (cl) | Hines,Earl 'Fatha' (p) | Carr,Mancy (bj) | Singleton,Zutty (dr)

Louis Armstrong And His Orchestra
Basin Street Blues
Chicago,Ill, rec. 4.12.1928
Armstrong,Louis (tp,voc) | Robinson,Fred (tb) | Strong,Jimmy (cl,ts) | Hines,Earl 'Fatha' (p) | Carr,Mancy (bj) | Singleton,Zutty (dr)

Louis Armstrong And His Savoy Ballroom Five
No One Else But You
Chicago,Ill, rec. 5.12.1928
Armstrong,Louis (tp,voc) | Robinson,Fred (tb) | Strong,Jimmy (cl,ts) | Redman,Don (cl,as) | Hines,Earl 'Fatha' (p) | Carr,Mancy (bj) | Singleton,Zutty (dr)

Louis Armstrong With Earl Hines
Weather Bird
Armstrong,Louis (tp) | Hines,Earl 'Fatha' (p)

Louis Armstrong And His Orchestra
Muggles
Chicago,Ill, rec. 7.12.1928
Armstrong,Louis (tp) | Robinson,Fred (tb) | Strong,Jimmy (cl) | Hines,Earl 'Fatha' (p) | Cara,Mancy (bj) | Singleton,Zutty (dr)

Louis Armstrong And His Savoy Ballroom Five
Tight Like That
Chicago,Ill, rec. 12.12.1928
Armstrong,Louis (tp,voc) | Robinson,Fred (tb) | Strong,Jimmy (cl) | Redman,Don (cl,as,voc) | Hines,Earl 'Fatha' (p) | Cara,Mancy (bj) | Singleton,Zutty (dr)

Mahogany Hall Stomp
NYC, rec. 5.3.1929
Armstrong,Louis (tp,voc) | Higginbotham,J.C. (tb) | Nicholas,Albert (cl,as) | Holmes,Charlie (as) | Hill,Teddy (ts) | Russell,Luis (p) | Condon,Eddie (bj) | Johnson,Lonnie (g) | Foster,George 'Pops' (b) | Barbarin,Paul (dr)

Louis Armstrong And His Orchestra
St.Louis Blues
NYC, rec. 13.12.1929
Armstrong,Louis (tp,voc) | Allen,Henry Red (tp) | Johnson,Otis (tp) | Higginbotham,J.C. (tb) | Nicholas,Albert (cl,as) | Holmes,Charlie (as) | Hill,Teddy (ts) | Russell,Luis (p,arr) | Johnson,Willie (g) | Foster,George 'Pops' (b) | Barbarin,Paul (dr)

I Got A Right To Sing The Blues
Chicago,Ill, rec. 25.1.1933
Armstrong,Louis (tp,voc) | Whitlock,Ellis (tp) | Randolph,Zilmer (tp,arr) | Johnson,Keg (tb) | Brown,Scoville (cl,as) | Oldham,George (cl,as) | Johnson,Budd (cl,ts) | Wilson,Teddy (p) | McKendrick,Mike (g,bj) | Oldham,Bill (b,tuba) | Porter,Yank (dr)

Struttin' With Some Barbecue
Los Angeles,CA, rec. 12.1.1938
Armstrong,Louis (tp,voc) | Higginbotham,J.C. (tb) | Holmes,Charlie (as) | Madison,Bingie (cl,ts) | Russell,Luis (p) | Blair,Lee (g) | Foster,George 'Pops' (b) | Barbarin,Paul (dr)

When The Saints Go Marching In
NYC, rec. 13.5.1938
Armstrong,Louis (tp,voc) | Hemphill,Shelton (tp) | Higginbotham,J.C. (tb) | Holmes,Charlie (as) | Cole,Rupert (cl,as) | Madison,Bingie (ts) | Russell,Luis (p) | Blair,Lee (g) | Foster,George 'Pops' (b) | Barbarin,Paul (dr) | unkn. (chorus)

Savoy Blues
NYC, rec. 5.4.1939
Armstrong,Louis (tp,voc) | Allen,Henry Red (tp) | Johnson,Otis (tp) | Hemphill,Shelton (tp) | Higginbotham,J.C. (tb) | DeParis,Wilbur (tb) | Washington,George (tb) | Garland,Joe (ts) | Holmes,Charlie (as) | Cole,Rupert (cl,as) | Madison,Bingie (ts) | Russell,Luis (p,arr) | Blair,Lee (g) | Foster,George 'Pops' (b) | Catlett,Big Sid (dr)

Wolverine Blues
NYC, rec. 14.3.1940
Armstrong,Louis (tp) | Allen,Henry Red (tp) | Flood,Bernard (tp) | Hemphill,Shelton (tp) | Higginbotham,J.C. (tb) | DeParis,Wilbur (tb) | Washington,George (tb) | Garland,Joe (ts) | Holmes,Henry (reeds) | Cole,Rupert (reeds) | Madison,Bingie (reeds) | Russell,Luis (p) | Blair,Lee (g) | Foster,George 'Pops' (b) | Catlett,Big Sid (dr)

2:19 Blues
NYC, rec. 27.5.1940
Armstrong,Louis (tp,voc) | Jones,Claude (tb) | Bechet,Sidney (cl,as) | Russell,Luis (p) | Addison,Bernard (g) | Braud,Wellman (b) | Singleton,Zutty (dr)

Coal Cart Blues
Armstrong,Louis (tp) | Bechet,Sidney (cl,as) | Addison,Bernard (g) | Braud,Wellman (b)

When It's Sleepy Time Down South
Chicago,Ill, rec. 16.11.1941
Armstrong,Louis (tp,voc) | Hemphill,Shelton (tp) | Prince,Gene (tp) | Galbraith,Frank (tp) | Washington,George (tb) | Chambers,Henderson (tb) | Greene,Norman (tb) | Cole,Rupert (as) | Frye,Carl (as) | Garland,Joe (cl,ts) | Madison,Bingie (ts,bs) | Robinson,Prince (cl,ts) | Russell,Luis (p,arr) | Lucie,Lawrence (g) | Alvis,Hayes (b) | Catlett,Big Sid (dr)

Duke Ellington And His Kentucky Club Orchestra
East St.Louis Toodle-Oo
NYC, rec. 14.3.1927
Ellington,Duke (p) | Miley,Bubber (tp) | Metcalf,Louis (tp) | Nanton,Joe 'Tricky Sam' (tb) | Hardwicke,Otto (reeds) | Robinson,Prince prob. (reeds) | unkn. (reeds) | Guy,Fred (bj) | Shaw,Mack prob. (tuba) | Greer,William 'Sonny' (dr)

Duke Ellington And His Orchestra
Creole Love Call
NYC, rec. 26.10.1927
Ellington,Duke (p) | Metcalf,Louis (tp) | Miley,Bubber (tp) | Nanton,Joe 'Tricky Sam' (tb) | Hardwicke,Otto (cl,ss,as,bs) | Jackson,Rudy (cl,ts) | Guy,Fred (bj) | Braud,Wellman (b) | Greer,William 'Sonny' (dr) | Hall,Adelaide (voc)

Black And Tan Fantasy
Ellington,Duke (p) | Metcalf,Louis (tp) | Miley,Bubber (tp) | Nanton,Joe 'Tricky Sam' (tb) | Hardwicke,Otto (cl,ss,as,bs) | Jackson,Rudy (cl,ts) | Guy,Fred (bj) | Braud,Wellman (b) | Greer,William 'Sonny' (dr)

The Mooche | Hot And Bothered
NYC, rec. 1.10.1928
Ellington,Duke (p) | Miley,Bubber (tp) | Whetsol,Arthur (tp) | Nanton,Joe 'Tricky Sam' (tb) | Hodges,Johnny (cl,ss,as) | Carney,Harry (cl,as,bs) | Bigard,Barney (cl,ts) | Guy,Fred (bj) | Johnson,Lonnie (g) | Braud,Wellman (b) | Greer,William 'Sonny' (dr)

Duke Ellington And His Cotton Club Orchestra
Mood Indigo | Echoes Of The Jungle
Camden,NJ, rec. 16.6.1931
Ellington,Duke (p) | Whetsol,Arthur (tp) | Jenkins,Freddie (tp) | Williams,Cootie (tp) | Nanton,Joe 'Tricky Sam' (tb) | Tizol,Juan (tb) | Hodges,Johnny (as) | Bigard,Barney (cl) | Carney,Harry (cl,bs) | Guy,Fred (bj) | Braud,Wellman (b) | Greer,William 'Sonny' (dr)

Duke Ellington And His Orchestra
The Mystery Song
Camden,NJ, rec. 17.6.1931
Ellington,Duke (p) | Williams,Cootie (tp) | Jenkins,Freddie (tp) | Whetsol,Arthur (tp) | Nanton,Joe 'Tricky Sam' (tb) | Tizol,Juan (tb) | Bigard,Barney (cl,ts) | Hodges,Johnny (cl,ss,as) | Carney,Harry (cl,ss,as,bs) | Guy,Fred (g,bj) | Braud,Wellman (b) | Greer,William 'Sonny' (dr)

Clarinet Lament(Barney's Concerto)
NYC, rec. 27.2.1936
Ellington,Duke (p) | Stewart,Rex (co) | Williams,Cootie (tp) | Whetsol,Arthur (tp) | Nanton,Joe 'Tricky Sam' (tb) | Tizol,Juan (tb) | Brown,Lawrence (tb) | Bigard,Barney (cl,ts) | Hodges,Johnny (cl,ss,as) | Webster,Ben (ts) | Carney,Harry (cl,ss,as,bs) | Guy,Fred (g,bj) | Alvis,Hayes (b) | Greer,William 'Sonny' (dr)

Duke Ellington And His Famous Orchestra
New East St.Louis Toodle Oo
NYC, rec. 5.3.1937
Ellington,Duke (p) | Stewart,Rex (co) | Williams,Cootie (tp) | Jones,Wallace (tp) | Nanton,Joe 'Tricky Sam' (tb) | Tizol,Juan (tb) | Brown,Lawrence (tb) | Bigard,Barney (cl,ts) | Hodges,Johnny (cl,ss,as) | Hardwicke,Otto (ss,as) | Carney,Harry (cl,ss,as,bs) | Guy,Fred (g,bj) | Alvis,Hayes (b) | Greer,William 'Sonny' (dr)

Battle Of Swing(Le Jazz Hot) | Old King Dooji | Portrait Of The Lion
NYC, rec. 19.12.1938
Ellington,Duke (p) | Whetsol,Arthur (tp) | Williams,Cootie (tp) | Jones,Wallace (tp) | Stewart,Rex (co) | Nanton,Joe 'Tricky Sam' (tb) | Brown,Lawrence (tb) | Hodges,Johnny (cl,ss,as) | Hardwicke,Otto (cl,as,bs) | Bigard,Barney (cl) | Carney,Harry (cl,as,bs) | Guy,Fred (bj) | Taylor,Billy (b) | Greer,William 'Sonny' (dr)

Jack The Bear | Ko-Ko
Chicago,Ill, rec. 6.3.1940
Ellington,Duke (p) | Stewart,Rex (co) | Williams,Cootie (tp) | Jones,Wallace (tp) | Nanton,Joe 'Tricky Sam' (tb) | Tizol,Juan (tb) | Brown,Lawrence (tb) | Bigard,Barney (cl,ts) | Hodges,Johnny (ss,as) | Hardwicke,Otto (as,bass-s) | Webster,Ben (ts) | Carney,Harry (cl,as,bs) | Guy,Fred (g) | Blanton,Jimmy (b) | Greer,William 'Sonny' (dr)

Concerto For Cootie
Chicago,Ill, rec. 15.3.1940
Ellington,Duke (p) | Stewart,Rex (co) | Williams,Cootie (tp) | Jones,Wallace (tp) | Nanton,Joe 'Tricky Sam' (tb) | Tizol,Juan (tb) | Brown,Lawrence (tb) | Bigard,Barney (cl,ts) | Hodges,Johnny (ss,as) | Hardwicke,Otto (as,bass-s) | Webster,Ben (ts) | Carney,Harry (cl,as,bs) | Guy,Fred (g) | Blanton,Jimmy (b) | Greer,William 'Sonny' (dr)

Dusk
Chicago,Ill, rec. 28.5.1940
Ellington,Duke (p,arr) | Jones,Wallace (tp) | Williams,Cootie (tp) | Stewart,Rex (co) | Nanton,Joe 'Tricky Sam' (tb) | Brown,Lawrence (tb) | Tizol,Juan (v-tb) | Bigard,Barney (cl) | Hodges,Johnny (cl,ss,as) | Hardwicke,Otto (as,bass-s) | Webster,Ben (ts) | Carney,Harry (cl,as,bs) | Guy,Fred (g) | Blanton,Jimmy (b) | Greer,William 'Sonny' (dr)

Harlem Air Shaft(Rumpus In Richmond) | Sepia Panorama(Night House)
NYC, rec. 22.& 24.7.1940
Ellington,Duke (p,arr) | Jones,Wallace (tp) | Williams,Cootie (tp) | Stewart,Rex (co) | Nanton,Joe 'Tricky Sam' (tb) | Brown,Lawrence (tb) | Tizol,Juan (v-tb) | Bigard,Barney (cl) | Hodges,Johnny (cl,ss,as) | Hardwicke,Otto (as,bass-s) | Webster,Ben (ts) | Carney,Harry (cl,as,bs) | Guy,Fred (g) | Blanton,Jimmy (b) | Greer,William 'Sonny' (dr)

Blue Serge
Hollywood,CA, rec. 15.2.1941
Ellington,Duke (ld) | Jones,Wallace (tp) | Williams,Cootie (tp) | Stewart,Rex (co) | Nanton,Joe 'Tricky Sam' (tb) | Brown,Lawrence (tb) | Tizol,Juan (v-tb) | Bigard,Barney (cl) | Hodges,Johnny (cl,ss,as) | Hardwicke,Otto (as,bass-s) | Webster,Ben (ts) | Carney,Harry (cl,as,bs) | Strayhorn,Billy (p,arr) | Guy,Fred (g) | Blanton,Jimmy (b) | Greer,William 'Sonny' (dr)

Chelsea Bridge
Hollywood,CA, rec. 26.9.1941
Ellington,Duke (ld) | Jones,Wallace (tp) | Williams,Cootie (tp) | Stewart,Rex (co) | Nanton,Joe 'Tricky Sam' (tb) | Brown,Lawrence (tb) | Tizol,Juan (v-tb) | Bigard,Barney (cl) | Hodges,Johnny (cl,ss,as) | Hardwicke,Otto (as,bass-s) | Webster,Ben (ts) | Carney,Harry (cl,as,bs) | Strayhorn,Billy (p,arr) | Guy,Fred (g) | Blanton,Jimmy (b) | Greer,William 'Sonny' (dr)

Duke Ellington And His Orchestra
Hiawatha
NYC, rec. 5.12.1946
Ellington,Duke (ld) | Jordan,Taft (tp) | Hemphill,Shelton (tp) | Anderson,Cat (tp) | Baker,Harold 'Shorty' (tp) | Nance,Ray (tp) | Brown,Lawrence (tb) | Jones,Claude (tb) | DeParis,Wilbur (tb) | Hamilton,Jimmy (cl,ts) | Hodges,Johnny (cl,ss,as) | Procope,Russell (cl,as) | Sears,Al (ts) | Carney,Harry (cl,as,bs) | Guy,Fred (g) | Pettiford,Oscar (b) | Greer,William 'Sonny' (dr)

Minnehaha
Ellington,Duke (ld) | Jordan,Taft (tp) | Hemphill,Shelton (tp) | Anderson,Cat (tp) | Baker,Harold 'Shorty' (tp) | Nance,Ray (tp) | Brown,Lawrence (tb) | Jones,Claude (tb) | DeParis,Wilbur (tb) | Hamilton,Jimmy (cl,ts) | Hodges,Johnny (cl,ss,as) | Procope,Russell (cl,as) | Sears,Al (ts) | Carney,Harry (cl,as,bs) | Guy,Fred (g) | Pettiford,Oscar (b) | Greer,William 'Sonny' (dr) | Davis,Kay (voc)

Earl Hines
Off Time Blues | Chicago High Life | Stowaway | Chimes In Blues | Panther Rag | Just Too Soon
Long Island,NY, rec. 8.12.1928
Hines,Earl 'Fatha' (p-solo)

Caution Blues | A Monday Date
Chicago,Ill, rec. 9.12.1928
Hines,Earl 'Fatha' (p-solo)

I Ain't Got Nobody | 57 Varieries
Chicago,Ill, rec. 12.12.1928
Hines,Earl 'Fatha' (p-solo)

Glad Rag Doll
Chicago,Ill, rec. 25.2.1929
Hines,Earl 'Fatha' (p-solo)

Earl Hines And His Orchestra
Grand Piano Blues
Chicago,Ill, rec. 25.10.1929
Hines,Earl 'Fatha' (p) | Clay,Shirley (co) | Mitchell,George (co) | Franklin,William (tb) | Boone,Lester (cl,as,bs) | Turner,Toby (cl,as) | Irwin,Cecil (cl,ts,arr) | Roberts,Claude (bj) | Alvis,Hayes (tuba) | Washington,Benny (dr)

Earl Hines
Love Me Tonight | Down Among The Sheltering Palms
NYC, rec. 14.7.1932
Hines,Earl 'Fatha' (p-solo)

Earl Hines And His Orchestra
Maple Leaf Rag | Sweet Georgia Brown
Chicago,Ill, rec. 12.9.1934
Hines,Earl 'Fatha' (p) | Allen,Charlie (tp) | Dixon,George (tp) | Fuller,Walter (tp) | Taylor,Louis (tb) | Howard,Darnell (cl,as,v) | Simeon,Omer (cl,as,bs) | Irwin,Cecil (cl,ts) | Dixon,Lawrence (g) | Wilson,Quinn (b) | Bishop,Wallace (dr)

Earl Hines
The Fatha's Getaway | Reminiscing At Blue Note
NYC, rec. 29.7.1939
Hines,Earl 'Fatha' (p-solo)

Earl Hines And His Orchestra
Riff Medley | X Y Z | 'Gator Swing
Chicago,Ill, rec. 6.10.1939
Hines,Earl 'Fatha' (p) | Fletcher,Milton (tp) | Simms,Edward (tp) | Fuller,Walter (tp) | Dixon,George (tp,as,bs) | Burke,Edward (tb) | Ewing,John 'Steamline' (tb) | McLewis,Joe (tb) | Simeon,Omer (cl,as) | Harris,Leroy (cl,as) | Johnson,Budd (as,ts,arr) | Crowder,Robert (ts,arr) | Roberts,Claude (g) | Wilson,Quinn (b) | Burroughs,Alvin (dr)

Earl Hines
Rosetta
Chicago,Ill, rec. 21.10.1939
Hines,Earl 'Fatha' (p-solo)

Child Of A Disordered Brain
NYC, rec. 26.2.1940
Hines,Earl 'Fatha' (p-solo)

On The Sunny Side Of The Street | My Melancholy Baby
Chicago,Ill, rec. 3.4.1941
Hines,Earl 'Fatha' (p-solo)

The Wolverines
Royal Garden Blues | Tiger Rag
Richmond, Indiana, rec. 20.6.1924
Wolverines,The | Beiderbecke,Bix (co) | Hartwell,Jimmy (cl,as) | Johnson,George (ts) | Voynow,Dick (p) | Gillette,Bob (bj) | Leibrock,Min (tuba) | Moore,Vic (dr)

Big Boy
NYC, rec. 7.10.1924
Wolverines,The | Beiderbecke,Bix (co) | Hartwell,Jimmy (cl,as) | Johnson,George (ts) | Voynow,Dick (p) | Gillette,Bob (bj) | Leibrock,Min (tuba) | Moore,Vic (dr)

Bix And His Rhythm Jugglers
Toodlin' Blues
Richmond, Indiana, rec. 26.1.1925
Beiderbecke,Bix (co) | Dorsey,Tommy (tb) | Murray,Don (cl) | Mertz,Paul (p) | Gargano,Tom (dr)

Davenport Blues
Beiderbecke,Bix (co) | Dorsey,Tommy (tb) | Murray,Don (cl) | Mertz,Paul (p) | Quicksell,Howdy (bj) | Gargano,Tom (dr)

Frankie Trumbauer And His Orchestra
Clarinet Marmalade | Singin' The Blues
NYC, rec. 4.2.1927
Trumbauer,Frank (c-mel-sax) | Beiderbecke,Bix (co) | Rank,Bill (tb) | Dorsey,Jimmy (cl,as) | Riskin,Itzy (p) | Lang,Eddie (g,bj) | Morehouse,Chauncey (dr)

Ostrich Walk | Riverboat Shuffle
NYC, rec. 9.5.1927
Trumbauer,Frank (c-mel-sax) | Beiderbecke,Bix (co) | Rank,Bill (tb) | Murray,Don (cl,bs) | Ingle,Ernest 'Red' (as) | Riskin,Itzy (p) | Lang,Eddie (g,bj) | Morehouse,Chauncey (dr)

I'm Coming Virginia | Way Down Yonder In New Orleans
NYC, rec. 13.5.1927
Trumbauer,Frank (c-mel-sax) | Beiderbecke,Bix (co) | Rank,Bill (tb) | Murray,Don (cl,bs) | Ingle,Ernest 'Red' (as) | Riskin,Itzy (p) | Lang,Eddie (g,bj) | Morehouse,Chauncey (dr)

Bix Beiderbecke
In A Mist
NYC, rec. 9.9.1927
Beiderbecke,Bix (p-solo)

Frankie Trumbauer And His Orchestra
Humpty Dumpty | Krazy Kat | Baltimore
NYC, rec. 28.9.1927
Trumbauer,Frankie (c-mel-sax) | Beiderbecke,Bix (co) | Rank,Bill (tb) | Murray,Don (bs) | Davis,Bobby (as) | Rollini,Adrian (bass-sax) | Venuti,Joe (v) | Lang,Eddie (g) | Signorelli,Frank (p) | Morehouse,Chauncey (dr)

Bix Beiderbecke And His Gang
At The Jazz Band Ball | Royal Garden Blues | Jazz Me Blues
NYC, rec. 5.10.1927
Beiderbecke,Bix (co) | Rank,Bill (tb) | Murray,Don (cl) | Rollini,Adrian (bass-sax) | Signorelli,Frank (p) | Morehouse,Chauncey (dr)

Goose Pimples | Sorry | Since My Best Gal Turned Me Down
NYC, rec. 25.10.1927
Beiderbecke,Bix (co) | Rank,Bill (tb) | Murray,Don (cl) | Rollini,Adrian (bass-sax) | Signorelli,Frank (p) | Morehouse,Chauncey (dr) | Quicksell,Howdy (arr)

Somebody Stole My Gal | Thou Swell
NYC, rec. 17.4.1928
Beiderbecke,Bix (co) | Rank,Bill (tb) | Friedman,Irving 'Izzy' (cl) | Leibrock,Min (bass-sax) | Satterfield,Tommy (p) | McDonald,Harold (dr)

Wa-Da-Da
Chicago,Ill, rec. 7.7.1928
Beiderbecke,Bix (co) | Rank,Bill (tb) | Friedman,Irving 'Izzy' (cl) | Leibrock,Min (bass-sax) | Satterfield,Tommy (p) | Gale,Harry (dr)

Rhythm King
NYC, rec. 21.9.1928
Beiderbecke,Bix (co) | Rank,Bill (tb) | Friedman,Irving 'Izzy' (cl) | Leibrock,Min (bass-sax) | Bargy,Roy (p) | Marsh,George (dr)

Art Tatum

Cocktails For Two
NYC, rec. 22.8.1934
Tatum,Art (p-solo)
The Shout | Liza
NYC, rec. 24.8.1924
Tatum,Art (p-solo)
I Ain't Got Nobody
NYC, rec. 9.10.1934
Tatum,Art (p-solo)
Gone With The Wind | Stormy Weather | Chloe | The Sheik Of Araby
NYC, rec. 29.11.1937
Tatum,Art (p-solo)
Tea For Two | Deep Purple
Los Angeles,CA, rec. 12.4.1939
Tatum,Art (p-solo)
Elegie | Humoresque | Sweet Lorraine | Get Happy | Lullaby Of The Leaves | Tiger Rag
Los Angeles,CA, rec. 22.2.1940
Tatum,Art (p-solo)
St.Louis Blues | Begin The Beguine | Rosetta | Back Home Again In Indiana
Los Angeles,CA, rec. 26.7.1940
Tatum,Art (p-solo)

Leonard Feather's Esquire All Stars
Esquire Bounce | Boff Boff(Mop Mop) | My Ideal | Esquire Blues
NYC, rec. 4.12.1943
Esquire All Stars | Williams,Cootie (tp) | Hall,Edmond (cl) | Hawkins,Coleman (ts) | Tatum,Art (p) | Casey,Al (g) | Pettiford,Oscar (b) | Catlett,Big Sid (dr)

78013-2 | 5 CD | Jazz:The Essential Collection Vol.3

McKinney's Cotton Pickers
Miss Hannah
NYC, rec. 6.1.1929
McKinney's Cotton Pickers | Smith,Joe (tp) | DeParis,Sidney (tp) | Davis,Leonard (tp) | Jones,Claude (tb) | Hawkins,Coleman (cl,ts) | McCord,Theodore (cl,ts) | Redman,Don (cl,as,bs,arr,voc) | Carter,Benny (cl,as) | Waller,Thomas 'Fats' (p,celeste) | Wilborn,Dave (bj) | Taylor,Billy (tuba) | Marshall,Kaiser (dr)

Mound City Blue Blowers
One Hour
NYC, rec. 14.11.1929
Mound City Blue Blowers | McKenzie,Red (blue-blowing) | Miller,Glenn (tb) | Russell,Pee Wee (cl) | Hawkins,Coleman (ts) | Condon,Eddie (bj) | Bland,Jack (g) | Morgan,Albert 'Al' (b) | Krupa,Gene (dr)

Chocolate Dandies
Dee Blues
NYC, rec. 31.12.1930
Chocolate Dandies,The | Stark,Bobby (tp) | Harrison,Jimmy (tb) | Carter,Benny (cl,as,arr) | Hawkins,Coleman (ts) | Henderson,Horace (p) | Jackson,Benny (g) | Kirby,John (tuba)

Spike Hughes And His Negro Orchestra
Donegal Cradle Song
NYC, rec. 19.5.1933
Allen,Henry Red (tp) | Scott,Howard or Bill Dillard (tp) | Wells,Dicky (tb) | DeParis,Wilbur (tb) | Washington,George (tb) | Carter,Benny (cl,as) | Carver,Wayman (fl,as,ts) | Johnson,Howard (cl,as) | Hawkins,Coleman (cl,ts) | Berry,Leon 'Chu' (ts) | Rodriguez,Nicholas (p) | Lucie,Lawrence (bj) | Hill,Ernest (b) | Catlett,Big Sid (dr)

Fletcher Henderson And His Orchestra
Yeah Man
NYC, rec. 18.8.1933
Henderson,Fletcher (p) | Smith,Russell (tp) | Stark,Bobby (tp) | Allen,Henry Red (tp) | Wells,Dicky (tb) | Procope,Russell (cl,as) | Jefferson,Hilton (cl,as) | Hawkins,Coleman (ts) | Addison,Bernard (g) | Kirby,John (b) | Johnson,Walter (dr)

Coleman Hawkins And His Orchestra
Jamaica Shout
NYC, rec. 29.9.1933
Hawkins,Coleman (ts) | Allen,Henry Red (tp) | Higginbotham,J.C. (tb) | Jefferson,Hilton (cl,as) | Henderson,Horace (p) | Addison,Bernard (g) | Kirby,John (b) | Johnson,Walter (dr)

Coleman Hawkins With The Ramblers
After You've Gone
Den Haag,Holland, rec. 4.2.1935
Hawkins,Coleman (ts) | Hinrichs,Henk (tp) | Van Helvoirt,George (tp) | Thielemans,Marcel (tb) | Poppink,Wim (cl,as) | Vanderouderaa,Andre (cl,ts) | Masman,Theo Uden (p) | Pet,Jacques 'Jack' (g) | Limbach,Tonny (b) | Kranenburg,Cornelius 'Cees' (dr)

Coleman Hawkins Trio
Stardust
Paris,France, rec. 2.3.1935
Hawkins,Coleman (ts) | Reinhardt,Django (g) | Grappelli,Stephane (p)
Smiles
Laren,Holland, rec. 26.4.1937
Hawkins,Coleman (ts) | Van Helvoirt,George (tp) | Bulterman,Jack (tp) | Thielemans,Marcel (tb) | Doof,Sal (as) | Poppink,Wim (cl,as) | Vanderouderaa,Andre (cl,ts) | De Rooy,Nico (p) | Reinders,Frits (g) | Pet,Jacques 'Jack' (b) | Kranenburg,Cornelius 'Cees' (dr)

Coleman Hawkins And His All Star Jam Band
Honeysuckle Rose
Paris,France, rec. 28.4.1937
Hawkins,Coleman (ts) | Carter,Benny (as) | Ekyan,Andre (as) | Reinhardt,Django (g) | Grappelli,Stephane (p) | D'Hellemmes,Eugene (b) | Benford,Tommy (dr)

Lionel Hampton And His Orchestra
When Lights Are Low
NYC, rec. 11.9.1939
Hampton,Lionel (vib) | Gillespie,Dizzy (tp) | Carter,Benny (as,arr) | Hawkins,Coleman (ts) | Webster,Ben (ts) | Berry,Leon 'Chu' (ts) | Hart,Clyde (p) | Christian,Charlie (g) | Hinton,Milt (b) | Cole,William 'Cozy' (dr)

Coleman Hawkins And His Orchestra
Body And Soul
NYC, rec. 11.10.1939
Hawkins,Coleman (ts) | Lindsey,Tommy (tp) | Guy,Joe (tp) | Hardy,Earl (tb) | Fields,Jackie (as) | Moore,Eustis (as) | Rodgers,Gene (p) | Smith,William Oscar (b) | Herbert,Arthur (dr)

Lionel Hampton And His Orchestra
Singin' The Blues
NYC, rec. 21.12.1939
Hampton,Lionel (vib) | Carter,Benny (tp) | Hall,Edmond (cl) | Hawkins,Coleman (ts) | Sullivan,Joe (p) | Green,Freddie (g) | Bernstein,Artie (b) | Singleton,Zutty (dr)

Coleman Hawkins And His Rhythm
Dedication
NYC, rec. 25.5.1940
Hawkins,Coleman (ts) | Addison,Bernard (g) | Kirby,John (b) | Catlett,Big Sid (dr)

Coleman Hawkins And His Orchestra
How Deep Is The Ocean
NYC, rec. 8.12.1943
Hawkins,Coleman (ts) | Coleman,Bill (tp) | Fitzgerald,Andy (cl) | Larkins,Ellis (p) | Casey,Al (g) | Pettiford,Oscar (b) | Manne,Shelly (dr)

Coleman Hawkins' Swing Four
The Man I Love
NYC, rec. 23.12.1943
Hawkins,Coleman (ts) | Heywood,Eddie (p) | Pettiford,Oscar (b) | Manne,Shelly (dr)

Coleman Hawkins Quintet
Bean At The Met
NYC, rec. 31.1.1944
Hawkins,Coleman (ts) | Eldridge,Roy (tp) | Wilson,Teddy (p) | Taylor,Billy (b) | Cole,William 'Cozy' (dr)

Coleman Hawkins And His Orchestra
Buh-De-Daht
NYC, rec. 16.2.1944
Hawkins,Coleman (ts) | Gillespie,Dizzy (tp) | Coulson,Victor (tp) | Vandever,Ed (tp) | Parker,Leo (as) | Lowry,Leonard (as) | Byas,Don (ts) | Abrams,Ray (ts) | Johnson,Budd (bs) | Hart,Clyde (p) | Pettiford,Oscar (b) | Roach,Max (dr)

Coleman Hawkins Quartet
On The Bean
NYC, rec. 19.10.1944
Hawkins,Coleman (ts) | Monk,Thelonious (p) | Robinson,Edward 'Bass' (b) | Best,Denzil (dr)

Coleman Hawkins
Hawk's Variation
NYC, rec. prob.January 1945
Hawkins,Coleman (ts-solo)

Coleman Hawkins And His Orchestra
Stuffy
Hollywood,CA, rec. 23.2.1945
Hawkins,Coleman (ts) | McGhee,Howard (tp) | Thompson,Sir Charles (p) | Reuss,Allan (g) | Pettiford,Oscar (b) | Best,Denzil (dr)
What Is There To Say
Hollywood,CA, rec. 2.3.1945
Hawkins,Coleman (ts) | McGhee,Howard (tp) | Thompson,Sir Charles (p) | Reuss,Allan (g) | Pettiford,Oscar (b) | Best,Denzil (dr)

Coleman Hawkins And His 52nd Street All Stars
Spotlite
NYC, rec. 27.2.1946
Hawkins,Coleman (ts) | Shavers,Charlie (tp) | Brown,Pete (as) | Eager,Allen (ts) | Jones,Jimmy (p) | Osborne,Mary (g) | McKibbon,Al (b) | Manne,Shelly (dr)

Coleman Hawkins And His All Stars
Half Step Down Please
NYC, rec. 11.12.1947
Hawkins,Coleman (ts) | Navarro,Fats (tp) | Johnson,J.J. (tb) | Johnson,Budd (as) | De Veta,Marion (bs) | Jones,Hank (p) | Wayne,Chuck (g) | Lesberg,Jack (b) | Roach,Max (dr)

Benny Moten's Kansas City Orchestra
The Blue Room
Camden,NJ, rec. 13.12.1932
Moten,Benny (ld) | Keyes,Joe (tp) | Stewart,Dee (tp) | Page,Oran 'Hot Lips' (tp) | Minor,Dan (tb) | Durham,Eddie (tb,el-g,arr) | Barefield,Eddie (cl,as) | Washington Jr.,Jack (as,bs) | Basie,Count (p,arr) | Berry,Leroy (g) | Page,Walter (b) | McWashington,Willie (dr)

Fletcher Henderson And His Orchestra
Limehouse Blues
NYC, rec. 11.9.1934
Henderson,Fletcher (p) | Smith,Russell (tp) | Randolph,Irving 'Mouse' (tp) | Allen,Henry Red (tp) | Jones,Claude (tb) | Johnson,Keg (tb) | Bailey,Buster (cl) | Jefferson,Hilton (cl,as) | Procope,Russell (cl,as) | Webster,Ben (ts) | Lucie,Lawrence (g) | James,Elmer (b) | Johnson,Walter (dr)

Teddy Wilson And His All Stars
A Sunbonnet Blue
NYC, rec. 2.7.1935
Wilson,Teddy (p) | Eldridge,Roy (tp) | Webster,Ben (ts) | Trueheart,John (g) | Kirby,John (b) | Cole,William 'Cozy' (dr) | Holiday,Billie (voc)

Duke Ellington And His Orchestra
Truckin'
NYC, rec. 19.8.1935
Ellington,Duke (p) | Williams,Cootie (tp) | Stewart,Rex (tp) | Whetsol,Arthur (tp) | Nanton,Joe 'Tricky Sam' (tb) | Tizol,Juan (tb) | Brown,Lawrence (tb) | Bigard,Barney (cl,ts) | Hodges,Johnny (ss,as) | Hardwicke,Otto (ss,as) | Webster,Ben (ts) | Carney,Harry (cl,as,bs) | Guy,Fred (g) | Alvis,Hayes (b) | Taylor,Billy (b) | Greer,William 'Sonny' (dr) | Anderson,Ivie (voc)

Teddy Wilson And His Orchestra
I'll See You In My Dreams
NYC, rec. 16.12.1936
Wilson,Teddy (p) | Randolph,Irving 'Mouse' (tp) | Musso,Vido (cl) | Webster,Ben (ts) | Reuss,Allan (g) | Kirby,John (b) | Cole,William 'Cozy' (dr)

Fletcher Henderson And His Orchestra
Sing You Sinners
NYC, rec. 25.10.1937
Henderson,Fletcher (p,arr) | Vance,Dick (tp) | Smith,Russell (tp) | Berry,Emmett (tp) | McConnell,John (tb) | Wynn,Albert (tb) | Cuffee,Ed (tb) | Blake,Jerry (cl,as) | Jefferson,Hilton (as) | Webster,Ben (ts) | Williams,Elmer (ts) | Lucie,Lawrence (g) | Crosby,Israel (b) | Suggs,Pete (dr)

Duke Ellington And His Famous Orchestra
Conga Brava
Chicago,Ill, rec. 15.3.1940
Ellington,Duke (p) | Stewart,Rex (co) | Williams,Cootie (tp) | Jones,Wallace (tp) | Nanton,Joe 'Tricky Sam' (tb) | Tizol,Juan (tb) | Brown,Lawrence (tb) | Bigard,Barney (cl,ts) | Hodges,Johnny (ss,as) | Hardwicke,Otto (as,bass-s) | Webster,Ben (ts) | Carney,Harry (cl,as,bs) | Guy,Fred (g) | Blanton,Jimmy (b) | Greer,William 'Sonny' (dr)
Cotton Tail
Hollywood,CA, rec. 4.5.1940
Ellington,Duke (p,arr) | Jones,Wallace (tp) | Williams,Cootie (tp) | Stewart,Rex (co) | Nanton,Joe 'Tricky Sam' (tb) | Brown,Lawrence (tb) | Tizol,Juan (v-tb) | Bigard,Barney (cl) | Hodges,Johnny (cl,ss,as) | Hardwicke,Otto (as,bass-s) | Webster,Ben (ts) | Carney,Harry (cl,as,bs) | Guy,Fred (g) | Blanton,Jimmy (b) | Greer,William 'Sonny' (dr)
All Too Soon
NYC, rec. 22.7.1940
Ellington,Duke (p,arr) | Jones,Wallace (tp) | Williams,Cootie (tp) | Stewart,Rex (co) | Nanton,Joe 'Tricky Sam' (tb) | Brown,Lawrence (tb) | Tizol,Juan (v-tb) | Bigard,Barney (cl) | Hodges,Johnny (cl,ss,as) | Hardwicke,Otto (as,bass-s) | Webster,Ben (ts) | Carney,Harry (cl,as,bs) | Guy,Fred (g) | Blanton,Jimmy (b) | Greer,William 'Sonny' (dr)

Barney Bigard And His Orchestra
Lament For Javanette
Chicago,Ill, rec. 11.11.1940
Bigard,Barney (cl) | Nance,Ray (tp) | Tizol,Juan (v-tb) | Webster,Ben (ts) | Ellington,Duke (p) | Blanton,Jimmy (b) | Greer,William 'Sonny' (dr)

Rex Stewart And His Orchestra
Some Saturday
Hollywood,CA, rec. 3.7.1941
Stewart,Rex (co) | Brown,Lawrence (tb) | Webster,Ben (ts) | Carney,Harry (bs) | Ellington,Duke (p) | Blanton,Jimmy (b) | Greer,William 'Sonny' (dr)

Duke Ellington And His Orchestra
Have You Changed
Hollywood,CA, rec. 3.12.1941
Ellington,Duke (p) | Jones,Wallace (tp) | Nance,Ray (tp,v) | Stewart,Rex (tp) | Nanton,Joe 'Tricky Sam' (tb) | Tizol,Juan (tb) | Brown,Lawrence (tb) | Haughton,Chauncey (cl) | Hardwicke,Otto (as) | Hodges,Johnny (as) | Webster,Ben (ts) | Carney,Harry (cl,bs) | Guy,Fred (g) | Raglin,Alvin 'Junior' (b) | Greer,William 'Sonny' (dr)
What Am I Here For
NYC, rec. 26.2.1942
Ellington,Duke (p) | Jones,Wallace (tp) | Stewart,Rex (co) | Nance,Ray (tp) | Brown,Lawrence (tb) | Nanton,Joe 'Tricky Sam' (tb) | Tizol,Juan (v-tb) | Hardwicke,Otto (as) | Hodges,Johnny (as) | Webster,Ben (ts) | Bigard,Barney (cl,ts) | Carney,Harry (cl,bs) | Guy,Fred (g) | Raglin,Alvin 'Junior' (b) | Greer,William 'Sonny' (dr)
The Blues
NYC, rec. 23.1.1943
Ellington,Duke (p) | Jones,Wallace (tp) | Stewart,Rex (co) | Nance,Ray (tp) | Baker,Harold 'Shorty' (tp) | Brown,Lawrence (tb) | Nanton,Joe 'Tricky Sam' (tb) | Tizol,Juan (v-tb) | Hardwicke,Otto (as) | Hodges,Johnny (as) | Webster,Ben (ts) | Haughton,Chauncey (cl,as) | Carney,Harry (cl,bs) | Guy,Fred (g) | Raglin,Alvin 'Junior' (b) | Greer,William 'Sonny' (dr) | Roche,Betty (voc)

Ben Webster Quintet
Tea For Two
NYC, rec. 8.2.1944
Webster,Ben (ts) | Page,Oran 'Hot Lips' (tp) | Hart,Clyde (p) | Drayton,Charlie (b) | Best,Denzil (dr)

James P.Johnson's Blue Note Jazzmen
Blue Mizz
NYC, rec. 4.3.1944
Johnson,James P. (p) | DeParis,Sidney (tp) | Dickenson,Vic (tb) | Webster,Ben (ts) | Shirley,Jimmy (g) | Simmons,John (b) | Catlett,Big Sid (dr)

Cozy Colo All Stars
Body And Soul
NYC, rec. 13.3.1944
Cole,William 'Cozy' (dr) | Webster,Ben (ts) | Guarnieri,Johnny (p) | Walters,Teddy (g) | Taylor,Billy (b)

Sidney Catlett Quartet
Memories Of You
NYC, rec. 18.3.1944
Catlett,Big Sid (dr) | Webster,Ben (ts) | Morris,Marlowe (p) | Simmons,John (b)

Ben Webster Quartet
I Surrender Dear
NYC, rec. 17.4.1944
Webster,Ben (ts) | Guarnieri,Johnny (p) | Pettiford,Oscar (b) | Booth,David (dr)

Benny Morton's All Stars
Conversing In Blue
NYC, rec. 31.1.1945
Morton,Benny (tb) | Bigard,Barney (cl) | Webster,Ben (ts) | Benskin,Sammy (p) | Crosby,Israel (b) | Dougherty,Eddie (dr)

Pete Johnson's Housewarmin'
Ben Rides Out
NYC, rec. 31.1.1946
Johnson,Pete (p) | Nicholas,Albert (cl) | Webster,Ben (ts) | Shirley,Jimmy (g) | Hall,Al (b) | Heard,J.C. (dr)

Tony Scott And His Down Beat Club Sextet
All Too Soon
NYC, rec. 6.3.1946
Scott,Tony (cl,as) | Gillespie,Dizzy (tp) | Young,Trummy (tb) | Webster,Ben (ts) | Jones,Jimmie (p) | Ramey,Gene (b) | Nicholson,Edward 'Eddie' (dr) | Vaughan,Sarah (voc)

Benny Carter And His Chocolate Dandies
Sweet Georgia Brown
NYC, rec. 23.8.1946
Carter,Benny (cl,as,arr) | Clayton,Buck (tp) | Grey,Al (tb) | Webster,Ben (ts) | White,Sonny (p) | Simmons,John (b) | Catlett,Big Sid (dr)

Jones-Smith Incorporated
Oh! Lady Be Good
Chicago,Ill, rec. 9.11.1936
Basie,Count (p) | Smith,Carl (tp) | Young,Lester (ts) | Page,Walter (b) | Jones,Jo (dr)

Teddy Wilson And His Orchestra
This Year's Kisses
NYC, rec. 25.1.1937
Wilson,Teddy (p) | Clayton,Buck (tp) | Goodman,Benny (cl) | Young,Lester (ts) | Green,Freddie (g) | Page,Walter (b) | Jones,Jo (dr) | Holiday,Billie (voc)

Billie Holiday And Her Orchestra
A Sailboat In The Moonlight
NYC, rec. 15.6.1937
Holiday,Billie (voc) | Clayton,Buck (tp) | Hall,Edmond (cl) | Young,Lester (ts) | Sherman,James (p) | Green,Freddie (g) | Page,Walter (b) | Jones,Jo (dr)

Count Basie And His Orchestra
Time Out
NYC, rec. 9.8.1937
Basie,Count (p) | Lewis,Ed (tp) | Clayton,Buck (tp) | Moore,Bobby (tp) | Morton,Benny (tb) | Minor,Dan (tb) | Durham,Eddie (el-g) | Warren,Earl (cl,as) | Evans,Hershel (cl,ts) | Young,Lester (cl,ts) | Washington Jr.,Jack (bs) | Green,Freddie (g) | Page,Walter (b) | Jones,Jo (dr)
Texas Shuffle
NYC, rec. 22.8.1938
Basie,Count (p) | Lewis,Ed (tp) | Clayton,Buck (tp) | Edison,Harry 'Sweets' (tp) | Wells,Dicky (tb) | Minor,Dan (tb) | Morton,Benny (tb) | Warren,Earl (cl,as) | Evans,Hershel (cl,ts) | Young,Lester (cl,ts) | Washington Jr.,Jack (bs) | Green,Freddie (g) | Page,Walter (b) | Jones,Jo (dr)

Kansas City Six
Way Down Yonder In New Orleans
NYC, rec. 27.9.1938
Kansas City Six,The | Clayton,Buck (tp) | Durham,Eddie (el-g) | Young,Lester (cl,ts) | Green,Freddie (g,voc) | Page,Walter (b) | Jones,Jo (dr)

Count Basie And His Orchestra
Dark Rapture
NYC, rec. 16.11.1938
Basie,Count (p) | Clayton,Buck (tp) | Smith,Eddie (tp) | Edison,Harry 'Sweets' (tp) | Morton,Benny (tb) | Wells,Dicky (tb) | Minor,Dan (tb) | Durham,Eddie (tb,el-g) | Warren,Earl (as) | Evans,Hershel (cl,ts) | Young,Lester (cl,ts) | Washington Jr.,Jack (bs) | Green,Freddie (g) | Page,Walter (b) | Jones,Jo (dr) | Humes,Helen (voc)

Count Basie Sextet
You Can Depend On Me
NYC, rec. 2.2.1939
Basie,Count (p) | Collins,Lester 'Shad' (tp) | Young,Lester (ts) | Green,Freddie (g) | Page,Walter (b) | Jones,Jo (dr) | Rushing,Jimmy (voc)

Count Basie And His Orchestra
Taxi War Dance
NYC, rec. 19.3.1939
Basie,Count (p,org) | Lewis,Ed (tp) | Clayton,Buck (tp) | Edison,Harry 'Sweets' (tp) | Collins,Lester 'Shad' (tp) | Wells,Dicky (tb) | Morton,Benny (tb) | Minor,Dan (tb) | Warren,Earl (as) | Washington Jr.,Jack (as,bs) | Young,Lester (ts) | Tate,Buddy (ts) | Green,Freddie (g) | Page,Walter (b) | Jones,Jo (dr)

Count Basie's Kansas City Seven
Lester Leaps In
NYC, rec. 5.9.1939
Basie,Count (p) | Clayton,Buck (tp) | Wells,Dicky (tb) | Young,Lester (ts) | Green,Freddie (g) | Page,Walter (b) | Jones,Jo (dr)

Count Basie And His Orchestra
Tickle Toe
NYC, rec. 19.3.1940
Basie,Count (p,org) | Lewis,Ed (tp) | Clayton,Buck (tp) | Edison,Harry 'Sweets' (tp) | Killian,Al (tp) | Wells,Dicky (tb) | Dickenson,Vic (tb) | Minor,Dan (tb) | Warren,Earl (as) | Washington Jr.,Jack (as,bs) | Young,Lester (ts) | Tate,Buddy (ts) | Green,Freddie (g) | Page,Walter (b) | Jones,Jo (dr)

Benny Goodman Septet
Ad Lib Blues
NYC, rec. 28.10.1940
Clayton,Buck (tp) | Young,Lester (ts) | Christian,Charlie (g) | Basie,Count (p) | Green,Freddie (g) | Page,Walter (b) | Jones,Jo (dr) | Goodman,Benny (ld)

Count Basie And His Orchestra
Broadway
NYC, rec. 19.11.1940
Clayton,Buck (tp) | Lewis,Ed (tp) | Edison,Harry 'Sweets' (tp) | Killian,Al (tp) | Dickenson,Vic (tb) | Wells,Dicky (tb) | Minor,Dan (tb) | Warren,Earl (as) | Young,Lester (ts) | Tate,Buddy (ts) | Washington Jr.,Jack (as,bs) | Basie,Count (p) | Green,Freddie (g) | Page,Walter (b) | Jones,Jo (dr)

Una Mae Carlisle Quintet
Blitzkrieg Baby(You Can't Bomb Me)
NYC, rec. 10.3.1941
Carlisle,Una Mae (voc) | Collins,Lester 'Shad' (tp) | Young,Lester (ts) | Hart,Clyde (p) | Fenton,Nick (b) | West,Harold 'Doc' (dr)

Sammy Price Septet
Just Jivin' Around
NYC, rec. 3.4.1941
Price,Sammy (p) | Collins,Lester 'Shad' (tp) | Johnson,Bill (tp) | Stovall,Don (as) | Young,Lester (ts) | Jones,Duke (b) | West,Harold 'Doc' (dr)

Dicky Wells And His Orchestra

I Got Rhythm
NYC, rec. 21.12.1943
Wells,Dicky (tb) | Coleman,Bill (tp) | Young,Lester (ts) | Larkins,Ellis (p) | Green,Freddie (g) | Hall,Al (b) | Jones,Jo (dr)

Lester Young Quartet
Sometimes I'm Happy
NYC, rec. 28.12.1943
Young,Lester (ts) | Guarnieri,Johnny (p) | Stewart,Slam (b) | Catlett,Big Sid (dr)

Count Basie's Kansas City Seven
Lester Leaps Again
NYC, rec. 22.3.1944
Basie,Count (p) | Clayton,Buck (tp) | Wells,Dicky (tb) | Young,Lester (ts) | Green,Freddie (g) | Richardson,Rodney (b) | Jones,Jo (dr)

Lester Young Quintet
Jump Lester Jump
NYC, rec. 1.5.1944
Young,Lester (ts) | Basie,Count (p) | Green,Freddie (g) | Richardson,Rodney (b) | Wilson,Shadow (dr)

Lester Young And His Band
These Foolish Things Remind Me On You
Los Angeles,CA, rec. December 1945
Young,Lester (ts) | Marmarosa,Dodo (p) | Green,Freddie (g) | Callender,Red (b) | Green,Henry (dr)

Lester Young-Nat King Cole
Peg O' My Heart
Los Angeles,CA, rec. March/April 1946
Young,Lester (ts) | Cole,Nat King (p)

Lester Young And His Band
You're Driving Me Crazy
Los Altos Hill,CA, rec. August 1946
Young,Lester (ts) | Albany,Joe (p) | Ashby,Irving (g) | Callender,Red (b) | Hamilton,Forrest 'Chico' (dr)

Jumpin' With Symphony Sid
Chicago,Ill, rec. 18.2.1947
Young,Lester (ts) | McConnell,Shorty (tp) | Thornton,Argonne (p) | Lacey,Fred (g) | Richardson,Rodney (b) | Marshall,Lyndell (dr)

Eddie Condon's Hot Shots
I'm Gonna Stomp Mr.Henry Lee
NYC, rec. 8.2.1929
Condon,Eddie (bj) | Davis,Leonard (tp) | Teagarden,Jack (tb,voc) | Mezzrow,Milton Mezz (c-mel-sax) | Caldwell,Happy (ts) | Sullivan,Joe (p) | Stafford,George (dr)

Louis Armstrong And His Orchestra
Knockin' A Jug
NYC, rec. 5.3.1929
Armstrong,Louis (tp) | Teagarden,Jack (tb) | Caldwell,Happy (ts) | Sullivan,Joe (p) | Lang,Eddie (g) | Marshall,Kaiser (dr)

Ben Pollack And His Park Central Orchestra
My Kinda Love
Pollack,Ben (voc) | McPartland,Jimmy (co) | Weinstein,Ruby (tp) | Teagarden,Jack (tb) | Goodman,Benny (cl,as) | Mezzrow,Milton Mezz (as) | Binyon,Larry (fl,cl,ts) | Beller,Alex 'Al' (v) | Bergman,Eddie (v) | Schulmann,Bill (cello) | Breidis,Vic (p) | Morgan,Dick (bj) | Goodman,Harry (tuba) | Bauduc,Ray (dr)

Fats Waller And His Buddies
Ridin' But Walkin'
NYC, rec. 18.12.1929
Waller,Thomas 'Fats' (p) | Allen,Henry Red (tp) | Davis,Leonard (tp) | Teagarden,Jack (tb) | Higginbotham,J.C. (tb) | Nicholas,Albert (cl) | Holmes,Charlie (cl,as) | Binyon,Larry (ts) | Johnson,Will (bj) | Foster,George 'Pops' (b) | Marshall,Kaiser (dr)

Irving Mills And His Hotsy Totsy Gang
Loved One
NYC, rec. 6.6.1930
Mills,Irving | Beiderbecke,Bix (co) | Lodwig,Ray (tp) | Teagarden,Jack (tb) | Goodman,Benny (cl) | Leibrock,Min (bass-sax) | Malneck,Matty (v) | Venuti,Joe prob. (v) | Russin,Jack or Frank Signorelli (p) | unkn. (g) | Krupa,Gene (dr)

Jack Teagarden And His Orchestra
I'll Be Glad When You're Dead You Rascal You
NYC, rec. 14.10.1931
Teagarden,Jack (tb,voc) | Teagarden,Charlie (tp) | Bose,Sterling (tp) | Russell,Pee Wee (cl) | Catalyne,Joe (cl,ts) | Farley,Max (cl,as,ts) | Rollini,Adrian (bass-sax) | Waller,Thomas 'Fats' (p) | Lamare,Hilton Napoleon 'Nappy' (g) | Bernstein,Artie (b) | King,Stan (dr)

Eddie Lang-Joe Venuti And Their Allstars Orchestra
After You've Gone
NYC, rec. 22.10.1931
Teagarden,Jack (tb,voc) | Lang,Eddie (g) | Venuti,Joe (v) | Teagarden,Charlie (tp) | Goodman,Benny (cl) | Signorelli,Frank (p) | Lay,Ward (b) | Marshall,Neil (dr)

Jack Teagarden With Orchestra
A Hundred Years From Today
NYC, rec. 11.11.1933
Teagarden,Jack (tb,voc) | Guarente,Frank (tp) | Bose,Sterling (tp) | Hazlett,Chester (cl,as) | Dorsey,Jimmy (cl,as) | Hayes,Mutt (cl,ts) | Edelstein,Walter (v) | Meresco,Joe (p) | Botkin,Perry (g) | Bernstein,Artie (b) | Gomar,Larry (dr) | Young,Victor (ld)

Bessie Smith And Her Band
Do Your Duty
NYC, rec. 24.11.1933
Smith,Bessie (voc) | Newton,Frankie (tp) | Teagarden,Jack (tb) | Goodman,Benny (cl) | Berry,Chuck (g) | Washington,Buck (p) | Johnson,Bobby (g) | Taylor,Billy (b)

Benny Goodman And His Orchestra
Your Mother's Son-In-Law
NYC, rec. 27.11.1933
Goodman,Benny (cl) | Teagarden,Charlie (tp) | Clay,Shirley (tp) | Teagarden,Jack (tb) | Karle,Art (ts) | Sullivan,Joe (p) | McDonough,Dick (g) | Bernstein,Artie (b) | Krupa,Gene (dr) | Holiday,Billie (voc)

Adrian Rollini And His Orchestra
Riverboat Shuffle
NYC, rec. 23.10.1934
Rollini,Adrian (bass-sax) | Klein,Manny (tp) | Klein,Dave (tp) | Teagarden,Jack (tb) | Goodman,Benny (cl) | Rollini,Arthur (ts) | Smith,Howard (p) | Van Eps,George (g) | Bernstein,Artie (b) | King,Stan (dr)

Paul Whiteman And His Orchestra
Ain't Misbehavin'
NYC, rec. 9.7.1935
Whiteman,Paul (ld) | prob.personal: | Wade,Eddie (tp) | Teagarden,Charlie (tp) | Goldfield,Harry (tp) | Teagarden,Jack (tb,voc) | Fulton,Jack (tb) | Rank,Bill (tb) | Bonaccio,Benny (cl,as) | Cordaro,Joe (cl,as) | Strickfaden,Charles (as,bs) | Trumbauer,Frank (c-mel-sax) | Bargy,Roy (p) | Davis,Ramona (p) | Pingitore,Mike (g,bj) | McPherson,Norman (tuba) | Miller,Art (b) | Gomar,Larry (vib,dr)

The Three T's
I'se A Muggin'
NYC, rec. 10.3.1936
The Three T's | Teagarden,Charlie (tp) | Teagarden,Jack (tb,voc) | Cordaro,Jack (cl) | Trumbauer,Frank (c-mel-sax) | Freeman,Bud (ts) | Bargy,Roy (p) | Kress,Carl (g) | Miller,Art (b) | White,Bobby (dr)

Jack Teagarden And His Orchestra
Swingin' On The Teagarden Gate
NYC, rec. 1.11.1939
Teagarden,Jack (tb) | Ryerson,Frank (tp) | Garvin,Carl (tp) | Castle,Lee (tp) | Gutierrez,Jose (tb) | Bennett,Mark (tb) | Dudley,Eddie (tb) | Caceres,Ernie (cl,ts,bs) | Van Eps,Johnny (cl,ts) | Lytle,Hub (cl,ts) | Garvin,Clint (cl,as) | St.John,Art (cl,as) | Russin,Jack (p) | Reuss,Allan (g) | Pottle,Benny (b) | Tough,Dave (dr)

The Metronome All-Star Nine
All-Star Strut
NYC, rec. 7.2.1940
Metronome All-Star Nine | James,Harry (tp) | Teagarden,Jack (tb) | Goodman,Benny (cl) | Carter,Benny (as) | Miller,Eddie (ts) | Stacy,Jess (p) | Christian,Charlie (g) | Haggart,Bob (b) | Krupa,Gene (dr)

Bud Freeman And His Famous Chicagoans
Jack Hits The Road
NYC, rec. 23.7.1940
Freeman,Bud (ts) | Teagarden,Jack (tb,voc) | Russell,Pee Wee (cl) | Bowman,Dave (p) | Condon,Eddie (g) | Stuhlmaker,Mort (b) | Tough,Dave (dr)

Jack Teagarden's Big Eight
Big Eight Blues
NYC, rec. 15.12.1940
Teagarden,Jack (tb,voc) | Stewart,Rex (co) | Bigard,Barney (cl) | Webster,Ben (ts) | Kyle,Billy (p) | Fleagle,Brick (g) | Taylor,Billy (b) | Tough,Dave (dr)

Jack Teagarden And His Orchestra
Blues To The Lonely(Lonely Blues)
NYC, rec. 31.1.1941
Teagarden,Jack (tb,voc) | Falstitch,John (tp) | Carrière,Pokey (tp) | Feller,Sid (tp,arr) | Gutierrez,Jose (tb) | Goldfinger,Seymour (tb) | Ferall,Joe (tb) | Polo,Danny (cl,as) | Antonelli,Tony (as) | Ferdinando,Joe (as) | Moore,Art (ts) | Beck,Art (ts) | Hughes,Ernie (p) | Fishkin,Arnold (b) | Collins,Paul (dr)

The Capitol Jazzmen
Clambake In B Flat
Hollywood,CA, rec. 16.11.1943
Capitol Jazzmen,The | May,Billy (tp) | Teagarden,Jack (tb,voc) | Noone,Jimmie (cl) | Matthews,Dave (ts) | Sullivan,Joe (p) | Barbour,Dave (g) | Shapiro,Artie (b) | Singleton,Zutty (dr)

Jack Teagarden's Chicagoans
Stars Fell On Alabama
Teagarden,Jack (tb,voc) | May,Billy (tp) | Beau,Heinie (cl) | Matthews,Dave (ts) | Sullivan,Joe (p) | Barbour,Dave (g) | Shapiro,Artie (b) | Singleton,Zutty (dr)

Esquire Metropolitan Opera House Jam Session
The Blues
NYC, rec. 18.1.1944
Esquire All Stars | Eldridge,Roy (tp) | Teagarden,Jack (tb) | Bigard,Barney (cl) | Hawkins,Coleman (ts) | Tatum,Art (p) | Casey,Al (g) | Pettiford,Oscar (b) | Catlett,Big Sid (dr)

V-Disc All Stars
Jack-Armstrong Blues
NYC, rec. 7.12.1944
V-Disc All Stars | Armstrong,Louis (tp) | Butterfield,Billy (tp) | Hackett,Bobby (tp) | Teagarden,Jack (tb,voc) | McGarity,Lou (tb,voc) | Caceres,Ernie (cl) | Caiazza,Nick (ts) | Guarnieri,Johnny (p) | Ellis,Herb (g) | Cole,William 'Cozy' (dr)

George Wettling's New Yorkers
Somebody Loves Me
NYC, rec. 12.12.1944
Wettling,George (dr) | Thomas,Joe (tp) | Teagarden,Jack (tb) | D'Amico,Hank (cl) | Hawkins,Coleman (ts) | Chittison,Herman (p) | Taylor,Billy (b)

Eddie Condon And His Orchestra
Impromptu Ensemble(No.1)
Condon,Eddie (g) | Hackett,Bobby (co) | Butterfield,Billy (tp) | Kaminsky,Max (tp) | Teagarden,Jack (tb) | Russell,Pee Wee (cl,as) | Caceres,Ernie (bs) | Schroeder,Gene (p) | Haggart,Bob (b) | Wettling,George (dr)

Benny Moten's Kansas City Orchestra
Moten Swing
Camden,NJ, rec. 13.12.1932
Moten,Benny (ld) | Keyes,Joe (tp) | Stewart,Dee (tp) | Page,Oran 'Hot Lips' (tp) | Minor,Dan (tb) | Durham,Eddie (tb,el-g,arr) | Barefield,Eddie (cl,as) | Washington Jr.,Jack (as,bs) | Webster,Ben (ts) | Basie,Count (p,arr) | Berry,Leroy (g) | Page,Walter (b) | McWashington,Willie (dr)

Jones-Smith Incorporated
Evenin'
NYC, rec. 9.11.1936
Smith,Carl (tp) | Young,Lester (ts) | Basie,Count (p) | Page,Walter (b) | Jones,Jo (dr) | Rushing,Jimmy (voc)

Count Basie And His Orchestra
Swingin' At The Daisy Chain | Roseland Shuffle
NYC, rec. 21.1.1937
Basie,Count (p) | Clayton,Buck (tp) | Keyes,Joe (tp) | Smith,Carl (tp) | Hunt,George (tb) | Minor,Dan (tb) | Roberts,Caughey (as) | Evans,Hershel (ts) | Young,Lester (ts) | Washington Jr.,Jack (as,bs) | Williams,Claude (g) | Page,Walter (b) | Jones,Jo (dr)

They Can't Take That Away From Me
NYC, rec. 30.6.1937
Basie,Count (p) | Clayton,Buck (tp) | Lewis,Ed (tp) | Moore,Bobby (tp) | Hunt,George (tb) | Minor,Dan (tb) | Warren,Earl (as) | Evans,Hershel (ts) | Young,Lester (ts) | Washington Jr.,Jack (as,bs) | Green,Freddie (g) | Page,Walter (b) | Jones,Jo (dr) | Holiday,Billie (voc)

One O'Clock Jump
NYC, rec. 7.7.1937
Basie,Count (p) | Clayton,Buck (tp) | Lewis,Ed (tp) | Moore,Bobby (tp) | Smith,Carl (tp) | Hunt,George (tb) | Minor,Dan (tb) | Warren,Earl (as) | Washington Jr.,Jack (as,bs) | Young,Lester (ts) | Evans,Hershel (cl,ts) | Green,Freddie (g) | Page,Walter (b) | Jones,Jo (dr)

Sent For You Yesterday And Here You Come Today
NYC, rec. 16.2.1938
Basie,Count (p) | Lewis,Ed (tp) | Clayton,Buck (tp) | Edison,Harry 'Sweets' (tp) | Morton,Benny (tb) | Minor,Dan (tb) | Warren,Earl (cl,as) | Evans,Hershel (cl,ts) | Young,Lester (cl,ts) | Washington Jr.,Jack (bs) | Green,Freddie (g) | Page,Walter (b) | Jones,Jo (dr) | Rushing,Jimmy (voc)

Count Basie Quartet
Your Red Wagon
NYC, rec. 26.1.1939
Basie,Count (p) | Green,Freddie (g) | Page,Walter (b) | Jones,Jo (dr)

Count Basie And His Orchestra
Jive At Five
NYC, rec. 4.2.1939
Basie,Count (p) | Clayton,Buck (tp) | Edison,Harry 'Sweets' (tp) | Collins,Lester 'Shad' (tp) | Wells,Dicky (tb) | Young,Lester (ts) | Washington Jr.,Jack (as,bs) | Green,Freddie (g) | Page,Walter (b) | Jones,Jo (dr)

12th Street Rag
NYC, rec. 5.4.1939
Basie,Count (p,org) | Lewis,Ed (tp) | Clayton,Buck (tp) | Edison,Harry 'Sweets' (tp) | Collins,Lester 'Shad' (tp) | Wells,Dicky (tb) | Morton,Benny (tb) | Minor,Dan (tb) | Warren,Earl (as) | Washington Jr.,Jack (as,bs) | Young,Lester (ts) | Tate,Buddy (ts) | Green,Freddie (g) | Page,Walter (b) | Jones,Jo (dr)

You Can Count On Me
Chicago,Ill, rec. 24.6.1939
Basie,Count (p,org) | Lewis,Ed (tp) | Clayton,Buck (tp) | Edison,Harry 'Sweets' (tp) | Collins,Lester 'Shad' (tp) | Wells,Dicky (tb) | Morton,Benny (tb) | Minor,Dan (tb) | Warren,Earl (as) | Washington Jr.,Jack (as,bs) | Young,Lester (ts) | Tate,Buddy (ts) | Green,Freddie (g) | Page,Walter (b) | Jones,Jo (dr) | Humes,Helen (voc)

Song Of The Islands
NYC, rec. 4.8.1939
Basie,Count (p,org) | Lewis,Ed (tp) | Clayton,Buck (tp) | Edison,Harry 'Sweets' (tp) | Collins,Lester 'Shad' (tp) | Wells,Dicky (tb) | Morton,Benny (tb) | Minor,Dan (tb) | Warren,Earl (as) | Washington Jr.,Jack (as,bs) | Young,Lester (ts) | Tate,Buddy (ts) | Green,Freddie (g) | Page,Walter (b) | Jones,Jo (dr)

Easy Does It
NYC, rec. 20.3.1940
Basie,Count (p) | Lewis,Ed (tp) | Clayton,Buck (tp) | Edison,Harry 'Sweets' (tp) | Killian,Al (tp) | Wells,Dicky (tb) | Dickenson,Vic (tb) | Minor,Dan (tb) | Warren,Earl (as) | Washington Jr.,Jack (as,bs) | Young,Lester (ts) | Tate,Buddy (ts) | Green,Freddie (g) | Page,Walter (b) | Jones,Jo (dr)

Feather Merchant
NYC, rec. 17.11.1941
Basie,Count (p) | Lewis,Ed (tp) | Clayton,Buck (tp) | Edison,Harry 'Sweets' (tp) | Killian,Al (tp) | Wells,Dicky (tb) | Robinson,Eli (tb) | Scott,Robert (tb) | Warren,Earl (as) | Byas,Don (ts) | Washington Jr.,Jack (as,bs) | Tate,Buddy (ts) | Green,Freddie (g) | Page,Walter (b) | Jones,Jo (dr) | Mundy,Jimmy (arr)

Harvard Blues
Basie,Count (p) | Lewis,Ed (tp) | Clayton,Buck (tp) | Edison,Harry 'Sweets' (tp) | Killian,Al (tp) | Wells,Dicky (tb) | Robinson,Eli (tb) | Scott,Robert (tb) | Warren,Earl (as) | Byas,Don (ts) | Washington Jr.,Jack (as,bs) | Tate,Buddy (ts) | Green,Freddie (g) | Page,Walter (b) | Jones,Jo (dr) | Rushing,Jimmy (voc)

It's Sand Man
Los Angeles,CA, rec. 27.7.1942
Basie,Count (p) | Lewis,Ed (tp) | Clayton,Buck (tp) | Edison,Harry 'Sweets' (tp) | Killian,Al (tp) | Wells,Dicky (tb) | Robinson,Eli (tb) | Scott,Robert (tb) | Roberts,Caughey (as) | Warren,Earl (as) | Byas,Don (ts) | Washington Jr.,Jack (as,bs) | Tate,Buddy (ts) | Green,Freddie (g) | Page,Walter (b) | Jones,Jo (dr)

Kansas City Seven
After Theatre Jump
NYC, rec. 22.3.1944
Kansas City Seven,The | Clayton,Buck (tp) | Wells,Dicky (tb) | Young,Lester (ts) | Basie,Count[as 'Prince Charming'] (p) | Green,Freddie (g) | Richardson,Rodney (b) | Jones,Jo (dr)

Count Basie And His Orchestra
Taps Miller
NYC, rec. 11.1.1945
Basie,Count (p) | Killian,Al (tp) | Edison,Harry 'Sweets' (tp) | Newman,Joe (tp) | Lewis,Ed (tp) | Wells,Dicky (tb) | Donelly,Ted (tb) | Robinson,Eli (tb) | Taylor,Louis (tb) | Warren,Earl (as) | Powell,Jimmy (as) | Tate,Buddy (ts) | Thompson,Lucky (ts) | Rutherford,Rudy (bs) | Green,Freddie (g) | Richardson,Rodney (b) | Marshall,Joe (dr) | Clayton,Buck (arr)

Avenue C
NYC, rec. 26.2.1945
Basie,Count (p) | Killian,Al (tp) | Edison,Harry 'Sweets' (tp) | Newman,Joe (tp) | Lewis,Ed (tp) | Wells,Dicky (tb) | Donelly,Ted (tb) | Robinson,Eli (tb) | Taylor,Louis (tb) | Warren,Earl (as) | Powell,Jimmy (as) | Tate,Buddy (ts) | Thompson,Lucky (ts) | Rutherford,Rudy (bs) | Green,Freddie (g) | Richardson,Rodney (b) | Wilson,Shadow (dr) | Clayton,Buck (arr)

Rambo | The King
NYC, rec. 4.& 6.2.1946
Basie,Count (p) | Edison,Harry 'Sweets' (tp) | Lewis,Ed (tp) | Berry,Emmett (tp) | Newman,Joe (tp) | Donnelly,Ted (tb) | Robinson,Eli (tb) | Johnson,J.J. (tb) | Matthews,George (tb) | Powell,Jimmy (as) | Love,Preston (as) | Tate,Buddy (ts) | Jacquet,Illinois (ts) | Rutherford,Rudy (bs) | Green,Freddie (g) | Richardson,Rodney (b) | Jones,Jo (dr)

Count Basie,His Instrumentals & Rhyhtm
Swingin' The Blues
NYC, rec. 20.4.1947
Basie,Count (p) | Berry,Emmett (tp) | Price,Charles Q. (as) | Gonsalves,Paul (ts) | Green,Freddie (g) | Page,Walter (b) | Jones,Jo (dr)

Count Basie And His Orchestra
Just A Minute
Los Angeles,CA, rec. 9.12.1947
Basie,Count (p) | Lewis,Ed (tp) | Berry,Emmett (tp) | Young,Eugene 'Snooky' (tp) | Edison,Harry 'Sweets' (tp) | Donnelly,Ted (tb) | Wells,Dicky (tb) | Matthews,George (tb) | Johnson,Bill (tb) | Love,Preston (as) | Price,Charles Q. (as) | Tate,Buddy (ts) | Gonsalves,Paul (ts) | Washington Jr.,Jack (bs) | Green,Freddie (g) | Page,Walter (b) | Jones,Jo (dr)

Indigo-Records | Matthias Petzold

1001 CD | CD | Lifelines
Matthias Petzold Esperanto-Music
Lifelines | Erinnerung An Die Opfer Des Golfkrieges(1) | Dans Des Grenouilles | Mobile Für Katharina | Ming Blue | Erinnerung An Die Opfer Des Golfkrieges(2) | Birth Of A Butterfly | Heaven | Talk To Me. Talk To Me
Zuelpich, rec. 30.5.1992
Petzold,Matthias (ts,cello) | Dörner,Axel (tp) | Petzold,Joachim (tb) | Bolte,Peter (fl,ss,as) | Heinze,Volker (b) | Kahlenborn,Peter (dr)

1002 CD | CD | Psalmen und Lobgesänge für Chor und Jazz-Enseble
Matthias Petzold Group With Choir
Psalm 33 | Psalm 139 | Psalm 131 | Vogelpredigt | Psalm 42 | Jesaja 40(Wer Mißt Das Meer Mit Der Hohlen Hand) | Franziskuspsalm 7(All Ihr Völker Klatscht In Die Hände) | Come Sunday | Psalm 118 | Der Sonnengesang Des Franziskus
Brühl, rec. 18.6.1994
Petzold,Matthias (cl,ts,cello) | Dörner,Axel (tp) | Leicht,Bruno (tp) | Petzold,Joachim (tb) | Gratkowski,Frank (b-cl) | Döring,Stefan (fl,ss,as) | Lindemann,Gregor (b) | Rückert,Jochen (dr) | Jugendchor Wellenbrecher | Kirchenchor St. Margareta | Koll,Michael (ld)

1003 CD | CD | Ulysses
Matthias Petzold Septett
Neujahrslied | Don Quijote Und Die Warteschlangen | Der Himmel Über Pingsdorf | Yussufs Traum | Strange Fruit | Ulysses 95 | Nun Laube,Lindlein,Laube
Brühl, rec. 25./26.3.& 15.6.1996
Petzold,Matthias (fl,cl,ss,ts,cello) | Leicht,Bruno (tp) | Kruse,Dietmar (tb) | Döring,Stefan (b-cl,as) | Friedrich,Jürgen (p) | Lindemann,Gregor (b) | Schläger,Ralph (dr)

Trentadue Panini | Eleanor Rigby
Petzold,Matthias (fl,cl,ss,ts,cello) | Leicht,Bruno (tp) | Petzold,Joachim (tb) | Döring,Stefan (b-cl,as) | Friedrich,Jürgen (p) | Lindemann,Gregor (b) | Schläger,Ralph (dr)

1004 CD | CD | Pangäa
Bigband Der Musikschule Der Stadt Brühl Mit Gastsolisten
Pangäa: | Part 1(Featherdance) | Part 2(What Passes,Passes Like Clouds) | Part 3(Mulanga) | Part 4(Millenium Blues) | Part 5(Roma Termini)
Live in Brühl, rec. 6.6.1999
Bigband Der Musikschule Der Stadt Brühl | Dulisch,Frank (tp) | Gregor,Tobia (tp) | Winninghoff,Christian (tp) | Kaminski,Klaus (tp) | Scheuermann,Michael (tb) | Schickentanz,Andreas (tb) | Stadler,Marcus (tb) | Deponte,Reiner (b-tb) | Lackner,Marko (ss,as) | Esser,Christian (as) | Deribeaupierre,Pierre (b-cl,ts) | Gering,Guido (ts) | Timmer,Sabine (bs) | Winter,Stefan (p) | Tölkes,Christian (g) | Imhorst,Nils (b) | Höppner,Roland (dr) | Klose,Markus (perc) | Frey,Elmar (ld)

1005 CD | CD | Elements | EAN 4260019890054
Matthias Petzold Working Band
Yellow Earth | Water Music | Try It Again | Weathercock's Call | Left Handed Blues | Behind The Clouds-Your Face
Köln, rec. 3./4.1.2002
Petzold,Matthias (ss,ts,cello) | Winninghoff,Christian (tp,fl-h) | Busch,Hanno (g) | Imhorst,Nils (b,el-b) | Höppner,Roland (dr) | Peil,Roland (perc)

Dragon City
Petzold,Matthias (ss,ts,cello) | Winninghoff,Christian (tp,fl-h) | Schmitz,Marion (fl) | Busch,Hanno (g) | Imhorst,Nils (b,el-b) | Höppner,Roland (dr) | Peil,Roland (perc)

Romeo
Petzold,Matthias (ss,ts,cello) | Winninghoff,Christian (tp,fl-h) | Schickentanz,Andreas (tb) | Busch,Hanno (g) | Imhorst,Nils (b,el-b) | Höppner,Roland (dr) | Peil,Roland (perc)

People | People(radio edit)
Petzold,Matthias (ss,ts,cello) | Winninghoff,Christian (tp,fl-h) | Schickentanz,Andreas (tb) | Busch,Hanno (g) | Imhorst,Nils (b,el-b) | Höppner,Roland (dr) | Peil,Roland (perc) | Baumgartner,Ariane (voc)

I Fall In Love Too Easily | Summertime | Sidewalk Stories
Petzold,Matthias (ss,ts,cello) | Winninghoff,Christian (tp,fl-h) |

Busch,Hanno (g) | Imhorst,Nils (b,el-b) | Höppner,Roland (dr) | Peil,Roland (perc) | Baumgartner,Ariane (voc)

Intuition Records | sunny moon Musikvertrieb

INN 1101-2 | CD | Battangó
Lewis Trio With Guests
Obba-In | Battangó | Notas Da Habana | Salsera | Amanda | Punto Neutro | Be | Góngo | Timba-Tumba
Madrid, Spain, rec. December 1999-January 2000
Lewis,Ricardo G. (v) | Lewis,Irván (p,el-p,keyboards) | Pérez,Alain (b,voc) | Pico,Georvis (dr,timbales,voc) | Nogueras,Yuri (congas,perc) | Mirabal,Linda (voc)

INT 2042-2 | CD | Behind Eleven Deserts
Stephan Micus
Salima's Dance | Behind Eleven Deserts | Katut | I Went On Your Wing | Over Crimson Stones | Pour La Fille Du Soleil | The Song Of Danijar
details unknown, rec. 1978
Micus,Stephan (g,bodhran,sitar,suling,voc)

INT 2044-2 | CD | Berlin 1991 Part 1
Lounge Lizards
Tibet | One Big Yes | No Pain For Cakes | Not A Rondo | Calvin | Big Heart
Live at The 'Quartier Latin',Berlin, rec. 28.-31.3.1991
Lounge Lizards,The | Berstein,Steven (tp,co) | Lurie,John (ss,as) | Blake,Michael (ss,ts) | Carrott,Bryan (vib) | Navazio,Michele (g) | Scarpantoni,Jane (cello) | Bloedow,Oren (b) | Weston,Grant Calvin (dr) | Martin,Billy (perc)

INT 2055-2 | CD | Live In Berlin 1991-Vol.2
Remember | Evan's Drive To Mombasa | King Precious | Mr.Stinky's Blues | Welcome Herr Lazaro | What Else Is In There
Lounge Lizards,The | Bernstein,Steven (tp,co) | Lurie,John (ss,as) | Blake,Michael (ss,ts) | Carrott,Bryan (vib,marimba,tympany) | Navazio,Michele (g) | Scarpantoni,Jane (cello) | Bloedow,Oren (b) | Weston,Grant Calvin (dr) | Martin,Bill (perc)

INT 2073-2 | CD | Always,Never And Forever
Oregon
Beppo | Balahto | Reneval | Oleander | Rapid Transit | When The Fire Burns Low | Aurora | Playground In Nuclear Winter | Guitarra Picante | Apology Nicaragua | Big Fat Orange | Always,Never And Forever
Köln, rec. details unknown
Oregon | McCandless,Paul (b-cl,oboe,ss,sopranino,whistles) | Towner,Ralph (g,p,synth) | Moore,Glen (p,b) | Gurtu,Trilok (perc,voice)

INT 3007-2 | CD | N.Y.C.
Steps Ahead
Lust For Life | Senegal Calling | Get It | N.Y.C. | Stick Jam | Absolutely Maybe | Paradiso
NYC, rec. details unknown
Steps Ahead | Bendik (sax,keyboards) | Mainieri,Mike (p,perc,midi-vib,synclavier) | Khan,Steve (g,el-g) | Levin,Tony (b,chapman-stick) | Smith,Steve (dr) | Martin,Bruce (keyboards,perc,arr,synclavier-programming)
Well In That Case | Festival
Steps Ahead | Bendik (sax,keyboards) | Mainieri,Mike (p,perc,midi-vib,synclavier) | Khan,Steve (g,el-g) | Gomez,Raymond (el-g) | Levin,Tony (b,chapman-stick) | Smith,Steve (dr) | Martin,Bruce (keyboards,perc,arr,synclavier-programming)
Red Neon, Go Or Give
Steps Ahead | Bendik (sax,keyboards) | Mainieri,Mike (p,perc,midi-vib,synclavier) | Khan,Steve (g,el-g) | Pantoja,Rique (p) | Levin,Tony (b,chapman-stick) | Smith,Steve (dr) | Martin,Bruce (keyboards,perc,arr,synclavier-programming)
Charanga
Steps Ahead | Bendik (sax,keyboards) | Mainieri,Mike (p,perc,midi-vib,synclavier) | Khan,Steve (g,el-g) | Levin,Tony (b,chapman-stick) | Smith,Steve (dr) | Martin,Bruce (keyboards,perc,arr,synclavier-programming) | Barber,Stephen (string-orchestration)

INT 3009-2 | CD | Flash Of The Spirit
Jon Hassell & Farafina
Flash On The Spirit(Laughter) | Night Moves(Fear) | Air Afrique(Wind) | Out Pours(Kongo) | Blue(Prayer) | Like Warriors Everywhere(Courage) -(Like) Warriors Everywhere(Courage) | Tales Of The Near Future(Clairvoyance) | A Vampire Dances(Symmetry) | Masque(Strehgth)
London,GB/Los Angeles,CA, rec. September & October 1987/February & June 1988
Hassell,Jon (tp,keyboards,synth) | Deane,J.A. (synth,perc,electronics) | Farafina | Konate,Mahama (balafon,voc) | Yé,Paco (dr,perc) | Coulibaly,Soungalo (fl,perc,maracas,voc) | Keita,Tiawara (soucou,tama) | Quattara,Seydou (bara) | Palm,Beh (bara) | Diara,Baba (perc,balafon) | Sanou,Souleyname (dancer,maracas)
Dreamworld(Dance)
Hassell,Jon (tp,keyboards,synth) | Deane,J.A. (synth,perc,electronics) | Schwartz,Daniel (el-b) | Farafina | Konate,Mahama (balafon,voc) | Yé,Paco (dr,perc) | Coulibaly,Soungalo (fl,perc,maracas,voc) | Keita,Tiawara (soucou,tama) | Quattara,Seydou (bara) | Palm,Beh (bara) | Diara,Baba (perc,balafon) | Sanou,Souleyname (dancer,maracas)

INT 3052-2 | CD | Come In Spinner
Vince Jones With Orchestra
I've Got You Under My Skin | Mood Indigo | Lil' Darlin' | You Go To My Head | Body And Soul
Sidney,Austalia, rec. details unknown
Jones,Vince (voc) | Motz,Dick (tp) | Hoffman,John (tp) | Panichi,Paul (tp) | McIver,Bob (tb) | Loughlan,Col (cl,as) | Hutchings,Lee (cl,ts) | Morphett,Jason (cl,ts) | Buchanon,Tony (cl,bs) | Kelly,Jim (g) | Lambert,Max (p) | Swanton,Lloyd (b) | Gander,Andrew (dr)
I Get Along Without You Very Well
Jones,Vince (voc) | Motz,Dick (tp) | Hoffman,John (tp) | Panichi,Paul (tp) | McIver,Bob (tb) | Loughlan,Col (cl,as) | Hutchings,Lee (cl,ts) | Morphett,Jason (cl,ts) | Buchanon,Tony (cl,bs) | Kelly,Jim (g) | Lambert,Max (p) | Swanton,Lloyd (b) | Gander,Andrew (dr) | Strings | Hartl,Phil (cond)
Grace Knight With Orchestra
The Man I Love | Don't Get Around Much Anymore | Sophisticated Lady | Loose Lips | Joy Juice | Lover Come Back To Me | Don't Know Much Abou Love
Knight,Grace (voc) | Motz,Dick (tp) | Hoffman,John (tp) | Panichi,Paul (tp) | McIver,Bob (tb) | Loughlan,Col (cl,as) | Hutchings,Lee (cl,ts) | Morphett,Jason (cl,ts) | Buchanon,Tony (cl,bs) | Kelly,Jim (g) | Lambert,Max (p) | Swanton,Lloyd (b) | Gander,Andrew (dr)
In A Sentimental Mood
Motz,Dick (tp) | Hoffman,John (tp) | Panichi,Paul (tp) | McIver,Bob (tb) | Loughlan,Col (cl,as) | Hutchings,Lee (cl,ts) | Morphett,Jason (cl,ts) | Buchanon,Tony (cl,bs) | Kelly,Jim (g) | Lambert,Max (p) | Swanton,Lloyd (b) | Gander,Andrew (dr)

INT 3067-2 | CD | Spell
Vince Jones Group
Tenderly | Better Than The Average Man | I Put A Spell On You | You're Gonna Hear From Me | Crazy She Calls Me | Let's Call This | My Funny Valentine | Night And Day | Fish Farm | Do Nothin' Till You Hear From Me
Melbourne, Australia, rec. 1983
Jones,Vince (tp,fl-h,voc) | Smith,Russell (v-tb) | DeVries,Doug (g,el-g) | Fitzgibbon,Mark (p) | Schwaiger,Herman (b) | Jones,Peter (dr)

INT 3068-2 | CD | On The Brink Of It
Vince Jones Septet
On The Brink Of It | Losing Hand | My Ideal | Like Young | Nature Boy | Boys On The Corner | My Baby Comes To Me | Come On Home(Comin' Home) | Pablo(Lady Z) | Funny How Time Slips Away | Everything Happens To Me
Melbourne, Australia, rec. June/Aug.1985
Jones,Vince (tp,perc,pocket-tp,voc) | Williamson,Paul (ts,bs) | Chindamo,Joe (p,accordeon) | DeVries,Doug (g,el-g) | Costello,Gary (b) | Browne,Allan (dr) | Pereira,Ray (perc)

INT 3069-2 | CD | It All Ends Up In Tears
Vince Jones Group
If You're Goin' To The City
Melbourne, Australia, rec. May & July 1987
Jones,Vince (tp,voc) | Smith,Russell (v-tb) | Williamson,Paul (ts) | Sandell,Bruce (ts) | DeVries,Doug (el-g) | McCall,Barney (p) | Hadley,Steve (b) | Floyd,Tony (dr) | Pereira,Ray (perc)
Jettison
Jones,Vince (tp,voc) | Smith,Russell (v-tb) | Chaplin,Ian (as) | Sandell,Bruce (ts) | DeVries,Doug (el-g) | McCall,Barney (p) | Hadley,Steve (b) | Floyd,Tony (dr)
Budgie
Jones,Vince (tp,voc) | Smith,Russell (v-tb) | Chaplin,Ian (as) | Sandell,Bruce (ts) | DeVries,Doug (el-g) | Hadley,Steve (b) | Floyd,Tony (dr) | Pereira,Ray (perc)
You Don't Know What Love Is
Jones,Vince (tp,voc) | Smith,Russell (v-tb) | Chaplin,Ian (as) | Sandell,Bruce (fl) | DeVries,Doug (el-g) | McCall,Barney (p) | Hadley,Steve (b) | Floyd,Tony (dr) | Pereira,Ray (congas)
Rainbow Cake
Jones,Vince (voc) | DeVries,Doug (g) | McCall,Barney (p) | Hadley,Steve (b) | Pereira,Ray (bells) | McTaggert,Steve (v) | Heath,Shelley (v) | Robertson,Angie (viola) | Johnson,Jacqueline (cello)
But Beautiful
Jones,Vince (voc) | DeVries,Doug (g) | McCall,Barney (p) | Hadley,Steve (b) | Floyd,Tony (dr) | McTaggert,Steve (v) | Heath,Shelley (v) | Robertson,Angie (viola) | Johnson,Jacqueline (cello)
Comes Love
Jones,Vince (tp,voc) | Sandell,Bruce (fl,ts) | Williamson,Paul (ts,bs) | DeVries,Doug (g) | Hadley,Steve (b) | Floyd,Tony (dr) | Pereira,Ray (perc)
A Sweet Defeat
Jones,Vince (tp,voc) | Sandell,Bruce (fl) | DeVries,Doug (g) | McCall,Barney (p) | Hadley,Steve (b) | Floyd,Tony (dr) | Pereira,Ray (perc)
Circle In The Square
Jones,Vince (tp,voc) | Smith,Russell (v-tb) | Chaplin,Ian (as) | Sandell,Bruce (ts) | Williamson,Paul (bs) | DeVries,Doug (g) | Grabowsky,Paul (p) | Hadley,Steve (b) | Floyd,Tony (dr) | Pereira,Ray (perc)
It All Ends Up In Tears
Jones,Vince (voc) | Sandell,Bruce (cl,voc) | DeVries,Doug (g) | Grabowsky,Paul (p,voc) | Hadley,Steve (b) | Floyd,Tony (dr) | Smith,Russell (vov)

INT 3070-2 | CD | Watch What Happens
Dream | I've Got You Under My Skin | When I Fall In Love | Loose Bloose | Martini Time | You Don't Know Me | Watch What Happens | As Time Goes By
Richmond Recorders,?, Australia, rec. Nov.1981
Jones,Vince (tp,fl-h,voc) | DeVries,Doug (g) | Saarelaht,Mart (p) | details unknown

INT 3071-2 | CD | For All Colours
For All Colours | Old For The New | Party Time | Blue | Call Of The West
Melbourne, Australia, rec. April/August 1984
Jones,Vince (tp,fl-h,perc,voc) | Williamson,Paul (ts) | Jones,Peter (p) | DeVries,Doug (g,el-g) | Costello,Gary (b) | Brown,Alan (dr)
Never Let Me Go | All Or Nothing At All | C'Est La Vie | Drinking Again
Jones,Vince (tp,fl-h,perc,voc) | Williamson,Paul (ts) | Jones,Peter (p) | DeVries,Doug (g,el-g) | Costello,Gary (b) | Whitford,Peter (dr)
Straighten Up And Fly Right
Jones,Vince (tp,fl-h,perc,voc) | Wilde,Wilbur (ts) | Jones,Peter (p) | DeVries,Doug (g,el-g) | Costello,Gary (b) | Whitford,Peter (dr)

INT 3072-2 | CD | Tell Me A Secret
Don't Worry 'Bout A Thing | Stop This World
Melbourne, Australia, rec. June/Aug.1986
Jones,Vince (voc) | Williamson,Paul (ts,bs) | Sandell,Bruce (ts) | DeVries,Doug (el-g) | Chindamo,Joe (p) | Costello,Gary (b) | Browne,Allan (dr)
Two Sleepy People | I've Never Been In Love Before
Jones,Vince (tp,voc) | Hope,Steven (p) | Costello,Gary (b) | Browne,Allan (dr)
Second Item
Jones,Vince (perc,voc) | DeVries,Doug (g) | Chindamo,Joe (p) | Costello,Gary (b) | Browne,Allan (dr) | Periera,Ray (perc)
I've Been Used
Jones,Vince (voc) | DeVries,Doug (el-g) | Hope,Steven (p) | Costello,Gary (b) | Browne,Allan (dr)
Too Much Too Soon
Jones,Vince (tp,voc) | Williamson,Paul (bs) | DeVries,Doug (el-g) | Costello,Gary (b) | Browne,Allan (dr)
Tell Me A Secret | It's Hard To Be Good
Jones,Vince (voc) | Williamson,Paul (ts,voc) | Sandell,Bruce (ts,voc) | DeVries,Doug (el-g) | Costello,Gary (b) | Browne,Allan (dr)
Harolds Land
Jones,Vince (tp,perc) | Sandell,Bruce (fl) | Williamson,Paul (ts) | Chindamo,Joe (p) | Costello,Gary (b) | Browne,Allan (dr) | Perlera,Ray (perc)
Some Say You Win
Jones,Vince (tp,voc) | DeVries,Doug (g) | Costello,Gary (b) | Browne,Allan (dr)
All The Way
Jones,Vince (voc) | Sandell,Bruce (ts) | Hope,Steven (p) | Costello,Gary (b) | Browne,Allan (dr)

INT 3080-2 | CD | Cantos
Lazaro Ros Con Mezcla
Barasuayo | Ikiri Adda | Iya Maasé Lobi Shango | Imbe Imbé | Aketé Oba Oba | Addé Oya | Ibanlayé | Echubelekéo
Havana,Cuba & Sinzig,Germany, rec. details unknown
Ros,Lazaro (voc) | Grupo Mezcla: | Menendez,Pablo (g,arr,voc) | Huergo,Lucia (sax,keyboards,arr,voc) | Cornuchet,Sonia (keyboards,voc) | Acosta,Jose Antonio (keyboards,b,arr,voc) | Abreu,Juan Carlos (dr,perc) | Rodriguez,Octavio (perc,bata-dr) | Pedroso,Miguel (voc)

INT 3087-2 | CD | One Day Spent
Vince Jones With The Benny Green Quartet
Detour Ahead | Let's Get Lost | I Wish You Love | Since I Fell For You | The After Thought | I Thought About You | Time After Time | Never Let Me Go | Save Your Love For Me
NYC, rec. details unknown
Jones,Vince (voc) | Green,Benny (p) | Barlow,Dale (ts) | Moffett,Charnett (b) | Allen,Carl (dr)
Vince Jones Quartet
There'll Never Be Another You
Richmond,Vic.,Australia, rec. details unknown
Jones,Vince (tp,voc) | McAll,John (p) | Swanton,Lloyd (b) | Gander,Andrew (dr)

INT 3109-2 | CD | Future Girl
Vince Jones Group
Hindered On His Way To Heaven | Drunk With Majic | Mirror On Yourself | Future Girl | Irreplacable | Nature Of Power | Lobster | Fortunes Pet | False Knot
Melbourne, Australia, rec. details unknown
Jones,Vince (tp,voc) | Barlow,Dale (ts) | DeVries,Doug (g) | McCall,Barney (p) | Swanton,Lloyd (b) | Gander,Andrew (dr) | Periera,Ray (perc)

INT 3174-2 | CD | Shifting Sands
Barbara Thompson Group
Shifting Sands | In The Shadow Of The Moon | Guardians Of The Deep | The Whisper In The Shell | The Wave Police | Sun Shapes | Head In The Sand
Temple Music Studios,?, rec. Summer 1998
Thompson,Barbara (fl,as,ts) | Thompson,Billy (v) | Lerner,Pete (keyboards) | Westwood,Paul (el-b) | Hiseman,Jon (dr)

INT 3175-2 | CD | Heavy Cairo Trafic
Koch-Schütz-Studer & El Nil Troop
Alaschaan Aref Albi Ma'ak | Makana | Tulli Men Al Maschkabeia | 18,Maamal El Sokar | Nightclubbing With Hatschepsud(dedicated to Grace Jones) | Oissa | Heavy Cairo Trafic(dedicated to Sun Ra) | El Ghalla Ghalletna- | Malaib Schina- | Belly Button Rave | Vice Versa | Nubian Bonus Track
Cairo,Egypt, rec. 14.-17.6.1995
Koch,Hans (cl,sax,sampling,sequencer-programming,tape) | Schütz,Martin (el-5-string-cello,electronics,sampling) | Studer,Freddy (dr,perc) | El Nil Troop | Ismail,Shaker (rababa) | Sadek,Ragab (tablas) | Aziz,Moustapha Abdel (arghoul) | Shaheen,Ibrahim (gaula) | Haggag,Ismail (duff) | Kholossy,Mohamed (saggat) | Abbas,Ihab (re) | Schiba,Reda (voc)

INT 3189-2 | CD | Kingdom Of Champa
Michael Blake Group
The Champa Theme | Dislocated In Natran | Folksong | Purple City | Mekong | Hué Is Hué? | Perfume River
NYC, rec. 20./21.8.1996
Blake,Michael (b-cl,ss,ts) | Bernstein,Steven (tp,co,slide-tp) | Rojas,Marcus (tuba) | Chapin,Thomas[Tom] (fl,bs,b-fl,piccolo) | Carrott,Bryan (vib) | Tronzo,David (el-slide-g) | Cappadocia,Rufus (cello) | Scherr,Tony (b,el-b,moonlute) | Neumann,Scott (dr) | Martin,Billy (perc)

INT 3191-2 | CD | Northwest Passage
Oregon
Take Heart | Claridade | Joyful Departure | Under A Dorian Sky | Under The Mountain | L'Assassino Che Suona(The Musical Assassin)
Chicago,Ill, rec. September/October 1996
Oregon | Towner,Ralph (g,p,keyboards,12-string-g) | McCandless,Paul (engl-h,ss,oboe,sopranino) | Moore,Glen (b) | Tuncboyaci[Boyaciyan],Arto (dr,perc,hand-dr)
Lost In The Hours | Nightfall | Fortune Cookie | Yes To Be | Northwest Passage
Oregon | Towner,Ralph (g,p,keyboards,12-string-g) | McCandless,Paul (engl-h,ss,oboe,sopranino) | Moore,Glen (b) | Walker,Mark (dr,perc,hand-dr)
Ralph Towner-Mark Walker
Over Your Shoulder
Towner,Ralph (12-string-g) | Walker,Mark (dr,hand-dr)
Ralph Towner-Glen Moore
Intro
Towner,Ralph (p,keyboards) | Moore,Glen (b)
Glen Moore-Arto Tuncboyaciyan
Don't Knock On My Door
Moore,Glen (b) | Tuncboyaci[Boyaciyan],Arto (dr,perc,voice)

INT 3192-2 | CD | Nude Bass Ascending...
Glen Moore -Rabih Abou-Khalil
Silk | Euphrates | Kubla Khan | Cicconi | Inky | Olivewood | Golden Penciled Paradise | Baida | Nude Bass Descending | The Stream Is Stony
details unknown, rec. May 1996
Moore,Glen (b) | Abou-Khalil,Rabih (oud)
Glen Moore Group
Moot | Roots In The Sky(1) | It Takes A Village | Mayday | Bloomination | Roots In The Sky(2)
details unknown, rec. April 1997
Moore,Glen (p,b) | Bley,Carla (org) | Swallow,Steve (el-b) | Tuncboyaci[Boyaciyan],Arto (perc,voc)

INT 3198-2 | CD | Here's To The Miracles
Vince Jones Group
Luncheon With The President | Bye Bye Love
Sidney,Austalia, rec. details unknown
Jones,Vince (tp,voc) | McAll,Barney (p) | Zwartz,Jonathan (b) | Jones,Peter (dr)
Here's To The Miracles
Jones,Vince (tp,voc) | McAll,Barney (p,org) | Zwartz,Jonathan (b) | Gander,Andrew (dr) | Backhouse,Tony (voc) | Davis,Stuart (voc) | Papademetriou,Alice (voc) | Allayialis,Toni (voc)
We're Still Friends | Can't Afford To Live,Can't Afford To Die
Jones,Vince (tp,voc) | Hopkins,Tim (ts) | McAll,Barney (p,org) | Zwartz,Jonathan (b) | Gander,Andrew (dr)
Love Comes Back
Jones,Vince (tp,voc) | McAll,Barney (p,claps) | Zwartz,Jonathan (b) | Jones,Peter (dr,claps) | Pereira,Ray (perc,claps)
Lost In The Stars | A Tribute Two
Jones,Vince (voc) | McAll,Barney (p) | Zwartz,Jonathan (b) | Stuart,Hamish (dr)
Take A Love Song
Jones,Vince (tp,voc) | Greening,James (tb) | Hopkins,Tim (ts) | McAll,Barney (p,el-p,synth) | Zwartz,Jonathan (b) | Jones,Peter (dr)
America
Jones,Vince (tp,voc) | Hopkins,Tim (ts) | McAll,Barney (p) | Zwartz,Jonathan (b) | Jones,Peter (dr) | Stuart,Hamish (bells) | Hevia,Fabian (perc)

INT 3210-2 | CD | Other Worlds
David Friedman Trio
New Los Them | Vorstellung | Carolyn V. | O Grande Amor | Czar | Tango
Ludwigsburg, rec. details unknown
Friedman,David (vib,marimba,perc) | Martinier,Jean-Louis (accordeon) | Cox,Anthony (b)
David Friedman Quartet
Triptych | Gold- | Alchemy- | Fleure De L'Eau | Le Chat | From The Distance
Friedman,David (vib,marimba) | Martinier,Jean-Louis (accordeon) | Cox,Anthony (b) | Verly,Francois (perc)

INT 3211-2 | CD | Affairs:Rolf Kühn & Friends
Rolf Kühn And Friends
Into The Pocket | Off A Bird
details unknown, rec. details unknown
Kühn,Rolf (cl) | Liebman,Dave (ss) | Loeb,Chuck (g) | Ilg,Dieter (b) | Haffner,Wolfgang (dr)
Easy Living
Kühn,Rolf (cl) | Brecker,Randy (tp,fl-h) | Loeb,Chuck (g)
There Is A Mingus Amonk Us
Kühn,Rolf (cl) | Brecker,Randy (tp,fl-h) | Loeb,Chuck (g) | Ilg,Dieter (b) | Haffner,Wolfgang (dr)
Just Friends | Three Bopeteers
rec. details unknown
Kühn,Rolf (cl) | Daniels,Eddie (cl) | DeFranco,Buddy (cl) | Loeb,Chuck (g) | Ilg,Dieter (b) | Haffner,Wolfgang (dr)
Lover Man(Oh,Where Can You Be?)
details unknown, rec. details unknown
Kühn,Rolf (cl) | DeFranco,Buddy (cl) | Loeb,Chuck (g) | Ilg,Dieter (b) | Haffner,Wolfgang (dr)
Polka Dots And Moonbeams- | Like Someone In Love-
Kühn,Rolf (cl) | Daniels,Eddie (cl) | Loeb,Chuck (g)
Fractions
Leipzig, rec. details unknown
Kühn,Rolf (cl) | Mangelsdorff,Albert (tb)
The Verticale Circle
NYC, rec. January 1997
Kühn,Rolf (cl) | Coleman,Ornette (as)

INT 3212-2 | CD | Drift
Michael Blake Group
Drift | Mean As A Swan | Toque | The Creep | Teo Walks | Lady Red | Duty Free Suite | Dry Socket | Afro Blake | Maria | Residence
NYC, rec. 4./5.9.1998 & 6.1.1999
Blake,Michael (ss,ts) | Horton,Ron (tp,fl-h) | Bernstein,Steven (slide-tp) | Rojas,Marcus (tuba) | Krauss,Briggan (as,bs) | Allmond,Peck (tp,peck-horn,ts) | Kimbrough,Frank (p) | Scherr,Tony (el-g) | Allison,Ben (b) | Wilson,Matt (dr) | Refosco,Mauro (perc)

INT 3218-2 | CD | Where We Come From

Vital Information
Dr.Demento | Moby Dick | Craniac Trilogy-Part 1:Transport | Listen Up! | Swamp Stomp | Craniac Trilogy-Part 2:The Extraction | First Thing This Morning | Take Eight | Craniac Trilogy-Part 3:The Implant | Bob | Cranial Joy:Completion | Happy House | Cranial Meltdown:Dementia | Blow Fish Blues | Sitting Ducks | One In A Lifetime | 008
Marin Country,CA, rec. 24.4-3.5.1997
Vital Information | Gambale,Frank (g) | Coster,Tom (el-p,org,accordeon) | Andrews,Jeff (b,el-b) | Smith,Steve (dr)

INT 3223-2 | CD | Hair Of The Dog
Dogslyde
Phoena Intro | 1,2,3, | Phoena | Buzzard Breath | Death Blues | I Still Miss You | Watanabe | Attack Of Sharon The Herbovore | Phoena Reprise
Oakland,CA, rec. 23.6.1996
Dogslyde | Clyde,'The Slide' (tp,el-p) | Graham,Ron (as) | Marshall,Joshi (ts) | Silverman,Mike (b) | Leinbach,Ben (dr)

INT 3224-2 | CD | 4+1 Ensemble
Wayne Horvitz Group
Step Aside | Up All Night | Cotton Club | First Light | Trouble | AFAP | Exit Laughing | Take Me Home | Calder- | Snake Eyes-
Bear Creek Studios,?, rec. details unknown
Horvitz,Wayne (p,keyboards) | Priester,Julian (tb) | Kang,Eywind (v) | Watts,Reggie (keyboards) | Martine,Tucker (processing)

INT 3228-2 | CD | If Trees Could Fly
Marc Johnson-Eric Longsworth
Reve-A-Ca | A Blues | Ton Sur Ton | Dancin' To The Coffee Machine | Lullaby | Longworld | Au Clair De La Femme | Spanish Fly | Her Majesty(The Turtle) | Seulement | Ton Sur Ton(reprise)
NYC, rec. 26.11.1996 & 12.6.1997
Longsworth,Eric (el-cello) | Johnson,Marc (b)

INT 3242-2 | CD | Driving While Black...
Bennie Maupin-Dr. Patrick Gleeson
Smiling Faces | Riverside Drive | The Work | The Lookout | Driving While Black | Bank Float | Miles To Go | In Re:Nude Orbit | Vutu
details unknown, rec. details unknown
Maupin,Bennie (reeds) | Gleeson,Pat (rhythm-instruments)

INT 3249-2 | CD | Port Of Entry
Ned Rothenberg Trio
Gamalong | Dad Can Dig | Lost In A Blue Forest | FoFela- | Misterioso- | The Hotel Lazard Cafe | Trip To The Bar | Port Of Entry | Rad-At
NYC, rec. 23./24.10.1997 & 3./4.3.1998
Rothenberg,Ned (cl,b-cl,as,shakuhachi) | Harris,Jerome (g,b-g) | Chatterjee,Samir (perc,dumbek,table)

INT 3257-2 | CD | Live At The Jazz Bakery
Denny Zeitlin-David Friesen
Equinox | Nefertiti | Other Times,Other Places | Triptych | Epiphany | The Touch Of Your Lips | Upon Tho Swing | Goal In Mind
Live at The Jazz Bakery,Los Angeles,CA, rec. 10./11.5.1996
Zeitlin,Denny (p) | Friesen,David (b)

INT 3258-2 | CD | Alter Ego
Miriam Alter Quintet
No More Stress | Warmness | Funny Story | Worry | Stay Close To Me | Change In Rhythm | Slow Waltz | Getting Dark | Carousel | Calm Down
NYC, rec. 8.12.1997
Miles,Ron (tp) | Drewes,Billy (cl,sax) | Werner,Kenny (p) | Johnson,Marc (b) | Baron,Joey (dr) | Alter,Myriam (comp)

INT 3260-2 | CD | Redemption
Slow Poke
Johnny Hornet | Sixth Sense | Jar Of Hair | Cilantro | God Don't Never Change | Dear Ear | Been A Son | Redemption | Breeze Valley | Shine A Light
Zerkall, rec. 16.-22.8.1998
Slow Poke | Blake,Michael (ss,ts,fingersnaps,handclaps,melodica) | Tronzo,David (bar-g,dobro,slide-g,waste-basket) | Scherr,Tony (g,b-g,dobro) | Wollesen,Kenny (dr,perc,samples)

INT 3264-2 | CD | Nomad's Notebook
Andy Middleton Group
Loyalsock | Mount Rundle | Lothlorien | I'll Remember August | Simone
Brooklyn,NY, rec. 17./18.9.1998
Middleton,Andy (ss,ts) | Towner,Ralph (g,grand-p,12-string-g) | Holland,Dave (b) | Jones,Alan (dr)
Lizbet
Middleton,Andy (ss,ts) | Hey,Henry (grand-p) | Towner,Ralph (g,12-string-g) | Holland,Dave (b) | Jones,Alan (dr)
Raffish
Middleton,Andy (ss,ts) | Towner,Ralph (g,12-string-g) | Holland,Dave (b) | Jones,Alan (dr) | Haddad,Jamey (perc,voc)
Kasbah Tadla | Songs Of Struggle And Songs Of Love
Middleton,Andy (ss,ts) | Bless,Noah (tb) | Towner,Ralph (g,12-string-g) | Holland,Dave (b) | Jones,Alan (dr) | Haddad,Jamey (perc,voc)

INT 3272-2 | CD | Point Of View
Susan Weinert Band
Liebman | The Kobayashi Syndrom | Knock On Wood | Trust Me | Day | Did I Get You Right | The Proof | Les Trois Arbres | Fort Carré | La Fuerza Del Viento | No Warm-Ups
Köln, rec. December 1998/January 1999
Weinert,Susan (g,el-g) | Weinert,Martin (b) | Fischötter,Hardy (dr) | Bertrand,Pierre (ts) | Jung,Jean-Yves (p) | Schiefel,Michael (voice)

INT 3276-2 | CD | Inside Out
Rolf Kühn Group
Working Inside | Second Visit
Zerkall, rec. 1999
Kühn,Rolf (cl) | Brecker,Michael (ts) | Schröder,John (g) | Beier,Detlev (b) | Haffner,Wolfgang (dr)
I Got It Bad And That Ain't Good
Kühn,Rolf (cl) | Brönner,Till (tp) | Schröder,John (g) | Beier,Detlev (b)
Go From Here
Kühn,Rolf (cl) | Brönner,Till (tp) | Kühn,Joachim (p) | Beier,Detlev (b) | Rückert,Jochen (dr)
Roulette | Ornette
Kühn,Rolf (cl) | Kühn,Joachim (p) | Beier,Detlev (b) | Rückert,Jochen (dr)
Kary's Trance
Kühn,Rolf (cl) | Konitz,Lee (as) | Chastenier,Frank (p) | Beier,Detlev (b) | Haffner,Wolfgang (dr)
Seeing Salinas Again
Kühn,Rolf (cl) | Chastenier,Frank (p) | Beier,Detlev (b) | Haffner,Wolfgang (dr)
Leeaison
Kühn,Rolf (cl) | Konitz,Lee (as)

INT 3290-2 | CD | Thompson's Tangos
Barbara Thompson's Paraphernalia
Tango 1 | Tango 2 | Tango 3 | Tango 4 | Naima | Regga Ragga | Smokey Embrace | The Slider | The Real Softshoe
Temple Music Studios,?, rec. 2000
Thompson,Barbara (ss,as,ts) | Thompson,Billy (v) | Lemer,Pete (keyboards) | Hiseman,Jon (dr)

INT 3296-2 | 2 CD | Live Around The World Where We Come From Tour '98-'99
Vital Information
Dr.Demento | Moby Dick | Swamp Stomp | Cranial Jam | Happy House | Fortaleza | First Thing This Morning | The Perfect Date | It's A Jungle Out There | The Drum Also Waltzes | Take Eight | Listen Up! | Europa | Do You Read Me? | Over And Out | Mr.P.C. | Soulful Drums
different Places, rec. 1998/1999
Vital Information | Gambale,Frank (g) | Coster,Tom (el-p,org,accordeon) | Browne,Baron (b) | Smith,Steve (dr)

INT 3306-2 | CD | Show 'Em Where You Live
Cranial No.1 Right Now | Mr. T.C. | Shagadelic Boogaloo | Cranial No.2 The Jinx | Soul Principle | Our Man In Louisiana | Cat And Mouse | Cranial No.3 Sizzy Blues | Sideway Blues | The Blackhawk | Cranial No.4 Where We Live | The Fire Still Bums(for Jimi) | Cranial No.5 Awaken The Hoodoo | Cranial No. 6 Mata Hari | Gingerbread Boy | Cranial No.7 Brake Failure
Marin Country,CA, rec. 4.-17.10.1999
Vital Information | Gambale,Frank (g) | Coster,Tom (org,el-p,accordeon) | Browne,Baron (b) | Smith,Steve (dr)

INT 3309-2 | CD | Brutto Tempo
Jasper Van't Hof-Charlie Mariano-Steve Swallow
Brutto Tempo | Away | Lied Der Mignon | Dry Four | Dhatuvardhani | Close Near | Ladies In Mercedes | Carnation | Ghost Guests | Not Quiet A Ballad
Arnhem, Holland, rec. November 2000
Mariano,Charlie (sax) | Van't Hof,Jasper (p,keyboards) | Swallow,Steve (el-b)

INT 3328-2 | CD | Internal Eyes
Rolf Kühn Group
Runferyerlife | Time For A Rainy Day | Total Refections | Groove Town | Re-Re | Lover Man(Oh,Where Can You Be?) | Freaky Eyes | The Way You Are | For All We Know | Total Reflections
different Places, rec. 2001
Kühn,Rolf (cl) | Mintzer,Bob (ts) | Loeb,Chuck (g) | Solal,Martial (p) | Crona,Claes (p) | Chastenier,Frank (org) | Beier,Detlev (b) | Erskine,Peter (dr) | Haffner,Wolfgang (dr)

INT 3334-2 | 2 CD | The Name Of A Woman
David Friesen Trio
I Love You | Beatrice | Delores | In The Wee Small Hours Of The Morning | Very Early | I Have Dreamed | Elsa | Ceora | My One And Only Love | Kirsten | My Funny Valentine | Rachel | Emily | Audrey | My Foolish Heart
Lake Oswego,Oregon, rec. May 1999-January 2000
Friesen,David (b) | Porter,Randy (p) | Jones,Alan (dr)

INT 3339-2 | CD | Balkan Jazz
Nicolas Simion Group
Fighting Song | Slovakian Peasant Song | One For Kisser | That's The Evening For Santa Claus | Balkanale | Cheremies Folk Song | Antiphon | Looking Back | May I Dance | Gankino Horo
Live at Stadtgarten,Köln, rec. 18./19.3.1999
Simion,Nicolas (b-cl,ss,ts) | Goykovich,Dusko (tp,fl-h) | Goodman,Geoff (g,mando-cello) | Scholly,Norbert (g,waldzither) | Gjakonovski,Martin (b,oud) | Skinner,Tom (dr) | Shotham,Ramesh (perc)

INT 3507-2 | CD | Story In,Story Out
Rinde Eckert Group
The Sign Says 'West' | Indian Summer | Bad Feelin' | Hit The Desert | Day By Day | Out Of The Mesa | Whatever The Reason | Slow Train Breakdown | Last Rite | Amnesia
San Francisco,CA, rec. details unknown
Eckert,Rinde (org,harm,pipe,10-string-slide-g,voc) | Granelli,Jerry (dr,perc) | Kögel,Christian (g,el-g) | Brücker,Kai (g,el-g) | Walter,Andreas (b)
Carlo Dreams | 5 AM:Locked In Amazement | Thin Walls | Street Don't Sleep | Beyond These Walls | The Mechanical Bird | Fearful Dark Streets | In The Morning Light | Winding The World
Eckert,Rinde (p,org,bar-h,voc) | Bernard,Will (el-g) | Suprynowicz,Clark (b,el-b) | Kassis,Jim (vib,dr,perc)

INT 3515-2 | CD | We'll Soon Find Out
Joey Baron Quartet
Slow Charleston | Closer Than You Think | Junior | Time To Cry | Wisely | Bit O'Water | M | Equaled | Contact
NYC, rec. details unknown
Baron,Joey (dr) | Blythe,Arthur (as) | Frisell,Bill (g,el-g) | Carter,Ron (b)

JA & RO | Jaro Medien GmbH

JARO 4101-2 | CD | Live In Der Balver Höhle
Piirpauke
Swedish Reggae | Mi Ardillitá | Azerbaizan Albatross | Flight | Tin Tin Deo | Lento
Live at Balver Höhle,Balve, rec. 22.6.1980
Piirpauke | Kukko,Sakari (sax,keyboards) | Oksala,Timo (g-synth) | Nylund,Pekka (g) | Koivulehto,Jorma (b) | Neklijudow,Tom (dr)

JARO 4113-2 | CD | Life Road
Oriental Wind
Gide Gide | Veli Aga | Ababa | Gypsy Song | Cergah Sirto | Life Road
Stockholm,Sweden, rec. June 1983
Oriental Wind | Aberg,Lennart (ss,ts) | Alsberg,Mats (el-b) | Temiz,Okay (dr,congas,bells,berimbau,cowbell,gopi-jantra,kalibas,sticks,talking-dr) | Svensson,Harald (synth)
Griot Song
Oriental Wind | Aberg,Lennart (fl,alto-fl,ss,ts) | Walters,Ted (el-b) | Temiz,Okay (dr,bells,berimbau) | Svensson,Harald (synth)
Azeri
Oriental Wind | Aberg,Lennart (fl,ss,ts) | Walters,Ted (b) | Temiz,Okay (dr,bells,sticks,talking-dr) | Svensson,Harald (synth)

JARO 4128-2 | CD | The Wild East
Piirpauke
Into The Wilderness | Lullaby | Forgotten Joys,Forsaken Songs | The Journey | The Law Of Nature | So Few OfUs | Temptation | My Songs Remain In Darkness Hidden | I Shouldn't Be Singing | Rites Of Passage
Helsinki, Finland, rec. 1984
Piirpauke | Kukko,Sakari (fl,sax,keyboards,perc,kantele,voc) | Rechardt,Pekka (g) | Ndjay,Badu (g,voc) | Railo,Tauno (b,voc) | Nyyssönen,Aku (dr,perc,timbales,voc)
Time For Joy,Time Of Song
Piirpauke | Kukko,Sakari (fl,sax,keyboards,perc,kantele,voc) | Rechardt,Pekka (g) | Ndjay,Badu (g,voc) | Railo,Tauno (b,voc) | Nyyssönen,Aku (dr,perc,timbales,voc) | Itkonen,Timo (voc)

JARO 4131-2 | CD | Jakko
Pili-Pili
Jakko Jakko | Vite Ayi | Sugu Mugu Jakakai | Vodoun Amon | The Break Tapper | Ambandru | Djamo Djamo | I Nan Djole
details unknown, rec. 1987
Pili-Pili | Van't Hof,Jasper (keyboards) | Schoof,Manfred (tp) | Fiszman,Nicolas (g,b) | Klein,Marlon (dr) | Samson (perc,voc) | Batta,Amancio (african-perc,voc) | Kidjo,Angelique (dance,voice)
Fusion De Souvenirs
Pili-Pili | Van't Hof,Jasper (keyboards) | Schoof,Manfred (tp) | Kooymans,George (g) | Fiszman,Nicolas (g,b) | Klein,Marlon (dr) | Samson (perc,voc) | Batta,Amancio (african-perc,voc) | Kidjo,Angelique (dance,voice)

JARO 4134-2 | CD | Be In Two Minds
Crush Dance | Les Demoiselles D'Avignon | Life Size | Be In Two Minds | Exaltation | One Mind
Amsterdam,Holland, rec. 1988
Pili-Pili | Van't Hof,Jasper (keyboards) | Klein,Marlon (dr,lyrics) | Sylla,Salifou (perc,voc) | Camara,Alpha (perc,voc) | Camara,Gilbert (perc,voc) | Kidjo,Angelique (dance,voice)
Black Gammon
Pili-Pili | Van't Hof,Jasper (keyboards) | Albers,Eef (g) | Klein,Marlon (dr,lyrics) | Sylla,Salifou (perc,voc) | Camara,Alpha (perc,voc) | Camara,Gilbert (perc,voc) | Kidjo,Angelique (dance,voice)
Talking Round | Post Scriptum
Pili-Pili | Van't Hof,Jasper (keyboards) | Sisi (v) | Klein,Marlon (dr,lyrics) | Sylla,Salifou (perc,voc) | Camara,Alpha (perc,voc) | Camara,Gilbert (perc,voc) | Kidjo,Angelique (dance,voice)

JARO 4136-2 | CD | Sparta
Johannes Cernota
Sparta: | Aura- | Prisma- | Dance- | Menelaos(King of Sparta) | Vorspiel | Pause | Nachspiel | Di-Ta-Tedo | Petite Overture A Danser(Erik Satie) | Embryons Desseches(Erik Satie): | D'Holothuries- | D'Eedriophtalma- | D'Podophtalma- | Nocturne Premier(Erik Satie) | Children's Songs(No.3,6,17,18,19) | For Alene(Arvo Pärt)
details unknown, rec. details unknown
Cernota,Johannes (p-solo)

JARO 4139-2 | CD | Pili-Pili Live 88
Pili-Pili
Vodoun Amon | Kibassa | Be In Two Minds | Ilé | Dixital
Live at different places, rec. 1988
Pili-Pili | Van't Hof,Jasper (keyboards) | Lakatos,Tony (sax) | Fiszman,Nicolas (g,b) | Allaert,Philippe (dr) | Samson (perc) | Kidjo,Angelique (perc,voice) | N'Diaye,Bachir (perc)

JARO 4141-2 | CD | Pili-Pili
Pili Pili
London,GB, rec. 1989
Pili-Pili | Van't Hof,Jasper (keyboards,synth) | Schoof,Manfred (tp,fl-h) | Isaac Tagul Group,The (perc,voc)
Kalungu Talks | Virgin Jungle
Pili-Pili | Van't Hof,Jasper (keyboards,synth) | Fiszman,Nicolas (g,b) | Schellekens,Shell (dr) | Batta,Amancio (perc) | O'Brian,Ponda (perc) | Ulrichi,Carlo (perc) | Youla,Fode (perc) | Kidjo,Angelique (voice)
Ilé | My Gongoma | Kinshasa Im Boté | Kiba
Pili-Pili | Van't Hof,Jasper (keyboards,synth) | Schoof,Manfred (tp,fl-h) | Fiszman,Nicolas (g,b) | Batta,Amancio (perc) | O'Brian,Ponda (perc) | Ulrichi,Carlo (perc) | Youla,Fode (perc) | Kidjo,Angelique (voice)
Afro Timento
Pili-Pili | Van't Hof,Jasper (keyboards,synth) | Fiszman,Nicolas (g,b) | Batta,Amancio (perc) | O'Brian,Ponda (perc) | Ulrichi,Carlo (perc) | Youla,Fode (perc) | Kidjo,Angelique (voice)
Smiling Lingala
Pili-Pili | Van't Hof,Jasper (keyboards,synth) | Fiszman,Nicolas (g,b) | Batta,Amancio (perc) | O'Brian,Ponda (perc) | Ulrichi,Carlo (perc) | Kidjo,Angelique (voice)

JARO 4142-2 | CD | Zerenade
Piirpauke
Nergiz | La Luna | La Gitana(Hevi Bülbül) | Zerenade | Kerelele | Para Mi Nina(para angeles) | Hattara Hääraa(para mi nina) | Lähtetään Kulkemaan(Vamonos) | Arbolé | Vauva(Baby) | Orava(Squirrel) | Noche De Tormenta(Sevillanas) | Ural-Caravana(Bajot Soi 1) | Paris-Dakar(Banjot 2)
Helsinki, Finland, rec. 1988-1989
Piirpauke | Kukko,Sakari (fl,sax,keyboards,voc) | Hermo,Cinta (g,perc,voc) | Tolonen,Jukka (g,el-g) | Ndjay,Badu (el-g,congas,talking-dr,voc) | Railo,Tauno (b) | Ounaskari,Markku (dr)

JARO 4146-2 | CD | Human Market
Toshinori Kondo & Ima plus Guests
Last Lost | Banana Plantation | Yellow Flag | H-Woman | Tokyo Girl | Moon Noom | Hoppoh | A Town In Your Heart
NYC/LA/Tokyo, rec. details unknown
Kondo,Toshinori (tp,electronics,voice) | Reck (el-g) | Sakai,Taizo (el-g) | Togashi,Haruo (keyboards,voc) | Yamaki,Hideo (dr,perc) | Thomas,Cybil (voc) | Livingstone,Annie (voc) | Bianchi Chiols,Janaina (voc) | Isso,Yukihiro (nohkan) | Shirasaka,Nobuyuki (ohtsuzumi)

JARO 4147-2 | CD | Hotel Babo
Pili-Pili
Hotel Babo | Uneven Image | Forbidden Drums | Dahomey Dance | Yoraba Gospel | Lon Lon
Amsterdam,Holland, rec. June 1989
Pili-Pili | Van't Hof,Jasper (p,keyboards,dr-programming) | Lakatos,Tony (sax) | Fiszman,Nicolas (g,b,dr-programming) | Yeltes,Gerhard (dr) | Vermie,Bart (perc) | Kidjo,Angelique (voice) | Komkommer,Joel (computer-programming)
Dance On The Water
Pili-Pili | Van't Hof,Jasper (p,keyboards,dr-programming) | Lakatos,Tony (sax) | Knapper,Jean Louis (g,computer-programming) | Fiszman,Nicolas (g,b,dr-programming) | Yeltes,Gerhard (dr) | Vermie,Bart (perc) | Komkommer,Joel (computer-programming) | Kidjo,Angelique (voice)
No Money No Tolerance
Pili-Pili | Van't Hof,Jasper (p,keyboards,dr-programming,sax-sampler) | Lakatos,Tony (sax) | Knapper,Jean Louis (g,computer-programming) | Fiszman,Nicolas (g,b,dr-programming) | Yeltes,Gerhard (dr) | Vermie,Bart (perc) | Kidjo,Angelique (voice) | Riebeek,Peter (voc)
Whitewash
Pili-Pili | Van't Hof,Jasper (p,keyboards,dr-programming) | Lakatos,Tony (sax) | Knapper,Jean Louis (g,computer-programming) | Fiszman,Nicolas (g,b,dr-programming) | Yeltes,Gerhard (dr) | Vermie,Bart (perc) | Kidjo,Angelique (voice) | Ellen (voc)

JARO 4150-2 | CD | Piirpauke-Global Servisi
Piirpauke
Konevitsan Kirkonkellot
Helsinki, Finland, rec. 1975
Piirpauke | Kukko,Sakari (p) | Walli,Hasse (g) | Hytti,Antti (b) | Wasama,Jukka (dr)
Imala Maika
Helsinki, Finland, rec. 1976
Piirpauke | Kukko,Sakari (p,indian-fl) | Walli,Hasse (g) | Hytti,Antti (b) | Wasama,Jukka (dr)
Yö Kyöpelinvuorella
Helsinki, Finland, rec. 1979
Piirpauke | Kukko,Sakari (p) | Björninen,Juha (g) | Wasama,Oli Pekka (b) | Wasama,Jukka (dr)
2 Bulgarische Zigeunerlieder
rec. 1983
Piirpauke | Kukko,Sakari (sax,keyboards) | Nylund,Pekka (g) | Saastamoinen,Ilpo (b) | Nekljudow,Tom (dr,perc)
Ranalla Istrusa
rec. 1979
Piirpauke | Kukko,Sakari (sax,p) | Walli,Hasse (g,perc) | Hytti,Antti (b) | Lehtimäki,Arja (voc) | Lehtimäki,Merja (voc)
Joropo Llandero
rec. 1981
Piirpauke | Kukko,Sakari (fl,sax,keyboards) | Nylund,Pekka (g) | Koivukoski,Karri (v) | Saastamoinen,Ilpo (b) | Nekljudow,Tom (dr,perc)
Swedish Reggae
Live at Balver Höhle,Balve, rec. 1981
Piirpauke | Kukko,Sakari (sax,keyboards) | Oksala,Timo (g-synth) | Nylund,Pekka (g) | Koivulehto,Jorma (b) | Nekljudow,Tom (dr)
Lamb's Polka
rec. 1981
Piirpauke | Kukko,Sakari (fl,p) | Nylund,Pekka (g) | Saastamoinen,Ilpo (b) | Nekljudow,Tom (dr,perc)
Forgotten Joys,Forsaken Songs
rec. 1986
Piirpauke | Kukko,Sakari (fl,sax,keyboards,perc,kantele,voc) | Rechardt,Pekka (g) | Ndjay,Badu (g,voc) | Railo,Tauno (b,voc) | Nyyssönen,Aku (dr,perc,timbales,voc)
Maam Bamba
rec. 1984
Piirpauke | Kukko,Sakari (p) | Ndjay,Badu (g,voc) | Walli,Hasse (g) | Moreno,Luis (b) | Nyyssönen,Aku (dr) | Bah,Hassan (congas)
Arbolé
rec. 1989
Piirpauke | Kukko,Sakari (fl) | Hermo,Cinta (g,perc,voc) | Ndjay,Badu (congas,talking-dr)
Crazy Sakari
rec. 1987
Piirpauke | Kukko,Sakari (sax,keyboards) | Hermo,Cinta (perc,voc) | Ndjay,Badu (g) | Railo,Tauno (b) | Ounaskari,Markku (dr)

JARO 4158-2 | CD | Tuku Tuku
Primavera(Kevät) | Primavera(II) | Girasol | Cheri(Dudu) | Mariama | Serimeni | Wami | Tuku Tuku | Tuku Tuku(II) | Dugub | Foroya | Carrosso | Mansali
Porvoo,Finland, rec. Autumn 1990
Piirpauke | Kukko,Sakari (fl,sax,keyboards,voc) | Hermo,Cinta (g,perc,voc) | Sane,Ismaila (perc,voc) | Cissokho,Malang (b,kora,voc) | Ndjay,Badu (el-g,tama,voc)
Marita
Piirpauke | Kukko,Sakari (fl,sax,keyboards,voc) | Hermo,Cinta (g,perc,voc) | Sane,Ismaila (perc,voc) | Cissokho,Malang (b,kora,voc) | Ndjay,Badu (el-g,tama,voc) | Lahti,Marja-Sisko (v) | Pihlasviita,Rea (voc)

JARO 4159-2 | CD | Stolen Moments

LABELVERZEICHNIS

Pili-Pili
Fingerlips | Mister Tarzan | Hippo Hips | Going Jungle | Liberata | Stolen Moments
Spitsbergen Studio,Zuidbroek,NL, rec. 1991
Pili-Pili | Van't Hof,Jasper (keyboards,synth,perc) | Lakatos,Tony (ss,ts) | Gasama,Samson (african-dr) | Haisma,Yelke (timbales) | Diara,Dra (perc,voc) | Balrak,Patricia (voc) | Camara,Damoyé Titti (voc) | Sylla,Kadia Tou (voc) | Traore,Kaloga (voc)
Bambra
Pili-Pili | Van't Hof,Jasper (keyboards,synth,perc) | Lakatos,Tony (ss,ts) | Holkenborg,Tom (g) | Gasama,Samson (african-dr) | Haisma,Yelke (timbales) | Diara,Dra (perc,voc) | Balrak,Patricia (voc) | Camara,Damoyé Titti (voc) | Sylla,Kadia Tou (voc) | Traore,Kaloga (voc)
Pili Pili(new version)
Pili-Pili | Van't Hof,Jasper (keyboards,synth,perc) | Lakatos,Tony (ss,ts) | Schoof,Manfred (tp) | Gasama,Samson (african-dr) | Haisma,Yelke (timbales) | Diara,Dra (perc,voc) | Balrak,Patricia (voc) | Camara,Damoyé Titti (voc) | Sylla,Kadia Tou (voc) | Traore,Kaloga (voc)
Our Neighbours Party
Pili-Pili | Van't Hof,Jasper (keyboards,synth,perc) | Lakatos,Tony (ss,ts) | Gasama,Samson (african-dr) | Haisma,Yelke (timbales) | Diara,Dra (perc,voc) | Balrak,Patricia (voc) | Camara,Damoyé Titti (voc) | Sylla,Kadia Tou (voc) | Traore,Kaloga (voc) | Ludolf,Jacques (voc) | Ludolf,Jasper (voc)

JARO 4172-2 | CD | Touchstone
Toshinori Kondo
Love Stone | Beat Stone | Doom Stone | Water Stone | Talk Stone | Dream Stone | Call Stone | Dance Stone | Mortal Stone | Time Sublime Stone
Kawasaki City,Japan, rec. 1993
Kondo,Toshinori (synth,el-tp)

JARO 4173-2 | CD | Red City Smoke
Toshinori Kondo & Ima
Space Killer | Temptation Flower | New Girl | Lovers,Hold Up | Blue Sky Battlezone | Red City Smoke | Sea 57 | Big Joy | Beyond The Sorrow
Kawasaki City,Japan, rec. April-July 1993
Kondo,Toshinori (el-tp,keyboard-b,voc) | Sakai,Taizo (g) | Togashi,Haruo (keyboards,keyboard-b) | Watanabe,Takahiro (keyboard-b) | Yamaki,Hideo (dr) | Beckett,Paul C. (computer-programming) | Ando,Naoki (synth-programming)
Moon Dream
Kawasaki City,Japan, rec. April-July 1993)
Kondo,Toshinori (el-tp,keyboard-b,voc) | Sakai,Taizo (g) | Nishizono,Mari (g,voc) | Togashi,Haruo (keyboards,keyboard-b) | Watanabe,Takahiro (keyboard-b) | Yamaki,Hideo (dr) | Beckett,Paul C. (computer-programming) | Ando,Naoki (synth-programming)

JARO 4174-2 | CD | Boogaloo
Pili-Pili
The Headpeeper | A Presi Dee | Summer Dance | Pilansberg | Live Is Not A Video | Blind Date | Jump To Dive | Rag Bag | Tight Lips | Boogaloo | Studio 150.?
rec. October 1993
Pili-Pili | Van't Hof,Jasper (p,keyboards) | Whitehead,Annie (tb) | Lakatos,Tony (sax) | Itt,Frank (el-b) | Klein,Marlon (dr) | Simmerl,Thomas (dr) | Diara,Dra (perc,djebe) | Maidman,Ian (cora-strings) | Balrak,Patricia (voc)

JARO 4187-2 | CD | Folk Dreams
Mikhail Alperin's Moscow Art Trio
Russian Raga(Za Nashey Derevney) | Pri Doline | Kalina | Wedding In The Wild Forest(part 1&2)
Moscow, rec. 1992
Alperin,Mikhail 'Misha' (p,keyboards,perc,voice) | Shilkloper,Arkady (fl-h,fr-h) | Starostin,Sergey (reeds,voc)
Mikhail Alperin's Moscow Art Trio With The Russkaja Pesnja Folk Choir
Oh Ne Budite | Sad Song | Dancing Meadow(suite in 5 parts)
Alperin,Mikhail 'Misha' (p,keyboards,perc,voice) | Shilkloper,Arkady (fl-h,fr-h) | Starostin,Sergey (reeds,voc) | Russkaja Pesnja Folk Choir | Babkina,Nadezhda (ld)

JARO 4189-2 | CD | Dance Jazz Live 1995
Pili-Pili
Summer Dance | No Money No Tolerance | Head Peeper | Pilansberg | Hotel Babo | Jim Jam | Jeez | Boogaloo
Live at different places, rec. 1995
Pili-Pili | Van't Hof,Jasper (keyboards) | Whitehead,Annie (tb) | Lakatos,Tony (sax) | Itt,Frank (el-b) | Klein,Marlon (dr) | Diara,Dra (perc,djebe) | Calister,Isaline (voc)

JARO 4192-2 | CD | Hoomba-Hoomba
Hoomba-Hoomba | Ilé | My Gongoma | Kinshasa Im Boté | Kiba
details unknown, rec. 1985
Pili-Pili | Van't Hof,Jasper (p,keyboards) | Fiszman,Nicolas (g,b-g) | Schoof,Manfred (tp) | Kidjo,Angelique (perc,voc) | Youla,Fode (perc,voc) | Batta,Amancio (perc,voc) | O'Brian,Ponda (perc,voc) | Ulrichi,Carlo (perc,voc)

JARO 4193-2 | CD | Prayer
Mikhail Alperin's Moscow Art Trio
Talk For Trio | Song From Mountains | Singing Wood | Troika | Talk For Three
Moscow, rec. 1991
Alperin,Mikhail 'Misha' (p,perc,melodica,voice) | Shilkloper,Arkady (fl-h,fr-h,voice) | Starostin,Sergey (reeds,voc)
Mikhail Alperin's Moscow Art Trio With The Tuva Folk & Russian Folk Ensemble
Prayer(part 1) | Prayer(part 2)
Alperin,Mikhail 'Misha' (p,perc,melodica,voice) | Shilkloper,Arkady (fl-h,fr-h,voice) | Starostin,Sergey (reeds,voc) | Tuva Folk Ensemble | Russian Folk Ensemble

JARO 4200-2 | CD | Jazzy World
Tam 'Echo' Tam
La Fruite De Jazz
Tam 'Echo' Tam (a capella voc-group)
Cash
Chicharera
Cash (jazz-rock-group)
Toshinori Kondo
Round About Midnight
Kondo,Toshinori (tp)
Charles
Can You Fee The Subway
Charles
Hannes Beckmann Group
Prager Schlüsselklingeln
Beckmann,Hannes (v)
The Meta Four
The Wind Beneath Your Wings
Meta Four (voc-group)
Moscow Art Trio
Sad Song
Moscow Art Trio | Alperin,Mikhail 'Misha' (p,keyboards,perc,voice)
Oriental Wind
Veli Aga
Oriental Wind | Aberg,Lennart (ss,ts) | Alsberg,Mats (el-b) | Temiz,Okay (dr,congas,bells,berimbau,cowbell,gopi-jantra,kalibas,sticks,talking-dr) | Svensson,Harald (synth)
Piirpauke
Swedish Reggae
Piirpauke | Kukko,Sakari (sax,keyboards) | Oksala,Timo (g-synth) | Nylund,Pekka (g) | Koivulehto,Jorma (b) | Nekljudow,Tom (dr)
Pili-Pili
Fingerlips
Pili-Pili | Van't Hof,Jasper (keyboards,synth,perc) | Lakatos,Tony (ss,ts) | Gasama,Samson (african-dr) | Haisma,Yelke (timbales) | Diara,Dra (perc,voc) | Balrak,Patricia (voc) | Camara,Damoyé Titti (voc) | Sylla,Kadia Tou (voc) | Traore,Kaloga (voc)

Johannes Cernota
Gnossienne(No.6)
Cernota,Johannes (p-solo)

JARO 4201-2 | CD | Hamburg Concert
Mikhail Alperin's Moscow Art Trio
Introduction & Kalina | South Etude | Skomorohi | Ironical Evening | Russian In China | Mountains Polka | Singing Wood | Talk For Trio | Wedding In The Wild Forest(part 2)
Live at NDR Studio,Hamburg, rec. 26.1.1996
Moscow Art Trio | Alperin,Mikhail 'Misha' (p,melodica,voice) | Shilkloper,Arkady (fl-h,fr-h,voice) | Starostin,Sergey (cl,reeds,voc)

JARO 4208-2 | CD | La Voce-Music For Voices,Trumpet And Bass
The Touch Of Your Hands | Tango Tragico | How It Was Then | Gülhan | Alore Domore | Canto Das Tres Racas | She Speak Her Name | Rap | La Voce | Samba Em Preludio | Gardsjenta | New And Again And Again
Bremen, rec. February 1997
Beckerhoff,Uli (tp,fl-h) | Kracht,Hartmut (b) | Winstone,Norma (voice) | Reis,Rosani (voice) | Di Benedetto,Giacomo (voice)

JARO 4209-2 | CD | Nomans Land
Pili-Pili
Mihiyo Ha Bohimara(Nomansland) | Gno Hon Mouna(No Time To Live) | Marabout | N'Ga Bohe(Motherland) | M'Bogne Mou Ra Fanhe M'Ma(I Am Sad) | N'Diaraby(Friendship) | Libertad(Freedom) | Saja Teriké(My Brother Died) | Anos Despues(Years Later) | Get Down | Get Up
details unknown, rec. 1997
Pili-Pili | Van't Hof,Jasper (p,keyboards) | Whitehead,Annie (tb) | Lakatos,Tony (sax) | Diara,Dra (perc,voc) | Sakho,Mabinthy (voc) | Camara,Manfrain (voc) | Kalister,Izaline (voc)

JARO 4214-2 | CD | Music
Moscow Art Trio
Den Endelause(The Eternal One) | Back Home | By The Sea | Wild Village Dance | Funeral
Norwegian State Academy Of Music,Oslo,N, rec. 29./30.6.1998
Moscow Art Trio | Shilkloper,Arkady (fl-h,fr-h) | Starostin,Sergey (cl,alto-cl,reeds,voc) | Alperin,Mikhail 'Misha' (p,claviola,melodica,plastic-tubes)
Grand Prolog | Jeg Er Norsk I Dag(Today,I'm Norwegian) | Almost Unisons | Almost Epilog
Moscow Art Trio | Shilkloper,Arkady (fl-h,fr-h) | Starostin,Sergey (cl,alto-cl,reeds,voc) | Alperin,Mikhail 'Misha' (p,claviola,melodica,plastic-tubes) | Sorensen,Hans-Kristian Kjos (perc)

JARO 4215-2 | CD | Oglinda
Trigon
The Lame Dance(Schiopatata) | The Belt(Brau) | Autumn Day In Balkans(O Zi De Toamna In Balcani) | Dance In The Cart(Sabra In Caruta) | Blues | Haulita | Doda | The Mirror(Oglinda)
Oslo,N, rec. 1997
Trigon | Testemiteanu,Sergiu (b-g) | Stefanet,Anatol (reeds,viola) | Baltaga,Oleg (dr) | Alperin,Mikhail 'Misha' (claviola)

JARO 4222-2 | CD | The Farlander
Farlanders
Gathering Grass | Fly | Twilight | Song Without Words | Keep Silent | Easter Song | Blok | Northern Dances | Mirror | Through The Orchard | Grey Eyes | Lullaby | Poppy
Metslawier,Friesland, rec. 1998
Farlanders,The | Zhelannaya,Inna (g,voc) | Starostin,Sergey (reeds,voc) | Klevensky,Sergey (reeds) | Kalachev,Sergey (b) | Timofeev,Pavel (dr)

JARO 4226-2 | CD | Journey
Sergey Starostin's Vocal Family
Suite For Five Voices In 6 Parts Without Intermission: | At Night- | Traveling Tatars- | Sun Prayer- | Sergey's Ballad- | I Was Fooling The Turkish- | Not The Last One-
Edinburgh,GB, rec. 13.-15.8.1999
Starostin,Sergey (voc) | Iovkova,Sonia (voc) | Douparinova,Tatiana (voc) | Koleva,Youlia (voc) | Vladimirova,Nadia (voc)

JARO 4227-2 | CD | Portrait
Mikhail Alperin-Vegar Vardal
Stolen From Norway(1) | Stolen From Norway(2) | Stolen From Norway(3)
Oslo,N, rec. 28.11.1999
Alperin,Mikhail 'Misha' (p) | Vardal,Vegar (v,harding-vele)
Moscow Art Trio
Russian Winter
Hamburg, rec. 18.5.1999
Alperin,Mikhail 'Misha' (p) | Shilkloper,Arkady (fl-h,fr-h) | Starostin,Sergey (cl,voc)
Cry
Live at The Jazzfestival Zürich,CH, rec. June 1992
Alperin,Mikhail 'Misha' (p) | Shilkloper,Arkady (fl-h,fr-h) | Starostin,Sergey (cl,voc)
Moscow Art Trio And The Bulgarian Voices Angelite
New Skomorohi
Louisville,KY, rec. November 1997
Alperin,Mikhail 'Misha' (p) | Shilkloper,Arkady (fl-h,fr-h) | Starostin,Sergey (cl) | Bulgarian Voices Angelie (voc)
Misha Alperin
Nostalgia
Asker,Norway, rec. January 1998
Alperin,Mikhail 'Misha' (p-solo)
Misha Alperin Group With The Brazz Brothers
Jewish Dance
Lillehammer,Norway, rec. 11.10.1997
Alperin,Mikhail 'Misha' (p) | Förde,Jarle (tp,fl-h) | Förde,Jan Magne (tp,fl-h) | Tafjord,Runar (fr-h) | Förde,Helge (tb) | Tafjord,Stein Erik (tuba) | Johansson,Egil (dr)
Movement
Lillehammer,Norway, rec. 11.10.1998
Alperin,Mikhail 'Misha' (p) | Förde,Jarle (tp,fl-h) | Förde,Jan Magne (tp,fl-h) | Tafjord,Runar (fr-h) | Förde,Helge (tb) | Tafjord,Stein Erik (tuba)

JARO 4238-2 | CD | Once Upon A Time
Moscow Art Trio
The Cat Is Crying | Once Upon A Time | Morning Talk | Village Voice | On The Green Grass A Cup Of Cottage Cheese | Dream | The Cat Is Crying(continued)
Oslo,N, rec. October/November 2000
Moscow Art Trio | Shilkloper,Arkady (fl-h,fr-h,voice) | Starostin,Sergey (cl,reeds,voc) | Alperin,Mikhail 'Misha' (p,claviola,voice)
Early Sunrise Over Cambodia | My Dance | Opera Rap
Moscow Art Trio | Shilkloper,Arkady (fl-h,fr-h,voice) | Starostin,Sergey (cl,reeds,voc) | Alperin,Mikhail 'Misha' (p,claviola,voice) | Hovdsveen Hagen,Eli Kristin (voice)

JARO 4240-2 | CD | Ballads Of Timbuktu
Pili-Pili
Maternal Love(N'unga) | My Son M'Ball Jo(M'Ball Jo) | The Vampire(Soubacha) | The Niger Oar(Niger Lalaba) | Incredible Astonishment(Ka Ba Ko) | Pure Village(Kangaba) | You Cannot Take My Dignity(Jinga Horonja) | Backbiting(Ton Soni) | Our Cow Pat Pride(Mi Si Bo Kolo Kagele) | The Tuareg's Desert(Tseng Tseng Can) | They Speak Their Heart Freely(Kanajoro Ka Kouma) | The Griots Song(Djelilou)
Suaucourt,France, rec. Summer 2001
Pili-Pili | Van't Hof,Jasper (keyboards) | Vloeimans,Eric (tp) | Diarra,Dra (perc,koni,voc) | Sakho,Mabinthy (voc) | Jungmair,Stefan (programming)

JARO 4250-2 | CD | Axioma | EAN 4006180425028
Jasper Van't Hof
The Countdown | Shadow | Gnashing | Uxorious | Trespass | Although | The Improvizer | Axioma | Famone Mumone | Tizzy | The Parry Game | Zeal | Boomerang | Peace Tongues
Radio Bremen, rec. 25.-27.11.2002 & 7.1.2003
Van't Hof,Jasper (p-solo)

JARO 4251-2 | CD | Müller Q[kju] | EAN 4006180425127

Lothar Müller Trio
Quiet I | Quiet II | Manha De Carnaval(Morning Of The Carnival) | Stay With Me | September | Niemandsland | River | Song For Agnes | Prepare Your Shoes | Kindercountry | MiniRock | Fetter Mond | Leave Me Paralysed
Hannover, rec. September 2001
Müller,Lothar (g,el-g,loops) | Henze,Andreas (b) | Hempel,Thomas (dr)

Japo | ECM Export

60015 | CD | Daybreak/The Dark Side Of Twilight
Herbert Joos With Strings
Why? | When Were You Born? | Leicester Court | Daybreak | Black Trees | Fasten Your Seatbelt
rec. Oct.1976
Joos,Herbert (tp,fl-h) | Schwarz,Thomas (oboe) | Members of Radio Symphony Orchestra Stuttgart (strings)

60031 | CD | It Had Been An Ordinary Enough Day In Pueblo, Colorado
AMM III
Radio-Activity | Convergence | Kline | Spittlefoelds' Slide | For A
rec. December 1979
AMM III | Rowe,Keith (g,prep.-p,transistor-radio) | Prevost,Eddie (dr)

60040 | CD | Listen To The Rain
Stephan Micus
Dancing With The Morning | Listen To The Rain | White Paint On Silver Wood
Ludwigsburg, rec. July 1983
Micus,Stephan (dilruba,shakuhachi,suling)
For Abai And Togshan
Köln, rec. June 1980
Micus,Stephan (dilruba,spanish-g)

Japo | Universal Music Germany

60002(835020-2) | CD | African Piano
60002(2360002) | LP | African Piano
Dollar Brand
Bra Joe From Kilimanjaro | Selby That The Eternal Spirit Is The Only Realty | The Moon | Xaba | Sunset In Blue | Kippy | Jabulani-Easter Joy | Tintinyana
rec. 22.10.1969
Brand,Dollar[Abdullah Ibrahim] (p-solo)

60017(2360017) | LP | Implosions
60017(829201-2) | CD | Implosions
60017(3106017) | MC | Implosions
Stephan Micus
As I Crossed A Bridge Of Dreams | Borkenkind | Amarchaj | For The Beautiful Changing Child | For M'schr And Djingis Khan
rec. March 1977
Micus,Stephan (g,rabab,shkuhachi,sho,sitar,thai-fl,zither)

60026(513786-2) | CD | Till The End Of Times
60026(3106026) | MC | Till The End Of Times
60026(2360026) | LP | Till The End Of Times
Till The End Of Times | For Wise And Ramin
Ludwigsburg, rec. June 1978
Micus,Stephan (g,kortholt,tischharfe,voc,zither)

60038(831058-2) | CD | Wings Over Water
60038(831058-4) | MC | Wings Over Water
60038(2360038) | LP | Wings Over Water
Wings Over Water | part 1-6
rec. Jan.&Oct.1981
Micus,Stephan (g,flower pots,nay,sarangi,suling,voice,zither)

60041(825655-2) | CD | East Of The Night
60041(825655-4) | MC | East Of The Night
60041(825655-1) | LP | East Of The Night
East Of The Night | For Nobuko
Ludwigsburg, rec. Jan.1985
Micus,Stephan (10&14-string-g,bamboo-fl)

Jardis Records | Jazz Network

JRCD 20027 | CD | I Wished On The Moon
Louis Stewart-Heiner Franz Quartet
I Wished On The Moon | Witchcraft | It Could Happen To You | O Grande Amor | I'll Take Romance | Speak Low | If I Had You | Jeannine
Neunkirchen, rec. 23.11.1999
Stewart,Louis (g) | Franz,Heiner (g) | Goldsby,John (b) | Strauch,Oliver (dr)
Louis Stewart-Heiner Franz
Invitation | Israel | I Fall In Love Too Easily
Neunkirchen, rec. 24.11.1999
Stewart,Louis (g) | Franz,Heiner (g)

JRCD 20028 | CD | Elle
John Stowell-Bebo Ferra
Punto | Juan E Il Cinque | In Your Own Sweet Way | Diciembre | Lazy Bird | Dreamsville | How My Heart Sings | Tramonto | Sundance | Elle | I Remember You
Milano,Italy, rec. 1998
Stowell,John (g) | Ferra,Bebo (g)

JRCD 20029 | CD | Portraits And Landscapes
John Stein Quintet
Samba Nights | Moonlight In Vermont | Be Ooo Ba | Sarlat | Mister Dave | Madelyn | Sammy | Rio Con Brio | Ben J Man | Switch-A-Roo
Westwood,MA, rec. 16.12.1999
Stein,John (g) | Thompson,Bill (fl,as,ts) | Goldings,Larry (org) | Kaumeheiwa,Keala (b) | Conroy,Greg (dr,perc)

JRCD 20030 | CD | Let's Have A Ball
Heiner Franz & Friends
Israel | Easy Living | Afternoon In Paris | Tiger Rag | Moonlight In Vermont | It Had To Be You
Live at Saarländischer Rundfunk, rec. 29.3.2000
Franz,Heiner (g) | Paquette,Pierre (cl,as,ts) | Huppertsberg,Lindy 'Lady Bass' (b)
Little Niles | Dexter's Minor Mad | Almost A Simple Blues | Funky Sweet | Invention In D-Moll | Pequeno Passeio | Broadway | Tears In The Moonlight | Blues Quodlibet | Para-Graffiti
Saarbrücken, rec. 21./22.8.2000
Franz,Heiner (g) | Paquette,Pierre (cl,as,ts) | Huppertsberg,Lindy 'Lady Bass' (b)

JRCD 20031 | CD | Flashes
Helmut Nieberle-Helmut Kagerer
In A Mist | Flashes | Hackensack | About Birds And Bees | Jitterbug Waltz | Milano | Mango | Prelude No.3 | Bucky Bucky Pizzarelli | Scrambled Eggs | Swing For Django
Abensberg, rec. August 1999-August 2000
Nieberle,Helmut (g) | Kagerer,Helmut (g)
Helmut Nieberle-Helmut Kagerer Quartet
Lullaby Of Birdland | From A To Z | Mind The Step | Courtship | Valse A Nieb
Nieberle,Helmut (g) | Kagerer,Helmut (g) | Kriener,Wolfgang (b) | Keul,Michael (dr)

JRCD 20032 | CD | Affinity
Ray Walker-John Pisano
The Touch Of Your Lips | If You Never Came To Me
Los Angeles,CA, rec. 13.& 20.2.2000
Walker,Ray (g) | Pisano,John (g)
Ray Walker-John Pisano Trio
Singin' In The Rain | Dearly Beloved | Johann's Step | Sweet Georgia Fame | Priscilla's Blues | Gentlefolk
Walker,Ray (g) | Pisano,John (g) | Berghofer,Chuck (b)
Como Voa As Coisas? | For Emily
Walker,Ray (g) | Pisano,John (g) | Leftwich,John (b)

JRCD 20133 | CD | Otherwise
Steve Rochinski Quartet
God And The Devil In The Land Of The Sun | Summer Night | I'm All Smiles | Almost Like Being In Love
Boston,MA, rec. 9./10.9.2000
Rochinski,Steve (g) | Stephens,Chip (p) | Stinnett,Jim (b) | Hunt,Joe (dr)

The Thrill Of It All
Rochinski,Steve (g) | Stephens,Chip (p) | Stinnett,Jim (b) | Hunt,Joe (dr) | McElroy,Donna (voc)
Steve Rochinski-Jim Stinnett
Swedish Pastry | I Let A Song Go Out Of My Heart | All The Shirts I Own
Rochinski,Steve (g) | Stinnett,Jim (b)
Steve Rochinski
Continuation On An Afterthought | Love Song
Rochinski,Steve (g-solo)

JRCD 20134 | CD | As We Are
Marcus Klossek Imagination
First Bird | Trainer | Time | Bluesy | Get Loose | 006 | Are You Surprised? | As We Are
Berlin, rec. 3./4.12.2000
Klossek,Marcus (g,el-g) | Wiesner,Klaus (ts) | Axenkopf,Klaus (b) | Martin,Kenny (dr)

JRCD 20135 | CD | How 'Bout It?
Mitch Seidman Quartet
Lee | How About It | Echo | Anouman | Hungarian Jazz Rhapsody | Meeting | Your Host | Struwelpeter | And She Remembers Me
Boston,MA, rec. 22./23.3.2001
Seidman,Mitch (g,el-g) | Shilansky,Mark (p) | Delnero,Paul (b) | Gray,Luther (dr)

JRCD 20136 | CD | Milan In Minor
Lorenzo Petrocca Organ Trio
Steeplechase | East Of The Sun West Of The Moon | The Gipsy | Love For Sale | Fotografia | Milan In Minor | Maurizio | Billie's Bounce
Klangküche Studio,?, rec. 28.3.2001
Petrocca,Lorenzo (g) | Marsico,Alberto (org) | Fischer,Armin (dr)

JRCD 20137 | CD | Two Sides To Every Story
Derrick James & Wesley 'G' Quintet
Dangerous Ground | Misunderstood | Standard Procedure | Two Sides To Every Story | Waltz For Wasili | Waiting For Summer | Sneaking In The Backdoor | Hanging On Sunday
Sandhausen, rec. 30.1.-2.2.2001
James,Derrick (sax) | 'G',Wesley (g) | Jung,Jean-Yves (p) | Imbert,Diego (b) | Strauch,Oliver (dr)
Destiny
'G',Wesley (g) | Jung,Jean-Yves (p) | Imbert,Diego (b) | Strauch,Oliver (dr)
Right Before My Eyes
James,Derrick (sax) | Jung,Jean-Yves (p) | Imbert,Diego (b) | Strauch,Oliver (dr)
Jackpot
James,Derrick (sax) | 'G',Wesley (g) | Hammes,Ernie (tp) | Menendez,Alberto (ts) | Jung,Jean-Yves (p) | Imbert,Diego (b) | Strauch,Oliver (dr)

JRCD 20138 | CD | Beauty
Thomas Brendgens-Mönkemeyer
Wisdom Of Notes | I Thought About You | You Don't Know What Love Is | It Could Happen To You | Muddy Waters Blues | George M. | Blame It On My Youth | The Beatles | Blues No.2 | Beauty | Footprints | Small Window Room | My Romance | Slippin' And Slidin'
Langwedel, rec. 2001
Brendgens-Mönkemeyer,Thomas (g-solo & overdubbing)

JRCD 20139 | CD | Manhattan Walls
Torsten Goods Group
Intimate Desire | I'll Remember April
Thorstadl,Obing, rec. 1./2.& 17.2.2001
Goods,Torsten (g,el-g,voc) | Lakatos,Tony (sax) | Gazarov,David (p) | Petrocca,Davide (b) | Terzic,Dejan (dr)
Carnaval De La Gente | Rosemonday Blues
Goods,Torsten (g,el-g,voc) | Keller,Rick (sax) | Eschke,Jan (p) | Kurz,Andreas (b) | May,Guido (dr)
Once Upon A Summertime
Goods,Torsten (g,el-g,voc) | Eschke,Jan (p) | Kurz,Andreas (b) | May,Guido (dr)
Jeannine | I'm Afraid The Masquerade Is Over - (I'm Afraid) The Masquerade Is Over | Got A Match? | On A Clear Day You Can See Forever | Speak Italian | In A Sentimental Mood
Goods,Torsten (g,el-g,voc) | Gazarov,David (p) | Petrocca,Davide (b) | Terzic,Dejan (dr)

JRCD 20140 | CD | Conversation Pieces
John Stein Quintet
Up And At 'Em | Serengeti | Half Minor | Oak Bluffs | September | Stepping Stones | Sao Paulo | Bb Blues | Lucy Lou | The Willie Walk
details unknown, rec. 18.& 23.3.2001
Stein,John (g) | Newman,David Fathead (sax) | Kaumeheiwa,Keala (b) | Conroy,Greg (dr)

JRCD 20141 | CD | Jazz Guitar Highlights 1
Helmut Kagerer-Peter Bernstein Quartet
All The Chords I Know
Kagerer,Helmut (g) | Bernstein,Peter (g) | Burno,Dwayne (b) | Parson,Dion (dr)
John Stowell-Bebo Ferra
Dreamsville
Stowell,John (g) | Ferra,Bebo (g)
Louis Stewart-Heiner Franz Quartet
It Could Happen To You
Stewart,Louis (g) | Franz,Heiner (g) | Goldsby,John (b) | Strauch,Oliver (dr)
Nicola Puglielli Group
In The Middle
Puglielli,Nicola (g-solo)
Louis Stewart
Blue Bossa
Stewart,Louis (g-solo)
Marcus Klossek Imagination
First Bird
Klossek,Marcus (g,el-g) | Wiesner,Klaus (ts) | Axenkopf,Klaus (b) | Martin,Kenny (dr)
Heiner Franz Trio
I Hear A Rhapsody
Franz,Heiner (g) | Krisch,Thomas (b) | Heitz,Uwe (dr)
John Stein Quintet
Ben J Man
Stein,John (g) | Thompson,Bill (fl,as,ts) | Goldings,Larry (org) | Kaumeheiwa,Keala (b) | Conroy,Greg (dr,perc)
Mitch Seidman-Fred Fried
This Over That
Seidman,Mitch (g) | Fried,Fred (7-string-g)
Helmut Kagerer 4 & Roman Schwaller
Samba For Bob
Kagerer,Helmut (g) | Schwaller,Roman (ts) | Jost,Tizian (p) | Apostolidis,Eugen (b) | May,Guido (dr)
Heiner Franz & Friends
Easy Living
Franz,Heiner (g) | Paquette,Pierre (cl,as,ts) | Huppertsberg,Lindy 'Lady Bass' (b)
Helmut Nieberle & Cordes Sauvages
Lady G's Delight
Nieberle,Helmut (g) | Holstein,Stephan (cl) | Schlick,Frederic (accordeon) | Kienastl,Max (v) | Baierl,Ferry (g) | Gnettner,Kartsten (b)
Thomas Brendgens-Mönkemeyer & Jochen Voss
How My Heart Sings
Brendgens-Mönkemeyer,Thomas (g) | Voss,Jochen (ss,as)
Lorenzo Petrocca Organ Trio
Love For Sale
Petrocca,Lorenzo (g) | Marsico,Alberto (org) | Fischer,Armin (dr)
Ray Walker-John Pisano Trio
Priscilla's Blues
Walker,Ray (g) | Pisano,John (g) | Berghofer,Chuck (b)
Steve Rochinski Solo/Duo/Trio/Quartet
Powder Your Face With Sunshine
Rochinski,Steve (g) | Thomas,Bruce (p) | Lee,Scott (b) | Hunt,Joe (dr)
Dieter Fischer Trio
Caravan
Fischer,Dieter (g) | Höfler,Karoline (b) | Schumacher,Dieter (dr)

Louis Stewart-Heiner Franz Quartet
Chelsea Bridge
Stewart,Louis (g) | Franz,Heiner (g) | Heieck,Fritz (b) | Berg,Thilo (dr)

JRCD 8801 | CD | A Window To The Soul
Heiner Franz Trio
Angel Eyes | It Could Happen To You | Pensativa | Walking In The Afternoon | A Window To The Soul | I Hear A Rhapsody | Days Of Wine And Roses | Autumn Leaves
details unknown, rec. 1988
Franz,Heiner (g) | Krisch,Thomas (b) | Heitz,Uwe (dr)

JRCD 8904 | CD | Gouache
Jardis Blues | Con Alma | Chega De Saudade(No More Blues) | Gouache | Lush Life | If I Should Lose You | Pequeno Passeio | Body And Soul | Ballad To J.S.B. | Solar | Polka Dots And Moonbeams | Summertime
details unknown, rec. 1989
Franz,Heiner (g) | Krisch,Thomas (b) | Heitz,Uwe (dr)

JRCD 9005 | CD | Winter Song
JRLP 9005 | LP | Winter Song
Louis Stewart-Heiner Franz Quartet
Almost A Simple Blues | Like Someone In Love | Winter Song | I Should Care | Bluesette | Just In Time | Joy Spring | Chelsea Bridge
Spiesen, rec. 1990
Stewart,Louis (g) | Franz,Heiner (g) | Heieck,Fritz (b) | Berg,Thilo (dr)

JRCD 9206 | CD | In A Mellow Tone
Louis Stewart-Heiner Franz
In A Mellow Tone | Jive Hot | Blue Daniel | Just Squeeze Me(But Don't Tease Me) | Nica's Dream | The More I See You | Star Eyes | There'll Never Be Another You | In A Sentimental Mood | Triste
details unknown, rec. June 1992
Stewart,Louis (g) | Franz,Heiner (g)
Louis Stewart
As Long As I Live
Stewart,Louis (g-solo)

JRCD 9307 | CD | The European Jazz Guitar Orchestra
The European Jazz Guitar Orchestra
Bye Bye Booze | Little Niles | Diabolo | Bits For Bitz | Unit 7 | The Dolphin | Hamp's Blues | The Lamp Is Low | Skylark | Everblue | Recto Verso | Weps | Turn Out The Stars | Wholly Cats
Saarländischer Rundfunk, rec. January 1993
European Jazz Guitar Orchestra,The | Stewart,Louis (g) | Raney,Doug (g) | Sylvestre,Frederic (g) | Van Der Grinten,Maarten (g) | Franz,Heiner (g) | Schädlich,Johannes (b) | Bings,Herbert (dr)

JRCD 9409 | CD | Invisible
Klaus Spencker Trio
Don't Know What To Say | You And The Night And The Music | Invisible | Finally | Visa | Alles Quart | Late Afternoon | Wie Leif Erikson Amerika Entdeckte | Farewell | Things Ain't What They Used To Be
Hannover, rec. 24.-27.11.1993 & 10./11.2.1994
Spencker,Klaus (g) | Casimir,Olaf (b) | Hanne,Willi (dr)

JRCD 9510 | CD | One Note Bossa
Tobias Langguth Band
One Note Bossa | Baiao Blues | Salsa Corrupti | Arabeske | Piano Bossa | Etude 22 | Sechser II | Minor Jazz Waltz | Choro | Fantasy In G
Dielheim, rec. July 1994
Langguth,Tobias (g,b,piccolo-g) | Reiter,Peter (cl,keyboards) | Schilgen,Dirik (dr)

JRCD 9611 | CD | At First Sight
Peter Leitch-Heiner Franz
Juris Blues | I Remember You | Body And Soul | Hall Mark | Para-Graffiti | April In Paris | Duality | Billie's Bounce- | Au Privave- | My Romance | Song For Jobim | Bit Bytes Bugs | On The Trail(From The Grand Canyon Suite)
details unknown, rec. 1996
Leitch,Peter (g) | Franz,Heiner (g)

JRCD 9612 | CD | Out On His Own
Louis Stewart
Blue Bossa | Windows | Darn That Dream | Wave | She Moved Through The Fair | Make Someone Happy | I'm All Smiles | Stella By Starlight | Lazy Afternoon | Invitation | I'm Old Fashioned | General Mojo's Well-Laid Plan | What's New? | I'll Remember April | Spring Is Here | Blues
details unknown, rec. November 1976/January 1977
Stewart,Louis (g-solo)

JRCD 9613 | CD | Acoustic Guitar Duets
Louis Stewart-Martin Taylor
Pick Yourself Up | Morning Of The Carnival | Jive At Five | Billie's Bounce | Coming Through The Rye | Cherokee | Stompin' At The Savoy | Darn That Dream | Bernie's Tune | Farewell To Erin
Dublin,Ireland, rec. July 1985
Stewart,Louis (g) | Taylor,Martin (g)

JRCD 9714 | CD | Gamblin'
Helmut Kagerer 4 & Roman Schwaller
Charlies Fingers | Confrontation | Waltz For Jim | Let's Go Wes | Tradition Trap | Round About Midnight | Gamblin' | Samba For Bob | Pocket Book | Take The Wess Trane
München, rec. January 1997
Kagerer,Helmut (g) | Schwaller,Roman (ts) | Jost,Tizian (p) | Apostolidis,Eugen (b) | May,Guido (dr)

JRCD 9816 | CD | This Over That
Mitch Seidman-Fred Fried
Dream Sequence | Reflecting On Jimmy | Late Again | Pannonica | This Over That
Westwood,MA, rec. 28.2.1998
Seidman,Mitch (g) | Fried,Fred (7-string-g)
Mitch Seidman-Fred Fried-Harvie Swartz
Wisdom Of Notes | Nobody Else But Me | No Walls | Careful | Jordu
NYC, rec. 18.4.1998
Seidman,Mitch (g) | Fried,Fred (7-string-g) | Swartz,Harvie (b)

JRCD 9817 | CD | Heiner Franz' Swing Connection
Heiner Franz' Swing Connection
Just You Just Me | All Of Me | C Jam Blues | China Boy | Basin Street Blues | Struttin' With Some Barbecue | If I Had You | 'S Wonderful | Baby Won't You Please Come Home | Sweet Georgia Brown
Live at '50 Jahre FATOL-Arzneimittel',Schiffweiler,Saar, rec. 28.8.1998
Franz,Heiner (g,bj) | Dawson,Colin (tp) | Lohfink,Charly (tb) | Höllering,Charles (cl) | Petrocca,Davide (b) | Beck,Gregor (dr)

JRCD 9818 | CD | April In New York
Helmut Kagerer-Peter Bernstein Quartet
Heidiology | I Remember You | Cookin' At The Continental | Joy For Joy | The Way You Look Tonight | Ballad For Attila | A Sound For Sore Ears | All The Chords I Know | Alone Together
Brooklyn,NY, rec. 25.4.1998
Kagerer,Helmut (g) | Bernstein,Peter (g) | Burno,Dwayne (b) | Parson,Dion (dr)

JRCD 9920 | CD | Textures
Thomas Brendgens-Mönkemeyer & Jochen Voss
It Could Happen To You | Perhaps | New & Average | Noch Einmal | Alone Together | How My Heart Sings | Unerwünscht | Special Days | Bone | Since You Asked | O.K. | Hymn For Joshua
Langwedel, rec. November/December 1998
Brendgens-Mönkemeyer,Thomas (g) | Voss,Jochen (ss,as)

JRCD 9921 | CD | Mood Pieces
Joseph Warner Quartet
Too Much Sake | Invitation | Isfahan | Gingerbread Boy | A Flower Is A Lovesome Thing | Witch Hunt | Infant Eyes
Live at 'Striese',Augsburg & 'Da Gianni',Germering, rec. 4.9. & 17.12.1998
Warner,Joseph (b) | Kagerer,Helmut (g) | Scales,Martin (g) | Baudisch,Joe (dr)

JRCD 9922 | CD | A Bird In The Hand
Steve Rochinski Solo/Duo/Trio/Quartet
Beautiful Love | Monk's Dream | House Party Starting | A Bird In The Hand | Round About Midnight | Tina | Go Little Boat | Get Out Of Town | They Didn't Believe Me | Hassan's Dream | Stardust- | Body And Soul- | Powder Your Face With Sunshine

Boston,MA, rec. 13./14.9.1997
Rochinski,Steve (g) | Thomas,Bruce (p) | Lee,Scott (b) | Hunt,Joe (dr)

JRCD 9923 | CD | Four Friends
Florin Niculescu Quartet
Balkanals | Laura | If I Were A Bell | Valse Tzigane | Bresilien | My Funny Valentine | Moose The Mooche | Ballad For Friends | Caravan | Sometime Ago | Just One Of Those Things
Vigneux,France, rec. 29./30.11.1998 & 2.1.1999
Niculescu,Florin (v) | Azzola,Marcel (accordeon) | Sylvestre,Frederic (g) | Vidal,Jacques (b)

JRCD 9924 | CD | In The Middle
Nicola Puglielli Group
Strollin'
Rome,Italy, rec. 6./7.3.1999
Puglielli,Nicola (g) | Ghigliordini,Elvio (fl) | Bartoccini,Gerardo (b)
What Is This Thing Called Love
Puglielli,Nicola (g) | Ghigliordini,Elvio (fl) | Beneventano,Andrea (p) | Bartoccini,Gerardo (b) | Sciommeri,Armando (dr)
Aspettando Caterina
Puglielli,Nicola (g) | Bartoccini,Gerardo (b)
My Shining Hour
Puglielli,Nicola (g) | Beneventano,Andrea (p)
Ritrovarsi | Ask Me Now
Rome,Italy, rec. 6.7.3.1999
Puglielli,Nicola (g) | Bartoccini,Gerardo (b) | Sciommeri,Armando (dr)
I Piaceri D'Amore | Stumbop | Inutil Paisagem(Useless Landscape)
Rome,Italy, rec. 6./7.3.1999
Puglielli,Nicola (g) | Beneventano,Andrea (p) | Bartoccini,Gerardo (b) | Sciommeri,Armando (dr)
In The Middle
Puglielli,Nicola (g-solo)

JRCD 9925 | CD | Trio Music
Dieter Fischer Trio
All The Things You Are | Samba Da Una Nota So(One Note Samba) | Cute | In A Sentimental Mood | Take The Coltrane | I Remember Wes | Autumn Leaves | Bossa Rocka | Borgia's Stick | I Hear A Rhapsody | Caravan | Mr.P.C. | Night And Day | Hello Dolly | Old Folks
Stuttgart, rec. 12.2.1999
Fischer,Dieter (g) | Höfler,Karoline (b) | Schumacher,Dieter (dr)

JRCD 9926 | CD | Salut To Django
Helmut Nieberle & Cordes Sauvages
It's You Or No One
Abensberg, rec. 17.2.1999
Nieberle,Helmut (g) | Holstein,Stephan (cl) | Baierl,Ferry (g) | Gnettner,Kartsten (b)
It Had To Be You
Nieberle,Helmut (ukelele) | Holstein,Stephan (cl) | Kienastl,Max (v) | Baierl,Ferry (g) | Gnettner,Kartsten (b)
Sweet And Lovely | Lady G's Delight | Says You
Nieberle,Helmut (g) | Holstein,Stephan (cl) | Schlick,Frederic (accordeon) | Kienastl,Max (v) | Baierl,Ferry (g) | Gnettner,Kartsten (b)
Augustine
Nieberle,Helmut (g) | Holstein,Stephan (cl) | Schlick,Frederic (accordeon) | Baierl,Ferry (g) | Gnettner,Kartsten (b)
The Song Is You
Nieberle,Helmut (g) | Holstein,Stephan (cl) | Kienastl,Max (v) | Baierl,Ferry (g) | Gnettner,Kartsten (b)
Romeno Baschepen
Nieberle,Helmut (g) | Baierl,Ferry (g) | Gnettner,Kartsten (b)
Swing For Django | Bob's Chops | Danny Boy (Londonderry Air) | Pra Dizer Adeus | You Do Something To Me
Abensberg, rec. 16.9.1999
Nieberle,Helmut (g) | Baierl,Ferry (g) | Gnettner,Kartsten (b) | Gottwald,Scotty (snare-dr)

Jazz 4 Ever Records:Jazz Network | jazz4everrecordsjazznetwork

J4E 4714 | CD | Whatever It Is
Wolfgang Haffner International Jazz Quintet
Ready Set Go | For The Time Being | Love Someone You Like | La Mesha | 1.2.79 | Whatever It Is | Sno' Peas | Cute | Bolivia
details unknown, rec. 27.2.1991
Haffner,Wolfgang (dr) | Joris,Bert (fl-h) | Schwaller,Roman (ts) | Moroni,Dado (p) | Stabenow,Thomas (b)

J4E 4718 | CD | Are You Serious?
Brodmann-Pausch Percussion Duo
Thomas Wartet | Der Alte Und Der Kranke | Giro | Zapzarap | Die Wende | Mach 1 | Softly | Karabenemdusi | F.D.H. | Gelbsucht | Wenn Nix Höre,Muß Spille | Kind Of Blue Period | Heavy Mädel | Vor Elise | Ein Flug Über's Kuckucksnest | TE TIMA TATANGA | Warten Auf Thomas
details unknown, rec. details unknown
Brodmann,Hans-Günter (perc) | Pausch,Yogo (perc)

J4E 4719 | CD | Pure
Straight Talk
Resistor | The Meaning Of The Blues | Outside | Two Stories | Woman On A Train | Mescalin | Solid | No Talk | Wet Point | Another Meaning Of The Blues
details unknown, rec. March 1993
Straight Talk | Sampson,Beate (voc) | Grassner,Hans (g) | Werb,Rainer (b) | Heider,Peter (synth,dr,perc) | Mahall,Rudi (b-cl)

J4E 4721 | CD | Room 626
Piludu Quattro
Mean Blues | Deviation Lozari | Beedees | Room 626 | Suite: Bafiology- | Mrs.D.P.- | Alba- | Hugo | Mazu
details unknown, rec. December 1993
Piludu,Marco (g) | Seefelder,Jürgen (sax) | Apostolidis,Eugen (b) | Kersting,Michael (dr)

J4E 4722 | CD | Pete Yellin's European Connection:Live!
Pete Yellin Quartet
Yesterdays | Song For Lynn | How Long Has This Been Going On | Almost Gently | Seatic | Blues For Jackie
Live at The Kulturfabrik Roth,Nürnberg, rec. 27.5.1994
Yellin,Pete (ss,as) | Pichl,Bernhard (p) | Rissmann,Gunther (b) | Terzic,Dejan (dr)

J4E 4723 | CD | Ass Bedient
Association Urbanetique
Harem Shuffle | Urbanetique | Red Black And Blue | Teneriffa-Kakerlaken | Revolution II | Tanz Der Tse Tse Fliegen | Ears4Evol | Sunday Morning Fast Break | Sanf Kanf | Turribo | OGM
Berlin, rec. 1990-1993
Association Urbanetique | Brennecke,Rainer (tp) | Dallmayer,Klaus (tp) | Boukouya,Marc (tb) | Wrase,Tina (b-cl) | Wahnschaffe,Felix (sax) | Schimmelpfennig,Frank (g) | Prill,Robert (g) | Kersthold,Andreas (p) | Nonnenmacher,Horst (b) | Robben,Rainer (dr)
-> Verschiedene Besetzungen, keine genauen Angaben auf dem Cover!

J4E 4726 | CD | On The Corner
Bernhard Pichl Trio
Check It Out | You And The Night And The Music | Satin Doll | Soul Eyes
Monster,NL, rec. 15.-17.8.1995
Pichl,Bernhard (p) | Engel,Rudi (b) | Netta,Sebastian (dr)
Benny Bailey With The Bernhard Pichl Trio
North Star Street | The Night We Called It A Day | Blues For Lady J.
Bailey,Benny (tp) | Pichl,Bernhard (p) | Engel,Rudi (b) | Netta,Sebastian (dr)

J4E 4729 | CD | Reflections Of South Africa
Johannes Enders Group
Johannesburg | Dark Before Dawn | Gingerbread Boy | Reflections Of South Aftica | Toenails | Second Thoughts | Passion Dance
Seapoint,Capetown,South Africa, rec. 1./2.9.1992
Enders,Johannes (ts) | Schilder,Hilton (p) | Moses,Basil (b) | Gibson,Kevin (dr)

J4E 4730 | CD | Back Home
Wolfgang Haffner Project
Intro | Flip Flop | Long Stories | Goodbye Again | Forever | The Journey | Song For Bam Bam | Back Home | Cascatas | There And Back Again

Nürnberg, rec. 20.1.1995
Haffner,Wolfgang (dr) | Tiehuis,Peter (g) | Di Gioia,Roberto (p,keyboards) | Diener,Christian (b) | Doctor,Marcio (perc)

J4E 4731 | CD | Silent Dances
Peter Fulda Trio With Céline Rudolph
Poravi | Continental Songlines | Islands Smiling | Fado | Ragavardhana | Candratala | Allemande
BR,Studio Franken, rec. 15.1.1998
Fulda,Peter (p) | Gier,Thomas (b) | Gandela,Andreas (dr) | Rudolph,Céline (voc)
Santeria Sunrise | Kotekan | Pavane | Tango | Drum Interlude | Bolero
Bürgerhaus,Schwabach, rec. 2.-5.9.1998
Fulda,Peter (p) | Gier,Thomas (b) | Gandela,Andreas (dr) | Rudolph,Céline (voc)

J4E 4733 | CD | New York Travels
Marco Piludu International Quartet
Tre Abandonati | It's Probably Me | Aisokey | Bible Travels | Fragile | Yucan 2 | Good Bye
NYC, rec. 28.2.1997
Piludu,Marco (g) | Hagans,Tim (tp) | Scherr,Tony (b) | Kersting,Michael (dr)
Synchronicity
Piludu,Marco (g) | Hagans,Tim (tp) | Hübner,Gregor (v) | Scherr,Tony (b) | Kersting,Michael (dr)
Finally
Piludu,Marco (g) | Hagans,Tim (tp) | Möck,Uli 'Ull' (keyboards) | Scherr,Tony (b) | Kersting,Michael (dr)

J4E 4735 | CD | Axis
Axis
Pocket Symphony: | Introduction | Trio No.2 | Interludium | Eye Of The Fly | In | Sequenz
Musikhochschule,Frankfurt, rec. November 1994 & March 1997
Axis | Stötter,Claus (tp,fl-h) | Read,Hugo (fl,as) | Kaenzig,Heiri (b) | Cremer,Thomas (dr)
Vom Wind | Chick On The Water | Blues!
Axis | Michel,Matthieu (tp,fl-h) | Read,Hugo (fl,as) | Kaenzig,Heiri (b) | Cremer,Thomas (dr)
Coda | Land Of Desolation,Land Of Mist(part 1&2)
Live at 'Alte Schmiede',Düsseldorf, rec. March 1997
Axis | Stötter,Claus (tp,fl-h) | Read,Hugo (fl,as) | Kaenzig,Heiri (b) | Cremer,Thomas (dr)

J4E 4737 | CD | Weave
Achim Kaufmann Trio
Ritual | The Night Sky Is A Rock | Hidden Sevens-Thinking Backwards | Three Thimbles | Asking For Trouble | Carnies | Redmm Saat | The Sinner's March | Koen(da kaze ga dandan tsuyoku ni naru yo ni...) | The Embalmers' Waltz
Hannover, rec. 1./2.7.1997
Kaufmann,Achim (p) | Heller,Ingmar (b) | Rückert,Jochen (dr)

J4E 4739 | CD | Music 4 Food
Michael Lutzeier Quartet
My Heart Belongs To Daddy | Nobody Else But Me | Little Waltz | Music 4 Food | Alone Together | I Wam You | Tricotism | Warm Valley
München, rec. 18.3.1998
Lutzeier,Michael (bs) | McKenna,Steve (g) | Sieverts,Henning (b) | Willis,Falk (dr)

J4E 4740 | CD | Der Rote Bereich 3
Der Rote Bereich
Schleckereien Auf Der Flucht | Das Geht Doch Nicht | Holzfällermedley: | Auf In Den Wald- | Die Axt Geschwungen- | Epilog:Da Ist Holz Vor Der Hütte- | Lustiger Tiroler | Feijoada De Chocos | Most Wanted Marathon Weekend | Eine Kleine Sekunde Vor 4 | Abendlich Erfolgt Die... | Pastilja Elastica | Autodienst Mitte | Heino Und Hannelore | Konäsörs
Hannover, rec. 7.5.1997
Der Rote Bereich | Mahall,Rudi (b-cl) | Möbus,Frank (g) | Schröder,John (dr)

J4E 4743 | CD | Tesoro
Rolf Römer Trio
Tesoro | Song For Patrick | Mesa Verde | Penta Chang | RoJoJo | Secret Love
Köln, rec. 26./27.5.1998
Römer,Rolf (b-cl,ss,ts) | Goldsby,John (b) | Riley,John (dr)
Rolf Römer Quartet
Scooter | My One And Only Love
Römer,Rolf (b-cl,ss,ts) | Dobbins,Bill (p) | Goldsby,John (b) | Riley,John (dr)

J4E 4744 | CD | Melodies Of '98
Rainer Tempel Big Band
3X3 | I Know,You Know | Miles Away | Ohne Worte(I) | Oslo Sun | Abendlich... | Melodies Of '98 | Ohne Worte(II)
Albstadt, rec. 20./21.4.1999
Ehringer,Christian (tp) | Schlosser,Axel (tp) | Studnitzky,Sebastian (tp) | Siffling,Thomas (tp) | Sell,Rainer (tb) | Gschößl,Gerhard (tb) | Budziat,Eberhard (tb) | Partyka,Edward (b-tb,tuba) | Lauber,Frank (reeds) | Trübsbach,Florian (reeds) | Erlewein,Matthias (reeds) | Wyand,Mark (reeds) | Steiner,Michael (reeds) | Eberle,Frank (p) | Möbus,Frank (g) | Bodenseh,Markus (b) | Gmelin,Matthias (dr) | Hammer,Thomas (perc) | Tempel,Rainer (arr,ld)

J4E 4745 | CD | ...On The Right Track
Edith Steyer... Posterity Quintet
Mellow Alto | The Kakapo | Night Has Come | Charlie's Tone | Flip Side | Scarborough Fair- | Skal Boyz | Taddlin' Awhile | Jug's Jug
München, rec. 10./11.4.1999
Steyer,Edith (cl,sax) | Hahn,Jürgen (tp,fl-h) | Wegele,Peter (p) | Lewalter,Rainer (b) | Malik,Hubert (dr)
Old Acquaintance | Bird's Perspective
Steyer,Edith (cl,sax) | Hahn,Jürgen (tp,fl-h) | Spiegelberg,Martin (g) | Wegele,Peter (p) | Lewalter,Rainer (b) | Malik,Hubert (dr)

J4E 4746 | CD | ...In Motion
Joachim Raffel Trio
Definitions | Circlesong No.5(Where To Go...) | Blues For Eric(Dolphy)
Hannover, rec. 4./5.11.1999
Raffel,Joachim (p) | Morsey,Alexander (b) | Schoenefeld,Christian (dr,perc)
Joachim Raffel Sextet
Move | Better Not Now | This Is | Nothing Of All | Split | There And Now | Blue Motion
Raffel,Joachim (p) | Struck,Stephan (tp) | Klare,Jan (as) | Kretzschmar,Robert (ts) | Morsey,Alexander (b) | Schoenefeld,Christian (dr,perc)

J4E 4747 | CD | Voyage Out
Friedrich-Herbert-Moreno Trio
Are We There Yet | Voyage Out | Autumn In New York | Fair Grounds | English Waltz | Do Not Disturb | Streams
NYC, rec. 2.1.1998
Friedrich,Jürgen (p) | Herbert,John (b) | Moreno,Anthony 'Tony' (dr)

J4E 4748 | CD | Gans Normal
Horst Faigle's Jazzkrement
Hangover In Hannover
Fürth, rec. August 1999
Faigle,Horst (dr,voice) | Alonso,Robert (tp) | Sell,Rainer (tb) | Emminger,Norbert (fl) | Hiller,Norbert (fl) | Häfner,Lutz (as) | Flügel,Michael (p,melodica) | Rissmann,Gunther (b)
Sushi My Love | Blackbird
Faigle,Horst (dr,voice) | Alonso,Robert (tp) | Sell,Rainer (tb) | Hiller,Norbert (fl) | Häfner,Lutz (as) | Möbus,Frank (g) | Flügel,Michael (p,melodica) | Rissmann,Gunther (b) | Sieverts,Henning (b)
Die Letzten Helden
Faigle,Horst (dr,voice) | Alonso,Robert (tp) | Sell,Rainer (tb) | Häfner,Lutz (as) | Möbus,Frank (g) | Flügel,Michael (p,melodica) | Rissmann,Gunther (b) | Sieverts,Henning (b)
Rosiwalzer
Fürth, rec. Augusrt 1999
Faigle,Horst (dr,voice) | Alonso,Robert (tp) | Sell,Rainer (tb) | Häfner,Lutz (as) | Flügel,Michael (p,melodica) | Rissmann,Gunther (b) | Sieverts,Henning (b)
Der Polizwar
Fürth, rec. August 1999
Faigle,Horst (dr,voice) | Alonso,Robert (tp) | Sell,Rainer (tb) | Brinkmann,Georg (cl-aditiv) | Häfner,Lutz (as) | Flügel,Michael (p,melodica) | Rissmann,Gunther (b)
The Chick From Ipanema
Faigle,Horst (dr,p,voice) | Alonso,Robert (tp) | Sell,Rainer (tb) | Häfner,Lutz (as) | Flügel,Michael (p,melodica) | Rissmann,Gunther (b)
Neger Karl
Faigle,Horst (dr,voice) | Alonso,Robert (tp) | Sell,Rainer (tb) | Häfner,Lutz (as) | Emminger,Norbert (b-cl,bs) | Flügel,Michael (p,melodica) | Rissmann,Gunther (b)
Fishland Curse | Don't | Peter Und Der Golf | Bluesy Sue
Faigle,Horst (dr,voice) | Alonso,Robert (tp) | Sell,Rainer (tb) | Häfner,Lutz (as) | Flügel,Michael (p,melodica) | Rissmann,Gunther (b)

J4E 4749 | CD | Meet You In Chicago
Jens Bunge Group
Morning Song | Invitation | Hurry Up! | Elsa | Meet You In Chicago | Chan's Song
Morton Grove,Ill., rec. 18./19.4.2000
Bunge,Jens (harm) | Guenther,Thomas (p) | Arnopol,Michael (b) | Jones,Rusty (dr)
Emily | The Summer Knows
Bunge,Jens (harm) | Guenther,Thomas (p) | Arnopol,Michael (b) | Jones,Rusty (dr) | Allen,Jackie (voc)
Skylark | What A Difference A Day Made
Bunge,Jens (harm) | Guenther,Thomas (p) | Arnopol,Michael (b) | Jones,Rusty (dr) | Roberts,Judy (p,voc)
The Loop
Bunge,Jens (harm) | Fishman,Greg (ts) | Guenther,Thomas (p) | Arnopol,Michael (b) | Jones,Rusty (dr)
Virginia
Bunge,Jens (harm) | Fishman,Greg (ts) | Delin,Diane (v) | Guenther,Thomas (p) | Arnopol,Michael (b) | Jones,Rusty (dr) | Pardon,Joe (perc)

J4E 4750 | CD | Recovering From y2k
Erdmann 2000
Sein AKG | The Desert Story | Naf Naf Naf | Väter Und Mutter Erde | Namderyew.ed! | Drugstore B. | Morgengrauen In Hafen Von Piräus | Gunn 2001 | Miss Mayenne | 3/4 & 1/4 8 | Ein Tag Im Leben Des Jungen L.
Hannover, rec. 21.1.2000
Erdmann,Daniel (ts) | Möbus,Frank (g) | Fink,Johannes (b) | Schröder,John (dr)

J4E 4751 | CD | Alfonsina
Gabriel Pérez Group
Pan Con Pan | Nos Da | Turquesa | El Portenito | Alta Paz | Merceditas | Alfonsina Y El Mar- | Cadencia- | Milonga Para Grela | Los Carnavales | El Dia Que Me Quieras | El Firulete | Otra Dia | Alfonsina Y El Mar(Tema)
Bonn, rec. details unknown
Pérez,Gabriel (fl,cl,sax) | Neudert,Jürgen (tb) | Sinesi,Quinque (g,spanish-g,charango) | Friedrich,Jürgen (p) | Heinze,Volker (b) | Mussawisade,Afro (perc) | Arte String Quartet

J4E 4752 | CD | La Leggenda Del Pescatore
Takabanda
Hupfdohlen Im Gleißenden Neonlicht | Tartaros | Lundi Au Lit | In A Sentimental Mood | Quartetto 1 | Quartetto 2
Berlin, rec. 2001
Takabanda | Schwingenschlögl,Paul (tp,fl-h) | Von Kleewitz,Jack (as) | Burkard,Thilo (b) | Eleodori,Paolo (dr)
Pension Lotterman | La Legenda Del Pescatore | Alesia | Vilshofen | Endless Journey
Takabanda | Schwingenschlögl,Paul (tp,fl-h) | Von Kleewitz,Jack (as) | Ande,Akira (b) | Eleodori,Paolo (dr)

J4E 4753 | CD | The Music Of Chance
Frank Sackenheim Quartet
The Music Of Chance | Wayne's World | Herbst | And Then It Had To Be You - ...And Then It Had To Be You | Reger
Hannover, rec. 5./6.2.2001
Sackenheim,Frank (ts) | Ross,Florian (p) | Fuhr,Dietmar (b) | Kornmaier,Mathias (dr)
Frank Sackenheim Quintet
Broken Arrow In A Bathub | Ciftik | May The Fourth Be With You | Stream Walk | Prince Vaillant
Sackenheim,Frank (as,ts) | Bergman,Matthias (fl-h) | Ross,Florian (p) | Fuhr,Dietmar (b) | Kornmaier,Mathias (dr)

J4E 4754 | CD | Future Of The Smallest Form
Christopher Dell D.R.A.
Einundvierzig | Dreiundvierzig | Vierundvierzig A | Neunundsiebzig | Fünfunddreissig | Sechsundvierzig | Siebenundvierzig | Dreiundvierzig A | Vierundfünfzig | Einunddreissig | Fünfundvierzig | Zweiundvierzig | Achtundvierzig | Siebenunddreissig | Fünfundsiebzig | Dreiunddreissig
Topaz Audio Studio,?, rec. November/December 2000
Dell,Christopher (vib) | Ramond,Christian (b) | Astor,Felix (dr,perc)

J4E 4755 | CD | Fantasia | EAN 4016761047556
Melanie Bong With Band
The Colour Of Love | Pansies | Let Us | The Voice | Don't Say Goodbye | You Are My Tree | The Secret | Darling | Soft Song | The Song Of Rosebuds | What? Where? Why? | Fantasia
Radio Studios Maribor, rec. 1996-2001
Bong,Melanie (voc) | Enders,Johannes (sax) | Correa,Fernando (g) | Wöss,Martin (p,keyboards) | Roidinger,Adelhard (el-b) | Hilbe,Gregor (dr) | Grieshofer,Ernst (perc) | Nobili,Maurizio (voc,arr)

J4E 4756 | CD | Stories
Thomas Stiffling Group
Course Of A Stream | Trilogie Über Gewisse Situationen Im Leben Eines Menschen: | Kurzer Ausbruch | Endlos | Change Of Colours | Remember(take 1) | Open Sea | Movements | Remember(take 2) | Movements(pocket radio edition)
Hannover, rec. 7.6.2001
Stiffling,Thomas (tp,fl-h) | Böhm,Rainer (p) | Lange,Uwe (b) | Faller,Markus (dr)
Die Frage Nach Dem Warum
Stiffling,Thomas (tp,fl-h) | Möbus,Frank (g) | Böhm,Rainer (p) | Lange,Uwe (b) | Faller,Markus (dr)

J4E 4757 | CD | Way In Way Out | EAN 4016761047570
Lutz Häfner Quartet
Way In | If You'd Know Me | Out | In A Rush | My Lady | Zone | I Mean! | Instru (For The) Mental | Way Out
Realistic Sound Studio,?/Mo' Swing Studio,?, rec. November 2001/February 2002
Häfner,Lutz (fl,b-cl,ss,ts,talk-box) | Enders,Johannes (fl,b-cl,ss,ts,CR-78) | Schieferdecker,Markus (b) | Smock,Hendrik (dr)

J4E 4758 | CD | Left Handed | EAN 4016761047587
New On The Corner
Dick Is Slick | Surabaya Johnny | Left Handed | Do You Know Why Stars Come Out At Night | Almost Gentle | Old Devil Moon | Green Eyes | The Touch Of Your Lips | Sneakin' Out
Sandhausen, rec. 18.9.2001
New On The Corner | Pichl,Bernhard (p) | Engel,Rudi (b) | Elgart,Billy (dr)

J4E 4759 | CD | Manson & Dixon | EAN 4016761047594
Florian Trübsbach Quintet
Maseru | Quixotic | Manson & Dixon | 200 Horses | Epoque | Non Stop City | Interlude | Buffalo Rhythm | Melody
Thorstadl,Obing, rec. 10.7.2001
Trübsbach,Florian (ss,as) | Hesse,Ralph (tp,fl-h) | Eschke,Jan (p) | Sieverts,Henning (b) | Willis,Falk (dr)

J4E 4760 | CD | L 14,16 | EAN 4016761047600
Schlosser/Weber/Böhm/Huber/Binder
Introduction: | Miniature 1-Blauer Jatz | Staircase To The Future | Hymn For Christine | All The Things You Are | Miniature 2-Masha | Sideburns | We'll See Yaw'll After While Ya Heah | Swingo | Miniature 3-Blues For Hub | In A Sentimental Mood | Rostock,Wir Kommen!
Monster,NL, rec. 3./4.1.2002
Schlosser,Axel (tp) | Weber,Steffen 'Larose' (ss,ts) | Böhm,Rainer (p) | Huber,Arne (b) | Binder,Lars (dr)

J4E 4761 | CD | Tough Tenors | EAN 4016761047617
The Tough Tenors With The Antonio Farao European Trio
Voyage | Time Tunel | Cherokee | Virgo | I Mean You
Live at The Jazzkeller Frankfurt/M., rec. 16.12.2001
Tough Tenors,The | Latatos,Tony (ss,ts) | Enders,Johannes (ts) | Farao,Antonio (p) | Gjakonovski,Martin (b) | Terzic,Dejan (dr)

J4E 4762 | CD | Martin Auer Quintett | EAN 4016761047624
Martin Auer Quintet
Evan | Wasserzeichen | Ex 7,2 | Bica | Exercise 13 | Watsoning
Live at 'Leerer Beutel',Regensburg, rec. 15.10.2002
Auer,Martin (tp,fl-h) | Trübsbach,Florian (cl,ss,as) | Eschke,Jan (p) | Kurz,Andreas (b) | Jütte,Bastian (dr)
Never Give Up | Mr. Wu | The End Of A Book | Woody & Wu
?,by Martin Fux, rec. 2003
Auer,Martin (tp,fl-h) | Trübsbach,Florian (cl,ss,as) | Eschke,Jan (p) | Kurz,Andreas (b) | Jütte,Bastian (dr)

J4E 4763 | CD | Duo 1 | EAN 4016761047631
Matthias Rosenbauer-Gerhard Gschößl
Maus,Raus,Aus | Hymne | Ein Dunkles Helles | Die Mücke | Television | Das Morsealphabet | Der Landwal | Stimmung | Seit Jahren | Das Virus | 18 Grad Minus | Reprise
Fürth, rec. 23.10.2001/23.7.2002
Gschößl,Gerhard (tb,harmonisierungsgerät,tonschleifen) | Rosenbauer,Matthias (dr,perc)

J4E 4764 | CD | endlich Jazz...? | EAN 4016761047648
Florian Bührich Quintet
Whisper Not | All Of Me | Tin Tin Deo | A Japanese Waltze | Django | Reunion Blues | Work Song | Softly As In A Morning Sunrise | Bebop
Nürnberg, rec. October/December 2001
Bührich,Florian (vib) | Wiersich,Andreas (g) | Adamietz,Peter (p) | Kühnl,Peter (b) | Seegel,Stefan (dr)

Jazz Connaisseur | Jörg Koran

JCCD 0029-2 | CD | Stridewalk
Bernd Lhotzky
Yacht Club Swing | Smashing Thirds | April In My Heart | S' Posin' | Honey Hush | Hold My Hand | I Surrender Dear | You Took Advantage Of Me | Morning Air | Lonesome Reverie | Harlem Strut | Blueswil | It's All Right With Me | Concentrating | The Mule Walk | If I Could Be With You One Hour Tonight | Candelights
Alte Kirche Boswil,CH, rec. 17./18.10.2000
Lhotzky,Bernd (p-solo)

JCCD 0140-2 | CD | Barrel Of Keys | EAN 7619961014020
Dick Hyman
I'm Coming Virginia | Aunt Hagar's Blues
Live,at 'Alte Kirche', Boswil,CH, rec. 29.10.2001
Hyman,Dick (p-solo)
Louis Mazetier
Pork And Beans | Nostalgic Walk | Mecca Flat
Mazetier,Louis (p-solo)
Dick Hyman-Louis Mazetier Duo
Sweetie Dear | Barrel Of Keys | Good Bait | Easy Living | South | 'Tain't So Honey 'Tain't So | Because My Baby Don't Mean May Be Now | Groovin' High | Dancers In Love | Dancing In The Dark | I'm A Little Blackbird Looking For A Little Bluebird | Mandy Make Up Your Mind | Cakewalkin' Babies From Home
Hyman,Dick (p) | Mazetier,Louis (p)

JCCD 0243-2 | CD | The Piano Starts Talking | EAN 7619967024320
Louis Mazetier
Keep Your Temper | Warm Valley | Just Before Daybreak | Morning Air | Feeling Lonesome | F Minor Stride | Sweet Smile | Reflections In D | Mister Joe | Pinetop's Boogie Woogie | Music On My Mind | I Ain't Got Nobody | Nothin' | Memories Of You | Sweet Patootie(Blues) | Erroll's Bounce
Live,at 'Alte Kirche', Boswil,CH, rec. 2.12.2002
Mazetier,Louis (p-solo)

JCCD 8701-2 | CD | Live At Swiss Radio Studio Zürich
JCLP 8701 | LP | Live At Swiss Radio Studio Zürich
Wild Bill Davis Quartet
Meridian | Honeysuckle Rose | Azure-Te | Stolen Sweets | Pompton Turnpike | This Is All I Ask | Caravan | Some More | Atlantic City | Jive Samba | Get Your Kicks On Route 66 | Lester Leaps In | April In Paris
Live at Radio DRS,Zürich, rec. 1.11.1986
Davis,Wild Bill (el-p,org,voc) | Scott,Clifford (fl,as,ts) | Thompson,Dickie (g,voc) | Lucas,Clyde (dr)

JCCD 8702-2 | CD | Greatest Organ Solos Ever!
JCLP 8702 | LP | Greatest Organ Solos Ever!
Wild Bill Davis
Blues Before Midnight | Azure-Te | Misty | On The Sunny Side Of The Street | Girl Of My Dreams | Give Me The Simple Life | For All We Know | Blues After Midnight | Chelsea Bridge | Lush Life | Spiritual Medley: | Sometimes I Feel Like A Motherless Child- | Deep River- | By The Bend Of The River- | April In Paris | In A Mellow Tone | Mood Indigo | Lotus Blossom | Warm Valley | Don't Get Around Much Anymore | Passion Flower | Heaven | Come Sunday
Studio Radio DRS,Zürich, rec. 17.12.1986
Davis,Wild Bill (org,voc)

JCCD 8803-2 | CD | Trombone Tradition
JCMC 8803-4 | MC | Trombone Tradition
Lucien Barbarin With The Henri Chaix Trio
Bye Bye Blackbird | Yes Sir That's My Baby | Black And Blue | Just A Closer Walk With Thee | After You've Gone | When You're Smiling | Do You Know What It Means To Miss New Orleans | Mood Indigo | Lucien's Blues
Studio Radio DRS,Zürich, rec. 8.7.1988
Barbarin,Lucien (tb) | Chaix,Henri (p) | Du Bois,Alain (b) | Cavicchiolo,Romano (dr)
Lucien Barbarin-Henri Chaix Duo
Baby Won't You Please Come Home | Rosetta | Georgia On My Mind | Basin Street Blues | Ain't She Sweet | On The Sunny Side Of The Street
Studio Radio DRS,Zürich, rec. 9.7.1988
Barbarin,Lucien (tb) | Chaix,Henri (p)
Henri Chaix
Sugar | Lulu's Back In Town
Chaix,Henri (p-solo)

JCCD 8904-2 | CD | My Pal Basie
Nat Pierce
Sweet Lorraine | I Can't Get Started | Mood Indigo | Blue Flame | What's New? | Mean To Me
Studio Radio DRS,Zürich, rec. 18.11.1989
Pierce,Nat (p-solo)
Nat Pierce-Irving Stokes
My Melancholy Baby | Just Friends | You've Changed
Pierce,Nat (p) | Stokes,Irving (tp)
Nat Pierce Trio
My Pal Basie | I Want A Little Girl | Lil' Darlin'
Pierce,Nat (p) | Woode,Jimmy (b) | Jackson,Oliver (dr)
Nat Pierce Quartet
Jive At Five
Pierce,Nat (p) | Stokes,Irving (tp) | Woode,Jimmy (b) | Jackson,Oliver (dr)

JCCD 9005-2 | CD | That's All
Wild Bill Davis Super Trio
Love Me Or Leave Me | I'm Just A Lucky So-And-So | Secret Love | I Only Have Eyes For You | Where Or When | That's All | My Ideal | Night Train | Girl Talk | Please Save Your Love For Me | Low Bottom
Studio Radio DRS,Zürich, rec. 26.3.1990
Davis,Wild Bill (org) | Johnson,Plas (ts) | Miles,Buddy (dr)

JCCD 9106-2 | CD | The Giant Of Stride Piano In Switzerland
Joe Turner
I've Found A New Baby | Honey Hush | Tea For Two | I'm Crazy 'Bout My Baby | Royal Garden Blues | Honeysuckle Rose | Carolina Shout | Sunday Girl

Basel,CH, rec. 26.4.1955
Turner,Joe (p-solo,voc)
Love Me | Smashing Thirds | Ready For The River
Basel,CH, rec. 18.4.1958
Turner,Joe (p-solo,voc)
Isn't It Romantic | Rosetta
Zürich,CH, rec. 2.10.1959
Turner,Joe (p-solo)
Joe Turner-Claude Dunson
How High The Moon | Begin The Beguine | 12th Street Rag | Royal Garden Blues- | Honeysuckle Rose-
Zürich,CH, rec. 1950
Turner,Joe (p) | Dunson,Claude (b)
Joe Turner-Albert Nicholas Quartet
Honeysuckle Rose | Ain't Misbehavin' | I'm Crazy 'Bout My Baby | Joe's Blues
Schlieren,CH, rec. 24.2.1958
Turner,Joe (p,voc) | Nicholas,Albert (cl) | Cizmek,Rolf (b) | Antolini,Charly (dr)
Joe Turner And Friends
Ready For The River | No Idea | Sweet Georgia Brown
Riehen,CH, rec. 7.5.1958
Turner,Joe (p,voc) | Dies,Werner (cl) | Armitage,Dennis (ts) | Prina,Curt (vib) | Lang,Sunny (b) | Ward,John (dr)

JCCD 9107-2 | CD | Ray Bryant Plays Blues And Ballads
Ray Bryant
Basin Street Blues | I Gotta Right To Sing The Blues | Medley: | She's Funny That Way- | Memories Of You- | I Surrender Dear- | In De Back Room | My One And Only Love | Black And Blue | If I Can Just Make It Into Heaven | I Can't Get Started | Tin Roof Blues | Gee Baby Ain't I Good To You | Blues In The Pulpit
Alte Kirche Boswil,CH, rec. 27.3.1991
Bryant,Ray (p-solo)

JCCD 9313-2 | CD | Playing My Way
Sir Charles Thompson
Medley: | I Got Rhythm- | Solitude- | Snowfall- | Some Other Spring- | Isn't It Romantic- | Body And Soul- | St.Louis Blues- | Robbin's Nest-
Basel,CH, rec. 3.5.1961
Thompson,Sir Charles (p-solo)
You Don't Know What Love Is | Shiny Stockings | So Blue | Strange Hours | An Affair Ro Remember | Churchhouse Blues | But Beautiful | Robbin's Nest
Zürich,CH, rec. 28.4.1967
Thompson,Sir Charles (p-solo)

JCCD 9415-2 | CD | With Duke In Mind
Dado Moroni
What Am I Here For(spoken introduction by Dado Moroni) | There Was Nobody Looking | Main Stem | All Too Soon | Pleadin' For Love | So | Black Beauty | Day Dream | Cotton Tail | Istahan | Caravan | Warm Valley | Don't Get Around Much Anymore | What Am I Here For(spoken closing by Dado Moroni)
Alte Kirche Boswil,CH, rec. 7.4.1994
Moroni,Dado (p-solo)

JCCD 9430-2 | CD | Inimitable
Ray Bryant
Lullaby Petite | Moanin' | Willow Weep For Me- | Back To The Blues- | Con Alma | Slow Freight | Jungle Town Jubilee | Django | Gotta Travel On | When I Look In Your Eyes | After Hours | The Impossible Rag | Georgia On My Mind | Good Morning Heartache | Until It's Time For You To Go | Little Susie
Live,at 'Alte Kirche', Boswil,CH, rec. details unknown
Bryant,Ray (p-solo)

JCCD 9518-2 | CD | The Way I Am
Dado Moroni
The Cup Bearers | Not Without You | Wrap Your Troubles In Dreams | I Can't Get Started | Improvisation In G Minor | Medley: | Time Will Tell- | The Man From Potters Crossing- | Yesterdays | Blue Dado | Thelonious Monk Medley: | Ruby My Dear- | Pannonica- | Round About Midnight- | What Am I Here For | Lotus Blossom | S.K.J.
Alte Kirche Boswil,CH, rec. 7.4.1994
Moroni,Dado (p-solo)

JCCD 9521-2 | CD | Good Vibrations
Louis Mazetier
Truckin' | I've Got The World On A String | Look Out,Lion,I've Got You | Waltz Medley: | A Child Is Born- | Nicolas- | Someday My Prince Will Come- | Sweet Lorraine | 'Deed I Do | A Single Petal Of A Rose | Sophie | Here Comes The Band | Ticklin' The Blues | If I Could Be With You One Hour Tonight | Sweet And Slow | Just One Of Those Things | Mr.Freddie Blues | Marianne | There Is Nobody Looking | Over The Rainbow | Handful Of Keys
Alte Kirche Boswil,CH, rec. 9.12.1995
Mazetier,Louis (p-solo)

JCCD 9522-2 | CD | In Concert:What A Treat!
Viper's Drag | I've Got The World On A String | I've Found A New Baby | Fats Waller Medley: | Lonesome Me- | How Can You Face Me?- | My Fate Is In Your Hands- | The Mule Walk | Cold Afternoon Blues | Echoes Of Spring | Look Out,Lion,I've Got You | Kansas City Stomps | Yesterdays | Overnight | Medley: | Nicolas- | Marianne- | Lotus Blossom | Carolina Shout | That's All
Alte Kirche Boswil,CH, rec. 10.12.1995
Mazetier,Louis (p-solo)

JCCD 9523-2 | CD | Swiss Air
Willy Bischof Jazztet
Air Mail Special | A Smooth One | Undecided | Ain't She Sweet | Sweet Georgia Brown | Way Down Yonder In New Orleans | Lullaby Of Birdland | Swiss Air | Asi | Moonglow | Slipped Disc | Avalon
Restaurant 'Bierhübeli',Bern,CH, rec. 2.11.1995
Bischof,Willy (p) | Schmid,Willy (cl,voc) | Osterwald,Hazy (vib,voc) | Kurmann,Stephan (b) | Schmidlin,Peter (dr)
Willy Bischof Trio
France Medley: | Autumn Leaves- | La Vie En Rose- | C'Est Si Bon-
Bischof,Willy (p) | Kurmann,Stephan (b) | Schmidlin,Peter (dr)

JCCD 9726-2 | CD | Live In Concert:Jon Weber Flying Keys
Jon Weber
Topsy | Snuggled On Your Shoulder | I'm Always Drunk In San Francisco | Lover Man(Oh,Where Can You Be?)- | Fascinating Rhythm- | As Time Goes By | A Smooth One | Igloo | In My Solitude | Between The Devil And The Deep Blue Sea | Gone With The Wind | Please Send Me Someone To Love | Here Lies Love | It Ain't Necessarily So | Take Five | Black And Blue | Willow Weep For Me | Smile
Live,at 'Alte Kirche', Boswil,CH, rec. 15.6.1997
Weber,Jon (p-solo)

JCCD 9728-2 | CD | Stridin' High
Ralph Sutton
Love Lies | In The Dark | Clothes Line Ballet | Ralph's Very Special Bonus Track
Live at Schloss Elmau, rec. 4.11.1997
Sutton,Ralph (p-solo)
Bernd Lhotzky
Drop Me Off In Harlem | Lover | Lush Life
Lhotzky,Bernd (p-solo)
Ralph Sutton-Bernd Lhotzky
Keepin' Out Of Mischief Now | Jeepers Creepers | Until The Real Thing Comes Along | A Porter's Love Song To A Chambermaid | Lulu's Back In Town | Taking A Chance On Love | I'm Gonna Sit Right Down And Write Myself A Letter | Back Home Again In Indiana
Sutton,Ralph (p) | Lhotzky,Bernd (p)

JCCD 9831-2 | CD | There Will Never Be Another You
Dick Hyman
Here's That Rainy Day | Blue Skies | Spring Is Here | Sobbin' Blues | Jungle Blues | Undecided | Shine | Yesterdays | Send In The Clowns | Skylark | There'll Never Be Another You | Boswil Boogie
Live,at 'Alte Kirche', Boswil,CH, rec. 25.10.1998
Hyman,Dick (p-solo)

JCCD 9932-2 | CD | A Friendly Chat
Louis Mazetier-Peter Ecklund
Jelly Roll Blues | I'll Never Be The Same | Everybody Loves My Baby | East St.Louis Toodle-Oo | Martinique | I'm In The Mood For Love | Blue Lou | Wherever There's Love | Lulu's Back In Town | Awful Sad | Waiting For Katy | Blues Chat | Swing It Easy | Ain't Misbehavin'
Live,at 'Alte Kirche', Boswil,CH, rec. 24.4.1999
Mazetier,Louis (p) | Ecklund,Peter (tp)
Louis Mazetier
Blue Turning Grey Over Me | Hallelujah
Mazetier,Louis (p-solo)

JCCD 9935-2 | CD | Prime Cuts
John Colianni
Straighten Up And Fly Right | Autumn In New York | Azure-Te(Paris Blues) | Moonlight In Vermont | Fascinating Rhythm | Slow Blues No.2(take 2) | Dancing In The Dark | Avalon | I Cover The Waterfront(take 2) | Mean To Me | I've Got A Crush On You | Lulu's Back In Town | Easy Living | Willow Weep For Me
details unknown, rec. 10.10.1999
Colianni,John (p-solo)

Jazz Haus Musik | Jazz Haus Musik

JHM 0029 CD | CD | Helix
Dioko
ANC | P.O.B. | I.C. | Tuuna | 15 W 40
Köln, rec. 27./28.6.1986
Dioko | Ruby,Georg (p) | Manderscheid,Dieter (cello,b) | Kobialka,Reinhard (dr)

JHM 0036 CD | CD | Saxfiguren
Kölner Saxophon Mafia
Mafia Indikativ | Elephant's Walk | Wayne War Schneller | Barry McGuigan | Stompin' At The Philharmonie | Phoenix | Fake Fuge | Ruby Domesticus | Fegefeuer | Süper | Mafia Blues | Mafia Indikativ(alt.take) | Lonely From Sky It's A Home For Benefit Within Sixty Lovely Good Hearts A Day
Köln, rec. August 1989
Kölner Saxophon Mafia | Hanschel,Roger (fl,alto-cl,as,sopranino) | Ullrich,Joachim (cl,b-cl,ss,ts) | Kaiser,Wollie (fl,b-cl,contra-b-cl,ss,ts,bass-sax,piccolo) | Raulf,Dirk (cl,ss,ts,bs) | Veeck,Gerhard (fl,alto-fl,ss,as,bs)

JHM 0037 CD | CD | Blaufrontal
Blaufrontal
Das Jagen Ist Des Saxophonisten Lust | Bilder,Köpfe,Gesichte | Der Blaue Reiter | Im August | Prinz | Der Almanach | Nr.2
Köln, rec. June 1989
Blaufrontal | Hanschel,Roger (alto-cl,as,sopranino) | Lüdemann,Hans (p) | Linke,Rainer (b)

JHM 0038 CD | CD | Chicago Breakdown:The Music Of Jelly Roll Morton
Thomas Heberer-Dieter Manderscheid
Chicago Breakdown | King Porter Stomp | Buddy Bolden's Blues | The Pearls | Black Bottom Stomp | Freakish
Köln, rec. October 1989
Heberer,Thomas (tp) | Manderscheid,Dieter (b)

JHM 0040 CD | CD | Directors
Directors
Sambady | Pleasure | Tom-Song | Cut | Pas De Deux | Silky Landscape | Mouse In History | In My Rays | Tonight
Köln, rec. details unknown
Directors | Maurer,Albrecht (keyboards,v,voice) | Witzmann,Thomas (keyboards,dr,midi-pads)
Take The Rest
Directors | Maurer,Albrecht (keyboards,v,voice) | Witzmann,Thomas (dr,darabuka,midi-pads) | Ernst,Thomas (g)
Deja
Directors | Maurer,Albrecht (keyboards,v,voice) | Witzmann,Thomas (dr,midi-pads) | Grabosch,Horst (tp)
Happy Hour
Directors | Maurer,Albrecht (keyboards,v,voice) | Witzmann,Thomas (dr,midi-pads) | Heupel,Michael (fl)
Fabrik
Directors | Maurer,Albrecht (keyboards,v,voice) | Witzmann,Thomas (dr,midi-pads) | Heupel,Michael (fl) | Grabosch,Horst (tp) | Ernst,Thomas (g)

JHM 0045 CD | CD | Faces Of The Duke
Joachim Ullrich Orchestra
Decrescendo Suite: | Decrescendo- | Cotton Tail- | Mood Indigo- | Finale- | Mr.Gentle And Mr.Cool | Just Missed The 'A'-Train | Everything But You | Sophisticated Lady | Don't Get Around Much Anymore
Köln, rec. January 1991
Ullrich,Joachim (arr,ld) | Winterschladen,Reiner (tp) | Berg,Henning (tb) | Puntin,Claudio (cl,b-cl) | Gratkowski,Frank (fl,b-cl,as) | Schubert,Matthias (ts) | Adams,Christoph (p) | Hoffmann,Hajo (viola) | Schaub,Brigitte (cello) | Berns,Pepe (b) | Soll,Hendrik (dr) | Schneider,Susanne (voc)

JHM 0046 CD | CD | Kölner Saxophon Mafia Proudly Presents
Kölner Saxophon Mafia With Bad Little Dynamos
H.R.H.
Kölner Saxophon Mafia | Kaiser,Wollie (reeds) | Veeck,Gerhard (reeds) | Hanschel,Roger (reeds) | Ulrich,Joachim (reeds) | Raulf,Dirk (reeds) | Herweg,Dirk (g) | Röhm,Jojo (b) | Ginsberg,Kerstin (dr) | Schumacher,Nils (voc)
Kölner Saxophon Mafia With V.Nick Nikitakis
A Fat Morgana
Kölner Saxophon Mafia | Kaiser,Wollie (reeds) | Veeck,Gerhard (reeds) | Hanschel,Roger (reeds) | Ulrich,Joachim (reeds) | Raulf,Dirk (reeds) | Nikitakis,V.Nick (bouzouki)
Kölner Saxophon Mafia With Klaus Der Geiger
Mein Automobil
Kölner Saxophon Mafia | Kaiser,Wollie (reeds) | Veeck,Gerhard (reeds) | Hanschel,Roger (reeds) | Ulrich,Joachim (reeds) | Raulf,Dirk (reeds) | Klaus Der Geiger (v,voc)
Kölner Saxophon Mafia With Blasorchester Dicke Luft
Requiem Für Ein Phänomen
Kölner Saxophon Mafia | Kaiser,Wollie (reeds) | Veeck,Gerhard (reeds) | Hanschel,Roger (reeds) | Ulrich,Joachim (reeds) | Raulf,Dirk (reeds) | Blasorchester Dicke Luft
Kölner Saxophon Mafia With Hans Süper
Blues For The Flitsch
Kölner Saxophon Mafia | Kaiser,Wollie (reeds) | Veeck,Gerhard (reeds) | Hanschel,Roger (reeds) | Ulrich,Joachim (reeds) | Raulf,Dirk (reeds) | Süper,Hans (mand,voc)
Kölner Saxophon Mafia With Irene Lorenz
Keep On Moving
Kölner Saxophon Mafia | Kaiser,Wollie (reeds) | Veeck,Gerhard (reeds) | Hanschel,Roger (reeds) | Ulrich,Joachim (reeds) | Raulf,Dirk (reeds) | Lorenz,Irene (voc)
Kölner Saxophon Mafia With Jacki Liebezeit
Jaki
Kölner Saxophon Mafia | Kaiser,Wollie (reeds) | Veeck,Gerhard (reeds) | Hanschel,Roger (reeds) | Ulrich,Joachim (reeds) | Raulf,Dirk (reeds) | Liebezeit,Jacki (dr)
Kölner Saxophon Mafia With Fleisch
La Boe La Boe
Kölner Saxophon Mafia | Kaiser,Wollie (reeds) | Veeck,Gerhard (reeds) | Hanschel,Roger (reeds) | Ulrich,Joachim (reeds) | Raulf,Dirk (reeds) | Fleisch: | Deistler,Gaga (g) | Bonnen,Dietmar (p,hardpaper-box) | Schilling,Andreas (cubes,metal-plate) | Leue,Eckhard (chair,el-saw)
Kölner Saxophon Mafia With Clarence Barlow
GVK 1 alt
Kölner Saxophon Mafia | Kaiser,Wollie (reeds) | Veeck,Gerhard (reeds) | Hanschel,Roger (reeds) | Ulrich,Joachim (reeds) | Raulf,Dirk (reeds) | Barlow,Clarence (computer-programming)
Kölner Saxophon Mafia With Arno Steffen
Supergut Ne
Kölner Saxophon Mafia | Kaiser,Wollie (reeds) | Veeck,Gerhard (reeds) | Hanschel,Roger (reeds) | Ulrich,Joachim (reeds) | Raulf,Dirk (reeds) | Steffen,Arno (voc)
Kölner Saxophon Mafia With The Auryn Quartet
Tod Auf Deutsch
Kölner Saxophon Mafia | Kaiser,Wollie (reeds) | Veeck,Gerhard (reeds) | Hanschel,Roger (reeds) | Ulrich,Joachim (reeds) | Raulf,Dirk (reeds) | Auryn String Quartet | Lingenfelder,Matthias (v) | Oppermann,Jens (v) | Eaton,Steuart (viola) | Arndt,Andreas (cello)
Kölner Saxophon Mafia With Triviatas(1.Schwuler Männerchor Köln)
Zaubertrick
Kölner Saxophon Mafia | Kaiser,Wollie (reeds) | Veeck,Gerhard (reeds) | Hanschel,Roger (reeds) | Ulrich,Joachim (reeds) | Raulf,Dirk (reeds) | Triviatas (1.Schwuler Männerchor Köln)
Kölner Saxophon Mafia With Rick E. Loef
Ohne Titel
Kölner Saxophon Mafia | Kaiser,Wollie (reeds) | Veeck,Gerhard (reeds) | Hanschel,Roger (reeds) | Ulrich,Joachim (reeds) | Raulf,Dirk (reeds) | Loef,Rick E. (paintbrushes,pencilsharper,percil,toothbrush)
Kölner Saxophon Mafia With Ina Stachelhaus And Erik Schneider
Enfant Terrible
Kölner Saxophon Mafia | Kaiser,Wollie (reeds) | Veeck,Gerhard (reeds) | Hanschel,Roger (reeds) | Ulrich,Joachim (reeds) | Raulf,Dirk (reeds) | Stachelhaus,Ina (voc) | Schneider,Erik (p)
Kölner Saxophon Mafia With Willie Gräff
All Of Me
Kölner Saxophon Mafia | Kaiser,Wollie (reeds) | Veeck,Gerhard (reeds) | Hanschel,Roger (reeds) | Ulrich,Joachim (reeds) | Raulf,Dirk (reeds) | Gräff,Willie (accordeon)
Kölner Saxophon Mafia With Dieter Wellershoff
Das Ich Und Seine Augenblicke
Kölner Saxophon Mafia | Kaiser,Wollie (reeds) | Veeck,Gerhard (reeds) | Hanschel,Roger (reeds) | Ulrich,Joachim (reeds) | Raulf,Dirk (reeds) | Wellershoff,Dieter (recitation)
Kölner Saxophon Mafia With Lydie Auvray
Differentes Planetes
Kölner Saxophon Mafia | Kaiser,Wollie (reeds) | Veeck,Gerhard (reeds) | Hanschel,Roger (reeds) | Ulrich,Joachim (reeds) | Raulf,Dirk (reeds) | Auvray,Lydie (accordeon)
Kölner Saxophon Mafia With Nedim Hazar And Orhan Temur
Kökler-Die Wurzeln
Kölner Saxophon Mafia | Kaiser,Wollie (reeds) | Veeck,Gerhard (reeds) | Hanschel,Roger (reeds) | Ulrich,Joachim (reeds) | Raulf,Dirk (reeds) | Hazar,Nedim (recitation) | Temur,Orhan (perc,saz)
Kölner Saxophon Mafia With Kristina Würminghausen
Tiger No.33
Kölner Saxophon Mafia | Kaiser,Wollie (reeds) | Veeck,Gerhard (reeds) | Hanschel,Roger (reeds) | Ulrich,Joachim (reeds) | Raulf,Dirk (reeds) | Würminghausen,Kristina (voice)
Kölner Saxophon Mafia With Ramesh Shotham
Inner Circle
Kölner Saxophon Mafia | Kaiser,Wollie (reeds) | Veeck,Gerhard (reeds) | Hanschel,Roger (reeds) | Ulrich,Joachim (reeds) | Raulf,Dirk (reeds) | Shotham,Ramesh (ghatam,tavil,voice)
Kölner Saxophon Mafia With Ingo Kümmel And Frank Köllges
Kümmel's Traum Oder Die Rheinische Republik
Kölner Saxophon Mafia | Kaiser,Wollie (reeds) | Veeck,Gerhard (reeds) | Hanschel,Roger (reeds) | Ulrich,Joachim (reeds) | Raulf,Dirk (reeds) | Kümmel,Ingo (recitation) | Köllges,Frank (dr)

JHM 0047 CD | CD | The Red Snapper
Tome XX
The Boyish Chest | The Red Snapper | On Borrowed Time | Cara Lucia | Inner Circle | Les Jeux Sont Faits | Villa Air Bell | O.T. | Love Streams | To Be Continued | Bao Ding | Obstinate Isles | Claudia Luna | The Years | One For Bill | The Clown | Monsieur Loyal | Nightmare Of A White Elephant | Forms | The Sword-Swallower | Icarus | Akkaya | Obstinate Isles(No.2) | Mex
Köln, rec. May/Junes 1991
Tome XX | Heberer,Thomas (tp) | Raulf,Dirk (ss,bs) | Manderscheid,Dieter (b) | Wittek,Fritz (dr)

JHM 0049 CD | CD | Aph-o-Rism's
Hans Lüdemann Rism
Wie Du(Like You) | Stella By Star Wars | Prinz | X-Rism | Ruck Än Ruul | Geschichte(His Story) | Let's Twist Again | Roll | Schabertnack | Heimkehr(Homecoming)
Köln, rec. 9./10.4.1991
Lüdemann,Hans (p) | Kracht,Hartmut (b) | Lehan,Marc (dr)

JHM 0051 CD | CD | Südamerika Sept. 90
Sotto In Su
Tunnelflug Mit Klimawechsel | Asphaltwirbel, Fleisch Vom Rind, Smogalarm | Tango Corrientes 319 | Sierraflimmern-Föhn Stufe 3 | Schrott, Charmante Erscheinungen, Fieber | Luna, Luna, Luna | Vandalis Electrica | El Lugar Y El Momento | Rock Beat Alemania | Warten Auf Die Pinguine | Nationalfeiertag | Epilog Mit Umgedrehter Sichel
Live in ?,Südamerika, rec. September 1990
Sotto In Su | Heberer,Thomas (tp) | Tuchacek,Alexander (synth,computer) | Schulte,Frank (synth,records,sampling,tapes,toys,voc) | Breuer,Reinhold (dr,perc) | Hanzer,Boris (recording,sound-effects)

JHM 0052 CD | CD | Beyond Janis
Ulla Oster Group
Blues Ar Easy To Write | Babe(1) | Babe(2) | Some Moon | Left | Me And Ornette C. | Trau Schau Wem | Thet's It
Köln, rec. January 1992
Oster,Ulla (b) | Winterschladen,Reiner (tp) | Von Kleewitz,Jack (as) | Raulf,Dirk (bs) | Sacher,Buddy (g) | Kübert,Martin (keyboards,sampling) | Eisold,Peter (dr)

JHM 0054 CD | CD | Dufte
Franck Band
Opener | Der Musikant | Zu Doof | Vivien | Connection | Kicker | Bauerntanz(7) | Nimmich | Positive | Bauerntanz(8) | Quieck! | Wir Sind Dufte | Good Bye, Good Bye, Good Bye
Stadtgarten,Köln, rec. June 1992
Franck,Hinrich (keyboards,voc) | Heberer,Thomas (tp) | Gratkowski,Frank (fl,as) | Fuhr,Wolfgang (fl,ts,bs) | Neumann,Werner (g,voc) | Fischer,Claus (b,voc) | Fischötter,Hardy (dr) | Engelke,Anke (voc) | Lorenz,Irene (voc) | Köllges,Frank (voc)

JHM 0056 CD | CD | King Kong
Reiner Winterschladen-Manos Tsangaris
Rappell | Procession | Still 99 | Station Monica | TRM'PT FLY FLY | Queeker | Clockwork Lemon | Mu | No Panama | So So | King Kong | Ekpyrosis
Stadtgarten,Köln, rec. details unknown
Winterschladen,Reiner (tp) | Tsangaris,Manos (dr,perc)

JHM 0057 CD | CD | Stange Loops
Georg Ruby Group
Drull 4
Köln, rec. 4.5.1992
Ruby,Georg (p) | Puntin,Claudio (cl,b-cl)
Mr.Lampshade
Köln, rec. 29.9.1992
Ruby,Georg (p) | Puntin,Claudio (cl,b-cl)
Metalog 1 | Metalog 2 | Metalog 3 | Metalog 4
Ruby,Georg (p) | Grabosch,Horst (tp,fl-h)
Metalog 5 | Supernova
Ruby,Georg (p) | Grabosch,Horst (tp,fl-h) | Kaiser,Wollie (ts) | Puntin,Claudio (cl)
Rubum Allorans | Aila | Aquamarin | Secret Codes | Bruschetta
Köln, rec. 24.-26.8.1992
Ruby,Georg (p) | Kaiser,Wollie (b-cl,contra-b-cl,ss) | Hasler,Gabriele (voice)
P.O.B. 499 | Strange Loop
Ruby,Georg (p-solo)

JHM 0058 CD | CD | Mafia Years 1982-86
Kölner Saxophon Mafia
Roots | Giant Steps
Live, rec. 1982
Kölner Saxophon Mafia | Tretter,Armin (as,sopranino) | Veeck,Gerhard

(fl,ss,as) | Schneider,Florian (fl,cl,ss) | Kaiser,Wollie (fl,b-cl,ss,ts) | Ullrich,Joachim (cl,ss,ts,bass-sax) | Clark,Dave (b-cl,bs)

Caran | Scorpio | KSM

details unknown, rec. 1984

Kölner Saxophon Mafia | Veeck,Gerhard (ss,as) | Tretter,Armin (cl,as,sopranino) | Stein,Norbert (ss,ts) | Ullrich,Joachim (cl,ss,ts) | Zoepf,Joachim (b-cl,bs) | Kaiser,Wollie (fl,b-cl,ss,ts)

Lebenslänglich | Rudophplatz 04:30 Uhr | Rudolphplatz 17:00 Uhr | Rudolphplatz 02:00

Köln, rec. 1985

Kölner Saxophon Mafia | Stein,Norbert (cl,ss,ts,koffer-perc,voice) | Tretter,Armin (cl,as,alukoffer-perc,sopranino) | Kaiser,Wollie (fl,b-cl,ss,ts,pappkoffer-perc) | Ullrich,Joachim (cl,ss,ts,präp.tom-tom) | Veeck,Gerhard (fl,alto-fl,ss,as,dr-computer) | Zoepf,Joachim (fl,bs,kontra-b-cl,saxophonkoffer-perc) | Stadt-Geräusche

Leo | B B 5 | Sophisticated Lady

details unknown, rec. 1986

Kölner Saxophon Mafia | Ullrich,Joachim (cl,b-cl,ts) | Veeck,Gerhard (fl,ss,as,bs) | Stein,Norbert (ss,ts) | Tretter,Armin (fl,cl,alto-cl,as,bs) | Kaiser,Wollie (b-cl,contra-b-cl,ts,piccolo)

Südstadt Shuffle | Die Matriarchin | Erich, Der Grüne Delphin | Erich, Der Grüne Delphin Tanzt | Erich, Der Dicke Grüne Delphin Tanzt | Sneakin'

Stadtgarten,Köln, rec. 1992

Kölner Saxophon Mafia | Ullrich,Joachim (cl,b-cl,ts) | Veeck,Gerhard (fl,ss,as,bs) | Raulf,Dirk (cl,ss,ts,bs) | Hanschel,Roger (alto-cl,as,sopranino) | Kaiser,Wollie (b-cl,contra-b-cl,ts,piccolo)

JHM 0060 CD | CD | Tust Du Fühlen Gut

Wollie Kaiser Timeghost

Feelgood | Fuckin' You Know Man | Axes 'N X-Legs | Wir Sind Die Sieger | Ruby Domesticus | Tex Mex Teevee | Damned I Love You Not | Freude Am Fahren | Are You Lonesome Tonight | Fühlgut

Stadtgarten,Köln, rec. January 1993

Kaiser,Wollie (b-cl,ss,ts,bass-sax,voc) | Oster,Ulla (b,voc) | Kobialka,Reinhard (dr,perc) | Beracz,Gerti (voc)

Male Couple

Kaiser,Wollie (b-cl,ss,ts,bass-sax,voc) | Oster,Ulla (b,voc) | Kobialka,Reinhard (dr,perc) | Beracz,Gerti (voc) | Franck,Hinrich (voc)

JHM 0061 CD | CD | Bad Times Roll

Blaufrontal With Hank Roberts & Mark Feldman

Warming Up | Staffel Shuffle | Zerkall Bleu | No Hau | Bad Times Roll | Teilquintet | The Slur | The Winner's Tears

Köln, rec. 4./5.1.1993

Blaufrontal | Hanschel,Roger (alto-cl,as,sopranino) | Lüdemann,Hans (p,manipulations) | Feldman,Mark (v) | Roberts,Hank (cello) | Linke,Rainer (b)

JHM 0062 CD | CD | Menschbilder

Double You

Machtspiele | Swansong | Schlehmil | Main Street | Pharao | Mutterliebe | Bagatelle | Kon-Tiki | Nacht Eines Fauns | Ländler | Sintra | Courage | Der Alptraum

Stadtgarten,Köln, rec. 26.-28.7.1993

Double You | Fuhr,Wolfgang (ts) | Neumann,Werner (g) | Heinze,Volker (b) | Höppner,Roland (dr)

JHM 0063 CD | CD | Third Degree

Tome XX

Thursday 2:55 p.m. | 4 Berth Out Front | Atsui Sugoku | The XX Meter Decoder | Alfred In Wonderland | Tuesday 8:12 p.m. | If You Leave Them Cats Alone,They'll Play Nothin' But Shit | Bunch Of Banners | Inner Logic | Jump Over! And Join The Party | Tuesday 3:35 p.m. | Sometimes It Snows In April | Guiro | Rumpuvalssi(Drum Waltz) | Allusion I | Finale(Friday 12:15 a.m.)

Stadtgarten,Köln, rec. July/August 1993

Tome XX | Heberer,Thomas (tp) | Raulf,Dirk (reeds) | Manderscheid,Dieter (b) | Wittek,Fritz (dr)

JHM 0065 CD | CD | Go Commercial...

Kölner Saxophon Mafia

Elephant's Walk | Nice Lines Man | Cultural Value | Kill Your Darlings | Hip Hop Hammer | The Fisherman's Wife's Friend | The Shuttle | Supergutne | Ali Shuffle | A Funkful Of House | Ragga Muffia | Chromatic Mousetrap | Odd Job | Floor Dance | Hekkto Tekkno | Anyday

Köln, rec. September 1993

Kölner Saxophon Mafia | Hanschel,Roger (fl,ss,as) | Veeck,Gerhard (as) | Kaiser,Wollie (b-cl,contra-b-cl,ts,bass-sax) | Raulf,Dirk (ss,ts,bs) | Ulrich,Joachim (cl,b-cl,ts)

JHM 0066 CD | CD | Pulsation

Christoph Haberer Group

Snow...Melting

Rüsselsheim-Bauschheim, rec. 1992/1993.

Haberer,Christoph (dr,perc,electronics) | Heberer,Thomas (tp) | Heupel,Michael (fl) | Bauer,Stefan (marimba) | Shotham,Ramesh (ghatam)

Live Pulse | Den Lille Sang(Til Gerd): | Noget Om Helte- | Den Lille Sang-

Haberer,Christoph (dr,perc,electronics) | Heupel,Michael (fl,alto-fl) | Van Kemenade,Paul (as)

Swing Cars

Haberer,Christoph (dr,perc,electronics) | Heberer,Thomas (tp)

Arco Iris

Haberer,Christoph (dr,perc,electronics) | Van Kemenade,Paul (as) | Bauer,Stefan (vib,marimba) | Shotham,Ramesh (dholak,kanjira,konakol,talking-dr,tavil)

Ta-Ka-Ta-Ki-Ta

Haberer,Christoph (dr,perc,electronics) | Heberer,Thomas (tp) | Heupel,Michael (fl,alto-fl,piccolo)

Hidden Pulse

Haberer,Christoph (dr,perc,electronics) | Heupel,Michael (fl) | Van Kemenade,Paul (as) | Shotham,Ramesh (kanjira,tavil)

Knitting Harmonix

Haberer,Christoph (dr,perc,electronics) | Heupel,Michael (fl,alto-fl,didgeridoo)

In Fragranti

Haberer,Christoph (dr,perc,electronics) | Heberer,Thomas (tp) | Shotham,Ramesh (kanjira)

Fin De Chantier

Haberer,Christoph (dr,perc,electronics) | Van Kemenade,Paul (as) | Bauer,Stefan (marimba)

The Deccan Queen SKB Express

Haberer,Christoph (dr,perc,electronics) | Heupel,Michael (sub-contra-b-fl) | Shotham,Ramesh (ghatam)

La Valse Virgin

Haberer,Christoph (dr,perc,electronics) | Heupel,Michael (fl,alto-fl,didgeridoo) | Bauer,Stefan (marimba) | Shotham,Ramesh (ghatam)

JHM 0067 CD | CD | Unitarism

Hans Lüdemann Rism

Second Symphony:Zerkall Bleu | Second Symphony:No Hau(Prolog) | Second Symphony:Johannes Braun | Canvas 1:Y-Rism | Terz | Second Symphony:No Hau | Canvas 2:Die Musik Des Erich Zann | Primpin(Salif Keita) | Die Vereinigung-The Unification | Die Lieder Der Deutschen- | Engführung- | Schnell Und Schmerzhaft- | Marlene(Ich Bin Von Kopf Bis Fuß Auf Liebe Eingestellt) | Canvas 3:Ungeist Und Geist | Second Symphony:No Hau(Epilog) | Second Symphony:Zerkall Bleu(Version 2)

Zerkall, rec. 24.5.1992

Lüdemann,Hans (p,bechstein-v,birds) | Ducret,Marc (g,melodica,switches) | Kracht,Hartmut (b,big-muff,ethno-beat) | Lehan,Marc (dr,perc,hi-hat)

JHM 0069 CD | CD | The Remedy

The Remedy

Improvised Songs(1-20)

details unknown, rec. November 1993

Remedy,The | Dörner,Axel (tp) | Schubert,Matthias (sax) | Gramss,Sebastian (g,cello,b,casio,electronics,voc) | Cora,Tom (cello) | Kowald,Peter (b,voice) | Wagner,Claus (dr,perc)

JHM 0070 CD | CD | Can I Go Like This?

Andreas Willers

Jan Lukas | Darizm | Von Allen Guten Geistern | Eden

Berlin, rec. January 1994

Willers,Andreas (g,el-g,melodica,steel-g)

2 Stromland | Off Range, No Hands | Cityscapes | Kaputt For Keeps | Mehr Licht | Tired But Not Sleepy | Far East | Nefertiti | Walz'er | Can I Go Like This | Pas De Deux

Berlin, rec. February-June 1994

Willers,Andreas (g,el-g,melodica,steel-g)

JHM 0071 CD | CD | Alien Lunatic

Planet Blow

Pretended Alien | Hip And Hop | Ich Warte,Ich Warte | Afraid Of What Might Be | Gautamas Dream | One Day | Lunatic | Alpha Centauri | Oregon | Quiet Place | Ionic Velocity | Verdammter Atlantic | The Slur | Mad Quasar

Biosphere Studio,?, rec. December 1994

Planet Blow | Hanschel,Roger (as) | Hübsch,Carl Ludwig 'Lu' (tuba) | Schipper,Jörn (dr)

JHM 0072 CD | CD | Eat Time

Agog

Sinnen | Piec | Nissen Hut | To Be Agog | White With Eyes | Dutch Rain | Eat Time | Kismet | Trinkle Tinkle | Umanqoba | Einmal Ist Keinmal | Good Bye | To Be Agog(II)

Stadtgarten,Köln, rec. May 1995

Agog | Wingold,Frank (g,el-g,g-synth) | Lucas,Boudewijn (b-g) | Lijbaart,Joost (dr,perc,amadinda)

JHM 0073 CD | CD | Go In Green

Roger Hanschel/Gabriele Hasler

Tillie | Study Nature | Interlude 1 | Curtains Dream | Bird Jet | Interlude 1 B | Go In Green | I Expressed My Opinion | Won | Old Dogs | Interlude 2 | Then Steal | Can Call Us | Interlude 1

Biosphere Studio,?, rec. March/April 1995

Hanschel,Roger (ss,as) | Hasler,Gabriele (voice)

JHM 0074 CD | CD | KontraSax

Christian Fuchs-Romy Herzberg

8,5 | Radio Days | Heartbeat Stories | Suite-Kontrabaß oder Die Kunst die Reisens | Arco Saltando | Spiralnebel(I,II) | O wie schön ist die Karibik

Köln, rec. May 1995

Fuchs,Christina (b-cl,ss,as) | Herzberg,Romy (b)

JHM 0075 CD | CD | The Natural Piano

Hans Lüdemann

Three Worlds(based on Akazehe Greeting from Burundi) | Rava-Tanz | Piece Of Soul | Piece Of Heart | Moving Hearts | Johann Brown(Hommage à James Brown) | Primpin | Piece Of Mind | Tu-Le | The Natural Piano | Wie Du | Alles Ist Hin(Song of the Mbuti Pygmies-German Folk Song) | Heimkehr

Live at The 'Loft', Köln, rec. 30.4.& 7.5.1994

Lüdemann,Hans (p-solo)

JHM 0076 CD | CD | Goldfischgesänge

Sieverts-Mahall-Elgart

Solo Dancing | Hören Sie Nicht? | Swing Low | Most Wanted | Cafe Subway Blues | Goldfischgesänge(IV) | A.B. | New Delhi, New Delhi | Goldfischgesänge(II) | Almost Fast | Goldfischgesänge(III) | Im Wald | But It's O.K.

Nürnberg, rec. 5.10.1994

Sieverts,Henning (cello,b) | Mahall,Rudi (cl,b-cl,turntable) | Elgart,Billy (dr,perc)

Dschungelschweiß | Zweifünfeins

Berlin, rec. 18./19.9.1994

Sieverts,Henning (cello,b) | Mahall,Rudi (cl,b-cl,turntable) | Elgart,Billy (dr,perc)

JHM 0077 CD | CD | Post Art Core

Wollie Kaiser Timeghost

Idole | 'Scuse Me | Worte | Time Is Now | Gnocci In Germania | Six Is Nine | MTV-Revolution Handmade Version | Hackenzack | Imaginationen | The Spirit Of Life | Midlife

Köln, rec. July-September 1995

Kaiser,Wollie (b-cl,ss,ts,el-b-cl,el-ss,el-ts,voc) | Lottermann,Stefan (tb,el-tb) | Oster,Ulla (b,voc) | Kobialka,Reinhard (dr)

A Melody

Kaiser,Wollie (b-cl,ss,ts,el-b-cl,el-ss,el-ts,voc) | Lottermann,Stefan (tb,el-tb) | Oster,Ulla (b,voc) | Kobialka,Reinhard (dr) | Harris,Paul (voc)

MTV-Revolution Nomal Version

Kaiser,Wollie (b-cl,ss,ts,el-b-cl,el-ss,el-ts,voc) | Lottermann,Stefan (tb,el-tb) | Oster,Ulla (b,voc) | Kobialka,Reinhard (dr) | Franck,Hinrich (computer-programming)

JHM 0078 CD | CD | Bonehenge Suite

Jan Von Klewitz Quintet

Bonehenge Suite: | Part 1:Dünung | Part 2:Treppenhaus | Part 3:Wahnfried | Interlude | Part 4:Tirolerhut | Intro | Bogenlampe | Novo Skopje | Sehnsucht Der Heringe | Tango | Epilog

Stadtgarten,Köln, rec. 5./6.7.1995

Von Kleewitz,Jan (sax) | Lottermann,Stefan (tb) | Hausmann,Iven (tb) | Berns,Pepe (b) | Schröder,John (dr)

JHM 0079 CD | CD | Evocation

Peter Bolte Quartet

Miss J. | Prof. Genessier | B.B. | Flora | Quint | Eighteen | Couples

Sandhausen, rec. 10/11.7.1994

Bolte,Peter (as) | Kaufmann,Achim (p) | Imm,Paul (b) | Jones,Alan (dr)

JHM 0081 CD | CD | Circe

Hayden Chisholm

Dance | Web | Didg. | Dance(2) | Beast | Dance(3) | Molly | Dance(4) | Wing | Dance(5) | Enchantress | Dance(6) | Feast | Dance(7) | Didg.(2) | O Circe,Guide Me

Karthäuser Church,Köln, rec. March 1996

Chisholm,Hayden (ss,didgeridoo)

JHM 0082 CD | CD | Place For Lovers

Kölner Saxophon Mafia

A Deserting Love Affair | The Love That Walked By | Seitensprung(amerikanisch) | Honeymoon For Two Elephants | Lovemachine | Seitensprung(karibisch) | The Lovesick Bassplayer's Bassplaying | Lover's X-Dream | Seitensprung(indisch) | Inner Vibes Of Love | Loverwoman | Seitensprung(brasilianisch) | M&F PNZ(Männer & Frauen passen nicht zusammen)

Köln, rec. Summer 1996

Kölner Saxophon Mafia | Hanschel,Roger (alto-fl,as,f-mezzo-sax,sopranino) | Kaiser,Wollie (b-cl,ss,ts,bass-sax) | Ullrich,Joachim (cl,ss,ts) | Schorn,Steffen (fl,alto-fl,b-cl,contra-b-cl,bs,bass-sax,piccolo) | Veeck,Gerhard (alto-cl,as)

JHM 0083 CD | CD | Gestalten

Frank Gratkowski Trio

Gesti | Blazing | Gloaming | Con Affetto | Dancing Derwish | Stag Rustler | Ernestine | Duck Hunt | Movements

Loft,Köln, rec. 22./23.9.1995

Gratkowski,Frank (b-cl,as) | Manderscheid,Dieter (b) | Hemingway,Gerry (dr,perc)

JHM 0084 CD | CD | She Could Do Nothing By Halves

Tome XX

She Could Do Tothing By Halves

Köln, rec. details unknown

Tome XX | details not on the cover

JHM 0085 CD | CD | Tango & Company

Henning Berg & John Taylor With 'Tango'

Landmark | Earspace | Duo Derdoo | Confluence | Lineage | The Heart Of The Matter | Inside Out | Garden | Solosol | Hey Presto!

Köln, rec. 2.-4.1.1996

Berg,Henning (tb) | Taylor,John (p) | Tango[Interactive Computer Program] (keyboard,sampling)

JHM 0086 CD | CD | Norbert Scholly Quartet

Norbert Scholly Quartet

Loopline | Holidays In Skopje | Personal Exstenz(for Ornette) | Ballad | Doors(Very Short Tales) | Nice! | King Kong- | Falling In Love- | Tribute To E.W. | Farmer's Dance

Monster,NL, rec. December 1996

Scholly,Norbert (g) | Von Kleewitz,Jan (sax) | Fuhr,Dietmar (b) | Rückert,Jochen (dr)

JHM 0087 CD | CD | Planet Blow Chill

Hanschel-Hübsch-Schipper

NGC 4755 | Al Kaphra | NGC 7541 | Mist | Days Of The Fifth Period | Reprise 4755 | Flow | NGC 221 | Reprise D.o.t.F.P. | Burst | Love Machine | Chill | Jandor

'Scheune',Treis, rec. June 1977

Hanschel,Roger (as) | Hübsch,Carl Ludwig 'Lu' (tuba) | Schipper,Jörn (dr)

JHM 0088 CD | CD | We Can Do It On Stage Any Time!

Ulla Oster-Wollie Kaiser

I Wanna Have Fun | X-Dream | Manic Musical Depression | Tapetenwechsel | Never Will I Marry | Super Sex | Isn't It Romantic | Mr.Unison | Sosolo | To Live & Let Die | Tex Mex Teevee | UB 40 | Südsee

Stadtgarten,Köln, rec. Summer 1997

Oster,Ulla (b,sampler,voc) | Kaiser,Wollie (b-cl,ss,ts,el-ss,el-ts,sampler,voc)

JHM 0089 CD | CD | Diary Of A Working Band

Blue Collar

Found Footage | Psalm | Dröttbom Hus | Morgenlied | Construct ß 32

Hannover, rec. 9.4.1997

Blue Collar | Willers,Andreas (g,el-g,bj,el-sitar) | Nonnenmacher,Horst (b) | Griener,Michael (dr,perc)

Sort Of A Tap Dance- | Arm In Arm- | Days Like Open Wounds | Ready-made:Torrid Zone | October 21th | Troubled Skies | Second-line Beckmann

Live at 'Schmuckkästchen',Köln, rec. 20./21.10.1997

Blue Collar | Willers,Andreas (g,el-g,bj,el-sitar) | Nonnenmacher,Horst (b) | Griener,Michael (dr,perc)

Liquid Stone | Mythos Berlin

Blue Collar | Willers,Andreas (g,el-g,bj,el-sitar) | Nonnenmacher,Horst (b) | Griener,Michael (dr,perc) | Puntin,Claudio (cl,b-cl)

A Blue Collection: | I Repeat Myself II- | Perking Lot Blues-

Blue Collar | Willers,Andreas (g,el-g,bj,el-sitar) | Nonnenmacher,Horst (b) | Griener,Michael (dr,perc) | Sudmann,Rolf (theremin)

JHM 0090 CD | CD | Garagenjazz

Dirk Berger Quartet

Garagenjazz | Der Buschmeister | I.G. | Blues Für Hendricks Mama | Time- | Life- | Dick | Intro To Song For... | Zugabe | Little Marie And The Wolf

Wuppertal, rec. 23.9.1997

Berger,Dirk (g) | Franck,Hinrich (keyboards) | Nendza,André (b) | Rückert,Jochen (dr)

JHM 0091 CD | CD | Auf Und Davon

Klaus Müller-Ekkehard Rössle

Blue Bossa

details unknown, rec. November 1995

Rössle,Ekkehard (ss,ts) | Müller,Klaus (p,el-p)

Blaues Wunder | Mind Reader | Leben Und Schlafen | Walking

Live at 'Treffpunkt Rotebühlplatz',Stuttgart, rec. 8.8.1997

Rössle,Ekkehard (ss,ts) | Müller,Klaus (p,el-p)

R&B | Sweet Rain

Ludwigsburg, rec. 11.8.1997

Rössle,Ekkehard (ss,ts) | Müller,Klaus (p,el-p)

In Einem Fernen Land(dedicated to Gary McFarland)

Rössle,Ekkehard (ss,ts) | Müller,Klaus (p,el-p) | Student,Mariola (v)

JHM 0092/93 CD | 2 CD | FutuRISM

Hans Lüdemann Rism 7

Futurism 1 | Futurism 2(Mysterious Call) | Futurism 6(Schöne Neue Welt) | Futurism 3(The Mism Rism) | Futurism 4(No Hau) | Futurism 5(Das Wahre Clavier) | Futurism 7(Wilde Augen) | Futurism 10(Malawi)

Köln, rec. 14./15.3.1997

Lüdemann,Hans (p,org,synth,clavichord,prepared-p) | Winterschladen,Reiner (tp) | Chisholm,Hayden (ss,as,bs,voice) | Ducret,Marc (g,el-g) | Feldman,Mark (v) | Kracht,Hartmut (b) | Pallemaerts,Dré (dr,perc)

JHM 0094 CD | CD | Fine Music With New Instruments

Stephan Froleyks

Sine Nomine | Hout(1) | Fünfzig Messer | Hout(2) | Aus | Hout(3) | Two Men,Two Boats | Hout(4) | Nirgendwohin,Hartnäckig

Deutschland Radio/Loft,Köln, rec. details unknown

Froleyks,Stephan (bambusstäbe,fötenmaschine,geschweifte-tuba,messertisch,saitenwanne)

JHM 0095 CD | CD | Trio

Peter Bolte Trio

O Willow Waly | Karin | My Old Man | Game | All I Want | O Willow Waly(2)

Hannover, rec. May 1998

Bolte,Peter (as) | Kaufmann,Achim (p) | Heller,Ingmar (b)

Peter Bolte-Imgmar Heller

Do I Love You

Hannover, rec. July 1998

Bolte,Peter (as) | Heller,Ingmar (b)

Peter Bolte

Eleanor Vance | Maria Cardona | Family Values

Sandhausen, rec. July 1998

Bolte,Peter (fl,cl,ss,as,p,el-p,dr,perc,as-b,el-b,sopranino) | street-noise

JHM 0096 CD | CD | KontraSax Plays Getrude Stein

KontaSax

Rose(1) | Sayo | Keine-Keiner | Lzw(1) | Rosenholz | Milk | Specht(1) | Rose(3) | Rose Arco | Sehr Reizend | Schlamm | Kanon Á Deux | Etwas | Specht(2) | Lzw(2) | Still A Rose

Loft,Köln, rec. June 1998

Fuchs,Christina (b-cl,ss,as,ts) | Herzberg,Romy (b) | Fuhrmann,Renate (rezitation) | Hahne,Dorothee (electronic-voice,samples)

Glasrosen

details unknown, rec. 2.7.1998

Fuchs,Christina (b-cl,ss,as,ts) | Herzberg,Romy (b) | Fuhrmann,Renate (rezitation)

JHM 0097 CD | CD | Plüschtier

Franz Bauer Quintet

Stolpern | Das Schweigen Des R. | East Seventh | Plüschtier | Neothis And Neothat | Good News | Breakfast With A. | Zoo 23:28 | Must I,Miss Sophie?

Monster,NL, rec. 1999

Bauer,Franz (vib,marimba) | Anderson,Michael (tp) | Thieke,Michael (cl,alto-cl,as) | Gunkel,Johannes (b) | Black,Jim (dr)

JHM 0099 CD | CD | The Blue One

The United Women's Orchestra

Lydisch Blau | Torch Song | Serenade For Leonie | Self Portrait | Netsuke | Siringo Road | Tiebreak

Köln, rec. November 1998

United Women's Orchestra,The | Riemer,Susanne (tp) | Horn,Sandra (tp) | Meßollen,Gisela (tp) | Ercklentz,Sabine (tp) | Barsby,Helen (tp) | Engelbrecht,Viola (tb) | Von Lenthe,Henriette (tb) | Roelofs,Annemarie (tb) | Struzyk,Janni (tuba) | Eberhard,Silke (as) | Goosmann,Meike (reeds) | Danzer,Corinna (reeds) | Schröck,Marie-Christine (reeds) | Leach,Hazel (reeds,ld) | Fuchs,Christina (reeds,ld) | Hörmann,Christine (reeds) | Pastuszyk,Regina (reeds) | Ilgner,Caroline (p) | Bosch,Ilse (b) | Kayser,Annette (dr) | Bigge,Carolina (dr) | Leigh-Brown,Sam (voc) | Duncan,Christine (voc)

JHM 0100 CD | CD | Licence To Thrill

Kölner Saxophon Mafia

Maigret's Letzter Fall | Ode An Erik | Für Immer Steif(1) | Possibly A Mission Impossible | Für Immer Steif(2) | The Snooper | The Fricticious Motive Of An Imaginary Murder | Für Immer Steif(3) | Racing Max | Jailbreaker's Nightmare | Für Immer Steif(4) | Creeps,Bloodhounds And Badies | The Trap | Für Immer Steif(5) | Derrick's Delight | Für Immer Steif(6)

different Places, rec. details unknown

Kölner Saxophon Mafia | Hanschel,Roger (fl,as,f-mezzo-sax,sopranino) |

Kaiser,Wollie (alto-fl,b-cl,ss,ts) | Schorn,Steffen (alto-fl,cl,b-cl,contra-b-cl,bs,bass-sax,bass-fl,contra-alt-cl) | Ullrich,Joachim (cl,ts) | Veeck,Gerhard (alto-cl,as)

JHM 0101 CD | CD | Haupstrom
Tomatic 7
Summertime | Birthday With Oliver | Naima | Ob Ich Spartacus Kenne? | König Der Gemeinheiten | Dwell On
Köln, rec. May 1998
Thomé,Christian (dr) | Meinberg,Stephan (tp,fl-h) | Pérez,Gabriel (cl,sax) | Portugall,Manfred (el-g) | Friedrich,Jürgen (p) | Räther,Sebastian (b) | Brown,Sam Leigh (voc)

JHM 0102 CD | CD | New Traces For Old Aces
Wollie Kaiser Timeghost
Talk To You | After Glow | Runnin' Wild | Feeling Lonely | I Can't Dance With You | Tin Soldier | Just Passing | My Mind's Eye | Itchycoo Park | Lazy Sunday Afternoon
Köln, rec. Summer 1999
Kaiser,Wollie (reeds,el-reeds,voc) | Nies,Joker (electronics) | Oster,Ulla (b,voc) | Beigang,Klaus Martell (dr,voc) | Lorenz,Irene (voc)

JHM 0103 CD | CD | Kontrabass Pur
Hartmut Kracht
Les Feuilles Mortes | Arco | E | I Mean You | Rubato | Sonanzen | Okonkolé Y Trompa | Köln Blues | Budapest | Donner-Träume | Ich Bin Von Kopf Bis Fuß Auf Liebe Eingestellt | Arco(reprise)
Köln, rec. 11./12.8.1999
Kracht,Hartmut (b-solo)

JHM 0104 CD | CD | State Of Things
Jürgen Knieper Quintet
Goon | Alleh Hopp! | State Of Things | Pentium | Hypopotamus | Limerick | Bread And Tears | Bird Feathers
Knieper,Jürgen (p,arr) | Harich,Matthias (tp,fl-h) | Engelhardt,Dirk (ss,ts) | Bahner,Michael (b) | Timm,Stefan (dr)

JHM 0105 CD | CD | Die Hintere Vase
Nickendes Perlgras
Wiener Dog-| Milz | Dante Extra Vergine | Glänzender Lügner | Lingus | Stroh-Alm | Fanfare | Flavoids | Stöckchen In Speiche | Und Plasikschweine | Ovulus | Wo Die Vasen Grasen
Nickendes Perlgras | Anderson,Michael (tp) | Thieke,Michael (cl,alto-cl,as) | Schäfer,Eric (dr)

JHM 0106 CD | CD | Horizontal
Stephan Meinberg VITAMINE
Keep Dein Heart Richtig | Freuden Der Verweigerung | In Weiter Entfernung | Bingolngo | Hard-Waich-Spyler
Vitamine | Meinberg,Stephan (tp,fl-h,toy-duck) | Niescier,Angelika (ss,as) | Kulenkampff,Heiko (p,accordeon) | Räther,Sebastian (b,el-b) | Thomé,Christian (dr,p.voc)

JHM 0107 CD | CD | knoM.T
Sebastian Gramss-Lömsch Lehmann
Hackensack | 52nd Street Theme | Consecutive Seconds | Japanese Folk Song | Little Rootie Tootie | Criss Cross- | Bye-Ya- | Epistrophy | Functional | Straight No Chaser(I)- | Well You Needn't- | Straight No Chaser(II)
Köln, rec. July 1999
Lehmann,Lömsch (reeds) | Gramss,Sebastian (b)

JHM 0108 CD | CD | Palindrome
Lars Duppler Quartet
And Now The Queer | Alone Again Suite | Global Player | The Beast Inside | May The Fourth Be With You | Palindrome | Lili Marlene | L'Ennui
Hannover, rec. 21./22.12.1999
Duppler,Lars (p) | Sackenheim,Frank (sax) | Speer,Daniel (b) | Glüsenkamp,Benno (dr)

JHM 0109 CD | CD | Kannenberg On Purpose
Ute Kannenberg Quartet
Intro | Some Cats Know | A Hard Day's Night | Angel Eyes(Intro)- | Angel Eyes | How Insensitive(Insensatez) | Let's Face The Music And Dance | Watch What Happens | Short Cut | The Good Life
Berlin, rec. 26.-29.10.1999
Kannenberg,Ute (voc) | Schmidt,Arthur (p,synth,CD-sounds) | Cordes,Daniel 'Danda' (b) | Wasdaris,Christian[Kristian] (dr,perc,wave-dr)
Ute Kannenberg Quartet With Guests
Hommage To Paul Bowles: | Lonesome Man | Caravan(Intro)- | Caravan-
Kannenberg,Ute (voc) | Schmidt,Arthur (p,synth,CD-sounds) | Cordes,Daniel 'Danda' (b) | Wasdaris,Christian[Kristian] (dr,perc,wave-dr) | Askari,Mohamed (nay) | Litty,Joachim (b-cl) | Al-Assi,Ali (oud) | Bowles,Paul (narration)

JHM 0110 CD | CD | Low And Behold
European Tuba Quartet
Bird | Desert Song | 'Round The Block | Duett Duell | Red Thread | Angels | Four Miniatures | Reed Hornets | Material Girls | Trash Dance | Moonlight Elephants | Moving Clusters
Schloß Ostrau, rec. 16.-18.4.1999
European Tuba Quartet | Moschner,Pinguin (F-tuba) | Hübsch,Carl Ludwig 'Lu' (Eb-tuba) | Wauschke,Bettina (C-tuba) | Fishkind,Larry (C-tuba)

JHM 0111 CD | CD | Lühning
Inga Lühning With Trio
Aquarius | Sunmaker | Black Crow | Candelight | Hyperballad | Wingman | Naima | Libertango | Cream
Köln, rec. 29.-31.8.2000
Lühning,Inga (voc) | Mammone,Mario (g) | Fass,Helmut (b) | Thomé,Christian (dr)

JHM 0112 CD | CD | Carl Ludwig Hübsch's Longrun Development Of The Universe
Carl Ludwig Hübsch Trio
Epizykel(part 1-4) | Tenuto | NGC 7541
Heidelberg, rec. October 1999
Hübsch,Carl Ludwig 'Lu' (tuba) | Schubert,Matthias (ts) | Wierbos,Wolter (tb)

JHM 0113 CD | CD | Zeitraum
Peter Bolte-Marcio Doctor
Stima | Doppelbelastung | Dienstag | Once | Sommerrest | Espai | Dark Matter | Contenance | Chain Reaction | Slick Willie | Die Unzertrennlichen | Strata | The Lombardo Method | When I Fall In Love
Mehmed Ergin Studios,?, rec. 2000
Bolte,Peter (as,woodwinds) | Doctor,Marcio (perc,hand-dr)
Autumn Into Fall | Hotel Strandlust | Over Silence And Secrecy
Bolte,Peter (as,woodwinds) | Doctor,Marcio (perc,hand-dr) | Heller,Ingmar (b)

JHM 0114 CD | CD | Der Verkauf Geht Weiter
Frank Paul Schubert Quartet
Dishes | Zappenduster | Der Verkauf Geht Weiter | Thamar | Betrum Narfoli | Umbrella Bob | Right Shoes | Love Choir | Bouché | Brückenpfeiler
Hannover, rec. 26./27.3.2001
Schubert,Frank Paul (ss,as) | Bauer,Franz (vib) | Gunkel,Johannes (b) | Merk,Sebastian (dr)

JHM 0115 CD | CD | Kölner Saxophon Mafia: 20 Jahre Saxuelle Befreiung
Kölner Saxophon Mafia With Guests
Hefegründe | Burnleigh | Under My Thumb | Downtown Waltz | Double Weasel | Prelude And Scurrying | Fitting | Walk | Die Matriarchin | Die Aura Des Wahns | Der Alb | Seven Wojos | In The Speed Mode | Anywhere I Lay My Head
different Places, rec. details unknown
Kölner Saxophon Mafia | Hanschel,Roger (fl,reeds) | Kaiser,Wollie (fl,reeds) | Schorn,Steffen (fl,reeds) | Ullrich,Joachim (fl,reeds) | Veeck,Gerhard (fl,reeds) | Tremontana,Sebi (tb) | Landgren,Nils (tb) | Kennel,Hans (alphorn) | Massot,Michel (tuba) | Seattle,Matt (bagpipe) | Mistry,Jagdish (v) | Bica,Carlos (b) | Kavina,Lydia (theremin) | France,Martin (dr) | Nies,Joker (electronics) | Becker,Meret (voc) | Blonk,Jaap (voice) | Ars Vitale (band) | Kroyt (band)

JHM 0116 CD | CD | Lingo
Stefan Bauer-Claudio Puntin-Marcio Doctor
N'diaye | Lights,Receding | Überall Und Nirgands | Istics | Slope Stomp | Mutation | Bizarre | Seduction | En Passant
Köln, rec. details unknown
Puntin,Claudio (cl,b-cl) | Bauer,Stefan (vib,marimba) | Doctor,Marcio (perc,hand-dr)

JHM 0117 CD | CD | Eric Schaefer & Demontage | EAN 4013205011708
Eric Schaefer & Demontage
DinA3 | Pose Nude | Jerry | Le Binz | Groschenotto | Flyjam | Kammerflirren | Könn't Ich Sie Trinken,Ich Wollt' An Ihr Ersticken | Ladenball
details unknown, rec. 15.6.2001
Schäfer,Eric (dr) | Anderson,Michael (tp) | Thieke,Michael (cl,alto-cl,as) | Erdmann,Daniel (ts,bs) | Fink,Johannes (b)

JHM 0118 CD | CD | What A Wonderful World | EAN 4013205011807
Thomas Heberer-Dieter Manderscheid
I'm Not Rough | Have The Stones Been Here? | It's Always Some Kind Of A Freak | Gully Low Blues- | West End Blues- | From Dipper To Satchmo | Comet Chop Suey | Okuka Lokole | Daddy Dig | Struttin' With Some Barbecue | Educating People- | Blueberry Hill | Hello Dolly | New Orleans Function- | When The Saints Go Marching In- | The Boon Companions | Kazue | Mack The Knife(Moritat)
Köln, rec. 2001
Heberer,Thomas (tp) | Manderscheid,Dieter (b)

JHM 0119 CD | CD | Movietalks | EAN 4013205011906
Albrecht Maurer Trio Works
Jour De Fete-Avant | Cyberola | Lola Rennt...Nicht Immer | A Mandala To Liberation | Horizontal Shower | Delicatessen | The Unbearable Lightness Of Beeing | To Unknown Movies | Jour De Fete-Passe
Erholungsheim der Bayer AG, rec. 9.11.1999
Maurer,Albrecht (v,prepared-v) | Wierbos,Wolter (tb) | Delbecq,Benoit (p,prepared-p)

JHM 0120 CD | CD | Pigeon | EAN 4013205012002
Gabriele Hasler-Roger Hanschel Duo
Paperballs | A Red Hat | Bit Of Blue | Air | Wood | Sea | By The Time | How Can I Thank You | Pigeon
Biosphere Studio,?, rec. June 2002
Hasler,Gabriele (voice) | Hanschel,Roger (as)

JHM 0121 CD | CD | Mackeben Revisited:The Ufa Years | EAN 4013205012101
Georg Ruby Village Zone
Frauen Sind Keine Engel | Wenn Ich Mir Was Wünschen Dürfte | Zwei In Einer Großen Stadt | Und Über Uns Der Himmel
Saarbrücken, rec. 18./19.2.2002
Ruby,Georg (p) | Manderscheid,Dieter (b) | Thomé,Christian (dr,perc,glockenspiel,electronics)
Bei Dir War Es Immer So Schön | Akkaya | Für Eine Nacht Voller Seligkeit | Wenn Verliebte Bummeln Gehen
Köln, rec. 6./7.4.2002
Ruby,Georg (p) | Manderscheid,Dieter (b) | Thomé,Christian (dr,perc,glockenspiel,electronics)

JHM 0122 CD | CD | Quartetto Pazzo | EAN 4013205012200
Christof Thewes-Rudi Mahall Duo
'Ne Handvoll Duos: | No.17 | No.2 | No.16753 | No.0 | No.11
Live at Stadtgarten,Köln, rec. 27.4.2002
Thewes,Christoph (tb) | Mahall,Rudi (b-cl)
Christoph Thewes-Rudi Mahall Quartet
Ging Ganz | Tiefseejahrmarkt | A Hard Night's Day | Postamt | Fast Desaster | Silence | Squak | Wie Man's Macht,Man Macht's Verkehrt
Thewes,Christoph (tb) | Mahall,Rudi (b-cl) | Scheib,Stefan (b) | Fischer,Jörg (dr)

JHM 0123 CD | CD | Virgo Supercluster | EAN 4013205012309
United Women's Orchestra
Shadow & Light | Sweet For Evie | Cerasarda | The Virgo Supercluster Suite: | Big Bang- | The First Glimmer Of Dawn- | Crescent Moon- | Orion Nebula- | Silent Room- | Man On Mars- | Lost One | Double Trouble: | Hubble Bubble- | Toil And Truble- | Hurly Burly- | A La Mode
Köln, rec. 1.-3.3.2002
United Women's Orchestra,The | Jensen,Ingrid (tp) | Horn,Sandra (tp) | Schneider,Hermine (tp) | Gildner,Nancy (tp) | Barsby,Helen (tp) | Roelofs,Annemarie (tb) | Engelbrecht,Viola (tb) | Steen,Teddy (tb) | Struzyk,Janni (tuba) | Danzer,Corinna (fl,as) | Goosmann,Meike (cl,ss,as) | Schröck,Marie-Christine (cl,ts) | Fuchs,Christina (fl,b-cl,ts,comp,ld) | Leach,Hazel (fl,b-cl,ts,comp,ld) | Hörmann,Christine (fl,bs) | Eberhard,Silke (cl,b-cl) | Hülsmann,Julia (p) | Oster,Ulla (b) | Bigge,Carolina (dr) | Rudolph,Céline (voc)
-> Note: Intro & Swing '42 plus extras only on DVD

JHM 0125 CD | CD | September | EAN 4013205012507
Matzeit-Daerr
September | Manchmal, Manchmal Lieber Nicht | Tight-Rope-Walker | Thinx | For Kenny Kirkland | Baskenmütze | Dümpeln | Intro | Der Regenmann | Bilbao | Der Indianer
Berlin, rec. March 2003
Matzeit,Friedemann (b-cl,ss,ts) | Daerr,Carsten (p)

JHM 0126 CD | CD | Bhavam | EAN 4013205012606
Matthias Müller Quartet
Prologue | Cella/No Quiere Postre) | Dialogue | Bhavan Rock | CFK | Bhavan Ballade | One Small Day | Catalogue | Palm | Untitled-Undefined | Epilogue
Perspektive Medienproduktion,?, rec. December 2002
Müller,Matthias (tb,electronics) | Klare,Jan (cl,as,electronics) | Wahl,Andreas (g,el-g,frettless-g) | Eisold,Peter (dr,perc)

JHM 0127 CD | CD | Minnola | EAN 4013205012705
Henning Berg Quartet
Ich Seh' Die Welt So Gern Durch Meine Sonnenbrille | Minnola | Chaconne | It's You Or No One | Links Und Rechts Vom Bahnhof | Reasons To Play | Summer Samba Für Die Dunklen Herrn | Bilder Einer Umstellung | Stablemates
Bonn, rec. 2./3.3.2003
Berg,Henning (tb) | Soll,Hendrik (p) | Ramond,Christian (b) | Schröteler,Daniel 'Danny' (dr)

JHM 0128 CD | CD | Away With Words:The Music Of John Scofield | EAN 4013205012804
Peter Ehwald Trio
I'll Catch You | But For Love | Hold That Thought | After The Fact | Bedside Manner | Rolf And The Gang | Let's Say We Did
Köln, rec. 12.3.2003
Ehwald,Peter (reeds) | Störmer,Friedrich (b) | Höhn,Wolfgang (dr)

JHM 0129 CD | CD | Sussurro | EAN 4013205012903
Lirico
Sussurro(1) | Tarantella(3) | Sittin' On The Dock Of The Bay - (Sittin' On) The Dock Of The Bay | Miniatura(6) | Si Se Calla El Cantor | A New Spirit(für Michael)
Bonn, rec. July 2003
Lirico | Lemke,Johannes (cl,ss,as) | Mammone,Mario (g,el-g) | Flubacher,Jan (b)
Ventidue
Lirico | Lemke,Johannes (cl,ss,as) | Mammone,Mario (g,el-g) | Flubacher,Jan (b) | Nendza,André (b)
Sussurro(2) | Go Down Moses | The Times They Are A-Changin'
Lirico | Lemke,Johannes (cl,ss,as) | Mammone,Mario (g,el-g) | Flubacher,Jan (b) | Nendza,André (b) | Lühning,Inga (voc)

JHM 0130 CD | CD | Zanshin/Kontrasax | EAN 4013205013009
Kontrasax
Bleu Et Blue | Yin | Zanshin | Africa | Blue And Orange | Yang | Sommerballade
Köln, rec. September 2003
Kontrasax | Fuchs,Christina (b-cl,ss) | Herzberg,Romy (b)
Elfzehn | Raga
Kontrasax | Fuchs,Christina (b-cl,ss) | Herzberg,Romy (b) | Gupta,Arup Sen (tablas)

JHM 0131 CD | CD | Palindrome 6tet
Lars Duppler Sextet
Booker | Squares | Douglas 64(part 1-3) | Forfait | The Sinner | Prelude
details unknown, rec. 2003
Duppler,Lars (p) | Meinberg,Stephan (tp,fl-h) | Klein,Niels (cl,ts) | Sackenheim,Frank (ts) | Fuhr,Dietmar (b) | Rieck,Marcus (dr)

JHM 0132 CD | CD | Space Player
Kölner Saxophon Mafia
The Loss Of The Human Soul | Schwein Im Weltall | Klingonenträume | The Disappearance Of Space And Time | The Unwelcome Morbidy Of Replicant Pris | Alles Roger,Buck? | Evas Pflug | The Adventures Of Hasso Sigbjörnsen | Last Picture Of Solaris
details unknown, rec. 2004
Kölner Saxophon Mafia | Kaiser,Wollie (reeds) | Hanschel,Roger (reeds) | Ullrich,Joachim (reeds) | Schorn,Steffen (reeds)

JHM 0133 CD | CD | Greyhound
Christof Thewes Little Big Band
Gegen K. | It Was You | Too Much At Once | I Got To Know | How You Held It | Too Soon-Exit
details unknown, rec. 2002
Thewes,Christoph (tb,cond,comp) | Gulden,Alfred (voc)

JHM 0134 CD | CD | Mondo
Claudio Puntin Quartet
Nouveau Odeur | Der Glöckner | Opera Meditativa | Cavallette | Lotus | Encore | Remember Radio Hanoi | Between Two Islands | Insects | Another Language | Encore
details unknown, rec. 2000
Puntin,Claudio (cl) | Gunnarsdóttir,Gerdur (v) | Yong-Gu Zheng,Wang (chin-zither) | Doctor,Marcio (perc)

LJBB 9104 | CD | Kazzou
Jazz Orchester Rheinland-Pfalz
Opening
Köln, rec. 31.7.-3.8.1991
Jazz Orchester Rheinland-Pfalz | Ruby,Georg (ld) | Himmler,Ralf (tp,fl-h) | Grimminger,Andreas (tp,fl-h) | Schünemann,Uli (tp,fl-h) | Bechtel,Dirk (tp,fl-h) | Schuh,Michael (tp,fl-h) | Becker,Adi (tb) | Casper,Peter (tb) | Sassenroth,Thomas (tb) | Busch,Thomas (b-tb) | Sonnenschein,Simone (fl,ss,as) | Steffen,Andreas (fl,ss,as) | Jakoby,Frank (fl,ss,ts) | Lehmann,Bernd (cl,ts) | Busch,Oliver (fl,b-cl,bs,piccolo) | Lindroth,Frank (g) | Burger,Markus (p,keyboards) | Gramss,Sebastian (b,el-b) | Busch,Heiko (dr)
Big Foot
Jazz Orchester Rheinland-Pfalz | Ruby,Georg (ld) | Himmler,Ralf (tp,fl-h) | Grimminger,Andreas (tp,fl-h) | Schünemann,Uli (tp,fl-h) | Bechtel,Dirk (tp,fl-h) | Fink,Achim (tb) | Becker,Adi (tb) | Casper,Peter (tb) | Sassenroth,Thomas (tb) | Busch,Thomas (b-tb) | Sonnenschein,Simone (fl,ss,as) | Steffen,Andreas (fl,ss,as) | Jakoby,Frank (fl,ss,ts) | Lehmann,Bernd (cl,ts) | Lemmert,Simon (ts) | Busch,Oliver (fl,b-cl,bs,piccolo) | Lindroth,Frank (g) | Mohr,Maike (p) | Gramss,Sebastian (b,el-b) | Kölsch,Dirk Peter (dr)
Attention- | Spontaneous Energy-
Jazz Orchester Rheinland-Pfalz | Ruby,Georg (ld) | Himmler,Ralf (tp,fl-h) | Grimminger,Andreas (tp,fl-h) | Schünemann,Uli (tp,fl-h) | Bechtel,Dirk (tp,fl-h) | Becker,Adi (tb) | Casper,Peter (tb) | Sassenroth,Thomas (tb) | Busch,Thomas (b-tb) | Sonnenschein,Simone (fl,ss,as) | Steffen,Andreas (fl,ss,as) | Jakoby,Frank (fl,ss,ts) | Lehmann,Bernd (cl,ts) | Lemmert,Simon (ts) | Busch,Oliver (fl,b-cl,bs,piccolo) | Lindroth,Frank (g) | Mohr,Maike (p) | Gramss,Sebastian (b,el-b) | Kölsch,Dirk Peter (dr) | Schomisch,Markus (perc)
Discovering Metal
Jazz Orchester Rheinland-Pfalz | Ruby,Georg (ld) | Himmler,Ralf (tp,fl-h) | Grimminger,Andreas (tp,fl-h) | Schünemann,Uli (tp,fl-h) | Bechtel,Dirk (tp,fl-h) | Becker,Adi (tb) | Casper,Peter (tb) | Sassenroth,Thomas (tb) | Busch,Thomas (b-tb) | Sonnenschein,Simone (fl,ss,as) | Steffen,Andreas (fl,ss,as) | Jakoby,Frank (fl,ss,ts) | Lehmann,Bernd (cl,ts) | Lemmert,Simon (ts) | Busch,Oliver (fl,b-cl,bs,piccolo) | Lindroth,Frank (g) | Burger,Markus (p,keyboards) | Gramss,Sebastian (b,el-b) | Kölsch,Dirk Peter (dr) | Schomisch,Markus (perc)
Kazzou
Jazz Orchester Rheinland-Pfalz | Ruby,Georg (ld) | Himmler,Ralf (tp,fl-h) | Grimminger,Andreas (tp,fl-h) | Schünemann,Uli (tp,fl-h) | Bechtel,Dirk (tp,fl-h) | Becker,Adi (tb) | Casper,Peter (tb) | Sassenroth,Thomas (tb) | Busch,Thomas (b-tb) | Sonnenschein,Simone (fl,ss,as) | Steffen,Andreas (fl,ss,as) | Jakoby,Frank (fl,ss,ts) | Lehmann,Bernd (cl,ts) | Busch,Oliver (fl,b-cl,bs,piccolo) | Lindroth,Frank (g) | Mohr,Maike (p) | Gramss,Sebastian (b,el-b) | Kölsch,Dirk Peter (dr) | Schomisch,Markus (perc)
Hunzenbach
Jazz Orchester Rheinland-Pfalz | Ruby,Georg (ld) | Himmler,Ralf (tp,fl-h) | Grimminger,Andreas (tp,fl-h) | Schünemann,Uli (tp,fl-h) | Bechtel,Dirk (tp,fl-h) | Becker,Adi (tb) | Casper,Peter (tb) | Sassenroth,Thomas (tb) | Busch,Thomas (b-tb) | Sonnenschein,Simone (fl,ss,as) | Steffen,Andreas (fl,ss,as) | Jakoby,Frank (fl,ss,ts) | Lehmann,Bernd (cl,ts) | Busch,Oliver (fl,b-cl,bs,piccolo) | Lindroth,Frank (g) | Mohr,Maike (p) | Gramss,Sebastian (b,el-b) | Busch,Heiko (dr) | Schomisch,Markus (perc)
Brownie Meets Bee Tee
Jazz Orchester Rheinland-Pfalz | Ruby,Georg (ld) | Himmler,Ralf (tp,fl-h) | Grimminger,Andreas (tp,fl-h) | Schünemann,Uli (tp,fl-h) | Bechtel,Dirk (tp,fl-h) | Becker,Adi (tb) | Casper,Peter (tb) | Sassenroth,Thomas (tb) | Busch,Thomas (b-tb) | Sonnenschein,Simone (fl,ss,as) | Steffen,Andreas (fl,ss,as) | Jakoby,Frank (fl,ss,ts) | Lehmann,Bernd (cl,ts) | Busch,Oliver (fl,b-cl,bs,piccolo) | Lindroth,Frank (g) | Mohr,Maike (p) | Gramss,Sebastian (b,el-b) | Kölsch,Dirk Peter (dr)
Fluorescent Stones In The River
Jazz Orchester Rheinland-Pfalz | Ruby,Georg (ld) | Himmler,Ralf (tp,fl-h) | Grimminger,Andreas (tp,fl-h) | Schünemann,Uli (tp,fl-h) | Bechtel,Dirk (tp,fl-h) | Becker,Adi (tb) | Casper,Peter (tb) | Sassenroth,Thomas (tb) | Busch,Thomas (b-tb) | Sonnenschein,Simone (fl,ss,as) | Steffen,Andreas (fl,ss,as) | Jakoby,Frank (fl,ss,ts) | Lehmann,Bernd (cl,ts) | Busch,Oliver (fl,b-cl,bs,piccolo) | Lindroth,Frank (g) | Mohr,Maike (p) | Gramss,Sebastian (b,el-b) | Busch,Heiko (dr)
Blues Forever Variations
Jazz Orchester Rheinland-Pfalz | Ruby,Georg (ld) | Himmler,Ralf (tp,fl-h) | Grimminger,Andreas (tp,fl-h) | Schünemann,Uli (tp,fl-h) | Bechtel,Dirk (tp,fl-h) | Becker,Adi (tb) | Casper,Peter (tb) | Sassenroth,Thomas (tb) | Busch,Thomas (b-tb) | Sonnenschein,Simone (fl,ss,as) | Steffen,Andreas (fl,ss,as) | Jakoby,Frank (fl,ss,ts) | Lehmann,Bernd (cl,ts) | Busch,Oliver (fl,b-cl,bs,piccolo) | Lindroth,Frank (g) | Burger,Markus (p,keyboards) | Gramss,Sebastian (b,el-b) | Busch,Heiko (dr)
Alkuin
Jazz Orchester Rheinland-Pfalz | Ruby,Georg (ld) | Himmler,Ralf (tp,fl-h) | Grimminger,Andreas (tp,fl-h) | Schünemann,Uli (tp,fl-h) | Bechtel,Dirk (tp,fl-h) | Becker,Adi (tb) | Casper,Peter (tb) | Sassenroth,Thomas (tb) | Busch,Thomas (b-tb) | Sonnenschein,Simone (fl,ss,as) | Steffen,Andreas (fl,ss,as) | Jakoby,Frank (fl,ss,ts) | Lehmann,Bernd (cl,ts) | Busch,Oliver (fl,b-cl,bs,piccolo) | Lindroth,Frank (g) | Burger,Markus (p,keyboards) | Gramss,Sebastian (b,el-b) | Kölsch,Dirk Peter (dr)

LJBB 9405 | CD | Like Life
Night At The Circus | Lennie's Pennies | Naima
Stadtgarten,Köln, rec. July 1994
Jazz Orchester Rheinland-Pfalz | Ruby,Georg (ld) | Himmler,Ralf (tp,fl-h) | Kämmerling,Roland (tp,fl-h) | Schuh,Michael (tp,fl-h) | Ryschka,Jurij (tp,fl-h) | Kordel,Guido (tp,fl-h) | Becker,Adi (tb) | Sassenroth,Thomas (tb) | Lechtenfeld,Bernd (tb) | Martin,Frederic (b-tb) | Caspar,Peter (tuba) | Sonnenschein,Simone (fl,ss,as) | Steffens,Andreas (fl,ss,as) | Willach,Thilo (fl,cl,ts) | Thomas,Torten (fl,cl,ts) | Busch,Oliver

LABELVERZEICHNIS

(fl,b-cl,bs,piccolo) | Wingold,Frank (g) | Mohr,Maike (p,synth) | Bebelaar,Patrick (p,synth) | Schwab,Guido (b,el-b) | Kölsch,Dirk Peter (dr) | Schomisch,Markus (perc)

Like Life
Jazz Orchester Rheinland-Pfalz | Ruby,Georg (ld) | Himmler,Ralf (tp,fl-h) | Kämmerling,Roland (tp,fl-h) | Schuh,Michael (tp,fl-h) | Ryschka,Jurij (tp,fl-h) | Kordel,Guido (tp,fl-h) | Becker,Adi (tb) | Sassenroth,Thomas (tb) | Lechtenfeld,Bernd (tb) | Martin,Frederic (b-tb) | Caspar,Peter (tuba) | Sonnenschein,Simone (fl,ss,as) | Steffens,Andreas (fl,ss,as) | Willach,Thilo (fl,cl,ts) | Thomas,Torten (fl,cl,ts) | Busch,Oliver (fl,b-cl,bs,piccolo) | Wingold,Frank (g) | Mohr,Maike (p,synth) | Bebelaar,Patrick (p,synth) | Schwab,Guido (b,el-b) | Kölsch,Dirk Peter (dr) | Busch,Heiko (dr) | Schomisch,Markus (perc)

Wabun
Jazz Orchester Rheinland-Pfalz | Ruby,Georg (ld) | Himmler,Ralf (tp,fl-h) | Kämmerling,Roland (tp,fl-h) | Schuh,Michael (tp,fl-h) | Ryschka,Jurij (tp,fl-h) | Kordel,Guido (tp,fl-h) | Becker,Adi (tb) | Sassenroth,Thomas (tb) | Lechtenfeld,Bernd (tb) | Martin,Frederic (b-tb) | Caspar,Peter (tuba) | Sonnenschein,Simone (fl,ss,as) | Steffens,Andreas (fl,ss,as) | Willach,Thilo (fl,cl,ts) | Thomas,Torten (fl,cl,ts) | Busch,Oliver (fl,b-cl,bs,piccolo) | Wingold,Frank (g) | Mohr,Maike (p,synth) | Bebelaar,Patrick (p,synth) | Gramss,Sebastian (b) | Schwab,Guido (b,el-b) | Kölsch,Dirk Peter (dr) | Schomisch,Markus (perc)

Better Days Ahead
Jazz Orchester Rheinland-Pfalz | Ruby,Georg (ld) | Himmler,Ralf (tp,fl-h) | Kämmerling,Roland (tp,fl-h) | Schuh,Michael (tp,fl-h) | Ryschka,Jurij (tp,fl-h) | Kordel,Guido (tp,fl-h) | Becker,Adi (tb) | Sassenroth,Thomas (tb) | Lechtenfeld,Bernd (tb) | Martin,Frederic (b-tb) | Sonnenschein,Simone (fl,ss,as) | Steffens,Andreas (fl,ss,as) | Willach,Thilo (fl,cl,ts) | Thomas,Torten (fl,cl,ts) | Busch,Oliver (fl,b-cl,bs,piccolo) | Wingold,Frank (g) | Mohr,Maike (p,synth) | Bebelaar,Patrick (p,synth) | Schwab,Guido (b,el-b) | Kölsch,Dirk Peter (dr) | Busch,Heiko (dr) | Schomisch,Markus (perc)

Nefertiti | Gentle Piece | Aila | Chelsea Bridge
Jazz Orchester Rheinland-Pfalz | Ruby,Georg (ld) | Himmler,Ralf (tp,fl-h) | Kämmerling,Roland (tp,fl-h) | Schuh,Michael (tp,fl-h) | Ryschka,Jurij (tp,fl-h) | Kordel,Guido (tp,fl-h) | Becker,Adi (tb) | Sassenroth,Thomas (tb) | Lechtenfeld,Bernd (tb) | Martin,Frederic (b-tb) | Sonnenschein,Simone (fl,ss,as) | Steffens,Andreas (fl,ss,as) | Willach,Thilo (fl,cl,ts) | Thomas,Torten (fl,cl,ts) | Busch,Oliver (fl,b-cl,bs,piccolo) | Wingold,Frank (g) | Mohr,Maike (p,synth) | Bebelaar,Patrick (p,synth) | Gramss,Sebastian (cello,b) | Schwab,Guido (b,el-b) | Kölsch,Dirk Peter (dr) | Busch,Heiko (dr) | Schomisch,Markus (perc)

LJBB 9706 | CD | Last Season
Black Hills
Köln, rec. March 1997
Jazz Orchester Rheinland-Pfalz | Ruby,Georg (ld) | Himmler,Ralf (tp,fl-h) | Kämmerling,Roland (tp,fl-h) | Schuh,Michael (tp,fl-h) | Kordel,Guido (tp,fl-h) | Schmauch,Davis (tp,fl-h) | Sassenroth,Thomas (tb) | Muche,Matthias (tb) | Trottenberg,Florian (tb) | Martin,Frederic (b-tb) | Caspar,Peter (tuba) | Steffens,Andreas (fl,cl,ss,as) | Reffgen,Alexander (fl,cl,ss,as) | Thomas,Torten (fl,cl,ts) | Torkewitz,Chris (fl,ts) | Busch,Oliver (fl,cl,b-cl,bs,piccolo) | Mohr,Maike (p) | Rautenbach,Gernot (synth) | Wingold,Frank (g) | Imhorst,Nils (b,el-b) | Scherzer,Derek (dr)

Dance,You Monster,To My Soft Song!
Jazz Orchester Rheinland-Pfalz | Ruby,Georg (ld) | Himmler,Ralf (tp,fl-h) | Kämmerling,Roland (tp,fl-h) | Schuh,Michael (tp,fl-h) | Kordel,Guido (tp,fl-h) | Schmauch,Davis (tp,fl-h) | Sassenroth,Thomas (tb) | Muche,Matthias (tb) | Martin,Frederic (b-tb) | Caspar,Peter (tuba) | Steffens,Andreas (fl,cl,ss,as) | Reffgen,Alexander (fl,cl,ss,as) | Thomas,Torten (fl,cl,ts) | Torkewitz,Chris (fl,ts) | Busch,Oliver (fl,cl,b-cl,bs,piccolo) | Mohr,Maike (p) | Rautenbach,Gernot (synth) | Wingold,Frank (g) | Imhorst,Nils (b,el-b) | Busch,Heiko (dr)

Gush
Jazz Orchester Rheinland-Pfalz | Ruby,Georg (ld) | Himmler,Ralf (tp,fl-h) | Kämmerling,Roland (tp,fl-h) | Schuh,Michael (tp,fl-h) | Kordel,Guido (tp,fl-h) | Schmauch,Davis (tp,fl-h) | Sassenroth,Thomas (tb) | Muche,Matthias (tb) | Martin,Frederic (b-tb) | Caspar,Peter (tuba) | Steffens,Andreas (fl,cl,ss,as) | Reffgen,Alexander (fl,cl,ss,as) | Thomas,Torten (fl,cl,ts) | Torkewitz,Chris (fl,ts) | Busch,Oliver (fl,cl,b-cl,bs,piccolo) | Mohr,Maike (p) | Rautenbach,Gernot (synth) | Wingold,Frank (g) | Imhorst,Nils (b,el-b) | Wehr,Daniel (dr) | Langer,Ameli (voc)

Last Season
Jazz Orchester Rheinland-Pfalz | Ruby,Georg (ld) | Himmler,Ralf (tp,fl-h) | Kämmerling,Roland (tp,fl-h) | Schuh,Michael (tp,fl-h) | Kordel,Guido (tp,fl-h) | Schmauch,Davis (tp,fl-h) | Sassenroth,Thomas (tb) | Muche,Matthias (tb) | Martin,Frederic (b-tb) | Caspar,Peter (tuba) | Steffens,Andreas (fl,cl,ss,as) | Reffgen,Alexander (fl,cl,ss,as) | Thomas,Torten (fl,cl,ts) | Torkewitz,Chris (fl,ts) | Busch,Oliver (fl,cl,b-cl,bs,piccolo) | Mohr,Maike (p) | Rautenbach,Gernot (synth) | Wingold,Frank (g) | Schwab,Guido (b,el-b) | Busch,Heiko (dr)

St.Vitus Dance
Jazz Orchester Rheinland-Pfalz | Ruby,Georg (ld) | Himmler,Ralf (tp,fl-h) | Kämmerling,Roland (tp,fl-h) | Schuh,Michael (tp,fl-h) | Kordel,Guido (tp,fl-h) | Schmauch,Davis (tp,fl-h) | Sassenroth,Thomas (tb) | Muche,Matthias (tb) | Martin,Frederic (b-tb) | Caspar,Peter (tuba) | Steffens,Andreas (fl,cl,ss,as) | Schröter,Achim (as) | Thomas,Torten (fl,cl,ts) | Torkewitz,Chris (fl,ts) | Busch,Oliver (fl,cl,b-cl,bs,piccolo) | Mohr,Maike (p) | Rautenbach,Gernot (synth) | Wingold,Frank (g) | Schwab,Guido (b,el-b) | Scherzer,Derek (dr) | Langer,Ameli (voc)

Quetschuan
Jazz Orchester Rheinland-Pfalz | Ruby,Georg (ld) | Himmler,Ralf (tp,fl-h) | Kämmerling,Roland (tp,fl-h) | Schuh,Michael (tp,fl-h) | Kordel,Guido (tp,fl-h) | Schmauch,Davis (tp,fl-h) | Sassenroth,Thomas (tb) | Muche,Matthias (tb) | Martin,Frederic (b-tb) | Caspar,Peter (tuba) | Steffens,Andreas (fl,cl,ss,as) | Schröter,Achim (as) | Thomas,Torten (fl,cl,ts) | Torkewitz,Chris (fl,ts) | Busch,Oliver (fl,cl,b-cl,bs,piccolo) | Mohr,Maike (p) | Rautenbach,Gernot (synth) | Wingold,Frank (g) | Schwab,Guido (b,el-b) | Wehr,Daniel (dr)

Waltz
Jazz Orchester Rheinland-Pfalz | Ruby,Georg (ld) | Himmler,Ralf (tp,fl-h) | Kämmerling,Roland (tp,fl-h) | Schuh,Michael (tp,fl-h) | Kordel,Guido (tp,fl-h) | Schmauch,Davis (tp,fl-h) | Sassenroth,Thomas (tb) | Muche,Matthias (tb) | Trottenberg,Florian (tb) | Martin,Frederic (b-tb) | Caspar,Peter (tuba) | Steffens,Andreas (fl,cl,ss,as) | Schröter,Achim (as) | Thomas,Torten (fl,cl,ts) | Torkewitz,Chris (fl,ts) | Busch,Oliver (fl,cl,b-cl,bs,piccolo) | Mohr,Maike (p) | Rautenbach,Gernot (synth) | Wingold,Frank (g) | Imhorst,Nils (b,el-b) | Busch,Heiko (dr)

Metalog 5
Jazz Orchester Rheinland-Pfalz | Ruby,Georg (ld) | Himmler,Ralf (tp,fl-h) | Kämmerling,Roland (tp,fl-h) | Schuh,Michael (tp,fl-h) | Kordel,Guido (tp,fl-h) | Schmauch,Davis (tp,fl-h) | Sassenroth,Thomas (tb) | Trottenberg,Florian (tb) | Martin,Frederic (b-tb) | Caspar,Peter (tuba) | Steffens,Andreas (fl,cl,ss,as) | Reffgen,Alexander (fl,cl,ss,as) | Thomas,Torten (fl,cl,ts) | Torkewitz,Chris (fl,ts) | Busch,Oliver (fl,cl,b-cl,bs,piccolo) | Mohr,Maike (p) | Rautenbach,Gernot (synth) | Wingold,Frank (g) | Schwab,Guido (b,el-b) | Wehr,Daniel (dr) | Langer,Ameli (voc)

Priestess
Jazz Orchester Rheinland-Pfalz | Ruby,Georg (ld) | Himmler,Ralf (tp,fl-h) | Kämmerling,Roland (tp,fl-h) | Schuh,Michael (tp,fl-h) | Kordel,Guido (tp,fl-h) | Schmauch,Davis (tp,fl-h) | Sassenroth,Thomas (tb) | Muche,Matthias (tb) | Martin,Frederic (b-tb) | Caspar,Peter (tuba) | Steffens,Andreas (fl,cl,ss,as) | Reffgen,Alexander (fl,cl,ss,as) | Thomas,Torten (fl,cl,ts) | Torkewitz,Chris (fl,ts) | Busch,Oliver (fl,cl,b-cl,bs,piccolo) | Mohr,Maike (p) | Rautenbach,Gernot (synth) | Wingold,Frank (g) | Schwab,Guido (b,el-b) | Wehr,Daniel (dr)

Consolation | Yellow Hill
Jazz Orchester Rheinland-Pfalz | Ruby,Georg (ld) | Himmler,Ralf (tp,fl-h) | Kämmerling,Roland (tp,fl-h) | Schuh,Michael (tp,fl-h) | Kordel,Guido (tp,fl-h) | Schmauch,Davis (tp,fl-h) | Sassenroth,Thomas (tb) | Muche,Matthias (tb) | Martin,Frederic (b-tb) | Caspar,Peter (tuba) | Steffens,Andreas (fl,cl,ss,as) | Reffgen,Alexander (fl,cl,ss,as) | Thomas,Torten (fl,cl,ts) | Torkewitz,Chris (fl,ts) | Busch,Oliver (fl,cl,b-cl,bs,piccolo) | Mohr,Maike (p) | Rautenbach,Gernot (synth) | Wingold,Frank (g) | Imhorst,Nils (b,el-b) | Busch,Heiko (dr) | Langer,Ameli (voc)

ohne Nummer | CD | A Night In Tunisia Suite(7 Variationen über Dizzy Gillespie's 'A Night In Tunisia') | EAN 4013205000207
Marcus Sukiennik Big Band
A Night In Tunisia Suite: | Ausrichtung | Anlauf | Überleitung
Köln, rec. 1999
Sukiennik,Marcus (p,arr)

Variation 1:Verschleierung
Sukiennik,Marcus (p,arr) | Schuh,Michael (tp) | Schwanitz,Bernie (tp) | Kämmerling,Roland (tp) | Konietzny,Jürgen (tp) | Lechtenfeld,Bernd (tb) | Kruse,Dietmar (tb) | Becker,Rüdiger (tb) | Schollmeyer,Harald (tb) | Gebhard,Thomas (sax) | Freytag,Guntram (sax) | Tjong-Ayong,Georg (sax) | Jahner,Mathias (sax) | Hörmann,Christine (sax) | Nendza,André (b) | Classen,Martin (ld)

Variation 2:Erstarrung und Befreiung
Sukiennik,Marcus (p,arr) | Schuh,Michael (tp) | Schwanitz,Bernie (tp) | Kämmerling,Roland (tp) | Konietzny,Jürgen (tp) | Engel,Frank (tp) | Lechtenfeld,Bernd (tb) | Kruse,Dietmar (tb) | Becker,Rüdiger (tb) | Schollmeyer,Harald (tb) | Becker,Adi (tb) | Heidl,Peter (fl) | Gebhard,Thomas (sax) | Freytag,Guntram (sax) | Tjong-Ayong,Georg (sax) | Jahner,Mathias (sax) | Hörmann,Christine (sax) | Nendza,André (b) | Soll,Hendrik (dr) | Classen,Martin (ld) | Ruby,Georg (ld)

Variation 3:Atem
Sukiennik,Marcus (p,arr) | Schuh,Michael (tp) | Schwanitz,Bernie (tp) | Kämmerling,Roland (tp) | Konietzny,Jürgen (tp) | Lechtenfeld,Bernd (tb) | Kruse,Dietmar (tb) | Becker,Rüdiger (tb) | Schollmeyer,Harald (tb) | Gebhard,Thomas (sax) | Freytag,Guntram (sax) | Tjong-Ayong,Georg (sax) | Jahner,Mathias (sax) | Hörmann,Christine (sax) | Classen,Martin (ld)

Variation 4:Geselligkeit
Sukiennik,Marcus (p,arr) | Schuh,Michael (tp) | Schwanitz,Bernie (tp) | Kämmerling,Roland (tp) | Engel,Frank (tp) | Lechtenfeld,Bernd (tb) | Kruse,Dietmar (tb) | Schollmeyer,Harald (tb) | Becker,Adi (tb) | Gebhard,Thomas (sax) | Freytag,Guntram (sax) | Tjong-Ayong,Georg (sax) | Jahner,Mathias (sax) | Hörmann,Christine (sax) | Nendza,André (b) | Soll,Hendrik (dr) | Ruby,Georg (ld)

Variation 5:Der Kern
Sukiennik,Marcus (p,arr) | Schuh,Michael (tp) | Kämmerling,Roland (tp) | Winninghoff,Christian (tp) | Konietzny,Jürgen (tp) | Lechtenfeld,Bernd (tb) | Kruse,Dietmar (tb) | Muche,Matthias (tb) | Tull,Thomas (tb) | Heidl,Peter (fl) | Gebhard,Thomas (sax) | Fahlenbock,Thomas (sax) | Tjong-Ayong,Georg (sax) | Briegleb,Christian (sax) | Hörmann,Christine (sax) | Nendza,André (b) | Soll,Hendrik (dr) | Ruby,Georg (ld)

Variation 6:Das Fest
Sukiennik,Marcus (p,arr) | Schuh,Michael (tp) | Kämmerling,Roland (tp) | Winninghoff,Christian (tp) | Konietzny,Jürgen (tp) | Lechtenfeld,Bernd (tb) | Kruse,Dietmar (tb) | Muche,Matthias (tb) | Luis,Ingo (tb) | Gebhard,Thomas (sax) | Fahlenbock,Thomas (sax) | Tjong-Ayong,Georg (sax) | Briegleb,Christian (sax) | Hörmann,Christine (sax) | Nendza,André (b) | Soll,Hendrik (dr) | Ruby,Georg (ld)

Variation 7:Ausklang
Sukiennik,Marcus (p,arr) | Gebhard,Thomas (sax)

Jazz 'n' Arts Records | Jazz Network

0100 | CD | Jazz Changes?
Changes
Hands Off The Wheel | For Bobby | Kastanie | Changes | One Bird, One Stone | Ce Qu'elle Dit | Out In The Fields | Maulbeerbaumbeerblues | Michael's Blues | For You
details unknown, rec. 30.7.-1.8.2000
Changes | Schönborn,Olaf (as) | Nölle,Sebastian (g) | Böhm,Rainer (p) | Steudinger,Torsten (b) | Binder,Lars (dr)

0200 | CD | Blue Ideas
Fritz Münzer Tentet
Introduction No.1 | Take Off | A Lot Of Things | Ode To D | Blue Ideas | Daydreaming | Juicy Blues | Trane Up | Westwind | Kiki's Last Farewell | Heading Home
Monster,NL, rec. 9.10.2000
Münzer,Fritz (as,comp,ld) | Ehringer,Christian (tp,fl-h) | Sauter,Thomas (tb) | Schönborn,Olaf (as) | Bothner,Jürgen (ts) | Steiner,Michael (bs) | Eckert,Christian (g) | Böhm,Rainer (p) | Simon,Jan-Martin (b) | Binder,Lars (dr)

0300 | CD | Alarm
Polyphonix
Band Introductions | Alarm | Time And More | Beacon Park | Newark Experience | Restless | Speak Like A Child | Monster | The Vision
Hannover, rec. 28./29.2.2000
Polyphonix | Siffling,Thomas (tp,fl-h) | Spaniol,Frank (ts) | Bodenseh,Markus (b) | Merk,Sebastian (dr)

C 01 | CD | Jazz für junge Leute:Live im HR 1962 | EAN 4042064001698
V 01 | VHS | Jazz für junge Leute:Live im HR 1962
Fritz Münzer Quintet
Grasshopper | Interview I | Night At Ghandi's | Interview II | Blue Ideas | Interview III | Asthma | Interview IV | Amen | Interview V | For Minors Only
Live at Hessischer Rundfunk, rec. ?,1962(broadcast 20.3.1963)
Münzer,Fritz (as) | Schoof,Manfred (tp) | Haider,Joe (p) | Peter,Eric (b) | Bartz,Hartwig (dr) | Hudtwalcker,Olaf (interviews)

JNA 0401 | CD | Suite Ellington | EAN 4042064000776
Rainer Tempel Band
The Duke's King | I Let A Song Go Out Of My Heart | It Don't Mean A Thing If It Ain't Got That Swing | I Got It Bad And That Ain't Good | Take The 'A' Train
Klangküche Studio,?, rec. January-Mai 2001
Tempel,Rainer (p) | Stötter,Claus (tp) | Uhl,Alex (keyboards) | Dohrmann,Florian (b) | Krill,Torsten (dr) | Marquardt,Klaus (v) | Borel,Felix (v) | Brutsch,Alex (viola) | Ströble,Tim (cello)

In A Sentimental Mood
Live in Mössingen, rec. 2.5.1999
Tempel,Rainer (p) | Stötter,Claus (tp) | Uhl,Alex (keyboards) | Dohrmann,Florian (b) | Krill,Torsten (dr) | Marquardt,Klaus (v) | Borel,Felix (v) | Brutsch,Alex (viola) | Ströble,Tim (cello)

JNA 0502 | CD | Little Girl Blue | EAN 4042064001063
Jutta Glaser & Bernhard Sperrfechter
Moondance | Don't Know Blues | Blue Moon | Talk 1 | Undecided | Talk 2 | Tasane Maa | Talk 3 | Little Girl Blue | Cement Mixer Putti Putti | Talk 4 | Over The Rainbow
Rothenberg, rec. 2001
Glaser,Jutta (voc) | Sperrfechter,Bernhard (g)

JNA 0602 | CD | Rolf Zielke Trio Feat. Mustafa Boztüy | EAN 4042064001070
Rolf Zielke Trio Feat. Mustafa Boztüy
Lalo Bossa Nova | Hadulangdan | La Lugubre Gondola | Indian River | East Of The Sun West Of The Moon | The Glow Of Temptation | Rolfing | Peping
Berlin, rec. Autumn 2001
Zielke,Rolf (p) | Bems,Pepe (b) | Köbberling,Heinrich (dr) | Boztüy,Mustafa (bendir,darbouka,udu)

JNA 0702 | CD | Meetings | EAN 4042064001094
The Groenewald Newnet
K&K | Five | Minor Affairs | Humbold Street | Fantasy Für Eine Alte Zugsäge | Lorraine | Blues For Cindy | Pindakaas | Meeting
Stuttgart, rec. 2001
Groenewald,Oliver (tp,fl-h) | Hesse,Ralph (tp,fl-h) | Grocott,Shawn (tb) | Lackner,Marko (b-cl,ss,as) | Studenroth,Kurt (cl,ts) | Gomersall,Anatole (ss,as,bs) | Sitter,Primus (g) | Senst,Ingo (b) | Schoenefeld,Christian (dr)

JNA 0802 | CD | Debut | EAN 4042064001506
Trio Larose
Lampoon | Swingo | We'll See | Devil's Pulpit | Poppin' Pop | Lady Face
details unknown, rec. 15.4.2002
Trio Larose | Weber,Steffen 'Larose' (ss,ts) | Huber,Arne (b) | Jütte,Bastian (dr)

Trio Larose With Toni Lakatos
Harlem Nocturne | Blues For Lucky Lakatos
Trio Larose | Weber,Steffen 'Larose' (ss,ts) | Lakatos Toni (ts) | Huber,Arne (b) | Jütte,Bastian (dr)

JNA 1002 | CD | Lunar Oder Solar? | EAN 4042064001629
Mathias Götz-Windstärke 4
Lunar Oder Solar? | Der Fels | Siebzehn | Die Augenbraue | Überverbot Am Richard-Strauss-Konservatorium
Thorstadl,Obing, rec. 6./7.3.2002
Goetz,Mathias (tb) | Schlosser,Axel (tp) | Fischer,Kay (ss) | Glatzel,Daniel (b-cl,ts) | Schmolling,Marc (p) | Leininger,Ludwig (b) | Pattusch,Nick (dr)

JNA 1102 | CD | Album 03 | EAN 4042064001636
Rainer Tempel Big Band
Metropol | White Song | The Night Comes Down | Soft Wind | Der Professor | I Got It Bad And That Ain't Good | At The Movies
details unknown, rec. 2002
Tempel,Rainer (arr,ld) | Ehringer,Christian (tp,fl-h) | Schlosser,Axel (tp,fl-h) | Auer,Martin (tp,fl-h) | Siffling,Thomas (tp,fl-h) | Gschößl,Gerhard (tb) | Sell,Rainer (tb) | Röser,Uli (tb) | Budziat,Eberhard (b-tb,tuba) | Leicht,Oliver (fl,piccolo-fl,cl,ss,as) | Francke,Andreas (cl,ss,as) | Wyand,Mark (fl,cl,ts) | Feucht,Jochen (alto-fl,ts) | Zimmermann,Jurek (b-cl,bs) | Eberle,Frank (p,synth) | Möbus,Frank (g) | Bodenseh,Markus (b,el-b) | Hammer,Thomas (perc)

JNA 1202 | CD | In The Mean Time | EAN 4042064001643
Arnulf Ochs Group
In The Meantime | Nomen Est Omen | Livingo | Hugo | L'Apres Midi
Amsterdam,Holland, rec. 12./13.12.2001
Ochs,Arnulf (g) | Erian,Michael (ss,ts) | Brederode,Wolfert (p) | Loh,Jens (b) | Grau,Thorsten (dr)

Odd | Lesmiante-The Forest Tale
Ochs,Arnulf (g) | Erian,Michael (ss,ts) | Brederode,Wolfert (p) | Loh,Jens (b) | Grau,Thorsten (dr) | Kurek,Natasza (voc)

JNA 1303 | CD | Mira | EAN 4042064001681
Acoustic Affaire
Mira | Assszonyság | Doubts | Lost Time | Wandring Eyes | Goodbye For Now | A Present With A View | Cobra | Strollin' | Too Much
Pforzheim, rec. 2002
Kienzle,Annette (voc) | Schönborn,Olaf (sax) | Blaschke,Ralf (g) | Engel,Holger (p,keyboards) | Engels,Stefan (b) | Hammer,Thomas (dr,perc)

JNA 1403 | CD | Die Entdeckung Der Banane | EAN 4042064001735
Claus Stötter's Nevertheless
Lethargend | Die Entdeckung Der Banane | At Swim Two Birds | Mad Africa | Bonjour Tristesse, Ca Va? | Poggibonsi | Mon Four | Le Trois Carton Corton Cartoon | Zu Guter Letzt | At Swin Two Birds(final theme)
Albstadt, rec. March 2001
Stötter,Claus (tp,fl-h,alt-h) | Erlewein,Matthias (cl,sax) | Krisch,Dizzy (vib) | Torchinsky,Yves (b) | Laizeau,Francois (dr)

JNA 1503 | CD | Winnetou | EAN 4042064001742
Couch Ensemble
Perpetuum | Prima Vista Sofa Pub | Winetou | Funky Donkey | Sweet Lake City Blues | Tunnel | A New Job | Jugandträume
Fuzzman Studio,?, rec. 2000-2002
Couch Ensemble | Nösig,Daniel (tp) | Erian,Michael (fl,ss,ts) | Sitter,Primus (g) | Asatrian,Karen (keyboards,synth,programming,voice) | Loh,Jens (b) | Marktl,Klemens (dr) | Lippitsch,Klaus (perc) | Deisenberger,Stefan (sound,groove programming)

Boogalule | Stingl & Wadl
Couch Ensemble | Nösig,Daniel (tp) | Vavti,Mario (tb) | Erian,Michael (fl,ss,ts) | Sitter,Primus (g) | Asatrian,Karen (keyboards,synth,programming,voice) | Loh,Jens (b) | Marktl,Klemens (dr) | Lippitsch,Klaus (perc) | Deisenberger,Stefan (sound,groove programming)

What Cames Out Of A Dog | One For Brahms
Couch Ensemble | Nösig,Daniel (tp) | Erian,Michael (fl,ss,ts) | Sitter,Primus (g) | Asatrian,Karen (keyboards,synth,programming,voice) | Loh,Jens (b) | Marktl,Klemens (dr) | Lippitsch,Klaus (perc) | Deisenberger,Stefan (sound,groove programming) | Turnovsky,Michael (oboe) | Habokyan,Anna (v) | Turnovsky,Regine (v) | Gerrits,Angela (viola) | Nemeth,Eva (cello)

JNA 1603 | CD | Dedicated | EAN 4042064001834
Uwe Oberg Quartet
Elastische Dinge(to Anthony Braxton) | Luhsbluhs | Nr. 74(to Morton Feldman) | Quartet Ghost[incl. After The Rain](to John Coltrane) | Supreme Loop(to Randy Weston) | Huhcks | Der Arumatische Klangbefeuchter(to Paul Bley) | Kelvin & Sophia
Wiesbaden, rec. June 2002
Oberg,Uwe (p) | Schubert,Matthias (ts) | Wuchner,Jürgen (b) | Fischer,Jörg (dr)

Uwe Oberg
Vor-Nach I | Vor-Nach II
Oberg,Uwe (p-solo)

JNA 1803 | CD | Crash Test | EAN 4042064001940
Palo Alto
Enigma | Il Grande Fave | Zacinto | Zeno's Dream | Crash Test No.1 | The Lemons's Tree | In The Cave Of Pan | Crash Test No.2 | L'Ombra Di Frisell | Lopa Tola | Classifica Avulsa
Cavalicco(Udine),Italy, rec. 15.11.2002
Palo Alto | Fazzini,Nicola (ss,as) | Volpi,Dario (g) | Gallo,Danilo (b) | De Rossi,Zeno (dr)

Jazz Unlimited | Fenn Music

JUCD 2037 | CD | The Dixieland All Stars
The Dixieland All Stars
Someone To Watch Over Me | Strike Up The Band | Sweet Sue Just You | Billboard March | Ballin' The Jack | Muskrat Ramble | Somebody Loves Me | Bugle Call Rag | Synthetic Blues | When The Saints Go Marching In | Embraceable You | Fascinating Rhythm | St.James Infirmary
Boston,MA, rec. 6./18.6.1959
Dixieland All Stars,The | Clayton,Buck (tp) | Dickenson,Vic (tb) | Russell,Pee Wee (cl) | Freeman,Bud (ts) | Carter,Lou (p) | Jones,Champ (b) | Jones,Jo (dr)

'Deed I Do | Dinah | Sunday
Boston Dateline,Telecast, rec. 3.6.1959
Dixieland All Stars,The | Clayton,Buck (tp) | Dickenson,Vic (tb) | Russell,Pee Wee (cl) | Freeman,Bud (ts) | Carter,Lou (p) | Jones,Champ (b) | Jones,Jo (dr)

JUCD 2044 | CD | The Hollywood Session:The Capitol Jazzmen
The Capitol Jazzmen
Clambake In B Flat | Casanova's Lament | In My Solitude | I'm Sorry I Made You Cry
Los Angeles,CA, rec. 16.11.1943
Capitol Jazzmen,The | May,Billy (tp) | Teagarden,Jack (tb,voc) | Noone,Jimmie (cl) | Matthews,Dave (ts) | Sullivan,Joe (p) | Barbour,Dave (g) | Shapiro,Artie (b) | Singleton,Zutty (dr)

Jack Teagarden's Chicagoans

Mighty Like A Rose
Teagarden,Jack (tb) | Sullivan,Joe (p) | Barbour,Dave (g) | Shapiro,Artie (b) | Singleton,Zutty (dr)
Stars Fell On Alabama | 'Deed I Do
Teagarden,Jack (tb,voc) | May,Billy (tp) | Beau,Heinie (cl) | Matthews,Dave (ts) | Sullivan,Joe (p) | Barbour,Dave (g) | Shapiro,Artie (b) | Singleton,Zutty (dr)

The Capitol Jazzmen
Sugar | Ain't Goin' No Place
Los Angeles,CA, rec. 7.1.1944
Capitol Jazzmen,The | Sherock,Shorty (tp) | Bigard,Barney (cl) | Robinson,Les (as) | Miller,Eddie (ts) | Johnson,Pete (p) | Lamare,Hilton Napoleon 'Nappy' (g) | Wayland,Hank (b) | Fatool,Nick (dr) | Lee,Peggy (voc)
Someday Sweetheart | That Old Feeling
Capitol Jazzmen,The | Sherock,Shorty (tp) | Bigard,Barney (cl) | Robinson,Les (as) | Miller,Eddie (ts) | Wrightsman,Stan (p) | Lamare,Hilton Napoleon 'Nappy' (g) | Wayland,Hank (b) | Fatool,Nick (dr) | Lee,Peggy (voc)
You Can Depend On Me | If I Could Be With You One Hour Tonight | Stormy Weather | Riffamarole
Los Angeles,CA, rec. 30.3.1945
Capitol Jazzmen,The | Coleman,Bill (tp) | Bigard,Barney (cl) | Carter,Benny (as) | Hawkins,Coleman (ts) | Cole,Nat King (p) | Moore,Oscar (g) | Kirby,John (b) | Roach,Max (dr) | Starr,Kay (voc)

The Hollywood Hucksters
Them There Eyes | Happy Blues
Los Angeles,CA, rec. 29.5.1947
Hollywood Hucksters,The | Shavers,Charlie (tp) | Goodman,Benny (cl,voc) | Carter,Benny (as) | Cavanaugh,Dave (ts) | Kock,Joe (bs) | Norvo,Red (vib,xylophone) | Rowles,Jimmy (p) | Ashby,Irving (g) | Callender,Red (b) | Young,Lee (dr) | Kenton,Stan (voc)

Ten Cats And A Mouse
Ja-Da | Three O'Clock Jump
Los Angeles,CA, rec. 14.10.1947
Ten Cats And A Mouse | May,Billy (tp) | Sherwood,Bobby (tp) | Barbour,Dave (tb) | Weston,Paul (cl) | Carter,Benny (as) | Miller,Eddie (ts) | Cavanaugh,Dave (bs) | Norvo,Red (p) | Derwin,Hal (g) | DeVol,Frank (b) | Lee,Peggy (dr)

Frank Trumbauer And His Orchestra
Between The Devil And The Deep Blue Sea | China Boy
NYC, rec. 25.3.1946
Trumbauer,Frank (c-mel-sax) | Erwin,Pee Wee (tp) | Lacey,Jack (tb) | Stegmeyer,Bill (sax) | Bowman,Dave (p) | Kress,Carl (g) | Alpert,Trigger (b) | Haggart,Bob (b) | Blowers,Johnny (dr)

JUCD 2048 | CD | Louis Armstrong-Jack Teagarden-Woody Herman:Midnights At V-Disc
V-Disc All Star Jam Session
Jack-Armstrong Blues | Jack-Armstrong Blues(alt.take)
NYC, rec. 6.12.1944
V-Disc All Stars | Hackett,Bobby (co) | Armstrong,Louis (tp) | Butterfield,Billy (tp) | McGarity,Lou (tb,voc) | Teagarden,Jack (tb,voc) | Caceres,Ernie (cl) | Caiazza,Nick (ts) | Guarnieri,Johnny (p) | Ellis,Herb (g) | Hall,Al (b) | Cole,William 'Cozy' (dr)
Rosetta | Rosetta(alt.take)
V-Disc All Stars | Shavers,Charlie (tp) | Young,Trummy (tb) | Caceres,Ernie (cl) | Byas,Don (ts) | Clifton,Bill (p) | Ellis,Herb (g) | Haggart,Bob (b) | Powell,Specs (dr)
Miss Martingale(incomplete) | Miss Martingale
V-Disc All Stars | Butterfield,Billy (tp) | Page,Oran 'Hot Lips' (tp) | McGarity,Lou (tb) | Teagarden,Jack (tb) | Caceres,Ernie (cl) | Caiazza,Nick (ts) | Guarnieri,Johnny (p) | Ellis,Herb (g) | Hall,Al (b) | Powell,Specs (dr)
Can't We Talk It Over
V-Disc All Stars | Hackett,Bobby (co) | McGarity,Lou (tb) | Teagarden,Jack (tb) | Caceres,Ernie (cl) | Caiazza,Nick (ts) | Clifton,Bill (p) | Ellis,Herb (g) | Weiss,Sid (b) | Cole,William 'Cozy' (dr) | McKenzie,Red (voc)
The Sheik Of Araby
V-Disc All Stars | Hackett,Bobby (co) | Page,Oran 'Hot Lips' (tp) | McGarity,Lou (tb) | Teagarden,Jack (tb) | Caceres,Ernie (cl) | Caiazza,Nick (ts) | Guarnieri,Johnny (p) | Ellis,Herb (g) | Hall,Al (b) | Powell,Specs (dr)
If I Could Be With You One Hour Tonight(incomplete) | If I Could Be With You One Hour Tonight
V-Disc All Stars | Hackett,Bobby (co) | McGarity,Lou (tb) | Teagarden,Jack (tb) | Caceres,Ernie (cl) | Caiazza,Nick (ts) | Clifton,Bill (p) | Ellis,Herb (g) | Giobbe,Felix (b) | Cole,William 'Cozy' (dr)
I'm Confessin'(That I Love You) | I'm Confessin'(That I Love You)(alt.take)
NYC, rec. 7.12.1944
V-Disc All Stars | Hackett,Bobby (co) | Armstrong,Louis (tp,voc) | Butterfield,Billy (tp) | McGarity,Lou (tb) | Teagarden,Jack (tb) | Caceres,Ernie (cl) | Caiazza,Nick (ts) | Guarnieri,Johnny (p) | Ellis,Herb (g) | Hall,Al (b) | Cole,William 'Cozy' (dr)

Woody Herman And The Vanderbilt All Stars
The Jeep Is Jumpin'
Vanderbilt Theatre,NYC, rec. 24.1.1945
Vanderbilt All Stars | Shavers,Charlie (tp) | Byas,Don (ts) | Jaffe,Nat (p) | Bryan,Mike prob. (g) | Taylor,Billy prob. (p) | West,Harold 'Doc' prob. (dr)
Northwest Passage
Vanderbilt All Stars | Harris,Bill (tb) | Herman,Woody (cl) | Fields,Herbie (as) | Phillips,Flip (ts) | Auld,Georgie (ts) | Hyams,Marjorie (vib) | Burns,Ralph (p) | Bauer,Billy (g) | Jackson,Chubby (b) | Blowers,Johnny (dr)
Somebody Loves Me
Vanderbilt All Stars | Harris,Bill (tb) | Herman,Woody (cl,voc) | Webster,Ben (ts) | Hyams,Marjorie (vib) | Burns,Ralph (p) | Bauer,Billy (g) | Jackson,Chubby (b) | Blowers,Johnny (dr)
John Hardy's Wife
Vanderbilt All Stars | Harris,Bill (tb) | Webster,Ben (ts) | Burns,Ralph (p) | Bauer,Billy (g) | Jackson,Chubby (b) | Blowers,Johnny (dr)
Just You Just Me
Vanderbilt All Stars | unkn. (tp) | Harris,Bill (tb) | Phillips,Flip (ts) | Webster,Ben (ts) | Hyams,Marjorie (vib) | Burns,Ralph (p) | Bauer,Billy (g) | Jackson,Chubby (b) | Blowers,Johnny (dr)

Woody Herman And His Orchestra
Billy Bauer's Tune
NYC, rec. 24.1.1945
Herman,Woody (as) | Berman,Sonny (tp) | Frankhauser,Charles (tp) | Wetzel,Ray (tp) | Candoli,Pete (tp) | Warwick,Carl (tp) | Pfeffner,Ralph (tb) | Harris,Bill (tb) | Kiefer,Ed (tb) | Marowitz,Sam (as) | LaPorta,John (as) | Phillips,Flip (ts) | Mondello,Pete (ts) | DeSair,Skippy (bs) | Burns,Ralph (p,arr) | Bauer,Billy (g) | Jackson,Chubby (b) | Tough,Dave (dr)

JUCD 2049 | CD | Muggsy Spanier And Bud Freeman:V-Discs 1944-45
Muggsy Spanier And His V-Disc All Stars
That's A Plenty | Just Squeeze Me(But Don't Tease Me) | Jazz Me Blues | Pee Wee Speaks | Pat's Blues
NYC, rec. 17.10.1944
Spanier,Francis 'Muggsy' (co) | McGarity,Lou (tb) | Russell,Pee Wee (cl,voc) | Richmond,Boomie (ts) | Stacy,Jess (p) | White,Hy (g) | Haggart,Bob (b,whistling) | Wettling,George (dr)
Tin Roof Blues | Tin Roof Blues(alt.take 1) | Tin Roof Blues(alt.take 2) | Tin Roof Blues(false start 1) | Tin Roof Blues(false start 2) | Cherry | China Boy | China Boy(false start 1) | China Boy(false start 2) | China Boy(false start 3) | Royal Garden Blues | You Took Advantage Of Me(false start) | You Took Advantage Of Me | You Took Advantage Of Me(alt.take 1) | You Took Advantage Of Me(alt.take 2)
NYC, rec. 22.10.1945
Spanier,Francis 'Muggsy' (co) | McGarity,Lou (tb) | Hucko,Peanuts (cl) | Freeman,Bud (ts) | Bowman,Dave (p) | White,Hy (g) | Alpert,Trigger (b) | Wettling,George (dr)

The V-Disc Jumpers
Love Is Just Around The Corner
NYC, rec. 4.10.1945
V-Disc Jumpers,The | Lawson,Yank (tp) | Mustarde,Bill (tb) | Hucko,Peanuts (cl) | Freeman,Bud (ts) | Weed,Buddy (p) | Mastren,Carmen (g) | Alpert,Trigger (b) | McKinley,Ray (dr)

Bud Freeman And His Stars
Coquette
Freeman,Bud (ts) | Lawson,Yank (tp) | Mustarde,Bill (tb) | Hucko,Peanuts (cl) | Weed,Buddy (p) | Mastren,Carmen (g) | Alpert,Trigger (b) | McKinley,Ray (dr)

Bud Freeman And The V-Disc Jumpers
For Musicians Only
V-Disc Jumpers,The | Lawson,Yank (tp) | Mustarde,Bill (tb) | Hucko,Peanuts (cl) | Freeman,Bud (ts,talking) | Weed,Buddy (p) | Mastren,Carmen (g) | Alpert,Trigger (b) | McKinley,Ray (dr)

Eight Squares And A Critic
The Latest Thing In HotJazz
Eight Squares And A Critic | Lawson,Yank (tp) | Mustarde,Bill (tb) | Hucko,Peanuts (cl) | Freeman,Bud (ts,talking) | Weed,Buddy (p) | Mastren,Carmen (g) | Alpert,Trigger (b) | McKinley,Ray (dr)

JUCD 2065 | CD | The Radio Years 1940 | EAN 717101206520
Ella Fitzgerald And Her Famous Orchestra
A-Tisket A-Tasket(Theme) | Traffic Jam | A Lover Is Blue | Dodgin' The Dean | 'Tain't What You Do (It's How You Do It) | Confessin' | Blue Lou | What's The Matter With Me | I Want The Waiter With The Water | Let's Go Together
Live at The 'Savoy Ballroom',NYC, rec. 22.1.1940
Fitzgerald,Ella (ld,voc) | Vance,Dick (tp,arr,voc) | Randolph,Irving 'Mouse' (tp) | Jordan,Taft (tp,voc) | Williams,Sandy (tb) | Story,Nat (tb) | Matthews,George (tb) | Barefield,Eddie (cl,as) | Jefferson,Hilton (as) | McRae,Teddy (ts,bs,arr) | Carver,Wayman (fl,as,ts,arr) | Ramirez,Roger 'Ram' (p) | Trueheart,John (g) | Peer,Beverley (b) | Beason,Bill (dr)
A-Tisket A-Tasket(Theme) | Limehouse Blues | This Changing World | Oh Johnny Oh Johnny | Diga Diga Do | Thank Your Stars | Take It From The Top | Vagabond Dreams | Break 'Em Down | Let's Get Together(Theme)
Live at The 'Savoy Ballroom',NYC, rec. 25.1.1940
Fitzgerald,Ella (ld,voc) | Vance,Dick (tp,arr,voc) | Randolph,Irving 'Mouse' (tp) | Jordan,Taft (tp,voc) | Williams,Sandy (tb) | Story,Nat (tb) | Matthews,George (tb) | Barefield,Eddie (cl,as) | Jefferson,Hilton (as) | McRae,Teddy (ts,bs,arr) | Carver,Wayman (fl,as,ts,arr) | Ramirez,Roger 'Ram' (p) | Trueheart,John (g) | Peer,Beverley (b) | Beason,Bill (dr)

JUCD 2076 | 2 CD | Fats Waller:The Complete Associated Transcription Sessions 1935-1939 | EAN 717101207626
Fats Waller
The Viper's Drag | Down Home Blues | Handful Of | I'm Crazy 'Bout My Baby | Tea For Two | Believe It Beloved | Sweet Sue Just You | Somebody Stole My Gal | Honeysuckle Rose | Night Wind | African Ripples | Because Of Once Upon A Time | Where Were You On The Night Of June The Third? | Clothes Line Ballet | Don't Let It Bother You | E-Flat Blues | Alligator Crawl | Zonky | Hallelujah | Do Me A Favour | California Here I Come | I've Got A Feeling I'm Falling | My Fate Is In Your Hands | Ain't Misbehavin' | You're The Top | Blue Turning Grey Over You | Russian Fantasy
NYC, rec. 11.3.1935
Waller,Thomas 'Fats' (p,voc)

Fats Waller-Rudy Powell
Baby Brown | How Can You Face Me?
Waller,Thomas 'Fats' (p,voc) | Powell,Rudy (cl,as)

Fats Waller-Cedric Wallace
Dinah | In My Solitude
Waller,Thomas 'Fats' (p,voc) | Wallace,Cedric (b)

Fats Waller And His Rhythm
The Moon Is Low | The Moon Is Low(alt.take) | The Sheik Of Araby | E-Flat Blues | E-Flat Blues(alt.take) | Honeysuckle Rose | Honeysuckle Rose(alt.take) | Ain't Misbehavin' | Sweet Sue Just You | Nagasaki | I'm Crazy 'Bout My Baby | I'm Crazy 'Bout My Baby(alt.take) | The Spider And The Fly | Lonesome Me | After You've Gone | After You've Gone(alt.take)
NYC, rec. 7.8.1939
Waller,Thomas 'Fats' (p,voc) | Hamilton,John (tp) | Sedric,Gene (cl,ts) | Smith,John (g) | Jones,Wilmore 'Slick' (dr)

Fats Waller
Dinah | Poor Butterfly | St.Louis Blues | Hallelujah | Tea For Two | Handful Of Keys
Waller,Thomas 'Fats' (org-solo)

JUCD 2079 | CD | Old Gold Rehearsals 1944 | EAN 717101207923
Woody Herman And His Orchestra
Blue Flame(Theme) | Is You Is Or Is You Ain't My Baby | It Must Be Jelly('Cause Jam Don't Shake Like That) | Woodshopper's Ball
NYC, rec. 2.8.1944
Herman,Woody (cl,as,voc) | Hefti,Neal (tp,arr) | Robbins,Billy (tp) | Wetzel,Ray (tp) | Candoli,Pete (tp) | Candoli,Conte (tp) | Pfeffner,Ralph (tb) | Harris,Bill (tb) | Kiefer,Ed (tb) | Marowitz,Sam (as) | Shine,Bill (as) | Phillips,Flip (ts) | Mondello,Pete (bs) | DeSair,Skippy (bs) | Burns,Ralph (p,arr) | Bauer,Billy (g) | Jackson,Chubby (b) | Tough,Dave (dr)
G.I.Jive | Red Top | Yeah,Man(Amen)
NYC, rec. 16.8.1944
Herman,Woody (cl,as,voc) | Hefti,Neal (tp,arr) | Robbins,Billy (tp) | Wetzel,Ray (tp) | Candoli,Pete (tp) | Candoli,Conte (tp) | Pfeffner,Ralph (tb) | Munson,Dick (tp) | Harris,Bill (tb) | Kiefer,Ed (tb) | Marowitz,Sam (as) | Shine,Bill (as) | Phillips,Flip (ts) | Mondello,Pete (ts) | DeSair,Skippy (bs) | Burns,Ralph (p,arr) | Bauer,Billy (g) | Jackson,Chubby (b) | Tough,Dave (dr)
Noah | Sweet Lorraine | The Golden Wedding | Blue Flame(Theme)
NYC, rec. 23.8.1944
Herman,Woody (cl,as,voc) | Hefti,Neal (tp,arr) | Robbins,Billy (tp) | Wetzel,Ray (tp) | Candoli,Pete (tp) | Candoli,Conte (tp) | Pfeffner,Ralph (tb) | Munson,Dick (tp) | Harris,Bill (tb) | Kiefer,Ed (tb) | Marowitz,Sam (as) | Shine,Bill (as) | Phillips,Flip (ts) | Mondello,Pete (ts) | DeSair,Skippy (bs) | Burns,Ralph (p,arr) | Bauer,Billy (g) | Jackson,Chubby (b) | Tough,Dave (dr)
I've Got The World On A String | Jones Beachhead | Four Or Five Times
NYC, rec. 30.8.1944
Herman,Woody (cl,as,voc) | Hefti,Neal (tp,arr) | Robbins,Billy (tp) | Wetzel,Ray (tp) | Candoli,Pete (tp) | Candoli,Conte (tp) | Pfeffner,Ralph (tb) | Munson,Dick (tp) | Harris,Bill (tb) | Kiefer,Ed (tb) | Marowitz,Sam (as) | Shine,Bill (as) | Phillips,Flip (ts) | Mondello,Pete (ts) | DeSair,Skippy (bs) | Burns,Ralph (p,arr) | Bauer,Billy (g) | Jackson,Chubby (b) | Tough,Dave (dr)
Somebody Loves Me | 125th Street Prophet | 'Taint Me | Blues On Parade
NYC, rec. 13.9.1944
Herman,Woody (cl,as,voc) | Hefti,Neal (tp,arr) | Wetzel,Ray (tp) | Candoli,Pete (tp) | Frankhauser,Chuck (tp) | Warwick,Carl (tp) | Pfeffner,Ralph (tb) | Munson,Dick (tp) | Harris,Bill (tb) | Kiefer,Ed (tb) | Marowitz,Sam (as) | LaPorta,John (ts) | Phillips,Flip (ts) | Mondello,Pete (ts) | DeSair,Skippy (bs) | Burns,Ralph (p,arr) | Bauer,Billy (g) | Jackson,Chubby (b) | Tough,Dave (dr)
There Is No Greater Love | Basie's Basement | There'll Be A Hot Time In The Old Town Tonight
NYC, rec. 20.9.1944
Herman,Woody (cl,as,voc) | Hefti,Neal (tp,arr) | Wetzel,Ray (tp) | Candoli,Pete (tp) | Frankhauser,Chuck (tp) | Warwick,Carl (tp) | Pfeffner,Ralph (tb) | Munson,Dick (tp) | Harris,Bill (tb) | Kiefer,Ed (tb) | Marowitz,Sam (as) | LaPorta,John (ts) | Phillips,Flip (ts) | Mondello,Pete (ts) | DeSair,Skippy (bs) | Hyams,Marjorie (vib) | Burns,Ralph (p,arr) | Bauer,Billy (g) | Jackson,Chubby (b) | Tough,Dave (dr)
1-2-3-4-Jump
NYC, rec. 27.9.1944
Herman,Woody (cl) | Hefti,Neal (tp) | Harris,Bill (tb) | Phillips,Flip (ts) | Hyams,Marjorie (vib) | Burns,Ralph (p) | Bauer,Billy (g) | Jackson,Chubby (b) | Tough,Dave (dr)
Apple Honey
NYC, rec. 4.10.1944
Herman,Woody (cl) | Hefti,Neal (tp) | Frankhauser,Chuck (tp) | Warwick,Carl (tp) | Candoli,Pete (tp) | Wetzel,Ray (tp) | Harris,Bill (tb) | Pfeffner,Ralph (tb) | Kiefer,Ed (tb) | Marowitz,Sam (as) | LaPorta,John (ts) | Mondello,Pete (ts) | Phillips,Flip (ts) | DeSair,Skippy (bs) | Hyams,Marjorie (vib) | Burns,Ralph (p) | Bauer,Billy (g) | Jackson,Chubby (b) | Tough,Dave (dr)

JUCD 2084 | CD | June Christy And The Johnny Guarnieri Quintet (1949) | EAN 717101208425
June Christy With The Johnny Guarnieri Quintet
Introduction by Johnny Guarnieri | September In The Rain | I Can't Believe That You're In Love With Me | Dancing On The Ceiling | Get Happy | Lucky In Love | Bewitched Bothered And Bewildered | One O'Clock Jump | Cheek To Cheek | Lullaby In Rhythm | S' Posin' | September Song | Nice Work If You Can Get It | Yesterdays | They Didn't Believe Me | I Didn't Know What Time It Was | Robins And Roses | Alice Blue Gown | I'm Thrilled | Wy Oh Why? | Reckon I'm In Love | Brother Leo | How High The Moon | There's A Small Hotel | Zing! Went The Strings Of My Heart | Too Marvelous For Words | Idaho | I'm Glad There Is You | Cross Your Heart | So Long- | Between The Devil And The Deep Blue Sea-
Hollywood,CA, rec. 1949
Christy,June (voc) | Guarnieri,Johnny (p) | Walters,George (tp) | DiMaggio,Charlie (cl,as) | Guarnieri,Leo (b) | Garisto,Frank (dr)

Jazzland | ZYX Music GmbH

JZSA 946-6 | SACD | Thelonious Monk With John Coltrane | EAN 025218730921
Thelonious Monk Quartet
Nutty | Ruby My Dear | Trinkle Tinkle
NYC, rec. 16.4.1957
Monk,Thelonious (p) | Coltrane,John (ts) | Ware,Wilbur (b) | Wilson,Shadow (dr)

Thelonious Monk Septet
Epistrophy(alt.take) | Off Minor(alt.take)
NYC, rec. 26.6.1957
Monk,Thelonious (p) | Copeland,Ray (tp) | Gryce,Gigi (as) | Hawkins,Coleman (ts) | Coltrane,John (ts) | Ware,Wilbur (b) | Blakey,Art (dr)

Thelonious Monk
Functional(alt.take)
NYC, rec. 12.4.1957
Monk,Thelonious (p-solo)

Jazzpoint | Jazzpoint

JP 1009 CD | CD | Bireli Swing '81
Bireli Lagrene Ensemble
B.L. | Swing Valse | Djangology | Bireli Hi Gogoro | Oh! Lady Be Good | Thundering Noise | Erster Tango (Sountrack Querelle) | September Song | Schwarze Augen | I Can't Give You Anything But Love | Carlos | Limehouse Blues | Nuages | How High The Moon | Night And Day
Ludwigsburg, rec. April 1981
Lagrene,Bireli (g) | Lagrene,Gaiti (g) | Loeffler,Tschirglo (g) | Rabe,Bernd (ss) | Jankeje,Jan (b) | Blairman,Allen (dr)

JP 1016 CD | CD | Zum Trotz
Jan Jankeje Quintet
Doo In Peru | Zum Trotz | Mitti | Rue De Pierre | Paris | Berga | Reinsburgstrasse | Down In Town | 3rd Type Blues | Elsa-Maria
Stuttgart, rec. May 1983
Jankeje,Jan (b) | Wagenleiter,Klaus (p) | Buck,Matthias (v,viola) | Lagrene,Bireli (g) | Braun,Werner (dr)

JP 1017 CD | CD | Serenity
Subroto Roy Chowdhury Group
Gurjari Todi | Raga Desh | Tabla Solo
Ludwigsburg, rec. 17./18.3.1986
Chowdhury,Subroto Roy (sitar) | Popatkar,Manikrao (tabla) | Martin,Patricia (tanpura)

JP 1020 CD | CD | Explorations
Subroto Roy Chowdhury-Steve Lacy Group
Explorations
Ludwigsburg, rec. 21.22.4.1987
Lacy,Steve (ss) | Chowdhury,Subroto Roy (sitar) | Ray,Shibsankar (tabla) | Martin,Patricia (tanpura)
Saxoraga
Lacy,Steve (ss) | Ray,Shibsankar (tabla) | Martin,Patricia (tanpura)

Subroto Roy Chowdhury Group
Spontaneity
Ludwigsburg, rec. 21./22.4.1987
Chowdhury,Subroto Roy (sitar) | Ray,Shibsankar (tabla) | Martin,Patricia (tanpura)

JP 1021 CD | CD | Dedicated To Bill Evans And Scott LaFaro
Larry Coryell-Miroslav Vitous
Someday My Prince Will Come | Nardis | Solar | Some Other Time | Corcovado(Quiet Nights) | Autumn Leaves | My Romance | Stella By Starlight | The Peacocks
March-Hugstetten, rec. 13.5.1987
Coryell,Larry (g) | Vitous,Miroslav (b)

JP 1023 CD | CD | Bohemia
Vic Juris-John Etheridge
You've Changed | Con Alma | Chips | A Keen Bat
March-Hugstetten, rec. 21.-24.4.1988
Juris,Vic (g) | Etheridge,John (g)

Vic Juris-John Etheridge Quartet
There Is No Greater Love | L | Georgeiana | Sim
Juris,Vic (g) | Etheridge,John (g) | Vitous,Miroslav (b) | Pellitteri,Marcello (dr)

JP 1025 CD | CD | Air Dancing
Larry Coryell Quartet
Prayer For Peace | Air Dancing | Impressions | Sienna: Welcome My Darling | Rhapsody In Blue | Zimbabwe | Dual Force
Live at Magnetic Terrace,Paris,France, rec. 4.6.1988
Coryell,Larry (g) | Cowell,Stanley (p) | Williams,Buster (b) | Hart,Billy (dr)

JP 1027 CD | CD | Bireli Lagrene 'Highlights'
Bireli Lagrene-Philip Catherine
Fisco Place
Alte Oper,Frankfurt/M, rec. July 1981
Lagrene,Bireli (g) | Catherine,Philip (g)

Bireli Lagrene
Bireli Hi Gogoro
Ludwigsburg, rec. April 1981
Lagrene,Bireli (g)

Bireli Lagrene-Vic Juris
Sim
Staufen im Breisgau, rec. June 1985
Lagrene,Bireli (g) | Juris,Vic (g)

Bireli Lagrene Group
Berga
Mühle Huntziken,Rubigen,CH, rec. May 1986
Lagrene,Bireli (g) | Coryell,Larry (g) | Vitous,Miroslav (b)
Erster Tango (Sountrack Querelle)
Ludwigsburg, rec. March 1982
Lagrene,Bireli (g) | Lagrene,Gaiti (g) | Loeffler,Tschirglo (g) | Jankeje,Jan (b)
Boxer's Boogie | Bireli Swing 1979
Krokodil,Kirchheim/Teck, rec. 29./30.5.1980
Lagrene,Bireli (g) | Reiter,Joerg (p) | Lagrene,Gaiti (g) | Loeffler,Tschirglo (g) | Jankeje,Jan (b)
Schwarze Augen
Ludwigsburg, rec. April 1981
Lagrene,Bireli (g) | Lagrene,Gaiti (g) | Loeffler,Tschirglo (g) | Jankeje,Jan (b)
Jaco Reggae

Stuttgart, rec. March 1986
Lagrene,Bireli (g) | Pastorius,Jaco (el-b) | Sendecki,Vladislaw (keyboards,synth) | Lübke,Peter (dr) | Bringolf,Serge (perc)
Teresa
Lagrene,Bireli (g) | Pastorius,Jaco (el-b) | Sendecki,Vladislaw (keyboards,synth) | Jankeje,Jan (b) | Lübke,Peter (dr)

JP 1028 CD | CD | Mother Nature
Things
Turn To East | Dancing Dolls | Basking Tiger | Kid Song | Good Luck | Osteria
Budapest, rec. April 1990
Things | Lakatos,Tony (sax,synth) | Laszlo,Attila (g) | Olah,Kalman (keyboards) | Lattmann,Bela (b) | Solti,Janos (dr) | Horvath,Kornel (perc)
When You Come... | Mother Nature
Things | Lakatos,Tony (sax,synth) | Laszlo,Attila (g) | Olah,Kalman (keyboards) | Lattmann,Bela (b) | Solti,Janos (dr) | Horvath,Kornel (perc) | Quick,Torita (voc)
Ballet On The Moon | Slow River
Things | Lakatos,Tony (sax,synth) | Laszlo,Attila (g) | Olah,Kalman (keyboards) | Lattmann,Bela (b) | Solti,Janos (dr) | Horvath,Kornel (perc)

JP 1029 CD | CD | Surprise
Fun Horns
Ankunft Des Orchesters Der Deutschen Jazzpolizei- | Ele-Fun(t)-Horn(s)- | Abreise Des O.D.D.J.P.- | Ein Jahr Später | Free Notes | Berceuse | Blinde Kuh | From Mexico To Bali | Fast Foot | 1989 Song | Last Dream | For John T | Königin Der Nacht-Oder Eine Kleine Horn-Musik
Burgsinn, rec. July 1990
Fun Horns | Schlott,Volker (fl,alto-fl,ss,as) | Klemm,Thomas (fl,ts,voc) | Huke,Jörg (tb) | Hesse,Joachim (tp,fl-h)

JP 1030 CD | CD | Really!
Matthew Brubeck & David Widelock
Boogie Bored | You Don't Know What Love Is | Big Foot | Really | Airwaves | Psyche's Springs
Los Gatos,CA, rec. April 1990
Brubeck,Matthew (cello) | Widelock,David (g,el-g,12-string-g)

JP 1031 CD | CD | Live In Italy
Jaco Pastorius Trio
Improvisation No.1- | Teen Town- | I Shot The Sheriff | Continuum | Fannie Mae | Black Market | Satin Doll
Live in Italy, rec. March 1986
Pastorius,Jaco (el-b) | Lagrene,Bireli (g) | Böröcz,Thomas (dr)

JP 1032 CD | CD | Jaco Pastorius Honestly
Jaco Pastorius
Honestly(part 1-10)
Pastorius,Jaco (el-b)

JP 1034 CD | CD | For The Music
Vic Juris Quartet
Victim | Sim | For The Music | If I Should Lose You | Folk Song | A Weaver Of Dreams | You Don't Know What Love Is | For Emily | Back Row Hi Jinx
NYC, rec. 1991/1992
Juris,Vic (g) | Hagans,Tim (tp) | Anderson,Jay (b) | Hirshfield,Jeff (dr)

JP 1035 CD | CD | Poema
Eduardo Niebla-Antonio Forcione Group
Poema | Superlatino | Ronnie | Primavera | Sunrise | Snow | Haciendo Camino | The Long Winter
London,GB, rec. 15.-25.5.1992
Niebla,Eduardo (g) | Forcione,Antonio (g) | Philpott (b-g) | Clavies,Paul (perc) | Lee,Simon (perc,clapping)

JP 1036 CD | CD | Heavy'n Jazz
Jaco Pastorius Trio
Broadway Blues | Bluma | Smoke On The Water | Medley: | Purple Haze- | The Third Stone From The Sun- | Teen Town- | Star Spangled Banner | Reza | Honestly | Invitation
Live in Rome,Italy, rec. December 1986
Pastorius,Jaco (el-b) | Lagrene,Bireli (g) | Bringolf,Serge (dr)
Jaco Reggae
Melody Tonstudio,?, rec. March 1986
Pastorius,Jaco (el-b) | Lagrene,Bireli (g) | Bringolf,Serge (dr)

JP 1037 CD | CD | Swinging Again
Benny Waters Quartet
Benny's Bounced Blues | Please Don't Talk About Me When I'm Gone | Autumn Leaves | Them There Eyes | Just One Of Those Things | The Nearness Of You | Strike Up The Band | Blue Waters | Undecided | Wham
Ludwigsburg, rec. 4.5.1993
Waters,Benny (as,voc) | Wagner,Thilo (p) | Jankeje,Jan (b) | Beck,Gregor (dr)

JP 1039 CD | CD | Benny Waters Plays Songs Of Love
Benny Waters Quintet
What Is This Thing Called Love | You Are The Sunshine Of My Life | I'm In The Mood For Love | The Love Nest | When Your Lover Has Gone | Almost Like Being In Love | Always | I Love You | Love Me Or Leave Me | Takin' A Chance On Love
Bioya,Paterson,NJ, rec. 28.7.1993
Waters,Benny (as) | Juris,Vic (g) | Richards,Charles 'Red' (p) | Williams Jr.,John (b) | Williams,Jackie (dr)

JP 1040 CD | CD | Live At The Carnegie Hall: A Tribute To Django Reinhardt
Bireli Lagrene Trio
Mirage
Live at Alte Oper,Frankfurt/M., rec. July 1981
Lagrene,Bireli (g) | Disley,William 'Diz' (g) | Jankeje,Jan (b)
Minor Swing | Paris | Toulouse Blues | September Song | Rue De Pierre | Djangology
Live at Carnegie Hall,NYC, rec. 22.6.1984
Lagrene,Bireli (g) | Disley,William 'Diz' (g) | Jankeje,Jan (b)
Daphne | Ornithology- | How High The Moon-
Live at The 'Zelt Musik Festival,Freiburg', rec. June 1985
Lagrene,Bireli (g) | Juris,Vic (g) | Jankeje,Jan (b)

JP 1041 CD | CD | Swingtime
Red Richards Quartet
Ounce To The Bounce | Once In A While | Black Butterfly | I Miss You | Them There Eyes | Soft Buns | There'll Never Be Another You | Go Red
NYC, rec. 15.11.1993
Richards,Charles 'Red' (p,voc) | Kelly,George (ts) | Ray,Carline (b) | Bean,Clarence 'Tootsie' (dr)

JP 1042 CD | CD | My Romance
Red Richards
I Wished On The Moon | Dorothy | I Would Do Most Anything For You | Drop Me Off In Harlem | I Should Care | Darn That Dream | My Romance | Idaho | It's Over Because We're Through | Louisiana | Three Little Words
NYC, rec. 17.11.1993
Richards,Charles 'Red' (p,voc)

JP 1043 CD | CD | Oscar Klein's Jazz Show
Oscar Klein's Jazz Show
You Are My Sunshine | Blues For Peter Schilperoort | O Sole Mio | Tribute To Wild Bill | Bratislava Fantasy | To My Mother | Bye Bye Blackbird | Me And My Guitar | The Roman Swing Of Mrs. Stone | Don't Get Around Much Anymore | The Sheik Of Araby | The New Harmonica Shuffle
Stuttgart, rec. 27.4.1994
Klein,Oscar (tp,cl,g,harm) | Mussolini,Romano (p) | Jankeje,Jan (b) | Beck,Gregor (dr)

JP 1044 CD | CD | A Tribute To Fats
Al Casey Quartet
It Don't Mean A Thing If It Ain't Got That Swing | Just Squeeze Me(But Don't Tease Me) | Holey Moley | Jit It | Like It Ji's | Cute | After You've Gone | Just The Blues | Honeysuckle Rose | How Long Has This Been Going On | Cheek To Cheek
Heeze,NL, rec. 22.5.1994
Casey,Al (g) | Richards,Charles 'Red' (p) | Jankeje,Jan (b) | Köszegi,Imre (dr)

JP 1045 CD | CD | Groove Move
Red Richards-George Kelly Sextet With Doc Cheatham
Groove Move | I Want A Little Girl | Like Mama | Right On | Lullaby Of Love | Up Stream | Idaho | Stella By Starlight | Sunday | It's A Little Thing | This Means So Much | Strike Up The Band | Sweet Sue Just You | Oh! Lady Be Good
Oberursel, rec. 2.10.1994
Richards,Charles 'Red' (p) | Kelly,George (ts) | Cheatham,Doc (tp) | Lindgreen,Ole 'Fessor' (tb) | Casey,Al (g) | Jankeje,Jan (b) | Köszegi,Imre (dr)

JP 1046 CD | CD | Great Traditionalists
Quartier Latin Jazz Band
Blues In The Air | When The Saints Go Marching In | Tommy's Blues | Texas Moaner Blues | St.Louis Blues | After You've Gone | Mood Indigo | Creole Love Call | I've Found A New Baby
different Places, rec. different Dates
Quartier Latin Jazz Band | Waters,Benny (as) | Holland,Peanuts (tp) | Mezzrow,Milton Mezz (cl) | Williams,Nelson (tp) | Schneider,Hans Wolf 'Hawe' (tb) | Attenoux,Michel (as)
Michel Attenoux And His Dream Band
After You've Gone | Ain't Misbehavin' | Stardust
Attenoux,Michel (as) | Daly,Geo (vib)
Dieter Antritter And His Traveling Jazz Band
You GotTo See Your Mama | Who's Sorry Now | Trouble In Mind | I'm Gonna Sit Right Down And Write Myself A Letter | What A Difference A Day Made
Antritter,Dieter (cl,sax) | Williams,Peter Seige (p,voc) | Armstrong,Jim (tb) | Francis,Susie (voc)
Great Traditionalists In Europe
C Jam Blues
Karlsruhe, rec. 4.10.1969
Williams,Nelson (tp) | Fleming,Herb (tb) | Bader,Klaus (sax) | Chaix,Henri (p) | Woode,Jimmy (b) | Bishop,Wallace (dr)

JP 1047 CD | CD | Live
Bireli Lagrene Ensemble
Bireli | Minor Swing | Spain | Paris | Rue De Pierre | Ornithology | Sim | St.Germain Des Pres | The Night Of A Champion | I Can't Give You Anything But Love | Moll-Blues
Live at The 'Zelt Musik Festival,Freiburg', rec. 1./2.6.1985
Lagrene,Bireli (g) | Juris,Vic (g) | Lagrene,Gaiti (g) | Disley,William 'Diz' (g) | Jankeje,Jan (b)

JP 1048 CD | CD | Oscar Klein's Jazz Show Vol.2
Oscar Klein's Jazz Show
Oscar's Theme | Stardust | Swinging For Mezz | Last Lost Love | Salute To Gene Krupa | Blue Reed | New Harmonica Breakdown | When The Saints Go Marching In | Blind Blake's Rag | Back Home Again In Indiana
Slovak Radio,Bratislava, rec. 14.1.1997
Klein,Oscar (tp,cl,g,harm) | Mussolini,Romano (p) | Jankeje,Jan (b) | Beck,Gregor (dr)

JP 1049 CD | CD | Bireli Lagrene
Bireli Lagrene Group
PSP Nr.2 | Berga | All The Things You Are | Albi | Solo(No.1) | Gloria's Step | All Blues
Mühle Huntziken,Rubigen,CH, rec. 3.5.1986
Lagrene,Bireli (g) | Coryell,Larry (g) | Vitous,Miroslav (b)

JP 1050 CD | CD | Travelling
Robert Balzar Trio
The Patriot | Ginette | Thanks To Isidor | Traveling | Wintertime | B.E. | Willy Nilly | For Your Sound
Ostrava, rec. 21./22.7.1997
Balzar,Robert (b) | Macha,Stanislav (p) | Partman,Marek (dr)

JP 1052 CD | CD | Live at The San Marino Jazz Festival
Oscar Klein-Lino Patruno European Jazz Stars
All Of Me | Up A Lazy River | Back Home Again In Indiana | Stealin' Apples | The World Is Waiting For The Sunrise | When You're Smiling | Mood Indigo | Come On | St.Louis Blues | Organ Grinder's Blues | Royal Garden Blues
Live at The San Marino Jazz Festival, rec. 16.7.1995
Klein,Oscar (cl,co) | Patruno,Lino (g,bj) | Katz,Alexander (tb) | Wrobel,Engelbert (cl,ss) | Barton,Bob (p,voc) | Jankeje,Jan (b) | Beck,Gregor (dr) | Gillespie,Dana (voc)

JP 1053 CD | 2 CD | Jaco Pastorius Broadway Blues & Theresa
Jaco Pastorius Trio
Bluma | Teresa | Jaco Reggae | Berga | Medley | Reza | Broadway Blues | Chicken | Medley | Donna Lee- | Days Of Wine And Roses | Teresa(track 1-3)
Stuttgart, rec. March 1986
Pastorius,Jaco (p,el-b,voc) | Lagrene,Bireli (el-g) | Lübke,Peter (dr)

JP 1054 CD | CD | A' Portrait Of Jan Jankeje
Doc Cheatham Sextet
I Wanna Little Girl Like Mama
Cheatham,Doc (tp,voc) | Kelly,George (ts) | Casey,Al (g) | Richards,Charles 'Red' (p) | Jankeje,Jan (b) | Köszegi,Imre (dr)
Jan Jankeje Trio
Zum Trotz
Jankeje,Jan (b) | Wagenleiter,Klaus (p) | Braun,Werner (dr)
Bireli Lagrene Group
Paris
Live at Carnegie Hall,NYC, rec. 22.6.1984
Lagrene,Bireli (g) | Disley,William 'Diz' (g) | Jankeje,Jan (b)
Bireli Lagrene Quartet
My Melancholy Baby
Lagrene,Bireli (g) | Kling,Schmitto (v) | Lagrene,Gaiti (g) | Jankeje,Jan (b)
Tschirglo Waltz | Erster Tango (Sountrack Querelle)
Lagrene,Bireli (g) | Loeffler,Tschirglo (g) | Lagrene,Gaiti (g) | Jankeje,Jan (b)
Al Casey Quartet
It Don't Mean A Thing If It Ain't Got That Swing | Jit It
Casey,Al (g) | Richards,Charles 'Red' (p) | Jankeje,Jan (b) | Köszegi,Imre (dr)
Bireli Lagrene Trio
Moll-Blues
Lagrene,Bireli (g) | Juris,Vic (g) | Jankeje,Jan (b)
Jan Jankeje Septet
Weinsberg Dance With Me
Jankeje,Jan (b) | Marquart,Bernd (tp) | Cumming,Ian (tb) | Schwarz,Ulrich C. (fl) | Beck,Fred (ts) | Fischer,Dieter (g) | Braun,Werner (dr)
Oscar Klein's Jazz Show
Bratislava Fantasy
Klein,Oscar (cl,g,harm) | Jankeje,Jan (b) | Beck,Gregor (dr)
The Roman Swing Of Mrs. Stone
Klein,Oscar (tp) | Mussolini,Romano (p) | Jankeje,Jan (b) | Beck,Gregor (dr)
Benny Waters Quartet
Benny's Bounced Blues
Waters,Benny (as) | Wagner,Thilo (p) | Jankeje,Jan (b) | Beck,Gregor (dr)
George Kelly Quintet
Right On
Kelly,George (ts) | Richards,Charles 'Red' (p) | Casey,Al (g) | Jankeje,Jan (b) | Köszegi,Imre (dr)
Bireli Lagrene Quartet
Boxer Boogie
Lagrene,Bireli (g) | Reiter,Joerg (p) | Lagrene,Gaiti (g) | Jankeje,Jan (b)
Benny Waters Sextet
When The Saints Go Marching In
Waters,Benny (as,voc) | Lawrence,Andy (tp) | Katz,Alexander (tb) | Graf,Klaus (sax) | Polziehn,Olaf (keyboards) | Jankeje,Jan (b) | Ritz,Ellen (voc)
Hans Kumpf-Jan Jankeje
Bassclarinet
details unknown, rec. 1993
Kumpf,Hans (cl) | Jankeje,Jan (b)

JP 1055 CD | 2 CD | Routes To Django & Bireli Swing '81
Bireli Lagrene Ensemble
Fisco Place
Krokodil,Kirchheim/Teck, rec. 29./30.5.1980
Lagrene,Bireli (g) | Lagrene,Gaiti (g)
Bireli Swing 1979 | Boxer's Boogie
Lagrene,Bireli (g) | Reiter,Joerg (p) | Lagrene,Gaiti (g) | Loeffler,Tschirglo (g) | Jankeje,Jan (b)
All Of Me | Tschirglo Waltz | Bireli Blues 1979 | Wave | Don't Worry 'Bout Me
Lagrene,Bireli (g,b) | Lagrene,Gaiti (g) | Loeffler,Tschirglo (g) | Jankeje,Jan (b)
Latches
Lagrene,Bireli (g,b) | Lackerschmid,Wolfgang (vib) | Lagrene,Gaiti (g) | Loeffler,Tschirglo (g) | Jankeje,Jan (b)
I've Found A New Baby
Lagrene,Bireli (g,b) | Marquart,Bernd (tp) | Lagrene,Gaiti (g) | Loeffler,Tschirglo (g) | Jankeje,Jan (b)
My Melancholy Baby
Lagrene,Bireli (g,b) | Kling,Schmitto (v) | Lagrene,Gaiti (g) | Loeffler,Tschirglo (g) | Jankeje,Jan (b)
Bluma | Mirage
Lagrene,Bireli (g-solo)
B.L. | Swing Valse | Djangology | Bireli Hi Gogoro | Oh! Lady Be Good | Thundering Noise | Erster Tango (Sountrack Querelle) | September Song | Schwarze Augen | I Can't Give You Anything But Love | Carlos | Limehouse Blues | Nuages | How High The Moon | Night And Day
Ludwigsburg, rec. April 1981
Lagrene,Bireli (g) | Lagrene,Gaiti (g) | Loeffler,Tschirglo (g) | Rabe,Bernd (ss) | Jankeje,Jan (b) | Blairman,Allen (dr)

JP 1056 CD | CD | Routs To Django-Live At The 'Krokodil'
Fisco Place
Krokodil,Kirchheim/Teck, rec. 29./30.5.1980
Lagrene,Bireli (g) | Lagrene,Gaiti (g)
Bireli Swing 1979 | Boxer's Boogie
Lagrene,Bireli (g) | Reiter,Joerg (p) | Lagrene,Gaiti (g) | Loeffler,Tschirglo (g) | Jankeje,Jan (b)
All Of Me | Tschirglo Waltz | Bireli Blues 1979 | Wave | Don't Worry 'Bout Me
Lagrene,Bireli (g,b) | Lagrene,Gaiti (g) | Loeffler,Tschirglo (g) | Jankeje,Jan (b)
Latches
Lagrene,Bireli (g,b) | Lackerschmid,Wolfgang (vib) | Lagrene,Gaiti (g) | Loeffler,Tschirglo (g) | Jankeje,Jan (b)
I've Found A New Baby
Lagrene,Bireli (g,b) | Marquart,Bernd (tp) | Lagrene,Gaiti (g) | Loeffler,Tschirglo (g) | Jankeje,Jan (b)
My Melancholy Baby
Lagrene,Bireli (g,b) | Kling,Schmitto (v) | Lagrene,Gaiti (g) | Loeffler,Tschirglo (g) | Jankeje,Jan (b)
Bluma | Mirage
Lagrene,Bireli (g-solo)

JP 1058 CD | 2 CD | Jaco Pastorius Heavy'n Jazz & Stuttgart Aria
Jaco Pastorius Trio
Broadway Blues | Bluma- | Smoke On The Water- | Medley: | Purple Haze- | The Third Stone From The Sun- | Teen Town- | Star Spangled Banner | Reza | Honestly | Invitation
Live in Rome,Italy, rec. December 1986
Pastorius,Jaco (p,el-p,el-b,voc) | Lagrene,Bireli (g,el-g,voc) | Sendecki,Vladislaw (keyboards,synth) | Lübke,Peter (dr) | Bringolf,Serge (perc,voc)
Jaco Reggae
Stuttgart, rec. March 1986
Pastorius,Jaco (el-b) | Lagrene,Bireli (g) | Bringolf,Serge (dr)
American Boy | Donna Lee | Stuttgart Aria-1 | Jaco Reggae | Stuttgart Aria-2
Pastorius,Jaco (p,el-b,voc) | Lagrene,Bireli (el-g) | Lübke,Peter (dr)
Teresa | Days Of Wine And Roses
Pastorius,Jaco (p,el-b,voc) | Lagrene,Bireli (el-g) | Jankeje,Jan (b-synth,voc) | Lübke,Peter (dr)

JP 1059 CD | 2 CD | Live In Italy & Honestly
Improvisation No.1 | Teen Town | I Shot The Sheriff | Continuum | Fannie Mae | Black Market | Satin Doll | Part 1-10
rec. 1986
Pastorius,Jaco (el-b) | Lagrene,Bireli (el-g) | Börcsök,Aliosa (dr)

JP 1061 CD | 2 CD | A Tribute To Django Reinhardt
Bireli Lagrene Group
Minor Swing | Paris | Toulouse Blues | September Song | Rue De Pierre | Djangology
Live at Carnegie Hall,NYC, rec. 22.6.1984
Lagrene,Bireli (g) | Disley,William 'Diz' (g) | Jankeje,Jan (b)
Mirage
Live at Alte Oper,Frankfurt/M., rec. July 1981
Lagrene,Bireli (g) | Disley,William 'Diz' (g) | Jankeje,Jan (b)
Daphne | Ornithology- | How High The Moon- | Bireli | Minor Swing | Spain | Paris | Rue De Pierre | Ornithology | Sim | Nuits De St.Germain-Des-Pres | The Night Of A Champion | I Can't Give You Anything But Love | Moll-Blues
Live at The Jazz Festival Freiburg, rec. 1./2.6.1985
Lagrene,Bireli (g,el-b) | Juris,Vic (g) | Disley,William 'Diz' (g) | Lagrene,Gaiti (g) | Jankeje,Jan (b)

JP 1062 CD | CD | Live In Berlin/Friedrichstadtpalast
Louis Armstrong And His All Stars
When It's Sleepy Time Down South | Mack The Knife(Moritat) | Blueberry Hill | Without A Song | Struttin' With Some Barbecue | The Faithfull Husar | Memories Of You | Hello Dolly | The Faithfull Husar(radio-version)
Live at Friedrichstadtpalast,Berlin, rec. 20.-22.3.1965
Armstrong,Louis (tp,voc) | Glenn,Tyree (tb) | Shu,Eddie (cl,sax) | Kyle,Billy (p) | Shaw,Arvell (b) | Barcelona,Danny (dr)

JP 1063 CD | CD | The Legendary Berlin Concert Part 2
Back Home Again In Indiana | Tiger Rag | Black And Blue | When I Grow Too Old To Dream | Lover Come Back To Me | Can't Help Lovin' Dat Man | When The Saints Go Marching In | Royal Garden Blues | How High The Moon | Stompin' At The Savoy | I Left My Heart In San Francisco | My Man | Mop Mop | When It's Sleepy Time Down South | Hello Dolly
Live at Friedrichstadtpalast,Berlin, rec. 22.3.1965
Armstrong,Louis (tp,voc) | Glenn,Tyree (tb) | Shu,Eddie (cl) | Kyle,Billy (p) | Shaw,Arvell (b) | Barcelona,Danny (dr) | Brown,Jewel (voc)

JP 1064 CD | CD | Another Side Of Jaco Pastorius
Jaco Pastorius Groups
Fannie Mae | Honestly(part 2) | Chicken | Jaco Reggae | Reza | Days Of Wine And Roses | Invitation | Stuttgart 2 | Teresa | Continuum
different Places, rec. details unknown
Pastorius,Jaco (el-b) | Lagrene,Bireli (el-g) | Sendecki,Vladislaw (keyboards,synth) | Jankeje,Jan (b-synth) | Böröcz,Thomas (dr) | Lübke,Peter (dr) | Bringolf,Serge (dr,perc)

JP 1065 CD | CD | Pick-A-Blues
Oscar Klein & Katie Kern Group
Going To New York | Moods | Long Lost Love | Honky Tonk Train Blues | Free My Mind | Blues For Django And Mezz | Pick That Thing(dedicated to Albert Lee) | Cotton Field Boogie | When The Saints Go Marching In | Boxer Boogie | Goin' To Chicago | C Jam Blues | Caravan(A Tribute to Charlie Antolini) | Blue Dreams
Wernau, rec. 27.8.2001
Klein,Oscar (tp,cl,g,harm) | Kern,Katie (el-g,voc) | Nemet,Chris (p,body-perc) | Jankeje,Jan (b) | Altbart,Heini (dr)

JP 1067 CD | CD | Swing & Folk | EAN 722746706724
Wedeli Köhler Group
Nuages | Avalon | Somewhere Over The Rainbow | I Got Rhythm
Walldorf, rec. 2002
Köhler,Wedeli (v,g) | Köhler,Sascha (g) | Wagner,Thilo (p) | Jankeje,Jan (b) | Lindfors,Will (dr) | Balogh,Elemar (cymbal)
Alter Be Tyar | Heycigany | Zyghanigili & Zimto Cardas
Köhler,Wedeli (v) | Köhler,Benjamin (p) | Köhler,Sascha (g) | Reinhardt,Bruno (b) | Lindfors,Will (dr) | Balogh,Elemar (cymbal)
Sindengo Walzare | See You In My Dreams | Fate

Köhler,Wedeli (g) | Köhler,Sascha (g) | Gropp,Peter (b) | Lindfors,Will (dr) | Balogh,Elemar (cymbal)
Wals De Fantasia
Köhler,Wedeli (g) | Köhler,Sascha (g) | Lindfors,Will (dr) | Balogh,Elemar (cymbal)
A Boy On A Dolphin(Tina Tue)
Köhler,Wedeli (v) | Köhler,Benjamin (v) | Köhler,Sascha (g) | Lindfors,Will (dr) | Balogh,Elemar (cymbal)
Wien Wien Nur Du Allein | Somewhere In My Dreams
Köhler,Wedeli (v) | Köhler,Sascha (g) | Lindfors,Will (dr) | Balogh,Elemar (cymbal)

JP 1068 CD | CD | Mobil | EAN 722746706823
Jan Jankeje's Party And Swingband
Petite Fleur | Bye Bye Blues | Honky Tonk Blues | Wild Cat Blues | What A Wonderful World | When The Saints Go Marching In | Blueberry Hill | Boxer Boogie | Sentimental Journey | Creole Jazz | Ain't She Sweet | St.Louis Blues | When You're Smiling | Stranger On The Shore | Schwarze Augen | Du Hast Glück Bei Den Frau'n Bel Ami | I Can't Give You Anything But Love | Happy Birthday
Wernau, rec. 2002
Jankeje,Jan (b) | Havlicek,Franta (cl,sax) | Klimes,Mirko (bj)

JP 1069 CD | CD | It's The Talk Of The Town
Stuttgarter Dixieland All Stars
Aunt Hagar's Blues | Potato Head Blues | What A Wonderful World | Someday You'll Be Sorry | Martinique | Down In Honky Tonk Town | Hotter Than That | Black And Blue | Weary Blues | Gee Baby Ain't I Good To You | Once In A While | It's The Talk Of The Town | Slow Boat To China | Bed And Breakfast | From Monday On
Karlsdorf, rec. 1.11.2002
Stuttgarter Dixieland All Stars | Lange,Peter (tp,voc,arr) | Katz,Alexander (tb,voc) | Lamparter,Peter (cl) | Schwer,Harald (p) | Lamparter,Jochen (g,bj,voc) | Jankeje,Jan (b) | Braun,Werner (dr)

JP 1070 CD | CD | Still Young | EAN 722746707028
Katie Kern
Bad Feeling | Jammin' With Jimmy | Goin' Where The Moonon Crosses The Yellow Dog
Wernau, rec. 24.-26.2.2003
Kern,Katie (g,voc)
Katie Kern-Werner Dannemann
'Til I Can Gain Control Again
Kern,Katie (g,voc) | Dannemann,Werner (g)
Katie Kern-Oscar Klein
He's Fine
Kern,Katie (g,voc) | Klein,Oscar (cl)
Katie Kern Group
Still Young
Kern,Katie (g,el-g,voc) | Harriman,Paul (b) | Grant,Steve (dr)
Last Waltz
Kern,Katie (g,el-g,voc) | Marquardt,Klaus (v) | Harriman,Paul (b) | Grant,Steve (dr)
Restless
Kern,Katie (g,voc) | Marquardt,Klaus (v) | Dannemann,Werner (g) | Harriman,Paul (b) | Grant,Steve (dr)
Rainy Day Blues
Kern,Katie (g,,voc) | Reiter,Joerg (fender-rhodes) | Harriman,Paul (b) | Grant,Steve (dr)
Route 66
Kern,Katie (g,,voc) | Dannemann,Werner (g) | Reiter,Joerg (fender-rhodes) | Harriman,Paul (b) | Grant,Steve (dr)
Hey Porter | Prosecutor
Kern,Katie (g,,voc) | Dannemann,Werner (g) | Harriman,Paul (b) | Grant,Steve (dr)
The Man I Love
Kern,Katie (g,,voc) | Marquardt,Klaus (v) | Reiter,Joerg (fender-rhodes) | Jankeje,Jan (b) | Grant,Steve (dr)
Cherokee
Kern,Katie (g,,el-g,voc) | Marquardt,Klaus (v) | Jankeje,Jan (b) | Grant,Steve (dr)

JP 1071 | DVD | Pick-A-Blues Live | EAN 722746707196
Oscar Klein Band
Going To New York | Pick That Thing(dedicated to Albert Lee) | Moods | Long Lost Love | Honky Tonk Train Blues | Free My Mind | Weinsberg Dance With Me | When The Saints Go Marching In | Caravan(A Tribute to Charlie Antolini) | Me And My Guitar | Shake That Boogie | Look On Yonder Wall | Kurhadanadur
Oeringen, rec. 11.7.2003
Klein,Oscar (tp,g,harm) | Kern,Katie (el-g,voc) | Nemet,Chris (p) | Jankeje,Jan (b) | Altbart,Heini (dr)
Extras: | Interview | Biography

JCOA | Universal Music Germany

1001/2 | CD | Comminications
The Jazz Composer's Orchestra
Communications No.8
rec. 24.1.1968
Jazz Composer's Orchestra,The | Mantler,Michael (cond,comp) | Cherry,Don (co) | Barbieri,Gato (ts) | Michels,Lloyd (fl-h) | Brecker,Randy (fl-h) | Knepper,Jimmy (tb) | Jeffers,Jack (b-tb) | Northern,Bob (fr-h) | Watkins,Julius (fr-h) | Johnson,Howard (tuba) | Lacy,Steve (ss) | Gibbons,Al (ss) | Hull,Gene (as) | Donovan,Bob (as) | Tabackin,Lew (ts) | Barrow,George (ts) | Davis,Charles (bs) | Bley,Carla (p) | Carter,Kent (b) | Carter,Ron (b) | Davis,Richard (b) | Haden,Charlie (b) | Workman,Reggie (b) | Cyrille,Andrew (dr)
Communications No.9
rec. 8.5.1968
Jazz Composer's Orchestra,The | Mantler,Michael (cond,comp) | Coryell,Larry (g) | Michels,Lloyd (fl-h) | Furtado,Steve (fl-h) | Knepper,Jimmy (tb) | Jeffers,Jack (b-tb) | Northern,Bob (fr-h) | Watkins,Julius (fr-h) | Johnson,Howard (tuba) | Gibbons,Al (ss) | Marcus,Steve (ss) | Wess,Frank (as) | Donovan,Bob (as) | Tabackin,Lew (ts) | Barrow,George (ts) | Davis,Charles (bs) | Bley,Carla (p) | Carter,Ron (b) | Gomez,Eddie (b) | Haden,Charlie (b) | Swallow,Steve (b) | Workman,Reggie (b) | Harris,Beaver (dr)
Communications No.10
Jazz Composer's Orchestra,The | Mantler,Michael (cond,comp) | Rudd,Roswell (tb) | Michels,Lloyd (fl-h) | Furtado,Steve (fl-h) | Knepper,Jimmy (tb) | Jeffers,Jack (b-tb) | Northern,Bob (fr-h) | Watkins,Julius (fr-h) | Johnson,Howard (tuba) | Gibbons,Al (ss) | Marcus,Steve (ss) | Wess,Frank (as) | Donovan,Bob (as) | Tabackin,Lew (ts) | Barrow,George (ts) | Davis,Charles (bs) | Bley,Carla (p) | Carter,Ron (b) | Gomez,Eddie (b) | Haden,Charlie (b) | Swallow,Steve (b) | Workman,Reggie (b) | Harris,Beaver (dr) | played by Steve Swallow,The bassintroduction is
Preview
Jazz Composer's Orchestra,The | Mantler,Michael (cond,comp) | Sanders,Pharoah (ts) | Michels,Lloyd (fl-h) | Furtado,Steve (fl-h) | Knepper,Jimmy (tb) | Jeffers,Jack (b-tb) | Northern,Bob (fr-h) | Watkins,Julius (fr-h) | Johnson,Howard (tuba) | Gibbons,Al (ss) | Marcus,Steve (ss) | Wess,Frank (as) | Donovan,Bob (as) | Tabackin,Lew (ts) | Barrow,George (ts) | Davis,Charles (bs) | Bley,Carla (p) | Carter,Ron (b) | Gomez,Eddie (b) | Haden,Charlie (b) | Swallow,Steve (b) | Workman,Reggie (b) | Harris,Beaver (dr)
Communications No.11-part 1 | Communications No.11-part 2
rec. 20./21.6.1968
Jazz Composer's Orchestra,The | Mantler,Michael (cond,comp) | Taylor,Cecil (p) | Michels,Lloyd (fl-h) | Furtado,Steve (fl-h) | Knepper,Jimmy (tb) | Jeffers,Jack (b-tb) | Northern,Bob (fr-h) | Watkins,Julius (fr-h) | Johnson,Howard (tuba) | Gibbons,Al (ss) | Marcus,Steve (ss) | Donovan,Bob (as) | Lyons,Jimmy (as) | Tabackin,Lew (ts) | Barbieri,Gato (ts) | Davis,Charles (bs) | Cunningham,Bob (b) | Haden,Charlie (b) | Workman,Reggie (b) | Johnson,Reggie (b) | Silva,Alan (b) | Cyrille,Andrew (dr)

JHM Records | sunny moon Musikvertrieb

JHM 3601 | CD | Magic Box
Joe Haider Quintet
Magic Box | Fragile Youth | Ni Deklaw Evol | Moving Out | Epitaph For Tom | Jumpin' At The Lochness | Once Again | No Samba
Kreuzlingen,Schweiz, rec. 26./27.11.1994
Haider,Joe (p) | Joris,Bert (tp,fl-h) | Schwaller,Roman (ts) | Eckinger,Isla (b) | Haffner,Wolfgang (dr)

JHM 3602 | CD | Conte Candoli Meets The Joe Haider Trio
Conte Candoli With The Joe Haider Trio
What Is This Thing | Woody'n You | Blue Daniel | Confirmation | All The Things You Are
Live at Jazzclub Moods,Zürich,CH, rec. 20.3.1994
Candoli,Conte (tp) | Haider,Joe (p) | Eckinger,Isla (b) | Haffner,Wolfgang (dr)
Tin Tin Deo | Darn That Dream
Live at Kantonsschule,Baden,CH, rec. 21.3.1994
Candoli,Conte (tp) | Haider,Joe (p) | Eckinger,Isla (b) | Haffner,Wolfgang (dr)

JHM 3605 | CD | Welcome Back From Outer Space
The New Roman Schwaller Jazzquartet
The Tag In F | Horacio Hieronymus | Parker 51 | Ali's Nest | Reflections | Brütsch Over Troubled Water | Mannix | Jumpin' With Symphony Sid | Groove Merchant | Bebop | Pacic | Trinkle Tinkle | The Tag In Bb
München, rec. 16.10.1995
Schwaller,Roman (ts) | Kent,Oliver (p) | Stabenow,Thomas (b) | Gonzi,Mario (dr)

JHM 3608 | CD | Bilein
Don Menza And The Joe Haider Trio
Bilein | It's April Again | Broadbottom | Karen's Birthday Waltz | Processional | Royal | B-4-U Leave
Bad Kissingen, rec. 17.3.1997
Menza,Don (sax) | Haider,Joe (p) | Gordan,Christopher (b) | Kreibich,Paul (dr)

JHM 3609 | CD | Visionary
Thomas Faist Jazzquartet
Late Spring | You Call-We Fly | Nina | Visionary | Childhood | Selffulfilling Prophecys | Involved | The Song Is You | After All
München, rec. 25.7.1995
Faist,Thomas (ts) | Lang,Walter (p) | Woodard,Will (b) | Hollander,Rick (dr)

JHM 3610 | CD | Hot Mallets...Live!
Hot Mallets
Stuffy
Radio Suisse Romand,Geneve, rec. 5.3.1981
Hot Mallets | Scherrer,Andy (ts) | Pilet,Michel (ts) | Eckinger,Isla (tb,vib) | Schmidli,Peter (g) | Chaix,Henri (p) | Du Bois,Alain (b)
Lay-By | Sophisticated Lady | Jack's Blues | Ring Dem Bells | Jumpin' At The Woodside | Lover Man(Oh,Where Can You Be?) | Bean And The Boys | Such Sweet Thunder | Caravan
Live at The Widder Bar,Zürich,CH, rec. 10./11.1983
Hot Mallets | Scherrer,Andy (ts) | Eckinger,Isla (tb,vib) | Schmidli,Peter (g) | Chaix,Henri (p) | Du Bois,Alain (b)
Jumpin' Punkins | Tickle Toe
Radio L., rec. 22.9.1984
Hot Mallets | Scherrer,Andy (ts) | Eckinger,Isla (tb,vib) | Schmidli,Peter (g) | Chaix,Henri (p) | Du Bois,Alain (b)

JHM 3611 | 2 CD | Three Generations Of Tenorsaxophone
Johnny Griffin-Sal Nistico-Roman Schwaller Sextet
Rue Chaptal | I Should Have Known | Waltz For Sweetie | Backlog | My Little Brown Book- | The Things I Leave Behind- | Bean And The Boys
Live at The Allotria,München, rec. 11.1.1985
Griffin,Johnny (ts) | Nistico,Sal (ts) | Schwaller,Roman (ts) | Grabowsky,Paul (p) | Stabenow,Thomas (b) | Dudli,Joris (dr)

JHM 3612 | CD | Some Changes In Life
Roman Schwaller Jazz Quartet
Tramline | Johnny Comes Lately | I Got A Crush On You | Brütsch Over Troubled Water | Some Changes In Life | The Loco Motif(Jimmy Cobb And The Locomotive) | In A Sentimental Mood | In Your Own Sweet Way
Live at Bisi's Piano Bar & Eisenbeiz,Frauenfeld,CH, rec. 10.& 17.11.1996
Schwaller,Roman (ts) | Kent,Oliver (p) | Stabenow,Thomas (b) | Cobb,Jimmy (dr)

JHM 3613 | CD | Survival Song
Munich Saxophone Family
Timezone Earth | La Paloma Revisited | Survival Song | Lotus | Drehung Inform | 100+8 | Illusion | Turnaround | Abenteuer Unter Wasser | Profile Of Jackie | Orange Blue
Zürich,CH, rec. 19./20.1.1999
Munich Saxophone Family | Trübsbach,Florian (ss,as) | Seefelder,Jürgen (ss,ts) | Schwaller,Roman (ts) | Zoller,Thomas (bs)

JHM 3614 | CD | A Night Of Blues & Ballads
Red Holloway With The Matthias Bätzel Trio
Teach Me Tonight | I Wish You Love | The Lamp Is Low | Nothin' I Do Is Right | You Don't Know What Love Is | Good Groove | Lazy Daisy
Weimar, rec. 1999
Holloway,Red (as,ts,voc) | Bätzel,Matthias (org) | Kagerer,Helmut (g) | Keul,Michael (dr)

JHM 3615 | CD | The Best Of Four For Jazz & Benny Bailey
Four For Jazz & Benny Bailey
What Is Happening | Music For A Quintet | Prompt
Stuttgart, rec. 12.-14.12.1970
Four For Jazz | Bailey,Benny (tp) | Bigler,Heinz (as) | Haider,Joe (p,el-p) | Eckinger,Isla (b) | Giger,Hans-Peter (dr)
Four For Jazz
All Them Chicken
Four For Jazz | Bigler,Heinz (as) | Haider,Joe (p) | Eckinger,Isla (b) | Giger,Hans-Peter (dr)
Power Of Nature | Mademoiselle Martine | For John Coltrane
Stuttgart, rec. 1971
Four For Jazz | Bigler,Heinz (as) | Haider,Joe (p,el-p) | Eckinger,Isla (b) | Giger,Hans-Peter (dr)

JHM 3616 | CD | Levitation | EAN 7619954036169
Domenic Landolf Quartet
Le Modulor | The Flight Back | Parthenope | If I Love Again | Levitation | Liberty Belle | Slow River | Tell Me The Truth
Zürich,CH, rec. 1./2.9.1999
Landolf,Domenic (ss,ts) | Brodbeck,Jean-Paul (p) | Gisler,Fabian (b) | Egli,Dominik (dr)
-> Note: The Piano was recorded in the late 1960's

JHM 3617 | CD | Clifford Jordan Meets Klaus Weiss | EAN 7619954036176
Clifford Jordan Quintet
Blue 'N' Boogie | Eye Witness Blues | Lush Life | Highest Mountain | L.A. Calling | Lover Man(Oh,Where Can You Be?) | Don't Get Around Much Anymore | Una Noche Con Francis
Live at 'Opus One',Wien, rec. 9.2.1987
Weiss,Klaus (dr) | Stabenow,Thomas (b) | Di Gioia,Roberto (p) | Schröder,John (g) | Jordan,Clifford (ts)

JHM 3618 | CD | Green Dumplings | EAN 7619954036183
Matthias Bätzel Trio
Green Dumplings | Yesterdays | First Rain | Wenn's Mailüfterl Weht | Blue Eyes | A Short Story | Play Of Colours | I'll Never Forget That | Jack's Theme
Weimar, rec. January 2000
Bätzel,Matthias (p,org) | Kagerer,Helmut (g) | Keul,Michael (dr)
Matthias Bätzel-Michael Keul
How Deep Is The Ocean
Bätzel,Matthias (org) | Keul,Michael (dr)

JHM 3619 | CD | Grandfather's Garden
Joe Haider Trio
Grandfather's Garden | Bilein | Blues For Alf | You And The Night And The Music | Sunday Child | Bright Angel Falls | You | T(h)ree
Zürich,CH, rec. 19./20.2.2000
Haider,Joe (p) | Antoniou,Giorgos (b) | Aebi,Daniel (dr)

JHM 3620 | CD | Something About Water
Matthias Spillmann Septet
Something About Water | Suite Of Gold And Blue(part 1-3) | Midsummer Night | Air | With A Little Help From My Friends | Kinderlied No.1 | Hale-Bop
Zürich-Altstetten,CH, rec. 3./4.2.2000
Spillmann,Matthias (tp) | Bamert,Bernhard (tb) | Landolf,Domenic (b-cl,ts) | Lüthi,Thomas (ss,ts) | Tardin,Léo (p) | Gisler,Fabian (b) | Egli,Dominik (dr)

JHM 3621 | CD | That's A Plenty
International Chicago-Jazz Orchestra
That's A Plenty | Petite Fleur | When My Sugar Walks Down The Street | Hindustan | Baby Won't You Please Come Home | Muskrat Ramble | If I Could Be With You One Hour Tonight | I Found A New Baby | Save It Pretty Mama | Black Coffee | At The Jazz Band Ball | Jazz Me Blues | Just Another Blues | I Ain't Gonna Give Nobody None Of My Jelly Roll | Liza | Big Butter And Egg Man From The West
Bubicon,CH, rec. 10.-12.7.2000
International Chicago-Jazz Orchestra | Saunders,Tom (co,voc) | Allred,Bill (tb) | Bigler,Heinz (cl) | Varro,Johnny (p) | Eckinger,Isla (b) | Rebmann,Rolf (dr)

JHM 3622 | CD | Katzenvilla
Joe Haider Trio
My Little Darling | Fate Of A Child | Katzenvilla | EJP | And Now | Capricorn
Stuttgart, rec. 12.10.1971
Haider,Joe (p) | Eckinger,Isla (b) | Favre,Pierre (dr)

JHM 3623 | CD | Michael Beck Trio
Michael Beck Trio
Loose Ends | 928 | Point Turnagain | Farewell | The Theme Of The Defeat | Open Doors | Three Men In A Boat | Everything I Love | Detour Ahead | Loose Ends(alt.take)
Zürich,CH, rec. 12./13.2.2000
Beck,Michael (p) | Oester,Bänz (b) | Rohrer,Samuel (dr)

JHM 3624 | CD | Consequences
Brigitte Dietrich-Joe Haider Jazz Orchestra
Waltz For My Lady | Consequences | Bilein | Obvious | Suite Of Gold And Blue(part 3) | Abstract | You | Blues For Alf | Caravan
Zürich,CH, rec. 1.-3.5.2000
Haider,Joe (p) | Burkart,Ingolf (tp) | Schenker,Daniel 'Dani' (tp) | Spillmann,Matthias (tp) | Mosele,René (tb) | Bamert,Bernhard (tb) | Weber,Adrian (tb) | Blanc,Daniel 'Dani' (fl,as) | Geiger,Thomi (cl,ss,ts) | Landolf,Domenic (b-cl,ss,ts) | Wettstein,Ruedi (cl,as,bs) | Antoniou,Giorgos (b) | Aebi,Daniel (dr) | Dietrich,Brigitte (co-ld)

JHM 3625 | CD | The Song Is You
Horn Knox
Maria | Arco I | The Song Is You | Iris | Michelle | Angie | Laura | Chan's Song | Pizzicato | Beatrice | Jeannine | Arco II
Zürich,CH, rec. 29.-31.1.2001
Horn Knox | Spillmann,Matthias (tp) | Bamert,Bernhard (tb) | Widmer,Klaus (ss,ts) | Zisman,Michael (bandoneon) | Beck,Michael (p,el-p) | Antoniou,Giorgos (b) | Aebi,Daniel (dr) | Frauchinger,Katrin (voc)

JHM 3626 | CD | A Magyar-The Hungarian-Die Ungarische
Joe Haider Trio
A Magyar-The Hungarian-Die Ungarische | A Moment In Montreux | Tante Nelly | Bolero In D | Moving Out | Friends | Someday My Prince Will Come | One For Trule
Zürich,CH, rec. 10./11.4.2001
Haider,Joe (p) | Antoniou,Giorgos (b) | Aebi,Daniel (dr)

JHM 3627 | 2 CD | Give Me A Double
Slide Hampton-Joe Haider Jazz Orchestra
Tribute | Grandfather's Garden | Think | Like A Blues | Tante Nelly | What Is Happening | Quiet Night | Petaluma | Waltz For My Lady | Time For Love
Live at The 'Domicile', München, rec. 17.-19.1.1974
Hampton,Slide (tb) | Haider,Joe (p) | Bailey,Benny (tp) | Sulieman[Leonard Graham],Idrees (tp) | Van Rooyen,Ack (tp) | Burgess,Bob 'Bobby' (tb) | Van Lier,Erik (tb) | Gordon,Dexter (ts) | Povel,Ferdinand (ts) | Scherrer,Andy (ts) | Eckinger,Isla (b) | Brooks,Billy (dr)

JHM 3628 | CD | Monk's Mood | EAN 7619954036282
Matthias Bätzel Trio
Work | Ugly Beauty | Monk's Mood | Pannonica | Green Chimneys | Ruby My Dear | Off Minor | Humph | Bolivar Blues | Crepuscule With Nellie | Japanese Folk Song
Worbboden,CH, rec. 17./18.11.2001
Bätzel,Matthias (org) | Kagerer,Helmut (g) | Keul,Michael (dr)

JHM 3629 | CD | The Original Tunes | EAN 7619954036299
Roman Schwaller Nonet
Love Someone You | Some Changes In Life | Pacific View Drive | Epitaph For Tom | Ready Set Go | A Line For Two | La Ballade Pour Pipette | I Should Have Known
Live at Psychiatric Clinic Muensterlingen and Kartause Ittingen,CH, rec. 19./20.10.2001
Schwaller,Roman (ts) | Tuscher,Peter (tp) | Herrlich,Johannes (tb) | Varner,Tom (fr-h) | Landolf,Domenic (b-cl) | Partyka,Edward (tuba) | Raible,Claus (p) | Stabenow,Thomas (b) | Gonzi,Mario (dr)

JMT Edition | Edel Contraire

514001-2 | CD | After The Beginning Again
Cassandra Wilson Group
There She Goes | Round About Midnight | Yazoo Moon | Sweet Black Night | My Corner Of The Sky | Baubles Bangles And Beads | Summerwind
NYC, rec. July/August 1991
Wilson,Cassandra (voc) | Weidman,James (p,synth) | Harris,Kevin Bruce (el-b) | Johnson,Mark (dr,perc) | Haynes,Jeff (perc)
Redbone
Wilson,Cassandra (perc,voc) | Weidman,James (p,synth,perc) | Harris,Kevin Bruce (perc,el-b) | Johnson,Mark (dr,perc) | Haynes,Jeff (perc)

919001-2 | CD | Motherland Pulse
Steve Coleman Group
Another Level | Cüd Ba-Rith | Wights Waits For Weights | On This | The Glide Was In The Ride | Motherland Pulse
NYC, rec. March 1985
Coleman,Steve (as) | Allen,Geri (p) | Plaxico,Lonnie (b) | Smith,Marvin 'Smitty' (dr,perc)
Irate Blues
Coleman,Steve (as) | Haynes,Graham (tp) | Allen,Geri (p) | Plaxico,Lonnie (b) | Smith,Marvin 'Smitty' (dr,perc)
No Goodtime Fairies
Coleman,Steve (as) | Haynes,Graham (tp) | Allen,Geri (p) | Plaxico,Lonnie (b) | Johnson,Mark (dr) | Wilson,Cassandra (voc)

919003-2 | CD | As One
Jane Ira Bloom-Fred Hersch Duo
Waiting For Daylight | Desert | A Child's Song(For Charlie Haden) | Miyako | Inside | Winter Of My Discontent | Janeology
NYC, rec. September 1984
Bloom,Jane Ira (ss) | Hersch,Fred (p)

919004-2 | CD | Point Of View
Cassandra Wilson And Her Quintet
Square Roots | Blue In Green | Never | Desperate Move | Love And Hate | I Am Waiting | I Wished On The Moon | I Thought You Knew
NYC, rec. 14./15.12.1985
Wilson,Cassandra (voc) | Moncur III,Grachan (tb) | Coleman,Steve (as,perc) | Bourelly,Jean-Paul (el-g) | Plaxico,Lonnie (b,el-b) | Johnson,Mark (dr)

919005-2 | CD | On The Edge Of Tomorrow
Steve Coleman And Five Elements
I Am Going Home | Change The Guard | Little One I'll Miss You | Almost There | Nine The Five | Fat Layback | Fire Revisited | Profile Man | Metaphysical Phunktion | Stone Bone | Perfect Union | It Is Time | T-T-Tim

Brooklyn,NY, rec. 28./29.1.& 1.2.1986
Coleman,Steve (as,voc) | Five Elements | Haynes,Graham (tp) | Bell,Kelvyn (el-g,voc) | Harris,Kevin Bruce (el-b,voc) | Allen,Geri (synth) | Smith,Marvin 'Smitty' (dr,perc) | Johnson,Mark (dr,perc) | Wilson,Cassandra (voc)

919006-2 | CD | Sound Songs
Jay Clayton-Jerry Granelli
Four Tom-Toms | Goodbye Pork Pie Hat | Togi | Joyous March | Somewhere Else | I'm Nobody | Forgotten Song | Everything Machine | Crystals
Seattle,WA, rec. December 1985
Clayton,Jay (voice) | Granelli,Jerry (dr,perc)

919007-2 | CD | The Little Trumpet
Herb Robertson Group
The Little Trumpet: | Panacoustica(Overture) | Despairing Little Trumpet | Friendship | The Wellcoming | Sad Fate | Lullaby | Wild Disputes | Harmony | The Night | The Marvelous Event | Panacoustica
Brooklyn,NY, rec. July 1986
Robertson,Herb (fl-h,co,pocket-tp) | Berne,Tim (as) | Eubanks,Robin (tb) | Stewart,Robert 'Bob' (tuba) | Frisell,Bill (g,el-g) | Smith,Warren (vib,marimba) | Cox,Anthony (b) | Nicholson,Reggie (dr)

919008-2 | CD | Shelter
Craig Harris And Tailgater's Tales
Shelter Suite: | Subway Scenarios- | Sea Of Swollen Hands- | Three Hots And A Cot- | Shelter(Reprise)- | Bags And Rags | Cootie | Reminiscing | Sound Sketches
NYC, rec. November/December 1986
Harris,Craig (tb,didjeridoo) | Allen,Eddie E.J. (tp) | Byron,Don (cl,b-cl) | Cox,Anthony (b) | AkLaff,Pheeroan (dr)
Shelter
NYC, rec. Nov./Dec.1986
Harris,Craig (tb,didjeridoo) | Allen,Eddie E.J. (tp) | Byron,Don (cl,b-cl) | Cox,Anthony (b) | AkLaff,Pheeroan (dr) | Samuel,Tunde (voc)
Africans Unite
Harris,Craig (tb,didjeridoo) | Allen,Eddie E.J. (tp) | Byron,Don (cl,b-cl) | Williams,Rod (p) | Cox,Anthony (b) | AkLaff,Pheeroan (dr) | Samuel,Tunde (voc)

919009-2 | CD | Jungle Cowboy
Jean-Paul Bourelly Group
Love Line | Tryin' To Get Over | Drifter | Jungle Cowboy | No Time To Share | Can't Get Enough | Parade | Groove With Me
NYC, rec. December 1986
Bourelly,Jean-Paul (g,voc) | Hemphill,Julius (as) | Bell,Kelvyn (g,voc) | Bourelly,Carl (synth,voc) | Cash,Freddie (b,voc) | Johnson,Kevin (dr,voc) | Caramouche,Greg (perc,voc)
Hope You Find Your Way
Bourelly,Jean-Paul (g,voc) | Hemphill,Julius (as) | Bell,Kelvyn (g,voc) | Bourelly,Carl (synth,voc) | Cash,Freddie (b,voc) | Johnson,Kevin (dr,voc) | Caramouche,Greg (perc,voc) | Williams,Alyson (voc)
Mother Earth
Bourelly,Jean-Paul (g,voc) | Hemphill,Julius (as) | Bell,Kelvyn (g,voc) | Bourelly,Carl (synth,voc) | Cash,Freddie (b,voc) | Johnson,Kevin (dr,voc) | Cyrille,Andrew (dr) | Caramouche,Greg (perc,voc)

919013-2 | CD | 'X'-cerpts:Live At Willisau | EAN 025091901326
Herb Robertson Quintet
Karmic Ramifications: | Vibration | Formation | Dissipation | Transformation | Flocculus
Mohren,Willisau, rec. 31.1.1987
Robertson,Herb (tp,fl-h,pocket-tp) | Berne,Tim (as) | Tsilis,Gust William (vib) | Horner,Lindsey (b) | Baron,Joey (dr)

919014-2 | CD | First Line | EAN 025091901425
Bob Stewart First Line Band
First Line | C.J. | Metamorphosis | Sometimes I Feel Like A Motherless Child | Nonet | Hey! Mama! | Bush Baby | Surinam | Hambone
NYC, rec. November 1997
Stewart,Bob (tuba) | Davis,Stanton (tp) | Turre,Steve (tb,shells) | Bell,Kelvyn (el-g) | Muhammad,Idris[Leo Morris] (dr) | Tuncboyaci[Boyaciyan],Arto (perc)

919015-2 | CD | Blackout In The Square Root Of Soul | EAN 025091901524
Craig Harris And Tailgater's Tales
Blackout In The Square Root Of Soul | Phase I- | Phase II- | Congratulations- | Fase I | Love Joy | Blues Dues | Dingo | Awakening Ancestores
NYC, rec. Nov.1987
Harris,Craig (tb,didjeridoo,voc) | Allen,Eddie E.J. (tp) | Byron,Don (cl,bs) | Bourelly,Jean-Paul (g) | Criner,Clyde (keyboards) | Cox,Anthony (b) | Peterson,Ralph (dr)

919016-2 | CD | Black Pastels | EAN 025091901623
Hank Roberts Group
Black Pastels | Jamil(For Jane) | Mountain Speaks | Rain Village | Choqueno(For Chuck Smart) | This Quietness | Grandpappy's Barn Dance Death Dance(For Daddy Ben Besson) | Scarecrow Shakedown
NYC, rec. Nov./Dec.1987
Roberts,Hank (cello,fiddle,12-string-g,voice) | Anderson,Ray (tb) | Eubanks,Robin (tb) | Taylor,Dave (b-tb) | Berne,Tim (as) | Frisell,Bill (g,bj,12-string-g) | Baron,Joey (dr,perc)
Lucky's Lament
Roberts,Hank (cello,fiddle,12-string-g,voice) | Anderson,Ray (tb) | Eubanks,Robin (tb) | Taylor,Dave (b-tb) | Berne,Tim (as) | Frisell,Bill (g,bj,12-string-g) | Dresser,Mark (b) | Baron,Joey (dr,perc)

919017-2 | CD | Peter Herborn's Acute Insights | EAN 025091901722
Peter Herborn's Acute Insights
Free Forward And Ahead | All Along The Sunstream | Beauty Is... | Love In Tune(For B.A. part 1-4) | Love In Tune(For B.A.) | Live Force- | Living Yet-
Ludwigsburg, rec. Nov.1987/Jan.1988
Herborn,Peter (tb) | Wheeler,Kenny (tp,fl-h) | Read,Hugo (fl,as) | Kaiser,Wollie (alto-fl,b-cl,ss,ts,b-fl) | Walter,Peter (keyboards) | Wells,Tim (b) | Thönes,Jo (dr,perc) | Hüttner,Raimund (sound-sampling,synth-programming)

919018-2 | CD | Blue Skies | EAN 025091901821
Cassandra Wilson With The Mulgrew Miller Trio
Shall We Dance? | Polka Dots And Moonbeams | I've Grown Accustomed To His Face | I Didn't Know What Time It Was | I'm Old Fashioned | Sweet Lorraine | My One And Only Love | Autumn Nocturne | Blue Skies(Trumpets No End)
NYC, rec. Feb.1988
Wilson,Cassandra (voc) | Miller,Mulgrew (p) | Plaxico,Lonnie (b) | Carrington,Terri Lyne (dr)

919019-2 | CD | Shades Of Bud Powell | EAN 025091901920
Herb Robertson Brass Ensemble
Un Poco Loco | I'll Keep Loving You | Hallucinations | Glass Enclosure | The Fruit | Shades Of Bud
NYC, rec. Jan./Feb.1988
Robertson,Herb (tp,fl-h) | Lynch,Brian (tp) | Eubanks,Robin (tb) | Chancey,Vincent (fr-h) | Stewart,Robert 'Bob' (tuba) | Baron,Joey (dr,perc)

919020-2 | CD | Monk In Motian | EAN 025091902026
Paul Motian Trio
Crepuscule With Nellie | Justice(Evidence) | Bye-Ya | Ugly Beauty | Trinkle Tinkle | Reflections
NYC, rec. March 1988
Motian,Paul (dr) | Lovano,Joe (ts) | Frisell,Bill (g)
Paul Motian Quartet
Ruby My Dear | Off Minor
Motian,Paul (dr) | Lovano,Joe (ts) | Allen,Geri (p) | Frisell,Bill (g)
Straight No Chaser | Epistrophy
Motian,Paul (dr) | Lovano,Joe (ts) | Redman,Dewey (ts) | Frisell,Bill (g)

919021-2 | CD | Mindgames | EAN 025091902125
Greg Osby Quartet
This Is Not A Test | Chin Lang
NYC, rec. May 1988
Osby,Greg (ss,as,perc,voice) | McNeal,Kevin (g) | Plaxico,Lonnie (b) | Samuels,Paul (dr,perc)
Greg Osby Quintet
Dolemite | Silent Attitude | All That Matters
Osby,Greg (ss,as,perc,voice) | McNeal,Kevin (g) | Allen,Geri (p,synth) | Plaxico,Lonnie (b) | Samuels,Paul (dr,perc)
Mindgames | Thinking Inside | Excuse Not | Mirror Mirror | Altered Ego
Osby,Greg (ss,as,perc,voice) | McNeal,Kevin (g) | Simon,Edward (p,synth) | Plaxico,Lonnie (b) | Samuels,Paul (dr,perc)

919025-2 | CD | Cold Sweat Plays J.B. | EAN 025091902521
Cold Sweat
Brown Prance | Try Me
NYC, rec. November 1988
Cold Sweat | Harris,Craig (tb,voc) | Allen,Eddie E.J. (tp) | Rogers,Kenny (ss,as) | Williams,Booker T. (ts) | Ross,Brandon (el-g) | Wells,Fred (el-g) | Criner,Clyde (keyboards) | Gardner,Alonzo (el-b) | Mendes,Damon (dr) | Agyapon,Kweyao (perc)
Give It Up Or Turn It A Loose
Cold Sweat | Dara,Olu (co) | Harris,Craig (tb,voc) | Allen,Eddie E.J. (tp) | Blythe,Arthur (as) | Rogers,Kenny (ss,as) | Williams,Booker T. (ts) | Ross,Brandon (el-g) | Wells,Fred (el-g) | Criner,Clyde (keyboards) | Gardner,Alonzo (el-b) | Mendes,Damon (dr) | Agyapon,Kweyao (perc) | Sundita,Sekou (voc)
It's A Man's World
Cold Sweat | Harris,Craig (tb,voc) | Allen,Eddie E.J. (tp) | Blythe,Arthur (as) | Rogers,Kenny (ss,as) | Williams,Booker T. (ts) | Ross,Brandon (el-g) | Wells,Fred (el-g) | Criner,Clyde (keyboards) | Gardner,Alonzo (el-b) | Agyapon,Kweyao (perc)
Please Please Please
Cold Sweat | Harris,Craig (tb,voc) | Allen,Eddie E.J. (tp) | Dara,Olu (co) | Rogers,Kenny (ss,as) | Williams,Booker T. (ts) | Ross,Brandon (el-g) | Wells,Fred (el-g) | Criner,Clyde (keyboards) | Gardner,Alonzo (el-b) | Agyapon,Kweyao (perc)
Showtime Medley: | Funky Good Time- | I Got The Feelin'- | I Can't Stand It- | Licking Stick- | There Was A Time-
Cold Sweat | Harris,Craig (tb,voc) | Allen,Eddie E.J. (tp) | Rogers,Kenny (ss,as) | Williams,Booker T. (ts) | Ross,Brandon (el-g) | Wells,Fred (el-g) | Criner,Clyde (keyboards) | Gardner,Alonzo (el-b) | Agyapon,Kweyao (perc) | Abdur-Rahman,Kenyatte (perc) | Sundita,Sekou (voc)
Brown's Dance | Cold Sweat
Cold Sweat | Harris,Craig (tb,voc) | Allen,Eddie E.J. (tp) | Rogers,Kenny (ss,as) | Murray,David (ts) | Williams,Booker T. (ts) | Ross,Brandon (el-g) | Wells,Fred (el-g) | Criner,Clyde (keyboards) | Gardner,Alonzo (el-b) | Agyapon,Kweyao (perc)
I Got The Feelin'
Cold Sweat | Harris,Craig (tb) | Allen,Eddie E.J. (tp) | Rogers,Kenny (ss,as) | Williams,Booker T. (ts)

919027-2 | CD | In The Year Of The Dragon | EAN 025091902729
Geri Allen/Charlie Haden/Paul Motian
Oblivion | For John Malachi | See You At Per Tutti's | Last Call | No More Mr. Nice Guy | Invisible | First Song | In The Year Of The Dragon
NYC, rec. March 1989
Allen,Geri (p) | Haden,Charlie (b) | Motian,Paul (dr)
Geri Allen/Charlie Haden/Paul Motian & Guest
Rollano
Allen,Geri (p) | Haden,Charlie (b) | Motian,Paul (dr) | Mendolas,Juan Lazaro (quena)

919028-2 | CD | Arcado-String Trio | EAN 025091902828
Arcado-String Trio
Gartman's | Griffin' Leroy | Subtonium No.Three | Kraine | Living Bicycles | Pastoral | Curveball | Ethel | West Bank City
Ludwigsburg, rec. February 1989
Arcado String Trio | Feldman,Mark (v) | Roberts,Hank (cello) | Dresser,Mark (b)

919029-2 | CD | Paul Motian On Broadway Vol.1 | EAN 025091902927
Paul Motian Quartet
Liza | Somewhere Over The Rainbow | They Didn't Believe Me | What Is This Thing Called Love | My Heart Belongs To Daddy | Last Night When We Were Young | I Concentrate On You | Someone To Watch Over Me | So In Love
NYC, rec. November 1988
Motian,Paul (dr) | Lovano,Joe (ts) | Frisell,Bill (g) | Haden,Charlie (b)

Koch Records | Universal Music Germany

238678-2 | CD | New York City | EAN 099923867821
Peter Malick Group feat. Norah Jones
New York City | Strange Transmissions | Deceptively Yours | All Your Love | Heart Of Mine | Things You Don't Have To Do | New York City(Radio Edit)
Boston,MA, rec. August 2000
Malick,Peter (g) | Jones,Norah (p,voc) | McGouch,Danny (keyboards) | Thompson,Mike (p,accordeon) | West,Tom (p) | Turmes,Jeff (el-b) | Gardner,Eric (dr) | Richards,Marty (dr)

Konnex Records | Connexion Agency(Ali Haurand)

KCD 5055 | CD | Pulque
Dudek-Van Den Broek-Haurand
Brother Joe | Round About Midnight | Slow Blues | Joachim's B Part | Slow Motion | Pannonica | Pulque | Tuesday's Death | Open End | My Foolish Heart | Soul Eyes
Live at Festhalle Viersen, rec. 7.7.1993
Dudek,Gerd (fl,ss,ts) | Van Den Broeck,Rob (p) | Haurand,Ali (b)

KCD 5064 | CD | European Trumpet Summit
European Trumpet Summit
Interaction | Pulque
Vredenburg Utrecht, rec. April 1993
European Trumpet Summit | Rava,Enrico (tp) | Heberer,Thomas (tp) | Hoogendijk,Jarmo (tp) | Botschinsky,Allan (tp) | Van Den Broeck,Rob (p) | Haurand,Ali (b) | Levin,Tony (dr)
Anna Sophia | Brother Joe | Cobra | Blaublusen
Alte Post,Neuss, rec. 22.4.1994
European Trumpet Summit | Rava,Enrico (tp) | Heberer,Thomas (tp) | Hoogendijk,Jarmo (tp) | Botschinsky,Allan (tp) | Van Den Broeck,Rob (p) | Haurand,Ali (b) | Levin,Tony (dr)

KCD 5068 | CD | Bordertalk
Stivin-Van Den Broeck-Haurand
In The Folk Tune | No More Chains | Moments | Fire | Silence | Memories | Rumour | Relation | Round Trip | Bordertalk | Birds | Mouse | Ballad For W.L. | Waves
Live at Festhalle Viersen, rec. 13.11.1994
Stivin,Jiri (fl,cl,as,ts) | Van Den Broeck,Rob (p) | Haurand,Ali (b)

KCD 5077 | CD | Crossing Level
Dudek-Van Den Broek-Haurand
Old Folks | Don Cherry | Wishing Well | Wave(Intro) | String Thing | No More Chains | You Don't Know What Love Is
Monster,NL, rec. 12.12.1996
Dudek,Gerd (sax) | Van Den Broeck,Rob (p) | Haurand,Ali (b)
The Quartet
Expressions | The Meaning Of The Blues | Melancholia
Monster,NL, rec. 8.2.1997
Dudek,Gerd (sax) | Van Den Broeck,Rob (p) | Haurand,Ali (b) | Levin,Tony (dr)

KCD 5078 | CD | 20th Anniversary Tour
European Jazz Ensemble
Para | Telisi Rama | The Double Rainbow Over Heeper Street | Pulque
Live at Freilichtbühne Burg Wilhelmstein, rec. 28.6.1996
European Jazz Ensemble | Hogendijk,Jarmo (tp) | Botschinsky,Allan (tp,fl-h) | Rava,Enrico (tp) | Schoof,Manfred (tp,fl-h) | Heberer,Thomas (tp) | Bauer,Conrad (tb) | Kühn,Rolf (cl) | Petrowsky,Ernst-Ludwig (fl,as) | Mariano,Charlie (as) | Stivin,Jiri (fl,b-cl,as,bs) | Sulzman,Stan (fl,ss,ts) | Dudek,Gerd (fl,ss,ts) | Lakatos,Tony (fl,ts) | Van Den Broeck,Rob (p) | Kühn,Joachim (p) | Haurand,Ali (b) | Humair,Daniel (dr) | Levin,Tony (dr)

KCD 5095 | CD | Just The Two Of Us | EAN 4031851990529
Jiri Stivin-Ali Haurand
Two Old Ships | Bazalicka | Toronto Experience | Don Cherry | Polka Dots And Moonbeams | Interplay | Dedications | Crystall Bells | Children Song No.8 | Brother Joe | Up Hahn The Swing | My Garden | Fuhrmann | Good Night
Düsseldorf, rec. 6.4.2000
Stivin,Jiri (fl,cl,as) | Haurand,Ali (b)

KCD 5100 | CD | European Jazz Ensemble 25th Anniversary | EAN 4017867030206
European Jazz Ensemble
Brother Joe
Sonic Yard Studio,?, rec. details unknown
European Jazz Ensemble | Botschinsky,Allan (tp) | Fresu,Paolo (tp) | Hoogendijk,Jarmo (tp) | Bauer,Conrad (tb) | Stivin,Jiri (fl,sax) | Mariano,Charlie (sax) | Skidmore,Alan (sax) | Sulzman,Stan (sax) | Dudek,Gerd (sax) | Van Den Broeck,Rob (p) | Haurand,Ali (b) | Roidinger,Adelhard (b) | Levin,Tony (dr)
Fellini
Live, ?, rec. details unknown
European Jazz Ensemble | Fresu,Paolo (tp) | Stivin,Jiri (fl,sax) | Mariano,Charlie (sax) | Van Den Broeck,Rob (p) | Roidinger,Adelhard (b) | Levin,Tony (dr)
Green Table Speech
European Jazz Ensemble | Skidmore,Alan (sax) | Dudek,Gerd (sax) | Van Den Broeck,Rob (p) | Haurand,Ali (b) | Levin,Tony (dr)
Traveller
European Jazz Ensemble | Botschinsky,Allan (tp) | Hoogendijk,Jarmo (tp) | Mariano,Charlie (sax) | Sulzman,Stan (sax) | Dudek,Gerd (sax) | Kühn,Joachim (p) | Roidinger,Adelhard (b) | Humair,Daniel (dr)
Salinas- | Missing A Page-
European Jazz Ensemble | Dudek,Gerd (sax) | Kühn,Joachim (p) | Haurand,Ali (b) | Humair,Daniel (dr)
Three In One
European Jazz Ensemble | Botschinsky,Allan (tp) | Fresu,Paolo (tp) | Hoogendijk,Jarmo (tp) | Bauer,Conrad (tb) | Stivin,Jiri (fl,sax) | Skidmore,Alan (sax) | Mariano,Charlie (sax) | Sulzman,Stan (sax) | Dudek,Gerd (sax) | Van Den Broeck,Rob (p) | Haurand,Ali (b) | Roidinger,Adelhard (b) | Levin,Tony (dr)
Conrad Bauer
Bötz
Bauer,Conrad (tb-solo)

KCD 5108 | CD | Jazz Und Lyrik:Schinderkarren Mit Buffet | EAN 4017867030213
Paul Eßer-Gerd Dudek-Ali Haurand-Jiri Strivin
Ballad For W.L. | Der Taugenichts | Verlorene Liebesmüh: | Glück- | Wild And Free- | Es War Ein Zauberer- | Exponiert- | Inuit Erzählung- | Ein Liebes Paar- | Heimaterde | Zug & Druck: | Fester Kurs- | Rache Akt- | Schlaflose- | Letzter Trip- | Trau Schau Wem | Niederrheinsonntag | Platzangst | Kulturaustausch | Dedications | Heinrich Böll | Sinn Isch D'r Dom... - ...Sinn Isch D'r Dom... | KeinOrt: | Diogenes- | Immigrant- | Exil- | Entwicklungshelfer- | Toleranz- | Friedhof In Jerusalem- | Die Diebe Von Bagdad | Über Die Wahrheit Des Schönen Scheins | Inspiration 2 | Kinderprogramm | Abendlandabend: | Ausklang- | Verhallt- | Unterwegs: | Tödlicher Irrtum- | Straßen Plätze- | Lösung- | Carpe Noctem- | Naturgeschichte | Der Hut-Trick- | Ausstellung- | Bilderfluß: | Chagall- | William Turner- | Salvador Dali- | Pound Underground- | Hamlet- | Locus Amoenus- | Saubersinn- | Schinderkarren Mit Büffet | A Delta So Old | Blue Rose | Gedichtmachen | Be Ass Em Dorp | Am Rande: | Abschiedsgeschenk Eines Obdachlosen- | Ausgetragen- | Religion | Francois Villon | Letzten Wille
Düsseldorf, rec. Juli 2001
Eßer,Paul (recitation) | Dudek,Gerd (sax) | Stivin,Jiri (fl,sax) | Haurand,Ali (b)

KCD 5110 | CD | Frontier Traffic | EAN 4017867030275
Mariano-Humair-Haurand
Plum Island | My Foolish Heart | Yagapriya | Round Trip | No More Chains | Everything Happens To Me | Pulque | Goodbye Pork Pie Hat
details unknown, rec. March 2002
Mariano,Charlie (as) | Haurand,Ali (b) | Humair,Daniel (dr)

Konnex Records | Jazz Network

KCD 5027 | CD | Re-Touch & Quartet
John Stevens Quartet
No Fear
London,GB, rec. 18.5.1977
Stevens,John (dr) | Holdsworth,Allan (g) | Young,Jeff (p) | Guy,Barry (b)
Re-Touch
Stevens,John (dr) | Holdsworth,Allan (g) | Young,Jeff (p) | Mathewson,Ron (b) | Guy,Barry (b)
One, Two- | Albert Ayler- | Birds Of A Feather- | Nothing-
Live at Notre Dame Hall,London,GB, rec. 7.5.1971
Stevens,John (dr) | Watts,Trevor (ss) | Tippetts,Julie (g,voc) | Herman,Ron (b)

KCD 5032 | CD | Alpharian
Wilton Gaynair Quintet
Spotlight | One For Joan | Blues For Erica | Sophisticated Lady | St.Petrian | Quick Sand | Song For Helga
Köln, rec. 1982
Gaynair,Wilton (ts) | Botschinsky,Allan (tp) | Van Den Broeck,Rob (p) | Haurand,Ali (b) | Nay,Joe (dr)

KCD 5042 | CD | Last Day In May
Ed Sarath Quintet
Solidarity | Crystal Palace | Dance Of Gaia | Old Age | As Is | Folk Song | Last Day In May | Sambananda
NYC, rec. 22./23.12.1991
Sarath,Ed (fl-h) | Liebman,Dave (ss) | Goodrick,Mick (g) | Swartz,Harvie (b) | Smith,Marvin 'Smitty' (dr)

KCD 5047 | CD | 3-Ology
Debriano-Hart-Blythe
Hipnotism | Elaborations | Our Thing | Jitterbug Waltz | A Nightingale Sang In Berkeley Square | Portrait | Get Out If You Can
Monster,NL, rec. 27.1.1993
3-Ology | Blythe,Arthur (as) | Debriano,Santi Wilson (b) | Hart,Billy (dr)

KCD 5048 | CD | Monk's Mood
Sonny Fortune Quartet
Little Rootie Tootie | Nutty | Monk's Mood | In Walked Bud | Misterioso | I Mean You | Ruby My Dear | Off Minor
NYC, rec. 25./26.1.1993
Fortune,Sonny (as) | Lightsey,Kirk (p) | Williams,David (b) | Chambers,Joe (dr)

KCD 5049 | CD | 4,4,4,
Evan Parker-Paul Rutherford-Barry Guy-John Stevens
1,4,4, | 2,4,4, | 3,4,4, | 4,4,4, | 5,4,4,
London,GB, rec. August 1979
Rutherford,Paul (tb,euphonium) | Parker,Evan (ss) | Guy,Barry (b,electronics) | Stevens,John (perc,voice)
John Stevens Trio
S.M.E.
London,GB, rec. 18.8.1992
Stevens,John (dr) | Smith,Roger (g) | Coombes,Nigel (v)

KCD 5051 | CD | Sunday Train
Bill Lowe/Philippe Crettien Quintet
Mister B.C. | Sunday Train | Radiator | Miles Magic | Meta | Blue Whale | Joone | Gentle Force
details unknown, rec. 10./11.1.1993
Lowe,Bill (b-tb,tuba) | Crettien,Philippe (ts) | Medeski,John (p) | Zino,Dave (b) | Gullotti,Bob (dr)

KCD 5059 | CD | The Eighth Wonder & More
Dick Griffin Septet
Eighth Wonder | It Could Be | Girl,I Really Love You So | Jakubu's Dance | Flying Back Home | Come Be With Me
NYC, rec. details unknown
Griffin,Dick (tb) | Rivers,Sam (fl,reeds) | Smith,Warren (vib) | Burton,Ron (p) | McBee,Cecil (b) | Waits,Freddie (dr) | Smith,Leopolodo F. (perc)
Waltz My Son | Multiphone Blues | Oree Me(alt.take)
NYC, rec. 1979
Griffin,Dick (tb) | Smith,Don (fl,p) | Jordan,Clifford (ts) | Saxton,Bill (ts) | Eaves,Hubert (p) | Hill,Calvin (b) | Waits,Freddie (dr) | Hart,Billy (dr) | Killian,Lawrence (perc)

Now Is The Time
Griffin,Dick (tb,voc) | Smith,Don (p,voc) | Jordan,Clifford (ts) | Saxton,Bill (ts,voc) | Eaves,Hubert (p) | Hill,Calvin (b) | Waits,Freddie (dr) | Hart,Billy (dr) | Killian,Lawrence (perc) | Griffin,Geraldine (voc)

Laika Records | Zomba

35100742 | CD | Live In Budapest
Tony Lakatos Quartet
The Duke | Filene's | Recycling | There Is No Greater Love
Live at PE.CSA,Budapest, rec. 7.3.1995
Lakatos,Tony (sax) | Brackeen,JoAnne (p) | McBee,Cecil (b) | Foster,Al (dr)

35100752 | CD | Imagination
Christoph Sänger Trio
Skyride | Caribbean Connection | Farewell To B.J. | Las Brisas | Imagination | You And The Night And The Music | Tres Palabras
Brooklyn,NY, rec. details unknown
Sänger,Christof (p) | Mraz,George 'Jiri' (b) | Foster,Al (dr)
Fancy Place | Brandyn | Maybe Tomorrow
Sänger,Christof (p) | Lakatos,Tony (ss,ts) | Mraz,George 'Jiri' (b) | Foster,Al (dr)

35100762 | CD | I Thought About You
Benny Bailey Quartet
Yardbird Suite | This One Is For Trunk(In Memoriam Peter Trunk) | Prelude To A Kiss | North Star Street | I Thought About You | Eukalypso
Köln, rec. January 1996
Bailey,Benny (tp) | Wunsch,Frank (p) | Krisse,Fritz (b) | Becton,Clarence (dr)
Benny Bailey Quartet With Wayne Bartlett
I Got It Bad And That Ain't Good | Don't Get Around Much Anymore
Bailey,Benny (tp) | Wunsch,Frank (p) | Krisse,Fritz (b) | Becton,Clarence (dr) | Bartlett,Wayne (voc)

35100782 | CD | Soulcolours
Fritz Krisse Quartet
Alvin | Soulcolours | Colleen | Carrer De Campos | Fruitcase | This One Is For Trunk(In Memoriam Peter Trunk) | Ubique | Left Alone
Monster,NL, rec. details unknown
Krisse,Fritz (b) | Lakatos,Tony (sax) | Degen,Bob (p) | Sides,Douglas 'Doug' (dr)

35100792 | CD | Ruino Vino
Mara!
Ruino Vino | Men Suffer Too | Fair Kop | Adje | The Big Dance | Dance Of Dospat | Lambkin | Jove | Past Carin' | Llew's Blues | Tu Madre
Sidney,Austalia, rec. May 1995
Mara | Kiek,Mara (tapan,voc) | Kiek,Llew (baglama,bouzouki,g,el-g,voc) | Evans,Sandy (ss,ts) | Gorman,Tony (cl,as) | Elphick,Steve (b)

35100802 | CD | Simple
The Catholics
Smoked Oysters | Ah-Kah-Kah | Uncle Bob's Your Uncle | Gumboot | Home | Good Morning,Freedom Fighter | Esprit De L'Escalier | Brothers And Sisters | DPM
St.Peters,NSW, rec. details unknown
Catholics,The | Greening,James (tb) | Evans,Sandy (ss,ts,tambourine) | Brewer,Dave (g,guira) | Swanton,Lloyd (b,cabasa,el-b,shaker,tambourine) | Hall,Toby (dr,surdo,timbales) | Rose,Michel (pedal-steel-g,shaker) | Sithole,Samila (perc,congas,timbales)

35100812 | CD | Border Crossing
Wanderlust
Year Of The Pig | Mambo Gumbo | La Belle Afrique | Some Heroes | Odalisque | Sabar Dance | Songo Baiao | El Tata | 34° South
Sidney,Austalia, rec. 26./27.5.1995
Wanderlust | Bukovsky,Miroslav (tp,fl-h,perc) | Greening,James (tb) | Orr,Carl (g) | Spence,Alister (p,keyboards) | Armstrong,Adam (b,el-b) | Hevia,Fabian (dr,perc)
Pentimento
Wanderlust | Bukovsky,Miroslav (tp,fl-h,perc) | Greening,James (tb) | Gough,Julian (ts) | Orr,Carl (g) | Spence,Alister (p,keyboards) | Armstrong,Adam (b,el-b) | Hevia,Fabian (dr,perc)
Until
Wanderlust | Bukovsky,Miroslav (tp,fl-h,perc) | Greening,James (tb) | Orr,Carl (g) | Spence,Alister (p,keyboards) | Armstrong,Adam (b,el-b) | Hevia,Fabian (dr,perc) | Geyer,Renée (voc)

35100822 | CD | Live At The Montreal Jazz Festival
Christoph Sänger
Ellington Medley: | In A Sentimental Mood- | Satin Doll- | Prelude To A Kiss- | Caravan- | Stella By Starlight | Security Blues | Body And Soul | Tico Tico | Lullaby Of Birdland | Condorito | Gershwin Medley: | Nice Work If You Can Get It- | I Loves You Porgy- | It Ain't Necessarily So-
Live at The Montreal Jazz Festival, rec. 5.7.1996
Sänger,Christof (p-solo)

35100832 | CD | Brandyn
Al Foster Quartet
The Chief | Brandyn | Monk Up And Down | Barney Rose | Amsterdam Blues | Hope | No Title | Black Nile
Monster,NL, rec. 14.10.1996
Foster,Al (dr) | Potter,Chris (ts) | Kikoski,David 'Dave' (p) | Weiss,Doug (b)

35100852 | CD | Alter Ego
Deborah Henson-Conant
996 | Bring It All Down | Dance The Way You Dance | Beck's Blues | Wild Mountain Thyme- | Summertime- | Congratulations,You Made It This Far(The Birthday Song) | Belinda | Siana's Dream:The Music Box | Nobody Half As Strong | Cindy Cindy | There's A Boat | Irene Goodnight
Somerville,MA., rec. 1996
Henson-Conant,Deborah (synth,harp,voc)

35100882 | CD | Sumblo
Doug Sides Ensemble
Sumblo | Mar | Pensive | Dialogue No.1 | Story Of E. | Samba D'Esprit | Zenith | Balancing Act
Monster,NL, rec. February 1997
Sides,Douglas 'Doug' (dr) | Head,Marilyn (fl,piccolo) | King,Peter (as) | Stagnitta,Frank (p) | Milosevic,Aleksandar (b)

35100902 | CD | The Art Of Time
Eda Zari With The Mark Joggerst Trio
Song For Eda | You Don't Know What Love Is | Dancing Alone | Come Rain Or Come Shine | Remember The Time | Once I Loved | Time To Tell The Truth | Body And Soul | Falling Back | The Man I Love | Never Again
Köln, rec. 29.5.-1.6.1997
Zari,Eda (voc) | Joggerst,Mark (p) | Gjakonovski,Martin (b) | Hillmann,Christoph (dr)

35100962 | CD | Alterd Ego
Deborah Henson-Conant
Bring It All Down | 996 | Congratulations,You Made It This Far | The Nightingale | Nobody Half As Strong | Siana's Dream:The Music Box | Cindy Cindy | Altered Ego | Beck's Blues | Dogs Of Somerville | Belinda | Wild Mountain Thyme- | Summertime- | Goodnight Irene
Crisis Island,Somerville,MA, rec. details unknown
Henson-Conant,Deborah (keyboards,synth,harp,voc) | Archibald,Tim (b)

35100992 | CD | The Gift:15 Weihnachtslieder der Erde
Joy To The World- | El Nino Jesus- | God Rest Ye Merry Gentlemen | We Three Kings Of Orient Are | Angels We Have Heard On High | Stille Nacht | Carol Of The Bells | Deck The Halls | What Child Is This(Greensleeves) | Un Flambeau,Jeannette Isabella | Slava- | Coventry Carol- | O Tannenbaum | Ain't That A Rockin' | Pag A-Tao | Fum Fum Fum | Dona Nobis Pacem- | Leanabh An Ai Auld Lang Syne-
details unknown, rec. 1995
Henson-Conant,Deborah (harp)

35101022 | CD | The Celtic Album
The Ash Grove | Comin' Through The Rye | The Drunken Sailor | Siobeg Siomor- | Ye Banks & Braes- | Planxty Irwin- | All Through The Night- | Kira's Lullabye- | Off She Hoes & She's Gone | She Moved Through The Fair | Gussie's Great Escape | Loch Lomond | The Mason's Apron | My Love Is Like A Red, Red Rose
Somerville,MA., rec. 1998
Henson-Conant,Deborah (keyboards,synth,harp,voc)
Slieve Russell | St.Annes's Reel- | Here In The Sun-
Henson-Conant,Deborah (synth,harp,voc) | Barnes,Peter (fl)

35101042 | CD | Human Bass
Benni Chaves-Laszlo Gardony
Perfect Touch | Entrance | For My Father | Rhymes | One Line(Is Enough) | Precious | Autumn Leaves
NYC, rec. 20./21.6.1998
Chawes,Benni (voice) | Gardonyi,Laszlo (p)

35101052 | CD | Beauty Of Silence
Alex Gunia-Philipp Van Endert Group
Number One | Tribute To Glenn Miller | Even Plains | Like The Morning Sunrise | Master Mind | Medicine Man | Gimmes Never Get
Köln, rec. 1998
Gunia,Alex (g) | Van Endert,Philipp (g) | Nendza,André (b) | Küttner,Michael (dr,perc)
Lullababy
Gunia,Alex (g) | Van Endert,Philipp (g) | Mat Jr. (org) | Nendza,André (b) | Küttner,Michael (dr,perc)

35101102 | CD | Sonateskas
Josep Maria Balanyà
Sonatesca Prensil Polyphonica(part 1-3) | Y Cuando Oigas El Agua Caer... | No Jungle? | Good Works For Bad Pianos | Ancestral Spring(part 1-3) | Sonatesca Gutural(part 1-3)
Zerkall, rec. 24.4.1998
Balanyà,Josep Maria (p-solo)

35101112 | CD | There Is More
Elke Reiff Quartett
There Is More | Arrival At The Castle | No Tomorrow | Never Will I Marry | Diebstahl Im Basar | Dubidap | Paris In The Rain | Carlypso | Getting On My Nerves | Out Of Silence | Blues For Ruurd
Köln, rec. 22./23.7.1998
Reiff,Elke (voc) | Bertram,Walter (p) | Ruck,Roland (b) | Breuer,Gerd (dr)

35101122 | CD | Source
Loft Line
Teu(tone)ntanz | Line Up | Source | Flowers | African Line | Celians Song | Live Steps | Song For Mike | Dream Walk(1) | Dream Walk(2)
Berlin, rec. March 1999
Loft Line | Raake,Christian (ss,ts,bass-fl) | Schenderlein,Peter (p,synth) | Procop,Alexander (b) | Von Thiem[Vonthiem],Max (dr,perc)

35101132 | CD | Soloquitar
Ulli Bögershausen
Ombrellino | Roots | 20.000 Dominosteine | Rushhour | Sunny Afternoon | Ich Weiß Nicht,Woran In Bin | Es Wäre Schön Gewesen | Tango | Walking Around | Gegen Die Zeit | Ganz Bestimmt Vielleicht | Frühling,Sommer,Herbst | Fragile | Weißt Du Noch? | Children's Song
Bielefeld, rec. March-June 1999
Bögershausen,Ulli (g-solo,12-string-g)

35101152 | CD | Briefcase
Ronnie Taheny Group
Read My Mind | Farewell To Fools | Home | Solo | Black And Blind | My Haven | The Princess And The Frog | Moving Door | Into The Night | Toyland | Think Of Me | Versailles
Adelaide,Australia, rec. December 1998
Taheney,Ronnie (g,p,keyboards,voc) | Wordley,Mick (g,perc,dobro,mando-g,voc) | Lehmann,Glyn (altonium,rog) | Todd,Steve (perc)

35101172 | CD | What's New
Ed Kröger Quartet
Speak Low | What's New? | Whisper Not | Estate(Summer) | It's You Or No One | For All We Know | Black Nile | Old Folks | Alone Together
Hannover, rec. 29./30.3.1999
Kröger,Ed (tb) | Bätzel,Matthias (p) | Gühlke,Lars (b) | Keul,Michael (dr) | Camerun,Romy (voc)

35101182 | CD | Sweet Relief
Swim Two Birds
All I Want | Whatever | Tango No.3 | Lonely | Too Little Too Late | Maybe | Dinner | The Rhyme | Wanna See Me Down
details unknown, rec. details unknown
Swim Two Birds | Gross,Michael (tp) | Gätjen,Achim (as) | Benesch,Rolf (ts,bs) | Lueers,Tammo (g,lap-steel,6-string-b) | Hart,Willy (b,noise) | Faerber,Achim (dr,perc) | GU (voc)
Rather Dead
Swim Two Birds | Gross,Michael (tp) | Gätjen,Achim (as) | Benesch,Rolf (ts,bs) | Kirschbaum,Rolf (g) | Lueers,Tammo (g,lap-steel,6-string-b) | Hart,Willy (b,noise) | Faerber,Achim (dr,perc) | GU (voc)

35101212 | CD | Tokyo Blues
Wayne Bartlett With The Thomas Hufschmidt Group
I Have To Say No | Dat Dere
Essen, rec. August & December 1999
Bartlett,Wayne (voc) | Hufschmidt,Thomas (p,keyboards) | Queck,Roman (ss,ts) | Krämer,Bernd (g) | Foltynowicz,Jens (b,voc) | Welle,Jochen (dr,perc)
Everything Matters
Bartlett,Wayne (voc) | Hufschmidt,Thomas (p,keyboards) | Schwatlo,Peter (tb) | Böhlke,Andreas (fl,as) | Queck,Roman (ss,ts) | Krämer,Bernd (g) | Foltynowicz,Jens (b,voc) | Welle,Jochen (dr,perc) | Laux,Carola (voc)
Waiting On A Sign From You
Bartlett,Wayne (voc) | Hufschmidt,Thomas (p,keyboards) | Schwatlo,Peter (tb) | Böhlke,Andreas (fl,as) | Queck,Roman (ss,ts) | Krämer,Bernd (g) | Foltynowicz,Jens (b,voc) | Welle,Jochen (dr,perc)
Everybody Plays The Game
Bartlett,Wayne (voc) | Hufschmidt,Thomas (p,keyboards) | Krüger,Olaf (tp) | Striepens,Ansgar (tb) | Queck,Roman (ss,ts) | Krämer,Bernd (g) | Foltynowicz,Jens (b,voc) | Welle,Jochen (dr,perc)
Old Man-Old Country
Bartlett,Wayne (voc) | Hufschmidt,Thomas (p,keyboards) | Beckerhoff,Uli (tp) | Striepens,Ansgar (tb) | Queck,Roman (ss,ts) | Krämer,Bernd (g) | Foltynowicz,Jens (b,voc) | Welle,Jochen (dr,perc)
Song For My Father
Bartlett,Wayne (voc) | Hufschmidt,Thomas (p,keyboards) | Beckerhoff,Uli (tp) | Striepens,Ansgar (tb) | Queck,Roman (ss,ts) | Bauer,Stefan (vib,marimba) | Krämer,Bernd (g) | Foltynowicz,Jens (b,voc) | Welle,Jochen (dr,perc) | Laux,Carola (voc)
Something Special
Bartlett,Wayne (voc) | Hufschmidt,Thomas (p,keyboards) | Queck,Roman (ss,ts) | Bauer,Stefan (vib,marimba) | Krämer,Bernd (g) | Foltynowicz,Jens (b,voc) | Welle,Jochen (dr,perc) | Laux,Carola (voc)
Tokyo Blues
Bartlett,Wayne (voc) | Hufschmidt,Thomas (p,keyboards) | Queck,Roman (ss,ts) | Bauer,Stefan (vib,marimba) | Krämer,Bernd (g) | Foltynowicz,Jens (b,voc) | Welle,Jochen (dr,perc)
It's Allright | Don't Go
Bartlett,Wayne (voc) | Hufschmidt,Thomas (p,keyboards) | Queck,Roman (ss,ts) | Krämer,Bernd (g) | Foltynowicz,Jens (b,voc) | Welle,Jochen (dr,perc) | Laux,Carola (voc)
Something In You
Bartlett,Wayne (voc) | Hufschmidt,Thomas (p,keyboards) | Beckerhoff,Uli (tp) | Queck,Roman (ss,ts) | Krämer,Bernd (g) | Foltynowicz,Jens (b,voc) | Welle,Jochen (dr,perc) | Laux,Carola (voc)
Filthy McNasty
Bartlett,Wayne (voc) | Hufschmidt,Thomas (p,keyboards) | Beckerhoff,Uli (tp) | Queck,Roman (ss,ts) | Krämer,Bernd (g) | Foltynowicz,Jens (b,voc) | Welle,Jochen (dr,perc)

35101222 | CD | Klezmer Stories
Paul Brody's Tango Toy
Chava Meets The Tango Man | Klezmer In Black | Taxi Story | Sheking | Tarra's Freilach | Mein Sohn,Was Immer Aus Dir Werde | Oif'n Pripitchik | New Klezmer Band | The Schlemiel As A Modern Hero
details unknown, rec. details unknown
Brody,Paul (tp) | Thomas,Jens (p) | Bica,Carlos (b) | Winch,Rainer (dr)

35101322 | CD | Deborah Henson-Conant:Best Of Instrumental Music
Deborah Henson-Conant Group
Take Five | The Phoenix | Siana's Dream | The Day It Rained Forever | Baroque Flamenco | Summertime | Nature Girl | Just For You | Budapest | Pava Diablo | 996 | The Danger Zone | Slieve Russell | Georgia On My Mind
different Places, rec. different Dates
Henson-Conant,Deborah (harp)

35101332 | CD | Movin' On
Ed Kröger Quartet plus Guests
On A Misty Night | Latin Steps | Goodbye | Groovin' At Chico's | The Neamess Of You | Movin' On | Day Dream | Loose Blues | High Wire | Tiny Tune
Hannover, rec. 6.11.2000
Kröger,Ed (tb) | Dinné,Ignaz (as) | Bätzel,Matthias (p) | Gühlke,Lars (b) | Keul,Michael (dr) | Camerun,Romy (voc)

35101342 | CD | No Regrets
Swim Two Birds
Drunk | The Return Of The Undead Mescalworm | Darkness | The Showliness Of Beeing Sane | Lovely How I Let My Mind Float | Murder One | Theme From Perry Mason | Hubcaps & Taillights
Bremen, rec. 2001
Swim Two Birds | Gross,Michael (tp) | Gätjen,Achim (as) | Benesch,Rolf (ts,bs) | Lueers,Tammo (g) | Hart,Willy (b,noise) | Faerber,Achim (dr,perc) | GU (voc)
It's Hard | Simple & True
Swim Two Birds | Gross,Michael (tp) | Hube,Mareike (tb) | Gätjen,Achim (as) | Benesch,Rolf (ts,bs) | Lueers,Tammo (g) | Hart,Willy (b,noise) | Faerber,Achim (dr,perc) | GU (voc)
Dream Come True
Swim Two Birds | Gross,Michael (tp) | Hube,Mareike (tb) | Gätjen,Achim (as) | Benesch,Rolf (ts,bs) | Lueers,Tammo (g) | Scheibe,Mark (p) | Hart,Willy (b,noise) | Faerber,Achim (dr,perc) | GU (voc)
Moon | Clean
Swim Two Birds | Gross,Michael (tp) | Gätjen,Achim (as) | Benesch,Rolf (ts,bs) | Lueers,Tammo (g) | Scheibe,Mark (p) | Hart,Willy (b,noise) | Faerber,Achim (dr,perc) | GU (voc)

35101352 | CD | Blue Topaz
Ernie Watts-Christof Sänger
Soul Eyes(I) | Days Of Wine And Roses | My Foolish Heart | Saudade | In Your Own Sweet Way | Like Someone In Love | Oriental Spring | Have You Met Miss Jones | I Hear A Rhapsody | I Didn't Know Until You Told Me | Blue Topaz | Somebody Loves Me | Soul Eyes(II)
Köln, rec. 19./20.12.2000
Watts,Ernie (as,ts) | Sänger,Christof (p)

35101382 | CD | Spring
ULG
Femskaft- | Amager-Dans- | Femspring | Craigie Hill | Jeg Gik Mig Ud Spadserende | Polsk Dans- | Springdans- | Oh No Not I | How Can I Live At The Top Of A Mountain | Den Gamle Gjonne | Where The Mulchair River Flows | Englis- | Frederiks Contra- | Topspring
Vestiysk Musikkonservatorium,Denmark, rec. April 2000
ULC | Uhrbrand,Peter (fiddle) | Lydom,Sonnich (accordeon,harm) | Cahill,Seamus (bouzouki,g,voc) | Rosendal,Peter (p,synth) | Vinding,Mads (b)
Dansk Morgenzarrar- | Kierlighed Pa Prove-
ULC | Uhrbrand,Peter (fiddle) | Lydom,Sonnich (accordeon,harm) | Cahill,Seamus (bouzouki,g,voc) | Rosendal,Peter (p,synth) | Vinding,Mads (b) | Friis-Holm,Joakim (irish-harp)

35101402 | CD | Waltz For The Red Fiddle
Susanne Lundeng Quartet
Lende(Homeground) | Refsetufsa(Wild Child) | Vals Til Den Rode Fela(Waltz For The Red Fiddle) | Marmor I | En Dance Tel Han Harald(Dance For Harald) | Brun Halling(Brown Halling) | Marmor II | I Et Skrin(In A Jewelry Box) | Utaforr Skapet(In Front Of The Cupboard) | Ingenting Sakralt(Sanctimonious) | Marmor III
Rosvik Church,Sorfold,Norway, rec. 2000
Lundeng,Susanne (v,voc) | Drage,Björn Andor (p,org,harmonium,keyboards) | Bendiksen,Havar (g,mand,accordeon) | Sletten,Finn (perc)
Rod Halling(Red Halling)
Live at Sogndal Kulturhus,Norway, rec. 2000
Lundeng,Susanne (v,voc) | Drage,Björn Andor (p,org,harmonium,keyboards) | Bendiksen,Havar (g,mand,accordeon) | Sletten,Finn (perc)

35101412 | CD | Full Bronte
Wanderlust + Guests
The Full Bronte | Twilight Rain | Fast Boat To China | Eleven Elvises | Landscape | Manchao | Four Miles | Where Does Love Come From(for My Father) | Plain Talk
Sidney,Austalia, rec. 2000
Wanderlust | Bukovsky,Miroslav (tp,fl-h) | Greening,James (tb,didjeridu) | Cutlan,Paul (b-cl) | Spence,Alister (p,keyboards) | Sawkins,Jeremy (g,el-g) | Armstrong,Adam (b) | Elphick,Steve (b) | Hevia,Fabian (dr,perc)

35101462 | CD | Sliding Affairs
Trombonefire
Fuller & Fuller | Caravan | The Blessing Of A Beautiful Bride | No Rules Allowed | On The Edge | 1.2.79 | The Bus Blues | Once Or Twice | Big Alice
Thorstadl,Obing, rec. 13.-15.2.2001
Trombonefire | Herrlich,Johannes (tb) | Mears,Adrian (tb) | Breuer,Hermann (tb) | Budziat,Eberhard (b-tb) | Lang,Walter (p) | Stabenow,Thomas (b) | Gmelin,Matthias (dr)

35101502 | CD | Eastern Moods
For Free Hands
Lyasata | Habar N-Am | Dracula's Breakfast | Guardian Angel | Bulgarskie Devoitsche | Ballade | East Side Story | Spanish Fly | Bulgarian Suite
Berlin, rec. 2001
For Free Hands | Karparov,Vladimir (fl,sax) | Hartmann,Hans (chapmanstick) | Brunn,Andreas (7-string-g,el-g,e-bow) | De Martin,Maurice (perc,sampler,shruti-box)

35101512 | CD | Resurection Lounge
booMbooM meets Uli Beckerhoff
Resurrection Lounge | Les Insecteurs | Un Instand | Space Party | Lonely Hours | Home
Bremen, rec. December 2000/January 2001
booMbooM | Beckerhoff,Uli (tp) | Schinkopf,Matthias (sax) | Berger,Michael (keyboards,samples,voc) | Albrecht,Marcello (b,sequencer) | Dahm,Stefan (dr,perc) | Ulrich,Stephan (dr,perc,voc) | Saby,Lea (voc)

35101542 | CD | Private Stories | EAN 4011786021543
Ulli Bögershausen
Secret Story | Pensive | Steam | No Rest InTainan | You Are The Sunshine Of My Life | Ulla | On Tour | Herbstallee | Zvoncekova Koleda | Besame Mucho | So Alt Wie Nina | Bärchen
details unknown, rec. details unknown
Bögershausen,Ulli (g-solo)

35101562 | CD | Ngoma | EAN 4011786021567
The Brazz Brothers
Zawose | Ejala | Kongolela | Hey Hey Beautiful Girl | Maasai | Tintiyana | African Marketplace | Maraba Blue | Chisa | My Kind Of Jazz
Vagnhared,Sweden, rec. 1999
Brazz Brothers,The | Forde,Jan Magne (tp,fl-h,kalimba,marimba) | Forde,Jarle (tp,voc) | Forde,Helge (tb,voc) | Tafjord,Runar (fr-h,voc) | Tafjord,Stein Erik (tuba,voc) | Lewin,Marcus (dr,perc)

35101622 | CD | Christmas Carols | EAN 4011786021628
Ulli Bögershausen
Alle Jahre Wieder | Fröhliche Weihnacht Überall | Morgen Kinder Wird's Was

LABELVERZEICHNIS

Geben | Schneeflöckchen.Weißröckchen | Jingle Bells | Il Est Né Le Divin Enfant | Leise Rieselt Der Schnee | Lulajze Jezuniu | Les Anges Dans Nos Campagnes | Am Weihnachtsbaum Die Lichter Brennen | Stille Nacht Heilige Nacht | Christmas Lullaby | Maria Durch Den Dornwald Ging | Hark! The Herald Angels Sing | Komet Ihr Hirten | Tu Scendi Dalle Stelle | We Wish You A Merry Christmas | Ihr Kinderlein Kommet | Entre Le Boeuf Et L'Ane Gris | Zwoncekova Koleda- | Carol Of The Bells- | What Child Is This(Greensleeves)
details unknown, rec. details unknown
Bögershausen,Ulli (g-solo)

35101632 | CD | The Nature Suite | EAN 4011786021635
David Jean-Baptiste Group
Frankincense & Rosewood | Tropical Storm | Unity
Jean-Baptiste,David (b-fl,b-cl,contra-b-cl) | Cumberbache,Williams (perc)
Rain Forest Breeze | Coconut & Banana | Puszczykowo
Jean-Baptiste,David (as,basset-h) | Joseph,Julian (p) | Olatunja,Michael (b,el-b) | Mondesir,Mark (dr)
Moonlight Cello Rivers
Jean-Baptiste,David (b-cl) | Joseph,Julian (p) | Dos Santos,Ricardo (b) | Olatunja,Michael (b,el-b)
Sky & Ocean
Jean-Baptiste,David (cl) | Robinson,Orphy (marimba) | Remi,Tony (el-g) | Dos Santos,Ricardo (b) | Mondesir,Mark (dr) | Arnold,Marcina (voc)
Cascade Infinity
Jean-Baptiste,David (b-cl,contra-b-cl) | Sutherland,Rowland (fl) | Robinson,Orphy (marimba) | Remi,Tony (g) | Dos Santos,Ricardo (b) | Mondesir,Mark (dr) | Cumberbache,Williams (perc) | Arnold,Marcina (voc)
Camden Maret
Jean-Baptiste,David (b-cl) | Scott,Sarah (cl) | Joseph,Julian (p) | Dos Santos,Ricardo (b) | Mondesir,Mark (dr)
Silence So Loud
Jean-Baptiste,David (b-fl.basset-h)

35101642 | CD | Dreams And Realities | EAN 4011786021642
Ansgar Striepens Quintet
Dreams And Realities
Köln, rec. September 2001
Striepens,Ansgar (tb) | Beckerhoff,Uli (tp) | Nuß,Hubert (p) | Heller,Ingmar (b) | Hollenbeck,John (dr)
John Abercrombie With The Ansgar Striepens Quintet
Zoe | Wait! | Now That You Are Gone | Ralph's Piano Waltz | The Pointsman's Contract | Waltz For Wheeler
Abercrombie,John (g) | Striepens,Ansgar (tb) | Beckerhoff,Uli (tp) | Nuß,Hubert (p) | Heller,Ingmar (b) | Hollenbeck,John (dr)
Lee Konitz With The Ed Partyka Jazz Orchestra
Zoe
Ludwigsburg, rec. September 1999
Konitz,Lee (as) | Partyka,Edward (ld) | Gansch,Thomas (tp) | Strempel,Sebastian (tp) | Benkenstein,Thorsten (tp) | Maaß,Torsten (tp) | Striepens,Ansgar (tb) | Stöger,Dominik (tb) | Jaksjo,Christian (tb) | Henry,Richard (b-tb) | Van De Wiele,Isabelle (fr-h) | Chapman,Christine (fr-h) | List,Pip (fr-h) | McKreel.Andy (tuba) | Lackner,Marko (reeds) | Leicht,Oliver (reeds) | Erlewein,Matthias (reeds) | Delle,Frank (reeds) | Herzog,Edgar (reeds) | Heller,Ingmar (b) | Hollenbeck,John (dr)

35101652 | CD | The Art Of The Bass Vol.1 | EAN 4011786021659
Wayne Darling Group
Bass Encounters | Stinky Pooh! | Here I Am | Basses Three-O | Speak Low | O,Tysta Ensamhet | St.Thomas | To Dorette
Graz, Austria, rec. 29./30.11.2001
Darling,Wayne (b) | Orsted-Pedersen,Niels-Henning (b) | Egilsson,Arni (b) | Pauer,Fritz (p) | Elgart,Billy (dr)
No Moe | Future Child
Live at Wist Hall,Graz,Austria, rec. 30.11.2001
Darling,Wayne (b) | Orsted-Pedersen,Niels-Henning (b) | Egilsson,Arni (b) | Pauer,Fritz (p) | Elgart,Billy (dr)

35101752 | CD | I Remember Love | EAN 4011786031757
Benny Bailey Quartet With Strings
I'm Never Happy Anymore | I Remember Love | Home | Peruvian Nights | Why Try To Change Ne Now | There's No You | They Didn't Believe Me | If You Could See Me Now | Will You Still Be Mine
Prag,CSFR, rec. June 2002
Bailey,Benny (tp) | Lightsey,Kirk (p) | Balzar,Robert (b) | Vejvoda,Josef (dr) | Petrasek Epoque String Orchestra | Laughlin,Richard (arr,cond)

8695067 | CD | Mosaic
Asita Hamidi & Arcobaleno
Deep Blue | Stella | Il Khan | Kilele(Intro) | Kilele | Nordlicht | Amoebe | Circle(Solo)
Ostermundingen, rec. March 1994
Hamidi,Asita (harp) | Grossniklaus,Melchior (sax) | Abbühl,Martin (v) | Doblies,Günther (g) | Gisinger,Nicolas (synth,el-b) | Eigensatz,Andreas (polychord,tanpura) | Rigert,Stephan (dr,perc)

8695068 | CD | Angel Eyes
Benny Bailey Quartet
Will You Still Be Mine | Angel Eyes | Quarters And Dimes | Johanna's Waltz | My Blues | I'm Afraid | Peruvian Nights | Blues For Lady J.
Live at Schüttbau Tagungs- und Kulturzentrum,Rügheim, rec. March 1995
Bailey,Benny (tp) | Wunsch,Frank (p) | Krisse,Fritz (b) | Krause,Jo (dr)

8695069 | CD | On Earth
Thomas Kessler Group
Into Darkness | A Smile In The Subway | Violet Song | Short Film On Diving | Bleue | '62 | Rain | Dance | Traveling By Flying Carpet | Urban Music(Vol.2)
Bielefeld/Ars-en-Rè,France, rec. 1995
Kessler,Thomas (p,keyboards,synth,perc,auto-harp,loops,programming,samples,treated-g) | Diekmann,Wolfgang (b-g) | Klein,Marlon (clay-bongos,darabuka,djembe,shaker) | Ingenhag,Harald (bells,vase-dr) | Carter,Neil (bodhran)

8695070 | CD | Elements Of Development
Josep Maria Balanyà
Elements Of Development Number Three | Side Effects | Macaccos Macaccos | Elements Of Development Number Four | Introspecció Stomacal | Estudi Per A Piano, Pinxitos | Tub De Plastic | Impromptus Interruptus | Mar | Profundus Tremens | Free Energy | Gentle Ghost & Ganso
Zerkall, rec. 13./14.11.1994
Balanyà,Josep Maria (p-solo)

8695071 | CD | Ageless Guitar Solos
Ulli Bögershausen
Children's Dance | The Fisherman | Das Loch In Der Banane | Morgen Ist Alles Wieder Gut | Samba An Einem Ruhigen Sonntag | Petite Valse | Santa Cruz | Angie | Montpellier | Classical Gas | Opus 20 | Ein Anflug Von Sehnsucht
details unknown, rec. details unknown
Bögershausen,Ulli (g-solo)

LK 190-015 | CD | Thomas Kessler & Group
Thomas Kessler & Group
Elements & Context | N 2.21 | Song For A(part 1&2) | Orchids | Blues F-T | Still Belonging To You | A Waste Land | N 2.21(reprise)
Mühlheim/Ruhr, rec. details unknown
Kessler,Thomas (synth,programming,samples) | Diekmann,Wolfgang (b-g) | Ingenhag,Harald (dr,perc)

LK 35100932 | CD | Pictures
Ulli Bögershausen-Reinhold Westerheide
Sprudelde Wasser | Von Irgendwo Nach Nirgendwo | Toccata | L'Orient Est Grand | Sunny Windo | Zu Allein | Teclado Marfil | Rydbo | Mistral | Roots(part 2) | Kundarra | Dedicated
details unknown, rec. March 1998
Bögershausen,Ulli (g) | Westerheide,Reinhold (g)

LK 689-012 | CD | Melodic Travel
Philippe Caillat Special Project
Slalom
Rheda, rec. details unknown
Caillat,Philippe (g) | Fiszman,Nicolas (b) | Michiels,Frank (perc)
Dark Space | Sahara Romance
Caillat,Philippe (g) | Van't Hof,Jasper (keyboards) | Fiszman,Nicolas (b) | Michiels,Frank (perc)
Relax | Tango Salsa
Caillat,Philippe (g) | Fiszman,Nicolas (b) | Brand,Dirk (dr) | Michiels,Frank (perc)
Relax
Caillat,Philippe (g) | Gouirand,Doudou (sax) | Fiszman,Nicolas (b) | Lühr,Willi (b) | Godejohann,Karl (dr,perc) | Michiels,Frank (perc)
Bouboule
Caillat,Philippe (g) | Fiszman,Nicolas (b) | Lühr,Willi (b) | Allouche,Joel (dr) | Michiels,Frank (perc)
Smooth Cha Cha | Dark Space | Paris Nostalgie | Winter Sun
Caillat,Philippe (g) | Fiszman,Nicolas (b) | Allouche,Joel (dr) | Michiels,Frank (perc)

LK 87-203 | CD | 'Round The Corner
Deborah Henson-Conant Trio
'Round The Corner | Georgia On My Mind | Blue Bossa | Swingin' Shepherd Blues | Take Five | Over The Rainbow | Summertime
Boston,MA, rec. 1987
Henson-Conant,Deborah (harp) | Lockwood,John (b) | Gullotti,Bob (dr,log-dr)

LK 90-021 | CD | Vaina
Serge Forté Trio
Vaina | Song For Magali | H.B.V. | Simba Samba
Studio Davout,?, rec. details unknown
Forté,Serge (p) | Chayeb,Philippe (el-b) | Pontieux,Loic (dr)
B.B.Bemol
Forté,Serge (p) | Racoupeau,Philippe (el-b) | Pontieux,Loic (dr)
Roots Of Love
Forté,Serge (p) | Mineau,Thierry (el-b) | Pontieux,Loic (dr)
Serge Forté-Michel Petrucciani
O Nana Oye
Forté,Serge (p) | Petrucciani,Michel (p)
Serge Forté
Kin's
Forté,Serge (p-solo)

LK 92-027 | CD | Untitled
Thomas Kessler Group
Talk(An Introduction) | Saints & Science | Islands | Falcon Hunting, Fishing Methods | Lost In Main Street | Satori | When The Work Is Done | Urban Music
Mühlheim/Ruhr, rec. details unknown
Kessler,Thomas (synth,digital-perc,programming,samples) | Ingenhag,Harald (dr,perc,vase-dr) | Diekmann,Wolfgang (b,b-g)

LK 92-030 | CD | Stream Of Time
Philippe Caillat Group
Stream Of Time
Rheda, rec. 1992
Caillat,Philippe (el-g) | Mariano,Charlie (ss) | Kochbeck,Georg (keyboards) | Fiszman,Nicolas (b) | Krisse,Fritz (b) | Allaert,Philippe (dr) | Michiels,Frank (perc)
Geisha
Caillat,Philippe (el-g) | Mariano,Charlie (as) | Kochbeck,Georg (keyboards) | Fiszman,Nicolas (b) | Allaert,Philippe (dr) | Michiels,Frank (perc) | Brand,Dirk (chicken shake)
First Day Of Spring
Caillat,Philippe (g) | Mariano,Charlie (sax) | Matinier,Jean-Louis (accordeon) | Kochbeck,Georg (keyboards) | Fiszman,Nicolas (b) | Allaert,Philippe (dr) | Michiels,Frank (perc)
I Think Of You
Caillat,Philippe (el-g) | Mariano,Charlie (sax) | Matinier,Jean-Louis (accordeon) | Kochbeck,Georg (p,keyboards) | Chaudagne,Remy (el-b) | Allaert,Philippe (dr)
Billy The Bowl
Caillat,Philippe (el-g) | Lakatos,Tony (ts) | Matinier,Jean-Louis (accordeon) | Rox,Georg (keyboards) | Fiszman,Nicolas (b) | Allaert,Philippe (dr) | Michiels,Frank (perc)
Round And Round
Caillat,Philippe (el-g) | Lakatos,Tony (ts) | Fiszman,Nicolas (b) | Allaert,Philippe (dr) | Michiels,Frank (perc)
Bivalence
Caillat,Philippe (el-g) | Matinier,Jean-Louis (accordeon) | Kochbeck,Georg (keyboards) | Krisse,Fritz (b) | Fiszman,Nicolas (b) | Allaert,Philippe (dr) | Michiels,Frank (perc)
16 Bars
Caillat,Philippe (g,el-g) | Lakatos,Tony (ts) | Matinier,Jean-Louis (accordeon) | Kochbeck,Georg (keyboards) | Krisse,Fritz (b) | Fiszman,Nicolas (b) | Allaert,Philippe (dr)
Bouboule
Caillat,Philippe (g) | Mariano,Charlie (as) | Matinier,Jean-Louis (accordeon) | Rox,Georg (keyboards) | Fiszman,Nicolas (b) | Allaert,Philippe (dr)

LK 93-033 | CD | Chorinho
Christof Sänger Trio
Montego | Soul Eyes | Body And Soul | Chorinho(Speedy Gonzales) | The Way You Look Tonight | Giant Steps | City Scape | Blues | The End Of A Love Affair | Saudade
Frankfurt/M, rec. 20.8.1992
Sänger,Christof (p) | Van Kaphengst,Christian (b) | Köbberling,Heinrich (dr)

LK 93-036 | CD | Frank Kirchner
Frank Kirchner Group
Scotch And Women | Children's Garden | Jah Man | Dose Hassiu | Downtown Blues | That's Because | Morning Sun | Ecstasy | Hymn | Autumn Leaves | Risk Of Electric Shock
Remscheid, rec. 1992
Kirchner,Frank (ss,ts) | Wienstroer,Markus (g,el-g,12-string-g) | Steinhauer,Dietmar (p,keyboards,synth) | Rademacher,Stefan (el-b) | Billker,Kurt (dr) | Ginzberg,Leonhard (perc)

LK 93-039 | CD | Budapest
Deborah Henson-Conant Group
Coqueta | Budapest | Inevitability Of You | Fool Of The World | Pava Diablo | Nature Girl | Swamp Ballet | Tiger Dreams | Daphne's Madness | Kerry Dance
Budapest, rec. 1992
Henson-Conant,Deborah (harp) | Johnson,Mark (sax) | Minucci,Chieli (g,el-g,synth) | Bailey,Victor (b) | Jinda,George (perc)

LK 93-043 | CD | About Time
Tim Sund Quartet
About TimeTo Begin | Dr. Dee Dee | Waltz For The Night | Yours | Adventures | Levrette | Turn Over The Musket | Retrospective | Darn That Dream
Monster,NL, rec. 11.-13.4.1993
Sund,Tim (p) | Valk,Claudius (ss,ts) | Foltynowicz,Jens (b) | Schönburg,Kai (dr)

LK 93-045 | CD | Best Of Ulli Bögershausen
Ulli Bögershausen
Von Irgendwo Nach Nirgendwo
details unknown, rec. 1991
Bögershausen,Ulli (g) | Diekmann,Wolfgang (b) | Kessler,Thomas (synth,samples)
Im Nebel Nach Brüssel
Bögershausen,Ulli (g) | Kirchner,Frank (sax) | Westerheide,Reinhold (marimba) | Diekmann,Wolfgang (b) | Kessler,Thomas (synth,samples) | Ingenhag,Harald (dr)
April
Bögershausen,Ulli (g) | Westerheide,Reinhold (vib,marimba) | Diekmann,Wolfgang (b) | Kessler,Thomas (synth) | Ingenhag,Harald (dr)
Zu Allein
details unknown, rec. 1993
Bögershausen,Ulli (g) | Leslie,Chris (v) | Diekmann,Wolfgang (b)
Domani
details unknown, rec. 1991
Bögershausen,Ulli (g) | Westerheide,Reinhold (perc) | Kessler,Thomas (synth,samples)
Weißt Du Noch? | Baman Bia
details unknown, rec. 1988
Bögershausen,Ulli (g) | Tahmasebi,Mohammad (dombac)
Autogen | Ombrellino | Frühling,Sommer,Herbst | Ganz Bestimmt Vielleicht | Ich Weiß Nicht,Woran In Bin | Ulla | Herbstallee | Montpellier | Ich Kann Nicht Länger Warten | Ein Anflug Von Sehnsucht | Fragile | Gentle Breeze
details unknown, rec. 1982-1993
Bögershausen,Ulli (g-solo,12-string-g)

LK 93-048 | CD | Contemporary Klezmer
Kol Simcha
Zipor | Shpiel Es | Nigun | Hip Hip Hora | Why | Everbody's Freilach | Folk Song | Negev | Long Live The Nigun | Josef's Freilach | Dybbuk | Lullaby | Sher | Tarra's Freilach | Shir Hamaalot
Zürich,CH, rec. details unknown
Koi Simcha | Reiser,Niki (fl) | Heitzler,Michael (cl) | Truan,Oliver (p) | Fricker,Daniel (b) | Klein,David (dr)

LK 94-051 | CD | Naked Music
Deborah Henson-Conant
Nataliana | Baroque Flamenco | Danger Zone | Home In Your Arms Again | Johnny Ramsay | Love Is On Your Side | New Blues | Dance With Me | All Through The Night | Closer To You | Noche
Wellspring Sound Concord,MA, rec. details unknown
Henson-Conant,Deborah (perc,harp,voc)

LK 94-054 | CD | Puasong Daffriek
Lotz Of Music
Rappin' Donna | Mean MC Mudda | Pygmies In The Dark | Ojos Chinos De Santa Ana | Aerofloz | Quasimodo | Dr.Kimble | Begona-Blues | Mogigrafisch Einerlei | Puasing Daffriek
Amsterdam,Holland, rec. 29./30.12.1993
Lotz Of Music | Lotz,Mark Alban (fl,b-fl,didjeridoo,hand-clapping) | Ornstein,Maarten (b-cl,ts,hand-clapping) | Schmid,Stefan (p,perc,hand-clapping) | Beets,Marius (b) | Kruger,Stefan (dr)

LK 94-057 | CD | Caprice
Christoph Sänger Trio
Buenavista | Bailando | Darn That Dream | Piranha | Biff Baff Buff | Tram | Everything Happens To Me | Maytanca | Lost | Caprice Francis(por F.Poulenc) | Solar | Waves
Frankfurt/M, rec. 30./31.3.1994
Sänger,Christof (p) | Von Kaphengst,Christian (b) | Köbberling,Heinrich (dr)

LK 94-060 | CD | Long Distance
Mario Neunkirchen Quintet
Night | Detailed Instructions | Long Distance | Twilight | Drug Waltz | Mirrors | Quiet Afternoon
Düsseldorf, rec. details unknown
Neunkirchen,Mario (g) | Scheunemann,Karsten (sax) | Poffo,Christian (keyboards,programming) | Mayer,Capo (b) | Pilger,Andreas (dr,perc)

LK 95-063 | CD | Just For You
Deborah Henson-Conant
Closer To You
Live in Baden-Baden/Düsseldorf/Bielefeld, rec. 1./10.& 12.6.1994
Henson-Conant,Deborah (harp,voc)
Deborah Henson-Conant Trio
Just For You | Budapest | The Rain King | Baroque Flamenco | Dance With Me | Danger Zone | Under The Bed | The Phoenix | Watermelon Boogie
Henson-Conant,Deborah (perc,harp,prepared-harp,voc) | Diekmann,Wolfgang (b-g) | Tulloch,Davey (perc)

LK 95-066 | CD | Senor Blues
Wayne Bartlett With The Thomas Hufschmidt Trio And Wolfgang Engstfeld
Senor Blues | I Walk With Music | I Betcha A Rainbow | I'd Rather Ride An Elephant | I Don't Know You | Cheaper To Keep Her | Unchain My Heart | Going To Chicago Blues | Ruby | I Wanna Know | On Green Dolphin Street | Just A Little Kiss | Stormy Monday Blues(They Call It Stormy Monday)
Monster,NL, rec. April/May 1994
Bartlett,Wayne (arr,voc) | Engstfeld,Wolfgang (ts) | Hufschmidt,Thomas (p,arr) | Foltynowicz,Jens (b) | Schilgen,Dirik (dr)

LK 990-018 | CD | Daniel Guggenheim Group feat. Jasper van't Hof
Daniel Guggenheim Group
One For Sonny | For Ute | Bangu Jabour | Dromedar | Back Home | Happiness | Foolish Dancer | No Rest
Frankfurt/M, rec. April 1990
Guggenheim,Daniel (ss,as) | Feil,Peter (tb) | Van't Hof,Jasper (p,keyboards) | Kistner,Udo (b) | Henkel,Roland (dr) | Nicholas,Tom (perc)

Laserlight | Delta Music

17249 | CD | Paris Jazz Concert:Jimmy Giuffre | EAN 4006408172499
Jimmy Giuffre Trio
The Boy Next Door | Mack The Knife(Moritat) | My Funny Valentine | Two For Timbuctu
Live at The Olympia,Paris,France, rec. 23.2.1960
Giuffre,Jimmy (cl) | Hall,Jim (g) | Middlebrooks,Wilfred (b)
Drive | Cry Want | Cross Roads | Syncopate | Ictus
Live at The Olympia,Paris,France, rec. 27.2.1965
Giuffre,Jimmy (cl,ss,ts) | Friedman,Don (p) | Phillips,Barre (b)

17250 | CD | Paris Jazz Concert:Theloniuos Monk And His Quartet | EAN 4006408172505
Thelonious Monk Quartet
Rhythm-A-Ning | Body And Soul | I Mean You | April In Paris | Well You Needn't | Bright Mississippi | Epistrophy
Live at The Olympia,Paris,France, rec. 7.3.1965
Monk,Thelonious (p) | Rouse,Charlie (ts) | Gales,Larry (b) | Riley,Ben (dr)

17433 | CD | Paris Jazz Concert:Gerry Mulligan And His Quartet | EAN 4006408174332
Gerry Mulligan Quartet
Spring Is Sprung | Five Brothers | Subterranean Blues | Darn That Dream | Blueport | Utter Chaos
Live at The Olympia,Paris,France, rec. 6.10.1962
Mulligan,Gerry (bs,p) | Brookmeyer,Bob (v-tb,p) | Crow,Bill (b) | Johnson,Gus (dr)

17445 | CD | Paris Jazz Concert:Miles Davis | EAN 4006408174455
Miles Davis Group
Turnaroundphrase- | Tune In 5- | Unidentified Title- | Ife- | Unidentified Title- | Unidentified Title
Live at The Olympia,Paris,France, rec. 11.7.1973
Davis,Miles (tp,org) | Liebman,Dave (fl,ss,ts) | Cosey,Pete (g) | Lucas,Reggie (g) | Henderson,Michael (el-b) | Foster,Al (dr) | M'tume,James[Forman] (perc)

24321 | 2 CD | Boogie Woogie
Boogie Woogie Trio
Cavalcade Of Boogie
Live at Carnegie Hall,NYC, rec. 23.12.1938
Ammons,Albert (p) | Lewis,Meade Lux (p) | Johnson,Pete (p) | Page,Walter (b) | Jones,Jo (dr)
Albert Ammons
Boogie Woogie Stomp | Boogie Woogie Blues | Suitcase Blues
NYC, rec. 6.1.1939
Ammons,Albert (p-solo)
Chicago In Mind
NYC, rec. 6.5.1939
Ammons,Albert (p-solo)
Shout For Joy
Chicago,Ill, rec. 31.10.1939
Ammons,Albert (p-solo)
Charles Avery
Dearborn St. Breakdown
Chicago,Ill, rec. October 1929

Avery,Charles (p-solo)
Henry Brown
Henry Brown Blues
Richmond, Indiana, rec. 16.8.1929
Brown,Henry (p-solo)
Deep Morgan Blues | Eastern Chimes Blues
Grafton,Wis., rec. February 1930
Brown,Henry (p-solo)
Cow Cow Davenport
Slow Drag | Chimes Blues | Atlanta Rag
Richmond, Indiana, rec. 1.4.1929
Davenport,Cow Cow (p,speech)
Will Ezell
Barrelhouse Woman | Heifer Dust
Chicago,Ill, rec. February 1929
Ezell,Will (p-solo)
Blind Leroy Garnett
Chain 'Em Down | Louisiana Glide
Richmond, Indiana, rec. 12.10.1929
Garnett,Blind Leroy (p-solo) | Wiggins,James 'Boodle It' (speech)
Meade Lux Lewis
Honky Tonk Train Blues
Chicago,Ill, rec. December 1927
Lewis,Meade Lux (p-solo)
Albert Ammons-Meade Lux Lewis
Twos And Fews
NYC, rec. 6.1.1939
Ammons,Albert (p) | Lewis,Meade Lux (p)
Albert Ammons
Boogie Woogie | Bass Goin' Crazy
Ammons,Albert (p-solo)
Wesley Wallace
Fanny Lee Blues | No.29
Grafton,Wis., rec. February 1930
Wallace,Wesley (p,voc)
Jabo Williams
Jab Blues | Pratt City Blues
Grafton,Wis., rec. May 1932
Williams,Jabo (p-solo,voc)

24327 | 2 CD | Miles Davis Live From His Last Concert In Avignon
Miles Davis Group
Intruders | New Blues | One Phone Call- | Street Scenes- | Perfect Way | The Senate- | Me And You- | Tutu | Movie Star | Splash | Time After Time | Wayne's Tune | Full Nelson
Live in Avignon,France, rec. Summer 1988
Davis,Miles (tp) | Garrett,Kenny (fl,as) | Foley (el-g) | Irving III,Robert (keyboards) | Holzman,Adam (keyboards) | Jones,Darryl (el-b) | Wellman,Ricky (dr) | Bird,Rudy (perc)

24338 | 2 CD | First Revolution Gospel Singers:A Capella
First Revolution Singers
Down By The Riverside | Oh! Freedom | Glory Glory Hallelujah | Family Circle | At The Cross | He's Okay | Hey Sinner | Please Remember Me | He Really Cares | Hymn Book,Holy Book And Pocket Book | I'm Gonna Serve The Lord | I Made Up My Mind | It's Gonna Rain | Balm In The Gilead | I Shall Not Be Moved | Good Lord I Have Done | Jesus Hits Like The Atom Bomb | Lord I Want To Be A Christian | Old Time Religion | I'll Be Somewhere Listening For My Name | Ezekiel Saw 'De Wheel | Deep River | The People Don't Do Like They Used To Do | Dry Bones In The Valley | Amazing Grace | Didn't It Rain | Wade In The Water | Wake Nicodemus | Woke Up This Morning | Back To The Church | Straighten Up And Fly Right | Sometimes I Feel Like A Motherless Child
New Orleans,Louisiana, rec. details unknown
First Revolution Singers,The | Alexander,Jerome (voc) | Bell,Larry (voc) | Coulon,Cornell (voc) | Hunter,George (voc) | Miller,Harold (voc) | Hicks,Jimmie (voc) | Marshall,Raymond (voc) | Gordon,Dennis (voc)

24366 | 2 CD | Jazz Collection:Louis Armstrong
Louis Armstrong And His All Stars
Mahogany Hall Stomp | Black And Blue | Royal Garden Blues | Muskrat Ramble | On The Sunny Side Of The Street | High Society
Live at Symphony Hall,Boston, rec. 20.11.1947
Armstrong,Louis (tp,voc) | Teagarden,Jack (tb,voc) | Bigard,Barney (cl) | Cary,Dick (p) | Shaw,Arvell (b) | Catlett,Big Sid (dr) | Middleton,Velma (voc)
Panama | Blue Skies | Lover | Whispering | A Song Was Born | Jack-Armstrong Blues
Armstrong,Louis (tp,voc) | Teagarden,Jack (tb,voc) | Bigard,Barney (cl) | Hines,Earl 'Fatha' (p) | Shaw,Arvell (b) | Catlett,Big Sid (dr) | Middleton,Velma (voc)
Mack The Knife(Moritat) | Blueberry Hill | Cabaret | A Kiss To Build A Dream On | Hello Dolly | That's My Desire
Armstrong,Louis (tp,voc) | Glenn,Tyree (tb,voc) | Muranyi,Joe (cl) | Napoleon,Marty (p) | Cattlett,Buddy (b) | Barcelona,Danny (dr)
Louis Armstrong With Sy Oliver's Choir And Orchestra
Down By The Riverside
rec. 4.2.1958
Armstrong,Louis (tp,voc) | Oliver,Sy (cond,arr) | Young,Trummy (tb) | McRae,Dave (cl) | Tragg,Nickie (org) | Kyle,Billy (p) | Barnes,George (g) | Herbert,Mort (b) | Deems,Barrett (dr) | 10-voice-choir
Swing Low Sweet Chariot
NYC, rec. 7.2.1958
Armstrong,Louis (tp,voc) | Oliver,Sy (cond,arr) | Young,Trummy (tb) | D'Amico,Hank (cl) | Tragg,Nickie (org) | Kyle,Billy (p) | Barksdale,Everett (g) | Herbert,Mort (b) | Deems,Barrett (dr)
Louis Armstrong With Orchestra
What A Wonderful World
Armstrong,Louis (tp,voc) | Studio Orchestra | details unknown
When The Saints Go Marching In | Georgia On My Mind | C'Est Si Bon | La Vie En Rose | Sweet Georgia Brown
Armstrong,Louis (tp,voc) | details unknown

24367 | 2 CD | Jazz Collection:Glenn Miller
Glenn Miller And His Orchestra
Moonlight Serenade | St.Louis Blues | American Patrol | Little Brown Jug | Serenade In Blue | In The Mood | Tuxedo Junction | String Of Pearls | At Last | Is You Is Or Is You Ain't My Baby | Great Day | Sun Valley Jump | I Got Rhythm | My Blue Heaven | A-Tisket A-Tasket | Solitude | Here We Go Again | Jeep Jockey Jump | Over There | Peggy The Pin Up Girl | Georgia On My Mind | In A Sentimental Mood | Jeannie With The Light Brown Hair | Woodpecker Song | Moon Love | Stardust | Anchors Aweigh | Caribbean Clipper | Glen Island Special | Perfidia
Miller,Glenn (tb,ld) | details unknown

24368 | 2 CD | Jazz Collection:Count Basie
Count Basie And His Orchestra
Little Pony | One O'Clock Jump | Blues | Indian Summer | Who Me | Jumpin' At The Woodside | Spring Is Here | Teddy The Toad | Pensive Miss | Corner Pocket | Sweet Cakes | Cute
Basie,Count (p) | Jones,Thad (tp) | Young,Eugene 'Snooky' (tp) | Culley,Wendell (tp) | Newman,Joe (tp) | Coker,Henry (tb) | Grey,Al (tb) | Powell,Benny (tb) | Royal,Marshall (as) | Wess,Frank (fl,as) | Mitchell,Billy (ts) | Foster,Frank (ts) | Fowlkes,Charlie (bs) | Green,Freddie (g) | Jones,Eddie (b) | Payne,Sonny (dr)
Lil' Darlin' | One O'Clock Jump | Dance Of The Gremlins | Let's Jump | Slow But Sure | Jazz Me Blues | Five O'Clock In The Morning | Flight Of The Foo Birds | Chestnut Street Ramble(Vine Street Ramble) | Dinah | Basie Boogie | Rock-A-Bye Basie
Live at different places
Basie,Count (p) | Jones,Thad (tp) | Young,Eugene 'Snooky' (tp) | Culley,Wendell (tp) | Jones,Reunald (tp) | Lewis,Ed (tp) | Killian,Al (tp) | Edison,Harry 'Sweets' (tp) | Clayton,Buck (tp) | Cohn[Cohen],Sonny (tp) | Coker,Henry (tb) | Grey,Al (tb) | Powell,Benny (tb) | Hughes,Bill (tb) | Donelly,Ted (tb) | Wells,Dicky (tb) | Robinson,Eli (tb) | Jackson,Quentin (tb) | Royal,Marshall (as) | Wess,Frank (fl,as) | Washington Jr.,Jack (as) | Mitchell,Billy (ts) | Foster,Frank (ts) | Dixon,Eric (ts) | Warren,Earl (as) | Powell,Jimmy (ts) | Byas,Don (ts) | Tate,Buddy (ts) | Wilkins,Ernie (ts) | Fowlkes,Charlie (bs) | Green,Freddie (g) | Jones,Eddie (b) | Alley,Vernon (b) | Payne,Sonny (dr) | Jones,Jo (dr) | Johnson,Gus (dr)

24369 | 2 CD | Jazz Collection:Duke Ellington
Duke Ellington And His Orchestra
Take The 'A' Train | Black And Tan Fantasy | Perdido | Raincheck | Satin Doll | Diminuendo In Blue | Happy-Go-Lucky Local(part 1) | Happy-Go-Lucky Local(part 2) | Flippant Flurry | Glory | Cool Rock | Chinoiserie | Vancouver Lights | Things Ain't What They Used To Be | Lullaby Of Birdland | Liza(All The Clouds'll Roll Away) | Creole Love Call | Hy' A Sue | Sophisticated Lady | Caravan | Perdido | C Jam Blues | Coffee & Kisses | Johnny Comes Lately | Honeysuckle Rose | Theme For Trambean | V.I.P.'s Boogie | Jam With Sam
different Places
Ellington,Duke (p) | personal included: | Baker,Harold 'Shorty' (tp) | Anderson,Cat (tp) | Terry,Clark (tp,fl-h) | Nance,Ray (tp,v,voc) | Jackson,Quentin (tb) | Sanders,John (tb) | Woodman,Britt (tb) | Hodges,Johnny (as) | Procope,Russell (cl,as) | Hamilton,Jimmy (cl,ts) | Gonsalves,Paul (ts) | Carney,Harry (cl,bs) | Woode,Jimmy (b) | Woodyard,Sam (dr)

24396 | 2 CD | Jazz Collection:Benny Goodman
Benny Goodman And His Orchestra
Sing Sing Sing | Jumpin' At The Woodside | Stompin' At The Savoy | Seven Come Eleven | Lonely Moments | Mahzel | Let's Dance | Somebody Stole My Gal | Sent For You Yesterday And Here You Come Today | Mission To Moscow | Henderson Stomp | After You've Gone | Down South Camp Meeting | One O'Clock Jump | Memories Of You | Avalon
different Places, rec. details unknown
Goodman,Benny (cl) | Orchestra | details unknown
Benny Goodman Trio
Oh! Lady Be Good | Who | After You've Gone | Body And Soul | Someday Sweetheart | China Boy
details unknown, rec. details unknown
Goodman,Benny (cl) | Wilson,Teddy (p) | Krupa,Gene (dr)
Benny Goodman Quartet
Dinah | Vibraphone Blues | Sweet Sue Just You | My Melancholy Baby | Close Your Eyes | You're Blasé | The World Is Waiting For The Sunrise | That's A Plenty
Goodman,Benny (cl) | Hampton,Lionel (vib,voc) | Wilson,Teddy (p) | Krupa,Gene (dr)

24397 | 2 CD | Jazz Collection:Ella Fitzgerald
Ella Fitzgerald And Her Orchestra
A-Tisket A-Tasket | We Can't Go On This Way | Basin Street Blues | That Old Black Magic | Sing Song Swing
Fitzgerald,Ella (voc) | Vance,Dick (tp) | Jordan,Taft (tp) | Stark,Bobby (tp) | Matthews,George (tb) | Story,Nat (tb) | Williams,Sandy (tb) | Bushell,Garvin (cl,ss) | Jefferson,Hilton (as) | Carver,Wayman (fl,as,ts) | McRae,Teddy (ts,bs) | Fulford,Tommy (p) | Trueheart,John (g) | Peer,Beverley (b) | Beason,Bill (dr)
Ella Fitzgerald With The Chick Webb Orchestra
Rock It For Me | My Heart Belongs To Daddy | Crying My Heart Out For You | Under The Spell Of The Blues | When I Get Low I Get High
Fitzgerald,Ella (voc) | Webb,Chick (dr) | Bauza,Mario (tp) | Stark,Bobby (tp) | Jordan,Taft (tp) | Williams,Sandy (tb) | Story,Nat (tb) | Haughton,Chauncey (cl,as) | Jordan,Louis (as) | McRae,Teddy (ts) | Carver,Wayman (fl,ts) | Fulford,Tommy (p) | Johnson,Bobby (g) | Peer,Beverley (b)
Ella Fitzgerald And Barney Kessel
Lover Come Back To Me | Starlight Hour | Flying Home
Fitzgerald,Ella (voc) | Orchestra | details unknown
Ella Fitzgerald And Her Orchestra
Oh Johnny Oh Johnny | Chew Chew Chew
details unknown, rec. details unknown
Fitzgerald,Ella (voc) | Orchestra | details unknown
Ella Fitzgerald With The Tommy Flanagan Trio
Alright,Okay,You Win | I Love You Madly | It Happened In Monterey- | No Regrets- | It's A Wonderful World- | Cabaret | I Concentrate On You | Mr.Paganini | Just One Of Those Things | I Can't Give You Anything But Love
Fitzgerald,Ella (voc) | Flanagan,Tommy (p) | Betts,Keter (b) | Durham,Bobby (dr)
Ella Fitzgerald And Her Be-Bop Boys
Love That Boy | Heat Wave | Bop Boogie
details unknown, rec. details unknown
Fitzgerald,Ella (voc) | details unknown
Ella Fitzgerald And Her Orchestra
Hallelujah | Love And Kisses
Fitzgerald,Ella (voc) | Orchestra | details unknown

24652 | 2 CD | The Art Of Saxophone
Lester Young Quintet
Jump Lester Jump
rec. 1.5.1944
Young,Lester (ts) | Basie,Count (p) | Green,Freddie (g) | Richardson,Rodney (b) | Wilson,Shadow (dr)
Coleman Hawkins Quartet
Body And Soul
London,GB, rec. 26.11.1967
Hawkins,Coleman (ts) | Carter,Benny (p) | Cranshaw,Bob (b) | Bellson,Louie (dr)
Ben Webster With The Kenny Drew Trio
Pennies From Heaven
Copenhagen,Denmark, rec. 4.3.1965
Webster,Ben (ts) | Drew,Kenny (p) | Orsted-Pedersen,Niels-Henning (b) | Riel,Alex (dr)
Benny Carter And His Orchestra
Blue Lou
?,Germany, rec. 1968
Carter,Benny (as) | Gagliardi,Joe (tp) | Faist,Andre (tb) | Zufferey,Roger (as) | Pilet,Michel (ts) | Erbetta,Marc (bs) | Chaix,Henri (p) | Du Bois,Alain (b) | Cavicchiolo,Romano (dr)
Don Byas Quartet
All The Things You Ain't
rec. 1959
Byas,Don (ts) | Axen,Bent (p) | Orsted-Pedersen,Niels-Henning (b) | Schiöppfe,William (dr)
Dexter Gordon Quintet
Settin' The Pace
rec. 11.12.1947
Gordon,Dexter (ts) | Parker,Leo (bs) | Dameron,Tadd (p) | Boyd,Nelson (b) | Blakey,Art (dr)
Sonny Stitt Quartet
Duty Free
Paris/Berikon,CH, rec. 1979
Stitt,Sonny (as,ts,voc) | Price,Gerald (p) | Mosley,Don (b) | Durham,Bobby (dr)
Duke Ellington And His Orchestra
I Got It Bad And That Ain't Good
?,Europe, rec. 1961
Ellington,Duke (p) | Anderson,Cat (tp) | Williams,Cootie (tp) | Jones,Herbie (tp) | Ellington,Mercer (tp) | Brown,Lawrence (tb) | Connors,Chuck (tb) | Cooper,Frank 'Buster' (tb) | Hodges,Johnny (as) | Hamilton,Jimmy (cl,ts) | Procope,Russell (cl,as) | Gonsalves,Paul (ts) | Carney,Harry (bs) | Lamb,John (b) | Woodyard,Sam (dr)
Eddie Lockjaw Davis Quartet
Leapin' At The Lennox
?,France, rec. 1974
Davis,Eddie 'Lockjaw' (ts) | Buckner,Milt (org) | Leary,Jimmy (b) | Johnson,Gus (dr)
Cannonball Adderley Quintet
Still Talkin' To Ya
rec. 26.7.1955
Adderley,Julian \'Cannonball\' (as) | Adderley,Nat (co) | Jones,Hank (p) | Chambers,Paul (b) | Clarke,Kenny (dr)
Phil Woods-Benny Carter Quintet
Out Of Nowhere
Woods,Phil (as) | Carter,Benny (as) | Arvanitas,Georges (p) | Trussardi,Luigi (b) | Babualt,Michel (dr)
Stan Getz Quartet
Desafinado
rec. February 1969
Getz,Stan (ts) | Cowell,Stanley (p) | Vitous,Miroslav (b) | DeJohnette,Jack (dr)
Hank Mobley Quintet
B For BB
rec. 23.7.1956
Mobley,Hank (ts) | Byrd,Donald (tp) | Harris,Barry (p) | Watkins,Doug (b) | Clarke,Kenny (dr)
Lucky Thompson Quartet
Soul Lullaby
NYC, rec. 1972
Thompson,Lucky (ss) | Walton,Cedar (p,el-p) | Ridley,Larry (b) | Hayes,Louis (dr)
Zoot Sims-Bucky Pizzarelli Duo
Come Rain Or Come Shine
Sims,Zoot (ss,ts) | Pizzarelli,Bucky (g)
Wilbur Harden Quintet
Wells Fargo
rec. 13.3.1958
Harden,Wilbur (fl-h) | Coltrane,John (ts) | Flanagan,Tommy (p) | Watkins,Doug (b) | Hayes,Louis (dr)
Gerry Mulligan Quartet
Jeru
rec. 1960
Mulligan,Gerry (bs) | Williamson,Claude (p) | Clarke,Buddy (b) | Lewis,Mel (dr)
Lee Konitz Orchestra
Me And My Baby
NYC, rec. 6.5.1975
Konitz,Lee (as) | Michels,Lloyd (tp) | Hurwitz,Richard (tp) | Maur,Barry (tb) | Ralph,Alan (tb) | Palmer,Don (ts) | Farrell,Joe (ts) | Katz,Dick (p,el-p) | Longo,Michael (keyboards,synth) | Davis,George (g) | Holley,Major (b,voice) | Locke,Eddie (dr) | Armando,Ray (perc)
Art Pepper Quartet
Patricia
Atlanta,GA, rec. May 1960
Pepper,Art (as) | Leviev,Milcho (p) | Magnusson,Bob (b) | Burnett,Carl (dr)
Yusef Lateef Sextet
Yusef
Detroit, rec. 23.8.1955
Lateef,Yusef (ts) | Byrd,Donald (tp) | McKinney,Bernard (euphonium) | Harris,Barry (p) | Jackson,Alvin 'Al' (b) | Gant,Frank (dr)
Archie Shepp-Dollar Brand Duo
Left Alone
Tokyo, Japan, rec. 5.6.1978
Shepp,Archie (ss,ts) | Brand,Dollar[Abdullah Ibrahim] (p)
Gato Barbieri Quintet
OC-DC
Paris,France, rec. May 1965
Barbieri,Gato (ts) | Cherry,Don (tp) | Berger,Karl (vib) | Jenny-Clark,Jean-Francois (b) | Romano,Aldo (dr)
Bob Berg Quintet
Autumn Leaves
rec. 1990
Berg,Bob (ts) | Stern,Mike (g) | Beard,Jim (keyboards) | Goines,Lincoln (el-b) | Chambers,Dennis (dr)

24653 | 2 CD | The Story Of Jazz Piano
James P.Johnson
Liza
NYC, rec. May 1945
Johnson,James P. (p-solo)
Jelly Roll Morton
Dead Man Blues
rec. 1924
Morton,Jelly Roll (p-solo)
Earl Hines
Once In A While
Santa Monica,CA, rec. 29.1.1974
Hines,Earl 'Fatha' (p-solo)
Teddy Wilson Trio
You Go To My Head
?,France, rec. 1976
Wilson,Teddy (p) | Hinton,Milt (b) | Jackson,Oliver (dr)
Art Tatum
Back Home Again In Indiana
Los Angeles,CA, rec. 1939
Tatum,Art (p-solo)
Duke Ellington And His Orchestra
Take The 'A' Train
Live at McElroy's Ballroom,Portland,OR
Ellington,Duke (p) | Orchestra | details unknown
Count Basie Trio
Basie Thought
?,France, rec. 1968
Basie,Count (p) | Keenan,Norman (b) | Jones,Harold (dr)
Erroll Garner Trio
Body And Soul
rec. 29.3.1949
Garner,Erroll (p) | Simmons,John (b) | Stoller,Alvin (dr)
George Shearing Trio
Have You Met Miss Jones
rec. 3.2.1947
Shearing,George (p) | Ramey,Gene (b) | Best,Denzil (dr)
Mary Lou Williams Quartet
Rosa Mae
rec. 17.1.1974
Williams,Mary Lou (p) | Carco,Zito (p) | Cranshaw,Bob (b) | Roker,Granville 'Mickey' (dr)
Bud Powell Quintet
Miguel's Party
?,France, rec. 1957
Powell,Bud (p) | Terry,Clark (tp) | Wilen,Barney (ts) | Peter,Eric (b) | Clarke,Kenny (dr)
Thelonious Monk
Round About Midnight
?,France, rec. 1954
Monk,Thelonious (p-solo)
Lennie Tristano Trio
Supersonic
rec. 23.10.1947
Tristano,Lennie (p) | Bauer,Billy (g) | Levy,John (b)
Horace Silver Sextet
Hear Me Talkin' To Ya
rec. 26.6.1955
Silver,Horace (p) | Adderley,Nat (co) | Byrd,Donald (tp) | Adderley,Julian \'Cannonball\' (as) | Chambers,Paul (b) | Clarke,Kenny (dr)
Wynton Kelly Trio
Kelly's Blues
rec. 4.8.1968
Kelly,Wynton (p) | Chambers,Paul (b) | Cobb,Jimmy (dr)
Hank Jones Trio With The Meridian String Quartet
Caravan
NYC, rec. 15.11.1990
Jones,Hank (p) | Reid,Rufus (b) | Mackrel,Dennis (dr) | Meridian String Quartet | Sirinian,Sebu (v) | Tipton,Lisa (v) | Evans,Rachel (viola) | Assael,Deborah (cello)
Cedar Walton Quartet
Home Comin'
NYC, rec. 1972
Walton,Cedar (p) | Thompson,Lucky (ts) | Ridley,Larry (b) | Higgins,Billy (dr)
Tommy Flanagan/Kenny Barron
Stella By Starlight
NYC, rec. 12.6.1978
Flanagan,Tommy (p) | Barron,Kenny (p)
Ben Webster With The Kenny Drew Trio
Blues In B Flat
Copenhagen,Denmark, rec. 4.3.1965
Webster,Ben (ts) | Drew,Kenny (p) | Orsted-Pedersen,Niels-Henning (b) | Riel,Alex (dr)

Bill Evans Trio
Autumn Leaves
NYC, rec. 1961
Evans,Bill (p) | LaFaro,Scott (b) | Motian,Paul (dr)
Roland Hanna Quartet
The Night Before
NYC, rec. 2.8.1991
Hanna,Sir Roland (p) | Easley,Bill (ts) | Burr,Jon (b) | Burrage,Ronnie (dr)
McCoy Tyner Quartet
Rotunda
NYC, rec. 11.2.1991
Tyner,McCoy (p) | Sharpe,Avery (b) | Scott,Aaron (dr) | Cruz,Rafael (perc)
Paul Bley Trio
When Will The Blues Leave
rec. 17.8.1962
Bley,Paul (p) | Swallow,Steve (b) | LaRoca,Pete (dr)
Chick Corea Trio
Blues Connotation
NYC, rec. 7.4.1970
Corea,Chick (p) | Holland,Dave (b) | Altschul,Barry (dr)
Eliane Elias Trio
Illusions
Elias,Eliane (p) | Gomez,Eddie (b) | Gadd,Steve (dr)
Bill Mays Quartet
Daydream
NYC, rec. February 1991
Mays,Bill (p) | Appleyard,Peter (vib) | Seaton,Lynn (b) | Maricle,Sherrie (dr)

24654 | 2 CD | Swingin' The Blues-Jumpin' The Blues
Jimmy McGriff Orchestra
Every Day | Lil' Darlin' | Splanky | Slow But Sure
NYC, rec. 28.2.1966
McGriff,Jimmy (org) | Nottingham,Jimmy (tp) | Collins,Bert (tp) | Markowitz,Irving 'Marky' (tp) | Newman,Joe (tp) | Johnson,J.J. (tb) | Andre,Wayne (tb) | Hixon,Richard (tb) | Studd,Tony (b-tb) | Richardson,Jerome (as) | Wess,Frank (as) | Johnson,Budd (ts) | Foster,Frank (ts) | Powell,Seldon (bs) | Burrell,Kenny (g) | Schwartz,Thornel (g) | Davis,Richard (b) | Amsterdam,Chet (b) | Tate,Grady (dr)
Cherry Point | Swingin' The Blues
NYC, rec. 1966
McGriff,Jimmy (org) | Nottingham,Jimmy (tp) | Collins,Bert (tp) | Jones,Thad (tp) | Royal,Ernie (tp) | Newman,Joe (tp) | Bert,Eddie (tb) | McIntosh,Tom (tb) | Andre,Wayne (tb) | Studd,Tony (b-tb) | Richardson,Jerome (as) | Wess,Frank (as) | Johnson,Budd (ts) | Foster,Frank (ts) | Powell,Seldon (bs) | Burrell,Kenny (g) | Schwartz,Thornel (g) | Davis,Richard (b) | Amsterdam,Chet (b) | Lewis,Mel (dr)
Hob Nail Boogie | Cute | Blues Go Away | Avenue C
NYC, rec. 14.4.1966
McGriff,Jimmy (org) | Nottingham,Jimmy (tp) | Williams,Richard (tp) | Royal,Ernie (tp) | Newman,Joe (tp) | Faulise,Paul (tb) | McIntosh,Tom (tb) | Andre,Wayne (tb) | Studd,Tony (b-tb) | Richardson,Jerome (as) | Wess,Frank (as) | Johnson,Budd (ts) | Mitchell,Billy (ts) | Powell,Seldon (bs) | Galbraith,Barry (g) | Davis,Richard (b) | Lewis,Mel (dr)
Buddy Rich Septet
Sweet Georgia Brown | How Long | Racquet Club | Loot To Boot | Soft Winds
NYC, rec. 1974
Rich,Buddy (dr) | Jacquet,Illinois (ts) | McGriff,Jimmy (org) | Barron,Kenny (el-p) | Freeman,George (g) | Cranshaw,Bob (el-b)
Jimmy McGriff Quintet
Groove Fly | Cotton Boy Blues
NYC, rec. 1972
McGriff,Jimmy (org) | Arnold,Ronald (ts) | Freeman,George (g) | Thomas,John (g) | Booker Jr.,Marion (dr)
Jimmy McGriff Orchestra
Shuckin' And Jivin' | Dig On It | Bug Out | Fat Cakes | Super Funk | Plain Brown Bag | Jumpin' The Blues | Tiki | These Foolish Things Remind Me On You | The Worm Turns | The Sermon
NYC, rec. 1973
McGriff,Jimmy (org) | unkn. (tp,ts,g,el-b,dr)

24655 | 2 CD | Backwoods Siseman/Pieces Of Dream
Buddy Rich Big Band
Kilimandjaro Cookout | Time Check | Backwoods Sideman | Nuttville | Payhouse | Senator Sam | Big Mac | Waltz For The Mushroom Hunters | Senator Sam
NYC, rec. October 1973
Rich,Buddy (dr) | Hopkins,Greg (tp) | Davis,Charlie (tp) | Hoffman,John (tp) | Hall,Larry (tp) | Kaplan,Alan (tb) | O'Quinn,Keith (tb) | Leys,John (b-tb) | Romano,Joe (fl,as) | Martin,Bob (fl,as) | LaBarbera,Pat (ss,ts) | Crea,Bob (ts) | Laws,John (bs) | Budson,Buddy (p) | Beck,Joe (g) | Levin,Tony (b) | Woodyard,Sam (perc)
Three Day Sucker | Ease On Down The Road | Tommy Medley: | Eyesight To The Blind- | Champagne- | See Me Fel Me- | Pieces Of Dreams | Lush Life | West Side Story(Medley)
NYC, rec. June 1974
Rich,Buddy (dr) | Michels,Lloyd (tp) | Hurwitz,Richard (tp) | Konikoff,Ross (tp) | Hayes,Danny (tp) | Camilleri,Charles (tp) | Maur,Barry (tb) | Chamberlain,Gerald (tb) | Salvaton,Anthony (b-tb) | Yellin,Pete (as) | Blaut,Bill (as) | Marcus,Steve (ss,ts) | Mintzer,Bob (ts) | Rosenberg,Roger (bs) | Wright,Wayne (g) | Dupree,Cornell (g) | Morris,Cliff (g) | Kogan,Greg (p) | Brown,Benjamin 'Ben' (b) | Armando,Ray (congas)
Nik-Nik | Layin' It Down
rec. details unknown
Rich,Buddy (dr) | details unknown

24656 | 2 CD | The Groove Merchant/The Second Race
Thad Jones-Mel Lewis Orchestra
Tow Zone Away | Quietude | Jive Samba | The Groove Merchant | The Big Dipper | Central Park North
NYC, rec. 25.7.1969
Jones,Thad (fl-h,arr) | Lewis,Mel (dr) | Moore,Danny (tp) | Nottingham,Jimmy (tp) | Williams,Richard (tp) | Young,Eugene 'Snooky' (tp) | Bert,Eddie (tb) | Knepper,Jimmy (tb) | Powell,Benny (tb) | Heather,Cliff (b-tb) | Richardson,Jerome (cl,ss,as,piccolo) | Dodgion,Jerry (fl,as) | Daniels,Eddie (cl,ts) | Farrell,Joe (ss,ts) | Temperley,Joe (bs) | Hanna,Sir Roland (p) | Brown,Sam (g) | Galbraith,Barry (g) | Davis,Richard (b,el-b)
Dedication
NYC, rec. 20.1.1970
Jones,Thad (fl-h,arr) | Lewis,Mel (dr) | Moore,Danny (tp) | Porcino,Al (tp) | Stamm,Marvin (tp) | Young,Eugene 'Snooky' (tp) | Bert,Eddie (tb) | Knepper,Jimmy (tb) | Powell,Benny (tb) | Heather,Cliff (b-tb) | Berg,Dick (fr-h) | Buffington,Jimmy (fr-h) | Chapin,Earl (fr-h) | Watkins,Julius (fr-h) | Johnson,Howard (tuba) | Richardson,Jerome (fl,ss,as) | Dodgion,Jerry (fl,as) | Daniels,Eddie (cl,ts) | Harper,Billy (fl,ss,as) | Kamuca,Richie (bs) | Hanna,Sir Roland (p) | Davis,Richard (b,el-b)
It Only Happens Every Time | Tiptoe
NYC, rec. 21.1.1970
Jones,Thad (fl-h,arr) | Lewis,Mel (dr) | Moore,Danny (tp) | Porcino,Al (tp) | Stamm,Marvin (tp) | Young,Eugene 'Snooky' (tp) | Bert,Eddie (tb) | Knepper,Jimmy (tb) | Powell,Benny (tb) | Heather,Cliff (b-tb) | Richardson,Jerome (fl,ss,as) | Dodgion,Jerry (fl,as) | Daniels,Eddie (cl,ts) | Harper,Billy (fl,ss,as) | Kamuca,Richie (bs) | Hanna,Sir Roland (p) | Davis,Richard (b,el-b)
A Child Is Born
NYC, rec. 25.5.1970
Jones,Thad (fl-h,arr) | Lewis,Mel (dr) | Moore,Danny (tp) | Porcino,Al (tp) | Stamm,Marvin (tp) | Young,Eugene 'Snooky' (tp) | Bert,Eddie (tb) | Knepper,Jimmy (tb) | Powell,Benny (tb) | Heather,Cliff (b-tb) | Richardson,Jerome (fl,ss,as) | Dodgion,Jerry (fl,as) | Daniels,Eddie (cl,ts) | Harper,Billy (fl,ss,as) | Adams,Pepper (cl,bs) | Hanna,Sir Roland (p) | Davis,Richard (b,el-b)
Gettin' Sassy | Little Pixie | Willow Tree | Ah' That's Freedom | Bachafillen
Live at The 'Village Vanguard',NYC, rec. 1.6.1967
Jones,Thad (fl-h) | Lewis,Mel (dr) | Berry,Bill (tp) | Nottingham,Jimmy (tp) | Stamm,Marvin (tp) | Williams,Richard (tp) | Young,Eugene 'Snooky' (tp) | Brookmeyer,Bob (v-tb) | Brown,Garnett (tb) | Heather,Cliff (tb) | McIntosh,Tom (tb) | Dodgion,Jerry (as) | Richardson,Jerome (as) | Daniels,Eddie (ts) | Farrell,Joe (ts) | Adams,Pepper (bs) | Hanna,Sir Roland (p) | Herman,Sam (g) | Davis,Richard (b)
The Second Race
Live at The 'Village Vanguard',NYC, rec. 4.12.1968
Jones,Thad (fl-h) | Lewis,Mel (dr) | Berry,Bill (tp) | Nottingham,Jimmy (tp) | Stamm,Marvin (tp) | Williams,Richard (tp) | Young,Eugene 'Snooky' (tp) | Brookmeyer,Bob (v-tb) | Brown,Garnett (tb) | Heather,Cliff (tb) | McIntosh,Tom (tb) | Dodgion,Jerry (as) | Richardson,Jerome (as) | Daniels,Eddie (ts) | Farrell,Joe (ts) | Adams,Pepper (bs) | Hanna,Sir Roland (p) | Herman,Sam (g) | Davis,Richard (b)
Quietude
Live at The 'Village Vanguard',NYC, rec. 17/18.6.1969
Jones,Thad (fl-h) | Lewis,Mel (dr) | Nottingham,Jimmy (tp) | Moore,Danny (tp) | Williams,Richard (tp) | Young,Eugene 'Snooky' (tp) | Bert,Eddie (tb) | Knepper,Jimmy (tb) | Powell,Benny (tb) | Heather,Cliff (b-tb) | Dodgion,Jerry (as) | Richardson,Jerome (as) | Daniels,Eddie (ts) | Farrell,Joe (ts) | Temperley,Joe (bs) | Hanna,Sir Roland (p) | Herman,Sam (g) | Galbraith,Barry (g) | Davis,Richard (el-b)

24657 | 2 CD | Stan Getz In Europe
Stan Getz With Ib Glindemann And His Orchestra
Don't Get Around Much Anymore | Cherokee
Live at Sonderjyllands Hallen,Aabenraa, rec. 13.12.1958
Getz,Stan (ts) | Glindemann,Ib (cond,arr) | Bolvig,Palle (tp) | Lundvig,Svend (tp) | Botschinsky,Allan (tp) | Ronak,Bent (tb) | Lind,John (tb) | Jorgensen,Johannes (as) | Karskov,Uffe (as) | Lewkovitch,Karl (ts) | Moller,Paul Martin (ts) | Mathiesen,Kai (bs) | Axen,Bent (p) | Rigou,Marcel (b) | Elniff,Jorn (dr)
My Funny Valentine
Live at Aalborg Hallen,Aalborg, rec. 7.12.1958
Getz,Stan (ts) | Glindemann,Ib (cond,arr) | Bolvig,Palle (tp) | Lundvig,Svend (tp) | Botschinsky,Allan (tp) | Ronak,Bent (tb) | Lind,John (tb) | Jorgensen,Johannes (as) | Karskov,Uffe (as) | Lewkovitch,Karl (ts) | Moller,Paul Martin (ts) | Mathiesen,Kai (bs) | Axen,Bent (p) | Rigou,Marcel (b) | Elniff,Jorn (dr)
Stan Getz With The Kurt Edelhagen Orchestra
Stan's Tune | Blues In Suburbia
Köln, rec. 1959
Getz,Stan (ts) | Edelhagen,Kurt (ld) | prob.personal: | Pavlovic,Milo (tp) | Goykovich,Dusko (tp) | Weichbrodt,Fritz (tp) | Deuchar,Jimmie (tp) | Wray,Ken (tb) | Hauck,Helmut (tb) | Gätjens,Manfred (tb) | Kellens,Christian (tb) | Humble,Derek (as) | Von Klenck,Franz (as) | Aderhold,Bubi (ts) | Chautemps,Jean-Louis (ts) | Busnello,Eddie (bs) | Coppieters,Francis (p) | Fischer,Johnny (b) | Combe,Stuff (dr)
Stan Getz With The Danish Radio Big Band
Two Little Pearls | Yesterdays | Song Without Words | Old Folks
Copenhagen,Denmark, rec. 29.1.1977
Danish Radio Big Band,The | Getz,Stan (ts) | Rosenfeld,Benny (tp,fl-h) | Bolvig,Palle (tp,fl-h) | Sulieman[Leonard Graham],Idrees (tp,fl-h) | Botschinsky,Allan (tp,fl-h) | Knudsen,Perry (tp,fl-h) | Nilsson,Vincent (tb) | Kroner,Erling (tb) | Boone,Richard (tb) | Jensen,Ole Kurt (tb,b-tb) | Windfeld,Axel (b-tb,tuba) | Thilo,Jesper (fl,cl,ss,as) | Petersen,Per Carsten (fl,ss,as) | Jaedig,Bent (fl,ts) | Karskov,Uffe (fl,cl,as,ts) | Madsen,Flemming (cl,b-cl,bs) | Hansen,Ole Kock (p) | Sylven,Bo (g) | Orsted-Pedersen,Niels-Henning (b) | Gruvstedt,Lennart (dr) | Weisgard,Ethan (perc,congas) | Ziegler Holm,Finn (cond)
Stan Getz Quartet
All God's Chillun Got Rhythm | Broadway | East Of The Sun West Of The Moon | They All Fall In Love
Paris,France, rec. 1958
Getz,Stan (ts) | Solal,Martial (p) | Michelot,Pierre (b) | Clarke,Kenny (dr)
Stan Getz Quintet
Dear Old Stockholm | Lady Bird
Paris,France, rec. 1959
Getz,Stan (ts) | Urtreger,René (p) | Gourley,Jimmy (g) | Ingrand,Jean-Marie (b) | Clarke,Kenny (dr)
Stan Getz Quartet
Theme For Manuel | Our Kind Of Sabi
Getz,Stan (ts) | Louiss,Eddie (org) | Thomas,Rene (g) | Lubat,Bernard (dr)

24659 | 2 CD | The Legends Of Swing
Benny Goodman And His Orchestra
Henderson Stomp
Broadcast from Hotel 'New Yorker', rec. November/December 1943
Goodman,Benny (cl) | prob.personal: | Muzillo,Ralph (tp) | Castaldo,Lee (tp) | Frankhauser,Charles (tp) | Harris,Bill (tb) | Bennett,Mark (tb) | Kaye,Leonard (as) | Schertzer,Hymie (as) | Sims,Zoot (ts) | Klink,Al (ts) | Caceres,Ernie (bs) | Stacy,Jess (p) | Reuss,Allan (g) | Weiss,Sid (b) | Krupa,Gene (dr)
Benny Goodman And His V-Disc All Star Band
After You've Gone | There'll Be A Jubilee
NYC, rec. July/August 1944
Goodman,Benny (cl) | Lawson,Yank (tp) | Eldridge,Roy (tp) | Mickle,Mickey (tp) | Brown,Vernon (tb) | Silloway,Ward (tb) | Merrill,Reggie (as) | Schertzer,Hymie (as) | Rollini,Arthur (ts) | Taye,Wolfe (ts) | Caceres,Ernie (bs) | Wilson,Teddy (p) | Kaye,Tommy (g) | Traxler,Gene (b) | Powell,Specs (dr)
Benny Goodman And His Orchestra
Mission To Moscow | King Porter Stomp
NYC, rec. 25./26.4.1962
Goodman,Benny (cl) | Terry,Clark (tp) | Severinsen,Doc (tp) | Fosk,John (tp) | Maxwell,Jimmy (tp) | Alexander,Bob (tb) | Knepper,Jimmy (tb) | Dennis,Willie (tb) | Woods,Phil (as) | Dodgion,Jerry (as) | Sims,Zoot (ts) | Newsom,Tommy (ts) | Allen,Gene (bs) | Bunch,John (p) | Van Lake,Turk (g) | Crow,Bill (b) | Lewis,Mel (dr)
Jimmy Lunceford And His Orchestra
Margie | Four Or Five Times
NYC, rec. 8.8.1946
Lunceford,Jimmie (ld) | Jones,Reunald (tp) | Mitchell,Bob (tp) | Scott,William (tp) | Green,Russell (tp) | Young,Trummy (tb,voc) | Bowles,Russell (tb) | King,Alphonso (tb) | Simeon,Omer (cl,as) | Bradford,Kirkland (as) | Thomas,Joe (ts) | Cobbs,Al (ts) | Horner,William (ts) | Caruthers,Earl (cl,bs) | Wilcox,Eddie (p) | Mitchell,John (g) | Parham,Charles 'Truck' (b) | Marshall,Joe (dr)
Woody Herman And His Orchestra
Bijou
rec. 20.8.1945
Herman,Woody (cl,as,ld) | Berman,Sonny (tp) | Hefti,Neal (tp) | Candoli,Pete (tp) | Candoli,Conte (tp) | Lewis,Irving (tp) | Pfeffner,Ralph (tb) | Harris,Bill (tb) | Kiefer,Ed (tb) | Marowitz,Sam (as) | LaPorta,John (as) | Phillips,Flip (ts) | Mondello,Pete (ts) | DeSair,Skippy (bs) | Aless,Tony (p) | Bauer,Billy (g) | Jackson,Chubby (b) | Tough,Dave (dr)
Woodshopper's Ball
Chicago,Ill, rec. 10./11.12.1946
Herman,Woody (cl,as) | Porcino,Al (tp) | Peterson,Chuck (tp) | Lewis,Cappy (tp) | Gozzo,Conrad (tp) | Peck,Bob (tp) | Harris,Bill (tb) | Kiefer,Ed (tb) | Pfeffner,Ralph (tb) | Marowitz,Sam (as) | LaPorta,John (as) | Folus,Mickey (ts) | Phillips,Flip (ts) | Rubinowitch,Sam (bs) | Rowles,Jimmy (p) | Wayne,Chuck (g) | Mondragon,Joe (b) | Lamond,Don (dr) | Hefti,Neal (arr)
Four Brothers
Los Angeles,CA, rec. 27.12.1947
Herman,Woody (cl,as) | Royal,Ernie (tp) | Glow,Bernie (tp) | Fishelson,Stan (tp) | Rogers,Shorty (tp) | Markowitz,Irving 'Marky' (tp) | Swope,Earl (tb) | Wilson,Ollie (tb) | Swift,Bob (b-tb) | Marowitz,Sam (as) | Stewart,Herbie (as,ts) | Getz,Stan (ts) | Sims,Zoot (ts) | Chaloff,Serge (bs) | Otis,Fred (p) | Sargent,Gene (g) | Yoder,Walt (b) | Lamond,Don (dr) | Giuffre,Jimmy (arr)
Caldonia | Wildroot | Northwest Passage
NYC, rec. 30.7.1958
Herman,Woody (cl,as) | Royal,Ernie (tp) | Glow,Bernie (tp) | Stewart,Al (tp) | Travis,Nick (tp) | Markowitz,Irving 'Marky' (tp) | Brookmeyer,Bob (tb) | Byers,Billy (tb) | Rehak,Frank (tb) | Marowitz,Sam (as) | Cohn,Al (ts) | Donahue,Sam (ts) | Quinichette,Paul (ts) | Bank,Danny (bs) | Pierce,Nat (p) | Bauer,Billy (g) | Jackson,Chubby (b) | Lamond,Don (dr)
Harry James And His Orchestra
Life Goes To A Party
NYC, rec. 1.12.1937
James,Harry (tp) | Clayton,Buck (tp) | Durham,Eddie (tb) | Warren,Earl (as) | Washington Jr.,Jack (as,bs) | Evans,Hershel (ts) | Stacy,Jess (p) | Page,Walter (b) | Jones,Jo (dr)
Feet Draggin' Blues
NYC, rec. 31.8.1939
James,Harry (tp) | Gonsoulin,Tommy (tp) | Bowen,Claude (tp) | Palmer,Jack (tp) | Brown,Russell (tb) | Jones,Truett (tb) | Matthews,Dave (as) | Lakey,Claude (as) | Page,Drew (ts) | Luther,Bill (ts) | Gardner,Jack (p) | Kent,Bryan (g) | Teague,Thurman (b) | Hawkins,Ralph (dr)
Back Beat Boogie
Los Angeles,CA, rec. 30.11.1939
James,Harry (tp) | Schaeffer,Jack (tp) | Bowen,Claude (tp) | Palmer,Jack (tp) | Rizzotto,Dalton (tb) | Jones,Truett (tb) | Squires,Bruce (tb) | Matthews,Dave (as) | Lakey,Claude (as) | Page,Drew (ts) | Luther,Bill (ts) | Gardner,Jack (p) | Kent,Bryan (g) | Teague,Thurman (b) | Scrima,Mickey (dr)
Artie Shaw And His Orchestra
Oh! Lady Be Good
rec. 27.8.1939
Shaw,Artie (cl) | Peterson,Chuck (tp) | Geller,Harry (tp) | Privin,Bernie (tp) | Arus,George (tb) | Jenkins,Les (tb) | Rodgers,Harry (tb) | Robinson,Les (as) | Freeman,Hank (as) | Pastor,Tony (ts) | Auld,Georgie (ts) | Kitsis,Bob (p) | Avola,Al (g) | Weiss,Sid (b) | Wettling,George (dr)
Begin The Beguine
rec. 24.7.1938
Shaw,Artie (cl) | Peterson,Chuck (tp) | Best,John (tp) | Bowen,Claude (tp) | Arus,George (tb) | Vesely,Ted (tb) | Rogers,Harry (tb) | Robinson,Les (as) | Freeman,Hank (as) | Pastor,Tony (ts) | Perry,Ronnie (ts) | Burness,Lester (p) | Avola,Al (g) | Weiss,Sid (b) | Leeman,Cliff (dr)
Nat King Cole Trio
Honeysuckle Rose | Early Morning Blues
Los Angeles,CA, rec. 6.12.1849
Cole,Nat King (p) | Moore,Oscar (g) | Prince,Wesley (b)
Jumpin' At Capitol
Los Angeles,CA, rec. November 1943
Cole,Nat King (p) | Moore,Oscar (g) | Prince,Wesley (b)
Woody Herman And His Orchestra
I've Got My Love To Keep Me Warm | Stars Fell On Alabama | Moonlight In Vermont
Herman,Woody (cl,as,ld) | Orchestra | details unknown
Earl Hines And His Orchestra
Keep On Jumpin' | Boogie Woogie On St. Louis Blues | Rockin' The Blues
NYC, rec. 1947/1948
Hines,Earl 'Fatha' (p) | prob.personal: | Fuller,Walter (tp) | Fletcher,Milton (tp) | Smith,Eddie (tp) | Dixon,George (tb,as) | Burke,Edward (tb) | Ewing,John 'Steamline' (tb) | McLewis,Joe (tb) | Simeon,Omer (cl,bs) | Harris,Leroy (as) | Mundy,Jimmy (ts) | Crowder,Robert (ts) | Roberts,Claude (g) | Wilson,Quinn (b) | Burroughs,Alvin (dr)
Duke Ellington And His Orchestra
Blue Skies
NYC, rec. 25..12.1946
Ellington,Duke (p) | Jordan,Taft (tp) | Hemphill,Shelton (tp) | Williams,Francis (tp) | Anderson,Cat (tp) | Nance,Ray (tp) | Brown,Lawrence (tb) | Jones,Claude (tb) | DeParis,Wilbur (tb) | Procope,Russell (cl,as) | Hodges,Johnny (as) | Hamilton,Jimmy (cl,ts) | Sears,Al (ts) | Carney,Harry (bs) | Guy,Fred (g) | Pettiford,Oscar (b) | Greer,William 'Sonny' (dr)
Jam-A-Ditty
NYC, rec. 18.12.1946
Ellington,Duke (p) | Baker,Harold 'Shorty' (tp) | Williams,Francis (tp) | Jordan,Taft (tp) | Nance,Ray (tp,v) | Jones,Claude (tb) | DeParis,Wilbur (tb) | Brown,Lawrence (tb) | Hamilton,Jimmy (cl,ts) | Procope,Russell (cl,as) | Hodges,Johnny (as) | Sears,Al (ts) | Carney,Harry (cl,b-cl,bs) | Guy,Fred (g) | Pettiford,Oscar (b) | Greer,William 'Sonny' (dr)
Lullaby Of Birdland | Summertime | Solitude
Ellington,Duke (p) | Terry,Clark (tp) | Cook,Willie (tp) | Anderson,Cat (tp) | Nance,Ray (tp) | Tizol,Juan (tb) | Woodman,Britt (tb) | Jackson,Quentin (tb) | Hamilton,Jimmy (cl,ts) | Henderson,Rick (as) | Procope,Russell (as) | Gonsalves,Paul (ts) | Carney,Harry (bs) | Marshall,Wendell (b) | Ballard,Butch (dr)
V.I.P.'s Boogie
Live at McElroy's Ballroom,Portland,OR, rec. 29.4.1954
Ellington,Duke (p) | Terry,Clark (tp) | Cook,Willie (tp) | Anderson,Cat (tp) | Nance,Ray (tp) | Woodman,Britt (tb) | Jackson,Quentin (tb) | Sanders,John (tb) | Hamilton,Jimmy (cl,ts) | Henderson,Rick (as) | Procope,Russell (as) | Gonsalves,Paul (ts) | Carney,Harry (bs) | Marshall,Wendell (b) | Black,Dave (dr)
Count Basie All Stars
Ain't Misbehavin'
NYC, rec. 16.10.1958
Basie,Count (org) | Green,Freddie (g) | Duvivier,George (b) | Crawford,James 'Jimmy' (dr) | Williams,Joe (voc)
Count Basie And His Orchestra
Dinah | Basie Boogie
Basie,Count (p) | prob.personal: | Culley,Wendell (tp) | Cohn[Cohen],Sonny (tp) | Jones,Thad (tp) | Young,Eugene Edward (tp) | Newman,Joe (tp) | Coker,Henry (tb) | Powell,Benny (tb) | Grey,Al (tb) | Jackson,Quentin (tb) | Royal,Marshall (as) | Wess,Frank (as) | Foster,Frank (ts) | Mitchell,Billy (ts) | Dixon,Eric (ts) | Fowlkes,Charlie (bs) | Green,Freddie (g) | Jones,Eddie (b) | Payne,Sonny (dr)

24906 | 2 CD | 100 Years Duke
Duke Ellington And His Orchestra
Take The 'A' Train | Lullaby Of Birdland | Time On My Hands | Creole Love Call | Happy-Go-Lucky Local | Sultry Serenade | Hyacinth Rag | Sophisticated Lady | Caravan | C Jam Blues | Tenderly | All The Things You Are | Mood Indigo | Coffee And Kisses | Johnny Comes Lately | Change My Ways | Satin Doll | Blue Jean Beguine | Tulip Or Turnip | Honeysuckle Rose | Theme From Trambean | Bunny Hop Mambo | Isle Of Capri | Primpin' At The Prom | Band Call | Take The 'A' Train
Live at McElroy's Ballroom,Portland,OR, rec. 26.-29.4.1954
Ellington,Duke (p) | Anderson,Cat (tp) | Cook,Willie (tp) | Terry,Clark (tp) | Nance,Ray (co,v,voc) | Woodman,Britt (tb) | Jackson,Quentin (tb) | Sanders,John (tb) | Procope,Russell (cl,as) | Hamilton,Jimmy (cl,ts) | Henderson,Rick (as) | Gonsalves,Paul (ts) | Carney,Harry (bs) | Marshall,Wendell (b) | Black,Dave (dr)

36056 | 2 CD | Louis Armstrong:Swing That Music
Louis Armstrong And His Orchestra
I'm In The Mood For Love | La Cucaracha
NYC, rec. 3.10.1935
Armstrong,Louis (tp,voc) | Davis,Leonard (tp) | Aiken,Gus (tp) | Bacon,Louis (tp) | White,Harry (tb) | Archey,Jimmy (tb) | Holmes,Charlie

(as) | Jones,Henry (as) | Madison,Bingie (ts) | Walton,Greely (ts) | Russell,Luis (p) | Blair,Lee (g) | Foster,George 'Pops' (b) | Barbarin,Paul (dr)
Old Man Mose | I'm Shooting High
NYC, rec. 21.11.1935
Armstrong,Louis (tp,voc) | Davis,Leonard (tp) | Aiken,Gus (tp) | Bacon,Louis (tp) | Archey,Jimmy (tb) | White,Harry (tb) | Jones,Henry (as) | Holmes,Charlie (as) | Madison,Bingie (cl,ts) | Walton,Greely (cl,ts) | Russell,Luis (p) | Blair,Lee (g) | Foster,George 'Pops' (b) | Barbarin,Paul (dr)
I Hope Gabriel Likes My Music | Rhythm Saved The World
NYC, rec. 13.12.1935 & 18.1.1936
Armstrong,Louis (tp,voc) | Davis,Leonard (tp) | Aiken,Gus (tp) | Bacon,Louis (tp) | Archey,Jimmy (tb) | White,Harry (tb) | Jones,Henry (as) | Holmes,Charlie (as) | Madison,Bingie (cl,ts) | Walton,Greely (cl,ts) | Russell,Luis (p) | Blair,Lee (g) | Foster,George 'Pops' (b) | Barbarin,Paul (dr)
Putting All My Eggs In One Basket
NYC, rec. 4.2.1936
Armstrong,Louis (tp,voc) | Berigan,Bunny (tp) | Mayhew,Bob (tp) | Philburn,Al (tb) | Tucker,Sid (cl,bs) | Waltzer,Phil (as) | Ricci,Paul (ts) | McGrath,Fulton (p) | Barbour,Dave (g) | Peterson,Pete (b) | King,Stan (dr)
I Come From A Musical Family | Somebody Stole My Break
NYC, rec. 28.& 29.4.1936
Armstrong,Louis (tp,voc) | Davis,Leonard (tp) | Aiken,Gus (tp) | Bacon,Louis (tp) | Archey,Jimmy (tb) | White,Harry (tb) | Jones,Henry (as) | Holmes,Charlie (as) | Madison,Bingie (cl,ts) | Walton,Greely (cl,ts) | Russell,Luis (p) | Blair,Lee (g) | Foster,George 'Pops' (b) | Barbarin,Paul (dr)
Swing That Music | Mahogany Hall Stomp
NYC, rec. 18.5.1936
Armstrong,Louis (tp,voc) | Davis,Leonard (tp) | Aiken,Gus (tp) | Bacon,Louis (tp) | Henry Jones (tb) | Archey,Jimmy (tb) | Jones,Henry (as) | Holmes,Charlie (as) | Madison,Bingie (ts) | Walton,Greely (ts) | Russell,Luis (p) | Blair,Lee (g) | Foster,George 'Pops' (b) | Barbarin,Paul (dr)
Louis Armstrong With Jimmy Dorsey And His Orchestra
Skeleton In The Closet | When Ruben Swings The Cuban | Dippermouth Blues
Los Angeles,CA, rec. 7.8.1936
Armstrong,Louis (tp,voc) | Dorsey,Jimmy (cl,as) | Thow,George (tp) | Camarata,Toots (tp) | Byrne,Bobby (tb) | Yukl,Joe (tb) | Mattison,Don (tb) | Stacey,Jack (as) | Livingston,Fud (ts) | Herfurt,Arthur 'Skeets' (ts) | Van Eps,Bobby (p) | Hillman,Roscoe (g) | Taft,Jim 'Slim' (b) | McKinley,Ray (dr)
Louis Armstrong And His Orchestra
Public Melody Number One | She's The Daughter Of A Planter From Havana | Alexander's Ragtime Band | I've Got A Heart Full Of Rhythm
NYC, rec. 2.& 7.7.1937
Armstrong,Louis (tp,voc) | Hemphill,Shelton (tp) | Bacon,Louis (tp) | Allen,Henry Red (tp) | Matthews,George (tb) | Washington,George (tb) | Higginbotham,J.C. (tb) | Clark,Pete (as) | Holmes,Charlie (as) | Nicholas,Albert (cl,ts) | Madison,Bingie (cl,ts) | Russell,Luis (p) | Blair,Lee (g) | Foster,George 'Pops' (b) | Barbarin,Paul (dr)
On The Sunny Side Of The Street
Los Angeles,CA, rec. 15.11.1937
Armstrong,Louis (tp,voc) | Higginbotham,J.C. (tb) | Holmes,Charlie (as) | Madison,Bingie (cl,ts) | Russell,Luis (p) | Blair,Lee (g) | Callender,Red (b) | Barbarin,Paul (dr)
Louis Armstrong And The Mills Brothers
My Darling Nellie Gray
NYC, rec. 7.4.1938
Armstrong,Louis (tp,voc) | Mills Brothers,The (voc) | Mills,Harry (voc) | Mills,Donald (voc) | Mills,Herbert (voc) | Mills Sr.,John (g,voc)
My Walking Stick
NYC, rec. 13.6.1938
Armstrong,Louis (tp,voc) | Mills Brothers,The (voc) | Mills,Harry (voc) | Mills,Donald (voc) | Mills,Herbert (voc) | Mills Sr.,John (g) | Brown,Norman (g)
Louis Armstrong And His Orchestra
Satchel Mouth Swing | The Trumpet Player's Lament | I Double Dare You
Los Angeles,CA, rec. 12.1.1938
Armstrong,Louis (tp,voc) | Hemphill,Shelton (tp) | Bacon,Louis (tp) | Allen,Henry Red (tp) | DeParis,Wilbur (tb) | Washington,George (tb) | Higginbotham,J.C. (tb) | Clark,Pete (as) | Holmes,Charlie (as) | Nicholas,Albert (cl,ts) | Madison,Bingie (cl,ts) | Russell,Luis (p) | Blair,Lee (g) | Foster,George 'Pops' (b) | Barbarin,Paul (dr)
So Little Time | When The Saints Go Marching In | 'S Wonderful | Love Walked In
NYC, rec. 13.& 18.5.1938
Armstrong,Louis (tp,voc) | Hemphill,Shelton (tp) | Higginbotham,J.C. (tb) | Cole,Rupert (cl,as) | Holmes,Charlie (as) | Madison,Bingie (cl,ts) | Russell,Luis (p) | Blair,Lee (g) | Callender,Red (b) | Barbarin,Paul (dr)
I Can't Give You Anything But Love | Ain't Misbehavin'
NYC, rec. 24.6.1938
Armstrong,Louis (tp,voc) | Cusumano,Bob (tp) | McGee,Johnny (tp) | Philburn,Al (tb) | Stoneburn,Sid (cl) | Jaffe,Nat (p) | Barbour,Dave (g) | Stevens,Haig (b) | Weiss,Sam (dr)
What Is This Thing Called Love
Los Angeles,CA, rec. 18.1.1939
Armstrong,Louis (tp,voc) | Hemphill,Shelton (tp) | Johnson,Otis (tp) | Allen,Henry Red (tp) | DeParis,Wilbur (tb) | Washington,George (tb) | Higginbotham,J.C. (tb) | Clark,Pete (as) | Holmes,Charlie (as) | Nicholas,Albert (cl,ts) | Madison,Bingie (cl,ts) | Russell,Luis (p) | Blair,Lee (g) | Foster,George 'Pops' (b) | Catlett,Big Sid (dr)
Louis Armstrong With The Casa Loma Orchestra
Rockin' Chair
NYC, rec. 20.2.1939
Armstrong,Louis (tp,voc) | Zullo,Frank (tp) | Watts,Grady (tp) | Dunham,Sonny (tp) | Rauch,Russell (tb) | McEachern,Murray (tb) | Hunt,Pee Wee (tb) | Ralston,Art (cl,as) | Hutchinson,Clarence (cl,as) | Davis,Pat (cl,ts) | D'Andrea,Dan (ts) | Sargent,Kenny (bs) | Hall,Howard (p) | Blanchette,Jack (g) | Dennis,Stanley (b) | Briglia,Tony (dr)
Louis Armstrong And His Orchestra
Hear Me Talkin' To Ya | West End Blues | Savoy Blues
NYC, rec. 5.4.1939
Armstrong,Louis (tp,voc) | Hemphill,Shelton (tp) | Johnson,Otis (tp) | Allen,Henry Red (tp) | DeParis,Wilbur (tb) | Washington,George (tb) | Higginbotham,J.C. (tb) | Clark,Pete (as) | Holmes,Charlie (as) | Garland,Joe (ts) | Madison,Bingie (cl,ts) | Russell,Luis (p) | Blair,Lee (g) | Foster,George 'Pops' (b) | Catlett,Big Sid (dr)
Baby Won't You Please Come Home
NYC, rec. 15.6.1939
Armstrong,Louis (tp,voc) | Allen,Henry Red (tp) | Flood,Bernard (tp) | Hemphill,Shelton (tp) | Higginbotham,J.C. (tb) | DeParis,Wilbur (tb) | Washington,George (tb) | Holmes,Charlie (as) | Clark,Pete (as) | Madison,Bingie (ts) | Garland,Joe (ts) | Russell,Luis (p) | Blair,Lee (g) | Foster,George 'Pops' (b) | Catlett,Big Sid (dr)
Hey Lawdy Mama | I'll Get Mine Bye And Bye | Do You Call That A Buddy | Yes Suh
NYC, rec. 11.4.1941
Armstrong,Louis (tp,voc) | Washington,George (tb) | Robinson,Prince (cl,ts) | Russell,Luis (p) | Lucie,Lawrence (g) | Williams,John (b) | Catlett,Big Sid (dr)
When It's Sleepy Time Down South | Leap Frog
Chicago,Ill, rec. 16.11.1941
Armstrong,Louis (tp,voc) | Hemphill,Shelton (tp) | Prince,Gene (tp) | Galbraith,Frank (tp) | Washington,George (tb) | Chambers,Henderson (tb) | Greene,Norman (tb) | Cole,Rupert (as) | Frye,Carl (as) | Garland,Joe (cl,ts) | Madison,Bingie (ts,bs) | Robinson,Prince (cl,ts) | Russell,Luis (p) | Lucie,Lawrence (g) | Alvis,Hayes (b) | Catlett,Big Sid (dr)
I'll Be Glad When You're Dead You Rascal You | Jodie Man
NYC, rec. 14.1.1945
Armstrong,Louis (tp,voc) | Butterfield,Billy (tp) | Stoneburn,Sid (as) | Rubin,Jules (as) | Stegmeyer,Bill (cl,ts) | Rollini,Arthur (ts) | Ricci,Paul (bs) | Bowman,Dave (p) | Kress,Carl (g) | Haggart,Bob (b) | Blowers,Johnny (dr)

36126 | 2 CD | Julian Cannonball Adderley: Salle Pleyel/Olympia
Cannonball Adderley Quintet
Jeannine | The Chant | Work Song | Big Pea
Live at Salle Pleyel,Paris,France, rec. 25.11.1960
Adderley,Julian \'Cannonball\' (as) | Adderley,Nat (co) | Feldman,Victor (p) | Jones,Sam (b) | Hayes,Louis (dr)
Arriving Soon | Serenity | Sack O'Woe | Bohemia After Dark
Live at The Olympia,Paris,France, rec. 15.4.1961
Adderley,Julian \'Cannonball\' (as) | Adderley,Nat (co) | Feldman,Victor (p) | Jones,Sam (b) | Hayes,Louis (dr)
Cannonball Adderley Sextet
In Walked Ray
Adderley,Julian \'Cannonball\' (as) | Adderley,Nat (co) | Feldman,Victor (vib) | Jones,Sam (cello) | Carter,Ron (b) | Hayes,Louis (dr)
Cannonball Adderley Quintet
Rufus Still Skinned | Black Orpheus | Work Song | Experience In E | Walk Tall | The Blooz | Mercy, Mercy, Mercy | End Title
Live at Salle Pleyel,Paris,France, rec. 27.3.1969
Adderley,Julian \'Cannonball\' (as) | Adderley,Nat (co) | Zawinul,Joe (p,keyboards) | Gaskin,Victor (b) | McCurdy,Roy (dr)

36127 | 2 CD | Count Basie: Salle Pleyel, April 17th, 1972
Count Basie And His Orchestra
Basie Power | Big Stuff | Fun Time | Meeting | The Python | Yellow Days | From This Moment On | It Could Happen To Me | The Spirit Is Willing | Cherry Point | Lover | I Need To Be Bee'd With | Meditation | Whirly Bird | Cleanhead Blues | Cherry Red | Person To Person | Hold It Right There
Live at Salle Pleyel,Paris,France, rec. 17.4.1972
Basie,Count (p) | Cohen,Paul (tp) | Cohn[Cohen],Sonny (tp) | Minger,George (tp) | Reed,Waymon (tp) | Grey,Al (tb) | Wanzo,Mel (tb) | Hughes,Bill (tb) | Watson Sr.,John (tb) | Peagler,Curtis (as) | Plater,Bobby (as) | Vinson,Eddie 'Cleanhead' (as,voc) | Dixon,Eric (fl,ts) | Williams,J.C. (sax) | Davis,Eddie 'Lockjaw' (ts) | Green,Freddie (g) | Keenan,Norman (b) | Jones,Harold (dr)
Count Basie And The Kansas City 7
Broadway | Just The Blues | Makin' Whoopee- | If I Had You- | I Surrender Dear | K.C.Blues | Everyday | In The Evening | The Comeback | Roll 'Em Pete
Basie,Count (p) | Eldridge,Roy (tp) | Grey,Al (tb) | Vinson,Eddie 'Cleanhead' (as,voc) | Davis,Eddie 'Lockjaw' (ts) | Green,Freddie (g) | Keenan,Norman (b) | Jones,Harold (dr) | Williams,Joe (voc)

36128 | 2 CD | Art Blakey & The Jazz Messengers: Olympia, May 13th, 1961
Art Blakey And The Jazz Messengers
The Summit | Yama | Close Your Eyes | Dat Dere | Lost And Found | Round About Midnight | Kozo's Waltz | Unidentified Title | A Night In Tunisia | The Theme
Live at The Olympia,Paris,France, rec. 13.5.1961
Blakey,Art (dr) | Morgan,Lee (tp) | Shorter,Wayne (ts) | Timmons,Bobby (p) | Merritt,Jymie (b)

36129 | 2 CD | Clark-Boland Big Band: TNP, October 29th, 1969
Kenny Clarke-Francy Boland Big Band
Pentonville | All Through The Night | Gloria | Now Hear My Meaning | New Box | You Stepped Out Of A Dream | Volcano | Box 702 | The Jamfs Are Coming | Doin' Time | Evanesque | Sonor | Sax No End
Live at T.N.P.,Paris, France, rec. 29.10.1969
Clarke,Kenny (dr) | Boland,Francy (p,arr) | Bailey,Benny (tp) | Farmer,Art (tp) | Watkins,Derek (tp) | Sulieman[Leonard Graham],Idrees (tp) | Persson,Ake (tb) | Peck,Nat (tb) | Van Lier,Bart (tb) | Humble,Derek (as) | Shihab,Sahib (fl,ts) | Griffin,Johnny (ts) | Coe,Tony (fl,cl,ts) | Scott,Ronnie (bs) | Woode,Jimmy (b) | Clare,Kenny (dr)

36130 | 2 CD | Miles Davis: Olympia, March 29th,1960
Miles Davis Quintet
All Of You | So What | On Green Dolphin Street | Walkin' | Bye Bye Blackbird | Round About Midnight | Oleo | The Theme
Live at The Olympia,Paris,France, rec. 20.3.1960
Davis,Miles (p) | Coltrane,John (ts) | Kelly,Wynton (p) | Chambers,Paul (b) | Cobb,Jimmy (dr)

36131 | 2 CD | Duke Ellington: The Champs-Elysees Theater January 29-30th,1965
Duke Ellington And His Orchestra
Boo-Dah | Afro-Bossa | Ad Lib On Nippon | The Opener | Chelsea Bridge | Happy-Go-Lucky Local | Satin Doll | Sophisticated Lady | Black Brown And Beige: | The Work Song- | Come Sunday- | Light- | Midriff | Take The 'A' Train | Meow | Passion Flower | Things Ain't What They Used To Be | Jeep's Blues | Perdido | Tutti For Cootie | East St.Louis Toodle-Oo | Carolina Shout- | Rockin' In Rhythm- | Jump For Joy | He Huffed And Puffed | Just Squeeze Me(But Don't Tease Me) | Just A-Sittin' And A-Rockin' | Jam With Sam | C Jam Blues
Live at The Theatre Des Champs-Elysees,Paris,France, rec. 29./30.1.1965
Ellington,Duke (p) | Anderson,Cat (tp) | Ellington,Mercer (tp) | Jones,Herbie (tp) | Nance,Ray (tp,voc) | Williams,Cootie (tp) | Brown,Lawrence (tb) | Cooper,Frank 'Buster' (tb) | Connors,Chuck (tb) | Hodges,Johnny (as) | Procope,Russell (as) | Hamilton,Jimmy (cl,ts) | Gonsalves,Paul (ts) | Carney,Harry (bs) | Lamb,John (b) | Woodyard,Sam (dr)

36132 | 2 CD | Dizzie Gillespie: Salle Pleyel/Olympia
Dizzy Gillespie Quintet
Gillespiana: | Prelude | Blues | Panamericana | Americana | Toccata
Live at Salle Pleyel,Paris,France, rec. 25.11.1960
Gillespie,Dizzy (tp) | Wright,Leo (fl,as) | Schifrin,Lalo (p) | Davis,Art (b) | Lampkin,Chuck (dr)
Dizzy Gillespie Sextet
Caravan | Coda
Gillespie,Dizzy (tp) | Wright,Leo (fl,as) | Schifrin,Lalo (p) | Davis,Art (b) | Lampkin,Chuck (dr) | Candido[Camero] (congas)
Dizzy Gillespie Quintet
One Note Samba | Con Alma | Umh, Umh | Tin Tin Deo | Oh Joe | Chega De Saudade(No More Blues)
Live at The Olympia,Paris,France, rec. 24.11.1965
Gillespie,Dizzy (tp,voc) | Moody,James (fl,ts) | Barron,Kenny (p) | White,Chris (b) | Collins,Rudy (dr)

36133 | CD | Lionel Hampton: Salle Pleyel, March 9th, 1971
Lionel Hampton And His All Star Jazz Inner Circle
Opening Theme | Air Mail Special | Big Joe | Summertime | On The Sunny Side Of The Street | The Mess Is Here | I Don't Stand A Ghost Of A Chance With You | Robbin's Nest | Avalon | Tenderly | Who Can I Turn To- | The Shadow Of Your Smile- | A Taste Of Honey | Stardust | Midnight Sun | How High The Moon | Flying Home- | Hamp's Boogie Woogie | C Jam Blues | I Don't Stand A Ghost Of A Chance With You(alt.take)
Live at Salle Pleyel,Paris,France, rec. 9.3.1971
Hampton,Lionel (vib,p,dr,voc) | Connors,Roland (tp) | Snyder,Bob (cl) | Gambino,Tommy (ss,as) | Jacquet,Illinois (ts) | McClendon,Chuck (ts) | Mackel,Billy (g) | Buckner,Milt (p,org) | Spruill,John (p,org) | Guillemet,Eustis (b) | Bolds,Kenny (dr)

36134 | CD | Oscar Peterson Trio: Olympia/Theatre Des Champs-Elysees
Oscar Peterson Sextet
The Man I Love | School Days | Bugle Call Rag
Live at The Olympia,Paris,France, rec. 8.5.1957
Peterson,Oscar (p) | Eldridge,Roy (tp) | Smith,Stuff (v) | Ellis,Herb (g) | Brown,Ray (b) | Jones,Jo (dr)
Oscar Peterson Trio
Daahoud | Soft Winds | After Hours
Live at The Olympia,Paris,France, rec. 30.4.1960
Peterson,Oscar (p) | Ellis,Herb (g) | Brown,Ray (b)
On Green Dolphin Street | Band Call | I Remember Clifford | Where Do I Go From Here | Satin Doll
Live at The Olympia,Paris,France, rec. 28.2.1961
Peterson,Oscar (p) | Brown,Ray (b) | Thigpen,Ed (dr)
Six And Four
Peterson,Oscar (p) | Brown,Ray (b) | Thigpen,Ed (dr)
Oscar Peterson Trio With Roy Eldridge
But Not For Me | Main Stem | I've Got A Crush On You- | Little Girl Blue- | Bonzo Blues
Live at The Olympia,Paris,France, rec. 22.3.1963
Eldridge,Roy (tp) | Peterson,Oscar (p) | Brown,Ray (b) | Thigpen,Ed (dr)
Oscar Peterson Trio
Reunion Blues | Wheatland | Nightingale | Hymn To Freedom- | Blues For Big Scotia-
Live at The Theatre Des Champs-Elysees,Paris,France, rec. 25./26.4.1964
Peterson,Oscar (p) | Brown,Ray (b) | Thigpen,Ed (dr)

36135 | 2 CD | Jimmy Smith Trio: Salle Pleyel, May 28th, 1965
Jimmy Smith Trio
Blue Bash | The Sermon | Mack The Knife(Moritat) | Who's Afraid Of Virginia Woolf | Goldfinger | Some Of My Best Friends Are Blues | Satin Doll(part 1) | Walk On The Wild Side | More | Back At The Chicken Shack | I Got A Woman | Organ Grinder's Swing | When Johnny Comes Marching Home | Delon's Blues | Satin Doll(part 2)
Live at Salle Pleyel,Paris,France, rec. 28.5.1965
Smith,Jimmy (org) | Warren,Quentin (g) | Hart,Billy (dr)
A Night In Tunisia
Live at Salle Pleyel,Paris,France, rec. 24.11.1965
Smith,Jimmy (org) | Warren,Quentin (g) | Hart,Billy (dr)

36155 | 2 CD | Paris Jazz Concert:Oscar Peterson | EAN 4006408361558
Oscar Peterson Trio
Hogtown Blues | Waltz For Debby | Between The Devil And The Deep Blue Sea | My One And Only Love | In A Mellow Tone
Live at Salle Pleyel,Paris,France, rec. 29.3.1966
Peterson,Oscar (p) | Jones,Sam (b) | Hayes,Louis (dr)
The Lamp Is | On A Clear Day You Can See Forever | Triste | Down Here On The Ground | Tristeza | By The Time I Get To Phoenix- | I Concentrate On You- | Let's Fall In Love | Someday My Prince Will Come | Lined With A Groove | Days Of Wine And Roses | Waltzing Is Hip | Blues Etude(Concert closing)
Live at Salle Pleyel,Paris,France, rec. 18.3.1969
Peterson,Oscar (p) | Jones,Sam (b) | Durham,Bobby (dr)
Oscar Peterson Quartet
Billie's Bounce | Fly Me To The Moon | Squeaky's Blues
Peterson,Oscar (p) | Watanabe,Butch (tb) | Jones,Sam (b) | Durham,Bobby (dr)

36158 | CD | Paris Jazz Concert:Art Blakey & The Jazz Messengers | EAN 4006408361589
Art Blakey And The Jazz Messengers
Round About Midnight | So Tired | My Funny Valentine | It's Only A Paper Moon | Noise In The Attic | Moanin' | I Didn't Know What Time It Was | Blues March | A Night In Tunisia
Live at The Olympia,Paris,France, rec. 13.5.1961
Blakey,Art (dr) | Morgan,Lee (tp) | Shorter,Wayne (ts) | Timmons,Bobby (p) | Merritt,Jymie (b)

36159 | 2 CD | Paris Jazz Concert:Jimmy Smith And The Trio | EAN 4006408361596
Jimmy Smith Trio
Sunny | By The Time I Get To Phoenix | High-Heel Sneakers | See See Rider | Quiet Nights Of Quiet Stars(Corcovado) | Misty | Got My Mojo Working | Satin Doll
Live at Salle Pleyel,Paris,France, rec. 20.11.1968
Smith,Jimmy (org) | Page,Nathan (g) | Bailey,Donald (dr)
Sunnymoon For Two | Ode To Billy Joe | Days Of Wine And Roses | Got My Mojo Working | See See Rider | A Funky Blues Called I Don't Know | My Romance | Satin Doll
Live at Salle Pleyel,Paris,France, rec. 1.12.1969
Smith,Jimmy (org) | McFadden,Eddie (g) | Crosby,Anthony (dr)

Limelight | Universal Music Germany

510439-2 | CD | Soul Espanol | EAN 731451043925
Oscar Peterson Sextet
Soulville Samba | How Insensitive(Insensatez) | Call Me | Carioca | Amanha(Tomorrow) | Samba De Orfeu | Meditacao(Meditation) | Mas Que Nada | Manha De Carnaval(Morning Of The Carnival) | Samba Sensitive
Chicago,Ill, rec. 12.-14.12.1966
Peterson,Oscar (p) | Jones,Sam (b) | Hayes,Louis (dr) | Jones,Harold (perc) | Gibson,Henley (congas) | Thompson,Marshall (timbales)

Lipstick Records | Efa-Medien GmbH

LIP 8970 | CD | Between The Words
Sabine&Markus Setzer
Welcome To Our World | For Earth And Stars | The First Twinkle | My Celtic Heart | The Dance | Dear Mr. P. | Little Wing | Between Our Eeys | One Couple-Two Heads | Child Of The Sea | My Heart Is Dancing | Lullaby For Jule
Hamburg, rec. January/February 2001
Setzer,Sabine (voice) | Setzer,Markus (b)

LIP 8971-2 | CD | Special Treatment | EAN 4015098897124
Jazz Pistols
Special Treatment | Odd Blues | Bugs | Dirty Sanchez | Vix 9 | Mr. Smithers | Borderline | Angry Dragon | Palladium
Cherrytown Studio,?, rec. April-August 2001
Jazz Pistols | Schäfer,Stefen Ivan (g) | Kaiser,Christoph Victor (el-b) | Ludwig,Thomas Lui (dr)

Loma | Warner Classics & Jazz Germany

936248277-2 | CD | Yaya 3 | EAN 093624827726
Yaya 3
Slow Orbit | Switch Blade | The Spirit Lives On | One More Once | Hometown | Aeolio | Two Remember, One Forgets | The Scribe | Confronting Our Fears
NYC, rec. January 2002
Redman,Joshua (ss,ts) | Yahel,Sam (org) | Blade,Brian (dr)

London | Universal Music Germany

820178-2 IMS | CD | The Golden Trumpet Of Harry James
Harry James And His Orchestra
Ciribiribin | You Made Me Love You | Two O'Clock Jump | I've Heard That Song Before | Ultra | By The Sleepy Lagoon | All Or Nothing At All | Cherry | Take The 'A' Train | I Heard You Cried Last Night | The Mole | Satin Doll | Ciribiribin
rec. details unknown
James,Harry (tp) | details unknown

820349-2 | 2 CD | 40th Anniversary Concert-Live At Carnegie Hall
Benny Goodman And His Orchestra
Let's Dance (Theme) | I Found A New Baby | Send In The Clowns | Loch Lomond | Stardust | I Love A Piano | Roll 'Em | King Porter Stomp | Rocky Raccoon | Yesterday | That's A Plenty | How High The Moon | Moonglow | Oh! Lady Be Good | Jersey Bounce | Seven Come Eleven | Someone To Watch Over Me | Please Don't Talk About Me When I'm Gone | Benny Goodman Medley: | Don't Be That Way- | Stompin' At The Savoy- | And The Angels Sing- | Why Don't You Do Right- | A String Of Pearls- | Sing Sing Sing- | Christopher Columbus- | Good Bye
Live at Carnegie Hall,NYC, rec. 17.1.1978
Goodman,Benny (cl) | Paz,Victor (tp) | Vaché,Warren (tp) | Sheldon,Jack (tp) | Andre,Wayne (tb) | Masso,George (tb) | Messner,John (tb) | Young,George (as) | Rodnon,Mel (as) | Tate,Buddy (ts) | Wess,Frank (ts) | Schlinger,Sol (bs) | Collins,Cal (g) | Wright,Wayne (g) | Hampton,Lionel (vib) | Williams,Mary Lou (p) | Rowles,Jimmy (p) | Bunch,John (p) | Moore,Michael (b) | Kay,Connie (dr) | Tilton,Martha (voc) | Craig,Debi (voc)

820878-2 | CD | The Best Of Dixieland-Live in 1954/55

Chris Barber's Jazz Band
All The Girls Go Crazy About The Way I Walk | I Never Knew Just What A Girl Could Do | St.Louis Blues | Salutation March | I Hate A Man Like You | The World Is Waiting For The Sunrise | Reckless Blues
Royal Festival Hall,London, rec. 9.1.1955
Barber,Chris (tb) | Halcox,Pat (co) | Sunshine,Monty (cl) | Donegan,Tony 'Lonnie' (bj) | Bray,Jim (b) | Bowden,Ron (dr) | Patterson,Ottilie (voc)
Storyville Blues | Ice Cream | Oh Didn't He Ramble | It's Tight Like That
Royal Festival Hall,London, rec. 30.10.1954
Barber,Chris (tb,voc) | Halcox,Pat (co,voc) | Sunshine,Monty (cl,voc) | Donegan,Tony 'Lonnie' (bj) | Bray,Jim (b,sousaphone) | Bowden,Ron (dr)
I'd Love It | Merrydown Blues | Skokiaan
Barber,Chris (tb) | Halcox,Pat (co) | Sunshine,Monty (cl) | King,Bertie (as) | Donegan,Tony 'Lonnie' (bj) | Bray,Jim (b,sousaphone) | Bowden,Ron (dr)
Lonnie Donegan Skiffle Group
Diggin' My Potatoes
Donegan,Tony 'Lonnie' (g,voc) | Halcox,Pat (p) | Bray,Jim (bj) | Barber,Chris (b) | Bowden,Colin (dr)
Burn My Body
Donegan,Tony 'Lonnie' (g,voc) | Halcox,Pat (voc) | Barber,Chris (voc)

M.A Music | M.A Music International

A 628-2 | CD | She Touched Me
Thomas Clausen Trio
Smoke Gets In Your Eyes | She Touched Me | Round About Midnight | All I Touch | Exactly Like A Blues | The Man I Love | Moon River | Steve | O Grande Amor | All The Things You Are | Prelude To A Kiss
rec. 1988
Clausen,Thomas (p) | Vinding,Mads (b) | Riel,Alex (dr)

A 800-2 | CD | European Jazz Ensemble At The Philharmonic Cologne
European Jazz Ensemble
Three In Four Or More | Flee Jazz | The Ballad | A Spire | Ein Unsel In Ali's Bus | Past Time
Live at The 'Philharmonie',Köln, rec. 27.4.1989
European Jazz Ensemble | Botschinsky,Allan (tp,fl-h) | Rava,Enrico (tp,fl-h) | Schoof,Manfred (tp,fl-h) | Sulzman,Stan (ss,ts) | Dudek,Gerd (ss,ts) | Petrowsky,Ernst-Ludwig (cl,ss,as,ts) | Catherine,Philip (g) | Van Den Broeck,Rob (p) | Haurand,Ali (b) | Levin,Tony (dr) | Brüning,Uschi (voc)

A 801-2 | CD | Pianomusic
Thomas Clausen
What Is This Thing Called Love | You And The Night And The Music | I Fall In Love Too Easily | Nice Work If You Can Get It | My Funny Valentine | Ballad In G-Major | Sous Les Ponts De Paris | Where Am I Going | Lullaby | Liza | Dankeschoen | Pomona | Stella By Starlight | Hymn To A Better World
?,Denmark, rec. 1989
Clausen,Thomas (p-solo)

A 802-2 | CD | Maasai Mara
Akili
Maasai Mara | Speak Low | The Moon Is Full Tonight | Amourette | Blue Afternoon | Promenade | Children's Song
rec. 1990
Akili | Van Lier,Bart (tb) | Ruocco,John (sax) | Albers,Eef (g) | Schön,Peter (p,keyboards) | Schirmsheimer,Marcel (b) | Lewis,Victor (dr) | Conrad,Eddie (perc,voice)

A 804-2 | CD | Last Summer
Allan Botschinsky Quartet
Last Summer | Silver Blues | The Lady From 300 Central Park West | Do You Know What It Means To Miss New Orleans | Forgotten Melody | Twenty-Seven-91 | Back To Eternity | Around The World
details unknown, rec. 1991
Botschinsky,Allan (fl-h) | Stryker,Dave (g) | Mraz,George 'Jiri' (b) | Lewis,Victor (dr)

A 805-2 | CD | Flowers And Trees
Thomas Clausen Trio With Gary Burton
Spanish Blue | Dream | Autumn Leaves | Blue In Green | Flowers And Trees | Moonlight | Holidays | Choral | The Lion And The Virgin | Play Time | Four On The Floor
Clausen,Thomas (p) | Burton,Gary (vib) | Vinding,Mads (b) | Riel,Alex (dr)

A 807-2 | CD | European Jazz Ensemble Meets The Khan Family
European Jazz Ensemble & The Khan Family feat. Joachim Kühn
Milab | Keshan | Indian Summer | Jashad
European Jazz Ensemble | Heberer,Thomas (tp,fl-h) | Schoof,Manfred (tp,fl-h) | Winterschladen,Reiner (tp,fl-h) | Petrowsky,Ernst-Ludwig (fl,as) | Dudek,Gerd (fl,ss,ts) | Sulzman,Stan (fl,ts) | Catherine,Philip (g) | Van Den Broeck,Rob (p) | Kühn,Joachim (p) | Haurand,Ali (b) | Levin,Tony (dr) | Khan,Ustad Zamir Ahmed (sitar,tablas) | Khan,Ishad Hussain (tabla) | Khan,Ustad Munir (sarangi)

A 916-2 | CD | I've Got Another Rhythm
Allan Botschinsky Quartet
Ray's Delight | Summertime | Blues In E Flat | The Rook | A Song For Anna Sophia | I'ver Got Another Rhythm | My Little Suede Shoes | Bright Eyes | First Strike
details unknown, rec. 1994
Botschinsky,Allan (fl-h) | Stryker,Dave (g) | Fambrough,Charles (b) | Hirshfield,Jeff (dr)

INTCD 004 | CD | Café Noir
Thomas Clausen Trio With Gary Burton
Julie | Sad | Night | Very Slow | Cafe Noir | In My Heart | Green Grass | Gary | Bells
details unknown, rec. 1991
Burton,Gary (vib) | Clausen,Thomas (p) | Vinding,Mads (b) | Riel,Alex (dr)

NU 158-3 | CD | First Brass
First Brass
Interlude No.4 | October Sunshine | Kubismus 502 | Wiegenlied | Don't Shoot The Banjo Player('Cause We've Done It Already) | Toot Your Roots | The Lady In Blue | Alster Promenade | Chops A La Salsa | Love Waltz
details unknown, rec. 1986
First Brass | Watkins,Derek (tp,fl-h) | Botschinsky,Allan (tp,fl-h) | Van Lier,Bart (tb,euphonium) | Van Lier,Erik (tb,b-tb,tuba)

NU 206-3 | CD | Duologue
Allan Botschinsky/Niels-Henning Orsted-Pedersen
The Bench | My One And Only Love | St.Louis Blues | Love Waltz | Samba Petite | Tre Sma Soldater | I've Got Another Rhythm | Shalom | Flamingo Struttin' | Subconscious-Lee | Jeanie With The Light Brown Hair
details unknown, rec. 1987
Botschinsky,Allan (tp,fl-h) | Orsted-Pedersen,Niels-Henning (b)

NU 730-2 | CD | Akili
Akili
Flowers In Bloom | Friday The 16th | Estuary | No.8
Akili | Van Lier,Bart (tb) | Albers,Eef (g) | Van Baal,Koen (p,keyboards) | King,Dave (b) | Lewis,Victor (dr)
Little Black Coot
Akili | Van Lier,Bart (tb) | Albers,Eef (g) | Van Baal,Koen (p,keyboards) | King,Dave (b) | Lewis,Victor (dr) | Conrad,Eddie (perc)
African River
Akili | Van Lier,Bart (tb) | Albers,Eef (g) | Van Baal,Koen (p,keyboards) | Schön,Peter (keyboards) | King,Dave (b) | Lewis,Victor (dr) | Conrad,Eddie (perc,voice)

Manhattan | EMI Germany

748059-2 | CD | Simple Pleasures
Bobby McFerrin
Don't Worry Be Happy | All I Want | Drive My Car | Simple Pleasures | Good Lovin' | Come To Me | Suzie Q | Drive | Them Changes | Sunshine Of Your Love
NYC, rec. details unknown
McFerrin,Bobby (voice) | details unknown

MCA | Universal Music Germany

951176-2 | CD | I Just Dropped By To Say Hello
Johnny Hartman And His Quintet
Charade | Our Time | In The Wee Small Hours Of The Morning | Sleeping Bee | Don't You Know I Care (Or Don't You Care I Know) | Kiss And Run | If I'm Lucky | I Just Dropped By To Say Hello | Stairway To The Stars | Don't Call It Love | How Sweet It Is To Be In Love
rec. 9.& 17.10.1963
Hartman,Johnny (voc) | Jacquet,Illinois (ts) | Jones,Hank (p) | Burrell,Kenny or Jim Hall (g) | Hall,Jim or Kenny Burrell (g) | Hinton,Milt (b) | Jones,Elvin (dr)

MCD 01876 | CD | What A Wonderful World
Louis Armstrong And His Orchestra
What A Wonderful World
NYC, rec. 16.8.1967
Armstrong,Louis (voc) | Wilder,Joe (tp) | Terry,Clark (tp) | Green,Urbie (tb) | Johnson,J.J. (tb) | Marowitz,Sam (fl,cl,as) | Trimboli,Dan (fl,sax) | Richardson,Jerome (fl,cl,ts) | Jones,Hank (p) | Hanlon,Allen (g) | Ryerson,Arthur 'Art' (g) | Suyker,Willard 'Bill' (g) | Savakus,Russell (b) | Tate,Grady (dr) | Hard,Warren (perc) | Goodman,Tommy (cond,arr) | Strings
The Sunshine Of Love
Armstrong,Louis (voc) | Wilder,Joe (tp) | Terry,Clark (tp) | Green,Urbie (tb) | Johnson,J.J. (tb) | Marowitz,Sam (fl,cl,as) | Trimboli,Dan (fl,sax) | Richardson,Jerome (fl,cl,ts) | Jones,Hank (p) | Hanlon,Allen (g) | Ryerson,Arthur 'Art' (g) | Suyker,Willard 'Bill' (g) | Savakus,Russell (b) | Tate,Grady (dr) | Hard,Warren (perc) | Goodman,Tommy (cond,arr) | Strings | Chorus
Louis Armstrong And His All Stars
Cabaret | Hellzapoppin'
Armstrong,Louis (tp,voc) | Glenn,Tyree (tb) | Muranyi,Joe (cl) | Napoleon,Marty (p) | Ryerson,Arthur 'Art' (g) | Catlett,Buddy (b) | Barcelona,Danny (dr)
Dream A Little Dream Of Me | Give Me Your Kisses | There Must Be A Way | I Guess I'll Take The Papers And Go Home
Las Vegas,NV, rec. 23.7.1968
Armstrong,Louis (tp,voc) | Glenn,Tyree (tb) | Muranyi,Joe (cl) | Napoleon,Marty (p) | Catlett,Buddy (b) | Barcelona,Danny (dr)
Louis Armstrong And His All Stars With A Studio Orchestra
The Home Fire | Hello Brother | Fantastic That's You
Armstrong,Louis (tp,voc) | Glenn,Tyree (tb) | Muranyi,Joe (cl) | Napoleon,Marty (p) | Catlett,Buddy (b) | Barcelona,Danny (dr) | Big Band | Butler,Art (cond) | details unknown

MCD 06103 | CD | Live At San Quentin
B.B.King And His Band
B.B.King Intro | Let The Good Times Roll | Everyday I Have The Blues | Whole Lotta Loving | Sweet Little Angel | Never Make A Move Too Soon | Into The Night | Ain't Nobody's Bizness If I Do | The Thrill Is Gone | Nobody Loves Me But My Mother | Sweet Sixteen | Rock Me Baby
Live at San Quentin, rec. 25.5.19??
King,B.B. (g,voc) | Bolden,James 'Buddy' (tp) | King,Walter (sax,ld) | Synigal,Edgar (sax) | Warren,Leon (g) | Carrier,Eugene (keyboards) | Doster,Michael (b-g) | Emphrey Jr.,Calep (dr)
Peace To The World
Studio,?, rec. details unknown
King,B.B. (g,voc) | similar pers. | Bolden,James 'Buddy' (tp) | King,Walter (sax,ld) | Synigal,Edgar (sax) | Warren,Leon (g) | Carrier,Eugene (keyboards) | Doster,Michael (b-g) | Emphrey Jr.,Calep (dr)

MCD 09337 | 2 CD | Buddy Guy-The Complete Chess Studio Recordings
Buddy Guy Blues Band
First Time I Met The Blues | Slop Around | I Got My Eyes On You | Broken Hearted Blues
Chicago,Ill, rec. 2.3.1960
Guy,Buddy (g,voc) | Gibson,Jarrett (ts) | Neely,Bob (ts) | Hawkins,Donald (bs) | Montgomery,Little Brother (p) | Meyers,Jack (el-b) | Below,Freddie (dr)
Let Me Love You Baby | I Got A Strange Feeling | Gully Hully | Ten Years Ago
Chicago,Ill, rec. 16.12.1960
Guy,Buddy (g,voc) | Gibson,Jarrett (ts) | Neely,Bob (ts) | Hawkins,Donald (bs) | Wells,Junior (harm) | Spann,Otis (p) | Meyers,Jack (el-b) | Below,Freddie (dr)
Watch Yourself | Stone Crazy | Skippin' | I Found A True Love
Chicago,Ill, rec. 7.12.1961
Guy,Buddy (g,voc) | Gibson,Jarrett (ts) | Neely,Bob (ts) | Hawkins,Donald (bs) | Spann,Otis (p) | unkn. (g) | Meyers,Jack (el-b) | Below,Freddie (dr)
Hard But It's Fair | Baby(Baby, Baby, Baby) | When My Left Eye Jumps | That's It
Chicago,Ill, rec. 12.8.1962
Guy,Buddy (g,voc) | Turner,Sunny (tp) | Watson,Murray (tp) | Locke,Abe (ts) | Gibson,Jarrett (ts) | Leake,Lafayette (org) | Bates,Lefty (g) | Meyers,Jack (el-b) | Thomas,Philip (dr) | unkn. (background-voc)
The Treasure Untold
Chicago,Ill, rec. 9.9.1962
Guy,Buddy (g,voc) | details unknown
American Bandstand(aka American Bandstand Thing) | No Lic | 100 Dollar Bill | My Love Is Real
Chicago,Ill, rec. 8.2.1963
Guy,Buddy (g,voc) | Neely,Bob (ts) | Gibson,Jarrett (ts) | Leake,Lafayette (p) | Gibson,Lacy (g) | Meyers,Jack (el-b) | Duncan,Al (dr)
Buddy's Boogie | Worried Mind(aka Stick Around) | Untitled Instrumental | Moanin'
Chicago,Ill, rec. 14.8.1963
Guy,Buddy (g,voc) | Hawkins,Donald (ts) | Gibson,Jarrett (ts) | Leake,Lafayette (p) | Meyers,Jack (el-b) | James,Clifton (dr)
I Dig Your Wig
Chicago,Ill, rec. 30.4.1964
Guy,Buddy (g,voc) | Williamson,Sonny Boy [Rice Miller] (harm) | Leake,Lafayette (p) | Meyers,Jack (el-b) | James,Clifton (dr)
My Time After A While | My Time After A While(alt.take)
Chicago,Ill, rec. 10.6.1954
Guy,Buddy (g,voc) | Gibson,Jarrett (ts) | Hawkins,Donald (bs) | Caston,Leonard (p) | Meyers,Jack (el-b) | James,Clifton (dr)
Night Flight
Chicago,Ill, rec. 30.6.1964
Guy,Buddy (g,voc) | Nighthawk,Robert (g) | Caston,Leonard (p) | Meyers,Jack (el-b) | James,Clifton (dr)
Crazy Love(Crazy Music) | Every Girl I See | Too Many Ways | Too Many Ways(alt.take)
Chicago,Ill, rec. April 1965
Guy,Buddy (g,voc) | Barge,Gene (ts) | Murphy,Matt (g) | Boyd,Reggie (b-g) | rest unkn.
Leave My Girl Alone | Go To Use You Head
Chicago,Ill, rec. 23.5.1965
Guy,Buddy (g,voc) | Reed,G.T. (ts) | Bland,Milton (ts) | Caston,Leonard (org) | Murphy,Matt (g) | Stewart,Leroy (el-b) | unkn. (dr)
Keep It To Myself(aka Keep It To Yourself) | My Mother | She Quits Me To A Tee | Mother-In-Law Blues | Keep It To Myself(aka Keep It To Yourself-alt.take) | I Didn't Know My Mother(She Suits Me To A Tee-alt.take)
Chicago,Ill, rec. August 1966
Guy,Buddy (g,voc) | Barge,Gene (ts) | Murphy,Matt (g) | Upchurch,Phil (el-b) | Stepney,Bill (dr) | rest unkn.
Buddy's Groove | Going To School | I Cry And Sing The Blues | Going Home | I Suffer With The Blues | Lip Lap Louie
Chicago,Ill, rec. July 1967
Guy,Buddy (g,voc) | details unknown

MCD 10413 | CD | Endless Boogie
John Lee Hooker Group
Pots On, Gas On High | We Might As Well Call It Thrtough(I Didn't Get Married To Your Two-Timing Mother)
San Francisco,CA, rec. 10.11.1970
Hooker,John Lee (g,voc) | Naftalin,Mark (p) | Coulter,Cliff (el-p) | Davis,Jesse Edwin (g) | Radle,Carl (el-b) | Gordon,Jim (dr)
I Got A Good 'Un - (I Got) A Good 'Un
San Francisco,CA, rec. 11.11.1970
Hooker,John Lee (g,voc) | Coulter,Cliff (el-p) | Miller,Steve (g) | Brown,Mel (g) | Skaggs,Chester 'Gino' (el-b) | Ingram,Billy (dr)
Sittin' In My Dark Room
Hooker,John Lee (g,voc) | Naftalin,Mark (p) | Coulter,Cliff (el-p) | Miller,Steve (g) | Brown,Mel (g) | Skaggs,Chester 'Gino' (el-b) | Ingram,Billy (dr)
Standing At The Crossroads
Hooker,John Lee (g,voc) | Naftalin,Mark (p) | Miller,Steve (g) | Skaggs,Chester 'Gino' (el-b) | Ingram,Billy (dr)
Kick Hit 4 Hit Kix U(Blues For Jimi And Janis)
Hooker,John Lee (g,voc) | Coulter,Cliff (el-p) | Naftalin,Mark (g) | Skaggs,Chester 'Gino' (el-b) | Ingram,Billy (dr)
House Rent Boogie
San Francisco,CA, rec. 12.11.1970
Hooker,John Lee (g,voc) | Naftalin,Mark (p) | Berger,Dave (harm) | Miller,Steve (g) | Alexander,Dan (g) | Skaggs,Chester 'Gino' (el-b) | Swank,Ken (dr)
Doin' The Shout
Hooker,John Lee (g,voc) | Miller,Steve (g) | Skaggs,Chester 'Gino' (el-b) | Swank,Ken (dr)
A Sheep Out Of A Foam
Hooker,John Lee (g,voc) | Coulter,Cliff (el-p) | Alexander,Dan (g) | Skaggs,Chester 'Gino' (el-b) | Swank,Ken (dr)
I Don't Need No Steam Heat
Hooker,John Lee (g,voc) | Naftalin,Mark (p) | Turk,John (el-p) | Miller,Steve (g) | Brown,Mel (g) | Coulter,Cliff (el-b) | Lanzara,Reno (dr)
Endless Boogie(part 27&28)
Hooker,John Lee (g,voc) | Naftalin,Mark (p) | Turk,John (org) | Berger,Dave (harm) | Miller,Steve (g) | Brown,Mel (g) | Coulter,Cliff (g) | Perez,Jerry (g) | Lanzara,Reno (dr) | Swank,Ken (tambourine)

MCD 18347 | CD | Louis Armstrong-My Greatest Songs
Louis Armstrong And His Orchestra
Struttin' With Some Barbecue
Los Angeles,CA, rec. 12.1.1938
Armstrong,Louis (tp) | Hemphill,Shelton (tp) | Bacon,Louis (tp) | Allen,Henry Red (tp) | DeParis,Wilbur (tb) | Washington,George (tb) | Higginbotham,J.C. (tb) | Clark,Pete (as) | Holmes,Charlie (as) | Nicholas,Albert (cl) | Madison,Bingie (cl,ts) | Russell,Luis (p) | Blair,Lee (g) | Foster,George 'Pops' (b) | Barbarin,Paul (dr)
When The Saints Go Marching In
NYC, rec. 13.5.1938
Armstrong,Louis (tp,voc) | Hemphill,Shelton (tp) | Higginbotham,J.C. (tb) | Holmes,Charlie (as) | Cole,Rupert (as) | Madison,Bingie (ts) | Russell,Luis (p) | Blair,Lee (g) | Foster,George 'Pops' (b) | Barbarin,Paul (dr)
Louis Armstrong With Gordon Jenkins And His Orchestra And Choir
That Lucky Old Sun(Just Rolls Around Heaven) | Blueberry Hill
NYC, rec. 6.9.1949
Armstrong,Louis (tp,voc) | Butterfield,Billy (tp) | Poole,Carl (tp) | Lawson,Yank (tp) | Bradley,Will (tb) | Yaner,Milt (as) | Schertzer,Hymie (as) | Parshley,Tom (ts) | Drellinger,Art (ts) | Leighton,Bernie (p) | Kress,Carl (g) | Lesberg,Jack (b) | Blowers,Johnny (dr) | Choir | Jenkins,George (cond,arr)
Louis Armstrong And His All Stars
New Orleans Function: | Flee As A Bird- | Oh Didn't He Ramble-
NYC, rec. 26./27.4.1950
Armstrong,Louis (tp,voc) | Teagarden,Jack (tb) | Bigard,Barney (cl) | Hines,Earl 'Fatha' (p) | Shaw,Arvell (b) | Cole,William 'Cozy' (dr)
Louis Armstrong With Sy Oliver And His Orchestra
C'Est Si Bon
NYC, rec. 26.6.1950
Armstrong,Louis (tp,voc) | Solomon,Melvin (tp) | Privin,Bernie (tp) | Webster,Paul (tp) | Bullman,Morton (tb) | Schertzer,Hymie (as) | Yaner,Milt (as) | Drellinger,Art (ts) | Holcombe,Bill (ts) | Hines,Earl 'Fatha' (p) | Barksdale,Everett (g) | Duvivier,George (b) | Blowers,Johnny (dr) | Oliver,Sy (cond,arr)
A Kiss To Build A Dream On
NYC, rec. 24.7.1951
Armstrong,Louis (tp,voc) | Cutshall,Cutty (tb) | Yaner,Milt (as) | Dorsey,George (as) | Williams,Freddy (cl,as) | Klink,Al (ts) | Kyle,Billy (p) | Block,Sandy (b) | Shawker,Norris 'Bunny' (dr) | Oliver,Sy (cond,arr)
Louis Armstrong And His All Stars
Otchi-Tchor-Ni-Ya[Dark Eyes]
NYC, rec. 19.3.1954
Armstrong,Louis (tp,voc) | Young,Trummy (tb) | Bigard,Barney (cl) | Freeman,Bud (ts) | Kyle,Billy (p) | Shaw,Arvell (b) | Johns,Kenny (dr)
Basin Street Blues
NYC, rec. 25.3.1954
Armstrong,Louis (tp,voc) | Young,Trummy (tb) | Bigard,Barney (cl) | Freeman,Bud (ts) | Kyle,Billy (p) | Shaw,Arvell (b) | Johns,Kenny (dr)
Louis Armstrong With Sy Oliver And His Orchestra
Skokiaan(part 1)
NYC, rec. 13.8.1954
Armstrong,Louis (tp,voc) | Shavers,Charlie (tp) | Jordan,Taft (tp) | Salaam,Abdul[William 'Chieftie' Scott] (tp) | Cobbs,Alfred (tb) | Crumbley,Elmer (tb) | Seldon,Paul (tb) | Bigard,Barney (cl) | Simeon,Omer (ss) | Martin,David (p) | Barker,Danny (g) | Shaw,Arvell (b) | Deems,Barrett (dr) | Oliver,Sy (cond,arr)
Louis Armstrong And Gary Crosby With Sonny Burke's Orchestra
Ko Ko Mo(I Love You So)
Los Angeles,CA, rec. 18.1.1955
Armstrong,Louis (tp,voc) | Candoli,Pete (tp) | Young,Trummy (tb) | Bigard,Barney (cl) | Ruffell,Donald (ts) | Gentry,Chuck (sax) | Koch,Joe (sax) | Kyle,Billy (p) | Deems,Barrett (dr) | Crosby,Gary (voc) | Judd Conlin Rhythmaires,The (voc-group)
Louis Armstrong With Benny Carter's Orchestra
Moments To Remember
Los Angeles,CA, rec. 8.9.1955
Armstrong,Louis (tp,voc) | Klein,Manny (tp) | Candoli,Pete (tp) | Mangano,Vito (tp) | Young,Trummy (tb) | Zentner,Si (tb) | Bigard,Barney (cl) | Herfurt,Arthur 'Skeets' (as) | Klee,Harry (as) | Russin,Irving 'Babe' (ts) | Ruffell,Donald (ts) | Kyle,Billy (p) | Shaw,Arvell (b) | Deems,Barrett (dr) | Carter,Benny (cond,arr)

MCD 18767 | CD | My Greatest Songs
Billie Holiday
Lover Man(Oh,Where Can You Be?) | Big Stuff | Don't Explain | Baby, I Don't Cry Over You | Good Morning Heartache | The Blues Are Brewin' | My Man | 'Tain't Nobody's Bizness If I Do | In My Solitude | Them There Eyes | Crazy He Calls Me | Keep On Rainin' | You're My Thrill | My Sweet Hank O'Trash | I Loves You Porgy | God Bless The Child
different Places, rec. 1940s
Holiday,Billie (voc) | details not on the cover

MCD 18961 | CD | Muddy Waters-The Collection
Muddy Waters Blues Band
Rolling Stone | I Can't Be Satisfied | Baby Please Don't Go | Hoochie Coochie Man | I Just Want To Make Love To You | I'm Ready | Smokestack Lightnin' | Forty Days And Forty Nights | I Love The Life I Live | I Got My Mojo Working | Southbound Train | Good Morning Little School Girl | Going Down Slow | Gypsy Woman | I Feel Like Going Home | Walkin' Blues | You Shook Me | Lonesome Road Blues
different Places, rec. details unknown
Muddy Waters[McKinley Morganfield] (g,voc) | personal included: | Horton,Big Walter 'Shakey' (harm) | Little Walter (harm) | Cotton,James (harm) | Rodgers,Jimmy (g) | Spann,Otis (p) | Dixon,Willie (b) | Clay,Francis (dr) | details not on the cover

Mercury | Universal Music Germany

074394-2 | CD | Nana Swings | EAN 044007739426
Nana Mouskouri With The Berlin Radio Big Band
Come Rain Or Come Shine | No Moon At All | Love Me Or Leave Me | Almost

Like Being In Love | Nature Boy | I Get A Kick Out Of You | Makin' Whoopee
| Lover Man(Oh,Where Can You Be?) | Moondance | Blues In The Night | Someone To Watch Over Me | A Foggy Day(In London Town) | Our Love Is Here To Stay | Bill | Over The Rainbow | Black Coffee | Without A Song | Come Rain Or Come Shine(alt.take)
Live at The Jazzopen Festival,Stuttgart, rec. 13.7.2002
Mouskouri,Nana (voc) | Berlin Radio Big Band,The | Bowen,Gregg (tp) | Brohm,Jörg (tp) | Grabandt,Christian (tp) | Burkhardt,Ingolf (tp) | Gallardo,Joe (tb) | Herrlich,Johannes (tb) | Fischer,Sören (tb) | Hartmann,Achim (tb) | Pfeiffer,Stephan (reeds) | Trübsbach,Florian (reeds) | Gauchel,Walter (reeds) | Wyand,Mark (reeds) | Bartelt,Marcus (reeds) | Köhler,Wolfgang (p) | Schmid,Ralf (p) | Busch,Hanno (g) | Diener,Christian (b) | Nell,Holger (dr)

512214-2 | CD | Mad About The Boy-The Best Of Dinah Washington
Dinah Washington With Orchestra
Mad About The Boy | What A Difference A Day Made | Unforgettable | Baby You Got What It Takes | A Rockin' Good Way | September In The Rain | Love For Sale | Every Time We Say Goodbye | Makin' Whoopee | All Of Me | Let's Do It(Let's Fall In Love) | If I Where A Bell | Teach Me Tonight | Manhattan | Everybody Loves Somebody | Our Love Is Here To Stay | Cry Me A River
different Places, rec. details unknown
Washington,Dinah (voc) | Orchestra | details not on the cover

522747-2 | CD | Feeling Good-The Very Best Of Nina Simone
Nina Simone Groups
Feeling Good | My Baby Just Cares For Me | Don't Let Me Be Misunderstood | Ne Me Quitte Pas | Take Me To The Water | I Put A Spell On You | Don't Explain | Mississippi Goddam | Don't Smoke In Bed | I Loves You Porgy | Work Song | Love Me Or Leave Me | Strange Fruit | Nobody Knows You When You're Down And Out | I'm Going Back Home | The Other Woman | Sinnerman | Mood Indigo | I'm Gonna Leave You | See Line Woman
different Places, rec. 1964-1987
Simone,Nina (p,voc) | details not on the cover

534598-2 | CD | Watch What Happens
Laura Fygi Meets Michel Legrand
Where's The Love | The First Time | You Had To Be There | Watch What Happens | Et Si Demain | The Windmills Of Your Mind | I Will Wait For You | Once Upon A Summertime | What Are You Doing The Rest Of Your Life | How Do You Keep The Music Playing | Summer Me Winter Me | The Way He Makes Me Feel | Ask Yourself Why | Rachel
details unknown, rec. details unknown
Fygi,Laura (voc) | Van Dijk,Louis (p) | Laurence,Chris (b) | Fisher,Harold (dr) | Legrand,Michel (cond,arr,voc) | Davis,Michael (concert-master) | Strings & Brass | details unknown

549374-2 | CD | !Viva! Vaughan | EAN 731454937429
Sarah Vaughan With Orchestra
Fascinating Rhythm | Tea For Two | Stompin' At The Savoy | Moment Of Truth
NYC, rec. 15.8.1964
Vaughan,Sarah (voc) | Winding,Kai (tb) | Powell,Benny (tb) | Byers,Billy (tb) | Andre,Wayne (tb) | Cleveland,Jimmy (tb) | Hixon,Richard 'Dick' (b-tb) | Richardson,Jerome (fl) | James,Bob (p) | Rodriguez,Roberto (b) | Bobo,Willie (perc) | Cadavieco,Juan (perc) | Donaldson,Bobby (perc) | Mangual,Jose (perc) | Sierra,Rafael (perc) | Foster,Frank (arr,ld)
Night Song | Shiny Stockings | A Taste Of Honey
Vaughan,Sarah (voc) | Winding,Kai (tb) | Powell,Benny (tb) | Byers,Billy (tb) | Andre,Wayne (tb) | Hixon,Richard 'Dick' (b-tb) | Richardson,Jerome (fl) | James,Bob (p) | Rodriguez,Roberto (b) | Bobo,Willie (perc) | Cadavieco,Juan (perc) | Donaldson,Bobby (perc) | Mangual,Jose (perc) | Sierra,Rafael (perc) | Eichen,Bernard (v) | Eley,Lewis (v) | Green,Emmanuel (v) | Kruczek,Leo (v) | Libove,Charles (v) | Nadien,David (v) | Samaroff,Tosha (v) | Lookofsky,Harry (tenor-v) | Foster,Frank (arr,ld)
Fever | Avalon
Vaughan,Sarah (voc) | Winding,Kai (tb) | Powell,Benny (tb) | Watrous,Bill (tb) | Andre,Wayne (tb) | Hixon,Richard 'Dick' (b-tb) | James,Bob (p) | Rodriguez,Roberto (b) | Bobo,Willie (perc) | Cadavieco,Juan (perc) | Donaldson,Bobby (perc) | Mangual,Jose (perc) | Sierra,Rafael (perc) | Foster,Frank (arr,ld)
Fascinating Rhythm | Jive Samba
NYC, rec. 14.8.1964
Vaughan,Sarah (voc) | Winding,Kai (tb) | Powell,Benny (tb) | Watrous,Bill (tb) | Byers,Billy (tb) | Cleveland,Jimmy (tb) | Hixon,Richard 'Dick' (b-tb) | James,Bob (p) | Rodriguez,Roberto (b) | Bobo,Willie (perc) | Cadavieco,Juan (perc) | Donaldson,Bobby (dr) | Mangual,Jose (perc) | Sierra,Rafael (perc) | Strings | Foster,Frank (arr,ld)
Quiet Nights Of Quiet Stars(Corcovado)
Vaughan,Sarah (voc) | Winding,Kai (tb) | Powell,Benny (tb) | Watrous,Bill (tb) | Byers,Billy (tb) | Cleveland,Jimmy (tb) | Hixon,Richard 'Dick' (b-tb) | James,Bob (p) | Galbraith,Barry (g) | Rodriguez,Roberto (b) | Bobo,Willie (perc) | Cadavieco,Juan (perc) | Donaldson,Bobby (dr) | Mangual,Jose (perc) | Sierra,Rafael (perc) | Strings | Foster,Frank (arr,ld)

589487-2 | CD | It's A Man's World | EAN 731458948728
Sarah Vaughan With The Hal Mooney Orchestra
Jim | The Man That Got Away | My Man | Happiness Is A Thing Called Joe | Trouble Is A Man | He's Funny That Way | For Every Man There's A Woman | I'm Just Wild About Harry | Danny Boy (Londonderry Air) | Alfie
NYC, rec. 20.-22.1.1967
Vaughan,Sarah (voc) | personal included: | Terry,Clark (tp) | Shavers,Charlie (tp) | Newman,Joe (tp) | Hubbard,Freddie (tp) | Johnson,J.J. (tb) | Winding,Kai (tb) | Woods,Phil (as) | Golson,Benny (ts) | James,Bob (p,arr) | Mooney,Hal (arr,ld) | Strings | details unknown

589673-2 | CD | Jewis Melodies In Jazztime | EAN 731458967323
Terry Gibbs Octet
Papirossen | Shaine Une Zees | My Yiddish Momma | And The Angels Sing
NYC, rec. 11.1.1963
Gibbs,Terry (vib,marimba) | Kutcher,Sam (tb) | Musiker,Ray (cl) | McLeod,Alice (p) | Logan,Alan (p) | Wright,Herman (b) | Pike,Bobby (dr) | Gaye,Sol (dr)
S And S | Kazochock | Bei Mir Bist Du Schön | Nyah Shore | Veiloch
NYC, rec. 11.3.1963
Gibbs,Terry (vib,marimba) | Kutcher,Sam (tb) | Musiker,Ray (cl) | McLeod,Alice (p) | Logan,Alan (p) | Wright,Herman (b) | Pike,Bobby (dr) | Gaye,Sol (dr)

841134-2 | CD | Gospel Train | EAN 042284113427
Sister Rosetta Tharpe And Her Group
Two Little Fishes Five Loaves Of Bread | All Alone | How About You | Ninety-Nine And A Half A Won't Do | Precious Memories | Beams On Heaven | Can't No Grave Hold My Body Down
NYC, rec. 2.7.1958
Tharpe,Sister Rosetta (g,voc) | Hayes,Ernest 'Ernie' (p) | Bagby,Doc (org) | Richardson,Ernest (g) | Trottman,Lloyd (b) | Francis,David 'Panama' (dr)
Joshua Fit The Battle Of Jericho
NYC, rec. 5.7.1958
Tharpe,Sister Rosetta (g,voc) | Hayes,Ernest 'Ernie' (p) | Bagby,Doc (org) | Richardson,Ernest (g) | Trottman,Lloyd (b) | Francis,David 'Panama' (dr)
Sister Rosetta Tharpe And Her Group With The Harmonizing Four
When They Ring The Golden Bell | Up Abow My Head There's Music In The Air | I Shall Know Him | Fly Away
Tharpe,Sister Rosetta (g,voc) | Hayes,Ernest 'Ernie' (p) | Bagby,Doc (org) | Richardson,Ernest (g) | Trottman,Lloyd (b) | Francis,David 'Panama' (dr) | Harmonizing Four,The

842409-2 | CD | My Kinda Swing | EAN 042284240925
Ernestine Anderson With Orchestra
My Kinda Love | Lazy Afternoon | Mound Bayou | Trouble Is A Man | All My Life | They Didn't Believe Me | I'll Never Be The Same | Land Of Dreams | Black Moonlight- | See See Rider | It Don't Mean A Thing If It Ain't Got That Swing | Moonlight In Vermont
NYC, rec. 1960
Anderson,Ernestine (voc) | Terry,Clark (tp) | Royal,Ernie (tp) | Rehak,Frank (tb) | Lateef,Yusef (fl,ts) | Houston,Tate (bs) | Jones,Hank (p) | Burrell,Kenny (g) | Ceppos,Mac (v) | Davis,Art (b) | Persip,Charles (dr) | Rodriguez,Willie (perc)

843454-2 | CD | Loads Of Love + Shirley Horn With Horns
Shirley Horn With Orchestra
Wild Is Love | Loads Of Love | My Future Just Passed | There's A Boat Dat's Leavin' Soon For New York | Ten Cents A Dance | Only The Lonely | The Second Time Around | Do It Again | It's Love | That's No Joke | Love For Sale | Who Am I
NYC, rec. early 1963
Horn,Shirley (voc) | personal included: | Royal,Ernie (tp) | Newman,Joe (tp) | Cohn,Al (sax) | Wess,Frank (reeds) | Richardson,Jerome (reeds) | Mulligan,Gerry (bs) | Jones,Hank (p) | Jones,Jimmy (p) | Burrell,Kenny (g) | Hinton,Milt (b) | Johnson,Osie (dr) | Orloff,Gene (v) | details unknown
Shirley Horn With The Quincy Jones Orchestra
On The Street Where You Live | The Great City | That Old Black Magic | Mack The Knife(Moritat) | Come Dance With Me | Let Me Love You | After You've Gone | Wouldn't It Be Loverly | Go Away Little Boy | I'm In The Mood For Love | The Good Life | In The Wee Small Hours Of The Morning
NYC, rec. 1963
Horn,Shirley (p,voc) | personal included: | Cleveland,Jimmy (tb) | Jones,Jimmy (p) | Jones,Quincy (arr,ld) | details unknown

846543-2 | CD | In Concert/I Put A Spell On You
Nina Simone Quartet
I Loves You Porgy | Plain Gold Ring | Pirate Jenny | Old Jim Crow | Don't Smoke In Bed | Go Limp | Mississippi Goddam
Live in Concert,NYC, rec. 21.3./1.& 6.4.1964
Simone,Nina (p,voc) | Stevenson,Rudy (fl,g) | Atkinson,Lisle (b) | Hamilton,Bobby (dr)
Nina Simone With Hal Mooney's Orchestra
I Put A Spell On You | Ne Me Quitte Pas | Marriage Is For Old Folks | Feeling Good | One September Day | Beautiful Land
NYC, rec. January 1965
Simone,Nina (p,voc) | Stevenson,Rudy (g) | Mooney,Hal (arr,ld) | details unknown
Nina Simone With Horace Ott's Orchestra
Tomorrow Is My Turn | Gimme Some | Blues On Purpose | You've Got To Learn | Take Care Of Business
Simone,Nina (p,voc) | Stevenson,Rudy (g) | Ott,Horace (cond,arr) | details unknown

846630-2 | 10 CD | Rahsaan/The Complete Mercury Recordings Of Roland Kirk
Roland Kirk Quartet
Blues For Alice | Blues For Alice(alt.take) | My Delight | The Haunted Melody | A Sack Full Of Soul
NYC, rec. 16.8.1961
Kirk,Rahsaan Roland (fl,ts,manzello,siren,stritch) | Wyands,Richard (p) | Davis,Art (b) | Persip,Charles (dr)
We Free Kings | Spring Will Be A Little Late This Year | Moon Song | Some Kind Of Love | Three For The Festival | You Did It You Did It
NYC, rec. 17.8.1961
Kirk,Rahsaan Roland (fl,ts,manzello,siren,stritch) | Jones,Hank (p) | Marshall,Wendell (b) | Persip,Charles (dr)
Get Out Of Town | Rolando | I Believe In You | Where Monk And Mingus Live | Let's Call This | Domino | E.D. | I Didn't Know What Time It Was | Someone To Watch Over Me | Termini's Corner | When The Sun Comes Out | Ad Lib
NYC, rec. 17./18.4.1962
Kirk,Rahsaan Roland (fl,ts,manzello,stritch) | Kelly,Wynton (p) | Martin,Vernon (b) | Haynes,Roy (dr)
Tubby Hayes And The All Stars
Stitt's Tune | I See With My Third 'I' | If I Had You- | Alone Together- | For Heaven's Sake- | Afternoon In Paris | Lady 'E'
NYC, rec. 23.6.1962
Hayes,Tubby (ts,vib) | Moody,James[as Jimmy Gloomy] (fl,ts) | Kirk,Rahsaan Roland (ts,manzello,nose-fl,stritch) | Bishop Jr.,Walter (p) | Jones,Sam (b) | Hayes,Louis (dr)
Roland Kirk Quartet
Meeting On Termini's Corner | Domino | Time | 3-In-1 Without The Oil | A Strich In Time | Lament
Chicago,Ill, rec. 6.9.1962
Kirk,Rahsaan Roland (fl,ts,manzello,stritch) | Hill,Andrew (p,celeste) | Martin,Vernon (b) | Duncan,Henry (dr)
Eddie Baccus Quartet
A Breath In The Wind
Chicago,Ill, rec. October 1962
Baccus,Eddie (org) | Kirk,Rahsaan Roland (fl) | Fowler,Mose (g) | Cook,George or Charles Crosby (dr)
Roland Kirk All Stars
Land Of Peace | Lonesome August Child | Limbo Boat | Hay Ro | Waltz Of The Friends
NYC, rec. 25.2.1963
Kirk,Rahsaan Roland (fl,ts,manzello,siren,stritch) | Jones,Virgil (tp) | Greenlee,Charles (tb) | Mabern,Harold (p) | Rafik,Abdullah (b) | Perkins,Walter (dr)
This Is Always | Reeds And Deeds | Song Of The Countrymen
NYC, rec. 26.2.1963
Kirk,Rahsaan Roland (fl,ts,manzello,siren,stritch) | Jones,Virgil (tp) | McIntosh,Tom (tb) | Mabern,Harold (p) | Davis,Richard (b) | Perkins,Walter (dr)
Roland Kirk With The Benny Golson Orchestra
Ecclusiastics | By Myself | Roland Speaks | A Nightingale Sang In Berkeley Square | Variations On A Theme Of Hindemith
NYC, rec. 11.6.1963
Kirk,Rahsaan Roland (fl,ts,manzello,siren,stritch) | Golson,Benny (arr) | Jones,Virgil (tp) | Williams,Richard (tp) | McIntosh,Tom (tb) | Greenlee,Charles (tb) | Butterfield,Don (tuba) | Mabern,Harold (p) | Davis,Richard (b) | Heath,Albert 'Tootie' (dr) | rest unkn.
Roland Kirk Quartet
I've Got Your Number | Between The Fourth And Fifth Step | April Morning | Get In The Basement
NYC, rec. 12.6.1963
Kirk,Rahsaan Roland (fl,ts,manzello,stritch) | Mabern,Harold (p) | Rafik,Abdullah (b) | Brown,Sonny (dr)
Roland Kirk
Abstract Improvisation
Kirk,Rahsaan Roland (manzello,stritch)
Roland Kirk Quintet
Narrow Bolero | Narrow Bolero(alt.take) | My Heart Stood Still | No Title No.1 | Mood Indigo | Cabin In The Sky | On The Corner Of King And Scott Streets | Untitled Blues | Will You Still Be Mine | One For My Baby(And One More For The Road) | We'll Be Together Again | Mingus-Griff Song | Mood Indigo | Rock-A-Bye Basie- | The Nearness Of You- | No Title No.3- | Half A Triple
Live at The 'Jazzhus' Montmartre,Copenhagen, rec. October 1963
Kirk,Rahsaan Roland (fl,ts,manzello,siren,stritch) | Montoliu,Tete (p) | Orsted-Pedersen,Niels-Henning (b) | Moore,Don (b) | Moses,J.C. (dr)
The Monkey Thing
Kirk,Rahsaan Roland (fl,ts,manzello,siren,stritch) | Montoliu,Tete (p) | Orsted-Pedersen,Niels-Henning (b) | Moore,Don (b) | Moses,J.C. (dr) | Williamson[as 'Big Skol'],Sonny Boy [Rice Miller] (harm)
Roland Kirk Quartet
Japan | Japan(take 2) | Japan(take 3) | Birkshire Blues | Dirty Money Blues | Dirty Money Blues(alt.take) | Ad Lib(Hip Chops)
details unknown, rec. 26.5.1964
Kirk,Rahsaan Roland (fl,ts,manzello,siren,stritch,voc) | details unknown
The Things I Love | Petite Fleur | March On Swan Lake | Tears Sent By You | My Heart At Thy Sweet Voice | Gifts And Messages | Hip Chops | Blues For C.T. | Where Does The Blame Lie | Vertigo Ro | Jive Elephant
Los Angeles,CA, rec. 22.7.1964
Kirk,Rahsaan Roland (fl,ts,manzello,oboe,siren,stritch) | Parlan,Horace (p) | Fleming,Michael (b) | Ellington,Steve (dr)
Roland Kirk Quintet
I Talk With The Spirits | Serenade To A Cuckoo | We'll Be Together Again- | People From Funny Girl- | Ruined Castles | Trees | Fugue'n And Alludin' | Django | My Ship | A Quote From Clifford Brown | The Business Ain't Nothin' But The Blues
Kirk,Rahsaan Roland (fl,african-fl) | Moses,Bobby (vib) | Parlan,Horace (p,celeste) | Fleming,Michael (b) | Perkins,Walter (dr) | Albert,Miss C.J. (voc)
Roland Kirk Quartet
No Tonic Press | From Bechet,Fats And Byas | Slippery,Hippery,Flippery | Black Diamond | Rip,Rig And Panic | Once In A While | Mystical Dream
New Jersey,NJ, rec. 13.1.1965
Kirk,Rahsaan Roland (fl,ts,castanets,manzello,oboe,siren,stritch) | Byard,Jaki (p) | Davis,Richard (b) | Jones,Elvin (dr)
Roland Kirk And His Orchestra
Walk On By | Juarez | Shakey Money | Safari | It's All In The Game | And I Love Her
NYC, rec. 16./17.11.1965
Kirk,Rahsaan Roland (fl,piccolo-fl,ts,bs,bagpipe,manzello,siren,stritch) | Jones,Virgil (tp) | Banks,Martin (fl-h) | Brown,Garnett (tb) | Parlan,Horace (p,celeste) | Mathias,Eddie (b) | Brown,Sonny (dr) | Montego Joe (congas) | Ramos,Manny (perc)
Ebrauqs | Raouf | Nothing But The Truth
Kirk,Rahsaan Roland (fl,piccolo-fl,ts,bs,bagpipe,manzello,siren,stritch) | Jones,Virgil (tp) | Banks,Martin (fl-h) | Brown,Garnett (tb) | Parlan,Horace (p,celeste) | Mathias,Eddie (b) | Brown,Sonny (dr,nagoya-harp) | Montego Joe (congas) | Ramos,Manny (perc) | Choir | Perkinson,Coleridge (dir) | details unknown
Quincy Jones And His Orchestra
A Taste Of Honey | Dyna-Soar
details unknown, rec. 1962
Kirk,Rahsaan Roland (fl,ts,strich) | Jones,Quincy (arr,ld) | Holley,Major (b) | details unknown
Soul Bossa Nova
NYC, rec. 13.8.1962
Kirk,Rahsaan Roland (fl,ts,strich) | Jones,Quincy (arr,ld) | Terry,Clark (tp) | Woods,Phil (as) | Schifrin,Lalo (p) | Hall,Jim (g) | White,Chris (b) | Collins,Rudy (dr) | Paula,Jose (perc) | Gomez,Carlos 'Bala' (perc) | Del Rio,Jack (perc) | details unknown
Comin' Home Baby
NYC, rec. 9.4.1963
Kirk,Rahsaan Roland (fl,ts,strich) | Jones,Quincy (arr,ld) | details unknown
Days Of Wine And Roses | Moon River | Dreamsville | I Love You And Don't You Forget It - (I Love You) And Don't You Forget It
NYC, rec. 5.2.1964
Kirk,Rahsaan Roland (fl,ts,manzello,siren,stritch) | Jones,Quincy (arr,ld) | Terry,Clark (tp) | Young,Eugene 'Snooky' (tp) | Maxwell,Jimmy (tp) | Royal,Ernie (tp) | Hixon,Richard (tb) | Green,Urbie (tb) | Byers,Billy (tb) | Jackson,Quentin (tb) | Studd,Tony (b-tb) | Buffington,Jimmy (fr-h) | Miranda,Tony (fr-h) | Northern,Bob (fr-h) | Alonge,Ray (fr-h) | Phillips,Harvey (tuba) | Richardson,Jerome (reeds) | Webb,Stanley (reeds) | Burton,Gary (vib) | Scott,Bobby (p) | Lowe,Mundell (g) | Hinton,Milt (b) | Johnson,Osie (dr) | Groupp,Martin (perc) | Ross,Margaret (harp)
Charade | Peter Gunn
NYC, rec. 6.2.1964
Kirk,Rahsaan Roland (fl,ts,manzello,siren,stritch) | Jones,Quincy (arr,ld) | Bello,John (tp) | Young,Eugene 'Snooky' (tp) | Maxwell,Jimmy (tp) | Royal,Ernie (tp) | Hixon,Richard (tb) | Green,Urbie (tb) | Byers,Billy (tb) | Jackson,Quentin (tb) | Studd,Tony (b-tb) | Richardson,Jerome (reeds) | Woods,Phil (as) | Powell,Seldon (reeds) | Penque,Romeo (reeds) | Borg,George (reeds) | Burton,Gary (vib) | Scott,Bobby (p) | Bell,Vincent (g) | Holley,Major (b) | Hinton,Milt (b) | Johnson,Osie (dr) | Kraus,Phil (perc)
Quincy Jones Big Band
I Had A Ball | Addie's At It Again
NYC, rec. 20.12.1964
Kirk,Rahsaan Roland (ts) | Jones,Quincy (ld) | Gillespie,Dizzy (tp) | Adderley,Nat (tp) | Maxwell,Jimmy (tp) | Hubbard,Freddie (tp) | Nottingham,Jimmy (tp) | Newman,Joe (tp) | Fuller,Curtis (tb) | Johnson,J.J. (tb) | Winding,Kai (tb) | Liston,Melba (tb) | Dodgion,Jerry (as) | Woods,Phil (as) | Moody,James (fl,as,ts) | Golson,Benny (ts,arr) | Thompson,Lucky (ts) | Adams,Pepper (bs) | Jackson,Milt (vib) | Scott,Bobby (p) | Cranshaw,Bob (b) | Blakey,Art (dr) | Byers,Billy (arr)

9861061 | CD | I Love John Frigo...He Swings | EAN 602498610619
Johnny Frigo Duo
Moonlight In Vermont
Chicago,Ill, rec. 1957
Frigo,John (v) | Jeffries,Norman (dr)
Johnny Frigo Quartet
Blue Orchid | If Love Is Good To Me | Be Me-Little Me
Frigo,John (v) | Marx,Dick (p) | Brown,Ray (b) | Jeffries,Norman (dr)
Johnny Frigo Sextet
Gone With The Wind | What A Difference A Day Made | Just Squeeze Me(But Don't Tease Me) | Polka Dots And Moonbeams
Frigo,John (v) | Touff,Cy (bass-tp) | Val,Vic (ts) | Marx,Dick (p) | Brown,Ray (b) | Faieta,Phil (dr)
Blow Fiddle Blow | You Stepped Out Of A Dream
Frigo,John (v) | Simpson,Mike (fl,ts) | Ellis,Herb (g) | Marx,Dick (p) | Brown,Ray (b) | Faieta,Phil (dr)

Metro Blue | EMI Germany

852699-0 | CD | It Happened One Night
Holly Cole And Her Quartet
Get Out Of Town | Cry(If You Want To) | Train Song | Losing My Mind | Tango 'Til They're Sore | Don't Let The Teardrops Rust Your Shining Heart | Que Sera Sera | Calling You
Live at St.Denis Theatre,Montreal,PQ, rec. 28.6.1995
Cole,Holly (voc) | Breit,Kevin (g) | Davis,Aaron (p) | Piltch,Dave (b) | Bowie,Dougie (dr,perc)
-> This CD contains a CD-ROM part!

MicNic Records | MicNic Records

MN 2 | CD | String Thing:Alles Wird Gut
String Thing
Alles Wird Gut | Drachentanz | Clouds Over Bew York | Aerofunk | Pluto | Am Meer | Dessacy | Administratosphäre | FM 9X.2 | Herbstkristalle | Störungsstelle | Auf Dem Jahrmarkt | Astorlogie | Herr Martin Skripinski | Just A Cappuccino
St.Martini,Estebrügge, rec. 1995
String Thing | Kruse,Nicola (v) | Rutledge,Mike (viola) | Kuhr,Hagen (cello) | Skriptschinski,Frank (b)

MN 4 | CD | String Thing:Turtifix
Reggae For Donald | Metall | Und Ewig Dröhnt Der Orient | Perlon Sweet | The Preacher And The Voodoo Woman | Sherlock Holmes Junior | Vogel Jakob | Höllenhund | S.K. | Twelve Months | B-Movie Bang Bang Bang | Frühlingsvorhersage | Friesel | Back To A Place
München, rec. 26.-30.10.1998
String Thing | Kruse,Nicola (v) | Rutledge,Mike (viola) | Kuhr,Hagen (cello) | Skriptschinski,Frank (b)

Milestone | ZYX Music GmbH

8MCD 4413-2 | 8 CD | Joe Henderson:The Milestone Years
Joe Henderson Sextet
Mamacita | The Kicker | Chelsea Bridge | If | Nardis | Without A Song | Moe' Joe

NYC, rec. 10.8.1967
Henderson,Joe (ts) | Lawrence,Mike (tp) | Moncur III,Grachan (tb) | Barron,Kenny (p) | Carter,Ron (b) | Hayes,Louis (dr)
Joe Henderson Quartet
O Amor En Paz(Once I Loved) | Tetragon | First Trip | I've Got You Under My Skin
NYC, rec. 27.9.1967
Henderson,Joe (ts) | Barron,Kenny (p) | Carter,Ron (b) | Hayes,Louis (dr)
Invitation | R.J. | Waltz For Zweetie | The Bad Game
NYC, rec. 16.5.1968
Henderson,Joe (ts) | Friedman,Don (p) | Carter,Ron (b) | DeJohnette,Jack (dr)
Lee Konitz-Joe Henderson
You Don't Know What Love Is
NYC, rec. 25.9.1967
Konitz,Lee (as) | Henderson,Joe (ts)
Nat Adderley Sextet
The Scavenger
NYC, rec. 19.1.1968
Adderley,Nat (co) | Steig,Jeremy (fl) | Henderson,Joe (ts) | Zawinul,Joe (p) | Gaskin,Victor (b) | McCurdy,Roy (dr)
Nat Adderley Quintet
Unilateral | But Not For Me
Adderley,Nat (co) | Henderson,Joe (ts) | Zawinul,Joe (p) | Gaskin,Victor (b) | McCurdy,Roy (dr)
Joe Henderson Quintet
Power To The People | Afro-Centric
NYC, rec. 23.5.1969
Henderson,Joe (ts) | Lawrence,Mike (tp) | Hancock,Herbie (el-p) | Carter,Ron (el-b) | DeJohnette,Jack (dr)
Joe Henderson Quartet
Black Narcissus | Isotope | Opus One-Point-Five | Lazy Afternoon
NYC, rec. 29.5.1969
Henderson,Joe (ts) | Hancock,Herbie (p,el-p) | Carter,Ron (b) | DeJohnette,Jack (dr)
Joe Henderson Trio
Foresight And Afterthought
Henderson,Joe (ts) | Carter,Ron (b) | DeJohnette,Jack (dr)
Joe Henderson Quintet
Recorda-Me | A Shade Of Jade | Isotope | Round About Midnight | Mode For Joe | Invitation | If You're Not Part Of The Solution, You're Part Of The Problem
Live at The Lighthouse,Hermosa Beach,CA, rec. 24.-26.9.1970
Henderson,Joe (ts) | Shaw,Woody (tp,fl-h) | Cables,George (el-p) | McClure,Ron (b,el-b) | White,Lenny (dr)
Joe Henderson Sextet
Caribbean Firedance | Blue Bossa | Gazelle
Henderson,Joe (ts) | Shaw,Woody (tp,fl-h) | Cables,George (el-p) | McClure,Ron (b) | White,Lenny (dr) | Waters,Tony (congas)
Mind Over Matter | No Me Esqueca | A Shade Of Jade
NYC, rec. 12.5.1971
Henderson,Joe (ts) | Fuller,Curtis (tb) | Yellin,Pete (fl,b-cl,as) | Cables,George (el-p) | Clarke,Stanley (b) | White,Lenny (dr)
Joe Henderson Quartet
Round About Midnight | Out 'N In | Blue Bossa | Junk Blues
Live at The Junk Club,Tokyo,Japan, rec. 4.8.1971
Henderson,Joe (ts) | Ichikawa,Hideo (el-p) | Inaba,Kunimitsu (b) | Hino,Motohiko (dr)
Vis-A-Vis
NYC, rec. March/April 1972
Henderson,Joe (ts) | Cables,George (el-p) | Holland,Dave (b) | DeJohnette,Jack (dr)
Joe Henderson Sextet
Foregone Conclusion
Henderson,Joe (fl,alto-fl,ss,ts,perc-overdubbing) | Wadenius,George (g) | Cables,George (el-p) | Holland,Dave (b) | DeJohnette,Jack (dr) | Moreira,Airto (perc)
Black Is The Color(Of My True Love's Mind)
Henderson,Joe (ts) | Wadenius,George (g) | Cables,George (el-p) | Holland,Dave (b) | DeJohnette,Jack (el-p,dr) | Moreira,Airto (perc)
Joe Henderson And His Orchestra
Terra Firma | Current Event
Henderson,Joe (ts) | Wadenius,George (g) | Cables,George (el-p) | Horowitz,David (synth) | Holland,Dave (b) | Carter,Ron (el-b) | DeJohnette,Jack (dr) | MacDonald,Ralph (perc)
Tres-Cun-Deo-La
NYC, rec. 30.1./5.4.1973
Henderson,Joe (fl,ss,ts,voice-overdubbing) | Willis,Larry (el-p,echoplex,ring-modulator) | Ulmer,James Blood (el-g) | Holland,Dave (b,el-b) | DeJohnette,Jack (dr) | Jenkins,Arthur (perc)
Me Among Others | Bwaata
NYC, rec. 30.1.1973
Henderson,Joe (ts) | Willis,Larry (el-p,echoplex,ring-modulator) | Holland,Dave (b,el-b) | DeJohnette,Jack (dr) | Jenkins,Arthur (perc)
Song For Sinners
NYC, rec. 31.1./2.2.& 13.4.1993
Henderson,Joe (ts,perc,voice-overdubbing) | Willis,Larry (el-p,echoplex,ring-modulator) | Thomas,John (g) | Holland,Dave (b,el-b) | DeJohnette,Jack (dr) | Jenkins,Arthur (perc)
Turned Around
NYC, rec. 31.1.1973
Henderson,Joe (ts) | Willis,Larry (el-p,echoplex,ring-modulator) | Holland,Dave (b,el-b) | DeJohnette,Jack (dr) | Jenkins,Arthur (perc)
Las Palmas
Berkeley,CA, rec. 3.10.1973
Henderson,Joe (ts) | Gasca,Luis (tp) | Duke,George (el-p) | Levine,Mark (p) | Heard,John (b) | Gravatt,Eric (dr) | Garcia,Hungaria 'Carmelo' (timbales) | Pantoja,Victor (congas)
Canyon Lady
Henderson,Joe (ts) | Gasca,Luis (tp,fl-h) | Duke,George (el-p) | Levine,Mark (p) | Heard,John (b) | Gravatt,Eric (dr) | Garcia,Hungaria 'Carmelo' (timbales) | Pantoja,Victor (congas) | Brashear,Oscar (tp) | Priester,Julian (tb) | Caliman,Hadley (ts)
All Things Considered
Henderson,Joe (ts) | Gasca,Luis (tp,fl-h) | Duke,George (el-p) | Levine,Mark (p) | Heard,John (b) | Gravatt,Eric (dr) | Garcia,Hungaria 'Carmelo' (timbales) | Pantoja,Victor (congas) | Brashear,Oscar (tp) | Priester,Julian (tb) | Aguabella,Francisco (congas)
Tres Palabras
Berkeley,CA, rec. 1.10.1973
Henderson,Joe (ts) | Brashear,Oscar (tp) | Hunt,John (tp) | Priester,Julian (tb) | TenBroek,Nicholaas (tb) | Caliman,Hadley (fl) | Pizzi,Ray (fl) | Denham,Vince (fl) | Duke,George (el-p) | Levine,Mark (p) | Heard,John (b) | Gravatt,Eric (dr) | Garcia,Hungaria 'Carmelo' (timbales) | Pantoja,Victor (congas)
In The Beginning There Was Africa
Berkeley,CA, rec. 3.10.1973
Henderson,Joe (ts) | Garcia,Hungaria 'Carmelo' (timbales) | Aguabella,Francisco (congas) | Pantoja,Victor (congas)
Alice Coltrane Quintet
Air
Los Angeles,CA, rec. 15.10.1973
Coltrane,Alice (p,harmonium,harp,tamboura) | Henderson,Joe (ts,p) | Haden,Charlie (b) | Nash,Kenneth (dr) | Oshun,Baba Duru (perc,tabla)
Alice Coltrane Sextet
Water
Coltrane,Alice (p,harmonium,harp,tamboura) | Henderson,Joe (ts) | White,Michael (v) | Haden,Charlie (b) | Nash,Kenneth (perc,wooden-fl) | Oshun,Baba Duru (perc,tabla)
Fire | Earth
Los Angeles,CA, rec. 16.10.1973
Coltrane,Alice (p,harmonium,harp,tamboura) | Henderson,Joe (ts) | Haden,Charlie (b) | Ndugu[Leon Chancler] (dr) | Nash,Kenneth (perc,narration) | Oshun,Baba Duru (perc,tabla) | White,Michael (v-overdubbing)
Flora Purim And Her Quartet
Butterfly Dreams
Berkeley,CA, rec. 3.12.1973
Purim,Flora (voc) | Henderson,Joe (ts) | Duke,George (keyboards) | Clarke,Stanley (b) | Moreira,Airto (dr,perc)
Flora Purim And Her Sextet
Light As A Feather
Purim,Flora (voc) | Henderson,Joe (fl) | Duke,George (keyboards) | Amaro,David (g) | Hood,Ernie (zither) | Clarke,Stanley (b) | Moreira,Airto (dr,perc)
Summer Night
Berkeley,CA, rec. 4.12.1973
Purim,Flora (voc) | Henderson,Joe (ts) | Duke,George (keyboards) | Amaro,David (g) | Hood,Ernie (zither) | Clarke,Stanley (b) | Moreira,Airto (dr,perc)
Flora Purim And Her Quintet
Love Reborn
Purim,Flora (voc) | Henderson,Joe (ts) | Duke,George (keyboards) | Amaro,David (g) | Clarke,Stanley (b) | Moreira,Airto (dr,perc)
Joe Henderson Quintet
Black Narcissus | Hindsight And Forethought | Power To The People
Paris,France, rec. October 1974
Henderson,Joe (ts) | Kühn,Joachim (p) | Jenny-Clark,Jean-Francois (b) | Humair,Daniel (dr) | Summers,Bill (perc)
Joe Henderson Sextet
The Other Side Of Right
Henderson,Joe (ts) | Kühn,Joachim (p) | Gleeson,Pat (synth) | Jenny-Clark,Jean-Francois (b) | Humair,Daniel (dr) | Summers,Bill (perc)
Good Morning Heartache
Berkeley,CA, rec. 26.4.1976
Henderson,Joe (ts) | Kühn,Joachim (p) | Gleeson,Pat (synth) | Friesen,David (b) | DeJohnette,Jack (dr) | Summers,Bill (perc)
Joe Henderson Trio
Amoeba
Berkeley,CA, rec. 26.4.1975
Henderson,Joe (ts,b-synth) | DeJohnette,Jack (dr) | Summers,Bill (perc)
Joe Henderson And His Orchestra
My Cherie Amour | Old Slippers
Berkeley,CA, rec. 13.2.1975
Henderson,Joe (ts) | Brashear,Oscar (tp,fl-h) | Young,Eugene 'Snooky' (tp,fl-h) | Bohanon,George (tb) | Waldrop,Don (b-tb,tuba) | Caliman,Hadley (fl,ts) | Gonga,Dawilli (el-p,synth,clavinet) | Carter,Ron (el-b) | Mason,Harvey (dr) | Summers,Bill (perc,congas)
Gazelle | Immaculate Deception
Berkeley,CA, rec. 13.2.1995
Henderson,Joe (ts) | Brashear,Oscar (tp,fl-h) | Young,Eugene 'Snooky' (tp,fl-h) | Bohanon,George (tb) | Waldrop,Don (b-tb,tuba) | Caliman,Hadley (fl,ts) | Ritenour,Lee (g) | Gonga,Dawilli (el-p,synth,clavinet) | Carter,Ron (el-b) | Mason,Harvey (dr) | Summers,Bill (perc,congas)
Soulution
Berkeley,CA, rec. 14.2.1975
Henderson,Joe (ts) | Brashear,Oscar (tp,fl-h) | Young,Eugene 'Snooky' (tp,fl-h) | Bohanon,George (tb) | Waldrop,Don (b-tb,tuba) | Caliman,Hadley (fl,ts) | Ritenour,Lee (g) | Gonga,Dawilli (el-p,synth,clavinet) | Carter,Ron (el-b) | Mason,Harvey (dr) | Summers,Bill (perc,congas)
Black Miracle
Henderson,Joe (ts) | Brashear,Oscar (tp,fl-h) | Young,Eugene 'Snooky' (tp,fl-h) | Bohanon,George (tb) | Waldrop,Don (b-tb,tuba) | Caliman,Hadley (fl,ts) | Gonga,Dawilli (el-p,synth,clavinet) | Carter,Ron (el-b) | Mason,Harvey (dr) | Summers,Bill (perc,congas)
Flora Purim With Orchestra
What Can I Say | Windows
Los Angeles,CA, rec. 30./31.8.1976
Purim,Flora (voc) | Brashear,Oscar (tp) | Bohanon,George (tb) | Watts,Ernie (fl) | Henderson,Joe (ts) | Graydon,Jay (g) | Duke,George (grand-p) | Miller,Byron (b) | Ndugu[Leon Chancler] (dr)
Black Narcissus
Los Angeles,CA, rec. 26.9.1976
Purim,Flora (voc) | Henderson,Joe (ts) | Duke,George (p) | Johnson,Alphonso (b) | Moreira,Airto (dr)

8MCD 4421-2 | 8 CD | Bill Evans:The Secret Sessions
Bill Evans Trio
Very Early | Round About Midnight | One For Helen | Blue In Green | Turn Out The Stars | Waltz For Debby | Time Remembered | Autumn Leaves
Live at The 'Village Vanguard',NYC, rec. March 1966
Evans,Bill (p) | Kotick,Teddy (b) | Wise,Arnold (dr)
I Should Care | Elsa | Who Can I Turn To | My Foolish Heart | In Your Own Sweet Way | Five(Closing Theme)
Live at The 'Village Vanguard',NYC, rec. 3.7.1966
Evans,Bill (p) | Gomez,Eddie (b) | Wise,Arnold (dr)
Gloria's Step | Nardis | Someday My Prince Will Come
Live at The 'Village Vanguard',NYC, rec. 21.10.1966
Evans,Bill (p) | Gomez,Eddie (b) | Wise,Arnold (dr)
Who Can I Turn To | Come Rain Or Come Shine | If You Could See Me Now | Spring Is Here | Re:Person I Knew | A Sleeping Bee
Live at The 'Village Vanguard',NYC, rec. 10.11.1966
Evans,Bill (p) | Gomez,Eddie (b) | Wise,Arnold (dr)
Emily | Alfie | Walkin' Up | You're Gonna Hear From Me | Some Other Time | I'll Remember April | Alice In Wonderland | I Love You
Live at The 'Village Vanguard',NYC, rec. 12.11.1966
Evans,Bill (p) | Gomez,Eddie (b) | Wise,Arnold (dr)
Very Early | Time Remembered | Round About Midnight | Stella By Starlight | Turn Out The Stars
Live at The 'Village Vanguard',NYC, rec. 8.1.1967
Evans,Bill (p) | Gomez,Eddie (b) | Hunt,Joe (dr)
My Man's Gone Now | In A Sentimental Mood | When I Fall In Love | Nardis
Live at The 'Village Vanguard',NYC, rec. 26.2.1967
Evans,Bill (p) | Gomez,Eddie (b) | Hunt,Joe (dr)
Come Rain Or Come Shine | Gloria's Step | Round About Midnight
Live at The 'Village Vanguard',NYC, rec. 5.3.1967
Evans,Bill (p) | Gomez,Eddie (b) | Hunt,Joe (dr)
Blue In Green | Waltz For Debby | Detour Ahead | On Green Dolphin Street
Live at The 'Village Vanguard',NYC, rec. 19.5.1967
Evans,Bill (p) | Gomez,Eddie (b) | Jones,Philly Joe (dr)
My Foolish Heart | If You Could See Me Now | Elsa
Live at The 'Village Vanguard',NYC, rec. 21.5.1967
Evans,Bill (p) | Gomez,Eddie (b) | Jones,Philly Joe (dr)
How Deep Is The Ocean | Polka Dots And Moonbeams | I'm Getting Sentimental Over You | I Should Care
Live at The 'Village Vanguard',NYC, rec. 26.5.1967
Evans,Bill (p) | Gomez,Eddie (b) | Jones,Philly Joe (dr)
Star Eyes | Peri's Scope | Haunted Heart | Airegin | Little Lulu | Five(Closing Theme)
Live at The 'Village Vanguard',NYC, rec. 28.5.1967
Evans,Bill (p) | Gomez,Eddie (b) | Jones,Philly Joe (dr)
Turn Out The Stars | Nardis | California Here I Come | Very Early | Easy Living | Wonder Why
Live at The 'Village Vanguard',NYC, rec. 1.6.1967
Evans,Bill (p) | Gomez,Eddie (b) | Jones,Philly Joe (dr)
Time Remembered | You And The Night And The Music
Live at The 'Village Vanguard',NYC, rec. 3.9.1967
Evans,Bill (p) | Gomez,Eddie (b) | Jones,Philly Joe (dr)
Beautiful Love | Waltz For Debby | I Fall In Love Too Easily
Live at The 'Village Vanguard',NYC, rec. 4.2.1968
Evans,Bill (p) | Gomez,Eddie (b) | Wise,Arnold (dr)
My Man's Gone Now | Who Can I Turn To | Polka Dots And Moonbeams | Emily
Live at The 'Village Vanguard',NYC, rec. 23.8.1968
Evans,Bill (p) | Gomez,Eddie (b) | DeJohnette,Jack (dr)
Everything I Love | Someday My Prince Will Come | The Shadow Of Your Smile
Live at The 'Village Vanguard',NYC, rec. 15.9.1968
Evans,Bill (p) | Gomez,Eddie (b) | Dentz,John (dr)
A Sleeping Bee | Blue In Green
Live at The 'Village Vanguard',NYC, rec. 13.12.1968
Evans,Bill (p) | Gomez,Eddie (b) | Morell,Marty (dr)
For Heaven's Sake | Our Love Is Here To Stay
Live at The 'Village Vanguard',NYC, rec. 22.12.1968
Evans,Bill (p) | Gomez,Eddie (b) | Morell,Marty (dr)
In A Sentimental Mood | How My Heart Sings | On Green Dolphin Street
Live at The 'Village Vanguard',NYC, rec. 2.2.1969
Evans,Bill (p) | Gomez,Eddie (b) | Morell,Marty (dr)
My Foolish Heart | Stella By Starlight
Live at The 'Village Vanguard',NYC, rec. 15.2.1970
Evans,Bill (p) | Gomez,Eddie (b) | Morell,Marty (dr)
Midnight Mood | What Are You Doing The Rest Of Your Life | I Should Care | Autumn Leaves
Live at The 'Village Vanguard',NYC, rec. 18.4.1970
Evans,Bill (p) | Gomez,Eddie (b) | Morell,Marty (dr)
Re:Person I Knew | Alfie | Very Early
Live at The 'Village Vanguard',NYC, rec. December 1971
Evans,Bill (p) | Gomez,Eddie (b) | Morell,Marty (dr)
Polka Dots And Moonbeams | Morning Glory | Yesterday I Heard The Rain | Emily | Time Remembered
Live at The 'Village Vanguard',NYC, rec. 12.8.1973
Evans,Bill (p) | Gomez,Eddie (b) | Morell,Marty (dr)
Who Can I Turn To | Dolphin Dance
Live at The 'Village Vanguard',NYC, rec. 12.1.1974
Evans,Bill (p) | Gomez,Eddie (b) | Morell,Marty (dr)
Sugar Plum | Turn Out Of The Stars | Quiet Now | Waltz For Debby
Live at The 'Village Vanguard',NYC, rec. 26.1.1975
Evans,Bill (p) | Gomez,Eddie (b) | Zigmund,Eliot (dr)

8MCD 4430-2 | 8 CD | Bill Evans Trio:The Last Waltz
After You | Like Someone In Love | Polka Dots And Moonbeams | Emily | Turn Out The Stars | I Do It For Your Love | Nardis | But Beautiful
Live at Keystone Korner,SF, rec. 31.8.1980
Evans,Bill (p) | Johnson,Marc (b) | LaBarbera,Joe (dr)
Yet Never Broken | Knit For Mary F | The Touch Of Your Lips | My Man's Gone Now | Turn Out The Stars | Your Story | Nardis
Live at Keystone Korner,SF, rec. 1.9.1980
Evans,Bill (p) | Johnson,Marc (b) | LaBarbera,Joe (dr)
Peau Douce | Yet Never Broken | My Foolish Heart | Up With The Lark | Turn Out The Stars | I Do It For Your Love
Live at Keystone Korner,SF, rec. 2.9.1980
Evans,Bill (p) | Johnson,Marc (b) | LaBarbera,Joe (dr)
Nardis | Noelle's Theme- | I Loves You Porgy- | Yet Never Broken | Spring Is Here | Who Can I Turn To | Letter To Evan | If You Could See Me Now | The Two Lonely People | A Sleeping Bee | Haunted Heart | Five
Live at Keystone Korner,SF, rec. 3.9.1980
Evans,Bill (p) | Johnson,Marc (b) | LaBarbera,Joe (dr)
Re:Person I Knew | Tiffany | Polka Dots And Moonbeams | Like Someone In Love | Your Story | Someday My Prince Will Come | Letter To Evan | My Romance | But Beautiful
Live at Keystone Korner,SF, rec. 4.9.1980
Evans,Bill (p) | Johnson,Marc (b) | LaBarbera,Joe (dr)
Mornin' Glory | Emily | For Mary F | Days Of Wine And Roses
Live at Keystone Korner,SF, rec. 5.9.1980
Evans,Bill (p) | Johnson,Marc (b) | LaBarbera,Joe (dr)
Up With The Lark | My Foolish Heart | Nardis | But Beautiful
Live at Keystone Korner,SF, rec. 6.9.1980
Evans,Bill (p) | Johnson,Marc (b) | LaBarbera,Joe (dr)
My Foolish Heart | Nardis | Mother Of Earl | If You Could See Me Now | My Man's Gone Now | Who Can I Turn To | Waltz For Debby | Spring Is Here | Five
Live at Keystone Korner,SF, rec. 7.9.1980
Evans,Bill (p) | Johnson,Marc (b) | LaBarbera,Joe (dr)
Letter To Evan | My Man's Gone Now | Skidoo | Spring Is Here | Autumn Leaves | Knit For Mary F | Nardis
Live at Keystone Korner,SF, rec. 8.9.1980
Evans,Bill (p) | Johnson,Marc (b) | LaBarbera,Joe (dr)

MCD 47005-2 | CD | Latin Byrd
Charlie Byrd Quartet
O Pato(The Duck) | Azul Tiple | Manha De Carnaval(Morning Of The Carnival) | Homage A Villa-Lobos | Samba Da Una Nota So(One Note Samba)
NYC, rec. May 1962
Byrd,Charlie (g) | Byrd,Gene (g) | Betts,Keter (b) | Reichenbach,Bill (dr,perc)
Charlie Byrd
Amor Flamenco | Cancion Di Argentna | Mexican Song No.1 | Mexican Song No.2 | Galopera | Valse(Opus 8 No.4)
Byrd,Charlie (g-solo)
Charlie Byrd Orchestra
Outra Vez | How Insensitive(Insensatez) | Three Note Samba | Saudade Da Bahia | Socegadamente(Softly) | Chega De Saudade(No More Blues)
Englewood Cliffs,NJ, rec. April 1963
Byrd,Charlie (g,arr) | Ramsey,Samuel (fr-h) | Byrd,Gene (g,b) | Betts,Keter (b) | Reichenbach,Bill (dr) | Deppenschmidt,Buddy (dr,perc) | Martin,John (cello) | Stahl,Dorothy (cello) | Vlasek,Frank (cello) | Kirschbaum,Morris (cello)
Charlie Byrd Quintet
Limehouse Blues
Englewood Cliffs,NJ, rec. 4.4.1963
Byrd,Charlie (g) | Byrd,Gene (g,b) | Betts,Keter (b) | Reichenbach,Bill (dr) | Deppenschmidt,Buddy (dr,perc)
Charlie Byrd Septet
Presente De Natal | Samba Of My Country | Anna | Lullaby For Carol
Byrd,Charlie (g) | Byrd,Gene (g,b) | Betts,Keter-(b) | Reichenbach,Bill (dr) | Deppenschmidt,Buddy (dr,perc) | Posey,Hal (tp,fl-h) | Gwaltney,Tommy (vib)

MCD 47069-2 | CD | Dizzy's Business-Live In Concert
Cannonball Adderley Sextet
Never Say Yes | Peter And The Goats | New Delhi
Live at The Jazz Workshop,San Francisco,CA, rec. 21.9.1962
Adderley,Julian \'Cannonball\' (as) | Adderley,Nat (co) | Lateef,Yusef (fl,ts,oboe) | Zawinul,Joe (p) | Jones,Sam (b) | Hayes,Louis (dr)
Autumn Leaves | Bohemia After Dark
Live at Sankei Hall,Osaka,Japan, rec. 14.7.1963
Adderley,Julian \'Cannonball\' (as) | Adderley,Nat (co) | Lateef,Yusef (fl,ts,oboe) | Zawinul,Joe (p) | Jones,Sam (b) | Hayes,Louis (dr)
Dizzy's Business | Primitivo | Jive Samba | This Here
Live at Kosei-Nenkin Hall,Tokyo,Japan, rec. 19.7.1963
Adderley,Julian \'Cannonball\' (as) | Adderley,Nat (co) | Lateef,Yusef (fl,ts,oboe) | Zawinul,Joe (p) | Jones,Sam (b) | Hayes,Louis (dr)

MCD 47077-2 | CD | Libra/Another Earth
Gary Bartz Quintet
Eastern Blues | Cabin In The Sky | Air And Fire | Libra | Bloomdido | Deep River | Freedom One Day
NYC, rec. 31.5./15.6.1967
Bartz,Gary (as) | Owens,Jimmy (tp,fl-h) | Dailey,Albert (p) | Davis,Richard (b) | Higgins,Billy (dr)
Gary Bartz Quartet
Dark Nebula | Ufo | Lost In The Stars | Perihelion And Aphelion
NYC, rec. 25.6.1968
Bartz,Gary (as) | Cowell,Stanley (p) | Workman,Reggie (b) | Waits,Freddie (dr)
Gary Bartz Sextet
Another Earth
NYC, rec. 19.6.1968
Bartz,Gary (as) | Cowell,Stanley (p) | Workman,Reggie (b) | Waits,Freddie (dr) | Tolliver,Charles (tp) | Sanders,Pharoah (ts)

MCD 47084-2 | CD | Blues Up And Down
Eddie Lockjaw Davis-Johnny Griffin Quintet
Last Train From Overbrook | Hey Lock | Midnight At Mintons | Second Balcony Jump | I'll Remember April | Good Bait
NYC, rec. 4.& 10.11.1960
Davis,Eddie 'Lockjaw' (ts) | Griffin,Johnny (ts) | Mance,Junior[Julian C.] (p) | Gales,Larry (b) | Riley,Ben (dr)
Blues Up And Down | Nice And Easy | Walkin' | Leapin' On Lenox | Layin' On Mellow
NYC, rec. 5.6.1961

Davis,Eddie 'Lockjaw' (ts) | Griffin,Johnny (ts) | Mayers,Lloyd (p) | Gales,Larry (b) | Riley,Ben (dr)
Camp Meeting | Oh Gee
NYC, rec. 17.8.1961
Davis,Eddie 'Lockjaw' (ts) | Griffin,Johnny (ts) | Mayers,Lloyd (p) | Gales,Larry (b) | Riley,Ben (dr)

MCD 47085-2 | CD | Randy Weston:Solo,Duo,Trio
Randy Weston-Sam Gill
What Is This Thing Called Love | I Love You | Night And Day | I Get A Kick Out Of You | In The Still Of The Night | Get Out Of Town | Just One Of Those Things | I've Got You Under My Skin
Hackensack,NJ, rec. 27.4.1954
Weston,Randy (p) | Gill,Sam (b)
Randy Weston Trio
Sweet Sue Just You | Pam's Waltz | Solemn Meditation | Again | Zulu | If You Could See Me Now
Hackensack,NJ, rec. 25.1.1955
Weston,Randy (p) | Gill,Sam (b) | Blakey,Art (dr)
Randy Weston
Little Girl Blue | We'll Be Together Again | Softness | Lover
Hackensack,NJ, rec. 10.9.1956
Weston,Randy (p-solo)

MCD 47086-2 | CD | Red,Blue & Green
Sonny Red (Kyner) Quartet
I Like The Likes Of You | Bye Bye Blues | Never Never Land | Ko-Kee
NYC, rec. 29.5.1961
Red (Kyner) | Walton,Cedar (p) | Tucker,George (b) | Cobb,Jimmy (dr)
Sonny Red (Kyner) Quintet
Images | Blues For Donna | Dodge City
NYC, rec. 25.6.1961
Red (Kyner) | Mitchell,Blue (tp) | Harris,Barry (p) | Tucker,George (b) | Humphries,Lex (dr)
Moon River | Super-20 | The Mode | Blue Sonny | The Rhythm Thing
NYC, rec. 14.12.1961
Red (Kyner) | Green,Grant (g) | Harris,Barry (p) | Tucker,George (b) | Cobb,Jimmy (dr)
Sonny Red (Kyner) Quartet
Bewitched Bothered And Bewildered
Red (Kyner) | Harris,Barry (p) | Tucker,George (b) | Cobb,Jimmy (dr)

MCD 47087-2 | CD | Out Of This World
Julian Priester Sextet
Chi Chi | Blue Stride | It Might As Well Be Spring | Excursion | Spiritsville | My Romance | Donna's Waltz
NYC, rec. 12.7.1960
Priester,Julian (tb) | Benton,Walter (ts) | Davis,Charles (bs) | Tyner,McCoy (p) | Jones,Sam (b) | Taylor,Arthur 'Art' (dr)
Walter Benton Quintet
Out Of This World | Night Movements | A Blues Mood | Lover Man(Oh,Where Can You Be?)
NYC, rec. 19.9.1960
Benton,Walter (ts) | Hubbard,Freddie (tp) | Kelly,Wynton (p) | Chambers,Paul (b) | Heath,Albert 'Tootie' (dr)
Walter's Altar | Azil
NYC, rec. 21.9.1960
Benton,Walter (ts) | Hubbard,Freddie (tp) | Kelly,Wynton (p) | Chambers,Paul (b) | Cobb,Jimmy (dr)

MCD 47089-2 | CD | Open House
Johnny 'Hammond' Smith Septet
Open House | Cyra | I Remember You | Theme From Cleopatra | Why Was I Born | I Love You
NYC, rec. 1963
Smith,Johnny 'Hammond' (org) | Jones,Thad (co,tp) | Powell,Seldon (fl,ts) | McFadden,Eddie (g) | Cranshaw,Bob (b) | Stevens,Leo (dr) | Barretto,Ray (congas)
Johnny 'Hammond' Smith Sextet
Blues For De-De
Smith,Johnny 'Hammond' (org) | Jones,Thad (co,tp) | Powell,Seldon (fl,ts) | McFadden,Eddie (g) | Cranshaw,Bob (b) | Taylor,Arthur 'Art' (dr)
Johnny 'Hammond' Smith Quartet
Nica's Dream | Cleopatra And The African Knight | Bennie's Diggin' | Eloise | A Little Taste | Twixt The Sheets
Smith,Johnny 'Hammond' (org) | Jones,Virgil (tp) | Person,Houston (ts) | Taylor,Luis (dr)

MCD 47090-2 | CD | Pick 'Em/Super Strings
Ron Carter Quartet
All Blues | Opus 2 | B And A | Pick 'Em | Tranquil | Eight
Englewood Cliffs,NJ, rec. December 1978
Carter,Ron (b,piccolo-b) | Barron,Kenny (p) | Williams,Buster (b) | Riley,Ben (dr)
Ron Carter Quintet With Strings
Bom Dia | Don't Misunderstand | Super Strings | Bitin' | No Flower Please | Uptown Conversation
NYC, rec. 14./15.4.1981
Carter,Ron (b,piccolo-b) | Barron,Kenny (p) | Tropea,John (g) | DeJohnette,Jack (dr) | McDonald,Ralph (perc) | Allen,Sanford (v,concertmaster) | Cykman,Harry (v) | Gordon,Kenneth (v) | Dicterow,Glenn (v) | Pintavalle,John (v) | Pinheiro,Marion (v) | Billingslea,Sandra 'Sandy' (v) | Young,Richard (v) | Micci,Alfio (v) | Hunte,Stanley (v) | Alsop,LaMar (viola) | Roach,Maxine (viola) | Levine,Jesse (viola) | Zaratzian,Harry (viola) | Moore,Kermit (cello) | Moye,Eugene (cello) | McCracken,Charles (cello) | Makeson,Leon (b)

MCD 47091-2 | CD | Quartet And Orchestra
Bobby Timmons Orchestra
If You Ain't Got It(I Got To Get It Somewhere) | Come Sunday | So Tired
NYC, rec. 20.11.1967
Timmons,Bobby (p) | Owens,Jimmy (tp,fl-h) | Laws,Hubert (reeds) | Moody,James (reeds) | Farrell,Joe (reeds) | Barrow,George (reeds) | Gale,Eric (g) | Carter,Ron (b) | Higgins,Billy (dr) | Voices
Up Up And Away | Straight No Chaser
NYC, rec. 21.11.1967
Timmons,Bobby (p) | Owens,Jimmy (tp,fl-h) | Laws,Hubert (reeds) | Moody,James (reeds) | Farrell,Joe (reeds) | Barrow,George (reeds) | Collins,Howard (g) | Carter,Ron (b) | Cobb,Jimmy (dr)
Bobby Timmons Quartet
Travelin' Light | One Down | Here's That Rainy Day | Booker's Bossa
NYC, rec. 4.12.1967
Timmons,Bobby (p) | Beck,Joe (g) | Carter,Ron (b) | Cobb,Jimmy (dr)
I Won't Be Back | Last Night When We Were Young | Do You Know The Way To San Jose? | Come Together | This Guy's In Love With You
NYC, rec. August 1968
Timmons,Bobby (p) | Beck,Joe (g) | Cranshaw,Bob (el-b) | DeJohnette,Jack (dr)
Bobby Timmons Trio
The Spanish Count | Something To Live For | Soul Time
NYC, rec. November 1968
Timmons,Bobby (p) | Cranshaw,Bob (el-b) | DeJohnette,Jack (dr)

MCD 47092-2 | CD | Mosaic
Clifford Jordan Quintet
Sunrise In Mexico | Extempore | Down Through The Years | Quittin' Time | One Flight Down | Windmill | Don't You Know I Care (Or Don't You Care I Know) | Mosaic
NYC, rec. 14./15.6.1961
Jordan,Clifford (ts) | Dorham,Kenny (tp) | Walton,Cedar (p) | Ware,Wilbur (b) | Heath,Albert 'Tootie' (dr)
Cumberland Court | A Story Tale | If I Didn't Care
NYC, rec. 14.2.1961
Jordan,Clifford (ts) | Red (Kyner) | Matthews,Ronnie (p) | Davis,Art (b) | Jones,Elvin (dr)
You're Driving Me Crazy | Defiance | Prints | Hip Pockets | They Say It's Wonderful
Jordan,Clifford (ts) | Red (Kyner) | Flanagan,Tommy (p) | Davis,Art (b) | Jones,Elvin (dr)

MCD 47093-2 | CD | Got That Feeling/Moon Child
Johnny Lytle Trio(Quartet)
Got That Feeling | Pow-Wow | In The Wee Small Hours Of The Morning | Big John Grady | The Breeze And I | It Ain't Necessarily So | Lela | Our Love Is Here To Stay | The Soulful One
NYC, rec. 1963
Lytle,Johnny (vib) | Harris,Milt (org) | Hinton,Milt (b) | Hinnant,Peppy (dr)
Johnny Lytle Quintet
Worksong | The Moor Man | When My Dreamboat Comes Home | The House Of Winchester
NYC, rec. 2.7.1962
Lytle,Johnny (vib) | Harris,Milt (org) | Cooper,Steve (b) | Hinnant,Peppy (dr) | Barretto,Ray (congas)
Johnny Lytle Quartet
Moon Child | A Taste Of Honey
Lytle,Johnny (vib) | Harris,Milt (org) | Hinnant,Peppy (dr) | Barretto,Ray (congas)
The Nearness Of You | Moonlight In Vermont
Lytle,Johnny (vib) | Harris,Milt (org) | Cooper,Steve (b) | Hinnant,Peppy (dr)

MCD 47095-2 | CD | Long Night | EAN 090204971268
Frank Strozier Sextet
Long Night | The Need For Love | The Crystal Ball | Just Think It Over
NYC, rec. 12.9.1961
Strozier,Frank (fl,as) | Coleman,George (ts) | Patrick,Pat (bs) | Anderson,Chris (p) | Lee,Bill (b) | Perkins,Walter (dr)
Frank Strozier Quartet
How Little We Know | The Man That Got Away | Happiness Is A Thing Called Joe | Pacemaker
Strozier,Frank (as) | Anderson,Chris (p) | Lee,Bill (b) | Perkins,Walter (dr)
March Of The Siamese Children | Extension | Something I Dreamed Last Night | Don't Follow The Crowd | Our Waltz | Will I Forget? | Lap | Hey,Lee!
NYC, rec. 28.3.1962
Strozier,Frank (as) | Mabern,Harold (p) | Lee,Bill (b) | Dreares,Al (dr)

MCD 47096-2 | CD | Heavyweights | EAN 090204942145
Sal Nistico Quintet
Seconds,Anyone? | Mamblue | Shoutin' | Au Privave | Heavyweights
NYC, rec. 20.12.1961
Nistico,Sal (ts) | Adderley,Nat (co) | Harris,Barry (p) | Jones,Sam (b) | Perkins,Walter (dr)
Sal Nistico Quartet
My Old Flame
Nistico,Sal (ts) | Harris,Barry (p) | Jones,Sam (b) | Perkins,Walter (dr)
Easy Living
NYC, rec. 17.10.1962
Nistico,Sal (ts) | Harris,Barry (p) | Cranshaw,Bob (b) | Ruggieri,Vinnie (dr)
Sal Nistico Quintet
Cheryl | Ariescene | By Myself | Samicotico | Comin' On Up | Down
Nistico,Sal (ts) | Amico,Sal (tp) | Harris,Barry (p) | Cranshaw,Bob (b) | Ruggieri,Vinnie (dr)

MCD 47097-2 | CD | That Lovin' Feelin' | EAN 090204942114
Junior Mance Trio & Orchestra
Never On Sunday | Maria | Tara's Theme | Funny | On Green Dolphin Street | One-Eyed Jack | Exodus | Invitation | The Apartment | Goodbye Again | Spellbound
NYC, rec. December 1961/January 1962
Mance,Junior[Julian C.] (p) | Duvivier,George (b) | Johnson,Osie (dr) | Terry,Clark (tp) | Royal,Ernie (tp) | Cleveland,Jimmy (tb) | Woodman,Britt (tb) | Richardson,Jerome (fl,ts) | Bank,Danny (b-cl,bs) | Liston,Melba (arr,cond)
Junior Mance Quartet
You've Lost That Lovin' Feelin' | Mean Old Frisco | Out South | Cubano Chant | Boss Blues | Blowin' In The Wind
NYC, rec. spring 1972
Mance,Junior[Julian C.] (p) | Cranshaw,Bob (b) | White,Harold (dr) | McDonald,Ralph (perc)
Junior Mance Trio
The Good Life | When Sunny Gets Blue | Lee's Lament
Mance,Junior[Julian C.] (p) | Bell,Aaron or Bob Cunningham (b) | Jackson,Oliver or Jimmy Lovelace (dr)

MCD 47098-2 | CD | Bottom Groove | EAN 090204942152
Wild Bill Moore Quintet
Heavy Soul | A Good 'Un | Tearin' Out | Wild Bill's Beat | Things Are Getting Better | Bubbles | Just You Just Me
NYC, rec. 25.1.1961
Moore,'Wild' Bill (ts) | Mance,Junior[Julian C.] (p) | Benjamin,Joe (b) | Riley,Ben (dr) | Barretto,Ray (congas)
Sister Caroline | Bottom Groove | My Little Girl | Down With It | Sea Breezes | Caravan
NYC, rec. 7.7.1961
Moore,'Wild' Bill (ts) | Smith,Johnny 'Hammond' (org) | Benjamin,Joe (b) | Riley,Ben (dr) | Barretto,Ray (congas)

MCD 47099-2 | CD | Songs For You | EAN 090204933853
Ron Carter Group
Song For You
Englewood Cliffs,NJ, rec. June 1978
Carter,Ron (b) | Berliner,Jay (el-g) | Pendarvis,Leon (p) | Moore,Kermit (cello) | McCracken,Charles (cello) | Abramowitz,Jonathan (cello) | Locker,Richard (cello) | DeJohnette,Jack (dr) | McDonald,Ralph (perc)
A Quiet Place
Carter,Ron (b) | Berliner,Jay (el-g) | Barron,Kenny (p) | Moore,Kermit (cello) | McCracken,Charles (cello) | Abramowitz,Jonathan (cello) | Locker,Richard (cello) | DeJohnette,Jack (dr) | McDonald,Ralph (perc)
El Ojo De Dios
Carter,Ron (b) | Berliner,Jay (el-g) | Barron,Kenny (p) | Moore,Kermit (cello) | McCracken,Charles (cello) | Abramowitz,Jonathan (cello) | Locker,Richard (cello) | DeJohnette,Jack (dr) | McDonald,Ralph (perc)
Someday My Prince Will Come | N.O.Blues
Englewood Cliffs,NJ, rec. June 1958
Carter,Ron (b) | Barron,Kenny (p) | Moore,Kermit (cello) | McCracken,Charles (cello) | Abramowitz,Jonathan (cello) | Locker,Richard (cello) | DeJohnette,Jack (dr) | McDonald,Ralph (perc)
Good Time
Englewood Cliffs,NJ, rec. June 1978
Carter,Ron (b) | Barron,Kenny (p) | Moore,Kermit (cello) | McCracken,Charles (cello) | Abramowitz,Jonathan (cello) | Locker,Richard (cello) | DeJohnette,Jack (dr)
Ron Carter Quartet
Parfait | New Waltz | Receipt Please | Blues For D.P. | Round About Midnight
Englewood Cliffs,NJ, rec. 29.9.1980
Carter,Ron (b) | Lo,Ted (p) | Maleson,Leon (b) | Fletcher,Wilby (dr)

MCD 55005-2 | CD | Don't Stop The Carnival
Sonny Rollins Quintet
Don't Stop The Carnival | Silver City | Autumn Nocturne | Camel
Live at The Great American Muisc Hall,San Francisco,CA, rec. 13.-15.4.1978
Rollins,Sonny (ts) | Soskin,Mark (p,el-p) | Ray,Aurell (el-12-string-g) | Harris,Jerry (el-b) | Williams,Tony (dr)
Sonny Rollins Sextet
Introducing The Band | Nobody Else But Me | Non-Cents | A Child's Prayer | President Hayes | Sais
Rollins,Sonny (ts) | Byrd,Donald (tp,fl-h) | Soskin,Mark (p,el-p) | Ray,Aurell (el-12-string-g) | Harris,Jerry (el-b) | Williams,Tony (dr)

MCD 9122-2 | CD | Sunny Days,Starry Nights
Sonny Rollins Quintet
I'm Old Fashioned | Wynton | Tell Me You Love Me | I'll See You Again
Berkeley,CA, rec. 23.-27.1.1984
Rollins,Sonny (ts) | Anderson,Clifton (tb) | Soskin,Mark (keyboards) | Blake,Russell (el-b) | Campbell,Tommy (dr)
Sonny Rollins Sextet
Mave Mave | Kilauea
Rollins,Sonny (ts) | Anderson,Clifton (tb) | Soskin,Mark (keyboards) | Blake,Russell (el-b) | Campbell,Tommy (dr) | Rollins,Lucille (cowbell)

MCD 9185-2 | CD | Blue In Green
Bill Evans Trio
One For Helen | The Two Lonely People | What Are You Doing The Rest Of Your Life | So What | Very Early | If You Could See Me Now | 34 Skidoo | Blue In Green | T.T.T.(Twelve Tone Tune)
Camp Fortune,Hull,Canada, rec. August 1974
Evans,Bill (p) | Gomez,Eddie (b) | Morell,Marty (dr)

MCD 9194-2 | CD | Here's To The People
Sonny Rollins Sextet
Here's To The People | Lucky Day
NYC, rec. 10.8.1991
Rollins,Sonny (ts) | Anderson,Clifton (tb) | Harris,Jerome (g) | Soskin,Mark (p) | Cranshaw,Bob (el-b) | Jordan,Steve (dr)
Doc Phil
NYC, rec. 17.8.1991
Rollins,Sonny (ts) | Anderson,Clifton (tb) | Harris,Jerome (g) | Soskin,Mark (p) | Cranshaw,Bob (el-b) | DeJohnette,Jack (dr)
Sonny Rollins Quintet
Why Was I Born | Someone To Watch Over Me | Long Ago And Far Away
NYC, rec. 24.8.1991
Rollins,Sonny (ts) | Harris,Jerome (g) | Soskin,Mark (p) | Cranshaw,Bob (el-b) | Jordan,Steve (dr)
I Wish I Knew | Young Roy
NYC, rec. 27.8.1991
Rollins,Sonny (ts) | Hargrove,Roy (tp) | Soskin,Mark (p) | Cranshaw,Bob (el-b) | Foster,Al (dr)

MCD 9215-2 | CD | Old Flames
Where Or When | My Old Flame | Times Slimes | I See Your Face Before Me | Delia
NYC, rec. July/August 1993
Rollins,Sonny (ts) | Anderson,Clifton (tb) | Flanagan,Tommy (p) | Cranshaw,Bob (b,el-b) | DeJohnette,Jack (dr)
Sonny Rollins Quintet With Brass
Dam That Dream | Prelude To A Kiss
Rollins,Sonny (ts) | Faddis,Jon (fl-h) | Stripling,Byron (fl-h) | Anderson,Clifton (tb) | Brofsky,Alex (fr-h) | Stewart,Robert 'Bob' (tuba) | Flanagan,Tommy (p) | Cranshaw,Bob (b,el-b) | DeJohnette,Jack (dr)

MCD 9235-2 | CD | On Green Dolphin Street
Bill Evans Trio
You And The Night And The Music | How Am I To Know? | Woody'n You | Woody'n You(alt.take) | My Heart Stood Still | On Green Dolphin Street
NYC, rec. 19.1.1959
Evans,Bill (p) | Chambers,Paul (b) | Jones,Philly Joe (dr)
All Of You(alt.take)
Live at The 'Village Vanguard',NYC, rec. 25.6.1961
Evans,Bill (p) | LaFaro,Scott (b) | Motian,Paul (dr)

MCD 9244-2 | CD | Prelude And Sonata
McCoy Tyner Quartet
Loss Of Love | I Will Wait For You | Soul Eyes | Smile | Good Morning Heartache | Piano Sonata No.8 In C Minor
NYC, rec. 26./27.11.1994
Tyner,McCoy (p) | Hart,Antonio Maurice (as) | McBride,Christian (b) | Smith,Marvin 'Smitty' (dr)
McCoy Tyner Quintet
Prelude In E Minor | Contemplation | For All We Know
Tyner,McCoy (p) | Hart,Antonio Maurice (as) | Redman,Joshua (ts) | McBride,Christian (b) | Smith,Marvin 'Smitty' (dr)

MCD 9247-2 | CD | Rip A Dip
Pucho & His Latin Soul Brothers
Sex Machine | Trouble Man | Caravan | Slippin' Into Darkness | Zebula | Pucho's Descarga II | Greasy Greens | Milestones | Mambo With Me | Hot Barbeque | Rip A Dip | Good News Blues | Guaganco | Ritmo Nueva York
NYC, rec. June 1995
Pucho (timbales) | Pazant,Al (tp) | Kwock,Robbie (tp) | Wallace,Wayne (tb) | Pazant,Edward (fl,as) | Martin,Mel (fl,ss,as,ts,piccolo) | Magdalayo,Melecio (bs) | Home,Marvin (g) | Sparks,Melvin (g,voc) | Bivens,William 'Yam' (vib) | Spruill,John (p,org) | Hart,Jon (b) | Colon,Ernesto (dr,congas,bongos) | Killian,Lawrence (congas) | James,Ricky 'Bongo' (congas,bongos) | Massamba (african-dr) | Berrios,Steve (congas,bongos,bells,chekere,claves,coro,guiro)

MCD 9249-2 | CD | But Beautiful
Stan Getz With The Bill Evans Trio
Grandfather's Waltz | Stan's Blues | See Saw | The Two Lonely People
Live at The Jazz Festival,Laaren,NL, rec. 9.8.1974
Getz,Stan (ts) | Evans,Bill (p) | Gomez,Eddie (b) | Morell,Marty (dr)
But Beautiful | Emily | Lover Man(Oh,Where Can You Be?) | Funkallero | The Peacocks | You And The Night And The Music
Antverp,B, rec. 16.8.1974
Getz,Stan (ts) | Evans,Bill (p) | Gomez,Eddie (b) | Morell,Marty (dr)

MCD 9250-2 | CD | Sonny Rollins + 3
Sonny Rollins Plus 3
They Say It's Wonderful | Cabin In The Sky
NYC, rec. 30.8.1995
Rollins,Sonny (ts) | Scott,Stephen (p) | Cranshaw,Bob (el-b) | DeJohnette,Jack (dr)
What A Difference A Day Made | Biji | Mona Lisa | H.S. | I've Never Been In Love Before
NYC, rec. 7.10.1995
Rollins,Sonny (ts) | Flanagan,Tommy (p) | Cranshaw,Bob (el-b) | Foster,Al (dr)

MCD 9251-2 | CD | All The Way
Jimmy Smith-Eddie Harris Trio
You'll See | Autumn Leaves | A Child Is Born | 8 Counts For Rita | Old Folks | The Sermon
Live at Keystone Korner,SF, rec. 29.8.1991
Harris,Eddie (el-sax) | Smith,Jimmy (org) | Dixon,Kenny (dr)

MCD 9269-2 | CD | Friends Forever
Niels-Henning Orsted-Pedersen Trio
Hush-A-Bye | Kenny | Someday My Prince Will Come | Theme From Elvira Madigan | Lullaby Of The Leaves | The Shadow Of Your Smile | Sometime Ago | Days Of Wine And Roses | Future Child- | Friends Forever-
Copenhagen,Denmark, rec. 27./28.8.1995
Orsted-Pedersen,Niels-Henning (b) | Rosnes,Renee (p) | Johansen,Jonas (dr)

MCD 9272-2 | CD | Bottom Line
George Mraz Quartet
Three Views Of A Secret | San Felice | Christina | Lisa Marie | Mr.Pastorius | Little Waltz | Strange Blues | Goodbye Pork Pie Hat | Falling Grace
NYC, rec. 1./2.4.1997
Mraz,George 'Jiri' (b) | Perry,Richard 'Rich' (ts) | Chestnut,Cyrus (p) | Foster,Al (dr)

MCD 9279-2 | CD | After Dark
Hank Crawford Quintet
My Babe | Our Day Will Come | Mother Nature | Beale Street After Dark | Amazing Grace
Englewood Cliffs,NJ, rec. 23./24.2.1998
Crawford,Hank (as) | Sparks,Melvin (g) | Mixon,Danny (p,org) | Bascomb,Wilbur (b) | Purdie,Bernard 'Pretty' (dr)
Git It | Share Your Love With Me | Ain't Nobody's Bizness If I Do | That's All | St.Louis Blues
Crawford,Hank (as) | Sparks,Melvin (g) | Mixon,Danny (p,org) | Banks,Stanley (b) | Purdie,Bernard 'Pretty' (dr)

MCD 9280-2 | CD | Global Warming
Sonny Rollins Quartet
Echo-Side Blue | Mother Nature's Blues | Change Partners
NYC, rec. 7.1.1998
Rollins,Sonny (ts) | Scott,Stephen (p) | Cranshaw,Bob (el-b) | Muhammad,Idris[Leo Morris] (dr)
Sonny Rollins Sextet
Island Lady | Global Warming | Clear-Cut Boogie
NYC, rec. 28.2.1998
Rollins,Sonny (ts) | Anderson,Clifton (tb) | Scott,Stephen (p,kalimba) | Cranshaw,Bob (el-b) | Wilson,Perry (dr) | See Yuen,Victor (perc)

MCD 9282-2 | CD | Half Moon Bay
Bill Evans Trio
Introductions | Waltz For Debby | Sareen Jurer | Very Early | Autumn Leaves

| What Are You Doing The Rest Of Your Life | Quiet Now | Who Can I Turn To | Elsa | Someday My Prince Will Come
Half Moon Bay,CA, rec. 4.11.1973
Evans,Bill (p) | Gomez,Eddie (b) | Morell,Marty (dr)

MCD 9283-2 | CD | Solid!
Eric Alexander Quartet
Solid | Theme For Ernie | Four | The Star-Crossed Lovers | My Conception | Light Blue
NYC, rec. 25.4.1998
Alexander,Eric (ts) | Hicks,John (p) | Mraz,George 'Jiri' (b) | Muhammad,Idris[Leo Morris] (dr)
Eric Alexander Quintet
Fire Waltz
Alexander,Eric (ts) | Locke,Joe (vib) | Hicks,John (p) | Mraz,George 'Jiri' (b) | Muhammad,Idris[Leo Morris] (dr)
Little Melonae | Straight Street
Alexander,Eric (ts) | Rotondi,Jim (tp) | Hicks,John (p) | Mraz,George 'Jiri' (b) | Muhammad,Idris[Leo Morris] (dr)

MCD 9286-2 | CD | Trumpet Legacy
Nicholas Payton With The Mulgrew Miller Trio
So What | Fire Waltz
NYC, rec. 14./15.5.1997
Payton,Nicholas (tp) | Miller,Mulgrew (p) | Washington,Peter (b) | Allen,Carl (dr)
Lew Soloff With The Mulgrew Miller Trio
Lotus Blossom | Nostalgia
Soloff,Lew (tp) | Miller,Mulgrew (p) | Washington,Peter (b) | Allen,Carl (dr)
Tom Harrell With The Mulgrew Miller Trio
Jordu | The Sidewinder | That's Earl Brother
Harrell,Tom (tp) | Miller,Mulgrew (p) | Washington,Peter (b) | Allen,Carl (dr)
Eddie Henderson With The Mulgrew Miller Trio
My Funny Valentine | There's No You
Henderson,Eddie (tp) | Miller,Mulgrew (p) | Washington,Peter (b) | Allen,Carl (dr)

MCD 9290-2 | CD | With A Song In My Heart
Lew Soloff Quartet
Come Rain Or Come Shine | The Way You Look Tonight | I'm A Fool To Want You | Mea Culpa | Istanbul | One For Emily | With A Song In My Heart
NYC, rec. 13./14.1.1998
Soloff,Lew (tp) | Miller,Mulgrew (p) | Mraz,George 'Jiri' (b) | Lewis,Victor (dr)
Lew Soloff Quintet
Andantino From Tchaikovsky Symphony No.4(2nd movement) | Degnello
Soloff,Lew (tp) | Miller,Mulgrew (p) | Mitchell,Emily (harp) | Mraz,George 'Jiri' (b) | Lewis,Victor (dr)

MCD 9291-2 | CD | Homecoming
Bill Evans Trio
Re:Person I Knew | Midnight Mood | Song From M.A.S.H. | Turn Out The Stars | Very Early | But Beautiful | I Loves You Porgy | Up With The Lark | Minha(All Mine) | I Do It For You | Someday My Prince Will Come | Interview(6:00) With Bill Evans by Rod Starns
Live at Southeastern University,Hammond,LA, rec. 6.11.1979
Evans,Bill (p) | Johnson,Marc (b) | LaBarbera,Joe (dr)

MCD 9292-2 | CD | Duke's Place
George Mraz Trio
In A Sentimental Mood | Angelica | Lotus Blossom | The Star-Crossed Lovers | Caravan
NYC, rec. 25.11.1998
Mraz,George 'Jiri' (b) | Rosnes,Renee (p) | Drummond,Billy (dr)
Satin Doll | Come Sunday | Mood Indigo | Take The 'A' Train | Don't Get Around Much Anymore
Mraz,George 'Jiri' (b) | Chestnut,Cyrus (p) | Drummond,Billy (dr)
George Mraz Quartet
Duke's Place(C Jam Blues)
Mraz,George 'Jiri' (b) | Rosnes,Renee (p) | Chestnut,Cyrus (p) | Drummond,Billy (dr)

MCD 9293-2 | CD | Man With A Horn
Eric Alexander Quartet
Man With A Horn | Unsung Hero | A Time For Love | My Shining Hour | Stars Fell On Alabama | Fiesta Espanola
NYC, rec. 20./21.1.1997
Alexander,Eric (ts) | Walton,Cedar (p) | Burno,Dwayne (b) | Farnsworth,Joe (dr)
Eric Alexander Sextet
GCCJ | Midnight Waltz | I Found You
Alexander,Eric (ts) | Rotondi,Jim (tp) | Davis,Steve (tb) | Walton,Cedar (p) | Burno,Dwayne (b) | Farnsworth,Joe (dr)

MCD 9297-2 | CD | In A New York Minute
Ian Shaw With The Cedar Walton Trio
In A New York Minute | Standing In The Dark | Wouldn't It Be Loverly | I Thought About You | Furry Sings The Blues | Grandma's Hands | Alfie | All Or Nothing At All | Shake Down The Stars | No One Ever Tells You | Last Night When We Were Young | That's Life
NYC, rec. September 1998
Shaw,Ian (voc) | Walton,Cedar (p) | Williams,David (b) | Ballamy,Iain (sax)

MCD 9300-2 | CD | McGriff's House Party
Jimmy McGriff Quintet
Neckbones A La Carte | Blues For Stitt | Red Roses For A Blue Lady | Grits,Gravy And Groove
Englewood Cliffs,NJ, rec. 28./29.9.1999
McGriff,Jimmy (org) | Easley,Bill (ts) | Alexander,Eric (ts) | Jones,Rodney (g) | Purdie,Bernard 'Pretty' (dr)
Jimmy McGriff Sextet
Red Cadillac Boogaloo | That's All | McGriff's House Party | Dishin' The Dirt
McGriff,Jimmy (org) | Rampton,Kenny (tp) | Alexander,Eric (ts) | Jones,Rodney (g) | Smith,Lonnie (org) | Purdie,Bernard 'Pretty' (dr)

MCD 9302-2 | CD | The First Milestone
Eric Alexander Quartet
No.34 Was Sweetness(for Walter Payton) | Night Song | Last Night When We Were Young | I'm Glad There Is You
NYC, rec. 3./4.11.1999
Alexander,Eric (ts) | Mabern,Harold (p) | Washington,Peter (b) | Farnsworth,Joe (dr)
Eric Alexander Quintet
Stand Pat | The First Milestone | The Towering Inferno | The Phineas Train
Alexander,Eric (ts) | Martino,Pat (g) | Mabern,Harold (p) | Washington,Peter (b) | Farnsworth,Joe (dr)

MCD 9304-2 | CD | The World Of Hank Crawford
Hank Crawford Septet
Grab The World | Way Back Home | Good Bait
Englewood Cliffs,NJ, rec. 8./9.2.2000
Crawford,Hank (as) | Belgrave,Marcus (tp,fl-h) | Cuber,Ronnie (bs) | Sparks,Melvin (g) | Mixon,Danny (p) | Banks,Stanley (b) | Washington,Kenny (dr)
Hank Crawford Quartet
Good Bait
Crawford,Hank (as) | Mixon,Danny (p) | Banks,Stanley (b) | Washington,Kenny (dr)
Trust In Me | Sonnymoon For Two
Crawford,Hank (as) | Sparks,Melvin (g) | Mixon,Danny (org) | Washington,Kenny (dr)
Hank Crawford Quintet
Back In The Day | Love For Sale | Come Sunday
Crawford,Hank (as) | Sparks,Melvin (g) | Mixon,Danny (p,org) | Banks,Stanley (b) | Washington,Kenny (dr)

MCD 9305-2 | CD | Mood Indigo
(Little)Jimmy Scott And His Band
Smile | Mood Indigo
NYC, rec. 15.-17.3.2000
Scott,Jimmy[Little] (voc) | Crawford,Hank (as) | Chestnut,Cyrus (p) | Mraz,George 'Jiri' (b) | Tate,Grady (dr)
Imagination | Without A Song
Scott,Jimmy[Little] (voc) | Crawford,Hank (as) | Maret,Gregoire (harm) | Chestnut,Cyrus (p) | Mraz,George 'Jiri' (b) | Tate,Grady (dr)
How Deep Is The Ocean | Blue Skies
Scott,Jimmy[Little] (voc) | Maret,Gregoire (harm) | Kanan,Michael 'Mike' (p) | Greene,Hillard (b) | Jones,Victor (dr)
Time After Time
Scott,Jimmy[Little] (voc) | Kanan,Michael 'Mike' (p)
Day By Day
Scott,Jimmy[Little] (voc) | Beck,Joe (g) | Chestnut,Cyrus (p) | Mraz,George 'Jiri' (b) | Tate,Grady (dr)
There'll Never Be Another You | Mood Indigo
NYC, rec. 15.-17.3.2000
Scott,Jimmy[Little] (voc) | Beck,Joe (alto-g)

MCD 9309-2 | CD | Morava
George Mraz Quartet
Aspen Leaf | Oh,Mountain | Gray Pigeon | Up In A Fir Tree | Myjava | She Walks In A Meadow | Little Black Swallow | Desire | Wine,Oh Wine | Gray Falcon | The Sun Goes Down | Jurenko,Jurenko
NYC, rec. 9.-11.6.2000
Mraz,George 'Jiri' (b) | Viklicky,Emil (p) | Hart,Billy (dr) | Lapcikova,Zuzana (cymbalon,voc)

MCD 9310-2 | CD | This Is What I Do
Sonny Rollins Quartet
Salvador | The Moon Of Manakoora
NYC, rec. 8./9.5.2000
Rollins,Sonny (ts) | Scott,Stephen (p) | Cranshaw,Bob (el-b) | DeJohnette,Jack (dr)
Sonny Rollins Quintet
Sweet Leilani | A Nightingale Sang In Berkeley Square
Rollins,Sonny (ts) | Anderson,Clifton (tb) | Scott,Stephen (p) | Cranshaw,Bob (el-b) | DeJohnette,Jack (dr)
Did You See Harold Vick? | Charles M.
NYC, rec. 29.7.2000
Rollins,Sonny (ts) | Anderson,Clifton (tb) | Scott,Stephen (p) | Cranshaw,Bob (el-b) | Wilson,Perry (dr)

MCD 9311-2 | CD | Fourmost Return
Jimmy Smith Quartet
Sonnymoon For Two | Mood Indigo | Ain't She Sweet | Back At The Chicken Shack | Laura | Blues For Stanley
NYC, rec. 16./17.11.1990
Smith,Jimmy (org,voc) | Turrentine,Stanley (ts) | Burrell,Kenny (g) | Tate,Grady (dr)

MCD 9312-2 | CD | Back To Bach
David Matthews & The Manhattan Jazz Orchestra
Toccata And Fugue | Air On The G String | Invention No.4 | Kyrie | Minuet(A Lover's Concerto) | Siciliano | Fugue No.2
NYC, rec. 5./6.2.2000
Matthews,David (cond,arr) | Soloff,Lew (tp) | Kisor,Ryan (tp) | Shepley,Joe (tp) | Wendholt,Scott (tp) | Pugh,Jim (tb) | Farrell,Larry (tb) | Johnson,Birch (tb) | Taylor,Dave (b-tb) | Griffin,Fred (fr-h) | Clark,John (fr-h) | Price,Tony (tuba) | Hunger,Chris (fl,as) | Evans,Bill (fl,ss,ts) | Rosenberg,Roger (b-cl) | Jackson,Charles 'Chip' (b) | Silverlight,Terry (dr)

MCD 9313-2 | CD | Feelin' It
Jimmy McGriff Quartet
Us | All Blues | Just In Time | City Lights
Englewood Cliffs,NJ, rec. 17.10.2000
McGriff,Jimmy (org) | Easley,Bill (ts) | Boyd,Wayne (g) | Williams,Don (dr)
Jimmy McGriff Sextet
Stan's Shuffle | Hard Times | Feelin' It | Sermonizing
Englewood Cliffs,NJ, rec. 19.10.2000
McGriff,Jimmy (org) | Easley,Bill (as) | Newman,David Fathead (ts) | Cuber,Ronnie (bs) | Sparks,Melvin (g) | Washington,Kenny (dr)

MCD 9314-2 | CD | Over The Rainbow
Jimmy Scott With Band
Pennies From Heaven | P.S.I Love You
NYC, rec. October/November 2000
Scott,Jimmy[Little] (voc) | Kindred,Bob (ts) | Beck,Joe (g) | Willis,Larry (p) | Mraz,George 'Jiri' (b) | Tate,Grady (dr)
Over The Rainbow | Everybody's Somebody's Fool
Scott,Jimmy[Little] (voc) | Locke,Joe (vib) | Beck,Joe (g)
Don't Take Your Love From Me
Scott,Jimmy[Little] (voc) | Locke,Joe (vib) | Beck,Joe (g) | Mraz,George 'Jiri' (b) | Tate,Grady (dr)
All Or Nothing At All
Scott,Jimmy[Little] (voc) | Robinson,Justin (as) | Beck,Joe (g) | Kanan,Michael 'Mike' (p) | Mraz,George 'Jiri' (b) | Tate,Grady (dr)
Strange Fruit
Scott,Jimmy[Little] (voc) | Newman,David Fathead (ts) | Beck,Joe (g) | Willis,Larry (p) | Mraz,George 'Jiri' (b) | Penn,Clarence (dr)
Just Friends
Scott,Jimmy[Little] (voc) | Maret,Gregoire (harm) | Willis,Larry (p)
If You Only Knew
Scott,Jimmy[Little] (voc) | Maret,Gregoire (harm) | Kanan,Michael 'Mike' (p) | Mraz,George 'Jiri' (b) | Tate,Grady (dr)
I'll Close My Eyes
Scott,Jimmy[Little] (voc) | Maret,Gregoire (harm) | Locke,Joe (vib) | Beck,Joe (g) | Mraz,George 'Jiri' (b) | Tate,Grady (dr)
I Got It Bad And That Ain't Good | When Did You Leave Heaven
Scott,Jimmy[Little] (voc) | Kanan,Michael 'Mike' (p)

MCD 9315-2 | CD | The Second Milestone
Eric Alexander Quartet
Matchmaker Matchmaker | The Second Milestone | Moment To Moment | Estate(Summer) | John Neely Beautiful People
Englewood Cliffs,NJ, rec. December 2000
Alexander,Eric (ts) | Mabern,Harold (p) | Washington,Peter (b) | Farnsworth,Joe (dr)
Eric Alexander Quintet
The Man From Hydepark | Luna Naranja | The Cliffs Of Asturias
Alexander,Eric (ts) | Rotondi,Jim (tp) | Mabern,Harold (p) | Washington,Peter (b) | Farnsworth,Joe (dr)

MCD 9316-2 | CD | Soho Stories
Ian Shaw With Band
Comes Love
NYC, rec. September 2000
Shaw,Ian (voc) | Alexander,Eric (ts) | Pearson,James (p) | Jackson,Charles 'Chip' (b) | Fletcher,Mark (dr)
I Never Went Away | I Wished On The Moon
Shaw,Ian (voc) | Kindred,Bob (ts) | Pearson,James (p) | Jackson,Charles 'Chip' (b) | Fletcher,Mark (dr)
Ruby
Shaw,Ian (voc) | Beck,Joe (g) | Pearson,James (p) | Jackson,Charles 'Chip' (b) | Fletcher,Mark (dr)
Dearly Beloved
Shaw,Ian (voc) | Soloff,Lew (tp) | Vasquez,Papo (tb) | Rubie,Steve (fl) | Alexander,Eric (ts) | Pearson,James (p) | Jackson,Charles 'Chip' (b) | Fletcher,Mark (dr)
How Little We Know
Shaw,Ian (voc) | Soloff,Lew (tp) | Pearson,James (p) | Jackson,Charles 'Chip' (b) | Fletcher,Mark (dr)
A Little Piece Of Heaven | If You Could See Me Now | I Keep Goin' Back To Joe's
Shaw,Ian (voc) | Pearson,James (p) | Jackson,Charles 'Chip' (b) | Fletcher,Mark (dr)
Be Sure I'll Let You Know
Shaw,Ian (voc) | Walton,Cedar (p) | Jackson,Charles 'Chip' (b) | Fletcher,Mark (dr)
Tomorrow Never Came
Shaw,Ian (voc) | Kindred,Bob (ts) | Pearson,James (p) | Jackson,Charles 'Chip' (b) | Fletcher,Mark (dr)
Happy With The Blues
NYC, rec. Deptember 2000
Shaw,Ian (voc) | Alexander,Eric (ts) | Pearson,James (p) | Jackson,Charles 'Chip' (b) | Fletcher,Mark (dr)
Rainbow Sleeves
NYC, rec. September 2000
Shaw,Ian (p,voc) | Jackson,Charles 'Chip' (b) | Fletcher,Mark (dr)

MCD 9317-2 | CD | Tenderly
Bill Evans-Don Elliott
Tenderly | I'll Take Romance | Laura | Blues No.1 | I'll Know | Like Someone In Love | Love Letters | Thou Swell | Airegin | Everything Happens To Me | Blues No.2 | Stella By Starlight | Funkallero
Connecticut, rec. 1956/1957
Evans,Bill (p) | Elliott,Don (vib,perc)

MCD 9319-2 | CD | Keep That Groove Going!
Plas Johnson-Red Holloway Quintet
Keep That Groove Going | Stuffy | Serenade In Blue | Go Red Go | Brethreren! | Pass The Gravy | Jammin' For Mr. Lee | Cry Me A River | Dream A Little Dream Of Me
Englewood Cliffs,NJ, rec. 24./25.4.2001
Johnson,Plas (ts) | Holloway,Red (ts) | Ludwig,Gene (org) | Sparks,Melvin (g) | Washington,Kenny (dr)

MCD 9320-2 | CD | Hey Duke!
David Matthews & The Manhattan Jazz Orchestra
Satin Doll | Cotton Tail
NYC, rec. 28./29.7.1999
Matthews,David (p,arr) | Soloff,Lew (tp) | Kisor,Ryan (tp) | Shepley,Joe (tp) | Wendholt,Scott (tp) | Pugh,Jim (tb) | Farrell,Larry (tb) | Johnson,Birch (tb) | Taylor,Dave (b-tb) | Griffin,Fred (fr-h) | Clark,John (fr-h) | Price,Tony (tuba) | Heick,Aaron (cl,ss) | Rosenberg,Roger (b-cl) | Hunter,Chris (as) | Jackson,Charles 'Chip' (b) | Silverlight,Terry (dr)
It Don't Mean A Thing If It Ain't Got That Swing | Prelude To A Kiss | In A Sentimental Mood
Matthews,David (p,arr) | Soloff,Lew (tp) | Kisor,Ryan (tp) | Shepley,Joe (tp) | Wendholt,Scott (tp) | Pugh,Jim (tb) | Farrell,Larry (tb) | Johnson,Birch (tb) | Taylor,Dave (b-tb) | Griffin,Fred (fr-h) | Comer,Chris (fr-h) | Price,Tony (tuba) | Heick,Aaron (cl,ss) | Rosenberg,Roger (b-cl) | Hunter,Chris (as) | Jackson,Charles 'Chip' (b) | Silverlight,Terry (dr)
Mood Indigo | Come Sunday | Song For Edward
Matthews,David (p,arr) | Soloff,Lew (tp) | Kisor,Ryan (tp) | Shepley,Joe (tp) | Wendholt,Scott (tp) | Pugh,Jim (tb) | Farrell,Larry (tb) | Johnson,Birch (tb) | Taylor,Dave (b-tb) | Griffin,Fred (fr-h) | Clark,John (fr-h) | Price,Tony (tuba) | Feldman,Lawrence (cl,ss) | Rosenberg,Roger (b-cl) | Hunter,Chris (as) | Jackson,Charles 'Chip' (b) | Silverlight,Terry (dr) | Sperry,Christine (voc)

MCD 9321-2 | CD | But Beautiful
Jimmy Scott With Band
You Don't Know What Love Is
NYC, rec. 16.-19.8.2001
Scott,Jimmy[Little] (voc) | Beck,Joe (g) | Rosnes,Renee (p) | Mraz,George 'Jiri' (b) | Nash,Lewis (dr)
Darn That Dream
Scott,Jimmy[Little] (voc) | Marsalis,Wynton (tp) | Rosnes,Renee (p) | Mraz,George 'Jiri' (b) | Nash,Lewis (dr)
It Had To Be You | Please Send Me Someone To Love | But Beautiful
Scott,Jimmy[Little] (voc) | Alexander,Eric (ts) | Beck,Joe (g) | Rosnes,Renee (p) | Mraz,George 'Jiri' (b) | Nash,Lewis (dr)
This Bitter Earth
Scott,Jimmy[Little] (voc) | Kindred,Bob (ts) | Rosnes,Renee (p) | Mraz,George 'Jiri' (b) | Nash,Lewis (dr)
When You Wish Upon A Star
Scott,Jimmy[Little] (voc) | Cole,Freddy (voc) | Rosnes,Renee (p) | Mraz,George 'Jiri' (b) | Nash,Lewis (dr)
Bye Bye Blackbird
Scott,Jimmy[Little] (voc) | Soloff,Lew (tp) | Beck,Joe (g) | Rosnes,Renee (p) | Mraz,George 'Jiri' (b) | Nash,Lewis (dr)
I'll Be Seeing You
Scott,Jimmy[Little] (voc) | Kindred,Bob (cl,ts) | Rosnes,Renee (p) | Mraz,George 'Jiri' (b) | Broadnax,Dwayne 'Cook' (dr)
Jimmy Scott
Take My Hand Precious Lord
Scott,Jimmy[Little] (voc)

MCD 9322-2 | CD | Summit Meeting
Eric Alexander Quartet
Summit Meeting | The Sweetest Sounds | I Haven't Got Anything Better To Do | This Girl's In Love With You | Something's Gotta Give | After The Rain
NYC, rec. 19./20.12.2001
Alexander,Eric (ts) | Mabern,Harold (p) | Webber,John (b) | Farnsworth,Joe (dr)
Eric Alexander Quintet
There But For The Grace Of... | A House Is Not A Home | Andre's Turn
Alexander,Eric (ts) | Payton,Nicholas (tp,fl-h) | Mabern,Harold (p) | Webber,John (b) | Farnsworth,Joe (dr)

MCD 9324-2 | CD | Eddie 'Cleanhead' Vinson With The Cannonball Adderley Quintet | EAN 090204962044
Eddie Cleanhead Vinson With The Cannonball Adderley Quintet
Hold It | Arriving Soon | Kidney Stew | Back Door Blues | Just A Dream | Audrey | Vinsonology | Cannonizing | Bernice's Bounce
Chicago,Ill, rec. 19.9.1961
Vinson,Eddie 'Cleanhead' (as,voc) | Adderley,Julian \'Cannonball\' (as) | Adderley,Nat (co) | Zawinul,Joe (p) | Jones,Sam (b) | Hayes,Louis (dr)
Bright Lights Big City | This Time | Person To Person
NYC, rec. 14.2.1962
Vinson,Eddie 'Cleanhead' (as,voc) | Adderley,Julian \'Cannonball\' (as) | Adderley,Nat (co) | Zawinul,Joe (p) | Jones,Sam (b) | Hayes,Louis (dr)

MCD 9325-2 | CD | McGriff Avenue | EAN 090204932412
Jimmy McGriff Septet
All About My Girl | Soul Street | The Great Unknown | The Worm | America The Beautiful
Englewood Cliffs,NJ, rec. 22./23.10.2001
McGriff,Jimmy (org) | Easley,Bill (ts) | Beadle,Gordon (ts) | Cuber,Ronnie (bs) | Sparks,Melvin (g) | Bascomb,Wilbur (b) | Purdie,Bernard 'Pretty' (dr)
McGriff Avenue | The Answer Is The Blues | Dissertation On The Blues
McGriff,Jimmy (org) | Easley,Bill (ts) | Beadle,Gordon (ts) | Cuber,Ronnie (bs) | Jones,Rodney (g) | Bascomb,Wilbur (b) | Williams,Don (dr)

MCD 9326-2 | CD | Strings | EAN 090204934065
Jim Snidero Quartet With Strings
Slipping Away | River Suite: | Dawn | On The Bank | Torrent | Theme For Ernie | Forever Gone | Ventura | It's The Talk Of The T
Brooklyn,NY, rec. 25.10.& 13.11.2001
Snidero,Jim (fl,as) | Rosnes,Renee (p) | Gill,Paul (b) | Drummond,Billy (dr) | Seaton,Laura (v) | Feldman,Mark (v) | Hammann,Joyce (v) | Cummings,Genovia (v) | Woodiel,Paul (v) | Lorentsen,Sue (v) | Farris,Ralph (viola) | Bunch,Kenji (viola) | Ulrich,Thomas (cello) | Wooten,Mary (cello)

MCD 9327-2 | CD | Love Dance:The Ballad Album | EAN 090204922451
Ithamara Koorax With Band
Ligia
NYC/New Jersey/Rio de Janeiro, rec. 2000-2002
Koorax,Ithamara (voc) | Araujo,Juarez (cl) | Bertrami,Jose Roberto (el-p,synth) | Barrosa,Sergio (b) | Palma,Joao (dr) | Romao,Dom Um (perc)
I Loved You
Koorax,Ithamara (voc) | Friedrich,Jürgen (p)
Love Dance
Koorax,Ithamara (voc) | Bertrami,Jose Roberto (el-p) | Malheiros,Alex (el-b) | Conti,Ivan (dr) | Moreira,Sidinho (perc)
La Puerta | Amparo
Koorax,Ithamara (voc) | Rubalcaba,Gonzalo (p)
Man Alone
Koorax,Ithamara (voc) | Carlos,Ze (fl) | Bigorna (fl) | Ramos,J.C. (fl) | Ramos,Carlos 'Big Horn' (ss) | Bonfa,Luiz (g) | Angelo,Nelson (g,p,arr) | McLaughlin,John (el-g) | Carvalho,Jorjao (el-b) | Palma,Joao (dr) | Moreira,Sidinho (perc)
Someday
Koorax,Ithamara (voc) | Castro-Neves,Mario (p,keyboards) | Gusmano,Manuel

(b) | Pescara,Jorge (fretless-b,stick) | Machado,Cesar (dr) | DeSouteiro,Arnaldo (perc)

MCD 9328-2 | CD | State Of Mind | EAN 090204922468
Dave Ellis Quartet
Something To Live For
Berkeley,CA, rec. 17.3.2001
Ellis,Dave (ts) | Miller,Mulgrew (p) | Washington,Peter (b) | Allen,Carl (dr)
Dave Ellis Quintet
Soul-Leo | Grand Central | IsabelleBlue
Ellis,Dave (ts) | Herring,Vincent (as) | Miller,Mulgrew (p) | Washington,Peter (b) | Allen,Carl (dr)
Dave Ellis Quartet
Not That You Asked | Barbados | Sunshowers | Don't Blame Me | Peace | Summertime
Berkeley,CA, rec. 30.11.2001
Ellis,Dave (ts) | Miller,Mulgrew (p) | McBride,Christian (b) | Nash,Lewis (dr)

MCD 9329-2 | CD | Live-Lee | EAN 090204922673
Lee Konitz With Alan Broadbent
I'll Remember April | Sweet And Lovely | Sequentialee | If You Could See Me Now | Cherokee | Gundula | Keepin' The News | Easy Living | 317 East 32nd Street | Ex Temp | Subconscious-Lee
Los Angeles,CA, rec. 20.-22.10.2000
Konitz,Lee (as) | Broadbent,Alan (p)

MCD 9330-2 | CD | Nightlife In Tokyo | EAN 025218933025
Eric Alexander Quartet
Nemesis | I Can Dream Can't I | Nightlife In Tokyo | I'll Be Around | Cold Smoke | Island Anthem | Big R.C. | Lock Up And Bow Out
NYC, rec. 19.12.2002
Alexander,Eric (ts) | Mabern,Harold (p) | Carter,Ron (b) | Farnsworth,Joe (dr)

MCD 9331-2 | CD | Flatjacks | EAN 025218933144
Willie Rodriguez Jazz Quartet
Moliendo Cafe | Serenata | Nanigo Soul | Mr. Yosso | Brasileira | On Foot In The Gutter | It Happened In Monterey | Flatjacks(Just A Minor Bass-A Nova) | Seafood Wally | After Words | Tasty | El Sueno DeFrances
NYC, rec. July/August 1963
Rodriguez,Willie (dr,perc) | Powell,Seldon (fl,cl,as,ts) | Galbraith,Barry (g) | Duvivier,George (b)

MCD 9332-2 | CD | Moon Glow | EAN 090204922796
Jimmy Scott With Band
Moonglow
NYC, rec. March 2000-August 2001
Scott,Jimmy[Little] (voc) | Alexander,Eric (ts) | Beck,Joe (g) | Mraz,George 'Jiri' (b)
Since I Fell For You
Scott,Jimmy[Little] (voc) | Newman,David Fathead (ts) | Locke,Joe (vib) | Beck,Joe (g) | Willis,Larry (p) | Mraz,George 'Jiri' (b) | Penn,Clarence (dr)
Those Who Were
Scott,Jimmy[Little] (voc) | Willis,Larry (p)
Yesterday
Scott,Jimmy[Little] (voc) | Maret,Gregoire (harm) | Chestnut,Cyrus (p) | Mraz,George 'Jiri' (b) | Tate,Grady (dr)
How Long Has This Been Going On
Scott,Jimmy[Little] (voc) | Crawford,Hank (as) | Beck,Joe (g) | Chestnut,Cyrus (p) | Mraz,George 'Jiri' (b) | Tate,Grady (dr)
I Thought About You
Scott,Jimmy[Little] (voc) | Soloff,Lew (tp) | Beck,Joe (g) | Rosnes,Renee (p) | Mraz,George 'Jiri' (b) | Nash,Lewis (dr)
Time On My Hands
Scott,Jimmy[Little] (voc) | Kindred,Bob (ts) | Kanan,Michael 'Mike' (p)
If I Should Lose You
Scott,Jimmy[Little] (voc) | Chestnut,Cyrus (p) | Mraz,George 'Jiri' (b) | Tate,Grady (dr)
Solitude
Scott,Jimmy[Little] (voc) | Maret,Gregoire (harm) | Willis,Larry (p)
We'll Be Together Again
Scott,Jimmy[Little] (voc) | Kindred,Bob (ts) | Rosnes,Renee (p) | Mraz,George 'Jiri' (b) | Nash,Lewis (dr)

MCD 9334-2 | CD | Cobb's Groove | EAN 090204923304
Jimmy Cobb's Mob
Cob's Groove | I Miss You, My Love | Willow Tree | Sweet And Lovely | Jet Stream | Moment To Moment | Minor Changes | Bobblehead | Simone
NYC, rec. 5.1.2003
Cobb,Jimmy (dr) | Alexander,Eric (ts) | Wyands,Richard (p) | Bernstein,Peter (g) | Webber,John (b)

MCD 9335-2 | CD | Coast To Coast | EAN 025218933520
Red Holloway Quintet
Still Groovin' | Avalon | 3 Steps Up Clark | Indian Summer | Struttin' With Julie | Water Jug | Million Dollar Secret | Good To Go
Englewood Cliffs,NJ, rec. 11./12.2.2003
Holloway,Red (as,ts,voc) | Wess,Frank (ts) | Smith,Lonnie (org) | Sparks,Melvin (g) | Humphrey,Paul (dr)

MCD 9346-2 | CD | Getting Sentimental | EAN 090204923151
Bill Evans Trio
I Should Care | How My Heart Sings | Gary's Theme | I'm Getting Sentimental Over You | Quiet Now | Re:Person I Knew | The Peacocks | Emily | Song From M.A.S.H. | Turn Out The Stars | When I Fall In Love | In Your Own Sweet Way | But Beautiful | I Love You
Live at The 'Village Vanguard',NYC, rec. 15.1.1978
Evans,Bill (p) | Moore,Michael (b) | Jones,Philly Joe (dr)

Minor Music | Minor Music Records Gmbh

801015 | CD | Roots Revisited
Maceo Parker Group
Children's World | Better Git It In Your Soul | People Get Ready | Up And Down East Street(For Ulysee Hardy) | Over The Rainbow | Jumpin' The Blues
NYC, rec. details unknown
Parker,Maceo (as) | Wesley,Fred (tb) | Ellis,Pee Wee (ts) | Pullen,Don (org) | Jones,Rodney (g) | Stuart,Billy (dr)
Them That Got
Parker,Maceo (as) | Wesley,Fred (tb) | Henry,Vince (as) | Ellis,Pee Wee (ts) | Pullen,Don (org) | Jones,Rodney (g) | Stuart,Billy (dr)
In Time
Parker,Maceo (p,org) | Wesley,Fred (tb) | Ellis,Pee Wee (ts) | Jones,Rodney (g) | Collins,William 'Bootsy' (b-g) | Stuart,Billy (dr)

801016 | CD | New Friends
Fred Wesley Group
Rockin' In Rhythm | Honey Love | Bright Mississippi | Plenty Plenty Soul | Blue Monk | Birk's Works | D-Cup And Up
Wesley,Fred (tb,voc) | Davis,Stanton (tp) | Parker,Maceo (as,perc) | Green,Tim (ss,ts,perc) | Allen,Geri (p,keyboards) | Cox,Anthony (b) | Stewart,Bill (dr)
Eyes So Beautiful As Yours | The Love We Had
Wesley,Fred (tb,voc) | Davis,Stanton (tp) | Parker,Maceo (as,perc) | Green,Tim (ss:ts,perc) | Allen,Geri (p,keyboards) | Cox,Anthony (b) | Stewart,Bill (dr) | Lundy,Carmen (voc)
For The Elders | Peace Fugue
Wesley,Fred (tb,voc) | Davis,Stanton (tp) | Eubanks,Robin (tb) | Turre,Steve (tb) | Parker,Maceo (as,perc) | Green,Tim (ss,ts,perc) | Allen,Geri (p,keyboards) | Cox,Anthony (b) | Stewart,Bill (dr)

801018 | CD | Mo' Roots
Maceo Parker Group
Hallelujah I Love Her So | Chicken | Let's Get It On | Hamp's Boogie Woogie | Sister Sadie | Daddy's Home | Down By The Riverside | Southwick
NYC, rec. March 1991
Parker,Maceo (as) | Wesley,Fred (tb) | Ellis,Pee Wee (ts) | Jones,Rodney (g,el-g) | Goldings,Larry (org,keyboards) | Stewart,Bill (dr)
Jack's Back
Parker,Maceo (as) | Wesley,Fred (tb) | Williamson,Steve (as) | Ellis,Pee Wee (ts) | Jones,Rodney (g,el-g) | Goldings,Larry (org,keyboards) | Stewart,Bill (dr)
Fa Fa Fa(The Sad Song)
Parker,Maceo (as,voc) | Wesley,Fred (tb) | Ellis,Pee Wee (ts) | Jones,Rodney (g,el-g) | Goldings,Larry (org,keyboards) | Madison,Jimmy (dr) | Mazelle,Kym (voc)

801022 | CD | Call Me
Hans Theessink Group
Late Last Night | Soul Of Song | Call Me | Mabellene | Lonely Days And Lonely Nights | Ain't Got No Home | Rock The Boat | New Orleans | The Planet | Bluesdoctor | Cuckoo | Sail On
München, rec. details unknown
Theessink,Hans (g,mand,harm,mandocello,steel-g,voc) | Wesley,Fred (tb) | Goldberg,Morris (as,thin-whistle) | Parker,Maceo (as) | Ellis,Pee Wee (ts) | Sass,Jon (tuba) | Bell,Richard (p,org) | Linden,Colin (g,voc) | Hudson,Garth (accordeon) | Graig,Gary (dr,perc) | King,Bobby (voc) | Evans,Terry (voc) | Danko,Rick (voc)

801027 | CD | Swing & Be Funky
Fred Wesley Group
For The Elders | Just Like That | On Green Dolphin Street | In Love In L.A. | Swing & Be Funky | Bop To The Boogie
Live at Stadtgarten,Köln, rec. 11.5.1992
Wesley,Fred (tb,voc) | Ragin,Hugh (tp,fl-h,voc) | Denson,Karl (ss,as,ts,voc) | Madsen,Peter (p,keyboards,voc) | Dolphin,Dwayne (b,el-b,voc) | Cox,Bruce (dr,voc)

801033 | CD | Southern Exposure
Maceo Parker Group
Blues For Shorty Bill | Keep On Marching | Splashin' | Fun In The Sun
Los Angeles,CA, rec. details unknown
Parker,Maceo (as) | Nocentelli,Leo (g) | Boulware,Will (org) | Porter Jr.,George (b) | Ernest III,Herman (dr)
Sister Sanctified
Parker,Maceo (as) | Nocentelli,Leo (g) | Boulware,Will (org) | Porter Jr.,George (b) | Ernest III,Herman (dr) | Ward,Michael (perc)
Every Saturday Night | The Way You Look Tonight
NYC, rec. details unknown
Parker,Maceo (as) | Wesley,Fred (tb) | Ellis,Pee Wee (ts) | Jones,Rodney (g) | Boulware,Will (org) | Stewart,Bill (dr)
Maceo Parker With The Rebirth Brass Band
Mercy, Mercy, Mercy | Walking Home Together
New Orleans,Louisiana, rec. details unknown
Parker,Maceo (as) | Rebirth Brass Band | Ruffins,Kermit (tp) | Shezbie,Derrick (tp) | Agee,Stafford (tb) | Steward,Reginald (tb) | Frazier,Philip (tuba) | Paulin,Roderick (ts) | Mallory,Ajay (snare-dr) | Frazier,Keith (bass-dr)

801034 | CD | Twelve And More Blues
Pee Wee Ellis Trio
There Is No Greater Love | Doxy | My Wife My Friend(As Each Day Goes By) | Pistachio | In The Middle | Bye Bye Blackbird- | I Love You- | My Neighbourhood | In A Sentimental Mood | Twelve And More Blues
Live at 'Schmuckkästchen',Köln, rec. 10./11.5.1993
Ellis,Pee Wee (ts,bs) | Dolphin,Dwayne (b) | Cox,Bruce (dr)

801037 | CD | Generations Of Jazz
Till Brönner-Gregoire Peters Quintet
Dejection Blues | Ku'Damm 1:30 A.M. | Smile | Sambà Per La Gamba | Bein' Green | Why Change | Lina's Waltz | I Want To Be Happy | Bye Bye Blackbird | Piccolo Blues
Köln, rec. 1./2.5.1993
Börner,Till (tp) | Peters,Gregoire (as,bs,piccolo) | Chastenier,Frank (p) | Brown,Ray (b) | Hamilton,Jeff (dr)

801040 | CD | Sepia Tonality
Pee Wee Ellis Quartet
What Are You Doing The Rest Of Your Life | I Should Care | Stardust | Cleaning Windows | Cherry Red | Body And Soul | Prayer Of Love | Why Not? | Come Rain Or Come Shine
NYC, rec. January 1994
Ellis,Pee Wee (ts) | Jones,Rodney (g) | Boulware,Will (org) | Tate,Grady (dr)
Pee Wee Ellis Quintet
Sepia Tonality
Ellis,Pee Wee (ts) | Jones,Rodney (g) | Boulware,Will (org) | Johnson,Howard (tuba) | Tate,Grady (dr)

801045 | CD | Amalgamation
Fred Wesley Group
No One | Peace Power | My Neighbourhood | Careless Whisper | Herbal Turkey Breast | The Next Thing I Knew | Trick Bag | Soft Soul And All That Jazz
Köln, rec. February 1994
Wesley,Fred (tb,voc) | Ragin,Hugh (tp,fl-h,voc) | Denson,Karl (ss,as,ts,voc) | Madsen,Peter (p,org,keyboards) | Dolphin,Dwayne (b,el-b) | Cox,Bruce (dr)

801046 | CD | Maceo(Soundtrack)
Maceo Parker Group
Cold Sweat | New Moon | House Party | New Song | Do Right Woman, Do Right Man | Make It Funky- | Funky Good Time- | There Was A Time
Live at The Fabrik,Hamburg, rec. 12.-14.4.1994
Parker,Maceo (as,voc) | Wesley,Fred (tb,voc) | Ellis,Pee Wee (ts,voc) | Speight,Ed (el-g) | Boulware,Will (org) | Speight,Bruno (g) | Preston,Jerry (b) | Thomas,Jamal (dr)
Knock On Wood
Parker,Maceo (as,voc) | Wesley,Fred (tb,voc) | Ellis,Pee Wee (ts,voc) | Speight,Ed (el-g) | Boulware,Will (org) | Speight,Bruno (g) | Preston,Jerry (b) | Thomas,Jamal (dr) | Mazelle,Kym (voc)
C Jam Funk
Parker,Maceo (as,voc) | Wesley,Fred (tb,voc) | Ellis,Pee Wee (ts,voc) | Speight,Ed (el-g) | Boulware,Will (org) | Speight,Bruno (g) | Preston,Jerry (b) | Thomas,Jamal (dr) | Mazelle,Kym (voc) | Clinton,George (voc)
Maceo Parker With The Rebirth Brass Band
Chameleon
Parker,Maceo (as,voc) | Wesley,Fred (tb,voc) | Ellis,Pee Wee (ts,voc) | Speight,Ed (el-g) | Boulware,Will (org) | Speight,Bruno (g) | Preston,Jerry (b) | Thomas,Jamal (dr) | Rebirth Brass Band

801047 | CD | Hans Theessink:Solo
Hans Theessink
Big Bill's Guitar | Hard Road Blues | You Make Me Feel So Good | Prison Blues | Two Trains | Blind Willie | Sugar Babe | Minnibelle | Vicksburg Is My Home | One Kind Of Favor | Shotgun Blues | Cypress Grove Blues | Sittin' On The Top Of The World
Judendorf,Austria, rec. Fall 1994
Theessink,Hans (g,el-g-mand,voc)

801051 | CD | My Secret Love
Till Brönner Quintet
Mer Loss D'r Dom In Kölle | My Secret Love | Caught In Love | Give Him What He Wants | Manteca | Screwed Up | This Can't Be Love | How Long Has This Been Going On
Köln, rec. 17./18.1.1995
Brönner,Till (tp,fl-h) | Gauchel,Walter (ts) | Nuß,Hubert (p) | Heller,Ingmar (b) | Dekker,Hans (dr)
Till Brönner Quintet With Annette Lowman
Don't Take Your Love From Me | For All We Know
Brönner,Till (tp,fl-h) | Gauchel,Walter (ts) | Nuß,Hubert (p) | Heller,Ingmar (b) | Dekker,Hans (dr) | Lowman,Annette (voc)

801052 | CD | Crazy Moon
Hans Theessink Group
Rolling Stone
Judendorf,Austria, rec. details unknown
Theessink,Hans (g,voc) | Bell,Richard (org) | Thelfa,Ali (dr) | Art Of Brass Vienna: | Gansch,Hans (tp) | Bruckner,Heinrich (tp) | Bieber,Thomas (fr-h) | Kojeder,Erich (tb)
Paint The Town
Theessink,Hans (g,voc) | Morales,Joe (as,ts) | Sass,Jon (tuba) | Bone,Ponty (accordeon) | Ball,Marcia (p,voc) | Thelfa,Ali (dr) | Pischel,Christian (dr) | Traenor,John 'Mambo' (triangle,wbd)
Lazy, Long Hot Summer's Day
Theessink,Hans (g,bj,jews-harp,kalimba,voc) | Sass,Jon (tuba) | Bell,Richard (org) | Thelfa,Ali (dr,voc) | Carter,Doretta (voc)
Power Of Love
Theessink,Hans (g,mand,voc) | Sass,Jon (tuba) | Bell,Richard (org,wurlitzer-p) | Traenor,John 'Mambo' (perc) | Pischel,Christian (dr) | Evans,Terry (voc) | Williams,Ray (voc) | Greene Jr.,Willie (voc) | Reese,Olivia (voc) | Kyle,Janet (voc) | Williams-Miller,Birdia (voc)
Home Cooking
Theessink,Hans (g,voc) | Sass,Jon (tuba) | Bell,Richard (p,org) | Thelfa,Ali (dr) | Evans,Terry (voc) | Williams,Ray (voc) | Greene Jr.,Willie (voc)
Homeless
Theessink,Hans (g,bj,mando-g,mandola,voc) | Sass,Jon (tuba) | Bell,Richard (org) | Thelfa,Ali (dr) | Evans,Terry (voc) | Williams,Ray (voc) | Greene Jr.,Willie (voc) | Art Of Brass Vienna: | Gansch,Hans (tp) | Bruckner,Heinrich (tp) | Bieber,Thomas (fr-h) | Kojeder,Erich (tb)
Sail Away
Theessink,Hans (g,voc) | Sheahan,John (fiddle,thin-whistle) | Bell,Richard (accordeon) | Cannon,Sean (voc)
Roll With The Punches
Theessink,Hans (g,bj,voc) | Morales,Joe (as,ts) | Sass,Jon (tuba) | Bell,Richard (org) | Bone,Ponty (accordeon) | Traenor,John 'Mambo' (wbd) | Thelfa,Ali (dr) | Evans,Terry (voc) | Williams,Ray (voc) | Greene Jr.,Willie (voc) | Reese,Olivia (voc) | Kyle,Janet (voc) | Williams-Miller,Birdia (voc)
Crazy Moon
Theessink,Hans (g,12-string-bj,voc) | Sass,Jon (tuba) | Bell,Richard (org) | Fabianek,Andreas (b) | Traenor,John 'Mambo' (perc) | Thelfa,Ali (dr)
Train
Theessink,Hans (g,steel-g,voc) | Thelfa,Ali (bass-dr,tambourine) | Evans,Terry (voc) | Williams,Ray (voc) | Greene Jr.,Willie (voc) | Reese,Olivia (voc) | Kyle,Janet (voc) | Williams-Miller,Birdia (voc)
Tears Are Rolling
Theessink,Hans (g,voc) | Bell,Richard (org) | Thelfa,Ali (dr)
Get Down 'N Play The Blues
Theessink,Hans (g,mand,voc) | Sass,Jon (tuba) | Thelfa,Ali (snare-dr)
Man With A Broken Heart
Theessink,Hans (g,voc) | Cashdollar,Cindy (dobro) | Starnes,Spencer (b)

801055 | CD | Stick To It
Bruce Cox Quartet With Guests
Monkey | Malcolm's Mood | Serenghetti Slide | Marie-Line | Strode Rode | Like Someone In Love | Happy House | Calaba
NYC, rec. details unknown
Cox,Bruce (dr) | Coltrane,Ravi (ss,ts) | Harrison,Donald (as) | Kikoski,David 'Dave' (p) | Madsen,Peter (p) | Essiet,Essiet Okon (b) | Dolphin,Dwayne (b) | Williams,Jeff (perc) | Lowman,Annette (voc)

801056 | CD | Drip Some Grease
Three Of A Kind
Cherokee
Stamford,CT, rec. January 1996
Three Of A Kind: | Madsen,Peter (p) | Dolphin,Dwayne (b) | Cox,Bruce (dr)
Gee Baby Ain't I Good To You
Three Of A Kind: | Madsen,Peter (p) | Dolphin,Dwayne (b) | Cox,Bruce (dr) | Daniels,Dee (voc)
Autumn Leaves
Golson,Benny (ts) | Three Of A Kind: | Madsen,Peter (p) | Dolphin,Dwayne (b) | Cox,Bruce (dr) | Daniels,Dee (voc)
Joren's Dance | The Theory Of Monkness | Panacea | Drip Some Grease
Brönner,Till (tp) | Golson,Benny (ts) | Three Of A Kind: | Madsen,Peter (p) | Dolphin,Dwayne (b) | Cox,Bruce (dr)
Killer Joe
Brönner,Till (tp) | Herwig,Conrad (tb) | Golson,Benny (ts) | Three Of A Kind: | Madsen,Peter (p) | Dolphin,Dwayne (b) | Cox,Bruce (dr)
Broken House | Rub A Dub Dub | The Way Home
Golson,Benny (ts) | Three Of A Kind: | Madsen,Peter (p) | Dolphin,Dwayne (b) | Cox,Bruce (dr)

801057 | CD | German Songs
Till Brönner Quartet & Deutsches Symphonieorchester Berlin
Ich Bin Von Kopf Bis Fuß Auf Liebe Eingestellt | Für Eine Nacht Voller Seligkeit | Wenn Ein Junger Mann Kommt | Not Yet | Mime | I Werde Jede Nacht Von Ihnen Träumen | The Never Ending Process | Schmetterlinge Weinen Nicht | Bare Necessities
Berlin, rec. 6./7.3.1996
Brönner,Till (tp,fl-h) | Di Gioia,Roberto (p) | Anderson,Reid (b) | Rossy,Jorge 'Jordi' (dr) | Deutsches Symphonieorchester Berlin | Maile,Hans (concertmaster) | Dittberner,Heidrun (v) | Roither,Gerhard (v) | Dean,Mladen (v) | Saad,Antoine (v) | Bitto,Stefan (v) | Grünkorn,Isabel (v) | Musat,Ioana (v) | Schwalke,Dagmar (v) | Michler,Sarah (v) | Schumann,Andreas (v) | De Nordstrom,Myrna Glanz (v) | Fournes,Rainer (v) | Grau,Tarla (v) | Van Schalk,Jan (v) | Woznak,Uta (v) | Sutinen,Kirsti (v) | Hartling,Betram (v) | Krüger,Erich (viola) | Heidrich,Peter (viola) | Vogt,Dieter (viola) | Reinke,Andreas (viola) | Pieper,Henry (viola) | Mühlnickel,Joachim (viola) | Donderer,Georg (cello) | Donderer,Mathias (cello) | Noack,Pierre (cello) | Blaise,Catherine (cello) | Akahoshi,Akira (b) | Schmidt,Christian (b) | Peters,Gregoire (fl,alto-fl) | Ingwersen,Kerstin (engl-h,oboe) | Welz,Joachim (cl) | Lemke,Hans (bassoon) | Keller,Jörg Achim (cond,arr) | Brand,Helmut (arr)

801058 | CD | Foot Prints
Peter Fessler Quartet
You Go To My Head | Fly Me To The Moon | Night And Day | Castles Of Spain | Laura | Come Rain Or Come Shine | Day By Day | All The Things You Are | I Fall In Love Too Easily | I Concentrate On You | You Don't Know What Love Is | Morning Light
Monster,NL, rec. details unknown
Fessler,Peter (voc) | Malschal,Berthold (p) | Von Kaphengst,Christian (b) | Jörris,Guido (dr)

801060 | CD | A New Shift
Pee Wee Ellis Quintet With Guests
It's A Funky Thing | Chicken Soup | What A Wonderful World | I'm So Tired Of Being Alone | A New Shift | Back Home | How Can You Mend A Broken Heart | Inarticulate Spech Of The Heart | Spring Like | New Moon | Come On In The House
Köln, rec. details unknown
Ellis,Pee Wee (ss,ts,voc) | Brönner,Till (tp) | Wesley,Fred (tb) | Scales,Martin (g) | Di Gioia,Roberto (org,keyboards) | Scales,Patrick (el-b) | May,Guido (dr)

801061 | CD | Brown Baby:A Tribute To Oscar Brown Jr.
Annette Lowman With Three Of A Kind, Fred Wesley And Rodney Jones
The Joneses | Excuse Me For Livin' | A Dime Away From A Hotdog | Tower Of Time | Forbidden Fruit | Brown Baby | Signifying Monkey | Dat Dere | The Lone Ranger | Brother Where Are You | Rags And Old Iron | Let's Get Drunk(And Be Somebody)
NYC, rec. details unknown
Lowman,Annette (voc) | Wesley,Fred (tb) | Jones,Rodney (g) | Three Of A Kind: | Madsen,Peter (p,arr,voc) | Dolphin,Dwayne (b,voc) | Cox,Bruce (dr,voc)

801062 | CD | Journey On
Hans Theessink Group
Where The Southern Crosses The Dog
different Places, rec. 1996
Theessink,Hans (g,bj,voc) | Sass,Jon (tuba) | Dozzler,Christian (harm) | Cashdollar,Cindy (dobro) | Bell,Richard (org,wurlitzer-p) | Thomas,Angus (b) | Thelfa,Ali (dr,tambourine) | Evans,Terry (voc)
Journey Of
Theessink,Hans (g,dobro,voc) | Sass,Jon (tuba) | Thelfa,Ali (dr,tambourine,voc) | Evans,Terry (voc) | Williams,Ray (voc)
Set Me Free
Theessink,Hans (g,voc) | Sass,Jon (tuba) | Pearlman,David (dobro) | Thelfa,Ali (dr,perc,djembe,voc) | Evans,Terry (voc) | Carter,Doretta (voc)

Storm Warning
Theessink,Hans (g,dobro,voc) | Sass,Jon (tuba) | Bell,Richard (org) | Thomas,Angus (b) | Thelfa,Ali (dr,perc,voc) | Carter,Doretta (voc)
Wings
Theessink,Hans (g,harm,dobro,voc) | Thomas,Angus (b) | Thelfa,Ali (dr) | Evans,Terry (voc)
Louisiana Man
Theessink,Hans (g,voc) | Sass,Jon (tuba) | Dozzler,Christian (harm) | Cashdollar,Cindy (dobro) | Thelfa,Ali (dr,voc) | Evans,Terry (voc) | Carter,Doretta (voc)
Run The Human Race
Theessink,Hans (g,dobro,voc) | Dozzler,Christian (accordeon) | Thomas,Angus (b) | Thelfa,Ali (dr,voc) | Gillespie,Dana (voc) | Evans,Terry (voc)
Bourgeois Blues
Theessink,Hans (mand,12-string-g,voc) | Sass,Jon (tuba) | Thelfa,Ali (bass-dr,tambourine) | Evans,Terry (voc)
Walking The Dog | 29 Ways
Theessink,Hans (g,voc) | Evans,Terry (voc) | Williams,Ray (voc) | Thelfa,Ali (voc)
Feel Like Going Home
Theessink,Hans (g,mand,dobro,voc)

801063 | CD | Colours Of My Mind
Peter Fessler Quartet
Here's That Rainy Day | Lush Life | Nature Boy | The Way We Were | It's De-Lovely | Easier Said Than Done | One Note Samba 'Waltz' | Lullaby
Monster,NL, rec. details unknown
Fessler,Peter (voc) | Matschat,Berthold (p,harp) | Van Kaphengst,Christian (b) | Jöris,Guido (dr)
Peter Fessler Quintet
Nothing But The Truth | Just One Of Those Things | My Foolish Heart | Nothing Comes From Fighting This Way
Fessler,Peter (voc) | Eidens,Christoph (vib) | Matschat,Berthold (p,harp) | Van Kaphengst,Christian (b) | Jöris,Guido (dr)

801064 | CD | What You Like
Pee Wee Ellis & NDR Bigband
The Prophet | Soul Pride | Far From Home
Hamburg, rec. 12.-16.5.1997
Ellis,Pee Wee (ts) | NDR Big Band | Axelsson,Lennart (tp) | Burkhardt,Ingolf (tp) | Stötter,Claus (tp) | Winterschladen,Reiner (tp) | Gallardo,Joe (tb) | Ahlers,Wolfgang (tb) | Christmann,Egon (tb) | Schmid,Lucas (tb) | Felsch,Fiete (reeds) | Bolte,Peter (reeds) | Herzog,Edgar (reeds) | Büchner,Lutz (reeds) | Schorn,Steffen (reeds) | Rémy,Tony (g) | Mondesir,Michael (b) | Mondesir,Mark (dr) | Keller,Jörg Achim (cond,arr)
Tune With A View
Ellis,Pee Wee (ts) | NDR Big Band | Axelsson,Lennart (tp) | Burkhardt,Ingolf (tp) | Stötter,Claus (tp) | Winterschladen,Reiner (tp) | Wesley,Fred (tb) | Gallardo,Joe (tb) | Ahlers,Wolfgang (tb) | Christmann,Egon (tb) | Schmid,Lucas (tb) | Felsch,Fiete (reeds) | Bolte,Peter (reeds) | Herzog,Edgar (reeds) | Büchner,Lutz (reeds) | Schorn,Steffen (reeds) | Rémy,Tony (g) | Mondesir,Michael (b) | Mondesir,Mark (dr) | Keller,Jörg Achim (cond)
I Will Be There
Ellis,Pee Wee (ts,bs) | NDR Big Band | Axelsson,Lennart (tp) | Burkhardt,Ingolf (tp) | Stötter,Claus (tp) | Winterschladen,Reiner (tp) | Wesley,Fred (tb) | Gallardo,Joe (tb) | Christmann,Egon (tb) | Schmid,Lucas (tb) | Felsch,Fiete (reeds) | Bolte,Peter (reeds) | Herzog,Edgar (reeds) | Büchner,Lutz (reeds) | Schorn,Steffen (reeds) | Rémy,Tony (g) | Beier,Detlev (b) | Mondesir,Mark (dr) | Keller,Jörg Achim (cond) | Sylven,Bo (arr)
I Get Along Without You Very Well | Dock 'C' | What You Like
Ellis,Pee Wee (ts) | NDR Big Band | Axelsson,Lennart (tp) | Burkhardt,Ingolf (tp) | Stötter,Claus (tp) | Winterschladen,Reiner (tp) | Gallardo,Joe (tb) | Welch,Jon (tb) | Christmann,Egon (tb) | Schmid,Lucas (tb) | Felsch,Fiete (reeds) | Bolte,Peter (reeds) | Herzog,Edgar (reeds) | Büchner,Lutz (reeds) | Schorn,Steffen (reeds) | Rémy,Tony (g) | Beier,Detlev (b) | Mondesir,Mark (dr) | Keller,Jörg Achim (cond,arr)
Take Me To The River | Your Love Is So Doggone Good - (Your Love Is) So Doggone Good | Step
Ellis,Pee Wee (ts) | NDR Big Band | Axelsson,Lennart (tp) | Burkhardt,Ingolf (tp) | Stötter,Claus (tp) | Winterschladen,Reiner (tp) | Gallardo,Joe (tb) | Ahlers,Wolfgang (tb) | Christmann,Egon (tb) | Schmid,Lucas (tb) | Felsch,Fiete (reeds) | Bolte,Peter (reeds) | Herzog,Edgar (reeds) | Büchner,Lutz (reeds) | Schorn,Steffen (reeds) | Rémy,Tony (g) | Mondesir,Michael (b) | Mondesir,Mark (dr) | Evans,Jenny (voc) | Keller,Jörg Achim (cond,arr)

801068 | CD | Timeless
Chuck Brown And The Second Chapter Band
Nature Boy | Tenderly
Uncle Punchy Studios,?, rec. details unknown
Brown,Chuck (g,voc) | Williams,Lenny (keyboards) | Betts,Keter (b) | Wood,Kent (vib) | Fisher,Ralph (dr)
Never Make Your Move Too Soon
Brown,Chuck (g,voc) | Holloway,Ron (sax) | Williams,Lenny (keyboards) | Biondo,Chris (b) | Wood,Kent (vib) | Fisher,Ralph (dr)
A Foggy Day(In London Town)
Brown,Chuck (g,voc) | Williams,Lenny (keyboards) | Betts,Keter (b) | Fisher,Ralph (dr)
I Only Have Eyes For You
Brown,Chuck (g,voc) | Williams,Lenny (keyboards) | Porecki,Benji (org) | Betts,Keter (b) | House,Ju Ju Julius (dr)
Love Won't Let Me Wait
Brown,Chuck (g,voc) | Pruitt,Skip (sax) | Williams,Lenny (keyboards) | Porecki,Benji (org) | Betts,Keter (b) | McLeod,Raice (dr)
Blue Skies
Brown,Chuck (g,voc) | Williams,Lenny (keyboards) | Biondo,Chris (b) | McLeod,Raice (dr) | Green,Robert (perc)
Wild Is The Wind
Brown,Chuck (voc) | Williams,Lenny (keyboards) | Holloway,Ron (sax) | Diggs,Elmore (b) | House,Ju Ju Julius (dr)
Autumn Leaves
Brown,Chuck (g,voc) | Williams,Lenny (keyboards) | Wood,Kent (vib) | Diggs,Elmore (b) | Robinson,Lenny (dr)
You'd Be So Nice To Come Home To
Brown,Chuck (voc) | Williams,Lenny (keyboards) | Betts,Keter (b) | McLeod,Raice (dr)
Hey There
Brown,Chuck (voc) | Williams,Lenny (keyboards,strings) | Betts,Keter (b) | House,Ju Ju Julius (dr)
Caravan
Brown,Chuck (g,voc) | Pruitt,Skip (sax) | Williams,Lenny (keyboards) | Betts,Keter (b) | Fisher,Ralph (dr) | Green,Robert (dr)

801071 | CD | Live Every Minute
Oscar Brown Jr. And His Group
Long As You're Living | Haven't I Loved You Somewhere
Hamburg, rec. 15.-17.6.1998
Brown Jr.,Oscar (voc) | Turrentine,Stanley (ts) | Graves,Aaron (p) | Diez,Stephan (g) | Lindholm,Lucas (b) | Brown,Gerry (dr)
It's October
Brown Jr.,Oscar (voc) | Ellis,Pee Wee (ss,ts) | Graves,Aaron (p) | Diez,Stephan (g) | Lindholm,Lucas (b) | Brown,Gerry (dr)
The Snake
Brown Jr.,Oscar (voc) | Burkhardt,Ingolf (tp) | Gallardo,Joe (tb) | Ellis,Pee Wee (ss,ts) | Graves,Aaron (p) | Diez,Stephan (g) | Lindholm,Lucas (b) | Brown,Gerry (dr)
A Column Of Birds
Brown Jr.,Oscar (voc) | Ellis,Pee Wee (ss,ts) | Graves,Aaron (p) | Lindholm,Lucas (b) | Brown,Gerry (dr)
Old Lovers Song
Brown Jr.,Oscar (voc) | Graves,Aaron (p)
Oscar Brown Jr. with The NDR Big Band
Dat Dere | Mr.Kicks | World Full Of Gray | Hazel's Hip | Billie's Bounce
Brown Jr.,Oscar (voc) | NDR Big Band | Axelsson,Lennart (tp) | Burkhardt,Ingolf (tp) | Stötter,Claus (tp) | Winterschladen,Reiner (tp) | Gallardo,Joe (tb) | Landgren,Nils (tb) | Lottermann,Stefan (tb) | Schweitzer,Christoph (tb) | Felsch,Fiete (reeds) | Bolte,Peter (reeds) | Lauer,Christof (reeds) | Büchner,Lutz (reeds) | Schorn,Steffen (reeds) | Diez,Stephan (g) | Sendecki,Vladislaw (p) | Lindholm,Lucas (b) | Brown,Gerry (dr) | Gray,Steve (cond)

801073 | CD | Gentle Men Blue
Pee Wee Ellis-Horace Parlan
Mercedes Benz(take 1) | I Love You For Sentimental Reasons | Someone To Watch Over Me | Party Time | Crazy | Old Folks | Parlaying | Cottage For Sale | Hamburg'n | Rock Of Ages | Mercedes Benz(take 2)
Hamburg, rec. 24./25.10.1998
Ellis,Pee Wee (ts) | Parlan,Horace (p)

801078 | CD | Eastside Moments
Peter Fessler Group
All The Things You Are | September Song | The Shadow Of Your Smile | Give Me One More Chance | What Now My Love | Love And Laughter | Remembering | So Danco Samba(I Only Dance The Samba) | Oh Sonho | Rainbow Songs | Dindi | Night Song
NYC, rec. details unknown
Fessler,Peter (g,voc) | Henry,Vince (ss,harm,b) | Café[Edson Café Adasilva] (perc)

801091 | CD | Going Home
Lisa Bassenge Trio
Like A Virgin | Caravan | I'm Thru With Love | Besame Mucho | Ways To Leave Your Lover | Fly Me To The Moon | Gee Baby Ain't I Good To You | I Hope I Don't Fall In Love With You | Gigolo | A Hard Day's Night | Guess Who I Saw Today | De Doo Doo Doo De Da Da | Going Home
SFB Radio,?, rec. June 2000
Bassenge,Lisa (voc) | Schmidt,Andreas (p) | Kieber,Paul (b)

801092 | CD | Feels Like Home
Steve Klink Trio
Lucinda | Have You Seen My Baby? | I'll Be Home | I Gotta Be Your Man | Memo To My Son | You've Got A Friend In Me | Texas Girl At The Funeral Of Her Father | A Wedding In Cherokee County | Short People
Köln, rec. 2.& 7.10.2000
Klink,Steve (p) | Führ,Dietmar (b) | Rieck,Marcus (dr)
Steve Klink-Alex Olivari
What Have You Done To Me | Louisiana 1927 | Guilty
Klink,Steve (p) | Olivari,Alex (g)
Steve Klink-Mia Znidaric
Feels Like Home | Dayton,Ohio 1903
Ljubljana,Slovenia, rec. 22.9.2000
Klink,Steve (p) | Znidaric,Mia (voc)

801093 | CD | Guardia Li
Francesca Simone Trio
Cantu Un Pucnu | Chi Ventu | Come To Me | Bella Ciao | Une Casa Leccera | Volare | Fantasia | Sento Freddo | So Allright | Magica | Si Continua | Here, There And Anywhere | Cry Me A River | Guarda Li
Bonn, rec. April 2001
Simone,Francesca (voc) | Mensebach,Robert (g,el-g,voc) | Kappler,Andreas (perc,voc)

801094 | CD | Lady Moon
Thärichens Tentett
Song To Aurore | She Opened The Door | Sunken Boat | Out Of The Blue
Berlin, rec. 2000/2001
Thärichen,Nicolai (p) | Wülker,Nils (tp,fl-h) | Fischer,Sören (tb) | Von Kleewitz,Jan (cl,as) | Spannagel,Andreas (fl,alto-fl,ts) | Willecke,Claas (bs) | Brückner,Kai (g) | Gunkel,Johannes (b) | Schönburg,Kai (dr) | Schiefel,Michael (voice)
When We Two Walked | Lady Moon | One Of Us Two | We'll Go No More A-Roving | Like The Touch Of Rain | I Can Tell | No | Too Late
Thärichen,Nicolai (p) | Klammer,Sven (tp,fl-h) | Fischer,Sören (tb) | Von Kleewitz,Jan (cl,as) | Spannagel,Andreas (fl,alto-fl,ts) | Willecke,Claas (bs) | Brückner,Kai (g) | Gunkel,Johannes (b) | Schönburg,Kai (dr) | Schiefel,Michael (voice)

801095 | CD | Songs For Joy And Sadness
Tuey Connell Group
When Joy Hits Town | Strawberries At Midnight | I'll Live Another Day | This Has To Be The One | Skylark | Love Just Took A Bow | Our Love Will Never End | That's The Trouble With Us | Life's Too Short To Be Unhappy Without You | When I Grow Too Old To Dream | What Is Love?
Chicago,Ill, rec. 27.-29.8.2000
Connell,Tuey (g,voc) | Bradfield,Geoff (ss,ts) | Luxion,Dennis (p) | Ferguson,Matt (b) | Hall,Dana (dr)

801096 | CD | Cafe Du Sport Jazzquartett
Cafe Du Sport Jazzquartett
Waves | On Ice | Still Missing | Hat Trick | Speedboats | Topspin | Soulmate | Slow Motion | Tiefseetaucher | Home Run
Köln, rec. August 2000
Cafe Du Sport Jazzquartett | Lauber,Frank (b-cl,as) | Müller,Bruno (g) | Von Kaphengst,Christian (b) | May,Guido (dr)
Like Eddie | Snorkelling Red Sea
Cafe Du Sport Jazzquartett | Lauber,Frank (b-cl,as) | Müller,Bruno (g) | Von Kaphengst,Christian (b) | May,Guido (dr) | Peil,Roland (bongos,skaker,perc)

801097 | CD | Armenonville
Flor De Tango
Armenonville | Garufa | Tu Olvido | Milonga Sentimental | Zorro Gris | El Esquinazo | Cuesta Abajo | Nostalgias | Caminito | A Madia Luz | La Cumparsita | Victoria | Milonga Del 900
Potsdam/Buenos Aires, rec. details unknown
Flor De Tango | Huber,Josef (bandoneon) | Sur,André (v) | Notrica,Eduardo (g,voice) | Janek,Klaus (b)

801098 | CD | Places To Come From,Places To Go
Steve Klink Trio
Ray's Dad's Cadillac | That Song About The Midway | Cotton Avenue | A Case Of You | Night Ride Home | Both Sides Now
Köln, rec. 5.11.2001
Klink,Steve (p) | Gailing,Henning (b) | Rieck,Marcus (dr)
Night In The City | Blue Motel Room
Klink,Steve (p) | Gailing,Henning (b) | Rieck,Marcus (dr) | Znidaric,Mia (voc)
Steve Klink Funk Unit
Big Yellow Taxi | You Turn Me On I'm A Radio | California
Slovenia Gradec,Slovenia, rec. 2./3.9.2001
Klink,Steve (p,el-p,org) | Golob,Ziga (el-b) | Levacic,Kruno (dr)
The Gallery
Klink,Steve (p,el-p,org) | Golob,Ziga (el-b) | Levacic,Kruno (dr) | Znidaric,Mia (voc)
Steve Klink-Barbara Boyle
Woman Of Heart And Mind | Sweet Bird
Iowa City,Iowa, rec. 23.9.2001
Klink,Steve (p) | Boyle,Barbara (voc)
Steve Klink-Sasa Olenjuk
Cactus Tree
Slovenia Gradec,Slovenia, rec. 2./3.9.2001
Klink,Steve (p) | Olenjuk,Sasa (v)

801099 | CD | Tuesdays In Chinatown | EAN 033585509927
Andy Bey
Feelin' Low Down | River Man
Hillside Sound Studio,Englewood,NJ, rec. 6./7.6.& 11./12.12.2000
Bey,Andy (p,voc)
Andy Bey Group
Tuesdays In Chinatown
Bey,Andy (p,voc) | Sneider,John (fl-h) | Washington,Peter (b) | Lewis,Victor (dr)
Fragile
Bey,Andy (voc) | Turre,Steve (tb) | Meyers,Paul (g) | Washington,Peter (b) | Lewis,Victor (dr) | Cinelu,Mino (perc)
Bridges | I'll Remember April
Bey,Andy (voc) | Meyers,Paul (g) | Carter,Ron (b) | Lewis,Victor (dr)
Saidas Bandeiras
Bey,Andy (p,voc) | Gardner,Earl (fl-h) | Turre,Steve (tb) | Ehrlich,Marty (alto-fl) | Bey,Andy (voc) | Washington,Peter (b) | Cinelu,Mino (perc)
In A Mist
Bey,Andy (p,voc) | Gardner,Earl (tp) | Turre,Steve (tb) | Ehrlich,Marty (b-cl) | Washington,Peter (b) | Lewis,Victor (dr)
Invitation | Little Girl Blue
Bey,Andy (p,voc) | Washington,Peter (b) | Lewis,Victor (dr)
Just Friends
Bey,Andy (p,voc) | Carter,Ron (b) | Lewis,Victor (dr) | Stein,Andy (v) | Seaton,Laura (v) | Finclair,Barry (viola) | Sanders,Peter (cello)

801100 | CD | A Sight, A Song | EAN 033585510022
Lisa Bassenge Trio
Can't Get You Out Of My Head | Blue Suede Shoes | Shake The Disease | Blue | Ol' 55 | Junimond
details unknown, rec. details unknown
Bassenge,Lisa (voc) | Schmid,Andreas (p) | Kleber,Paul (b)
Lisa Bassenge Trio With Guests
My Guy
Bassenge,Lisa (voc) | Schmid,Andreas (p) | Kleber,Paul (b) | Mattar,Daniel (perc,voc)
My Heart Belongs To Daddy
Bassenge,Lisa (voc) | Schmid,Andreas (p) | Kleber,Paul (b) | Merkelbach,Michael (tp) | Winch,Rainer (perc)
A Sight A Song
Bassenge,Lisa (voc) | Schmid,Andreas (p) | Merkelbach,Michael (tp) | Kleber,Paul (b) | Winch,Rainer (perc)
Blue | Golden Earrings
Bassenge,Lisa (voc) | Schmid,Andreas (p) | Kleber,Paul (b) | Friedman,David (vib)
It's Now Or Never | Everybody Loves Somebody Sometime | Are You Lonesome Tonight | Interlude
Bassenge,Lisa (voc) | Schmid,Andreas (p) | Kleber,Paul (b) | Kretz,Julia-Maria (v) | Von Der Nahmer,Martin (viola) | Schirmer,Rouven (cello)
Adeus
Bassenge,Lisa (voc) | Schmid,Andreas (p) | Kleber,Paul (b) | Mattar,Daniel (voc) | Winch,Rainer (perc)

MMM Records | SALKO Productions

CD 1296 | CD | The Duo Live In Concert
Häns'che Weiss-Vali Mayer Duo
Präsentation | Les Feuilles Mortes | On A Clear Day You Can See Forever | Hommage À Hojok | Ain't Misbehavin' | Polka Dots And Moonbeams | What Is This Thing Called Love | Flowers | Vis-A-Vis | Nuages
Live at ?, rec. 1996
Weiss,Häns'che (g) | Mayer,Vali (b,voc)

CD 1298 | CD | Just Play
Myriam | Fall Of Leaves | Dans Ma Roulotte | Tenderly | Tenderly | Minor Swing | Flute Blues | Lil' Darlin' | Limehouse Blues | La Puerta | Historia De Un Amor | Sweet Georgia Brown | Bei Mir Bist Du Schön
Cayman Studios,?, rec. 1998
Weiss,Häns'che (g) | Mayer,Vali (b)

CD 1303 | CD | Just Play II | EAN 7611085313034
Melange | Blackbird | Pupa | Manoir- | Daphne- | Laura | Valse Oubliée | Ou Es Tu...? | Gloomy Sunday | Gerra | Kale Yaka | Zürich-Berlin
Caiman Studio,?, rec. 2003
Weiss,Häns'che (g) | Mayer,Vali (b)

MPS | Universal Music Germany

067375-2 | CD | Albert Mangelsdorff And His Friends | EAN 044006737522
Albert Mangelsdorff-Don Cherry
I Dig It, You Dig It
Baden-Baden, rec. 18.12.1967
Mangelsdorff,Albert (tb) | Cherry,Don (co)
Albert Mangelsdorff-Lee Konitz
Al-Lee
VS-Villingen, rec. 14.3.1968
Mangelsdorff,Albert (tb) | Konitz,Lee (as)
Albert Mangelsdorff-Elvin Jones
My Kind Of Time
Berlin, rec. 12.11.1968
Mangelsdorff,Albert (tb) | Jones,Elvin (dr)
Albert Mangelsdorff-Karl Berger
Way Beyond Cave
Baden-Baden, rec. 12.12.1968
Mangelsdorff,Albert (tb) | Berger,Karl (vib)
Outox
Stuttgart, rec. 16.1.1969
Mangelsdorff,Albert (tb) | Berger,Karl (vib)
Albert Mangelsdorff-Wolfgang Dauner
My Kind Of Beauty
Mangelsdorff,Albert (tb) | Dauner,Wolfgang (p)

519195-2 | 2 CD | Two Originals:Karuna Supreme/Rainbow
John Handy-Ali Akbar Khan Group
Ganesha's Jubilee Dance | Karuna Supreme | The Soul And The Atma
Ludwigsburg, rec. 1.11.1975
Handy,John (as) | Khan,Ali Akbar (sarod) | Hussain,Zakir (tabla) | Sahota,Yogish S. (tampura)
Rainbow
Rajashik-The Majesty Of Wisdom | Indian Boogie Shoes | Rainbow Serenade | Kali Dance
VS-Villingen, rec. 3./4.9.1980
Rainbow | Handy,John (as) | Khan,Ali Akbar (sarod) | Subramaniam,Dr. L. (v) | Kane,Shyram (tablas) | Johnson,Mary (tanpura)
Garland Of Flowers (Alap And Jod In Raga Mala)
Rainbow | Handy,John (as) | Khan,Ali Akbar (sarod) | Subramaniam,Dr. L. (v) | Johnson,Mary (tanpura)

519213-2 | 2 CD | Three Originals:The Wide Point/Trilogue/Albert Live In Montreux
Albert Mangelsdorff Trio
The Up And Down Man | Mayday Hymn | Oh Horn | I Mo' Take You To To My Hospital And Cut Your Liver Out | Mood Indigo | The Wild Point | For Peter (Dedicated To Peter Trunk)
Walldorf, rec. 1./2.5.1975
Mangelsdorff,Albert (tb) | Danielsson,Palle (b) | Jones,Elvin (dr)
Mangelsdorff-Pastorius-Mouzon
Trilogue | Zores Mores | Foreign Fun | Accidental Meeting | Ant Steps On An Elephant's Toe
Live at Berliner Jazztage, rec. 6.11.1976
Mangelsdorff,Albert (tb) | Pastorius,Jaco (el-b) | Mouzon,Alphonse (dr)
Albert Mangelsdorff Trio
Dear Mr.Palmer | Mood Azur | Stay Off The Carpet | Rip Off
Live at The Montreux Jazz Festival, rec. 30.11./1.12.1980
Mangelsdorff,Albert (tb) | Jenny-Clark,Jean-Francois (b) | Jackson,Ronald Shannon (dr)

519216-2 | 2 CD | Three Originals:Tristeza On Guitar/Poema On Guitar/Apaixonado
Baden Powell Solo/Group
Tristeza | Canto De Xango | Round About Midnight | Sarava | Canto De Ossanha | Manha De Carnaval(Morning Of The Carnival) | Invencao Em 7 1 | 2 | Das Rosas | Som Do Carnaval | O Astronauta
VS-Villingen, rec. 1./2.6.1966
Baden Powell (g,agogo,surdo) | Copinha (fl,agogo) | Sergio (b) | Bessa,Alfredo (atabaque,guica) | Coelho,Amauri (atabaque,pandeiro) | Banana,Milton (dr)
Baden Powell
Euridice
rec. 11.11.1967
Baden Powell (g-solo)
Sidney Smith & Eberhard Weber
Tristeza e Solidao
Smith,Sidney (fl) | Weber,Eberhard (b)
Baden Powell Quartet
Dindi | Samba Triste | Reza
Baden Powell (g) | Smith,Sidney (fl) | Weber,Eberhard (b) | Antolini,Charly (dr)
Baden Powell Trio

Feltinha Pro Poeta | Consolacao | All The Things You Are
Baden Powell (g) | Weber,Eberhard (b) | Antolini,Charly (dr)
Baden Powell Ensemble
Casa Velha | Alcantara | Igarape | Estorias De Alcantara | Waltzing | Lembrancas | Abstrato | As Flores | Balantofe | Brisa Do Mar
rec. 1973
Baden Powell (g) | Filho,Braz Limoge (oboe) | Da Silva,Jorge Ferreira (fl) | De Melo,Gabriel Bezerra (b) | Henriques,Joaquim Paes (dr) | Guimaraes,Nelson Franca (cuica) | Pizziali,Paulo Humberto (perc)

521059-2 | 2 CD | Three Originals:Motion&Emotions/Tristeza On Piano/Hello Herbie
Oscar Peterson Trio With The Claus Ogermann Orchestra
Sally's Tomato | Sunny | By The Time I Get To Phoenix | Wandering | This Guy's In Love With You | Wave | Dreamsville | Yesterday | Eleanor Rigby | Ode To Billy Joe
NYC, rec. late March 1969
Peterson,Oscar (p) | Jones,Sam (b) | Durham,Bobby (dr) | Ogerman,Claus (cond,arr) | details unknown
Oscar Peterson Trio With Herb Ellis
Naptown Blues | Exactly Like You | Day By Day | Hamp's Blues | Blues For H.G. | A Lovely Way To Spend An Evening | Seven Come Eleven
VS-Villingen, rec. 5./6.11.1969
Peterson,Oscar (p) | Ellis,Herb (g) | Jones,Sam (b) | Durham,Bobby (dr)
Oscar Peterson Trio
Tristeza | Nightingale | Porgy | Triste | You Stepped Out Of A Dream | Whatch What Happens | Down Here On The Ground | Fly Me To The Moon
VS-Villingen, rec. 1970
Peterson,Oscar (p) | Jones,Sam (b) | Durham,Bobby (dr)

523498-2 | CD | Tracks
Oscar Peterson
Give Me The Simple Life | Basin Street Blues | Honeysuckle Rose | Dancing On The Ceiling | A Child Is Born | If I Should Lose You | A Little Jazz Exercise | Django | Ja-Da | Just A Gigolo
VS-Villingen, rec. November 1970
Peterson,Oscar (p-solo)

523526-2 | 2 CD | Three Originals:Love And Sunshine/Estade/Cobilimbo
Monty Alexander Quartet
S.J.K. | Summer Of '42(The Summer Knows) | Now's The Time | You Are The Sunshine Of My Life | Feel Like Making Love | On A Clear Day You Can See Forever
VS-Villingen, rec. 25.10.1974
Alexander,Monty (p) | Ranglin,Ernest (g) | Weber,Eberhard (b) | Clare,Kenny (dr)
Too Marvelous For Words | Funny | You're My Everything | Gee Baby Ain't I Good To You | Isn't She Lovely | This Is The End Of... A Beautiful Friendship - (This Is The End Of...) A Beautiful Friendship | I Love You For Sentimental Reasons | Got To Go
VS-Villingen, rec. 14.-16.9.1977
Alexander,Monty (p) | Ranglin,Ernest (g) | Simpkins,Andrew (b) | Campbell,Charles (congas)
Monty Alexander Sextet
Out Of Many People, One | Muko | Too Many Rivers To Cross | Cobilimbo | Ripe Banana | Jammin' | Tropical Breeze | Caribea
VS-Villingen, rec. 8./9.9.1977
Alexander,Monty (p) | Ranglin,Ernest (g) | Taylor,Vincent (steel-dr) | Simpkins,Andrew (b) | Gant,Frank (dr) | Campbell,Charles (congas)

529093-2 | CD | Keep Going/Blue World
Art Van Damme Quintet
Turnabout | Sunday Kind Of Love | I Want To Be Happy | Tenderly | Gone With The Wind | Everything I've Got | Let Yourself Down | On Green Dolphin Street | I Saw Stars | Small World | It's Easy To Remember | The Man I Love | Blue Lou | It's A Blue World | My Kind A (Of) Love | Laura | Too Close For Comfort | When Your Lover Has Gone | The Song Is You | The Things We Did Last Summer | Cheek To Cheek | On The Alamo | Jim | Diane
VS-Villingen, rec. 8.-12.6.1970
Van Damme,Art (accordeon) | Pass,Joe (g) | Thusek,Heribert (vib) | Weber,Eberhard (b) | Clare,Kenny (dr)

529095-2 | CD | Three Latin Adventures
Kenny Clarke-Francy Boland Big Band
Latin Kaleidoscope: | Un Grao De Areia- | Duas Rosas- | A Rosa Negra- | Uma Fita De Tres Cores- | Olhos Negros- | Ramo Des Flores- | Cuban Fever: | Fiebre Cubana- | Mambo DeLas Brujas- | Extrano Sueno- | Cara Bruja- | Crepusculo Y Aurora- | Fellini 712: | Villa Radieuse- | 'Tween Dusk And Dawn In Via Urbana- | Rosati At Popolo Square-
Köln, rec. 28./29.8.1968
Clarke,Kenny (dr) | Boland,Francy (p,arr) | Bailey,Benny (tp) | Sulieman[Leonard Graham],Idrees (tp) | Pavlovic,Milo (tp) | Deuchar,Jimmie (tp) | Goykovich,Dusko (tp) | Persson,Ake (tb) | Peck,Nat (tb) | Van Lier,Erik (tb) | Humble,Derek (as) | Woods,Phil (as) | Griffin,Johnny (ts) | Scott,Ronnie (ts) | Coe,Tony (cl,sax) | Shihab,Sahib (bs) | Woode,Jimmy (b) | Warland,Jean (b) | Clare,Kenny (dr) | Keane,Shake (perc) | Heath,Albert 'Tootie' (perc) | Inzalaco,Tony (perc) | Martinez,Sabu (perc)

529096-2 | CD | Exclusively For My Friends-The Lost Tapes
Oscar Peterson Trio
Gravy Waltz | Three O'Clock In The Morning | Squeaky's Blues | Tenderly
VS-Villingen, rec. 10.5.1965
Peterson,Oscar (p) | Brown,Ray (b) | Thigpen,Ed (dr)
I Will Wait For You | Let's Fall In Love | Put On A Happy Face | Stella By Starlight | Moanin'
VS-Villingen, rec. 12.11.1967
Peterson,Oscar (p) | Jones,Sam (b) | Durham,Bobby (dr)
Never Say Yes | It's Impossible | My Romance
VS-Villingen, rec. 30.10.1968
Peterson,Oscar (p) | Jones,Sam (b) | Durham,Bobby (dr)

531848-2 | CD | Dave Pike Set:Masterpieces
Dave Pike Set
Regards From Freddie Horowitz | Noisy Silence-Gentle Noise | Mathar | Walkin' Down The Highway In A Raw Red Egg
VS-Villingen, rec. 21.1.1969
Pike,Dave (vib,tambourine) | Kriegel,Volker (g,sitar) | Rettenbacher,J.A. (b) | Baumeister,Peter (dr)
Greater Kalesh No.48 | Goodtime Charlie At The Big Washdown
VS-Villingen, rec. August 1969
Pike,Dave (vib,tambourine) | Kriegel,Volker (g,el-b,sitar) | Rettenbacher,J.A. (cello,b) | Baumeister,Peter (dr,perc)
Nobody's Afraid Of Howard Monster
Live at The 'Philharmonie',Berlin, rec. 7.11.1969
Pike,Dave (vib) | Kriegel,Volker (g) | Rettenbacher,J.A. (cello,b) | Baumeister,Peter (dr)
But Anyway | Rabbi Mogen's Hideout | Raga Jeeva Swara | Send Me The Yellow Guys
VS-Villingen, rec. 15./16.6.1970
Pike,Dave (vib) | Kriegel,Volker (g,sitar) | Rettenbacher,J.A. (b) | Baumeister,Peter (dr,perc)
Big Schlepp
VS-Villingen, rec. 15.3.1971
Pike,Dave (vib) | Kriegel,Volker (g) | Rettenbacher,J.A. (b) | Baumeister,Peter (dr,perc)
The New Dave Pike Set & Grupo Baiafra De Bahia
Salomao
Rio De Janeiro,Brazil, rec. 18.-21.6.1972
Pike,Dave (vib) | Kriegel,Volker (g) | Weber,Eberhard (b) | Hellman,Marc (dr) | Correa,Djalma (perc,agogo,atabaques,pinicos,timbales,triangle) | De Santana,Edson Emetério (atabaques,surdo) | Carmadell,Onias (atabaques,berimbau,pandeiro)

533102-2 | CD | Sunshine Of Your Love
Ella Fitzgerald With The Tommy Flanagan Trio
Unsuless Landscape | Old Devil Moon | Don't Cha Go 'Way Mad | A House Is Not A Home | Trouble Is A Man | Love You Madly
San Francisco,CA, rec. October 1968
Fitzgerald,Ella (voc) | Flanagan,Tommy (p) | De La Rosa,Frank (b) | Thigpen,Ed (dr)
Ella Fitzgerald And Her Orchestra
Hey Jude | Sunshine Of Your Love | The Girl's In Love With You | Watch What Happens | Alright,Okay,You Win | Give Me The Simple Life
Fitzgerald,Ella (voc) | Smith,Allan (tp) | Heckscher Band,members of the Ernie | Flanagan,Tommy (arr,ld) | details unknown

533549-2 | CD | Two Originals:Walking The Line/Another Day
Oscar Peterson Trio
Blues For Martha | Greensleeves | I'm Old Fashioned | All The Things You Are | Too Close For Comfort | The Jamfs Are Coming | It Never Entered My Mind | Carolina Shout | I Love You | Rock Of Ages | Once Upon A Summertime | Teach Me Tonight | The Windmills Of Your Mind | I Didn't Know What Time It Was | All Of You
VS-Villingen, rec. 10.-13.11.1970
Peterson,Oscar (p) | Mraz,George 'Jiri' (b) | Price,Ray (dr)

539085-2 | CD | Swinging Cooperations:Reunion Blues/Great Connection
Oscar Peterson-Milt Jackson Quartet
Satisfaction | Dream Of You | Someday My Prince Will Come | A Time For Love | Reunion Blues | When I Fall In Love | Red Top
VS-Villingen, rec. July 1971
Peterson,Oscar (p) | Jackson,Milt (vib) | Brown,Ray (b) | Hayes,Louis (dr)
Oscar Peterson Trio
Younger Than Springtime | Where Do We Go From Here | Smile | Soft Winds | Just Squeeze Me(But Don't Tease Me) | On The Trail(From The Grand Canyon Suite) | Wheatland
VS-Villingen, rec. October 1971
Peterson,Oscar (p) | Orsted-Pedersen,Niels-Henning (b) | Hayes,Louis (dr)

539130-2 | 7 CD | The Singers Unlimited:Magic Voices
Singers Unlimited + The Oscar Peterson Trio
Sesame Street | It Never Entered My Mind | Children's Games | The Gentle Rain (Chuva Delicada) | A Child Is Born | The Shadow Of Your Smile | Catherine | Once Upon A Summertime | Here's That Rainy Day
VS-Villingen, rec. July 1971
Singers Unlimited,The | Puerling,Gene (voc) | Shelton,Don (voc) | Dresslar,Len (voc) | Herman,Bonnie (voc) | Peterson,Oscar (p) | Mraz,George 'Jiri' (b) | Hayes,Louis (dr)
Singers Unlimited
Both Sides Now | London By Night | Here, There And Everywhere | Lullaby | Michelle | Try To Remember | Emily | Since You Asked | More I Can Not Wish You | The Fool On The Hill
Singers Unlimited,The | Puerling,Gene (voc) | Shelton,Don (voc) | Dresslar,Len (voc) | Herman,Bonnie (voc)
Singers Unlimited With The Roger Kellaway Cello Quartet
Just In Time | My Foolish Heart | Stone Ground Seven | Sleep Loved | Someone To Watch Over Me | Honeysuckle Rose | Zip-A-Dee-Doo-Dah | Prelude To A Kiss | It Had To Be You | Impossible
Los Angeles,CA/VS-Villingen, rec. 4.-7.4./April-May 1977
Singers Unlimited,The | Herman,Bonnie (voc) | Shelton,Don (voc) | Puerling,Gene (voc) | Dresslar,Len (voc) | Kellaway,Roger (p,celeste,hammerklavier) | Lustgarten,Edgar 'Ed' (cello) | Domanico,Chuck (b) | Pocaro,Joe (dr,perc) | Richards,Emil (perc)
Singers Unlimited With The Art Van Damme Quintet
Spring Is Here | But Beautiful | We Could Be Flying | Violets For Your Furs | Invitation | Cherry | Ecstasy | Let There Be Love | My One And Only Love | Wave | Good Bye
VS-Villingen, rec. June 1973
Singers Unlimited,The | Herman,Bonnie (voc) | Shelton,Don (voc) | Puerling,Gene (voc) | Dresslar,Len (voc) | Van Damme,Art (accordeon) | Thusek,Heribert (vib) | Schwab,Sigi (g) | Weber,Eberhard (b) | Antolini,Charly (dr)
Singers Unlimited With The Robert Farnon Orchestra
The More I See You | Sleepytime Gal | I Get Along Without You Very Well | Angel Eyes | As Time Goes By | I'll Remember April | If I Didn't Care | Sentimental Journey
London,GB/VS-Villingen, rec. August/September 1974
Singers Unlimited,The | Herman,Bonnie (voc) | Shelton,Don (voc) | Dresslar,Len (voc) | Puerling,Gene (arr,voc) | Farnon,Robert (cond,arr) | Orchestra | details unknown
Singers Unlimited
Clair | Killing Me Softly With His Song | Yesterdays | My Romance | Lost In The Stars | April In Paris | Girl Talk | Nature Boy | I Don't Know Where I Stand | Autumn In New York | Like Someone In Love | Indian Summer
VS-Villingen, rec. 10.-17.9.1974
Singers Unlimited,The | Herman,Bonnie (voc) | Shelton,Don (voc) | Dresslar,Len (voc) | Puerling,Gene (arr,voc)
Singers Unlimited With The Pat Williams Orchestra
You Are The Sunshine Of My Life | A Time For Love | On Green Dolphin Street | So Many Stars | Feeling Free With Patrick B. | Ja-Da | Skylark | On A Clear Day You Can See Forever | I'm Shadowing You | Where Is The Love
Los Angeles,CA/VS-Villingen, rec. 26.-31.5.1975
Singers Unlimited,The | Herman,Bonnie (voc) | Shelton,Don (voc) | Dresslar,Len (voc) | Puerling,Gene (arr,voc) | Williams,Patrick (cond,arr) | Findley,Chuck (tp,fl-h) | Shew,Bobby (tp,fl-h) | Welsch,Chauncey (tb) | Waldrop,Don (b-tb) | Shelton,Don (fl,as) | Christlieb,Pete (fl,ts) | Raffael,Donald (cl,ts) | Nimitz,Jack (b-cl,bs) | Feldman,Victor (vib,perc) | Fischer,Clare (el-p,arr) | Hughart,Jim (b,el-b) | West,Bobby (el-b) | Guerin,John (dr) | Bunker,Larry (dr) | Budimir,Dennis (g) | Elizalde,John (synth) | Vinci,Gerry (v)
Singers Unlimited With The Clare Fischer Orchestra
Round About Midnight | Mood Indigo | When I Fall In Love
Hollywood,CA, rec. 29.9.& 3.10.1975
Singers Unlimited,The | Herman,Bonnie (voc) | Shelton,Don (fl,cl,voc) | Dresslar,Len (voc) | Puerling,Gene (arr,voc) | Fischer,Clare (el-p) | Hughart,Jim (b) | Budimir,Dennis (g) | Guerin,John (dr)
Bye Bye Blues | Cry Me A River | Born To Be Blue
Singers Unlimited,The | Herman,Bonnie (voc) | Shelton,Don (fl,cl,voc) | Dresslar,Len (voc) | Puerling,Gene (arr,voc) | Findley,Chuck (tp) | Foster,Gary (ss,as) | Christlieb,Pete (ts) | Perkins,Bill (bs) | Fischer,Clare (el-p) | Hughart,Jim (b) | Budimir,Dennis (g) | Guerin,John (dr)
I Left My Heart In San Francisco | Gotcha | Why Don't You Do Right
Singers Unlimited,The | Herman,Bonnie (voc) | Shelton,Don (fl,cl,voc) | Dresslar,Len (voc) | Puerling,Gene (arr,voc) | Feldman,Victor (vib) | Morrell,John (g) | Fischer,Clare (el-p) | Hughart,Jim (b) | Mason,Harvey (dr)
Singers Unlimited With The Patrick Williams Orchestra
Just Friends | The Trouble With Hello Is Good-Bye | When The Sun Comes Out | Eleanor Rigby
Los Angeles,CA/VS-Villingen, rec. 22./23.9.& 25-29.10.1976
Singers Unlimited,The | Williams,Patrick (cond,arr) | Herman,Bonnie (voc) | Shelton,Don (voc) | Dresslar,Len (voc) | Puerling,Gene (arr,voc) | Childers,Buddy (tp) | Stiles,Danny (tp) | Watrous,Bill (tb) | Welsch,Chauncey (tb) | DeRosa,Vince (fr-h) | Duke,David (fr-h) | Johnson,Tommy (tuba) | Grusin,Dave (el-p) | Ferguson,Dan (g) | Hughart,Jim (el-b) | Schaeffer,Steve (dr) | Bunker,Larry (perc)
Sweet Georgia Brown | I Got Rhythm | Don't Get Around Much Anymore | I'm Gonna Go Fishin'
Singers Unlimited,The | Williams,Patrick (cond,arr) | Herman,Bonnie (voc) | Shelton,Don (voc) | Dresslar,Len (voc) | Puerling,Gene (arr,voc) | Childers,Buddy (tp) | Stiles,Danny (tp) | Watrous,Bill (tb) | Welsch,Chauncey (tb) | DeRosa,Vince (fr-h) | Duke,David (fr-h) | Johnson,Tommy (tuba) | Grusin,Dave (el-p) | Ferguson,Dan (g) | Rainey,Chuck (el-b) | Schaeffer,Steve (dr) | Bunker,Larry (perc) | Grant,Gary (tp) | McNab,Malcolm (tp) | Waldrop,Don (tb) | Roberts,George (tb) | Henderson,Bobby (fr-h) | Scott,Tom (ss,ts)
When April Comes Again | She Was Too Good To Me
Singers Unlimited,The | Williams,Patrick (cond,arr) | Herman,Bonnie (voc) | Shelton,Don (voc) | Dresslar,Len (voc) | Puerling,Gene (arr,voc) | Fischer,Clare (el-p) | Berghofer,Chuck (el-b) | Ferguson,Dan (g) | Schaeffer,Steve (dr)
Singers Unlimited With The Robert Farnon Orchestra
Deep Purple | Air From The Suite In D (Bach) | Put Your Dreams Away(For Another Day) | I Loved You | In The Still Of The Night | Mona Lisa | Feelings | Gymnopedie No.1 | How Beautiful Is Night | Eventide
VS-Villingen, rec. May 1976
Singers Unlimited,The | Herman,Bonnie (voc) | Shelton,Don (voc) | Dresslar,Len (voc) | Puerling,Gene (arr,voc) | String Orchestra | Farnon,Robert (cond,arr) | details unknown
Singers Unlimited With Roger Kellaway
Yours Truly Rosa
VS-Villingen, rec. May 1977
Singers Unlimited,The | Herman,Bonnie (voc) | Shelton,Don (voc) | Dresslar,Len (voc) | Puerling,Gene (arr,voc) | Kellaway,Roger (p)
Singers Unlimited
Marlies
VS-Villingen, rec. May 1975
Singers Unlimited,The | Herman,Bonnie (voc) | Shelton,Don (cl,voc) | Dresslar,Len (voc) | Puerling,Gene (arr,voc)
We've Only Just Begun | It Could Happen To You | Soon It's Gonna Rain | Where Is Love | My Ship | You've Got A Friend | Jennifer's Rabbit | Look Around | Snowfall | If
VS-Villingen, rec. June 1973
Singers Unlimited,The | Puerling,Gene (arr,voc) | Shelton,Don (fl,alto-fl,as,voc) | Lewis,Bobby (fl-h) | Ferreri,Pat (g,el-g) | Atlas,Jim (b,el-b) | Coleman,Jerry (dr) | Dresslar,Len (voc) | Herman,Bonnie (voc) | Hooper,Les (p,el-p)
Singers Unlimited With Rob McConnell And The Boss Brass
Tangerine | Laura | Lullaby Of The Leaves | You Are My Sunshine | Sophisticated Lady | This Is The End Of... A Beautiful Friendship - (This Is The End Of...) A Beautiful Friendship | It Might As Well Be Spring | Chelsea Morning | Dindi | Pieces Of Dreams
Toronto,Canada/VS-Villingen, rec. June/August 1978
Singers Unlimited,The | Herman,Bonnie (voc) | Shelton,Don (voc) | Dresslar,Len (voc) | Puerling,Gene (arr,voc) | McConnell,Rob (arr) | Chycoski,Arnie (tp,fl-h) | Traugott,Erich (tp,fl-h) | Basso,Guido (tp,fl-h) | Noto,Sam (tp,fl-h) | Cassidy,Bruce (tp,fl-h) | McDougall,Ian (tb) | Livingston,Bob (tb) | McMurdo,Dave (tb) | Hughes,Ron (b-tb) | Warnaar,Brad (fr-h) | Stimpson,George (fr-h) | Koffman,Moe (fl,ss,as,piccolo) | Toth,Jerry (fl,cl,as) | Amero,Eugene (fl,cl,ts) | Wilkins,Rick (cl,ts) | Morgan,Gary (cl,b-cl,ba) | Dale,James (p,el-p) | Bickert,Ed (g,el-g) | Thompson,Don (b,el-b) | Clarke,Terry (dr) | Morell,Marty (perc)
Singers Unlimited
Anything Goes | The Way We Were | One More Time Chuck Corea | Sweet Lorraine | Jeanie With The Light Brown Hair | Someone To Light Up My Life | Our Love Is Here To Stay | The Entertainer | All The Things You Are | Sometimes I Feel Like A Motherless Child | I Wish You Love
VS-Villingen, rec. June 1979
Singers Unlimited,The | Herman,Bonnie (voc) | Shelton,Don (voc) | Puerling,Gene (arr,voc) | Dresslar,Len (voc)
Singers Unlimited With Orchestra
Easy To Love | Where Or When | Close Enough For Love | Mountain Greenery | Lullaby Of Birdland | Falling In Love With Love | Nina Never Knew | Bass-Ically Speaking | Willow Weep For Me
Los Angeles,CA/VS-Villingen, rec. 3./4.9.& 29.9./3.10.1980
Singers Unlimited,The | Herman,Bonnie (voc) | Shelton,Don (fl,as,ts,voc) | Puerling,Gene (voc) | Dresslar,Len (voc) | Findley,Chuck (tp,fl-h) | Luening,Warren (tp,fl-h) | Watrous,Bill (tb) | DeRosa,Vince (fr-h) | Shank,Bud (fl,alto-fl,as) | Christlieb,Pete (cl,ts) | Tricarico,Bob (b-cl,bs) | Hooper,Les (p,el-p,cond,arr) | Magnusson,Bob (b,el-b) | Radtke,Tom (dr,perc)

557423-2 | CD | Reith On! | EAN 731455742329
Dieter Reith Group
Attention | Drum Organ | Yeah Man
VS-Villingen, rec. details unknown
Reith,Dieter (p) | Jackel,Conny (tp) | Lachmann,Gerhard (tb) | Fischer,Bernd (as) | Freund,Joki (sax) | Feigl,Johnny (sax) | Witte,Peter (b) | Antolini,Charly (dr)
Dieter Reith Trio
Wives And Lovers | A Happy Afternoon | Days Of Wine And Roses
Reith,Dieter (p) | Witte,Peter (b) | Antolini,Charly (dr)
Dieter Reith Quintet
Goofin Each Other
Reith,Dieter (p) | Witte,Peter (b) | Antolini,Charly (dr) | Mutschler,Hermann (timbales) | Bong,Kurt (bongos)
Knut Kiesewetter With The Dieter Reith Orchestra
Fool On The Hill | Sometimes In Winter | Roll On The Left Side
Kiesewetter,Knut (voc) | Van Rooyen,Ack (tp,fl-h) | Wright,Leo (fl,as) | Dudek,Gerd (fl,ts) | Reith,Dieter (org) | Kitschenberg,Heinz (g) | Weber,Eberhard (b) | Clare,Kenny (dr)
Dieter Reith Quartet
Follow Me | Open Drive
Reith,Dieter (org) | Kitschenberg,Heinz (g) | Weber,Eberhard (b) | Wittich,Roland (dr)

557656-2 | 2 CD | Black Myth/Out In Space
Sun Ra And His Intergalactic Research Arkestra
Black Forest Myth | Friendly Galaxy No.2 | Journey Through The Outer Darkness | Strange Worlds- | Black Myth- | It's After The End Of The World- | We'll Wait For You
Live at 'Donaueschinger Musiktage', rec. 17.10.1970
Sun Ra (p,clavinet,farfisa-org,hohner-electra,mini-moog,recitation,roksichord,sp | Hadi,Kwame (tp) | Ebah,Akh Tal (tp,mellophon) | Northern,Bob (fr-h) | Nur,Al Batin (engl-h) | Gilmore,John (ts,perc,voc) | Allen,Marshall (fl,as,perc,oboe,piccolo) | Patrick,Pat (fl,cl,b-cl,as,ts,bs,perc) | Davis,Danny (fl,cl,as) | Thompson,Danny (fl,as,bs,bassoon) | Cummings,Robert (b-cl) | Jackson,James (fl,dr,perc,lightning-dr,oboe) | Shlomo,Absholom Ben (fl,cl,as,perc) | Silva,Alan (v,viola,cello,b) | Blake,Alex (b) | Humphries,Lex (dr,perc) | Brister,William (dr,congas) | Hunt,Nimrod (perc,hand-dr) | Tyson,June (dancer,voc) | Tayo,Ife (perc,dancer) | Hazoumé,Roger Aralamon (african-perc,balafon,dancer) | Samba,Math (african-perc,dancer) | Wilkinson,Richard (light-show)
Out In Space | Discipline Seres | Walkin' On The Moon... | Outer Space Were I Cam From(recitation) | Watusa | Myth Versus Reality | Theme Of The Stargazers | Space Chants Medley: | Second Stop Is Jupiter- | Why Go To The Moon- | Neptun- | Mercury- | Venus- | Mars- | Jupiter- | Saturn- | Uranus- | Pluto- | We Travel The Spaceways
Live at Berliner Jazztage, rec. 7.11.1970
Sun Ra (p,clavinet,farfisa-org,hohner-electra,mini-moog,recitation,roksichord,sp | Hadi,Kwame (tp) | Ebah,Akh Tal (tp,mellophon) | Northern,Bob (fr-h) | Nur,Al Batin (engl-h) | Gilmore,John (ts,perc,voc) | Allen,Marshall (fl,as,perc,oboe,piccolo) | Patrick,Pat (fl,cl,b-cl,as,ts,bs,perc) | Davis,Danny (fl,cl,as) | Thompson,Danny (fl,as,bs,bassoon) | Cummings,Robert (b-cl) | Jackson,James (fl,dr,perc,lightning-dr,oboe) | Shlomo,Absholom Ben (fl,cl,as,perc) | Silva,Alan (v,viola,cello,b) | Blake,Alex (b) | Humphries,Lex (dr,perc) | Brister,William (dr,congas) | Hunt,Nimrod (perc,hand-dr) | Tyson,June (dancer,voc) | Tayo,Ife (perc,dancer) | Hazoumé,Roger Aralamon (african-perc,balafon,dancer) | Samba,Math (african-perc,dancer) | Wilkinson,Richard (light-show)

817487-2 | CD | Montreux Alexander-Live! At The Montreux Festival
Monty Alexander Trio
Nite Mist Blues | Feelings | Satin Doll | The Work Song | Drown In My Own Tears | Battle Hymn Of The Republic
Live at The Montreux Jazz Festival, rec. 10.6.1976
Alexander,Monty (p) | Clayton Jr.,John (b) | Hamilton,Jeff (dr)

817489-2 PMS | CD | Tristeza On Piano
Oscar Peterson Trio
Tristeza | Nightingale | Porgy | Triste | You Stepped Out Of A Dream | Whatch What Happens | Down Here On The Ground | Fly Me To The Moon

VS-Villingen, rec. 1970
Peterson,Oscar (p) | Jones,Sam (b) | Durham,Bobby (dr)

821846-2 | CD | Hello Herbie
Oscar Peterson Trio With Herb Ellis
Naptown Blues | Exactly Like You | Day By Day | Hamp's Blues | Blues For H.G. | A Lovely Way To Spend An Evening | Seven Come Eleven
VS-Villingen, rec. 5./6.11.1969
Peterson,Oscar (p) | Ellis,Herb (g) | Jones,Sam (b) | Durham,Bobby (dr)

841413-2 | CD | State Of Art
Art Van Damme Group
Gone With The Wind | I Want To Be Happy
VS-Villingen, rec. June 1970
Van Damme,Art (accordeon) | Pass,Joe (g) | Thusek,Heribert (vib) | Weber,Eberhard (b) | Clare,Kenny (dr)
When Your Lover Has Gone | Laura | The Song Is You
VS-Villingen, rec. 8.-12.6.1970
Van Damme,Art (accordeon) | Pass,Joe (g) | Thusek,Heribert (vib) | Weber,Eberhard (b) | Clare,Kenny (dr)
I Get A Kick Out Of You | All The Things You Are
VS-Villingen, rec. 4.-7.3.1968
Van Damme,Art (accordeon) | Thusek,Heribert (vib) | Rundquist,Fred (g) | Witte,Peter (b) | Antolini,Charly (dr)
My Little Boat | Shiny Stockings | Poor Butterfly
VS-Villingen, rec. May 1969
Van Damme,Art (accordeon) | Wolf,Hans (as) | Dauber,Werner (ts) | Prinz,Rolf (ts) | Loch,Heinz (bs) | Thusek,Heribert (fl,vib) | Rundquist,Fred (g) | Witte,Peter (b) | Antolini,Charly (dr)
Cheers | I Only Have Eyes For You
VS-Villingen, rec. June 1972
Van Damme,Art (accordeon) | Risavy,Rudi (fl) | Thusek,Heribert (fl) | Kümpel,Kurt (fl) | Wolf,Hans (fl) | Schwab,Sigi (g) | Pilar,Milan (b) | Kovacev,Branislav (dr)
Wave
VS-Villingen, rec. May 1969
Van Damme,Art (accordeon) | Thusek,Heribert (fl,vib) | Rundquist,Fred (g) | Witte,Peter (b) | Antolini,Charly (dr)
Cute | Autumn In New York | Ecstasy
VS-Villingen, rec. 8.-11.3.1967
Van Damme,Art (accordeon) | Thusek,Heribert (vib) | Rundquist,Fred (g) | Witte,Peter (b) | Antolini,Charly (dr)
Here's That Rainy Day | Ode To Cleavage Or The Camel
San Francisco,CA, rec. January 1966
Van Damme,Art (accordeon) | Rae,Johnny (vib,timbales) | Miller,Paul (g) | Mosher,John (b) | Markham,John (dr)

8431072 | CD | Zoller-Koller-Solal | EAN 042284310727
Zoller-Koller-Solal Trio
Mr.Heine's Blues | Away From The Crowd | H.J. Meets M.A.H.
VS-Villingen, rec. 16.1.1965
Koller,Hans (ts) | Zoller,Attila (g) | Solal,Martial (p)
Attila Zoller-Martial Solal
Stella By Starlight
Zoller,Attila (g) | Solal,Martial (p)
Attila Zoller-Hans Koller
All The Things You Are
Koller,Hans (ts) | Zoller,Attila (g)
Attila Zoller
After Glow
Zoller,Attila (g-solo)
Martial Solal
The End Of A Love Affair | My Old Flame | Stompin' At The Savoy
Solal,Martial (p-solo)

9808189 | CD | Jankowskinetik | EAN 602498081891
Horst Jankowski Quartet
Zerocasion | Satin Doll | Falling In Love With Love | I've Got You Under My Skin | 'Lady Eve | Speech Craft | Out'n Ground | No Troubles At All | Black Flower | Please Don't Talk About Me When I'm Gone
VS-Villingen, rec. 6.-8.4.1970
Jankowski,Horst (p) | Wenzel,Hans (g) | Wendlandt,Götz (g) | Kovacev,Branislav (dr)

9808190 | CD | Music Zounds | EAN 602498081907
Wolfgang Dauner Trio
Leap Tick | The Things We Did Last Summer | Diäthylaminoäthyl | Es Läuft | Here Comes De Honey Man | Blue Light | Golden Green
VS-Villingen, rec. February 1970
Dauner,Wolfgang (p) | Weber,Eberhard (b) | Wittich,Roland (dr)

9808191 | CD | Drum Beat | EAN 602498081914
Charly Antolini Orchestra
Yeah Man | The Preacher | Drum Organ | Cheers | Attention | Drum-Pet
VS-Villingen, rec. 12.6.1966
Antolini,Charly (dr) | Jackel,Conny (tp) | Lachmann,Gerhard (tb) | Fischer,Bernd (as) | Freund,Joki (ts) | Feigl,Johnny (bs) | Reith,Dieter (p,org,arr) | Witte,Peter (b)

9808699 | CD | Spectrum | EAN 602498086995
Volker Kriegel Quintet
Zoom | So Long For Now | More About D | Suspicious Child,Growing Up | Instand Judgement | Ach Kina | Strings Revisited
VS-Villingen, rec. 1./2.2.1971
Kriegel,Volker (g,sitar) | Taylor,John (hohner-electra-p) | Trunk,Peter (cello,b,el-b) | Baumeister,Peter (dr,perc) | See,Cees (perc)

9811257 | CD | Annie Ross & Pony Poindexter with The Berlin All Stars | EAN 602498112571
Annie Ross & PonyPoindexter With The Berlin All Stars
Saturday Night Fish Fry | All Blues | Home Cookin' | Jumpin' At The Woodside | Moody's Mood For Love | Goin' To Chicago | Twisted
Live at Volksbildungsheim,Frankfurt/M., rec. 1.5.1966
Ross,Annie (voc) | Poindexter,Pony (ss,as,voc) | Jones,Carmell (tp) | Wright,Leo (fl,as) | Condouant,André (g) | Pauer,Fritz (p) | Woode,Jimmy (b) | Nay,Joe (dr)

9811263 | CD | Live At The Berlin Jazz Galerie | EAN 602498112632
Fritz Pauer Trio
Albert's Waltz | Who'll Buy My Dreams | Understanding | Modal Forces(Suite In Three Movements: | Gratuliere- | Gentle Eyes- | Modal Forces-
Live at The Jazz Galerie,Berlin, rec. 3./4.1.1970
Pauer,Fritz (p) | Woode,Jimmy (b) | Brooks,Billy (dr)

9811443 | CD | From Vienna With Art | EAN 602498114438
Art Farmer Quintet
Cascavelo | The Day After | Con-Fab | The Gap Sealer | Cocodrilo | Whole Tone Stomp
VS-Villingen, rec. 7.9.1970
Farmer,Art (fl-h) | Heath,Jimmy (fl,ss,ts) | Pauer,Fritz (p) | Woode,Jimmy (b) | Bachträgl,Erich (dr)

9811446 | CD | Morning Song | EAN 602498114469
Don Menza Septet
Cinderella's Waltz | Morning Song | Oliver's Twist | When Johnny Comes Marching Home | New Spanish Boots | Devil's Disciples
München, rec. 22.12.1965
Menza,Don (ts) | Kiefer,Rick (tp) | Fuesers,Rudi (tb) | Spencer,Dick (as) | Pauer,Fritz (p) | Lenz,Günter (b) | Favre,Pierre (dr)

9813437 | CD | New York City | EAN 602498134375
Hans Koller Big Band
Opening | 52nd Street | Central Park | Manhattan | Brooklyn | Skyline | Harlem | Freedom | Black And White | Ending
VS-Villingen, rec. 18.1.1968
Koller,Hans (ts) | Aszodi,Ference (tp) | Bailey,Benny (tp) | Pavlicek,Arthur (tp) | Hnilicka,Jaromir (tp) | Schmid,Alfa (tp) | Herbolzheimer,Peter (tb) | Brom Jr.,Gustav (tb) | Bartek,Mosmir (tb) | Simons,Franz (tb) | Pelc,Josef (tb) | Mangelsdorff,Emil (fl,as) | Navratil,Frantisek (sax) | Horak,Bronislav (sax) | Novak,Zdenek (sax) | Freund,Joki (sax) | Auders,Josef (sax) | Konopasek,Jan (sax) | Blaha,Josef (p,oboe) | Mraz,George 'Jiri' (b) | Moody,Bill (dr)

9813438 | CD | Phoenix | EAN 602498134382
Hans Koller Free Sound
Nicolas 1-2 | Isus Mirror | CH & HC | Phoenix | Victor | LWS | Nicholas 3-4
VS-Villingen, rec. 25./26.9.1972
Koller,Hans (ss,ts) | Mair,Albert (el-p) | Roidinger,Adelhard (b,el-b) | Bally,Alex (dr)

9813439 | CD | Kunstkopfindianer | EAN 602498134399
Hans Koller Quintet
Kunstkopfindianer | Suomi | Nom | Ulla M. & 22-8 | Adea
Ludwigsburg, rec. 21.-23.1.1974
Koller,Hans (ss,ts) | Seifert,Zbigniew (as,v) | Dauner,Wolfgang (p,el-p,synth,nagoya-harp) | Roidinger,Adelhard (b,el-b) | Stefanski,Janusz (dr)

9813440 | CD | Exclusiv | EAN 602498134405
Hans Koller Quartet
Blues In The Closet | Chordless | Stalag | The Gentle Art Of Love
Baden-Baden, rec. 19.2.1959
Koller,Hans (as,ts) | Zoller,Attila (g) | Pettiford,Oscar (b) | Pratt,Jimmy (dr)
Hans Koller Nonet
Natalie | Egil | Painter's Lament | Muttnik | Plädoyer | It's Over | Pagode
VS-Villingen, rec. 26.11.1963
Koller,Hans (as,ts) | Spencer,Dick (as) | Flierl,Rudi (ts) | Wenig,Erhard (ts) | Reinhardt,Helmut (bs) | Ross,Ronnie (bs) | Kris,Ira (g) | Rettenbacher,Hans (b) | Ganley,Allan (dr) | Garcia,Russell (arr)

9813445 | CD | Relax With My Horns | EAN 602498134450
Hans Koller Trio
Relax | The Sweetest Girl I've Ever Known | Music For Pablo(I) | Music For Pablo(II) | The Twister(1) | Half And Half | Ziag Hin | Blues For Marina
VS-Villingen, rec. 4.-6.7.1966
Koller,Hans (ss,ts) | Rettenbacher,Hans (b) | Lüderitz,Rafi (dr)

9814789 | CD | More Smiles | EAN 602498147894
Kenny Clarke-Francy Boland Big Band
Johnny One Note | Lullaby Of The Leaves | Bei Dir War Es Immer So Schön | My Favorite Things | Just In Time | All Through The Night | November Girl | My Heart Belongs To Daddy | Love For Sale
Köln, rec. 28.5.1969
Clarke,Kenny (dr) | Boland,Francy (p,arr) | Bailey,Benny (tp) | Sulieman[Leonard Graham],Idrees (tp) | Fischer,Tony (tp) | Goykovich,Dusko (tp) | Persson,Ake (tb) | Peck,Nat (tb) | Van Lier,Erik (tb) | Humble,Derek (as) | Griffin,Johnny (ts) | Scott,Ronnie (ts) | Coe,Tony (cl,ts) | Shihab,Sahib (bs) | Woode,Jimmy (b) | Clare,Kenny (dr)

9814790 | CD | All Smiles | EAN 602498147900
Let's Face The Music And Dance | I'm All Smiles | You Stepped Out Of A Dream | I'm Glad There Is You | Get Out Of Town | By Strauss | When Your Lover Has Gone | Gloria's Theme(from Butterfield Eight) | Sweet And Lovely | High School Cadets
Köln, rec. 13./14.5.1968
Clarke,Kenny (dr) | Boland,Francy (p,arr) | Bailey,Benny (tp,fl-h) | Sulieman[Leonard Graham],Idrees (tp) | Deuchar,Jimmie (tp) | Grey,Sonny (tp) | Persson,Ake (tb) | Peck,Nat (tb) | Van Lier,Erik (tb) | Humble,Derek (as) | Griffin,Johnny (ts) | Scott,Ronnie (ts) | Coe,Tony (cl,ts) | Shihab,Sahib (fl,bs) | Pike,Dave (vib) | Woode,Jimmy (b) | Clare,Kenny (dr)

9814794 | CD | Changing Colors | EAN 602498147948
Nelson Riddle And His Orchestra
My Life | My Sweert Lord | Sao Paulo | Close To You | My One And Only Love | Lamento | When The World Was Young | Naomi | Changing Colors
München, rec. August 1971
Orchestra | details unknown | Riddle,Nelson (cond,arr)

9814795 | CD | Communication | EAN 602498147955
It's Your Turn | Uptown Dance | Time And Space | Romantic Places | Volcano's Daughter | Rachel | Bom Happy | A Night Of Love | Dedication | Greenwich Village
Orchestra | details unknown | Riddle,Nelson (cond,arr)

9814805 | CD | Francy Boland-Fellini 712 | EAN 602498148051
Kenny Clarke-Francy Boland Big Band
Fellini 712: | 1st Movement:Villa Radieuse | 2nd Movement:Tween Dusk And Down In Via Urbana | 3rd Movement:Rosati At Popolo Square
Köln, rec. 2./3.12.1968
Clarke,Kenny (dr) | Boland,Francy (p,arr) | Bailey,Benny (tp,fl-h) | Sulieman[Leonard Graham],Idrees (tp) | Deuchar,Jimmie (tp) | Goykovich,Dusko (tp,fl-h) | Persson,Ake (tb) | Peck,Nat (tb) | Van Lier,Erik (tb) | Humble,Derek (as) | Griffin,Johnny (ts) | Scott,Ronnie (ts) | Coe,Tony (cl,ts) | Shihab,Sahib (ss,bs) | Warland,Jean (b) | Clare,Kenny (dr)

9814806 | CD | Jankowskeynotes | EAN 602498148068
Horst Jankowski Orchestra With Voices
Baronesse | Soulful Strut | I'll Never Fall In Love Again | Preacherman's Daughter | Big Crwod | Elephant's Camp | How Short Is The Time For Love | Valdivia | Do You Know The Way To San Jose? | A Dance To Summer | Machribinia 4 5 | A Letter To Mr. B | Wichita Lineman
Stuttgart, rec. July 1970
Jankowski,Horst (p,clavinet) | Van Rooyen,Ack (tp,fl-h) | Herbolzheimer,Peter (tb) | Christmann,Egon (tb) | Rabe,Bernd (sax) | Wenzel,Hans (g) | Wendlandt,Götz (b) | Kovacev,Branislav (dr) | Gebhardt,Jörg (dr) | Jankowski Singers,The (voc-group)

Nabel Records:Jazz Network | nabelrecordsjazznetwork

CD 4601 | CD | Devil Dance
John Thomas & Lifeforce
Devil Dance | Mr.P | Vector | Maryke | Without Words(New Ballad) | Seven Kinds Of Jewels(Cha-Cha For A Jiyu) | The End
Köln, rec. 12.-23.5.1980
Thomas,John (g,comp) | Lumpp,Andy (p) | Plümer,Gunnar (b) | Kremer,Stefan (dr) | O'Bryan,Ponda (perc) | Linges,Monika (voc)

CD 4604 | CD | 3000 Worlds
3000 Worlds | 3 | 4 Ballade | As You Once Were | Promontory
Köln, rec. 22.-24.7.1981
Thomas,John (g) | Lumpp,Andy (p) | Plümer,Gunnar (b) | Morales,Garcia (dr) | O'Bryan,Ponda (perc) | Veldmann,Eddy (perc)
Like A Samba
Thomas,John (g) | Lumpp,Andy (p) | Plümer,Gunnar (b) | Morales,Garcia (dr) | O'Bryan,Ponda (perc) | Veldmann,Eddy (perc) | Linges,Monika (voc)

CD 4607 | CD | Floating
LP 4607(Audiophile) | LP | Floating
Monika Linges Quartet
Too Fond Samba | Till We Get There | Floating | Blues Triste | Running | La Danse Du Coeur | Prayer For The Newborn | The World Was Young
Aachen, rec. Jan.1982
Linges,Monika (voc) | Luxion,Dennis (p) | Schöneich,Michael (b) | Breuer,Gerd (dr)

CD 4612 | CD | Midnight Sun
LP 4612(Audiophile) | LP | Midnight Sun
Lumpp-Read-Küttner Trio
Der Kleine Prinz | Karin | Midnight Sun | Mondstein | Song For You | Fly On
Frankfurt/M, rec. 19.8.1983
Read,Hugo (ss,as) | Lumpp,Andy (p) | Küttner,Michael (perc)

CD 4613 | CD | Tango Subversivo
Jürgen Sturm's Ballstars
Tango Subversivo | Flick Flag | Tscha Tscha Para Abeja | Maybe We Should'nt | Rumba Meu Boi | 77 Throughshine Slip | Lotto Graf Lambsdorff | James' Bounce | Rann & Roll | Last Xango
Köln, rec. 19./20.3.1984
Sturm,Jürgen (g) | Jongen,Jel (tb) | Moschner,Pinguin (tuba) | Ramirez,Hugo (cl,ts) | Leuchter,Heribert (b-cl,as) | Sembritzki,Semel (ss,ts) | Bauer,Stefan (marimba) | Schöneich,Michael (b) | Rahier,Manfred (dr) | Leidner,Am (dr,perc)

CD 4614 | CD | The Spell
Klaus Ignatzek Group Feat.Dave Liebman
Trilogy(1) | Trilogy(2) | Trilogy(3) | A Taste Of Caramel | Mysterious Dream | The Spell | Katzenjammer
Stuttgart, rec. April/May 1984
Liebman,Dave (ss) | Ignatzek,Klaus (p) | Ilg,Dieter (b) | Ecker,Uwe (dr)

CD 4616 | CD | Tears Of Sound
Paul Shigihara-Charlie Mariano Quartet
Quasi Raga | N.C. Blues | Tango | Zana | Randy | Hymn | Lonely Woman
Köln, rec. 13.-15.11.1984
Shigihara,Paul (g,el-g,g-synth) | Mariano,Charlie (ss,as,wooden-fl) | Wells,Tim (b) | Küttner,Michael (dr,perc)

CD 4618 | CD | Drivin'
Engstfeld-Plümer-Weiss
Drivin' | Darn That Dream | Hackensack | Hills | Nardis | E.P.W. | Whims Of Chambers
Köln, rec. 8./9.5.1985
Engstfeld,Wolfgang (ts) | Plümer,Gunnar (b) | Weiss,Peter (dr)

CD 4623 | CD | Out To Lunch
Ullmann-Willers-Schäuble-Lorenz
Minus One | No Way | Crawler | No Rags | No Dinner | Kaspar Hauser | Concentration | Feels
Ludwigsburg, rec. 21.-23.11.1985
Ullmann Gebhard (ss,ts) | Willers,Andreas (g) | Lorenz,Hans-Dieter (b,el-b) | Schäuble,Nikolaus 'Niko' (dr)

CD 4624 | CD | Tomato Kiss
Tomato Kiss
Looking Out | Hanni And Her Cat | L'Italiana | Birds | Harry | Synchronicity | Nocturne | Get Lucky
Hamburg, rec. March 1986
Tomato Kiss | Beckerhoff,Uli (tp,piccolo-tp) | Schnelle,Rainer (synth,sequencer-programming) | Beier,Detlev (b) | Küttner,Michael (dr,perc)

CD 4628 | CD | Conversa
LP 4628 | LP | Conversa
Maria Joao Quintet
O Ronco Cuica- | Lush Life- | Them There Eyes | Closed System | Se Eu Quiser Falar Com Deus | A Uma Escrava Que Ihe Ocultou O Sol | Conversa
Köln, rec. April 1986
Joao,Maria (voc) | Fredebeul,Martin (fl,b-cl,ss,as) | Walter,Peter (marimba,p,tambourine) | Bica,Carlos (b) | Gröning,Peter (dr) | Küttner,Michael (perc,african-dr)

CD 4629 | CD | Camporondo
Uli Beckerhoff Trio
The Nature Line | Peter,The Genius And The Revolution | Somehow In September | Camporondo | Soft Movements | Farrah's Eye
details unknown, rec. details unknown
Beckerhoff,Uli (tp,keyboards) | Van't Hof,Jasper (keyboards) | Marshall,John (dr)

CD 4630 | CD | Live At Leverkusener Jazztage
Klaus Ignatzek Group
Blue Energy | In Good Spirits | Deformation | Conversation | A Wheel Within A Wheel | Ball Games
Jazz Festival,Leverkusen, rec. 1.11.1986
Ignatzek,Klaus (p) | Watson,Robert 'Bobby' (as) | Schwaller,Roman (ts) | Ilg,Dieter (b) | Gonzi,Mario (dr)

CD 4631 | CD | Gershwin Songs
Klaus Ignatzek
'S Wonderful | Summertime | But Not For Me | Liza | It Ain't Necessarily So | Oh! Lady Be Good | Strike Up The Band | Fascinating Rhythm | A Foggy Day(In London Town) | Someone To Watch Over Me
Monster,NL, rec. 27./28.7.1988
Ignatzek,Klaus (p-solo)

CD 4633 | CD | West End Avenue
Jim Pepper Quartet
Three For Gemini | Ballad For Nori | Traces Of Darkness | Hey New Day | Mr.R.B. | Sentimental Walk(Theme From Diva) | In The Hall
NYC, rec. 1.2.1989
Pepper,Jim (ts) | Spendel,Christoph (p) | McClure,Ron (b) | Hoch,Reuben (dr)

CD 4634 | CD | Wasserwüste
Die Elefanten
Rain | From The Beginning | The Flood | The Depth | Dream Of Plancton | Small Fish Big Fish | Inside The Whale | Man On Water | Winner? Loser? | Rain(take 2)
Berlin, rec. 8.6.1988
Elefanten,Die | Litty,Joachim (cl,as) | Ullmann Gebhard (fl,ss) | Rodach,Michael (g,el-g) | Kaulard,Gerd (b) | Moritz,Ulrich (perc) | Schäuble,Nikolaus 'Niko' (perc) | Staffa,Klaus M. (perc) | Weiser,Andreas (perc)

CD 4635 | CD | Forbidden City
Human Factor
Rainy Days | Jade Green | Abate Fetel | Canadian 4 | Taabo Taabo
Berlin, rec. details unknown
Human Factor | Heller,Volker (fl,ss,ts,keyboards) | Gertken,Klaus (keyboards)
Belfast Area
Human Factor | Heller,Volker (fl,ss,ts,keyboards) | Gertken,Klaus (keyboards) | Moritz,Ulrich (dr,perc,voc)
Tribute To S.M.
Human Factor | Heller,Volker (fl,ss,ts,keyboards) | Gertken,Klaus (keyboards) | Siebert,Stephan (b-g) | Moritz,Ulrich (dr,perc,voc)
Forbidden City
Human Factor | Heller,Volker (fl,ss,ts,keyboards) | Gertken,Klaus (keyboards) | Mieres,Sylvia (voc)
Fog In The Highlands
Human Factor | Heller,Volker (fl,ss,ts,keyboards) | Gertken,Klaus (keyboards)

CD 4636 | CD | Stay
Uli Beckerhoff Group
The Chinese Dog | Stay | Joe Is Watching You
Bremen, rec. details unknown
Beckerhoff,Uli (tp,piccolo-tp) | Berger,Michael (p,keyboards) | Beier,Detlev (b) | Ahlers,Jens (dr)
Dramatic Interplay | Critics,Promotors And Producers | Colours Of The Late Afternoon | Stop It
Beckerhoff,Uli (tp,piccolo-tp) | Nadolny,Matthias (ts) | Berger,Michael (p,keyboards) | Beier,Detlev (b) | Ahlers,Jens (dr)
Icy Desert
Beckerhoff,Uli (tp,piccolo-tp) | Weber,Serge (keyboards) | Berger,Michael (p,keyboards) | Beier,Detlev (b) | Ahlers,Jens (dr)

CD 4637 | CD | Mr. Max!
LP 4637 | LP | Mr. Max!
Randy Brecker-Wolfgang Engstfeld Quartet
Mr.Max | Bumble Bee Blues | Lover Man(Oh,Where Can You Be?) | Moonlift | Waltz For Pee Wee | Poinciana | Easy Living | Anika | On Green Dolphin Street | New Place
Monster,NL, rec. 22./23.5.1989
Brecker,Randy (tp) | Engstfeld,Wolfgang (ts) | Plümer,Gunnar (b) | Weiss,Peter (dr)

CD 4638 | CD | Das Kurt Weill Programm
Anirahtak und die Jürgen Sturm Band
Die Moritat Von Mackie Messer | Die Seeräuber Jenny | Die Zuhälter Ballade | Der Kanonsong | Und Was Bekam Des Soldaten Weib | Das Lied Von Den Braunen Inseln | Muschel Von Margate(Petroleum Song) | Klops Lied | Es Regnet
Aachen, rec. September 1989
Anirahtak (voc) | Sturm,Jürgen (g) | Singer,Ludger (tb,el-orchestrion) | Galle,Lothar (b) | Rahier,Manfred (dr)

CD 4639 | CD | Day For Night
LP 4639 | LP | Day For Night
Klaus Ignatzek Group
Day For Night | Three Wishes | New Surprise | Beautiful Colours | Blue Energy | Ballad For Vivi | Monk's Visit
Monster,NL, rec. 3./4.10.1989
Ignatzek,Klaus (p) | Henderson,Joe (ts) | Rassinfosse,Jean-Louis (b) | Dudli,Joris (dr)

CD 4640 | CD | Per-Dee-Doo
Gebhard Ullmann Quartet
Seven Come Eleven | Perdido | 502 Blues | St.Thomas | Ida Lupino | Satin Doll | Epistrophy | Fall | Blue In Green
Monster,NL, rec. 25./26.7.1989
Ullmann,Gebhard (fl,ts) | Rodach,Michael (g,el-g) | Lillich,Martin (b) | Schäuble,Nikolaus 'Niko' (dr)
Georgia On My Mind
Ullmann,Gebhard (ts) | Rodach,Michael (g) | Lillich,Martin (b) | Schäuble,Nikolaus 'Niko' (dr)

CD 4641 | CD | S'Nice
LP 4641 | LP | S'Nice
Lee Konitz-Frank Wunsch Quartet
October Walk | Remember | So Nice(Summer Samba) | February Waltz | The Nearness Of You | Trio Con Arco | Every Time We Say Goodbye | Impression(No.1-4) | It's You- | Match
Monster,NL, rec. 18./19.6.1990
Konitz,Lee (ss,as) | Wunsch,Frank (p) | Plümer,Gunnar (b) | Haberer,Christoph (dr)

CD 4642 | CD | Choral Concert
LP 4642(Audiophile) | LP | Choral Concert
Karl Scharnweber Trio
Erhalt Uns, Herr Bei Deinam Wort | Gott Ist Gegenwärtig | Herr Jesus, Gnadensonne | Ich Grüße Dich Am Kreuzesstamm | Nun Bitten Wir Den Heiligen Geist | Die Nacht Ist Kommen | Der Herr Ist Mein Getreuer Hirt | Der Du Die Zeit In Händen Hast
Johanneskirche, Neubrandenburg, rec. 26./28.7.1990
Scharnweber,Karl (church-org) | Klemm,Thomas (fl,ts) | Schmiedt,Wolfgang (g,el-g)

CD 4643 | CD | Plays Beatles Songs
Klaus Ignatzek
Penny Lane | Lucy In The Sky With Diamonds | Can't Buy Me Love | Yesterdays | Norwegian Wood | The Fool On The Hill | Lady Madonna | Eleanor Rigby | Hey Jude
Monster,NL, rec. 27./28.8.1990
Ignatzek,Klaus (p-solo)

CD 4644 | CD | West End Avenue II
Lance Bryant With The Christoph Spendel Trio
Fancy Colours | Back To Normal | Boulevard | Cosmic Song | West End Avenue | Monday Night | Carey Line | Brooklyn Bridge | Strange Times | City Speed
Brooklyn,NY, rec. September 1990
Bryant,Lance (ss,ts) | Spendel,Christoph (p,keyboards) | Plaxico,Lonnie (b,el-b) | Hoch,Reuben (dr)

CD 4646 | CD | Piano Solo | EAN 4011471464624
Andy Lumpp
Enter The Malesh(for Handy Van Baren) | Azimuth(for Renate Otta) | Enter The Malesh | Azimuth | Dancing With A Beautiful Lady(for Galel) | Wiener Peter | Angela | Dancing With A Beautiful Lady | Neuland(for Garcia Morales)
Köln, rec. June 1982
Borderline(for Paco Leva) | Endzeit | Wiener Gerd | Borderline | Neuland
Lumpp,Andy (p-solo)

CD 4647 | CD | Secret Obsession
LP 4647(Audiophile) | LP | Secret Obsession
Uli Beckerhoff Quartet
Secret Obsession | Follow Her Heart | Crisis Stuff | If You Look Far Enough | Lady M. | Monkey Monkey Do
Frankfurt/M, rec. 26.10.1990
Beckerhoff,Uli (tp) | Abercrombie,John (g) | Andersen,Arild (b) | Marshall,John (dr)

CD 4648 | CD | ToGether
LP 4648(Audiophile) | LP | ToGether
Brecker-Engstfeld-Plümer-Weiss
Uptown Downunder | Last Chance | When I Fall In Love | Moontide | Completely Different | Body And Soul | Canada | Tetris | I've Grown Accustomed To Her Face | Shiny Stockings
Köln, rec. June/July 1991
Brecker,Randy (tp,el-tp) | Engstfeld,Wolfgang (ts) | Plümer,Gunnar (b) | Weiss,Peter (dr)

CD 4649 | CD | Suite Noire
Gebhard Ullmann-Andreas Willers
Autumn Leaves | Blaues Lied | L'Aurá
NYC/Ludwigsburg, rec. January/August 1990
Ullmann Gebhard (alto-fl,b-cl,ss,ts,b-fl) | Willers,Andreas (g,el-g,g-synth)
Gebhard Ullmann Trio
Suite Noire: | Low-Liness- | Ein Denkmal Für Rosa Und Karl- | Sudan Airways Loop- | Solo- | La Prima Vera- | Twelve Tone Stomp-
Ullmann Gebhard (alto-fl,b-cl,ss,ts,b-fl) | Willers,Andreas (g,el-g,g-synth) | Stewart,Robert 'Bob' (tuba) (dr)
Lonely Woman- | Double Density- | Departure | Trapping The Foot, Trapping The Brain
Ullmann Gebhard (alto-fl,b-cl,ss,ts,b-fl) | Willers,Andreas (g,el-g,g-synth) | Smith,Marvin 'Smitty' (dr,perc,perc-sample)

CD 4650 | CD | Coral Concert II/Another View
LP 4650(Audiophile) | LP | Coral Concert II/Another View
Karl Scharnweber Trio
Ist Gott Für Mich | Komm,Gott Schöpfer,Heiliger Geist | Von Gott Will Ich Nicht Lassen | Oh Haupt Voll Blut Und Wunden | Mein Schönste Zier Und Kleinod | Befiehl Du Deine Wege | Vater Unser Im Himmelreich | Verleih Uns Frieden Gnädiglich
St.Petri Dom,Schleswig, rec. 5./8.2.1992
Scharnweber,Karl (church-org) | Klemm,Thomas (fl,ts) | Schmiedt,Wolfgang (g,el-g)

CD 4651 | CD | Airballoon
LP 4651(Audiophile) | LP | Airballoon
Klaus Ignatzek Trio
You And The Night And The Music | Airballoon | Come Back To Me | Portret De Iubire | 'S Wonderful | Everything Happens To Me | You Don't Know What Love Is | Too Soon Too Late | Our Blues
Monster,NL, rec. 31.3./1.4.1992
Ignatzek,Klaus (p) | Rassinfosse,Jean-Louis (b) | Parghel,Anca (voc)

CD 4652 | CD | Search
Martin Fredebeul Quartet
Nardis | Pee Wee | Night And Day | Leaving | You Don't Know What Love Is
Aachen, rec. 2./3.4.1992
Fredebeul,Martin (b-cl,ss) | Erbstösser,Christoph (p,synth) | Van Der Hoeven,Frans (b) | Lehan,Marc (dr)

CD 4653 | CD | Songs Of A Wayfarer
Hugo Read Group
Altonality | Song Of A Wayfarer | Music,After Stories From The 'Thousand And One Nights': | Sultan's Theme- | Scheherazade- | Arabian Night- | Young Prince And Princess- | Shipwreck On The Magnetic Rock- | Land Of Desolation,Land Of Mist | Hyperion's Song Of Destiny | The Light In The Dark | Alto Music
Köln, rec. April/May 1992
Read,Hugo (ss,as) | Winterschladen,Reiner (tp) | Fink,Achim (tb,tuba) | Walter,Peter (p) | Rogall,Volker (p,synth) | Plümer,Gunnar (b) | Thönes,Jo (dr)

CD 4654 | CD | Today Is Tomorrow/Live In Leverkusen
Klaus Ignatzek Quintet
Today Is Tomorrow | Yours Truly | Who's Smoking? | Flowers Around Midnight | Sunny Island | One Milestone | The Answer | What A B.T.
Live,at 'Jazztage' Leverkusen, rec. 19.10.1991
Ignatzek,Klaus (p) | Roditi,Claudio (tp) | Bergalli,Gustavo (tp) | Rassinfosse,Jean-Louis (b) | Dudli,Joris (dr)

CD 4655 | CD | Berlin-Paris-New York/Music By Kurt Weil
Anirahtak und die Jürgen Sturm Band
Denn Wovon Lebt Der Mensch | Matrosen Tango | Alabama Song | Youkali | Complainte De La Seine | Speak Low | September Song | Wie Lange Noch? | My Ship
Monster,NL, rec. 15./16.9.1992
Anirahtak (voc) | Sturm,Jürgen (g) | Singer,Ludger (tb,keyboards) | Galle,Lothar (el-b) | Rahier,Manfred (dr)

CD 4656 | CD | Carpathian Colors
Anca Parghel
Doina Olt | Sirba In Caruta | Maramu | Toaca De Paste | Rumanian Rapsody | Buco | Toccata | Vrancea | Oas | Bucovina | Andante | Cintec De Legan
Monster,NL, rec. 10./11.5.1993
Parghel,Anca (p,voc)

CD 4657 | CD | Private Life
Uli Beckerhoff Septet
Private Life | Elegia Cascais | It Could Be You | Milen | Victor | Dee Gee | Kindertraum | Don't Throw Your Heart Away | Omerta
Bremen, rec. 1992
Beckerhoff,Uli (tp) | Nadolny,Matthias (ts) | Abercrombie,John (g) | Taylor,John (p) | Berger,Michael (keyboards) | Plümer,Gunnar (b) | Thönes,Jo (dr)

CD 4658 | CD | Songs And Ballads
Wolfgang Engstfeld Quartet
Spring Can Really Hang You Up The Most | For You | Ode To Sammy Davis Jr. | Bad Girl | Never Ending Nights | Blue Ballad | Joy In A Scene From Sadness | Early Summer | Ballad | Parting | Spring
Düsseldorf, rec. May 1993
Engstfeld,Wolfgang (ts) | Degen,Bob (p) | Eckinger,Isla (b) | Weiss,Peter (dr)

CD 4659 | CD | Playful '93
Gebhard Ullmann-Andreas Willers
Mass Ritual | Hverdag | Macondo | The Listening Room | Beirut | Backyard Thang | Schlafende Hunde | Sleeping In | Berliner Zimmer
different Places, rec. 1988-1993
Ullmann Gebhard (alto-fl,b-cl,ss,ts,b-fl) | Willers,Andreas (g,perc)
Juliusstraße 25
Ullmann Gebhard (alto-fl,b-cl,ss,ts,b-fl) | Willers,Andreas (g,perc,tape) | Schoyble,Niko (dr-machine)
Sixty One
Ullmann Gebhard (alto-fl,b-cl,ss,ts,b-fl) | Willers,Andreas (g,perc) | Wasdanis,Christian[Kristian] (tablas)
Lam Earth
Ullmann Gebhard (alto-fl,b-cl,ss,ts,b-fl,tape) | Willers,Andreas (g,perc)
Petite Marché
Ullmann Gebhard (alto-fl,b-cl,ss,ts,b-fl) | Willers,Andreas (g,perc) | Stewart,Robert 'Bob' (tuba) | Smith,Marvin 'Smitty' (dr)

CD 4660 | CD | Son Of Gaudi
Klaus Ignatzek Quintet
What A B.T. | Son Of Gaudi | Ballad For G.B. | Nails | Number One | No More Troubles | There Is No Greater Love
Live at The 'Domicile',Dortmund, rec. December 1992
Ignatzek,Klaus (p) | Roditi,Claudio (tp) | Bergalli,Gustavo (tp) | Rassinfosse,Jean-Louis (b) | Rossy,Jorge 'Jordi' (dr)

CD 4661 | CD | Paintings
Céline Rudolph And Her Trio
I Feel The Ocean But She's On The Other Side | Frame-Up | Pintura Desse Mundo | Mystery Of Green And Black | Fuji Colors | Creep Into Your Dream | Dungo | And These Few Words - ...And These Few Words | Erotic Lines | Manu | Beyond The Horizon | Home
Ludwigsburg, rec. April/June 1993
Rudolph,Céline (voc) | Kottenhahn,Volker (p) | Strakhof,Dirk (b) | Bockholt,Johannes (dr)

CD 4662 | CD | Dreamin' Man
Andy Lumpp
Oliver | Summermorning | Anja | Ratte | Gerrit's Broken Silence | All The Things You Where | Diana | To Walk Back Home
Monster,NL, rec. 21.11.1993
Lumpp,Andy (p-solo)

CD 4663 | CD | Into The Afro-Latin Bag
Hipsters In The Zone
Ayola | Hipsters In The Zone | Peace To | Hellas | Waterloop
Düsseldorf, rec. August 1994
Hipsters In The Zone | Witzel,Reiner (fl,ts) | Haus,Matthias (vib,perc) | Fischer,Xaver (p) | Foltynowicz,Jens (b) | Weiss,Peter (dr,perc)
Tobago
Hipsters In The Zone | Witzel,Reiner (ts) | Haus,Matthias (vib) | Fischer,Xaver (p) | Foltynowicz,Jens (b) | Weiss,Peter (dr) | Zieburg,Martin (perc)
Stepping | Saudade | Time Of Change
Hipsters In The Zone | Witzel,Reiner (fl,ts) | Haus,Matthias (vib,perc) | Fischer,Xaver (p) | Foltynowicz,Jens (b) | Weiss,Peter (dr,perc) | Linges,Monika (voc)

CD 4664 | CD | Haiku
Lee Konitz Quartet
There Is A Sun Chase | The Man Who Came To Dinner | Fun Keys | Steinolphonk | Geraldo | Ittle Onk Usik | The Princess | Nuts | Egyptian Caravan | Rudimentär
Berlin, rec. November 1994
Konitz,Lee (as,voice) | Mahall,Rudi (b-cl,turntable) | Schmidt,Andreas (p,voice) | Granelli,Jerry (dr,perc,voice)
Hi-Lee | Uki-Ah | Freezoo
Konitz,Lee (as,voice) | Mahall,Rudi (b-cl,turntable) | Schmidt,Andreas (p,voice) | Granelli,Jerry (dr,perc,voice) | Yoshida,Sayumi (voice)

CD 4665 | CD | Andreas Willers & Friends Play Jimi Hendrix:Experience
Andreas Willers Group
Burning Of The Midnight Lamp | Manic Depression | Purple Haze | Burglar King
Berlin, rec. January 1995
Willers,Andreas (g,el-g) | Schippa,Jörg (g) | Stolterfoht,Jan (g) | Meinhold,Boris (g) | Nonnenmacher,Horst (b) | Schäuble,Nikolaus 'Niko' (dr)
If Six Was Nine
Willers,Andreas (el-sitar) | Nonnenmacher,Horst (b) | Schäuble,Nikolaus 'Niko' (perc)
Castles Made Of Sand | Lyric Collection-
Berlin, rec. November 1994
Willers,Andreas (g,el-g) | Nonnenmacher,Horst (b) | Black,Jim (dr,perc) | Hasler,Gabriele (voc)
Angel | Crack House Blues | Who Knows | Voodoo Chile- | Voodoo Child(Slight Return)-
Willers,Andreas (g,melodica) | Nonnenmacher,Horst (b) | Black,Jim (dr,perc)
Foxy Lady
Berlin, rec. January 1995
Willers,Andreas (g) | Huke,Jörg (tb) | Nonnenmacher,Horst (b) | Schäuble,Nikolaus 'Niko' (dr)
Sept. 21st, 1966 | Tricons
Willers,Andreas (g,el-g,sampling)

CD 4666 | CD | Original Motion Picture Soundtrack:Das Geheimnis(Secret Of Love)
Uli Beckerhoff Quintet
Das Geheimnis | Ankunft | Annäherung | Die Einladung | Die Liebe | Landpartie | Uckermark | Winter | Am See | Lydia | Der Mann Mit Dem Kreuz | Die Familie | Sarah
Bremen, rec. October 1994
Beckerhoff,Uli (tp) | Nadolny,Matthias (ts,melodica) | Berger,Michael (p,keyboards) | Plümer,Gunnar (b) | Thönes,Jo (dr)

CD 4667 | CD | You'll Never Walk Alone
Matthias Nadolny-Gunnar Plümer
Everything Happens To Me | Hüppekästchen | Conversation In A Flat | Fupsi | Ameckestr.29 | There Are Such Things | Okevi | For Dolphy | Nature Boy | Waltz For Pee Wee | There Is No Greater Love
Dortmund, rec. December 1993/January 1994
Nadolny,Matthias (ts,melodica) | Plümer,Gunnar (b)

CD 4668 | CD | Passage To The Ear
Reiner Witzel Group
The World Within | Distant Desire | Explorer
Monster,NL, rec. 27./28.6.& 7.7.1995
Witzel,Reiner (fl,ss,ts,didjeridoo) | Soloff,Lew (tp) | Adams,Christoph (p,keyboards) | Heinze,Volker (b) | Astor,Felix (dr)
T.K. On A Mission | Chillin' | A Night In Bongolia
Witzel,Reiner (fl,ss,ts,didjeridoo) | Soloff,Lew (tp) | Adams,Christoph (p,keyboards) | Heinze,Volker (b) | Astor,Felix (dr) | Peil,Roland (perc)
Passage To The Ear(part 1) | Late Night | Passage To The Ear(part 2)
Witzel,Reiner (fl,ss,ts,didjeridoo) | Soloff,Lew (tp) | Adams,Christoph (p,keyboards) | Heinze,Volker (b) | Astor,Felix (dr) | Peil,Roland (perc) | Duke T. (rap)

CD 4669 | CD | Personal Choice
Peter Weiss Quartet
In A Sentimental Mood
Live in Bremen, rec. May 1988
Weiss,Peter (dr) | Read,Hugo (as) | Lumpp,Andy (p) | Beier,Detlev (b)
Peter Weiss Sextet
Kairo
Bonn, rec. January 1988
Weiss,Peter (dr) | Pilz,Michel (b-cl) | Read,Hugo (as) | Plümer,Gunnar (b) | Schmidt,Jochen (el-b) | Gillmann,Andy (perc)
Peter Weiss Orchestra
Into The Light
Köln, rec. September 1990
Weiss,Peter (dr) | Gottschalk,Norbert (tp) | Beckerhoff,Uli (tp) | Read,Hugo (as) | Engstfeld,Wolfgang (ts) | Lumpp,Andy (p) | Kracht,Hartmut (b) | Küttner,Michael (perc)
Ballad
Weiss,Peter (dr) | Beckerhoff,Uli (tp) | Read,Hugo (as) | Engstfeld,Wolfgang (ts) | Lumpp,Andy (p) | Kracht,Hartmut (b) | Küttner,Michael (perc) | Gottschalk,Norbert (voc)
Peter Weiss Quartet
So In Love
Live in Köln, rec. October 1991
Weiss,Peter (dr) | Engstfeld,Wolfgang (ts) | Kaufmann,Achim (p) | Kracht,Hartmut (b)
I've Grown Accustomed To Her Face
Live at Stadtgarten,Köln, rec. September 1993
Weiss,Peter (dr) | Engstfeld,Wolfgang (ts) | Degen,Bob (p) | Plümer,Gunnar (b)
Peter Weiss
Interlude 1 | Interlude 2 | Interlude 3 | Interlude 4
Düsseldorf, rec. July 1995
Weiss,Peter (dr)
Peter Weiss-Paul Imm
Loop De Loop
Weiss,Peter (dr) | Imm,Paul (b)
Peter Weiss-Claus Fischer
Starter
Weiss,Peter (dr) | Fischer,Claus (el-b)

CD 4670 | CD | New Directions
Heinrich Von Kalnein Group
Melange | Arizona Stars(dedicated to Judith) | Drahtseilakt | Cosmic Chicken | Stainach Song | The Three Madonnas | Heitzmann's Delight | Place Pigalle | Dark Tales
Ludwigsburg, rec. May & July 1995
Von Kalnein,Heinrich (sax,EWI) | Lindvall,Lars (tp) | Spanyi,Emil (p) | Sieverts,Henning (b) | Salfellner,Christian (dr)

CD 4671 | CD | Welcome To The Maze:Puzzle
Welcome To The Maze
Two Magpies | I Didn't Know What Time It Was | Garden Of Devotion | She Expected A Caress | Waves | Breath | Say Yes | What Are Days For | My Favorite Things | Walking In A Maze
Monster,NL, rec. 13./14.1.1995
Welcome To The Maze | Fischer,Sören (tb) | Kottenhahn,Volker (p) | Cordes,Daniel 'Danda' (b) | Düwer,Sönke (dr) | Flex,Britta-Ann (voc)

CD 4672 | CD | Book Of Travels
Céline Rudolph And Her Trio
Solidao | Soumolé | Earth Chant | Der Betrunkene Pinguin | Drunken Penguin
A-Trane Club,Berlin, rec. 17./18.10.1995
Rudolph,Céline (voc) | Kottenhahn,Volker (p) | Strakhof,Dirk (b) | Bockholt,Johannes (dr)

CD 4673 | CD | Trad Corrosion
Ullmann-Wille-Haynes
Etude Part 3 | D.Nee No | Windchime | Princess | Heaven No.2.5 | Wealthy Clients | Etude Part 1 | Juliusstraße 25 | Gospel | Sit Sofort | Etude Part 2 | Variationen Über 'Rauch Und Moder' | Snaring A Yotte | Oberschöneweide | Diffusion 8 | Flying In A Nutshell | Jan Lukas | Heaven No.2.6 | Etude Part 4
Berlin, rec. 24.-26.4.1995
Ullmann Gebhard (woodwinds) | Willers,Andreas (g,el-g,melodica,sitar,slide-g) | Haynes,Phil (dr)

CD 4674 | CD | Frank Talk
House Five
Frank Talk | I Like That | Keep On | Rapid Speed | Brighter Days | Blow Your Mind | How Time Flies
Genk,Belgium, rec. 26./29.12.1995
House Five | Valk,Claudius (ss,ts) | Schimmeroth,Alex (p,el-p,synth) | Morsey,Alexander (b,el-b) | Maichel,Golo (dr) | Tunja F.M. (rap,voc)

CD 4675 | CD | Coast To Coast
Richard Carr Trio
In A Maze | Saranac By Starlight | Bypass | Headfake | A Chicken Named Fido | Too Much Grey | I Wanna Smell That Thing | Metal Winds | Abf
Brooklyn,NY, rec. 28.1.1996
Carr,Richard (v) | Nord,Mike (g,electronics) | Hofmann,Georg (perc)

CD 4676 | CD | On The Trail
Till Martin Quintet
Unfold Twice | Keep The Heavens Beautiful | I Like Fish | Late Afternoon | Hesitation | Soul Eyes | On The Trail(From The Grand Canyon Suite) | Small Feet
München, rec. 18.9.1996
Martin,Till (ts) | Mears,Adrian (tb) | Schmid,Stefan (p) | Stabenow,Thomas (b) | May,Guido (dr)

CD 4677 | CD | Pisces
Heinrich Köbberling-Matt Renzi Quartet
Grey Van Livelihood | Peggy's Blue Skylight | Trumpet | How Doo's | Nice Pants For Everybody | Pisces | Without A Song | Love Saves The Day | Time Remembered | Zapp
NYC, rec. 9.3.1997
Köbberling,Heinrich (dr) | Renzi,Matt (sax) | Monder,Ben (g) | Johnson,Marc (b)

CD 4678 | CD | Elegy For Africa
Nils Petter Molvaer Group
Batoru
Live at Passionskirche,Berlin, rec. 7.6.1996
Molvaer,Nils Petter (tp) | Moritz,Ulrich (perc)
Birds Of Passage | Doundounba | Ballad For Tinga Tinga
Molvaer,Nils Petter (tp) | Fischer,Sören (tb) | Goodhew,Denney (b-cl,ss,as,sopranino) | Bauer,Franz (vib,marimba) | Strakhof,Dirk (b) | Moritz,Ulrich (perc)
Drumbeats And Heartbeats | Africa And Aviation
Molvaer,Nils Petter (tp) | Fischer,Sören (tb) | Goodhew,Denney (b-cl,ss,as,sopranino) | Bauer,Franz (vib,marimba) | Strakhof,Dirk (b) | Moritz,Ulrich (perc) | Malik,Sharifa Dietra (voc)
Once Upon A Time
Molvaer,Nils Petter (tp) | Goodhew,Denney (b-cl) | Bauer,Franz (vib,marimba) | Strakhof,Dirk (b) | Moritz,Ulrich (perc) | Malik,Sharifa Dietra (voc)
Never Disturb A Ballaphon Player At Work
Goodhew,Denney (b-cl) | Bauer,Franz (marimba)

CD 4679 | CD | In The Midst Of Change
Tim Sund Quintet
Prologue | Lost Hills Road(Song Of The Seeker) | In The Traffic(Song For The Modern World) | Erilinda(Song Of Love) | Blue Trees(Song Of Fantasy) | In The Midst Of Change | Devi(Song Of The Childhood) | Ananta(Song Of Creation) | And Flowers Pick Themselves(Song Of Hope) | Traps(Song Of The Hidden Path) | Stralsund(Song Of Memories)

NYC, rec. 19./20.6.1997
Sund,Tim (p) | Frahm,Joel (ss,ts) | Hübner,Gregor (v) | Brown,Mark P. (b) | Griefingholt,Andreas (dr,perc)

CD 4680 | CD | Out Of Print
Volker Kottenhahn Trio
High Dee | Fishland Canyon | Joy | Confidence | His Last Wish | Cherry | Jerry's Mood | Waltz For Snoopy
Live at The A-Train Jazzclub,Berlin, rec. 8./9.9.& 18.11.1998
Kottenhahn,Volker (p) | Strakhof,Dirk (b) | Bockholt,Johannes (dr)

CD 4681 | CD | Orlando Fragments
Friedemann Graef Group
Reinforzamento..The Healing Force | Una Lotta Machinosa(And A New Delaying Tactic) | Canzone Dolce:Unresistable! | The Sunny Jingle Of The Camino De Cadaques | Impressione Impreciso | Il Monstro Saltando After Having Eaten The Turkish Dancer | Aqua Rapida | Simultanuos Images Of Queen Nofretete | Sonnifero Per Inamorati | The Soulful Turnaround Of Giovanni Sebastiano B. | Aterragio Africano:Do Not Remain Seated! | Il Canto Della Sierra
Berlin, rec. 3.9.1998
Graef,Friedemann (b-cl,ss,ts,bass-sax) | Schippa,Jörg (g,electronics) | Moritz,Ulrich (dr,perc)

CD 4682 | CD | Ostara
Andy Lumpp Trio
Michaela Sofia | Ostara | Mediane | Balladin | For 'M' Dance | Free Bop | Rast
Live at Kulturhaus Dormagen, rec. 27.3.1999
Lumpp,Andy (p) | Chastca,Heinrich (b) | Hoelker,Stefan (perc)

CD 4683 | CD | Along The Edge
Richard Carr Trio
In The Shade | Headline Suite:Lovers Shot On Bosnian Bridge | Appalachian Gamelan | Shep's Carr- | Heads- | Druids | David's Tumbao- | 32 Lunch- | Leavin' It | Fanfare For A Timeshare- | Muldoon In June- | Untitled Train- | Marie
Hardstudios,?,CH, rec. 1.7.?
Carr,Richard (v) | Nord,Mike (g,el-g,electronics) | Hofmann,Georg (perc)
Oilator
NYC, rec. 30.12.?
Carr,Richard (v) | Nord,Mike (g,el-g,electronics) | Hofmann,Georg (perc)

CD 4684 | CD | Das Lied
Erika Rojo & Tim Sund
Kennst Du Das Land | Nana | Asturiana | Silent Noon | In Der Fremde | Cancion- | Auf Erden Und Im Paradies- | Auf Erden | Und | Im Paradies | An Die Musik
Berlin, rec. 28.-30.5.1999
Rojo,Erika (voc) | Sund,Tim (p) | Heintz,David (g,el-g) | Strakhof,Dirk (b) | Schönburg,Kai (dr)

CD 4685 | CD | Tree Of Sounds
Batoru
Oriental Line | Mawdo | Zagreb | Slow Dark | Refugees | Right Shoes | Time For The Tupan | Katinka's Ballad | Bouché | Jimmy
Berlin, rec. 28./29.6.1999
Batoru | Bauer,Franz (vib,marimba) | Raichov,Peter (accordeon) | Strakhof,Dirk (b) | Yankoulov,Stoyan (perc,tupan) | Schiefel,Michael (voice)

CD 4686 | CD | The Rains From A Cloud Do Not Wet The Sky
Joel Frahm Quintet
Hunting Shadows | Beirach | Drifting | Dr. Dee Dee | The Hill Of Love | Jumping Jack | Uma Nuvam No Céu(Prelude To The Rains) | The Rains From A Cloud Do Not Wet The Sky | Towers Of Faith | Stretch The Match
Berlin, rec. 19./20.9.1999
Frahm,Joel (ss,ts) | Hübner,Gregor (v) | Sund,Tim (p) | Bica,Carlos (b) | Griefingholt,Andreas (dr)

CD 4687 | CD | Music From Planet Earth
Andy Lumpp Trio With Andy Przybielski
Hallo! | Andy & Andy | Crying In Hiroshima | Meloman | Action | Chet | Dance For M | Trubadur | Pepit | Carnival | Music From Planet Earth | Code
Kulturhaus Dormagen, rec. 8.3.2000
Lumpp,Andy (p) | Przybielski,Andy (tp) | Chastca,Heinrich (b) | Hoelker,Stefan (perc)

CD 4690 | CD | Orlando Frames | EAN 4011471469025
Graef-Schippa-Moritz
The Tiger Trap | Slamboat | Orlando's Evening Prayer | The Pakistani Fruit Box | Zep Di | Thought Of Happines | The Breeze From Orlando's Shore | Orlando's Midtown Anthem | Orlando's Endless Silver Wake | The Orinoco Paddle Stick | Mud On Face | The Funky Girl's Broken Heel | He Said | Teaching A Rat To Sing | Rapped From The Circus Tent | Punkoholic | Tröste Dich | Carved From The Monkey's Cage | NamNamSuri | Let Me Tell You A Xmas Night Farewell
SFB-Studio, rec. 3.5.2001
Graef,Friedemann (b-cl,ss,ts,bass-sax) | Schippa,Jörg (g,electronics) | Moritz,Ulrich (dr,perc)

CD 4691 | CD | Piano Solo | EAN 4011471469124
Klaus Ignatzek
Oh! Lady Be Good | Springdale | Norwegian Wood | But Not For Me | Penny Lane | Moin,Moin | It Ain't Necessarily So | Summertime | Liza | African Flower | Peace
Greifswald, rec. 29.11.2001
Ignatzek,Klaus (p-solo)

CD 4692 | CD | Trialogue | EAN 4011471469223
Tim Sund Trio
Nardis | Puzzle 1499 | Blue In Green | When Will The Blues Leave | Trialogue No.1: | The Cage Map | Hidden Rhapody | Trialogue No.2: | Let's Open The Year! | El Rojo | Trialogue No.3: | A Deeper Season | The Peacocks | Trialogue No.4: | The Evergreen Terrace | Ravi
SFB-Studio Berlin, rec. July 2001
Sund,Tim (p) | Lillich,Martin (b) | Kersting,Michael (dr)

CD 4693 | CD | Joe-Jack | EAN 4011471469322
Vasilic Nenad Balkan Band
Na Uskrs Sam Se Rodila | Nishijski Chochek-Joe-Jack | Stade Se | Oj Kceri Moja | Sila Kale Bal | Zapevala Sojka Ptica | Balld For Djole
Wien,Austria, rec. 30.6./1.7.2002
Nenad,Vasilic (b) | Simion,Nicolas (ss,ts) | Heckel,Stefan (p) | Novakov,Dusan (dr)
Jovane Mori Jovane | I Barval Pudela
Nenad,Vasilic (b) | Simion,Nicolas (ss,ts) | Heckel,Stefan (p) | Novakov,Dusan (dr) | Peric

CD 4694 | CD | Musica Ex Spiritu Sancto | EAN 4011471469421
Andy Lumpp Trio Feat. Andy Przybielski
Musica Ex Spiritu Sancto(part 1-8)
Kloster Knechtsteden, rec. 17.6.2001
Lumpp,Andy (p) | Przybielski,Andy (tp) | Chastca,Heinrich (b) | Hoelker,Stefan (perc)

CD 4696 | CD | Arabesque | EAN 4011471469629
Dirk Strakhof & Batoru
My Temple | Dogs From Afar | Kriv Sadosko | Donau | Kite | Holland | Home | Close To The Black Sea | Heat | At Last
Berlin, rec. 25./26.& 28.3.2002
Strakhof,Dirk (b) | Ralchev,Petar (accordeon) | Bauer,Franz (vib,marimba) | Yankoulov,Stoyan (perc,tupan) | Schiefel,Michael (voc)

CD 4697 | CD | Americana | EAN 4011471469728
Tim Sund & Tom Christensen Quartet
Americana | New Chances | The Watcher & The Moon | Akira | Vashkar | Pit Jazz | Nozomi(The Secret Garden) | The Cosmic Lawn
NYC, rec. 4./5.5.2002
Christensen,Thomas 'Tom' (alto-fl,engl-h,b-cl,ss,ts) | Sund,Tim (p) | Allison,Ben (b) | Kersting,Michael (dr)

CD 4698 | CD | Concentric Cycles | EAN 4011471469827
Kostas Konstantinou-Vassilis Tsabropoulos
Concentric Cycles | Apartement 103 | Remembrance | Bad Ladder | Isomnia | Guided Tour | In Thought... | Road Ends | Internal Affairs
Athens,Greece, rec. 13.3.2002
Tsabropoulos,Vassilis (p) | Konstantinou,Kostas (b)

Nagel-Heyer | Nagel Heyer Records GmbH

CD 001 | CD | The Wonderful World Of George Gershwin
George Masso Allstars
Strike Up The Band | But Not For Me | Summertime | Soon | Oh! Lady Be Good | Somebody Loves Me | Porgy And Bess Medley | I've Got A Crush On You | 'S Wonderful
Live at Musikhalle Hamburg, rec. 26.9.1992
Masso,George (tb) | Sandke,Randy (tp) | Davern,Kenny (cl) | Moss,Danny (ts) | Higgins,Eddie (p) | Skeat,Len (b) | Hanna,Jake (dr)

CD 003 | CD | Broadway
The New York Allstars
Broadway | Moten Swing | Round About Midnight | Rosetta | When It's Sleepy Time Down South | In A Mellow Tone | After You've Gone | Bye Bye Blackbird | On The Sunny Side Of The Street | It's All Right With Me | Basin Street Blues | Mack The Knife(Moritat)
Hamburg, rec. 2.5.1993
New York All Stars,The | Sandke,Randy (tp,ld) | Barrett,Dan (tb) | Robinson,Scott (ts,bs,co) | Shane,Mark (p) | Grosz,Marty (g,voc) | Milliman,Linc (b) | Ratajczak,Dave (dr) | Peplowski,Ken (dr)

CD 004 | CD | A Salute To Eddie Condon
A Salute To Eddie Condon
California Here I Come | Beale Street Blues | I Guess I'll Have To Change My Plans | Fidgety Feet | I Used To Love You(But It's All Over Now) | September In The Rain | Wherever There's Love | St.Louis Blues | I Believe In Miracles | Hindustan | Wabash Blues | South Rampart Street Parade
Live at Musikhalle Hamburg, rec. 25.9.1993
A Salute To Eddie Condon | Polcer,Ed (co) | Havens,Bob (tb) | Vaché,Allan (cl) | Barnes,John (bs,voc) | Varro,Johnny (p) | Douglas,Jim (g) | Haggart,Bob (b) | Miles,Butch (dr)

CD 005 | CD | Hapy Birthday Jazzwelle Plus
The Yamaha International Allstar Band
Happy Birthday- | Stompy Jones- | Will You Still Be Mine | A Ghost Of A Chance | Stealin' Apples | Jumpin' At The Woodside | What's New? | Kansas City | Chicago | Jeanie Lambe Talkin' | Willow Weep For Me | Satin Doll | If Dreams Come True | Sabine's Jazz Arena | For You For Me For Evermore | Just Squeeze Me(But Don't Tease Me) | Every Time We Say Goodbye | You Are My Heart's Delight | Crossing The Border | Get Out Of Town | All Of Me | Things Ain't What They Used To Be | It Don't Mean A Thing If It Ain't Got That Swing
Live at The Fabrik,Hamburg, rec. 16.11.1993
Yamaha International Allstar Band,The | Sandke,Randy (tp) | Tilitz,Jerry (tb) | Allen,Harry (ts) | Moss,Danny (ts) | Sarpila,Antti (cl,ts) | Dee,Brian (p) | Skeat,Len (b) | Jackson,Oliver (dr) | Lambe,Jeanie (voc)

CD 006 | CD | All The Cats Join In(Buck Clayton Remembered)
The Buck Clayton Legacy
All The Cats Join In | Come Again | Buckin' The Blues | Lester Leaps In | Fiesta In Blue | Toot Sweet | Christopher Columbus | Blue And Sentimental | Professor Jazz | Jumpin' At The Woodside | Robbin's Nest | Top Brass | Lean Baby
Live at Birdland,Hamburg, rec. 17./18.11.1993
Buck Clayton Legacy,The | Sandke,Randy (tp) | Tilitz,Jerry (tb) | Sarpila,Antti (cl,ss,ts) | Allen,Harry (ts) | Moss,Danny (ts) | Dee,Brian (p) | Skeat,Len (b) | Jackson,Oliver (dr)

CD 008 | CD | One Two Three
George Masso Allstars
Fascinating Rhythm | Liza | The Half Of It Deary Blues | Who Cares
Live at Musikhalle Hamburg, rec. 26.9.1992
Masso,George (tb) | Sandke,Randy (tp) | Davern,Kenny (cl) | Moss,Danny (ts) | Higgins,Eddie (p) | Skeat,Len (b) | Hanna,Jake (dr)
The New York Allstars
There Ain't No Sweet Man Worth The Salt Of My Tears | Mississippi Mud | In A Mist- | Candelight-
Live at Musikhalle Hamburg, rec. 1.5.1993
New York All Stars,The | Sandke,Randy (tp) | Barrett,Dan (tb) | Peplowski,Ken (cl) | Robinson,Scott (ts) | Shane,Mark (p) | Grosz,Marty (g,voc) | Milliman,Linc (b) | Ratajczak,Dave (dr)
A Salute To Eddie Condon
I Would Do Most Anything For You | I Can't Give You Anything But Love | Have You Met Miss Jones | Louisiana | Jitterbug Waltz | Sentimental Journey | Mandy Make Up Your Mind
Live at Musikhalle Hamburg, rec. 25.9.1993
A Salute To Eddie Condon | Polcer,Ed (co) | Havens,Bob (tb) | Vaché,Allan (cl) | Barnes,John (bs,voc) | Varro,Johnny (p) | Douglas,Jim (g) | Haggart,Bob (b) | Miles,Butch (dr)

CD 009 | CD | Jazz Party
The European Jazz Ginats
China Boy | Ballin' The Jack | Till There Was You | Handful Of Keys | When You're Smiling | Savoy Blues | Runnin' Wild | Harmonica Boogie | I Can't Give You Anything But Love | Royal Garden Blues | Sweet Georgia Brown | That's A Plenty | I Got Rhythm
Live at Musikhalle Hamburg, rec. 29.3.1994
European Jazz Giants,The | Klein,Oscar (tp,cl,harm) | Williams,Roy (tb,voc) | Sarpila,Antti (cl,ss) | Thilo,Jesper (ts,voc) | Chaix,Henri (p) | Meyer,Peter 'Banjo' (bj,voc) | Pitt,Vic (b) | Antolini,Charly (dr)

CD 010 | CD | A Night At Birdland
Harry Allen Quintet
Isn't It A Lovely Day | From This Moment On | My Foolish Heart | The Song Is You | Blues My Naughty Sweetie Gives To Me | Sweet Lorraine | All God's Chillun Got Rhythm | Stardust | Now's The Time | Sophisticated Lady | Lover Come Back To Me
Live at Birdland,Hamburg, rec. 19./20.11.1993
Allen,Harry (ts) | Sandke,Randy (tp) | Dee,Brian (p) | Skeat,Len (b) | Jackson,Oliver (dr)

CD 011 | CD | Jazz Im Amerika Haus,Vol.1
Harry Allen Quartet
'Deed I Do | Close Your Eyes | But Beautiful | The King | Did You Call Her Today | Honeysuckle Rose | This Time The Dream's On Me | My Heart Stood Still | Everyday I Have The Blues | Limehouse Blues
Live at The 'Amerikahaus',Hamburg, rec. 28.5.1994
Allen,Harry (ts) | Bunch,John (p) | Irwin,Dennis (b) | Jackson,Duffy (dr)

CD 012 | CD | Jazz Im Amerikahaus,Vol.2
Warren Vaché Quintet With Special Guest Allan Vaché
My Shining Hour | I Fall In Love Too Easily | You'd Be So Nice To Come Home To | Poor Butterfly | Purple Gazelle | Isfahan | My Romance | There'll Never Be Another You | The End Of A Love Affair | Cherokee
Live at The 'Amerikahaus',Hamburg, rec. 25.6.1994
Vaché,Warren (co) | Vaché,Allan (cl) | Lemon,Brian (p) | Cliff,Dave (g) | Green,Dave (b) | Ganley,Allan (dr)

CD 013 | CD | Jazz Im Amerikahaus,Vol.3
Allan Vaché Swingtet
There Is No Greater Love | I Hadn't Anyone 'Till Now | Can't We Be Friends | Perdido | Warm Valley | Speak Low | Blue Lou | The Song Is You | Raincheck | Georgia On My Mind | Summer Night | Idaho
Live at The 'Amerikahaus',Hamburg, rec. 6.8.1994
Vaché,Allan (cl) | Vaché,Warren (co) | Varro,Johnny (p) | Douglas,Jim (g) | Tate,Frank (b) | Masessa,Mike (dr)

CD 015 | CD | Jazz Im Amerikahaus,Vol.5
Summit Reunion
Oh! Lady Be Good | Beale Street Blues | If Dreams Come True | Back Home Again In Indiana | Comes Love | Rosetta | Yours Is My Heart Alone | Apex Blues | A Porter's Love Song To A Chambermaid
Live at The 'Amerikahaus',Hamburg, rec. 24.9.1994
Summit Reunion | Wilber,Bob (cl,ss) | Davern,Kenny (cl) | Cliff,Dave (g) | Green,Dave (b) | Worth,Bobby (dr)

CD 016 | CD | Keep Swingin'
Rex Allen's Swing Express
Take The 'A' Train | Pleasingly Plump | Back Bay Shuffle | Why | Opus 1 | When You're Smiling | Fine And Mellow | What A Little Moonlight Can Do | Blues For Mannie | Stompin' At The Savoy | Duke Ellington Medley: | In My Solitude- | Chelsea Bridge- | Do Nothin' Till You Hear From Me- | I Got It Bad And That Ain't Good- | Mood Indigo- | Flying Home
Live at Musikhalle Hamburg, rec. 20.10.1994
Allen,Rex (tb,vib) | Barrett,Dan (tp) | Rothermel,Jim (cl,ss,as) | Allen,Harry (ts) | Shane,Mark (p) | Pizzarelli,Bucky (g) | Tate,Frank (b) | Beck,Gregor (dr) | Richards[Alden],Terrie (voc)

CD 017 | CD | Weaver Of Dreams
Danny Moss Quartet
9:20 Special | This Heart Of Mine | Then I'll Be Tired Of You | Do Nothin' Till You Hear From Me | Smoke Gets In Your Eyes | A Gal In Calico | In A Mellow Tone | My Romance | Fine And Dandy | Weaver Of Dreams | I'm Glad There Is You | Poor Butterfly | There's No You | Blue Lou
Hamburg, rec. 17.11.1994
Moss,Danny (ts) | Lemon,Brian (p) | Skeat,Len (b) | Miles,Butch (dr)

CD 018 | CD | Encore Live
The Buck Clayton Legacy
All The Cats Join In | Buckin' The Blues | Toot Sweet | Robbin's Nest | Professor Jazz | Fiesta In Blue | Jumpin' At The Woodside | Blue And Sentimental | Sabine's Jazz Arena | Lean Baby | Rock-A-Bye Basie
Live at The Fabrik,Hamburg, rec. 15.11.1994
Buck Clayton Legacy,The | Sandke,Randy (tp) | Tilitz,Jerry (tb) | Sarpila,Antti (cl,ss,ts) | Allen,Harry (ts) | Moss,Danny (ts) | Robinson,Scott (bs) | Dee,Brian (p) | Skeat,Len (b) | Miles,Buddy (dr)

CD 019 | CD | Three Great Concerts:Live In Hamburg 1993-1995
Jeanie Lambe And The Danny Moss Quartet
Any Place I Hang My Hat Is Home | Can't We Be Friends | Little Girl Blue | I'm Glad There Is You | Stormy Weather | Blue Prelude | I Can't Give You Anything But Love | Bye Bye Blackbird | Stompin' At The Savoy
Live at Birdland,Hamburg, rec. 17./18.11.1993
Lambe,Jeanie (voc) | Moss,Danny (ts) | Dee,Brian (p) | Skeat,Len (b) | Jackson,Oliver (dr)
Teach Me Tonight | All Of You | My Funny Valentine | You Came A Long Way From St. Louis | Candy | Gee Baby Ain't I Good To You | 'Deed I Do | St.Louis Blues
Live at The Fabrik,Hamburg, rec. 15.11.1994
Lambe,Jeanie (voc) | Moss,Danny (ts) | Lemon,Brian (p) | Skeat,Len (b) | Miles,Buddy (dr)
Nobody Knows You When You're Down And Out
Hamburg, rec. 23.12.1995
Lambe,Jeanie (voc) | Moss,Danny (ts) | Varro,Johnny (p) | Eckinger,Isla (b) | Miles,Buddy (dr)
Jeanie Lambe And The Danny Moss Septet
Aunt Hagar's Blues
Lambe,Jeanie (voc) | Moss,Danny (ts) | Saunders,Tom (co) | Allred,Bill (tb) | Hedges,Chuck (cl) | Varro,Johnny (p) | Eckinger,Isla (b) | Miles,Buddy (dr)

CD 021 | CD | Moonglow
Oscar Klein's Anniversary Band
Oh! Lady Be Good | Moonglow | If I Had You | Honeysuckle Rose | Creole Love Call | Out Of Nowhere | All Of Me | Oscar's Blues | Mack The Knife(Moritat) | Impromptu Ensemble
Live at The 'Amerikahaus',Hamburg, rec. 6.1.1995
Klein,Oscar (tp,cl,g) | Meerwald,Willi (tb,bar-h,voc) | Keller,Werner (cl) | Wrobel,Engelbert (cl,ts) | Mussolini,Romano (p) | Patruno,Lino (g) | Van Oven,Bob (b) | Antolini,Charly (dr)

CD 022 | CD | Ring Dem Bells
Marty Grosz And His Swinging Fools
Rose Of The Rio Grande | Baby Won't You Please Come Home | Gee Baby Ain't I Good To You | Nobody's Sweetheart | I Must Have That Man | You Brought A New Kind Of Love To Me | Old Man Blues | Ain't Cha Glad | My Daddy Rocks Me | Swing That Music | More Than You Know | She's Crying For Me | Ring Dem Bells
Live at The 'Amerikahaus',Hamburg, rec. 25.2.1995
Grosz,Marty (g,voc) | Kellso,Jon-Erik (tp) | Robinson,Scott (cl,ss,bs) | Litton,Martin (p) | Cohen,Greg (b) | Riggs,Chuck (dr)

CD 023 | CD | Exactly Like You
Tom Saunders' 'Wild Bill Davison Band' & Guests
Sleep | Someday You'll Be Sorry | Milneberg Joys | Echoes Of Spring | Struttin' With Some Barbecue | I'm Crazy 'Bout My Baby | Smiles | If I Could Be With You One Hour Tonight | Doin' The New Low Down | Exactly Like You | Home | Beale Street Blues | I Never Knew
Live at Musikhalle Hamburg, rec. 23.9.1995
Saunders,Tom (co,voc) | Sudholter,Dick (tp,fl-h,co) | Allred,Bill (tb) | Williams,Roy (tb) | Hedges,Chuck (cl) | Moss,Danny (ts) | Barnes,John (cl,bs) | Varro,Johnny (p) | Grosz,Marty (g,voc) | Eckinger,Isla (b) | Miles,Butch (dr) | Lambe,Jeanie (voc)

CD 024 | CD | Absolutely
Bill Allred-Roy Williams Quintet
Constantly | Satin Doll | Isn't It A Pity | Gypsy In My Soul | Too Close For Comfort | Blues No.1 | If There Is Someone Lovelier Than You | Absolutely | Blue Bones | So Beats My Heart For You | It's Only A Paper Moon | Makin' Whoopee | Sometimes I'm Happy | You're Driving Me Crazy
Hamburg, rec. 28.9.1995
Allred,Bill (tb) | Williams,Roy (tb,voc) | Varro,Johnny (p) | Eckinger,Isla (b) | Miles,Butch (dr)

CD 025 | CD | The International Allstars Play Benny Goodman:Vol.1
International Allstars
You | Did I Remember | Stardust | You Brought A New Kind Of Love To Me | Limehouse Blues | Our Love Is Here To Stay
Live at The 'Amerikahaus',Hamburg, rec. 14.10.1995
International Allstars | Peplowski,Ken (cl,ts) | Erstrand,Lars (vib) | Alden,Howard (g) | Shane,Mark (p) | Skeat,Len (b) | Ascione,Joseph 'Joe' (dr)
Medley: | Memories Of You- | Poor Butterfly- | Moonglow- | After You've Gone
International Allstars | Peplowski,Ken (cl,ts) | Sarpila,Antti (cl) | Vaché,Allan (cl) | Erstrand,Lars (vib) | Alden,Howard (g) | Shane,Mark (p) | Skeat,Len (b) | Ascione,Joseph 'Joe' (dr)

CD 026 | CD | Swing Is Here
Allan Vaché-Antti Sarpila Quintet
As Long As I Live | Fidgety Feet | Careless Love Blues | Easy Living | Meet Me Tonight In Dreamland | Blues No.2 | Just One Of Those Things | How Am I To Know? | Swing Is Here | Up A Lazy River | Mama's Gone Goodbye | I Know That You Know | Goodnight My Love | Some Of These Days
Hamburg, rec. 15.10.1995
Vaché,Allan (cl) | Sarpila,Antti (cl,ss) | Shane,Mark (p) | Skeat,Len (b) | Ascione,Joseph 'Joe' (dr)

CD 027 | CD | Summit Meeting
Allan Vaché-Antti Sarpila & 1 Sextet
Original Dixieland One Step | What Can I Say After I Say I'm Sorry | Air Mail Special | These Foolish Things Remind Me On You | Cherry | Royal Garden Blues | You'll Always Be Mine | Nuages | A Shanty In Old Shanty Town | Yellow Dog Blues | Who's Sorry Now | I've Started All Over Again | Blues No.3 | Bye Bye Blues
Hamburg, rec. 16.10.1995
Vaché,Allan (cl) | Sarpila,Antti (cl,ss) | Peplowski,Ken (cl,ts) | Shane,Mark (p) | Skeat,Len (b) | Ascione,Joseph 'Joe' (dr)

CD 028 | CD | The Hamburg Concert-Tribute To A Legend
Bob Wilber's Bechet Legacy
Down In Honky Tonk Town | Promenade Aux Champs-Elysees | Oh Daddy | Miss Jennie's Ball | Egyptain Fantasy | Quincy Street Stomp | Georgia Cabin | I Had It But It's All Gone Now | Maryland My Maryland | Si Tu Vois Ma Mere | Dans Les Rues D'Antibes | Premier Bal | Reverie | Chloe | Petite Fleur | After You've Gone
Live at Musikhalle Hamburg, rec. 22.10.1995
Wilber,Bob (cl,ss) | Sandke,Randy (tp) | Shane,Mark (p,voc) | Cliff,Dave (g) | Green,Dave (b) | Miles,Buddy (dr) | Horton,Pug (voc)

CD 029 | CD | We Love You,Louis!

The New York Allstars
When It's Sleepy Time Down South(Theme) | Mabel's Dream | Sugarfoot Stomp | Big Butter And Egg Man From The West | Cornet Chop Suey | Wild Man Blues | Potato Head Blues | Muskrat Ramble | Savoy Blues | Struttin' With Some Barbecue | Basin Street Blues | Weather Bird | Ballad Medley: | Thanks A Million- | Rockin' Chair- | Do You Know What It Means To Miss New Orleans- | Swing That Music | If I Could Be With You One Hour Tonight | Mack The Knife(Moritat)- | The Faithfull Husar- | Ole Miss- | Mabel's Dream- | When It's Sleepy Time Down South
Live at The Congress Center Hamburg, rec. 5.-9.2.1996
New York All Stars,The | Sandke,Randy (tp,ld) | Stripling,Byron (tp,voc) | Helleny,Joel (tb) | Davern,Kenny (cl) | Ostwald,David (tuba) | Shane,Mark (p) | Cohen,Greg (b) | Ascione,Joseph 'Joe' (dr)

CD 031 | CD | Count Basie Remembered
Swingin' Back | Down For Double | Softly With Feeling | Shoe Shine Boy | Shiny Stockings | I Want A Little Girl | Lester Leaps In | How Long Blues | 9:20 Special | One O'Clock Jump
Live at The 'Amerikahaus',Hamburg, rec. 2.11.1996
New York All Stars,The | Sandke,Randy (tp,ld) | Barrett,Dan (tb) | Ogilvie,Brian (cl,as,ts) | Mitchell,Billy (ts) | Shane,Mark (p,voc) | Chirillo,James (g) | Haggart,Bob (b) | Ascione,Joseph 'Joe' (dr)

CD 032 | CD | Allan Vaché's Floridy Jazz Allstars
Allan Vaché's Florida Jazz Allstars
Meet Me Tonight In Dreamland | Spain | My Inspiration | My Honey's Lovin' Arms | Krazy Kapers | Baby Won't You Please Come Home | Breezin' Along With The Breeze | South Rampart Street Parade | What's New? | Jubilee | Poor Butterfly | Sleep
Orlando,Florida, rec. 27./28.3.1996
Vaché,Allan (cl) | Jones,David (co) | Allred,John (tb) | Varro,Johnny (p) | Leary,Bob (g) | Haggart,Bob (b) | Metz Jr.,Ed 'Eddie' (dr)

CD 033 | CD | Warren Plays Warrey
Warren Vaché Quintet
This Heart Of Mine | Would You Like To Take A Walk | Nagasaki | Serenade In Blue- | At Last- | I Only Have Eyes For You | The Girlfriend Of The Whirling Dervish | You're Getting To Be A Habit With Me | Lulu's Back In Town | I Remember You From Somewhere | Forty-Second Street | September In The Rain | Blues Times(2) | An Affair To Remember | I Had The Craziest Dream | Jeepers Creepers | You're Getting To Be A Habit With Me(vocal)
Hamburg, rec. 19.-21.6.1966
Vaché,Warren (co,voc) | Sandke,Randy (tp) | Drew Jr.,Kenny (p) | Wall,Murray (b) | Cobb,Jimmy (dr)

CD 034 | CD | A Swingin' Affair
Danny Moss Meets Buddha's Gamblers
Just You Just Me | Moten Swing | D.M. Blues | Moppin' And Boppin' | A Smooth One | The Jeep Is Jumpin' | Georgia On My Mind | Crazy Rhythm | Swingin' The Blues | Sweet And Lovely | The King
Hamburg, rec. 31.1.& 4.-6.2.1996
Moss,Danny (ts) | Buddha's Gamblers | Bühler,Heinz (tp) | Meier,Hans (tb) | Keller,Werner (cl) | Scheidegger,Buddha (p) | Schmidli,Peter (g) | Kummer,Vinzenz (b) | Capello,Carlo (dr)

CD 035 | CD | What Swing Is All About
Bob Wilber And Friends
Smiles | Tickle Toe | Someday You'll Be Sorry | I Gotta Right To Sing The Blues | I Want To Be Happy | You'd Be So Nice To Come Home To | Basiec Jump | Back Home Again In Indiana | Love Comes Along Once In A Lifetime | The Song Is You | I've Got A Feeling I'm Falling | I've Gotta Crush On You- | You Do Something To Me- | Bemfest '96 | This Is New | Goody Goody | Billie's Bounce | Doggin' Around
Live at The 'Amerikahaus',Hamburg, rec. 28.9.1996
Wilber,Bob (cl,ss) | Sarpila,Antti (cl,ts) | Shane,Mark (p) | Flanigan,Phil (b) | Ascione,Joseph 'Joe' (dr) | Horton,Pug (voc)

CD 036 | CD | My Buddy:A Tribute To Buddy Rich
Joe Ascione Octet
Cotton Tail | My Buddy | J.& B's Bag | Here's That Rainy Day | Limehouse Blues | Hi Fly | Nica's Dream | Straight No Chaser | Soft Winds | I Want To Be Happy | Love For Sale | Blues No.5(Blues For Kurtchen)
Hamburg, rec. 3.11.1996
Ascione,Joseph 'Joe' (dr) | Sandke,Randy (tp) | Barrett,Dan (tb) | Ogilvie,Brian (cl,as,ts) | Mitchell,Billy (ts) | Shane,Mark (p) | Chirillo,James (g) | Haggart,Bob (b)

CD 037 | CD | The Music Of The Trumpet Kings
Harry Allen And Randy Sandke Meets The RIAS Big Band Berlin
I Love Louis | Cloudy | Echoes Of Harlem | Little Jazz Boogie | I Can't Get Started | Melancholy Rhapsody | Randy's Rolls Royce | Shaw 'Nuff | All Blues | Turnstile | Relaxin' At Clifford's | The Moontrane | Birdlike
Berlin, rec. 5.-11.12.1996
Sandke,Randy (tp) | Allen,Harry (ts) | RIAS-Big Band | Bowen,Gregg (tp) | Bilsheim,Dieter (tp) | Brönner,Till (tp) | Grabandt,Christian (tp) | Loup,Thomas (tb) | Marshall,John (tb) | Fischer,Sören (tb) | Grossman,Andy (b-tb) | Nagel,Norbert (as) | Mamulla,Klaus (as) | Gauchel,Walter (ts) | Peters,Gregoire (ts) | Wenzel,Helmut (bs) | Cramer,Ingo (g) | Rautenberg,Kai (grand-p) | Lange,Hajo (b) | Nell,Holger (dr)

CD 038 | 2 CD | Echoes Of Spring:The Complete Hamburg Concert
Ralph Sutton And His Allstars
Fine And Dandy | Moonglow | California Here I Come | Clothes Line Ballet | Song Of The Wanderer | Sweet Lorraine | Happy Birthday- | Blame It On My Youth- | Limehouse Blues | My Gal Sal | Beale Street Blues | Some Of These Days | Runnin' Wild | Thanks A Million | Shine | Buddy Bolden's Blues
Live at The 'Amerikahaus',Hamburg, rec. 1.3.1997
Sutton,Ralph (p) | Kellso,Jon-Erik (tp) | Allred,Bill (tb) | Sarpila,Antti (cl,ss) | Lesberg,Jack (b) | Beck,Gregor (dr)

CD 039 | CD | Just For Fun!
Marty Grosz Quartet
All I Do Is Dream Of You | Just Friends | Love Is Just Around The Corner | It's The Talk Of The Town | How Can You Face Me? | Mood Indigo | Sweethearts On Parade | Ain't Misbehavin' | A Hundred Years From Today | If I Had A Talking Picture Of You | Memphis Blues | The Lady Is In Love With You
Live at The 'Amerikahaus',Hamburg, rec. 13.4.1996
Grosz,Marty (g,voc) | Elsdon,Alan (tp,voc) | Barnes,John (cl,as,bs,voc) | Wall,Murray (b)

CD 040 | CD | With Thee I Swing!
Mark Shane-Terry Blaine Group
I Never Knew | It's A Wonderful World | What A Little Moonlight Can Do | They Say That Falling In Love Is Wonderful | Why Don't You Do Right | Carolina Shout | St.Louis Blues | With Thee I Swing | Oh Daddy | What Is This Thing Called Love | I Would Do Anything For You | Dream- | Dream A Little Dream Of Me- | Getting Some Fun Out Of Life | Mama Don't Allow
Live at The Hanse-Merkur Auditorium,Hamburg, rec. 21.-24.10.1997
Blaine,Terry (voc) | Shane,Mark (p) | Polcer,Ed (co) | Artin,Tom (tb) | Vaché,Allan (cl,ts) | Flanigan,Phil (b) | Metz Jr.,Ed 'Eddie' (dr)

CD 041 | CD | Count Basie Remembered Vol.2
The New York Allstars
Swingin' The Blues | Moten Swing | Blue And Sentimental | April In Paris | Lil' Darlin' | Big Noise From Winnetka | Broadway | Baby Won't You Please Come Home | The King
Live at The 'Amerikahaus',Hamburg, rec. 2.11.1996
New York All Stars,The | Sandke,Randy (tp,ld) | Barrett,Dan (tb) | Ogilvie,Brian (cl,as,ts) | Mitchell,Billy (ts) | Shane,Mark (p) | Chirillo,James (g) | Haggart,Bob (b) | Ascione,Joseph 'Joe' (dr)

CD 042 | CD | Side By Side
The Vaché-Allred-Metz Family Jazz Band
Side By Side- | Ding Dong Daddy- | No One Else But You | Oh Daddy | Japanese Sandman | I Believe In Miracles | Zip-A-Dee-Doo-Dah | Sonny Boy | I Double Dare You | Blues For The Old Men | You Turned The Tables On Me | I Want A Little Girl | Come Back Sweet Papa | Old Fashioned Love
Orlando,Florida, rec. 14./15.1.1997
Vaché,Warren (co) | Allred,Bill (tb) | Allred,John (tb) | Vaché,Allan (cl) | Metz Sr.,Ed (p) | Vaché Sr.,Warren (b) | Metz Jr.,Ed 'Eddie' (dr)

CD 043 | CD | The Tremble Kids All Stars Play Chicago Jazz!
The Tremble Kids All Stars
Them There Eyes | Someday You'll Be Sorry | Way Down Yonder In New Orleans | Blues In The Air | I'm Crazy 'Bout My Baby | After You've Gone | Pretty Little Missy | I Cried For You(Now It's Your Turn To Cry Over Me) | Mama's Gone Goodbye | A Kiss To Build A Dream On | Everybody Loves My Baby | I May Be Wrong(But I Think You're Wonderful) | Tutti For Eddie
Winterthur,CH, rec. 16./17.12.1997
Tremble Kids All Stars,The | Lange,Peter (tp) | Leibundgut,Walter (tb,voc) | Keller,Werner (cl,voc) | Chaix,Henri (p) | Schmidli,Peter (g) | Kummer,Vinzenz (b) | Antolini,Charly (dr)

CD 044 | CD | Revisited!
Allan Vaché Big Four
That Da-Da Strain | Liza | Louisiana Fairytale | Promenade Aux Champs-Elysees | She's Just Perfect | I May Be Wrong(But I Think You're Wonderful) | Song Of Songs | China Boy | Relaxin' At The Touro | Four Or Five Times | Panama | Deep Henderson | Cherry
Orlando,Florida, rec. 3.6.1997
Vaché,Allan (cl) | Jones,David (co) | Leary,Bob (g,voc) | Flanigan,Phil (b)

CD 045 | CD | The International Allstars Play Benny Goodman Vol.1
The International Allstars
The Sheik Of Araby | I Must Have That Man | Jingles | Sleep | All The Things You Are | Jubilee | Everything I Love
Live at The 'Amerikahaus',Hamburg, rec. 14.10.1995
International Allstars | Peplowski,Ken (cl,ts) | Erstrand,Lars (vib) | Alden,Howard (g) | Shane,Mark (p) | Skeat,Len (b) | Ascione,Joseph 'Joe' (dr)
Stompin' At The Savoy | Body And Soul | Lulu's Back In Town
International Allstars | Vaché,Allan (cl) | Sarpila,Antti (cl) | Peplowski,Ken (cl,ts) | Erstrand,Lars (vib) | Alden,Howard (g) | Shane,Mark (p) | Skeat,Len (b) | Ascione,Joseph 'Joe' (dr)

CD 046 | CD | Oh,Yeah! The New York Allstars Play More Music Of Louis Armstrong
The New York Allstars
When It's Sleepy Time Down South- | Back Home Again In Indiana- | West End Blues | Weary Blues | Lazy 'Sippi' Steamer | I Double Dare You | Someday You'll Be Sorry | Mahogany Hall Stomp | On The Sunny Side Of The Street | St.Louis Blues | I'm A Ding Dong Daddy | Black And Blue | Ory's Creole Trombone | Samantha | Tiger Rag | When It's Sleepy Time Down South
Hamburg, rec. 28.2.1998
New York All Stars,The | Sandke,Randy (tp,ld) | Stripling,Byron (tp,voc) | Helleny,Joel (tb) | Vaché,Allan (cl) | Varro,Johnny (p) | Haggart,Bob (b) | Ascione,Joseph 'Joe' (dr)

CD 047 | CD | Hey Ba-Ba-Re-Bop!! The New York Allstars Play Lionel Hampton Vol.1
Air Mail Special | Moonglow | Ring Dem Bells | Indian Summer | Hey Ba-Ba-Re-Bop | A Nightingale Sang In Berkeley Square | Avalon | Rose Room | Body And Soul | Flying Home
Live at The Hanse-Merkur Auditorium,Hamburg, rec. 17.10.1998
New York All Stars,The | Sandke,Randy (tp,ld) | Williams,Roy (tb) | Sarpila,Antti (cl,sax) | Erstrand,Lars (vib) | Chirillo,James (g) | Wagner,Thilo (p) | Green,Dave (b) | Metz Jr.,Ed 'Eddie' (dr)

CD 048 | CD | Voice With Heart
Terrie Richard Alden And The Warren Vaché Quartet
Please Don't Talk About Me When I'm Gone | Comes Love | Sweet Substitute | Makin' Whoopee | Just One Of Those Things | Gee Baby Ain't I Good To You | Talk To Me Baby | Dindi | Ill Wind | It's All Right With Me | The Very Thought Of You | Am I Blue | Is You Is Or Is You Ain't My Baby | His Eye Is On The Sparrow
NYC, rec. 21./22.8.1996
Richards[Alden],Terrie (voc) | Vaché,Warren (fl-h,co,voc) | Alden,Howard (g,el-g) | Moore,Michael (b) | Williams,Jackie (dr)

CD 049 | CD | Steamers!
Danny Moss-Roy Williams Quintet
Justin Time | It's All Right With Me | Theme There Eyes | Too Late Now | It's A Wonderful World | Lil' Darlin' | You're My Everything | Isn't It Romantic | There Is No Greater Love | Mood Indigo | Hi 'Ya | Blues To Be There | I've Found A New Baby
Hamburg, rec. 10.10.1998
Moss,Danny (ts) | Williams,Roy (tb) | Pearce,John (p) | Skeat,Len (b) | Antolini,Charly (dr)

CD 050 | CD | Mrs.Vaché's Boys
Warren Vaché-Allen Vaché Sextet
Just Friends | Tangerine | London By Night | I'll Remember April | All Blues | Squeeze Me | The Eel's Nephew | Falando De Orlando | Cotton Tail | Danny Boy (Londonderry Air) | If Dreams Come True | What Am I Here For
Orlando,Florida, rec. 19./20.2.1998
Vaché,Warren (fl-h,co) | Vaché,Allan (cl) | Higgins,Eddie (p) | Alden,Howard (g) | Flanigan,Phil (b) | Metz Jr.,Ed 'Eddie' (dr)

CD 051 | CD | Blues In Your Heart
David Ostwald's Gully Low Jazz Band
Jubilee Stomp | When Day Is Done | Don't Forget To Mess Around | Lover Come Back To Me | Thou Swell | Someday Sweetheart | Panama | 'Tain't So Honey 'Tain't So | Blues In My Heart | New Orleans Stomp | Changes | Who' Sit | Home | Diga Diga Do
NYC, rec. 14.-16.12.1998
Ostwald,David (tuba) | Sandke,Randy (tp) | Gordon,Wycliffe (tb,voc) | Peplowski,Ken (cl,as) | Shane,Mark (p) | Alden,Howard (g,bj) | Riley,Herlin (dr)

CD 052 | CD | The Blue Noise Session
Jeanie Lambe And The Danny Moss Quartet
Long Ago And Far Away | Just Squeeze Me(But Don't Tease Me) | Black Coffee | Saturday Night Is The Loneliest Night Of The Week | I Get Along Without You Very Well | Don't You Go Way Mad | Just One Of Those Things | Mad About The Boy | Love For Sale | Honeysuckle Rose | The Thrill Is Gone | Day In Day Out | Here's That Rainy Day | A Foggy Day(In London Town) | It Never Entered My Mind | Come Rain Or Come Shine | Don't Worry 'Bout Me | Do I Love You
Hamburg, rec. 21.10.1998
Lambe,Jeanie (voc) | Moss,Danny (ts) | Pearce,John (p) | Skeat,Len (b) | Antolini,Charly (dr)

CD 053 | CD | Tough Assignment:A Tribute To Dave Tough
Eddie Metz And His Gang
Smiles | It All Belongs To Me | Moanin' Low | Waiting At The End Of The Road | Beale Street Blues | It's Been So Long | Sophisticated Swing | At The Codfish Ball | Why Begin Again | I Hadn't Anyone 'Til You | Lover Come Back To Me | Hindustan | Not Too Tough | Though Sledding
Ocoee,Florida, rec. 23./24.3.1999
Metz Jr.,Ed 'Eddie' (dr) | Sandke,Randy (tp) | Allred,John (tb) | Allen,Harry (ts) | Vaché,Allan (cl) | Varro,Johnny (p) | Flanigan,Phil (b)

CD 054 | CD | Raisin' The Roof:Allan Vaché Meets Jim Galloway
Allan Vaché-Jim Galloway Sextet
When I Grow Too Old To Dream | Cakewalkin' Babies From Home | Dream | Raisin' The Roof | Oh Sister Ain't That Hot | The Very Thought Of You | Lullaby In Rhythm | Hymn To Freedom | San | Si Tu Vois Ma Mere | Shag | Make Me A Pallet On The Floor
NYC, rec. 17./18.12.1998
Vaché,Allan (cl) | Galloway,Jim (ss) | Bunch,John (p) | Alden,Howard (g) | Moore,Michael (b) | Hanna,Jake (dr)

CD 055 | CD | What Would Santa Say?
Mark Shane's X-Mas Allstars
What Will Santa Claus Say | God Rest Ye Merry Gentlemen | Santa Claus Is Coming To Town | The Christmas Song | Santa Claus Came In The Spring | Silent Night | Joy To The World | 'Zat You,Zanta Claus? | Jingle Bells | Merry Christmas Baby | Sleigh Ride | Oh Christmas Tree(O Tannenbaum) | Hark! The Herald Angels Sing | Oh Du Fröhliche- | Alle Jahre Wieder-
Shane,Mark (p,voc) | Allen,Harry (ts) | Kellso,Jon-Erik (tp) | Chirillo,James (g,bj) | O'Leary,Pat (b) | Ratajczak,Dave (dr)

CD 056 | CD | What Is There To Say?
Warren Vaché Quartet
At Sundown | My Shining Hour | Deep In A Dream | Too Phat Blues | Samantha | Bossango | Pow-Wow | I'll Never See Maggie Alone | I've Grown Accustomed To Her Face | See Jim, See Joe, C-Jam Blues | Comes Love | What Is There To Say | It's A Blue World | Falling In Love Is Wonderful
NYC, rec. 18./19.5.1999
Vaché,Warren (tp,co,voc) | Puma,Joe (g) | Wall,Murray (b) | Locke,Eddie (dr)

CD 057 | CD | Sweet Sue-The Music Of Fats Waller Vol.1
Ralph Sutton And Friends
Moppin' And Boppin' | Lounging At The Waldorf | I'm Gonna Sit Right Down And Write Myself A Letter | Yacht Club Swing | Sweet Sue Just You | Black And Blue | Tea For Two | It's A Sin To Tell A Lie | Honeysuckle Rose
Live at The Hanse-Merkur Auditorium,Hamburg, rec. 12.-14.& 26.-27.10.1999
Sutton,Ralph (p) | Kellso,Jon-Erik (tp) | Ogilvie,Brian (cl,ts) | Grosz,Marty (g,voc) | Green,Dave (b) | Capp,Frank (dr)

CD 058 | CD | The Re-Discovered Louis And Bix
Randy Sandke And The New York Allstars
No One Knows What It's All About
NYC, rec. 24.6.1999
Sandke,Randy (co) | Barrett,Dan (tb) | Peplowski,Ken (cl) | Hyman,Dick (p) | Alden,Howard (bj) | Ascione,Joseph 'Joe' (dr)
Play It Red
Sandke,Randy (co) | Barrett,Dan (tb) | Peplowski,Ken (cl) | Robinson,Scott (bass-sax) | Hyman,Dick (p) | Alden,Howard (g) | Ascione,Joseph 'Joe' (dr)
Lily
Sandke,Randy (co) | Barrett,Dan (tb) | Peplowski,Ken (cl) | Robinson,Scott (bass-sax) | Hyman,Dick (p,celeste) | Alden,Howard (g) | Ascione,Joseph 'Joe' (dr)
Did You Mean It | Betcha' I Getcha'
Sandke,Randy (co) | Barrett,Dan (tb) | Peplowski,Ken (cl) | Robinson,Scott (c-mel-sax,bass-sax) | Hyman,Dick (p) | Alden,Howard (g) | Cohen,Greg (b) | Ascione,Joseph 'Joe' (dr)
Cloudy
Sandke,Randy (co) | Barrett,Dan (tb) | Peplowski,Ken (cl) | Robinson,Scott (bass-sax) | Hyman,Dick (p,celeste) | Alden,Howard (g) | Cohen,Greg (b) | Ostwald,David (tuba) | Ascione,Joseph 'Joe' (dr)
Stampede
NYC, rec. 14.6.1999
Sandke,Randy (co,tp) | Barrett,Dan (tb) | Peplowski,Ken (cl,ts) | Wilson,Chuck (as) | Robinson,Scott (c-mel-sax) | Hyman,Dick (p) | Alden,Howard (g) | Cohen,Greg (b) | Ascione,Joseph 'Joe' (dr)
Papa What Are You Trying To Do To Me I've Been Doing It For Years | When You Leave Me Alone To Pine
NYC, rec. 31.8./1.9.1999
Sandke,Randy (tp) | Kellso,Jon-Erik (tp) | Gordon,Wycliffe (tb) | Davern,Kenny (cl) | Hyman,Dick (p) | Chirillo,James (bj) | Ostwald,David (tuba) | Ascione,Joseph 'Joe' (dr)
Drop That Sack
Payton,Nicholas (tp) | Gordon,Wycliffe (tb) | Davern,Kenny (cl) | Hyman,Dick (p) | Chirillo,James (bj) | Ostwald,David (tuba) | Ascione,Joseph 'Joe' (dr)
Randy Sandke-Dick Hyman
Weather Bird
Sandke,Randy (tp) | Hyman,Dick (p)
The Jive Don't Come From Kokomo | Beyond A Shadow Of Doubt | Mr.Jackson From Jacksonville
Sandke,Randy (tp) | Kellso,Jon-Erik (tp) | Wilson,Chuck (as) | Peplowski,Ken (cl,ts) | Robinson,Scott (ts) | Hyman,Dick (p) | Chirillo,James (bj) | Washington,Peter (b) | Ascione,Joseph 'Joe' (dr)
I Got What It Takes- | I Need Your Kind Of Lovin'-
Sandke,Randy (tp) | Gordon,Wycliffe (tb) | Davern,Kenny (cl) | Hyman,Dick (p) | Chirillo,James (bj) | Washington,Peter (b) | Ascione,Joseph 'Joe' (dr)

CD 059 | CD | Swingtime!
Warren Vaché And The New York City All-Star Big Band
Swingtime! | From This Moment On | I've Got My Fingers Crossed | Mr.Bojangles | The Way You Look Tonight | Stompin' At The Savoy | B.D. Blues | Jumpin' At The Woodside | Portrait Of Jenny | Ain't Misbehavin' | Saturday Night Fish Fry | When You're Smiling | Let The Good Times Roll
NYC, rec. 11./12.1.2000
Vaché,Warren (tp,voc) | Reinhart,Randy (tp) | Allred,John (tb) | Bilyk,Matt (tb) | Wilson,Chuck (cl,as) | Allen,Harry (ts) | Woodard,Rickey (ts) | Barnes,Alan (cl,as,bs) | Ash,Steve (p) | Wall,Murray (b) | Hanna,Jake (dr)

CD 060 | CD | C'Est Magnifique!
George Masso Sextet
It's D'Lovely | It's All Right With Me | Why Shouldn't I | What Is This Thing Called Love | I Love You Samantha | Get Out Of Town | C'Est Magnifique
Live at The Hanse-Merkur Auditorium,Hamburg, rec. 6.3.1999
Masso,George (tb) | Colombo,Lou (tp,fl-h) | Allen,Harry (ts) | Varro,Johnny (p) | Flanigan,Phil (b) | Hanna,Jake (dr)

CD 061 | CD | Sultry Serenade
James Chirillo-Johnny Carisi
Counterpoise No.2 For Electric Guitar And Trumpet
NYC, rec. 12.5.1991
Chirillo,James (el-g) | Carisi,Johnny (tp)
James Chirillo Sextet
When Lights Are Low | Sultry Serenade | Move | Elend(Zemlinsky,from Op.27 No.7) | Can't We Be Friends | Bourbon Street Parade | Lush Life | I'm Always Chasing Rainbows | Fancifree | Blues For Valerie
NYC, rec. 4./5.10.1999
Chirillo,James (g,el-g) | Sandke,Randy (tp) | Robinson,Scott (ts,bass-sax) | Simon,Alan (p) | Cohen,Greg (b) | Ratajczak,Dave (dr,perc)
James Chirillo Quartet with Vera Mara
I Love You Samantha
NYC, rec. 4./5.10.1991
Chirillo,James (g) | Simon,Alan (p) | Cohen,Greg (b) | Ratajczak,Dave (dr) | Mara,Vera (voc)

CD 062 | CD | Fuse Blues
Marty Elkins And Her Sextet
Day In Day Out | Stars Fell On Alabama | Moon Ray- | No Moon At All- | In The Wee Small Hours Of The Morning | As Long As I Live | When Your Lover Has Gone | We'll Be Together Again | Fuse Blues | There's No You | Born To Be Blue | Soon | Never Never Land | You're Blasé
Brooklyn,NY, rec. 30./31.8.1999
Elkins,Marty (voc) | Pomeroy,Herb (tp) | Person,Houston (ts) | Hammer,Tardo (p) | Skaff,Greg (g) | Irwin,Dennis (b) | Taylor,Mark (dr)

CD 063 | CD | The Last Great Concert
Oliver Jackson Orchestra
Stompy Jones | Sabine's Jazz Arena | A Ghost Of A Chance | Jumpin' At The Woodside | Crossing The Border | What's New? | Stealin' Apples | If Dreams Come True | Will You Still Be Mine | Willow Weep For Me | Satin Doll | It Don't Mean A Thing If It Ain't Got That Swing
Live at The Fabrik,Hamburg, rec. 16.11.1993
Jackson,Oliver (dr) | Sandke,Randy (tp) | Tilitz,Jerry (tb) | Sarpila,Antti (cl,ts) | Allen,Harry (ts) | Moss,Danny (ts) | Dee,Brian (p) | Skeat,Len (b) | Lambe,Jeanie (voc)

CD 064 | CD | Keeper Of The Flame
Danny Moss Quartet
Three Little Words | When Your Lover Has Gone | Nancy(With The Laughing Face) | Speak Low | Where Or When | Moten Swing | Cry Me A River | It Only Happens When I Dance With You | I Should Care | Perdido | I Thought About You | Small Fry

Hamburg, rec. 20.10.1998
Moss,Danny (ts) | Pearce,John (p) | Skeat,Len (b) | Antolini,Charly (dr)

CD 065 | CD | Mundell's Moods
Mundell Lowe Quintet
Windy Wendy | Please Let The Sun Come Out Again | Shoreway | Darn That Dream | Seven Steps To Heaven | A Lad Named Charlie | Opus 1 | Body And Soul | You Say You Care | I'll Follow My Secret Heart | There Is No Greater Love
Hamburg, rec. 18.1.2000
Lowe,Mundell (g) | Meurkens,Hendrik (vib,harm) | Porter,Larry (p) | O'Leary,Pat (b) | Redd,Chuck (dr)

CD 066 | CD | Jammin' At The IAJRC Convention Hamburg 1999
Wrobel-Roberscheuten-Hopkins Jam Session
You Do Something To Me | Can't Help Lovin' Dat Man | Rose Room | I Can't Get Started | Robbin's Nest | Smiles | When I Grow Too Old To Dream | Mama Inez | I Surrender Dear | You Brought A New Kind Of Love To Me | I Can't Believe That You're In Love With Me | Candelights | El Salon De Gutbucket
Live at The Marriott Hotel, Hamburg, rec. 29.7.1999
Wrobel,Engelbert (cl,ss,ts) | Roberscheuten,Frank (cl,as,ts) | Hopkins,Chris (p) | Weston,Harvey (b) | Worth,Bobby (dr)

CD 067 | CD | Dan Barrett's International Swing Party
Dan Barrett Septet
Easy Street | Linger Awhile | 'Tain't Me | I'm On My Way From You | Vic's Spot | I Double Dare You | What Is This Thing Called Love | Early Session Hop | Jumpin' Punkins | Hindustan | Esquire Bounce | Dream A Little Dream Of Me
Live at Birdland,Hamburg, rec. 14.10.2000
Barrett,Dan (tb,co,voc) | Baker,Tom (tp,tb,as,ts) | Robinson,Scott (cl,as,ts,normaphone) | Hopkins,Chris (p) | Erickson,Eddie (bj,g,voc) | Forbes,Joel (b) | Hamilton,Jeff (dr)

CD 068 | CD | Herr Ober
Clark Terry Quintet
On The Alamo | Miss Thing | Lil' Darlin' | Herr Ober(I) | Taking A Chance On Love | Jumpin' At The Woodside | My Gal | Canadian Sunset | The Nearness Of You | Blue 'N' Boogie | Herr Ober(II)
Live at 'Birdland',Neuburg/Donau, rec. 20.5.2000
Terry,Clark (tp,fl-h,voc) | Glasser,David (as) | Friedman,Don (p) | McLaurine,Marcus (b) | Cuenca,Sylvia (dr)

CD 069 | CD | Live In Belfast
Frank Tate Quintet
Four Brothers | On The Alamo | I'll Only Miss Her When I Think Of Her | Fred | Chinatown My Chinatown | Oh! Lady Be Good | The Touch Of Your Lips | Willow Weep For Me | Just You Just Me | O Grande Amor
Live in Belfast, rec. 7./8.11.1996
Tate,Frank (b) | Allen,Harry (ts) | Alden,Howard (g) | McKenna,Dave (p) | Miles,Butch (dr)

CD 070 | CD | The Sound Of Alex Vol.1
The Alex Welsh Legacy Band
Oh! Baby | Home | At The Jazz Band Ball | Nobody Else But Me | Limehouse Blues | Someday You'll Be Sorry | Up A Lazy River | Chinatown My Chinatown
Live at The Marriott Hotel, Hamburg, rec. 31.7.1999
Saunders,Tom (co,voc) | Williams,Roy (tb) | Shepherd,Dave (cl) | Barnes,John (as,bs) | Lemon,Brian (p) | Douglas,Jim (g) | Weston,Harvey (b) | Worth,Bobby (dr)

CD 071 | CD | Love
Terrie Richard Alden-Howard Alden
The Lady Is In Love With You | Gone With The Wind | Miss Otis Regrets | Skylark | Justin Time | I Gotta Right To Sing The Blues | I Can't Give You Anything But Love | What A Little Moonlight Can Do | How Deep Is The Ocean | Travelin' Light | Everything I Have Is Yours | Almost Like Being In Love | Love Is The Thing
NYC, rec. 20.12.2000
Richards[Alden],Terrie (voc) | Alden,Howard (g)

CD 072 | CD | Face To Face:The Swingcats Live
The Swingcats
Good Queen Bess | I Want To Be Happy | Face To Face | Fascinating Rhythm | I Hear Music | Just One Of Those Things | Indian Summer | Corrine Corrina Blues | Someone To Watch Over Me | It All Depends On You | What Is This Thing Called Love | You're My Everything | I'll See You In My Dreams | Every Time We Say Goodbye
Live at Birdland,Hamburg, rec. 15.6.2001
Swingcats,The | Baker,Tom (co,tb,as) | Roberscheuten,Frank (cl,as,ts) | Van Der Linden,Dick (p) | Algoed,Karel (b) | De Bruyn,Onno (dr) | Hildabrand,Shaunette (voc)

CD 073 | CD | All Night Long
Dylan Cramer Quartet
Caruso | Estate(Summer) | Bumpin' | Black Orpheus | All Night Long | Stolen Moments | Lover Man(Oh,Where Can You Be?) | Clouds | My Funny Valentine | So What
Vancouver,Canada, rec. 7./8.10.1998
Cramer,Dylan (as) | Johnston,Ron (p) | Holy,Steve (b) | Nolan,John (dr)

CD 074 | CD | Allan And Allan
Allan Vaché-Harry Allen Quintet
Lover Come Back To Me | Jive At Five | Lake Ponchartrain Blues | Allen And Allen | Where Are You | What Can I Say After I Say I'm Sorry | Straighten Up And Fly Right | You Go To My Head | Tickle Toe | Corcovado(Quiet Nights) | Ben's Blues | Do Nothin' Till You Hear From Me | Stealin' Apples
Orlando,Florida, rec. 17./18.1.2000
Vaché,Allan (cl) | Allen,Harry (ts) | Higgins,Eddie (p) | Flanigan,Phil (b) | Metz,Eddie (dr)

CD 076 | CD | Jam Session Concert
The Sidney Bechet Society
'Deed I Do | Blues In The Air | Blues In Thirds | Basin Street Blues | Rosetta | Passport To Paradise | Do Nothin' Till You Hear From Me | St.Louis Blues | Bechet Medley: | Si Tu Vois Ma Mere- | Petite Fleur- | Summertime- | Mood Indigo- | Royal Garden Blues
NYC, rec. 13.9.1999
Sidney Bechet Society,The | Christopher,Evan (cl) | Davis,Spanky (tp) | Gordon,Wycliffe (tb) | Shane,Mark (p) | Lesberg,Jack (b) | Williams,Jackie (dr)

CD 077 | CD | The New York Allstars Play Lionel Hampton,Vol.2: Stompin' At The Savoy
The New York Allstars
Seven Come Eleven | Stompin' At The Savoy | Hamp's Boogie Woogie | Stardust | How High The Moon | Pennies From Heaven | Air Mail Special(alt.take) | Avalon(alt.take)
Live at The Hanse-Merkur Auditorium,Hamburg, rec. 17.10.1998
New York All Stars,The | Sandke,Randy (tp) | Williams,Roy (tb) | Sarpila,Antti (cl,ts) | Erstrand,Lars (vib) | Chirillo,James (g) | Wagner,Thilo (p) | Green,Dave (b) | Metz,Eddie (dr)

CD 078 | CD | Wagner,Mörike.Beck,Finally. | EAN 645347007826
Thilo Wagner Trio
Finally | I'll Be Seeing You | If I Were A Bell | My Romance | O Sole Mio | What Is This Thing Called Love | When You Wish Upon A Star | I'm Old Fashioned | Zelim | All Of You | Everything Happens To Me | Pennies From Heaven
Stuttgart, rec. 6./7.3.2001
Wagner,Thilo (p) | Mörike,Wolfgang (b) | Beck,Gregor (dr)

CD 079 | CD | That's Swing | EAN 645347007925
André Holst With Chris Dean's European Swing Orchestra
The Most Beautiful Girl In The World | Softly As I Leave You | Let's Face The Music And Dance | Please Don't Bug Me | All Or Nothing At All | Tribute To Valente(I Love Paris) | Fly Me To The Moon | Hit The Road Jack
London,GB, rec. 5.4.2000
Holst,André (voc) | Dean,Chris (tb) | Gibson,Dale (tp) | Greenwood,Andrew (tp) | Reaney,Terry (tp) | Dixon,Tony (tp) | Southcott,Derek (tb) | Moffat,Ian (tb) | Rae,Roger (tb) | Williams,Sarah (b-tb) | Taylor,Andy (reeds) | Thompson,Shaun (reeds) | Burney,Mike (reeds) | Ashworth.Nigel (reeds) | Nathaniel,Paul (reeds) | Brown,Trevor (p) | Messeder,André (b) | Verrell,Ronnie (dr)

Shiny Stockings | Route 66
Holst,André (voc) | Dean,Chris (tb) | Gibson,Dale (tp) | Greenwood,Andrew (tp) | Reaney,Terry (tp) | Dixon,Tony (tp) | Southcott,Derek (tb) | Moffat,Ian (tb) | Rae,Roger (tb) | Williams,Sarah (b-tb) | Taylor,Andy (reeds) | Thompson,Shaun (reeds) | Burney,Mike (reeds) | Ashworth.Nigel (reeds) | Nathaniel,Paul (reeds) | Brown,Trevor (p) | Messeder,André (b) | Verrell,Ronnie (dr) | Roos,Mary (voc)
-> Note:additional recordings,NYC,September 1992

CD 080 | CD | Tate Live | EAN 82750367
Buddy Tate With The Torsten Swingenberger Swintet
Tangerine | Shiny Stockings | Sweet Georgia Brown | Summertime | Jumpin' At The Woodside | She's Got It
Live at The Quasimodo,Berlin, rec. 15.4.1986
Tate,Buddy (fl,ts,voc) | Meurkens,Hendrik (vib,voc) | Weiss,Otto (p) | Gützkow,Dieter (b) | Zwingenberger,Torsten (dr)
-> Note: Es wurden diverse Armstrong-Original-Aufnahmen eingeblendet

CD 081 | CD | Standards For A New Century
Dunstan Coulber Quartet
You Do Something To Me | The Very Thought Of You | For All We Know | No Moon At All | I Love Paris | Blue Room | You Took Advantage Of Me | I Surrender Dear | Soon | I Got It Bad And That Ain't Good | Blues For Zain | It's All Right With Me | Dream A Little Dream Of Me
Ardingly,West Sussex,GB, rec. 24./25.9.2001
Coulber,Dunstan (cl) | Pearce,John (p) | Preston,Nik (b) | Brown,Steve (dr)

CD 082 | CD | Harlem 2000 | EAN 645347008229
Engelbert Wrobel-Chris Hopkins-Dan Barrett Sextet
Beyond The Blue Horizon | Four Or Five Times | Dreamy Mood | It's Been So Long | Solid Old Man | Angel's Idea | Echoes Of Harlem | Haven't Named It Yet | Drop Me Off In Harlem | Body And Soul | Harlem Sundown | I May Be Wrong(But I Think You're Wonderful) | B Flat Swing | Synthetic Love | A Lull At Dawn
Hamburg, rec. 12.-14.11.2000
Barrett,Dan (tb,co,voc) | Wrobel,Engelbert (cl,ts) | Hopkins,Chris (p) | Smith,John 'Butch' (ss,as,voc) | Ramond,Christian (b) | Mewes,Oliver (dr)

CD 2001 | CD | Slidin' Home
Wycliffe Gordon Group
Mood Indigo | Green Chimneys | It Don't Mean A Thing If It Ain't Got That Swing | Jolly June Jumey | Amazing Grace | What?! | Blooz...First Thaingh 'Dis Moanin' | The 'Hallelujah' Shout | My God
NYC, rec. 21./22.12.1998
Gordon,Wycliffe (tb,tuba) | Goines,Victor (cl,ts) | Reed,Eric (p) | Whitaker,Rodney Thomas (b) | Riley,Herlin (dr)

Do Nothin' Till You Hear From Me
Gordon,Wycliffe (tb,tuba) | Goines,Victor (cl,ts) | Reed,Eric (p) | Whitaker,Rodney Thomas (b) | Riley,Herlin (dr) | Grayson,Milt (voc)

Beauty's In The Eye
Gordon,Wycliffe (tb,tuba) | Goines,Victor (cl,ts) | Temperley,Joe (bs) | Reed,Eric (p) | Whitaker,Rodney Thomas (b) | Riley,Herlin (dr)

New Awlins'
Gordon,Wycliffe (tb,tuba) | Sandke,Randy (tp) | Goines,Victor (cl,ts) | Temperley,Joe (ss) | Reed,Eric (p) | Whitaker,Rodney Thomas (b) | Riley,Herlin (dr)

St.Louis Blues
Gordon,Wycliffe (tb,tuba) | Sandke,Randy (tp) | Goines,Victor (cl,ts) | Reed,Eric (p) | Whitaker,Rodney Thomas (b) | Riley,Herlin (dr)

CD 2002 | CD | Striplingnow!
Byron Stripling Sextet
Greasy Livin' | I Want To Be Happy | I Can't Get Started | Basie And Bean | East Of The Sun West Of The Moon | Julliette's Holiday | Rebop | Tired Of Pretty Women | Yesterdays | If I Had You | Glasstronic | My Ship
NYC, rec. 11.& 14.12.1998
Stripling,Byron (tp) | Glasser,David (as) | Wess,Frank (ts) | Charlap,Bill (p) | Washington,Peter (b) | Mackrel,Dennis (dr)

CD 2003 | CD | Uh! Oh!
The Dave Glasser/Clark Terry/Barry Harris Project
Uh! Oh! | Intimacy Of The Blues | The Nearness Of You | CT | Jumpin' At The Woodside
NYC, rec. 15./18.6.1999
Terry,Clark (tp) | Powell,Benny (tb) | Glasser,David (as) | Wess,Frank (ts) | Harris,Barry (p) | Washington,Peter (b) | Boyd,Curtis (dr)

Bye Bye Blackbird | Charise
Hargrove,Roy (tp,fl-h) | Powell,Benny (tb) | Glasser,David (as) | Wess,Frank (ts) | Harris,Barry (p) | Washington,Peter (b) | Boyd,Curtis (dr)

Bye-Yard | A Touch Of Kin | Blue Rose | 52nd Street Theme | FNH | Tranquility | Powell's Prances
Powell,Benny (tb) | Glasser,David (as) | Wess,Frank (ts) | Harris,Barry (p) | Washington,Peter (b) | Boyd,Curtis (dr)

CD 2004 | CD | Uptown Lowdown:A Jazz Salute To The Big Apple
The Nagel-Heyer Allstars
The Harlem Medley: | Echoes Of Harlem- | Drop Me Off In Harlem- | Jungle Nights In Harlem | Boys From Harlem | Sugar Hill Penthouse | Blue Bells Of Harlem | Harlem Speaks | Scrapple From The Apple | Nostalgia In Time Square | Grand Central | Take The 'A' Train
NYC, rec. 16.6.1999
Nagel-Heyer Allstars,The | Sandke,Randy (tp,ld) | Vaché,Warren (tp) | Vaché,Allan (cl) | Peplowski,Ken (cl,ts) | Robinson,Scott (fl,as,ts) | Temperley,Joe (bs) | Alden,Howard (g) | Reed,Eric (p) | Whitaker,Rodney Thomas (b) | Ascione,Joseph 'Joe' (dr)

Chinatown | Rose Of Washington Square- | Broadway Rose- | 42nd Street Theme | 52nd Street Theme
Nagel-Heyer Allstars,The | Sandke,Randy (tp,ld) | Vaché,Warren (tp) | Vaché,Allan (cl) | Peplowski,Ken (cl,ts) | Robinson,Scott (fl,as,ts) | Temperley,Joe (bs) | Alden,Howard (g) | Shane,Mark (p) | Whitaker,Rodney Thomas (b) | Ascione,Joseph 'Joe' (dr)

CD 2005 | CD | Fields Of Gold
Terell Stafford Quintet
Hey; It's Me You're Talkin' To | Minnesota | Dear Rudy | Ms.Shirley Scott | Ill Wind | If I Perish | Sagittarius | I Believe In You | His Eye Is On The Sparrow | Flashdance | That's All | September In The Rain
NYC, rec. 29./30.11.1999
Stafford,Terell (tp) | Hart,Antonio Maurice (ss,as) | Cunliffe,Bill (p,org) | Kitagawa,Kiyoshi (b) | Green,Rodney (dr)

CD 2006 | CD | Off Broadway
Frank Vignola Sextet
Funny How | Stars Fell On Alabama | Off Broadway | Limone's Blues | The Return | Stardust | Sing That | Cookin' At The Continental | Never Never | Annie | In The Hills | Frankly Speaking | Stars Fell On Alabama(alt.take) | It's All Right With Me | What's Up
NYC, rec. 1.&3.12.1999
Vignola,Frank (g) | Sandke,Randy (tp) | Wess,Frank (fl,ts) | Hanna,Sir Roland (p) | Goldsby,John (b) | Ascione,Joseph 'Joe' (dr)

CD 2007 | CD | The Search
Wycliffe Gordon Group
Cheeky | Touch It Lightly | Blues For Deac'n Cone
NYC, rec. 30.11./1.12.1999
Gordon,Wycliffe (tb) | Printup,Marcus (tp) | Nash,Ted (fl,as) | Blandings Jr.,Walter (ts) | Reed,Eric (p) | Whitaker,Rodney Thomas (b) | Harper,Winard (dr,perc)

The Search(part 1)-
Gordon,Wycliffe (didgeridoo) | Harper,Winard (dr,perc)

The Search(part 2)-
Gordon,Wycliffe (tb) | Westray,Ronald (tb) | Marsalis,Delfeayo (tb) | Krupa,Jen (tb) | Gibson,David 'Dave' (tb) | Nash,Ted (fl) | Reed,Eric (p) | Whitaker,Rodney Thomas (b) | Riley,Herlin (dr)

He Looked Beyond My Fault(Danny Boy)
Gordon,Wycliffe (tb) | Westray,Ronald (tb) | Krupa,Jen (tb) | Gibson,David 'Dave' (tb) | Floreska,Roger (b-tb)

Frantic Flight
Gordon,Wycliffe (tb) | Westray,Ronald (tb) | Marsalis,Delfeayo (tb) | Krupa,Jen (tb) | Gibson,David 'Dave' (tb) | Reed,Eric (p) | Whitaker,Rodney Thomas (b) | Riley,Herlin (dr)

Sign Me Up
Gordon,Wycliffe (tuba) | Westray,Ronald (tb) | Marsalis,Delfeayo (tb) | Reed,Eric (p) | Whitaker,Rodney Thomas (b) | Riley,Herlin (dr)

What Is This Thing Called Love | Ba-Lue Bolivar Ba-Lues-Are
Gordon,Wycliffe (tb) | Goines,Victor (ts) | Reed,Eric (p) | Whitaker,Rodney Thomas (b) | Riley,Herlin (dr)

Georgia On My Mind | Rhythm-A-Ning
Gordon,Wycliffe (tb) | Reed,Eric (p) | Whitaker,Rodney Thomas (b) | Riley,Herlin (dr)

Sweet Georgia Brown
Gordon,Wycliffe (tb) | Reed,Eric (p) | Whitaker,Rodney Thomas (b) | Harper,Winard (dr,perc)

Stardust
Gordon,Wycliffe (tb) | Reed,Eric (p)

CD 2008 | CD | Here We Come
Martin Sasse Trio
Groove Machine | The Modal Thing | Waltz For Katharina | Dear McCoy | Sail Away | On A Clear Day You Can See Forever | Ballade Für Juliane | I Had The Craziest Dream | Mr.K.
Köln, rec. 1.2.2000
Sasse,Martin (p) | Gailing,Henning (b) | Smock,Hendrik (dr)

CD 2009 | CD | In The Moment
Joachim Schoenecker Quartet
Better Than Words | Taxi Of The Desert | Analog Guy | Dawn | Do You Remember Me? | De Haan | Night Out | Dry Martino
Köln, rec. 19./20.2.2000
Schoenecker,Joachim (g) | Potter,Chris (ss,ts) | Goldsby,John (b) | Nussbaum,Adam (dr)

Joachim Schoenecker-Chris Potter
Three
Live at 'Alte Schmiede',Düsseldorf, rec. 18.2.2000
Schoenecker,Joachim (g) | Potter,Chris (ts) | Goldsby,John (b) | Nussbaum,Adam (dr)

Joachim Schoenecker
Day Dream
Hamburg, rec. 19.9.2000
Schoenecker,Joachim (g-solo)

CD 2010 | CD | Happiness
Eric Reed Orchestra
Three Dances | Island Grind- | Latin Bump- | Boogie Down- | Suite Sisters: | Fine & Brown- | Crazy Red- | Black Beauty- | Mood Indigo | Someone Else's Love
NYC, rec. 20./21.12.2000
Reed,Eric (p) | Printup,Marcus (tp) | Gordon,Wycliffe (tb) | Anderson,Wessell 'Wes' (as) | Escoffery,Wayne (ss,ts) | Mori,Barak (b) | Green,Rodney (dr)

Say You Care
Reed,Eric (p) | Printup,Marcus (tp) | Gordon,Wycliffe (tb) | Tolentino,Julius (as) | Anderson,Wessell 'Wes' (as) | Escoffery,Wayne (ss,ts) | Mori,Barak (b) | Green,Rodney (dr)

Devil In A Dress
Reed,Eric (p) | Printup,Marcus (tp) | Gordon,Wycliffe (tb) | Anderson,Wessell 'Wes' (as) | Escoffery,Wayne (ss,ts) | Mori,Barak (b) | Green,Rodney (dr) | Thoms,Renato (perc)

Happiness
Reed,Eric (p) | Printup,Marcus (tp) | Rodriguez,Mike (tp) | Tucker,Dion (tb) | Gordon,Wycliffe (tb) | Anderson,Wessell 'Wes' (as) | Escoffery,Wayne (ss,ts) | Mori,Barak (b) | Green,Rodney (dr)

Romantic Rag
Reed,Eric (p) | Printup,Marcus (tp) | Rodriguez,Mike (tp) | Tucker,Dion (tb) | Gordon,Wycliffe (tb) | Blandings Jr.,Walter (cl) | Anderson,Wessell 'Wes' (as) | Escoffery,Wayne (ss,ts) | Mori,Barak (b) | Green,Rodney (dr)

CD 2011 | CD | 2Gether
Warren Vaché And Bill Charlap
If I Should Lose You | You And The Night And The Music | Darn That Dream | What'll I Do | Easy Living | Nip-Hoc Waltz(Homage To Chopin) | Etude No.2 | Soon | Dancing On The Ceiling | Prelude To A Kiss | St.Louis Blues
Old Greenwich,CT, rec. 13./14.12.2000
Vaché,Warren (fl-h,co) | Charlap,Bill (p)

CD 2012 | CD | A Mooth One
Karl Schloz Quartet
Wholly Cats | Moonglow | Tricotism | In Love In Vain | Recado Bossa Nova | Girl Talk | Jersey Bounce | It Might As Well Be Spring | Lester Leaps In | Isn't It Romantic
NYC, rec. 23.10.2000
Schloz,Karl (g) | Allen,Harry (ts) | Monte,Tony (p) | LaSpina,Steve (b)

CD 2013 | CD | North By Northwest
Roy Powell Quartet
Social Intelligence | Paws | Vemond | Borrowed Time | Oxymoron | Somewhere | Scramble | A Simple Answer
London,GB, rec. 17./18.11.1998
Powell,Roy (p) | Walker,Mike (g) | Andersen,Arild (b) | Marshall,John (dr)

CD 2014 | CD | Viewpoint
John Goldsby Sextet
I Love Paris | Cup Bearers | Bohemia After Dark | Le Cannet | Mr.McGregor | Brazilian Hat Trick | Sleepy Boys | In The Hills | Every Time We Say Goodbye | Replaceable You | Annie | Seven For Twelve | The Folks Who Live On The Hill
Köln, rec. 12.-14.12.2000
Goldsby,John (b) | Marshall,John (tp,fl-h) | Peters,Oliver (ss,ts) | Chisholm,Hayden (as) | Chastenier,Frank (p) | Dekker,Hans (dr)

CD 2015 | CD | Time Changes
Wayne Escoffery Quartet
Come Back Lucky | Beatrice | After You've Gone | That's All | Times Change | Dawn | Triste | Water Pistol
NYC, rec. 4.1.2001
Escoffery,Wayne (ss,ts) | Goldberg,Aaron (p) | Forbes,Joel (b) | Allen,Carl (dr)

CD 2016 | CD | Byron,Get On Free
Byron Stripling Quintet
Back Home Again In Indiana | Gee Baby Ain't I Good To You | Sometimes I'm Happy
NYC, rec. 15.& 18.12.2000
Stripling,Byron (tp,voc) | Gordon,Wycliffe (tb) | Charlap,Bill (p) | Coleman,Ira (b) | Mackrel,Dennis (dr)

Byron Stripling Sextet
Frank's Magic
Stripling,Byron (tp) | Gordon,Wycliffe (tb) | Wess,Frank (ts) | Charlap,Bill (p) | Coleman,Ira (b) | Mackrel,Dennis (dr)

Byron Stripling Quintet
Con Alma | Lover Man(Oh,Where Can You Be?) | Byron Get One Free | Woody'n You
Stripling,Byron (tp) | Wess,Frank (ts) | Charlap,Bill (p) | Washington,Peter (b) | Mackrel,Dennis (dr)

Byron Stripling Quartet
I Can't Give You Anything But Love
Stripling,Byron (tp,voc) | Charlap,Bill (p) | Coleman,Ira (b) | Mackrel,Dennis (dr)

Byron Stripling Trio
I'm Old Fashioned
Stripling,Byron (tp,voc) | Charlap,Bill (p) | Mackrel,Dennis (dr)

CD 2017 | CD | Duet
Shinichi Kato-Masahiko Sato
Old Diary | Smiling Sunlight | Clouds In Green | You May Be Asked For | Bass Folk Song | Dr. R | Something Close To Love | Too Little Tenderness | You Are In My Thoughts | Blues For Pluto | A Song For Jack
Saitama,Japan, rec. 24./25.3.2000
Kato,Shinichi (b) | Sato,Masahiko (p)

CD 2018 | CD | Maya | EAN 645347201828

David Gibson Sextet
Big John | Solid State | Maya | Snide Remarks | Speak Low
NYC, rec. 17.6.2001
Gibson,David 'Dave' (tb) | Sneider,John (tp,fl-h) | Escoffery,Wayne (ts) | Manasia,Jeremy (p) | Hartman,Peter (b) | Leone,Tony (dr)
New Level | Tré | What's New? | Indomitable
NYC, rec. 9.9.2001
Gibson,David 'Dave' (tb) | Sneider,John (tp,fl-h) | Escoffery,Wayne (ts) | Manasia,Jeremy (p) | Burno,Dwayne (b) | Leone,Tony (dr)

CD 2019 | CD | The New Boogaloo
Marcus Printup Sextet
Sardinian Princess | In A Sentimental Mood | Printupian Prance | Speak Low
NYC, rec. 3.11.2001
Printup,Marcus (tp) | Gordon,Wycliffe (tb) | Blandings Jr.,Walter (ts) | Colligan,George (p) | Archer,Vincente (b) | Edwards,Donald (dr)
The Bullet Train | The Weeping Prince(for Malcolm) | The New Boogaloo | Soul Waltz | The Inception
NYC, rec. 5.11.2001
Printup,Marcus (tp) | Gordon,Wycliffe (tb) | Blandings Jr.,Walter (ts) | Lewis,Eric (p) | Archer,Vincente (b) | Edwards,Donald (dr)

CD 2020 | CD | Lost In The Stars | EAN 645347202023
Ken Peplowski Quartet
If This Isn't Love | Why Do I Love You | Ataraxi | My Ship | Ballad For Very Tired And Very Sad Lotus Eaters | People.Will Say We're In Love | Marchons | Lament | Good Morning Heartache | Sleep | Lost In The Stars- | When You Wish Upon A Star- | Piece No.8 From Benny's Gig
NYC, rec. 6./7.11.2001
Peplowski,Ken (cl,ts) | Aronov,Ben (p) | Cohen,Greg (b) | Nash,Lewis (dr)

CD 2021 | CD | Out Of This Mood | EAN 645347202122
Lyambiko And Her Trio
Some Other Time | If I Were A Bell | Chega De Saudade(No More Blues) | Afro Blue | Gone With The Wind | Can't Get Out Of This Mood | Our Love Is Here To Stay | I Ain't Got Nothin' But The Blues | Parakeet Prowl | Mean To Me | Worksong | Do Nothin' Till You Hear From Me | Miss Celie's Blues | You'd Be So Nice To Come Home To | Skylark
Berlin, rec. 19./20.12.2001
Lyambiko (voc) | Lowenthal,Marque (p) | Draganis,Robin (b) | Zwingenberger,Torsten (dr,perc)

CD 2023 | CD | We | EAN 645347202320
Wycliffe Gordon-Eric Reid
The Lord's Prayer | Paris Blues | This Rhythm On My Mind | Embraceable You | Cherokee | Precious Lord Take My Hand | Lament | Toast My Bread | He Looked Beyond My Fault(Danny Boy) | He Cares
NYC, rec. 29.10.2001
Gordon,Wycliffe (tb,voc) | Reed,Eric (p)

CD 2024 | CD | Candoli Live | EAN 645347202429
Conte Candoli Quartet
I Dig Fig | There Is No Greater Love | Lover Man(Oh,Where Can You Be?) | You And The Night And The Music | Black Orpheus | Just Friends
Live at 'Birdland',Neuburg/Donau, rec. 26.5.2000
Candoli,Conte (tp) | Pichl,Bernhard (p) | Zenker,Martin (b) | Hollander,Rick (dr)

CD 2031 | CD | How Swee It Is | EAN 645347203129
Loren Stillman Quartet
Between The Devil And God | Happy | Meat | Chicken | How Sweet It Is | Meat Snake | Darling Clementine | Chasing The White Rabbit
NYC, rec. 15.5.2001
Stillman,Loren (as) | Lossing,Russ (p) | Lee,Scott (b) | Hirshfield,Jeff (dr)

CD 2032 | CD | The Joyride | EAN 645347203228
Wycliffe Gordon Quintet
Blues Impromptus | The Island Boy | Bad Time | Let's Call This(Walkin' The Blues) | Rhythm Cole | Wishing Well | Just Going On | Blessed
NYC, rec. 16./17.12.2000
Gordon,Wycliffe (tp,tb,tuba,p,voc) | Goines,Victor (cl,ss,ts) | Barron,Farid (p) | Whitaker,Rodney Thomas (b) | Riley,Herlin (dr)

CD 2033 | CD | Echoes | EAN 645347203327
Stephan Noel Lang Trio
Allright ! | Kallipygos | Here's To Joy | Parting | Echoes | Lily Of The Valley | Verlangen | Mr.R.M. | You Don't Know What Love Is | What's My Name? | Prolog | Goodbye | 16-Bar-Blues
Berlin, rec. 15.-17.7.2002
Lang,Stephan Noel (p) | Draganic,Robin (b) | Winch,Rainer (dr)

CD 2035 | CD | Round And Round | EAN 645347203525
Marc Copland-Greg Osby
Silent Attitude | Balloonman | Round She Goes | Mentor's Praise | Whatever The Moon | The Wizzard | Copious | Deed-Lee-Yah | Easy Living
NYC, rec. 20.11.2002
Osby,Greg (as) | Copland,Marc (p)

CD 2037 | CD | Cliffhanger | EAN 645347203723
Randy Sandke Quintet
Let's Face The Music And Dance | Nobody Else But Me | What's New? | Come Rain Or Come Shine | One For Mulgrew | I Fall In Love Too Easily | One Fine Day In May | I Concentrate On You | Willow Weep For Me | No Moon At All | Limehouse Blues
NYC, rec. 6./7.12.1999
Sandke,Randy (tp,fl-h) | Allen,Harry (ts) | Miller,Mulgrew (p) | Washington,Peter (b) | Washington,Kenny (dr)
Randy Sandke Sextet
Cliffhanger
NYC, rec. 6./7.12.1999
Sandke,Randy (tp,fl-h) | Gordon,Wycliffe (tb) | Allen,Harry (ts) | Miller,Mulgrew (p) | Washington,Peter (b) | Washington,Kenny (dr)

CD 2038 | CD | Intuition | EAN 645347203822
Wayne Escoffery Quintet
Intuition | Tightrope | The Alchemist | The First One | Gazelle | Enduring Freedom | I'm Old Fashioned | Is This The Same Place I'm In?
NYC, rec. 2001
Escoffery,Wayne (ss,ts) | Pelt,Jeremy (tp) | Germanson,Rick (p,fender-rhodes) | Cannon,Gerald (b) | Peterson,Ralph (dr)
I Should Care
Escoffery,Wayne (ss,ts) | Pelt,Jeremy (tp) | Germanson,Rick (p,fender-rhodes) | Cannon,Gerald (b) | Peterson,Ralph (dr) | Leonhart,Carolyn (voc)

CD 2041 | CD | Heroes | EAN 645347204126
Donald Harrison Trio
Heroes | Blues For The New Millenium | My Funny Valentine | One OF A Kinf | Double Trouble | Receipt Please | Candelight | Solar | Freestyle | Iko-Iko | Straight No Chaser
Harrison,Donald (as) | Carter,Ron (b) | Cobham,Billy (dr)

CD 3002 | CD | Randy Sandke Meets Bix Beiderbecke
The New York Allstars
Fidgety Feet | Tia Juana | Davenport Blues | My Pretty Girl | Singin' The Blues- | I'm Coming Virginia- | Changes | When | Because My Baby Don't Mean May Be Now | Sorry | Wait 'Till You See My Cherie | Riverboat Shuffle | China Boy | My Melancholy Baby | At The Jazz Band Ball | I'll Be A Friend With Pleasure | Clarinet Marmalade | Sweet Sue Just You
Live at Musikhalle Hamburg, rec. 1.5.1993
New York All Stars,The | Sandke,Randy (tp) | Barrett,Dan (tp,tb) | Peplowski,Ken (cl) | Robinson,Scott (bass-sax,c-mel-sax,co) | Shane,Mark (p) | Grosz,Marty (g,voc) | Milliman,Linc (b,tuba) | Ratajczak,Dave (dr)

CD 3039 | CD | Pure Love | EAN 645347203921
Zona Sul
The Waters Of March(Aguas De Marco) | O Cantador | Dans Mon Ile | Vivo Sohando(Dreamer) | Falando De Amor | Eu Vim Da Bahia | Chovendo Na Roseira(Double Rainbow) | If You Never Come To Me | Estrada Do Sol | Bonita | Estate(Summer) | Retrato Em Branco E Preto | Dorme Profundo | The Waters Of March(Aguas De Marco-alt.take) | Vivo Sohando(Dreamer-alt.take) | Inutil Paisagem(Useless Landscape)
München, rec. 28./29.1.2003
Zona Zul | Wegener,Sophie (voc) | Tagliani,Pedro (g) | Jost,Tizian (p) | Medan,Sava (b) | v. Hadeln,Hajo (dr)

CD 5001 | CD | Just Friends
George Masso-Ken Peplowski Quintet
You'd Be So Nice To Come Home To | In A Mellow Tone | More Than You Know | Blue Monk | If I Were A Bell | It All Depends On You | Just Friends | I Thought About You | On The Alamo | Three Little Words
Live at The 'Amerikahaus',Hamburg, rec. 27.8.1994
Masso,George (tb) | Peplowski,Ken (cl) | Dee,Brian (p) | Skeat,Len (b) | Hanna,Jake (dr)

CD 5002 | CD | A Night At Birdland Vol. 1
Harry Allen Quintet
My Heart Stood Still | Slow Boat To China | Tickle Toe | You Took Advantage Of Me | Stardust | Sometimes I'm Happy | How Deep Is The Ocean | I Got It Bad And That Ain't Good | The Man I Love
Live at Birdland,Hamburg, rec. 19./20.11.1993
Allen,Harry (ts) | Sandke,Randy (tp) | Dee,Brian (p) | Skeat,Len (b) | Jackson,Oliver (dr)

CD 5003 | CD | Cookin'
Butch Miles-Howard Alden Sextet
Oh! Lady Be Good | Did You Call Her Today | The Claw | Azalea | Them There Eyes | I Can't Believe That You're In Love With Me | Tico Tico | Jubilee | Barney's Blues | What A Little Moonlight Can Do | Gone With The Wind | Funkallero | Tickle Toe
Live at The 'Amerikahaus',Hamburg, rec. 26.11.1994
Miles,Butch (dr) | Sandke,Randy (tp) | Allen,Harry (ts) | Alden,Howard (g) | Tate,Frank (b) | Richards[Alden],Terrie (voc)

CD 5004 | CD | Swing's The Village
Buck Clayton Swing Band
Scorpio | Swingin' On The State Line | Horn O'Plenty | Rise 'N' Shine | The One For Me | B.C.Special | Black Sheep Blues | Sparky | Song For Sarah | Cadillac Taxi | What A Beautiful Yesteryear | The Bowery Bunch
Live at The Greenwich Village,NYC, rec. 16.-18.2.1990
Clayton,Buck (arr,ld) | Eckert,John (tp) | Sandke,Jordan (tp) | Stripling,Byron (tp) | Vaché,Warren (tp) | Finders,Matt (tb) | Pring,Bob (tb) | Tibbs,Harvey (tb) | Dodgion,Jerry (as) | Lawrence,Doug (ts) | Wess,Frank (ts) | Robinson,Scott (bs) | Temperley,Joe (bs) | Chirillo,James (g) | Katz,Dick (p) | Seaton,Lynn (b) | Mackrel,Dennis (dr)

NH 1008 | CD | Christmas Jazz!
Mark Shane's X-Mas Allstars
Santa Claus Is Coming To Town | Hark! The Herald Angels Sing | Oh Christmas Tree(O Tannenbaum) | Sleigh Ride
NYC, rec. 17./18.12.1998
Shane,Mark (p,voc) | Allen,Harry (ts) | Kellso,Jon-Erik (tp) | Chirillo,James (g,bj) | O'Leary,Pat (b) | Ratajczak,Dave (dr)
Jim Galloway-Jay McShann Quartet
The Christmas Song | Auld Lang Syne | Rudolph The Red Nosed Reindeer
Toronto,Canada, rec. 8./9.11.1992
Galloway,Jim (ss,ts,bs) | McShann,Jay (p) | Swainson,Neil (b) | Alleyne,Archie (dr)
Sackville All Stars
Winter Wonderland | Good King Wenceslas | Santa Claus Came In The Spring
Toronto,Canada, rec. 29./30.3.1986
Sackville All Stars | Galloway,Jim (ss) | Sutton,Ralph (p) | Hinton,Milt (b) | Johnson,Gus (dr)
Jan Harrington Band
Christmas In New Orleans
Hamburg, rec. 6.12.1996
Harrington,Jan (ld) | Gürtler,Werner (tb) | Marks,Jon (p) | Bartels,Gerald (b) | Smith,Harold (dr,voc)
Chris Murrell-Bobby Irving III
Silent Night
Hamburg, rec. 10.12.1994
Murrell,Christopher 'Chris' (voc) | Irving III,Robert (p)

NH 1009 | CD | Ellington For Lovers
Harry Allen Quintet
Sophisticated Lady | I Got It Bad And That Ain't Good
Live at Birdland,Hamburg, rec. 19./20.11.1993
Allen,Harry (ts) | Sandke,Randy (tp) | Dee,Brian (p) | Skeat,Len (b) | Jackson,Oliver (dr)
Danny Moss-Roy Williams Quintet
Blues To Be There | Mood Indigo
Hamburg, rec. 19.10.1998
Moss,Danny (ts) | Williams,Roy (tb) | Pearce,John (p) | Skeat,Len (b) | Antolini,Charly (dr)
Wycliffe Gordon Group
Do Nothin' Till You Hear From Me
NYC, rec. 22.12.1998
Gordon,Wycliffe (tb) | Goines,Victor (cl) | Reed,Eric (p) | Whitaker,Rodney Thomas (b) | Riley,Herlin (dr) | Grayson,Milt (voc)
Allan Vaché Swingtet
Warm Valley
Live at The 'Amerikahaus',Hamburg, rec. 6.8.1994
Vaché,Allan (cl) | Vaché,Warren (co) | Varro,Johnny (p) | Douglas,Jim (g) | Tate,Frank (b) | Masessa,Mike (dr)
In A Mellow Tone
New York All Stars,The | Sandke,Randy (tp,ld) | Barrett,Dan (tb) | Robinson,Scott (bass-sax) | Shane,Mark (p) | Grosz,Marty (g) | Milliman,Linc (b) | Ratajczak,Dave (dr) | Peplowski,Ken (dr)
Bill Allred-Roy Williams Quintet
Satin Doll
Hamburg, rec. 28.9.1995
Allred,Bill (tb) | Williams,Roy (tb) | Varro,Johnny (p) | Eckinger,Isla (b) | Miles,Buddy (dr)
Warren Vaché-Allen Vaché Sextet
Squeeze Me
Orlando,Florida, rec. 20.2.1998
Vaché,Warren (fl-h,co) | Vaché,Allan (cl) | Higgins,Eddie (p) | Alden,Howard (g) | Flanigan,Phil (b) | Metz Jr.,Ed 'Eddie' (dr)
Randy Sandke-Howard Alden
Azalea
Hamburg, rec. 26.11.1994
Sandke,Randy (tp) | Alden,Howard (g)
Oscar Klein's Anniversary Band
Creole Love Call
Hamburg, rec. 6.1.1995
Klein,Oscar (cl) | Meerwald,Willi (tb) | Keller,Werner (cl) | Wrobel,Engelbert (cl) | Mussolini,Romano (p) | Patruno,Lino (g) | Van Oven,Bob (b) | Antolini,Charly (dr)
Rex Allen's Swing Express
Duke Ellington Medley: | In My Solitude- | Chelsea Bridge- | Do Nothin' Till You Hear From Me | I Got It Bad And That Ain't Good- | Mood Indigo-
Hamburg, rec. 20.10.1994
Allen,Rex (tb) | Barrett,Dan (tp) | Rothermel,Jim (cl,as) | Allen,Harry (ts) | Shane,Mark (p) | Pizzarelli,Bucky (g) | Tate,Frank (b) | Beck,Gregor (dr)

NH 1010 | CD | If I Could Be With You | EAN 645347101029
Byron Stripling And Friends
Struttin' With Some Barbecue | Ballad Medley: | Thanks A Million- | Rockin' Chair- | Do You Know What It Means To Miss New Orleans- | If I Could Be With You One Hour Tonight | Mack The Knife(Moritat)- | The Faithfull Husar- | Big Butter And Egg Man From The West | When It's Sleepy Time Down South
Live at The Congress Center Hamburg, rec. 18.11.1995
Stripling,Byron (tp,voc) | Sandke,Randy (tp) | Helleny,Joel (tb) | Davern,Kenny (cl) | Shane,Mark (p) | Cohen,Greg (b) | Ostwald,David (tuba) | Ascione,Joseph 'Joe' (dr)
On The Sunny Side Of The Street | I Double Dare You | I'm Confessin'(That I Love You) | St.Louis Blues | West End Blues | Tiger Rag
Live at The Hanse-Merkur Auditorium,Hamburg, rec. 28.2.1998
Stripling,Byron (tp,voc) | Sandke,Randy (tp) | Helleny,Joel (tb) | Vaché,Allan (cl) | Varro,Johnny (p) | Haggart,Bob (b) | Ascione,Joseph 'Joe' (dr)

NH 1011 | CD | Blues Of Summer
Danny Moss Meets Buddha's Gamblers
D.M. Blues
Winterthur,CH, rec. 20.-23.11.1996
Moss,Danny (ts) | Buddha's Gamblers | Bühler,Heinz (tp) | Meier,Hans (tb) | Keller,Werner (cl) | Scheidegger,Buddha (p) | Schmidli,Peter (g) | Kummer,Vinzenz (b) | Capello,Carlo (dr)
Allan Vaché-Antti Sarpila Quintet
Blues Of Summer
Hamburg, rec. 15.10.1995
Vaché,Allan (cl) | Sarpila,Antti (ss) | Shane,Mark (p) | Skeat,Len (b) | Ascione,Joseph 'Joe' (dr)
Warren Vaché With Joe Puma
Too Phat Blues
NYC, rec. 18./19.5.1999
Vaché,Warren (co,voc) | Puma,Joe (g) | Wall,Murray (b) | Locke,Eddie (dr)
Buck Clayton Swing Band
Black Sheep Blues
NYC, rec. 16.-18.2.1990
Clayton,Buck (arr,ld) | Eckert,John (tp) | Sandke,Jordan (tp) | Stripling,Byron (tp) | Vaché,Warren (tp) | Finders,Matt (tb) | Pring,Bob (tb) | Tibbs,Harvey (tb) | Dodgion,Jerry (as) | Lawrence,Doug (ts) | Wess,Frank (ts) | Robinson,Scott (bs) | Temperley,Joe (bs) | Chirillo,James (g) | Katz,Dick (p) | Seaton,Lynn (b) | Mackrel,Dennis (dr)
Butch Miles And Friends
Barney's Blues
Live at The 'Amerikahaus',Hamburg, rec. 26.11.1994
Miles,Buddy (dr) | Alden,Howard (g) | Tate,Frank (b)
Bill Allred-Roy Williams Quintet
Sunhat Blues
Hamburg, rec. 28.9.1995
Allred,Bill (tb) | Williams,Roy (tb) | Varro,Johnny (p) | Eckinger,Isla (b) | Miles,Buddy (dr)
The Dave Glasser/Clark Terry/Barry Harris Project
Intimacy Of The Blues
NYC, rec. 15./18.6.1999
Terry,Clark (tp) | Powell,Benny (tb) | Glasser,David (as) | Wess,Frank (ts) | Harris,Barry (p) | Washington,Peter (b) | Boyd,Curtis (dr)
Bob Wilber And Friends
I Gotta Right To Sing The Blues
Live at The 'Amerikahaus',Hamburg, rec. 28.9.1996
Wilber,Bob (ss) | Sarpila,Antti (cl) | Shane,Mark (p) | Flanigan,Phil (b) | Ascione,Joseph 'Joe' (dr) | Horton,Pug (voc)
Oscar Klein
Oscar's Blues
Live at The 'Amerikahaus',Hamburg, rec. 5.1.1995
Klein,Oscar (g)
Wycliffe Gordon Group
St.Louis Blues
NYC, rec. 21./22.12.1998
Gordon,Wycliffe (tb) | Sandke,Randy (tp) | Goines,Victor (cl,ts) | Reed,Eric (p) | Whitaker,Rodney Thomas (b) | Riley,Herlin (dr)
Warren Vaché Quintet
Blues Times(2)
NYC, rec. 13./14.5.1996
Vaché,Warren (co) | Sandke,Randy (tp) | Drew Jr.,Kenny (p) | Wall,Murray (b) | Cobb,Jimmy (dr)
Harry Allen Quartet
Everyday I Have The Blues
Live at The 'Amerikahaus',Hamburg, rec. 28.5.1994
Allen,Harry (ts) | Bunch,John (p) | Irwin,Dennis (b) | Jackson,Duffy (dr)

NH 1014 | CD | Love Songs Live!
But Beautiful | This Time The Dream's On Me
Allen,Harry (ts) | Bunch,John (p) | Irwin,Dennis (b) | Jackson,Duffy (dr)
Every Time We Say Goodbye
Live at The Fabrik,Hamburg, rec. 16.11.1993
Allen,Harry (ts) | Dee,Brian (p) | Skeat,Len (b) | Jackson,Oliver (dr)
Harry Allen Quintet
Once I Loved | Skycraper | The Touch Of Your Lips | O Grande Amor
Live in Belfast, rec. 1996
Allen,Harry (ts) | Alden,Howard (g) | McKenna,Dave (p) | Tate,Frank (b) | Miles,Buddy (dr)
Sweet Lorraine | Sophisticated Lady | Stardust
Live at Birdland,Hamburg, rec. 19./20.11.1993
Allen,Harry (ts) | Sandke,Randy (tp) | Dee,Brian (p) | Skeat,Len (b) | Jackson,Oliver (dr)

NH 1015 | CD | Girltalk
Caterina Valente-Catherine Michel
Chiquilin De Bachin | Martina(Les Enfants Qui Pleurent) | And So It Goes | Prelude No.3 | With A Song In My Heart | Andantino(Sonata In C-Mino)- | The Most Beautiful Sea- | All Of A Sudden My Heart Sings | Tout Ca(Count Every Star) | Eu Nao Exixte | Bolero | Papa N'as Pas Voulu
Fino Mornasco,Italy, rec. 1998
Valente,Caterina (g,voc,perc) | Michel,Catherine (harp)
Gigi
Valente,Caterina (g,voc,perc) | Michel,Catherine (harp) | Francesco,Silvio (pamdeiro,tambourine)
The Way We Were
Valente,Caterina (g,voc,perc) | Michel,Catherine (harp) | Mambretti,Sebastiano (shaker)

NHR SP 3 | CD | Full Circle:Gospels And Spirituals
Christopher Murrell-Robert Irving III
Amazing Grace | Go Tell It On The Mountain | Christopher Murrell Speaking | He Looked Beyond My Fault | How Great Thou Art | I'll Fly Away | Mighty Spirit | Hallelujah | I Surrender Dear | Silent Night | Precious Lord Take My Hand | Amen
Live at The 'Amerikahaus',Hamburg, rec. 10.12.1994
Murrell,Christopher 'Chris' (voc) | Irving III,Robert (p,org,voc)

NHR SP 4 | CD | Jan Harrington's Christmas In New Orleans
Jan Harrington Sextet
Christmas In New Orleans | Go Tell It On The Mountain | A Christmas Song | Love Train | Jingle Bells | Oh Tannenbaum | Santa Claus Is Coming To Town | Put A Little Love In Your Heart | Silver Bells | The First Noel | Is That You,Santa Claus? | When The Saints Go Marching In- | Encore:Amen- | Angels We Have Heard On High | Stille Nacht
Live at The 'Amerikahaus',Hamburg, rec. 6.12.1996
Harrington,Jan (voc) | Gürtler,Werner (tb) | Marks,Jon (p) | Bartels,Gerald (b) | Smith,Harold (dr,voc) | Fields,Linda (voc)

NHR SP 5 | CD | The First Sampler
George Masso Allstars
Soon
Live at Musikhalle Hamburg, rec. 26.9.1992
Masso,George (tb) | Sandke,Randy (tp) | Davern,Kenny (cl) | Moss,Danny (ts) | Higgins,Eddie (p) | Skeat,Len (b) | Hanna,Jake (dr)
The New York Allstars
Because My Baby Don't Mean May Be Now
Live at Musikhalle Hamburg, rec. 1.5.1993
New York All Stars,The | Sandke,Randy (tp) | Barrett,Dan (tb) | Peplowski,Ken (cl) | Robinson,Scott (bs) | Shane,Mark (p) | Grosz,Marty (g) | Milliman,Linc (b) | Ratajczak,Dave (dr)
Rosetta
Hamburg, rec. 2.5.1993
New York All Stars,The | Sandke,Randy (tp,ld) | Barrett,Dan (tb) | Robinson,Scott (ts) | Shane,Mark (p) | Grosz,Marty (g) | Milliman,Linc (b) | Ratajczak,Dave (dr) | Peplowski,Ken (dr)
A Salute To Eddie Condon
Wabash Blues
Live at Musikhalle Hamburg, rec. 25.9.1993
A Salute To Eddie Condon | Polcer,Ed (co) | Havens,Bob (tb) | Vaché,Allan (cl) | Barnes,John (bs) | Varro,Johnny (p) | Douglas,Jim (g) | Haggart,Bob (b) | Miles,Butch (dr)
The Yamaha International Allstar Band
Jumpin' At The Woodside
Live at The Fabrik,Hamburg, rec. 16.11.1993
Yamaha International Allstar Band,The | Sandke,Randy (tp) | Tilitz,Jerry (tb) | Allen,Harry (ts) | Moss,Danny (ts) | Sarpila,Antti (cl) | Dee,Brian (p) | Skeat,Len (b) | Jackson,Oliver (dr)

The Buck Clayton Legacy
Come Again
Live at Birdland,Hamburg, rec. 17./18.11.1993
Buck Clayton Legacy,The | Sandke,Randy (tp) | Tilitz,Jerry (tb) | Sarpila,Antti (cl) | Allen,Harry (ts) | Moss,Danny (ts) | Dee,Brian (p) | Skeat,Len (b) | Jackson,Oliver (dr)

Harry Allen Quintet
You Took Advantage Of Me
Live at Birdland,Hamburg, rec. 19./20.11.1993
Allen,Harry (ts) | Sandke,Randy (tp) | Dee,Brian (p) | Skeat,Len (b) | Jackson,Oliver (dr)

The European Jazz Ginats
When You're Smiling
Live at Musikhalle Hamburg, rec. 29.3.1994
European Jazz Giants,The | Klein,Oscar (tp) | Williams,Roy (tb,voc) | Sarpila,Antti (cl) | Thilo,Jesper (ts) | Chaix,Henri (p) | Meyer,Peter 'Banjo' (bj) | Pitt,Vic (b) | Antolini,Charly (dr)

Harry Allen Quartet
Everyday I Have The Blues
Live at The 'Amerikahaus',Hamburg, rec. 28.5.1994
Allen,Harry (ts) | Bunch,John (p) | Irwin,Dennis (b) | Jackson,Duffy (dr)

Warren Vaché Quintet
I Fall In Love Too Easily
Live at The 'Amerikahaus',Hamburg, rec. 25.6.1994
Vaché,Warren (co) | Lemon,Brian (p) | Cliff,Dave (g) | Green,Dave (b) | Ganley,Allan (dr)

Allan Vaché Swingtet
There Is No Greater Love
Live at The 'Amerikahaus',Hamburg, rec. 6.8.1994
Vaché,Allan (cl) | Vaché,Warren (co) | Varro,Johnny (p) | Douglas,Jim (g) | Tate,Frank (b) | Masessa,Mike (dr)

George Masso Quintet
In A Mellow Tone
Live at The 'Amerikahaus',Hamburg, rec. 27.8.1994
Masso,George (tb) | Peplowski,Ken (cl) | Dee,Brian (p) | Skeat,Len (b) | Hanna,Jake (dr)

Summit Reunion
If Dreams Come True
Live at The 'Amerikahaus',Hamburg, rec. 24.9.1994
Summit Reunion | Wilber,Bob (ss) | Davern,Kenny (cl) | Cliff,Dave (g) | Green,Dave (b) | Worth,Bobby (dr)

NHR SP 6 | CD | The Second Sampler

Rex Allen's Swing Express
Take The 'A' Train
Live at Musikhalle Hamburg, rec. 20.10.1994
Allen,Rex (tb) | Barrett,Dan (tp) | Rothermel,Jim (as) | Allen,Harry (ts) | Shane,Mark (p) | Pizzarelli,Bucky (g) | Tate,Frank (b) | Beck,Gregor (dr)

Danny Moss Quartet
I'm Glad There Is You
Hamburg, rec. 17.11.1994
Moss,Danny (ts) | Lemon,Brian (p) | Skeat,Len (b) | Miles,Butch (dr)

The Buck Clayton Legacy
Fiesta In Blue
Live at The Fabrik,Hamburg, rec. 15.11.1994
Buck Clayton Legacy,The | Sandke,Randy (tp) | Tilitz,Jerry (tb) | Sarpila,Antti (ss) | Allen,Harry (ts) | Moss,Danny (ts) | Robinson,Scott (bs) | Dee,Brian (p) | Skeat,Len (b) | Miles,Buddy (dr)

Jeanie Lambe And The Danny Moss Quartet
You Came A Long Way From St. Louis
Lambe,Jeanie (voc) | Moss,Danny (ts) | Lemon,Brian (p) | Skeat,Len (b) | Miles,Buddy (dr)

Butch Miles And Friends
Jubilee
Live at The 'Amerikahaus',Hamburg, rec. 26.11.1994
Miles,Butch (dr) | Sandke,Randy (tp) | Allen,Harry (ts) | Alden,Howard (g) | Tate,Frank (b)

Oscar Klein's Anniversary Band
Moonglow
Live at The 'Amerikahaus',Hamburg, rec. 6.1.1995
Klein,Oscar (tp) | Meerwald,Willi (tb) | Keller,Werner (cl) | Wrobel,Engelbert (ts) | Mussolini,Romano (p) | Patruno,Lino (g) | Van Oven,Bob (b) | Antolini,Charly (dr)

Marty Grosz And His Swinging Fools
Rose Of The Rio Grande
Live at The 'Amerikahaus',Hamburg, rec. 25.2.1995
Grosz,Marty (g) | Kellso,Jon-Erik (tp) | Robinson,Scott (bs) | Litton,Martin (p) | Cohen,Greg (b) | Riggs,Chuck (dr)

Tom Saunders' 'Wild Bill Davison Band' & Guests
Home
Live at Musikhalle Hamburg, rec. 23.9.1995
Saunders,Tom (co) | Sudholter,Dick (fl-h) | Allred,Bill (tb) | Williams,Roy (tb) | Hedges,Chuck (cl) | Moss,Danny (ts) | Barnes,John (bs) | Varro,Johnny (p) | Grosz,Marty (g) | Eckinger,Isla (b) | Miles,Butch (dr)

Bill Allred-Roy Williams Quintet
Constantly
Hamburg, rec. 28.9.1995
Allred,Bill (tb) | Williams,Roy (tb) | Varro,Johnny (p) | Eckinger,Isla (b) | Miles,Buddy (dr)

International Allstars
Did I Remember
Live at The 'Amerikahaus',Hamburg, rec. 14.10.1995
International Allstars | Peplowski,Ken (cl) | Erstrand,Lars (vib) | Alden,Howard (g) | Shane,Mark (p) | Skeat,Len (b) | Ascione,Joseph 'Joe' (dr)

Allan Vaché-Antti Sarpila Quintet
As Long As I Live
Hamburg, rec. 15.10.1995
Vaché,Allan (cl) | Sarpila,Antti (ss) | Shane,Mark (p) | Skeat,Len (b) | Ascione,Joseph 'Joe' (dr)

Bob Wilber's Bechet Legacy
Down In Honky Tonk Town
Live at Musikhalle Hamburg, rec. 22.10.1995
Wilber,Bob (ss) | Sandke,Randy (tp) | Shane,Mark (p) | Cliff,Dave (g) | Green,Dave (b) | Miles,Buddy (dr)

The New York Allstars
When It's Sleepy Time Down South
Live at The Congress Center Hamburg, rec. 5.-9.2.1996
New York All Stars,The | Sandke,Randy (tp,ld) | Stripling,Byron (tp) | Helleny,Joel (tb) | Davern,Kenny (cl) | Ostwald,David (tuba) | Shane,Mark (p) | Cohen,Greg (b) | Ascione,Joseph 'Joe' (dr)

NHR SP 7 | CD | I Feel The Spirit

Jan Harrington And Friends
Down By The Riverside | Follow Him | Nobody Knows The Trouble I've Seen | Battle Hymn Of The Republic | Summertime- | Sometimes I Feel Like A Motherless Child- | Will The Circle Be Unbroken | Christmas Time In New Orleans | Just A Closer Walk With Thee | Good News | How I Got Over | Over My Head | Swing Low Sweet Chariot | Didn't It Rain | He's Got The Whole World In His Hands
Hamburg, rec. 13.12.1997
Harrington,Jan (voc) | Gürtler,Werner (tb) | Luley,Jan (p,keyboards) | Bartels,Gerald (b) | Smith,Harold (dr,voc) | Fields,Linda (voc)

New Jazz | ZYX Music GmbH

NJSA 8276-2 | SACD | Kenny Burrell & John Coltrane | EAN 025218731461

Kenny Burrell-John Coltrane Duo
Why Was I Born
Hackensack,NJ, rec. 7.3.1958
Burrell,Kenny (g) | Coltrane,John (ts)

Kenny Burrell-John Coltrane Quintet
Big Paul | Freight Train | I Never Knew | Lyresto
Burrell,Kenny (g) | Coltrane,John (ts) | Flanagan,Tommy (p) | Chambers,Paul (b) | Cobb,Jimmy (dr)

NJSA 8252-6 | SACD | Out There | EAN 025218731362

Eric Dolphy Quartet
Out There | Serene | The Baron | Eclipse | 17 West | Sketch Of Melba | Feathers
Englewood Cliffs,NJ, rec. 16.8.1960
Dolphy,Eric (fl,cl,b-cl,as) | Carter,Ron (cello) | Duvivier,George (b) | Haynes,Roy (dr)

Nimbus Records | Naxos Deutschland

NI 2000 | CD | Billie's Love Songs

Billie Holiday With Teddy Wilson And His Orchestra
Twenty-Four Hours A Day
NYC, rec. 25.10.1935
Wilson,Teddy (p) | Eldridge,Roy (tp) | Goodman,Benny (cl) | Webster,Ben (ts) | Trueheart,John (g) | Kirby,John (b) | Cole,William 'Cozy' (dr) | Holiday,Billie (voc)

I Can't Give You Anything But Love
NYC, rec. 19.11.1936
Wilson,Teddy (p) | Jones,Jonah (tp) | Goodman,Benny (cl) | Webster,Ben (ts) | Reuss,Allan (g) | Kirby,John (b) | Cole,William 'Cozy' (dr) | Holiday,Billie (voc)

I'll Get By(As Long As I Have You)
NYC, rec. 11.5.1937
Holiday,Billie (voc) | Wilson,Teddy (p) | Clayton,Buck (tp) | Bailey,Buster (cl) | Hodges,Johnny (as) | Young,Lester (ts) | Reuss,Allan (g) | Bernstein,Artie (b) | Cole,William 'Cozy' (dr)

Billie Holiday And Her Band
He's Funny That Way
NYC, rec. 13.9.1937
Holiday,Billie (voc) | Clayton,Buck (tp) | Bailey,Buster (cl) | Young,Lester (ts) | Thornhill,Claude (p) | Green,Freddie (g) | Page,Walter (b) | Jones,Jo (dr)

Billie Holiday With Teddy Wilson And His Orchestra
You're So Desirable | Let's Dream In The Moonlight
NYC, rec. 28.11.1938
Wilson,Teddy (p) | Hackett,Bobby (co) | Young,Trummy (tb) | Mondello,Toots (as) | Buckner,Ted (as) | Freeman,Bud (ts) | Berry,Leon 'Chu' (ts) | Casey,Al (g) | Hinton,Milt (b) | Cole,William 'Cozy' (dr) | Holiday,Billie (voc)

Sugar | More Than You Know
NYC, rec. 30.1.1939
Wilson,Teddy (p) | Eldridge,Roy (tp) | Powell,Ernie (cl,ts) | Carter,Benny (as,ts) | Barker,Danny (g) | Hinton,Milt (b) | Cole,William 'Cozy' (dr) | Holiday,Billie (voc)

Billie Holiday With Frankie Newton And His Orchestra
Fine And Mellow
NYC, rec. 20.4.1939
Holiday,Billie (voc) | Newton,Frankie (tp) | Smith,Tab (as) | Hollon,Kenneth (ts) | Payne,Stanley (ts) | White,Sonny (p) | McLin,Jimmy (g) | Williams,John B. (b) | Dougherty,Eddie (dr)

Billie Holiday And Her Orchestra
Night And Day
NYC, rec. 13.12.1939
Holiday,Billie (voc) | Clayton,Buck (tp) | Edison,Harry 'Sweets' (tp) | Warren,Earl (as) | Washington Jr.,Jack (as,bs) | Young,Lester (ts) | Sullivan,Joe (p) | Green,Freddie (g) | Page,Walter (b) | Jones,Jo (dr)

Billie Holiday With Eddie Heywood And His Orchestra
All Of Me
NYC, rec. 21.3.1941
Holiday,Billie (voc) | Heywood,Eddie (p) | Collins,Lester 'Shad' (tp) | Johnakins,Leslie (as) | Barefield,Eddie (as) | Young,Lester (ts) | Collins,John (g) | Sturgis,Ted (b) | Clarke,Kenny (dr)

Billie Holiday With Teddy Wilson And His Orchestra
Until The Real Thing Comes Along
NYC, rec. 10.2.1942
Holiday,Billie (voc) | Wilson,Teddy (p) | Berry,Emmett (tp) | Hamilton,Jimmy (cl) | Schertzer,Hymie (as) | Russin,Irving 'Babe' (ts) | Fields,Gene (g) | Williams,John B. (b) | Heard,J.C. (dr)

Billie Holiday With Toots Camarata And His Orchestra
Lover Man(Oh,Where Can You Be?)
NYC, rec. 4.10.1944
Holiday,Billie (voc) | Camarata,Toots (arr,ld) | Chase,Russ (tp) | Schertzer,Hymie (as) | Cressey,Jack (as) | Binyon,Larry (ts) | Ricci,Paul (ts) | Bowman,Dave (p) | Kress,Carl (g) | Stephens,Haig (b) | Blowers,Johnny (dr) | Strings

Billie Holiday With The Bobby Tucker Quartet
My Man
NYC, rec. 10.12.1948
Holiday,Billie (voc) | Tucker,Bobby (p) | Lowe,Mundell (g) | Levy,John (b) | Best,Denzil (dr)

Billie Holiday With Sy Oliver And His Orchestra
Them There Eyes
NYC, rec. 29.8.1949
Holiday,Billie (voc) | Privin,Bernie (tp) | Vance,Dick (tp) | Faso,Tony (tp) | Chambers,Henderson (tb) | Bullman,Morton (tb) | Mince,Johnny (as) | Dorsey,George (as) | Johnson,Budd (ts) | Williams,Freddy (ts) | Henderson,Horace (p) | Barksdale,Everett (g) | Duvivier,George (b) | Cole,William 'Cozy' (dr) | Oliver,Sy (ld)

Now Or Never
NYC, rec. 30.9.1949
Holiday,Billie (voc) | Privin,Bernie (tp) | Vance,Dick (tp) | Faso,Tony (tp) | Chambers,Henderson (tb) | Bullman,Morton (tb) | Mince,Johnny (as) | Dorsey,George (as) | Johnson,Budd (ts) | Williams,Freddy (ts) | Henderson,Horace (p) | Barksdale,Everett (g) | Duvivier,George (b) | Cole,William 'Cozy' (dr) | Oliver,Sy (ld)

Billie Holiday With Gordon Jenkins And His Orchestra
You're My Thrill | Crazy He Calls Me | Somebody's On My Mind | Please Tell Me Now
NYC, rec. 19.10.1949
Holiday,Billie (voc) | Jenkins,Gordon (ld) | Hackett,Bobby (tp) | Yaner,Milt (cl,as) | Fulton,John (cl,ts) | Leighton,Bernie (p) | Mottola,Tony (g) | Lesberg,Jack (b) | Shawker,Norris 'Bunny' (dr) | Strings

NI 2001 | CD | Swing Legends

Glenn Miller And His Orchestra
Moonlight Serenade | Runnin' Wild | Pavane | Sliphorn Jive | Pagan Love Song | Glen Island Special | Farewell Blues | Johnson Rag | My Melancholy Baby | Stardust | Rug Cutter's Swing | Tuxedo Junction | Slow Freight | Pennsylvania Six Five Thousand | I Dreamt I Dwelt In Harlem | Boulder Buff | The Booglie Wooglie Piggy | A String Of Pearls | When Johnny Comes Marching Home | Here We Go Again
NYC/Hollywood, rec. 1939-1942
Miller,Glenn (tb) | prob.personal incl.: | Best,John (tp) | McMickle,Dale (tp) | Hurley,Clyde (tp) | Knowles,Legh (tp) | May,Billy (tp) | Hackett,Bobby (co) | Mack,Tommy (tb) | Mastren,Al (tb) | Tanner,Paul (tb) | Abato,Jimmy (sax) | Klink,Al (sax) | Caceres,Ernie (cl,sax) | Schwartz,Wilbur (cl,sax) | McIntyre,Hal (sax) | Beneke,Gordon 'Tex' (sax,voc) | Russin,Irving 'Babe' (reeds) | MacGregor,John Chalmers 'Chummy' (p) | Fisher,Richard (g) | Bundock,Rowland 'Rolly' (b) | Purtill,Maurice 'Moe' (dr) | Hutton,Marion (voc) | Eberle,Ray (voc) | Modernaires,The (voc-group)

NI 2010 | CD | Love Songs

Nat King Cole Trio
Sweet Lorraine
Los Angeles,CA, rec. 6.12.1940
Cole,Nat King (p,voc) | Moore,Oscar (g) | Prince,Wesley (b)

Slow Down
Chicago,Ill, rec. 14.3.1941
Cole,Nat King (p,voc) | Moore,Oscar (g) | Prince,Wesley (b)

This Will Make You Laugh
NYC, rec. 16.7.1941
Cole,Nat King (p,voc) | Moore,Oscar (g) | Prince,Wesley (b)

Gee Baby Ain't I Good To You | If You Can't Smile And Say Yes
Los Angeles,CA, rec. 30.11.1943
Cole,Nat King (p,voc) | Moore,Oscar (g) | Miller,Johnny (b)

I Just Can't See For Looking
Los Angeles,CA, rec. 15.12.1943
Cole,Nat King (p,voc) | Moore,Oscar (g) | Miller,Johnny (b)

I Realize Now
Los Angeles,CA, rec. 6.4.1944
Cole,Nat King (p,voc) | Moore,Oscar (g) | Miller,Johnny (b)

Come To Baby Do
Los Angeles,CA, rec. 11.10.1945
Cole,Nat King (p,voc) | Moore,Oscar (g) | Miller,Johnny (b)

You Call It Madness But I Call It Love
Los Angeles,CA, rec. 1.5.1946
Cole,Nat King (p,voc) | Moore,Oscar (g) | Miller,Johnny (b)

The Best Man
NYC, rec. 19.8.1946
Cole,Nat King (p,voc) | Moore,Oscar (g) | Miller,Johnny (b)

I Love You For Sentimental Reasons
NYC, rec. 22.8.1946
Cole,Nat King (p,voc) | Moore,Oscar (g) | Miller,Johnny (b)

Come In Out Of The Rain
NYC, rec. 18.12.1946
Cole,Nat King (p,voc) | Moore,Oscar (g) | Miller,Johnny (b)

Can You Look Me In The Eyes
NYC, rec. 30.12.1946
Cole,Nat King (p,voc) | Moore,Oscar (g) | Miller,Johnny (b)

Meet Me At No Special Place
NYC, rec. 21.1.1947
Cole,Nat King (p,voc) | Moore,Oscar (g) | Miller,Johnny (b)

This Is My Night To Dream | Makin' Whoopee
Los Angeles,CA, rec. 7.8.1947
Cole,Nat King (p,voc) | Moore,Oscar (g) | Miller,Johnny (b)

Nature Boy | Those Things Money Can't Buy
Los Angeles,CA, rec. 22.& 29.8.1947
Cole,Nat King (p,voc) | Moore,Oscar (g) | Miller,Johnny (b)

I Feel So Smoochie | I've Only Myself To Blame | It's The Sentimental Thing To Do
Los Angeles,CA, rec. 4./5.11.1947
Cole,Nat King (p,voc) | Ashby,Irving (g) | Miller,Johnny (b)

Put 'Em In A Box
NYC, rec. 24.11.1947
Cole,Nat King (p,voc) | Ashby,Irving (g) | Miller,Johnny (b)

NI 2011 | CD | Swing Legens:Bob Crosby

Bob Crosby And His Orchestra
Dixieland Shuffle | Savoy Blues
NYC, rec. 13.4.1936
Crosby,Bob (ld) | Hart,Phil (tp) | Lawson,Yank (tp) | Silloway,Ward (tb) | Foster,Artie (tb) | Rodin,Gil (cl,as) | Matlock,Matty (cl,as) | Bernardo,Noni (as) | Miller,Eddie (cl,ts) | Kincaide,Dean (ts) | Bowers,Gil (p) | Lamare,Hilton Napoleon 'Nappy' (g) | Haggart,Bob (b) | Bauduc,Ray (dr)

Gin Mill Blues
NYC, rec. 8.2.1937
Crosby,Bob (ld) | Ferretti,Andy (tp) | Lawson,Yank (tp) | Silloway,Ward (tb) | Bennett,Mark (tb) | Matlock,Matty (cl,as) | Bernardi,Noni (as) | Rodin,Gil (as) | Miller,Eddie (cl,ts) | Kincaide,Dean (ts) | Zurke,Bob (p) | Lamare,Hilton Napoleon 'Nappy' (g) | Haggart,Bob (b) | Bauduc,Ray (dr)

Just Squeeze Me(But Don't Tease Me)
Los Angeles,CA, rec. 5.11.1937
Crosby,Bob (ld) | Zarchy,Reuben 'Zeke' (tp) | Lawson,Yank (tp) | Butterfield,Billy (tp) | Silloway,Ward (tb) | Smith,Warren (tb) | Matlock,Matty (cl,as) | Kearns,Joe[Joey] (as) | Rodin,Gil (ts) | Miller,Eddie (cl,ts) | Zurke,Bob (p) | Lamare,Hilton Napoleon 'Nappy' (g) | Haggart,Bob (b) | Bauduc,Ray (dr)

South Rampart Street Parade | Dogtown Blues
Los Angeles,CA, rec. 16.11.1937
Crosby,Bob (ld) | Spivak,Charlie (tp) | Lawson,Yank (tp) | Butterfield,Billy (tp) | Silloway,Ward (tb) | Smith,Warren (tb) | Matlock,Matty (cl,as) | Kearns,Joe[Joey] (as) | Rodin,Gil (ts) | Miller,Eddie (cl,ts) | Zurke,Bob (p) | Lamare,Hilton Napoleon 'Nappy' (g) | Haggart,Bob (b) | Bauduc,Ray (dr)

Bob Crosby's Bobcats
Who's Sorry Now | Stumbling | Coquette | Fidgety Feet | You're Driving Me Crazy | Can't We Be Friends
Los Angeles,CA, rec. 13.11.1937
Crosby,Bob (ld) | Lawson,Yank (tp) | Smith,Warren (tb) | Matlock,Matty (cl) | Miller,Eddie (ts) | Zurke,Bob (p) | Lamare,Hilton Napoleon 'Nappy' (g) | Haggart,Bob (b) | Bauduc,Ray (dr)

Wolverine Blues | At The Jazz Band Ball
NYC, rec. 10.3.1938
Crosby,Bob (ld) | Spivak,Charlie (tp) | Lawson,Yank (tp) | Butterfield,Billy (tp) | Silloway,Ward (tb) | Smith,Warren (tb) | Fazola[Prestopnick],Irving (cl) | Matlock,Matty (cl,as) | Kearns,Joe[Joey] (as) | Rodin,Gil (ts) | Miller,Eddie (cl,ts) | Zurke,Bob (p) | Lamare,Hilton Napoleon 'Nappy' (g) | Haggart,Bob (b) | Bauduc,Ray (dr)

March Of The Bob Cats | Palestrina | Slow Mood | Big Foot Jump | The Big Crash From China | Five Point Blues
NYC, rec. 14.3.1938
Crosby,Bob (ld) | Lawson,Yank (tp) | Smith,Warren (tb) | Fazola[Prestopnick],Irving (cl) | Miller,Eddie (cl,ts) | Zurke,Bob (p) | Lamare,Hilton Napoleon 'Nappy' (g) | Stephens,Haig (b) | Bauduc,Ray (dr)

Bob Haggart/Ray Bauduc
Big Noise From Winnetka
Chicago,Ill, rec. 14.10.1938
Haggart,Bob (b,whistling) | Bauduc,Ray (dr)

Bob Crosby And His Orchestra
Swinging At The Sugar Bowl | Honky Tonk Train Blues
Chicago,Ill, rec. 19.10.1938
Crosby,Bob (ld) | Zarchy,Reuben 'Zeke' (tp) | Bose,Sterling (tp) | Butterfield,Billy (tp) | Silloway,Ward (tb) | Smith,Warren (tb) | Fazola[Prestopnick],Irving (cl) | Matlock,Matty (cl,as) | Kearns,Joe[Joey] (as) | Rodin,Gil (ts) | Miller,Eddie (cl,ts) | Zurke,Bob (p) | Lamare,Hilton Napoleon 'Nappy' (g) | Haggart,Bob (b) | Bauduc,Ray (dr)

Burnin' The Candle At Both Ends
Los Angeles,CA, rec. 16.12.1940
Crosby,Bob (ld) | Spanier,Francis 'Muggsy' (co) | Herman,Max (tp) | Peck,Bob (tp) | O'Brien,Floyd (tb) | Smithers,Elmer (tb) | D'Amico,Hank (cl) | Matlock,Matty (as) | Rando,Arthur (as) | Miller,Eddie (cl,ts) | Rodin,Gil (ts) | Stacy,Jess (p) | Lamare,Hilton Napoleon 'Nappy' (g) | Haggart,Bob (b) | Bauduc,Ray (dr)

NI 2012 | CD | Swing Legends:Louis Armstrong

Louis Armstrong And His Orchestra
Swing That Music
NYC, rec. 29.4.1936
Armstrong,Louis (tp,voc) | Davis,Leonard (tp) | Aiken,Gus (tp) | Bacon,Louis (tp) | Henry Jones (tb) | Archey,Jimmy (tb) | Jones,Henry (as) | Holmes,Charlie (as) | Madison,Bingie (ts) | Walton,Greely (ts) | Russell,Luis (p) | Blair,Lee (g) | Foster,George 'Pops' (b) | Barbarin,Paul (dr)

Rhythm Saved The World
NYC, rec. 18.1.1936
Armstrong,Louis (tp,voc) | Davis,Leonard (tp) | Aiken,Gus (tp) | Bacon,Louis (tp) | Archey,Jimmy (tb) | White,Harry (tb) | Jones,Henry (as) | Holmes,Charlie (as) | Madison,Bingie (cl,ts) | Walton,Greely (ts) | Russell,Luis (p,arr) | Blair,Lee (g) | Foster,George 'Pops' (b) | Barbarin,Paul (dr)

Louis Armstrong With Jimmy Dorsey And His Orchestra
Dippermouth Blues
Los Angeles,CA, rec. 7.8.1936
Armstrong,Louis (tp,voc) | Dorsey,Jimmy (cl,as) | Thow,George (tp) | Camarata,Toots (tp) | Byrne,Bobby (tb) | Yukl,Joe (tb) | Mattison,Don (tb) | Stacey,Jack (as) | Livingston,Fud (ts) | Herfurt,Arthur 'Skeets' (ts) | Van Eps,Bobby (p) | Hillman,Roscoe (g) | Taft,Jim 'Slim' (b) | McKinley,Ray (dr)

Louis Armstrong And His Orchestra
Public Melody Number One
NYC, rec. 2.7.1937
Armstrong,Louis (tp,voc) | Hemphill,Shelton (tp) | Bacon,Louis (tp) | Allen,Henry Red (tp) | Matthews,George (tb) | Washington,George (tb) | Higginbotham,J.C. (tb) | Clark,Pete (as) | Holmes,Charlie (as) | Nicholas,Albert (cl,ts) | Madison,Bingie (cl,ts) | Russell,Luis (p) | Blair,Lee (g) | Foster,George 'Pops' (b) | Barbarin,Paul (dr)

On The Sunny Side Of The Street
Los Angeles,CA, rec. 15.11.1937
Armstrong,Louis (tp,voc) | Higginbotham,J.C. (tb) | Holmes,Charlie (as) | Madison,Bingie (cl,ts) | Russell,Luis (p) | Blair,Lee (g) | Callender,Red (b) | Barbarin,Paul (dr)
When The Saints Go Marching In
NYC, rec. 13.5.1938
Armstrong,Louis (tp,voc) | Hemphill,Shelton (tp) | Higginbotham,J.C. (tb) | Holmes,Charlie (as) | Cole,Rupert (reeds) | Madison,Bingie (reeds) | Callender,Red (b) | Russell,Luis (p) | Blair,Lee (g) | Barbarin,Paul (dr) | Choir
Jeepers Creepers | What Is This Thing Called Swing
NYC, rec. 18.1.1939
Armstrong,Louis (tp,voc) | Hemphill,Shelton (tp) | Johnson,Otis (tp) | Allen,Henry Red (tp) | DeParis,Wilbur (tb) | Washington,George (tb) | Higginbotham,J.C. (tb) | Cole,Rupert (as) | Holmes,Charlie (as) | Nicholas,Albert (cl,ts) | Madison,Bingie (cl,ts) | Russell,Luis (p) | Blair,Lee (g) | Foster,George 'Pops' (b) | Catlett,Big Sid (dr)
Hear Me Talkin' To Ya | Save It Pretty Mama | West End Blues | Savoy Blues
NYC, rec. 5.4.1939
Armstrong,Louis (tp,voc) | Allen,Henry Red (tp) | Johnson,Otis (tp) | Hemphill,Shelton (tp) | Higginbotham,J.C. (tb) | DeParis,Wilbur (tb) | Washington,George (tb) | Garland,Joe (ts) | Holmes,Charlie (as) | Cole,Rupert (cl,as) | Madison,Bingie (ts) | Russell,Luis (p,arr) | Blair,Lee (g) | Foster,George 'Pops' (b) | Catlett,Big Sid (dr)
Confessin'(That I Love You) | Our Monday Date
NYC, rec. 25.4.1939
Armstrong,Louis (tp,voc) | Allen,Henry Red (tp) | Flood,Bernard (tp) | Hemphill,Shelton (tp) | Higginbotham,J.C. (tb) | DeParis,Wilbur (tb) | Washington,George (tb) | Garland,Joe (ts) | Holmes,Charlie (as) | Cole,Rupert (cl,as) | Madison,Bingie (ts) | Russell,Luis (p,arr) | Blair,Lee (g) | Foster,George 'Pops' (b) | Catlett,Big Sid (dr)
Sweethearts On Parade
NYC, rec. 1.5.1939
Armstrong,Louis (tp,voc) | Allen,Henry Red (tp) | Flood,Bernard (tp) | Hemphill,Shelton (tp) | Higginbotham,J.C. (tb) | DeParis,Wilbur (tb) | Washington,George (tb) | Garland,Joe (ts) | Holmes,Charlie (as) | Cole,Rupert (cl,as) | Madison,Bingie (ts) | Russell,Luis (p,arr) | Blair,Lee (g) | Foster,George 'Pops' (b) | Catlett,Big Sid (dr)
2:19 Blues
NYC, rec. 27.5.1940
Armstrong,Louis (tp,voc) | Jones,Claude (tb) | Bechet,Sidney (cl,as) | Russell,Luis (p) | Addison,Bernard (g) | Braud,Wellman (b) | Singleton,Zutty (dr)
Louis Armstrong And His Dixieland Seven
Do You Know What It Means To Miss New Orleans | Where The Blues Were Born In New Orleans | Mahogany Hall Stomp
Los Angeles,CA, rec. 17.10.1946
Armstrong,Louis (tp,voc) | Ory,Edward 'Kid' (tb) | Bigard,Barney (cl) | Beal,Charlie (p) | Scott,Bud (g) | Callender,Red (b) | Hall,Minor 'Ram' (dr)
Louis Armstrong And His Orchestra
You Don't Learn That In School
NYC, rec. 12.3.1947
Armstrong,Louis (tp,voc) | Mullens,Eddie (tp) | Scott,William (tp) | Grider,Thomas (tp) | Butler,Robert (tp) | Moore,Russel 'Big Chief' (tb) | Williams,Waddet (tb) | Whitney,James (tb) | Moore,Alton (tb) | Gordon,Amos (as) | Dennis,Arthur (as) | Garland,Joe (ts) | Thompson,Lucky (ts) | Sparrow,John (ts) | Mason,Earl (p) | Warner,Elmer (g) | Shaw,Arvell (b) | Harris,James (dr)
Jack-Armstrong Blues | Rockin' Chair
NYC, rec. 10.6.1947
Armstrong,Louis (tp,voc) | Hackett,Bobby (co) | Teagarden,Jack (tb,voc) | Hucko,Peanuts (cl) | Caceres,Ernie (cl,bs) | Guarnieri,Johnny (p) | Casey,Al (g) | Hall,Al (b) | Cole,William 'Cozy' (dr)
Louis Armstrong With Gordon Jenkins And His Orchestra And Choir
Blueberry Hill
NYC, rec. 6.9.1949
Armstrong,Louis (tp,voc) | Butterfield,Billy (tp) | Poole,Carl (tp) | Lawson,Yank (tp) | Bradley,Will (tb) | Yaner,Milt (as) | Schertzer,Hymie (as) | Parshley,Tom (ts) | Drellinger,Art (ts) | Leighton,Bernie (p) | Kress,Carl (g) | Lesberg,Jack (b) | Blowers,Johnny (dr) | Choir | Jenkins,George (cond,arr)
Louis Armstrong And His All Stars
That's For Me
NYC, rec. 26.4.1950
Armstrong,Louis (tp,voc) | Teagarden,Jack (tb) | Bigard,Barney (cl) | Hines,Earl 'Fatha' (p) | Shaw,Arvell (b) | Cole,William 'Cozy' (dr)

NI 5569 | CD | Ragatal
John Mayer's Indio-Jazz Fusions
Chhota Mitha | Partita | Dance Of The Pisachas | Multani | Miyan Ki Malhar | Serenade | Bengal Blues | Prayoga
Nimbus Foundation,?, rec. 4./5.10.1997
Mayer,John (v) | Smith,Dave (tp) | McDowall,James (fl) | Brooks,Anna (sax) | Mayer,Jonathan (sitar) | Tromans,Steve (p) | Featonby,Chris (b) | Bratt,Andrew (dr) | Matharu,Harjinder (tablas) | Young,Richard (perc)

Nonesuch | Warner Classics & Jazz Germany

7559-60843-2 | CD | Before We Were Born
Bill Frisell Band
Before We Were Born | Steady Girl
NYC, rec. August 1988
Frisell,Bill (g,el-g) | Lindsay,Arto (el-g,voice) | Scherer,Peter (keyboards,dr-programming) | Baron,Joey (dr)
The Lone Ranger
Frisell,Bill (g,el-g) | Lindsay,Arto (el-g,voice) | Scherer,Peter (keyboards,dr-programming) | Baron,Joey (dr) | Baptista,Cyro (shaker)
Hard Plains Drifter
NYC, rec. September 1988
Frisell,Bill (g,el-g) | Roberts,Hank (cello,voice) | Driscoll,Kermit (el-b) | Baron,Joey (dr,perc,electronics)
Some Song And Dance: | Freddy's Step- | Love Motel- | Pip, Squeak- | Good Bye-
Frisell,Bill (g,el-g) | Hemphill,Julius (as) | Drewes,Billy (as) | Wieselman,Doug (bs) | Roberts,Hank (cello) | Driscoll,Kermit (el-b) | Baron,Joey (dr)

7559-60844-2 | CD | Spy Vs. Spy-The Music Of Ornette Coleman
John Zorn Group
W.R.U. | Chronology | Word For Bird | Good Old Days | The Disguise | Enfant | Rejoicing | Blues Connotation | C&D | Chippie | Peace Warriors | Ecars | Feet Music | Broadway Blues | Space Church | Zig Zag | Mob Job
NYC, rec. 18./19.8.1988
Zorn,John (as) | Berne,Tim (as) | Dresser,Mark (b) | Baron,Joey (dr) | Vatcher,Michael (dr)

7559-60956-2 | CD | Is That You?
Bill Frisell Band
No Man's Land | Someone In My Backyard | Rag | Thy Way Home | Twenty Years | Days Of Wine And Roses | Yuba City | Half A Million | Hope And Fear
Seattle,WA, rec. August 1989
Frisell,Bill (cl,g,el-g,bj,b,ukulele) | Horvitz,Wayne (keyboards,b,dr-programming) | Baron,Joey (dr)
Is That You? | Hello Nellie | Chain Of Fools
NYC, rec. August 1989
Frisell,Bill (cl,g,el-g,bj,b,ukulele) | Horvitz,Wayne (keyboards,b,dr-programming) | Hofstra,David (b,tuba) | Baron,Joey (dr)

7559-61181-2 | CD | Where In The World
Unsung Heros | Rob Roy | Spell | Child At Heart | Beautiful E. | Again | Smilin' Jones | Where In The World | Worry Doll | Let Me In
Seattle,WA, rec. January 1991
Frisell,Bill (el-g,ukulele) | Roberts,Hank (cello,jazz-a-phone-fiddle) | Driscoll,Kermit (b) | Baron,Joey (dr)

7559-79137-2 | CD | Plays Duke Ellington
World Saxophone Quartet
Take The 'A' Train | Lush Life | Prelude To A Kiss | Sophisticated Lady | I Let A Song Go Out Of My Heart | Come Sunday | In A Sentimental Mood | Take The 'A' Train(alt.take)
NYC, rec. April 1986
World Saxophone Quartet | Hemphill,Julius (as) | Lake,Oliver (as) | Murray,David (ts) | Bluiett,Hamiet (bs)

7559-79159-2 | CD | Scott Joplin Piano Rags
Joshua Rifkin
Maple Leaf Rag | The Entertainer | Ragtime Dance | Gladiolus Rag | Fig Leaf Rag | Scott Joplin's New Rag | Euphonic Sounds-A Syncopeted Novelty | Magnetic Rag
NYC, rec. September 1970
Rifkin,Joshua (p-solo)
Elite Syncopations | Bethena-A Concert Waltz | Paragon Rag | Solance-A Mexican Serenade | Pineapple Rag
NYC, rec. January 1972
Rifkin,Joshua (p-solo)
Weeping Willow | The Cascades | Country Club | Stoptime Rag
NYC, rec. September 1974
Rifkin,Joshua (p-solo)

7559-79164-2 | CD | Dances And Ballads
World Saxophone Quartet
Sweet D | For Lester | Belly Up | Cool Red | Hattie Wall | Adjacent | West African Snap | Full Deep And Mellow | Dance Until Dawn | Fast Life
NYC, rec. April 1987
World Saxophone Quartet | Hemphill,Julius (fl,ss,as) | Lake,Oliver (ss,as) | Murray,David (b-cl,ts) | Bluiett,Hamiet (alto-cl,bs)

7559-79172-2 | CD | Spillane
John Zorn Group
Spillane
NYC, rec. June/Aug.1986
Zorn,John (cl,as) | Staley,Jim (tb) | Frisell,Bill (g) | Coleman,Anthony (p,org,celeste) | Emanuel,Carol (harp) | Hofstra,David (b,tuba) | James,Bob (tapes) | Previte,Robert 'Bobby' (dr,perc) | Weinstein,David (keyboards,celeste) | Lurie,John (voice) | Quine,Robert (voice)
Two-Lane Highway: | Preacher Man- | White Line Fever- | Nacogdoches Gumbo- | East Texas Freezeout- | San Angelo Release- | Rollin' To Killeen- | Blowout- | Devil's Highway- | Midnight Standoff- | Marchin' For Abilene- | Hico Killer- | Long Mile To Houston-
NYC, rec. June 1986
Zorn,John (arr,ld) | Collins,Albert (g,voc) | Quine,Robert (g) | Patton,Big John (org) | Horvitz,Wayne (p,keyboards) | Gibbs,Melvin (b) | Jackson,Ronald Shannon (dr) | Previte,Robert 'Bobby' (dr,perc)
John Zorn Group With The Kronos Quartet
Forbidden Fruit
San Francisco,CA, rec. September 1987
Zorn,John (arr,ld) | Kronos Quartet | Harrington,David (v) | Sherba,John (v) | Dutt,Hank (viola) | Jeanrenaud,Joan (cello) | Marclay,Christian (turntables) | Hiromi,Ohta (voice)

7559-79174-2 | CD | Concierto Para Bandoneon-Tres Tangos
Astor Piazzolla With Orchestra Of St. Luke's
Concierto Para Bandoneon: | Allegro Marcato- | Moderato- | Presto- | Tres Tangos For Bandoneon And Orchestra | Allegro Tranquillo- | Moderato Mistico- | Allegretto Molto Marcato-
Princetown,NJ., rec. September 1987
Piazzolla,Astor (bandoneon) | Orchestra Of St. Luke's | Schifrin,Lalo (cond) | details unknown

7559-79238-2 | CD | Naked City
Batman
The Sicilian Clan | You Will Be Shot | Latin Quarter | A Shot In The Dark | Reanimator | Snagglepuss | I Want To Live | Lonely Woman | Igneous Ejaculation | Blood Duster | Hammer Head | Demon Sanctuary | Obeah Man | Ujaku | Fuck The Facts | Speedball | Chinatown | Punk China Doll | N.Y. Flat Top Box | Saigon Pickup | The James Bond Theme | Den Of Sins | Contempt | Graveyard Shift | Inside Straight
details unknown, rec. details unknown
Naked City | Zorn,John (as) | Frisell,Bill (g) | Horvitz,Wayne (keyboards) | Frith,Fred (b) | Baron,Joey (dr) | Eye,Yamatsuka (voc)

7559-79280-2 | CD | Tuskegee Experiments
Don Byron
Waltz For Ellen
NYC, rec. November 1990 & July 1991
Byron,Don (cl-solo)
Don Byron-Reggie Workman
In Memoriam: Uncle Dan
Byron,Don (b-cl) | Workman,Reggie (b)
Don Byron-Joe Berkovitz
Auf Einer Burg(Robert Schumann)
Byron,Don (b-cl) | Berkovitz,Joe (p)
Don Byron Quartet
Tuskegee Strutter's Ball | Main Stem
Byron,Don (cl) | Frisell,Bill (el-g) | Plaxico,Lonnie (b) | Peterson,Ralph (dr)
Don Byron Quintet
Next Love | Tears
Byron,Don (cl) | Frisell,Bill (el-g) | Gomez,Edsel (p) | Plaxico,Lonnie (b) | Peterson,Ralph (dr)
Tuskegee Experiment
Byron,Don (cl) | Schwarz,Richard (marimba) | Berkovitz,Joe (p) | Davis,Kenneth 'Kenny' (el-b) | AkLaff,Pheeroan (dr) | Sadiq (recitation)
Don Byron Quartet
Diego Rivera
Byron,Don (cl,b-cl) | Buck,Greta (v) | Workman,Reggie (b) | AkLaff,Pheeroan (dr)

7559-79468-2 | CD | Bill Frisell:Songs We Know
A Band Of Friends
A>C

7559-79583-2 | CD | Ghost Town
Bill Frisell
Tell Your Ma,Tell Your Pa | Ghost Town- | Poem For Eva- | Wildwood Flower | Creep | Variation On A Theme(Tales From The Farside) | Follow Your Heart | I'm So Lonesome I Could Cry | What A World | My Man's Gone Now | Outlaw | When I Fall In Love | Big Bob | Winter Always Turns To Spring | Justice And Honor | Fingers Snappin' And Toes Tappin' | Under A Golden Sky
NYC, rec. 1999
Frisell,Bill (g,el-g,bass,loops,6-string-bj)

7559-79615-2 | CD | Blues Dream
Bill Frisell Band
Blues Dream | Ron Carter | Pretty Flowers Were Made For Blooming | Pretty Stars Were Made To Shine | Where Do We Go? | Like Dreamers Do(part 1) | Like Dreamers Do(part 2) | Outlaws | What Do We Do? | Episode | Soul Merchant | Greg Leisz | The Tractor | Fifty Years | Slow Dance | Things Will Never Be The Same | Dream On | Blues Dream(reprise)
Burbank,Los Angeles,CA, rec. 2000
Frisell,Bill (g,el-g,loops) | Miles,Ron (tp) | Fowlkes,Curtis (tb) | Drewes,Billy (as) | Leisz,Greg (steel-g,resonator-g) | Piltch,Dave (b) | Wollesen,Kenny (dr)

7559-79624-2 | CD | Bill Frisell With Dave Hollnad And Elvin Jones
Bill Frisell Trio
Always | Twenty Years | Coffaro's Theme | Blues Dream | Moon River | Tell Your Ma,Tell Your Pa | Strange Meeting | Convict 13 | Again | Hard Times | Justice And Honor | Smilin' Jones
NYC, rec. 2001
Frisell,Bill (g,el-g,loops) | Holland,Dave (b) | Jones,Elvin (dr)

Novus | BMG-Ariola Classics GmbH

2124747-2 | CD | A Tale Of 3 Cities,The EP
Steve Coleman And Metrics
Bebop | I Am Who I Am | Sience | Get Open | Slow Burn | Left Go Right
Brooklyn,NY, rec. details unknown
Coleman,Steve (as) | Alessi,Ralph (tp) | Coltrane,Ravi (ts) | Milne,Andy (p) | Washington,Reggie (el-b) | Lake,Gene (dr) | Wimberly,Michael (perc)

2131690-2 | CD | The Way Of The Cipher
Freestyle | Fast Lane | Slow Lane | S-Ludes | Black Genghis | Chaos(Tech Jump) | Hyped | Laxed & Warped | Night Breed
Live at The Hot Brass Club,Paris,France, rec. 26.& 28.3.1995
Coleman,Steve (as) | Alessi,Ralph (tp) | Milne,Andy (p,keyboards) | Washington,Reggie (b) | Lake,Gene (dr) | Jones,Josh (perc) | Laila (dance)

2131693-2 | CD | Curves Of Life
Steve Coleman And Five Elements
Multiplicity Of Approaches(The African Way Of Knowing) | The Streets | Round About Midnight | Drop Kick Live | The Gypsy
Live at The Hot Brass Club,Paris,France, rec. 29.3.1995
Coleman,Steve (as) | Milne,Andy (p,keyboards) | Washington,Reggie (b) | Lake,Gene (dr)
Country Bama
Coleman,Steve (as) | Murray,David (ts) | Milne,Andy (p,keyboards) | Washington,Reggie (b) | Lake,Gene (dr)
I'm Burnin' Up(Fire Theme)
Coleman,Steve (as) | Murray,David (ts) | Milne,Andy (p,keyboards) | Washington,Reggie (b) | Lake,Gene (dr) | Kokayi (lyricist) | Black Indian (lyricist) | Sub-Zero (lyricist)

4163182-2 | CD | Dear Mr.Cole
John Pizzarelli Trio
What Can I Say After I Say I'm Sorry | Little Girl | You Must Be Blind | Sweet Georgia Brown | It's Only A Paper Moon | September Song | On The Sunny Side Of The Street | Nature Boy | This Way Out | Too Marvelous For Words | Get Your Kicks On Route 66 | Sweet Lorraine | Straighten Up And Fly Right | Honeysuckle Rose | L.O.V.E. | Unforgettable | Portrait Of Jenny
NYC, rec. details unknown
Pizzarelli,John (g,voc) | Green,Benny (p) | McBride,Christian (b)
John Pizzarelli Quartet
Style Is Coming Back In Style
Pizzarelli,John (g,voc) | Kennedy,Ray (p) | Pizzarelli,Martin (b) | Guerin,John (dr)

Organic Music | Fenn Music

ORGM 9701 | CD | Basic Instinct
Grooveyard Meets Houston Person
Summertime | You've Changed | Houston Calling | Can't Buy Me Love
München, rec. 30.6.1996
Person,Houston (ts) | Grooveyard | Bätzel,Matthias (org) | Arlt,Michael (g) | Keul,Michael (dr)
Grooveyard Meets Roman Schwaller
Talkin' About J.C. | Fried Bananas | Samba For Pat And Billy
München, rec. 6.7.1996
Schwaller,Roman (ts) | Grooveyard | Bätzel,Matthias (org) | Arlt,Michael (g) | Keul,Michael (dr)
Grooveyard Meets Red Holloway
Song For Carlos | Basic Instinct | Smoke Gets In Your Eyes
München, rec. 6.12.1996
Holloway,Red (ts) | Grooveyard | Bätzel,Matthias (org) | Arlt,Michael (g) | Keul,Michael (dr)

ORGM 9702 | CD | East Coasting
We Three
Isn't She Lovely | My Girl Is Just Enough Woman For Me | The Triangle | Here, There And Everywhere | Soulmates | East Coasting | Estate(Summer)
München, rec. 4./5.11.1996
We Three | Kostelnik,Dan (org) | Arlt,Michael (g) | Scott,Duck (dr)
We Three With Roman Schwaller
Basic Instinct | You Say You Care | Fingersnappin',Foottappin'
Schwaller,Roman (ts) | We Three | Kostelnik,Dan (org) | Arlt,Michael (g) | Scott,Duck (dr)

ORGM 9703 | CD | VoceBasso
Sabina Sciubba-Paulo Cardoso
Lazy Afternoon | Cheerlessness | Seagulls Of Kristiansund | Blackbird | Lush Life | Dismal | Estate(Summer)
Dießen,Ammersee, rec. November 1996
Sciubba,Sabina (voc) | Cardoso,Paulo (b)
Paulo Cardoso
Tenderly
Cardoso,Paulo (b-solo)
Sabina Sciubbia
Monologue(Un Mondo De Dire)
Sciubbia,Sabina (voc)

ORGM 9704 | CD | Christian Rover Group-Live With Rhoda Scott At The Organ
Christian Rover Group feat. Rhoda Scott
Easter Blue | We'll Be Together Again | In A Mellow Tone | Mack The Knife(Moritat) | Stay With Me Lord | Tocata- | Impressions- | Splanky
Live at The 'Frauenfestival',Eisenach, rec. 4.6.1997
Rover,Christian (g) | Blume,Stanley (as) | Scott,Rhoda (org) | Bätzel,Alexander (dr)
Stay With Me Lord
Rover,Christian (g) | Blume,Stanley (as) | Scott,Rhoda (org,voc) | Bätzel,Alexander (dr)

ORGM 9705 | CD | Them That's Got
Alberto Marsico Quintet
She Came In Through The Bathroom Window | Bathman Blues | Chorar | Sassie Lassie | Giu La Testa | Am Südlichen Ende Der Bar | What's Going On | Yes Or No | Ain't No Love In Town | Them That's Got | Mercy Train
Thorstadl,Obing, rec. 17.-19.3.1998
Marsico,Alberto (org) | Blume,Stanley (as) | Kreitmeier,Thilo (ts) | Rover,Christian (g) | Bätzel,Alexander (dr)

ORGM 9706 | CD | Mo' Better Blues
Thilo Kreitmeier Quintet
Little Sheri | The Shadow Of Your Smile | Mo' Better Blues | Since I Fell For You | There Was A Time-Echo Of Harlem | Light Blue | Strings | Roots | Willow Weep For Me | Spicy Fried Chicken | Blues In Maude's Flat | Monty's Mood
München, rec. 7./8.3 & 19.4.1998
Kreitmeier,Thilo (as,ts) | Tuscher,Peter (tp,fl-h) | Frommeyer,Heinz (p) | Knauer,Rocky (b) | Diaz,Manolo (b) | Keul,Michael (dr)

ORGM 9707 | CD | The Drivin' Beat
We Three
Freddie Tooks Jr. | It's Easy To Remember | Duck's Room | Minority | This Is The End Of... A Beautiful Friendship - (This Is The End Of...) A Beautiful Friendship
Thorstadl,Obing, rec. 9./10.11.1998
We Three | Arlt,Michael (g) | Kostelnik,Dan (org) | Scott,Duck (dr)
So Danco Samba(I Only Dance The Samba) | Day Dream
Live at 'Eddy's',Rheine, rec. 6.11.1998
We Three | Arlt,Michael (g) | Kostelnik,Dan (org) | Scott,Duck (dr) | Cortijo,José (perc)
The Buzz | Tin Tin Deo | At The Rio Bar
Thorstadl,Obing, rec. 9./10.11.1998
We Three | Arlt,Michael (g) | Kostelnik,Dan (org) | Scott,Duck (dr) | Cortijo,José (perc)

ORGM 9708 | CD | A Little Taste Of Cannonball
Mike Turk With The Alkaline Jazz Trio
Sack O'Woe | Jeannine | Things Are Getting Better | This Yeah | Little Taste | Save You Love For Me | Hamba Nami | Wabash | Dat Dere | Cereal Killer
Thorstadl,Obing, rec. 29.11.-2.12.1998
Turk,Mike (harm) | Alkaline Jazz Trio | Marsico,Alberto (org) | Di Puccio,Alessandro (vib) | Fabbri,Alessandro (dr)

ORGM 9709 | CD | Movin' Up
Stanley Blume Quartet
Mr.Spirit | Thorstadlin' | Foundation | Brother Al | Soul Of A Stone - (Soul Of A) Stone
Thorstadl,Obing, rec. 14.-18.12.1998
Blume,Stanley (ss,as) | Bätzel,Matthias (org) | Gleim,Ecki (g) | Bätzel,Alexander (dr)
Stanley Blume Quintet

Movin' Up | Little Outsider | Song For J.&J. | Up And Down
Blume,Stanley (ss,as) | Burkhardt,Ingolf (tp) | Bätzel,Matthias (org) | Gleim,Ecki (g) | Bätzel,Alexander (dr)

ORGM 9710 | CD | Sketches
Jason Seizer With The Larry Goldings Trio
The Henhouse | Clarabell | Sketches | Cumi Cumi | What Do You See? | Porter's House | Body And Soul
Loosdrecht,NL, rec. 3.12.1999
Seizer,Jason (ts) | Goldings,Larry (org) | Bernstein,Peter (g) | Stewart,Bill (dr)

ORGM 9711 | CD | Soul Call
Thilo Kreitmeier & Group
Sneakin' In The Back | Soul Call | Besame Mucho | Cubano Chant | Yeah Yeah Yeah | Smoke Gets In Your Eyes | Soul Meeting | Way Back Home | Comin' Home Baby | Cookie Man | Movin' Out
Thorstadl,Obing, rec. 22.-24.5.1999
Kreitmeier,Thilo (fl,as,ts) | Tuscher,Peter (tp,fl-h) | Frommeyer,Heinz (p,el-p) | Knauer,Rocky (b,el-b) | Keul,Michael (dr,perc) | Roth,Rudi (perc,congas)

ORGM 9712 | CD | Let's Have A Merry Christmas With The David Gazarov Trio!
David Gazarov Trio
White Christmas | Stille Nacht | Kommet Ihr Hirten | Have Yourself A Merry Little Christmas | Wassail Song | Leise Rieselt Der Schnee- | A Child Is Born- | Es Ist Ein Ros Entsprungen | Oh Tannenbaum' | The Christmas Song | Santa Claus Is Coming To Town
Thorstadl,Obing, rec. 17.11.1998
Gazarov,David (p) | Cardoso,Paulo (b) | Gonzi,Mario (dr)

ORGM 9713 | CD | Dreamin' On The Hudson
John Marshall Quintet
Better To Know | Whatever Possessed Me | La Vita | Dream For Claudine | I'm A Dreamer Aren't We All | Dreamin' On The Hudson | Little Girl | Poor Butterfly | From This Moment On
Englewood Cliffs,NJ, rec. 6./7.1.1999
Marshall,John (tp,fl-h) | Fusco,Andy (as) | Hammer,Tardo (p) | Goldsby,John (b) | Williams,Leroy (dr)

ORGM 9714 | CD | Introducing The Exciting Claus Raible Trio
Claus Raible Trio
Lunar Web | Hammon Dex | I'll Remember April | Moon Mist | Little Leo | It's The Talk Of The Town | The Squirrel
Thorstadl,Obing, rec. 22./23.6.1999
Raible,Claus (p) | Cardoso,Paulo (b) | Gonzi,Mario (dr)
Claus Raible
Nici's Blues | I Should Care
Raible,Claus (p-solo)

ORGM 9715 | CD | Ghost Busters
Andreas Böttcher-Günter Heinz
Ghost Busters | Sunday Morning | Nothing Like This | Magic Lake | Blue Planet | Help! | Fata Morgana | Fata Morgana Kaputt
details unknown, rec. 30.5.1997
Heinz,Günter (tb) | Böttcher,Andreas (org)

ORGM 9716 | CD | Stabat Mater Inspirations
Victor Alcántara Trio
Stabat Mater | Cuius Animam | Quae Moerebat | Vidit Suum Dulcem | Eja Mater | Fac Ut Ardeat | Sancta Mater | Fac Ut Portem | Quando Corpus
Thorstadl,Obing, rec. 10.8.1999
Alcántara,Victor (p) | Stabenow,Thomas (b) | Jütte,Bastian (dr)

ORGM 9717 | CD | Al Porcino Big Band Live!
Al Porcino Big Band
Day In Day Out | Tape Worm | After You've Gone | Out Of Nowhere | The Big Cat | Lush Life | Get Me To The Church On Time | Groovin' High | TNT | Let's Dance | Whirly Bird
Live at The Nachtcafé,München, rec. 13.-15.12.1999
Porcino,Al (ld) | Weidinger,Tobias (tp) | Marshall,John (tp) | Hesse,Ralph (tp) | Strempel,Sebastian (tp) | Tuscher,Peter (tp) | Laughlin,Richard (tp) | Gregg,Erwin (tb) | Herrlich,Johannes (tb) | Fink,Gerhard (tb) | Gmelch,Leo (b-tb) | Keller,Rick (ss,as) | Faist,Thomas (as,ts) | Kühn,Axel (ts) | Koch,Claus (ts) | Lutzeier,Michael (bs) | Frommeyer,Heinz (p) | Zenker,Martin (b) | Keul,Michael (dr)
The Man With A Horn
Porcino,Al (ld) | Weidinger,Tobias (tp) | Marshall,John (tp) | Hesse,Ralph (tp) | Strempel,Sebastian (tp) | Tuscher,Peter (tp) | Laughlin,Richard (tp) | Gregg,Erwin (tb) | Herrlich,Johannes (tb) | Fink,Gerhard (tb) | Gmelch,Leo (b-tb) | Keller,Rick (ss,as) | Faist,Thomas (as,ts) | Kühn,Axel (ts) | Koch,Claus (ts) | Lutzeier,Michael (bs) | Frommeyer,Heinz (p) | Zenker,Martin (b) | Keul,Michael (dr) | Neuffer,Annette (voc)
The One I Love
Porcino,Al (ld,voc) | Weidinger,Tobias (tp) | Marshall,John (tp) | Hesse,Ralph (tp) | Strempel,Sebastian (tp) | Tuscher,Peter (tp) | Laughlin,Richard (tp) | Gregg,Erwin (tb) | Herrlich,Johannes (tb) | Fink,Gerhard (tb) | Gmelch,Leo (b-tb) | Keller,Rick (ss,as) | Faist,Thomas (as,ts) | Kühn,Axel (ts) | Koch,Claus (ts) | Lutzeier,Michael (bs) | Raible,Claus (p) | Zenker,Martin (b) | Keul,Michael (dr) | Frommeyer,Heinz (voc)

ORGM 9718 | CD | Standard Moods
Eckhard Weigt Quartet
Ars Vivendi | Rollinissimo | Sienna | Stille Stunden | Monky Tonky | Paul's Abschied | Standard Moods
Thorstadl,Obing, rec. 26./27.2.2000
Weigt,Eckhard (ts) | Schrack,Martin (p) | Stabenow,Thomas (b) | May,Guido (dr)

ORGM 9719 | CD | Theme Of No Repeat
John Marshall Quintet
With A Song In My Heart | Doggy Boy | Ballad For Very Tired And Very Sad Lotus Eaters | Theme Of No Repeat | Una Mas | That's Earl Brother | Philly J.J. | The Scene Is Clean | So In Love | I Can Dream Can't I | Sweet And Lovely
Thorstadl,Obing, rec. 2.-4.8.2000
Marshall,John (tp,fl-h) | Povel,Ferdinand (ts) | Hammer,Tardo (p) | Goldsby,John (b) | Sides,Douglas 'Doug' (dr)

ORGM 9720 | CD | Sandsee
Johannes Enders Quartet
Kind Of Now | Song For Ben | Taurus | Mother Song | Dual Force | Underground Dream | Please Stop Me Now | Herzog | Sandsee
Thorstadl,Obing, rec. 6.11.2000
Enders,Johannes (ss,ts) | Farao,Antonio (p) | Howard,Ed (b) | Hart,Bill (dr)

ORGM 9721 | CD | Future Days
Christian Elsässer Trio
Pas(s)ing Moments | Afterthoughts Of A Dream | Significant Decicions | Gossip Song | Something Special | The Story-Teller | My Foolish Heart
Thorstadl,Obing, rec. 3./4.1.2001
Elsässer,Christian (p) | Medan,Sava (b) | Sanguinetti,Alex (dr)
Conclusions Of A Dream | Future Days
Elsässer,Christian (p) | Schulz,Helmuth (b) | Sanguinetti,Alex (dr)

ORGM 9722 | CD | Earth Tones | EAN 4028164097229
Ron Ringwood's Crosscut Bluesband
Born Under A Bad Sign | Nobody Loves Me Like You Do | Next Time You See Me | Sittin' On The Dock Of The Bay - (Sittin' On) The Dock Of The Bay | Send Me Someone To Love | I'd Rather Drink Muddy Water | Rainy Night In Georgia | Turner Brown Blues | Goin' Down Slow | Lush Life(R.Ringwood) | Way Back Home | The Thrill Is Gone
Thorstadl,Obing, rec. 4.-6.12.2000
Ringwood,Ron (voc) | James,Derrick (sax) | Marsico,Alberto (p,org) | Kingue,J.C. Doo (g) | Zirelli,Enzo (dr)

ORGM 9723 | CD | Festa Do Olho | EAN 4028164097236
Marcio Tubino Group
Valsa Tupi | Ciranda(1) | Tangara | Trovas | Xiste | O Coreto | Ciranda(2)
Thorstadl,Obing, rec. 4.-6.2.2001
Tubino,Marcio (fl,ss,as,ts,perc) | Noschke,Regine (v) | Hoxha,Blerim (v) | Weber,Tobias (viola) | Weber,Ute (cello)
Entre Nos
Tubino,Marcio (fl,ss,as,ts,perc) | Kent,Oliver (p) | Noschke,Regine (v) | Hoxha,Blerim (v) | Weber,Tobias (viola) | Weber,Ute (cello)
Fresta Do Olho | Milonga
Tubino,Marcio (fl,ss,as,ts,perc) | Noschke,Regine (v) | Hoxha,Blerim (v) | Weber,Tobias (viola) | Weber,Ute (cello) | Cardoso,Paulo (b)

ORGM 9724 | CD | Loopin' With Lea | EAN 4028164097243
Claus Raible Sextet
Loopin' With Lea | Workshop | Jammin' At Duffield | Laird Turner Meteor | Gondwana | I Didn't Know What Time It Was | Petite Bel | Jive Bomber | If I Love You | Bebop In Pastel
Thorstadl,Obing, rec. 12./13.3.2000
Raible,Claus (p) | Nagorski,Grzegorz 'Greg' (tb) | Leali,Brad (as) | Gradischnig,Herwig 'Hank' (bs) | Abrams,Marc (b) | Coleman,Montez (dr)

ORGM 9725 | CD | Changes
Thilo Kreitmeier & Group
Funky Rabbits | Hide Out | Changes | Flying High | Blues For Charlie | Soulrider | Good News | I'll Never Do You Wrong | Sunny | The Wedding | Changes(reprise)
Thorstadl,Obing, rec. 16.-18.9.2000
Kreitmeier,Thilo (fl,as,ts,varitone) | Brunton,John 'Lee' (g) | Marsico,Alberto (org,el-p) | Knauer,Rocky (el-b) | Eppinger,Stephan (dr) | De Sousa,Borel (perc) | Bluesharp Slim (harm) | Laughlin,Richard (tp) | Kellem,Butch (tb)

ORGM 9726 | CD | Kyoto
Johannes Enders Quartet
Dawning Dance | Kyoto | Tainish | Eighty-One | Scientific | Faustino No.7 | Saturns Child | The Lost Lenore
Thorstadl,Obing, rec. 1.10.2001
Enders,Johannes (ts) | Locke,Joe (vib) | Stabenow,Thomas (b) | Salfellner,Christian (dr)

ORGM 9727 | CD | Venice | EAN 4028164097274
Christian Elsässer Trio
San Andrea | Never Will I Marry | Venice | But Not For Me | Spaces | At The Crossroad | Minor Importance | Skylark | Solution
Thorstadl,Obing, rec. 2./3.4.2002
Elsässer,Christian (p) | Abrams,Marc (b) | May,Guido (dr)

ORGM 9728 | CD | Who's Been Talkin'... | EAN 4028164097281
Dook Joint
Walkin' The Dog | Who's Been Talkin'? | Breakin' Down | Ma Jolie | No Computer Aid | Bad Times | Raincheck | Frankie And Johnny | You Can Stay But The Noise Must Go | Get Outta Yo Seat | Always Broke | Bright Lights Big City | When Something Is Wrong With My Baby | Funky Broadway
Thorstadl,Obing, rec. 2002
Dook Joint | Kingue,J.C. Doo (g,voc) | Marsico,Alberto (org,el-p) | DuVernay-Shipman,Kevin (b,voc) | Harris,Tommie (dr,voc) | Hurdle,Tony (tb) | Abdul-Khaliq,Fuasi (as,ts)

ORGM 9729 | CD | Jazz The Beatles | EAN 4028164097298
Scenario
Help! | I Am The Walrus | Blue Jay Way | Come Together | Happiness Is A Warm Gun | Lucy In The Sky With Diamonds | Julia | Dig A Pony- | Don't Let Me Down- | Norwegian Wood | Helter Skelter | Her Majesty
Thorstadl,Obing, rec. 23.-25.2.2002
Scenario | Santini,Simone (sopranino,as) | Marsico,Alberto (org) | Zirilli,Enzo (dr,perc)

ORGM 9730 | CD | Al Cohn Meets Al Porcino | EAN 4028164097304
Al Porcino Big Band
Tiny's Blues | I Cover The Waterfront | No Thanks | Body And Soul | Dancing In The Dark | Lover Come Back To Me | Music To Dance To | The Goof And I | My Heart Belongs To Daddy | Autumn In New York | Mambo Di Paulo | All The Things You Are | The Fuzz | Get Me To The Church On Time | Sophisticated Lady | Jumpin' With Symphony Sid
Live at Club Jubez,Karlsruhe, rec. 30.3.1987
Porcino,Al (tp,ld) | Weyerer,Franz (tp) | Reichstaller,Claus (tp) | Tuscher,Peter (tp) | Welch,Jon (tb) | Fink,Gerd (tb) | Gregg,Erwin (tb) | Geyer,Auwi (tb) | Staniloi,Otto (as) | Faist,Thomas (as) | Cohn,Al (ts,arr) | Kral,Petri (ts) | Martlreiter,Hermann (ts) | Zoller,Thomas (bs) | Di Gioia,Roberto (p) | Cardoso,Paulo (b) | Haffner,Wolfgang (dr)

ORGM 9731 | CD | Nostalgia Soul Ship | EAN 4028164097311
Marc Schmolling Trio
Nostalgia Soul Ship | Gummy Dummy | Silent Blue | Cinderella | Moonpower | Cautious Heart
Thorstadl,Obing, rec. 16.4.2002
Schmolling,Marc (p) | Medan,Sava (b) | Jütte,Bastian (dr)

ORGM 9732 | CD | Off Minor | EAN 4028164097328
Wanja Slavin-Matc Schmolling
The Duke | Encore | Off Minor | Isfahan | 26-2 | You Don't Know What Love Is | Widmung | One For Paulo
Thorstadl,Obing, rec. 23.4.2002
Slavin,Wanja (cl,sax) | Schmolling,Marc (p)

ORGM 9733 | CD | Bar Piano: Simon Schott Plays Your Favorite Evergreens Vol.1 | EAN 4028164097335
Simon Schott
As Time Goes By- | The Man I Love- | Summertime- | Flamingo- | Memory- | Sentimental Journey- | All The Things You Are- | On The Sunny Side Of The Street- | Body And Soul- | Blue Skies- | Embraceable You- | Oh! Lady Be Good- | Tea For Two- | Blue Moon- | Isn't It A Lovely Day- | Moon River- | Tenderly- | Night And Day- | Stardust- | September In The Rain- | Strangers In The Night- | Misty- | The Way You Look Tonight- | What A Wonderful World- | Over The Rainbow- | Stormy Weather- | Smoke Gets In Your Eyes- | Begin The Beguine- | There's A Small Hotel- | I Only Have Eyes For You- | 'S Wonderful- | I Left My Heart In San Francisco- | I'm Beginning To See The Light- | Confessin'- | East Of The Sun West Of The Moon- | Georgia On My Mind- | Two Sleepy People- | They Can't Take That Away From Me- | Sophisticated Lady- | Goodnight Sweetheart- | Everybody Loves Somebody- | Bye Bye Blues-
details unknown, rec. details unknown
Schott,Simon (p-solo)

ORGM 9734 | CD | Travelin' Man | EAN 4028164097342
J.C. Dook Quartet
A Little Push | Ooh Wee Baby | Ms. Raymona's House | Cissy Strut | She Got It Like That | I Want To Be Loved | Do You Remember?(Jimi) | Travelin' Man | People Get Ready | Down Down Down | New Friends
Thorstadl,Obing, rec. 2003
Dook,J.C. (g,el-g,voc) | Di Gioia,Roberto (keyboards) | Mills,Alvin (el-b) | Jackson,Jay (dr,perc,voc)

ORGM 9735 | CD | Bar Piano: Simon Schott Plays Your Favorite Evergreens Vol.2 | EAN 4028164097359
Simon Schott
Charmaine- | These Foolish Things Remind Me On You- | Someone To Watch Over Me- | Cherokee- | Cheek To Cheek- | Can't Help Lovin' Dat Man- | Prisoner Of Love- | I Got Rhythm- | Nice Work If You Can Get It- | Why Was I Born- | Goodnight My Love- | Laura- | I See You Again- | Red Sails In The Sunset- | Easy To Love- | Penthouse Serenade- | Dream- | Somebody Loves Me- | Ain't Misbehavin'- | True Love- | Fly Me To The Moon- | After You've Gone- | Memories Of You- | Manhattan- | Blue Room- | Sweet Sue Just You- | Don't Blame Me- | You Go To My Head- | Autumn In New York- | My Blue Heaven- | Whispering- | San Francisco- | Stars Fell On Alabama- | They Can't Take That Away From Me- | Long Ago And Far Away- | On The Street Where You Live- | Who Cares- | Deep Purple- | Satin Doll- | Mean To Me- | Moonlight Serenade-
München, rec. 2003
Schott,Simon (p-solo)

Orgel ist mehr! | Orgel Ist Mehr!

OIM/BA/1999-1 CD | CD | Orgel Ist Mehr!...In Bamberg,Vol.1
Natascha Majevskaja
Der Tag Ist Seiner Höhe Nah(Partita) | Allegretto Grazioso(Mozart:Klaviersonate B-Dur) | Präludium in e-Moll(Bach BWV 548) | Fuga in e-Moll(Bach BWV 548) | Psalm Nr.42,Arie(Mendelssohn-Bartholdy)
Bamberg, rec. details unknown
Majevskaja,Natascha (org)
Thomas Jäger
My One And Only Love | So Many Stars | Sister Sadie
Jäger,Thomas (org)
Natascha Majevskaja-Thomas Jäger
Overtüre(Rossini:Il Barbiere di Seviglia) | Overtüre(Mozart:Cosi fan tutte)
Majevskaja,Natascha (org) | Jäger,Thomas (org)

OIM/BA/1999-2 CD | CD | Orgel Ist Mehr...In Bamberg Vol.2
Natascha Majevskaja
Herr Geh' Nicht Ins Gericht,Arie(Bach) | Adagio(Haydn:Klaviersonate C-Dur) | Klavierkonzert in C-Dur,2.Satz(Mozart) | Agnus Dei(Mozart:Litaniae Lauretanae KV 195) | Regina Angelorum(Mozart)
Majevskaja,Natascha (org)
Thomas Jäger
Lil' Darlin' | Fly Me To The Moon | My Funny Valentine
Jäger,Thomas (org)
Natascha Majevskaja-Thomas Jäger
Overtüre(Mozart:Titus) | Symphonie in B-Dur(Schubert)
Majevskaja,Natascha (org) | Jäger,Thomas (org)

Original Blues Classics | ZYX Music GmbH

OBCCD 509-2(RLP 9417) | CD | Odetta And The Blues
Odetta With The Buck Clayton Sextet
Hard Oh Lord | Believe I'll Go | Oh Papa | How Long Blues | Hogan's Alley | Leavin' This Mornin' | Oh My Babe | Yonder Came The Blues | Make Me A Pallet On The Floor | Weeping Willow Blues | Go Down Sunshine | Nobody Knows You When You're Down And Out
NYC, rec. 1962
Odetta (voc) | Clayton,Buck (tp) | Dickenson,Vic (tb) | Hall,Herb (cl) | Wellstood,Dick (p) | Abdul-Malik,Ahmed (b) | Shepherd,Shep (dr)

OBCCD 517-2 | CD | Last Session
Blind Willie McTell
Baby, It Must be Love | The Dyin' Crapshooter's Blues | Don't Forget It | Kill It Kid | That Will Never Happen No More | Goodbye Blues | Salty Dog | Early Life | Beedle Um Bum | A Married Man's A Fool | A To Z Blues | Wabash Cannonball | Pal Of Mine
Atlanta,GA, rec. September 1956
McTell,Blind Willie (g,voc)
Kill It Kid | Broke Down Engine Blues
Atlanta,GA, rec. 1949
McTell,Blind Willie (g,voc)

OBCCD 520-2 | CD | Songs We Taught Your Mother
Alberta Hunter With Buster Bailey's Blues Blasters
I Got Myself A Workin' Man | I Got A Mind To Ramble | You Gotta Reap What You Sow | Chirpin' The Blues
Englewood Cliffs,NJ, rec. 16.8.1961
Hunter,Alberta (voc) | Bailey,Buster (cl) | Higginbotham,J.C. (tb) | DeParis,Sidney (tuba) | Jackson,Cliff (p) | Singleton,Zutty (dr)
Victoria Spivey With Buster Bailey's Blues Blasters
Got The Blues So Bad | Let Him Beat Me
Spivey,Victoria (voc) | Bailey,Buster (cl) | Higginbotham,J.C. (tb) | DeParis,Sidney (tuba) | Jackson,Cliff (p) | Singleton,Zutty (dr)
Black Snake Blues | Going Blues
Spivey,Victoria (p,voc) | Bailey,Buster (cl) | Higginbotham,J.C. (tb) | DeParis,Sidney (tuba) | Singleton,Zutty (dr)
Lucille Hegamin With Willie The Lion And His Cubs
St.Louis Blues | You'll Want My Love | Arkansas Blues | Has Anybody Seen My Corine
Hegamin[Nelson],Lucille (voc) | Smith,Willie 'The Lion' (p) | Goodwin,Henry (tp) | Scott,Cecil (cl) | Brooks,Gene (dr)

OBCCD 522-2(BV 1073) | CD | Going Away
Lightnin' Hopkins
Wake Up Old Lady | Don't Embarrass Me, Baby | Stranger Here | Little Sister's Boogie | Goin' Away | You Better Stop Here | Business You're Doin' | I'm Wit' It
Englewood Cliffs,NJ, rec. 4.6.1963
Hopkins,Sam Lightnin' (g,voc) | Gaskin,Leonard (b) | Lovelle,Herbie (dr)

OBCCD 527-2(P 7290) | CD | Baby, Baby, Baby
Jimmy Witherspoon And His Band
Mean Old Frisco | Rocks In My Bed | Bad Bad Whiskey | Baby Baby Baby | Sail On Little Girl Sail On | One Scotch One Bourbon One Beer | Lonely Boy Blues | Blues And Trouble
NYC, rec. 6.5.1963
Witherspoon,Jimmy (voc) | Wright,Leo (as,tambourine) | Burrell,Kenny (g) | Mahones,Gildo (p) | Tucker,George (b) | Smith,Jimmie (dr)
Endless Sleep | I'll Go On Living | I Can't Hardly See | It's A Lonesome Old World
Los Angeles,CA, rec. 8.7.1963
Witherspoon,Jimmy (voc) | Bryant,Bobby (tp,fl-h) | Allen,Jimmy (ts) | Wright,Arthur (harm) | Mitchell,Herman (g) | Freeman,Ernie (p) | Bond,Jimmy (b) | Miller,Jimmy (dr)

OBCCD 528-2(P 7368) | CD | Jesse Fuller's Favorites
Jesse Fuller
Red River Blues | How Long Blues | You Can't Keep A Good Man Down | Key To The Highway | Tickling The Strings | Midnight Special | Stranger Blues | Fables Aren't Nothing But Doggone Lies | Brownskin Gal (I Got My Eyes On You) | Cincinnati Blues | Hump In Your Back | Trouble If I Don't Use My Head
Berkeley,CA, rec. 13./14.5.1963
Fuller,Jesse (harm,fotdella,kazoo,12-string-g,voc,wbd)

OBCCD 529-2(P 7388) | CD | Blues On The Southside
Homesick James Quartet
The Woman I'm Lovin' | She May Be Your Woman | Goin' Down Swingin' | Homesick Shuffle | Johnny Mae | Gotta Move | Lonesome Road | Working With Homesick | The Cloud Is Crying | Homesick's Blues | Crawlin' | Stones In My Passway
Chicago,Ill, rec. 7.1.1964
Homesick James[William Henderson] (g,voc) | Leake,Lafayette (p) | Taylor,Eddie (b-g) | James,Clifton (dr)

OBCCD 530-2(P 7391) | CD | The Blues Never Die!
Otis Spann Band
One More Mile To Go | Feelin' Good | Dust My Broom | Straighten Up Baby | Lightnin' | I'm Ready
Chicago,Ill, rec. 21.11.1964
Spann,Otis (p,voc) | Cotton,James (harm,voc) | Madison,James (g) | Muddy Waters[McKinley Morganfield] (g) | Rector,Milton (b) | Leary,S.P. (dr)
The Blues Never Die | I Got A Feeling | After While | Come On | Must Have Been The Devil
Spann,Otis (p,voc) | Madison,James (g) | Muddy Waters[McKinley Morganfield] (g) | Rector,Milton (b) | Leary,S.P. (dr)

OBCCD 531-2(BV 1011) | CD | Blues And Ballads
Lonnie Johnson With Elmer Snowden
Haunted House | Memories Of You | Blues For Chris | I Found A Dream | St.Louis Blues | I'll Get Along Somehow | Savoy Blues | Back Water Blues | Elmer's Blues | Jelly Roll Baker
Englewood Cliffs,NJ, rec. 5.4.1960
Johnson,Lonnie (g,voc) | Snowden,Elmer (g) | Marshall,Wendell (b)

OBCCD 532-2(BV 1019) | CD | The Blues Of Lightnin' Hopkins
Lightnin' Hopkins Trio
Automobile Blues | You Better Watch Yourself | Mean Old Frisco | Shinin' Moon | Come Back Baby | Thinkin' 'Bout An Old Friend | The Walkin' Blues | Back To New Orleans | Katie Mae | Down There Baby
Englewood Cliffs,NJ, rec. 9.11.1960
Hopkins,Sam Lightnin' (g,voc) | Gaskin,Leonard (b) | Evans,Belton (dr)

OBCCD 535-2(M 93003) | CD | Long Way From Home-The Blues Of Fred McDowell
Fred McDowell
The Train I Ride | Poor Boy Long Way From Home | Milk Cow Blues | John Henry | Gravel Road Blues | Millionaire's Daughter Blues | Big Fat Mama | You Drove Me From Your Door | Sail On Little Girl Sail On
Los Angeles,CA, rec. 12.11.1966

McDowell,Mississippi Fred (g,voc)

OBCCD 536-2(F 8091) | CD | Sonny Terry And Brownie McGhee At Suger Hill

Sonny Terry & Brownie McGhee

Hooray, Hooray, This Woman Is Killing Me | Born To Live The Blues | Just About Crazy | Up, Sometimes Down | Baby, I Knocked On Your Door | Keep On Walkin' | Baby I Got My Eyes On You | I Got A Little Girl | I Feel Alright Now | Worry, Worry, Worry | Sweet Woman Blues

San Francisco,CA, rec. December 1961

Terry,Sonny (harm,voc) | McGhee,Brownie (g,voc)

OBCCD 538-2(RLP 12-321) | CD | That's My Story

John Lee Hooker

Come On Ahd See About Me | Democrat Man | That's My Story

NYC, rec. 9.2.1960

Hooker,John Lee (g,voc)

John Lee Hooker Trio

I Need Some Money | I'm Wanderin' | I Want To Talk About You | Gonna Use My Rod | Wednesday Evening Blues | No More Doggin' | One Of These Days | I Believe I'll Go Back Home | You're Leavin' Me, Baby

Hooker,John Lee (g,voc) | Jones,Sam (b) | Hayes,Louis (dr)

OBCCD 541-2(F 3296) | CD | Just A Closer Walk With Thee

Sonny Terry & Brownie McGhee

Just A Closer Walk With Thee | Children Go Where I Send Thee | What A Beautiful City | Glory Glory | If I Could Hear My Mother Pray Again | I'm Going To Shout | I Shall Not Be Moved | Packing Up | Get Right Church | Some Of These Days | If You See My Saviour | You Can't Hide

Jenny Lind Hall,Oakland, rec. 1957

Terry,Sonny (harm,voc) | McGhee,Brownie (g,voc)

OBCCD 542-2 | CD | The Country Blues Of John Lee Hooker

John Lee Hooker

Black Snake | How Long Blues | Wobblin' Baby | She's Long She's Tall She Weeps Like A Willow Tree | Pea Vine Special | Tupelo Blues | I'm Prison Bound | I Rowed A Little Boat | Water Boy | Church Bell Tone | Bundle Up And Go | Good Mornin' Lil' School Girl | Behind The Plow

Detroit, rec. April 1959

Hooker,John Lee (g,voc)

OBCCD 544-2(BV 1055) | CD | Bawdy Blues

Memphis Slim

Sweet Root Man | Churnin' Man Blues | Steady Rollin' Blues | If You See Kay

NYC, rec. 1960

Memphis Slim[Peter Chatman] (p,voc)

Tampa Red

Let Me Play With Your Poodle | Jelly Whipping Blues

Chicago,Ill(prob), rec. 1960

Tampa Red[Hudson Whitaker] (g,kazoo,voc)

Victoria Spivey

That Man

Englewood Cliffs,NJ, rec. 13.7.1961

Spivey,Victoria (p,voc)

I'm A Red Hot Mama

Spivey,Victoria (p,voc) | Johnson,Lonnie (g)

Lonnie Johnson Trio

Jelly Roll Baker

Englewood Cliffs,NJ, rec. 16.5.1960

Johnson,Lonnie (g) | Snowden,Elmer (g) | Marshall,Wendell (b)

Pink Anderson

Try Some Of That

NYC, rec. 1960

Anderson,Pink (g,voc)

Memphis Willie B.

Car Machine Blues

Memphis,Tenn., rec. 12.8.1961

Memphis Willie B.[Borum] (p,voc)

Blind Willie McTell

Beedle Um Bum

Atlanta,GA, rec. 1956

McTell,Blind Willie (g,voc)

OBCCD 545-2 | CD | Classic Delta Blues

Big Joe Williams

Rollin' And Tumblin' | Hellhound On My Trail | Bird's Nest Bound | Crossroads Blues | Special Rider | Pony Blues | Pea Vine Special | Walking Blues | Dirt Road Blues | Banty Rooster Blues | Terraplane Blues | Jinx Blues

Chicago,Ill, rec. 29.7.& 26.9.1964

Williams,Big Joe (g,voc)

OBCCD 548-2(BV 1029) | CD | Last Night Blues

Lightnin' Hopkins Trio With Sonny Terry

Rocky Mountain | Got To Move Your Baby | So Sorry To Leave You | Take A Trip With Me | Last Night Blues | Lightnin's Stroke | Hard To Love A Woman | Conversation Blues

Englewood Cliffs,NJ, rec. 26.10.1960

Hopkins,Sam Lightnin' (g,voc) | Terry,Sonny (harm,voc) | Gaskin,Leonard (b) | Evans,Belton (dr)

OBCCD 555-2(RLP 008) | CD | Burning Hell

John Lee Hooker

Burnin' Hell | Graveyard Blues | Baby Please Don't Go | Jackson,Tennessee | You Live Your Life And I'll Live Mine | Smokestack Lightnin' | How Can You Do It | I Don't Want No Woman If Her Hair Ain't No Longer Than Mine(Short-Haired Woman) | I Rolled And Turned And Cried The Whole Night Long | Blues For My Baby | Key To The Highway | Natchez Fire(Burnin')

Detroit, rec. 20.4.1959

Hooker,John Lee (g,voc)

OBCCD 583-2(BV 1013) | CD | Midnight Special

Al Smith With The King Curtis Quintet

Five Long Years | You're A Sweetheart | Baby Don't Worry 'Bout Me | Ride On Midnight Special | The Bells | Goin' To Alabama | I'll Never Let You Go | I Can't Make It By Myself

Englewood Cliffs,NJ, rec. 11.8.1960

Smith,Al (voc) | Curtis,King (ts) | Robinson,Jimmy Lee (g) | Banks,Robert (org) | Gaskin,Leonard (b) | Donaldson,Bobby (dr)

OBCCD 584-2(BV 1028) | CD | Goin' Down Slow

St.Louis Jimmy Oden Group

Poor Boy | Nothin' But The Blues | Mother's Day Blues | Some Sweet Day | Dog House Blues | My Heart Is Loaded With Trouble | I'm St.Louis Bound | Goin' Down Slow | Sweet As She Can Be | Monkey Face Woman

Englewood Cliffs,NJ, rec. 19.11.1960

Oden,James[St.Louis Jimmy] (voc) | Robinson,Jimmy Lee (g) | Banks,Robert (p) | Gaskin,Leonard (b) | Evans,Belton (dr)

OBCCD 585-2(PR 7475) | CD | Blues For Easy Livers

Jimmy Witherspoon And His All Stars

Lotus Blossom | Gee Baby Ain't I Good To You | Trav'lin' Light | P.S.I Love You | I'll Always Be In Love With You | Don't Worry 'Bout Me | Easy Living | Embraceable You | Blues In The Night | Trouble In Mind | How Long Will It Take To Be A Man? | I Got It Bad And That Ain't Good

NYC, rec. 1065/66

Witherspoon,Jimmy (voc) | Watrous,Bill (tb) | Adams,Pepper (bs) | Kellaway,Roger (p) | Davis,Richard (b) | Lewis,Mel (dr)

Original Jazz Classics | ZYX Music GmbH

OJC 056(P 7048) | LP | 4, 5 And 6

Jackie McLean Quartet

Sentimental Journey | Why Was I Born

Hackensack,NJ, rec. 13.7.1956

McLean,Jackie (as) | Waldron,Mal (p) | Watkins,Doug (b) | Taylor,Arthur 'Art' (dr)

When I Fall In Love

Hackensack,NJ, rec. 20.7.1956

McLean,Jackie (as) | Waldron,Mal (p) | Watkins,Doug (b) | Taylor,Arthur 'Art' (dr)

Jackie McLean Quintet

Contour

Hackensack,NJ, rec. 13.7.1956

McLean,Jackie (as) | Byrd,Donald (tp) | Waldron,Mal (p) | Watkins,Doug (b) | Taylor,Arthur 'Art' (dr)

Abstraction

Hackensack,NJ, rec. 20.7.1956

McLean,Jackie (as) | Byrd,Donald (tp) | Waldron,Mal (p) | Watkins,Doug (b) | Taylor,Arthur 'Art' (dr)

Jackie McLean Sextet

Confirmation

McLean,Jackie (as) | Byrd,Donald (tp) | Mobley,Hank (ts) | Waldron,Mal (p) | Watkins,Doug (b) | Taylor,Arthur 'Art' (dr)

OJC 075(P 7091) | LP | Back Country Suite

OJCCD 075-2(P 7091) | CD | Back Country Suite

Mose Allison Trio

Back Country Suite For Piano, Bass And Drums: | New Ground- | Train- | Warm Night- | Blues(Young Man)- | Saturday- | Scamper- | January- | Promised Land- | Spring Song- | Highway 49- | Blueberry Hill | I Thought About You | In Salah | You Won't Let Me Go | One Room Country Shack

NYC, rec. 7.3.1957

Allison,Mose (p,voc) | LaFargue,Taylor (b) | Isola,Frank (dr)

OJC 080(NJ 8243) | LP | Screamin' The Blues

OJCCD 080-2(NJ 8243) | CD | Screamin' The Blues

Oliver Nelson Sextet

Screamin' The Blues | March On March On | The Drive | The Meetin' | Three Seconds | Alto-Itis

NYC, rec. 27.5.1960

Nelson,Oliver (as,ts) | Williams,Richard (tp) | Dolphy,Eric (b-cl,as) | Wyands,Richard (p) | Duvivier,George (b) | Haynes,Roy (dr)

OJC 105(R 12-433) | LP | Know What I Mean?

OJC20 105-2 | CD | Know What I Mean?

Cannonball Adderley Quartet

Waltz For Debby | Good Bye | Who Cares | Who Cares(alt.take) | Venice | Toy | Elsa | Nancy(With The Laughing Face) | Know What I Mean | Know What I Mean (alt.take)

NYC, rec. 21.2.& 13.3.1961

Adderley,Julian \'Cannonball\' (as) | Evans,Bill (p) | Heath,Percy (b) | Kay,Connie (dr)

OJC 126(P 7064) | LP | A Garland Of Red

OJCCD 126-2(P 7064) | CD | A Garland Of Red

Red Garland Trio

A Foggy Day(In London Town) | My Romance | What Is This Thing Called Love | Makin' Whoopee | September In The Rain | Little Girl In Blue | Blue Red | Constellation

NYC, rec. 17.8.1956

Garland,Red (p) | Chambers,Paul (b) | Taylor,Arthur 'Art' (dr)

OJC 198(NJ 8237) | LP | The New Scene Of King Curtis

OJCCD 198-2(NJ 8237) | CD | The New Scene Of King Curtis

King Curtis Quintet

Have You Heard | Da-Duh-Dah | Little Brother Soul | In A Funky Groove

Englewood Cliffs,NJ, rec. 21.4.1960

Curtis,King (ts) | Adderley,Nat[as 'Little Brother'] (tp) | Kelly,Wynton (p) | Chambers,Paul (b) | Jackson,Oliver (dr)

King Curtis Quartet

Willow Weep For Me

Curtis,King (ts) | Kelly,Wynton (p) | Chambers,Paul (b) | Jackson,Oliver (dr)

OJC 231(RLP 1158) | LP | Alone In San Francisco

OJC20 231-2(RLP 1158) | CD | Alone In San Francisco

Thelonious Monk

Remember | Reflections | Pannonica | Bluehawk | You Took The Words Right Out Of My Heart | Everything Happens To Me | Round Lights | Ruby My Dear | Blue Monk | There's Danger In Your Eyes Cherie | There's Danger In Your Eyes Cherie(alt.take)

San Francisco,CA, rec. 18./20.& 22.10.1959

Monk,Thelonious (p-solo)

OJC 269(C 7563) | LP | Barney Kessel Plays Carmen

Barney Kessel And His Orchestra

Free As A Bird | A Pad On Edge Of Town | Viva El Toro | Flowersville | Like There's No Place Like... | Swingin' The Toreador

Los Angeles,CA, rec. 19.12.1958

Kessel,Barney (g) | Collette,Buddy (fl,cl) | Smith,Bill (cl,b-cl) | Jacobs,Jules (cl,oboe) | Terry,Pete (b-cl,bassoon) | Gordon,Justin (fl,alto-fl) | Previn,André (p) | Mondragon,Joe (b) | Manne,Shelly (dr)

The Gypsy's Hip

Kessel,Barney (g) | Linn,Ray (tp) | Betts,Harry (tb) | Geller,Herb (as) | Gordon,Justin (ts) | Gentry,Chuck (bs) | Previn,André (p) | Mondragon,Joe (b) | Manne,Shelly (dr)

Barney Kessel And His Quintet

If You Dig Me | Carmen's Cool

Los Angeles,CA, rec. 22.12.1958

Kessel,Barney (g) | Feldman,Victor (vib) | Previn,André (p) | Mondragon,Joe (b) | Manne,Shelly (dr)

OJC 302(R 12-271) | LP | In Orbit

OJCCD 302-2 | CD | In Orbit

Clark Terry-Thelonious Monk Quartet

In Orbit | One Foot In The Gutter | Trust In Me | Let's Cool One | Pea-Eye | Moonlight Fiesta | Argentia | Buck's Business | Very Near Blues

NYC, rec. 7.& 12.5.1958

Terry,Clark (fl-h) | Monk,Thelonious (p) | Jones,Sam (b) | Jones,Philly Joe (dr)

OJC 312 (M 9042) | LP | Next Album

Sonny Rollins Quartet

Skylark | Poinciana

rec. July 1972

Rollins,Sonny (ss,ts) | Cables,George (p,el-p) | Cranshaw,Bob (b,el-b) | Lee,David (dr)

Sonny Rollins Quintet

The Everywhere Calypso

Rollins,Sonny (ss,ts) | Cables,George (p,el-p) | Cranshaw,Bob (b,el-b) | Lee,David (dr) | Jenkins,Arthur (perc,congas)

Playin' In The Yard

Rollins,Sonny (ss,ts) | Cables,George (p,el-p) | Cranshaw,Bob (b,el-b) | DeJohnette,Jack (dr) | Jenkins,Arthur (perc,congas)

Sonny Rollins Quartet

Keep Hold Of Yourself

Rollins,Sonny (ss,ts) | Cables,George (p,el-p) | Cranshaw,Bob (b,el-b) | DeJohnette,Jack (dr)

OJC 316(C 3515) | LP | The Trio-Vol.1

OJCCD 316-2 | CD | The Trio-Vol.1

Hampton Hawes Trio

I Got Rhythm | What Is This Thing Called Love | Blues The Most | So In Love | Feelin' Fine | Hamp's Blues | Easy Living | All The Things You Are | These Foolish Things Remind Me On You | Carioca

Los Angeles,CA, rec. 28.6.1955

Hawes,Hampton (p) | Mitchell,Red (b) | Thompson,Chuck (dr)

OJC 336(C 7527) | LP | My Fair Lady

OJCCD 336-2 | CD | My Fair Lady

Shelly Manne And His Friends

Get Me To The Church On Time | On The Street Where You Live | I've Grown Accustomed To Her Face | Wouldn't It Be Loverly | Ascot Gavotte | Show Me | With A Little Bit Of Luck | I Could Have Danced All Night

Los Angeles,CA, rec. 17.8.1956

Manne,Shelly (dr) | Vinnegar,Leroy (b) | Previn,André (p)

OJC 346(P 7120) | LP | Gil Evans And Ten

Gil Evans And Ten

Remember

Hackensack,NJ, rec. 9.9.1957

Evans,Gil (p,arr) | Carisi,Johnny (tp) | Koven,Jack (tp) | Cleveland,Jimmy (tb) | Varsalona,Bart (tb) | Ruff,Willie (fr-h) | Konitz,Lee[as Zeke Tolin] (as) | Lacy,Steve (ss) | Kurtzer,Dave (bassoon) | Chambers,Paul (b) | Jones,Jo (dr)

Nobody's Heart | If You Could See Me Now

Hackensack,NJ, rec. 27.9.1957

Evans,Gil (p,arr) | Mucci,Louis (tp) | Koven,Jack (tp) | Cleveland,Jimmy (tb) | Varsalona,Bart (tb) | Ruff,Willie (fr-h) | Konitz,Lee[as Zeke Tolin] (as) | Lacy,Steve (ss) | Kurtzer,Dave (bassoon) | Chambers,Paul (b) | Stabulas,Nick (dr)

Ella Speed | Big Stuff | Just One Of Those Things | Jambangle

Hackensack,NJ, rec. 10.10.1957

Evans,Gil (p,arr) | Mucci,Louis (tp) | Koven,Jack (tp) | Cleveland,Jimmy (tb) | Varsalona,Bart (tb) | Ruff,Willie (fr-h) | Konitz,Lee[as Zeke Tolin] (as) | Lacy,Steve (ss) | Kurtzer,Dave (bassoon) | Chambers,Paul (b) | Stabulas,Nick (dr)

OJC 352(P 7316) | LP | Black Pearls

OJC20 352-2(P 7316) | CD | Black Pearls

John Coltrane Quintet

Black Pearls | Lover Come Back To Me | Sweet Sapphire Blues

Hackensack,NJ, rec. 23.5.1958

Coltrane,John (ts) | Byrd,Donald (tp) | Garland,Red (p) | Chambers,Paul (b) | Cobb,Jimmy (dr)

OJC 372(2308202) | LP | Montreux '77

OJCCD 372-2 | CD | Montreux '77

Tommy Flanagan 3

Barbados | Some Other Spring- | Easy Living- | Star Crossed Lovers- | Jump For Joy- | Woody'n You | Blue Bossa

rec. 13.7.1977

Flanagan,Tommy (p) | Betts,Keter (b) | Durham,Bobby (dr)

OJC 379(2308209) | LP | Montreux '77

OJC20 379-2(2308209) | CD | Montreux '77

Count Basie Jam

Bookie's Blues | She's Funny That Way | These Foolish Things Remind Me On You | Kidney Stew | Trio Blues | I Got It Bad And That Ain't Good | Jumpin' At The Woodside

Montreux,CH, rec. 14.7.1977

Basie,Count (p) | Eldridge,Roy (tp) | Dickenson,Vic (tb) | Grey,Al (tb) | Carter,Benny (as) | Sims,Zoot (ts) | Brown,Ray (b) | Smith,Jimmie (dr)

OJC 383(2308213) | LP | Montreux '77

OJC20 383-2 | CD | Montreux '77

Oscar Peterson And The Bassists

There Is No Greater Love | You Look Good To Me | People | Reunion Blues | Teach Me Tonight | Sweet Georgia Brown | Soft Winds

rec. 15.7.1977

Peterson,Oscar (p) | Brown,Ray (b) | Orsted-Pedersen,Niels-Henning (b)

OJC 385(2620105) | LP | Montreux '77

OJC20 385-2(2620105) | CD | Montreux '77

Oscar Peterson Jam

Perdido | Mack The Knife(Moritat)

Montreux,CH, rec. 14.7.1977

Peterson,Oscar (p) | Gillespie,Dizzy (tp) | Terry,Clark (tp) | Davis,Eddie 'Lockjaw' (ts) | Orsted-Pedersen,Niels-Henning (b) | Durham,Bobby (dr)

Milt Jackson-Ray Brown Jam

Red Top

Montreux,CH, rec. 13.7.1977

Jackson,Milt (vib) | Brown,Ray (b) | Terry,Clark (tp,fl-h) | Davis,Eddie 'Lockjaw' (ts) | Alexander,Monty (p) | Smith,Jimmie (dr)

Dizzy Gillespie Jam

Here's 'Tis

Montreux,CH, rec. 14.7.1977

Gillespie,Dizzy (tp) | Faddis,Jon (tp) | Jackson,Milt (vib,p) | Brown,Ray (b,dr)

Count Basie Jam

Freeport Jump

Basie,Count (p) | Eldridge,Roy (tp) | Dickenson,Vic (tb) | Grey,Al (tb) | Carter,Benny (as) | Sims,Zoot (ts) | Brown,Ray (b) | Smith,Jimmie (dr)

Pablo All Star Jam

Donna Lee

Pablo All Stars | Terry,Clark (tp,fl-h) | Scott,Ronnie (ts) | Jackson,Milt (vib) | Pass,Joe (g) | Peterson,Oscar (p) | Orsted-Pedersen,Niels-Henning (b) | Durham,Bobby (dr)

OJC 390(C 7646) | LP | At The Renaissance

OJC20 390-2 | CD | At The Renaissance

Ben Webster Quintet

Gone With The Wind | Georgia On My Mind | Caravan | Ole Miss Blues | Stardust | Mop Mop | What Is This Thing Called Love | Renaissance Blues

Live at The Renaissance Club,Hollywood,CA, rec. 14.10.1960

Webster,Ben (ts) | Rowles,Jimmy (p) | Hall,Jim (p) | Mitchell,Red (b) | Butler,Frank (dr)

OJC 394(P 7378) | LP | The Last Trane

OJC20 394-2(P 7378) | CD | The Last Trane | EAN 090204948154

John Coltrane Trio

Slowtrane

rec. 16.8.1957

Coltrane,John (ts) | May,Earl (b) | Taylor,Arthur 'Art' (dr)

John Coltrane Quintet

Lover | Come Rain Or Come Shine

rec. 10.1.1958

Coltrane,John (ts) | Byrd,Donald (tp) | Garland,Red (p) | Chambers,Paul (b) | Hayes,Louis (dr)

John Coltrane With The Red Garland Trio

By The Numbers

rec. 26.3.1958

Coltrane,John (ts) | Garland,Red (p) | Chambers,Paul (b) | Taylor,Arthur 'Art' (dr)

OJC 413(P 7304) | LP | Eric Dolphy in Europe, Vol.1

OJC20 413-2(P 7304) | CD | Eric Dolphy in Europe, Vol.1 | EAN 090204923076

Eric Dolphy With Erik Moseholm's Trio

Oleo | Glad To Be Unhappy

Copenhagen,Denmark, rec. 8.9.1961

Dolphy,Eric (fl,b-cl) | Moseholm,Erik (b) | Axen,Bent (p) | Elniff,Jorn (dr)

Eric Dolphy Duo

Hi Fly

Dolphy,Eric (fl,b-cl) | Israels,Chuck (b)

Eric Dolphy

God Bless The Child

Dolphy,Eric (b-cl-solo)

OJC 467(M 9045) | LP | Alone Together

OJC20 467-2(M 9045) | CD | Alone Together

Jim Hall-Ron Carter Duo

St.Thomas | Alone Together | Receipt Please | I'll Remember April | Softly As In A Morning Sunrise | Whose Blues | Prelude To A Kiss | Autumn Leaves

Live at The Playboy Club,NYC, rec. 4.8.1972

Hall,Jim (g) | Carter,Ron (b)

OJC 468(M 9059) | LP | The Cutting Edge

OJCCD 468-2 | CD | The Cutting Edge

Sonny Rollins Sextet

The Cuttin' Edge | To A Wild Rose | First Moves | A House Is Not A Home

Jazz Festival Montreux,CH, rec. 6.7.1974

Rollins,Sonny (ts) | Masuo,Yoshiaki (g) | Cowell,Stanley (p) | Cranshaw,Bob (el-b) | Lee,David (dr) | M'tume,James[Forman] (perc,congas)

Sonny Rollins Sextet With Rufus Harley

Swing Low Sweet Chariot

Rollins,Sonny (ts) | Harley,Rufus (bagpipes) | Masuo,Yoshiaki (g) | Cowell,Stanley (p) | Cranshaw,Bob (el-b) | Lee,David (dr) | M'tume,James[Forman] (perc,congas)

OJC 600(2310878) | LP | For The Second Time

OJCCD 600-2 | CD | For The Second Time

Count Basie Kansas City 3

Sandman | If I Could Be With You One Hour Tonight | Draw | On The Sunny Side Of The Street | The One I Love Belongs To Somebody Else | Blues For Eric | I Surrender Dear | Racehorse

Los Angeles,CA, rec. 28.8.1975

Basie,Count (p) | Brown,Ray (b) | Bellson,Louie (dr)

OJC 602(2312109) | LP | I Remember Charlie Parker

OJCCD 602-2 | CD | I Remember Charlie Parker

Joe Pass

Just Friends | Easy To Love | Summertime | April In Paris | Everything

Happens To Me | Laura | They Can't Take That Away From Me | I Didn't Know
What Time It Was | If I Should Lose You | Out Of Nowhere (Concept 1) | Out Of Nowhere (Concept 2)
Hollywood,CA, rec. 17.2.1979
Pass,Joe (g-solo)

OJC 607(C 7556) | LP | The Poll Winners Ride Again
OJCCD 607-2 | CD | The Poll Winners Ride Again
The Poll Winners
De Deele Dee Do | Volare (Nel Blu Dipinto Di Blu) | Spring Is Here | The Surrey With The Fringe On Top | Custard Puff | Whe The Red Red Robin Come Bob Bob Bobbin' Along | Foreign Intrigue | Angel Eyes | The Merry-Go-Round Broke Down
rec. 19./21.8.1958
Poll Winners,The | Kessel,Barney (g) | Brown,Ray (b) | Manne,Shelly (dr)

OJC 610(C 14010) | LP | Peter Erskine
OJCCD 610-2 | CD | Peter Erskine
Peter Erskine Orchestra
Leroy Street | In Statu Nascendi | E.S.P. | Change Of Mind | All's Well That Ends | My Ship | Coyote Blues
NYC, rec. 22./23.6.1982
Erskine,Peter (dr) | Brecker,Randy (tp,fl-h) | Brecker,Michael (ts) | Mintzer,Bob (b-cl,ts) | Grolnick,Don (el-p) | Kirkland,Kenny (p) | Mainieri,Mike (vib) | Gomez,Eddie (b) | Alias,Don (perc,congas)

OJC 622(F 9501) | LP | Since We Met
OJCCD 622-2(F 9501) | CD | Since We Met
Bill Evans Trio
Since We Met | Midnight Mood | See Saw | Sareen Jurer | Time Remembered | Turn Out The Stars | But Beautiful
Live at The 'Village Vanguard',NYC, rec. 11./12.1.1974
Evans,Bill (p) | Gomez,Eddie (b) | Morell,Marty (dr)

OJC 627(2308241) | LP | The Good Life
OJC20 627-2(2308241) | CD | The Good Life
Oscar Peterson Trio
Wheatland | Wave | For Count | The Good Life | On A Clear Day You Can See Forever
London House,Chicago,Ill., rec. 1973
Peterson,Oscar (p) | Pass,Joe (g) | Orsted-Pedersen,Niels-Henning (b)

OJC 808(2310901) | LP | 88 Basie Street
OJCCD 808-2(2310901) | CD | 88 Basie Street
Count Basie And His Orchestra
Bluesville | 88 Basie Street | The Blues Machine | Katy (Dizzier and Dizzier)
Hollywood,CA, rec. 11./12.5.1983
Basie,Count (p) | Summers,Bob (tp,fl-h) | Carley,Dale (tp) | Cohn[Cohen],Sonny (tp,fl-h) | Szabo,Frank (tp,fl-h) | Crawford,Jim (tp) | Wood,Booty (tb) | Mitchell,Grover (tb) | Wilson,Dennis (tb) | Hughes,Bill (tb) | Turner,Danny (fl,as) | Woods,Chris (fl,as) | Dixon,Eric (fl,ts) | Schneider,Eric (fl,ts) | Williams,John (bs) | Eaton,Cleveland (b) | Mackrel,Dennis (dr) | Nestico,Sam (arr,ld)
Count Basie's Small Band
Contractor's Blues | Sunday At The Savoy
Basie,Count (p) | Summers,Bob (tp,fl-h) | Woods,Chris (as) | Hing,Kenny (ts) | Pass,Joe (g) | Eaton,Cleveland (b) | Mackrel,Dennis (dr)

OJC20 001-2(P 7003) | CD | Milt Jackson
OJC 001(P 7003) | LP | Milt Jackson
Milt Jackson Quartet
Wonder Why | I Should Care | My Funny Valentine | Stonewall | Moon Ray | The Nearness Of You
NYC, rec. 20.5.1955
Jackson,Milt (vib) | Silver,Horace (p) | Heath,Percy (b) | Kay,Connie (dr)

OJC20 002-2 | CD | Concorde
OJC 002(P 7005) | LP | Concorde
Modern Jazz Quartet
Ralph's New Blues | All Of You | I'll Remember April | Gershwin Medley: | Soon- | For You For Me For Evermore- | Love Walked In- | Our Love Is Here To Stay- | Softly As In A Morning Sunrise | Concorde
Hackensack,NJ, rec. 2.7.1955
MJQ (Modern Jazz Quartet) | Jackson,Milt (vib) | Lewis,John (p) | Heath,Percy (b) | Kay,Connie (dr)

OJC20 005-2 | CD | Dig
OJC 005(P 7012) | LP | Dig
Miles Davis Sextet
Dig | It's Only A Paper Moon | Denial | Bluing | Out Of The Blue
NYC, rec. 5.10.1951
Davis,Miles (tp) | McLean,Jackie (as) | Rollins,Sonny (ts) | Bishop Jr.,Walter (p) | Potter,Tommy (b) | Blakey,Art (dr)

OJC20 006-2(P 7014) | CD | Miles
The New Miles Davis Quintet
Just Squeeze Me(But Don't Tease Me) | There Is No Greater Love | How Am I To Know? | S' Posin' | Miles' Theme | Stablemates
Hackensack,NJ, rec. 16.11.1955
Davis,Miles (tp) | Coltrane,John (ts) | Garland,Red (p) | Chambers,Paul (b) | Jones,Philly Joe (dr)

OJC20 007-2(P 7020) | CD | Worktime
OJC 007(P 7020) | LP | Worktime
Sonny Rollins Quartet
There's No Business Like Show Business | Paradox | Raincheck | There Are Such Things | It's All Right With Me
NYC, rec. 2.12.1955
Rollins,Sonny (ts) | Bryant,Ray (p) | Morrow,George (b) | Roach,Max (dr)

OJC20 010-2(P 7027) | CD | Thelonious Monk
Thelonious Monk Trio
Little Rootie Tootie | Sweet And Lovely | Bye-Ya | Monk's Dream
Hackensack,NJ, rec. 15.10.1952
Monk,Thelonious (p) | Mapp,Gary (b) | Blakey,Art (dr)
Trinkle Tinkle | These Foolish Things Remind Me On You | Bemsha Swing | Reflection
Hackensack,NJ, rec. 18.12.1952
Monk,Thelonious (p) | Mapp,Gary (b) | Roach,Max (dr)
Blue Monk
Hackensack,NJ, rec. 22.9.1954
Monk,Thelonious (p) | Heath,Percy (b) | Blakey,Art (dr)
Thelonious Monk
Just A Gigolo
Monk,Thelonious (p-solo)

OJC20 012-2(P 7034) | CD | Miles Davis And Milt Jackson
OJC 012(P 7034) | LP | Miles Davis And Milt Jackson
Miles Davis-Milt Jackson Quintet
Bitty Ditty | Changes
Hackensack,NJ, rec. 5.8.1955
Davis,Miles (tp) | Jackson,Milt (vib) | Bryant,Ray (p) | Heath,Percy (b) | Taylor,Arthur 'Art' (dr)
Miles Davis-Milt Jackson Sextet
Dr.Jackle | Minor March
Davis,Miles (tp) | Jackson,Milt (vib) | McLean,Jackie (as) | Bryant,Ray (p) | Heath,Percy (b) | Taylor,Arthur 'Art' (dr)

OJC20 017-2(P 7055) | CD | Clifford Brown Memorial
Tadd Dameron And His Orchestra
Philly J.J. | Choose Now | Choose Now(alt.take) | Dial 'B' For Beauty | Theme Of No Repeat
NYC, rec. 11.6.1953
Dameron,Tadd (p) | Brown,Clifford (tp) | Sulieman[Leonard Graham],Idrees (tp) | Mullins,Herb (tb) | Gryce,Gigi (as) | Golson,Benny (ts) | Estell,Oscar (bs) | Heath,Percy (b) | Jones,Philly Joe (dr)
Clifford Brown And Art Farmer With The Swedish All Stars
Stockholm Sweetnin' | 'Scuse These Blues | Falling In Love With Love | Lover Come Back To Me
Stockholm,Sweden, rec. 15.9.1953
Brown,Clifford (tp) | Farmer,Art (tp) | Persson,Ake (tb) | Domnerus,Arne (as) | Gullin,Lars (bs) | Hallberg,Bengt (p) | Johnson,Gunnar (b) | Noren,Jack (dr)

OJC20 020-2 | CD | Coltrane
OJC 020(P 7105) | LP | Coltrane
John Coltrane Quartet
Violets For Your Furs | Time Was
NYC, rec. 31.5.1957
Coltrane,John (ts) | Garland,Red (p) | Chambers,Paul (b) | Heath,Albert 'Tootie' (dr)
John Coltrane Sextet
Bakai
Coltrane,John (ts) | Splawn,Johnny (tp) | Shihab,Sahib (bs) | Garland,Red (p) | Chambers,Paul (b) | Heath,Albert 'Tootie' (dr)
Straight Street | Chronic Blues
Coltrane,John (ts) | Splawn,Johnny (tp) | Shihab,Sahib (bs) | Waldron,Mal (p) | Chambers,Paul (b) | Heath,Albert 'Tootie' (dr)
John Coltrane Quintet
While My Lady Sleeps
Coltrane,John (ts) | Splawn,Johnny (tp) | Waldron,Mal (p) | Chambers,Paul (b) | Heath,Albert 'Tootie' (dr)

OJC20 021-2 | CD | Soultrane
OJC 021(P 7142) | LP | Soultrane
John Coltrane Quartet
Good Bait | I Want To Talk About You | You Say You Care | Theme For Ernie | Russian Lullaby
NYC, rec. 7.2.1958
Coltrane,John (ts) | Garland,Red (p) | Chambers,Paul (b) | Taylor,Arthur 'Art' (dr)

OJC20 023-2(NJ 8252) | CD | Out There
OJC 023(NJ 8252) | LP | Out There
Eric Dolphy Quartet
Out There | Serene | The Baron | Eclipse | 17 West | Sketch Of Melba | Feathers
Englewood Cliffs,NJ, rec. 15.8.1960
Dolphy,Eric (fl,b-cl,as) | Carter,Ron (cello) | Duvivier,George (b) | Haynes,Roy (dr)

OJC20 024-2 | CD | Plays The Music Of Duke Ellington
OJC 024(R 201) | LP | Plays The Music Of Duke Ellington
Thelonious Monk Trio
It Don't Mean A Thing If It Ain't Got That Swing | Sophisticated Lady | I Got It Bad And That Ain't Good | Black And Tan Fantasy | Mood Indigo | I Let A Song Go Out Of My Heart | In My Solitude | Caravan
Hackensack,NJ, rec. 21.& 27.7.1955
Monk,Thelonious (p) | Pettiford,Oscar (b) | Clarke,Kenny (dr)

OJC20 025-2(RLP 223) | CD | New Jazz Conceptions
Bill Evans
I Got It Bad And That Ain't Good | Waltz For Debby | My Romance
NYC, rec. 18.9.1956
Evans,Bill (p-solo)
Bill Evans Trio
I Love You | Five | Conception | Easy Living | Displacement | Speak Low | Our Delight | No Cover No Minimum
NYC, rec. 27.9.1956
Evans,Bill (p) | Kotick,Teddy (b) | Motian,Paul (dr)

OJC20 026-2 | CD | Brilliant Corners
Thelonious Monk Quintet
Bemsha Swing
NYC, rec. 17.12.1956
Monk,Thelonious (p) | Terry,Clark (tp) | Rollins,Sonny (ts) | Chambers,Paul (b) | Roach,Max (dr,tympani)
Brilliant Corners | Ba-Lue Bolivar Ba-Lues-Are | Pannonica
NYC, rec. 23.12.1956
Monk,Thelonious (p,celeste) | Henry,Ernie (as) | Rollins,Sonny (ts) | Pettiford,Oscar (b) | Roach,Max (dr)
Thelonious Monk
I Surrender Dear
Monk,Thelonious (p-solo)

OJC20 029-2 | CD | The Sound Of Sonny
Sonny Rollins Quartet
Dearly Beloved | Every Time We Say Goodbye | What Is There To Say
NYC, rec. 11.6.1957
Rollins,Sonny (ts) | Clark,Sonny (p) | Heath,Percy (b) | Haynes,Roy (dr)
It Could Happen To You
Rollins,Sonny (ts-solo)
Sonny Rollins Trio
The Last Time I Saw Paris
NYC, rec. 12.6.1957
Rollins,Sonny (ts) | Chambers,Paul (b) | Haynes,Roy (dr)
Sonny Rollins Quartet
Just In Time | Toot Toot Tootsie | Mangoes | Cutie
NYC, rec. 19.6.1957
Rollins,Sonny (ts) | Clark,Sonny (p) | Heath,Percy (b) | Haynes,Roy (dr)

OJC20 032-2 | CD | Things Are Getting Better
OJC 032(R 1128) | LP | Things Are Getting Better
Cannonball Adderley-Milt Jackson Quintet
Blues Oriental | Things Are Getting Better | Serves Me Right | Groovin' High | The Sidewalks Of New York | Sounds For Sid | Just One Of Those Things
NYC, rec. 28.10.1958
Adderley,Julian \'Cannonball\' (as) | Jackson,Milt (vib) | Kelly,Wynton (p) | Heath,Percy (b) | Blakey,Art (dr)

OJC20 033-2(RLP 1142) | CD | Kelly Blue
OJC 033(R 1142) | LP | Kelly Blue
Wynton Kelly Sextet
Kelly Blue | Keep It Moving | Keep It Moving(alt.take)
NYC, rec. 19.2.1959
Kelly,Wynton (p) | Adderley,Nat (co) | Jaspar,Bobby (fl) | Golson,Benny (ts) | Chambers,Paul (b) | Cobb,Jimmy (dr)
Wynton Kelly Trio
Softly As In A Morning Sunrise | Do Nothin' Till You Hear From Me | On Green Dolphin Street | Willow Weep For Me | Old Clothes
NYC, rec. 10.3.1959
Kelly,Wynton (p) | Chambers,Paul (b) | Cobb,Jimmy (dr)

OJC20 035-2 | CD | Live In San Francisco
Cannonball Adderley Quintet
A Few Words By Cannonball... | Straight No Chaser
Live at The Jazz Workshop,San Francisco,CA, rec. 18.10.1959
Adderley,Julian \'Cannonball\' (as) | Adderley,Nat (co) | Timmons,Bobby (p) | Jones,Sam (b) | Hayes,Louis (dr)
This Here | Spontaneous Combustion | Hi Fly | You Got It | Bohemia After Dark
Live at The Jazz Workshop,San Francisco,CA, rec. 20.10.1959
Adderley,Julian \'Cannonball\' (as) | Adderley,Nat (co) | Timmons,Bobby (p) | Jones,Sam (b) | Hayes,Louis (dr)

OJC20 036-2 | CD | The Incredible Guitar Of Wes Montgomery
Wes Montgomery Quartet
Airegin | D-Natural Blues | Polka Dots And Moonbeams | Four On Six | West Coast Blues | In Your Own Sweet Way | Gone With The Wind
NYC, rec. 26.1.1960
Montgomery,Wes (g) | Flanagan,Tommy (p) | Heath,Percy (b) | Heath,Albert 'Tootie' (dr)
Mr.Walker
NYC, rec. 28.1.1960
Montgomery,Wes (g) | Flanagan,Tommy (p) | Heath,Percy (b) | Heath,Albert 'Tootie' (dr)

OJC20 037-2(RLP 9351) | CD | Explorations
OJC 037 (RLP 9351) | LP | Explorations
Bill Evans Trio
Israel | Haunted Heart | Beautiful Love | Beautiful Love(alt.take) | Elsa | Nardis | How Deep Is The Ocean | I Wish I Knew | Sweet And Lovely | The Boy Next Door
NYC, rec. 2.2.1961
Evans,Bill (p) | LaFaro,Scott (b) | Motian,Paul (dr)

OJC20 038-2 | CD | Caravan
OJC 038 (RLP 9438) | LP | Caravan
Art Blakey And The Jazz Messengers
Caravan | Sweet 'N' Sour | In The Wee Small Hours Of The Morning | This Is For Albert | Skylark | Thermo | Sweet 'N' Sour(alt.take) | Thermo(alt.take)
NYC, rec. 23./24.10.1962
Blakey,Art (dr) | Hubbard,Freddie (tp) | Fuller,Curtis (tb) | Shorter,Wayne (ts) | Walton,Cedar (p) | Workman,Reggie (b)

OJC20 039-2 | CD | Thelonious Monk With John Coltrane
OJC 039(JLP 946) | LP | Thelonious Monk With John Coltrane
Thelonious Monk Quartet
Nutty | Ruby My Dear | Trinkle Tinkle
NYC, rec. 16.4.1957
Monk,Thelonious (p) | Coltrane,John (ts) | Ware,Wilbur (b) | Wilson,Shadow (dr)
Thelonious Monk Septet
Epistrophy(alt.take) | Off Minor(alt.take)
NYC, rec. 26.6.1957
Monk,Thelonious (p) | Copeland,Ray (tp) | Gryce,Gigi (as) | Coltrane,John (ts) | Hawkins,Coleman (ts) | Ware,Wilbur (b) | Blakey,Art (dr)
Thelonious Monk
Functional(alt.take)
NYC, rec. 12.4.1957
Monk,Thelonious (p-solo)

OJC20 041-2(JWS 500) | CD | Bird At St. Nick's
OJC 041(JWS 500) | LP | Bird At St. Nick's
Charlie Parker Quintet
I Didn't Know What Time It Was | Ornithology | Embraceable You | Visa | I Cover The Waterfront | Scrapple From The Apple | Star Eyes- | 52nd Street Theme- | Confirmation | Out Of Nowhere | Hot House | What's New? | Now's The Time | Smoke Gets In Your Eyes- | 52nd Street Theme-
NYC, rec. 18.2.1950
Parker,Charlie (as) | Rodney,Red (tp) | Haig,Al (p) | Potter,Tommy (b) | Haynes,Roy (dr)

OJC20 043-2(DEB 120) | CD | Blue Moods
OJC- 043(DEB 120) | LP | Blue Moods
Miles Davis Quintet
Nature Boy | Alone Together | There Is No You | Easy Living
Hackensack,NJ, rec. 9.7.1955
Davis,Miles (tp) | Woodman,Britt (tb) | Charles,Teddy (vib) | Mingus,Charles (b) | Jones,Elvin (dr)

OJC20 044-2 | CD | The Quintet-Jazz At Massey Hall
OJC 044(DEB 124) | LP | The Quintet-Jazz At Massey Hall
Quintet Of The Year
Perdido | Salt Peanuts | Wee | Hot House | A Night In Tunisia | All The Things You Are | 52nd Street Theme
Live at Massey Hall,Toronto, rec. 15.5.1953
Quintet Of The Year | Gillespie,Dizzy (tp) | Parker[as 'Charlie Chan'],Charlie (as) | Powell,Bud (p) | Mingus,Charles (b) | Roach,Max (dr)

OJC20 045-2 | CD | Mingus At The Bohemia
OJC 045(DEB 123) | LP | Mingus At The Bohemia
Charles Mingus Quintet
Jump Monk | Jump Monk(alt.take) | Serenade In Blue | The Work Song | All The Things You Are In C Sharp Minor | All The Things You Are In C Sharp Minor(alt.take) | Septemberly
NYC, rec. 23.12.1955
Mingus,Charles (b) | Bert,Eddie (tb) | Barrow,George (ts) | Waldron,Mal (p) | Jones,Willie (dr)
Charles Mingus-Max Roach
Percussion Discussion
Mingus,Charles (cello,b) | Roach,Max (dr)

OJC20 047-2(F 3223) | CD | Jazz At The College Of The Pacific
OJC 047(F 3223) | LP | Jazz At The College Of The Pacific
Dave Brubeck Quartet
All The Things You Are | I'll Never Smile Again | Laura | Lullaby In Rhythm | I Remember You | For All We Know
College Of The Pacific,Stockton,CA, rec. 14.12.1953
Brubeck,Dave (p) | Desmond,Paul (as) | Crotty,Ron (b) | Dodge,Joe (dr)

OJC20 053-2(P 7025) | CD | Miles Davis And Horns
OJC 053(P 7025) | LP | Miles Davis And Horns
Miles Davis Sextet
Morpheus | Down | Blue Room | Blue Room(alt.take) | Whispering
NYC, rec. 17.1.1951
Davis,Miles (tp) | Green,Bennie (tb) | Rollins,Sonny (ts) | Lewis,John (p) | Heath,Percy (b) | Haynes,Roy (dr)
Miles Davis Septet
Tasty Pudding | Willie The Wailer | Floppy | For Adults Only
NYC, rec. 19.2.1953
Davis,Miles (tp) | Truitt,Sonny (tb) | Cohn,Al (ts) | Sims,Zoot (ts) | Lewis,John (p) | Gaskin,Leonard (b) | Clarke,Kenny (dr)

OJC20 057-2 | CD | Django
Modern Jazz Quartet
The Queen's Fancy | Delauney's Dilemma | Autumn In New York | But Not For Me
NYC, rec. 25.6.1953
MJQ (Modern Jazz Quartet) | Jackson,Milt (vib) | Lewis,John (p) | Heath,Percy (b) | Clarke,Kenny (dr)
La Ronde Suite: | Piano- | Bass- | Vibes- | Drums-
NYC, rec. 9.1.1955
MJQ (Modern Jazz Quartet) | Jackson,Milt (vib) | Lewis,John (p) | Heath,Percy (b) | Clarke,Kenny (dr)
Django | One Bass Hit | Milano
NYC, rec. 23.12.1954
MJQ (Modern Jazz Quartet) | Jackson,Milt (vib) | Lewis,John (p) | Heath,Percy (b) | Clarke,Kenny (dr)

OJC20 065-2(RLP 224) | CD | The Kenny Drew Trio
OJC 065(R 12- 224) | LP | The Kenny Drew Trio
Kenny Drew Trio
Caravan | Come Rain Or Come Shine | Ruby My Dear | Weird-O | Taking A Chance On Love | When You Wish Upon A Star | Blues For Nica | It's Only A Paper Moon
NYC, rec. 20./26.9.1956
Drew,Kenny (p) | Chambers,Paul (b) | Jones,Philly Joe (dr)

OJC20 068-2 | CD | Everybody Digs Bill Evans
OJC 068(RLP 1129) | LP | Everybody Digs Bill Evans
Bill Evans
Lucky To Be Me | Peace Piece | Epilogue
NYC, rec. 15.12.1958
Evans,Bill (p-solo)
Bill Evans Trio
Minority | Young And Foolish | Night And Day | Tenderly | What Is There To Say | Oleo | Some Other Time
Evans,Bill (p) | Jones,Sam (b) | Jones,Philly Joe (dr)

OJC20 069-2(RLP 1153) | CD | Abbey Is Blue
Abbey Lincoln With The Kenny Dorham Quintet
Lonely House | Thursday's Child | Brother Where Are You
NYC, rec. Spring&Fall 1959
Lincoln,Abbey (voc) | Dorham,Kenny (tp) | Spann,Les (fl,g) | Kelly,Wynton (p) | Jones,Sam (b) | Jones,Philly Joe (dr)
Come Sunday | Softly As In A Morning Sunrise | Lost In The Stars
Lincoln,Abbey (voc) | Dorham,Kenny (tp) | Spann,Les (fl,g) | Wright,Phillip (p) | Jones,Sam (b) | Jones,Philly Joe (dr)
Abbey Lincoln With The Max Roach Sextet
Afro Blue | Let Up | Laugh, Clown, Laugh
Lincoln,Abbey (voc) | Roach,Max (dr) | Turrentine,Tommy (tp) | Priester,Julian (tb) | Turrentine,Stanley (ts) | Walton,Cedar (p) | Boswell,Bobby (b)
Abbey Lincoln With The Max Roach Quintet
Long As You're Living
Lincoln,Abbey (voc) | Roach,Max (dr) | Turrentine,Tommy (tp) | Priester,Julian (tb) | Turrentine,Stanley (ts) | Boswell,Bobby (b)

OJC20 071-2(P 7044) | CD | Collector's Items
OJC 071(P 7044) | LP | Collector's Items
Miles Davis And His Orchestra
Compulsion | The Serpent's Tooth(I) | The Serpent's Tooth(II) | Round About Midnight

NYC, rec. 30.1.1953
Davis,Miles (tp) | Rollins,Sonny (ts) | Parker,Charlie (ts) | Bishop Jr.,Walter (p) | Heath,Percy (b) | Jones,Philly Joe (dr)
Miles Davis Quintet
No Line | Vierd Blues | In Your Own Sweet Way
NYC, rec. 16.3.1956
Davis,Miles (tp) | Rollins,Sonny (ts) | Flanagan,Tommy (p) | Chambers,Paul (b) | Taylor,Arthur 'Art' (dr)

OJC20 073-2(P 7086) | CD | Red Garland's Piano
Red Garland Trio
Please Send Me Someone To Love | Stompin' At The Savoy | The Very Thought Of You | Almost Like Being In Love | I Can't Give You Anything But Love | But Not For Me
Hackensack,NJ, rec. 22.3.1957
Garland,Red (p) | Chambers,Paul (b) | Taylor,Arthur 'Art' (dr)
If I Were A Bell | I Know Why
Hackensack,NJ, rec. 14.12.1956
Garland,Red (p) | Chambers,Paul (b) | Taylor,Arthur 'Art' (dr)

OJC20 078-2 | CD | Settin' The Pace
OJC 078(P 7213) | LP | Settin' The Pace
John Coltrane With The Red Garland Trio
I See Your Face Before Me | If There Is Someone Lovelier Than You | Little Malonae | Rise 'N' Shine
Englewood Cliffs,NJ, rec. 26.3.1958
Coltrane,John (ts) | Garland,Red (p) | Chambers,Paul (b) | Taylor,Arthur 'Art' (dr)

OJC20 084-2 | CD | Monk's Music
OJC 084(R 12- 242) | LP | Monk's Music
Thelonious Monk Septet
Well You Needn't | Off Minor | Off Minor(alt.take) | Epistrophy | Crepescule With Nellie | Crepuscule With Nellie(alt.take)
NYC, rec. 26.6.1957
Monk,Thelonious (p) | Copeland,Ray (tp) | Gryce,Gigi (as) | Hawkins,Coleman (ts) | Coltrane,John (ts) | Ware,Wilbur (b) | Blakey,Art (dr)
Coleman Hawkins Quartet
Ruby My Dear
Hawkins,Coleman (ts) | Monk,Thelonious (p) | Ware,Wilbur (b) | Blakey,Art (dr)
Quartet
Abide With Me
Copeland,Ray (tp) | Gryce,Gigi (as) | Hawkins,Coleman (ts) | Coltrane,John (ts)

OJC20 087-2 | CD | Chet
Chet Baker Septet
'Tis Autumn | You The Night And The Music
NYC, rec. March 1959
Baker,Chet (tp) | Mann,Herbie (fl) | Adams,Pepper (bs) | Evans,Bill (p) | Burrell,Kenny (g) | Chambers,Paul (b) | Jones,Philly Joe (dr)
Alone Together
Baker,Chet (tp) | Mann,Herbie (fl) | Adams,Pepper (bs) | Evans,Bill (p) | Burrell,Kenny (g) | Chambers,Paul (b) | Kay,Connie (dr)
Chet Baker Quartet
Time On My Hands
Baker,Chet (tp) | Evans,Bill (p) | Chambers,Paul (b) | Jones,Philly Joe (dr)
Chet Baker Sextet
How High The Moon | If You Could See Me Now | You'd Be So Nice To Come Home To | Early Morning(Before Daybreak)
Baker,Chet (tp) | Adams,Pepper (bs) | Evans,Bill (p) | Burrell,Kenny (g) | Chambers,Paul (b) | Kay,Connie (dr)
Chet Baker Quartet
September Song | It Never Entered My Mind
Baker,Chet (tp) | Burrell,Kenny (g) | Chambers,Paul (b) | Kay,Connie (dr)

OJC20 088-2 | CD | Portrait In Jazz
OJC 088(RLP 1162) | LP | Portrait In Jazz
Bill Evans Trio
Autumn Leaves | Someday My Prince Will Come | Come Rain Or Come Shine | Witchcraft | When I Fall In Love | Peri's Scope | What Is This Thing Called Love | Blue In Green | Autumn Leaves(mono version) | Blue In Green(alt.take)
NYC, rec. 28.12.1959
Evans,Bill (p) | LaFaro,Scott (b) | Motian,Paul (dr)

OJC20 089-2 | CD | Movin' Along
OJC 089(R 12-342) | LP | Movin' Along
Wes Montgomery Quartet
I Don't Stand A Ghost Of A Chance With You | Says You
Los Angeles,CA, rec. 12.10.1960
Montgomery,Wes (g) | Feldman,Victor (p) | Jones,Sam (b) | Hayes,Louis (dr)
Wes Montgomery Quintet
Movin' Along | Tune Up | Tune Up(alt.take) | Sandu | Body And Soul | Body And Soul(alt.take) | So Do It
Los Angeles,CA, rec. 11.10.1960
Montgomery,Wes (g) | Clay,James (fl,ts) | Feldman,Victor (p) | Jones,Sam (b) | Hayes,Louis (dr)

OJC20 090-2(RLP 9464) | CD | Ugetsu
OJC 090(RLP 9464) | LP | Ugetsu
Art Blakey And The Jazz Messengers
One By One | Ugetsu | Time Off | Ping Pong | I Didn't Know What Time It Was | On The Ginza | Eva | The High Priest | The Theme
Live at 'Birdland',NYC, rec. 16.6.1963
Blakey,Art (dr) | Hubbard,Freddie (tp) | Fuller,Curtis (tb) | Shorter,Wayne (ts) | Walton,Cedar (p) | Workman,Reggie (b)

OJC20 093-2(P 7054) | CD | Blue Haze
Miles Davis Quartet
When Lights Are Low | Tune Up | Miles Ahead
NYC, rec. 19.5.1953
Davis,Miles (tp) | Lewis,John (p) | Heath,Percy (b) | Roach,Max (dr)
Smooch
Davis,Miles (tp) | Mingus,Charles (p) | Heath,Percy (b) | Roach,Max (dr)
Four | That Old Devil Called Love | Blue Haze
NYC, rec. 15.3.1954
Davis,Miles (tp) | Silver,Horace (p) | Heath,Percy (b) | Blakey,Art (dr)
Miles Davis Quintet
I'll Remember April
NYC, rec. 3.4.1954
Davis,Miles (tp) | Schildkraut,Dave (as) | Silver,Horace (p) | Heath,Percy (b) | Clarke,Kenny (dr)

OJC20 096-2(P 7149) | CD | Soul
Coleman Hawkins Quintet
Soul Blues | I Hadn't Anyone 'Till You | Groovin' | Greensleeves | Sunday Morning | Until The Real Thing Comes Along | Sweetnin'
Hackensack,NJ, rec. 7.11.1958
Hawkins,Coleman (ts) | Burrell,Kenny (g) | Bryant,Ray (p) | Marshall,Wendell (b) | Johnson,Osie (dr)

OJC20 104-2(RLP 1164) | CD | This Here Is Bobby Timmons | EAN 090204948260
OJC 104(R 12-317) | LP | This Here Is Bobby Timmons
Bobby Timmons Trio
This Here | Moanin' | The Party's Over | Prelude To A Kiss | Dat Dere | My Funny Valentine | Come Rain Or Come Shine | Joy Ride
NYC, rec. 13./14.1.1960
Timmons,Bobby (p) | Jones,Sam (b) | Cobb,Jimmy (dr)
Bobby Timmons
Lush Life
Timmons,Bobby (p-solo)

OJC20 106-2 | CD | Full House
OJC 106(RLP 9434) | LP | Full House
Wes Montgomery Quintet
Full House | I've Grown Accustomed To Her Face | Blue 'N' Boogie | Cariba | Come Rain Or Come Shine | Come Rain Or Come Shine(alt.take) | S.O.S. | S.O.S.(alt.take) | Born To Be Blue
Live at Tsubo-Berkeley,CA, rec. 25.6.1962
Montgomery,Wes (g) | Griffin,Johnny (ts) | Kelly,Wynton (p) | Chambers,Paul (b) | Cobb,Jimmy (dr)

OJC20 1063(RS 9453) | CD | Blues Sonata
Charlie Byrd Trio
Blues Sonata: | Polonaise Pour Pietro- | Ballad In B Minor- | Scherzo For An Old Shoe-
NYC, rec. 23.10.1961
Byrd,Charlie (g,el-g) | Betts,Keter (b) | Deppenschmidt,Buddy (dr)
Charlie Byrd Quartet
Alexander's Ragtime Band | Jordu | That Old Devil Called Love | Zing! Went The Strings Of My Heart
NYC, rec. 24.10.1961
Byrd,Charlie (g,el-g) | Betts,Keter (b) | Deppenschmidt,Buddy (dr) | Harris,Barry (p)

OJC20 108-2(RLP 475) | CD | Great Times! | EAN 090204948277
OJC 108(R 12-475) | LP | Great Times!
Duke Ellington-Billy Strayhorn Trio
Cotton Tail | C Jam Blues | Flamingo | Bang-Up Blues | Tonk | Johnny Comes Lately | In A Blue Summer Garden | Great Times
NYC, rec. Oct./Nov.1950
Ellington,Duke (p) | Strayhorn,Billy (p) | Marshall,Wendell (b)
Duke Ellington Quartet
Perdido | Blues For Blanton
NYC, rec. 13.9.1950
Ellington,Duke (p) | Pettiford,Oscar (cello) | Trottman,Lloyd (b) | Jones,Jo (dr)
Duke Ellington-Billy Strayhorn Quintet
Take The 'A' Train | Oscalypso
Ellington,Duke (p) | Strayhorn,Billy (celeste) | Pettiford,Oscar (cello) | Trottman,Lloyd (b) | Jones,Jo (dr)

OJC20 121-2(P 7002) | CD | Stan Getz Quartets
Stan Getz Quartet
Long Island Sound | Mar-cia | Indian Summer | Crazy Chords
NYC, rec. 21.6.1949
Getz,Stan (ts) | Haig,Al (p) | Ramey,Gene (b) | Levey,Stan (dr)
There's A Small Hotel | I've Got You Under My Skin | What's New? | Too Marvelous For Words
NYC, rec. 6.1.1950
Getz,Stan (ts) | Haig,Al (p) | Potter,Tommy (b) | Haynes,Roy (dr)
The Lady In Red | My Old Flame | You Stepped Out Of A Dream | Wrap Your Troubles In Dreams
NYC, rec. 14.4.1950
Getz,Stan (ts) | Aless,Tony (p) | Heath,Percy (b) | Lamond,Don (dr)

OJC20 124-2 | CD | Tenor Madness
OJC 124(P 7047) | LP | Tenor Madness
Sonny Rollins Quartet
My Reverie | Most Beautiful Girl | Paul's Pal | When Your Lover Has Gone
Hackensack,NJ, rec. 24.5.1956
Rollins,Sonny (ts) | Garland,Red (p) | Chambers,Paul (b) | Jones,Philly Joe (dr)
Sonny Rollins Quintet
Tenor Madness
Rollins,Sonny (ts) | Coltrane,John (ts) | Garland,Red (p) | Chambers,Paul (b) | Jones,Philly Joe (dr)

OJC20 128-2 | CD | Cookin' With The Miles Davis Quintet
OJC 128(P 7094) | LP | Cookin' With The Miles Davis Quintet
Miles Davis Quintet
Airegin | Tune Up | When Lights Are Low | Blues By Five | My Funny Valentine
NYC, rec. 26.10.1956
Davis,Miles (tp) | Coltrane,John (ts) | Garland,Red (p) | Chambers,Paul (b) | Jones,Philly Joe (dr)

OJC20 131-2 | CD | Lush Life
OJC 131(P 7188) | LP | Lush Life
John Coltrane Trio
Like Someone In Love | I Love You | Trane's Slow Blues
NYC, rec. 16.8.1957
Coltrane,John (ts) | May,Earl (b) | Taylor,Arthur 'Art' (dr)
John Coltrane Quintet
Lush Life
NYC, rec. 10.1.1958
Coltrane,John (ts) | Byrd,Donald (tp) | Garland,Red (p) | Chambers,Paul (b) | Hayes,Louis (dr)
John Coltrane Quartet
I Hear A Rhapsody
NYC, rec. 24.5.1957
Coltrane,John (ts) | Garland,Red (p) | Chambers,Paul (b) | Heath,Albert 'Tootie' (dr)

OJC20 133-2 | CD | At The Five Spot,Vol.1
Eric Dolphy-Booker Little Quintet
Fire Waltz | Bee Vamp | The Prophet
Live at The Five Spot Cafe,NYC, rec. 16.7.1961
Dolphy,Eric (fl,b-cl,as) | Little,Booker (tp) | Waldron,Mal (p) | Davis,Richard (b) | Blackwell,Ed (dr)

OJC20 137-2 | CD | Chet Baker Plays The Best Of Lerner And Loewe
Chet Baker Quintet
Thank Heaven For The Little Girls
NYC, rec. 21.7.1959
Baker,Chet (tp) | Sims,Zoot (ts) | Evans,Bill (p) | May,Earl (b) | Jarvis,Clifford (dr)
Show Me
Baker,Chet (tp) | Adams,Pepper (bs) | Evans,Bill (p) | May,Earl (b) | Jarvis,Clifford (dr)
Chet Baker Septet
I Talk To The Trees | I Could Have Danced All Night
Baker,Chet (tp) | Mann,Herbie (fl,ts) | Sims,Zoot (as,ts) | Adams,Pepper (bs) | Evans,Bill (p) | May,Earl (b) | Jarvis,Clifford (dr)
The Heather On The Hill | I've Grown Accustomed To Her Face | On The Street Where You Live | Almost Like Being In Love
NYC, rec. 22.7.1959
Baker,Chet (tp) | Mann,Herbie (fl,ts) | Sims,Zoot (as,ts) | Adams,Pepper (bs) | Corwin,Bob (p) | May,Earl (b) | Jarvis,Clifford (dr)

OJC20 140-2 | CD | Sunday At The Village Vanguard
OJC 140(RLP 9376) | LP | Sunday At The Village Vanguard
Bill Evans Trio
Gloria's Step | Gloria's Step(alt.take) | My Man's Gone Now | Solar | Alice In Wonderland | Alice In Wonderland(alt.take) | All Of You | All Of You(alt.take) | Jade Visions | Jade Visions(alt.take)
Live at The 'Village Vanguard',NYC, rec. 25.6.1961
Evans,Bill (p) | LaFaro,Scott (b) | Motian,Paul (dr)

OJC20 142-2(RLP 9404) | CD | Cannonball Adderley In New York
OJC 142(RLP 9404) | LP | Cannonball Adderley In New York
Cannonball Adderley Sextet
Intruduction | Gemini | Dizzy's Business | Planet Earth | Synthesia | Scotch And Water | Cannon's Theme
Live at The 'Village Vanguard',NYC, rec. 12.-14.1.1962
Adderley,Julian \'Cannonball\' (as) | Adderley,Nat (co) | Lateef,Yusef (fl,ts,oboe) | Zawinul,Joe (p) | Jones,Sam (b) | Hayes,Louis (dr)

OJC20 149-2(F 3225) | CD | Vince Guaraldi Trio
OJC 149(F 3225) | LP | Vince Guaraldi Trio
Vince Guaraldi Trio
Django | Fenwyck's Farfel | Never Never Land | Chelsea Bridge | Fascinating Rhythm | The Lady Is In Love With You | Sweet And Lovely | Ossobucco | Three Coins In The Fountain | It's De-Lovely
San Francisco,CA, rec. April 1956
Guaraldi,Vince (p) | Duran,Eddie (g) | Reilly,Dean (b)

OJC20 163-2 | CD | The Music Of Ornette Coleman:Something Else!!
Ornette Coleman Quintet
Invisible | The Blessing | Jayne
Los Angeles,CA, rec. 10.2.1958
Coleman,Ornette (as) | Cherry,Don (tp) | Norris,Walter (p) | Payne,Don (b) | Higgins,Billy (dr)
Chippie | The Disguise | Angel Voice
Los Angeles,CA, rec. 22.2.1958
Coleman,Ornette (as) | Cherry,Don (tp) | Norris,Walter (p) | Payne,Don (b) | Higgins,Billy (dr)
Alpha | When Will The Blues Leave | The Sphinx
Los Angeles,CA, rec. 24.3.1958
Coleman,Ornette (as) | Cherry,Don (tp) | Norris,Walter (p) | Payne,Don (b) | Higgins,Billy (dr)

OJC20 167-2(C 7555) | CD | Jazz Giant
Benny Carter Sextet
Old Fashioned Love | Blue Lou
Los Angeles,CA, rec. 11.6.1957
Carter,Benny (tp,as) | Rosolino,Frank (tb) | Webster,Ben (ts) | Previn,André (p) | Vinnegar,Leroy (b) | Manne,Shelly (dr)
A Walking Thing | I'm Coming Virginia
Los Angeles,CA, rec. 22.7.1957
Carter,Benny (tp,as) | Rosolino,Frank (tb) | Webster,Ben (ts) | Rowles,Jimmy (p) | Vinnegar,Leroy (b) | Manne,Shelly (dr)
How Can You Lose
Los Angeles,CA, rec. 7.10.1957
Carter,Benny (tp,as) | Rosolino,Frank (tb) | Webster,Ben (ts) | Previn,André (p) | Vinnegar,Leroy (b) | Manne,Shelly (dr)
Benny Carter Quintet
Ain't She Sweet | Blues My Naughty Sweetie Gives To Me
Los Angeles,CA, rec. 21.4.1958
Carter,Benny (tp,as) | Previn,André (p) | Kessel,Barney (g) | Vinnegar,Leroy (b) | Manne,Shelly (dr)

OJC20 176-2 | CD | Smack Up
Art Pepper Quintet
Smack Up | Las Cuevas De Mario | A Bit Of Basie | How Can You Lose | Maybe Next Year | Tears Inside | Solid Citizens | Solid Citizens(alt.take)
Hollywood,CA, rec. 24./25.10.1960
Pepper,Art (as) | Sheldon,Jack (tp) | Jolly,Pete (p) | Bond,Jimmy (b) | Butler,Frank (dr)

OJC20 181-2(MV 7) | CD | At Easy
Coleman Hawkins Quartet
For You For Me For Evermore | While We're Young | Then I'll Be Tired Of You | Mighty Like A Rose | At Dawning | Trouble Is A Man | Poor Butterfly | I'll Get By(As Long As I Have You)
Englewood Cliffs,NJ, rec. 29.1.1960
Hawkins,Coleman (ts) | Flanagan,Tommy (p) | Marshall,Wendell (b) | Johnson,Osie (dr)

OJC20 190-2 | CD | Relaxin'
Miles Davis Quintet
It Could Happen To You | Woody'n You
Hackensack,NJ, rec. 11.5.1956
Davis,Miles (tp) | Coltrane,John (ts) | Garland,Red (p) | Chambers,Paul (b) | Jones,Philly Joe (dr)
If I Were A Bell | You Are My Everything | I Could Write A Book | Oleo
Hackensack,NJ, rec. 26.10.1956
Davis,Miles (tp) | Coltrane,John (ts) | Garland,Red (p) | Chambers,Paul (b) | Jones,Philly Joe (dr)

OJC20 192-2(P 7146) | CD | Blue Gene | EAN 090204923038
OJC 192(P 7146) | LP | Blue Gene
Gene Ammons And His All Stars
Blue Gene | Scamperin' | Blue Greens 'N Beans | Hip Tip
NYC, rec. 3.5.1958
Ammons,Gene (ts) | Sulieman[Leonard Graham],Idrees (tp) | Adams,Pepper (bs) | Waldron,Mal (p) | Watkins,Doug (b) | Taylor,Arthur 'Art' (dr) | Barretto,Ray (congas)

OJC20 206-2 | CD | Misterioso
OJC 206(RRLP 1133) | LP | Misterioso
Thelonious Monk Quartet
Nutty | Blues Five Spot | Let's Cool One | In Walked Bud | Misterioso | Round About Midnight | Evidence
Live at The Five Spot Cafe,NYC, rec. August 1958
Monk,Thelonious (p) | Griffin,Johnny (ts) | Abdul-Malik,Ahmed (b) | Haynes,Roy (dr)
Thelonious Monk
Just A Gigolo
Monk,Thelonious (p-solo)

OJC20 207-2 | CD | Chet Baker In New York
OJC 207(R 12- 281) | LP | Chet Baker In New York
Chet Baker Quartet
Polka Dots And Moonbeams | Solar | When Lights Are Low | Soft Winds
NYC, rec. September 1958
Baker,Chet (tp) | Haig,Al (p) | Chambers,Paul (b) | Jones,Philly Joe (dr)
Chet Baker Quintet
Fair Weather | Hotel 49 | Blue Thoughts
Baker,Chet (tp) | Griffin,Johnny (ts) | Haig,Al (p) | Chambers,Paul (b) | Jones,Philly Joe (dr)

OJC20 210-2 | CD | Waltz For Debby
OJC 210(RLP 9399) | LP | Waltz For Debby
Bill Evans Trio
My Foolish Heart | Waltz For Debby | Waltz For Debby(alt.take) | Detour Ahead | Detour Ahead(alt.take) | My Romance | My Romance(alt.take) | Some Other Time | Milestones | I Loves You Porgy
Live at The 'Village Vanguard',NYC, rec. 25.6.1961
Evans,Bill (p) | LaFaro,Scott (b) | Motian,Paul (dr)

OJC20 213-2 | CD | Walkin'
OJC 213(P 7076) | LP | Walkin'
Miles Davis Quintet
Solar | You Don't Know What Love Is | Love Me Or Leave Me
rec. 3.4.1954
Davis,Miles (tp) | Schildkraut,Dave (as) | Silver,Horace (p) | Heath,Percy (b) | Clarke,Kenny (dr)
Miles Davis All Star Sextet
Blue 'N' Boogie | Walkin'
rec. 29.4.1954
Davis,Miles (tp) | Johnson,J.J. (tb) | Thompson,Lucky (ts) | Silver,Horace (p) | Heath,Percy (b) | Clarke,Kenny (dr)

OJC20 233-2 | CD | So Much Guitar!
OJC 233(RLP 9382) | LP | So Much Guitar!
Wes Montgomery Quintet
I Wish I Knew | While We're Young | One For My Baby(And One More For The Road) | Twisted Blues | Cotton Tail | I'm Just A Lucky So-And-So | Repetition | Something Like Bags
NYC, rec. 4.8.1961
Montgomery,Wes (g) | Jones,Hank (p) | Carter,Ron (b) | Humphries,Lex (dr) | Barretto,Ray (congas)

OJC20 234-2(RLP 9407) | CD | Bags Meets Wes!
OJC 234(RLP 9407) | LP | Bags Meets Wes!
Milt Jackson-Wes Montgomery Quintet
S.J.K. | Stairway To The Stars | Stablemates | Blue Roz | Sam Sack | Jingles | Delilah
NYC, rec. 18./19.12.1961
Jackson,Milt (vib) | Montgomery,Wes (g) | Kelly,Wynton (p) | Jones,Sam (b) | Jones,Philly Joe (dr)

OJC20 243-2(P 7038) | CD | Sonny Rollins Plus 4
OJC 243(P 7038) | LP | Sonny Rollins Plus 4
Sonny Rollins Plus Four
Valse Hot | Kiss And Run | Count Your Blessings | I Feel A Song Coming On | Pent-Up House
Hackensack,NJ, rec. 22.3.1956
Rollins,Sonny (ts) | Brown,Clifford (tp) | Powell,Richie (p) | Morrow,George (b) | Roach,Max (dr)

OJC20 245-2 | CD | Bags' Groove
OJC 245 (P 7109) | LP | Bags' Groove
Miles Davis Quintet
Airegin | Oleo | But Not For Me(take 1) | But Not For Me(take 2) | Doxy
Hackensack,NJ, rec. 29.6.1954
Davis,Miles (tp) | Rollins,Sonny (ts) | Silver,Horace (p) | Heath,Percy (b,dr)
Miles Davis All Stars
Bag's Groove(take 1) | Bag's Groove(take 2)
Hackensack,NJ, rec. 24.12.1954
Davis,Miles (tp) | Jackson,Milt (vib) | Monk,Thelonious (p) | Heath,Percy (b) | Clarke,Kenny (dr)

OJC20 247-2(P 7294) | CD | Eric Dolphy At The Five Spot Vol.2
OJC 247(P 7294) | LP | Eric Dolphy At The Five Spot Vol.2

Eric Dolphy Quintet
Aggression | Like Someone In Love
Live at The Five Spot Cafe,NYC, rec. 16.7.1961
Dolphy,Eric (fl,b-cl) | Little,Booker (tp) | Waldron,Mal (p) | Davis,Richard (b) | Blackwell,Ed (dr)

OJC20 262-2 | CD | Byrd At The Gate
OJC 262(RLP 9467) | LP | Byrd At The Gate
Charlie Byrd Trio
Shiny Stockings | Blues For The Night People | I Left My Heart In San Francisco | Where Are The Hebrew Children
Live at The 'Village Gate',NYC, rec. 9.5.1963
Byrd,Charlie (g) | Betts,Keter (b) | Reichenbach,Bill (dr)
Charlie Byrd Trio And Guests
Broadway
Live at The 'Village Gate',NYC, rec. 10.5.1963
Byrd,Charlie (g) | Terry,Clark (tp) | Powell,Seldon (ts) | Betts,Keter (b) | Reichenbach,Bill (dr)
More | Ela Me Deixou
Byrd,Charlie (g) | Powell,Seldon (ts) | Betts,Keter (b) | Reichenbach,Bill (dr)
I Want A Big Butter And Egg Man | Some Other Spring
Byrd,Charlie (g) | Terry,Clark (tp) | Betts,Keter (b) | Reichenbach,Bill (dr)

OJC20 263-2(RLP 9487) | CD | At Shelly's Manne-Hole
OJC 263(RLP 9487) | LP | At Shelly's Manne-Hole
Bill Evans Trio
Isn't It Romantic | The Boy Next Door | Wonder Why | Swedish Pastry | Our Love Is Here To Stay | Round About Midnight | Stella By Starlight | All The Things You Are | Blues In F
Shelly's Manne-Hole,LA, rec. 14./19.5.1963
Evans,Bill (p) | Israels,Chuck (b) | Bunker,Larry (dr)

OJC20 275-2(F 3266) | CD | Stan Getz With Cal Tjader | EAN 090204948253
OJC 275(F 8348) | LP | Stan Getz With Cal Tjader
Stan Getz-Cal Tjader Sextet
For All We Know | I've Grown Accustomed To Her Face | Ginza | Crow's Nest | Liz-Anne | Big Bear | My Buddy
San Francisco,CA, rec. 8.2.1958
Getz,Stan (ts) | Tjader,Cal (vib) | Guaraldi,Vince (p) | Duran,Eddie (g) | LaFaro,Scott (b) | Higgins,Billy (dr)

OJC20 291-2 | CD | Saxophone Colossus
OJC 291(P 7079) | LP | Saxophone Colossus
Sonny Rollins Quartet
You Don't Know What Love Is | St.Thomas | Strode Rode | Blue Seven | Mack The Knife(Moritat)
NYC, rec. 22.6.1956
Rollins,Sonny (ts) | Flanagan,Tommy (p) | Watkins,Doug (b) | Roach,Max (dr)

OJC20 293-2(P-7130) | CD | All Mornin' Long
Red Garland Quintet
All Morning Long | Our Delight | They Can't Take That Away From Me
Hackensack,NJ, rec. 15.11.1957
Garland,Red (p) | Byrd,Donald (tp) | Coltrane,John (ts) | Nasser,Jamil[George Joyner] (b) | Taylor,Arthur 'Art' (dr)

OJC20 297-2(P-7180) | CD | Boss Tenor
Gene Ammons Quintet
Close Your Eyes | Savoy | Blue Ammons | Confirmation | Hittin' The Jug | Canadian Sunset | My Romance
Englewood Cliffs,NJ, rec. 16.6.1960
Ammons,Gene (ts) | Flanagan,Tommy (p) | Watkins,Doug (b) | Taylor,Arthur 'Art' (dr) | Barretto,Ray (congas)

OJC20 300-2 | CD | Kenny Burrell & John Coltrane
OJC 300 (NJ 8276) | LP | Kenny Burrell & John Coltrane
Kenny Burrell-John Coltrane Quintet
Lyresto | Freight Train | I Never Knew | Big Paul
NYC, rec. 7.3.1958
Burrell,Kenny (g) | Coltrane,John (ts) | Flanagan,Tommy (p) | Chambers,Paul (b) | Cobb,Jimmy (dr)
Kenny Burrell-John Coltrane Duo
Why Was I Born
Burrell,Kenny (g) | Coltrane,John (ts)

OJC20 301-2(RLP 1106) | CD | Mulligan Meets Monk
Gerry Mulligan-Thelonious Monk Quartet
Rhythm-A-Ning | I Mean You | I Mean You(alt.take) | Straight No Chaser | Straight No Chaser(alt.take) | Sweet And Lovely | Round About Midnight | Decidedly | Decidedly(alt.take)
NYC, rec. 12./13.8.1957
Mulligan,Gerry (bs) | Monk,Thelonious (p) | Ware,Wilbur (b) | Wilson,Shadow (dr)

OJC20 303-2 | CD | Sings/It Could Happen To You
Chet Baker Quartet
The More I See You | That Old Devil Moon
NYC, rec. August 1958
Baker,Chet (tp,voc) | Drew,Kenny (p) | Jones,Sam (b) | Jones,Philly Joe (dr)
You're Driving Me Crazy | How Long Has This Been Going On | It Could Happen To You | You Make Me Feel So Young
Baker,Chet (tp,voc) | Drew,Kenny (p) | Jones,Sam (b) | Richmond,Dannie (dr)
I'm Old Fashioned | Dancing On The Ceiling | Everything I Have Is Yours | My Heart Stood Still | Do It The Hard Way
Baker,Chet (tp,voc) | Drew,Kenny (p) | Morrow,George (b) | Jones,Philly Joe (dr)
While My Lady Sleeps
Baker,Chet (voc) | Drew,Kenny prob. (p)

OJC20 304-2(RLP 1122) | CD | Deeds Not Words | EAN 090204923090
OJC 304(R 12-280) | LP | Deeds Not Words
Max Roach Quintet
Deeds Not Words | Conversation | Filide | It's You Or No One | Larry Larue | Jodie's Cha-Cha | You Stepped Out Of A Dream
NYC, rec. 4.9.1958
Roach,Max (dr) | Little,Booker (tp) | Coleman,George (ts) | Draper,Ray (tuba) | Davis,Art (b)
Max Roach Sextet
There'll Never Be Another You
Roach,Max (dr) | Little,Booker (tp) | Coleman,George (ts) | Draper,Ray (tuba) | Davis,Art (b) | Pettiford,Oscar (b)

OJC20 306-2 | CD | Cannonball Adderley Quintet Plus
OJC 306(R 12-388) | LP | Cannonball Adderley Quintet Plus
Cannonball Adderley Quintet Plus
Well You Needn't | New Delhi | Winestone | Star Eyes
NYC, rec. 11.5.1961
Adderley,Julian \'Cannonball\' (as) | Adderley,Nat (co) | Feldman,Victor (vib) | Kelly,Wynton (p) | Jones,Sam (b) | Hayes,Louis (dr)
Cannonball Adderley Quintet
Arriving Soon | Lisa
Adderley,Julian \'Cannonball\' (as) | Adderley,Nat (co) | Feldman,Victor (p) | Jones,Sam (b) | Hayes,Louis (dr)

OJC20 311-2 | CD | Sahara
OJC 311 (M 9039) | LP | Sahara
McCoy Tyner Quartet
Ebony Queen | A Prayer For My Family | Valley Of Life | Rebirth | Sahara
NYC, rec. January 1992
Tyner,McCoy (fl,p,perc,koto) | Fortune,Sonny (fl,ss,as) | Hill,Calvin (b,perc) | Mouzon,Alphonse (tp,reeds,dr,perc)

OJC20 316-2(C 3505) | CD | Hampton Hawes Trio Vol.1
Hampton Hawes Trio
I Got Rhythm | What Is This Thing Called Love | Blues The Most | So In Love | Feelin' Fine | Hamp's Blues | Easy Living | All The Things You Are | These Foolish Things Remind Me On You | Carioca
Los Angeles,CA, rec. 28.6.1955
Hawes,Hampton (p) | Mitchell,Red (b) | Thompson,Chuck (dr)

OJC20 329-2(P 7435) | CD | Soul Message
Richard 'Groove' Holmes Trio
Groove's Groove | Daahoud | Misty | Song For My Father | The Things We Did Last Summer | Soul Message
Englewood Cliffs,NJ, rec. 3.8.1965
Holmes,Richard 'Groove' (org) | Edwards,Gene (g) | Smith,Jimmie (dr)

OJC20 332-2(P 7678) | CD | Goodness!
Houston Person Sextet
Hard Times | Goodness | Jamilah | Brother H. | Close Your Eyes | Hey Driver
Englewood Cliffs,NJ, rec. 25.8.1969
Person,Houston (ts) | Phillips,Sonny (org) | Butler,Billy (el-g) | Bushnell,Bob (el-b) | Jones,Frankie (dr) | Caldwell,Buddy (congas)

OJC20 337-2(S 7530) | CD | Way Out West | EAN 090204948284
OJC 337(C 7530) | LP | Way Out West
Sonny Rollins Trio
I'm An Old Cowhand | I'm An Old Cowhand(alt.take) | In My Solitude | Come Gone | Come Gone(alt.take) | Wagon Wheels | There Is No Greater Love | Way Out West | Way Out West(alt.take)
Los Angeles,CA, rec. 7.3.1957
Rollins,Sonny (ts) | Brown,Ray (b) | Manne,Shelly (dr)

OJC20 338-2 | CD | Art Pepper Meets The Rhythm Section
OJC 338(C 7532) | LP | Art Pepper Meets The Rhythm Section
Art Pepper Quartet
You'd Be So Nice To Come Home To | Red Pepper Blues | Imagination | Waltz Me Blues | Straight Life | Jazz Me Blues | Tin Tin Deo | Star Eyes | Birk's Works
Los Angeles,CA, rec. 19.1.1957
Pepper,Art (as) | Garland,Red (p) | Chambers,Paul (b) | Jones,Philly Joe (dr)

OJC20 341-2 | CD | Modern Jazz Classics
Art Pepper Plus Eleven
Opus De Funk | Round About Midnight | Walkin' Shoes | Airegin
Los Angeles,CA, rec. 14.3.1959
Pepper,Art (cl,as,ts) | Candoli,Pete (tp) | Sheldon,Jack (tp) | Nash,Dick (tb) | Enevoldsen,Bob (v-tb,ts) | DeRosa,Vince (fr-h) | Geller,Herb (as) | Perkins,Bill (ts) | Flory,Med (bs) | Freeman,Russ (p) | Mondragon,Joe (b) | Lewis,Mel (dr) | Paich,Marty (cond,arr)
Groovin' High | Shaw 'Nuff | Donna Lee | Donna Lee(alt.take) | Anthropology
Los Angeles,CA, rec. 28.3.1959
Pepper,Art (cl,as,ts) | Porcino,Al (tp) | Sheldon,Jack (tp) | Nash,Dick (tb) | Enevoldsen,Bob (v-tb,ts) | DeRosa,Vince (fr-h) | Shank,Bud (as) | Perkins,Bill (ts) | Flory,Med (bs) | Freeman,Russ (p) | Mondragon,Joe (b) | Lewis,Mel (dr) | Paich,Marty (cond,arr)
Move | Four Brothers | Walkin' | Walkin'(alt.take 1) | Walkin'(alt.take 2) | Bernie's Tune
Los Angeles,CA, rec. 12.5.1959
Pepper,Art (cl,as,ts) | Porcino,Al (tp) | Sheldon,Jack (tp) | Nash,Dick (tb) | Enevoldsen,Bob (v-tb,ts) | DeRosa,Vince (fr-h) | Kennedy,Charlie (as,ts) | Kamuca,Richie (ts) | Flory,Med (bs) | Freeman,Russ (p) | Mondragon,Joe (b) | Lewis,Mel (dr) | Paich,Marty (cond,arr)

OJC20 342-2(S 7569) | CD | Tomorrow Is The Question | EAN 090204948208
Ornette Coleman Quartet
Lorraine
Los Angeles,CA, rec. 16.1.1959
Coleman,Ornette (as) | Cherry,Don (tp) | Mitchell,Red (b) | Manne,Shelly (dr)
Turn Around | Endless
Los Angeles,CA, rec. 23.2.1959
Coleman,Ornette (as) | Cherry,Don (tp) | Mitchell,Red (b) | Manne,Shelly (dr)
Tears Inside | Tomorrow Is The Question | Compassion | Giggin | Rejoicing | Mind And Time
Los Angeles,CA, rec. 9./10.3.1959
Coleman,Ornette (as) | Cherry,Don (tp) | Heath,Percy (b) | Manne,Shelly (dr)

OJC20 347-2(P 7150) | CD | Miles Davis And The Modern Jazz Giants | EAN 090204923069
OJC 347(P 7150) | LP | Miles Davis And The Modern Jazz Giants
Miles Davis All Stars
The Man I Love (take 1) | The Man I Love (take 2) | Swing Spring | Bemsha Swing
Hackensack,NJ, rec. 24.12.1954
Davis,Miles (tp) | Jackson,Milt (vib) | Monk,Thelonious (p) | Heath,Percy (b) | Clarke,Kenny (dr)
Miles Davis Quintet
Round About Midnight
Hackensack,NJ, rec. 26.10.1956
Davis,Miles (tp) | Coltrane,John (ts) | Garland,Red (p) | Chambers,Paul (b) | Jones,Philly Joe (dr)

OJC20 351-2(P 7257) | CD | Bad! Bossa Nova
Gene Ammons Septet
Pagan Love Song | Ca' Purange(Jungle Soul) | Anna | Caé Caé | Moito Mato Grosso | Yellow Bird
Englewood Cliffs,NJ, rec. 9.9.1962
Ammons,Gene (ts) | Pizzarelli,Bucky (spanish-g) | Burrell,Kenny (g) | Jones,Hank (p) | Edge,Norman (b) | Jackson,Oliver (dr) | Hayes,Al (bongos)

OJC20 363-2 | CD | Work Song
Nat Adderley Quartet
Mean To Me
NYC, rec. 25.1.1960
Adderley,Nat (co) | Montgomery,Wes (g) | Betts,Keter (b) | Hayes,Louis (dr)
Nat Adderley Quintet
My Heart Stood Still
Adderley,Nat (co) | Montgomery,Wes (g) | Betts,Keter (cello) | Jones,Sam (b) | Hayes,Louis (dr)
Nat Adderley Sextet
Pretty Memory | Fall Out
Adderley,Nat (co) | Montgomery,Wes (g) | Betts,Keter (b) | Jones,Sam (cello) | Hayes,Louis (dr) | Timmons,Bobby (p)
The Work Song | Sack O'Woe | Scrambled Eggs
NYC, rec. 27.1.1960
Adderley,Nat (co) | Montgomery,Wes (g) | Timmons,Bobby (p) | Jones,Sam (cello) | Heath,Percy (b) | Hayes,Louis (dr)
Nat Adderley Trio
I've Got A Crush On You | Violets For Your Furs
Adderley,Nat (co) | Montgomery,Wes (g) | Jones,Sam (b)

OJC20 364-2(RLP 9391) | CD | In Person
Bobby Timmons Trio
Autumn Leaves | So Tired | Good Bye | Dat Dere(Theme) | They Didn't Believe Me | Dat Dere | Popsy | I Didn't Know What Time It Was | Softly As In A Morning Sunrise | Dat Dere(Theme)
Live at The 'Village Vanguard',NYC, rec. 1.10.1961
Timmons,Bobby (p) | Carter,Ron (b) | Heath,Albert 'Tootie' (dr)

OJC20 370-2(JLP 18) | CD | Chet Baker In Milan
Chet Baker Quartet
Indian Summer | My Old Flame
Milano,Italy, rec. October 1959
Baker,Chet (tp) | Sellani,Renato (p) | Serri,Franco (b) | Victory,Gene (dr)
Chet Baker Sextet
Lady Bird | Cheryl Blues | Tune Up | Line For Lyons | Pent-Up House | Look For The Silver Lining
Baker,Chet (tp) | Masetti,Glauco (as) | Basso,Gianni (ts) | Sellani,Renato (p) | Serri,Franco (b) | Victory,Gene (dr)

OJC20 374-2(2308204) | CD | Montreux '77
OJC 374(2308204) | LP | Montreux '77
Benny Carter 4
Three Little Words | In A Mellow Tone | Wave | Undecided | Body And Soul | On Green Dolphin Street | Here's That Rainy Day
Montreux,CH, rec. 13.7.1977
Carter,Benny (tp,as) | Bryant,Ray (p) | Orsted-Pedersen,Niels-Henning (b) | Smith,Jimmie (dr)

OJC20 375-2(2308205) | CD | Montreux '77
OJC 375(2308205) | LP | Montreux '77
Milt Jackson-Ray Brown Jam
Slippery | This Is The End Of... A Beautiful Friendship - (This Is The End Of...) A Beautiful Friendship | C.M.J. | Mean To Me | You Are My Sunshine | That's The Way It Is
Jackson,Milt (vib) | Brown,Ray (b) | Terry,Clark (tp,fl-h) | Davis,Eddie 'Lockjaw' (ts) | Alexander,Monty (p) | Smith,Jimmie (dr)

OJC20 376-2(2308206) | CD | Montreux '77
OJC 376(2308206) | LP | Montreux '77
Ella Fitzgerald With The Tommy Flanagan Trio
Too Close For Comfort | I Ain't Got Nothin' But The Blues | My Man | Come Rain Or Come Shine | Day By Day | Ordinary Fool | Samba Da Una Nota So(One Note Samba) | I Let A Song Go Out Of My Heart | Billie's Bounce | You Are The Sunshine Of My Life
Montreux,CH, rec. 14.7.1977
Fitzgerald,Ella (voc) | Flanagan,Tommy (p) | Betts,Keter (b) | Durham,Bobby (dr)

OJC20 378-2(2308208) | CD | Montreux '77
Oscar Peterson Jam
Ali And Frazier | If I Were A Bell | Things Ain't What They Used To Be | Just In Time | Bye Bye Blues
Peterson,Oscar (p) | Gillespie,Dizzy (tp) | Terry,Clark (tp) | Davis,Eddie 'Lockjaw' (ts) | Orsted-Pedersen,Niels-Henning (b) | Durham,Bobby (dr)

OJC20 381-2(2308211) | CD | Montreux '77
OJC 381(2308211) | LP | Montreux '77
Dizzy Gillespie Jam
Girl Of My Dreams | Get Happy | Once In A While- | But Beautiful- | Here's That Rainy Day- | The Champ
Gillespie,Dizzy (tp) | Faddis,Jon (tp) | Jackson,Milt (vib) | Alexander,Monty (p) | Brown,Ray (b) | Smith,Jimmie (dr)

OJC20 382-2(2308212) | CD | Montreux '77
OJC 382(2308212) | LP | Montreux '77
Joe Pass
Blues For Yano San | Blues For Sitges | Blues For Val | Wait 'Till You See Her | She's Funny That Way | Blues For Martin | Masquerade
Montreux,CH, rec. 15.7.1977
Pass,Joe (g-solo)

OJC20 391-2 | CD | Steamin'
Miles Davis Quintet
Surrey With The Fringe On Top | Salt Peanuts | Something I Dreamed Last Night | Diane | When I Fall In Love
Hackensack,NJ, rec. 11.5.1956
Davis,Miles (tp) | Coltrane,John (ts) | Garland,Red (p) | Chambers,Paul (b) | Jones,Philly Joe (dr)
Well You Needn't
Hackensack,NJ, rec. 26.10.1956
Davis,Miles (tp) | Coltrane,John (ts) | Garland,Red (p) | Chambers,Paul (b) | Jones,Philly Joe (dr)

OJC20 392-2(PR 7229) | CD | Dig It
OJC 392(P 7229) | LP | Dig It
John Coltrane With The Red Garland Trio
C.T.A.
Hackensack,NJ, rec. 22.3.1957
Garland,Red (p) | Coltrane,John (ts) | Nasser,Jamil[George Joyner] (b) | Taylor,Arthur 'Art' (dr)
Red Garland Quintet
Billie's Bounce | Lazy Mae
Hackensack,NJ, rec. 13.12.1957
Garland,Red (p) | Byrd,Donald (tp) | Coltrane,John (ts) | Nasser,Jamil[George Joyner] (b) | Taylor,Arthur 'Art' (dr)
Red Garland Trio
Crazy Rhythm
Hackensack,NJ, rec. 2.2.1958
Garland,Red (p) | Chambers,Paul (b) | Taylor,Arthur 'Art' (dr)

OJC20 393-2(P 7280) | CD | Dakar | EAN 090204923052
OJC 393(P 7280) | LP | Dakar
John Coltrane All Stars
Dakar | Mary's Blues | Route 4 | Velvet Scene | Witches Pit | Cat Walks
Hackensack,NJ, rec. 20.4.1957
Coltrane,John (ts) | Payne,Cecil (bs) | Adams,Pepper (bs) | Waldron,Mal (p) | Waltkins,Doug (b) | Taylor,Arthur 'Art' (dr)

OJC20 400-2 | CD | Far Cry
OJC 400(NJ 8270) | LP | Far Cry
Eric Dolphy Quintet
Mrs.Parker Of K.C. | Ode To Charlie Parker | Far Cry | Miss Ann | Left Alone | Tenderly | It's Magic | Serene
Englewood Cliffs,NJ, rec. 21.12.1960
Dolphy,Eric (fl,b-cl,as) | Little,Booker (tp) | Byard,Jaki (p) | Carter,Ron (b) | Haynes,Roy (dr)

OJC20 420-2(SV 2016) | CD | Night Hawk | EAN 090204948246
Coleman Hawkins With Eddie Lockjaw Davis And The Tommy Flanagan Trio
Night Hawk | There Is No Greater Love | In A Mellow Tone | Don't Take Your Love From Me | Pedalin'
Englewood Cliffs,NJ, rec. 30.12.1960
Hawkins,Coleman (ts) | Davis,Eddie 'Lockjaw' (ts) | Flanagan,Tommy (p) | Carter,Ron (b) | Johnson,Gus (dr)

OJC20 434-2(RLP 9428) | CD | Moonbeams | EAN 090204923106
Bill Evans Trio
If You Could See Me Now
NYC, rec. 17.5.1962
Evans,Bill (p) | Israels,Chuck (b) | Motian,Paul (dr)
Re:Person I Knew | Very Early
NYC, rec. 29.5.1962
Evans,Bill (p) | Israels,Chuck (b) | Motian,Paul (dr)
Polka Dots And Moonbeams | I Fall In Love Too Easily | Stairway To The Stars | It Might As Well Be Spring | In Love In Vain
NYC, rec. 2.6.1962
Evans,Bill (p) | Israels,Chuck (b) | Motian,Paul (dr)

OJC20 435-2(RLP 9477) | CD | Nippon Soul
Cannonball Adderley Sextet
Nippon Soul(Nihon No Soul) | Easy To Love | The Weaver | Tengo Tango | Come Sunday | Brother John | The Work Song
Live at Sankei Hall,Osaka,Japan, rec. 14./15.7.1963
Adderley,Julian \'Cannonball\' (as) | Adderley,Nat (co) | Lateef,Yusef (fl,ts,oboe) | Zawinul,Joe (p) | Jones,Sam (b) | Hayes,Louis (dr)

OJC20 439-2(F 9489) | CD | The Tony Bennett-Bill Evans Album
Tony Bennett-Bill Evans
Young And Foolish | The Touch Of Your Lips | Some Other Time | When In Rome | We'll Be Together Again | My Foolish Heart | Waltz For Debby | But Beautiful | Days Of Wine And Roses
Berkeley,CA, rec. 10.-13.6.1975
Bennett,Tony (voc) | Evans,Bill (p)

OJC20 440-2(F 6009) | CD | The Charles Mingus Quintet+Max Roach | EAN 090204923083
Charles Mingus Quintet
A Foggy Day(In London Town) | Haitian Fight Song | Lady Bird | Love Chant
Live at The Cafe Bohemia,Greenwich Village,NYC, rec. 23.12.1955
Mingus,Charles (b) | Bert,Eddie (tb) | Barrow,George (ts) | Waldron,Mal (p) | Jones,Willie (dr)
I'll Remember April | Drums
Mingus,Charles (b) | Bert,Eddie (tb) | Barrow,George (ts) | Waldron,Mal (p) | Roach,Max (dr)

OJC20 442-2 | CD | Ella A Nice
OJC 442(2308234) | LP | Ella A Nice
Ella Fitzgerald With The Tommy Flanagan Trio
Night And Day | The Many Faces Of Cole Porter: | Get Out Of Town- | Easy To Love- | You Do Something To Me- | The Ballad Medley: | Body And Soul- | The Man I Love- | Porgy- | The Bossa Scene: | Girl From Ipanema(Garota De Ipanema) | Fly Me To The Moon- | O Nosso Amor- | Cielito Lindo- | Magdalena- | Aqua De Beber- | Summertime | They Can't Take That Away From Me | Aspects Of Duke: | Mood Indigo- | Do Nothin' Till You Hear From Me- | It Don't Mean A Thing If It Ain't Got That Swing- | Something | St.Louis Blues | Close To You | Put A Little Love In Your Heart

Nice,France, rec. 21.7.1971
Fitzgerald,Ella (voc) | Flanagan,Tommy (p) | De La Rosa,Frank (b) | Thigpen,Ed (dr)

OJC20 444-2(2310744) | CD | Zoot Sims And The Gershwin Brothers
OJC 444(2310744) | LP | Zoot Sims And The Gershwin Brothers
Zoot Sims Quintet
The Man I Love | How Long Has This Been Going On | Oh! Lady Be Good | I've Got A Crush On You | I Got Rhythm | Embraceable You | 'S Wonderful | Someone To Watch Over Me | Isn't It A Pity | Summertime | They Can't Take That Away From Me
NYC, rec. 6.6.1975
Sims,Zoot (ts) | Pass,Joe (g) | Peterson,Oscar (p) | Mraz,George 'Jiri' (b) | Tate,Grady (dr)

OJC20 446-2(2310762) | CD | The Ellington Suites
Duke Ellington And His Orchestra
The Queen's Suite: | Lightning Bugs And Frogs- | Le Sucrier Velours- | Northern Lights-
NYC, rec. 25.2.1959
Ellington,Duke (p) | Terry,Clark (tp) | Anderson,Cat (tp) | Baker,Harold 'Shorty' (tp) | Nance,Ray (tp,v) | Woodman,Britt (tb) | Jackson,Quentin (tb) | Sanders,John (tb) | Hodges,Johnny (as) | Procope,Russell (cl,as) | Hamilton,Jimmy (cl,ts) | Gonsalves,Paul (ts) | Carney,Harry (b-cl,bs) | Woode,Jimmy (b) | Johnson,Jimmy (dr)
Sinset And The Mocking Birds- | Apes And Peacocks-
NYC, rec. 1.4.1959
Ellington,Duke (p) | Terry,Clark (tp) | Anderson,Cat (tp) | Baker,Harold 'Shorty' (tp) | Nance,Ray (tp,v) | Woodman,Britt (tb) | Jackson,Quentin (tb) | Sanders,John (tb) | Hodges,Johnny (as) | Procope,Russell (cl,as) | Hamilton,Jimmy (cl,ts) | Gonsalves,Paul (ts) | Carney,Harry (b-cl,bs) | Woode,Jimmy (b) | Johnson,Jimmy (dr)
Duke Ellington Duo
The Single Petal Of A Rose-
NYC, rec. 14.4.1959
Ellington,Duke (p) | Woode,Jimmy (b)
Duke Ellington And His Orchestra
The Goutelas Suite: | Fanfare- | Goutelas- | Get-With-Itness- | Something- | Having At It-
NYC, rec. 27.4.1971
Ellington,Duke (p) | Williams,Cootie (tp) | Ellington,Mercer (tp) | Johnson,Money (tp) | Preston,Eddie (tp) | Wood,Booty (tb) | Taylor,Malcolm (tb) | Connors,Chuck (tb) | Minerve,Harold (as) | Turney,Norris (as) | Gonsalves,Paul (ts) | Ashby,Harold (ts) | Carney,Harry (bs) | Benjamin,Joe (b) | Jones,Rufus (dr)
The Uwis Suite: | Uwis- | Klop- | Loco Madi-
NYC, rec. 5.10.1972
Ellington,Duke (p) | Williams,Cootie (tp) | Ellington,Mercer (tp) | Johnson,Money (tp) | Coles,Johnny (tp) | Wood,Booty (tb) | Prudente,Vince (tb) | Connors,Chuck (tb) | Procope,Russell (cl,as) | Minerve,Harold (as) | Turney,Norris (as) | Ashby,Harold (ts) | Andrews,Russ (ts) | Carney,Harry (bs) | Benjamin,Joe (b) | Freedman,Wulf (el-b) | Jones,Rufus (dr)

OJC20 447-2 | CD | Afro-Cuban Jazz Moods
Machito And His Orchestra
Oro Incienso Y Mirra
NYC, rec. 4./5.6.1975
Machito (Raul Grillo) | Gillespie,Dizzy (tp) | Paz,Victor (tp,fl-h) | Gonzales,Raul (tp,fl-h) | Gonzales Jr.,Ramon (tp,fl-h) | Duran,Manny (tp,fl-h) | Morrow,Barry (tb) | Kahn,Lewis (tb) | Chamberlain,Gerald (tb) | Tillotson,Brooks (fr-h) | Corrado,Donald (fr-h) | Stewart,Robert 'Bob' (tuba) | Bauza,Mario (cl,as) | Smith,Mauricio (fl,as,piccolo) | Madera,Jose (cl,ts) | Rivera,Mario (alto-fl,ts) | Dalto,Jorge (el-p) | Castillo,Carlos (el-b) | McCurdy,Dana (synth) | Roker,Granville 'Mickey' (dr) | Collazo,Julio (african-dr) | Hernandez,Rene (african-dr) | Grillo,Mario (perc,congas,bongos,bells) | Madera Jr.,Jose (perc,cabassa,timbales)
Three Afro-Cuban Jazz Moods: | Calidocopico- | Pensativa- | Exuberante-
Machito (Raul Grillo) | Gillespie,Dizzy (tp) | Paz,Victor (tp,fl-h) | Gonzales,Raul (tp,fl-h) | Gonzales Jr.,Ramon (tp,fl-h) | Duran,Manny (tp,fl-h) | Morrow,Barry (tb) | Kahn,Lewis (tb) | Chamberlain,Gerald (tb) | Jeffers,Jack (tb) | Bauza,Mario (cl,as) | Smith,Mauricio (fl,as,piccolo) | Madera,Jose (cl,ts) | Rivera,Mario (alto-fl,ts) | Yahonikan,Leslie (b-cl,bs) | Dalto,Jorge (el-p) | Castillo,Carlos (el-b) | McCurdy,Dana (synth) | Roker,Granville 'Mickey' (dr) | Collazo,Julio (african-dr) | Hernandez,Rene (african-dr) | Grillo,Mario (perc,congas,bongos,bells) | Madera Jr.,Jose (perc,cabassa,timbales)

OJC20 449-2(2310871) | CD | Count Basie:Kansas City 6
Kansas City 6
Walkin' The Blues | Blues For Little Jazz | Vegas Drag | Wee Baby Blues | Scooter | St.Louis Blues | Opus Six
Las Vegas,NV, rec. 1.11.1981
Kansas City Six,The | Basie,Count (p) | Cook,Willie (tp) | Vinson,Eddie 'Cleanhead' (as,voc) | Pass,Joe (g) | Orsted-Pedersen,Niels-Henning (b) | Bellson,Louie (dr)

OJC20 456-2(P 7081) | CD | All Day Long | EAN 090204948147
Prestige All Stars
Slim Jim | A.T. | Say Listen | All Day Long | C.P.W.
Hackensack,NJ, rec. 4.1.1957
Prestige All Stars | Byrd,Donald (tp) | Foster,Frank (ts) | Burrell,Kenny (g) | Flanagan,Tommy (p) | Watkins,Doug (b) | Taylor,Arthur 'Art' (dr)

OJC20 459-2(P 7210) | CD | Kirk's Work
Roland Kirk With The Jack McDuff Trio
Three For Dizzy | Makin' Whoopee | Funk Underneath | Kirk's Work | Doin' The Sixty-Eight | Too Late Now | Skater's Waltz
Englewood Cliffs,NJ, rec. 11.7.1961
Kirk,Rahsaan Roland (fl,ts,manzello,siren,stritch) | McDuff,Brother Jack (org) | Benjamin,Joe (b) | Taylor,Arthur 'Art' (dr)

OJC20 469-2 | CD | Latin America Suite
Duke Ellington And His Orchestra
Oclupaca | Chico Cuadradino | Eque | The Sleeping Lady And The Giant Who Watches Over Her | Latin American Sunshine | Brasilliance
NYC, rec. 5.11.1968
Ellington,Duke (p) | Anderson,Cat (tp) | Cook,Willie (tp) | Jones,Herbie (tp) | Ellington,Mercer (tp) | Williams,Cootie (tp) | Brown,Lawrence (tb) | Cooper,Frank 'Buster' (tb) | Connors,Chuck (tb) | Procope,Russell (cl,as) | Hodges,Johnny (as) | Gonsalves,Paul (ts) | Carney,Harry (bs) | Castleman,Jeff (b) | Jones,Rufus (dr)
Duke Ellington Quartet
Tina
Las Vegas,NV, rec. 7.1.1970
Ellington,Duke (p) | Gaskin,Victor (b) | Kondziela,Paul (b) | Jones,Rufus (dr)

OJC20 492-2(JLP 921) | CD | Chet Baker With Fifty Italian Strings
Chet Baker With String-Orchestra And Voices
I Should Care | Violets For Your Furs | The Song Is You | When I Fall In Love | Good Bye | Autumn In New York | Angel Eyes | Street Of Dreams | Forgetful | Deep In A Dream
Milano,Italy, rec. 28.9.& 5.10.1959
Baker,Chet (tp,voc) | unkn. (fl-h) | Pezzotta,Mario (as) | Massetti,Glauco (as) | Basso,Gianni (ts) | Papetti,Fausto (bs) | Libani,Giulio (p,celeste) | Cerri,Franco (b) | Voctory,Gene (dr) | unkn. (harp) | Strings | details unknown

OJC20 496-2 | CD | Skol
OJC 496(2308232) | LP | Skol
Oscar Peterson Quintet
Nuages | How 'Bout You | Someone To Watch Over Me | Makin' Whoopee | That's All | Skol Blues
Live at The 'Tivoli Gardens',Copenhagen, rec. 6.7.1979
Peterson,Oscar (p) | Grappelli,Stephane (v) | Pass,Joe (g) | Orsted-Pedersen,Niels-Henning (b) | Roker,Granville 'Mickey' (dr)

OJC20 612-2(P 7319) | CD | Eastern Sounds
Yusef Lateef Quartet
The Plum Blossom | Blues For The Orient | Chinq Miau | Don't Blame Me | Love Theme From Spartacus | Snafu | Purple Flower | Love Theme From The Robe | The Three Faces Of Balal
Englewood Cliffs,NJ, rec. 5.9.1961
Lateef,Yusef (fl,ts,oboe) | Harris,Barry (p) | Farrow,Ernie (b) | Humphries,Lex (dr)

OJC20 644-2(F 9510) | CD | Montreux III
Bill Evans-Eddie Gomez Duo
Elsa | Milano | Venutian Rhythm Dance | Django | Minha(All Mine) | Driftin' | I Love You | Summer Of '42(The Summer Knows)
Live at The Montreux Jazz Festival, rec. 20.7.1975
Evans,Bill (p,el-p) | Gomez,Eddie (b)

OJC20 652-2(P 7141) | CD | Cookbook Vol.1
Eddie Lockjaw Davis Quintet
Have Horn, Will Blow | The Chef | But Beautiful | In The Kitchen | Three Deuces
Hackensack,NJ, rec. 29.6.1958
Davis,Eddie 'Lockjaw' (ts) | Richardson,Jerome (fl,ts) | Scott,Shirley (org) | Duvivier,George (b) | Edgehill,Arthur (dr)

OJC20 653-2(P 7161) | CD | The Eddie Lockjaw Davis Cookbook Vol.2 | EAN 090204948239
Eddie Lockjaw Davis Quartet
Willow Weep For Me
Hackensack,NJ, rec. 12.9.1958
Davis,Eddie 'Lockjaw' (ts) | Scott,Shirley (org) | Duvivier,George (b) | Edgehill,Arthur (dr)
Eddie Lockjaw Davis Quintet
The Rev | Stardust | Skillet | I Surrender Dear | The Broilers
Hackensack,NJ, rec. 5.12.1958
Davis,Eddie 'Lockjaw' (ts) | Richardson,Jerome (fl) | Scott,Shirley (org) | Duvivier,George (b) | Edgehill,Arthur (dr)

OJC20 677-2(GXY 5140) | CD | Winter Moon
Art Pepper Quintet With Strings
Our Song | Here's That Rainy Day | That's Love | Winter Moon | When The Sun Comes Out | Blues In The Night | The Prisoner | Our Song(alt.take) | The Prisoner(alt.take) | Ol' Man River
Berkeley,CA, rec. 3.-4.9.1980
Pepper,Art (cl,as) | Roberts,Howard (g) | Cowell,Stanley (p) | McBee,Cecil (b) | Burnett,Carl (dr) | Rubin,Nathan (v,concertmaster) | Tenney,John (v) | Mazmanian,Greg (v) | Anderson,Patrice (v) | Foster,Clifton (v) | Smiley,Dan (v) | Desilva,Audrey (v) | Gibson,Elizabeth (v) | Gehl,Stephen (v) | Van Valkenburgh,Emily (v) | O'Connor,Sharon (cello) | Meredith,Mary Ann (cello) | Adams,Terry (cello)

OJC20 681-2(2308227) | CD | Bye Bye Blackbird
John Coltrane Quartet
Bye Bye Blackbird | Traneing In
Live,at Konserthuset,Stockholm, rec. 19.11.1962
Coltrane,John (ss,ts) | Tyner,McCoy (p) | Garrison,Jimmy (b) | Jones,Elvin (dr)

OJC20 684-2(2310805) | CD | Virtuoso No.3
Joe Pass
Offbeat | Trinidad | Nina's Blues | Sevenths | Ninths | Dissonance No.1 | Minor Detail | Paco De Lucia | Sultry | Passanova | Pasta Blues | Dissonance No.2
Los Angeles,CA, rec. 27.5.& 1.6.1977
Pass,Joe (g-solo)

OJC20 720-2(M 9063) | CD | Trident | EAN 090204923137
McCoy Tyner Trio
Celestial Chant | O Amor En Paz(Once I Loved) | Elvin (Sir) Jones | Land Of The Lonely | Impressions | Ruby My Dear
Berkeley,CA, rec. 18./19.2.1975
Tyner,McCoy (p,harpsichord) | Carter,Ron (b) | Jones,Elvin (dr)

OJC20 739-2(2310749) | CD | Dizzy-At The Montreux Jazz Festival 1975
Dizzy Gillespie Big 7
Lover Come Back To Me | I'll Remember April | What's New? | Cherokee
Live at The Montreux Jazz Festival, rec. 16.7.1975
Gillespie,Dizzy (tp) | Davis,Eddie 'Lockjaw' (ts) | Griffin,Johnny (ts) | Jackson,Milt (vib) | Flanagan,Tommy (p) | Orsted-Pedersen,Niels-Henning (b) | Roker,Granville 'Mickey' (dr)

OJC20 781-2(2308217) | CD | The Paris Concert
OJC 781(2308217) | LP | The Paris Concert
John Coltrane Quartet
Mr.P.C. | The Inch Worm | Every Time We Say Goodbye
Live at The Olympia,Paris,France, rec. 17.11.1962
Coltrane,John (ss,ts) | Tyner,McCoy (p) | Garrison,Jimmy (b) | Jones,Elvin (dr)

OJC20 789-2(2310751) | CD | Ella-At The Montreux Jazz Festival 1975
OJC 789(2310751) | LP | Ella-At The Montreux Jazz Festival 1975
Ella Fitzgerald With The Tommy Flanagan Trio
Caravan | Satin Doll | Teach Me Tonight | Wave | It's All Right With Me | Let's Do It(Let's Fall In Love) | How High The Moon | Girl From Ipanema(Garota De Ipanema) | 'Tain't Nobody's Bizness If I Do
Live at The Montreux Jazz Festival, rec. 17.7.1975
Fitzgerald,Ella (voc) | Flanagan,Tommy (p) | Betts,Keter (b) | Durham,Bobby (dr)

OJC20 790-2(2310896) | CD | The Timekeepers-Count Basie Meets Oscar Peterson
Count Basie-Oscar Peterson Quartet
I'm Confessin'(That I Love You) | Soft Winds | Rent Party | Back Home Again In Indiana | Hey Raymond | After You've Gone | That's The One
Hollywood,CA, rec. 21./22.2.1978
Basie,Count (p) | Peterson,Oscar (p) | Heard,John (b) | Bellson,Louie (dr)

OJC20 815-2(P 7680) | CD | More Power
Dexter Gordon-James Moody Quintet
Lady Bird | Sticky Wicket
Englewood Cliffs,NJ, rec. 2.4.1969
Gordon,Dexter (ts) | Moody,James (ts) | Harris,Barry (p) | Williams,Buster (b) | Heath,Albert 'Tootie' (dr)
Dexter Gordon Quartet
Meditation | Fried Bananas | Boston Bernie
Englewood Cliffs,NJ, rec. 4.4.1969
Gordon,Dexter (ts) | Harris,Barry (p) | Williams,Buster (b) | Heath,Albert 'Tootie' (dr)

OJC20 873-2(R 9468) | CD | Born To Be Blue! | EAN 090204923113
Bobby Timmons Trio
Sometimes I Feel Like A Motherless Child | Know Not One | Namely You
NYC, rec. 12.8.1963
Timmons,Bobby (p) | Carter,Ron (b) | Kay,Connie (dr)
Born To Be Blue | Malice Towards None | The Sit-In | Often Annie
NYC, rec. 10.9.1963
Timmons,Bobby (p) | Jones,Sam (b) | Kay,Connie (dr)

OJC20 884-2(2310753) | CD | Milt Jackson At The Montreux Jazz Festival 1975
Milt Jackson Big 4
Funji Mama | Everything Must Change | Speedball | Nature Boy | Stella By Starlight | Like Someone In Love | Night Mist Blues | Mack The Knife(Moritat)
Live at The Montreux Jazz Festival, rec. 17.7.1975
Jackson,Milt (vib) | Peterson,Oscar (p) | Orsted-Pedersen,Niels-Henning (b) | Roker,Granville 'Mickey' (dr)

OJC20 933-2(2310750) | CD | Count Basie Jam Session At The Montreux Jazz Festival 1975
2310750 | LP | Count Basie Jam Session At The Montreux Jazz Festival 1975
Count Basie Jam Session
Billie's Bounce | Festival Blues | Lester Leaps In
Live at The Montreux Jazz Festival, rec. 19.7.1975
Basie,Count (p) | Eldridge,Roy (tp) | Griffin,Johnny (ts) | Jackson,Milt (vib) | Orsted-Pedersen,Niels-Henning (b) | Bellson,Louie (dr)

OJC20 934-2(2310752) | CD | Joe Pass At The Montreux Jazz Festival 1975
Joe Pass
You Are The Sunshine Of My Life | The Very Thought Of You | Nobs | Lil' Darlin' | Blues For Nina | How Long Has This Been Going On | More Than You Know | Grete | Nuages | I'm Glad There Is You | Willow Weep For Me
Live at The Montreux Jazz Festival, rec. 17./18.7.1975
Pass,Joe (g-solo)

OJCC20 754-2(M 9105) | CD | Third Plane | EAN 090204923045
Ron Carter Trio
Third Plane | Quiet Times | Lawra | Stella By Starlight | United Blues | Dolphin Dance
San Francisco,CA, rec. 13.7.1977
Carter,Ron (b) | Hancock,Herbie (p) | Williams,Tony (dr)

OJCCD 004-2 | CD | The Musings Of Miles
OJC 004(P 7007) | LP | The Musings Of Miles
Miles Davis Quartet
Will You Still Be Mine | I See Your Face Before Me | I Didn't | A Gal In Calico | A Night In Tunisia | Green Haze
NYC, rec. 6.6.1955
Davis,Miles (tp) | Garland,Red (p) | Pettiford,Oscar (b) | Jones,Philly Joe (dr)

OJCCD 008-2 | CD | The Brothers
OJC 008(P 7022) | LP | The Brothers
Stan Getz And His Four Brothers
Five Brothers | Four And One More | Battleground | Battle Of The Saxes
NYC, rec. 8.4.1949
Getz,Stan (ts) | Sims,Zoot (ts) | Eager,Allen (ts) | Moore,Brew (ts) | Bishop Jr.,Walter (p) | Ramey,Gene (b) | Perry,Charlie (dr)
Zoot Sims-Al Cohn Sextet
Morning Fun | The Red Door | Tangerine | Zootcase
NYC, rec. 8.9.1952
Sims,Zoot (ts) | Cohn,Al (ts) | Winding,Kai (tb) | Wallington,George (p) | Heath,Percy (b) | Blakey,Art (dr)

OJCCD 009-2 | CD | Sonny Stitt
OJC 009(P 7024) | LP | Sonny Stitt
Sonny Stitt Quintet
Afternoon In Paris | Elora | Blue Mode(2 takes) | Teapot
NYC, rec. 17.10.1949
Stitt,Sonny (ts) | Johnson,J.J. (tb) | Lewis,John (p) | Boyd,Nelson (b) | Roach,Max (dr)
Sonny Stitt Quartet
All God's Chillun Got Rhythm | Sonnyside | Bud's Blues | Sunset
NYC, rec. 11.12.1949
Stitt,Sonny (ts) | Powell,Bud (p) | Russell,Curly (b) | Roach,Max (dr)
Strike Up The Band | I Want To Be Happy | Taking A Chance On Love | Fine And Dandy(2 takes)
rec. 26.1.1950
Stitt,Sonny (ts) | Powell,Bud (p) | Russell,Curly (b) | Roach,Max (dr)

OJCCD 011-2 | CD | Sonny Rollins With The Modern Jazz Quartet
Sonny Rollins Quartet
I Know
NYC, rec. 17.1.1951
Rollins,Sonny (ts) | Davis,Miles (p) | Heath,Percy (b) | Haynes,Roy (dr)
Mambo Bounce | Time On My Hands | This Love Of Mine | Shadrack | Slow Boat To China | Scoops | With A Song In My Heart | Newk's Fadeway
NYC, rec. 17.12.1951
Rollins,Sonny (ts) | Drew,Kenny (p) | Heath,Percy (b) | Blakey,Art (dr)
Sonny Rollins With The Modern Jazz Quartet
The Stopper | In A Sentimental Mood | No Moe | Almost Like Being In Love
NYC, rec. 7.10.1953
Rollins,Sonny (ts) | MJQ (Modern Jazz Quartet) | Jackson,Milt (vib) | Lewis,John (p) | Heath,Percy (b) | Clarke,Kenny (dr)

OJCCD 016-2 | CD | MONK
Thelonious Monk Quintet
Let's Call This | Think Of One(take 1+2)
NYC, rec. 13.11.1953
Monk,Thelonious (p) | Rollins,Sonny (ts) | Watkins,Julius (fr-h) | Heath,Percy (b) | Jones,Willie (dr)
We See | Smoke Gets In Your Eyes | Loco Motif | Hackensack
NYC, rec. 11.5.1954
Monk,Thelonious (p) | Copeland,Ray (tp) | Foster,Frank (ts) | Russell,Curly (b) | Blakey,Art (dr)

OJCCD 019-2(P 7088) | CD | Kenny Burrell
OJC 019(P 7088) | LP | Kenny Burrell
Kenny Burrell Quintet
Don't Cry Baby | Drum Boogie | Strictly Confidential | All Of You | Perception
Hackensack,NJ, rec. 1.2.1957
Burrell,Kenny (g) | Payne,Cecil (bs) | Flanagan,Tommy (p) | Watkins,Doug (b) | Jones,Elvin (dr)

OJCCD 028-2(RLP 239) | CD | Jazz Contrast
Kenny Dorham Quintet
La Villa | Falling In Love With Love | I'll Remember April
NYC, rec. 21.& 27.5.1957
Dorham,Kenny (tp) | Rollins,Sonny (ts) | Jones,Hank (p) | Pettiford,Oscar (b) | Roach,Max (dr)
Jarue | But Beautiful
rec. 21.& 27.5.1957
Dorham,Kenny (tp) | Glamman,Betty (harp) | Jones,Hank (p) | Pettiford,Oscar (b) | Roach,Max (dr)
Kenny Dorham Sextet
My Old Flame
Dorham,Kenny (tp) | Rollins,Sonny (ts) | Jones,Hank (p) | Pettiford,Oscar (b) | Roach,Max (dr) | Glamman,Betty (harp)

OJCCD 031-2(RLP 265) | CD | 10 To 4 At The 5-Spot
OJC 031 (RLP 265) | LP | 10 To 4 At The 5-Spot
Pepper Adams Quartet
You're My Thrill
Live at The Five Spot Cafe,NYC, rec. 15.4.1958
Adams,Pepper (bs) | Timmons,Bobby (p) | Watkins,Doug (b) | Jones,Elvin (dr)
Pepper Adams Quintet
'Tis(Theme) | The Long Two- | Four- | Hasting Street Bounce | Youma
Adams,Pepper (bs) | Byrd,Donald (tp) | Timmons,Bobby (p) | Watkins,Doug (b) | Jones,Elvin (dr)

OJCCD 034-2 | CD | A Dynamic New Jazz Sound
OJC 034 (RLP 1156) | LP | A Dynamic New Jazz Sound
Wes Montgomery Trio
Round About Midnight | Yesterdays | The End Of A Love Affair | Whisper Not | Ecaroh | Satin Doll | Missile Blues | Too Late Now | Jingles
rec. 5./6.10.1959
Montgomery,Wes (g) | Rhyne,Melvin (org) | Parker,Paul (dr)

OJCCD 040-2 | CD | George Shearing And The Montgomery Brothers
George Shearing With The Montgomery Brothers
Love Walked In | Love For Sale | No Hard Feelings | Enchanted | Double Deal | And Then I Wrote | Dam That Dream | Lois Ann
rec. 9./10.10.1961
Shearing,George (p) | Montgomery,Wes (g) | Montgomery,Buddy (vib) | Montgomery,Monk (b) | Perkins,Walter (dr)
The Lamp Is Low | Mambo In Chimes
Shearing,George (p) | Montgomery,Wes (g) | Montgomery,Buddy (vib) | Montgomery,Monk (b) | Peraza,Armando (congas,bongos) | Chimelis,Richard (bongoes,conga,timbales)
Stranger In Paradise
Shearing,George (p) | Montgomery,Wes (g) | Montgomery,Buddy (vib) | Montgomery,Monk (b) | Peraza,Armando (congas,bongos) | Chimelis,Richard (bongoes,conga,timbales) | Perkins,Walter (dr)

OJCCD 042-2 | CD | Town Hall Concert 1964, Vol.1
OJC 042(JWS 005) | LP | Town Hall Concert 1964, Vol.1
Charles Mingus Sextet
So Long Eric | Praying With Eric
NYC, rec. 4.4.1964
Mingus,Charles (b) | Coles,Johnny (tp) | Dolphy,Eric (fl,b-cl,as) | Jordan,Clifford (ts) | Byard,Jaki (p) | Richmond,Dannie (dr)

OJCCD 046-2 | CD | Jazz At Oberlin
OJC 046(F 3245) | LP | Jazz At Oberlin
Dave Brubeck Quartet
These Foolish Things Remind Me On You | The Way You Look Tonight | Perdido | Stardust | How High The Moon

Oberlin College,Oberlin,Ohio, rec. 2.3.1953
Brubeck,Dave (p) | Desmond,Paul (as) | Crotty,Ron (b) | Davis,Lloyd (dr)

OJCCD 050-2(P 7008) | CD | Wardell Gray Memorial Vol.1
Wardell Gray Quartet
Twisted | Twisted(alt.take 1) | Twisted(alt.take 2) | Twisted(alt.take 3) | Easy Living | Easy Living(alt.take) | South Side | South Side(alt.take 1) | South Side(alt.take 2) | South Side(alt.take 3) | South Side(alt.take 4) | South Side(alt.take 5) | South Side(alt.take 6) | Sweet Lorraine
NYC, rec. 11.11.1949
Gray,Wardell (ts) | Haig,Al (p) | Potter,Tommy (b) | Haynes,Roy (dr)
Teddy Charles' West Coasters
So Long Broadway | Paul's Cause | The Man I Love | Lavonne
Los Angeles,CA, rec. 20.2.1953
Charles,Teddy (vib) | Morgan,Frank (as) | Gray,Wardell (ts) | Clark,Sonny (p) | Nivison,Dick (b) | Marable,Lawrence (dr)

OJCCD 051-2(P 7009) | CD | Wardell Gray Memorial Vol.2
Wardell Gray's Los Angeles All Stars
Scrapple From The Apple
Los Angeles,CA, rec. 27.8.1950
Gray,Wardell (ts) | Terry,Clark (tp) | Criss,Sonny (as) | Bunn,Jimmy (p) | Hadnott,Billy (b) | Thompson,Chuck (dr)
Move
Gray,Wardell (ts) | Terry,Clark (tp) | Criss,Sonny (as) | Gordon,Dexter (ts) | Bunn,Jimmy (p) | Hadnott,Billy (b) | Thompson,Chuck (dr)
Wardell Gray Quintet
Farmer's Market | Jackie | Bright Boy | April Skies | Lover Man(Oh,Where Can You Be?)
Los Angeles,CA, rec. 21.1.1952
Gray,Wardell (ts) | Farmer,Art (tp) | Hawes,Hampton (p) | Crosby,Harper (b) | Marable,Lawrence (dr) | Collier,Robert (congas)
Wardell Gray Quartet
Sweet And Lovely
Gray,Wardell (ts) | Hawes,Hampton (p) | Crosby,Harper (b) | Marable,Lawrence (dr) | Collier,Robert (congas)

OJCCD 052-2 | CD | Woodlore
OJC 052(P 7018) | LP | Woodlore
Phil Woods Quartet
Slow Boat To China | Get Happy | Strollin' With Pam | Woodlore | Falling In Love All Over Again | Be My Love
NYC, rec. 25.11.1955
Woods,Phil (as) | Williams,John (p) | Kotick,Teddy (b) | Stabulas,Nick (dr)

OJCCD 054-2 | CD | Plays The Arrangements And Compositions Of Gigi Gryce And Quincy Jones
Art Farmer Septet
Work Of Art | The Little Bandmaster | Mau Mau | Up In Quincy's Room
NYC, rec. 2.7.1953
Farmer,Art (tp) | Cleveland,Jimmy (tb) | Solomon,Clifford (ts) | Estell,Oscar (bs) | Jones,Quincy (p,arr) | Montgomery,Monk (el-b) | Johnson,Sonny (dr)
Wildwood | Evening In Paris | Elephant Walk | Tia Juana
NYC, rec. 7.6.1954
Farmer,Art (tp) | Cleveland,Jimmy (tb) | Rouse,Charlie (ts) | Bank,Danny (bs) | Silver,Horace (p) | Heath,Percy (b) | Taylor,Arthur 'Art' (dr)
Art Farmer Quartet
When Your Lover Has Gone
Hackensack,NJ, rec. 3.8.1956
Farmer,Art (tp) | Harris,Barry (p) | Watkins,Doug (b) | Taylor,Arthur 'Art' (dr)

OJCCD 055-2 | CD | Fontainebleau
Tadd Dameron And His Orchestra
Fontainebleau | Delirium | The Scene Is Clean | Flossie Lou | Bula-Beige
NYC, rec. 9.3.1956
Dameron,Tadd (p) | Dorham,Kenny (tp) | Coker,Henry (tb) | Shihab,Sahib (as) | Alexander,Joe (ts) | Payne,Cecil (bs) | Simmons,John (b) | Wilson,Shadow (dr)

OJCCD 059-2 | CD | Thelonious Monk/Sonny Rollins
OJC 059(P 7075) | LP | Thelonious Monk/Sonny Rollins
Thelonious Monk Quintet
Friday The 13th
NYC, rec. 13.11.1953
Monk,Thelonious (p) | Rollins,Sonny (ts) | Watkins,Julius (fr-h) | Heath,Percy (b) | Jones,Willie (dr)
Thelonious Monk Trio
Work | Nutty
NYC, rec. 22.9.1954
Monk,Thelonious (p) | Heath,Percy (b) | Blakey,Art (dr)
Sonny Rollins Quartet feat.Thelonious Monk
The Way You Look Tonight | I Want To Be Happy
NYC, rec. 25.10.1954
Rollins,Sonny (ts) | Monk,Thelonious (p) | Potter,Tommy (b) | Taylor,Arthur 'Art' (dr)

OJCCD 060-2(P 7077) | CD | Kaleidoscope
Sonny Stitt Quartet
Later | Ain't Misbehavin'
NYC, rec. 17.2.1950
Stitt,Sonny (ts) | Drew,Kenny (p) | Potter,Tommy (b) | Blakey,Art (dr)
Imagination | Cherokee
NYC, rec. 15.12.1950
Stitt,Sonny (ts) | Mance,Junior[Julian C.] (p) | Wright,Eugene 'Gene' (b) | Blakey,Art (dr)
Liza | Can't We Be Friends
NYC, rec. 31.1.1951
Stitt,Sonny (ts) | Bateman,Charles (p) | Wright,Eugene 'Gene' (b) | Blakey,Art (dr)
P.S.I Love You | This Can't Be Love
NYC, rec. 1.2.1951
Stitt,Sonny (ts,bs) | Bateman,Charles (p) | Wright,Eugene 'Gene' (b) | Stewart,Teddy (dr)
Sonny Stitt Quintet
Sonny Sounds | Stitt's It
NYC, rec. 25.2.1952
Stitt,Sonny (ts) | Houston,John (p) | Shepard,Ernie (b) | Wilson,Shadow (dr) | Morales,Humberto (congas)
Sonny Stitt And His Band
Cool Mambo | Blue Mambo
Stitt,Sonny (ts) | Massey,Bill (tp) | Newman,Joe (tp) | Hunt,John (tp) | Houston,John (p) | Shepard,Ernie (b) | Wilson,Shadow (dr) | Morales,Humberto (congas)

OJCCD 061-2 | CD | Groovy
Red Garland Trio
Willow Weep For Me | What Can I Say After I Say I'm Sorry
Englewood Cliffs,NJ, rec. 14.12.1956
Garland,Red (p) | Chambers,Paul (b) | Taylor,Arthur 'Art' (dr)
Hey Now
Englewood Cliffs,NJ, rec. 24.5.1957
Garland,Red (p) | Chambers,Paul (b) | Taylor,Arthur 'Art' (dr)
Will You Still Be Mine | C Jam Blues | Gone Again
Englewood Cliffs,NJ, rec. 9.8.1957
Garland,Red (p) | Chambers,Paul (b) | Taylor,Arthur 'Art' (dr)

OJCCD 063-2 | CD | Reflections-Steve Lacy Plays Thelonious Monk
Steve Lacy Quartet
Four In One | Reflections | Hornin' In | Bye-Ya | Let's Call This | Ask Me Now | Skippy
NYC, rec. 17.10.1958
Lacy,Steve (ss) | Waldron,Mal (p) | Neidlinger,Buell (b) | Jones,Elvin (dr)

OJCCD 064-2 | CD | The Unique Thelonious Monk
OJC 064(R 12-209) | LP | The Unique Thelonious Monk
Thelonious Monk Trio
Liza | Honeysuckle Rose | Darn That Dream | Tea For Two | You Are Too Beautiful | Just You Just Me
Hackensack,NJ, rec. 17.3.& 3.4.1956
Monk,Thelonious (p) | Pettiford,Oscar (b) | Blakey,Art (dr)
Thelonious Monk
Memories Of You
Monk,Thelonious (p-solo)

OJCCD 067-2 | CD | Freedom Suite
OJC 067(RLP 258) | LP | Freedom Suite
Sonny Rollins Trio
The Freedom Suite | Someday I'll Find You | Will You Still Be Mine | Till There Was You(take 1) | Till There Was You(take 2) | Shadow Waltz
rec. Feb.1958
Rollins,Sonny (ts) | Pettiford,Oscar (b) | Roach,Max (dr)

OJCCD 070-2(RLP 9375) | CD | Ezz-thetics
OJC 070(RLP 9375) | LP | Ezz-thetics
George Russell Sextet
Ezz-thetic | Nardis | Lydiot | Thoughts | Honesty | Round About Midnight
NYC, rec. 8.5.1961
Russell,George (p) | Ellis,Don (tp) | Baker,Dave (tb) | Dolphy,Eric (b-cl,as) | Swallow,Steve (b) | Hunt,Joe (dr)

OJCCD 079-2(NJ 8217) | CD | The Cats
Prestige All Stars
Eclypso | Solacium | Minor Mishap | Tommy's Time
Hackensack,NJ, rec. 18.4.1957
Prestige All Stars | Sulieman[Leonard Graham],Idrees (tp) | Coltrane,John (ts) | Flanagan,Tommy (p) | Burrell,Kenny (g) | Watkins,Doug (b) | Hayes,Louis (dr)
Tommy Flanagan Trio
How Long Has This Been Going On
Flanagan,Tommy (p) | Watkins,Doug (b) | Hayes,Louis (dr)

OJCCD 082-2(NJ 8269) | CD | The Quest
Mal Waldron Sextet
Status Seeking | Duquility | Thirteen | We Diddit | Warm Canto | Warp And Woof | Fire Waltz
NYC, rec. 27.6.1961
Waldron,Mal (p) | Dolphy,Eric (cl,as) | Ervin,Booker (ts) | Carter,Ron (cello) | Benjamin,Joe (b) | Persip,Charles (dr)

OJCCD 085-2 | CD | That's Him!
Abbey Lincoln With Her Quintet
Strong Man | Happiness Is A Thing Called Joe | That's Him | I Must Have That Man | My Man | Porgy | When A Woman Loves A Man
NYC, rec. 28.10.1957
Lincoln,Abbey (voc) | Dorham,Kenny (tp) | Rollins,Sonny (ts) | Kelly,Wynton (p) | Chambers,Paul (b) | Roach,Max (dr)
Abbey Lincoln With Her Quartet
Don't Explain
Lincoln,Abbey (voc) | Dorham,Kenny (tp) | Rollins,Sonny (ts) | Kelly,Wynton (p) | Roach,Max (dr)
Abbey Lincoln
Tender As A Rose
Lincoln,Abbey (voc-solo)

OJCCD 095-2 | CD | Tour De Force
Sonny Rollins Quartet
Ee-Ah | B.Quick | B.Swift
rec. 7.12.1956
Rollins,Sonny (ts) | Drew,Kenny (p) | Morrow,George (b) | Roach,Max (dr)
Two Different Worlds | My Ideal
Rollins,Sonny (ts) | Drew,Kenny (p) | Morrow,George (b) | Roach,Max (dr) | Coleman,Earl (voc)

OJCCD 099-2 | CD | Straight Ahead
OJC 099(NJ 8255) | LP | Straight Ahead
Oliver Nelson Quintet
Images | Six And Four | Mama Lou | Ralph's New Blues | Straight Ahead | 111-44
NYC, rec. 1.3.1961
Nelson,Oliver (cl,as,ts) | Dolphy,Eric (fl,b-cl,as) | Wyands,Richard (p) | Duvivier,George (b) | Haynes,Roy (dr)

OJCCD 1000-2(RLP 9447) | CD | Junior's Blues
Junior Mance Trio
Down The Line | Creole Love Call | Rainy Mornin' Blues | Yancey Special | Gravy Waltz | Cracklin' | In The Evening | Blue Monk | The Jumpin' Blues
NYC, rec. 14.2.1963
Mance,Junior[Julian C.] (p) | Cranshaw,Bob (b) | Roker,Granville 'Mickey' (dr)

OJCCD 1001-2(R 9474) | CD | Little Big Horn!
Nat Adderley With Kenny Burrell And The Junior Mance Trio
Foo Foo | Loneliness | Little Big Horn | Hustle With Russell
NYC, rec. 23.9.1963
Adderley,Nat (co) | Burrell,Kenny (g) | Mance,Junior[Julian C.] (p) | Cranshaw,Bob (b) | Roker,Granville 'Mickey' (dr)
Nat Adderley With Jim Hall And The Junior Mance Trio
El Chico | Half-Time | Broadway Lady | Roses For Your Pillow
NYC, rec. 4.10.1963
Adderley,Nat (co) | Hall,Jim (g) | Mance,Junior[Julian C.] (p) | Cranshaw,Bob (b) | Roker,Granville 'Mickey' (dr)

OJCCD 100-2(F 3-222) | CD | The Brew Moore Quintet
Brew Moore Quintet
Fools Rush In
University Of California, rec. August 1955
Moore,Brew (ts) | Marabuto,Johnny (p) | unkn. (g) | Hartstein,Max (b) | Gustofson,Gus (dr)
Brew Moore Quartet
Them There Eyes | Tea For Two | Five Planets In Leo | I Can't Believe That You're In Love With Me
Live at The Marines Memorial Theatre,San Francisco,CA, rec. 15.1.1956
Moore,Brew (ts) | Marabuto,Johnny (p) | Hartstein,Max (b) | Gustofson,Gus (dr)
Brew Moore Quintet
Rose | Them Old Blues | Rotation | I Want A Little Girl
San Francisco,CA, rec. 22.2.1956
Moore,Brew (ts) | Mills,Dickie (tp) | Marabuto,Johnny (p) | Hartstein,Max (b) | Gustafsson,Gus (dr)

OJCCD 1002-2(1210890) | CD | Jazz Dance
OJC 1002(2310890) | LP | Jazz Dance
Zoot Sims Quartet feat.Count Basie
It's Only A Paper Moon
NYC, rec. 9.4.1975
Sims,Zoot (ts) | Basie,Count (p) | Heard,John (b) | Bellson,Louie (dr)
Count Basie-Oscar Peterson Quintet
Jumpin' At The Woodside
NYC, rec. 1975
Basie,Count (org) | Peterson,Oscar (p) | Green,Freddie (g) | Brown,Ray (b) | Bellson,Louie (dr)
Coleman Hawkins Quartet
Sweet And Lovely
NYC, rec. 20.12.1966
Hawkins,Coleman (ts) | Harris,Barry (p) | Cranshaw,Bob (b) | Locke,Eddie (dr)
Oscar Peterson Quintet With Strings
The Waltz I Blew For You
NYC, rec. Jan./Feb.1980
Peterson,Oscar (p) | Terry,Clark (tp) | Leitch,Peter (g) | Young,Dave (b) | Fuller,Jerry (dr) | Strings
Roy Eldridge And The Jimmy Ryan All Stars
Sing Sing Sing
NYC, rec. 7.4.1975
Eldridge,Roy (tp) | Pratt,Bobby (tb) | Muranyi,Joe (cl) | Katz,Dick (p) | Holley,Major (b) | Locke,Eddie (dr)
Count Basie And His Orchestra
Bundle O'Funk
NYC, rec. 18./20.1.1977
Basie,Count (p) | Minger,Pete (tp) | Biviano,Lyn (tp) | Mitchell,Bob (tp) | Cohn[Cohen],Sonny (tp) | Grey,Al (tb) | Fuller,Curtis (tb) | Hughes,Bill (tb) | Wanzo,Mel (tb) | Turner,Danny (as) | Plater,Bobby (as) | Forrest,Jimmy (ts) | Dixon,Eric (ts) | Fowlkes,Charlie (bs) | Green,Freddie (g) | Duke,John (b) | Press,Reiny (el-b) | Miles,Butch (dr)
Zoot Sims-Harry Edison Quintet
Nature Boy
NYC, rec. 18./20.12.1978
Edison,Harry 'Sweets' (tp) | Sims,Zoot (ts) | Kellaway,Roger (el-p) | Heard,John (b) | Smith,Jimmie (dr)
Oscar Peterson Quartet
The World Is Waiting For The Sunrise
NYC, rec. 28./29.1.1980
Peterson,Oscar (el-p) | Leitch,Peter (g) | Young,Dave (b) | Fuller,Jerry (dr)
Clark Terry Quintet
Jitterbug Waltz
NYC, rec. 15./16.5.1979
Terry,Clark (tp) | Woods,Chris (as) | Peterson,Oscar (p) | Sproles,Victor (b) | Hart,Billy (dr)
Ray Bryant
Take The 'A' Train
NYC, rec. 13.7.1977
Bryant,Ray (p-solo)

OJCCD 1003-2(JLP 962) | CD | The Nearness Of You
Red Garland Trio
Why I Was Born | The Nearness Of You | Where Or When | Long Ago And Far Away | I Got It Bad And That Ain't Good | Don't Worry 'Bout Me | All Alone
NYC, rec. 30.11.1961
Garland,Red (p) | Ridley,Larry (b) | Gant,Frank (dr)
Red Garland
Lush Life
Garland,Red (p-solo)

OJCCD 1004-2(P 7084) | CD | Olio
The Prestige All Stars
Potpourri | Blues Without Woe | Touche | Dakar | Embraceable You | Hello Frisco
Hackensack,NJ, rec. 16.2.1957
Prestige All Stars | Jones,Thad (tp) | Wess,Frank (fl,ts) | Charles,Teddy (vib) | Waldron,Mal (p) | Watkins,Doug (b) | Jones,Elvin (dr)

OJCCD 1007-2(C 7557) | CD | The Gambit
Shelly Manne And His Men
The Gambit: | Queen's Pawn
Los Angeles,CA, rec. 4.1.1957
Manne,Shelly (dr) | Williamson,Stu (tp,v-tb) | Mariano,Charlie (as) | Freeman,Russ (p) | Vinnegar,Leroy (b)
En Passant
Los Angeles,CA, rec. 17.7.1957
Manne,Shelly (dr) | Williamson,Stu (tp,v-tb) | Mariano,Charlie (as) | Freeman,Russ (p) | Vinnegar,Leroy (b)
Castling | Checkmate
Los Angeles,CA, rec. 25.7.1957
Manne,Shelly (dr) | Williamson,Stu (tp,v-tb) | Mariano,Charlie (as) | Freeman,Russ (p) | Vinnegar,Leroy (b)
Blu Gnu | Tom Brown's Buddy | Hugo Hurwey
Los Angeles,CA, rec. 24.2.1958
Manne,Shelly (dr) | Williamson,Stu (tp,v-tb) | Mariano,Charlie (as) | Freeman,Russ (p) | Vinnegar,Leroy (b)

OJCCD 1008-2(GXY 5120) | CD | A Little New York Midtown Music
Nat Adderley Quintet
Fortune's Child | A Little New York Midtown Music | Sunshine Sammy | Yeehaw Junction | Come Rain Or Come Shine | Whipitup | Saguaro
Berkeley,CA, rec. 18./19.9.1978
Adderley,Nat (co) | Griffin,Johnny (ts) | Feldman,Victor (p,el-p) | Carter,Ron (b) | McCurdy,Roy (dr)

OJCCD 1009-2(M 9072) | CD | Focal Point
McCoy Tyner Sextet
Mes Trois Fils | Parody | Indo-Serenade | Departure | Theme For Nana
Berkeley,CA, rec. 4.-7.8.1976
Tyner,McCoy (p) | Bartz,Gary (cl,ss,as,sopranino) | Ford,Joe (fl,ss,as) | Bridgewater,Ron (ss,ts) | Fambrough,Charles (b) | Gravatt,Eric (dr)
McCoy Tyner Septet
Mode For Dulcimer
Tyner,McCoy (dulcimer) | Bartz,Gary (cl,ss,as,sopranino) | Ford,Joe (fl,ss,as) | Bridgewater,Ron (ss,ts) | Fambrough,Charles (b) | Gravatt,Eric (dr) | Franco,Guilherme (perc,congas,tabla)

OJCCD 1011-2(2308221) | CD | Northsea Nights
Joe Pass/Niels-Henning Orsted-Pedersen Duo
If I Were A Bell | Round About Midnight | How Deep Is The Ocean | Stella By Starlight | I Can't Get Started | Blues For The Hague
Live at The Northsea Festival, rec. July 1979
Pass,Joe (g) | Orsted-Pedersen,Niels-Henning (b)

OJCCD 101-2(F 3239) | CD | The Dave Brubeck Octet
Dave Brubeck Octet
How High The Moon | I Hear A Rhapsody | Laura | Playland-At-The-Beach | Serenade's Suite | Prisoner's Song | Rondo | Schizophrenic Scherzo | You Go To My Head | Closing Theme
San Francisco,CA, rec. 1948-1949
Brubeck,Dave (p) | Collins,Dick (tp) | Collins,Bob (tb) | Desmond,Paul (as) | Van Kriedt,Dave (ts) | Smith,Bill (cl,bs) | Crotty,Ron (b) | Tjader,Cal (dr)
Love Walked In | IPCA | What Is This Thing Called Love | The Way You Look Tonight | September In The Rain | Prelude | Fugue In Bop Themes | Let's Fall In Love
San Francisco,CA, rec. July 1950
Brubeck,Dave (p) | Collins,Dick (tp) | Collins,Bob (tb) | Desmond,Paul (as) | Van Kriedt,Dave (ts) | Smith,Bill (cl,bs) | Crotty,Ron (b) | Tjader,Cal (dr)

OJCCD 1012-2(JLP 11) | CD | East Coast Sound
Trigger Alpert's Absolutely All Star Seven
Treat Me Rough | Love Me Tomorrow | Trigger Happy
NYC, rec. 29.10.1956
Alpert,Trigger (b) | Wilder,Joe (tp) | Green,Urbie (tb) | Sims,Zoot (as,ts) | Cohn,Al (ts,bs) | Scott,Tony (cl,ts) | Shaughnessy,Ed (dr)
Looking At You | Tranquilizer | I Like The Likes Of You
NYC, rec. 23.11.1956
Alpert,Trigger (b) | Wilder,Joe (tp) | Green,Urbie (tb) | Sims,Zoot (as,ts) | Cohn,Al (ts,bs) | Scott,Tony (cl,ts) | Shaughnessy,Ed (dr)
Trigger Fantasy | I Wish I Were In Love Again | I Don't Want To Be Alone Again | Where's That Rainbow
NYC, rec. 30.11.1956
Alpert,Trigger (b) | Wilder,Joe (tp) | Green,Urbie (tb) | Sims,Zoot (as,ts) | Cohn,Al (ts,bs) | Scott,Tony (cl,ts) | Shaughnessy,Ed (dr)

OJCCD 1014-2(M 9104) | CD | No Problem
Sonny Rollins Quintet
No Problem | Here You Come Again | Jo-Jo | Coconut Bread | Penny Saved | Illusions | Joyous Lake
Berkeley,CA, rec. 9.-15.12.1981
Rollins,Sonny (ts) | Hutcherson,Bobby (vib) | Broom,Bobby (el-g) | Cranshaw,Bob (el-b) | Williams,Tony (dr)

OJCCD 1015-2(C 7534) | CD | Music To Listen To Red Norvo By
Red Norvo Sextet
Poeme | Red Sails | The Red Broom
Los Angeles,CA, rec. 26.1.1957
Norvo,Red (vib) | Collette,Buddy (fl) | Smith,Bill (cl) | Kessel,Barney (g) | Mitchell,Red (b) | Manne,Shelly (dr)
Playing The Dues Blues
Los Angeles,CA, rec. 9.2.1957
Norvo,Red (vib) | Collette,Buddy (fl) | Smith,Bill (cl) | Kessel,Barney (g) | Mitchell,Red (b) | Manne,Shelly (dr)
Divertimento(in 4 movements)
Los Angeles,CA, rec. 2.3.1957
Norvo,Red (vib) | Collette,Buddy (fl) | Smith,Bill (cl) | Kessel,Barney (g) | Mitchell,Red (b) | Manne,Shelly (dr)

OJCCD 1026-2(P 7733) | CD | Magnificent!
Barry Harris Trio
Bean And The Boys | You Sweet And Fancy Lady | Rouge | Ah-Leu-Cha | Just Open Your Heart | Sun Dance | These Foolish Things Remind Me On You | Dexterity
NYC, rec. 25.11.1969
Harris,Barry (p) | Carter,Ron (b) | Williams,Leroy (dr)

OJCCD 1028-2(P 7838) | CD | It's A Blue World

Red Garland Trio
This Can't Be Love | Since I Fell For You | Crazy Rhythm | Teach Me Tonight | It's A Blue World
Hackensack,NJ, rec. 7.2.1958
Garland,Red (p) | Chambers,Paul (b) | Taylor,Arthur 'Art' (dr)

OJCCD 1030-2(2312108) | CD | Night Child
Oscar Peterson Quartet
Solar Winds | Dancin' Feet | Soliloquy (Blues For Dr.John) | Night Child | Charlie | Teenager
Toronto,Canada, rec. 11./12.4.1979
Peterson,Oscar (p,el-p) | Pass,Joe (g) | Orsted-Pedersen,Niels-Henning (b) | Bellson,Louie (dr)

OJCCD 103-2 | CD | Thelonious In Action
OJC 103(R 12-262) | LP | Thelonious In Action
Thelonious Monk Quartet
Light Blue | Coming On The Hudson | Rhythm-A-Ning | Blue Monk | Evidence | Epistrophy(theme)
Live at The Five Spot Cafe,NYC, rec. August 1958
Monk,Thelonious (p) | Griffin,Johnny (ts) | Abdul-Malik,Ahmed (b) | Haynes,Roy (dr)

OJCCD 1032-2(RS 3053) | CD | From The Bottom
Bobby Timmons Trio
From The Bottom | Corcovado(Quiet Nights) | If I Should Lose You | Samba Triste | Someone To Watch Over Me | Moanin'
NYC, rec. 1964
Timmons,Bobby (vib,p,org) | Jones,Sam (b) | Cobb,Jimmy (dr)
Bobby Timmons
You're Blasé- | Bewitched Bothered And Bewildered-
Timmons,Bobby (p-solo)

OJCCD 1033-2(P 7134) | CD | Overseas
Tommy Flanagan Trio
Relaxin' At The Camarillo | Chelsea Bridge | Eclypso | Beats Up | Skal Brother | Little Rock | Verdandi | Delarna | Willow Weep For Me | Delarna(alt.take) | Verdandi(alt.take) | Willow Weep For Me(alt.take)
Stockholm,Sweden, rec. 15.8.1957
Flanagan,Tommy (p) | Little,Wilbur (b) | Jones,Elvin (dr)

OJCCD 1035-2 | CD | Bird Song
Hampton Hawes Trio
Big Foot | Ray's Idea | Stella By Starlight | Blues For Jacque | I Should Care | Bird Song | Yesterdays | Just One Of Those Things | Cheryl
Los Angeles,CA, rec. 18.1.1956
Hawes,Hampton (p) | Chambers,Paul (b) | Marable,Lawrence (dr)
What's New? | I'll Remember April | Blue 'N' Boogie
Los Angeles,CA, rec. March 1958
Hawes,Hampton (p) | LaFaro,Scott prob. (b) | Butler,Frank (dr)

OJCCD 1036-2(2310743) | CD | Oscar Peterson & Jon Faddis
Oscar Peterson-Jon Faddis Duo
Things Ain't What They Used To Be | Autumn Leaves | Take The 'A' Train | Blues For Birks | Summertime | Leaster Leaps In
NYC, rec. 5.6.1975
Peterson,Oscar (p) | Faddis,Jon (tp)

OJCCD 1037-2(2310877) | CD | Eximious
Joe Pass Trio
A Foxy Chick And A Cool Cat | Robbin's Nest | Lush Life | Serenata | We'll Be Together Again | You Are To Me Everything | Love For Sale | Everything I've Got Belongs To You | Night And Day | Speak Low
Hollywood,CA, rec. 25.5.& 8.7.1982
Pass,Joe (g) | Orsted-Pedersen,Niels-Henning (b) | Drew,Martin (dr)

OJCCD 1038-2(2310920) | CD | Fancy Pants
Count Basie And His Orchestra
Put It Right Here | By My Side | Blue Chip | Fancy Pants | Hi-Five | Time Stream | Samantha | Strike Up The Band
Hollywood,CA, rec. December 1983
Basie,Count (p) | Carley,Dale (tp) | Cohn[Cohen],Sonny (tp) | Crawford,Jim (tp) | Summers,Bob (tp) | Szabo,Frank (tp) | Hughes,Bill (tb) | Mitchell,Grover (tb) | Wilson,Dennis (tb) | Wood,Booty (tb) | Woods,Chris (as) | Turner,Danny (as) | Dixon,Eric (ts) | Hing,Kenny (ts) | Williams,Johnny (bs) | Green,Freddie (g) | Eaton,Cleveland (b) | Mackrel,Dennis (dr)

OJCCD 1039-2(M 9079) | CD | Inner Voices
McCoy Tyner Group With Horns
Uptown
NYC, rec. 1.-8.9.1977
Tyner,McCoy (p) | Klugh,Earl (g) | Carter,Ron (b) | DeJohnette,Jack (dr) | Royal,Ernie (tp) | Faddis,Jon (tp) | Bridgewater,Cecil (tp) | Preston,Eddie (tp) | McIntyre,Earl (tb) | Stephens,Charles (tb) | Griffin,Dick (tb) | Robinson,Janice (tb) | Dodgion,Jerry (as) | Ford,Joe (as) | Foster,Alex (ts) | Xiques,Eddie (bs)
McCoy Tyner Group With Horns And Voices
Opus
Tyner,McCoy (p) | Klugh,Earl (g) | Carter,Ron (b) | DeJohnette,Jack (dr) | Franco,Guilherme (perc) | Royal,Ernie (tp) | Faddis,Jon (tp) | Bridgewater,Cecil (tp) | Preston,Eddie (tp) | McIntyre,Earl (tb) | Stephens,Charles (tb) | Griffin,Dick (tb) | Robinson,Janice (tb) | Dodgion,Jerry (as) | Ford,Joe (as) | Foster,Alex (ts) | Xiques,Eddie (bs) | Anderson,Adrienne (voc) | Dorsey,Fran (voc) | Scott,Bessye Ruth (voc) | Simmons,Suzanne (voc) | Taylor,Joan (voc) | Carter,Benjamin (voc) | Scott,Carl (voc)
Festival In Bahia
Tyner,McCoy (p) | Carter,Ron (b) | Gravatt,Eric (dr) | Royal,Ernie (tp) | McIntyre,Earl (tb) | Dodgion,Jerry (fl) | Xiques,Eddie (as) | Anderson,Adrienne (voc) | Dorsey,Fran (voc) | Scott,Bessye Ruth (voc) | Simmons,Suzanne (voc) | Taylor,Joan (voc) | Carter,Benjamin (voc) | Scott,Carl (voc)
McCoy Tyner Group With Voices
Rotunda
Tyner,McCoy (p) | Klugh,Earl (g) | Carter,Ron (b) | DeJohnette,Jack (dr) | Anderson,Adrienne (voc) | Dorsey,Fran (voc) | Scott,Bessye Ruth (voc) | Simmons,Suzanne (voc) | Taylor,Joan (voc) | Carter,Benjamin (voc) | Scott,Carl (voc)
For Tomorrow
Tyner,McCoy (p) | Carter,Ron (b) | Anderson,Adrienne (voc) | Dorsey,Fran (voc) | Scott,Bessye Ruth (voc) | Simmons,Suzanne (voc) | Taylor,Joan (voc) | Carter,Benjamin (voc) | Scott,Carl (voc)

OJCCD 1040-2(M 9047) | CD | Joe Henderson In Japan
Joe Henderson Quartet
Round About Midnight | Out 'N In | Blue Bossa | Junk Blues
Live at The Junk Club,Tokyo,Japan, rec. 4.8.1971
Henderson,Joe (ts) | Ichikawa,Hideo (el-p) | Inaba,Kunimitsu (b) | Hino,Motohiko (dr)

OJCCD 1041-2(P 10091) | CD | Tangerine
Dexter Gordon Quartet
Days Of Wine And Roses
Englewood Cliffs,NJ, rec. 22.6.1972
Gordon,Dexter (ts) | Walton,Cedar (p) | Williams,Buster (b) | Higgins,Billy (dr)
Dexter Gordon Quintet
The Group
Gordon,Dexter (ts) | Hubbard,Freddie (tp) | Walton,Cedar (p) | Williams,Buster (b) | Higgins,Billy (dr)
Tangerine | August Blues | What It Was
Englewood Cliffs,NJ, rec. 28.6.1972
Gordon,Dexter (ts) | Jones,Thad (tp,fl-h) | Jones,Hank (p) | Clarke,Stanley (b) | Hayes,Louis (dr)

OJCCD 1044-2(F 8414) | CD | Brand New
Woody Herman And His Orchestra
Sidewalk Stanley | Since I Fell For You | Proud Mary | Hitch Hike On The Possum Trot Line
San Francisco,CA, rec. March 1971
Herman,Woody (cl,ss,as,voc) | Klatka,Tony (tp) | Harrell,Tom (tp) | Powers,Buddy (tp) | Buchtel,Forrest (tp) | Byrne,Billy (tp) | Burgess,Bob 'Bobby' (tb) | Nepus,Ira (tb) | Switzer,Don (tb) | Nistico,Sal (ts) | Tiberi,Frank (ts) | Lederer,Steve (ts) | Smookler,Gene (bs) | Bloomfield,Mike (el-g) | Broadbent,Alan (p,el-p) | Read,Alan (el-b) | Soph,Ed (dr)
After Hours | Love In Silent Amber | I Almost Lost My Mind | Adam's Apple
Herman,Woody (cl,ss,as,voc) | Klatka,Tony (tp) | Harrell,Tom (tp) | Powers,Buddy (tp) | Buchtel,Forrest (tp) | Byrne,Billy (tp) | Burgess,Bob 'Bobby' (tb) | Nepus,Ira (tb) | Switzer,Don (tb) | Nistico,Sal (ts) | Tiberi,Frank (ts) | Lederer,Steve (ts) | Smookler,Gene (bs) | Broadbent,Alan (p,el-p) | Read,Alan (el-b) | Soph,Ed (dr)

OJCCD 1045-2(P 7566) | CD | Blue Odyssey
Houston Person Sextet
Blue Odyssey | Holy Land | I Love You Yes I Do | Funky London | Please Send Me Someone To Love | Starburst
NYC, rec. 12.3.1968
Person,Houston (ts) | Fuller,Curtis (tb) | Adams,Pepper (bs) | Walton,Cedar (p) | Cranshaw,Bob (b) | Jones,Frankie (dr)

OJCCD 1046-2(C 14052) | CD | Reflections
Frank Morgan All Stars
Old Bowl, New Grits | Reflections | Starting Over | Black Narcissus | Sonnymoon For Two | O.K. | Caravan
Berkeley,CA, rec. 11./12.1.1988
Morgan,Frank (as) | Henderson,Joe (ts) | Hutcherson,Bobby (vib) | Miller,Mulgrew (p) | Carter,Ron (b) | Foster,Al (dr)

OJCCD 1047-2(M 9088) | CD | Parade
Ron Carter Orchestra
Parade | A Theme In 3-4 | Tinderbox | G.T.J.
Englewood Cliffs,NJ, rec. March 1979
Carter,Ron (b,piccolo-b) | Shepley,Joe (tp,fl-h) | Faddis,Jon (tp,fl-h) | Frosk,John (tp,fl-h) | Green,Urbie (tb) | Malone,Tom (b-tb) | Dodgion,Jerry (fl,cl,as) | Wess,Frank (fl,cl,ts) | Henderson,Joe (ts) | Corea,Chick (p) | Williams,Tony (dr)
Sometimes I Feel Like A Motherless Child
Carter,Ron (b,piccolo-b) | Shepley,Joe (tp,fl-h) | Faddis,Jon (tp,fl-h) | Frosk,John (tp,fl-h) | Green,Urbie (tb) | Malone,Tom (b-tb) | Dodgion,Jerry (fl,cl,as) | Wess,Frank (fl,cl,ts)
Ron Carter Quartet
Gypsy
Carter,Ron (b) | Henderson,Joe (ts) | Corea,Chick | Williams,Tony (dr)

OJCCD 1048-2(M 9140) | CD | Roadhouse Symphony
Hank Crawford And His Orchestra
Roadhouse Symphony | Tragick Magick | Jubilee | Say It Isn't So | Time Is On Our Side | Precious Lord Take My Hand | Sugar Ditch
NYC, rec. 5./6.& 12.4.1985
Crawford,Hank (as) | Sparks,Melvin (g) | Dr.John[MacRebenack] (p,org,voc) | Bascomb,Wilbur (b) | Purdie,Bernard 'Pretty' (dr) | Brecker,Randy (tp) | Rubin,Alan (tp) | Newman,David Fathead (as,ts) | Person,Houston (ts) | Johnson,Howard (bs)

OJCCD 1050-2(P 7376) | CD | Blue Seven
Shirley Scott Quintet
Blue Seven | How Sweet | Don't Worry 'Bout It Baby,Here I Am | Nancy(With The Laughing Face) | Give Me The Simple Life
Englewood Cliffs,NJ, rec. 22.8.1961
Scott,Shirley (org) | Newman,Joe (tp) | Nelson,Oliver (ts) | Tucker,George (b) | Brooks,Roy (dr)

OJCCD 1051-2(P 7558) | CD | The Beat Goes On!
Sonny Criss Quartet
The Beat Goes On | Georgia Rose | Somewhere My Love | Calidad | Yesterdays | Ode To Billy Joe
NYC, rec. 12.1.1968
Criss,Sonny (as) | Walton,Cedar (p) | Cranshaw,Bob (b) | Dawson,Alan (dr)

OJCCD 1052-2(2310772) | CD | Fitzgerald & Pass... Again
Ella Fitzgerald-Joe Pass Duo
I Ain't Got Nothin' But The Blues | 'Tis Autumn | My Old Flame | That Old Feeling | Rain | I Didn't Know About You | You Took Advantage Of Me | I've Got The World On A String | All Too Soon | The One I Love Belongs To Somebody Else | In My Solitude | Nature Boy | Tennessee Waltz | Samba Da Una Nota So(One Note Samba)
Los Angeles,CA, rec. 29./30.1.& 8.2.1976
Fitzgerald,Ella (voc) | Pass,Joe (g)

OJCCD 1053-2(2310937) | CD | Flip Flop And Fly
Big Joe Turner With The Count Basie Orchestra
Hine And Seek | T.V.Mama | Corinne Corinna | Cherry Red | Shake Rattle And Roll | Since I Fell For You | Everyday I Have The Blues | Good Morning Blues
Paris,France/Frankfurt-Main, rec. 17.& 24.4.1972
Turner,Big Joe (voc) | Basie,Count (p) | Minger,Pete (tp) | Cohn[Cohen],Sonny (tp) | Cohen,Paul (tp) | Reed,Waymon (tp) | Grey,Al (tb) | Wanzo,Mel (tb) | Hughes,Bill (tb,b-tb) | Hooks,Bob (tb) | Peagler,Curtis (as) | Plater,Bobby (as) | Davis,Eddie 'Lockjaw' (ts) | Dixon,Eric (ts) | Williams,John (as,bs) | Green,Freddie (g) | Keenan,Norman (b) | Payne,Sonny (dr)
Flip Flop And Fly
Turner,Big Joe (voc) | Basie,Count (p) | Minger,Pete (tp) | Cohn[Cohen],Sonny (tp) | Cohen,Paul (tp) | Reed,Waymon (tp) | Grey,Al (tb) | Wanzo,Mel (tb) | Hughes,Bill (tb,b-tb) | Hooks,Bob (tb) | Peagler,Curtis (as) | Plater,Bobby (as) | Davis,Eddie 'Lockjaw' (ts) | Forrest,Jimmy (ts) | Dixon,Eric (ts) | Williams,John (as,bs) | Green,Freddie (g) | Keenan,Norman (b) | Payne,Sonny (dr)

OJCCD 1054-2(R 9448) | CD | Byrd's Word!
Charlie Byrd Sextet
Byrd's Word | Tri-X | What's New? | Buck's Hill
Washington,DC, rec. 1958
Byrd,Charlie (g) | Felder,Bobby (v-tb) | Hill,Buck (ts) | Carson,Tee (p) | Betts,Keter (b) | Knox,Bertell (dr)
Bobby In Bassoonville
Byrd,Charlie (g) | Felder,Bobby (v-tb) | Pasmanick,Kenneth (bassoon) | Carson,Tee (p) | Betts,Keter (b) | Knox,Bertell (dr)
Charlie Byrd Trio
Satin Doll
Byrd,Charlie (g) | Betts,Keter (b) | Phyfe,Eddie (dr)
Charlie Byrd Quartet
Stompin' At The Savoy
Byrd,Charlie (g) | Schneer,Charlie (p) | Betts,Keter (b) | Phyfe,Eddie (dr)
Charlie Byrd-Keter Betts
Conversation Piece
Byrd,Charlie (g) | Betts,Keter (cello)
Charlie Byrd-Ginny Byrd
Blue Turning Grey Over Me | Don't Explain
Byrd,Charlie (g) | Byrd,Ginny (voc)

OJCCD 1055-2(JLP 916) | CD | Organ-izing
Mel Rhyne Sextet
Things Ain't What They Used To Be | Blue Farouq | Barefoot Sunday Blues | Shoo-Shoo Baby
NYC, rec. 31.3.1960
Rhyne,Melvin (org) | Mitchell,Blue (tp) | Griffin,Johnny (ts) | Harris,Gene (p) | Simpkins,Andrew (b) | Heath,Albert 'Tootie' (dr)

OJCCD 1056-2(C 14030) | CD | By George
George Cables Trio
Bess You Is My Woman Now | My Man's Gone Now | I Got Rhythm | A Foggy Day(In London Town) | Summertime
Berkeley,CA, rec. 27.2.1987
Cables,George (p) | Heard,John (b) | Penland,Ralph (dr)
George Cables
Embraceable You | Someone To Watch Over Me
Cables,George (p-solo)

OJCCD 1058-2(DRE 1001) | CD | Little Jazz And The Jimmy Ryan All-Stars
Roy Eldridge And The Jimmy Ryan All Stars
Between The Devil And The Deep Blue Sea | St.James Infirmary | Beale Street Blues | Black And Blue | Sing Sing Sing(With A Swing) | Wynola | Cute | Bourbon Street Parade | All Of Me | Last Call At Jimmy Ryan's | Black And Blue(alt.take) | Between The Devil And The Deep Blue Sea(alt.take) | Last Call At Jimmy Ryan's(alt.take)
NYC, rec. 7.4.1975
Eldridge,Roy (tp,voc) | Pratt,Bobby (tb) | Muranyi,Joe (cl,as) | Katz,Dick (p) | Holley,Major (b) | Locke,Eddie (dr)

OJCCD 1059-2(2310900) | CD | Soul Route
Milt Jackson Quartet
Sittin' In The Sandtrap | Blues For Gene | How Long Has This Been Going On | Dejection Blues | Soul Route | Ne-Afterglow | In A Mellow Tone | My Romance | Chloe
NYC, rec. 30.11.& 1.12.1983
Jackson,Milt (vib) | Harris,Gene (p,el-keyboards) | Brown,Ray (b) | Roker,Granville 'Mickey' (dr)

OJCCD 1060-2(C 14045) | CD | Yardbird Suite
Frank Morgan Quartet
Yardbird Suite | A Night In Tunisia | Billie's Bounce | Star Eyes | Scrapple From The Apple | Skylark | Cheryl
Berkeley,CA, rec. 10./11.1.1988
Morgan,Frank (as) | Miller,Mulgrew (p) | Carter,Ron (b) | Foster,Al (dr)

OJCCD 1061(PR 7284) | CD | Hollar!
Etta Jones With The Oliver Nelson Quintet
I Got It Bad And That Ain't Good | The More I See You | Our Love Is Here To Stay | They Can't Take That Away From Me
Englewood Cliffs,NJ, rec. 16.9.1960
Jones,Etta (voc) | Nelson,Oliver (ts) | Winchester,Lem (vib) | Wyands,Richard (p) | Duvivier,George (b) | Haynes,Roy (dr)
Etta Jones And Her Quartet
And The Angels Sing | Give Me The Simple Life | Reverse The Charges | Answer My Love | Looking Back
Englewood Cliffs,NJ, rec. 30.3.1961
Jones,Etta (voc) | Richardson,Wally (g) | Neely,Jimmy (p) | Mulia,Michael (b) | Lawless,Rudy (dr)
Etta Jones With The Jerome Richardson Sextet
Nature Boy
Englewood Cliffs,NJ, rec. 29.11.1962
Jones,Etta (voc) | Richardson,Jerome (ts) | Burrell,Kenny (g) | Pizzarelli,Bucky (g) | Hayes,Ernest 'Ernie' (p) | Bruno,Sam (b) | Donaldson,Bobby (dr)

OJCCD 1062-2(RLP 9413) | CD | Never Than New
Barry Harris Quintet
Mucho Dinero | Easy To Love | Burgundy | The Last One | Anthropology | I Didn't Know What Time It Was | Make Haste | Nightingale
NYC, rec. 28.9.1961
Harris,Barry (p) | Hillyer,Lonnie (tp) | McPherson,Charles (as) | Farrow,Ernie (b) | Jarvis,Clifford (dr)

OJCCD 1064-2(987) | CD | Red's Good Groove
Red Garland Quintet
Red's Good Groove | Our Love Is Here To Stay | This Time The Dream's On Me | Take Me In Your Arms | Excerent! | Falling In Love With Love
NYC, rec. 22.3.1962
Garland,Red (p) | Mitchell,Blue (tp) | Adams,Pepper (bs) | Jones,Sam (b) | Jones,Philly Joe (dr)

OJCCD 1065-2(RLP 245) | CD | Great Ideas Of Western Man
Herbie Mann's Californians
The Theme | Lady Bird | Get Out Of Town | Is It True What They Say About Dixie | A Handful Of Stars | A Stella Performance | Blues For Tomorrow
Los Angeles,CA, rec. 3.7.1957
Mann,Herbie (b-cl) | Sheldon,Jack (tp) | Rowles,Jimmy (p) | Clark,Buddy (b) | Lewis,Mel (dr)

OJCCD 1066-2(S 7613) | CD | Barney Kessel's Swingin' Party At Contemporary
Barney Kessel Quartet
Bluesology | Lover Man(Oh,Where Can You Be?) | Joy Spring | Now's The Time | Miss Menphis | New Rhumba
Los Angeles,CA, rec. 19.7.1960
Kessel,Barney (g) | Jenkins,Marvin (fl,p) | Peacock,Gary (b) | Lundberg,Ron (dr)

OJCCD 1067-2(C 7653) | CD | The Sermon
Hampton Hawes Trio
Down By The Riverside | Just A Closer Walk With Thee | Swing Low Sweet Chariot | Nobody Knows The Trouble I've Seen | When The Roll Is Called Up Yonder | Go Down Moses | Joshua Fit The Battle Of Jericho | Blues N/C
Los Angeles,CA, rec. 24./25.11.1958
Hawes,Hampton (p) | Vinnegar,Leroy (b) | Levey,Stan (dr)

OJCCD 1068-2(F 9499) | CD | King Cobra
Woody Herman And His Orchestra
King Cobra | Don't You Worry 'Bout A Thing | Spain | Jazzman | Lake Taco | Come Rain Or Come Shine | Toothless
Berkeley,CA, rec. 7.-9.1.1975
Herman,Woody (cl,as,voc) | Porrello,Tom (tp) | Stahl,Dave (tp,fl-h) | Hatt,Nelson (tp,fl-h) | Powers,Buddy (tp,fl-h) | Dotson,Dennis (tp) | Byrne,Billy (tp,fl-h) | Pugh,Jim (tb) | Kirkland,Dale (tb) | Wiester,Vaughn (b-tb) | Tiberi,Frank (fl,ts,bassoon) | Anderson,Gary (fl,ts) | Herbert,Greg (fl,ts,piccolo) | Oslawski,John (bs) | LaVerne,Andy (el-p) | Paley,Ron (el-b) | Brillinger,Jeff (dr) | Nash,Kenneth (perc)

OJCCD 1069-2(F 9630) | CD | Bill Evans:From The 70's
Bill Evans Trio
Up With The Lark | Quiet Now | Gloria's Step
Live at Shelly's Manne Hole,Los Angeles,CA, rec. 15.11.1973
Evans,Bill (p) | Gomez,Eddie (b) | Morell,Marty (dr)
Elsa
Live at The 'Village Vanguard',NYC, rec. 11./12.1.1924
Evans,Bill (p) | Gomez,Eddie (b) | Morell,Marty (dr)
Bill Evans-Eddie Gomez | Gone With The Wind(take 3) | Hi Lili Hi Lo(take 6) | The Nature Of Things(take 9) | Show-Type Tune(take 1) | Are You All The Things(take 3)
Berkeley,CA, rec. 7.-10.11.1974
Evans,Bill (p) | Gomez,Eddie (b)

OJCCD 1070-2(GXY 5144) | CD | Carnaval
Ron Carter Quartet
Chelsea Bridge | Manha De Camaval(Morning Of The Carnival) | I'm Old Fashioned | Confirmation | Moose The Mooche
Denen Coliseum,Tokyo,Japan, rec. 30.7.1978
Carter,Ron (b) | Watanabe,Sadao (as) | Jones,Hank (p) | Williams,Tony (dr)

OJCCD 1071-2(M 9056) | CD | Sama Layuca
McCoy Tyner Orchestra
Sama Layuca | La Cubana | Desert Cry | Paradox
NYC, rec. 26.-28.3.1974
Tyner,McCoy (p) | Stubblefield,John (oboe,fl) | Bartz,Gary (as) | Lawrence,Azar (ss,ts) | Hutcherson,Bobby (vib,marimba) | Williams,Buster (b) | Hart,Billy (dr) | M'tume,James[Forman] (perc,congas) | Franco,Guilherme (perc)
McCoy Tyner-Bobby Hutcherson Duo
Above The Rainbow
Tyner,McCoy (p) | Hutcherson,Bobby (vib)

OJCCD 1072-2(2310814) | CD | Dream Dancing
Ella Fitzgerald With The Nelson Riddle Orchestra
I've Got You Under My Skin | I Concentrate On You | My Heart Belongs To Daddy | Love For Sale | So Near And Yet So Far | Down In The Depths | Just One Of Those Things | I Get A Kick Out Of You | All Of You | Anything Goes | At Long Last Love | C'Est Magnifique | Without Love
Hollywood,CA, rec. 9.6.1972
Fitzgerald,Ella (voc) | Riddle,Nelson (cond,arr) | Aarons,Albert 'Al' (tp) | Lewis,Carroll (tp) | Sherock,Shorty (tp) | Turner,Charlie (tp) | Johnson,J.J. (tb) | Noel,Dick (tb) | Watrous,Bill (tb) | Riddle,Christopher (b-tb) | Klee,Harry (fl) | Schwartz,Wilbur (fl) | Christlieb,Don (bassoon) | Tricarico,Bob (bassoon) | Clark,Mahlon (cl) | Green,Bill (cl) | Benno,Norman (oboe) | Schoenberg,Gordon (oboe) | Grasso,Ralph (g) | Smith,Paul (p) | Heard,John (b) | Bellson,Louie (dr)
Dream Dancing | After You
Hollywood,CA, rec. 13.2.1978
Fitzgerald,Ella (voc) | Riddle,Nelson (cond,arr) | Turner,Charlie (tp) | Aarons,Albert 'Al' (tp) | Lewis,Carroll (tp) | Sherock,Shorty (tp) | Johnson,J.J. (tb) | Watrous,Bill (tb) | Noel,Dick (tb) | Riddle,Christopher (b-tb) | Green,Bill (cl) | Clark,Mahlon (cl) | Tricarico,Bob (bassoon) | Christlieb,Don (bassoon) | Schoneberg,Gordon (oboe) | Benno,Norman (oboe) | Schwartz,Wilbur (fl) | Klee,Harry (fl) | Grasso,Ralph (g) | Smith,Paul (p) | Heard,John (b) | Bellson,Louie (dr)

OJCCD 1073-2(2310917) | CD | Topsy-This One's For Basie

Modern Jazz Quartet
Reunion Blues | Nature Boy | Topsy | D And E | Valeria | Milano | Le Cannet | D And E Blues(alt.take)
NYC, rec. 3./4.6.1985
MJQ (Modern Jazz Quartet) | Jackson,Milt (vib) | Lewis,John (p) | Heath,Percy (b) | Kay,Connie (dr)

OJCCD 1074-2(P 7216) | CD | Movin' Right Along
Arnett Cobb Quintet
Nitty Gritty | All I Do Is Dream Of You | I Don't Stand A Ghost Of A Chance With You | Exactly Like You | Walkin' | Softly As In A Morning Sunrise | The Shy One
Englewood Cliffs,NJ, rec. 16./17.2.1960
Cobb,Arnett (ts) | Timmons,Bobby (p) | Jones,Sam (b) | Taylor,Arthur 'Art' (dr) | Clark,Buck (congas)
Fast Ride
Cobb,Arnett (ts) | Flanagan,Tommy (p) | Jones,Sam (b) | Taylor,Arthur 'Art' (dr) | Barrajanos,Danny (congas)

OJCCD 1075-2(RLP 1178) | CD | The Sound Of The Wide Open Spaces
James Clay/David Fathead Newman Quintet
Wide Open Spaces | They Can't Take That Away From Me | Some Kinda Mean | What's New? | Figger-ration
NYC, rec. 26.4.1960
Clay,James (fl,ts) | Newman,David Fathead (ts) | Kelly,Wynton (p) | Jones,Sam (b) | Taylor,Arthur 'Art' (dr)

OJCCD 1076-2 | CD | Jazz At The College Of The Pacific Vol.2
Dave Brubeck Quartet
Crazy Rhythm | Let's Fall In Love | Stardust | How High The Moon | The Way You Look Tonight | Love Walked In.| Give A Little Whistle | I Found A New Baby
Live at The College Of Pacific,Stockton,CA, rec. 14.12.1953
Brubeck,Dave (p) | Desmond,Paul (as) | Crotty,Ron (b) | Dodge,Joe (dr)

OJCCD 1079-2(NJ 8287) | CD | Cymbalism | EAN 025218707923
Roy Haynes Quartet
Modette | I'm Getting Sentimental Over You | Go 'N' Git It! | La Palomeinding | Medley: | Hag- | Cymbalismn- | Oleo-
Englewood Cliffs,NJ, rec. 10.9.1963
Haynes,Roy (dr) | Strozier,Frank (fl,as) | Matthews,Ronnie (p) | Ridley,Larry (b)

OJCCD 1081-2(P 100939) | CD | Goodbye | EAN 025218708128
Gene Ammons Septet
Sticks | Alone Again(Naturally) | It Don't Mean A Thing If It Ain't Got That Swing | Jeannine | Geru's Blues | Goodbye
NYC, rec. 18.-20.3.1974
Ammons,Gene (ts) | Adderley,Nat (co) | Bartz,Gary (as) | Drew,Kenny (p) | Jones,Sam (b) | Hayes,Louis (dr) | Barretto,Ray (congas)

OJCCD 1082-2(P 7600) | CD | Bull's Eye! | EAN 025218708227
Barry Harris Trio
Clockwise | Off Minor
NYC, rec. 4.6.1968
Harris,Barry (p) | Chambers,Paul (b) | Higgins,Billy (dr)
Barry Harris Sextet
Bull's Eye | Off Monk | Barengo | Oh So Basal
Higgins,Billy (dr) | Chambers,Paul (b) | Adams,Pepper (bs) | McPherson,Charles (ts) | Dorham,Kenny (tp) | Harris,Barry (p)
-> Demo-Tape!

OJCCD 1084-2(P 2124) | CD | Flute Flight | EAN 025218708425
Herbie Mann-Bobby Jaspar Sextet
Tutti Flutti | Bo-Do
Hackensack,NJ, rec. 21.3 1957
Mann,Herbie (fl,alto-fl) | Jaspar,Bobby (fl) | Puma,Joe (g) | Flanagan,Tommy (p) | Marshall,Wendell (b) | Donaldson,Bobby (dr)
Bobby Jaspar Quintet
Flute Bass Blues | Flute Bob | Solacium
Jaspar,Bobby (fl) | Costa,Eddie (vib) | Flanagan,Tommy (p) | Watkins,Doug (b) | Donaldson,Bobby (dr)

OJCCD 1085(P7282) | CD | Battle Stations | EAN 025218708524
Eddie Lockjaw Davis-Johnny Griffin Quintet
What's Happening | Abundance | If I Had You | 632nd Street Theme | Pull My Coat | Hey Jim
Englewood Cliffs,NJ, rec. 2.9.1960
Riley,Ben (dr) | Sproles,Victor (b) | Simmons,Norman (p) | Griffin,Johnny (ts) | Davis,Eddie 'Lockjaw' (ts)
Billie's Bounce | Theme
Live at Minton's Play House,NYC, rec. 6.1.1961
Griffin,Johnny (ts) | Davis,Eddie 'Lockjaw' (ts) | Mance,Junior[Julian C.] (p) | Gales,Larry (b) | Riley,Ben (dr)

OJCCD 1086(RS 9449) | CD | Byrd In The Wind | EAN 025218708623
Charlie Byrd Group
Swing '59 | You're A Sweetheart
Washington,DC, rec. 1959
Byrd,Charlie (g) | Mann,Wallace (fl) | White,Richard (oboe) | Pasmanick,Kenneth (bassoon) | Knox,Bertell (dr)
Love Letters | Wait 'Till You See Her
Byrd,Charlie (g) | White,Richard (oboe) | Pasmanick,Kenneth (bassoon)
You Came A Long Way From St. Louis | Georgia On My Mind
Byrd,Charlie (g) | Schneer,Charlie (p) | Betts,Keter (b) | Knox,Bertell (dr) | Byrd,Ginny (voc)
Copacabana
Byrd,Charlie (g) | Hill,Buck (ts) | Schneer,Charlie (p) | Betts,Keter (b) | Knox,Bertell (dr)
Showboat Shuffle | Keter's Dirty Blues
Byrd,Charlie (g) | Hill,Buck (ts) | Betts,Keter (b) | Knox,Bertell (dr)
You'd Be So Nice To Come Home To | Cross Your Heart
Byrd,Charlie (g) | Byrd,Ginny (voc)
Stars Fell On Alabama
Byrd,Charlie (g-solo)

OJCCD 1087-2(S 7533) | CD | Li'l Abner | EAN 090204933617
Shelly Manne Trio
Jubilation T. Comepone | The Country's In The Very Best Hands | If I Had My Druthers | Unnecessary Town | Matrimonial Stomp | Progress Is The Root Of All Evil | Oh Happy Day | Namely You | Past My Prime
Los Angeles,CA, rec. 6./7.& 25.2.1957
Manne,Shelly (dr) | Previn,André (p) | Vinnegar,Leroy (b)

OJCCD 1088-2(JLP 947) | CD | Naturally! | EAN 090204933631
Nat Adderley Quartet
Naturly | Seventh Son(aka Lateef Minor Seventh) | Love Letters | This Man's Dream
NYC, rec. 20.6.1961
Adderley,Nat (co) | Zawinul,Joe (p) | Jones,Sam (b) | Hayes,Louis (dr)
Chloe | Images | Oleo | Scotch And Water
NYC, rec. 19.7.1961
Adderley,Nat (co) | Kelly,Wynton (p) | Chambers,Paul (b) | Jones,Philly Joe (dr)

OJCCD 1089-2(M 9102) | CD | 13th House | EAN 090204933648
McCoy Tyner Orchestra
Short Suite | 13th House | Search For Peace | Love Samba | Leo Rising
NYC, rec. October 1980
Tyner,McCoy (p) | Brashear,Oscar (tp,fl-h) | Sullivan,Charles (tp,fl-h) | Hampton,Slide (tb) | Williams,Gregory (fr-h) | Stewart,Bob (tuba) | Laws,Hubert (fl,piccolo) | Foster,Frank (ts) | Ford,Joe (fl,ss,as) | Ford,Ricky (ss,ts) | Carter,Ron (b) | DeJohnette,Jack (dr) | Moreira,Airto (perc,congas) | Romao,Dom Um (perc,congas)

OJCCD 1090-2(P 7178) | CD | Bacalao | EAN 090204933655
Eddie Lockjaw Davis-Shirley Scott Sextet
Last Train From Overbrook | Sometimes I'm Happy | That Old Black Magic | Fast Spiral | Dobbin' With Redd Foxx | Come Rain Or Come Shine | Dansero | When Your Lover Has Gone
Englewood Cliffs,NJ, rec. 20.12.1959
Perez,Luis (bongos,congas) | Barretto,Ray (congas) | Edgehill,Arthur (dr) | Duvivier,George (b) | Scott,Shirley (org) | Davis,Eddie 'Lockjaw' (ts)

OJCCD 1091-2(PR 10065) | CD | Chicago Concert | EAN 090204933662
Gene Ammons-James Moody Quintet
Just In Time | Work Song | Have You Met Miss Jones | Jim-Jam-Jug | I'll Close My Eyes | C Jam Blues | Yardbird Suite
Live at The North Park Hotel,Chicago,Ill, rec. 21.11.1971
Ammons,Gene (ts) | Moody,James (ts) | Christian,Jodie (p) | Eaton,Cleveland (b) | Thompson,Marshall (dr)

OJCCD 1092-2(RS 9481) | CD | Byrd Song | EAN 090204933679
Charlie Byrd Trio With Voices
I Left My Heart In San Francisco | Who Will Buy | The Night We Called It A Day | Wildcat | Felicidade | Action Painting | This Can't Be Love | Let's Do It | God Bless The Child | My Favorite Things | Swing '59 | Born To Be Blue
Los Angeles,CA, rec. 1965
Byrd,Charlie (g) | Betts,Keter (b) | Reichenbach,Bill (dr) | unkn. (voices)

OJCCD 1093-2(RS 9498) | CD | Solo Flight | EAN 025218709323
Charlie Byrd
Am I Blue | Easy Living | House Of The Rising Sun | Mood Indigo | You Took Advantage Of Me | Lil' Darlin' | Tears | Nocturne | Satin Doll | Blue Mobile | Sweet Sue Just You
details unknown, rec. 1965
Byrd,Charlie (g-solo)

OJCCD 1094-2(JLP 931) | CD | Tough Tenors | EAN 025218709422
Johnny Griffin-Eddie Lockjaw Davis Quintet
Tickle Toe | Save Your Love For Me | Twins | Funky Fluke | Imagination | Soft Winds
NYC, rec. 4.& 10.11.1960
Griffin,Johnny (ts) | Davis,Eddie 'Lockjaw' (ts) | Mance,Junior[Julian C.] (p) | Gales,Larry (b) | Riley,Ben (dr)

OJCCD 1095-2(C- 14054-2) | CD | Sail Away | EAN 025218709521
Tom Harrell Quintet
Sail Away
NYC, rec. 22./23.3.1989
Harrell,Tom (tp,fl-h) | Abercrombie,John (g,g-synth) | Williams,James (p) | Drummond,Ray (b) | Nussbaum,Adam (dr)
Tom Harrell Sextet
Dream In June | Visions Of Gaudi
Harrell,Tom (tp,fl-h) | Liebman,Dave (ss) | Abercrombie,John (g,g-synth) | Williams,James (p) | Drummond,Ray (b) | Nussbaum,Adam (dr)
Tom Harrell Quintet
Eons | Glass Mystery | Buffalo Wings | It Always Is | April Mist
Harrell,Tom (tp,fl-h) | Lovano,Joe (ts) | Williams,James (p) | Drummond,Ray (b) | Nussbaum,Adam (dr)
Dancing Trees
Harrell,Tom (tp,fl-h) | Pyle,Cheryl (fl) | Abercrombie,John (g) | Williams,James (p)
Hope St.
Harrell,Tom (tp,fl-h) | Liebman,Dave (ss) | Abercrombie,John (g) | Williams,James (p) | Drummond,Ray (b) | Nussbaum,Adam (dr)

OJCCD 1097-2(P-7367) | CD | Morning Mist | EAN 025218709729
Chuck Wayne Trio
Goodbye | See Saw | Lil' Darlin' | I'll Get Along | Things Ain't What They Used To Be | Shalimar | Someone To Watch Over Me | The Song Is You | Alone At Last | Lovely
Englewood Cliffs,NJ, rec. 8.12.1964
Wayne,Chuck (g,bj) | Williams,Joe (b) | Bedford,Ronnie (dr)

OJCCD 110-2(R 9480) | CD | The Village Caller
Johnny Lytle Quintet
The Village Caller | On Green Dolphin Street | Can't Help Lovin' Dat Man | Pedro Strodder | Kevin Devin | You Don't Know What Love Is | Unhappy Happy Soul | In My Solitude
NYC, rec. 18.9.1963
Lytle,Johnny (vib) | Harris,Milt (org) | Cranshaw,Bob (b) | Hinnant,Peppy (dr) | Rodriguez,Willie (perc)

OJCCD 125-2 | CD | MJQ
OJC 125(P 7059) | LP | MJQ
Modern Jazz Quartet
All The Things You Are | La Ronde | Vendome | Rose Of The Rio Grande
NYC, rec. 22.12.1952
MJQ (Modern Jazz Quartet) | Jackson,Milt (vib) | Lewis,John (p) | Heath,Percy (b) | Clarke,Kenny (dr)
Milt Jackson Quintet
Opus De Funk | I've Lost Your Love | Buhaina | Soma
NYC, rec. 16.6.1954
Jackson,Milt (vib) | Boozier,Henry (tp) | Silver,Horace (p) | Heath,Percy (b) | Clarke,Kenny (dr)

OJCCD 127-2 | CD | Tenor Conclave
OJC 127(P 7074) | LP | Tenor Conclave
Prestige All Stars
Just You Just Me | Tenor Conclave | How Deep Is The Ocean | Bob's Boys
NYC, rec. 7.9.1956
Prestige All Stars | Mobley,Hank (ts) | Cohn,Al (ts) | Sims,Zoot (ts) | Coltrane,John (ts) | Garland,Red (p) | Chambers,Paul (b) | Taylor,Arthur 'Art' (dr)

OJCCD 130-2(P 7125) | CD | Soprano Sax
OJC 130(P 7125) | LP | Soprano Sax
Steve Lacy Quartet
Day Dream | Alone Together | Work | Rockin' In Rhythm | Little Girl Your Daddy Is Calling You | Easy To Love
NYC, rec. 1.11.1957
Lacy,Steve (ss) | Kelly,Wynton (p) | Neidlinger,Buell (b) | Charles,Dennis (dr)

OJCCD 135-2 | CD | At Town Hall
OJC 135(RLP 1138) | LP | At Town Hall
Thelonious Monk And His Orchestra
Thelonious | Friday The 13th | Monk's Mood | Little Rootie Tootie | Off Minor | Crepescule With Nellie
Town Hall,NYC, rec. 28.2.1959
Monk,Thelonious (p) | Byrd,Donald (tp) | Bert,Eddie (tb) | Northern,Bob (fr-h) | McAllister,Jay (tuba) | Woods,Phil (as) | Rouse,Charlie (ts) | Adams,Pepper (bs) | Jones,Sam (b) | Taylor,Arthur 'Art' (dr)

OJCCD 139-2(R 9362) | CD | Groove Yard
Montgomery Brothers
Back To Back | If I Should Lose You | Groove Yard | Delirium | Just For Now | Doogie | Heart Strings | Remember
NYC, rec. 3.1.1961
Montgomery Brothers,The | Montgomery,Buddy (vib,p) | Montgomery,Wes (g) | Montgomery,Monk (b) | Thomas,Bobby (dr)

OJCCD 141-2(R 9395) | CD | RAH
OJC 141(R 9395) | LP | RAH
Mar Murphy With The Ernie Wilkins Orchestra
Angel Eyes | On Green Dolphin Street | Stoppin' The Clock | Spring Can Really Hang You Up The Most | No Tears For Me | Out Of This World | Milestones | My Favorite Things | Doodlin' | Lil' Darlin' | Twisted
NYC, rec. September/October 1961
Murphy,Mark (voc) | prob.personal: | Terry,Clark (tp) | Mitchell,Blue (tp) | Wilder,Joe (tp) | Glow,Bernie (tp) | Royal,Ernie (tp) | Cleveland,Jimmy (tb) | Green,Urbie (tb) | Liston,Melba (tb) | Kelly,Wynton or Bill Evans (p) | Galbraith,Barry or Sam Herman (g) | Duvivier,George or Art Davis (b) | Cobb,Jimmy (dr) | Wilkins,Ernie (arr,ld)

OJCCD 144-2 | CD | Portrait Of Wes
OJC 144(RLP 9492) | LP | Portrait Of Wes
Wes Montgomery Trio
Freddie Freeloader | Lolita | Movin' Along | Dangerous | Yesterday's Child | Moanin'
NYC, rec. 10.10.1963
Montgomery,Wes (g) | Rhyne,Melvin (org) | Brown,George (dr)

OJCCD 150-2 | CD | Reunion
OJC 150(F 3268) | LP | Reunion
Dave Brubeck Quintet
Chorale | Prelude | Divertimento | Shouts | Leo's Place | Darien Mode | Pieta | Strollin'
San Francisco,CA, rec. February 1957
Brubeck,Dave (p) | Desmond,Paul (as) | Van Kriedt,Dave (ts) | Bates,Norman (b) | Morello,Joe (dr)

OJCCD 152-2 | CD | Vol.1:The West Coast Sound
OJC 152(C 3507) | LP | Vol.1:The West Coast Sound
Shelly Manne And His Men
Grasshopper | Summer Night | Spring Is Here | You're Getting To Be A Habit With Me
Los Angeles,CA, rec. 13.9.1955
Manne,Shelly (dr) | Enevoldsen,Bob (v-tb) | Maini,Joe (as) | Holman,Bill (ts) | Giuffre,Jimmy (bs) | Freeman,Russ (p) | Pena,Ralph (b)

OJCCD 153-2 | CD | Easy Like
Barney Kessel Quintet
Vicky's Dream | Just Squeeze Me(But Don't Tease Me) | Bernardo | Tenderly
Los Angeles,CA, rec. 14.11.1953
Kessel,Barney (g) | Shank,Bud (fl,as) | Ross,Arnold (p) | Babasin,Harry (b) | Manne,Shelly (dr)
Lullaby Of Birdland | What Is There To Say | Salute To Charlie Christian | I Let A Song Go Out Of My Heart
Los Angeles,CA, rec. 19.12.1953
Kessel,Barney (g) | Shank,Bud (fl,as) | Ross,Arnold (p) | Babasin,Harry (b) | Manne,Shelly (dr)

OJCCD 154-2(C 3520) | CD | Oboe/Flute
Howard Rumsey's Lighthouse All-Stars
Albatros | Aquarium | Bag's Groove | Happy Town | A Night In Tunisia | Hermosa Summer | Still Life | Warm Winds
Los Angeles,CA, rec. 25./26.2.1954
Rumsey,Howard (b) | Cooper,Bob (engl-h,oboe) | Shank,Bud (fl,alto-fl) | Williamson,Claude (p) | Roach,Max (dr)
A Bit Of Basie | Blue Sands | Waikikian | Swing House
Los Angeles,CA, rec. 25.9.1956
Rumsey,Howard (b) | Cooper,Bob (engl-h,oboe) | Collette,Buddy (fl,alto-fl) | Clark,Sonny (p) | Levey,Stan (dr)

OJCCD 165-2 | CD | Four!!
OJC 165(C 7553) | LP | Four!!
Hampton Hawes Quartet
Yardbird Suite | There'll Never Be Another You | Bow Jest | Sweet Sue Just You | Love Is Just Around The Corner | Like Someone In Love | Up Blues
Los Angeles,CA, rec. 27.1.1958
Hawes,Hampton (p) | Kessel,Barney (g) | Mitchell,Red (b) | Manne,Shelly (dr)

OJCCD 169-2 | CD | Gettin' Together
OJC 169(C 7573) | LP | Gettin' Together
Art Pepper Quartet
Wy Are We Afraid | Softly As In A Morning Sunrise | Diane | Gettin' Together
Los Angeles,CA, rec. 29.2.1960
Pepper,Art (as,ts) | Kelly,Wynton (p) | Chambers,Paul (b) | Cobb,Jimmy (dr)
Art Pepper Quintet
Whims Of Chambers | Bijoy The Poodle | Rhythm-A-Ning
Pepper,Art (as,ts) | Candoli,Conte (tp) | Kelly,Wynton (p) | Chambers,Paul (b) | Cobb,Jimmy (dr)

OJCCD 1820-2(R 12-287) | CD | Jazz Sahara
Ahmed Abdul-Malik's Middle-Eastern Music
Ya Annas(Oh, People) | Isma'a(Listen) | El Haris(Anxious) | Farah' Alaiyna(Joy Upon Us)
NYC, rec. October 1958
Abdul-Malik,Ahmed (b,oud) | Griffin,Johnny (ts) | Karacand,Naim (v) | Ghanaim,Jack (kanoon) | Hamway,Mike (darabeka) | Abdurrahman,Bilal (duf,tambourine) | Harewood,Al (dr)

OJCCD 185-2(SV 2019) | CD | Good 'N' Groovy
Joe Newman Quintet
A.M. Romp | Lil' Darlin' | Mo-Lasses | To Rigmor | Just Squeeze Me(But Don't Tease Me) | Loop-D-Loop
Englewood Cliffs,NJ, rec. 17.3.1961
Newman,Joe (tp) | Foster,Frank (ts) | Flanagan,Tommy (p) | Jones,Eddie (b) | English,Bill (dr)

OJCCD 186-2(P 7004) | CD | Subconcious-Lee
Lenny Tristano Quintet
Subconscious-Lee | Tautology | Progression | Retrospection
NYC, rec. 11.1.1949
Tristano,Lennie (p) | Konitz,Lee (as) | Bauer,Billy (g) | Fishkin,Arnold (b) | Manne,Shelly (dr)
Lenny Tristano Quartet
Judy
Tristano,Lennie (p) | Konitz,Lee (as) | Bauer,Billy (g) | Fishkin,Arnold (b)
Lee Konitz Quintet
Marshmallow | Fishin' Around
NYC, rec. 28.6.1949
Konitz,Lee (as) | Marsh,Warne (ts) | Mosca,Sal (p) | Fishkin,Arnold (b) | Best,Denzil (dr)
Tautology | Sound Lee
NYC, rec. 27.9.1949
Konitz,Lee (as) | Marsh,Warne (ts) | Mosca,Sal (p) | Fishkin,Arnold (b) | Morton,Jeff (dr)
Ice Cream Konitz | Palo Alto
NYC, rec. 7.4.1950
Konitz,Lee (as) | Mosca,Sal (p) | Bauer,Billy (g) | Fishkin,Arnold (b) | Morton,Jeff (dr)
Lee Konitz Quartet
You Go To My Head
Konitz,Lee (as) | Bauer,Billy (g) | Fishkin,Arnold (b) | Morton,Jeff (dr)
Lee Konitz-Billy Bauer Duo
Rebecca
Konitz,Lee (as) | Bauer,Billy (g)

OJCCD 1884-2(RLP 221) | CD | Jazz By Gee!
Matthew Gee All-Stars
Out Of Nowhere | I'll Remember April | Joram | Sweet Georgia Brown | Lover Man(Oh,Where Can You Be?)
NYC, rec. 22.8.1956
Gee,Matthew (tb) | Henry,Ernie (as) | Knight,Joe (p) | Ware,Wilbur (b) | Taylor,Arthur 'Art' (dr)
Gee! | Kingston Lounge | The Boys From Brooklyn
NYC, rec. 19.7.1956
Gee,Matthew (tb) | Dorham,Kenny (tp) | Foster,Frank (ts) | Payne,Cecil (bs) | Knight,Joe (p) | Simmons,John (b) | Taylor,Arthur 'Art' (dr)

OJCCD 189-2 | CD | Traning In
OJC 189(P 7123) | LP | Traning In
John Coltrane With The Red Garland Trio
You Leave Me Breathless | Bass Blues | Soft Lights And Sweet Music | Traneing In | Slow Dance
NYC, rec. 23.8.1957
Coltrane,John (ts) | Garland,Red (p) | Chambers,Paul (b) | Taylor,Arthur 'Art' (dr)

OJCCD 1928-2(CPST 556) | CD | Juanita Hall Sings The Blues
Juanita Hall With The Claude Hopkins All Stars
Hold That Train | You've Been A Good Old Wagon(Daddy But You Done Broke Down) | After You've Gone | Nobody Wants You When You're Down And Out | I Don't Want It Second Hand | A Good Man Is Hard To Find | Baby Won't You Please Come Home | Gulf Coast Blues | I Ain't Gonna Play No Second Fiddle | Downhearted Blues | Gimme A Pigfoot | Lovin' Sam(The Sheik Of Alabam')
NYC, rec. 1958
Hall,Juanita (voc) | Hopkins,Claude (p,arr) | Cheatham,Doc (tp) | Bailey,Buster (cl) | Hawkins,Coleman (ts) | Duvivier,George (b) | Crawford,James 'Jimmy' (dr)

OJCCD 1929-2(SPL 1118) | CD | Al Haig Trio And Sextets
Al Haig Sextet
Skull Buster | Ante Room | Poop Deck | Pennies From Heaven
NYC, rec. 12.5.1949
Haig,Al (p) | Getz,Stan (ts) | Raney,Jimmy (g) | Ramey,Gene (b) | Perry,Charlie (dr) | Vidal,Carlos (congas)
Al Haig Sextet(Quintet)
Sugar Hill | Five Star | It's The Talk Of The Town | In A Pinch
NYC

Haig,Al (p) | Gray,Wardell (ts) | Raney,Jimmy (g) | Potter,Tommy (b) | Perry,Charlie (dr) | Swope,Terry (voc)

Al Haig Trio

Just One Of Those Things | Yardbird Suite | Taboo | Mighty Like A Rose | 'S Wonderful | Just You Just Me | The Moon Was Yellow | Round About Midnight

NYC, rec. 13.3.1954

Haig,Al (p) | Crow,Bill (b) | Abrams,Lee (dr)

OJCCD 1930-2 | CD | The Birdlanders Vol.1

Milt Jackson Septet

Jay Jay's Blues | I'll Remember April | Out Of Nowhere | If I Had You

NYC, rec. 7.3.1954

Johnson,J.J. (tb) | Winding,Kai (tb) | Cohn,Al (ts) | Jackson,Milt (vib) | Renaud,Henri (p) | Heath,Percy (b) | Smith,Charlie (dr)

Milt Jackson Sextet

Jerry's Old Man | There's No You | Lullaby Of The Leaves | Back Home Again In Indiana

Johnson,J.J. (tb) | Winding,Kai (tb) | Jackson,Milt (vib,p) | Renaud,Henri (p) | Heath,Percy (b) | Smith,Charlie (dr)

Duke Jordan Trio

Just One Of Those Things | Embraceable You | Minor Escamp(aka Jordu) | Scotch Blues | Confirmation

NYC, rec. 28.1.1954

Jordan,Duke (p) | Ramey,Gene (b) | Abrams,Lee (dr)

OJCCD 1931-2 | CD | The Birdlanders Vol.2

Oscar Pettiford Sextet

East Lag | Marcel The Furrier | Rhumblues | Stardust | Ondine | Burt's Pad

NYC, rec. 13.3.1954

Pettiford,Oscar (cello,b) | Winding,Kai (tb) | Cohn,Al (ts) | Farlow,Tal (g) | Renaud,Henri (p) | Roach,Max (dr)

Al Cohn Quartet

You Stepped Out Of A Dream | Lazy Things | Ny's Idea | Once In A While | Ny's Idea(alt.take)

NYC, rec. 5.3.1954

Cohn,Al (ts) | Renaud,Henri (p) | Ramey,Gene (b) | Roach,Max (dr)

OJCCD 1932-2(ES 548) | CD | Charlie Christian-Jazz Immortal/Dizzy Gillespie 1944

Charlie Christian All Stars

Swing To Bop

Live at Minton's Play House,NYC, rec. 12.5.1941

Christian,Charlie (g) | Guy,Joe (tp) | Monk,Thelonious (p) | Fenton,Nick (b) | Clarke,Kenny (dr)

Stompin' At The Savoy

Christian,Charlie (g) | unkn. (tp) | unkn. (ts) | Monk,Thelonious (p) | Fenton,Nick (b) | Clarke,Kenny (dr)

Up On Teddy's Hill

Live at Minton's Play House,NYC, rec. May 1941

Christian,Charlie (g) | Guy,Joe (tp) | Byas,Don (ts) | unkn. (p,b,dr)

Down On Teddy's Hill

Live at Clark Monroe's Uptown House, rec. 6.5.1941

Christian,Charlie (g) | Page,Oran 'Hot Lips' (tp) | Guy,Joe (tp) | Coulson,Victor (tp) | Williams,Rudy (as) | Byas,Don prob. (ts) | Scott,Kermit (ts) | Tinney,Allen (p) | Ebenezer,Paul (b) | Miller,Taps (dr)

Guy's Got To Go

Christian,Charlie (g) | Page,Oran 'Hot Lips' (tp) | Guy,Joe (tp) | Coulson,Victor (tp) | Williams,Rudy (as) | Byas,Don prob. (ts) | Scott,Kermit (ts) | Tinney,Allen (p) | Ebenezer,Paul (b) | unkn. (dr)

Lips Flips | Stardust(1) | Kerouac | Stardust(2)

Live at Clark Monroe's Uptown House, rec. 7.5.1941

Gillespie,Dizzy (tp) | Byas,Don (ts) | Kersey,Kenny (p) | House Band | details unknown

OJCCD 1933-2(C 3518) | CD | Lennie Niehaus Vol.1:The Quintets

Lennie Niehaus Quintet

Prime Ribs | Inside Out | I'll Take Romance | Bottoms Up

Los Angeles,CA, rec. 2.7.1954

Niehaus,Lennie (as) | Montrose,Jack (ts) | Gordon,Bob (bs) | Budwig,Monty (b) | Manne,Shelly (dr)

I Remember You | Whose Blues | You Stepped Out Of A Dream | Day By Day

Los Angeles,CA, rec. 9.7.1954

Niehaus,Lennie (as) | Montrose,Jack (ts) | Gordon,Bob (bs) | Budwig,Monty (b) | Manne,Shelly (dr)

Poinciana | I Should Care | I Can't Believe That You're In Love With Me | Happy Times

Los Angeles,CA, rec. 20.1.1956

Niehaus,Lennie (as) | Williamson,Stu (tp,v-tb) | Hawes,Hampton (p) | Mitchell,Red (b) | Manne,Shelly (dr)

OJCCD 1934-2(S 7597) | CD | Lookin' Good

Joe Gordon Quintet

Terra Firma Irma | A Song For Richard | Non-Viennese Waltz Blues | You're The Only Girl In The Next World For Me | Co-Op Blues | Marina | Heleen | Diminishing

Los Angeles,CA, rec. 11./12.& 18.7.1961

Gordon,Joe (tp) | Woods,Jimmy (as) | Wittington,Dick (p) | Bond,Jimmy (b) | Turner,Milton (dr)

OJCCD 1936-2(P 7096) | CD | Tuba Sounds

Ray Draper Sextet

Terry Anne | You're My Thrill | Pivot | Jackie's Dolly | Mimmi's Interlude | House Of Davis

Hackensack,NJ, rec. 15.3.1957

Draper,Ray (tuba) | Young,Webster (tp) | McLean,Jackie (as) | Waldron,Mal (p) | DeBrest,Jimmy 'Spanky' (b) | Dixon,Ben (dr)

OJCCD 1937-2(P 7108) | CD | The Prestige Jazz Quartet

The Prestige Jazz Quartet

Take Three Parts Jazz | Meta-Waltz | Dear Elaine | Friday The 13th

Hackensack,NJ, rec. 22.6.1957

Prestige Jazz Quartet,The | Charles,Teddy (vib) | Waldron,Mal (p) | Farmer,Addison (b) | Segal,Jerry (dr)

OJCCD 1938-2(P7401) | CD | Jay Hawk Talk

Carmel Jones Quintet

Jay Hawk Talk | What Is This Thing Called Love | Just In Time | Dance Of The Night Child | Beepdurple

NYC, rec. 8.5.1965

Jones,Carmell (tp) | Heath,Jimmy (ts) | Harris,Barry (p) | Tucker,George (b) | Humphries,Roger (dr)

Carmel Jones Quartet

Willow Weep For Me

Jones,Carmell (tp) | Harris,Barry (p) | Tucker,George (b) | Humphries,Roger (dr)

OJCCD 1939-2(P 7729) | CD | Dedication!

Duke Pearson Sextet

Minor Mishap | Number Five(aka Miss Bertha D.Blues) | The Nearness Of You | Apothegm | Lex | Blues For Alvina | Time After Time

NYC, rec. 2.8.1961

Pearson,Duke (p) | Hubbard,Freddie (tp) | Wilson,Willie (tb) | Adams,Pepper (bs) | Howard,Thomas (b) | Humphries,Lex (dr)

OJCCD 1940-(RLP 238) | CD | A Grand Night For Swinging

Mundell Lowe Quartet

It's A Grand Night For Swingin' | Easy To Love | It Could Happen To You | Crazy Rhythm

NYC, rec. 7.3.1957

Lowe,Mundell (g) | Taylor,Billy (p) | Grinage,Les (b) | Thigpen,Ed (dr)

Mundell Lowe Quintet

Blues Before Freud | Love Me Or Leave Me | You Turned The Tables On Me

NYC, rec. 10.4.1957

Lowe,Mundell (g) | Quill,Gene (as) | Taylor,Billy (p) | Grinage,Les (b) | Thigpen,Ed (dr)

OJCCD 1941-2(RLP 9437) | CD | Grab This!

Johnny Griffin Quintet

Grab This! | 63rd Street Theme | Don't Get Around Much Anymore | Offering Time | These Foolish Things Remind Me On You | Cherry Float

Los Angeles,CA, rec. 28.7.1962

Griffin,Johnny (ts) | Pass,Joe (g) | Bryant,Paul (org) | Bond,Jimmy (b) | Sides,Douglas 'Doug' (dr)

OJCCD 1942-2(NJ 8305) | CD | Curtis Fuller And Hampton Hawes With French Horns

Curtis Fuller And Hampton Hawes With French Horns

Ronnie's Tune | Roc And Troll | A-Drift | Five Spot | No Crooks

NYC, rec. 18.5.1957

Fuller,Curtis (tb) | Hawes,Hampton (p) | Watkins,Julius (fr-h) | Amram,David (fr-h) | Shihab,Sahib (as) | Farmer,Addison (b) | Segal,Jerry (dr)

Curtis Fuller And Teddy Charles With French Horns

Lyriste

Fuller,Curtis (tb) | Charles,Teddy (p) | Watkins,Julius (fr-h) | Amram,David (fr-h) | Shihab,Sahib (as) | Farmer,Addison (b) | Segal,Jerry (dr)

OJCCD 1943-2(F 3243) | CD | This Is Lucy Reed

Lucy Reed With Orchestra

There He Goes | Love For Sale | A Trout No Doubt | No Moon At All

NYC, rec. January 1957

Reed,Lucy (voc) | Cleveland,Jimmy (tb) | Mitchell,Tom (b-tb) | Penque,Romeo (engl-h,alto-fl) | Kurtzer,Dave (bassoon) | Lookofsky,Harry (tenor-v) | Evans,Gil (p) | Pemberton,Bill (b) | Russell,George (dr)

In The Wee Small Hours Of The Morning | Born To Blow The Blues | This Is New

Reed,Lucy (voc) | Farmer,Art (tp) | Penque,Romeo (engl-h,fl) | Schlinger,Sol (b-cl,bs) | Galbraith,Barry (g) | Abney,Don (p) | Hinton,Milt (b) | Russell,George (dr)

Lucy Reed With The Eddie Higgins Trio

Easy Come Easy Go | Little Boy Blue | You Don't Know What Love Is

Reed,Lucy (voc) | Higgins,Eddie (p) | Rammer,Verne (b) | Gaeto,William 'Billy' (dr)

Lucy Reed With The Eddie Higgins Quartet

Lucky To Be Me

Reed,Lucy (voc) | Higgins,Eddie (p) | Gray,John (g) | Rammer,Verne (b) | Gaeto,William 'Billy' (dr)

St.Louis Blues

Reed,Lucy (voc) | Higgins,Eddie (p) | Soderblom,Ken 'Kenny' (cl) | Rammer,Verne (b) | Gaeto,William 'Billy' (dr)

OJCCD 1944-2(C 3524) | CD | Lennie Niehaus Vol.5:The Sextet

Lennie Niehaus Sextet

Thou Swell | I Wished On The Moon | Knee Deep | Fond Memories | Take It From Me | Belle Of The Ball | As Long As I Live | Ill Wind(You're Blowin' Me No Good) | Three Of A Kind | Elbow Room

Los Angeles,CA, rec. 9./11.&12.1.1956

Niehaus,Lennie (as) | Williamson,Stu (tp,v-tb) | Perkins,Bill (fl,ts) | Giuffre,Jimmy (bs) | Clark,Buddy (b) | Manne,Shelly (dr)

OJCCD 1945-2(S 7610) | CD | The Cry

Prince Lasha Quintet

Congo Call | Green And Gold | Ghost Of The Past | Red's Mood | Juanita

Los Angeles,CA, rec. 21.11.1962

Lasha,Prince (fl) | Simmons,Sonny (as) | Peacock,Gary (b) | Proctor,Mark (b) | Stone,Gene (dr)

Prince Lasha Quartet

Bojangles | Lost Generations | A Y

Lasha,Prince (fl) | Simmons,Sonny (as) | Peacock,Gary (b) | Stone,Gene (dr)

OJCCD 1946-2(PR 7550) | CD | Sunshine Of My Soul

Jaki Byard Trio

Sunshine | Cast Away | Chandra | St.Louis Blues | Diane's Melody | Trendsition Zildjian

NYC, rec. 31.10.1967

Byard,Jaki (p,g) | Izenzon,David (b) | Jones,Elvin (dr,tympani)

OJCCD 1947-2(PR 7743) | CD | McPherson's Mood

Charles McPherson Quartet

Explorations | McPherson's Mood | Opalescence | My Cherie Amour | Mish-Mash-Bash | I Get A Kick Out Of You

NYC, rec. 23.12.1969

McPherson,Charles (as) | Harris,Barry (p) | Williams,Buster (b) | Brooks,Roy (dr)

OJCCD 1948-2(JLP 9355) | CD | Gemini

Les Spann Quintet

Smile | It Might As Well Be Spring | Blues For Gemini | Afterthought

NYC, rec. 8.12.1960

Spann,Les (fl) | Watkins,Julius (fr-h) | Flanagan,Tommy (p) | Jones,Sam (b) | Heath,Albert 'Tootie' (dr)

Con Alma | Q's Dues Blues | Stockholm Sweetnin' | There Is No Greater Love

NYC, rec. 16.12.1960

Spann,Les (g) | Watkins,Julius (fr-h) | Flanagan,Tommy (p) | Jones,Sam (b) | Hayes,Louis (dr)

OJCCD 1949-2(JLP 9455) | CD | All Members

Don Sleet Quintet

Brooklyn Bridge | Secret Love | Softly As In A Morning Sunrise | Fast Company | But Beautiful | All Members | The Hearing

NYC, rec. 16.3.1961

Sleet,Don (tp) | Heath,Jimmy (ts) | Kelly,Wynton (p) | Carter,Ron (b) | Cobb,Jimmy (dr)

OJCCD 1950-2(RLP 1186) | CD | The Texas Twister

Don Wilkerson Quartet

Easy To Love | Where Or When

San Francisco,CA, rec. 19./20.5.1960

Wilkerson,Don (ts) | Harris,Barry (p) | Jones,Sam (b) | Higgins,Billy (dr)

Don Wilkerson Quintet

The Twister | Jelly Roll | Morning Coffee | Idiom | Media

Wilkerson,Don (ts) | Adderley,Nat (co) | Harris,Barry (p) | Jones,Sam (b) | Higgins,Billy (dr)

OJCCD 1951-2(RLP 9360) | CD | It's Time For Dave Pike

Dave Pike Quartet

Cheryl | On Green Dolphin Street | It's Time | Hot House | Forward | Solar | Tendin' To Business

NYC, rec. 30.1./1.2.1961

Pike,Dave (vib) | Harris,Barry (p) | Workman,Reggie (b) | Higgins,Billy (dr)

Dave Pike

Little Girl Blue

Pike,Dave (vib-solo)

OJCCD 195-2(P 7513) | CD | El Hombre

Pat Martino Sextet

Waltz For Geri | O Amor En Paz(Once I Loved) | El Hombre | Cisco | One For Rose | A Blues For Mickey-O | Just Friends

Englewood Cliffs,NJ, rec. 1.5.1967

Martino,Pat (g) | Turner,Danny (fl) | Pitts,Tudy (org) | Fine,Mitch (dr) | Johnson,Abdu (conga) | Abderson,Vance (bongo)

OJCCD 1952-2(RLP 9420) | CD | The Kerry Dancers

Johnny Griffin Quartet

Black Is The Color Of My True Love's Hair | Oh Now I See | Hush-A-Bye

NYC, rec. 21.12.1961

Griffin,Johnny (ts) | Harris,Barry (p) | Carter,Ron (b) | Riley,Ben (dr)

25 1-2 Daze | Green Grow The Rushes | Ballad For Monsieur

NYC, rec. 5.1.1962

Griffin,Johnny (ts) | Harris,Barry (p) | Carter,Ron (b) | Riley,Ben (dr)

The Kerry Dancers | The Londonderry Air

NYC, rec. 29.1.1962

Griffin,Johnny (ts) | Harris,Barry (p) | Carter,Ron (b) | Riley,Ben (dr)

OJCCD 1954-2(S 7612) | CD | Conflict | EAN 090204922482

Jimmy Woods Sextet

Conflict | Coming Home | Aim | Pazmuerte | Conflict(alt.take)

Los Angeles,CA, rec. 25.3.1963

Woods,Jimmy (as) | Jones,Carmell (tp) | Land,Harold (ts) | Hill,Andrew (p) | Tucker,George (b) | Jones,Elvin (dr)

Apart Together | Look To Your Heart | Aim(alt.take) | Look To Your Heart(alt.take)

Los Angeles,CA, rec. 26.3.1963

Woods,Jimmy (as) | Jones,Carmell (tp) | Land,Harold (ts) | Hill,Andrew (p) | Tucker,George (b) | Jones,Elvin (dr)

OJCCD 1955-2(RS 9471) | CD | The Dynamic Sound Patterns Of The Rod Levitt Orchestra | EAN 090204922499

Rod Levitt Orchestra

Holler | Ah! Spain | Jelly Man | Upper Bay | El General | His Master's Voice

NYC, rec. July 1963

Renn,Buzz (fl,cl,as) | Ericson,Rolf (tp) | Renn,Buzz (cl,as) | Marge,George (piccolo,cl,engl-h,ts) | Allen,Gene (b-cl,bs) | Johnson,Sy (p) | Beal,John (b) | Bedford,Ronnie (dr)

OJCCD 1956-2(S 7591) | CD | Folk Jazz U.S.A. | EAN 090204922505

Bill Smith Quartet

Nobody Knows The Trouble I've Seen | Wayfaring Stranger | Three Blind Mice | Black Is The Color Of My True Love's Hair | Reuben, Reuben | Nobody Knows The Trouble I've Seen(alt.take) | Reuben, Reuben(alt.take)

Los Angeles,CA, rec. 16.2.1959

Smith,Bill (cl) | Hall,Jim (g) | Budwig,Monty (b) | Manne,Shelly (dr)

A-Roving | Greensleeves | John Henry | Go Down Moses | Blow That Man Down

Los Angeles,CA, rec. 24.11.1959

Smith,Bill (cl) | Hall,Jim (g) | Budwig,Monty (b) | Manne,Shelly (dr)

OJCCD 196-2(NJ 8210) | CD | We Three

OJC 196(NJ 8210) | LP | We Three

Roy Haynes Trio

Sneakin' Around | Reflection | Sugar Ray | Our Delight | Solitaire | After Hours

NYC, rec. 14.11.1958

Haynes,Roy (dr) | Newborn Jr.,Phineas (p) | Chambers,Paul (b)

OJCCD 199-2 | CD | Forest Fire

OJC 199(NJ 8250) | LP | Forest Fire

Jimmy Forrest Quartet

Remember | Dexter's Deck | Jim's Jam | Bag's Groove | When Your Lover Has Gone | Help

Englewood Cliffs,NJ, rec. 9.8.1960

Forrest,Jimmy (ts) | Young,Larry (org) | Schwartz,Thornel (g) | Smith,Jimmie (dr)

OJCCD 201-2(DEB 7) | CD | Introducing Paul Bley

Paul Bley Trio

Opus 1 | Opus 1(alt.take) | Teapot Walin' - (Teapot) Walin' | Like Someone In Love | Spontaneous Combustion | Split Kick | I Can't Get Started | Santa Claus Is Coming To Town | The Theme | This Time The Dream's On Me | Zootcase

NYC, rec. 30.11.1953

Bley,Paul (p) | Mingus,Charles (b) | Blakey,Art (dr)

OJCCD 203-2 | CD | Gettin' Together

OJC 203(JLP 936) | LP | Gettin' Together

Paul Gonsalves Quintet

Hard Groove | I Surrender Dear | I Cover The Waterfront | Walkin' | Yesterdays | J And B Blues | Low Gravy | Gettin' Together

NYC, rec. 20.12.1960

Gonsalves,Paul (ts) | Adderley,Nat (tp) | Kelly,Wynton (p) | Jones,Sam (b) | Cobb,Jimmy (dr)

OJCCD 205-2 | CD | It's Magic

Abbey Lincoln With The Benny Golson Septet

Just For Me | An Occasional Man | Music Maestro Please

NYC, rec. August 1958

Lincoln,Abbey (voc) | Golson,Benny (ts,arr) | Dorham,Kenny (tp) | Fuller,Curtis (tb) | Richardson,Jerome (fl,bs) | Kelly,Wynton (p) | Chambers,Paul (b) | Jones,Philly Joe (dr)

Abbey Lincoln With The Benny Golson Quintet

Ain't Nobody's Bizness If I Do | Exactly Like You

Lincoln,Abbey (voc) | Golson,Benny (ts,arr) | Dorham,Kenny (tp) | Kelly,Wynton (p) | Chambers,Paul (b) | Jones,Philly Joe (dr)

It's Magic | Out Of The Past | Little Niles

Lincoln,Abbey (voc) | Golson,Benny (ts,arr) | Farmer,Art (tp) | Kelly,Wynton (p) | Jones,Sam (b) | Jones,Philly Joe (dr)

Abbey Lincoln With The Benny Golson Septet

I Am In Love | Love

Lincoln,Abbey (voc) | Golson,Benny (ts,arr) | Farmer,Art (tp) | Fuller,Curtis (tb) | Shihab,Sahib (fl,bs) | Kelly,Wynton (p) | Jones,Sam (b) | Jones,Philly Joe (dr)

OJCCD 211-2(P 7060) | CD | Jammin' With Gene

OJC 211(P 7060) | LP | Jammin' With Gene

Gene Ammons And His All Stars

Jammin' With Gene | We'll Be Together Again | Not Really The Blues

NYC, rec. 13.7.1956

Ammons,Gene (ts) | Byrd,Donald (tp) | McLean,Jackie (as) | Waldron,Mal (p) | Watkins,Doug (b) | Taylor,Arthur 'Art' (dr)

OJCCD 212-2(P 7070) | CD | Mating Call

OJC 212(P 7070) | LP | Mating Call

John Coltrane-Tadd Dameron Quartet

Mating Call | Soultrane | Gnid | Super Jet | On A Misty Night | Romas

rec. 30.11.1956

Coltrane,John (ts) | Simmons,John (b) | Jones,Philly Joe (dr)

OJCCD 214-2 | CD | Sonny Rollins Plays For Bird

OJC 214(P 7095) | LP | Sonny Rollins Plays For Bird

Sonny Rollins Quintet

Bird Medley: | I Remember You- | My Melancholy Baby- | Old Folks- | They Can't Take That Away From Me- | Just Friends- | My Little Suede Shoes- | Star Eyes- | Kids Know | I've Grown Accustomed To Her Face

rec. 5.10.1966

Rollins,Sonny (ts) | Dorham,Kenny (tp) | Legge,Wade (p) | Morrow,George (b) | Roach,Max (dr)

OJCCD 218-2(P 7154) | CD | Jaws

Eddie Lockjaw Davis Quartet

I Let A Song Go Out Of My Heart | I'll Never Be The Same | You Stepped Out Of A Dream | Old Devil Moon | Too Close For Comfort | Body And Soul | But Not For Me | Tangerine

Hackensack,NJ, rec. 12.9.1958

Davis,Eddie 'Lockjaw' (ts) | Scott,Shirley (org) | Duvivier,George (b) | Edgehill,Arthur (dr)

OJCCD 221-2(P 7194) | CD | Something Nice

Etta Jones And Her Quartet

Easy Living | Canadian Sunset

NYC, rec. 16.9.1960

Jones,Etta (voc) | Winchester,Lem (vib) | Wyands,Richard (p) | Duvivier,George (b) | Haynes,Roy (dr)

Etta Jones With Her Trio

That's All There Is To That | I Only Have Eyes For You | Almost Like Being In Love

Jones,Etta (voc) | Wyands,Richard (p) | Duvivier,George (b) | Haynes,Roy (dr)

Etta Jones And Her Quartet

And Maybe You'll Be There | My Heart Tells Me | Till There Was You | Love Is The Thing | Fools Rush In | Trough A Long And Sleepless Night

NYC, rec. 30.3.1961

Jones,Etta (voc) | Neely,Jimmy (p) | Richardson,Wally (g) | Mulia,Michael (b) | Lawless,Rudy (dr)

OJCCD 222-2(P 7199) | CD | The Honeydripper

Jack McDuff Quartet

Whap! | I Want A Little Girl | The Honeydripper | Dink's Blues | Mr.Lucky | Blues And Tonic

Englewood Cliffs,NJ, rec. 3.2.1961

McDuff,Brother Jack (org) | Forrest,Jimmy (ts) | Green,Grant (g) | Dixon,Ben (dr)

OJCCD 223-2(P 7547) | CD | Strings!

OJC 223(P 7547) | LP | Strings!

Pat Martino Quintet

Querido | Lean Years | Mom | Minority

NYC, rec. 2.10.1967

Martino,Pat (g) | Farrell,Joe (fl,ts) | Walton,Cedar (p) | Tucker,Ben (b) | Perkins,Walter (dr)

Pat Martino Septet

Strings

Martino,Pat (g) | Farrell,Joe (fl,ts) | Walton,Cedar (p) | Tucker,Ben (b) | Perkins,Walter (dr) | Appleton,Ray (perc) | Levine,Dave (perc)

OJCCD 225-2(SV 2005) | CD | Coleman Hawkins All Stars

Coleman Hawkins All Stars

You Blew Out The Flame | I'm Beginning To See The Light | More Bounce To The Vonce | Cool Blues | Some Streching

Englewood Cliffs,NJ, rec. 8.1.1960
Hawkins,Coleman (ts) | Thomas,Joe (tp) | Dickenson,Vic (tb) | Flanagan,Tommy (p) | Marshall,Wendell (b) | Johnson,Osie (dr,tambourine)

OJCCD 226-2(NJ 8220) | CD | Groovin'
OJC 226(NJ 8220) | LP | Groovin'
Benny Golson Quintet
Drum Boogie | Yesterdays | I Didn't Know | My Blue House | The Broilers
NYC, rec. 28./29.8.1959
Golson,Benny (ts) | Fuller,Curtis (tb) | Bryant,Ray (p) | Chambers,Paul (b) | Blakey,Art (dr)

OJCCD 227-2(NJ 8224) | CD | Oliver Nelson Feat. Kenny Dorham
OJC 227(NJ 8224) | LP | Oliver Nelson Feat. Kenny Dorham
Oliver Nelson Quintet
Jams And Jellies | Ostinato | Passion Flower | Booze Baby Blues | Don't Stand Up | What's New?
NYC, rec. 30.10.1959
Nelson,Oliver (ts) | Dorham,Kenny (tp) | Bryant,Ray (p) | Marshall,Wendell (b) | Taylor,Arthur 'Art' (dr)

OJCCD 237-2 | CD | Right Now
OJC 237(F 6017) | LP | Right Now
Charles Mingus Quartet
Meditation On A Pair Of Wire Cutters
Jazz Workshop,San Francisco,CA, rec. 2./3.6.1964
Mingus,Charles (b) | Jordan,Clifford (ts) | Getz,Jane (p) | Richmond,Dannie (dr)
Charles Mingus Quintet
New Fables
Mingus,Charles (b) | Handy,John (as) | Jordan,Clifford (ts) | Getz,Jane (p) | Richmond,Dannie (dr)

OJCCD 238-2 | CD | Barney Kessel Plays Standards
Barney Kessel Quintet
Slow Boat To China | Speak Low | A Foggy Day(In London Town) | Prelude To A Kiss
Los Angeles,CA, rec. 4.6.1954
Kessel,Barney (g) | Cooper,Bob (ts,oboe) | Williamson,Claude (p) | Budwig,Monty (b) | Manne,Shelly (dr)
Our Love Is Here To Stay | How Long Has This Been Going On | 64 Bars On Wilshire Boulevard | Barney's Blues
Los Angeles,CA, rec. 1.7.1954
Kessel,Barney (g) | Cooper,Bob (ts,oboe) | Williamson,Claude (p) | Budwig,Monty (b) | Manne,Shelly (dr)

OJCCD 242-2(P 7026) | CD | Zoot Sims Quartets
Zoot Sims Quartet
My Silent Love | Jane-O | Dancing In The Dark | Memories Of You
NYC, rec. 16.9.1950
Sims,Zoot (ts) | Lewis,John (p) | Russell,Curly (b) | Lamond,Don (dr)
Trotting | Trotting(alt.take 1) | Trotting(alt.take 2) | It Had To Be You | I Wonder Who | Zoot Swings The Blues(take 1) | Zoot Swings The Blues(take 2) | East Of The Sun West Of The Moon
NYC, rec. 14.8.1951
Sims,Zoot (ts) | Biss,Harry (p) | Lombardi,Clyde (b) | Blakey,Art (dr)

OJCCD 246-2 | CD | Standard Coltrane
OJC 246(P 7243) | LP | Standard Coltrane
John Coltrane Quintet
Don't Take Your Love From Me | I'll Get By(As Long As I Have You) | Spring Is Here | Invitation
NYC, rec. 11.7.1958
Coltrane,John (ts) | Harden,Wilbur (tp) | Garland,Red (p) | Chambers,Paul (b) | Cobb,Jimmy (dr)

OJCCD 253-2(NJ 8253) | CD | A Long Drink Of The Blues
Jackie McLean Quartet
Embraceable You | I Cover The Waterfront | These Foolish Things Remind Me On You
NYC, rec. 15.2.1957
McLean,Jackie (as) | Waldron,Mal (p) | Phipps,Arthur (b) | Taylor,Arthur 'Art' (dr)
Jackie McLean Sextet
A Long Drink Of The Blues(take 1) | A Long Drink Of The Blues(take 2)
NYC, rec. 30.8.1957
McLean,Jackie (as,ts) | Young,Webster (tp) | Fuller,Curtis (tb) | Coggins,Gil (p) | Chambers,Paul (b) | Hayes,Louis (dr)

OJCCD 254-2 | CD | Thelonious Himself
OJC 254(R 12- 235) | LP | Thelonious Himself
Thelonious Monk
April In Paris | I Don't Stand A Ghost Of A Chance With You | Functional | I'm Getting Sentimental Over You | I Should Care | Round About Midnight | All Alone
NYC, rec. 12.4.1957
Monk,Thelonious (p-solo)
Thelonious Monk Quartet
Monk's Mood
NYC, rec. 16.4.1957
Monk,Thelonious (p) | Coltrane,John (ts) | Ware,Wilbur (b) | Wilson,Shadow (dr)

OJCCD 255-2(R 285) | CD | Branching Out
Nat Adderley Quintet(incl.The Three Sounds)
Sister Caroline | Well You Needn't | Branching Out | I Never Knew | Warm Blue Stream
NYC, rec. September 1958
Adderley,Nat (co) | Griffin,Johnny (ts) | Three Sounds,The | Harris,Gene (p) | Simpkins,Andrew (b) | Dowdy,Bill (dr)
Nat Adderley With The Three Sounds
Don't Get Around Much Anymore | I've Got Plenty Of Nothin'
Adderley,Nat (co) | Three Sounds,The | Harris,Gene (p) | Simpkins,Andrew (b) | Dowdy,Bill (dr)

OJCCD 261-2 | CD | Boss Guitar
OJC 261(RLP 9459) | LP | Boss Guitar
Wes Montgomery Trio
Besame Mucho | Dearly Beloved | Days Of Wine And Roses | The Trick Bag | Canadian Sunset | Fried Pies | The Breeze And I | For Heaven's Sake
NYC, rec. 22.4.1963
Montgomery,Wes (g) | Rhyne,Melvin (org) | Cobb,Jimmy (dr)

OJCCD 271-2(F 3202) | CD | Mambo With Tjader
OJC 271(F 3202) | LP | Mambo With Tjader
Cal Tjader's Modern Mambo Quintet(Sextet)
Chloe | Lucero | Sonny Boy | Mamblues | Midnight Sun | This Can't Be Love | I'll Remember April | Dearly Beloved | Tenderly
San Francisco,CA, rec. September 1954
Tjader,Cal (vib,timbales,voc) | Duran,Manuel (p) | Duran,Carlos (b) | Rosalies,Edward (perc) | Verlardi,Edward (perc) | Verlardi,Bernardo (perc)

OJCCD 274-2(F 3221) | CD | Tjader Plays Mambo | EAN 090204942565
Cal Tjader Quintet
Out Of Nowhere | The Lady Is A Tramp | Have You Met Miss Jones | East Of The Sun West Of The Moon
San Francisco,CA, rec. 11.9.1954
Tjader,Cal (vib,cencero) | Duran,Manuel (p,claves) | Duran,Carlos (b) | Velarde,Byardo (timbales,cencero,congas) | Miranda,Luis (congas)
Cal Tjader's Orchestra
Fascinating Rhythm | It Ain't Necessarily So | Mambo Macumba | I Concentrate On You
San Francisco,CA, rec. 21.9.1954
Tjader,Cal (vib,cencero) | Collins,Dick (tp) | Porcino,Al (tp) | Walp,Charlie (tp) | Howell,John (tp) | Duran,Manuel (p,claves) | Duran,Carlos (b) | Velarde,Byardo (timbales,cencero,congas) | Miranda,Luis (congas)
Cal Tjader Quintet
Yesterdays | Guarachi Guaro | For Heaven's Sake | Bei Mir Bist Du Schön
San Francisco,CA, rec. 21.2.1956
Tjader,Cal (vib,cencero) | Duran,Manuel (p,claves) | Duran,Carlos (b) | Velarde,Byardo (timbales,cencero,congas) | Rosales,Edgard (congas,maracas)

OJCCD 281-2 | CD | Sabroso
OJC 281(F 8058) | LP | Sabroso
Mongo Santamaria And His Band
Que Maravilloso | En La Felicidad | Pachanga Pa'ti | Tuli Bamba | Mambo Cuco | El Bote | Pito Pito | Guaguanco Mania | Ja Ja-Ja | Tula Hula | Dimelo | A La Luna | Para Ti
San Francisco,CA, rec. ca.1960
Santamaria,Mongo (perc,congas,bongos) | Valizan,Louis (tp) | Cabuto,Marcus (tp) | Lozano,Rolando (fl) | Silva,Jose (ts,v) | Legarreta,Felix (v) | Hernandez,Rene (p) | Venegas,Victor (b) | Bobo,Willie (timbales) | Velarde,Byardo (perc,voc) | Escovedo,Pete (perc,voc) | Calzado,Rudi (voc)

OJCCD 294-2 | CD | Hawk Eyes
Coleman Hawkins Sextet
Stealin' The Bean | Through For The Night | La Rosita | Hawk Eyes | C'Mon In
NYC, rec. 3.4.1959
Hawkins,Coleman (ts) | Shavers,Charlie (tp) | Bryant,Ray (p) | Grimes,Tiny (g) | Duvivier,George (b) | Johnson,Osie (dr)

OJCCD 295-2 | CD | Red In Bluesville
Red Garland Trio
Trouble In Mind | He's A Real Gone Guy | See See Rider | St.Louis Blues | M Squad | That's Your Red Wagon
NYC, rec. 17.4.1959
Garland,Red (p) | Jones,Sam (b) | Taylor,Arthur 'Art' (dr)

OJCCD 299-2(P 7623) | CD | Tower Of Power
OJC 299(P 7623) | LP | Tower Of Power
Dexter Gordon Quintet
Montmartre
NYC, rec. 2.4.1969
Gordon,Dexter (ts) | Moody,James (ts) | Harris,Barry (p) | Williams,Buster (b) | Heath,Albert 'Tootie' (dr)
Dexter Gordon Quartet
Those Were The Days | Stanley The Steamer | The Rainbow People
NYC, rec. 4.4.1969
Gordon,Dexter (ts) | Harris,Barry (p) | Williams,Buster (b) | Heath,Albert 'Tootie' (dr)

OJCCD 305-2 | CD | At The Blackhawk
OJC 305(R 12-323) | LP | At The Blackhawk
Thelonious Monk Quartet Plus Two
Let's Call This | Four In One | I'm Getting Sentimental Over You | Worry Later | Round About Midnight | Epistrophy
Live at The Black Hawk,San Francisco,CA, rec. 29.4.1960
Monk,Thelonious (p) | Gordon,Joe (tp) | Rouse,Charlie (ts) | Land,Harold (ts) | Ore,John (b) | Higgins,Billy (dr)

OJCCD 308-2 | CD | Interplay
OJC 308(RLP 9445) | LP | Interplay
Bill Evans Quintet
Interplay | You And The Night And The Music | When You Wish Upon A Star | I'll Never Smile Again | You Go To My Head | Wrap Your Troubles In Dreams
NYC, rec. 1.7.1962
Evans,Bill (p) | Hubbard,Freddie (tp) | Hall,Jim (g) | Heath,Percy (b) | Jones,Philly Joe (dr)

OJCCD 309-2 | CD | At The Village Gate
OJC 309(RLP 9495) | LP | At The Village Gate
Milt Jackson Quintet
Bags Of Blues | Little Girl Blue | Gemini | Gerri's Blues | Time After Time | Ignunt Oil
Live at The 'Village Gate',NYC, rec. December 1963
Jackson,Milt (vib) | Heath,Jimmy (ts) | Jones,Hank (p) | Cranshaw,Bob (b) | Heath,Albert 'Tootie' (dr)

OJCCD 310-2 | CD | Take Twelve
Lee Morgan Quintet
Raggedy Ann | A Waltz For Fran | Lee-Sure Time | Little Spain | Take Twelve | Second's Best
NYC, rec. 24.1.1962
Morgan,Lee (tp) | Jordan,Clifford (ts) | Harris,Barry (p) | Cranshaw,Bob (b) | Hayes,Louis (dr)

OJCCD 313-2 | CD | Song For My Lady
OJC 313 (M 9044) | LP | Song For My Lady
McCoy Tyner
A Silent Tear
rec. 27.11.1972
Tyner,McCoy (p-solo)
McCoy Tyner Quartet
The Night Has A Thousand Eyes | Song For My Lady
Tyner,McCoy (p) | Fortune,Sonny (fl,ss,as) | Hill,Calvin (b) | Mouzon,Alphonse (dr)
McCoy Tyner Septet
Native Song | Essence
rec. 6.9.1972
Tyner,McCoy (p) | Fortune,Sonny (fl,ss,as) | Hill,Calvin (b) | Mouzon,Alphonse (dr) | Tolliver,Charles (fl-h) | White,Michael (v) | M'tume,James[Forman] (perc,congas)

OJCCD 315-2 | CD | Butterfly Dreams
OJC 315 (M 9052) | LP | Butterfly Dreams
Flora Purim And Her Sextet
Dr.Jive(part 1) | Butterfly Dreams | Dindi | Summer Night | Love Reborn | Moon Dreams | Dr.Jive(part 2) | Light As A Feather
rec. December 1973
Purim,Flora (voc) | Henderson,Joe (fl,ts) | Duke,George (p,el-p,synth,clavinet) | Amaro,David (g,el-g) | Hood,Ernie (zither) | Clarke,Stanley (b,el-b) | Moreira,Airto (dr,perc)

OJCCD 317-2 | CD | To Swing Or Not To Swing
OJC 317(C 3513) | LP | To Swing Or Not To Swing
Barney Kessel And His Septet
Louisiana | Back Home Again In Indiana | Moten Swing | 12th Street Rag
Los Angeles,CA, rec. 26.6.1955
Kessel,Barney (g) | Edison,Harry 'Sweets' (tp) | Auld,Georgie (ts) | Rowles,Jimmy (p) | Hendrickson,Al (g) | Mitchell,Red (b) | Cottler,Irv (dr)
Barney Kessel And His Quintet
Begin The Blues | Embraceable You | Midnight Sun | Don't Blame Me
Kessel,Barney (g) | Rowles,Jimmy (p) | Hendrickson,Al (g) | Mitchell,Red (b) | Cottler,Irv (dr)

OJCCD 318-2 | CD | The Trio Vol.2
Hampton Hawes Trio
Just Squeeze Me(But Don't Tease Me)
Los Angeles,CA, rec. 28.6.1955
Hawes,Hampton (p) | Mitchell,Red (b) | Thompson,Chuck (dr)
Stella By Starlight | You And The Night And The Music | Yesterdays | Steeplechase | Autumn In New York | Section Blues
Los Angeles,CA, rec. 5.12.1955
Hawes,Hampton (p) | Mitchell,Red (b) | Thompson,Chuck (dr)
Blues For Jacques | Round About Midnight
Los Angeles,CA, rec. 25.1.1956
Hawes,Hampton (p) | Mitchell,Red (b) | Thompson,Chuck (dr)

OJCCD 320-2(C 7519) | CD | More Swinging Sounds
Shelly Manne And His Men
Quartet
Los Angeles,CA, rec. 16.7.1956
Manne,Shelly (dr) | Williamson,Stu (v-tb) | Mariano,Charlie (as) | Freeman,Russ (p) | Vinnegar,Leroy (b)
Moose The Mooche | Pint Of Blues | Tommy Hawk | The Wind
Los Angeles,CA, rec. 15./16.8.1956
Manne,Shelly (dr) | Williamson,Stu (tp) | Mariano,Charlie (as) | Freeman,Russ (p) | Vinnegar,Leroy (b)

OJCCD 322-2(P 7171) | CD | Jaws In Orbit
OJC 322(P 7171) | LP | Jaws In Orbit
Eddie Lockjaw Davis Quintet
Intermission Riff | Can't Get Out Of This Mood | Foxy | Our Delight | Bahia | Bingo Domingo
Hackensack,NJ, rec. 1.5.1959
Davis,Eddie 'Lockjaw' (ts) | Pulliam,Steve (tb) | Scott,Shirley (org) | Duvivier,George (b) | Edgehill,Arthur (dr)

OJCCD 323-2 | CD | Smooth Sailing
OJC 323(P 7184) | LP | Smooth Sailing
Arnett Cobb Quintet
Charmaine | Cobb's Mob | I Don't Stand A Ghost Of A Chance With You | Let's Split | Blues Around Dusk | Smooth Sailing | Blues In My Heart
Hackensack,NJ, rec. 27.2.1959
Cobb,Arnett (ts) | Cooper,Frank 'Buster' (tb) | Mitchell,Austin (org) | Duvivier,George (b) | Johnson,Osie (dr)

OJCCD 324-2(P 7185) | CD | Tough 'Duff
OJC 324(P 7185) | LP | Tough 'Duff
Jack McDuff Quartet
Smooth Sailing | Mean To Me | Tippin' In | Yeah Baby | Autumn Leaves | Tough 'Duff
Englewood Cliffs,NJ, rec. 12.7.1960
McDuff,Brother Jack (org) | Forrest,Jimmy (ts) | Winchester,Lem (vib) | Elliott,Bill (dr)

OJCCD 326-2(P 7228) | CD | Brother Jack Meets The Boss
Jack McDuff Quartet With Gene Ammons
Watch Out | Mellow Gravy | Christopher Columbus | Buzzin' Around | Mr.Clean
Englewood Cliffs,NJ, rec. 23.1.1962
McDuff,Brother Jack (org) | Ammons,Gene (ts) | Vick,Harold (ts) | Diehl,Eddie (g) | Dukes,Joe (dr)
Jack McDuff Quartet
Strollin'
McDuff,Brother Jack (org) | Vick,Harold (ts) | Diehl,Eddie (g) | Dukes,Joe (dr)

OJCCD 328-2(P 7338) | CD | Blue Flames
Shirley Scott Quartet
The Funky Fox | Hip Knees An' Legs | Five Spot After Dark | Grand Street | Flamingo
Englewood Cliffs,NJ, rec. 31.3.1964
Scott,Shirley (org) | Turrentine,Stanley (ts) | Cranshaw,Bob (b) | Finch,Otis 'Candy' (dr)

OJCCD 331-2(P 7626) | CD | Rusty Bryant Returns
OJC 331(P 7626) | LP | Rusty Bryant Returns
Rusty Bryant Quintet
Streak O' Clean | Night Flight | The Cat | All Day Long | Ready Rusty | Zoo Boogaloo
Englewood Cliffs,NJ, rec. 17.2.1969
Bryant,Rusty (as,varitone-as) | Phillips,Sonny (org) | Green,Grant (g) | Bushnell,Bob (el-b) | Lovelle,Herbie (dr)

OJCCD 335-2(P 7758) | CD | Black Talk!
OJC 335(P 7758) | LP | Black Talk!
Charles Earland Quintet
Here Comes Charlie | Black Talk | Aquarius
Englewood Cliffs,NJ, rec. 15.12.1969
Earland,Charles (org) | Jones,Virgil (tp) | Person,Houston (ts) | Sparks,Melvin (g) | Muhammad,Idris[Leo Morris] (dr)
Charles Earland Sextet
More Today Then Yesterday | The Mighty Burner
Earland,Charles (org) | Jones,Virgil (tp) | Person,Houston (ts) | Sparks,Melvin (g) | Muhammad,Idris[Leo Morris] (dr) | Caldwell,Buddy (congas)

OJCCD 340-2 | CD | Sonny Rollins & The Contemporary Leaders
Sonny Rollins & The Contemporary Leaders
I've Told Every Little Star | Rock-A-Bye Your Baby With A Dixie Melody | How High The Moon | I've Found A New Baby | Alone Together | In The Chapel In The Moonlight | The Song Is You
rec. 20.-22.10.1958
Rollins,Sonny (ts) | Hawes,Hampton (p) | Kessel,Barney (g) | Vinnegar,Leroy (b) | Manne,Shelly (dr)
You
Rollins,Sonny (ts) | Hawes,Hampton (p) | Kessel,Barney (g) | Vinnegar,Leroy (b) | Manne,Shelly (dr) | Feldman,Victor (vib)

OJCCD 343-2 | CD | The Fox
Harold Land Quintet
The Fox | Mirror-Mind Rose | One Second Please | Sims A-Plenty | Little Chris | One Down
Los Angeles,CA, rec. August 1959
Land,Harold (ts) | Bolton,Dupree (tp) | Hope,Elmo (p) | Lewis,Herbie (b) | Butler,Frank (dr)

OJCCD 345-2 | CD | The Tokyo Concert
Bill Evans Trio
Morning Glory | Up With The Lark | Yesterday I Heard The Rain | My Romance | When Autumn Comes | T.T.T.(Twelve Tone Tune) | Hullo Bolinas | Gloria's Step | On Green Dolphin Street
Live at Yubin Chokin Hall,Tokyo,Japan, rec. 20.1.1973
Evans,Bill (p) | Gomez,Eddie (b) | Morell,Marty (dr)

OJCCD 348-2(P 7207) | CD | Sonny Boy
Sonny Rollins Quintet
The House I Live In
Hackensack,NJ, rec. 5.10.1956
Rollins,Sonny (ts) | Dorham,Kenny (tp) | Legge,Wade (p) | Morrow,George (b) | Roach,Max (dr)
Sonny Rollins Quartet
Ee-Ah | B.Quick | B.Swift | Sonny Boy
Hackensack,NJ, rec. 7.12.1956
Rollins,Sonny (ts) | Drew,Kenny (p) | Morrow,George (b) | Roach,Max (dr)

OJCCD 349-2(P 7209) | CD | High Pressure
Red Garland Quintet feat.John Coltrane
Undecided | What Is There To Say
Hackensack,NJ, rec. 15.11.1957
Garland,Red (p) | Byrd,Donald (tp) | Coltrane,John (ts) | Nasser,Jamil[George Joyner] (b) | Taylor,Arthur 'Art' (dr)
Two Bass Hit | Soft Winds | In My Solitude
Hackensack,NJ, rec. 13.12.1957
Garland,Red (p) | Byrd,Donald (tp) | Coltrane,John (ts) | Nasser,Jamil[George Joyner] (b) | Taylor,Arthur 'Art' (dr)

OJCCD 353-2 | CD | Eric Dolphy Memorial Album
OJC 353(P 7334) | LP | Eric Dolphy Memorial Album
Eric Dolphy-Booker Little Quintet
Number Eight | Booker's Waltz
rec. 16.7.1961
Dolphy,Eric (b-cl,as) | Little,Booker (tp) | Waldron,Mal (p) | Davis,Richard (b) | Blackwell,Ed (dr)

OJCCD 356-2 | CD | The Return Of Tal Farlow/1969
Tal Farlow Quartet
Straight No Chaser | Darn That Dream | Summertime | Sometime Ago | I'll Remember April | My Romance | Crazy She Calls Me
NYC, rec. 23.9.1969
Farlow,Tal (g) | Scully,John (p) | Six,Jack (b) | Dawson,Alan (dr)

OJCCD 360-2(MV 1) | CD | Prestige Moodsville Vol.1
Red Garland Trio
Stella By Starlight | I Heard You Cried Last Night | Wonder Why | Blue Room | The Red Blues
Englewood Cliffs,NJ, rec. 11.12.1959
Garland,Red (p) | Jones,Sam (b) | Taylor,Arthur 'Art' (dr)
Eddie Lockjaw Davis With The Red Garland Trio
We'll Be Together Again | Softly Baby | When Your Lover Has Gone
Davis,Eddie 'Lockjaw' (ts) | Garland,Red (p) | Jones,Sam (b) | Taylor,Arthur 'Art' (dr)

OJCCD 361-2(RLP 269) | CD | Portrait Of Cannonball
Cannonball Adderley Quintet
Minority(take 1) | Minority(take 2) | Minority(take 3) | Straight Life | Blue Funk | A Little Taste | People Will Say We're In Love | Nardis | Nardis(alt.take)
NYC, rec. 1.7.1958
Adderley,Julian \'Cannonball\' (as) | Mitchell,Blue (tp) | Evans,Bill (p) | Jones,Sam (b) | Jones,Philly Joe (dr)

OJCCD 362-2 | CD | 5 By Monk By 5
Thelonious Monk Quintet
Jackie-Ing | Straight No Chaser | Played Twice(take 1) | Played Twice(take 2) | Played Twice(take 3) | I Mean You | Ask Me Now

NYC, rec. 1./2.6.1959
Monk,Thelonious (p) | Jones,Thad (co) | Rouse,Charlie (ts) | Jones,Sam (b) | Taylor,Arthur 'Art' (dr)

OJCCD 366-2(RLP 9429) | CD | Big Bags
Milt Jackson Orchestra
Round About Midnight | Round About Midnight(alt.take) | If You Could See Me Now | The Dream Is You
NYC, rec. 19.6.1962
Jackson,Milt (vib) | Terry,Clark (tp,fl-h) | Severinsen,Doc (tp) | Burns,Dave (tp) | Cleveland,Jimmy (tb) | Liston,Melba (tb) | Ruff,Willie (fr-h) | Moody,James (fl,as) | Dorsey,George (fl,as) | Richardson,Jerome (fl,ts) | Heath,Jimmy (ts) | Houston,Tate (bs) | Jones,Hank (p) | Carter,Ron (b) | Kay,Connie (dr) | Dameron,Tadd (arr) | Wilkins,Ernie (arr)
Old Devil Moon | You'd Be So Nice To Come Home To | Later Than You Think
NYC, rec. 5.7.1962
Jackson,Milt (vib) | Adderley,Nat (co) | Terry,Clark (tp,fl-h) | Glow,Bernie (tp) | Royal,Ernie (tp) | Cleveland,Jimmy (tb) | Liston,Melba (tb) | Faulise,Paul (tb) | Richardson,Jerome (as) | Dorsey,George (as) | Moody,James (fl,ts) | Heath,Jimmy (ts) | Clarke,Arthur (bs) | Jones,Hank (p) | Carter,Ron (b) | Jones,Philly Joe (dr) | Wilkins,Ernie (arr)
Echoes | Star Eyes | Star Eyes(alt.take) | Namesake | If I Should Lose You
Jackson,Milt (vib) | Terry,Clark (tp,fl-h) | Royal,Ernie (tp) | Young,Eugene Edward (tp) | McIntosh,Tom (tb) | Liston,Melba (tb) | Ruff,Willie (fr-h) | Warren,Earl (as) | Moody,James (fl,as) | Heath,Jimmy (ts) | Richardson,Jerome (fl,ts) | Houston,Tate (bs) | Jones,Hank (p) | Carter,Ron (b) | Kay,Connie (dr) | Dameron,Tadd (arr) | Wilkins,Ernie (arr)

OJCCD 369-2 | CD | How My Heart Sings!
Bill Evans Trio
How My Heart Sings | Summertime
NYC, rec. 17.5.1962
Evans,Bill (p) | Israels,Chuck (b) | Motian,Paul (dr)
Walking Up | 34 Skidoo | Show-Type Tune
NYC, rec. 29.5.1962
Evans,Bill (p) | Israels,Chuck (b) | Motian,Paul (dr)
I Should Care | In Your Own Sweet Way | In Your Own Sweet Way(alt.take) | Everything I Love
NYC, rec. 5.6.1962
Evans,Bill (p) | Israels,Chuck (b) | Motian,Paul (dr)

OJCCD 373-2 | CD | Montreux '77
OJC 373(2308203) | LP | Montreux '77
Roy Eldridge 4
Between The Devil And The Deep Blue Sea | Gofor | I Surrender Dear | Joie De Roy | Perdido | Bye Bye Blackbird
rec. 13.7.1977
Eldridge,Roy (tp) | Peterson,Oscar (p) | Orsted-Pedersen,Niels-Henning (b) | Durham,Bobby (dr)

OJCCD 377-2 | CD | Montreux '77
OJC 377(2308207) | LP | Montreux '77
Count Basie Big Band
The Heat's On | Freckle Face | Splanky | The More I See You | A Night In Tunisia | Hittin' 12 | Bag Of Dreams | Things Ain't What They Used To Be | I Need's To Bee'd With | Lil' Darlin' | Jumpin' At The Woodside | One O'Clock Jump
rec. 15.7.1977
Basie,Count (p) | Reed,Waymon (tp) | Biviano,Lyn (tp) | Cohn[Cohen],Sonny (tp) | Mitchell,Bob (tp) | Grey,Al (tb) | Wilson,Dennis (tb) | Wanzo,Mel (tb) | Hughes,Bill (tb) | Forrest,Jimmy (ts) | Dixon,Eric (fl,ts) | Turner,Danny (as) | Plater,Bobby (as) | Fowlkes,Charlie (bs) | Green,Freddie (g) | Duke,John (b) | Miles,Butch (dr)

OJCCD 386-2(C 3504) | CD | Howard Rumsey's Lighthouse All-Stars Vol.6
Howard Rumsey's Lighthouse All-Stars
Who's Sleepy | Mad At The World | Sad Sack
Hollywood,CA, rec. 3.12.1954
Rumsey,Howard (b) | Candoli,Conte (tp) | Rosolino,Frank (tb) | Shank,Bud (fl) | Cooper,Bob (ts) | Williamson,Claude (p) | Levey,Stan (dr)
Long Ago And Far Away | Dickie's Dream
Hollywood,CA, rec. 22.2.1955
Rumsey,Howard (b) | Candoli,Conte (tp) | Williamson,Stu (v-tb) | Shank,Bud (as) | Cooper,Bob (ts) | Williamson,Claude (p) | Levey,Stan (dr)
Isn't It Romantic | East Of The Sun West Of The Moon | If I Should Lose You | Prelude To A Kiss
Hollywood,CA, rec. 1.3.1955
Rumsey,Howard (b) | Candoli,Conte (tp) | Shank,Bud (as) | Cooper,Bob (ts) | Williamson,Claude (p) | Levey,Stan (dr)

OJCCD 387-2 | CD | Intensity
Art Pepper Quartet
I Can't Believe That You're In Love With Me | I Love You | Come Rain Or Come Shine | Long Ago And Far Away | Gone With The Wind | I Wished On The Moon | Too Close For Comfort
rec. 23.& 25.11.1960
Pepper,Art (as) | Coker,Dolo (p) | Bond,Jimmy (b) | Butler,Frank (dr)
rec. 23.11.1960
Pepper,Art (as) | Coker,Dolo (p) | Bond,Jimmy (b) | Butler,Frank (dr)

OJCCD 389-2 | CD | The Way It Is
OJC 389(C 7630) | LP | The Way It Is
Art Pepper-Warne Marsh Quintet
I Can't Believe That You're In Love With Me | I Can't Believe That You're In Love With Me(alt.take) | All The Things You Are | All The Things You Are(alt.take) | What's New? | Tickle Toe
Los Angeles,CA, rec. 26.11.1956
Pepper,Art (as) | Marsh,Warne (ts) | Ball,Ronnie (p) | Tucker,Ben (b) | Frommer,Gary (dr)
Art Pepper Quartet
The Man I Love
Los Angeles,CA, rec. 19.1.1957
Pepper,Art (as) | Garland,Red (p) | Chambers,Paul (b) | Jones,Philly Joe (dr)
Autumn Leaves
Los Angeles,CA, rec. 23.11.1960
Pepper,Art (as) | Coker,Dolo (p) | Bond,Jimmy (b) | Butler,Frank (dr)
The Way You Look Tonight
Los Angeles,CA, rec. 29.2.1960
Pepper,Art (as) | Kelly,Wynton (p) | Chambers,Paul (b) | Cobb,Jimmy (dr)

OJCCD 396-2(P 7619) | CD | Body And Soul
Eddie Jefferson With The James Moody Quintet
Introduction by Ed Williams | See If You Can Git To That | Body And Soul | Mercy, Mercy, Mercy | So What | There I Go There I Go Again | Psychedelic Sally | Now's The Time | Filthy McNasty | Oh Gee
NYC, rec. 27.9.1968
Jefferson,Eddie (voc) | Moody,James (fl,ts) | Burns,Dave (tp) | Harris,Barry (p) | Davis,Steve (b) | English,Bill (dr)

OJCCD 397-2(P 7795) | CD | Desperado
Pat Martino Quartet
Dearborn Walk | Oleo | Desperado | A Portrait Of Diana | Express
Englewood Cliffs,NJ, rec. 9.3.1970
Martino,Pat (12-string-g) | Green,Eddie (el-p) | Brown,Tyrone (el-b) | Ferguson,Sherman (dr,bells)
Pat Martino Quintet
Blackjack
Martino,Pat (12-string-g) | Kloss,Eric (ss) | Green,Eddie (el-p) | Brown,Tyrone (el-b) | Ferguson,Sherman (dr,bells)

OJCCD 399-2(NJ 8218) | CD | Other Sounds
Yusef Lateef Quintet
All Alone | Anastasia | Minor Mood | Taboo | Lambert's Point | Mahaba
Hackensack,NJ, rec. 11.10.1957
Lateef,Yusef (fl,ts,argol) | Harden,Wilbur (fl-h) | Lawson,Hugh (p,turkish-finger-cymbals) | Farrow,Ernie (b,earthboard) | Jackson,Oliver (dr,earthboard)

OJCCD 401-2(RLP 12-254) | CD | Wynton Kelly-Piano
Wynton Kelly Quartet
Whisper Not | Action | Dark Eyes | Dark Eyes(alt.take)
NYC, rec. 31.1.1958
Kelly,Wynton (p) | Burrell,Kenny (g) | Chambers,Paul (b) | Jones,Philly Joe (dr)
Wynton Kelly Trio
Strong Man | Ill Wind | Don't Explain | You Can't Get Away
Kelly,Wynton (p) | Burrell,Kenny (g) | Chambers,Paul (b)

OJCCD 403-2(RLP 9373) | CD | Afro-Jaws
Eddie Lockjaw Davis Orchestra
Wild Rice | Guanco Lament | Alma Alegre(Happy Soul) | Star Eyes | Afro-Jaws
NYC, rec. 4.& 12.5.1961
Davis,Eddie 'Lockjaw' (ts) | Terry,Clark (tp) | Royal,Ernie (tp) | Sunkel,Phil (tp) | Mayers,Lloyd (p) | Gales,Larry (b) | Riley,Ben (dr) | Barretto,Ray (perc,congas,bongos,quinto)
Tin Tin Deo | Jazz-A-Samba
Davis,Eddie 'Lockjaw' (ts) | Terry,Clark (tp) | Royal,Ernie (tp) | Sunkel,Phil (tp) | Bello,John (tp) | Mayers,Lloyd (p) | Gales,Larry (b) | Riley,Ben (dr) | Barretto,Ray (perc,congas,bongos,quinto)

OJCCD 405-2 | CD | Once Upon A Summertime
OJC 405(GXY 5150) | LP | Once Upon A Summertime
Chet Baker Quintet
Tidal Breeze | Shifting Down | E.S.P. | The Song Is You | Once Upon A Summertime
rec. 20.2.1977
Baker,Chet (tp) | Herbert,Greg (ts) | Danko,Harold (p) | Carter,Ron (b) | Lewis,Mel (dr)

OJCCD 408-2 | CD | Living Legend
OJC 408(C 7633) | LP | Living Legend
Art Pepper Quartet
Ophelia | Here's That Rainy Day | What Laurie Likes | Mr.Yohe | Lost Life | Samba Mom Mom
rec. 9.8.1975
Pepper,Art (as) | Hawes,Hampton (p) | Haden,Charlie (b) | Manne,Shelly (dr)

OJCCD 411-2 | CD | No Limit
OJC 411(C 7639) | LP | No Limit
Rita-San | Ballad Of The Sad Young Men | My Laurie | Mambo De La Pinta
rec. 26.3.1977
Pepper,Art (as,ts) | Cables,George (p) | Dumas,Tony (b) | Burnett,Carl (dr)

OJCCD 412-2 | CD | Something For Lester
OJC 412(C 7641) | LP | Something For Lester
Ray Brown Trio
Ojos De Rojo | Slippery | Something On Common | Love Walked In | Georgia On My Mind | Little Girl Blue | Sister Sadie
rec. 22.-24.6.1977
Brown,Ray (b) | Walton,Cedar (p) | Jones,Elvin (dr)

OJCCD 414-2 | CD | Eric Dolphy In Europe, Vol.2
Eric Dolphy With Erik Moseholm's Trio
Don't Blame Me | Miss Ann
rec. 6.9.1961
Dolphy,Eric (fl,as) | Moseholm,Erik (b) | Axen,Bent (p) | Elniff,Jorn (dr)
The Way You Look Tonight | Laura
rec. 8.9.1961
Dolphy,Eric (fl,as) | Moseholm,Erik (b) | Axen,Bent (p) | Elniff,Jorn (dr)

OJCCD 415-2 | CD | Bahia
OJC 415(P 7353) | LP | Bahia
John Coltrane Quintet
I'm Dreamer Aren't We All | My Ideal
rec. 11.7.1958
Coltrane,John (ts) | Harden,Wilbur (tp,fl-h) | Garland,Red (p) | Chambers,Paul (b) | Cobb,Jimmy (dr)
John Coltrane Quartet
Something I Dreamed Last Night | Bahia
rec. 26.12.1958
Coltrane,John (ts) | Garland,Red (p) | Chambers,Paul (b) | Taylor,Arthur 'Art' (dr)
John Coltrane Trio
Goldsboro Express
Coltrane,John (ts) | Chambers,Paul (b) | Taylor,Arthur 'Art' (dr)

OJCCD 416-2 | CD | Eric Dolphy In Europe, Vol.3
Eric Dolphy With Erik Moseholm's Trio
When Lights Are Low
rec. 6.9.1961
Dolphy,Eric (b-cl,as) | Moseholm,Erik (b) | Axen,Bent (p) | Elniff,Jorn (dr)
Woody'n You | In The Blues (1-2-3)
rec. 8.9.1961
Dolphy,Eric (b-cl,as) | Moseholm,Erik (b) | Axen,Bent (p) | Elniff,Jorn (dr)

OJCCD 418-2(SV 2001) | CD | Coleman Hawkins With The Red Garland Trio
Coleman Hawkins With The Red Garland Trio
It's A Blue World | I Want To Be Loved | Red Beans | Bean's Blues | Blues For Ron
Hackensack,NJ, rec. 12.8.1959
Hawkins,Coleman (ts) | Garland,Red (p) | Watkins,Doug (b) | Wright,Charles 'Specs' (dr)

OJCCD 424-2 | CD | Together Again!
OJC 424(C 7588) | LP | Together Again!
Teddy Edwards-Howard McGhee Quintet
Together Again | You Stepped Out Of A Dream | Up There | Perhaps | Misty | Sandy
Los Angeles,CA, rec. 15./17.5.1961
Edwards,Teddy (ts) | McGhee,Howard (tp) | Newborn Jr.,Phineas (p) | Brown,Ray (b) | Thigpen,Ed (dr)

OJCCD 428-2(PR 7139) | CD | Manteca
Red Garland Trio With Ray Barretto
Manteca | 'S Wonderful | Oh! Lady Be Good | Exactly Like You | Mort's Report | Portrait Of Jenny
Hackensack,NJ, rec. 11.4.1958
Garland,Red (p) | Chambers,Paul (b) | Taylor,Arthur 'Art' (dr) | Barretto,Ray (congas)

OJCCD 430-2(P 7511) | CD | This Is Criss
Sonny Criss Quartet
Black Coffee | Days Of Wine And Roses | When Sunny Gets Blue | Greasy | Sunrise Sunset | Steve's Blues | Skylark | Love For Sale
Englewood Cliffs,NJ, rec. 21.10.1966
Criss,Sonny (as) | Davis,Walter (p) | Chambers,Paul (b) | Dawson,Alan (dr)

OJCCD 432-2 | CD | Where
Ron Carter Quintet
Rally | Bass Duet | Softly As In A Morning Sunrise | Where | Yes Indeed | Saucer Eyes
rec. 20.6.1961
Carter,Ron (cello,b) | Dolphy,Eric (fl,b-cl,as) | Waldron,Mal (p) | Duvivier,George (b) | Persip,Charles (dr)

OJCCD 433-2(RLP 12-292) | CD | Chet Baker Introduces Johnny Pace
Johnny Pace With The Chet Baker Quintet
All Or Nothing At All | Crazy She Calls Me | It Might As Well Be Spring
NYC, rec. 23.12.1958
Pace,Johnny (voc) | Baker,Chet (tp) | Mann,Herbie (fl) | Berle,Joe (p) | Burke,Jimmie (b) | Jones,Philly Joe (dr)
The Way You Look Tonight | When The Sun Comes Out | What Is There To Say | Everything I've Got Belongs To You
NYC, rec. 29.12.1958
Pace,Johnny (voc) | Baker,Chet (tp) | Mann,Herbie (fl) | Berle,Joe (p) | Burke,Jimmie (b) | Thigpen,Ed (dr)
This Is Always | We Could Make Such Beautiful Music Together | Yesterdays
NYC, rec. 30.12.1958
Pace,Johnny (voc) | Baker,Chet (tp) | Mann,Herbie (fl) | Berle,Joe (p) | Burke,Jimmie (b) | Thigpen,Ed (dr)

OJCCD 436-2(F 8096) | CD | Jazz At The Blackhawk
Cal Tjader Quartet
Bill B. | Lands End | I'll Remember April | Blues In The Night | Thinking Of You, MJQ | I've Never Been In Love Before | Two For Blues Suite | When The Sun Comes Out | Lover Come Back To Me
Live at The Black Hawk,San Francisco,CA, rec. 20.1.1957
Tjader,Cal (vib) | Guaraldi,Vince (p) | Wright,Eugene 'Gene' (b) | Torre,Al (dr)

OJCCD 437-2(F 8089) | CD | Cast Your Fate To The Wind
Vince Guaraldi Trio
Samba De Orfeu | Manha De Carnaval(Morning Of The Carnival) | O Nosso Amor | Generique | Cast Your Fate To The Wind | Moon River | Alma-Ville | Since I Fell For You
San Francisco,CA, rec. 1962
Guaraldi,Vince (p) | Budwig,Monty (b) | Bailey,Colin (dr)

OJCCD 441-2 | CD | Tivoli Garders, Copenhagen, Denmark
OJC 441(2308220) | LP | Tivoli Garders, Copenhagen, Denmark
Stephane Grappelli Trio
It's Only A Paper Moon | Time After Time | Let's Fall In Love | Crazy Rhythm | How Deep Is The Ocean | I'll Remember April | I Can't Get Started | I Get A Kick Out Of You
rec. 6.7.1979
Grappelli,Stephane (v) | Pass,Joe (g) | Orsted-Pedersen,Niels-Henning (b)

OJCCD 457-2 | CD | Local Color
OJC 457(P 7121) | LP | Local Color
Mose Allison Trio
Carnival | Parchman Farm | Crepuscular Air | Mojo Woman | Town | Trouble In Mind | Lost Mind | I'll Never Be Free | Don't Ever Say Goodbye | Ain't You A Mess
Hackensack,NJ, rec. 8.11.1957
Allison,Mose (tp,p,voc) | Farmer,Addison (b) | Stabulas,Nick (dr)

OJCCD 458-2 | CD | Very Saxy
OJC 458(P 7167) | LP | Very Saxy
Very Saxy
Very Saxy | Lester Leaps In | Fourmost | Light And Lovely | Foot Pattin'
Hackensack,NJ, rec. 29.4.1959
Very Saxy | Davis,Eddie 'Lockjaw' (ts) | Hawkins,Coleman (ts) | Cobb,Arnett (ts) | Tate,Buddy (ts) | Scott,Shirley (org) | Duvivier,George (b) | Edgehill,Arthur (dr)

OJCCD 460-2 | CD | Cattin'
John Coltrane-Paul Quinichette Quintet
Cattin' | Anatomy | Sunday | Exactly Like You
rec. 17.5.1957
Coltrane,John (ts) | Quinichette,Paul (ts) | Waldron,Mal (p) | Euell,Julian (b) | Thigpen,Ed (dr)

OJCCD 461-2 | CD | The New Boss Guitar
George Benson With The Jack McDuff Quartet
Shadow Dancers | The Sweet Alice Blues | I Don't Know | Just Another Sunday | Will You Still Be Mine | Easy Living | Rock-A-Bye
NYC, rec. 1.5.1964
Benson,George (g) | McDuff,Brother Jack (p,org) | Holloway,Red (ts) | Boykins,Ronnie (b) | Montego Joe (dr)
My Three Sons
NYC, rec. 14.5.1954
Benson,George (g) | McDuff,Brother Jack (org) | Holloway,Red (ts) | Boykins,Ronnie (b) | Dukes,Joe (dr)

OJCCD 465-2 | CD | The Kicker
Joe Henderson Quartet
O Amor En Paz(Once I Loved)
rec. 10.8.1967
Henderson,Joe (ts) | Barron,Kenny (p) | Carter,Ron (b) | Hayes,Louis (dr)
Joe Henderson Sextet
Mamacita | The Kicker | Chelsea Bridge | Nardis | Without A Song | Mo' Joe
Henderson,Joe (ts) | Barron,Kenny (p) | Carter,Ron (b) | Hayes,Louis (dr) | Lawrence,Mike (tp) | Moncur III,Grachan (tb)

OJCCD 470-2 | CD | Intuition
OJC 470(F 9475) | LP | Intuition
Bill Evans Duo
Invitation | Blue Serge | Show-Type Tune | The Nature Of Things | Are You All The Things | A Face Without A Name | Falling Grace | Hi Lili Hi Lo
Berkeley,CA, rec. 7.-10.11.1974
Evans,Bill (p) | Gomez,Eddie (b)

OJCCD 475-2 | CD | Straight Life
OJC 475(GXY 5127) | LP | Straight Life
Art Pepper Quartet
Surf Ride | Nature Boy | Staight Life | September Song
rec. 21.9.1979
Pepper,Art (as) | Flanagan,Tommy (p) | Mitchell,Red (b) | Higgins,Billy (dr)
Art Pepper Quartet
Make A List Make A Wish
Pepper,Art (as) | Flanagan,Tommy (p) | Mitchell,Red (b) | Higgins,Billy (dr) | Nash,Kenneth (cowbell,reco-reco)

OJCCD 480-2 | CD | At Last!
Miles Davis And The Lighthouse All Stars
Infinity Promenade | A Night In Tunisia
Lighthouse,Hermosa Beach,CA, rec. 13.9.1953
Davis,Miles (tp) | Ericson,Rolf (tp) | Shank,Bud (as,bs) | Cooper,Bob (ts) | Geller,Lorraine (p) | Rumsey,Howard (b) | Roach,Max (dr)
Round About Midnight
Davis,Miles (tp) | Geller,Lorraine (p) | Rumsey,Howard (b) | Roach,Max (dr)
Max Roach
Drum Conversation
Roach,Max (dr-solo)
Chet Baker Quartet
At Last
Baker,Chet (tp) | Freeman,Russ (p) | Rumsey,Howard (b) | Roach,Max (dr)

OJCCD 481-2 | CD | Soul Junction
Red Garland Quintet
Soul Junction | Woody'n You | Birk's Works | I Got It Bad And That Ain't Good | Hallelujah
Hackensack,NJ, rec. 15.11.1957
Garland,Red (p) | Byrd,Donald (tp) | Coltrane,John (ts) | Nasser,Jamil[George Joyner] (b) | Taylor,Arthur 'Art' (dr)

OJCCD 488-2(RLP 9443) | CD | Thelonious Monk In Italy
Thelonious Monk Quartet
Jackie-Ing | Epistrophy | Body And Soul | Straight No Chaser | Bemsha Swing | San Francisco Holiday | Crepuscule With Nellie | Rhythm-A-Ning
Live at Teatro Lirico,Milano, rec. 21.4.1961
Monk,Thelonious (p) | Rouse,Charlie (ts) | Ore,John (b) | Dunlop,Frankie (dr)

OJCCD 489-2(RLP 9494) | CD | Guitar On The Go
Wes Montgomery Trio
Missile Blues
NYC, rec. 5.10.1959
Montgomery,Wes (g) | Rhyne,Melvin (org) | Parker,Paul (dr)
Fried Pies
NYC, rec. 22.4.1963
Montgomery,Wes (g) | Rhyne,Melvin (org) | Cobb,Jimmy (dr)
The Way You Look Tonight | Dreamsville | For All We Know
NYC, rec. 10.10.1963
Montgomery,Wes (g) | Rhyne,Melvin (org) | Brown,George (dr)
Geno | The Way You Look Tonight
NYC, rec. 27.11.1963
Montgomery,Wes (g) | Rhyne,Melvin (org) | Brown,George (dr)
Wes Montgomery
Unidentified Solo Guitar
NYC, rec. 10.10.1963
Montgomery,Wes (g)

OJCCD 490-2(RLP 9529) | CD | Mongo At The Village Gate
Mongo Santamaria And His Band
Introduction by 'Symphony Sid Torin' | El Toro | Fat Back | Mongo's Groove | Creole | The Jungle Bit | My Sound | The Morning After | Nothing For Nothing | Para Ti
Live at The 'Village Gate',NYC, rec. 2.9.1963
Santamaria,Mongo (congas) | Sheller,Marty (tp) | Patrick,Pat (fl,reeds) | Capers,Bob (fl,reeds) | Grant,Rodger (p) | Venegas,Victor (b) | Hernandez,Frank (dr) | Martinez,Osvaldo 'Chihuahua' (perc) | Cabrera,Julian (perc)

OJCCD 497-2 | CD | The Trumpet Kings Meet Joe Turner
Dizzy Gillespie's Trumpet Kings
Mornin', Noon And Night | I Know You Love Me Baby | 'Tain't Nobody's Bizness If I Do | T.V.Mama
rec. 19.9.1974
Turner,Big Joe (voc) | Gillespie,Dizzy (tp) | Eldridge,Roy (tp) | Edison,Harry 'Sweets' (tp) | Terry,Clark (tp) | Crayton,Connie C. (g) | Norris,Charles (b) | Robins,Jimmy (p) | Rucker,Washington (dr)

OJCCD 6004-2 | CD | Mose Allison:Greatest Hits
Mose Allison Trio
One Room Country Shack | Young Man's Blues | Blueberry Hill
Hackensack,NJ, rec. 7.3.1957
Allison,Mose (p,voc) | LaFargue,Taylor (b) | Isola,Frank (dr)
Lost Mind | Parchman Farm | Trouble In Mind
Hackensack,NJ, rec. 8.11.1957
Allison,Mose (tp,p,voc) | Farmer,Addison (b) | Stabulas,Nick (dr)
Baby Let Me Hold Your Hand | Don't Get Around Much Anymore | I Hadn't Anyone 'Till You
Hackensack,NJ, rec. 24.1.1958
Allison,Mose (p,voc) | Farmer,Addison (b) | Stabulas,Nick (dr)
I've Gotta Right To Cry
Hackensack,NJ, rec. 18.4.1958
Allison,Mose (p,voc) | Farmer,Addison (b) | Free,Ronnie (dr)
The Seventh Son | If You Live | Creek Bank
Hackensack,NJ, rec. 15.8.1958
Allison,Mose (p,voc) | Farmer,Addison (b) | Free,Ronnie (dr)
Eyesight To The Blind | Do Nothin' Till You Hear From Me | That's All Right
Hackensack,NJ, rec. 13.2.1959
Allison,Mose (p,voc) | Farmer,Addison (b) | Free,Ronnie (dr)

OJCCD 601-2 | CD | It Don't Mean A Thing If You Can't Tap Your Foot To It
OJC 601(2310909) | LP | It Don't Mean A Thing If You Can't Tap Your Foot To It
Milt Jackson-Ray Brown Quartet
Midnight Waltz | Ain't That Nothin' | Stess And Trauma | Used To Be Jackson | It Don't Mean A Thing If It Ain't Got That Swing | If I Were A Bell | Close Enough For Love
NYC, rec. July 1984
Jackson,Milt (vib) | Brown,Ray (b) | Walton,Cedar (p) | Roker,Granville 'Mickey' (dr)

OJCCD 603-2 | CD | The Trumpet Summit Meets The Oscar Peterson Big 4
OJC 603(2312114) | LP | The Trumpet Summit Meets The Oscar Peterson Big 4
The Trumpet Summit With The Oscar Peterson Big 4
Daahoud | Chicken Wings | Just Friends | The Champ
rec. 10.3.1980
Trumpet Summit | Gillespie,Dizzy (tp) | Hubbard,Freddie (tp) | Terry,Clark (tp) | Pass,Joe (g) | Peterson,Oscar (p) | Brown,Ray (b) | Durham,Bobby (dr)

OJCCD 609-2 | CD | Witch Doctor
Chet Baker And The Lighthouse All Stars
Loaded | I'll Remember April
Lighthouse,Hermosa Beach,CA, rec. 13.9.1953
Baker,Chet (tp) | Ericson,Rolf (tp) | Shank,Bud (as,bs) | Giuffre,Jimmy (ts) | Freeman,Russ (p) | Rumsey,Howard (b) | Roach,Max (dr)
Winter Wonderful
Baker,Chet (tp) | Ericson,Rolf (tp) | Shank,Bud (as,bs) | Cooper,Bob (ts) | Freeman,Russ (p) | Rumsey,Howard (b) | Roach,Max (dr)
Pirouette | Witchdoctor
Baker,Chet (tp) | Ericson,Rolf (tp) | Shank,Bud (as,bs) | Cooper,Bob (ts) | Williamson,Claude (p) | Rumsey,Howard (b) | Manne,Shelly (dr)

OJCCD 614-2(P 7731) | CD | The Blues That's Me!
Illinois Jacquet Quintet
The Blues, That's Me! | Still King | Round About Midnight | The Galloping Latin | For Once In My Life | Everyday I Have The Blues
NYC, rec. 16.9.1969
Jacquet,Illinois (ts,bassoon) | Grimes,Tiny (g) | Kelly,Wynton (p) | Williams,Buster (b) | Jackson,Oliver (dr)

OJCCD 615-2(RLP 12-273) | CD | Blue Mitchell Big 6
Blue Mitchell Sextet
Blues March | Big Six | There'll Never Be Another You | Brother 'Ball | Jamph | Sir John | Promenade
NYC, rec. 2./3.7.1958
Mitchell,Blue (tp) | Fuller,Curtis (tb) | Griffin,Johnny (ts) | Kelly,Wynton (p) | Ware,Wilbur (b) | Jones,Philly Joe (dr)

OJCCD 616-2(RLP 9440) | CD | The Outer View
George Russell Sextet
Au Privave | Zig Zag | The Outer View | The Outer View(alt.take) | D.C.Divertimento
NYC, rec. 27.8.1962
Russell,George (p) | Ellis,Don (tp) | Brown,Garnett (tb) | Plummer,Paul (ts) | Swallow,Steve (b) | LaRoca,Pete (dr)
You Are My Sunshine
Russell,George (p) | Ellis,Don (tp) | Brown,Garnett (tb) | Plummer,Paul (ts) | Swallow,Steve (b) | LaRoca,Pete (dr) | Jordan,Sheila (voc)

OJCCD 617-2 | CD | The DeJohnette Complex
Jack DeJohnette Quintet
Equipoise
NYC, rec. 26.12.1968
DeJohnette,Jack (melodica) | Maupin,Bennie (ts) | Cowell,Stanley (p) | Vitous,Miroslav (b) | Haynes,Roy (dr)
Miles' Mode | Papa-Daddy And Me
DeJohnette,Jack (melodica) | Maupin,Bennie (ts) | Cowell,Stanley (el-p) | Gomez,Eddie (b) | Haynes,Roy (dr)
Jack DeJohnette Sextet
Requiem(Number 1) | Requiem(Number 2)
DeJohnette,Jack (melodica) | Maupin,Bennie (wood-fl) | Cowell,Stanley (p) | Vitous,Miroslav (b) | Gomez,Eddie (b) | Haynes,Roy (dr,perc)
Jack DeJohnette Quartet
The Major General
NYC, rec. 27.12.1968
DeJohnette,Jack (dr) | Maupin,Bennie (ts) | Cowell,Stanley (p) | Vitous,Miroslav (b)
Mirror Image
DeJohnette,Jack (dr) | Cowell,Stanley (el-p) | Vitous,Miroslav (b) | Gomez,Eddie (b)
Brown Warm and Wintery
DeJohnette,Jack (dr) | Cowell,Stanley (el-p) | Maupin,Bennie (fl) | Gomez,Eddie (b)

OJCCD 621-2 | CD | Peg Leg
Ron Carter Group
Peg Leg
rec. 16/18./21.& 22.11.1977
Carter,Ron (piccolo-b) | Kane,Walter (fl,cl) | Dodgion,Jerry (fl) | Marge,George (fl) | Russo,Charles (cl) | Berliner,Jay (el-g) | Barron,Kenny (p) | Williams,Buster (b) | Riley,Ben (dr)
Sheila's Song
Carter,Ron (b,perc) | Dodgion,Jerry (fl) | Marge,George (fl,oboe) | Russo,Charles (cl) | Kane,Walter (bassoon) | Berliner,Jay (g) | Barron,Kenny (p) | Riley,Ben (dr,perc)
Chapter XI
Carter,Ron (piccolo-b) | Dodgion,Jerry (cl) | Marge,George (cl) | Kane,Walter (cl) | Russo,Charles (b-cl) | Barron,Kenny (p) | Williams,Buster (b) | Riley,Ben (dr)
Epistrophy
Carter,Ron (piccolo-b) | Dodgion,Jerry (fl) | Marge,George (oboe) | Kane,Walter (bassoon) | Russo,Charles (cl,b-cl) | Barron,Kenny (p) | Williams,Buster (b) | Riley,Ben (dr)
My Ship
Carter,Ron (b) | Dodgion,Jerry (alto-fl) | Marge,George (cl) | Kane,Walter (bassoon) | Russo,Charles (b-cl)
Patchouli
Carter,Ron (b) | Dodgion,Jerry (fl,alto-fl,piccolo) | Marge,George (fl,piccolo) | Kane,Walter (fl) | Russo,Charles (cl) | Berliner,Jay (g) | Barron,Kenny (p) | Riley,Ben (dr)

OJCCD 623-2 | CD | Duke Ellington And His Orchestra feat. Paul Gonsalves
Duke Ellington And His Orchestra
C Jam Blues | Take The 'A' Train | Happy-Go-Lucky Local | Jam With Sam | Caravan | Just A-Sittin' And A-Rockin' | Paris Blues | Ready Go
NYC, rec. 1.5.1962
Ellington,Duke (p) | Burrowes,Roy (tp) | Anderson,Cat (tp) | Berry,Bill (tp) | Nance,Ray (tp) | Brown,Lawrence (tb) | Cox,Leon (tb) | Connors,Chuck (tb) | Procope,Russell (as) | Hodges,Johnny (as) | Hamilton,Jimmy (cl,ts) | Gonsalves,Paul (ts) | Carney,Harry (bs) | Bell,Aaron (b) | Woodyard,Sam (dr)

OJCCD 624-2 | CD | The Intimacy Of The Blues
Duke Ellington Small Band
Combo Suite: | The Intimacy Of The Blues | Out South | Tell Me 'Bout My Baby | Kentucky Avenue,A.C. | Near North | Soul Country
NYC, rec. 15.3.1967
Ellington,Duke (p) | Anderson,Cat (tp) | Brown,Lawrence (tb) | Hodges,Johnny (as) | Gonsalves,Paul (ts) | Carney,Harry (bs) | Lamb,John (b) | Jones,Rufus (dr)
Noon Morning
Las Vegas,NV, rec. 7.1.1970
Ellington,Duke (p) | Cook,Willie (tp) | Brown,Lawrence (tb) | Gonsalves,Paul (ts) | Davis,Wild Bill (org) | Gaskin,Victor (b) | Kondziela,Paul (b) | Jones,Rufus (dr)
Rockochet
Ellington,Duke (p) | Gonsalves,Paul (ts) | Gaskin,Victor (b) | Kondziela,Paul (b) | Jones,Rufus (dr)
Tippy-Toeing Through The Jungle Garden
Cook,Willie (tp) | Brown,Lawrence (tb) | Gonsalves,Paul (ts) | Davis,Wild Bill (org) | Gaskin,Victor (b) | Kondziela,Paul (b) | Jones,Rufus (dr)
Just A-Sittin' And A-Rockin'
NYC, rec. 15.6.1970
Ellington,Duke (p) | Turney,Norris (fl) | Gonsalves,Paul (ts) | Davis,Wild Bill (org) | Benjamin,Joe (b) | Jones,Rufus (dr)
All Too Soon
Ellington,Duke (p) | Anderson,Cat (tp) | Ashby,Harold (ts) | Benjamin,Joe (b) | Jones,Rufus (dr)

OJCCD 626-2(2308229) | CD | Summertime-Digital At Montreux 1980
OJC 626(2308229) | LP | Summertime-Digital At Montreux 1980
Mongo Santamaria Group With Dizzy Gillespie And Toots Thielemans
Virtue | Afro Blue | Summertime | Mambo Mongo
Montreux,CH, rec. 19.7.1980
Santamaria,Mongo (congas,bongos) | Gillespie,Dizzy (tp) | Villariny,Tommy (tp,cow-bell) | Harris,Douglas (fl,ts) | Hoist,Allen (alto-fl,bs,cello) | Thielemans,Jean 'Toots' (harm) | Hamilton,Milton (p) | Smith,Lee (b) | Berrios,Steve (dr,timbales)

OJCCD 630-2(2310785) | CD | Agora
Paulinho Da Costa Orchestra
Simbora | Terra | Toledo Bagel | Berimbau Variations | Belisco | Ritmo Number One
Burbank,Los Angeles,CA, rec. 6.-16.8.1976
Da Costa,Paulinho (a-go-go,berimbau,cuica,pandeiro,reco-reco,surdo,tambourine) | Huffstetter,Steven (tp,fl-h) | Goe,Gene (tp,fl-h) | Rosolino,Frank (tb) | Julian,Mike (tb) | Williams,Larry (fl,sax) | Ritenour,Lee (g) | Slon,Claudio (synth,dr,perc,timbales,voc,water-dr) | Bailly,Octavio (b,voc) | Phillinganes,Gregory (p,el-p)

OJCCD 631-2(2310786) | CD | Basie Jam No. 2
Count Basie Band
Mama Don't Wear No Drawers | Doggin' Around | Kansas City Line | JJ Jump
Los Angeles,CA, rec. 6.5.1976
Basie,Count (p) | Terry,Clark (tp) | Grey,Al (tb) | Carter,Benny (as) | Davis,Eddie 'Lockjaw' (ts) | Pass,Joe (g) | Heard,John (b) | Bellson,Louie (dr)

OJCCD 642-2(F 8033) | CD | Cal Tjader's Latin Kick
Cal Tjader Sextet
Invitation | Lover Come Back To Me | September Song | Will You Still Be Mine | I Love Paris | Tropicville | Moonlight In Vermont | Bye Bye Blues | Manuel's Mambo | All The Things You Are | Blues From Havana
Los Angeles,CA, rec. 1956
Tjader,Cal (vib) | Moore,Brew (ts) | Duran,Manuel (p) | Duran,Carlos (b) | Miranda,Luis (congas) | Velarde,Byardo (timbales)

OJCCD 643-2(F 8014) | CD | Cal Tjader's Latin Concert
Cal Tjader Quintet
Viva Cepeda | Mood For Milt | The Continental | Lucero | Tu Crees Que | Mi Guaquanco | Cubano Chant | A Young Love | Theme
Live at The Black Hawk,San Francisco,CA, rec. 1958
Tjader,Cal (vib) | Guaraldi,Vince (p) | McKibbon,Al (b) | Bobo,Willie (dr,timbales) | Santamaria,Mongo (congas)

OJCCD 645-2(F 9498) | CD | The Afro-Eurasian Eclipse-A Suite In Eight Parts
Duke Ellington And His Orchestra
Afro-Eurasian Eclipse:,The | Chinoiserie | Didjeridoo | Afrique | Acht O'Clock Rock | Gong | Tang | True | Hard Way
NYC, rec. 17.2.1971
Ellington,Duke (p) | Williams,Cootie (tp) | Johnson,Money (tp) | Ellington,Mercer (tp) | Preston,Eddie (tp) | Wood,Booty (tb) | Taylor,Malcolm (tb) | Connors,Charles (b-tb) | Procope,Russell (cl,as) | Turney,Norris (fl,as cl) | Gonsalves,Paul (ts) | Ashby,Harold (ts) | Carney,Harry (bs) | Benjamin,Joe (b) | Jones,Rufus (dr)

OJCCD 646-2(F 86007) | CD | Speak, Brother, Speak
Max Roach Quartet
Speak Brother Speak | A Variation
Live at The Jazz Workshop,San Francisco,CA, rec. 27.10.1962
Roach,Max (dr) | Jordan,Clifford (ts) | Waldron,Mal (p) | Khan,Eddie (b)

OJCCD 648-2(JLP 975) | CD | In The Bag
Nat Adderley Sextet
In The Bag | Sister Wilson | R.S.V.P. | Low Brown | Mozart-In' | New Arrival | Chatterbox | The Popeye | The Gospel Truth
New Orleans,Louisiana, rec. 9.5.1962
Adderley,Nat (co) | Adderley,Julian \'Cannonball\' (as) | Perrilliat,Nat (ts) | Marsalis,Ellis (p) | Jones,Sam (b) | Black,James (dr)

OJCCD 650-2(M 9055) | CD | Echoes Of A Friend
McCoy Tyner
Naima | Promise | My Favorite Things | The Discovery | Folks
Tokyo, Japan, rec. 11.11.1972
Tyner,McCoy (p-solo)

OJCCD 651-2(P 7132) | CD | The Big Sound
Gene Ammons And His All Stars
Cheek To Cheek | Blue Hymn
Hackensack,NJ, rec. 3.1.1958
Ammons,Gene (ts) | Richardson,Jerome (fl) | Waldron,Mal (p) | Nasser,Jamil[George Joyner] (b) | Taylor,Arthur 'Art' (dr)
That's All
Ammons,Gene (ts) | Richardson,Jerome (fl) | Adams,Pepper (bs) | Waldron,Mal (p) | Nasser,Jamil[George Joyner] (b) | Taylor,Arthur 'Art' (dr)
The Real McCoy
Ammons,Gene (ts) | Richardson,Jerome (fl) | Coltrane,John (as) | Quinichette,Paul (ts) | Adams,Pepper (bs) | Waldron,Mal (p) | Nasser,Jamil[George Joyner] (b) | Taylor,Arthur 'Art' (dr)

OJCCD 654-2(P 7255) | CD | Early Stan
Jimmy Raney Quintet
Motion | Lee | Signal | Round About Midnight
NYC, rec. 23.4.1953
Getz,Stan (ts) | Faney,Jimmy (g) | Overton,Hal (p) | Mitchell,Red (b) | Isola,Frank (dr)
Terry Gibbs Septet
Michelle(part 1&2) | Michelle (alt.take 1) | Michelle (alt.take 2) | T & S | Terry's Tune | Terry's Tune(alt.take 1) | Terry's Tune(alt.take 2) | Cuddles
NYC, rec. 14.4.1949
Gibbs,Terry (vib) | Getz,Stan (ts) | Rogers,Shorty (tp) | Swope,Earl (tb) | Wallington,George (p) | Russell,Curly (b) | Wilson,Shadow (dr)

OJCCD 656-2(S 7577) | CD | At The Black Hawk Vol.1
Shelly Manne And His Men
Our Delight | Summertime | Poinciana
Live at The Black Hawk,San Francisco,CA, rec. 22.9.1959
Blue Daniel(alt.take)
Live at The Black Hawk,San Francisco,CA, rec. 23.9.1959
Blue Daniel | A Gem From Tiffany(Theme)
Live at The Black Hawk,San Francisco,CA, rec. 24.9.1959
Manne,Shelly (dr) | Gordon,Joe (tp) | Kamuca,Richie (ts) | Feldman,Victor (p) | Budwig,Monty (b)

OJCCD 657-2(S 7578) | CD | At The Black Hawk Vol.2
Step Lightly(alt.take)
Live at The Black Hawk,San Francisco,CA, rec. 22.9.1959
Step Lightly | What's New? | The Vamp's Blues | A Gem From Tiffany(Theme)
Live at The Black Hawk,San Francisco,CA, rec. 24.9.1959
Manne,Shelly (dr) | Gordon,Joe (tp) | Kamuca,Richie (ts) | Feldman,Victor (p) | Budwig,Monty (b)

OJCCD 658-2(S 7579) | CD | At The Black Hawk Vol.3
Blackhawk Blues
Live at The Black Hawk,San Francisco,CA, rec. 22.9.1959
Manne,Shelly (dr) | Gordon,Joe (tp) | Kamuca,Richie (ts) | Feldman,Victor (p) | Budwig,Monty (b)
Whisper Not
Live at The Black Hawk,San Francisco,CA, rec. 23.9.1959
Manne,Shelly (dr) | Gordon,Joe (tp) | Kamuca,Richie (ts) | Feldman,Victor (p) | Budwig,Monty (b)
I Am In Love | Whisper Not(alt.take)
Live at The Black Hawk,San Francisco,CA, rec. 24.9.1959
Manne,Shelly (dr) | Gordon,Joe (tp) | Kamuca,Richie (ts) | Feldman,Victor (p) | Budwig,Monty (b)

OJCCD 659-2(S 7580) | CD | At The Black Hawk Vol.4
A Gem From Tiffany | Cabu(alt.take)
Live at The Black Hawk,San Francisco,CA, rec. 22.9.1959
Manne,Shelly (dr) | Gordon,Joe (tp) | Kamuca,Richie (ts) | Feldman,Victor (p) | Budwig,Monty (b)
Cabu | Just Squeeze Me(But Don't Tease Me) | Nightingale
Live at The Black Hawk,San Francisco,CA, rec. 24.9.1959
Manne,Shelly (dr) | Gordon,Joe (tp) | Kamuca,Richie (ts) | Feldman,Victor (p) | Budwig,Monty (b)

OJCCD 660-2 | CD | At The Black Hawk Vol.5
How Deep Are The Roots | This Is Always
Live at The Black Hawk,San Francisco,CA, rec. 23.9.1959
Manne,Shelly (dr) | Gordon,Joe (tp) | Kamuca,Richie (ts) | Feldman,Victor (p) | Budwig,Monty (b)
A Gem From Tiffany(Theme) | Pullin' Strings
Live at The Black Hawk,San Francisco,CA, rec. 24.9.1959
Manne,Shelly (dr) | Gordon,Joe (tp) | Kamuca,Richie (ts) | Feldman,Victor (p) | Budwig,Monty (b)
Shelly Manne Trio
Wonder Why
Manne,Shelly (dr) | Feldman,Victor (p) | Budwig,Monty (b)

OJCCD 663-2(F 9416) | CD | The Raven Speaks
Woody Herman And His Orchestra
Fat Mama | Alone Again(Naturally) | Watermelon Man | It's Too Late | The Raven Speaks | Summer Of '42(The Summer Knows) | Reunion At Newport | Bill's Blues
NYC, rec. 28.-30.8.1972
Herman,Woody (cl,ss,as) | Porcino,Al (tp) | Davis,Charlie (tp) | Thomas,John (tp) | Stapleton,Bill (fl-h) | Byrne,Billy (tp) | Burgess,Bob 'Bobby' (tb) | Stepton,Rick (tb) | Garrett,Harold (b-tb) | Tiberi,Frank (fl,ts,bassoon,cowbell) | Herbert,Greg (fl,alto-fl,ts,piccolo) | Lederer,Steve (ts) | Anastas,Tom (bs) | Danko,Harold (p) | Martino,Pat (g) | Johnson,Al (dr) | LaBarbera,Joe (dr) | Pacheco,Johnny (congas)

OJCCD 664-2 | CD | Yale Concert
Duke Ellington And His Orchestra
The Little Purple Flower | Put-tin | A Chromatic Love Affair | Boola Boola | A Johnny Hodges Medley: | Warm Valley- | Drag- | Salome | Swamp Goo | Up Jump | Take The 'A' Train
Woolsey Hall,New Haven,CT, rec. 26.1.1968
Ellington,Duke (p) | Anderson,Cat (tp,fl-h) | Williams,Cootie (tp) | Ellington,Mercer (tp) | Jones,Herbie (tp) | Brown,Lawrence (tb) | Cooper,Frank 'Buster' (tb) | Connors,Chuck (tb) | Hodges,Johnny (as) | Procope,Russell (cl) | Hamilton,Jimmy (cl,ts) | Gonsalves,Paul (ts) | Carney,Harry (bs) | Castleman,Jeff (b) | Woodyard,Sam (dr)

OJCCD 665-2(M 9073) | CD | Pastels
Ron Carter With Strings
Woolaphant | Ballad | One Bass Rag | Pastels | 12 + 12
Berkeley,CA, rec. 18./19.10.1976
Carter,Ron (b,piccolo-b) | Barron,Kenny (p) | McCracken,Hugh (g,el-g,harm) | Mason,Harvey (dr) | Rubin,Nathan (v) | Baker,Virginia (v) | Kobialka,Daniel (v) | Volkert,Mark (v) | Bucky,Myra (v) | Van Valkenburgh,Emily (v) | Erickson,Ronald (v) | Ching,Fei-Pang (v) | Oakley Jr.,Roy (v) | Bauch,Arthur (viola) | DeCoteau,Denis (viola) | Yale,Daniel (viola) | Moore,Kermit (cello) | Ross,Melinda (cello) | Moore,Garfield (cello) | Allen,Sanford (v,concertmaster) | Sebesky,Don (cond,arr)

OJCCD 667-2(RLP 1131) | CD | Out Of The Blue
Blue Mitchell Quintet
Blues On My Mind | Boomerang | Sweet Cakes
NYC, rec. 5.1.1959
Mitchell,Blue (tp) | Golson,Benny (ts) | Kelly,Wynton (p) | Jones,Sam (b) | Blakey,Art (dr)
It Could Happen To You | When The Saints Go Marching In | Missing You
Mitchell,Blue (tp) | Golson,Benny (ts) | Kelly,Wynton (p) | Chambers,Paul (b) | Blakey,Art (dr)
Studio B
Mitchell,Blue (tp) | Golson,Benny (ts) | Walton,Cedar (p) | Chambers,Paul (b) | Blakey,Art (dr)

OJCCD 669-2(RLP 9452) | CD | At The Village Vanguard
Charlie Byrd Trio
Just Squeeze Me(But Don't Tease Me) | Why Was I Born | You Stepped Out Of A Dream | Fantasia On Which Side Are You On
Live at The 'Village Vanguard',NYC, rec. 15.1.1961
Byrd,Charlie (g) | Betts,Keter (b) | Deppenschmidt,Buddy (dr)

OJCCD 670-2 | CD | Monk In France
Thelonious Monk Quartet
Well You Needn't | Off Minor | I Mean You | Hackensack | I'm Getting Sentimental Over You | Crepuscule With Nellie
Live at The Olympia,Paris,France, rec. 18.4.1961
Monk,Thelonious (p) | Rouse,Charlie (ts) | Ore,John (b) | Dunlop,Frankie (dr)
Thelonious Monk
Just A Gigolo | Body And Soul
Live at The Olympia,Paris,France, rec. 18.1.1961
Monk,Thelonious (p-solo)

OJCCD 672-2(P7131) | CD | Wheelin' & Dealin'
Prestige All Stars
Things Ain't What They Used To Be | Wheelin'(take 1) | Wheelin'(take 2) | Robbin's Nest | Dealin'(take 1) | Dealin'(take 2)
Hackensack,NJ, rec. 20.9.1957
Prestige All Stars | Coltrane,John (ts) | Wess,Frank (fl,ts) | Quinichette,Paul (ts) | Waldron,Mal (p) | Watkins,Doug (b) | Taylor,Arthur 'Art' (dr)

OJCCD 680-2 | CD | Arthur's Blues
Art Pepper Quartet
Donna Lee
Live at The Maiden Voyage,LA, rec. 13.8.1981

Pepper,Art (as) | Cables,George (p) | Williams,David (b) | Burnett,Carl (dr)
Road Waltz | For Freddie | But Beautiful
Live at The Maiden Voyage,LA, rec. 14.8.1981
Pepper,Art (as) | Cables,George (p) | Williams,David (b) | Burnett,Carl (dr)
Arthur's Blues
Live at The Maiden Voyage,LA, rec. 15.8.1981
Pepper,Art (as) | Cables,George (p) | Williams,David (b) | Burnett,Carl (dr)

OJCCD 683-2(2310803) | CD | If I'm Lucky
Zoot Sims-Jimmy Rowles Quartet
I Wonder Where Our Love Has Gone | Legs | If I'm Lucky | Shadow Waltz | You're My Everything | It's All Right With Me | Gypsy Sweetheart | I Hear A Rhapsody
rec. 27./28.10.1977
Sims,Zoot (ts) | Rowles,Jimmy (p) | Mraz,George 'Jiri' (b) | Alexander,Mousie (dr)

OJCCD 689-2(2310881) | CD | Two Of The Few
Oscar Peterson-Milt Jackson Duo
Oh! Lady Be Good | Limehouse Blues | Reunion Blues | Just You Just Me | If I Had You | Mister Basie | More Than You Know | Here's Two Of The Few
NYC, rec. 20.1.1983
Peterson,Oscar (p) | Jackson,Milt (vib)

OJCCD 690-2(2310908) | CD | Count Basie Kansas City 7
Count Basie Kansas City 7
Jaylock | Exactly Like You | I'll Always Be In Love With You | If I Could Be With You One Hour Tonight | Honi Coles | Blues For Norman | Count Me In
Hollywood,CA, rec. 10.4.1980
Basie,Count (p) | Hubbard,Freddie (tp,fl-h) | Johnson,J.J. (tb) | Davis,Eddie 'Lockjaw' (ts) | Pass,Joe (g) | Heard,John (b) | Hanna,Jake (dr)

OJCCD 691-2(S 7570) | CD | King Size!
André Previn' s Jazz Trio
I'll Remember April | Much Too Late | You'd Be So Nice To Come Home To | It Could Happen To You | Low And Inside | I'm Beginning To See The Light
Los Angeles,CA, rec. 26.11.1958
Previn,André (p) | Mitchell,Red (b) | Capp,Frank (dr)

OJCCD 692-2(C 7576) | CD | Poll Winners Three
The Poll Winners
Soft Winds | Crisis | The Little Rhumba | Easy Living | It's All Right With Me | Mack The Knife(Moritat) | Raincheck | Minor Mystery | I'm Afraid The Masquerade Is Over - (I'm Afraid) The Masquerade Is Over | I Hear Music
Los Angeles,CA, rec. 2.11.1959
Poll Winners,The | Kessel,Barney (g) | Brown,Ray (b) | Manne,Shelly (dr)

OJCCD 694-2(7642) | CD | Thursday Night At The Village Vanguard
OJC 694(C 7642) | LP | Thursday Night At The Village Vanguard
Art Pepper Quartet
Valse Triste | Good Bye | Blues For Les | My Friend John
rec. 28.7.1977
Pepper,Art (as) | Cables,George (p) | Mraz,George 'Jiri' (b) | Jones,Elvin (dr)

OJCCD 695-2(C 7643) | CD | Friday Night At The Village Vanguard
OJC 695(C 7643) | LP | Friday Night At The Village Vanguard
Las Cuevas De Mario | But Beautiful | Caravan | Labyrinth | A Night In Tunisia
Live at The 'Village Vanguard',NYC, rec. 29.7.1977
Pepper,Art (as,ts) | Cables,George (p) | Mraz,George 'Jiri' (b) | Jones,Elvin (dr)

OJCCD 696-2(C 7644) | CD | Saturday Night At The Village Vanguard
OJC 696(C 7644) | LP | Saturday Night At The Village Vanguard
You Go To My Head | The Trip | Cherokee | For Freddie
Live at The 'Village Vanguard',NYC, rec. 30.7.1977
Pepper,Art (as,ts) | Cables,George (p) | Mraz,George 'Jiri' (b) | Jones,Elvin (dr)

OJCCD 698-2(F 9529) | CD | Quintessence
Bill Evans Quintet
Sweet Dulcinea | Martina | Second Time Around | A Child Is Born | Bass Face | Nobody Else But Me
Berkeley,CA, rec. May 1976
Evans,Bill (p) | Land,Harold (ts) | Burrell,Kenny (g) | Brown,Ray (b) | Jones,Philly Joe (dr)

OJCCD 700-2(NJ 8272) | CD | Into Something
Yusef Lateef Quintet
When You're Smiling | Water Pistol | Koko's Tune
Englewood Cliffs,NJ, rec. 29.12.1961
Lateef,Yusef (fl,ts,oboe) | Wright,Herman (b) | Jones,Elvin (dr)
Yusef Lateef Quartet
Rasheed | You've Changed | I'll Remember April | P-Bouk
Lateef,Yusef (fl,ts,oboe) | Harris,Barry (p) | Wright,Herman (b) | Jones,Elvin (dr)

OJCCD 703-2(P 7244) | CD | Stitt Meets Brother Jack
Sonny Stitt-Jack McDuff Quintet
All Of Me | Pam Ain't Blue | Time After Time | Ringin' In | 'Nother Fu'ther | When Sunny Gets Blue | Thirty-Three, Ninety-Six
Englewood Cliffs,NJ, rec. 16.2.1962
Stitt,Sonny (ts) | McDuff,Brother Jack (org) | Diehl,Eddie (g) | Taylor,Arthur 'Art' (dr) | Barretto,Ray (congas)

OJCCD 709-2(MV 15) | CD | The Hawk Relaxes
Coleman Hawkins Quintet
I'll Never Be The Same | When Day Is Done | Under A Blanket Of Blue | More Than You Know | Moonglow | Just A Gigolo | Speak Low
Englewood Cliffs,NJ, rec. 28.2.1961
Hawkins,Coleman (ts) | Bright,Ronnell (p) | Burrell,Kenny (g) | Carter,Ron (b) | Cyrille,Andrew (dr)

OJCCD 711-2(F 8082/P 7641) | CD | Gerry Mulligan Quartet feat.Chet Baker
Gerry Mulligan Quartet
Carioca | Line For Lyons | Bark For Barksdale | My Funny Valentine
Live at The Black Hawk,San Francisco,CA, rec. September 1952
Mulligan,Gerry (bs) | Baker,Chet (tp) | Smith,Carson (b) | Hamilton,Forrest 'Chico' (dr)
Moonlight In Vermont | Turnstile | The Lady Is A Tramp | Limelight | Gerry Mulligan Singing Off
Hollywood,CA, rec. January 1953
Mulligan,Gerry (bs) | Baker,Chet (tp) | Smith,Carson (b) | Hamilton,Forrest 'Chico' (dr)
Chubby Jackson Big Band
Flying The Coop | Why Not? | So What | I May Be Wrong(But I Think You're Wonderful) | New York | Leavin' Town | Hot Dog | Sax Appeal
NYC, rec. 15.3.1950
Jackson,Chubby (b) | Porcino,Al (tp) | McGhee,Howard (tp) | Ferrara,Don (tp) | Johnson,J.J. (tb) | Winding,Kai (tb) | Kennedy,Charlie (as) | Auld,Georgie (ts) | Sims,Zoot (ts) | Mulligan,Gerry (bs) | Aless,Tony (p) | Lamond,Don (dr)

OJCCD 712-2(F 3235/8082) | CD | Desmond
Paul Desmond Quintet
Jeruvian | Baroque(Chorale Prelude) | But Happy(Fugue IV) | Misty Window
Hollywood,CA, rec. October 1954
Desmond,Paul (as) | Collins,Dick (tp) | Van Kriedt,Dave (ts) | Bates,Bob (b) | Dodge,Joe (dr)
Paul Desmond Quartet With The Bill Bates Singers
Soon | Winky(Gigi) | Garden In The Rain
Desmond,Paul (as) | Kessel,Barney (g) | Bates,Bob (b) | Dodge,Joe (dr) | Bill Bates Singers: | Allen,Sue (voc) | Brown,Bill (voc) | Norman,Loulie Jean (voc) | Parke,Bernie (voc) | Thompson,Bill (voc) | Wood,Gloria (voc)
Will I Know
Desmond,Paul (as) | Weeks,Jack (tb) | Bates,Bob (b) | Dodge,Joe (dr) | Bill Bates Singers: | Allen,Sue (voc) | Brown,Bill (voc) | Norman,Loulie Jean (voc) | Parke,Bernie (voc) | Thompson,Bill (voc) | Wood,Gloria (voc)

Paul Desmond Quartet
Jazzabelle | A Watchman's Carroll | Everything Happens To Me | Let's Get Away From It All | Look For The Silver Lining | Sacre Blues | You Go To My Head | Line For Lyons
San Francisco,CA, rec. 14.2.1956
Desmond,Paul (as) | Elliott,Don (tp,mellophone) | Bates,Norman (b) | Dodge,Joe (dr)

OJCCD 714-2(S 7593) | CD | Live! At The Manne Hole Vol.1
Shelly Manne And His Men
Love For Sale | How Could I Happen To A Dream | Softly As In A Morning Sunrise | The Champ
Live at Shelly's Manne Hole,Los Angeles,CA, rec. 3.-5.3.1961
Manne,Shelly (dr) | Candoli,Conte (tp) | Kamuca,Richie (ts) | Freeman,Russ (p) | Berghofer,Chuck (b)

OJCCD 715-2(S 7594) | CD | Live! At The Manne Hole Vol.2
On Green Dolphin Street | What's New? | If I Were A Bell | Every Time We Say Goodbye | A Gem From Tiffany
Manne,Shelly (dr) | Candoli,Conte (tp) | Kamuca,Richie (ts) | Freeman,Russ (p) | Berghofer,Chuck (b)

OJCCD 716-2(F 3259) | CD | Dave Brubeck Plays And Plays And Plays...
Dave Brubeck
Sweet Cleo Brown | I'm Old Fashioned | Our Love Is Here To Stay | Indian Summer | In Search Of A Theme | You'd Be So Nice To Come Home To | I See Your Face Before Me | They Say It's Wonderful | Imagination | Two Sleepy People
Oakland,CA, rec. 8.2.1957
Brubeck,Dave (p-solo)

OJCCD 721-2(RLP 9337) | CD | The Centaur And The Phoenix
Yusef Lateef Orchestra
Revelation | Apathy | Everyday(I Fall In Love) | The Centaur And The Phoenix | Iqbal | Summer Song | The Philanthropist
NYC, rec. 4.& 6.10.1960
Lateef,Yusef (fl,ts,argol,oboe) | Terry,Clark (tp) | Williams,Richard (tp) | Fuller,Curtis (tb) | Taylor,Josea (bassoon) | Houston,Tate (bs) | Zawinul,Joe (p) | Tucker,Ben (b) | Humphries,Lex (dr)
Jungle Fantasy | Titora
NYC, rec. 23.6.1961
Lateef,Yusef (fl,ts,argol,oboe) | Harris,Barry (p) | Farrow,Ernie (b) | Humphries,Lex (dr) | Sanders,Roger (perc) | Masseaux,Garvin (perc) | unkn. (background-voc)

OJCCD 723-2(PR 7201) | CD | Groove Blues
Gene Ammons And His All Stars
Ammons' Joy | Groove Blues | It Might As Well Be Spring
Hackensack,NJ, rec. 3.1.1958
Ammons,Gene (ts) | Richardson,Jerome (fl) | Coltrane,John (as) | Quinichette,Paul (ts) | Adams,Pepper (bs) | Waldron,Mal (p) | Nasser,Jamil[George Joyner] (b) | Taylor,Arthur 'Art' (dr)
Jug Handle
Ammons,Gene (ts) | Richardson,Jerome (fl) | Quinichette,Paul (ts) | Adams,Pepper (bs) | Waldron,Mal (p) | Nasser,Jamil[George Joyner] (b) | Taylor,Arthur 'Art' (dr)

OJCCD 727-2(2310739) | CD | Oscar Peterson & Roy Eldridge
Oscar Peterson-Roy Eldridge Duo
Little Jazz | She's Funny That Way | The Way You Look Tonight | Sunday | Bad Hat Blues | Between The Devil And The Deep Blue Sea | Blues For Chu
Los Angeles,CA, rec. 8.12.1974
Peterson,Oscar (p,org) | Eldridge,Roy (tp)

OJCCD 731-2(2310804) | CD | Soul Fusion
Milt Jackson With The Monty Alexander Trio
Parking Lot Blues | 3000 Miles Ago | Isn't She Lovely | Soul Fusion | Compassion | O Amor En Paz(Once I Loved) | Yano | Bossa Nova Do Marilla
Los Angeles,CA, rec. 1./2.6.1977
Jackson,Milt (vib) | Alexander,Monty (p) | Clayton Jr.,John (b) | Hamilton,Jeff (dr)

OJCCD 732-2(2310874) | CD | Farmers Market Barbecue
Count Basie Big Band
Way Out Basie | St.Louis Blues | Beaver Junction | Lester Leaps In | Blues For The Barbecue | I Don't Know Yet | Ain't That Something | Jumpin' At The Woodside
Hollywood,CA, rec. 4.5.1982
Basie,Count (p) | Summers,Bob (tp) | Cohn[Cohen],Sonny (tp) | Carley,Dale (tp) | Albert,Chris (tp) | Hughes,Bill (tb) | Wilson,Dennis (tb) | Mitchell,Grover (tb) | Wood,Booty (tb) | Turner,Danny (as) | Plater,Bobby (as) | Hing,Kenny (ts) | Dixon,Eric (ts) | Williams,John B. (bs) | Green,Freddie (g) | Leary III,James (b) | Field,Gregg (dr)

OJCCD 734-2(2312134) | CD | Born To Be Blue
Freddie Hubbard And His Orchestra
Gibraltar | True Colors | Born To Be Blue | Joy Spring | Up Jumped Spring
Hollywood,CA, rec. 14.12.1981
Hubbard,Freddie (tp) | Land,Harold (ts) | Childs,Billy (keyboards) | Klein,Larry (b) | Houghton,Steve (dr) | Clarke,William 'Buck' (perc)

OJCCD 738-2(2310741) | CD | Oscar Peterson & Harry Edison
Oscar Peterson-Harry Edison Duo
Easy Living | Days Of Wine And Roses | Gee Baby Ain't I Good To You | Basie! | Mean To Me | Signify | Willow Weep For Me | The Man I Love | You Go To My Head
Los Angeles,CA, rec. 21.12.1974
Peterson,Oscar (p) | Edison,Harry 'Sweets' (tp)

OJCCD 740-2(2310822) | CD | Milt Jackson + Count Basie + Big Band Vol.1
Milt Jackson With The Count Basie Orchestra
The Comeback | Basie! | Corner Pocket | Lady In Lace | Blues For Joe Turner | Good Time Blues | Lil' Darlin' | Big Stuff | Blue And Sentimental
Hollywood,CA, rec. 18.1.1978
Jackson,Milt (vib) | Basie,Count (p) | Reed,Waymon (tp) | Biviano,Lyn (tp) | Cohn[Cohen],Sonny (tp) | Minger,Pete (tp) | Hughes,Bill (tb) | Wanzo,Mel (tb) | Wesley,Fred (tb) | Wilson,Dennis (tb) | Turner,Danny (as) | Plater,Bobby (as) | Dixon,Eric (ts) | Hing,Kenny (ts) | Fowlkes,Charlie (bs) | Green,Freddie (g) | Clayton Jr.,John (b) | Miles,Butch (dr)

OJCCD 741-2(2310823) | CD | Milt Jackson + Count Basie + Big Band Vol.2
9:20 Special | Moonlight Becomes You | Shiny Stockings | Blues For Me | Every Tub | Easy Does It | Lena And Lenny | On The Sunny Side Of The Street | Back To The Apple | I'll Always Be In Love With You
Jackson,Milt (vib) | Basie,Count (p) | Reed,Waymon (tp) | Biviano,Lyn (tp) | Cohn[Cohen],Sonny (tp) | Minger,Pete (tp) | Hughes,Bill (tb) | Wanzo,Mel (tb) | Wesley,Fred (tb) | Wilson,Dennis (tb) | Turner,Danny (as) | Plater,Bobby (as) | Dixon,Eric (ts) | Hing,Kenny (ts) | Fowlkes,Charlie (bs) | Green,Freddie (g) | Clayton Jr.,John (b) | Miles,Butch (dr)

OJCCD 742-2(2310898) | CD | Suddenly It's Spring
Zoot Sims Quartet
Brahm's...I Think | I Can't Get Started | MacGuffie's Blues | In The Middle Of A Kiss | So Long | Never Let Me Go | Suddenly It's Spring
NYC, rec. 26.5.1983
Sims,Zoot (ss,ts) | Rowles,Jimmy (p) | Mraz,George 'Jiri' (b) | Tana,Akira (dr)

OJCCD 744-2 | CD | Alternate Blues
All Stars
Alternate Blues One | Alternate Blues Two | Alternate Blues Three | Alternate Blues Four | Wrap Your Troubles In Dreams | Ballad Medley: | Here's That Rainy Day- | Gypsy- | If I Should Lose You-
Hollywood,CA, rec. 10.3.1980
Terry,Clark (tp) | Gillespie,Dizzy (tp) | Hubbard,Freddie (tp) | Peterson,Oscar (p) | Pass,Joe (g) | Brown,Ray (b) | Durham,Bobby (dr)

OJCCD 745-2(2312141) | CD | Things Are Getting Better All The Time
J.J. Johnson-Al Grey Sextet
Soft Winds | Let Me See | Softly As In A Morning Sunrise | It's Only A Paper Moon | Boy Meets Horn | Things Ain't What They Used To Be | Things Are Getting Better | Doncha Hear Me Callin' To Ya
NYC, rec. 28./29.11.1983
Johnson,J.J. (tb) | Grey,Al (tb) | Barron,Kenny (p,el-keyboards) | Brown,Ray (b) | Roker,Granville 'Mickey' (dr) | Carey,Dave (perc)

OJCCD 749-2(F 9608) | CD | Re: Person I Knew
Bill Evans Trio
Re:Person I Knew | Sugar Plum | Alfie | T.T.T. | Dolphin Dance-(Excerpts) | Very Early-(Excerpts) | 34 Skidoo | Emily | Are You All The Things
Live at The 'Village Vanguard',NYC, rec. 11./12.1.1974
Evans,Bill (p) | Gomez,Eddie (b) | Morell,Marty (dr)

OJCCD 750-2(F 9435) | CD | Inside Straight
Cannonball Adderley Septet
Introduction | Inside Straight | Saudade | Inner Journey | Snakin' The Grass | Five Of A Kind | Second Son | The End
Berkeley,CA, rec. 3.6.1973
Adderley,Julian \'Cannonball\' (as) | Adderley,Nat (co) | Galper,Hal (el-p) | Booker,Walter (b) | McCurdy,Roy (dr) | Errisson,King (perc)

OJCCD 757-2(SV 2017) | CD | Buck & Buddy
Buck Clayton-Buddy Tate Quintet
Highlife | When A Woman Loves A Man | Thou Swell | Can't We Be Friends | Birdland Betty | Kansas City Nights
Englewood Cliffs,NJ, rec. 20.12.1960
Clayton,Buck (tp) | Tate,Buddy (ts) | Thompson,Sir Charles (p) | Ramey,Gene (b) | Alexander,Mousie (dr)

OJCCD 760-2(P 7101) | CD | Flute Souflé
Herbie Mann-Bobby Jaspar Sextet
Tel-Aviv | Somewhere Else | Let's March | Chasing The Bird
Hackensack,NJ, rec. 21.3.1957
Mann,Herbie (fl,ts) | Jaspar,Bobby (fl,ts) | Puma,Joe (g) | Flanagan,Tommy (p) | Marshall,Wendell (b) | Donaldson,Bobby (dr)

OJCCD 761-2(F 9593) | CD | I Will Say Goodbye
Bill Evans Trio
I Will Say Goodbye | Dolphin Dance | Seascape | Peau Douce | Nobody Else But Me | I Will Say Goodbye(alt.take) | The Opener | Quiet Light | A House Is Not A Home | Orson's Theme
Berkeley,CA, rec. 11.-13.5.1977
Evans,Bill (p) | Gomez,Eddie (b) | Zigmund,Eliot (dr)

OJCCD 763-2(M 9050) | CD | Multiple
Joe Henderson Quintet
Bwaata | Turned Me Around | Me, Among Others
NYC, rec. 30./31.1.1973
Henderson,Joe (ts) | Willis,Larry (el-p,synth) | Holland,Dave (b,el-b) | DeJohnette,Jack (dr) | Jenkins,Arthur (perc,congas)
Joe Henderson Sextet
Tres-Cun-Deo-La
Henderson,Joe (fl,ss,ts,perc,voice) | Ulmer,James Blood (g) | Willis,Larry (el-p,synth) | Holland,Dave (b,el-b) | DeJohnette,Jack (dr) | Jenkins,Arthur (perc,congas)
Song For Sinners
Henderson,Joe (ts,perc,voice) | Thomas,John (g) | Willis,Larry (el-p,synth) | Holland,Dave (b,el-b) | DeJohnette,Jack (dr) | Jenkins,Arthur (perc,congas)

OJCCD 765-2(RLP 1155) | CD | Blue Soul
Blue Mitchell Sextet
Minor Vamp | The Head | Top Shelf | Waverly Street | Polka Dots And Moonbeams | Nica's Dream
NYC, rec. September 1959
Mitchell,Blue (tp) | Fuller,Curtis (tb) | Heath,Jimmy (ts) | Kelly,Wynton (p) | Jones,Sam (b) | Jones,Philly Joe (dr)
Jimmy Heath Quartet
The Way You Look Tonight | Park Avenue Petite | Blue Soul
Heath,Jimmy (ts) | Kelly,Wynton (p) | Jones,Sam (b) | Jones,Philly Joe (dr)

OJCCD 766-2(RLP 9340) | CD | Spellbound
Clifford Jordan Quartet
Toy | Lush Life | Moon-A-Tic | Spellbound | Hot Water | Last Night When We Were Young | Au Privave
NYC, rec. 10.8.1960
Jordan,Clifford (ts) | Walton,Cedar (p) | DeBrest,Jimmy 'Spanky' (b) | Heath,Albert 'Tootie' (dr)

OJCCD 770-2(P 10030) | CD | The Panther
Dexter Gordon Quartet
The Panther | Body And Soul | Valse Robin | Mrs.Miniver | The Christmas Song | The Blues Walk
NYC, rec. 7.7.1970
Gordon,Dexter (ts) | Flanagan,Tommy (p) | Ridley,Larry (b) | Dawson,Alan (dr)

OJCCD 773-2(S 7629) | CD | Alive In London
Shelly Manne Sextet
Three On A Match | Once Again | Big Oak Basin | Illusion | Don't Know
Live at Ronnie Scott's,London,GB, rec. 30./31.7.1970
Manne,Shelly (dr) | Barone,Gary (tp,fl-h) | Gross,John (ts) | Wofford,Mike (el-p) | Morell,John (g) | Haynes,Roland (b)

OJCCD 774-2(GXY 5142) | CD | Roadgame
Art Pepper Quartet
Roadgame | Road Waltz | When You're Smiling | Everything Happens To Me | Roadgame(alt.take)
Live at The Maiden Voyage,LA, rec. 15.8.1981
Pepper,Art (cl,as) | Cables,George (p) | Williams,David (b) | Burnett,Carl (dr)

OJCCD 776-2(C 14006) | CD | Relaxin' At Camarillo
Joe Henderson Quartet
Y Todavia La Quiero | My One And Only Love | Relaxin' At The Camarillo
rec. 20.8.1979
Henderson,Joe (ts) | Corea,Chick (p) | Dumas,Tony (b) | Erskine,Peter (dr)
Crimson Lake | Yes My Dear
rec. 29.12.1979
Henderson,Joe (ts) | Corea,Chick (p) | Davis,Richard (b) | Williams,Tony (dr)

OJCCD 779-2(P 7318) | CD | The Song Book
Booker Ervin Quartet
The Lamp Is Low | Come Sunday | All The Things You Are | Just Friends | Yesterdays | Our Love Is Here To Stay
Englewood Cliffs,NJ, rec. 27.2.1964
Ervin,Booker (ts) | Flanagan,Tommy (p) | Davis,Richard (b) | Dawson,Alan (dr)

OJCCD 780-2(P 7340) | CD | The Blues Book
Booker Ervin Quintet
Eerie Dearie | One For Mort | No Blooze Blooze | True Blue
Englewood Cliffs,NJ, rec. 30.6.1964
Ervin,Booker (ts) | Jones,Carmell (tp) | Mahones,Gildo (p) | Davis,Richard (b) | Dawson,Alan (dr)

OJCCD 782-2(2308219) | CD | Lester Young In Washington,DC 1956:Vol.1
Lester Young With The Bill Potts Trio
A Foggy Day(In London Town) | When You're Smiling | I Can't Get Started | Fast Bb Blues | D.B.Blues | Tea For Two | Jeepers Creepers
Live at Olivia Davis's Patio Lounge,Washington,DC, rec. 3.-9.12.1956
Young,Lester (ts) | Potts,Bill (p) | Williams,Norman (b) | Lucht,Jim (dr)

OJCCD 783-2(2312102) | CD | Happy People
Paulinho Da Costa Orchestra
Deja Vu | Take It On Up | Love Till The End Of Time | Seeing Is Believing | Dreamflow | Carnival Of Colors | Let's Go Together | Happy People | Put Your Mind On Vacation
Dayton Sound/Sunset Sound/Mom And Pops Co-Store, rec. January-March 1993
Da Costa,Paulinho (perc) | Findley,Charles (tp,fl-h,arr) | Madaio,Steven (tp,fl-h) | Grant,Gary (tp,fl-h) | Reichenbach,Bill (tb,arr) | Culver,Eric (tb) | Hyde,Dick (tb) | McCreary,Lou (tb) | Malone,Tom (tb) | Herbig,Gary (fl,sax,oboe) | Henderson,Marlo (g) | McKay,Al (g) | Carlton,Larry (g) | Barnes,John (keyboards,arr) | Phillinganes,Gregory (keyboards) | Boddicker,Michael (synth) | Watts,Nathan (b) | Gadson,James (dr) | Bailey,Philip (arr,voc) | Thompson,Deborah (voc) | Champlin,Bill (arr,voc)

| Carwell,Carl (arr,voc) | Hawes,Jeanette (voc) | Ford Jr.,Clarence (voc) | Cloud,Vennette (voc) | Twillie,Carmen (voc) | Bulling,Erich (arr) | Miller,Bruce (arr)

OJCCD 784-2(2310794) | CD | Free Ride
Dizzy Gillespie With The Lalo Schifrin Orchestra
Unicorn | Fire Dance | Incantation | Wrong Number | Free Ride | Ozone Madness | Love Poem For Donna | The Last Stroke Of Midnight
NYC, rec. 1./2.2.1977
Gillespie,Dizzy (tp) | Schifrin,Lalo (cond,arr,el-keyboards) | Brashear,Oscar (tp) | Laubach,Jack H. (tp) | McCreary,Lou (tb) | Horn,Jim (fl,sax) | Watts,Ernie (sax) | Richardson,Jerome (fl) | Burke,Sonny (p,el-p) | Spangler,Charles E. (synth) | Parker,Ray (el-g) | Ritenour,Lee (el-g) | Watson,Wah Wah (el-g) | Felder,Wilton (b) | Greene,Ed (dr) | Da Costa,Paulinho (perc)

OJCCD 785-2(2310873) | CD | Ain't But A Few Of Us Left
Milt Jackson Quartet
Ain't But A Few Of Us Left | A Time For Love | If I Should Lose You | Stuffy | Body And Soul | What Am I Here For
NYC, rec. 30.11.1981
Jackson,Milt (vib) | Peterson,Oscar (p) | Brown,Ray (b) | Tate,Grady (dr)

OJCCD 786-2(2310830) | CD | Chops
Joe Pass/Niels-Henning Orsted-Pedersen Duo
Have You Met Miss Jones | Oleo | Lover Man(Oh,Where Can You Be?) | 5 Blues | Come Rain Or Come Shine | Quiet Nights Of Quiet Stars(Corcovado) | Tricotism | Old Folks | Yardbird Suite | In Your Own Sweet Way
rec. 19.11.1978
Pass,Joe (g) | Orsted-Pedersen,Niels-Henning (b)

OJCCD 787-2(2310903) | CD | Quietly There-Zoot Sims Plays Johnny Mandel
OJC 787(2310903) | LP | Quietly There-Zoot Sims Plays Johnny Mandel
Zoot Sims Quintet
A Time For Love | Cinnamon And Clove | Low Life | Zoot | Emily | Quietly There
Hollywood,CA, rec. 20./21.3.1984
Sims,Zoot (ts) | Wofford,Mike (p) | Berghofer,Chuck (b) | Ceroli,Nick (dr) | Feldman,Victor (perc)

OJCCD 791-2(RLP 9330) | CD | That's Right
Nat Adderley And The Big Sax Section
Coordination | The Folks Who Live On The Hill | You Leave Me Breathless
NYC, rec. 9.8.1960
Adderley,Nat (co) | Adderley,Julian \'Cannonball\' (as) | Lateef,Yusef (fl,ts) | Heath,Jimmy (ts) | Rouse,Charlie (ts) | Houston,Tate (bs) | Hall,Jim (g) | Jones,Sam (b) | Cobb,Jimmy (dr)
The Old Country | Tadd | Night After Night | E.S.P. | That's Right
NYC, rec. 15.9.1960
Adderley,Nat (co) | Adderley,Julian \'Cannonball\' (as) | Lateef,Yusef (fl,ts,oboe) | Heath,Jimmy (ts) | Rouse,Charlie (ts) | Houston,Tate (bs) | Spann,Les (g) | Jones,Sam (b) | Cobb,Jimmy (dr)

OJCCD 792-2(P 7270) | CD | Preachin'
Gene Ammons Quartet
Sweet Hour | Yield Not | Abide With Me | Blessed Assurance | The Prayer | You'll Never Walk Alone | I Believe | Precious Memories | What A Friend We Have In Jesus | Holy Holy | The Light
Chicago,Ill, rec. 3.5.1962
Ammons,Gene (ts) | Anderson,Clarence 'Sleepy' (org) | Hickman,Sylvester (b) | Anderson,Dorral (dr)

OJCCD 793-2(P 7098) | CD | Ray Bryant Trio
Ray Bryant Trio
Golden Earrings | Angel Eyes | Blues Changes | Splittin' | Django | The Thrill Is Gone | Daahoud | Sonar
Hackensack,NJ, rec. 5.4.1957
Bryant,Ray (p) | Isaacs,Ike (b) | Wright,Charles 'Specs' (dr)

OJCCD 795-2(F 9542) | CD | Alone (Again)
Bill Evans
The Touch Of Your Lips | In Your Own Sweet Way | Make Someone Happy | What Kind Of Fool Am I | People
Berkeley,CA, rec. 16.-18.12.1975
Evans,Bill (p-solo)

OJCCD 799-2(C 14008) | CD | Destiny's Dance
Chico Freeman Sextet
Dextiny's Dance | C & M
Hollywood Bowl,CA, rec. 29./30.10.1981
Freeman,Chico (ss,ts) | Marsalis,Wynton (tp) | Hutcherson,Bobby (vib) | Moorman,Dennis (p) | McBee,Cecil (b) | Burrage,Ronnie (dr)
Chico Freeman Septet
Wilpan's Walk
Hollywood,CA, rec. 29./30.10.1981
Freeman,Chico (ss,ts) | Marsalis,Wynton (tp) | Hutcherson,Bobby (vib) | Moorman,Dennis (p) | McBee,Cecil (b) | Burrage,Ronnie (dr) | Da Costa,Paulinho (perc)
Chico Freeman Quartet
Same Shame | Embracing Oneness
Freeman,Chico (b-cl,ts) | Hutcherson,Bobby (vib) | McBee,Cecil (b) | Burrage,Ronnie (dr)
Chico Freeman Quintet
Crossing The Sudan
Freeman,Chico (b-cl,ts) | Marsalis,Wynton (tp) | Hutcherson,Bobby (vib) | McBee,Cecil (b) | Burrage,Ronnie (dr)

OJCCD 801-2(2308238) | CD | What Is This Thing Called Soul:In Europe-Live!
Cannonball Adderley-Nat Adderley Quintet
Azule Serape | Big 'P' | One For Daddy-O | The Chant | What Is This Thing Called Love | Cannonball's Theme
Paris/Stockholm/Göteborg, rec. November 1960
Adderley,Julian \'Cannonball\' (as) | Adderley,Nat (co) | Feldman,Victor (p) | Jones,Sam (b) | Hayes,Louis (dr)

OJCCD 802-2(2310838) | CD | Louie Bellson Jam
Louie Bellson Septet
Melody For Thelma | Stein On Vine | Shave Trail | Gonga Din | I Wonder Why | Ballad Medley: | All The Way Home- | Time To Ride A Moonbeam- | Bye Bye To All Birds- | Blue Invasion | A Gush Of Periwinkles
Hollywood,CA, rec. 28./29.9.1978
Bellson,Louie (dr) | Mitchell,Blue (tp,fl-h) | Christlieb,Pete (ts) | Tompkins,Ross (p,el-p) | Bain,Robert 'Bob' (g,el-g) | Pratt,Gary (b,el-b) | Richards,Emil (vib,perc,congas,bells,gong)

OJCCD 804-2(2310780) | CD | Edison's Light
Harry Edison Quintet
Edison's Lights | Ain't Misbehavin' | Avalon | 'E'
Los Angeles,CA, rec. 5.5.1976
Edison,Harry 'Sweets' (tp) | Davis,Eddie 'Lockjaw' (ts) | Basie,Count (p) | Heard,John (b) | Smith,Jimmie (dr)
Helena's Theme | Home Grown | Spring Is Here | On The Trail(From The Grand Canyon Suite)
Edison,Harry 'Sweets' (tp) | Davis,Eddie 'Lockjaw' (ts) | Coker,Dolo (p) | Heard,John (b) | Smith,Jimmie (dr)

OJCCD 805-2(2310757) | CD | The Big Three
The Big Three
The Pink Panther | Nuages | Blue Bossa | Come Sunday | Wave | Moonglow | You Stepped Out Of A Dream | Blues For Sammy
Los Angeles,CA, rec. 25.8.1975
Big Three,The | Jackson,Milt (vib) | Pass,Joe (g) | Brown,Ray (b)

OJCCD 806-2(2310742) | CD | Oscar Peterson & Clark Terry
Oscar Peterson-Clark Terry Duo
Slow Boat To China | But Beautiful | Shaw 'Nuff | Satin Doll | Chops | Makin' Whoopee | No Flugel Blues | Mack The Knife(Moritat)
Los Angeles,CA, rec. 18.5.1975
Peterson,Oscar (p) | Terry,Clark (tp)

OJCCD 807-2(2310816) | CD | Jazz Maturity... Where It's Coming From
Roy Eldridge-Dizzy Gillespie With The Oscar Peterson Quartet
Quasi-Boogaloo | Take The 'A' Train | I Cried For You(Now It's Your Turn To Cry Over Me) | Drebirks | When It's Sleepy Time Down South | Back Home Again In Indiana
rec. 3.6.1975
Eldridge,Roy (tp) | Gillespie,Dizzy (tp) | Peterson,Oscar (p) | Brown,Ray (b) | Roker,Granville 'Mickey' (dr)

OJCCD 814-2(F 9618) | CD | Eloquence
Bill Evans-Eddie Gomez Duo
Gone With The Wind | Saudade Do Brazil
Hollywood,CA, rec. 7.-10.11.1974
Evans,Bill (p,el-p) | Gomez,Eddie (b)
In A Sentimental Mood | But Beautiful
Live at The Montreux Jazz Festival, rec. 20.7.1975
Evans,Bill (p,el-p) | Gomez,Eddie (b)
Bill Evans
All Of You | Since We Met | But Not For Me- | Isn't It Romantic- | The Opener-
Hollywood,CA, rec. 16.-18.12.1975
Evans,Bill (p-solo)
When In Rome | It Amazes Me
Live at Shelly's Manne Hole,Los Angeles,CA, rec. November 1973
Evans,Bill (p-solo)

OJCCD 822-2(2310745) | CD | Basie & Zoot
Count Basie-Zoot Sims Quartet
I Never Knew | It's Only A Paper Moon | Blues For Nat Cole | Captain Bligh | Honeysuckle Rose | Hardav | Mean To Me | I Surrender Dear
NYC, rec. 9.4.1975
Basie,Count (p,org) | Sims,Zoot (ts) | Heard,John (b) | Bellson,Louie (dr)

OJCCD 824-2(2310767) | CD | I Told You So
OJC 824(2310767) | LP | I Told You So
Count Basie And His Orchestra
Tree Frog | Flirt | Blues For Alfy | Something To Live For | Plain Brown Wrapper | Swee'pea | Ticker | Too Close For Comfort | Told You So | The Gift
NYC, rec. 12.-14.1.1976
Basie,Count (p) | Cohn[Cohen],Sonny (tp) | Minger,Pete (tp) | Mitchell,Bob (tp) | Thomas,John (tp) | Feierman,Jack (tp) | Grey,Al (tb) | Fuller,Curtis (tb) | Hughes,Bill (tb) | Wanzo,Mel (tb) | Turner,Danny (as) | Plater,Bobby (as) | Forrest,Jimmy (ts) | Dixon,Eric (ts) | Fowlkes,Charlie (bs) | Green,Freddie (g) | Duke,John (b) | Miles,Butch (dr) | Holman,Bill (arr)

OJCCD 828-2(2312133) | CD | Ira George And Joe-Joe Pass Loves Gershwin
Joe Pass Quartet
Bidin' My Time | How Long Has This Been Going On | Soon | Oh! Lady Be Good | But Not For Me | Foggy Day | It Ain't Necessarily So | Our Love Is Here To Stay | 'S Wonderful | Nice Work If You Can Get It | Embraceable You
rec. 23.11.1981
Pass,Joe (g) | Pisano,John (g) | Hughart,Jim (b) | Manne,Shelly (dr)

OJCCD 829-2(2310779) | CD | Porgy And Bess
Oscar Peterson-Joe Pass Duo
Summertime | Bess You Is My Woman Now | My Man's Gone Now | It Ain't Necessarily So | I Loves You Porgy | I Got Plenty O'Nuttin' | Oh Bess Where's My Bess | They Pass By Singin' | There's A Boat Dat's Leavin' Soon For New York | Strawberry Woman
Los Angeles,CA, rec. 26.1.1976
Peterson,Oscar (clavichord) | Pass,Joe (g)

OJCCD 831-2(F 9465) | CD | Pieces Of Dream
Stanley Turrentine And His Orchestra
I Know It's You | Deep In Love | Midnight And You | Evil | Blanket On The Beach | I'm In Love | Blanket On The Beach(alt.take) | I'm In Love(alt.take)
Berkeley,CA, rec. 30./31.5.1974
Turrentine,Stanley (ts) | Parker Jr.,Ray (g) | Parks,Dean (g) | Walker,David T. (g) | Burke,Sonny (keyboards) | Miller,John (keyboards) | Page,Gene (keyboards) | Brown,Ron (b) | Greene,Ed (dr) | Coleman,Gary (perc) | Clayton,Joe (congas) | Matthews,Myrna (voc) | Willis,Carolyn (voc) | Wright,Edna (voc)
Pieces Of Dreams | Pieces Of Dreams(alt.take)
Turrentine,Stanley (ts) | Parker Jr.,Ray (g) | Parks,Dean (g) | Walker,David T. (g) | Burke,Sonny (keyboards) | Miller,John (keyboards) | Page,Gene (keyboards) | Brown,Ron (b) | Moore,Eddie (dr) | Coleman,Gary (perc) | Clayton,Joe (congas) | Matthews,Myrna (voc) | Willis,Carolyn (voc) | Wright,Edna (voc)

OJCCD 832-2(F 9638) | CD | Live At Vine Street
Dave Frishberg
You Would Rather Have The Blues | Zanzibar | One Horse Town | El Cajon | The Dear Departed Past | Johnny Hodges Medley: | Wanderlust- | Squatty Roo- | Day Dream- | I Got It Bad And That Ain't Good- | I'm Beginning To See The Light- | Don't Get Around Much Anymore- | Passion Flower- | Didn't Know About You- | The Star-Crossed Lovers- | Hodge Podge- | The Sports Page | Long Daddy Green | Eloise | Blizzard Of Lies
Vine Street Bar,Hollywood,CA, rec. October 1984
Frishberg,Dave (p,voc)

OJCCD 833-2(C 14013) | CD | Easy Living
Frank Morgan Quartet
Manha De Carnaval(Morning Of The Carnival) | Yes And No | Easy Living | The Rubber Man | Third Street Blues | Three Flowers | Embraceable You | Now's The Time
Glendale,CA, rec. 12./13.6.1985
Morgan,Frank (as) | Walton,Cedar (p) | Dumas,Tony (b) | Higgins,Billy (dr)

OJCCD 834-2(P 7153) | CD | Blue Stompin'
Hal Singer-Charlie Shavers Quintet
Blue Stompin' | Windy | With A Song In My Heart | Midnight | Fancy Pants | The Blast Off
Hackensack,NJ, rec. 20.2.1959
Shavers,Charlie (tp) | Singer,Hal (ts) | Bryant,Ray (p) | Marshall,Wendell (b) | Johnson,Gus (dr)

OJCCD 835-2(P 7293) | CD | Exultation!
Booker Ervin Quintet
Mooche Mooche | Black And Blue | Tune In | Just In Time | Just In Time(long take) | No Man's Land | No Man's Land(long take) | Mour
Englewood Cliffs,NJ, rec. 19.6.1963
Ervin,Booker (ts) | Strozier,Frank (as) | Parlan,Horace (p) | Warren,Edward 'Butch' (b) | Perkins,Walter (dr)

OJCCD 836-2(P 10069) | CD | Generation
Dexter Gordon Quintet
Milestones | Scared To Be Alone | We See | The Group | Milestones(alt.take)
Englewood Cliffs,NJ, rec. 22.7.1972
Gordon,Dexter (ts) | Hubbard,Freddie (tp,fl-h) | Walton,Cedar (p) | Williams,Buster (b) | Higgins,Billy (dr)

OJCCD 837-2 | CD | A Sure Thing
Blue Mitchell And His Orchestra
I Can't Get Started | A Sure Thing | Hootie Blues
NYC, rec. 7./8.& 28.3.1962
Mitchell,Blue (tp) | Terry,Clark (tp) | Watkins,Julius (fr-h) | Richardson,Jerome (fl,as) | Heath,Jimmy (ts) | Kelly,Wynton (p) | Jones,Sam (b) | Heath,Albert 'Tootie' (dr)
West Coast Blues
Mitchell,Blue (tp) | Terry,Clark (tp) | Watkins,Julius (fr-h) | Richardson,Jerome (fl,as) | Heath,Jimmy (ts) | Adams,Pepper (bs) | Kelly,Wynton (p) | Jones,Sam (b) | Heath,Albert 'Tootie' (dr)
Hip To It
Mitchell,Blue (tp) | Terry,Clark (tp) | Watkins,Julius (fr-h) | Richardson,Jerome (fl,as) | Heath,Jimmy (ts) | Patrick,Pat (bs) | Kelly,Wynton (p) | Jones,Sam (b) | Heath,Albert 'Tootie' (dr)
Gone With The Wind
Mitchell,Blue (tp) | Heath,Jimmy (ts) | Kelly,Wynton (p) | Jones,Sam (b) | Heath,Albert 'Tootie' (dr)

OJCCD 838-2(SV 2018) | CD | Swing's The Thing
Al Sears Quintet
Moving Out | Record Hop | Take Off Road | Already Alright | In A Mellow Tone | Out Of Nowhere | Ain't No Use | The Thrill Is Gone
Englewood Cliffs,NJ, rec. 29.11.1960
Sears,Al (ts) | Richardson,Wally (g) | Abney,Don (p) | Marshall,Wendell (b) | Marshall,Joe (dr)

OJCCD 839-2(SV 2021) | CD | Shorty & Doc
Shorty Baker-Doc Cheatham Quintet
Chitlin's | I Didn't Know What Time It Was | Baker's Dozen | Good Queen Bess | Night Train | Lullaby In Rhythm
Englewood Cliffs,NJ, rec. 17.1.1961
Baker,Harold 'Shorty' (tp) | Cheatham,Doc (tp) | Bishop Jr.,Walter (p) | Marshall,Wendell (b) | Heard,J.C. (dr)

OJCCD 840-2(F 9502) | CD | Amazonas
Cal Tjader Group
Amazonas | Flying | Corine
Los Angeles,CA, rec. June 1975
Tjader,Cal (vib,marimba) | Amaro,David (g,el-g) | Gismonti,Egberto (p,synth) | Gonga,Dawilli (keyboards) | Alves,Luiz (b) | Silva,Roberto (dr,perc)
Noa Noa
Tjader,Cal (vib,marimba) | De Souza,Raoul (tb) | Amaro,David (g,el-g) | Gismonti,Egberto (p,synth) | Gonga,Dawilli (keyboards) | Alves,Luiz (b) | Silva,Roberto (dr,perc)
Tamanco No Samba
Tjader,Cal (vib,marimba) | Amaro,David (g,el-g) | Milanez,Aloisio (p) | Gismonti,Egberto (p,synth) | Gonga,Dawilli (keyboards) | Alves,Luiz (b) | Silva,Roberto (dr,perc)
Mindoro | Xibaba | Cahuenga
Tjader,Cal (vib,marimba) | Pascoal,Hermeto (fl) | Amaro,David (g,el-g) | Gismonti,Egberto (p,synth) | Gonga,Dawilli (keyboards) | Alves,Luiz (b) | Silva,Roberto (dr,perc)

OJCCD 841-2 | CD | Woody Herman:Thundering Herd
Woody Herman And The New Thundering Herd
Lazy Bird | Blues For Poland | What Are You Doing The Rest Of Your Life | America Drinks And Goes Home | Naima | Come Saturday Morning
Berkeley,CA, rec. 2.-4.1.1974
Herman,Woody (ss,as) | Stahl,Dave (fl-h) | Powers,Buddy (fl-h) | Stapleton,Bill (fl-h) | Klatka,Tony (fl-h) | Byrne,Billy (tp) | Pugh,Jim (tb) | Kohlbacher,Steve (tb) | Garrett,Harold (b-tb) | Tiberi,Frank (fl,cl,ss,ts,bassoon) | Herbert,Greg (fl,ts,piccolo) | Anderson,Gary (fl,ts) | Konopasek,Jan (bs) | LaVerne,Andy (el-p) | Jackson,Charles 'Chip' (el-b) | Davis,Ron (dr) | Rae,Johnny (perc)
Corazon | Bass Folk Song
Herman,Woody (ss,as) | Stahl,Dave (fl-h) | Powers,Buddy (fl-h) | Stapleton,Bill (fl-h) | Klatka,Tony (fl-h) | Byrne,Billy (tp) | Pugh,Jim (tb) | Kohlbacher,Steve (tb) | Garrett,Harold (b-tb) | Tiberi,Frank (fl,cl,ss,ts,bassoon) | Herbert,Greg (fl,ts,piccolo) | Anderson,Gary (fl,ts) | Konopasek,Jan (bs) | LaVerne,Andy (el-p) | Jackson,Charles 'Chip' (el-b) | Davis,Ron (dr) | Rae,Johnny (perc) | Dollarhide,Richard (congas)

OJCCD 843-2(GXY 5147) | CD | Tete-A-Tete
Art Pepper-George Cables Duo
Body And Soul
Berkeley,CA, rec. 13.4.1982
Pepper,Art (as) | Cables,George (p)
Over The Rainbow | Tete-A-Tete | Darn That Dream | The Way You Look Tonight | Round About Midnight
Berkeley,CA, rec. 14.4.1982
Pepper,Art (as) | Cables,George (p)
You Go To My Head
Berkeley,CA, rec. 11.5.1982
Pepper,Art (as) | Cables,George (p)

OJCCD 844-2(M 9017) | CD | Tetragon
Joe Henderson Quartet
Invitation | R.J. | The Bad Game | Waltz For Sweetie
NYC, rec. 16.5.1968
Henderson,Joe (ts) | Friedman,Don (p) | Carter,Ron (b) | DeJohnette,Jack (dr)
Tetragon | First Trip | I've Got You Under My Skin
NYC, rec. 27.9.1967
Henderson,Joe (ts) | Barron,Kenny (p) | Carter,Ron (b) | Hayes,Louis (dr)

OJCCD 845-2(P 7295) | CD | The Freedom Book
Booker Ervin Quartet
A Lunar Tune | Cry Me Not | Grant's Stand | A Day To Mourn | Al's In
Englewood Cliffs,NJ, rec. 3.12.1963
Ervin,Booker (ts) | Byard,Jaki (p) | Davis,Richard (b) | Dawson,Alan (dr)

OJCCD 846-2(P 7315) | CD | Soul Call
Kenny Burrell Quintet
I'm Just A Lucky So-And-So | Mark One | A Sleeping Bee | Soul Call | Kenny's Theme | Here's That Rainy Day | Oh Henry
Englewood Cliffs,NJ, rec. 7.4.1964
Burrell,Kenny (g) | Davis,Will (p) | Rivera,Martin (b) | English,Bill (dr) | Barretto,Ray (congas)

OJCCD 847-2(P 7693) | CD | Soul Cycle
Cedar Walton Quintet
Sundown Express | Quiet Dawn | Pensativa | My Cherie Amour | Easy Walker | I Should Care
Englewood Cliffs,NJ, rec. 25.6.1969
Walton,Cedar (p,el-p) | Moody,James (fl,ts) | Stevenson,Rudy (g) | Workman,Reggie (b) | Heath,Albert 'Tootie' (dr)

OJCCD 848-2(R 1143) | CD | Much Brass
Nat Adderley Sextet
Blue Concept | Little Miss | Israel | What's Next? | Moving | Accent
NYC, rec. 23.& 27.3.1959
Adderley,Nat (co) | Hampton,Slide (tb) | Jackson,Laymon (tuba) | Kelly,Wynton (p) | Jones,Sam (b) | Heath,Albert 'Tootie' (dr)
Blue Concept
Adderley,Nat (co) | Hampton,Slide (tuba) | Jackson,Laymon (b) | Kelly,Wynton (p) | Jones,Sam (cello) | Heath,Albert 'Tootie' (dr)
Nat Adderley Quintet
Blue Grass Groove | Sometimes I Feel Like A Motherless Child
Adderley,Nat (co) | Jackson,Laymon (tuba) | Kelly,Wynton (p) | Jones,Sam (b) | Heath,Albert 'Tootie' (dr)

OJCCD 850-2(SV 2030) | CD | Buck & Buddy Blow The Blues
Buck Clayton-Buddy Tate Quintet
Rompin' At Red Bank | Blue Creek | A Swinging Doll | Dallas Delight | Don't Mind If I Do | Blue Breeze | Blue Ebony
Englewood Cliffs,NJ, rec. 15.9.1961
Clayton,Buck (tp) | Tate,Buddy (cl,ts) | Thompson,Sir Charles (p) | Ramey,Gene (b) | Johnson,Gus (dr)

OJCCD 861-2(2310707) | CD | Sirius
Coleman Hawkins Quartet
The Man I Love | Don't Blame Me | Just A Gigolo | The One I Love Belongs To Somebody Else | Time On My Hands | Sweet And Lovely | Exactly Like You | Street Of Dreams | Sugar
Berkeley,CA, rec. 20.12.1966
Hawkins,Coleman (ts) | Harris,Barry (p) | Cranshaw,Bob (b) | Locke,Eddie (dr)

OJCCD 864-2(2310825) | CD | Lady Time
Ella Fitzgerald With Jackie Davis And Louis Bellson
I'm Walkin' | All Or Nothing At All | I Never Had A Chance | I Cried For You(Now It's Your Turn To Cry Over Me) | What Will I Tell My Heart | Since I Fell For You | And The Angels Sing | I'm Confessin'(That I Love You) | Mack The Knife(Moritat) | That's My Desire | I'm In The Mood For Love
Los Angeles,CA, rec. 19.-20.6.1978
Fitzgerald,Ella (voc) | Davis,Jackie (org) | Bellson,Louie (dr)

OJCCD 867-2(2310915) | CD | Hark
Buddy DeFranco Meets The Oscar Peterson Quartet
All Too Soon | Summer Me Winter Me | Llovisna(Light Rain) | By Myself | Joy Spring | This Is All I Ask | Hark | Why Am I
Berkeley,CA, rec. 30.4.1985
DeFranco,Buddy (cl) | Peterson,Oscar (p) | Pass,Joe (g) | Orsted-Pedersen,Niels-Henning (b) | Drew,Martin (dr)

OJCCD 875-2(P 7259) | CD | Screamin'
Jack McDuff Quartet
He's A Real Gone Guy | Soulful Drums | After Hours | Screamin' | I Cover The Waterfront | One O'Clock Jump
Englewood Cliffs,NJ, rec. 23.10.1962
McDuff,Brother Jack (org) | Wright,Leo (as) | Burrell,Kenny (g) | Dukes,Joe (dr)

OJCCD 876-2(P 7292) | CD | The Believer
John Coltrane Quintet
The Believer | Nakatini Serenade
rec. 10.1.1958
Coltrane,John (ts) | Byrd,Donald (p) | Garland,Red (p) | Chambers,Paul (b) | Hayes,Louis (dr)
John Coltrane All Stars
Do I Love You Because You're Beautiful
rec. 26.12.1958
Coltrane,John (ts) | Hubbard,Freddie (tp) | Garland,Red (p) | Chambers,Paul (b) | Taylor,Arthur 'Art' (dr)

OJCCD 880-2(NJ 8258) | CD | Early Art
Art Farmer Quintet
Wisteria | Soft Shoe | Confab In Tempo | I'll Take Romance
rec. 20.1.1954
Farmer,Art (tp) | Rollins,Sonny (ts) | Silver,Horace (p) | Heath,Percy (b) | Clarke,Kenny (dr)
Art Farmer Quartet
I've Never Been In Love Before | I'll Walk Alone | Gone With The Wind | Alone Together | Preamp | Autumn Nocturne
rec. 9.11.1954
Farmer,Art (tp) | Kelly,Wynton (p) | Farmer,Addison (b) | Lovelle,Herbie (dr)

OJCCD 8805-2 | 4 CD | Workin',Steamin',Cookin',Relaxin' With The Miles Davis Quintet
Miles Davis New Quintet
In Your Own Sweet Way | Trane's Blues | It Never Entered My Mind | Four | The Theme | The Theme(alt.take) | Surrey With The Fringe On Top | Salt Peanuts | Something I Dreamed Last Night | Diane | When I Fall In Love
NYC, rec. 11.5.1956
Davis,Miles (tp) | Coltrane,John (ts) | Garland,Red (p) | Chambers,Paul (b) | Jones,Philly Joe (dr)
Half Nelson | Well You Needn't | My Funny Valentine | Blues By Five | Airegin | Tune Up | When Lights Are Low | If I Where A Bell | You're My Everything | I Could Write A Book | Oleo | It Could Happen To You | Woody'n You
NYC, rec. 26.10.1956
Davis,Miles (tp) | Coltrane,John (ts) | Garland,Red (p) | Chambers,Paul (b) | Jones,Philly Joe (dr)

OJCCD 8806-2 | 4 CD | Joe Pass:A Man And His Guitar
Ella Fitzgerald-Joe Pass Duo
Take Love Easy | O Amor En Paz(Once I Loved) | Don't Be That Way | You're Blasé | Lush Life | A Foggy Day(In London Town) | Gee Baby. Ain't I Good To You | You Go To My Head | I Want To Talk About You
Berkeley,CA, rec. 1973
Fitzgerald,Ella (voc) | Pass,Joe (g)
Joe Pass
Night And Day | Stella By Starlight | Here's That Rainy Day | My Old Flame | How High The Moon | Cherokee | Sweet Lorraine | Have You Met Miss Jones | Round About Midnight | All The Things You Are | Blues For Alician | The Song Is You
Los Angeles,CA, rec. December 1973
Pass,Joe (g-solo)
Joe Pass-Jimmy Rowles Duo
What's Your Story(Morning Glory) | So Rare | As Long As I Live | Marquita | Stardust | We'll Be Together Again | Can't We Be Friends | 'Deed I Do | 'Tis Autumn | God Bless The Child
Venice,CA, rec. 12.1.1981
Pass,Joe (g) | Rowles,Jimmy (p)
Joe Pass
Wave | Blues In G | All The Things You Are | Round About Midnight | Here's That Rainy Day | Duke Ellington's Sophisticated Lady Melange | Blues Dues | Bluesette | Honeysuckle Rose
Live at The City College,Long Beach,CA, rec. 20.1.1984
Pass,Joe (g-solo)

OJCCD 886-2(2310833) | CD | The Gifted Ones
Dizzy Gillespie-Count Basie Quartet
Back To The Land | Constantinople | You Got It | St.James Infirmary | Follow The Leader | Ow!
Las Vegas,NV, rec. 3.2.1977
Gillespie,Dizzy (tp) | Basie,Count (p) | Brown,Ray (b) | Roker,Granville 'Mickey' (dr)

OJCCD 889-2(2312138) | CD | The Best Is Yet To Come
Ella Fitzgerald With Orchestra
Don't Be That Way | God Bless The Child | You're Driving Me Crazy | Any Old Time | The Best Is Yet To Come
Hollywood,CA, rec. 4.2.1982
Fitzgerald,Ella (voc) | Aarons,Albert 'Al' (tp) | Watrous,Bill (tb) | Laws,Hubert (fl) | Schwartz,Wilbur (fl) | Green,Bill (fl) | Langinger,Ronald (fl) | Royal,Marshall (as) | Cooper,Bob (ts) | Duke,David (fr-h) | Robinson,Gale (fr-h) | Meyer,Joe (fr-h) | Klein,Richard G. (fr-h) | Pass,Joe (g) | Kessler,Jerome (cello) | Karmazyn,Dennis (cello) | Ermacoff,Christine (cello) | Hunter,Barbara Jane (cello) | Martin,Robert L. (cello) | Stein,Nancy (cello) | Seykora,Frederick (cello) | Perett,Judy (cello) | Rowles,Jimmy (p) | Hillery,Art (org) | Hughart,Jim (b) | Manne,Shelly (dr)
I Wonder Where Our Love Has Gone | Good Bye | Autumn In New York | Deep Purple | Somewhere In The Night
Hollywood,CA, rec. 5.2.1982
Fitzgerald,Ella (voc) | Aarons,Albert 'Al' (tp) | Watrous,Bill (tb) | Laws,Hubert (fl) | Schwartz,Wilbur (fl) | Green,Bill (fl) | Langinger,Ronald (fl) | Royal,Marshall (as) | Cooper,Bob (ts) | Duke,David (fr-h) | Robinson,Gale (fr-h) | Meyer,Joe (fr-h) | Klein,Richard G. (fr-h) | Tedesco,Tommy (g) | Kessler,Jerome (cello) | Karmazyn,Dennis (cello) | Ermacoff,Christine (cello) | Hunter,Barbara Jane (cello) | Martin,Robert L. (cello) | Stein,Nancy (cello) | Seykora,Frederick (cello) | Perett,Judy (cello) | Rowles,Jimmy (p) | Hillery,Art (org) | Hughart,Jim (b) | Manne,Shelly (dr)

OJCCD 893-2 | CD | Easy Living
Sonny Rollins Quintet
Down In The Line | My One And Only Love | Arroz Con Pollo | Hear What I'm Saying
Berkeley,CA, rec. 3.-6.8.1977
Rollins,Sonny (ss,ts) | Johnson,Charles Icarus (g) | Duke,George (p,el-p) | Jackson,Paul (el-b) | Williams,Tony (dr)
Sonny Rollins Sextet
Isn't She Lovely
Berkeley,CA/Los Angeles,CA, rec. 3.-6.8.1977
Rollins,Sonny (ts) | Johnson,Charles Icarus (g) | Duke,George (el-p) | Miller,Byron (el-b) | Williams,Tony (dr) | Summers,Bill (congas)
Sonny Rollins Quartet
Easy Living
Berkeley,CA, rec. 3.-6.8.1977
Rollins,Sonny (ts) | Duke,George (p) | Jackson,Paul (el-b) | Williams,Tony (dr)

OJCCD 896-2(PR 7386) | CD | The Space Book
Booker Ervin Quartet
Number Two | I Can't Get Started | Mojo | There Is No Greater Love
Englewood Cliffs,NJ, rec. 2.10.1964
Ervin,Booker (ts) | Byard,Jaki (p) | Davis,Richard (b) | Dawson,Alan (dr)

OJCCD 899-2(PR 10020) | CD | The Jumpin' Blues
Dexter Gordon Quartet
Evergreenish | I Love You For Sentimental Reasons | Star Eyes | Rhythm-A-Ning | If You Could See Me Now | The Jumpin' Blues
NYC, rec. 27.8.1970
Gordon,Dexter (ts) | Kelly,Wynton (p) | Jones,Sam (b) | Brooks,Roy (dr)

OJCCD 900-2(NJ 8211) | CD | Just Wailin'
Herbie Mann Sextet
Minor Groove | Blue Echo | Blue Dip | Gospel Truth | Jumpin' With Symphony Sid | Trinidad
Hackensack,NJ, rec. 14.2.1958
Mann,Herbie (fl) | Rouse,Charlie (ts) | Burrell,Kenny (g) | Waldron,Mal (p) | Nasser,Jamil[George Joyner] (b) | Taylor,Arthur 'Art' (dr)

OJCCD 912-2(M 9004) | CD | Full View
Wynton Kelly Trio
I Want A Little Girl | I Thought | What A Difference A Day Made | Autumn Leaves | Don't Cha Hear Me Callin' To Ya | On A Clear Day You Can See Forever | Scufflin' | Born To Be Blue | Walk On By
NYC, rec. 2./27.& 30.9.1966
Kelly,Wynton (p) | McClure,Ron (b) | Cobb,Jimmy (dr)

OJCCD 915-2(M 9090) | CD | Don't Ask
Sonny Rollins-Larry Coryell Duo
The File | My Ideal
Berkeley,CA, rec. 15.-18.5.1979
Rollins,Sonny (ts) | Coryell,Larry (g)
Sonny Rollins Quintet
Harlem Boys | Tai-Chi
Rollins,Sonny (ts,lyricon) | Soskin,Mark (p) | Harris,Jerome (el-b) | Foster,Al (dr) | Summers,Bill (perc,congas)
Sonny Rollins Sextet
Disco Monk | Don't Ask | And Then My Love I Found You
Rollins,Sonny (ts,p) | Coryell,Larry (el-g) | Soskin,Mark (p,el-p,synth,clavinet) | Harris,Jerome (el-b) | Foster,Al (dr) | Summers,Bill (perc,congas)

OJCCD 916-2(M 9096) | CD | New York Slick
Ron Carter Sextet
Ny Slik | A Slight Smile | Alternate Route | Aromatic
Englewood Cliffs,NJ, rec. December 1979
Carter,Ron (b) | Farmer,Art (fl-h) | Johnson,J.J. (tb) | Laws,Hubert (fl) | Barron,Kenny (p) | Cobham,Billy (dr)
Ron Carter Octet
Tierra Espanola
Carter,Ron (b) | Farmer,Art (fl-h) | Johnson,J.J. (tb) | Laws,Hubert (fl) | Barron,Kenny (p) | Cobham,Billy (dr) | Berliner,Jay (g) | McDonald,Ralph (perc)

OJCCD 918-2(PR 7276) | CD | Can't See For Lookin'
Red Garland Trio
Can't See For Lookin' | Soon | Black Out | Castle Rock
Hackensack,NJ, rec. June 1958
Garland,Red (p) | Chambers,Paul (b) | Taylor,Arthur 'Art' (dr)

OJCCD 920-2(P 7268) | CD | Stardust
John Coltrane Quintet
Love Thy Neighbor | Stardust
Hackensack,NJ, rec. 11.7.1958
Coltrane,John (ts) | Harden,Wilbur (tp,fl-h) | Garland,Red (p) | Chambers,Paul (b) | Cobb,Jimmy (dr)
John Coltrane All Stars
Then I'll Be Tired Of You
Hackensack,NJ, rec. 26.12.1958
Coltrane,John (ts) | Hubbard,Freddie (tp) | Garland,Red (p) | Chambers,Paul (b) | Taylor,Arthur 'Art' (dr)
John Coltrane Quartet
Time After Time
Coltrane,John (ts) | Garland,Red (p) | Chambers,Paul (b) | Taylor,Arthur 'Art' (dr)

OJCCD 930-2(2308233) | CD | Live In The Netherlands
Toots Thielemans Trio
Blues In The Closet | The Mooche | Thriving On A Riff | Autumn Leaves | Someday My Prince Will Come
Live at The Northsea Festival, rec. 13.7.1980
Thielemans,Jean 'Toots (harm,voc) | Pass,Joe (g) | Orsted-Pedersen,Niels-Henning (b)

OJCCD 935-2(2310842) | CD | Bag's Bag
Milt Jackson And His Colleagues
Slow Boat To China | I Cover The Waterfront
rec. details unknown
Jackson,Milt (vib) | Brown,Ray (b) | Walton,Cedar (p)
Blues For Roberta | How Are You | The Rev | Blues For Tomi-Oka
Jackson,Milt (vib) | Walton,Cedar (p) | Brown,Ray (b) | Higgins,Billy (dr)
Tour Angel
Jackson,Milt (vib) | Andre,Vaughn (g) | Walton,Cedar (p) | Brown,Ray (b) | Higgins,Billy (dr)
Groovin'
Jackson,Milt (vib) | Collins,John (g) | Walton,Cedar (p) | Brown,Ray (b) | Severino,Frank (dr)

OJCCD 937-2(2310876) | CD | Face To Face
Freddie Hubbard-Oscar Peterson Quintet
All Blues | Thermo | Weaver Of Dreams | Portrait Of Jenny | Tippin'
rec. 24.5.1982
Hubbard,Freddie (tp) | Peterson,Oscar (p) | Pass,Joe (g) | Orsted-Pedersen,Niels-Henning (b) | Drew,Martin (dr)

OJCCD 939-2(2312120) | CD | Passion Flower
Zoot Sims With Orchestra
In A Mellow Tone | I Got It Bad And That Ain't Good | It Don't Mean A Thing If It Ain't Got That Swing | I Let A Song Go Out Of My Heart | Black Butterfly
rec. 14.8.& 10./11.12.1979
Sims,Zoot (ts) | Bryant,Bobby (tp) | Aarons,Albert 'Al' (tp) | Brashear,Oscar (tp) | Gardner,Earl (tp) | Johnson,J.J. (tb) | Woodman,Britt (tb) | Mitchell,Grover (tb) | Powell,Benny (tb) | Royal,Marshall (as) | Wess,Frank (fl,as) | Johnson,Plas (ts) | Collette,Buddy (ts) | Collins,John (g) | Rowles,Jimmy (p) | Simpkins,Andrew (b) | Tate,Grady (dr) | Carter,Benny (cond,arr)
Passion Flower
Sims,Zoot (ts) | Bryant,Bobby (tp) | Aarons,Albert 'Al' (tp) | Brashear,Oscar (tp) | Gardner,Earl (tp) | Johnson,J.J. (tb) | Woodman,Britt (tb) | Mitchell,Grover (tb) | Powell,Benny (tb) | Royal,Marshall (as) | Wess,Frank (fl,as) | Johnson,Plas (ts) | Collette,Buddy (ts) | Collins,John (g) | Rowles,Jimmy (p) | Moore,Michael (b) | Clay,John (dr) | Carter,Benny (cond,arr)
Bojangles | Your Love Has Faded | Do Nothin' Till You Hear From Me
Sims,Zoot (ts) | Bryant,Bobby (tp) | Aarons,Albert 'Al' (tp) | Brashear,Oscar (tp) | Gardner,Earl (tp) | Johnson,J.J. (tb) | Woodman,Britt (tb) | Mitchell,Grover (tb) | Powell,Benny (tb) | Royal,Marshall (as) | Wess,Frank (fl,as) | Johnson,Plas (ts) | Collette,Buddy (ts) | Collins,John (g) | Rowles,Jimmy (p) | Heard,John (b) | Manne,Shelly (dr) | Carter,Benny (cond,arr)

OJCCD 941-2(P 7272) | CD | Love Shout
Etta Jones And Her Band
The Gal From Joe's | Hi Lili Hi Lo | If I Loved You
Englewood Cliffs,NJ, rec. 28.11.1962
Jones,Etta (voc) | Richardson,Jerome (fl,ts) | Burrell,Kenny (g) | Pizzarelli,Bucky (g) | Hayes,Ernest 'Emie' (p,org) | Bruno,Sam (b) | Donaldson,Bobby (dr)
There Are Such Things | Someday My Prince Will Come | Some Enchanted Evening
Englewood Cliffs,NJ, rec. 4.2.1963
Jones,Etta (voc) | Cox,Kenny (p) | Young,Larry (org) | Burrell,Kenny (g) | Tucker,George (b) | Smith,Jimmie (dr)
Old Folks
Jones,Etta (voc) | Burrell,Kenny (g) | Tucker,George (b) | Smith,Jimmie (dr)
Love Walked In | It's Magic | Like Someone In Love
Englewood Cliffs,NJ, rec. 12.2.1963
Jones,Etta (voc) | Cox,Kenny (p) | Young,Larry (org) | Burrell,Kenny (g) | Morrison,Peck (b) | Jackson,Oliver (dr)

OJCCD 954-2(M 9023) | CD | The Blues And Other Colors
James Moody Orchestra
Gone Are The Days | Feeling Low | You Got To Pay
NYC, rec. 14.8.1968
Moody,James (fl) | Woodman,Britt (tb) | Buffington,Jimmy (fr-h) | Brown,Alfred (viola) | McCracken,Charles (cello) | Moore,Kermit (cello) | Katz,Dick (p) | Carter,Ron (b) | Kay,Connie (dr) | November,Linda (voc)
Everyone Needs It | Savannah Calling | Old Folks
NYC, rec. 3.1.& 11.2.1969
Moody,James (fl,ss) | Coles,Johnny (tp,fl-h) | McIntosh,Tom (tb) | Farrell,Joe (alto-fl,as,oboe) | Payne,Cecil (bs) | Brown,Sam (el-g) | Barron,Kenny (p) | Tucker,Ben (b,el-b) | Waits,Freddie (dr)
Main Stem | A Statement
Moody,James (fl,ss) | Coles,Johnny (tp,fl-h) | McIntosh,Tom (tb) | Farrell,Joe (alto-fl,as,oboe) | Payne,Cecil (bs) | Barron,Kenny (p) | Carter,Ron (b) | Waits,Freddie (dr)

OJCCD 969-2(C 7581) | CD | Exploring The Scene
The Poll Winners
Little Susie | The Blessing | The Duke | So What | Misty | Doodlin' | The Golden Striker | Lil' Darlin' | This Here
Los Angeles,CA, rec. 30./31.8.& 1.9.1960
Poll Winners,The | Kessel,Barney (g) | Brown,Ray (b) | Manne,Shelly (dr)

OJCCD 972-2(S 2501) | CD | Sunday Jazz A La Lighthouse Vol.2
Howard Rumsey's Lighthouse All-Stars
Luau | Comin' Thru The Rye Bread | Taking A Chance On Love | The Big Top | The Duke You Say! | Sunset Eyes
Live at The Lighthouse,Hermosa Beach,CA, rec. 15.5.1953
Rumsey,Howard (b) | Rogers,Shorty (tp) | Bernhart,Milton 'Milt' (tb) | Giuffre,Jimmy (ts) | Cooper,Bob (ts) | Freeman,Russ (p) | Manne,Shelly (dr)
Glidin' Along | Beau Boy | Four Others
Live at The Lighthouse,Hermosa Beach,CA, rec. September 1953
Rumsey,Howard (b) | Baker,Chet (tp) | Ericson,Rolf (tp) | Shank,Bud (as) | Cooper,Bob (ts) | Geller,Lorraine or Claude Williamson (p) | Roach,Max (dr)

OJCCD 973-2(2312129) | CD | A Royal Wedding Suite
Oscar Peterson With Orchestra
A Royal Wedding Suite: | London Gets Ready | It's On | Jubilation | Let The World Sing
rec. 15.4.1981
Peterson,Oscar (p,arr,comp) | Orchestra | Wilkins,Rick (cond,arr) | details unknown
Announcement | When Summer Comes | Heraldry | Royal Honeymoon | Lady Di's Waltz | The Empty Cathedral
rec. 24./25.4.1981
Peterson,Oscar (p,arr,comp) | Orchestra | Wilkins,Rick (cond,arr) | details unknown

OJCCD 974-2(2310711) | CD | Ella In London
Ella Fitzgerald With The Tommy Flanagan Quartet
Sweet Georgia Brown | They Can't Take That Away From Me | Every Time We Say Goodbye | The Man I Love | It Don't Mean A Thing If It Ain't Got That Swing | You've Got A Friend | Lemon Drop | The Very Thought Of You | Happy Blues
Live at Ronnie Scott's,London,GB, rec. 11.4.1974
Fitzgerald,Ella (voc) | Flanagan,Tommy (p) | Pass,Joe (g) | Betts,Keter (b) | Durham,Bobby (dr)

OJCCD 975-2(2310865) | CD | Checkmate
Joe Pass-Jimmy Rowles Duo
What's Your Story(Morning Glory) | So Rare | As Long As I Live | Marquita | Stardust | We'll Be Together Again | Can't We Be Friends | 'Deed I Do | 'Tis Autumn | God Bless The Child
Venice,CA, rec. 12.1.1981
Pass,Joe (g) | Rowles,Jimmy (p)

OJCCD 979-2(P 7175) | CD | More Party Time
Arnett Cobb Quintet
Lover Come Back To Me | Blue Lou | Swanee River | Blue Me | Sometimes I'm Happy
Englewood Cliffs,NJ, rec. 16.2.1960
Cobb,Arnett (ts) | Flanagan,Tommy (p) | Jones,Sam (b) | Taylor,Arthur 'Art' (dr) | Barrajanos,Danny (congas)
Down By The Riverside
Englewood Cliffs,NJ, rec. 17.2.1960
Cobb,Arnett (ts) | Timmons,Bobby (p) | Jones,Sam (b) | Taylor,Arthur 'Art' (dr) | Clarke,Buck (congas)

OJCCD 981-2(P 7499) | CD | Heavy!!!
Booker Ervin Quartet
You Don't Know What Love Is
Englewood Cliffs,NJ, rec. 9.9.1966
Ervin,Booker (ts) | Byard,Jaki (p) | Davis,Richard (b) | Dawson,Alan (dr)
Booker Ervin Sextet
Bachafillen | Aluminum Baby | Not Quite That | Bei Mir Bist Du Schön | Ode To Charlie Parker
Ervin,Booker (ts) | Owens,Jimmy (tp,fl-h) | Brown,Garnett (tb) | Byard,Jaki (p) | Davis,Richard (b) | Dawson,Alan (dr)

OJCCD 983-2(P 7563) | CD | Boppin' & Burnin'
Don Patterson Quartet
Donna Lee
Englewood Cliffs,NJ, rec. 22.2.1968
Patterson,Don (org) | McGhee,Howard (tp) | Martino,Pat (g) | James,William 'Billy' (dr)
Don Patterson Quintet
Pisces Soul | Island Fantasy | Epistrophy | Now's The Time
Patterson,Don (org) | McGhee,Howard (tp) | McPherson,Charles (as) | Martino,Pat (g) | James,William 'Billy' (dr)

OJCCD 984-2(7479) | CD | Soul Outing!
Frank Foster Sextet
Show The Good Side | Night Song
Englewood Cliffs,NJ, rec. 27.6.1966
Foster,Frank (ts) | Jones,Virgil (tp) | Butler,Billy (g) | Rebillot,Pat (p) | Davis,Richard (b) | Dawson,Alan (dr,congas)
Frank Foster Quintet
While The City Sleeps | Skankaroony | Chiquito Loco
Englewood Cliffs,NJ, rec. 11.7.1966
Foster,Frank (ts) | Jones,Virgil (tp) | Rebillot,Pat (p) | Cunningham,Bob (b) | Dawson,Alan (dr,congas)

OJCCD 985-2(P 7658) | CD | Red Garland Revisited!
Red Garland Trio
Billy Boy | Everybody's Somebody's Fool | You Keep Coming Back Like A Song | Hey Now | I'm Afraid The Masquerade Is Over - (I'm Afraid) The Masquerade Is Over | It Could Happen To You
Hackensack,NJ, rec. 24.5.1957
Garland,Red (p) | Chambers,Paul (b) | Taylor,Arthur 'Art' (dr)
Red Garland Quartet
Four | Walkin'
Garland,Red (p) | Burrell,Kenny (g) | Chambers,Paul (b) | Taylor,Arthur 'Art' (dr)

OJCCD 986-2(F 3-211) | CD | Cal Tjader Plays Jazz
Cal Tjader Quartet
I've Never Been In Love Before | How About You | My One And Only Love | I'll Know
Live at The Marines Memorial Theatre,San Francisco,CA, rec. 4.12.1954
Tjader,Cal (dr) | Collins,Bob (tb) | Duran,Eddie (g) | McKibbon,Al (b)
Cal Tjader Quintet
Moten Swing | There'll Never Be Another You | Jeepers Creepers | A Minor Goof | Imagination | Brew's Blues
Live at Little Theatre,Berkeley,CA, rec. 6.6.1955
Tjader,Cal (vib) | Moore,Brew (ts) | Clark,Sonny (p) | Wright,Eugene 'Gene' (b) | White,Bobby (dr)

OJCCD 987-2(NJ 8293) | CD | Soul Street
Oliver Nelson Sextet
Soul Street
Hackensack,NJ, rec. 9.9.1960
Nelson,Oliver (ts) | Forrest,Jimmy (ts) | Curtis,King (ts) | Casey,Gene (p) | Duvivier,George (b) | Haynes,Roy (dr)
Jimmy Forrest Quintet
That's All
Hackensack,NJ, rec. 1.9.1961
Forrest,Jimmy (ts) | Lawson,Hugh (p) | Newborn,Calvin (g) | Potter,Tommy (b) | Johnston,Clarence (dr)
I Love You | Sonny Boy
Hackensack,NJ, rec. 19.10.1961

Forrest,Jimmy (ts) | Lawson,Hugh (p) | Potter,Tommy (b) | Johnston,Clarence (dr) | Barretto,Ray (congas)

Jimmy Forrest With The Oliver Nelson Orchestra
Soft Summer Breeze | Just A-Sittin' And A-Rockin' | Experiment In Terror
Hackensack,NJ, rec. 1.6.1962
Forrest,Jimmy (ts) | Royal,Ernie (tp) | Cleveland,Jimmy (tb) | Barrow,George (ts) | Powell,Seldon (ts) | Woods,Chris (p) | Lowe,Mundell (g) | Davis,Richard (b) | Shaughnessy,Ed (dr) | Nelson,Oliver (arr,ld)

Prestige Blues-Swingers
I Wanna Blow Blow Blow(alt.take)
Hackensack,NJ, rec. 29.8.1958
Prestige Blues-Swingers,The | Farmer,Art (tp) | Sulieman[Leonard Graham],Idrees (tp) | Cooper,Frank 'Buster' (tb) | Richardson,Jerome (fl,as) | Forrest,Jimmy (ts) | Adams,Pepper (bs) | Bryant,Ray (p) | Grimes,Tiny (g) | Marshall,Wendell (b) | Johnson,Osie (dr) | Valentine,Jerry (arr)

OJCCD 990-2(F 9417) | CD | 'Round Midnight
Kenny Burrel Quartet
A Streetcar Named Desire | Make Someone Happy | I Think It's Going To Rain Today | Since I Fell For You | I'm Gonna Laugh You Out Of My Life
Berkeley,CA, rec. 1972
Burrell,Kenny (g) | Wyands,Richard (p) | Johnson,Reggie (b) | McBrowne,Lennie (dr)
Round About Midnight
Burrell,Kenny (g) | Sample,Joe (p) | Johnson,Reggie (b) | Humphrey,Paul (dr)

Richard Wyands
Blues In The Night
Wyands,Richard (p-solo)

OJCCD 991-2(F 9470) | CD | Woody Herman Herd At Montreux
Woody Herman And His Orchestra
I Can't Get Next To You | Superstar | Fanfare For The Common Man | Montevideo | Tantum Ergo(in memoriam Edward Kennedy Ellington) | Crosswind
Live at The Montreux Jazz Festival, rec. 6.7.1974
Herman,Woody (ss) | Stahl,Dave (tp,fl-h) | Hatt,Nelson (tp,fl-h) | Powers,Buddy (tp,fl-h) | Pack,Gary (tp,fl-h) | Byrne,Billy (tp,fl-h) | Pugh,Jim (tb) | Kirkland,Dale (tb) | Linsner,Art (b-tb) | Tiberi,Frank (fl,ts) | Anderson,Gary (fl,ts) | Herbert,Greg (ts,piccolo) | Konopasek,Jan (bs) | LaVerne,Andy (p) | Jackson,Charles 'Chip' (b) | Brillinger,Jeff (dr)

OJCCD 992(2310101) | CD | The Trio
Oscar Peterson Trio
Blues Etude | Chicago Blues | Easy Listening Blues | Come Sunday | Secret Love
London House,Chicago,Ill., rec. 1973
Peterson,Oscar (p) | Pass,Joe (g) | Orsted-Pedersen,Niels-Henning (b)

OJCCD 993-2 | CD | Lester Young In Washington,DC 1956:Vol.5
Lester Young With The Bill Potts Trio
D.B.Blues | Three Little Words | Pennies From Heaven | When You're Smiling
Live at Olivia Davis's Patio Lounge,Washington,DC, rec. 3.-9.12.1956
Young,Lester (ts) | Potts,Bill (p) | Williams,Norman (b) | Lucht,Jim (dr)

Lester Young And Earl Swope With The Bill Potts Trio
Oh! Lady Be Good | Up 'N Adam | Jumpin' With Symphony Sid | Lullaby Of Birdland
Olivia Davis' Patio Lounge,Washington,DC, rec. 3.-9.12.1956
Young,Lester (ts) | Swope,Earl (tb) | Potts,Bill (p) | Williams,Norman (b) | Lucht,Jim (dr)

OJCCD 996-2(2308223) | CD | Digital III At Montreux
Count Basie And His Orchestra
I Can't Get Started | Good Mileage
Live at The Montreux Jazz Festival, rec. 12.7.1979
Basie,Count (p) | Minger,Pete (tp) | Cohn[Cohen],Sonny (tp) | Cohen,Paul (tp) | Brown,Raymond (tp) | Wood,Booty (tb) | Hughes,Bill (tb) | Wanzo,Mel (tb) | Wilson,Dennis (tb) | Dixon,Eric (as) | Plater,Bobby (as) | Turner,Danny (ts) | Hing,Kenny (ts) | Fowlkes,Charlie (bs) | Green,Freddie (g) | Clayton Jr.,John (b) | Miles,Butch (dr)

Ella Fitzgerald With Count Basie And His Orchestra
I Don't Stand A Ghost Of A Chance With You | Flying Home
Smith,Paul (p) | Minger,Pete (tp) | Cohn[Cohen],Sonny (tp) | Cohen,Paul (tp) | Brown,Raymond (tp) | Wood,Booty (tb) | Hughes,Bill (tb) | Wanzo,Mel (tb) | Wilson,Dennis (tb) | Dixon,Eric (as) | Plater,Bobby (as) | Turner,Danny (ts) | Hing,Kenny (ts) | Fowlkes,Charlie (bs) | Green,Freddie (g) | Betts,Keter (b) | Roker,Granville 'Mickey' (dr) | Fitzgerald,Ella (voc)

Joe Pass
I Cover The Waterfront | Lil' Darlin'
Pass,Joe (g-solo)

Joe Pass/Niels-Henning Orsted-Pedersen Duo
In Your Own Sweet Way | Oleo
Pass,Joe (g) | Orsted-Pedersen,Niels-Henning (b)

OJCCD 998-2(R 9450) | CD | Mr. Guitar Charlie Byrd
Charlie Byrd Trio
Blues For Felix | Gypsy In My Soul | In A Mellow Tone | Prelude To A Kiss | Travelin' On | Play Fiddle Play | Funky Flamenco | How My Heart Only | Mama I'll Be Home Someday | How Long Has This Been Going On | Who Cares | Lay The Lily Low
Washington,DC, rec. 30.11.1961
Byrd,Charlie (g) | Betts,Keter (b) | Knox,Bertell (dr)

Owl Records | Universal Music Germany

013425-2 | CD | Night On The City | EAN 044001342523
Paolo Fresu Quintet
Notti Eluse E Attese Deluse | Satie | Il Lungo Addio | La Danza Delle Ombre | Pour Une Femme(to Chet Baker) | Ninna Nanna Per Vale | Giuletta Degli Spiriti(to F.Fellini) | La Palazzina Americana | Slow Down John | Retro' | To Gil(to Gil Evans) | Prezzo X(to Miles Davis)To M. | To M. | Ossi Di Seppia
Milano,Italy, rec. 4.5.1994
Fresu,Paolo (tp) | Tracanna,Tino (ss,ts) | Cipelli,Roberto (p) | Zanchi,Attilio (b) | Fioravanti,Ettore (dr)

013426-2 | CD | After Hours | EAN 044001342622
Jeanne Lee-Mal Waldron
Caravan | You Go To My Head | I Could Write A Book | Goodbye Pork Pie Hat | Straight Ahead | Fire Waltz | I Let A Song Go Out Of My Heart | Every Time We Say Goodbye
Paris,France, rec. 25./26.5.1994
Lee,Jeanne (voice) | Waldron,Mal (p)

013427-2 | CD | Homage To Carla | EAN 044001342721
Paul Bley
Seven | Closer | Olhos De Gato | And Now The Queen | Vashkar | Around Again | Donkey | King Korn | Ictus | Turns | Overtoned
NYC, rec. 25.4.1992
Bley,Paul (p-solo)

013428-2 | CD | Oceans In The Sky
Steve Kuhn Trio
The Island | Lotus Blossom | La PlusQue Lente- | Passion Flower- | Do | Ocean In The Sky | Theme For Ernie | Angela | In Your Own Sweet Way | Ulla | The Music That Makes Me Dance
Paris,France, rec. 20./21.9.1989
Kuhn,Steve (p) | Vitous,Miroslav (b) | Romano,Aldo (dr)

013430-2 | CD | Happy Reunion
Stephane Grappelli-Martial Solal Duo
Shine | Valsitude | Sing For Your Supper | God Bless The Child | Nuages | Parisian Thoroughfare | Grandeur Et Cadence | Stumbling | Et Si L'on Improvisait
Paris,France, rec. 17./18.2.1980
Grappelli,Stephane (v) | Solal,Martial (p)

013431-2 | CD | Michel Petrucciani | EAN 044001343124
Michel Petrucciani Trio
Hommage A Enelram Atsenig | Days Of Wine And Roses | Christmas Dreams | Juste Un Moment | Gattito | Cherokee
rec. 3./4.4.1981
Petrucciani,Michel (p) | Jenny-Clark,Jean-Francois (b) | Romano,Aldo (dr)

013432-2 | CD | Toot Sweet
Lee Konitz-Michel Petrucciani Duo
I Hear A Rhapsody | To Erlinda | Round About Midnight | Lover Man(Oh,Where Can You Be?) | Ode | Lovelee
Paris,France, rec. 25.5.1982
Konitz,Lee (as) | Petrucciani,Michel (p)

013434-2 | CD | Dream Drops
Michel Graillier
Auroville | Keep On Kicking | Top Dance | Billie's Heart
Spitsbergen Studio,Zuidbroek,NL, rec. 1./2.4.1981
Graillier,Michel (p,el-p,synth)
Owl Blues
Graillier,Michel (p-solo)

Michel Graillier-Chet Baker
Dream Drops
Paris,France, rec. 13.11.1981
Graillier,Michel (p) | Baker,Chet (tp)

Michel Graillier-J.F. Jenny-Clark
L'Étranger
Spitsbergen Studio,Zuidbroek,NL, rec. 1./2.4.1981
Graillier,Michel (p) | Jenny-Clark,Jean-Francois (b)

Michel Graillier Trio
Nem Um Talvez
Graillier,Michel (p) | Jenny-Clark,Jean-Francois (b) | Romano,Aldo (dr)

Michel Graillier-Michel Petrucciani
Little Song
Paris,France, rec. 27.11.1981
Graillier,Michel (el-p) | Petrucciani,Michel (p)

013435-2 | CD | No Tears No Goodbyes
Helen Merrill-Gordon Beck
When I Look In Your Eyes | I Love Paris | I Love Paris Too | Poor Butterfly | Bye Bye Blackbird | I Got It Bad And That Ain't Good | I Got It Good | The Thrill Is Gone | By Myself
Paris,France, rec. 1.-3.11.1984
Merrill,Helen (voc) | Beck,Gordon (p,el-p,org)

013575-2 | CD | Il Piacere
Aldo Romano Duo
Francavilla | Nano Nano | Pioggoa Sul'Pineto
Paris,France, rec. 19.-21.12.1978
Romano,Aldo (g,dr,perc,voc) | Barthelmy,Claude (g,el-g,b)
Il Piacere | Il Camino
Romano,Aldo (g) | Portal,Michel (cl,bandoneon)

Aldo Romano Trio
La Panna | Ciao Ciao | Berceuse
Romano,Aldo (g,dr) | Barthelmy,Claude (el-g,b) | Jenny-Clark,Jean-Francois (b)

014727-2 | CD | Unleemited | EAN 044001472725
Lee Konitz-Kenny Werner
Unleemited(take 1) | Les Fesses Au Clair De Lune | O Gato | Monica | Ohad | Nota Della Notte | Brazilian Fondue | Baby I'm A Legend | La Valse Qui Rit | Scent Of Dream | Pick-A.Boo
Geneva,CH, rec. 21.-23.1.1992
Konitz,Lee (ss,as) | Werner,Kenny (p,celeste)

014730-2 | CD | Partners
Paul Bley-Gary Peacock Duet
Again Anew | Latin Genetics | Hand In Hand | Who's Who Is It? | No Pun Intended
NYC, rec. 18.12.1989
Bley,Paul (p) | Peacock,Gary (b)

Paul Bley
Octavon | Afternoon Of A Dawn(part 1-4) | Lull-A-Bye | Majestic
Bley,Paul (p-solo)

Gary Peacock
Pleiades Skirt | Workinoot | Satyr Satire | Twitter Pat | Gently,Gently | Pot Luck
Peacock,Gary (b-solo)

014731-2 | CD | The Life Of A Trio:Saturday
Paul Bley/Jimmy Giuffre/Steve Swallow
Turns | By The Way(part 1&2) | Clusters(part 1&2)
NYC, rec. 16.12.1989
Giuffre,Jimmy (cl) | Bley,Paul (p) | Swallow,Steve (el-b)

Paul Bley/Jimmy Giuffre
Black Ivory
Giuffre,Jimmy (cl) | Bley,Paul (p)

Paul Bley/Steve Swallow
Endless Melody
Bley,Paul (p) | Swallow,Steve (el-b)

Jimmy Giuffre/Steve Swallow
We Agree
Giuffre,Jimmy (ss) | Swallow,Steve (el-b)

Jimmy Giuffre
Clarinet Zone | Someone
Giuffre,Jimmy (cl-solo,ss-solo)

Paul Bley
Owl Eyes | Foreplay | Even Steven
Bley,Paul (p-solo)

Steve Swallow
December
Swallow,Steve (el-b-solo)

014733-2 | CD | Evening Song
Paolo Fresu-Furio Di Castri
Intro Per Stella | Stella By Starlight | El Barrio | Don't Open Here | Una Notte Sul Divano | My Funny Valentine | Il Sogno Del Pescecane | Intro Per Un Basso Nel Buio | Un Basso Nel Buio | Maree | Rolling Car | Stratotrumpet Blues
Bologna,Italy, rec. 14./15.4.1991
Fresu,Paolo (tp,fl-h,co,electronic-effects,pocket-tp) | Di Castri,Furio (b,perc,electronic-effects)

Paolo Fresu-Furio Di Castri Quintet
Ossi Di Seppia | Evening Song
Fresu,Paolo (tp,fl-h,co,electronic-effects,pocket-tp) | Di Castri,Furio (b,perc,electronic-effects) | Eletto,Michele (fr-h) | Longo,Alessandra Giura (fl) | Nobile,Mario (cello)

014734-2 | CD | Humair/Jeanneau/Texier
Daniel Humair Trio
Fluctuations | Suite Eolienne(part 1-3) | Bram Van Velde | Bas De Lou | Syotanka | Jackie-Ing
Paris,France, rec. 21./22.3.&18.6.1979
Humair,Daniel (dr,perc) | Jeanneau,Francois (fl,ss,as,ts) | Texier,Henri (b)

014735-2 | CD | The Life Of A Trio:Sunday
Paul Bley/Jimmy Giuffre/Steve Swallow
Sensing | Industrial Suite | Tango Del Mar | Where Were We? | Play Ball | The Life Of A trio
NYC, rec. 17.12.1989
Giuffre,Jimmy (cl,ss) | Bley,Paul (p) | Swallow,Steve (el-b)

Jimmy Giuffre/Steve Swallow
The Giant Guitar And The Black Stick | Two Singers
Giuffre,Jimmy (cl) | Swallow,Steve (el-b)

Paul Bley/Steve Swallow
Sanctuary Much | Scrambled Legs | Things
Bley,Paul (p) | Swallow,Steve (el-b)

Paul Bley/Jimmy Giuffre
Sweet Song | Fallen Statue
Giuffre,Jimmy (ss) | Bley,Paul (p)

Paul Bley
Monique | Mephisto
Bley,Paul (p-solo)

Jimmy Giuffre
The Hidden Voice
Giuffre,Jimmy (cl-solo)

014739-2 | CD | Moderne | EAN 044001473920
Claude Barthelmy Group
Mank De Monk | Hairache | Stay Quite | Late | Moderne | Catch A Satch | Between The Sheets | Wazemmes | Sumatra | S'Ornette Margareta
Paris,France, rec. 27.-31.12.1982
Barthelmy,Claude (g,el-g) | Padovani,Jean-Marc (ss,ts) | De Schepper,Philippe (g) | Buquet,Anthomy Bo Bo (b,tuba,tb) | Ponthieux,Jean-Luc (b,el-b) | Mahieux,Jacques (dr,p,voc) | Denizet,Manuel (dr)

014802-2 | CD | Easy To Read
Joachim Kühn Trio
Guyléne | Easy To Read | Habits | Sensitive Details | Open De Trio | Monday
Paris,France, rec. June 1985
Kühn,Joachim (p) | Jenny-Clark,Jean-Francois (b) | Humair,Daniel (dr)

018350-2 | CD | Ten Tales | EAN 044001835025
Joe Lovano-Aldo Romano
Remanence | Dragons Are | Yellow Shadow | Moon Moth | Rain Season | Eternal Youth | Monologue For Two | Return Match | Sediments | Koua 1 | Autumn In New York
Paris,France, rec. 8.5.1989
Lovano,Joe (ts) | Romano,Aldo (dr)

018351-2 | CD | Fly Away Little Bird | EAN 044001835124
Jimmy Giuffre-Paul Bley-Steve Swallow
Fly Away Littel Bird | Fits | I Can't Get Started | Qualude | Possibilities | Tumbleweed | All The Things You Are | Starts | Good Bye | Just Dropped By | Lover Man(Oh,Where Can You Be?) | Postlude | Sweet And Lovely | Bats In The Belfry
NYC, rec. 25.4.1992
Giuffre,Jimmy (cl,ss,voc) | Bley,Paul (p) | Swallow,Steve (b-g)

018352-2 | CD | Natural Affinities | EAN 044001835223
Jeanne Lee-Dave Holland
Mingus Meditations
NYC, rec. 13./14.24.1.& 6./7.7.1992
Lee,Jeanne (voc) | Holland,Dave (b)

Jeanne Lee Group
I Thought About You
NYC, rec. 13./14./24.1.& 6./7.7.1992
Lee,Jeanne (voc) | Broadnax,Paul (p,voc) | Atkinson,Lisle (b) | Baker,Newman (dr)
Journey To Edaneres
NYC, rec. 13./14./24.1.& 6./7.7.1992
Lee,Jeanne (voc) | Hampel,Gunter (fl,vib) | Myers,Amina Claudine (p,voc) | Atkinson,Lisle (b) | Baker,Newman (dr)
Peace Chorale- | Peace Chorale(II)-
Lee,Jeanne (voc) | Smith,Leo[Wadada] (tp) | Atkinson,Lisle (b) | Baker,Newman (dr)
Bushwhacked-
Lee,Jeanne (voc) | Smith,Nadja (newspeak) | Whitecage,Mark (as) | Atkinson,Lisle (b) | Baker,Newman (dr)
Free Space
Lee,Jeanne (voc) | Smith,Leo[Wadada] (tp) | Whitecage,Mark (as) | Atkinson,Lisle (b) | Baker,Newman (dr)
Trilogy: | Beauty Is Rarity- | I Move And Set The Ways- | Silent Dance-
Lee,Jeanne (voc) | Smith,Leo[Wadada] (tp) | Atkinson,Lisle (b) | Baker,Newman (dr)
Ambrosia Mama
Lee,Jeanne (voc) | Harris,Jerome (g) | Atkinson,Lisle (b) | Baker,Newman (dr)

018353-2 | CD | Longing | EAN 044001835322
Bob Mintzer-Gil Goldstein Duo
Overlap | Jaco | Angelique | Comotion | Longing | Your Story | What's The Word | Two To Tango | Three Little Initials | Everything Happens To Me
Stamford,CT, rec. 20.3.1995
Mintzer,Bob (b-cl,ts) | Goldstein,Gil (p,accordeon)

018356-2 | CD | African Drums | EAN 044001835629
Beaver Harris
Aurora | Godvin | Glo-Billy-Vee Vee | The Builder | South Stream Road
Paris,France, rec. 26.5.1977
Harris,Beaver (dr)

Beaver Harris & Davis S.Ware
African Drums
Harris,Beaver (dr) | Ware,David S. (ts)

018357-2 | CD | Homage To John Coltrane | EAN 044001835728
Dave Liebman Quintet
Untitled Original | Crescent | Love | Joy- | Selflessness- | After The Rain
NYC, rec. 27.1.1987
Liebman,Dave (ss) | Visentin,Caris (oboe) | McNeely,Jim (p) | Gomez,Eddie (b) | Nussbaum,Adam (dr,perc)
India | Welcome | Mr.Day | Dear Lord | Dahomey Dance
NYC, rec. 28.1.1987
Liebman,Dave (ss) | Visentin,Caris (oboe) | Beard,Jim (synth) | Egan,Mark (el-b) | Moses,Bobby (dr,perc)

018364-2 | CD | AlmaLatina | EAN 044001836428
Aldo Romano Group
Roanugo | Santa Maria Novella | C'era Una Volta | Tastiere | Cadenza | Una Volta, Danny | Amalgame | Alma Latina | Six Millions Dollars Song | La Derniere Chanson
Paris,France, rec. January 1983
Romano,Aldo (dr) | Giammarco,Maurizio (ts) | Kane,Danny (harm) | Fouquey,Jean-Pierre (p,el-p) | Widemann,Benoit (p,el-p,synth) | Goubert,Estelle (p,el-p) | Catherine,Philip (g) | Perrin,Gilles (vib,perc) | Sylvain,Marc (el-b)

159572-2 | CD | Full Metal Quartet
Eric Watson Quartet
Tryst | Wear And Tear | Dragonfly | Stitches | Secrets | Full Metal Quartet | The Big Dipper | Confessions | Tryst Revisited
Pernes Les Fontaines,France, rec. 4.-6.12.1999
Watson,Eric (p) | Wallace,Bennie (ts) | Dresser,Mark (b) | Thigpen,Ed (dr)

P&J Music | Connexion Agency(Ali Haurand)

P&J 101-1 CD | CD | The Quartet Live In Prague
The Quartet
Razzle Dazzle | Oderbruch | My One And Only | Dedications
Live at Jazz Art Club,Prague, rec. 24.3.1991
Quartet,The | Dudek,Gerd (ss,ts) | Van Den Broeck,Rob (p) | Haurand,Ali (b) | Lewis,Tony (dr)

Pablo | ZYX Music GmbH

2308231-2 | CD | Nigerian Marketplace
2308231 | LP | Nigerian Marketplace
Oscar Peterson Trio
Nigerian Marketplace | Au Privave | Nancy(With The Laughing Face) | Misty- | Waltz For Debby- | Cakewalk | You Look Good To Me
Montreux,CH, rec. 16.7.1981
Peterson,Oscar (p) | Orsted-Pedersen,Niels-Henning (b) | Clark,Terry (dr)

2308242-2 | CD | The Stockholm Concert 1966
2308242 | LP | The Stockholm Concert 1966
Ella Fitzgerald With The Duke Ellington Orchestra
Imagine My Frustration | Duke's Place(C Jam Blues) | Satin Doll | Something To Live For | Wives And Lovers | So Danco Samba(I Only Dance The Samba) | Let's Do It(Let's Fall In Love) | Lover Man(Oh,Where Can You Be?) | Cotton Tail
Live,at Konserthuset,Stockholm, rec. 1966
Fitzgerald,Ella (voc) | Ellington,Duke (p,ld) | Williams,Cootie (tp) | Jones,Herbie (tp) | Anderson,Cat (tp) | Ellington,Mercer (tp) | Brown,Lawrence (tb) | Cooper,Frank 'Buster' (tb) | Connors,Chuck (tb) | Hodges,Johnny (as) | Procope,Russell (as) | Hamilton,Jimmy (cl,ts) | Gonsalves,Paul (ts) | Carney,Harry (bs) | Jones,Jimmy (p) | Lamb,John (b) | Comfort,Joe (b) | Woodyard,Sam (dr) | Johnson,Gus (dr)

2310702 | LP | Take Love Easy
2310702-2 | CD | Take Love Easy
Ella Fitzgerald-Joe Pass Duo
Take Love Easy | O Amor En Paz(Once I Loved) | Don't Be That Way | You're Blasé | Lush Life | A Foggy Day(In London Town) | Gee Baby Ain't I Good To You | You Go To My Head | I Want To Talk About You
Berkeley,CA, rec. 1973
Fitzgerald,Ella (voc) | Pass,Joe (g)

2310708-2 | CD | Virtuoso

2310708 | LP | Virtuoso
Joe Pass
Night And Day | Stella By Starlight | Here's That Rainy Day | My Old Flame | How High The Moon | Cherokee | Sweet Lorraine | Have You Met Miss Jones | Round About Midnight | All The Things You Are | Blues For Alician | The Song Is You
Los Angeles,CA, rec. December 1973
Pass,Joe (g-solo)

2310722-2 | CD | Satch And Josh
2310722 | LP | Satch And Josh
Count Basie-Oscar Peterson Quintet
Bums | These Foolish Things Remind Me On You | RB | Burning | Exactly Like You | Jumpin' At The Woodside | Louie B. | Lester Leaps In | Big Stockings | S & J Blues
Los Angeles,CA, rec. 2.12.1974
Basie,Count (p,org) | Peterson,Oscar (p) | Green,Freddie (g) | Brown,Ray (b) | Bellson,Louie (dr)

2310759-2 | CD | Ella And Oscar
2310759 | LP | Ella And Oscar
Ella Fitzgerald-Oscar Peterson Duo
Mean To Me | How Long Has This Been Going On | When Your Lover Has Gone | More Than You Ever Know | There's A Lull In My Life
Los Angeles,CA, rec. 19.5.1975
Fitzgerald,Ella (voc) | Peterson,Oscar (p)
Ella Fitzgerald-Oscar Peterson Trio
Midnight Sun | I Hear Music | Street Of Dreams | April In Paris
Fitzgerald,Ella (voc) | Peterson,Oscar (p) | Brown,Ray (b)

2310821-2 | CD | How Long Has This Been Going On?
2310821 | LP | How Long Has This Been Going On?
Sarah Vaughan With The Oscar Peterson Quartet
I've Got The World On A String | Midnight Sun | How Long Has This Been Going On | You're Blasé | Easy Living | More Than You Know | My Old Flame | Teach Me Tonight | Body And Soul | When Your Lover Has Gone
Hollywood,CA, rec. 25.4.1978
Vaughan,Sarah (voc) | Peterson,Oscar (p) | Pass,Joe (g) | Brown,Ray (b) | Bellson,Louie (dr)

2310888 | LP | Speak Love
2310888-2 | CD | Speak Love
Ella Fitzgerald With Joe Pass
Speak Low | Comes Love | There's No You | I May Be Wrong(But I Think You're Wonderful) | At Last | The Thrill Is Gone(Medley) | Gone With The Wind | Blue And Sentimental | Girl Talk | Georgia On My Mind
Hollywood,CA, rec. 21./22.3.1983
Fitzgerald,Ella (voc) | Pass,Joe (g)

2310938-2 | CD | All That Jazz
Ella Fitzgerald And Her All Stars
My Last Affair | Baby Don't You Quit Now
Hollywood,CA, rec. 15.-22.3.1989
Fitzgerald,Ella (voc) | Edison,Harry 'Sweets' (tp) | Barron,Kenny (p) | Brown,Ray (b) | Durham,Bobby (dr)
Jersey Bounce | All That Jazz
Fitzgerald,Ella (voc) | Edison,Harry 'Sweets' (tp) | Carter,Benny (as) | Barron,Kenny (p) | Brown,Ray (b) | Durham,Bobby (dr)
Dream A Little Dream Of Me | Oh Look At Me Now | When You Lover Has Gone | That Old Devil Called Love | Just Wen We're Falling In Love(Robbin's Nest) | Good Morning Heartache | Little Jazz
Fitzgerald,Ella (voc) | Terry,Clark (tp) | Grey,Al (tb) | Wofford,Mike (p) | Brown,Ray (b) | Durham,Bobby (dr)
The Nearness Of You
Fitzgerald,Ella (voc) | Edison,Harry 'Sweets' (tp) | Carter,Benny (as) | Barron,Kenny (p) | Brown,Ray (b) | Durham,Bobby (dr)

2310940-2 | CD | Oscar Peterson Live!
2310940 | LP | Oscar Peterson Live!
Oscar Peterson Quartet
The Bach Suite: | Allegro- | Andante- | Bach's Blues- | City Lights | Perdido- | Caravan-
Los Angeles,CA, rec. 12.& 14.11.1986
Peterson,Oscar (p) | Pass,Joe (g) | Young,David (b) | Drew,Martin (dr)

2310945-2 | CD | Fun Time
Count Basie And His Orchestra
Fun Time | Why Not? | Lil' Darlin' | In A Mellow Tone | Body And Soul | Good Time Blues | Whirly Bird | One O'Clock Jump
Montreux,CH, rec. 19.7.1975
Basie,Count (p) | Minger,Pete (tp) | Stahl,Dave (tp) | Mitchell,Bob (tp) | Cohn[Cohen],Sonny (tp,fl-h) | Szabo,Frank (tp,fl-h) | Grey,Al (tb) | Fuller,Curtis (tb) | Hughes,Bill (tb) | Wanzo,Mel (tb) | Dixon,Eric (fl,as) | Turner,Danny (fl,as) | Plater,Bobby (fl,as) | Forrest,Jimmy (ts) | Fowlkes,Charlie (bs) | Green,Freddie (g) | Duke,John (b) | Miles,Butch (dr)
I Hate You Baby | Lonesome Blues
Basie,Count (p) | Minger,Pete (tp) | Stahl,Dave (tp) | Mitchell,Bob (tp) | Cohn[Cohen],Sonny (tp,fl-h) | Szabo,Frank (tp,fl-h) | Grey,Al (tb) | Fuller,Curtis (tb) | Hughes,Bill (tb) | Wanzo,Mel (tb) | Dixon,Eric (fl,as) | Turner,Danny (fl,as) | Plater,Bobby (fl,as) | Forrest,Jimmy (ts) | Fowlkes,Charlie (bs) | Green,Freddie (g) | Duke,John (b) | Miles,Butch (dr) | Caffey,Bill (voc)

2310946-2 | CD | Apassionato
Joe Pass Quartet
Relaxin' At The Camarillo | Groove Yard | Body And Soul | Nica's Dream | Tenderly | When It's Sleepy Time Down South | Red Door | Gee Baby Ain't I Good To You | Lil' Darlin' | That's Earl Brother | Stuffy | You're Driving Me Crazy
Hollywood,CA, rec. 9.-11.8.1990
Pass,Joe (g,el-g) | Pisano,John (g) | Hughart,Jim (b) | Bailey,Colin (dr)

2310947-2 | CD | Time After Time
Oscar Peterson Quartet
Cool Walk | Love Ballade | Soft Winds | Medley: | Who Can I Turn To- | With A Song In My Heart- | Time After Time- | On The Trail(From The Grand Canyon Suite)
Los Angeles,CA, rec. 12.& 14.11.1986
Peterson,Oscar (p) | Pass,Joe (g) | Young,Dave (b) | Drew,Martin (dr)

2310955-2 | CD | Songs For Ellen
Joe Pass
The Shadow Of Your Smile | Song For Ellen | I Only Have Eyes For You | Stars Fell On Alabama | That Old Feeling | Star Eyes | Robbin's Nest | Someone To Watch Over Me | Blues For Angel | There's A Small Hotel | How Deep Is The Ocean | Stormy Weather | Just Friends | Blue Moon | Satellite Village
Hollywood Bowl,CA, rec. 7./11.& 20.8.1992
Pass,Joe (g-solo)

2310957-2 | CD | Art 'N' Zoot
Art Pepper Quartet
Over The Rainbow
Live at Royce Hall,University Of California,Los Angels,CA, rec. 27.9.1981
Pepper,Art (as) | Feldman,Victor (p) | Haden,Charlie (b) | Higgins,Billy (dr)
Zoot Sims Quartet
In The Middle Of A Kiss
Live at Royce Hall,University Of California,Los Angels,CA, rec. 27.9.1081
Sims,Zoot (ts) | Feldman,Victor (p) | Brown,Ray (b) | Higgins,Billy (dr)
Zoot Sims Quintet
Broadway | Girl From Ipanema(Garota De Ipanema)
Live at Royce Hall,University Of California,Los Angels,CA, rec. 27.9.1981
Sims,Zoot (ts) | Kessel,Barney (g) | Feldman,Victor (p) | Brown,Ray (b) | Higgins,Billy (dr)
Art Pepper-Zoot Sims Quintet
Wee(Allen's Alley) | Breakdown Blues
Pepper,Art (as) | Sims,Zoot (ts) | Feldman,Victor (p) | Brown,Ray (b) | Higgins,Billy (dr)

2310959-2 | CD | Joe Pass-John Pisano:Duets
Joe Pass-John Pisano
Alone Together | Bailewick | S'il Vous Plait | Lonely Woman | Nina's Birthday Song | You Were Meant For Me | Blues For The Wee Folk | Satie | For Jim H. | Back To Back
Hollywood,CA, rec. 16./17.2.1991
Pass,Joe (g) | Pisano,John (g)

2310960-2 | CD | Bluella:Ella Fitzgerald Sings The Blues
Ella Fitzgerald And Count Basie With The JATP All Stars
C Jam Blues
Live at Santa Monica,CA, rec. 2.6.1972
Fitzgerald,Ella (voc) | JATP All Stars | Eldridge,Roy (tp) | Edison,Harry 'Sweets' (tp) | Grey,Al (tb) | Getz,Stan (ts) | Davis,Eddie 'Lockjaw' (ts) | Basie,Count (p) | Green,Freddie (g) | Brown,Ray (b) | Thigpen,Ed (dr)
Ella Fitzgerald Jam
Fine And Mellow
Los Angeles,CA, rec. 8.1.1974
Fitzgerald,Ella (voc) | Edison,Harry 'Sweets' (tp) | Terry,Clark (tp,fl-h) | Sims,Zoot (ts) | Davis,Eddie 'Lockjaw' (ts) | Pass,Joe (g) | Flanagan,Tommy (p) | Brown,Ray (b) | Bellson,Louie (dr)
Ella Fitzgerald With The Tommy Flanagan Quartet
Happy Blues
Live at Ronnie Scott's,London,GB, rec. 11.4.1974
Fitzgerald,Ella (voc) | Flanagan,Tommy (p) | Pass,Joe (g) | Betts,Keter (b) | Durham,Bobby (dr)
Ella Fitzgerald With The Tommy Flanagan Trio
Billie's Bounce
Montreux,CH, rec. 14.7.1977
Fitzgerald,Ella (voc) | Flanagan,Tommy (p) | Betts,Keter (b) | Durham,Bobby (dr)
Ella Fitzgerald With Jackie Davis And Louis Bellson
I'm Walkin'
Los Angeles,CA, rec. 19./20.6.1978
Fitzgerald,Ella (voc) | Davis,Jackie (org) | Bellson,Louie (dr)
Ella Fitzgerald With The Count Basie Orchestra
Fine And Mellow | St.Louis Blues | Basella
Montreux,CH, rec. 12.7.1979
Fitzgerald,Ella (voc) | Basie,Count (p) | Minger,Pete (tp) | Cohn[Cohen],Sonny (tp) | Cohen,Paul (tp) | Brown,Raymond (tp) | Wood,Booty (tb) | Hughes,Bill (tb) | Wanzo,Mel (tb) | Wilson,Dennis (tb) | Hing,Kenny (ts) | Turner,Danny (ts) | Dixon,Eric (as) | Plater,Bobby (as) | Fowlkes,Charlie (bs) | Smith,Paul (p) | Green,Freddie (g) | Betts,Keter (b) | Roker,Granville 'Mickey' (dr)

2310961-2 | CD | Nuages
Joe Pass Quartet
I Remember You | Repetition | September Song | Nuages | If I Had You | Love Letters | What Is This Thing Called Love | Blues For The Weasel | Cherokee
Live at Yoshi's Keystone Korner,Oakland,CA, rec. 30.1.-1.2.1982
Pass,Joe (g) | Pisano,John (g,el-g) | Budwig,Monty (b) | Bailey,Colin (dr)

2310964-2 | CD | Unforgettable
Joe Pass
My Romance | The Very Thought Of You | I Cover The Waterfront | Isn't It Romantic | Walkin' My Baby Back Home | Autumn Leaves | Round About Midnight | I Should Care | Unforgettable | Don't Worry 'Bout Me | Spring Is Here | Moonlight In Vermont | April In Paris | Stardust | You'll Never Know | After You've Gone | I Can't Believe That You're In Love With Me
Hollywood,CA, rec. 7./11.& 20.8.1992
Pass,Joe (g-solo)

2310966-2 | CD | Oscar Peterson Plays Duke Ellington
Oscar Peterson Trio
Main Stem | Don't Get Around Much Anymore
NYC, rec. 25.5.1974
Peterson,Oscar (p) | Jones,Sam (b) | Hayes,Louis (dr)
In A Sentimental Mood
NYC, rec. 14.2.1973
Peterson,Oscar (p) | Jones,Sam (b) | Durham,Bobby (dr)
Oscar Peterson
Lady Of The Lavender Mist
NYC, rec. 25.5.1974
Peterson,Oscar (p-solo)
I Got It Bad And That Ain't Good
Live in Tallin,Estonia, rec. 17.11.1974
Peterson,Oscar (p-solo)
Oscar Peterson-Clark Terry Duo
Satin Doll
Los Angeles,CA, rec. 18.5.1975
Peterson,Oscar (p) | Terry,Clark (tp)
Oscar Peterson Quartet
Cotton Tail
Berkeley,CA, rec. 8.11.1983
Peterson,Oscar (p) | Pass,Joe (g) | Orsted-Pedersen,Niels-Henning (b) | Drew,Martin (dr)
Rerdido- | Caravan-
Live at The Westwood Playhouse,Los Angeles,CA, rec. 14.11.1986
Peterson,Oscar (p) | Pass,Joe (g) | Young,David (b) | Drew,Martin (dr)
Oscar Peterson Jam
Things Ain't What They Used To Be
Montreux,CH, rec. 14.7.1977
Peterson,Oscar (p) | Gillespie,Dizzy (tp) | Terry,Clark (tp) | Davis,Eddie 'Lockjaw' (ts) | Orsted-Pedersen,Niels-Henning (b) | Durham,Bobby (dr)
Oscar Peterson With The Duke Ellington Orchestra
Take The 'A' Train
rec. 1.7.1967
Ellington,Duke (p) | Anderson,Cat (tp) | Ellington,Mercer (tp) | Jones,Herbie (tp) | Williams,Cootie (tp) | Cooper,Frank 'Buster' (tb) | Connors,Chuck (tb) | Brown,Lawrence (tb) | Hamilton,Jimmy (cl,ts) | Procope,Russell (cl,as) | Hodges,Johnny (as) | Gonsalves,Paul (ts) | Carney,Harry (bs) | Lamb,John (b) | Jones,Rufus (dr) | Peterson,Oscar (p)

2310967-2 | CD | To Bags...With Love:Memorial Album
Oscar Peterson-Milt Jackson Duo
Mister Basie
NYC, rec. 20.1.1983
Peterson,Oscar (p) | Jackson,Milt (vib)
Modern Jazz Quartet
Ralph's New Blues
NYC, rec. 2.7.1955
MJQ (Modern Jazz Quartet) | Jackson,Milt (vib) | Lewis,John (p) | Heath,Percy (b) | Kay,Connie (dr)
Milt Jackson With Strings
Blues For Edith
Hollywood,CA, rec. 12.4.1976
Jackson,Milt (vib) | Laws,Hubert (fl) | Richardson,Jerome (fl,alto-fl) | Flanagan,Tommy (p) | Brown,Ray (b) | Budimir,Dennis (g) | Vinci,Gerry (v) | Jones,Karen (v) | Van Dyke,Marcia (v) | Belnick,Arnold (v) | Vael Jr.,C. (v) | Neufeld,Erno (v) | Krachmalnick,Jacob (v) | Plummer,Stanley (v) | Clebanoff,Herman (v) | Kundell,Barnard (v) | Geller,J. (v) | Schaeffer,Ralph (v) | Harshman,Allan (v) | Frisina,Dave (v) | Dale,Rollice (viola) | Schwartz,David (viola) | Kramer,Raphael (cello) | Cooper,Ron (cello) | Gotthoffer,Catherine (harp) | Smith,Jimmie (dr) | Da Costa,Paulinho (perc)
Roy Eldridge Septet
Recado Bossa Nova
NYC, rec. 16.1.1976
Eldridge,Roy (tp) | Turney,Norris (as) | Johnson,Budd (ts) | Simmons,Norman (p) | Sturgis,Ted (b) | Locke,Eddie (dr) | Jackson,Milt (vib)
Milt Jackson-Wes Montgomery Quintet
S.K.J.
NYC, rec. 19.12.1961
Jackson,Milt (vib) | Montgomery,Wes (g) | Kelly,Wynton (p) | Jones,Sam (b) | Jones,Philly Joe (dr)
Milt Jackson Orchestra
If You Could See Me Now
NYC, rec. 20.6.1962
Jackson,Milt (vib) | Terry,Clark (tp,fl-h) | Severinsen,Doc (tp) | Burns,Dave (tp) | Cleveland,Jimmy (tb) | Liston,Melba (tb) | Ruff,Willie (fr-h) | Moody,James (fl,as) | Dorsey,George (fl,as) | Richardson,Jerome (fl,ts) | Heath,Jimmy (ts) | Houston,Tate (bs) | Jones,Hank (p) | Carter,Ron (b) | Kay,Connie (dr) | Dameron,Tadd (arr)
Miles Davis Quintet
Bag's Groove
Hackensack,NJ, rec. 24.12.1954
Davis,Miles (tp) | Jackson,Milt (vib) | Monk,Thelonious (p) | Heath,Percy (b) | Clarke,Kenny (dr)
Benny Carter Sextet
Easy Money
Los Angeles,CA, rec. 11.2.1976
Carter,Benny (as) | Jackson,Milt (vib) | Pass,Joe (g) | Flanagan,Tommy (p) | Williams,John B. (b) | Hanna,Jake (dr)
Cannonball Adderley-Milt Jackson Quintet
Things Are Getting Better
NYC, rec. 28.10.1958
Adderley,Julian \'Cannonball\' (as) | Jackson,Milt (vib) | Kelly,Wynton (p) | Heath,Percy (b) | Blakey,Art (dr)
Milt Jackson With The Monty Alexander Trio
Yano
Los Angeles,CA, rec. 2.6.1977
Jackson,Milt (vib) | Alexander,Monty (p) | Clayton Jr.,John (b) | Hamilton,Jeff (dr)
Milt Jackson With The Count Basie Orchestra
Corner Pocket
Hollywood,CA, rec. 18.1.1978
Jackson,Milt (vib) | Basie,Count (p) | Reed,Waymon (tp) | Biviano,Lyn (tp) | Cohn[Cohen],Sonny (tp) | Minger,Pete (tp) | Hughes,Bill (tb) | Wanzo,Mel (tb) | Wesley,Fred (tb) | Wilson,Dennis (tb) | Turner,Danny (as) | Plater,Bobby (as) | Dixon,Eric (ts) | Hing,Kenny (ts) | Fowlkes,Charlie (bs) | Green,Freddie (g) | Clayton Jr.,John (b) | Miles,Butch (dr)

2310968-2 | CD | Resonance
Joe Pass Trio
It Could Happen To You | Corcovado(Quiet Nights) | Too Late Now | Come Rain Or Come Shine | The Lamp Is Low | Yardbird Suite | N.E.C. Blues | Misty | Bloos For Baby B
Live at Donte's,Los Angeles,CA, rec. December 1974
Pass,Joe (el-g) | Hughart,Jim (el-b) | Severino,Frank (dr)
Joe Pass
How Deep Is The Ocean
Pass,Joe (g-solo)

2310970-2 | CD | Oscar Peterson:The Composer
Oscar Peterson With Orchestra
Jubilation
Toronto,Canada, rec. 15.4.1981
Peterson,Oscar (p,arr,comp) | Orchestra | Wilkins,Rick (cond,arr) | details unknown
Lady Di's Waltz
London,GB, rec. 24./25.4.1981
Peterson,Oscar (p,arr,comp) | Orchestra | Wilkins,Rick (cond,arr) | details unknown
Oscar Peterson Quartet
Night Child
Toronto,Canada, rec. 11./12.4.1979
Peterson,Oscar (p,el-p) | Pass,Joe (g) | Orsted-Pedersen,Niels-Henning (b) | Bellson,Louie (dr)
L'Impossible
Berkeley,CA, rec. 9.11.1983
Peterson,Oscar (p,el-p) | Pass,Joe (g) | Orsted-Pedersen,Niels-Henning (b) | Drew,Martin (dr)
City Lights | The Bach Suite: Allegro | If You Only Knew
Los Angeles,CA, rec. 12./14.11.1986
Peterson,Oscar (p,el-p) | Pass,Joe (g) | Young,David (b) | Drew,Martin (dr)
Oscar Peterson
Hogtown Blues | Place St.Henri
Tallinn,Estland, rec. 17.11.1974
Peterson,Oscar (p-solo)

2310971-2 | CD | What Is There To Say
Joe Pass
Django | Old Folks | I Concentrate On You | I'll Be Around | They Can't Take That Away From Me | Medley: | It's All In The Game- | Yesterdays- | Come Rain Or Come Shine | On Green Dolphin Street | What Is There To Say | Nobody Else But Me | Lush Life
Live at The Vine St.Bar,Los Angeles,CA, rec. 13./14.9.1990
Pass,Joe (g-solo)

2310974-2 | CD | Solo Guitar | EAN 025218097420
Meditation | Shadow Waltz | Mood Indigo | More Than You Know | When Your Lover Has Gone | Everything Happens To Me | It's All Right With Me | I'll Never Be The Same | You Stepped Out Of A Dream | All The Things You Are | How Deep Is The Ocean | They Can't Take That Away From Me
Live at Yoshi's Night Club,Oakland,CA, rec. 30..1.-1.2.1992
Pass,Joe (el-g-solo)

2310975-2 | CD | Solo | EAN 025218097529
Oscar Peterson
Yesterdays | Makin' Whoopee | Who Can I Turn To | Take The 'A' Train | Body And Soul | Blues Of The Prairies | Corcovado(Quiet Nights) | Blues Etude
Live at Baalbek,Lebanon, rec. 17.8.1972
Peterson,Oscar (p-solo)
Autumn Leaves | Here's That Rainy Day | Sweet Georgia Brown | Satin Doll | Mirage | Hogtown Blues
Live at Amsterdam, rec. 4.11.1972
Peterson,Oscar (p-solo)

2312101-2 | CD | I Love Brazil
Sarah Vaughan With Orchestra
If You Went Away | Triste | Roses And Roses | Empty Faces(Vera Cruz) | I Live To Love You | The Face I Love | Courage | The Day It Rained | A Little Tear | Like A Lover(Cantador) | Bridges(Travessia) | Someone To Light Up My Life
Rio De Janeiro,Brazil, rec. 31.10.& 3.-7.11.1977
Vaughan,Sarah (voc) | Caymmi,Danilo (fl,voc) | Jobim,Paulo (fl) | Delmiro,Helio (g) | Einhorn,Mauricio (harm) | Angelo,Nelson (el-g) | Frederico,Edson (p,arr) | Jobim,Tom (el-p) | Bertrami,Jose Roberto (el-p) | Barroso,Sergio (b) | Betrami,Claudio (b) | Novelli (el-b) | Das Neves,Wilson (dr) | Batera,Chico (perc) | Ariovaldo (perc) | Nascimento,Milton (g,voc)

2312144-2 | CD | Linger Awhile
Sarah Vaughan With The Jimmy Jones Trio
If This Isn't Love | I'm Afraid The Masquerade Is Over - (I'm Afraid) The Masquerade Is Over | All Of Me | Black Coffee | Sometimes I'm Happy | Poor Butterfly | Linger Awhile | Time- | Tenderly-
Live at Newport,Rhode Island, rec. 7.7.1957
Vaughan,Sarah (voc) | Jones,Jimmy (p) | Davis,Richard (b) | Haynes,Roy (dr)
Sarah Vaughan With The Joe Pass Quartet
I Didn't Know What Time It Was | That's All
NYC, rec. 1.3.1982
Vaughan,Sarah (voc) | Pass,Joe (g) | Hanna,Sir Roland (p) | Simpkins,Andrew (b) | Jones,Harold (dr)
Sarah Vaughan With Band
I Got It Bad And That Ain't Good | I Let A Song Go Out Of My Heart
NYC, rec. 13.9.1979
Vaughan,Sarah (voc) | Reed,Waymon (tp) | Foster,Frank (ts) | Pizzarelli,Bucky (g) | Wofford,Mike (p) | Simpkins,Andrew (b) | Tate,Grady (dr) | Byers,Billy (arr,ld)

2405431-2 | CD | The Art Tatum Group Masterpieces Vol.8
Art Tatum-Ben Webster Quartet
Gone With The Wind | All The Things You Are | Have You Met Miss Jones | My One And Only Love | Night And Day | My Ideal | Where Or When | Gone With The Wind(alt.take 1) | Gone With The Wind(alt.take-2) | Have You Met Miss Jones(alt.take)
Los Angeles,CA, rec. 11.9.1956
Tatum,Art (p) | Webster,Ben (ts) | Callender,Red (b) | Douglas,Bill (dr)

2620103-2 | CD | Milt Jackson At The Kosei Nenkin
Milt Jackson Quintet

Pablo | ZYX Music GmbH   Bielefelder Katalog   840   Jazz • Ausgabe 2004   Pablo | ZYX Music GmbH

Killer Joe | Get Happy | All Blues | St.Thomas | The Prophet Speaks | Bolivia | Birk's Works | Stolen Moments | Bye Bye Blackbird
Live at Kosei-Nenkin Hall,Tokyo,Japan, rec. 22./23.3.1976
Jackson,Milt (vib) | Edwards,Teddy (ts) | Walton,Cedar (p,el-p) | Brown,Ray (b) | Higgins,Billy (dr)

2620104-2 | 2 CD | JATP In Tokyo
JATP All Stars
Introduction by Norman Granz | Jam Session Blues | J.C.Heard Drum Solo | Cotton Tail | The Nearness Of You- | Someone To Watch Over Me- | Flamingo- | I Surrender Dear- | Sweet And Lovely- | Stardust- | Embraceable You-
rec. 4./7.& 8.11.1953
JATP All Stars | Eldridge,Roy (tp) | Harris,Bill (tb) | Smith,Willie (as) | Carter,Benny (as) | Phillips,Flip (ts) | Webster,Ben (ts) | Peterson,Oscar (p) | Ellis,Herb (g) | Brown,Ray (b) | Heard,J.C. (dr)
Oscar Peterson Trio
That Old Black Magic | Tenderly | Blues | Alone Together | Swingin' Till The Girls Come Home
Peterson,Oscar (p) | Ellis,Herb (g) | Brown,Ray (b)
JATP All Stars
Back Home Again In Indiana | Cocktails For Two | Don't Be That Way | Stompin' At The Savoy
JATP All Stars | Peterson,Oscar (p) | Krupa,Gene (dr)
On The Sunny Side Of The Street | Body And Soul | Why Don't You Do Right | Oh! Lady Be Good | I Got It Bad And That Ain't Good | How High The Moon | My Funny Valentine | Smooth Sailing | Frim Fram Sauce | Perdido
JATP All Stars | Tunia,Raymond (p) | Ellis,Herb (g) | Brown,Ray (b) | Heard,J.C. (dr)
After Hours Session: Sweethearts On Parade And Dixie
JATP All Stars | Shavers,Charlie (tp) | Harris,Bill (tb) | Carter,Benny (as) | Smith,Willie (as) | Webster,Ben (ts) | Phillips,Flip (ts) | Peterson,Oscar (p) | Ellis,Herb (g) | Brown,Ray (b) | Heard,J.C. (dr) | Fitzgerald,Ella (voc)

2620113-2 | CD | Live At The Northsea Jazz Festival
Freddie Hubbard Quintet
First Light | One Of Another Kind | One Of A Kind | Impressions | Happiness Is Now | Red Clay
Live at The Northsea Festival, rec. July 1980
Hubbard,Freddie (tp) | Schnitter,David (ts) | Childs,Billy (keyboards) | Klein,Larry (b) | Lott,Sinclair (dr)

2620114-2 | 2 CD | Live At Donte's
Joe Pass Trio
What Have They Done To My Song Ma | You Stepped Out Of A Dream | A Time For Love | Donte's Inferno | You Are The Sunshine Of My Life | Secret Love | Sweet Georgia Brown | Stompin' At The Savoy | Darn That Dream | Milestones | Lullaby Of The Leaves | What Are You Doing The Rest Of Your Life | Blues For Pam
Live at Donte's,Los Angeles,CA, rec. 8./9.12.1974
Pass,Joe (g) | Hughart,Jim (el-b) | Severino,Frank (dr)

2630201-2 | CD | Ella Abraca Jobim
2630201 | 2 LP | Ella Abraca Jobim
Ella Fitzgerald With Orchestra
Somewhere In The Hills | Girl From Ipanema(Garota De Ipanema) | Dindi | Desafinado | Wave | Agua De Beber(Water To Drink) | Fotografia | Triste | How Insensitive(Insensatez) | He's A Carioca | A Felicidade(Happiness) | This Love That I've Found | Corcovado(Quiet Nights) | Dreamer | Bonita | Samba Da Una Nota So(One Note Samba) | Useless Landscape
Hollywood,CA, rec. 17.-19.9.1980/18.-20.3.1981
Fitzgerald,Ella (voc) | Terry,Clark (tp) | Sims,Zoot (ts) | Thielemans,Jean 'Toots' (harm) | Pass,Joe (g) | Castro-Neves,Oscar (g) | Jackson,Paul (g) | Holder,Mitch (g) | Bautista,Roland (g) | Trotter,Terry (keyboards) | Lang,Mike (keyboards) | McDonald,Clarence (keyboards) | Laboriel,Abe (b) | Acuna,Alejandro Neciosup (dr) | Da Costa,Paulinho (perc) | Bulling,Erich (cond,arr)

2CD 2620102 | CD | Johnny Hodges At The Sportpalast, Berlin
Johnny Hodges Orchestra
Take The 'A' Train | In The Kitchen | Mood Indigo- | In My Solitude- | Satin Doll | I Got It Bad And That Ain't Good | Rockin' In Rhythm | Autumn Leaves | Stompy Jones | C Jam Blues | The Jeep Is Jumpin' | Good Queen Bess | Things Ain't What They Used To Be | I'll Get By(As Long As I Have You) | I Let A Song Go Out Of My Heart- | Don't Get Around Much Anymore- | Just Squeeze Me(But Don't Tease Me) | Do Nothin' Till You Hear From Me | Rose Of The Rio Grande | All Of Me | On The Sunny Side Of The Street | Blue Moon | Perdido
Live at The Sportpalast,Berlin, rec. March 1961
Hodges,Johnny (as) | Nance,Ray (v,co,voc) | Brown,Lawrence (tb) | Carney,Harry (bs) | Williams,Al (p) | Bell,Aaron (b) | Woodyard,Sam (dr)

2CD 2620111 | 2 CD | The London Concert
Oscar Peterson Trio
It's A Wonderful World | People | Ain't Misbehavin' | Jitterbug Waltz | Pennies From Heaven | I Get Along Without You Very Well | Sweet Georgia Brown | Falling In Love With Love | Hogtown Blues | Emily(The Americanization Of Emily) | Satin Doll | Duke Ellington Medley: | I Got It Bad And That Ain't Good- | Do Nothin' Till You Hear From Me- | C Jam Blues | Lush Life- | Take The 'A' Train- | Caravan- | Cute
Live at The Royal Festival Hall,London, rec. 21.10.1978
Peterson,Oscar (p) | Heard,John (b) | Bellson,Louie (dr)

2CD 2620118 | 2 CD | At Zardis'
Sunday | I've Got You Under My Skin | Herbie's Tune | There's A Small Hotel | How High The Moon | Noreen's Nocturne | I Was Doing Alright | Falling In Love With Love | Big Fat Mama | The Way You Look Tonight | Begin The Beguine | Easy Does It | Will You Still Be Mine | Laura | Roy's Tune | The Continental | You Are Too Beautiful | Pompton Turnpike | Surrey With The Fringe On Top | Swinging On A Star | I've Got You Under My Skin | Autumn Leaves | Love For Sale | Soft Winds | I Loves You Porgy- | Anything Goes- | It's A Marshmallow World | Tenderly | Honeysuckle Rose | Love You Madly | Have You Met Miss Jones
Live at Zardis',Hollywood,CA, rec. 1955
Peterson,Oscar (p) | Ellis,Herb (g) | Brown,Ray (b)

2CD 2620119 | 2 CD | J.A.T.P. In London 1969
JATP All Stars
Ow! | Stardust | Yesterdays | You Go To My Head | What Is This Thing Called Love | Tin Tin Deo | The Champ
London,GB, rec. March 1969
JATP All Stars | Gillespie,Dizzy (tp) | Terry,Clark (tp) | Sims,Zoot (ts) | Moody,James (fl,ts) | Wilson,Teddy (p) | Cranshaw,Bob (b) | Bellson,Louie (dr)
Woman You Must Be Crazy | Goin' To Chicago Blues | Stormy Monday Blues(They Call It Stormy Monday)
JATP All Stars | Gillespie,Dizzy (tp) | Terry,Clark (tp) | Sims,Zoot (ts) | Moody,James (fl,ts) | Walker,T-Bone (g,voc) | Wilson,Teddy (p) | Cranshaw,Bob (b) | Bellson,Louie (dr)
Teddy Wilson Trio
Shiny Stockings | Undecided | I've Got The World On A String | L.O.V.E.
Wilson,Teddy (p) | Cranshaw,Bob (b) | Bellson,Louie (dr)
JATP All Stars
Blue Lou | I Can't Get Started | September Song | Body And Soul | Bean Stalkin'
JATP All Stars | Carter,Benny (as) | Hawkins,Coleman (ts) | Wilson,Teddy (p) | Cranshaw,Bob (b) | Bellson,Louie (dr)

2CD 2625705 | 2 CD | Oscar Pterson Et Joe Pass A La Salle Pleyel
Oscar Peterson-Joe Pass Duo
I Gotta Right To Sing The Blues | Mirage | Tenderly | Back Home Again In Indiana | It Never Entered My Mind | Ellingtonia: | Take The 'A' Train- | In A Sentimental Mood- | Satin Doll- | Lady Of The Lavender Mist- | Things Ain't What They Used To Be- | Sweet Georgia Brown | Darn That Dream | Medley: | The Summer Knows- | What Are You Doing The Rest Of Your Life- | Everything I Love | It's All Right With Me | Stella By Starlight | Just You Just Me | If | Honeysuckle Rose | Blues For Bise | Pleyel Bis
Live at Salle Pleyel,Paris,France, rec. 17.3.1975
Pass,Joe (g) | Peterson,Oscar (p)

2CD 2625711 | 2 CD | Oscar Peterson In Russia
Oscar Peterson
I Got It Bad And That Ain't Good | I Concentrate On You | Hogtown Blues | Place St.Henri | Someone To Watch Over Me
Tallinn,Estland, rec. 17.11.1974
Peterson,Oscar (p-solo)
Oscar Peterson Duo
On Green Dolphin Street | You Stepped Out Of A Dream | Wave | On The Trail(From The Grand Canyon Suite)
Peterson,Oscar (p) | Orsted-Pedersen,Niels-Henning (b)
Oscar Peterson Trio
Take The 'A' Train | Summertime | Just Friends | Do You Know What It Means To Miss New Orleans | I Loves You Porgy- | Georgia On My Mind-
Peterson,Oscar (p) | Orsted-Pedersen,Niels-Henning (b) | Hanna,Jake (dr)

2PACD 2620101 | 2 CD | Afro Blue Impressions
John Coltrane Quartet
Spiritual | Impressions
Live,at Konserthuset,Stockholm, rec. 22.10.1963
Coltrane,John (ss,ts) | Tyner,McCoy (p) | Garrison,Jimmy (b) | Jones,Elvin (dr)
Lonnie's Lament | Naima | Chasin' The Trane | My Favorite Things | Afro Blue | Cousin Mary | I Want To Talk About You
?,Europe, rec. 1963
Coltrane,John (ss,ts) | Tyner,McCoy (p) | Garrison,Jimmy (b) | Jones,Elvin (dr)

2PACD 2620112 | 2 CD | The Paris Concert
Oscar Peterson Trio
Please Don't Talk About Me When I'm Gone | Who Can I Turn To | Benny's Bugle | Soft Winds | Good Bye | Plage St. Henri | Manha De Carnaval(Morning Of The Carnival)- | If- | Ornithology | Blue Lou | How Long Has This Been Going On | Gentle Tears | Lover Man(Oh,Where Can You Be?) | Samba De Orfeu(I Want To Live) | Donna Lee | Sweet Georgia Brown
Live at Salle Pleyel,Paris,France, rec. 5.10.1978
Peterson,Oscar (p) | Orsted-Pedersen,Niels-Henning (b) | Pass,Joe (g)

4 PACD 4423-2 | 4 CD | Joe Pass:Guitar Virtuoso
Joe Pass
Night And Day | Here's That Rainy Day | Indian Summer | Lush Life | Weaselocity
Los Angeles,CA, rec. 11./16.& 26.11.1973
Pass,Joe (el-g)
Giant Steps | Misty | Blues For Basie
Hollywood,CA, rec. 14.9.1976
Pass,Joe (el-g)
Have You Met Miss Jones | Passanova | Sultry
Los Angeles,CA, rec. 1.6.1977
Pass,Joe (el-g)
Gentle Tears | Lover Man(Oh,Where Can You Be?)
Live at Salle Pleyel,Paris,France, rec. 5.10.1978
Pass,Joe (el-g)
Tarde
University of Akron,Kent,Ohio, rec. March 1986
Pass,Joe (g-solo)
Cheek To Cheek | Blues For Fred- | They All Laughed-
Berkeley,CA, rec. 2./3.2.1988
Pass,Joe (el-g)
Eric's Smoozie Blues | Beautiful Love
Live at The Vine St.Bar,Los Angeles,CA, rec. 13.9.1991
Pass,Joe (g,el-g)
Star Eyes | Blues For Angel | Song For Ellen | How Deep Is The Ocean
Hollywood,CA, rec. 7./11.& 12.8.1992
Pass,Joe (g)
Duke Ellington Quartet
Cotton Tail
Hollywood,CA, rec. 8.1.1973
Ellington,Duke (p) | Pass,Joe (el-g) | Brown,Ray (b) | Bellson,Louie (dr)
Joe Pass-Herb Ellis
Samba De Orfeu | Seulb
Burbank,Los Angeles,CA, rec. 30.1./13.& 20.2.1973
Pass,Joe (g) | Ellis,Herb (g)
Joe Pass Trio
Do Nothin' Till You Hear From Me
Hollywood,CA, rec. 21.6.1974
Pass,Joe (el-g) | Brown,Ray (b) | Durham,Bobby (dr)
Time For Love | Stompin' At The Savoy
Live at Donte's,Los Angeles,CA, rec. 9.12.1974
Pass,Joe (el-g) | Hughart,Jim (el-b) | Severino,Frank (dr)
Joe Pass Sextet
O Barquinho(Little Boat) | The Gentle Rain (Chuva Delicada)
Hollywood,CA, rec. 8.5.1978
Pass,Joe (el-g) | Grusin,Don (keyboards) | Castro-Neves,Oscar (g) | Bailly,Octavio (b) | Slon,Claudio (dr) | Da Costa,Paulinho (perc)
Oscar Peterson Trio
Ornithology
Live at Salle Pleyel,Paris,France, rec. 5.10.1978
Peterson,Oscar (p) | Pass,Joe (el-g) | Orsted-Pedersen,Niels-Henning (b)
Joe Pass/Niels-Henning Orsted-Pedersen Duo
Samba De Orfeu | Donna Lee | Sweet Georgia Brown
Pass,Joe (el-g) | Orsted-Pedersen,Niels-Henning (b)
Joe Pass-Jimmy Rowles Duo
As Long As I Live
Venice,CA, rec. 12.1.1981
Pass,Joe (el-g) | Rowles,Jimmy (p)
Joe Pass Quartet
It Ain't Necessarily So
Hollywood,CA, rec. 23.11.1981
Pass,Joe (el-g) | Pisano,John (g) | Hughart,Jim (b) | Manne,Shelly (dr)
Joe Pass Quintet
Bluesology
Hollywood,CA, rec. 28.12.1988
Pass,Joe (el-g) | Johnson,Plas (ts) | Wiggins,Gerald 'Gerry' (p,org) | Simpkins,Andrew (b) | Heath,Albert 'Tootie' (dr)
Joe Pass Quartet
D-Joe | Anouman | Belleville
Hollywood,CA, rec. December 1989
Pass,Joe (el-g) | Pisano,John (g) | Hughart,Jim (b) | Bailey,Colin (dr)
Relaxin' At The Camarillo | Tenderly | Gee Baby Ain't I Good To You
Hollywood,CA, rec. 9.-11.8.1990
Pass,Joe (el-g) | Pisano,John (g) | Hughart,Jim (b) | Bailey,Colin (dr)
Oleo | Blues For Monty
Live at Yoshi's Keystone Korner,Oakland,CA, rec. 30.1.1992
Pass,Joe (el-g) | Pisano,John (g,el-g) | Hughart,Jim (b) | Bailey,Colin (dr)
Ella Fitzgerald With Joe Pass
You Go To My Head
Hollywood,CA, rec. 28.8.1973
Fitzgerald,Ella (voc) | Pass,Joe (g)
You Took Advantage Of Me | All Too Soon | I Didn't Know About You
Los Angeles,CA, rec. 29./30.1.1976
Fitzgerald,Ella (voc) | Pass,Joe (g)
Easy Living | Why Don't You Do Right
Hollywood,CA, rec. 21.3.1983
Fitzgerald,Ella (voc) | Pass,Joe (g)
Sarah Vaughan With The Oscar Peterson Quartet
My Old Flame
Hollywood,CA, rec. 25.4.1978
Vaughan,Sarah (voc) | Peterson,Oscar (p) | Pass,Joe (g) | Brown,Ray (b) | Bellson,Louie (dr)
Sarah Vaughan With The Joe Pass Quartet
I Didn't Know What Time It Was | Autumn Leaves
Hollywood,CA, rec. 1./2.3.1982
Vaughan,Sarah (voc) | Pass,Joe (g) | Hanna,Sir Roland (p) | Simpkins,Andrew (b) | Jones,Harold (dr)
Joe Pass/Niels-Henning Orsted-Pedersen Duo
Lover Man(Oh,Where Can You Be?) | Tricotism
London,GB, rec. 19.11.1978
Pass,Joe (el-g) | Orsted-Pedersen,Niels-Henning (b)
Zoot Sims-Joe Pass Duo
Blues For 2 | Dindi | Take-Off
NYC, rec. 6.3.& 23.6.1982
Sims,Zoot (ts) | Pass,Joe (el-g)
Joe Pass-John Pisano
Alone Together | Bailewick | S'il Vous Plait
Hollywood,CA, rec. 16./17.2.1991
Pass,Joe (el-g) | Pisano,John (g)

6 PACD 4401-2 | 6 CD | Art Tatum-The Complete Pablo Group Masterpieces
Tatum-Carter-Bellson Trio
Blues In C | Undecided | Under A Blanket Of Blue | Blues In B Flat | A Foggy Day(In London Town) | Street Of Dreams | 'S Wonderful | Makin' Whoopee | Old Fashioned Love | I'm Left With The Blues In My Heart | My Blue Heaven | Hands Across The Table | You're Mine You | Idaho
Los Angeles,CA, rec. 25.6.1954
Tatum,Art (p) | Carter,Benny (as) | Bellson,Louie (dr)
Art Tatum Quartet
Night And Day | I Won't Dance | In A Sentimental Mood | The Moon Is Low | Moon Song | You Took Advantage Of Me | This Can't Be Love | I Surrender Dear | I Won't Dance(alt.take) | In A Sentimental Mood(alt.take)
Los Angeles,CA, rec. 23.& 29.3.1955
Tatum,Art (p) | Eldridge,Roy (tp) | Simmons,John (b) | Stoller,Alvin (dr)
Tatum-Hampton-Rich Trio
What Is This Thing Called Love | I'll Never Be The Same | Makin' Whoopee | Hallelujah | Perdido | More Than You Know | How High The Moon | This Can't Be Love | Stars Fell On Alabama | Lover Man(Oh,Where Can You Be?) | Prisoner Of Love | Love For Sale (Concept 1) | Love For Sale (Concept 2) | Body And Soul | Please Be Kind | This Can't Be Love(alt.take) | Hallelujah(alt.take)
Los Angeles,CA, rec. 1.8.1955
Tatum,Art (p) | Hampton,Lionel (vib) | Rich,Buddy (dr)
Art Tatum Sextet
Verve Blues | Plaid | Somebody Loves Me | September Song | Deep Purple | September Song(alt.take) | What Is This Thing Called Love | What Is This Thing Called Love(alt.take)
Los Angeles,CA, rec. 7.9.1955
Tatum,Art (p) | Edison,Harry 'Sweets' (tp) | Hampton,Lionel (vib) | Kessel,Barney (g) | Callender,Red (b) | Rich,Buddy (dr)
Art Tatum Trio
Just One Of Those Things | More Than You Know | Some Other Spring | If | Blue Lou | Love For Sale | Isn't It Romantic | I'll Never Be The Same | I Guess I'll Have To Change My Plans | Trio Blues
Los Angeles,CA, rec. 27.1.1956
Tatum,Art (p) | Callender,Red (b) | Jones,Jo (dr)
Art Tatum-Buddy DeFranco Quartet
Deep Night | This Can't Be Love | Memories Of You | Once In A While | A Foggy Day(In London Town) | Lover Man(Oh,Where Can You Be?) | You're Mine You | Makin' Whoopee | Deep Night(alt.take) | Once In A While(alt.take) | This Can't Be Love(alt.take)
Los Angeles,CA, rec. 6.2.1956
Tatum,Art (p) | DeFranco,Buddy (cl) | Callender,Red (b) | Douglas,Bill (dr)
Art Tatum-Ben Webster Quartet
Gone With The Wind | All The Things You Are | Have You Met Miss Jones | My One And Only Love | Night And Day | My Ideal | Where Or When | Gone With The Wind(alt.take) | Gone With The Wind(alt.take-2) | Have You Met Miss Jones(alt.take)
Los Angeles,CA, rec. 11.9.1956
Tatum,Art (p) | Webster,Ben (ts) | Callender,Red (b) | Douglas,Bill (dr)

7 PACD 4404-2 | 7 CD | Art Tatum-The Complete Pablo Solo Masterpieces
Art Tatum
Can't We Be Friends | This Can't Be Love | Elegy | Memories Of You | Over The Rainbow | If You Hadn't Gone Away | Body And Soul | The Man I Love | Makin' Whoopee | September Song | Begin The Beguine | Humoresque | Louise | Love For Sale | Judy | I'm Coming Virginia | Wrap Your Troubles In Dreams | Dixieland Band | Embraceable You | Come Rain Or Come Shine | Just A-Sittin' And A-Rockin' | There'll Never Be Another You | Tenderly | What Does It Take | You Took Advantage Of Me | I've Got The World On A String | Yesterdays | I Hadn't Anyone 'Till You | Night And Day | Jitterbug Waltz | Someone To Watch Over Me | The Very Thought Of You | You're Driving Me Crazy | I Don't Stand A Ghost Of A Chance With You
Hollywood,CA, rec. 28.12.1953
Tatum,Art (p-solo)
Stardust | I Cover The Waterfront | Where Or When | Stay As Sweet As You Are | Fine And Dandy | All The Things You Are | Have You Met Miss Jones | In A Sentimental Mood | I'll See You Again | I'll See You In My Dreams | Ill Wind | Isn't It A Lovely Day | Blue Skies | Without A Song | Stompin' At The Savoy | My Last Affair | I'm In The Mood For Love | Taboo | Would You Like To Take A Walk | I've Got A Crush On You | Japanese Sandman | Too Marvelous For Words | Aunt Hagar's Blues | Just Like A Butterfly | Gone With The Wind | Danny Boy (Londonderry Air) | They Can't Take That Away From Me | Tea For Two | It's The Talk Of The Town | Blue Lou | When A Woman Loves A Man | Willow Weep For Me | Ain't Misbehavin' | Smoke Gets In Your Eyes | Mighty Like A Rose
Hollywood,CA, rec. 29.12.1953
Tatum,Art (p-solo)
Stars Fell On Alabama | Blue Moon | There's A Small Hotel | Caravan | The Way You Look Tonight | You Go To My Head | Lover Come Back To Me | Sophisticated Lady | Dancing In The Dark | Love Me Or Leave Me | Cherokee | These Foolish Things Remind Me On You | Deep Purple | After You've Gone | I Didn't Know What Time It Was | Somebody Loves Me | What's New? | Sweet Lorraine | Crazy Rhythm | Isn't It Romantic | You're Blasé | You're Mine You | Back Home Again In Indiana | That Old Feeling | Heat Wave | She's Funny That Way
Hollywood,CA, rec. 22.4.1954
Tatum,Art (p-solo)
I Surrender Dear | Happy Feet | Mean To Me | Boulevard Of Broken Dreams | Moonlight On The Ganges | Moon Song | When You Lover Has Gone | The Moon Is Low | If I Had You | S' Posin' | Don't Worry 'Bout Me | Prisoner Of Love | Moonlow | I Won't Dance | I Can't Give You Anything But Love | Lullaby Of Rhythm | Out Of Nowhere | I Gotta Right To Sing The Blues | It's Only A Paper Moon | Everything I Have Is Yours | I Only Have Eyes For You | On The Sunny Side Of The Street | Do Nothin' Till You Hear From Me | So Beats My Heart For You | If You Hadn't Gone Away | Please Be Kind
Hollywood,CA, rec. 19.1.1955
Tatum,Art (p-solo)
Someone To Watch Over Me | Begin The Beguine | Willow Weep For Me | Humoresque
Live at The Hollywood Bowl,Los Angeles,CA, rec. 15.8.1956
Tatum,Art (p-solo)

7PACD 4433-2 | 7 CD | John Coltrane-Live Trane:The European Tours
John Coltrane Quintet With Eric Dolphy
Impressions | My Favorite Things
Live at The Olympia,Paris,France, rec. 18.11.1961
Coltrane,John (ts) | Dolphy,Eric (fl,as) | Tyner,McCoy (p) | Workman,Reggie (b) | Jones,Elvin (dr)
Blue Train | Naima | My Favorite Things
Live,at Konserthuset,Stockholm, rec. 23.11.1961
Coltrane,John (ss,ts) | Dolphy,Eric (fl,b-cl,as) | Tyner,McCoy (p) | Workman,Reggie (b) | Jones,Elvin (dr)
Mr.P.C. | My Favorite Things | Miles' Mode
Live at Musikhalle Hamburg, rec. 25.11.1961
Coltrane,John (ss,ts) | Dolphy,Eric (fl,as) | Tyner,McCoy (p) | Workman,Reggie (b) | Jones,Elvin (dr)
John Coltrane Quartet
Introduction by Norman Granz | Bye Bye Blackbird | The Inch Worm | Every Time We Say Goodbye | Mr.P.C. | My Favorite Things | The Inch Worm | Mr.P.C.(2)
Live at The Olympia,Paris,France, rec. 17.11.1962
Coltrane,John (ss,ts) | Tyner,McCoy (p) | Garrison,Jimmy (b) | Jones,Elvin (dr)

Naima | Traneing In | Bye Bye Blackbird | Impressions
Live,at Konserthuset,Stockholm, rec. 19.11.1962
Coltrane,John (ss,ts) | Tyner,McCoy (p) | Garrison,Jimmy (b) | Jones,Elvin (dr)
Introduction in Swedish | Traneing In | Mr.P.C. | Naima | The Promise | Spiritual | I Want To Talk About You | My Favorite Things
Live,at Konserthuset,Stockholm, rec. 22.10.1963
Coltrane,John (ss,ts) | Tyner,McCoy (p) | Garrison,Jimmy (b) | Jones,Elvin (dr)
Mr.P.C.
Live at Salle Pleyel,Paris,France, rec. 1.11.1963
Coltrane,John (ts) | Tyner,McCoy (p) | Garrison,Jimmy (b) | Jones,Elvin (dr)
Lonnie's Lament | Naima | Chasin' The Trane | My Favorite Things | Afro Blue | Cousin Mary | I Want To Talk About You
Live at Auditorium Maximum,Universität Berlin, rec. 2.11.1963
Coltrane,John (ss,ts) | Tyner,McCoy (p) | Garrison,Jimmy (b) | Jones,Elvin (dr)
Impressions
Live at Liederhalle,Stuttgart, rec. 4.11.1963
Coltrane,John (ts) | Tyner,McCoy (p) | Garrison,Jimmy (b) | Jones,Elvin (dr)

CD 2310976-2 | CD | Parisian Thoroughfare | EAN 090204922871
Bud Powell Trio
Yesterdays
Live at Club St.Germain,Paris,France, rec. 1.-14.11.1957
Powell,Bud (p) | Michelot,Pierre (b) | Clarke,Kenny (dr)
Bud Powell Quintet
No Problem | Miguel's Party
Live at Club St.Germain,Paris,France, rec. 7.11.1959
Powell,Bud (p) | Terry,Clark (fl-h) | Wilen,Barney (ts) | Michelot,Pierre (b) | Clarke,Kenny (dr)
Bud Powell Quartet
Pie Eye
Live at Club St.Germain,Paris,France, rec. 1959
Powell,Bud (p) | Terry,Clark (fl-h) | Michelot,Pierre (b) | Clarke,Kenny (dr)
52nd Street Theme
Powell,Bud (p) | Wilen,Barney (ts) | Michelot,Pierre (b) | Clarke,Kenny (dr)
Bud Powell Trio
John's Abbey | Shaw 'Nuff
Live at The Blue Note,Paris,France, rec. 12.12.1959
Powell,Bud (p) | Michelot,Pierre (b) | Clarke,Kenny (dr)
Just One Of Those Things
Live at The Blue Note,Paris,France, rec. 1959
Powell,Bud (p) | Michelot,Pierre (b) | Clarke,Kenny (dr)
Bud Powell Quartet
Omicron
Studios De La Radio Television Francaise,Paris , rec. 1959
Powell,Bud (p) | Wilen,Barney (ts) | Peter,Eric (b) | Humair,Daniel (dr)
Bud Powell Trio
Anthropology(incomplete)
Studio De La Radio Television Francaise,Paris, rec. 1959
Powell,Bud (p) | Peter,Eric (b) | Humair,Daniel (dr)
Bud Powell Quintet
Buzzy
Live at Club St.Germain,Paris,France, rec. 1959
Powell,Bud (p) | Holland,Peanuts (tp) | Wilen,Barney (ts) | Thomas,Rene prob. (g) | Michelot,Pierre (b) | Clarke,Kenny (dr)
Bud Powell Quartet
Groovin' High | Blue Bud Blues- | 52nd Street Theme-
Live at The Blue Note,Paris,France, rec. January 1961
Powell,Bud (p) | Sims,Zoot (ts) | Michelot,Pierre (b) | Clarke,Kenny (dr)

CD 2312111 | CD | Duke Ellington Song Book One
Sarah Vaughan With Small Group & Orchestra
I'm Just A Lucky So-And-So | In My Solitude | I Didn't Know About You | All Too Soon | Sophisticated Lady | Day Dream
Hollywood,CA, rec. 15./16.8.1979
Vaughan,Sarah (voc) | Reed,Waymon (tp,fl-h) | Johnson,J.J. (tb) | Wess,Frank (fl,ts) | Foster,Frank (ts) | Sims,Zoot (ts) | Rowles,Jimmy (p) | Wofford,Mike (p) | Pass,Joe (g) | Pizzarelli,Bucky (g) | Simpkins,Andrew (b) | Tate,Grady (dr) | Byers,Billy (arr,ld) | details unknown
In A Sentimental Mood | I Let A Song Go Out Of My Heart | Lush Life | In A Mellow Tone
NYC, rec. 12./13.9.1979
Vaughan,Sarah (voc) | Reed,Waymon (tp,fl-h) | Johnson,J.J. (tb) | Wess,Frank (fl,ts) | Foster,Frank (ts) | Sims,Zoot (ts) | Rowles,Jimmy (p) | Wofford,Mike (p) | Pass,Joe (g) | Pizzarelli,Bucky (g) | Simpkins,Andrew (b) | Tate,Grady (dr) | Byers,Billy (arr,ld) | details unknown

CD 2312116 | CD | Duke Ellington Song Book Two
Sarah Vaughan And Her Band
I Ain't Got Nothin' But The Blues | Everything But You | Prelude To A Kiss
NYC/Hollywood, rec. 15/16.8.& 12/13.9.1977
Vaughan,Sarah (voc) | Reed,Waymon (tp,fl-h) | Wess,Frank (fl) | Vinson,Eddie 'Cleanhead' (as,voc) | Pass,Joe (g) | Wofford,Mike (p) | Simpkins,Andrew (b) | Tate,Grady (dr)
What Am I Here For
NYC/Hollywood, rec. 15/16.8.& 12/13.9.1979
Vaughan,Sarah (voc) | Reed,Waymon (tp,fl-h) | Wess,Frank (fl) | Vinson,Eddie 'Cleanhead' (as,voc) | Pass,Joe (g) | Rowles,Jimmy (p) | Wofford,Mike (p) | Simpkins,Andrew (b) | Tate,Grady (dr)
Black Butterfly | Tonight I Shall Sleep With A Smile On My Face | I Got It Bad And That Ain't Good | It Don't Mean A Thing If It Ain't Got That Swing
Vaughan,Sarah (voc) | Reed,Waymon (tp,fl-h) | Wess,Frank (fl) | Vinson,Eddie 'Cleanhead' (as,voc) | Pizzarelli,Bucky (g) | Wofford,Mike (p) | Simpkins,Andrew (b) | Tate,Grady (dr)
Rocks In My Bed
Vaughan,Sarah (voc) | Reed,Waymon (tp,fl-h) | Wess,Frank (fl) | Vinson,Eddie 'Cleanhead' (as,voc) | Crayton,Pee Wee (g) | Glenn,Lloyd (p) | Walker,Bill (b) | Randall,Charles (dr)
Chelsea Bridge | Mood Indigo
Vaughan,Sarah (voc) | Reed,Waymon (tp,fl-h) | Wess,Frank (fl) | Vinson,Eddie 'Cleanhead' (as,voc) | Pass,Joe (g) | Wofford,Mike (p) | Simpkins,Andrew (b) | McCurdy,Roy (dr)

PACD 2310972-2 | CD | Bud Powell Paris Sessions | EAN 025218097222
Bud Powell Trio
Bud On Bach | Bebop
Live at Club St.Germain,Paris,France, rec. 1957
Powell,Bud (p) | Michelot,Pierre (b) | Clarke,Kenny (dr)
Bud Powell Quintet
How High The Moon
Powell,Bud (p) | Gillespie,Dizzy (tp) | Wilen,Barney (ts) | Michelot,Pierre (b) | Clarke,Kenny (dr)
Bud Powell Trio
Crossing The Channel
Paris,France, rec. 7.11.1959
Powell,Bud (p) | Michelot,Pierre (b) | Clarke,Kenny (dr)
Get Happy | John's Abbey
Live at The Blue Note,Paris,France, rec. 15.6.1960
Powell,Bud (p) | Michelot,Pierre (b) | Clarke,Kenny (dr)
Taking A Chance On Love
Live at The Blue Note,Paris,France, rec. January 1961
Powell,Bud (p) | Michelot,Pierre (b) | Clarke,Kenny (dr)
Tune For Duke | I Got It Bad And That Ain't Good | Satin Doll | For My Friends | Perdido | Rue De Clichy
Paris,France, rec. February 1963
Powell,Bud (p) | Rovere,Gilbert 'Bibi' (b) | Fields,Kansas (dr)
Bud Powell Quartet
Body And Soul
Edenville,France, rec. 10.-12.8.1964
Powell,Bud (p) | Griffin,Johnny (ts) | Hayat,Guy (b) | Gervais,Jacques (dr)

PACD 2310977-2 | CD | Live At Falcon Lair | EAN 025218097727
Zoot Sims With The Joe Castro Trio
A Night In Tunisia | Pennies From Heaven | I'll See You In My Dreams | It's Always You | Blues For Nat | Swinging With Rudolph | East Of The Sun West Of The Moon | J.C. Blues
Live at Falcon Lair,Beverly Hills,CA, rec. 1.4.1956
Sims,Zoot (as) | Castro,Joe (p) | Vinnegar,Leroy (b) | Jefferson,Ron (dr)

PACD 2310978-2 | CD | Bebop | EAN 025218097826
Bud Powell Orchestra
Introduction by Leonard Feather | Perdido | Back Home Again In Indiana | Jumpin' With Symphony Sid | I'll Be Seeing You | 52nd Street Theme | Ornithology
Live at The Royal Roost,NYC, rec. 19.12.1948
Powell,Bud (p) | Harris,Benny (tp) | Johnson,J.J. (tb) | DeFranco,Buddy (cl) | Konitz,Lee (as) | Johnson,Budd (ts) | Payne,Cecil (bs) | Wayne,Chuck (g) | Boyd,Nelson (b) | Roach,Max (dr)
Bud Powell Trio
Blues In The Closet
Live at Club St.Germain,Paris,France, rec. 7.11.1959
Powell,Bud (p) | Michelot,Pierre (b) | Clarke,Kenny (dr)
Now's The Time | Confirmation
Paris,France, rec. 12.3.1960
Powell,Bud (p) | Michelot,Pierre (b) | Clarke,Kenny (dr)
Salt Peanuts | Lady Bird | I Remember Clifford
Live at The Hotel Restaurant 'La Belle Escale',Edenville,France, rec. 8.-14.8.1964
Powell,Bud (p) | Hayat,Guy (b) | Gervais,Jacques (dr)
Johnny Griffin With The Bud Powell Trio
Hot House
Griffin,Johnny (ts) | Powell,Bud (p) | Hayat,Guy (b) | Gervais,Jacques (dr)

PACD 2620121-2 | CD | Yokohama Concert Vol.2:Chain Reaction | EAN 025218212120
J.J.Johnson-Nat Adderley Quintet
Colors | Chain Reaction | Mr.Clean | Walkin' | Mohawk
Tokyo, Japan, rec. 16.4.1977
Adderley,Nat (tp) | Johnson,J.J. (tb) | Childs,Billy (keyboards) | Dumas,Tony (b) | Johnson,Kevin (dr)
Blue 'N' Boogie | Modaji | Song From M.A.S.H.
Live at Kanagawa Kenritsu Ongakudo,Yokohama,Japan, rec. 20.4.1977
Adderley,Nat (tp) | Johnson,J.J. (tb) | Childs,Billy (keyboards) | Dumas,Tony (b) | Johnson,Kevin (dr)

PACD 5302-2 | CD | Muddy Waters:Paris 1972
Muddy Waters Band
Introduction | Clouds In My Heart | Lovin' Man | County Jail | Hoochie Coochie Man | Blow Wind Blow | Honey Bee | Walking Through The Park | Rollin' And Tumblin' | Walkin' Blues | Got My Mojo Working
Live in Paris,France, rec. 1972
Muddy Waters[McKinley Morganfield] (g,voc) | Bufford,George 'Mojo' (harm) | Myers,Louis (g) | Perkins,'Pinetop' Joe (p) | Jones,Calvin (b) | Smith,Willie 'Big Eyes' (dr)

PACD 5303-2 | CD | The Cannonball Adderley Quintet:Paris 1960
The Cannonball Adderley Quintet
Introduction by Norman Granz | Jeannine | This Here | Blue Daniel | The Chant | Bohemia After Dark | Work Song
Live at Salle Pleyel,Paris,France, rec. 25.11.1960
Adderley,Julian \'Cannonball\' (as) | Adderley,Nat (co) | Feldman,Victor (p) | Jones,Sam (b) | Hayes,Louis (dr)

PACD 5304-2 | CD | Jazz At The Philharmonis Berlin '65/Paris '67
Duke Ellington And His Orchestra
Midriff | Ad Lib On Nippon | Chelsea Bridge | Happy-Go-Lucky Local
Live at The Sportpalast,Berlin, rec. 3.2.1965
Ellington,Duke (p) | Anderson,Cat (tp) | Williams,Cootie (tp) | Jones,Herbie (tp) | Ellington,Mercer (tp) | Nance,Ray (tp) | Johnson,Money (tp) | Brown,Lawrence (tb) | Cooper,Frank 'Buster' (tb) | Connors,Chuck (tb) | Procope,Russell (as) | Hodges,Johnny (as) | Hamilton,Jimmy (cl,ts) | Gonsalves,Paul (ts) | Carney,Harry (cl,bs) | Lamb,John (b) | Woodyard,Sam (dr)
Blood Count | Harmony In Harlem | Things Ain't What They Used To Be | Drag | Rockin' In Rhythm | Portrait Of The Lion(The Second)
Live at Salle Pleyel,Paris,France, rec. 10.3.1967
Ellington,Duke (p) | Anderson,Cat (tp) | Williams,Cootie (tp) | Jones,Herbie (tp) | Ellington,Mercer (tp) | Nance,Ray (tp) | Johnson,Money (tp) | Brown,Lawrence (tb) | Cooper,Frank 'Buster' (tb) | Connors,Chuck (tb) | Procope,Russell (as) | Hodges,Johnny (as) | Hamilton,Jimmy (cl,ts) | Gonsalves,Paul (ts) | Carney,Harry (cl,bs) | Lamb,John (b) | Jones,Rufus (dr)

PACD 5305-2 | CD | Jazz At The Philharmonic-Frankfurt 1952
JATP All Stars
Introduction by Norman Granz | How High The Moon | Undecided | Ballad Medley: | Deep Purple- | Rockin' Chair- | This Is Always- | I Cover The Waterfront- | Dre's Blues
Live at Frankfurt/M., rec. 20.11.1952
JATP All Stars | Eldridge,Roy (tp) | Young,Lester (ts) | Phillips,Flip (ts) | Jones,Hank (p) | Brown,Ray (b) | Roach,Max (dr)

PACD 5306-2 | CD | Jazz At The Philharmonic:The Montreux Collection
Oscar Peterson
Cubano Chant
Montreux,CH, rec. 19.7.1975
Peterson,Oscar (p-solo)
Count Basie Sextet
Collection Blues
Basie,Count (p) | Eldridge,Roy (tp) | Griffin,Johnny (ts) | Jackson,Milt (vib) | Orsted-Pedersen,Niels-Henning (b) | Bellson,Louie (dr)
Benny Carter And His Orchestra
Sunday
Montreux,CH, rec. 16.7.1975
Carter,Benny (as) | Eldridge,Roy (tp) | Terry,Clark (tp) | Sims,Zoot (ts) | Pass,Joe (g) | Flanagan,Tommy (p) | Betts,Keter (b) | Durham,Bobby (dr)
Joe Pass
Alison
Montreux,CH, rec. 19.7.1975
Pass,Joe (g-solo)
Milt Jackson Quartet
Slow Death
Montreux,CH, rec. 16.7.1975
Jackson,Milt (vib) | Peterson,Oscar (p) | Orsted-Pedersen,Niels-Henning (b) | Roker,Granville 'Mickey' (dr)
Ella Fitzgerald With The Tommy Flanagan Trio
The Man I Love
Montreux,CH, rec. 17.7.1975
Fitzgerald,Ella (voc) | Flanagan,Tommy (p) | Betts,Keter (b) | Durham,Bobby (dr)
Oscar Peterson All Stars
Woody'n You
Montreux,CH, rec. 16.7.1975
Peterson,Oscar (p) | Jackson,Milt (vib) | Thielemans,Jean 'Toots' (harm) | Pass,Joe (g) | Orsted-Pedersen,Niels-Henning (b) | Bellson,Louie (dr)
Dizzy Gillespie All Stars
I'll Remember April
Gillespie,Dizzy (tp) | Griffin,Johnny (ts) | Davis,Eddie 'Lockjaw' (ts) | Jackson,Milt (vib) | Flanagan,Tommy (p) | Orsted-Pedersen,Niels-Henning (b) | Roker,Granville 'Mickey' (dr)

PACD 5308-2 | CD | Ella Fitzgerald In Budapest
Ella Fitzgerald With The Tommy Flanagan Trio
Crazy Rhythm | This Guy's In Love With You- | I'm Gonna Sit Right Down And Write Myself A Letter- | Open Your Window | Satin Doll | Spinning Wheel | As Time Goes By | You Better Love Me | I'll Never Fall In Love Again | Hello Young Lovers | I Concentrate On You- | You Go To My Head- | Girl From Ipanema(Garota De Ipanema) | Cabaret | Dancing In The Dark | Raindrops Keep Fallin' On My Head | The Lady Is A Tramp | Summertime | Mr.Paganini | Mack The Knife(Moritat) | People
Live in Budapest,Hungary, rec. 20.5.1970
Fitzgerald,Ella (voc) | Flanagan,Tommy (p) | De La Rosa,Frank (b) | Thigpen,Ed (dr)

PACD 5309-2 | CD | Jazz At The Philharmonic: The Gerry Mulligan Quartets In Concert
Gerry Mulligan Quartet
Introduction by Norman Granz | Come Out Wherever You Are | Baubles Bangles And Beads | Laura | Bweebida Bwobbida | Utter Chaos
Live at The Hollywood Bowl,Los Angeles,CA, rec. 27.8.1957
Mulligan,Gerry (bs) | Brookmeyer,Bob (v-tb) | Benjamin,Joe (b) | Bailey,Donald (dr)
Introduction by Norman Granz | Open Country | Love In New Orleans | Four For Three | Subterranean Blues
Live in Paris,France, rec. 6.10.1962
Mulligan,Gerry (bs) | Brookmeyer,Bob (v-tb,p) | Crow,Bill (b) | Johnson,Gus (dr)

PACD 5310-2 | CD | Sophisticated Lady
Ella Fitzgerald With Joe Pass
Introduction by Ella Fitzgerald | I'm Beginning To See The Light | I Got It Bad And That Ain't Good- | Sophisticated Lady- | Georgia On My Mind | Gone With The Wind | Bluesette
Live in Tokyo,Japan, rec. 1983
Fitzgerald,Ella (voc) | Pass,Joe (el-g)
Joe Pass
Samba Da Una Nota So(One Note Samba)
Pass,Joe (el-g-solo)
Old Folks | Wave | Cherokee
Live in Hamburg, rec. 1975
Pass,Joe (el-g-solo)
Ella Fitzgerald With Joe Pass
Take Love Easy | Mood Indigo | Satin Doll
Fitzgerald,Ella (voc) | Pass,Joe (el-g)

PACD 5311-2 | CD | Norman Granz' JATP: Carnegie Hall 1949
JATP All Stars
Introduction by Norman Granz | Leap Here | Back Home Again In Indiana | Lover Come Back To Me
Live at Carnegie Hall,NYC, rec. 2.11.1949
JATP All Stars | Navarro,Fats | Turk,Tommy (tb) | Parker,Charlie (as) | Phillips,Flip (ts) | Jones,Hank (p) | Brown,Ray (b) | Manne,Shelly (dr)
Introduction by Norman Granz | Rifftide | Sophisticated Lady | Things We Did Last Summer | Stuffy
JATP All Stars | Navarro,Fats | Hawkins,Coleman (ts) | Jones,Hank (p) | Brown,Ray (b) | Manne,Shelly (dr)

PACD 5312-2 | CD | Stompin' At Newport | EAN 025218531221
Stan Kenton Orchestra
The Opener | Artistry In Rhythm | Stompin' At The Savoy | Yesterdays | Intermission Riff | 23 Degrees North-82 Degrees West | Everything Happens To Me | The Peanut Vendor | The End Of A Love Affair | Young Blood | La Suerte De Los Tontos(Fortune Of Fools) | The Big Chase
Live at Newport,Rhode Island, rec. 5.7.1957
Kenton,Stan (p) | Leddy,Ed (tp) | Noto,Sam (tp) | Katzman,Lee (tp) | Gilbert,Phil (tp) | Catalano,Billy (tp) | Larsen,Kent (tb) | LeCoque,Archie (tb) | Reed,Don (tb) | Amlotte,Jim (tb,b-tb) | Shroyer,Kenny (tb,b-tb) | Niehaus,Lennie (as) | Perkins,Bill (ts) | Dunstan,Wayne (ts) | Perlow,Steve (bs) | Robinson,Billy (bs) | Kelly,Red (b) | McKenzie,Jerry (dr)

PACD 5313-2 | CD | Duke Ellington At The Alhambra | EAN 025218531320
Duke Ellington And His Orchestra
Take The 'A' Train | Black And Tan Fantasy- | Creole Love Call- | The Mooche- | Newport Up | Tenderly | Juniflí | Frustration | Rockin' In Rhythm | Jeep's Blues | All Of Me | Things Ain't What They Used To Be | Jam With Sam | Hi-Fi Fo Fums | Diminuendo And Crescendo In Blue
Live at The Alhambra,Paris,France, rec. 29.10.1958
Ellington,Duke (p) | Baker,Harold 'Shorty' (tp) | Anderson,Cat (tp) | Terry,Clark (tp,fl-h) | Nance,Ray (tp,v,voc) | Jackson,Quentin (tb) | Sanders,John (tb) | Woodman,Britt (tb) | Hodges,Johnny (as) | Procope,Russell (cl,as) | Hamilton,Jimmy (cl,ts) | Gonsalves,Paul (ts) | Carney,Harry (cl,bs) | Woode,Jimmy (b) | Woodyard,Sam (dr)

PACD 5314-2 | CD | Decidedly | EAN 025218531429
Roy Eldridge Quintet
Undecided
Live at The Antibes Jazz Festival, rec. 20.7.1975
Eldridge,Roy (tp) | Griffin,Johnny (ts) | Bryant,Ray (p) | Orsted-Pedersen,Niels-Henning (b) | Bellson,Louie (dr)
Roy Eldridge Sextet
Bee's Blues | Lover Man(Oh,Where Can You Be?)
Live at The Antibes Jaz Festival, rec. 20.7.1975
Eldridge,Roy (tp) | Griffin,Johnny (ts) | Pass,Joe (g) | Bryant,Ray (p) | Orsted-Pedersen,Niels-Henning (b) | Bellson,Louie (dr)
Hackensack
Live at The Antibes Jazz Festival, rec. 20.7.1975
Eldridge,Roy (tp) | Griffin,Johnny (ts) | Pass,Joe (g) | Bryant,Ray (p) | Jackson,Milt (p) | Orsted-Pedersen,Niels-Henning (b) | Bellson,Louie (dr)

PACD 5315-2 | CD | At Newport | EAN 090204932733
Cannonball Adderley Quintet
Wee Dot | A Foggy Day(In London Town) | Sermonette | Sam's Tune | Hurricane Connie
Live at Newport,Rhode Island, rec. 5.7.1957
Adderley,Julian \'Cannonball\' (as) | Adderley,Nat (tp) | Mance,Junior[Julian C.] (p) | Jones,Sam (b) | Cobb,Jimmy (dr)
George Shearing Quintet
Pawn Ticket | It Never Entered My Mind | There'll Never Be Another You
Shearing,George (p) | Richards,Emil (vib,perc) | Thielemans,Jean 'Toots' (g) | McKibbon,Al (b) | Brice,Percy (dr)
George Shearing Quintet With Cannonball And Nat Adderley
Soul Station
Shearing,George (p) | Adderley,Nat (tp) | Adderley,Julian \'Cannonball\' (as) | Richards,Emil (vib,perc) | Thielemans,Jean 'Toots' (g) | McKibbon,Al (b) | Brice,Percy (dr)
George Shearing Sextet
Old Devil Moon | Nothin'' But De Best
Shearing,George (p) | Richards,Emil (vib,perc) | Thielemans,Jean 'Toots' (g) | McKibbon,Al (b) | Brice,Percy (dr) | Peraza,Armando (congas)

PACD 5316-2 | CD | Paris Blues | EAN 090204932740
Horace Silver Quintet
Introduction by Norman Granz And Horace Silver | Where You At? | The Tokyo Blues | Filthy McNasty | Sayonara Blues | Doin' The Thing
Live at The Olympia,Paris,France, rec. 6.10.1962
Silver,Horace (p) | Mitchell,Blue (tp) | Cook,Junior (ts) | Taylor,Gene (b) | Brooks,Roy (dr)

PACD 5317-2 | CD | Montreux Heat! | EAN 090204933792
Mongo Santamaria And His Band
T.V. | Havana | Sofrito | Pajaro Canter | Come Candela | Amanecer | Para Ti
Live at The Montreux Jazz Festival, rec. 19.7.1980
Santamaria,Mongo (congas,bongos) | Villarini,Tommy (tp,perc,cowbell) | Harris,Douglas (fl,ss,ts) | Hoist,Allen (fl,as,bs,cello) | Hamilton,Milton (p) | Smith,Lee (b) | Berrios,Steve (dr,perc)
Mongo Santamaria Group With Dizzy Gillespie And Toots Thielemans
Watermelon Man
Santamaria,Mongo (congas,bongos) | Gillespie,Dizzy (tp) | Thielemans,Jean 'Toots' (harm) | Villarini,Tommy (tp,perc,cowbell) | Harris,Douglas (fl,ss,ts) | Hoist,Allen (fl,as,bs,cello) | Hamilton,Milton (p) | Smith,Lee (b) | Berrios,Steve (dr,perc)

PACD 5318-2 | CD | Jazz At The Philharmonic-Yesterdays | EAN 025218531825
Shelly Manne And His Men
Cabu | Bag's Groove | Poinciana
Live In Zürich,Ch, rec. 22.2.1960
Manne,Shelly (dr) | Gordon,Joe (tp) | Kamuca,Richie (ts) | Freeman,Russ (p) | Budwig,Monty (b)
Straight No Chaser | Yesterdays
Live In Copenhagen,Denmark, rec. 2.3.1960
Manne,Shelly (dr) | Gordon,Joe (tp) | Kamuca,Richie (ts) | Freeman,Russ (p) | Budwig,Monty (b)

PACD20 244-2(2308244) | CD | Together Again

Modern Jazz Quartet
Django | The Cylinder | The Martyr | Really True Blues | Odds Against Tomorrow | The Jasmin Tree | Monterey Mist | Bags New Groove | Woody'n You
Live at The Montreux Jazz Festival, rec. 25.7.1982
MJQ (Modern Jazz Quartet) | Jackson,Milt (vib) | Lewis,John (p) | Heath,Percy (b) | Kay,Connie (dr)

PACD20 431-2 | CD | The Tatum Group Masterpieces Vol.8
Art Tatum-Ben Webster Quartet
Gone With The Wind | All The Things You Are | Have You Met Miss Jones | My One And Only Love | Night And Day | My Ideal | Where Or When | Gone With The Wind(alt.take 1) | Gone With The Wind(alt.take 2) | Have You Met Miss Jones(alt.take)
Los Angeles,CA, rec. 11.9.1956
Tatum,Art (p) | Webster,Ben (ts) | Callender,Red (b) | Douglas,Bill (dr)

PASA 2310-744-6 | SACD | Zoot Sims And The Gershwin Brothers | EAN 025218730822
Zoot Sims Quintet
The Man I Love | How Long Has This Been Going On | Oh! Lady Be Good | I've Got A Crush On You | I Got Rhythm | Embraceable You | 'S Wonderful | Someone To Watch Over Me | Isn't It A Pity | Summertime | They Can't Take That Away From Me
NYC, rec. 6.6.1975
Sims,Zoot (ts) | Pass,Joe (g) | Peterson,Oscar (p) | Mraz,George 'Jiri' (b) | Tate,Grady (dr)

Pacific Jazz | EMI Germany

494106-2 | CD | Picture Of Heath
Chet Baker-Art Pepper-Phil Urso Sextet
Picture Of Heath | For Miles And Miles | C.T.A. | For Minors Only | Minor Yours | Resonant Emotions | Tynan Tyme
Los Angeles,CA, rec. 31.10.1956
Baker,Chet (tp) | Pepper,Art (as) | Urso,Phil (ts) | Perkins,Carl (p) | Counce,Curtis (b) | Marable,Lawrence (dr)

494507-2 | CD | The New One!
Buddy Rich Big Band
New Blues | I Can't Get Started | Group Shot
Hollywood,CA, rec. 16.6.1967
Rich,Buddy (dr) | Findley,Chuck (tp) | Mitchell,Ollie (tp) | Sotille,John (tp) | Murakami,Yoshito (tp) | Trimble,James (tb) | Boice,Johnny (tb) | Brawn,Robert (tb) | Watts,Ernie (fl,cl,as) | Mosher,Jimmy (fl,cl,as) | Corre,Jay (cl,ts) | Keller,Robert (fl,cl,ts) | Hirsh,Meyer (b-cl,bs) | Resnicoff,Richie (g) | Starling,Ray (p) | Gannon,Jimmy (b)
Old Timey
Hollywood,CA, rec. 23.6.1967
Rich,Buddy (dr) | Findley,Chuck (tp) | Mitchell,Ollie (tp) | Sotille,John (tp) | Murakami,Yoshito (tp) | Trimble,James (tb) | Boice,Johnny (tb) | Brawn,Robert (tb) | Watts,Ernie (fl,cl,as) | Mosher,Jimmy (fl,cl,as) | Corre,Jay (cl,ts) | Keller,Robert (fl,cl,ts) | Hirsh,Meyer (b-cl,bs) | Resnicoff,Richie (g) | Starling,Ray (p) | Gannon,Jimmy (b)
Chicago | Luv | The Rotten Kid(alt.take) | Diabolus(alt.take)
Hollywood,CA, rec. 26.6.1967
Rich,Buddy (dr) | Findley,Chuck (tp) | Mitchell,Ollie (tp) | Sotille,John (tp) | Murakami,Yoshito (tp) | Trimble,James (tb) | Boice,Johnny (tb) | Brawn,Robert (tb) | Watts,Ernie (fl,cl,as) | Mosher,Jimmy (fl,cl,as) | Corre,Jay (cl,ts) | Keller,Robert (fl,cl,ts) | Hirsh,Meyer (b-cl,bs) | Resnicoff,Richie (g) | Starling,Ray (p) | Gannon,Jimmy (b)
Away We Go | Machine | Something For Willie | Standing Up In A Hammock | Naptown Blues
Hollywood,CA, rec. 27.6.1967
Rich,Buddy (dr) | Findley,Chuck (tp) | Mitchell,Ollie (tp) | Sotille,John (tp) | Murakami,Yoshito (tp) | Trimble,James (tb) | Boice,Johnny (tb) | Brawn,Robert (tb) | Watts,Ernie (fl,cl,as) | Mosher,Jimmy (fl,cl,as) | Corre,Jay (cl,ts) | Keller,Robert (fl,cl,ts) | Hirsh,Meyer (b-cl,bs) | Resnicoff,Richie (g) | Starling,Ray (p) | Gannon,Jimmy (b)
The Rotten Kid | Diabolus | Away We Go(alt.take)
Hollywood,CA, rec. 5.12.1967
Rich,Buddy (dr) | Findley,Chuck (tp) | Iverson,Russ (tp) | Sotille,John (tp) | Murakami,Yoshito (tp) | Spurlock,Jack (tb) | Burtis,Sam (tb) | Brawn,Robert (b-tb) | Watts,Ernie (fl,cl,as) | Owens,Charles (fl,cl,as) | Corre,Jay (cl,ts) | LaBarbera,Pat (fl,cl,ts) | Capi,Frank (b-cl,bs) | Resnicoff,Richie (g) | Turner Jr.,Russell (p) | Fudoli,Ron (b)

524567-2 | CD | The Original Ellington Suite
Chico Hamilton Quintet
In A Mellow Tone | In A Sentimental Mood | I'm Just A Lucky So-And-So | Just A-Sittin' And A-Rockin' | Everything But You | Day Dream | I'm Beginning To See The Light | Azure | It Don't Mean A Thing If It Ain't Got That Swing
Los Angeles,CA, rec. 22.8.1958
Hamilton,Forrest 'Chico' (dr) | Dolphy,Eric (fl,cl,as) | Pisano,John (g) | Gershman,Nathan (cello) | Gaylor,Hal (b)

525248-2 | CD | Chet Baker Quartet Live Vol.1:This Time The Dreams's On Me
Chet Baker Quartet
All The Things You Are | Isn't It Romantic | Maid In Mexico | My Funny Valentine | This Time The Dream's On Me
Live at The Carlton Theatre,Los Angeles, rec. 12.8.1953
Baker,Chet (tp) | Freeman,Russ (p) | Smith,Carson (b) | Bunker,Larry (dr)
Introduction | Line For Lyons | Lover Man(Oh,Where Can You Be?) | My Funny Valentine | Maid In Mexico | Stella By Starlight | My Old Flame | Headline | Russ Job
Live at Masonic Temple,Ann Arbour, rec. 9.5.1954
Baker,Chet (tp) | Freeman,Russ (p) | Smith,Carson (b) | Neel,Bob (dr)

531573-2 | CD | Chet Baker Quartet Live Vol.3: May Old Flame
My Little Suede Shoes | Line For Lyons | Lullaby Of The Leaves | My Old Flame | Russ Job | The Wind | Zing! Went The Strings Of My Heart | Everything Happens To Me | A Dandy Line | Frenesi | Moonlight In Vermont | Carson City Stage
Live at The Tiffany Club,Los Angeles,CA, rec. 10.8.1954
Baker,Chet (tp,boo-bam) | Freeman,Russ (p) | Smith,Carson (b) | Neal,Bob (dr)

582671-2 | CD | Chet Baker & Crew | EAN 724358267129
Chet Baker Quintet
Jumpin' Off A Clef | Chippyn' | Lucius Lou | Line For Lyons
Forum Theatre,Los Angeles,CA, rec. 24.7.1956
Baker,Chet (tp,voc) | Urso,Phil (ts) | Timmons,Bobby (p) | Bond,Jimmy (b) | Littman,Peter (dr)
Helena | Music To Dance By | Medium Rock | Revelation | Slightly Above Moderate | Something For Liza | Worryin' The Life Out Of Me
Forum Theatre,Los Angeles,CA, rec. 31.7.1956
Baker,Chet (tp) | Urso,Phil (ts) | Timmons,Bobby (p) | Bond,Jimmy (b) | Littman,Peter (dr)
Chet Baker Sextet
To Mickey's Memory | To Mickey's Memory(alt.take) | Pawnee Junction
Baker,Chet (tp) | Urso,Phil (ts) | Timmons,Bobby (p) | Bond,Jimmy (b) | Littman,Peter (dr) | Loughbrough,Bill (chromatic-tympani)

590957-2 | CD | Chile Con Soul | EAN 724359095721
Jazz Crusaders
Agua Dulce | Soul Bourgeoisie | Ontem A Note | Tough Talk | Tecos | Latin Bit | The Breeze And I | Dulzura
Los Angeles,CA, rec. 2.7.1965
Jazz Crusaders,The | Henderson,Wayne (tb) | Laws,Hubert (fl) | Felder,Wilton (ts) | Sample,Joe (p) | Fischer,Clare (org) | McKibbon,Al (b) | Hooper,Nesbert 'Stix' (dr) | Vidal,Carlos (congas) | Garcia,Hungaria 'Carmelo' (cowbell,timbales)

746847-2 | CD | Konitz Meets Mulligan
Lee Konitz & The Gerry Mulligan Quartet
Too Marvelous For Words | Lover Man(Oh,Where Can You Be?) | I'll Remember April | These Foolish Things Remind Me On You | All The Things You Are | Bernie's Tune | Almost Like Being In Love | Sextet | Broadway
Los Angeles,CA, rec. late January 1953
Konitz,Lee (as) | Mulligan,Gerry (bs) | Baker,Chet (tp) | Smith,Carson (b) | Bunker,Larry (dr)
I Can't Believe That You're In Love With Me | Oh! Lady Be Good | Oh! Lady Be Good(alt.take)
Konitz,Lee (as) | Mulligan,Gerry (bs) | Baker,Chet (tp) | Mondragon,Joe (b) | Bunker,Larry (dr)

792932-2 | CD | Let's Get Lost: The Best Of Chet Baker Sings
Chet Baker Quartet
The Thrill Is Gone
Los Angeles,CA, rec. 27.10.1953
Baker,Chet (tp,voc) | Freeman,Russ (p) | Mondragon,Joe (b) | Manne,Shelly (dr)
But Not For Me | Time After Time | I Get Along Without You Very Well | There'll Never Be Another You | Look For The Silver Lining | My Funny Valentine | I Fall In Love Too Easily | Daybreak | Just Friends | I Remember You | Let's Get Lost | Long Ago And Far Away | You Don't Know What Love Is
Los Angeles,CA, rec. 15.2.& 7.3.1953
Baker,Chet (tp,voc) | Freeman,Russ (p) | Smith,Carson (b) | Neal,Bob (dr)
That Old Feeling | It's Always You | I've Never Been In Love Before
Forum Theatre,Los Angeles,CA, rec. 23.7.1956
Baker,Chet (tp,voc) | Freeman,Russ (p) | Bond,Jimmy (b) | Littman,Peter (dr)
My Buddy | Like Someone In Love | My Ideal
Forum Theatre,Los Angeles,CA, rec. 30.7.1956
Baker,Chet (tp,voc) | Freeman,Russ (p) | Bond,Jimmy (b) | Marable,Lawrence (dr)

795481-2 | CD | The Best Of The Gerry Mulligan Quartet With Chet Baker
A Band Of Friends
Bernie's Tune
Los Angeles,CA, rec. 16.8.1952
Baker,Chet (tp) | Mulligan,Gerry (bs) | Whitlock,Bob (b) | Hamilton,Forrest 'Chico' (dr)
Nights At The Turntable | Freeway | Soft Shoe | Walkin' Shoes
Los Angeles,CA, rec. 15./16.10.1952
Baker,Chet (tp) | Mulligan,Gerry (bs) | Whitlock,Bob (b) | Hamilton,Forrest 'Chico' (dr)
Makin' Whoopee | Carson City Stage
Los Angeles,CA, rec. 24.2.1953
Baker,Chet (tp) | Mulligan,Gerry (bs) | Smith,Carson (b) | Bunker,Larry (dr)
My Old Flame | Love Me Or Leave Me | Swing House | Jeru
Los Angeles,CA, rec. 27.4.1953
Baker,Chet (tp) | Mulligan,Gerry (bs) | Smith,Carson (b) | Bunker,Larry (dr)
Darn That Dream | I'm Beginning To See The Light
Los Angeles,CA, rec. 29./30.4.1953
Baker,Chet (tp) | Mulligan,Gerry (bs) | Smith,Carson (b) | Bunker,Larry (dr)
My Funny Valentine
Los Angeles,CA, rec. 20.5.1953
Baker,Chet (tp) | Mulligan,Gerry (bs) | Smith,Carson (b) | Bunker,Larry (dr)
Festive Minor
NYC, rec. December 1957
Baker,Chet (tp) | Mulligan,Gerry (bs) | Grimes,Henry (b) | Bailey,Dave (dr)

797161-2 | CD | The Best Of Chet Baker Plays
Chet Baker Quartet
Carson City Stage | Imagination
Los Angeles,CA, rec. 29./30.7.1953
Baker,Chet (tp) | Freeman,Russ (p) | Smith,Carson (b) | Bunker,Larry (dr)
All The Things You Are | Bea's Flat | Happy Little Sunbeam
Los Angeles,CA, rec. 3.10.1953
Baker,Chet (tp) | Freeman,Russ (p) | Smith,Carson (b) | Bunker,Larry (dr)
Chet Baker Septet
Prodefunctus | Moonlight Becomes You
Los Angeles,CA, rec. 22.12.1953
Baker,Chet (tp) | Geller,Herb (as,ts) | Montrose,Jack (ts,arr) | Gordon,Bob (bs) | Freeman,Russ (p) | Mondragon,Joe (b) | Manne,Shelly (dr)
Chet Baker Sextet
Stella By Starlight
Los Angeles,CA, rec. 15.9.1954
Baker,Chet (tp) | Brookmeyer,Bob (v-tb) | Shank,Bud (bs) | Freeman,Russ (p) | Smith,Carson (b) | Manne,Shelly (dr)
Chet Baker Big Band
Darn That Dream
Los Angeles,CA, rec. 26.10.1956
Baker,Chet (tp) | Candoli,Conte (tp) | Faye,Norman (tp) | Rosolino,Frank (tb) | Pepper,Art (as) | Shank,Bud (as,bs) | Perkins,Bill (ts) | Urso,Phil (ts) | Timmons,Bobby (p) | Bond,Jimmy (b) | Marable,Lawrence (dr)
Chet Baker Quartet
Sweet Lorraine
Los Angeles,CA, rec. 26.7.1956
Baker,Chet (tp) | Jolly,Pete (p) | Vinnegar,Leroy (b) | Levey,Stan (dr)
Chet Baker Sextet
Minor Yours
Baker,Chet (tp) | Pepper,Art (as) | Kamuca,Richie (ts) | Jolly,Pete (p) | Vinnegar,Leroy (b) | Levey,Stan (dr)
C.T.A.
Los Angeles,CA, rec. 31.10.1956
Baker,Chet (tp) | Pepper,Art (as) | Urso,Phil (ts) | Perkins,Carl (p) | Counce,Curtis (b) | Marable,Lawrence (dr)
To Mickey's Memory | Jumpin' Off A Clef
Los Angeles,CA, rec. 31.7.1956
Baker,Chet (tp) | Urso,Phil (ts) | Timmons,Bobby (p) | Bond,Jimmy (b) | Littman,Peter (dr) | Loughbrough,Bill (chromatic-tympani)

831676-2 | CD | Embraceable You
Chet Baker Trio
The Night We Called It A Day | Little Girl Blue | Embraceable You | They All Laughed | There's A Lull In My Life | What Is There To Say | While My Lady Sleeps | Forgetful | How Long Has This Been Going On | Come Rain Or Come Shine | On Green Dolphin Street | Little Girl Blue(vocal-version) | Trav'lin' Light
NYC, rec. 9.12.1957
Baker,Chet (tp,voc) | Wheat,David (g) | Savakus,Russell (b)

833575-2 | CD | The Gerry Mulligan Songbook
Gerry Mulligan And The Sax Section
Four And One More | Crazy Day | Turnstile | Sextet | Disc Jockey Jump | Venus De Milo | Revelation
NYC, rec. 4./5.12.1957
Mulligan,Gerry (bs) | Konitz,Lee (as) | Eager,Allen (as,ts) | Sims,Zoot (as,ts) | Cohn,Al (ts,bs) | Green,Freddie (g) | Grimes,Henry (b) | Bailey,Dave (dr) | Holman,Bill (arr)
Gerry Mulligan Sextet
Mayreh | The Preacher | Good Bait | Bag's Groove
NYC, rec. 5.12.1957
Mulligan,Gerry (bs) | Palmieri,Paul (g) | Wetmore,Dick (v) | Scott,Calo (cello) | Burke,Vinnie (b) | Bailey,Dave (dr)

835232-2 | CD | Swingin' New Big Band | EAN 724383523221
Buddy Rich And His Orchestra
Basically Blues | My Man's Gone Now | Up Tight(Everything's Alright) | More Soul | What'd I Say | Chicago
Live at The Chez Club,Hollywood,CA, rec. 29.9.1966
Rich,Buddy (dr) | Shew,Bobby (tp) | Scottile,John (tp) | Murakami,Yoshito (tp) | Batagello,Walter (tp) | Trimble,James (tb) | Boice,Johnny (tb) | Good,Dennis Allen (b-tb) | Waverley,Mike (b-tb) | Quill,Daniel (cl,as) | Yellin,Pete (fl,cl,as) | Corre,Jay (fl,cl,ts) | Flax,Marty (fl,cl,ts) | Perlow,Steve (b-cl,bs) | Bunch,John (p) | Zweig,Barry (g) | Smith,Carson (b)
Critic's Choice | Step Right Up | Apples(aka Gino) | Never Will I Marry
Live at The Chez Club,Hollywood,CA, rec. 30.9.1966
Rich,Buddy (dr) | Shew,Bobby (tp) | Scottile,John (tp) | Murakami,Yoshito (tp) | Batagello,Walter (tp) | Trimble,James (tb) | Boice,Johnny (tb) | Good,Dennis Allen (b-tb) | Waverley,Mike (b-tb) | Quill,Daniel (cl,as) | Yellin,Pete (fl,cl,as) | Corre,Jay (fl,cl,ts) | Flax,Marty (fl,cl,ts) | Perlow,Steve (b-cl,bs) | Bunch,John (p) | Zweig,Barry (g) | Smith,Carson (b)
Up Tight(Everything's Alright) | Lament For Lester
Live at The Chez Club,Hollywood,CA, rec. 1.10.1966
Rich,Buddy (dr) | Shew,Bobby (tp) | Scottile,John (tp) | Murakami,Yoshito (tp) | Batagello,Walter (tp) | Trimble,James (tb) | Boice,Johnny (tb) | Good,Dennis Allen (b-tb) | Waverley,Mike (b-tb) | Quill,Daniel (cl,as) | Yellin,Pete (fl,cl,as) | Corre,Jay (fl,cl,ts) | Flax,Marty (fl,cl,ts) | Perlow,Steve (b-cl,bs) | Bunch,John (p) | Zweig,Barry (g) | Smith,Carson (b)
Hoe Down | In A Mellow Tone
Live at The Chez Club,Hollywood,CA, rec. 2.10.1966
Rich,Buddy (dr) | Shew,Bobby (tp) | Scottile,John (tp) | Murakami,Yoshito (tp) | Batagello,Walter (tp) | Trimble,James (tb) | Boice,Johnny (tb) | Good,Dennis Allen (b-tb) | Waverley,Mike (b-tb) | Quill,Daniel (cl,as) | Yellin,Pete (fl,cl,as) | Corre,Jay (fl,cl,ts) | Flax,Marty (fl,cl,ts) | Perlow,Steve (b-cl,bs) | Bunch,John (p) | Zweig,Barry (g) | Smith,Carson (b)
Sister Sadie | West Side Story Medley: | Overture- | Cool- | Something's Coming- | Somewhere- | Naptown Blues
Hollywood,CA, rec. 10.10.1966
Rich,Buddy (dr) | Shew,Bobby (tp) | Scottile,John (tp) | Murakami,Yoshito (tp) | Batagello,Walter (tp) | Trimble,James (tb) | Boice,Johnny (tb) | Good,Dennis Allen (b-tb) | Waverley,Mike (b-tb) | Quill,Daniel (cl,as) | Yellin,Pete (fl,cl,as) | Corre,Jay (fl,cl,ts) | Flax,Marty (fl,cl,ts) | Perlow,Steve (b-cl,bs) | Bunch,John (p) | Zweig,Barry (g) | Smith,Carson (b)

837989-2 | CD | Big Swing Face | EAN 724383798926
Norwegian Wood | Wack Wack | Love For Sale | Bugle Call Rag
Live at The Chez Club,Hollywood,CA, rec. 22.2.1967
Rich,Buddy (dr) | Findley,Charles (tp) | Murakami,Yoshito (tp) | Scottile,John (tp) | Shew,Bobby (tp) | Myers,Ronald (tb) | Trimble,James (tb) | Wimberley,Bill (tb) | Davis,Quin (sax) | Flax,Marty (sax) | Corre,Jay (fl,sax) | Keller,Robert (fl,sax) | Watts,Ernie (fl,ts) | Resnicoff,Richie (g) | Starling,Ray (p) | Gannon,Jimmy (b)
Big Swing Face | Willowcrest | New Blues
Live at The Chez Club,Hollywood,CA, rec. 23.2.1967
Rich,Buddy (dr) | Findley,Charles (tp) | Murakami,Yoshito (tp) | Scottile,John (tp) | Shew,Bobby (tp) | Myers,Ronald (tb) | Trimble,James (tb) | Wimberley,Bill (tb) | Davis,Quin (sax) | Flax,Marty (sax) | Corre,Jay (fl,sax) | Keller,Robert (fl,sax) | Watts,Ernie (fl,ts) | Resnicoff,Richie (g) | Starling,Ray (p) | Gannon,Jimmy (b)
Mexicali Nose | Standing Up In A Hammock | Silver Threads Among The Blues
Live at The Chez Club,Hollywood,CA, rec. 24.2.1967
Rich,Buddy (dr) | Findley,Charles (tp) | Murakami,Yoshito (tp) | Scottile,John (tp) | Shew,Bobby (tp) | Myers,Ronald (tb) | Trimble,James (tb) | Wimberley,Bill (tb) | Davis,Quin (sax) | Flax,Marty (sax) | Corre,Jay (fl,sax) | Keller,Robert (fl,sax) | Watts,Ernie (fl,ts) | Resnicoff,Richie (g) | Starling,Ray (p) | Gannon,Jimmy (b)
Lament For Lester | Machine | Loose | Apples(aka Gino)
Live at The Chez Club,Hollywood,CA, rec. 25.2.1967
Rich,Buddy (dr) | Findley,Charles (tp) | Murakami,Yoshito (tp) | Scottile,John (tp) | Shew,Bobby (tp) | Myers,Ronald (tb) | Trimble,James (tb) | Wimberley,Bill (tb) | Davis,Quin (sax) | Flax,Marty (sax) | Corre,Jay (fl,sax) | Keller,Robert (fl,sax) | Watts,Ernie (fl,ts) | Resnicoff,Richie (g) | Starling,Ray (p) | Gannon,Jimmy (b)
The Beat Goes On
Rich,Buddy (dr) | Findley,Charles (tp) | Murakami,Yoshito (tp) | Scottile,John (tp) | Shew,Bobby (tp) | Myers,Ronald (tb) | Trimble,James (tb) | Wimberley,Bill (tb) | Davis,Quin (sax) | Flax,Marty (sax) | Corre,Jay (fl,sax) | Keller,Robert (fl,sax) | Watts,Ernie (fl,ts) | Resnicoff,Richie (g) | Starling,Ray (p) | Gannon,Jimmy (b) | unkn. (voices)
Monitor Theme | Chicago | Old Timey
Hollywood,CA, rec. 10.3.1967
Rich,Buddy (dr) | Findley,Charles (tp) | Murakami,Yoshito (tp) | Scottile,John (tp) | Shew,Bobby (tp) | Myers,Ronald (tb) | Trimble,James (tb) | Wimberley,Bill (tb) | Davis,Quin (sax) | Flax,Marty (sax) | Corre,Jay (fl,sax) | Keller,Robert (fl,sax) | Watts,Ernie (fl,ts) | Resnicoff,Richie (g) | Starling,Ray (p) | Gannon,Jimmy (b)
-> Note:The voices recorded March,10.1967)

855452-2 | CD | Somethin' Special | EAN 724385545221
Richard 'Groove' Holmes Sextet
Satin Doll
Los Angeles,CA, rec. March 1961
Holmes,Richard 'Groove' (org) | Lofton,Lawrence 'Tricky' (tb) | Webster,Ben (ts) | Freeman,George (g) | McCann,Les (p) | Jefferson,Ron (dr)
Richard 'Groove' Holmes Trio
Blow That Man Down
Los Angeles,CA, rec. 20.2.1962
Holmes,Richard 'Groove' (org) | Edwards,Gene (g) | Henderson,Leroy (dr)
Richard 'Groove' Holmes Quintet
Something Special | Black Groove | Me & Groove | Comin' Through The Apple | I Thought I Knew You | Carma
Los Angeles,CA, rec. April 1961
Holmes,Richard 'Groove' (org) | Scott,Clifford (as,ts) | Pass,Joe (g) | McCann,Les (p) | Jefferson,Ron (dr)

Pata Musik | Pata Musik

PATA 10 CD | 2 CD | News Of Roi Ubu
Pata Music Meets Arfi
Introduction | Chat Imaginaire | Maitre De Plaisir | Treomphe | Ubu's Talking | Autism Cap | Die Ultravioletten Dinge,Die Uns Verboten Waren | Absinth | Speak Yomm | Lip Tone Galaxy | Chaboud | La Fete Surreale | Nut Is Wahn | Von Der Tönenden Insel(Carnet De La Vie) | Enige Nurksen | Yomm L'Amour Absolu | Ubu's Logbook | Pata In Rouen | Elektrische Libellen | Ubu's Love | Just Rave In A Bin Bar
Live at Jazz im Foyer,Leverkusen, rec. 1997
Pata Music | Arfi | Grabosch,Horst (tp) | Méreu,Jean (tp,voice) | Charbonnier,Patrick (tb) | Veille,Jacques (tb) | Heupel,Michael (fl) | Riessler,Michael (b-cl,sopranino) | Merle,Maurice (ss,as) | Autin,Jean-Paul (as,sopranino) | Stein,Norbert (ts,electronics,ld) | Maurer,Albrecht (v,prepared-v) | Bolato,Jean (b,voice) | Rollet,Christian (dr,perc) | Spirli,Alfred (dr,perc) | Mages,Klaus (dr,perc) | Haberer,Christoph (dr,electronics) | Köllges,Frank (synth,dr) | Garcia,Xavier (synth,machines) | Von Welck,Matthias (bass-slit-dr,gongs) | Buhs,Han (voc)

PATA 11 CD | CD | Pata-Bahia
Pata Masters
Maria Fumaca | Cats On The Roof | Santissima Trinidade | I Ching Das Aguas | Roda De Sete | Osho Ibi | Ode | Wildes Denken | Aguas De Oxala | Coco Quebrado | Alaude
Live at Goethe Institut,Salvador-Bahia,Brazil, rec. 4.-21.9.1997
Pata Masters | Winterschladen,Reiner (tp) | Heupel,Michael (fl) | Stein,Norbert (ts) | Bastos,Ivan (b) | Mages,Klaus (dr) | Von Welck,Matthias (bass-slit-dr) | D'Amatta,Cinho (g,voice) | Araujo,Lourival (berimbau,voice) | Guedes,Gabi (congas,atabaques,djembe,voice) | Millet,Monica (atabaques,djembe,udu) | Lins,Alexandre (caxixi,cuica,djembe,pandeiro) | Lopo,Angela (agogo,voice)

PATA 12(AMF 1063) | CD | Pata Maroc
Norbert Stein Pata Masters
Railships To Rabat | White Birds On Bare Trees | Parliament Of Music | Marasouks | Absinth In Oudayas | Bamboo Interior | Outside Balimba | Storks Over Rabat | Inside Chella | Djema Voices | Navratil | Atonal Citizen | Nightgarden
Rabat/Marrakesh,Morocco, rec. May 1998 & February 1999

Stein,Norbert (sax,electronics) | Zeroual,Rachid (kawala,nei) | Heupel,Michael (fl,sub-contra-b-fl) | Mages,Klaus (dr) | Von Welck,Matthias (bass-slit-dr,deep-,mallets) | Hillmann,Christoph (dr,electronics) | Buhrs,Han (voice) | Rüsenberg,Michael (soundscapes)

PATA 13(amf 1064) | CD | Pata Blue Chip
Pata Blue Chip
Continental Breakfast | You Be You | Blue Chip | Otherlands
Studio u.b.u.&klarsicht,?, rec. 2000
Pata Blue Chip | Stein Norbert (electronic-composer) | Knieps,Reinhold (videotraces)
-> Note: This Is A CD-ROM

PATA 14(amf 1066) | CD | La Belle Et La Bête
Pata Music Meets Arfi
Auf Dem Meere | Zwei Schwestern | Die Schöne | Ruin, Klatsch Und Tratsch | Der Verzauberte Garten | Die Fee | Das Gespräch Im Schloss | Pas Si Belle | Das Biest | Versprechen Und Neid | Die Liebe | Dance
Bonn, rec. 2000
Pata Music | Stein,Norbert (tsax,electronics,ld) | Méreu,Jean (tp,narration) | Gibert,Alain (tb) | Heupel,Michael (fl) | Hillmann,Christoph (perc,electronics) | Rollet,Christian (dr,perc) | Hofman,Josef (narration)

PATA 15 CD | CD | Live In Australia | EAN 4017071000156
Nornert Stein Pata Masters
Parliament Of Music | Monks | Wildes Denken | Liquid Bird | Atonal Citizen II | Chat Imaginaire | Blue Stomp
Live at The Wangaratta Festival Of Jazz,Australia, rec. 3./4.11.2001
Stein,Norbert (ts) | Heupel,Michael (fl,sub-contra-b-fl) | Mages,Klaus (dr,perc) | Von Welck,Matthias (bass-slit-dr,deep-,mallets) | Hillmann,Christoph (perc,electronics)

PATA 16 CD | CD | Pata Java | EAN 4017071000163
Norbert Stein Pata Masters meets Djaduk Ferianto Kua Etnika
Sing A Pure Song | Jiwa | Dialog | Speak Yomm | Juzzla Juzzli | Code Carnival | Cublak Cublak Suweng | Sound Theatre Of Tukang Pijad | Wulang Sunu
Jakarta, rec. 31.10.-2.11.2003
Pata Masters | Stein,Norbert (ts) | Heupel,Michael (fl,alto-fl,b-fl,sub-contra-b-fl) | Mages,Klaus (dr) | Von Welck,Matthias (bass-slit-dr,deep-mallets) | Hillmann,Christoph (electronics) | Kua Etnika | Ferianto,Djaduk (srompet,kendang,beduk,klunthung,kemanak,ketipung,krincing,triangle | Purwanto (bonang,klunthung,calung,rebana,rebeb,kemanak,voc) | Suvarjiyo (demung,klunthung,rebana,demung,voc) | Suharjono (saron,klunthung,calung,rebana,siter,voc) | Pardiman,Fredy (saron,klunthung,rebana,rebab,voc) | Wardoye (peking,krincing,kendang,rebana,klunthung,voc) | Sukoco (gender,kendang,calung,ketipung,beduk) | Suprapto,Sony (kempul,gong,beduk,rebana,voc)

PATA 5(JHM 50) CD | CD | Ritual Life
Norbert Stein Pata Orchester
Arise | Mother Earth | Beautiful Life | Die Mühle | Old Folks Not At Home | Es Wird Einmal Gewesen Sein | Norden | Weird Poetry | Josebas Traum | Atomic Cafe | Last Ballad | Die Namen | Ritual Life | Huomaamaton
Bonn-Beuel, rec. October 1991
Stein,Norbert (ss,ts) | Winterschladen,Reiner (tp) | Gellert,Joachim (tb,b-tb) | Fink,Achim (tb,ten-h,tuba) | Gilgenberg,Andreas (fl,alto-cl,b-cl,as) | Hehn,Hennes (cl,ts) | Maurer,Albrecht (synth,v) | Kramer,Viola (synth) | Köllges,Frank (dr) | Vujin-Stein,Basa (voc) | Stühlen,Peter (soundsculptures)

PATA 7 CD | CD | The Secret Act Of Painting
Introduction | Helden | Unterste Zeit | Africain | Liquid Bird | Gentle Mental Journey | Königskinder | In A Woman's Mood | Di Wing | Kymenlaakson Laulu | The People Of Yomm | Petruschka | The Path | Israel Adventi | The Bridge Of Iron Roses | Glucklich | Dunkle Wolken | Iron Painting
Sherwood Studio/Hansahaus Studio,?, rec. Spring 1993
Pata Orchestra | Stein,Norbert (b-cl,ss,ts,synth,perc) | Winterschladen,Reiner (tp) | Fink,Achim (tb,tuba) | Gratkowski,Frank (b-cl) | Heupel,Michael (fl,alto-fl,sub-contra-b-fl) | Gilgenberg,Andreas (b-cl,as,falto-cl,gongs,slit-dr) | Kramer,Viola (synth,live-electronics) | Köllges,Frank (dr,tympani)

PATA 8 CD | CD | Blue Slit
Norbert Stein Pata Masters
Ruth Is Back To Joseph | Stille Menschen | Fremde | Niding Summer | Lowena | Es War Einmal | Mein Halblächelnder Freund | Mother Earth | Call Me | The Zennuugh People | Bastard | The Light | Blue Slit
Köln, rec. March 1994
Stein,Norbert (ss,ts,bass-slit-dr,khaen,marimbula,silversticks) | Winterschladen,Reiner (tp,kalimba) | Heupel,Michael (fl,alto-fl,b-fl,sub-contra-b-fl) | Mages,Klaus (dr,perc,bass-slit-dr,berimbao)

PATA 9 CD | CD | Graffiti
Community | Liquid Bird | Sharkey's | Blue Stomp | Thermidor | DuduWawa | Basic Instinct | Graffiti | X-Mas
Köln, rec. November 1995
Stein,Norbert (ts) | Grabosch,Horst (tp) | Heupel,Michael (fl,alto-fl,sub-contra-b-fl) | Von Welck,Matthias (bass-slit-dr) | Mages,Klaus (dr)

Philips | Universal Music Germany

542552-2 | CD | Jazz Sebastian Bach
Swingle Singers
Fugue In D Minor(BWV 1080) | Choral No.1 'Wachet Auf Ruft Uns Die Stimme'(BWV 645) | Aria(from Orchestra Suite No.3 In D Major BWV 1068) | Prelude No.11 In F Major(BWV 880) | Bourree(BWV 807) | Fugue No.2 In C Minor(BWV 871) | Prelude No.9(BWV 878) | Sinfonia(BWV 826) | Prelude No.1 In C Major(BWV 870) | Two Part Invention No.1 In C Major(BWV 772) | Fugue No.5 In D Major(BWV 874)
Paris,France, rec. 1963
Swingle Singers (voc-group) | Legrand,Christiane (voc) | Baucomont,Jeanette (voc) | Meunier,Claudine (voc) | Germain,Anne (voc) | Germain,Claude (voc) | Swingle,Ward (ld,voc) | Briodin,Jean-Claude (voc) | Cussac,Jean (voc) | Michelot,Pierre (b) | Wallez,Gus (dr)
Fugue No.5 In D Major(BWV 850) | Canon
Swingle Singers (voc-group) | Legrand,Christiane (voc) | Baucomont,Jeanette (voc) | Meunier,Claudine (voc) | Germain,Anne (voc) | Germain,Claude (voc) | Swingle,Ward (ld,voc) | Briodin,Jean-Claude (voc) | Cussac,Jean (voc) | Michelot,Pierre (b) | Arpino,André (dr)

542553-2 | CD | Jazz Sebastian Bach Vol.2
Vivace-Concerto for two Violins In D Minor(BWV 1043) | Prelude And Fugue No.10 In E Minor(BWV 855) | Choral Jesus Bleibet Meine Freude(BWV 147) | Gavotte from Partita No.3 In E Major(BWV 1006) | Fugue No.21 In B Flat Major(BWV 866)
Paris,France, rec. 1968
Swingle Singers (voc-group) | Legrand,Christiane (voc) | Baucomont,Jeanette (voc) | Meunier,Claudine (voc) | Devos,Hélène (voc) | Germain,José (voc) | Swingle,Ward (ld,voc) | Noves,Joseph (voc) | Cussac,Jean (voc) | Pedersen,Guy (b) | Lubat,Bernard (dr)
Prelude And Fugue No.1 In C Major(BWV 846) | Fugue In G Major(BWV 541) | Adagio From Sonate No.3 In E Major(BWV 1016) | Prelude And Fugue No.3 In C Sharp Major(BWV 848) | Chorale(BWV 859)
Swingle Singers (voc-group) | Legrand,Christiane (voc) | Baucomont,Jeanette (voc) | Meunier,Claudine (voc) | Devos,Hélène (voc) | Germain,José (voc) | Swingle,Ward (ld,voc) | Noves,Joseph (voc) | Cussac,Jean (voc) | Pedersen,Guy (b) | Humair,Daniel (dr)

546746-2 | CD | Swingle Singers Going Baroque | EAN 731454674621
Badinerie from Suite No.2 in B Minor(BWV 1067) | Aria And Variations from Suite for Harpsichord in E Major(Haendel) | Giga from Cello Suite No.1 in F Minor(BWV 1009) | Largo from Harpsichord Concerto in F Minor(BWV 1056) | Prelude No.19 in A Major(BWV 864) | Präambulum from Partita No.5 in G Major(BWV 829) | Fugue from Concert Op.3 No.11 in D Minor(Vivaldi) | Allegro from Concerto Grosso Op.6 No.4 in A Minor(Haendel) | Prelude No.7 in E Flat Major(BWV 876) | Solfiegietto in C Minor(C.P.E.Bach) | Der Frühling(W.F.Bach) | Prelude No.24 in B Minor(BWV 893)
Paris,France, rec. 1964
Swingle Singers (voc-group) | Legrand,Christiane (voc) | Baucomont,Jeanette (voc) | Meunier,Claudine (voc) | Germain,Anne (voc) | Germain,Claude (voc) | Swingle,Ward (ld,voc) | Briodin,Jean-Claude (voc) | Cussac,Jean (voc)

548538-2 | CD | Swingle Singers Singing Mozart | EAN 731454853828
Variations on Ah! Vous Dirais-Je Maman(KV 265) | Fugue from Sonata for Violin and Piano in A Major (KV 402) | Piano Sonata No.15 in C Major(KV 545): | Allegro-Andante-Finale | Andante- | Allegretto- | Serenade No.13 in G Major 'Eine Kleine Nachtmusik'(KV 525): | Allegro- | Romance- | Menuetto- | Rondo- | Allegro from Piano Sonata No.5 in G Major(KV 283)
Paris,France, rec. September/October 1964
Swingle Singers (voc-group) | Legrand,Christiane (voc) | Baucomont,Jeanette (voc) | Herald,Alice (voc) | Germain,Anne (voc) | Germain,Claude (voc) | Swingle,Ward (ld,voc) | Germain,José (voc) | Cussac,Jean (voc) | Pedersen,Guy (b) | Humair,Daniel (dr)

586735-2 | CD | Swingling Telemann | EAN 731458673521
Concerto A Six: | Allegro- | Adagio- | Presto- | Adagio- | Allegro- | La Couperin from Pieces For Harpsichord, Book 4(Francois Couperin) | Gigue from Suite For Strings 'La Lyra' | Fugue In D Minor(Georg Muffat) | Presto from Trio Sonata In E Major | Larghetto from Concerto In A Major For Oboe D'Amore And Strings | Le Coucou from Pieces For Harpsichórd,Book 1(Louis-Claude Daguin) | Presto from Sonata No.4 For Flute And Continuo In E Minor(Benedetto Marcello) | Sonata In C Minor(Johann Joachim Quantz): | Allegro- | Andante Moderato- | Vivace-
Paris,France, rec. 1966
Swingle Singers (voc-group) | Legrand,Christiane (voc) | Baucomont,Jeanette (voc) | Herald,Alice (voc) | Meunier,Claudine (voc) | Germain,Claude (voc) | Swingle,Ward (ld,voc) | Germain,José (voc) | Cussac,Jean (voc) | Pedersen,Guy (b) | Humair,Daniel (dr)

586736-2 | CD | Swingle Singers Getting Romantic | EAN 731458673620
Scherzo from Sonata for Violin And Piano Op.24 In F Major(L.v.Beethoven) | Allegro from Piano Sonata Op.26 In A Flat Major(L.v.Beethoven) | Etude Op.10 No.6 In E Flat Major(Chopin) | Etude Op.25 No.2 In F Minor(Chopin) | Waktz Op.64 No.2 In C Sharp Minor(Chopin) | Short Fugue from Album For The Young Op.68(Robert Schuman) | Spinning Song from Songs Without Words Op.67 No.4(Mendelssohn-Bartholdy) | Limoges, The Market from Pictures At An Exhibition(Mussorsky) | Andante from String Quartet Op.44 No.1 In D Major(Mendelssohn-Bartholdy) | Zortzico(Albinez) | Andante from String Quartet Op.29 No.13 in A Minor(Schubert,D 804)
Paris,France, rec. 1967
Swingle Singers (voc-group) | Legrand,Christiane (voc) | Baucomont,Jeanette (voc) | Herald,Alice (voc) | Meunier,Claudine (voc) | Germain,Claude (voc) | Swingle,Ward (ld,voc) | Germain,José (voc) | Cussac,Jean (voc) | Pedersen,Guy (b) | Humair,Daniel (dr)

589490-2 | CD | Woody Herman-1963 | EAN 731458949022
Woody Herman And His Orchestra
Mo-Lasses | Sister Sadie | Sig Ep
NYC, rec. 15.10.1962
Herman,Woody (cl,as,voc) | Harrell,Ziggy (tp) | Gale,Dave (tp) | Chase,Bill (tp) | Lamy,Gerald (tp) | Fontaine,Paul (tp) | Gale,Jack (tb) | Wilson,Phil (tb) | Morgan,Eddie (tb) | Nistico,Sal (ts) | Brisker,Gordon (ts) | Covelli,Larry (ts) | Allen,Gene (bs) | Pierce,Nat (p) | Andrus,Chuck (b) | Hanna,Jake (dr)
Camel Walk | It's A Lonesome Old Town When You're Not Around | Blues For J.P. | Don't Get Around Much Anymore | Tunin' In
NYC, rec. 16.10.1962
Herman,Woody (cl,voc) | Harrell,Ziggy (tp) | Gale,Dave (tp) | Chase,Bill (tp) | Lamy,Gerald (tp) | Fontaine,Paul (tp) | Gale,Jack (tb) | Wilson,Phil (tb) | Morgan,Eddie (tb) | Nistico,Sal (ts) | Brisker,Gordon (ts) | Covelli,Larry (ts) | Allen,Gene (bs) | Pierce,Nat (p) | Andrus,Chuck (b) | Hanna,Jake (dr)

800064-2 | CD | Night In Tunisia
Art Blakey And The Jazz Messengers
A Night In Tunisia | Moanin' | Blues March
Tokyo, Japan, rec. 12.2.1979
Blakey,Art (dr) | Ponomarev,Valery (tp) | Watson,Robert 'Bobby' (as) | Schnitter,David (ts) | Williams,James (p) | Irwin,Dennis (b)

824256-2 PMS | CD | Swinging Studio Sessons
Dutch Swing College Band
At The Jazz Band Ball | Savoy Blues | Fidgety Feet | See See Rider | Royal Garden Blues | Some Of These Days
Hilversum,NL, rec. 9.6.1960
Dutch Swing College Band | Klein,Oscar (co) | Kaart,Dick (tb) | Morks,Jan (cl,dr) | Schilperoort,Peter (cl,bs) | Lighthart,Arie (g,bj) | Van Oven,Bob (b) | Beenen,Martin (tp,dr)
Tiger Rag | Just A Closer Walk With Thee | March Of The Indians
Hilversum,NL, rec. 14.12.1959
Dutch Swing College Band | Klein,Oscar (co) | Kaart,Dick (tb) | Morks,Jan (cl) | Schilperoort,Peter (cl,bs) | Lighthart,Arie (g,bj) | Van Oven,Bob (b) | Beenen,Martin (dr)
Mood Indigo
Eindhoven,NL, rec. 27.4.1960
Dutch Swing College Band | Klein,Oscar (co) | Kaart,Dick (tb) | Morks,Jan (cl) | Lighthart,Arie (bj) | Van Oven,Bob (b)
I Wish I Could Shimmy Like My Sister Kate | I've Been Working On The Railroad | East St.Louis Toodle-Oo
Hilversum,NL, rec. 30.12.1960 & 11.9.1962
Dutch Swing College Band | Klein,Oscar (co) | Kaart,Dick (tb) | Schilperoort,Peter (ss) | Lighthart,Arie (bj) | Van Oven,Bob (b) | De Lussanet,Louis (dr)
Cornet Chop Suey | When It's Sleepy Time Down South | Dippermouth Blues
Den Haag,Holland, rec. 27.1.1966
Dutch Swing College Band | Kaart,Ray (tp) | Kaart,Dick (tb,bar-h) | Schilperoort,Peter (cl,bs) | Lighthart,Arie (bj) | Van Oven,Bob (b) | Ypma,Peter (dr)
Davenport Blues | Shake It And Break It
Hilversum,NL, rec. 11.6.1969
Dutch Swing College Band | De Kort,Bert (co) | Kaart,Dick (tb) | Kaper,Bob (cl) | Schilperoort,Peter (bs) | Lighthart,Arie (g,bj) | Schmidger,Chris (b) | Janssen,Huub (dr)

824585-2 PMS | CD | Digital Anniversary
Bourbon Street Parade | Wabash Blues | Caribbean Parade | Is It True What They Say About Dixie | Saturday Night Is The Loneliest Night Of The Week | Double Bass Hit | Coal Black Shine | Third Street Blues | Gladiolus Rag | Columbus Stockade Blues | Original Dixieland One Step | Swing '36
Hilversum,NL, rec. 31.10.1985
Dutch Swing College Band | Van Duin,Sytze (co) | Boeren,Bert (tb,co) | Kaper,Bob (cl,as) | Schilperoort,Peter (cl,ss,ts,bs,bj) | Murray,Fred (p) | Van Drakenstein,Henk Bosch (b) | Janssen,Huub (dr,maracas,tambourin,wbd)
Rose Room
Dutch Swing College Band | Van Duin,Sytze (co) | Schilperoort,Peter (g) | Murray,Fred (p) | Van Drakenstein,Henk Bosch (b) | Janssen,Huub (dr)
Clarinet Games
Dutch Swing College Band | Schilperoort,Peter (cl) | Kaper,Bob (cl) | Murray,Fred (p) | Van Drakenstein,Henk Bosch (b) | Janssen,Huub (dr)
Devil In The Moon
Dutch Swing College Band | Schilperoort,Peter (cl) | Murray,Fred (p) | Van Drakenstein,Henk Bosch (b) | Janssen,Huub (dr)

824664-2 | CD | The Best Of Play Bach
Jacques Loussier Trio
Air On The G String | Siciliano In G Minor | Toccata And Fugue In D Minor(BWV 565) | Prelude No.1 | Chorale:Jesu You Of Man's Desiring | Italien Concerto: | Allegro- | Adagio- | Presto- | Chorale No.1 | Chromatic Fantasy | D Minor Concerto: | Allegro Risoluto- | Adagio- | Allegro Moderato-
London,GB, rec. December 1984
Loussier,Jacques (p) | Michelot,Pierre (b) | Garros,Christian (dr)

838765-2 | CD | Dutch Swing College Band Live In 1960
Dutch Swing College Band
Way Down Yonder In New Orleans | South Rampart Street Parade | Apex Blues | Ory's Creole Trombone | King Of The Zulus | Freeze And Melt | Please Don't Talk About Me When I'm Gone | Jazz Me Blues | Weary Blues | Way Down Yonder In New Orleans(Theme)
Eindhoven,NL, rec. 27.4.1960
Dutch Swing College Band | Klein,Oscar (co) | Kaart,Dick (tb) | Schilperoort,Peter (cl,bs) | Morks,Jan (cl) | Lighthart,Arie (g,bj) | Van Oven,Bob (b) | Beenen,Martin (dr)
Mood Indigo
Dutch Swing College Band | Klein,Oscar (co) | Kaart,Dick (tb) | Morks,Jan (cl) | Lighthart,Arie (g,bj) | Van Oven,Bob (b)
Opus 5
Dutch Swing College Band | Morks,Jan (cl) | Lighthart,Arie (g) | Van Oven,Bob (b) | Beenen,Martin (dr)
Out Of The Gallion
Dutch Swing College Band | Schilperoort,Peter (cl) | Morks,Jan (cl) | Lighthart,Arie (g) | Van Oven,Bob (b) | Beenen,Martin (dr)
Carry Me Back To Old Virginia
Dutch Swing College Band | Klein,Oscar (co) | Schilperoort,Peter (cl) | Lighthart,Arie (g) | Van Oven,Bob (b) | Beenen,Martin (dr)
Tin Roof Blues
Dutch Swing College Band | Klein,Oscar (co) | Beenen,Martin (tp) | Kaart,Dick (tb) | Schilperoort,Peter (cl) | Lighthart,Arie (bj) | Van Oven,Bob (b) | Morks,Jan (dr)

Phontastic | Fenn Music

NCD 7532 | CD | Hallberg's Hot Accordion In The Foreground
Bengt Hallberg Quartet
St.Louis Blues | Sweet Sue Just You | Novelty Accordion | Penséer,Waltz | Pillen
Live at Grünevald Room,Konserthus,Stockholm,Sweden, rec. 6./7.5.1980
Hallberg,Bengt (accordeon) | Domnerus,Arne (cl) | Gustafsson,Rune (g) | Riedel,Georg (b)
Fjorton Ar Tror Jag Visst Att Jag Var | Truddelutter | Sillsaltarvisan
Sundbyberg,Sweden, rec. 4.-6.6.1981
Hallberg,Bengt (accordeon) | Domnerus,Arne (cl) | Gustafsson,Rune (g) | Riedel,Georg (b)
Tiger Rag | Bye Bye Blues | Farewell Blues | Limehouse Blues | Tva Solröda Segel | How High The Moon | Blue Moon | Some Of These Days
Sundbyberg,Sweden, rec. 3.6.1981
Hallberg,Bengt (accordeon) | Domnerus,Arne (cl) | Gustafsson,Rune (g) | Riedel,Georg (b)

NCD 7555 | CD | Count On The Coast Vol.1
Count Basie And His Orchestra
Moten Swing | Cute | Sweetie Cakes | Indian Summer | Jumpin' At The Woodside | Plymouth | Flight Of The Foo Birds | Lil' Darlin' | Low Life | Whirly Bird | Swingin' The Blues | Blue On Blue | No Moon At All | Allright Okay You Win | Fancy Meeting You | Slats
rec. 24.6.-3.7.1958
Basie,Count (p) | Newman,Joe (tp) | Jones,Thad (tp) | Culley,Wendell (tp) | Young,Eugene 'Snooky' (tp) | Powell,Benny (tb) | Coker,Henry (tb) | Grey,Al (tb) | Wess,Frank (fl,as) | Royal,Marshall (as) | Mitchell,Billy (ts) | Foster,Frank (ts) | Fowlkes,Charlie (bs) | Green,Freddie (g) | Jones,Eddie (b) | Payne,Sonny (dr) | Williams,Joe (voc)

NCD 7575 | CD | Count On The Coast Vol.2
PHONT 7575 | LP | Count On The Coast Vol.2
H.R.H. | Duet | Teddy The Toad | Smack Dab In The Middle | Pensive Miss | One O'Clock Jump | Countin' The Blues | Lullaby Of Birdland | I've Got A Girl | You're A Memory | Scoot | Who Me | Kid From Red Bank | Late Date | Stop Pretty Baby | Gee Baby Ain't I Good To You | Shiny Stockings | April In Paris
Basie,Count (p) | Newman,Joe (tp) | Jones,Thad (tp) | Culley,Wendell (tp) | Young,Eugene 'Snooky' (tp) | Powell,Benny (tb) | Coker,Henry (tb) | Grey,Al (tb) | Wess,Frank (fl,as) | Royal,Marshall (as) | Mitchell,Billy (ts) | Foster,Frank (ts) | Fowlkes,Charlie (bs) | Green,Freddie (g) | Jones,Eddie (b) | Payne,Sonny (dr) | Williams,Joe (voc)

NCD 8804 | CD | Svend Asmussen At Slukafter
Svend Asmussen Sextet
Believe It Beloved | Nadja | Exactly Like You | Hot House | Body And Soul | Cocoanut Calypso | Someone To Watch Over Me | Barney Goin' Easy(I'm Checkin' Out Goin' Bye) | Out Of Nowhere | Pent-Up House | Things Ain't What They Used To Be
Live at Slukafter,Copenhagen, rec. 3.9.1984
Asmussen,Svend (v) | Domnerus,Arne (cl,as) | Hallberg,Bengt (p) | Gustafsson,Rune (g) | Orsted-Pedersen,Niels-Henning (b) | Thigpen,Ed (dr)

NCD 8813 | CD | Newport Jazz Festival 1958,July 3rd-6th,Vol.1:Mostly Miles
Miles Davis Quintet
Introduction | Ah-Leu-Cha | Straight No Chaser | Fran-Dance | Two Bass Hit | Bye Bye Blackbird | The Theme
Live at Newport,Rhode Island, rec. 3.7.1958
Davis,Miles (p) | Adderley,Julian \'Cannonball\' (as) | Coltrane,John (ts) | Evans,Bill (p) | Chambers,Paul (b) | Cobb,Jimmy (dr)
Lee Konitz Trio
Lover Man(Oh,Where Can You Be?) | Will You Still Be Mine
Live at Newport,Rhode Island, rec. 6.7.1958
Konitz,Lee (as) | Grimes,Henry (b) | Levinson,Ed (dr)
Horace Silver Quintet
Tippin'
Silver,Horace (p) | Smith,Louis (tp) | Cook,Junior (ts) | Taylor,Gene (b) | Hayes,Louis (dr)

NCD 8814 | CD | Newport Jazz Festival 1958,July 3rd-6th Vol.2:Mulligan The Main Man
Gerry Mulligan Quartet
Introduction | The Festive Minor | Bernie's Tune | Baubles Bangles And Beads | Blueport | Moonlight In Vermont | News From Blueport | As Catch Can
Live at Newport,Rhode Island, rec. 5.7.1958
Mulligan,Gerry (bs) | Farmer,Art (tp) | Grimes,Henry (b) | Bailey,Dave (dr)
Gerry Mulligan With The Marian McPartland Trio
Don't Get Around Much Anymore | C Jam Blues
Live at Newport,Rhode Island, rec. 3.7.1958
Mulligan,Gerry (bs) | McPartland,Marian (p) | Hinton,Milt (b) | Shaughnessy,Ed (dr)
Chico Hamilton Quintet
Chrissie | Nice Day
Live at Newport,Rhode Island, rec. 6.7.1958
Hamilton,Forrest 'Chico' (dr) | Dolphy,Eric (fl,cl,as) | Pisano,John (g) | Gershman,Nathan (cello) | Gaylor,Hal (b)
Sonny Stitt-Sal Salvador Quintet
Cherokee
Stitt,Sonny (as) | Salvador,Sal (g) | Mahones,Gildo (p) | Rivera,Martin (b) | Hayes,Louis (dr)
Urbie Green Sextet
Original Blues
Green,Urbie (tb) | Elliott,Don (mellophone) | Gibbs,Terry (vib) | Kelly,Wynton (p) | West,Paul (b) | Roach,Max (dr)
Dinah Washington With The Urbie Green Sextet
All Of Me
Washington,Dinah (voc) | Green,Urbie (tb) | Elliott,Don (mellophone) | Gibbs,Terry (vib) | Kelly,Wynton (p) | West,Paul (b) | Roach,Max (dr)

NCD 8815 | CD | Newport Jazz Festival 1958,July 3rd-6th Vol.3:Blues In The Night No.1

Chuck Berry With The Blues Band
Introduction | School Days | No Money Down | Sweet Little Sixteen | Johnny Be Good
Live at Newport,Rhode Island, rec. 5.7.1958
Berry,Chuck (g,voc) | Clayton,Buck (tp) | Teagarden,Jack (tb) | Scott,Tony (cl) | Tate,Buddy (ts) | Rutherford,Rudy (as) | Auld,Georgie (ts) | Bryant,Ray (p) | Burrell,Kenny (g) | Bryant,Tommy (b) | Jones,Jo (dr)

Big Maybelle With The Blues Band
Baby Please Don't Go | Cherry | Let's Roll It | One Hour | The Blues
Big Maybelle[Mabel Smith] (voc) | Clayton,Buck (tp) | Teagarden,Jack (tb) | Scott,Tony (cl) | Tate,Buddy (ts) | Rutherford,Rudy (as) | Auld,Georgie (ts) | Bryant,Ray (p) | Burrell,Kenny (g) | Bryant,Tommy (b) | Jones,Jo (dr)

Big Joe Turner And Pete Johnson With The Blues Band
Boogie Woogie | Feeling Happy | Corinne Corinna | Honey Hush | Shake Rattle And Roll
Turner,Big Joe (voc) | Johnson,Pete (p) | Clayton,Buck (tp) | Teagarden,Jack (tb) | Scott,Tony (cl) | Tate,Buddy (ts) | Rutherford,Rudy (as) | Auld,Georgie (ts) | Bryant,Ray (p) | Burrell,Kenny (g) | Bryant,Tommy (b) | Jones,Jo (dr)

Jack Teagarden Sextet
Aunt Hagar's Blues | High Society | Handful Of Keys
Teagarden,Jack (tb) | Goldie,Don (tp) | Fuller,Jerry (cl) | Ewell,Don (p) | Pulch,Stan prob. (b) | Deems,Barrett (dr)

Jack Teagarden Sextet With Bobby Hackett
What's New?
Teagarden,Jack (tb) | Hackett,Bobby (co) | Goldie,Don (tp) | Fuller,Jerry (cl) | Ewell,Don (p) | Pulch,Stan prob. (b) | Deems,Barrett (dr)

NCD 8816 | CD | Newport Jazz Festival 1958,July 3rd-6th Vol.4:Blues In The Night No.2

Dinah Washington And Her Sextet
Love Come Back To Me | Crazy Love(Crazy Music) | Send Me To The 'Lectric Chair | Gimme A Pigfoot | Back Water Blues
Washington,Dinah (voc) | Mitchell,Blue (tp) | Liston,Melba (tb) | Shihab,Sahib (sax) | Kelly,Wynton (p) | West,Paul (b) | Roach,Max (dr)

Ray Charles Sextet With The Raylets
Hot Rod | Sherry | The Blues Waltz | The Blues | Yes Indeed | Night Time Is The Right Time | I Feel Alright- | I Got A Woman-
Charles,Ray (as,p,voc) | Harper,Lee (tp) | Belgrave,Marcus (tp) | Newman,David Fathead (ts) | Crawford,Bennie (bs) | Wills,Edgar L. (b) | Goldberg,Richie (dr)

NCD 8817 | CD | Camel Caravan Broadcast 1939 Vol.1

Benny Goodman And His Orchestra
Let's Dance (Theme) | I Can't Believe That You're In Love With Me | Deep In A Dream | Fraligh In Swing(And The Angels Sing) | I Cried For You(Now It's Your Turn To Cry Over Me) | Jeepers Creepers | Hold Tight
NYC, rec. 17.1.1939
Goodman,Benny (cl) | Elman,Ziggy (tp) | Griffin,Chris (tp) | Baker,Cy (tp) | Ballard,Red (tb) | Brown,Vernon (tb) | Schertzer,Hymie (as) | Barnardi,Noni (as) | Rollini,Arthur (ts) | Jerome,Jerry (ts) | Stacy,Jess (p) | Heller,Benny 'Ben' (g) | Goodman,Harry (b) | Schutz,Buddy (dr) | Hampton,Lionel (dr) | Tilton,Martha (voc) | Mercer,Johnny (voc) | Holiday,Billie (voc) | Watson,Leo (voc)
Gypsy Love Song | My Heart Belongs To Daddy | Undecided | Stompin' At The Savoy | Wrappin' It Up
NYC, rec. 24.1.1939
Goodman,Benny (cl) | Elman,Ziggy (tp) | Griffin,Chris (tp) | Baker,Cy (tp) | Ballard,Red (tb) | Brown,Vernon (tb) | Schertzer,Hymie (as) | Barnardi,Noni (as) | Rollini,Arthur (ts) | Jerome,Jerry (ts) | Stacy,Jess (p) | Heller,Benny 'Ben' (g) | Goodman,Harry (b) | Schutz,Buddy (dr) | Hampton,Lionel (dr) | Tilton,Martha (voc) | Mercer,Johnny (voc)
Shadrack
Goodman,Benny (cl) | Elman,Ziggy (tp) | Griffin,Chris (tp) | Baker,Cy (tp) | Ballard,Red (tb) | Brown,Vernon (tb) | Schertzer,Hymie (as) | Barnardi,Noni (as) | Rollini,Arthur (ts) | Jerome,Jerry (ts) | Stacy,Jess (p) | Heller,Benny 'Ben' (g) | Goodman,Harry (b) | Schutz,Buddy (dr) | Hampton,Lionel (dr) | Tilton,Martha (voc) | Mercer,Johnny (voc) | Quintones,The (voc)
And The Angels Sing | I Gotta Right To Sing The Blues | Basin Street Blues | Smoke House | Two Sleepy People | Roll 'Em | Good Bye
NYC, rec. 31.1.1939
Goodman,Benny (cl) | Elman,Ziggy (tp) | Griffin,Chris (tp) | Baker,Cy (tp) | Teagarden,Jack (tb,voc) | Ballard,Red (tb) | Brown,Vernon (tb) | Schertzer,Hymie (as) | Barnardi,Noni (as) | Rollini,Arthur (ts) | Jerome,Jerry (ts) | Stacy,Jess (p) | Johnson,Pete (p) | Heller,Benny 'Ben' (g) | Goodman,Harry (b) | Schutz,Buddy (dr) | Hampton,Lionel (dr) | Tilton,Martha (voc) | Mercer,Johnny (voc) | Quintones,The (voc)

Benny Goodman Quartet
Lillie Stomp
NYC, rec. 17.1.1939
Goodman,Benny (cl) | Hampton,Lionel (vib) | Wilson,Teddy (p) | Schutz,Buddy (dr)
Umbrella Man
NYC, rec. 31.1.1939
Goodman,Benny (cl) | Hampton,Lionel (vib) | Wilson,Teddy (p) | Schutz,Buddy (dr)

NCD 8818 | CD | Camel Caravan Broadcast 1939 Vol.2

Benny Goodman And His Orchestra
Let's Dance (Theme) | Honolulu | Hurry Home | When Buddah Smiles | Gone For Nothing But Love | Together- | Anything Can Swing- | Farewell Blues
Shubert Theater,Newark,NJ, rec. 21.2.1939
Goodman,Benny (cl) | Elman,Ziggy (tp) | Griffin,Chris (tp) | Goodman,Irving (tp) | Ballard,Red (tb) | Brown,Vernon (tb) | Schertzer,Hymie (as) | Barnardi,Noni (as) | Rollini,Arthur (ts) | Jerome,Jerry (ts) | Stacy,Jess (p) | Heller,Benny 'Ben' (g) | Goodman,Harry (b) | Schutz,Buddy (dr) | Tilton,Martha (voc) | Mercer,Johnny (voc)
Singing In The Rain | Deep Purple | In The Shade Of The Old Apple Tree | Big John's Special | What's The Reason(I'm Not Pleasing You) | Bugle Call Rag
Fox Theatre,Detroit, rec. 28.2.1939
Goodman,Benny (cl) | Elman,Ziggy (tp) | Griffin,Chris (tp) | Baker,Cy (tp) | Ballard,Red (tb) | Brown,Vernon (tb) | Schertzer,Hymie (as) | Barnardi,Noni (as) | Rollini,Arthur (ts) | Jerome,Jerry (ts) | Stacy,Jess (p) | Heller,Benny 'Ben' (g) | Goodman,Harry (b) | Schutz,Buddy (dr) | Hampton,Lionel (dr) | Tilton,Martha (voc) | Mercer,Johnny (voc)
Gypsy Love Song | I Get Along With You Very Well | Spring Beautiful Spring | Bach Goes To Town | Them There Eyes | The Kingdom Of Swing | Good Bye
Earl Theatre,Washington,DC, rec. 21.3.1939
Goodman,Benny (cl) | Elman,Ziggy (tp) | Griffin,Chris (tp) | Baker,Cy (tp) | Ballard,Red (tb) | Brown,Vernon (tb) | Schertzer,Hymie (as) | Barnardi,Noni (as) | Rollini,Arthur (ts) | Jerome,Jerry (ts) | Stacy,Jess (p) | Heller,Benny 'Ben' (g) | Goodman,Harry (b) | Schutz,Buddy (dr) | Hampton,Lionel (dr) | Tilton,Martha (voc) | Mercer,Johnny (voc)

Benny Goodman Trio
The World Is Waiting For The Sunrise
Shubert Theater,Newark,NJ, rec. 21.2.1939
Goodman,Benny (cl) | Wilson,Teddy (p) | Hampton,Lionel (dr)

Benny Goodman Quartet
I Cried For You(Now It's Your Turn To Cry Over Me)
Fox Theatre,Detroit, rec. 28.2.1939
Goodman,Benny (cl) | Hampton,Lionel (vib) | Wilson,Teddy (p) | Schutz,Buddy (dr)
Deep Purple
Earl Theatre,Washington,DC, rec. 21.3.1939
Goodman,Benny (cl) | Hampton,Lionel (vib) | Stacy,Jess (p) | Schutz,Buddy (dr)

NCD 8819 | CD | Camel Caravan Broadcast 1939 Vol.3

Benny Goodman And His Orchestra
Let's Dance (Theme) | Clap Yo' Hands | And The Angels Sing | Paradise- | Anything Can Swing- | 'Tain't What You Do (It's How You Do It) | Goodnight My Love | Swingtime In The Rockies
Palace Theater,Akron,Ohio, rec. 28.3.1939
Goodman,Benny (cl) | Elman,Ziggy (tp) | Griffin,Chris (tp) | Goodman,Irving (tp) | Ballard,Red (tb) | Brown,Vernon (tb) | Schertzer,Hymie (as) | Barnardi,Noni (as) | Rollini,Arthur (ts) | Jerome,Jerry (ts) | Stacy,Jess (p) | Heller,Benny 'Ben' (g) | Goodman,Harry (b) | Schutz,Buddy (dr) | Tilton,Martha (voc) | Mercer,Johnny (voc)
Rose Of Washington Square | Show Your Linen,Miss Richardson | Who'll Buy My Bublitckki? | Pick-A-Rib
Jefferson County,Armory,Louisville, rec. 18.4.1939
Goodman,Benny (cl) | Elman,Ziggy (tp) | Griffin,Chris (tp) | Cornelius,Corky (tp) | Baker,Cy (tp) | Ballard,Red (tb) | Brown,Vernon (tb) | Schertzer,Hymie (as) | Barnardi,Noni (as) | Rollini,Arthur (ts) | Jerome,Jerry (ts) | Stacy,Jess (p) | Heller,Benny 'Ben' (g) | Goodman,Harry (b) | Schutz,Buddy (dr) | Hampton,Lionel (dr) | Tilton,Martha (voc) | Mercer,Johnny (voc)
Night Must Fall | You And Your Love | Beer Barrel Polka | Carolina In The Morning | Don't Worry 'Bout Me | Madhouse | Good Bye
Tobacco Warehouse,Asherville,N.C., rec. 25.4.1939
Goodman,Benny (cl,voc) | Elman,Ziggy (tp) | Griffin,Chris (tp) | Baker,Cy (tp) | Cornelius,Corky (tp) | Ballard,Red (tb) | Brown,Vernon (tb) | Schertzer,Hymie (as) | Barnardi,Noni (as) | Rollini,Arthur (ts) | Jerome,Jerry (ts) | Stacy,Jess (p) | Heller,Benny 'Ben' (g) | Goodman,Harry (b) | Schutz,Buddy (dr) | Hampton,Lionel (dr) | Tilton,Martha (voc) | Mercer,Johnny (voc)

Benny Goodman Trio
She's Funny That Way
Palace Theater,Akron,Ohio, rec. 28.3.1939
Goodman,Benny (cl) | Stacy,Jess (p) | Hampton,Lionel (dr)

Benny Goodman Quartet
The Man I Love
Jefferson County,Armory,Louisville, rec. 18.4.1939
Goodman,Benny (cl) | Hampton,Lionel (vib) | Stacy,Jess (p) | Schutz,Buddy (dr)
Opus 3-4
Tobacco Warehouse,Asherville,N.C., rec. 25.4.1939
Goodman,Benny (cl) | Hampton,Lionel (vib) | Stacy,Jess (p) | Schutz,Buddy (dr)

NCD 8831 | CD | Sugar Fingers

Arne Domnerus Quartet
Bye Bye Blackbird | Thursday's Child | Flamingo | Short Life | It Could Happen To You | Lover Man(Oh,Where Can You Be?)
Stockholm,Sweden, rec. 20./21.7.1993
Domnerus,Arne (cl,as) | Lundgren,Jan (p) | Akerberg,Sture (b) | Löfcrantz,Johan (dr)

Arne Domnerus Quintet
Avalon | That's All | Jeep's Blues | Tea For Two | Memories Of You
Domnerus,Arne (cl,as) | Erstrand,Lars (vib) | Lundgren,Jan (p) | Akerberg,Sture (b) | Löfcrantz,Johan (dr)

Jan Lundgren Trio
Sugar Finger
Lundgren,Jan (p) | Akerberg,Sture (b) | Löfcrantz,Johan (dr)

NCD 8841/2 | 2 CD | More Camel Caravans

Benny Goodman And His Orchestra
Let's Dance (Theme) | Remember | Me Myself And I(Are All In Love With You) | Mother Goose Marches On | Swing Benny Swing | Sing Sing Sing | Good Bye
Los Angeles,CA, rec. 10.8.1937
Goodman,Benny (cl) | James,Harry (tp) | Elman,Ziggy (tp) | Griffin,Chris (tp) | Ballard,Red (tb) | McEachern,Murray (tb) | Schertzer,Hymie (as) | Koenig,George (as) | Rollini,Arthur (ts) | Musso,Vido (ts) | Stacy,Jess (p) | Reuss,Allan (g) | Goodman,Harry (b) | Krupa,Gene (dr)
Let's Dance (Theme) | That Naughty Waltz | Satan Takes A Holiday | Let's Have Another Cigarette | Russian Swing | Chloe (Song Of The Swamp) | Caravan | Good Bye
Los Angeles,CA, rec. 17.8.1937
Goodman,Benny (cl) | James,Harry (tp) | Elman,Ziggy (tp) | Griffin,Chris (tp) | Ballard,Red (tb) | McEachern,Murray (tb) | Schertzer,Hymie (as) | Koenig,George (as) | Rollini,Arthur (ts) | Musso,Vido (ts) | Stacy,Jess (p) | Reuss,Allan (g) | Goodman,Harry (b) | Krupa,Gene (dr)
Let's Dance (Theme) | Sometimes I'm Happy | Minnie The Moocher's Wedding Day | Bye Bye Pretty Baby | Swing High Swing Low | Sailboat In The Moonlight | Roll 'Em | Good Bye
Los Angeles,CA, rec. 24.8.1937
Goodman,Benny (cl) | James,Harry (tp) | Elman,Ziggy (tp) | Griffin,Chris (tp) | Ballard,Red (tb) | McEachern,Murray (tb) | Schertzer,Hymie (as) | Koenig,George (as) | Rollini,Arthur (ts) | Musso,Vido (ts) | Stacy,Jess (p) | Reuss,Allan (g) | Goodman,Harry (b) | Krupa,Gene (dr)
Let's Dance (Theme) | Camel Hop | La Cucaracha | The Blue Danube | Swing Song | The Dixieland Band | House Hop | Good Bye
Los Angeles,CA, rec. 31.8.1937
Goodman,Benny (cl) | James,Harry (tp) | Elman,Ziggy (tp) | Griffin,Chris (tp) | Ballard,Red (tb) | McEachern,Murray (tb) | Schertzer,Hymie (as) | Koenig,George (as) | Rollini,Arthur (ts) | Musso,Vido (ts) | Stacy,Jess (p) | Reuss,Allan (g) | Goodman,Harry (b) | Krupa,Gene (dr)

Benny Goodman Quartet
Shine
Los Angeles,CA, rec. 10.8.1937
Goodman,Benny (cl) | Hampton,Lionel (vib) | Wilson,Teddy (p) | Krupa,Gene (dr)
Liza
Los Angeles,CA, rec. 17.8.1937
Goodman,Benny (cl) | Hampton,Lionel (vib) | Wilson,Teddy (p) | Krupa,Gene (dr)
Stompin' At The Savoy
Los Angeles,CA, rec. 24.8.1937
Goodman,Benny (cl) | Hampton,Lionel (vib) | Wilson,Teddy (p) | Krupa,Gene (dr)
Vibraphone Blues
Los Angeles,CA, rec. 31.8.1937
Goodman,Benny (cl) | Hampton,Lionel (vib) | Wilson,Teddy (p) | Krupa,Gene (dr)

Benny Goodman Trio
Sailboat In The Moonlight
Los Angeles,CA, rec. 10.8.1937
Goodman,Benny (cl) | Wilson,Teddy (p) | Krupa,Gene (dr)
So Rare
Los Angeles,CA, rec. 17.8.1937
Goodman,Benny (cl) | Wilson,Teddy (p) | Krupa,Gene (dr)
My Cabin Of Dreams
Los Angeles,CA, rec. 24.8.1937
Goodman,Benny (cl) | Wilson,Teddy (p) | Krupa,Gene (dr)
Whispers In The Dark
Los Angeles,CA, rec. 31.8.1937
Goodman,Benny (cl) | Wilson,Teddy (p) | Krupa,Gene (dr)

NCD 8843/4 | 2 CD | More Camel Caravans

Benny Goodman And His Orchestra
Let's Dance (Theme) | Stardust | If It's The Last Thing I Do | You Took The Words Right Out Of My Heart | Laughing At Life | Mama That Moon Is Here Again | Big John's Special | Good Bye
Kansas City,MO, rec. 20.9.1937
Goodman,Benny (cl) | James,Harry (tp) | Elman,Ziggy (tp) | Griffin,Chris (tp) | Ballard,Red (tb) | Bradley,Will (tb) | Schertzer,Hymie (as) | Koenig,George (as) | Rollini,Arthur (ts) | Musso,Vido (ts) | Stacy,Jess (p) | Reuss,Allan (g) | Goodman,Harry (b) | Krupa,Gene (dr) | Tilton,Martha (voc)
Let's Dance (Theme) | The March Of The Swing Parade | I Used To Be Colour Blind | At Sundown | Liza | Russian Lullaby | When I Go A-Dreamin' | The Yam | Good Bye
Los Angeles,CA, rec. 17.8.1937
Goodman,Benny (cl) | James,Harry (tp) | Elman,Ziggy (tp) | Griffin,Chris (tp) | Ballard,Red (tb) | Brown,Vernon (tb) | Matthews,Dave (as) | Bernardi,Noni (as) | Rollini,Arthur (ts) | Freeman,Buzz (dr) | Stacy,Jess (p) | Heller,Benny 'Ben' (g) | Goodman,Harry (b) | Tough,Dave (dr) | Tilton,Martha (voc)
Let's Dance (Theme) | Chicago | I've Got A Date With A Dream | Margie | In A Mist | The Lambeth Walk | You Go To My Head | Madhouse | Good Bye
Los Angeles,CA, rec. 24.8.1937
Goodman,Benny (cl) | James,Harry (tp) | Elman,Ziggy (tp) | Griffin,Chris (tp) | Ballard,Red (tb) | Brown,Vernon (tb) | Matthews,Dave (as) | Bernardi,Noni (as) | Rollini,Arthur (ts) | Freeman,Bud (ts) | Stacy,Jess (p) | Heller,Benny 'Ben' (g) | Goodman,Harry (b) | Tough,Dave (dr) | Tilton,Martha (voc)
Let's Dance (Theme) | A-Tisket A-Tasket | You're Driving Me Crazy | Blue Skies(and Fletcher Henderson) | I Used To Be Colour Blind | Big John's Special | Good Bye
Los Angeles,CA, rec. 31.8.1937
Goodman,Benny (cl) | James,Harry (tp) | Elman,Ziggy (tp) | Griffin,Chris (tp) | Ballard,Red (tb) | Brown,Vernon (tb) | Matthews,Dave (as) | Bernardi,Noni (as) | Rollini,Arthur (ts) | Freeman,Bud (ts) | Stacy,Jess (p) | Heller,Benny 'Ben' (g) | Goodman,Harry (b) | Tough,Dave (dr) | Tilton,Martha (voc)

Benny Goodman Quartet
Nagasaki
Kansas City,MO, rec. 20.9.1937
Goodman,Benny (cl) | Hampton,Lionel (vib) | Wilson,Teddy (p) | Krupa,Gene (dr)
Benny Sent Me
Los Angeles,CA, rec. 17.8.1937
Goodman,Benny (cl) | Hampton,Lionel (vib) | Wilson,Teddy (p) | Tough,Dave (dr)
Shine
Los Angeles,CA, rec. 24.8.1937
Goodman,Benny (cl) | Hampton,Lionel (vib) | Wilson,Teddy (p) | Tough,Dave (dr)
Some Of These Days
Los Angeles,CA, rec. 31.8.1937
Goodman,Benny (cl) | Hampton,Lionel (vib) | Wilson,Teddy (p) | Tough,Dave (dr)

Benny Goodman Trio
After You've Gone
Kansas City,MO, rec. 20.9.1937
Goodman,Benny (cl) | Wilson,Teddy (p) | Krupa,Gene (dr)
I Surrender Dear
Los Angeles,CA, rec. 31.8.1937
Goodman,Benny (cl) | Wilson,Teddy (p) | Hampton,Lionel (dr)

NCD 8845/6 | 2 CD | More Camel Caravans

Benny Goodman And His Orchestra
Let's Dance (Theme) | Russian Lullaby | I've Got A Pocket Full Of Dreams | Moten Swing | Oh! Lady Be Good | Margie | Bumble Bee Stomp | Good Bye
Kansas City,MO, rec. 20.9.1938
Goodman,Benny (cl) | James,Harry (tp) | Elman,Ziggy (tp) | Griffin,Chris (tp) | Ballard,Red (tb) | Brown,Vernon (tb) | Matthews,Dave (as) | Bernardi,Noni (as) | Rollini,Arthur (ts) | Freeman,Bud (ts) | Stacy,Jess (p) | Heller,Benny 'Ben' (g) | Goodman,Harry (b) | Tough,Dave (dr)
Let's Dance (Theme) | Rose Of The Rio Grande | Lullaby In Rhythm | The Yam | Ciribiribin | Sometimes I'm Happy | One O'Clock Jump | Good Bye
Chicago,Ill, rec. 27.9.1938
Goodman,Benny (cl) | James,Harry (tp) | Elman,Ziggy (tp) | Griffin,Chris (tp) | Ballard,Red (tb) | Brown,Vernon (tb) | Matthews,Dave (as) | Bernardi,Noni (as) | Rollini,Arthur (ts) | Freeman,Buzz (dr) | Stacy,Jess (p) | Heller,Benny 'Ben' (g) | Goodman,Harry (b) | Tough,Dave (dr)
Let's Dance (Theme) | If I Could Be With You One Hour Tonight | Day In Day Out | The Jumpin' Jive | Sent For You Yesterday And Here You Come Today | Boy Meets Horn | I've Been There Before | Pick-A-Rib | Good Bye
Detroit, rec. 2.9.1939
Goodman,Benny (cl) | Elman,Ziggy (tp) | Griffin,Chris (tp) | Cornelius,Corky (tp) | Ballard,Red (tb) | Brown,Vernon (tb) | Squires,Bruce (tb) | Mondello,Toots (as) | Estes,Buff (as) | Bassey,Bus (ts) | Jerome,Jerry (ts) | Henderson,Fletcher (p) | Covey,Arnold (g) | Bernstein,Artie (b) | Fatool,Nick (dr) | Tobin,Louise (voc)
Let's Dance (Theme) | Spring Song | Over The Rainbow | Jumpin' At The Woodside | Moonlight Serenade | Put That Down In Writing | Mozart Matriculates | Stealin' Apples | Good Bye
Detroit, rec. 9.9.1939
Goodman,Benny (cl) | Elman,Ziggy (tp) | Griffin,Chris (tp) | Cornelius,Corky (tp) | Ballard,Red (tb) | Brown,Vernon (tb) | Squires,Bruce (tb) | Mondello,Toots (as) | Estes,Buff (as) | Bassey,Bus (ts) | Jerome,Jerry (ts) | Henderson,Fletcher (p) | Covey,Arnold (g) | Bernstein,Artie (b) | Fatool,Nick (dr) | Tobin,Louise (voc)

Benny Goodman Sextet
Stardust
Detroit, rec. 2.9.1939
Goodman,Benny (cl) | Hampton,Lionel (vib) | Christian,Charlie (g) | Henderson,Fletcher (p) | Bernstein,Artie (b) | Fatool,Nick (dr)
Flying Home
Detroit, rec. 9.9.1939
Goodman,Benny (cl) | Hampton,Lionel (vib) | Christian,Charlie (g) | Henderson,Fletcher (p) | Bernstein,Artie (b) | Fatool,Nick (dr)

Benny Goodman Quartet
The Sheik Of Araby
Chicago,Ill, rec. 27.9.1938
Goodman,Benny (cl) | Hampton,Lionel (vib) | Wilson,Teddy (p) | Tough,Dave (dr)

Benny Goodman Trio
Don't Let That Moon Get Away
Kansas City,MO, rec. 20.9.1938
Goodman,Benny (cl) | Wilson,Teddy (p) | Hampton,Lionel (dr)
You're Blasé
Chicago,Ill, rec. 27.9.1938
Goodman,Benny (cl) | Wilson,Teddy (p) | Hampton,Lionel (dr)

Lionel Hampton/Jess Stacy
Chinatown My Chinatown
Kansas City,MO, rec. 20.9.1938
Hampton,Lionel (p) | Stacy,Jess (p)

-> Die Nummern 8841-8846 sind auch in einem 6-CD-Schuber erhältlich!

Planet Jazz | BMG-Ariola Classics GmbH

2152052-2 | CD | Planet Jazz:Louis Armstrong

Louis Armstrong And His Orchestra
I'll Be Glad When You're Dead You Rascal You- | When It's Sleepy Time Down South- | Nobody's Sweetheart-
Camden,NJ, rec. 21.12.1932
Armstrong,Louis (tp,voc) | Gaines,Charlie (tp) | unkn. (tp) | unkn. (tb) | Jordan,Louis (as) | Davey,Arthur (as) | Blake,Ellsworth (ts) | Robinson,Wesley (p) | unkn. (g) | Hayes,Ed (b) | Hill,Benny (dr)
I Got A Right To Sing The Blues
Chicago,Ill, rec. 26.1.1933
Armstrong,Louis (tp,voc) | Whitlock,Ellis (tp) | Randolph,Zilmer (tp,arr) | Johnson,Keg (tb) | Brown,Scoville (cl,as) | Oldham,George (cl,as) | Johnson,Budd (cl,ts) | Wilson,Teddy (p) | McKendrick,Mike (g,bj) | Oldham,Bill (b,tuba) | Porter,Yank (dr)
Basin Street Blues
Chicago,Ill, rec. 26.4.1933
Armstrong,Louis (tp,voc) | Whitlock,Ellis (tp) | Randolph,Zilmer (tp,arr) |

Johnson,Keg (tb) | Brown,Scoville (cl,as) | Oldham,George (cl,as) | Johnson,Budd (cl,ts) | Wilson,Teddy (p) | McKendrick,Mike (g,bj) | Oldham,Bill (b,tuba) | Porter,Yank (dr)

St.Louis Blues

Armstrong,Louis (tp,voc) | Randolph,Zilmer (tp) | Whitlock,Elmer (tp) | Johnson,Keg (tb) | Johnson,Budd (sax) | Brown,Scoville (sax) | Oldham,George (sax) | Beal,Charlie (p) | McKendrick,Mike (bj) | Oldham,Bill (b) | Dial,Harry (dr)

Louis Armstrong And His Hot Seven

Sugar

Los Angeles,CA, rec. 6.9.1946

Armstrong,Louis (tp,voc) | Dickenson,Vic (tb) | Bigard,Barney (cl) | Beal,Charlie (p) | Reuss,Allan (g) | Callender,Red (b) | Singleton,Zutty (dr)

Louis Armstrong And His Dixieland Seven

Do You Know What It Means To Miss New Orleans

Los Angeles,CA, rec. 17.10.1946

Armstrong,Louis (tp,voc) | Ory,Edward 'Kid' (tb) | Bigard,Barney (cl) | Beal,Charlie (p) | Scott,Bud (g) | Callender,Red (b) | Hall,Minor 'Ram' (dr)

Louis Armstrong And His All Stars

Ain't Misbehavin'

Live at Town Hall,NYC, rec. 17.5.1947

Armstrong,Louis (tp,voc) | Hackett,Bobby (tp) | Teagarden,Jack (tb) | Hucko,Peanuts (cl) | Cary,Dick (p) | Haggart,Bob (b) | Catlett,Big Sid (dr)

Rockin' Chair | Someday You'll Be Sorry

NYC, rec. 10.6.1947

Armstrong,Louis (tp,voc) | Hackett,Bobby (tp) | Teagarden,Jack (tb,voc) | Hucko,Peanuts (cl) | Caceres,Ernie (cl,bs) | Guarnieri,Johnny (p,celeste) | Casey,Al (g) | Hall,Al (b) | Cole,William 'Cozy' (dr)

Louis Armstrong And His Friends

Mood Indigo | What A Wonderful World | My One And Only Love

NYC, rec. 26.5.1970

Armstrong,Louis (voc) | Spaulding,James (fl) | Owens,Frank (p) | Brown,Sam (g) | Burrell,Kenny (g) | Davis,Richard (b) | Duvivier,George (b) | Williams Jr.,John (el-b) | Purdie,Bernard 'Pretty' (dr) | Black,Arnold (v) | Clarke,Selwart (v) | Collymore,Winston (v) | Gersham,Paul (v) | Green,Manny (v) | Lookofsky,Harry (v) | Orloff,Gene (v) | Malin,Joe (v) | Pollikoff,Max (v) | Barber,Julian (viola) | Brown,Alfred (viola) | Schwartz,David (viola) | Vardi,Emanuel (viola) | McCracken,Charles (cello) | Moore,Kermit (cello) | Ricci,George (cello) | Schulman,Allan (cello) | Nelson,Oliver (arr,ld)

Everybody's Talkin'(Echoes)

NYC, rec. 27.5.1970

Armstrong,Louis (voc) | Spaulding,James (fl) | Owens,Frank (p) | Brown,Sam (g) | Burrell,Kenny (g) | Davis,Richard (b) | Duvivier,George (b) | Williams Jr.,John (el-b) | Purdie,Bernard 'Pretty' (dr) | Black,Arnold (v) | Clarke,Selwart (v) | Collymore,Winston (v) | Gersham,Paul (v) | Green,Manny (v) | Lookofsky,Harry (v) | Raimondi,Matthew (v) | Malin,Joe (v) | Pollikoff,Max (v) | Barber,Julian (viola) | Brown,Alfred (viola) | Schwartz,David (viola) | Vardi,Emanuel (viola) | McCracken,Charles (cello) | Moore,Kermit (cello) | Ricci,George (cello) | Schulman,Allan (cello) | Golden,Gene (congas) | Nelson,Oliver (arr,ld)

2152053-2 | CD | Planet Jazz:Duke Ellington

Duke Ellington And His Cotton Club Orchestra

I Can't Give You Anything But Love

NYC, rec. 26.3.1928

Ellington,Duke (p) | Jenkins,Freddie (tp) | Whetsol,Arthur (tp) | Nanton,Joe 'Tricky Sam' (tb) | Hodges,Johnny (cl,ss,as) | Carney,Harry (cl,as,bs) | Bigard,Barney (cl,ts) | Guy,Fred (bj) | Braud,Wellman (tuba) | Greer,William 'Sonny' (dr) | Cox,Baby (voc) | Mills,Irving (voc)

Duke Ellington And His Famous Orchestra

Take The 'A' Train

Hollywood,CA, rec. 15.2.1941

Ellington,Duke (ld) | Jones,Wallace (tp) | Williams,Cootie (tp) | Stewart,Rex (co) | Nanton,Joe 'Tricky Sam' (tb) | Brown,Lawrence (tb) | Tizol,Juan (v-tb) | Bigard,Barney (cl) | Hodges,Johnny (cl,ss,as) | Hardwicke,Otto (as,bass-s) | Webster,Ben (ts) | Carney,Harry (cl,as,bs) | Strayhorn,Billy (p,arr) | Guy,Fred (g) | Blanton,Jimmy (b) | Greer,William 'Sonny' (dr)

I Got It Bad And That Ain't Good

Hollywood,CA, rec. 26.6.1941

Ellington,Duke (p,arr) | Jones,Wallace (tp) | Nance,Ray (tp) | Stewart,Rex (co) | Nanton,Joe 'Tricky Sam' (tb) | Brown,Lawrence (tb) | Tizol,Juan (v-tb) | Bigard,Barney (cl) | Hodges,Johnny (cl,ss,as) | Hardwicke,Otto (as,bass-s) | Webster,Ben (ts) | Carney,Harry (cl,as,bs) | Guy,Fred (g) | Blanton,Jimmy (b) | Greer,William 'Sonny' (dr) | Anderson,Ivie (voc)

Perdido

Chicago,Ill, rec. 21.1.1942

Ellington,Duke (p,arr) | Jones,Wallace (tp) | Nance,Ray (tp) | Stewart,Rex (co) | Nanton,Joe 'Tricky Sam' (tb) | Brown,Lawrence (tb) | Tizol,Juan (v-tb) | Bigard,Barney (cl) | Hodges,Johnny (cl,ss,as) | Hardwicke,Otto (as,bass-s) | Webster,Ben (ts) | Carney,Harry (cl,as,bs) | Guy,Fred (g) | Blanton,Jimmy (b) | Greer,William 'Sonny' (dr)

Duke Ellington And His Orchestra

I'm Beginning To See The Light

NYC, rec. 1.12.1944

Ellington,Duke (p) | Hemphill,Shelton (tp) | Jordan,Taft (tp) | Anderson,Cat (tp) | Nance,Ray (tp) | Nanton,Joe 'Tricky Sam' (tb) | Jones,Claude (tb) | Brown,Lawrence (tb) | Hodges,Johnny (as) | Hardwicke,Otto (as) | Sears,Al (ts) | Hamilton,Jimmy (cl,ts) | Carney,Harry (cl,bs) | Guy,Fred (g) | Raglin,Alvin 'Junior' (b) | Greer,William 'Sonny' (dr) | Sherrill,Joya (voc)

Prelude To A Kiss

NYC, rec. 10.5.1945

Ellington,Duke (p,arr) | Jordan,Taft (tp) | Hemphill,Shelton (tp) | Anderson,Cat (tp) | Nance,Ray (v,co) | Nanton,Joe 'Tricky Sam' (tb) | Brown,Lawrence (tb) | Jones,Claude (tb) | Hamilton,Jimmy (cl,ts) | Hodges,Johnny (cl,ss,as) | Hardwicke,Otto (as,bass-s) | Sears,Al (ts) | Carney,Harry (cl,as,bs) | Guy,Fred (g) | Raglin,Alvin 'Junior' (b) | Greer,William 'Sonny' (dr) | Sherrill,Joya (voc)

Caravan | Mood Indigo

NYC, rec. 11.5.1945

Ellington,Duke (p,arr) | Jordan,Taft (tp) | Hemphill,Shelton (tp) | Anderson,Cat (tp) | Nance,Ray (v,co) | Nanton,Joe 'Tricky Sam' (tb) | Brown,Lawrence (tb) | Jones,Claude (tb) | Hamilton,Jimmy (cl,ts) | Hodges,Johnny (cl,ss,as) | Hardwicke,Otto (as,bass-s) | Sears,Al (ts) | Carney,Harry (cl,as,bs) | Guy,Fred (g) | Raglin,Alvin 'Junior' (b) | Greer,William 'Sonny' (dr) | Davis,Kay (voc)

In A Sentimental Mood | It Don't Mean A Thing If It Ain't Got That Swing | Sophisticated Lady

NYC, rec. 14.5.1945

Ellington,Duke (p) | Hemphill,Shelton (tp) | Jordan,Taft (tp) | Anderson,Cat (tp) | Nance,Ray (tp) | Stewart,Rex (co) | Nanton,Joe 'Tricky Sam' (tb) | Jones,Claude (tb) | Brown,Lawrence (tb) | Hodges,Johnny (as) | Hardwicke,Otto (as) | Sears,Al (ts) | Hamilton,Jimmy (cl,ts) | Carney,Harry (cl,bs) | Guy,Fred (g) | Haggart,Bob (b) | Greer,William 'Sonny' (dr) | Davis,Kay (voc) | Sherrill,Joya (voc) | Ellington,Marie (voc)

Solitude

NYC, rec. 15.5.1945

Ellington,Duke (p) | Hemphill,Shelton (tp) | Jordan,Taft (tp) | Anderson,Cat (tp) | Nance,Ray (tp) | Stewart,Rex (co) | Nanton,Joe 'Tricky Sam' (tb) | Jones,Claude (tb) | Brown,Lawrence (tb) | Hodges,Johnny (as) | Hardwicke,Otto (as) | Sears,Al (ts) | Hamilton,Jimmy (cl,ts) | Carney,Harry (cl,bs) | Guy,Fred (g) | Weiss,Sid (b) | Greer,William 'Sonny' (dr) | Davis,Kay (voc) | Sherrill,Joya (voc) | Ellington,Marie (voc) | Hibbler,Al (voc)

Duke Ellington-Billy Strayhorn Duo

Drawing Room Blues

NYC, rec. 10.1.1946

Ellington,Duke (p) | Strayhorn,Billy (p)

Duke Ellington And His Orchestra

Lover Man(Oh,Where Can You Be?)

NYC, rec. 26.8.1946

Ellington,Duke (p) | Jordan,Taft (tp) | Hemphill,Shelton (tp) | Anderson,Cat (tp) | Williams,Francis (tp) | Baker,Harold 'Shorty' (tp) | Nance,Ray (v,co,voc) | DeParis,Wilbur (tb) | Jones,Claude (tb) | Brown,Lawrence (tb) | Hamilton,Jimmy (cl,ts) | Procope,Russell (as) | Hodges,Johnny (as) | Sears,Al (ts) | Carney,Harry (cl,bs) | Guy,Fred (g) | Pettiford,Oscar (b) | Greer,William 'Sonny' (dr) | Cox,Marion (voc)

Duke Ellington

Lotus Blossom

NYC, rec. 1.9.1967

Ellington,Duke (p-solo)

2152054-2 | CD | Planet Jazz:Benny Goodman

Benny Goodman And His Orchestra

Always

NYC, rec. 19.4.1935

Goodman,Benny (cl) | Erwin,Pee Wee (tp) | Kazebier,Nate (tp) | Neary,Jerry (tp) | Teagarden,Jack (tb) | Lacey,Jack (tb) | Mondello,Toots (as) | Schertzer,Hymie (as) | Rollini,Arthur (ts) | Clark,Dick (ts) | Froeba,Frank (p) | Reuss,Allan (g) | Goodman,Harry (b) | Krupa,Gene (dr) | Henderson,Horace (arr)

King Porter Stomp

NYC, rec. 1.7.1935

Goodman,Benny (cl) | Berigan,Bunny (tp) | Kazebier,Nate (tp) | Muzillo,Ralph (tp) | Ballard,Red (tb) | Lacey,Jack (tb) | Mondello,Toots (as) | Schertzer,Hymie (as) | Clark,Dick (ts) | Rollini,Arthur (ts) | Froeba,Frank (p) | Van Eps,George (g) | Goodman,Harry (b) | Krupa,Gene (dr) | Henderson,Fletcher (arr)

Good Bye

Goodman,Benny (cl) | Berigan,Bunny (tp) | Kazebier,Nate (tp) | Muzillo,Ralph (tp) | Ballard,Red (tb) | Lacey,Jack (tb) | Harris,Joe (tb) | DePew,Bill (as) | Schertzer,Hymie (as) | Clark,Dick (ts) | Rollini,Arthur (ts) | Stacy,Jess (p) | Reuss,Allan (g) | Goodman,Harry (b) | Krupa,Gene (dr) | Jenkins,Gordon (arr)

Benny Goodman Trio

After You've Gone | Body And Soul

NYC, rec. 13.7.1935

Goodman,Benny (cl) | Wilson,Teddy (p) | Krupa,Gene (dr)

Benny Goodman And His Orchestra

Stompin' At The Savoy

Chicago,Ill, rec. 24.1.1936

Goodman,Benny (cl) | Geller,Harry (tp) | Kazebier,Nate (tp) | Muzillo,Ralph (tp) | Ballard,Red (tb) | Harris,Joe (tb) | Mondello,Toots (as) | Schertzer,Hymie (as) | DePew,Bill (as) | Clark,Dick (ts) | Rollini,Arthur (ts) | Stacy,Jess (p) | Reuss,Allan (g) | Goodman,Harry (b) | Krupa,Gene (dr) | Sampson,Edgar (arr)

Get Happy

Chicago,Ill, rec. 20.3.1936

Goodman,Benny (cl) | Geller,Harry (tp) | Kazebier,Nate (tp) | Muzillo,Ralph (tp) | Ballard,Red (tb) | Harris,Joe (tb) | Mondello,Toots (as) | Schertzer,Hymie (as) | DePew,Bill (as) | Clark,Dick (ts) | Rollini,Arthur (ts) | Stacy,Jess (p) | Reuss,Allan (g) | Goodman,Harry (b) | Krupa,Gene (dr) | Murphy,Spud (arr)

In A Sentimental Mood

NYC, rec. 15.6.1936

Goodman,Benny (cl) | Geller,Harry (tp) | Kazebier,Nate (tp) | Griffin,Chris (tp) | Ballard,Red (tb) | McEachern,Murray (tb) | DePew,Bill (as) | Schertzer,Hymie (as) | Rollini,Arthur (ts) | Clark,Dick (ts) | Stacy,Jess (p) | Reuss,Allan (g) | Goodman,Harry (b) | Krupa,Gene (dr) | Mundy,Jimmy (arr)

You Turned The Tables On Me

Hollywood,CA, rec. 13.8.1936

Goodman,Benny (cl) | Geller,Harry (tp) | Klein,Manny (tp) | Griffin,Chris (tp) | Ballard,Red (tb) | McEachern,Murray (tb) | DePew,Bill (as) | Schertzer,Hymie (as) | Rollini,Arthur (ts) | Clark,Dick (ts) | Stacy,Jess (p) | Reuss,Allan (g) | Goodman,Harry (b) | Krupa,Gene (dr) | Ward,Helen (voc) | Henderson,Fletcher (arr)

Love Me Or Leave Me

Hollywood,CA, rec. 21.8.1936

Goodman,Benny (cl) | Griffin,Gordon (tp) | Bose,Sterling (tp) | Erwin (Irvin) | Ballard,Red (tb) | McEachern,Murray (tb) | Schertzer,Hymie (as) | DePew,Bill (as) | Clark,Dick (ts) | Rollini,Arthur (ts) | Musso,Vido (ts) | Stacy,Jess (p) | Reuss,Allan (g) | Goodman,Harry (b) | Krupa,Gene (dr) | Henderson,Fletcher (arr)

Benny Goodman Quartet

Moonglow

Goodman,Benny (cl) | Hampton,Lionel (vib) | Wilson,Teddy (p) | Krupa,Gene (dr)

Benny Goodman And His Orchestra

'Tain't No Use | Bugle Call Rag | Goodnight My Love

NYC, rec. 5.11.1936

Goodman,Benny (cl,voc) | Elman,Ziggy (tp) | Griffin,Gordon (tp) | Zarchy,Reuben 'Zeke' (tp) | Ballard,Red (tb) | McEachern,Murray (tb) | Schertzer,Hymie (as) | DePew,Bill (as) | Musso,Vido (ts) | Rollini,Arthur (ts) | Stacy,Jess (p) | Reuss,Allan (g) | Goodman,Harry (b) | Krupa,Gene (dr) | Fitzgerald,Ella (voc) | Mundy,Jimmy (arr)

Benny Goodman Quartet

Tea For Two

NYC, rec. 3.2.1937

Goodman,Benny (cl) | Hampton,Lionel (vib) | Wilson,Teddy (p) | Krupa,Gene (dr)

Benny Goodman And His Orchestra

Sing Sing Sing(part 1) | Sing Sing Sing(part 2)

Hollywood,CA, rec. 6.7.1937

Goodman,Benny (cl) | James,Harry (tp) | Griffin,Gordon (tp) | Elman,Ziggy (tp) | Ballard,Red (tb) | McEachern,Murray (tb) | Schertzer,Hymie (as) | Koenig,George (as) | Rollini,Arthur (ts) | Musso,Vido (ts) | Stacy,Jess (p) | Reuss,Allan (g) | Goodman,Harry (b) | Krupa,Gene (dr) | Mundy,Jimmy (arr)

2152055-2 | CD | Planet Jazz:Coleman Hawkins

Connie's Inn Orchestra

Sugarfoot Stomp

Camden,NJ, rec. 29.4.1931

Connie's Inn Orchestra | Smith,Russell (tp) | Stark,Bobby (tp) | Stewart,Rex (co) | Jones,Claude (tb) | Morton,Benny (tb) | Procope,Russell (cl,as) | Boone,Harvey (cl,as) | Hawkins,Coleman (cl,ts) | Henderson,Fletcher (p,arr,ld) | Holiday,Clarence (g) | Kirby,John (tuba) | Johnson,Walter (dr)

Lionel Hampton And His Orchestra

When Lights Are Low

NYC, rec. 11.9.1939

Hampton,Lionel (vib) | Gillespie,Dizzy (tp) | Carter,Benny (as,arr) | Hawkins,Coleman (ts) | Webster,Ben (ts) | Berry,Leon 'Chu' (ts) | Hart,Clyde (p) | Christian,Charlie (g) | Hinton,Milt (b) | Cole,William 'Cozy' (dr)

Coleman Hawkins And His Orchestra

She's Funny That Way | Body And Soul

NYC, rec. 11.10.1939

Hawkins,Coleman (ts) | Lindsey,Tommy (tp) | Guy,Joe (tp) | Hardy,Earl (tb) | Fields,Jackie (as) | Moore,Eustis (as) | Rodgers,Gene (tp) | Smith,William Oscar (b) | Herbert,Arthur (dr) | Carpenter,Thelma (voc)

Lionel Hampton And His Orchestra

Dinah

NYC, rec. 21.12.1939

Hampton,Lionel (vib) | Carter,Benny (tp) | Hall,Edmond (cl) | Hawkins,Coleman (ts) | Sullivan,Joe (p) | Green,Freddie (g) | Bernstein,Artie (b) | Singleton,Zutty (dr)

Coleman Hawkins All Star Octet

My Blue Heaven

NYC, rec. 3.1.1940

Hawkins,Coleman (ts) | Carter,Benny (tp) | Higginbotham,J.C. (tb) | Polo,Danny (cl) | Rodgers,Gene (p) | Lucie,Lawrence (g) | Williams,John B. (b) | Johnson,Walter (dr)

Coleman Hawkins' Fifty-Second Street All-Stars

Say It Isn't So | Spotlite

NYC, rec. 27.2.1946

Hawkins,Coleman (ts) | Shavers,Charlie (tp) | Brown,Pete (as) | Eager,Allen (ts) | Jones,Jimmy (p) | Osborne,Mary (g) | McKibbon,Al (b) | Manne,Shelly (dr)

Coleman Hawkins And His All Stars

April In Paris | How Strange | Angel Face

NYC, rec. 11.12.1947

Hawkins,Coleman (ts) | Navarro,Fats (tp) | Johnson,J.J. (tb) | Johnson,Budd (as) | De Veta,Marion (bs) | Jones,Hank (p) | Wayne,Chuck (b) | Lesberg,Jack (b) | Roach,Max (dr)

Coleman Hawkins With Billy Byers And His Orchestra

There'll Never Be Another You

NYC, rec. 17.1.1956

Hawkins,Coleman (ts) | Nottingham,Jimmy (tp) | Green,Urbie (tb) | Satterfield,Jack (tb) | Ohms,Freddie (tb) | Mitchell,Tom (tb) | Baker,Julius (fl) | Jekowsky,Sidney (cl) | Bodner,Phil (oboe) | Wilson,Marty (vib) | Jones,Hank (p) | Galbraith,Barry (g) | Hinton,Milt (b) | Johnson,Osie (dr) | Orloff,Gene (concertmaster) | unkn. (7 strings) | Byers,Billy (arr,ld)

Coleman Hawkins With Many Albam And His Orchestra

I Love Paris | Under Paris Skies

NYC, rec. 9.7.1956

Hawkins,Coleman (ts) | Albam,Manny (cond,arr) | Travis,Nick (tp) | Welsch,Chauncey (tb) | Beckenstein,Ray (fl) | Penque,Romeo (sax) | Epstein[Young],Al (sax) | Galbraith,Barry (g) | Jones,Hank (p) | Fishkin,Arnold (b) | Johnson,Osie (dr)

Henry Red Allen's All Stars

Sweet Lorraine | I've Got The World On A String

NYC, rec. 10.4.1957

Allen,Henry Red (tp,voc) | Higginbotham,J.C. (tb) | Bailey,Buster (cl) | Hawkins,Coleman (ts) | Napoleon,Marty (p) | Barksdale,Everett (g) | Trottman,Lloyd (b) | Cole,William 'Cozy' (dr)

2152056-2 | CD | Planet Jazz:Glenn Miller

Glenn Miller And His Orchestra

King Porter Stomp

NYC, rec. 27.9.1938

Miller,Glenn (tb) | Peck,Bob (tp) | Price,Bob (tp) | Austin,Johnny (tp) | Mastren,Al (tb) | Tanner,Paul (tb) | Schwartz,Wilbur (cl,as) | McIntyre,Hal (as) | Stegmeyer,Bill (as) | Beneke,Gordon 'Tex' (ts) | Aronson,Stanley (ts) | MacGregor,John Chalmers 'Chummy' (p) | Bundock,Rowland 'Rolly' (b) | Spangler,Bob (dr)

Moonlight Serenade

NYC, rec. 4.4.1939

Miller,Glenn (tb) | Price,Bob (tp) | Knowles,Legh (tp) | McMickle,Dale (tp) | Mastren,Al (tb) | Tanner,Paul (tb) | McIntyre,Hal (as) | Aronson,Stanley (as,bs) | Schwartz,Wilbur (cl,as) | Beneke,Gordon 'Tex' (ts) | Klink,Al (ts) | MacGregor,John Chalmers 'Chummy' (p) | Reuss,Allan (g) | Bundock,Rowland 'Rolly' (b) | Carlson,Frank (dr)

Sunrise Serenade | Little Brown Jug

NYC, rec. 10.4.1939

Miller,Glenn (tb) | Knowles,Legh (tp) | Price,Bob (tp) | McMickle,Dale (tp) | Mastren,Al (tb) | Tanner,Paul (tb) | Schwartz,Wilbur (cl,as) | McIntyre,Hal (as) | Aronson,Stanley (as) | Beneke,Gordon 'Tex' (ts) | Klink,Al (ts) | MacGregor,John Chalmers 'Chummy' (p) | Reuss,Allan (g) | Bundock,Rowland 'Rolly' (b) | Purtill,Maurice 'Moe' (dr) | Finegan,Bill (arr)

Moon Love

NYC, rec. 25.5.1939

Miller,Glenn (tb) | Knowles,Legh (tp) | Hurley,Clyde (tp) | McMickle,Dale (tp) | Mastren,Al (tb) | Tanner,Paul (tb) | Schwartz,Wilbur (cl,as) | McIntyre,Hal (as) | Gelinas,Gabe (as,bs) | Beneke,Gordon 'Tex' (ts) | Klink,Al (ts) | MacGregor,John Chalmers 'Chummy' (p) | Ens,Arthur (g) | Bundock,Rowland 'Rolly' (b) | Purtill,Maurice 'Moe' (dr) | Eberle,Ray (voc)

In The Mood

NYC, rec. 1.8.1939

Miller,Glenn (tb) | Knowles,Legh (tp) | Hurley,Clyde (tp) | McMickle,Dale (tp) | Mastren,Al (tb) | Tanner,Paul (tb) | Schwartz,Wilbur (cl,as) | McIntyre,Hal (as) | Tennyson,Hal (as,bs) | Beneke,Gordon 'Tex' (ts) | Klink,Al (ts) | MacGregor,John Chalmers 'Chummy' (p) | Fisher,Richard (g) | Bundock,Rowland 'Rolly' (b) | Purtill,Maurice 'Moe' (dr)

When You Wish Upon A Star

NYC, rec. 6.1.1940

Miller,Glenn (tb) | Knowles,Legh (tp) | Hurley,Clyde (tp) | McMickle,Dale (tp) | Best,John (tp) | Mastren,Al (tb) | Tanner,Paul (tb) | D'Annolfo,Frank (tb) | Schwartz,Wilbur (cl,as) | McIntyre,Hal (as) | Abato,Jimmy (as,bs) | Beneke,Gordon 'Tex' (ts) | Klink,Al (ts) | MacGregor,John Chalmers 'Chummy' (p) | Fisher,Richard (g) | Bundock,Rowland 'Rolly' (b) | Purtill,Maurice 'Moe' (dr) | Eberle,Ray (voc)

Tuxedo Junction

NYC, rec. 5.2.1940

Miller,Glenn (tb) | Knowles,Legh (tp) | Hurley,Clyde (tp) | McMickle,Dale (tp) | Best,John (tp) | Mack,Tommy (tb) | Tanner,Paul (tb) | D'Annolfo,Frank (tb) | Schwartz,Wilbur (cl,as) | McIntyre,Hal (as) | Abato,Jimmy (as,bs) | Beneke,Gordon 'Tex' (ts) | Klink,Al (ts) | MacGregor,John Chalmers 'Chummy' (p) | Bundock,Rowland 'Rolly' (b) | Purtill,Maurice 'Moe' (dr) | Gray,Jerry (arr)

Pennsylvania Six Five Thousand

NYC, rec. 28.4.1940

Miller,Glenn (tb) | Knowles,Legh (tp) | Hurley,Clyde (tp) | Zarchy,Reuben 'Zeke' (tp) | Best,John (tp) | Priddy,Jimmy (tb) | Tanner,Paul (tb) | D'Annolfo,Frank (tb) | Schwartz,Wilbur (cl,as) | McIntyre,Hal (as) | Caceres,Ernie (cl,as,bs) | Beneke,Gordon 'Tex' (ts) | Klink,Al (ts) | MacGregor,John Chalmers 'Chummy' (p) | Lathrop,Jack (g) | Bundock,Rowland 'Rolly' (b) | Purtill,Maurice 'Moe' (dr) | Gray,Jerry (arr)

Chattanooga Choo Choo

Hollywood,CA, rec. 7.5.1941

Miller,Glenn (tb) | McMickle,Dale (tp) | Anthony,Ray (tp) | May,Billy (tp) | Best,John (tp) | Priddy,Jimmy (tb) | Tanner,Paul (tb) | D'Annolfo,Frank (tb) | Schwartz,Wilbur (cl,as) | McIntyre,Hal (as) | Caceres,Ernie (cl,as,bs) | Beneke,Gordon 'Tex' (ts) | Klink,Al (ts) | MacGregor,John Chalmers 'Chummy' (p) | Lathrop,Jack (g) | Alpert,Trigger (b) | Purtill,Maurice 'Moe' (dr) | Gray,Jerry (arr) | Modernaires,The (voc-group)

A String Of Pearls

NYC, rec. 3.11.1941

Miller,Glenn (tb) | Best,John (tp) | McMickle,Dale (tp) | Fila,Alex (tp) | May,Billy (tp) | Hackett,Bobby (g,co) | Priddy,Jimmy (tb) | Tanner,Paul (tb) | Smith,Warren (tb) | Feman,Ben (as) | Schwartz,Wilbur (cl,as) | Beneke,Gordon 'Tex' (ts) | Klink,Al (ts) | Caceres,Ernie (cl,as,bs) | MacGregor,John Chalmers 'Chummy' (p) | Goldberg,Edward 'Doc' (b) | Purtill,Maurice 'Moe' (dr) | Gray,Jerry (arr)

Don't Sit Under The Apple Tree

NYC, rec. 18.2.1942

Miller,Glenn (tb) | Best,John (tp) | McMickle,Dale (tp) | Lipkins,Steve (tp) | May,Billy (tp) | Hackett,Bobby (g,co) | Priddy,Jimmy (tb) | Tanner,Paul (tb) | D'Annolfo,Frank (tb) | Martin,Skippy (as) | Schwartz,Wilbur (cl,as) | Beneke,Gordon 'Tex' (ts,voc) | Klink,Al (ts) | Caceres,Ernie (cl,as,bs) | MacGregor,John Chalmers 'Chummy' (p) | Goldberg,Edward 'Doc' (b) | Purtill,Maurice 'Moe' (dr) | Modernaires,The (voc-group)

American Patrol

NYC, rec. 2.4.1942

Miller,Glenn (tb) | Best,John (tp) | McMickle,Dale (tp) | Lipkins,Steve (tp) | May,Billy (tp) | Hackett,Bobby (g,co) | Priddy,Jimmy (tb) | Tanner,Paul (tb) | D'Annolfo,Frank (tb) | Martin,Skippy (as) | Schwartz,Wilbur (cl,as) | Beneke,Gordon 'Tex' (ts,voc) | Klink,Al (ts) | Caceres,Ernie (cl,as,bs) | MacGregor,John Chalmers 'Chummy' (p) | Goldberg,Edward 'Doc' (b) | Purtill,Maurice 'Moe' (dr) | Modernaires,The (voc-group) | Gray,Jerry (arr)

I've Got A Girl In Kalamazoo
Hollywood,CA, rec. 20.5.1942
Miller,Glenn (tb) | Best,John (tp) | McMickle,Dale (tp) | Lipkins,Steve (tp) | May,Billy (tp) | Hackett,Bobby (g,co) | Priddy,Jimmy (tb) | Tanner,Paul (tb) | D'Annolfo,Frank (tb) | Martin,Skippy (as) | Schwartz,Wilbur (cl,as) | Beneke,Gordon 'Tex' (ts,voc) | Klink,Al (ts) | Caceres,Ernie (cl,as,bs) | MacGregor,John Chalmers 'Chummy' (p) | Goldberg,Edward 'Doc' (b) | Purtill,Maurice 'Moe' (dr) | Hutton,Marion (voc) | Modernaires,The (voc-group) | Gray,Jerry (arr)

That Old Black Magic
NYC, rec. 15.7.1942
Miller,Glenn (tb) | Best,John (tp) | McMickle,Dale (tp) | Lipkins,Steve (tp) | May,Billy (tp) | Hackett,Bobby (g,co) | Priddy,Jimmy (tb) | Tanner,Paul (tb) | D'Annolfo,Frank (tb) | Martin,Skippy (as) | Schwartz,Wilbur (cl,as) | Beneke,Gordon 'Tex' (ts) | Klink,Al (ts) | Caceres,Ernie (cl,as,bs) | MacGregor,John Chalmers 'Chummy' (p) | Goldberg,Edward 'Doc' (b) | Purtill,Maurice 'Moe' (dr) | Nelson,Skip (voc) | Modernaires,The (voc-group) | Gray,Jerry (arr)

2152057-2 | CD | Planet JazzArtie Shaw

Artie Shaw And His Orchestra
Begin The Beguine | Indian Love Call | Any Old Time
NYC, rec. 24.7.1938
Shaw,Artie (cl) | Peterson,Chuck (tp) | Best,John (tp) | Bowen,Claude (tp) | Arus,George (tb) | Vesely,Ted (tb) | Rodgers,Harry (tb) | Robinson,Les (as) | Freeman,Hank (as) | Pastor,Tony (ts,voc) | Perry,Ronnie (ts) | Burness,Lester (p) | Avola,Al (g) | Weiss,Sid (b) | Leeman,Cliff (dr) | Holiday,Billie (voc) | Gray,Jerry (arr)

Lover Come Back To Me
NYC, rec. 17.1.1939
Shaw,Artie (cl) | Peterson,Chuck (tp) | Best,John (tp) | Privin,Bernie (tp) | Arus,George (tb) | Jenkins,Les (tb) | Rodgers,Harry (tb) | Robinson,Les (as) | Freeman,Hank (as) | Pastor,Tony (ts) | Auld,Georgie (ts) | Kitsis,Bob (p) | Avola,Al (g) | Weiss,Sid (b) | Rich,Buddy (dr) | Gray,Jerry (arr)

Deep Purple
NYC, rec. 12.3.1939
Shaw,Artie (cl) | Peterson,Chuck (tp) | Best,John (tp) | Privin,Bernie (tp) | Arus,George (tb) | Jenkins,Les (tb) | Rodgers,Harry (tb) | Robinson,Les (as) | Freeman,Hank (as) | Pastor,Tony (ts,voc) | Auld,Georgie (ts) | Kitsis,Bob (p) | Avola,Al (g) | Weiss,Sid (b) | Rich,Buddy (dr) | Forrest,Helen (voc)

Comes Love
Hollywood,CA, rec. 12.6.1939
Shaw,Artie (cl) | Peterson,Chuck (tp) | Best,John (tp) | Privin,Bernie (tp) | Arus,George (tb) | Jenkins,Les (tb) | Rodgers,Harry (tb) | Robinson,Les (as) | Freeman,Hank (as) | Pastor,Tony (ts) | Auld,Georgie (ts) | Kitsis,Bob (p) | Avola,Al (g) | Weiss,Sid (b) | Rich,Buddy (dr) | Forest,Helen (voc)

Oh! Lady Be Good
NYC, rec. 27.8.1939
Shaw,Artie (cl) | Peterson,Chuck (tp) | Geller,Harry (tp) | Privin,Bernie (tp) | Arus,George (tb) | Jenkins,Les (tb) | Rodgers,Harry (tb) | Robinson,Les (as) | Freeman,Hank (as) | Pastor,Tony (ts) | Auld,Georgie (ts) | Kitsis,Bob (p) | Avola,Al (g) | Weiss,Sid (b) | Rich,Buddy (dr) | Gray,Jerry (arr)

St.Louis Blues
Live at Hotel Pennsylvania's Café Rouge,NYC, rec. 28.11.1939
Shaw,Artie (cl) | Peterson,Chuck (tp) | Geller,Harry (tp) | Privin,Bernie (tp) | Arus,George (tb) | Jenkins,Les (tb) | Rogers,Harry (tb) | Robinson,Les (as) | Freeman,Hank (as) | Pastor,Tony (ts) | Auld,Georgie (ts) | Kitsis,Bob (p) | Barbour,Dave (g) | Weiss,Sid (b) | Rich,Buddy (dr)

Frenesi
Hollywood,CA, rec. 3.3.1940
Shaw,Artie (cl) | Margulis,Charlie (tp) | Klein,Manny (tp) | Thow,George (tp) | Miller,Randall (tb) | Rank,Bill (tb) | Bowman,Babe (tb) | Reynolds,Blake (as) | Carlton,Bud (as) | Stacey,Jack (as) | Clark,Dick (ts) | Krechter,Joe (b-cl) | Cave,Jack (fr-h) | Ruderman,Morton (fl) | Nemoli,Phil (oboe) | Levant,Mark (v) | Bluestone,Harry (v) | Eisenburg,Peter (v) | Barene,Robert (v) | Brokaw,Sid (v) | Cracov,Dave (v) | Law,Alex (v) | Joyce,Jerry (v) | Sturkin,David (viola) | Spiegelman,Stanley (viola) | Gray,Jack (viola) | Lipschultz,Irving (cello) | Tannenbaum,Jules (cello) | Wrightsman,Stan (p) | Sherwood,Bobby (g) | DeNaut,Jud (b) | Maus,Carl (dr)

Temptation
Hollywood,CA, rec. 7.9.1940
Shaw,Artie (cl) | Wendt,George (tp) | Cathcart,Jack (tp) | Butterfield,Billy (tp) | Jenney,Jack (tb) | Brown,Vernon (tb) | Bassey,Bus (as) | Plumb,Neely (as) | Robinson,Les (ts) | Jerome,Jerry (ts) | Guarnieri,Johnny (p) | Hendrickson,Al (el-g) | DeNaut,Jud (b) | Fatool,Nick (dr) | Lamas,E. (v) | Klages,T. (v) | Morrow,Bob (v) | Bower,B. (v) | Beller,Alex 'Al' (v) | Harshman,Allan (viola) | Collins,K. (viola) | Goerner,F. (cello)

Stardust
Hollywood,CA, rec. 7.10.1840
Shaw,Artie (cl) | Wendt,George (tp) | Cathcart,Jack (tp) | Butterfield,Billy (tp) | Jenney,Jack (tb) | Brown,Vernon (tb) | Bassey,Bus (as) | Plumb,Neely (as) | Robinson,Les (ts) | Jerome,Jerry (ts) | Guarnieri,Johnny (p) | Hendrickson,Al (el-g) | DeNaut,Jud (b) | Fatool,Nick (dr) | Lamas,E. (v) | Klages,T. (v) | Morrow,Bob (v) | Bower,B. (v) | Beller,Alex 'Al' (v) | Harshman,Allan (viola) | Collins,K. (viola) | Goerner,F. (cello)

I Cover The Waterfront | Moonglow
Hollywood,CA, rec. 23.1.1941
Shaw,Artie (cl) | Wendt,George (tp) | Cathcart,Jack (tp) | Butterfield,Billy (tp) | Jenney,Jack (tb) | Conniff,Ray (tb) | Brown,Vernon (tb) | Bassey,Bus (as) | Plumb,Neely (as) | Robinson,Les (ts) | Jerome,Jerry (ts) | Guarnieri,Johnny (p) | Hendrickson,Al (el-g) | DeNaut,Jud (b) | Fatool,Nick (dr) | Lamas,E. (v) | Klages,T. (v) | Morrow,Bob (v) | Bower,B. (v) | Beller,Alex 'Al' (v) | Harshman,Allan (viola) | Collins,K. (viola) | Goerner,F. (cello)

To A Broadway Rose
NYC, rec. 12.11.1941
Shaw,Artie (cl) | Castle,Lee (tp) | Kaminsky,Max (tp) | Lipkins,Steve (tp) | Page,Oran 'Hot Lips' (tp) | Jenney,Jack (tb) | Samuel,Morey (tb) | Brown,Vernon (tb) | Conniff,Ray (tb) | DiMaggio,Charlie (as) | Robinson,Les (as) | Auld,Georgie (ts) | Folus,Mickey (ts) | Guarnieri,Johnny (p) | Bryant,Mike (el-g) | McKimmey,Eddie (b) | Tough,Dave (dr) | unkn. (15 strings)

2152058-2 | CD | Planet Jazz:Fats Waller

Fats Waller
Handful Of Keys
NYC, rec. 1.3.1929
Waller,Thomas 'Fats' (p-solo)

Smashing Thirds
NYC, rec. 24.9.1929
Waller,Thomas 'Fats' (p-solo)

Fats Waller And His Rhythm
Lulu's Back In Town
NYC, rec. 8.5.1935
Waller,Thomas 'Fats' (p,voc) | Autrey,Herman (tp) | Powell,Rudy (cl,as) | Casey,Al (g) | Turner,Charles (b) | Dial,Harry (dr)

I'm Crazy 'Bout My Baby
NYC, rec. 1.8.1936
Waller,Thomas 'Fats' (p,voc) | Autrey,Herman (tp) | Sedric,Gene (cl) | Casey,Al (g) | Turner,Charles (b) | Jones,Wilmore 'Slick' (dr)

S' Posin'
NYC, rec. 9.9.1936
Waller,Thomas 'Fats' (p,voc) | Autrey,Herman (tp) | Sedric,Gene (cl) | Casey,Al (g) | Turner,Charles (b) | Jones,Wilmore 'Slick' (dr)

A Jam Session At Victor
Honeysuckle Rose
NYC, rec. 31.3.1937
A Jam Session At Victor | Berigan,Bunny (tp) | Dorsey,Tommy (tb) | Waller,Thomas 'Fats' (p) | McDonough,Dick (g) | Wettling,George (dr)

Fats Waller
Keepin' Out Of Mischief Now | Tea For Two | I Ain't Got Nobody
NYC, rec. 11.6.1937
Waller,Thomas 'Fats' (p-solo)

Fats Waller And His Rhythm
The Joint Is Jumpin'
NYC, rec. 7.10.1937
Waller,Thomas 'Fats' (p,voc) | Autrey,Herman (tp) | Sedric,Gene (cl,ts) | Casey,Al (g) | Turner,Charles (b) | Jones,Wilmore 'Slick' (dr)

Your Feet's Too Big
NYC, rec. 3.11.1939
Waller,Thomas 'Fats' (p,voc) | Hamilton,John (tp) | Sedric,Gene (cl,ts) | Smith,John (g) | Wallace,Cedric (b) | Jones,Wilmore 'Slick' (dr)

Fats Waller
Carolina Shout | Ring Dem Bells
NYC, rec. 13.5.1941
Waller,Thomas 'Fats' (p-solo)

Fats Waller And His Rhythm
Ain't Misbehavin'
Los Angeles,CA, rec. 23.1.1943
Waller,Thomas 'Fats' (p) | Carter,Benny (tp) | Moore,Alton (tb) | Porter,Gene (cl) | Ashby,Irving (g) | Stewart,Slam (b) | Singleton,Zutty (dr)

2152059-2 | CD | Planet Jazz:Lionel Hampton

Lionel Hampton And His Orchestra
The Munson Street Breakdown | I've Found A New Baby | I Can't Get Started
NYC, rec. 30.10.1939
Hampton,Lionel (vib,p) | Elman,Ziggy (tp) | Mondello,Toots (cl,as) | Webster,Ben (ts) | Jerome,Jerry (ts) | Hart,Clyde (p) | Casey,Al (g) | Bernstein,Artie (b) | Jones,Wilmore 'Slick' (dr)

Dinah
NYC, rec. 21.12.1939
Hampton,Lionel (vib) | Carter,Benny (tp) | Hall,Edmond (cl) | Hawkins,Coleman (ts) | Sullivan,Joe (p) | Green,Freddie (g) | Bernstein,Artie (b) | Singleton,Zutty (dr)

Tempo And Swing
Chicago,Ill, rec. 26.2.1940
Hampton,Lionel (vib) | Elman,Ziggy (tp) | Mondello,Toots (as) | Estes,Buff (as) | Jerome,Jerry (ts) | Johnson,Budd (ts) | Odun,Spencer (p) | Ashley,Ernest (g) | Bernstein,Artie (b) | Fatool,Nick (dr)

Central Avenue Breakdown | Jack The Bellboy
Hollywood,CA, rec. 10.5.1940
Hampton,Lionel (p,dr) | Cole,Nat King (p) | Moore,Oscar (g) | Prince,Wesley (b) | Spieldock,Al (dr)

Jivin' With Jarvis | Blue Because Of You
Hollywood,CA, rec. 17.7.1940
Hampton,Lionel (vib) | Cole,Nat King (p) | Moore,Oscar (g) | Prince,Wesley (b) | Spieldock,Al (dr) | Hampton Rhythm Boys,The (voc)

Flamenco Soul | Hot Club Madrid Serenade | Bop City Flamenco
Madrid, Spain, rec. 28.6.1956
Hampton,Lionel (vib) | Gonzales,Dave (tp) | Morris,Walter 'Phatz' (tb) | Brown,Scoville (cl) | Plater,Bobby (as) | Chamblee,Eddie (ts) | Lowe,Curtis (bs) | Denard,Oscar (p) | Mackel,Billy (g) | Badie,Peter (b) | Gordner,June (dr) | Angelica,Maria (castanets) | unkn. (large band) | unkn. (perc,voc) | Warner,Eddie (ld)

Lionel Hampton Quintet
Tenderly | Toledo Blade
Hampton,Lionel (vib) | Montoliu,Tete (p) | Mackel,Billy (g) | Badie,Peter (b) | Gordner,June (dr) | Angelica,Maria (castanets)

2152060-2 | CD | Planet Jazz:Jelly Roll Morton

Jelly Roll Morton's Red Hot Peppers
Black Bottom Stomp | Smokehouse Blues
Chicago,Ill, rec. 15.9.1926
Morton,Jelly Roll (p) | Mitchell,George (co) | Ory,Edward 'Kid' (tb) | Simeon,Omer (cl) | St.Cyr,Johnny (bj) | Lindsey,Johny (b) | Hilaire,Andrew (dr)

Sidewalk Blues | Dead Man Blues
Chicago,Ill, rec. 21.9.1926
Morton,Jelly Roll (p,voc) | Mitchell,George (co) | Ory,Edward 'Kid' (tb) | Simeon,Omer (cl) | Bigard,Barney (cl) | Howard,Darnell (cl) | St.Cyr,Johnny (bj) | Lindsey,Johny (b) | Hilaire,Andrew (dr) | Bloom,Marty (voc)

Steamboat Stomp
Morton,Jelly Roll (p) | Mitchell,George (co) | Ory,Edward 'Kid' (tb) | Simeon,Omer (cl) | St.Cyr,Johnny (bj) | Lindsey,Johny (b) | Hilaire,Andrew (dr)

Original Jelly Roll Blues | Dr.Jazz
Chicago,Ill, rec. 16.12.1926
Morton,Jelly Roll (p) | Mitchell,George (co) | Ory,Edward 'Kid' (tb) | Simeon,Omer (cl,b-cl) | St.Cyr,Johnny (g) | Lindsey,Johny (b) | Hilaire,Andrew (dr)

Wild Man Blues
Chicago,Ill, rec. 4.6.1927
Morton,Jelly Roll (p,voc) | Mitchell,George (co) | Reeves,Gerald (tb) | Dodds,Johnny (cl) | Evans,Paul 'Stump' (as) | Scott,Bud (g) | Wilson,Quinn (tuba) | Dodds,Warren 'Baby' (dr)

The Pearls
Chicago,Ill, rec. 10.6.1927
Morton,Jelly Roll (p) | Mitchell,George (co) | Reeves,Gerald (tb) | Dodds,Johnny (cl) | Evans,Paul 'Stump' (as) | Scott,Bud (g) | Wilson,Quinn (tuba) | Dodds,Warren 'Baby' (dr)

Georgia Swing | Kansas City Stomps | Shreveport Stomp
NYC, rec. 11.6.1928
Morton,Jelly Roll (p) | Pinkett,Ward (tp) | Fields,Geechie (tb) | Simeon,Omer (cl) | Blair,Lee (bj) | Benford,Bill (tuba) | Benford,Tommy (dr)

Jelly Roll Morton And His Orchestra
Red Hot Pepper | Deep Creek
NYC, rec. 6.12.1928
Morton,Jelly Roll (p) | Anderson,Edward (tp) | Swayzee,Edwin (tp) | Kato,William G. (tb) | Procope,Russell (cl,as) | Barnes,Paul (ss) | Garland,Joe (ts) | Blair,Lee (g) | Moore,William (tuba) | Johnson,Manzie (dr)

Burnin' The Iceberg | Pretty Lil
Camden,NJ, rec. 9.7.1929
Morton,Jelly Roll (p) | Rossiter,Red (tp) | Draper,Briscoe (tp) | Irvis,Charlie (tb) | Baquet,George (cl) | Barnes,Paul (ss) | Thomas,Joe (as) | Thomas,Walter 'Foots' (ts) | Rodriguez,Red (p) | Barney ? (bj) | Prather,Harry (tuba) | Laws,William (dr)

Jelly Roll Morton Trio
Turtle Twist
NYC, rec. 17.12.1929
Morton,Jelly Roll (p) | Bigard,Barney (cl) | Singleton,Zutty (dr)

2152061-2 | CD | Planet Jazz:Paul Desmond

Paul Desmond With Strings
Desmond Blue
NYC, rec. 2.10.1961
Desmond,Paul (as) | Richman,Albert (fr-h) | Penque,Romeo (woodwinds) | Webb,Stanley (woodwinds) | Agostini,Gloria (harp) | Hall,Jim (g) | Hinton,Milt (b) | Thomas,Robert C. (dr) | Strings | Prince,Bob (cond) | details unknown

Paul Desmond-Gerry Mulligan Quartet
All The Things You Are
NYC, rec. 3.7.1962
Desmond,Paul (as) | Mulligan,Gerry (bs) | Marshall,Wendell (b) | Kay,Connie (dr)

Paul Desmond Quartet
Polka Dots And Moonbeams
NYC, rec. 5.6.1963
Desmond,Paul (as) | Hall,Jim (g) | Cherico,Gene (b) | Kay,Connie (dr)

Theme From Black Orpheus
NYC, rec. 10.6.1963
Desmond,Paul (as) | Hall,Jim (g) | Cherico,Gene (b) | Kay,Connie (dr)

El Prince | Alone Together
NYC, rec. 12.6.1963
Desmond,Paul (as) | Hall,Jim (g) | Cherico,Gene (b) | Kay,Connie (dr)

Embarcadero
NYC, rec. 14.6.1963
Desmond,Paul (as) | Hall,Jim (g) | Cherico,Gene (b) | Kay,Connie (dr)

Take Ten
NYC, rec. 25.6.1963
Desmond,Paul (as) | Hall,Jim (g) | Wright,Eugene 'Gene' (b) | Kay,Connie (dr)

A Taste Of Honey
NYC, rec. 14.7.1963
Desmond,Paul (as) | Hall,Jim (g) | Wright,Eugene 'Gene' (b) | Kay,Connie (dr)

O Gato
NYC, rec. 20.8.1964
Desmond,Paul (as) | Hall,Jim (g) | Wright,Eugene 'Gene' (b) | Kay,Connie (dr)

Hi Lili Hi Lo
NYC, rec. 8.9.1964
Desmond,Paul (as) | Hall,Jim (g) | Wright,Eugene 'Gene' (b) | Kay,Connie (dr)

I've Grown Accustomed To Her Face
NYC, rec. 1.6.1965
Desmond,Paul (as) | Hall,Jim (g) | Heath,Percy (b) | Kay,Connie (dr)

2152062-2 | CD | Planet Jazz:Sonny Rollins

Sonny Rollins Quartet
You Do Something To Me
NYC, rec. 13.2.1962
Rollins,Sonny (ts) | Hall,Jim (g) | Cranshaw,Bob (b) | Riley,Ben (dr)

Brownskin Gal (I Got My Eyes On You) | Don't Stop The Carnival
NYC, rec. 26.4.1962
Rollins,Sonny (ts) | Hall,Jim (g) | Cranshaw,Bob (b) | Riley,Ben (dr) | Charles,Dennis (perc) | Charles,Frank (perc) | Rodriguez,Willie (perc) | Chorus | Jones,Jimmy (cond)

Sonny Rollins & Co.
There'll Never Be Another You
NYC, rec. 20.2.1963
Rollins,Sonny (ts) | Cherry,Don (co) | Grimes,Henry (b) | Higgins,Billy (dr)

Sonny Rollins-Coleman Hawkins Quintet
Just Friends
NYC, rec. 18.7.1963
Hawkins,Coleman (ts) | Rollins,Sonny (ts) | Bley,Paul (p) | Grimes,Henry (b) | McCurdy,Roy (dr)

Sonny Rollins & Co.
St.Thomas | Four
NYC, rec. 14.2.1964
Rollins,Sonny (ts) | Carter,Ron (b) | McCurdy,Roy (dr)

Sonny Rollins Quartet
Now's The Time | Round About Midnight
Rollins,Sonny (ts) | Hancock,Herbie (p) | Carter,Ron (b) | McCurdy,Roy (dr)

Sonny Rollins Trio
Night And Day
NYC, rec. 24.6.1964
Rollins,Sonny (ts) | Cranshaw,Bob (b) | Roker,Granville 'Mickey' (dr)

Sonny Rollins Quartet
My One And Only Love
NYC, rec. 2.7.1964
Rollins,Sonny (ts) | Hancock,Herbie (p) | Cranshaw,Bob (b) | Roker,Granville 'Mickey' (dr)

2152063-2 | CD | Planet Jazz:Sidney Bechet

Sidney Bechet With Claude Luter And His Orchestra
Les Oignons
Paris,France, rec. 14.10.1949
Bechet,Sidney (ss) | Luter,Claude (cl) | Dervaux,Pierre (tp) | Philippe,Claude (tp,bj) | Jospin,Mowgli (tb) | Azzi,Christian (p) | Bianchini,Roland (b) | Galepides,Francois 'Moustache' (dr)

Sidney Bechet Quartet
Mon Homme(My Man)
Paris,France, rec. 20.10.1949
Bechet,Sidney (ss) | Lewis,Charles (p) | Michelot,Pierre (b) | Clarke,Kenny (dr)

Sidney Bechet All Stars
Petite Fleur
Paris,France, rec. 21.1.1952
Bechet,Sidney (ss) | Longnon,Guy (tp) | Zacharias,Bernard (tb) | Lewis,Charles (p) | Masselier,Alf (b) | Molinetti,Armand (dr)

Sidney Bechet With Claude Luter And His Orchestra
Maryland My Maryland | Royal Garden Blues
Live at Salle Pleyel,Paris,France, rec. 31.1.1952
Bechet,Sidney (ss) | Luter,Claude (cl) | Longnon,Guy (tp) | Rabanit,Claude (tp) | Zacharias,Bernard (tb) | Azzi,Christian (p) | Philippe,Claude (bj) | Bianchini,Roland (b) | Galepides,Francois 'Moustache' (dr)

Le Marchand De Poisson | Dans Les Rues D'Antibes
Live at Salle Pleyel,Paris,France, rec. 12.3.1952
Bechet,Sidney (ss) | Luter,Claude (cl) | Longnon,Guy (tp) | Rabanit,Claude (tp) | Zacharias,Bernard (tb) | Fol,Raimond (p) | Bianchini,Roland (b) | Galepides,Francois 'Moustache' (dr)

As-Tu Le Cafard | When The Saints Go Marching In
Live at La Chaux-De-Fonds,CH, rec. 30.5.1952
Bechet,Sidney (ss) | Luter,Claude (cl) | Longnon,Guy (tp) | Rabanit,Claude (tp) | Zacharias,Bernard (tb) | Fol,Raimond (p) | Bianchini,Roland (b) | Galepides,Francois 'Moustache' (dr)

Si Tu Vois Ma Mere
Live at La Chaux-De-Fonds,CH, rec. 31.5.1952
Bechet,Sidney (ss) | Luter,Claude (cl) | Longnon,Guy (tp) | Rabanit,Claude (tp) | Zacharias,Bernard (tb) | Fol,Raimond (p) | Bianchini,Roland (b) | Galepides,Francois 'Moustache' (dr)

Sidney Bechet Trio
Rockin' Chair
Paris,France, rec. 7.10.1952
Bechet,Sidney (ss) | Armstrong [Hardin],Lil (p) | Singleton,Zutty (dr)

Sidney Bechet With Michel Attenoux And His Orchestra
Summertime
Live in Saarbrücken, rec. November 1954
Bechet,Sidney (ss) | Attenoux,Michel (as) | Longnon,Guy (tp) | Zacharias,Bernard (tb) | Badini,Gerard (cl) | Persiany,Andre (p) | Banks,Alvin 'Buddy' (b) | David,Jacques (dr)

Sidney Bechet With Sammy Price's Bluesicians
St.Louis Blues
Paris,France, rec. 16.5.1956
Bechet,Sidney (ss) | Price,Sammy (p) | Berry,Emmett (tp) | Stevenson,George (tb) | Hall,Herb (cl) | Foster,George 'Pops' (b) | Moore,Fred[Freddie] (dr)

Sidney Bechet-Teddy Buckner Sextet
Souvenirs De La Nouvelle-Orleans
Paris,France, rec. 4.7.1958
Bechet,Sidney (ss) | Buckner,Teddy (tp) | Guerin,Christian (tb) | Bernard,Eddie (p) | Bianchini,Roland (b) | Fields,Kansas (dr)

2152064-2 | CD | Planet Jazz:Bud Powell

Bud Powell Trio
There'll Never Be Another You | I Cover The Waterfront | Topsy Turvy | Elegy | Coscrane | Jump City | Blues For Bessie
NYC, rec. 5.10.1956
Powell,Bud (p) | Duvivier,George (b) | Taylor,Arthur 'Art' (dr)

Salt Peanuts | Swedish Pastry | Shaw 'Nuff | Midway | Oblivion | Get It | Another Dozen | Birdland Blues
NYC, rec. 11.2.1957
Powell,Bud (p) | Duvivier,George (b) | Taylor,Arthur 'Art' (dr)

2152065-2 | CD | Planet Jazz:Johnny Hodges

Duke Ellington And His Famous Orchestra
Never No Lament(Don't Get Around Much Anymore)
Hollywood,CA, rec. 4.5.1940
Ellington,Duke (p,arr) | Jones,Wallace (tp) | Williams,Cootie (tp) | Stewart,Rex (co) | Nanton,Joe 'Tricky Sam' (tb) | Brown,Lawrence (tb) | Tizol,Juan (v-tb) | Hodges,Johnny (cl,ss,as) | Hardwicke,Otto (as,bass-s) | Bigard,Barney (ts) | Webster,Ben (ts) | Carney,Harry (cl,as,bs) | Guy,Fred (g) | Blanton,Jimmy (b) | Greer,William 'Sonny' (dr)

In A Mellow Tone
Chicago,Ill, rec. 5.9.1940
Ellington,Duke (p,arr) | Jones,Wallace (tp) | Williams,Cootie (tp) | Stewart,Rex (co) | Nanton,Joe 'Tricky Sam' (tb) | Brown,Lawrence (tb) | Tizol,Juan (v-tb) | Bigard,Barney (cl) | Hodges,Johnny (cl,ss,as) | Hardwicke,Otto (as,bass-s) | Webster,Ben (ts) | Carney,Harry (cl,as,bs) | Guy,Fred (g) | Blanton,Jimmy (b) | Greer,William 'Sonny' (dr)
Johnny Hodges Orchestra
That's The Blues Old Man
Chicago,Ill, rec. 2.11.1940
Hodges,Johnny (ss,as) | Williams,Cootie (tp) | Brown,Lawrence (tb) | Carney,Harry (bs) | Ellington,Duke (p) | Blanton,Jimmy (b) | Greer,William 'Sonny' (dr)
Passion Flower | Things Ain't What They Used To Be
Hollywood,CA, rec. 3.7.1941
Hodges,Johnny (as) | Nance,Ray (tp) | Brown,Lawrence (tb) | Carney,Harry (bs) | Ellington,Duke (p) | Blanton,Jimmy (b) | Greer,William 'Sonny' (dr)
Duke Ellington And His Famous Orchestra
Come Sunday
NYC, rec. 12.12.1944
Ellington,Duke (p,arr) | Jordan,Taft (tp) | Hemphill,Shelton (tp) | Anderson,Cat (tp) | Nance,Ray (tp,v) | Nanton,Joe 'Tricky Sam' (tb) | Brown,Lawrence (tb) | Jones,Claude (tb) | Hamilton,Jimmy (cl,ts) | Hardwicke,Otto (as) | Hodges,Johnny (as) | Sears,Al (ts) | Carney,Harry (bs) | Guy,Fred (g) | Raglin,Alvin 'Junior' (b) | Greer,William 'Sonny' (dr)
Johnny Hodges-Wild Bill Davis Sextet
On The Sunny Side Of The Street | I'm Beginning To See The Light | Sophisticated Lady
NYC, rec. 7.1.1965
Hodges,Johnny (as) | Davis,Wild Bill (org) | Thompson,Dickie (g) | Lowe,Mundell (g) | Hinton,Milt (b) | Johnson,Osie (dr)
Good Queen Bess | It's Only A Paper Moon
Live at Grace's Little Belmont,Atlantic City, rec. 10.8.1966
Hodges,Johnny (as) | Davis,Wild Bill (org) | Brown,Lawrence (tb) | Brown,Bob 'Bobby' (fl,ts) | Thompson,Dickie (g) | Durham,Bobby (dr)
Duke Ellington And His Orchestra
Isfahan
NYC, rec. 20.12.1966
Ellington,Duke (p) | Williams,Cootie (tp) | Anderson,Cat (tp) | Jones,Herbie (tp) | Ellington,Mercer (tp) | Brown,Lawrence (tb) | Connors,Chuck (tb) | Cooper,Frank 'Buster' (tb) | Hodges,Johnny (as) | Procope,Russell (cl,as) | Gonsalves,Paul (ts) | Hamilton,Jimmy (cl,ts) | Carney,Harry (bs) | Lamb,John (b) | Jones,Rufus (dr)
Johnny Hodges Orchestra
Big Boy Blues
NYC, rec. 10.1.1967
Hodges,Johnny (as) | Eldridge,Roy (tp) | Powell,Benny (tb) | Carney,Harry (bs) | Pierce,Nat (p) | Jones,Jimmie (p) | Butler,Billy (g) | Benjamin,Joe (b) | Jackson,Oliver (dr)
Duke Ellington And His Orchestra
Snibor
NYC, rec. 1.9.1967
Ellington,Duke (p) | Brisbois,Wilbur 'Bud' (tp) | Anderson,Cat (tp) | Ellington,Mercer (tp) | Jones,Herbie (tp) | Brown,Lawrence (tb) | Cooper,Frank 'Buster' (tb) | Connors,Chuck (tb) | Hodges,Johnny (as) | Procope,Russell (as) | Hamilton,Jimmy (cl,ts) | Gonsalves,Paul (ts) | Carney,Harry (bs) | Bell,Aaron (b) | Little,Steve (dr)

2152066-2 | CD | Planet Jazz:Art Blakey
Art Blakey And The Jazz Messengers
On The Street Where You Live
NYC, rec. 13.3.1957
Blakey,Art (dr) | Hardman,Bill (tp) | Griffin,Johnny (ts) | Dockery,Sam (p) | DeBrest,Jimmy 'Spanky' (b)
A Night In Tunisia | Theory Of Art
NYC, rec. 8.4.1957
Blakey,Art (dr) | Hardman,Bill (tp) | McLean,Jackie (as) | Griffin,Johnny (ts) | Dockery,Sam (p) | DeBrest,Jimmy 'Spanky' (b)
Moanin' With Hazel
Live at Club St.Germain,Paris,France, rec. 21.12.1958
Blakey,Art (dr) | Morgan,Lee (tp) | Golson,Benny (ts) | Timmons,Bobby (p) | Merritt,Jymie (b)
Lester Left Town
Live at The Theatre Des Champs-Elysees,Paris,France, rec. 15.11.1959
Blakey,Art (dr) | Morgan,Lee (tp) | Shorter,Wayne (ts) | Davis Jr.,Walter (p) | Merritt,Jymie (b)

2152067-2 | CD | Planet Jazz:Frank Sinatra & Tommy Dorsey
Tommy Dorsey And His Orchestra
The Sky Fell Down
Chicago,Ill, rec. 1.2.1940
Dorsey,Tommy (tb) | Zarchy,Reuben 'Zeke' (tp) | Blake,Jimmy (tp) | Castle,Lee (tp) | Silloway,Ward (tb) | Jacobs,Dave (tb) | Smithers,Elmer (tb) | Mince,Johnny (cl,as) | Stulce,Fred (as) | Kincaide,Dean (ts) | Zimmer,Tony (ts) | Smith,Howard (p) | Mastren,Carmen (g) | Traxler,Gene (b) | Rich,Buddy (dr) | Sinatra,Frank (voc)
Polka Dots And Moonbeams
NYC, rec. 4.3.1940
Dorsey,Tommy (tb) | Berigan,Bunny (tp) | Zarchy,Reuben 'Zeke' (tp) | Linn,Ray (tp) | Blake,Jimmy (tp) | Jacobs,Dave (tb) | Arus,George (tb) | Martin,Lowell (tb) | Mince,Johnny (cl,as) | Schertzer,Hymie (as) | Stulce,Fred (as) | Mason,Paul (ts) | Russin,Irving 'Babe' (ts) | Kitsis,Bob (p) | Avola,Al (g) | Leatherwood,Ray (b) | Rich,Buddy (dr) | Sinatra,Frank (voc) | Stordahl,Axel (arr)
Fools Rush In
NYC, rec. 29.3.1940
Dorsey,Tommy (tb) | Berigan,Bunny (tp) | Conselman,Bob (tp) | Blake,Jimmy (tp) | Jacobs,Dave (tb) | Jenkins,Les (tb) | Arus,George (tb) | Mince,Johnny (cl,as) | Schertzer,Hymie (as) | Stulce,Fred (as) | Mason,Paul (ts) | Lodice,Don (ts) | Kitsis,Bob (p) | Heller,Benny 'Ben' (g) | Weiss,Sid (b) | Rich,Buddy (dr) | Sinatra,Frank (voc)
Imagination
NYC, rec. 10.4.1940
Dorsey,Tommy (tb) | Berigan,Bunny (tp) | Linn,Ray (tp) | Dillard,John (tp) | Blake,Jimmy (tp) | Martin,Lowell (tb) | Jenkins,Les (tb) | Arus,George (tb) | Mince,Johnny (cl,as) | Schertzer,Hymie (as) | Stulce,Fred (as) | Mason,Paul (ts) | Bushkin,Joe (p) | Yocum,Clark (g) | Weiss,Sid (b) | Rich,Buddy (dr) | Sinatra,Frank (voc)
I'll Never Smile Again
NYC, rec. 23.5.1940
Dorsey,Tommy (tb) | Berigan,Bunny (tp) | Linn,Ray (tp) | Debrow,Leon (tp) | Blake,Jimmy (tp) | Martin,Lowell (tb) | Jenkins,Les (tb) | Arus,George (tb) | Mince,Johnny (cl,as) | Schertzer,Hymie (as) | Stulce,Fred (as) | Mason,Paul (ts) | Lodice,Don (ts) | Bushkin,Joe (p) | Yocum,Clark (g) | Weiss,Sid (b) | Rich,Buddy (dr) | Sinatra,Frank (voc) | Pied Piepers,The (voc) | Stordahl,Axel (arr)
The One I Love Belongs To Somebody Else
NYC, rec. 27.6.1940
Dorsey,Tommy (tb) | Berigan,Bunny (tp) | Linn,Ray (tp) | Hurley,Clyde (tp) | Blake,Jimmy (tp) | Martin,Lowell (tb) | Jenkins,Les (tb) | Arus,George (tb) | Mince,Johnny (cl,as) | Schertzer,Hymie (as) | Stulce,Fred (as) | Mason,Paul (ts) | Lodice,Don (ts) | Bushkin,Joe (p) | Yocum,Clark (g) | Weiss,Sid (b) | Rich,Buddy (dr) | Sinatra,Frank (voc) | Pied Piepers,The (voc) | Stordahl,Axel (arr)
Once In A While
NYC, rec. 27.7.1940
Dorsey,Tommy (tb) | Berigan,Bunny (tp) | Linn,Ray (tp) | Hurley,Clyde (tp) | Blake,Jimmy (tp) | Martin,Lowell (tb) | Jenkins,Les (tb) | Arus,George (tb) | Mince,Johnny (cl,as) | Schertzer,Hymie (as) | Stulce,Fred (as) | Mason,Paul (ts) | Lodice,Don (ts) | Bushkin,Joe (p) | Yocum,Clark (g) | Weiss,Sid (b) | Rich,Buddy (dr) | Sinatra,Frank (voc) | Pied Piepers,The (voc)
Stardust
Hollywood,CA, rec. 11.11.1940
Dorsey,Tommy (tb) | Linn,Ray (tp) | Peterson,Chuck (tp) | Elman,Ziggy (tp) | Jenkins,Les (tb) | Arus,George (tb) | Martin,Lowell (tb) | Mince,Johnny (cl,as) | Stulce,Fred (as) | Schertzer,Hymie (as) | Beau,Heinie (ts) | Lodice,Don (ts) | Bushkin,Joe (celeste) | Yocum,Clark (g,voc) | Weiss,Sid (b) | Rich,Buddy (dr) | Sinatra,Frank (voc) | Pied Piepers,The (voc)
How Am I To Know?
Hollywood,CA, rec. 28.11.1940
Dorsey,Tommy (tb) | Linn,Ray (tp) | Peterson,Chuck (tp) | Elman,Ziggy (tp) | Jenkins,Les (tb) | Arus,George (tb) | Martin,Lowell (tb) | Mince,Johnny (cl,as) | Stulce,Fred (as) | Schertzer,Hymie (as) | Beau,Heinie (ts) | Lodice,Don (ts) | Bushkin,Joe (p) | Yocum,Clark (g) | Weiss,Sid (b) | Rich,Buddy (dr) | Sinatra,Frank (voc)
Without A Song
NYC, rec. 20.1.1941
Dorsey,Tommy (tb) | Elman,Ziggy (tp) | Linn,Ray (tp) | Peterson,Charlie (tp) | Blake,Jimmy (tp) | Jenkins,Les (tb) | Arus,George (tb) | Martin,Lowell (tb) | Mince,Johnny (cl,as) | Stulce,Fred (as) | Beau,Heinie (as) | Lodice,Don (ts) | Mason,Paul (ts) | Bushkin,Joe (p) | Yocum,Clark (g) | Weiss,Sid (b) | Rich,Buddy (dr) | Sinatra,Frank (voc) | Oliver,Sy (arr)
This Love Of Mine
NYC, rec. 28.5.1941
Dorsey,Tommy (tb) | Elman,Ziggy (tp) | Sherock,Shorty (tp) | Peterson,Charlie (tp) | Blake,Jimmy (tp) | Mercurio,Walter (tb) | Arus,George (tb) | Martin,Lowell (tb) | Schertzer,Hymie (cl,as) | Gershman,Manny (cl,as) | Beau,Heinie (as) | Lodice,Don (ts) | Mason,Paul (ts) | Bushkin,Joe (p) | Yocum,Clark (g) | Kelleher,Jack (b) | Rich,Buddy (dr) | Sinatra,Frank (voc) | Stordahl,Axel (arr)
Blue Skies
NYC, rec. 15.7.1941
Dorsey,Tommy (tb) | Elman,Ziggy (tp) | Stearns,Al (tp) | Peterson,Chuck (tp) | Blake,Jimmy (tp) | Jacobs,Dave (tb) | Arus,George (tb) | Martin,Lowell (tb) | Snyders,Bruce (cl,as) | Gershman,Manny (cl,as) | Stulce,Fred (as) | Mason,Paul (ts) | Lodice,Don (ts) | Bushkin,Joe (p) | Yocum,Clark (g) | Weiss,Sid (b) | Rich,Buddy (dr) | Sinatra,Frank (voc) | Oliver,Sy (arr)
I Think Of You
NYC, rec. 18.9.1941
Dorsey,Tommy (tb) | Elman,Ziggy (tp) | Stearns,Al (tp) | Peterson,Chuck (tp) | Blake,Jimmy (tp) | Jacobs,Dave (tb) | Arus,George (tb) | Skiles,Jimmy (tb) | Snydors,Bruce (cl,as) | Gershman,Manny (cl,as) | Stulce,Fred (as) | Beau,Heinie (ts) | Lodice,Don (ts) | Bushkin,Joe (p) | Yocum,Clark (g) | Weiss,Sid (b) | Rich,Buddy (dr) | Sinatra,Frank (voc)
Frank Sinatra With Orchestra
Night And Day
Hollywood,CA, rec. 19.1.1942
Sinatra,Frank (voc) | Stordahl,Axel (arr,ld) | Stulce,Fred (as) | Gershman,Manny (as) | Beau,Heinie (ts) | Lodice,Don (ts) | Strickfaden,Charles (oboe) | Mason,Ann (harp) | Bluestone,Harry (v) | Russell,Mischa (v) | Pisani,Nick (v) | Freed,Sam (v) | Bernard,Cy (cello) | Henderson,Skitch (p) | Yokum,Clark (g) | Stern,Hank (b)
Tommy Dorsey And His Orchestra
In The Blue Of The Evening
NYC, rec. 6.8.1942
Dorsey,Tommy (tb) | Elman,Ziggy (tp) | Peterson,Charlie (tp) | Blake,Jimmy (tp) | Zito,Jimmy (tp) | Arus,George (tb) | Jacobs,Dave (tb) | Skiles,Jimmy (tb) | Stulce,Fred (as) | Schuchman,Harry (as) | Beau,Heinie (ts) | Lodice,Don (ts) | Snyder,Bruce (ts) | Atkins,Leonard (v) | Beller,Alex 'Al' (v) | Ehrenkranz,William (v) | Posner,Leonard (v) | Raymond,Irving (v) | Ross,Sam (v) | Tinterow,Bernard (v) | Bemko,Harold (cello) | Hill,Ruth (harp) | Raskin,Milt (p) | Yokum,Clark (g) | Stephens,Phil (b) | Rich,Buddy (dr) | Sinatra,Frank (voc)

2152068-2 | CD | Planet Jazz:Count Basie
Count Basie And His Orchestra
Bill's Mill | Brand New Wagon
Hollywood,CA, rec. 3.1.1947
Basie,Count (p) | Lewis,Ed (tp) | Berry,Emmett (tp) | Young,Eugene 'Snooky' (tp) | Edison,Harry 'Sweets' (tp) | Johnson,Bill (tb) | Donnelly,Ted (tb) | Matthews,George (tb) | Robinson,Eli (tb) | Love,Preston (as) | Rutherford,Rudy (as) | Gonsalves,Paul (ts) | Tate,Buddy (ts) | Washington Jr.,Jack (bs) | Green,Freddie (g) | Richardson,Rodney (b) | Wilson,Shadow (dr) | Rushing,Jimmy (voc)
One O'Clock Boogie
NYC, rec. 13.3.1947
Basie,Count (p) | Lewis,Ed (tp) | Berry,Emmett (tp) | Young,Eugene 'Snooky' (tp) | Edison,Harry 'Sweets' (tp) | Donnelly,Ted (tb) | Matthews,George (tb) | Robinson,Eli (tb) | Johnson,Bill (tb) | Love,Preston (as) | Rutherford,Rudy (cl,as) | Tate,Buddy (ts) | Gonsalves,Paul (ts) | Washington Jr.,Jack (bs) | Green,Freddie (g) | Richardson,Rodney (b) | Wilson,Shadow (dr)
Count Basie,His Instrumentals & Rhyhtm
Swingin' The Blues
NYC, rec. 20.5.1947
Basie,Count (p) | Berry,Emmett (tp) | Price,Charles Q. (as) | Gonsalves,Paul (ts) | Green,Freddie (g) | Page,Walter (b) | Jones,Jo (dr)
Basie's Basement
Basie,Count (p) | Green,Freddie (g) | Page,Walter (b) | Jones,Jo (dr)
Shine On Harvest Moon
NYC, rec. 21.5.1947
Basie,Count (org) | Berry,Emmett (tp) | Matthews,George (tb) | Price,Charles Q. (as) | Gonsalves,Paul (ts) | Washington Jr.,Jack (bs) | Green,Freddie (g) | Page,Walter (b) | Jones,Jo (dr)
Sugar
Basie,Count (p) | Gonsalves,Paul (ts) | Green,Freddie (g) | Page,Walter (b) | Jones,Jo (dr)
Count Basie And His Orchestra
Seventh Avenue Express | Mr.Roberts' Roost
Chicago,Ill, rec. 19.10.1947
Basie,Count (p) | Lewis,Ed (tp) | Berry,Emmett (tp) | Young,Eugene 'Snooky' (tp) | Edison,Harry 'Sweets' (tp) | Donnelly,Ted (tb) | Wells,Dicky (tb) | Simon,George (tb) | Johnson,Bill (tb) | Love,Preston (as) | Price,Charles Q. (as) | Tate,Buddy (ts) | Gonsalves,Paul (ts) | Washington Jr.,Jack (bs) | Green,Freddie (g) | Page,Walter (b) | Jones,Jo (dr)
Just A Minute
Los Angeles,CA, rec. 9.12.1947
Basie,Count (p) | Lewis,Ed (tp) | Berry,Emmett (tp) | Young,Eugene 'Snooky' (tp) | Edison,Harry 'Sweets' (tp) | Donnelly,Ted (tb) | Wells,Dicky (tb) | Matthews,George (tb) | Johnson,Bill (tb) | Love,Preston (as) | Price,Charles Q. (as) | Tate,Buddy (ts) | Gonsalves,Paul (ts) | Washington Jr.,Jack (bs) | Green,Freddie (g) | Page,Walter (b) | Jones,Jo (dr)
Hey Pretty Baby | Bye Bye Baby
Los Angeles,CA, rec. 12.12.1947
Basie,Count (p) | Lewis,Ed (tp) | Berry,Emmett (tp) | Young,Eugene 'Snooky' (tp) | Edison,Harry 'Sweets' (tp) | Donnelly,Ted (tb) | Washington,George (tb) | Matthews,George (tb) | Johnson,Bill (tb) | Love,Preston (as) | Price,Charles Q. (as) | Tate,Buddy (ts) | Gonsalves,Paul (ts) | Washington Jr.,Jack (bs) | Green,Freddie (g) | Page,Walter (b) | Jones,Jo (dr) | Rushing,Jimmy (voc)
After You've Gone
NYC, rec. 13.7.1949
Basie,Count (p) | Edison,Harry 'Sweets' (tp) | Berry,Emmett (tp) | Terry,Clark (tp) | Nottingham,Jimmy (tp) | Wilson,Gerald (tp) | Donnelly,Ted (tb) | Wells,Dicky (tb) | Matthews,George (tb) | Warren,Earl (as) | Price,Charles Q. (as) | Gonsalves,Paul (ts) | Parker,Bill (ts) | Washington Jr.,Jack (bs) | Green,Freddie (g) | Palmer,Singleton (b) | Ballard,George (dr) | Rushing,Jimmy (voc)
Count Basie Octet
If You See My Baby | Sweets
NYC, rec. 6.2.1950
Basie,Count (p) | Edison,Harry 'Sweets' (tp) | Wells,Dicky (tb) | Auld,Georgie (ts) | Ammons,Gene (ts) | Green,Freddie (g) | McKibbon,Al (b) | Johnson,Gus (dr) | 'Google Eyes' (voc)

2152069-2 | CD | Planet Jazz:Dizzy Gillespie
Dizzy Gillespie And His Orchestra
52nd Street Theme | A Night In Tunisia(Interlude)
NYC, rec. 22.2.1946
Gillespie,Dizzy (tp) | Byas,Don (ts) | Jackson,Milt (vib) | Haig,Al (p) | De Arango,Bill (g) | Brown,Ray (b) | Heard,J.C. (dr)
Anthropology
Gillespie,Dizzy (tp) | Jackson,Milt (vib) | Haig,Al (p) | De Arango,Bill (g) | Brown,Ray (b) | Heard,J.C. (dr)
Two Bass Hit | Stay On It
NYC, rec. 22.8.1947
Gillespie,Dizzy (tp) | Burns,Dave (tp) | McKay,Matthew (tp) | Orr,Raymond (tp) | Wright,Elmon (tp) | Baird,Taswell (tb) | Shepherd,William 'Bill' (tb) | Brown,John (as) | Johnson,Howard (as) | Gayles,Joe (ts) | Moody,James (ts) | Payne,Cecil (bs) | Jackson,Milt (vib) | Lewis,John (p) | Collins,John (g) | Brown,Ray (b) | Harris,Joe (dr) | Dameron,Tadd (arr)
Manteca | Good Bait | Ool-Ya-Koo | Minor Walk
NYC, rec. 30.12.1947
Gillespie,Dizzy (tp,voc) | Burns,Dave (tp) | Bailey,Benny (tp) | Wright,Lammar (tp) | Wright,Elmon (tp) | Kelly,Ted (tb) | Shepherd,William 'Bill' (tb) | Brown,John (as) | Johnson,Howard (as) | Gayles,Joe (ts) | Nicholas,George 'Big Nick' (ts) | Payne,Cecil (bs) | Lewis,John (p) | Collins,John (g) | McKibbon,Al (b) | Clarke,Kenny (dr) | Pozo,Chano (congas,voc) | Hagood,Kenny (voc) | Garner,Linton (arr) | Fuller,Gil (arr) | Dameron,Tadd (arr)
Lover Come Back To Me | I'm Be Boppin' Too
NYC, rec. 29.12.1948
Gillespie,Dizzy (tp,voc) | Burns,Dave (tp) | Cook,Willie (tp) | Wright,Elmon (tp) | Duryea,Andy (tb) | Hurt,Sam (tb) | Tarrant,Jesse (tb) | Brown,John (as) | Henry,Ernie (as) | Gayles,Joe (ts) | Johnson,Budd (ts) | Payne,Cecil (bs) | Forman,James (p,celeste) | McKibbon,Al (b) | Stewart,Teddy (dr) | Harris,Joe (congas) | Martinez,Sabu (bongos)
The Metronome All Stars
Victory Ball
NYC, rec. 3.1.1949
Metronome All Stars,The | Gillespie,Dizzy (tp) | Davis,Miles (tp) | Navarro,Fats (tp) | Johnson,J.J. (tb) | Winding,Kai (tb) | DeFranco,Buddy (cl) | Parker,Charlie (as) | Ventura,Charlie (ts) | Caceres,Ernie (bs) | Tristano,Lennie (p) | Bauer,Billy (g) | Safranski,Eddie (b) | Manne,Shelly (dr) | Rugolo,Pete (cond,arr)
Dizzy Gillespie And His Orchestra
St.Louis Blues
NYC, rec. 14.4.1949
Gillespie,Dizzy (tp,voc) | Harris,Benny (tp) | Cook,Willie (tp) | Wright,Elmon (tp) | Duryea,Andy (tb) | Hurt,Sam (tb) | Tarrant,Jesse (tb) | Brown,John (as) | Henry,Ernie (as) | Gayles,Joe (ts) | Lateef,Yusef (ts) | Gibson,Al (bs) | Forman,James (p) | McKibbon,Al (b) | Stewart,Teddy (dr) | Guerra,Vince (congas)
You Go To My Head | Jump Did-Le-Ba
NYC, rec. 6.5.1949
Gillespie,Dizzy (tp,voc) | Harris,Benny (tp) | Cook,Willie (tp) | Wright,Elmon (tp) | Duryea,Andy (tb) | Hurt,Sam (tb) | Tarrant,Jesse (tb) | Brown,John (as) | Henry,Ernie (as) | Gayles,Joe (ts) | Lateef,Yusef (ts) | Gibson,Al (bs) | Forman,James (p) | McKibbon,Al (b) | Stewart,Teddy (dr) | Carroll,Joe (voc) | Hartman,Johnny (voc)
Jumpin' With Symphony Sid | In The Land Of Oo-Bla-Dee
NYC, rec. 6.7.1949
Gillespie,Dizzy (tp,voc) | Harris,Benny (tp) | Cook,Willie (tp) | Wright,Elmon (tp) | Duryea,Andy (tb) | Greenlee,Charles (tb) | Johnson,J.J. (tb) | Brown,John (as) | Henry,Ernie (as) | Gayles,Joe (ts) | Lateef,Yusef (ts) | Gibson,Al (bs) | Forman,James (p) | McKibbon,Al (b) | Steward,Teddy (dr) | Carroll,Joe (voc) | Mundy,Jimmy (arr)

2152070-2 | CD | Planet Jazz:Gerry Mulligan
Gerry Mulligan Quartet
Bernie's Tune | Walkin' Shoes | The Nearness Of You | Soft Shoe | Bark For Barksdale
Live at Salle Pleyel,Paris,France, rec. 1.6.1954
Mulligan,Gerry (bs) | Brookmeyer,Bob (v-tb) | Mitchell,Red (b) | Isola,Frank (dr)
I May Be Wrong(But I Think You're Wonderful) | Gold Rush | Makin' Whoopee | The Lady Is A Tramp | Laura
Live at Salle Pleyel,Paris,France, rec. 3.6.1954
Mulligan,Gerry (bs) | Brookmeyer,Bob (v-tb) | Mitchell,Red (b) | Isola,Frank (dr)
Love Me Or Leave Me | Moonlight In Vermont
Live at Salle Pleyel,Paris,France, rec. 7.6.1954
Mulligan,Gerry (bs) | Brookmeyer,Bob (v-tb) | Mitchell,Red (b) | Isola,Frank (dr)

2152071-2 | CD | Planet Jazz:Django Reinhardt
Django Reinhardt And The Quintet Du Hot Club De France
Swing Guitars | Viper's Dream | Blues En Mineur
Paris,France, rec. 25.8.1947
Quintet Du Hot Club De France | Reinhardt,Django (g) | Meunier,Maurice (cl) | Bernard,Eddie (p) | Vees,Eugene (g) | Soudieux,Emmanuel (b) | Martinon,Jacques (dr)
Minor Swing | Swing '39 | Les Yeux Noirs
Paris,France, rec. 28.8.1947
Quintet Du Hot Club De France | Reinhardt,Django (g) | Meunier,Maurice (cl) | Vees,Eugene (g) | Soudieux,Emmanuel (b) | Jourdan,Andre (dr)
Louise | Swingtime In Springtime | Crepuscule
Paris,France, rec. 7./15.& 22.9.1947
Quintet Du Hot Club De France | Reinhardt,Django (g) | Rostaing,Hubert (cl) | Vees,Eugene (g) | Soudieux,Emmanuel (b) | Jourdan,Andre (dr)
Dinette | Belleville | St.Louis Blues
Paris,France, rec. 21.11.1947
Quintet Du Hot Club De France | Reinhardt,Django (g) | Leveque,Gerard (cl) | Vees,Eugene (g) | Soudieux,Emmanuel (b) | Jourdan,Andre (dr)
Ol' Man River
Quintet Du Hot Club De France | Reinhardt,Django (g) | Grappelli,Stephane (v) | Vees,Eugene (g) | Reinhardt,Joseph (g) | Ermelin,Fred (b)
Dinah | Daphne
Paris,France, rec. late November 1947
Quintet Du Hot Club De France | Reinhardt,Django (g) | Grappelli,Stephane (v) | Vees,Eugene (g) | Reinhardt,Joseph (g) | Ermelin,Fred (b)
Nuages
Geneve, CH, rec. 25.10.1949
Quintet Du Hot Club De France | Reinhardt,Django (g) | Eykan,André (cl) | Vermeille,Francois (p) | Bouchety,Jean (b) | Leonard,Gaston (dr)

2152326-2 | CD | Planet Jazz Sampler
Louis Armstrong And His Friends
What A Wonderful World
NYC, rec. 26.5.1970
Armstrong,Louis (voc) | Spaulding,James (fl) | Owens,Frank (p) | Brown,Sam (g) | Burrell,Kenny (g) | Davis,Richard (b) | Duvivier,George (b) | Williams Jr.,John (el-b) | Purdie,Bernard 'Pretty' (dr) | Black,Arnold (v) | Clarke,Selwart (v) | Collymore,Winston (v) | Gersham,Paul (v) | Green,Manny (v) | Lookofsky,Harry (v) | Orloff,Gene (v) | Malin,Joe (v) | Pollikoff,Max (v) | Barber,Julian (viola) | Brown,Alfred (viola) | Schwartz,David (viola) | Vardi,Emanuel (viola) | McCracken,Charles (cello) | Moore,Kermit (cello) | Ricci,George (cello) | Schulman,Allan (cello)
Tommy Dorsey And His Orchestra
Blue Skies
NYC, rec. 15.7.1941

Dorsey,Tommy (tb) | Elman,Ziggy (tp) | Stearns,Al (tp) | Peterson,Chuck (tp) | Blake,Jimmy (tp) | Jacobs,Dave (tb) | Arus,George (tb) | Martin,Lowell (tb) | Snyders,Bruce (cl,as) | Gershman,Manny (cl,as) | Stulce,Fred (as) | Mason,Paul (ts) | Lodice,Don (ts) | Bushkin,Joe (p) | Yocum,Clark (g) | Weiss,Sid (b) | Rich,Buddy (dr) | Sinatra,Frank (voc) | Oliver,Sy (arr)

Duke Ellington And His Famous Orchestra
Take The 'A' Train
Hollywood,CA, rec. 15.2.1941
Ellington,Duke (ld) | Jones,Wallace (tp) | Williams,Cootie (tp) | Stewart,Rex (co) | Nanton,Joe 'Tricky Sam' (tb) | Brown,Lawrence (tb) | Tizol,Juan (v-tb) | Bigard,Barney (cl) | Hodges,Johnny (cl,ss,as) | Hardwicke,Otto (as,bass-s) | Webster,Ben (ts) | Carney,Harry (cl,as,bs) | Strayhorn,Billy (p,arr) | Guy,Fred (g) | Blanton,Jimmy (b) | Greer,William 'Sonny' (dr)

Benny Goodman And His Orchestra
Stompin' At The Savoy
Chicago,Ill, rec. 24.1.1936
Goodman,Benny (cl) | Geller,Harry (tp) | Kazebier,Nate (tp) | Muzillo,Ralph (tp) | Ballard,Red (tb) | Harris,Joe (tb) | Mondello,Toots (as) | Schertzer,Hymie (as) | DePew,Bill (as) | Clark,Dick (ts) | Rollini,Arthur (ts) | Stacy,Jess (p) | Reuss,Allan (g) | Goodman,Harry (b) | Krupa,Gene (dr) | Sampson,Edgar (arr)

Count Basie And His Orchestra
Seventh Avenue Express
Chicago,Ill, rec. 19.10.1947
Basie,Count (p) | Lewis,Ed (tp) | Berry,Emmett (tp) | Young,Eugene 'Snooky' (tp) | Edison,Harry 'Sweets' (tp) | Donnelly,Ted (tb) | Wells,Dicky (tb) | Simon,George (tb) | Johnson,Bill (tb) | Love,Preston (as) | Price,Charles Q. (as) | Tate,Buddy (ts) | Gonsalves,Paul (ts) | Washington Jr.,Jack (bs) | Green,Freddie (g) | Page,Walter (b) | Jones,Jo (dr)

Coleman Hawkins And His Orchestra
Body And Soul
NYC, rec. 11.10.1939
Hawkins,Coleman (ts) | Lindsey,Tommy (tp) | Guy,Joe (tp) | Hardy,Earl (tb) | Fields,Jackie (as) | Moore,Eustis (as) | Rodgers,Gene (tp) | Smith,William Oscar (b) | Herbert,Arthur (dr)

Sidney Bechet All Stars
Petite Fleur
Paris,France, rec. 21.1.1952
Bechet,Sidney (ss) | Longnon,Guy (tp) | Zacharias,Bernard (tb) | Lewis,Charles (p) | Masselier,Alf (b) | Molinetti,Armand (dr)

Art Blakey And The Jazz Messengers
On The Street Where You Live
NYC, rec. 13.3.1957
Blakey,Art (dr) | Hardman,Bill (tp) | Griffin,Johnny (ts) | Dockery,Sam (p) | DeBrest,Jimmy 'Spanky' (b)

Paul Desmond Quartet
Take Ten
NYC, rec. 25.6.1963
Desmond,Paul (as) | Hall,Jim (g) | Wright,Eugene 'Gene' (b) | Kay,Connie (dr)

Sonny Rollins & Co.
St.Thomas
NYC, rec. 14.2.1964
Rollins,Sonny (ts) | Carter,Ron (b) | McCurdy,Roy (dr)

Jelly Roll Morton's Red Hot Peppers
Black Bottom Stomp
Chicago,Ill, rec. 15.9.1926
Morton,Jelly Roll (p) | Mitchell,George (co) | Ory,Edward 'Kid' (tb) | Simeon,Omer (cl) | St.Cyr,Johnny (bj) | Lindsey,Johny (b) | Hilaire,Andrew (dr)

Glenn Miller And His Orchestra
In The Mood
NYC, rec. 1.8.1939
Miller,Glenn (tb) | Knowles,Legh (tp) | Hurley,Clyde (tp) | McMickle,Dale (tp) | Mastren,Al (tb) | Tanner,Paul (tb) | Schwartz,Wilbur (cl,as) | McIntyre,Hal (as) | Tennyson,Hal (as,bs) | Beneke,Gordon 'Tex' (ts) | Klink,Al (ts) | MacGregor,John Chalmers 'Chummy' (p) | Fisher,Richard (g) | Bundock,Rowland 'Rolly' (b) | Purtill,Maurice 'Moe' (dr)

Artie Shaw And His Orchestra
Begin The Beguine
NYC, rec. 24.7.1938
Shaw,Artie (cl) | Peterson,Chuck (tp) | Best,John (tp) | Bowen,Claude (tp) | Arus,George (tb) | Vesely,Ted (tb) | Rodgers,Harry (tb) | Robinson,Les (as) | Freeman,Hank (as) | Pastor,Tony (ts) | Perry,Ronnie (ts) | Burness,Lester (p) | Avola,Al (g) | Weiss,Sid (b) | Leeman,Cliff (dr)

Fats Waller And His Rhythm
I'm Crazy 'Bout My Baby
NYC, rec. 1.8.1936
Waller,Thomas 'Fats' (p,voc) | Autrey,Herman (tp) | Sedric,Gene (cl,ts) | Casey,Al (g) | Turner,Charles (b) | Bolden,Arnold (dr)

Lionel Hampton And His Orchestra
I've Found A New Baby
NYC, rec. 30.10.1939
Hampton,Lionel (p) | Elman,Ziggy (tp) | Mondello,Toots (cl,as) | Webster,Ben (ts) | Jerome,Jerry (ts) | Hart,Clyde (p) | Casey,Al (g) | Bernstein,Artie (b) | Jones,Wilmore 'Slick' (dr)

Dizzy Gillespie And His Orchestra
A Night In Tunisia
NYC, rec. 22.2.1946
Gillespie,Dizzy (tp) | Byas,Don (ts) | Jackson,Milt (vib) | Haig,Al (p) | De Arango,Bill (g) | Brown,Ray (b) | Heard,J.C. (dr)

Johnny Hodges Orchestra
Passion Flower
Hollywood,CA, rec. 3.7.1941
Hodges,Johnny (as) | Nance,Ray (tp) | Brown,Lawrence (tb) | Carney,Harry (bs) | Ellington,Duke (p) | Blanton,Jimmy (b) | Greer,William 'Sonny' (dr)

Gerry Mulligan Quartet
Makin' Whoopee
Live at Salle Pleyel,Paris,France, rec. 3.6.1954
Mulligan,Gerry (bs) | Brookmeyer,Bob (v-tb) | Mitchell,Red (b) | Isola,Frank (dr)

Bud Powell Trio
I Cover The Waterfront
NYC, rec. 5.10.1956
Powell,Bud (p) | Duvivier,George (b) | Taylor,Arthur 'Art' (dr)

Django Reinhardt And The Quintet Du Hot Club De France
Swing Guitars
Paris,France, rec. 25.8.1947
Reinhardt,Django (g) | Meunier,Maurice (cl) | Bernard,Eddie (p) | Vees,Eugene (g) | Soudieux,Emmanuel (b) | Martinon,Jacques (dr)

2159972-2 | CD | Planet Jazz:Tommy Dorsey
Tommy Dorsey And His Orchestra
I'm Getting Sentimental Over You
NYC, rec. 18.10.1935
Dorsey,Tommy (tb) | Ferretti,Andy (tp) | Bose,Sterling (tp) | Graham,Bill (tp) | Weston,Cliff (tp) | Jacobs,Dave (tb) | Pickering,Ben (tb) | Stoneburn,Sid (cl,as) | Bernardi,Noni (as) | Rounds,Clyde (as,ts) | Van Eps,Johnny (ts) | Mitchell,Paul (p) | Cheikes,Mac (g) | Traxler,Gene (b) | Rosen,Sam (dr)

Tommy Dorsey And His Clambake Seven
The Music Goes 'Round And 'Round
NYC, rec. 9.12.1935
Dorsey,Tommy (tb,voc) | Bose,Sterling (tp) | Stoneburn,Sid (cl) | Van Eps,Johnny (ts) | Jones,Dick (p) | Schaffer,William (g) | Traxler,Gene (b) | Weiss,Sam (dr) | Wright,Edythe (voc)

Tommy Dorsey And His Orchestra
You
NYC, rec. 25.3.1936
Dorsey,Tommy (tb) | Kaminsky,Max (tp) | Skolnick,Sam (tp) | Bauer,Joe (tp) | Pickering,Ben (tb) | Mercurio,Walter (tb) | Dixon,Joe (cl,as) | Stulce,Fred (as) | Rounds,Clyde (as,ts) | Block,Sid (ts) | Jones,Dick (p) | Schaffer,William (g) | Traxler,Gene (b) | Tough,Dave (dr) | Wright,Edythe (voc) | Weiss,Sam (dr)

Song Of India | Marie
NYC, rec. 29.1.1937
Dorsey,Tommy (tb) | Berigan,Bunny (tp) | Welch,Jimmy (tp) | Bauer,Joe (tp) | Cusumano,Bob (tp) | Jenkins,Les (tb) | Bone,E.W. 'Red' (tb) | Dixon,Joe (cl,as) | Stulce,Fred (as) | Rounds,Clyde (as) | Freeman,Bud (ts) | Jones,Dick (p) | Mastren,Carmen (g) | Traxler,Gene (b) | Tough,Dave (dr) | Leonard,Jack (voc)

Once In A While
NYC, rec. 21.7.1937
Dorsey,Tommy (tb) | Erwin,Pee Wee (tp) | Ferretti,Andy (tb) | Bauer,Joe (tp) | Jenkins,Les (tb) | Mercurio,Walter (tb) | Bone,E.W. 'Red' (tb) | Stulce,Fred (as) | Mince,Johnny (cl,as) | Herfurt,Arthur 'Skeets' (as) | Freeman,Bud (ts) | Smith,Howard (p) | Mastren,Carmen (g) | Traxler,Gene (b) | Tough,Dave (dr) | Four Esquires,The (voc)

Little White Lies
NYC, rec. 6.12.1937
Dorsey,Tommy (tb) | Erwin,Pee Wee (tp) | Ferretti,Andy (tb) | Castle,Lee (tp) | Jenkins,Les (tb) | Hagen,Earle (tb) | Bone,E.W. 'Red' (tb) | Stulce,Fred (as) | Mince,Johnny (cl,as) | Herfurt,Arthur 'Skeets' (as) | Freeman,Bud (ts) | Smith,Howard (p) | Mastren,Carmen (g) | Traxler,Gene (b) | Tough,Dave (dr)

Our Love
Chicago,Ill, rec. 15.3.1939
Dorsey,Tommy (tb) | Ferretti,Andy (tb) | Lawson,Yank (tp) | Blake,Jimmy (tp) | Silloway,Ward (tb) | Jacobs,Dave (tb) | Smithers,Elmer (tb) | Stulce,Fred (as) | Mince,Johnny (cl,as) | Herfurt,Arthur 'Skeets' (as) | Russin,Irving 'Babe' (ts) | Smith,Howard (p) | Mastren,Carmen (g) | Traxler,Gene (b) | Tough,Dave (dr) | Leonard,Jack (voc)

Indian Summer
NYC, rec. 27.9.1939
Dorsey,Tommy (tb) | Ferretti,Andy (tb) | Lawson,Yank (tp) | Erwin,Pee Wee (tp) | Silloway,Ward (tb) | Jacobs,Dave (tb) | Smithers,Elmer (tb) | Mince,Johnny (cl,as) | Bernardi,Noni (as) | Russin,Irving 'Babe' (ts) | Smith,Howard (p) | Mastren,Carmen (g) | Traxler,Gene (b) | Leeman,Cliff (dr) | Leonard,Jack (voc)

All The Things You Are
Chicago,Ill, rec. 20.10.1939
Dorsey,Tommy (tb) | Ferretti,Andy (tb) | Lawson,Yank (tp) | Blake,Jimmy (tp) | Silloway,Ward (tb) | Jacobs,Dave (tb) | Smithers,Elmer (tb) | Mince,Johnny (cl,as) | Stulce,Fred (as) | Russin,Irving 'Babe' (ts) | Smith,Howard (p) | Mastren,Carmen (g) | Traxler,Gene (b) | Leeman,Cliff (dr) | Leonard,Jack (voc)

Stardust
Hollywood,CA, rec. 11.11.1940
Dorsey,Tommy (tb) | Linn,Ray (tp) | Peterson,Chuck (tp) | Elman,Ziggy (tp) | Jenkins,Les (tb) | Arus,George (tb) | Martin,Lowell (tb) | Mince,Johnny (cl,as) | Stulce,Fred (as) | Schertzer,Hymie (as) | Beau,Heinie (ts) | Lodice,Don (ts) | Bushkin,Joe (celeste) | Yocum,Clark (g) | Weiss,Sid (b) | Rich,Buddy (dr) | Sinatra,Frank (voc) | Pied Piepers,The (voc)

In The Blue Of The Evening
NYC, rec. 17.11.1942
Dorsey,Tommy (tb) | Petersen,Chuck (tp) | Elman,Ziggy (tp) | Zito,Jimmy (tp) | Blake,Jimmy (tp) | Arus,George (tb) | Jacobs,Dave (tb) | Skiles,Jimmy (tb) | Stulce,Fred (as) | Schuchman,Harry (as) | Beau,Heinie (ts) | Lodice,Don (ts) | Raskin,Milt (p) | Yocum,Clark (g) | Stevens,Phil (b) | Rich,Buddy (dr) | Sinatra,Frank (voc) | Strings

Opus 1
Hollywood,CA, rec. 14.11.1944
Dorsey,Tommy (tb) | Ellick,Roger (tp) | Mangano,Mickey (tp) | Pierce,Dale (tp) | Seaberg,George (tp) | Benson,Walt (tb) | Riddle,Nelson (tb) | Satterwhite,Tex (tb) | DeFranco,Buddy (cl) | Cooper,Sid (as) | Curtis,Gale (as) | Klink,Al (ts) | Branson,Bruce (bs) | Park,Joe (tuba) | Golden,Milt (p) | Bain,Bob (g) | Block,Sid (b) | Rich,Buddy (dr) | Oliver,Sy (arr) | Strings

The Song Is You
Hollywood,CA, rec. 8.4.1946
Dorsey,Tommy (tb) | Mangano,Mickey (tp) | Seaberg,George (tp) | Dougherty,Jack (tp) | Elman,Ziggy (tp) | Shavers,Charlie (tp) | Phillips,Greg (tb) | Siegel,Bill (tb) | Satterwhite,Tex (tb) | DeFranco,Buddy (cl,as) | Cooper,Sid (as) | Lodice,Don (ts) | Fresk,Livio 'Babe' (ts) | Branson,Bruce (bs) | Potoker,Johnny (p) | Herman,Sam (g) | Block,Sid (b) | Stoller,Alvin (dr) | Strings

Summertime | I'm In The Mood For Love
Hollywood,CA, rec. 7.4.1949
Dorsey,Tommy (tb) | Dougherty,Jack (tp) | Arslan,Vern (tp) | Peterson,Chuck (tp) | Solomon,Red (tp) | Shavers,Charlie (tp,voc) | Bradley,Will (tb) | DiMaio,Nick (tb) | Noel,Dick (tb) | Ainsworth,William 'Billy' (as) | Kennon,George (as) | Richman,Abe 'Boomie' (ts) | Fresk,Livio 'Babe' (ts) | Berman,Marty (bs) | Smith,Paul (p) | Herman,Sam (g) | Seelig,Norman (b) | Bellson,Louie (dr)

Birmingham Bounce
Hollywood,CA, rec. 13.4.1950
Dorsey,Tommy (tb) | Amarosa,John (tp) | DePew,Art (tp) | Mangano,Mickey (tp) | Shavers,Charlie (tp,voc) | DiMaio,Nick (tb) | Harris,Sidney (tb) | Lowenstein,Hugo (as) | Winner,Jerry (as) | Richman,Abe 'Boomie' (ts) | Fresk,Livio 'Babe' (ts) | Bank,Danny (bs) | Gibbs,Terry (vib) | Levy,Lou (p) | Herman,Sam (g) | Baldwin,Bob (b) | Bellson,Louie (dr)

2159973-2 | CD | Planet Jazz:Earl Hines
Earl Hines And His Orchestra
G.T. Stomp | Grand Terrace Shuffle | Father Steps In | Piano Man
NYC, rec. 12.7.1939
Hines,Earl 'Fatha' (p) | Fletcher,Milton (tp) | Simms,Edward (tp) | Fuller,Walter (tp) | Dixon,George (tp,as,bs) | Burke,Edward (tb) | Ewing,John 'Steamline' (tb) | McLewis,Joe (tb) | Simeon,Omer (cl,as) | Harris,Leroy (cl,as) | Johnson,Budd (as,ts,arr) | Crowder,Robert (ts,arr) | Roberts,Claude (g) | Wilson,Quinn (b) | Burroughs,Alvin (dr)

Riff Medley
Chicago,Ill, rec. 6.10.1939
Hines,Earl 'Fatha' (p) | Fuller,Walter (tp) | Fletcher,Milton (tp) | Simms,Edward (tp) | Dixon,George (tp,as) | Burke,Edward (tb) | Ewing,John 'Steamline' (tb) | McLewis,Joe (tb) | Simeon,Omer (cl,bs) | Johnson,Budd (cl,as,ts) | Harris,Leroy (as) | Crowder,Robert (ts) | Roberts,Claude (g) | Wilson,Quinn (b) | Burroughs,Alvin (dr)

Earl Hines
Rosetta
Chicago,Ill, rec. 21.10.1939
Hines,Earl 'Fatha' (p-solo)

Earl Hines And His Orchestra
Boogie Woogie On St. Louis Blues | Deep Forest | Number 19
NYC, rec. 13.2.1940
Hines,Earl 'Fatha' (p) | Fletcher,Milton (tp) | Simms,Edward (tp) | Fuller,Walter (tp) | Dixon,George (tp,as,bs) | Burke,Edward (tb) | Ewing,John 'Steamline' (tb) | McLewis,Joe (tb) | Simeon,Omer (cl,as) | Harris,Leroy (as) | Mundy,Jimmy (ts,arr) | Crowder,Robert (ts,arr) | Roberts,Claude (g) | Wilson,Quinn (b) | Burroughs,Alvin (dr)

Call Me Happy | Tantalizing A Cuban
NYC, rec. 19.6.1940
Hines,Earl 'Fatha' (p) | Clay,Shirley (tp) | Simms,Edward (tp) | Fuller,Walter (tp) | Dixon,George (tp,as,bs) | Burke,Edward (tb) | Ewing,John 'Steamline' (tb) | McLewis,Joe (tb) | Simeon,Omer (cl,as) | Harris,Leroy (cl,as) | Mundy,Jimmy (ts,arr) | Crowder,Robert (ts) | Roberts,Claude (g) | Wilson,Quinn (b) | Burroughs,Alvin (dr)

Jelly Jelly
Hollywood,CA, rec. 2.12.1940
Hines,Earl 'Fatha' (p) | Jackson,Harry (tp) | Reese,Rostelle (tp) | White,Leroy (tp) | McLewis,Joe (tb) | Ewing,John 'Steamline' (tb) | Fant,Edward (tb) | Harris,Leroy (as) | Carry,George (as) | Randall,William (cl,ts) | Johnson,Budd (cl,ts) | Jackson,Franz (ts,arr) | Ramey,Hurley (g) | Parham,Charles 'Truck' (b) | Burroughs,Alvin (dr) | Eckstine,Billy (voc)

Up Jumped The Devil
NYC, rec. 3.4.1941
Hines,Earl 'Fatha' (p) | Jackson,Harry (tp) | Dixon,George (tp,as) | Enoch,Tommy (tp) | Harris,Benny (tp) | McLewis,Joe (tb) | Hunt,George (tb) | Fant,Edward (tb) | Harris,Leroy (as) | Carry,George (as) | Randall,William (cl,ts) | Johnson,Budd (cl,ts) | Jackson,Franz (ts) | Ramey,Hurley (g) | Parham,Charles 'Truck' (b) | Taylor,Rudolph (dr)

Windy City Jive
Hollywood,CA, rec. 20.8.1941
Hines,Earl 'Fatha' (p) | Jackson,Harry (tp) | Dixon,George (tp,as) | Enoch,Tommy (tp) | Webster,Freddie (tp) | McLewis,Joe (tb) | Hunt,George (tb) | Ewing,John 'Steamline' (tb) | Harris,Leroy (as) | Carry,George (as) | Randall,William (cl,ts) | Johnson,Budd (cl,ts) | Jackson,Franz (ts) | Ramey,Hurley (g) | Parham,Charles 'Truck' (b) | Taylor,Rudolph (dr)

The Father Jumps
Chicago,Ill, rec. 28.10.1941
Hines,Earl 'Fatha' (p) | Jackson,Harry (tp) | Dixon,George (tp) | Enoch,Tommy (tp) | Miller,Jesse (tp) | McLewis,Joe (tb) | Hunt,George (tb) | Atkins,Nat (tb) | Harris,Leroy (as) | Carry,George (as) | Randall,William (cl,ts) | Johnson,Budd (cl,ts) | Jackson,Franz (ts) | Ramey,Hurley (g) | Parham,Charles 'Truck' (b) | Taylor,Rudolph (dr)

Second Balcony Jump | Stormy Monday Blues(They Call It Stormy Monday)
NYC, rec. 19.3.1942
Hines,Earl 'Fatha' (p) | Jackson,Harry (tp) | Dixon,George (tp,as) | McConnell,Maurice (tp) | Miller,Jesse (tp) | McLewis,Joe (tb) | Hunt,George (tb) | Valentine,Gerry (tb,arr) | Harris,Leroy (cl,as) | Carry,George (cl,as) | Randall,William (cl,ts) | Johnson,Budd (cl,ts) | Crowder,Robert (ts) | Best,Skeeter (g) | Parham,Charles 'Truck' (b) | Taylor,Rudolph (dr) | Eckstine,Billy (voc)

2159974-2 | CD | Planet Jazz:J.J.Johnson
J.J.Johnson And His Orchestra
My Little Suede Shoes | Stratusphunk | So What | Bemsha Swing
NYC, rec. 7.12.1964
Johnson,J.J. (tb) | Terry,Clark (tp,fl-h) | Royal,Ernie (tp) | Cleveland,Jimmy (tb) | Studd,Tony (b-tb) | Dodgion,Jerry (fl,as) | Nelson,Oliver (as,ts) | Richardson,Jerome (fl,ts,bs) | Jones,Hank (p) | Cranshaw,Bob (b) | Tate,Grady (dr)

Stolen Moments | Swing Spring
NYC, rec. 8.12.1964
Johnson,J.J. (tb) | Jones,Thad (tp) | Royal,Ernie (tp) | Cleveland,Jimmy (tb) | Studd,Tony (b-tb) | Dodgion,Jerry (fl,as) | Nelson,Oliver (as,ts) | Beckenstein,Ray (fl,b-cl,bs) | Jones,Hank (p) | Cranshaw,Bob (b) | Tate,Grady (dr)

El Camino Real
NYC, rec. 9.12.1964
Johnson,J.J. (tb) | Jones,Thad (tp) | Royal,Ernie (tp) | Maxwell,Jimmy (tp) | Wilder,Joe (tp) | Cleveland,Jimmy (tb) | Studd,Tony (b-tb) | Mitchell,Tom (b-tb) | Buffington,Jimmy (fr-h) | Stanley,Bill (tuba) | Dodgion,Jerry (fl,as) | Nelson,Oliver (as,ts) | Johnson,Budd (ts,bs) | Estrin,Harvey (mouthpiece) | Jones,Hank (p) | Cranshaw,Bob (b) | Tate,Grady (dr)

Say When | Ballade
NYC, rec. 30.11.1966
Johnson,J.J. (tb) | Farmer,Art (tp) | Young,Eugene 'Snooky' (tp) | Stiles,Danny (tp) | Powell,Benny (tb) | Faulise,Paul (tb) | Richardson,Jerome (reeds) | Bodner,Phil (reeds) | Newsom,Tommy (reeds) | Jones,Hank (p) | Carter,Ron (b) | Tate,Grady (dr)

Space Walk | Little Dave | In Walked Horace
NYC, rec. 2.12.1966
Johnson,J.J. (tb) | Farmer,Art (tp) | Royal,Ernie (tp) | Collins,Bert (tp) | Powell,Benny (tb) | Faulise,Paul (tb) | Richardson,Jerome (reeds) | Bodner,Phil (reeds) | Newsom,Tommy (reeds) | Jones,Hank (p) | Carter,Ron (b) | Tate,Grady (dr) | Rosengarden,Bobby (perc)

2159976-2 | CD | PLanet Jazz:Shorty Rogers
Shorty Rogers And His Giants
Powder Puff | The Pesky Serpent | Bunny | Pirouette
Los Angeles,CA, rec. 12.1.1953
Rogers,Shorty (tp,arr) | Bernhart,Milton 'Milt' (tb) | Graas,John (fr-h) | Englund,Gene (tuba) | Pepper,Art (as) | Giuffre,Jimmy (ts) | Hawes,Hampton (p) | Mondragon,Joe (b) | Manne,Shelly (dr)

Morpho | Diablo's Dance | Mambo Del Crow | Indian Club
Los Angeles,CA, rec. 15.1.1953
Rogers,Shorty (tp) | Bernhart,Milton 'Milt' (tb) | Graas,John (fr-h) | Englund,Gene (tuba) | Pepper,Art (as) | Giuffre,Jimmy (ts) | Hawes,Hampton (p) | Mondragon,Joe (b) | Manne,Shelly (dr)

Shorty Rogers And His Orchestra Feat. The Giants
Coop De Graas | Infinity Promenade | Short Stop | Boar Jibu
Los Angeles,CA, rec. 26.3.1953
Rogers,Shorty (tp) | Gozzo,Conrad (tp) | Ferguson,Maynard (tp) | Candoli,Pete (tp) | Howell,John (tp) | Bernhart,Milton 'Milt' (tb) | Halliburton,John (tb) | Betts,Harry (tb) | Graas,John (fr-h) | Englund,Gene (tuba) | Pepper,Art (as,ts) | Shank,Bud (as) | Giuffre,Jimmy (ts,bs) | Cooper,Bob (ts,bs) | Paich,Marty (p) | Counce,Curtis (b) | Manne,Shelly (dr)

Tale Of An African Lobster | Contours | Chiquito Loco | The Sweetheart Of Sigmund Freud
Los Angeles,CA, rec. 2.4.1953
Rogers,Shorty (tp) | Gozzo,Conrad (tp) | Ferguson,Maynard (tp) | Candoli,Pete (tp) | Howell,John (tp) | Bernhart,Milton 'Milt' (tb) | Halliburton,John (tb) | Betts,Harry (tb) | Graas,John (fr-h) | Englund,Gene (tuba) | Pepper,Art (as,ts) | Shank,Bud (as,bs) | Giuffre,Jimmy (ts,bs) | Cooper,Bob (ts) | Paich,Marty (p) | Counce,Curtis (b) | Manne,Shelly (dr)

2161236-2 | CD | Planet Jazz:Jack Teagarden
Roger Wolfe Kahn And His Orchestra
She's A Great,Great Girl
NYC, rec. 14.3.1928
Kahn,Roger Wolfe (ld) | Gott,Tommy (tp) | Klein,Manny (tp) | Teagarden,Jack (tb) | Evans,Alfie (cl,as,bs) | Brillhart,Arnold (fl,cl,as) | unkn. (ts) | Venuti,Joe (v) | Raymond,Joe (v) | Schutt,Arthur (p) | Colucci,Tony (bj) | Lang,Eddie (g) | Campbell,Arthur (tuba) | Berton,Vic (dr)

Eddie's Hot Shots
I'm Gonna Stomp Mr.Henry Lee | That's A Serious Thing
NYC, rec. 8.2.1929
Condon,Eddie (bj) | Davis,Leonard (tp) | Teagarden,Jack (tb,voc) | Mezzrow,Milton Mezz (c-mel-sax) | Caldwell,Happy (ts) | Sullivan,Joe (p) | Stafford,George (dr)

Ben Pollack And His Park Central Orchestra
My Kinda Love
NYC, rec. 5.3.1929
Pollack,Ben (voc) | McPartland,Jimmy (co) | Weinstein,Ruby (tp) | Teagarden,Jack (tb) | Goodman,Benny (cl,as) | Mezzrow,Milton Mezz (as) | Binyon,Larry (fl,cl,ts) | Beller,Alex 'Al' (v) | Bergman,Eddie (v) | Schulmann,Bill (cello) | Breidis,Vic (p) | Morgan,Dick (bj) | Goodman,Harry (tuba) | Bauduc,Ray (dr)

Mound City Blue Blowers
Tailspin Blues | Never Had A Reason To Believe In You
NYC, rec. 25.9.1929
Mound City Blue Blowers | McKenzie,Red (comb,voc) | Teagarden,Jack (tb,voc) | Bland,Jack (g,voc) | Condon,Eddie (bj) | Foster,George 'Pops' (b) | Billings,Frank 'Josh' (dr)

Fats Waller And His Buddies
Looking' Good But Feelin' Bad
NYC, rec. 30.9.1929
Waller,Thomas 'Fats' (p,voc) | Allen,Henry Red (tp) | Teagarden,Jack (tb) | Nicholas,Albert (as) | Hardwicke,Otto (as) | Binyon,Larry (ts) | Condon,Eddie (bj) | Morgan,Albert 'Al' (b) | Krupa,Gene (dr) | Four Wanderers,The (voc) | Hughes,Herman (voc) | Clinkscales,Charles (voc) | Johnson,Maceo (voc) | Childs,Oliver (voc)

Paul Whiteman And His Orchestra
Fare Thee Well To Harlem
NYC, rec. 16.2.1934
Whiteman,Paul (ld) | Natoli,Nat (tp) | Teagarden,Charlie (tp) | Goldfield,Harry (tp) | Fulton,Jack (tb) | Teagarden,Jack (tb,voc) | Bonaccio,Benny (reeds) | Cordaro,Jack (reeds) | Strickfaden,Charles (reeds) | Trumbauer,Frank (reeds) | Bargy,Roy (p) | Pirro,Vincent (accordeon) | Pingitore,Mike (g) | Miller,Art (b) | McPherson,Norman (tuba) | Quigley,Herb (dr) | Mercer,Johnny (voc)
Nobody's Sweetheart
NYC, rec. 9.7.1935
Whiteman,Paul (ld) | Wade,Eddie (tp) | Teagarden,Charlie (tp) | Goldfield,Harry (tp) | Rank,Bill (tb) | Teagarden,Jack (tb,voc) | Matthews,Hal (tb) | Bonaccio,Benny (cl,b-cl,as) | Cordaro,John (cl,b-cl,as,bs) | Strickfaden,Charles (cl,as,ts,bs) | Trumbauer,Frankie (c-mel-sax) | Bargy,Roy (p) | Pingitore,Mike (g) | Miller,Art (b) | Gomar,Larry (vib,dr)

All Star Band
Blue Lou
NYC, rec. 11./12.1.1939
Berigan,Bunny (tp) | Spivak,Charlie (tp) | Dunham,Sonny (tp) | Teagarden,Jack (tb) | Dorsey,Tommy (tb) | Goodman,Benny (cl) | Schertzer,Hymie (as) | Rollini,Arthur (ts) | Miller,Eddie (ts) | Zurke,Bob (p) | Mastren,Carmen (g) | Haggart,Bob (b) | Bauduc,Ray (dr) | Henderson,Fletcher (arr)
The Blues
James,Harry (tp) | Berigan,Bunny (tp) | Dunham,Sonny (tp) | Teagarden,Jack (tb) | Dorsey,Tommy (tb) | Goodman,Benny (cl) | Schertzer,Hymie (as) | Rollini,Arthur (ts) | Miller,Eddie (ts) | Zurke,Bob (p) | Mastren,Carmen (g) | Haggart,Bob (b) | Bauduc,Ray (dr)

Jack Teagarden's Big Eight
St.Louis Blues
NYC, rec. 14.3.1947
Teagarden,Jack (tb,voc) | Kaminsky,Max (tp) | Hucko,Peanuts (cl) | Stickland,Clifton (ts) | Schroeder,Gene (p) | Wayne,Chuck (g) | Lesberg,Jack (b) | Tough,Dave (dr)

Louis Armstrong And His All Stars
St.James Infirmary
Live at Town Hall,NYC, rec. 17.5.1947
Armstrong,Louis (tp) | Teagarden,Jack (tb,voc) | Cary,Dick (p) | Haggart,Bob (b) | Catlett,Big Sid (dr)
Jack-Armstrong Blues
NYC, rec. 10.6.1947
Armstrong,Louis (tp,voc) | Hackett,Bobby (tp) | Teagarden,Jack (tb,voc) | Hucko,Peanuts (cl) | Caceres,Ernie (sax) | Guarnieri,Johnny (p) | Casey,Al (g) | Hall,Al (b) | Cole,William 'Cozy' (dr)

Bud Freeman And His Summa Cum Laude Orchestra
Jack Hits The Road | There'll Be Some Changes Made
NYC, rec. 8.7.1957
Freeman,Bud (ts) | Butterfield,Billy (tp) | Teagarden,Jack (tb,voc) | Hucko,Peanuts (cl) | Schroeder,Gene (p) | Gaskin,Leonard (b) | Wettling,George (dr)

2161237-2 | CD | Planet Jazz:Cab Calloway

Cab Calloway And His Orchestra
The Lady With The Fan | Harlem Camp Meeting | Zaz Zuh Zaz | Father's Got His Glasses On
NYC, rec. 2.11.1933
Calloway,Cab (ld,voc) | Wright,Lammar (tp) | Cheatham,Doc (tp) | Swayzee,Edwin (tp) | Wheeler,De Priest (tb) | White,Harry (tb) | Barefield,Eddie (cl,as,bs) | Brown,Andrew (b-cl,as,bs) | Harris,Arville (cl,as) | Thomas,Walter 'Foots' (fl,cl,ts) | Payne,Benny (p) | White,Morris (g,bj) | Morgan,Albert 'Al' (b) | Maxey,Leroy (dr)
The Scat Song | There's A Cabin In The Cotton
NYC, rec. 18.12.1933
Calloway,Cab (ld,voc) | Wright,Lammar (tp) | Cheatham,Doc (tp) | Swayzee,Edwin (tp) | Wheeler,De Priest (tb) | White,Harry (tb) | Barefield,Eddie (cl,as,bs) | Brown,Andrew (b-cl,as,bs) | Harris,Arville (cl,as) | Thomas,Walter 'Foots' (fl,cl,ts) | Payne,Benny (p,voc) | White,Morris (g,bj) | Morgan,Albert 'Al' (b) | Maxey,Leroy (dr)
Little Town Gal
NYC, rec. 19.12.1933
Calloway,Cab (ld,voc) | Wright,Lammar (tp) | Cheatham,Doc (tp) | Swayzee,Edwin (tp) | Wheeler,De Priest (tb) | White,Harry (tb) | Barefield,Eddie (cl,as,bs) | Brown,Andrew (b-cl,as,bs) | Harris,Arville (cl,as) | Thomas,Walter 'Foots' (fl,cl,ts) | Payne,Benny (p) | White,Morris (g,bj) | Morgan,Albert 'Al' (b) | Maxey,Leroy (dr)
Long About Midnight | Moonglow | Jitterbug
NYC, rec. 2.1.1934
Calloway,Cab (ld,voc) | Wright,Lammar (tp) | Cheatham,Doc (tp) | Swayzee,Edwin (tp) | Wheeler,De Priest (tb) | White,Harry (tb) | Barefield,Eddie (cl,as,bs) | Brown,Andrew (b-cl,as,bs) | Harris,Arville (cl,as) | Thomas,Walter 'Foots' (fl,cl,ts) | Payne,Benny (p) | White,Morris (g,bj) | Morgan,Albert 'Al' (b) | Maxey,Leroy (dr)
Margie
NYC, rec. 23.1.1934
Calloway,Cab (ld,voc) | Wright,Lammar (tp) | Cheatham,Doc (tp) | Swayzee,Edwin (tp) | Wheeler,De Priest (tb) | White,Harry (tb) | Barefield,Eddie (cl,as,bs) | Brown,Andrew (b-cl,as,bs) | Harris,Arville (cl,as) | Thomas,Walter 'Foots' (fl,cl,ts) | Payne,Benny (p) | White,Morris (g,bj) | Morgan,Albert 'Al' (b) | Maxey,Leroy (dr)

Cab Calloway And His Cab Jivers
Rooming House Boogie
NYC, rec. 29.11.1949
Calloway,Cab (ld,voc) | Jones,Jonah (tp) | Glenn,Tyree (tb) | Jefferson,Hilton (as) | Taylor,Sam 'The Man' (ts) | Rivera,Dave (p) | Hinton,Milt (b) | Francis,Panama (dr)

Cab Calloway And His Orchestra
Minnie The Moocher | It Ain't Necessarily So
NYC, rec. 5.12.1958
Calloway,Cab (voc) | Glow,Bernie (tp) | Maxwell,Jimmy (tp) | Wilder,Joe (tp) | Green,Urbie (tb) | Welsch,Chauncey (tb) | Mitchell,Tom (tb) | Marowitz,Sam (reeds) | O'Kane,Charles (sax) | Richman,Abe 'Boomie' (reeds) | Donahue,Sam (ts) | Webb,Stanley (sax) | Jones,Hank (p) | Barksdale,Everett (g) | Hinton,Milt (b) | Heard,J.C. (dr) | Reisman,Joe (ld)
Kickin' The Gong Around | Stormy Weather
NYC, rec. 16.12.1958
Calloway,Cab (voc) | Glow,Bernie (tp) | Severinsen,Doc (tp) | Wilder,Joe (tp) | Green,Urbie (tb) | Welsch,Chauncey (tb) | Hixon,Richard (tb) | Marowitz,Sam (reeds) | O'Kane,Charles (sax) | Richman,Abe 'Boomie' (reeds) | Donahue,Sam (ts) | Webb,Stanley (sax) | Jones,Hank (p) | Barksdale,Everett (g) | Hinton,Milt (b) | Heard,J.C. (dr) | Reisman,Joe (ld)

2161238-2 | CD | Planet Jazz:Lee Morgan

Art Blakey And The Jazz Messengers
Whisper Not | Blues March For Europe No.1 | Along Came Betty
Live at Club St.Germain,Paris,France, rec. 21.12.1958
Blakey,Art (dr) | Morgan,Lee (tp) | Golson,Benny (ts) | Timmons,Bobby (p) | Merritt,Jymie (b)

Ahmed Abdul-Malik Orchestra
El-Lail(Night)
NYC, rec. 16.3.1959
Abdul-Malik,Ahmed (b,oud) | Morgan,Lee (tp) | Fuller,Curtis (tb) | Richardson,Jerome (fl) | Golson,Benny (ts) | Griffin,Johnny (ts) | Karacand,Naim (v) | Yetman,Ahmed (kanon) | Harewood,Al (dr) | Hamway,Mike (darabeka) | Abdurrahman,Bilal (darabeka)

Art Blakey And The Jazz Messengers
Close Your Eyes | Goldie
Live at The Theatre Des Champs-Elysees,Paris,France, rec. 15.11.1959
Blakey,Art (dr) | Morgan,Lee (tp) | Shorter,Wayne (ts) | Davis Jr.,Walter (p) | Merritt,Jymie (b)

2161239-2 | CD | Planet Jazz:Clifford Brown

Gigi Gryce-Clifford Brown Sextet
Conception | All The Things You Are
Paris,France, rec. 29.9.1953
Brown,Clifford (tp) | Gryce,Gigi (as) | Renaud,Henri (p) | Gourley,Jimmy (g) | Michelot,Pierre (b) | Viale,Jean-Louis (dr)
Minority
Paris,France, rec. 8.10.1953
Brown,Clifford (tp) | Gryce,Gigi (as) | Gourley,Jimmy (g) | Renaud,Henri (p) | Michelot,Pierre (b) | Viale,Jean-Louis (dr)

Gigi Gryce-Clifford Brown Octet
No Start No End | Chez Moi
Paris,France, rec. 10.8.1953
Brown,Clifford (tp) | Gryce,Gigi (as) | Cleveland,Jimmy (tb) | Solomon,Clifford (ts) | Gourley,Jimmy (g) | Renaud,Henri (p) | Michelot,Pierre (b) | Viale,Jean-Louis (dr)

Clifford Brown Quartet
Blue And Brown | I Can Dream Can't I | The Song Is You | Come Rain Or Come Shine | It Might As Well Be Spring
Paris,France, rec. 15.10.1953
Brown,Clifford (tp) | Renaud,Henri (p) | Michelot,Pierre (b) | Bennett,Benny (dr)

2161240-2 | CD | Planet Jazz:Bud Freeman

Hoagy Carmichael And His Orchestra
Bessie Couldn't Help It
NYC, rec. 15.9.1930
Carmichael,Hoagy (voc) | Beiderbecke,Bix (co) | Lodwig,Ray (tp) | Cullen,Boyce (tb) | Teagarden,Jack (tb) | Dorsey,Jimmy (as) | Brilhart,Arnold (as) | Russell,Pee Wee (cl,ts) | Freeman,Bud (ts) | Venuti,Joe (b) | Brodsky,Irving (p) | Lang,Eddie (g) | Leibrock,Min (tuba) | Morehouse,Chauncey (dr)

Mezz Mezzrow And His Orchestra
Apologies
NYC, rec. 7.5.1934
Mezzrow,Milton Mezz (cl,as,arr) | Kaminsky,Max (tp) | Jones,Reunald (tp) | Quealey,Chelsea (tp) | O'Brien,Floyd (tb,arr) | Carter,Benny (as) | Freeman,Bud (ts) | Smith,Willie 'The Lion' (p) | Kirby,John (b) | Webb,Chick (dr) | Hill,Alex (arr)

Gene Gifford And His Orchestra
New Orleans Twist
NYC, rec. 13.5.1935
Gifford,Gene (arr,ld) | Berigan,Bunny (tp) | Samuel,Morey (tb) | Matlock,Matty (cl) | Freeman,Bud (ts) | Thornhill,Claude (p) | McDonough,Dick (g) | Peterson,Pete (b) | Bauduc,Ray (dr)

Mezz Mezzrow And His Swing Band
The Panic Is On
NYC, rec. 12.3.1936
Mezzrow,Milton Mezz (cl) | Newton,Frankie (tp) | Freeman,Bud (ts) | Smith,Willie 'The Lion' (p) | Casey,Al (g) | Braud,Wellman (b) | Stafford,George (dr)

Tommy Dorsey And His Clambake Seven
At The Codfish Ball
NYC, rec. 15.4.1936
Dorsey,Tommy (tb) | Kaminsky,Max (tp) | Dixon,Joe (cl) | Freeman,Bud (ts) | Jones,Dick (p) | Schaffer,William (g) | Traxler,Gene (b) | Tough,Dave (dr) | Wright,Edythe (voc)

Bud Freeman And His Summa Cum Laude Orchestra
Easy To Get | China Boy | The Eel
NYC, rec. 19.7.1939
Freeman,Bud (ts) | Kaminsky,Max (tp) | Gowans,Brad (tb) | Russell,Pee Wee (cl) | Bowman,Dave (p) | Condon,Eddie (g) | Newcomb,Clyde (b) | Alvin,Danny (dr)
Sugar | Nobody's Sweetheart
NYC, rec. 7.3.1957
Freeman,Bud (ts) | McPartland,Jimmy (co) | Russell,Pee Wee (cl) | Cary,Dick (p) | Hinton,Milt (b) | Wettling,George (dr)
At Sundown
NYC, rec. 3.4.1957
Freeman,Bud (ts) | Butterfield,Billy (tp) | Glenn,Tyree (tb) | Russell,Pee Wee (cl) | Cary,Dick (p) | Casamenti,Al (g) | Hall,Al (b) | Wettling,George (dr)
You Took Advantage Of Me
NYC, rec. 8.7.1957
Freeman,Bud (ts) | Butterfield,Billy (tp) | Teagarden,Jack (tb) | Hucko,Peanuts (cl) | Schroeder,Gene (p) | Gaskin,Leonard (b) | Wettling,George (dr)

The Chicago All Stars
I've Found A New Baby | At The Jazz Band Ball
Live at Newport,Rhode Island, rec. 2.7.1964
Chicago All Stars,The | Kaminsky,Max (tp) | McGarity,Lou (tb) | Hucko,Peanuts (cl) | Freeman,Bud (ts) | Wein,George (p) | Haggart,Bob (b) | Drootin,Buzzy (dr) | Wettling,George prob. (dr)

2165369-2 | CD | Planet Jazz:Tito Puente

Tito Puente Orchestra
What Is This Thing Called Love | Tiny-Not Ghengis
NYC, rec. 2.5.1956
Puente,Tito (ld) | Glow,Bernie (tp) | LoPinto,Frank (tp) | Rapetti,Gene (tp) | Frisaura,Vincent (tp) | Lehrfeld,Allen (sax) | Kurtzer,Dave (sax) | Holmes,Martin (sax) | Schildkraut,David (sax) | Gellers,Alvin (p) | Rodriguez,Roberto (b) | Sommer,Ted (dr) | Correa,William (bongo) | Santamaria,Ramon (congas)
What Are You Doin' Honey | Lucky Dog | That's Puente
NYC, rec. 25.5.1956
Puente,Tito (ld) | Glow,Bernie (tp) | LoPinto,Frank (tp) | Rapetti,Gene (tp) | Frisaura,Vincent (tp) | Williams,Francis (tp) | Travis,Nick (tp) | Lehrfeld,Allen (sax) | Kurtzer,Dave (sax) | Holmes,Martin (sax) | Quill,Gene (sax) | Gellers,Alvin (p) | Galbraith,Barry (el-g) | Rodriguez,Roberto (b) | Sommer,Ted (dr) | Correa,William (bongo) | Santamaria,Ramon (congas)
Lotus Land
NYC, rec. 2.6.1956
Puente,Tito (ld) | Glow,Bernie (tp) | LoPinto,Frank (tp) | Rapetti,Gene (tp) | Frisaura,Vincent (tp) | Williams,Francis (tp) | Travis,Nick (tp) | Lehrfeld,Allen (sax) | Kurtzer,Dave (sax) | Holmes,Martin (sax) | Quill,Gene (sax) | Gellers,Alvin (p) | Galbraith,Barry (el-g) | Sanfino,Gerald (b) | Sommer,Ted (dr) | Correa,William (bongo) | Santamaria,Ramon (congas)
Birdland After Dark | Yesterdays | Terry Cloth | Tito'in
details unknown, rec. details unknown
Puente,Tito (ld) | details unknown

2165370-2 | CD | Planet Jazz:Joe Williams

Joe Williams With The Jimmy Jones Orchestra
Just A-Sittin' And A-Rockin'
NYC, rec. 1.2.1963
Williams,Joe (voc) | Jones,Jimmy (arr,ld) | Terry,Clark (tp) | Green,Urbie (tb) | Woods,Phil (as) | Richardson,Jerome (fl,ts) | Bodner,Phil (fl,reeds) | Leighton,Bernie (p) | Burrell,Kenny (g) | Hinton,Milt (b) | Gubin,Sol (dr)
Jump For Joy
NYC, rec. 6.2.1963
Williams,Joe (voc) | Jones,Jimmy (arr,ld) | Terry,Clark (tp) | Green,Urbie (tb) | Woods,Phil (as) | Richardson,Jerome (fl,ts) | Bank,Danny (bs) | Jones,Hank (p) | Burrell,Kenny (g) | Hinton,Milt (b) | Johnson,Osie (dr)

Joe Williams,With The Oliver Nelson Orchestra
Wrap Your Troubles In Dreams
NYC, rec. 4.2.1963
Williams,Joe (voc) | Nelson,Oliver (arr,ld) | Terry,Clark (tp) | Glow,Bernie (tp) | Jones,Thad (tp) | Young,Eugene 'Snooky' (tp) | Jackson,Quentin (tb) | Green,Urbie (tb) | Dorsey,George (as) | Levinsky,Walt (as) | Bodner,Phil (fl,reeds) | Penque,Romeo (fl,ts) | Jones,Hank (p) | Burrell,Kenny (g) | Hinton,Milt (b) | Rodriguez,Willie (perc)

Joe Williams And His Band
Come Back Baby | Every Day | April In Paris | In The Evening
Live at Newport,Rhode Island, rec. 5.7.1963
Williams,Joe (voc) | Terry,Clark (tp) | McGhee,Howard (tp) | Hawkins,Coleman (ts) | Sims,Zoot (ts) | Mance,Junior[Julian C.] (p) | Cranshaw,Bob (b) | Roker,Granville 'Mickey' (dr)
All God's Chillun Got Rhythm- | Do You Wanna Jump Children-
NYC, rec. 17.7.1963
Williams,Joe (voc) | Terry,Clark (tp) | Hawkins,Coleman (ts) | Webster,Ben (ts) | Mance,Junior[Julian C.] (p) | Cranshaw,Bob (b) | Roker,Granville 'Mickey' (dr)

Joe Williams With The Jimmy Jones Orchestra
Every Night
NYC, rec. 18.11.1963
Williams,Joe (voc) | Jones,Jimmy (cond,arr) | Terry,Clark (tp) | Green,Urbie (tb) | Woods,Phil (as) | Powell,Seldon (ts) | Bank,Danny (bs) | Jones,Hank (p) | Galbraith,Barry (g) | Hinton,Milt (b) | Johnson,Osie (dr)
Rocks In My Bed
NYC, rec. 20.11.1963
Williams,Joe (voc) | Jones,Jimmy (cond,arr) | Jones,Thad (tp) | Webster,Ben (ts) | Jones,Hank (p) | Galbraith,Barry (g) | Hinton,Milt (b) | Johnson,Osie (dr)
Early In The Morning | Kansas City
NYC, rec. 5.12.1963
Williams,Joe (voc) | Jones,Jimmy (cond,arr) | Jones,Thad (tp) | Green,Urbie (tb) | Richardson,Jerome (as) | Powell,Seldon (ts) | Bank,Danny (bs) | Jones,Hank (p) | Galbraith,Barry (g) | Hinton,Milt (b) | Johnson,Osie (dr)

Joe Williams With The Frank Hunter Orchestra
Prelude To A Kiss
NYC, rec. 11.11.1964
Williams,Joe (voc) | Green,Urbie (tb) | Jones,Hank (p) | Lowe,Mundell (g) | Block,Sandy (b) | Lewis,Mel (dr) | Strings | Background Vocals | Hunter,Frank (arr,cond) | details unknown
You Stepped Out Of A Dream
NYC, rec. 12.11.1964
Williams,Joe (voc) | Royal,Ernie (tp) | Glow,Bernie (tp) | Ferrante,Joe (tp) | Reasinger,Clyde (tp) | Cooper,Sid (reeds) | Cohen,Leon (reeds) | Bodner,Phil (reeds) | Richardson,Jerome (reeds) | Penque,Romeo (reeds) | Devens,George (vib) | Hyman,Dick (p) | Lowe,Mundell (g) | Block,Sandy (b) | Lewis,Mel (dr) | Background Vocals | Hunter,Frank (arr,cond)
Gypsy In My Soul | I Wonder Who's Kissing Her Now
NYC, rec. 31.3.1965
Williams,Joe (voc) | Royal,Ernie (tp) | Glow,Bernie (tp) | Ferrante,Joe (tp) | Nottingham,Jimmy (tp) | Green,Urbie (tb) | Gravine,Mickey (tb) | Morrow,Buddy (tb) | Johnson,J.J. (tb) | Ralph,Alan (b-tb) | Cohen,Leon (reeds) | Dorsey,George (reeds) | Richardson,Jerome (reeds) | Tricarico,Bob (reeds) | Bank,Danny prob (bs) | Jones,Hank (p) | Lowe,Mundell (g) | Block,Sandy (b) | Gubin,Sol (dr) | Powell,Gordon (perc) | Hunter,Frank (arr,cond)
On The Sunny Side Of The Street
NYC, rec. 18.6.1965
Williams,Joe (voc) | Alonge,Ray (fr-h) | Richardson,Jerome (fl,cl,ts) | Jones,Hank (p) | Caiola,Al (g) | Block,Sandy (b) | Igoe,Sonny (dr) | Strings | Hunter,Frank (arr,cond)

2165372-2 | CD | Planet Jazz:Nina Simone

Nina Simone And Orchestra
Day And Night | Do I Move You?
NYC, rec. 19.12.1966
Simone,Nina (p,voc) | Lucas,Buddy (harm) | Hayes,Ernest 'Ernie' (org) | Stevenson,Rudy (g) | Gale,Eric (g) | Bushnell,Bob (el-b) | Purdie,Bernard 'Pretty' (dr) | unkn. (chorus)
Blues For Mama | Real Real
NYC, rec. 22.12.1966
Simone,Nina (p,voc) | Lucas,Buddy (harm) | Hayes,Ernest 'Ernie' (org) | Stevenson,Rudy (g) | Gale,Eric (g) | Bushnell,Bob (el-b) | Purdie,Bernard 'Pretty' (dr)
Since I Fell For You | I Want A Little Sugar In My Bowl | Backlash Blues | The House Of The Rising Sun | In The Dark | Buck
NYC, rec. 5.1.1967
Simone,Nina (p,voc) | Lucas,Buddy (ts,harm) | Hayes,Ernest 'Ernie' (org) | Stevenson,Rudy (g) | Gale,Eric (g) | Bushnell,Bob (el-b) | Purdie,Bernard 'Pretty' (dr)

Nina Simone-Bob Bushnell
My Man's Gone Now
Simone,Nina (p,voc) | Bushnell,Bob (el-b)

Nina Simone And Orchestra
The Pusher
details unknown, rec. details unknown
Simone,Nina (p,voc) | details unknown
Turn Me On
NYC, rec. 13.6.1967
Simone,Nina (p,voc) | Tax,Melvin (reeds) | Richardson,Jerome (reeds) | Stevenson,Rudy (g) | Gale,Eric (g) | Taylor,Calvin (el-b) | Purdie,Bernard 'Pretty' (dr)
Go To Hell
NYC, rec. 21.6.1967
Simone,Nina (p,voc) | Markowitz,Irving 'Marky' (tp) | Davis,Mel (tp) | Tax,Melvin (fl) | Richardson,Jerome (b-fl) | Stevenson,Rudy (g) | Gale,Eric (g) | Taylor,Calvin (el-b) | Purdie,Bernard 'Pretty' (dr)
Gin House Blues
NYC, rec. 7.4.1968
Simone,Nina (p,voc) | unkn. (g) | Taylor,Gene (b) | unkn. (dr)

Nina Simone
Nobody's Fault But Mine
NYC, rec. 16.9.1968
Simone,Nina (p,voc)

Nina Simone Quintet
I Shall Be Released
NYC, rec. 8.1.1969
Simone,Nina (p,voc) | Irvine,Weldon (org) | Shackman,Al (g) | Perla,Gene (el-b) | Davis,Charles (dr) | Willingham,Doris (voc) | Crawford,Virdia (voc)

2165373-2 | CD | Planet Jazz:Lena Horne

Lena Horne With The Lou Bring Orchestra
Stormy Weather | What Is This Thing Called Love | Ill Wind | The Man I Love
Hollywood,CA, rec. 15.12.1941
Horne,Lena (voc) | Klein,Manny (tp) | Mayhew,Jack (sax) | Friedman,Morty (sax) | Rosati,Archie (sax) | Russell,Mischa (v) | Pisano,Nick (v) | Botkin,Perry (g) | Bernstein,Artie (b) | Freeman,Ned (arr) | Bring,Lou (cond)
Where Or When | I Gotta Right To Sing The Blues | Moanin' Low
Hollywood,CA, rec. 17.12.1941
Horne,Lena (voc) | Klein,Manny (tp) | Mayhew,Jack (sax) | Friedman,Morty (sax) | Rosati,Archie (sax) | Russell,Mischa (v) | Pisano,Nick (v) | Botkin,Perry (g) | Bernstein,Artie (b) | Freeman,Ned (arr) | Bring,Lou (cond)

Lena Horne With The Horace Henderson Orchestra
I Didn't Know About You | One For My Baby(And One More For The Road) | As Long As I Live | I Ain't Got Nothin' But The Blues
Hollywood,CA, rec. 21.11.1944
Horne,Lena (voc) | Hurley,Clyde (tp) | Porter,Jake (tp) | Trainer,Freddie (tp) | Miller,Randall (tb) | Robinson,Lester (tb) | Songer,Wayne (as) | Jacquet,Illinois (ts) | Stacey,Jack (ts) | Plumb,Neely (cl,bs) | Lutcher,Nellie or Horace Henderson (p) | Barbour,Dave (g) | Simmons,John (b) | Catlett,Big Sid (dr) | Hayton,Lennie (arr) | Henderson,Horace (ld)

Lena Horne With The Phil Moore Four
How Long Has That Train Been Gone
NYC, rec. 9.4.1945
Horne,Lena (voc) | Letman,Johnny (tp) | Sedric,Gene (cl) | Moore,Phil (p) | Palmieri,Remo (g) | Gibbs,Edward (g) | Dickens,Doles (b) | Bishop,Wallace (dr)

Lena Horne With The Lennie Hayton Orchestra
It's Love | Let Me Love You
NYC, rec. 31.5.1955
Horne,Lena (voc) | Wilder,Joe (tp) | Baker,Harold 'Shorty' (tp) | DeRisi,Al (tp) | Alexander,Bob (tb) | Welsch,Chauncey (tb) | Marowitz,Sam (sax) | O'Kane,Charles (sax) | Penque,Romeo (sax) | Richman,Abe 'Boomie' (sax) | Strayhorn,Billy (p) | Lowe,Mundell (g) | Duvivier,George (b) | Crawford,Jimmy (dr) | Strings | Hayton,Lennie (arr,ld)

It's All Right With Me
NYC, rec. 7.6.1955
Horne,Lena (voc) | Maxwell,Jimmy (tp) | Baker,Harold 'Shorty' (tp) | DeRisi,Al (tp) | Byrne,Bobby (tb) | D'Agostino,John (tb) | Welsch,Chauncey (tb) | Marowitz,Sam (sax) | O'Kane,Charles (sax) | Cohn,Al (sax) | Webb,Stanley (sax) | Richman,Abe 'Boomie' (sax) | Strayhorn,Billy (p) | Mottola,Tony (g) | Duvivier,George (b) | Lamond,Don (dr) | Rodriguez,Willie (bongos) | Hayton,Lennie (arr,ld)

People Will Say We're In Love
NYC, rec. 3.6.1958
Horne,Lena (voc) | Glow,Bernie (tp) | Travis,Nick (tp) | DeRisi,Al (tp) | Byers,Billy (tb) | Forchetti,Vinvent (tb) | Bert,Eddie (tb) | Welsch,Chauncey (tb) | Penque,Romeo (sax) | Gershman,Manny (sax) | Gilbert,Al (sax) | Caine,Eddie (sax) | Banks,Danny (sax) | DiNovi,Gene (p) | Duvivier,George (b) | Johnson,Osie (dr) | Burns,Ralph (arr) | Hayton,Lennie (arr,ld)

Justin Time
NYC, rec. 9.6.1958
Horne,Lena (voc) | Maxwell,Jimmy (tp) | Severinsen,Doc (tp) | DeRisi,Al (tp) | Byers,Billy (tb) | Forchetti,Vinvent (tb) | Bert,Eddie (tb) | Rehak,Frank (tb) | Gershman,Manny (sax) | Cohn,Al (sax) | Caine,Eddie (sax) | Epstein[Young],Al (sax) | Banks,Danny (sax) | DiNovi,Gene (p) | Duvivier,George (b) | Johnson,Osie (dr) | Burns,Ralph (arr) | Hayton,Lennie (arr,ld)

2169648-2 | CD | Planet Jazz:Jazz Greatest Hits

Glenn Miller And His Orchestra
Chattanooga Choo Choo
Hollywood,CA, rec. 7.5.1941
Miller,Glenn (tb) | McMickle,Dale (tp) | Anthony,Ray (tp) | May,Billy (tp) | Best,John (tp) | Priddy,Jimmy (tb) | Tanner,Paul (tb) | D'Annolfo,Frank (tb) | Schwartz,Wilbur (cl,as) | McIntyre,Hal (as) | Caceres,Ernie (cl,as,bs) | Beneke,Gordon 'Tex' (ts) | Klink,Al (ts) | MacGregor,John Chalmers 'Chummy' (p) | Lathrop,Jack (g) | Alpert,Trigger (b) | Purtill,Maurice 'Moe' (dr) | Gray,Jerry (arr) | Modernaires,The (voc-group)

Coleman Hawkins And His Orchestra
Body And Soul
NYC, rec. 11.10.1939
Hawkins,Coleman (ts) | Lindsey,Tommy (tp) | Guy,Joe (tp) | Hardy,Earl (tb) | Fields,Jackie (as) | Moore,Eustis (as) | Rodgers,Gene (tp) | Smith,William Oscar (b) | Herbert,Arthur (dr)

Tommy Dorsey And His Orchestra
Opus 1
Hollywood,CA, rec. 14.11.1944
Dorsey,Tommy (tb) | Ellick,Roger (tp) | Mangano,Mickey (tp) | Pierce,Dale (tp) | Seaberg,George (tp) | Benson,Walt (tb) | Riddle,Nelson (tb) | Satterwhite,Tex (tb) | DeFranco,Buddy (cl) | Cooper,Sid (as) | Curtis,Gale (as) | Klink,Al (ts) | Branson,Bruce (bs) | Park,Joe (tuba) | Golden,Milt (p) | Bain,Bob (g) | Block,Sid (b) | Krupa,Gene (dr) | Oliver,Sy (arr) | Strings

Louis Armstrong And His Dixieland Seven
Do You Know What It Means To Miss New Orleans
Los Angeles,CA, rec. 17.10.1946
Armstrong,Louis (tp,voc) | Ory,Edward 'Kid' (tb) | Bigard,Barney (cl) | Beal,Charlie (p) | Scott,Bud (g) | Callender,Red (b) | Hall,Minor 'Ram' (dr)

Paul Desmond-Gerry Mulligan Quartet
All The Things You Are
NYC, rec. 3.7.1962
Desmond,Paul (as) | Mulligan,Gerry (bs) | Marshall,Wendell (b) | Kay,Connie (dr)

Benny Goodman And His Orchestra
Sing Sing Sing
Hollywood,CA, rec. 6.7.1937
Goodman,Benny (cl) | James,Harry (tp) | Elman,Ziggy (tp) | Griffin,Chris (tp) | Ballard,Red (tb) | McEachern,Murray (tb) | Schertzer,Hymie (as) | Koenig,George (as) | Rollini,Arthur (ts) | Musso,Vido (ts) | Stacy,Jess (p) | Reuss,Allan (g) | Goodman,Harry (b) | Krupa,Gene (dr)

A Jam Session At Victor
Honeysuckle Rose
NYC, rec. 31.3.1937
A Jam Session At Victor | Berigan,Bunny (tp) | Dorsey,Tommy (tb) | Waller,Thomas 'Fats' (p) | McDonough,Dick (g) | Wettling,George (dr)

Sonny Rollins Quartet
God Bless The Child
NYC, rec. 30.1.1962
Rollins,Sonny (ts) | Hall,Jim (g) | Cranshaw,Bob (b) | Saunders,Harry (dr)

Duke Ellington And His Orchestra
It Don't Mean A Thing If It Ain't Got That Swing
NYC, rec. 14.5.1945
Ellington,Duke (p) | Hemphill,Shelton (tp) | Jordan,Taft (tp) | Anderson,Cat (tp) | Nance,Ray (tp) | Stewart,Rex (co) | Nanton,Joe 'Tricky Sam' (tb) | Jones,Claude (tb) | Brown,Lawrence (tb) | Hodges,Johnny (as) | Hardwicke,Otto (as) | Sears,Al (ts) | Hamilton,Jimmy (cl,ts) | Carney,Harry (cl,bs) | Guy,Fred (g) | Haggart,Bob (b) | Greer,William 'Sonny' (dr) | Davis,Kay (voc) | Sherrill,Joya (voc) | Ellington,Marie (voc)

Lionel Hampton And His Quintet
Tenderly
Madrid, Spain, rec. 30.6.1956
Hampton,Lionel (vib) | Montoliu,Tete (p) | Mackel,Billy (g) | Badie,Peter (b) | Gordner,June (dr) | Angelica,Maria (castanets)

Artie Shaw And His Orchestra
Frenesi
Hollywood,CA, rec. 3.3.1940
Shaw,Artie (cl) | Margulis,Charlie (tp) | Klein,Manny (tp) | Thow,George (tp) | Miller,Randall (tb) | Rank,Bill (tb) | Bowman,Babe (tb) | Reynolds,Blake (as) | Carlton,Bud (as) | Stacey,Jack (as) | Clark,Dick (ts) | Krechter,Joe (b-cl) | Cave,Jack (fr-h) | Ruderman,Morton (fl) | Nemoli,Phil (oboe) | Wrightsman,Stan (p) | Sherwood,Bobby (g) | DeNaut,Jud (b) | Maus,Carl (dr) | Levant,Mark (v) | Bluestone,Harry (v) | Eisenburg,Peter (v) | Barene,Robert (v) | Brokaw,Sid (v) | Cracov,Dave (v) | Law,Alex (v) | Joyce,Jerry (v) | Sturkin,David (viola) | Spiegelman,Stanley (viola) | Gray,Jack (viola) | Lipschultz,Irving (cello) | Tannenbaum,Jules (cello)

Dizzy Gillespie And His Orchestra
A Night In Tunisia
NYC, rec. 22.2.1946
Gillespie,Dizzy (tp) | Byas,Don (ts) | Jackson,Milt (vib) | Haig,Al (p) | De Arango,Bill (g) | Brown,Ray (b) | Heard,J.C. (dr)

Count Basie And His Orchestra
Bill's Mill
Hollywood,CA, rec. 3.1.1947
Basie,Count (p) | Lewis,Ed (tp) | Berry,Emmett (tp) | Young,Eugene 'Snooky' (tp) | Edison,Harry 'Sweets' (tp) | Johnson,Bill (tb) | Donnelly,Ted (tb) | Matthews,George (tb) | Robinson,Eli (tb) | Love,Preston (as) | Rutherford,Rudy (as) | Gonsalves,Paul (ts) | Tate,Buddy (ts) | Washington Jr.,Jack (bs) | Green,Freddie (g) | Page,Walter (b) | Jones,Jo (dr)

2169649-2 | CD | Planet Jazz:Big Bands

Glenn Miller And His Orchestra
Chattanooga Choo Choo
Hollywood,CA, rec. 7.5.1941
Miller,Glenn (tb) | McMickle,Dale (tp) | Anthony,Ray (tp) | May,Billy (tp) | Best,John (tp) | Priddy,Jimmy (tb) | Tanner,Paul (tb) | D'Annolfo,Frank (tb) | Schwartz,Wilbur (cl,as) | McIntyre,Hal (as) | Caceres,Ernie (cl,as,bs) | Beneke,Gordon 'Tex' (ts) | Klink,Al (ts) | MacGregor,John Chalmers 'Chummy' (p) | Lathrop,Jack (g) | Alpert,Trigger (b) | Purtill,Maurice 'Moe' (dr) | Gray,Jerry (arr) | Modernaires,The (voc-group)

Erskine Hawkins And His Orchestra
Tuxedo Junction
NYC, rec. 18.7.1939
Hawkins,Erskine (tp,arr) | Lowe,Sam (tp,arr) | Bascomb,Wilbur (tp) | Green,Marcellus (tp) | Sims,Edward (tb) | Range,Robert (tb) | Johnson,Bill (as,arr) | Mitchell,Jimmy (as,voc) | Dash,Julian (ts) | Henry,Haywood (cl,bs) | Parrish,Avery (p,arr) | McLemore,William (g) | Stanfield,Leemie (b) | Morrison,James (dr)

Charlie Barnet And His Orchestra
Cherokee
NYC, rec. 17.7.1939
Barnet,Charlie (ss,as,ts) | Owens,Johnny (tp) | Burnet,Bobby (tp) | May,Billy (tp) | Hall,Ben (tb) | Ruppersberg,Don (tb) | Robertson,Bill (tb) | McCook,Don (as) | Kinsey,Gene (as) | Bloom,Kurt (ts) | Lamare,Jimmy (as,bs) | Miller,Bill (p) | Etri,Bus (g) | Stephens,Phil (b) | Michaels,Ray (dr)

Duke Ellington And His Famous Orchestra
Take The 'A' Train
Hollywood,CA, rec. 15.2.1941
Ellington,Duke (p) | Jones,Wallace (tp) | Williams,Cootie (tp) | Stewart,Rex (co) | Nanton,Joe 'Tricky Sam' (tb) | Brown,Lawrence (tb) | Tizol,Juan (v-tb) | Bigard,Barney (cl) | Hodges,Johnny (cl,ss,as) | Hardwicke,Otto (as,bass-s) | Webster,Ben (ts) | Carney,Harry (cl,as,bs) | Guy,Fred (g) | Blanton,Jimmy (b) | Greer,William 'Sonny' (dr) | Strayhorn,Billy (arr)

Artie Shaw And His Orchestra
Stardust
Hollywood,CA, rec. 7.10.1940
Shaw,Artie (cl) | Wendt,George (tp) | Cathcart,Jack (tp) | Butterfield,Billy (tp) | Jenney,Jack (tb) | Brown,Vernon (tb) | Bassey,Bus (as) | Plumb,Neely (as) | Robinson,Les (ts) | Jerome,Jerry (ts) | Guarnieri,Johnny (p) | Hendrickson,Al (el-g) | DeNaut,Jud (b) | Fatool,Nick (dr) | Lamas,E. (v) | Klages,T. (v) | Morrow,Bob (v) | Bower,B. (v) | Beller,Alex 'Al' (v) | Harshman,Allan (viola) | Collins,K. (viola) | Goerner,F. (cello)

Benny Goodman And His Orchestra
One O'Clock Jump
NYC, rec. 16.2.1938
Goodman,Benny (cl) | Kazebier,Nate (tp) | James,Harry (tp) | Elman,Ziggy (tp) | Ballard,Red (tb) | Brown,Vernon (tb) | Koenig,George (as) | Schertzer,Hymie (as) | Russin,Irving 'Babe' (ts) | Rollini,Arthur (ts) | Stacy,Jess (p) | Reuss,Allan (g) | Goodman,Harry (b) | Krupa,Gene (dr)

Count Basie And His Orchestra
Hey Pretty Baby
Los Angeles,CA, rec. 12.12.1947
Basie,Count (p) | Lewis,Ed (tp) | Berry,Emmett (tp) | Young,Eugene 'Snooky' (tp) | Edison,Harry 'Sweets' (tp) | Donnelly,Ted (tb) | Washington,George (tb) | Matthews,George (tb) | Johnson,Bill (tb) | Love,Preston (as) | Price,Charles Q. (as) | Tate,Buddy (ts) | Gonsalves,Paul (ts) | Washington Jr.,Jack (bs) | Green,Freddie (g) | Page,Walter (b) | Jones,Jo (dr) | Rushing,Jimmy (voc)

Tommy Dorsey And His Orchestra
I'll Never Smile Again
NYC, rec. 23.5.1940
Dorsey,Tommy (tb) | Berigan,Bunny (tp) | Linn,Ray (tp) | Debrow,Leon (tp) | Blake,Jimmy (tp) | Martin,Lowell (tb) | Jenkins,Les (tb) | Arus,George (tb) | Mince,Johnny (cl,as) | Schertzer,Hymie (as) | Stulce,Fred (as) | Mason,Paul (ts) | Lodice,Don (ts) | Bushkin,Joe (p) | Yocum,Clark (g) | Weiss,Sid (b) | Rich,Buddy (dr) | Sinatra,Frank (voc) | Pied Piepers,The (voc)

Lionel Hampton And His Orchestra
Flying Home
Live at Newport,Rhode Island, rec. 3.7.1967
Hampton,Lionel (vib) | Young,Eugene 'Snooky' (tp) | Nottingham,Jimmy (tp) | Newman,Joe (tp) | Davenport,Wallace (tp) | Grey,Al (tb) | Brown,Garnett (tb) | Woodman,Britt (tb) | Powell,Benny (tb) | Pazant,Edward (fl,as) | Dorsey,George (as) | Young,David (ts) | Foster,Frank (ts) | Jacquet,Illinois (ts) | Richardson,Jerome (bs) | Buckner,Milt (p) | Mackel,Billy (g) | Duvivier,George (b) | Little,Steve (dr) | Dawson,Alan (dr)

Turn Me Loose
Hampton,Lionel (vib) | Young,Eugene 'Snooky' (tp) | Nottingham,Jimmy (tp) | Newman,Joe (tp) | Davenport,Wallace (tp) | Grey,Al (tb) | Brown,Garnett (tb) | Woodman,Britt (tb) | Powell,Benny (tb) | Pazant,Edward (fl,as) | Dorsey,George (as) | Young,David (ts) | Foster,Frank (ts) | Richardson,Jerome (bs) | Spruill,John (p) | Mackel,Billy (g) | Duvivier,George (b) | Little,Steve (dr)

Woody Herman And The New Thundering Herd
Four Brothers
Live at Carnegie Hall,NYC, rec. 26.11.1976
Herman,Woody (cl,ss) | Vizutti,Alan (tp) | Hatt,Nelson (tp) | Hoffman,John (tp) | Dotson,Dennis (tp) | Byrne,Billy (tp) | Pugh,Jim (tb) | Kirkland,Dale (tb) | Daniels,Jim (b-tb) | Giuffre,Jimmy (ts) | Cohn,Al (ts) | Getz,Stan (ts) | Sims,Zoot (ts) | Coil,Pat (p) | Jackson,Chubby (b) | Lamond,Don (dr) | Hanna,Jake (dr)

Tommy Dorsey And His Orchestra
Song Of India
NYC, rec. 29.1.1937
Dorsey,Tommy (tb) | Berigan,Bunny (tp) | Welch,Jimmy (tp) | Bauer,Joe (tp) | Cusumano,Bob (tp) | Jenkins,Les (tb) | Bone,E.W. 'Red' (tb) | Dixon,Joe (cl,as) | Stulce,Fred (as) | Rounds,Clyde (as) | Freeman,Bud (ts) | Jones,Dick (p) | Mastren,Carmen (g) | Traxler,Gene (b) | Tough,Dave (dr)

Benny Goodman And His Orchestra
Sing Sing Sing
Hollywood,CA, rec. 6.7.1937
Goodman,Benny (cl) | James,Harry (tp) | Elman,Ziggy (tp) | Griffin,Chris (tp) | Ballard,Red (tb) | McEachern,Murray (tb) | Schertzer,Hymie (as) | Koenig,George (as) | Rollini,Arthur (ts) | Musso,Vido (ts) | Stacy,Jess (p) | Reuss,Allan (g) | Goodman,Harry (b) | Krupa,Gene (dr)

Glenn Miller And His Orchestra
In The Mood
NYC, rec. 1.8.1939
Miller,Glenn (tb) | Knowles,Legh (tp) | Hurley,Clyde (tp) | McMickle,Dale (tp) | Mastren,Al (tb) | Tanner,Paul (tb) | Schwartz,Wilbur (cl,as) | McIntyre,Hal (as) | Tennyson,Hal (as,bs) | Beneke,Gordon 'Tex' (ts) | Klink,Al (ts) | MacGregor,John Chalmers 'Chummy' (p) | Fisher,Richard (g) | Bundock,Rowland 'Rolly' (b) | Purtill,Maurice 'Moe' (dr)

2169651-2 | CD | Planet Jazz:Swing

Benny Goodman And His Orchestra
Life Goes To A Party
NYC, rec. 12.11.1937
Goodman,Benny (cl) | James,Harry (tp,arr) | Griffin,Gordon (tp) | Elman,Ziggy (tp) | Ballard,Red (tb) | McEachern,Murray (tb) | Schertzer,Hymie (as) | Koenig,George (as) | Rollini,Arthur (ts) | Musso,Vido (ts) | Stacy,Jess (p) | Reuss,Allan (g) | Goodman,Harry (b) | Krupa,Gene (dr)

Benny Moten's Kansas City Orchestra
Moten Swing
Camden,NJ, rec. 13.12.1932
Moten,Benny | Keyes,Joe (tp) | Stewart,Dee (tp) | Page,Oran 'Hot Lips' (tp) | Minor,Dan (tb) | Durham,Eddie (tb,el-g,arr) | Barefield,Eddie (cl,as) | Washington Jr.,Jack (as,bs) | Webster,Ben (ts) | Basie,Count (p) | Berry,Leroy (g) | Page,Walter (b) | McWashington,Willie (dr)

Tommy Dorsey And His Clambake Seven
The Music Goes 'Round And 'Round
NYC, rec. 9.12.1935
Dorsey,Tommy (tb,voc) | Bose,Sterling (tp) | Stoneburn,Sid (cl) | Van Eps,Johnny (ts) | Jones,Dick (p) | Schaffer,William (g) | Traxler,Gene (b) | Weiss,Sam (dr) | Wright,Edythe (voc)

Charlie Barnet And His Orchestra
Cherokee
NYC, rec. 17.7.1939
Barnet,Charlie (ss,as,ts) | Owens,Johnny (tp) | Burnet,Bobby (tp) | May,Billy (tp) | Hall,Ben (tb) | Ruppersberg,Don (tb) | Robertson,Bill (tb) | McCook,Don (as) | Kinsey,Gene (as) | Bloom,Kurt (ts) | Lamare,Jimmy (as,bs) | Miller,Bill (p) | Etri,Bus (g) | Stephens,Phil (b) | Michaels,Ray (dr)

Glenn Miller And His Orchestra
Sunrise Serenade
NYC, rec. 10.4.1939
Miller,Glenn (tb) | Knowles,Legh (tp) | Price,Bob (tp) | McMickle,Dale (tp) | Mastren,Al (tb) | Tanner,Paul (tb) | Schwartz,Wilbur (cl,as) | McIntyre,Hal (as) | Aronson,Stanley (as) | Beneke,Gordon 'Tex' (ts) | Klink,Al (ts) | MacGregor,John Chalmers 'Chummy' (p) | Ens,Arthur (g) | Bundock,Rowland 'Rolly' (b) | Purtill,Maurice 'Moe' (dr) | Finegan,Bill (arr)

Artie Shaw And His Orchestra
Any Old Time | Begin The Beguine
NYC, rec. 24.7.1938
Shaw,Artie (cl) | Peterson,Chuck (tp) | Best,John (tp) | Bowen,Claude (tp) | Arus,George (tb) | Vesely,Ted (tb) | Rodgers,Harry (tb) | Robinson,Les (as) | Freeman,Hank (as) | Pastor,Tony (ts,voc) | Perry,Ronnie (ts) | Burness,Lester (p) | Avola,Al (g) | Weiss,Sid (b) | Leeman,Cliff (dr) | Holiday,Billie (voc) | Gray,Jerry (arr)

Benny Goodman Trio
Body And Soul
NYC, rec. 13.7.1935
Goodman,Benny (cl) | Wilson,Teddy (p) | Krupa,Gene (dr)

Gene Krupa's Swing Band
Swing Is Here
Chicago,Ill, rec. 29.2.1926
Krupa,Gene (dr) | Eldridge,Roy (tp) | Goodman,Benny (cl) | Berry,Leon 'Chu' (ts) | Stacy,Jess (p) | Reuss,Allan (g) | Crosby,Israel (b)

Lionel Hampton And His Orchestra
I'm In The Mood For Swing
NYC, rec. 21.7.1938
Hampton,Lionel (vib) | James,Harry (tp) | Carter,Benny (cl,as,arr) | Matthews,Dave (as) | Evans,Hershel (ts) | Russin,Irving 'Babe' (ts) | Kyle,Billy (p) | Kirby,John (b) | Jones,Jo (dr)

Benny Goodman And His Orchestra
Stompin' At The Savoy
Chicago,Ill, rec. 24.1.1935
Goodman,Benny (cl) | Geller,Harry (tp) | Kazebier,Nate (tp) | Muzillo,Ralph (tp) | Ballard,Red (tb) | Lacey,Jack (tb) | Harris,Joe (tb) | Schertzer,Hymie (as) | DePew,Bill (as) | Rollini,Arthur (ts) | Clark,Dick (bs) | Stacy,Jess (p) | Reuss,Allan (g) | Goodman,Harry (b) | Krupa,Gene (dr) | Sampson,Edgar (arr)

Tommy Dorsey And His Orchestra
Song Of India
NYC, rec. 29.1.1937
Dorsey,Tommy (tb) | Berigan,Bunny (tp) | Welch,Jimmy (tp) | Bauer,Joe (tp) | Cusumano,Bob (tp) | Jenkins,Les (tb) | Bone,E.W. 'Red' (tb) | Dixon,Joe (cl,as) | Stulce,Fred (as) | Rounds,Clyde (as) | Freeman,Bud (ts) | Jones,Dick (p) | Mastren,Carmen (g) | Traxler,Gene (b) | Tough,Dave (dr)

Glenn Miller And His Orchestra
In The Mood
NYC, rec. 1.8.1939
Miller,Glenn (tb) | Knowles,Legh (tp) | Hurley,Clyde (tp) | McMickle,Dale (tp) | Mastren,Al (tb) | Tanner,Paul (tb) | Schwartz,Wilbur (cl,as) | McIntyre,Hal (as) | Tennyson,Hal (as,bs) | Beneke,Gordon 'Tex' (ts) | Klink,Al (ts) | MacGregor,John Chalmers 'Chummy' (p) | Fisher,Richard (g) | Bundock,Rowland 'Rolly' (b) | Purtill,Maurice 'Moe' (dr)

Jimmy Lunceford And His Orchestra
Swingin' Uptown
NYC, rec. 26.1.1934
Lunceford,Jimmie (arr,ld) | Tompkins,Eddie (tp) | Stevenson,Tommy (tp) | Oliver,Sy (tp,arr) | Wells,Henry (tb) | Bowles,Russell (tb) | Smith,Willie (cl,as,bs) | Carruthers,Earl (cl,as,bs) | Thomas,Joe (cl,ts) | Wilcox,Edwin (p) | Norris,Al (g) | Allen,Moses (tuba) | Crawford,Jimmy (dr)

Benny Goodman And His Orchestra
King Porter Stomp
NYC, rec. 1.7.1935
Goodman,Benny (cl) | Berigan,Bunny (tp) | Kazebier,Nate (tp) | Muzillo,Ralph (tp) | Ballard,Red (tb) | Lacey,Jack (tb) | Mondello,Toots (as) | Schertzer,Hymie (as) | Clark,Dick (ts) | Rollini,Arthur (ts) | Froeba,Frank (p) | Van Eps,George (g) | Goodman,Harry (b) | Krupa,Gene (dr) | Ward,Helen (voc) | Henderson,Fletcher (arr)

2169652-2 | CD | Planet Jazz

Original Dixieland 'Jass' Band
Dixieland Jass Band One Step
NYC, rec. 26.2.1917
Original Dixieland 'Jass' Band | La Rocca,Nick (co) | Edwards,Edwin (tb) | Shields,Larry (cl) | Ragas,Henry (p) | Sbarbaro,Tony (dr)

New Orleans Feetwarmers
Maple Leaf Rag
NYC, rec. 15.9.1932
New Orleans Feetwarmers,The | Ladnier,Tommy (tp) | Nixon,Teddy (tb) | Bechet,Sidney (cl,ss) | Duncan,Hank (p) | Myers,Wilson Ernest (b) | Morand,Morris (dr)

Tommy Ladnier And His Orchestra
Weary Blues
NYC, rec. 28.11.1939
Ladnier,Tommy (tp) | Bechet,Sidney (cl,ss) | Mezzrow,Milton Mezz (cl,ts) | Jackson,Cliff (p) | Bunn,Teddy (g) | James,Elmer (b) | Johnson,Manzie (dr)

Muggsy Spanier And His Ragtime Band
Big Butter And Egg Man From The West
Chicago,Ill, rec. 7.7.1939
Spanier,Francis 'Muggsy' (co) | Brunies,George (tb,voc) | Cless,Rod (cl) | McKinstry,Ray (ts) | Zack,George (p) | Casey,Bob (g) | Pattison,Pat (b) | Greenberg,Marty (dr)

Jimmy McPartland And His Dixielanders
That's A Plenty | When The Saints Go Marching In
NYC, rec. 27.5.1959
McPartland,Jimmy (co,voc) | Shavers,Charlie (tp,voc) | Cutshall,Cutty (tb) | Wilber,Bob (cl,ts) | Caceres,Ernie (cl,bs) | Cary,Dick (alto-h,p) | Barnes,George (el-g) | Phillips,Harvey (tuba) | Burriesce,Joe (b) | Wettling,George (dr)

Jelly Roll Morton's New Orleans Jazzmen
High Society
NYC, rec. 14.9.1939
Morton,Jelly Roll (p) | DeParis,Sidney (tp) | Jones,Claude (tb) | Nicholas,Albert (cl) | Bechet,Sidney (ss) | Caldwell,Happy (ts) | Lucie,Lawrence (g) | Braud,Wellman (b) | Singleton,Zutty (dr)

Sidney Bechet And His New Orleans Feetwarmers
Indian Summer
NYC, rec. 5.2.1940
Bechet,Sidney (cl,ss,voc) | White,Sonny (p) | Howard,Charlie (g) | Myers,Wilson Ernest (b,voc) | Clarke,Kenny (dr)

Bob Scobey's Frisco Band
Down By The Riverside
NYC, rec. 4.6.1958
Scobey,Bob (tp) | Beebe,Jim (tb) | Shanley,Brian (cl) | Schroeder,Gene (p) | Hayes,Clancy (bj) | Duvivier,George (b) | Matteson,Richard (tuba) | Black,Dave (dr)

Muggsy Spanier And His Ragtime Band
At The Jazz Band Ball
NYC, rec. 10.11.1939
Spanier,Francis 'Muggsy' (co) | Brunies,George (tb,voc) | Cless,Rod (cl) | Billings,Bernie (ts) | Bushkin,Joe (p) | Casey,Bob (b) | Carter,Don (dr)

Max Kaminsky And His Dixieland Bashers
Shim-Me-Sha-Wabble
NYC, rec. 24.5.1954
Kaminsky,Max (tp) | Diehl,Ray (tb) | D'Amico,Hank (cl) | Cary,Dick (alto-h,p,arr) | Condon,Eddie prob. (g) | Lesberg,Jack (b) | Leeman,Cliff (dr)

Dr. Henry Levine's Barefoot Dixieland Philharmonic feat.Prof. Sidney Bechet
Muskrat Ramble
NYC, rec. 11.11.1940
Levine,Henry 'Hot-Lips' (tp) | Epstein,Jack (tb) | Evans,Alfie (cl) | Bechet,Sidney (ss) | Adler,Rudolph (ts) | Janarro,Mario (p) | Colucci,Tony (g) | Patent,Harry (b) | Levine,Nat (dr)

George Wein's Dixie Victors
Struttin' With Some Barbecue
NYC, rec. 28.5.1956
Wein,George (p) | Braff,Ruby (tp) | Dickenson,Vic (tb) | Stegmeyer,Bill (cl) | Caceres,Ernie (bs) | Barker,Danny (bj) | Hinton,Milt (b) | Drootin,Buzzy (dr)

Turk Murphy And His Jazz Band
Sweet Georgia Brown
Los Angeles,CA, rec. 2.5.1961
Murphy,Turk (tb) | Carson,Everett Ernest (tp,co) | Helm,Bob (cl) | Clute,Pete (p) | Short,Bob (b) | Capp,Frank (dr)

Muggsy Spanier And His Ragtime Band
Black And Blue
NYC, rec. 12.12.1939
Spanier,Francis 'Muggsy' (co) | Brunies,George (tb,voc) | Cless,Rod (cl) | Caiazza,Nick (ts) | Bushkin,Joe (p) | Casey,Bob (b) | Sidell,Al (dr)

Jack Teagarden's Big Eight
St.Louis Blues
NYC, rec. 14.3.1947
Teagarden,Jack (tb,voc) | Kaminsky,Max (tp) | Hucko,Peanuts (cl) | Stickland,Clifton (ts) | Schroeder,Gene (p) | Wayne,Chuck (g) | Lesberg,Jack (b) | Tough,Dave (dr)

Sidney Bechet And His New Orleans Feetwarmers
12th Street Rag
NYC, rec. 24.10.1941
Bechet,Sidney (cl,ss) | Shavers,Charlie (tp) | Smith,Willie 'The Lion' (p) | Barksdale,Everett (el-g) | Braud,Wellman (b) | Catlett,Big Sid (dr)

2169653-2 | CD | Planet Jazz:Jazz Saxophone

Lionel Hampton And His Orchestra
Dinah
NYC, rec. 21.12.1939
Hampton,Lionel (vib) | Carter,Benny (tp) | Hall,Edmond (cl) | Hawkins,Coleman (ts) | Sullivan,Joe (p) | Green,Freddie (g) | Bernstein,Artie (b) | Singleton,Zutty (dr)
Early Session Hop
NYC, rec. 11.9.1939
Hampton,Lionel (vib) | Gillespie,Dizzy (tp) | Carter,Benny (as,arr) | Hawkins,Coleman (ts) | Berry,Leon 'Chu' (ts) | Webster,Ben (ts) | Hart,Clyde (p) | Christian,Charlie (g) | Hinton,Milt (b) | Cole,William 'Cozy' (dr)
Wizzin' The Wizz
NYC, rec. 5.4.1939
Hampton,Lionel (vib,p,voc) | Berry,Leon 'Chu' (ts) | Hart,Clyde (p) | Reuss,Allan (g) | Hinton,Milt (b) | Cole,William 'Cozy' (dr)
I'm In The Mood For Swing
NYC, rec. 21.7.1938
Hampton,Lionel (vib) | James,Harry (tp) | Carter,Benny (cl,as,arr) | Matthews,Dave (as) | Evans,Hershel (ts) | Russin,Irving 'Babe' (ts) | Kyle,Billy (p) | Kirby,John (b) | Jones,Jo (dr)

Henry Allen Jr. And His New York Orchestra
It Should Be You
NYC, rec. 16.7.1929
Allen,Henry Red (tp) | Higginbotham,J.C. (tb) | Nicholas,Albert (cl,as) | Holmes,Charlie (cl,ss,as) | Hill,Teddy (cl,ts,bs) | Russell,Luis (p,celeste) | Johnson,Will (g,bj) | Foster,George 'Pops' (b) | Barbarin,Paul (vib,dr)

Johnny Hodges Orchestra
Things Ain't What They Used To Be
Hollywood,CA, rec. 3.7.1941
Hodges,Johnny (as) | Nance,Ray (tp) | Brown,Lawrence (tb) | Carney,Harry (bs) | Ellington,Duke (p) | Blanton,Jimmy (b) | Greer,William 'Sonny' (dr)

Bud Freeman And His Summa Cum Laude Orchestra
The Eel
NYC, rec. 19.7.1939
Freeman,Bud (ts) | Kaminsky,Max (tp) | Gowans,Brad (tb) | Russell,Pee Wee (cl) | Bowman,Dave (p) | Condon,Eddie (g) | Newcomb,Clyde (b) | Alvin,Danny (dr)

Lucky Thompson With The Gerard Pochonet All-Stars
Don't Blame Me
Paris,France, rec. 14.3.1956
Thompson,Lucky (ts) | Pochonet,Gerard 'Dave' (dr) | Gerard,Fred (tp) | Guerin,Roger (tp) | Vasseur,Benny (tb) | Hameline,Teddy (as) | Chautemps,Jean-Louis (ts) | Boucaya,William (bs) | Solal,Martial (p) | Quersin,Benoit (b) | Paraboschi,Roger (dr)

Eddie Lockjaw Davis Sextet feat. Paul Gonsalves
Time After Time
NYC, rec. 3.8.1967
Davis,Eddie 'Lockjaw' (ts) | Gonsalves,Paul (ts) | Hanna,Sir Roland (p) | Barksdale,Everett (g) | Tucker,Ben (b) | Tate,Grady (dr)

The Four Brothers
Four Brothers
NYC, rec. 11.2.1957
Four Brothers,The | Cohn,Al (ts) | Sims,Zoot (ts) | Steward,Herbie (ts) | Chaloff,Serge (bs) | Lawrence,Elliot (p) | Jones,Buddy (b) | Lamond,Don (dr) | Albam,Manny (arr)

Don Byas Quartet
Lover Man(Oh,Where Can You Be?)
Paris,France, rec. 24.11.1953
Byas,Don (ts) | Solal,Martial (p) | Michelot,Pierre (b) | Bennett,Benny (dr)

Woody Herman's Thundering Herd
Early Autumn
Live at Carnegie Hall,NYC, rec. 26.11.1976
Herman,Woody (cl,ss) | Vizutti,Alan (tp) | Hatt,Nelson (tp) | Hoffman,John (tp) | Dotson,Dennis (tp) | Byrne,Billy (tp) | Pugh,Jim (euphonium) | Kirkland,Dale (tb) | Daniels,Jim (b-tb) | Getz,Stan (ts) | Tiberi,Frank (sax) | Anderson,Gary (sax) | Lovano,Joe (sax) | Oslawski,John (sax) | Burns,Ralph (p) | Jackson,Charles 'Chip' (b) | Lamond,Don (dr) | Hanna,Jake (dr)

Al Cohn-Zoot Sims Quintet
Somebody Loves Me
NYC, rec. 24.1.1956
Cohn,Al (ts) | Sims,Zoot (ts) | Jones,Hank (p) | Hinton,Milt (b) | Johnson,Osie (dr)

Paul Desmond Orchestra
My Funny Valentine
NYC, rec. 14.9.1961
Desmond,Paul (as) | Richman,Albert (fr-h) | Marge,George (woodwinds) | Doty,Robert (woodwinds) | Hall,Jim (g) | Bianco,Gene (harp) | Cherico,Gene (b) | Kay,Connie (dr) | Strings

Gerry Mulligan Quartet
Walkin' Shoes
Live at Salle Pleyel,Paris,France, rec. 1.6.1954
Mulligan,Gerry (bs) | Brookmeyer,Bob (v-tb) | Mitchell,Red (b) | Isola,Frank (dr)

Sonny Rollins Trio
St.Thomas
NYC, rec. 14.2.1964
Rollins,Sonny (ts) | Cranshaw,Bob (b) | McCurdy,Roy (dr)

2169654-2 | CD | Planet Jazz:Jazz Trumpet

Louis Armstrong And His Dixieland Seven
Mahogany Hall Stomp
Los Angeles,CA, rec. 17.10.1946
Armstrong,Louis (tp,voc) | Ory,Edward 'Kid' (tb) | Bigard,Barney (cl) | Beal,Charlie (p) | Scott,Bud (g) | Callender,Red (b) | Hall,Minor 'Ram' (dr)

King Oliver And His Orchestra
West End Blues
NYC, rec. 16.1.1929
Oliver,Joseph 'King' (ld) | Metcalf,Louis (co) | Higginbotham,J.C. (tb) | Holmes,Charlie (as) | Hill,Teddy (ts) | Russell,Luis (p) | Johnson,Willie (bj) | Moore,William (tuba) | Barbarin,Paul (dr)

Bunk Johnson And His New Orleans Band
Snag It
NYC, rec. 6.12.1945
Johnson,Bunk (tp) | Robinson,Jim (tb) | Lewis,George (cl) | Purnell,Alton (p) | Marrero,Lawrence (bj) | Pavageau,Alcide 'Slow Drag' (b) | Dodds,Warren 'Baby' (dr)

Mezzrow-Ladnier Quintet
Everybody Loves My Baby
NYC, rec. 19.12.1938
Ladnier,Tommy (tp) | Mezzrow,Milton Mezz (cl) | Bunn,Teddy (g) | Foster,George 'Pops' (b) | Johnson,Manzie (dr)

Henry Allen Jr. And His New York Orchestra
Feeling Drowsy
NYC, rec. 17.7.1929
Allen,Henry Red (tp) | Higginbotham,J.C. (tb) | Nicholas,Albert (cl,as) | Holmes,Charlie (cl,ss,as) | Hill,Teddy (cl,ts,bs) | Russell,Luis (p) | Johnson,Will (bj) | Foster,George 'Pops' (b) | Barbarin,Paul (vib,dr)

Louisiana Sugar Babes
'Sippi
Camden,NJ, rec. 27.3.1928
Louisiana Sugar Babes | Smith,Jabbo (tp) | Bushell,Garvin (cl,as,bs) | Johnson,James P. (p) | Waller,Thomas 'Fats' (org)

Paul Whiteman And His Orchestra
Lonely Melody
NYC, rec. 4.1.1928
Whiteman,Paul (ld) | Beiderbecke,Bix (co) | Busse,Henry (tp) | Mayhew,Bob or Charlie Margulis (tp) | Rank,Bill (tb) | Fulton,Jack (tb) | Dorsey,Jimmy (cl,as) | Hazlett,Chester (cl,as) | Trumbauer,Frankie (c-mel-sax) | Strickfaden,Charles (as,bs) | Mayhew,Nye (as,ts) | Dieterle,Kurt (v) | Russell,Mischa (v) | Perry,Mario (v) | Gaylord,Charles (v) | Perella,Harry (p) | Pingitore,Mike (bj) | Trafficante,Mike (tuba) | Brown,Steve (b) | Hall,Wilbur (g) | McDonald,Harold (dr) | Challis,William 'Bill' (arr)

Red And Miff's Stompers
Davenport Blues
NYC, rec. 11.2.1927
Nichols,Red (tp) | Mole,Miff (tb) | Dorsey,Jimmy (cl,as) | Schutt,Arthur (p) | Colucci,Tony (bj) | Berton,Vic (dr)

Muggsy Spanier And His Ragtime Band
Black And Blue
NYC, rec. 12.12.1939
Spanier,Francis 'Muggsy' (co) | Brunies,George (tb,voc) | Cless,Rod (cl) | Caiazza,Nick (ts) | Bushkin,Joe (p) | Casey,Bob (b) | Sidell,Al (dr)

Wingy Mannone And His Orchestra
Jumpy Nerves
NYC, rec. 26.4.1939
Mannone,Joe 'Wingy' (tp) | Bailey,Buster (cl) | Berry,Leon 'Chu' (ts) | Lanoue,Conrad (p) | Julian,Zeb (g) | Cassard,Jules (b) | Cole,William 'Cozy' (dr)

Benny Goodman And His Orchestra
Peckin'
Hollywood,CA, rec. 6.7.1937
Goodman,Benny (cl) | Elman,Ziggy (tp) | Griffin,Gordon (tp) | James,Harry (tp,arr) | Ballard,Red (tb) | McEachern,Murray (tb) | Schertzer,Hymie (as) | Koenig,George (as) | Musso,Vido (ts) | Rollini,Arthur (ts) | Stacy,Jess (p) | Reuss,Allan (bj) | Goodman,Harry (b) | Krupa,Gene (dr)

Duke Ellington And His Famous Orchestra
Concerto For Cootie
NYC, rec. 14.2.1940
Ellington,Duke (p) | Stewart,Rex (co) | Jones,Wallace (tp) | Williams,Cootie (tp) | Nanton,Joe 'Tricky Sam' (tb) | Brown,Lawrence (tb) | Tizol,Juan (v-tb) | Bigard,Barney (cl) | Hodges,Johnny (cl,ss,as) | Carney,Harry (cl,as,bs) | Hardwicke,Otto (as,bass-s) | Webster,Ben (ts) | Guy,Fred (g) | Blanton,Jimmy (b) | Greer,William 'Sonny' (dr)

Rex Stewart And His Orchestra
Subtle Slough
Hollywood,CA, rec. 3.7.1941
Stewart,Rex (co) | Brown,Lawrence (tb) | Webster,Ben (ts) | Carney,Harry (bs) | Ellington,Duke (p) | Blanton,Jimmy (b) | Greer,William 'Sonny' (dr)

Artie Shaw And His Orchestra
Little Jazz
Hollywood,CA, rec. 5.4.1945
Shaw,Artie (cl,arr) | Glow,Bernie (tp) | Schwartz,George (tp) | Cohen,Paul (tp) | Eldridge,Roy (tp) | Rodgers,Harry (tb) | Swift,Bob (tb) | Wilson,Ollie (tb) | Dixon,Gus (tb) | Tanza,Rudolph 'Rudy' (as) | Prisby,Lou (as) | Walton,Jon (ts) | Stewart,Herbie (ts) | Gentry,Chuck (bs) | Marmarosa,Dodo (p) | Kessel,Barney (g) | Rayman,Morris (b) | Fromm,Louis 'Lou' (dr) | Harding,Buster (arr)

Hot Lips Page Band
Skull Duggery
NYC, rec. 27.4.1938
Page,Oran 'Hot Lips' (tp) | Mullens,Eddie (tp) | Moore,Bobby (tp) | Stevenson,George (tb) | White,Harry (tb,arr) | Scott,Ulysses (as) | Smith,Ben (cl,as) | Waters,Benny (ts) | Powell,Ernie (ts) | Reynolds,James (p) | Wainwright,Connie (g) | Bolar,Abe (b) | Taylor,Alfred (dr)

Esquire All-American Award Winners
Buckin' The Blues
NYC, rec. 4.12.1946
Esquire All Stars | Shavers,Charlie (tp) | Clayton,Buck (tp) | Johnson,J.J. (tb) | Hawkins,Coleman (ts) | Carney,Harry (bs) | Wilson,Teddy (p) | Collins,John (g) | Jackson,Chubby (b) | Wilson,Shadow (dr)

Roy Hargrove Quintet
Wee
NYC, rec. December 1989
Hargrove,Roy (tp) | Hart,Antonio Maurice (as) | Hicks,John (p) | Colley,Scott (b) | Foster,Al (dr)

2169656-2 | CD | Planet Jazz:Female Jazz Vocalists

Alberta Hunter
Beale Street Blues
Camden,NJ, rec. 20.5.1927
Hunter,Alberta (voc) | Waller,Thomas 'Fats' (org)

Artie Shaw And His Orchestra
Any Old Time
NYC, rec. 24.7.1938
Shaw,Artie (cl) | Peterson,Chuck (tp) | Best,John (tp) | Bowen,Claude (tp) | Arus,George (tb) | Vesely,Ted (tb) | Rodgers,Harry (tb) | Robinson,Les (as) | Freeman,Hank (as) | Pastor,Tony (ts,voc) | Perry,Ronnie (ts) | Burness,Lester (p) | Avola,Al (g) | Weiss,Sid (b) | Leeman,Cliff (dr) | Holiday,Billie (voc)

Benny Goodman And His Orchestra
Goodnight My Love
NYC, rec. 5.11.1936
Goodman,Benny (cl,voc) | Elman,Ziggy (tp) | Griffin,Gordon (tp) | Zarchy,Reuben 'Zeke' (tp) | Ballard,Red (tb) | McEachern,Murray (tb) | Schertzer,Hymie (as) | DePew,Bill (as) | Musso,Vido (ts) | Rollini,Arthur (ts) | Stacy,Jess (p) | Reuss,Allan (g) | Goodman,Harry (b) | Krupa,Gene (dr) | Fitzgerald,Ella (voc) | Mundy,Jimmy (arr)

Mildred Bailey With The Ellis Larkins Trio
That Ain't Right
NYC, rec. 20.2.1947
Bailey,Mildred (voc) | Larkins,Ellis (p) | Fields,Gene (g) | Peer,Beverley (b)

Lee Wiley With The Dean Kincaide Dixieland Band
Stars Fell On Alabama
NYC, rec. 12.6.1956
Wiley,Lee (voc) | Kincaide,Dean (bs) | Butterfield,Billy (tp) | Cutshall,Cutty (tb) | Hucko,Peanuts (cl) | Stein,Lou (p) | Galbraith,Barry (g) | Haggart,Bob (b) | Leeman,Cliff (dr)

Benny Goodman And His Orchestra
Loch Lomond
NYC, rec. 12.11.1937
Goodman,Benny (cl) | James,Harry (tp) | Griffin,Gordon (tp) | Elman,Ziggy (tp) | Ballard,Red (tb) | McEachern,Murray (tb) | Schertzer,Hymie (as) | Koenig,George (as) | Rollini,Arthur (ts) | Musso,Vido (ts) | Stacy,Jess (p) | Reuss,Allan (g) | Goodman,Harry (b) | Krupa,Gene (dr) | Tilton,Martha (voc) | Thornhill,Claude (arr)

Una Mae Carlisle Septet
There'll Be Some Changes Made
NYC, rec. 10.3.1941
Carlisle,Una Mae (voc) | Collins,Lester 'Shad' (tp) | Young,Lester (ts) | Hart,Clyde (p) | Collins,John (g) | Fenton,Nick (b) | West,Harold 'Doc' (dr)

Duke Ellington And His Famous Orchestra
I Got It Bad And That Ain't Good
Hollywood,CA, rec. 26.6.1941
Ellington,Duke (p,arr) | Jones,Wallace (tp) | Nance,Ray (tp) | Stewart,Rex (co) | Nanton,Joe 'Tricky Sam' (tb) | Brown,Lawrence (tb) | Tizol,Juan (v-tb) | Bigard,Barney (cl) | Hodges,Johnny (cl,ss,as) | Hardwicke,Otto (as,bass-s) | Webster,Ben (ts) | Carney,Harry (cl,as,bs) | Guy,Fred (g) | Blanton,Jimmy (b) | Greer,William 'Sonny' (dr) | Anderson,Ivie (voc)

Red Norvo And His Orchestra
I Sing The Blues
Los Angeles,CA, rec. 28.1.1958
Norvo,Red (vib,xylophone) | Fagerquist,Don (tp) | Leddy,Ed (tp) | Linn,Ray (tp) | Paladino,Don (tp) | Sims,Ray (tb) | Smith,Willie (as) | Land,Harold (ts) | Gentry,Chuck (bs) | Rowles,Jimmy (p) | Wyble,Jimmy (g) | Wooten,Red (b) | Lewis,Mel (dr) | Humes,Helen (voc)

Lena Horne With The Lou Bring Orchestra
Stormy Weather
Hollywood,CA, rec. 15.12.1941
Horne,Lena (voc) | Klein,Manny (tp) | Mayhew,Jack (sax) | Friedman,Morty (sax) | Rosati,Archie (sax) | Russell,Mischa (v) | Pisano,Nick (v) | Botkin,Perry (g) | Bernstein,Artie (b) | Freeman,Ned (arr) | Bring,Lou (cond)

Nina Simone-Bob Bushnell
My Man's Gone Now
NYC, rec. 5.1.1967
Simone,Nina (p,voc) | Bushnell,Bob (el-b)

Carmen McRae With The Shirley Horn Trio
Tenderly
NYC, rec. 12.-14.10.1990
McRae,Carmen (voc) | Horn,Shirley (p) | Ables,Charles (b) | Williams,Stephen E. 'Steve' (dr)

Monica Zetterlund With The Zoot Sims Quartet
He's My Guy
NYC, rec. 10.3.1960
Zetterlund,Monica (voc) | Sims,Zoot (ts) | Jones,Jimmie (p) | Hinton,Milt (b) | Johnson,Osie (dr)

Sarah Vaughan With Dizzy Gillespie And His Orchestra
Embraceable You
Live at Salle Pleyel,Paris,France, rec. 9.2.1953
Vaughan,Sarah (voc) | Gillespie,Dizzy (tp) | Graham,Bill (as,bs) | Legge,Wade (p) | Hackney,Lou (b) | Jones,Al (dr)

Helen Merrill And Her Band
Night And Day
Rome,Italy, rec. October-November 1960
Merrill,Helen (voc) | Rosso,Nino (tp) | Marinacci,Gino (fl,bs) | Umiliani,Piero (p) | Grillini,Enzo (g) | Pisano,Berto (b) | Conti,Sergio (dr)

2169657-2 | CD | Planet Jazz:Male Jazz Vocalists

Louis Armstrong And His Dixieland Seven
Do You Know What It Means To Miss New Orleans
Los Angeles,CA, rec. 17.10.1946
Armstrong,Louis (tp,voc) | Ory,Edward 'Kid' (tb) | Bigard,Barney (cl) | Beal,Charlie (p) | Scott,Bud (g) | Callender,Red (b) | Hall,Minor 'Ram' (dr)

Fats Waller And His Rhythm
I'm Gonna Sit Right Down And Write Myself A Letter
NYC, rec. 8.5.1935
Waller,Thomas 'Fats' (p,voc) | Autrey,Herman (tp) | Powell,Rudy (cl,as) | Casey,Al (g) | Turner,Charles (b) | Dial,Harry (dr)

Louis Armstrong And His All Stars
St.James Infirmary
Live at Town Hall,NYC, rec. 17.5.1947
Armstrong,Louis (tp,voc) | Teagarden,Jack (tb,voc) | Cary,Dick (p) | Haggart,Bob (b) | Catlett,Big Sid (dr)

Jelly Roll Morton's New Orleans Jazzmen
I Thought I Heard Buddy Bolden Say
NYC, rec. 14.9.1939
Morton,Jelly Roll (p,voc) | DeParis,Sidney (tp) | Jones,Claude (tb) | Nicholas,Albert (cl) | Bechet,Sidney (ss) | Caldwell,Happy (ts) | Lucie,Lawrence (g) | Braud,Wellman (b) | Singleton,Zutty (dr)

Wingy Mannone And His Orchestra
When My Sugar Walks Down The Street
NYC, rec. 6.9.1939
Mannone,Joe 'Wingy' (tp,voc) | Scott,Buck (tb) | Fetterer,Gus (cl) | Berry,Leon 'Chu' (ts) | Hughes,Ernie (p) | Julian,Zeb (g) | Jacobs,Sid (b) | Cole,William 'Cozy' (dr)

Artie Shaw And His Orchestra
Take Your Shoes Off Baby
Chicago,Ill, rec. 30.10.1941
Shaw,Artie (cl) | Page,Oran 'Hot Lips' (tp,voc) | Castle,Lee (tp) | Lipkins,Steve (tp) | Kaminsky,Max (tp) | Jenney,Jack (tb) | Samuels,Morey (tb) | Conniff,Ray (tb) | Robinson,Les (as) | Kinsey,Gene (as) | Auld,Georgie (ts) | Folus,Mickey (ts) | DiMaggio,Charlie (bs) | Guarnieri,Johnny (p) | Bryan,Mike (g) | McKimmey,Eddie (b) | Tough,Dave (dr)

Lionel Hampton And His Orchestra
On The Sunny Side Of The Street
NYC, rec. 26.4.1937
Hampton,Lionel (vib,voc) | Bailey,Buster (cl) | Hodges,Johnny (as) | Stacy,Jess (p) | Reuss,Allan (g) | Kirby,John (b) | Cole,William 'Cozy' (dr)

Joe Williams And Friends
Everyday I Have The Blues
Live at Newport,Rhode Island, rec. 5.7.1963
Williams,Joe (voc) | Terry,Clark (tp,fl-h) | McGhee,Howard (tp) | Hawkins,Coleman (ts) | Sims,Zoot (ts) | Mance,Junior[Julian C.] (p) | Cranshaw,Bob (b) | Roker,Granville 'Mickey' (dr)

Big Joe Turner And His Orchestra
Careless Love Blues
Los Angeles,CA, rec. 18.8.1969
Turner,Big Joe (voc) | Smith,George Harmonica (harm) | Butler,Artie (p) | Shelton,Louie (g) | Page,Gene (cond) | details unknown

Jimmy Rushing And His Band
Fine And Mellow
NYC, rec. 29.4.1971
Rushing,Jimmy (voc) | Nance,Ray (v,co) | Sims,Zoot (ts) | Frishberg,Dave (p,arr) | Hinton,Milt (b) | Lewis,Mel (dr)

Dizzy Gillespie And His Orchestra
I'm Be Boppin' Too
NYC, rec. 6.5.1949
Gillespie,Dizzy (tp,voc) | Cook,Willie (tp) | Harris,Little Benny (tp) | Wright,Elmon (tp) | Duryea,Andy (tb) | Hurt,Sam (tb) | Tarrant,Jesse (tb) | Brown,John (as) | Henry,Ernie (as) | Gales,Joe (ts) | Lateef,Yusef (ts) | Gibson,Al (bs) | Forman,James (p) | McKibbon,Al (b) | Stewart,Teddy (dr)

Lambert, Hendricks And Bavan
One O'Clock Jump
NYC, rec. 8.9.1962
Lambert,Dave (voc) | Hendricks,Jon (voc) | Bavan,Yolanda (voc) | Mahones,Gildo (p) | Tucker,George (b) | Smith,Jimmie (dr)

Jimmy Witherspoon With Jay McShann And His Band
Piney Brown Blues
NYC, rec. 4.12.1957
Witherspoon,Jimmy (voc) | McShann,Jay (p) | Copeland,Ray (tp) | Higginbotham,J.C. (tb) | Jefferson,Hilton (as) | Powell,Seldon (ts) | Henry,Haywood (bs) | Burrell,Kenny (g) | Ramey,Gene (b) | Alexander,Mousie (dr)

Cab Calloway And His Orchestra
It Ain't Necessarily So
NYC, rec. 5.12.1958
Calloway,Cab (ld,voc) | Glow,Bernie (tp) | Maxwell,Jimmy (tp) | Wilder,Joe (tp) | Green,Urbie (tb) | Welsch,Chauncey (tb) | Mitchell,Tom (tb) | Marowitz,Sam (reeds) | O'Kane,Charles (sax) | Richman,Abe 'Boomie' (reeds) | Donahue,Sam (ts) | Webb,Stanley (sax) | Jones,Hank (p) | Barksdale,Everett (g) | Hinton,Milt (b) | Heard,J.C. (dr) | Reisman,Joe (ld)

Tommy Dorsey And His Orchestra
East Of The Sun West Of The Moon
NYC, rec. 23.4.1940
Dorsey,Tommy (tb) | Berigan,Bunny (tp) | Linn,Ray (tp) | Dillard,John (tp) | Blake,Jimmy (tp) | Martin,Lowell (tb) | Jenkins,Les (tb) | Arus,George (tb) | Mince,Johnny (cl,as) | Schertzer,Hymie (as) | Stulce,Fred (as) | Mason,Paul (ts) | Lodice,Don (ts) | Bushkin,Joe (p) | Yocum,Clark (g) | Weiss,Sid (b) | Rich,Buddy (dr) | Sinatra,Frank (voc)

Louis Armstrong And His All Stars
Jack-Armstrong Blues
NYC, rec. 10.6.1947
Armstrong,Louis (tp,voc) | Hackett,Bobby (tp) | Teagarden,Jack (tb,voc) | Hucko,Peanuts (cl) | Caceres,Ernie (cl,bs) | Guarnieri,Johnny (p) | Casey,Al (g) | Hall,Al (b) | Cole,William 'Cozy' (dr)

Poise | Jazz Haus Musik

Poise 01 | CD | Teatime Vol.1
A Band Of Friends
Prolog | Gleißender Ruhm | Teetanz | Diary:26.11.1995 | Die Maus Und Die Auster | 1-2 Spoon | Es Ist Schön,Viel Zu Schön | Pic Du Midi D'Ossau | Mei | Diary:26.12.1995 | What Does The Snail Say? | Monollith | Planetenfahrer | Last Service | Diary:28.1.1996 | Die Drei Faulen | Better Than Anything | Der Zufallsgenerator III | Diary:25.2.1996 | No Title | Visur Vatnsenda-Rósu | Jöklabaen | Hvert Örstutt Spor | Diary:31.3.1996 | Sokrates:Der Skorpion Und Der Alligator | R | Aus:Philipp Keller 'Ärmliche Verhältnisse' | Diary:28.4.1996 | Epilog
Schmuckkästchen,Stadtgarten,Köln, rec. 1995-1996

Poise 02 | CD | Das Digitale Herz
Kodexx Sentimental
Digitales Herz(1) | Digitales Herz(2) | Re | Dein Herz(1) | Dein Herz(2) | Fressn(1) | Fressn(2) | Mein Herz | Herzleid | Bleibender Ruhm | Im Internet | Porno Hirn | Second Hand | Ich Bin Hi-Fi | Neue Stadt
Loft,Köln, rec. 14./15.12.1995
Kodexx Sentimental | Ritzenhoff,Jörg (org,recitation) | Raulf,Dirk (sax) | Peil,Roland (perc)

Poise 03 | CD | Die Welt Ist Immer Wieder Schön
Dirk Raulf Group
Die Welt Ist Immer Wieder Schön(Hörspiel-Collage)
Berlin/Köln, rec. 7.5.& 20.12.1995
Raulf,Dirk (b-cl,sax) | Anzenhofer,Thomas (recitation) | Willers,Andreas (g) | Heuss,Oliver (p,keyboards) | Manderscheid,Dieter (b) | Köllges,Frank (dr) | Schulte,Frank (electronics) | Ritzenhoff,Jörg (voc)

Poise 04 | CD | Vanitas
Sotto In Su
Invocation | Death Chant | Red Is My Blood | The Timeless Space | Revenge | Moonspell For Pleasure | A Full Moon Ritual | Sickness | Illumination | Epilog
Köln, rec. details unknown
Sotto In Su | Heberer,Thomas (tp) | Breuer,Reinhold (dr,perc) | Deyhim,Sussan (voc) | Tuchacek,Alexander (electronics) | Schulte,Frank (synth,concept.mix,records,sampling,tapes)

Poise 05 | CD | Kill Yr Darlins
Thomas Heberer
This Is A Hard Hat Area | Les Moutons(Su Le Lit) | Paul's Pal | Get Your Ticket Here | Buy This Record | This Is A Hard Hat Area(reprise remix) | The Gunslingers Delight | Where Is My Yellow Lighter? | Handic Apped Rabbits | M-M-M-M-Milkers | Tana
Heberer,Thomas (tp,computer,electronics,sampling)

Poise 06/2 | 2 CD | Teatime Vol.2
A Band Of Friends
Das Haus: | Prolog | Love Or Infatuation | You Leave Me Breathless | Moon Story(1-2) | Fugitive Fandangos | BB 9 | Bei Dir War Es Immer So Schön | Escapades For Twice | Tisch Und Bett | Reich Und Berühmt | Couch Potato | Solo Z | Moon Story(3) | Aus:Morgenstern-Lieder | BB 35 | Venedig | Die Stadt: | Prolog | As Time Goes By | Petra Vom Finanzamt | BB 14 | Handful Of Keys | Torrid Zone | Es Gescheh'n Noch Wunder | Girl From Ipanema(Garota De Ipanema) | Der Richter Brief | Ain't Misbehavin' | Unstable Symetry | Dialing In | BB 45 | Jesus Un St.Johänneken | Come Sunday | Come Rain Or Come Shine | Die Jodlerin Von Teheran | Epilog
Schmuckkästchen,Stadtgarten,Köln, rec. 1996-1997

Poise 07 | CD | Theater I (Bühnenmusik) | EAN 4028878000072
Dirk Raulf Group
Hermann Und Dorothea(Schauspielhaus Bochum) | Paco Und Die Tiere(Schauspielhaus Bochum) | Baal(Theater Oberhausen) | Maß Für Maß(Schauspielhaus Zürich) | Endstation Sehnsucht(Theater Oberhausen) | Viel Lärm Um Nichts(Schauspielhaus Graz)
rec. 1994-2000
Raulf,Dirk (sax,comp) | Engels,Jorg (tp) | Franck,Hinrich (keyboards) | Grabosch,Horst (tp) | Grimshaw,Stuart (b) | Hanschel,Roger (sax) | Lenardt,Jörg | Lüdemann,Hans (keyboards) | Manderscheid,Dieter (cello,b) | Neumann,Werner (g,el-g) | Peil,Roland (dr,perc) | Puntin,Claudio (reeds) | Schulte,Frank (electronics) | Shotham,Ramesh (perc) | Temur,Orhan (perc) | Wienstroer,Markus (g,el-g) | Wittek,Fritz (dr,perc)

Poise 08 | CD | Stella | EAN 4028878000089
Thomas Heberer
Stella | German Measles | Nuggets | Twins | Natalie | Seven | Sams | Kayak | Courses | Osmosis
Köln, rec. 2001
Heberer,Thomas (tp,computer,electronics,sampling)

Poise 09 | CD | Mouth | EAN 4028878000096
Najat(2002) | Nadja(2001) | Nods(2000) | Irene(2002) | Deeds(2002) | June(2002) | Liv(2001) | Bucket(2001) | Blue(2000) | Najat(2002 Reprise) | Selim(Coda 2000)
Köln, rec. 2000-2002
Heberer,Thomas (tp,computer,electronics,sampling)

Poise 10 | CD | Theater II(Bühnenmusik)
Dirk Raulf Group
Cymbeline(Schaupielhaus Bonn)
rec. 2001
Raulf,Dirk (comp) | Rodenkirchen,Norbert (fl) | Wienstroer,Markus (g,trumscheit) | Queck,Holger (voc)

Poise 11 | CD | Theater III(Bühnenmusik)
Dirk Raulf-Frank Shulte
Kampfhunde
rec. 2000
Raulf,Dirk (comp) | Schulte,Frank (comp,electronics)

Polydor | Universal Music Germany

521414-2 | CD | Getz/Gilberto
Getz-Gilberto Quintet
Girl From Ipanema(Garota De Ipanema) | Doralice | Para Machuchar Meu Conancao | Desafinado | Corcovado(Quiet Nights) | So Danco Samba(I Only Dance The Samba) | O Grande Amor | Vivo Sohando | Girl From Ipanema(Garota De Ipanema,45 rpm issue) | Corcovado(Quiet Nights,45rpm issue)
NYC, rec. 18./19.3.1963
Getz,Stan (ts) | Jobim,Antonio Carlos (p) | Gilberto,Joao (g,voc) | Williams,Tommy (b) | Banana,Milton (dr) | Gilberto,Astrud (voc)

543303-3 | CD | My Spanish Heart
Chick Corea And His Orchestra
Love Castle | The Gardens | Day Danse | My Spanish Heart | Night Street | The Hilltop | The Sky | Wind Danse | Prelude To El Bozo | El Bozo(part 1-3) | Spanish Fantasy(part 1-4) | The Clouds
Burbank,Los Angeles,CA, rec. October 1976
Corea,Chick (p,el-p,org,synth,footstomping,handclapping,voc) | Thomas,John (tp) | Rosenburg,John (tp) | Blumberg,Stuart (tp) | Mass,Ron (tb) | Clarke,Stanley (b,el-b) | Gadd,Steve (dr) | Alias,Don (perc) | Arriaga Quartet | Sacher,Barry (v) | Kupke,Connie (v) | Mukogava,Carol (viola) | Speltz,David (cello) | Morgan,Gayle (voc)

Chick Corea Quartet
Armando's Rhumba
Corea,Chick (p,handclapping) | Ponty,Jean-Luc (v) | Clarke,Stanley (el-b) | Walden,Narada Michael (handclapping)

543393-2 | CD | Night Train
Max Greger Quintet
Perdido | Harlem Nocturne | Route 66 | Will You Still Be Mine | Stardust | Cute | Night Train | I Got Rhythm | As Time Goes By | Jet Propulsion | In A Sentimental Mood | Take The 'A' Train | Misty | Flamingo | One O'Clock Jump | Caravan
München, rec. 13./14.10.1999
Greger,Max (ts) | Bailey,Benny (tp,voc) | Greger Jr.,Max (p,voc) | Knauer,Rocky (b) | Antolini,Charly (dr)

549581-2 | CD | Suenos Gitanos
The Rosenberg Trio
Moon Flower | The Shadow Of Your Smile
Oegstgeest,NL, rec. 2000
Rosenberg,Stochelo (g) | Rosenberg,Nou'che (g) | Rosenberg,Nonnie (b) | Corsen,Randal (p,keyboards) | Amuedo,Leonardo (g,el-b) | Rosales,Gerardo (perc)

Moonlight Serenade
Rosenberg,Stochelo (g) | Rosenberg,Nou'che (g) | Rosenberg,Nonnie (b) | Thielemans,Jean 'Toots' (harm) | Corsen,Randal (p,keyboards) | Amuedo,Leonardo (g,el-b) | Rosales,Gerardo (perc)

Bolero Triste
Rosenberg,Stochelo (g) | Rosenberg,Nou'che (g) | Rosenberg,Nonnie (b) | Thielemans,Jean 'Toots' (harm) | Amuedo,Leonardo (g,el-b) | Rosales,Gerardo (perc)

Party In The Ghetto | Les Yeux Noirs | Tocata Para Billy Blanco
Rosenberg,Stochelo (g) | Rosenberg,Nou'che (g) | Rosenberg,Nonnie (b) | Beets,Peter (p) | Amuedo,Leonardo (g,el-b) | Rosales,Gerardo (perc)

Mediterranean Sundance | Pepito | Gitano | Troublant Bolero | Just Relax
Rosenberg,Stochelo (g) | Rosenberg,Nou'che (g) | Rosenberg,Nonnie (b) | Amuedo,Leonardo (g,el-b) | Rosales,Gerardo (perc)

557115-2 | 2 CD | Light As A Feather
Chick Corea And Return To Forever
You're Everything | Light As A Feather | Captain Marvel | 500 Miles High | Children's Song | Spain | Matrix | Light As A Feather(alt.take) | 500 Miles High(alt.take) | Children's Song(alt.take) | Spain(alt.take 1) | Spain(alt.take 2) | What Game Shall We Play Today | What Game Shall We Play Today(alt.take 1) | What Game Shall We Play Today(alt.take 2) | What Game Shall We Play Today(alt.take 3)
London,GB, rec. October 1972
Return To Forever | Corea,Chick (el-p) | Farrell,Joe (fl,ts) | Clarke,Stanley (b) | Moreira,Airto (dr,perc) | Purim,Flora (perc,voc)

825086-2 PMS | CD | The Silver Collection: Toots Thielemans
Toots Thielemans Quintet
I Do It For Your Love | My Little Suede Shoes
Laren,Holland, rec. 10.4.1975
Thielemans,Jean 'Toots' (g,harm) | Franken,Rob (keyboards) | Overgaauw,Wim (g) | Orsted-Pedersen,Niels-Henning (b) | Castellucci,Bruno (dr)

Toots Thielemans
You're My Blues Machine
Laren,Holland, rec. 4.4.1974
Thielemans,Jean 'Toots' (g-solo)

Toots Thielemans Quintet
Dirty Old Man | Theme From 'Summer Of 42' (The Summer Knows) | Bluesette
Thielemans,Jean 'Toots' (g,harm) | Franken,Rob (el-p,org) | Scholten,Joop (g) | Kaihatu,Victor (b) | Overweg,Evert (dr)

Toots Thielemans
Muskrat Ramble | The Mooche
Laren,Holland, rec. 10.4.1974
Thielemans,Jean 'Toots' (g-solo)

Toots Thielemans With The Ruud Bos Orchestra
What Are You Doing The Rest Of Your Life | The Gentle Rain (Chuva Delicada) | The First Time Ever I Saw Your Face | Big Bossa | Ben | You've Got It Bad Girl | Love Remembered | Old Friend
rec. details unknown
Thielemans,Jean 'Toots' (harm) | Povel,Ferdinand (ts) | Bos,Ruud (cond,arr) | details unknown

825206-2 | CD | Where Have I Known You Before
Return To Forever
Vulcan Worlds | Where Have I Loved You Before | The Shadow Of Lo | Where Have I Danced With You Before | Beyond The Seventh Galaxy | Earth Juice | Where Have I Known You Before | Song Of The Pharoah Kings
NYC, rec. July/Aug.1974
Return To Forever | Corea,Chick (p,el-p,org,synth,perc,clavinet) | Di Meola,Al (g,el-g) | Clarke,Stanley (org,bell-tree,chimes,el-b) | White,Lenny (dr,perc,congas,bongos)

825336-2 | CD | Hymn Of The Seventh Galaxy
Hymn Of The Seventh Galaxy | After The Cosmic Rain | Captain Senor Mouse | Theme To The Mothership | Space Circus(part 1&2) | The Game Maker
NYC, rec. August 1973
Return To Forever | Corea,Chick (p,el-p,org,gongs,harpsichord) | Connors,Bill (g,el-g) | Clarke,Stanley (bell-tree,el-b) | White,Lenny (dr,perc,congas,bongos)

833394-2 | CD | Byrd In Paris Vol.1
Donald Byrd Quintet
Dear Old Stockholm | Paul's Pal | Flute Blues | Ray's Idea | The Blues Walk
Live at The Olympia,Paris,France, rec. 22.10.1958
Byrd,Donald (tp) | Jaspar,Bobby (ts) | Davis Jr.,Walter (p) | Watkins,Doug (b) | Taylor,Arthur 'Art' (dr)

835680-2 | CD | An Evening Wirh Chick Corea & Herbie Hancock
Chick Corea-Herbie Hancock Duo
Homecoming | Ostinato | The Hook | Bouquet | Maiden Voyage | La Fiesta
Live at San Francisco/Los Angeles & Ann Arbor,CA, rec. Feb.1978
Corea,Chick (p) | Hancock,Herbie (p)

841598-2 | CD | Extrapolation
John McLaughlin Quartet
Extrapolation | It's Funny | Argen's Bag | Pete The Poet | This Is For Us To Share | Spectrum | Binky's Beam | Really You Know | Two For Two | Peace Piece
London,GB, rec. 18.1.1969
McLaughlin,John (g,el-g) | Surman,John (ss,bs) | Odges,Brian (b) | Oxley,Tony (dr)

847913-2 | CD | Dee Dee Bridgewater In Montreux | EAN 042284791328
Dee Dee Bridgewater With Her Trio
All Of Me | How Insensitive(Insensatez) | Just Friends | A Child Is Born | Strange Fruit | A Night In Tunisia | Horace Silver Medley: | Sister Sadie- | Next Time I Fall In Love- | Senor Blues-
Montreux,CH, rec. 18.7.1990
Bridgewater,Dee Dee (voc) | Van Den Brink,Bert (p) | Van De Geyn,Hein (b) | Ceccarelli,André (dr)

Prestige | ZYX Music GmbH

16 PCD 4405-2 | 16 CD | John Coltrane-The Prestige Recordings
Sonny Rollins Quintet
Tenor Madness
Hackensack,NJ, rec. 24.5.1956
Rollins,Sonny (ts) | Coltrane,John (ts) | Garland,Red (p) | Chambers,Paul (b) | Jones,Philly Joe (dr)

Elmo Hope Sextet
Weeja | Polka Dots And Moonbeams | On It | Avalon
Hackensack,NJ, rec. 7.5.1956
Hope,Elmo (p) | Byrd,Donald (tp) | Coltrane,John (ts) | Mobley,Hank (ts) | Chambers,Paul (b) | Jones,Philly Joe (dr)

Prestige All Stars
Tenor Conclave | How Deep Is The Ocean | Just You Just Me | Bob's Boys
Hackensack,NJ, rec. 7.9.1956
Prestige All Stars | Coltrane,John (ts) | Mobley,Hank (ts) | Cohn,Al (ts) | Sims,Zoot (ts) | Garland,Red (p) | Chambers,Paul (b) | Taylor,Arthur 'Art' (dr)

Tadd Dameron Quartet
Mating Call | Soultrane | Gnid | Super Jet | On A Misty Night | Romas
Hackensack,NJ, rec. 30.11.1956
Dameron,Tadd (p) | Coltrane,John (ts) | Simmons,John (b) | Jones,Philly Joe (dr)

Prestige All Stars
Soul Eyes | Anatomy | Interplay | Light Blue
Hackensack,NJ, rec. 22.3.1957
Prestige All Stars | Sulieman[Leonard Graham],Idrees (tp) | Young,Webster (co) | Coltrane,John (ts) | Jaspar,Bobby (ts) | Waldron,Mal (p) | Burrell,Kenny (g) | Chambers,Paul (b) | Taylor,Arthur 'Art' (dr)

Taylor's Wailers
C.T.A.
Taylor,Arthur 'Art' (dr) | Coltrane,John (ts) | Garland,Red (p) | Chambers,Paul (b)

Prestige All Stars
Eclypso | Solacium | Minor Mishap | Tommy's Time
Hackensack,NJ, rec. 18.4.1957
Prestige All Stars | Sulieman[Leonard Graham],Idrees (tp) | Coltrane,John (ts) | Flanagan,Tommy (p) | Burrell,Kenny (g) | Watkins,Doug (b) | Hayes,Louis (dr)

Dakar | Mary's Blues | Route 4 | Velvet Scene | Witches Pit | Catwalk
Hackensack,NJ, rec. 20.4.1957
Prestige All Stars | Coltrane,John (ts) | Payne,Cecil (bs) | Adams,Pepper (bs) | Waldron,Mal (p) | Watkins,Doug (b) | Taylor,Arthur 'Art' (dr)

Mal Waldron Sextet
Potpourri | J.M.'s Dream Doll | Don't Explain | Falling In Love With Love | Blue Calypso
Hackensack,NJ, rec. 19.4.1957
Waldron,Mal (p) | Hardman,Bill (tp) | McLean,Jackie (as) | Coltrane,John (ts) | Euell,Julian (b) | Taylor,Arthur 'Art' (dr)

The Way You Look Tonight | From This Moment On | One By One
Hackensack,NJ, rec. 17.5.1957
Waldron,Mal (p) | Sulieman[Leonard Graham],Idrees (tp) | Shihab,Sahib (as,bs) | Coltrane,John (ts) | Euell,Julian (b) | Thigpen,Ed (dr)

John Coltrane-Paul Quinichette Quintet
Cattin' | Anatomy | Vodka | Sunday
Coltrane,John (ts) | Quinichette,Paul (ts) | Waldron,Mal (p) | Euell,Julian (b) | Thigpen,Ed (dr)

John Coltrane Quintet
While My Lady Sleeps
Hackensack,NJ, rec. 31.5.1957
Coltrane,John (ts) | Splawn,Johnny (tp) | Waldron,Mal (p) | Chambers,Paul (b) | Heath,Albert 'Tootie' (dr)

John Coltrane Sextet
Straight Street | Chronic Blues
Coltrane,John (ts) | Splawn,Johnny (tp) | Shihab,Sahib (bs) | Waldron,Mal (p) | Chambers,Paul (b) | Heath,Albert 'Tootie' (dr)

Bakai
Coltrane,John (ts) | Splawn,Johnny (tp) | Shihab,Sahib (bs) | Garland,Red (p) | Chambers,Paul (b) | Heath,Albert 'Tootie' (dr)

John Coltrane Quartet
Violets For Your Furs | Time Was | I Hear A Rhapsody
Coltrane,John (ts) | Garland,Red (p) | Chambers,Paul (b) | Heath,Albert 'Tootie' (dr)

John Coltrane Trio
Trane's Slow Blues | Slowtrane | Like Someone In Love | I Love You
Hackensack,NJ, rec. 18.8.1957
Coltrane,John (ts) | May,Earl (b) | Taylor,Arthur 'Art' (dr)

Prestige All Stars
Dealin'(take 1) | Dealin'(take 2) | Wheelin'(take 1) | Wheelin'(take 2) | Robbin's Nest | Things Ain't What They Used To Be
Hackensack,NJ, rec. 20.9.1957
Prestige All Stars | Wess,Frank (as,ts) | Coltrane,John (ts) | Quinichette,Paul (ts) | Waldron,Mal (p) | Watkins,Doug (b) | Taylor,Arthur 'Art' (dr)

John Coltrane With The Red Garland Trio
You Leave Me Breathless | Bass Blues | Soft Lights And Sweet Music | Traneing In | Slow Dance
Hackensack,NJ, rec. 23.8.1957
Coltrane,John (ts) | Garland,Red (p) | Chambers,Paul (b) | Taylor,Arthur 'Art' (dr)

Red Garland Quintet
Our Delight | They Can't Take That Away From Me | Woody'n You | I Got It Bad And That Ain't Good | Undecided | Soul Junction | What Is There To Say | Birk's Works | Halle Hallelujah | All Morning Long
Hackensack,NJ, rec. 15.11.1957
Garland,Red (p) | Byrd,Donald (tp) | Coltrane,John (ts) | Nasser,Jamil[George Joyner] (b) | Taylor,Arthur 'Art' (dr)

Billie's Bounce | In My Solitude | Two Bass Hit | Soft Winds | Lazy Mae
Hackensack,NJ, rec. 13.12.1957
Garland,Red (p) | Byrd,Donald (tp) | Coltrane,John (ts) | Nasser,Jamil[George Joyner] (b) | Taylor,Arthur 'Art' (dr)

Ray Draper Quintet
Under Paris Skies | Two Sons | Clifford's Kappa | Filide | Paul's Pal
Hackensack,NJ, rec. 20.12.1957
Draper,Ray (tuba) | Coltrane,John (ts) | Coggins,Gil (p) | DeBrest,Jimmy 'Spanky' (b) | Ritchie,Larry (dr)

Gene Ammons And His All Stars
Ammons' Joy | Groove Blues | The Real McCoy
Hackensack,NJ, rec. 3.1.1958
Ammons,Gene (ts) | Richardson,Jerome (fl) | Coltrane,John (as) | Quinichette,Paul (ts) | Adams,Pepper (bs) | Waldron,Mal (p) | Nasser,Jamil[George Joyner] (b) | Taylor,Arthur 'Art' (dr)

It Might As Well Be Spring
Ammons,Gene (ts) | Coltrane,John (as) | Waldron,Mal (p) | Nasser,Jamil[George Joyner] (b) | Taylor,Arthur 'Art' (dr)

John Coltrane Quintet
Lush Life | The Believer | Nakatini Serenade | Come Rain Or Come Shine | Lover
Hackensack,NJ, rec. 10.1.1958
Coltrane,John (ts) | Byrd,Donald (tp) | Garland,Red (p) | Chambers,Paul (b) | Hayes,Louis (dr)

John Coltrane Quartet
Russian Lullaby | Theme For Ernie | You Say You Care | Good Bait | I Want To Talk About You
Hackensack,NJ, rec. 7.2.1958
Coltrane,John (ts) | Garland,Red (p) | Chambers,Paul (b) | Taylor,Arthur 'Art' (dr)

Kenny Burrell Quintet
Lyresto | Why Was I Born | Freight Train | I Never Knew | Big Paul
Hackensack,NJ, rec. 7.3.1958
Burrell,Kenny (g) | Coltrane,John (ts) | Garland,Red (p) | Chambers,Paul (b) | Cobb,Jimmy (dr)

John Coltrane Quartet
Rise 'N' Shine | I See Your Face Before Me | If There Is Someone Lovelier Than You | Little Malonae | By The Numbers
Hackensack,NJ, rec. 26.3.1958
Coltrane,John (ts) | Garland,Red (p) | Chambers,Paul (b) | Taylor,Arthur 'Art' (dr)

John Coltrane Quintet

Black Pearls | Lover Come Back To Me | Sweet Sapphire Blues
Hackensack,NJ, rec. 23.5.1958
Coltrane,John (ts) | Byrd,Donald (tp) | Garland,Red (p) | Chambers,Paul (b) | Taylor,Arthur 'Art' (dr)
Spring Is Here | Invitation | I'm A Dreamer Aren't We All | Love Thy Neighbor | Don't Take Your Love From Me | Stardust | My Idea | I'll Get By(As Long As I Have You)
Hackensack,NJ, rec. 11.7.1958
Coltrane,John (ts) | Harden,Wilbur (tp,fl-h) | Garland,Red (p) | Chambers,Paul (b) | Cobb,Jimmy (dr)
Do I Love You Because You're Beautiful | Then I'll Be Tired Of You | Something I Dreamed Last Night
Hackensack,NJ, rec. 26.12.1958
Coltrane,John (ts) | Hubbard,Freddie (tp) | Garland,Red (p) | Chambers,Paul (b) | Taylor,Arthur 'Art' (dr)
John Coltrane Quartet
Bahia | Time After Time
Coltrane,John (ts) | Garland,Red (p) | Chambers,Paul (b) | Taylor,Arthur 'Art' (dr)
John Coltrane Trio
Goldsboro Express
Coltrane,John (ts) | Chambers,Paul (b) | Taylor,Arthur 'Art' (dr)

2PCD 24073-2 | 2 CD | Carnegie Hall Concert December 1944
Duke Ellington And His Orchestra
Blutopia | Midriff | Creole Love Call | Suddenly It Jumped | Pitter Panther Patter | It Don't Mean A Thing If It Ain't Got That Swing | Things Ain't What They Used To Be | Perfume Suite: | Introduction | Sonata- | Strange Feeling- | Dancers In Love- | Coloratura- | Black Brown And Beige: | The Work Song- | The Blues- | Three Dances(West Indian Dance-Creamy Brown-Emancipation Celebration)- | Come Sunday- | The Mood To Be Wooed | Blue Cellophane | Blue Skies(Trumpets No End) | Frankie And Johnny
Live at Carnegie Hall,NYC, rec. 19.12.1944
Ellington,Duke (p,arr) | Stewart,Rex (tp) | Jordan,Taft (tp) | Anderson,Cat (tp) | Hemphill,Shelton (tp) | Nance,Ray (tp,v) | Nanton,Joe 'Tricky Sam' (tb) | Brown,Lawrence (tb) | Jones,Claude (tb) | Hamilton,Jimmy (cl,ts) | Hardwicke,Otto (as) | Hodges,Johnny (as) | Sears,Al (ts) | Carney,Harry (cl,b-cl,bs) | Guy,Fred (g) | Raglin,Alvin 'Junior' (b) | Brown,Hillard (dr) | Davis,Kay (voc) | Ellington,Marie (voc) | Hibbler,Al (voc) | Strayhorn,Billy (arr)

2PCD 24074-2 | 2 CD | Carnegie Hall Concert January 1946
Caravan | In A Mellow Tone | Solid Old Man | Black Brown And Beige (Excerpts) | Come Sunday(Spiritual)- | The Work Song- | The Blues- | Rugged Romeo | Sono | Air-Conditioned Jungle | Pitter Panther Patter | Take The 'A' Train | A Tonal Group: | Mello-Ditti- | Fugue-A-Ditty- | Jam-A-Ditty- | Magenta Haze | Diminuendo And Crescendo In Blue- | Transblucency- | Crescendo In Blue | Suburbanite | I'm Just A Lucky So-And-So | Riffin' Drill
Live at Carnegie Hall,NYC, rec. 4.1.1946
Ellington,Duke (p,arr) | Jordan,Taft (tp) | Anderson,Cat (tp) | Williams,Francis (tp) | Hemphill,Shelton (tp) | Brown,Lawrence (tb) | Jones,Claude (tb) | DeParis,Wilbur (tb) | Hodges,Johnny (as) | Hardwicke,Otto (as) | Hamilton,Jimmy (cl,ts) | Sears,Al (ts) | Carney,Harry (cl,b-cl,bs) | Lucas,Al (g) | Pettiford,Oscar (b) | Greer,William 'Sonny' (dr) | Sherrill,Joya (voc) | Davis,Kay (voc) | Hibbler,Al (voc) | Strayhorn,Billy (arr)

2PCD 24075-2 | 2 CD | Carnegie Hall Concert December 1947
The New Look(Snibor) | Blue Serge | Triple Play | Harlem Air Shaft | A Johnny Hodges Medley: | Wanderlust- | Junior Hop- | Jeep's Blues- | Jeep Is Jumpin'- | Squatty Roo- | The Mood To Be Wooed- | Mella Brava | Kickapoo Joy Juice | On A Turquoise Cloud | Bakiff | Cotton Tail | Liberian Suite: | Dance No.1 | Dance No.2 | Dance No.3 | Dance No.4 | Dance No.5 | Theme Medley: | East St.Louis Toodle-Oo- | Echoes Of Harlem- | Black And Tan Fantasy- | Things Ain't What They Used To Be- | Basso Profundo | New York City Blues | The Clothed Woman | Trumpets No End(Blue Skies)
Live at Carnegie Hall,NYC, rec. 27.12.1947
Ellington,Duke (p,arr) | Baker,Harold 'Shorty' (tp) | Killian,Al (tp) | Williams,Francis (tp) | Hemphill,Shelton (tp) | Nance,Ray (tp,v) | Brown,Lawrence (tb) | Jones,Claude (tb) | Glenn,Tyree (tb,vib) | Hamilton,Jimmy (cl,ts) | Procope,Russell (cl,as) | Hodges,Johnny (as) | Sears,Al (ts) | Carney,Harry (b-cl,bs) | Guy,Fred (g) | Pettiford,Oscar (b) | Raglin,Alvin 'Junior' (b) | Greer,William 'Sonny' (dr) | Davis,Kay (voc) | Hibbler,Al (voc) | Strayhorn,Billy (arr)

2PCD 34004-2 | 2 CD | Carnegie Hall Concert January 1943
The Star Spangled Banner | Black And Tan Fantasy | Rockin' In Rhythm | Moon Mist | Jumpin' Punkins | Portrait Of Bert Williams | Portrait Of Bojangles | Portrait Of Florence Mills(Black Beauty) | Ko-Ko | Dirge | Stomp(Johnny Come Lately) | Are You Stickin' | Black Brown And Beige: | First Movement-Black- | Second Movement-Brown- | Third Movement-Beige- | Bakiff | Jack The Bear | Blue Belles Of Harlem | Cotton Tail | Day Dream | Boy Meets Horn | Rose Of The Rio Grande | Don't Get Around Much Anymore | Goin' Up | Mood Indigo
Live at Carnegie Hall,NYC, rec. 23.1.1943
Ellington,Duke (p,arr) | Stewart,Rex (tp) | Baker,Harold 'Shorty' (tp) | Jones,Wallace (tp) | Nance,Ray (tp,v) | Nanton,Joe 'Tricky Sam' (tb) | Tizol,Juan (tb) | Brown,Lawrence (tb) | Hodges,Johnny (as) | Hardwicke,Otto (as) | Webster,Ben (ts) | Haughton,Chauncey (ts) | Carney,Harry (bs) | Guy,Fred (g) | Raglin,Alvin 'Junior' (b) | Greer,William 'Sonny' (dr) | Roche,Betty (voc) | Strayhorn,Billy (arr)

3 PRCD 4428-2 | 3 CD | Thelonious Monk:The Complete Prestige Recordings
Coleman Hawkins Quartet
Flyin' Hawk | Recollections | Drifting On A Reed | On The Bean
NYC, rec. 19.10.1944
Hawkins,Coleman (ts) | Monk,Thelonious (p) | Robinson,Edward 'Bass' (b) | Best,Denzil (dr)
Thelonious Monk Trio
Bye-Ya | Monk's Dream | Sweet And Lovely | Little Rootie Tootie
NYC, rec. 15.10.1952
Monk,Thelonious (p) | Mapp,Gary (b) | Blakey,Art (dr)
Bemsha Swing | Reflections | These Foolish Things Remind Me On You | Trinkle Tinkle
NYC, rec. 18.12.1952
Monk,Thelonious (p) | Mapp,Gary (b) | Roach,Max (dr)
Thelonious Monk Quintet
Think Of One | Let's Call This | Think Of One(alt.take) | Friday The 13th
NYC, rec. 13.11.1953
Monk,Thelonious (p) | Rollins,Sonny (ts) | Watkins,Julius (fr-h) | Heath,Percy (b) | Jones,Willie (dr)
We See | Locomotive | Smoke Gets In Your Eyes | Hackensack
Hackensack,NJ, rec. 11.5.1954
Monk,Thelonious (p) | Copeland,Ray (tp) | Foster,Frank (ts) | Russell,Curly (b) | Blakey,Art (dr)
Thelonious Monk Trio
Nutty | Work | Blue Monk
Hackensack,NJ, rec. 22.9.1954
Monk,Thelonious (p) | Heath,Percy (b) | Blakey,Art (dr)
Thelonious Monk
Just A Gigolo
Monk,Thelonious (p-solo)
Sonny Rollins Quartet
I Want To Be Happy | The Way You Look Tonight | More Than You Know
Hackensack,NJ, rec. 25.10.1954
Rollins,Sonny (ts) | Monk,Thelonious (p) | Potter,Tommy (b) | Taylor,Arthur 'Art' (dr)
Miles Davis Quintet
Bag's Groove | Bemsha Swing | The Man I Love | Swing Spring | Bag's Groove(alt.take) | The Man I Love(alt.take)
Hackensack,NJ, rec. 24.12.1954
Davis,Miles (tp) | Jackson,Milt (vib) | Monk,Thelonious (p) | Heath,Percy (b) | Clarke,Kenny (dr)

4PRCD 4438-2 | 4 CD | The Complete Modern Jazz Quartet Prestige & Pablo Recordings | EAN 090204922901
Modern Jazz Quartet
All The Things You Are | La Ronde | Vendome | Rose Of The Rio Grande
NYC, rec. 22.12.1952
MJQ (Modern Jazz Quartet) | Jackson,Milt (vib) | Lewis,John (p) | Heath,Percy (b) | Clarke,Kenny (dr)
The Queen's Fancy | Delauney's Dilemma | Autumn In New York | But Not For Me
NYC, rec. 25.6.1953
MJQ (Modern Jazz Quartet) | Jackson,Milt (vib) | Lewis,John (p) | Heath,Percy (b) | Clarke,Kenny (dr)
Sonny Rollins With The Modern Jazz Quartet
In A Sentimental Mood | The Stopper | Almost Like Being In Love | No Moe
NYC, rec. 7.10.1953
Rollins,Sonny (ts) | MJQ (Modern Jazz Quartet) | Jackson,Milt (vib) | Lewis,John (p) | Heath,Percy (b) | Clarke,Kenny (dr)
Modern Jazz Quartet
Django | One Bass Hit | Milano
Hackensack,NJ, rec. 23.12.1954
MJQ (Modern Jazz Quartet) | Jackson,Milt (vib) | Lewis,John (p) | Heath,Percy (b) | Clarke,Kenny (dr)
La Ronde Suite
Hackensack,NJ, rec. 9.1.1955
MJQ (Modern Jazz Quartet) | Jackson,Milt (vib) | Lewis,John (p) | Heath,Percy (b) | Clarke,Kenny (dr)
Ralph's New Blues | All Of You | I'll Remember April | Gershwin Medley: | Soon- | For You For Me For Evermore- | Love Walked In- | Our Love Is Here To Stay- | Concorde | Softly As In A Morning Sunrise
Hackensack,NJ, rec. 2.7.1955
MJQ (Modern Jazz Quartet) | Jackson,Milt (vib) | Lewis,John (p) | Heath,Percy (b) | Kay,Connie (dr)
Softly As In A Morning Sunrise | The Cylinder | Really True Blues | The Golden Striker | Odds Against Tomorrow | The Jasmine Tree | Bag's Groove | Django
Live at Budokan, Tokyo, Japan, rec. 19./20.10.1981
MJQ (Modern Jazz Quartet) | Jackson,Milt (vib) | Lewis,John (p) | Heath,Percy (b) | Kay,Connie (dr)
Django | The Jasmine Tree | Odds Against Tomorrow | The Cylinder | The Martyr | Really True Blues | Monterey Mist | Bags New Groove | Woody'n You
Live at The Montreux Jazz Festival, rec. 25.7.1982
MJQ (Modern Jazz Quartet) | Jackson,Milt (vib) | Lewis,John (p) | Heath,Percy (b) | Kay,Connie (dr)
Echoes | The Watergate Blues | The Horn Pipe | Connie's Blues | Sacha's March | That Slavic Smile
NYC, rec. 5.3.1984
MJQ (Modern Jazz Quartet) | Jackson,Milt (vib) | Lewis,John (p) | Heath,Percy (b) | Kay,Connie (dr)
Reunion Blues | D And E Blues(alt.take) | Rockin' In Rhythm(alt.take)
NYC, rec. 4.6.1985
MJQ (Modern Jazz Quartet) | Jackson,Milt (vib) | Lewis,John (p) | Heath,Percy (b) | Kay,Connie (dr)
Valeria | Le Cannet | Nature Boy | Milano | Topsy | D And E Blues
NYC, rec. 5.6.1985
MJQ (Modern Jazz Quartet) | Jackson,Milt (vib) | Lewis,John (p) | Heath,Percy (b) | Kay,Connie (dr)

9 PRCD-4418-2 | 9 CD | Eric Dolphy:The Complete Prestige Recordings
Eric Dolphy Quintet
G.W. | On Green Dolphin Street | Les | 245 | Glad To Be Unhappy | Miss Toni | April Fool | GW(alt.take) | 245(alt.take)
Englewood Cliffs,NJ, rec. 1.4.1960
Dolphy,Eric (fl,b-cl,as) | Hubbard,Freddie (tp) | Byard,Jaki (p) | Tucker,George (b) | Haynes,Roy (dr)
Oliver Nelson Sextet
Screamin' The Blues | March On March On | The Drive | The Meetin' | Three Seconds | Alto-Itis
Englewood Cliffs,NJ, rec. 27.5.1960
Nelson,Oliver (as,ts) | Williams,Richard (tp) | Dolphy,Eric (b-cl,as) | Wyands,Richard (p) | Duvivier,George (b) | Haynes,Roy (dr)
Ken McIntyre Quintet feat.Eric Dolphy
Lautir | Curtsy | Geo's Tune | They All Laughed | Head Shakin' | Diana
Englewood Cliffs,NJ, rec. 28.6.1960
McIntyre,Ken (fl,as) | Dolphy,Eric (fl,b-cl,as) | Bishop Jr.,Walter (p) | Jones,Sam (b) | Taylor,Arthur 'Art' (dr)
Eric Dolphy Quartet
Out There | Serene | The Baron | Eclipse | 17 West | Sketch Of Melba | Feather
Englewood Cliffs,NJ, rec. 15.8.1960
Dolphy,Eric (fl,cl,b-cl,as) | Carter,Ron (cello) | Duvivier,George (b) | Haynes,Roy (dr)
The Latin Jazz Quintet Plus Guest: Eric Dolphy
Caribé | Blues In 6-8 | First Bass Line | Mambo Ricci | Spring Is Here | Sunday Go Meetin'
Englewood Cliffs,NJ, rec. 19.8.1960
Latin Jazz Quintet,The | Dolphy,Eric (fl,b-cl,as) | Simons,Charles (vib) | Casey,Gene (p) | Ellington,Bill (b) | Amalbert,Juan (conga) | Ramos,Manny (dr,timbales)
Eddie Lockjaw Davis And His Orchestra
Trane Whistle | Whole Nelson | You Are Too Beautiful | Stolen Moments | Walk Away | Jaws
Englewood Cliffs,NJ, rec. 20.9.1960
Davis,Eddie 'Lockjaw' (ts) | Terry,Clark (tp) | Williams,Richard (tp) | Bryant,Bobby (tp) | Liston,Melba (tb) | Cleveland,Jimmy (tb) | Dolphy,Eric (as) | Nelson,Oliver (as) | Richardson,Jerome (ts) | Ashton,Bob (ts) | Barrow,George (bs) | Wyands,Richard (p) | Marshall,Wendell (b) | Haynes,Roy (dr)
Eric Dolphy-Booker Little Quintet
Mrs.Parker Of K.C. | Ode To Charlie Parker | Far Cry | Left Alone | It's Magic | Serene
Englewood Cliffs,NJ, rec. 21.12.1960
Dolphy,Eric (fl,b-cl,as) | Little,Booker (tp) | Byard,Jaki (p) | Carter,Ron (b) | Haynes,Roy (dr)
Eric Dolphy
Tenderly
Dolphy,Eric (as-solo)
Oliver Nelson Quintet
Images | Six And Four | Mama Lou | Ralph's New Blues | Straight Ahead | 111-44
Englewood Cliffs,NJ, rec. 1.3.1961
Nelson,Oliver (cl,as,ts) | Dolphy,Eric (fl,b-cl,as) | Wyands,Richard (p) | Duvivier,George (b) | Haynes,Roy (dr)
Ron Carter Quintet
Rally | Bass Duet | Softly As In A Morning Sunrise | Where? | Yes Indeed | Saucer Eyes
Englewood Cliffs,NJ, rec. 20.6.1961
Carter,Ron (cello,b) | Dolphy,Eric (fl,b-cl,as) | Waldron,Mal (p) | Duvivier,George (b) | Persip,Charles (dr)
Mal Waldron Sextet
Status Seeking | Duquility | Thirteen | We Diddit | Warm Canto | Warp And Woof | Fire Waltz
Englewood Cliffs,NJ, rec. 27.6.1961
Waldron,Mal (p) | Dolphy,Eric (cl,as) | Ervin,Booker (ts) | Carter,Ron (cello) | Benjamin,Joe (b) | Persip,Charles (dr)
Eric Dophy Quintet
Like Someone In Love | God Bless The Child | Aggression | Fire Waltz | Bee Vamp | The Prophet | Booker's Waltz | Status Seeking | Number Eight | Bee Vamp(alt.take)
Live at The Five Spot Cafe,NYC, rec. 16.7.1961
Dolphy,Eric (fl,b-cl,as) | Little,Booker (tp) | Waldron,Mal (p) | Davis,Richard (b) | Blackwell,Ed (dr)
Eric Dolphy With Erik Moseholm's Trio
Don't Blame Me | When Lights Are Low | Don't Blame Me(alt.take)
Live at The Berlingske Has,Copenhagen, rec. 6.9.1961
Dolphy,Eric (fl,as) | Moseholm,Erik (b) | Axen,Bent (p) | Elniff,Jorn (dr)
Les | The Way You Look Tonight | Woody'n You | Laura | Glad To Be Unhappy | In The Blues (1-2-3) | Hi Fly | Oleo
Copenhagen,Denmark, rec. 8.9.1961
Dolphy,Eric (fl,as) | Moseholm,Erik (b) | Axen,Bent (p) | Elniff,Jorn (dr)
Eric Dolphy-Chuck Israels
Hi Fly
Dolphy,Eric (fl) | Israels,Chuck (b)
Eric Dolphy
God Bless The Child
Dolphy,Eric (b-cl-solo)

PCD 11018-2 | CD | L.T.D.
Dexter Gordon Quartet
Broadway | Boston Bernie | In A Sentimental Mood | Blues Up And Down
Live at The Famous Ballroom,Baltimore.MD, rec. 4.5.1969
Gordon,Dexter (ts) | Timmons,Bobby (p) | Gaskin,Victor (b) | Brice,Percy (dr)

PCD 11019-2 | CD | God Bless Jug And Sonny
Gene Ammons Quartet
God Bless The Child
Live at The Famous Ballroom,Baltimore,MD, rec. 24.6.1973
Ammons,Gene (ts) | Walton,Cedar (p) | Jones,Sam (b) | Higgins,Billy (dr)
Sonny Stitt Quartet
Autumn In New York
Stitt,Sonny (as) | Walton,Cedar (p) | Jones,Sam (b) | Higgins,Billy (dr)
Gene Ammons-Sonny Stitt Quintet
Blue 'N' Boogie | Stringin' The Jug | Bye Bye Blackbird
Ammons,Gene (ts) | Stitt,Sonny (ts) | Walton,Cedar (p) | Jones,Sam (b) | Higgins,Billy (dr)
Cedar Walton Trio
Ugetsu
Walton,Cedar (p) | Jones,Sam (b) | Higgins,Billy (dr)

PCD 11020-2 | CD | Discovery:Grover Washington Jr.-The First Recordings
Boogaloo Joe Jones Quintet
No Way
NYC, rec. 23.11.1970
Jones,Boogaloo Joe (g) | Washington Jr.,Grover (ts) | Phillips,Sonny (org) | Lewis,Jimmy (b) | Purdie,Bernard 'Pretty' (dr)
Sunshine Alley
Jones,Boogaloo Joe (g) | Washington Jr.,Grover (ts) | Cornell,Butch (org) | Lewis,Jimmy (b) | Purdie,Bernard 'Pretty' (dr)
Boogaloo Joe Jones Sextet
Feel The Earth Move | Inside Job | Fadin'
NYC, rec. 16.8.1971
Jones,Boogaloo Joe (g) | Washington Jr.,Grover (ts) | Cornell,Butch (org) | Lewis,Jimmy (b) | Purdie,Bernard 'Pretty' (dr) | Caldwell,Buddy (congas)
Johnny 'Hammond' Smith Quintet
Between The Sheets | L&J
NYC, rec. 12.4.1971
Smith,Johnny 'Hammond' (keyboards) | Washington Jr.,Grover (ts) | Clark,James (g) | Lewis,Jimmy (b) | Gee,Eddie (dr)
Leon Spencer Sextet
Our Love Will Never Die
NYC, rec. 7.7.1971
Spencer Jr.,Leon (org) | Jones,Virgil (tp) | Washington Jr.,Grover (fl) | Sparks,Melvin (g) | Muhammad,Idris[Leo Morris] (dr) | Caldwell,Buddy (congas)

PCD 11033-2 | CD | XXL | EAN 025218312325
Dexter Gordon Quartet
Rhythm-A-Ning | Misty | Love For Sale
Live at The Famous Ballroom,Baltimore.MD, rec. 4.5.1969
Gordon,Dexter (ts) | Timmons,Bobby (p) | Gaskin,Victor (b) | Brice,Percy (dr)

PCD 24163-2 | CD | Keystone Bop Vol.2:Friday/Saturday
Freddie Hubbard Sextet
Spoken Introduction | One Of Another Kind
Live at Keystone Korner,SF, rec. 28.11.1981
Hubbard,Freddie (tp,fl-h) | Henderson,Joe (ts) | Hutcherson,Bobby (vib) | Childs,Billy (p) | Klein,Larry (b) | Houghton,Steve (dr)
Red Clay | Spoken Introduction | First Light
Hubbard,Freddie (tp,fl-h) | Henderson,Joe (ts) | Hutcherson,Bobby (vib) | Childs,Billy (p) | Klein,Larry (b) | Houghton,Steve (dr)
Joe Henderson Quartet
Round About Midnight
Live at Keystone Korner,SF, rec. 27.11.1981
Henderson,Joe (ts) | Childs,Billy (p) | Klein,Larry (b) | Houghton,Steve (dr)

PCD 24201-2 | CD | The Jazz Giants Play Harold Arlen:Blues In The Night
Red Garland Trio
Blues In The Night
Englewood Cliffs,NJ, rec. 15.7.1960
Garland,Red (p) | Jones,Sam (b) | Taylor,Arthur 'Art' (dr)
Miles Davis Sextet
It's Only A Paper Moon
NYC, rec. 5.10.1951
Davis,Miles (tp) | McLean,Jackie (as) | Rollins,Sonny (ts) | Bishop Jr.,Walter (p) | Potter,Tommy (b) | Blakey,Art (dr)
Art Tatum
I Gotta Right To Sing The Blues
Hollywood,CA, rec. 19.1.1955
Tatum,Art (p-solo)
Count Basie Trio
As Long As I Live
Los Angeles,CA, rec. 22.5.1974
Basie,Count (p) | Brown,Ray (b) | Bellson,Louie (dr)
Joe Pass
My Shining Hour
Los Angeles,CA, rec. November 1973
Pass,Joe (g-solo)
Milt Jackson Quartet
Ill Wind(You're Blowin' Me No Good)
NYC, rec. 17.5.1985
Jackson,Milt (vib) | Walton,Cedar (p) | Cranshaw,Bob (b) | Roker,Granville 'Mickey' (dr)
Wes Montgomery Quartet
One For My Baby(And One More For The Road)
NYC, rec. 4.8.1961
Montgomery,Wes (g) | Jones,Hank (p) | Carter,Ron (b) | Humphries,Lex (dr)
John Coltrane Quintet
Come Rain Or Come Shine
Hackensack,NJ, rec. 10.1.1958
Coltrane,John (ts) | Byrd,Donald (tp) | Garland,Red (p) | Chambers,Paul (b) | Hayes,Louis (dr)
Bill Perkins-Bud Shank Quintet
Out Of This World
Berkeley,CA, rec. 4.12.1986
Shank,Bud (as) | Perkins,Bill (ts) | Broadbent,Alan (p) | Heard,John (b) | Ferguson,Sherman (dr)
André Previn
That Old Black Magic
Los Angeles,CA, rec. 5.5.1960
Previn,André (p-solo)
Art Pepper Quartet
Over The Rainbow
Live at The 'Village Vanguard',NYC, rec. 28.7.1977
Pepper,Art (ts) | Cables,George (p) | Mraz,George 'Jiri' (b) | Jones,Elvin (dr)
Bill Evans Trio
A Sleeping Bee
Live at The 'Jazzhus' Montmartre,Copenhagen, rec. 24.11.1969
Evans,Bill (p) | Gomez,Eddie (b) | Morell,Marty (dr)
Dizzy Gillespie Sextet
Get Happy
Montreux,CH, rec. 14.7.1977
Gillespie,Dizzy (tp) | Faddis,Jon (tp) | Jackson,Milt (vib) | Alexander,Monty (p) | Brown,Ray (b) | Smith,Jimmie (dr)

PCD 24202-2 | CD | The Jazz Giants Play Jerome Kern:Yesterdays
Art Tatum-Ben Webster Quartet
All The Things You Are
Hollywood,CA, rec. 11.9.1956
Tatum,Art (p) | Webster,Ben (ts) | Callender,Red (b) | Douglas,Bill (dr)

Thelonious Monk Quintet
Smoke Gets In Your Eyes
Hackensack,NJ, rec. 11.5.1954
Monk,Thelonious (p) | Copeland,Ray (tp) | Foster,Frank (ts) | Russell,Curly (b) | Blakey,Art (dr)

Sonny Rollins Quartet
Dearly Beloved
NYC, rec. 1./12.6.1957
Rollins,Sonny (ts) | Clark,Sonny (p) | Heath,Percy (b) | Haynes,Roy (dr)

Hampton Hawes Trio
Yesterdays
Los Angeles,CA, rec. 3.12.1955
Hawes,Hampton (p) | Mitchell,Red (b) | Thompson,Chuck (dr)

Gene Ammons Quintet
Ol' Man River
Englewood Cliffs,NJ, rec. 27.1.1961
Ammons,Gene (ts) | Wyands,Richard (p) | Watkins,Doug (b) | Heard,J.C. (dr) | Barretto,Ray (congas)

Art Pepper Quartet
Long Ago And Far Away
Los Angeles,CA, rec. 23.11.1960
Pepper,Art (as) | Coker,Dolo (p) | Bond,Jimmy (b) | Butler,Frank (dr)

Art Farmer Quartet
The Folks Who Live On The Hill
NYC, rec. 1.5.1958
Farmer,Art (tp) | Jones,Hank (p) | Farmer,Addison (b) | Haynes,Roy (dr)

Blue Mitchell And His Orchestra
A Sure Thing
NYC, rec. 7.3.1962
Mitchell,Blue (tp) | Terry,Clark (tp) | Watkins,Julius (fr-h) | Richardson,Jerome (fl,as) | Heath,Jimmy (ts) | Kelly,Wynton (p) | Jones,Sam (b) | Heath,Albert 'Tootie' (dr)

Mal Waldron Sextet
The Way You Look Tonight
Hackensack,NJ, rec. 17.5.1957
Waldron,Mal (p) | Sulieman[Leonard Graham],Idrees (tp) | Shihab,Sahib (as) | Coltrane,John (ts) | Euell,Julian (b) | Thigpen,Ed (dr)

Paul Desmond Quartet
Look For The Silver Lining
rec. 1956
Desmond,Paul (as) | Elliott,Don (mellophone) | Bates,Norman (b) | Dodge,Joe (dr)

Bill Evans Quintet
Nobody Else But Me
Englewood Cliffs,NJ, rec. 8.3.1963
Evans,Bill (p) | Land,Harold (ts) | Burrell,Kenny (g) | Brown,Ray (b) | Jones,Philly Joe (dr)

Jackie McLean Quartet
Why Was I Born
Hackensack,NJ, rec. 13.7.1956
McLean,Jackie (as) | Waldron,Mal (p) | Watkins,Doug (b) | Taylor,Arthur 'Art' (dr)

Terry Gibbs Dream Band
The Song Is You
Live at Sundown,Hollywood,CA, rec. November 1959
Gibbs,Terry (vib) | Audino,Johnny (tp) | Candoli,Conte (tp) | Higgins,Frank (tp) | Williamson,Stu (tp) | Burgess,Bob 'Bobby' (tb) | Fryley,Vern (tb) | Smiley,Bill (tb) | Maini,Joe (as) | Kennedy,Charlie (as) | Perkins,Bill (ts) | Flory,Med (ts,arr) | Schwartz,Jack (bs) | Levy,Lou (p) | Clark,Buddy (b) | Lewis,Mel (dr) | Holman,Bill (arr)

PCD 24203-2 | CD | The Jazz Giants Play Cole Porter:Night And Day

Zoot Sims Quartet
Dream Dancing
NYC, rec. 18./19.9.1978
Sims,Zoot (ss,ts) | Rowles,Jimmy (p) | Cranshaw,Bob (b) | Roker,Granville 'Mickey' (dr)

Gil Evans And Ten
Just One Of Those Things
Hackensack,NJ, rec. 10.10.1957
Evans,Gil (p,arr) | Mucci,Louis (tp) | Koven,Jack (tp) | Cleveland,Jimmy (tb) | Varsalona,Bart (tb) | Ruff,Willie (fr-h) | Konitz,Lee (as) | Lacy,Steve (ss) | Kurtzer,Dave (bassoon) | Chambers,Paul (b) | Stabulas,Nick (dr)

Art Pepper Quartet
You'd Be So Nice To Come Home To
Los Angeles,CA, rec. 19.1.1957
Pepper,Art (as) | Garland,Red (p) | Chambers,Paul (b) | Jones,Philly Joe (dr)

Herb Ellis-Joe Pass
Love For Sale
rec. 13.2.1973
Ellis,Herb (g) | Pass,Joe (g)

Modern Jazz Quartet
All Of You
Hackensack,NJ, rec. 2.7.1955
MJQ (Modern Jazz Quartet) | Jackson,Milt (vib) | Lewis,John (p) | Heath,Percy (b) | Kay,Connie (dr)

Bill Evans Trio
Night And Day
NYC, rec. 15.12.1958
Evans,Bill (p) | Jones,Sam (b) | Jones,Philly Joe (dr)

Cal Tjader Sextet
I Love Paris
Hollywood,CA, rec. 1956
Tjader,Cal (vib) | Silva,Joe (ts) | Guaraldi,Vince (p) | McKibbon,Al (b) | Bobo,Willie (congas,bongos) | Santamaria,Mongo (congas,bongos)

Joe Henderson Quartet
I've Got You Under My Skin
NYC, rec. 27.9.1967
Henderson,Joe (ts) | Barron,Kenny (p) | Carter,Ron (b) | Hayes,Louis (dr)

Art Tatum
Begin The Beguine
Hollywood,CA, rec. 28.12.1953
Tatum,Art (p-solo)

John Coltrane Trio
I Love You
Hackensack,NJ, rec. 16.8.1957
Coltrane,John (ts) | May,Earl (b) | Taylor,Arthur 'Art' (dr)

Gene Ammons Quintet
Easy To Love
Englewood Cliffs,NJ, rec. 27.1.1961
Ammons,Gene (ts) | Wyands,Richard (p) | Watkins,Doug (b) | Heard,J.C. (dr) | Barretto,Ray (congas)

Sonny Rollins Quartet
Every Time We Say Goodbye
NYC, rec. 11./12.or 19.6.1957
Rollins,Sonny (ts) | Clark,Sonny (p) | Heath,Percy (b) | Haynes,Roy (dr)

Eddie Lockjaw Davis-Johnny Griffin Quintet
From This Moment On
NYC, rec. 5.2.1962
Davis,Eddie 'Lockjaw' (ts) | Griffin,Johnny (ts) | Parlan,Horace (p) | Catlett,Buddy (b) | Riley,Ben (dr)

PCD 24204-2 | CD | The Jazz Giants Play Harry Warren:Lullaby Of Broadway

Art Pepper Quartet
There'll Never Be Another You
Berkeley,CA, rec. 5.9.1980
Pepper,Art (as) | Cowell,Stanley (p) | McBee,Cecil (b) | Burnett,Carl (dr)

Kenny Dorham Quartet
I Had The Craziest Dream
Englewood Cliffs,NJ, rec. 13.11.1959
Dorham,Kenny (tp) | Flanagan,Tommy (p) | Chambers,Paul (b) | Taylor,Arthur 'Art' (dr)

Sonny Rollins Quintet
I'll String Along With You
Berkeley,CA, rec. 19.9.1987
Rollins,Sonny (ts) | Anderson,Clifton (tb) | Soskin,Mark (el-p) | Harris,Jerome (g) | Smith,Marvin 'Smitty' (dr)

Kenny Drew-Wilbur Ware
Lullaby Of Broadway
NYC, rec. February 1947
Drew,Kenny (p) | Ware,Wilbur (b)

Leroy Vinnegar Sextet
Would You Like To Take A Walk
Los Angeles,CA, rec. 23.9.1957
Vinnegar,Leroy (b) | Wilson,Gerald (tp) | Edwards,Teddy (ts) | Feldman,Victor (vib) | Perkins,Carl (p) | Bazley,Tony (dr)

Art Tatum
Boulevard Of Broken Dreams
Hollywood,CA, rec. 22.4.1954
Tatum,Art (p-solo)

Zoot Sims-Jimmy Rowles Quartet
Shadow Waltz
NYC, rec. 27.10.1977
Sims,Zoot (as) | Rowles,Jimmy (p) | Mraz,George 'Jiri' (b) | Alexander,Mousie (dr)

Shelly Manne And His Men
You're Getting To Be A Habit With Me
Los Angeles,CA, rec. 13.9.1955
Manne,Shelly (dr) | Enevoldsen,Bob (v-tb) | Maini,Joe (as) | Holman,Bill (ts) | Giuffre,Jimmy (bs) | Freeman,Russ (p) | Pena,Ralph (b)

Bill Evans Trio
I Wish I Knew
NYC, rec. 2.2.1961
Evans,Bill (p) | LaFaro,Scott (b) | Motian,Paul (dr)

Red Garland Trio
You'll Never Know
NYC, rec. 19.7.1961
Garland,Red (p) | Jones,Sam (b) | Persip,Charles (dr)

The Poll Winners
Nagasaki
Los Angeles,CA, rec. 18./19.3.1957
Poll Winners,The | Kessel,Barney (g) | Brown,Ray (b) | Manne,Shelly (dr)

Eddie Lockjaw Davis Quintet
I Only Have Eyes For You
Englewood Cliffs,NJ, rec. 15.11.1962
Davis,Eddie 'Lockjaw' (ts) | Weeden,Paul (g) | Patterson,Don (org) | Duvivier,George (b) | James,William 'Billy' (dr)

Lester Young With The Bill Potts Trio
Jeepers Creepers
Live at Olivia Davis's Patio Lounge,Washington,DC, rec. 7.12.1956
Young,Lester (ts) | Potts,Bill (p) | Williams,Norman (b) | Lucht,Jim (dr)

Chet Baker And The Lighthouse All Stars
At Last
Live at The Lighthouse,Hermosa Beach,CA, rec. 13.9.1953
Baker,Chet (tp) | Shank,Bud (as) | Cooper,Bob (ts) | Freeman,Russ (p) | Rumsey,Howard (b) | Roach,Max (dr)

Count Basie And His Orchestra
The More I See You
Montreux,CH, rec. 15.7.1977
Basie,Count (p) | Cohn[Cohen],Sonny (tp) | Mitchell,Bob (tp) | Biviano,Lyn (tp) | Reed,Waymon (tp) | Wanzo,Mel (tb) | Hughes,Bill (tb) | Grey,Al (tb) | Wilson,Dennis (tb) | Plater,Bobby (as) | Turner,Danny (as) | Forrest,Jimmy (ts) | Dixon,Eric (ts) | Fowlkes,Charlie (bs) | Green,Freddie (g) | Duke,John (b) | Miles,Butch (dr)

Johnny Hodges Orchestra
Rose Of The Rio Grande
Live at The Sportpalast,Berlin, rec. March 1961
Hodges,Johnny (as) | Nance,Ray (co) | Brown,Lawrence (tb) | Carney,Harry (bs) | Williams,Al (p) | Bell,Aaron (b) | Woodyard,Sam (dr)

PCD 24205-2 | CD | The Jazz Giants Play Rodgers & Hart:Blue Moon

Chet Baker Quintet
Have You Met Miss Jones
Englewood Cliffs,NJ, rec. 23./25.8.1965
Baker,Chet (fl-h) | Coleman,George (ts) | Lightsey,Kirk (p) | Wright,Herman (b) | Brooks,Roy (dr)

Stephane Grappelli-McCoy Tyner Duo
I Didn't Know What Time It Was
NYC, rec. 18.4.1990
Grappelli,Stephane (v) | Tyner,McCoy (p)

Art Tatum Trio
Isn't It Romantic
Hollywood,CA, rec. 27.1.1956
Tatum,Art (p) | Callender,Red (b) | Jones,Jo (dr)

Miles Davis Quintet
Blue Room
NYC, rec. 17.1.1951
Davis,Miles (p) | Green,Bennie (tb) | Lewis,John (p) | Heath,Percy (b) | Haynes,Roy (dr)

Gene Ammons Quartet
Little Girl Blue
Englewood Cliffs,NJ, rec. 26.1.1961
Ammons,Gene (ts) | Wyands,Richard (p) | Watkins,Doug (b) | Heard,J.C. (dr)

Milt Jackson Quartet
My Funny Valentine
Hackensack,NJ, rec. 20.5.1955
Jackson,Milt (vib) | Silver,Horace (p) | Heath,Percy (b) | Kay,Connie (dr)

Joe Pass
Blue Moon
Hollywood,CA, rec. 26.8.1992
Pass,Joe (g-solo)

Stan Getz Quartet
There's A Small Hotel
NYC, rec. 6.1.1950
Getz,Stan (ts) | Haig,Al (p) | Potter,Tommy (b) | Haynes,Roy (dr)

Gerry Mulligan Quartet
The Lady Is A Tramp
Hollywood,CA, rec. January 1953
Mulligan,Gerry (bs) | Baker,Chet (tp) | Smith,Carson (b) | Hamilton,Forrest 'Chico' (dr)

Red Garland Quartet
Lover
Englewood Cliffs,NJ, rec. 27.6.1958
Garland,Red (p) | Chambers,Paul (b) | Taylor,Arthur 'Art' (dr) | Barretto,Ray (congas)

Benny Carter Quartet
Thou Swell
Los Angeles,CA, rec. 2.11.1958
Carter,Benny (as) | Hines,Earl 'Fatha' (p) | Vinnegar,Leroy (b) | Manne,Shelly (dr)

Wes Montgomery With The Jimmy Jones Orchestra
My Romance
NYC, rec. 18.4.1963
Montgomery,Wes (g) | Jones,Jimmy (cond,arr) | Jones,Hank (p,celeste) | Burrell,Kenny (g) | Hinton,Milt (b) | Johnson,Osie (dr) | Bodner,Phil (woodwinds) | Agostini,Gloria (harp) | Orloff,Gene (v,concertmaster) | Lookofsky,Harry (v) | Nadien,David (v) | Collymore,Winston (v) | Ceppos,Mac (v) | Eidus,Arnold (v) | Kruczek,Leo (v) | Poliakin,Raoul (v) | Zir,Isadore (v) | Brown,Alfred (viola) | Fisch,Burt (viola) | McCracken,Charles (cello) | Ricci,George (cello)

Bill Evans Trio
My Heart Stood Still
NYC, rec. 19.1.1959
Evans,Bill (p) | Chambers,Paul (b) | Jones,Philly Joe (dr)

Mal Waldron Trio
With A Song In My Heart
Englewood Cliffs,NJ, rec. 20.3.1959
Waldron,Mal (p) | Farmer,Addison (b) | Heath,Albert 'Tootie' (dr)

Barney Kessel And His Orchestra
Mountain Greenery
Los Angeles,CA, rec. 4.12.1956
Kessel,Barney (g) | Collette,Buddy (cl) | Terry,Howard (cl,b-cl) | Jacob,Julie (oboe) | Nash,Ted (fl) | Gordon,Justin (cl,b-cl) | Williamson,Claude (p) | Mitchell,Red (b) | Manne,Shelly (dr)

Hampton Hawes Trio
Spring Is Here
Los Angeles,CA, rec. 1.5.1966
Hawes,Hampton (p) | Mitchell,Red (b) | Bailey,Donald (dr)

Oscar Peterson Trio
Falling In Love With Love
London,GB, rec. 21.10.1978
Peterson,Oscar (p) | Heard,John (b) | Bellson,Louie (dr)

PCD 24223-2 | CD | The Jazz Giants Play Rodgers & Hammerstein:My Favorite Things

Bill Evans Trio
It Might As Well Be Spring
NYC, rec. 5.6.1962
Evans,Bill (p) | Israels,Chuck (b) | Motian,Paul (dr)

John Coltrane Quintet
Do I Love You Because You're Beautiful
Hackensack,NJ, rec. 26.12.1958
Coltrane,John (ts) | Byrd,Freddie (tp) | Garland,Red (p) | Chambers,Paul (b) | Taylor,Arthur 'Art' (dr)

Gene Ammons Quartet
You'll Never Walk Alone
Chicago,Ill, rec. 3.5.1962
Ammons,Gene (ts) | Anderson,Clarence 'Sleepy' (org) | Hickman,Sylvester (b) | Anderson,Dorral (dr)

McCoy Tyner
My Favorite Things
Tokyo, Japan, rec. 11.11.1972
Tyner,McCoy (p-solo)

Miles Davis Quintet
Surrey With The Fringe On Top
Hackensack,NJ, rec. 11.5.1956
Davis,Miles (tp) | Coltrane,John (ts) | Garland,Red (p) | Chambers,Paul (b) | Jones,Philly Joe (dr)

Coleman Hawkins Quartet
Climb Every Mountain
Englewood Cliffs,NJ, rec. 16.8.1962
Hawkins,Coleman (ts) | Flanagan,Tommy (p) | Holley,Major (b) | Locke,Eddie (dr)

Charles McPherson Quintet
If I Loved You
Englewood Cliffs,NJ, rec. 20.11.1964
McPherson,Charles (as) | Jones,Carmell (tp) | Harris,Barry (p) | Boyd,Nelson (b) | Heath,Albert 'Tootie' (dr)

Red Garland Trio
We Kiss In The Shadow
Hackensack,NJ, rec. 22.8.1958
Garland,Red (p) | Nasser,Jamil[George Joyner] (b) | Persip,Charles (dr)

Cannonball Adderley Quintet
People Will Say We're In Love
NYC, rec. 1.7.1958
Adderley,Julian \'Cannonball\' (as) | Mitchell,Blue (tp) | Evans,Bill (p) | Jones,Sam (b) | Jones,Philly Joe (dr)

Oscar Peterson Trio
Younger Than Springtime
Montreux,CH, rec. 16.7.1979
Peterson,Oscar (p) | Orsted-Pedersen,Niels-Henning (b) | Hayes,Louis (dr)

PCD 24225-2 | CD | The Jazz Giants Play Miles Davis:Milestones

Oscar Peterson Quartet
Vierd Blues
Berkeley,CA, rec. 9.11.1983
Peterson,Oscar (p) | Pass,Joe (g) | Orsted-Pedersen,Niels-Henning (b) | Drew,Martin (dr)

Dexter Gordon Quintet
Milestones
Englewood Cliffs,NJ, rec. 22.7.1972
Gordon,Dexter (ts) | Hubbard,Freddie (tp,fl-h) | Walton,Cedar (p) | Williams,Buster (b) | Higgins,Billy (dr)

Bill Evans Trio
So What
Hull,Canada, rec. August 1974
Evans,Bill (p) | Gomez,Eddie (b) | Morell,Marty (dr)

Sonny Stitt Quartet
Tune Up
Englewood Cliffs,NJ, rec. 15.9.1969
Stitt,Sonny (ts) | Green,Grant (g) | Patterson,Don (org) | James,William 'Billy' (dr)

Chet Baker Quartet
Solar
NYC, rec. September 1958
Baker,Chet (tp) | Haig,Al (p) | Chambers,Paul (b) | Jones,Philly Joe (dr)

Hampton Hawes Trio
Blue In Green
Los Angeles,CA, rec. 14.8.1976
Hawes,Hampton (p) | Brown,Ray (b) | Manne,Shelly (dr)

Wes Montgomery Trio
Freddie Freeloader
NYC, rec. 10.10.1963
Montgomery,Wes (g) | Rhyne,Melvin (org) | Brown,George (dr)

George Russell Sextet
Nardis
NYC, rec. 8.5.1961
Russell,George (p) | Ellis,Don (tp) | Baker,Dave (tb) | Dolphy,Eric (b-cl) | Swallow,Steve (b) | Hunt,Joe (dr)

Miles Davis Sextet
Compulsion | The Serpent's Tooth(I)
Hackensack,NJ, rec. 30.1.1953
Davis,Miles (tp) | Rollins,Sonny (ts) | Parker,Charlie (ts) | Bishop Jr.,Walter (p) | Heath,Percy (b) | Jones,Philly Joe (dr)

Phineas Newborn Jr. Trio
Four
Los Angeles,CA, rec. 21.11.1961
Newborn Jr.,Phineas (p) | Jones,Sam (b) | Hayes,Louis (dr)

Ray Bryant Trio
All Blues
NYC, rec. 10.4.1978
Bryant,Ray (p) | Jones,Sam (b) | Tate,Grady (dr)

Ron Affif Quartet
Seven Steps To Heaven
Hollywood,CA, rec. 28.12.1993
Affif,Ron (g) | O'Bourke,Brian (p) | Simpkins,Andrew (b) | Bailey,Colin (dr)

PCD 24226-2 | CD | The Jazz Giants Play Sammy Cahn:It's Magic

Milt Jackson Quartet
Wonder Why
Hackensack,NJ, rec. 20.5.1955
Jackson,Milt (vib) | Silver,Horace (p) | Heath,Percy (b) | Kay,Connie (dr)

Kenny Dorham Quintet
Be My Love(take 2)
NYC, rec. 15.12.1953
Dorham,Kenny (tp) | Heath,Jimmy (ts) | Bishop Jr.,Walter (p) | Heath,Percy (b) | Clarke,Kenny (dr)

Coleman Hawkins Quintet
Until The Real Thing Comes Along
Hackensack,NJ, rec. 7.11.1958
Hawkins,Coleman (ts) | Burrell,Kenny (g) | Bryant,Ray (p) | Marshall,Wendell (b) | Johnson,Osie (dr)

Art Tatum
Please Be Kind
Hollywood,CA, rec. 19.1.1955
Tatum,Art (p-solo)

Art Farmer Quartet
I'll Walk Alone
Hackensack,NJ, rec. 9.11.1954
Farmer,Art (tp) | Kelly,Wynton (p) | Farmer,Addison (b) | Lovelle,Herbie (dr)

Joe Pass
I Should Care
Hollywood,CA, rec. 20.8.1992
Pass,Joe (g-solo)

Oliver Nelson Quintet
All The Way
Englewood Cliffs,NJ, rec. 22.3.1960
Nelson,Oliver (as,ts) | Winchester,Lem (vib) | Smith,Johnny 'Hammond' (org) | Tucker,George (b) | Haynes,Roy (dr)
John Coltrane Quartet
Time After Time
Hackensack,NJ, rec. 26.12.1958
Coltrane,John (ts) | Garland,Red (p) | Chambers,Paul (b) | Taylor,Arthur 'Art' (dr)
Max Roach Quintet
It's You Or No One
NYC, rec. 4.9.1958
Roach,Max (dr) | Little,Booker (tp) | Coleman,George (ts) | Draper,Ray (tuba) | Davis,Art (b)
Bill Holman Octet
The Things We Did Last Summer
Los Angeles,CA, rec. 1959
Holman,Bill (bs,arr) | Candoli,Conte (dr) | Leddy,Ed (tp) | Rosolino,Frank (tb) | Kamuca,Richie (ts) | Guaraldi,Vince (p) | Budwig,Monty (b) | Levey,Stan (dr)
Hank Crawford Quintet
If It's The Last Thing I Do
Englewood Cliffs,NJ, rec. 5.4.1996
Crawford,Hank (as) | Mixon,Danny (org) | Sparks,Melvin (g) | Banks,Stanley (b) | Muhammad,Idris[Leo Morris] (dr)
Count Basie-Oscar Peterson
Teach Me Tonight
Hollywood,CA, rec. 21.2.1978
Basie,Count (p) | Peterson,Oscar (p)
Bill Evans Quintet
Second Time Around
Berkeley,CA, rec. May 1976
Evans,Bill (p) | Land,Harold (ts) | Burrell,Kenny (g) | Brown,Ray (b) | Jones,Philly Joe (dr)
Cal Tjader Quintet
Pete Kelly's Blues
San Francisco,CA, rec. Spring 1956
Tjader,Cal (vib) | Duran,Manuel (p) | Duran,Carlos (b) | Miranda,Luis (congas) | Velarde,Byardo (timbales)

PCD 24227-2 | CD | The Jazz Giants Play Duke Ellington:Caravan
Clark Terry Five
Things Ain't What They Used To Be
Hollywood,CA, rec. 11.3.1980
Terry,Clark (tp) | Pass,Joe (g) | Wilson,Jack (p) | Brown,Ray (b) | Severino,Frank (dr)
Miles Davis Quintet
Just Squeeze Me(But Don't Tease Me)
Hackensack,NJ, rec. 16.11.1955
Davis,Miles (tp) | Coltrane,John (ts) | Garland,Red (p) | Chambers,Paul (b) | Jones,Philly Joe (dr)
Joe Pass Quartet
Solitude
Hollywood,CA, rec. December 1989
Pass,Joe (el-g) | Pisano,John (g) | Hughart,Jim (b) | Bailey,Colin (dr)
Ben Webster Quartet
Come Sunday
NYC, rec. 1963
Webster,Ben (ts) | Zawinul,Joe (p) | Davis,Richard (b) | Jones,Philly Joe (dr)
Sonny Rollins With The Modern Jazz Quartet
In A Sentimental Mood
NYC, rec. 7.10.1953
Rollins,Sonny (ts) | MJQ (Modern Jazz Quartet) | Jackson,Milt (vib) | Lewis,John (p) | Heath,Percy (b) | Clarke,Kenny (dr)
Duke Ellington Quartet
Everything But You
Los Angeles,CA, rec. 8.1.1973
Ellington,Duke (p) | Pass,Joe (g) | Brown,Ray (b) | Bellson,Louie (dr)
Red Garland Quintet
I Got It Bad And That Ain't Good
Hackensack,NJ, rec. 15.11.1957
Garland,Red (p) | Byrd,Donald (tp) | Coltrane,John (ts) | Nasser,Jamil[George Joyner] (b) | Taylor,Arthur 'Art' (dr)
Art Tatum
Caravan
Hollywood,CA, rec. 29.12.1953
Tatum,Art (p-solo)
Wes Montgomery Quintet
Cotton Tail
NYC, rec. 4.8.1961
Montgomery,Wes (g) | Jones,Hank (p) | Carter,Ron (b) | Humphries,Lex (dr) | Barretto,Ray (congas)
Duke Ellington And His Orchestra
Just A-Sittin' And A-Rockin'
NYC, rec. 1.5.1962
Ellington,Duke (p) | Burrowes,Roy (tp) | Anderson,Cat (tp) | Berry,Bill (tp) | Nance,Ray (tp) | Brown,Lawrence (tb) | Cox,Leon (tb) | Connors,Chuck (tb) | Procope,Russell (as) | Hodges,Johnny (as) | Hamilton,Jimmy (cl,ts) | Gonsalves,Paul (ts) | Carney,Harry (bs) | Bell,Aaron (b) | Woodyard,Sam (dr)
Zoot Sims And His Orchestra
Main Stem
Los Angeles,CA, rec. 20./21.9.1976
Sims,Zoot (ts) | Brashear,Oscar (tp) | Young,Eugene 'Snooky' (tp) | Rosolino,Frank (tb) | Kamuca,Richie (ts) | Richardson,Jerome (ss) | Hood,Bill (bs) | Tompkins,Ross (p) | Budwig,Monty (b) | Ceroli,Nick (dr) | Holman,Bill (cond,arr)
Duke Ellington And His Orchestra
Prelude To A Kiss | Satin Doll
Live in New York, rec. July 1967
Ellington,Duke (p) | Anderson,Cat (tp) | Ellington,Mercer (tp) | Jones,Herbie (tp) | Williams,Cootie (tp) | Cooper,Frank 'Buster' (tb) | Connors,Chuck (tb) | Brown,Lawrence (tb) | Hamilton,Jimmy (cl,as) | Procope,Russell (as) | Hodges,Johnny (as) | Carter,Benny (as) | Gonsalves,Paul (ts) | Carney,Harry (bs) | Lamb,John (b) | Jones,Rufus (dr)
Benny Carter-Coleman Hawkins-Johnny Hodges With The Oscar Peterson Trio
C Jam Blues
Hodges,Johnny (as) | Carter,Benny (as) | Hawkins,Coleman (ts) | Peterson,Oscar (p) | Jones,Sam (b) | Hayes,Louis (dr)

PCD 24242-2 | CD | Silken Soul
Jack McDuff Quartet
Around The Corner | There Is No Greater Love | Almost Like Being In Love
NYC, rec. 1965/66
McDuff,Brother Jack (org) | Holloway,Red (ts) | Martino,Pat (g) | Dukes,Joe (dr)
Song Of The Soul | More (Theme From Mondo Cane)
NYC, rec. February 1966
McDuff,Brother Jack (org) | Ousley,Harold (ts) | Martino,Pat (g) | Dukes,Joe (dr)
Jack McDuff Quintet
For Those Who Choose | Haitian Lady | The Live People | Stop It | How High The Moon
McDuff,Brother Jack (org) | Holloway,Red (ts) | Ousley,Harold (ts) | Martino,Pat (g) | Dukes,Joe (dr)
Jack McDuff Sextet
Chicken Feet
McDuff,Brother Jack (org) | Holloway,Red (ts) | Ousley,Harold (ts) | Martino,Pat (g) | Dukes,Joe (dr) | Montego Joe (congas)
Silk 'N' Soul
NYC, rec. 196
McDuff,Brother Jack (org) | Holloway,Red (ts) | Benson,George (g) | Gales,Larry (b) | Dukes,Joe (dr) | Montego Joe (congas)
That's When We Thought Of Love
NYC, rec. February 1966
McDuff,Brother Jack (org) | Holloway,Red (ts) | Ousley,Harold (ts) | Benson,George (g) | Gales,Larry (b) | Dukes,Joe (dr)

PCD 24243-2 | CD | At Large
Willis Jackson Quintet
A Twist Of Blues | Sweet Peter Charleston | Cat Meal | He Said,She Said,I Said
Englewood Cliffs,NJ, rec. 10.1.1961
Jackson,Willis (ts) | Neely,Jimmy (p) | Marshall,Wendell (b) | Johnson,Gus (dr) | Amalbert,Juan (conga)
Willis Jackson Quartet
Nobody Knows The Trouble I've Seen | Sometimes I Feel Like A Motherless Child
Englewood Cliffs,NJ, rec. 11.4.1961
Jackson,Willis (ts) | Wyands,Richard (p) | Morrison,Peck (b) | Roker,Granville 'Mickey' (dr)
Willis Jackson Group
Shuckin' | Cachita | I Left My Heart In San Francisco | What Kind Of Fool Am I | Mama Inez
Englewood Cliffs,NJ, rec. 30.10.1962
Jackson,Willis (ts) | Burrell,Kenny (g) | Flanagan,Tommy (p) | Calhoun,Eddie (b) | Haynes,Roy (dr,cabasa) | Amalbert,Juan (conga,timbales) | Montego Joe (congas) | Paulo,Jose (perc)
Willis Jackson Sextet
Arrivederci Roma | Neapolitan Nights
Englewood Cliffs,NJ, rec. 19.12.1962
Jackson,Willis (ts) | Pizzarelli,Bucky (g) | Mahones,Gildo (p) | Tucker,George (b) | Donaldson,Bobby (dr) | Montego Joe (congas)
By The Time I Get To Phoenix | Florence Of Arabia
Englewood Cliffs,NJ, rec. 9.9.1968
Jackson,Willis (ts,gator-horn) | Ivory,Jackie (org) | Jennings,Bill (g) | Tucker,Ben (b,el-b) | Potter,Jerry (dr) | Dorsey,Ralph (congas)

PCD 24244-2 | CD | The Soulful Blues
Johnny 'Hammond' Smith Sextet
The Sin-In | Stand By Me | Knock On Wood | The Soulful Blues | Ebb Tide | Summertime | Gettin' Up | The 'In' Crowd
Englewood Cliffs,NJ, rec. 3.3.1967
Smith,Johnny 'Hammond' (org) | Jones,Virgil (tp) | Person,Houston (ts) | Schwartz,Thornel (g) | Lewis,Jimmy (el-b) | Harris,John 'Ironman' (dr)
Johnny 'Hammond' Smith Quartet
If I Were A Bell | Song For My Father | Speak Low | Unchained Melody | Nasty | Four Bowls Of Soup
NYC, rec. 18.6.1968
Smith,Johnny 'Hammond' (org) | Person,Houston (ts) | Abercrombie,John (g) | Tate,Grady (dr)

PCD 24245-2 | CD | Andy Bey And The Bey Sisters
Andy And The Bey Sisters
Corcovado(Quiet Nights) | Besame Mucho | Since I Fell For You | September In The Rain | Smiles
NYC, rec. 17.8.1964
Bey,Andy (p,voc) | Richardson,Jerome (fl,ts) | Galbraith,Barry (g) | Hinton,Milt (b) | Jones,Jo (dr) | Bey,Salome (voc) | Bey,Geraldine (voc)
A Taste Of Honey | Night Song | The Swinging Preacher | Willow Weep For Me | Sister Sadie
NYC, rec. 20.8.1964
Bey,Andy (p,voc) | Richardson,Jerome (fl,ts) | Burrell,Kenny (g) | Davis,Richard (b) | Johnson,Osie (dr) | Bey,Salome (voc) | Bey,Geraldine (voc)
Feeling Good | Tammy | Everybody Loves My Baby | Hallelujah I Love Her So | Round About Midnight
NYC, rec. 26.2.1965
Bey,Andy (p,voc) | Burrell,Kenny (g) | Hinton,Milt (b) | Johnson,Osie (dr) | Bey,Salome (voc) | Bey,Geraldine (voc)
Squeeze Me | God Bless The Child | Every Time We Say Goodbye | Solitude | Love Is Just Around The Corner- | I Love You- | Love You Madly-
NYC, rec. 27.5.1965
Bey,Andy (p,voc) | Hinton,Milt (b) | Johnson,Osie (dr) | Bey,Salome (voc) | Bey,Geraldine (voc)

PCD 24246-2 | CD | Jaki Byard:Solo/Strings
Jaki Byard Sextet
Falling Rains Of Life | Music To Watch Girls By | Ray's Blues | How High The Moon | Cat's Cradle Conference Rag
NYC, rec. 2.4.1968
Byard,Jaki (p,org) | Benson,George (g) | Nance,Ray (v) | Carter,Ron (cello) | Davis,Richard (b) | Dawson,Alan (vib,dr)
Jaki Byard
Spanish Tinge(No.2) | Do You Know What It Means To Miss New Orleans | I Know A Place- | Let The Good Times Roll- | New Orleans Strut | Top Of The Gate Rag | Seasons | A Basin Street Ballad | The Hollis Stomp
NYC, rec. 31.7.1969
Byard,Jaki (p-solo)

PCD 24247-2 | CD | The Long Road
Frank Wess And His Orchestra
Southern Comfort | Blue Skies | Gin's Beguine | Blues For Butterball | Summer Frost | Dancing In The Dark | Shufflin'
Englewood Cliffs,NJ, rec. 22.3.1962
Wess,Frank (alto-fl,fl,ts) | Aarons,Albert 'Al' (tp) | Nelson,Oliver (ts) | Barrow,George (bs) | Flanagan,Tommy (p) | Duvivier,George (b) | Johnson,Osie (dr) | Barretto,Ray (congas)
Frank Wess Quintet
The Lizard | Little Me | Yo Ho | Cold Miner | Poor You | The Long Road
Englewood Cliffs,NJ, rec. 24.1.1963
Wess,Frank (fl,ts) | Jones,Thad (tp) | Mahones,Gildo (p) | Catlett,Buddy (b) | Haynes,Roy (dr)

PCD 24248-2 | CD | Carnavals
Dave Pike Sextet
Sono | Carnival Samba(aka Carnaval) | Philumba | Ginha
NYC, rec. 6.9.1962
Pike,Dave (vib,marimba) | Terry,Clark (fl-h) | Burrell,Kenny (g) | Paulo,Jose (cabasa,bandero) | White,Chris (b) | Collins,Rudy (dr)
Dave Pike Quintet
Sambolero | Serenidade | Melvalita | Sausalito
NYC, rec. 7.9.1962
Pike,Dave (vib,marimba) | Burrell,Kenny (g) | Paulo,Jose (cabasa,bandero) | White,Chris (b) | Collins,Rudy (dr)
Dave Pike Sextet
La Bamba | Mathilda,Mathilda | Limbo Rock | Jamaica Farewell
Englewood Cliffs,NJ, rec. 12.12.1962
Pike,Dave (vib,marimba) | Wright,Leo (fl,as) | Raney,Jimmy (g) | Duvivier,George (b) | Correa,William (dr) | Barretto,Ray (congas)
Dave Pike Quintet
My Little Suede Shoes | Mambo Bounce | Calypso Blues | Cattin' Latin | St.Thomas
Pike,Dave (vib,marimba) | Flanagan,Tommy (p) | Abdul-Malik,Ahmed (b) | Correa,William (dr) | Barretto,Ray (congas)

PCD 24249-2 | CD | Gentle Jug Vol.3
Gene Ammons Quartet
Didn't We | Blue Velvet
Englewood Cliffs,NJ, rec. 11.11.1969
Ammons,Gene (ts) | Phillips,Sonny (org) | Bushnell,Bob (el-b) | Purdie,Bernard 'Pretty' (dr)
Gene Ammons Quintet
I'm Afraid The Masquerade Is Over - (I'm Afraid) The Masquerade Is Over | You Better Go Now
Chicago,Ill, rec. 27.4.1962
Ammons,Gene (ts) | Anderson,Clarence 'Sleepy' (org) | unkn. (g,b,dr)
Gene Ammons-Sonny Stitt Quartet
Out In Cold Again
Englewood Cliffs,NJ, rec. 19.2.1962
Ammons,Gene (ts) | Stitt,Sonny (ts) | McDuff,Brother Jack (org) | Persip,Charles (dr)
Gene Ammons Quintet
Let It Be You
Englewood Cliffs,NJ, rec. 27.1.1961
Ammons,Gene (ts) | Anderson,Clarence 'Sleepy' (p,org) | Watkins,Doug (b) | Heard,J.C. (dr) | Barretto,Ray (congas)
Gene Ammons-Sonny Stitt Quintet
My Foolish Heart | We'll Be Together Again
Chicago,Ill, rec. 26.1.1961
Ammons,Gene (ts) | Stitt,Sonny (as,ts) | Houston,John (p) | Williams,Buster (b) | Brown,George (dr)
Gene Ammons Quartet
Lush Life
Englewood Cliffs,NJ, rec. 2.2.1970
Ammons,Gene (ts) | Kelly,Wynton (p) | Duvivier,George (b) | Collins,Rudy (dr)
Gene Ammons Quintet
Angel Eyes
Englewood Cliffs,NJ, rec. 17.6.1960
Ammons,Gene (ts) | Wess,Frank (fl,ts) | Smith,Johnny 'Hammond' (org) | Watkins,Doug (b) | Taylor,Arthur 'Art' (dr)
Gene Ammons Sextet
Born To Be Blue
Englewood Cliffs,NJ, rec. 28.11.1961
Ammons,Gene (ts) | Newman,Joe (tp) | McDuff,Brother Jack (org) | Marshall,Wendell (b) | Perkins,Walter (dr) | Barretto,Ray (congas)

PCD 24250-2 | CD | Charlie's Greatest Hits
Charles Earland Sextet
More Today Then Yesterday
Englewood Cliffs,NJ, rec. 15.12.1969
Earland,Charles (org) | Jones,Virgil (tp) | Person,Houston (ts) | Sparks,Melvin (g) | Muhammad,Idris[Leo Morris] (dr) | Caldwell,Buddy (congas)
Boogaloo Joe Jones Quintet
Someday We'll Be Together
Englewood Cliffs,NJ, rec. 16.2.1970
Jones,Boogaloo Joe (g) | Bryant,Rusty (ts) | Earland,Charles (org) | Lewis,Jimmy (el-b) | Purdie,Bernard 'Pretty' (dr)
Charles Earland Sextet
Raindrops Keep Fallin' On My Head
Englewood Cliffs,NJ, rec. 1.6.1970
Earland,Charles (org) | Jones,Virgil (tp) | Pruden,Layton (tb) | Heath,Jimmy (fl,ss) | Parker,Maynard (g) | Turner,Jimmy (dr)
More Today Then Yesterday | Don't Let Me Lose This Dream
Live at The Key Club,Newark,NJ, rec. 17.9.1970
Earland,Charles (org) | Chandler,Gary (tp) | Washington Jr.,Grover (ts) | Parker,Maynard (g) | Kilpatrick Jr.,Jesse (dr) | Caldwell,Buddy (congas)
Charles Earland Orchestra
Morgan
Englewood Cliffs,NJ, rec. 17.2.1972
Earland,Charles (org) | Morgan,Lee (tp) | Jones,Virgil (tp) | Laws,Hubert (piccolo) | Harper,Billy (ts) | Parker,Maynard (g) | Thorpe,William (b) | Cobham,Billy (dr) | Morgan,Sonny (congas)
Charles Earland Septet
Leaving This Planet
Berkeley,CA, rec. 11.12.1973
Earland,Charles (org) | Henderson,Eddie (tp) | Henderson,Joe (ts) | Gleeson,Pat (synth) | Arkin,Eddie (g) | Mason,Harvey (dr) | Killian,Lawrence (perc) | Copeland,Rudy (voc)

PCD 24251-2 | CD | The Prestige Legacy Vol.1:The High Priests
Miles Davis Sextet
Down
NYC, rec. 17.1.1951
Davis,Miles (tp) | Green,Bennie (tb) | Rollins,Sonny (ts) | Lewis,John (p) | Heath,Percy (b) | Haynes,Roy (dr)
Sonny Rollins Quartet
Mambo Bounce
NYC, rec. 17.12.1951
Rollins,Sonny (ts) | Drew,Kenny (p) | Heath,Percy (b) | Blakey,Art (dr)
Thelonious Monk Trio
Little Rootie Tootie
NYC, rec. 15.10.1952
Monk,Thelonious (p) | Mapp,Gary (b) | Blakey,Art (dr)
Bemsha Swing
NYC, rec. 18.12.1952
Monk,Thelonious (p) | Mapp,Gary (b) | Roach,Max (dr)
Miles Davis Sextet
Compulsion
Hackensack,NJ, rec. 30.1.1953
Davis,Miles (tp) | Rollins,Sonny (ts) | Parker,Charlie (ts) | Bishop Jr.,Walter (p) | Heath,Percy (b) | Jones,Philly Joe (dr)
Miles Davis Quartet
When Lights Are Low
Hackensack,NJ, rec. 19.5.1953
Davis,Miles (tp) | Lewis,John (p) | Heath,Percy (b) | Roach,Max (dr)
Thelonious Monk Quintet
Let's Call This
Hackensack,NJ, rec. 13.11.1953
Monk,Thelonious (p) | Rollins,Sonny (ts) | Watkins,Julius (fr-h) | Heath,Percy (b) | Jones,Willie (dr)
Miles Davis Quintet
Solar
Hackensack,NJ, rec. 3.4.1954
Davis,Miles (tp) | Schildkraut,Dave (as) | Silver,Horace (p) | Heath,Percy (b) | Blakey,Art (dr)
Thelonious Monk Quintet
Hackensack
Hackensack,NJ, rec. 11.5.1954
Monk,Thelonious (p) | Copeland,Ray (tp) | Foster,Frank (ts) | Russell,Curly (b) | Blakey,Art (dr)
Thelonious Monk
Just A Gigolo
Hackensack,NJ, rec. 22.9.1954
Monk,Thelonious (p-solo)
Sonny Rollins Quartet
The Way You Look Tonight
Hackensack,NJ, rec. 25.10.1954
Rollins,Sonny (ts) | Monk,Thelonious (p) | Potter,Tommy (b) | Taylor,Arthur 'Art' (dr)
Sonny Rollins Plus Four
Valse Hot
Hackensack,NJ, rec. 22.3.1956
Rollins,Sonny (ts) | Brown,Clifford (tp) | Powell,Richie (p) | Morrow,George (b) | Roach,Max (dr)
Prestige All Stars
Sunday
Hackensack,NJ, rec. 17.5.1957
Prestige All Stars | Coltrane,John (ts) | Quinichette,Paul (ts) | Waldron,Mal (p) | Euell,Julian (b) | Thigpen,Ed (dr)
John Coltrane Sextet
While My Lady Sleeps
Hackensack,NJ, rec. 31.5.1957
Coltrane,John (ts) | Splawn,Johnny (tp) | Shihab,Sahib (bs) | Waldron,Mal (p) | Chambers,Paul (b) | Heath,Albert 'Tootie' (dr)
John Coltrane Quartet
Bass Blues
Hackensack,NJ, rec. 23.8.1957
Coltrane,John (ts) | Garland,Red (p) | Chambers,Paul (b) | Taylor,Arthur 'Art' (dr)
You Say You Care
Hackensack,NJ, rec. 7.2.1958
Coltrane,John (ts) | Garland,Red (p) | Chambers,Paul (b) | Taylor,Arthur 'Art' (dr)

PCD 24252-2 | CD | The Prestige Legacy Vol.2:Battles Of Saxes
Stan Getz And His Four Brothers
Battle Of The Saxes
NYC, rec. 8.4.1949
Getz,Stan (ts) | Sims,Zoot (ts) | Eager,Allen (ts) | Moore,Brew (ts) | Bishop Jr.,Walter (p) | Ramey,Gene (b) | Perry,Charlie (dr)
Gene Ammons-Sonny Stitt Quintet
You Can Depend On Me
NYC, rec. 5.3.1950
Ammons,Gene (ts) | Stitt,Sonny (ts) | Jordan,Duke (p) | Potter,Tommy (b) | Jones,Jo (dr)
Wardell Gray Sextet
Scrapple From The Apple
Liveat The Hula Hut Club,Los Angeles,CA, rec. 27.8.1950
Gray,Wardell (ts) | Terry,Clark (tp) | Criss,Sonny (as) | Bunn,Jimmy (p) | Hadnott,Billy (b) | Thompson,Chuck (dr)

Sonny Rollins Quintet
Tenor Madness
Hackensack,NJ, rec. 24.5.1956
Rollins,Sonny (ts) | Coltrane,John (ts) | Garland,Red (p) | Chambers,Paul (b) | Jones,Philly Joe (dr)

Prestige All Stars
Kinda Kanonic
Hackensack,NJ, rec. 9.2.1957
Prestige All Stars | Woods,Phil (as) | Quill,Gene (as) | Stein,Hal (as) | Shihab,Sahib (as) | Waldron,Mal (p) | Potter,Tommy (b) | Hayes,Louis (dr)

Windy City
Hackensack,NJ, rec. 3.5.1957
Prestige All Stars | McLean,Jackie (as) | Jenkins,John (as) | Legge,Wade (p) | Watkins,Doug (b) | Taylor,Arthur 'Art' (dr)

Gene Ammons And His All Stars
Groove Blues
Hackensack,NJ, rec. 3.1.1958
Ammons,Gene (ts) | Richardson,Jerome (fl) | Coltrane,John (as,ts) | Quinichette,Paul (ts) | Adams,Pepper (bs) | Waldron,Mal (p) | Nasser,Jamil[George Joyner] (b) | Taylor,Arthur 'Art' (dr)

Very Saxy
Lester Leaps In
Hackensack,NJ, rec. 29.4.1959
Very Saxy | Davis,Eddie 'Lockjaw' (ts) | Hawkins,Coleman (ts) | Cobb,Arnett (ts) | Tate,Buddy (ts) | Scott,Shirley (org) | Duvivier,George (b) | Edgehill,Arthur (dr)

Oliver Nelson Sextet
Alto-Itis
Englewood Cliffs,NJ, rec. 27.5.1960
Nelson,Oliver (as,ts) | Williams,Richard (tp) | Dolphy,Eric (b-cl,as) | Wyands,Richard (p) | Duvivier,George (b) | Haynes,Roy (dr)

Eddie Lockjaw Davis-Johnny Griffin Quintet
Dee Dee's Dance
Live at Minton's Play House,NYC, rec. 6.1.1961
Davis,Eddie 'Lockjaw' (ts) | Griffin,Johnny (ts) | Mance,Junior[Julian C.] (p) | Gales,Larry (b) | Riley,Ben (dr)

Sonny Stitt Quartet
Sonny's Book
Englewood Cliffs,NJ, rec. 25.8.1964
Stitt,Sonny (as) | Ervin,Booker (ts) | Patterson,Don (org) | James,William 'Billy' (dr)

PCD 24253-2 | CD | The Boss Men
Sonny Stitt Trio
All God's Chillun Got Rhythm | Answering Service | Tangerine | Night Crawler | Who Can I Turn To | Star Eyes
Englewood Cliffs,NJ, rec. 21.9.1965
Stitt,Sonny (as) | Patterson,Don (org) | James,William 'Billy' (dr)
Diane | Someday My Prince Will Come | Easy To Love | What's New? | Big C's Rock | They Say It's Wonderful | Please Don't Talk About Me When I'm Gone | 42639
Englewood Cliffs,NJ, rec. 28.12.1965
Stitt,Sonny (as,ts) | Patterson,Don (org) | James,William 'Billy' (dr)

PCD 24254-2 | CD | Gravy
Willis Jackson Quintet
Brother Elijah | Doot Dat
Englewood Cliffs,NJ, rec. 23.5.1963
Jackson,Willis (ts) | Robinson,Frank (tp) | Martino,Pat (g) | Wilson,Carl (org) | Hadrick,Joe (dr)

Willis Jackson Sextet
The Good Life | Days Of Wine And Roses | As Long As She Needs Me | Fly Me To The Moon | Angel Eyes
Jackson,Willis (ts) | Robinson,Frank (tp) | Martino,Pat (g) | Wilson,Carl (org) | Gaskin,Leonard (b) | Hadrick,Joe (dr)
Stompin' At The Savoy | Gra-a-a-vy | Troubled Times | Walk Right In
Englewood Cliffs,NJ, rec. 24.5.1963
Jackson,Willis (ts) | Robinson,Frank (tp) | Martino,Pat (g) | Wilson,Carl (org) | Gaskin,Leonard (b) | Hadrick,Joe (dr)

Willis Jackson Quintet
Grease
Jackson,Willis (ts) | Robinson,Frank (tp) | Martino,Pat (g) | Wilson,Carl (org) | Hadrick,Joe (dr)

PCD 24256-2 | CD | The Soulful Drums
Jack McDuff Quartet
Soulful Drums | Two Bass Hit | Greasy Drums | Moohah The D.J. | Moanin' Bench | My Three Sons
Englewood Cliffs,NJ, rec. 14.5.1964
McDuff,Brother Jack (org) | Holloway,Red (as,ts) | Benson,George (g) | Dukes,Joe (dr)
Hot Barbeque | The Party's Over | Briar Patch | Hippy Dip | 601 1-2 North Polar St. | Cry Me A River | The Three Day Thang
Englewood Cliffs,NJ, rec. 19.10.1965
McDuff,Brother Jack (org) | Holloway,Red (as,ts) | Benson,George (g) | Dukes,Joe (dr)

Jack McDuff Sextet
Redwood City
Los Angeles,CA, rec. 6./7.2.1964
McDuff,Brother Jack (org) | Holloway,Red (ts) | Tyler,Alvin 'Red' (bs) | Benson,George (g) | Shelvin,Tommy (el-b) | Dukes,Joe (dr)

PCD 24257-2 | CD | The Soul Brotherhood
Charles Kynard Sextet
The Soul Brotherhood | Big City | Jealjon | Piece O'Pisces | Blue Farouq
Englewood Cliffs,NJ, rec. 10.3.1969
Kynard,Charles (org) | Mitchell,Blue (tp) | Newman,David Fathead (ts) | Green,Grant (g) | Lewis,Jimmy (el-b) | Roker,Granville 'Mickey' (dr)

Charles Kynard Quintet
Reelin' With The Feelin' | Soul Reggae | Slow Burn | Boogalooin' | Be My Love | Stomp
NYC, rec. 11.8.19969
Kynard,Charles (org) | Felder,Wilton (ts) | Pass,Joe (g) | Kaye,Carol (b) | Humphrey,Paul (dr)

PCD 24258-2 | CD | Like Cozy
Shirley Scott Trio
Sweet Lorraine | I Should Care | Gee Baby Ain't I Good To You | Until The Real Thing Comes Along
Hackensack,NJ, rec. 23.10.1958
Scott,Shirley (org) | Duvivier,George (b) | Edgehill,Arthur (dr)
I Thought I'd Let You Know | Spring Is Here | I Didn't Know What Time It Was | Lover Man(Oh,Where Can You Be?)
Englewood Cliffs,NJ, rec. 8.4.1960
Scott,Shirley (p) | Tucker,George (b) | Edgehill,Arthur (dr)
Like Cozy | Little Girl Blue | Laura | You Do Something To Me | Once In A While | 'Deed I Do | More Than You Know | My Heart Stood Still
Englewood Cliffs,NJ, rec. 27.9.1960
Scott,Shirley (org) | Duvivier,George (b) | Edgehill,Arthur (dr)

PCD 24260-2 | CD | Night Life
Billy Butler Quintet
Blow For The Crossing | Golden Earrings | The Thumb | Honky Tonk | B+B Calypso | Seven Come Eleven | Medley | Autumn Nocturne- | You Go To My Head-
Englewood Cliffs,NJ, rec. 22.9.1969
Butler,Billy (g,el-g,b-g) | Powell,Seldon (fl,varisax) | Philips,Sonny (org) | Bushnell,Bob (el-b) | Powell,Specs (dr)
Yesterday, Today And Tomorrow | Girl Talk | Dancing On The Ceiling | Hold It | Sweet Georgia Brown
Englewood Cliffs,NJ, rec. 29.6.1970
Butler,Billy (g,b-g) | Person,Houston (ts) | Hayes,Ernest 'Ernie' (org) | Lewis,Jimmy (el-b) | Johnson,Jimmy (dr)

Jerome Richardson Sextet
Evening Dreams | The Butler Did It
Englewood Cliffs,NJ, rec. 27.4.1970
Richardson,Jerome (fl,ts) | Philips,Sonny (el-p,org) | Suyker,Willard 'Bill' (g) | Barksdale,Everett (g) | Rainey,Chuck (el-b) | Johnson,Jimmy (dr)

PCD 24261-2 | CD | Brothers 4
Sonny Stitt Quintet
Brothers 4 | Creepin' Home | Alexander's Ragtime Band | Walk On By | Donnybrook | St.Thomas | Mud Turtle | Good Bait | Starry Night
Englewood Cliffs,NJ, rec. 15.9.1969
Stitt,Sonny (ts-varitone) | Green,Grant (g) | Patterson,Don (org) | James,William 'Billy' (dr)
Tune Up
Stitt,Sonny (as) | Green,Grant (g) | Patterson,Don (org) | James,William 'Billy' (dr)

PCD 24262-2 | CD | Uptown And Lowdown
Dick Wellstood's Wallerites
Yacht Club Swing | Brush Lightly | Blook's Dues
Englewood Cliffs,NJ, rec. 27.7.1961
Wellstood,Dick (p) | Autrey,Herman (tp) | Sedric,Gene (cl,ts) | Hinton,Milt (b) | Singleton,Zutty (dr)

Dick Wellstood-Tommy Benford
Old Fashioned Love | Mule Walk | Closed Mouth Blues | The Shout | Toodlin' Home | Alligator Crawl | Oh Baby, Watcha Doing To Me | Liza(All The Clouds'll Roll Away)
NYC, rec. 25.10.1954
Wellstood,Dick (p) | Benford,Tommy (dr)

Cliff Jackson's Washboard Wanderers
The Sheik Of Araby | I Found A New Baby | Wolverine Blues | Blues In Englewood Cliffs
Englewood Cliffs,NJ, rec. 20.7.1961
Jackson,Cliff (p) | Allen,Ed (tp) | Powell,Rudy (cl) | Snowden,Elmer (bj) | Bolar,Abe (b) | Casey,Floyd (wbd,kazoo)

PCD 24263-2 | CD | Disciples Blues
The Modern Jazz Disciples
After You've Gone | Disciples Blues | Slippin' And Slidin' | A Little Taste | Perhaps | Huck's Delight | Dottie
Englewood Cliffs,NJ, rec. 8.9.1959
Modern Jazz Disciples | Kelly,William 'Hicky' (normaphone,euphonium) | Peagler,Curtis (as) | Brown,William 'Billy' (p) | Tucker,Lee (b) | McCurdy,Roy (dr)
Hapnin's
Modern Jazz Disciples | Kelly,William 'Hicky' (normaphone) | Peagler,Curtis (as) | Brown,William 'Billy' (p) | Tucker,Lee (b) | Jackson,Wilber 'Slim' (dr)
Right Down Front | Along Come Cheryl | Ros-Al | The Happy Blues | My Funny Valentine | Kelley's Line
Englewood Cliffs,NJ, rec. 24.5.1960
Modern Jazz Disciples | Kelly,William 'Hicky' (normaphone) | Peagler,Curtis (as) | Brown,William 'Billy' (p) | Tucker,Lee (b) | McCurdy,Roy (dr)

PCD 24264-2 | CD | Trust In Me
Houston Person Quintet
Chocomotive | You're Gonna Hear From Me | Close Quarters | Since I Fell For You | More(Theme From Mondo Cane)
NYC, rec. 14.6.1967
Person,Houston (ts) | Dawson,Alan (vib) | Walton,Cedar (p) | Cranshaw,Bob (b) | Jones,Frankie (dr)
Airegin | One Mint Julep | Trust In Me | Hey There | My Little Suede Shoes | That Old Black Magic | Sometimes I Feel Like A Motherless Child | The Second Time Around
Englewood Cliffs,NJ, rec. 13.10.1967
Person,Houston (ts) | Walton,Cedar (p) | Cranshaw,Bob (b) | Jones,Frankie (dr) | Dorsey,Ralph (congas)

PR20 7174-2 | CD | Brother Jack
Jack McDuff Quartet
Brother Jack | Mr.Wonderful | Noon Train | Drowsy | Organ Grinder's Swing | Mack 'N' Duff | You're Driving Me Crazy | Light Blues
Englewood Cliffs,NJ, rec. 25.1.1960
McDuff,Brother Jack (org) | Jennings,Bill (g) | Marshall,Wendell (b) | Johnson,Alvin (dr)

PR20 7279-2 | CD | Mose Allison Sings The 7th Son
Mose Allison Trio
One Room Country Shack | Young Man
NYC, rec. 7.3.1957
Allison,Mose (p,voc) | LaFargue,Taylor (b) | Isola,Frank (dr)
Lost Mind | Parchman Farm
NYC, rec. 8.11.1957
Allison,Mose (p,voc) | Farmer,Addison (b) | Stabulas,Nick (dr)
Don't Get Around Much Anymore | I Hadn't Anyone 'Till You | Baby Let Me Hold Your Hand
NYC, rec. 24.1.1958
Allison,Mose (p,voc) | Farmer,Addison (b) | Stabulas,Nick (dr)
I Gotta Right To Cry
NYC, rec. 18.4.1958
Allison,Mose (p,voc) | Farmer,Addison (b) | Free,Ronnie (dr)
The Seventh Son | If You Live
NYC, rec. 15.8.1958
Allison,Mose (p,voc) | Farmer,Addison (b) | Free,Ronnie (dr)
Eyesight To The Blind | Do Nothin' Till You Hear From Me | That's All Right
NYC, rec. 13.2.1959
Allison,Mose (p,voc) | Farmer,Addison (b) | Free,Ronnie (dr)

PR20 7460-2 | CD | Groovin' With The Chet Baker Quintet
Chet Baker Quintet
Madison Avenue | Lonely Star | Wee,Too | Tan Gaugin | Cherokee | Bevan Beeps
Englewood Cliffs,NJ, rec. 23./25.& 29.8.1965
Baker,Chet (fl-h) | Coleman,George (ts) | Lightsey,Kirk (p) | Wright,Herman (b) | Brooks,Roy (dr)

PR20 7478-2 | CD | Comin' On With The Chet Baker Quintet
Comin' On | Stairway To The Stars | No Fair Lady | When You're Gone | Choose Now | Chabootie | Carpsie's Groove
Baker,Chet (fl-h) | Coleman,George (ts) | Lightsey,Kirk (p) | Wright,Herman (b) | Brooks,Roy (dr)

PR20 7496-2 | CD | Cool Burnin' With The Chet Baker Quintet
Hurry | I Waited For You | The 490 | Cut Plug | Boudoir | Etude In Three | Sleeping Susan
Baker,Chet (fl-h) | Coleman,George (ts) | Lightsey,Kirk (p) | Wright,Herman (b) | Brooks,Roy (dr)

PR20 7512-2 | CD | Boppin' With The Chet Baker Quintet
Go-Go | Lament For The Living | Pot Luck | Bud's Blues | Romas | On A Misty Night
Baker,Chet (fl-h) | Coleman,George (ts) | Lightsey,Kirk (p) | Wright,Herman (b) | Brooks,Roy (dr)

PR20 7749-2 | CD | Smokin' With The Chet Baker Quintet
Grade 'A' Gravy | Serenity | Fine And Dandy | Have You Met Miss Jones | Rearin' Back | So Easy
Baker,Chet (fl-h) | Coleman,George (ts) | Lightsey,Kirk (p) | Wright,Herman (b) | Brooks,Roy (dr)

PR20 7792-2 | CD | Brother Jug!
Gene Ammons Quintet
Ger-Ru
Chicago,Ill, rec. 10.11.1969
Ammons,Gene (ts) | James,Prince (ts) | Mance,Junior[Julian C.] (p) | Williams,Buster (b) | Jones,Frankie (dr)

Gene Ammons Quartet
Didn't We | He's A Real Gone Guy | Blue Velvet
Chicago,Ill, rec. 11.11.1969
Ammons,Gene (ts) | Phillips,Sonny (org) | Bushnell,Bob (el-b) | Purdie,Bernard 'Pretty' (dr)

Gene Ammons Quintet
Son Of A Preacher Man | Jungle Strut
Chicago,Ill, rec. 11.11.1979
Ammons,Gene (ts) | Butler,Billy (g) | Phillips,Sonny (org) | Bushnell,Bob (el-b) | Purdie,Bernard 'Pretty' (dr)

PRCD 11022-2 | CD | Left Bank Encores | EAN 025218312226
Gene Ammons-Sonny Stitt Quintet
Just In Time | They Can't Take That Away From Me | Autumn Leaves | Blues Up And Down
Live at The Famous Ballroom,Baltimore.MD, rec. 24.6.1973
Ammons,Gene (ts) | Stitt,Sonny (as,ts) | Walton,Cedar (p) | Jones,Sam (b) | Higgins,Billy (dr)
Exactly Like You | Don't Go To Strangers
Ammons,Gene (ts) | Stitt,Sonny (as,ts) | Walton,Cedar (p) | Jones,Sam (b) | Higgins,Billy (dr) | Jones,Etta (voc)

Cedar Walton Trio
Theme From Love Story
Walton,Cedar (p) | Jones,Sam (b) | Higgins,Billy (dr)

PRCD 11024-2 | CD | The Mal Waldron Memorial Album:Soul Eyes | EAN 090204922635
Mal Waldron
A Portrait Of Bud Powell
Live at The Cafe Bohemia,Greenwich Village,NYC, rec. 23.12.1955
Waldron,Mal (p-solo)

Prestige All Stars
Soul Eyes
Hackensack,NJ, rec. 22.3.1957
Prestige All Stars | Sulieman[Leonard Graham],Idrees (tp) | Young,Webster (co) | Coltrane,John (ts) | Jaspar,Bobby (ts) | Waldron,Mal (p) | Burrell,Kenny (g) | Chambers,Paul (b) | Taylor,Arthur 'Art' (dr)

Mal Waldron Sextet
Potpourri
Hackensack,NJ, rec. 19.4.1957
Waldron,Mal (p) | Hardman,Bill (tp) | McLean,Jackie (as) | Coltrane,John (ts) | Euell,Julian (b) | Taylor,Arthur 'Art' (dr)

John Coltrane Sextet
Dakar
Hackensack,NJ, rec. 20.4.1957
Coltrane,John (ts) | Payne,Cecil (bs) | Adams,Pepper (bs) | Waldron,Mal (p) | Watkins,Doug (b) | Taylor,Arthur 'Art' (dr)

John Coltrane Quintet
While My Lady Sleeps
Hackensack,NJ, rec. 31.5.1957
Coltrane,John (ts) | Splawn,Johnny (tp) | Waldron,Mal (p) | Chambers,Paul (b) | Heath,Albert 'Tootie' (dr)

Prestige All Stars
God Bless The Child
Hackensack,NJ, rec. 14.6.1957
Prestige All Stars | Young,Webster (co) | Quinichette,Paul (ts) | Puma,Joe (g) | Waldron,Mal (p) | May,Earl (b) | Thigpen,Ed (dr)

Prestige Jazz Quartet
Dear Elaine
Hackensack,NJ, rec. 22.6.1957
Prestige Jazz Quartet,The | Charles,Teddy (vib) | Waldron,Mal (p) | Farmer,Addison (b) | Segal,Jerry (dr)

Mal Waldron Trio
Splidium-Dow(alt.take)
Hackensack,NJ, rec. 26.9.1958
Farmer,Addison (b) | Segal,Jerry (dr) | Dennis,Kenny (dr)

Steve Lacy Quartet
Bye-Ya
Hackensack,NJ, rec. 17.10.1958
Lacy,Steve (ss) | Waldron,Mal (p) | Neidlinger,Buell (b) | Jones,Elvin (dr)

Mal Waldron Sextet
Fire Waltz
Englewood Cliffs,NJ, rec. 27.6.1961
Waldron,Mal (p) | Dolphy,Eric (cl,as) | Ervin,Booker (ts) | Carter,Ron (cello) | Benjamin,Joe (b) | Persip,Charles (dr)

Gene Ammons Quartet
Light'n Up
Englewood Cliffs,NJ, rec. 5.9.1962
Ammons,Gene (ts) | Waldron,Mal (p) | Marshall,Wendell (b) | Thigpen,Ed (dr)

PRCD 11025-2 | CD | The J.J.Johnson Memorial Album | EAN 090204922680
Coleman Hawkins All Stars
I Mean You
NYC, rec. December 1946
Hawkins,Coleman (ts) | Navarro,Fats (tp) | Johnson,J.J. (tb) | Kilbert,Porter (as) | Jones,Hank (p) | Russell,Curly (b) | Roach,Max (dr)

J.J.Johnson Sextet
Elysee
NYC, rec. 26.5.1949
Johnson,J.J. (tb) | Dorham,Kenny (tp) | Rollins,Sonny (ts) | Lewis,John (p) | Boyd,Nelson (b) | Roach,Max (dr)

J.J.Johnson Quintet
Blue Mode
NYC, rec. 17.10.1949
Johnson,J.J. (tb) | Stitt,Sonny (ts) | Lewis,John (p) | Boyd,Nelson (b) | Roach,Max (dr)

Four Trombones
Chazzanova
NYC, rec. 18.9.1953
Johnson,J.J. (tb) | Winding,Kai (tb) | Green,Bennie (tb) | Dennis,Willie (tb) | Lewis,John (p) | Mingus,Charles (b) | Taylor,Arthur 'Art' (dr)

Miles Davis All Stars
Blue 'N' Boogie
Hackensack,NJ, rec. 29.4.1954
Davis,Miles (tp) | Johnson,J.J. (tb) | Thompson,Lucky (ts) | Silver,Horace (p) | Heath,Percy (b) | Clarke,Kenny (dr)

J.J.Johnson-Kai Winding Quintet (Jay&Kai)
Bag's Groove
Hackensack,NJ, rec. 3.12.1954
Johnson,J.J. (tb) | Winding,Kai (tb) | Katz,Dick (p) | Morrison,Peck (b) | Harewood,Al (dr)

Coleman Hawkins All Stars
Laura
NYC, rec. 12.3.1957
Hawkins,Coleman (ts) | Sulieman[Leonard Graham],Idrees (tp) | Johnson,J.J. (tb) | Galbraith,Barry (g) | Jones,Hank (p) | Pettiford,Oscar (b) | Jones,Jo (dr)

Benny Golson Sextet
Hymn To The Orient
NYC, rec. 19.12.1957
Golson,Benny (ts) | Dorham,Kenny (tp) | Johnson,J.J. (tb) | Kelly,Wynton (p) | Chambers,Paul (b) | Roach,Max (dr)

J.J.Johnson-Nat Adderley Quintet
Horace
Live at Kanagawa Kenritsu Ongakudo,Yokohama,Japan, rec. 20.4.1977
Johnson,J.J. (tb) | Adderley,Nat (tp) | Childs,Billy (keyboards) | Dumas,Tony (b) | Johnson,Kevin (dr)

J.J.Johnson Quintet
Pinnacles
Berkeley,CA, rec. 18.9.1979
Johnson,J.J. (tb) | Henderson,Joe (ts) | Flanagan,Tommy (p,clavinet) | Carter,Ron (b) | Higgins,Billy (dr)

Kansas City Seven
Jaylock
Hollywood,CA, rec. 10.4.1980
Kansas City Seven,The | Johnson,J.J. (tb) | Davis,Eddie 'Lockjaw' (ts) | Pass,Joe (g) | Basie,Count (p) | Heard,John (b) | Hanna,Jake (dr)

J.J.Johnson Sextet
Concepts In Blue
Hollywood,CA, rec. 23.9.1980
Johnson,J.J. (tb) | Terry,Clark (tp) | Watts,Ernie (as,ts) | Childs,Billy (p) | Brown,Ray (b) | Johnson,Kevin (dr)

JATP All Stars
Misty
Live at The Tokyo Yoyogi National Stadium,Japan, rec. 17.10.1983
Johnson,J.J. (tb) | Pass,Joe (g)
What's New?
Johnson,J.J. (tb) | Peterson,Oscar (p) | Pass,Joe (g)

J.J.Johnson-Joe Pass
Nature Boy
Hollywood,CA, rec. 26.10.1983
Johnson,J.J. (tb) | Pass,Joe (g)

J.J. Johnson-Al Grey Sextet
Soft Winds
NYC, rec. 29.11.1983
Johnson,J.J. (tb) | Grey,Al (tb) | Barron,Kenny (keyboards) | Brown,Ray (b) | Roker,Granville 'Mickey' (dr) | Carey,Dave (perc)

PRCD 11026-2 | CD | The New Folk Sound Of Terry Callier | EAN 090204922642
Terry Callier Duo
900 Miles | Oh Dear,What Can The Matter Be | Johnny Be Gay If You Can Be |

Cotton Eyed Joe | It's About Time | Promenade In Greed | Spin Spin Spin |
I'm Drifter | Be My Woman | Jack O'Diamonds
Chicago,Ill, rec. 29.7.1964
Callier,Terry (g,voc) | Tweedle,John (b)
The Golden Apples Of The Sun
Callier,Terry (g,voc) | Attenbourough,Terbour (b)

PRCD 11027-2 | CD | Queen Of The Organ-Shirley Scott Memorial Album | EAN 090204922833
Shirley Scott Trio
It Could Happen To You
Hackensack,NJ, rec. 27.5.1958
Scott,Shirley (org) | Duvivier,George (b) | Edgehill,Arthur (dr)
Eddie Lockjaw Davis Quintet
The Chef
Hackensack,NJ, rec. 20.6.1958
Davis,Eddie 'Lockjaw' (ts) | Richardson,Jerome (fl,ts) | Scott,Shirley (org) | Duvivier,George (b) | Edgehill,Arthur (dr)
Shirley Horn Trio
Caravan
Hackensack,NJ, rec. 24.4.1959
Scott,Shirley (org) | Duvivier,George (b) | Edgehill,Arthur (dr)
Shirley Scott All Stars
Fourmost
Hackensack,NJ, rec. 29.4.1959
Scott,Shirley (org) | Davis,Eddie 'Lockjaw' (ts) | Hawkins,Coleman (ts) | Cobb,Arnett (ts) | Tate,Buddy (ts) | Duvivier,George (b) | Edgehill,Arthur (dr)
Al Smith With The Eddie Lockjaw Davis Quartet
Night Time Is The Right Time
Englewood Cliffs,NJ, rec. 20.9.1959
Smith,Al (voc) | Davis,Eddie 'Lockjaw' (ts) | Scott,Shirley (org) | Marshall,Wendell (b) | Edgehill,Arthur (dr)
Mildred Anderson With The Eddie Lockjaw Davis Quartet
Person To Person
Englewood Cliffs,NJ, rec. 22.1.1960
Anderson,Mildred (voc) | Davis,Eddie 'Lockjaw' (ts) | Scott,Shirley (org) | Duvivier,George (b) | Edgehill,Arthur (dr)
Eddie Lockjaw Davis Quartet
The Moon Of Manakoora
Englewood Cliffs,NJ, rec. 12.4.1960
Davis,Eddie 'Lockjaw' (ts) | Scott,Shirley (org) | Duvivier,George (b) | Edgehill,Arthur (dr)
Shirley Scott Quartet
Sonnymoon For Two
Englewood Cliffs,NJ, rec. 23.6.1960
Scott,Shirley (org) | Winchester,Lem (vib) | Duvivier,George (b) | Edgehill,Arthur (dr)
Shirley Scott Quintet
Travelin' Light
Englewood Cliffs,NJ, rec. 24.3.1961
Scott,Shirley (org) | Richardson,Wally (g) | Bright,Ronnell (p) | Morrison,Peck (b) | Haynes,Roy (dr)
Blue Seven
Englewood Cliffs,NJ, rec. 22.8.1961
Scott,Shirley (org) | Newman,Joe (tp) | Nelson,Oliver (ts) | Tucker,George (b) | Brooks,Roy (dr)
Shirley Scott Trio
Senor Blues
Englewood Cliffs,NJ, rec. 17.11.1961
Scott,Shirley (org) | Grimes,Henry (b) | Finch,Otis 'Candy' (dr)
Shirley Scott Quartet
Soul Shoutin'
Englewood Cliffs,NJ, rec. 15.10.1963
Scott,Shirley (org) | Turrentine,Stanley (ts) | May,Earl (b) | Oliphant,Grasselle (dr)
Solar
Englewood Cliffs,NJ, rec. 17.2.1964
Scott,Shirley (org) | Burrell,Kenny (g) | Kahn,Eddie (b) | Finch,Otis 'Candy' (dr)
Five Spot After Dark
Englewood Cliffs,NJ, rec. 31.3.1964
Scott,Shirley (org) | Turrentine,Stanley (ts) | Cranshaw,Bob (b) | Finch,Otis 'Candy' (dr)

PRCD 11028-2 | CD | On Basie's Bandstand | EAN 090204923502
Richard 'Groove' Holmes Trio
Back Home Again In Indiana | Moanin' | When I Grow Too Old To Dream | Rifftide | This Here | Nica's Dream | Night Train
Live at Count Basie's,Harlem,NY, rec. 22.4.1966
Holmes,Richard 'Groove' (org) | Edwards,Gene (g) | Randall,George (dr)

PRCD 11029-2 | CD | The Last From Lennie's | EAN 090204923533
Jaki Byard Quartet
Twelve(alt.take) | Dolphy No.1 | After You've Gone- | Strolling Along- | St. Mark's Place Among The Sewers | Dolphy No.2 | Jaki Byard's Ballad Medley: | Tea For Two- | Lover- | Strolling Along- | Cherokee- | Shiny Stockings- | King David
Live at Lennie's At The Tumpike,West Peabody,MA, rec. 15.4.1965
Byard,Jaki (p) | Farrell,Joe (fl,ss,ts) | Tucker,George (b) | Dawson,Alan (dr)

PRCD 24043-2 | CD | Another Monday Date | EAN 025218544320
Earl Hines Quartet
Jitterbug Waltz | Black And Blue | Blue Turning Grey Over Me | Honeysuckle Rose | Squeeze Me | Ain't Misbehavin' | Keepin' Out Of Mischief Now | I Can't Give You Anything But Love | I'm Gonna Sit Right Down And Write Myself A Letter
Live at Marines' Memorial Auditorium,San Francisco,CA, rec. December 1955/January 1956
Hines,Earl 'Fatha' (p) | Duran,Eddie (g) | Reilly,Dean (b) | Watkins,Earl (dr)
Earl Hines
Deep Forest | Everything Depends On Me | Am I Too Late? | Blues For Tatum | In San Francisco | Ann | You Can Depend On Me | When I Dream Of You | R.R.Blues | Straight To Love | Piano Man | My Monday Date
San Francisco,CA, rec. December 1956
Hines,Earl 'Fatha' (p-solo)

PRCD 24265-2 | CD | Nuther'n Like Thuther'n | EAN 025218526524
Willis Jackson Sextet
Pool Shark | Somewhere Along The Way | Stuffin' | Nuther'n Like Thuther'n | More Gravy | Fiddlin'
Englewood Cliffs,NJ, rec. 24.10.1963
Jackson,Willis (ts) | Robinson,Frank (tp) | Wilson,Carl (org) | Martino,Pat (g) | Jones,Sam (b) | Hadrick,Joe (dr)
St.Louis Blues | Que Sera,Sweetie | Shoutin' | Nice 'N' Easy | Your Wonderful Love
Englewood Cliffs,NJ, rec. 9.1.1964
Jackson,Willis (ts) | Robinson,Frank (tp) | Wilson,Carl (org) | Martino,Pat (g) | Tucker,George (b) | Hadrick,Joe (dr)

PRCD 24266-2 | CD | A Stranger In Town | EAN 025218526623
Gene Ammons And His Orchestra
The Song Is You
NYC, rec. 13.6.1928
Ammons,Gene (ts) | Terry,Clark (tp) | Dotson,Hobart (tp) | Nelson,Oliver (as) | Holloway,Red (ts) | Barrow,George (ts) | Ashton,Bob (bs) | Wyands,Richard (p) | Marshall,Wendell (b) | English,Bill (dr) | Barretto,Ray (congas)
Gene Ammons Quartet
Light'n Up | Short Stop | They Say You're Laughing At Me | A Stranger In Town | Blue Coolade | Salome's Tune
NYC, rec. 5.9.1962
Ammons,Gene (ts) | Waldron,Mal (p) | Marshall,Wendell (b) | Thigpen,Ed (dr)
Scam
NYC, rec. 13.4.1962
Ammons,Gene (ts) | Bown,Patti (p) | Duvivier,George (b) | Perkins,Walter (dr)
Gene Ammons Septet
Count Your Blessings | Cara Mia
NYC, rec. 26.11.1954
Ammons,Gene (ts) | Woodward,Nate (tp) | Chambers,Henderson (tb) | Easton,Gene (bs) | Houston,John (p) | Steuberville,Ben (b) | Brown,George (dr)
Gene Ammons Quartet
Night Lights | Nature Boy
Englewood Cliffs,NJ, rec. 2.2.1970
Ammons,Gene (ts) | Kelly,Wynton (p) | Duvivier,George (b) | Collins,Rudy (dr)
Gene Ammons Quintet
Calypso Blues
Ammons,Gene (ts) | Kelly,Wynton (p) | Duvivier,George (b) | Collins,Rudy (dr) | Brown,Henry 'Pucho' (congas)

PRCD 24267-2 | CD | Charles Earland In Concert | EAN 025218526722
Charles Earland Septet
Smilin' | We've Only Just Begun | Black Gun | Spinky | Freedom Jazz Dance | The Moontrane
Live at The Lighthouse,Hermosa Beach,CA, rec. 1972
Earland,Charles (org) | Coles,Elmer (tp) | Adams,Clifford (tb) | Vass,James 'Jimmy' (ss,as) | Parker,Maynard (g) | Washington,Darryl (dr) | Nash,Kenneth (congas)
Kharma | Suite For Martin Luther King: | Mode For Martin-
Live at The Montreux Jazz Festival, rec. 6.7.1974
Earland,Charles (org,el-p,synth) | Faddis,Jon (tp) | Adams,Clifford (tb) | Hubbard,Dave (fl,ss,ts) | Ray,Aurell (g) | Carter,Ron (el-b) | Johnson,George (dr)
Charles Earland Sextet
Joe Brown | Morgan | Suite For Martin Luther King: | Offering-
Earland,Charles (org,el-p) | Faddis,Jon (tp) | Adams,Clifford (tb) | Hubbard,Dave (fl,ss,ts) | Ray,Aurell (g) | Johnson,George (dr)

PRCD 24268-2 | CD | About Time | EAN 025218526821
Eric Kloss Quartet
Close Your Eyes | Old Folks | 'S 'Bout Time | That's The Way It Is | All Blues | Embraceable You
Englewood Cliffs,NJ, rec. 1.9.1965
Kloss,Eric (as,ts) | Patterson,Don (org) | Martino,Pat (g) | James,Billy (dr)
You'd Be So Nice To Come Home To | Just For Fun-K | N.O.Blues | Love For Sale | I'm Glad There Is You
Englewood Cliffs,NJ, rec. 11.4.1966
Kloss,Eric (as,ts) | Patterson,Don (org) | Corrao,Vinnie (g) | James,Billy (dr)
The Shadow Of Your Smile | Gemini
Kloss,Eric (as,ts) | Holmes,Richard 'Groove' (org) | Edwards,Gene (g) | Tate,Grady (dr)

PRCD 24269-2 | CD | For The Good Times | EAN 025218526920
Rusty Bryant Sextet
For The Good Times | Killing Me Softly With His Song | The Last One Out | Appalachian Green | A Night In Tunisia | Looking Through The Eyes Of Love | Theme From Deep Throat
Englewood Cliffs,NJ, rec. 9.3.1973
Bryant,Rusty (as,ts) | Beck,Joe (g) | McCracken,Hugh (g) | Jones,Hank (el-p) | Levin,Tony (b,el-b) | Gadd,Steve (dr)
Rusty Bryant Group
The Hump Bump | Troubles | Until It's Time For You To Go
NYC, rec. 1./2.8.1974
Bryant,Rusty (as,ts) | Ott,Horace (p,clavinet) | Spinozza,David (g) | McCracken,Hugh (g) | Hayes,Ernest 'Ernie' (org) | Bascomb,Wilbur (b) | Purdie,Bernard 'Pretty' (dr) | Devens,George (vib,perc)
The Red-Eye Special
Bryant,Rusty (as,ts) | Faddis,Jon (tp) | Shepley,Joe (tp) | Ott,Horace (el-p) | Spinozza,David (g) | Resnicoff,Richie (g) | Hayes,Ernest 'Ernie' (org) | Bascomb,Wilbur (b) | Purdie,Bernard 'Pretty' (dr) | Devens,George (vib,perc)
Ga Gang Gang Gong
Bryant,Rusty (as,ts) | Faddis,Jon (tp) | Shepley,Joe (tp) | Ott,Horace (clavinet) | Spinozza,David (g) | Resnicoff,Richie (g) | Hayes,Ernest 'Ernie' (org) | Bascomb,Wilbur (b) | Purdie,Bernard 'Pretty' (dr) | Devens,George (vib,perc)
Draggin' In The Line
Bryant,Rusty (as,ts) | Ott,Horace (clavinet) | Spinozza,David (g) | Hayes,Ernest 'Ernie' (org) | Bascomb,Wilbur (b) | Purdie,Bernard 'Pretty' (dr) | Devens,George (vib,perc)

PRCD 24270-2 | CD | The Concert McDuff | EAN 025218527026
Jack McDuff Quartet
Undecided(alt.take) | Love Walked In | Midnight Sun
Newark,NJ, rec. 5.6.1963
McDuff,Brother Jack (org) | Holloway,Red (ts) | Benson,George (g) | Dukes,Joe (dr)
Swedenin' | Girl From Ipanema(Garota De Ipanema) | Another Goodun' | 'Sokay | Save Your Love For Me | Four Brothers | Lew's Piece
Live at The Golden Circle,Stockholm, rec. July 1964
McDuff,Brother Jack (org) | Holloway,Red (ts) | Benson,George (g) | Dukes,Joe (dr)
Spoonin'
Hackensack,NJ, rec. 1965/1966
McDuff,Brother Jack (org) | Holloway,Red (ts) | Martino,Pat (g) | Dukes,Joe (dr)

PRCD 24271-2 | CD | Ronnie Mathews-Roland Alexander-Freddie Hubbard | EAN 025218527125
Ronnie Mathews Quintet
The Thang | Ichi-Ban | The Orient | Let's Get Down | 1239A
Englewood Cliffs,NJ, rec. 17.12.1963
Mathews,Ronnie (p) | Hubbard,Freddie (tp) | Davis,Charles (bs) | Kahn,Eddie (b) | Heath,Albert 'Tootie' (dr)
Ronnie Mathews Trio
Prelude To A Kiss
Mathews,Ronnie (p) | Kahn,Eddie (b) | Heath,Albert 'Tootie' (dr)
Roland Alexander Quintet
Lil's Blues | Orders To Take Out | My Melancholy Baby | Pleasure Bent | I'll Be Around | Dorman Road
Englewood Cliffs,NJ, rec. 17.6.1961
Alexander,Roland (ts) | Belgrave,Marcus (tp) | Mathews,Ronnie (p) | Taylor,Gene (b) | Stroman,Clarence 'Scoby' (dr)

PRCD 24272-2 | CD | Stretching Out | EAN 025218527224
Red Garland Trio
Satin Doll | The Man I Love | A Little Bit Of Basie
Englewood Cliffs,NJ, rec. 12.8.1959
Garland,Red (p) | Watkins,Doug (b) | Wright,Charles 'Specs' (dr)
It's A Blue World | M-Squad Theme | Lil' Darlin' | We Kiss In The Shadow | Blues In The Closet | Like Someone In Love
Live at The Prelude Club,NYC, rec. 2.10.1959
Garland,Red (p) | Rowser,Jimmy (b) | Wright,Charles 'Specs' (dr)

PRCD 24273-2 | CD | Soul Night Live! | EAN 025218527323
Willis Jackson Quintet
Jumpin' With Symphony Sid | Tangerine | Ebb Tide | Blue Gator | Secret Love
Live at The Allegro,NYC, rec. 21.3.1964
Jackson,Willis (ts) | Robinson,Frank (tp) | Martino,Pat (g) | Wilson,Carl (org) | Hadrick,Joe (dr)

PRCD 24274-2 | CD | The Last Goodun' | EAN 025218527422
Jack McDuff Quartet
It's Alvin Again
Englewood Cliffs,NJ, rec. 21.8.1959
McDuff,Brother Jack (org) | Jennings,Bill (g) | Marshall,Wendell (b) | Dukes,Joe (dr)
Your Nose Is Open | The Last Goodun' | Scram | Dink's Dream | Groanin' | Hey Lawdy Mama | Drown In My
Englewood Cliffs,NJ, rec. 1.12.1961
McDuff,Brother Jack (org) | Vick,Harold (ts) | Diehl,Eddie (g) | Dukes,Joe (dr)
Ballad For Baby
Englewood Cliffs,NJ, rec. 23.1.1962
McDuff,Brother Jack (org) | Ammons,Gene (ts) | Diehl,Eddie (g) | Dukes,Joe (dr)
Jack McDuff Orchestra
9:20 Special
Englewood Cliffs,NJ, rec. 2.1.1963
McDuff,Brother Jack (org) | Mitchell,Blue (tp) | Cooper,Frank 'Buster' (tb) | Turner,Danny (as) | Vick,Harold (ts) | Diehl,Eddie (g) | Dukes,Joe (dr)
Jack McDuff Trio
Easy To Love
Englewood Cliffs,NJ, rec. 1964/1965
McDuff,Brother Jack (org) | Vick,Harold (ts) | Dukes,Joe (dr)
Jack McDuff Quintet
What's Shakin'
Englewood Cliffs,NJ, rec. 1965
McDuff,Brother Jack (org) | Holloway,Red (ts) | Benson,George (g) | Dukes,Joe (dr) | Montego Joe (congas)
The Morning Song
McDuff,Brother Jack (org) | Holloway,Red (fl) | Gales,Larry (b) | Benson,George (g) | Montego Joe (congas)
Jack McDuff Quartet
Twelve Inches Wide
McDuff,Brother Jack (org) | Holloway,Red (ts) | Benson,George (g) | Dukes,Joe (dr)

PRCD 24276-2 | CD | Goin' Down Slow | EAN 090204933808
Sonny Stitt Quartet
Back Door | Your Love Is So Doggone Good - (Your Love Is) So Doggone Good | Orange Ashtray | I Don't Know Yet | The More I See You | Speculation
Berkeley,CA, rec. 13./14.9.1972
Stitt,Sonny (as,ts) | Hawes,Hampton (p) | Johnson,Reggie (b) | McBrowne,Lennie (dr)
Sonny Stitt With Orchestra
Miss Ann,Lisa,Sue And Sadie | Where Is Love | Living Without You | Goin' Down Slow | Moving Beauty
Englewood Cliffs,NJ, rec. 5.2.1972
Stitt,Sonny (as,ts) | Jones,Thad (tp,arr) | Butler,Billy (g) | Richardson,Wally (g) | Jones,Hank (p) | Duvivier,George (b) | Muhammad,Idris[Leo Morris] (dr) | Caldwell,Buddy (perc,congas) | Nadien,David (strings) | Ellen,Max (strings) | Brand,Julius (strings) | Baumel,Herbert (strings) | VerPlanck,Billy (arr)

PRCD 24277-2 | CD | Bobby Timmons:The Prestige Trio Sessions | EAN 090204933815
Bobby Timmons Trio
A Little Barefoot Soul | Walkin' Wadin' Sittin' Ridin' | Little One | Cut Me Loose,Charlie | Ain't Thinkin' 'Bout It | Nobody Knows The Trouble I've Seen
Englewood Cliffs,NJ, rec. 18.6.1964
Timmons,Bobby (p) | Jones,Sam (b) | Lucas,Ray (dr)
Chun-King | Walking Death | O Grande Amor | Gettin' It Togetha' | I Could Have Danced All Night | Someone To Watch Over Me
Englewood Cliffs,NJ, rec. 12.8.1964
Timmons,Bobby (p) | Betts,Keter (b) | Heath,Albert 'Tootie' (dr)

PRCD 24278-2 | CD | Northern Windows Plus | EAN 090204933839
Hampton Hawes Trio
Playin' In The Yard | Double Trouble | Pink Peaches | De De | Stella By Starlight
Live at The Montreux Jazz Festival, rec. 7.7.1973
Hawes,Hampton (p,el-p) | Cranshaw,Bob (el-b) | Clarke,Kenny (dr)
Hampton Hawes Orchestra
Sierra Morena | Go Down Moses | Bach | Web | Tune Axle Grease | C & H Sugar
Berkeley,CA, rec. 18./19.7.1974
Hawes,Hampton (p,el-p) | De Rienzo,Allen (tp) | Young,Eugene 'Snooky' (tp) | Bohanon,George (tb) | Kelso,Jack (fl,reeds) | Green,William (fl,reeds) | Migliori,Jay (fl,reeds) | Kaye,Carol (b) | Webb,Spider (dr)

PRCD 24279-2 | CD | Jazz Sounds Of Africa | EAN 090204933846
Ahmed Abdullah Sextet
Nights On Saturn | The Hustlers | Oud Blues | La Ibkey | Don't Blame Me | Hannibal's Carnivals | Out Of Nowhere
Englewood Cliffs,NJ, rec. 23.5.1961
Abdul-Malik,Ahmed (b,oud) | Turrentine,Tommy (tp) | Abdurrahman,Bilal (cl,darabeka,perc) | Dixon,Eric (ts) | Scott,Calo (cello) | Cyrille,Andrew (dr)
Ahmed Abdul-Malik Orchestra
Wakida Hena | African Bossa Nova | Nadusilma | Communication | Suffering
Englewood Cliffs,NJ, rec. 22.8.1962
Abdul-Malik,Ahmed (b,oud) | Alleyne,Rupert (fl) | Williams,Richard (tp) | Abdurrahman,Bilal (cl,darabeka,perc) | Steede,Erwin (as) | Chandler,Taft (ts) | Scott,Calo (v,cello) | Collins,Rudy (dr) | Montego Joe (congas,bongos) | Bey,Chief (african-dr)

PRCD 24281-2 | CD | Fine And Mellow | EAN 090204923335
Gene Ammons Sextet With Strings
Lady Sings The Blues | Play Me | Ben
Englewood Cliffs,NJ, rec. 28.10.1972
Ammons,Gene (ts) | Beck,Joe (g) | Jones,Hank (el-p) | Hayes,Ernest 'Ernie' (org) | Carter,Ron (b,el-b) | Muhammad,Idris[Leo Morris] (dr) | Strings | Bogas,Ed (cond,arr)
Gene Ammons Sextet
Fly Me | Fuzz
Ammons,Gene (ts) | Beck,Joe (g) | Jones,Hank (el-p) | Hayes,Ernest 'Ernie' (org) | Carter,Ron (b,el-b) | Muhammad,Idris[Leo Morris] (dr)
Fine And Mellow | Big Bad Jug
Englewood Cliffs,NJ, rec. 30.10.1972
Ammons,Gene (ts) | Beck,Joe (g) | Jones,Hank (el-p) | Hayes,Ernest 'Ernie' (org) | Carter,Ron (b,el-b) | Roker,Granville 'Mickey' (dr)
Gene Ammons Quartet
Strange Fruit
Ammons,Gene (ts) | Jones,Hank (el-p) | Carter,Ron (b,el-b) | Muhammad,Idris[Leo Morris] (dr)
Gene Ammons Quintet
God Bless The Child | Tin Shack Out Back | Lady Mama | Can't Help Myself | Lucille | Papa Was A Rolling Stone
Englewood Cliffs,NJ, rec. 1.11.1972
Ammons,Gene (ts) | Parker,Maynard (g) | Phillips,Sonny (el-p,org) | Carter,Ron (b,el-b) | Cobham,Billy (dr)

PRCD 24282-2 | CD | Good 'Nuff | EAN 025218528221
Johnny 'Hammond' Smith Quartet
Good 'Nuff | Sonja's Dreamland | Besame Mucho | Neck Bones | Delicious | Y'all
Englewood Cliffs,NJ, rec. 12.6.1962
Smith,Johnny 'Hammond' (org) | Jackson,Willis (ts) | McFadden,Eddie (g) | Stevens,Leo (dr)
Johnny 'Hammond' Smith Trio
Nobody Knows The Trouble I've Seen
Smith,Johnny 'Hammond' (org) | McFadden,Eddie (g) | Stevens,Leo (dr)
Johnny 'Hammond' Smith Quartet
The Stinger | Cleopatra And The African Knight | Benny's Diggin'
Englewood Cliffs,NJ, rec. 7.5.1965
Smith,Johnny 'Hammond' (org) | Person,Houston (ts) | Smith,Floyd (g) | Harris,John 'Ironman' (dr)
There Is No Greater Love | Brother John | You Don't Know What Love Is
Smith,Johnny 'Hammond' (org) | Edwards,Earl (ts) | Smith,Floyd (g) | Harris,John 'Ironman' (dr)

PRCD 24283-2 | CD | Prelude:Jack McDuff Big Band | EAN 090204923182
Jack McDuff Quartet With Orchestra
A Kettle Of Fish | Candlelight | Put On A Happy Face | Prelude | Mean To Me | Carry Me Home | Easy Living | Oh Look At Me Now | Dig Cousin Will
Englewood Cliffs,NJ, rec. 24.12.1963
McDuff,Brother Jack (org) | Holloway,Red (ts) | Benson,George (g) | Dukes,Joe (dr) | Stiles,Danny (tp) | Kail,Jerome (tp) | Byers,Billy (tb) | Collins,Burt (tb) | McIntosh,Tom (tb) | Ashworth,Don (fr-h) | Northern,Bob (fr-h) | Marge,George (sax) | Holladay,Marvin (sax) | Davis,Richard (b) | Lewis,Mel (dr) | Rodriguez,Willie (perc) | Golson,Benny (arr,ld)
Theme From The Carpetbaggers | Theme From The Pink Panther | You'd Better Love Me | Once In A Lifetime | Rock-A-Bye

Englewood Cliffs,NJ, rec. 7.4.1964
McDuff,Brother Jack (org) | Holloway,Red (as,ts) | Benson,George (g) | Dukes,Joe (dr) | Stiles,Danny (tp) | Kail,Jerome (tp) | Byers,Billy (tb) | Collins,Burt (tb) | McIntosh,Tom (tb) | Ashworth,Don (fr-h) | Northern,Bob (fr-h) | Marge,George (sax) | Holladay,Marvin (sax) | Davis,Richard (b) | Lewis,Mel (dr) | Rodriguez,Willie (perc) | Golson,Benny (arr,ld)

English Country Gardens | Shortnin' Bread
Englewood Cliffs,NJ, rec. early 1965
McDuff,Brother Jack (org) | Holloway,Red (as,ts) | Benson,George (g) | Dukes,Joe (dr) | Stiles,Danny (tp) | Kail,Jerome (tp) | Byers,Billy (tb) | Collins,Burt (tb) | McIntosh,Tom (tb) | Ashworth,Don (fr-h) | Northern,Bob (fr-h) | Marge,George (sax) | Holladay,Marvin (sax) | Davis,Richard (b) | Lewis,Mel (dr) | Rodriguez,Willie (perc) | Golson,Benny (arr,ld)

Walk On By | Talking 'Bout My Woman
Englewood Cliffs,NJ, rec. February 1966

Jersey Bounce | Too Many Fish In The Sea
McDuff,Brother Jack (org) | Holloway,Red (ts) | Ousley,Harold (ts) | Benson,George (g) | Dukes,Joe (dr) | prob.personal: | Stiles,Danny (tp) | Kail,Jerome (tp) | Byers,Billy (tb) | Collins,Burt (tb) | McIntosh,Tom (tb) | Ashworth,Don (fr-h) | Northern,Bob (fr-h) | Marge,George (sax) | Holladay,Marvin (sax) | Davis,Richard (b) | Lewis,Mel (dr) | Rodriguez,Willie (perc) | Golson,Benny (arr,ld)

PRCD 24284-2 | CD | Together Again: Willis Jackson With Jack McDuff | EAN 090204923489

Willis Jackson Quintet

Gil's Pills | Angel Eyes | Three Little Words | Glad 'A See Ya'
Hackensack,NJ, rec. 25.5.1959
Jackson,Willis (ts) | Jennings,Bill (g) | McDuff,Brother Jack (org) | Potter,Tommy (b) | Johnson,Al (dr)

Medley | September Song- | Easy Living- | Deep Purple-
Englewood Cliffs,NJ, rec. 9.11.1959
Jackson,Willis (ts) | Jennings,Bill (g) | McDuff,Brother Jack (org) | Marshall,Wendell (b) | Johnson,Al (dr)

Willis Jackson Sextet

Dancing On The Ceiling | It Might As Well Be Spring | This'll Get To Ya
Englewood Cliffs,NJ, rec. 26.2.1960
Jackson,Willis (ts) | Jennings,Bill (g) | McDuff,Brother Jack (org) | Hinton,Milt (b) | Johnson,Al (dr) | Clarke,Buck (congas)

Willis Jackson Quintet

Tu' Gether
Englewood Cliffs,NJ, rec. 16.8.1960
Jackson,Willis (ts) | Jennings,Bill (g) | McDuff,Brother Jack (org) | Marshall,Wendell (b) | Elliott,Bill (dr)

Jambalaya(On The Bayou) | Backtrack(Twistin' Train) | Without A Song | Snake Crawl
Englewood Cliffs,NJ, rec. 13.12.1961
Jackson,Willis (ts) | Jennings,Bill (g) | McDuff,Brother Jack (org) | Lewis,Jimmy (b) | Shea,Frank (dr)

PRCD 24285-2 | CD | Billy Taylor Trio | EAN 090204923496

Billy Taylor Trio

A Foggy Day(In London Town) | I'll Remember April | Sweet Georgia Brown | Theodora | How High The Moon
Hackensack,NJ, rec. 17.12.1954
Taylor,Billy (p) | May,Earl (b) | Brice,Percy (dr)

Early Bird | A Bientot | Memories Of Spring | Ever So Easy | Day Dreaming | Radio-Activity | Purple Mood | Long Tom | It's A Grand Night For Swingin' | Blue Clouds | Live It Up | Daddy-O
Hackensack,NJ, rec. 10.4.1955
Taylor,Billy (p) | May,Earl (b) | Brice,Percy (dr)

PRCD 24286-2 | CD | The Bud Freeman All-Star Sessions | EAN 090204923472

Bud Freeman All Stars

I Let A Song Go Out Of My Heart | S' Posin' | March On March On | Shorty's Blues | Love Me Or Leave Me | Something To Remember You By | Hector's Dance | But Not For Me
Englewood Cliffs,NJ, rec. 13.5.1960
Freeman,Bud (ts) | Baker,Harold 'Shorty' (tp) | Hopkins,Claude (p) | Duvivier,George (b) | Heard,J.C. (dr)

Darktown Strutters Ball
Englewood Cliffs,NJ, rec. 23.8.1962
Freeman,Bud (ts) | Autrey,Herman (tp) | Wells,Dicky (tb) | Hall,Herb (cl) | Richards,Charles 'Red' (p) | Gaskin,Leonard (b,ld) | Lovelle,Herbie (dr)

It Had To Be You | Farewell Blues
Freeman,Bud (ts) | Erwin,Pee Wee (tp) | Moore,Russel 'Big Chief' (tb) | Richards,Charles 'Red' (p) | Gaskin,Leonard (b,ld) | Lovelle,Herbie (dr)

Keep Smiling At Trouble | The Buzzard | What Is There To Say | Tillie's Downtown Now
Freeman,Bud (ts) | Berigan,Bunny (tp) | Condon,Eddie (g) | Thornhill,Claude (p) | Moncur,Grachan (b) | Cole,William 'Cozy' (dr)

PRCD 24387-2 | CD | Jack McDuff:The Prestige Years | EAN 025218528726

Jack McDuff Quartet

Brother Jack | Organ Grinder's Swing
Englewood Cliffs,NJ, rec. 25.1.1960
McDuff,Brother Jack (org) | Jennings,Bill (g) | Marshall,Wendell (b) | Johnson,Alvin (dr)

Yeah Baby | Tough 'Duff
Englewood Cliffs,NJ, rec. 12.7.1960
McDuff,Brother Jack (org) | Forrest,Jimmy (ts) | Winchester,Lem (vib) | Elliott,Bill (dr)

The Honeydripper
Englewood Cliffs,NJ, rec. 3.2.1961
McDuff,Brother Jack (org) | Forrest,Jimmy (ts) | Green,Grant (g) | Dixon,Ben (dr)

Sanctified Waltz
Englewood Cliffs,NJ, rec. 14.7.1961
McDuff,Brother Jack (org) | Vick,Harold (ts) | Green,Grant (g) | Dukes,Joe (dr)

Jack McDuff Quintet

Mellow Gravy
Englewood Cliffs,NJ, rec. 23.1.1962
McDuff,Brother Jack (org) | Ammons,Gene (ts) | Vick,Harold (ts) | Diehl,Eddie (g) | Dukes,Joe (dr)

Jack McDuff Quartet

He's A Real Gone Guy | Screamin'
Englewood Cliffs,NJ, rec. 23.10.1962
McDuff,Brother Jack (org) | Wright,Leo (as) | Burrell,Kenny (g) | Dukes,Joe (dr)

Rock Candy
Englewood Cliffs,NJ, rec. 5.6.1963
McDuff,Brother Jack (org) | Holloway,Red (ts) | Benson,George (g) | Dukes,Joe (dr)

Grease Monkey | Jive Samba
Live at The Jazz Workshop,San Francisco,CA, rec. 3.10.1963
McDuff,Brother Jack (org) | Vick,Harold (ts) | Benson,George (g) | Dukes,Joe (dr)

Opus De Funk
NYC, rec. July 1964
McDuff,Brother Jack (org) | Holloway,Red (ts) | Benson,George (g) | Dukes,Joe (dr)

Hot Barbeque
Englewood Cliffs,NJ, rec. 19.10.1965
McDuff,Brother Jack (org) | Holloway,Red (as,ts) | Benson,George (g) | Dukes,Joe (dr)

PRCD 24770-2 | CD | The Mastersounds | EAN 025218247023

The Mastersounds

Golden Earrings | People Will Say We're In Love | There Is No Greater Love | West Coast Blues | I've Never Been In Love Before- | Don't Blame Me- | I Could Write A Book
NYC, rec. 10.8.1960
Mastersounds,The | Montgomery,Buddy (vib) | Crabtree,Richie (p) | Montgomery,Monk (b) | Barth,Benny (dr)

Whisper Not | Fink-Fank-Funk | It Could Happen To You | Try It | Alone Together | For Now | Surrey With The Fringe On Top
NYC, rec. 2.11.1960
Mastersounds,The | Montgomery,Buddy (vib) | Crabtree,Richie (p) | Montgomery,Monk (b) | Barth,Benny (dr)

PRSA 7047-6 | SACD | Tenor Madness | EAN 025218731560

Sonny Rollins Quartet

When Your Lover Has Gone | Paul's Pal | My Reverie | The Most Beautiful Girl In The World
Hackensack,NJ, rec. 24.5.1956
Rollins,Sonny (ts) | Garland,Red (p) | Chambers,Paul (b) | Jones,Philly Joe (dr)

Sonny Rollins Quintet

Tenor Madness
Rollins,Sonny (ts) | Coltrane,John (ts) | Garland,Red (p) | Chambers,Paul (b) | Jones,Philly Joe (dr)

PRSA 7120-6 | SACD | Gil Evans And Ten | EAN 025218730426

Gil Evans And Ten

Remember
Hackensack,NJ, rec. 9.9.1957
Evans,Gil (p,arr) | Carisi,Johnny (tp) | Koven,Jack (tp) | Cleveland,Jimmy (tb) | Varsalona,Bart (tb) | Ruff,Willie (fr-h) | Konitz,Lee[as Zeke Tolin] (as) | Lacy,Steve (ss) | Kurtzer,Dave (bassoon) | Chambers,Paul (b) | Jones,Jo (dr)

Nobody's Heart | If You Could See Me Now
Hackensack,NJ, rec. 27.9.1957
Evans,Gil (p,arr) | Mucci,Louis (tp) | Koven,Jack (tp) | Cleveland,Jimmy (tb) | Varsalona,Bart (tb) | Ruff,Willie (fr-h) | Konitz,Lee[as Zeke Tolin] (as) | Lacy,Steve (ss) | Kurtzer,Dave (bassoon) | Chambers,Paul (b) | Stabulas,Nick (dr)

Ella Speed | Big Stuff | Just One Of Those Things | Jambangle
Hackensack,NJ, rec. 10.10.1957
Evans,Gil (p,arr) | Mucci,Louis (tp) | Koven,Jack (tp) | Cleveland,Jimmy (tb) | Varsalona,Bart (tb) | Ruff,Willie (fr-h) | Konitz,Lee[as Zeke Tolin] (as) | Lacy,Steve (ss) | Kurtzer,Dave (bassoon) | Chambers,Paul (b) | Stabulas,Nick (dr)

PRSA 7129-6 | SACD | Relaxin' | EAN 025218731669

Miles Davis Quintet

It Could Happen To You | Woody'n You•
Hackensack,NJ, rec. 11.5.1956
Davis,Miles (tp) | Coltrane,John (ts) | Garland,Red (p) | Chambers,Paul (b) | Jones,Philly Joe (dr)

If I Were A Bell | You're My Everything | I Could Write A Book | Oleo
Hackensack,NJ, rec. 26.10.1956
Davis,Miles (tp) | Coltrane,John (ts) | Garland,Red (p) | Chambers,Paul (b) | Jones,Philly Joe (dr)

Ray Blue Music | Jazz Network

JN 007(RMB 01) | CD | Always With A Purpose | EAN 4042064001476

Ray Blue Quartet

Anazing Grace | Always With A Purpose | Okay Now | Two Kings | Desirée | Stuff'n Such | In A Sentimental Mood | Little Sunflower | Precious Lord Take My Hand
Berlin, rec. 2001
Blue,Ray (ts) | Zielke,Rolf (p) | Lillich,Martin (b) | Martin,Kenny (dr)

RCA | BMG-Ariola Classics GmbH

2112587-2 | CD | Friedrich Gulda At Birdland

Friedrich Gulda Septet

Vienna Discussion(Theme Song) | Introduction by Pee-Wee Marquette | Scruby | Dark Glow | Dodo | Air From Other Planets | New Shoes | Bernie's Tune
Live at 'Birdland',NYC, rec. 28.8.1956
Gulda,Friedrich (p,arr) | Sulieman[Leonard Graham],Idrees (tp) | Cleveland,Jimmy (tb) | Woods,Phil (as) | Powell,Seldon (ts) | Bell,Aaron (b) | Stabulas,Nick (dr)

Friedrich Gulda Trio

A Night In Tunisia
Gulda,Friedrich (p,arr) | Bell,Aaron (b) | Stabulas,Nick (dr)

2113038-2 | CD | The Magic Horn

George Wein's Dixie Victors

Just Squeeze Me(But Don't Tease Me) | Struttin' With Some Barbecue | The Magic Horn | A Monday Date
NYC, rec. 28.5.1956
Wein,George (p) | Braff,Ruby (tp) | Dickenson,Vic (tb) | Stegmeyer,Bill (cl) | Caceres,Ernie (bs) | Barker,Danny (bj) | Hinton,Milt (b) | Drootin,Buzzy (dr)

Sugar
Wein,George (p) | Braff,Ruby (tp) | Dickenson,Vic (tb) | Hucko,Peanuts (cl) | Caceres,Ernie (bs) | Barker,Danny (bj) | Hinton,Milt (b) | Drootin,Buzzy (dr)

Dippermouth Blues
Wein,George (p) | Braff,Ruby (tp) | McPartland,Jimmy (co) | Dickenson,Vic (tb) | Hucko,Peanuts (cl) | Caceres,Ernie (bs) | Barker,Danny (bj) | Hinton,Milt (b) | Drootin,Buzzy (dr)

Loveless Love
Wein,George (p) | McPartland,Jimmy (co) | Dickenson,Vic (tb) | Hucko,Peanuts (cl) | Caceres,Ernie (bs) | Barker,Danny (bj) | Hinton,Milt (b) | Drootin,Buzzy (dr)

I Ain't Gonna Give Nobody None Of My Jelly Roll | On The Sunny Side Of The Street
Wein,George (p) | Braff,Ruby (tp) | Dickenson,Vic (tb) | Hucko,Peanuts (cl) | Caceres,Ernie (bs) | Barker,Danny (bj) | Hinton,Milt (b) | Drootin,Buzzy (dr)

2113137-2 | CD | The Ultimate Glenn Miller-22 Original Hits From The King Of Swing

Glenn Miller And His Orchestra

In The Mood | Little Brown Jug | Sliphorn Jive | My Prayer | Tuxedo Junction | Fools Rush In | Pennsylvania Six Five Thousand | Blueberry Hill | Song Of The Volga Boatmen | Perfidia | Chattanooga Choo Choo | I Know Why | Adios | A String Of Pearls | Skylark | Don't Sit Under The Apple Tree | American Patrol | Serenade In Blue | I've Got A Girl In Kalamazoo | St.Louis Blues March | At Last | Moonlight Serenade
different Places, rec. 1939-1942
Miller,Glenn (tb,arr,ld) | personal included: | Claire,Dorothy (voc) | Beneke,Gordon 'Tex' (ts,voc) | Kelly,Paula (voc) | Eberle,Ray (voc) | Hutton,Marion (voc) | Modernaires,The (voc-group) | details not on the cover

2119255-2 | CD | A Genuine Tong Funeral(Dark Opera Without Words)

Gary Burton Quartet With Orchestra

The Opening- | Interlude:Shovels- | The Survivors- | Grave Train- | Death Rolls | Morning(part 1) | Interlude:Lament-Intermission Music- | Silent Spring | Fanfare- | Mother Of The Dead Man- | Some Dirge | Morning(part 2) | The New Funeral March | The New National Anthem- | The Survivors-
NYC, rec. 20.11.1967
Burton,Gary (vib) | Mantler,Michael (tp) | Knepper,Jimmy (tb,b-tb) | Johnson,Howard (bs,tuba) | Lacy,Steve (ss) | Barbieri,Gato (ts) | Bley,Carla (p,org,cond) | Coryell,Larry (g) | Swallow,Steve (el-b) | Moses,Bobby (dr)

2119257-2 | CD | Heavy Metal Be-Bop

The Brecker Brothers

Inside Out | Some Skunk Funk | Sponge | Funky Sea, Funky Dew | Squids
Live at My Father's Place,Roslyn,Long Island, rec. 1978
Brecker,Randy (tp,keyboards) | Brecker,Michael (el-ts) | Finnerty,Barry (g,g-synth,voc) | Jason,Neil (b,voc) | Bozzio,Terry (dr,voc) | Figueroa,Sammy (perc) | Cruz,Rafael (perc)

East River
Brecker Brothers,The | Brecker,Randy (tp,handclaps) | Brecker,Michael (el-ts,handclaps) | Finnerty,Barry (g) | Schaeffer,Paul (el-p) | Jason,Neil (b,voc) | Bozzio,Terry (dr) | Schwartzberg,Alan (dr) | Monet,Kash (perc,handclaps,voc) | Victoria (tambourine) | Schoen,Jeff (voc) | Herring,Roy (voc) | Clearmountain,Bob (handclaps) | various Friends (handclaps)

2119541-2 | 2 CD | Jazz Gallery:Lester Young Vol.2(1946-59)

JATP All Stars

I Can't Get Started
Los Angeles,CA, rec. 28.1.1946
JATP All Stars | McGhee,Howard (tp) | Killian,Al (tp) | Smith,Willie (as) | Parker,Charlie (as) | Young,Lester (ts) | Ross,Arnold (p) | Hadnott,Billy (b) | Young,Lee (dr)

Lester Young And His Band

It's Only A Paper Moon
Los Angeles,CA, rec. January 1946
Young,Lester (ts) | McGhee,Howard (tp) | Dickenson,Vic (tb) | Smith,Willie (as) | Jones,Wesley (p) | Counce,Curtis (b) | Otis,Johnny (dr)

Jubilee All Stars

Oh! Lady Be Good
Hollywood,CA, rec. early April 1946
Jubilee All Stars,The | Clayton,Buck (tp) | Young,Lester (ts) | Hawkins,Coleman (ts) | Kersey,Kenny (p) | Ashby,Irving (g) | Hadnott,Billy (b) | Wilson,Shadow (dr)

Jumpin' With Symphony Sid
Chicago,Ill, rec. 18.2.1947
Young,Lester (ts) | Hakim,Sadik[Argonne Thornton] (p) | Lacey,Fred (g) | Richardson,Rodney (b) | Marshall,Lyndell (dr)

I'm Confessin'(That I Love You)
NYC, rec. 28.-30.12.1947
Young,Lester (ts) | Hakim,Sadik[Argonne Thornton] (p) | Lacey,Fred (g) | Briscoe,Ted (b) | Haynes,Roy (dr)

Lester Smooths It Out
Young,Lester (ts) | McConnell,Shorty (tp) | Hakim,Sadik[Argonne Thornton] (p) | Lacey,Fred (g) | Briscoe,Ted (b) | Haynes,Roy (dr)

Just You Just Me
Live at The Royal Roost,NYC, rec. 27.11.1948
Young,Lester (ts) | Drakes,Jesse (tp) | Kelly,Ted (tb) | Jefferson,Freddy (p) | Briscoe,Ted (b) | Haynes,Roy (dr)

Something To Remember You By
NYC, rec. 29.12.1948
Young,Lester (ts) | DiNovi,Gene (p) | Wayne,Chuck (g) | Russell,Curly (b) | Kahn,Tiny (dr)

Tea For Two
Live at The Royal Roost,NYC, rec. 26.3.1949
Young,Lester (ts) | Drakes,Jesse (tp) | Elliot,Jerry (tb) | Mance,Junior[Julian C.] (p) | Briscoe,Ted (b) | Haynes,Roy (dr)

Blues 'N' Bells
NYC, rec. 23.6.1949
Young,Lester (ts) | Drakes,Jesse (tp) | Elliot,Jerry (tb) | Mance,Junior[Julian C.] (p) | Jackson,Leroy (b) | Haynes,Roy (dr)

Lester Young Quartet

Up 'N Adam
NYC, rec. March 1950
Young,Lester (ts) | Jones,Hank (p) | Brown,Ray (b) | Rich,Buddy (dr)

Lester Young Quintet

Body And Soul
Chicago,Ill, rec. 2.4.1950
Young,Lester (ts) | Drakes,Jesse (tp) | unkn. (p,b,dr)

Lester Young Quartet

Neenah
NYC, rec. July 1950
Young,Lester (ts) | Lewis,John (p) | Shulman,Joe (b) | Clark,Bill (dr)

I Cover The Waterfront
NYC, rec. 6.1.1951
Young,Lester (ts) | Lewis,John (p) | Ramey,Gene (b) | Jones,Jo (dr)

Undercover Girl Blues
NYC, rec. 16.1.1951
Young,Lester (ts) | Lewis,John (p) | Ramey,Gene (b) | Jones,Jo (dr)

I Don't Stand A Ghost Of A Chance With You
Live Broadcast,NYC, rec. 20.1.1951
Young,Lester (ts) | Lewis,John (p) | Ramey,Gene (b) | Jones,Jo (dr)

Lester Young With The Oscar Peterson Quartet

Back Home Again In Indiana
NYC, rec. 28.11.1952
Young,Lester (ts,voc) | Peterson,Oscar (p) | Kessel,Barney (g) | Brown,Ray (b) | Heard,J.C. (dr)

Count Basie And His Orchestra

Prez
Live at 'Birdland',NYC, rec. 8.1.1953
Basie,Count (p) | Campbell,Paul (tp) | Culley,Wendell (tp) | Jones,Reunald (tp) | Newman,Joe (tp) | Coker,Henry (tb) | Powell,Benny (tb) | Wilkins,Jimmy (tb) | Royal,Marshall (as) | Wilkins,Ernie (as) | Young,Lester (ts) | Davis,Eddie 'Lockjaw' (ts) | Quinichette,Paul (ts) | Fowlkes,Charlie (bs) | Green,Freddie (g) | Ramey,Gene (b) | Johnson,Gus (dr)

Lester Young Quintet

Too Marvelous For Words
NYC, rec. 15.4.1953
Young,Lester (ts) | Drakes,Jesse (tp) | Silver,Horace (p) | Skeete,Frank (b) | Kay,Connie (dr)

The Metronome All Stars

St.Louis Blues(part 2)
NYC, rec. 9.7.1953
Metronome All Stars,The | Eldridge,Roy (tp) | Winding,Kai (tb) | LaPorta,John (cl) | Young,Lester (ts) | Marsh,Warne (ts) | Gibbs,Terry (vib) | Wilson,Teddy (p) | Bauer,Billy (g) | Safranski,Eddie (b) | Roach,Max (dr) | Eckstine,Billy (voc)

Lester Young With The Oscar Peterson Quartet

Lester's Blues
Live at Carnegie Hall,NYC, rec. 19.9.1953
Young,Lester (ts) | Peterson,Oscar (p) | Ellis,Herb (g) | Brown,Ray (b) | Heard,J.C. (dr)

Lester Young Quintet

Tenderly
NYC, rec. 11.12.1953
Young,Lester (ts) | Drakes,Jesse (tp) | Mahones,Gildo (p) | Ramey,Gene (b) | Kay,Connie (dr)

Lester Young-Harry Edison With The Oscar Peterson Quartet

Pennies From Heaven
NYC, rec. 1.12.1955
Edison,Harry 'Sweets' (tp) | Young,Lester (ts) | Peterson,Oscar (p) | Ellis,Herb (g) | Brown,Ray (b) | Rich,Buddy (dr)

The Jazz Giants '56

Gigantic Blues
NYC, rec. 12.1.1956
Jazz Giants '56,The | Eldridge,Roy (tp) | Dickenson,Vic (tb) | Young,Lester (ts) | Wilson,Teddy (p) | Ramey,Gene (b) | Jones,Jo (dr)

Lester Young-Teddy Wilson Quartet

Pres Returns
NYC, rec. 13.1.1956
Young,Lester (ts) | Wilson,Teddy (p) | Ramey,Gene (b) | Jones,Jo (dr)

Lester Young Quintet

Three Little Words
Live at 'Birdland',NYC, rec. 5.9.1956
Young,Lester (ts) | Drakes,Jesse prob. (tp) | unkn. (p,b,dr)

Count Basie And His Orchestra

Polka Dots And Moonbeams | Lester Leaps In
Live at Newport,Rhode Island, rec. 7.7.1957
Basie,Count (p) | Culley,Wendell (tp) | Jones,Reunald (tp) | Jones,Thad (tp) | Newman,Joe (tp) | Coker,Henry (tb) | Hughes,Bill (tb) | Powell,Benny (tb) | Royal,Marshall (as) | Graham,Bill (as) | Young,Lester (ts) | Foster,Frank (ts) | Wess,Frank (fl,ts) | Fowlkes,Charlie (bs) | Green,Freddie (g) | Jones,Eddie (b) | Jones,Jo (dr) | Hammond,John (announcements)

Jam Session

Chris 'N' Diz
Live at Carnegie Hall,NYC, rec. 14.9.1957
Jam Session | Gillespie,Dizzy (tp) | Young,Lester (ts) | Peterson,Oscar (p) | Ellis,Herb (g) | Brown,Ray (b) | Rich,Buddy (dr)

Lester Young-Roy Eldridge-Harry Edison Band

They Can't Take That Away From Me
NYC, rec. 8.2.1958
Eldridge,Roy (tp) | Edison,Harry 'Sweets' (tp) | Young,Lester (ts) | Jones,Hank (p) | Ellis,Herb (g) | Duvivier,George (b) | Sheen,Mickey (dr)

Lester Young Quartet
There'll Never Be Another You
Paris,France, rec. March 1959
Young,Lester (ts) | Kauffman,Harold (p) | Gourley,Jimmy (g) | Ingrand,Jean-Marie (b) | Clarke,Kenny (dr)

2122103-2 | CD | The Becker Bros
The Brecker Brothers
Some Skunk Funk | Sponge | A Creature Of Many Faces | Twilight | Rocks | Levitate | D.B.B.
NYC, rec. January 1975
Brecker Brothers,The | Brecker,Randy (tp,fl-h,el-tp) | Brecker,Michael (ts) | Sanborn,David (as) | Grolnick,Don (keyboards) | Mann,Bob (g) | Lee,Will (b) | Mason,Harvey (dr) | MacDonald,Ralph (perc)
Oh My Stars
Brecker Brothers,The | Brecker,Randy (tp,voc) | Brecker,Michael (ts) | Sanborn,David (as) | Grolnick,Don (keyboards) | Mann,Bob (g) | Lee,Will (b,voc) | Mason,Harvey (dr) | MacDonald,Ralph (perc)
Sneakin' Up Behind You
Brecker Brothers,The | Brecker,Randy (tp) | Brecker,Michael (ts) | Sanborn,David (as) | Grolnick,Don (keyboards) | Mann,Bob (g) | Lee,Will (b) | Mason,Harvey (dr) | Parker,Chris (dr) | MacDonald,Ralph (perc)

2131392-2 | CD | There Comes A Time
Gil Evans Orchestra
Buzzard Variation | Joy Spring
NYC, rec. 6.3.1975
Evans,Gil (el-p,arr) | Soloff,Lew (tp,fl-h,piccolo-tp) | Royal,Ernie (tp,fl-h) | Malone,Tom (tb,b-tb,synth,tuba) | Johnson,Howard (b-cl,tuba) | Stewart,Robert 'Bob' (tuba) | Gordon,Peter (fr-h) | Clark,John (fr-h) | Sanborn,David (fl,ss,as) | Adams,George (fl,ts) | Horowitz,David (el-p) | Levin,Pete (synth) | Gallivan,Joe (g,synth,perc,congas) | Kawasaki,Ryo (pedals) | Metzke,Paul (el-b) | Ditmas,Bruce (dr) | Evans,Suzan 'Sue' (perc,congas)
So Long | There Comes A Time
NYC, rec. 12.3.1975
Evans,Gil (keyboards,arr) | Soloff,Lew (tp,fl-h,piccolo-tp) | Royal,Ernie (tp,fl-h) | Malone,Tom (tb,b-tb,synth,tuba) | Johnson,Howard (tb,b-cl,bs,tuba) | Daley,Joe (tuba) | Gordon,Peter (fr-h) | Clark,John (fr-h) | Sanborn,David (fl,ss,as) | Harper,Billy (fl,ts) | Horowitz,David (org,synth) | Levin,Pete (fr-h,org,synth) | Kawasaki,Ryo (g) | Gallivan,Joe (g,synth,perc) | Metzke,Paul (el-b) | Ditmas,Bruce (dr) | Smith,Warren (bongos,mallet-instruments) | Evans,Suzan 'Sue' (perc,congas,tympani)
King Porter Stomp | The Meaning Of The Blues | Anita's Dance | Makes Her Move | Aftermath The Fourth Movement- | Children Of The Fire-
NYC, rec. 11.4 1975
Evans,Gil (keyboards,arr) | Soloff,Lew (tp,fl-h,piccolo-tp) | Royal,Ernie (tp,fl-h) | Malone,Tom (tb,synth,tuba) | Johnson,Howard (b-cl,bs) | Stewart,Robert 'Bob' (tuba) | Gordon,Peter (fr-h) | Clark,John (fr-h) | Sanborn,David (fl,ss,as) | Adams,George (fl,ts) | Horowitz,David (org,synth) | Levin,Pete (fr-h,synth) | Kawasaki,Ryo (g) | Bushler,Herb (b) | Gallivan,Joe (synth,perc,bells,steel-g) | Metzke,Paul (synth) | Williams,Tony (dr) | Ditmas,Bruce (perc,snare-dr,tabla) | Peterson,Hanibal Marvin (perc,koto) | Smith,Warren (marimba,perc) | Evans,Suzan 'Sue' (dr,perc,congas,mallet-instruments,tympani)
Little Wing
NYC, rec. 14.4.1975
Evans,Gil (keyboards,arr) | Soloff,Lew (tp,fl-h,piccolo-tp) | Royal,Ernie (tp,fl-h) | Malone,Tom (tb,synth,tuba) | Johnson,Howard (b-cl,bs) | Stewart,Robert 'Bob' (tuba) | Gordon,Peter (fr-h) | Clark,John (fr-h) | Sanborn,David (fl,ss,as) | Adams,George (fl,ts) | Horowitz,David (org,synth) | Levin,Pete (fr-h,synth) | Kawasaki,Ryo (g) | Bushler,Herb (b) | Gallivan,Joe (synth,perc,bells,steel-g) | Metzke,Paul (synth) | Ditmas,Bruce (perc,snare-dr,tabla) | Peterson,Hanibal Marvin (perc,koto) | Smith,Warren (marimba,perc) | Evans,Suzan 'Sue' (dr,perc,congas,mallet-instruments,tympani)

21429372 | CD | The Ballad Of Paul Desmond
Paul Desmond Quartet
I've Got You Under My Skin
NYC, rec. 19.6.1961
Desmond,Paul (as) | Hall,Jim (g) | Duvivier,George (b) | Kay,Connie (dr)
Paul Desmond With Strings
Autumn Leaves
NYC, rec. 15.3.1962
Desmond,Paul (as) | Orchestra | Strings | details unknown
Paul Desmond-Gerry Mulligan Quartet
Easy Living
NYC, rec. 26.6.1962
Desmond,Paul (as) | Mulligan,Gerry (bs) | Beal,John (b) | Kay,Connie (dr)
All The Things You Are
NYC, rec. 3.7.1962
Desmond,Paul (as) | Mulligan,Gerry (bs) | Marshall,Wendell (b) | Kay,Connie (dr)
The One I Love
NYC, rec. 5.6.1963
Desmond,Paul (as) | Mulligan,Gerry (bs) | Cherico,Gene (b) | Kay,Connie (dr)
Samba De Orfeu | Theme From Black Orpheus
NYC, rec. 10.6.1963
Desmond,Paul (as) | Hall,Jim (g) | Cherico,Gene (b) | Kay,Connie (dr)
The Night Has A Thousand Eyes
NYC, rec. 14.6.1963
Desmond,Paul (as) | Hall,Jim (g) | Cherico,Gene (b) | Kay,Connie (dr)
Take Ten
NYC, rec. 25.6.1963
Desmond,Paul (as) | Hall,Jim (g) | Wright,Eugene 'Gene' (b) | Kay,Connie (dr)
Rude Old Man
NYC, rec. 13.7.1964
Desmond,Paul (as) | Hall,Jim (g) | Wright,Eugene 'Gene' (b) | Kay,Connie (dr)
A Taste Of Honey
NYC, rec. 14.7.1964
Desmond,Paul (as) | Hall,Jim (g) | Wright,Eugene 'Gene' (b) | Kay,Connie (dr)
The Girl From East 9th Street
NYC, rec. 28.7.1964
Desmond,Paul (as) | Hall,Jim (g) | Wright,Eugene 'Gene' (b) | Kay,Connie (dr)
Curacao Dolorosa
NYC, rec. 20.8.1964
Desmond,Paul (as) | Hall,Jim (g) | Wright,Eugene 'Gene' (b) | Kay,Connie (dr)
By The River Saint Marie
NYC, rec. 4.9.1964
Desmond,Paul (as) | Hall,Jim (g) | Wright,Eugene 'Gene' (b) | Kay,Connie (dr)

2143175-2 | CD | When Did You Leave Heaven
Lisa Ekdahl With The Peter Nordahl Trio
When Did You Leave Heaven | But Not For Me | Cry Me A River | Lush Life | You're Gonna See A Lot Of Me | Just One Of Those Things | The Boy Next Door | I'm A Fool To Want You | My Heart Belongs To Daddy | Blame It On My Youth
Studio Atlantis,?, rec. details unknown
Ekdahl,Lisa (voc) | Nordahl,Peter (p) | Boman,Patrik (b) | Gardiner,Ronnie (dr)
Love For Sale
Ekdahl,Lisa (voc) | Koverhult,Tommy (ts) | Nordahl,Peter (p) | Boman,Patrik (b) | Wartel,Henrik (dr)

2147794-2 | CD | Combo!
Henry Mancini And His Orchestra
Sidewalks Of Cuba | Castle Rock | Charleston Alley
Hollywood,CA, rec. 14.6.1960
Mancini,Henry (cond,arr) | Candoli,Pete (tp) | Nash,Dick (tb) | Pepper,Art (cl) | Nash,Ted (fl,as) | Lang,Ronnie (alto-fl,bs) | Bunker,Larry (vib,marimba) | Williams,Johnny (p,harpsichord) | Bain,Bob (g,b-g) | Bundock,Rowland 'Rolly' (b) | Manne,Shelly (dr) | Rivera,Ramon (congas)
Dream Of You | Playboy's Theme | Far East Blues | Scandinavian Shuffle
Hollywood,CA, rec. 17.6.1960
Mancini,Henry (cond,arr) | Candoli,Pete (tp) | Nash,Dick (tb) | Pepper,Art (cl) | Nash,Ted (fl,as) | Lang,Ronnie (alto-fl,bs) | Bunker,Larry (vib,marimba) | Williams,Johnny (p,harpsichord) | Bain,Bob (g,b-g) | Bundock,Rowland 'Rolly' (b) | Manne,Shelly (dr) | Rivera,Ramon (congas)
Moanin' | Swing Lightly | A Powdered Wig | Tequila | Everybody Blow!
Hollywood,CA, rec. 21.6.1960
Mancini,Henry (cond,arr) | Candoli,Pete (tp) | Nash,Dick (tb) | Pepper,Art (cl) | Nash,Ted (fl,as) | Lang,Ronnie (alto-fl,bs) | Bunker,Larry (vib,marimba) | Williams,Johnny (p,harpsichord) | Bain,Bob (g,b-g) | Bundock,Rowland 'Rolly' (b) | Manne,Shelly (dr) | Rivera,Ramon (congas)

2147797-2 | CD | Yesterdays
Gato Barbieri Septet
Yesterdays | A John Coltrane Blues | Mamie | Carinoso
details unknown, rec. 1974
Barbieri,Gato (ts) | Dalto,George (p,el-p) | Metzke,Paul (el-g) | Carter,Ron (el-b) | Purdie,Bernard 'Pretty' (dr) | Babafemi (congas) | Mantilla,Ray (timbales)

2151694-2 | CD | A Delicate Ballace
Kenny Werner Trio
Amonkst | Work Song | Ivoronics | Footsteps | Trio Imitation | The Look | Lorraine | Melodies Of 1997
NYC, rec. 15.-17.6.1997
Werner,Kenny (p) | Holland,Dave (b) | DeJohnette,Jack (dr)

2152934-2 | 2 CD | Genesis & The Opening Of The Way
Steve Coleman And The Council Of Balance
Day One | Day Two | Day Three | Day Four | Day Five
Brooklyn,NY, rec. 24.-27.4./9.10.& 18.6.1997
Coleman,Steve (as) | Alessi,Ralph (tp) | Endsley,Shane (tp) | Isles,Nabate (tp) | Lewis,George (tb) | Albright,Tim (tb) | Roseman,Joshua 'Josh' (tb) | Atkins,André (tb) | Haines,Jamal (tb) | Osby,Greg (as) | Coltrane,Ravi (ss,ts) | Stewart,Aaron (ts) | Cabera,Yosvany Terry (ts) | Tardy,Greg (ts) | Gilmore,David (g) | Milne,Andy (p) | Davis,Kenneth 'Kenny' (b) | Washington,Reggie (b) | Rickman,Sean (dr) | Morales,Luis Cancino (perc,congas) | Perez,Ramon Garcia (perc,congas) | Jones,Josh (perc) | Diaz Zayas,Miguel 'Anga' (perc) | Aldazabar,Barbaro Ramos (claves) | Kurtis-Stewart,Elektra (v) | Rice,Marlene (v) | Insell-Stack,Judith (viola) | Workman,Nioka (cello)
Day Six | Awareness
Coleman,Steve (as) | Alessi,Ralph (tp) | Endsley,Shane (tp) | Isles,Nabate (tp) | Lewis,George (tb) | Albright,Tim (tb) | Roseman,Joshua 'Josh' (tb) | Atkins,André (tb) | Haines,Jamal (tb) | Osby,Greg (as) | Coltrane,Ravi (ss,ts) | Stewart,Aaron (ts) | Cabera,Yosvany Terry (ts) | Tardy,Greg (ts) | Gilmore,David (g) | Milne,Andy (p) | Davis,Kenneth 'Kenny' (b) | Washington,Reggie (b) | Lake,Gene (dr) | Morales,Luis Cancino (perc,congas) | Perez,Ramon Garcia (perc,congas) | Jones,Josh (perc) | Diaz Zayas,Miguel 'Anga' (perc) | Aldazabar,Barbaro Ramos (claves) | Kurtis-Stewart,Elektra (v) | Rice,Marlene (v) | Insell-Stack,Judith (viola) | Workman,Nioka (cello)
Day Seven
NYC, rec. 24.-27.4./9.10.& 18.6.1997
Coleman,Steve (as) | Alessi,Ralph (tp) | Endsley,Shane (tp) | Isles,Nabate (tp) | Lewis,George (tb) | Albright,Tim (tb) | Roseman,Joshua 'Josh' (tb) | Atkins,André (tb) | Haines,Jamal (tb) | Osby,Greg (as) | Coltrane,Ravi (ss,ts) | Stewart,Aaron (ts) | Cabera,Yosvany Terry (ts) | Tardy,Greg (ts) | Gilmore,David (g) | Iyer,Vijay (p) | Davis,Kenneth 'Kenny' (b) | Washington,Reggie (b) | Rickman,Sean (dr) | Morales,Luis Cancino (perc,congas) | Perez,Ramon Garcia (perc,congas) | Jones,Josh (perc) | Diaz Zayas,Miguel 'Anga' (perc) | Aldazabar,Barbaro Ramos (claves) | Kurtis-Stewart,Elektra (v) | Rice,Marlene (v) | Insell-Stack,Judith (viola) | Workman,Nioka (cello)
Steve Coleman And Five Elements
Birth Death Regeneration | Law Of Ballance | Pi | First Cause | Wheel Of Nature | Rite Of Passage | Regeneration | Organic Movement | The Law | Fortitude And Chaos | Seti I | Polar Shift | Third Dynasty
Brooklyn,NY, rec. 7.-10.1997
Coleman,Steve (as) | Gilmore,David (g) | Milne,Andy (p) | Washington,Reggie (b) | Dyson,Dave (el-b) | Rickman,Sean (dr) | Diaz Zayas,Miguel 'Anga' (perc) | Silvestre,Rosangela (dance)

2155864-2 | CD | Angel
Paolo Fresu Quartet
Everything Happens To Me | Walkabout | Fellini | Elogio Del Discanto | Saigon | Variazione Cinque | El Saola | Song One | Suenos | Dove Niente Accade | Il Gatto E La Volpe | Real Time | Angel | I Fall In Love Too Easily
Rubiera,Italy, rec. 25.-29.9.1997
Fresu,Paolo (tp,fl-h,electronics) | Le,Nguyen (el-g,g-synth) | Di Castri,Furio (b) | Gatto,Roberto (dr)
Accarezzame
Fresu,Paolo (tp,fl-h,electronics) | Le,Nguyen (el-g,g-synth) | Di Castri,Furio (b) | Gatto,Roberto (dr) | Vanoni,Ornella (voc)

2159144-2 | CD | The RCA Victor Jazz Workshop
George Russell Smalltet
Ye Hypocrite,Ye Beelzebub | Jack's Blues | Livingstone I Presume | Ezz-thetic
NYC, rec. 31.3.1956
Russell,George (arr,ld) | Farmer,Art (tp) | McKusick,Hal (as) | Evans,Bill (p) | Galbraith,Barry (g) | Hinton,Milt (b) | Harris,Joe (dr)
Night Sound | Round Johnny Ronde | Witch Hunt | Concerto For Billy The Kid | Concerto For Billy The Kid(alt.take)
NYC, rec. 17.10.1956
Russell,George (arr,ld) | Farmer,Art (tp) | McKusick,Hal (as) | Evans,Bill (p) | Galbraith,Barry (g) | Hinton,Milt (b) | Motian,Paul (dr)
Fellow Delegates | The Sad Sergeant | Knights Of The Steamtable | Ballad Of Hix Blewitt | Ballad Of Hix Blewitt(alt.take)
NYC, rec. 21.12.1956
Russell,George (arr,ld) | Farmer,Art (tp) | Evans,Bill (p) | Galbraith,Barry (g) | Kotick,Teddy (b) | Motian,Paul (dr)

2161463-2 | CD | Back To Earth
Lisa Ekdahl With The Peter Nordahl Trio
Stranger On Earth | Nature Boy | Now Or Never | Laziest Girl In Town | It Had To Be You | Down With Love | What Is This Thing Called Love | Tea For Two | The Lonely One | I Get A Kick Out Of You | Just For A Thrill | Night And Day | Plaintive Rumba
details unknown, rec. 1999
Ekdahl,Lisa (voc) | Nordahl,Peter (p) | Boman,Patrik (b) | Gardiner,Ronnie (dr)

2164123-2 | CD | The Sonic Language Of Myth
Steve Coleman And Five Elements
Precession
NYC, rec. 6.-11.4.1998
Coleman,Steve (as) | Alessi,Ralph (tp) | Albright,Tim (tb) | Handy,Craig (ts) | Moran,Jason (p) | Washington,Reggie (b) | Tidd,Anthony (el-b) | Rickman,Sean (dr) | Diaz,Miguel (perc) | Reynolds,Todd (v) | Rowell,Mary (v) | Gold,David (viola) | Lawson,Dorothy (cello)
Maat
Coleman,Steve (as) | Endsley,Shane (tp) | Albright,Tim (tb) | Coltrane,Ravi (ts) | Washington,Reggie (b) | Reynolds,Todd (v) | Rowell,Mary (v) | Gold,David (viola) | Lawson,Dorothy (cello) | Rickman,Sean (dr) | Diaz,Miguel (perc) | McVoy,Karen (voc) | Ricks,Jeanne (voc) | Palmore,Eugene (voc) | Charleston,Erik (voc)
The Twelve Powers
Coleman,Steve (as) | Alessi,Ralph (tp) | Albright,Tim (tb) | Coltrane,Ravi (ts) | Harris,Stefon (vib) | Moran,Jason (p) | Washington,Reggie (el-b) | Rickman,Sean (dr) | Diaz,Miguel (perc)
The Gate
Coleman,Steve (as) | Albright,Tim (tb) | Coltrane,Ravi (ts) | Moran,Jason (p)
Seth
Coleman,Steve (as) | Endsley,Shane (tp) | Coltrane,Ravi (ts) | Iyer,Vijay (p) | Tidd,Anthony (el-b) | Rickman,Sean (dr) | Diaz,Miguel (perc) | Parkins,Sara (v) | Gold,David (viola) | Lawson,Dorothy (cello) | Silvestre,Rosangela (voc) | Charleston,Erik (voc)
Ausar(Reincarnation)
Coleman,Steve (as) | Endsley,Shane (tp) | Iyer,Vijay (p) | Washington,Reggie (b) | Tidd,Anthony (el-b) | Rickman,Sean (dr) | Diaz,Miguel (perc) | Gold,David (viola) | Lawson,Dorothy (cello) | Parkins,Sara (v) | McVoy,Karen (voc) | Ricks,Jeanne (voc) | Charleston,Erik (voc)
Heru(Redemption)
Coleman,Steve (as) | Alessi,Ralph (tp) | Albright,Tim (tb) | Mitchell,Robert (p) | Moran,Jason (keyboards) | Washington,Reggie (b) | Tidd,Anthony (el-b) | Rickman,Sean (dr) | Diaz,Miguel (perc) | Reynolds,Todd (v) | Gold,David (viola) | Lawson,Dorothy (cello)

2164314-2 | CD | Les Double Six
Les Double Six
Evening In Paris | Count 'Em | Walkin'
Paris,France, rec. late 1959
Les Double Six | Aldebert,Monique (voc) | Aldebert,Louis (voc) | Conrozier,Jean-Louis (voc) | Guerin,Roger (voc) | Perrin,Mimi (voc) | Swingle,Ward (voc) | Simmons,Art (p) | Michelot,Pierre (b) | Clarke,Kenny (dr)
For Lena And Lennie | Rat Race | Meet Benny Bailey
Paris,France, rec. early 1960
Les Double Six | Briodin,Jean-Claude (voc) | Denjean,Jacques (voc) | Germain,Claude (voc) | Legrand,Christiane (voc) | Perrin,Mimi (voc) | Swingle,Ward (voc) | Simmons,Art (p) | Bacsik,Elek (g) | Gaudry,Michel (b) | Humair,Daniel (dr)
Stockholm Sweetnin' | Boo's Bloos | Doodlin'
Les Double Six | Briodin,Jean-Claude (voc) | Denjean,Jacques (voc) | Germain,Claude (voc) | Legrand,Christiane (voc) | Perrin,Mimi (voc) | Swingle,Ward (voc) | Simmons,Art (p) | Gaudry,Michel (b) | Garros,Christian (dr)
Early Autumn
Paris,France, rec. late 1960
Les Double Six | Aldebert,Monique (voc) | Aldebert,Louis (voc) | Briodin,Jean-Claude (voc) | Germain,Claude (voc) | Louiss,Eddie (vib,voc) | Perrin,Mimi (voc) | Simmons,Art (p) | Gaudry,Michel (b) | Humair,Daniel (dr)
Moanin'
Les Double Six | Aldebert,Monique (voc) | Aldebert,Louis (voc) | Briodin,Jean-Claude (voc) | Germain,Claude (voc) | Louiss,Eddie (vib,voc) | Perrin,Mimi (voc) | Arvanitas,Georges (p) | Gaudry,Michel (b) | Humair,Daniel (dr)
Fascinating Rhythm
Les Double Six | Aldebert,Monique (voc) | Aldebert,Louis (voc) | Briodin,Jean-Claude (voc) | Germain,Claude (voc) | Louiss,Eddie (voc) | Perrin,Mimi (voc) | Gaudry,Michel (b) | Humair,Daniel (dr)
Boplicity
Les Double Six | Aldebert,Monique (voc) | Aldebert,Louis (voc) | Briodin,Jean-Claude (voc) | Germain,Claude (voc) | Louiss,Eddie (voc) | Perrin,Mimi (voc) | Urtreger,René (p) | Gaudry,Michel (b) | Humair,Daniel (dr)
Tickle Toe
Paris,France, rec. late 1961
Les Double Six | Barge,Claudine (voc) | Briodin,Jean-Claude (voc) | Germain,Claude (voc) | Louiss,Eddie (voc) | Perrin,Mimi (voc) | Swingle,Ward (voc) | Arvanitas,Georges (p) | Piguilhem,Paul (g) | Gaudry,Michel (b) | Humair,Daniel (dr)
Sweets
Les Double Six | Briodin,Jean-Claude (voc) | Germain,Claude (voc) | Louiss,Eddie (voc) | Perrin,Mimi (voc) | Arvanitas,Georges (p) | Gaudry,Michel (b) | Humair,Daniel (dr)
A Night In Tunisia
Les Double Six | Barge,Claudine (voc) | Briodin,Jean-Claude (voc) | Germain,Claude (voc) | Louiss,Eddie (voc) | Perrin,Mimi (voc) | Swingle,Ward (voc) | Gaudry,Michel (b) | Humair,Daniel (dr) | Drouet,Jean-Pierre (bongos)
Westwood Walk | A Ballad
Paris,France, rec. early 1962
Les Double Six | Barge,Claudine (voc) | Briodin,Jean-Claude (voc) | Germain,Claude (voc) | Louiss,Eddie (voc) | Perrin,Mimi (voc) | Swingle,Ward (voc) | Michelot,Pierre (b) | Garros,Christian (dr)
Scrapple From The Apple
Les Double Six | Barge,Claudine (voc) | Perrin,Mimi (voc) | Arvanitas,Georges (p) | Michelot,Pierre (b) | Garros,Christian (dr)

2165202-2 | CD | Metamorfosi
Paolo Fresu Angel Quartet
Elegio Del Discanto | Nightly | Pong | The Open Trio | Giravolta | Adagio | Bee | Don't Ask | Note Di Un Libretto Per Un'Opera Mai Scitta | Little Willie Leaps
Rubiera,Italy, rec. 7.-10.12.1998
Fresu,Paolo (tp,fl-h,electronics) | Le,Nguyen (g,el-g,g-synth) | Di Castri,Furio (b) | Gatto,Roberto (dr)
Si Dolce E Il Tormento | Metamorfosi | Abbamele | Nympheas
Fresu,Paolo (tp,fl-h,electronics) | Salis,Antonello (fisarmonica,voc,whistle) | Le,Nguyen (g,el-g,g-synth) | Di Castri,Furio (b) | Gatto,Roberto (dr)

2165364-2 | CD | Planet Jazz:Gato Barbieri
Gato Barbieri Group
Tupac Amaru | Bahia
NYC, rec. 27./28.4.1971
Barbieri,Gato (ts) | Beck,Joe (g) | Smith,Lonnie Liston (p,el-p) | Carter,Ron (el-b) | White,Lenny (dr) | Vasconcelos,Nana (congas,berimbau) | Golden,Gene (bongo,conga)
Maria Domingas
NYC, rec. 1971
Barbieri,Gato (ts) | Abercrombie,John (g) | Smith,Lonnie Liston (p) | Clarke,Stanley (b) | Moreira,Airto (dr) | M'tume,James[Forman] (congas) | Hafid,Moulay Ali (dumbeg)
El Gato
Barbieri,Gato (ts) | Nelson,Oliver (as) | Penque,Romeo (engl-h,fl) | Bodner,Phil (fl,alto-fl) | Bank,Danny (b-cl) | Jones,Hank (p) | Spinozza,David (g) | Carter,Ron (b) | Purdie,Bernard 'Pretty' (dr) | Moreira,Airto (perc)
Brazil
Live at The Montreux Jazz Festival, rec. 18.6.1971
Barbieri,Gato (ts) | Smith,Lonnie Liston (p) | Rainey,Chuck (el-b) | Purdie,Bernard 'Pretty' (dr) | Morgan,Sonny (congas) | Vasconcelos,Nana (perc,berimbau)
Yesterdays
NYC, rec. 1974
Barbieri,Gato (ts) | Dalto,George (p) | Carter,Ron (el-b) | Metzke,Paul (el-g) | Purdie,Bernard 'Pretty' (dr) | Babafemi (congas) | Mantilla,Ray (perc)

2165365-2 | CD | Planet Music:Oscar Peterson
Oscar Peterson Trio
Back Home Again In Indiana | Margie | I Surrender Dear | I Don't Stand A Ghost Of A Chance With You
Montreal,Canada, rec. 7.4.1947
Peterson,Oscar (p) | King,Albert (b) | Wilkinson,Mark 'Wilkie' (dr)
Oscar's Boogie | Smiles | Stairway To The Stars | Poor Butterfly
Montreal,Canada, rec. 15.12.1947
Peterson,Oscar (p) | Roberts,Auston (b) | Jones,Clarence (dr)
Oscar Peterson Quartet
Oop-Bop-Sh-Bam | Sweet Georgia Brown | Sleepytime Gal | Rockin' In Rhythm
Montreal,Canada, rec. 1.3.1949
Peterson,Oscar (p) | Sampson,Armand (g) | Brown,Bert (b) | Verdon,Roland (dr) | unkn. (voc)

Oscar Peterson Trio
Fine And Dandy | My Heart Stood Still | Somebody Loves Me | At Sundown
Montreal,Canada, rec. 14.11.1949
Peterson,Oscar (p) | Johnson,Ben (g) | Roberts,Auston (b)

2165366-2 | CD | Planet Jazz:Stephane Grappelli
Django Reinhardt And The Quintet Du Hot Club De France
Hallelujah | I'll Never Be The Same | Honeysuckle Rose | Beyond The Sea(La Mer) | I Surrender Dear | Minor Swing
Rome,Italy, rec. January-February 1949
Quintet Du Hot Club De France | Reinhardt,Django (g) | Grappelli,Stephane (v) | Safred,Gianni (p) | Pecori,Carlo (b) | De Carolis,Aurelio (dr)
Stephane Grappelli Quintet
What Am I Here For | Flamingo | Time On My Hands
Paris,France, rec. 28.1.1969
Grappelli,Stephane (v) | Ovio,Tony (g) | Fol,Raimond (p) | Sewing,Jack (b) | Hartmann,André (dr)
Stephane Grappelli Quartet
Tea For Two | Danny Boy (Londonderry Air) | I Hear Music | Smoke Gets In Your Eyes
Paris,France, rec. 13.12.1870
Grappelli,Stephane (v) | Hemmeler,Marc (p) | Sewing,Jack (b) | Clarke,Kenny (dr)
Stephane Grappelli-Kenny Clarke
Body And Soul
Paris,France, rec. 13.12.1970
Grappelli,Stephane (v) | Clarke,Kenny (dr)

2165367-2 | CD | Planet Jazz:Gary Burton
Gary Burton Trio
Like Someone In Love | Over The Rainbow | Joy Spring | Sir John
NYC, rec. 6.7.1961
Burton,Gary (vib) | Cherico,Gene (b) | Morello,Joe (dr)
Gary Burton Sextet
Storm | One Note
NYC, rec. 14.9.1962
Burton,Gary (vib) | Terry,Clark (tp) | Woods,Phil (cl,as) | Flanagan,Tommy (p) | Neves,John (b) | Morello,Joe (dr)
Gary Burton Quartet
Stella By Starlight | Blue Comedy | Hello Young Lovers | Gentle Wind And Falling Tear
Los Angeles,CA, rec. 14.2.1963
Burton,Gary (vib) | Sheldon,Jack (tp) | Budwig,Monty (b) | Fournier,Vernell (dr)
Sing Me Softly Of The Blues | Reponse | One, Two, 1-2-3-4 | General Mojo's Well-Laid Plan
NYC, rec. 20.4.1967
Burton,Gary (vib) | Coryell,Larry (g) | Swallow,Steve (b) | Haynes,Roy (dr)

2165368-2 | CD | Planet Jazz:Ben Webster
Benny Moten's Kansas City Orchestra
Lafayette
Camden,NJ, rec. 13.12.1932
Moten,Benny | Keyes,Joe (tp) | Stewart,Dee (tp) | Page,Oran 'Hot Lips' (tp) | Minor,Dan (tb) | Durham,Eddie (tb,el-g,arr) | Barefield,Eddie (cl,as) | Washington Jr.,Jack (as,bs) | Webster,Ben (ts) | Basie,Count (p,arr) | Berry,Leroy (g) | Page,Walter (b) | McWashington,Willie (dr)
Willie Bryant And His Orchestra
The Voice Of Old Man River
NYC, rec. 1.8.1935
Bryant,Willie (v,ld) | Johnson,Otis (tp) | Clarke,Dick (tp) | Battle,Edgar (tp) | Houghton,John (tb) | Matthews,George (tb) | Paque,Glyn (cl,as) | Payne,Stanley (as) | Russell,Johnny (ts) | Webster,Ben (ts) | Ramirez,Roger 'Ram' (p) | Adams,Arnold (g) | Hill,Ernest (b) | Cole,William 'Cozy' (dr)
Lionel Hampton And His Orchestra
Early Session Hop
NYC, rec. 11.9.1939
Hampton,Lionel (vib,voc) | Gillespie,Dizzy (tp) | Carter,Benny (as,arr) | Hawkins,Coleman (ts) | Berry,Leon 'Chu' (ts) | Webster,Ben (ts) | Hart,Clyde (p) | Christian,Charlie (g) | Hinton,Milt (b) | Cole,William 'Cozy' (dr)
Duke Ellington And His Famous Orchestra
Cotton Tail
Hollywood,CA, rec. 4.5.1940
Ellington,Duke (p) | Jones,Wallace (tp) | Williams,Cootie (tp) | Stewart,Rex (co) | Nanton,Joe 'Tricky Sam' (tb) | Brown,Lawrence (tb) | Tizol,Juan (tb) | Bigard,Barney (cl) | Hodges,Johnny (as) | Hardwicke,Otto (as,bass-s) | Webster,Ben (ts) | Carney,Harry (bs) | Guy,Fred (g) | Blanton,Jimmy (b) | Greer,William 'Sonny' (dr)
All Too Soon
NYC, rec. 22.7.1940
Ellington,Duke (p) | Jones,Wallace (tp) | Williams,Cootie (tp) | Stewart,Rex (co) | Nanton,Joe 'Tricky Sam' (tb) | Brown,Lawrence (tb) | Tizol,Juan (tb) | Bigard,Barney (cl) | Hodges,Johnny (as) | Hardwicke,Otto (as,bass-s) | Webster,Ben (ts) | Carney,Harry (bs) | Guy,Fred (g) | Blanton,Jimmy (b) | Greer,William 'Sonny' (dr)
Rex Stewart And His Orchestra
Linger Awhile
Chicago,Ill, rec. 2.11.1940
Stewart,Rex (co) | Brown,Lawrence (tb) | Webster,Ben (ts) | Carney,Harry (bs) | Strayhorn,Billy (p) | Blanton,Jimmy (b) | Greer,William 'Sonny' (dr)
Benny Carter And His Chocolate Dandies
Cadillac Slim
NYC, rec. 23.8.1946
Carter,Benny (cl) | Clayton,Buck (tp) | Grey,Al (tb) | Webster,Ben (ts) | White,Sonny (p) | Simmons,John (b) | Catlett,Big Sid (dr)
Red Norvo Sextet
Sunrise Blues | The Night Is Blue
Los Angeles,CA, rec. 18.1.1957
Norvo,Red (vib,xylophone) | Edison,Harry 'Sweets' (tp) | Webster,Ben (ts) | Rowles,Jimmy (p) | Carter,Bob (b) | Douglas,Bill (dr)
Mundell Lowe And His All Stars
My Man's Gone Now | Bess You Is My Woman Now | Summertime | I Got Plenty O'Nuttin'
NYC, rec. 16.7.1958
Lowe,Mundell (g,arr) | Farmer,Art (tp) | Elliott,Don (vib,mellophone) | Duvivier,George (b) | Johnson,Oliver (dr) | Shaughnessy,Ed (vib,dr) | Scott,Tony (cl,bs) | Webster,Ben (ts)

2165371-2 | CD | Planet Jazz:Jimmy Rushing
Benny Moten's Kansas City Orchestra
That Too Do Blues
Kansas City,MO, rec. 28.10.1930
Moten,Benny (ld) | Page,Oran 'Hot Lips' (tp) | Lewis,Ed (co) | Washington,Booker (co) | Hayes,Thamon (tb) | Durham,Eddie (tb,el-g) | Leonard,Harlan (reeds) | Washington Jr.,Jack (reeds) | Waller,Woody (reeds) | Basie,Count (p) | Moten,Buster prob. (p) | Berry,Leroy (bj) | Page,Vernon (tuba) | McWashington,Willie (dr) | Rushing,Jimmy (voc)
New Orleans
Camden,NJ, rec. 13.12.1932
Moten,Benny | Keyes,Joe (tp) | Stewart,Dee (tp) | Page,Oran 'Hot Lips' (tp) | Minor,Dan (tb) | Durham,Eddie (tb,el-g,arr) | Barefield,Eddie (cl,as) | Washington Jr.,Jack (as,bs) | Basie,Count (p,arr) | Berry,Leroy (g) | Page,Walter (b) | McWashington,Willie (dr) | Rushing,Jimmy (voc)
Count Basie And His Orchestra
Your Red Wagon
NYC, rec. 8.12.1947
Basie,Count (p) | Lewis,Ed (tp) | Berry,Emmett (tp) | Young,Eugene 'Snooky' (tp) | Edison,Harry 'Sweets' (tp) | Donnelly,Ted (tb) | Wells,Dicky (tb) | Matthews,George (tb) | Johnson,Bill (tb) | Love,Preston (as) | Price,Charles Q. (as) | Tate,Buddy (ts) | Gonsalves,Paul (ts) | Washington Jr.,Jack (bs) | Green,Freddie (g) | Page,Walter (b) | Jones,Jo (dr) | Rushing,Jimmy (voc)
Jimmy Rushing And His Band
My Last Affair | When I Grow Too Old To Dream | Home | Fine And Mellow | Linger Awhile
NYC, rec. 29.4.1971
Rushing,Jimmy (voc) | Nance,Ray (v,co) | Sims,Zoot (ts) | Frishberg,Dave (p,arr) | Hinton,Milt (b) | Lewis,Mel (dr)
Jimmy Rushing/Dave Frishberg
I Surrender Dear
Rushing,Jimmy (voc) | Frishberg,Dave (p,arr)
Jimmy Rushing And His Band
The You And Me That Used To Be | Bei Mir Bist Du Schön | All God's Chillun Got Rhythm | Thanks A Million
NYC, rec. 30.4.1971
Rushing,Jimmy (voc) | Johnson,Budd (ss) | Cohn,Al (ts) | Frishberg,Dave (p,arr) | Hinton,Milt (b) | Lewis,Mel (dr)
Jimmy Rushing/Dave Frishberg
More Than You Know
Rushing,Jimmy (voc) | Frishberg,Dave (p,arr)

2168206-2 | CD | Juan's Again
Juan Garcia Esquivel Orchestra
Boulevard Of Broken Dreams | Sentimental Journey | Third Man Theme | All Of Me | Guantanamera | Carioca | Surfboard | Begin The Beguine | Mini Skirt | Turkish March | Besame Mucho | Fantasy | Mucha Muchacha | Who's Sorry Now | My Blue Heaven | Anna(El Negro Zumbo) | Lazy Bones | Question Mark
details unknown, rec. 1959-1968
Esquivel,Juan Garcia (arr,ld) | Orchestra | details unknown

2168452-2 | CD | Portraits In Jazz And Clave
Ray Barretto Orchestra
The Mooche | Johnny Comes Lately | I Mean You | Go | Like Sonny | Oclupaca
NYC, rec. 6.-14.3.1999
Barretto,Ray (congas) | Bailey,John (tp) | Turre,Steve (tb,shells) | Lovano,Joe (ts) | Kolker,Adam (ss,ts) | Burrell,Kenny (g) | DiMartino,Bobby (p) | Gomez,Eddie (b) | Cherico,Vince (dr)
Cotton Tail | Cancion Del Fuego Fatuo | Lamento Borincano
Barretto,Ray (congas) | Bailey,John (tp) | Turre,Steve (tb,shells) | Lovano,Joe (ts) | Kolker,Adam (ss,ts) | Burrell,Kenny (g) | DiMartino,Bobby (p) | Gomez,Eddie (b) | Cherico,Vince (dr) | Sanabria,Bobby (perc)

2169309-2 | CD | Sound Of Surprise
Lee Konitz Quintet
Hi-Beck | Gundula | Mr. 88 | Bits And Pieces | Blues Suite | Friend Lee | Soddy And Bowl | Singin' | Wingin' | Thingin' | Crumbles | Subconscious-Lee
NYC, rec. 21./22.5.1999
Konitz,Lee (as,voice) | Brown,Ted (ts) | Abercrombie,John (g) | Johnson,Marc (b) | Baron,Joey (dr)

2169310-2 | CD | Fast Mood
Michel Portal-Martial Solal
Fast Mood | Duo À 3 Voix | Solitudes | BMG No.5 | Quand Les Chlamydes Sont Fatiguées | Long Space | Domimonk | Zag-Zig | Rien D'un Blues | Petite Phrases | Allegro Spiritual | Walkin'
Boulogne,France, rec. 1.-4.3.1999
Portal,Michel (cl,b-cl,ss,as) | Solal,Martial (p)

2169650-2 | CD | Planet Jazz:Bebop
Dizzy Gillespie And His Orchestra
A Night In Tunisia(Interlude) | 52nd Street Theme
NYC, rec. 22.2.1946
Gillespie,Dizzy (tp) | Byas,Don (ts) | Jackson,Milt (vib) | Haig,Al (p) | De Arango,Bill (g) | Brown,Ray (b) | Heard,J.C. (dr)
Anthropology
Gillespie,Dizzy (tp) | Jackson,Milt (vib) | Haig,Al (p) | De Arango,Bill (g) | Brown,Ray (b) | Heard,J.C. (dr)
52nd Street All Stars
Allen's Alley
NYC, rec. 27.2.1946
52nd Street All Stars | Brown,Pete (as) | Eager,Allen (ts) | Jones,Jimmy (p) | Osborne,Mary (g) | McKibbon,Al (b) | Manne,Shelly (dr)
Kenny Clarke And His 52nd Street Boys
Epistrophy | Oop-Bop-Sh-Bam
NYC, rec. 5.9.1946
Clarke,Kenny (dr) | Navarro,Fats (tp) | Dorham,Kenny (tp) | Stitt,Sonny (as) | Abrams,Ray (ts) | De Verteuil,Eddie (bs) | Powell,Bud (p) | Collins,John (g) | Hall,Al (b) | Fuller,Gil (arr)
Lucky Thompson And His Lucky Seven
Boppin' The Blues
Hollywood,CA, rec. 22.4.1947
Thompson,Lucky (ts) | Hefti,Neal (tp) | Carter,Benny (as) | Lawson,Bob (bs) | Marmarosa,Dodo (p) | Kessel,Barney (g) | Callender,Red (b) | Mills,Jackie (dr)
Coleman Hawkins And His All Stars
Half Step Down Please
NYC, rec. 11.12.1947
Hawkins,Coleman (ts) | Navarro,Fats (tp) | Johnson,J.J. (tb) | Johnson,Budd (as) | De Veta,Marion (bs) | Jones,Hank (p) | Wayne,Chuck (g) | Lesberg,Jack (b) | Roach,Max (dr)
Dizzy Gillespie And His Orchestra
Ow! | Two Bass Hit
NYC, rec. 22.8.1947
Gillespie,Dizzy (tp,voc) | Burns,Dave (tp) | McKay,Matthew (tp) | Orr,Raymond (tp) | Wright,Elmon (tp) | Baird,Taswell (tb) | Shepherd,William 'Bill' (tb) | Brown,John (as) | Johnson,Howard (as) | Gayles,Joe (ts) | Moody,James (ts) | Payne,Cecil (bs) | Jackson,Milt (vib) | Lewis,John (p) | Collins,John (g) | Brown,Ray (b) | Harris,Joe (dr)
Algo Bueno(Woody'n You) | Cubana Be | Cubana Bop
NYC, rec. 22.12.1947
Gillespie,Dizzy (tp,voc) | Burns,Dave (tp) | Bailey,Benny (tp) | Wright,Lammar (tp) | Wright,Elmon (tp) | Kelly,Ted (tb) | Shepherd,William 'Bill' (tb) | Brown,John (as) | Johnson,Howard (as) | Gayles,Joe (ts) | Nicholas,George 'Big Nick' (ts) | Payne,Cecil (bs) | Lewis,John (p) | Collins,John (g) | McKibbon,Al (b) | Clarke,Kenny (dr) | Pozo,Chano (congas,voc)
Manteca | Good Bait
NYC, rec. 30.12.1947
Gillespie,Dizzy (tp,voc) | Burns,Dave (tp) | Bailey,Benny (tp) | Wright,Lammar (tp) | Wright,Elmon (tp) | Kelly,Ted (tb) | Shepherd,William 'Bill' (tb) | Brown,John (as) | Johnson,Howard (as) | Gayles,Joe (ts) | Nicholas,George 'Big Nick' (ts) | Payne,Cecil (bs) | Lewis,John (p) | Collins,John (g) | McKibbon,Al (b) | Clarke,Kenny (dr) | Pozo,Chano (congas)
Dizzier and Dizzier
NYC, rec. 6.5.1949
Gillespie,Dizzy (tp,voc) | Harris,Benny (tp) | Cook,Willie (tp) | Wright,Elmon (tp) | Duryea,Andy (tb) | Hurt,Sam (tb) | Tarrant,Jesse (tb) | Brown,John (as) | Henry,Ernie (as) | Gayles,Joe (ts) | Lateef,Yusef (ts) | Gibson,Al (bs) | Forman,James (p) | McKibbon,Al (b) | Stewart,Teddy (dr)
Jumpin' With Symphony Sid
NYC, rec. 6.7.1949
Gillespie,Dizzy (tp,voc) | Cook,Willie (tp) | Harris,Benny (tp) | Wright,Elmon (tp) | Duryea,Andy (tb) | Johnson,J.J. (tb) | Mageed,Harneefan (tb) | Brown,John (as) | Henry,Ernie (as) | Gayles,Joe (ts) | Lateef,Yusef (ts) | Gibbons,Al (bs) | Forman,James (p) | McKibbon,Al (b) | Stewart,Teddy (dr)

2169655-2 | CD | Planet Jazz:Jazz Piano
Willie 'The Lion' Smith
Contrary Motion
NYC, rec. 2.2.1966
Smith,Willie 'The Lion' (p-solo)
Art Tatum
Out Of Nowhere
NYC, rec. 20.1.1947
Tatum,Art (p-solo)
Benny Goodman Trio
Where Or When
NYC, rec. 29.10.1937
Goodman,Benny (cl) | Wilson,Teddy (p) | Krupa,Gene (dr)
Jess Stacy And His Orchestra
Daybreak Serenade
NYC, rec. 29.6.1945
Stacy,Jess (p) | Butterfield,Billy (tp) | Erwin,Pee Wee (tp) | Natoli,Nat (tp) | Bradley,Will (tb) | Satterfield,Jack (tb) | Ross,Hank (as) | Schertzer,Hymie (as) | Binyon,Larry (ts) | Bradley,Julius (bs) | Worrell,Frank (g) | Haggart,Bob (b) | Toscarelli,Mario (dr)
Duke Ellington
Solitude
NYC, rec. 14.5.1941
Ellington,Duke (p-solo)
Count Basie Quartet
Shine On Harvest Moon
NYC, rec. 21.5.1947
Basie,Count (p) | Green,Freddie (g) | Page,Walter (b) | Jones,Jo (dr)
Mary Lou Williams Trio
All God's Chillun Got Rhythm
NYC, rec. 7.10.1946
Williams,Mary Lou (p) | Rotenberg,June (b) | Flynn,Bridget (dr)
Erroll Garner
Erroll's Bounce
NYC, rec. 1.10.1946
Garner,Erroll (p-solo)
Oscar Peterson Trio
Poor Butterfly
Montreal,Canada, rec. 15.12.1947
Peterson,Oscar (p) | Roberts,Auston (b) | Jones,Clarence (dr)
Lennie Tristano
I Don't Stand A Ghost Of A Chance With You
NYC, rec. 23.9.1947
Tristano,Lennie (p-solo)
Bud Powell Trio
Shaw 'Nuff
NYC, rec. 11.2.1957
Powell,Bud (p) | Duvivier,George (b) | Taylor,Arthur 'Art' (dr)

2173925-2 | CD | Fantasm
Stephan Oliva Trio
Interieur Jour | Five Miles To Wrentham | Dance | Sables | Fantasm | Blue Midnight | Fiasco | Impromede | Etude | M | Folk Song For Rosie | It Should've Happened A Long Time Ago
Pernes Les Fontaines,France, rec. 18./19.10.1999
Oliva,Stephan (p) | Chevillon,Bruno (b) | Motian,Paul (dr)

2174795-2 | CD | Bossa Antigua
Paul Desmond Quartet
Bossa Antigua | Samba Cantina | Samba Cepeda
NYC, rec. 28.7.1964
Desmond,Paul (as) | Hall,Jim (g) | Wright,Eugene 'Gene' (b) | Kay,Connie (dr)
The Night Has A Thousand Eyes | A Ship Without A Sail | The Girl From East 9th Street
NYC, rec. 29.7.1964
Desmond,Paul (as) | Hall,Jim (g) | Wright,Eugene 'Gene' (b) | Kay,Connie (dr)
The Night Has A Thousand Eyes(alt.take)
Desmond,Paul (as) | Hall,Jim (g) | Cherico,Gene (b) | Kay,Connie (dr)
O Gato | O Gato(alt.take) | Curacao Dolorosa
NYC, rec. 20.8.1964
Desmond,Paul (as) | Hall,Jim (g) | Wright,Eugene 'Gene' (b) | Kay,Connie (dr)
Alianca
NYC, rec. 8.9.1964
Desmond,Paul (as) | Hall,Jim (g) | Wright,Eugene 'Gene' (b) | Kay,Connie (dr)

2174796-2 | CD | Easy Living
Polka Dots And Moonbeams
NYC, rec. 5.6.1963
Desmond,Paul (as) | Hall,Jim (g) | Cherico,Gene (b) | Kay,Connie (dr)
Blues For Fun
NYC, rec. 14.6.1963
Desmond,Paul (as) | Hall,Jim (g) | Cherico,Gene (b) | Kay,Connie (dr)
That Old Feeling
NYC, rec. 25.6.1963
Desmond,Paul (as) | Hall,Jim (g) | Wright,Eugene 'Gene' (b) | Kay,Connie (dr)
Rude Old Man
NYC, rec. 13.7.1964
Desmond,Paul (as) | Hall,Jim (g) | Wright,Eugene 'Gene' (b) | Kay,Connie (dr)
When Joanna Loved Me | Polka Dots And Moonbeams
NYC, rec. 14.7.1964
Desmond,Paul (as) | Hall,Jim (g) | Wright,Eugene 'Gene' (b) | Kay,Connie (dr)
Easy Living
NYC, rec. 9.9.1964
Desmond,Paul (as) | Hall,Jim (g) | Wright,Eugene 'Gene' (b) | Kay,Connie (dr)
Bewitched Bothered And Bewildered
NYC, rec. 16.9.1964
Desmond,Paul (as) | Hall,Jim (g) | Wright,Eugene 'Gene' (b) | Kay,Connie (dr)
Here's That Rainy Day | Bewitched Bothered And Bewildered | I've Grown Accustomed To Her Face
NYC, rec. 1.6.1965
Desmond,Paul (as) | Hall,Jim (g) | Heath,Percy (b) | Kay,Connie (dr)

2174797-2 | CD | Duke Ellington's Far East Suite
Duke Ellington And His Orchestra
Tourist Point Of View | Amad | Tourist Point Of View(alt.take) | Amad(alt.take)
NYC, rec. 19.12.1966
Ellington,Duke (p) | Williams,Cootie (tp) | Anderson,Cat (tp) | Jones,Herbie (tp) | Ellington,Mercer (tp) | Brown,Lawrence (tb) | Connors,Chuck (tb) | Cooper,Frank 'Buster' (tb) | Hodges,Johnny (as) | Procope,Russell (cl,as) | Gonsalves,Paul (ts) | Hamilton,Jimmy (cl,ts) | Carney,Harry (bs) | Lamb,John (b) | Jones,Rufus (dr)
Isfahan | Agra | Ad Lib On Nippon | Isfahan(alt.take)
NYC, rec. 20.12.1966
Ellington,Duke (p) | Williams,Cootie (tp) | Anderson,Cat (tp) | Jones,Herbie (tp) | Ellington,Mercer (tp) | Brown,Lawrence (tb) | Connors,Chuck (tb) | Cooper,Frank 'Buster' (tb) | Hodges,Johnny (as) | Procope,Russell (cl,as) | Gonsalves,Paul (ts) | Hamilton,Jimmy (cl,ts) | Carney,Harry (bs) | Lamb,John (b) | Jones,Rufus (dr)
Bluebird Of Delhi(Mynah) | Depk | Mount Harissa | Blue Pepper(Far East Of The Blues) | Bluebird Of Delhi(alt.take)
NYC, rec. 21.12.1966
Ellington,Duke (p) | Williams,Cootie (tp) | Anderson,Cat (tp) | Jones,Herbie (tp,fl-h) | Ellington,Mercer (tp,fl-h) | Brown,Lawrence (tb) | Connors,Chuck (tb) | Cooper,Frank 'Buster' (tb) | Hodges,Johnny (as) | Procope,Russell (cl,as) | Gonsalves,Paul (ts) | Hamilton,Jimmy (cl,ts) | Carney,Harry (bs) | Lamb,John (b) | Jones,Rufus (dr)

2174798-2 | CD | Parole E Musica
Helen Merrill With The Piero Umilliani Group
Night And Day | Everything Happens To Me | Autumn In New York | These Foolish Things Remind Me On You | I've Got You Under My Skin
Rome,Italy, rec. 1960
Merrill,Helen (voc) | Umiliani,Piero (p,celeste) | Rosso,Nino (tp) | Marinacci,Gino (fl,bs) | Grillini,Enzo (g) | Pisano,Berto (b) | Conti,Sergio (dr) | Caiati,Fernando (spoken lyrics in Italian)
Why Don't You Do Right | You Don't Know What Love Is | April In Paris | Solitude | Willow Weep For Me | When Your Lover Has Gone
Merrill,Helen (voc) | Umiliani,Piero (p,celeste) | Culasso,Nino (tp) | Ferelli,Tonino (b) | Ferraro,Ralph (dr) | Caiati,Fernando (spoken lyrics in Italian)

2174800-2 | CD | Sonny Meets Hawk!
Sonny Rollins-Coleman Hawkins Quintet
Yesterdays | All The Things You Are | Lover Man(Oh,Where Can You Be?)
NYC, rec. 15.7.1963
Hawkins,Coleman (ts) | Rollins,Sonny (ts) | Bley,Paul (p) | Cranshaw,Bob (b) | McCurdy,Roy (dr)

Summertime | Just Friends | At McKies'
NYC, rec. 18.7.1963
Hawkins,Coleman (ts) | Rollins,Sonny (ts) | Bley,Paul (p) | Grimes,Henry (b) | McCurdy,Roy (dr)

2174801-2 | CD | The Standard Sonny Rollins
Sonny Rollins Sextet
Trav'lin' Light | Trav'lin' Light(alt take)
NYC, rec. 11.6.1964
Rollins,Sonny (ts) | Hall,Jim (g) | Hancock,Herbie (p) | Izenzon,David (b) | Smith,Teddy (b) | Martin,Stu (dr)
Sonny Rollins Trio
I'll Be Seeing You
NYC, rec. 23.6.1964
Rollins,Sonny (ts) | Cranshaw,Bob (b) | Roker,Granville 'Mickey' (dr)
Three Little Words | Night And Day
NYC, rec. 24.6.1964
Rollins,Sonny (ts) | Cranshaw,Bob (b) | Roker,Granville 'Mickey' (dr)
Sonny Rollins Quartet
My Ship
Rollins,Sonny (ts) | Hall,Jim (g) | Cranshaw,Bob (b) | Roker,Granville 'Mickey' (dr)
Love Letters | Long Ago And Far Away
NYC, rec. 26.6.1964
Rollins,Sonny (ts) | Hall,Jim (g) | Cranshaw,Bob (b) | Roker,Granville 'Mickey' (dr)
It Could Happen To Me | My One And Only Love | Winter Wonderland | When You Wish Upon A Star
NYC, rec. 2.7.1964
Rollins,Sonny (ts) | Hancock,Herbie (p) | Cranshaw,Bob (b) | Roker,Granville 'Mickey' (dr)
Sonny Rollins Trio
Autumn Nocturne
NYC, rec. 9.7.1964
Rollins,Sonny (ts) | Cranshaw,Bob (b) | Roker,Granville 'Mickey' (dr)

2174803-2 | CD | Martial Solal At Newport '63
Martial Solal Trio
Poinciana(Song Of The Tree) | Clouds(Nuages) | Suite Pour Une Frise | Stella By Starlight | What Is This Thing Called Love | Round About Midnight | Boplicity | All God's Chillun Got Rhythm | Fine And Dandy | I Got Rhythm | I Got Rhythm(alt.take 1) | I Got Rhythm(alt.take 2)
NYC, rec. 11./15.& 16.7.1963
Solal,Martial (p) | Kotick,Teddy (b) | Motian,Paul (dr)

2177829-2 | 2 CD | 100 Ans De Jazz:Fats Waller
Fats Waller Groups
My Mommie Sent Me To The Store | Fats Waller's Original E-Flat Blues | Hey! Stop Kissin' My Sister | Everybody Loves My Baby | Ain't Nobody's Business If I Do | Abercrombie Had A Zombie | Scream | My Melancholy Baby | Mamacita | Pantin' In The Panther Room | Shortnin' Bread | Pan Pan | I Wanna Hear Swing Songs | All That Meat And No Potatoes | Carolina Shout | Twenty-Four Robbers | Sad Sap Sucker Am I | Chant Of The Groove | Come And Get It | Rump Steak Serenade | Buck Jumpin' | Winter Weather | Cash For Your Trash | Don't Give Me That Jive | Your Socks Don't Match | Really Fine | Jitterbug Waltz | By The Light Of The Silver Moon | Swing Out To Victory | Moppin' And Boppin' | Ain't Misbehavin'
different Places, rec. 1940-1043
Waller,Thomas 'Fats' (p,org,voc) | details not on the cover

2177830-2 | 2 CD | 100 Ans De Jazz:Paul Desmond
Paul Desmond With Different Groups
My Funny Valentine | Desmond Blue | Then I'll Be Tired Of You | I've Got You Under My Skin | Late Lament | I Should Care | Like Someone In Love | Ill Wind | Body And Soul | Advise And Consent | Autumn Leaves | Imagination | Take Ten | El Prince | El Prince(alt.take) | Alone Together | Embracadero | Embracadero(alt.take) | Theme From Black Orpheus | The Night Has A Thousand Eyes | Nancy | Samba De Orfeu | The One I Love Belongs To Somebody Else
different Places, rec. 1062-1987?
Desmond,Paul (as) | details not on the cover

2177831-2 | 2 CD | 100 Ans De Jazz:Count Basie
Count Basie And His Orchestra
Bill's Mill | Brand New Wagon | One O'Clock Boogie | Futile Frustration | Swingin' The Blues | St.Louis Boogie | Basie Basement | Backstage At Stuff's | My Buddy | Shine On Harvest Moon | Lopin' | I Never Knew | Sugar | The Jungle King | I Ain't Mad At You | After You've Gone | House Rent Boogie | South | Don't You Want A Man Like Me | Seventh Avenue Express | Sophisticated Swing | Guest In A Nest | Your Red Wagon | Money Is Honey | Just A Minute | Robbin's Nest | Hey Pretty Baby | Just An Old Manuscript | She's A Wine-O | Shoutin' Blues | Wonderful Thing | Mine Too | Walking Slow Behind You | Normania | Rat Race | Sweets
different Places, rec. 1947-1950
Basie,Count (p,ld) | details not on the cover

2177832-2 | 2 CD | 100 Ans De Jazz:Coleman Hawkins
Coleman Hawkins With Different Bands
St.Louis Shuffle | Wherever There's A Will There's A Way(My Baby) | Hello Lola | One Hour | Sugarfoot Stomp | Hocus Pocus | One Sweet Letter From You | Meet Doctor Foo | Fine Dinner | She's Funny That Way | Body And Soul | When Day Is Done | The Sheik Of Araby | My Blue Heaven | Bouncing With Bean | One O'Clock Jump | Bugle Call Rag | Say It Isn't So | Spotlite | Low Flame | Allen's Alley | Indian Summer | You Were Meant For Me | April In Paris | How Strange | Half Step Down Please | Angel Face | Jumpin' Jane | I Love You | 39-25-39 | Body And Soul | Essence Of Jazz
different Places, rec. 1927-1956
Hawkins,Coleman (ts) | details not on the cover

2178289-2 | CD | Melos
Paolo Fresu Quintet
Que Reste-T-Il De Nos Amours | Melos(Variazione Nove) | Amerino | On Second Line | Ammazare Il Tempo | Per Toda Minha Vida | Solstizie D'Estate(from the movie Il Prezzo) | Luiza | Variazione Otto | Tutto E Il Contrario Di Tutto | Lester | Cosi- | E' Quasi L'Alba- | Variazione Sei | Prayer For Sibylle
Pernes Les Fontaines,France, rec. 8.-11.5.2000
Fresu,Paolo (tp) | Tracanna,Tino (ss,ts) | Cipelli,Roberto (p) | Zanchi,Attilo (b) | Fioravanti,Ettore (dr)

2179617-2 | CD | The Third World
Gato Barbieri Sextet
Introduction- | Cancion Del Llamero- | Tango- | Zelao | Antonio Das Mortes | Bachianas Brasileiras- | The Aloe And The Wild Rose-
NYC, rec. 24./25.11.1969
Barbieri,Gato (fl,ts,voc) | Rudd,Roswell (tb) | Smith,Lonnie Liston (p) | Haden,Charlie (b) | Harris,Beaver (dr) | Landrum,Richard 'Pablo' (perc)

2179618-2 | CD | Afrique
Count Basie And His Orchestra
Hobo Flats | Gypsy Queen | African Sunrise
NYC, rec. 22.12.1970
Basie,Count (p) | Cohen,Paul (tp) | Cohn,George (tp) | Minger,Pete (tp) | Reed,Waymon (tp,fl-h) | Galloway,Steve (tb) | Hughes,William (tb) | Wanzo,Mel (tb) | Watson Sr.,John (tb) | Laws,Hubert (fl) | Adkins,Bill (sax) | Plater,Bobby (sax) | Davis,Eddie 'Lockjaw' (ts) | Dixon,Eric (sax) | Payne,Cecil (bs) | Green,Freddie (g) | Williams,John B. (el-b) | Jones,Harold (dr) | Landrum,Richard 'Pablo' (congas) | Morgan,Sonny (bongos) | Nelson,Oliver (arr,ld)
Step Right Up | Love Flower | Afrique | Kilimanjaro | Japan
NYC, rec. 23.12.1970
Basie,Count (p) | Cohen,Paul (tp) | Cohn,George (tp) | Minger,Pete (tp) | Reed,Waymon (tp) | Galloway,Steve (tb) | Hughes,William (tb) | Wanzo,Mel (tb) | Watson Sr.,John (tb) | Laws,Hubert (fl) | Adkins,Bill (sax) | Plater,Bobby (sax) | Ashton,Bob (ts) | Dixon,Eric (sax) | Payne,Cecil (bs) | Green,Freddie (g) | Keenan,Norman (b) | Jones,Harold (dr) | Landrum,Richard 'Pablo' (congas) | Morgan,Sonny (bongos) | Smith,Warren (marimba) | Nelson,Oliver (as,arr,ld)

2179620-2 | CD | Two Of A Mind
Paul Desmond-Gerry Mulligan Quartet
Blight Of The Fumble Bee
NYC, rec. 26.6.1962
Demond,Paul (as) | Mulligan,Gerry (bs) | Beal,John (b) | Kay,Connie (dr)
All The Things You Are | Stardust
NYC, rec. 3.7.1962
Demond,Paul (as) | Mulligan,Gerry (bs) | Marshall,Wendell (b) | Kay,Connie (dr)
Two Of A Mind | The Way You Look Tonight | Out Of Nowhere
NYC, rec. 13.8.1962
Demond,Paul (as) | Mulligan,Gerry (bs) | Benjamin,Joe (b) | Lewis,Mel (dr)

2179621-2 | CD | Take Ten
Paul Desmond Quartet
The One I Love
NYC, rec. 5.6.1963
Desmond,Paul (as) | Hall,Jim (g) | Cherico,Gene (b) | Kay,Connie (dr)
Theme From Black Orpheus | Samba De Orfeu
NYC, rec. 10.6.1963
Desmond,Paul (as) | Hall,Jim (g) | Cherico,Gene (b) | Kay,Connie (dr)
El Prince | Alone Together | Embarcadero
NYC, rec. 12.6.1963
Desmond,Paul (as) | Hall,Jim (g) | Cherico,Gene (b) | Kay,Connie (dr)
El Prince | Embarcadero | Out Of Nowhere | Nancy
NYC, rec. 14.6.1963
Desmond,Paul (as) | Hall,Jim (g) | Cherico,Gene (b) | Kay,Connie (dr)
Take Ten
NYC, rec. 25.6.1963
Desmond,Paul (as) | Hall,Jim (g) | Wright,Eugene 'Gene' (b) | Kay,Connie (dr)

2179622-2 | CD | Fabulous Phineas
Phineas Newborn Jr.
What's New? | Cherokee
NYC, rec. 34.1958
Newborn Jr.,Phineas (p-solo)
Phineas Newborn Jr. Trio
Pamela
NYC, rec. 28.3.1958
Newborn Jr.,Phineas (p) | Newborn,Calvin (g) | Nasser,Jamil[George Joyner] (b)
Phineas Newborn Jr. Quartet
Sugar Ray | I'll Remember April | Back Home
Newborn Jr.,Phineas (p) | Newborn,Calvin (g) | Nasser,Jamil[George Joyner] (b) | Best,Denzil (dr)
45Grad Angle | No Moon At All
NYC, rec. 3.4.1958
Newborn Jr.,Phineas (p) | Newborn,Calvin (g) | Nasser,Jamil[George Joyner] (b) | Best,Denzil (dr)

2179623-2 | CD | Together Again!
The Four Brothers
The Swinging Door | Four In Hand | Four Brothers | Ten Years Later | Here We Go Again
NYC, rec. 11.2.1957
Four Brothers,The | Cohn,Al (ts) | Sims,Zoot (ts) | Steward,Herbie (ts) | Chaloff,Serge (bs) | Lawrence,Elliot (p) | Jones,Buddy (b) | Lamond,Don (dr) | Albam,Manny (arr)
Aged In Wood | So Blue | The Pretty One | Four And One More | A Quick One
Four Brothers,The | Cohn,Al (ts) | Sims,Zoot (ts) | Steward,Herbie (ts) | O'Kane,Charles (bs) | Lawrence,Elliot (p) | Jones,Buddy (b) | Lamond,Don (dr) | Albam,Manny (arr)

2179624-2 | CD | I Hear Music
Stephane Grappelli Quartet
Tea For Two | Danny Boy (Londonderry Air) | Let's Fall In Love | Coltrane | I Hear Music | Dany | Smoke Gets In Your Eyes | Gary
Paris,France, rec. 13.12.1970
Grappelli,Stephane (v) | Hemmeler,Marc (p) | Sewing,Jack (b) | Clarke,Kenny (dr)
Flower For Kenny
Grappelli,Stephane (p) | Hemmeler,Marc (org) | Sewing,Jack (b) | Clarke,Kenny (dr)
Stephane Grappelli Trio
Dear Ben
Grappelli,Stephane (p) | Sewing,Jack (b) | Clarke,Kenny (dr)
Body And Soul
Grappelli,Stephane (v) | Clarke,Kenny (p) | Sewing,Jack (b)

2179625-2 | CD | The Bridge
Sonny Rollins Quartet
God Bless The Child
NYC, rec. 30.1.1962
Rollins,Sonny (ts) | Hall,Jim (g) | Cranshaw,Bob (b) | Saunders,Harry (dr)
John S. | You Do Something To Me | Where Are You
NYC, rec. 13.2.1962
Rollins,Sonny (ts) | Hall,Jim (g) | Cranshaw,Bob (b) | Riley,Ben (dr)
Without A Song | The Bridge
NYC, rec. 14.2.1962
Rollins,Sonny (ts) | Hall,Jim (g) | Cranshaw,Bob (b) | Riley,Ben (dr)

2179626-2 | CD | What's New?
If Ever I Would Leave You
NYC, rec. 18.4.1962
Rollins,Sonny (ts) | Hall,Jim (g) | Cranshaw,Bob (b) | Riley,Ben (dr)
Sonny Rollins Group
Brownskin Gal (I Got My Eyes On You) | Don't Stop The Carnival
rec. 26.4.1962
Rollins,Sonny (ts) | Hall,Jim (g) | Cranshaw,Bob (b) | Riley,Ben (dr) | Charles,Dennis (congas) | Charles,Frank (bongos) | Rodriguez,Willie (shakers) | Roberts,H. (voc) | Stewart,M. (voc) | Spencers,C. (voc) | Burton,M. (voc) | Wright,N. (voc) | Glover,W. (voc) | Jones,Jimmy (cond)
Sonny Rollins Quartet
The Night Has A Thousand Eyes
NYC, rec. 8.5.1962
Rollins,Sonny (ts) | Hall,Jim (g) | Cranshaw,Bob (b) | Riley,Ben (dr)
Jungoso | Bluesongo
NYC, rec. 14.5.1962
Rollins,Sonny (ts) | Cranshaw,Bob (b) | Riley,Ben (dr) | Candido[Camero] (congas,bongos)

2179681-2 | CD | Lisa Ekdahl Sings Salvadore Poe
Lisa Ekdahl With The Salvador Poe Quartet, Strings And Guests
Daybreak | Rivers Of Love | Sunny Weather | Only You | The Color Of You | How Many More Times | I Will Be Blessed | Since You've Been Gone | I've Never Seen Anythning Like You | I Don't Miss You Anymore | Nightingale | The Rhythm Of Our Hearts | Sun Rose | Of My Conceit
Stockholm,Sweden, rec. details unknown
Ekdahl,Lisa (voc) | Poe,Salvadore (g) | Lindgren,Magnus (fl,alto-fl,bass-fl,cl,b-cl,ts,bs,p,el-p) | Johnsson,Fredrik (b,el-b) | Holgersson,Jones (dr) | Strings

2185157-2 | CD | While My Lady Sleeps
Phineas Newborn Jr. With Dennis Farnon And His Orchestra
Moonlight In Vermont | Don't You Know I Care (Or Don't You Care I Know) | Lazy Mood | Black Is The Color Of My True Love's Hair | While My Lady Sleeps | Bali Ha'i
Hollywood,CA, rec. 23.4.1957
Newborn Jr.,Phineas (p) | Nasser,Jamil[George Joyner] (b) | Stoller,Alvin (dr) | Gasselin,Jaques (v) | Atkins,Leonard (v) | Lustgarten,Alfred (v) | Wennermark,Eunice (v) | Arno,Victor (v) | Lube,Dan (v) | Vinci,Gerry (v) | La Magna,Carl (v) | Hill,Henry (v) | Gill,Ben (v) | Baker,Ysrael (v) | Limonick,Marvin (v) | Robyn,Paul (viola) | Figelski,Cecil (viola) | Harshman,Allan (viola) | Klevman,Louis (viola) | Lustgarten,Edgar 'Ed' (cello) | Kramer,Raphael (cello)
I'm Old Fashioned | It's Easy To Remember | If I Should Lose You
Hollywood,CA, rec. 24.4.1957
Newborn Jr.,Phineas (p) | Nasser,Jamil[George Joyner] (b) | Stoller,Alvin (dr) | Gasselin,Jaques (v) | Atkins,Leonard (v) | Lustgarten,Alfred (v) | Wennermark,Eunice (v) | Arno,Victor (v) | Lube,Dan (v) | Vinci,Gerry (v) | La Magna,Carl (v) | Hill,Henry (v) | Gill,Ben (v) | Baker,Ysrael (v) | Schaeffer,Ralph (v) | Robyn,Paul (viola) | Hochstein,Abraham (viola) | Hyams,Harry A. (viola) | Reilich,Joe (viola) | Lustgarten,Edgar 'Ed' (cello) | Neikrug,George (cello)

21951952 | CD | Kind Of Porgy & Bess | EAN 743219519528
Paolo Fresu Trio
I Got Plenty O'Nuttin' | Oh, Doctor Jesus- | Oh, De Lawd Shake De Heavens-
Rubiera,Italy, rec. 10.-16.3.2002
Fresu,Paolo (tp) | Salis,Antonello (p) | Di Castri,Furio (b)
Lo Bess Goin' To The Picnic?
Fresu,Paolo (tp) | Le,Nguyen (el-g,g-synth) | Di Castri,Furio (b)
Paolo Fresu Quartet
Oh Bess Where's My Bess | Bess You Is My Woman Now | What You Want Wid Bess
Fresu,Paolo (tp) | Le,Nguyen (el-g,g-synth) | Di Castri,Furio (b) | Gatto,Roberto (dr)
I Loves You Porgy
Fresu,Paolo (tp) | Salis,Antonello (el-p) | Salis,Antonello (el-p,fisarmonica) | Gatto,Roberto (dr)
Paolo Fresu Quintet
The Buzzard Song | Gone Gone Gone | My Man's Gone Now
Fresu,Paolo (tp) | Le,Nguyen (el-g,g-synth) | Salis,Antonello (p) | Di Castri,Furio (b) | Gatto,Roberto (dr)
Fishermen,Strawberry And Devil Crab: | Here Comes De Honey Man- | Crab Man- | Oh Dey's So Fresh And Fine-
Fresu,Paolo (tp) | Le,Nguyen (el-g,g-synth) | Di Castri,Furio (b) | Gatto,Roberto (dr) | Youssef,Dhafer (voc)
Summertime
Fresu,Paolo (tp) | Le,Nguyen (el-g,g-synth) | Salis,Antonello (p) | Di Castri,Furio (b) | Youssef,Dhafer (voc)
Paolo Fresu Sextet
Clara,Don't You Be Downhearted
Fresu,Paolo (tp) | Le,Nguyen (el-g,g-synth) | Salis,Antonello (fisarmonica) | Di Castri,Furio (b) | Gatto,Roberto (dr) | Youssef,Dhafer (oud,voc)

2663113-2 | CD | The Chesterfield Broadcasts Vol.1
Glenn Miller And His Orchestra
Indian Summer | In The Mood | I Love You Too Much | Tuxedo Junction | The Rhumba Jumps | One O'Clock Jump
NYC, rec. December 1939-March 1940
Miller,Glenn (tb,arr,ld) | Hurley,Clyde (tp) | Knowles,Legh (tp) | McMickle,Dale (tp) | Best,John (tp) | Tanner,Paul (tb) | Mastandrea,Alex (tb) | D'Annolfo,Frank (tb) | Mack,Tommy (tb) | Gibeling,Howard (tb) | Priddy,Jimmy (tb) | McIntyre,Hal (cl,as) | Schwartz,Wilbur (cl,as) | Abato,Jimmy (cl,as,bs) | Beneke,Gordon 'Tex' (cl,ts,voc) | Klink,Al (b-cl,ts) | Caceres,Ernie (cl,as,bs) | MacGregor,John Chalmers 'Chummy' (p) | Fisher,Richard (g) | Bundock,Rowland 'Rolly' (b) | Purtill,Maurice 'Moe' (dr) | Eberle,Ray (voc) | Hutton,Marion (voc) | Andrews,Patti (voc)
The Andrew Sisters With The Glenn Miller Orchestra
Introduction | Oh Johnny Oh Johnny | I've Got No Strings | Begin The Beguine | Chico's Love Song | Bei Mir Bist Du Schön | Beer Barrel Polka | The Donkey Serenade | Say Si Si | Hold Tight | Yodelin' Jive | Closing Announcement
Miller,Glenn (tb,arr,ld) | Hurley,Clyde (tp) | Knowles,Legh (tp) | McMickle,Dale (tp) | Best,John (tp) | Tanner,Paul (tb) | Mastandrea,Alex (tb) | D'Annolfo,Frank (tb) | Mack,Tommy (tb) | Gibeling,Howard (tb) | Priddy,Jimmy (tb) | McIntyre,Hal (cl,as) | Schwartz,Wilbur (cl,as) | Abato,Jimmy (cl,as,bs) | Beneke,Gordon 'Tex' (cl,ts,voc) | Klink,Al (b-cl,ts) | Caceres,Ernie (cl,as,bs) | MacGregor,John Chalmers 'Chummy' (p) | Fisher,Richard (g) | Bundock,Rowland 'Rolly' (b) | Purtill,Maurice 'Moe' (dr) | Andrew Sisters,The | Andrews,Laverne (voc) | Andrews,Maxine (voc) | Andrews,Patti (voc)

2663353-2 | CD | Wild Man Blues
Woody Allen Trio
Lonesome Blues | After You've Gone | Martha(aka Mazie) | Lead Me Saviour | Last Night On The Back Porch | Shake That Thing | In The Evening When The Sun Goes Down | Come On And Stomp Stomp Stomp
NYC, rec. February-March 1998
Allen,Woody (cl) | Davis,Eddy (bj,voc) | Cohen,Greg (b)
Woody Allen And His New Orleans Jazz Band
Dippermouth Blues | Swing A Lullaby | Yaaka Hula Hickey Dula | Wild Man Blues | Tie Me To Your Apron String Again | Pappy's B Flat Blues | Hear Me Talkin' To Ya
Allen,Woody (cl) | Wettenhall,Simon (tp) | Zigmont,Jerry (tb) | Sayer,Cynthia (p) | Davis,Eddy (bj,ld) | Cohen,Greg (b) | Garcia,Rob (dr)

2663455-2 | CD | Take The A Train
Canadian Brass
It Don't Mean A Thing If It Ain't Got That Swing | Echoes Of Harlem | Sophisticated Lady | The Cotton Tail Caper | Pitter Panther Patter | Come Sunday | I've Got To Be A Rug Cutter | Solitude | Blood Count | Lush Life Variations: | Live Is Lonely | Come What May Places | A Week In Paris | Portrait Of Cootie | Portrait Of Johnny | New World A-Coming | Harlem- | Sunday Morning- | Take The 'A' Train
Toronto,Canada, rec. 26.-28.10.1998
Canadian Brass | Lindemann,Jens (tp,piccolo-tp) | Romm,Ronald (tp,fl-h) | Watts,Gene (tb) | Cooper,Chris (fr-h) | Daellenbach,Chuck (tuba)

2663523-2 | CD | Gato Barbieri:The Best Of The Early Years
Gato Barbieri Group
Bahia | Falsa Bahiana | El Dia Que Me Quieras
NYC, rec. 27./28.4.1971
Barbieri,Gato (ts) | Beck,Joe (g) | Smith,Lonnie Liston (p,el-p) | Carter,Ron (el-b) | White,Lenny (dr) | Vasconcelos,Nana (congas,berimbau) | Golden,Gene (bongo,conga)
Bolivia
NYC, rec. 1973
Barbieri,Gato (fl,ts,handclaps,voice) | Abercrombie,John (g) | Smith,Lonnie Liston (p) | Clarke,Stanley (b) | M'tume,James[Forman] (congas) | Moreira,Airto (dr)
Eclypse | Michellina
Barbieri,Gato (ts) | Smith,Lonnie Liston (p) | Clarke,Stanley (b) | Jenny-Clark,Jean-Francois (b) | Moreira,Airto (dr) | Golden,Gene (congas)
Antonico
NYC, rec. 1971
Barbieri,Gato (ts) | Abercrombie,John (g) | Smith,Lonnie Liston (p) | Clarke,Stanley (b) | Moreira,Airto (dr) | M'tume,James[Forman] (congas) | Hafid,Moulay Ali (dumbeg)
Yo Le Canto A La Luna
Barbieri,Gato (ts) | Smith,Lonnie Liston (p) | Clarke,Stanley (b) | Moreira,Airto (dr) | M'tume,James[Forman] (congas) | Hafid,Moulay Ali (dumbeg)
El Gato
Barbieri,Gato (ts) | Nelson,Oliver (as) | Penque,Romeo (engl-h,fl) | Bodner,Phil (fl,alto-fl) | Bank,Danny (b-cl) | Jones,Hank (p) | Spinozza,David (g) | Carter,Ron (b) | Purdie,Bernard 'Pretty' (dr) | Moreira,Airto (perc)

2663524-2 | CD | Time's Mirror
Tom Harrell Orchestra
Shapes | Autumn Leaves | Daily Affirmation | Dream | Chasin' The Bird | Sao Paulo | Time's Mirror | Train Shuffle
NYC, rec. 11./12.3.1999
Harrell,Tom (tp,fl-h) | Gardner,Earl (tp) | Magnarelli,Joe (tp,fl-h) | Rogers,Chris (tp,fl-h) | Weiss,David (tp,fl-h) | Zollar,James (tp,fl-h) | Herwig,Conrad (tb) | Fahn,Mike (tb) | Hasselbring,Curtis (tb) | Purviance,Douglas (b-tb) | Bailey,Craig (fl,as) | Foster,Alex (fl,ts) | Braden,Don (ts) | Schumacher,Dave (bs) | Davis,Xavier (p) | Davis,Kenneth 'Kenny' (b) | Allen,Carl (dr)

2663563-2 | CD | P.S. Mr.Cole

John Pizzarelli Trio
Walkin' My Baby Back Home | Candy | Welcome To The Club | Back Home Again In Indiana | I Love You For Sentimental Reasons | Meet Me At No Special Place | The Late Late Show | Smile | Tenderly | I Was A Little Too Lonely | I'm An Errand Boy For Rhythm | That's Nat | Azure-Te | I Know That You Know | Embraceable You | I Like Jersey Best
NYC, rec. January 1996
Pizzarelli,John (g,voc) | Kennedy,Ray (p) | Pizzarelli,Martin (b)
John Pizzarelli Trio With Harry Allen
Don't Let It Go To Your Head | Then I'll Be Tired Of You
Allen,Harry (ts) | Pizzarelli,John (g,voc) | Kennedy,Ray (p) | Pizzarelli,Martin (b)

2663603-2 | CD | Soul On Soul
Dave Douglas Group
Blue Heaven | Waltz Boogie
NYC, rec. 11./12.8.1999
Douglas,Dave (tp) | Roseman,Joshua 'Josh' (tb) | Tardy,Greg (cl,ts) | Caine,Uri (p) | Genus,James (b) | Baron,Joey (dr)
Ageless
Douglas,Dave (tp) | Speed,Chris (ts) | Caine,Uri (p) | Genus,James (b) | Baron,Joey (dr)
Soul On Soul | Canticle | Aries | Mary's Idea | Multiples | Kyrie | Zonish
Douglas,Dave (tp) | Roseman,Joshua 'Josh' (tb) | Speed,Chris (cl,ts) | Caine,Uri (p) | Genus,James (b) | Baron,Joey (dr)
Moon In The West
Douglas,Dave (tp) | Roseman,Joshua 'Josh' (tb) | Speed,Chris (ts) | Tardy,Greg (b-cl,ts) | Caine,Uri (p) | Genus,James (b) | Baron,Joey (dr)
Eleven Years Old
Douglas,Dave (tp) | Roseman,Joshua 'Josh' (tb) | Speed,Chris (cl)
Play It Momma
Douglas,Dave (tp) | Genus,James (b) | Baron,Joey (dr)

2663636-2 | CD | Best Of The Complete RCA Victor Recordings
Louis Armstrong With Chick Webb's Orchestra
That's My Home | Medley Of Armstrong's Hits: | I'll Be Glad When You're Dead You Rascal You- | When It's Sleepy Time Down South- | Nobody's Sweetheart-
Camden,NJ, rec. 8.12.1932
Armstrong,Louis (tp,voc) | Bacon,Louis (tp) | Hunt,Louis (tp) | Hicks,Billy (tp) | Green,Charlie (tb) | Clark,Pete (cl,as) | Sampson,Edgar (as,v) | Williams,Elmer (ts) | Kirkpatrick,Don (p) | Trueheart,John (g) | James,Elmer (b,tuba) | Webb,Chick (dr)
Louis Armstrong And His Orchestra
I've Got The World On A String | I've Got A Right To Sing The Blues | High Society
Chicago,Ill, rec. 26.1.1933
Armstrong,Louis (tp,voc) | Whitlock,Elmer (tp) | Randolph,Zilmer (tp) | Johnson,Keg (tb) | Brown,Scoville (cl,as) | Oldham,George (as) | Johnson,Budd (ts) | Wilson,Teddy (p) | McKendrick,Mike (bj) | Oldham,Bill (b) | Porter,Yank (dr)
Basin Street Blues
Chicago,Ill, rec. 27.1.1933
Armstrong,Louis (tp,voc) | Whitlock,Ellis (tp) | Randolph,Zilmer (tp) | Johnson,Keg (tb) | Browne,Scoville (as) | Oldham,George (as) | Johnson,Budd (ts) | Wilson,Teddy (p) | McKendrick,Mike (bj) | Oldham,Bill (tb,b,tuba) | Porter,Yank (dr)
Mahogany Hall Stomp
Chicago,Ill, rec. 28.1.1933
Armstrong,Louis (tp,voc) | Whitlock,Ellis (tp) | Randolph,Zilmer (tp) | Johnson,Keg (tb) | Browne,Scoville (as) | Oldham,George (as) | Johnson,Budd (ts) | Wilson,Teddy (p) | McKendrick,Mike (bj) | Oldham,Bill (b) | Porter,Yank (dr)
St.Louis Blues
Chicago,Ill, rec. 26.4.1933
Armstrong,Louis (tp,voc) | Randolph,Zilmer (tp) | Whitlock,Elmer (tp) | Johnson,Keg (tb) | Johnson,Budd (sax) | Brown,Scoville (sax) | Oldham,George (sax) | Beal,Charlie (p) | McKendrick,Mike (bj) | Oldham,Bill (tuba) | Dial,Harry (dr)
Jimmy Rodgers With Louis And Lil Armstrong
Blue Yodel No.9 (Standin' On The Corner)
Los Angeles,CA, rec. 16.7.1930
Rodgers,Jimmy (voc) | Armstrong,Louis (co) | Armstrong [Hardin],Lil (p)
Esquire All-American Award Winners
Long Long Journey
NYC, rec. 10.1.1946
Esquire All Stars | Armstrong,Louis (tp,voc) | Shavers,Charlie (tp) | Hamilton,Jimmy (cl) | Hodges,Johnny (as) | Byas,Don (ts) | Ellington,Duke (p) | Strayhorn,Billy (p) | Palmieri,Remo (g) | Jackson,Chubby (b) | Greer,William 'Sonny' (dr)
Louis Armstrong And His Orchestra
Back O'Town Blues
NYC, rec. 27.4.1946
Armstrong,Louis (tp,voc) | Jordan,Ludwig (tp) | Mullens,Eddie (tp) | Ford,Fats (tp) | Scott,William (tp) | Moore,Russel 'Big Chief' (tb) | Martin,Adam (tb) | Powe,Norman (tb) | Cobbs,Alfred (tb) | Hill,Don (as) | Gordon,Amos (as) | Sparrow,John (ts) | Garland,Joe (ts) | Thompson,Ernest (bs) | Swanston,Ed (p) | Warner,Elmer (g) | Shaw,Arvell (b) | Ballard,Butch (dr)
Louis Armstrong And His Hot Seven
Sugar
Los Angeles,CA, rec. 6.9.1946
Armstrong,Louis (tp,voc) | Dickenson,Vic (tb) | Bigard,Barney (cl) | Beal,Charlie (p) | Reuss,Allan (g) | Callender,Red (b) | Singleton,Zutty (dr)
Louis Armstrong And His Dixieland Seven
Do You Know What It Means To Miss New Orleans
Los Angeles,CA, rec. 17.10.1946
Armstrong,Louis (tp,voc) | Ory,Edward 'Kid' (tb) | Bigard,Barney (cl) | Beal,Charlie (p) | Scott,Bud (g) | Callender,Red (b) | Hall,Minor 'Ram' (dr)
Louis Armstrong And His All Stars
Ain't Misbehavin' | Rockin' Chair
Live at Town Hall,NYC, rec. 17.5.1947
Armstrong,Louis (tp,voc) | Hackett,Bobby (tp) | Teagarden,Jack (tb,voc) | Hucko,Peanuts (cl,ts) | Cary,Dick (p) | Haggart,Bob (b) | Catlett,Big Sid (dr)
Jack-Armstrong Blues
NYC, rec. 10.6.1947
Armstrong,Louis (tp,voc) | Hackett,Bobby (tp) | Teagarden,Jack (tb,voc) | Hucko,Peanuts (cl) | Caceres,Ernie (sax) | Guarnieri,Johnny (p) | Casey,Al (g) | Hall,Al (b) | Cole,William 'Cozy' (dr)

2663672-2 | 3 CD | Highlights From The Duke Ellington Centennial Edition
Duke Ellington And His Orchestra
Black And Tan Fantasy | Black Beauty
Camden,NJ, rec. 26.10.1927
Ellington,Duke (p) | Whetsol,Arthur (tp) | Jenkins,Freddie (tp) | Williams,Cootie (tp,voc) | Nanton,Joe 'Tricky Sam' (tb) | Hodges,Johnny (cl,ss,as) | Bigard,Barney (cl,ts) | Carney,Harry (cl,as,bs) | Guy,Fred (bj) | Braud,Wellman (b) | Greer,William 'Sonny' (dr,voc)
The Mooche
NYC, rec. 26.3.1928
Ellington,Duke (p) | Whetsol,Arthur (tp) | Jenkins,Freddie (tp) | Williams,Cootie (tp,voc) | Nanton,Joe 'Tricky Sam' (tb) | Hodges,Johnny (cl,ss,as) | Bigard,Barney (cl,ts) | Carney,Harry (cl,as,bs) | Guy,Fred (bj) | Braud,Wellman (b) | Greer,William 'Sonny' (dr,voc)
Cotton Club Stomp
NYC, rec. 12.4.1929
Ellington,Duke (p) | Whetsol,Arthur (tp) | Jenkins,Freddie (tp) | Williams,Cootie (tp,voc) | Nanton,Joe 'Tricky Sam' (tb) | Hodges,Johnny (ss,as) | Carney,Harry (cl,as,bs) | Bigard,Barney (cl,ts) | Guy,Fred (bj) | Braud,Wellman (b) | Greer,William 'Sonny' (dr)
Jungle Nights In Harlem
rec. 4.6.1930
Ellington,Duke (p) | Williams,Cootie (tp) | Jenkins,Freddie (tp) | Whetsol,Arthur (tp) | Nanton,Joe 'Tricky Sam' (tb) | Tizol,Juan (tb) | Bigard,Barney (cl,ts) | Hodges,Johnny (cl,ss,as) | Carney,Harry (cl,as,as,bs) | Guy,Fred (g,bj) | Braud,Wellman (b) | Greer,William 'Sonny' (dr)
Ring Dem Bells
Hollywood,CA, rec. 20.8.1930
Ellington,Duke (p) | Williams,Cootie (tp) | Jenkins,Freddie (tp) | Whetsol,Arthur (tp) | Nanton,Joe 'Tricky Sam' (tb) | Tizol,Juan (tb) | Bigard,Barney (cl,ts) | Hodges,Johnny (cl,ss,as) | Carney,Harry (cl,ss,as,bs) | Guy,Fred (g,bj) | Braud,Wellman (b) | Greer,William 'Sonny' (dr)
Mood Indigo
NYC, rec. 10.12.1930
Ellington,Duke (p) | Williams,Cootie (tp) | Jenkins,Freddie (tp) | Whetsol,Arthur (tp) | Nanton,Joe 'Tricky Sam' (tb) | Tizol,Juan (tb) | Bigard,Barney (cl,ts) | Hodges,Johnny (cl,ss,as) | Carney,Harry (cl,ss,as,bs) | Guy,Fred (g,bj) | Braud,Wellman (b) | Greer,William 'Sonny' (dr)
Rockin' In Rhythm
NYC, rec. 16.1.1931
Ellington,Duke (p) | Jenkins,Freddie (tp) | Williams,Cootie (tp) | Whetsol,Arthur (tp) | Nanton,Joe 'Tricky Sam' (tb) | Tizol,Juan (tb) | Bigard,Barney (cl,ts) | Hodges,Johnny (cl,ss,as) | Carney,Harry (cl,bs) | Guy,Fred (bj) | Braud,Wellman (b) | Greer,William 'Sonny' (dr)
Creole Rhapsody(part 1) | Creole Rhapsody(part 2)
Camden,NJ, rec. 11.6.1931
Ellington,Duke (p) | Williams,Cootie (tp) | Jenkins,Freddie (tp) | Whetsol,Arthur (tp) | Nanton,Joe 'Tricky Sam' (tb) | Tizol,Juan (tb) | Bigard,Barney (cl,ts) | Hodges,Johnny (cl,ss,as) | Carney,Harry (cl,ss,as,bs) | Guy,Fred (g,bj) | Braud,Wellman (b) | Greer,William 'Sonny' (dr)
Echoes Of The Jungle
Camden,NJ, rec. 16.6.1931
Ellington,Duke (p) | Williams,Cootie (tp) | Jenkins,Freddie (tp) | Whetsol,Arthur (tp) | Nanton,Joe 'Tricky Sam' (tb) | Tizol,Juan (tb) | Bigard,Barney (cl,ts) | Hodges,Johnny (cl,ss,as) | Carney,Harry (cl,ss,as,bs) | Guy,Fred (g,bj) | Braud,Wellman (b) | Greer,William 'Sonny' (dr)
Daybreak Express
Chicago,Ill, rec. 4.12.1933
Ellington,Duke (p,arr) | Whetsol,Arthur (tp) | Jenkins,Freddie (tp) | Williams,Cootie (tp) | Bacon,Louis (tp) | Nanton,Joe 'Tricky Sam' (tb) | Brown,Lawrence (tb) | Bigard,Barney (cl,ts) | Hodges,Johnny (cl,ss,as) | Hardwicke,Otto (cl,as,bass-s) | Carney,Harry (cl,as,bs) | Guy,Fred (g) | Braud,Wellman (b) | Greer,William 'Sonny' (dr)
My Old Flame
Hollywood,CA, rec. 9.5.1934
Ellington,Duke (p) | Williams,Cootie (tp) | Whetsol,Arthur (tp) | Bacon,Louis (tp) | Nanton,Joe 'Tricky Sam' (tb) | Brown,Lawrence (tb) | Tizol,Juan (v-tb) | Hodges,Johnny (as) | Royal,Marshall (as) | Bigard,Barney (cl,ts) | Carney,Harry (cl,bs) | Guy,Fred (g) | Braud,Wellman (b) | Greer,William 'Sonny' (dr) | Anderson,Ivie (voc)
Jack The Bear
Chicago,Ill, rec. 6.3.1940
Ellington,Duke (p) | Jones,Wallace (tp) | Stewart,Rex (tp) | Williams,Cootie (tp) | Brown,Lawrence (tb) | Nanton,Joe 'Tricky Sam' (tb) | Tizol,Juan (v-tb) | Hodges,Johnny (ss,as) | Hardwicke,Otto (as) | Bigard,Barney (cl,ts) | Webster,Ben (ts) | Carney,Harry (cl,b-cl,as,bs) | Guy,Fred (g) | Blanton,Jimmy (b) | Greer,William 'Sonny' (dr)
Cotton Tail | Never No Lament
Hollywood,CA, rec. 4.5.1940
Ellington,Duke (p) | Stewart,Rex (co) | Williams,Cootie (tp) | Jones,Wallace (tp) | Nanton,Joe 'Tricky Sam' (tb) | Brown,Lawrence (tb) | Tizol,Juan (tb) | Bigard,Barney (cl) | Hodges,Johnny (ss,as) | Hardwicke,Otto (as,bass-s) | Webster,Ben (ts) | Carney,Harry (b-cl,bs) | Guy,Fred (g) | Blanton,Jimmy (b) | Greer,William 'Sonny' (dr)
Duke Ellington And His Famous Orchestra
Sepia Panorama
NYC, rec. 24.7.1940
Ellington,Duke (p,arr) | Jones,Wallace (tp) | Williams,Cootie (tp) | Stewart,Rex (co) | Nanton,Joe 'Tricky Sam' (tb) | Brown,Lawrence (tb) | Tizol,Juan (v-tb) | Bigard,Barney (cl) | Hodges,Johnny (cl,ss,as) | Hardwicke,Otto (as,bass-s) | Webster,Ben (ts) | Carney,Harry (cl,as,bs) | Guy,Fred (g) | Blanton,Jimmy (b) | Greer,William 'Sonny' (dr)
Duke Ellington/Jimmy Blanton
Sophisticated Lady
Chicago,Ill, rec. 1.10.1940
Ellington,Duke (p) | Blanton,Jimmy (b)
Johnny Hodges Orchestra
Day Dream
Chicago,Ill, rec. 2.11.1940
Hodges,Johnny (as) | Berry,Emmett (tp) | Brown,Lawrence (tb) | Sears,Al (ts) | Lovett,Leroy (p,celeste) | Trottman,Lloyd (b) | Greer,William 'Sonny' (dr)
Barney Bigard And His Orchestra
A Lull At Dawn
Chicago,Ill, rec. 11.11.1940
Bigard,Barney (cl) | Nance,Ray (tp) | Tizol,Juan (v-tb) | Webster,Ben (ts) | Ellington,Duke (p) | Blanton,Jimmy (b) | Greer,William 'Sonny' (dr)
Duke Ellington And His Orchestra
Take The 'A' Train
Hollywood,CA, rec. 15.2.1941
Ellington,Duke (p) | Jones,Wallace (tp) | Stewart,Rex (co) | Nance,Ray (tp) | Brown,Lawrence (tb) | Nanton,Joe 'Tricky Sam' (tb) | Tizol,Juan (v-tb) | Hardwicke,Otto (as) | Hodges,Johnny (as) | Webster,Ben (ts) | Bigard,Barney (cl,ts) | Carney,Harry (cl,bs) | Guy,Fred (g) | Blanton,Jimmy (b) | Greer,William 'Sonny' (dr)
Just A-Sittin' And A-Rockin'
Hollywood,CA, rec. 5.6.1941
Ellington,Duke (p) | Jones,Wallace (tp) | Nance,Ray (tp) | Stewart,Rex (tp) | Nanton,Joe 'Tricky Sam' (tb) | Brown,Lawrence (tb) | Tizol,Juan (tb) | Bigard,Barney (cl,ts) | Hodges,Johnny (ss,as) | Webster,Ben (ts) | Carney,Harry (cl,as,bs) | Guy,Fred (g) | Blanton,Jimmy (b) | Greer,William 'Sonny' (dr)
I Got It Bad And That Ain't Good
Hollywood,CA, rec. 26.6.1941
Ellington,Duke (p) | Jones,Wallace (tp) | Stewart,Rex (co) | Nance,Ray (tp) | Brown,Lawrence (tb) | Nanton,Joe 'Tricky Sam' (tb) | Tizol,Juan (v-tb) | Hardwicke,Otto (as) | Hodges,Johnny (as) | Webster,Ben (ts) | Bigard,Barney (cl,ts) | Carney,Harry (cl,bs) | Guy,Fred (g) | Blanton,Jimmy (b) | Greer,William 'Sonny' (dr) | Anderson,Ivie (voc)
Johnny Hodges Orchestra
Passion Flower | Things Ain't What They Used To Be
Hollywood,CA, rec. 3.7.1941
Hodges,Johnny (as) | Nance,Ray (tp) | Brown,Lawrence (tb) | Carney,Harry (bs) | Ellington,Duke (p) | Blanton,Jimmy (b) | Greer,William 'Sonny' (dr)
Duke Ellington And His Orchestra
Rocks In My Bed | Chelsea Bridge
Hollywood,CA, rec. 26.9.1941
Ellington,Duke (p) | Jones,Wallace (tp) | Stewart,Rex (co) | Nance,Ray (tp) | Brown,Lawrence (tb) | Nanton,Joe 'Tricky Sam' (tb) | Tizol,Juan (v-tb) | Hardwicke,Otto (as) | Hodges,Johnny (as) | Webster,Ben (ts) | Bigard,Barney (cl,ts) | Carney,Harry (cl,bs) | Guy,Fred (g) | Blanton,Jimmy (b) | Greer,William 'Sonny' (dr) | Anderson,Ivie (voc)
Perdido
Chicago,Ill, rec. 21.1.1942
Ellington,Duke (p) | Jones,Wallace (tp) | Stewart,Rex (co) | Nance,Ray (tp) | Brown,Lawrence (tb) | Nanton,Joe 'Tricky Sam' (tb) | Tizol,Juan (v-tb) | Hardwicke,Otto (as) | Hodges,Johnny (as) | Webster,Ben (ts) | Bigard,Barney (cl,ts) | Carney,Harry (cl,bs) | Guy,Fred (g) | Raglin,Alvin 'Junior' (b) | Greer,William 'Sonny' (dr)
I'm Beginning To See The Light
NYC, rec. 1.12.1944
Ellington,Duke (p) | Hemphill,Shelton (tp) | Jordan,Taft (tp) | Anderson,Cat (tp) | Nance,Ray (tp) | Nanton,Joe 'Tricky Sam' (tb) | Jones,Claude (tb) | Brown,Lawrence (tb) | Hodges,Johnny (as) | Hardwicke,Otto (as) | Sears,Al (ts) | Hamilton,Jimmy (cl,ts) | Carney,Harry (cl,bs) | Guy,Fred (g) | Raglin,Alvin 'Junior' (b) | Greer,William 'Sonny' (dr) | Sherrill,Joya (voc)
Work Song
NYC, rec. 11.12.1944
Ellington,Duke (p) | Hemphill,Shelton (tp) | Jordan,Taft (tp) | Anderson,Cat (tp) | Nance,Ray (tp,v) | Brown,Lawrence (tb) | Jones,Claude (tb) | Nanton,Joe 'Tricky Sam' (tb) | Hamilton,Jimmy (cl,ts) | Hodges,Johnny (as) | Hardwicke,Otto (as) | Sears,Al (ts) | Carney,Harry (bs) | Guy,Fred (g) | Raglin,Alvin 'Junior' (b) | Greer,William 'Sonny' (dr)
Caravan
NYC, rec. 11.5.1945
Ellington,Duke (p,arr) | Jordan,Taft (tp) | Hemphill,Shelton (tp) | Anderson,Cat (tp) | Nance,Ray (v,co) | Nanton,Joe 'Tricky Sam' (tb) | Brown,Lawrence (tb) | Jones,Claude (tb) | Hamilton,Jimmy (cl,ts) | Hodges,Johnny (cl,ss,as) | Hardwicke,Otto (as,bass-s) | Sears,Al (ts) | Carney,Harry (cl,as,bs) | Guy,Fred (g) | Raglin,Alvin 'Junior' (b) | Greer,William 'Sonny' (dr) | Davis,Kay (voc)
Duke Ellington With Tommy Dorsey And His Orchestra
The Minor Goes Muggin'
NYC, rec. 14.5.1945
Ellington,Duke (p) | Dorsey,Tommy (tb) | Goff,Gerry (tp) | Mangano,Mickey (tp) | Seaberg,George (tp) | Shavers,Charlie (tp) | De Karske,Karl (tb) | Satterwhite,Tex (tb) | Noel,Dick (tb) | Bivona,Gus (cl,as) | Cooper,Sid (as) | Fresk,Livio 'Babe' (ts) | Musso,Vido (ts) | Branson,Bruce (as,bs) | Bain,Bob (g) | Block,Sid (b) | Rich,Buddy (dr) | Strings | unkn. (harp,tuba) | Oliver,Sy (arr)
Duke Ellington-Billy Strayhorn Duo
Tonk
NYC, rec. 10.1.1946
Ellington,Duke (p) | Strayhorn,Billy (p)
Duke Ellington And His Orchestra
Just Squeeze Me(But Don't Tease Me)
NYC, rec. 9.7.1946
Ellington,Duke (p) | Anderson,Cat (tp) | Baker,Harold 'Shorty' (tp) | Hemphill,Shelton (tp) | Jordan,Taft (tp) | Nance,Ray (tp) | Williams,Francis (tp) | Jones,Claude (tb) | Brown,Lawrence (tb) | DeParis,Wilbur (tb) | Nanton,Joe 'Tricky Sam' (tb) | Hodges,Johnny (as) | Procope,Russell (as) | Hamilton,Jimmy (cl,ts) | Sears,Al (ts) | Carney,Harry (b-cl,bs) | Guy,Fred (g) | Pettiford,Oscar (b) | Greer,William 'Sonny' (dr)
Esquire All-American Award Winners
Long Long Journey
NYC, rec. 10./11.1.1946
Esquire All Stars | Armstrong,Louis (tp,voc) | Shavers,Charlie (tp) | Hamilton,Jimmy (cl) | Hodges,Johnny (as) | Byas,Don (ts) | Ellington,Duke (p) | Strayhorn,Billy (p) | Palmieri,Remo (g) | Jackson,Chubby (b) | Greer,William 'Sonny' (dr)
Duke Ellington And His Orchestra
Perdido
Live in Seattle,Washington, rec. 25.3.1952
Ellington,Duke (p) | Terry,Clark (tp) | Anderson,Cat (tp) | Cook,Willie (tp) | Nance,Ray (tp,v) | Jackson,Quentin (tb) | Woodman,Britt (tb) | Tizol,Juan (v-tb) | Hamilton,Jimmy (cl,ts) | Smith,Willie (as) | Procope,Russell (as) | Gonsalves,Paul (ts) | Carney,Harry (bs) | Marshall,Wendell (b) | Bellson,Louie (dr)
Come Sunday | New World A-Coming
Live at The Presbyterian Church,NYC, rec. 26.12.1965
Ellington,Duke (p) | Williams,Cootie (tp) | Anderson,Cat (tp) | Ellington,Mercer (tp) | Jones,Herbie (tp) | Brown,Lawrence (tb) | Cooper,Frank 'Buster' (tb) | Jackson,Quentin (tb) | Connors,Chuck (tb) | Procope,Russell (cl,as) | Hodges,Johnny (as) | Gonsalves,Paul (ts) | Hamilton,Jimmy (cl,ts) | Carney,Harry (bs) | Lamb,John (b) | Bellson,Louie (dr) | Peters,Brock (voc) | Marrow,Esther (voc) | McPhail,Jimmy (voc) | McCoy Choir,The Herman (voc)
Ain't Nobody Nowhere Nothin' Without God
Live at Westminster Abbey,London,GB, rec. 24.10.1973
Ellington,Duke (p) | Orchestra | Watkins,Tony (voc)
Isfahan
NYC, rec. 20.12.1966
Ellington,Duke (p) | Williams,Cootie (tp) | Anderson,Cat (tp) | Jones,Herbie (tp) | Ellington,Mercer (tp) | Brown,Lawrence (tb) | Connors,Chuck (tb) | Cooper,Frank 'Buster' (tb) | Hodges,Johnny (as) | Procope,Russell (cl,as) | Gonsalves,Paul (ts) | Hamilton,Jimmy (cl,ts) | Carney,Harry (bs) | Lamb,John (b) | Jones,Rufus (dr)
Blue Pepper(Far East Of The Blues)
NYC, rec. 21.12.1966
Ellington,Duke (p) | Williams,Cootie (tp) | Anderson,Cat (tp) | Jones,Herbie (tp,fl-h) | Ellington,Mercer (tp,fl-h) | Brown,Lawrence (tb) | Connors,Chuck (tb) | Cooper,Frank 'Buster' (tb) | Hodges,Johnny (as) | Procope,Russell (cl,as) | Gonsalves,Paul (ts) | Hamilton,Jimmy (cl,ts) | Carney,Harry (bs) | Lamb,John (b) | Jones,Rufus (dr)
Take The 'A' Train
Hollywood,CA, rec. 9.5.1966
Ellington,Duke (p) | Williams,Cootie (tp) | Anderson,Cat (tp) | Ellington,Mercer (tp) | Jones,Herbie (tp) | Brown,Lawrence (tb) | Cooper,Frank 'Buster' (tb) | Connors,Chuck (tb) | Procope,Russell (cl,as) | Hodges,Johnny (as) | Hamilton,Jimmy (cl,ts) | Gonsalves,Paul (ts) | Carney,Harry (bs) | Lamb,John (b) | Woodyard,Sam (dr)
Duke Ellington Trio
Second Portrait Of The Lion
Live at The Pittsburgh Jaz Festival, rec. 20.6.1965
Ellington,Duke (p) | Gales,Larry (b) | Riley,Ben (dr)
Duke Ellington Trio With The Boston Pops Orchestra
Sophisticated Lady
Tanglewood,Lenox MAS, rec. 28.7.1965
Ellington,Duke (p) | Lamb,John (b) | Bellson,Louie (dr) | Boston Pops Orchestra | Fiedler,Arthur (cond)
Duke Ellington And His Orchestra
Blood Count
San Francisco,CA, rec. 1.9.1967
Ellington,Duke (p) | Anderson,Cat (tp) | Ellington,Mercer (tp) | Jones,Herbie (tp) | Williams,Cootie (tp) | Cooper,Frank 'Buster' (tb) | Connors,Chuck (tb) | Brown,Lawrence (tb) | Hamilton,Jimmy (cl,ts) | Procope,Russell (cl,as) | Hodges,Johnny (as) | Gonsalves,Paul (ts) | Carney,Harry (bs) | Lamb,John (b) | Jones,Rufus (dr)
Raincheck
San Francisco,CA, rec. 30.8.1967
Ellington,Duke (p) | Anderson,Cat (tp) | Ellington,Mercer (tp) | Jones,Herbie (tp) | Williams,Cootie (tp) | Cooper,Frank 'Buster' (tb) | Connors,Chuck (tb) | Brown,Lawrence (tb) | Hamilton,Jimmy (cl,ts) | Procope,Russell (cl,as) | Hodges,Johnny (as) | Gonsalves,Paul (ts) | Carney,Harry (bs) | Lamb,John (b) | Jones,Rufus (dr)
Basin Street Blues | Don't You Know I Care (Or Don't You Care I Know)
Live at The Congress Theatre,Eastbourne,GB, rec. 1.12.1973
Ellington,Duke (p) | Ellington,Mercer (tp) | Johnson,Money (tp,voc) | Coles,Johnny (tp) | Hall,Barry Lee (tp) | Prudente,Vince (tb) | Baron,Art (tb) | Connors,Chuck (tb) | Procope,Russell (reeds) | Marion,Percy (reeds) | Minerve,Harold (reeds) | Ashby,Harold (cl,ts) | Carney,Harry (b-cl,bs) | Benjamin,Joe (b) | White,Rocky (dr)

2663694-2 | 2 CD | Louis Armstrong:A 100th Birthday Celebration
Louis Armstrong With Chick Webb's Orchestra
Hobo You Can't Ride This Train | That's My Home
Camden,NJ, rec. 8.12.1932
Armstrong,Louis (tp,voc) | Bacon,Louis (tp) | Hunt,Louis (tp) | Hicks,Billy (tp) | Green,Charlie (tb) | Clark,Pete (cl,as) | Sampson,Edgar (as,v) | Williams,Elmer (ts) | Kirkpatrick,Don (p) | Trueheart,John (g) | James,Elmer (b,tuba) | Webb,Chick (dr)
Louis Armstrong And His Orchestra
Medley Of Armstrong's Hits: | When You're Smiling- | St.James Infirmary- | Dinah- | I'll Be Glad When You're Dead You Rascal You- | When It's Sleepy Time Down South- | Nobody's Sweetheart-
Camden,NJ, rec. 21.12.1932

Armstrong,Louis (tp,voc) | Gaines,Charlie (tp) | unkn. (tp,tb) | Jordan,Louis (as) | Davey,Arthur (as) | Blake,Ellsworth (ts) | Robinson,Wesley (p) | unkn. (g,bj) | Hayes,Ed (tuba) | Hill,Benny (dr)
I've Got The World On A String | He's A Son Of The South | Sittin' In The Dark | High Society | Hustlin' And Bustlin' For Baby | I Gotta Right To Sing The Blues | Mahogany Hall Stomp
Chicago,Ill, rec. 26.1.1933
Armstrong,Louis (tp,voc) | Whitlock,Ellis (tp) | Randolph,Zilmer (tp) | Johnson,Keg (tb) | Browne,Scoville (as) | Oldham,George (as) | Johnson,Budd (ts) | Wilson,Teddy (p) | McHendrick,Mike (bj) | Oldham,Bill (tb,b,tuba) | Porter,Yank (dr)
Honey Do | Basin Street Blues
Chicago,Ill, rec. 27.1.1933
Armstrong,Louis (tp,voc) | Whitlock,Ellis (tp) | Randolph,Zilmer (tp) | Johnson,Keg (tb) | Browne,Scoville (as) | Oldham,George (as) | Johnson,Budd (ts) | Wilson,Teddy (p) | McHendrick,Mike (bj) | Oldham,Bill (tb,b,tuba) | Porter,Yank (dr)
Honey Don't You Love Me Anymore | Laughin' Louie | There's A Cabin In The Pines
Chicago,Ill, rec. 24.4.1933
Armstrong,Louis (tp,voc) | Whitlock,Ellis (tp) | Randolph,Zilmer (tp) | Johnson,Keg (tb) | Browne,Scoville (as) | Oldham,George (as) | Johnson,Budd (ts) | Beal,Charlie (p) | McHendrick,Mike (bj) | Oldham,Bill (tb,b,tuba) | Catlett,Big Sid (dr)
St.Louis Blues | Sweet Sue Just You
Chicago,Ill, rec. 26.4.1933
Armstrong,Louis (tp,voc) | Randolph,Zilmer (tp) | Whitlock,Elmer (tp) | Johnson,Keg (tb) | Johnson,Budd (cl,ts,voc) | Brown,Scoville (cl,as) | Oldham,George (cl,as) | Wilson,Teddy (p) | McKendrick,Mike (bj) | Oldham,Bill (b) | Dial,Harry (dr)
Whatta Ya Gonna Do | Linger In My Arms A Little Longer Baby | Joseph 'n His Brudders
NYC, rec. 27.4.1946
Armstrong,Louis (tp,voc) | Jordan,Ludwig (tp) | Mullens,Eddie (tp) | Ford,Fats (tp) | Scott,William (tp) | Moore,Russel 'Big Chief' (tb) | Martin,Adam (tb) | Powe,Norman (tb) | Cobbs,Alfred (tb) | Hill,Don (as) | Gordon,Amos (as) | Sparrow,John (ts) | Garland,Joe (ts) | Thompson,Ernest (bs) | Swanston,Ed (p) | Warner,Elmer (g) | Shaw,Arvell (b) | Ballard,Butch (dr)
Louis Armstrong And His Hot Seven
Blues For Yesterday | I Want A Little Girl | Sugar
Los Angeles,CA, rec. 6.9.1946
Armstrong,Louis (tp,voc) | Dickenson,Vic (tb) | Bigard,Barney (cl) | Beal,Charlie (p) | Reuss,Allan (g) | Callender,Red (b) | Singleton,Zutty (dr)
Louis Armstrong And His Dixieland Seven
Do You Know What It Means To Miss New Orleans | Where The Blues Were Born In New Orleans
Los Angeles,CA, rec. 17.10.1946
Armstrong,Louis (tp,voc) | Ory,Edward 'Kid' (tb) | Bigard,Barney (cl) | Beal,Charlie (p) | Scott,Bud (g) | Callender,Red (b) | Hall,Minor 'Ram' (dr)
Louis Armstrong And His All Stars
Back O'Town Blues | Rockin' Chair
Live at Town Hall,NYC, rec. 17.5.1947
Armstrong,Louis (tp,voc) | Hackett,Bobby (tp) | Teagarden,Jack (tb,voc) | Hucko,Peanuts (cl,ts) | Cary,Dick (p) | Haggart,Bob (b) | Catlett,Big Sid (dr)
Jack-Armstrong Blues
NYC, rec. 10.6.1947
Armstrong,Louis (tp,voc) | Hackett,Bobby (tp) | Teagarden,Jack (tb,voc) | Hucko,Peanuts (cl) | Caceres,Ernie (sax) | Guarnieri,Johnny (p) | Casey,Al (g) | Hall,Al (b) | Cole,William 'Cozy' (dr)

2663698-2 | CD | A Thousand Evenings
Dave Douglas Quartet
A Thousand Evenings | The Branches(for Dave Tarras-part 1) | The Branches(for Dave Tarras-part 2) | Words For A Loss | Variety(for Guy Klucevsek) | The Little Boy With The Sad Eyes | In So Many Wordls(for Jaki Byard): | Ecstatic | Mournful | In Praise | Goldfinger | On Our Way Home | Memories Of A Pure Spring
Douglas,Dave (tp) | Feldman,Mark (v) | Klucevsek,Guy (accordeon) | Cohen,Greg (b)

2663738-2 | CD | Paradise
Tom Harrell Group
Daybreak | Sunrise
NYC, rec. 13.-15.11.200
Harrell,Tom (tp) | Greene,Jimmy (ts) | Bryant,Freddie (el-g) | Colin,Lois (harp) | Davis,Xavier (p) | Okegwo,Ugonna (b) | Parker,Leon (dr)
Wind Chant
NYC, rec. 13.-15.11.2000
Harrell,Tom (tp) | Greene,Jimmy (ts) | Bryant,Freddie (el-g) | Colin,Lois (harp) | Davis,Xavier (p) | Okegwo,Ugonna (b) | Parker,Leon (dr) | Café[Edson Café Adasilva] (perc)
Baroque Steps
Harrell,Tom (fl-h) | Greene,Jimmy (ts) | Okegwo,Ugonna (b) | Parker,Leon (dr) | Cummings,Genovia (v) | Whitney-Barratt,Belinda (v) | Haffner,Juliet (viola) | Miller,Daniel (cello) | Szabo,Jeffrey (cello)
Nighttime
Harrell,Tom (fl-h) | Greene,Jimmy (ts) | Colin,Lois (harp) | Okegwo,Ugonna (b) | Cruz,Adam (dr) | Cummings,Genovia (v) | Whitney-Barratt,Belinda (v) | Haffner,Juliet (viola) | Miller,Daniel (cello) | Szabo,Jeffrey (cello)
Wishing Well
Harrell,Tom (fl-h) | Colin,Lois (harp) | Davis,Xavier (p) | Okegwo,Ugonna (b) | Parker,Leon (dr) | Cummings,Genovia (v) | Whitney-Barratt,Belinda (v) | Haffner,Juliet (viola) | Miller,Daniel (cello) | Szabo,Jeffrey (cello)
Paradise Sring
Harrell,Tom (tp) | Greene,Jimmy (ts) | Bryant,Freddie (el-g) | Colin,Lois (harp) | Davis,Xavier (p) | Okegwo,Ugonna (b) | Cruz,Adam (dr) | Café[Edson Café Adasilva] (perc) | Cummings,Genovia (v) | Whitney-Barratt,Belinda (v) | Haffner,Juliet (viola) | Miller,Daniel (cello) | Szabo,Jeffrey (cello)
Morning Prayer(part 1)
Cummings,Genovia (v) | Whitney-Barratt,Belinda (v) | Haffner,Juliet (viola) | Miller,Daniel (cello) | Szabo,Jeffrey (cello)
Morning Prayer(part)
Harrell,Tom (fl-h) | Bryant,Freddie (g) | Colin,Lois (harp) | Okegwo,Ugonna (b) | Cruz,Adam (dr) | Cummings,Genovia (v) | Whitney-Barratt,Belinda (v) | Haffner,Juliet (viola) | Miller,Daniel (cello) | Szabo,Jeffrey (cello)

2663763-2 | CD | Witness | EAN 090266376322
Dave Douglas Group
Witness | One More News | Kidnapping Kissinger | Episode For Taslima Nasrin | Child Of All Nations
NYC, rec. 13./14.12.2000
Douglas,Dave (tp,processed-tp,AM-radio) | Speed,Chris (cl,ts) | Daley,Joe (tuba) | Carrott,Bryan (vib,marimba,glockenspiel) | Feldman,Mark (v) | Friedlander,Erik (cello) | Gress,Drew (b) | Sarin,Michael (dr) | Mori,Ikue (electronic-perc) | Gress,Drew | Carrott,Bryan (vib,marimba,tympany)
Sozaboy | Woman At Point Zero
Douglas,Dave (tp,processed-tp,AM-radio) | Roseman,Joshua 'Josh' (tb) | Speed,Chris (cl,ts) | Daley,Joe (tuba) | Carrott,Bryan (vib,marimba,glockenspiel) | Feldman,Mark (v) | Friedlander,Erik (cello) | Gress,Drew (b) | Sarin,Michael (dr) | Mori,Ikue (electronic-perc) | Gress,Drew | Carrott,Bryan (vib,marimba,tympany)
Ruckus
Douglas,Dave (tp,processed-tp,AM-radio) | Roseman,Joshua 'Josh' (tb) | Speed,Chris (cl,ts) | Daley,Joe (tuba) | Carrott,Bryan (vib,marimba,glockenspiel) | Feldman,Mark (v) | Friedlander,Erik (cello) | Gress,Drew (b) | Sarin,Michael (dr) | Mori,Ikue (electronic-perc) | Gress,Drew | Carrott,Bryan (vib,marimba,tympany) | Honda,Yuka (sampler)
Mahfouz
Douglas,Dave (tp,processed-tp,AM-radio) | Roseman,Joshua 'Josh' (tb) | Speed,Chris (cl,ts) | Daley,Joe (tuba) | Carrott,Bryan (vib,marimba,glockenspiel) | Feldman,Mark (v) | Friedlander,Erik (cello) | Gress,Drew (b) | Sarin,Michael (dr) | Mori,Ikue (electronic-perc) | Gress,Drew | Carrott,Bryan (vib,marimba,tympany) | Honda,Yuka (sampler) | Waits,Tom (voc)

2663840-2 | 2 CD | Tijuana Moods(The Complete Edition) | EAN 090266384020
Charles Mingus Orchestra
Dizzy Moods | Ysabel's Table Dance | Ysabel's Table Dance(alt.take) | Ysabel's Table Dance(alt.take-2) | Los Mariachis(The Street Musicians) | Los Mariachis(The Street Musicians-alt.take) | Los Mariachis(The Street Musicians-alt.take-2) | Los Mariachis(The Street Musicians-alt.take-3) | Los Mariachis(The Street Musicians-short-take) | Dizzy Moods(short-take-1) | Dizzy Moods(short-take-2) | A Colloquial Dream(Scenes In The City-alt.take)
NYC, rec. 18.7.1957
Mingus,Charles (b) | Shaw,Clarence (tp) | Knepper,Jimmy (tb) | Hadi [Curtis Porter],Shafti (as) | Triglia,Bill (p) | Richmond,Dannie (dr) | Dunlop,Frankie (perc) | Morel,Ysabel (castanets) | Elder,Connie (voice)
Tijuana Gift Shop | Tijuana Gift Shop(alt.take) | Flamingo | Flamingo(alt.take) | A Colloquial Dream(Scenes In The City) | A Colloquial Dream(Scenes In The City-alt.take) | A Colloquial Dream(Scenes In The City-short-take-1) | A Colloquial Dream(Scenes In The City-alt.take) | Tijuana Gift Shop(alt.take-2) | Tijuana Gift Shop(short-take)
NYC
Mingus,Charles (b) | Shaw,Clarence (tp) | Knepper,Jimmy (tb) | Porter,Curtis[Shafi Hadi] (as) | Triglia,Bill (p) | Richmond,Dannie (dr) | Dunlop,Frankie (perc)

2663841-2 | CD | Carmen Sings Monk
Carmen McRae And Her Quartet
Get It Straight(Straight No Chaser) | Suddenly(In Walked Bud)
Live at The Great American Muisc Hall,San Francisco,CA, rec. 30.1./1.2.1988
McRae,Carmen (voc) | Rouse,Charlie (ts) | Willis,Larry (p) | Mraz,George 'Jiri' (b) | Foster,Al (dr)
Monkery's The Blues(Blue Monk) | You Know Who(I Mean You) | Little Butterfly(Pannonica) | Listen To Monk(Rhythm-A-Ning) | Looking Back(Reflections) | Get It Straight(Straight No Chaser) | Round About Midnight(alt.take) | Listen To Monk(Rhythm-A-Ning-alt.take) | Man,That Was A Dream(Monk's Dream-alt.take)
NYC, rec. 12.4.1988
McRae,Carmen (voc) | Jordan,Clifford (ss,ts) | Gunnison,Eric (p) | Mraz,George 'Jiri' (b) | Foster,Al (dr)
Dear Ruby(Ruby My Dear) | It's Over Now(Well You Needn't) | How I Wish(Ask Me Now) | Man,That Was A Dream(Monk's Dream) | Round About Midnight | Still We Dream(Ugly Beauty) | Suddenly(In Walked Bud)
NYC, rec. 13.4.1988
McRae,Carmen (voc) | Jordan,Clifford (ts) | Gunnison,Eric (p) | Mraz,George 'Jiri' (b) | Foster,Al (dr)

2663842-2 | CD | The Hawk In Hi-Fi
Coleman Hawkins With Billy Byers And His Orchestra
Little Girl Blue | I Never Knew | Dinner For One Please James | There'll Never Be Another You | There'll Never Be Another You(alt.take 1) | There'll Never Be Another You(alt.take 2) | Little Girl Blue(alt.take) | Dinner For One Please James(alt.take) | I Never Knew(alt.take)
NYC, rec. 17.1.1956
Hawkins,Coleman (ts) | Nottingham,Jimmy (tp) | Green,Urbie (tb) | Satterfield,Jack (tb) | Ohms,Freddie (tb) | Mitchell,Tom (tb) | Baker,Julius (fl) | Jekowsky,Sidney (cl) | Bodner,Phil (oboe) | Wilson,Marty (vib) | Jones,Hank (p) | Galbraith,Barry (g) | Hinton,Milt (b) | Johnson,Osie (dr) | Orloff,Gene (concertmaster) | Samaroff,Tosha (v) | Kruczek,Leo (v) | Lookofsky,Harry (v) | Gershman,Paul (v) | Zir,Isadore (viola) | Shulman,Alan (cello) | Byers,Billy (arr,ld)
The Bean Stalks Again | His Very Own Blues | I'm Shooting High | Bean And The Boys
NYC, rec. 18.1.1956
Hawkins,Coleman (ts) | Glow,Bernie (tp) | Shavers,Charlie (tp) | Oles,Louis (tp) | Royal,Ernie (tp) | Travis,Nick (tp) | Green,Urbie (tb) | Satterfield,Jack (tb) | Ohms,Freddie (tb) | Welsch,Chauncey (tb) | Marowitz,Sam (as) | McKusick,Hal (as) | Cohn,Al (ts) | Sims,Zoot (ts) | Schlinger,Sol (bs) | Wilson,Marty (vib) | Jones,Hank (p) | Galbraith,Barry (g) | Hinton,Milt (b) | Johnson,Osie (dr) | Byers,Billy (arr,ld)
Body And Soul | The Day You Came Along | Have You Met Miss Jones | The Essence Of You | Have You Met Miss Jones(alt.take 1) | Have You Met Miss Jones(alt.take 2) | Have You Met Miss Jones(incomplet) | The Day You Came Along(alt.take)
NYC, rec. 20.1.1956
Hawkins,Coleman (ts) | Baker,Julius (fl) | Rodney,Phil (oboe) | Jekowsky,Sidney (cl) | Buffington,Jimmy (fr-h) | Wilson,Marty (xylophone,glockenspiel) | Jones,Hank (p,celeste) | Lesberg,Jack (b) | Johnson,Osie (dr) | Kraus,Phil (bells) | Orloff,Gene (v) | Samaroff,Tosha (v) | Gersham,Paul (v) | Newman,Dave (v) | Rudnitsky,Alvin (v) | Eidus,Arnold (v) | Hollander,Max (v) | Cahn,Max (v) | Miroff,Seymour (v) | Kraft,Stan (viola) | Sarser,Dave (viola) | Fish,Bert (viola) | Ricci,George (cello) | Greenhouse,Bernhard (cello) | Sodaro,Edgardo (cello) | Byers,Billy (arr,ld)

2663859-2 | CD | Fancy Meeting You Here | EAN 090266385928
Bing Crosby And Rosemarie Clooney With The Billy May Orchestra
Fancy Meeting You Here | Slow Boat To China | I Can't Get Started | Hindustan | It Happened In Monterey | You Came A Long Way From St. Louis | Love Won't Let You Get Away | How About You | Brazil | Isle Of Capri | Say Si Si | Calcutta | Love Won't Let You Get Away(alt.take 1) | Ain't A-Hankerin' | Protection | Love Won't Let You Get Away(alt.take 2) | Fancy Meeting You Here- | Slow Boat To China- | Hindustan- | Ol' Man River | When It's Twilight On The Trail
Los Angeles,CA, rec. July 1958
Clooney,Rosemary (voc) | Crosby,Bing (voc) | Orchestra | May,Billy (arr,ld) | details unknown

2663872-2 | CD | PLay The Music Of Jimi Hendrix
Gil Evans Orchestra
Up From The Skies | Castles Made Of Sand | Up From The Skies(alt.take)
NYC, rec. 11.6.1974
Evans,Gil (cond,arr) | Peterson,Hanibal Marvin (tp,voc) | Soloff,Lew (tp) | Malone,Tom (tb,b-tb,fl,synth) | Gordon,Peter (fr-h) | Levin,Pete (fr-h,synth) | Johnson,Howard (b-cl,el-b,tuba) | Sanborn,David (fl,ss,as) | Harper,Billy (fl,ts) | Koehler,Trevor (fl,as,ts) | Horowitz,David (el-p,synth) | Abercrombie,John (el-g) | Kawasaki,Ryo (el-g) | Loving,Keith (g) | Pate,Don (b) | Moore,Michael (b,el-b) | Ditmas,Bruce (dr) | Smith,Warren (vib,marimba,perc,chimes) | Evans,Suzan 'Sue' (dr,perc,congas)
Crosstown Trafic | Voodoo Chile | Gypsy Eyes | Gypsy Eyes(alt.take)
NYC, rec. 12.6.1974
Evans,Gil (keyboards,arr) | Peterson,Hanibal Marvin (tp,voc) | Soloff,Lew (tp) | Gordon,Peter (fr-h) | Levin,Pete (fr-h,synth) | Malone,Tom (tb,b-tb,fl,synth) | Johnson,Howard (b-cl,tuba) | Sanborn,David (fl,ss,as) | Harper,Billy (fl,ts) | Koehler,Trevor (fl,ss,as,ts,bs) | Horowitz,David (el-p,synth) | Abercrombie,John (el-g) | Kawasaki,Ryo (el-g) | Loving,Keith (g) | Pate,Don (b) | Moore,Michael (b-g) | Ditmas,Bruce (dr) | Smith,Warren (vib,marimba,perc,chimes) | Evans,Suzan 'Sue' (dr,perc,congas)
Angel | Castles Made Of Sand- | Foxy Lady- | 1983 A Merman I Should Turn To Be | Angel(alt.take)
NYC, rec. 13.6.1974
Evans,Gil (keyboards,arr) | Peterson,Hanibal Marvin (tp,voc) | Soloff,Lew (tp) | Gordon,Peter (fr-h) | Levin,Pete (fr-h,synth) | Malone,Tom (tb,b-tb,fl,synth) | Johnson,Howard (b-cl,tuba) | Sanborn,David (fl,ss,as) | Harper,Billy (fl,ts) | Koehler,Trevor (fl,ss,as,ts,bs) | Horowitz,David (el-p,synth) | Abercrombie,John (el-g) | Kawasaki,Ryo (el-g) | Loving,Keith (g) | Pate,Don (b) | Moore,Michael (b-g) | Ditmas,Bruce (dr) | Smith,Warren (vib,marimba,perc,chimes) | Evans,Suzan 'Sue' (dr,perc,congas)

2663873-2 | CD | Birdland Dream Band
Birdland Dream Band
The Wailing Boat | Somebody Wants Me Down There | Maynard The Fox | Great Guns | More West | That Jones Boy | Button Nose | Little Girl Kimbi
NYC, rec. 11.9.1956
Birdland Dreamband,The | Ferguson,Maynard (tp,v-tb) | DeRisi,Al (tp) | Ferrante,Joe (tp) | Travis,Nick (tp) | Bert,Eddie (tb) | Cleveland,Jimmy (tb) | Russo,Sonny (tb) | Geller,Herb (as) | Cohn,Al (ts) | Johnson,Budd (ts) | Wilkins,Ernie (bs) | Jones,Hank (p) | Hinton,Milt (b) | Campbell,Jimmy (dr)
Blue Birdland | Lady Bug | Still Water Stomp | Rosebud | Blue Birdland(alt.take) | Lady Bug(alt.take) | Lady Bug(incompl.take) | Still Water Stomp(alt.take 1) | Still Water Stomp(alt.take 2) | Rosebud(alt.take 1) | Rosebud(alt.take 2)
NYC, rec. 8.9.1956
Birdland Dreamband,The | Ferguson,Maynard (tp,v-tb) | DeRisi,Al (tp) | Ferrante,Joe (tp) | Travis,Nick (tp) | Royal,Ernie (tp) | Bert,Eddie (tb) | Cleveland,Jimmy (tb) | Geller,Herb (as) | Cohn,Al (ts) | Johnson,Budd (ts) | Wilkins,Ernie (bs) | Jones,Hank (p) | Hinton,Milt (b) | Campbell,Jimmy (dr)
Little Girl Kimbi | Little Girl Kimbi(alt.take)
NYC, rec. 25.9.1956
Birdland Dreamband,The | Ferguson,Maynard (tp,v-tb) | DeRisi,Al (tp) | Ferrante,Joe (tp) | Travis,Nick (tp) | Royal,Ernie (tp) | Stewart,Al (tp) | Bert,Eddie (tb) | Cleveland,Jimmy (tb) | Geller,Herb (as) | Cohn,Al (ts) | Johnson,Budd (ts) | Wilkins,Ernie (bs) | Jones,Hank (p) | Fishkin,Arnold (b) | Lamond,Don (dr)

2663874-2 | CD | Super Black Blues Vol.II
Super Black Blues Band
Cleanhead Blues | I Had A Dream | Person To Person | Stormy Monday Blues(They Call It Stormy Monday) | Sail On
Live at Carnegie Hall,NYC, rec. May 1970
Super Black Blues Band | Vinson,Eddie 'Cleanhead' (as,voc) | Andrews,Russ (ts) | Walker,T-Bone (g,voc) | Kelly,Wynton (p) | Lucie,Lawrence (g) | Hall,Al (b) | Jones,Elvin (dr)
Honey Hush | Yakety Yak
Super Black Blues Band | Vinson,Eddie 'Cleanhead' (as) | Andrews,Russ (ts) | Walker,T-Bone (g) | Kelly,Wynton (p) | Lucie,Lawrence (g) | Hall,Al (b) | Jones,Elvin (dr) | Turner,Big Joe (voc)
Leon Thomas With Band
Welcome To New York | Disillusion Blues | Damn Nam
Thomas,Leon (voc) | Creque,Neal Earl (p) | Phillips,James 'Jimmy' (b) | Ferguson,Sherman (dr) | Landrum,Richard 'Pablo' (congas) | Morgan,Sonny (bongos)

2663876-2 | CD | Spirits Known And Unknown
The Creator Has A Master Plan(Peace) | One | Echoes | Song For My Father | Damn Nam | Let The Rain Fall On Me
NYC, rec. 21./22.10.1969
Thomas,Leon (perc,voc,wood-fl) | Spaulding,James (fl,as) | Smith,Lonnie Liston (p) | Davis,Richard (b) | McBee,Cecil (b) | Haynes,Roy (dr) | Landrum,Richard 'Pablo' (bongos)
Malcolm's Gone | Um,Um,Um | A Night In Tunisia
Thomas,Leon (perc,voc,wood-fl) | Spaulding,James (fl,as) | Sanders,Pharoah (ts) | Smith,Lonnie Liston (p) | Davis,Richard (b) | McBee,Cecil (b) | Haynes,Roy (dr) | Landrum,Richard 'Pablo' (bongos)
Leon Thomas With Orchestra
Take The 'A' Train | Take The 'A' Train(alt.take) | Walkin' | Walkin'(alt.take) | Willow Weep For Me | Willow Weep For Me(alt.take) | If It Didn't Hurt So Much | If It Didn't Hurt So Much(alt.take)
NYC, rec. 12.11.1958
Thomas,Leon (voc) | Brown,Vernon (tb) | Bullman,Morton (tb) | Mitchell,Tom (tb) | Welsch,Chauncey (tb) | Socarras,Albert (fl) | Merkin,Lester (reeds) | Mondello,Toots (reeds) | Ricci,Paul (reeds) | Penque,Romeo (reeds) | Leighton,Bernie (p) | Perri,Danny (g) | Ryerson,Arthur 'Art' (g) | Baker,Abe (b) | Leeman,Cliff (dr) | Divigard,Jala (voc) | Workman,Miriam (voc) | Treadwell,Constance (voc) | Steiff,Helen (voc) | Steiff,Pete (voc) | McCulloh,Bob (voc) | Herst,Lou (voc) | Hale,Lee (voc) | Martin,Dave (arr,ld)

2663877-2 | CD | Leon Thomas In Berlin
Leon Thomas With The Oliver Nelson Quintet
Straight No Chaser | Pharoah's Tune- | Echoes- | Umbo Weti | The Creator Has A Master Plan(Peace)
Live at The 'Philharmonie',Berlin, rec. 6.11.1970
Thomas,Leon (perc,voc,wood-fl) | Nelson,Oliver (as) | Sterling,Arthur (p) | Lenz,Günter (b) | Humphries,Lex (dr) | Morgan,Sonny (congas)
Leon Thomas
Oo Whee!! Hidewe
Thomas,Leon (voc,wood-fl)
Leon Thomas With Band
Damn Nam(Ain't Goin' To Vietnam)
Live at Filmore East,NYC, rec. 15.3.1970
Thomas,Leon (voc,perc) | Alexander,Honey (fl) | Smith,Lonnie Liston (p) | Phillips,James 'Jimmy' (b) | Queen,Alvin (dr) | Landrum,Richard 'Pablo' (perc) | Morgan,Sonny (perc)

2663878-2 | CD | Astral Travelling
Lonnie Liston Smith & His Cosmic Echoes
Astral Traveling | Let Us Go Into The House Of The Lord | Rejuvenation | I Mani(Faith) | In Search Of Truth | Aspirations | Astral Traveling(alt.take) | Rejuvenation(alt.take) | I Mani(Faith-alt.take) | In Search Of Truth(alt.take)
NYC, rec. 24.4.1973
Smith,Lonnie Liston (p,el-p) | Barron,George (ss,ts) | Beck,Joe (g) | McBee,Cecil (b) | Lee,David (dr) | Roy,Badal (tablas) | Morgan,Sonny (congas,perc) | M'tume,James[Forman] (perc,congas) | Vashi,Geeta (taboura)

2663880-2 | CD | The Popular Duke Ellington
Duke Ellington And His Orchestra
Take The 'A' Train | I Got It Bad And That Ain't Good | The Mooche | Caravan | Do Nothin' Till You Hear From Me
Hollywood,CA, rec. 9.5.1966
Ellington,Duke (p) | Williams,Cootie (tp) | Anderson,Cat (tp) | Ellington,Mercer (tp) | Jones,Herbie (tp) | Brown,Lawrence (tb) | Cooper,Frank 'Buster' (tb) | Connors,Chuck (tb) | Procope,Russell (cl,as) | Hodges,Johnny (as) | Hamilton,Jimmy (cl,ts) | Gonsalves,Paul (ts) | Carney,Harry (bs) | Lamb,John (b) | Woodyard,Sam (dr)
Black And Tan Fantasy | The Twitch | Sophisticated Lady
Hollywood,CA, rec. 10.5.1966
Ellington,Duke (p) | Williams,Cootie (tp) | Anderson,Cat (tp) | Ellington,Mercer (tp) | Jones,Herbie (tp) | Brown,Lawrence (tb) | Cooper,Frank 'Buster' (tb) | Connors,Chuck (tb) | Procope,Russell (cl,as) | Hodges,Johnny (as) | Hamilton,Jimmy (cl,ts) | Gonsalves,Paul (ts) | Carney,Harry (bs) | Lamb,John (b) | Woodyard,Sam (dr)
Perdido | Mood Indigo | In My Solitude | Do Nothin' Till You Hear From Me | Creole Love Call | Wings And Things
Hollywood,CA, rec. 11.5.1966
Ellington,Duke (p) | Brisbois,Wilbur 'Bud' (tp) | Anderson,Cat (tp) | Ellington,Mercer (tp) | Jones,Herbie (tp) | Brown,Lawrence (tb) | Cooper,Frank 'Buster' (tb) | Connors,Chuck (tb) | Procope,Russell (cl,as) | Hodges,Johnny (as) | Hamilton,Jimmy (cl,ts) | Gonsalves,Paul (ts) | Carney,Harry (cl,bs) | Lamb,John (b) | Woodyard,Sam (dr)

2663881-2 | CD | Together Again!
Benny Goodman Quartet
Who Cares
NYC, rec. 13.2.1963
Goodman,Benny (cl) | Hampton,Lionel (vib) | Wilson,Teddy (p) | Krupa,Gene (dr)

Dearest
NYC, rec. 14.2.1963
Goodman,Benny (cl) | Hampton,Lionel (vib) | Wilson,Teddy (p) | Krupa,Gene (dr)
Seven Come Eleven | I've Found A New Baby | Somebody Loves Me | I'll Get By(As Long As I Have You)
NYC, rec. 26.8.1963
Goodman,Benny (cl) | Hampton,Lionel (vib) | Wilson,Teddy (p) | Krupa,Gene (dr)
Say It Isn't So | Runnin' Wild | I Got It Bad And That Ain't Good | Four Once More
NYC, rec. 27.8.1963
Goodman,Benny (cl) | Hampton,Lionel (vib) | Wilson,Teddy (p) | Krupa,Gene (dr)

2663896-2 | LP | A Night In Tunisia | EAN 090266389629
Art Blakey And The Jazz Messengers
A Night In Tunisia | A Night In Tunisia(alt.take)
NYC, rec. 8.4.1957
Blakey,Art (dr) | Hardman,Bill (tp,perc) | McLean,Jackie (as,perc) | Griffin,Johnny (ts,perc) | Dockery,Sam (p) | DeBrest,Jimmy 'Spanky' (b)
Off The Wagon | Theory Of Art | Couldn't It Be You | Evans | Off The Wall(alt.take) | Theory Of Art(alt.take)
Blakey,Art (dr) | Hardman,Bill (tp) | McLean,Jackie (as) | Griffin,Johnny (ts) | Dockery,Sam (p) | DeBrest,Jimmy 'Spanky' (b)

2663898-2 | CD | Desmond Blue | EAN 090266389827
Paul Desmond With Strings
I've Got You Under My Skin
NYC, rec. 19.6.1961
Desmond,Paul (as) | Richman,Albert (fr-h) | Penque,Romeo (woodwinds) | Webb,Stanley (woodwinds) | Agostini,Gloria (harp) | Duvivier,George (b) | Kay,Connie (dr) | Strings | Prince,Bob (arr,cond)
My Funny Valentine
NYC, rec. 14.9.1961
Desmond,Paul (as) | Richman,Albert (fr-h) | Marge,George (woodwinds) | Doty,Robert (woodwinds) | Bianco,Gene (harp) | Hall,Jim (g) | Cherico,Gene (b) | Kay,Connie (dr) | Strings | Prince,Bob (arr,cond)
Late Lament | I Should Care | Like Someone In Love
NYC, rec. 28.9.1961
Desmond,Paul (as) | Richman,Albert (fr-h) | Bodner,Phil (woodwinds) | Penque,Romeo (woodwinds) | Agostini,Gloria (harp) | Hall,Jim (g) | Hinton,Milt (b) | Thomas,Robert C. (dr) | Strings | Prince,Bob (arr,cond)
Desmond Blue | Then I'll Be Tired Of You | Ill Wind | Body And Soul
NYC, rec. 2.10.1961
Desmond,Paul (as) | Richman,Albert (fr-h) | Penque,Romeo (woodwinds) | Webb,Stanley (woodwinds) | Agostini,Gloria (harp) | Hall,Jim (g) | Hinton,Milt (b) | Thomas,Robert C. (dr) | Strings | Prince,Bob (cond) | details unknown
Advise And Consent | Autumn Leaves | Imagination | Autumn Leaves(alt.take 1) | Autumn Leaves(alt.take 2) | Imagination(alt.take) | Advise And Consent(alt.take)
NYC, rec. 15.3.1962
Desmond,Paul (as) | Miranda,Tony (fr-h) | Bodner,Phil (woodwinds) | Penque,Romeo (woodwinds) | Agostini,Gloria (harp) | Hinton,Milt (b) | Johnson,Osie (dr) | Strings | Prince,Bob (arr,cond)

2663910-2 | CD | Live At The Village Vanguard | EAN 090266391028
Tom Harrell Quintet
Asia Minor | Manhattan,3 A.M. | Where The Rain Begins | Blues In Una Sea | A Child Is Born | Design | Party Song
Live at The 'Village Vanguard',NYC, rec. 15.-18.11.2001
Harrell,Tom (tp) | Greene,Jimmy (ts) | Davis,Xavier (p) | Okegwo,Ugonna (b) | Davis,Quincy (dr)
Tom Harrell-Xavier Davis Duo
Everything Happens To Me
Harrell,Tom (tp) | Davis,Xavier (p)

2663912-2 | CD | Della | EAN 090266391226
Della Reese With The Neal Hefti Orchestra
The Lady Is A Tramp | If I Could Be With You One Hour Tonight | Let's Get Away From It All | Thou Swell | You're Driving Me Crazy | Goody Goody | And The Angels Sing | Baby Won't You Please Come Home | I'm Beginning To See The Light | I'll Get By(As Long As I Have You) | Blue Skies | Someday(You'll Want Me To Want You)
NYC, rec. 19.-22.10.1959
Reese,Della (voc) | Royal,Ernie (tp) | Glenn,Tyree (tb) | Green,Urbie (tb) | Hefti,Neal (arr,ld) | details unknown
Los Angeles,CA, rec. 2.10.1959
Reese,Della (voc) | Butcher,George prob. (tp) | details unknown | McPherson,Charles (ts)
-> Demo-Tape!

2663916-2 | CD | Heartfelt | EAN 090266391622
Fourplay
Galaxia | That's The Time | Break It Out | Rollin' | Let's Make Love | Heatfelt | Tally Ho! | Cafe L'amour | Juju | Goin' Back Home | Karma | Making Up
Hollywood/Burbank CA, rec. 2002
Fourplay | East,Nathan (b,voc) | Carlton,Larry (g) | James,Bob (keyboards) | Mason,Harvey (dr)

2663918-2 | CD | The Infinite | EAN 090266391820
Dave Douglas Group
Poses | The Infinite | Penelope | Crazy Games | Waverly | Yorke | Unison | Deluge | Argo
NYC, rec. 16.-18.12.2001
Douglas,Dave (tp) | Potter,Chris (ts) | Caine,Uri (el-p) | Genus,James (b) | Penn,Clarence (dr)

2663919-2 | CD | At Newport '63 | EAN 090266391929
Joe Williams And Friends
Spoken Introduction by Joe Williams | She's Warm She's Willing She's Wonderful | Wayfaring Stranger | Every Day | Any Time Any Day Any Where
Live at Newport,Rhode Island, rec. 5.7.1963
Williams,Joe (voc) | Terry,Clark (tp,fl-h) | McGhee,Howard (tp) | Hawkins,Coleman (ts) | Sims,Zoot (ts) | Mance,Junior[Julian C.] (p) | Cranshaw,Bob (b) | Roker,Granville 'Mickey' (dr)
Without A Song
Williams,Joe (voc) | Mance,Junior[Julian C.] (p) | Cranshaw,Bob (b) | Roker,Granville 'Mickey' (dr)
Come Back Baby
Williams,Joe (voc) | Terry,Clark (tp,fl-h) | Hawkins,Coleman (ts) | Mance,Junior[Julian C.] (p) | Cranshaw,Bob (b) | Roker,Granville 'Mickey' (dr)
April In Paris
Williams,Joe (voc) | McGhee,Howard (tp) | Hawkins,Coleman (ts) | Mance,Junior[Julian C.] (p) | Cranshaw,Bob (b) | Roker,Granville 'Mickey' (dr)
In The Evening When The Sun Goes Down | Roll 'Em Pete
Williams,Joe (voc) | McGhee,Howard (tp) | Sims,Zoot (ts) | Mance,Junior[Julian C.] (p) | Cranshaw,Bob (b) | Roker,Granville 'Mickey' (dr)
Gravy Waltz | All God's Chillun Got Rhythm- | Do You Wanna Jump Children-
NYC, rec. 17.7.1963
Williams,Joe (voc) | Terry,Clark (tp,fl-h) | McGhee,Howard (tp) | Hawkins,Coleman (ts) | Sims,Zoot (ts) | Mance,Junior[Julian C.] (p) | Cranshaw,Bob (b) | Roker,Granville 'Mickey' (dr)
Gravy Waltz | All God's Chillun Got Rhythm- | Do You Wanna Jump Children- | Some Of This 'N' Some Of That
Williams,Joe (voc) | Terry,Clark (tp,fl-h) | Jones,Thad (tp) | Hawkins,Coleman (ts) | Webster,Ben (ts) | Mance,Junior[Julian C.] (p) | Cranshaw,Bob (b) | Roker,Granville 'Mickey' (dr)

2663990-2 | 2 CD | This Is Oscar Peterson | EAN 090266399024
Oscar Peterson Trio
I Got Rhythm | Louise | My Blue Heaven | The Sheik Of Araby | Louise(alt.take)
Montreal,Canada, rec. 30.4.1945
Peterson,Oscar (p) | Brown,Bert (b) | Gariepy,Frank (dr)
Oscar Peterson Quartet
Flying Home | C Jam Blues | If I Could Be With You One Hour Tonight | Humoresque
Montreal,Canada, rec. 17.8.1945
Peterson,Oscar (p) | Sampson,Armand (g) | Brown,Bert (b) | Verdon,Roland (dr)
Oscar Peterson Trio
Blue Moon | In A Little Spanish Town | Time On My Hands | China Boy | In A Little Spanish Town(alt.take) | Blue Moon(alt.take) | Time On My Hands(alt.take) | China Boy(alt.take)
Montreal,Canada, rec. 3.4.1946
Peterson,Oscar (p) | Brown,Bert (b) | Dufort,Russ (dr)
Runnin' Wild | Sweet Lorraine | The Honeydripper | East Of The Sun West Of The Moon | Runnin' Wild(alt.take) | Sweet Lorraine(alt.take) | The Honeydripper(alt.take) | East Of The Sun West Of The Moon(alt.take)
Montreal,Canada, rec. 23.7.1946
Peterson,Oscar (p) | Brown,Bert (b) | Dufort,Russ (dr)
Back Home Again In Indiana | Margie | I Surrender Dear | I Don't Stand A Ghost Of A Chance With You | Back Home Again In Indiana(alt.take) | Margie(alt.take) | I Surrender Dear(alt.take) | I Don't Stand A Ghost Of A Chance With You(alt.take)
Montreal,Canada, rec. 17.4.1947
Peterson,Oscar (p) | King,Albert (b) | Wilkinson,Mark 'Wilkie' (dr)
Oscar's Boogie | Smiles | Stairway To The Stars | Poor Butterfly | Oscar's Boogie(alt.take) | Smiles(alt.take) | Stairway To The Stars(alt.take) | Poor Butterfly(alt.take)
Montreal,Canada, rec. 15.12.1947
Peterson,Oscar (p) | Roberts,Auston (b) | Jones,Clarence (dr)
Oop-Bop-Sh-Bam | Sweet Georgia Brown | Sleepy Time Gal
Montreal,Canada, rec. 1.3.1949
Peterson,Oscar (p) | Roberts,Auston (b) | Jones,Clarence (dr)
Rockin' In Rhythm
Peterson,Oscar (p,voc) | Roberts,Auston (b,voc) | Jones,Clarence (dr,voc)
Fine And Dandy | My Heart Stood Still | Somebody Loves Me | At Sundown
Montreal,Canada, rec. 14.11.1949
Peterson,Oscar (p) | Johnson,Ben (g) | Roberts,Auston (b)

2668701-2 | CD | Frank Sinatra And The Tommy Dorsey Orchestra
Tommy Dorsey And His Orchestra
I'll Never Smile Again
NYC, rec. 23.5.1940
Dorsey,Tommy (tb) | Berigan,Bunny (tp) | Linn,Ray (tp) | Debrow,Leon (tp) | Blake,Jimmy (tp) | Martin,Lowell (tb) | Jenkins,Les (tb) | Arus,George (tb) | Mince,Johnny (cl,as) | Schertzer,Hymie (as) | Stulce,Fred (as) | Mason,Paul (ts) | Lodice,Don (ts) | Bushkin,Joe (p) | Yocum,Clark (g) | Weiss,Sid (b) | Rich,Buddy (dr) | Sinatra,Frank (voc) | Pied Piepers,The (voc)
Only Forever
Hollywood,CA, rec. 17.10.1940
Dorsey,Tommy (tb) | Sinatra,Frank (voc) | details not on the cover
Stardust
Hollywood,CA, rec. 11.11.1940
Dorsey,Tommy (tb) | Linn,Ray (tp) | Peterson,Chuck (tp) | Elman,Ziggy (tp) | Jenkins,Les (tb) | Arus,George (tb) | Martin,Lowell (tb) | Mince,Johnny (cl,as) | Stulce,Fred (as) | Schertzer,Hymie (as) | Beau,Heinie (ts) | Lodice,Don (ts) | Bushkin,Joe (celeste) | Yocum,Clark (g,voc) | Weiss,Sid (b) | Rich,Buddy (dr) | Sinatra,Frank (voc) | Pied Piepers,The (voc) | Lowrey,Chuck (voc) | Huddleston,Floyd (voc) | Stafford,Jo (voc) | Weston,Paul (arr)
Dolores
NYC, rec. 20.1.1941
Dorsey,Tommy (tb) | Sinatra,Frank (voc) | Pied Piepers,The (voc) | Lowrey,Chuck (voc) | Huddleston,Floyd (voc) | Stafford,Jo (voc) | details not on the cover
Everything Happens To Me
NYC, rec. 7.2.1941
Dorsey,Tommy (tb) | Elman,Ziggy (tp) | Linn,Ray (tp) | Peterson,Charlie (tp) | Blake,Jimmy (tp) | Jenkins,Les (tb) | Arus,George (tb) | Martin,Lowell (tb) | Mince,Johnny (cl,as) | Stulce,Fred (as) | Beau,Heinie (as) | Lodice,Don (ts) | Mason,Paul (ts) | Bushkin,Joe (p) | Yocum,Clark (g) | Weiss,Sid (b) | Rich,Buddy (dr) | Sinatra,Frank (voc)
This Love Of Mine
NYC, rec. 28.5.1941
Dorsey,Tommy (tb) | Elman,Ziggy (tp) | Sherock,Shorty (tp) | Peterson,Charlie (tp) | Blake,Jimmy (tp) | Mercurio,Walter (tb) | Arus,George (tb) | Martin,Lowell (tb) | Schertzer,Hymie (cl,as) | Gershman,Manny (cl,as) | Beau,Heinie (as) | Lodice,Don (ts) | Mason,Paul (ts) | Bushkin,Joe (p) | Yocum,Clark (g) | Kelleher,Jack (b) | Rich,Buddy (dr) | Sinatra,Frank (voc)
I Guess I'll Have To Dream The Rest
NYC, rec. 27.6.1941
Dorsey,Tommy (tb) | Sinatra,Frank (voc) | Pied Piepers,The (voc) | details not on the cover
Violets For Your Furs
NYC, rec. 19.8.1941
Dorsey,Tommy (tb) | Sinatra,Frank (voc) | details not on the cover
The Night We Called It A Day | The Lamplighter's Serenade | The Song Is You | Night And Day
Hollywood,CA, rec. 19.1.1942
Sinatra,Frank (voc) | Members of The Dorsey Band | Stordahl,Axel (arr,ld) | details not on the cover
There Are Such Things | Daybreak | It Started All Over Again
NYC, rec. 1.7.1942
Dorsey,Tommy (tb) | Sinatra,Frank (voc) | Pied Piepers,The (voc) | details not on the cover
Just As Though You Were Here
NYC, rec. 6.8.1942
Dorsey,Tommy (tb) | Sinatra,Frank (voc) | Pied Piepers,The (voc) | details not on the cover

2668713-2 | CD | The Collected Carmen McRae
Carmen McRae with the Clifford Jordan Quartet
Dear Ruby(Ruby My Dear) | Still We Dream(Ugly Beauty)
NYC, rec. April 1988
McRae,Carmen (voc) | Jordan,Clifford (ts) | Gunnison,Eric (p) | Mraz,George 'Jiri' (b) | Foster,Al (dr)
Carmen McRae With The Shirley Horn Trio
It's Magic | Dedicated To You | Poor Butterfly | Misty | Tenderly
NYC, rec. October 1990
McRae,Carmen (voc) | Horn,Shirley (p) | Ables,Charles (el-b) | Williams,Stephen E. 'Steve' (dr)
Carmen McRae And Her Trio
Don't Explain | My Old Flame | If You Were Mine- | It's Like Reaching For The Moon-
Live at The 'Blue Note',NYC, rec. December 1993
McRae,Carmen (voc) | Otwell,Marshall (p) | Leftwich,John (b) | Bailey,Donald (dr)
Carmen McRae And Her Trio With Zoot Sims
Lover Man(Oh,Where Can You Be?) | I'm Pulling Through
NYC, rec. December 1963
McRae,Carmen (p,voc) | Sims,Zoot (ts) | Otwell,Marshall (p) | Leftwich,John (b) | Bailey,Donald (dr)

2668716-2 | CD | Candelight Miller
Glenn Miller And His Orchestra
Moonlight Serenade
details unknown, rec. 4.4.1939
Miller,Glenn (tb) | McMickle,Dale (tp) | Price,Bob (tp) | Knowles,Legh (tp) | Mastren,Al (tb) | Tanner,Paul (tb) | McIntyre,Hal (as) | Klink,Al (ts) | Schwartz,Wilbur (cl,as) | Beneke,Gordon 'Tex' (ts) | Aronson,Stanley (as) | MacGregor,John Chalmers 'Chummy' (p) | Reuss,Allan (g) | Bundock,Rowland 'Rolly' (b) | Carlson,Frank (dr) | Eberle,Ray (voc) | Hutton,Marion (voc) | Finegan,Bill (arr)
Stairway To The Stars
details unknown, rec. 9.5.1939
Miller,Glenn (tb) | McMickle,Dale (tp) | Knowles,Legh (tp) | Prince,Bob (tp) | Mastren,Al (tb) | Tanner,Paul (tb) | McIntyre,Hal (as) | Gelinas,Gabe (as,bs) | Schwartz,Wilbur (cl,as) | Beneke,Gordon 'Tex' (ts) | MacGregor,John Chalmers 'Chummy' (p) | Ens,Arthur (g) | Bundock,Rowland 'Rolly' (b) | Purtill,Maurice 'Moe' (dr) | Eberle,Ray (voc) | Hutton,Marion (voc) | Finegan,Bill (arr)
Indian Summer
details unknown, rec. 5.11.1939
Miller,Glenn (tb) | prob.personal: | McMickle,Dale (tp) | Knowles,Legh (tp) | Prince,Bob (tp) | Mastren,Al (tb) | Tanner,Paul (tb) | McIntyre,Hal (as) | Gelinas,Gabe (as,bs) | Schwartz,Wilbur (cl,as) | Beneke,Gordon 'Tex' (ts) | MacGregor,John Chalmers 'Chummy' (p) | Ens,Arthur (g) | Bundock,Rowland 'Rolly' (b) | Purtill,Maurice 'Moe' (dr) | Eberle,Ray (voc) | Hutton,Marion (voc) | Finegan,Bill (arr)
Careless
details unknown, rec. 18.11.1939
Miller,Glenn (tb) | prob.personal: | McMickle,Dale (tp) | Knowles,Legh (tp) | Prince,Bob (tp) | Mastren,Al (tb) | Tanner,Paul (tb) | McIntyre,Hal (as) | Gelinas,Gabe (as,bs) | Schwartz,Wilbur (cl,as) | Beneke,Gordon 'Tex' (ts) | MacGregor,John Chalmers 'Chummy' (p) | Ens,Arthur (g) | Bundock,Rowland 'Rolly' (b) | Purtill,Maurice 'Moe' (dr) | Eberle,Ray (voc) | Hutton,Marion (voc) | Finegan,Bill (arr)
It's A Blue World
details unknown, rec. 6.12.1939
Miller,Glenn (tb) | prob.personal: | McMickle,Dale (tp) | Knowles,Legh (tp) | Prince,Bob (tp) | Mastren,Al (tb) | Tanner,Paul (tb) | McIntyre,Hal (as) | Gelinas,Gabe (as,bs) | Schwartz,Wilbur (cl,as) | Beneke,Gordon 'Tex' (ts) | MacGregor,John Chalmers 'Chummy' (p) | Ens,Arthur (g) | Bundock,Rowland 'Rolly' (b) | Purtill,Maurice 'Moe' (dr) | Eberle,Ray (voc) | Hutton,Marion (voc) | Finegan,Bill (arr)
When You Wish Upon A Star
details unknown, rec. 15.1.1940
Miller,Glenn (tb) | prob.personal: | McMickle,Dale (tp) | Knowles,Legh (tp) | Prince,Bob (tp) | Mastren,Al (tb) | Tanner,Paul (tb) | McIntyre,Hal (as) | Gelinas,Gabe (as,bs) | Schwartz,Wilbur (cl,as) | Beneke,Gordon 'Tex' (ts) | MacGregor,John Chalmers 'Chummy' (p) | Ens,Arthur (g) | Bundock,Rowland 'Rolly' (b) | Purtill,Maurice 'Moe' (dr) | Eberle,Ray (voc) | Hutton,Marion (voc) | Finegan,Bill (arr)
Danny Boy (Londonderry Air)
details unknown, rec. 29.1.1940
Miller,Glenn (tb) | prob.personal: | McMickle,Dale (tp) | Knowles,Legh (tp) | Prince,Bob (tp) | Mastren,Al (tb) | Tanner,Paul (tb) | McIntyre,Hal (as) | Gelinas,Gabe (as,bs) | Schwartz,Wilbur (cl,as) | Beneke,Gordon 'Tex' (ts) | MacGregor,John Chalmers 'Chummy' (p) | Ens,Arthur (g) | Bundock,Rowland 'Rolly' (b) | Purtill,Maurice 'Moe' (dr) | Eberle,Ray (voc) | Hutton,Marion (voc) | Finegan,Bill (arr)
Fools Rush In
details unknown, rec. 31.3.1940
Miller,Glenn (tb) | prob.personal: | McMickle,Dale (tp) | Knowles,Legh (tp) | Prince,Bob (tp) | Mastren,Al (tb) | Tanner,Paul (tb) | McIntyre,Hal (as) | Gelinas,Gabe (as,bs) | Schwartz,Wilbur (cl,as) | Beneke,Gordon 'Tex' (ts) | MacGregor,John Chalmers 'Chummy' (p) | Ens,Arthur (g) | Bundock,Rowland 'Rolly' (b) | Purtill,Maurice 'Moe' (dr) | Eberle,Ray (voc) | Hutton,Marion (voc) | Finegan,Bill (arr)
The Nearness Of You
details unknown, rec. 28.4.1940
Miller,Glenn (tb) | details not on the cover
A Nightingale Sang In Berkeley Square
details unknown, rec. 11.10.1940
Miller,Glenn (tb) | details not on the cover
You Stepped Out Of A Dream
details unknown, rec. 17.1.1941
Miller,Glenn (tb) | details not on the cover
It's Always You
details unknown, rec. 20.2.1941
Miller,Glenn (tb) | Eberle,Ray (voc) | Beneke,Gordon 'Tex' (voc) | Kelly,Paula (voc) | Hutton,Marion (voc) | details not on the cover
I Guess I'll Have To Dream The Rest
details unknown, rec. 28.5.1941
Miller,Glenn (tb) | Eberle,Ray (voc) | Beneke,Gordon 'Tex' (voc) | Kelly,Paula (voc) | Hutton,Marion (voc) | details not on the cover
Moonlight Cocktail
details unknown, rec. 8.12.1941
Miller,Glenn (tb) | Eberle,Ray (voc) | Beneke,Gordon 'Tex' (voc) | Kelly,Paula (voc) | Hutton,Marion (voc) | details not on the cover
Serenade In Blue | At Last
details unknown, rec. 20.5.1942
Miller,Glenn (tb) | Beneke,Gordon 'Tex' (ts,voc) | Eberle,Ray (voc) | Modernaires,The (voc-group) | Finegan,Bill (arr) | details not on the cover
Moonlight Becomes You
details unknown, rec. 15.7.1942
Miller,Glenn (tb) | Beneke,Gordon 'Tex' (ts,voc) | Nelson,Skip (voc) | Modernaires,The (voc-group) | Finegan,Bill (arr) | details not on the cover
Rhapsody In Blue
details unknown, rec. 16.7.1942
Miller,Glenn (tb) | Kelly,Paula (voc) | Caceres,Ernie (voc) | Modernaires,The (voc-group) | details not on the cover

3411633-2 | CD | Burnin' Down he House | EAN 019341163329
Etta James & The Roots Band
Introduction | Come To Mama | I Just Want To Make Love To You | Born To Be Wild | I'd Rather Go Blind | All The Way Down | At Last | You Can Leave Your Hat On | Something's Got A Hold On Me | Your Good Thing Is About To End | Rock Me Baby | Love And Happiness | Take Me To The River | My Funny Valentine | Sugar On The Floor
Hollywood,CA, rec. 9.12.2001
James,Etta (voc) | Roots Band,The | Poole,Tom (tp) | Buttacavoli,Ronnie (tp,fl-h) | Thornburg,Lee R. (tp,fl-h,tb,arr) | Zavala,Jimmy Z. (ts,harm) | Woodford,David L. (bs) | Sklair,Josh (g,ld) | Murray,Bobby (g) | Matthews,David (keyboards) | Finnigan,Mike (org) | James,Sametto (b) | James,Donto (dr,MVP) | Conte,Luis (perc)

ND 74897(2) | 2 CD | At The Club St.Germain
Art Blakey And The Jazz Messengers
Politely | Whisper Not | Now's The Time | The First Theme | Moanin' With Hazel | Evidence(We Named It Justice) | Blues March For Europe No.1 | Like Someone In Love
Live at Club St.Germain,Paris,France, rec. 21.12.1958
Blakey,Art (dr) | Morgan,Lee (tp) | Golson,Benny (ts) | Timmons,Bobby (p) | Merritt,Jymie (b)
Along Came Manon | Out Of The Past | A Night In Tunisia | Ending With The Theme
Paris,France, rec. 21.12.1958
Blakey,Art (dr) | Morgan,Lee (tp) | Golson,Benny (ts) | Timmons,Bobby (p) | Merritt,Jymie (b) | Clarke,Kenny (dr) | M'Bow,Gana (congas)

ND 89221 | CD | The Glenn Miller Story Vol. 2
Glenn Miller And His Orchestra
Johnson Rag
rec. 5.11.1939
Miller,Glenn (tb) | McIntyre,Hal (as) | Beneke,Gordon 'Tex' (ts,voc) | Hutton,Marion (voc) | details unknown
King Porter Stomp
rec. 12.3.1940
Miller,Glenn (tb) | McIntyre,Hal (as) | Beneke,Gordon 'Tex' (ts,voc) | Hutton,Marion (voc) | details unknown
One O'Clock Jump
rec. 4.4.1940
Miller,Glenn (tb) | McIntyre,Hal (as) | Beneke,Gordon 'Tex' (ts,voc) | Hutton,Marion (voc) | details unknown
Under A Blanket Of Blue
rec. 19.12.1940
Miller,Glenn (tb) | McIntyre,Hal (as) | Beneke,Gordon 'Tex' (ts,voc) | Hutton,Marion (voc) | details unknown
Sun Valley Jump
rec. 17.1.1941
Miller,Glenn (tb) | McIntyre,Hal (as) | Beneke,Gordon 'Tex' (ts,voc) | Hutton,Marion (voc) | details unknown

The Hop
rec. 10.4.1942
Miller,Glenn (tb) | McIntyre,Hal (as) | Beneke,Gordon 'Tex' (ts,voc) | Hutton,Marion (voc) | details unknown

Here We Go Again
rec. 14.7.1942
Miller,Glenn (tb) | McIntyre,Hal (as) | Beneke,Gordon 'Tex' (ts,voc) | Hutton,Marion (voc) | details unknown

Rhapsody In Blue
rec. 16.7.1942
Miller,Glenn (tb) | McIntyre,Hal (as) | Beneke,Gordon 'Tex' (ts,voc) | Hutton,Marion (voc) | details unknown

Flying Home | In My Solitude | A-Tisket A-Tasket | I Got Rhythm
rec. details unknown
Miller,Glenn (tb) | McIntyre,Hal (as) | Beneke,Gordon 'Tex' (ts,voc) | Hutton,Marion (voc) | details unknown

ND 89222 | CD | The Glenn Miller Story Vol. 3
Sunrise Serenade
rec. 10.4.1939
Miller,Glenn (tb) | Beneke,Gordon 'Tex' (ts,voc) | Hutton,Marion (voc) | Eberle,Ray (voc) | Modernaires,The (voc-group) | Finegan,Bill (arr) | details unknown

My Melancholy Baby
rec. 29.1.1940
Miller,Glenn (tb) | Beneke,Gordon 'Tex' (ts,voc) | Hutton,Marion (voc) | Eberle,Ray (voc) | Modernaires,The (voc-group) | Finegan,Bill (arr) | details unknown

Say It
rec. 24.2.1940
Miller,Glenn (tb) | Beneke,Gordon 'Tex' (ts,voc) | Hutton,Marion (voc) | Eberle,Ray (voc) | Modernaires,The (voc-group) | Finegan,Bill (arr) | details unknown

My Blue Heaven
rec. 28.4.1940
Miller,Glenn (tb) | Beneke,Gordon 'Tex' (ts,voc) | Hutton,Marion (voc) | Eberle,Ray (voc) | Modernaires,The (voc-group) | Finegan,Bill (arr) | details unknown

Yes My Darling Daughter
rec. 14.11.1940
Miller,Glenn (tb) | Beneke,Gordon 'Tex' (ts,voc) | Hutton,Marion (voc) | Eberle,Ray (voc) | Modernaires,The (voc-group) | Finegan,Bill (arr) | details unknown

Perfidia
rec. 19.2.1941
Miller,Glenn (tb) | Beneke,Gordon 'Tex' (ts,voc) | Hutton,Marion (voc) | Eberle,Ray (voc) | Modernaires,The (voc-group) | Finegan,Bill (arr) | details unknown

Cradle Song
rec. 20.5.1941
Miller,Glenn (tb) | Beneke,Gordon 'Tex' (ts,voc) | Hutton,Marion (voc) | Eberle,Ray (voc) | Modernaires,The (voc-group) | Finegan,Bill (arr) | details unknown

Elmer's Tune
rec. 11.8.1941
Miller,Glenn (tb) | Beneke,Gordon 'Tex' (ts,voc) | Hutton,Marion (voc) | Eberle,Ray (voc) | Modernaires,The (voc-group) | Finegan,Bill (arr) | details unknown

Beethoven's Moonlight Sonata
rec. 24.11.1941
Miller,Glenn (tb) | Beneke,Gordon 'Tex' (ts,voc) | Hutton,Marion (voc) | Eberle,Ray (voc) | Modernaires,The (voc-group) | Finegan,Bill (arr) | details unknown

Don't Sit Under The Apple Tree
rec. 18.2.1942
Miller,Glenn (tb) | Beneke,Gordon 'Tex' (ts,voc) | Hutton,Marion (voc) | Eberle,Ray (voc) | Modernaires,The (voc-group) | Finegan,Bill (arr) | details unknown

Sweet Eloise
rec. 2.4.1942
Miller,Glenn (tb) | Beneke,Gordon 'Tex' (ts,voc) | Hutton,Marion (voc) | Eberle,Ray (voc) | Modernaires,The (voc-group) | Finegan,Bill (arr) | details unknown

I've Got A Girl In Kalamazoo | Serenade In Blue
rec. 20.5.1942
Miller,Glenn (tb) | Beneke,Gordon 'Tex' (ts,voc) | Hutton,Marion (voc) | Eberle,Ray (voc) | Modernaires,The (voc-group) | Finegan,Bill (arr) | details unknown

Caribbean Clipper
rec. 14.7.1942
Miller,Glenn (tb) | Beneke,Gordon 'Tex' (ts,voc) | Hutton,Marion (voc) | Eberle,Ray (voc) | Modernaires,The (voc-group) | Finegan,Bill (arr) | details unknown

Reprise | Warner Classics & Jazz Germany

7599-25670-2 | CD | Goldmine
Take 6
Gold Mine | Spread Love | If We Ever | A Quiet Place | Mary | David And Goliath | Get Away Jordan | He Never Sleeps | Milky White Way | Let The Words
Nashville,TN, rec. details unknown
Take 6 (voc-group) | Chea,Alvin (voc) | Kibble,Mark (voc) | Thomas,David (voc) | Dent,Cedric (voc) | McKnight,Claude V. (voc) | Warren,Mervyn (voc) | Humphries,David (finger-snaps,sound-effects)

7599-25892-2 | CD | So Much To Say
Not Again? | So Much 2 Say | Human Body | I L-o-v-e U | Something Within' Me | Time After Time(The Savior Is Waiting) | Come Unto Me | Pre-Rise: I'm On My Way | I Believe | Sunday's On The Way | I'm On My Way | That's The Law | Where Do The Children Play?
Take 6 (voc-group) | Chea,Alvin (voc) | Kibble,Mark (voc) | Thomas,David (voc) | Dent,Cedric (voc) | McKnight,Claude V. (voc) | Warren,Mervyn (voc)

7599-26665-2 | CD | He Is Christmas
Silent Night | Oh! He Is Christmas | Hark! The Herald Angels Sing | Away In The Manger | Amen | Little Drummer Boy | 'T Was Da Nite | Sweet Little Jesus Boy | O Come All Ye Faithful
Take 6 (voc-group) | Chea,Alvin (voc) | Kibble,Mark (voc) | Thomas,David (voc) | Dent,Cedric (voc) | McKnight,Claude V. (voc) | Warren,Mervyn (voc)

Take 6 With The Yellow Jackets
God Rest Ye Merry Gentlemen
Take 6 (voc-group) | Chea,Alvin (voc) | Kibble,Mark (voc) | Thomas,David (voc) | Dent,Cedric (voc) | McKnight,Claude V. (voc) | Warren,Mervyn (voc) | Yellowjackets | Ferrante,Russell (keyboards) | Haslip,Jimmy (el-b) | Kennedy,William (dr) | Mintzer,Bob (sax)

7599-27023-2 | CD | Sinatra-Basie:An Historic Musical First
Frank Sinatra With The Count Basie Orchestra
Pennies From Heaven | Please Be Kind | Love Is The Tender Trap - (Love Is) The Tender Trap | Looking At The World Thru Rose Colored Glassas | My Kind Of Girl | I Only Have Eyes For You | Nice Work If You Can Get It | Learnin' The Blues | I'm Gonna Sit Right Down And Write Myself A Letter | I Won't Dance
Los Angeles,CA, rec. 2./3.10.1962
Sinatra,Frank (voc) | Basie,Count (p) | Jones,Thad (tp) | Ricard,Fip (tp) | Cohn[Cohen],Sonny (tp) | Aarons,Albert 'Al' (tp) | Porcino,Al (tp) | Coker,Henry (tb) | Wagner,Rufus (tb) | Powell,Benny (tb) | Royal,Marshall (cl,as) | Wess,Frank (fl,as,ts) | Dixon,Eric (fl,ts) | Foster,Frank (ts) | Fowlkes,Charlie (bs) | Green,Freddie (g) | Catlett,Buddy (b) | Payne,Sonny (dr)

7599-27027-2 | CD | It Might As Well Be Spring
Fly Me To The Moon | I Believe In You | Hello Dolly | I Wanna Be Around | The Best Is Yet To Come
Los Angeles,CA, rec. 8.6.1964
Sinatra,Frank (voc) | Basie,Count (p) | Rader,Don (tp) | Porcino,Al (tp) | Davenport,Wallace (tp) | Aarons,Albert 'Al' (tp) | Cohn[Cohen],Sonny (tp) | Edison,Harry 'Sweets' (tp) | Coker,Henry (tb) | Mitchell,Grover (tb) | Hughes,Bill (tb) | Chambers,Henderson (tb) | Shroyer,Kenny (b-tb) | Royal,Marshall (cl,as) | Wess,Frank (fl,as,ts) | Dixon,Eric (fl,ts) | Foster,Frank (ts) | Fowlkes,Charlie (bs) | Green,Freddie (g) | Catlett,Buddy (b) | Payne,Sonny (dr) | Richards,Emil (vib,perc) | Jones,Quincy (arr)

The Good Life | I Wish You Love | I Can't Stop Loving You | More | Wives And Lovers
Los Angeles,CA, rec. 9.6.1964
Sinatra,Frank (voc) | Basie,Count (p) | Rader,Don (tp) | Porcino,Al (tp) | Davenport,Wallace (tp) | Aarons,Albert 'Al' (tp) | Cohn[Cohen],Sonny (tp) | Edison,Harry 'Sweets' (tp) | Coker,Henry (tb) | Mitchell,Grover (tb) | Hughes,Bill (tb) | Chambers,Henderson (tb) | Shroyer,Kenny (b-tb) | Royal,Marshall (cl,as) | Wess,Frank (fl,as,ts) | Dixon,Eric (fl,ts) | Foster,Frank (ts) | Fowlkes,Charlie (bs) | Green,Freddie (g) | Catlett,Buddy (b) | Payne,Sonny (dr) | Richards,Emil (vib,perc) | Vinci,Gerry (v,concertmaster) | Baker,Israel (v) | Gasselin,Jaques (v) | Beach,Thelma (v) | Sosson,Marshall (v) | Neufeld,Erno (v) | Douglas,Bonnie (v) | Raderman,Lou (v) | Shure,Paul (v) | Getzoff,James (v) | Majewski,Virginia (viola) | Robyn,Paul (viola) | Dinkin,Alvin (viola) | Harris,Stan (viola) | Lustgarten,Edgar 'Ed' (cello) | Goodman,Anne (cello) | Jones,Quincy (arr)

7599-27222-2 | CD | We Got By
Al Jarreau With Band
Spirit | We Got By | Susan's Song | You Don't See Me | Lock All The Gates | Raggedy Ann | Letter Perfect | Sweet Potato Pie | Aladdin's Lamp
Hollywood,CA, rec. details unknown
Jarreau,Al (fl,perc,voice) | Bunker,Larry (vib) | Canning,Tom (keyboards) | Grusin,Dave (keyboards) | Adams,Arthur (g) | Stallworth,Paul (b) | Correro,Joe (dr) | Strings | Background Vocals

9362-45204-2 | CD | Reverence And Compassion
Milt Jackson And His Orchestra
Reverence | Young And Foolish | Little Girl Blue | This Masquerade | J.C. | Cedar Lane | How Do You Keep The Music Playing | Newest Blues | It Never Entered My Mind | Bullet Bag | Compassion | Here's That Rainy Day
Jackson,Milt (vib) | Brashear,Oscar (tp) | Bohanon,George (tb) | Clayton,Jeff (as) | Foster,Gary (ss,ts) | Brown,Ronald (ts) | Nimitz,Jack (b-cl,bs) | Walton,Cedar (p) | Clayton,John (b) | Higgins,Billy (dr) | Vinci,Gerry (v,concertmaster) | Drori,Assa (v) | Daskoff,Isabelle (v) | Derouin,Joel (v) | Ferber,Henry (v) | Geller,Irv (v) | Kent,Peter (v) | Marron,Gordon (v) | Palmer,Don (v) | Shamban,Kwihee (v) | Sprecher,Eve (v) | Sushel,Robert (v) | Wilson,Elizabeth (v) | Zippert,Shari (v) | Boghossian,Sam (viola) | Baker,Marilyn (viola) | MacLaine,Margot (viola) | Wise,Hershel (viola) | Seykora,Frederick (cello) | Katayama,Suzie (cello) | Ehrhardt,Ernie (cello) | Karam,Anne (cello) | Corbett,Larry (cello) | Shamban,David (cello) | Hughart,Jim (b) | Storer,Margaret (b) | Slone,David (b)

9362-45946-2 | CD | Live at The Sands
Count Basie And His Orchestra
Introduction | Splanky | I Can't Stop Loving You | I Need To Be Bee'd With | Flight Of The Foo Birds | Satin Doll | Makin' Whoopee | Corner Pocket | One O'Clock Jump | Hello Little Girl | Whirly Bird | Blues For Ilene | This Could Be The Start Of Something Big | Jumpin' At The Woodside
Live at The Sands Hotel,Las Vegas, rec. 26.-29.1.& 1.2.1966
Basie,Count (p) | Aarons,Albert 'Al' (tp) | Cohn[Cohen],Sonny (tp) | Davenport,Wallace (tp) | Guilbeau,Phil (tp) | Chambers,Henderson (tb) | Grey,Al (tb) | Mitchell,Grover (tb) | Hughes,Bill (b-tb) | Royal,Marshall (cl,as) | Plater,Bobby (fl,as) | Dixon,Eric (fl,ts) | Davis,Eddie 'Lockjaw' (ts) | Fowlkes,Charlie (bs) | Green,Freddie (g) | Keenan,Norman (b) | Payne,Sonny (dr)

9362-47876-2 | CD | Afro-Bossa
Duke Ellington And His Orchestra
Volupte
Chicago,Ill, rec. 29.11.1962
Ellington,Duke (p) | Anderson,Cat (tp,perc) | Burrowes,Roy (tp,perc) | Williams,Cootie (tp,perc) | Nance,Ray (v,co) | Brown,Lawrence (tb) | Cooper,Frank 'Buster' (tb) | Connors,Chuck (b-tb) | Procope,Russell (cl,as) | Hodges,Johnny (as) | Hamilton,Jimmy (cl,ts) | Gonsalves,Paul (ts) | Carney,Harry (cl,b-cl,bs) | Strayhorn,Billy (p,perc) | Shepard,Ernie (b) | Woodyard,Sam (dr)

Silk Lake | Eighth Veil
NYC, rec. 14.12.1962
Ellington,Duke (p) | Anderson,Cat (tp,perc) | Burrowes,Roy (tp,perc) | Williams,Cootie (tp,perc) | Nance,Ray (v,co) | Brown,Lawrence (tb) | Cooper,Frank 'Buster' (tb) | Connors,Chuck (b-tb) | Procope,Russell (cl,as) | Hodges,Johnny (as) | Hamilton,Jimmy (cl,ts) | Gonsalves,Paul (ts) | Carney,Harry (cl,b-cl,bs) | Strayhorn,Billy (p,perc) | Shepard,Ernie (b) | Woodyard,Sam (dr)

Pyramid
NYC, rec. 20.12.1962
Ellington,Duke (p) | Anderson,Cat (tp,perc) | Burrowes,Roy (tp,perc) | Williams,Cootie (tp,perc) | Nance,Ray (v,co) | Brown,Lawrence (tb) | Cooper,Frank 'Buster' (tb) | Connors,Chuck (b-tb) | Procope,Russell (cl,as) | Hodges,Johnny (as) | Hamilton,Jimmy (cl,ts) | Gonsalves,Paul (ts) | Carney,Harry (cl,b-cl,bs) | Strayhorn,Billy (p,perc) | Shepard,Ernie (b) | Woodyard,Sam (dr)

Bonga
NYC, rec. 3.1.1963
Ellington,Duke (p) | Anderson,Cat (tp,perc) | Burrowes,Roy (tp,perc) | Williams,Cootie (tp,perc) | Nance,Ray (v,co) | Brown,Lawrence (tb) | Cooper,Frank 'Buster' (tb) | Connors,Chuck (b-tb) | Procope,Russell (cl,as) | Hodges,Johnny (as) | Hamilton,Jimmy (cl,ts) | Gonsalves,Paul (ts) | Carney,Harry (cl,b-cl,bs) | Strayhorn,Billy (p,perc) | Shepard,Ernie (b) | Woodyard,Sam (dr)

Angu | Purple Gazelle | Absinthe | Moonbow | Tigress | Afro-Bossa
NYC, rec. 5.1.1963
Ellington,Duke (p) | Anderson,Cat (tp,perc) | Burrowes,Roy (tp,perc) | Williams,Cootie (tp,perc) | Nance,Ray (v,co) | Brown,Lawrence (tb) | Cooper,Frank 'Buster' (tb) | Connors,Chuck (b-tb) | Procope,Russell (cl,as) | Hodges,Johnny (as) | Hamilton,Jimmy (cl,ts) | Gonsalves,Paul (ts) | Carney,Harry (cl,b-cl,bs) | Strayhorn,Billy (p,perc) | Shepard,Ernie (b) | Woodyard,Sam (dr)

Island Virgin | Virgin Jungle | Fiddler On The Diddle | Jungle Kitty | Things Ain't What They Used To Be | Big Fat Alice's Blues | Chelsea Bridge | The Opener | Mysterious Chick | Barefoot Stomper | Fade Up
Live in The Virgin Island, rec. 14.4.1965
Ellington,Duke (p) | Anderson,Cat (tp) | Williams,Cootie (tp) | Williams,Richard (tp) | Jones,Herbie (tp) | Nance,Ray (tp,v) | Brown,Lawrence (tb) | Cooper,Frank 'Buster' (tb) | Connors,Chuck (tb) | Procope,Russell (cl,as) | Hodges,Johnny (as) | Hamilton,Jimmy (cl,ts) | Gonsalves,Paul (ts) | Carney,Harry (bs) | Lams,John (b) | Woodyard,Sam (dr)

Rhino | Warner Classics & Jazz Germany

8122-71256-2 | CD | Atlantic Saxophones
Rahsaan Roland Kirk Sextet
If I Loved You
Live at Keystone Korner,SF, rec. 9.6.1973
Kirk,Rahsaan Roland (fl,ts,perc,manzello,nose-fl,strich) | Burton,Ron (p) | Barkan,Todd (synth) | Pearson,Henry 'Metathius' (b) | Shy,Robert (dr) | Habao,Joe (perc)

Eddie Harris Quintet
Freedom Jazz Dance
NYC, rec. 30.4.1965
Harris,Eddie (ts) | Codrington,Ray (tp) | Walton,Cedar (p) | Carter,Ron (b) | Higgins,Billy (dr)

David Fathead Newman Sextet
Willow Weep For Me
NYC, rec. 5.11.1958
Newman,David Fathead (as) | Belgrave,Marcus (tp) | Crawford,Hank (bs) | Charles,Ray (p) | Willis,Edgar (b) | Turner,Milton (dr)

Yusef Lateef Ensemble
Russell And Eliot
NYC, rec. 4.2.1969
Lateef,Yusef (ts) | Jones,Thad (tp) | Owens,Jimmy (tp) | Young,Eugene 'Snooky' (tp) | Gale,Eric (el-g) | Lawson,Hugh (p) | McBee,Cecil (b) | Rainey,Chuck (el-b) | Purdie,Bernard 'Pretty' (dr) | Barretto,Ray (congas) | Heath,Albert 'Tootie' (perc)

Hank Crawford And His Orchestra
Lorelei's Lament
NYC, rec. 2.5.1961
Crawford,Hank (as) | Guilbeau,Phil (tp) | Hunt,John (tp) | Newman,David Fathead (ts) | Cooper,Leroy 'Hog' (bs) | Willis,Edgar (b) | Carr,Bruno (dr)

Sonny Stitt Quintet
Confirmation
NYC, rec. 29.1.1963
Stitt,Sonny (as) | Hall,Jim (g) | Lewis,John (p) | Davis,Richard (b) | Kay,Connie (dr)

John Coltrane Quartet
Giant Steps
NYC, rec. 5.5.1959
Coltrane,John (ts) | Flanagan,Tommy (p) | Chambers,Paul (b) | Taylor,Arthur 'Art' (dr)

Ornette Coleman Quartet
Lonely Woman
Los Angeles,CA, rec. 22.5.1959
Coleman,Ornette (as) | Cherry,Don (co) | Haden,Charlie (b) | Higgins,Billy (dr)

Charles Lloyd Quartet
Forest Flower(Sunrise) | Forest Flower(Sunset)
Live at The Monterey Jazz Festival,CA, rec. 18.9.1966
Lloyd,Charles (ts) | Jarrett,Keith (p) | McBee,Cecil (b) | DeJohnette,Jack (dr)

8122-71403-2 | CD | Changes One
Charles Mingus Quintet
Remember Rockefeller At Attica | Sue's Changes | Devil Blues | Duke Ellington's Sound Of Love
NYC, rec. 27.-30.12.1974
Mingus,Charles (b) | Walrath,Jack (tp) | Adams,George (ts,voc) | Pullen,Don (p) | Richmond,Dannie (dr)

8122-71404-2 | CD | Changes Two
Free Cell Block F 'Tis Nazi U.S.A. | Orange Was The Colour Of Her Dress Then Blue Silk | Black Bats And Poles | For Harry Carney
Mingus,Charles (b) | Walrath,Jack (tp) | Adams,George (ts,voc) | Pullen,Don (p) | Richmond,Dannie (dr)

Charles Mingus Sextet
Duke Ellington's Sound Of Love
Mingus,Charles (b) | Walrath,Jack (tp) | Belgrave,Marcus (tp) | Adams,George (ts,voc) | Pullen,Don (p) | Richmond,Dannie (dr) | Paris,Jackie (voc) | Johnson,Sy (arr)

8122-71407-2 | CD | Volunteered Slavery
Rahsaan Roland Kirk Sextet
On Ton | A Tribute To John Coltrane: | Lush Life- | Afro Blues- | Bessie's Blues- | Thre For The Festival
Live at Newport,Rhode Island, rec. 7.7.1968
Kirk,Rahsaan Roland (fl,ts,manzello,stritch,voc) | McGhee,Charles (tp) | Griffin,Dick (tb) | Burton,Ron (p) | Martin,Vernon (b) | Hopps,Jimmy (dr)

Volunteered Slavery | Spirits Up Above | My Cherie Amour | Search For The Reason Why | I Say A Little Prayer | Roland's Opening Remarks
Kirk,Rahsaan Roland (fl,ts,manzello,stritch,voc) | McGhee,Charles (tp) | Griffin,Dick (tb) | Burton,Ron (p) | Martin,Vernon (b) | Brown,Sonny or Crosby,Charles (dr) | Roland Kirk Spirit Choir,The (background-voc)

8122-71408-2 | CD | Blacknuss
Ain't No Sunshine
NYC, rec. 31.8.1971
Kirk,Rahsaan Roland (fl,ts,gong,manzello,police-whistle,strich,voc) | Butler,Billy (g) | Smith,Sonelius (p) | Pearson,Henry 'Metathius' (b) | Mhadi,Khalil (dr) | Landrum,Richard 'Pablo' (congas) | Texidor,Joe Habad (perc)

Never Can Say Goodbye | Blacknuss
Kirk,Rahsaan Roland (fl,ts,gong,manzello,police-whistle,strich,voc) | Butler,Billy (g) | Smith,Sonelius (p) | Pearson,Henry 'Metathius' (b) | Mhadi,Khalil (dr) | Landrum,Richard 'Pablo' (congas) | Texidor,Joe Habad (perc) | Houston,Cissy (voc)

Rahsaan Roland Kirk And His Orchestra
What's Going On- | Mercy, Mercy Me(The Ecology)- | I Love You Yes I Do | Take Me Girl, I'm Ready | My Girl | Which Way Is It Going | The Old Rugged Cross | Make It With You
NYC, rec. 8.9.1971
Kirk,Rahsaan Roland (fl,ts,gong,manzello,police-whistle,strich,voc) | McGee,Charles (tp) | Griffin,Dick (tb) | Tee,Richard (p) | Tucker,Mickey (org) | Dupree,Cornell (g) | Salter,Bill (b) | Purdie,Bernard 'Pretty' (dr) | Jenkins,Arthur (cabassa,conga) | Texidor,Joe Habad (perc)

One Nation
Kirk,Rahsaan Roland (fl,ts,gong,manzello,police-whistle,strich,voc) | McGee,Charles (tp) | Griffin,Dick (tb) | Tee,Richard (p) | Tucker,Mickey (org) | Dupree,Cornell (g) | Salter,Bill (b) | Purdie,Bernard 'Pretty' (dr) | Jenkins,Arthur (cabassa,conga) | Texidor,Joe Habad (perc) | Burton,Princess Patience (voc)

8122-71410-2 | 6 CD | Ornette Coleman-Beauty Is A Rare Thing
A Band Of Friends
A>C

8122-71417-2 | CD | I Don't Worry About A Thing
Mose Allison Trio
I Don't Worry About A Thing | It Didn't Turn Out That Way | Your Mind Is On Vacation | Let Me See | Everything I Have Is Yours | Stand By | Idyll | The Well | Meet Me At No Special Place | The Song Is Ended
NYC, rec. 15.3.1962
Allison,Mose (p,voc) | Farmer,Addison (b) | Johnson,Osie (dr)

8122-71984-2 | 7 CD | John Coltrane:The Heavy Weight Champion
A Band Of Friends
A>C

812273670-2 | CD | New Orleans Suite
Duke Ellington And His Orchestra
Bourbon Street Jingling Jollies | Thanks For The Beautiful Land On The Delta | Second Line | Aristocracy A La Jean Lafitte
NYC, rec. 27.4.1970
Ellington,Duke (p) | Williams,Cootie (tp) | Johnson,Money (tp,fl-h) | Ellington,Mercer (tp,fl-h) | Rubin,Alan (tp,fl-h) | Stone,Fred (tp,fl-h) | Wood,Booty (tb) | Priester,Julian (tb) | Taylor,Dave (b-tb) | Procope,Russell (cl,as) | Hodges,Johnny (as) | Turney,Norris (fl,cl,as) | Ashby,Harold (cl,ts) | Gonsalves,Paul (ts) | Carney,Harry (cl,b-cl,bs) | Benjamin,Joe (b) | Jones,Rufus (dr)

Blues For New Orleans
Ellington,Duke (p) | Williams,Cootie (tp) | Johnson,Money (tp,fl-h) | Ellington,Mercer (tp,fl-h) | Rubin,Alan (tp,fl-h) | Stone,Fred (tp,fl-h) | Wood,Booty (tb) | Priester,Julian (tb) | Taylor,Dave (b-tb) | Procope,Russell (cl,as) | Hodges,Johnny (as) | Turney,Norris (fl,cl,as) | Ashby,Harold (cl,ts) | Gonsalves,Paul (ts) | Carney,Harry (cl,b-cl,bs) | Davis,Wild Bill (org) | Benjamin,Joe (b) | Jones,Rufus (dr)

Portrait Of Louis Armstrong | Portrait Of Wellman Braud | Portrait Of Sidney Bechet | Portrait Of Mahalia Jackson
NYC, rec. 13.5.1970
Ellington,Duke (p) | Williams,Cootie (tp) | Anderson,Cat (tp) | Ellington,Mercer (tp,fl-h) | Rubin,Alan (tp,fl-h) | Stone,Fred (tp,fl-h) | Wood,Booty (tb) | Connors,Chuck (b-tb) | Procope,Russell (cl,as) | Turney,Norris (fl,cl,as) | Ashby,Harold (cl,ts) | Gonsalves,Paul (ts) | Carney,Harry (cl,b-cl,bs) | Benjamin,Joe (b) | Jones,Rufus (dr)

8122-73678-2 | CD | Movin' On
Oscar Brown Jr. And His Group
A Dime Away From A Hotdog | Walk Away | No PLace To Be Somebody | Gang Bang | First Lady

NYC, rec. 1972
Brown Jr.,Oscar (voc) | Dupree,Cornell (g) | Tee,Richard (p) | Salter,Bill (b) | Johnson,Jimmy (dr) | McDonald,Ralph (perc) | Eaton,William (arr)
Feel The Fire
Brown Jr.,Oscar (voc) | Dupree,Cornell (g) | Tee,Richard (p) | Salter,Bill (b) | McDonald,Ralph (perc) | Eaton,William (arr) | Houston,Cissy (voc) | Tender Loving Care (background-voc)
A Ladiesman
Brown Jr.,Oscar (voc) | Jones,Thad (tp,fl-h) | Williams,Ed (tp,fl-h) | Lewis,Charles (tp,fl-h) | Newman,David Fathead (fl,ts) | Beckenstein,Ray (as,piccolo) | Clarke,Arthur (b-cl,bs) | Dupree,Cornell (g) | Tee,Richard (p) | Edwards,Gourdine (b) | Purdie,Bernard 'Pretty' (dr) | McDonald,Ralph (perc) | Eaton,William (arr) | Houston,Cissy (voc) | Tender Loving Care (background-voc)
Young Man
Brown Jr.,Oscar (voc) | Jones,Thad (tp,fl-h) | Williams,Ed (tp,fl-h) | Lewis,Charles (tp,fl-h) | Newman,David Fathead (fl,ts) | Beckenstein,Ray (as,piccolo) | Clarke,Arthur (b-cl,bs) | Dupree,Cornell (g) | Tee,Richard (p) | Edwards,Gourdine (b) | Purdie,Bernard 'Pretty' (dr) | McDonald,Ralph (perc) | Eaton,William (arr)
To Stay In Good With You
Brown Jr.,Oscar (voc) | Jones,Thad (tp,fl-h) | Williams,Ed (tp,fl-h) | Lewis,Charles (tp,fl-h) | Newman,David Fathead (fl,ts) | Beckenstein,Ray (as,piccolo) | Clarke,Arthur (b-cl,bs) | Dupree,Cornell (g) | Tee,Richard (p) | Edwards,Gourdine (b) | Purdie,Bernard 'Pretty' (dr) | McDonald,Ralph (perc) | Eaton,William (arr) | Pace,Jean (voc)

812273679-2 | CD | Pyramid
Modern Jazz Quartet
Django
NYC, rec. 22.8.1959
MJQ (Modern Jazz Quartet) | Jackson,Milt (vib) | Lewis,John (p) | Heath,Percy (b) | Kay,Connie (dr)
Romaine
NYC, rec. 25.8.1959
MJQ (Modern Jazz Quartet) | Jackson,Milt (vib) | Lewis,John (p) | Heath,Percy (b) | Kay,Connie (dr)
Pyramid | It Don't Mean A Thing If It Ain't Got That Swing
NYC, rec. 21.12.1959
MJQ (Modern Jazz Quartet) | Jackson,Milt (vib) | Lewis,John (p) | Heath,Percy (b) | Kay,Connie (dr)
How High The Moon | Vendome
NYC, rec. 15.1.1960
MJQ (Modern Jazz Quartet) | Jackson,Milt (vib) | Lewis,John (p) | Heath,Percy (b) | Kay,Connie (dr)

8122-73685-2 | CD | Bags & Trane
John Coltrane-Milt Jackson Quintet
Bag's & Trane | Three Little Words | The Night We Called It A Day | Bebop | The Late Late Blues | Stairway To The Stars | Blues Legacy | Centerpiece
NYC, rec. 15.1.1959
Coltrane,John (ts) | Jackson,Milt (vib) | Jones,Hank (p) | Chambers,Paul (b) | Kay,Connie (dr)

8122-73687-2 | CD | Fontessa
Modern Jazz Quartet
Versailles | Angel Eyes | Fontessa
NYC, rec. 22.1.1956
MJQ (Modern Jazz Quartet) | Jackson,Milt (vib) | Lewis,John (p) | Heath,Percy (b) | Kay,Connie (dr)
Willow Weep For Me | Woody'n You | Bluesology | Over The Rainbow
NYC, rec. 14.2.1956
MJQ (Modern Jazz Quartet) | Jackson,Milt (vib) | Lewis,John (p) | Heath,Percy (b) | Kay,Connie (dr)

8122-73699-2 | CD | Olé Coltrane
John Coltrane Group
Olé | Dahomey Dance | Aisha | To Her Ladyship
NYC, rec. 25.5.1961
Coltrane,John (ss,ts) | Hubbard,Freddie (tp) | Dolphy,Eric[as George Lane] (fl,as) | Tyner,McCoy (p) | Workman,Reggie (b) | Davis,Art (b) | Jones,Elvin (dr)

8122-73717-2 | CD | The Blue Yusef Lateef
Yusef Lateef Orchestra
Othelia | Moon Cup | Get Over Get Off And Get On | Six Miles Next Door | Sun Dog
NYC, rec. 23./24.4.1968
Lateef,Yusef (fl,ts,bamboo-fl,koto,pneumatic-fl,scratcher,shannie,tamboura,voc) | Mitchell,Blue (tp) | Red (Kyner) | Lucas,Buddy (harm) | Lawson,Hugh (p) | Burrell,Kenny (g) | McBee,Cecil (b) | Cranshaw,Bob (el-b) | Brooks,Roy (dr)
Juba Juba | Back Home
Lateef,Yusef (fl,ts,bamboo-fl,koto,pneumatic-fl,scratcher,shannie,tamboura) | Mitchell,Blue (tp) | Red (Kyner) | Lucas,Buddy (harm) | Lawson,Hugh (p) | Burrell,Kenny (g) | McBee,Cecil (b) | Cranshaw,Bob (el-b) | Brooks,Roy (dr) | Sweet Inspirations,The (voc-group)
Like It Is
NYC, rec. 23.4.1968
Lateef,Yusef (fl,ts,bamboo-fl,koto,pneumatic-fl,scratcher,shannie,tamboura) | Mitchell,Blue (tp) | Red (Kyner) | Lucas,Buddy (harm) | Lawson,Hugh (p) | Burrell,Kenny (g) | McBee,Cecil (b) | Cranshaw,Bob (el-b) | Brooks,Roy (dr) | Clarke,Selwart (v) | Tryon,James (v) | Brown,Alfred (viola) | Moore,Kermit (cello)

812273719-2 | CD | You Must Believe In Spring
Bill Evans Trio
B Minor Waltz (For Ellaine) | You Must Believe In Spring | Gary's Theme | We Will Met Again (For Harry) | The Peacocks | Some Time Ago | Theme From M.A.S.H.
Hollywood,CA, rec. 23.-25.8.1977
Evans,Bill (p) | Gomez,Eddie (b) | Zigmund,Eliot (dr)

8122-73720-2 | CD | Svengali
Gil Evans Orchestra
Thoroughbred | Blues In Orbit | Eleven | Cry Of Hunger | Summertime
NYC, rec. 30.5.1973
Evans,Gil (p,el-p,arr) | Allen,Tex (tp) | Williams,Richard (tp) | Daley,Joe (tb,tuba) | Freeman,Sharon (fr-h) | Levin,Pete (fr-h) | Johnson,Howard (fl-h,bs,tuba) | Sanborn,David (as) | Harper,Billy (fl,ts) | Koehler,Trevor (fl,ss,bs) | Horowitz,David (synth) | Dunbar,Ted (g) | Bushler,Herb (el-b) | Ditmas,Bruce (dr) | Evans,Suzan 'Sue' (perc)
Zee Zee
NYC, rec. 30.6.1973
Evans,Gil (p,el-p,arr) | Peterson,Hanibal Marvin (tp) | Williams,Richard (tp) | Daley,Joe (tb) | Freeman,Sharon (fr-h) | Levin,Pete (fr-h) | Johnson,Howard (tuba) | Sanborn,David (as) | Harper,Billy (fl,ts) | Koehler,Trevor (fl,ss,bs) | Horowitz,David (synth) | Bushler,Herb (el-b) | Dunbar,Ted (g) | Ditmas,Bruce (dr) | Evans,Suzan 'Sue' (perc)

8122-73721-2 | CD | The Warm Moods-With Strings
Ben Webster With Strings
The Sweetheart Of Sigma Chi | Stella By Starlight | With Every Breath I Take | Accent On Youth | But Beautiful | Time After Time | Nancy(With The Laughing Face) | I'm Beginning To See The Light | It Was So Beautiful | The Wiffenproof Song | It's Easy To Remember | There's No You
Radio Recorders,?, rec. 18./19.1.1960
Webster,Ben (ts) | Richards,Johnny (arr,ld) | Lustgarten,Alfred (v) | Minghetti,Lisa (v) | Kaproff,Armand (cello) | Figelski,Cecil (viola) | Trenner,Don (p) | Bagley,Don (b) | Capp,Frank (dr)

8122-79778-2 | CD | The Very Best Of John Coltrane
John Coltrane Quartet
Giant Steps | Cousin Mary | Naima
NYC, rec. 5.5.1959
Coltrane,John (ts) | Flanagan,Tommy (p) | Chambers,Paul (b) | Taylor,Arthur 'Art' (dr)
Like Sonny | My Shining Hour
NYC, rec. 2.12.1959
Coltrane,John (ts) | Kelly,Wynton (p) | Chambers,Paul (b) | Cobb,Jimmy (dr)
My Favorite Things | Central Park West | Summertime | Mr.Syms
NYC, rec. 21.10.1960
Coltrane,John (ss,ts) | Tyner,McCoy (p) | Davis,Steve (b) | Jones,Elvin (dr)
Body And Soul
NYC, rec. 24.10.1960
Coltrane,John (ts) | Tyner,McCoy (p) | Davis,Steve (b) | Jones,Elvin (dr)
Equinox
NYC, rec. 26.10.1960
Coltrane,John (ts) | Tyner,McCoy (p) | Davis,Steve (b) | Jones,Elvin (dr)

8122-79862-2 | CD | The Very Best Of Jean-Luc Ponty
Jean-Luc Ponty Quintet
Bowing Bowing
Hollywood,CA, rec. January 1975
Ponty,Jean-Luc (synth,v,el-v,violectra) | Sawyer,Dan (el-g) | Rushen,Patrice (p,el-p,org,synth,clavinet) | (Leon Chandler),Ndugu(dr,perc,toms) | Armstrong,Ralphe (b-g,el-b)
Aurora(part 2) | Renaissance
Hollywood,CA, rec. December 1975
Ponty,Jean-Luc (v,el-v,autoharp,violectra) | Stuermer,Daryl (g,el-g) | Rushen,Patrice (p,el-p,synth) | Fowler,Tom (b-g) | Flarrington,Norman (dr,perc)
New Country
Burbank,Los Angeles,CA, rec. July/August 1975
Ponty,Jean-Luc (org,synth,v,el-v) | Stuermer,Daryl (g,el-g) | Zavod,Allan (p,el-keyboards) | Towler,Tom (el-b) | Craney,Mark (perc)
Jean-Luc Ponty Sextet
Enigmatic Ocean(part 3) | Mirage
Burbank,Los Angeles,CA, rec. June/July 1977
Ponty,Jean-Luc (el-v,bells,grand-p,violectra) | Holdsworth,Allan (el-g) | Stuermer,Daryl (el-g) | Zavod,Allan (el-p,org,synth,clavinet,grand-p) | Armstrong,Ralphe (el-b) | Smith,Steve (dr,perc)
Egocentric Molecules | Cosmic Messenger
Hollywood,CA, rec. April 1978
Ponty,Jean-Luc (org,v,el-v) | Maunu,Peter (el-g) | Lievano,Joaquin (g,el-g) | Armstrong,Ralphe (el-b) | Zavod,Allan (el-p,org,synth) | Scheurell,Casey (dr,perc)
Jean-Luc Ponty Quartet
I Only Feel Good With You
Ponty,Jean-Luc (org,v,el-v) | Armstrong,Ralphe (el-b) | Zavod,Allan (el-p,org,synth) | Scheurell,Casey (dr,perc)
Jean-Luc Ponty
No Strings Attached
Live in Santa Barbera,CA, rec. December 1978
Ponty,Jean-Luc (synth,el-v-solo)
Jean-Luc Ponty Sextet
A Taste For Passion
Los Angeles,CA, rec. June/July 1979
Ponty,Jean-Luc (org,el-p,v) | Zavod,Allan (keyboards) | Lievano,Joaquin (g,g-synth) | Glaser,Jamie (g) | Armstrong,Ralphe (b) | Scheurell,Casey (dr,perc)
Jean-Luc Ponty
Forms Of Life
Los Angeles,CA, rec. June/July 1980
Ponty,Jean-Luc (keyboards,synth,v)
Jean-Luc Ponty Quintet
Final Truth(part 1)
Hollywood,CA, rec. August/September 1981
Ponty,Jean-Luc (v,violectra,p,b-synth) | Rhyne,Chris (p,synth) | Glaser,Jamie (g) | Jackson,Randy (b) | Griffin,Rayford (dr)
Jean-Luc Ponty Sextet
Rhythms Of Hope
Ponty,Jean-Luc (v,violectra,p,b-synth) | Rhyne,Chris (p,synth) | Glaser,Jamie (g) | Jackson,Randy (b) | Griffin,Rayford (dr) | Da Costa,Paulinho (perc)
Jean-Luc Ponty-Raymond Griffin
Individual Choice
Hollywood,CA, rec. March/May 1993
Ponty,Jean-Luc (v,synth,org) | Griffin,Rayford (perc)
Jean-Luc Ponty Quartet
Infinite Pursuit
Los Angeles,CA, rec. July/August 1985
Ponty,Jean-Luc (synth,v,effects,electronic-perc,sequencer,synclavier) | Henderson,Scott (g) | Browne,Baron (b) | Griffin,Rayford (dr)

8122-79892-2 | CD | The Avantgarde
John Coltrane-Don Cherry Quartet
Cherryco | The Blessing
NYC, rec. 28.6.1960
Cherry,Don (tp) | Coltrane,John (ss,ts) | Haden,Charlie (b) | Blackwell,Ed (dr)
Focus On Sanity | The Invisible | Bemsha Swing
NYC, rec. 8.7.1960
Cherry,Don (tp) | Coltrane,John (ss,ts) | Heath,Percy (b) | Blackwell,Ed (dr)

8122-79966-2 | CD | Coltrane Plays The Blues
John Coltrane Quartet
Blues To Elvin | Mr.Day | Mr.Syms | Mr.Knight | Untitled Original(Exotica) | Blues To Elvin(alt.take 1) | Blues To Elvin(alt.take 2)
NYC, rec. 24.10.1960
Coltrane,John (ss,ts) | Tyner,McCoy (p) | Davis,Steve (b) | Jones,Elvin (dr)
John Coltrane Trio
Blues To Bechet | Blues To You | Blues To You(alt.take 1) | Blues To You(alt.take 2)
Coltrane,John (ss,ts) | Davis,Steve (b) | Jones,Elvin (dr)

8122-79988-2 | CD | The Very Best Of Charles Mingus
Charles Mingus Jazz Workshop
Pithecanthropus Erectus | Profile Of Jackie
NYC, rec. 30.1.1956
Mingus,Charles (b) | McLean,Jackie (as) | Monterose,J.R. (ts) | Waldron,Mal (p) | Jones,Willie (dr)
Charles Mingus Quintet
Tonight At Noon | Haitian Fight Song | Re-Incarnation Of A Love Bird
NYC, rec. 12.3.1957
Mingus,Charles (b) | Knepper,Jimmy (tb) | Hadi [Curtis Porter],Shafti (as) | Legge,Wade (p) | Richmond,Dannie (dr)
Charles Mingus Orchestra
Moanin' | Cryin' Blues | Wednesday Night Prayer Meeting
NYC, rec. 4.2.1959
Mingus,Charles (b) | Knepper,Jimmy (tb) | Dennis,Willie (tb) | Handy,John (as) | McLean,Jackie (as) | Adams,Pepper (bs) | Parlan,Horace (p) | Richmond,Dannie (dr)
Charles Mingus Quintet With Roland Kirk
Ecclusiastics | Passions Of A Man | Wham Bam Thank You Ma'Am
NYC, rec. 6.11.1961
Mingus,Charles (p,voc) | Kirk,Rahsaan Roland (fl,ts,manzello,siren,strich,voice) | Ervin,Booker (ts) | Knepper,Jimmy (tb) | Watkins,Doug (b) | Richmond,Dannie (dr)

81273726-2 | CD | Spellbound
Joe Sample Group
Seven Years Of Good Luck | Spellbound | All God's Children | Bones Jive | Luna En New York | Sermonized
Los Angeles,CA, rec. 1988
Sample,Joe (p,synth) | Landau,Michael (g) | Miller,Marcus (el-b) | Hakim,Omar (dr) | Castro,Lenny (perc) | Hey,Jerry (synth-programming) | Buchanan,Robbie (synth-programming)
Leading Me Back To You
Sample,Joe (p,synth) | Landau,Michael (g) | Miller,Marcus (el-b) | Hakim,Omar (dr) | Castro,Lenny (perc) | Hey,Jerry (synth-programming) | Buchanan,Robbie (synth-programming) | Franks,Michael (voc)
Looking Glass
Sample,Joe (p,synth) | Landau,Michael (g) | Domanico,Chuck (b) | Miller,Marcus (el-b) | Hakim,Omar (dr) | Castro,Lenny (perc) | Hey,Jerry (synth-programming) | Buchanan,Robbie (synth-programming)
Somehow Our Love Survives
Sample,Joe (p,synth) | Landau,Michael (g) | Pena,John (b) | Robinson,John (dr) | Castro,Lenny (perc) | Hey,Jerry (synth-programming) | Buchanan,Robbie (synth-programming) | Jarreau,Al (voice)
U Turn
Sample,Joe (p,synth) | Landau,Michael (g) | East,Nathan (b) | Robinson,John (dr) | Castro,Lenny (perc) | Hey,Jerry (synth-programming) | Buchanan,Robbie (synth-programming) | Take 6 (voc-group)

Riverside | ZYX Music GmbH

12 RCD 4408-2 | 12 CD | Wes Montgomery-The Complete Riverside Recordings
Wes Montgomery Trio
Round About Midnight | Satin Doll | Satin Doll(alt.take) | Missile Blues | Missile Blues(alt.take)
NYC, rec. 5.10.1959
Montgomery,Wes (g) | Rhyne,Melvin (org) | Parker,Paul (dr)
Jingles | Whisper Not | The End Of A Love Affair | Too Late Now | Ecaroh | Yesterdays
NYC, rec. 6.10.1959
Montgomery,Wes (g) | Rhyne,Melvin (org) | Parker,Paul (dr)
Wes Montgomery Quartet
Airegin | West Coast Blues | Four On Six | D Natural Blues | In Your Own Sweet Way
NYC, rec. 26.1.1960
Montgomery,Wes (g) | Flanagan,Tommy (p) | Heath,Percy (b) | Heath,Albert 'Tootie' (dr)
Mister Walker | Polka Dots And Moonbeams | Gone With The Wind
NYC, rec. 28.1.1960
Montgomery,Wes (g) | Flanagan,Tommy (p) | Heath,Percy (b) | Heath,Albert 'Tootie' (dr)
Nat Adderley Sextet
Sack O'Woe | The Work Song | Scrambled Eggs
NYC, rec. 25.1.1960
Adderley,Nat (co) | Montgomery,Wes (g) | Timmons,Bobby (p) | Jones,Sam (cello) | Heath,Percy (b) | Hayes,Louis (dr)
Pretty Memory | Fall Out
NYC, rec. 27.1.1960
Adderley,Nat (co) | Montgomery,Wes (g) | Timmons,Bobby (p) | Betts,Keter (cello,b) | Jones,Sam (cello,b) | Hayes,Louis (dr)
Nat Adderley Quintet
My Heart Stood Still
Adderley,Nat (co) | Montgomery,Wes (g) | Betts,Keter (cello,b) | Jones,Sam (cello,b) | Hayes,Louis (dr)
Nat Adderley Quartet
Mean To Me
Adderley,Nat (co) | Montgomery,Wes (g) | Betts,Keter (cello,b) | Hayes,Louis (dr)
Nat Adderley Trio
Violets For Your Furs | I've Got A Crush On You
NYC, rec. 28.1.1960
Adderley,Nat (co) | Montgomery,Wes (g) | Jones,Sam (b)
Harold Land Sextet
Compulsion | Terrain
San Francisco,CA, rec. 17.5.1960
Land,Harold (ts) | Gordon,Joe (tp) | Montgomery,Wes (g) | Harris,Barry (p) | Jones,Sam (b) | Hayes,Louis (dr)
Klact-Oveedseds-Tene | Ursula | West Coast Blues | Don't Explain
San Francisco,CA, rec. 18.5.1960
Land,Harold (ts) | Gordon,Joe (tp) | Montgomery,Wes (g) | Harris,Barry (p) | Jones,Sam (b) | Hayes,Louis (dr)
Cannonball Adderley Quintet
Lolita | The Chant | Azule Serape
San Francisco,CA, rec. 21.5.1960
Adderley,Julian \'Cannonball\' (as) | Feldman,Victor (vib,p) | Montgomery,Wes (g) | Brown,Ray (b) | Hayes,Louis (dr)
Never Will I Marry | Yours Is My Heart Alone | Au Privave | Au Privave(alt.take)
San Francisco,CA, rec. 5.6.1960
Adderley,Julian \'Cannonball\' (as) | Feldman,Victor (vib,p) | Montgomery,Wes (g) | Brown,Ray (b) | Hayes,Louis (dr)
Wes Montgomery Quintet
Tune Up | Tune Up(alt.take) | Body And Soul | Body And Soul(alt.take) | Sandu | So Do It | So Do It(alt.take) | Movin' Along | Movin' Along(alt.take)
Los Angeles,CA, rec. 12.10.1960
Montgomery,Wes (g) | Clay,James (fl,ts) | Feldman,Victor (p) | Jones,Sam (b) | Hayes,Louis (dr)
Wes Montgomery Quartet
I Don't Stand A Ghost Of A Chance With You | Says You
Montgomery,Wes (g) | Feldman,Victor (p) | Jones,Sam (b) | Hayes,Louis (dr)
The Montgomery Brothers
Doujie | Doujie(alt.take) | Just For Now | Groove Yard | Heart Strings | Remember | Delirium | Back To Bock(Back To Back) | If I Should Lose You | If I Should Lose You(alt.take) | Doujie(take 8)
NYC, rec. 3.1.1961
Montgomery,Wes (g) | Montgomery,Buddy (vib,p) | Montgomery,Monk (b) | Thomas,Bobby (dr)
Wes Montgomery Quartet
Something Like Bags | Cotton Tail | Twisted Blues | Repetition
NYC, rec. 4.8.1961
Montgomery,Wes (g) | Jones,Hank (p) | Carter,Ron (b) | Humphries,Lex (dr)
Wes Montgomery Quintet
I'm Just A Lucky So-And-So | One For My Baby(And One More For The Road)
Montgomery,Wes (g) | Jones,Hank (p) | Carter,Ron (b) | Humphries,Lex (dr) | Barretto,Ray (congas)
Wes Montgomery
I Wish I Knew
Montgomery,Wes (g-solo)
George Shearing With The Montgomery Brothers
Dam That Dream | Dam That Dream(alt.take) | And Then I Wrote | Double Deal | No Hard Feelings | Love Walked In | Love Walked In(alt.take) | Lois Ann | Enchanted | Love For Sale
Los Angeles,CA, rec. 9.10.1961
Shearing,George (p) | Montgomery,Buddy (vib) | Montgomery,Wes (g) | Montgomery,Monk (b) | Perkins,Walter (dr)
Mambo In Chimes | Mambo In Chimes(alt.take) | The Lamp Is Low
Los Angeles,CA, rec. 10.10.1961
Shearing,George (p) | Montgomery,Buddy (vib) | Montgomery,Wes (g) | Montgomery,Monk (b) | Perkins,Walter (dr)
Stranger In Paradise
Shearing,George (p) | Montgomery,Buddy (vib) | Montgomery,Wes (g) | Montgomery,Monk (b) | Perkins,Walter (dr) | Peraza,Armando (congas) | Chimelis,Richard (bongoes,timbales)
Milt Jackson-Wes Montgomery Quintet
Blue Roz | Blue Roz(alt.take) | Jingles | Jingles(alt.take) | Stairway To The Stars | Stairway To The Stars(alt.take) | Stablemates | Stablemates(alt.take)
NYC, rec. 18.12.1961
Jackson,Milt (vib) | Montgomery,Wes (g) | Kelly,Wynton (p) | Jones,Sam (b) | Jones,Philly Joe (dr)
Sam Sack | Sam Sack(alt.take) | S.K.J. | S.K.J.(alt.take) | Delilah | Delilah(alt.take)
NYC, rec. 19.12.1961
Jackson,Milt (vib) | Montgomery,Wes (g) | Kelly,Wynton (p) | Jones,Sam (b) | Jones,Philly Joe (dr)
Wes Montgomery Quartet
Come Rain Or Come Shine | Blue 'N' Boogie | Cariba | S.O.S. | Born To Be Blue | Full House | Cariba(alt.take) | Blue 'N' Boogie(alt.take) | S.O.S.(alt.take)
Berkeley,CA, rec. 25.6.1962
Montgomery,Wes (g) | Griffin,Johnny (ts) | Kelly,Wynton (p) | Chambers,Paul (b) | Cobb,Jimmy (dr)

Wes Montgomery Quartet
Born To Be Blue
Montgomery,Wes (g) | Kelly,Wynton (p) | Chambers,Paul (b) | Cobb,Jimmy (dr)
Wes Montgomery Trio
I've Grown Accustomed To Her Face
Montgomery,Wes (g) | Chambers,Paul (b) | Cobb,Jimmy (dr)
Wes Montgomery With The Jimmy Jones Orchestra
The Girl Next Door | The Girl Next Door(alt.take)
NYC, rec. 18.4.1963
Montgomery,Wes (g) | Jones,Jimmy (cond,arr) | Hyman,Dick (p,celeste) | Burrell,Kenny (g) | Hinton,Milt (b) | Johnson,Osie (dr) | Bodner,Phil (woodwinds) | Agostini,Gloria (harp) | Orloff,Gene (v,concertmaster) | Lookofsky,Harry (v) | Nadien,David (v) | Collymore,Winston (v) | Ceppos,Mac (v) | Eidus,Arnold (v) | Kruczek,Leo (v) | Poliakin,Raoul (v) | Zir,Isadore (v) | Brown,Alfred (viola) | Fisch,Burt (viola) | McCracken,Charles (cello) | Ricci,George (cello)
Pretty Blue | Pretty Blue(alt.take)
Montgomery,Wes (g) | Jones,Jimmy (cond,arr) | Hyman,Dick (p,celeste) | Burrell,Kenny (g) | Hinton,Milt (b) | Johnson,Osie (dr) | Agostini,Gloria (harp) | Orloff,Gene (v,concertmaster) | Lookofsky,Harry (v) | Nadien,David (v) | Collymore,Winston (v) | Ceppos,Mac (v) | Eidus,Arnold (v) | Kruczek,Leo (v) | Poliakin,Raoul (v) | Zir,Isadore (v) | Brown,Alfred (viola) | Fisch,Burt (viola) | McCracken,Charles (cello) | Ricci,George (cello)
God Bless The Child | God Bless The Child(alt.take) | My Romance | Prelude To A Kiss | Prelude To A Kiss(alt.take) | All The Way
NYC, rec. 18.4.1963
Montgomery,Wes (g) | Jones,Jimmy (cond,arr) | Jones,Hank (p,celeste) | Burrell,Kenny (g) | Hinton,Milt (b) | Johnson,Osie (dr) | Bodner,Phil (woodwinds) | Agostini,Gloria (harp) | Orloff,Gene (v,concertmaster) | Lookofsky,Harry (v) | Nadien,David (v) | Collymore,Winston (v) | Ceppos,Mac (v) | Eidus,Arnold (v) | Kruczek,Leo (v) | Poliakin,Raoul (v) | Zir,Isadore (v) | Brown,Alfred (viola) | Fisch,Burt (viola) | McCracken,Charles (cello) | Ricci,George (cello)
Somewhere | Tune Up | Tune Up(alt.take) | Tune-Up(take 4) | Tune Up(take 5) | Baubles Bangles And Beads | Baubles Bangles And Beads(alt.take)
NYC, rec. 19.4.1963
Montgomery,Wes (g) | Jones,Jimmy (cond,arr) | Hyman,Dick (p,celeste) | Burrell,Kenny (g) | Hinton,Milt (b) | Johnson,Osie (dr) | Bodner,Phil (woodwinds) | Ross,Margaret (harp) | Orloff,Gene (v,concertmaster) | Lookofsky,Harry (v) | Nadien,David (v) | Collymore,Winston (v) | Ceppos,Mac (v) | Rand,Sam (v) | Shulman,Sylvan (v) | Winter,Paul (v) | Zir,Isadore (v) | Hersh,Ralph (viola) | Fisch,Burt (viola) | Schmit,Lucien (cello) | Moore,Kermit (cello)
Wes Montgomery Trio
The Trick Bag | The Trick Bag(alt.take) | Days Of Wine And Roses | Canadian Sunset | Dearly Beloved | For Heaven's Sake | Besame Mucho | Besame Mucho(alt.take) | Fried Pies | Fried Pies(alt.take) | The Breeze And I
NYC, rec. 22.4.1963
Montgomery,Wes (g) | Rhyne,Melvin (org) | Cobb,Jimmy (dr)
Moanin' | Dreamsville | Freddie Freeloader | Movin' Along
NYC, rec. 10.10.1963
Montgomery,Wes (g) | Rhyne,Melvin (org) | Brown,George (dr)
Wes Montgomery
Mi Cosa
Montgomery,Wes (g-solo)
Wes Montgomery Trio
For All We Know | The Way You Look Tonight | The Way You Look Tonight(alt.take) | Yesterday's Child | Geno | Dangerous | Lolita | Blues Riff | Blues Riff(alt.take) | Moanin'(alt.take)
rec. 27.11.1963
Montgomery,Wes (g) | Rhyne,Melvin (org) | Brown,George (dr)

3RCD 1961-2 | 3 CD | Bill Evans:The Complete Live At The Village Vanguard 1961 | EAN 090204923144
Bill Evans Trio
Spoken Introduction | Gloria's Step | Alice In Wonderland | My Foolish Heart | All Of You | Announcement | My Romance | Some Other Time | Solar | Gloria's Step(alt.take-1) | My Man's Gone Now | All Of You | Detour Ahead | Discussing Repertoire | Waltz For Debby | Alice In Wonderland(alt.take) | Porgy | My Romance(alt.take) | Milestones | Detour Ahead(alt.take) | Gloria's Step(alt.take-2) | Waltz For Debby(alt.take) | All Of You(alt.take) | Jade Visions | Jade Visions(alt.take) | A Final Bars
Live at The 'Village Vanguard',NYC, rec. 25.6.1961
Evans,Bill (p) | LaFaro,Scott (b) | Motian,Paul (dr)

5 RCD 4427-2 | 5 CD | Sonny Rollins-The Freelance Years:The Complete Riverside & Contemporary Recordings
Thelonious Monk Quintet
Brilliant Corners | Ba-Lue Bolivar Ba-Lues-Are | Pannonia
NYC, rec. 1956
Monk,Thelonious (p,celeste) | Henry,Ernie (as) | Rollins,Sonny (ts) | Pettiford,Oscar (b) | Roach,Max (dr)
Bemsha Swing
Monk,Thelonious (p) | Terry,Clark (tp) | Rollins,Sonny (ts) | Chambers,Paul (b) | Roach,Max (dr)
Sonny Rollins Trio
I'm An Old Cowhand | Way Out West | Come Gone | There Is No Greater Love | Wagon Wheels | Solitude | I'm An Old Cowhand(alt.take) | Come Gone(alt.take) | There Is No Greater Love(alt.take) | Way Out West(alt.take)
NYC, rec. 7.3.1957
Rollins,Sonny (ts) | Brown,Ray (b) | Manne,Shelly (dr)
Kenny Dorham Quintet
Falling In Love With Love | My Old Flame | La Villa | I'll Remember April
NYC, rec. 21.& 27.5.1957
Dorham,Kenny (tp) | Rollins,Sonny (ts) | Jones,Hank (p) | Pettiford,Oscar (b) | Roach,Max (dr)
Sonny Rollins Quartet
Just In Time | Toot Toot Tootsie | Dearly Beloved | Every Time We Say Goodbye | Cutie | Mangoes
NYC, rec. 11./12.6.1957
Rollins,Sonny (ts) | Clark,Sonny (p) | Chambers,Paul (b) | Haynes,Roy (dr)
The Last Time We Saw Paris | What Is There To Say | Funky Hotel Blues
NYC, rec. 19.6.1957
Rollins,Sonny (ts) | Clark,Sonny (p) | Heath,Percy (b) | Haynes,Roy (dr)
Sonny Rollins
It Could Happen To You
NYC, rec. 11./12.6.1957
Rollins,Sonny (ts-solo)
Abbey Lincoln With Her Quintet
Porgy | I Must Have That Man | When A Woman Loves A Man | Strong Man | Happiness Is A Thing Called Joe | That's Him | My Man | Don't Explain | I Must Have That Man(alt.take) | Porgy(alt.take)
NYC, rec. 28.10.1957
Lincoln,Abbey (voc) | Dorham,Kenny (tp) | Rollins,Sonny (ts) | Kelly,Wynton (p) | Chambers,Paul (b) | Roach,Max (dr)
Sonny Rollins Quintet
Sonnymoon For Two | Like Someone In Love | Theme From Tchaikovsky's Symphony Pathetic
NYC, rec. 4.11.1957
Rollins,Sonny (ts) | Cleveland,Jimmy (tb) | Coggins,Gil (p) | Marshall,Wendell (b) | Dennis,Kenny (dr)
Sonny Rollins Trio
Till There Was You | Someday I'll Find You | Will You Still Be Mine | Shadow Waltz | Till There Was You(alt.take) | The Freedom Suite
NYC, rec. February 1958
Rollins,Sonny (ts) | Pettiford,Oscar (b) | Roach,Max (dr)
Sonny Rollins And The Contemporary Leaders
I've Told Every Little Star | Rock-A-Bye Your Baby With A Dixie Melody | How High The Moon | You | I've Found A New Baby | Alone Together | The Song Is You | In The Chapel In The Moonlight | You(alt.take) | I've Found A New Baby(alt.take) | The Song Is You(alt.take)
Los Angeles,CA, rec. 20.-22.10.1958
Rollins,Sonny (ts) | Kessel,Barney (g) | Hawes,Hampton (p) | Vinnegar,Leroy (b) | Manne,Shelly (dr)

RISA 1142-6 | SACD | Kelly Blue | EAN 025218731768
Wynton Kelly Sextet
Kelly Blue | Keep It Moving | Keep It Moving(alt.take)
NYC, rec. 19.2.1959
Kelly,Wynton (p) | Adderley,Nat (co) | Jaspar,Bobby (fl) | Golson,Benny (ts) | Chambers,Paul (b) | Cobb,Jimmy (dr)
Wynton Kelly Trio
Softly As In A Morning Sunrise | Do Nothin' Till You Hear From Me | On Green Dolphin Street | Willow Weep For Me | Old Clothes
NYC, rec. 10.3.1959
Kelly,Wynton (p) | Chambers,Paul (b) | Cobb,Jimmy (dr)

RISA 1157-6 | SACD | Live In San Francisco | EAN 025218731867
Cannonball Adderley Quintet
A Few Words By Cannonball... | Straight No Chaser
Live at The Jazz Workshop,San Francisco,CA, rec. 18.10.1959
Adderley,Julian \'Cannonball\' (as) | Adderley,Nat (co) | Timmons,Bobby (p) | Jones,Sam (b) | Hayes,Louis (dr)
This Here | Hi Fly | Bohemia After Dark | Spontaneous Combustion | You Got It
Live at The Jazz Workshop,San Francisco,CA, rec. 20.10.1959
Adderley,Julian \'Cannonball\' (as) | Adderley,Nat (co) | Timmons,Bobby (p) | Jones,Sam (b) | Hayes,Louis (dr)

Rockwerk Records | Jazz Network

CD 011001 | CD | Boone Up Blues | EAN 4042064001087
Uli Binetsch's Own Bone
Bone Up Blues | Ballad For Two Girls | Jazz Tools | Quartet | First Step | Hallelujah | Calypsodelic | Breath | Play Your Own Bone
Dornbirn,Austria, rec. 2001
Binetsch,Uli (tb,shell) | Fesselé,Joe (keyboards) | Ketterl,Apri (b,el-b) | Jenne,Meinhard (dr)
Monday Blues
Binetsch,Uli (tb,shell) | Madsen,Peter (p) | Fesselé,Joe (keyboards) | Ketterl,Apri (b,el-b) | Jenne,Meinhard (dr)

Roulette | EMI Germany

497871-2 | CD | Atomic Swing
Count Basie And His Orchestra
Teddy The Toad | The Late Late Show | Lil' Darlin'
NYC, rec. 21./22.10.1957
Basie,Count (p) | Newman,Joe (tp) | Jones,Thad (tp) | Culley,Wendell (tp) | Young,Eugene 'Snooky' (tp) | Powell,Benny (tb) | Coker,Henry (tb) | Grey,Al (tb) | Wess,Frank (fl,as) | Royal,Marshall (as) | Davis,Eddie 'Lockjaw' (ts) | Foster,Frank (ts) | Fowlkes,Charlie (bs) | Green,Freddie (g) | Jones,Eddie (b) | Payne,Sonny (dr)
Fair And Warmer | Moten Swing
NYC, rec. 28./29.4.1958
Basie,Count (p) | Newman,Joe (tp) | Jones,Thad (tp) | Cohn[Cohen],Sonny (tp) | Young,Eugene 'Snooky' (tp) | Powell,Benny (tb) | Coker,Henry (tb) | Grey,Al (tb) | Wess,Frank (fl,as) | Royal,Marshall (as) | Mitchell,Billy (ts) | Foster,Frank (ts) | Fowlkes,Charlie (bs) | Green,Freddie (g) | Jones,Eddie (b) | Payne,Sonny (dr)
The Midnight Sun Will Never Set
NYC, rec. 19.12.1958
Basie,Count (p) | Newman,Joe (tp) | Jones,Thad (tp) | Culley,Wendell (tp) | Young,Eugene 'Snooky' (tp) | Powell,Benny (tb) | Coker,Henry (tb) | Grey,Al (tb) | Wess,Frank (fl,as) | Royal,Marshall (as) | Mitchell,Billy (ts) | Foster,Frank (ts) | Fowlkes,Charlie (bs) | Green,Freddie (g) | Jones,Eddie (b) | Payne,Sonny (dr)
Back To The Apple
NYC, rec. 16.12.1959
Basie,Count (p) | Newman,Joe (tp) | Jones,Thad (tp) | Culley,Wendell (tp) | Young,Eugene 'Snooky' (tp) | Powell,Benny (tb) | Coker,Henry (tb) | Grey,Al (tb) | Wess,Frank (fl,as) | Royal,Marshall (as) | Mitchell,Billy (ts) | Foster,Frank (ts) | Fowlkes,Charlie (bs) | Green,Freddie (g) | Jones,Eddie (b) | Payne,Sonny (dr)
The Daly Jump | Out The Window
NYC, rec. 7.6.1960
Basie,Count (p) | Newman,Joe (tp) | Jones,Thad (tp) | Cohn[Cohen],Sonny (tp) | Young,Eugene 'Snooky' (tp) | Powell,Benny (tb) | Coker,Henry (tb) | Grey,Al (tb) | Wess,Frank (fl,as) | Royal,Marshall (as) | Mitchell,Billy (ts) | Foster,Frank (ts) | Fowlkes,Charlie (bs) | Green,Freddie (g) | Jones,Eddie (b) | Payne,Sonny (dr)
9:20 Special | Rock-A-Bye Basie | Taps Miller
NYC, rec. 12./16.& 22..7.1960
Basie,Count (p) | Newman,Joe (tp) | Jones,Thad (tp) | Cohn[Cohen],Sonny (tp) | Young,Eugene 'Snooky' (tp) | Powell,Benny (tb) | Coker,Henry (tb) | Grey,Al (tb) | Wess,Frank (fl,as) | Royal,Marshall (as) | Mitchell,Billy (ts) | Foster,Frank (ts) | Fowlkes,Charlie (bs) | Green,Freddie (g) | Jones,Eddie (b) | Payne,Sonny (dr)
I Got It Bad And That Ain't Good
NYC, rec. 3.7.1962
Basie,Count (p) | Aarons,Albert 'Al' (tp) | Cohn[Cohen],Sonny (tp) | Jones,Thad (tp) | Ricard,Fip (tp) | Powell,Benny (tb) | Coker,Henry (tb) | Jackson,Quentin (tb) | Wess,Frank (fl,as) | Royal,Marshall (as) | Dixon,Eric (ts) | Foster,Frank (ts) | Fowlkes,Charlie (bs) | Green,Freddie (g) | Davis,Art (b) | Johnson,Gus (dr)

524546-2 | 2 CD | Louis Armstrong-Duke Ellington:The Great Summit-Complete Session
Louis Armstrong And His All Stars With Duke Ellington
Duke's Place(C Jam Blues) | I'm Just A Lucky So-And-So | Cotton Tail | Mood Indigo | Do Nothin' Till You Hear From Me | The Beautiful American | Black And Tan Fantasy | Drop Me Off In Harlem | The Mooche | In A Mellow Tone | It Don't Mean A Thing If It Ain't Got That Swing | Solitude | Don't Get Around Much Anymore | I'm Beginning To See The Light | Just Squeeze Me(But Don't Tease Me) | I Got It Bad And That Ain't Good | Azalea | In A Mellow Tone(alt.take) | I'm Beginning To See The Light(alt.take) | Do Nothin' Till You Hear From Me(alt.take) | Don't Get Around Much Anymore(alt.take) | Duke's Place(C Jam Blues-alt.take) | Drop Me Off In Harlem(alt.take) | I'm Just A Lucky So-And-So(alt.take) | Azalea(alt.take) | Black And Tan Fantasy(alt.take) | Band discussion on Cotton Tail
NYC, rec. 3./4.4.1961
Armstrong,Louis (tp,voc) | Young,Trummy (tb) | Bigard,Barney (cl) | Ellington,Duke (p) | Herbert,Mort (b) | Barcelona,Danny (dr)

531790-2 | CD | Together/Have A Good Time
Joe Williams With The Harry 'Sweets' Edison Sextet
Winter Weather | I Don't Know Why(I Just Do) | There's A Small Hotel | Out Of Nowhere | Aren't You Glad You're You | Remember | Together | Deep Purple | Always | Lover Come Back To Me | By The River Saint Marie | Alone Together
Los Angeles,CA, rec. 31.1.-2.2.1961
Williams,Joe (voc) | Edison,Harry 'Sweets' (tp) | Forrest,Jimmy (ts) | unkn. (g) | Thompson,Sir Charles (p) | Potter,Tommy (b) | Johnston,Clarence (dr) | Wilkins,Ernie (arr)
Joe Williams With The Harry 'Sweets' Edison Band
Have A Good Time | Sometimes I'm Happy | Old Folks | Until I Met You | I Won't Cry Anymore | S' Posin' | A Blues Serenade | September In The Rain | Summertime | Moonlight In Vermont | Falling In Love With Love
NYC, rec. July 1961
Williams,Joe (voc) | Edison,Harry 'Sweets' (tp) | Jones,Jimmie (p) | Benjamin,Joe (b) | Persip,Charles (dr) | Wilkins,Ernie (arr) | details unknown

531791-2 | CD | Breakfast Dance And Barbecue
Count Basie And His Orchestra
The Deacon | Cute | In A Mellow Tone | No Moon At All | Cherry Red | Roll 'Em Pete | Cherry Point | Splanky | Counter Block | Lil' Darlin' | Who Me | Five O'Clock In The Morning | Everyday I Have The Blues | Back To The Apple | Let's Have A Taste | Moten Swing | Hallelujah I Love Her So | One O'Clock Jump
Live at The Americana Hotel,Miami,Florida, rec. 31.5.1959
Basie,Count (p) | Jones,Thad (tp) | Newman,Joe (tp) | Culley,Wendell (tp) | Young,Eugene 'Snooky' (tp) | Edison,Harry 'Sweets' (tp) | Grey,Al (tb) | Coker,Henry (tb) | Powell,Benny (tb) | Royal,Marshall (as) | Wess,Frank (fl,as,ts) | Foster,Frank (ts) | Mitchell,Billy (ts) | Fowlkes,Charlie (bs) | Green,Freddie (g) | Jones,Eddie (b) | Payne,Sonny (dr) | Williams,Joe (voc)

531792-2 | CD | The Sound Of The Johnny Smith Guitar
Johnny Smith Quartet
Come Rain Or Come Shine | Gypsy In My Soul | Embraceable You | Misty | As Long As There's Music | Round About Midnight | This Can't Be Love | Blues Chorale | Prelude
NYC, rec. 1960
Smith,Johnny (g) | Jones,Hank (p) | Duvivier,George (b) | Shaughnessy,Ed (dr)
I Got It Bad And That Ain't Good | Let's Fall In Love | I Can't Get Started | Some Of These Days | You Took Advantage Of Me | Over The Rainbow | Out Of Nowhere | Prelude To A Kiss | Un Poco Loco | Hippo The Sentimental Hippy | It's You Or No One
NYC, rec. 1961
Smith,Johnny (g) | Pancoast,Bob (p) | Roumanis,George (b) | Alexander,Mousie (dr)

531793-2 | CD | Sweet 'N' Sassy
Sarah Vaughan With Orchestra
I Didn't Know About You | More Than You Know | Thanks For The Ride | Come Spring | I Wish I Were In Love Again | Lazy Afternoon | Just Married Today | Something I Dreamed Last Night | I Got Rhythm | This Can't Be Love | Slowly | Just You Just Me | This Can't Be Love(alt.take)
Chicago,Ill, rec. June 1963
Vaughan,Sarah (voc) | Orchestra | details unknown | Schifrin,Lalo (arr)

537559-2 | CD | Ballads | EAN 724353755928
Dinah Washington With Orchestra
Lover Man(Oh,Where Can You Be?) | I Wanne Be Around My Baby All The Time | I Don't Know About You | Funny Thing | I'll Close My Eyes | The Show Must Go On | If It's The Last Thing I Do | He's Gone Again | These Foolish Things Remind Me On You | For All We Know | What's New? | Baby Won't You Please Come Home | A Stranger On Earth
NYC, rec. 1962-1963
Washington,Dinah (voc) | Orchestra & Strings | Costa,Don (cond,arr) | Norman,Fred (arr) | Manning,Marty (arr) | details unknown

537561-2 | CD | Ballads | EAN 724353756123
Sarah Vaughan With The Jimmy Jones Orchestra
Dreamy
NYC, rec. 19.4.1960
Vaughan,Sarah (voc) | Edison,Harry 'Sweets' (tp) | Sanfino,Gerald (fl,ts) | Bright,Ronnell (p) | Galbraith,Barry (g) | Davis,Richard (b) | Duvivier,George (b) | Brice,Percy (dr) | Soyer,Janet (harp) | Strings
Sarah Vaughan And The Count Basie Orchestra
You Go To My Head | Lover Man(Oh,Where Can You Be?)
NYC, rec. 15.5.1960
Cohn[Cohen],Sonny (tp) | Strings | Jones,Thad (tp,arr) | Newman,Joe (tp) | Young,Eugene 'Snooky' (tp) | Coker,Henry (tb) | Grey,Al (tb) | Powell,Benny (tb) | Royal,Marshall (as) | Wess,Frank (as) | Foster,Frank (ts) | Mitchell,Billy (ts) | Fowlkes,Charlie (bs) | Basie,Count (p) | Green,Freddie (g) | Jones,Eddie (b) | Payne,Sonny (dr)
Sarah Vaughan With Mundell Lowe And George Duvivier
In A Sentimental Mood
NYC, rec. June 1961
Vaughan,Sarah (voc) | Lowe,Mundell (g) | Duvivier,George (b)
Sarah Vaughan With The Quincy Jones Orchestra
Second Time Around
NYC, rec. 1962
Vaughan,Sarah (voc) | Jones,Quincy (arr,ld) | details unknown
Sarah Vaughan With Orchestra
I Fall In Love Too Easily
Vaughan,Sarah (voc) | Costa,Don (cond,arr) | details unknown
Sarah Vaughan With The Benny Carter Orchestra
If I Had You | Solitude
Los Angeles,CA, rec. January 1963
Vaughan,Sarah (voc) | Wilson,Gerald (tp) | Orchestra & Strings | Carter,Benny (arr,ld) | details unknown
Sarah Vaughan With The Gerald Wilson Orchestra
I Guess I'll Hang My Tears Out To Dry | Round About Midnight | Midnight Sun
NYC, rec. 1963
Vaughan,Sarah (voc) | Jones,Carmell (tp) | Edwards,Teddy (ts) | Freeman,Ernie (org) | Collins,John (g) | McKibbon,Al (b) | Turner,Milton (dr) | Wilson,Gerald (arr,ld)
Sarah Vaughan Plus Two
Key Largo | All Or Nothing At All
Vaughan,Sarah (voc) | Kessel,Barney (g) | Comfort,Joe (b)

581664-2 | CD | Chairman Of The Board | EAN 724358166422
Count Basie And His Orchestra
Blues In Hoss' Flat | H.R.H.
Chicago,Ill, rec. 4.3.1958
Basie,Count (p) | Young,Eugene 'Snooky' (tp) | Culley,Wendell (tp) | Jones,Thad (tp,arr) | Coker,Henry (tb) | Grey,Al (tb) | Powell,Benny (tb) | Royal,Marshall (cl,as) | Wess,Frank (fl,as) | Foster,Frank (ts,arr) | Mitchell,Billy (ts) | Fowlkes,Charlie (b-cl,bs) | Green,Freddie (g) | Jones,Eddie (b) | Payne,Sonny (dr)
Who Me | Half Moon Street | Moten Swing
NYC, rec. 28.4.1958
Basie,Count (p) | Young,Eugene 'Snooky' (tp) | Culley,Wendell (tp) | Jones,Thad (tp) | Coker,Henry (tb) | Grey,Al (tb) | Powell,Benny (tb) | Royal,Marshall (cl,as) | Wess,Frank (fl,as,arr) | Foster,Frank (ts,arr) | Mitchell,Billy (ts) | Fowlkes,Charlie (b-cl,bs) | Green,Freddie (g) | Jones,Eddie (b) | Payne,Sonny (dr) | Wilkins,Ernie (arr)
Kansas City Shout | Mutt And Jeff | Fair And Warmer
NYC, rec. 29.4.1958
Basie,Count (p) | Young,Eugene 'Snooky' (tp) | Culley,Wendell (tp) | Jones,Thad (tp,arr) | Coker,Henry (tb) | Grey,Al (tb) | Powell,Benny (tb) | Royal,Marshall (cl,as) | Wess,Frank (fl,as) | Foster,Frank (ts) | Mitchell,Billy (ts) | Fowlkes,Charlie (b-cl,bs) | Green,Freddie (g) | Jones,Eddie (b) | Payne,Sonny (dr) | Wilkins,Ernie (arr)
Speaking Of Sounds | The Deacon
NYC, rec. 10.12.1958
Basie,Count (p) | Young,Eugene 'Snooky' (tp) | Culley,Wendell (tp) | Jones,Thad (tp,arr) | Coker,Henry (tb) | Grey,Al (tb) | Powell,Benny (tb) | Royal,Marshall (cl,as) | Wess,Frank (fl,as) | Foster,Frank (ts) | Mitchell,Billy (ts) | Fowlkes,Charlie (b-cl,bs) | Green,Freddie (g) | Jones,Eddie (b) | Payne,Sonny (dr)
Segue In C | T.V.Time
NYC, rec. 11.12.1958
Basie,Count (p) | Young,Eugene 'Snooky' (tp) | Jones,Thad (tp) | Culley,Wendell (tp) | Newman,Joe (tp) | Powell,Benny (tb) | Coker,Henry (tb) | Grey,Al (tb) | Royal,Marshall (as) | Wess,Frank (fl,as,arr) | Foster,Frank (ts,arr) | Mitchell,Billy (ts) | Fowlkes,Charlie (bs) | Green,Freddie (g) | Jones,Eddie (b) | Payne,Sonny (dr)

581829-2 | CD | Chet Baker:The Most Important Jazz Album Of 1964/65 | EAN 724358182927
Chet Baker Quintet
Soultrane | Walkin' | Tadd's Delight | Whatever Possessed Me | Retsim B. | Gnid | Ann,Wonderful One | Mating Call | Margerine | Flight To Jordan
NYC, rec. April/May 1964
Baker,Chet (fl-h,voc) | Urso,Phil (ts) | Galper,Hal (p) | Merritt,Jymie (b) | Rice,Charlie (dr)

581830-2 | CD | Five Feet Of Soul | EAN 724358183023

Jimmy Rushing And His Orchestra
Just Because | 'Tain't Nobody's Bizness If I Do | Heartaches | I'm Walking Through Heaven With You | Trouble In Mind | Oooh! Look-A-There Ain't She Pretty | Please Come Back | You Always Hurt The One You Love | Did You Ever | My Bucket's Got A Hole In It
NYC, rec. 22./23.1.1963
Rushing,Jimmy (voc) | Glow,Bernie (tp) | Markowitz,Irving 'Marky' (tp) | Newman,Joe (tp) | Young,Eugene Edward (tp) | Byers,Billy (tb) | Cleveland,Jimmy (tb) | Dennis,Willie (tb) | Green,Urbie (tb) | Quill,Gene (as) | Woods,Phil (as) | Johnson,Budd (ts) | Sims,Zoot (ts) | Schlinger,Sol (bs) | Bown,Patti (p) | Green,Freddie (g) | Hinton,Milt (b) | Johnson,Gus (dr)

581862-2 | CD | Once More With Feeling | EAN 724358186222
Billy Eckstine With The Billy May Orchestra
Once More With Feeling | Cottage For Sale | As Time Goes By | I Apologize | With Every Breath I Take | Secret Love
Los Angeles,CA, rec. 28./29.1.1960
Eckstine,Billy (voc) | Collette,Buddy (reeds) | Jacob,Julie (reeds) | Gleghorn,Arthur (fl) | DeRosa,Vince (fr-h) | Cave,Jack (fr-h) | Decker,Jim (fr-h) | Stephen,Phil (tuba) | Gibbons,Bobby (g) | Raskin,Milt (p) | Rubin,Mike (b) | Cottler,Irv (dr) | unkn. (strings) | May,Billy (cond,arr)
Stormy Weather | Blues In The Night | I Hear A Rhapsody | That Old Black Magic | I Love You | I'm Beginning To See The Light
Eckstine,Billy (voc) | Gozzo,Conrad (tp) | Candoli,Pete (tp) | Rasey,Uan (tp) | Triscari,Joe (tp) | Noel,Dick (tb) | Ulyate,Lloyd (tb) | Schaefer,Bill (tb) | Kusby,Eddie (tb) | Carter,Benny (as) | Schwartz,Wilbur (as) | Falensby,Fred (ts) | Gordon,Justin (ts) | Gentry,Chuck (bs) | Gibbons,Bobby (g) | Rowles,Jimmy (p) | Callender,Red (b) | Cottler,Irv (dr) | May,Billy (cond,arr)
Anything You Wanna Do(I Wanna Do With You) | Like Wow
NYC, rec. 29./30.7.1959
Eckstine,Billy (voc) | details unknown

590954-2 | CD | Bobo's Beat | EAN 724359095424
Willie Bobo Group
Bon Sueno | Naked City Theme | Felicidade | Bossa Nova In Blue | Boroquinho | Crisis | Mi Fas Y Recordar | Capers | Let Your Hair Down Blues
NYC, rec. 11.10.1962
Bobo,Willie (timbales,perc) | Terry,Clark (tp) | Farrell,Joe (ts) | Anderson,Frank (p,org) | others unknown
Trinidad | Timbale Groove
NYC, rec. 27./28.5.1964
Bobo,Willie (timbales,perc) | details unknown

596593-2 | CD | Moonlight In Vermont
Johnny Smith Quintet
Where Or When | Tabu | Moonlight In Vermont | Jaguar | Jaguar(alt.take)
NYC, rec. 11.3.1952
Smith,Johnny (g) | Getz,Stan (ts) | Gold,Sanford (p) | Safranski,Eddie (b) | Lamond,Don (dr)
A Ghost Of A Chance | Vilia
NYC, rec. April 1952
Smith,Johnny (g) | Sims,Zoot (ts) | Gold,Sanford (p) | Safranski,Eddie (b) | Lamond,Don (dr)
Sometimes I'm Happy | Stars Fell On Alabama | Nice Work If You Can Get It | Tenderly
NYC, rec. November 1952
Smith,Johnny (g) | Getz,Stan (ts) | Gold,Sanford (p) | Carter,Ron (b) | Feld,Morey (dr)
My Funny Valentine
NYC, rec. 6.6.1953
Smith,Johnny (g) | Sims,Zoot (ts) | Gold,Sanford (p) | Safranski,Eddie (b) | Lamond,Don (dr)
Cavu | I'll Be Around
NYC, rec. July 1953
Smith,Johnny (g) | Sims,Zoot (ts) | Gold,Sanford (p) | Fishkin,Arnold (b) | Lamond,Don (dr)
Yesterdays | Cherokee
NYC, rec. August 1953
Smith,Johnny (g) | Quinichette,Paul (ts) | Gold,Sanford (p) | Fishkin,Arnold (b) | Lamond,Don (dr)
Johnny Smith Trio
Lullaby Of Birdland
NYC, rec. 1953
Smith,Johnny (g) | Fishkin,Arnold (b) | Lamond,Don (dr)
Johnny Smith Quartet
What's New? | I'll Remember April
Smith,Johnny (g) | unkn. (g) | Fishkin,Arnold (b) | Lamond,Don (dr)

828635-2 | CD | The Complete Atomic Basie
Count Basie And His Orchestra
Kid From Red Bank | Duet | After Supper | Flight Of The Foo Birds | Double-O | Teddy The Toad | Whirly Bird | Midnite Blue | Splanky | Fantail | Lil' Darlin' | Silks And Satins | Sleepwalker's Serenade | Sleepwalker's Serenade(alt.take) | The Late Late Show
NYC, rec. 21./22.10.1957
Basie,Count (p) | Newman,Joe (tp) | Jones,Thad (tp) | Culley,Wendell (tp) | Young,Eugene 'Snooky' (tp) | Powell,Benny (tb) | Coker,Henry (tb) | Grey,Al (tb) | Wess,Frank (fl,as) | Royal,Marshall (as) | Davis,Eddie 'Lockjaw' (ts) | Foster,Frank (ts) | Fowlkes,Charlie (bs) | Green,Freddie (g) | Jones,Eddie (b) | Payne,Sonny (dr) | Hefti,Neal (arr) | Mundy,Jimmy (arr)
The Late Late Show
Basie,Count (p) | Newman,Joe (tp) | Jones,Thad (tp) | Culley,Wendell (tp) | Young,Eugene 'Snooky' (tp) | Powell,Benny (tb) | Coker,Henry (tb) | Grey,Al (tb) | Wess,Frank (fl,as) | Royal,Marshall (as) | Davis,Eddie 'Lockjaw' (ts) | Foster,Frank (ts) | Fowlkes,Charlie (bs) | Green,Freddie (g) | Jones,Eddie (b) | Payne,Sonny (dr) | Williams,Joe (voc)

837201-2 | CD | Two's Company
Maynard Ferguson Orchestra With Chris Connor
I Feel A Song Coming On | The Wind | New York's My Home | Guess Who I Saw Today | When The Sun Comes Out | Send For Me | Where Do You Go | Something's Coming | Deep Song | Can't Get Out Of This Mood
NYC, rec. June 1961
Ferguson,Maynard (tp,tb,fr-h) | Feretti,Chet (tp) | Berry,Bill (tp) | Ericson,Rolf (tp) | Winslow,Ray (tb) | Rupp,Kenny (tb) | Morgan,Lanny (fl,as) | Maiden,Willie (cl,ts) | Farrell,Joe (fl,ss,ts) | Hittner,Frank (b-cl,bs) | Byard,Jaki (p) | Neves,John (b) | Jones,Rufus (dr) | Connor,Chris (voc)

855468-2 | CD | After Hours | EAN 724385546822
Sarah Vaughan With Mundell Lowe And George Duvivier
My Favorite Things | Every Time We Say Goodbye | Wonder Why | Easy To Love | Sophisticated Lady | Great Day | Ill Wind | If Love Is Good To Me | In A Sentimental Mood | Vanity | Through The Years
NYC, rec. 18.7.1961
Vaughan,Sarah (voc) | Lowe,Mundell (g) | Duvivier,George (b)

Satin Doll Productions | Jazz Network

SDP 1011-1 CD | CD | Just In Time
Thilo Wagner Trio
Just In Time | Georgia On My Mind | Bag's Groove | I Can't Get Started | You Don't Know What Love Is
Ettlingen, rec. 24.10.1994
Wagner,Thilo (p) | Mörike,Wolfgang (b) | Brunner,Giga (dr)
Thilo Wagner Quintet
Count's Blues | So You Don't | Autumn Leaves | Del Sasser
Ettlingen, rec. 28.12.1994
Wagner,Thilo (p) | Studnitzky,Sebastian (tp,fl-h) | Graf,Klaus (as) | Mörike,Wolfgang (b) | Brunner,Giga (dr)

SDP 1013-1 CD | CD | My Own
Werner Lener Trio
Happy With Friends | Turnaround | Buckie Wuckie | Nearly The Blues | Talk With The Band | In A Mist | Joy Of Life | Danny Boy (Londonderry Air) | Stammba | Bass Hit | Cubano Chant
Altensteig, rec. 9./10.3.1996
Lener,Werner (p) | Krisch,Thomas (b) | Wachter,Herbert (dr)
Werner Lener Quartet
My Own | Waltz For Bette | Just Friends
Lener,Werner (p) | Graf,Klaus (sax) | Krisch,Thomas (b) | Wachter,Herbert (dr)

SDP 1015-1 CD | CD | Panonien
Gregor Hübner Quartet
Panonien | Nur Ein Schatten | Russian Impressions | Truce | Golden Earrings
NYC, rec. 5./6.4.1996
Hübner,Gregor (p,v) | Maile,Andreas 'Andi' (sax) | Swartz,Harvie (b) | Nell,Holger (dr)
Gregor Hübner Quintet
Handwork | Reflections | Something | Underneath It All
Hübner,Gregor (p,v) | Hagans,Tim (tp) | Maile,Andreas 'Andi' (sax) | Swartz,Harvie (b) | Nell,Holger (dr)

SDP 1017-1 CD | CD | Jazz 4 Fun
Regina Büchner's Jazz 4 Fun
Groove Merchant | Night And Day | A Matter Of Intensity | The Lady Is A Tramp | St.Thomas | In A Sentimental Mood- | Girl From Ipanema(Garota De Ipanema)- | Cantaloupe Island | All Of Me | Where's The Exit
Auenwald, rec. April1995/August 1996/February 1997
Büchner,Regina (ts) | Berlin,Frieder (p) | Fröschlin,Rolf Dieter (b) | Oliva,Reiner (dr,voc)

SDP 1018-1 CD | CD | Bach Lives!!
Matthias Stich & Whisper Not
Drei Fragmente Aus der Markus-Pasion | Agnus Dei Plus
Live at Kaufhaussaal,Freiburg, rec. 24.11.1996
Stich,Matthias (cl,b-cl,ss,sopranino,as,voc) | Mayer,Wolf (p,voc) | Fernow,Wolfgang (b,voc) | Bockius,Frank (dr,tambourine,voc) | de Galgoczy-Mecher,Viola (voc)
PräludiumIn C-Moll Únd Dur | Rhythm Fugue | BA(e)SF,Oder Die Kunst Der Fugendichting | Präludium Aus Der Cello-Suite Nr.2 | Variationen Über BWV 38 | Vom Himmel Hoch...
Live at SWF-Landesstudio, rec. 15.2.1997
Stich,Matthias (cl,b-cl,ss,sopranino,as,voc) | Mayer,Wolf (p,voc) | Fernow,Wolfgang (b,voc) | Bockius,Frank (dr,tambourine,voc) | de Galgoczy-Mecher,Viola (voc)
Donna Inventia | Wachet Auf Ruft Uns Die Stimme | Der Die Das Blueneon
SWF-Landesstudio

SDP 1019-1 CD | CD | Signs On Lines
Jochen Feucht Trio
Signs On Lines | Nardis | Time Game | By Heart | Tune For The Moon | Blues No.2
Ludwigsburg, rec. 2.3.1997
Feucht,Jochen (alto-fl,ss,ts) | Ramond,Christian (b) | Rückert,Jochen (dr)
Jochen Feucht Quartet
Little Waltz | Meje | Beacons | Between Now And Then
Feucht,Jochen (alto-fl,ss,ts) | Studnitzky,Sebastian (tp,fl-h) | Ramond,Christian (b) | Rückert,Jochen (dr)
Jochen Feucht
Lines 1
Feucht,Jochen (ss-solo)

SDP 1020-1 CD | CD | Hallelujah Time
Patrick Tompert Trio
Hallelujah Time | Someday My Prince Will Come | Uli's Delight | Blues For Charles | Intermezzo | Spragare | First Romance | It Don't Mean A Thing If It Ain't Got That Swing | Old Folks | Now's The Time
Böblingen, rec. 16.-18.4.1997
Tompert,Patrick (p) | Petrocca,Davide (b) | Braun,Werner (dr)

SDP 1022-1 CD | CD | Mailensteine
Andreas Maile Quartet
Love Chant | Mailensteine | March Of Destiny | Drum Intro- | Something- | Listen To Me | Deep In Green | At The Regency | Walkin' In Brussels
Albstadt, rec. 29./30.10.1996
Maile,Andreas 'Andi' (ss,ts) | Stötzler,Olaf (g) | Thys,Nicolas 'Nic' (b) | Manzecchi,Patrick (dr)

SDP 1023-1 CD | CD | Drilling
Uli Möck Trio
In Suspense | Dr.Bär(für Onkel Manfred) | After Eight | Waiting | Drilling | Swing Low | Bad Habit | Ethnolog | Balanced Time | Living In Chelsea | When Will I See You Again
Ludwigsburg, rec. 27./28.10.1997
Möck,Uli 'Ull' (p) | Höfler,Karoline (b) | Fickelscher,Hans (dr)

SDP 1024-1 CD | CD | Heavy Rotation
Peter Lehel Quartet
Finale | Papa Groove | Bits Of Blues | Waiting | Kiss & Fly | Lost April | Heavy Rotation | This Is New | Because Of The Bass | Prison Changes | Little Lady | I Feel Good
Lammroad Studios,?, rec. 28./29.12.1997
Lehel,Peter (b-cl,ss,ts) | Möck,Uli 'Ull' (p) | Schulz,Mini (b) | Schumacher,Dieter (dr)

SDP 1025-1 CD | CD | Memories
The Huebner Brothers
Memories | Am Fluss | Kathedrale Im Dunkeln(Hans Koller gewidmet) | Short Cuts | Wise One | Un Machito | Elfe | Riddles
Englewood Cliffs,NJ, rec. 27.4.1997
Hübner,Gregor (p,v) | Hübner,Veit (b) | Rössle,Ekkehard (ss,ts) | Beirach,Richard (p) | Köbberling,Heinrich (dr)

SDP 1026-1 CD | CD | Personal Moments
Werner Lener Trio
Bird Flight | Holiday Scenes | My Own | Rain,Sun,Grass And Flowers | Boogie Bop | Pianofighter Rag
Hirschhorn-Langenthal, rec. 21.5.1998
Lener,Werner (p) | Krisch,Thomas (b) | Wachter,Herbert (dr)
Werner Lener Quartet
Take A Bebop | Straight No Chaser | The Peacocks | Come Spring
Lener,Werner (p) | Paquette,Pierre (cl,as) | Krisch,Thomas (b) | Wachter,Herbert (dr)

SDP 1027-1 CD | CD | Obsecion
Tango Five feat. Raul Jaurena
Mi Vida Contigo | Obsecion | Desesperacion | Tango Para Lajuana | Mi Tristeza | La Cumparsita | Tango Madrugada | Te Acuerdas | Ochiata | Resignacion | New York Tango
Digital Masters Studio,?, rec. 6.-9.8.1997
Tango Five | Jaurena,Raul (bandoneon) | Ruf,Bernd (cl) | Hübner,Gregor (v) | Fischer,Karl Albrecht (p,viola) | Hübner,Veit (b)

SDP 1029-1 CD | CD | Patrick Tompert Trio Live
Patrick Tompert Trio
If I Where A Bell | Song For My Parents- | Blues For Charles | Manha De Carnaval(Morning Of The Carnival) | Autumn Leaves | Au Privave | Beautiful Love | Bye Bye Blackbird | On Danish Shore | Hymn To Freedom- | Hallelujah Time-
Live at Kunstatelier Zimmermann,Arberg-Mörsach, rec. 24.10.1998
Tompert,Patrick (p) | Petrocca,Davide (b) | Braun,Werner (dr)

SDP 1030-1 CD | CD | Soft Winds
Thomas Siffling Jazz Quartet
For Dad | Open Eyes | Latin Dreaming | Fall Fog | Soft Winds
Monster,NL, rec. 8.-10.2.1999
Siffling,Thomas (tp,fl-h) | Böhm,Rainer (p) | Lange,Uwe (b) | Faller,Markus (dr)

SDP 1031-1 CD | CD | All That Jazz & Helena Paul
All That Jazz & Helena Paul
The Lady Is A Tramp | Let The Good Times Roll | On Green Dolphin Street | Teach Me Tonight | Bogey's Blues | Wave | Spain | In My Live(Walt's Walz) | Don't Get Around Much Anymore | Dr.Feelgood | Lover Man(Oh,Where Can You Be?) | I Can't Stop Loving You
Albstadt, rec. 30.11./1.12.1999
All That Jazz | Zimmermann,Stephan (tp,fl-h) | Nuß,Ludwig (tb) | Erlewein,Matthias (fl,as,ts) | Acker,Werner (g) | Dollmann,Jürgen (p,keyboards) | Killinger,Johannes (b,el-b) | Kersting,Michael (dr) | Paul,Helena (voc)

SDP 1032-1 CD | CD | American Songbook
Olaf Polziehn Trio
Dinah | But Not For Me | Moonlight Serenade | April In Paris | Girl Of My Dreams | Cheek To Cheek
Köln, rec. 20.2.1999
Polziehn,Olaf (p) | Heller,Ingmar (b) | Mewes,Oliver (dr)
Teach Me Tonight | Strike Up The Band | The Party's Over | Just You Just Me | Manhattan | Wrap Your Troubles In Dreams | Blues
Köln, rec. 20.1.2000
Polziehn,Olaf (p) | Heller,Ingmar (b) | Mewes,Oliver (dr)

SDP 1033-1 CD | CD | Colours | EAN 4019487103315
Werner Lener Trio
Walking Foreward,Not Back | Colours Of Sky | Leaves In The Wind | Classic Emotion | Flower Song | Leise Leise,Fromme Weise(from Freischütz) | Fooling Around Blues | Just Comming Home | Partly Raggy
Stuttgart, rec. 30.3./1.4.2000
Lener,Werner (p) | Krisch,Thomas (b) | Wachter,Herbert (dr)
My Own
Lener,Werner (p) | Krisch,Thomas (b) | Wachter,Herbert (dr) | Württemberger,Eva (voc)
Werner Lener Quartet
Going For A Walk | Waltz Beautiful | Light Shadows | Quintessential | Soap Bubbles
Lener,Werner (p) | Paquette,Pierre (cl,as) | Krisch,Thomas (b) | Wachter,Herbert (dr)

SDP 1034-1 CD | CD | Januschke's Time | EAN 4019487103414
Gregor Hübner Quintet
910,Columbus Ave | Jazz Like | Short Cuts | La Juana | Air-Lines | Hidden Enemies | Havana Manana | In Line Again
details unknown, rec. 7./8.2.1998
Hübner,Gregor (p,v) | Hagans,Tim (tp) | Maile,Andreas 'Andi' (sax) | Swartz,Harvie (b) | Noll,Holger (dr)

SDP 1035-1 CD | CD | Moche! | EAN 4019487103513
Patrick Tompert Trio
On Green Dolphin Street | Sam's Blues | Moche! | Song For My Parents | Just Don't | Cute | Secret Love | On The Highway | A Few Words For Galileo | Softly As In A Morning
Stuttgart, rec. 12.-14.8.2000
Tompert,Patrick (p) | Petrocca,Davide (b) | Braun,Werner (dr)

SDP 1037-1 CD | CD | Niceland | EAN 4019487103711
Vesna Skorija Band
My One And Only Love | Just One Of Those Things | O Pato(The Duck) | Willow Weep For Me | The Boy From Ipanema | On A Clear Day You Can See Forever | Niceland | Send In The Clowns | The Jody Grind | Since I Fell For You
Remshalden, rec. details unknown
Skorija,Vesna (voc) | Höfer,Armin (sax) | Geisler,Chris (p) | Sieb,Lothar (b) | Settelmeyer,Bernd (dr)

SDP 1038-1 CD | CD | ...mehrschichtig | EAN 4019487103810
Matthias Stich Sevensenses
Head Heart And 'Hands | Phanta | Minor Seconds | Downbeats | Comino Island | Flügelflug | Making Sense | Half-,Whole-,Tritone-Funk | Elegie | Mehrschichtig...Mehrschichtig...Mehrschichtig | Der 7.Sinn-Jay Jay
Freiburg,Brg., rec. 20.-22.1.2001
Stich,Matthias (b-cl,ss,as) | Barone,Gary (fl-h) | Schweizer,Mike (ss,ts) | Welander,Jörgen (tuba) | Daneck,Matthias (dr)

SDP 1039-1 CD | CD | Soul Fingers | EAN 4019487103919
Frieder Berlin Trio
Route 66 | Lullaby Of Birdland | 'S Wonderful | Learnin' The Blues | Soul Fingers | My Funny Valentine | Days Of Wine And Roses | Yesterdays | My Romance | Caravan | A Foggy Day(In London Town) | Lignano | Blues For Lennie
Auenwald, rec. 24.-26.2.2000
Berlin,Frieder (p) | Schuller,Hansi (b) | Schmidt,Peter (dr)

SDP 1040-1 CD | CD | Sorry,It's Jazz! | EAN 4019487104015
Sorry,It's Jazz
GQFS | Spanish Go-Round | The Way You Look Tonight | Not Really Sorry | I Fall In Love Too Easily | Back To Brooklyn | Claudia | Tigri-Bing | I Hear A Rhapsody
Stuttgart, rec. 19.-21.11.2000
Sorry It's Jazz | Haas,Arno (ss,as) | Tompert,Patrick (p) | Klaiber,German (b) | Frey,Elmar (dr,perc)

SDP 1041-1 CD | CD | Scarlet Sunrise | EAN 4019487104114
Frank Eberle Septet
Grasshoppers | Scarlet Sunrise | The Funeral | Resignation | Under The Surface
details unknown, rec. 2000
Eberle,Frank (p) | Schlosser,Axel (tp,fl-h) | Mears,Adrian (tb) | Cimiotti,André (ss,as) | Bothner,Jürgen (ts) | Bodenseh,Markus (b) | Gandela,Andreas (dr)
Vibrations | Fatal Passions | Party In The Pentagon | Catch The Blues
details unknown, rec. 2002
Eberle,Frank (p) | Schlosser,Axel (tp,fl-h) | Mears,Adrian (tb) | Cimiotti,André (ss,as) | Bothner,Jürgen (ts) | Glaszmann,Uli (b) | Grau,Thorsten (dr)
Oh Lord,Give Me A Cigarette
Eberle,Frank (p) | Schlosser,Axel (tp,harmon mute fills) | Mears,Adrian (tb) | Francke,Andreas (as) | Bothner,Jürgen (ts) | Glaszmann,Uli (b) | Grau,Thorsten (dr)
The Return Of The Pleasures
Eberle,Frank (p) | Schlosser,Axel (tp,fl-h) | Mears,Adrian (tb) | Francke,Andreas (ss) | Bothner,Jürgen (ts) | Bodenseh,Markus (b) | Gandela,Andreas (dr)

SDP 1042-1 CD | CD | Mr. B's Time Machine | EAN 4019487104213
Ralph Abelein Group
Mr. B's Time Machine | Try To Fly | Catch Up With The Count | Deancing
Ludwigsburg, rec. 2002
Abelein,Ralph (p,el-p,org,voc) | Seyler,Jürgen (tb,voc) | Francke,Andreas (cl,as,voc) | Wekenmann,Frank (g,bj,voc) | Blümlein,Dirk (b,voc) | Stromer,Rckhard (dr,voc)
Cantus Interruptus
Remshalden, rec. 2002
Abelein,Ralph (p,el-p,org,voc) | Metzler,Jochen (tp) | Seyler,Jürgen (tb,voc) | Francke,Andreas (cl,as,voc) | Malikova,Alisa (ts) | Birkle,Markus (g) | Wekenmann,Frank (g,bj,voc) | Blümlein,Dirk (b,voc) | Stromer,Rckhard (dr,voc)
Brother B
Abelein,Ralph (p,el-p,org,voc) | Metzler,Jochen (fl-h) | Nell,Thomas (tp,piccolo-tp) | Röser,Uli (euphonium) | Seyler,Jürgen (tb,voc) | Francke,Andreas (cl,as,voc) | Malikova,Alisa (ts) | Wekenmann,Frank (g,bj,voc) | Blümlein,Dirk (b,voc) | Stromer,Rckhard (dr,voc)

SDP 1043-1 CD | CD | Abendlieder | EAN 4019487104213
Tilman Jäger Tape 4
Guten Abend | Abend Wird Es Wieder | Ade Zur Guten Nacht | Ach Lieber Herre Jesu Christ | Die Nacht Ist Gekommen,Drin Wir Ruhen Sollen | Guter Mond Du Gehst So Stille | Wer Nur Den Lieben Gott Lässt Walten | Jesu Meine | Gehe Ein In Deinen Frieden | Gott Ist Gegenwärtig | Nun Ruhen Alle Wälder | Der Mond Ist Aufgegangen
Ludwigsburg, rec. 5./6.8.2002
Jäger,Tilman (p) | Rössle,Ekkehard (sax) | Müller,Paul (b) | Witte,Andy (dr)

Smash | Universal Music Germany

065507-2 | CD | This Is Billy Mitchell | EAN 044006550725
Billy Mitchell Quintet
Just Waiting | Charlie's Song | Sophisticated Lady | J & B
Chicago,Ill, rec. 29.10.1962
Mitchell,Billy (ts) | Hutcherson,Bobby (vib) | Anderson,Clarence 'Sleepy' (org) | Wright,Herman (b) | Finch,Otis 'Candy' (dr)
Billy Mitchell Sextet
Automation | Siam | Passionnova | You Turned The Tables On Me | Tamara
Chicago,Ill, rec. 30.10.1962

Mitchell,Billy (ts) | Burns,Dave (tp) | Hutcherson,Bobby (vib) | Wallace,Billy (p) | Wright,Herman (b) | Finch,Otis 'Candy' (dr)

somethin'else | EMI Germany

494442-2 | CD | The Trio
Gonzalo Rubalcaba Trio
Maiden Voyage | Caravan | On Green Dolphin Street | Hot House | Yesterdays | Woody'n You | Manha De Carnaval(Morning Of The Carnival)
NYC, rec. 1997
Rubalcaba,Gonzalo (p) | Bromberg,Brian (b) | Chambers,Dennis (dr)

537813-2 | CD | Stardust | EAN 724353781323
Ron Carter-Roland Hanna
Stardust
NYC, rec. 6.4.2001
Carter,Ron (b) | Hanna,Sir Roland (p)
Ron Carter Trio
Blues In The Closet
Carter,Ron (b) | Hanna,Sir Roland (p) | White,Lenny (dr)
Ron Carter Quartet
That's Deep
Carter,Ron (b) | Locke,Joe (vib) | Hanna,Sir Roland (p) | White,Lenny (dr)
Ron Carter Quintet
Tamalpais | Nearly | Bohemia After Dark | Tail Feathers
Carter,Ron (b) | Golson,Benny (ts) | Locke,Joe (vib) | Hanna,Sir Roland (p) | White,Lenny (dr)

Specialty | ZYX Music GmbH

SPCD 2170-2 | CD | Little Jimmy Scott | EAN 090204923373
Little Jimmy Scott With The Paul Gayten Band | All Of Me | When Your Lover Has Gone | Everybody's Somebody's Fool | The Loneliest House In the Street | Anytime Anyplace Anywhere | Band Intro | Flying Home
New Orleans,Louisiana, rec. 1951
Scott,Jimmy[Little] (voc) | Hunt,John (tp) | Abrams,Ray (ts) | Numa-Moore,Pee Wee (bs) | Brannon,Teddy (p) | Legange,Thomas (b) | Landis,Wesley (dr)
Dueling Tenors | Body And Soul
Scott,Jimmy[Little] (voc) | Hunt,John (tp) | Butera,Sam (ts) | Abrams,Ray (ts) | Numa-Moore,Pee Wee (bs) | Brannon,Teddy (p) | Legange,Thomas (b) | Landis,Wesley (dr)

Spectra | Universal Music Germany

9811207 | DVD | Laura Fygi Live At The North Sea Jazz | EAN 602498112076
Laura Fygi With Band
That Old Feeling | Let There Be Love | Bewitched Bothered And Bewildered | Don't It Make My Brown Eyes Blue | Guess Who I Saw Today | I Will Wait For You | The First Time | Just One Of Those Things | For Me Formidable | Autumn Leaves | Diamonds Are A Girl's Best Friend | The Nearness Of You | Triste | Corcovado(Quiet Nights) | Como Fué | Rhythm Is Our Business | Almost Like Being In Love | I Get A Kick Out Of You | Extras: | Behind The Scenes | Photogallery
Live at The Northsea Festival, rec. July 2000
Fygi,Laura (voc) | Band

9811660 | DVD | Festival International De Jazz De Montreal | EAN 602498116609
Stanley Jordan Trio
Flying Home | Cousin Mary | Autumn Leaves | All The Children | One Less Bell To Answer | Eleanor Rigby | Willow Weep For Me | What's Going On | Lady In My Life | Stairway To Heaven
Live at The Montreal Jazz Festival, rec. details unknown
Jordan,Stanley (g,el-g) | Moffett,Charnett (b) | Campbell,Tommy (dr)

9811661 | DVD | Festival International De Jazz De Montreal | EAN 602498116616
Lee Ritenour With Special Guests
Night Rhythms | 24th Street Blues | Solo Flute | Zephyr | Rio Sol | Etude | Uptown | Rio Funk
Ritenour,Lee (g) | Valentine,Dave (fl) | Watts,Ernie (ts) | Benoit,David (keyboards) | Grusin,Don (keyboards) | Laboriel,Abe (b) | Novak,Gary (dr)

Stax | ZYX Music GmbH

SCD 8517-2(STS 2040) | CD | Lovejoy
Albert King Blues Band
Honky Tonk Woman | Bay Area Blues | From The Love Of A Woman | Everybody Wants To Go To Heaven
Hollywood,CA, rec. December 1970
King,Albert (g,voc) | Murphy,Matt (g) | Davis,Jesse Edwin (g) | Gallie,John (keyboards) | Dunn,Donald 'Duck' (b) | Keltner,Jim (dr) | Konikoff,Sandy (perc)
Corinne Corinna | She Caught The Katy And Left A Mule To Ride | Lovejoy,Ill. | Going Back To Iuka | Like A Road Leading Home
Muscle Shoals,AL, rec. January 1971
King,Albert (g,voc) | Armstrong,Tippy (g) | Perkins,Wayne (g) | Beckett,Barry (keyboards) | Hood,David (b) | Hawkins,Roger (dr) | Green,Jeannie (voc) | Mt.Zion Singers (voc)

SCD 8534-2 | CD | The Lost Session
She Won't Gimme No Lovin' | Cold In Hand | Stop Lying | All The Way Down | Tell Me What True Love Is | Down The Road I Go | Money Lovin' Women | Sun Gone Down(take 1) | Brand New Razor | Sun Gone Down(take 2)
Los Angeles,CA, rec. 28.8.1971
King,Albert (g,voc) | Mitchell,Blue (tp) | Solomon,Clifford (as,ts) | Watts,Ernie (ts) | Mayall,John (p,org,harm,12-string-g) | Kevin (org) | King,Lee (g) | Taylor,Larry (b) | Selico,Ron (dr)

SCD 8556-2 | CD | Wednesday Night In San Francisco
Watermelon Man | Why You So Mean To Me | I Get Evil | Got To Be Some Changes Made | Personal Manager | Born Under A Bad Sign | Don't Throw Your Love On Me So Strong
Live at The Filmore Auditorium,San Francisco,CA, rec. 26.6.1968
King,Albert (g,voc) | Exon,Willie James (g) | Washington,James (org) | Pointer,Roosevelt (b) | Morgan,Theotis (dr)

SCD 8612-2 | CD | Windy City Blues
Albert King With The Willie Dixon Band
The Lovin'est Woman In Town | Put All In There | Need More Mamma | Love Me To Death
Chicago,Ill, rec. February/March 1970
King,Albert (g,voc) | Murphy,Matt (g) | Young,Mighty Joe (g) | Leake,Lafayette (p) | Upchurch,Phil (b) | Jennings,Morris (dr) | Watson,Murray (tp) | Cameron,John (ts) | Barge,Gene (ts) | Board,Johnny (ts) | Galloway,Tomothy (?)
Otis Spann Band
Dust My Broom | Must Have Been The Devil
Chicago,Ill, rec. 21.11.1964
Spann,Otis (p,voc) | Cotton,James (harm,voc) | Madison,James (g) | Muddy Waters[McKinley Morganfield] (g) | Rector,Milton (b) | Leary,S.P. (dr)
Willie Dixon-Memphis Slim Quintet
Move Me | That's My Baby
Englewood Cliffs,NJ, rec. 3.12.1959
Dixon,Willie (b,voc) | Memphis Slim[Peter Chatman] (p) | Ashby,Harold (ts) | Richardson,Wally (g) | Johnson,Gus (dr)
Billy Boy Arnold Group
Two Drinks Of Wine | Playing With The Blues | Billy Boy's Blues
Chicago,Ill, rec. 30.12.1963
Arnold,Billy Boy (harm,voc) | Young,Mighty Joe (g) | Leake,Lafayette (p) | Arnold,Jerome (el-b) | Blackmon,Junior (dr)
Sunnyland Slim Band
The Devil Is A Busy Man | Every Time I Get To Drinking(take 3) | Tired Of You Clowning
Englewood Cliffs,NJ, rec. 15.9.1960
Sunnyland Slim[Albert Luandrew] (p,voc) | Curtis,King (ts) | Banks,Robert (org) | Gaskin,Leonard (b) | Evans,Belton (dr)
Homesick James Quartet
Gotta Move(alt.take) | The Cloud Is Crying(alt.take) | Homesick Shuffle(alt.take)
Chicago,Ill, rec. 7.1.1964
Homesick James[William Henderson] (g,voc) | Leake,Lafayette (p) | Taylor,Eddie (b-g) | James,Clifton (dr)

Steeplechase | Fenn Music

SCCD 31008 | CD | My Man-Live At The Montmartre
SCS 1008(Audiophile Pressing) | LP | My Man-Live At The Montmartre
Ben Webster Quartet
Sunday | Willow Weep For Me | Exactly Like You | Old Folks | I Got Rhythm | Set Call
rec. Jan./April 1973
Webster,Ben (ts) | Hansen,Ole Kock (p) | Stief,Bo (b) | Riel,Alex (dr)

SCCD 31029 | CD | Tete!
SCS 1029(Audiophile Pressing) | LP | Tete!
Tete Montoliu Trio
Giant Steps | Theme For Ernie | Body And Soul | Solar | I Remember Clifford | Hot House
Copenhagen,Denmark, rec. 28.5.1974
Montoliu,Tete (p) | Orsted-Pedersen,Niels-Henning (b) | Heath,Albert 'Tootie' (dr)

SCCD 31033 | CD | Firm Roots
SCS 1033(Audiophile Pressing) | LP | Firm Roots
Clifford Jordan Quartet
Firm Roots | Angel In The Night | Scorpio | Inga | Voices Deep Within Me | One For Amos
rec. 18.4.1975
Jordan,Clifford (fl,ts) | Walton,Cedar (p) | Jones,Sam (b) | Higgins,Billy (dr)

SCCD 31050 | CD | Swiss Nights-Vol. 1
SCS 1050(Audiophile Pressing) | LP | Swiss Nights-Vol. 1
Dexter Gordon Quartet
Tenor Madness | Wave | You've Changed | Days Of Wine And Roses
rec. 23.8.1975
Gordon,Dexter (ts) | Drew,Kenny (p) | Orsted-Pedersen,Niels-Henning (b) | Riel,Alex (dr)

SCCD 31059 | CD | Don't Look Back
SCS 1059(Audiophile Pressing) | LP | Don't Look Back
Nat Adderley Septet
Funny Funny | K.High | Just A Quickie | I Think I Got It | Home | Don't Look Back
rec. 9.8.1976
Adderley,Nat (co) | McIntyre,Ken (fl,b-cl,as,oboe) | Stubblefield,John (ss,ts) | Gumbs,Onaje Allen (p,el-p,clavinet) | Gumbs,Fernando (b) | Williams,Ira Buddy (dr) | See Yuen,Victor (perc)

SCCD 31079 | CD | Goin' Home
SCS 1079(Audiophile Pressing) | LP | Goin' Home
Archie Shepp-Horace Parlan Duo
Deep River | My Lord What A Morning | Amazing Grace | Sometimes I Feel Like A Motherless Child | Swing Low Sweet Chariot | Goin' Home | Nobody Knows The Trouble I've Seen | Go Down Moses | Steal Away To Jesus
rec. 25.4.1977
Shepp,Archie (ss,ts) | Parlan,Horace (p)

SCCD 31085 | CD | First Set
SCS 1085(Audiophile Pressing) | LP | First Set
Cedar Walton Quartet
Introduction by Cedar Walton | Off Minor | For All We Know | Holy Land | I'm Not So Sure | Ojos De Rojo
rec. 1.10.1977
Walton,Cedar (p) | Berg,Bob (ts) | Jones,Sam (b) | Higgins,Billy (dr)

SCCD 31087 | CD | Brighter Days For You
SCS 1087(Audiophile Pressing) | LP | Brighter Days For You
Monnette Sudler Sextet
Brighter Days For You | To Be Exposed | Natural Accurance | Rightousness | Congo | Moments Of Love | Family
details unknown, rec. 7.11.1977
Sudler,Monnette (g,voc) | Jamal,Khan (marimba) | Collins,Oliver (p) | Brown,Tyrone (b) | Baker,Newman (dr) | Wilson,William Duke (perc,congas)

SCCD 31090 | CD | Swiss Nights Vol.2
SCS 1090(Audiophile Pressing) | LP | Swiss Nights Vol.2
Dexter Gordon Quartet
There Is No Greater Love | Sticky Wicket | Dam That Dream | Montmartre
rec. 23./24.8.1975
Gordon,Dexter (ts) | Drew,Kenny (p) | Orsted-Pedersen,Niels-Henning (b) | Riel,Alex (dr)

SCCD 31110 | CD | Swiss Nights Vol.3
SCS 1110(Audiophile Pressing) | LP | Swiss Nights Vol.3
Jelly Jelly | Didn't We | Sophisticated Lady | Rhythm-A-Ning
Gordon,Dexter (ts,voc) | Drew,Kenny (p) | Orsted-Pedersen,Niels-Henning (b) | Riel,Alex (dr)

SCCD 31111 | CD | A Lazy Afternoon
SCS 1111(Audiophile Pressing) | LP | A Lazy Afternoon
Shirley Horn Trio
I'm Old Fashioned | There's No You | New York's My Home | Why Did I Choose You | Take A Little Time To Smile | Lazy Afternoon | Gentle Rain | Gra'Ma's Hands | I'll Go My Way By Myself
rec. 9.7.1978
Horn,Shirley (p,voc) | Williams,Buster (b) | Hart,Billy (dr)

SCCD 31122 | CD | The Touch Of Your Lips
SCS 1122(Audiophile Pressing) | LP | The Touch Of Your Lips
Chet Baker Trio
I Waited For You | But Not For Me | Autumn In New York | Blue Room | The Touch Of Your Lips | Star Eyes
rec. 21.6.1979
Baker,Chet (tp,voc) | Raney,Doug (g) | Orsted-Pedersen,Niels-Henning (b)

SCCD 31139 | CD | Trouble In Mind
SCS 1139(Audiophile Pressing) | LP | Trouble In Mind
Archie Shepp-Horace Parlan Duo
Back Water Blues | Trouble In Mind | Nobody Knows You When You're Down And Out | Careless Love Blues | How Long Blues | Goin' Down Slow | Courthouse Blues | See See Rider | Make Me A Pallet On The Floor | St.James Infirmary
rec. 6.2.1980
Shepp,Archie (ss,ts) | Parlan,Horace (p)

SCCD 31163 | CD | Mbizo
SCS 1163(Audiophile Pressing) | LP | Mbizo
Johnny Dyani Quartet
Dorkay House | House Arrest | Musician's Musician | Dedicated To Mingus
Live at 'Third Eye',Glasgow,Scotland, rec. 24.2.1981
Dyani,Johnny (b) | Pukwana,Dudu (ss,as) | Epstein,Ed (as,bs) | Jolobe,Churchill (dr)

SCCD 31164 | CD | Violets For Your Furs
SCS 1164(Audiophile Pressing) | LP | Violets For Your Furs
Shirley Horn Trio
Our Love Is Here To Stay | Georgia On My Mind | Gee Baby Ain't I Good To You | Lover Man(Oh,Where Can You Be?) | Violets For Your Furs | Baby Won't You Please Come Home | My Man | More Than You Know | I Didn't Know What Time It Was
North Sea Festival,Den Haag, rec. 10.-12.7.1981
Horn,Shirley (p,voc) | Ables,Charles (b) | Hart,Billy (dr)

SCCD 31168 | CD | This Is Always
SCS 1168(Audiophile Pressing) | LP | This Is Always
Chet Baker Trio
How Deep Is The Ocean | House Of Jade | Love For Sale | This Is Always
rec. 4.10.1979
Baker,Chet (tp,voc) | Raney,Doug (g) | Orsted-Pedersen,Niels-Henning (b)

SCCD 31169 | CD | Mama Rose
SCS 1169(Audiophile Pressing) | LP | Mama Rose
Archie Shepp-Jasper Van't Hof Duo
Contrasts | Mama Rose | Pipo | Kalimba | Recovered Residence
rec. 5.2.1982
Shepp,Archie (ss,ts,recitation) | Van't Hof,Jasper (el-p,keyboards,synth,grand,kalimba,prep.-organ)

SCCD 31179 | CD | Third Set
SCS 1179(Audiophile Pressing) | LP | Third Set
Cedar Walton Quartet
Angel In The Night | Bolivia | Fantasy In D | Blue Monk | Rhythm-A-Ning
Live at The 'Jazzhus' Montmartre,Copenhagen, rec. 1.10.1977
Walton,Cedar (p) | Berg,Bob (ts) | Jones,Sam (b) | Higgins,Billy (dr)

SCCD 31236 | CD | Solo Piano
Paul Bley
Tin Tin Deo | Mariona | Lady Of Chet | Peace Pipe | Blues Reconstruction | Slipping | Gee Baby Ain't I Good To You | And Now The Queen | You Go To My Head | Carla | Clopin Clopant | Finale | If I Loved You | So Hard It Hurts | If I Should Lose You | Gladys | Someone To Watch Over Me | Ostinato II
Copenhagen,Denmark, rec. 2.4.1988
Bley,Paul (p-solo)

SCCD 31373 | CD | Revelation
Dexter Gordon-Benny Bailey Quintet
At Ronnie's | Medley: | Polka Dots And Moonbeams- | I Can't Get Started- | Days Of Wine And Roses | The Shadow Of Your Smile | Revelation
details unknown, rec. Fall 1974
Bailey,Benny (tp) | Gordon,Dexter (ts) | Sjösten,Lars (p) | Hultcrantz,Torbjörn (b) | Curtis,Jual (dr)

SCCD 31514 | CD | Rascality
Tony Purrone Trio
Remember Me | Blue In Green | After PM | Black Narcissus | Body And Soul | Petits Machines | Afro-Centric | Twelve More Bars To Go
details unknown, rec. March 2001
Purrone,Tony (g) | Anderson,Dave (el-b,fretless-b) | Arpino,Thierry (dr)

SCCD 31515 | CD | Hearsay
Rich Perry Quartet
King Baby | Hearsay | Sam | Penance | Bigos | Gymel | Then From Now | On Clouds,Danced
Perry,Richard 'Rich' (ts) | Lampert,Steve (tp) | Irwin,Dennis (b) | Hirshfield,Jeff (dr)

SCCD 31516 | CD | Songbook 2
Vic Juris Trio
Long Ago And Far Away | Poor Butterfly | Django | Swedish Pastry | You Won't Forget Me | Gloria's Step | Giant Steps | One True Friend | Golden Earrings | Peace | Locomotive
Juris,Vic (g) | Formanek,Michael (b) | Hirshfield,Jeff (dr)

SCCD 31517 | CD | Match Point
Ron McClure Quartet
Mainstay | Walter Davis | Shorter Story | Moon Ray | Cellular Expansions | West Side Blues | In Search Of Times Lost | Something New For You | The Day After Christmas | Match Point
details unknown, rec. August 2001
McClure,Ron (b) | Levy,Jed (ts) | DeVos,Bob (g) | Brillinger,Jeff (dr)

SCCD 31518 | CD | United
Ari Ambrose Trio
Blue Daniel | My Ideal | Four And One | Once I Loved | Mr.Day | How Can You Believe | Star Crossed Lovers | United
details unknown, rec. December 2000
Ambrose,Ari (ts) | Anderson,Jay (b) | Williams,Jeff (dr)

SCCD 31519 | CD | Return To Copenhagen
George Colligan
Return To Copenhagen | What Is The Meaning Of This | Underground Emotions(Way Way Down) | Abandon All Hope Ye Who Enter Here | Chelsea Bridge | Inner Urge | When You Love A Woman But She Don't Love You Back Blues | Living In A Dream World | Better Days Ahead | Chance | Everything Happens To Me
SteepleChase Digital Studio,Ganlose,Denmark, rec. March 1999
Colligan,George (p-solo)

SCCD 31520 | CD | Shades Of Light
Conrad Herwig-Andy LaVerne
Three Flowers | Tones For Joan's Bones | Crystal Silence | Bessie's Blues | If You Never Came To Me | Shades Of Light | Black Narcissus | Think Of Me | African Flower | In Your Own Sweet Way
SteepleChase Digital Studio,Ganlose,Denmark, rec. April 2000
Herwig,Conrad (tb) | LaVerne,Andy (p)

SCCD 31521 | CD | The Rainbow People
Dexter Gordon-Benny Bailey Quintet
The Rainbow People | I Can't Get Started | C Jam Blues | Montmartre
details unknown, rec. November 1974
Bailey,Benny (tp) | Gordon,Dexter (ts) | Sjösten,Lars (p) | Hultcrantz,Torbjörn (b) | Curtis,Jual (dr)

SCCD 31522 | CD | Jam Session Vol.1
Jam Session
Change Up | Triplicate | Old Folks- | Lush Life- | I'm Old Fashioned- | Sticks Up | Go Tenor
details unknown, rec. March 1996
Jam Session | Schneider,Larry (ss,ts) | Margitza,Rick (ss,ts) | Potter,Chris (b-cl,ts) | LaVerne,Andy (p) | Andersen,Jay (b) | Hart,Billy (dr)

SCCD 31523 | CD | Jam Session Vol.2
Billie's Bounce | Strike Zone | Who Cares | Subway | Bluebird | Twenty-Five | Wee
Jam Session | Juris,Vic (g) | Stryker,Dave (g) | Purrone,Tony (g) | Colley,Scott (b) | Copeland,Keith (dr)

SCCD 31524 | CD | Blue To The Bone III | EAN 716043152421
Dave Stryker Octet
Stan's Shuffle | Complicity | Crazy House | If 6 Was 9 | For Jack And T | Going Home | So Long Eric | Soulful Mr. Timmons | Doin' The Bone
SteepleChase Digital Studio,Ganlose,Denmark, rec. March 2001
Stryker,Dave (g) | Lynch,Brian (tp,fl-h) | Gayton,Clark (tb) | Slagle,Steve (as) | Parsons,Bob (bs) | Williams,James (p) | Anderson,Jay (b) | Horner,Tim (dr)

SCCD 31525 | CD | Rothko | EAN 716043152520
Dave Ballou Quartet
The Nearness Of You | No.5 | Stella By Starlight | Rothko | I Should Care | Ivan Illych | Herb | Art Deco | Solar
SteepleChase Digital Studio,Ganlose,Denmark, rec. August 2001
Ballou,Dave (tp) | Colligan,George (p) | Brown,Cameron (b) | Sarin,Michael (dr)

SCCD 31526 | CD | Jam Session Vol.3 | EAN 716043152629
Jam Session
Jamboree | Private Eye | You Are Too Beautiful | April | I Can't Get Started | Hat Trick | My One And Only Love | How High The Mood | Airegin
SteepleChase Digital Studio,Ganlose,Denmark, rec. April 1997
Oatts,Dick (as,ts) | Herring,Vincent (as,ts) | Braden,Don (ts) | LaVerne,Andy (p) | Anderson,Jay (b) | Drummond,Billy (dr)

SCCD 31527 | CD | Jam Session Vol.4 | EAN 716043152728
Invitation | A Brilliant Madness | Touch Her Soft Lips And Part | Chief Crazy Horse | Juju | Four Openers
SteepleChase Digital Studio,Ganlose,Denmark, rec. September 1997
Jensen,Ingrid (tp,fl-h) | Newsome,Sam (ss) | Turner,Mark (ts) | Colligan,George (p) | Weidenmüller,Johannes (b) | Rückert,Jochen (dr)

SCCD 31528 | CD | Gone With The Wind | EAN 716043152827
Lee Konitz-Matt Wilson
Gone With The Wind | Song With Wind | Winding Up | Brush-Wind | No Ill Wind | Brush Thing | Rhythmic Wind | Stickin' | Snare Rattle | Rapids | Foxtrot | Tommin' | Winding Town
SteepleChase Digital Studio,Ganlose,Denmark, rec. March 2002
Konitz,Lee (as) | Wilson,Matt (dr)

SCCD 31529 | CD | Round And Round | EAN 716043152926
Jed Levy Quartet
Round And Round | Subtle Rebuttal | Holiday | People In Time | Hillside | Cherokee | These Are My Dreams | Buck's County Blues | Projectile

Levy,Jed (ts) | Gerhardt,Bill (p) | McGuirk | Brillinger,Jeff (dr)

SCCD 31530 | CD | Fantasy Exit | EAN 716043153022
Harold Danko Trio
Hi Fly | Mrs.Parker Of K.C. | Fantasy Exit | Born To Be Blue | Smoke House | Rocker | Tea Time | In And Out | Lullababy
Danko,Harold (p) | Formanek,Michael (b) | Hirschfield,Jeff (dr)

SCCD 31531 | CD | Inside Chicago Vol.3 | EAN 716043153121
Brad Goode-Von Freeman Sextet
The Blues Walk | You And The Night And The Music | Just You Just Me | A Night In Tunisia | Star Eyes | Blue Moon | What Is This Thing Called Love
Live at The Green Mill Jazz Club,Chicagi,Ill, rec. January/February 1993
Goode,Brad (tp) | Freeman,Von (ts) | McKee,Paul (tb) | Perrillo,Ron (p) | Miller,Stewart (b) | Rummage,Bob (dr)

SCCD 31532 | CD | Inside Chicago Vol.4 | EAN 716043153220
You Stepped Out Of A Dream | Speak Low | Bye Bye Blackbird | You And The Night And The Music | Just You Just Me | I Hear A Rhapsody | Oleo
Goode,Brad (tp) | Freeman,Von (ts) | McKee,Paul (tb) | Perrillo,Ron (p) | Miller,Stewart (b) | Rummage,Bob (dr)

SCCD 31533 | CD | At Eastman | EAN 716043153329
Rich Perry Quintet
Doxy | How Deep Is The Ocean | Acquiescence | Bemsha Swing | You Don't Know What Love Is | Stella By Starlight
Live at Kilbourn Hall,Eastman School Of Music,Rocheste,NY, rec. 21.3.2001
Perry,Richard 'Rich' (ts) | Jenkins,Clay (tp) | Danko,Harold (p) | Campbell,Jeff (b) | Thompson,Rich (dr)

SCCD 31534 | CD | My Foolish Heart | EAN 716043153428
Don Friedman Quartet
Positivity | My Foolish Heart | Desafinado | Memory Of Scotty | Bye Bye Blackbird | Petite Fleur | Swans | Almost Everything
SteepleChase Digital Studio,Ganlose,Denmark, rec. April 2000
Friedman,Don (p) | Levy,Jed (ts) | Ferguson,Tim (b) | Jefferson,Tony (dr)

SCCD 31535 | CD | Jazmin | EAN 716043153527
Ari Ambrose Quartet
Jazmin | When Your Lover Has Gone | Ila | Along Came Betty | Dollar Shot | Baubles | Who Knows
SteepleChase Digital Studio,Ganlose,Denmark, rec. March 2001
Ambrose,Ari (ts) | Leonhart,Michael 'Mike' (tp) | Martin,Joe (b) | Montalbano,Rick (dr)

SCCD 31536 | CD | Jam Session Vol.5 | EAN 716043153626
Jam Session
Dig | Up Jumped Spring | Body And Soul | Strike Zone | If You Could See Me Now | Afterthought | Duke Ellington's Sound Of Love | World Wide Web | Onion Straw
SteepleChase Digital Studio,Ganlose,Denmark, rec. April 1997
Wendholt,Scott (tp) | Ballou,Dave (tp) | Gisbert,Gregory 'Greg' (tp) | LaVerne,Andy (p) | Anderson,Jay (b) | Drummond,Billy (dr)

SCCD 31537 | CD | Jam Session Vol.6 | EAN 716043153725
It's You Or No One | Short Hare | El Gaucho | S.K.J.
SteepleChase Digital Studio,Ganlose,Denmark, rec. September 1997
Norris,Alex (tp) | Frahm,Joel (ss) | Ambrose,Ari (ts) | Colligan,George (p) | Ephross,David (b) | Hoenig,Ari (dr)

SCCD 31538 | CD | Timeline | EAN 716043153824
John Abercrombie-Andy LaVerne
My Funny Valentine | Darn That Dream | You Go To My Head | Skating In Central Park | Inner Voice | Stairway To The Stars | I'm Getting Sentimental Over You | All Across The City | Chance Meeting | Turn Out The Stars | Adagio
SteepleChase Digital Studio,Ganlose,Denmark, rec. September 2002
Abercrombie,John (g) | LaVerne,Andy (p)

SCCD 31539 | CD | Preservation | EAN 716043153923
Ted Brown Quartet
Three Little Words | Yesterdays | The Man I Love | Preservation | Lover Man(Oh,Where Can You Be?) | Broadway | Willow Weep For Me | Somebody Loves Me | Little Girl
SteepleChase Digital Studio,Ganlose,Denmark, rec. November 2002
Brown,Ted (ts) | Danko,Harold (p) | Irwin,Dennis (b) | Hirshfield,Jeff (dr)

SCCD 31540 | CD | Remember When | EAN 716043154029
Steve LaSpina Quintet
Madness | A Better Place | Foreward Motion | Remember When | When There's Nothing Left To Do Or Say | Lost In The Abyss | How I Miss You | Seduction | When The Time Comes
LaSpina,Steve (b) | Ballou,Dave (tp) | Rathbun,Andrew (ss,ts) | Juris,Vic (g) | Hirshfield,Jeff (dr)

SCCD 31541 | CD | Walkin' Up | EAN 716043154128
LeeAnn Ledgerwood Trio
This Is For Albert | Lonnie's Lament | Out Of This World | Black Nile | Ida Lupino | Walkin' Up | If You Could See Me Now | Passion Dance
SteepleChase Digital Studio,Ganlose,Denmark, rec. September 2002
Ledgerwood,Lee Ann (p) | Davis,John Graham (b) | Lewis,Brandon (dr)

SCCD 31542 | CD | Path Ways | EAN 716043154227
Michael Cochrane Quartet
When Will The Blues Leave | Samba Do Aviao(Song Of The Jet) | Thinking Of Wayne | Pathways | Visions | Stars Fell On Alabama | Nocturnal | Broken Wing | Samba Two Step | The Line Forms At The End
SteepleChase Digital Studio,Ganlose,Denmark, rec. November 2002
Cochrane,Michael (p) | Malach,Bob (ts) | Hill,Calvin (b) | Hirshfield,Jeff (dr)

SCCD 31543 | CD | Flight To Norway | EAN 716043154326
Duke Jordan Trio
Jealous Blues | Undecided Lady | If I Did-Would You | The Bullet | I Should Care | I Remember April | Ornithology | Dancer's Call | Misty | On Green Dolphin Street | My Heart Skips A Beat | A Night In Tunisia
Live at Kunstsentret,Hoevikodden,Norway, rec. 10.11.1978
Jordan,Duke (p) | Little,Wilbur (b) | Richmond,Dannie (dr)

SCCD 31545 | CD | My Foolish Heart | EAN 716043153428
Don Friedman Quartet
Positivity | My Foolish Heart | Desafinado | Memory Of Scotty | Bye Bye Blackbird | Petite Fleur | Swans | Almost Everything
SteepleChase Digital Studio,Ganlose,Denmark, rec. April 2000
Friedman,Don (p) | Levy,Jed (ts) | Ferguson,Tim (b) | Jefferson,Tony (dr)

SCCD 31551 | CD | Trilix | EAN 716043155125
Harold Danko Trio
Flight To Jordan | Pee Wee | Elm | I Wished On The Moon | Blood Count | Monk's Dream | What Was | Damned If I Know | Sister Salvation
SteepleChase Digital Studio,Ganlose,Denmark, rec. April 2003
Danko,Harold (p) | Formanek,Michael (b) | Hirshfield,Jeff (dr)

SCCD 31552 | CD | Louisville | EAN 716043155224
Louis Smith Quintet
Buzzy | Isfahan | Algo Bueno | I'll Close My Eyes | Ande | For All We Know | Days Of Wine And Roses | Scrapple From The Apple
Smith,Louis (tp) | Gordon,Jon (as) | Cochrane,Michael (p) | Hill,Calvin (b) | Hirshfield,Jeff (dr)

SCCD 31553 | CD | While My Guitar Gently Weeps | EAN 716043155323
Vic Juris Trio
Do You Hear The Voices That You Left Behind | Magenta | While My Guitar Gently Weeps | The Visit | Ladies Choice | Careful | Action | Road Song | Soulful Spirit | Jean De Fleur
SteepleChase Digital Studio,Ganlose,Denmark, rec. November 2002
Juris,Vic (g) | Chandler,Jesse (org) | Horner,Tim (dr)

SCCD 31554 | CD | Jam Session Vol.9 | EAN 716043155422
Jam Session
Lady Bird | Triplicate | Watermelon Man | Ballad Medley: | The Nearness Of You- | Old Folks- | Here's That Rainy Day- | Body And Soul | Fourth Waltz | Cedar's Blues
SteepleChase Digital Studio,Ganlose,Denmark, rec. April 1998
Jam Session | Turner,Mark (ts) | Braden,Don (ts) | Greene,Jimmy (ts) | LaVerne,Andy (p) | LaSpina,Steve (b) | Drummond,Billy (dr)

SCCD 31555 | CD | Jam Session Vol.10 | EAN 716043155521
Seven Come Eleven | Nardis | My Little Suede Shoes | Orchids | Sippin' At Bells | The Three Muscateers | Better Git It In Your Soul | Half Nelson
SteepleChase Digital Studio,Ganlose,Denmark, rec. December 1998
Jam Session | Raney,Doug (g) | Stryker,Dave (g) | Bryant,Freddie (g) | LaSpina,Steve (b) | Drummond,Billy (dr)

SCCD 31556 | CD | Dancing Foot | EAN 716043155620
Dave Ballou Quartet
Dancing Foot | Pinky | Bobblehead | Sadhana | Skippy | Prayer | Stagnate | Norton Utilities | Anya Goes East
SteepleChase Digital Studio,Ganlose,Denmark, rec. April 2003
Ballou,Dave (tp,fl-h) | Formanek,Michael (b) | Herbert,John (b) | Norton,Kevin (vib,dr,perc)

SCCD 31557 | CD | Venus Perplexed | EAN 716043155729
Steve Lampert Group
Venus Perplexed Suite: | R U There? | Music Box | Wbirl | Aftershock | Still There | Metaphor Of Travel
Brooklyn,NY, rec. Spring 2000
Lampert,Steve (tp) | Perry,Richard 'Rich' (ts) | Torres,Gene (el-b) | Cutler,Rick (dr) | Gomez,Carlos 'Bala' (congas)
Geometry
Lampert,Steve (tp) | Perry,Richard 'Rich' (ts) | Blenzig,Charles (p) | Torres,Gene (el-b) | Cutler,Rick (dr) | Gomez,Carlos 'Bala' (congas)
Either Or
Lampert,Steve (p) | Perry,Richard 'Rich' (ts) | Locke,Joe (vib) | Torres,Gene (el-b) | Cutler,Rick (dr) | Gomez,Carlos 'Bala' (congas)
Telephony
Locke,Joe (vib)
Held In Reflection | Venus Perplexed | Water Test With Question
Lampert,Steve (synth,samples)

SCCD 36032 | CD | Loose Walk | EAN 716043603220
Dexter Gordon With The Kenny Drew Trio
There'll Never Be Another You | Introduction by Dexter Gordon | Come Rain Or Come Shine | Introduction by Dexter Gordon | I Should Care | Introduction by Dexter Gordon | Loose Walk
Live at The 'Jazzhus' Montmartre,Copenhagen, rec. 24.6.1965
Gordon,Dexter (ts) | Drew,Kenny (p) | Orsted-Pedersen,Niels-Henning (b) | Riel,Alex (dr)

SCCD 37021/22 | 2 CD | Live At Montmartre(CD=Stan's Party)
SCS 1073/74(Audiophile Pressing) | 2 LP | Live At Montmartre(CD=Stan's Party)
Stan Getz Quartet
Morning Star | Lady Sings The Blues | Cancao Do Sol | Lush Life | Stan's Blues | Infant Eyes | Lester Left Town | Eiderdown | Blues For Dorte | Cancao Do Sol | La Fiesta | Con Alma
Live at The 'Jazzhus' Montmartre,Copenhagen, rec. 27.-29.1.1977
Getz,Stan (ts) | Brackeen,JoAnne (p,el-p) | Orsted-Pedersen,Niels-Henning (b) | Hart,Billy (dr)

SCS 1055(Audiophile Pressing) | LP | Double Bass
SCCD 31055 | CD | Double Bass
Niels-Henning Orsted-Pedersen/Sam Jones Quartet
Falling In Love With Love | Giant Steps | Miss Morgan | Au Privave | Yesterdays
rec. 15./16.2.1976
Orsted-Pedersen,Niels-Henning (b) | Jones,Sam (b) | Catherine,Philip (g) | Higgins,Billy (dr)
Niels-Henning Orsted-Pedersen/Sam Jones Quintet
A Notation | I Fall In Love Too Easily | Little Train
Orsted-Pedersen,Niels-Henning (b) | Jones,Sam (b) | Catherine,Philip (g) | Higgins,Billy (dr) | Heath,Albert 'Tootie' (dr,perc)

SCS 1125(Audiophile Pressing) | LP | Dancing On The Tables
SCCD 31125 | CD | Dancing On The Tables
Niels-Henning Orsted-Pedersen Quartet
Dancing On The Tables | Future Child | Jeg Gik Mig Ud En Sommerdag | Evening Song | Clouds
rec. 3./4.7.& 30.8.1979
Orsted-Pedersen,Niels-Henning (b) | Liebman,Dave (alto-fl,ss,ts) | Scofield,John (g) | Hart,Billy (dr)

SCS 1142(Audiophile Pressing) | LP | Daybreak
SCCD 31142 | CD | Daybreak
Chet Baker Trio
For Minors Only | Daybreak | Broken Wing | Down
rec. 4.10.1979
Baker,Chet (tp,voc) | Raney,Doug (g) | Orsted-Pedersen,Niels-Henning (b)

SCS 1149(Audiophile Pressing) | LP | Looking At Bird
SCCD 31149 | CD | Looking At Bird
Archie Shepp/Niels-Henning Orsted-Pedersen Duo
Moose The Mooche | Embraceable You | Ornithology | Billie's Bounce | Yardbird Suite | Blues For Alice | How Deep Is The Ocean | Confirmation
rec. 7.2.1980
Shepp,Archie (ss,ts) | Orsted-Pedersen,Niels-Henning (b)

SCS 1186(Audiophile Pressing) | LP | Afrika
SCCD 31186 | CD | Afrika
Johnny Dyani Septet
Blame It On The Boers | Appear | Pretoria Three | Needle Children | Kalahari Lives | Grandmother's Teaching | Funk Dem Dudu | Kippieology | Dedicated Abdullah Ibrahim | Grandmother's Teaching(take 1)
Copenhagen,Denmark, rec. 1.10.1983
Dyani,Johnny (p,b) | Epstein,Ed (as,ts) | Davis,Charles (as) | Ostergren,Thomas (b) | Mathews,Gilbert (dr) | Smith,Rudy (steel-dr) | Dyani,Thomas Akuru (congas)

Stony Plain | Fenn Music

SPCD 1260 | CD | Conversation In Swing Guitar
Duke Robillard-Herb Ellis Quintet
Flying Home | Easin' In | Jivin' In Rhythm | Just Squeeze Me(But Don't Tease Me) | Avalon | Blue Brew | Stuffy
West Greenwich,Rhode Island, rec. 1999
Ellis,Herb (g) | Robillard,Duke (g) | Holmes,Terry (g) | Ballou,Marty (b) | Richards,Marty (dr)

SPCD 1286 | CD | Goin' To Kansas City | EAN 772532128629
Jay McShann Quartet
Kansas City | Trouble In Mind | When I Grow Too Old To Dream | Nasty Attitude | My Chile | Wrong Neighborhood | Just For You | One Woman's Man | Doo Wah Doo | 'Fore Day Rider | Ain't Nobody's Business | The Fish Fry Boogie | Crying Won't Make Me Stay
Kansas City,MO, rec. details unknown
McShann,Jay (p,voc) | Robillard,Duke (g,el-g) | Able,Milt (b) | Ruskin,Tommy (dr)
Confessin' The Blues
McShann,Jay (p,voc) | Robillard,Duke (g,el-g) | Able,Milt (b) | Ruskin,Tommy (dr) | Muldaur,Maria (voc)
Kansas City(revisited) | Some Kinda Crazy | Jay And Johnnie Conversation
McShann,Jay (p,voc) | Johnson,Johnnie (p,voc) | Robillard,Duke (g,el-g) | Able,Milt (b) | Ruskin,Tommy (dr)
Jay at home and at his Piano(Interview 19:51)
McShann,Jay (p,talking)

SPCD 1292 | CD | More Conversations In Swing Guitar | EAN 772532129220
Duke Robillard-Herb Ellis Quintet
Moten Swing | Train To Texas | Robbin's Nest | Just You Just Me | Blues For Terry | End Of Session Jump
Rhode Island, rec. details unknown
Ellis,Herb (g) | Robillard,Duke (g) | Holmes,Terry (g) | Ballou,Marty (b) | Richards,Marty (dr)

Storyville | Fenn Music

109 1001 | CD | The Golden Years Of Revival Jazz,Sampler
Adrian Bentzon's Jazzband
That's A Plenty
Copenhagen,Denmark, rec. 16.11.1953
Bentzon,Adrian (p) | Johnsson,Gunnar (co) | Johansen,Henrik (cl) | Bentzon,Fridolin (b) | Karn,Ole (dr)
Perdido Street Blues
Aarhus, Denmark, rec. 2.1.1955
Bentzon,Adrian (p) | Johnsson,Gunnar (co) | Johansen,Henrik (cl) | Bentzon,Fridolin (b) | Karn,Ole (dr)
Albert Nicholas With Adrian Bentzon's Jazzband
Basin Street Blues
Nicholas,Albert (cl) | Bentzon,Adrian (p) | Johnsson,Gunnar (co) | Johansen,Henrik (cl) | Bentzon,Fridolin (b) | Karn,Ole (dr)
Cy Laurie Jazz Band
Don't Go 'Way Nobody
London,GB, rec. July 1954
Laurie,Cy (cl) | Fairweather,Al (tp) | Picard,John (tb) | Thomas,Alan (p) | Potter,John (bj) | Wood,Dave (b) | McKay,Ron (dr)
Sandy Brown's Jazz Band
Everybody Loves Saturday Night
London,GB, rec. 1.4.1955
Brown,Sandy (cl,voc) | Fairweather,Al (tp) | Davies,John R.T. (tb) | Thomas,Alan (p) | Umansky,Mo (bj) | Parker,Brian (b) | Burbidge,Graham (dr)
Henrik Johansen With The City Ramblers
Trouble In Mind
Copenhagen,Denmark, rec. 12.9.1956
Johansen,Henrik (cl) | City Ramblers | Bateson,Chris (tp) | Quaye,Russell (kazoo,g) | Sims,Hylda (g,voc) | Elliot,Jack (g) | Buquet,Anthomy Bo Bo (b,tuba) | Sutton,Alan 'Little Bear' (wbd)
Graham Stewart And His New Orleans Band
Shake That Thing
London,GB, rec. 2.1.1958
Stewart,Graham (tb,voc) | Elsdon,Alan (tp) | McKerrow,Ian (cl) | Root,Alan (p) | Barton,Johnny (bj) | Johnson,Johnny (b) | Mawford,Peter (dr)
Adrian Bentzon's Jazzband
Struttin' With Some Barbecue
Live at K.B. Hallen,Copenhagen, rec. 1960
Bentzon,Adrian (p) | Jensen,Theis (tp) | Andersen,Erik 'Krolle' (cl) | Poulsen,Freddy 'Freak' (b) | Jensen,Henrik Eigil (dr)
Ricardo's Jazzmen
Dusty Rag
Copenhagen,Denmark, rec. 6.11.1961
Hansen,Niels Richard (bj) | Thomsen,Jorn L. (tp) | Lindgreen,Ole 'Fessor' (tb) | Holbroe,Hans (cl) | Johansen,Arne Birger (b) | Moller,Thorkild (dr)
Papa Benny's Jazzband
King Of The Zulus
Copenhagen,Denmark, rec. 9.12.1961
Nielsen,Benny 'Papa' (tb) | Rasmussen,Kai 'Satch' (tp) | Hagemann,Per (cl) | Schiorring,Erik (bj) | Engberg,Alf (b) | Madsen,Knud Ryskov (dr)
Lennie Baldwin's Dauphin Street Six
Ace In The Hole(alt.take)
Copenhagen,Denmark, rec. 13.2.1962
Baldwin,Lennie (tb,voc) | Barrett,Dave (tp) | Crocker,John (cl) | Hart,Roy (bj) | Mason,Dick (b) | Prince,Viv (dr)
Papa Bue's Viking Jazzband
Annie Laurie
Copenhagen,Denmark, rec. 16.1.1962
Papa Bue's Viking Jazzband | Hansen,Finn Otto (tp) | Jensen,Arne Bue (tb,ld) | Svare,Jorgen (cl) | Petersen,Bjarne Liller (bj) | Lindschouw,Ib (dr)
Tweed And Tropical
Copenhagen,Denmark, rec. 11.4.1962
Papa Bue's Viking Jazzband | Hansen,Finn Otto (tp) | Jensen,Arne Bue (tb,ld) | Svare,Jorgen (cl) | Petersen,Bjarne Liller (bj) | Lindschouw,Ib (dr)
Finn Air
Copenhagen,Denmark, rec. August 1962
Papa Bue's Viking Jazzband | Hansen,Finn Otto (tp) | Jensen,Arne Bue (tb,ld) | Svare,Jorgen (cl) | Petersen,Bjarne Liller (bj) | Madsen,Knud Ryskov (dr)
Leonardo Pedersen's Jazzkapel
Muggin' Lightly
Copenhagen,Denmark, rec. 3.3.1963
Pedersen,Hans Leonardo (cl,as) | Moller,Jorgen (co) | Eghjort,Mogens (co) | Bredberg,Arne (tb) | Hansen,Hans J. (cl,as) | Tvaergard,Per (p) | Nielsen,Ove (bj) | Kuhn,Karsten (b) | Larsen,John (tuba) | Jensen,Flemming (dr)
Doug Richford's London Jazzmen
Spooky Takes A Holiday | Runnin' Wild | Beedle Um Bum
Copenhagen,Denmark, rec. 10.10.1963
Richford,Doug (cl,voc) | Tatum,Dick (tp) | Hayres,Bill (tb) | Sealey,Paul (bj) | Herman,Mookie (b) | Bowden,Colin (dr)
Theis/Nyegaard Jazzband
Ory's Creole Trombone
Copenhagen,Denmark, rec. 24.10.1964
Jensen,Theis (tp) | Nyegaard,Peter (tb) | Andersen,Erik 'Krolle' (cl) | Jorgensen,Orla Levin (bj) | Poulsen,Freddy 'Freak' (b) | Bodker,Niels (dr)

STCD 4203 | CD | Will You Make My Soup Hot & Silver
Carsten Dahl Trio
Autumn Leaves | Giant Steps | Will You Make My Soup Hot And Silver | On Green Dolphin Street | Take Five | All Blues | Caravan | Freddie Freeloader | I Thought About You | There Is No Greater Love | Someday My Prince Will Come | Ain't Sorry Blues
Copenhagen,Denmark, rec. 7.12.1996
Dahl,Carsten (p,org) | Ginman,Lennart V. (b) | Rifbjerk,Frands (dr,perc)

STCD 4212 | CD | Some Aspects Of Water
Geri Allen Trio
Feed The Fire | This Is The End Of... A Beautiful Friendship - (This Is The End Of...) A Beautiful Friendship | Slin
Live at SAS Falconer Center,Copenhagen,Denmark, rec. 17.3.1996
Allen,Geri (p) | Danielsson,Palle (b) | White,Lenny (dr)
Geri Allen Trio With Johny Coles
Old Folks
Live at Kulturhus,Tonder,Denmark, rec. 15.3.1996
Allen,Geri (p) | Coles,Johnny (tp) | Danielsson,Palle (b) | White,Lenny (dr)
Geri Allen And The Jazzpar 1996 Nonet
Smooth Attitudes | Some Aspects Of Water
Jazzpar 1996 Nonet | Coles,Johnny (fl-h) | Bolberg Pedersen,Herik (tp,fl-h) | Ipsen,Kjeld (tb) | Windfeld,Axel (tuba) | Hove,Michael (fl,cl,ss) | Markussen,Uffe (fl,cl,b-cl,ss,ts) | Allen,Geri (p) | Danielsson,Palle (b) | White,Lenny (dr)

STCD 4230 | CD | Jazzpar 98
Jim Hall Jazzpar Quartet
Stella By Starlight | Chelsea Bridge | Mr.Blues
Copenhagen,Denmark, rec. 3.& 5.4.1998
Hall,Jim (g) | Potter,Chris (ts) | Ovesen,Thomas (b) | Clarke,Terry (dr)
Jim Hall Jazzpar Quartet +4
Quartet + 4
Hall,Jim (g) | Potter,Chris (ts) | Ovesen,Thomas (b) | Clarke,Terry (dr) | Zapolski String Quartet | Zapolski,Alexander (v) | Soelberg,Jacob (v) | Teilmann,Iben Bramsnaes (viola) | Louro,Vanja (cello)
Jim Hall With The Zapolski Quartet
Thesis | Purple Haze | In A Sentimental Mood
Hall,Jim (g) | Zapolski String Quartet | Zapolski,Alexander (v) | Soelberg,Jacob (v) | Teilmann,Iben Bramsnaes (viola) | Louro,Vanja (cello)

STCD 4245 | CD | This Will Be
Chris Potter Quartet
This Will Be | Okinawa | In A Sentimental Mood
Live at The Jazzpar Concerts,Copenhagen, rec. 9.-12.3.2000
Potter,Chris (ts) | Hays,Kevin (p) | Colley,Scott (b) | Drummond,Billy (dr)
Chris Potter & Jazzpar Septet
Jazzpar Suite: | Chorale- | Medium- | Rubato- | Tribute To Hodges & Ellington- | Ballad- | Folk Tune-
Live at The Jazzpar Concerts,Copenhagen, rec. 10.& 12.3.2000
Potter,Chris (fl,ss,ts) | Tranberg,Kasper (co) | Fuglsang,Peter (fl,b-cl) | Hays,Kevin (p) | Fischer,Jacob (g) | Colley,Scott (b) | Drummond,Billy (dr)

STCD 4252 | CD | Still Fiddling | EAN 717101425228
Svend Asmussen Quartet
The Best Things In Life Are Free | How Deep Is The Ocean | My Yiddish Momma | Silly Shuffle | Jeg Elsker Dig | Down South Camp Meeting | My Man Is Gone Now | Hallelujah | Sermon For Stuff | It Had To Be You | Shalom Elechem | Memories Of You
Allerod,Denmark, rec. June-November 1999
Asmussen,Svend (v) | Fischer,Jacob (g) | Lundgaard,Jesper (b) | Tanggaard,Aage (dr)

STCD 4253 | CD | Headin' Home | EAN 717101425327
Martin Schrack Quartet
The City | My Blues | Keep Them Chords Comin' | Alone Together
details unknown, rec. 26./27.2.2001
Schrack,Martin (p) | Ellis,John (ss,ts) | Ginsburg,Josh (b) | Campagnol,Niclas (dr)
Martin Schrack Quintet feat.Tom Harrell
Summer Bossa | To Elvin And Cleve | Dedication To Tom Harrell | Headin' Home
Schrack,Martin (p) | Harrell,Tom (tp,fl-h) | Ellis,John (ss,ts) | Ginsburg,Josh (b) | Campagnol,Niclas (dr)

STCD 5506 | CD | The Golden Years Of Revival Jazz,Vol.1
Chris Barber's Jazz Band
Tiger Rag | Ice Cream | Saratoga Swing | Precious Lord Take My Hand
Studenterforeningen,Copenhagen,Denmark, rec. 9.10.1954
Barber,Chris (tb) | Halcox,Pat (tp,voc) | Sunshine,Monty (cl) | Donegan,Tony 'Lonnie' (bj,voc) | Bray,Jim (b) | Bowden,Ron (dr)
Cy Laurie's New Orleans Septet
Weather Bird | Minor Drag | Margie
Det Nye Casino,Arhus,Denmark, rec. 22.8.1954
Laurie,Cy (cl) | Fairweather,Al (tp) | Picard,John (tb) | Thomas,Alan (p) | Potter,John (bj) | Christiansen,Ole (b) | McKay,Ron (dr,wbd,voc) | Banks,Billy (voc)
Adrian Bentzon's Jazzband
Creole Love Call
Copenhagen,Denmark, rec. 21.6.1957
Bentzon,Adrian (p) | Jensen,Theis (co) | Andersen,Erik 'Krolle' (cl) | Poulsen,Freddy 'Freak' (b) | Jensen,Henrik Eigil (dr)
Minor Drag | Georgia Grind | Shim-Me-Sha-Wabble
Copenhagen,Denmark, rec. 22.6.1957
Bentzon,Adrian (p) | Jensen,Theis (co) | Andersen,Erik 'Krolle' (cl) | Poulsen,Freddy 'Freak' (bj) | Jensen,Henrik Eigil (dr)
Ken Colyer's Jazzmen
If I Ever Cease To Love You | Wabash Blues
Gentofte Hotel,Copenhagen,Denmark, rec. 19.4.1953
Colyer,Ken (tp) | Barber,Chris (tb) | Sunshine,Monty (cl) | Donegan,Tony 'Lonnie' (bj) | Bray,Jim (b) | Bowden,Ron (dr)
Henrik Johansen's Jazzband
Go Tell It On The Mountain | Precious Memories
Copenhagen,Denmark, rec. 18.4.1963
Johansen,Henrik (cl) | Thomsen,Jorn H. (tp) | Nyegaard,Peter (tb) | Solund,Jens (b) | Krogh,Per (bj) | Bodker,Niels (dr)
Lennie Baldwin's Dauphin Street Six
Ace In The Hole | Sweet Like This
Copenhagen,Denmark, rec. 13.2.1962
Baldwin,Lennie (tb,voc) | Barrett,Dave (tp) | Crocker,John (cl) | Hart,Roy (bj) | Mason,Dick (b) | Prince,Viv (dr)
Papa Bue's Viking Jazzband
Chinatown | Yes Sir That's My Baby
Copenhagen,Denmark, rec. 31.8.1962
Papa Bue's Viking Jazzband | Hansen,Finn Otto (tp) | Jensen,Arne Bue (tb) | Svare,Jorgen (cl) | Petersen,Bjarne Liller (bj,voc) | Seidelin,Mogens 'Basse' (b) | Madsen,Knud Ryskov (dr)

STCD 5507 | CD | The Golden Years Of Revival Jazz,Vol.2
Chris Barber's Jazz Band
Makin' Whoopee
Live at Odd Fellow Palast,Copenhagen, rec. 10.10.1954
Barber,Chris (tb) | Halcox,Pat (co) | Sunshine,Monty (cl) | Donegan,Tony 'Lonnie' (bj,voc) | Bray,Jim (b) | Bowden,Ron (dr)
Hush-A-Bye
Sunshine,Monty (cl) | Donegan,Tony 'Lonnie' (bj) | Bray,Jim (b) | Bowden,Ron (dr)
Over In The Burying Ground
Donegan,Tony 'Lonnie' (bj,voc)
Long Deep And Wide | Bill Bailey Won't You Please Come Home | Close Fit Blues
Copenhagen,Denmark, rec. 30.12.1956
Jensen,Arne Bue (tb) | Vohwinkel,Gerhard (tp) | Svare,Jorgen (cl) | Petersen,Bjarne Liller (bj) | Seidelin,Mogens 'Basse' (b,sousaphone) | Lindschouw,Ib (dr)
Adrian Bentzon's Jazzband
Sensation Rag | St.James Infirmary | Rockin' In Rhythm | Rachmaninoff's Prelude In C-Sharp Minor
Copenhagen,Denmark, rec. 9.6.1958
Bentzon,Adrian (p) | Jensen,Theis (co) | Andersen,Erik 'Krolle' (cl) | Poulsen,Freddy 'Freak' (bj) | Jensen,Henrik Eigil (dr)
Henrik Johansen's Jazzband
Cakewalkin' Babies From Home | Miss Otis Regrets | I Ain't Gonna Give Nobody None Of My Jelly Roll | Cool Water
Copenhagen,Denmark, rec. 18.4.1963
Johansen,Henrik (cl) | Thomsen,Jorn H. (tp) | Nyegaard,Peter (tb) | Krogh,Per (bj) | Solund,Jens (b) | Bodker,Niels (dr)
Mr.Acker Bilk And His Paramount Jazz Band
The Old Rugged Cross
Metro Club,London,GB, rec. 1.8.1957
Bilk,Bernhard 'Mr.Acker' (cl) | Wallis,Bob (tp) | Avison,Keith (tb) | Hawkins,Jay (bj) | Macey,John (b) | Carter,Viv Clambake (dr)
Over The Rainbow
Bilk,Bernhard 'Mr.Acker' (cl) | Hawkins,Jay (bj) | Macey,John (b) | Carter,Viv Clambake (dr)
Papa Benny's Jazzband
Cheerin' Rag
Copenhagen,Denmark, rec. 11.11.1956
Nielsen,Benny 'Papa' (tb) | Hansen,Finn Otto (co) | Moller,Jorgen (co) | Elmoe,Torben (p) | Jensen,Bjorn (bj) | Jorgensen,John (b) | Hougaard,Erling (dr)
Just A Day
Copenhagen,Denmark, rec. Fall 1960
Nielsen,Benny 'Papa' (tb) | Jorgensen,Orla Levin (co) | McKerrow,Ian (cl) | Hoyer,Peter (bj) | Engberg,Alf (b) | Madsen,Knud Ryskov (dr)

STCD 5508 | CD | The Golden Years Of Revival Jazz,Vol.3
Chris Barber's Jazz Band
Lord Lord Lord | The Martinique | Panama Rag
Live at Old Fellow Palaet's Store Sal,Kopenhagen, rec. 10.10.1954
Barber,Chris (tb) | Halcox,Pat (co) | Sunshine,Monty (cl) | Donegan,Tony 'Lonnie' (bj) | Bray,Jim (b) | Bowden,Ron (dr)
Papa Bue's Viking Jazzband
Bogalusa
Copenhagen,Denmark, rec. 7.11.1957
Jensen,Arne Bue (tb) | Hansen,Finn Otto (tp) | Svare,Jorgen (cl) | Petersen,Bjarne Liller (bj) | Seidelin,Mogens 'Basse' (b) | Lindschouw,Ib (dr)
Nyboder's Pris | When I Leave This World Behind | 1919 March
Copenhagen,Denmark, rec. 12.11.1957
Jensen,Arne Bue (tb) | Hansen,Finn Otto (tp) | Svare,Jorgen (cl) | Petersen,Bjarne Liller (bj) | Seidelin,Mogens 'Basse' (b) | Lindschouw,Ib (dr)
Adrian Bentzon's Jazzband
Save It Pretty Mama
Copenhagen,Denmark, rec. 30.8.1960
Bentzon,Adrian (p) | Jensen,Theis (tp) | Andersen,Erik 'Krolle' (cl) | Poulsen,Freddy 'Freak' (bj) | Fonlev,Kurt (b) | Jensen,Henrik Eigil (dr)
Gatemouth | Mahogany Hall Stomp
Copenhagen,Denmark, rec. 15.10.1960
Bentzon,Adrian (p) | Jensen,Theis (tp) | Andersen,Erik 'Krolle' (cl) | Poulsen,Freddy 'Freak' (bj) | Fonlev,Kurt (b) | Jensen,Henrik Eigil (dr)
Save It Pretty Mama
Copenhagen,Denmark, rec. 4.2.1961
Bentzon,Adrian (celeste) | Jensen,Theis (tp) | Andersen,Erik 'Krolle' (cl) | Poulsen,Freddy 'Freak' (bj) | Fonlev,Kurt (b) | Jensen,Henrik Eigil (dr)
Ken Colyer Trio
Breeze
Copenhagen,Denmark, rec. 12.4.1953
Colyer,Ken (tp,voc) | Donegan,Tony 'Lonnie' (bj) | Barber,Chris (b)
Monty Sunshine Trio
Bill Bailey Won't You Please Come Home
Sunshine,Monty (cl) | Donegan,Tony 'Lonnie' (bj) | Barber,Chris (b)
Lennie Baldwin's Dauphin Street Six
All That Meat And No Potatoes | Is It True What They Say About Dixie
Copenhagen,Denmark, rec. 13.2.1962
Baldwin,Lennie (tb,voc) | Barrett,Dave (tp) | Crocker,John (cl) | Hart,Roy (bj) | Mason,Dick (b) | Prince,Viv (dr)
Theis/Nyegaard Jazzband
Yes I'm In The Barrel
Copenhagen,Denmark, rec. 24.10.1964
Jensen,Theis (tp) | Nyegaard,Peter (tb) | Andersen,Erik 'Krolle' (cl) | Poulsen,Freddy 'Freak' (bj) | Jorgensen,Orla Levin (b) | Bodker,Niels (dr)
That's My Home
Copenhagen,Denmark, rec. 31.3./1.4.1965
Jensen,Theis (tp,voc) | Nyegaard,Peter (tb) | Andersen,Erik 'Krolle' (cl) | Poulsen,Freddy 'Freak' (bj) | Jorgensen,Orla Levin (b) | Bodker,Niels (dr)
Avalon
Andersen,Erik 'Krolle' (cl) | Poulsen,Freddy 'Freak' (bj) | Jorgensen,Orla Levin (b) | Bodker,Niels (dr)
21th Street Stomp
Copenhagen,Denmark, rec. 31.3/1.4.1965
Nyegaard,Peter (tb) | Poulsen,Freddy 'Freak' (bj,voc) | Bodker,Niels (wbd)

STCD 5509 | CD | The Golden Years Of Revival Jazz,Vol.4
Chris Barber's Jazz Band
Bugle Boy March | Down Home Rag | South
Live at Odd Fellow Palast,Copenhagen, rec. 10.10.1954
Barber,Chris (tb) | Halcox,Pat (tp) | Sunshine,Monty (cl) | Donegan,Tony 'Lonnie' (bj) | Bray,Jim (b) | Bowden,Ron (dr)
Papa Bue's New Orleans Band
Moten Shake | Tell Me Your Dreams | Bourbon Street Parade | My Mama Rocks Me
Copenhagen,Denmark, rec. 30.12.1956
Jensen,Arne Bue (tb) | Vohwinkel,Gerhard (tp) | Svare,Jorgen (cl) | Petersen,Bjarne Liller (bj,voc) | Seidelin,Mogens 'Basse' (b,sousaphone) | Lindschouw,Ib (dr)
Ricardo's Jazzmen
Just A Little While To Stay Here | Black Cat On The Fence | Big Chief Battle Axe | Chicago Buzz
Copenhagen,Denmark, rec. 6.11.1961
Hansen,Ricardo (bj) | Thomsen,Jorn L. (tp) | Lindgreen,Ole 'Fessor' (tb) | Holbroe,Hans (cl) | Birger,Arne (b) | Moller,Thorkild (dr)
Dick Charlesworth And His City Gents
Diga Diga Do
London,GB, rec. 25.6.1959
Charlesworth,Dick (cl) | Masters,Bob (tp) | Preston,Cyril (tb) | Dixon,Bill (bj) | Beazley,Graham (b) | Darby,Ron (dr)
Adrian Bentzon's Jazzband
Oh Didn't He Ramble | Bill Bailey Won't You Please Come Home | Sensation Rag
Copenhagen,Denmark, rec. 4.2.1961
Bentzon,Adrian (p) | Jensen,Theis (co,voc) | Andersen,Erik 'Krolle' (cl) | Poulsen,Freddy 'Freak' (bj) | Jensen,Henrik Eigil (dr)
Graham Stewart And His New Orleans Band
Snag It | Black Bottom Stomp | Keyhole Blues | Cushion Foot Stomp
Copenhagen,Denmark, rec. 14.11.1958
Stewart,Graham (tb) | Elsdon,Alan (tp) | Cooper,Alan (cl) | Parker,Johnny (p) | Bray,Jim (b,sousaphone) | Barton,Johnny (g,bj) | Scriven,Tony (dr,wbd)

STCD 5510 | CD | The Golden Years Of Revival Jazz,Vol.5
Papa Bue's Viking Jazzband
Washington Post March | Roll Jordan Roll
Copenhagen,Denmark, rec. 11.1.1962
Papa Bue's Viking Jazzband | Hansen,Finn Otto (tp) | Jensen,Arne Bue (tb) | Svare,Jorgen (cl) | Petersen,Bjarne Liller (bj) | Seidelin,Mogens 'Basse' (b) | Madsen,Knud Ryskov (dr)
Lead Me Saviour
Papa Bue's Viking Jazzband | Jensen,Arne Bue (tb) | Svare,Jorgen (cl) | Petersen,Bjarne Liller (bj) | Seidelin,Mogens 'Basse' (b) | Madsen,Knud Ryskov (dr)
Chiri-Biri-Bin
Copenhagen,Denmark, rec. 13.1.1961
Papa Bue's Viking Jazzband | Hansen,Finn Otto (tp) | Jensen,Arne Bue (tb) | Svare,Jorgen (cl) | Petersen,Bjarne Liller (bj) | Seidelin,Mogens 'Basse' (b) | Madsen,Knud Ryskov (dr)
Sandy Brown's Jazz Band
Swingin' The Blues | Dreamed I Hand The Blues | Skinnie Minnie | St.James Infirmary
Copenhagen,Denmark, rec. 2.9.1957
Brown,Sandy (cl,voc) | Fairweather,Al (tp) | French,Jeremy (tb) | Greig,Stan (p) | McPake,Al (g) | Mahn,Tim (b) | Burbidge,Graham (dr)
Johnny Parker Trio
Boogie | What Me Worry | Feline Stomp | Honeysuckle Rose
Copenhagen,Denmark, rec. 15.11.1958
Parker,Johnny (p) | Bray,Jim (b) | Scriven,Tony (dr,wbd)
Theis/Nyegaard Jazzband
Wild Man Blues | I Ain't Got Nobody
Copenhagen,Denmark, rec. 31.3/1.4.1965
Jensen,Theis (tp,voc) | Nyegaard,Peter (tb) | Andersen,Erik 'Krolle' (cl) | Poulsen,Freddy 'Freak' (bj) | Jorgensen,Orla Levin (b) | Bodker,Niels (dr)
Mr.Acker Bilk And His Paramount Jazz Band
We Shall Walk Through The Streets Of The City | Climax Rag
London,GB, rec. 10.12.1957
Bilk,Bernhard 'Mr.Acker' (cl) | Wallis,Bob (tp) | Mortimer,John (tb) | Hawkins,Jay (bj) | Price,Ernest (b) | McKay,Ron (dr)
Ricardo's Jazzmen
Sentimental Journey | Oriental Strut
Copenhagen,Denmark, rec. 6.11.961
Hansen,Ricardo (bj) | Thomsen,Jorn L. (tp) | Lindgreen,Ole 'Fessor' (tb) | Holbroe,Hans (cl) | Birger,Arne (b) | Moller,Thorkild (dr)
Cy Laurie's New Orleans Septet
King Of The Zulus | S.O.L.Blues
Det Nye Casino,Arhus,Denmark, rec. 22.8.1954
Laurie,Cy (cl) | Fairweather,Al (tp) | Picard,John (tb) | Thomas,Alan (p) | Potter,John (bj) | Christiansen,Ole (b) | McKay,Ron (dr)

STCD 5511 | CD | The Golden Years Of Revival Jazz,Vol.6
Sandy Brown's Jazz Band
Everybody Loves Saturday Night | Tree Top Tall Papa | Something Blue | Too Bad
London,GB, rec. 1.4.1955
Brown,Sandy (cl,voc) | Fairweather,Al (tp) | Davies,John R.T. (tb) | Thomas,Alan (p) | Umansky,Mo (bj) | Parker,Brian (b) | Burbidge,Graham (dr)
Papa Bue's Viking Jazzband
She's No Trouble | Gatemouth | Savoy Blues
Copenhagen,Denmark, rec. 25.1.1958
Papa Bue's Viking Jazzband | Vohwinkel,Gerhard (tp) | Jensen,Arne Bue (tb) | Svare,Jorgen (cl) | Petersen,Bjarne Liller (bj) | Seidelin,Mogens 'Basse' (b,sousaphone) | Madsen,Knud Ryskov (dr)
Creole Song
Papa Bue's Viking Jazzband | Vohwinkel,Gerhard (tp) | Lassen,Helmuth (tb,voc) | Svare,Jorgen (cl) | Petersen,Bjarne Liller (bj) | Seidelin,Mogens 'Basse' (b,sousaphone) | Madsen,Knud Ryskov (dr)
Cy Laurie's New Orleans Septet
Forty And Tight | Pleading The Blues | Blues Mess Around | Skit Dat De Dat
London,GB, rec. 22.9.1954
Laurie,Cy (cl) | Fairweather,Al (tp) | Picard,John (tb) | Thomas,Alan (p) | Potter,John (bj) | Wood,Dave (b) | McKay,Ron (dr)
Mr.Acker Bilk And His Paramount Jazz Band
Goodnight Sweet Prince
Metro Club,London,GB, rec. 22.8.1957
Bilk,Bernhard 'Mr.Acker' (cl) | Wallis,Bob (tp) | Avison,Keith (tb) | Hawkins,Jay (bj) | Macey,John (b) | Carter,Viv Clambake (dr)
Postman's Lament
Metro Club,London,GB, rec. 10.12.1957
Bilk,Bernhard 'Mr.Acker' (cl,voc) | Wallis,Bob (tp) | Mortimer,John (tb) | Hawkins,Jay (bj) | Price,Ernest (b) | McKay,Ron (dr)
Henrik Johansen's Jazzband
At Sundown
London,GB, rec. 5.7.1956
Johansen,Henrik (cl) | Fairweather,Al (tp) | Davies,John R.T. (tb) | Disley,William 'Diz' (g) | Holley,Major (b) | Burbidge,Graham (dr)
Theis/Nyegaard Jazzband
Walk Right In
Copenhagen,Denmark, rec. 31.3.1965
Jensen,Theis (voc) | Poulsen,Freddy 'Freak' (bj,voc) | Jorgensen,Orla Levin (b) | Bodker,Niels (wbd)
Dick Charlesworth And His City Gents
Kitty's Dream | Take Her To Jamaica
Metro Club,London,GB, rec. late 1959
Charlesworth,Dick (cl) | Masters,Bob (tp) | Preston,Cyril (tb) | Dixon,Bill (bj) | Beazley,Graham (b) | O'Malley,Ernie (dr)
Bohana Jazzband
You Always Hurt The One You Love
Copenhagen,Denmark, rec. 26.2.1954
Bohana Jazzband | Hansen,Hans Borge (tp) | Jensen,Arne Bue (tb) | Bruun,Buster (cl) | Hansen,Niels Richard (bj) | Christiansen,Ole (b) | Rasmussen,Allan (dr)
Lennie Baldwin's Dauphin Street Six
Down Home Rag | Do What Ory Say
Copenhagen,Denmark, rec. 13.2.1962
Baldwin,Lennie (tb,voc) | Barrett,Dave (tp) | Crocker,John (cl) | Hart,Roy (bj) | Mason,Dick (b) | Prince,Viv (dr)

STCD 5512 | CD | The Golden Years Of Revival Jazz,Vol.7
Chris Barber's Jazz Band
Ice Cream | Down By The Riverside
Copenhagen,Denmark, rec. 9.10.1954
Barber,Chris (tb,voc) | Halcox,Pat (tp,voc) | Sunshine,Monty (cl) | Donegan,Tony 'Lonnie' (bj) | Bray,Jim (b) | Bowden,Ron (dr)
It's Tight Like That
Live at Old Fellow Palaet's Store Sal,Kopenhagen, rec. 10.10.1954
Barber,Chris (tb,voc) | Halcox,Pat (tp) | Sunshine,Monty (cl) | Donegan,Tony 'Lonnie' (bj) | Bray,Jim (b) | Bowden,Ron (dr)
Papa Bue's Viking Jazzband
Silver Threads Among The Gold | Old Spinning Wheel
Copenhagen,Denmark, rec. 27.10.1959
Papa Bue's Viking Jazzband | Hansen,Finn Otto (tp) | Jensen,Arne Bue (tb,ld) | Svare,Jorgen (cl) | Petersen,Bjarne Liller (bj) | Seidelin,Mogens 'Basse' (b) | Lindschouw,Ib (dr)
Es War In Schöneberg | Beautiful Dreamer
Copenhagen,Denmark, rec. 26.4.1960
Papa Bue's Viking Jazzband | Hansen,Finn Otto (tp) | Jensen,Arne Bue (tb,ld) | Svare,Jorgen (cl) | Petersen,Bjarne Liller (bj) | Seidelin,Mogens 'Basse' (b) | Lindschouw,Ib (dr)
Bob Wallis Storyville Jazzmen
Jerusalem Blues | Blanche Touquatuox | Willie The Weeper | Over The Waves
Metro Club,London,GB, rec. 23.1.1958
Wallis,Bob (tp,voc) | Davies,John R.T. (tb) | Wood,Less (cl) | Graham,Peter (p) | Rainey,Hugh (bj) | Winsey,Stu (b) | Baker,Ginger (dr)
Henrik Johansen's Jazzband
New Orleans Hop Scop Blues
London,GB, rec. 5.7.1956
Johansen,Henrik (cl) | Fairweather,Al (tp) | Davies,John R.T. (tb) | Disley,William 'Diz' (g) | Holley,Major (b) | Burbidge,Graham (dr)
Adrian Bentzon's Jazzband
Stomp Off-Let's Go | Black And Tan Fantasy | Cherry Red
Copenhagen,Denmark, rec. 30.8.1960
Bentzon,Adrian (p) | Jensen,Theis (tp,voc) | Poulsen,Freddy 'Freak' (tb) | Andersen,Erik 'Krolle' (cl) | Fronlev,Kurt (b) | Jensen,Henrik Eigil (dr)
Ken Colyer's Jazzmen
Saturday Night Function
Gentofte Hotel,Copenhagen,Denmark, rec. 19.3.1953
Colyer,Ken (tp) | Barber,Chris (tb) | Sunshine,Monty (cl) | Donegan,Tony 'Lonnie' (bj) | Bray,Jim (b) | Bowden,Ron (dr)
Mr.Acker Bilk And His Paramount Jazz Band
St.Louis Blues | Travelin' Blues
London,GB, rec. 1.8.1957
Bilk,Bernhard 'Mr.Acker' (cl) | Wallis,Bob (tp) | Davies,John R.T. (tb) | Hawkins,Jay (bj) | Macey,John (b) | Carter,Viv Clambake (dr)
Papa Benny's Jazzband
Something Blues | Thriller Rag
Copenhagen,Denmark, rec. 29.12.1962
Nielsen,Benny 'Papa' (tb) | Rasmussen,Kai 'Satch' (tp) | Holbroe,Hans (cl) | Ibsen,John (b) | Jensen,Bjorn (bj) | Moller,Thorkild (dr)

STCD 5513 | CD | The Golden Years Of Revival Jazz,Vol.8
Papa Bue's Viking Jazzband
All The Girls Go Crazy | The Entertainer | Pass Out Lightly | Stockyard Strut
Copenhagen,Denmark, rec. 15.1.1958
Papa Bue's Viking Jazzband | Vohwinkel,Gerhard (tp) | Jensen,Arne Bue (tb) | Svare,Jorgen (cl) | Petersen,Bjarne Liller (bj,voc) | Seidelin,Mogens 'Basse' (b,sousaphon) | Lindschouw,Ib (dr)
Sandy Brown's Jazz Band
Black Six Blues | Blues Stampede | Fifty-Fifty Blues
Live at Royal Festival Hall,London,GB, rec. 18.2.1956
Brown,Sandy (cl) | Fairweather,Al (tp) | Davies,John R.T. (tb) | Thomas,Alan (p) | Umansky,Mo (bj) | Parker,Brian (b) | Burbidge,Graham (dr)
Graham Stewart Seven
Yes Sir That's My Baby | Yellow Dog Blues | Shake That Thing | The Boy Friend
London,GB, rec. 2.1.1958
Stewart,Graham (tb,voc) | Elsdon,Alan (tp) | McKerrow,Ian (cl) | Root,Alan (p) | Johnson,Johnny (b) | Barton,Johnny (bj,voc) | Mawford,Peter (dr)
Mr.Acker Bilk And His Paramount Jazz Band
Darkness On The Delta | King Joe
Burnham,GB, rec. 31.8.1957
Bilk,Bernhard 'Mr.Acker' (cl) | Davies,John R.T. (as) | Hawkins,Jay (bj) | Macey,John (b) | Carter,Viv Clambake (dr)
Arne Birger's Jazzsjak
Everybody Loves My Baby | Mr.Joe | Close Fit Blues | Over In The Gloryland
Copenhagen,Denmark, rec. 30.1.1965
Johansen,Arne Birger (tuba) | Mortensen,John Wellejs (co) | Mortensen,Finn Wellejus (tb) | Hansen,Steen Vig (ss) | Madsen,Thorkild Edgar (bj)
Cy Laurie's New Orleans Septet
Old Stack O'Lee Blues | Wipe It Off
Det Nye Casino,Arhus,Denmark, rec. 22.8.1954
Laurie,Cy (cl) | Fairweather,Al (tp) | Picard,John (tb) | Thomas,Alan (p) | Potter,John (bj) | Christiansen,Ole (b) | McKay,Ron (dr)

STCD 5514 | CD | The Golden Years Of Revival Jazz,Vol.9
Chris Barber's Jazz Band
Maryland My Maryland | St.George's Rag | Wabash Blues
Live at Odd Fellow Palast,Copenhagen, rec. 10.10.1954
Barber,Chris (tb,voc) | Halcox,Pat (tp) | Sunshine,Monty (cl) | Donegan,Tony 'Lonnie' (bj) | Bray,Jim (b) | Bowden,Ron (dr)
Papa Bue's Viking Jazzband
O Sole Mio
Copenhagen,Denmark, rec. 2.5.1960
Papa Bue's Viking Jazzband | Hansen,Finn Otto (tp) | Jensen,Arne Bue (tb,ld) | Svare,Jorgen (cl) | Petersen,Bjarne Liller (bj) | Seidelin,Mogens 'Basse' (b) | Lindschouw,Ib (dr)
White Cliffs Of Dover | When Irish Eyes Are Smiling
Copenhagen,Denmark, rec. 18.5.1960

Papa Bue's Viking Jazzband | Hansen,Finn Otto (tp) | Jensen,Arne Bue (tb,ld) | Svare,Jorgen (cl) | Petersen,Bjarne Liller (bj,voc) | Seidelin,Mogens 'Basse' (b) | Lindschouw,Ib (dr)
Dark Eyes
Copenhagen,Denmark, rec. 2.9.1960
Papa Bue's Viking Jazzband | Hansen,Finn Otto (tp) | Jensen,Arne Bue (tb,ld) | Svare,Jorgen (cl) | Petersen,Bjarne Liller (bj) | Seidelin,Mogens 'Basse' (b) | Lindschouw,Ib (dr)
Hylda Sims And The Citty Ramblers Skiffle Group With Henrik Johansen
I Want A Girl | 2:19 Blues | Mama Don't Allow
Copenhagen,Denmark, rec. 12.9.1956
Johansen,Henrik (cl) | Rambler's Skiffle Group | Quaye,Russell (kazoo,g,voc) | Bateson,Chris (tp-mouthpiece) | Buquet,Anthomy Bo Bo (b,tuba) | Sutton,Alan 'Little Bear' (wbd) | Sims,Hylda (g,voc)
900 Miles
Rambler's Skiffle Group | Quaye,Russell (kazoo,g,voc) | Bateson,Chris (tp-mouthpiece) | Buquet,Anthomy Bo Bo (b,tuba) | Sutton,Alan 'Little Bear' (wbd) | Sims,Hylda (g,voc)
Mr.Acker Bilk And His Paramount Jazz Band
St.Louis Blues
London,GB, rec. 22.8.1957
Bilk,Bernhard 'Mr.Acker' (cl) | Wallis,Bob (tp) | Davies,John R.T. (as) | Hawkins,Jay (bj) | Macey,John (b) | Carter,Viv Clambake (dr)
Swing Low Sweet Chariot
Metro Club,London,GB, rec. 10.12.1957
Bilk,Bernhard 'Mr.Acker' (cl,voc) | Wallis,Bob (tp) | Mortimer,John (tb) | Hawkins,Jay (bj) | Price,Ernest (b) | McKay,Ron (dr)
Lennie Baldwin's Dauphin Street Six
Fish Seller | Old Man Mose
Copenhagen,Denmark, rec. 13.2.1962
Baldwin,Lennie (tb,voc) | Barrett,Dave (tp) | Crocker,John (cl) | Hart,Roy (bj) | Mason,Dick (b) | Prince,Viv (dr)
Cy Laurie's New Orleans Septet
Wild Man Blues | Gravier Street Blues | Stockyard Strut | Mamie's Blues
Det Nye Casino,Arhus,Denmark, rec. 22.8.1954
Laurie,Cy (cl) | Fairweather,Al (tp) | Picard,John (tb) | Thomas,Alan (p) | Potter,John (bj) | Christiansen,Ole (b) | McKay,Ron (dr)

STCD 5515 | CD | The Golden Years Of Revival Jazz,Vol.10
Papa Bue's Viking Jazzband
Lil' Liza Jane | Royal Telephone
Copenhagen,Denmark, rec. 31.8.1962
Papa Bue's Viking Jazzband | Hansen,Finn Otto (tp) | Jensen,Arne Bue (tb,ld) | Svare,Jorgen (cl) | Petersen,Bjarne Liller (bj,voc) | Seidelin,Mogens 'Basse' (b) | Madsen,Knud Ryskov (dr)
Sibiria(Kosakken Borge)
Copenhagen,Denmark, rec. 31.5.1963
Papa Bue's Viking Jazzband | Hansen,Finn Otto (tp) | Jensen,Arne Bue (tb,ld) | Svare,Jorgen (cl) | Petersen,Bjarne Liller (bj) | Seidelin,Mogens 'Basse' (b) | Madsen,Knud Ryskov (dr)
Un Claire De Lune(Moonlight Tango)
Copenhagen,Denmark, rec. 3.6.1963
Papa Bue's Viking Jazzband | Hansen,Finn Otto (tp) | Jensen,Arne Bue (tb,ld) | Svare,Jorgen (cl) | Petersen,Bjarne Liller (bj) | Seidelin,Mogens 'Basse' (b) | Madsen,Knud Ryskov (dr)
Sandy Brown's Jazz Band
African Queen | Special Delivery | Nothing Blues | Africa Blues
London,GB, rec. 1.4.1955
Brown,Sandy (cl,voc) | Fairweather,Al (tp) | Davies,John R.T. (tb) | Thomas,Alan (p) | Umansky,Mo (bj) | Parker,Brian (b) | Burbidge,Graham (dr)
Graham Stewart And His New Orleans Band
Canal Street Blues | Working Man Blues | Tears | Sweet Lovin' Man
Copenhagen,Denmark, rec. 2.1.1958
Stewart,Graham (tb) | Elsdon,Alan (tp) | McKerrow,Ian (cl) | Root,Alan (p) | Barton,Johnny (bj) | Johnson,Johnny (b) | Mawford,Peter (dr)
Mr.Acker Bilk And His Paramount Jazz Band
Darkness On The Delta(alt.take) | King Joe(alt.take)
Burnham,GB, rec. 31.8.1957
Bilk,Bernhard 'Mr.Acker' (cl) | Davies,John R.T. (as) | Hawkins,Jay (bj) | Macey,John (b) | Carter,Viv Clambake (dr)
Arne Birger's Jazzsjak
Funny Feathers Man | Stepping On The Blues | Cementary Blues | Travelin' Blues
Copenhagen,Denmark, rec. 30.1.1965
Johansen,Arne Birger (tuba) | Mortensen,John Wellejs (co) | Mortensen,Finn Wellejus (tb) | Hansen,Steen Vig (ss,ts) | Madsen,Thorkild Edgar (bj)
Bohana Jazzband
Franklin Street Blues
Copenhagen,Denmark, rec. 26.2.1954
Bohana Jazzband | Hansen,Hans Borge (tp) | Jensen,Arne Bue (tb) | Bruun,Buster (cl) | Hansen,Niels Richard (bj) | Christiansen,Ole (b) | Rasmussen,Allan (dr)
Lennie Baldwin's Dauphin Street Six
Riverside Blues | You Are My Sunshine
Copenhagen,Denmark, rec. 13.2.1962
Baldwin,Lennie (tb,voc) | Barrett,Dave (tp) | Crocker,John (cl) | Hart,Roy (bj) | Mason,Dick (b) | Prince,Viv (dr)

STCD 5516 | CD | The Golden Years Of Revival Jazz,Vol.11
Papa Bue's Viking Jazzband
Gentle Annie
Copenhagen,Denmark, rec. 4.1.1960
Papa Bue's Viking Jazzband | Hansen,Finn Otto (tp) | Jensen,Arne Bue (tb,ld) | Svare,Jorgen (cl) | Petersen,Bjarne Liller (bj) | Seidelin,Mogens 'Basse' (b) | Lindschouw,Ib (dr)
On A Little Bamboo Bridge
Copenhagen,Denmark, rec. 23.12.1960
Papa Bue's Viking Jazzband | Jensen,Arne Bue (tb) | Hansen,Finn Otto (tp) | Svare,Jorgen (cl) | Petersen,Bjarne Liller (bj,voc) | Seidelin,Mogens 'Basse' (b) | Lindschouw,Ib (dr)
Copenhagen | Up A Lazy River
Copenhagen,Denmark, rec. 17.2.1961
Papa Bue's Viking Jazzband | Jensen,Arne Bue (tb) | Hansen,Finn Otto (tp) | Svare,Jorgen (cl) | Petersen,Bjarne Liller (bj,voc) | Seidelin,Mogens 'Basse' (b) | Lindschouw,Ib (dr)
Monty Sunshine Trio
Wild Cat Blues
Gentofte Hotel,Copenhagen,Denmark, rec. 12.4.1953
Sunshine,Monty (cl) | Donegan,Tony 'Lonnie' (bj) | Barber,Chris (b)
Ken Colyer's Jazzmen
Blue Bells Goodbye
Gentofte Hotel,Copenhagen,Denmark, rec. 19.4.1953
Colyer,Ken (tp) | Barber,Chris (tb) | Sunshine,Monty (cl) | Donegan,Tony 'Lonnie' (bj) | Bray,Jim (b) | Bowden,Ron (dr)
Dick Charlesworth And His City Gents
Salty Dog | Blue Blood Blues | Yes We Have No Bananas | Salutation March
Metro Club,London,GB, rec. 25.6.1959
Charlesworth,Dick (cl,voc) | Masters,Bob (tp) | Preston,Cyril (tb,voc) | Dixon,Bill (bj) | Beazley,Graham (b) | Darby,Ron (dr)
Chris Barber's Jazz Band
Over In The Gloryland
Live at Old Fellow Palaet's Store Sal,Kopenhagen, rec. 10.10.1954
Barber,Chris (tb) | Halcox,Pat (co) | Sunshine,Monty (cl) | Donegan,Tony 'Lonnie' (bj) | Bray,Jim (b) | Bowden,Ron (dr)
St.Phillip Street Breakdown
Live at Odd Fellow Palast,Copenhagen, rec. 10.10.1954
Sunshine,Monty (cl) | Donegan,Tony 'Lonnie' (bj) | Bray,Jim (b) | Bowden,Ron (dr)
Leonardo Pedersen's Jazzkapel
Give Me Your Telephone Number | St.Louis Shuffle | Zonky | Saratoga Shout
Copenhagen,Denmark, rec. 3.3.1963
Pedersen,Leonardo (cl,as) | Moller,Jorgen (co) | Eghjort,Mogens (co) | Bredberg,Arne (tb) | Hansen,Hans J. (cl,as) | Tvaergard,Per (p) | Nielsen,Ove (bj) | Kuhn,Karsten (b) | Larsen,John (sousaphone) | Jensen,Flemming (dr)
Papa Benny's Jazzband
March Hare
Copenhagen,Denmark, rec. 19.12.1962
Nielsen,Benny 'Papa' (tb) | Rasmussen,Kai 'Satch' (tp) | Holbroe,Hans (cl) | Ibsen,John (b) | Jensen,Bjorn (bj) | Moller,Thorkild (dr)
The Old Rugged Cross
Copenhagen,Denmark, rec. 29.12.1962
Holbroe,Hans (cl) | Ibsen,John (b) | Jensen,Bjorn (bj)
Cy Laurie's New Orleans Septet
2:19 Blues | Jazz Lips
Det Nye Casino,Arhus,Denmark, rec. 22.8.1954
Laurie,Cy (cl) | Fairweather,Al (tp) | Picard,John (tb) | Thomas,Alan (p) | Potter,John (bj) | Christiansen,Ole (b) | McKay,Ron (dr)

STCD 5517 | CD | The Golden Years Of Revival Jazz,Vol.12
Papa Bue's Viking Jazzband
South Rampart Street Parade | Bucket's Got A Hole In It
Copenhagen,Denmark, rec. 2.& 18.5.1960
Papa Bue's Viking Jazzband | Hansen,Finn Otto (tp) | Jensen,Arne Bue (tb,ld) | Svare,Jorgen (cl) | Petersen,Bjarne Liller (bj) | Seidelin,Mogens 'Basse' (b) | Lindschouw,Ib (dr)
At A Georgia Camp Meeting | Walking With The King
Copenhagen,Denmark, rec. 13.1.& 17.2.1961
Papa Bue's Viking Jazzband | Hansen,Finn Otto (tp) | Jensen,Arne Bue (tb,ld) | Svare,Jorgen (cl) | Petersen,Bjarne Liller (bj,voc) | Seidelin,Mogens 'Basse' (b) | Lindschouw,Ib (dr)
Mr.Acker Bilk And His Paramount Jazz Band
Travelin' Blues | Franklin Street Blues
Metro Club,London,GB, rec. 1.8.1957
Bilk,Bernhard 'Mr.Acker' (cl) | Wallis,Bob (tp,voc) | Avison,Keith (tb) | Hawkins,Jay (bj) | Macey,John (b) | Carter,Viv Clambake (dr)
St.Phillip Street Breakdown
Metro Club,London,GB, rec. 22.8.1957
Bilk,Bernhard 'Mr.Acker' (cl) | Wallis,Bob (tp) | Davies,John R.T. (as) | Hawkins,Jay (bj) | Macey,John (b) | Carter,Viv Clambake (dr)
Swing Low Sweet Chariot
Metro Club,London,GB, rec. 10.12.1957
Bilk,Bernhard 'Mr.Acker' (cl) | Wallis,Bob (tp) | Mortimer,John (tb) | Hawkins,Jay (bj) | Price,Ernest (b) | McKay,Ron (dr)
Papa Benny's Jazzband
Ice Cream | Saratoga Swing | Bye Bye Blackbird | Wrap Your Troubles In Dreams
Copenhagen,Denmark, rec. September 1959
Nielsen,Benny 'Papa' (tb) | Hansen,Finn Otto (co) | Runov,John (cl) | Hansen,Niels Richard (bj) | Johansen,Arne Birger (b) | Madsen,Knud Ryskov (dr,voc)
Chris Barber & The Ramblers
Sweet Lovin' Man | Down By The Riverside | At The Jazz Band Ball | Buddy Bolden's Blues
Copenhagen,Denmark, rec. 16.9.1952
Barber,Chris (tb,voc) | Larsen,Jeppe Esper (co,voc) | Bruun,Buster (cl,voc) | Ramsby,Poul Erik (p) | Albrechtsen,Claus (dr)
Graham Stewart And His New Orleans Band
Lou-Easy-An-I-A | Dinah
Copenhagen,Denmark, rec. 19.2.1960
Stewart,Graham (tb,voc) | Peters,Mike (tp) | Cooper,Nick (cl,voc) | Stevenson,Joe (bj) | King,Geoff (b) | Darby,Ron (dr)
Theis/Nyegaard Jazzband
On The Sunny Side Of The Street | When You're Smiling
Copenhagen,Denmark, rec. 31.3./1.4.1965
Jensen,Theis (co,voc) | Nyegaard,Peter (tb) | Andersen,Erik 'Krolle' (cl) | Jorgensen,Orla Levin (b) | Poulsen,Freddy 'Freak' (bj) | Bodker,Niels (dr)

STCD 5518 | CD | The Golden Years Of Revival Jazz,Vol.13
Mr.Acker Bilk And His Paramount Jazz Band
A Monday Date
Burnham,GB, rec. 31.8.1957
Bilk,Bernhard 'Mr.Acker' (cl) | Wallis,Bob (tp) | Davies,John R.T. (as) | Hawkins,Jay (bj) | Macey,John (b) | Carter,Viv Clambake (dr)
Sweetie Dear | Salutation March | Savoy Blues
London,GB, rec. 10.12.1957
Bilk,Bernhard 'Mr.Acker' (cl) | Wallis,Bob (tp) | Mortimer,John (tb) | Hawkins,Jay (bj) | Price,Ernest (b) | McKay,Ron (dr)
Ken Colyer's Jazzmen
Isle Of Capri | Shine
Gentofte Hotel,Copenhagen,Denmark, rec. 19.4.1953
Colyer,Ken (co) | Barber,Chris (tb) | Sunshine,Monty (cl) | Donegan,Tony 'Lonnie' (bj) | Bray,Jim (b) | Bowden,Ron (dr)
Gentofte Blues
Barber,Chris (tb) | Sunshine,Monty (cl) | Donegan,Tony 'Lonnie' (bj) | Bray,Jim (b) | Bowden,Ron (dr)
Monty Sunshine Trio
St.Phillip Street Breakdown
Copenhagen,Denmark, rec. 12.4.1953
Sunshine,Monty (cl) | Donegan,Tony 'Lonnie' (bj) | Barber,Chris (b)
Henrik Johansen's Jazzband
Oriental Man | Blues My Naughty Sweetie Gives To Me | Bimbo | Camp Meeting Blues
Copenhagen,Denmark, rec. 23.6.1956
Johansen,Henrik (cl) | Jensen,Theis (co) | Eriksen,Bent 'Kid' (p) | Poulsen,Freddy 'Freak' (bj) | Jensen,Henrik Eigil (dr)
Lennie Baldwin's Dauphin Street Six
Un Claire De Lune A Maubeuge | John Brown's Body
Copenhagen,Denmark, rec. 13.2.1962
Baldwin,Lennie (tb,voc) | Barrett,Dave (tp) | Crocker,John (cl) | Hart,Roy (bj) | Mason,Dick (b) | Prince,Viv (dr)
Adrian Bentzon's Jazzband
Tiger Rag
Copenhagen,Denmark, rec. 5.2.1960
Bentzon,Adrian (p) | Jensen,Theis (tp) | Poulsen,Freddy 'Freak' (tb) | Andersen,Erik 'Krolle' (cl) | Fonlev,Kurt (b) | Jensen,Henrik Eigil (dr)
Four Or Five Times
Copenhagen,Denmark, rec. 4.2.1961
Bentzon,Adrian (p) | Jensen,Theis (tp) | Poulsen,Freddy 'Freak' (tb) | Andersen,Erik 'Krolle' (cl) | Fonlev,Kurt (b) | Jensen,Henrik Eigil (dr)
Papa Bue's Viking Jazzband
Hawaiian Hospitality
Copenhagen,Denmark, rec. 16.2.1961
Papa Bue's Viking Jazzband | Hansen,Finn Otto (tp) | Jensen,Arne Bue (tb,ld) | Svare,Jorgen (cl) | Petersen,Bjarne Liller (bj,voc) | Seidelin,Mogens 'Basse' (b) | Lindschouw,Ib (dr)
Chris Barber's Jazz Band
When The Saints Go Marching In
Det Nye Casino,Arhus,Denmark, rec. 1.10.1954
Barber,Chris (tb,voc) | Halcox,Pat (co) | Sunshine,Monty (cl) | Donegan,Tony 'Lonnie' (bj) | Bray,Jim (b) | Bowden,Ron (dr)
The Bucket's Got A Hole In It
Live at Odd Fellow Palast,Copenhagen, rec. 10.10.1954
Barber,Chris (tb,voc) | Halcox,Pat (co,voc) | Sunshine,Monty (cl,voc) | Donegan,Tony 'Lonnie' (bj) | Bray,Jim (b) | Bowden,Ron (dr)

STCD 5519 | CD | The Golden Years Of Revival Jazz,Vol.14
Mr.Acker Bilk And His Paramount Jazz Band
Bye And Bye | All The Gifts Go Crazy | East Coast Trot | Careless Love Blues
Metro Club,London,GB, rec. 1.8.1957
Bilk,Bernhard 'Mr.Acker' (cl,voc) | Wallis,Bob (tp) | Avison,Keith (tb) | Hawkins,Jay (bj) | Macey,John (b) | Carter,Viv Clambake (dr)
Ken Colyer's Jazzmen
I Can't Escape From You
Copenhagen,Denmark, rec. 12.4.1953
Colyer,Ken (tp) | Barber,Chris (tb) | Sunshine,Monty (cl) | Donegan,Tony 'Lonnie' (bj) | Bray,Jim (b) | Bowden,Ron (dr)
The Bucket's Got A Hole In It | We Sure Do Need Him
Gentofte Hotel,Copenhagen,Denmark, rec. 19.4.1953
Colyer,Ken (tp,voc) | Barber,Chris (tb) | Sunshine,Monty (cl) | Donegan,Tony 'Lonnie' (bj) | Bray,Jim (b) | Bowden,Ron (dr)
Henrik Johansen's Jazzband
Doctor Jazz | Moonlight Bay | Lord Lord Lord | Gamblin' Man
Copenhagen,Denmark, rec. 6.3.1955
Johansen,Henrik (cl) | Hansen,Hans Borge (tp) | Jensen,Arne Bue (tb) | Poulsen,Freddy 'Freak' (bj) | Christiansen,Ole (b) | Karn,Ole (dr)
Adrian Bentzon's Jazzband
I'll Be Glad When You're Dead You Rascal You | Sidewalk Blues
Copenhagen,Denmark, rec. 4.2.1961
Bentzon,Adrian (p) | Jensen,Theis (co) | Andersen,Erik 'Krolle' (cl) | Poulsen,Freddy 'Freak' (tb) | Fonlev,Kurt (b) | Jensen,Henrik Eigil (dr)
Graham Stewart And His New Orleans Band
Pretty Baby
Copenhagen,Denmark, rec. 19.2.1960
Stewart,Graham (tb) | Peters,Mike (tp) | Cooper,Nick (cl) | Stevenson,Joe (bj) | King,Geoff (b) | Darby,Ron (dr)
Papa Bue's Viking Jazzband
Egyptian Fantasy
Copenhagen,Denmark, rec. 31.5.1962
Papa Bue's Viking Jazzband | Hansen,Finn Otto (tp) | Jensen,Arne Bue (tb,ld) | Svare,Jorgen (cl) | Petersen,Bjarne Liller (bj) | Seidelin,Mogens 'Basse' (b) | Madsen,Knud Ryskov (dr)
Belelia | My Little Bimbo | Just A Gigolo
Copenhagen,Denmark, rec. 30.10.1963
Papa Bue's Viking Jazzband | Hansen,Finn Otto (tp) | Jensen,Arne Bue (tb,ld) | Svare,Jorgen (cl) | Petersen,Bjarne Liller (bj,voc) | Seidelin,Mogens 'Basse' (b) | Madsen,Knud Ryskov (dr)
Magic Horn
Copenhagen,Denmark, rec. 30.10.1962
Papa Bue's Viking Jazzband | Svare,Jorgen (cl) | Petersen,Bjarne Liller (g) | Seidelin,Mogens 'Basse' (b) | Madsen,Knud Ryskov (dr)
Chris Barber's Jazz Band
Precious Lord Take My Hand
Aarhus, Denmark, rec. 1.10.1954
Barber,Chris (tb) | Halcox,Pat (tb) | Sunshine,Monty (cl) | Donegan,Tony 'Lonnie' (bj) | Bray,Jim (b) | Bowden,Ron (dr)

STCD 5520 | CD | The Golden Years Of Revibal Jazz,Vol.15
Mr.Acker Bilk And His Paramount Jazz Band
Breeze
Metro Club,London,GB, rec. 1.8.1957
Bilk,Bernhard 'Mr.Acker' (cl) | Wallis,Bob (tp) | Avison,Keith (tb) | Hawkins,Jay (bj) | Macey,John (b) | Carter,Viv Clambake (dr)
Gladiolus Rag
London,GB, rec. 22.8.1957
Bilk,Bernhard 'Mr.Acker' (cl) | Wallis,Bob (tp) | Avison,Keith (tb) | Hawkins,Jay (bj) | Macey,John (b) | Carter,Viv Clambake (dr)
Bei Mir Bist Du Schön | Shine
Bilk,Bernhard 'Mr.Acker' (cl) | Wallis,Bob (tp) | Mortimer,John (tb) | Hawkins,Jay (bj) | Price,Ernest (b) | McKay,Ron (dr,voc)
Ken Colyer's Jazzmen
Tiger Rag
Gentofte Hotel,Copenhagen,Denmark, rec. 11.4.1953
Colyer,Ken (tp) | Barber,Chris (tb) | Sunshine,Monty (cl) | Donegan,Tony 'Lonnie' (bj) | Bray,Jim (b) | Bowden,Ron (dr)
Just A Closer Walk With Thee | The Sheik Of Araby
Gentofte Hotel,Copenhagen,Denmark, rec. 19.4.1953
Colyer,Ken (tp,voc) | Barber,Chris (tb) | Sunshine,Monty (cl) | Donegan,Tony 'Lonnie' (bj) | Bray,Jim (b,sousaphone) | Bowden,Ron (dr)
Henrik Johansen's Jazzband
New Orleans Hop Scop Blues | Yama Yama Blues | Margie | Pauline's Blues
London,GB, rec. 5.6.1956
Johansen,Henrik (cl) | Fairweather,Al (tp) | Davies,John R.T. (tb) | Disley,William 'Diz' (g) | Holley,Major (b) | Burbidge,Graham (b)
Papa Bue's Viking Jazzband
When The Saints Go Marching In
Copenhagen,Denmark, rec. 23.7.1959
Papa Bue's Viking Jazzband | Hansen,Finn Otto (tp) | Jensen,Arne Bue (tb,ld) | Svare,Jorgen (cl) | Petersen,Bjarne Liller (bj) | Seidelin,Mogens 'Basse' (b) | Madsen,Knud Ryskov (dr)
Chris Barber's Jazz Band
Ice Cream | We Shall Walk Through The Streets Of The City
Copenhagen,Denmark, rec. 9./10.10.1954
Barber,Chris (tb) | Halcox,Pat (tb) | Sunshine,Monty (cl) | Donegan,Tony 'Lonnie' (bj) | Bray,Jim (b) | Bowden,Ron (dr)
Monty Sunshine Trio
Blue Blood Blues
Copenhagen,Denmark, rec. 12.4.1953
Sunshine,Monty (cl) | Donegan,Tony 'Lonnie' (bj) | Barber,Chris (b)
Theis/Nyegaard Jazzband
High Society | Mabel's Dream | Winin' Boy Blues | Shine
Copenhagen,Denmark, rec. 31.3./1.4.1965
Jensen,Theis (tp,voc) | Nyegaard,Peter (tb) | Andersen,Erik 'Krolle' (cl) | Poulsen,Freddy 'Freak' (bj) | Jorgensen,Orla Levin (b) | Bodker,Niels (dr)

STCD 5522 | CD | Albert Nicholas & The Dutch Swing College Band
Albert Nicholas With The Dutch Swing College Band
Black And Blue | I Found A New Baby | Weary Blues
Live at Old Fellow Palaet's Store Sal,Kopenhagen, rec. 5.9.1954
Nicholas,Albert (cl) | Buma,Wybe (tp) | Kolstee,Wim (tb) | Schilperoort,Peter (cl) | Kesber,Dim (cl) | Schrier,Joop (p) | Braxhoofden,Dick (bj) | Van Oven,Bob (b) | Westendorp,André (dr)
Albert Nicholas With Adrian Bentzon's Jazzband
Royal Garden Blues | Winin' Boy Blues | Rose Room | Ostrich Walk
Nicholas,Albert (cl) | Bentzon,Adrian (p) | Fairweather,Al (tp) | Bentzon,Fridolin (b) | Karn,Ole (dr)
Dutch Swing College Band
Fidgety Feet | Tin Roof Blues | Tears | Basin Street Blues | Dippermouth Blues | Room Rent Blues
Buma,Wybe (tp) | Kolstee,Wim (tb) | Schilperoort,Peter (cl,ss,dr) | Kesber,Dim (cl) | Schrier,Joop (p) | Braxhoofden,Dick (bj) | Van Oven,Bob (b) | Westendorp,André (dr,co)
Lulu's Back In Town
Kesber,Dim (cl) | Schrier,Joop (p) | Van Oven,Bob (b) | Schilperoort,Peter (dr)

STCD 6033 | CD | Muggsy Spanier At Club Hangover 1953/54
Muggsy Spanier And His Dixieland All Stars
Royal Garden Blues | Basin Street Blues | Dippermouth Blues | Just Squeeze Me(But Don't Tease Me) | Rose Room
Live at Club Hangover,San Francisco,CA, rec. 11.4.1953
Spanier,Francis 'Muggsy' (co) | Hutchinson,Ralph (tb) | Howard,Darnell (cl) | Grant,Mel (p) | Parham,Charles 'Truck' (b) | Deems,Barrett (dr)
St.Louis Blues | Riverside Blues | Farewell Blues | If I Had You | That's A Plenty | Relaxin' At The Touro (Theme)
Live at Club Hangover,San Francisco,CA, rec. 18.4.1953
Spanier,Francis 'Muggsy' (co) | Hutchinson,Ralph (tb) | Howard,Darnell (cl) | Grant,Mel (p) | Parham,Charles 'Truck' (b) | Deems,Barrett (dr)
Memphis Blues | I Wish I Could Shimmy Like My Sister Kate
Live at Club Hangover,San Francisco,CA, rec. 13.11.1954
Spanier,Francis 'Muggsy' (co) | Hutchinson,Ralph (tb) | Gomez,Chico (cl) | Richards,Charles 'Red' (p) | Parham,Charles 'Truck' (b) | Cozeneau,Coz (dr)
Moonglow | That Da-Da Strain | Relaxin' At The Touro (Theme)
Live at Club Hangover,San Francisco,CA, rec. 27.11.1954
Spanier,Francis 'Muggsy' (co) | Hutchinson,Ralph (tb) | Gomez,Chico (cl) | Richards,Charles 'Red' (p) | Parham,Charles 'Truck' (b) | Cozeneau,Coz (dr)

STCD 6037 | CD | Earl Hines/Muggsy Spanier All Stars:The Chicago Dates
Earl Hines-Muggsy Spanier All Stars
My Monday Date | Mood Indigo | Wang Wang Blues | Pop's Blues | Apex Blues | Caravan | I Ain't Got Nobody | Mahogany Hall Stomp | Savoy Blues | I Found A New Baby | Relaxin' At The Touro | Bugle Call Rag- | Ole Miss- | I'm Coming Virginia | It's Right Here For You | When The Saints Go Marching In
Chicago,Ill, rec. 1954
Spanier,Francis 'Muggsy' (tp,co) | Hines,Earl 'Fatha' (p) | Archey,Jimmy (tb) | Howard,Darnell (cl) | Foster,George 'Pops' (b) | Watkins,Earl (dr)

STCD 6051 | CD | Muggsy Spanier-Manhattan Masters,1945
Muggsy Spanier And His Dixieland Band
Tin Roof Blues | Muskrat Ramble
NYC, rec. 1.3.1945
Spanier,Francis 'Muggsy' (co) | McGarity,Lou (tb) | Russell,Pee Wee (cl) | Schroeder,Gene (p) | Kress,Carl (g) | Casey,Bob (b) | Grauso,Joe (dr)

Miff Mole And His Dixieland Band
Original Dixieland One Step | I Can't Give You Anything But Love | Three Little Words
NYC, rec. 2.3.1945
Mole,Miff (tb) | Spanier,Francis 'Muggsy' (co) | Russell,Pee Wee (cl) | Schroeder,Gene (p) | Sharp,Fred (g) | Lesberg,Jack (b) | Carroll,Charles (dr)
Livery Stable Blues | I'm Sorry I Made You Cry | Miff's Blues
Mole,Miff (tb) | Spanier,Francis 'Muggsy' (co) | Russell,Pee Wee (cl) | Schroeder,Gene (p) | Hanlon,Allen (g) | Lesberg,Jack (b) | Carroll,Charles (dr)
Muggsy Spanier And His Dixieland Band
Bugle Call Rag | Feather Brain Blues | You're Lucky To Me
Spanier,Francis 'Muggsy' (co) | McGarity,Lou (tb) | Russell,Pee Wee (cl) | Caceres,Ernie (bs) | Schroeder,Gene (p) | Kress,Carl (g) | Haggart,Bob (b,whistling) | Carroll,Charles (dr)
That's A Plenty
Spanier,Francis 'Muggsy' (co) | McGarity,Lou (tb) | Russell,Pee Wee (cl) | Caceres,Ernie (bs) | Rongetti,Nick (p) | Kress,Carl (g) | Haggart,Bob (b) | Carroll,Charles (dr)
Pee Wee Russell And His Dixieland Band
Back Home Again In Indiana | I Ain't Gonna Give Nobody None Of My Jelly Roll | Clarinet Marmalade | Mama's In The Groove | My Honey's Lovin' Arms | Fidgety Feet
Russell,Pee Wee (cl) | Spanier,Francis 'Muggsy' (co) | McGarity,Lou (tb) | Schroeder,Gene (p) | Casey,Bob (b) | Grauso,Joe (dr)

STCD 6052 | CD | Edmond Hall With The Ralph Sutton Group
Edmond Hall With The Ralph Sutton Group
Oh! Baby | Keepin' Out Of Mischief Now | Basin Street Blues | I Found A New Baby | Dardanella
Live at Club Hangover,San Francisco,CA, rec. 24.7.1954
Hall,Edmond (cl) | Sutton,Ralph (p) | Page,Walter (b) | Lodice,Charlie (dr)
Checkin' With Chuck(theme) | St.Louis Blues | Sweet And Lovely | Blues My Naughty Sweetie Gives To Me | Up Jumped You With Love
Live at Club Hangover,San Francisco,CA, rec. 31.7.1954
Hall,Edmond (cl) | Sutton,Ralph (p) | Page,Walter (b) | Lodice,Charlie (dr)
Black And Blue | Between The Devil And The Deep Blue Sea | Honeysuckle Rose | The Sheik Of Araby
Live at Club Hangover,San Francisco,CA, rec. 7.8.1954
Hall,Edmond (cl) | Hurley,Clyde (tp) | Sutton,Ralph (p) | Page,Walter (b) | Lodice,Charlie (dr)
Tin Roof Blues | Love Is Just Around The Corner | I Got Rhythm
Live at Club Hangover,San Francisco,CA, rec. 14.8.1954
Hall,Edmond (cl) | Hurley,Clyde (tp) | Sutton,Ralph (p) | Page,Walter (b) | Lodice,Charlie (dr)

STCD 8221 | CD | Tivoli Encounter
Phineas Newborn Jr. Trio
Oh! Lady Be Good | Don't Blame Me | Daahoud | Billie's Bounce- | Walkin'- | Sweet And Lovely | On Green Dolphin Street | Nica's Dream | Trees- | Tea For Two- | Oleo | A Night In Tunisia | I'll Remember April
Live at Jazzhus Slukefter,Tivoli Gardens,Copenhagen, rec. 16.7.1979
Newborn Jr.,Phineas (p) | Lundgaard,Jesper (b) | Rostvold,Bjarne (dr)

STCD 8222 | CD | Earl Hines Live!
Earl Hines Trio
Monday Date- | Blues In Thirds- | You Can Depend On Me- | Tea For Two | Keepin' Out Of Mischief Now- | Two Sleepy People- | Ain't Misbehavin'- | Jitterbug Waltz- | Just Squeeze Me(But Don't Tease Me)- | Honeysuckle Rose- | Shiny Stockings | Perdido | Black Coffee | Canadian Sunset- | Lullaby Of Birdland- | Misty- | Satin Doll- | Boogie Woogie On St. Louis Blues
Live at East Park Jazz Club,Aalborg,Denmark, rec. 22.4.1965
Hines,Earl 'Fatha' (p) | Hansen,Morten (b) | Kureer,Jorgen (dr)

STCD 8236 | CD | The Complete Associated Transcriptions,1944
Teddy Wilson Sextet
Flying Home | Back Home Again In Indiana | Embraceable You | A Touch Of Boogie Woogie | B Flat Swing | Don't Be That Way | Honeysuckle Rose | Mop Mop | I Got Rhythm | Rose Room | Oh! Lady Be Good | The Way You Look Tonight | Stompin' At The Savoy | You're My Favorite Memory | The Sheik Of Araby
NYC, rec. 15.6.1944
Wilson,Teddy (p) | Berry,Emmett (tp) | Morton,Benny (tb) | Hall,Edmond (cl) | Stewart,Slam (b) | Catlett,Big Sid (dr)

STCD 8238 | CD | Elegiac
Zoot Sims-Bucky Pizzarelli Duo
Lester Leaps In | Willow Weep For Me | Limehouse Blues | My Old Flame | In A Mellow Tone | I Got It Bad And That Ain't Good | Satin Doll | Take The 'A' Train | Fred | Jean | Stompin' At The Savoy | Memories Of You | Softly As In A Morning Sunrise | Girl From Ipanema(Garota De Ipanema)
NYC, rec. 6.11.1980
Sims,Zoot (ss,ts) | Pizzarelli,Bucky (g)

STCD 8242 | CD | Louis Armstrong:Wintergarden 1947/Blue Note 1948
Louis Armstrong And His All Stars
Introduction by Fred Murray | Way Down Yonder In New Orleans | Basin Street Blues | Muskrat Ramble | Dear Old Southland | Do You Know What It Means To Miss New Orleans | Someday You'll Be Sorry | Tiger Rag
Live at The Winter Garden Theatre,NYC, rec. 19.6.1947
Armstrong,Louis (tp,voc) | Hackett,Bobby (co) | Teagarden,Jack (tb,voc) | Hucko,Peanuts (cl,ts) | Caceres,Ernie (bs,bass-s) | Cary,Dick (p) | Lesberg,Jack (b) | Wettling,George (dr)
When It's Sleepy Time Down South(Theme) | Muskrat Ramble | A Song Was Born | Basin Street Blues | St.Louis Blues | High Society | Royal Garden Blues | I've Got A Right To Sing The Blues
Live Broadcast 'Blue Note,Chicago,Ill', rec. 11.12.1948
Armstrong,Louis (tp,voc) | Teagarden,Jack (tb,voc) | Bigard,Barney (cl) | Hines,Earl 'Fatha' (p) | Shaw,Arvell (b) | Catlett,Big Sid (dr)

STCD 8246 | CD | The Ralph Sutton Quartet With Ruby Braff,Vol.2
Ralph Sutton Quartet
I'm Gonna Sit Right Down And Write Myself A Letter | Oh! Baby | Ain't Misbehavin' | Don't Blame Me | What A Little Moonlight Can Do | Can't We Be Friends | I Wished On The Moon- | If You Were Mine- | I've Got A Pocket Full Of Money | Diane- | All By Myself- | You Are My Lucky Star- | The Sheik Of Araby
Live at Sunnie's Rendezvous,Aspen,Colorado, rec. 28.2.1968
Sutton,Ralph (p) | Braff,Ruby (co) | Hinton,Milt (b) | Alexander,Mousie (dr)

STCD 8253 | CD | Art Tatum-The Complete Jazz Chronicle Solo Session | EAN 717101825325
Art Tatum
Wrap Your Troubles In Dreams | Sittin' And Rockin' | You're Driving Me Crazy | Tenderly | Over The Rainbow | In A Sentimental Mood | You Took Advantage Of Me | It's The Talk Of The Town | She's Funny That Way | I'll Never Be The Same | Night And Day | Over The Rainbow | Over The Rainbow(alt.take) | It's The Talk Of The Town(alt.take) | I'll Never Be The Same(alt.take) | Night And Day(alt.take)
Los Angeles,CA, rec. ca.1948
Tatum,Art (p-solo)
Someone To Watch Over Me | Smoke Gets In Your Eyes | Begin The Beguine | I Cover The Waterfront | Body And Soul | I Know That You Know | If I Should Lose You
Radio Broadcast, taped in NY, 26.11.1955
Tatum,Art (p-solo,narration)

STCD 8258 | CD | The Keystone Transcriptions 1939-1940
Teddy Wilson
A Ghost Of A Chance | Sunday | More Than You Know | Summers End | Goin' Home Blues | Minute Steak | Sugar | At Sundown | Tuesday Jump | The Moon Is Low | Afternoon Blues | The LittleThings That Mean So Much | You're My Favorite Memory | Rhythmatics | Almost Blues | Tempo Positioned | Out Of Nowhere | Night And Day | Oh! Lady Be Good | Jumpin' Off | You'll Be Sorry | Chinatown My Chinatown | Twilight Blue | Love Is The Sweetest Thing | Rose Room | Why Shouldn't I
NYC, rec. ca.1939-1940
Wilson,Teddy (p-solo)

STCD 8264 | CD | Hurry On Down
Benny Waters Quartet
Hurry On Down | Up A Lazy River | Topsy | Blue Moon | On The Sunny Side Of The Street | I'm Beginning To See The Light | As Time Goes By | Oh! Lady Be Good | Autumn Leaves | It Had To Be You
Blackbird Close,Basingstoke,GB, rec. 21.4.1981
Waters,Benny (cl,as,ts,voc) | Sealey,Paul (g) | Howard,Erica (b) | Cox,John (dr)
Have You Met Miss Jones | Fuzzy Blues(take 1)
Blackbird Close,Basingstoke,GB, rec. 28.4.1981
Waters,Benny (cl,as,ts,voc) | Sealey,Paul (g) | Howard,Erica (b) | Cox,John (dr)

STCD 8269 | CD | Then Here And Now
Richard Wyands Trio
Yes It Is | Lament | As Long As There's Music | Leonora | Never Let Me Go | Yesterdays | Blue Rose | Leonora(alt.take) | Blue Rose(alt.take)
NYC, rec. 12.10.1978
Wyands,Richard (p) | Atkinson,Lisle (b) | Lee,David (dr)

STCD 8270 | CD | Bass Contra Bass
Lisle Atkinson Quartet
Sweet And Lovely | Tranquility | Hit It | Samba De Amor | Lush Life | C'Mon Baby | C'Mon Baby(alt.take) | Hit It(alt.take)
NYC, rec. 13.10.1978
Atkinson,Lisle (b) | Wyands,Richard (p) | West,Paul (b) | Harewood,Al (dr)
Lisle Atkinson Quintet
Karen
Atkinson,Lisle (b) | Atkinson,Karen (fl) | Wyands,Richard (p) | West,Paul (b) | Harewood,Al (dr)

STCD 8274 | CD | Kenny Drew/Solo-Duo
Kenny Drew/Niels-Henning Orsted-Pedersen Duo
Everything I Love | Ode To Mariann | Willow Weep For Me | Swingin' Till The Girls Come Home
Copenhagen,Denmark, rec. 1966
Drew,Kenny (p) | Orsted-Pedersen,Niels-Henning (b)
Kenny Drew
Yesterdays | Blues For Nils | A Simple Need | Whisper Not
Copenhagen,Denmark, rec. 15.12.1978
Drew,Kenny (p-solo)
Kenny Drew-Bo Stief Duo
Blues For Nils | There Is No Greater Love | Ack Värmeland Du Sköna | Bluesology
Live at 'Grock',Copenhagen,Denmark, rec. 29.9.1983
Drew,Kenny (p) | Stief,Bo (b)

STCD 8275 | CD | No More Brew
Brew Moore Quartet
It Could Happen To You | Manny's Tune | No More Brew | Blue Monk
Live at 'Stampen',Stockholm, rec. 25.2.1971
Moore,Brew (ts) | Sjösten,Lars (p) | Nordin,Sture (b) | Noren,Fredrik (dr)
Special Brew | I Remember You | Samba De Orfeu | Straight No Chaser
Copenhagen,Denmark, rec. March 1971
Moore,Brew (ts) | Bjorn,Atli (p) | Molbak,Erik (b) | Curtis,Jual (dr)

STCD 8278 | CD | The Unissued Copenhagen Studio Recordings
Warne Marsh Trio
Confirmation | I Can't Give You Anything But Love | Without A Song | Just One Of Those Things | All The Things You Are | I Should Care | The More I See You | When You're Smiling | Takin' A Chance On Love | Little Willie Leaps | Every Time We Say Goodbye | I Want To Be Happy
Copenhagen,Denmark, rec. 29.12.1975
Marsh,Warne (ts) | Orsted-Pedersen,Niels-Henning (b) | Levitt,Al (dr)

STCD 8280 | CD | Live At Sunnie's Rendezvous Vol.1
Ralph Sutton Quartet
I'm Gonna Sit Right Down And Write Myself A Letter | What A Little Moonlight Can Do | Everything Happens To Me | Sweet And Lovely | I Found A New Baby | Street Of Dreams | Blue Turning Grey Over You | Oh! Lady Be Good | Keepin' Out Of Mischief Now | Blue And Broken Hearted | St.Louis Blues
Live at Sunnie's Rendezvous,Aspen,Colorado, rec. 18.2.1969
Sutton,Ralph (p) | Wilber,Bob (cl,ss) | Hall,Al (b) | Leeman,Cliff (dr)

STCD 8283 | CD | Thelonious Monk In Copenhagen
Thelonious Monk Quartet
Jackie-Ing | Crepuscule With Nellie | I Mean You | Rhythm-A-Ning | Epistrophy | Well You Needn't | Round About Midnight | Off Minor | Blue Monk
Live at Odd Fellow Palast,Copenhagen, rec. 17.5.1961
Monk,Thelonious (p) | Rouse,Charlie (ts) | Ore,John (b) | Dunlop,Frankie (dr)
Thelonious Monk
Body And Soul
Monk,Thelonious (p-solo)

STCD 8284 | CD | Frank Talks!
Frank Rosolino Quartet
Blue Daniel | How About You | Straight No Chaser | There Is No Greater Love | Waltz For Diana
Live at Slukafter,Copenhagen, rec. 30.8.1978
Rosolino,Frank (tb) | Clausen,Thomas (p) | Stief,Bo (b) | Rostvold,Bjarne (dr)

STCD 8285 | CD | May Lou Williams Trio At Rick's Cafe Americain,Chicago,Ill.
Mary Lou Williams Trio
Autumn Leaves | I Can't Get Started | You Can't Take That Away From Me | Satin Doll | The Jeep Is Jumpin' | St.James Infirmary | Surrey With The Fringe On Top | My Funny Valentine | Mack The Knife(Moritat) | What's Your Story(Morning Glory) | Without A Song | Caravan | A Grand Night For Swinging
Live at Rick's Cafe Americain,Chicago,Ill., rec. 14.11.1979
Williams,Mary Lou (p) | Suggs,Milton (b) | Khalid,Drashear (dr)

STCD 8287 | CD | Jimmy Rowles/Subtle Legend Vol.1
Jimmy Rowles
Devastating Cherub | Limehouse Blues | Now That You'r Gone | Some Other Spring | Jitterbug Waltz | Tell It Like It Is | Do You Know Why Stars Come Out At Night | Looking At You | Sweet Lorraine | Devil's Island | Humoresque
Live at Chappy's,Los Angeles,CA, rec. 15.10.1972
Rowles,Jimmy (p,voc)
Jimmy Rowles Trio
Isfahan | Ballad Of Thelonious Monk
Live at Danshean Residence,Stems House,Glendale,CA, rec. 8.1.1972
Rowles,Jimmy (p,voc) | Budwig,Monty (b) | Bailey,Donald (dr)

STCD 8292 | CD | Old Friends
Bob Brookmeyer Quartet
I Hear A Rhapsody | Stella By Starlight | Polka Dots And Moonbeams | Who Cares | All Blues
Copenhagen Jazz House,Copenhagen,Denmark, rec. 30.11.1994
Brookmeyer,Bob (v-tb) | Clausen,Thomas (p) | Vinding,Mads (b) | Riel,Alex (dr)

STCD 8298 | CD | Tough Tenors Back Again!
Eddie Lockjaw Davis-Johnny Griffin Quintet
Blues Up And Down | Oh Gee | Call It What You Wanna | Funky Fluke | Hey Lock | Lester Leaps In | Intermission Riff
Live at The 'Jazzhus' Montmartre,Copenhagen, rec. 10.7.1984
Griffin,Johnny (ts) | Davis,Eddie 'Lockjaw' (ts) | Pickins,Harry (p) | Lundy,Curtis (b) | Washington,Kenny (dr)

STCD 8300 | CD | Johnny Griffin/Art Taylor In Copenhagen
Johnny Griffin-Art Taylor Quartet
What Is This Thing Called Love | Body And Soul | Wee Dot | Doctor's Blues | Exactly Like You | A Night In Tunisia
Live at The 'Jazzhus' Montmartre,Copenhagen, rec. 14.4./28.11.& 12.12.1964
Griffin,Johnny (ts,voc) | Drew,Kenny (p) | Orsted-Pedersen,Niels-Henning (b) | Taylor,Arthur 'Art' (dr)

STCD 8316/17 | 2 CD | The Duke At Fargo 1940
Duke Ellington And His Orchestra
It's Glory | The Mooche | The Sheik Of Araby | Sepia Panorama | Ko-Ko | There Shall Be No Night | Pussy Willow | Chatterbox | Mood Indigo | Harlem Air Shaft | Ferryboat Serenade | Warm Valley | Stompy Jones | Chloe | Bojangles | On The Air | Rumpus In Richmond | Chaser | The Sidewalks Of New York | The Flaming Sword | Never No Lament | Caravan | Clarinet Lament | Slap Happy | Sepia Panorama | Boy Meets Horn | Way Down Yonder In New Orleans | Oh Babe! Maybe Someday | Five O'Clock Whistle | Fanfare | Call Of The Canyon | Unidentified Title | All This And Heaven Too | Rockin' In Rhythm | Sophisticated Lady | Cotton Tail | Whispering Grass | Conga Brava | I Never Felt This Way Before | Across The Track Blues | Honeysuckle Rose | Wham | Stardust | Rose Of The Rio Grande | St.Louis Blues | Warm Valley | God Bless America
Live at The Crystal Ballroom,Fargo,North Dakota, rec. 7.11.1940
Ellington,Duke (p) | Stewart,Rex (co) | Jones,Wallace (tp) | Nance,Ray (tp,v,voc) | Nanton,Joe 'Tricky Sam' (tb) | Tizol,Juan (tb) | Brown,Lawrence (tb) | Bigard,Barney (cl,ts) | Hodges,Johnny (cl,ss,as) | Hardwicke,Otto (cl,as) | Webster,Ben (cl,ts) | Carney,Harry (cl,bs) | Guy,Fred (g,whistle) | Blanton,Jimmy (b) | Greer,William 'Sonny' (dr) | Anderson,Ivie (voc) | Jeffries,Herb (voc)

STCD 8322 | CD | Clark Terry And His Orchestra Feat. Paul Gonsalves
Clark Terry And His Orchestra
Serenade To A Bus Seat | Pannonica | Pea-Eyes | Satin Doll | Daniel's Blues | Mean To Me | Blues For The Champ Of The Champs | Circeo | Clark Bars | Pannonica No.2 | Lonely One
Paris,France, rec. October 1959
Terry,Clark (tp) | Gonsalves,Paul (ts) | Fol,Raimond (p) | Woode,Jimmy (b) | Woodyard,Sam (dr)

STCD 8323 | CD | Togo Brava Swuite
Duke Ellington And His Orchestra
Peke
NYC, rec. 3.2.1971
Ellington,Duke (p) | Williams,Cootie (tp) | Preston,Eddie (tp) | Johnson,Money (tp) | Ellington,Mercer (tp) | Wood,Booty (tb) | Taylor,Malcolm (tb) | Connors,Chuck (tb) | Procope,Russell (cl,as) | Turney,Norris (cl,as) | Ashby,Harold (ts) | Gonsalves,Paul (ts) | Carney,Harry (b-cl,bs) | Davis,Wild Bill (org) | Benjamin,Joe (b) | Jones,Rufus (dr)
Checkered Hat | There's A Place
NYC, rec. 23.1.1971
Ellington,Duke (p) | Williams,Cootie (tp) | Preston,Eddie (tp) | Johnson,Money (tp) | Ellington,Mercer (tp) | Wood,Booty (tb) | Taylor,Malcolm (tb) | Connors,Chuck (tb) | Procope,Russell (cl,as) | Turney,Norris (cl,as) | Ashby,Harold (ts) | Gonsalves,Paul (ts) | Carney,Harry (b-cl,bs) | Davis,Wild Bill (org) | Benjamin,Joe (b) | Jones,Rufus (dr) | Brookshire,Nell (voc) | Watkins,Tony (voc)
Duke Ellington Quartet
Blues
NYC, rec. 23.2.1971
Ellington,Duke (p) | Davis,Wild Bill (org) | Benjamin,Joe (b) | Jones,Rufus (dr)
Duke Ellington And His Orchestra
Hick | Grap(The Giggling Rapsids) | Something | Making The Scene(Love Scenes)
NYC, rec. 28.4.1971
Ellington,Duke (p) | Williams,Cootie (tp) | Preston,Eddie (tp) | Johnson,Money (tp) | Ellington,Mercer (tp) | Wood,Booty (tb) | Taylor,Malcolm (tb) | Connors,Chuck (tb) | Minerve,Harold (fl,as) | Turney,Norris (cl,as) | Ashby,Harold (ts) | Gonsalves,Paul (ts) | Carney,Harry (b-cl,bs) | Benjamin,Joe (b) | Jones,Rufus (dr) | Watkins,Tony (voc)
Lover Man(Oh,Where Can You Be?) | Perdido
NYC, rec. 13.5.1951
Ellington,Duke (p) | Williams,Cootie (tp) | Preston,Eddie (tp) | Johnson,Money (tp) | Ellington,Mercer (tp) | Wood,Booty (tb) | Taylor,Malcolm (tb) | Connors,Chuck (tb) | Pearson,Buddy (as) | Turney,Norris (cl,as) | Ashby,Harold (ts) | Gonsalves,Paul (ts) | Carney,Harry (b-cl,bs) | Davis,Wild Bill (org) | Benjamin,Joe (b) | Jones,Rufus (dr)
Togo Brava Suite: | Mkis(Soul Soothing Beach) | Tego | Togo Or Yoyo(Naturellement)
NYC, rec. 28.6.1971
Ellington,Duke (p) | Williams,Cootie (tp) | Williams,Richard (tp) | Johnson,Money (tp) | Ellington,Mercer (tp) | Wood,Booty (tb) | Taylor,Malcolm (tb) | Connors,Chuck (tb) | Procope,Russell (cl,as) | Pearson,Buddy (as) | Turney,Norris (cl,as) | Ashby,Harold (ts) | Gonsalves,Paul (ts) | Carney,Harry (b-cl,bs) | Davis,Wild Bill (org) | Benjamin,Joe (b) | Jones,Rufus (dr)
Too Kee(Amour.Amour) | Buss(Right On Togo) | Soso | Toto(Afrique)
NYC, rec. 29.6.1971
Ellington,Duke (p) | Williams,Cootie (tp) | Williams,Richard (tp) | Johnson,Money (tp) | Ellington,Mercer (tp) | Wood,Booty (tb) | Taylor,Malcolm (tb) | Connors,Chuck (tb) | Procope,Russell (cl,as) | Pearson,Buddy (as) | Turney,Norris (cl,as) | Ashby,Harold (ts) | Gonsalves,Paul (ts) | Carney,Harry (b-cl,bs) | Davis,Wild Bill (org) | Benjamin,Joe (b) | Jones,Rufus (dr)

STCD 8328 | CD | Late Woman Blues
Stuff Smith With The Henri Chaix Trio
C Jam Blues | Perdido | Late Woman Blues | How High The Moon | On The Sunny Side Of The Street | Take The 'A' Train | Body And Soul | After You've Gone | Oh! Lady Be Good | Rosetta
Live at Jazz in der Aula,Baden,CH, rec. 29.5.1965
Smith,Stuff (v,voc) | Chaix,Henri (p) | Guillemin,Michel (b) | Bishop,Wallace (dr)

STCD 8340 | CD | Stan Kenton With The Danish Radio Big Band | EAN 717101834020
Stan Kenton With The Danish Radio Big Band
Artistry In Rhythm | Malaguena | I'm Glad There Is You | The Blues Story | Love For Sale | Stella By Starlight | Limehouse Blues | Interlude | Dragonwyck | Yesterdays | Artemis And Apollo | Cuban Fire Suite | Talk | It's The Talk Of The Town | Fanfare
Live at Radio Concert Hall,Copenhagen,Denmark, rec. 20.3.1966
Kenton,Stan (p,ld) | Mikkelborg,Palle (tp) | Sulieman[Leonard Graham],Idrees (tp) | Botschinsky,Allan (tp) | Bolvig,Palle (tp) | Lundvig,Svend (tp) | Molgaard,Torolf (tb) | Lind,John (tb) | Jensen,Ole Kurt (tb) | Kjaeldgaard,Poul (tb) | Engelholt,Steen (tb) | Hansen,Helmuth Hjort (tb) | Garnov, | Sternbach,David (fr-h) | Larsen,Per (fr-h) | Billberg,Rolf (as) | Christensen,Erling (as) | Karskov,Uffe (as,ts) | Jaedig,Bent (ts) | Nielsen,Bent (bs) | Molin,Ole (g) | Orsted-Pedersen,Niels-Henning (b) | Rostvold,Bjarne (dr) | Steffensen,John (perc) | Nielsen,Per (perc) | Glindemann,Ib (cond)

STCD 8359 | CD | At The Hurricane:Original 1943 Broadcasts | EAN 717101835928
Duke Ellington And His Orchestra
Take The 'A' Train(theme) | Hayfoot Strawfoot | It Can't Be Wrong | What Am I Here For | Main Stem | Could It Be You | Goin' Up | Don't Get Around Much Anymore | Nevada | Things Ain't What They Used To Be
Live at The Hurricane.NYC, rec. 3.4.1943
Ellington,Duke (p) | Nance,Ray (tp) | Stewart,Rex (tp) | Baker,Harold 'Shorty' (tp) | Jones,Wallace (tp) | Brown,Lawrence (tb) | Nanton,Joe 'Tricky Sam' (tb) | Hodges,Johnny (as) | Mallard,Oett 'Sax' (cl,as) | Haughton,Chauncey (cl) | Webster,Ben (ts) | Carney,Harry (b-cl,bs) | Guy,Fred (g) | Raglin,Alvin 'Junior' (b) | Greer,William 'Sonny' (dr)
Take The 'A' Train(theme) | Don't Get Around Much Anymore | Main Stem | I Don't Want Anybody At All | Johnny Comes Lately | Things Ain't What They Used To Be
Live at The Hurricane,NYC, rec. 4.4.1943
Ellington,Duke (p) | Jones,Wallace (tp) | Nance,Ray (tp) | Stewart,Rex (tp) | Baker,Harold 'Shorty' (tp) | Tizol,Juan (tb) | Nanton,Joe 'Tricky Sam' (tb) | Brown,Lawrence (tb) | Hodges,Johnny (as) | Mallard,Oett 'Sax' (cl,as) | Haughton,Chauncey (cl) | Webster,Ben (ts) | Carney,Harry (bs) | Guy,Fred (g) | Raglin,Alvin 'Junior' (b) | Greer,William 'Sonny' (dr)

Moon Mist | You'll Never Know | Tonight I Shall Sleep With A Smile On My Face | I Don't Know What Kind Of Blues I Got | Don't Get Around Much Anymore | Moon Mist(theme)

Live at The Hurricane,NYC, rec. 6,6,1943

Ellington,Duke (p) | Jones,Wallace (tp) | Nance,Ray (tp) | Jordan,Taft (tp) | Baker,Harold 'Shorty' (tp) | Tizol,Juan (tb) | Nanton,Joe 'Tricky Sam' (tb) | Williams,Sandy (tb) | Hodges,Johnny (as) | Jones,Nat (cl,as) | Hamilton,Jimmy (cl,ts) | Webster,Ben (ts) | Carney,Harry (b-cl,bs) | Guy,Fred (g) | Raglin,Alvin 'Junior' (b) | Greer,William 'Sonny' (dr)

STCD 8362 | CD | The Many Faces Of Dorothy Donegan | EAN 717101836222

Dorothy Donegan Trio

Introduction | St.Louis Blues | Mack The Knife(Moritat) | Just In Time

Live at The London House,Chicago,Ill., rec. 14.4.1961

Donegan,Dorothy (p) | unkn. (b,dr)

Misty | Some Of These Days | Begin The Beguine | Bill Bailey Won't You Please Come Home | 12th Street Rag | Liza

Live at The London House,Chicago,Ill., rec. details unknown

Donegan,Dorothy (p) | unkn. (b,dr)

I Just Want To Sing | You Are The Sunshine Of My Life | Donegan's Blues | Lift Every Voice And Sing | Dorothy Runs Away | Willow Weep For Me | Minuet In G | I Love You | Stop The World,I Want To Get Off!

Antibes,France, rec. 22.7.1975

Donegan,Dorothy (p) | Shaw,Arvell (b) | Francis,Panama (dr)

STCD 8363 | CD | Dexter Gordon:Atlanta Georgia May 5,1981 | EAN 717101836321

Dexter Gordon Quartet

Tangerine | I Told You So | Skylark | It's You Or No One | Backstairs | As Time Goes By | Jumpin' Blues

Atlanta,GA, rec. 5.5.1981

Gordon,Dexter (ts) | Lightsey,Kirk (p) | Reid,Rufus (b) | Gladden,Eddie (dr)

STCD 8367 | CD | Zoot Sims | EAN 717101836727

Zoot Sims Quartet

That Old Devil Called Love | Jitterbug Waltz | Softly As In A Morning Sunrise | Over The Rainbow | In A Mellow Tone | I Got It Bad And That Ain't Good | Caravan

Live at E.J.'s,Atlanta, rec. 9.8.1981

Sims,Zoot (ss,ts) | Korosi,Yancey (p) | Sampson,Devey (b) | Martin,James (dr)

Zoot Sims Quintet

Groovin' High | Take The 'A' Train | Lester Leaps In

Sims,Zoot (ss,ts) | Bell,Rick (ts) | Korosi,Yancey (p) | Sampson,Devey (b) | Martin,James (dr)

STCD 8374 | CD | Kinnings | EAN 717101837427

Ulf Meyer & Martin Wind Group

O Grande Amor | Biji | Pete's Repeat | Fuglsang | Groove Merchant | Taylor's Test | Do You Know What It Means To Miss New Orleans

Hamburg, rec. September/October 2002

Meyer,Ulf (g) | Wind,Martin (b) | Riel,Alex (dr)

Kinnings | The Soccerball | Ain't Got Nothing But The Blues | Birkelunden

Meyer,Ulf (g) | Wind,Martin (b) | Kerschek,Wolf (grand-p,fender-rhodes) | Riel,Alex (dr)

STCD 8378 | CD | OW | EAN 717101837823

Clark Terry Quartet

Secret Love | Ow! | Just An Old Manuscript | Georgia On My Mind | Mack The Knife(Moritat) | Take The 'A' Train | Straight No Chaser | God Bless The Child | Rebecca

Live at E.J.'s,Atlanta, rec. 18.12.1981

Terry,Clark (tp,voc) | O'Neal,Johnny (p) | Sampson,Devey (b) | Martin,James (dr)

Storyville | ZYX Music GmbH

4960043 | DVD | The Big Bands Vol.1.The Snader Telescriptions | EAN 5708812960042

Duke Ellington And His Orchestra

Sophisticated Lady | Caravan | The Mooche | V.I.P.'s Boogie | Solitude | Mood Indigo | The Hawk Talks

details unknown, rec. 1952

Ellington,Duke (p) | Anderson,Cat (tp) | Terry,Clark (tp) | Coock,Willie (tp) | Nance,Ray (tp,v) | Jackson,Quentin (tb) | Woodman,Britt (tb) | Tizol,Juan (tb) | Procope,Russell (as) | Smith,Willie (as) | Gonsalves,Paul (ts) | Hamilton,Jimmy (cl,ts) | Carney,Harry (b-cl,bs) | Marshall,Wende | Bellson,Louie (dr)

Lionel Hampton Orchestra

Midnight Sun | Beulah's Boogie | Cobb's Idea | T.V. Special

details unknown, rec. 1950

Hampton,Lionel (vib,p) | Mullens,Eddie (tp) | Shepherd,Leo (tp) | Garrette,Duke (tp) | Williams,Walter (tp) | Bailey,Benny (tp) | Higaki,Paul (tb) | Grey,Al (tb) | Powell,Benny (tb) | Warwick,Jimmy (tb) | Plater,Bobby (as) | Richardson,Jerome (as) | Board,Johnny (ts) | Lowe,Curtis (ts) | Kynard,Ben (bs) | Buckner,Milt (p) | Mackel,Billy (g) | Johnson,Roy (b) | Bartee,Ellis (dr)

Love You Like Mad | Ding Dong Baby | Vibe Boogie | Bongo Interlude | Air Mail Special | Slide Hamp Slide | Who Cares

details unknown, rec. 1951

Hampton,Lionel (vib,p) | Mullens,Eddie (tp) | Shepherd,Leo (tp) | Jones,Quincy (tp) | Williams,Walter (tp) | Bailey,Benny (tp) | Higaki,Paul (tb) | Grey,Al (tb) | Powell,Benny (tb) | Cleveland,Jimmy (tb) | Plater,Bobby (as) | Richardson,Jerome (as) | Board,Johnny (ts) | Bernal,Gil (ts) | Kynard,Ben (bs) | Buckner,Milt (p) | Mackel,Billy (g) | Johnson,Roy (b) | Bartee,Ellis (dr)

4960103 | DVD | Nat King Cole:The Snader Telescriptions | EAN 5708812960103

Nat King Cole And His Trio

Route 66 | Sweet Lorraine | Little Girl | Home | The Trouble With Me Is You | That's My Girl | This Is My Night To Dream | Nature Boy | Sweet Lorraine(alt.take)

details unknown, rec. prob.1951

Cole,Nat King (p,voc) | Ashby,Irving (g) | Comfort,Joe (b) | Costanza,Jack (bongos)

Nat King Cole Trio

You Call It Madness But I Call It Love | For Sentimental Reasons

Cole,Nat King (p,voc) | Ashby,Irving (g) | Comfort,Joe (b)

Nat King Cole Duo

Calypso Blues

Cole,Nat King (p,voc) | Costanza,Jack (bongos)

Nat King Cole And His Trio With Strings

Mona Lisa | Because Of Rain | Too Young | Always You | Home | Nature Boy

Cole,Nat King (p,voc) | Ashby,Irving (g) | Comfort,Joe (b) | Costanza,Jack (bongos) | unkn. (strings)

4960213 | DVD | Monterey Jazz Festival 1975 | EAN 5708812960219

Toshiko Akiyoshi-Lew Tabackin Big Band

Henpecked Old Man

Live at The Monterey Jazz Festival,CA, rec. 1975

Tabackin,Lew (reeds) | Akiyoshi,Toshiko (p,arr) | Terry,Clark (tp)

Paul Desmond Quartet

Emily

Desmond,Paul (as)

Bill Evans Trio

Up With The Lark

Evans,Bill (p)

Dizzy Gillespie Orchestra

Improvisation- | Blues-

Gillespie,Dizzy (tp,voc) | Tjader,Cal (vib)

Bobby Bland And His Band

I Wouldn't Tread A Dog

Bland,Bobby (g,voc)

Etta James And The Outlaws

Woman

James,Etta (voc) | Outlaws,The

Marion McPartland

Afterglow

McPartland,Marian (p-solo)

Marion McPartland-Bill Evans-John Lewis-Patrice Rushen

Billie's Bounce

McPartland,Marian (p) | Evans,Bill (p) | Lewis,John (p) | Rushen,Patrice (p)

Blood,Sweat And Tears

One Room Country Shack | And When I Die

Blood,Sweat And Tears | Clayton Thomas,David (voc)

John Lewis Sextet

Lyon's Head

Lewis,John (p) | Asmussen,Svend (v)

Chuck Mangione Quartet

Ichano

Mangione,Chuck (tp)

4960233 | DVD | The Mills Brothers Story | EAN 5708812960233

The Mills Brothers

Paper Doll | You Alway | Till Then | You're Nobody 'Til Somebody Loves You | Glow Worm | Nevertheless | Opus One | Yellow Bird | Dinah | Bye Bye Blackbird | Documentation

different Places, rec. different Dates

Mills Brothers,The (voc) | Mills,Harry (voc) | Mills,Donald (voc) | Mills,Herbert (voc)

4960263 | DVD | Jazz Legends:Eddie Lockjaw Davis Quartet Vol.1&2 | EAN 5708812960264

Eddie Lockjaw Davis Quartet

Take The 'A' Train | Just Friends | Out Of Nowhere | The Shadow Of Your Smile | If I Had You | Light And Lovely | 'S Wonderful | Shiny Stockings | Meditation | I Can't Get Started | Don't Get Around Much Anymore

Live at The Jazzhus Slukefter,Copenhagen,Denmark, rec. 1985

Davis,Eddie 'Lockjaw' (ts) | Stehen,Niels Jorgen (p) | Lundgaard,Jesper (b) | Thigpen,Ed (dr)

4960283 | DVD | Jazz Legends:Clark Terry-Duke Jordan | EAN 5708812960288

Clark Terry Quartet

In A Mellow Tone | Mood Indigo | Just Squeeze Me(But Don't Tease Me) Intro | Just Squeeze Me(But Don't Tease Me) | God Bless The Child | Satin Doll | Oh! Lady Be Good

Live at The 'Jazzhus' Montmartre,Copenhagen, rec. 7.4.1985

Terry,Clark (tp,fl-h) | Jordan,Duke (p) | Woode,Jimmy (b) | Norregaard,Svend Erik (dr)

Duke Jordan Trio

Dancesaball | Medley: | Lush Life- | Solitude- | Gone With The Wind | Jordu

Jordan,Duke (p) | Lundgaard,Jesper (b) | Tanggaard,Aage (dr)

4960323 | DVD | The Blues | EAN 5708812960325

Bessie Smith With The James P.Johnson Orchestra And The Hal Johnson Choir

St.Louis Blues

Gramercy Studio(RCA), rec. 1929

Smith,Bessie (voc) | Johnson,James P. (p) | Smith,Joe (co) | DeParis,Sidney prob. (tp) | Smith,Russell (tp) | Bailey,Buster (cl) | Caldwell,Happy (ts) | Addison,Bernard prob. (g) | Dixon,Charlie (bj) | Hull,Harry (tuba) | Marshall,Kaiser (dr) | Hall Johnson Choir,The | Handy,W.C. (arr)

Mamie Smith WithThe Lucky Millinder Orchestra

Tell To Mama

details unknown, rec. 1940

Smith,Mamie (voc) | Orchestra | Millinder,Lucky (ld) | details unknown

Ida Cox With Jesse Crump

Kentucky Man Blues | 'Fore Day Creep

details unknown, rec. 1947

Cox,Ida (voc) | Crump,Jesse 'Tiny' (p)

Big Bill Broonzy

John Henry | Stump Blues | Guitar Blues No.1 | Guitar Blues No.2

Field, rec. 1938-1942

Broonzy,Big Bill (g,voc)

Sonny Boy Williamson Group

Tell Me Baby | You're My Baby | Goin' Back Home

Stockholm,Sweden, rec. 1962

Williamson,Sonny Boy [Rice Miller] (harm,voc) | Nordin,Sture (b) | Nyten,Lennart (g)

4960333 | DVD | Duke Ellington And His Orchestra 1929-1943 | EAN 5708812960332

Duke Ellington And His Orchestra

Black And Tan Fantasy | The Duke Steps Out | Black Beauty | Cotton Club Stomp | Flaming Youth | Same Train | Black And Tan Fantasy(alt.take) | Check And Double Check | Symphony In Black: | The Laborers- | A Triangle(Dance,Jealousy,Blues)- | A Hymn Of Sorrow- | Harlem Rhythm- | Daybreak Express | Oh Babe! Maybe Someday | I've Got To Be A Rug Cutter | Mood Indigo | Sophisticated Lady | It Don't Mean A Thing If It Ain't Got That Swing | Don't Get Around Much Anymore

different Places,USA, rec. 1929-1943

Ellington,Duke (p,ld) | Orchestra

4960343 | DVD | Swing Vol.1 | EAN 5708812960349

Benny Goodman And His Orchestra

Auld Lang Syne: | I've Got A Heartful Of Music | Avalon | House Hop

Hollywood,CA, rec. 1937

personal included: | Goodman,Benny (cl) | James,Harry (tp) | Hampton,Lionel (vib) | Krupa,Gene (dr)

Artie Shaw And His Orchestra

Class In Swing: | Nightmare | Table D'Hote | I Have Eyes | Shoot The Likker To Me,John Boy

Hollywood,CA, rec. 1939

personal included: | Shaw,Artie (cl) | Auld,Georgie (sax) | Pastor,Tony (sax) | Rich,Buddy (dr) | Forest,Helen (voc)

Second Chorus: | Concerto For Clarinet(edited)

Hollywood,CA, rec. 1940

personal included: | Shaw,Artie (cl) | Hackett,Bobby (co) | Butterfield,Billy (tp) | Guarnieri,Johnny (p) | Fatool,Nick (dr)

Jimmy Dorsey And His Orchestra

Contrasts(Opening Theme) | Beebe | Rubber Dolly | Only A Rose | John Silver

personal included: | Dorsey,Jimmy (as,ld) | O'Connell,Helen (voc) | Eberle,Bob (voc)

Hoagy Carmichael With Jack Teagarden And His Big Band

Two Sleepy People | That's Right I'm Wrong | Washboard Blues | Lazy Bones | Small Fry | Rockin' Chair | Stardust

Hollywood,CA, rec. 1939

personal included: | Carmichael,Hoagy (voc) | Teagarden,Jack (tb,voc) | Blake,Meredith (voc)

Stan Kenton And His Orchestra

Let's Make Rhythm: | Artistry In Rhythm | Down In Chihuahua | Just A-Sittin' And A-Rockin' | Concerto To End All Concertos | Tampico | Pastels

Hollywood,CA, rec. 1947

personal included: | Kenton,Stan (p,ld) | Childers,Buddy (tp) | Wetzel,Ray (tp) | Alvarez,Chico (tp) | Anderson,John (tp) | Hanna,Ken (tp) | Winding,Kai (tb) | Layton,Skip (tb) | Bernhart,Milton 'Milt' (tb) | Forbes,Harry (tb) | Varsalona,Bart (b-tb) | Meyers,Eddie (as) | Mussulli,Boots (as) | Musso,Vido (ts) | Cooper,Bob (ts) | Gioga,Bob (bs) | Ahern,Bob (g) | Safranski,Eddie (b) | Manne,Shelly (dr)

4960363 | DVD | Steps Ahead:Copenhagen Live | EAN 5708812960363

Steps Ahead

Island Anthem | Pools | Skyward Bound | Northern Cross | Loxodrome | Sara's Touch | Duo(In Two Parts) | Both Sides Of The Coin

Live at The Ny Carlsberg Glyptotek, rec. 1.4.1983

Steps Ahead | Brecker,Michael (sax) | Mainieri,Mike (vib) | Elias,Eliane (p) | Gomez,Eddie (b) | Erskine,Peter (dr)

4960383 | DVD | Champion Jack Dupree | EAN 5708812960387

Champion Jack Dupree

Dupree Special | When I Was One Year Old | Crossroads | When I Got Married | Mean Old Lone Train | My Home In Louisiana | Alberta | Champion Jack's Boogie | You Can Make It

Hannover/Copenhagen/? Europe, rec. 1986

Dupree,Champion Jack (g,voc) | Lending,Kenn (g) | Svafnisson,Svenni (?) | Lauritsen,Kjeld (?) | Larsen,Frank (?) | Lang,Jorgen (?) | Louisiana Red (g,voc)

4960423 | DVD | Rockin' Dopsie And The Zydeco Twister | EAN 5708812960424

Rockin' Dopsie And The Zydeco Twisters

Ay-Tete-Fee | O,O,Ba,Ba | Tous Demandaient Pour Toi | I'm In The Mood For Love | Lucille | Please Don't Leave Me | The Louisiana Two Step | Keep A-Knockin' | Allons A Lafayette | I Got A Woman

Live at The Maple Leaf Bar,New Orleans, rec. 24.3.1984

Rockin' Dopsie (accordeon,voc) | Band

4960483 | DVD | A Tribute To Charlie Parker Vol.1 | EAN 5708812960486

Red Rodney All Stars

Confirmation | Round About Midnight | My Little Suede Shoes | Love Letters | 52nd Street | Snap Crackle | Parker's Mood | Blues For Alice | Chasin' The Bird | Quasimodo | Buzzy

Live at the Palais Des Festival,Cannes,France, rec. January 1990

Rodney,Red (tp) | Morgan,Frank (as) | Alexander,Monty (p) | Reid,Rufus (b) | Haynes,Roy (dr)

4960493 | DVD | A Tribute To Charlie Parker Vol.2 | EAN 5708812960493

Phil Woods Quartet

Repetition | My Old Flame | Steeplechase | All Bird's Children

Live at Palais Des Festival,Cannes,France, rec. January 1990

Woods,Phil (as) | Galper,Hal (p) | Gilmore,Steve (b) | Goodwin,Bill (dr)

Jon Hendricks Group

Hootie's Blues | Now's The Time | Billy's Bounce | Parker's Mood | What Price Love | Everything Happens To Me | Night And Day | Jumpin' At The Woodside

Live at the Palais Des Festival,Cannes,France, rec. January 1990

Hendricks,Jon (voc) | Burke,Kevin Fitzgerald (voc) | Hendricks,Aria (voc) | Hendricks,Judith (voc) | Hendricks,Michelle (voc) | Goldings,Larry (p) | Mitchell,Tyler (b) | Cobb,Jimmy (dr)

4960523 | DVD | The Small Black Groups | EAN 5708812960523

Nat King Cole Trio

Is You Is Or Is You Ain't My Baby | I'm A Shy Guy | Who's Been Eatin' My Porridge | Frim Fram Sauce

Los Angeles,CA, rec. 1944-1946

Cole,Nat King (p,voc) | Moore,Oscar (g) | Miller,Johnny (b) | James,Ida (voc)

Oh Kickeroony | Now He Tells Me | Breezy And The Bass

details unknown, rec. 1947

Cole,Nat King (p,voc) | Moore,Oscar (g) | Miller,Johnny (b)

John Kirby Band

Broad Jump | Can't Find A Word To Say

Kirby,John (b) | Shavers,Charlie (tp,arr) | Bailey,Buster (cl) | Holmes,Charlie (as) | Kyle,Billy (p) | Catlett,Big Sid (dr)

Big Sid Catlett And His Orchestra

Just A Riff | Crazy Riffin

details unknown, rec. 1948

Catlett,Big Sid (dr) | Vance,Dick (tp,arr) | Morton,Benny (tb) | Stovall,Don (as) | Davis,Eddie 'Lockjaw' (ts) | Ramirez,Roger 'Ram' (p) | Simmons,John (b) | Krupa,Gene (dr) | Mays,Betti (voc)

Slam Stewart Trio

Oh Me, Oh My, Oh Gosh

Stewart,Slam (b,voice) | Booker,Beryl (p) | Collins,John (g)

Slim Gaillard Trio

O'Rooney's Overture Hoboken Bounce | Dynamite's O'Rooney | Spanish Melody And Swing | Chile And Beans O'Voutee | Dunkin' Bagel | Laguna

At Billy Berg's,?, rec. 1946

Gaillard,Slim (g,p,voc) | Brown,Tiny Bam (b,voc) | Crothers,Scat Man (dr)

Louis Jordan And His Tympany Five

Old Man Mose

Hollywood,CA, rec. 1942

Jordan,Lewis (as,voc) | Roane,Eddie (tp) | Thomas,Arnold (p) | Bartley,Dallas (b) | Martin,Walter (dr)

Jordan Jive

Hollywood,CA, rec. 1944

Jordan,Lewis (as) | Roane,Eddie (tp) | Thomas,Arnold (p) | Morgan,Albert 'Al' (b) | Jones,Wilmore 'Slick' (dr)

Nat King Cole Trio

Solid Potato Salad | It's Better To Be By Yourself

Hollywood,CA, rec. 1946

Cole,Nat King (p,voc) | Moore,Oscar (g,voc) | Miller,Johnny (b,voc)

4960543 | DVD | Ruby Braff Trio:In Concert | EAN 5708812960547

Ruby Braff Trio

It's Only A Paper Moon | Miss Brown To | Lonely Moments | I've Grown Accustomed To Her Face | When A Man Loves A Woman | Black Beauty- | Liza | Do It Again | Them There Eyes

Live at The Brecon Jazz Festival 1991, rec. 1991

Braff,Ruby (tp) | Alden,Howard (g) | Tate,Frank (b)

4960563 | DVD | The Blues Of Clarence 'Gatemouth Brown | EAN 5708812960561

Clarence Gatemouth Brown Band

I Feel Airlight Again | I Wonder | Gate Walks To Board | Sunrise Cajun Style | Song For René | Six Levels Below Olat Life | Frosty | One More Mile | Pressure Cooker | Catfish | Up Jumped The Devil

Live at The Maple Leaf Bar,New Orleans, rec. 4.2.1984

Brown,Clarence Gatemouth (g,v,voc) | Band

4960603 | DVD | Lennie Tristano:The Copenhagen Concert | EAN 5708812960608

Lennie Tristano

Darn That Dream | Lullaby Of The Leaves | Expressions | You Don't Know What Love Is | Tivoli Gardens Swing | I Don't Stand A Ghost Of A Chance With You | It's You Or No One | Imagination | Tangerine

Live at The 'Tivoli Gardens',Copenhagen, rec. 31.10.1965

Tristano,Lennie (p-solo)

4960633 | DVD | Kenny Drew Trio At The Brewhouse | EAN 5708812960639

Kenn Drew Trio

My Shing Hour | You Don't Know What Love Is | Oleo | Bluesology | In Your Own Sweet Way | All Blues | Blues In The Closet

Brewhose,GB, rec. 22.7.1992

Drew,Kenny (p) | Orsted-Pedersen,Niels-Henning (b) | Queen,Alvin (dr)

4960683 | DVD | Chris Barber On The Road:A Jazz Documentary | EAN 5708812960684

Chris Barber's Jazz And Blues Band

Music & Interviews-Documentation

different Places, rec. 1988

Barber,Chris (tb,bar-h,voc) | Halcox,Pat (tp,voc) | Crocker,John (cl,as,ts,voc) | Wheeler,Ian (cl,sax,harm) | McCullum,Johnny (bj,snare-dr) | Hill,Roger (g) | Pitt,Vic (b) | Emberson,Norman (dr)

4960723 | DVD | Stephane Grappelli:Live In San Francisco | EAN 5708812960721

Stephane Grappelli Group

California Here I Come | I've Got Rhythm | Fascinating Rhythm | Let's Fall In Love | Tea For Two | Swing '42 | Honeysuckle Rose | After You've Gone | You Are The Sunshine Of My Life | Minor Swing | Here, There And Everywhere | St.Louis Blues | Danny Boy (Londonderry Air) | Them There Eyes | After You've Gone

Live at Paul Manson Wineyard,Saratoga & The Great American Muisc Hall,San Francisco,CA, rec. 4.& 7.7.1982

Grappelli,Stephane (v,el-v,p) | Disley,William 'Diz' (g) | Taylor,Martin (g) | Sewing,Jack (b)

Stephane Grappelli-David Grisman Group

Sweet Georgia Brown

Live at The Great American Muisc Hall,San Francisco,CA, rec. 7.7.1982

Grappelli,Stephane (v,el-v,p) | Disley,William 'Diz' (g) | Taylor,Martin (g) | Sewing,Jack (b) | Grisman,David (mand) | Marshall,Mike (mand) | Anger,Darol (v) | Wasserman,Rob (b)

4960733 | DVD | Jazz Festival Vol.1 | EAN 5708812960738

Louis Armstrong And His All Stars

When It's Sleepy Time Down South | C'Est Si Bon | Some Day | Jerry | Nobody
Knows The Trouble I've Seen | When The Saints Go Marching In
NYC, rec. 2.4.1962
Armstrong,Louis (tp,voc) | Young,Trummy (tb) | Darensbourg,Joe (cl) | Kyle,Billy (p) | Cronck,Billy (p) | Barcelona,Danny (dr) | Brown,Jewel (voc)

Eddie Condon All Stars
Royal Garden Blues | Blue And Broken Hearted | Big Ben Blues | Stealin' Apples | Little Ben Blues | Muskrat Ramble
NYC, rec. 1962
Condon,Eddie (g) | Davison,Wild Bill (co) | Cutshall,Cutty (tb) | Hucko,Peanuts (cl) | Varro,Johnny (p) | Williams,Joe (b) | Drootin,Buzzy (dr)

Bobby Hackett Sextet
Bill Bailey, Won't You Please Come Home | Struttin' With Some Barbecue | When The Saints Go Marching In
Hackett,Bobby (co) | Green,Urbie (tb) | Wilber,Bob (cl) | McKenna,Dave (p) | Totah,Nabil 'Knobby' (b) | Feld,Morey (dr)

4960743 | DVD | Jazz Festival Vol.2 | EAN 5708812960745
Duke Ellington And His Orchestra
Take The 'A' Train | Satin Doll | Blow By Blow | Things Ain't What They Used To Be | V.I.P.'s Boogie- | Jam With Sam-
NYC, rec. 9.1.1962
Ellington,Duke (p) | Baker,Harold 'Shorty' (tp) | Berry,Bill (tp) | Mullens,Eddie (tp) | Anderson,Cat (tp) | Nance,Ray (tp,v) | Cox,Leon (tb) | Brown,Lawrence (tb) | Connors,Chuck (tb) | Hamilton,Jimmy (cl,ts) | Procope,Russell (cl,as) | Hodges,Johnny (as) | Gonsalves,Paul (ts) | Carney,Harry (cl,b-cl,bs) | Bell,Aaron (b) | Woodyard,Sam (dr)

Mike Bryan Sextet
Benny's Bugle | Blues In G | Seven Come Eleven | Ain't Got Time | Sweet Lorraine | Air Mail Special
NYC, rec. August 1962
Mike Bryan Sextet,The | Severinsen,Doc (tp) | Auld,Georgie (ts) | Sheppard,Harry (vib) | Smith,Derek (p) | Lesberg,Jack (b) | Alexander,Mousie (dr)

Bobby Hackett Sextet
'Deed I Do | The Sentimental Blues | Swing That Music
NYC, rec. January 1962
Hackett,Bobby (co) | Green,Urbie (tb) | Wilber,Bob (cl) | McKenna,Dave (p) | Totah,Nabil 'Knobby' (b) | Feld,Morey (dr)

4960753 | DVD | Jazz Life Vol.1:From Village Vanguard | EAN 5708812960752
Johnny Griffin Quartet
Opening- | Blues For Gonzi- | A Monk's Dream | 56- | Closing-
details unknown, rec. 1981
Griffin,Johnny (ts) | Matthews,Ronnie (p) | Drummond,Ray (b) | Washington,Kenny (dr)

Richie Cole Group
Opening- | Hi Fly | I Can't Get Started | Punishment Blues | Yardbird Suite | Red Top
Cole,Richie (as) | Forman,Bruce (g) | Enriquez,Bobby (p) | Hawkins,Marshall (b) | Morris,Scott (dr)

4960763 | DVD | Jazz Life Vol.2:From Seventh At Avenue South | EAN 5708812960769
Art Blakey And The Jazz Messengers
Fuller Love | MX'B,C. | My Ship | Theme
Live at Seventh At Avenue South, rec. 1982
Blakey,Art (dr) | Marsalis,Wynton (tp) | Marsalis,Branford (as) | Pierce,Billy (ts) | Brown,Donald (p) | Fambrough,Charles (b)

Mike Mainieri Group
Sara's Touch | Bamboo | Bullet Train
Mainieri,Mike (vib) | Mintzer,Bob (ts) | Bernhardt,Warren (p) | Gomez,Eddie (b) | Hakim,Omar (dr)

4990013 | DVD | Chris Barber:40 Years Jubilee Concert | EAN 5708812990018
Chris Barber Original Jazzband Of 1954
Isle Of Capri | Chimes Blues | Hiawatha Rag | We Sure Do Need Him Now | It's Tight Like That | The Old Rugged Cross | Bill Bailey Won't You Please Come Home | Hush-A-Bye | Can't You Line 'Em | Over in The New Burying Ground | Worried Man Blues | Lonnie's Blues | Grand Collie Dam | Ice Cream
Musikhuset Aarhus,Denmark, rec. 27.6.1995
Barber,Chris (tb,voc) | Halcox,Pat (tp,co,voc) | Sunshine,Monty (cl,voc) | Donegan,Tony 'Lonnie' (g,bj,voc) | Bray,Jim (b,sousaphone) | Bowden,Ron (dr)

Chris Barber's Jazz And Blues Band
Bourbon Street Parade | All The Girls Go Crazy | Ellingtonia: | Double Check Stomp- | Stevedore Stomp- | Goin' To Town- | Big Noise From Winnetka | St.Louis Blues | Goin' Up The River | Petite Fleur | Sweet Georgia Brown | High Society
Barber,Chris (tb,voc) | Halcox,Pat (tp,co,voc) | Wheeler,Ian (cl,as,harmonica) | Crocker,John (cl,as,ts) | Sealey,Paul (g,bj) | Slaughter,John (el-g) | Pitt,Vic (b) | Wickett,Alan 'Sticky' (dr)

String Jazz | Jazz Network

SJRCD 1002 | CD | Hands Across The Water | EAN 651009100224
Royce Campbell-Adrian Ingram Group
Wes | My Romance | Serenade To A Cuckoo | In A Sentimental Mood | Boplics | Little Bossa | Weaver Of Dreams | Monkish Business | Polka Dots And Moonbeams | Crooked Blues
Sale,Cheshire, rec. 24./25.2.1998
Campbell,Royce (g) | Ingram,Adrian (g) | Linane,Dave (b) | Hassell,Dave (dr,perc)

SJRCD 1006 | CD | West Coast Sessions | EAN 651009100620
John Pisano-Billy Bean-Dennis Budimir
The Hippie | My Old Flame | Have You Met Miss Jones | Airegin | Two Five Jive | Every Time We Say Goodbye
Los Angeles,CA, rec. 1957-1959
Pisano,John (g) | Bean,Billy (g) | Budimir,Dennis (g) | Estes,Gene (vib) | details unknown

Billy Bean-Dennis Budimir
I Love You | All The Things You Are
Los Angeles,CA, rec. 1959
Bean,Billy (g) | Budimir,Dennis (g)

SJRCD 1007 | CD | The Trio:Rediscovered | EAN 651009100729
The Trio
Motivation | Lush Life | All Of You | Porgy And Bess Medley | Lands End | Have You Met Miss Jones | Groove Yard | Ohe-Low | Safari
NYC, rec. June 1961
Trio,The | Norris,Walter (p) | Bean,Billy (g) | Gaylor,Hal (b)

SJRCD 1013 | CD | Live At Boomers | EAN 651009101320
Greg Clayton Trio
This Is New | There Is No Greater Love | You Don't Know What Love Is | You've Changed | My Shining Hour | Misdemeanor | I Don't Stand A Ghost Of A Chance With You | I Thought About You
Live at Café Boomers,Pointe Claire,Quebec,Canada, rec. 9.-11.1.1997
Clayton,Greg (g) | Young,Dave (b) | Fuller,Jerry (dr)

SJRCD 102 | CD | Modern Memory | EAN 659057360324
Rez Abbasi Group
Serie De Arco | Next Year | Modern Memory 1(Improvisation for John Coltrane) | Depiction | Modern Memory 2(Improvisation For Jim Hall) | Every Sunday | Modern Memory 3(Improvisation for Keith Jarrett) | Third Ear | Rise Above | Four In One
NYC, rec. June 1996
Abbasi,Rez (g,el-g) | Hagans,Tim (tp) | Whitfield,Scott (tb) | Thomas,Gary (fl,ts) | Formanek,Michael (b) | Moreno,Anthony 'Tony' (dr)

SJRCD 1021 | CD | Out Of Body | EAN 656613748022
To Your Perfection | Out Of Body | Winners Circle | Phosphor Colors | Ganges Gang | Gold Rush | Halt The Battle | Smile At Darkness | Dark Bones
Brooklyn,NY, rec. 1999
Abbasi,Rez (g,el-g,tablas,perc) | Horton,Ron (tp,fl-h) | Malaby,Tony (ss,ts) | Herbert,John (b) | Hall,Bruce (dr)

Stunt Records | sunny moon Musikvertrieb

STUCD 01212 | CD | Meeting Monty
Kristian Jorgensen Quartet With Monty Alexander
The Mill | Squeb | A Flower Is A Lovesome Thing | Astor Samba | Be Nice | The Stuffed Monk | Jespers Vuggevise | Oriental Shuffle | Willow Weep For Me
Copenhagen,Denmark, rec. July/August 2001
Jorgensen,Kristian Bagge (v) | Fischer,Jacob (g) | Alexander,Monty (p) | Fonnesbaek,Thomas (b) | Osgood,Kresten (dr)
Estate(Summer)
Jorgensen,Kristian Bagge (v) | Fischer,Jacob (g) | Alexander,Monty (p) | Fonnesbaek,Thomas (b) | Osgood,Kresten (dr) | Zapponi,Caterina (voc)

T&P Records | Universal Music Germany

9815810 | CD | A Gift Of Love | EAN 602498158104
Tuck And Patti
Up On the Roof | Can't Help Falling In Love | Sukiyaki | Just The Way You Are | Loving You | I Was Born To Love You | Hold Me Tight And Don't Let Go | Song For You | Close To You | Time After Time
San Francisco,CA/Menlo Park,CA, rec. details unknown
Tuck And Patti: | Cathcart,Patti (voc) | Andress,Tuck (el-g) | Hébert,Joseph (cello) | Martin,Frank (keyboards,string-arrangements)

Take Twelve On CD | Georg Löffler Musikverlag

TT 007-2 | CD | Piano Moments
Cornelius Claudio Kreusch/Hans Poppel
Music For Two Pianos(part 3+9)
Kreusch,Cornelius Claudio (p) | Poppel,Hans (p)

Chris Jarrett
Fire | Down South | Paprika Lady | Blue Nights- | White Nights-
Jarrett,Chris (p)

Cornelius Claudio Kreusch
Taiga | Stella Backstage | One Way In Harlem
Kreusch,Cornelius Claudio (p-solo)

Rade Soric Trio
Nahend | Lucyna | Ahaha
Soric,Rade (p) | Rotter,Thomas (b) | Fickelscher,Hans (dr)

TT 008-2 | CD | Vocal Moments
Mind Games With Claudio Roditi
As Everybody Sees I'm Oldfashioned | Trip To Your Town | Caravan
Mind Games | Roditi,Claudio (tp,fl-h) | Binder,Andreas 'Andi' (fr-h) | Franzl,Andy Mulo (cl,ss,ts) | Wangenheim,Ulrich (fl,as) | Pusch,Bastian (p,keyboards) | Lowka,Didi 'D.D.' (b) | Schmitz,Csaba (dr) | Maass,Stephan (perc) | Wahlandt,Lisa (voc)

Dogs Don't Sing In The Rain
Georgia On My Mind | U Always Know | Tinka's Dreams
Dogs Don't Sing In The Rain | Wennemar,Harald (as) | Van Beek,Romain (g) | Pütz,Mark (synth,grand-p) | Jaegers,Marcus (b) | Cox,Luuk (dr,perc) | Janssen,Digna (voc)

Maximilian Goller Quartet feat. Melanie Bong
How Insensitive(Insensatez) | Smile | Beautiful Love | The Very Thought Of You
Geller,Maximilian (sax) | Mihilic,Peter (p) | Mariella,Fracesco (b) | Lesczak,Vito (dr) | Bong,Melanie (voc)

TT 009-2 | CD | Wind Moments
Peter O'Mara Quartet
Seven Up | Blues Dues | Catalyst
O'Mara,Peter (g,el-g) | Mintzer,Bob (ss,ts) | Johnson,Marc (b) | Willis,Falk (dr)

Colin Dunwoodie Quartet
Afro Blue | Bop Or Not To Be | Four Bars Short
Dunwoodie,Colin (fl,ss,as,ts) | Seitz,Ernst (p) | Brenner,Udo (b) | Bozem,Günter (dr,perc)

Dogs Don't Sing In The Rain
Out Of A Bandbox | Did You Expect That...?
Dogs Don't Sing In The Rain | Wennemar,Harald (as) | Van Beek,Romain (g) | Pütz,Mark (synth,grand-p) | Jaegers,Marcus (b) | Cox,Luuk (dr,perc) | Janssen,Digna (voc)

Uli Gutscher Quintet
Shut Your Mouth | Cariffity
Gutscher,Uli (tb,bass-fl-h) | Acker,Werner (g,el-g) | Schrack,Martin (p) | Krisch,Thomas (b) | Wachter,Herbert (dr,perc)

Mind Games
Los Uncoolos
Mind Games | Binder,Andreas 'Andi' (fr-h) | Sterzer,Philipp (fl) | Franzl,Andy Mulo (ss,ts) | Despot,Dalio (p,keyboards) | Lowka,Didi 'D.D.' (b) | Schmitz,Csaba (dr) | Rupcic,Hrvoje (perc) | Hupfauer,Pidi (voc)

Tom Bennecke & Space Gurilla
Vinz
Mind Games | Binder,Andreas 'Andi' (fr-h) | Sterzer,Philipp (fl) | Franzl,Andy Mulo (ss,ts) | Despot,Dalio (p,keyboards) | Lowka,Didi 'D.D.' (b) | Schmitz,Csaba (dr) | Rupcic,Hrvoje (perc) | Hupfauer,Pidi (voc)

Talkin' Loud | Universal Music Germany

518166-2 | CD | United Future Organization
United Future Organizatio
The Sixth Sense
details unknown, rec. details unknown
United Future Organization | Yabe,Tadashi (?) | Matsuura,Toshio (?) | Sebbag,Raphael (voc) | Sanshiro (as) | Obinata,Ayumi (keyboards,programming) | Genta (perc) | Galliano (voc)
On Est Ensemble Sans Se Parler-L.O.V.E.
United Future Organization | Yabe,Tadashi (?) | Matsuura,Toshio (?) | Sebbag,Raphael (voc) | Obinata,Ayumi (keyboards,programming)
Vinyl Junkie
United Future Organization | Yabe,Tadashi (?) | Matsuura,Toshio (?) | Sebbag,Raphael (?) | Nagoya,Kimiyoshi (tp) | Sanshiro (as) | Tachibana,Hajime (g) | Aoki,Tatsuyuki (dr) | Obinata,Ayumi (keyboards,programming)
Upa Nequinho
United Future Organization | Yabe,Tadashi (?) | Matsuura,Toshio (?) | Sebbag,Raphael (?) | Nagoya,Kimiyoshi (tp) | Komagata,Hiroyuki (g) | Obinata,Ayumi (keyboards,programming)
I'll Bet You Thought I'd Never Find You
United Future Organization | Yabe,Tadashi (?) | Matsuura,Toshio (?) | Sebbag,Raphael (?) | Sanshiro (fl) | Komagata,Hiroyuki (g) | Grey,Alex (v) | Obinata,Ayumi (keyboards,programming) | Hendricks,Jon (voc)
Poetry And All That Jazz
United Future Organization | Yabe,Tadashi (?) | Matsuura,Toshio (?) | Sebbag,Raphael (?) | Sanshiro (fl) | Komagata,Hiroyuki (g) | Banchi (v) | Obinata,Ayumi (keyboards,programming)
Be Here Now
United Future Organization | Yabe,Tadashi (?) | Matsuura,Toshio (?) | Sebbag,Raphael (?) | Sanshiro (fas) | Obinata,Ayumi (keyboards,programming)
My Foolish Dream?
rec. details unknown
United Future Organization | Yabe,Tadashi (?) | Matsuura,Toshio (?) | Sebbag,Raphael (?) | Nugier,Patrick (accordeon) | Obinata,Ayumi (keyboards,programming) | Michiru,Monday (voc)
Off Road
details unknown, rec. details unknown
United Future Organization | Yabe,Tadashi (?) | Matsuura,Toshio (?) | Sebbag,Raphael (?) | Ohi,Takashi (vib) | Obinata,Ayumi (keyboards,programming)

Timescrapper | Timbre Records

TSCR 9611 | CD | At Night When You Go To Sleep
Ernst Bier-Mack Goldsbury Quartet
Crossing Over | Paradoxical Conversation | Duke's Voice | Surgin' | At Night When You Go To Sleep | Leba,Si? | J.G.'s Dance | Tatort
Berlin, rec. June 1996
Goldsbury,Mack (ss,ts) | Biel,Ernst (dr) | Möbus,Frank (g) | Schuller,Ed (b)

Ernst Bier-Mack Goldsbury Quintet
Rachel's Song
Goldsbury,Mack (ss,ts) | Biel,Ernst (dr) | Möbus,Frank (g) | Schuller,Ed (b) | Gioia,Topo (perc)

TSCR 9612 | CD | Neal Kirkwood Octet
Neal Kirkwood Octet
Baghdad By The Bay | Portrait Of Pony Poindexter | Portrait Of Sidney Bechet | The Dog Who Smokes | Passion Flower | Bye-Ya | Ghost Shadows | The Dream | Genarek's Tango | Chopin's Waterloo
NYC, rec. 21./22.7.1995
Kirkwood,Neal (p) | Walrath,Jack (tp) | Neumeister,Ed (tb) | Varner,Tom (fr-h) | Furnace,Sam (sax) | Drewes,Billy (sax) | Horner,Lindsey (b) | Rainey,Tom (dr)

TSCR 9613 | CD | Perry Robinson Quartet
Perry Robinson Quartet
The Call | Wahaila | Son Of Alfalfa | Interlude(1) | My Gypsy Baby | For Django | Walk On | Touch Of Strange | Interlude(2) | Harem Dance | Angels | Angelology | The Call(2)
Berlin, rec. December 1996
Robinson,Perry (cl,ss,sopranino) | Nabatov,Simon (p,accordeon) | Schuller,Ed (b) | Bier,Ernst (dr)

TSCR 9614 | CD | Ed Neumeister Quartet/Quintet
Ed Neumeister Quintet
A Nightingale Sang In Berkeley Square | Relative Lightness | Weeping Willow | Negrin | Happy Coincidence | Sadie Hall
details unknown, rec. 1997
Neumeister,Ed (tb) | Drewes,Billy (cl,sax) | McNeely,Jim (p) | Irwin,Dennis (b) | Haddad,Jamey (dr)

Ed Neumeister Quartet
Row To Tow | Herbie Nichols | Longing
Neumeister,Ed (tb) | Werner,Kenny (p) | Irwin,Dennis (b) | Clark,Mike (dr)

TSCR 9615 | CD | Songs I Love To Play
Mack Goldsbury And The New York Connection
Without A Song | Tin Tin Deo | The First Snow | Like Sonny | The Nearness Of You | The Smile Of Menja | Meant To Be | Karen(Intro) | Karen | Scrjabin | Time On Monday
NYC, rec. 1997
Goldsbury,Mack (ss,ts) | Werner,Kenny (p) | Schuller,Ed (b) | Hart,Billy (dr)

TSCR 9617 | CD | The Chromatic Persuaders
The Chromatic Persuaders
Arthur's Seat | The Chromatic Persuaders | Drums Of Heaven | Nova | Gloria's Step | Monolithic Attidude | Providence | Low Life
Chromatic Persuaders,The | Feldman,Mark (v) | Kirkwood,Neal (p) | Horner,Lindsey (b) | Rainey,Tom (dr)

TSCR 9618 | CD | Rated X
Unit X
The Norm | Who Are You | Bird Brain | Inside Out | Ryokam | CMW | Apeiron | Hakuin | Hablo | A+B+C+D
Unit X | Noriega,Oscar (b-cl,as) | Lossing,Russ (p) | Schuller,Ed (b) | Meyer,Bob (dr)

TSCR 9811 | CD | Maniakisses
Schlothauer's Maniacs
Peace
Berlin, rec. May 1997
Schlothauer,Burkhard (v) | Hensel,Lothar (bandoneon) | Hauser,Michael (b,el-b) | Kaczynski,Ray (dr,perc)
Lugar Comun I
Schlothauer,Burkhard (v,viola) | Hensel,Lothar (bandoneon) | Mello,Chico (g,voc) | Hauser,Michael (b,el-b) | Kaczynski,Ray (dr,perc)
Think Low
Schlothauer,Burkhard (v,viola,voc) | Chouraqui,Ahmed (el-g) | Hauser,Michael (b,el-b) | Kaczynski,Ray (dr,perc) | Mello,Chico (g,voc)
Minor Reggae | Somethink | Happy People | Summertime
Schlothauer,Burkhard (v,viola,voc) | Hensel,Lothar (bandoneon) | Chouraqui,Ahmed (el-g) | Hauser,Michael (b,el-b) | Kaczynski,Ray (dr,perc)
My Foolish Heart | My Funny Valentine
Schlothauer,Burkhard (v) | Hensel,Lothar (bandoneon) | Hauser,Michael (b,el-b) | Kaczynski,Ray (dr,perc)
Monster Mobbin'
Schlothauer,Burkhard (v) | Strien,Ary (accordeon) | Chouraqui,Ahmed (el-g) | Hauser,Michael (b,el-b) | Kaczynski,Ray (dr,perc)

TipToe | Enja Eigenvertrieb

TIP-888805 2 | CD | Off Abbey Road
Mike Westbrook Band
Come Together | Something | Maxwell's Silver Hammer | Oh Darling | Octopus's Garden | I Want You (She's So Heavy) | Here Comes The Sun | Because | You Never Give Me Your Money | Sun King | Mean Mr.Mustard | Polythene Pam | She Came In Through The Bathroom Window | Golden Slumbers | Carry That Weight | The End
Willisau,CH, rec. 31.8.1989
Westbrook,Mike (p) | Westbrook,Kate (ten-horn,voc) | Minton,Phil (tp,voc) | Wakeman,Alan (ss,ts) | Whyman,Peter (sax) | Grappy,Andy (tuba) | Godding,Brian (g) | Fairclough,Peter (dr)

TIP-888806 2 | CD | The Way We Used To Do
Michael Gregory
Cowboys Cartoons & Assorted Candy | The Way We Used To Do | This Life A Road | Closer | Where I Come From | American Dream | It's Just A Flesh Wound | Steel Your Heart | Share My Love | Mr.Cool
NYC, rec. 2./3.5.1982
Jackson,Michael Gregory (g,el-g,voc)

TIP-888808 2 | CD | Tales Of A Voice
Greetje Bijma Kwintet
Dyani | The Pharoah | The Coach | Sunshine Mama | Amy Camus | La Donna | Haden | Pops | Turn
Köln, rec. 3./4.10.1990
Bijma,Greetje (voice) | Laurillard,Alan (fl,reeds,perc) | Kuiper,Jan (g) | Ammerlaan,Gerard (b,perc) | Huffstadt,Charles (dr,kalimba)

TIP-888809 2 | CD | No Filters
Wolfgang Schmid's Kick
Black Baroness | Panama
Ludwigsburg, rec. August 1990
Schmid,Wolfgang (el-b) | Keller,Robert (fl,sax) | Wölpl,Peter (g) | Falk,Dieter (keyboards) | Cobham,Billy (dr,timbales) | Noya,Nippy (perc)
Mango On The Rocks | No Filters
Schmid,Wolfgang (el-b) | Keller,Robert (fl,sax) | Wölpl,Peter (g) | Falk,Dieter (keyboards) | Cobham,Billy (dr,timbales) | Richter,Kay (dr) | Noya,Nippy (perc)
New Block For The Kids
Schmid,Wolfgang (el-b) | Keller,Robert (fl,sax) | Wölpl,Peter (g) | Falk,Dieter (keyboards) | Cobham,Billy (dr,timbales) | Richter,Kay (dr) | Noya,Nippy (perc) | Hussain,Zakir (tabla)
Funk In Spain | Gospel News | Land Of The Morning Sun
Schmid,Wolfgang (el-b) | Keller,Robert (fl,sax) | Wölpl,Peter (g) | Falk,Dieter (keyboards) | Richter,Kay (dr) | Noya,Nippy (perc)
What's The News
Schmid,Wolfgang (el-b) | Keller,Robert (fl,sax) | Wölpl,Peter (g) | Falk,Dieter (keyboards) | Noya,Nippy (perc) | Haenning,Gitte (voc)

TIP-888811 2 | CD | The Funk Stops Here
Mike Clark-Paul Jackson Quartet
Steady Freddy | Four String Drive | Spider Man | Swamp Thing | Hotel Domingo | Jurasic Park | Funk Is...Bill Doggett | Pitt & The Pendulum | Slinky | Steady Freddy(reprise)
Altamonte Springs,Florida, rec. April 1991
Clark,Mike (dr) | Jackson,Paul (el-b,voc) | Garrett,Kenny (sax) | Pittson,Jeff (keyboards)

TIP-888822 2 | CD | Diario De Bordo
Raiz De Pedra
Sao Sepé | Linha Azul | Munique | Tempos De Minuano

Ludwigsburg, rec. 3./4.7.1995
Raiz De Pedra | Tubino,Marcio (fl,ss,as,voice) | Tagliani,Pedro (g,triangle,voice) | Pecoits,Conrado (p,el-p,voice) | Mombelli,Carlo (b,fretless-b,voice) | Audi,Cesar (dr,surdo,voice) | Do O,Fernando (perc)
As Historias De Domingos
Raiz De Pedra | Tubino,Marcio (fl) | Tagliani,Pedro (g) | Pecoits,Conrado (p) | Mombelli,Carlo (b) | Audi,Cesar (dr) | Pereira,Domingo (berimbau) | Do O,Fernando (perc)
O Navio
Raiz De Pedra | Tubino,Marcio (ts) | Tagliani,Pedro (g-synth,surdo) | Mombelli,Carlo (fretless-b) | Audi,Cesar (dr,effects) | Do O,Fernando (perc)

Raiz De Pedra feat. Egberto Gismonti
O Quem Tai! | Amigos De Longe | Levando A Vida
Raiz De Pedra | Tubino,Marcio (ss,caxixis,tssurdo) | Tagliani,Pedro (g,triangle) | Gismonti,Egberto (p) | Mombelli,Carlo (b,fretless-b) | Audi,Cesar (dr) | Do O,Fernando (perc,cabassa)

TIP-888829 2 | CD | Dejala En La Puntica
Conjunto Clave Y Guaguanco
Para Clave Y Guaguando | Mamaita..What You've Got | La Voz Del Congo | Tyawo | Avisale A La Vecina | Chevere | Capricho DeAbuela | Para Rita Montaner | La Terigonza | Na Francisca | Dejala En La Puntica
Havana,Cuba, rec. 1996
Hernandez,Amado De Jesus Dedeu (ld) | Montalvo,Mabel De La Caridad Dedeu (voc,perc) | Rodriguez,Damarys Driggs (voc,perc) | Garcia,Amadeo Dedeu (voc,perc) | Rodriguez Pedrosa,Mario Facundo (voc,perc) | Rill,Santiago Garzon (perc,voc) | Cabrera,Arturo Martinez (voc,perc) | Lara,Leonardo Planches (perc,voc) | Berriel,Almeida Pedro F. (perc,voc) | Manreza,Jose Perez (perc,voc) | Garcia,Silva Amaro (voc) | Navarrete,Banguela (voc)

TIP-888830 2 | CD | SheshBesh
SheshBesh
Jonona | Nelson | Romance | Kramim | Longa Yurgo | Amman Amman | Segoh | Wared | Kumran | Shortwave
Bene Brak,Israel, rec. 21.-24.8.1997
SheshBesh | Arnheim,Yossi (fl) | Dalal,Yair (oud) | Massarik,Amir (b) | Zimbalista,Chen (perc)

TIP-888831 2 | CD | Perfume Light...
Greenfish
Perfume Light: | Perfume Worlds- | The Deep High- | Earth Sky- | Remember | Shaking Lights | Flower Clouds | SingendesBlau | Vienna
Köln, rec. 25.2.-2.3.1997
Greenfish | Kott,Alois (p,b) | Petzold,Lars (g) | Zehrt,Holger (dr,perc)

TIP-888833 2 | CD | The First Second
Paradox
Parablue | Mozaik | Twistedology | Pandora's Box | Subwayer | Serengeti Plains | Once In A Blue Mood | Nu Mess
Live at 'The Feierwerk',München, rec. details unknown
Paradox | Bickford,Bill (el-g) | Schmid,Wolfgang (el-b) | Cobham,Billy (dr)

TIP-888835 2 | CD | Nuqta
Mahmoud Turkmani
Hanin | Hdiye | Nuqta | Halba | Diwen
details unknown, rec. February 1999
Turkmani,Mahmoud (g,oud)

Mahmoud Turkmani With The Ludus Guitar Quartet
Pointing At The Moon | Point II | Piece For Guitar Quartet | Point III
details unknown, rec. Febryary 1999
Turkmani,Mahmoud (g,oud) | Ludus Guitar Quartet | Estermann,Thomas (g) | Kuen,Stefan (g) | Meneghelli,Claudio (g)

TIP-888837 2 | CD | Ocean
NuNu!
Tkanje | De Grine Kusine | Yo M'enamori D'un Aire | Joschke Fort Avek | Bessarabia | Mondom | Si Verias | Shine | Papirossn | Csardas | Fliesse Wasser- | Ondas Do Mar- | Schlof Majn Kind | Bolgar Ritmus | Nardis | Hommage A Jacques Tati
München, rec. January 1999
NuNu! | Jacob,Willie (as,bottleneck-bouzouki,steel-g,voc) | Oechsner,Mic (accordeon,v,voc) | Gmelch,Leo (b-tb,tuba) | Graner,Ulrich (g) | Schwidewski,Uwe (b,el-b) | Falk,Marika (bandir,cajon,cuica,daff,darabuka,dombak,ghatam,rick,talking-dr,voc)

TIP-888838 2 | CD | Rainbow Mountain | EAN 063757783824
Lew Soloff Group
Frog Legs | Don't Speak | Up From The Skies | Quiero No Puedo | Suzie Q | Starmaker | Born On The Bayou | Stairway To Heaven | Tout Va Lew
NYC, rec. January/February 1999
Soloff,Lew (tp) | Marini,Lou (fl,sax) | Beck,Joe (as,g) | Egan,Mark (b,el-b) | Gottlieb,Dan 'Danny' (dr)
Rainbow Mountain
Soloff,Lew (tp) | Evans,Miles (tp) | Marini,Lou (fl,sax) | Bullock,Hiram (g) | Brown,Delmar (synth) | Lee,Will (b) | Chulo (b) | Beck,Joe (g) | Shaffer,Paul (org) | Egan,Mark (b,el-b) | Gottlieb,Dan 'Danny' (dr) | Watts,Jeff 'Tain' (dr)

TipToe | Soulfood

TIP-888812 2 | CD | Water From An Ancient Well
Abdullah Ibrahim And Ekaya
Mandela | Song For Sathima(Daughter Of Cape Town) | Manenberg Revisited(Cape Town Fringe) | Tuang Guru | Water From An Ancient Well | The Wedding | The Mountain | Sameeda
Englewood Cliffs,NJ, rec. Oct.1985
Brand,Dollar[Abdullah Ibrahim] (p) | Griffin,Dick (tb) | Ward,Carlos (fl,as) | Ford,Ricky (ts) | Davis,Charles (bs) | Williams,David (b) | Riley,Ben (dr)

TIP-888815 2 | CD | No Fear, No Die(S'en Fout La Mort):Original Soundtrack
Abdullah Ibrahim Septet
Calypso Minor | Angelica | Meditation II | Nisa | Kata | Meditation I | Calypso Major
Englewood Cliffs,NJ, rec. 18.7.1990
Brand,Dollar[Abdullah Ibrahim] (p) | Lacy,Ku-umba Frank (tb) | Young,Horace Alexander (fl,ss,as) | Ford,Ricky (ts) | Cozier,Jimmy (cl,bs) | Williams,Buster (b) | Riley,Ben (dr)

TIP-888820 2 | CD | Yarona
Abdullah Ibrahim Trio
Nisa | Duke 88 | Cherry | Mannenberg | African River | Tuang Guru | Star Dance | African Marketplace | Tintinyana | Barakaat
Live at Sweet Basil, NYC, rec. 13./14.1.1995
Brand,Dollar[Abdullah Ibrahim] (p) | McLaurine,Marcus (b) | Johnson,George (dr)

TIP-888823 2 | CD | The Budapest Concert
Ferenc Snétberger
Budapest Mood | Springtime In Winter | Song Of The East | Brazil | The Dolphin | Little Bossa | Variation(dedicated to Django Reinhardt) | Tangoa Free | Bossa For Egberto | Manha De Carnaval(Morning Of The Carnival) | Budapest Encore
Live at Music Academy 'Ferenc Liszt',Budapest, rec. 26.11.1995
Snétberger,Ferenc (g-solo)

TIP-888826 2 | CD | Cape Town Flowers
Abdullah Ibrahim Trio
Excursion | Eleventh Hour | Koffifi Blue | Chisa | Song For Aggerey | The Stride | The Call | African Marketplace | Joan-Capetown Flower | Maraba Blue | Monk In Harlem
Englewood Cliffs,NJ, rec. 15.8.1996
Brand,Dollar[Abdullah Ibrahim] (p) | McLaurine,Marcus (b) | Gray,George (dr)

TIP-888832 2 | CD | African Suite
Abdullah Ibrahim Trio And A String Orchestra
Mindif | Ishmael | Tsakwe | The Call | Damara Blue | The Wedding | Barakaat | Tintinyana | The Mountain Of Night
L'Abbatiale De Payerne,CH, rec. 12.-16.11.1997
Brand,Dollar[Abdullah Ibrahim] (p) | Bullock,Belden (b) | Gray,George (dr) | Members of The Youth Orchestra of The European Community | Mertes,Wolfgang (concertmaster) | Alvares,Enrico (v) | Mancel,Ghislaine Benabdalla (v) | Bertz,Simone (v) | Dragus,Rogdan (v) | De Groot,Ilona (v) | Peters,Chie (v) | Sauvaire,Alexandre (v) | Waterhouse,Lucy (v) | Adamopoulos,Dahlia (viola) | Bruil,Michelle (viola) | Reber,Raphael (viola) | Villotte,Estelle (viola) | Caron,Natalie (cello) | Duret,Lea (cello) | Lüthi,Eva (cello) | Spencer,Kristin (cello) | Adriaansen,Charice (b) | Sundquist,Knut Eric (b) | Schnyder,Daniel (arr)

String Orchestra
Blanton
Members of The Youth Orchestra of The European Community | Mertes,Wolfgang (concertmaster) | Alvares,Enrico (v) | Mancel,Ghislaine Benabdalla (v) | Bertz,Simone (v) | Dragus,Rogdan (v) | De Groot,Ilona (v) | Peters,Chie (v) | Sauvaire,Alexandre (v) | Waterhouse,Lucy (v) | Adamopoulos,Dahlia (viola) | Bruil,Michelle (viola) | Reber,Raphael (viola) | Villotte,Estelle (viola) | Caron,Natalie (cello) | Duret,Lea (cello) | Lüthi,Eva (cello) | Spencer,Kristin (cello) | Adriaansen,Charice (b) | Sundquist,Knut Eric (b) | Schnyder,Daniel (arr)

Dollar(Abdullah Ibrahim) Brand
Aspen
Brand,Dollar[Abdullah Ibrahim] (p-solo)

TIP-888834 2 | CD | Obsession
Ferenc Snétberger Trio
Wanton Spirit | E-Bossa | Szivarvany(for Attila Zoller) | FS Five | Gypsy | Hanging Out | Obsession | I Remember | Song To The East
Zerkall, rec. 29.-31.10.1997
Snétberger,Ferenc (g) | Egri,Janos (b) | Balazs,Elemer (dr)
Pava
Snétberger,Ferenc (g) | Egri,Janos (b) | Balazs,Elemer (dr) | Lovasz,Iren (voc)

TIP-888836 2 | CD | Cape Town Revisited
Abdullah Ibrahim Trio
Damara Blue | Someday Soon | African Street Parade | District Six | Song For Sathima | Too-Kah | Tuang Guru | Eleventh Hour | Water From An Ancient Well | The Mountain | The Wedding | Barakaat(The Blessing)
Cape Town,South Africa, rec. December 1997
Brand,Dollar[Abdullah Ibrahim] (p) | McLaurine,Marcus (b) | Gray,George (dr)

Abdullah Ibrahim Quartet
Tintinyana | Tsakwe-Royal Blue | Soweto
Brand,Dollar[Abdullah Ibrahim] (p) | Faku,Fezile 'Feya' (tp) | McLaurine,Marcus (b) | Gray,George (dr)

TIP-888839 2 | CD | Gilad Atzmon & The Orient House Ensemble
Gilad Atzmon & The Orient House Ensemble
Pardonnez Nous | Shir | Miron Dance | Nard-ish | Rai Print | Miserlou | Orient House | Balladi
London,GB, rec. details unknown
Atzmon,Gilad (cl,ss,sol) | Harrison,Frank (p,melodica) | Hayhurst,Oli (b) | Sirkis,Asaf (dr,bandir)

TIP-888840 2 | CD | Ekapa Lodumo
Abdullah Ibrahim With The NDR Big Band
Kramat | Mindif | Black And Brown Cherries | Pule | African Market | Whoza Mtwana | Duke
Hamburg, rec. 24.6.2000
Brand,Dollar[Abdullah Ibrahim] (p) | NDR Big Band | Axelsson,Lennart (tp,fl-h) | Burkhardt,Ingolf (tp,fl-h) | Stötter,Claus (tp,fl-h) | Winterschladen,Reiner (tp,fl-h) | Gallardo,Joe (tb) | Danner,Michael (tb) | Neudert,Jürgen (tb) | Schweizer,Christoph (tb,b-tb) | Felsch,Fiete (fl,as) | Bolte,Peter (fl,ss,as) | Delle,Frank (cl,ss,ts) | Büchner,Lutz (cl,ts) | Herzog,Edgar (b-cl,bs) | Diez,Stephan (g) | Lindholm,Lucas (b) | Riel,Alex (dr) | Cortijo,José (perc) | Glawischnig,Dieter (cond)

TIP-888843 2 | CD | World Quintet | EAN 063757784326
World Quintet
Send In The World Quintet | Flatbush Mioyan Bulgar(Star Trek Edit) | Wedding Suite | Naphtule Is Having A Bad Boy | Lied Ohne Worte
different Places, rec. different Dates
World Quintet,The | Zuckermann,Ariel (fl) | Heitzler,Michael (cl) | Truan,Oliver (p) | Fricker,Daniel (b) | Klein,David (dr)
The Chase
Zuckermann,Ariel (fl) | Heitzler,Michael (cl)

World Quintet With The London Mozart Players
Vergebung | Intermezzo No.3 | The Rod | Intermezzo No.1
World Quintet,The | Zuckermann,Ariel (fl) | Heitzler,Michael (cl) | Truan,Oliver (p) | Fricker,Daniel (b) | Klein,David (dr) | London Mozart Players,The | details unknown

World Quintet With The London Mozart Players And Herbert Grönemeyer
Trauer
World Quintet,The | Zuckermann,Ariel (fl) | Heitzler,Michael (cl) | Truan,Oliver (p) | Fricker,Daniel (b) | Klein,David (dr) | Grönemeyer,Herbert (voc) | London Mozart Players,The | details unknown

TIP-888845 2 | CD | African Magic | EAN 063757784524
Abdullah Ibrahim Trio
Blue Bolero(fragment 1) | Third Line Samba | Blue Bolero(fragment 2) | Blues For A Hip King | District Six | Tuang Guru | Blue Bolero(fragment 3) | Joan-Capetown Flower | Pule | The Stride | Thaba Bhosigo | The Mountain | Machopi- | Jabulani- | Black Lightning | Duke 88 | Solitude | Eleventh Hour | Blue Bolero(fragment 4) | In A Sentimental Mood | Moten Swing | For Coltrane | Whoza Mtwana | Tsakwe- | Royal Blue- | Blue Bolero
Live at 'Haus der Kulturen',Berlin, rec. 13.7.2001
Brand,Dollar[Abdullah Ibrahim] (p) | Bullock,Belden (b) | Kunene,Sipho (dr)

Touché Music | ZYX Music GmbH

TMcCD 001 | CD | Skiss
Knud Jorgensen-Bengt Hanson
Skiss | Prelude To A Kiss | I Thought About You | Teddy The Toad | You've Changed | I Should Care
Live at Maxim,Stockholm,Sweden, rec. 15./15.3.1983
Jorgensen,Knud (p) | Hanson,Bengt (b)

Knud Jorgensen-Bengt Hanson-Gustavo Bergalli
Have You Met Miss Jones | EKE Blues | Gone With The Wind | 2 Degrees East 3 Degrees West
Live at Castle Hotel,Stockholm,Sweden, rec. 24./25.8.1992
Bergalli,Gustavo (tp) | Jorgensen,Knud (p) | Hanson,Bengt (b)

TMcCD 002 | CD | Bojangles
Knud Jorgensen-Bengt Hanson
Softly As In A Morning Sunrise | My Heart Stood Still | Sophisticated Lady | What Is This Thing Called Love | She's Funny That Way | There Is No Greater Love | Days Of Wine And Roses | The Touch Of Your Lips | Bojangles
Live at Maxim,Stockholm,Sweden, rec. 15./16.3.1983
Jorgensen,Knud (p) | Hanson,Bengt (b)

TMcCD 003 | CD | Day Dream
Knud Jorgensen-Bengt Hanson-Gustavo Bergalli
What's New? | Day Dream | The Touch Of Your Lips | Lover Man(Oh,Where Can You Be?) | Look For The Silver Lining | My Ideal | Yesterdays | Old Folks | Angel Eyes
Live at Castle Hotel,Stockholm,Sweden, rec. 24./25.8.1992
Bergalli,Gustavo (tp) | Jorgensen,Knud (p) | Hanson,Bengt (b)

TMcCD 004 | CD | Close
Lina Nyberg-Esbjörn Svensson
Little Unhappy Boy | Close | Here, There And Everywhere | Never Let Me Go | In Your Own Sweet Way | You Can Have Him | Waiting | Ruby My Dear | I Wish I Didn't Love You So | You Let My Love Grow Cold | Spring Can Really Hang You Up The Most | I Hadn't Anyone 'Till You | May I Come In? | Waltz For The Lonely Ones
Gothenburg, Schweden, rec. 28./29.8.1993
Nyberg,Lina (voc) | Svensson,Esbjörn (p)

TMcCD 005 | CD | Cry Me A River
Anders Lindskog Quartet
Blues Changes | Old Folks | Time After Time | Falling In Love With Love | Cry Me A River | Tickle Toe | I'm Afraid The Masquerade Is Over - (I'm Afraid) The Masquerade Is Over | Israel | Angel Eyes | The Man I Love
Kungälv,Sweden, rec. 26./27.8.1995
Lindskog,Anders (ts) | Johansson,Ake (p) | Jansson,Kjell (b) | Gran,Magnus (dr)

TMcCD 006 | CD | A Time For Love
Agneta Baumann And Her Quintet
A Time For Love | I Get Along Without You Very Well | He Was Too Good To Me | Here's That Rainy Day | More Than You Know | If You Love Me | The Good Life | When The World Was Young | I Fall In Love Too Easily | I'm Afraid The Masquerade Is Over - (I'm Afraid) The Masquerade Is Over | The Party's Over | Everything Happens To Me | All My Tomorrows | The Best Is Yet To Come | That's All
Stockholm,Sweden, rec. 24./25.8.1996
Baumann,Agneta (voc) | Hallgren,Staffan (fl) | Lindskog,Anders (ts) | Orrje,Carl Fredrik (p) | Gadd,Per-Ola (b) | Stark,Bengt (dr)

TMcCD 007 | CD | Tango In Jazz
Gustavo Bergalli Group
Maleva | Nada | Grisel | Los Mareados | Naranjo En Flor | Soledad
Stockholm,Sweden, rec. 11./12.3.1996
Bergalli,Gustavo (tp) | Bergalli,Facundo (g) | Paglia,Gustavo (bandoneon) | Spering,Christian (b) | Gran,Magnus (dr)
La Casita De Mis Viejos | El Ultimo Café | Volver | Nunca Tuvo Novio
Stockholm,Sweden, rec. 30.4.1997
Bergalli,Gustavo (tp) | Bergalli,Facundo (g) | Paglia,Gustavo (bandoneon) | Spering,Christian (b) | Gran,Magnus (dr)

TMcCD 008 | CD | Sketches Of Roses
Elise Einarsdotter-Olle Steinholz
Vanja | Time Remembered | Nardis | Come Bright Sunshine | Blue Haze | Impulse(1) | Impulse(2) | Falling Grace | Else-Britt's Blues | Sketches Of Roses | You Must Believe In Spring | Israel | In Your Own Sweet Way | Scared Hearts | Song Of Ra | You Understand | The Little Girl With The Shells | I Fall In Love Too Easily
Stockholm,Sweden, rec. 14./15.1.1998
Einarsdotter,Elise (p) | Steinholz,Olle (b)

TMcCD 009 | CD | Back From Where We Came
Kjell Jansson Quartet
Sing Me A Song | To Hip For Your Own Good | Well Hello There | The Ice Is Breaking | The Inside Lane | Brother G. | On Crutches | Song For Stina | Outside The Grotto | To Vana | Back From Where We Came
Kungälv,Sweden, rec. 6./7.6.1998
Jansson,Kjell (b) | Holmström,Gilbert (ts) | Johansson,Ake (p) | Lowe,Leroy (dr)

Kjell Jansson Quintet
Blind Faith
Jansson,Kjell (b) | Holmström,Gilbert (ts) | Lindgren,Gunnar (ts) | Johansson,Ake (p) | Lowe,Leroy (dr)

TMcCD 010 | CD | Fine Together
Anders Lindskog Trio
Fine Together | I'll Close My Eyes | Tickle Toe | When Lights Are Low | Blame It On My Youth | Three And One | Strollin' | Peace | Love You Madly | Swingin' Till The Girls Come Home | I Got It Bad And That Ain't Good | They Can't Take That Away From Me | Do Nothin' Till You Hear From Me
Copenhagen,Denmark, rec. 14.8.1998
Lindskog,Anders (ts) | Fischer,Jacob (g) | Lundgaard,Jesper (b)

TMcCD 011 | CD | Comes Love...
Agneta Baumann And Her Quartet
That Old Devil Called Love | Comes Love | Blame It On My Youth | I'm Just A Lucky So-And-So | Easy Living | Thou Swell | Every Time We Say Goodbye | Who Cares | I Have The Feeling I've Been Here Before | Get Out Of Town | There's No You | It Never Entered My Mind | In Love In Vain | What's New?
Stockholm,Sweden, rec. 5./6.5.1999
Baumann,Agneta (voc) | Broberg,Bosse (tp) | Rundquist,Gösta (p) | Backenroth,Hans (b) | Löfcrantz,Johan (dr)

TMcCD 012 | CD | Monk By Five
Monk By Five
Let's Call This | Worry Later | Pannonica | Think Of One | Light Blue | Evidence | Ugly Beauty | Locomotive | Bemsha Swing | Ruby My Dear | Bye-Ya | Monk's Dream
Sundbyberg,Sweden, rec. 2.9.& 2.10.2000
Monk By Five | Adaker,Ulf (tp) | Milder,Joakim (ts) | Stenson,Bobo (p) | Danielsson,Palle (b) | Holgersson,Jones (dr)

TMcCD 014 | CD | Yiddish'n Jazz
Rebecka Gordon Quartet
By The Wayside Stand A Tree | Rabbi Motenyu | Beneath The Little Green Trees | What Will Happen When The Messiah Comes? | Our Father Abraham | By The Fireside | There Once Was A Jew | Little Boots | Hi,Little Goats | Yidl With The Fiddle | A Little Gypsy | Morning Prayer | My Childhood Years
Stockholm,Sweden, rec. 18./19.1.2001
Gordon,Rebecka (voc) | Von Heijne,Claes (p) | Augustsson,Filip (b) | Matthews,Gilbert (dr)

TMcCD 015 | CD | Song For A Willow
Irene Sjögren Group
Isn't That The Thing To Do | Round About Midnight | We'll Be Together Again | The Two Lonely People | If You Could See Me Now | Cry To The Stars | Every Time We Say Goodbye
Stockholm,Sweden, rec. 14.-16.3.2001
Sjögren,Irene (voc) | Lundin,Ove (p) | Steinholtz,Olle (b)
Yesterdays | Song For A Willow | I Didn't Know About You | I Concentrate On You
Sjögren,Irene (voc) | Bergalli,Gustavo (tp) | Lundin,Ove (p) | Steinholtz,Olle (b)
The Folks Who Live On The Hill | Meaning Of The Blues
Sjögren,Irene (voc) | Lundin,Ove (p)

TMcCD 016 | CD | Reflections
Ulf Adaker Quartet
East Of The Sun West Of The Moon | Gallop's Gallop | Reflections | How About You | Over The Rainbow | Manhattan | La Mano | And More... | A Flower Is A Lovesome Thing | The Cape Of Good Hope | Loose Changes
Stockholm,Sweden, rec. 3./4.5.2001
Adaker,Ulf (tp) | Stenson,Bobo (p) | Danielsson,Palle (b) | Löfcrantz,Johan (dr)

TMcCD 017 | CD | Sentimental Lady
Agneta Baumann Group
Close Enough For Love | I'm Glad There Is You | What Are You Doing The Rest Of Your Life | Only Trust You Heart | Where Do You Start
Stockholm,Sweden, rec. 29./30.11.2001
Baumann,Agneta (voc) | Rundquist,Gösta (p) | Danielsson,Palle (b)
Born To Be Blue | I Didn't Know About You Sentimental Lady | If You Could See Me Now | My Ship | Young And Foolish
Baumann,Agneta (voc) | Broberg,Bosse (tp) | Rundquist,Gösta (p) | Danielsson,Palle (b)

TMcCD 018 | CD | Jonas Knutsson Quartet
Jonas Knutsson Quartet
Fly Away | Horn's Street | I Loves You Porgy- | On The Lee Side- | Anglar(Angels) | The Kangaroo Woman | Trädet(The Tree) | Eine Kleine März Muzik | Smiles | Loriken(Polska Altributed To Lorns Anders Ersson)
Pernes Les Fontaines,France, rec. 18./19.2.2002
Knutsson,Jones (sax) | Persson,Anders (p) | Dubé,Sebastién (b) | Sida,Rafael (perc)

TMcCD 019 | CD | Mingus By Five | EAN 7330081000198
Mingus By Five
Dizzy Moods | Peggy's Blue Skylight | Smooch | What Love | Goodbye Pork Pie Hat | Orange Was The Colour Of Her Dress Then Blue Silk | Self-Portrait In 3 Colors | Re-Incarnation Of A Love Bird
Stockholm,Sweden, rec. 6./7.5.2002
Mingus By Five | Adaker,Ulf (tp) | Milder,Joakim (ts) | Stenson,Bobo (p) | Danielsson,Palle (b) | Holgersson,Jones (dr)

-> *Note: The Piano was recorded in the late 1960's*

TMcCD 020 | CD | Two Basses | EAN 7330081000204
Jesper Lundgaard & MadsVinding
God Bless The Child | Secret Love | Trubbel (Trouble) | Top Of The Mountain | Don't Get Around Much Anymore | A Child Is Born | I Can See The Bright Islands | Lover Man(Oh,Where Can You Be?) | Basslines | Nocturne
Copenhagen,Denmark, rec. June, 2002
Lundgaard,Jesper (b) | Vinding,Mads (b)

TMcCD 021 | CD | Reunion | EAN 7330081000211
Amanda Sedgwick Quintet
Silvia | To My Friends | I've Never Been In Love Before | Rue Hamra | Blue Jay | Stay As Sweet As You Are | When Did You Stop Loving Me,When Did I Stop Loving You | Sorcerer Of Antiquity | Ugetsu | Brown Silk | Reunion
Stockholm,Sweden, rec. 11./12.12.2003
Sedgwick,Amanda (as) | Harper,Phillip (tp) | Tilling,Daniel (p) | Sjöstedt,Martin (b) | Matthews,Gilbert (dr)

Traumton Records | Indigo

2406-2 | CD | Air Sculpture
David Friedman
The Snake | Bees | Lunch With Pancho Villa | On Green Dolphin Street | Behind Bars | Air Sculpture | The Search | Green House Fables | Hand Dance | Song For Starsy
Berlin, rec. details unknown
Friedman,David (vib,marimba)

2412-2 | CD | Looking-Glass River
Theo Bleckman & Kirk Nurock
Looking-Glass River | Lost In Loving You | To Me,Fair Friend | Norwegian Wood | Kaba Nestra | Side By Side | It Was The Lark | Sojourn
Berlin/NYC, rec. details unknown
Bleckmann,Theo (voice) | Nurock,Kirk (p)
Theo Bleckman & Kirk Nurock Quartet
My Verse | 7-4 | The More I See You
NYC, rec. details unknown
Bleckmann,Theo (voice) | Nurock,Kirk (p) | Richmond,Mike (b) | Hirshfield,Jeff (dr)

2413-2 | CD | Sand
Rudi Neuwirth Group
Mogli | Der Taucher | Jaca | Das Raumschiff | Seven Cherries | Famoudou's Bone | He Left The Planet | Wang Tang | Sand | Majon | Der Tisch Ist Gedeckt
Hamburg, rec. 6.-8.2.1995
Neuwirth,Rudi (dr,wonder-tb) | Von Kleewitz,Jan (as) | Breitkreuz,Falk (ts) | Jordi,Thomas 'Thomy' (b) | Gioia,Topo (perc)

2415-2 | CD | Under Water
Jazz Indeed
Late Nite | Der Ägypter | So Far So Near | Umsonst Und Draußen | Funky 94 | Under Water | Joey | Summer | Time Bandits | Encore
Senden, rec. details unknown
Jazz Indeed | Dehnhard,Tilmann (fl,ts) | Aperdannier,Bene (p) | Cordes,Daniel 'Danda' (b) | Winch,Rainer (dr) | Schiefel,Michael (electronics,voice)

2428-2 | CD | Birds Of A Feather
David Friedman-Jasper Van't Hof
For Now | Savanna Rainbow | Pampas Fugue | Birds Of A Feather | Mordogan Köj | Twomblish | Picnic At The Mozarteum
Berlin, rec. 1998
Friedman,David (vib,marimba) | Van't Hof,Jasper (p)

4425-2 | CD | Azul
Carlos Bica Group
Azul É O Mar | Simple Melody | Cancao De Embalar | Dagobert | M.J. | Two | Pet Shop | Tea For Two
Ludwigsburg, rec. 20.-22.11.1995
Bica,Carlos (b) | Möbus,Frank (el-g) | Black,Jim (dr,perc)
I Think I've Met You Before | Red Cadillac
Bica,Carlos (b) | Anderson,Ray (tb) | Möbus,Frank (el-g) | Black,Jim (dr,perc)
A Tragédia De Um Homem Condenado A Ser Um Poeta | Planicies
Bica,Carlos (b) | Möbus,Frank (el-g) | Black,Jim (dr,perc) | Joao,Maria (voc)

4427-2 | CD | Who The Moon Is
Jazz Indeed
Clouseau | Coda | Softache(My Darling Since) | Port Authority | Waltz 4 | In A Dream | Your Little Voice | Guzzi | Tefka | Naxotique | Pop
details unknown, rec. details unknown
Jazz Indeed | Dehnhard,Tilmann (fl,ss,ts) | Aperdannier,Bene (p,el-p,org) | Kleber,Paul (b) | Winch,Rainer (dr) | Schiefel,Michael (voice)

4430-2 | CD | Right Now
Martin Koller's Third Movement
Right Now | What | Subharmonic Dawn(Liquid Mix) | Trippin' | No.13 Haviland Street | Right Now(Core Mix)
Libra Sound,?, rec. 1998-1999
Koller,Martin (g,el-g,fretless-g,g-synth,electronis) | Preinfalk,Gerald (cl,b-cl,ss,as,bs,sopranino)
Hope
Koller,Martin (g,el-g,fretless-g,g-synth,electronis) | Preinfalk,Gerald (cl,b-cl,ss,as,bs,sopranino) | Wilson,Willsingh (voice-perc)

4432-2 | CD | Fragmentary Blues
David Moss-Michael Rodach
Fragmentary Blues | Boys | Story Time | Blues For Tango | Wittgenstein Blues | No Way,Ohhh! | Is That My Bizness? | Down Deep | Light Sweet Crude | Working | Gimme Gimme Blues | Unmade Films | A Question Of Doing It | Fellini | Say You Blues | Song For Elswhere | Blue Loop Garow | Just Don't Go | Somewhere In The South | Highly Artifical Blues
Berlin, rec. 29.-31.1.1999
Rodach,Michael (g,el-g,b,slide-g) | Moss,David (dr,perc,electronics,voice)

4433-2 | CD | I Don't Belong
Michael Schiefel
A Delicate Atmosphere | In The Theatre | I Have Nothing To Say | So I Better | Shut Up | On The Highway | Remember | I Don't Belong | Breathing | In The City | It's Time For A Change | Synchronicity | There Are So Many | Things To Do
Berlin, rec. details unknown
Schiefel,Michael (electronics,voice)

4434-2 | CD | Himmel Und Hölle-Heaven And Hell
Rodach
Himmel Und Hölle | Eskimo Märchen | Devil With The Blue Herrt | Georgia On My Mind | Hot Turbes | Medea | Golden Era | Shake Your Fish | Anna's Cat | Hysterie | Fruit Of The Bottom | Spoons | Hybrid Cods | Zeitlupenländler | Einsturz | The 'Don't Know Mind' | Maschinenherz | Open 12
details unknown, rec. details unknown
Rodach,Michael (gb,keyboards) | Nissl,Anton (dr) | Kilada,Nasser (voc)

4446-2 | CD | Cantar A Vida
Jorge Degas-Wolfgang Loos
Eu Ja Sei | Cantar A Vida | O Poeta Beija Flor | Brasil Postal | Cedo D'Amanhã | Sinto Ela Chegar | Terra Branca | Fäm Fäm | Outono | Vem Morena | Sempre Sonhei | Meu Jardim | Sinto Sempre Assim | O Tempo Passou | Um Dia Mama
Degas,Jorge (g,voc) | Loos,Wolfgang (cello)

4451-2 | CD | Music Has Its Way With Me
Jerry Granelli Group
Visitors | Papp Joe | Bad Ass | Sew It Seems | Music Has Its Way With Me | Heavy Metal | Darth Songs | Jo Mo | Dynaelo | Sunday At Jack's | Richie's Secret World | Giants
Granelli,Jerry (dr,perc) | Kögel,Christian (g,el-g) | Granelli,J.Anthony (el-b) | Saft,Jamie (el-p,moog) | Stinkin' Rich (voc,turntables)

4472-2 | CD | PurpleCoolCarSleep | EAN 705304300923
Carsten Daerr Trio
Dümpeln | Shuhyata | Pygmi Up! | Der Regenmann | Stuffed Piano | Nonen Est | Omen | Papa | September | Nardism | PurpleCoolCarSleep | Ludens Ludentis |
For Kenny Kirkland | Standard Imitation(My Funny Valentine) | Drum Interlude
Hamburg, rec. details unknown
Daerr,Carsten (p) | Potratz,Oliver (b) | Schäfer,Eric (dr)

4474-2 | CD | Red & Blue Days | EAN 705304480922
Yakou Tribe
Hurt | Ocean | News From Home | Heute Jedoch Nicht | Texas Girl At The Funeral Of Her Father | Little Giant | Kiruna | Don Camelone | Mellenthin | Mr. 4,5 Volt | Freaky Deaky | Niebo | Companero | Moment
details unknown, rec. details unknown
Yakou Tribe | Von Kleewitz,Jan (sax) | Brückner,Kai (g,dobro) | Gunkel,Johannes (b) | Winch,Rainer (dr)

Trick Music | Trick Music Records & Production

TM 0112 CD | CD | Big little Gigs: First Takes Live
Klaus Kreuzeder & Franz Benton
Blue | Unter Den Linden | Leaving Home | Much More | Brown Eyes | Fragile Feeling | Why | Indian Summer | How I Wish | Love Song
different Places, rec. 2000
Kreuzeder,Klaus (ss) | Benton,Franz (g,voc)

TM 8712 CD | CD | Sax As Sax Can
TM 8713 MC | MC | Sax As Sax Can
TM 8711 LP | LP | Sax As Sax Can
Klaus Kreuzeder & Willi Herzinger
Crystal Beat | Cuckoo's Egg | Summertime | Orpheo Negro | No Contract | First Take | Mental Surf | Karatschan | Autumn Leaves | Take Five | Box The Music | Sax As Sax Can
Transformer/Hartman Digital Studios, Bavaria, rec. ca.1987
Kreuzeder,Klaus (ss,sopranino) | Herzinger,Willi (g)

TM 9013 MC | MC | Saxappeal
TM 9011 LP | LP | Saxappeal
TM 9012 CD | CD | Saxappeal
Klaus Kreuzeder & Henry Sincigno
Ede Pustefix | Fullmoon(in Fuhlsbüttel) | Big Bop | Swinging St. Fu | Indian Summer | Liebeslied(Love Song) | Saxappeal | Is This True(dedicated to Jimi Hendrix) | Red River | Deep Sea | Floating | Unter Den Linden
Hilpoltstein, rec. 1989/1990
Kreuzeder,Klaus (ss,as,sopranino) | Sincigno,Henry (g)

TM 9202 CD | CD | Conversations
Jamenco
Sogno D'Amore | Tellaro | Bahia | Il Campo | Neapolitaner | Firedance | Praha | Elephant Business
Hilpoltstein, rec. April 1992
Jamenco | Pröbstl,Peter (g,el-g) | Kieslich,Klaus (g) | Remold,Michael (p,keyboards) | Hergenröder,Stefan (el-b) | Bildhauer,Shekilua (perc)
Kalimba
Jamenco | Pröbstl,Peter (g,el-g) | Kieslich,Klaus (g) | Remold,Michael (p,keyboards) | Geßner,Volker (keyboards) | Hergenröder,Stefan (el-b) | Bildhauer,Shekilua (perc)
Perfect Time
Jamenco | Pröbstl,Peter (g,el-g) | Kieslich,Klaus (g) | Remold,Michael (p,keyboards) | Hergenröder,Stefan (el-b) | Bildhauer,Shekilua (perc) | Yannic (dog-voices)
Mai Tai
Jamenco | Mensching,Fritz (sax) | Pröbstl,Peter (g,el-g) | Kieslich,Klaus (g) | Remold,Michael (p,keyboards) | Hergenröder,Stefan (el-b) | Nickola,Mario (dr) | Bildhauer,Shekilua (perc)

TM 9312 CD | CD | Sax As Sax Can-Alive
TM 9313 MC | MC | Sax As Sax Can-Alive
Klaus Kreuzeder & Henry Sincigno
Tumbling Derwish | G-Spot | Deep Sea | Jungle Groove | Brown Eyes | Georgia On My Mind | Serafina | White City Kids | Manaus Fever | Alive | The Blue | Take Five
Hilpoltstein, rec. 1992/1998
Kreuzeder,Klaus (ss,as,sopranino) | Sincigno,Henry (g)

Triptychon | Triptychon GmbH

300201 | CD | Roots And Wings
Wolf Mayer Dialects
Choral Fantasie I | Barcarole | For A.M.B. | Für Glenn Gould | Directed-Undirected | Bach In Mind | Choral | Vom Himmel Hoch | Orgelpunkt 34 Grad F | Ein Feste Burg
Live at Schwarzwald Musikfestival,Freudenstadt, rec. 21.6.2000
Mayer,Wolf (p) | Read,Hugo (ss,as) | Schmolck,Stefan (b) | Schilgen,Dirik (dr)

400403 | CD | I Do Believe In Spring
Wolf Mayer Trio
I Do Believe In Spring | Daydream | What Is This Thing Called Love | Vom Himmel Hoch | Ein Feste Burg | So Oder So | Wacked Cat 'Lisa' | Solar | Deauville | Rites Of Passage | Boston Summer
Sandhausen, rec. 11.-13.9.1997
Mayer,Wolf (p) | Schmolck,Stefan (b) | Schilgen,Dirik (dr)

true muze | True Muze Rec.

TUMU CD 9801 | CD | Goldstein-Wilson
Malcolm Goldstein-Peter Niklas Wilson
Monsun Vibrations I | From 'Configurations In Darkness' | Kraniche Im Zweireiher | The Space Of The Bass | Soundings For Solo Violin | Monsun Vibrations II | Monsun Afterthoughts
Hamburg, rec. 29.10.1996
Goldstein,Malcolm (v) | Wilson,Peter Niklas (b)

TUMU CD 9802 | CD | The Collective 3 +
The Collective 3 +
Micro-Orka | Revolving Door | Nagaraja | Grüblein | Aarti
Amsterdam,Holland, rec. 14./15.4.1997
Collective 3 +,The | Metha,Rajesh (tp,b-tp,hybrid-tp) | Provan,Felicity (co,pocket-tp,voice) | Fryer,Tom (el-g) | Stouthamer,Paul (cello) | Purves,Alan (dr,perc)

TUMU CD 9803 | CD | Vlatko Kucan Group
Vlatko Kucan Group
Dance Of The Robot People | Gigolo | Paris Blues | Floating | Tuba Tune | Round About Midnight
Hannover, rec. 19.3.1991
Kucan,Vlatko (b-cl,ss,ts) | Stanko,Tomasz (tp) | Danner,Michael (tb,tuba) | Oliver,Jay (b) | Elgart,Billy (dr)

Tutu Records | Tutu(alle mit einem * markierten CD's über Fenn Music)

888102-2* | CD | Mal, Dance And Soul
888002 | LP | Mal, Dance And Soul
Mal Waldron Trio
Dancing On The Flames | A Bow To The Classics | Little One | From A Little Acorns | Blood And Guts
München, rec. 25.11.1987
Waldron,Mal (p) | Schuller,Ed (b) | Betsch,John (dr)
Mal Waldron Quartet feat.Jim Pepper
Soulmates
Waldron,Mal (p) | Pepper,Jim (ts) | Schuller,Ed (b) | Betsch,John (dr)

888104-2* | CD | Inside Lookin' Out
Simon Nabatov, String Gang & Percussion
Bottom Of The Mirror | So Near | Clave For Collin | Say It | Sundial | In-Side Out
München, rec. 26./27.4.1988
Nabatov,Simon (p) | Schuller,Ed (b) | Betsch,John (dr,perc) | Tuncboyaci[Boyaciyan],Arto (perc,voice)
Papa Willy Rhumba
München, rec. 27.4.1988
Betsch,John (dr,perc) | Tuncboyaci[Boyaciyan],Arto (perc,voice)
Simon Nabatov-Ed Schuller
Purple On Gold
Nabatov,Simon (p) | Schuller,Ed (b)

888106-2* | CD | Art Of The Duo
888006 | LP | Art Of The Duo
Mal Waldron & Jim Pepper
Ticket To Tokyo | Ruby My Dear | Bathing Beauties | Somewhere Over The Rainbow | What Is This Thing Called Love | You're No Bunny Unless Some Bunny Loves You | Good Bait | A Pepper Poem | Willy's Blues | Indian Water
München, rec. 1988
Pepper,Jim (ss,ts) | Waldron,Mal (p)

888110-2* | CD | Internationales Jazzfestival Münster
Albert Mangelsdorff-John Scofield
The Eternal Turn-On | Gray And Visceral | Alfie's Theme
Münster, rec. 17.6.1988
Mangelsdorff,Albert (tb) | Scofield,John (el-g)
Marty Cook Group feat. Jim Pepper
Comin' To Git You | Face The Nation
Münster, rec. 18.6.1988
Cook,Marty (tb) | Pepper,Jim (ts,voc) | Schuller,Ed (b) | Betsch,John (dr)
Günther Klatt Quartet
Chelsea Bridge | Kuriosita
Münster, rec. 17.6.1988
Klatt,Günther (ts) | Drewing,Jörg (tb) | Wuchner,Jürgen (b) | Krieger,Andreas (dr)
Aki Takase-Alexander von Schlippenbach
Frictitious Paragon
Takase,Aki (p) | Von Schlippenbach,Alexander (p)

888112-2* | CD | Tonal Weights & Blue Fire
Frank Ku-Umba Lacy Group
Requiem | Apostle Man | Random Vibrations | Namasté- | I Bow To The Light With You- | The Little Child
NYC, rec. 13./14.4.1990
Lacy,Ku-umba Frank (fl-h,tb,p,org,voc) | Hopkins,Fred (b) | Carvin,Michael (dr,tympani)
Robot | Yesterdays | Tenderly
Lacy,Ku-umba Frank (fl-h,tb,p,org,voc) | Lacy Sr.,Frank (g) | Hopkins,Fred (b) | Carvin,Michael (dr,tympani)

888116-2* | CD | Art Of The Duo: Plays Ballads Of Duke Ellington:
Gunther Klatt & Aki Takase
In A Sentimental Mood | Sophisticated Lady | Prelude To A Kiss | Chelsea Bridge | Strangehorn | Warm Valley | Warm Blue | Lush Life | Giudecca
München, rec. 25./26.4.1990
Klatt,Günther (ts) | Takase,Aki (p)

888118-2* | CD | Quadrologue At Utopia Vol.1
Mal Waldron Quartet feat.Jim Pepper
Ticket To Utopia | Time For Duke | Never In Hurry | Mistral Breeze No. One | Funny Glasses & A Moustache
Live at Utopia Jazz Club,Innsbruck,Austia, rec. 25./26.10.1989
Waldron,Mal (p) | Pepper,Jim (ts) | Schuller,Ed (b) | Betsch,John (dr)

888120-2* | CD | Three Or Four Shades Of Dannie Richmond Quintet
Dannie Richmond Quintet
Introduction by Dannie Richmond | Soft Seas | Theme For Lester Young: Goodbye Pork Pie Hat | Announcement by Dannie Richmond | Big Alice & John Henry | Cumbia & Jazz Fusion | Audience's Excitement
Live at The Jazzfestival Münster, rec. 12.7.1981
Richmond,Dannie (dr) | Walrath,Jack (tp) | Garrett,Kenny (as) | Nellums,Bob (p) | Brown,Cameron (b)

888122-2* | CD | Borderlines
Marty Cook Group feat. Monty Waters
Water Dream | Full Moon | O.C. & Montville
München, rec. 17./18.12.1990
Cook,Marty (tb) | Waters,Monty (as) | Schuller,Ed (b) | Lewis,Art (dr)
Strauss' Last Waltz | Borderlines No. One | Bordercross | Sweet Pea | Aware | Borderlines No. Two | Theme For Martha
Cook,Marty (tb) | Waters,Monty (as) | Grabowsky,Paul (p) | Schuller,Ed (b) | Lewis,Art (dr)

888124-2* | CD | The Eleventh Hour
Ed Schuller & Band
O-Zone | PM In The AM | Keeping Still- | Mountain- | Love Lite | Shamal | For Dodo
Hoboken,NJ, rec. 21./22.2.1991
Schuller,Ed (b) | Valente,Gary (tb) | Osby,Greg (ss,as) | Bickford,Bill (g) | Jones,Victor (dr)
The Eleventh Hour(part 1) | The Eleventh Hour(part 2)
Schuller,Ed (b) | Valente,Gary (tb) | Osby,Greg (ss,as) | Bickford,Bill (g) | Jones,Victor (dr) | Tuncboyaci[Boyaciyan],Arto (perc,voice)

888128-2* | CD | ...You Don't Need To Know...If You Have To Ask
Hamiet Bluiett Group
Black Danube(James Brown In 3-4 Time) | Wide Open | If You Have To Ask, You Don't Need To Know | Theme For Lester Young: Goodbye Pork Pie Hat | The Gift: One Shot From The Hip
NYC, rec. 18./19.2.1991
Bluiett,Hamiet (alto-fl,bs) | Hopkins,Fred (b) | Carvin,Michael (dr)
If Only We Knew & T.S. Monk, Sir | The King In The Pallenquin | Children At Play | Circle Of Prayer
Bluiett,Hamiet (alto-fl,bs) | Hopkins,Fred (b) | Asante,Okeryema (perc,voc)
El Owora Befame-Ko(So, I'll Come Back)
Bluiett,Hamiet (alto-fl,bs) | Hopkins,Fred (b) | Ansah,Thomas Ebow (g,voc) | Asante,Okeryema (perc,voc)

888134-2* | CD | Black Sea
Nicolas Simion Group
Black Sea | Blues For Bird | Africa | Red | Song For Leo(dedicated to Leo Wright) | Solomon
Wien,Austria, rec. 25.4.1991
Simion,Nicolas (ss,ts) | Haynes,Graham (co) | Plaxico,Lonnie (b) | Burrage,Ronnie (dr)
Mr.McCoy
Simion,Nicolas (ss,ts) | Haynes,Graham (co) | Burton,Ron (p) | Plaxico,Lonnie (b) | Burrage,Ronnie (dr)

888136-2* | CD | Landwhales In New York
Gordon Lee Quartet feat. Jim Pepper
Jumpin' Gemini | Insomnia | Autumn In New York | Three-Quarter Gemini | Indian Water | Land Whales | Gone
details unknown, rec. 21./22.12.1982
Lee,Gordon (p) | Pepper,Jim (ss,ts) | Hill,Calvin (b) | Moses,Bobby (dr)

888140-2* | CD | Live In Paris, Duc Des Lombards, Volume One
Monty Waters' Hot House
Money Blues | Six-Four My Singer | Seidah's Eyes | Without You | Montville No. One | You And Me
Paris/Berikon,CH, rec. 6./7.12.1991
Waters,Monty (ss,as) | weitere Angaben lagen bei Redaktionsschluß nicht vor

888142-2* | CD | Colours Of A Ferghana Bazar-Live At The International Jazzfestival Münster
Enver Ismailov
The Legend Of A Tartar | Crimian Dance | Haitarma | Eternal Heavy Metal | Sittin' And Drinkin' | Scholocho | At A Fergana Bazar | The Girl Of Meexor | Impressions Of Turkey | Champak Odours | Enver Left Town
Münster, rec. 29.6.1991
Ismailov,Enver (el-g)

888144-2* | CD | Art Of The Duo: Trouble In Paradise
Noma Kosazana & Uli Lenz
What A Little Moonlight Can Do | Master Of TheWar | Trouble In Paradise | All One Can Get | Come, Come Crazy | Maduna | Amamponda | NongQongQo | Heart Still Alive | Hamba Khale | Kalahari Song
details unknown, rec. 19./20.12.1992
Kosazana,Noma (voc) | Lenz,Uli (p)

888146-2* | CD | Dinner For Don Carlos
Nicolas Simion Quartet feat. Tomasz Stanko
Nicolas' Blues | Ornette | Chiacona For Chet | Go-Go | Relaxin' With Lonnie | One For Michael(No.1) | Don Carlos | Open Windows | One For Michael(No.2)

details unknown, rec. 6.12.1991
Simion,Nicolas (ts) | Stanko,Tomasz (tp) | Schuller,Ed (b) | Heral,Patrice (dr)

888148-2* | CD | The Git-Go At Utopia,Volume Two
Mal Waldron Quartet feat. Jim Pepper
Dancing On The Flames | The Git Go | Mistral Breeze No. Two | You Open My Eyes | Warm Puppies
details unknown, rec. 25.6.& 26.10.1989
Waldron,Mal (p) | Pepper,Jim (ss,ts) | Schuller,Ed (b) | Betsch,John (dr)

888150-2* | CD | Songs From The Musical 'Poker'
Ku-umba Frank Lacy & The Poker Bigband
Overture | Nobody Helps You- | Rap- | Dreamstuff | Combination | Supermarket | I'm Only Trying | Money, Money | Interlude 2- | Cold Turkey- | Come, Come Crazy | Open Up The Pearly Gates | Take It! | Ballad- | I Wish I Were A Child Again- | Forgive Me | Princess | You Owe Me | Here We All Are | My Pleasure | Don't Let The Sun | Poker Finale- | Play Out-
München, rec. November 1991 & October 1994
Poker Bigband,The | Lacy,Ku-umba Frank (tp,tb,keyboards,perc,arr,ld,voc) | Waters,Monty (as) | Simion,Nicolas (b-cl,ss,ts) | Warren,Geoff (fl,keyboards) | Jost,Tizian (p) | Bickford,Bill (el-g) | Clarke,Kim (el-b) | Schuller,Ed (b) | Ditmas,Bruce (keyboards,dr) | Nomakozasana (keyboards,voc)

888152-2* | CD | Remembrance-Live At The International Jazzfestival Münster
Jim Pepper & Eagle Wing
Trapeze | Comin' & Goin' | Three-Quarter Gemini | Dakota Song | Legacy Of The Flying Eagle | Ticket To Tokyo | Malinyea | Native Amarican Visions: Remembrance-Ya Na Ho-Four Winds
details unknown, rec. 19.5.1990
Pepper,Jim (ts,perc,voc) | Bickford,Bill (el-g) | Schuller,Ed (b) | Betsch,John (dr)

888154-2* | CD | Mu-Point
Ed Schuller Quartet feat. Dewey Redman
Mu-Point | Ghana Song | I See You Now(for Jim Pepper) | Paradoxical Conversation | B-Well(for Ed Blackwell) | I-Pimp | Folk Song For Rosie | Quasar | Remembrance
Hoboken,NJ, rec. 9./10.1.1993
Schuller,Ed (b) | Redman,Dewey (ts) | Bickford,Bill (el-g) | Motian,Paul (dr,perc)

888158-2* | CD | Volume One:Fa Mozzo
Gunther Klatt & New York Razzmatazz
Fa Mozzo | Otok Is Around | Love Song From A Movie Never Made | We Like It | Pompeiian Tango | Les Enfants Des Dubrovnik | Giudecca | Eddie's Razzmatazz Rap
Live at The Unterfahrt,München, rec. 1.12.1991
Klatt,Günther (ts,perc,voc) | Lacy,Ku-umba Frank (tp,tb,perc,voc) | Schuller,Ed (b,voc) | Burrage,Ronnie (dr,voc)

888160-2* | CD | Phases Of The Moon
Marty Cook Conspiracy
Kicking Monster And The Vagina Girls | Princess | 2:25 | Soft Touch | The Duck And The Dodo | Third Street | Carefree | Universal Trains | Endless | Princess Of Third Street
München, rec. 3./4.11.1993
Cook,Marty (tb) | Mahall,Rudi (b-cl,record-player) | Bickford,Bill (el-g) | Schuller,Ed (b) | Black,Jim (dr,perc)
Phases Of The Moon | One Way Out
Cook,Marty (tb) | Mahall,Rudi (b-cl) | Porter,Larry (p) | Bickford,Bill (el-g) | Schuller,Ed (b) | Black,Jim (dr,perc)

888162-2* | CD | Settegast Strut
Ku-Umba Frank Lacy & His Quartet
Caroline's Dance | Jordan's Mood | Tonal Weights & Blue Fire(No.Two) | Welcome | What's The Resolution | Settegast Strut | A.D. 2016:The Comet
Live at The Jazz Club 'Moods',Zürich,CH, rec. 3./4.6.1994
Lacy,Ku-umba Frank (tp,tb,voc) | Roberts,Katy (p) | Williams,Richard 'Radu' (b) | Hammond,Doug (dr)
Hip Hop Swing, A Love Supreme
Lacy,Ku-umba Frank (tp,tb,p,voc) | Roberts,Katy (p) | Williams,Richard 'Radu' (b) | Whittaker,Sebastian (dr)

888164-2* | CD | Transylvanian Dance
Nicolas Simion Quartet feat. Tomasz Stanko
That's Dope | I Got Changes | You'll Never Know(dedicated to my Father) | Peasant Flute Song Round About Underground No.One | Transylvanian Dance | When The Shepherd Lost His Sheep | Mozy's Land | Longing | Bride's March
Wien,Austria, rec. 16./17.5.1994
Simion,Nicolas (b-cl,ss,ts,caval,kalimba) | Stanko,Tomasz (tp) | Schuller,Ed (b) | Jones,Victor (dr)

888166-2* | CD | The Force
Ed Schuller Group feat. Dewey Redman
Warm Puppies | Playing For Keeps | 4 KH | The Force | Star Crossed Lovers | Jumpin' Gemini | Bathing Beauties | Kyyoi | Ohadi
NYC, rec. 12./13.9.1994
Schuller,Ed (b) | Valente,Gary (tb) | D'Angelo,Andrew (b-cl) | Noriega,Oscar (as) | Redman,Dewey (ts) | Black,Jim (dr,perc)

888168-2* | CD | Art Of The Duo:Dancing Over The Moon
Enver Ismailov & Geoff Warren
Terrain Turquoise | Touch Down At Falconara | Ancona Danza | Among The Hops | Near The Grapes | Boina | Dolu | Lonely Dancer | Enver's Mood No.2 | Departure | White Minarets
Live at 'Loft Hinkelstein',Essen, rec. 19./20.6.1995
Warren,Geoff (fl,ss) | Ismailov,Enver (el-g)

888170-2* | CD | Mal,Verve,Black & Blue
Mal Waldron Quartet
Judy Full Grown | Transylvanian Dance | Here Comes Mikey | Soul Eyes | I See You Now(for Jim Pepper) | The Last Go Pepper Blues
Live at The Theatre 'Satiricon',Essen, rec. 11.10.1994
Waldron,Mal (p) | Simion,Nicolas (ts) | Schuller,Ed (b) | Jones,Victor (dr)

888172-2* | CD | Walkin' & Talkin'
Hamiet Bluiett
Daddy Banks- | Doll Baby- | A View From My Mind's Eye | Full Deep And Mellow- | Mighty Denn- | Talkin' To Myself | Black Yard Sonata- | Traditional New Orleans Tune- | Overtones Song- | Hard Bottom- | Oasis- | Ballad For My People- | Foot Stompin' Blues- | Departure- | Mangalam-
Live at Stadttheater Basel,CH, rec. 22.4.1991
Bluiett,Hamiet (alto-fl,b-cl,bs)

888174-2* | CD | Red,White,Black & Blue
Marty Cook Group feat. Jim Pepper
It's About That Time | Sweet-No Regrets Now | Mr.D.C. | Face The Nation
München, rec. 23./24.11.1987
Cook,Marty (tb) | Pepper,Jim (ss,ts) | Schuller,Ed (b) | Betsch,John (dr)
Spirit War | Love Life | Grab Bag | Trapeze
Cook,Marty (tb) | Pepper,Jim (ss,ts) | Waldron,Mal (p) | Schuller,Ed (b) | Betsch,John (dr)

888176-2 | CD | Back To The Roots
Nicolas Simion Trio
Walking The Fish | Bella Ragazza | Transylvanian Dance | Jenny's Dream | Mountain Talk | Unfinished Column | Prelude A L'Unisson | Tales Retold | Happy House
Wien,Austria, rec. 16.12.1992
Simion,Nicolas (ts) | Fisher,Glen (b) | Perfido,Peter (dr)

888178-2* | CD | Art Of The Duo: Endless Radiance
Badal Roy & Amit Chatterjee
Village Dance No.1 | Endless Radiance | The Origin | Geeta's Shuffle | Seven Past Midnight | Restless Moon | Village Dance- | Goin' Home-
Paterson,NJ, rec. October 1993
Chatterjee,Amit (el-g) | Roy,Badal (perc,tablas)

888180-2* | CD | Echoes Of Mandela
Uli Lenz Trio
Love Channel | There Is No Greater Love | Blue Lips | Soul Eyes | L.B. And Me | Whims Of Chambers | Free For Mandela | Don't Trust The Mirror
Live at The 'Loft', Köln, rec. 17.6.1996
Lenz,Uli (p) | Schuller,Ed (b) | Jones,Victor (dr)

888182-2* | CD | Monty Waters New York Calling Vol.2
Monty Waters Quartet
New York Chicago And Rhythm Burrage | Aparajita,The Lady From The East | Monteville No.2 | You And Me
Live at Duc Des Lombardes,Paris
Waters,Monty (as,voc) | Porter,Larry (p) | James,Stafford (b) | Burrage,Ronnie (dr)
One Full Moon Night | Road To Moroco | Dancing With Daniela | Jump'n Jive,Still Alive
Senftenberg
Waters,Monty (as,voc) | Porter,Larry (p) | James,Stafford (b) | Burrage,Ronnie (dr) | Nicholas,Tom (perc)

888184-2* | CD | Art Of The Duo:Live In Mexico City
Günther Klatt-Tizian Jost
Prelude To A Kiss | Lost In The Stars | Day Dream | Solitude | Strangehorn | Warm Valley | Star Crossed Lovers | Mexico City | Speak Low | Giudecca | In A Sentimental Mood
Live at Concert Hall Nezahualcoyotl,Mexico City, rec. 18.4.1993
Klatt,Günther (ss,ts,p) | Jost,Tizian (p,melodica)

888186-2* | CD | Art Of The Duo:The Big Rochade
Mal Waldron-Nicolas Simion
Open Windows | Monk's Dream | Minor Mode For Majors | Dinosaurus' Dispute | Song For Leo | From Dark Into The Light | Search For Euridice | Slovakian Folk Song | Singing Red
Köln, rec. 19.12.1995
Simion,Nicolas (b-cl,ss,ts) | Waldron,Mal (p)

888188-2* | CD | Snake Dancing
Ed Schuller & The Eleventh Hour Band
Just Say | Zoology | Qualify Your Funk | Wave Forms No. One | Wave Forms No. Two | Is There A Beauty In The Beast | Clave For Collin | Life Circle | Snake Dancing
Köln, rec. 1./2.12.1996
Schuller,Ed (b,voc) | Valente,Gary (tb) | Goldsbury,Mack (sax) | Bickford,Bill (el-g) | Burrage,Ronnie (dr,perc)
Koch's Curve
Schuller,Ed (b,voc) | Valente,Gary (tb) | Goldsbury,Mack (sax) | Bickford,Bill (el-g) | Burrage,Ronnie (dr,perc) | Kämpgen,Nicole (voice) | Irving,Nat (computer-sequencing)

888190-2* | CD | Brecht Songs
Brass Attack
Ballade Von Der Sexuellen Hörigkeit | Die Zuhälter Ballade | Ruf Aus Der Gruft | Anstatt-Dass Song(II)
Berlin, rec. 16.-20.11.1997
Brass Attack | Wolf,Lutz (tp) | Bergmann,Thomas (tb) | Wahnschaffe,Felix (as) | Erdmann,Daniel (ss,ts) | Gocht,Stefan (tuba) | Tinwa,Joshua (dr)
Grabschrift
Brass Attack | Wolf,Lutz (tp) | Dörner,Axel (tp) | Bergmann,Thomas (tb) | Wahnschaffe,Felix (as) | Erdmann,Daniel (ss,ts) | Gocht,Stefan (tuba) | Tinwa,Joshua (dr)
Die Moritat Von Mackie Messer(II)
Brass Attack | Wolf,Lutz (tp) | Bergmann,Thomas (tb) | Zickerick,Ralf 'Zicke' (tb) | Wahnschaffe,Felix (as) | Erdmann,Daniel (ss,ts) | Gocht,Stefan (tuba) | Tinwa,Joshua (dr)
Die Moritat Von Mackie Messer(I)
Brass Attack | Wolf,Lutz (tp) | Bergmann,Thomas (tb) | Zickerick,Ralf 'Zicke' (tb) | Wahnschaffe,Felix (as) | Erdmann,Daniel (ss,ts) | Gocht,Stefan (tuba) | Tinwa,Joshua (dr) | Maza,Diseur Diserable (voc)
Morgenchoral Des Peachum | Lied Vom Achten Elefanten
Brass Attack | Wolf,Lutz (tp) | Bergmann,Thomas (tb) | Wahnschaffe,Felix (as) | Erdmann,Daniel (ss,ts) | Gocht,Stefan (tuba) | Tinwa,Joshua (dr) | Maza,Diseur Diserable (voc)
Anstatt-Dass Song(I)
Brass Attack | Wolf,Lutz (tp) | Bergmann,Thomas (tb) | Wahnschaffe,Felix (as) | Erdmann,Daniel (ss,ts) | Gocht,Stefan (tuba) | Tinwa,Joshua (dr) | Maza,Diseur Diserable (voc) | Muza,Celina (voc)
Alabama Song
Brass Attack | Wolf,Lutz (tp) | Bergmann,Thomas (tb) | Wahnschaffe,Felix (as) | Erdmann,Daniel (ss,ts) | Gocht,Stefan (tuba) | Tinwa,Joshua (dr) | Maza,Diseur Diserable (voc) | Muza,Celina (voc) | Ries,Tanja (voc)
Ballade Über Die Frage:Wovon Lebt Der Mensch
Brass Attack | Wolf,Lutz (tp) | Bergmann,Thomas (tb) | Wahnschaffe,Felix (as) | Erdmann,Daniel (ss,ts) | Gocht,Stefan (tuba) | Tinwa,Joshua (dr) | Maza,Diseur Diserable (voc) | Ries,Tanja (voc)
Das Lied Vom Surabaya-Johnny
Brass Attack | Wolf,Lutz (tp) | Bergmann,Thomas (tb) | Wahnschaffe,Felix (as) | Erdmann,Daniel (ss,ts) | Gocht,Stefan (tuba) | Tinwa,Joshua (dr) | Ries,Tanja (voc)

888192-2* | CD | Viaggio Imaginario
Nicolas Simion Quartet feat. Tomasz Stanko
Saint Nick's Groove
Wien,Austria, rec. 23./24.4.1995
Simion,Nicolas (b-cl,ss,ts,wooden-fl) | Stanko,Tomasz (tp) | Muthspiel,Christian (tb) | Schuller,Ed (b) | Thomas,Angus (el-b) | Perfido,Peter (dr) | Haddad,Jamey (perc)
Geamparale | Viaggio Imaginario
Simion,Nicolas (b-cl,ss,ts,wooden-fl) | Stanko,Tomasz (tp) | Muthspiel,Christian (tb) | Schuller,Ed (b) | Perfido,Peter (dr) | Haddad,Jamey (perc)
Poem For Paula | Requiem For Flying Eagle | In & Out Underground
Simion,Nicolas (b-cl,ss,ts,wooden-fl) | Stanko,Tomasz (tp) | Schuller,Ed (b) | Perfido,Peter (dr) | Haddad,Jamey (perc)
Allegro Furioso | Jumpin' Kalushary | Promenade Avec Christine
Simion,Nicolas (b-cl,ss,ts,wooden-fl) | Stanko,Tomasz (tp) | Schuller,Ed (b) | Perfido,Peter (dr)

888194-2* | CD | Live At New Morning,Paris
Jim Pepper Flying Eagle
Flying At New Morning | Three-Quarter Gemini | Somewhere Over The Rainbow | Ski Jumping Blues | Soul Mates | Green Pepper- | Freewheelin' At Utopia- | Legacy Of The Flying Eagle: | Remembrance- | Ya Na Ho- | Four Winds- | Witchi-Tai-To-
Live at The New Morning,Paris,France, rec. 10.5./26.10.& 4.11.1989
Pepper,Jim (ts,voc) | Waldron,Mal (p) | Schuller,Ed (b) | Betsch,John (dr)

888196-2* | CD | Jazzoerty
Monty Waters' Hot Rhythm Junction
The Song You Sing | Lift Off | Spanish Harlem,125th Esat Street | Buddy Bolden | Run Joe,A Hit When I Was A Kid | Basket Of Fruit | You Don't Know What Love Is(No.2) | Jazzmine | Keep Your Beat Alive | You Don't Know What Love Is(No.1) | The Dark Side Of The Moon | San Domingo Night
Loft,Köln, rec. 1./2.11.1997
Waters,Monty (as,voc) | Cardoso,Paulo (b,voc) | Nicolas,Tom (perc,voc)

888198-2* | CD | Tenderness
Nomakozasana-Uli Lenz
Pula | Tenderness | Blow My Friend | Dream Of Muskogee | Poor Little Music Boy | Ameva | Biko In Bonn | Hamba Jam | Broken Heart | Tell Someone
Schloss Hallberg/Saarbrücken/München, rec. December 1997/18.5.1998/26.3.2000
Nomakozasana (voc) | Lenz,Uli (p)
Ngekengiye Kwazulu | Ya Na Ho | Umamoya Jabula
Schloss Hallberg/Saarbrücken/München, rec. December 1997/16.5.1998/26.3.2000
Nomakozasana (voc) | Lenz,Uli (p) | Ott,Tobias (ghatam,tablas)

888202-2* | CD | Violin Tales
Hannes Beckmann Quartet
March For My Friend Blam | Speedy Edgar | Walk With My Father | Afro Dio | The Cab Driver | Imre,The Gambler | Turn To G
Radio Beograd, rec. 6.1.1998
Beckmann,Hannes (v) | Wilson,Edgar (p) | Blam,Michael 'Mischa' (b) | Köszegi,Imre (dr)

888204-2* | 2 CD | Witchi Tia To, The Music Of Jim Pepper
Gunther Schuller With The WDR Radio Orchestra & Rememberance Band
Inter Tribal(I) | Comin' And Goin' | Feathers Dance | I See You Now | Wichi-Tai-To | Mr.D.C. | Reflection | Dra Kumba | Malinyea | Fancy Dance Song | A Pepper Poem | Lakoda Song | Goin' Down To Muskogee | Dance No.1 | So Long Jim | Memorial Song | Funny Glasses & A Moustache | Inter Tribal(II) | Remembrance | Jim | Legacy Of The Flying Eagle No.3
WDR Köln, rec. 15.-22.3.1998
WDR Radio Orchestra & Rememrerance Band | Simion,Nicolas (b-cl,ss,ts) | Kämpgen[Schuller],Nicole (as,voc) | Bickford,Bill (el-g) | Lightsey,Kirk (p,celesta) | Schuller,Ed (b,voc) | Schuller,George (dr) | Gioia,Topo (perc) | Knight[Pepper],Caren (voc,perc) | Bender,Pete 'Wyoming' (voc) | Moore,Pat (dance,voc,pow-wow-dr) | Garland,Kent (dance,voc,pow-wow-dr) | Pepper,Floy (narration) | Schuller,Gunther (cond,arr)

888206-2* | CD | Art Of The Duo: Savignyplatz
Ed Schuller & Mack Goldbury
Parody No.Two | Odwalla | Skylark | Bath Thing | What Love | Fly Down Low
Live at The A-Train Jazzclub,Berlin, rec. 29.9.1999
Goldsbury,Mack (ss,ts) | Schuller,Ed (b)
Mutab Ali | Jennifer Marie | Love Irgendwie | A Tribute To Munir
On Air Studio,?, rec. 6.3.2000
Goldsbury,Mack (ss,ts) | Schuller,Ed (b)

888208-2* | CD | Islands Everywhere
Tabla & Strings
Tiger Walk | Disappearing Act
Live at Studio Hofbräuhaus,Traunstein, rec. 30.10.1999
Tablas & Strings | Goodman,Geoff (g,el-g,el-mand,mando-cello) | Hess,Bernd (g,el-g) | Lal,Shankar (tablas,voc) | Ott,Tobias (ghatam,tanpura)
Blood
Live at Künstlerwerkstatt,Pfaffenhofen, rec. 23.3.2000
Tablas & Strings | Goodman,Geoff (g,el-g,el-mand,mando-cello) | Hess,Bernd (g,el-g) | Lal,Shankar (tablas,voc) | Ott,Tobias (ghatam,tanpura)
Islands Everywhere | Umpachene Falls | Dim Light Raga | Aquarium Suite | Vishnu Blues | Once Again & Far Away
München, rec. 7.& 9.4.2000
Tablas & Strings | Goodman,Geoff (g,el-g,el-mand,mando-cello) | Hess,Bernd (g,el-g) | Lal,Shankar (tablas,voc) | Ott,Tobias (ghatam,tanpura)
Of Winter
Tablas & Strings | Goodman,Geoff (g,el-g,el-mand,mando-cello) | Hess,Bernd (g,el-g) | Haas,Alex (b) | Lal,Shankar (tablas,voc) | Ott,Tobias (ghatam,tanpura)

888210-2* | CD | Marty Cook Trio/Quintet
Marty Cook Trio
F No.6 | Raise Four & Monk's Point | Last Time Around
Live at The Unterfahrt,München, rec. 4.4.2000
Cook,Marty (tb) | Geisse,Gunnar (el-g) | Goodman,Geoff (el-g)
Marty Cook Quintet
B.T. | Balkan Blues | Fractual Gumbo | Wee See | Y II | True Romance | Yor Ladab | Sweet-No Regrets | Sweet Fifteen
München, rec. 31.7./1.8.2000
Cook,Marty (tb) | Geisse,Gunnar (el-g) | Goodman,Geoff (el-g) | Schuller,Ed (b,voc) | Perfido,Peter (dr)

888212-2* | CD | Oriental Gates:Live In Vienna
Nicolas Simion Quartet
Bartók Goes New Orleans | An Evening In Thessaloniki-At The Oriental Gates | Dear Arnold | Bird Talk | Afro-Transdabubian Groove | Slovakian Folk Song
Live at 'Porgy & Bess',Wien, rec. 4.4.1996
Simion,Nicolas (b-cl,ss,ts) | Tiberian,Mircea (p) | Schuller,Ed (b) | Jones,Victor (dr)
Nicolas Simion Trio
Blues Connotation
Simion,Nicolas (b-cl,ss,ts) | Schuller,Ed (b) | Jones,Victor (dr)

888214-2* | CD | Naked Eye | EAN 4015728882148
Geoff Goodman Quintet
Strip Poker | Raffedore | John Lennnon's Assassination | Who Is Heinz? | Naked Eye | Two Fishes In A Foreign City | Tengelman Girls | Time Dust Gathered | Topsy | I'm A Woman Locked Inside A Man's Body
München, rec. 27./28.11.2002
Goodman,Geoff (g) | Mahall,Rudi (b-cl) | Wahnschaffe,Felix (as) | Sieverts,Henning (cello,b) | Perfido,Peter (dr)

Vagabond | Edel Contraire

VRCD 8.00027 | CD | Kansas City Boogie Jam
Axel Zwingenberger With Big Joe Duskin
Boogie Out In The Field | Just Before The Breath Of Day | Cincinnati Baby
Cincinatti,OH, rec. 20.7.1999
Zwingenberger,Axel (p) | Duskin,Big Joe (voc)
Goin' Down To The River | When I'm With My Baby | Baby,Rub My Achin' Head | Little Girl Boogie | So Tired,So Lonely Too | I Love My Baby
Ann Arbor,Michigan, rec. 3.9.1999
Zwingenberger,Axel (p) | Duskin,Big Joe (voc)
Axel Zwingenberger
PC Bounce | Indian Summer Boogie
Zwingenberger,Axel (p-solo)
Axel Zwingenberger-Sam Price
Slow Storm | High Price Boogie | Mr.Freddie Boogie
Frankfurt/M, rec. 30.10.1985
Zwingenberger,Axel (p) | Price,Sammy (p)
Axel Zwingenberger-Jay McShann Quartet
Kansas City Boogie Jam | Doo Wah Doo
Live at The Jazzland,Wien, rec. 31.3.1990
Zwingenberger,Axel (p) | McShann,Jay (p,voc) | Gugolz,Dani (b) | Strasser,Michael (dr)

VRCD 8.78013 | CD | Boogie Woogie Breakdown
Axel Zwingenberger
Boogie Woogie Breakdown | Steady Roll Boogie | Slow Motion Blues | Told My Story | Tell Me More | Celeste Rocks | Two O'Clock Mood | Boogie De Lux | Honky Tonk Train Blues | Suitcase Blues | Boogie Woogie Dream | Introvert Blues | Walking The Basses | Bouncing The Celeste
Hamburg, rec. 25.8./1.2.&..9.1976
Zwingenberger,Axel (celeste-solo,p-solo)
Axel Zwingenberger With Teddy Ibing
Holler Stomp | Turk Street Boogie
Zwingenberger,Axel (p) | Ibing,Teddy (dr)

VRCD 8.79012 | CD | Let's Boogie Woogie All Night Long
Big Joe Turner With Axel Zwingenberger
Roll 'Em Boy | New Goin' Away Blues | In The Evening | Corinne Corinna Boogie | Arbor Place Blues | Rock The Joint Boogie | John's And Louis' Blues | Jelly Jelly Blues | The L.A.Boogie Chase | On Your Daddy's Knee | The Chicken And The Hawk Boogie | Lown Down Dog
Los Angeles,CA, rec. 22.5.1978
Turner,Big Joe (voc) | Zwingenberger,Axel (p) | Zwingenberger,Torsten (dr)

VRCD 8.81010 | CD | Boogie Woogie Jubilee
VRLP 8.81010 | 2 LP | Boogie Woogie Jubilee
Hide And Seek Boogie | Back Door Getaway | Chains Of Love | Flip Flop And Fly | California Crawl | Cherry Red | St.Louis Blues | Boogie Woogie Round The Clock | Piney Brown Blues | Wee Baby Blues | Backyard Boogie | Back Door Getaway (2nd version) | Rolling On Western Ave. | Boogie Woogie Jubilee | Cimarrob St.Breakdown
rec. 1981
Turner,Big Joe (voc) | Zwingenberger,Axel (p) | details unknown

VRCD 8.84002 | CD | Sippie Wallace/Axel Zwingenberger And The Friends Of Boogie Woogie Vol.1

Sippie Wallace With Axel Zwingenberger
Shake It To A Jelly | T.B. Blues | How Long Blues | Bedroom Blues | Underworld Blues | Dago Hill | Nobody Knows | Suitcase Blues | Fan It & Cool It | My Man's In Trouble | Black Gal | Nervous Blues | Shorty George | You Really Don't Know | Black Snake Blues | Rocks & Mountains | You Really Don't Know | Electric Light
Ann Arbor,USA, rec. August 1983
Wallace,Sippie (voc) | Zwingenberger,Axel (p)
Axel Zwingenberger
Arkansas Blues | Ann Arbor Boogie
Zwingenberger,Axel (p-solo)

VRCD 8.85005 | CD | Axel Zwingenberger And The Friends Of Boogie Woogie Vol.2
VRLP 8.85005 | LP | Axel Zwingenberger And The Friends Of Boogie Woogie Vol.2
Joe Newman With Axel Zwingenberger
Boogie Call Blues | Joe's Lonesome Blues | Don't Be Mad At Me Pretty Mama
Hamburg, rec. 9.1.1982
Newman,Joe (tp) | Zwingenberger,Axel (p) | Zwingenberger,Torsten (dr)
Axel Zwingenberger
Palm Tree | Funky Stuff | Freeway Driver
Hollywood,CA, rec. 28.5.1981
Zwingenberger,Axel (p-solo)
Lloyd Glenn-Axel Zwingenberger
Struttin' The Boogie | Hollywood Special | L & A Groove | Boogie Woogie Mess Around | Lonesome Sundown
Glenn,Lloyd (p) | Zwingenberger,Axel (p)
Big Joe Turner With Axel Zwingenberger
Crawdad Hole | Watch The Boogie
Los Angeles,CA, rec. 22.5.1978
Turner,Big Joe (voc) | Zwingenberger,Axel (p) | Zwingenberger,Torsten (dr)

VRCD 8.85007 | CD | Boogie Woogie Live
VRLP 8.85007 | LP | Boogie Woogie Live
Axel Zwingenberger
Boogie Woogie Be With Me | Jump And Jive | April Mood | Blues For Sippie Wallace | Sunset Special | Eldorado Stomp | In The Heat | Make Me Call California | My Style | Blues On Top | Boogie Du Printemps | Goodnight Blues
Live,Drehleier/Theaterfabrik, rec. details unknown
Zwingenberger,Axel (p-solo)

VRCD 8.86006 | CD | An Evening With Sippie Wallace
Sippie Wallace With Axel Zwingenberger
Mighty Tight Woman | Gambler's Dream | Electric Light | Woman Be Wise | Fan It & Cool It | T.B. Blues | My Man's In Trouble | Mr.Freddie Blues | The Fives | Suitcase Blues | You Got To Know How | You Really Don't Know | Nobody Knows | You've Been A Good Old Wagon(Daddy But You Done Broke Down) | Shake It To A Jelly | How Long Blues
Live at The Drehleier,Munich, rec. October 1984
Wallace,Sippie (voc) | Zwingenberger,Axel (p)
Axel Zwingenberger
Play It, Maestro
Zwingenberger,Axel (p-solo)

VRCD 8.88008 | CD | The Boogie Woogie Album
VRLP 8.88008 | LP | The Boogie Woogie Album
Axel Zwingenberger With The Lionel Hampton Big Band
Graffiti Express | Rolling Slow | Central Avenue Breakdown | Whiskey Blues | Mr.Freddie Blues | The Sheik Of Araby Boogie | New York Shuffle | Central Avenue Breakdown(2nd version) | Jivin' In Jazzland | Hamp's Boogie Woogie
NYC, rec. 28.1.1982
Zwingenberger,Axel (p) | Hampton,Lionel (vib) | Malta,Yoshi (as) | Chapin,Thomas[Tom] (as) | Cobb,Arnett (ts) | Ford,Ricky (ts) | Kelly,George (ts) | Reis,Barry (tp) | Walker,Johnny (tp) | Jacquet,Illinois (ts) | Hamperian,Ralph (b) | Shaw,Arvell (b) | Francis,Panama (dr) | details unknown

VRCD 8.88009 | CD | Axel Zwingenberger And The Friends Of Boogie Woogie Vol.4: The Blues Of Mama Yancey
Estella Mama Yancey With Axel Zwingenberger
Make Me A Pallet On The Floor | How Long Will It Be | Monkey Woman Blues | Santa Fe Blues | Weekly Blues | Four O'Clock Blues
Chicago,Ill, rec. 19.10.1982
Yancey Estella 'Mama' (voc) | Zwingenberger,Axel (p)
Crying In My Sleep | Stella Yancey Blues | Blues In The Burying Ground | Midnight Plea | 2:19 Blues
Chicago,Ill, rec. 24.8.1982
Yancey Estella 'Mama' (voc) | Zwingenberger,Axel (p)
Axel Zwingenberger
Chicago Melodie
Chicago,Ill, rec. 24.8.1983
Zwingenberger,Axel (p-solo)

VRCD 8.88014 | CD | Champ's Housewarming
Champion Jack Dupree Group
Champ's Housewarming | Mean Mistreater | Tricks Ain't Walkin' No More | Come Back Baby | When I'm Drinking
Live at Jazzland,Wien, rec. 11./12.2.1988
Dupree,Champion Jack (voc) | Dozzler,Christian (harm) | Trauner,Erik (g) | Zwingenberger,Axel (p) | Toyfl,Markus (g) | Gugolz,Dani (b) | Strasser,Michael (dr)
Hungarian Stew
Live at Jazzland,Wien, rec. 12.2.1988
Dupree,Champion Jack (voc) | Dozzler,Christian (harm) | Trauner,Erik (g) | Zwingenberger,Axel (p) | Toyfl,Markus (g) | Gugolz,Dani (b) | Zwingenberger,Torsten (dr)
Shim Sham Shimmy
Dupree,Champion Jack (voc) | Dozzler,Christian (accordeon) | Trauner,Erik (g) | Zwingenberger,Axel (p) | Toyfl,Markus (g) | Gugolz,Dani (b) | Strasser,Michael (dr)
Shake Baby Shake
Dupree,Champion Jack (voc) | Trauner,Erik (g) | Zwingenberger,Axel (p) | Gugolz,Dani (b) | Zwingenberger,Torsten (dr)
When I Was One Year Old | No Future
Live at Jazzland,Wien, rec. 11./12.2.1988
Dupree,Champion Jack (voc) | Trauner,Erik (g) | Zwingenberger,Axel (p)
Whiskey Headed Woman
Live at Jazzland,Wien, rec. 11.2.1988
Dupree,Champion Jack (voc) | Trauner,Erik (g) | Zwingenberger,Axel (p) | Gugolz,Dani (b) | Strasser,Michael (dr)

VRCD 8.88015 | CD | Boogie Woogie Bros.
VRLP 8.89015 | LP | Boogie Woogie Bros.
Axel Zwingenberger-Torsten Zwingenberger
Ballade Pour Adrenalin | Solid Sending Boogie | Jazzland Blues | Little Eva's Dance | Farewell To Peter | Two Eels Waltzing On An Icecake | Walking Down The Keys | Jive For Johnson | Eva's Pleasure | Brothers Boogie
Live at Jazzland,Wien, rec. February 1988
Zwingenberger,Axel (p) | Zwingenberger,Torsten (dr)

VRCD 8.92018 | CD | Axel Zwingenberger And The Friends Of Boogie Woogie Vol.7: Champion Jack Dupree Sings Blues Classics
Champion Jack Dupree-Axel Zwingenberger Group
School Days | Who's Been Here | Blues Before Sunrise | Alberta | See See Rider | Rocky Mountains | That's All Right | Professor Boogie | I Wouldn't Be Where I Am | Midnight Hour Blues | How Long Blues | Louise Louise Blues | Hand Me Down My Walkin' Cane | Fine And Mellow | 44 Blues | Shakin' Mother For You | Night Time Is The Right Time | The Lock On My Door | Keep A-Knockin' | Goin' Down Slow | Hell On Earth
Live at The Drehleier,Munich, rec. September 1990
Dupree,Champion Jack (voc) | Zwingenberger,Axel (p) | Seidelin,Mogens 'Basse' (b) | Strasser,Michael (dr)

VRCD 8.92023 | CD | Boogie Woogie Classics
Axel Zwingenberger
Pinetop's Blues | Mr.Freddie Blues | Honky Tonk Train Blues | Boogie Woogie Jump | Suitcase Blues(part 1+2) | Cow Cow Blues | Boogie Woogie Stomp | Yancey Special | Chicago Flyer | Bass Goin' Crazy | New Blues On The Dark Side | The Boogie Rocks | Roll 'Em Pete | Swanee River Boogie
Hamburg, rec. June & August 1991
Zwingenberger,Axel (p-solo)

VRCD 8.93019 | CD | Axel Zwingenberger And The Friends Of Boogie Woogie,Vol.8
Axel Zwingenberger With The Mojo Blues Band And Red Holloway
Heatin' It Up | Smack Dab In The Middle | The Hoochi Coochi Coo | Hoodoo Man | Ooeeh Train | The Boogie Hop | Let Her Go | Summer Breeze Boogie | Ramblin' In You Dresser Drawers | Papa Wants To Knock A Jug | Dream Train | Barrelhouse Woman | Fried Buzzard | Ice Cream Freezer | Chasing Chicken | Closedown
Live at The Jazzland,Wien, rec. July 1992
Zwingenberger,Axel (p,voc) | Holloway,Red (ts,voc) | Mojo Bluesband,The | Dozzler,Christian (accordeon,voc) | Trauner,Erik (slide-g,voc) | Toyfl,Markus (g,voc) | Gugolz,Dani (b,voc) | Müller,Peter (dr,voc)

VRCD 8.99026 | CD | The Boogiemeisters
Axel Zwingenberger
Fantasy In Blues
Leutkirch, rec. 7.11.1996
Zwingenberger,Axel (p-solo)
Low Down Dog
Dresden, rec. 19.11.1996
Zwingenberger,Axel (p-solo)
Boogie For Real
Zürich,CH, rec. 7.11.1997
Zwingenberger,Axel (p-solo)
Vince Weber
I've Got To Move
Leutkirch, rec. 7.11.1996
Weber,Vince (p,voc)
The Dirty Dozen
Zürich,CH, rec. 7.11.1997
Weber,Vince (p,voc)
Axel Zwingenberger-Vince Weber
The Higher We Jump
Friedrichshafen, rec. 8.11.1996
Zwingenberger,Axel (p) | Weber,Vince (p,voc)
The Boogiemeisters | Roll 'Em Pete
Ludwigsburg, rec. 11.11.1996
Zwingenberger,Axel (p) | Weber,Vince (p)
Foot Pedal Boogie | Sixth Avenue Express | Midnight Hour Blues
Freudenstadt, rec. 12.11.1996
Zwingenberger,Axel (p) | Weber,Vince (p,voc)
Welcome To Boogie City
Nürtingen, rec. 13.11.1996
Zwingenberger,Axel (p) | Weber,Vince (p,voc)
Boogie Woogie Country Girl
Tübingen, rec. 16.11.1996
Zwingenberger,Axel (p) | Weber,Vince (p,voc)

VRLP 8.90016 | LP | Axel Zwingenberger & The Friends Of Boogie Woogie Vol.6
VRCD 8.90016 | CD | Axel Zwingenberger & The Friends Of Boogie Woogie Vol.6
Axel Zwingenberger With Champion Jack Dupree & Torsten Zwingenberger
I Hate To Be Alone | No Dog No More | Do You Thing Of Me? | Jack's Boogie Woogie | Driftin' Boogie | I Left My Mother | Everyday I Have The Blues | Diggin' My Potatoes | Bring Me Flowers While I'm Living | The Drinker
Live at Jazzland,Wien, rec. 12.2.1988
Dupree,Champion Jack (voc) | Zwingenberger,Axel (p) | Zwingenberger,Torsten (dr)

Vanguard | ZYX Music GmbH

VCD 169/71 | 3 CD | From Spiritual To Swing
Count Basie And His Orchestra
Swingin' The Blues | One O'Clock Jump | Every Tub
Live at Carnegie Hall,NYC, rec. 23.12.1938
Basie,Count (p) | Lewis,Ed (tp) | Edison,Harry 'Sweets' (tp) | Clayton,Buck (tp) | Collins,Lester 'Shad' (tp) | Wells,Dicky (tb) | Minor,Dan (tb) | Morton,Benny (tb) | Warren,Earl (as) | Evans,Hershel (cl,ts) | Young,Lester (ts) | Washington Jr.,Jack (bs) | Green,Freddie (g) | Page,Walter (b) | Jones,Jo (dr)
Jimmy Rushing With Count Basie And His Orchestra
Stealin' Blues
Basie,Count (p) | Lewis,Ed (tp) | Edison,Harry 'Sweets' (tp) | Clayton,Buck (tp) | Collins,Lester 'Shad' (tp) | Wells,Dicky (tb) | Minor,Dan (tb) | Morton,Benny (tb) | Warren,Earl (as) | Evans,Hershel (cl,ts) | Young,Lester (ts) | Washington Jr.,Jack (bs) | Green,Freddie (g) | Page,Walter (b) | Jones,Jo (dr) | Rushing,Jimmy (voc)
Introduction by John Hammond | Blues With Lips
Basie,Count (p) | Page,Oran 'Hot Lips' (tp) | Lewis,Ed (tp) | Edison,Harry 'Sweets' (tp) | Clayton,Buck (tp) | Collins,Lester 'Shad' (tp) | Wells,Dicky (tb) | Minor,Dan (tb) | Morton,Benny (tb) | Warren,Earl (as) | Evans,Hershel (cl,ts) | Young,Lester (ts) | Washington Jr.,Jack (bs) | Green,Freddie (g) | Page,Walter (b) | Jones,Jo (dr)
Kansas City Five
I Never Knew | Don't Be That Way | Oh! Lady Be Good | Allez Oop | Mortgage Stomp
NYC, rec. 3.6.1938
Kansas City Five,The | Basie,Count (p) | Clayton,Buck (tp) | Young,Lester (cl,ts) | Page,Walter (b) | Jones,Jo (dr)
Helen Humes With The Kansas City Five
Introduction by John Hammond | Blues With Helen
Kansas City Five,The | Basie,Count (p) | Clayton,Buck (tp) | Young,Lester (cl,ts) | Page,Walter (b) | Jones,Jo (dr) | Humes,Helen (voc)
Kansas City Six
After You've Gone
Live at Carnegie Hall,NYC, rec. 23.12.1938
Kansas City Six,The | Clayton,Buck (tp) | Young,Lester (ts) | Ware,Leonard (el-g) | Green,Freddie (g) | Page,Walter (b) | Jones,Jo (dr)
Count Basie Trio
Introduction by John Hammond | I Ain't Got Nobody
NYC, rec. 3.6.1938
Basie,Count (p) | Page,Walter (b) | Jones,Jo (dr)
Albert Ammons-Pete Johnson-Meade Lux Lewis
Jumpin' The Blues
Live at Carnegie Hall,NYC, rec. 23.12.1938
Ammons,Albert (p) | Johnson,Pete (p) | Lewis,Meade Lux (p)
Cavalcade Of Boogie
Ammons,Albert (p) | Johnson,Pete (p) | Lewis,Meade Lux (p) | Page,Walter (b) | Jones,Jo (dr)
Meade Lux Lewis
Honky Tonk Train Blues
Lewis,Meade Lux (p-solo)
Big Joe Turner With Pete Johnson
Low Down Dog | It's All Right Baby
Turner,Big Joe (voc) | Johnson,Pete (p)
Albert Ammons
Boogie Woogie
Ammons,Albert (p-solo)
Sister Rosetta Tharpe With Albert Ammons
Rock Me | That's All
Tharpe,Sister Rosetta (g,voc) | Ammons,Albert (p)
Mitchell's Christian Singers
What More Can Jesus Do | My Poor Mother Died A'Shoutin' | Are You Living Humble
Mitchell's Christian Singers: | Brown,William (voc) | Davis,Julius (voc) | David,Louis (voc) | Bryant,Sam (voc)
New Orleans Feetwarmers
Weary Blues | Milneberg Joys | I Wish I Could Shimmy Like My Sister Kate
New Orleans Feetwarmers,The | Ladnier,Tommy (tp) | Minor,Dan (tb) | Bechet,Sidney (cl,ss) | Johnson,James P. (p) | Page,Walter (b) | Jones,Jo (dr)
Big Bill Broonzy With Albert Ammons
It Was Just A Dream
Broonzy,Big Bill (g,voc) | Ammons,Albert (p)
Sonny Terry
Fox Chase
Terry,Sonny (harm,voc)
James P.Johnson
Carolina Shout
Johnson,James P. (p-solo)
Golden Gate Quartet
Introduction by Sterling A.Brown | Gospel Train | I'm On My Way | Noah
Live at Carnegie Hall,NYC, rec. 24.12.1939
Golden Gate Quartet: | Johnson,Willie (voc) | Owens,Henry (voc) | Langford,William (voc) | Wilson,Arlandus (voc)
Benny Goodman Sextet
I Got Rhythm | Flying Home | Memories Of You | Stompin' At The Savoy | Honeysuckle Rose
Goodman,Benny (cl) | Hampton,Lionel (vib) | Henderson,Fletcher (p) | Christian,Charlie (g) | Bernstein,Artie (b) | Fatool,Nick (dr)
James P.Johnson
Blueberry Rhyme | The Mule Walk
Johnson,James P. (p-solo)
Ida Cox With The James P. Johnson Septet
Low Down Dirty Shame | 'Fore Day Creep
Cox,Ida (voc) | Johnson,James P. (p) | Collins,Lester 'Shad' (tp) | Wells,Dicky (tb) | Tate,Buddy (ts) | Green,Freddie (g) | Page,Walter (b) | Jones,Jo (dr)
Big Bill Broonzy With Albert Ammons
Done Got Wise | Louise Louise
Broonzy,Big Bill (g,voc) | Ammons,Albert (p)
Sonny Terry
Mountain Blues
Terry,Sonny (harm,voc)
Sonny Terry-Bull City Red
The New John Henry
Terry,Sonny (harm,voc) | Bull City Red[George Washington] (wbd)
Kansas City Six
Pagin' The Devil | Way Down Yonder In New Orleans | Good Momin' Blues
Kansas City Six,The | Clayton,Buck (tp) | Young,Lester (ts) | Christian,Charlie (g) | Green,Freddie (g) | Page,Walter (b) | Jones,Jo (dr)
Helen Humes With James P. Johnson And The Count Basie Orchestra
Old Fashioned Love | If I Could Be With You One Hour Tonight
Humes,Helen (voc) | Johnson,James P. (p) | Basie,Count (ld) | Lewis,Ed (tp) | Edison,Harry 'Sweets' (tp) | Clayton,Buck (tp) | Collins,Lester 'Shad' (tp) | Wells,Dicky (tb) | Minor,Dan (tb) | Morton,Benny (tb) | Warren,Earl (as) | Tate,Buddy (ts) | Young,Lester (ts) | Washington Jr.,Jack (bs) | Green,Freddie (g) | Page,Walter (b) | Jones,Jo (dr)
Count Basie And His Orchestra
That Rhythm Man
Basie,Count (p) | Lewis,Ed (tp) | Edison,Harry 'Sweets' (tp) | Clayton,Buck (tp) | Collins,Lester 'Shad' (tp) | Wells,Dicky (tb) | Minor,Dan (tb) | Morton,Benny (tb) | Warren,Earl (as) | Tate,Buddy (ts) | Young,Lester (ts) | Washington Jr.,Jack (bs) | Green,Freddie (g) | Page,Walter (b) | Jones,Jo (dr)
Oh! Lady Be Good(Jam Session)
Basie,Count (p) | Lewis,Ed (tp) | Edison,Harry 'Sweets' (tp) | Clayton,Buck (tp) | Collins,Lester 'Shad' (tp) | Wells,Dicky (tb) | Minor,Dan (tb) | Morton,Benny (tb) | Goodman,Benny (cl) | Warren,Earl (as) | Tate,Buddy (ts) | Young,Lester (ts) | Washington Jr.,Jack (bs) | Hampton,Lionel (vib) | Christian,Charlie (g) | Lewis,Meade Lux (p) | Ammons,Albert (p) | Henderson,Fletcher (p) | Green,Freddie (g) | Page,Walter (b) | Bernstein,Artie (b) | Fatool,Nick (dr) | Jones,Jo (dr)

VCD 79609-2 | CD | Duets Vol.1
Ruby Braff-Ellis Larkins
Thou Swell | Where Or When | Mountain Greenery | I Married An Angel | Blue Moon | My Romance | Blues For Ruby | Love For Sale | Please | What Is There To Say | Skylark | Sailboat In The Moonlight
NYC, rec. 1956
Braff,Ruby (co) | Larkins,Ellis (p)

VCD 79610-2 | CD | Nice Work
Vic Dickenson Septet
Jeepers Creepers | Russian Lullaby
NYC, rec. 29.12.1953
Dickenson,Vic (tb) | Braff,Ruby (tp) | Hall,Edmond (cl) | Thompson,Sir Charles (p) | Jordan,Steve (g) | Page,Walter (b) | Erskine,Les (dr)
Vic Dickenson Septet With Ruby Braff
When You And I Were Young Maggie | Everybody Loves My Baby | Old Fashioned Love | Nice Work If You Can Get It | Suspension Blues | Running Wild | You Brought A New Kind Of Love To Me
NYC, rec. 29.11.1954
Dickenson,Vic (tb) | Braff,Ruby (tp) | Collins,Lester 'Shad' (tp) | Hall,Edmond (cl) | Thompson,Sir Charles (p) | Jordan,Steve (g) | Page,Walter (b) | Jones,Jo (dr)

VCD 79611-2 | CD | Duets Vol.2
Ruby Braff-Ellis Larkins
You Took Advantage Of Me | The Girl Friend | I Could Write A Book | My Funny Valentine | Little Girl Blue | I Didn't Know What Time It Was | Old Folks | Pocket Full Of Dreams | I've Got The World On A String | When A Woman Loves A Man | You Are Too Beautiful | A City Called Heaven | Blues For Ellis
NYC, rec. 1956
Braff,Ruby (co) | Larkins,Ellis (p)

VCD 79612-2 | CD | Key One Up
Bobby Henderson
Ain't Misbehavin' | Blue Turning Grey Over Me | Handful Of Keys | Jitterbug Waltz | Keepin' Out Of Mischief Now | Squeeze Me | Sugar
NYC, rec. 5.7.1957
Henderson,Bobby (p-solo)
Sir Charles Thompson Quartet
Swingtime In The Rockies | Honeysuckle Rose | These Foolish Things | Remind Me On You | Sweet Georgia Brown
NYC, rec. 1954
Thompson,Sir Charles (p) | Green,Freddie (g) | Page,Walter (b) | Jones,Jo (dr)
Jo Jones Trio
Sweet Lorraine | Bicycle Built For Two | Sometimes I'm Happy | Little Susie | Spider Kelly's Blues
NYC, rec. May 1959
Jones,Jo (dr) | Bryant,Ray (p) | Bryant,Tommy (b)

VeraBra Records | sunny moon Musikvertrieb

CDVBR 2005-2 | CD | Mother Earth
Barbara Thompson's Paraphernalia
Aspects Of Mother Earth | Country Dance | The Adventures Of Water | Fear Of Spiders | Humaira | Castles In The Air
rec. Summer 1982
Thompson,Barbara (fl,alto-fl,ss,as,ts) | Oldridge,Anthony (v,el-v) | Dudman,Colin (el-p,synth) | Katz,Dill (b-g) | Hiseman,Jon (dr,perc,gong)

CDVBR 2011-2 | CD | The Bear Walks
Hugh Marsh Duo/Quartet/Orchestra
Versace | My Brother | At The Top Of The Hill(A Double Left) | San Calimero | La Carezza | Znefu For Y'All | Big Fun | The Bear Walks | Laura With The Laughing Eyes | The Doctor Is Out
rec. details unknown
Marsh,Hugh (v) | Dorge,Vern (fl,as,ts) | Brecker,Michael (ts) | Cockburn,Bruce (g) | Mann,Bob (g) | Pomanti,Lou (p,synth,synclavier) | Goldsmith,Jon (p) | Riley,Doug (p) | Cardinali,Peter (b) | McKenzie,Kevan (dr) | Andersen,Jorn (dr) | Marsh,Fergus (sticks) | Smith,Dick (perc) | Morell,Marty (marimba) | Seymour,Earl (fl,ts) | Johnson,Johnny (fl,ts) | Moses,Kathy (b-fl) | Riley,Doug (p,org)

CDVBR 2014-2 | CD | About Time Too!
Jon Hiseman With The United Jazz & Rock Ensemble And Babara Thompson's Paraphernalia
Solo Berlin | Ganz Schön Heiss Man | Ganz Schön Heiss Man-2 | Solo Hannover
Hiseman,Jon (dr,perc) | United Jazz & Rock Ensemble | Carr,Ian (tp,fl-h) | Van Rooyen,Ack (tp,fl-h) | Wheeler,Kenny (tp,fl-h) | Mangelsdorff,Albert (tb) | Mariano,Charlie (sax) | Thompson,Barbara (fl,sax) | Dauner,Wolfgang (p,synth) | Melling,Steve (keyboards) | Kriegel,Volker (g) | Weber,Eberhard (b) | Bell,Dave (b-g) | Dorothy,Rod (v)

CDVBR 2015-2 | CD | Heavenly Bodies
Barbara Thompson Group
'Horizons New
Sutton,Surrey,GB, rec. August 1986
Thompson,Barbara (reeds,keyboards) | Hiseman,Jon (dr,perc)
Le Grand Voyage
Thompson,Barbara (reeds,keyboards) | Melling,Steve (keyboards) | Dunne,Paul (g) | Ball,Dave (b-g) | Hiseman,Jon (dr,perc)
Requiem Pour Deux Pilotes
Thompson,Barbara (reeds,keyboards) | Cullen,David (keyboards) | Lemer,Pete (keyboards) | Paak,Andy (b-g) | Halling,Patrick (v) | Williams,Robin (v) | Harris,Tony (viola) | Williams,Quentin (cello) | Hiseman,Jon (dr,perc)
Entre Les Trous De La Memoire
Thompson,Barbara (reeds,keyboards) | Lemer,Pete (keyboards) | Dunne,Paul (g) | Paak,Andy (b-g) | Hiseman,Jon (dr,perc)
Elysian Fields
Thompson,Barbara (reeds,keyboards) | Dunne,Paul (g) | Paak,Andy (b-g) | Hiseman,Jon (dr,perc) | Dorothy,Rod (v) | Williams,Quentin (cello)
Tibetan Sunrise
Thompson,Barbara (reeds,keyboards) | Barker,Guy (tp) | Brooks,Stuart (tp) | Thirkell,John (tp) | Geldard,Bill (b-tb) | Paak,Andy (b-g) | Dorothy,Rod (v) | Halling,Patrick (v) | Williams,Robin (v) | Harris,Tony (viola) | Williams,Quentin (cello) | Hiseman,Jon (dr,perc)
Entre Les Trous De La Memoire
Thompson,Barbara (reeds,keyboards) | Barker,Guy (tp) | Brooks,Stuart (tp) | Thirkell,John (tp) | Geldard,Bill (b-tb) | Lemer,Pete (keyboards) | Dunne,Paul (g) | Paak,Andy (b-g) | Hiseman,Jon (dr,perc)
Flights Of Fancy
Thompson,Barbara (reeds,keyboards) | Barker,Guy (tp) | Brooks,Stuart (tp) | Thirkell,John (tp) | Geldard,Bill (b-tb) | Lemer,Pete (keyboards) | Paak,Andy (b-g) | Hiseman,Jon (dr,perc)
Heavenly Bodiesy
Thompson,Barbara (reeds,keyboards) | Cullen,David (keyboards) | Paak,Andy (b-g) | Hiseman,Jon (dr,perc)
Love On The Edge Of Life
Thompson,Barbara (reeds,keyboards) | Cullen,David (keyboards) | Dorothy,Rod (v) | Paak,Andy (b-g) | Hiseman,Jon (dr,perc)
Extreme Jonction
Thompson,Barbara (reeds,keyboards) | Lemer,Pete (keyboards) | Paak,Andy (b-g) | Hiseman,Jon (dr,perc)

CDVBR 2016-2 | CD | Hearts And Numbers
Don Grolnick Group
Pointing At The Moon
rec. details unknown
Grolnick,Don (p,synth) | Brecker,Michael (ts) | Carter,Clifford (synth-programming) | Mironov,Jeff (g) | Lee,Will (b) | Jordan,Steve (dr)
More Pointing
Grolnick,Don (p,synth) | Brecker,Michael (ts) | Carter,Clifford (synth-programming)
Pools
Grolnick,Don (p,el-p) | Brecker,Michael (ts) | Mironov,Jeff (g) | Lee,Will (b) | Erskine,Peter (dr)
Regrets
Grolnick,Don (p,synth) | Brecker,Michael (ts) | Carter,Clifford (synth-programming) | Mann,Bob (g) | Kennedy,Tom (b) | Erskine,Peter (dr)
The Four Sleepers
Grolnick,Don (p,synth) | Brecker,Michael (ts) | Carter,Clifford (synth-programming) | Mironov,Jeff (g) | Miller,Marcus (b) | Erskine,Peter (dr)
Human Bites
Grolnick,Don (synth) | Brecker,Michael (ts) | Carter,Clifford (synth-programming) | Bullock,Hiram (g) | Jordan,Steve (dr) | Erskine,Peter (dr)
Act Natural
Grolnick,Don (synth) | Brecker,Michael (ts) | Carter,Clifford (synth-programming) | Mironov,Jeff (g) | Erskine,Peter (cymbals)
Hearts And Numbers
Grolnick,Don (p,synth) | Carter,Clifford (synth-programming)

CDVBR 2017-2 | CD | Barbara Thompson's Special Edition
Barbara Thompson's Paraphernalia
Country Dance | Fear Of Spiders | City Lights
details unknown, rec. details unknown
Thompson,Barbara (ss,as,ts) | Dudman,Colin (keyboards) | Katz,Dill (b-g) | Oldridge,Anthony (v,el-v) | Hiseman,Jon (dr)
Little Annie-Ooh | Out To Lunch
Live at The Pavillon,Hannover, rec. 12.6.1985
Thompson,Barbara (ss) | Melling,Steve (keyboards) | Dorothy,Rod (v) | Ball,Dave (b-g) | Hiseman,Jon (dr)
Voices Behind Locked Doors
Live at The Metropol,Berlin, rec. 19.6.1985
Thompson,Barbara (ss) | Melling,Steve (keyboards) | Dorothy,Rod (v) | Ball,Dave (b-g) | Hiseman,Jon (dr)
Fields Of Flowers | Dusk: Nightwatch | Listen To The Plants
details unknown, rec. details unknown
Thompson,Barbara (fl,ss,ts,recorder) | Worrall,Bill (keyboards) | Dorothy,Rod (v) | Ball,Dave (b-g) | Hiseman,Jon (dr)
Sleepwalker | Midday Riser | Times Past
Thompson,Barbara (ss,as) | Argent,Rod (keyboards) | Clempson,Clem (keyboards) | Mole,John (b-g) | Hiseman,Jon (dr) | Kettel,Gary (perc)

CDVBR 2021-2 | CD | A Cry From The Heart
Joy Ride | L'extreme Jonction | A Cry From The Heart | Entre Les Trous De La Memoire | Out To Lunch | Close To The Edge | Voices Behind Locked Doors | Eastern Western Promise(part 1&2)
Live at London,GB, rec. 7./8.11.1987
Thompson,Barbara (alto-fl,ss,as,ts,piccolo) | Dunne,Paul (el-g) | Lemer,Pete (keyboards,synth) | Mulford,Phil (el-b) | Hiseman,Jon (dr,electronic-perc)

CDVBR 2034-2 | CD | Live
Charlie Mariano & The Karnataka College Of Percussion
Yagapriya | Mr.Mani | Arun | Varshini | Kartik | Bhajan
Köln, rec. February 1989
Mariano,Charlie (as) | Karnataka College of Percussion,The | Ramamani,R.A. (kopakko,voc) | Mani,T.A.S. (mridamgam) | Shashikumar,T.N. (kanjeera) | Shotham,Ramesh (ghatam,morsing,tavil)

CDVBR 2039-2 | CD | Random And Providence
Marco Cerletti Group
Setting The Sailes | Glasshouse In The Desert | La Ville Blanche | Sundown | Random And Providence | Light Oer Darkness | Encore Toi | The Web | Birds Of Paradise | The Art Of Weathering November
Wohlen,CH, rec. details unknown
Cerletti,Marco (synth,el-b,sticks,voc) | Grieder,Andreas (fl,p,org,bassoon,horns) | Hopkins,David (claves,didjeridu,horns) | Öcal,Burhan (cabassa,calebasse,darabuka,dombek,ghatam,gong,kancira,rainmaker

CDVBR 2048-2 | CD | 45th Parallel
Oregon
Pageant | Hand In Hand | King Font | Riding On The D Train | Beneath An Evening Sky | Urumchi | Les Douzilles | Bombay Vice | Pageant(Epilogue)
Portland,Oregon, rec. August/September 1988
Oregon | Towner,Ralph (g,p,synth,12-string-g) | McCandless,Paul (engl-h,b-cl,ss,oboe,piccolo-sax) | Moore,Glen (b) | Gurtu,Trilok (dr,perc,tabla,voice)
Chihuahua Dreams
Oregon | Towner,Ralph (g,p,synth,12-string-g) | McCandless,Paul (engl-h,b-cl,ss,oboe,piccolo-sax) | Moore,Glen (b) | Gurtu,Trilok (dr,perc,tabla,voice) | King,Nancy (voc)

CDVBR 2051-2 | CD | Vitalive!
Steve Smith & Vital Information
Looks Bad Feels Good | Jave And A Nail | What Lies Beyond - (What Lies) Beyond | I Should Care | Mac Attack | Johnny Cat | The Perfect Date | Island Holiday | Europa(Earth Cry-Heaven's Smile)
Live at 'Club Nova 2',Ignacio,CA, rec. 21.8.1989
Smith,Steve (dr) | Schneider,Larry (sax) | Gambale,Frank (g,voc) | Coster,Tom (keyboards) | Grenadier,Larry (b)
One Flight Up
Smith,Steve (dr) | Schneider,Larry (sax) | Gambale,Frank (g,voc) | Coster,Tom (keyboards) | Coster Jr.,Tom (keyboards) | Grenadier,Larry (b)

CDVBR 2052-2 | CD | World Trio
World Trio
The Palantir | The Whirling Dervish | Over There | Will O'The Wisp | Dr.Do-Right | The Arch Mage | Blue Jean | Seven Rings | Eulogy
NYC, rec. 1995
World Trio | Eubanks,Kevin (g) | Holland,Dave (b) | Cinelu,Mino (perc)

CDVBR 2056-2 | CD | Seven Songs
Freddy Studer Orchestra
Sans Titre | Ein Blindenhund Und Ein Spazierhund | Bellydance On A Chessboard | Hajime!(Dedicated to Jimi Hendrix, John Coltrane And Edgar Varese) | Sol Y Sombra | I Don't Hear Anything | S.F.K.
Luzern,CH, rec. 12.8.1982-27.1.1988
Studer,Freddy (dr) | Mariano,Charlie (ss,as,bamboo-fl,bassoon) | Doran,Christy (g,el-g,slide-g,12-string-g) | Wittwer,Stephan (g,el-g,prepared-g) | Brüninghaus,Rainer (p,synth) | Zerlett,Helmut (synth) | Vitous,Miroslav (b) | Gee,Rosco (el-b) | Gurtu,Trilok (perc,cymbals,gongs,log-dr,tabla,voice) | Vasconcelos,Nana (perc,bells,berimbau,cuica,gongs,tambourine,voice) | Romao,Dom Um (perc,bells,claves,voice,whistles,wooden-fl) | Tamia (voice)

CDVBR 2057-2 | CD | Breathless
Barbara Thompson's Paraphernalia
Jaunty | You Must Be Jokin' | Squiffy | Bad Blues | Gracey
Sutton,Surrey,GB, rec. Autumn 1990/Spring 1991
Thompson,Barbara (alto-fl,ss,as) | Lemer,Pete (p,el-p,keyboards,synth) | Macfarlane,Malcolm (g,el-g,g-synth) | Mulford,Phil (b-g) | Hiseman,Jon (dr,cymbals)
Breathless | Breathless(short cut)
Thompson,Barbara (alto-fl,ss,as) | Lemer,Pete (p,el-p,keyboards,synth) | Macfarlane,Malcolm (g,el-g,g-synth) | Mulford,Phil (b-g) | Hiseman,Jon (dr,cymbals) | Ramzy,Hossam (perc)
Sax Rap | Sax Rap(short cut)
Thompson,Barbara (alto-fl,ss,as) | Langley,Noel (tp) | Slater,Ashley (tb) | Lemer,Pete (p,el-p,keyboards,synth) | Macfarlane,Malcolm (g,el-g,g-synth) | Mulford,Phil (b-g) | Hiseman,Jon (dr,cymbals)
Cheeky | Cheeky(short cut)
Thompson,Barbara (alto-fl,ss,as) | Langley,Noel (tp) | Slater,Ashley (tb) | Lemer,Pete (p,el-p,keyboards,synth) | Macfarlane,Malcolm (g,el-g,g-synth) | Mulford,Phil (b-g) | Hiseman,Jon (dr,cymbals) | Holder,Frank (congas,bongos)

CDVBR 2074-2 | CD | Dark & Curious
Mike Nock Quartet
Dance Of The Global Village | Nata Lagal | Embracing You | Resurrection | Tango For Gretchen Rodriguez | Oz Blu | Dark And Curious | Nature Boy | Upline
Sidney,Austalia, rec. 1990
Nock,Mike (p) | Hopkins,Tim (ts,recorder) | Undy,Cameron (b) | Dickeson,Andrew (dr)

CDVBR 2075-2 | CD | Blue Shift
Clarion Fracture Zone
Blue Shift | Moeshoeshoe The First | The Wild Uproar | Feather Star | La Mar Esta Enferma | Samba Nova | Spice Island
Sidney,Austalia, rec. March 1990
Clarion Fracture Zone | Evans,Sandy (ss,ts) | Gorman,Tony (cl,as,ts,perc) | Spence,Alister (p,synth) | Elphick,Steve (b) | Dickeson,Andrew (dr,perc)

CDVBR 2076-2 | CD | Encounters
Mark Isaacs/Dave Holland/Roy Haynes
First Encounter | Exclamation | Incantation | Rumours | Jewelette | Direct Input | Ringside | Tai-Min
NYC, rec. December 1988
Isaacs,Mark (p) | Holland,Dave (b) | Haynes,Roy (dr)

CDVBR 2093-2 | CD | The International Commission For The Prevention Of Musical Border Control
International Commission For The Prevention Of Musical Border Control,The
Introduction | Smoke The Carribbean | Sol Di Gioia | China Party | Down The River | Lifeline
Bochum, rec. November 1991
International Commission For The Prevention Of Musical Border Control,The | Heberer,Thomas (tp) | Mariano,Charlie (sax) | Shigihara,Paul (g) | Herting,Michael (p,keyboards) | Stanley,Emanuel (b) | Smaak,Bert (dr) | Harari,Vened (voc) | Marreiro,Nicky (congas,timbales) | Gassama,Samson (bougadabou,djembe) | Brause Horns,The
Down The River | Metamorfose | Mars | Arabian Hip | The Plains | The Gathering | The Tribe
International Commission For The Prevention Of Musical Border Control,The | Heberer,Thomas (tp) | Mariano,Charlie (sax) | Shigihara,Paul (g) | Herting,Michael (p,keyboards) | Mathieu,Konny (b) | Smaak,Bert (dr) | Harari,Vened (voc) | Marreiro,Nicky (congas,timbales) | Gassama,Samson (bougadabou,djembe) | Brause Horns,The

CDVBR 2102-2 | CD | Different Places
Scetches
Ricky's Living Room | Soundlotion | Slowtrack | Tribute | Bert | Reefer | Bild An Der Wand
Köln, rec. 20.-24.5.1991
Scetches | Titz,Christoph (tp,fl-h,keyboards) | Lauscher,Werner (el-b) | Federkeil,Elmar (dr) | Peil,Roland (keyboards,perc,synth-b)
Sau
Scetches | Titz,Christoph (tp) | Lauscher,Werner (el-b) | Federkeil,Elmar (dr) | Peil,Roland (perc) | Z.,Marq (voc)
Hypnotized
Scetches | Titz,Christoph (tp,keyboards) | Malischewski,Uwe (sax) | Lauscher,Werner (el-b) | Federkeil,Elmar (dr) | Peil,Roland (perc,synth-b) | Z.,Marq (voc)
Song Of The Whales
Scetches | Titz,Christoph (fl-h) | Lauscher,Werner (b)

CDVBR 2105-2 | CD | Marilyn Mazure's Future Song
Marilyn Mazur's Future Song
First Dream
Copenhagen,Denmark, rec. 28.3.1991
Mazur,Marilyn (dr,perc,voice) | Molvaer,Nils Petter (tp) | Plenar,Elvira (p,keyboards) | Hovman,Klavs (b) | Kleive,Audun (dr) | Kemanis,Aina (voice)
Saturn Song | When I Get To The Mountain | Urstrom | Rainbow Birds Suite(part 1b) | Aina's Travels | Rainbow Birds Suite(part 2b) | Well Of Clouds | Rainbow Birds Suite(part 1a) | Seventh Dream
Copenhagen,Denmark, rec. 21.-24.7.1990
Mazur,Marilyn (dr,perc,voice) | Molvaer,Nils Petter (tp) | Plenar,Elvira (p,keyboards) | Hovman,Klavs (b) | Kleive,Audun (dr) | Kemanis,Aina (voice)

CDVBR 2111-2 | CD | Mysterious Stories
Susan Weinert Band
Mysterious Phonecall(dedicated to Klaus Kinski) | Never Looking Back | Wrong Time, Wrong Place | Three Coices | Feel Free To Come By Any Time You Want | A Short Story About Tofu | Put Me In Coach, 'Cause I'm The Right Man | For That Job | We've Made Some Good Money, Man | Off Limit | Gangster Groove
Köln, rec. June/July 1992
Weinert,Susan (g,g-synth) | Weinert,Martin (b,el-b) | Fischötter,Hardy (dr)

CDVBR 2124-2 | CD | Mariano
Charlie Mariano Trio
Alvorada | Al Hadji | Fourth Sun | El Colibri | The Path | Daria | Kalimba | Pink Lady | Pavane(Pour Une Infante Defunte)
Köln/Bochum, rec. ca.1987
Mariano,Charlie (ss,as) | Shigihara,Paul (g,el-g) | Herting,Michael (keyboards,synth,grand-p)

CDVBR 2146-2 | CD | News From The Street
Jerry Granelli UFB
Honey Boy | Big Love | Rainbow's Cadillac | The Swamp | Sad Hour | Akicita | Ellen Waltzing | Brilliant Corners | Little Wing
Münster, rec. details unknown
UFB | Granelli,Jerry (dr,perc) | Brücker,Kai (g,el-g) | Kögel,Christian (g,el-g) | Walter,Andreas (b)
Blue Spanish Eyes
UFB | Granelli,Jerry (dr,perc) | Brücker,Kai (g,el-g) | Kögel,Christian (g,el-g) | Walter,Andreas (b) | Eckert,Rinde (voice)

CDVBR 2154-2 | CD | Dragonetti's Dream
Glen Moore
Oxeye | Beautiful Swan Lady | If You Can't Beat 'Em,Beat 'Em! | Red And Black | Dragonetti's Dream | Jade Visions | Walcott's Pendulum | Enter The King | Vertebra | Travels With My Foot | Appalachian Dance | Four Queasy Pieces | Fat Horse | Burning Fingers | Put In A Qaurter
Calliano,Italy, rec. 17.-19.7.1995
Moore,Glen (p,b)

CDVBR 2156-2 | CD | Rios
Dino Saluzzi-Anthony Cox-David Friedman
Los Them | Minguito | Fulano De Tal... | Sketch No.1 | And He Loved His Brother Till The End - ...And He Loved His Brother Till The End | Penta Y Uno | Jad | Lunch With Pancho Villa | My One And Only Love | Rios
Münster, rec. 1995
Saluzzi,Celso (perc,bandoneon,voice) | Friedman,David (vib,marimba,perc) | Cox,Anthony (b,el-b)

CDVBR 2161-2 | CD | Ray Of Hope
Vital Information
Clouds | Celebrate Life | Rio-Lize | Lorenzo's Soul | Sacred Treasure | Sixth Sense | Ray Of Hope | Maxed Out | All My Love,Always | Peace | Fit To Be Tired | Over And Out
Marin Country,CA, rec. details unknown
Vital Information | Gambale,Frank (g) | Coster,Tom (keyboards) | Andrews,Jeff (b) | Smith,Steve (dr)

CDVBR 2166-2 | CD | Lady Saxophone
Barbara Thompson's Paraphernalia
In Memory | All In Love Is Fair | Falling Stars | I Do It For Your Love | Reuben, Reuben | Out On A Limb | Wastelands | Waiting For The Rain | What Am I Here For | Lady S.
London,GB, rec. Winter 1995
Thompson,Barbara (ss,as,ts) | Lemer,Pete (keyboards) | Westwood,Paul (el-b) | Hiseman,Jon (dr)

CDVBR 2177-2 | CD | The Bottom Line
Susan Weinert Band
Hombre | Triple X | Tribute To Fitzcaraldo | Don't Smile Too Soon | Masters Of The Midiverse | That's For You | Kluski Theory | Dakota Kid | Nothing | Trabucco | Vinnie
Köln, rec. February/March 1996
Weinert,Susan (g,el-g,g-synth) | Z.,Rachel (p,keyboards) | Weinert,Martin (b,el-b) | Fischötter,Hardy (dr)

CDVBR 2184-2 | CD | Brothers
Rolf Kühn-Joachim Kühn
Lover Man Express | Saturday Blues | Walk | Opal | What Is Left | Love | Brothers | Every Time We Say Goodbye
Berlin, rec. 5.-7.7.1994
Kühn,Rolf (cl) | Kühn,Joachim (p)

Verve | Universal Music Germany

014184-2 | CD | Saturday Night In Bombay | EAN 044001416422
Remember Shakti
Luki
Bombay,India, rec. 8./9.12.2000
Remember Shakti | McLaughlin,John (g,el-g) | Shrinivas,U. (mand) | Hussain,Zakir (tabla) | Selvaganesh (kanjira,ghatam,mridangam) | Bhattacharya,Debashish (hindustani-slide-g) | Sivamani (dr,perc) | Shankar,Bhavani (cholak,pakhawaj) | Ali,Roshan (cholek) | Aziz (cholak) | Qureshi,Taufik (clef,dafi,perc) | Mahadevan,Shankar (voc)
Shringar
Remember Shakti | McLaughlin,John (g,el-g) | Hussain,Zakir (tabla) | Selvaganesh (kanjira,ghatam,mridangam) | Sharma,Shiv Kumar (santur)
Giriraj Sudha
Remember Shakti | McLaughlin,John (g,el-g) | Shrinivas,U. (mand) | Hussain,Zakir (tabla) | Selvaganesh (kanjira,ghatam,mridangam) | Pallanivel,A.K. (tavil) | Mahadevan,Shankar (voc)
Bell' Alla
Remember Shakti | McLaughlin,John (g,el-g) | Shrinivas,U. (mand) | Hussain,Zakir (tabla) | Selvaganesh (kanjira,ghatam,mridangam) | Bhattacharya,Debashish (hindustani-slide-g) | Sivamani (dr,perc) | Mahadevan,Shankar (voc)

014317-2 | CD | Live In Paris | EAN 044001431722
Dee Dee Bridgewater With Her Trio
All Blues | Misty | On A Clear Day You Can See Forever | Dr.Feelgood | There Is No Greater Love | Here's That Rainy Day | Medley Blues | Cherokee | How High The Moon
Live at The New Morning,Paris,France, rec. 24./25.11.1986
Bridgewater,Dee Dee (voc) | Sellin,Hervé (p) | Bonfils,Tony (b-g) | Ceccarelli,André (dr)

016884-2 | CD | This Is New | EAN 044001688423
Dee Dee Bridgewater With Band
This Is New | My Ship | Alabama Song | The Saga Of Jenny | I'm A Stranger Here Myself | Speak Low | Here I'll Stay
Paris,France/Los Angeles,CA, rec. 19./20.11.& 28./29.12.2001
Bridgewater,Dee Dee (voc) | Folmer,Nicolas (tp) | Leloup,Denis (tb) | Scannapieco,Daniele (fl,as) | Eliez,Thierry (p,voc) | Winsberg,Louis (g) | Coleman,Ira (b) | Ceccarelli,André (dr) | Garay,Minino (perc) | Bridgewater Kowalski,Tulani (voc) | Moses,China (voc)
Lost In The Stars | Bilbao Song | September Song
Bridgewater,Dee Dee (voc) | Folmer,Nicolas (tp) | Leloup,Denis (tb) | Hart,Antonio Maurice (fl,as) | Scannapieco,Daniele (fl,as) | Eliez,Thierry (p,voc) | Winsberg,Louis (g) | Coleman,Ira (b) | Ceccarelli,André (dr) | Garay,Minino (perc) | Bridgewater Kowalski,Tulani (voc) | Moses,China (voc)
Youkali
Bridgewater,Dee Dee (voc) | Folmer,Nicolas (tp) | Leloup,Denis (tb) | Scannapieco,Daniele (fl,as) | Mosalini,Juan Jose (bandoneon) | Eliez,Thierry (p,voc) | Winsberg,Louis (g) | Coleman,Ira (b) | Ceccarelli,André (dr) | Garay,Minino (perc) | Bridgewater Kowalski,Tulani (voc) | Moses,China (voc)

018243-2 | CD | Traveling Mercies | EAN 044001824326
Chris Potter Group
Children Go | Any Moment Now | Highway One | Just As I Am
NYC, rec. 27.-29.1.2002
Potter,Chris (alto-fl,b-cl,ss,as,ts,reed-org,sampler) | Hays,Kevin (p,el-b,clavinet) | Colley,Scott (b) | Stewart,Bill (dr)
Snake Oil
Potter,Chris (alto-fl,b-cl,ss,as,ts,reed-org,sampler) | Hays,Kevin (p,el-b,clavinet) | Colley,Scott (b) | Stewart,Bill (dr) | Binney,David 'Dave' (sampler)

Invisible Man | Azalea
Potter,Chris (alto-fl,b-cl,ss,as,ts,sampler,voc) | Rogers,Adam (g) | Hays,Kevin (p,el-b,clavinet) | Colley,Scott (b) | Stewart,Bill (dr)
Megalopolis | Washed Ashore
Potter,Chris (alto-fl,b-cl,ss,as,ts,sampler) | Scofield,John (g) | Hays,Kevin (p,el-b,clavinet) | Colley,Scott (b) | Stewart,Bill (dr)
Migrations
Potter,Chris (alto-fl,b-cl,ss,as,ts,sampler) | Scofield,John (g) | Hays,Kevin (p,el-b,clavinet) | Colley,Scott (b) | Stewart,Bill (dr) | Dotson-Westphalen,Elizabeth (voc-sample)

021906-2 | CD | Treasure | EAN 044002190628
Makoto Ozone Group
Bienvenidos Al Mundo | My Lazy Uncle | Tanglewood '63 | Three Wishes | Only We Know | Rainbow's End | Samba D'Rivera | Margaret | Might As Well | Where Do We Go From Here
NYC, rec. 15.-17.4.2002
Hendricks,Jon (voc) | Penn,Clarence (dr) | Genus,James (b) | Corea,Chick (p) | Burton,Gary (vib) | Brecker,Michael (sax) | Ozone,Makoto (p)
La Fiesta | Pandora
NYC, rec. 27.4.2002
Ozone,Makoto (p) | Brecker,Michael (sax) | Burton,Gary (vib) | Corea,Chick (p) | Genus,James (b) | Penn,Clarence (dr)

050293-2 | CD | Jazz Has... A Sense Of Humor
Horace Silver Quintet
Satisfaction Guaranteed | The Mama Suite: | Not Enough Mama- | Too Much Mama- | Just Right Mama- | Philley Millie | Ah-Ma-Tell | I Love Annie's Fanny | Gloria | Where Do I Go From Here
NYC, rec. 17./18.12.1998
Silver,Horace (p) | Kisor,Ryan (tp) | Greene,Jimmy (ss,ts) | Webber,John (b) | Jones III,Willie (dr)

064096-2 | CD | American Dreams | EAN 044006409627
Charlie Haden Quartet With Orchestra
American Dreams | Travels | No Lonely Nights | It Might Be You | Prism | America The Beautiful | Nightfall | Ron's Place | Bittersweet | Young And Foolish | Bird Food | Sotto Voce | Love Like Ours
Los Angeles,CA, rec. 14.-17.5.2002
Haden,Charlie (b) | Brecker,Michael (ts) | Mehldau,Brad (p) | Blade,Brian (dr) | Orchestra & Strings | details unknown

065510-2 | CD | Motion | EAN 044006551029
Lee Konitz Trio
I Remember You | All Of Me | Foolin' Myself | You'd Be So Nice To Come Home To | I'll Remember April
NYC, rec. 29.8.1961
Konitz,Lee (as) | Dallas,Sonny (b) | Jones,Elvin (dr)

065512-2 | CD | At The Montreux Jazz Festival | EAN 044006551227
Phil Woods And His European Rhythm Machine
Capricci Cavalleschi | I Remember Bird | Ad Infinitum | Riot
Live at The Montreux Jazz Festival, rec. 19.6.1969
Woods,Phil (as) | Gruntz,George (p) | Texier,Henri (b) | Humair,Daniel (dr)

065513-2 | CD | Gerry Mulligan Meets Johnny Hodges | EAN 044006551326
Gerry Mulligan-Johnny Hodges Quintet
Bunny | What's The Rush | Back Beat | What It's All About | 18 Carrots For Rabbit | Shady Side
Los Angeles,CA, rec. 17.11.1959
Hodges,Johnny (as) | Mulligan,Gerry (bs) | Williamson,Claude (p) | Clark,Buddy (b) | Lewis,Mel (dr)

076028-2 | CD | May The Music Never End | EAN 044007602829
Shirley Horn And Her Trio
Forget Me | If You Go Away | Yesterday | Never Let Me Go | Watch What Happens | Everything Must Change | May The Music Never End
NYC, rec. 3.-5.2.2003
Horn,Shirley (voc) | Mesterhazy,George (p) | Howard,Ed (b) | Williams,Steve (dr)
Shirley Horn And Her Quartet
Take Love | Ill Wind
Horn,Shirley (voc) | Hargrove,Roy (fl-h) | Mesterhazy,George (p) | Howard,Ed (b) | Williams,Steve (dr)
Shirley Horn And Her Trio
Maybe September | This Is All I Ask
Horn,Shirley (voc) | Jamal,Ahmad (p) | Howard,Ed (b) | Williams,Steve (dr)

0760562 | CD | After Hours With Miss D | EAN 044007605622
Dinah Washington And Her Band
Am I Blue
NYC, rec. 17.6.1953
Washington,Dinah (voc) | Quinichette,Paul (ts) | Anderson,Clarence 'Sleepy' (p) | Davis,Jackie (org) | Betts,Keter (b) | Thigpen,Ed (dr)
Pennies From Heaven
Washington,Dinah (voc) | Quinichette,Paul (ts) | Anderson,Clarence 'Sleepy' (p) | Davis,Jackie (org) | Betts,Keter (b) | Thigpen,Ed (dr) | Candido[Camero] (congas)
Our Love Is Here To Stay
NYC, rec. 5.2.1954
Washington,Dinah (voc) | unkn. (g) | Davis,Jackie (org) | Betts,Keter (b) | Thigpen,Ed (dr)
Love For Sale
Washington,Dinah (voc) | Terry,Clark (tp) | Chamblee,Eddie (ts) | Davis,Jackie (org) | Mance,Junior[Julian C.] (p) | unkn. (g) | Betts,Keter (b) | Thigpen,Ed (dr)
Blue Skies | Bye Bye Blues | A Foggy Day(In London Town) | I Let A Song Go Out Of My Heart | Blue Skies(unedited version)
NYC, rec. 15.6.1954
Washington,Dinah (voc) | Terry,Clark (tp) | Chappell,Gus (tb) | Henderson,Rick (as) | Davis,Eddie 'Lockjaw' (ts) | Mance,Junior[Julian C.] (p) | Betts,Keter (b) | Thigpen,Ed (dr)

0760942 | CD | How About Uke? | EAN 044007609422
Lyle Ritz Quartet
Don't Get Around Much Anymore | Ritz Cracker
Hollywood,CA, rec. 18.9.1957
Ritz,Lyke (ukelele) | Shelton,Don (fl) | Mitchell,Red (b) | Estes,Gene (dr)
Lyke Ritz Trio
Have You Met Miss Jones | Little Girl Blue
Ritz,Lyke (ukelele) | Mitchell,Red (b) | Estes,Gene (dr)
Lyke Ritz Quartet
Solamente Una Vez(You Belong To My Heart) | Moonlight In Vermont
Hollywood,CA, rec. 28.9.1957
Ritz,Lyke (ukelele) | Shelton,Don (fl) | Mitchell,Red (b) | Estes,Gene (dr)
Lyke Ritz Trio
Lulu's Back In Town | How About You
Ritz,Lyke (ukelele) | Mitchell,Red (b) | Estes,Gene (dr)
Playmates | I'm Beginning To See The Light | Sunday | Tangerine | Sweet Joan
Hollywood,CA, rec. 1.10.1957
Ritz,Lyke (ukelele) | Mitchell,Red (b) | Estes,Gene (dr)

076142-2 | CD | Wide Angles | EAN 044007614228
Michael Brecker Quindectet
Broadland | Cool Day In Hell | Angle Of Repose | Timbiktu | Night Jessamine | Scylla | Brexterity | Evening Faces | Modus Operandy | Never Alone
Englewood Cliffs,NJ, rec. 22.-24.1.2003
Brecker,Michael (ts) | Sipiagin,Alex (tp) | Eubanks,Robin (tb) | Gordon,Peter (fr-h) | Wilson,Steve (fl,alto-fl) | Dixon,Iain (cl,b-cl) | Pillow,Charles (oboe,engl-h) | Feldman,Mark (v) | Hammann,Joyce (v) | Martin,Lois (viola) | Friedlander,Erik (cello) | Rogers,Adam (g) | Patitucci,John (b) | Sanchez,Antonio (dr) | Sadownick,Daniel (perc)

157534-2 | CD | Chattin' With Chet
Till Brönner Group
You Don't Know What Love Is
NYC/Berlin, rec. 1999
Brönner,Till (tp,keyboards,programming) | Peters,Grégoire (alto-fl) | Chastenier,Frank (el-p) | Lake,Gene (dr) | Charles,David (perc) | Kawamura,Samon (turntables)
She Was Too Good To Me
Brönner,Till (tp,keyboards,programming) | Chastenier,Frank (el-p) | Lefebvre,Tim (b,programming) | Charles,David (perc)
Everything Happens To Me
Brönner,Till (tp,keyboards,programming,voc) | Lefebvre,Tim (el-b,programming) | Danzinger,Zachary (dr-programming) | Schroeder,Wiebke (voice) | Kawamura,Samon (turntables)
Have You Met Chet?
Brönner,Till (tp,fl-h,keyboards,ride-cymbal,voc) | Peters,Gregoire (ts) | Loeb,Chuck (g) | Schloz,Karl (rh-g) | Lefebvre,Tim (b) | Haffner,Wolfgang (dr)
When I Fall In Love
Brönner,Till (tp,voc) | Chastenier,Frank (el-p) | Ilg,Dieter (b) | Haffner,Wolfgang (dr)
My Funny Valentine | Not Like This
Brönner,Till (tp,fl-h) | Chastenier,Frank (p,el-p)
Every Time We Say Goodbye
Brönner,Till (tp,keyboards,programming,voc) | Peters,Gregoire (ts) | Brown,Dean (g) | Lefebvre,Tim (el-b) | Lake,Gene (dr) | Kawamura,Samon (turntables) | Supernatural (rap)
Tell Me
Brönner,Till (tp,fl-h,keyboards,programming,voc) | Loeb,Chuck (g) | Chastenier,Frank (p,el-p) | Lake,Gene (dr) | Charles,David (perc) | Cuesta,Carmen (voc)
But Not For Me
Brönner,Till (tp,keyboards,programming) | Brown,Dean (g) | Chastenier,Frank (el-p) | Lefebvre,Tim (b,el-b,programming) | Lake,Gene (dr) | Kawamura,Samon (turntables)
Chattin' With Chet
Brönner,Till (tp,programming) | Loeb,Chuck (g) | Chastenier,Frank (el-p) | Ilg,Dieter (b) | Haffner,Wolfgang (dr)
-> Note: Contains sampled Chet Baker Solo, rec. Live at The Subway,Köln, 22.3.1980

394915-2 | CD | 1975-The Duets
Dave Brubeck-Paul Desmond Duo
You Got To My Head
NYC, rec. 10.6.1975
Brubeck,Dave (p) | Desmond,Paul (as)
Alice In Wonderland | These Foolish Things Remind Me On You | Blues Dove | Stardust | Koto Song | Balcony Rock | Summer Song
rec. 15./16.9.1975
Brubeck,Dave (p) | Desmond,Paul (as)

397000-2 | CD | Closeness Duets
Charlie Haden-Alice Coltrane
For Turiya
Burbank,Los Angeles,CA, rec. 26.1.1976
Haden,Charlie (b) | Coltrane,Alice (harp)
Charlie Haden-Keith Jarrett
Ellen David
NYC, rec. 18.3.1976
Haden,Charlie (b) | Jarrett,Keith (p)
Charlie Haden-Ornette Coleman
O.C.
NYC, rec. 21.3.1976
Haden,Charlie (b) | Coleman,Ornette (as)
Charlie Haden-Paul Motian
For A Free Portugal
Haden,Charlie (b) | Motian,Paul (dr)

511036-2 PMS | CD | Gitanes Jazz 'Round Midnight: Oscar Peterson
Oscar Peterson-Ray Brown Duo
Laura
NYC, rec. 19.1.1951
Peterson,Oscar (p) | Brown,Ray (b)
Oscar Peterson Trio
It Ain't Necessarily So
Los Angeles,CA, rec. prob.December 1952
Peterson,Oscar (p) | Kessel,Barney (g) | Brown,Ray (b)
These Foolish Things Remind Me On You | You Go To My Head
Los Angeles,CA, rec. 26.1.1952
Peterson,Oscar (p) | Ashby,Irving (g) | Brown,Ray (b)
I Loves You Porgy
Los Angeles,CA, rec. 12.10.1959
Peterson,Oscar (p) | Brown,Ray (b) | Thigpen,Ed (dr)
On The Sunny Side Of The Street
Chicago,Ill, rec. 14.7.-9.8.1959
Peterson,Oscar (p) | Brown,Ray (b) | Thigpen,Ed (dr)
Bag's Groove
Los Angeles,CA, rec. 15./16.12.1962
Peterson,Oscar (p) | Brown,Ray (b) | Thigpen,Ed (dr)
Little Right Foot
NYC, rec. 27.2.1964
Peterson,Oscar (p) | Brown,Ray (b) | Thigpen,Ed (dr)
Blues Of The Prairies
NYC, rec. 9.9.1964
Peterson,Oscar (p) | Brown,Ray (b) | Thigpen,Ed (dr)
Angel Eyes
NYC, rec. 27.4.1954
Peterson,Oscar (p) | Ellis,Herb (g) | Brown,Ray (b)
Milt Jackson With The Oscar Peterson Trio
Heart Strings
NYC, rec. 15.9.1961
Peterson,Oscar (p) | Jackson,Milt (vib) | Brown,Ray (b) | Thigpen,Ed (dr)
When I Fall In Love
VS-Villingen, rec. July 1971
Peterson,Oscar (p) | Jackson,Milt (vib) | Brown,Ray (b) | Hayes,Louis (dr)
Oscar Peterson
Just A Gigolo
VS-Villingen, rec. November 1970
Peterson,Oscar (p-solo)

511110-2 | CD | You Gotta Pay The Band
Abbey Lincoln With The Stan Getz Quartet
I'm In Love | You Gotta Pay The Band | Brother Can You Spare A Dime | You Made Me Funny | An How I Hoped For Your Love | When I'm Called Home | Summer Wishes,Winter Dreams | Up Jumped Spring
NYC, rec. 25./26.2.1991
Lincoln,Abbey (voc) | Getz,Stan (ts) | Jones,Hank (p) | Haden,Charlie (b) | Johnson,Mark (dr)
Abbey Lincoln With The Stan Getz Quintet
Bird Alone | A Time For Love
Lincoln,Abbey (voc) | Getz,Stan (ts) | Jones,Hank (p) | Roach,Maxine (viola) | Haden,Charlie (b) | Johnson,Mark (dr)

511385-2 | CD | Swingin' On The Moon
Mel Tormé With The Russell Garcia Orchestra
Swingin' On The Moon | Don't Let The Moon Get Away | No Moon At All | The Moon Was Yellow
Hollywood,CA, rec. 4.8.1960
Tormé,Mel (voc) | Nash,Dick (tb) | Pederson,Pullman 'Tommy' (tb) | Roberts,George (tb) | Shepard,Tom (tb) | DeRosa,Vince (fr-h) | Shank,Bud (as) | Roberts,Howard (g) | Callender,Red (b) | Pena,Ralph (b) | Lewis,Mel (dr) | Garcia,Russell (cond,arr)
Moonlight Cocktail | Moon Song | Moonlight In Vermont
Hollywood,CA, rec. 3.8.1960
Tormé,Mel (voc) | Shank,Bud (as) | Roberts,Howard (g) | Pena,Ralph (b) | Lewis,Mel (dr) | La Magna,Carl (v) | Lube,Dan (v) | Neiman,Alex (v) | Reher,Kurt (cello) | Garcia,Russell (cond,arr)
I Wished On The Moon | How High The Moon | Blue Moon | A Velvet Affair | Oh! You Crazy Moon
Hollywood,CA, rec. 5.8.1960
Tormé,Mel (voc) | Fagerquist,Don (tp) | Jolly,Pete (p) | Roberts,Howard (g) | Pena,Ralph (b) | Lewis,Mel (dr) | Frisina,Dave (v) | Lube,Dan (v) | Marino,Rickey (v) | Miller,William (v) | Neiman,Alex (v) | Raderman,Lou (v) | Shubring,Clarence (v) | Vinci,Gerry (v) | Harshman,Allan (viola) | Sandler,Myron (viola) | Neikrug,George (cello) | Reher,Kurt (cello) | Johnstone,Marcia (harp) | Garcia,Russell (cond,arr)

511524-2 | CD | Like Someone In Love
Ella Fitzgerald With Frank De Vol And His Orchestra
There's A Lull In My Life | More Than You Know | What Will I Tell My Heart | I Never Had A Chance | Close Your Eyes | We'll Be Together Again | Then I'll Be Tired Of You | Like Someone In Love | Midnight Sun | I Thought About You | You're Blasé
Los Angeles,CA, rec. 15.10.1957
Fitzgerald,Ella (voc) | Nash,Ted (as) | Getz,Stan (ts) | DeVol,Frank (cond,arr) | details unknown
Night Wind | What's New? | Hurry Home | How Long Has This Been Going On | I'll Never Be The Same | Lost In A Fog | Everything Happens To Me | So Rare
Los Angeles,CA, rec. 28.10.1957
Fitzgerald,Ella (voc) | Nash,Ted (as) | Getz,Stan (ts) | DeVol,Frank (cond,arr) | details unknown

511779-2 | CD | Lush Life-The Music Of Billy Strayhorn
Joe Henderson
Lush Life
Englewood Cliffs,NJ, rec. 3.& 8.9.1991
Henderson,Joe (ts-solo)
Joe Henderson/Christian McBride
Isfahan
Englewood Cliffs,NJ, rec. 3./6.& 8.9.1991
Henderson,Joe (ts) | McBride,Christian (b)
Joe Henderson Trio
Drawing Room Blues
Henderson,Joe (ts) | Scott,Stephen (p) | McBride,Christian (b)
Raincheck
Henderson,Joe (ts) | McBride,Christian (b) | Hutchinson,Gregory (dr)
Joe Henderson Quartet
Blood Count
Henderson,Joe (ts) | Scott,Stephen (p) | McBride,Christian (b) | Hutchinson,Gregory (dr)
Joe Henderson/Stephen Scott
Lotus Blossom
Henderson,Joe (ts) | Scott,Stephen (p)
Joe Henderson/Gregory Hutchinson
Take The 'A' Train
Henderson,Joe (ts) | Hutchinson,Gregory (dr)
Joe Henderson Quintet
Johnny Comes Lately | A Flower Is A Lovesome Thing | U.M.M.G.(Upper Manhattan Medical Group)
Henderson,Joe (ts) | Marsalis,Wynton (tp) | Scott,Stephen (p) | McBride,Christian (b) | Hutchinson,Gregory (dr)

511879-2 | CD | Here's To Life
Shirley Horn With Strings
Here's To Life | Come A Little Closer- | Wild Is The Wind- | How Am I To Know? | A Time For Love | Where Do You Start | You're Nearer | Return To Paradise | Isn't It A Pity | Quietly There | If You Love Me | Summer(Estate)
NYC/Hollywood/Los Angeles, rec. 1992
Horn,Shirley (p,voc) | Ables,Charles (b) | Williams,Stephen E. 'Steve' (dr) | Marsalis,Wynton (tp) | Orchestra | Strings | Mandel,Johnny (cond,arr)

513078-2 | CD | Haunted Heart
Charlie Haden Quartet West
Introduction | Hello My Lovely | Haunted Heart | Dance Of The Infidels | The Long Goodbye | Moonlight Serenade | Lennie's Pennies | Every Time We Say Goodbye | Lady In The Lake | Segment | The Bad And The Beautiful | Deep Song
Sete,France, rec. 27./28.10.1991
Haden,Charlie (b) | Watts,Ernie (ts) | Broadbent,Alan (p) | Marable,Lawrence (dr)
-> feat. The Original Voices of Jo Stafford, Jeri Southern and Billie Holiday

513752-2 | CD | At The Stratford Shakespearean Festival
Oscar Peterson Trio
Falling In Love With Love | How About You | Flamingo | Swinging On A Star | Noreen's Nocturne | Gypsy In My Soul | Nuages | How High The Moon | Love You Madly | 52nd Street Theme | Daisy 's Dream
Live at The Stratford Shakepearean Festival,Ontario,CA, rec. 8.8.1956
Peterson,Oscar (p) | Ellis,Herb (g) | Brown,Ray (b)

514724-2 | CD | Bewitched
Laura Fygi With Band
Dream A Little Dream Of Me | It's Crazy | Good Morning Heartache | Let There Be Love | I Only Have Eyes For You | Bewitched Bothered And Bewildered | The End Of A Love Affair | I Love You For Sentimental Reasons | Just One Of Those Things | Girl Talk | Willow Weep For Me
details unknown, rec. details unknown
Fygi,Laura (voc) | Terry,Clark (fl-h) | Griffin,Johnny (ts) | Povel,Ferdinand (fl,sax) | Thielemans,Jean 'Toots' (harm) | Micault,Gwénael (keybords) | Van Eyk,John (keyboards) | Vroomans,Hans (p) | Meulendijk,Bert (g) | Goya,Francis (g) | Catherine,Philip (g) | Lee,Phil (g) | Creese,Malcolm (b) | Jacobs,Ruud (b) | Ypma,Peter (dr) | Fischer,Harold (dr) | Landesbergen,Frits (perc) | London Studio Symphony Orchestra,The | Rothstein,Jack (v,concertmaster)

515807-2 | 2 CD | Grapelli Story
Quintet Du Hot Club De France
Stompin' At Decca | My Sweet
London,GB, rec. 31.1.1938
Quintet Du Hot Club De France | Grappelli,Stephane (v) | Reinhardt,Django (g) | Chaput,Roger (g) | Vees,Eugene (g) | Vola,Louis (b)
Stephane Grappelli-Django Reinhard
It Had To Be You | Nocturne
London,GB, rec. 1.2.1938
Grappelli,Stephane (p,v) | Reinhardt,Django (g)
Arthur Young And Hatchett's Swingtette
Alexander's Ragtime Band
London,GB, rec. 29.12.1939
Hatchett's Swingtette | Shakespeare,Bill (tp) | Moonan,Dennis (cl,ts) | unkn. (cl,ts) | Grappelli,Stephane (v) | Young,Arthur (novachord) | Llewellyn,Jack (g) | D'Amato,Chappie (g) | Senior,George (b) | Spurgin,Tony (dr) | Davis,Beryl (voc)
Blue Ribbon Rag
London,GB, rec. 25.5.1940
Hatchett's Swingtette | Andrews,Stanley (tp,v) | Weir,Frank (cl) | Moonan,Dennis (cl,viola) | Grappelli,Stephane (v) | Young,Arthur (novachord) | Pudel,Charlie (p) | Llewellyn,Jack (g) | D'Amato,Chappie (g) | Senior,George (b) | Spurgin,Tony (dr)
Oh! Lady Be Good
London,GB, rec. 19.3.1940
Hatchett's Swingtette | Andrews,Stanley (tp,v) | Moonan,Dennis (viola) | Grappelli,Stephane (v) | Young,Arthur (novachord) | Baron,Frank (p) | Llewellyn,Jack (g) | D'Amato,Chappie (g) | Senior,George (b) | Spurgin,Tony (dr)
Stephane Grappelli And His Musicians
Stephane's Tune
London,GB, rec. 30.7.1940
Grappelli,Stephane (v) | Andrews,Stanley (v) | Chapman,Harry (harp) | Conray,Reg (vib) | Shearing,George (p) | Llewellyn,Jack (g) | Hobson,Hank (b) | Philcock,Al (dr)
Tiger Rag | Stephane's Blues
London,GB, rec. 28.2.1941
Grappelli,Stephane (v) | Pini,Eugene (v) | Andrews,Stanley (v) | Moonan,Dennis (viola) | unkn. (cello) | Chapman,Harry (harp) | Conray,Reg (vib) | Shearing,George (p) | Jacobson,Syd (g) | Gibbs,George (b) | Jacobson,Jack (dr)
Stephane Grappelli Quartet
Jive Bomber | Body And Soul
London,GB, rec. 9.4.1941
Grappelli,Stephane (v) | Shearing,George (p) | Llewellyn,Jack (g) | Gibbs,George (b) | Fullerton,Dave (dr)
Stephane Grappelli Quintet
Liza(All The Clouds'll Roll Away) | The Folks Who Live On The Hill
London,GB, rec. 20.8.1942
Grappelli,Stephane (v) | Marsh,Roy (vib) | De Sousa,Yorke (p) | Deniz,Joe (g) | Nussbaumn,Joe (b) | Fullerton,Dave (dr,voc)

Weep No More,My Lady
London,GB, rec. 7.7.1943
Grappelli,Stephane (v) | Shearing,George (p) | Wilkins,Dave (g) | Nussbaumn,Joe (b) | Fullerton,Dave (dr) | Davis,Beryl (voc)
Quintet Du Hot Club De France
Nuages
London,GB, rec. 1.2.1946
Quintet Du Hot Club De France | Grappelli,Stephane (v) | Reinhardt,Django (g) | Llewellyn,Jack (g) | Hodgkiss,Allan (g) | Goode,Coleridge (b)
Stephane Grappelli Sextet
The Nearness Of You
Paris,France, rec. 12.4.1955
Grappelli,Stephane (v) | Hauser,Michel (vib) | Vander,Maurice (p) | Duchaussoir,Rene (g) | Quersin,Benoit (b) | Viale,Jean-Louis (dr)
Stephane Grappelli Quartet
'S Wonderful | Fascinating Rhythm | Just One Of Those Things | Dans La Vie
Paris,France, rec. 6.2.1956
Grappelli,Stephane (v) | Vander,Maurice (p) | Michelot,Pierre (b) | Reilles,Jean-Baptiste 'Mac Kac' (dr)
The Lady Is A Tramp
Paris,France, rec. 14.2.1956
Grappelli,Stephane (v) | Vander,Maurice (p) | Michelot,Pierre (b) | Reilles,Jean-Baptiste 'Mac Kac' (dr)
I Want To Be Happy
Paris,France, rec. 10.4.1956
Grappelli,Stephane (v) | Vander,Maurice (p) | Michelot,Pierre (b) | Reilles,Jean-Baptiste 'Mac Kac' (dr)
It's Only A Paper Moon | A Flower Is A Lovesome Thing
Paris,France, rec. 17.7.1957
Grappelli,Stephane (v) | Fol,Raimond (p) | Michelot,Pierre (b) | Levitt,Al (dr)
Stephane Grappelli Quintet
Daphne
Paris,France, rec. 7.3.1962
Grappelli,Stephane (v) | Cavalli,Pierre (g) | Petit,Leo (g) | Pedersen,Guy (b) | Humair,Daniel (dr)
Makin' Whoopee
Paris,France, rec. 8.3.1962
Grappelli,Stephane (v) | Cavalli,Pierre (g) | Petit,Leo (g) | Pedersen,Guy (b) | Humair,Daniel (dr)
Minor Swing | Pent-Up House | Django
Paris,France, rec. 9.3.1962
Grappelli,Stephane (v) | Cavalli,Pierre (g) | Petit,Leo (g) | Pedersen,Guy (b) | Humair,Daniel (dr)
Stephane Grappelli And Friends
Darling Je Vous Aime Beaucoup | How High The Moon | More
London,GB, rec. 29.6.1970
Grappelli,Stephane (v,voc) | Hemmeler,Marc (p) | Disley,William 'Diz' (g) | Bush,Lennie (b) | Spooner,John (dr)
Willow Weep For Me
Grappelli,Stephane (v) | Hemmeler,Marc (p) | Bush,Lennie (b) | Spooner,John (dr)
Lonely Street
Grappelli,Stephane (v) | Hemmeler,Marc (org)
Stephane Grappelli Quartet
Time After Time | Misty
VS-Villingen, rec. March 1971
Grappelli,Stephane (v) | Hemeler,Marc (p) | Weber,Eberhard (b) | Clare,Kenny (dr)
Stephane Grappelli With The Diz Disley Trio
Shine
VS-Villingen, rec. March 1975
Grappelli,Stephane (v) | Disley,William 'Diz' (g) | Isaacs,Ike (g) | Eckinger,Isla (b)
Stephane Grappelli-Ike Isaacs
Lover Man(Oh,Where Can You Be?)
Grappelli,Stephane (v) | Isaacs,Ike (g)
Stephane Grappelli With The George Shearing Trio
I'm Coming Virginia
VS-Villingen, rec. 11.4.1976
Grappelli,Stephane (v) | Shearing,George (p) | Simpkins,Andrew (b) | Jones,Rusty (dr)
Stephane Grappelli-George Shearing
La Chanson Des Rues
Grappelli,Stephane (v) | Shearing,George (p)
Stephane Grappelli Quartet
Sweet Chorus
Stuttgart, rec. 19.-21.1.1979
Grappelli,Stephane (v) | Catherine,Philip (g) | Coryell,Larry (g) | Orsted-Pedersen,Niels-Henning (b)
Stephane Grappelli With The Michel Legrand Orchestra
Mon Homme
Paris,France, rec. 27.5.1992
Grappelli,Stephane (v) | Cervera,Bertrand (v,concertmaster) | Arnaud,Francois (v) | Beridot,Marie-Hélène (v) | Bisquay,Yann (v) | Brunon,Karen (v) | Carlucci,Nathalie (v) | Chavauché,Corinne (v) | De Nattes,Valérie (v) | Dupuis,Laurence (v) | Fontanarosa,Guillaume (v) | Gates,Pamela (v) | Goloboff,Sofia (v) | Granjon,Stéphane (v) | Juchors,Dominique (v) | Le Bars,Marie-Anne (v) | Moyal,Sandrine (v) | Pierre,Catherine (v) | Saint-Arroman,Nathalie (v) | Arap,Jean-Marc (viola) | Briquet,Christoph (viola) | Jaboulay,Christine (viola) | Jaboulay,Laurence (viola) | Lenert,Pierre (viola) | Allalah,Laurence (cello) | Boissenin,Anne-Sophie (cello) | Caron,Natalie (cello) | Petit,Emmanuel (cello) | Marillier,Daniel (b) | Noharet,Philippe (b) | Legrand,Michel (p,cond,arr) | Le Bevillon,Marc-Michel (el-b) | Ceccarelli,André (dr) | Cevero,Maurice (contractor)

516319-2 | CD | Verve Jazz Masters 10:Dizzy Gillespie
Charlie Parker Quintet
Leap Frog(take 5)
NYC, rec. 6.6.1950
Parker,Charlie (as) | Gillespie,Dizzy (tp) | Monk,Thelonious (p) | Russell,Curly (b) | Rich,Buddy (dr)
Dizzy Gillespie Group
A Night In Tunisia
NYC, rec. 3.6.1954
Gillespie,Dizzy (tp) | Valdez,Gilbert (fl) | Hernandez,Rene (p) | Rodriguez,Roberto (b) | Candido[Camero] (perc) | Mangual,Jose (perc) | Miranda,Ralph (perc) | Nieto,Ubaldo (perc) | unkn. (perc)
Dizzy Gillespie Sextet
Trumpet Blues
NYC, rec. 29.10.1954
Gillespie,Dizzy (tp) | Eldridge,Roy (tp) | Peterson,Oscar (p) | Ellis,Herb (g) | Brown,Ray (b) | Bellson,Louie (dr)
Dizzy Gillespie Orchestra
Birk's Works
Los Angeles,CA, rec. 23.3.1957
Gillespie,Dizzy (tp) | Dawud,Talib (tp) | Morgan,Lee (tp) | Perry,Ermit V. (tp) | Warwick,Carl (tp) | Grey,Al (tb) | Levitt,Rod (tb) | Liston,Melba (tb) | Henry,Ernie (as) | Powell,Jimmy (as) | Golson,Benny (ts) | Mitchell,Billy (ts) | Root,Billy (bs) | Kelly,Wynton (p) | West,Paul (b) | Persip,Charles (dr)
Tour De Force
NYC, rec. 25.5.-6.6.1956
Gillespie,Dizzy (tp) | Gordon,Joe (tp) | Jones,Quincy (tp) | Perry,Ermit V. (tp) | Warwick,Carl (tp) | Levitt,Rod (tb) | Liston,Melba (tb) | Rehak,Frank (tb) | Powell,Jimmy (as) | Woods,Phil (as) | Mitchell,Billy (ts) | Wilkins,Ernie (ts) | Flax,Marty (bs) | Davis Jr.,Walter (p) | Boyd,Nelson (b) | Persip,Charles (dr)
Manteca
Live at Newport,Rhode Island, rec. 6.7.1957
Gillespie,Dizzy (tp) | Dawud,Talib (tp) | Morgan,Lee (tp) | Perry,Ermit V. (tp) | Warwick,Carl (tp) | Liston,Melba (tb) | Connors,Ray (tb) | Grey,Al (tb) | Powell,Jimmy (as) | Henry,Ernie (as) | Mitchell,Billy (ts) | Golson,Benny (ts) | Moore,Numa 'Pee Wee' (bs) | Kelly,Wynton (p) | West,Paul (b) | Persip,Charles (dr)
Dizzy Gillespie-Sonny Stitt Quintet
Con Alma
NYC, rec. 11.12.1957
Gillespie,Dizzy (tp) | Stitt,Sonny (ts) | Bryant,Ray (p) | Bryant,Tommy (b) | Persip,Charles (dr)
Dizzy Gillespie Quintet
Swing Low Sweet Cadillac
NYC, rec. 18.2.1959
Gillespie,Dizzy (tp,voc) | Mance,Junior[Julian C.] (p) | Spann,Les (g) | Jones,Sam (b) | Humphries,Lex (dr)
Dizzy Gillespie And His Orchestra
Africana
NYC, rec. 14./15.11.1960
Gillespie,Dizzy (tp) | Frosk,John (tp) | Royal,Ernie (tp) | Terry,Clark (tp) | Wilder,Joe (tp) | Green,Urbie (tb) | Rehak,Frank (tb) | Woodman,Britt (tb) | Faulise,Paul (b-tb) | Buffington,Jimmy (fr-h) | Richman,Albert (fr-h) | Schuller,Gunther (fr-h) | Watkins,Julius (fr-h) | Butterfield,Don (tuba) | Wright,Leo (fl,as) | Schifrin,Lalo (p,arr) | Davis,Art (b) | Lampkin,Chuck (dr) | Candido[Camero] (congas) | Rodriguez,Willie (tympani) | Del Rio,Jack (bongos)
Dizzy Gillespie Sextet
Desafinado
NYC, rec. May 1962
Gillespie,Dizzy (tp) | Wright,Leo (fl) | Schifrin,Lalo (p) | White,Chris (b) | Collins,Rudy (dr) | Pepito,Rietria (perc)
Dizzy Gillespie Quintet
November Afternoon | I Can't Get Started- | Round About Midnight-
NYC, rec. 25.4.1963
Gillespie,Dizzy (tp) | Moody,James (as,ts) | Barron,Kenny (p) | White,Chris (b) | Collins,Rudy (dr)

516320-2 | CD | Verve Jazz Masters 16:Oscar Peterson
Oscar Peterson Trio
Willow Weep For Me
Los Angeles,CA, rec. 1952
Peterson,Oscar (p) | Kessel,Barney (g) | Brown,Ray (b)
Noreen's Nocturne
Live at The Stratford Shakespearean Festival,Ontario,CA, rec. 8.8.1956
Peterson,Oscar (p) | Ellis,Herb (g) | Brown,Ray (b)
Gal In Calico
Live at Newport,Rhode Island, rec. 7.7.1957
Peterson,Oscar (p) | Ellis,Herb (g) | Brown,Ray (b)
Evrev
Live at The Concertgebouw,Amsterdam, rec. 12.4.1958
Peterson,Oscar (p) | Brown,Ray (b) | Thigpen,Ed (dr)
Love For Sale
Chicago,Ill, rec. 14.7.-9.8.1959
Peterson,Oscar (p) | Brown,Ray (b) | Thigpen,Ed (dr)
Woody'n You
Chicago,Ill, rec. August 1959
Peterson,Oscar (p) | Brown,Ray (b) | Thigpen,Ed (dr)
Oscar Peterson Trio With The Russell Garcia Orchestra
O.P.
Los Angeles,CA, rec. 5.9.1959
Peterson,Oscar (p) | Brown,Ray (b) | Thigpen,Ed (dr) | Garcia,Russell (cond,arr) | details unknown
Night Train | Honey Dripper
Los Angeles,CA, rec. 15./16.12.1962
Peterson,Oscar (p) | Brown,Ray (b) | Thigpen,Ed (dr)
Oscar Peterson With The Ernie Wilkins Orchestra
West Coast Blues
NYC, rec. 1962
Peterson,Oscar (p) | Adderley,Nat[as 'Pat Brotherly'] (tp) | Eldridge,Roy (tp) | Royal,Ernie (tp) | Terry,Clark (tp) | Young,Eugene 'Snooky' (tp) | Nottingham,Jimmy (tp) | Cleveland,Jimmy (tb) | Faulise,Paul (tb) | Liston,Melba (tb) | Woodman,Britt (tb) | Hampton,Slide (tb) | Alonge,Ray (fr-h) | Ruff,Willie (fr-h) | Watkins,Julius (fr-h) | Buffington,Jimmy (fr-h) | Butterfield,Don (tuba) | Adderley,Julian 'Cannonball'[as 'Jud Brotherly'] (as) | Moody,James (reeds) | Richardson,Jerome (reeds) | Turney,Norris (reeds) | Dorsey,George (reeds) | Powell,Seldon (reeds) | Brown,Ray (b) | Thigpen,Ed (dr) | Wilkins,Ernie (arr,ld)
Oscar Peterson Trio With The Nelson Riddle Orchestra
Someday My Prince Will Come
Los Angeles,CA, rec. November 1963
Peterson,Oscar (p) | Brown,Ray (b) | Thigpen,Ed (dr) | Riddle,Nelson (arr,ld) | details unknown
Oscar Peterson Trio
D & E
NYC, rec. 20.10.1964
Peterson,Oscar (p) | Brown,Ray (b) | Thigpen,Ed (dr)
Younger Than Springtime
Live at The 'Tivoli Gardens',Copenhagen, rec. 29.5.1965
Peterson,Oscar (p) | Brown,Ray (b) | Thigpen,Ed (dr)
Bossa Beguine
NYC, rec. 3.12.1965
Peterson,Oscar (p) | Brown,Ray (b) | Hayes,Louis (dr)
Blues Etude
NYC, rec. 4.5.1966
Peterson,Oscar (p) | Jones,Sam (b) | Hayes,Louis (dr)

516338-2 | CD | Verve Jazz Masters 4:Duke Ellington
Duke Ellington And His Orchestra
Take The 'A' Train | Flirtbird | Perdido | Rockin' In Rhythm
Live at Newport,Rhode Island, rec. 4.7.1959
Ellington,Duke (p) | Anderson,Cat (tp) | Baker,Harold 'Shorty' (tp) | Ford,Fats (tp) | Nance,Ray (tp,v) | Terry,Clark (tp) | Woodman,Britt (tb) | Jackson,Quentin (tb) | Sanders,John (tb) | Hamilton,Jimmy (cl,ts) | Procope,Russell (cl,as) | Hodges,Johnny (as) | Gonsalves,Paul (ts) | Carney,Harry (bs) | Woode,Jimmy (b) | Johnson,Jimmy (dr) | Woodyard,Sam (dr)
Caravan
NYC, rec. 25.-27.6.1957
Ellington,Duke (p) | Anderson,Cat (tp) | Cook,Willie (tp) | Nance,Ray (tp,v) | Terry,Clark (tp) | Woodman,Britt (tb) | Jackson,Quentin (tb) | Sanders,John (tb) | Hamilton,Jimmy (cl,ts) | Procope,Russell (cl,as) | Hodges,Johnny (as) | Foster,Frank (ts) | Gonsalves,Paul (ts) | Carney,Harry (bs) | Woode,Jimmy (b) | Woodyard,Sam (dr) | Fitzgerald,Ella (voc)
Total Jazz(Final Movement Of 'Portrait Of Ella Fitzgerald'
Ellington,Duke (p) | Anderson,Cat (tp) | Cook,Willie (tp) | Nance,Ray (tp,v) | Terry,Clark (tp) | Woodman,Britt (tb) | Jackson,Quentin (tb) | Sanders,John (tb) | Hamilton,Jimmy (cl,ts) | Procope,Russell (cl,as) | Hodges,Johnny (as) | Foster,Frank (ts) | Gonsalves,Paul (ts) | Carney,Harry (bs) | Woode,Jimmy (b) | Woodyard,Sam (dr)
La Plus Belle Africaine | Jam With Sam
Live at Juan Les Pins,France, rec. 29.7.1966
Ellington,Duke (p) | Anderson,Cat (tp) | Williams,Cootie (tp) | Jones,Herbie (tp) | Ellington,Mercer (tp) | Nance,Ray (tp,v) | Terry,Clark (tp) | Connors,Chuck (tb) | Cooper,Frank 'Buster' (tb) | Hamilton,Jimmy (cl,ts) | Procope,Russell (as) | Hodges,Johnny (as) | Gonsalves,Paul (ts) | Carney,Harry (bs) | Lamb,John (b) | Woodyard,Sam (dr)
Diminuendo In Blue- | Blow By Blow-
Live at Juan Les Pins,France, rec. 26./27.7.1966
Ellington,Duke (p) | Anderson,Cat (tp) | Williams,Cootie (tp) | Jones,Herbie (tp) | Ellington,Mercer (tp) | Nance,Ray (tp,v) | Connors,Chuck (tb) | Cooper,Frank 'Buster' (tb) | Hamilton,Jimmy (cl,ts) | Procope,Russell (as) | Hodges,Johnny (as) | Gonsalves,Paul (ts) | Carney,Harry (bs) | Lamb,John (b) | Woodyard,Sam (dr)
Duke Ellington-Johnny Hodges All Stars
Loveless Love | Going Up | St.Louis Blues | Stompy Jones
NYC, rec. 20.2.1959
Hodges,Johnny (as) | Ellington,Duke (p) | Edison,Harry 'Sweets' (tp) | Spann,Les (g) | Jones,Sam (b) | Jones,Jo (dr)

516409-2 | CD | Verve Jazz Masters 13:Antonio Carlos Jobim
Getz-Gilberto Quintet
Quiet Nights Of Quiet Stars(Corcovado) | O Grande Amor
NYC, rec. 18./19.3.1963
Getz,Stan (ts) | Jobim,Antonio Carlos (p) | Gilberto,Joao (g,voc) | Williams,Tommy (b) | Banana,Milton (dr) | Gilberto,Astrud (voc)
Antonio Carlos Jobim With The Claus Ogerman Orchestra
Vivo Sohando(Dreamer) | Desafinado | Agua De Beber(Water To Drink) | Insensatez(How Insensitive) | Favela
NYC, rec. 9./10.5.1963
Jobim,Antonio Carlos (p) | Cleveland,Jimmy (tb) | Wright,Leo (fl) | Strings | Ogerman,Claus (cond,arr) | details unknown
Stan Getz-Luiz Bonfa Orchestra
So Danco Samba(I Only Dance The Samba) | O Morro Nao Tem Vez(One I Loved)
NYC, rec. 8.2.1963
Getz,Stan (ts) | Bonfa,Luiz (g) | Jobim,Antonio Carlos (g,p) | Duvivier,George (b) | Williams,Tommy (b) | Ferreira,Paulo (dr) | Carlos,Jose (dr) | Toledo,Maria (voc)
Antonio Carlos Jobim Group
Aguas De Marco(Waters Of March) | Chovendo Na Roseira(Double Rainbow) | Por Toda A Minha Vida | Triste
Los Angeles,CA, rec. 22.2./9.3.1974
Jobim,Antonio Carlos (g,voc) | Mariano,Cesar Camargo (p,keyboards) | Delmiro,Helio (g) | Neves,Oscar Castro (g) | Maia,Luizao (b) | Braga,Paulo (dr) | Regina,Elis (voc)
Inutil Paisagem(Useless Landscape)
Jobim,Antonio Carlos (p,voc) | Regina,Elis (voc)
Antonio Carlos Jobim With Orchestra
Fascinating Rhythm
Rio De Janeiro,Brazil, rec. November 1986/March 1987
Jobim,Antonio Carlos (p,voc) | Caymmi,Danilo (fl,voc) | Jobim,Paul (g,voc) | Morelenbaum,Jacques (cello) | Neto,Sebastiao (b) | Braga,Paulo (dr) | Adnet,Maucha (voc) | Caymmi,Simone (voc) | Jobim,Ana Lontra (voc) | Jobim,Elizabeth (voc) | Morelenbaum,Paul (voc)
Borzeguim
Jobim,Antonio Carlos (birdcalls,voc) | Morelenbaum,Jacques (cello,arr) | Braga,Ohana (perc) | Braga,Paulo (perc) | Adnet,Maucha (voc) | Caymmi,Danilo (voc) | Caymmi,Simone (voc) | Jobim,Ana Lontra (voc) | Jobim,Elizabeth (voc) | Morelenbaum,Paul (voc)

516758-2 | CD | Verve Jazz Masters 11:Stéphane Grappelli
Stephane Grappelli Trio
Pennies From Heaven
Basel,CH, rec. 30.9.1966
Grappelli,Stephane (v) | Orsted-Pedersen,Niels-Henning (b) | Riel,Alex (dr)
Stephane Grappelli Quartet
Manoir De Mes Reves- | Daphne-
VS-Villingen, rec. March 1971
Grappelli,Stephane (v) | Hemmeler,Marc (p) | Weber,Eberhard (b) | Clare,Kenny (dr)
In My Solitude | Ain't Misbehavin' | Shine | A Nightingale Sang In Berkeley Square
VS-Villingen, rec. March 1975
Grappelli,Stephane (v) | Disley,William 'Diz' (g) | Isaacs,Ike (g) | Eckinger,Isla (b)
Stephane Grappelli With The George Shearing Trio
Star Eyes | The Folks Who Live On The Hill
VS-Villingen, rec. 11.4.1976
Grappelli,Stephane (v) | Shearing,George (p) | Simpkins,Andrew (b) | Jones,Rusty (dr)
Stephane Grappelli Quartet
Are You In The Mood | Djangology
Stuttgart, rec. 19.-21.1.1979
Grappelli,Stephane (v) | Catherine,Philip (g) | Coryell,Larry (g) | Orsted-Pedersen,Niels-Henning (b)
Stephane Grappelli With The Michel Legrand Orchestra
Insensiblement | Nuages
Paris,France, rec. 25.-27.5.1992
Grappelli,Stephane (v) | Legrand,Michel (p,cond,arr) | Le Bevillon,Marc-Michel (b) | Ceccarelli,André (dr) | Orchestra & Chorus | details unknown
Stephane Grappelli Quartet
Tears | Someone To Watch Over Me- | I Got Rhythm-
Colombes,France, rec. 27./28.3.1992
Grappelli,Stephane (v) | Catherine,Philip (g) | Fosset,Marc (g) | Orsted-Pedersen,Niels-Henning (b)

516893-2 | CD | Verve Jazz Masters 37:Oscar Peterson Plays Broadway
Oscar Peterson-Ray Brown Duo
Lover Come Back To Me | All The Things You Are
NYC, rec. March 1950
Peterson,Oscar (p) | Brown,Ray (b)
I Get A Kick Out Of You
NYC, rec. August 1950
Peterson,Oscar (p) | Brown,Ray (b)
Oscar Peterson Trio
There's A Small Hotel
Los Angeles,CA, rec. 26.1.1952
Peterson,Oscar (p) | Ashby,Irving (g) | Brown,Ray (b)
Oscar Peterson Quartet
Body And Soul
Los Angeles,CA, rec. February 1952
Peterson,Oscar (p) | Kessel,Barney (g) | Brown,Ray (b) | Stoller,Alvin (dr)
Oscar Peterson Trio
Easter Parade | Strike Up The Band
Los Angeles,CA, rec. December 1952
Peterson,Oscar (p) | Kessel,Barney (g) | Brown,Ray (b)
I Want To Be Happy
Los Angeles,CA, rec. 10.12.1953
Peterson,Oscar (p) | Ellis,Herb (g) | Brown,Ray (b)
Come Rain Or Come Shine
Los Angeles,CA, rec. 15.11.1954
Peterson,Oscar (p) | Ellis,Herb (g) | Brown,Ray (b)
Wouldn't It Be Loverly
NYC, rec. 20./21.11.1958
Peterson,Oscar (p) | Brown,Ray (b) | Gammage,Gene (dr)
Just In Time
Paris,France, rec. 18.5.1959
Peterson,Oscar (p) | Brown,Ray (b) | Thigpen,Ed (dr)
Surrey With The Fringe On Top
Chicago,Ill, rec. late July 1959
Peterson,Oscar (p) | Brown,Ray (b) | Thigpen,Ed (dr)
Little Tin Box
Los Angeles,CA, rec. January 1960
Peterson,Oscar (p) | Brown,Ray (b) | Thigpen,Ed (dr)
Maria
NYC, rec. 24./25.1.1962
Peterson,Oscar (p) | Brown,Ray (b) | Thigpen,Ed (dr)
Baubles Bangles And Beads
Chicago,Ill, rec. 26.9.1962
Peterson,Oscar (p) | Brown,Ray (b) | Thigpen,Ed (dr)
Clark Terry With The Oscar Peterson Trio
Brotherhood Of Man
NYC, rec. 17.8.1964
Terry,Clark (tp) | Peterson,Oscar (p) | Brown,Ray (b) | Thigpen,Ed (dr)

516931-2 | CD | Verve Jazz Masters 38:Django Reinhardt
Quintet Du Hot Club De France
Daphne | Souvenirs | Honeysuckle Rose | Sweet Georgia Brown
London,GB, rec. 31.1.1938
Quintet Du Hot Club De France | Grappelli,Stephane (v) | Reinhardt,Django (g) | Chaput,Roger (g) | Vees,Eugene (g) | Vola,Louis (b)
Please Be Kind
London,GB, rec. 1.9.1938
Grappelli,Stephane (p) | Reinhardt,Django (g)
H.C.Q. Strut
London,GB, rec. 25.8.1939
Quintet Du Hot Club De France | Grappelli,Stephane (v) | Reinhardt,Django (g) | Ferret,Pierre (g) | Vees,Eugene (g) | Soudieux,Emmanuel (b)
The Man I Love
Quintet Du Hot Club De France | Grappelli,Stephane (v) | Reinhardt,Django (g) | Reinhardt,Joseph (g) | Vees,Eugene (g) | Soudieux,Emmanuel (b)
Vous Et Moi

Brussels,Belgium, rec. 16.4.1942
Reinhardt,Django (g,v) | De Bie,Ivon (p)
Django Reinhardt With Stan Brenders Et Son Grand Orchestre
Djangology
Brussels,Belgium, rec. 8.5.1942
Chantrain,Raymond (tp) | Clais,George (tp) | D'Hondt,Paul (tp) | Damm,Jean (tb) | Van Camp,Sus (tb) | Demany,Jack (ts,v) | Billen,Louis (cl,as) | Magis,Joe (as) | Saguets,Arthur (cl,ts,bars) | Van Herswingle,Jeff (ts) | Douilliez,Jean (v) | Deltour,Emile (v) | Dolne,Chas (v) | Reinhardt,Django (g) | Ouwerckx,John (p) | Van Der Jeught,Jim (g) | Peeters,Arthur (b) | Aerts,Jos (d) | Brenders,Stan (cond,arr)
Quintet Du Hot Club De France
Nuages | Love's Melody(Melodie Au Crepuscule) | Belleville | Liza(All The Clouds'll Roll Away)
London,GB, rec. 1.2.1946
Quintet Du Hot Club De France | Grappelli,Stephane (v) | Reinhardt,Django (g) | Llewellyn,Jack (g) | Hodgkiss,Allan (g) | Goode,Coleridge (b)
Anniversary Song | Swing '48
Paris,France, rec. 6.7.1947
Quintet Du Hot Club De France | Rostaing,Hubert (cl) | Reinhardt,Django (g) | Reinhardt,Joseph (g) | Czabancyk,Ladislas (b) | Jourdan,Andre (dr)
Django Reinhardt And His Rhythm
Night And Day
Paris,France, rec. 10.3.1953
Reinhardt,Django (g) | Vander,Maurice (p) | Michelot,Pierre (b) | Viale,Jean-Louis (dr)

517052-2 | CD | Afro | EAN 731451705229
Dizzy Gillespie And His Orchestra
Manteca | Contraste | Jungle | Rhumba Finale
NYC, rec. 24.5.1954
Gillespie,Dizzy (tp) | Jones,Quincy (tp) | Royal,Ernie (tp) | Nottingham,Jimmy (tp) | Comegys,Leon (tb) | Johnson,J.J. (tb) | Matthews,George (tb) | Jefferson,Hilton (as) | Dorsey,George (as) | Mobley,Hank (ts) | Thompson,Lucky (ts) | Bank,Danny (bs) | Legge,Wade (p) | Concepcion,Ray (p) | Hackney,Lou (b) | Rodriguez,Bobby (b) | Persip,Charles (dr) | Candido[Camero] (congas) | Santamaria,Ramon (congas) | Mangual,Jose (bongos) | Nieto,Ubaldo (timbales) | O'Farrill,Chico (arr)
Dizzy Gillspie And His Latin American Rhythm
A Night In Tunisia | Caravan | Con Alma
NYC, rec. 3.6.1954
Gillespie,Dizzy (tp) | Valdez,Gilbert (fl) | Hernandez,Rene (p) | Rodriguez,Roberto (b) | Candido[Camero] (congas) | Mangual,Jose (bongos) | Nieto,Ubaldo (timbales) | Miranda,Ralph (perc)

517065-2 | CD | All The Sad Youn Men
Anita O'Day With The Gary McFarland Orchestra
Boogie Blues | You Came A Long Way From St. Louis | I Want To Sing A Song | A Woman Alone With The Blues | The Ballad Of All The Sad Young Men | Do Nothin' Till You Hear From Me | One More Mile | Night Bird | Up State | Senor Blues
NYC/Los Angeles,CA, rec. 15.10.1961
O'Day,Anita (voc) | Glow,Bernie (tp) | Pomeroy,Herb (tp) | Severinsen,Doc (tp) | Brookmeyer,Bob (v-tb) | Byers,Billy (tb) | Dennis,Willie (tb) | Levinsky,Walt (reeds) | Woods,Phil (reeds) | Richardson,Jerome (reeds) | Sims,Zoot (reeds) | Jones,Hank (p) | Galbraith,Barry (g) | Duvivier,George (b) | Lewis,Mel (dr) | McFarland,Gary (cond,arr)
-> Note: Anita O'Day(voc) overdubbed November/December 1961

517067-2 | CD | Give Him The Ooh-La-La
Blossom Dearie Quartet
Just One Of Those Things | Like Someone In Love | Between The Devil And The Deep Blue Sea | They Say It's Spring | Try Your Wings | Bang Goes The Drum | The Riviera | The Middle Of Love | Plus Je T'Embrasse | Give Him The Ooh-La-La | Let Me Love You | I Walk A Little Faster | Give Him The Ooh-La-La(alt.take)
NYC, rec. 12./13.9.1957
Dearie,Blossom (p,voc) | Ellis,Herb (g) | Brown,Ray (b) | Jones,Jo (dr)

517329-2 | CD | Pick Yourself Up
Anita O'Day With The Buddy Bregman Orchestra
The Rock 'N' Roll Waltz | I'm With You
Los Angeles,CA, rec. 4.1.1956
O'Day,Anita (voc) | Bregman,Buddy (cond,arr) | details unknown
The Getaway And The Chase | Your Picture Hanging Crooked On The Wall | We Laughed At Love | I'm Not Lonely
Los Angeles,CA, rec. 23.2.1956
O'Day,Anita (voc) | Bregman,Buddy (cond,arr) | details unknown
Anita O'Day And Her Combo
Don't Be That Way | Let's Face The Music And Dance | I Used To Be Colour Blind | Pick Yourself Up | Let's Face The Music And Dance(alt.take)
Los Angeles,CA, rec. 15.9.1956
O'Day,Anita (voc) | Edison,Harry 'Sweets' (tp) | Bunker,Larry (vib) | Smith,Paul (p) | Kessel,Barney (g) | Mondragon,Joe (b) | Stoller,Alvin (dr)
Anita O'Day With The Buddy Bregman Orchestra
Man With The Horn | Stars Fell On Alabama | There's A Lull In My Life | Ivy | Stars Fell On Alabama(alt.take)
Los Angeles,CA, rec. 19.12.1956
O'Day,Anita (voc) | prob.personal: | Candoli,Conte (tp) | Candoli,Pete (tp) | Gozzo,Conrad (tp) | Linn,Ray (tp) | Bernhart,Milton 'Milt' (tb) | Elliot,Lloyd (tb) | Rosolino,Frank (tb) | Roberts,George (tb) | Geller,Herb (as) | Shank,Bud (as) | Auld,Georgie (ts) | Cooper,Bob (ts) | Giuffre,Jimmy (bs) | Smith,Paul (p) | Hendrickson,Al (g) | Mondragon,Joe (b) | Stoller,Alvin (dr) | Bregman,Buddy (cond,arr) | Strings
I Never Had A Chance | Stompin' At The Savoy | Sweet Georgia Brown | I Won't Dance | Let's Begin
Los Angeles,CA, rec. 20.12.1956
O'Day,Anita (voc) | prob.personal: | Candoli,Conte (tp) | Candoli,Pete (tp) | Gozzo,Conrad (tp) | Linn,Ray (tp) | Bernhart,Milton 'Milt' (tb) | Elliot,Lloyd (tb) | Rosolino,Frank (tb) | Roberts,George (tb) | Geller,Herb (as) | Shank,Bud (as) | Auld,Georgie (ts) | Cooper,Bob (ts) | Giuffre,Jimmy (bs) | Smith,Paul (p) | Hendrickson,Al (g) | Mondragon,Joe (b) | Stoller,Alvin (dr) | Bregman,Buddy (cond,arr) | Strings

517330-2 | 2 CD | Stan Getz Highlights:The Best Of The Verve Years Vol.2
Stan Getz Quintet
Thanks For The Memory
NYC, rec. 29.12.1952
Getz,Stan (ts) | Raney,Jimmy (g) | Jordan,Duke (p) | Crow,Bill (b) | Isola,Frank (dr)
Rustic Hop
NYC, rec. 16.4.1953
Getz,Stan (ts) | Brookmeyer,Bob (v-tb) | Williams,John (p) | Crow,Bill (b) | Levitt,Al (dr)
Roundup Time
NYC, rec. 31.1.1955
Getz,Stan (ts) | Fruscella,Tony (tp) | Williams,John (p) | Anthony,Bill (b) | Isola,Frank (dr)
Stan Getz-Lionel Hampton Quintet
Cherokee
Los Angeles,CA, rec. 1.8.1955
Getz,Stan (ts) | Hampton,Lionel (vib) | Levy,Lou (p) | Vinnegar,Leroy (b) | Manne,Shelly (dr)
Stan Getz Quintet
East Of The Sun West Of The Moon
Los Angeles,CA, rec. 15.8.1955
Getz,Stan (ts) | Candoli,Conte (tp) | Levy,Lou (p) | Vinnegar,Leroy (b) | Manne,Shelly (dr)
Stan Getz Quartet
Serenade In Blue
Los Angeles,CA, rec. 19.8.1955
Getz,Stan (ts) | Levy,Lou (p) | Vinnegar,Leroy (b) | Manne,Shelly (dr)
Dizzy Gillespie Septet
Dark Eyes
Los Angeles,CA, rec. 16.10.1956
Gillespie,Dizzy (tp) | Stitt,Sonny (as) | Getz,Stan (ts) | Lewis,John (p) | Ellis,Herb (g) | Brown,Ray (b) | Levey,Stan (dr)
Stan Getz Quartet
Where Or When
Los Angeles,CA, rec. 2.8.1957
Getz,Stan (ts) | Levy,Lou (p) | Vinnegar,Leroy (b) | Levey,Stan (dr)
J.J.Johnson & Stan Getz With The Oscar Peterson Quartet
Billie's Bounce
Live at Shrine Auditorium,Los Angeles,CA, rec. 7.10.1957
Johnson,J.J. (tb) | Getz,Stan (ts) | Peterson,Oscar (p) | Ellis,Herb (g) | Brown,Ray (b) | Kay,Connie (dr)
Herb Ellis Quintet
Blues For Junior
Los Angeles,CA, rec. 11.10.1957
Ellis,Herb (g) | Eldridge,Roy (tp) | Getz,Stan (ts) | Brown,Ray (b) | Levey,Stan (dr)
Stan Getz And The Swedish All Stars
Honeysuckle Rose
Stockholm,Sweden, rec. 26.8.1958
Getz,Stan (ts) | Bailey,Benny (tp) | Persson,Ake (tb) | Nordstrom,Erik (ts) | Gullin,Lars (bs) | Johansson,Ake (p) | Johnson,Gunnar (b) | Schiöppfe,William (dr)
JATP All Stars
All The Things You Are
Live,at Konserthuset,Stockholm, rec. 21.11.1960
JATP All Stars | Eldridge,Roy (tp) | Getz,Stan (ts) | Byas,Don (ts) | Hawkins,Coleman (ts) | Schifrin,Lalo (p) | Davis,Art (b) | Jones,Jo (dr)
Stan Getz Quartet
The Folks Who Live On The Hill
Copenhagen,Denmark, rec. 14.-18.1.1960
Getz,Stan (ts) | Johansson,Jan (p) | Jordan,Daniel (b) | Schiöppfe,William (dr)
Airegin
NYC, rec. 21.2.1961
Getz,Stan (ts) | Kuhn,Steve (p) | LaFaro,Scott (b) | LaRoca,Pete (dr)
Stan Getz-Bob Brookmeyer Quintet
Who Could Care
San Francisco,CA, rec. 12./13.9.1961
Getz,Stan (ts) | Brookmeyer,Bob (v-tb) | Kuhn,Steve (p) | Neves,John (b) | Haynes,Roy (dr)
Stan Getz With The Gary McFarland Orchestra
Chega De Saudade(No More Blues)
NYC, rec. 27.8.1962
Getz,Stan (ts) | Severinsen,Doc (tp) | Glow,Bernie (tp) | Terry,Clark (tp) | Brookmeyer,Bob (tb) | Studd,Tony (tb) | Alonge,Ray (fr-h) | Beckenstein,Ray (cl) | Clark,Babe (cl) | Sanfino,Jerry (fl) | Caine,Eddie (fl) | Penque,Romeo (fl) | Jones,Hank (p) | Hall,Jim (g) | William,Tommy (sb) | Rae,Johnny (dr) | Costa,Carmen (perc) | Paulo,Jose (perc)
Getz-Gilberto Quintet
Corcovado(Quiet Nights)
NYC, rec. 18./19.3.1963
Getz,Stan (ts) | Jobim,Antonio Carlos (p) | Gilberto,Joao (g,voc) | Williams,Tommy (b) | Banana,Milton (dr) | Gilberto,Astrud (voc)
Stan Getz-Laurindo Almeida Orchestra
Maria Moca
NYC, rec. 22.3.1963
Getz,Stan (ts) | Almeida,Laurindo (g) | Kuhn,Steve (p) | Duvivier,George (b) | Bailey,Dave (dr) | Machado,Edison (perc) | Paolo,Jose (perc) | Parga,Luiz (perc) | Soorez,Jose (perc)
Stan Getz-Bill Evans Quartet
My Heart Stood Still
NYC, rec. 5.5.1964
Getz,Stan (ts) | Evans,Bill (p) | Davis,Richard (b) | Jones,Elvin (dr)
Stan Getz New Quartet
When The World Was Young
Live at Salle Pleyel,Paris,France, rec. 13.11.1966
Getz,Stan (ts) | Burton,Gary (vib) | Swallow,Steve (b) | Haynes,Roy (dr)
Stan Getz Quartet
Litha
Englewood Cliffs,NJ, rec. 21.3.1967
Getz,Stan (ts) | Corea,Chick (p) | Carter,Ron (b) | Tate,Grady (dr)
I Remember Clifford
Live at Ronnie Scott's,London,GB, rec. 15./17.3.1971
Getz,Stan (ts) | Louiss,Eddie (org) | Thomas,Rene (g) | Lubat,Bernard (dr)

517535-2 | CD | Ella Swings Lightly
Ella Fitzgerald With Marty Paich's Dektette
You Hit The Spot | What's Your Story(Morning Glory) | Just You Just Me | Teardrops From My Eyes | My Kinda Love | Blues In The Night | If I Were A Bell
Los Angeles,CA, rec. 22.11.1958
Fitzgerald,Ella (voc) | Paich,Marty (cond,arr) | Fagerquist,Don (tp) | Porcino,Al (tp) | Enevoldsen,Bob (v-tb,ts) | DeRosa,Vince (fr-h) | Kitzmiller,John (tuba) | Shank,Bud (as) | Holman,Bill (ts) | Flory,Med (bs) | Levy,Lou (p) | Mondragon,Joe (b) | Lewis,Mel (dr)
Little White Lies | As Long As I Live | Gotta Be This Or That | Moonlight On The Ganges | You're An Old Smoothie | Little Jazz | You Brought A New Kind Of Love To Me | Knock Me A Kiss | 720 In The Book | Oh What A Night For Love(long version) | Little Jazz(alt.take) | Dreams Are Made For Children | Oh What A Night For Love(single version)
Los Angeles,CA, rec. 23.11.1958
Fitzgerald,Ella (voc) | Paich,Marty (cond,arr) | Fagerquist,Don (tp) | Porcino,Al (tp) | Enevoldsen,Bob (v-tb,ts) | DeRosa,Vince (fr-h) | Kitzmiller,John (tuba) | Shank,Bud (as) | Holman,Bill (ts) | Flory,Med (bs) | Levy,Lou (p) | Mondragon,Joe (b) | Lewis,Mel (dr)

517898-2 | 3 CD | Ella Fitzgerald-First Lady Of Song
Ella Fitzgerald With The JATP All Stars
Perdido
NYC, rec. 18.9.1949
Fitzgerald,Ella (voc) | JATP All Stars | Eldridge,Roy (tp) | Turk,Tommy (tb) | Parker,Charlie (as) | Young,Lester (ts) | Phillips,Flip (ts) | Jones,Hank (p) | Brown,Ray (b) | Rich,Buddy (dr)
Lullaby Of Birdland
Hartford,Conn., rec. 17.9.1954
Fitzgerald,Ella (voc) | Tunia,Raymond (p) | Ellis,Herb (g) | Brown,Ray (b) | Rich,Buddy (dr)
Ella Fitzgerald With The Buddy Bregman Orchestra
Too Young For The Blues
Los Angeles,CA, rec. 25.1.1956
Fitzgerald,Ella (voc) | prob.personal: | Candoli,Pete (tp) | Edison,Harry 'Sweets' (tp) | Gozzo,Conrad (tp) | Linn,Ray (tp) | Bernhart,Milton 'Milt' (tb) | Howard,Joe (tb) | Ulyate,Lloyd (tb) | Roberts,George (b-tb) | Geller,Herb (as) | Shank,Bud (as) | Cooper,Bob (ts) | Nash,Ted (ts) | Gentry,Chuck (bs) | Smith,Paul (p) | Kessel,Barney (g) | Mondragon,Joe (b) | Stoller,Alvin (dr) | Bregman,Buddy (cond,arr)
Too Darn Hot
Los Angeles,CA, rec. 7.2.1956
Fitzgerald,Ella (voc) | prob.personal: | Candoli,Pete (tp) | Edison,Harry 'Sweets' (tp) | Gozzo,Conrad (tp) | Linn,Ray (tp) | Bernhart,Milton 'Milt' (tb) | Howard,Joe (tb) | Ulyate,Lloyd (tb) | Roberts,George (b-tb) | Geller,Herb (as) | Shank,Bud (as) | Cooper,Bob (ts) | Nash,Ted (ts) | Gentry,Chuck (bs) | Smith,Paul (p) | Kessel,Barney (g) | Mondragon,Joe (b) | Stoller,Alvin (dr) | Bregman,Buddy (cond,arr)
Ella Fitzgerald With The Paul Smith Quartet
Miss Otis Regrets
Fitzgerald,Ella (voc) | Smith,Paul (p) | Kessel,Barney (g) | Mondragon,Joe (b) | Stoller,Alvin (dr)
Ella Fitzgerald With The Count Basie Orchestra
April In Paris
NYC, rec. 25.6.1956
Fitzgerald,Ella (voc) | Basie,Count (p) | Culley,Wendell (tp) | Jones,Reunald (tp) | Jones,Thad (tp) | Newman,Joe (tp) | Coker,Henry (tb) | Hughes,Bill (tb) | Powell,Benny (tb) | Foster,Frank (reeds) | Fowlkes,Charlie (reeds) | Graham,Bill (reeds) | Royal,Marshall (reeds) | Wess,Frank (reeds) | Green,Freddie (g) | Jones,Eddie (b) | Payne,Sonny (dr)
Ella Fitzgerald With Louis Armstrong And The All Stars
Undecided
Live at The Hollywood Bowl,Los Angeles,CA, rec. 15.8.1956
Fitzgerald,Ella (voc) | Armstrong,Louis (tp) | Young,Trummy (tb) | Hall,Edmond (cl) | Kyle,Billy (p) | Jones,Dale (b) | Deems,Barrett (dr)
Ella Fitzgerald And Louis Armstrong With The Oscar Peterson Quartet
Can't We Be Friends
Los Angeles,CA, rec. 16.8.1956
Fitzgerald,Ella (voc) | Armstrong,Louis (tp,voc) | Peterson,Oscar (p) | Ellis,Herb (g) | Brown,Ray (b) | Rich,Buddy (dr)
Ella Fitzgerald With The Paul Smith Quartet
Bewitched Bothered And Bewildered
Los Angeles,CA, rec. 29.8.1956
Fitzgerald,Ella (voc) | Smith,Paul (p) | Kessel,Barney (g) | Mondragon,Joe (b) | Stoller,Alvin (dr)
Ella Fitzgerald And Her Sextet
Just A-Sittin' And A-Rockin'
Los Angeles,CA, rec. 4.9.1956
Fitzgerald,Ella (voc) | Webster,Ben (ts) | Smith,Stuff (v) | Smith,Paul (p) | Kessel,Barney (g) | Mondragon,Joe (b) | Stoller,Alvin (dr)
Ella Fitzgerald With The Duke Ellington Orchestra
I'm Just A Lucky So-And-So
NYC, rec. 26.6.1957
Fitzgerald,Ella (voc) | Ellington,Duke (p) | Anderson,Cat (tp) | Cook,Willie (tp) | Terry,Clark (tp) | Nance,Ray (tp,v) | Jackson,Quentin (tb) | Woodman,Britt (tb) | Sanders,John (tb) | Hamilton,Jimmy (cl,ts) | Procope,Russell (cl,as) | Hodges,Johnny (as) | Gonsalves,Paul (ts) | Carney,Harry (b-cl,bs) | Woode,Jimmy (b) | Woodyard,Sam (dr)
Ella Fitzgerald With The Don Abney Trio
Air Mail Special
Live at Newport,Rhode Island, rec. 4.7.1957
Fitzgerald,Ella (voc) | Abney,Don (p) | Marshall,Wendell (b) | Jones,Jo (dr)
Ella Fitzgerald With The Frank DeVol Orchestra
A-Tisket A-Tasket
Los Angeles,CA, rec. 24.7.1957
Fitzgerald,Ella (voc) | DeVol,Frank (cond,arr) | details unknown
Ella Fitzgerald And Her Sextet
Baby Don't You Go Way Mad
Fitzgerald,Ella (voc) | prob.personal: | Edison,Harry 'Sweets' (tp) | Webster,Ben (ts) | Kessel,Barney (g) | Smith,Paul (p) | Mitchell,Red (b) | unkn (dr)
Ella Fitzgerald And Barney Kessel
Angel Eyes
Fitzgerald,Ella (voc) | Kessel,Barney (g)
Ella Fitzgerald And Louis Armstrong With The Oscar Peterson Quartet
I Won't Dance
Los Angeles,CA, rec. 13.8.1957
Fitzgerald,Ella (voc) | Armstrong,Louis (tp,voc) | Peterson,Oscar (p) | Ellis,Herb (g) | Brown,Ray (b) | Bellson,Louie (dr)
Ella Fitzgerald And Louis Armstrong With The Russell Garcia Orchestra
Summertime
Los Angeles,CA, rec. 18.8.1957
Fitzgerald,Ella (voc) | Armstrong,Louis (tp,voc) | Garcia,Russell (cond,arr) | details unknown
Ella Fitzgerald With The JATP All Stars
Oh! Lady Be Good
Live at Shrine Auditorium,Los Angeles,CA, rec. 7.10.1957
Fitzgerald,Ella (voc) | JATP All Stars | Eldridge,Roy (tp) | Johnson,J.J. (tb) | Stitt,Sonny (as) | Young,Lester (ts) | Jacquet,Illinois (ts) | Hawkins,Coleman (ts) | Getz,Stan (ts) | Phillips,Flip (ts) | Peterson,Oscar (p) | Ellis,Herb (g) | Brown,Ray (b) | Jones,Jo (dr)
Ella Fitzgerald With The Frank DeVol Orchestra feat. Stan Getz
More Than You Know
Los Angeles,CA, rec. 15.10.1957
Fitzgerald,Ella (voc) | Getz,Stan (ts) | DeVol,Frank (cond,arr) | details unknown
Ella Fitzgerald And Oscar Peterson
Lush Life
Los Angeles,CA, rec. 17.10.1957
Fitzgerald,Ella (voc) | Peterson,Oscar (p)
Ella Fitzgerald With The Paul Weston Orchestra
Blue Skies | Swingin' Shepherd Blues
Los Angeles,CA, rec. 18.3.1958
Fitzgerald,Ella (voc) | Edison,Harry 'Sweets' (tp) | Weston,Paul (cond,arr) | details unknown
Ella Fitzgerald With The Lou Levy Trio
These Foolish Things Remind Me On You | Travelin' Light
Live in Rome,Italy, rec. 25.4.1958
Fitzgerald,Ella (voc) | Levy,Lou (p) | Bennett,Max (b) | Johnson,Gus (dr)
Ella Fitzgerald With The Marty Paich Dek-tette
You're An Old Smoothie
Los Angeles,CA, rec. 22.11.1958
Fitzgerald,Ella (voc) | Fagerquist,Don (tp) | Porcino,Al (tp) | Enevoldsen,Bob (v-tb,ts) | DeRosa,Vince (fr-h) | Kitzmiller,John (tuba) | Shank,Bud (as) | Holman,Bill (ts) | Flory,Med (bs) | Levy,Lou (p) | Mondragon,Joe (b) | Lewis,Mel (dr) | Paich,Marty (arr,ld)
Ella Fitzgerald With The Frank DeVol Orchestra
Makin' Whoopee
Los Angeles,CA, rec. 24.11.1958
Fitzgerald,Ella (voc) | Edison,Harry 'Sweets' (tp) | DeVol,Frank (cond,arr) | details unknown
Ella Fitzgerald With The Nelson Riddle Orchestra
How Long Has This Been Going On
Los Angeles,CA, rec. 5.1.1959
Fitzgerald,Ella (voc) | Fagerquist,Don (tp) | Cooper,Bob (ts) | Stoller,Alvin (dr) | Riddle,Nelson (arr,ld) | details unknown
Ella Fitzgerald And Herb Ellis
Detour Ahead
Los Angeles,CA, rec. 25.3.1959
Fitzgerald,Ella (voc) | Ellis,Herb (g)
Ella Fitzgerald With The Paul Smith Quartet
Mack The Knife(Moritat) | How High The Moon
Live at The Deutschlandhalle, Berlin, rec. 13.2.1960
Fitzgerald,Ella (voc) | Smith,Paul (p) | Hall,Jim (g) | Middlebrooks,Wilfred (b) | Johnson,Gus (dr)
Ella Fitzgerald And Paul Smith
Black Coffee
Los Angeles,CA, rec. 14.4.1960
Fitzgerald,Ella (voc) | Smith,Paul (p)
Ella Fitzgerald With The Frank DeVol Orchestra
Let It Snow, Let It Snow, Let It Snow
Los Angeles,CA, rec. 16.7.1960
Fitzgerald,Ella (voc) | DeVol,Frank (cond,arr) | details unknown
Ella Fitzgerald With The Billy May Orchestra
Get Happy | Heart And Soul
Los Angeles,CA, rec. 2.8.1960
Fitzgerald,Ella (voc) | May,Billy (arr,ld) | Fagerquist,Don (tp) | Bernhart,Milton 'Milt' (tb) | Nash,Dick (tb) | Carter,Benny (as) | Nash,Ted (as) | Johnson,Plas (ts) | Bunker,Larry (vib) | Smith,Paul (p) | Hendrickson,Al (g) | Collins,John (g) | Mondragon,Joe (b) | Stoller,Alvin (dr) | details unknown
Ella Fitzgerald With The Lou Levy Quartet
Mr.Paganini
Live at The Crescendo Club,Los Angeles,CA, rec. 12.5.1961
Fitzgerald,Ella (voc) | Levy,Lou (p) | Ellis,Herb (g) | Middlebrooks,Wilfred (b) | Johnson,Gus (dr)
A Night In Tunisia
Los Angeles,CA, rec. 23.1.1961
Fitzgerald,Ella (voc) | Levy,Lou (p) | Ellis,Herb (g) | Middlebrooks,Wilfred (b) | Johnson,Gus (dr)
Ella Fitzgerald With The Nelson Riddle Orchestra
I Can't Get Started
Los Altos Hill,CA, rec. 13.11.1961
Fitzgerald,Ella (voc) | Lang,Ronnie (as) | Riddle,Nelson (arr,ld) | details unknown
Don't Be That Way
Los Angeles,CA, rec. 27.12.1961
Fitzgerald,Ella (voc) | Lang,Ronnie (as) | Riddle,Nelson (arr,ld) | details unknown

Ella Fitzgerald With The Bill Doggett Orchestra
After You've Gone
Los Angeles,CA, rec. 30.1.1962
Fitzgerald,Ella (voc) | Royal,Ernie (tp) | Jordan,Taft (tp) | Copeland,Ray (tp) | Wilder,Joe (tp) | Liston,Melba (tb) | Winding,Kai (tb) | Woodman,Britt (tb) | Davis,Charles (reeds) | Dodgion,Jerry (reeds) | Shakesnider,Wilmer (reeds) | Taylor,Les (reeds) | Woods,Phil (as) | Jones,Hank (p) | Lowe,Mundell (g) | Dixon,Lucille (b) | Johnson,Gus (dr) | Doggett,Bill (arr,ld)

Ella Fitzgerald With Orchestra
Hernando's Hideaway
Los Angeles,CA, rec. 2.10.1962
Fitzgerald,Ella (voc) | Orchestra | details unknown

Ella Fitzgerald With The Nelson Riddle Orchestra
A Fine Romance
Los Angeles,CA, rec. 5.1.1963
Fitzgerald,Ella (voc) | Riddle,Nelson (arr,ld) | details unknown

Ella Fitzgerald With The Count Basie Orchestra
'Deed I Do
NYC, rec. 15/16.7.1963
Fitzgerald,Ella (voc) | Basie,Count (p) | Newman,Joe (tp) | Al Aarons (tp) | Cohn[Cohen],Sonny (tp) | Rader,Don (tp) | Ricard,Fip (tp) | Coker,Henry (tb) | Mitchell,Grover (tb) | Powell,Benny (tb) | Green,Urbie (tb) | Royal,Marshall (cl,as) | Dixon,Eric (fl,ts) | Wess,Frank (fl,as,ts) | Foster,Frank (ts) | Fowlkes,Charlie (bs) | Green,Freddie (g) | Catlett,Buddy (b) | Payne,Sonny (dr)

Ella Fitzgerald And Her All Stars
Hear Me Talkin' To Ya
NYC, rec. 28.10.1963
Fitzgerald,Ella (voc) | Eldridge,Roy (tp) | Davis,Wild Bill (org) | Ellis,Herb (g) | Brown,Ray (b) | Johnson,Gus (dr)

Ella Fitzgerald With The Johnny Spence Orchestra
Can't Buy Me Love
London,GB, rec. 7.4.1964
Fitzgerald,Ella (voc) | Spence,Johnny (arr,ld) | details unknown

Ella Fitzgerald And Her All Stars
Day In Day Out
Live at Juan Les Pins,France, rec. 28.7.1964
Fitzgerald,Ella (voc) | Eldridge,Roy (tp) | Flanagan,Tommy (p) | Yancey,Bill (b) | Johnson,Gus (dr)

Ella Fitzgerald With The Nelson Riddle Orchestra
Something's Gotta Give
Los Angeles,CA, rec. October 1964
Fitzgerald,Ella (voc) | DeFranco,Buddy (cl) | Smith,Willie (as) | Johnson,Plas (ts) | Flynn,Frank (vib) | Smith,Paul (p) | Riddle,Nelson (cond,arr) | details unknown

Ella Fitzgerald With The Tommy Flanagan Trio
Here's That Rainy Day
Live in Hamburg, rec. 26.3.1965
Fitzgerald,Ella (voc) | Flanagan,Tommy (p) | Betts,Keter (b) | Johnson,Gus (dr)

Ella Fitzgerald With The Duke Ellington Orchestra
Something To Live For
Los Angeles,CA, rec. October 1965
Fitzgerald,Ella (voc) | Ellington,Duke (p,ld) | Williams,Cootie (tp) | Jones,Herbie (tp) | Anderson,Cat (tp) | Ellington,Mercer (tp) | Brown,Lawrence (tb) | Cooper,Frank 'Buster' (tb) | Connors,Chuck (tb) | Hodges,Johnny (as) | Procope,Russell (as) | Hamilton,Jimmy (cl,ts) | Gonsalves,Paul (ts) | Carney,Harry (bs) | Jones,Jimmy (p) | Lamb,John (b) | Bellson,Louie (dr)

Ella Fitzgerald With The Marty Paich Orchestra
You've Changed
Los Angeles,CA, rec. Summer 1966
Fitzgerald,Ella (voc) | Williamson,Stu (tp) | Perkins,Bill (ts) | Rowles,Jimmy (p) | Viola,Al (g) | Mondragon,Joe (b) | Manne,Shelly (dr) | Paich,Marty (arr,ld) | details unknown

Ella Fitzgerald With The Jimmy Jones Trio
Jazz Samba
Live at Juan Les Pins,France, rec. 27.-29.7.1966
Fitzgerald,Ella (voc) | Jones,Jimmy (p) | Hughart,Jim (b) | Tate,Grady (dr)

Ella Fitzgerald With The Duke Ellington Orchestra
It Don't Mean A Thing If It Ain't Got That Swing
Fitzgerald,Ella (voc) | Ellington,Duke (p) | Williams,Cootie (tp) | Anderson,Cat (tp) | Jones,Herbie (tp) | Nance,Ray (tp,v) | Ellington,Mercer (tp) | Brown,Lawrence (tb) | Cooper,Frank 'Buster' (tb) | Connors,Chuck (tb) | Hamilton,Jimmy (cl,ts) | Hodges,Johnny (as) | Procope,Russell (as) | Gonsalves,Paul (ts) | Webster,Ben (ts) | Carney,Harry (bs) | Lamb,John (b) | Woodyard,Sam (dr)

518197-2 | CD | Verve Jazz Masters 7:Erroll Garner
Erroll Garner Quartet
I've Got To Be A Rug Cutter | Misty | All Of A Sudden My Heart Sings | 7-11 Jump | Don't Worry 'Bout Me | Part Time Blues | I've Got The World On A String | Oh! Lady Be Good
Chicago,Ill, rec. 27.7.1954
Garner,Erroll (p) | Ruther,Wyatt (b) | Heard,Eugene 'Fats' (dr) | Candido[Camero] (congas)

Erroll Garner
Smooth One | Love In Bloom | Don't Be That Way | St.James Infirmary | Is You Is Or Is You Ain't My Baby | Yesterdays | Fandango
NYC, rec. 14.3.1955
Garner,Erroll (p-solo)

518198-2 | CD | Verve Jazz Masters 17:Nina Simone
Nina Simone
Black Is The Color Of My True Love's Hair
NYC, rec. March/April 1964
Simone,Nina (p,voc)

Strange Fruit
NYC, rec. 19./20.5.1964
Simone,Nina (p,voc)

Nina Simone With Hal Mooney's Orchestra
I Put A Spell On You | Ne Me Quitte Pas
NYC, rec. January 1965
Simone,Nina (p,voc) | Stevenson,Rudy (g) | Mooney,Hal (arr,ld) | details unknown

The Work Song | I Hold No Grudge
details unknown, rec. 1966
Simone,Nina (p,voc) | Mooney,Hal (arr,ld) | details unknown

Nina Simone Quartet
Little Girl Blue | See Line Woman
NYC, rec. ca.1964
Simone,Nina (p,voc) | Stevenson,Rudy (g) | Atkinson,Lisle (b) | Hamilton,Bobby (dr)

I Loves You Porgy | Wild Is The Wind | Pirate Jenny | Mississippi Goddam
NYC, rec. March/April 1964
Simone,Nina (p,voc) | Stevenson,Rudy (g) | Atkinson,Lisle (b) | Hamilton,Bobby (dr)

Love Me Or Leave Me | Four Women
NYC, rec. 30.9./1.10.1964
Simone,Nina (p,voc) | Stevenson,Rudy (g) | Atkinson,Lisle (b) | Hamilton,Bobby (dr)

Nina Simone With Horace Ott's Orchestra
Don't Let Me Be Misunderstood
NYC, rec. 1964
Simone,Nina (p,voc) | Orchestra | Ott,Horace (cond,arr) | details unknown

Nina Simone Trio
My Baby Just Cares For Me
Live at The Vine St.Bar,Los Angeles,CA, rec. 1987
Simone,Nina (p,voc) | Adams,Arthur (b) | McFadden,Cornell (dr)

519564-2 | CD | Mack The Knife-The Complete Ella In Berlin
Ella Fitzgerald With The Paul Smith Quartet
That Old Black Magic | Our Love Is Here To Stay | Gone With The Wind | Misty | The Lady Is A Tramp | The Man I Love | Love For Sale | Just One Of Those Things | Summertime | Too Darn Hot | Lorelei | Mack The Knife(Moritat) | How High The Moon
Live,Deutschlandhalle,Berlin, rec. 13.2.1960
Fitzgerald,Ella (voc) | Smith,Paul (p) | Hall,Jim (g) | Middlebrooks,Wilfred (b) | Johnson,Gus (dr)

519607-2 | CD | Keeping Tradition
Dee Dee Bridgewater With Her Trio
Just One Of Those Things | Fascinating Rhythm | The Island | Angel Eyes | What Is This Thing Called Love | Autumn Leaves | I'm A Fool To Want You- | I Fall In Love Too Easily- | Lullaby Of Birdland | What A Little Moonlight Can Do | Love Vibrations | Polka Dots And Moonbeams | Sister Sadie
Paris,France, rec. 8.-10.12.1992
Bridgewater,Dee Dee (voc) | Eliez,Thierry (p) | Van De Geyn,Hein (b) | Ceccarelli,André (dr)

519703-2 | CD | Light Out Of Darkness(A Tribute To Ray Charles)
Shirley Horn Quartet
Hit The Road Jack
NYC, rec. 30.4.-3.5.1993
Horn,Shirley (p,voc) | Ables,Charles (g) | Mitchell,Tyler (b) | Williams,Stephen E. 'Steve' (dr) | Hornettes,The (background-voc)

Shirley Horn Quintet
Just A Little Lovin' | Makin' Whoopee | Bye Bye Love | If You Were Mine
Horn,Shirley (p,voc) | Bartz,Gary (as) | Ables,Charles (g) | Mitchell,Tyler (b) | Williams,Stephen E. 'Steve' (dr)

Shirley Horn Quartet
Drown In My Own Tears | Hard Hearted Hannah
Horn,Shirley (p,org,voc) | Bartz,Gary (as) | Ables,Charles (b) | Williams,Stephen E. 'Steve' (dr)

I Got A Man
Horn,Shirley (p,voc) | Ables,Charles (g) | Mitchell,Tyler (b) | Williams,Stephen E. 'Steve' (dr)

Shirley Horn Trio
You Don't Know Me | Georgia On My Mind | The Sun Died | How Long Has This Been Going On | Just For A Thrill | Light Out Of Darkness
Horn,Shirley (p,org,voc) | Ables,Charles (b) | Williams,Stephen E. 'Steve' (dr)

Shirley Horn
Green(It's Not Easy Being Green)
Horn,Shirley (p)

519800-2 | CD | Getz/Gilberto No.2
Stan Getz Quartet
Grandfather's Waltz | Tonight I Shall Sleep With A Smile On My Face | Stan's Blues | Here's That Rainy Day
Live at Carnegie Hall,NYC, rec. 9.10.1964
Getz,Stan (ts) | Burton,Gary (vib) | Cherico,Gene (b) | Milito,Helcio (dr)

Joao Gilberto Trio
Samba Da Minha Terra | Rosa Morena | Um Braco No Bronfa | Bim Bom | Meditation | O Pato(The Duck)
Gilberto,Joao (g,voc) | Betts,Keter (b) | Milito,Helcio (dr)

Getz-Gilberto Quintet
It Might As Well Be Spring | Only Trust Your Heart | Corcovado(Quiet Nights) | Girl From Ipanema(Garota De Ipanema) | Eu E Voce
Getz,Stan (ts) | Gilberto,Joao (g,voc) | Burton,Gary (vib) | Cherico,Gene (b) | Hunt,Joe (dr) | Gilberto,Astrud (voc)

519804-2 | CD | The Best Of The Song Books
Ella Fitzgerald With The Nelson Riddle Orchestra
Something's Gotta Give
Los Angeles,CA, rec. October 1964
Fitzgerald,Ella (voc) | DeFranco,Buddy (cl) | Smith,Willie (as) | Johnson,Plas (ts) | Flynn,Frank (vib) | Smith,Paul (p) | Riddle,Nelson (cond,arr) | details unknown

Our Love Is Here To Stay | They Can't Take That Away From Me
Los Angeles,CA, rec. 5.-8.1.1959
Fitzgerald,Ella (voc) | Fagerquist,Don (tp) | Cooper,Bob (ts) | Stoller,Alvin (dr) | Strings | Riddle,Nelson (cond,arr) | details unknown

Why Was I Born
Los Angeles,CA, rec. 6.1.1963
Fitzgerald,Ella (voc) | Riddle,Nelson (cond,arr) | details unknown

Midnight Sun
Los Angeles,CA, rec. October 1964
Fitzgerald,Ella (voc) | DeFranco,Buddy (cl) | Smith,Willie (as) | Flynn,Frank (vib) | Smith,Paul (p) | Riddle,Nelson (cond,arr) | details unknown

'S Wonderful
Los Angeles,CA, rec. 16.7.1959
Fitzgerald,Ella (voc) | Riddle,Nelson (cond,arr) | details unknown

Ella Fitzgerald And The Paul Smith Quartet
Bewitched Bothered And Bewildered
Los Angeles,CA, rec. 29.8.1956
Fitzgerald,Ella (voc) | Smith,Paul (p) | Kessel,Barney (g) | Mondragon,Joe (b) | Stoller,Alvin (dr)

Miss Otis Regrets
Los Angeles,CA, rec. 7.2.1956
Fitzgerald,Ella (voc) | Smith,Paul (p) | Kessel,Barney (g) | Mondragon,Joe (b) | Stoller,Alvin (dr)

Ella Fitzgerald With Paul Weston And His Orchestra
I've Got My Love To Keep Me Warm
Los Angeles,CA, rec. 18.3.1958
Fitzgerald,Ella (voc) | Edison,Harry 'Sweets' (tp) | Weston,Paul (cond) | details unknown

Ella Fitzgerald With The Buddy Bregman Orchestra
The Lady Is A Tramp
Los Angeles,CA, rec. 21.8.1956
Fitzgerald,Ella (voc) | Bregman,Buddy (cond,arr) | details unknown

Love For Sale
Los Angeles,CA, rec. 8.2.1956
Fitzgerald,Ella (voc) | Bregman,Buddy (cond,arr) | details unknown

Every Time We Say Goodbye
Los Angeles,CA, rec. 7.2.1957
Fitzgerald,Ella (voc) | Bregman,Buddy (cond,arr) | details unknown

Ella Fitzgerald With The Duke Ellington Orchestra
I Got It Bad And That Ain't Good
NYC, rec. 25.6.1957
Fitzgerald,Ella (voc) | Ellington,Duke (p) | Anderson,Cat (tp) | Cook,Willie (tp) | Terry,Clark (tp) | Nance,Ray (tp,v) | Jackson,Quentin (tb) | Woodman,Britt (tb) | Sanders,John (tb) | Hamilton,Jimmy (cl,ts) | Procope,Russell (cl,as) | Hodges,Johnny (as) | Gonsalves,Paul (ts) | Carney,Harry (b-cl,bs) | Woode,Jimmy (b) | Woodyard,Sam (dr)

Ella Fitzgerald With The Billy May Orchestra
Between The Devil And The Deep Blue Sea
Los Angeles,CA, rec. 16.1.1961
Fitzgerald,Ella (voc) | May,Billy (arr,ld) | Fagerquist,Don (tp) | Bernhart,Milton 'Milt' (tb) | Nash,Dick (tb) | Carter,Benny (as) | Nash,Ted (as) | Johnson,Plas (ts) | Bunker,Larry (vib) | Smith,Paul (p) | Hendrickson,Al (g) | Collins,John (g) | Mondragon,Joe (b) | Stoller,Alvin (dr) | details unknown

Hooray For Love
Los Angeles,CA, rec. 1.8.1960
Fitzgerald,Ella (voc) | May,Billy (arr,ld) | Fagerquist,Don (tp) | Bernhart,Milton 'Milt' (tb) | Nash,Dick (tb) | Carter,Benny (as) | Nash,Ted (as) | Johnson,Plas (ts) | Bunker,Larry (vib) | Smith,Paul (p) | Hendrickson,Al (g) | Collins,John (g) | Mondragon,Joe (b) | Stoller,Alvin (dr) | details unknown

Ella Fitzgerald And Her Sextet
Cotton Tail
Los Angeles,CA, rec. 4.9.1957
Fitzgerald,Ella (voc) | Webster,Ben (ts) | Smith,Stuff (v) | Smith,Paul (p) | Kessel,Barney (g) | Mondragon,Joe (b) | Stoller,Alvin (dr)

519806-2 | CD | King Of The Tenors
Ben Webster With The Oscar Peterson Quartet
Bounce Blues | Cotton Tail | Danny Boy (Londonderry Air) | Poutin' | Bounce Blues(alt.take)
NYC, rec. 21.5.1953
Webster,Ben (ts) | Peterson,Oscar (p) | Kessel,Barney (g) | Brown,Ray (b) | Heard,J.C. (dr)

Tenderly
Los Angeles,CA, rec. 8.12.1953
Webster,Ben (ts) | Peterson,Oscar (p) | Ellis,Herb (g) | Brown,Ray (b) | Stoller,Alvin (dr)

Ben Webster All Stars
Jive At Six | Don't Get Around Much Anymore | That's All | Pennies From Heaven | That's All(single version)
Webster,Ben (ts) | Edison,Harry 'Sweets' (tp) | Carter,Benny (as) | Peterson,Oscar (p) | Ellis,Herb (g) | Brown,Ray (b) | Stoller,Alvin (dr)

519807-2 | CD | Porgy And Bess
Oscar Peterson Trio
I Got Plenty O'Nuttin' | I Wants To Stay Here(aka I Loves You Porgy) | Summertime | Oh Dey's So Fresh An' Fine (Strawberry Woman) | Oh Lawd I'm On My Way | It Ain't Necessarily So | There's A Boat Dat's Leavin' Soon For New York | Oh Bess Where's My Bess | Here Comes De Honey Man | Bess You Is My Woman Now
Los Angeles,CA, rec. 12.10.1959
Peterson,Oscar (p) | Brown,Ray (b) | Thigpen,Ed (dr)

519809-2 | CD | Gillespiana And Carnegie Hall Concert
Dizzy Gillespie And His Orchestra
Gillespiana: | Prelude- | Blues- | Panamericana-
NYC, rec. 14./15.11.1960
Gillespie,Dizzy (tp) | Frosk,John (tp) | Royal,Ernie (tp) | Terry,Clark (tp) | Wilder,Joe (tp) | Green,Urbie (tb) | Rehak,Frank (tb) | Woodman,Britt (tb) | Faulise,Paul (b-tb) | Buffington,Jimmy (fr-h) | Richman,Albert (fr-h) | Schuller,Gunther (fr-h) | Watkins,Julius (fr-h) | Butterfield,Don (tuba) | Wright,Leo (fl,as) | Schifrin,Lalo (p,arr) | Davis,Art (b) | Lampkin,Chuck (dr) | Del Rio,Jack (bongos) | Candido[Camero] (congas) | Rodriguez,Willie (timbales)

Africana- | Toccata-
NYC, rec. 16.11.1960
Gillespie,Dizzy (tp) | Frosk,John (tp) | Royal,Ernie (tp) | Terry,Clark (tp) | Wilder,Joe (tp) | Green,Urbie (tb) | Rehak,Frank (tb) | Woodman,Britt (tb) | Faulise,Paul (b-tb) | Lister,William (fr-h) | Scott,Morris (fr-h) | Schuller,Gunther (fr-h) | Watkins,Julius (fr-h) | Butterfield,Don (tuba) | Wright,Leo (fl,as) | Schifrin,Lalo (p,arr) | Davis,Art (b) | Lampkin,Chuck (dr) | Del Rio,Jack (bongos) | Candido[Camero] (congas) | Rodriguez,Willie (timbales)

Manteca | This Is The Way | Ool-Ya-Koo | Kush | Tunisian Fantasy
Live at Carnegie Hall,NYC, rec. 4.3.1961
Gillespie,Dizzy (tp,voc) | Frosk,John (tp) | Terry,Clark (tp) | Travis,Nick (tp) | Warwick,Carl (tp) | Matthews,George (tb) | Sparrow,Arnett (tb) | Woodman,Britt (tb) | Faulise,Paul (b-tb) | Buffington,Jimmy (fr-h) | Schuller,Gunther (fr-h) | Barrows,John (fr-h) | Berg,Richard (fr-h) | Butterfield,Don (tuba) | Wright,Leo (fl,as) | Schifrin,Lalo (p,arr) | Davis,Art (b) | Lampkin,Chuck (dr) | Barretto,Ray (congas) | Colazo,Julio (perc) | Mangual,Jose (perc) | Carroll,Joe (voc)

519810-2 | CD | Solitude
Billie Holiday And Her Orchestra
East Of The Sun West Of The Moon | Blue Moon | I Only Have Eyes For You
Los Angeles,CA, rec. 26.3.1952
Holiday,Billie (voc) | Shavers,Charlie (tp) | Phillips,Flip (ts) | Peterson,Oscar (p) | Kessel,Barney (g) | Stoller,Alvin (dr)

You Turned The Tables On Me
Holiday,Billie (voc) | Phillips,Flip (ts) | Peterson,Oscar (p) | Kessel,Barney (g) | Stoller,Alvin (dr)

Easy To Love | In My Solitude
Holiday,Billie (voc) | Shavers,Charlie (tp) | Peterson,Oscar (p) | Kessel,Barney (g) | Stoller,Alvin (dr)

You Go To My Head
Holiday,Billie (voc) | Peterson,Oscar (p) | Kessel,Barney (g) | Brown,Ray (b) | Stoller,Alvin (dr)

Billie Holiday-Oscar Peterson
These Foolish Things Remind Me On You
Holiday,Billie (voc) | Peterson,Oscar (p)

Love For Sale
Los Angeles,CA, rec. April 1952
Holiday,Billie (voc) | Peterson,Oscar (p)

Billie Holiday And Her Orchestra
If The Moon Turns Green
Holiday,Billie (voc) | Shavers,Charlie (tp) | Phillips,Flip (ts) | Peterson,Oscar (p) | Kessel,Barney (g) | Brown,Ray (b) | Heard,J.C. (dr)

Everything I Have Is Yours
Holiday,Billie (voc) | Phillips,Flip (ts) | Peterson,Oscar (p) | Kessel,Barney (g) | Brown,Ray (b) | Heard,J.C. (dr)

Moonglow
Holiday,Billie (voc) | Shavers,Charlie (tp) | Peterson,Oscar (p) | Kessel,Barney (g) | Brown,Ray (b) | Heard,J.C. (dr)

Tenderly | Remember | Autumn In New York | Autumn In New York(78 rpm-take)
Holiday,Billie (voc) | Peterson,Oscar (p) | Kessel,Barney (g) | Brown,Ray (b) | Heard,J.C. (dr)

519818-2 | CD | Verve Jazz Masters 1:Louis Armstrong
Louis Armstrong And His All Stars
When The Saints Go Marching In
Live at The Hollywood Bowl,Los Angeles,CA, rec. 15.8.1956
Armstrong,Louis (tp,voc) | Young,Trummy (tb) | Hall,Edmond (cl) | Kyle,Billy (p) | Jones,Dale (b) | Deems,Barrett (dr)

Louis Armstrong With The Oscar Peterson Quartet
Just One Of Those Things | That Old Feeling | Let's Do It(Let's Fall In Love) | Blues In The Night | I Was Doing Alright
Chicago,Ill, rec. 14.10.1957
Armstrong,Louis (tp,voc) | Peterson,Oscar (p) | Ellis,Herb (g) | Brown,Ray (b) | Bellson,Louie (dr)

Louis Armstrong With The Russell Garcia Orchestra
I Got A Right To Sing The Blues | You're The Top | Body And Soul | When Your Lover Has Gone | Home | I've Got The World On A String
Los Angeles,CA, rec. 14.8.1957
Armstrong,Louis (tp,voc) | Garcia,Russell (cond,arr) | details unknown

There's A Boat Dat's Leavin' Soon For New York
Los Angeles,CA, rec. 19.8.1957
Armstrong,Louis (tp,voc) | Garcia,Russell (cond,arr) | details unknown

Ella Fitzgerald And Louis Armstrong With The Oscar Peterson Quartet
Learnin' The Blues
Los Angeles,CA, rec. 22.7.1957
Armstrong,Louis (tp,voc) | Fitzgerald,Ella (voc) | Peterson,Oscar (p) | Ellis,Herb (g) | Brown,Ray (b) | Bellson,Louie (dr)

A Fine Romance
Los Angeles,CA, rec. 13.8.1957
Fitzgerald,Ella (voc) | Armstrong,Louis (voc) | Peterson,Oscar (p) | Ellis,Herb (g) | Brown,Ray (b) | Bellson,Louie (dr)

519819-2 | CD | Verve Jazz Masters 2:Count Basie
Count Basie And His Orchestra
Big Red
NYC, rec. 5.1.1956
Basie,Count (p) | Culley,Wendell (tp) | Jones,Quincy (tp) | Jones,Reunald (tp) | Jones,Thad (tp) | Newman,Joe (tp) | Coker,Henry (tb) | Hughes,Bill (tb) | Powell,Benny (tb) | Wess,Frank (fl,ts) | Royal,Marshall (cl,as) | Graham,Bill (as) | Foster,Frank (ts) | Fowlkes,Charlie (bs) | Green,Freddie (g) | Jones,Eddie (b) | Payne,Sonny (dr)

Polka Dots And Moonbeams | Sent For You Yesterday And Here You Come Today
Live at Newport,Rhode Island, rec. 7.7.1957
Basie,Count (p) | Culley,Wendell (tp) | Jones,Reunald (tp) | Jones,Thad (tp) | Newman,Joe (tp) | Coker,Henry (tb) | Hughes,Bill (tb) | Powell,Benny (tb) | Royal,Marshall (as) | Graham,Bill (as) | Young,Lester (ts) | Foster,Frank (ts) | Wess,Frank (fl,ts) | Fowlkes,Charlie (bs) | Green,Freddie (g) | Jones,Eddie (b) | Jones,Jo (dr) | Rushing,Jimmy (voc)

One O'Clock Jump
Basie,Count (p) | Eldridge,Roy (tp) | Culley,Wendell (tp) | Jones,Reunald (tp) | Jones,Thad (tp) | Newman,Joe (tp) | Coker,Henry (tb) | Hughes,Bill (tb) | Powell,Benny (tb) | Royal,Marshall (as) | Graham,Bill (as) | Young,Lester (ts) | Jacquet,Illinois (ts) | Foster,Frank (ts) | Wess,Frank (fl,ts) | Fowlkes,Charlie (bs) | Green,Freddie (g) | Jones,Eddie (b) | Jones,Jo (dr)

April In Paris | Shiny Stockings
NYC, rec. 26.7.1955
Basie,Count (p) | Culley,Wendell (tp) | Jones,Reunald (tp) | Jones,Thad (tp) | Newman,Joe (tp) | Coker,Henry (tb) | Hughes,Bill (tb) | Powell,Benny

(tb) | Royal,Marshall (as) | Graham,Bill (as) | Foster,Frank (ts) | Wess,Frank (fl,ts) | Fowlkes,Charlie (bs) | Green,Freddie (g) | Jones,Eddie (b) | Payne,Sonny (dr) | Davis,Wild Bill (arr)
Two Franks | Sterephonic
NYC, rec. 17.8.1954
Basie,Count (p) | Culley,Wendell (tp) | Jones,Reunald (tp) | Jones,Thad (tp) | Newman,Joe (tp) | Coker,Henry (tb) | Hughes,Bill (tb) | Powell,Benny (tb) | Royal,Marshall (cl,as) | Wilkins,Ernie (as,ts) | Foster,Frank (ts) | Wess,Frank (ts) | Fowlkes,Charlie (bs) | Green,Freddie (g) | Jones,Eddie (b) | Johnson,Gus (dr)
Count Basie Sextet
Royal Garden Blues | Blue And Sentimental | K.C.Organ Blues
NYC, rec. 15.12.1952
Basie,Count (p,org) | Newman,Joe (tp) | Quinichette,Paul (ts) | Green,Freddie (g) | Ramey,Gene (b) | Rich,Buddy (dr)
Midgets
NYC, rec. 4.1.1956
Basie,Count (p) | Newman,Joe (tp) | Wess,Frank (fl) | Green,Freddie (g) | Jones,Eddie (b) | Payne,Sonny (dr)
Count Basie And His Orchestra
Everyday I Have The Blues
NYC, rec. 17.5.1955
Basie,Count (p) | Culley,Wendell (tp) | Jones,Reunald (tp) | Jones,Thad (tp) | Newman,Joe (tp) | Coker,Henry (tb) | Hughes,Bill (tb) | Powell,Benny (tb) | Wess,Frank (fl,ts) | Royal,Marshall (cl,as) | Graham,Bill (as) | Foster,Frank (ts) | Fowlkes,Charlie (bs) | Green,Freddie (g) | Jones,Eddie (b) | Payne,Sonny (dr) | Wilkins,Ernie (arr) | Williams,Joe (voc)
Paradise Squat
NYC, rec. 22./23.7.1952
Basie,Count (org) | Culley,Wendell (tp) | Jones,Reunald (tp) | Campbell,Paul (tp) | Newman,Joe (tp) | Coker,Henry (tb) | Wilkins,Jimmy (tb) | Powell,Benny (tb) | Royal,Marshall (cl,as) | Davis,Eddie 'Lockjaw' (ts) | Wilkins,Ernie (as,ts) | Quinichette,Paul (ts) | Fowlkes,Charlie (bs) | Green,Freddie (g) | Lewis,Jimmy (b) | Johnson,Gus (dr)
Every Tub
NYC, rec. 25.1.1952
Basie,Count (p) | Culley,Wendell (tp) | Shavers,Charlie (tp) | Campbell,Paul (tp) | Newman,Joe (tp) | Coker,Henry (tb) | Wilkins,Jimmy (tb) | Powell,Benny (tb) | Royal,Marshall (cl,as) | Johnson,Floyd (ts) | Wilkins,Ernie (as,ts) | Quinichette,Paul (ts) | Fowlkes,Charlie (bs) | Green,Freddie (g) | Lewis,Jimmy (b) | Johnson,Gus (dr) | Hefti,Neal (arr)
Kansas City Wrinkles
NYC, rec. 21.4.1963
Basie,Count (tack-p) | Aarons,Albert 'Al' (tp) | Cohn[Cohen],Sonny (tp) | Rader,Don (tp) | Ricard,Fip (tp) | Young,Eugene 'Snooky' (tp) | Coker,Henry (tb) | Green,Urbie (tb) | Mitchell,Grover (tb) | Powell,Benny (tb) | Royal,Marshall (cl,as) | Dixon,Eric (as,ts) | Foster,Frank (ts) | Wess,Frank (ts) | Fowlkes,Charlie (bs) | Green,Freddie (g) | Catlett,Buddy (b) | Payne,Sonny (dr)

519820-2 | CD | Verve Jazz Masters 3:Chick Corea
Chick Corea's Return To Forever
You're Everything | Spain | Light As A Feather | Captain Marvel
London,GB, rec. October 1972
Corea,Chick (p,el-p) | Farrell,Joe (fl) | Clarke,Stanley (b) | Moreira,Airto (dr,perc) | Purim,Flora (voc)
Chick Corea
Space Circus(part 1)
NYC, rec. August 1973
Corea,Chick (keyboards)
Chick Corea-Stanley Clarke
Interplay
NYC, rec. July/August 1974
Corea,Chick (p) | Clarke,Stanley (b)
Chick Corea Quartet
Nite Sprite
NYC, rec. 1975
Corea,Chick (keyboards) | Farrell,Joe (ss) | Jackson,Anthony (b) | Gadd,Steve (dr)
Chick Corea Group
Lenore
Corea,Chick (keyboards) | Gadd,Steve (dr) | Moran,Gayle (voc)
Wind Danse
Burbank,Los Angeles,CA, rec. October 1976
Corea,Chick (keyboards) | Gadd,Steve (dr) | Moran,Gayle (voc)
My Spanish Heart
Corea,Chick (keyboards) | Moran,Gayle (voc)
Night Street
Corea,Chick (keyboards) | Blumberg,Stuart (tp) | Rosenberg,John (tp) | Thomas,John (tp) | Moss,Ron (tb) | Clarke,Stanley (b) | Gadd,Steve (dr) | Alias,Don (perc)
Chick Corea With String Quartet
Tweedle Dee
Burbank,Los Angeles,CA, rec. 1978
Corea,Chick (p) | Veal Jr.,Charles (v) | Yerke,Ken (v) | Buffum,Denyse (viola) | Karmazyn,Dennis (cello)
Chick Corea Trio
Children's Song(No.15)
Corea,Chick (p) | Farrell,Joe (fl) | Gomez,Eddie (b)
Chick Corea Quartet
Friends
Corea,Chick (el-p) | Farrell,Joe (fl) | Gomez,Eddie (b) | Gadd,Steve (dr)

519821-2 | CD | Verve Jazz Masters 5:Bill Evans
Bill Evans Trio
Let's Go Back To The Waltz
NYC, rec. 14.8.1962
Evans,Bill (p) | Budwig,Monty (b) | Manne,Shelly (dr)
Bill Evans
N.Y.C.'s No Lark
NYC, rec. 6.2.1963
Evans,Bill (p,overdubbed)
Just You Just Me | Bemsha Swing
NYC, rec. 9.2.1963
Evans,Bill (p,overdubbed)
Bill Evans Trio
A Sleeping Bee
NYC, rec. 18.12.1963
Evans,Bill (p) | Peacock,Gary (b) | Motian,Paul (dr)
Stan Getz With The Bill Evans Trio
Funkallero
NYC, rec. 6.5.1964
Getz,Stan (ts) | Evans,Bill (p) | Carter,Ron (b) | Jones,Elvin (dr)
Bill Evans Trio
Israel
NYC, rec. 3.2.1965
Evans,Bill (p) | Israels,Chuck (b) | Bunker,Larry (dr)
Bill Evans-Jim Hall
Angel Face
Englewood Cliffs,NJ, rec. 10.5.1966
Evans,Bill (p) | Hall,Jim (g)
Bill Evans
Quiet Now
NYC, rec. 9.8.1967
Evans,Bill (p,overdubbed)
Bill Evans Trio
Alfie | On Green Dolphin Street
Live at The 'Village Vanguard',NYC, rec. 17./18.8.1967
Evans,Bill (p) | Gomez,Eddie (b) | Jones,Philly Joe (dr)
Mother Of Earl
Live at The Montreux Jazz Festival, rec. 15.6.1968
Evans,Bill (p) | Gomez,Eddie (b) | DeJohnette,Jack (dr)
Bill Evans
Here's That Rainy Day
NYC, rec. 12.12.1969
Evans,Bill (p-solo)

519822-2 | CD | Verve Jazz Masters 6:Ella Fitzgerald
Ella Fitzgerald And The Paul Smith Quartet
Everything I've Got
Los Angeles,CA, rec. 4.9.1956
Fitzgerald,Ella (voc) | Smith,Paul (p) | Kessel,Barney (g) | Mondragon,Joe (b) | Stoller,Alvin (dr)
Ella Fitzgerald With The Duke Ellington Orchestra
I Ain't Got Nothin' But The Blues
NYC, rec. 25.6.1957
Fitzgerald,Ella (voc) | Ellington,Duke (p) | Anderson,Cat (tp) | Cook,Willie (tp) | Terry,Clark (tp) | Nance,Ray (tp,v) | Jackson,Quentin (tb) | Woodman,Britt (tb) | Sanders,John (tb) | Hamilton,Jimmy (cl,ts) | Procope,Russell (cl,as) | Hodges,Johnny (as) | Gonsalves,Paul (ts) | Foster,Frank (ts) | Carney,Harry (cl,b-cl,bs) | Woode,Jimmy (b) | Woodyard,Sam (dr)
Ella Fitzgerald With The Oscar Peterson Quartet
These Foolish Things Remind Me On You
Los Angeles,CA, rec. 23.7.1957
Fitzgerald,Ella (voc) | Peterson,Oscar (p) | Ellis,Herb (g) | Brown,Ray (b) | Bellson,Louie (dr)
Ella Fitzgerald With Frank De Vol And His Orchestra
A-Tisket A-Tasket
Los Angeles,CA, rec. 24.7.1957
Fitzgerald,Ella (voc) | DeVol,Frank (cond,arr) | details unknown
Ella Fitzgerald And Louis Armstrong With The Oscar Peterson Quartet
I'm Putting All My Eggs In One Basket
Los Angeles,CA, rec. 13.8.1957
Fitzgerald,Ella (voc) | Armstrong,Louis (tp,voc) | Peterson,Oscar (p) | Ellis,Herb (g) | Brown,Ray (b) | Bellson,Louie (dr)
Ella Fitzgerald With Russell Garcia And His Orchestra
I Loves You Porgy
Los Angeles,CA, rec. 28.8.1957
Fitzgerald,Ella (voc) | Garcia,Russell (cond,arr) | details unknown
Ella Fitzgerald With Frank De Vol And His Orchestra
I Never Had A Chance
Los Angeles,CA, rec. 15.10.1957
Fitzgerald,Ella (voc) | DeVol,Frank (cond,arr) | details unknown
Ella Fitzgerald With Paul Weston And His Orchestra
Heat Wave
Los Angeles,CA, rec. 18.3.1958
Fitzgerald,Ella (voc) | Weston,Paul (cond,arr) | details unknown
Ella Fitzgerald With The Marty Paich Dek-tette
Just You Just Me
Los Angeles,CA, rec. 22.11.1958
Fitzgerald,Ella (voc) | Fagerquist,Don (tp) | Porcino,Al (tp) | DeRosa,Vince (fr-h) | Enevoldsen,Bob (v-tb,ts) | Kitzmiller,John (tuba) | Shank,Bud (as) | Holman,Bill (ts) | Flory,Med (bs) | Levy,Lou (p) | Mondragon,Joe (b) | Lewis,Mel (dr) | Paich,Marty (arr,ld)
Ella Fitzgerald With The Paul Smith Quartet
Mack The Knife(Moritat) | How High The Moon
Berlin, rec. 13.2.1960
Fitzgerald,Ella (voc) | Smith,Paul (p) | Hall,Jim (g) | Middlebrooks,Wilfred (b) | Johnson,Gus (dr)
Ella Fitzgerald With The Billy May Orchestra
The Man That Got Away | I've Got The World On A String
Los Angeles,CA, rec. 1.8.1960
Fitzgerald,Ella (voc) | May,Billy (arr,ld) | Fagerquist,Don (tp) | Bernhart,Milton 'Milt' (tb) | Nash,Dick (tb) | Carter,Benny (as) | Nash,Ted (as) | Johnson,Plas (ts) | Bunker,Larry (vib) | Smith,Paul (p) | Hendrickson,Al (g) | Collins,John (g) | Mondragon,Joe (b) | Stoller,Alvin (dr) | details unknown
Ella Fitzgerald With The Lou Levy Quartet
Signing Off
Los Angeles,CA, rec. 23.6.1961
Fitzgerald,Ella (voc) | Levy,Lou (p) | Ellis,Herb (g) | Mondragon,Joe (b) | Levey,Stan (dr)
Ella Fitzgerald With The Nelson Riddle Orchestra
I Hear Music
Los Angeles,CA, rec. 14.11.1961
Fitzgerald,Ella (voc) | Lang,Ronnie (as) | Riddle,Nelson (arr,ld) | details unknown
Ella Fitzgerald And Her All Stars
In The Evening When The Sun Goes Down
NYC, rec. 29.10.1963
Fitzgerald,Ella (voc) | Eldridge,Roy (tp) | Davis,Wild Bill (org) | Ellis,Herb (g) | Brown,Ray (b) | Johnson,Gus (dr)

519823-2 | CD | Verve Jazz Masters 8:Stan Getz
Stan Getz Quintet
Body And Soul
NYC, rec. 12.12.1952
Getz,Stan (ts) | Jordan,Duke (p) | Raney,Jimmy (g) | Crow,Bill (b) | Isola,Frank (dr)
Gladys
Los Angeles,CA, rec. 1.8.1955
Getz,Stan (ts) | Hampton,Lionel (vib) | Levy,Lou (p) | Vinnegar,Leroy (b) | Manne,Shelly (dr)
Shine
Los Angeles,CA, rec. 15.8.1955
Getz,Stan (ts) | Candoli,Conte (tp) | Levy,Lou (p) | Vinnegar,Leroy (b) | Manne,Shelly (dr)
Stan Getz With The Oscar Peterson Quartet
It Never Entered My Mind
Live at The 'Opera House',Chicago,Ill, rec. 19.10.1957
Getz,Stan (ts) | Peterson,Oscar (p) | Ellis,Herb (g) | Brown,Ray (b) | Kay,Connie (dr)
Stan Getz Quartet
Jordu
Chicago,Ill, rec. 16.2.1958
Getz,Stan (ts) | Christian,Jodie (p) | Sproles,Victor (b) | Thompson,Marshall (dr)
Stan Getz With The Eddie Sauter Orchestra
Her
NYC, rec. Fall 1961
Getz,Stan (ts) | Beaux-Arts String Quartet,The | Martin,Allan (v) | Tarack,Gerald (v) | unkn. (v) | Glick,Jacob (viola) | Rogers,Buce (cello) | unkn. (cello) | Sauter,Eddie (arr) | Kay,Hershy (ld) | details unknown
Stan Getz Sextet
Desafinado
Washington,DC, rec. 13.2.1962
Getz,Stan (ts) | Byrd,Charlie (g) | Betts,Keter (b) | Byrd,Gene (b) | Deppenschmidt,Buddy (dr) | Reichenbach,Bill (dr)
Stan Getz Quintet Feat. Astrud Gilberto
Girl From Ipanema(Garota De Ipanema)
NYC, rec. 18./19.3.1963
Getz,Stan (ts) | Gilberto,Joao (g,voc) | Jobim,Antonio Carlos (p) | Williams,Tommy (b) | Banana,Milton (dr) | Gilberto,Astrud (voc)
Stan Getz Quartet
Window
NYC, rec. 30.3.1967
Getz,Stan (ts) | Corea,Chick (p) | Carter,Ron (b) | Tate,Grady (dr)
Dynasty
Live at Ronnie Scott's,London,GB, rec. 15.-17.3.1971
Getz,Stan (ts) | Louiss,Eddie (org) | Thomas,Rene (g) | Lubat,Bernard (dr)

519824-2 | CD | Verve Jazz Masters 9:Astrud Gilberto
Astrud Gilberto With The Marty Paich Orchestra
Vivo Sohando | Agua De Beber(Water To Drink) | Dindi
Los Angeles,CA, rec. 27./28.1.1965
Gilberto,Astrud (voc) | Williamson,Stu (tp) | Bernhart,Milton 'Milt' (tb) | Shank,Bud (fl,as) | Donato,Joao (p) | Mondragon,Joe (b) | Jobim,Antonio Carlos (g,voc) | Paich,Marty (arr,ld) | details unknown
Astrud Gilberto With The New Stan Getz Quartet
Girl From Ipanema(Garota De Ipanema) | Corcovado(Quiet Nights)
Live at Carnegie Hall,NYC, rec. 9.10.1964
Gilberto,Astrud (voc) | Getz,Stan (ts) | Burton,Gary (vib) | Gilberto,Joao (g,voc) | Cherico,Gene (b) | Hunt,Joe (dr)
Astrud Gilberto With The Gil Evans Orchestra
Once Upon A Summertime | Berimbau
NYC, rec. 23.12.1965
Gilberto,Astrud (voc) | Coles,Johnny (tp) | Brookmeyer,Bob (tb) | Burrell,Kenny (g) | Evans,Gil (p,cond,arr) | Tate,Grady (dr) | details unknown
Frevo
NYC, rec. 22.11.1965
Gilberto,Astrud (voc) | Coles,Johnny (tp) | Brookmeyer,Bob (tb) | Burrell,Kenny (g) | Evans,Gil (p,cond,arr) | Tate,Grady (dr) | details unknown
Astrud Gilberto With The Al Cohn Orchestra
Felicidade | Look To The Rainbow
NYC, rec. 6.12.1965
Gilberto,Astrud (voc) | Coles,Johnny (tp) | Brookmeyer,Bob (tb) | Burrell,Kenny (g) | Tate,Grady (dr) | Cohn,Al (arr,ld) | details unknown
Astrud Gilberto With The Walter Wanderley Quuitet
A Certain Sadness | Tristeza
NYC, rec. 21.9.1966
Gilberto,Astrud (voc) | Wanderley,Walter (org) | unkn. (g) | Marino,Jose (b) | Slon,Claudio (dr) | Rosengarden,Bobby (perc)
Astrud Gilberto With The Claus Ogerman Orchestra
Day By Day
NYC, rec. 4.2.1965
Gilberto,Astrud (voc) | Green,Urbie (tb) | Ogerman,Claus (cond,arr) | details unknown
Astrud Gilberto With The Don Sebesky Orchestra
The Shadow Of Your Smile | Take Me To Aruanda | The Gentle Rain (Chuva Delicada)
Los Angeles,CA, rec. 3.6.1965
Gilberto,Astrud (voc) | Winding,Kai (tb) | Strings | Sebesky,Don (cond,arr) | details unknown

519825-2 | CD | Verve Jazz Masters 12:Billie Holiday
Billie Holiday And Her All Stars
Blue Moon | Remember | Autumn In New York
Los Angeles,CA, rec. Late Spring 1952
Holiday,Billie (voc) | Shavers,Charlie (tp) | Phillips,Flip (ts) | Peterson,Oscar (p) | Kessel,Barney (g) | Brown,Ray (b) | Stoller,Alvin (dr)
Yesterdays
NYC, rec. 27.7.1952
Holiday,Billie (voc) | Quinichette,Paul (ts) | Peterson,Oscar (org) | Green,Freddie (g) | Brown,Ray (b) | Johnson,Gus (dr)
Lover Come Back To Me
Holiday,Billie (voc) | Newman,Joe (tp) | Quinichette,Paul (ts) | Peterson,Oscar (p) | Green,Freddie (g) | Brown,Ray (b) | Johnson,Gus (dr)
What A Little Moonlight Can Do
NYC, rec. 14.4.1954
Holiday,Billie (voc) | Shavers,Charlie (tp) | Ellis,Herb (g) | Peterson,Oscar (p) | Brown,Ray (b) | Shaughnessy,Ed (dr)
Willow Weep For Me | P.S.I Love You | Los Angeles Blues
rec. 3.9.1954
Holiday,Billie (voc) | Edison,Harry 'Sweets' (tp) | Smith,Willie (as) | Tucker,Bobby (p) | Kessel,Barney (g) | Callender,Red (b) | Hamilton,Forrest 'Chico' (dr)
Nice Work If You Can Get It | Please Don't Talk About Me When I'm Gone
Los Angeles,CA, rec. 23.8.1955
Holiday,Billie (voc) | Edison,Harry 'Sweets' (tp) | Carter,Benny (as) | Rowles,Jimmy (p) | Kessel,Barney (g) | Simmons,John (b) | Bunker,Larry (dr)
A Fine Romance
Los Angeles,CA, rec. 25.8.1955
Holiday,Billie (voc) | Edison,Harry 'Sweets' (tp) | Carter,Benny (as) | Rowles,Jimmy (p) | Kessel,Barney (g) | Simmons,John (b) | Bunker,Larry (dr)
Some Other Spring | Good Morning Heartache | God Bless The Child
NYC, rec. 6./7.7.1956
Holiday,Billie (voc) | Shavers,Charlie (tp) | Scott,Tony (cl) | Quinichette,Paul (ts) | Kelly,Wynton (p) | Burrell,Kenny (g) | Bell,Aaron (b) | McBrowne,Lennie (dr)
Speak Low
Los Angeles,CA, rec. 14.8.1956
Holiday,Billie (voc) | Webster,Ben (ts) | Rowles,Jimmy (p) | Kessel,Barney (g) | Mondragon,Joe (b) | Stoller,Alvin (dr)
All Or Nothing At All
Los Angeles,CA, rec. 18.8.1956
Holiday,Billie (voc) | Edison,Harry 'Sweets' (tp) | Webster,Ben (ts) | Rowles,Jimmy (p) | Kessel,Barney (g) | Mitchell,Red (b) | Stoller,Alvin (dr)

519826-2 | CD | Verve Jazz Masters 14:Wes Montgomery
Wes Montgomery With The Johnny Pate Orchestra
Caravan | Twisted Blues
NYC, rec. 11.or 16.11.1964
Montgomery,Wes (g) | Pate,Johnny (cond,arr) | Royal,Ernie (tp) | Terry,Clark (tp) | Young,Eugene 'Snooky' (tp) | Cleveland,Jimmy (tb) | Green,Urbie (tb) | Jackson,Quentin (tb) | Welsch,Chauncey (tb) | Butterfield,Don (tuba) | Richardson,Jerome (reeds) | Scott,Bobby (p) | Cranshaw,Bob (b) | Tate,Grady (dr) | Bobo,Willie (perc)
Wes Montgomery With The Oliver Nelson Orchestra
Goin' Out Of My Head
Englewood Cliffs,NJ, rec. 20.11.1965
Montgomery,Wes (g) | Nelson,Oliver (arr,ld) | Byrd,Donald (tp) | Newman,Joe (tp) | Royal,Ernie (tp) | Andre,Wayne (tb) | Cleveland,Jimmy (tb) | Jackson,Quentin (tb) | Moore,Danny (tp) | Studd,Tony (tb) | Ashton,Bob (reeds) | Woods,Phil (as) | Dodgion,Jerry (as) | Penque,Romeo (ts) | Bank,Danny (bs) | Hancock,Herbie (p) | Duvivier,George (b) | Tate,Grady (dr) | Candido[Camero] (congas)
Wes Montgomery Quartet
Impressions | No Blues
Live at The Half Note Cafe,NYC, rec. June 1965
Montgomery,Wes (g) | Kelly,Wynton (p) | Chambers,Paul (b) | Cobb,Jimmy (dr)
Wes Montgomery With The Don Sebesky Orchestra
My One And Only Love | Bumpin' | The Shadow Of Your Smile | Con Alma
Englewood Cliffs,NJ, rec. 20.5.1965
Montgomery,Wes (g) | Kellaway,Roger (p) | Eidus,Arnold (v) | Eley,Lewis (v) | Gershman,Paul (v) | Haber,Louis (v) | Held,Julius (v) | Lookofsky,Harry (v) | Malignaggi,Joseph (v) | Orloff,Gene (v) | Shapiro,Sol (v) | Coletta,Harold (viola) | Schwartz,David (viola) | McCracken,Charles (cello) | Ricci,George (cello) | Cranshaw,Bob (b) | Ross,Margaret (harp) | Candido[Camero] (congas,bongos) | Milito,Helcio or Grady Tate (dr) | Sebesky,Don (cond,arr)
Wes Montgomery Quartet
Tequilla | The Thumb
Englewood Cliffs,NJ, rec. 21.3.1966
Montgomery,Wes (g) | Carter,Ron (b) | Tate,Grady (dr) | Barretto,Ray (congas)
What The World Needs Now Is Love
Englewood Cliffs,NJ, rec. March 1966
Montgomery,Wes (g) | Devens,George (vib) | Carter,Ron (b) | Tate,Grady (dr)
Wes Montgomery With The Claus Ogerman Orchestra
Bumpin' On Sunset
Englewood Cliffs,NJ, rec. 17.3.1966
Montgomery,Wes (g) | Ogerman,Claus (cond,arr) | Devens,George (vib) | Carter,Ron (b) | Tate,Grady (dr) | Barretto,Ray (perc) | Eichen,Bernard (v) | Eidus,Arnold (v) | Gersham,Paul (v) | Green,Emmanuel (v) | Held,Julius (v) | Lookofsky,Harry (v) | Malin,Joe (v) | Orloff,Gene (v) | Kessler,Abe (cello) | McCracken,Charles (cello) | Ricci,George (cello) | Shapiro,Harvey (cello)
Wes Montgomery With The Don Sebesky Orchestra
Oh! You Crazy Moon
Englewood Cliffs,NJ, rec. 16.9.1966
Montgomery,Wes (g) | Davis,Mel (tp) | Glow,Bernie (tp) | Nottingham,Jimmy (tp) | Andre,Wayne (tb) | Messner,John (tb) | Watrous,Bill (tb) | Buffington,Jimmy (fr-h) | Butterfield,Don (tuba) | Beckenstein,Ray (reeds) | Webb,Stanley (reeds) | Kane,Walter (reeds) | Casamenti,Al (g) | Pizzarelli,Bucky (g) | Jennings,Jack (vib,perc) | Davis,Richard (b) | Tate,Grady (dr,perc) | Barretto,Ray (perc)

519850-2 | CD | Gerry Mulligan-Paul Desmond Quartet
Gerry Mulligan-Paul Desmond Quartet

Blues In Time | Body And Soul | Winter Song | Tea For Two | Winter Song(alt.take) | Lover
Los Angeles,CA, rec. 2.8.1957
Desmond,Paul (as) | Mulligan,Gerry (bs) | Benjamin,Joe (b) | Bailey,Dave (dr)
Stand Still | Line For Lyons | Battle Hymn Of The Republican | Fall Out
NYC, rec. 27.8.1957
Desmond,Paul (as) | Mulligan,Gerry (bs) | Benjamin,Joe (b) | Bailey,Dave (dr)

519852-2 | CD | Count Basie Swings-Joe Williams Sings
Count Basie And His Orchestra
Everyday I Have The Blues | The Comeback | Allright Okay You Win | In The Evening When The Sun Goes Down | Roll 'Em Pete | Teach Me Tonight | My Baby Upsets Me | Please Send Me Someone To Love | Everyday(I Fall In Love)
NYC, rec. 26./27.7.1955
Basie,Count (p) | Culley,Wendell (tp) | Jones,Reunald (tp) | Jones,Thad (tp) | Newman,Joe (tp) | Coker,Henry (tb) | Hughes,Bill (tb) | Powell,Benny (tb) | Royal,Marshall (cl,as) | Graham,Bill (as) | Wess,Frank (fl,ts) | Foster,Frank (ts,arr) | Fowlkes,Charlie (bs) | Green,Freddie (g) | Jones,Eddie (b) | Payne,Sonny (dr) | Williams,Joe (voc)
As I Love You | Stop! Don't!
Chicago,Ill, rec. 23.1.1956
Basie,Count (p) | Culley,Wendell (tp) | Jones,Reunald (tp) | Jones,Thad (tp) | Newman,Joe (tp) | Coker,Henry (tb) | Hughes,Bill (tb) | Powell,Benny (tb) | Royal,Marshall (cl,as) | Graham,Bill (as) | Wess,Frank (fl,ts) | Foster,Frank (ts,arr) | Fowlkes,Charlie (bs) | Green,Freddie (g) | Jones,Eddie (b) | Payne,Sonny (dr) | Williams,Joe (voc)
Too Close For Comfort
NYC, rec. 27.6.1956
Basie,Count (p) | Culley,Wendell (tp) | Jones,Reunald (tp) | Jones,Thad (tp) | Newman,Joe (tp) | Coker,Henry (tb) | Hughes,Bill (tb) | Powell,Benny (tb) | Royal,Marshall (cl,as) | Graham,Bill (as) | Wess,Frank (fl,ts) | Foster,Frank (ts,arr) | Fowlkes,Charlie (bs) | Green,Freddie (g) | Jones,Eddie (b) | Payne,Sonny (dr) | Williams,Joe (voc)

519853-2 | CD | Verve Jazz Masters 20:Introducing
Louis Armstrong With The Oscar Peterson Quartet
Just One Of Those Things
Chicago,Ill, rec. 14.10.1957
Armstrong,Louis (tp,voc) | Peterson,Oscar (p) | Ellis,Herb (g) | Brown,Ray (b) | Bellson,Louie (dr)
Oscar Peterson Trio
Woody'n You
Chicago,Ill, rec. August 1957
Peterson,Oscar (p) | Brown,Ray (b) | Thigpen,Ed (dr)
Sarah Vaughan With The Clifford Brown All Stars
Lullaby Of Birdland
NYC, rec. 16.12.1954
Vaughan,Sarah (voc) | Brown,Clifford (tp) | Mann,Herbie (fl) | Quinichette,Paul (ts) | Jones,Jimmy (p) | Benjamin,Joe (b) | Haynes,Roy (dr) | Wilkins,Rick (cond,arr)
Dizzy Gillespie And His Orchestra
Tour De Force
NYC, rec. 25.5./6.6.1956
Gillespie,Dizzy (tp,voc) | Gordon,Joe (tp) | Perry,Ermit V. (tp) | Warwick,Carl (tp) | Jones,Quincy (tp) | Liston,Melba (tb) | Rehak,Frank (tb) | Levitt,Rod (tb) | Powell,Jimmy (as) | Woods,Phil (as) | Michell,Billy (ts) | Wilkins,Ernie (ts) | Flax,Marty (bs) | Davis Jr.,Walter (p) | Boyd,Nelson (b) | Persip,Charles (dr)
Getz-Gilberto Quintet
Girl From Ipanema(Garota De Ipanema)
NYC, rec. 18./19.3.1963
Getz,Stan (ts) | Jobim,Antonio Carlos (p) | Gilberto,Joao (g,voc) | Williams,Tommy (b) | Banana,Milton (dr) | Gilberto,Astrud (voc)
Duke Ellington And His Orchestra
Diminuendo In Blue- | Blow By Blow-
Juan Les Pins,France, rec. 26./27.7.1956
Ellington,Duke (p) | Anderson,Cat (tp) | Williams,Cootie (tp) | Jones,Herbie (tp) | Ellington,Mercer (tp) | Nance,Ray (tp,v) | Connors,Chuck (tb) | Cooper,Frank 'Buster' (tb) | Hamilton,Jimmy (cl,ts) | Procope,Russell (as) | Hodges,Johnny (as) | Gonsalves,Paul (ts) | Carney,Harry (bs) | Lamb,John (b) | Woodyard,Sam (dr)
Chick Corea Quartet
Captain Marvel
London,GB, rec. October 1972
Corea,Chick (el-p) | Farrell,Joe (fl) | Clarke,Stanley (b) | Moreira,Airto (dr,perc) | Purim,Flora (voc)
Ella Fitzgerald With The Paul Smith Quartet
Everything I've Got
Los Angeles,CA, rec. 4.9.1956
Fitzgerald,Ella (voc) | Smith,Paul (p) | Kessel,Barney (g) | Mondragon,Joe (b) | Stoller,Alvin (dr)
Wes Montgomery Quartet
Impressions
Live at The Half Note Cafe,NYC, rec. June 1965
Montgomery,Wes (g) | Kelly,Wynton (p) | Chambers,Paul (b) | Cobb,Jimmy (dr)
Nina Simone Quartet
Love Me Or Leave Me
NYC, rec. 30.9./1.10.1965
Simone,Nina (p,voc) | Stevenson,Rudy (fl,g) | Atkinson,Lisle (b) | Hamilton,Bobby (dr)
Charlie Parker Quartet
Star Eyes
NYC, rec. March/April 1950
Parker,Charlie (as) | Jones,Hank (p) | Brown,Ray (b) | Rich,Buddy (dr)
Bill Evans
Here's That Rainy Day
NYC, rec. 12.12.1959
Evans,Bill (p-solo)
Dinah Washington With The Belford Hendricks Orchestra
What A Difference A Day Made
NYC, rec. 19.2.1959
Washington,Dinah (voc) | Richardson,Jerome (reeds) | Davis,Charles (bs) | Hinton,Milt (b) | Francis,Panama (dr) | Hendricks,Belford (arr,ld) | details unknown
Erroll Garner Quartet
Misty
Chicago/Hollywood/NYC, rec. 27.7.1954
Garner,Erroll (p) | Ruther,Wyatt (b) | Heard,Eugene 'Fats' (dr) | Candido[Camero] (congas)
Billie Holiday And Her All Stars
A Fine Romance
Los Angeles,CA, rec. 25.8.1955
Holiday,Billie (voc) | Edison,Harry 'Sweets' (tp) | Carter,Benny (as) | Rowles,Jimmy (p) | Kessel,Barney (g) | Simmons,John (b) | Bunker,Larry (dr)
Count Basie And His Orchestra
April In Paris
NYC, rec. 26.7.1955
Basie,Count (p) | Culley,Wendell (tp) | Jones,Reunald (tp) | Jones,Thad (tp) | Newman,Joe (tp) | Coker,Henry (tb) | Hughes,Bill (tb) | Powell,Benny (tb) | Royal,Marshall (as) | Graham,Bill (as) | Foster,Frank (ts) | Wess,Frank (fl,ts) | Fowlkes,Charlie (bs) | Green,Freddie (g) | Jones,Eddie (b) | Payne,Sonny (dr)

519857-2 | CD | Juicy
Willie Bobo Group
Knock On Wood | Mating Call | Mercy, Mercy, Mercy | Felicidade | La Descarga Del Bobo | Juicy | Ain't Too Proud To Beg | Music To Watch Girls By | Dreams | Dis-Advantages | Roots | Shing-A-Ling Baby | Juicy(alt.take) | Music To Watch Girls By(alt.take) | Dis-Advantages(alt.take) | Shing-A-Ling Baby(alt.take)
NYC, rec. January 1967
Bobo,Willie (timbales,voc) | prob.personal: | Lastie,Melvin (co) | unkn. (tb) | Brown,Bob 'Bobby' (as,ts) | Henry,Sonny (g) | unkn. (b,dr,guiro)

519861-2 | CD | Time Remembered:John McLaughlin Plays Bill Evans
John McLaughlin With The Aighette Quartet And Yan Marez
Prologue | Very Early | Only Child | Waltz For Debby | Homage | My Bells | Time Remembered | SongFor Helen | Turn Out The Stars | We Will Met Again | Epilogue
Milano,Italy, rec. 25.-28.3.1993
McLaughlin,John (g) | Aighetta Quartet,The | Szonyi,Francois (g) | Rabatti,Pascal (g) | Del Fa,Alexandre (g) | Loli,Philippe (g) | Maresz,Yan (b-g)

519905-2 | CD | My Gentleman Friend | EAN 731451990526
Blossom Dearie Quintet
Chez Moi | Boum | L'Etang
NYC, rec. 8./9.4.1959
Dearie,Blossom (p,voc) | Jaspar,Bobby (fl) | Burrell,Kenny (g) | Brown,Ray (b) | Thigpen,Ed (dr)
Blossom Dearie Quartet
Little Jazz Bird | My Gentleman Friend | It's Too Good To Talk About Now | You Fascinate Me So | You've Got Something I Want | Hello Love | Someone To Watch Over Me
NYC, rec. 1.5.1959
Dearie,Blossom (p,voc) | Burrell,Kenny (g) | Brown,Ray (b) | Thigpen,Ed (dr)

521402-2 | CD | April In Paris
Count Basie And His Orchestra
April In Paris | April In Paris(alt.take) | Corner Pocket | Corner Pocket(alt.take) | Didn't You | Didn't You(alt.take) | Sweety Cakes
rec. 26./27.7.1955
Basie,Count (p) | Culley,Wendell (tp) | Jones,Reunald (tp) | Jones,Thad (tp) | Newman,Joe (tp) | Coker,Henry (tb) | Hughes,Bill (tb) | Powell,Benny (tb) | Royal,Marshall (as) | Graham,Bill (as) | Wess,Frank (fl,ts) | Foster,Frank (ts) | Fowlkes,Charlie (bs) | Green,Freddie (g) | Jones,Eddie (b) | Payne,Sonny (dr)
Magic | Magic(alt.take 1) | Magic(alt.take 2) | Shiny Stockings | What Am I Here For | What Am I Here For(alt.take)
rec. 4.1.1956
Basie,Count (p) | Culley,Wendell (tp) | Jones,Reunald (tp) | Jones,Thad (tp) | Newman,Joe (tp) | Coker,Henry (tb) | Hughes,Bill (tb) | Powell,Benny (tb) | Royal,Marshall (as) | Graham,Bill (as) | Wess,Frank (fl,ts) | Foster,Frank (ts) | Fowlkes,Charlie (bs) | Green,Freddie (g) | Jones,Eddie (b) | Payne,Sonny (dr)
Midgets | Midgets(alt.take)
NYC, rec. 4.1.1956
Basie,Count (p) | Newman,Joe (tp) | Wess,Frank (fl,ts) | Green,Freddie (g) | Jones,Eddie (b) | Payne,Sonny (dr)
Mambo Inn | Dinner With Friends
rec. 5.1.1956
Basie,Count (p) | Culley,Wendell (tp) | Jones,Reunald (tp) | Jones,Thad (tp) | Newman,Joe (tp) | Baker,Harold 'Shorty' (tp) | Coker,Henry (tb) | Hughes,Bill (tb) | Powell,Benny (tb) | Royal,Marshall (as) | Graham,Bill (as) | Wess,Frank (fl,ts) | Foster,Frank (ts) | Fowlkes,Charlie (bs) | Green,Freddie (g) | Jones,Eddie (b) | Payne,Sonny (dr)

521403-2 | CD | Guitar Forms
Kenny Burrell With The Gil Evans Orchestra
Lotus Land | Moon And Sand | Loie | Greensleeves | Last Night When We Were Young
Englewood Cliffs,NJ, rec. 4 & 15.12.1964/5 & 12.4.1965
Burrell,Kenny (g) | Coles,Johnny (tp) | Mucci,Louis (tp) | Cleveland,Jimmy (tb) | Knepper,Jimmy (tb) | Fitzgerald,Andy (engl-h,fl) | Beckenstein,Ray (fl,as) | Marge,George (engl-h,fl) | Kamuca,Richie (ts,oboe) | Konitz,Lee (as) | Lacy,Steve (ss) | Tricarico,Bob (fl,ts,bassoon) | Alonge,Ray (fr-h) | Watkins,Julius (fr-h) | Barber,Bill (tuba) | Carter,Ron (b) | Jones,Elvin (dr) | Persip,Charles (dr)
Kenny Burrell Quintet
Downstairs | Downstairs(alt.take 1) | Downstairs(alt.take 2) | Downstairs(alt.take 3) | Downstairs(alt.take 4) | Terrace Theme | Terrace Theme(alt.take 1) | Terrace Theme(alt.take 2) | Terrace Theme(alt.take 3) | Bread Winner | Bread Winner(alt.take 1) | Bread Winner(alt.take 2) | Bread Winner(alt.take 3) | Bread Winner(alt.take 4)
Burrell,Kenny (g) | Kellaway,Roger (p) | Benjamin,Joe (b) | Tate,Grady (dr) | Rodriguez,Willie (congas)
Excerpts From Prelude No.2
Burrell,Kenny (g-solo)

521404-2 | CD | Back To Back
Duke Ellington-Johnny Hodges All Stars
Basin Street Blues | Beale Street Blues | St.Louis Blues | Loveless Love | Royal Garden Blues
NYC, rec. 20.2.1959
Hodges,Johnny (as) | Ellington,Duke (p) | Edison,Harry 'Sweets' (tp) | Spann,Les (g) | Jones,Sam (b) | Jones,Jo (dr)
Wabash Blues | Weary Blues
Hodges,Johnny (as) | Ellington,Duke (p) | Edison,Harry 'Sweets' (tp) | Spann,Les (g) | Hall,Al (b) | Jones,Jo (dr)

521405-2 | CD | Side By Side
Duke Ellington And Johnny Hodges Orchestra
Stompy Jones | Squeeze Me | Going Up
Hodges,Johnny (as) | Ellington,Duke (p) | Edison,Harry 'Sweets' (tp) | Spann,Les (g) | Hall,Al (b) | Jones,Jo (dr)
Johnny Hodges Orchestra
Big Shoe | Just A Memory | Let's Fall In Love | Ruint | Bend One | You Need To Rock
NYC, rec. 14.8.1958
Hodges,Johnny (as) | Eldridge,Roy (tp) | Brown,Lawrence (tb) | Webster,Ben (ts) | Strayhorn,Billy (p) | Marshall,Wendell (b) | Jones,Jo (dr)

521409-2 | CD | Conversations With Myself
Bill Evans
Round About Midnight | How About You | Spartacus Love Theme | Blue Monk | Stella By Starlight | Hey There | N.Y.C.'s No Lark | Just You Just Me | Bemsha Swing | A Sleeping Bee
NYC, rec. 6./9.& 20.2.1963
Evans,Bill (p,overdubbed)

521413-2 | CD | Jazz Samba
Stan Getz-Charlie Byrd Sextet
Desafinado | Samba Dees Days | O Pato(The Duck) | Samba Triste | Samba Da Una Nota So(One Note Samba) | E Luxo So | Baia | Desafinado(45rpm issue)
Washington,DC, rec. 13.2.1962
Getz,Stan (ts) | Byrd,Charlie (g) | Byrd,Gene (g,b) | Betts,Keter (b) | Deppenschmidt,Buddy (dr) | Reichenbach,Bill (dr)

521426-2 | CD | Sonny Side Up
Dizzy Gillespie-Sonny Rollins-Sonny Stitt Sextet
On The Sunny Side Of The Street | The Eternal Triangle | After Hours | I Know That You Know
NYC, rec. 19.12.1957
Gillespie,Dizzy (tp,voc) | Rollins,Sonny (ts) | Stitt,Sonny (ts) | Bryant,Ray (p) | Bryant,Tommy (b) | Persip,Charles (dr)

521427-2 | CD | Coleman Hawkins Encounters Ben Webster
Coleman Hawkins And Ben Webster With The Oscar Peterson Quartet
Blues For Yolanda(Stereo take) | It Never Entered My Mind | Rosita | You'd Be So Nice To Come Home To | Prisoner Of Love | Tangerine | Shine On Harvest Moon | Blues For Yolanda(Mono take) | Blues For Yolanda(incompl.take)
Hollywood,CA, rec. 16.10.1957
Hawkins,Coleman (ts) | Webster,Ben (ts) | Peterson,Oscar (p) | Ellis,Herb (g) | Brown,Ray (b) | Stoller,Alvin (dr)

521429-2 | CD | Billie Holiday Story Vol.4:Lady Sings The Blues
Billie Holiday And Her All Stars
I Wished On The Moon | Ain't Misbehavin' | Everything Happens To Me | Say It Isn't So | I've Got My Love To Keep Me Warm | Always | Do Nothin' Till You Hear From Me
NYC, rec. 14.2.1955
Holiday,Billie (voc) | Shavers,Charlie (tp) | Scott,Tony (cl) | Johnson,Budd (ts) | Drinkard,Carl (p) | Bauer,Billy (g) | Gaskin,Leonard (b) | Cole,William 'Cozy' (dr)

Travelin' Light | I Must Have That Man | Some Other Spring | Lady Sings The Blues
NYC, rec. 6.6.1956
Holiday,Billie (voc) | Shavers,Charlie (tp) | Scott,Tony (cl) | Quinichette,Paul (ts) | Kelly,Wynton (p) | Burrell,Kenny (g) | Bell,Aaron (b) | McBrowne,Lennie (dr)
God Bless The Child | Good Morning Heartache | No Good Man
NYC, rec. 7.6.1956
Holiday,Billie (voc) | Shavers,Charlie (tp) | Scott,Tony (cl) | Quinichette,Paul (ts) | Kelly,Wynton (p) | Burrell,Kenny (g) | Bell,Aaron (b) | McBrowne,Lennie (dr)
Strange Fruit
Holiday,Billie (voc) | Shavers,Charlie (tp) | Kelly,Wynton (p) | Burrell,Kenny (g) | McBrowne,Lennie (dr)
God Bless The Child(Rehersal)
NYC, rec. 30.5.1956
Holiday,Billie (voc) | Scott,Tony (p)

521431-2 | CD | The Composer Of 'Desafinado' Plays
Antonio Carlos Jobim With The Claus Ogerman Orchestra
Insensatez(How Insensitive) | Corcovado(Quiet Nights) | Chega De Saudade(No More Blues)
NYC, rec. 9.5.1963
Jobim,Antonio Carlos (g,p) | Wright,Leo (fl) | Duvivier,George (b) | Strings | Ogerman,Claus (cond,arr) | details unknown
Vivo Sohando(Dreamer) | Meditation | Desafinado
Jobim,Antonio Carlos (p) | Cleveland,Jimmy (tb) | Wright,Leo (fl) | Strings | Ogerman,Claus (cond,arr) | details unknown
Agua De Beber(Water To Drink)
Jobim,Antonio Carlos (p) | Cleveland,Jimmy (tb) | Wright,Leo (fl) | Ogerman,Claus (cond,arr) | details unknown
O Morro Nao Tem Vez(One I Loved) | So Danco Samba(I Only Dance The Samba)
NYC, rec. 10.5.1963
Jobim,Antonio Carlos (p) | Wright,Leo (fl) | Ogerman,Claus (cond,arr) | details unknown
Girl From Ipanema(Garota De Ipanema) | Amor En Paz(Once I Loved) | Samba Da Una Nota So(One Note Samba)
Jobim,Antonio Carlos (p) | Wright,Leo (fl) | Strings | Ogerman,Claus (cond,arr) | details unknown

521433-2 | CD | Movin' Wes
Wes Montgomery Orchestra
People | Matchmaker Matchmaker | Senza Fine | Theodora | Born To Be Blue | West Coast Blues
NYC, rec. 16.& 18.11.1964
Montgomery,Wes (g) | Royal,Ernie (tp) | Young,Eugene 'Snooky' (tp) | Terry,Clark (tp) | Cleveland,Jimmy (tb) | Green,Urbie (tb) | Jackson,Quentin (tb) | Welsch,Chauncey (tb) | Butterfield,Don or Harvey Phillips (tuba) | Richardson,Jerome (fl,as,ts) | Scott,Bobby (p) | Cranshaw,Bob (b) | Tate,Grady (dr) | Pate,Johnny (cond,arr)
Caravan | Movin' Wes(part 1) | Movin' Wes(part 2) | Moca Flor | In And Out
Montgomery,Wes (g) | Royal,Ernie (tp) | Young,Eugene 'Snooky' (tp) | Terry,Clark (tp) | Cleveland,Jimmy (tb) | Green,Urbie (tb) | Jackson,Quentin (tb) | Welsch,Chauncey (tb) | Butterfield,Don or Harvey Phillips (tuba) | Richardson,Jerome (fl,as,ts) | Scott,Bobby (p) | Cranshaw,Bob (b) | Tate,Grady (dr) | Bobo,Willie (perc) | Pate,Johnny (cond,arr)

521436-2 | CD | Bird And Diz
Charlie Parker Quintet
Bloomdido | An Oscar For Treadwell | An Oscar For Treadwell(alt.take) | Mohawk | Mohawk(alt.take) | My Melancholy Baby | My Melancholy Baby(alt.take) | Leap Frog | Leap Frog(alt.take 1) | Leap Frog(alt.take 2) | Leap Frog(alt.take 3) | Leap Frog(7 incompl.takes) | Relaxin' With Lee | Relaxin' With Lee(alt.take) | Relaxin' With Lee(4 incompl.takes)
NYC, rec. 6.6.1950
Parker,Charlie (as) | Gillespie,Dizzy (tp) | Monk,Thelonious (p) | Russell,Curly (b) | Rich,Buddy (dr)

521440-2 | CD | Night Train
Oscar Peterson Trio
Happy-Go-Lucky Local(aka 'Night Train') | C Jam Blues | Georgia On My Mind | Bag's Groove | Moten Swing | Easy Does It | Honey Dripper | Things Ain't What They Used To Be | I Got It Bad And That Ain't Good | Band Call | Hymn To Freedom | Happy-Go-Lucky Local(aka 'Night Train' alt.take) | Volare | My Heart Belongs To Daddy | Moten Swing(rehersal take) | Now's The Time | This Could Be The Start Of Something
rec. 15./16.12.1962
Peterson,Oscar (p) | Brown,Ray (b) | Thigpen,Ed (dr)

521442-2 | CD | We Get Request
Quiet Nights Of Quiet Stars(Corcovado) | Days Of Wine And Roses | My One And Only Love | People | Have You Met Miss Jones | You Look Good To Me | Girl From Ipanema(Garota De Ipanema) | D & E
NYC, rec. 19./20.10.1964
Peterson,Oscar (p) | Brown,Ray (b) | Thigpen,Ed (dr)
Goodbye J.D.
NYC, rec. 19.11.1964
Peterson,Oscar (p) | Brown,Ray (b) | Thigpen,Ed (dr)
Time And Again
NYC, rec. prob.1964
Peterson,Oscar (p) | Brown,Ray (b) | Thigpen,Ed (dr)

521444-2 | CD | Music For Zen Meditation
Tony Scott Trio
Is Not All One | The Murmuring Sound Of The Mountain Stream | A Quivering Sound Of The Mountain Stream | After The Snow The Fragrance | To Drift Like Clouds | Za-Zen(Meditation) | Prajna-Paramita-Hridaya Sutra(Sutra Chant) | Sanzen(Moment Of The Truth) | Satori(Enlightenment)
Tokyo, Japan, rec. February 1964
Scott,Tony (cl) | Yamamoto,Hozan (shakuhachi) | Yuize,Shinichi (koto)

521445-2 | CD | Jimmy & Wes-The Dynamic Duo
Jimmy Smith And Wes Montgomery With Orchestra
13 (Death March)
NYC, rec. 21.9.1966
Montgomery,Wes (g) | Smith,Jimmy (org) | Maxwell,Jimmy (tp) | Newman,Joe (tp) | Royal,Ernie (tp) | Terry,Clark (tp) | Cleveland,Jimmy (tb) | Liston,Melba (tb) | Hixon,Richard 'Dick' (tb) | Ashton,Bob (fl,cl,ts) | Bank,Danny (fl,b-cl,bs) | Dodgion,Jerry (fl,cl,as) | Richardson,Jerome (fl,cl) | Woods,Phil (cl,as) | Davis,Richard (b) | Tate,Grady (dr) | Barretto,Ray (perc) | Nelson,Oliver (arr)
Night Train | Down By The Riverside
NYC, rec. 23.9.1966
Montgomery,Wes (g) | Smith,Jimmy (org) | Maxwell,Jimmy (tp) | Newman,Joe (tp) | Royal,Ernie (tp) | Terry,Clark (tp) | Cleveland,Jimmy (tb) | Liston,Melba (tb) | Studd,Tony (b-tb) | Ashton,Bob (fl,cl,ts) | Bank,Danny (fl,b-cl,bs) | Dodgion,Jerry (fl,cl,as) | Richardson,Jerome (fl,cl) | Woods,Phil (cl,as) | Davis,Richard (b) | Tate,Grady (dr) | Nelson,Oliver (arr)
Jimmy Smith-Wes Montgomery Quartet
Baby It's Cold Outside | James And Wes | O.G.D.(alt.take)
NYC, rec. 28.9.1966
Smith,Jimmy (org) | Montgomery,Wes (g) | Tate,Grady (dr) | Barretto,Ray (perc)

521448-2 | CD | Ben Webster Meets Oscar Peterson
Ben Webster With The Oscar Peterson Trio
The Touch Of Your Lips | When Your Lover Has Gone | Bye Bye Blackbird | How Deep Is The Ocean | In The Wee Small Hours Of The Morning | Sunday | This Can't Be Love
Los Angeles,CA, rec. 6.11.1959
Webster,Ben (ts) | Peterson,Oscar (p) | Brown,Ray (b) | Thigpen,Ed (dr)

521449-2 | CD | Soulville | EAN 731452144928
Ben Webster Quintet
Soulville | Late Date | Time On My Hands | Lover Come Back To Me | Where Are You | Makin' Whoopee | Ill Wind
Los Angeles,CA, rec. 15.10.1957
Webster,Ben (ts) | Peterson,Oscar (p) | Ellis,Herb (g) | Brown,Ray (b) | Levey,Stan (dr)

Ben Webster Quartet
Who | Boogie Woogie | Roses Of Picardy
Webster,Ben (p) | Ellis,Herb (g) | Brown,Ray (b) | Levey,Stan (dr)

521451-2 | CD | Lester Young With The Oscar Peterson Trio
Lester Young With The Oscar Peterson Quartet
Ad Lib Blues | I Can't Get Started | Just You Just Me | Almost Like Being In Love | Tea For Two | There'll Never Be Another You | Back Home Again In Indiana | On The Sunny Side Of The Street | Stardust | I'm Confessin'(That I Love You) | I Can't Give You Anything But Love | These Foolish Things Remind Me On You | Two To Tango | I Can't Get Started(false start)
NYC, rec. 4.8.1952
Young,Lester (ts) | Peterson,Oscar (p) | Kessel,Barney (g) | Brown,Ray (b) | Heard,J.C. (dr)

521501-2 | CD | Always Say Goodbye
Charlie Haden Quartet West
Introduction | Always Say Goodbye | Nice Eyes | Relaxin' At The Camarillo | Sunset Afternoon | Alone Together | Our Spanish Love Song | Background Music | Avenue Of Stars | Low Key Lightly(Variation On The Theme Of Here To Zero) | Celia | Ending
Hollywood,CA, rec. 30.7./1.8.1993
Haden,Charlie (b) | Watts,Ernie (ts) | Broadbent,Alan (p) | Marable,Lawrence (dr)
Ou Es-Tu Mon Amour
Haden,Charlie (b) | Watts,Ernie (ts) | Grappelli,Stephane (v) | Broadbent,Alan (p) | Marable,Lawrence (dr)
My Love And I(Love Song From Apache) | Everything Happens To Me
Haden,Charlie (b) | Watts,Ernie (ts) | Broadbent,Alan (p,cond,arr) | Marable,Lawrence (dr) | Strings | Adler,Murray (concertmaster) | details unknown

521642-2 | CD | Billie Holiday Story Vol.1:Jazz At The Philharmonic
Billie Holiday With The JATP All Stars
Body And Soul | Strange Fruit
Philharmonic Auditorium,LA, rec. 12.2.1945
Holiday,Billie (voc) | JATP All Stars | McGhee,Howard (arr) | unkn. (tb) | Smith,Willie (as) | Gray,Wardell or Illinois Jacquet or Charlie Ventura (ts) | Raskin,Milt prob. (p) | Barbour,Dave prob. (g) | Mingus,Charles (b) | Coleman,Dave (dr)
I Cried For You(Now It's Your Turn To Cry Over Me) | Fine And Mellow | He's Funny That Way
Live at Carnegie Hall,NYC, rec. 27.5.1946
Holiday,Billie (voc) | JATP All Stars | Clayton,Buck (tp) | Young,Trummy (tb) | unkn. (tb) | Hawkins,Coleman (ts) | Jacquet,Illinois (ts) | Young,Lester (ts) | Kersey,Kenny (p) | Collins,John or Tiny Grimes (g) | Russell,Curly prob. (b) | Heard,J.C. (dr)
The Man I Love | Gee Baby Ain't I Good To You | All Of Me | Billie's Blues(aka I Love My Man)
Live at Carnegie Hall,NYC, rec. 3.6.1946
Holiday,Billie (voc) | JATP All Stars | Guy,Joe (tp) | Auld,Georgie (as) | Jacquet,Illinois (ts) | Young,Lester (ts) | Kersey,Kenny (p) | Grimes,Tiny prob. (g) | McKibbon,Al (b) | Heard,J.C. (dr)
Travelin' Light | He's Funny That Way
Live at Shrine Auditorium,Los Angeles,CA, rec. 7.10.1946
Holiday,Billie (voc) | JATP All Stars | McGhee,Howard prob. (tp) | Young,Trummy (tb) | Jacquet,Illinois prob. (ts) | Kersey,Kenny (p) | Kessel,Barney (g) | Drayton,Charlie (b) | Mills,Jackie (dr)
Billie Holiday With Bobby Tucker
Announcement by Norman Granz | You Better Go Now | You're Driving Me Crazy | There Is No Greater Love | I Cover The Waterfront
Live at Carnegie Hall,NYC, rec. 24.5.1947
Holiday,Billie (voc) | Tucker,Bobby (p)
Billie Holiday With The Mal Waldron Trio
Announcement by Norman Granz | Announcement by Willis Connover | Announcement by Johnny Mercer | Oh! Lady Be Good(Fanfare) | Nice Work If You Can Get It | Willow Weep For Me | My Man | Lover Come Back To Me | Lady Sings The Blues | What A Little Moonlight Can Do | Oh! Lady Be Good(Fanfare with announcements)
Live at Newport,Rhode Island, rec. 6.7.1957
Holiday,Billie (voc) | Waldron,Mal (p) | Benjamin,Joe (b) | Jones,Jo (dr)
Billie Holiday With Buck Clayton And The Mal Waldron Trio
Announcement by Leonard Feather | I Wished On The Moon | Lover Man(Oh,Where Can You Be?)
Live at The Seven Ages Festival,Wallingford,Conn., rec. 26.9.1958
Holiday,Billie (voc) | Clayton,Buck (tp) | Hawkins,Coleman or Grorgie Auld (ts) | Waldron,Mal (p) | Hinton,Milt (b) | Lamond,Don (dr)

521643-2 | CD | Krupa And Rich
Gene Krupa Orchestra
Gene's Blues
Los Angeles,CA, rec. 1.11.1955
Krupa,Gene (dr) | Eldridge,Roy (tp) | Gillespie,Dizzy (tp) | Jacquet,Illinois (ts) | Phillips,Flip (ts) | Peterson,Oscar (p) | Ellis,Herb (g) | Brown,Ray (b)
Buddy Rich Orchestra
Buddy's Blues
Rich,Buddy (dr) | Eldridge,Roy (tp) | Gillespie,Dizzy (tp) | Jacquet,Illinois (ts) | Phillips,Flip (ts) | Peterson,Oscar (p) | Ellis,Herb (g) | Brown,Ray (b)
Buddy Rich-Gene Krupa Orchestra
Bernie's Tune | I Never Knew | Sweethearts On Parade | Sunday | The Monster
Krupa,Gene (dr) | Rich,Buddy (dr) | Eldridge,Roy (tp) | Gillespie,Dizzy (tp) | Jacquet,Illinois (ts) | Phillips,Flip (ts) | Peterson,Oscar (p) | Ellis,Herb (g) | Brown,Ray (b)

521649-2 | CD | The Oscar Peterson Trio At The Concertgebouw
Oscar Peterson Trio
The Lady Is A Tramp | We'll Be Together Again | Bluesology | Budo | I've Got The World On A String | Daahoud | When Lights Are Low | Evrev
Live at The 'Opera House',Chicago,Ill, rec. 29.12.1957
Peterson,Oscar (p) | Ellis,Herb (g) | Brown,Ray (b)
Should I | Big Fat Mama | Back Home Again In Indiana | Joy Spring | Elevation
Live at Shrine Auditorium,Los Angeles,CA, rec. 9.10.1957
Peterson,Oscar (p) | Ellis,Herb (g) | Brown,Ray (b)

521674-2 | CD | Nothing But The Blues
Herb Ellis Quintet
Pap's Blues | Big Red's Boogie Woogie | Tin Roof Blues | Soft Winds | Royal Garden Blues | Patti Cake | Blues For Janet | Blues For Junior
Hollywood,CA, rec. 11./12.10.1957
Ellis,Herb (g) | Eldridge,Roy (tp) | Getz,Stan (ts) | Brown,Ray (b) | Levey,Stan (dr)
JATP All Stars
Les Tricheurs
Paris,France, rec. 1.5.1958
JATP All Stars | Eldridge,Roy (tp) | Getz,Stan (ts) | Peterson,Oscar (p) | Ellis,Herb (g) | Brown,Ray (b) | Johnson,Gus (dr)
Phil's Tune
JATP All Stars | Eldridge,Roy (tp) | Peterson,Oscar (p) | Ellis,Herb (g) | Brown,Ray (b) | Johnson,Gus (dr)
Clo's Blues
JATP All Stars | Hawkins,Coleman (ts) | Peterson,Oscar (p) | Ellis,Herb (g) | Brown,Ray (b) | Johnson,Gus (dr)
Mic's Jump
JATP All Stars | Gillespie,Dizzy (tp) | Peterson,Oscar (p) | Ellis,Herb (g) | Brown,Ray (b) | Johnson,Gus (dr)

521690-2 | 2 CD | Wes Montgomery:The Verve Jazz Sides
Wes Montgomery With The Johnny Pate Orchestra
West Coast Blues
Englewood Cliffs,NJ, rec. 18.11.1964
Montgomery,Wes (g) | Royal,Ernie (tp) | Young,Eugene 'Snooky' (tp) | Terry,Clark (tp) | Cleveland,Jimmy (tb) | Green,Urbie (tb) | Jackson,Quentin (tb) | Welsch,Chauncey (tb) | Butterfield,Don (tuba) | Richardson,Jerome (fl,as,ts) | Scott,Bobby (p) | Cranshaw,Bob (b) | Tate,Grady (dr) | Pate,Johnny (arr,ld)
Caravan
Montgomery,Wes (g) | Royal,Ernie (tp) | Young,Eugene 'Snooky' (tp) | Terry,Clark (tp) | Cleveland,Jimmy (tb) | Green,Urbie (tb) | Jackson,Quentin (tb) | Welsch,Chauncey (tb) | Butterfield,Don (tuba) | Richardson,Jerome (fl,as,ts) | Scott,Bobby (p) | Cranshaw,Bob (b) | Tate,Grady (dr) | Bobo,Willie (perc) | Pate,Johnny (arr,ld)
Wes Montgomery With The Oliver Nelson Orchestra
Twisted Blues | Golden Earrings | Naptown Blues
Englewood Cliffs,NJ, rec. 7.12.1965
Montgomery,Wes (g) | Byrd,Donald (tp) | Newman,Joe (tp) | Royal,Ernie (tp) | Andre,Wayne (tb) | Cleveland,Jimmy (tb) | Jackson,Quentin (tb) | Moore,Danny (tp) | Studd,Tony (tb) | Ashton,Bob (reeds) | Woods,Phil (as) | Dodgion,Jerry (as) | Penque,Romeo (reeds) | Bank,Danny (reeds) | Hancock,Herbie (p) | Duvivier,George (b) | Tate,Grady (dr) | Nelson,Oliver (arr,ld)
Wes Montgomery With The Don Sebesky Orchestra
Sundown
Englewood Cliffs,NJ, rec. 16.9.1966
Montgomery,Wes (g) | Davis,Mel (tp) | Glow,Bernie (tp) | Nottingham,Jimmy (tp) | Andre,Wayne (tb) | Messner,John (tb) | Watrous,Bill (tb) | Butterfield,Don (tuba) | Buffington,Jimmy (fr-h) | Beckenstein,Ray (reeds) | Webb,Stanley (sax) | Knie,Walter (reeds) | Hancock,Herbie (p) | Pizzarelli,Bucky (g) | Davis,Richard (b) | Tate,Grady (dr) | Barretto,Ray (congas) | Sebesky,Don (cond,arr)
Jimmy Smith And Wes Montgomery With The Oliver Nelson Orchestra
Milestones | Round About Midnight
Montgomery,Wes (g) | Smith,Jimmy (org) | Maxwell,Jimmy (tp) | Newman,Joe (tp) | Royal,Ernie (tp) | Terry,Clark (tp) | Cleveland,Jimmy (tb) | Jackson,Quentin (tb) | Studd,Tony (tb) | Liston,Melba (tb) | Ashton,Bob (reeds) | Woods,Phil (as) | Dodgion,Jerry (reeds) | Richardson,Jerome (reeds) | Bank,Danny (reeds) | Davis,Richard (b) | Tate,Grady (dr) | Nelson,Oliver (arr,ld)
Jimmy Smith-Wes Montgomery Quartet
Mellow Mood | James And Wes | OGD(Road Song)
Englewood Cliffs,NJ, rec. 28.9.1966
Montgomery,Wes (g) | Smith,Jimmy (org) | Tate,Grady (dr) | Barretto,Ray (perc)
Wes Montgomery Trio
Wives And Lovers
Englewood Cliffs,NJ, rec. 17.3.1966
Montgomery,Wes (g) | Carter,Ron (b) | Tate,Grady (dr)
Wynton Kelly Trio With Wes Montgomery
Portrait Of Jenny | Surrey With The Fringe On Top | Surrey With The Fringe On Top(reconstructed version) | Willow Weep For Me | Oh! You Crazy Moon | Misty | Impressions | Four On Six | No Blues | If You Could See Me Now
Live at The Half Note Cafe,NYC, rec. 22.-27.6.1965
Montgomery,Wes (g) | Kelly,Wynton (p) | Chambers,Paul (b) | Cobb,Jimmy (dr)
Unit 7 | Four On Six | What's New?
Englewood Cliffs,NJ, rec. 22.9.1965
Montgomery,Wes (g) | Kelly,Wynton (p) | Chambers,Paul (b) | Cobb,Jimmy (dr)

521851-2 | CD | Verve Jazz Masters 24:Ella Fitzgerald & Louis Armstrong
Ella Fitzgerald And Louis Armstrong With The Oscar Peterson Quartet
Isn't It A Lovely Day | Moonlight In Vermont | Under A Blanket Of Blue | April In Paris | Tenderly
Los Angeles,CA, rec. 16.8.1956
Fitzgerald,Ella (voc) | Armstrong,Louis (tp,voc) | Peterson,Oscar (p) | Ellis,Herb (g) | Brown,Ray (b) | Rich,Buddy (dr)
Learnin' The Blues | Our Love Is Here To Stay
Los Angeles,CA, rec. 23.7.1957
Fitzgerald,Ella (voc) | Armstrong,Louis (tp,voc) | Peterson,Oscar (p) | Ellis,Herb (g) | Brown,Ray (b) | Bellson,Louie (dr)
I've Got My Love To Keep Me Warm | I'm Putting All My Eggs In One Basket
Los Angeles,CA, rec. 13.8.1957
Fitzgerald,Ella (voc) | Armstrong,Louis (tp,voc) | Peterson,Oscar (p) | Ellis,Herb (g) | Brown,Ray (b) | Bellson,Louie (dr)
Ella Fitzgerald With The Oscar Peterson Quartet
They All Laughed
Los Angeles,CA, rec. 23.7.1957
Fitzgerald,Ella (voc) | Peterson,Oscar (p) | Ellis,Herb (g) | Brown,Ray (b) | Bellson,Louie (dr)
Ella Fitzgerald And Louis Armstrong With The Russell Garcia Orchestra
I Got Plenty O'Nuttin' | Bess You Is My Woman Now
Los Angeles,CA, rec. 18.8.1957
Fitzgerald,Ella (voc) | Armstrong,Louis (tp,voc) | Garcia,Russell (cond,arr) | details unknown

521852-2 | CD | Verve Jazz Masters 25:Stan Getz & Dizzy Gillespie
Dizzy Gillespie-Stan Getz Sextet
It Don't Mean A Thing If It Ain't Got That Swing | It's The Talk Of The Town
Los Angeles,CA, rec. 9.12.1953
Gillespie,Dizzy (tp) | Getz,Stan (ts) | Peterson,Oscar (p) | Ellis,Herb (g) | Brown,Ray (b) | Roach,Max (dr)
Dizzy Gillespie Septet
Dark Eyes | Bebop
Los Angeles,CA, rec. 16.10.1956
Gillespie,Dizzy (tp) | Stitt,Sonny (as) | Getz,Stan (ts) | Lewis,John (p) | Ellis,Herb (g) | Brown,Ray (b) | Levey,Stan (dr)
JATP All Stars
The Mooche
Live,at Konserthuset,Stockholm, rec. 21.11.960
JATP All Stars | Gillespie,Dizzy (tp) | Johnson,J.J. (tb) | Getz,Stan (ts) | Schifrin,Lalo (p) | Davis,Art (b) | Lampkin,Chuck (dr) | Candido[Camero] (perc)
Dizzy Gillespie All Stars
The Way You Look Tonight
NYC, rec. 26.6.1957
Gillespie,Dizzy (tp) | Getz,Stan (ts) | Gonsalves,Paul (ts) | Hawkins,Coleman (ts) | Kelly,Wynton (p) | Marshall,Wendell (b) | Heard,J.C. (dr)

521853-2 | CD | Verve Jazz Masters 26:Lionel Hampton with Oscar Peterson
Lionel Hampton With The Oscar Peterson Trio
Always | Soft Winds
NYC, rec. 2.9.1953
Hampton,Lionel (vib) | Peterson,Oscar (p) | Brown,Ray (b) | Rich,Buddy (dr)
Stardust
NYC, rec. 12.4.1954
Hampton,Lionel (vib) | Peterson,Oscar (p) | Brown,Ray (b) | Rich,Buddy (dr)
Tenderly | Hallelujah
NYC, rec. 13.9.1954
Hampton,Lionel (vib) | Peterson,Oscar (p) | Brown,Ray (b) | Rich,Buddy (dr)
Lionel Hampton With The Oscar Peterson Quartet
Sweethearts On Parade | Date With Oscar
NYC, rec. 15.9.1954
Hampton,Lionel (vib,voc) | Peterson,Oscar (p) | Ellis,Herb (g) | Brown,Ray (b) | Rich,Buddy (dr)
Lionel Hampton With Buddy DeFranco And The Oscar Peterson Trio
Je Ne Sais Pas
NYC, rec. 13.4.1954
Hampton,Lionel (vib) | DeFranco,Buddy (cl) | Peterson,Oscar (p) | Brown,Ray (b) | Rich,Buddy (dr)
Norman Granz Jam Session
Jam Blues
NYC, rec. 2.9.1953
Norman Granz Jam Session | Eldridge,Roy (tp) | Gillespie,Dizzy (tp) | Harris,Bill (tb) | Phillips,Flip (ts) | Webster,Ben (ts) | Hampton,Lionel (vib) | Peterson,Oscar (p) | Brown,Ray (b) | Rich,Buddy (dr)

521854-2 | CD | Verve Jazz Masters 28:Charlie Parker Plays Standards
Charlie Parker Quintet
Love For Sale | I Love Paris
NYC, rec. 10.12.1954
Parker,Charlie (as) | Bishop Jr.,Walter (p) | Bauer,Billy (g) | Kotick,Teddy (b) | Taylor,Arthur 'Art' (dr)
Charlie Parker With Strings
If I Should Lose You
NYC, rec. 30.11.1949
Parker,Charlie (as) | Miller,Mitch (oboe) | Gimpel,Bronislaw (v) | Hollander,Max (v) | Lomask,Milt (v) | Brieff,Frank (viola) | Miller,Frank (cello) | Rosen,Myoer (harp) | Freeman,Stan (p) | Brown,Ray (b) | Rich,Buddy (dr) | Carroll,Jimmy (cond,arr)
Charlie Parker With The Joe Lipman Orchestra
Almost Like Being In Love | What Is This Thing Called Love
NYC, rec. 25.3.1952
Parker,Charlie (as) | Maxwell,Jimmy (tp) | Poole,Carl (tp) | Porcino,Al (tp) | Privin,Bernie (tp) | Harris,Bill (tb) | McGarity,Lou (tb) | Varsalona,Bart (tb) | Terrill,Harry (as) | Williams,Murray (as) | Phillips,Flip (ts) | Ross,Hank (ts) | Bank,Danny (bs) | Peterson,Oscar (p) | Green,Freddie (g) | Brown,Ray (b) | Lamond,Don (dr) | Lippman,Joe (cond,arr)
Laura
NYC, rec. late Summer 1950
Parker,Charlie (as) | Singer,Joe (fr-h) | Brown,Eddie (oboe) | Caplan,Sam (v) | Kay,Howard (v) | Melnikoff,Harry (v) | Rand,Sam (v) | Smirnoff,Kelly (v) | Zir,Isadore (viola) | Brown,Maurice (cello) | Mills,Verley (harp) | Leighton,Bernie (p) | Brown,Ray (b) | Rich,Buddy (dr) | Lippman,Joe (cond,arr)
Charlie Parker Sextet
Why Do I Love You
NYC, rec. 12.3.1951
Parker,Charlie (as) | Bishop Jr.,Walter (p) | Kotick,Teddy (b) | Haynes,Roy (dr) | Mangual,Jose (bongos) | Miranda,Luis (congas)
Estrellita(Little Star)
NYC, rec. 23.1.1952
Parker,Charlie (as) | Harris,Benny (tp) | Bishop Jr.,Walter (p) | Kotick,Teddy (b) | Roach,Max (dr) | Mangual,Jose (bongos) | Miranda,Luis (congas)
Charlie Parker Quartet
I Remember You
NYC, rec. 30.7.1953
Parker,Charlie (as) | Haig,Al (p) | Heath,Percy (b) | Roach,Max (dr)
Charlie Parker With Strings
Easy To Love
Live at Carnegie Hall,NYC, rec. 17.9.1950
Parker,Charlie (as) | Mace,Tommy (oboe) | Caplan,Sam (v) | Feller,Al (v) | Kraft,Stan (v) | Uchitel,Dave (viola) | Bundy,Bill (cello) | McManus,Wallace (harp) | Haig,Al (p) | Potter,Tommy (b) | Haynes,Roy (dr) | Mundy,Jimmy (arr)
Charlie Parker With Orchestra & The Dave Lambert Singers
Old Folks
NYC, rec. 25.5.1953
Parker,Charlie (as) | Collins,Junior (fr-h) | McKusick,Hal (cl) | Mace,Tommy (oboe) | Thaler,Manny (bassoon) | Aless,Tony (p) | Mingus,Charles (b) | Roach,Max (dr) | Lambert Singers,The Dave | Birdsall,Butch (voc) | Parker,Jerry (voc) | Ross,Annie (voc) | unkn. (2 voc) | Evans,Gil (cond,arr)
JATP All Stars
I Got Rhythm
Los Angeles,CA, rec. 22.4.1946
JATP All Stars | Smith,Willie (as) | Young,Lester (ts) | Hawkins,Coleman (ts) | Kersey,Kenny (p) | Ashby,Irving (g) | Hadnott,Billy (b) | Rich,Buddy (dr)
Embraceable You
Live at Carnegie Hall,NYC, rec. 18.9.1949
JATP All Stars | Eldridge,Roy (tp) | Turk,Tommy (tb) | Parker,Charlie (as) | Phillips,Flip (ts) | Young,Lester (ts) | Jones,Hank (p) | Brown,Ray (b) | Rich,Buddy (dr) | Granz,Norman (announcer)
How High The Moon
JATP All Stars | Eldridge,Roy (tp) | Turk,Tommy (tb) | Parker,Charlie (as) | Phillips,Flip (ts) | Young,Lester (ts) | Jones,Hank (p) | Brown,Ray (b) | Rich,Buddy (dr) | Fitzgerald,Ella (voc) | Granz,Norman (announcer)

521855-2 | CD | Verve Jazz Masters 29:Jimmy Smith
Jimmy Smith Trio
Organ Grinder's Swing | I'll Close My Eyes
Englewood Cliffs,NJ, rec. 14./15.6.1965
Smith,Jimmy (org,voc) | Burrell,Kenny (g) | Tate,Grady (dr)
Jimmy Smith With The Oliver Nelson Orchestra
The Preacher | Hobo Flats
NYC, rec. 20.3.1963
Smith,Jimmy (org) | Newman,Joe (fl-h) | Royal,Ernie (tp) | Terry,Clark (tp) | Cleveland,Jimmy (tb) | Green,Urbie (tb) | Jackson,Quentin (tb) | Dorsey,Bob (as) | Woods,Phil (as) | Cohn,Al (ts) | Sims,Zoot (ts) | Duvivier,George (b) | Rodriguez,Bill (dr) | Nelson,Oliver (arr,ld)
Meditation
NYC, rec. 15.3.1963
Smith,Jimmy (org) | Newman,Joe (fl-h) | Royal,Ernie (tp) | Terry,Clark (tp) | Cleveland,Jimmy (tb) | Green,Urbie (tb) | Jackson,Quentin (tb) | Dorsey,Bob (as) | Woods,Phil (as) | Cohn,Al (ts) | Sims,Zoot (ts) | Hinton,Milt (b) | Johnson,Jimmy (dr) | Nelson,Oliver (arr,ld)
Jimmy Smith With Orchestra
Side Mouthin'
Live at Jimmy Smith' Super Club,North Hollywood, rec. 6./7.7.1977
Smith,Jimmy (p,org,arr) | Mitchell,Blue (tp) | Behrens,Stanley (fl) | Phillips,John (fl,reeds) | Land,Harold (ts) | Edwards,Teddy (ts) | Crawford,Ray (g) | Brandon,Kevin (b) | Dixon,Kenny (dr) | Clarke,Buck (perc)
Jimmy Smith With The Oliver Nelson Orchestra
Blues And The Abstract Truth
NYC, rec. 14.6.1966
Smith,Jimmy (org) | Newman,Joe (tp) | Royal,Ernie (tp) | Williams,Richard (tp) | Young,Eugene 'Snooky' (tp) | Jackson,Quentin (tb) | Liston,Melba (tb) | McIntosh,Tom (tb) | Woodman,Britt (tb) | Corrado,Donald (fr-h) | Ruff,Willie (fr-h) | Butterfield,Don (tuba) | Agee,Jack (reeds) | Ashton,Bob (reeds) | Dodgion,Jerry (reeds) | Richardson,Jerome (reeds) | Woods,Phil (reeds) | Lucas,Buddy (harm) | Burrell,Kenny (g) | Butler,Billy (g) | Galbraith,Barry (g) | Suyker,Willard 'Bill' (g) | Cranshaw,Bob (b) | Davis,Richard (b) | Tate,Grady (dr) | Rosengarden,Bobby (perc) | Nelson,Oliver (arr,ld)
Jimmy Smith-Wes Montgomery Quartet
O.G.D.(alt.take) | Maybe September
NYC, rec. 28.9.1966
Smith,Jimmy (org) | Montgomery,Wes (g) | Tate,Grady (dr) | Barretto,Ray (congas)
Jimmy Smith Trio
Bashin'
NYC, rec. 28.3.1962
Smith,Jimmy (org) | Warren,Quentin (g) | Bailey,Donald (dr)
Jimmy Smith With The Oliver Nelson Orchestra
Walk On The Wild Side
Smith,Jimmy (org) | Newman,Joe (tp) | Royal,Ernie (tp) | Severinsen,Doc (tp) | Wilder,Joe (tp) | Cleveland,Jimmy (tb) | Green,Urbie (tb) | Woodman,Britt (tb) | Mitchell,Tom (b-tb) | Dodgion,Jerry (as) | Woods,Phil (as) | Ashton,Bob (ts) | Clarke,Babe (ts) | Barrow,George (bs) | Galbraith,Barry (g) | Duvivier,George (b) | Shaughnessy,Ed (dr) | Nelson,Oliver (arr,ld)
Johnny Comes Lately
Englewood Cliffs,NJ, rec. 17..12.1965
Smith,Jimmy (org) | Royal,Ernie (tp) | Woods,Phil (as) | Penque,Romeo (fl,ts) | Richardson,Jerome (bs) | Burrell,Kenny (g) | Duvivier,George (b) | Tate,Grady (dr) | Nelson,Oliver (arr,ld)
Jimmy Smith With The Claus Ogerman Orchestra
G'wan Train
Englewood Cliffs,NJ, rec. 10.7.1963
Smith,Jimmy (org) | Maxwell,Jimmy (tp) | Newman,Joe (tp) | Shavers,Charlie (tp) | Cleveland,Jimmy (tb) | Liston,Melba (tb) | Winding,Kai (tb) | Faulise,Paul (b-tb) | Dodgion,Jerry (as) | Woods,Phil (as) | Johnson,Budd (ts) | Powell,Seldon (ts) | Halladay,Marvin (bs) | Burrell,Kenny (g) | Davis,Art (b) | Lovelle,Herbie (dr) | Devens,George (perc) | Ogerman,Claus (cond,arr)

521856-2 | CD | Verve Jazz Masters 43:Coleman Hawkins
Coleman Hawkins Quintet
I Only Have Eyes For You | 'S Wonderful
NYC, rec. 31.1.1944
Hawkins,Coleman (ts) | Eldridge,Roy (tp) | Wilson,Teddy (p) | Taylor,Billy (b) | Cole,William 'Cozy' (dr)
Coleman Hawkins Quartet
Night And Day
NYC, rec. 17.2.1944
Hawkins,Coleman (ts) | Wilson,Teddy (p) | Crosby,Israel (b) | Cole,William 'Cozy' (dr)
Coleman Hawkins' All-American Four
Just One Of Those Things | Hallelujah
NYC, rec. 29.5.1944
Hawkins,Coleman (ts) | Wilson,Teddy (p) | Kirby,John (b) | Catlett,Big Sid (dr)
Coleman Hawkins
Picasso
NYC, rec. 1948
Hawkins,Coleman (ts-solo)
Coleman Hawkins All Stars
The Big Head
NYC, rec. 29.8.1949
Hawkins,Coleman (ts) | Payne,Cecil (bs) | Haig,Al (p) | Collins,John (el-g) | Boyd,Nelson (b) | Wilson,Shadow (dr)
Coleman Hawkins Quartet
Body And Soul | Rifftide(aka Disorder At The Border)
Live at Carnegie Hall,NYC, rec. 18.9.1949
Hawkins,Coleman (ts) | Jones,Hank (p) | Brown,Ray (b) | Rich,Buddy (dr)
Coleman Hawkins-Roy Eldridge Quintet
Time On My Hands
Live at Opera House,Chicago,Ill, rec. 29.9.1957
Eldridge,Roy (tp) | Hawkins,Coleman (ts) | Lewis,John (p) | Heath,Percy (b) | Kay,Connie (dr)
Coleman Hawkins And Ben Webster With The Oscar Peterson Quartet
Cocktails For Two
Los Angeles,CA, rec. 16.10.1957
Hawkins,Coleman (ts) | Webster,Ben (ts) | Peterson,Oscar (p) | Ellis,Herb (g) | Brown,Ray (b) | Stoller,Alvin (dr)
Coleman Hawkins With The Oscar Peterson Quartet
Ill Wind(You're Blowin' Me No Good) | The World Is Waiting For The Sunrise | I Wished On The Moon
Hawkins,Coleman (ts) | Peterson,Oscar (p) | Ellis,Herb (g) | Brown,Ray (b) | Stoller,Alvin (dr)
Coleman Hawkins-Roy Eldridge Quintet
Hanid
NYC, rec. 7.2.1958
Eldridge,Roy (tp) | Hawkins,Coleman (ts) | Jones,Hank (p) | Duvivier,George (b) | Sheen,Mickey (dr)
Coleman Hawkins Quartet
Bean And The Boys
Live at The 'Village Gate',NYC, rec. 15.8.1962
Hawkins,Coleman (ts) | Flanagan,Tommy (p) | Holley,Major (b) | Locke,Eddie (dr)

521857-2 | CD | Verve Jazz Masters 35:Johnny Hodges
Johnny Hodges And His Band
Jeep's Blues | Castle Rock
NYC, rec. 28.2.1951
Hodges,Johnny (as) | Berry,Emmett (tp) | Brown,Lawrence (tb) | Sears,Al (ts) | Lovett,Leroy (p) | Trottman,Lloyd (b) | Greer,William 'Sonny' (dr)
Norman Granz Jam Session
Funky Blues
Los Angeles,CA, rec. 22.7.1952
Shavers,Charlie (tp) | Carter,Benny (as) | Hodges,Johnny (as) | Parker,Charlie (as) | Phillips,Flip (ts) | Webster,Ben (ts) | Peterson,Oscar (p) | Kessel,Barney (g) | Brown,Ray (b) | Heard,J.C. (dr)
Johnny Hodges And His Band
Passion Flower(aka A Flower Is A Lovesome Thing)
NYC, rec. 8.9.1955
Hodges,Johnny (as) | Terry,Clark (tp) | Brown,Lawrence (tb) | Hamilton,Jimmy (cl,ts) | Carney,Harry (bs) | Strayhorn,Billy (p,arr) | Woode,Jimmy (b) | Greer,William 'Sonny' (dr)
Johnny Hodges And The Ellington All-Stars Without Duke
Duke's In Bed
Chicago,Ill, rec. 1.9.1956
Hodges,Johnny (as) | Terry,Clark (tp) | Nance,Ray (tp,v) | Jackson,Quentin (tb) | Hamilton,Jimmy (cl,ts) | Carney,Harry (bs) | Strayhorn,Billy (p) | Woode,Jimmy (b) | Woodyard,Sam (dr)
Johnny Hodges And The Ellington Men
Little Rabbit Blues
NYC, rec. 25.7.1957
Hodges,Johnny (as) | Terry,Clark (tp) | Nance,Ray (tp,v) | Jackson,Quentin (tb) | Sanders,John (tb) | Woodman,Britt (tb) | Procope,Russell (cl,as) | Hamilton,Jimmy (cl,ts) | Carney,Harry (bs) | Strayhorn,Billy (p) | Woode,Jimmy (b) | Woodyard,Sam (dr)
Early Morning Rock
Chicago,Ill, rec. 3.9.1957
Hodges,Johnny (as) | Terry,Clark (tp) | Nance,Ray (tp,v) | Anderson,Cat (tp) | Baker,Harold 'Shorty' (tp) | Cook,Willie (tp) | Jackson,Quentin (tb) | Sanders,John (tb) | Woodman,Britt (tb) | Procope,Russell (cl,as) | Hamilton,Jimmy (cl,ts) | Gonsalves,Paul (ts) | Carney,Harry (bs) | Strayhorn,Billy (p) | Woode,Jimmy (b) | Woodyard,Sam (dr)
Johnny Hodges And His Band
Honey Hill
NYC, rec. 5.4.1958
Hodges,Johnny (as) | Dickenson,Vic (tb) | Webster,Ben (ts) | Strayhorn,Billy (p) | Woode,Jimmy (b) | Woodyard,Sam (dr)
The Last Time I Saw Paris
NYC, rec. 10.9.1958
Hodges,Johnny (as) | Strayhorn,Billy (p) | Woode,Jimmy (b) | Woodyard,Sam (dr)
Not So Dukish
Hodges,Johnny (as) | Eldridge,Roy (tp) | Brown,Lawrence (tb) | Webster,Ben (ts) | Strayhorn,Billy (p) | Woode,Jimmy (b) | Woodyard,Sam (dr)
Johnny Hodges With The Dizzy Gillespie Quintet
Squatty Roo
NYC, rec. 20.2.1959
Hodges,Johnny (as) | Gillespie,Dizzy (tp) | Mance,Junior[Julian C.] (p) | Spann,Les (g) | Jones,Sam (b) | Humphries,Lex (dr)
Gerry Mulligan-Johnny Hodges Quintet
Back Beat
Los Angeles,CA, rec. 17.11.1959
Hodges,Johnny (as) | Mulligan,Gerry (bs) | Williamson,Claude (p) | Clark,Buddy (b) | Lewis,Mel (dr)
Johnny Hodges With Billy Strayhorn And The Duke Ellington Orchestra
The Gal From Joe's
NYC, rec. 14.1.1966
Hodges,Johnny (as) | Anderson,Cat (tp) | Baker,Harold 'Shorty' (tp) | Berry,Bill (tp) | Mullens,Eddie (tp) | Brown,Lawrence (tb) | Connors,Chuck (tb) | Jackson,Quentin (tb) | Procope,Russell (cl,as) | Hamilton,Jimmy (cl,ts) | Gonsalves,Paul (ts) | Carney,Harry (bs) | Jones,Jimmie (p) | Bell,Aaron (b) | Woodyard,Sam (dr) | Strayhorn,Billy (arr,ld)
Johnny Hodges-Earl Hines Quintet
Rosetta
Hodges,Johnny (as) | Hines,Earl 'Fatha' (p) | Burrell,Kenny (g) | Davis,Richard (b) | Marshall,Joe (dr)
Johnny Hodges Orchestra
Don't Sleep In The Subway
NYC, rec. 21.8.1967
Hodges,Johnny (as) | Royal,Ernie (tp) | Young,Eugene 'Snooky' (tp) | Berry,Bill (tp,vib) | Studd,Tony (b-tb) | Richardson,Jerome (cl,as) | Wess,Frank (cl,as) | Hamilton,Jimmy (cl,ts) | Bank,Danny (cl,bs) | Jones,Hank (p) | Barksdale,Everett (g) | Hinton,Milt (b) | Tate,Grady (dr) | Jones,Jimmy (cond,arr)

521858-2 | CD | Verve Jazz Masters 39:Cal Tjader
Cal Tjader Group
Triste
Los Angeles,CA, rec. 28./29.8.1961
Tjader,Cal (vib) | Horn,Paul (fl,as) | Hewitt,Lonnie (p) | McKibbon,Al (b) | Rae,Johnny (dr) | Peraza,Armando (bongos) | Vincente,Wilfredo (congas)
Lalo Schifrin And His Orchestra
China Nights | Borneo | Tokyo Blue
NYC, rec. 23.4.1963
Schifrin,Lalo (p,cond,arr) | Royal,Ernie (tp) | Terry,Clark (tp) | Green,Urbie (tb) | Northern,Bob (fr-h) | Butterfield,Don (tuba) | Levinsky,Walt (fl,woodwinds) | Cohen,Leon (oboe) | Horowitz,Irving (oboe) | Berg,George (b-cl,bassoon) | Bodner,Phil (woodwinds) | Kraus,Phil (woodwinds) | Webb,Stanley (woodwinds) | Tjader,Cal (vib) | Eidus,Arnold (v) | Kruczek,Leo (v) | Vardi,Emanuel (viola) | McCracken,Charles (strings) | Maxwell,Robert (harp) | Raney,Jimmy (g) | Duvivier,George (b) | Shaughnessy,Ed (dr) | Del Rio,Jack (congas,tambourine) | Rae,Johnny (perc,timbales)
Cal Tjader's Orchestra
The Way You Look Tonight
NYC, rec. 11.5.1964
Tjader,Cal (vib) | Powell,Seldon or Jerome Richardson (ts) | Jones,Hank or Patti Bown or Bernie Leighton (p) | Burrell,Kenny or Jimmy Raney (g) | Duvivier,George (b) | Shaughnessy,Ed (dr) | Rodriguez,Willie (perc) | Strings | Ogerman,Claus (cond,arr) | details unknown
Soul Sauce | Leyte
NYC, rec. 20.11.1964
Tjader,Cal (vib) | Hewitt,Lonnie (p) | Hilliard,John (b) | Rae,Johnny (dr) | Peraza,Armando (perc) | Valdes,Alberto (perc) | unkn. (voc)
Whiffenproof Song | Daddy Wong Legs
NYC, rec. 1./2.6.1965
Tjader,Cal (vib) | Griffin,Paul (p) | Davis,Richard (b) | Tate,Grady or Sol Gubin (dr) | Peraza,Armando (perc)
Soul Bird(aka Tin Tin Deo)
Englewood Cliffs,NJ, rec. 22.6.1965
Tjader,Cal (vib) | Hewitt,Lonnie (p) | Hilliard,John (b) | Rae,Johnny (dr) | Peraza,Armando (perc)
Curacao | Cuchy Frito Man
NYC, rec. 10./11.2.1966
Tjader,Cal (vib) | Dodgion,Jerry or Jerome Richardson (fl) | Powell,Seldon (fl) | Corea,Chick (p) | Zoller,Attila (g) | Davis,Richard or Bobby Rogriguez (b) | Tate,Grady (dr) | Valdez,Carlos 'Patato' (congas) | Mangual,Jose (timbales) | Pantoja,Victor (perc) | Nelson,Oliver (arr)
The Prophet | Cal's Bluedo
Los Angeles,CA, rec. 19.9.1967
Tjader,Cal (vib) | Orchestra | details unknown
Hip Vibrations
NYC, rec. 12.12.1967
Tjader,Cal (vib) | Royal,Ernie (tp) | Stamm,Marvin (tp,fl-h) | Johnson,J.J. (tb) | Ralph,Alan (b-tb) | Richardson,Jerome (bs) | Bown,Patti (p) | Davis,Richard (b) | Lewis,Mel (dr) | Barretto,Ray (congas) | Rosengarden,Bobby (perc) | Bryant,Bobby (arr)
Moanin'
Tjader,Cal (vib) | Royal,Ernie (tp) | Stamm,Marvin (tp,fl-h) | Johnson,J.J. (tb) | Ralph,Alan (b-tb) | Richardson,Jerome (bs) | Hancock,Herbie (p) | Carter,Ron (b) | Lewis,Mel (dr) | Barretto,Ray (congas) | Rosengarden,Bobby (perc) | Bryant,Bobby (arr)

521859-2 | CD | Verve Jazz Masters 30:Lester Young
Lester Young Quartet
Love Me Or Leave Me | Prisoner Of Love | All Of Me
NYC, rec. 13.1.1956
Young,Lester (ts) | Wilson,Teddy (p) | Ramey,Gene (b) | Jones,Jo (dr)
Sometimes I'm Happy | Just You Just Me | I Never Knew
NYC, rec. 28.12.1943
Young,Lester (ts) | Guarnieri,Johnny (p) | Stewart,Slam (b) | Catlett,Big Sid (dr)
Lester Young Trio
I've Found A New Baby | Mean To Me
NYC, rec. March/April 1946
Young,Lester (ts) | Cole,Nat King (p) | Rich,Buddy (dr)
Peg O' My Heart
Young,Lester (ts) | Cole,Nat King (p)
Lester Young Quartet
Polka Dots And Moonbeams | Too Marvelous For Words
NYC, rec. 17.9.1949
Young,Lester (ts) | Jones,Hank (p) | Brown,Ray (b) | Rich,Buddy (dr)
Lester Young With The Oscar Peterson Quartet
On The Sunny Side Of The Street | Back Home Again In Indiana | I'm Confessin'(That I Love You)
NYC, rec. 28.11.1952
Young,Lester (ts) | Peterson,Oscar (p) | Kessel,Barney (g) | Brown,Ray (b) | Heard,J.C. (dr)
Lester Young Quartet
In A Little Spanish Town
NYC, rec. 8.3.1951
Young,Lester (ts) | Lewis,John (p) | Ramey,Gene (b) | Jones,Jo (dr)

521860-2 | CD | Verve Jazz Masters 23:Gil Evans
Gil Evans Orchestra
Time Of The Baracudas
Englewood Cliffs,NJ, rec. 9.7.1964
Evans,Gil (p,arr) | Rehak,Frank (tb) | Alonge,Ray (fr-h) | Watkins,Julius (fr-h) | Barber,Bill (tuba) | Block,Al (reeds) | Fitzgerald,Andy (reeds) | Marge,George (reeds) | Tricarico,Bob (reeds) | Shorter,Wayne (ts) | Mackwell,Bob (harp) | Burrell,Kenny (g) | Peacock,Gary (b) | Jones,Elvin (dr)
The Barbara Song
Evans,Gil (p,arr) | Rehak,Frank (tb) | Alonge,Ray (fr-h) | Watkins,Julius (fr-h) | Barber,Bill (tuba) | Block,Al (reeds) | Fitzgerald,Andy (reeds) | Marge,George (reeds) | Tricarico,Bob (reeds) | Shorter,Wayne (ts) | Mackwell,Bob (harp) | Peacock,Gary (b) | Jones,Elvin (dr)
Kenny Burrell With The Gil Evans Orchestra
Greensleeves | Last Night When We Were Young | Moon And Sand
Englewood Cliffs,NJ, rec. 4.12.1964
Burrell,Kenny (g) | Evans,Gil (p,arr) | Coles,Johnny (tp) | Mucci,Louis (tp) | Cleveland,Jimmy (tb) | Knepper,Jimmy (tb) | Alonge,Ray (fr-h) | Watkins,Julius (fr-h) | Barber,Bill (tuba) | Fitzgerald,Andy (engl-h,fl) | Marge,George (engl-h,fl) | Beckenstein,Ray (fl,b-cl) | Lacy,Steve (ss) | Konitz,Lee (as) | Kamuca,Richie (ts,oboe) | Tricarico,Bob (fl,ts,bassoon) | Carter,Ron (b) | Persip,Charles (dr) | Jones,Elvin (dr)
Astrud Gilberto With The Gil Evans Orchestra
She's A Carioca | I Will Wait For You
NYC, rec. 6.12.1965
Gilberto,Astrud (voc) | Evans,Gil (p,arr) | Coles,Johnny (tp) | Brookmeyer,Bob (v-tb) | Burrell,Kenny (g) | Tate,Grady (dr) | details unknown
Gil Evans Orchestra
Las Vegas Tango
NYC, rec. September/December 1963
Evans,Gil (p,arr) | Coles,Johnny (tp) | Glow,Bernie (tp) | Cleveland,Jimmy (tb) | Studd,Tony (tb) | Alonge,Ray (fr-h) | Barber,Bill (tuba) | Bushell,Garvin (reeds) | Dolphy,Eric (fl,b-cl,as) | Tricarico,Bob (reeds) | Lacy,Steve (ss) | Burrell,Kenny (g) | Carter,Ron (b) | Chambers,Paul (b) | Jones,Elvin (dr)
Spoonful | Concorde
NYC, rec. 25.5.1964
Evans,Gil (p,arr) | Jones,Thad (tp) | Glow,Bernie (tp) | Mucci,Louis (tp) | Cleveland,Jimmy (tb) | Knepper,Jimmy (tb) | Alonge,Ray (fr-h) | Watkins,Julius (fr-h) | Barber,Bill (tuba) | Fitzgerald,Andy (reeds) | Marge,George (reeds) | Tricarico,Bob (reeds) | Woods,Phil (reeds) | Lookofsky,Harry (v) | Burrell,Kenny (g) | Chambers,Paul (b) | Jones,Elvin (dr)

521861-2 | CD | Verve Jazz Masters 21:George Benson
George Benson Quintet
Thunder Walk | Billie's Bounce | Low Down & Dirty | What's New?
NYC, rec. 7.2.1968
Benson,George (g) | Hancock,Herbie (p) | Carter,Ron (b) | Cobham,Billy (dr) | Pacheco,Johnny (congas)
George Benson Orchestra
Sack O'Woe
NYC, rec. 6.2.1968
Benson,George (g) | Owens,Jimmy (tp,fl-h) | Royal,Ernie (tp) | Young,Eugene 'Snooky' (tp) | Ralph,Alan (b-tb) | Adams,Pepper (bs) | Hancock,Herbie (p) | Carter,Ron (b) | Cobham,Billy (dr)
Jimmy Smith Trio
Tuxedo Junction | The Boss
Live at Paschal's La Carousel Club,Atlanta,GA, rec. 1968
Smith,Jimmy (org) | Benson,George (g) | Bailey,Donald (dr)
George Benson With The Don Sebesky Orchestra
Something- | Octopus's Garden-
NYC, rec. October/November 1969
Benson,George (g,voc) | Davis,Mel (tp) | Glow,Bernie (tp) | Hubbard,Freddie (tp) | Stamm,Marvin (tp) | Andre,Wayne (tb) | Ashworth,Don (reeds) | Bodner,Phil (reeds) | Fortune,Sonny (reeds) | Laws,Hubert (fl,reeds) | Richardson,Jerome (reeds) | Hancock,Herbie (el-p) | Hayes,Ernest 'Ernie' (p,org) | James,Bob (el-p) | Carter,Ron (b) | Jemmott,Jerry (el-b) | Muhammad,Idris[Leo Morris] (dr) | Shaughnessy,Ed (dr) | Barretto,Ray (perc) | Gonzalez,Andy (perc) | Strings | Sebesky,Don (cond,arr)
Shape Of Things(To Come)
NYC, rec. 5.9.1968
Benson,George (g) | Marge,George (fl) | Penque,Romeo (fl) | Webb,Stanley (fl) | Jennings,Jack (vib) | Jones,Hank (p) | Covington,Charles (org) | Davis,Richard (b) | Muhammad,Idris[Leo Morris] (dr) | Pacheco,Johnny (perc) | Eichen,Bernard (v) | Libove,Charles (v) | Markowitz,Dave (viola) | Ricci,George (cello) | Sebesky,Don (cond,arr)
George Benson With Orchestra
I Remember Wes
NYC, rec. 18.11.1969
Benson,George (g) | Terry,Clark (tp) | Brown,Garnett (tb) | Clark,Arthur (fl,ts) | Marge,George (fl,ts) | Lucas,Buddy (harm) | Jennings,Jack (vib) | Griffin,Paul (p,celeste) | Rainey,Chuck (el-b) | Muhammad,Idris[Leo Morris] (dr) | Barretto,Ray (perc) | Gonzalez,Andy (perc) | Strings | Ott,Horace (arr)
George Benson Group
Out Of The Blue
details unknown, rec. 1969
Benson,George (g,voc) | details unknown

521867-2 | CD | The Best Of The Song Books:The Ballads
Ella Fitzgerald With The Nelson Riddle Orchestra
How Long Has This Been Going On
Los Angeles,CA, rec. 5.1.1959
Fitzgerald,Ella (voc) | Fagerquist,Don (tp) | Klein,Manny (tp) | McMickle,Dale (tp) | Sherock,Shorty (tp) | Bernhart,Milton 'Milt' (tb) | Noel,Richard (tb) | Pederson,Pullman 'Tommy' (tb) | De Karske,Karl (b-tb) | DeRosa,Vince (fr-h) | Nash,Ted (ts) | Collette,Buddy (reeds) | Klee,Harry (reeds) | Koch,Joe (reeds) | Webb,Champ (reeds) | Baker,Israel (v) | Bay,Victor (v) | Beller,Alex 'Al' (v) | Edelstein,Walter (v) | Getzoff,James (v) | Gill,Ben (v) | Kellner,Murray (v) | Ross,Nathan 'Nat' (v) | Sosson,Marshall (v) | Vinci,Gerry (v) | Dinkin,Alvin (viola) | Robyn,Paul (viola) | Simons,Barbara (viola) | Greenschpoon,Elizabeth (cello) | Neikrug,George (cello) | Reher,Kurt (cello) | Julyie,Katharine 'Kathryn' (harp) | Smith,Paul (p) | Ellis,Herb (g) | Comfort,Joe (b) | Stoller,Alvin (dr) | Flynn,Fred (perc) | Riddle,Nelson (arr,ld)
Oh! Lady Be Good
Hollywood,CA, rec. 8.1.1959
Fitzgerald,Ella (voc) | Arno,Victor (v) | Bay,Victor (v) | Beller,Alex 'Al' (v) | Gasselin,Jaques (v) | Gill,Ben (v) | Hill,Henry (v) | Kellner,Murray (v) | Russell,Mischa (v) | Shure,Paul (v) | Neufeld,Erno (v) | Sosson,Marshall (v) | Vinci,Gerry (v) | Dinkin,Alvin (viola) | Robyn,Paul (viola) | Simons,Barbara (viola) | Sterkin,David (viola) | Arkatov,James (cello) | Greenschpoon,Elizabeth (cello) | Neikrug,George (cello) | Reher,Kurt (cello) | Julyie,Katharine 'Kathryn' (harp) | Smith,Paul (p) | Ellis,Herb (g) | Mondragon,Joe (b) | Richmond,Bill (dr) | Riddle,Nelson (arr,ld)
I'm Old Fashioned
Los Angeles,CA, rec. 5.1.1963
Fitzgerald,Ella (voc) | Fagerquist,Don (tp) | Lewis,Carroll (tp) | Seaberg,George (tp) | Sherock,Shorty (tp) | Nash,Dick (tb) | Shepard,Tom (tb) | Pederson,Pullman 'Tommy' (tb) | Roberts,George (b-tb) | Johnson,Plas (ts) | Klee,Harry (reeds) | Koch,Joe (reeds) | Schwartz,Wilbur (reeds) | Webb,Champ (reeds) | Arno,Victor (v) | Baker,Israel (v) | Bay,Victor (v) | Beller,Alex 'Al' (v) | Neufeld,Erno (v) | Raderman,Lou (v) | Ross,Nathan 'Nat' (v) | Slatkin,Felix (v) | Sosson,Marshall (v) | Vinci,Gerry (v) | Neiman,Alex (viola) | Robyn,Paul (viola) | Simons,Barbara (viola) | Kaproff,Armand (cello) | Lustgarten,Edgar 'Ed' (cello) | Slatkin,Eleanor (cello) | Stockton[Mason],Ann (harp) | Smith,Paul (p) | Bain,Robert 'Bob' (g) | Comfort,Joe (b) | Stoller,Alvin (dr) | Flynn,Fred (perc) | Riddle,Nelson (arr,ld)
Let's Begin
Los Altos Hill,CA, rec. 7.1.1963
Fitzgerald,Ella (voc) | Fagerquist,Don (tp) | Lewis,Carroll (tp) | Seaberg,George (tp) | Sherock,Shorty (tp) | Nash,Dick (tb) | Shepard,Tom (tb) | Pederson,Pullman 'Tommy' (tb) | Roberts,George (b-tb) | Johnson,Plas (ts) | Klee,Harry (reeds) | Koch,Joe (reeds) | Schwartz,Wilbur (reeds) | Webb,Champ (reeds) | Arno,Victor (v) | Baker,Israel (v) | Bay,Victor (v) | Beller,Alex 'Al' (v) | Lube,Dan (v) | Neufeld,Erno (v) | Raderman,Lou (v) | Ross,Nathan 'Nat' (v) | Slatkin,Felix (v) | Sosson,Marshall (v) | Sharp,Sidney 'Sid' (v) | Vinci,Gerry (v) | Neiman,Alex (viola) | Robyn,Paul (viola) | Simons,Barbara (viola) | Kaproff,Armand (cello) | Kramer,Ray (cello) | Slatkin,Eleanor (cello) | Smith,Paul (p) | Bain,Robert 'Bob' (g) | Comfort,Joe (b) | Stoller,Alvin (dr) | Flynn,Fred (perc) | Riddle,Nelson (arr,ld)
Laura
Los Angeles,CA, rec. 21.10.1964
Fitzgerald,Ella (voc) | Lewis,Carroll (tp) | Mangano,Vito (tp) | Seaberg,George (tp) | Sherock,Shorty (tp) | Bernhart,Milton 'Milt' (tb) | Shepard,Tom (tb) | Pederson,Pullman 'Tommy' (tb) | Roberts,George (b-tb) | Cave,John (fr-h) | Decker,James 'Jimmy' (fr-h) | Hinshaw,William 'Bill' (fr-h) | Collette,Buddy (fl) | Klee,Harry (fl) | Benno,Norman (oboe) | Schoneberg,Seymour (oboe) | DeFranco,Buddy (cl) | Smith,George (cl) | Johnson,Plas (ts) | Russin,Irving 'Babe' (ts) | Hildebrandt,Lloyd (bs) | Terry,Howard (bs) | Koch,Joe (reeds) | Schwartz,Wilbur (reeds) | Smith,Willie (as) | Julyie,Katharine 'Kathryn' (harp) | Smith,Paul (p) | Kessel,Barney (g) | Comfort,Joe (b) | Cottler,Irv (dr) | Radocchia,Emil (perc) | Riddle,Nelson (arr,ld)
Travelin' Light
Los Angeles,CA, rec. 19.10.1964
Fitzgerald,Ella (voc) | Lewis,Carroll (tp) | Mangano,Vito (tp) | Seaberg,George (tp) | Sherock,Shorty (tp) | Nash,Dick (tb) | Shepard,Tom (tb) | Pederson,Pullman 'Tommy' (tb) | Roberts,George (b-tb) | Cave,John (fr-h) | Decker,James 'Jimmy' (fr-h) | Hinshaw,William 'Bill' (fr-h) | Collette,Buddy (fl) | Klee,Harry (fl) | Benno,Norman (oboe) | Schoneberg,Seymour (oboe) | DeFranco,Buddy (cl) | Smith,George (cl) | Johnson,Plas (ts) | Russin,Irving 'Babe' (ts) | Hildebrandt,Lloyd (bs) | Terry,Howard (bs) | Koch,Joe (reeds) | Schwartz,Wilbur (reeds) | Smith,Willie (as) | Julyie,Katharine 'Kathryn' (harp) | Smith,Paul (p) | Kessel,Barney (g) | Comfort,Joe (b) | Cottler,Irv (dr) | Radocchia,Emil (perc) | Riddle,Nelson (arr,ld)
Ella Fitzgerald With The Billy May Orchestra
It Was Written In The Stars | Ill Wind | This Time The Dream's On Me
Los Angeles,CA, rec. 15.1.1961

Fitzgerald,Ella (voc) | Fagerquist,Don (tp) | Bernhart,Milton 'Milt' (tb) | Carter,Benny (as) | Johnson,Plas (ts) | Gentry,Chuck (bs) | Baker,Israel (v) | Gasselin,Jaques (v) | Gill,Ben (v) | Kellner,Murray (v) | Lube,Dan (v) | Neufeld,Erno (v) | Sosson,Marshall (v) | Stepansky,Joe (v) | Vinci,Gerry (v) | Raderman,Lou (v) | Ross,Nathan 'Nat' (v) | Russell,Mischa (v) | Dinkin,Alvin (viola) | Kievman,Louis (viola) | Majewski,Virginia (viola) | Robyn,Paul (viola) | Kaproff,Armand (cello) | Kramer,Ray (cello) | Lustgarten,Edgar 'Ed' (cello) | Slatkin,Eleanor (cello) | Brilhart,Verlye (harp) | Levy,Lou (p) | Ellis,Herb (g) | Middlebrooks,Wilfred (b) | Mondragon,Joe (b) | Stoller,Alvin (dr) | Sheet,Walter (arr) | May,Billy (arr,ld)

Ella Fitzgerald With The Buddy Bregman Orchestra
There's A Small Hotel
Los Angeles,CA, rec. 29.8.1956
Fitzgerald,Ella (voc) | DeRosa,Vince (fr-h) | unkn. (2 fr-h) | Nash,Ted (fl) | Schwartz,Wilbur (fl) | Shank,Bud (fl) | Koblenz,Arnold (engl-h,oboe) | Gentry,Chuck (b-cl,bs) | unkn. (2 bs) | Russell,Mischa (concertmaster) | unkn. (12 v) | unkn. (2 violas) | La Marchina,Robert 'Bob' (cello) | Lustgarten,Edgar 'Ed' (cello) | unkn. (2 cellos) | Hale,Corky (harp) | Smith,Paul (p) | Kessel,Barney (g) | Mondragon,Joe (b) | Holland,Milt (vib,perc) | Stoller,Alvin (dr) | Bregman,Buddy (cond,arr)

A Ship Without A Sail
Los Angeles,CA, rec. 30.8.1956
Fitzgerald,Ella (voc) | DeRosa,Vince (fr-h) | Nash,Ted (fl) | Cooper,Bob (engl-h,oboe) | unkn. (8 v) | unkn. (2 violas) | La Marchina,Robert 'Bob' (cello) | Lustgarten,Edgar 'Ed' (cello) | Hale,Corky (harp) | Smith,Paul (p) | Kessel,Barney (g) | Mondragon,Joe (b) | Holland,Milt (vib,perc) | Stoller,Alvin (dr) | Bregman,Buddy (cond,arr)

Ella Fitzgerald With The Duke Ellington Orchestra
Day Dream
NYC, rec. 24.6.1957
Fitzgerald,Ella (voc) | Anderson,Cat (tp) | Baker,Harold 'Shorty' (tp) | Cook,Willie (tp) | Terry,Clark (tp) | Jackson,Quentin (tb) | Sanders,John (tb) | Woodman,Britt (tb) | Hamilton,Jimmy (cl,ts) | Hodges,Johnny (as) | Procope,Russell (as) | Foster,Frank (ts) | Gonsalves,Paul (ts) | Carney,Harry (bs) | Strayhorn,Billy (p) | Woode,Jimmy (b) | Woodyard,Sam (dr)

Ella Fitzgerald With The Paul Smith Quartet
Easy To Love
Los Angeles,CA, rec. 7.2.1956
Fitzgerald,Ella (voc) | Smith,Paul (p) | Kessel,Barney (g) | Mondragon,Joe (b) | Stoller,Alvin (dr)

Ella Fitzgerald And Her All Stars
Do Nothin' Till You Hear From Me
Los Angeles,CA, rec. 4.9.1956
Fitzgerald,Ella (voc) | Webster,Ben (ts) | Smith,Stuff (v) | Smith,Paul (p) | Kessel,Barney (g) | Mondragon,Joe (b) | Stoller,Alvin (dr)

Ella Fitzgerald With The Paul Weston Orchestra
Now It Can Be Told | You're Laughing At Me
Los Angeles,CA, rec. 17.3.1958
Fitzgerald,Ella (voc) | Orchestra | Weston,Paul (cond,arr) | details unknown

522055-2 | CD | Verve Jazz Masters 40:Dinah Washington

Dinah Washington With The Jimmy Cobb Orchestra
Trouble In Mind
Los Angeles,CA, rec. 18.1.1952
Washington,Dinah (voc) | Cobb,Jimmy (dr) | Webster,Ben (ts) | Gray,Wardell (ts) | Kelly,Wynton (p) | details unknown

Clifford Brown All Stars With Dinah Washington
I'll Remember April | You Go To My Head
Los Angeles,CA, rec. 14.8.1954
Washington,Dinah (voc) | Brown,Clifford (tp) | Ferguson,Maynard (tp) | Terry,Clark (tp) | Geller,Herb (as) | Land,Harold (ts) | Powell,Richie (p) | Morrow,George (b) | Roach,Max (dr)

Dinah Washington And Her Band
Love For Sale
NYC, rec. 5.2.1954
Washington,Dinah (voc) | Terry,Clark (tp) | Chamblee,Eddie (ts) | Davis,Jackie (org) | Mance,Junior[Julian C.] (p) | unkn. (g) | Betts,Keter (b) | Thigpen,Ed (dr)

Blue Skies
NYC, rec. 15.6.1954
Washington,Dinah (voc) | Terry,Clark (tp) | Chappell,Gus (tb) | Henderson,Rick (as) | Davis,Eddie 'Lockjaw' (ts) | Mance,Junior[Julian C.] (p) | Betts,Keter (b) | Roach,Max (dr)

I've Got You Under My Skin
Los Angeles,CA, rec. 14.8.1954
Washington,Dinah (voc) | Ferguson,Maynard (tp) | Mance,Junior[Julian C.] (p) | Betts,Keter (b) | Roach,Max (dr)

Crazy He Calls Me
Washington,Dinah (voc) | Geller,Herb (as) | Powell,Richie (p) | Morrow,George (b) | Roach,Max (dr)

Dinah Washington And Her Orchestra
Teach Me Tonight
NYC, rec. 2.11.1954
Washington,Dinah (voc) | Orchestra | details unknown

Dinah Washington With The Quincy Jones Orchestra
They Didn't Believe Me | Never Let Me Go
NYC, rec. 5.12.1956
Washington,Dinah (voc) | Glow,Bernie (tp) | Maxwell,Jimmy (tp) | Severinsen,Doc (tp) | Shavers,Charlie (tp) | Terry,Clark (tp) | Travis,Nick (tp) | Cleveland,Jimmy (tb) | Green,Urbie (tb) | Jackson,Quentin (tb) | Mitchell,Tom (b-tb) | McKusick,Hal (as) | Ortega,Anthony (as) | Richardson,Jerome (ts) | Thompson,Lucky (ts) | Bank,Danny (bs) | Elliott,Don (vib,mellophone) | Anderson,Clarence 'Sleepy' (p) | Galbraith,Barry (g) | Hinton,Milt (b) | Johnson,Osie (dr) | Jones,Quincy (arr,ld)

Dinah Washington With The Eddie Chamblee Orchestra
After You've Gone
Chicago,Ill, rec. 7.1.1958
Washington,Dinah (voc) | Chamblee,Eddie (ts) | Ricard,Fip (tp) | Priester,Julian (tb) | Davis,Charles (bs) | Wilson,Jack (p) | Wilson,Robert (b) | Slaughter,James (dr) | Edmondson,Bob (arr)

Dinah Washington With The Terry Gibbs Band
All Of Me
Live at Newport,Rhode Island, rec. 6.7.1958
Washington,Dinah (vib,voc) | Gibbs,Terry (vib) | Elliott,Don (mellophone) | Green,Urbie (tb) | Kelly,Wynton (p) | West,Paul (b) | Roach,Max (dr)

522651-2 | CD | Verve Jazz Masters 31:Cannonball Adderley

Cannonball Adderley And His Orchestra
The Song Is You | Cynthia's In Love
NYC, rec. 21.7.1955
Adderley,Julian \'Cannonball\' (as) | Adderley,Nat (tp) | Cleveland,Jimmy (tb) | Richardson,Jerome (ts) | Payne,Cecil (bs) | Williams,John (p) | Chambers,Paul (b) | Clarke,Kenny (dr)

You'd Be So Nice To Come Home To
NYC, rec. 29.7.1955
Adderley,Julian \'Cannonball\' (as) | Adderley,Nat (tp) | Johnson,J.J. (tb) | Richardson,Jerome (ts) | Payne,Cecil (bs) | Williams,John (p) | Chambers,Paul (b) | Clarke,Kenny (dr)

I'm Afraid The Masquerade Is Over - (I'm Afraid) The Masquerade Is Over | Street Of Dreams | Falling In Love With Love
NYC, rec. 27./28.10.1955
Adderley,Julian \'Cannonball\' (as) | Hayman,Richard (arr,ld) | details unknown

I'm Glad There Is You | Little Girl Blue
NYC, rec. 18.6.1956
Adderley,Julian \'Cannonball\' (as) | Adderley,Nat (co) | Royal,Ernie (tp) | Byrne,Bobby (tb) | Cleveland,Jimmy (tb) | Richardson,Jerome (fl,ts) | Bank,Danny (bs) | Mance,Junior[Julian C.] (p) | Betts,Keter (b) | Wright,Charles 'Specs' (dr)

Cannonball Adderley Quintet
Lover Man(Oh,Where Can You Be?) | The Way You Look Tonight
NYC, rec. 7.2.1957
Adderley,Julian \'Cannonball\' (as) | Adderley,Nat (co) | Mance,Junior[Julian C.] (p) | Jones,Sam (b) | Cobb,Jimmy (dr)

Spring Is Here
NYC, rec. 11.2.1957
Adderley,Julian \'Cannonball\' (as) | Adderley,Nat (co) | Mance,Junior[Julian C.] (p) | Jones,Sam (b) | Cobb,Jimmy (dr)

What's New? | Straight No Chaser
NYC, rec. 4.3.1958
Adderley,Julian \'Cannonball\' (as) | Adderley,Nat (co) | Mance,Junior[Julian C.] (p) | Jones,Sam (b) | Cobb,Jimmy (dr)

Cannonball Adderley And His Orchestra
I Got It Bad And That Ain't Good
NYC, rec. 20.8.1958
Adderley,Julian \'Cannonball\' (as) | Berry,Emmett (tp) | Kruczek,Leo (v) | Orloff,Gene (v) | Schwartz,David (viola) | Ricci,George (cello) | Evans,Bill (p) | Galbraith,Barry (g) | Hinton,Milt (b) | Cobb,Jimmy (dr) | Russo,Bill (cond,arr)

Cannonball Adderley Quintet
Limehouse Blues | Stars Fell On Alabama
Chicago,Ill, rec. 3.2.1959
Adderley,Julian \'Cannonball\' (as) | Coltrane,John (ts) | Kelly,Wynton (p) | Chambers,Paul (b) | Cobb,Jimmy (dr)

523019-2 | CD | Roy Hargrove Quintet With The Tenors Of Our Time

Roy Hargrove Quintet With Stanley Turrentine
Soppin' The Biscuit | Wild Is Love
NYC, rec. 16./17.1.1994
Hargrove,Roy (tp,fl-h) | Turrentine,Stanley (ts) | Blake,Ron (ss,ts) | Chestnut,Cyrus (p) | Whitaker,Rodney Thomas (b) | Hutchinson,Gregory (dr)

Roy Hargrove Quintet With Johnny Griffin
When We Were One | Greens At The Chicken Shack
Hargrove,Roy (tp,fl-h) | Griffin,Johnny (ts) | Blake,Ron (ss,ts) | Chestnut,Cyrus (p) | Whitaker,Rodney Thomas (b) | Hutchinson,Gregory (dr)

Roy Hargrove Quintet With Branford Marsalis
Valse Hot
Hargrove,Roy (tp,fl-h) | Marsalis,Branford (ts) | Blake,Ron (ss,ts) | Chestnut,Cyrus (p) | Whitaker,Rodney Thomas (b) | Hutchinson,Gregory (dr)

Roy Hargrove Quintet With Joe Henderson
Shade Of Jade | Serenity
Hargrove,Roy (tp,fl-h) | Henderson,Joe (ts) | Blake,Ron (ss,ts) | Chestnut,Cyrus (p) | Whitaker,Rodney Thomas (b) | Hutchinson,Gregory (dr)

Roy Hargrove Quintet With Joshua Redman
Across The Pond | Mental Phrasing
Hargrove,Roy (tp,fl-h) | Blake,Ron (ss,ts) | Chestnut,Cyrus (p) | Whitaker,Rodney Thomas (b) | Hutchinson,Gregory (dr)

Roy Hargrove Quintet
Once Forgotten | April's Fool
Hargrove,Roy (tp,fl-h) | Blake,Ron (ss,ts) | Chestnut,Cyrus (p) | Whitaker,Rodney Thomas (b) | Hutchinson,Gregory (dr)

523260-2 | CD | The Montreal Tapes Vol.1

Charlie Haden Trio
The Sphinx | Art Deco | Happy House | Lonely Woman | Mopti | The Blessing | When Will The Blues Leave | Law Years
Live at The Jazzfestival Montreal, rec. 2.7.1989
Haden,Charlie (b) | Cherry,Don (pocket-tp) | Blackwell,Ed (dr)

523321-2 | CD | Get Happy!

Ella Fitzgerald With The Frank DeVol Orchestra
You Turned The Tables On Me | Gypsy In My Soul | Goody Goody | St.Louis Blues | A-Tisket A-Tasket
Hollywood,CA, rec. 24.7.1957
Fitzgerald,Ella (voc) | Edison,Harry 'Sweets' (tp) | Candoli,Pete (tp) | Linn,Ray (tp) | Werth,George (tp) | Bernhart,Milton 'Milt' (tb) | Roberts,George (tb) | Ulyate,Lloyd (tb) | Ruderman,Morton (fl) | Ruderman,Sylvia (fl) | Naegly,Clint (as) | Webster,Ben (ts) | Herfurt,Arthur 'Skeets' (reeds) | Koch,Joe (reeds) | Romersa,Ernest (reeds) | Gassman,Bert (oboe) | Koblenz,Arnold (oboe) | Schoenberg,Gordon (oboe) | Herzberg,Norman (bassoon) | Lowman,Kenneth (bassoon) | Marsh,Jack (bassoon) | Albert,Sam (v) | Raderman,Lou (v) | Baker,Israel (v) | Barene,Robert (v) | Dicterow,Harold (v) | Freed,Sam (v) | Frisina,Dave (v) | Gill,Ben (v) | Herbert,Mort (v) | Hill,Henry (v) | Kaminsky,Anatol (v) | Lube,Dan (v) | Lustgarten,Alfred (v) | Miller,Bill (v) | Russo,Ambrose (v) | Saparoff,Albert (v) | Henhennick,G.R. (viola) | Hinka,Jan (viola) | Majewski,Virginia (viola) | Ostrowsky,Bob (viola) | Schonbach,Sanford (viola) | Thomas,Milton (viola) | DiTullio,Justin (cello) | Kaproff,Armand (cello) | Kramer,Raphael (cello) | Rosso,Nino (cello) | Ross,Arnold (p) | Remsen,Dorothy (harp) | Kessel,Barney (g) | Luboff,Abe (b) | Mondragon,Joe (b) | Stephens,Phil (b) | Stoller,Alvin (dr) | Holland,Milt (perc) | DeVol,Frank (cond,arr)

Ella Fitzgerald With The Paul Weston Orchestra
Blue Skies
Hollywood,CA, rec. 18.3.1958
Fitzgerald,Ella (voc) | Best,John (tp) | Candoli,Pete (tp) | Edison,Harry 'Sweets' (tp) | Fagerquist,Don (tp) | Klein,Manny (tp) | Kusby,Eddie (tb) | Noel,Dick (tb) | Schaefer,Bill (tb) | Tizol,Juan (v-tb) | Gentry,Chuck (reeds) | Matlock,Matty (reeds) | Nash,Ted (reeds) | Russin,Irving 'Babe' (reeds) | Stulce,Fred (reeds) | Smith,Paul (p) | Kessel,Barney (g) | Mondragon,Joe (b) | Stoller,Alvin (dr) | Weston,Paul (cond,arr)

Swingin' Shepherd Blues
Hollywood,CA, rec. 19.3.1958
Fitzgerald,Ella (voc) | Edison,Harry 'Sweets' (tp) | Hartman,Leonard 'Lennie' (reeds) | Matlock,Matty (reeds) | Nash,Ted (reeds) | Stulce,Fred (reeds) | Smith,Paul (p) | Kessel,Barney (g) | Mondragon,Joe (b) | Stoller,Alvin (dr) | Weston,Paul (cond,arr)

Ella Fitzgerald With The Nelson Riddle Orchestra
Somebody Loves Me | Cheerful Little Earful
Hollywood,CA, rec. 7.1.1959
Fitzgerald,Ella (voc) | Gozzo,Conrad (tp) | Lewis,Cappy (tp) | Mangano,Vito (tp) | Sherock,Shorty (tp) | Noel,Dick (tb) | Pederson,Pullman 'Tommy' (tb) | Roberts,George (tb) | Tizol,Juan (v-tb) | Carter,Benny (reeds) | Gordon,Justin (reeds) | Johnson,Plas (reeds) | Koch,Joe (reeds) | Nash,Ted (reeds) | Smith,Paul (p) | Ellis,Herb (g) | Mondragon,Joe (b) | Richmond,Bill (dr) | Riddle,Nelson (cond)

Ella Fitzgerald With Frank De Vol And His Orchestra
You Make Me Feel So Young | Moonlight Becomes You
Hollywood,CA, rec. 11.7.1959
Fitzgerald,Ella (voc) | Beach,Frank (tp) | Candoli,Pete (tp) | Lewis,Cappy (tp) | Porcino,Al (tp) | Betts,Harry (tb) | Noel,Dick (tb) | Roberts,George (tb) | Ulyate,Lloyd (tb) | Cipriano,Gene (reeds) | Collette,Buddy (reeds) | Gentry,Chuck (reeds) | Johnson,Plas (reeds) | Langinger,Ronald (reeds) | Feldman,Victor (vib) | Levy,Lou (p) | Ellis,Herb (g) | Mondragon,Joe (b) | Stoller,Alvin (bongos) | Garcia,Russell (arr) | DeVol,Frank (cond)

Ella Fitzgerald With The Marty Paich Orchestra
Beat Me Daddy Eight To The Bar | Like Young | Cool Breeze
Hollywood,CA, rec. 3.9.1958
Fitzgerald,Ella (voc) | Candoli,Pete (tp) | Candreva,Philip (tp) | Childers,Buddy (tp) | Williamson,Stu (tp) | McEachern,Murray (tb) | Roberts,George (tb) | Shepard,Tom (tb) | Ulyate,Lloyd (tb) | Corre,Jay (reeds) | Gentry,Chuck (reeds) | Holman,Bill (reeds) | Nash,Ted (reeds) | Frisina,Dave (v) | Lube,Dan (v) | Miller,William (v) | Shapiro,Eunice (v) | Slatkin,Felix (v) | Williamson,Claude (p) | Barton,Mary Jane (harp) | Ellis,Herb (g) | Mitchell,Red (b) | Sperling,Jack (dr) | Paich,Marty (arr,ld) | Garcia,Russell (cond,arr)

523322-2 | CD | Reflections | EAN 731452332226

Stan Getz With Strings And Voices
Spring Can Really Hang You Up The Most | Charade | Early Autumn | Reflections | Sleeping Bee | Penthouse Serenade | Love | Nitetime Street
NYC, rec. 21./22.10.1963
Getz,Stan (ts) | Burton,Gary (vib) | Burrell,Kenny (g) | Duvivier,George (b) | Hunt,Joe (dr) | Ogerman,Claus (arr) | Schifrin,Lalo (cond,arr) | unkn. (perc) | unkn. (brass) | unkn. (choir)

Moonlight In Vermont | If Ever I Would Leave You | Blowin' In The Wind
NYC, rec. 28.10.1963
Getz,Stan (ts) | Burrell,Kenny (g) | Duvivier,George (b) | Ogerman,Claus (cond,arr) | unkn. (strings) | unkn. (perc) | unkn. (choir)

523342-2 | CD | Verve Jazz Masters 36:Gerry Mulligan

Gerry Mulligan Concert Jazz Band
You Took Advantage Of Me | Manoir De Mes Reves(aka Django's Castle)
NYC, rec. 25./27.7.1960
Mulligan,Gerry (bs) | Candoli,Conte (tp) | Ferrara,Don (tp) | Travis,Nick (tp) | Andre,Wayne (tb) | Brookmeyer,Bob (v-tb,arr) | Ralph,Alan (b-tb) | Quill,Gene (cl,as) | Meldonian,Dick (as) | Sims,Zoot (as) | Allen,Gene (bs) | Clark,Buddy (b) | Lewis,Mel (dr)

Barbara's Theme
Milano,Italy, rec. November 1960
Mulligan,Gerry (bs) | Travis,Nick (tp) | Ferrara,Don (tp) | Candoli,Conte (tp) | Brookmeyer,Bob (v-tb) | Dennis,Willie (tb) | Ralph,Alan (tb) | Quill,Gene (cl,as) | Donovan,Bob (as) | Sims,Zoot (ts) | Reider,Jimmy (ts) | Allen,Gene (b-cl,bs) | Clark,Buddy (b) | Lewis,Mel (dr) | Mandel,Johnny (arr)

Lady Chatterley's Mother | Blueport
Live at The 'Village Vanguard',NYC, rec. December 1960
Mulligan,Gerry (bs) | Travis,Nick (tp) | Ferrara,Don (tp) | Terry,Clark (tp) | Brookmeyer,Bob (v-tb) | Dennis,Willie (tb) | Ralph,Alan (tb) | Quill,Gene (cl,as) | Donovan,Bob (as) | Reider,Jimmy (ts) | Allen,Gene (b-cl,bs) | Crow,Bill (b) | Lewis,Mel (dr) | Cohn,Al (arr)

Weep | All About Rosie | Chuggin' | Summer's Over | Israel
NYC, rec. 10./11.7.1961
Mulligan,Gerry (bs,p) | Travis,Nick (tp) | Ferrara,Don (tp) | Severinsen,Doc (tp) | Brookmeyer,Bob (v-tb,arr) | Dennis,Willie (tb) | Ralph,Alan (tb) | Quill,Gene (cl,as) | Donovan,Bob (as) | Reider,Jimmy (ts) | Allen,Gene (b-cl,bs) | Crow,Bill (b) | Lewis,Mel (dr) | McFarland,Gary (arr) | Russell,George (arr)

Ballad | Big City Blues
NYC, rec. 18.-21.12.1962
Mulligan,Gerry (cl,bs) | Travis,Nick (tp) | Ferrara,Don (tp) | Severinsen,Doc (tp) | Terry,Clark (fl-h) | Brookmeyer,Bob (v-tb,p,arr) | Dennis,Willie (tb) | Studd,Tony (b-tb) | Quill,Gene (cl,as) | Caine,Eddie (as) | Reider,Jimmy (ts) | Allen,Gene (bs) | Hall,Jim (g) | Crow,Bill (b) | Johnson,Gus (dr)

523392-2 | CD | The Best Of Bud Powell On Verve

Bud Powell Trio
Tempus Fugit | Celia | All God's Chillun Got Rhythm
NYC, rec. January/February 1949
Powell,Bud (p) | Brown,Ray (b) | Roach,Max (dr)

So Sorry Please | Sweet Georgia Brown | April In Paris
NYC, rec. February 1950
Powell,Bud (p) | Russell,Curly (b) | Roach,Max (dr)

Tea For Two
NYC, rec. June/July 1950
Powell,Bud (p) | Brown,Ray (b) | Rich,Buddy (dr)

Bud Powell
Just One Of Those Things | Parisian Thoroughfare
NYC, rec. February 1951
Powell,Bud (p-solo)

Bud Powell Trio
It Never Entered My Mind
NYC, rec. 10.6.1954
Powell,Bud (p) | Heath,Percy (b) | Taylor,Arthur 'Art' (dr)

Tenderly
NYC, rec. 11.1.1955
Powell,Bud (p) | Trottman,Lloyd (b) | Blakey,Art (dr)

Dance Of The Infidels
NYC, rec. 13.1.1955
Powell,Bud (p) | Heath,Percy (b) | Clarke,Kenny (dr)

Lady Bird | Willow Groove | Bean And The Boys | Star Eyes | Stairway To The Stars
NYC, rec. 27.4.1955
Powell,Bud (p) | Duvivier,George (b) | Taylor,Arthur 'Art' (dr)

523893-2 | 10 CD | The Complete Jazz At The Philharmonic On Verve 1944-1949

JATP All Stars
Lester Leaps In | Tea For Two | Blues | Body And Soul
Live at Philharmonic Auditorium,Los Angeles,CA, rec. 2.7.1944
JATP All Stars | Johnson,J.J. (tb) | Jacquet,Illinois (ts) | McVea,Jack (ts) | Cole,Nat King (p) | Paul,Les (g) | Miller,Johnny (b) | Young,Lee (dr)

Meade Lux Lewis
Yancey Special | Fast Boogie | Dupree Blues | Honky Tonk Train Blues
Lewis,Meade Lux (p-solo)

JATP All Stars
C Jam Blues
Live at Philharmonic Auditorium,Los Angeles,CA, rec. 2.7.194
JATP All Stars | Sherock,Shorty (tp) | Myers,Bumps (ts) | Thomas,Joe (ts) | Cole,Buddy (p) | Callender,Red (b) | Marshall,Joe (dr)

Sweet Lorraine
Live at Philharmonic Auditorium,Los Angeles,CA, rec. 2.7.1944
JATP All Stars | Cole,Nat King (p) | Paul,Les (g) | Miller,Johnny (b) | Young,Lee (dr)

I've Found A New Baby | Rosetta | Bugle Call Rag
JATP All Stars | Sherock,Shorty (tp) | Jacquet,Illinois (ts) | McVea,Jack (ts) | Cole,Nat King (p) | Paul,Les (g) | Callender,Red (b) | Miller,Johnny (b) | Young,Lee (dr)

The Man I Love
JATP All Stars | Sherock,Shorty (tp) | Jacquet,Illinois (ts) | McVea,Jack (ts) | Cole,Nat King (p) | Paul,Les (g) | Callender,Red (b) | Miller,Johnny (b) | Young,Lee (dr) | Richards,Carolyn (voc)

One O'Clock Jump | Oh! Lady Be Good
Live at Philharmonic Auditorium,Los Angeles,CA, rec. 30.7.1944
JATP All Stars | Jacquet,Illinois (ts) | Cole,Nat King (p) | Callender,Red (b) | Young,Lee (dr)

Introduction by Al Jarvis | Stompin' At The Savoy | I've Found A New Baby | Body And Soul
Live at Philharmonic Auditorium,Los Angeles,CA, rec. 12.2.1945
JATP All Stars | Hefti,Neal (tp) | Sherock,Shorty (tp) | Corcoran,Corky (ts) | Hawkins,Coleman (ts) | Raskin,Milt (p) | Barbour,Dave (g) | Mingus,Charles (b) | Coleman,Dave (dr)

Billie Holiday With The JATP All Stars
Body And Soul
Holiday,Billie (voc) | JATP All Stars | McGhee,Howard (arr) | unkn. (tb) | Smith,Willie (as) | Gray,Wardell or Illinois Jacquet or Charlie Ventura (ts) | Raskin,Milt prob. (p) | Barbour,Dave prob. (g) | Mingus,Charles (b) | Coleman,Dave (dr)

Strange Fruit
Holiday,Billie (voc) | Raskin,Milt (p)

JATP All Stars
I Don't Stand A Ghost Of A Chance With You
JATP All Stars | Hefti,Neal (tp) | Sherock,Shorty (tp) | Jacquet,Illinois (ts) | Corcoran,Corky (ts) | Ventura,Charlie (ts) | Raskin,Milt (p) | Barbour,Dave (g) | Mingus,Charles (b) | Coleman,Dave (dr)

Oh! Lady Be Good | How High The Moon
JATP All Stars | Guy,Joe (tp) | McGhee,Howard (tp) | Smith,Willie (as) | Jacquet,Illinois (ts) | Ventura,Charlie (ts) | Finney,Garland (p) | Livingstone,Ulysses (g) | Callender,Red (b) | Krupa,Gene (dr)

Slim Gaillard-Bam Brown
Opera In Vout(Groove Juice Symphony) | Introduzione Pianissimo(Softly Most Softly)- | Recitativo E Finale(Of Much Scat)- | Andante Cantabile In Modo De Blues- | Presto Con Stomp(With A Floy Floy)- | The Flat Foot Floogie | Big Noise From Winnetka | Yancey Special
Gaillard,Slim (g,p,voc) | Brown,Tiny Bam (b,dr,voc)

JATP All Stars
Blues For Norman | Oh! Lady Be Good | I Can't Get Started | After You've Gone
Live at Philharmonic Auditorium,Los Angeles,CA, rec. 28.1.1946
JATP All Stars | Killian,Al (tp) | McGhee,Howard (tp) | Parker,Charlie (as) | Smith,Willie (as) | Young,Lester (ts) | Ross,Arnold (p) | Hadnott,Billy (b) | Young,Lee (dr)

Gene Krupa Trio

Stompin' At The Savoy | Idaho
Krupa,Gene (dr) | Ventura,Charlie (ts) | Napoleon,Teddy (p)
JATP All Stars
Crazy Rhythm
JATP All Stars | Gillespie,Dizzy (tp) | Smith,Willie (as) | Ventura,Charlie (ts) | Young,Lester (ts) | Powell,Mel (p) | Hadnott,Billy (b) | Young,Lee (dr)
The Man I Love
JATP All Stars | Gillespie,Dizzy (tp) | Killian,Al (tp) | Smith,Willie (as) | Ventura,Charlie (ts) | Young,Lester (ts) | Powell,Mel (p) | Hadnott,Billy (b) | Young,Lee (dr)
Sweet Georgia Brown
JATP All Stars | Gillespie,Dizzy (tp) | Killian,Al (tp) | Parker,Charlie (as) | Smith,Willie (as) | Ventura,Charlie (ts) | Young,Lester (ts) | Powell,Mel (p) | Hadnott,Billy (b) | Young,Lee (dr)
Meade Lux Lewis
Blues De Lux | Announcement by Norman Granz | Honky Tonk Train Blues
Live at Embassy Auditorium,LA, rec. 22.4.1946
Lewis,Meade Lux (p-solo)
JATP All Stars
Announcement by Norman Granz | JATP Blues | I Got Rhythm | I Surrender Dear | I've Found A New Baby
JATP All Stars | Clayton,Buck (tp) | Parker,Charlie (as) | Smith,Willie (as) | Young,Lester (ts) | Hawkins,Coleman (ts) | Kersey,Kenny (p) | Ashby,Irving (g) | Hadnott,Billy (b) | Rich,Buddy (dr)
Bugle Call Rag
JATP All Stars | Clayton,Buck (tp) | Linn,Ray (tp) | Smith,Willie (as) | Corcoran,Corky (ts) | Hawkins,Coleman (ts) | Russin,Irving 'Babe' (ts) | Young,Lester (ts,voc) | Kersey,Kenny (p) | Ashby,Irving prob. (g) | Hadnott,Billy (b) | Rich,Buddy (dr)
Philharmonis Blues(Carnegie Blues) | Oh! Lady Be Good | I Can't Get Started | Sweet Georgia Brown
Live at Carnegie Hall,NYC, rec. 27.5.1946
JATP All Stars | Clayton,Buck (tp) | Hawkins,Coleman (ts) | Jacquet,Illinois (ts) | Young,Lester (ts) | Kersey,Kenny (p) | Russell,Curly (b) | Heard,J.C. (dr)
Gene Krupa Trio
The Man I Love
Krupa,Gene (dr) | Ventura,Charlie (ts) | Napoleon,Teddy (p)
JATP All Stars
Slow Drag
JATP All Stars | Clayton,Buck (tp) | Hawkins,Coleman (ts) | Young,Lester (ts) | Kersey,Kenny (p) | Russell,Curly (b) | Heard,J.C. (dr)
Billie Holiday With The JATP All Stars
The Man I Love | Gee Baby Ain't I Good To You | All Of Me | Billie's Blues | Announcement by Al Anderson
Live at Carnegie Hall,NYC, rec. 3.6.1846
Holiday,Billie (voc) | JATP All Stars | Guy,Joe (tp) | Auld,Georgie (as) | Jacquet,Illinois (ts) | Young,Lester (ts) | Kersey,Kenny (p) | Grimes,Tiny (g) | McKibbon,Al (b) | Heard,J.C. (dr)
Lester Young Quintet
Tea For Two
Live at Carnegie Hall,NYC, rec. 3.6.1946
Young,Lester (ts) | Guy,Joe (tp) | Kersey,Kenny (p) | McKibbon,Al (b) | Heard,J.C. (dr)
Coleman Hawkins Quartet
It's The Talk Of The Town
Hawkins,Coleman (ts) | Kersey,Kenny (p) | McKibbon,Al (b) | Heard,J.C. (dr)
Buck Clayton Quartet
My Honey's Lovin' Arms
Clayton,Buck (tp) | Kersey,Kenny (p) | McKibbon,Al (b) | Heard,J.C. (dr)
Kenny Kersey Trio
Boogie Woogie Cocktail
Kersey,Kenny (p) | McKibbon,Al (b) | Heard,J.C. (dr)
Lester Young Quartet
D.B.Blues | Sax-O-Be-Bop | Lester Blows Again
Young,Lester (ts) | Kersey,Kenny (p) | Richardson,Rodney (b) | West,Harold 'Doc' (dr)
Billie Holiday With The JATP All Stars
I Cried For You(Now It's Your Turn To Cry Over Me) | Fine And Mellow | He's Funny That Way
Holiday,Billie (voc) | JATP All Stars | Clayton,Buck (tp) | unkn. (tb) | Hawkins,Coleman (ts) | Jacquet,Illinois (ts) | Young,Lester (ts) | Kersey,Kenny (p) | Collins,John or Tiny Grimes (g) | Russell,Curly prob. (b) | Heard,J.C. (dr)
JATP All Stars
Blues
Live at Carnegie Hall,NYC, rec. 17.6.1946
JATP All Stars | Gillespie,Dizzy (tp) | Johnson,J.J. (tb) | Eager,Allen (ts) | Jacquet,Illinois (ts) | Kersey,Kenny (p) | Collins,John (g) | Jackson,Chubby (b) | Heard,J.C. (dr)
Blues(Pres) | Just You Just Me | I Got Rhythm
JATP All Stars | Clayton,Buck (tp) | Young,Trummy (tb) | Young,Lester (ts) | Kersey,Kenny (p) | Collins,John (g) | Russell,Curly or Rodney Richardson (g) | Heard,J.C. (dr)
Slam Stewart Trio
My Blue Heaven | Play Fiddle Play
Stewart,Slam (b,voice) | Kersey,Kenny (p) | Heard,J.C. (dr)
JATP All Stars
Flying Home
Jacquet,Illinois (ts) | Kersey,Kenny (p) | Collins,John (g) | Russell,Curly or Rodney Richardson (g) | Heard,J.C. (dr)
Billie Holiday With The JATP All Stars
He's Funny That Way
Live at Shrine Auditorium,Los Angeles,CA, rec. 7.10.1946
Holiday,Billie (voc) | JATP All Stars | prob.personal: | McGhee,Howard (tp) | Young,Trummy (tb) | Jacquet,Illinois (ts) | Kersey,Kenny (p) | Kessel,Barney (g) | Drayton,Charlie (b) | Mills,Jackie (dr)
Trav'lin' Light
Holiday,Billie (voc) | Young,Trummy (tb) | Kersey,Kenny (p)
JATP All Stars
How High The Moon
Live at Syria Mosque,Pittsburgh, rec. 5.3.1947
JATP All Stars | Young,Trummy (tb) | Smith,Willie (as) | Hawkins,Coleman (ts) | Phillips,Flip (ts) | Kersey,Kenny (p) | Fonville,Benny (b) | Rich,Buddy (dr)
Bell Boy Blues
JATP All Stars | Clayton,Buck (tp) | Young,Trummy (tb) | Smith,Willie (as) | Phillips,Flip (ts) | Kersey,Kenny (p) | Fonville,Benny (b) | Rich,Buddy (dr)
Kenny Kersey Trio
Boogie Woogie Cocktail | Sweet Lorraine
Kersey,Kenny (p) | Fonville,Benny (b) | Rich,Buddy (dr)
JATP All Stars
Characteristically B.H.
Live at Carnegie Hall,NYC, rec. 5.4.1947
JATP All Stars | Harris,Bill (tb) | Ventura,Charlie (ts) | Burns,Ralph (p) | De Arango,Bill (g) | Russell,Curly (b) | Tough,Dave (dr)
Summertime | Sid Flips His Lid
Shavers,Charlie (tp) | Jones,Hank (p) | Russell,Curly (b) | Catlett,Big Sid (dr)
Medley: | Lover Come Back To Me- | I Don't Stand A Ghost Of A Chance With You- | Just You Just Me-
Shavers,Charlie (tp) | Harris,Bill (tb) | Ventura,Charlie (ts) | Burns,Ralph (p) | De Arango,Bill (g) | Russell,Curly (b) | Catlett,Big Sid (dr)
Blues
Live at Carnegie Hall,NYC, rec. 24.5.1947
JATP All Stars | Eldridge,Roy (tp) | Brown,Pete (as) | Smith,Willie (as) | Phillips,Flip (ts) | Paul,Les (g) | Jones,Hank (p) | Fonville,Benny (b) | Stoller,Alvin (dr)
Billie Holiday With Bobby Tucker
Announcement by Norman Granz | You'd Better Go Now | You're Driving Me Crazy | There Is No Greater Love | I Cover The Waterfront
Holiday,Billie (voc) | Tucker,Bobby (p)
JATP All Stars
Perdido | Mordido | I Surrender Dear | Endido
Live at Carnegie Hall,NYC, rec. 27.9.1947
JATP All Stars | McGhee,Howard (tp) | Harris,Bill (tb) | Jacquet,Illinois (ts) | Phillips,Flip (ts) | Jones,Hank (p) | Brown,Ray (b) | Jones,Jo (dr)
Introduction by Norman Granz | The Opener | Lester Leaps In | Embraceable You | The Closer | Ow! | Announcement by Norman Granz | Flying Home
Live at Carnegie Hall,NYC, rec. 18.9.1949
JATP All Stars | Eldridge,Roy (tp) | Turk,Tommy (tb) | Parker,Charlie (as) | Phillips,Flip (ts) | Young,Lester (ts) | Jones,Hank (p) | Brown,Ray (b) | Rich,Buddy (dr)
Oscar Peterson-Ray Brown Duo
Introduction by Norman Granz | Fine And Dandy | I Only Have Eyes For You | Carnegie Blues
Peterson,Oscar (p) | Brown,Ray (b)
Coleman Hawkins Quartet
Introduction by Norman Granz | Body And Soul | Rifftide | The Big Head | Stuffy | Sophisticated Lady
Hawkins,Coleman (ts) | Jones,Hank (p) | Brown,Ray (b) | Rich,Buddy (dr)
Hank Jones Trio
Introduction by Norman Granz | Ol' Man River | Air Mail Special
Jones,Hank (p) | Brown,Ray (b) | Rich,Buddy (dr)
Ella Fitzgerald With The Hank Jones Trio
Introduction by Norman Granz | Robbin's Nest | A New Shade Of Blues | Old Mother Hubbard | I'm Just A Lucky So-And-So | Basin Street Blues | Introduction by Norman Granz | Oh! Lady Be Good | Black Coffee | A-Tisket A-Tasket
Fitzgerald,Ella (voc) | Jones,Hank (p) | Brown,Ray (b) | Rich,Buddy (dr)
JATP All Stars
Announcement by Norman Granz | How High The Moon | Perdido
JATP All Stars | Eldridge,Roy (tp) | Turk,Tommy (tb) | Parker,Charlie (as) | Phillips,Flip (ts) | Young,Lester (ts) | Jones,Hank (p) | Brown,Ray (b) | Rich,Buddy (dr) | Fitzgerald,Ella (voc)
Gene Krupa Trio
Stompin' At The Savoy | Body And Soul | Dark Eyes
details unknown, rec. March 1952
Krupa,Gene (dr) | Ventura,Charlie (ts) | Napoleon,Marty (p)

523984-2 | CD | Charlie Parker With Strings:The Master Takes
Charlie Parker With Strings
Repetition
Live at Carnegie Hall,NYC, rec. December 1947
Parker,Charlie (as) | Porcino,Al (tp) | Wetzel,Ray (tp) | Mettome,Doug (tp) | Harris,Bill (tb) | Varsalona,Bart (tb) | Jacobs,Vinnie (fr-h) | LaPorta,John (cl) | Williams,Murray (as) | Salad,Sonny (as) | Phillips,Flip (ts) | Mondello,Pete (ts) | Caplan,Sam (v) | Katzman,Harry (v) | Orloff,Gene (v) | Smirnoff,Ziggy (v) | Harris,Sid (v) | Fidler,Manny (v) | Benaventi,Joe (cello) | Aless,Tony (p) | Russell,Curly (b) | Manne,Shelly (dr) | Iborra,Diego (congas,bongos) | Hefti,Neal (cond,arr)
April In Paris | Summertime | If I Should Lose You | I Didn't Know What Time It Was | Everything Happens To Me | Just Friends
NYC, rec. 30.11.1949
Parker,Charlie (as) | Miller,Mitch (oboe) | Gimpel,Bronislaw (v) | Hollander,Max (v) | Lomask,Milt (v) | Brieff,Frank (viola) | Miller,Frank (cello) | Rosen,Myoer (harp) | Freeman,Stan (p) | Brown,Ray (b) | Rich,Buddy (dr) | Carroll,Jimmy (cond,arr)
Charlie Parker With The Joe Lipman Orchestra
Dancing In The Dark | Laura | East Of The Sun West Of The Moon | They Can't Take That Away From Me | Easy To Love | I'm In The Mood For Love | I'll Remember April
NYC, rec. late summer 1950
Parker,Charlie (as) | Singer,Joe (fr-h) | Brown,Eddie (oboe) | Caplan,Sam (v) | Kay,Howard (v) | Melnikoff,Harry (v) | Rand,Sam (v) | Smirnoff,Kelly (v) | Zir,Isadore (viola) | Brown,Maurice (cello) | Mills,Verley (harp) | Leighton,Bernie (p) | Brown,Ray (b) | Rich,Buddy (dr) | Lippman,Joe (cond,arr)
Out Of Nowhere
Parker,Charlie (as) | Singer,Joe (fr-h) | Brown,Eddie (oboe) | Caplan,Sam (v) | Kay,Howard (v) | Melnikoff,Harry (v) | Rand,Sam (v) | Smirnoff,Kelly (v) | Zir,Isadore (viola) | Brown,Maurice (cello) | Mills,Verley (harp) | unkn. (xyl) | Leighton,Bernie (p) | Brown,Ray (b) | Rich,Buddy (dr) | Lippman,Joe (cond,arr)
Charlie Parker With Strings
What Is This Thing Called Love | April In Paris | Repetition | Easy To Love | Rocker
Live at Carnegie Hall,NYC, rec. 17.9.1950
Parker,Charlie (as) | Mace,Tommy (oboe) | Caplan,Sam (v) | Bloom,Ted (v) | Karpenia,Stan (v) | Uchitel,Dave (viola) | Bundy,Bill (cello) | McManus,Wallace (harp) | Haig,Al (p) | Potter,Tommy (b) | Haynes,Roy (dr)
Charlie Parker With The Joe Lipman Orchestra
Temptation | Lover | Autumn In New York | Stella By Starlight
NYC, rec. 22./23.1.1952
Parker,Charlie (as) | Porcino,Al (tp) | Griffin,Chris (tp) | Privin,Bernie (tp) | Bradley,Will (tb) | Williams,Murray (as) | Mondello,Toots (as) | Ross,Hank (ts) | Webb,Stanley (bs) | Drellinger,Art (reeds) | unkn. (2 reeds) | Caplan,Sam prob. (v) | Shulman,Sylvan prob. (v) | Zayde,Jack prob. (v) | unkn. (5 v,2 viola,2 cello) | Mills,Verley (harp) | Stein,Lou (p) | Ryerson,Arthur 'Art' (g) | Haggart,Bob (b) | Lamond,Don (dr) | Lippman,Joe (cond,arr)

523989-2 | CD | Gettin' To It
Christian McBride Group
In A Hurry | Gettin' To It
NYC, rec. 30./31.8.& 1.9.1994
McBride,Christian (b) | Hargrove,Roy (tp) | Turre,Steve (tb) | Redman,Joshua (ts) | Chestnut,Cyrus (p) | Nash,Lewis (dr)
The Shade Of The Cedar Tree | King Freddie Of Hubbard
McBride,Christian (b) | Hargrove,Roy (tp) | Redman,Joshua (ts) | Chestnut,Cyrus (p) | Nash,Lewis (dr)
Black Moon
McBride,Christian (b) | Redman,Joshua (ts) | Chestnut,Cyrus (p) | Nash,Lewis (dr)
Sitting On A Cloud
McBride,Christian (b) | Hargrove,Roy (tp) | Chestnut,Cyrus (p) | Nash,Lewis (dr)
Too Close For Comfort | Stars Fell On Alabama
McBride,Christian (b) | Chestnut,Cyrus (p) | Nash,Lewis (dr)
Christian McBride
Night Train
McBride,Christian (b)
Christian McBride/Ray Brown/Milt Hinton
Splanky
McBride,Christian (b) | Brown,Ray (b) | Hinton,Milt (b)

523990-2 | CD | Essential Ella
Ella Fitzgerald With Orchestra
Manhattan | With A Song In My Heart | Every Time We Say Goodbye | Let's Face The Music And Dance | The Man I Love | A Fine Romance | Blue Moon | Mack The Knife(Moritat) | Let's Do It(Let's Fall In Love) | Love For Sale | It's All Right With Me | What Is This Thing Called Love | But Not For Me | 'S Wonderful | I Could Write A Book | The Lady Is A Tramp | My Funny Valentine | Bewitched Bothered And Bewildered | There's A Small Hotel | Our Love Is Here To Stay
different Places, rec. different Dates
Fitzgerald,Ella (voc) | details not on the cover

525431-2 | CD | Verve Jazz Masters 43:Ben Webster
Johnny Hodges Orchestra
Meet The Fog
NYC, rec. 8.4.1959
Hodges,Johnny (as) | Baker,Harold 'Shorty' (tp) | Jackson,Quentin or John Sanders (tb) | Hamilton,Jimmy (cl,ts) | Webster,Ben (ts) | Jones,Jimmie (p) | Spann,Les (g) | Brown,Ray (b) | Jones,Jo (dr)
Ben Webster And His Orchestra
That's All | Pennies From Heaven
Hollywood,CA, rec. 8.,12.1953
Webster,Ben (ts) | Edison,Harry 'Sweets' (tp) | Carter,Benny (as) | Peterson,Oscar (p) | Ellis,Herb (g) | Brown,Ray (b) | Stoller,Alvin (dr)
Ben Webster With Orchestra And Strings
Come Rain Or Come Shine | Do Nothin' Till You Hear From Me
NYC, rec. 15.12.1954
Webster,Ben (ts) | Hamilton,Jimmy (cl) | Bank,Danny (fl,cl,b-cl) | Deutsch,Solomon (v) | Kruczek,Leo (v) | Schachter,Julius (v) | Zayde,Jack (v) | Fisch,Burt (viola) | Greenhouse,Bernhard (cello) | Wilson,Teddy (p) | Marshall,Wendell (b) | Bellson,Louie (dr) | Burns,Ralph (cond,arr)
Ben Webster Sextet
Old Folks
Hollywood Bowl,CA, rec. 21.12.1951
Webster,Ben (ts) | Ferguson,Maynard (tp) | Carter,Benny (as) | Wiggins,Gerald 'Gerry' (p) | Kirby,John (b) | Jenkins,George (b)
Coleman Hawkins And Ben Webster With The Oscar Peterson Quartet
You'd Be So Nice To Come Home To
Hollywood,CA, rec. 16.10.1957
Hawkins,Coleman (ts) | Webster,Ben (ts) | Peterson,Oscar (p) | Ellis,Herb (g) | Brown,Ray (b) | Stoller,Alvin (dr)
Ben Webster With The Teddy Wilson Trio
You're Mine You | Love's Away
NYC, rec. 30.3.1954
Webster,Ben (ts) | Wilson,Teddy (p) | Brown,Ray (b) | Jones,Jo (dr)
Ben Webster And His Associates
De-Dar
NYC, rec. 9.4.1959
Webster,Ben (ts) | Eldridge,Roy (tp) | Hawkins,Coleman (ts) | Johnson,Budd (ts) | Jones,Jimmy (p) | Spann,Les (g) | Brown,Ray (b) | Jones,Jo (dr)
Ben Webster With The Oscar Peterson Trio
Bye Bye Blackbird
Hollywood,CA, rec. 6.11.1959
Webster,Ben (ts) | Peterson,Oscar (p) | Brown,Ray (b) | Thigpen,Ed (dr)
Ella Fitzgerald With The Oscar Peterson Quartet And Ben Webster
In A Mellow Tone
Hollywood,CA, rec. 17.10.1957
Webster,Ben (ts) | Peterson,Oscar (p) | Ellis,Herb (g) | Brown,Ray (b) | Stoller,Alvin (dr) | Fitzgerald,Ella (voc)
Gerry Mulligan-Ben Webster Quintet
Chelsea Bridge
Hollywood,CA, rec. 3.11.1959
Webster,Ben (ts) | Mulligan,Gerry (bs) | Rowles,Jimmy (p) | Vinnegar,Leroy (b) | Lewis,Mel (dr)
Ben Webster With The Oscar Peterson Quartet
Soulville
Hollywood,CA, rec. 15.10.1957
Webster,Ben (ts) | Peterson,Oscar (p) | Ellis,Herb (g) | Brown,Ray (b) | Levey,Stan (dr)
Johnny Otis And His Orchestra
Stardust
Los Angeles,CA, rec. 16.12.1951
Otis,Johnny (vib) | Johnson,Don (tp) | Wilson,Gerald (tp) | Pettigrew,John (tb) | Washington,George (tb) | Turnham,Floyd (as) | Webster,Ben (ts) | Holderness,Lorenzo (ts) | Lowe,Curtis (bs) | Williams,Devonia (p) | Lewis,Pete (g) | Delagarde,Mario (b) | Bell,Leard (dr) | Vaharandes,Emmanuel (congas)

525472-2 | CD | The Antonio Carlos Jobim Songbook
Stan Getz-Joao Gilberto Quintet
Girl From Ipanema(Garota De Ipanema)
NYC, rec. 18./19.3.1963
Getz,Stan (ts) | Gilberto,Joao (g) | Jobim,Antonio Carlos (p) | Williams,Tommy (b) | Banana,Milton (dr) | Gilberto,Astrud (voc)
Sarah Vaughan With The Frank Foster Orchestra
Corcovado(Quiet Nights)
NYC, rec. 14.8.1964
Vaughan,Sarah (voc) | Andre,Wayne (tb) | Byers,Billy (tb) | Cleveland,Jimmy (tb) | Faulise,Paul (tb) | Hixon,Richard 'Dick' (tb) | Richardson,Jerome (fl) | James,Bob (p) | Galbraith,Barry (g) | Rodriguez,Roberto (b) | Donaldson,Bobby (dr) | Cadavieco,Juan (perc) | Mangual,Jose (perc) | Sierra,Rafael (perc) | Foster,Frank (arr,ld)
Billy Eckstine With Bobby Tucker And His Orchestra
Felicidade
Rio De Janeiro,Brazil, rec. 1963
Eckstine,Billy (voc) | Byers,Billy (arr) | Tucker,Bobby (cond) | details unknown
Stan Getz-Luiz Bonfa Group
Favela(O Morro Nao Tem Vez)
NYC, rec. 9.2.1963
Getz,Stan (ts) | Bonfa,Luiz (g) | Jobim,Antonio Carlos (g) | Duvivier,George (b) | Williams,Tommy (b) | Ferreira,Paulo (dr) | Carlos,Jose (dr,perc)
Astrud Gilberto With Antonio Carlos Jobim And The Marty Paich Orchestra
Agua De Beber(Water To Drink)
Los Angeles,CA, rec. 28.1.1965
Gilberto,Astrud (voc) | Jobim,Antonio Carlos (g,p) | Bernhart,Milton 'Milt' (tb) | Shank,Bud (fl) | Donato,Joao (p) | Mondragon,Joe (b) | unkn. (perc) | Paich,Marty (arr,ld) | details unknown
Antonio Carlos Jobim Group
So Danco Samba(I Only Dance The Samba)
NYC, rec. 10.5.1963
Jobim,Antonio Carlos (g) | Wright,Leo (fl) | details unknown
Wes Montgomery Quintet With The Claus Ogerman Orchestra
Insensatez(How Insensitive)
Englewood Cliffs,NJ, rec. 17.3.1966
Montgomery,Wes (g) | Eichen,Bernard (v) | Eidus,Arnold (v) | Gershman,Paul (v) | Green,Emmanuel (v) | Held,Julius (v) | Lookofsky,Harry (v) | Malin,Joe (v) | Orloff,Gene (v) | Kessler,Abe (cello) | McCracken,Charles (cello) | Ricci,George (cello) | Shapiro,Harvey (cello) | Carter,Ron (b) | Tate,Grady (dr) | Barretto,Ray (congas) | Ogerman,Claus (cond,arr)
Shirley Horn Trio
Once I Loved
NYC, rec. 14.-16.11.1988
Horn,Shirley (p,voc) | Ables,Charles (b) | Williams,Stephen E. 'Steve' (dr)
Stan Getz-Charlie Byrd Sextet
Samba Da Una Nota So(One Note Samba)
All Souls Unitarian Church,Washington,DC, rec. 13.2.1962
Getz,Stan (ts) | Byrd,Charlie (g) | Byrd,Gene (g) | Betts,Keter (b) | Reichenbach,Bill (perc) | Deppenschmidt,Buddy (perc)
Joao Gilberto Trio
Meditacao(Meditation)
Live at Carnegie Hall,NYC, rec. 9.10.1964
Gilberto,Joao (g,voc) | Betts,Keter (b) | Melito,Helcio (dr)
Ella Fitzgerald With The Marty Paich Orchestra
Desafinado
NYC, rec. 1.10.1962
Fitzgerald,Ella (voc) | Orchestra | Paich,Marty (arr,ld) | details unknown
Astrud Gilberto With Antonio Carlos Jobim And The Marty Paich Orchestra
Dindi
Los Angeles,CA, rec. 27.1.1965
Gilberto,Astrud (voc) | Jobim,Antonio Carlos (g,voc) | Williamson,Stu (tp) | Bernhart,Milton 'Milt' (tb) | Shank,Bud (fl,as) | Donato,Joao (p) | Mondragon,Joe (b) | Paich,Marty (arr,ld) | Strings | details unknown
Oscar Peterson Trio With The Claus Ogermann Orchestra
Wave
NYC, rec. March 1969
Peterson,Oscar (p) | Jones,Sam (b) | Durham,Bobby (dr) | Orchestra | Ogerman,Claus (cond,arr) | details unknown
Antonio Carlos Jobim-Elis Regina Group
Aguas De Marco(Waters Of March)
Los Angeles,CA, rec. 22.2./9.3.1974
Jobim,Antonio Carlos (p,voc) | Regina,Elis (voc) | Mariano,Cesar Camargo (p) | Delmiro,Helio (g) | Castro-Neves,Oscar (g) | Maia,Luizao (b) | Braga,Paulo (dr)
Dizzy Gillespie Septet
Chega De Saudade(No More Blues)

Live at Juan Les Pins,France, rec. 24.7.1962
Gillespie,Dizzy (tp) | Wright,Leo (as,voc) | Schifrin,Lalo (p,arr) | Bacsik,Elek (g) | White,Chris (b) | Collins,Rudy (dr) | Riestra,Pepito (perc)

526373-2 | 2 CD | Clifford Brown-Max Roach:Alone Together-The Best Of The Mercury Years
Clifford Brown-Max Roach Quintet
Cherokee | What Am I Here For | Sandu | Daahoud | Jordu
NYC, rec. 25.2.1955
Brown,Clifford (tp) | Land,Harold (ts) | Powell,Richie (p) | Morrow,George (b) | Roach,Max (dr)
Joy Spring | Mildama | Daahoud | Parisian Thoroughfare | Blues Walk
Hollywood,CA, rec. 6.8.1954
Brown,Clifford (tp) | Land,Harold (ts) | Powell,Richie (p) | Morrow,George (b) | Roach,Max (dr)
Clifford Brown With Strings
What's New? | Stardust
NYC, rec. 18.1.1955
Brown,Clifford (tp) | Powell,Richie (p) | Galbraith,Barry (g) | Morrow,George (b) | Roach,Max (dr) | Hefti,Neal (arr) | Strings | details unknown
Sarah Vaughan With The Clifford Brown All Stars
September Song
NYC, rec. 16.12.1954
Vaughan,Sarah (voc) | Brown,Clifford (tp) | Mann,Herbie (fl) | Quinichette,Paul (ts) | Jones,Jimmy (p) | Benjamin,Joe (b) | Haynes,Roy (dr) | Wilkins,Rick (cond,arr)
Helen Merrill With The Quincy Jones Orchestra
Born To Be Blue
NYC, rec. 22.12.1954
Merrill,Helen (voc) | Brown,Clifford (tp) | Bank,Danny (fl,bs) | Jones,Jimmy (p) | Galbraith,Barry (g) | Hinton,Milt (b) | Johnson,Osie (dr) | Jones,Quincy (arr,ld)
Clifford Brown-Max Roach Quintet
Gertrude's Bounce
NYC, rec. 4.1.1956
Brown,Clifford (tp) | Rollins,Sonny (ts) | Powell,Richie (p) | Morrow,George (b) | Roach,Max (dr)
Max Roach Plus Four
Dr. Free-Zee | Just One Of Those Things
NYC, rec. 19.9.1956
Roach,Max (dr,overdubbed tympani) | Dorham,Kenny (tp) | Rollins,Sonny (ts) | Bryant,Ray (p) | Morrow,George (b)
Max Roach Quintet
Valse Hot
NYC, rec. 20.3.1957
Roach,Max (dr) | Dorham,Kenny (tp) | Rollins,Sonny (ts) | Wallace,Billy (p) | Morrow,George (b)
Max Roach Quartet
Tune Up
NYC, rec. 20.12.1957
Roach,Max (dr) | Dorham,Kenny (tp) | Mobley,Hank (ts) | Morrow,George (b)
Yardbird Suite
NYC, rec. 23.12.1957
Roach,Max (dr) | Dorham,Kenny (tp) | Mobley,Hank (ts) | Boyd,Nelson (b)
Max Roach Plus Four
A Night In Tunisia | La Villa
Live at Newport,Rhode Island, rec. 6.7.1958
Roach,Max (dr) | Little,Booker (tp) | Draper,Ray (tuba) | Coleman,George (ts) | Davis,Art (b)
Max Roach With The Boston Percussion Ensemble
Max's Variations
Lenox,Massachusette, rec. August 1958
Roach,Max (dr) | Boston Percussion Ensemble,The | Faberman,Irvin (perc,cond) | Firth,Everett (perc) | MacClausland,Lloyd (perc) | Press,Arthur (perc) | Smith,Charles (perc) | Thompson,Harold (perc) | Tobarczyk,Walter (perc)
Max Roach Quintet
Prelude
Chicago,Ill, rec. 22.9.1959
Roach,Max (dr) | Little,Booker (tp) | Priester,Julian (tb) | Coleman,George (ts) | Davis,Art (b)
Juliano | Lotus Blossom
NYC, rec. January 1960
Roach,Max (dr) | Turrentine,Tommy (tp) | Priester,Julian (tb) | Turrentine,Stanley (ts) | Boswell,Bobby (b)
The Left Bank
Paris,France, rec. 1.3.1960
Roach,Max (dr) | Turrentine,Tommy (tp) | Priester,Julian (tb) | Turrentine,Stanley (ts) | Boswell,Bobby (b)
Max Roach Sextet
Never Leave Me
Chicago,Ill, rec. October 1960
Roach,Max (dr) | Turrentine,Tommy (tp) | Priester,Julian (tb) | Turrentine,Stanley (ts) | Bryant,Ray (p) | Boswell,Bobby (b) | Lincoln,Abbey (voc)

526702-2 | CD | Nina Simone After Hours
Nina Simone With Hal Mooney's Orchestra
Night Song | Nobody
NYC, rec. 1964
Simone,Nina (p,voc) | Orchestra | Mooney,Hal (arr,ld) | details unknown
Nina Simone
Lilac Wine
NYC, rec. 30.9.1965
Simone,Nina (p,voc)
Nina Simone Quintet
Tell Me More And More And Then Some | If I Should Lose You
NYC, rec. 19./20.5.1965
Simone,Nina (p,voc) | Shackman,Al (g,harm) | Stevenson,Rudy (g) | Atkinson,Lisle (b) | Hamilton,Bobby (dr)
Nina Simone Quartet
End Of The Line
Simone,Nina (p,voc) | Stevenson,Rudy (g) | Atkinson,Lisle (b) | Hamilton,Bobby (dr)
The Other Woman
NYC, rec. 1./6.4.1964
Simone,Nina (p,voc) | Stevenson,Rudy (fl) | Atkinson,Lisle (b) | Hamilton,Bobby (dr)
Don't Explain
NYC, rec. 30.9.1965
Simone,Nina (p,voc) | Stevenson,Rudy (fl) | Atkinson,Lisle (b) | Hamilton,Bobby (dr)
Nina Simone
Black Is The Color Of My True Love's Hair
NYC, rec. 1./6.4.1964
Simone,Nina (p,voc)
Nina Simone Trio
Wild Is The Wind | Little Girl Blue
Simone,Nina (p,voc) | Atkinson,Lisle (b) | Hamilton,Bobby (dr)
Nina Simone With Hal Mooney's Orchestra
Keeper Of The Flame
details unknown, rec. August 1966
Simone,Nina (p,voc) | Orchestra & Chorus | Mooney,Hal (arr,ld) | details unknown
Nina Simone
Images
Live at Carnegie Hall,NYC, rec. 21.3.1964
Simone,Nina (p,voc)
Nina Simone Trio
I Loves You Porgy
Simone,Nina (p,voc) | Atkinson,Lisle (b) | Hamilton,Bobby (dr)
Nina Simone With Horace Ott's Orchestra
For Myself
NYC, rec. 1.10.1965
Simone,Nina (p,voc) | Stevenson,Rudy (fl) | Atkinson,Lisle (b) | Hamilton,Bobby (dr) | Orchestra | Ott,Horace (cond,arr) | details unknown

526817-2 | CD | Verve Jazz Masters 42:Sarah Vaughan-The Jazz Sides
Sarah Vaughan And Her Trio
I Cried For You(Now It's Your Turn To Cry Over Me) | The More I See You | Over The Rainbow | I Feel Pretty | Misty | Tenderly
Live at The 'Tivoli Gardens',Copenhagen, rec. 18.& 21.7.1963
Vaughan,Sarah (voc) | Stuart,Kirk (p) | Williams,Charles (b) | Hughes,George (dr)
Words Can't Describe | Pennies From Heaven
NYC, rec. 14.2.1957
Vaughan,Sarah (voc) | Jones,Jimmie (p) | Davis,Richard (b) | Haynes,Roy (dr)
It's Got To Be Love | Dancing In The Dark
Live at Mister Kelly's,Chicago, rec. 7./8.8.1957
Vaughan,Sarah (voc) | Jones,Jimmie (p) | Davis,Richard (b) | Haynes,Roy (dr)
Prelude To A Kiss | Polka Dots And Moonbeams | Body And Soul
NYC, rec. 2.4.1954
Vaughan,Sarah (voc) | Malachi,John (p) | Benjamin,Joe (b) | Haynes,Roy (dr)
Sarah Vaughan And The Thad Jones Orchestra
Doodlin'
NYC, rec. 5.1.1958
Vaughan,Sarah (voc) | Jones,Thad (tp) | Culley,Wendell (tp) | Newman,Joe (tp) | Young,Eugene 'Snooky' (tp) | Coker,Henry (tb) | Grey,Al (tb) | Powell,Benny (tb) | Wess,Frank (as,ts) | Royal,Marshall (as) | Foster,Frank (ts) | Mitchell,Billy (ts) | Fowlkes,Charlie (bs) | Bright,Ronnell (p) | Green,Freddie (g) | Davis,Richard (b) | Payne,Sonny (dr)
I Left My Heart In San Francisco
NYC, rec. 24.1.1967
Vaughan,Sarah (voc) | Jones,Thad (arr) | Newman,Joe (tp) | Hubbard,Freddie (tp) | Shavers,Charlie (tp) | Terry,Clark (tp) | Johnson,J.J. (tb) | Winding,Kai (tb) | Woods,Phil (as) | Golson,Benny (ts) | James,Bob (p) | details unknown
Sarah Vaughan With Her Quartet
Like Someone In Love
Live at London House,Chicago, rec. 7.3.1958
Vaughan,Sarah (voc) | Wess,Frank (ts) | Bright,Ronnell (p) | Davis,Richard (b) | Haynes,Roy (dr)

527222-2 | CD | Double Rainbow
Joe Henderson Group
Boto | Ligia
NYC, rec. 5./6.11.1994
Henderson,Joe (ts) | Elias,Eliane (p) | Assumpcao,Nico (b) | Braga,Paulo (dr)
Felicidade | Dreamer(Vivo Sohando)
Henderson,Joe (ts) | Castro-Neves,Oscar (g) | Elias,Eliane (p) | Assumpcao,Nico (b) | Braga,Paulo (dr)
Once I Loved
Henderson,Joe (ts) | Castro-Neves,Oscar (g)
Triste | Photograph | Chega De Saudade(No More Blues) | Passarim
Los Angeles,CA, rec. 19./20.9.1994
Henderson,Joe (ts) | Hancock,Herbie (p) | McBride,Christian (b) | DeJohnette,Jack (dr)
Portrait In Black And White
Henderson,Joe (ts) | Hancock,Herbie (p) | McBride,Christian (b)
Happy Madness
Henderson,Joe (ts) | Hancock,Herbie (p)
Modinha
Henderson,Joe (ts) | McBride,Christian (b)

527249-2 | CD | Steal Away
Charlie Haden-Hank Jones
It's Me Oh Lord | Nobody Knows The Trouble I've Seen | Spiritual | Wade In The Water | Swing Low Sweet Chariot | Sometimes I Feel Like A Motherless Child | L'Amour De Moy | Danny Boy (Londonderry Air) | I've Got A Robe, You Got A Robe(Goin' To Shout All Over God's Heaven) | Steal Away | We Shall Overcome | Go Down Moses | My Lord What A Morning | Hymn Medley: | Abide With Me- | Just As I Am Without One Plea- | What A Friend We Have In Jesus- | Amazing Grace-
Montreal,Canada, rec. 29./30.6.1994
Jones,Hank (p) | Haden,Charlie (b)

527365-2 | CD | Verve Jazz Masters 41:Tal Farlow
Tal Farlow Quartet
Everything I've Got | The Love Nest | With The Wind And The Rain In Your Hair
NYC, rec. 2.6.1954
Farlow,Tal (g) | Galbraith,Barry (g) | Pettiford,Oscar (b) | Morello,Joe (dr)
Little Girl Blue | Autumn In New York | Cherokee
Hollywood,CA, rec. 15./16.11.1954
Farlow,Tal (g) | Wiggins,Gerald 'Gerry' (p) | Brown,Ray (b) | Hamilton,Forrest 'Chico' (dr)
It's You Or No One | I Remember You
Hollywood,CA, rec. 17.1.1955
Farlow,Tal (g) | Williamson,Claude (p) | Mitchell,Red (b) | Levey,Stan (dr)
Tal Farlow
Autumn Leaves
Farlow,Tal (g-solo)
Tal Farlow Sextet
Out Of Nowhere | Lorinesque | Moonlight Becomes You
Hollywood,CA, rec. 4.5.1955
Farlow,Tal (g) | Enevoldsen,Bob (tb) | Perkins,Bill (ts) | Gordon,Bob (bs) | Budwig,Monty (b) | Marable,Lawrence (dr)
Tal Farlow Trio
Meteor
NYC, rec. 31.5.1956
Farlow,Tal (g) | Costa,Eddie (p) | Burke,Vinnie (b)
Isn't It Romantic | Yesterdays
NYC, rec. 5.6.1946
Farlow,Tal (g) | Costa,Eddie (p) | Burke,Vinnie (b)
Tal Farlow Quartet
Stella By Starlight
NYC, rec. 17./18.2.or 10.3.1958
Farlow,Tal (g) | Costa,Eddie (p) | Totah,Nabil 'Knobby' or Bill Takas (b) | Campbell,Jimmy (dr)

527382-2 | CD | A Turtle's Dream
Abbey Lincoln With The Rodney Kendrick Trio And Guests
Nature Boy | Storywise
NYC, rec. May/August & November 1994
Lincoln,Abbey (voc) | Hargrove,Roy (tp) | Lourau,Julien (ts) | Kendrick,Rodney (p) | McBride,Christian (b) | Lewis,Victor (dr)
A Turtle's Dream
Lincoln,Abbey (voc) | Lourau,Julien (ts) | Kendrick,Rodney (p) | Haden,Charlie (b) | Lewis,Victor (dr)
My Love Is You
Lincoln,Abbey (voc) | Lourau,Julien (ts) | Kendrick,Rodney (p) | Bowie,Michael (b) | Lewis,Victor (dr)
Hey Lordy Mama
Lincoln,Abbey (voc) | Kendrick,Rodney (p) | Peterson,Lucky (g,voc) | Bowie,Michael (b) | Lewis,Victor (dr)
Down Here Below
Lincoln,Abbey (voc) | Barron,Kenny (p) | Haden,Charlie (b) | Lewis,Victor (dr) | Billingslea,Sandra 'Sandy' (v) | Robinson,John (cello) | Noel,Randolph (string-arr)
Being Me
Lincoln,Abbey (voc) | Barron,Kenny (p) | Metheny,Pat (g) | Haden,Charlie (b) | Lewis,Victor (dr)
Throw It Away
Lincoln,Abbey (voc) | Metheny,Pat (g) | Haden,Charlie (b) | Lewis,Victor (dr) | Blanchard,Pierre (v) | Pagliarin,Vincent (v) | Fymard,Frederic (viola) | Bisquay,Anne-Gaelle (cello) | Gilet,Marc (cello) | Cugny,Laurent (string-arr)
Alec Le Temps
Lincoln,Abbey (voc) | Metheny,Pat (g,el-g) | Haden,Charlie (b) | Lewis,Victor (dr)
Should've Been
Lincoln,Abbey (voc) | Kendrick,Rodney (p) | Metheny,Pat (el-g) | Haden,Charlie (b) | Lewis,Victor (dr)
Not To Worry
Lincoln,Abbey (voc) | Lourau,Julien (ss) | Kendrick,Rodney (p) | Haden,Charlie (b) | Lewis,Victor (dr)

527452-2 | CD | Charlie Parker:Bird's Best Bop On Verve
Charlie Parker Quintet
Passport
NYC, rec. 5.5.1949
Parker,Charlie (as) | Dorham,Kenny (tp) | Haig,Al (p) | Potter,Tommy (b) | Roach,Max (dr)
Bloomdido | Leap Frog | Relaxin' With Lee
NYC, rec. 6.6.1950
Parker,Charlie (as) | Gillespie,Dizzy (tp) | Monk,Thelonious (p) | Russell,Curly (b) | Rich,Buddy (dr)
Au Privave | She Rote | K.C.Blues | Star Eyes
NYC, rec. 17.1.1951
Parker,Charlie (as) | Davis,Miles (tp) | Bishop Jr.,Walter (p) | Kotick,Teddy (b) | Roach,Max (dr)
Blues For Alice | Swedish Schnapps
NYC, rec. 8.8.1951
Parker,Charlie (as) | Rodney,Red (tp) | Lewis,John (p) | Brown,Ray (b) | Clarke,Kenny (dr)
Charlie Parker Quartet
The Song Is You | Laird Baird | Kim
NYC, rec. December 1952 or January 1953
Parker,Charlie (as) | Jones,Hank (p) | Kotick,Teddy (b) | Roach,Max (dr)
Chi Chi | Now's The Time | Confirmation
NYC, rec. 30.7.1953
Parker,Charlie (as) | Haig,Al (p) | Heath,Percy (b) | Roach,Max (dr)

527467-2 | CD | After The Rain
John McLaughlin Trio
Take The Coltrane | My Favorite Things | Sing Me Softly Of The Blues | Encuentros | Naima | Tones For Elvin Jones | Crescent | Afro Blue | After The Rain
NYC, rec. 4./5.10.1994
McLaughlin,John (g) | DeFrancesco,Joey (org) | Jones,Elvin (dr)

527469-2 | CD | The Montreal Tapes:Liberation Music Orchestra
Charlie Haden And The Liberation Music Orchestra
La Pasionara | Silence | Sandino | We Shall Overcome
Live at The Festival International De Jazz De Montreal,Canada, rec. 8.7.1989
Haden,Charlie (b) | Harrell,Tom (tp) | Davis,Stanton (tp) | Anderson,Ray (tb) | Freeman,Sharon (fr-h) | Daley,Joe (tuba) | McIntyre,Ken (as) | Watts,Ernie (as) | Watts,Ernie (ts) | Lovano,Joe (ts) | Goodrick,Mick (g) | Allen,Geri (p) | Motian,Paul (dr)

527470-2 | CD | Love And Peace-A Tribute To Horace Silver
Dee Dee Bridgewater With Her Quintet
Permit Me To Introduce You To Yourself | The Tokyo Blues | Pretty Eyes | Saint Vitus Dance | You Happened My Way | Soulville | Doodlin' | Lonely Woman | Blowin' The Blues Away
Paris,France, rec. December 1994
Bridgewater,Dee Dee (voc) | Belmondo,Stephane (tp) | Belmondo,Lionel (ts) | Eliez,Thierry (p) | Van De Geyn,Hein (b) | Ceccarelli,André (dr)
Dee Dee Bridgewater With Her Quintet With Jimmy Smith
Filthy McNasty | The Jody Grind
Bridgewater,Dee Dee (voc) | Belmondo,Stephane (tp) | Belmondo,Lionel (ts) | Smith,Jimmy (org) | Eliez,Thierry (p) | Van De Geyn,Hein (b) | Ceccarelli,André (dr)
Dee Dee Bridgewater With Her Quartet With Horace Silver
Nica's Dream | Song For My Father
Bridgewater,Dee Dee (voc) | Belmondo,Stephane (tp) | Belmondo,Lionel (ts) | Silver,Horace (p) | Van De Geyn,Hein (b) | Ceccarelli,André (dr)

527475-2 | 2 CD | The Soul Of Ben Webster
Ben Webster Septet
Fajista | Chelsea Bridge | Charlotte's Piccolo | Coal Train | When I Fall In Love | Ev's Mad | Ash
NYC, rec. July 1958
Webster,Ben (ts) | Farmer,Art (tp) | Ashby,Harold (ts) | Jones,Jimmy (p) | Lowe,Mundell (g) | Hinton,Milt (b) | Bailey,Dave (dr)
Harry Sweets Edison Sextet
Blues For The Blues | Blues For Piney Brown | Blues For The Blues(alt.take) | Gee Baby Ain't I Good To You | Blues For Bill Basie | You're Getting To Be A Habit With Me
Hollywood,CA, rec. 5.3.1957
Edison,Harry 'Sweets' (tp) | Webster,Ben (ts) | Peterson,Oscar (p) | Kessel,Barney (g) | Brown,Ray (b) | Stoller,Alvin (dr)
Moonlight In Vermont | Taste On The Place
Hollywood,CA, rec. 29.3.1957
Edison,Harry 'Sweets' (tp) | Webster,Ben (ts) | Peterson,Oscar (p) | Ellis,Herb (g) | Brown,Ray (b) | Stoller,Alvin (dr)
Johnny Hodges Orchestra
Reelin' And Rockin' | Honey Hill | Blues-A-Plenty | Saturday Afternoon Blues | Cool Your Motor | Reelin' And Rockin'(alt.take)
NYC, rec. 5.4.1958
Hodges,Johnny (as) | Eldridge,Roy (tp) | Dickenson,Vic (tb) | Webster,Ben (ts) | Strayhorn,Billy (p) | Woode,Jimmy (b) | Woodyard,Sam (dr)
I Didn't Know About You | Gone With The Wind | Don't Take Your Love From Me | Satin Doll | Don't Take Your Love From Me(alt.take)
Hodges,Johnny (as) | Strayhorn,Billy (p) | Woode,Jimmy (b) | Woodyard,Sam (dr)

527630-2 | CD | Family
Roy Hargrove-Walter Booker
Ethiopia
NYC, rec. 26.-29.1.1995
Hargrove,Roy (tp) | Booker,Walter (b)
Roy Hargrove Quartet
Lament For Love
Hargrove,Roy (tp) | Matthews,Ronnie (p) | Booker,Walter (b) | Cobb,Jimmy (dr)
Pas De Trois
Hargrove,Roy (tp) | Hicks,John (p) | Booker,Walter (b) | Cobb,Jimmy (dr)
The Challenge
Hargrove,Roy (tp) | Scott,Stephen (p) | Whitaker,Rodney Thomas (b) | Riggins,Karriem (dr)
A Dream Of You
Hargrove,Roy (tp) | Scott,Stephen (p) | McBride,Christian (b) | Hutchinson,Gregory (dr)
Roy Hargrove Quintet
Velera | Roy Allen | Brian's Bounce | Another Level
Hargrove,Roy (tp) | Blake,Ron (ts) | Scott,Stephen (p) | Whitaker,Rodney Thomas (b) | Hutchinson,Gregory (dr)
Polka Dots And Moonbeams
Hargrove,Roy (fl-h) | Davis,Jesse (as) | Willis,Larry (p) | Booker,Walter (b) | Cobb,Jimmy (dr)
Thirteenth Floor
Hargrove,Roy (tp) | Newman,David Fathead (fl) | Scott,Stephen (p) | Whitaker,Rodney Thomas (b) | Cobb,Jimmy (dr)
Firm Roots
Hargrove,Roy (tp) | Blake,Ron (ts) | Scott,Stephen (p) | Whitaker,Rodney Thomas (b) | Nash,Lewis (dr)
Roy Hargrove Sextet
The Nearness Of You
Hargrove,Roy (tp) | Newman,David Fathead (ts) | Blake,Ron (ts) | Scott,Stephen (p) | Whitaker,Rodney Thomas (b) | Cobb,Jimmy (dr)
Nostalgia
Hargrove,Roy (tp) | Marsalis,Wynton (tp) | Blake,Ron (ts) | Scott,Stephen (p) | Whitaker,Rodney Thomas (b) | Hutchinson,Gregory (dr)
The Trial
Hargrove,Roy (tp) | Davis,Jesse (as) | Blake,Ron (ss,ts) | Scott,Stephen (p) | Whitaker,Rodney Thomas (b) | Hutchinson,Gregory (dr)

527632-2 | CD | Angel Eyes-Ballads & Slow Jams
Jimmy Smith Sextet
Stolen Moments | You Better Go Now | Angel Eyes | Bess Oh Where's My Bess | Slow Freight | Tenderly | Days Of Wine And Roses | Lil' Darlin' | What A Wonderful World
NYC, rec. 25./26.1.1995
Smith,Jimmy (org) | Hargrove,Roy (tp,fl-h) | Payton,Nicholas (tp) | Whitfield,Mark (g) | McBride,Christian (b) | Hutchinson,Gregory (dr)

527650-2 | CD | Verve Jazz Masters 47:Billie Holiday Sings Standards
Billie Holiday And Her Band
But Not For Me | Darn That Dream
Hollywood,CA, rec. 7.1.1957
Holiday,Billie (voc) | Edison,Harry 'Sweets' (tp) | Webster,Ben (ts) | Rowles,Jimmy (p) | Kessel,Barney (g) | Mitchell,Red (b) | Stoller,Alvin (dr)
Our Love Is Here To Stay
Hollywood,CA, rec. 8.1.1957
Holiday,Billie (voc) | Edison,Harry 'Sweets' (tp) | Webster,Ben (ts) | Rowles,Jimmy (p) | Kessel,Barney (g) | Mitchell,Red (b) | Stoller,Alvin (dr)
April In Paris | We'll Be Together Again
Hollywood,CA, rec. 18.8.1956
Holiday,Billie (voc) | Edison,Harry 'Sweets' (tp) | Webster,Ben (ts) | Rowles,Jimmy (p) | Kessel,Barney (g) | Mitchell,Red (b) | Stoller,Alvin (dr)
Gee Baby Ain't I Good To You
Hollywood,CA, rec. 9.1.1957
Holiday,Billie (voc) | Edison,Harry 'Sweets' (tp) | Webster,Ben (ts) | Rowles,Jimmy (p) | Kessel,Barney (g) | Mitchell,Red (b) | Bunker,Larry (dr)
When Your Lover Has Gone | It Had To Be You
Hollywood,CA, rec. 23.8.1955
Holiday,Billie (voc) | Edison,Harry 'Sweets' (tp) | Carter,Benny (as) | Rowles,Jimmy (p) | Kessel,Barney (g) | Simmons,John (b) | Bunker,Larry (dr)
What's New?
Hollywood,CA, rec. 25.8.1955
Holiday,Billie (voc) | Carter,Benny (as) | Rowles,Jimmy (celeste) | Kessel,Barney (g) | Simmons,John (b) | Bunker,Larry (dr)
Billie Holiday With The JATP All Stars
All Of Me
Holiday,Billie (voc) | JATP All Stars | Guy,Joe (tp) | Auld,Georgie (as) | Jacquet,Illinois (ts) | Young,Lester (ts) | Kersey,Kenny (p) | Grimes,Tiny prob. (g) | McKibbon,Al (b) | Heard,J.C. (dr)
Billie Holiday And Her Quintet
Stormy Weather
NYC, rec. 27.7.1952
Holiday,Billie (voc) | Newman,Joe (tp) | Peterson,Oscar (p) | Green,Freddie (g) | Brown,Ray (b) | Johnson,Gus (dr)
Billie Holiday And Her All Stars
East Of The Sun West Of The Moon | Tenderly
Hollywood,CA, rec. late Spring 1952
Holiday,Billie (voc) | Shavers,Charlie (tp) | Phillips,Flip (ts) | Peterson,Oscar (p) | Kessel,Barney (g) | Brown,Ray (b) | Stoller,Alvin (dr)
You Turned The Tables On Me
Holiday,Billie (voc) | Phillips,Flip (ts) | Peterson,Oscar (p) | Kessel,Barney (g) | Brown,Ray (b) | Stoller,Alvin (dr)
Billie Holiday With The JATP All Stars
Body And Soul
Los Angeles,CA, rec. 12.2.1945
Holiday,Billie (voc) | JATP All Stars | McGhee,Howard (arr) | unkn. (tb) | Smith,Willie (as) | Gray,Wardell or Illinois Jacquet or Charlie Ventura (ts) | Raskin,Milt prob. (p) | Barbour,Dave prob. (g) | Mingus,Charles (b) | Coleman,Dave (dr)
Billie Holiday With The Ray Ellis Orchestra
When It's Sleepy Time Down South
NYC, rec. 4./5.3.1954
Holiday,Billie (voc) | Edison,Harry 'Sweets' (tp) | Cleveland,Jimmy (tb) | Quill,Gene (as) | Jones,Hank (p) | Galbraith,Barry (g) | Hinton,Milt (b) | Johnson,Osie (dr) | unkn. (12 strings) | Ellis,Ray (cond,arr)

527651-2 | CD | Verve Jazz Masters 50:Sonny Sitt
Sonny Stitt Quartet
I Got Rhythm
Hollywood,CA, rec. 9.2.1959
Stitt,Sonny (as) | Trice,Amos (p) | Morrow,George (b) | McBrowne,Lennie (dr)
Modern Jazz Sextet
Mean To Me
NYC, rec. 12.1.1956
Modern Jazz Sextet,The | Gillespie,Dizzy (tp) | Stitt,Sonny (as) | Lewis,John (p) | Best,Skeeter (g) | Heath,Percy (b) | Persip,Charles (dr)
Sonny Stitt Quartet
Sonny's Tune
NYC, rec. 14.9.1956
Stitt,Sonny (as) | Jones,Jimmy (p) | Brown,Ray (b) | Jones,Jo (dr)
Sonny Stitt With The Ralph Burns Orchestra
Time After Time
details unknown, rec. 6./7.3.1961
Stitt,Sonny (as) | Burns,Ralph (cond,arr) | details unknown
Gene Ammons-Sonny Stitt Quintet
Walkin'
NYC, rec. February 1962
Ammons,Gene (ts) | Stitt,Sonny (ts) | Patterson,Don (org) | Weeden,Paul (g) | James,William 'Billy' (dr)
Sonny Stitt Quartet
Do Nothing Till You're True
Hollywood,CA, rec. 20.6.1960
Stitt,Sonny (ts) | Levy,Lou (p) | Chambers,Paul (b) | Levey,Stan (dr)
Sonny Stitt With The Oscar Peterson Trio
Easy Does It
Paris,France, rec. 18.5.1959
Stitt,Sonny (ts) | Peterson,Oscar (p) | Brown,Ray (b) | Thigpen,Ed (dr)
Sonny Stitt Quartet
Just Friends
Hollywood,CA, rec. 23.12.1959
Stitt,Sonny (ts) | Levy,Lou (p) | Vinnegar,Leroy (b) | Lewis,Mel (dr)
Easy Living
NYC, rec. 12.5.1957
Stitt,Sonny (ts) | Timmons,Bobby (p) | Willis,Edgar (b) | Dennis,Kenny (dr)
Dizzy Gillespie Sextet
On The Sunny Side Of The Street
NYC, rec. 19.12.1957
Gillespie,Dizzy (tp,voc) | Rollins,Sonny (ts) | Stitt,Sonny (ts) | Bryant,Ray (p) | Bryant,Tommy (b) | Persip,Charles (dr)
Sonny Stitt Orchestra
Laura
Hollywood,CA, rec. 16.2.1959
Stitt,Sonny (as) | Katzman,Lee (tp) | Sheldon,Jack (tp) | Rosolino,Frank (tb) | Pollen,Al (tuba) | Rowles,Jimmy (p) | Clark,Buddy (b) | Marable,Lawrence (dr) | Giuffre,Jimmy (arr)
Sonny Stitt Sextet
The String
Hollywood,CA, rec. 10./11.10.1957
Stitt,Sonny (as) | Eldridge,Roy (tp) | Peterson,Oscar (p) | Ellis,Herb (g) | Brown,Ray (b) | Levey,Stan (dr)

527652-2 | CD | Verve Jazz Masters 45:Kenny Burrell
Kenny Burrell Sextet
Wholly Cats
NYC, rec. 16.12.1966
Burrell,Kenny (g) | Mainieri,Mike (vib) | Wyands,Richard (p) | Carter,Ron (b) | Tate,Grady (dr)
Kenny Burrell With The Don Sebesky Orchestra
The Common Ground | Angel Eyes
NYC, rec. 15.12.1967
Burrell,Kenny (g) | Nottingham,Jimmy (tp) | Jones,Thad (tp) | Royal,Ernie (tp) | Andre,Wayne (tb) | Cleveland,Jimmy (tb) | Green,Urbie (tb) | Studd,Tony (tb,b-tb) | Phillips,Harvey (tuba) | Richardson,Jerome (woodwinds) | Hancock,Herbie (p) | Carter,Ron (b) | Tate,Grady (dr) | Pacheco,Johnny (perc) | Sebesky,Don (cond,arr)
Wonder Why | Everyday I Have The Blues
NYC, rec. 12.2.1968
Burrell,Kenny (g) | Owens,Jimmy (tp) | Glow,Bernie (tp) | Young,Eugene 'Snooky' (tp) | Andre,Wayne (tb) | Cleveland,Jimmy (tb) | Faulise,Paul (b-tb) | Watrous,Bill (tb) | Butterfield,Don (tuba) | Richardson,Jerome (woodwinds) | Hancock,Herbie (p) | Carter,Ron (b) | McDonald,Donald (dr) | Pacheco,Johnny (perc) | Sebesky,Don (cond,arr)
Love You Madly
NYC, rec. 18.4.1968
Burrell,Kenny (g) | Glow,Bernie (tp) | Stamm,Marvin (tp) | Shepley,Joe (tp) | Andre,Wayne (tb) | Cleveland,Jimmy (tb) | Green,Urbie (tb) | Ralph,Alan (b-tb) | Butterfield,Don (tuba) | Richardson,Jerome (fl,piccolo) | Bernhardt,Warren (p) | Carter,Ron (b) | McDonald,Donald (dr) | Pacheco,Johnny (perc) | Sebesky,Don (cond,arr)
Kenny Burrell Quintet
Greensleeves
NYC, rec. 6.4.1965
Burrell,Kenny (g) | Kellaway,Roger (p) | Benjamin,Joe (b) | Tate,Grady (dr) | Rodriguez,Willie (perc)
Kenny Burrell
Just A-Sittin' And A-Rockin'
NYC, rec. 6.1.1969
Burrell,Kenny (g-solo)
Kenny Burrell With The Johnny Pate Orchestra
Sugar Hill
NYC, rec. 16.10.1969
Burrell,Kenny (g) | Orchestra | Pate,Johnny (arr,ld) | details unknown
Kenny Burrell With The Gil Evans Orchestra
Lotus Land
NYC, rec. 15.12.1964
Burrell,Kenny (g) | Coles,Johnny (tp) | Mucci,Louis (tp) | Cleveland,Jimmy (tb) | Knepper,Jimmy (tb) | Alonge,Ray (fr-h) | Watkins,Julius (fr-h) | Barber,Bill (tuba) | Konitz,Lee (as) | Kamuca,Richie (engl-h,fl) | Tricarico,Bob (fl,ts,bassoon) | Carter,Ron (b) | Jones,Elvin (dr) | Persip,Charles (dr) | Evans,Gil (cond,arr)
Last Night When We Were Young
NYC, rec. 4.12.1964
Burrell,Kenny (g) | Coles,Johnny (tp) | Mucci,Louis (tp) | Cleveland,Jimmy (tb) | Knepper,Jimmy (tb) | Alonge,Ray (fr-h) | Watkins,Julius (fr-h) | Barber,Bill (tuba) | Fitzgerald,Andy (engl-h,fl) | Marge,George (engl-h,fl) | Beckenstein,Ray (fl,b-cl) | Lacy,Steve (ss) | Konitz,Lee (as) | Kamuca,Richie (ts,oboe) | Tricarico,Bob (fl,ts,bassoon) | Carter,Ron (b) | Jones,Elvin (dr) | Persip,Charles (dr) | Evans,Gil (cond,arr)
Kenny Burrell Quartet
Seven Come Eleven
Englewood Cliffs,NJ, rec. 1966/1967
Burrell,Kenny (g) | Woods,Phil (as) | Carter,Ron (b) | Tate,Grady (dr)
Soulful Brothers | Were You There
NYC, rec. 19.2.1968
Burrell,Kenny (g) | Hancock,Herbie (p) | Carter,Ron (b) | Tate,Grady (dr)
Kenny Clarke Quintet
Bread Winner
NYC, rec. 12.4.1965
Burrell,Kenny (g) | Kellaway,Roger (p) | Benjamin,Joe (b) | Tate,Grady (dr) | Rodriguez,Willie (congas)
Jimmy Smith Quartet
Blue Bash
NYC, rec. 10.7.1963
Smith,Jimmy (org) | Burrell,Kenny (g) | Gambella,Vince (b) | Lewis,Mel (dr)

527653-2 | CD | Verve Jazz Masters 49:Anita O'Day
Anita O'Day With The Russ Garcia Orchestra
That Old Feeling | Waiter, Make Mine Blues
Los Angeles,CA, rec. 1.8.1960
O'Day,Anita (voc) | Betts,Harry (tb) | Nash,Dick (tb) | Rosolino,Frank (tb) | Wells,Dicky (tb) | Shroyer,Kenny (tb,b-tb) | Shank,Bud (fl,as) | Clarkson,Geoff (p) | Hendrickson,Al (g) | McKibbon,Al (b) | Lewis,Mel (dr) | Garcia,Russell (cond,arr)
Angel Eyes
Los Angeles,CA, rec. 4.10.1960
O'Day,Anita (voc) | prob.personal incl.: | Shank,Bud (as) | Kessel,Barney (g) | Roberts,Howard (g) | Garcia,Russell (cond,arr) | details unknown
Anita O'Day With The Gary McFarland Orchestra
Boogie Blues
NYC, rec. 16.10.1961
O'Day,Anita (voc) | prob.personal incl.: | Pomeroy,Herb (tp) | Brookmeyer,Bob (v-tb) | Dennis,Willie (tb) | Levinsky,Walt (cl,as) | Woods,Phil (as) | Richardson,Jerome (ts) | Sims,Zoot (ts) | Jones,Hank (p) | Galbraith,Barry (g) | McFarland,Gary (cond,arr) | details unknown
Anita O'Day With The Three Sounds
Fly Me To The Moon | When The World Was Young
NYC, rec. 12.10.1962
O'Day,Anita (voc) | Three Sounds,The | Harris,Gene (p) | Simpkins,Andrew (b) | Dowdy,Bill (dr)
Anita O'Day With The Billy May Orchestra
Ten Cents A Dance
Hollywood,CA, rec. 8.6.1960
O'Day,Anita (voc) | Candoli,Pete (tp) | Gozzo,Conrad (tp) | Rasey,Uan (tp) | Kusby,Eddie (tb) | McEachern,Murray (tb) | Pederson,Pullman 'Tommy' (tb) | Schaefer,Bill (tb) | Falensby,Fred (ts) | Gentry,Chuck (as) | Gordon,Justin (ts) | Nash,Ted (as) | Schwartz,Wilbur (bs) | Castro,Joe (p) | Hendrickson,Al (g) | Pena,Ralph (b) | Cottler,Irv (dr) | May,Billy (arr,ld)
Johnny One Note
Hollywood,CA, rec. 6.6.1960
O'Day,Anita (voc) | Candoli,Pete (tp) | Gozzo,Conrad (tp) | Rasey,Uan (tp) | Kusby,Eddie (tb) | McEachern,Murray (tb) | Shepard,Tom (tb) | Schaefer,Bill (tb) | Falensby,Fred (ts) | Gentry,Chuck (as) | Gordon,Justin (ts) | Nash,Ted (as) | Schwartz,Wilbur (bs) | Castro,Joe (p) | Hendrickson,Al (g) | Pena,Ralph (b) | Cottler,Irv (dr) | May,Billy (arr,ld)
What Is This Thing Called Love
Hollywood,CA, rec. 9.4.1959
O'Day,Anita (voc) | May,Billy (arr,ld) | details unknown
Anita O'Day With The Jimmy Giuffre Orchestra
Easy Come Easy Go
Hollywood,CA, rec. 6.4.1959
O'Day,Anita (voc) | Rosolino,Frank (tb) | Giuffre,Jimmy (cl,ts,bs,arr,ld) | Harding,Al (ts) | Shank,Bud (woodwinds) | unkn. (g) | Morrow,George (b) | Lewis,Mel (dr)
Anita O'Day And Her Combo
No Soap, No Hope Blues
Chicago,Ill, rec. July 1952
O'Day,Anita (voc) | Kral,Roy (p) | Backus,Earl (g) | Frigo,Johnny (b) | Lionberg,Red (dr) | Wilson,Jim (bongos)
Anita O'Day With The Cal Tjader Quartet
Just In Time
Hollywood,CA, rec. 27.2.1962
O'Day,Anita (voc) | Tjader,Cal (vib) | Corwin,Bob or Lonnie Hewitt (p) | Schreiber,Freddy (b) | Rae,Johnny (dr)
Anita O'Day With The Bill Holman Orchestra
Old Devil Moon
Hollywood,CA, rec. 23.8.1960
O'Day,Anita (voc) | prob.personal incl.: | Katzman,Lee (tp) | Porcino,Al (tp) | Rosolino,Frank (tb) | Maini,Joe (as) | Perkins,Bill (ts) | Levy,Lou (p) | Mondragon,Joe (b) | Lewis,Mel (dr) | Holman,Bill (arr,ld) | details unknown
Anita O'Day With The Buddy Bregman Orchestra
A Nightingale Sang In Berkeley Square
Hollywood,CA, rec. 7.12.1955
O'Day,Anita (voc) | prob.personal incl.: | Dan Lube (v) | Raderman,Lou (v) | Majewski,Virginia (viola) | Hale,Corky (harp) | Smith,Paul (p) | Kessel,Barney (g) | Mondragon,Joe (b) | Stoller,Alvin (dr) | Bregman,Buddy (cond,arr) | details unknown
Anita O'Day With The Oscar Peterson Quartet
Them There Eyes
Chicago,Ill, rec. 31.1.1957
O'Day,Anita (voc) | Peterson,Oscar (p) | Ellis,Herb (g) | Brown,Ray (b) | Poole,John (dr)

527655-2 | CD | Verve Jazz Masters 46:Ella Fitzgerald-The Jazz Sides
Ella Fitzgerald And The Paul Smith Quartet
Let's Do It(Let's Fall In Love)
Hollywood,CA, rec. 9.2.1956
Fitzgerald,Ella (voc) | Smith,Paul (p) | Kessel,Barney (g) | Mondragon,Joe (b) | Stoller,Alvin (dr)
Everything I've Got
Hollywood,CA, rec. 29.8.1956
Fitzgerald,Ella (voc) | Smith,Paul (p) | Kessel,Barney (g) | Mondragon,Joe (b) | Stoller,Alvin (dr)
Ella Fitzgerald With The Duke Ellington Orchestra
Caravan
NYC, rec. 27.6.1957
Fitzgerald,Ella (voc) | Ellington,Duke (p) | Anderson,Cat (tp) | Cook,Willie (tp) | Terry,Clark (tp) | Nance,Ray (tp,v) | Jackson,Quentin (tb) | Woodman,Britt (tb) | Sanders,John (tb) | Hamilton,Jimmy (cl,ts) | Procope,Russell (cl,as) | Hodges,Johnny (as) | Gonsalves,Paul (ts) | Foster,Frank (ts) | Carney,Harry (cl,b-cl,bs) | Woode,Jimmy (b) | Woodyard,Sam (dr)
Passion Flower
Los Angeles,CA, rec. November 1965
Fitzgerald,Ella (voc) | Ellington,Duke (ld) | Anderson,Cat (tp) | Ellington,Mercer (tp) | Jones,Herbie (tp) | Williams,Cootie (tp) | Brown,Lawrence (tb) | Cooper,Frank 'Buster' (tb) | Connors,Chuck (b-tb) | Hamilton,Jimmy (cl,ts) | Procope,Russell (cl,as) | Hodges,Johnny (as) | Gonsalves,Paul (ts) | Carney,Harry (cl,b-cl,bs) | Jones,Jimmy (p) | Lamb,John (b) | Bellson,Louie (dr)
Ella Fitzgerald And Louis Armstrong With The Oscar Peterson Quartet
They Can't Take That Away From Me
Los Angeles,CA, rec. 16.8.1956
Fitzgerald,Ella (voc) | Armstrong,Louis (tp,voc) | Peterson,Oscar (p) | Ellis,Herb (g) | Brown,Ray (b) | Rich,Buddy (dr)
Ella Fitzgerald And Her Quintet
In A Mellow Tone
NYC, rec. 17.10.1957
Fitzgerald,Ella (voc) | Webster,Ben (ts) | Peterson,Oscar (p) | Ellis,Herb (g) | Brown,Ray (b) | Stoller,Alvin (dr)
Ella Fitzgerald And Paul Smith
One For My Baby(And One More For The Road) | Black Coffee
Los Angeles,CA, rec. 19.4.1960
Fitzgerald,Ella (voc) | Smith,Paul (p)
Ella Fitzgerald With The Marty Paich Dek-tette
You Hit The Spot | Knock Me A Kiss
Los Angeles,CA, rec. 22.11.1958
Fitzgerald,Ella (voc) | Fagerquist,Don (tp) | Porcino,Al (tp) | Enevoldsen,Bob (v-tb,ts) | DeRosa,Vince (fr-h) | Kitzmiller,John (tuba) | Shank,Bud (as) | Holman,Bill (ts) | Flory,Med (bs) | Levy,Lou (p) | Mondragon,Joe (b) | Lewis,Mel (dr) | Paich,Marty (arr,ld)
Ella Fitzgerald With The Lou Levy Quartet
Born To Be Blue | Jersey Bounce
Los Angeles,CA, rec. 23.6.1961
Fitzgerald,Ella (voc) | Levy,Lou (p) | Ellis,Herb (g) | Mondragon,Joe (b) | Levey,Stan (dr)
The Music Goes 'Round And 'Round
Los Angeles,CA, rec. 24.6.1961
Fitzgerald,Ella (voc) | Levy,Lou (p) | Ellis,Herb (g) | Mondragon,Joe (b) | Levey,Stan (dr)
Ella Fitzgerald With The Count Basie Orchestra
Them There Eyes
NYC, rec. 15./16.7.1963
Fitzgerald,Ella (voc) | Newman,Joe (tp) | Green,Urbie (tb) | Foster,Frank (ts) | Basie,Count (p,ld) | Green,Freddie (g) | Catlett,Buddy (b) | Payne,Sonny (dr)
Ella Fitzgerald And Her Quintet
Hear Me Talkin' To Ya
NYC, rec. 28.10.1963
Fitzgerald,Ella (voc) | Eldridge,Roy (tp) | Davis,Wild Bill (org) | Ellis,Herb (g) | Brown,Ray (b) | Johnson,Gus (dr)
Ella Fitzgerald With The Billy May Orchestra
It's Only A Paper Moon
Los Angeles,CA, rec. 1.8.1960
Fitzgerald,Ella (voc) | May,Billy (arr,ld) | Fagerquist,Don (tp) | Bernhart,Milton 'Milt' (tb) | Nash,Dick (tb) | Carter,Benny (as) | Nash,Ted (as) | Johnson,Plas (ts) | Bunker,Larry (vib) | Smith,Paul (p) | Hendrickson,Al (g) | Collins,John (g) | Mondragon,Joe (b) | Stoller,Alvin (dr) | details unknown

527664-2 | CD | Take Off
Barbara Dennerlein Group
Victory Blues
NYC, rec. March 1995
Dennerlein,Barbara (org) | Sim,Mike (bs) | Locke,Joe (vib) | Watkins,Mitch (el-g) | Chambers,Dennis (dr) | Alias,Don (perc)
Take-Off
Dennerlein,Barbara (org) | Hargrove,Roy (tp) | Sim,Mike (ss,ts) | Locke,Joe (midi-vib) | Watkins,Mitch (el-g) | Plaxico,Lonnie (b) | Chambers,Dennis (dr) | Alias,Don (perc)
Fast Food
Dennerlein,Barbara (org) | Hargrove,Roy (fl-h) | Anderson,Ray (tb) | Sim,Mike (ts) | Watkins,Mitch (el-g) | Plaxico,Lonnie (b) | Chambers,Dennis (dr) | Alias,Don (perc)
Fata Morgana
Dennerlein,Barbara (org,synth) | Anderson,Ray (tb) | Sim,Mike (ss) | Locke,Joe (midi-vib) | Watkins,Mitch (el-g) | Plaxico,Lonnie (b) | Chambers,Dennis (dr) | Alias,Don (perc)
Hot House
Dennerlein,Barbara (org) | Hargrove,Roy (fl-h) | Sim,Mike (as) | Chambers,Dennis (dr)
Purple
Dennerlein,Barbara (org,synth) | Sim,Mike (ss) | Watkins,Mitch (el-g) | Chambers,Dennis (dr) | Alias,Don (perc)
Fly Away
Dennerlein,Barbara (org,synth) | Hargrove,Roy (tp) | Sim,Mike (ss,ts) | Locke,Joe (midi-vib) | Watkins,Mitch (g,el-g) | Plaxico,Lonnie (b) | Chambers,Dennis (dr) | Alias,Don (perc)
Bo-Peep
Dennerlein,Barbara (org) | Hargrove,Roy (tp) | Anderson,Ray (tb) | Sim,Mike (ts) | Watkins,Mitch (el-g) | Chambers,Dennis (dr)
Green Paradise
Dennerlein,Barbara (p,org) | Sim,Mike (ss) | Watkins,Mitch (g,el-g) | Chambers,Dennis (dr) | Alias,Don (perc)
Give It Up
Dennerlein,Barbara (org) | Hargrove,Roy (tp) | Anderson,Ray (tb) | Sim,Mike (ss,ts,bs) | Watkins,Mitch (g,el-g) | Plaxico,Lonnie (b) | Chambers,Dennis (dr) | Alias,Don (perc)

527715-2 | CD | Herbie Hancock The New Standards
Herbie Hancock Group
New York Minute | You Got It Bad Girl | Scarborough Fair | All Apologies | Manhattan | Your Good Teath(II)
NYC, rec. 1995
Hancock,Herbie (p) | Brecker,Michael (ss,ts) | Scofield,John (g,el-g,el-sitar) | Holland,Dave (b) | DeJohnette,Jack (dr,el-perc) | Alias,Don (perc)
Herbie Hancock Group With String Quartet
When Can I See You | Thieves In The Temple
Hancock,Herbie (p) | Brecker,Michael (ss,ts) | Scofield,John (g,el-g,el-sitar) | Holland,Dave (b) | DeJohnette,Jack (dr,el-perc) | Alias,Don (perc) | Haydn,Lilli R. (v) | Wootn,Margaret R. (v) | Green,Richard S. (viola) | Stone,Cameron L. (cello)
Herbie Hancock Group With String Quartet,Woodwinds And Brass

Norwegian Wood | Mercy Street
Hancock,Herbie (p) | Brecker,Michael (ss,ts) | Scofield,John (g,el-g,el-sitar) | Holland,Dave (b) | DeJohnette,Jack (dr,el-perc) | Alias,Don (perc) | Haydn,Lilli R. (v) | Wootn,Margaret R. (v) | Green,Richard S. (viola) | Stone,Cameron L. (cello) | Lovitt,Lester 'Les' (tp,fl-h) | Brashear,Oscar (tp,fl-h) | Moriarty,Suzette (fr-h) | Spears,Maurice (b-tb) | Riney,Sam (fl,alto fl) | Herbig,Gary (cl,b-cl) | Cipriano,Gene (engl-h,oboe) | Green,William (fl,alto-fl)
Herbie Hancock Group With Woodwinds And Brass
Love Is Stronger Than Pride
Hancock,Herbie (p) | Brecker,Michael (ss,ts) | Scofield,John (g,el-g,el-sitar) | Holland,Dave (b) | DeJohnette,Jack (dr,el-perc) | Alias,Don (perc) | Lovitt,Lester 'Les' (tp,fl-h) | Brashear,Oscar (tp,fl-h) | Moriarty,Suzette (fr-h) | Spears,Maurice (b-tb) | Riney,Sam (fl,alto-fl) | Herbig,Gary (cl,b-cl) | Cipriano,Gene (engl-h,oboe) | Green,William (fl,alto-fl)

527774-2 | 2 CD | Music For Loving:Ben Webster With Strings
Ben Webster With Orchestra And Strings
Chelsea Bridge | All Too Soon | Our Love Is Here To Stay | It Happens To Be Me | Our Love Is Here To Stay(alt.take 1) | Our Love Is Here To Stay(alt.take 2)
NYC, rec. 28.5.1954
Webster,Ben (ts) | Scott,Tony (cl) | Ceppos,Mac (v) | Novales,David (v) | Russell,Mischa (v) | Dickler,Richard (viola) | Sims,Rudolph (cello) | Strayhorn,Billy (p,arr,ld) | Duvivier,George (b) | Bellson,Louie (dr)
Willow Weep For Me | Do Nothin' Till You Hear From Me | Prelude To A Kiss | Come Rain Or Come Shine
NYC, rec. 15.12.1954
Webster,Ben (ts) | Hamilton,Jimmy (cl) | Bank,Danny (fl,cl,b-cl) | Deutsch,Solomon (v) | Kruczek,Leo (v) | Schachter,Julius (v) | Zayde,Jack (v) | Fisch,Burt (viola) | Greenhouse,Bernhard (cello) | Wilson,Teddy (p) | Marshall,Wendell (b) | Bellson,Louie (dr) | Burns,Ralph (cond,arr)
There Is No Greater Love | Teach Me Tonight | Until Tonight | We'll Be Together Again | Blue Moon | Early Autumn | My Greatest Mistake | What Am I Here For
NYC, rec. 9.9.1955
Webster,Ben (ts) | Epstein[Young],Al (engl-h,cl,b-cl) | Bank,Danny (fl,cl) | Colletta,Harold (v) | Donegan,Martin (v) | Kruczek,Leo (v) | Lookofsky,Harry (v) | Orloff,Gene (v) | Samaroff,Tosha (v) | Winter,Paul (v) | Fish,Bert (viola) | Borodkin,Abram (cello) | Ricci,George (cello) | Schmit,Lucien (cello) | Jones,Hank (p) | Amsterdam,Chet (b) | Marshall,Wendell (b) | Johnson,Osie (dr) | Burns,Ralph (cond,arr)
Some Other Spring | When Your Lover Has Gone | Stars Fell On Alabama | Under A Blanket Of Blue | Stars Fell On Alabama(alt.take) | Under A Blanket Of Blue(alt.take 1) | Under A Blanket Of Blue(alt.take 2)
NYC, rec. 3.2.1955
Webster,Ben (ts) | Wilson,Teddy (p) | Orchestra | Strings | details unknown
Ben Webster With The Teddy Wilson Trio
My Funny Valentine | You're Mine You | Sophisticated Lady | Love's Away
NYC, rec. 30.3.1954
Webster,Ben (ts) | Wilson,Teddy (p) | Brown,Ray (b) | Jones,Jo (dr)
Ben Webster With The Billy Strayhorn Trio
Almost Like Being In Love
NYC, rec. 28.5.1954
Webster,Ben (ts) | Strayhorn,Billy (p) | Duvivier,George (b) | Bellson,Louie (dr)
Harry Carney And His Orchestra With Strings
I Don't Stand A Ghost Of A Chance With You | Take The 'A' Train | We're In Love Again | Chalmeau | Moonlight On The Ganges | It Had To Be You | My Fantasy | I Got It Bad And That Ain't Good
NYC, rec. 13.12.1954
Carney,Harry (b-cl,bs) | Nance,Ray (tp,v) | Miranda,Tony (fr-h) | Hamilton,Jimmy (cl,ts) | Ceppos,Mac (v) | Donegan,Martin (v) | Gerrard,Ben (v) | Kay,Howard (v) | Orloff,Gene (v) | Shulman,Sylvan (v) | Smirnoff,Ziggy (v) | Zir,Isadore (v) | Edwards,Sidney (cello) | Johnson,Doris (cello) | Shulman,Alan (cello) | Lovett,Leroy (p) | Bauer,Billy (g) | Marshall,Wendell (b) | Bellson,Louie (dr)

527806-2 | CD | Gypsy Swing
The Rosenberg Trio
It Don't Mean A Thing If It Ain't Got That Swing | Cherokee | Hungaria | Yours Is My Heart Alone | Latscheben
Hilversum,NL, rec. Spring 1995
Rosenberg,Stochelo (g) | Rosenberg,Nou'che (g) | Rosenberg,Nonnie (b)
The Rosenberg Trio With Frits Landesbergen
Miro Tat Mimer(For My Dad Mimer)
Rosenberg,Stochelo (g) | Rosenberg,Nou'che (g) | Rosenberg,Nonnie (b) | Landesbergen,Frits (vib)
Guitar Boogie
Rosenberg,Stochelo (g) | Rosenberg,Nou'che (g) | Rosenberg,Nonnie (b) | Schrama,Cees (p) | Landesbergen,Frits (dr) | Conrad,Eddie (perc)
Silk And Steel | Begin The Beguine
Rosenberg,Stochelo (g) | Rosenberg,Nou'che (g) | Rosenberg,Nonnie (b) | Landesbergen,Frits (vib,dr) | Conrad,Eddie (perc)
Stochelo Rosenberg Group
Django
Rosenberg,Stochelo (g) | Jansen,Hans (p) | Landesbergen,Frits (vib,dr) | Van Der Hoeven,Frans (b) | Conrad,Eddie (perc)
Rosemary's Baby
Rosenberg,Stochelo (g) | Jansen,Hans (keyboards) | Meulendijk,Bert (g) | Van Der Hoeven,Frans (b) | Serierse,Marcel (dr) | Conrad,Eddie (perc)
How Insensitive(Insensatez)
Rosenberg,Stochelo (g) | Jansen,Hans (keyboards) | Landesbergen,Frits (vib) | Meulendijk,Bert (g) | Van Der Hoeven,Frans (b) | Serierse,Marcel (dr) | Conrad,Eddie (perc)
Children Of Sanchez
Rosenberg,Stochelo (g) | Both,Wim (tp) | Godfroit,Marc (tb) | Jansen,Hans (p) | Meulendijk,Bert (g) | Van Der Hoeven,Frans (b) | Serierse,Marcel (dr) | Conrad,Eddie (perc)
Tequilla
Rosenberg,Stochelo (g) | Both,Wim (tp) | Godfroit,Marc (tb) | Kolb,Philip (as,ts) | Jansen,Hans (p) | Landesbergen,Frits (vib) | Meulendijk,Bert (g) | Van Der Hoeven,Frans (b) | Serierse,Marcel (dr) | Conrad,Eddie (perc)
Bluesette
Rosenberg,Stochelo (g) | Both,Wim (fl-h) | Kolb,Philip (fl) | Jansen,Hans (p) | Landesbergen,Frits (vib) | Meulendijk,Bert (g) | Van Der Hoeven,Frans (b) | Serierse,Marcel (dr) | Conrad,Eddie (perc)
Stochelo Rosenberg Group With Strings
Theme From Mahogany
Rosenberg,Stochelo (g) | Kolb,Philip (as) | Jansen,Hans (keyboards) | Meulendijk,Bert (g) | Van Der Hoeven,Frans (b) | Serierse,Marcel (dr) | Conrad,Eddie (perc) | Terlouw,P.M. (v) | Korthals Altes,Erica (v) | Munk,A.J. (v) | Koenders,Dennis (v) | Illes,J. (v) | Viestra,Simone (v) | Illes,E. (v) | Jowett,J.A. (viola) | De Munk,J. (viola) | Bonsel,Hans (cello) | Grin,Wim (cello) | Olah,E.L. (concertmaster)
Cavatina(Theme From The Deerhunter)
Rosenberg,Stochelo (g) | Jansen,Hans (p) | Meulendijk,Bert (g) | Van Der Hoeven,Frans (b) | Serierse,Marcel (dr) | Conrad,Eddie (perc) | Terlouw,P.M. (v) | Korthals Altes,Erica (v) | Munk,A.J. (v) | Koenders,Dennis (v) | Illes,J. (v) | Viestra,Simone (v) | Illes,E. (v) | Jowett,J.A. (viola) | De Munk,J. (viola) | Bonsel,Hans (cello) | Grin,Wim (cello) | Olah,E.L. (concertmaster)

527815-2 | CD | Charlie Parker:The Best Of The Verve Years
Charlie Parker With Strings
Just Friends | April In Paris | I Didn't Know What Time It Was
NYC, rec. 30.11.1949
Parker,Charlie (as) | Miller,Mitch (engl-horn,oboe) | Gimpel,Bronislaw (v) | Hollander,Max (v) | Lamask,Milton (v) | Brieff,Frank (viola) | Miller,Frank (cello) | Rosen,Meyer (harp) | Freeman,Stan (p) | Brown,Ray (b) | Rich,Buddy (dr) | Carroll,Jimmy (arr,dir)
Laura
NYC, rec. Summer 1950
Parker,Charlie (as) | Singer,Joe (fr-h) | Brown,Eddie (oboe) | Caplan,Sam (v) | Kay,Howard (v) | Melnikoff,Harry (v) | Rand,Sam (v) | Smirnoff,Kelly (v) | Zir,Isadore (viola) | Brown,Maurice (cello) | Mills,Verley (harp) | Leighton,Bernie (p) | Brown,Ray (b) | Rich,Buddy (dr) | Lippman,Joe (cond,arr)
Charlie Parker Quintet
Swedish Schnapps | Lover Man(Oh,Where Can You Be?) | Blues For Alice
NYC, rec. 8.8.1951
Parker,Charlie (as) | Rodney,Red (tp) | Lewis,John (p) | Brown,Ray (b) | Clarke,Kenny (dr)
K.C.Blues | Au Privave | She Rote | Star Eyes
NYC, rec. 17.1.1951
Parker,Charlie (as) | Davis,Miles (tp) | Bishop Jr.,Walter (p) | Kotick,Teddy (b) | Roach,Max (dr)
Charlie Parker Quartet
Laird Baird | The Song Is You | Kim
NYC, rec. December 1952/January 1953
Parker,Charlie (as) | Jones,Hank (p) | Kotick,Teddy (b) | Roach,Max (dr)
JATP All Stars
Embraceable You | How High The Moon
Live at Carnegie Hall,NYC, rec. 18.9.1949
JATP All Stars | Eldridge,Roy (tp) | Turk,Tommy (tb) | Parker,Charlie (as) | Phillips,Flip (ts) | Young,Lester (ts) | Jones,Hank (p) | Brown,Ray (b) | Rich,Buddy (dr)
Charlie Parker All Stars
Ballade
NYC, rec. Fall 1950
Parker,Charlie (as) | Hawkins,Coleman (ts) | Jones,Hank (p) | Brown,Ray (b) | Rich,Buddy (dr)
Charlie Parker With Machito And His Orchestra
Mango Mangue
NYC, rec. 20.12.1948
Parker,Charlie (as) | Machito (Raul Grillo) | Bauza,Mario (tp) | Davilla,Frank 'Paquito' (tp) | Woodlen,Bob (tp) | Johnson,Gene (as) | Skerritt,Fred (as) | Madera,Jose (ts) | Johnakins,Leslie (bs) | Fernandez,Rene (p) | Rodriguez,Roberto (b) | Mangual,Jose (bongos) | Miranda,Luis (dr,congas) | Nieto,Ubaldo (timbales)
Charlie Parker Quartet
Confirmation | Now's The Time | Chi Chi
NYC, rec. 30.7.1953
Parker,Charlie (as) | Haig,Al (p) | Heath,Percy (b) | Roach,Max (dr)
Charlie Parker Quintet
Segment
NYC, rec. 5.5.1949
Parker,Charlie (as) | Dorham,Kenny (tp) | Haig,Al (p) | Potter,Tommy (b) | Roach,Max (dr)
Charlie Parker And His Orchestra
In The Still Of The Night | Old Folks
NYC, rec. 25.5.1953
Parker,Charlie (as) | Collins,Junior (fr-h) | Block,Al (fl) | McKusick,Hal (cl) | Mace,Tommy (oboe) | Thaler,Manny (bassoon) | Aless,Tony (p) | Mingus,Charles (b) | Roach,Max (dr) | Lambert Singers,The Dave | Ross,Annie (voc) | Evans,Gil (cond,arr)
Cardboard
NYC
Parker,Charlie (as) | Dorham,Kenny (tp) | Turk,Tommy (tb) | Haig,Al (p) | Potter,Tommy (b) | Roach,Max (dr) | Vidal,Carlos (bongos)
JATP All Stars
Oh! Lady Be Good
Live at Philharmonic Auditorium,Los Angeles,CA, rec. 28.1.1946
JATP All Stars | Killian,Al (tp) | McGhee,Howard (tp) | Parker,Charlie (as) | Smith,Willie (as) | Young,Lester (ts) | Ross,Arnold (p) | Hadnott,Billy (b) | Young,Lee (dr)
Charlie Parker With Orchestra
I Can't Get Started | What Is This Thing Called Love
NYC, rec. 25.3.1952
Parker,Charlie (as) | Maxwell,Jimmy (tp) | Poole,Carl (tp) | Porcino,Al (tp) | Privin,Bernie (tp) | Harris,Bill (tb) | McGarity,Lou (tb) | Varsalona,Bart (b-tb) | Terrill,Harry (as) | Williams,Murray (as) | Phillips,Flip (ts) | Ross,Hank (ts) | Bank,Danny (bs) | Peterson,Oscar (p) | Green,Freddie (g) | Brown,Ray (b) | Lamond,Don (dr) | Lippman,Joe (cond,arr)
Norman Granz Jam Session
Funky Blues
Hollywood,CA, rec. June 1952
Shavers,Charlie (tp) | Carter,Benny (as) | Hodges,Johnny (as) | Parker,Charlie (as) | Phillips,Flip (ts) | Webster,Ben (ts) | Peterson,Oscar (p) | Kessel,Barney (g) | Brown,Ray (b) | Heard,J.C. (dr)
Charlie Parker Sextet
Tico Tico | My Little Suede Shoes
NYC, rec. 12.3.1951
Parker,Charlie (as) | Bishop Jr.,Walter (p) | Kotick,Teddy (b) | Haynes,Roy (dr) | Mangual,Jose (bongos) | Miranda,Luis (congas)
Charlie Parker Quintet
Leap Frog | Bloomdido
NYC, rec. 6.6.1950
Parker,Charlie (as) | Gillespie,Dizzy (tp) | Monk,Thelonious (p) | Russell,Curly (b) | Rich,Buddy (dr)
Charlie Parker With The Neal Hefti Orchestra
Repetition
Live at Carnegie Hall,NYC, rec. December 1947
Parker,Charlie (as) | Porcino,Al (tp) | Mettome,Doug (tp) | Wetzel,Ray (tp) | Harris,Bill (tb) | Varsalona,Bart (b-tb) | Jacobs,Vinnie (fr-h) | LaPorta,John (cl) | Williams,Murray (as) | Salad,Sonny (as) | Mondello,Pete (ts) | Phillips,Flip (ts) | Albam,Manny (bs) | Orloff,Gene (v) | Caplan,Sam (v) | Fidler,Manny (v) | Harris,Sid (v) | Katzman,Harry (v) | Smirnoff,Kelly (v) | Nathanson,Nat (viola) | Ruzilla,Fred (viola) | Benaventi,Joe (cello) | Aless,Tony (p) | Russell,Curly (b) | Manne,Shelly (dr) | Iborra,Diego (perc) | Hefti,Neal (cond,arr)

527827-2 | CD | Now Is The Hour
Charlie Haden Quartet West
Back Home Blues | All Through The Night | Blue Pearl | Palo Alto | Marable's Parade
Paris,France, rec. 18.-20.7.1995
Haden,Charlie (b) | Watts,Ernie (ts) | Broadbent,Alan (p) | Marable,Lawrence (dr)
Charlie Haden Quartet West With Strings
Here's Looking At You! | The Left Hand Of God | When Tomorrow Comes | Now Is The Hour(Haere Ra-Maori Farewell Song)
Paris,France, rec. 18.-20.7.1005
Haden,Charlie (b) | Watts,Ernie (ts) | Broadbent,Alan (p,cond,arr) | Marable,Lawrence (dr) | Cavelier,Hervé (concertmaster) | Cadé,Thierry (v) | Canier,Charles (v) | Carlucci,Nathalie (v) | Dato,Daniel (v) | Huchin,Thierry (v) | Lisiecki,Claire (v) | Maubré,Jocelyne (v) | Melon,Yves (v) | Metry-Travail,Lysiane (v) | Persiaux,Alain (v) | Tcheuredkjan,Jean-Claude (v) | Tétard,Christian (v) | Visconte,Fréderic (v) | Kaspar,Olivier (viola) | Borsarello,Jacques (viola) | Dufour,Christian (viola) | Grimoin,Olivier (viola) | Lacrouts,Cyrille (cello) | Audin,Jean-Philippe (cello) | Chérond,Philippe (cello) | Derrien,Hervé (cello) | Féret,Philippe (cello) | Nadal,Philippe (cello) | Noharet,Philippe (b) | Berbé,Thierry (cello)
Requiem | There In A Dream | Detour Ahead
Paris,France, rec. 18.-20.7.1995
Haden,Charlie (b) | Watts,Ernie (ts) | Broadbent,Alan (p,cond,arr) | Marable,Lawrence (dr) | Cavelier,Hervé (concertmaster) | Dupuis,Laurence (v) | Naudy,Sandrine (v) | Carlucci,Nathalie (v) | Dato,Daniel (v) | Huchin,Thierry (v) | Lisiecki,Claire (v) | Maubré,Jocelyne (v) | Melon,Yves (v) | Metry-Travail,Lysiane (v) | Persiaux,Alain (v) | Tcheuredkjan,Jean-Claude (v) | Tétard,Christian (v) | Visconte,Fréderic (v) | Kaspar,Olivier (viola) | Borsarello,Jacques (viola) | Dufour,Christian (viola) | Grimoin,Olivier (viola) | Lacrouts,Cyrille (cello) | Audin,Jean-Philippe (cello) | Chérond,Philippe (cello) | Derrien,Hervé (cello) | Féret,Philippe (cello) | Nadal,Philippe (cello) | Noharet,Philippe (b) | Berbé,Thierry (cello)

527900-2 | 2 CD | Dizzy Gillespie:Birks Works-The Verve Big Band Sessions
Dizzy Gillespie And His Orchestra
Dizzy's Business | Jessica's Day | Tour De Force | I Can't Get Started | Stella By Starlight | Doodlin' | A Night In Tunisia | The Champ | Hey Pete | Yesterdays | Tin Tin Deo | Groovin' For Nat | My Reverie | Dizzy's Blues | Annie's Dance | Cool Breeze | School Days
NYC, rec. 6.6.1956
Gillespie,Dizzy (tp,voc) | Gordon,Joe (tp) | Perry,Ermit V. (tp) | Warwick,Carl (tp) | Jones,Quincy (tp) | Liston,Melba (tb) | Rehak,Frank (tb) | Levitt,Rod (tb) | Powell,Jimmy (as) | Woods,Phil (as) | Mitchell,Billy (ts) | Wilkins,Ernie (ts) | Flax,Marty (bs) | Davis Jr.,Walter (p) | Boyd,Nelson (b) | Persip,Charles (dr)
Jordu | Yo No Quiero Bailar | Birk's Works | Autumn Leaves | Tangorine | Over The Rainbow | Umbrella Man | If You Could See Me Now
NYC, rec. 7.4.1957
Gillespie,Dizzy (tp,voc) | Morgan,Lee (tp) | Perry,Ermit V. (tp) | Warwick,Carl (tp) | Daawood,Talib (tp) | Liston,Melba (tb) | Grey,Al (tb) | Levitt,Rod (tb) | Powell,Jimmy (as) | Henry,Ernie (as) | Mitchell,Billy (ts) | Golson,Benny (ts) | Root,Billy (bs) | Kelly,Wynton (p) | West,Paul (b) | Persip,Charles (dr) | Cromer,Austin (voc)
Left Hand Corner(false start 1) | Left Hand Corner(false start 2) | Left Hand Corner | Left Hand Corner(alt.take 1) | Left Hand Corner(alt.take 2) | Whisper Not | Whisper Not(alt.take 1) | Whisper Not(alt.take 2) | Stablemates | That's All | Groovin' High | Mayflower Rock | Mayflower Rock(alt.take)
NYC, rec. 8.4.1957
Gillespie,Dizzy (tp) | Morgan,Lee (tp) | Perry,Ermit V. (tp) | Warwick,Carl (tp) | Daawood,Talib (tp) | Liston,Melba (tb) | Grey,Al (tb) | Levitt,Rod (tb) | Powell,Jimmy (as) | Henry,Ernie (as) | Mitchell,Billy (ts) | Golson,Benny (ts) | Root,Billy (bs) | Kelly,Wynton (p) | West,Paul (b) | Persip,Charles (dr) | Cromer,Austin (voc)
Joogie Boogie | I Remember Clifford | You'll Be Sorry | Wonder Why
NYC, rec. 8.7.1957
Gillespie,Dizzy (tp) | Morgan,Lee (tp) | Perry,Ermit V. (tp) | Warwick,Carl (tp) | Daawood,Talib (tp) | Liston,Melba (tb,voc) | Grey,Al (tb) | Connor,Ray (tb) | Powell,Jimmy (as) | Henry,Ernie (as) | Mitchell,Billy (ts) | Golson,Benny (ts) | Moore,Numa 'Pee Wee' (bs) | Kelly,Wynton (p) | West,Paul (b) | Persip,Charles (dr) | Cromer,Austin (voc)

527907-2 | CD | Parker's Mood
Roy Hargrove Trio
Klact-Oveedseds-Tene | Parker's Mood | Marmaduke | Steeplechase | Laura | Dexterity | Repetition | Cardboard | Bongo Beep | Star Eyes
NYC, rec. 12.-14.4.1995
Hargrove,Roy (tp,fl-h) | Scott,Stephen (p) | McBride,Christian (b)
Roy Hargrove-Stephen Scott
Yardbird Suite
Hargrove,Roy (tp) | Scott,Stephen (p)
Roy Hargrove-Christian McBride
Chasin' The Bird
Hargrove,Roy (tp) | McBride,Christian (b)
Stephen Scott-Christian McBride
Laird Baird
Scott,Stephen (p) | McBride,Christian (b)
Stephen Scott
April In Paris
Scott,Stephen (p-solo)
Christian McBride
Red Cross
McBride,Christian (b-solo)
Roy Hargrove
Dewey Square
Hargrove,Roy (tp-solo)

527950-2 | 2 CD | Jimmy Smith:Best Of The Verve Years
Jimmy Smith With The Oliver Nelson Orchestra
Walk On The Wild Side
NYC, rec. 28.3.1962
Smith,Jimmy (org) | Newman,Joe (tp) | Royal,Ernie (tp) | Severinsen,Doc (tp) | Wilder,Joe (tp) | Cleveland,Jimmy (tb) | Green,Urbie (tb) | Woodman,Britt (tb) | Mitchell,Tom (b-tb) | Dodgion,Jerry (as) | Woods,Phil (as) | Ashton,Bob (ts) | Clarke,Babe (ts) | Barrow,George (bs) | Galbraith,Barry (g) | Duvivier,George (b) | Shaughnessy,Ed (dr) | Nelson,Oliver (arr,ld)
Jimmy Smith Trio
Blues For J | Organ Grinder's Swing
Englewood Cliffs,NJ, rec. 14.6.1965
Smith,Jimmy (org) | Burrell,Kenny (g) | Tate,Grady (dr)
Jimmy Smith With The Lalo Schifrin Orchestra
The Cat | Delon's Blues
NYC, rec. 29.4.1964
Smith,Jimmy (org) | Jones,Thad (tp) | Markowitz,Irving 'Marky' (tp) | Glow,Bernie (tp) | Maxwell,Jimmy (tp) | Royal,Ernie (tp) | Young,Eugene 'Snooky' (tp) | Cleveland,Jimmy (tb) | Green,Urbie (tb) | Studd,Tony (b-tb) | Alonge,Ray (fr-h) | Buffington,Jimmy (fr-h) | Chapin,Earl (fr-h) | Correa,Bill (fr-h) | Butterfield,Don (tuba) | Burrell,Kenny (g) | Duvivier,George (b) | Tate,Grady (dr) | Kraus,Phil (perc) | Schifrin,Lalo (cond,arr) | details unknown
Jimmy Smith With The Oliver Nelson Orchestra
Trouble In Mind
NYC, rec. 15.3.1963
Smith,Jimmy (org) | Terry,Clark (tp) | Newman,Joe (tp) | Royal,Ernie (tp) | Jackson,Quentin (tb) | Green,Urbie (tb) | Cleveland,Jimmy (tb) | Woods,Phil (as) | Dorsey,George (as) | Sims,Zoot (ts) | Cohn,Al (ts) | Hinton,Milt (b) | Johnson,Jimmy (dr) | Nelson,Oliver (arr,ld)
Hobo Flats
NYC, rec. 20.3.1963
Smith,Jimmy (org) | Newman,Joe (fl-h) | Royal,Ernie (tp) | Terry,Clark (tp) | Cleveland,Jimmy (tb) | Green,Urbie (tb) | Jackson,Quentin (tb) | Dorsey,Bob (as) | Woods,Phil (as) | Cohn,Al (ts) | Sims,Zoot (ts) | Duvivier,George (b) | Rodriguez,Bill (dr) | Nelson,Oliver (arr,ld)
Jimmy Smith Quartet
Funky Broadway
NYC, rec. 2.6.1967
Smith,Jimmy (org) | Gale,Eric (g) | Carter,Ron (b) | Tate,Grady (dr)
Jimmy Smith And Wes Montgomery With The Oliver Nelson Orchestra
Milestones
Englewood Cliffs,NJ, rec. 21.9.1966
Montgomery,Wes (g) | Smith,Jimmy (org) | Maxwell,Jimmy (tp) | Newman,Joe (tp) | Royal,Ernie (tp) | Terry,Clark (tp) | Cleveland,Jimmy (tb) | Jackson,Quentin (tb) | Hixon,Richard 'Dick' (tb) | Liston,Melba (tb) | Ashton,Bob (reeds) | Woods,Phil (as) | Dodgion,Jerry (reeds) | Richardson,Jerome (reeds) | Bank,Danny (reeds) | Davis,Richard (b) | Tate,Grady (dr) | Barretto,Ray (perc) | Nelson,Oliver (arr,ld)
Down By The Riverside
Englewood Cliffs,NJ, rec. 23.9.1966
Montgomery,Wes (g) | Smith,Jimmy (org) | Maxwell,Jimmy (tp) | Newman,Joe (tp) | Royal,Ernie (tp) | Terry,Clark (tp) | Cleveland,Jimmy (tb) | Jackson,Quentin (tb) | Studd,Tony (b-tb) | Liston,Melba (tb) | Ashton,Bob (reeds) | Woods,Phil (as) | Dodgion,Jerry (reeds) | Richardson,Jerome (reeds) | Bank,Danny (reeds) | Davis,Richard (b) | Tate,Grady (dr) | Nelson,Oliver (arr,ld)
Jimmy Smith With The Billy Byers Orchestra
The Christmas Song
Englewood Cliffs,NJ, rec. 29.9.1964
Smith,Jimmy (org) | Royal,Ernie (tp) | Glow,Bernie (tp) | Stiles,Danny (tp) | Wilder,Joe (tp) | Newman,Joe (fl-h) | Cleveland,Jimmy (tb) | Welsch,Chauncey (tb) | Faulise,Paul (b-tb) | Mitchell,Tom (b-tb) |

Chapin,Earl (fr-h) | Corrado,Donald (fr-h) | Secon,Morris (fr-h) | Buffington,Jimmy (fr-h) | Phillips,Harvey (tuba) | Burrell,Kenny (g) | Ross,Margaret (harp) | Davis,Art (b) | Tate,Grady (dr) | Devens,George (perc) | Byers,Billy (arr,ld)

Jimmy Smith Quartet
Kenny's Sound
Englewood Cliffs,NJ, rec. 17.7.1963
Smith,Jimmy (org) | Burrell,Kenny (g) | Gambella,Vince (b) | Lewis,Mel (dr)

Jimmy Smith With The Oliver Nelson Orchestra
St.James Infirmary | Monlope
Englewood Cliffs,NJ, rec. 19./20.1.1965
Smith,Jimmy (org) | Ashton,Bob (reeds) | Bank,Danny (reeds) | Beckenstein,Ray (reeds) | Dorsey,George (reeds) | Estrin,Harvey (reeds) | Johnson,Budd (reeds) | Richardson,Jerome (reeds) | Woods,Phil (reeds) | Burrell,Kenny (g) | Davis,Richard (b) | Smith,Warren (tympani) | Tate,Grady (dr) | Nelson,Oliver (arr,ld)
Refractions
Los Angeles,CA, rec. 13.5.1968
Smith,Jimmy (org) | Candoli,Conte (tp) | Childers,Buddy (tp) | Byers,Billy (tb) | Tack,Ernie (tb) | Johnson,Plas (reeds) | Scott,Tom (reeds) | unkn. (14 strings) | Roberts,Howard (g) | Brown,Ray or Carol Kaye (b) | Bunker,Larry (dr,perc) | Nelson,Oliver (arr,ld) | details unknown

Jimmy Smith Trio
The Champ
NYC, rec. 31.5.1963
Smith,Jimmy (org) | Warren,Quentin (g) | Hart,Billy (dr)

Jimmy Smith Sextet
Sags Shootin' His Arrow
Los Angeles,CA, rec. 8.2.1972
Smith,Jimmy (org) | Williams,Steve (harm) | Adams,Arthur (g) | Felder,Wilton (b) | Humphrey,Paul (dr) | Clarke,Buck (perc,congas)

Jimmy Smith With Orchestra
And I Love You So | Ritual
NYC, rec. 8.2.1973
Smith,Jimmy (org) | Orchestra | details unknown | Jones,Thad (cond)

Jimmy Smith Trio
The Boss
Live at Paschal's La Carousel Club,Atlanta,GA, rec. 20.11.1968
Smith,Jimmy (org) | Benson,George (g) | Bailey,Donald (dr)

Jimmy Smith With The Oliver Nelson Orchestra
Got My Mojo Working
Englewood Cliffs,NJ, rec. 17.12.1965
Smith,Jimmy (org,voc) | Royal,Ernie (tp) | Richardson,Jerome (bs) | Penque,Romeo (ts) | Woods,Phil (as) | Burrell,Kenny (g) | Duvivier,George (b) | Tate,Grady (dr) | Nelson,Oliver (arr,ld)

Jimmy Smith With The Johnny Pate Orchestra
Groove Drops
NYC, rec. 22.12.1969
Smith,Jimmy (org,voc) | Orchestra | Pate,Johnny (arr,ld) | details unknown

Jimmy Smith-Wes Montgomery Quartet
OGD(Road Song-alt.take)
Englewood Cliffs,NJ, rec. 28.9.1966
Montgomery,Wes (g) | Smith,Jimmy (org) | Tate,Grady (dr) | Barretto,Ray (congas)

Jimmy Smith Trio
When Johnny Comes Marching Home
Paris,France, rec. 28.5.1965
Montgomery,Wes (g) | Warren,Quentin (g) | Hart,Billy (dr)

Jimmy Smith With The Oliver Nelson Orchestra
Blues And The Abstract Truth
Englewood Cliffs,NJ, rec. 14.6.1966
Smith,Jimmy (org) | Newman,Joe (tp) | Royal,Ernie (tp) | Williams,Richard (tp) | Young,Eugene 'Snooky' (tp) | Jackson,Quentin (tb) | Liston,Melba (tb) | McIntosh,Tom (tb) | Woodman,Britt (tb) | Corrado,Donald (fr-h) | Ruff,Willie (fr-h) | Butterfield,Don (tuba) | Agee,Jack (reeds) | Ashton,Bob (reeds) | Dodgion,Jerry (reeds) | Richardson,Jerome (reeds) | Woods,Phil (reeds) | Lucas,Buddy (harm) | Burrell,Kenny (g) | Butler,Billy (g) | Galbraith,Barry (g) | Suyker,Willard 'Bill' (g) | Cranshaw,Bob (b) | Davis,Richard (b) | Tate,Grady (dr) | Rosengarden,Bobby (perc) | Nelson,Oliver (arr,ld)

527953-2 | 18 CD | The Complete Bill Evans On Verve

Bill Evans Trio
The Washington Twist | Danny Boy (Londonderry Air) | Let's Go Back To The Waltz | With A Song In My Heart | Good Bye | I Believe In You
NYC, rec. 20.8.1962
Evans,Bill (p) | Budwig,Monty (b) | Manne,Shelly (dr)

Gary McFarland And His Orchestra
Reflections In The Park | Tree Patterns | Peach Tree | Misplaced Cowpoke
NYC, rec. 24.1.1963
Woods,Phil (cl) | Sinatra,Spencer (fl,alto-fl) | Barber,Julian (viola) | Goldberg,Allan (viola) | Juvelier,Aaron (cello) | Tekula,Joe (cello) | Hall,Jim (g) | McFarland,Gary (vib,cond,arr) | Evans,Bill (p) | Davis,Richard (b) | Shaughnessy,Ed (dr)
Night Images | A Moment Alone
Woods,Phil (cl) | Sinatra,Spencer (fl,alto-fl) | Barber,Julian (viola) | Goldberg,Allan (viola) | Juvelier,Aaron (cello) | Tekula,Joe (cello) | McFarland,Gary (vib,cond,arr) | Evans,Bill (p) | Davis,Richard (b) | Shaughnessy,Ed (dr)

Bill Evans
N.Y.C.'s No Lark
NYC, rec. 6.2.1963
Evans,Bill (p,overdubbed)
Round About Midnight | How About You | Stella By Starlight | Hey There | Just You Just Me | Bemsha Swing | A Sleeping Bee
NYC, rec. 9.2.1963
Evans,Bill (p,overdubbed)
Spartacus Love Theme | Blue Monk
NYC, rec. 20.2.1963
Evans,Bill (p,overdubbed)

Bill Evans Trio
For Heaven's Sake | A Sleeping Bee | Always | Always(alt.take 1) | Always(alt.take 2) | Everything Happens To Me | Dancing In The Dark | Santa Claus Is Coming To Town | I'll See You Again | I'll See You Again(alt.take) | I'll See You Again(incompl.take) | Little Lulu | Little Lulu(alt.take 1) | Little Lulu(alt.take 2) | My Heart Stood Still | My Heart Stood Still(alt.take)
NYC, rec. 18.12.1963
Evans,Bill (p) | Peacock,Gary (b) | Motian,Paul (dr)

Stan Getz With The Bill Evans Trio
My Heart Stood Still | My Heart Stood Still(alt.take) | My Heart Stood Still(incompl.take) | My Heart Stood Still(rehersal fragments) | Grandfather's Waltz | Grandfather's Waltz(alt.take) | Grandfather's Waltz(incomplete take 2) | Grandfather's Waltz(incomplete take 1) | Melinda | Dark Eyes
Englewood Cliffs,NJ, rec. 5.5.1964
Getz,Stan (ts) | Evans,Bill (p) | Davis,Richard (b) | Jones,Elvin (dr)
Funkallero | Funkallero(rehersal fragments) | But Beautiful | Theme From The Carpetbaggers | Theme From The Carpetbaggers(alt.take 1) | Theme From The Carpetbaggers(alt.take 2) | Theme From The Carpetbaggers(alt.take 3) | Theme From The Carpetbaggers(alt.take 4) | Theme From The Carpetbaggers(incomplete take) | Night And Day | Night And Day(alt.take 1) | Night And Day(alt.take 2) | WNEW
Englewood Cliffs,NJ, rec. 6.5.1964
Getz,Stan (ts) | Evans,Bill (p) | Carter,Ron (b) | Jones,Elvin (dr)

Bill Evans Trio
How Deep Is The Ocean | Our Love Is Here To Stay | Baubles Bangles And Beads | Nardis | Time Remembered | Someday My Prince Will Come | What Is This Thing Called Love | Stella By Starlight | Round About Midnight | Make Someone Happy | The Boy Next Door | Spoken Introduction | Little Lulu | My Love Is An April Song | What Kind Of Fool Am I | What Is This Thing Called Love | The Touch Of Your Lips
Live at The Trident Club,Sausolito,CA, rec. 7.7.1964
Evans,Bill (p) | Israels,Chuck (b) | Bunker,Larry (dr)
Spoken Introduction | The Boy Next Door | Time Remembered | Stella By Starlight | 'Deed I Do | Baubles Bangles And Beads | What Kind Of Fool Am I | Spoken Introduction | Come Rain Or Come Shine | How My Heart Sings | Alone Together | Israel | Spoken Introduction | Alone Together(2) | Make Someone Happy | My Love Is An April Song | 'Deed I Do | Our Love Is Here To Stay | California Here I Come | Warming Up(These Things Called Changes) | What Kind Of Fool Am I(2) | What Is This Thing Called Love | Alone Together(3) | California Here I Come(2)
Live at The Trident Club,Sausolito,CA, rec. 9.7.1964
Evans,Bill (p) | Israels,Chuck (b) | Bunker,Larry (dr)

Monica Zetterlund With The Bill Evans Trio
Come Rain Or Come Shine | Jag Vet En Deglig Rosa(A Beautiful Rose) | Once Upon A Summertime | So Long,Big Time | Monica Vals(aka Waltz For Debby) | Lucky To Be Me | Vindarna Sucka(Sorrow Wind) | It Could Happen To You | Some Other Time | On Natten(In The Night) | Come Rain Or Come Shine(alt.take 1) | Come Rain Or Come Shine(alt.take 2) | Lucky To Be Me(alt.take) | It Could Happen To You(alt.take 1) | It Could Happen To You(alt.take 2)
Stockholm,Sweden, rec. 23.8.1964
Zetterlund,Monica (voc) | Evans,Bill (p) | Israels,Chuck (b) | Bunker,Larry (dr)

Bill Evans Trio
Santa Claus Came In The Spring
Evans,Bill (p) | Israels,Chuck (b) | Bunker,Larry (dr)
Israel | Elsa | Round About Midnight | Our Love Is Here To Stay | How My Heart Sings | Who Can I Turn To | Come Rain Or Come Shine | If You Could See Me Now
Englewood Cliffs,NJ, rec. 3.2.1965
Evans,Bill (p) | Israels,Chuck (b) | Bunker,Larry (dr)

Bill Evans Trio With The Claus Ogerman Orchestra
Granados | Prelude(No.15 in D-Flat Major[Scriabin]) | Pavane | Elegia
Englewood Cliffs,NJ, rec. 29.9.1965
Evans,Bill (p) | Israels,Chuck (b) | Tate,Grady (dr) | Orchestra | Ogerman,Claus (cond,arr) | details unknown
Valse(Siciliano in G Minor[Bach]) | Time Remembered | My Bells | Blue Interlude(C-Minor Prelude[Chopin])
Englewood Cliffs,NJ, rec. 18.10.1965
Evans,Bill (p) | Israels,Chuck (b) | Tate,Grady (dr) | Orchestra | Ogerman,Claus (cond,arr) | details unknown

Bill Evans Trio
I Should Care | Spring Is Here | Who Can I Turn To | Make Someone Happy | Beautiful Love | My Foolish Heart | One For Helen
Live at Town Hall,NYC, rec. 21.2.1966
Evans,Bill (p) | Israels,Chuck (b) | Wise,Arnold (dr)

Bill Evans
In Memory Of My Father: | Prologue- | Story Line- | Turn Out The Stars- | Epilogue-
Evans,Bill (p-solo)

Bill Evans-Jim Hall
Turn Out The Stars | All Across The City
Englewood Cliffs,NJ, rec. 7.4.1966
Evans,Bill (p) | Hall,Jim (g)
My Man's Gone Now | I've Got You Under My Skin | Angel Face | Jazz Samba
Englewood Cliffs,NJ, rec. 10.5.1966
Evans,Bill (p) | Hall,Jim (g)

Bill Evans Trio
A Simple Matter Of Conviction | Stella By Starlight | Orbit(Unless It's You) | Laura | My Melancholy Baby | I'm Getting Sentimental Over You | Star Eyes | Only Child | These Things Called Changes
Englewood Cliffs,NJ, rec. 4.10.1966
Evans,Bill (p) | Gomez,Eddie (b) | Manne,Shelly (dr)

Bill Evans
Emily | Yesterdays | Santa Claus Is Coming To Town | Funny Man | The Shadow Of Your Smile | Little Lulu | Quiet Now
NYC, rec. 9.8.1967
Evans,Bill (p,overdubbed)

Bill Evans Trio
Happiness Is A Thing Called Joe | In A Sentimental Mood | Re:Person I Knew | California Here I Come | Alfie | Gone With The Wind | Turn Out The Stars | Polka Dots And Moonbeams | Stella By Starlight | Very Early | You're Gonna Hear From Me | Emily | Wrap Your Troubles In Dreams | Round About Midnight | On Green Dolphin Street | If You Could See Me Now | I'm Getting Sentimental Over You | G Waltz | California Here I Come(2) | Emily(2) | Alfie(2) | Wrap Your Troubles In Dreams(2)
Live at The 'Village Vanguard',NYC, rec. 17.8.1967
Evans,Bill (p) | Gomez,Eddie (b) | Jones,Philly Joe (dr)
In A Sentimental Mood | California Here I Come | You're Gonna Hear From Me | Alfie | Gone With The Wind | Emily | G Waltz | Wrap Your Troubles In Dreams | In A Sentimental Mood(2) | California Here I Come(2) | You're Gonna Hear From Me(2) | Alfie(2) | Gone With The Wind(2) | Emily(2) | G Waltz(2) | Wrap Your Troubles In Dreams(2) | On Green Dolphin Street | G Waltz(3) | You're Gonna Hear From Me(3) | Wrap Your Troubles In Dreams(3) | Gone With The Wind(3) | G Waltz(4)
Live at The 'Village Vanguard',NYC, rec. 18.8.1967
Evans,Bill (p) | Gomez,Eddie (b) | Jones,Philly Joe (dr)
Spoken Introduction | One For Helen | A Sleeping Bee | Mother Of Earl | Nardis | The Touch Of Your Lips | Embraceable You | Someday My Prince Will Come | Walkin' Up
Montreux,CH, rec. 15.6.1968
Evans,Bill (p) | Gomez,Eddie (b) | DeJohnette,Jack (dr)

Bill Evans
Quiet Now | I Loves You Porgy
Evans,Bill (p-solo)
Here's That Rainy Day | A Time For Love | Midnight Mood | On A Clear Day You Can See Forever | Never Let Me Go | A Time For Love | Midnight Mood(alt.take) | All The Things You Are- | Midnight Mood-
NYC, rec. 23./24./30.9.& 8./14./21.10.1968
Evans,Bill (p-solo)

Bill Evans Trio With Jeremy Steig
Straight No Chaser | Lover Man(Oh,Where Can You Be?) | What's New? | Autumn Leaves | Time Out For Chris | Spartacus Love Theme | So What
NYC, rec. 30.1./3.& 5.2./11.3.1969
Evans,Bill (p) | Steig,Jeremy (fl) | Gomez,Eddie (b) | Morell,Marty (dr)

Bill Evans Quartet
Why Did I Choose You | Why Did I Choose You(alt.take 1) | Why Did I Choose You(alt.take 2) | Why Did I Choose You(alt.take 3) | Why Did I Choose You(alt.take 4) | Why Did I Choose You(alt.take 5) | Why Did I Choose You(alt.take 6)
San Francisco,CA, rec. 26.3.1970
Evans,Bill (p,el-p) | Brown,Sam (g) | Gomez,Eddie (b) | Morell,Marty (dr)

Bill Evans Quartet With Orchestra
Why Did I Choose You
NYC, rec. April/May 1970
Evans,Bill (p,el-p) | Brown,Sam (g) | Gomez,Eddie (b) | Morell,Marty (dr) | Orchestra | Leonard,Mickey (cond,arr) | details unknown
I'm All Smiles | Like Someone In Love | Children's Play Song
NYC, rec. 23.& 29.4./1.5./14.& 21.10./13.11.1970
Evans,Bill (p,el-p) | Kait,Jerome (tp) | Triffon,George (tp,fr-h) | Andre,Wayne (tb) | Gravine,Mickey (tb) | Messner,John (tb) | Faulise,Paul (b-tb) | Alonge,Ray (fr-h) | D'Angelis,Joseph (fr-h) | Estrin,Harvey (fl) | Ashworth,Don (reeds) | Soldo,Joe (reeds) | Penque,Romeo (reeds) | Slapin,Bill (reeds) | Brown,Sam (g) | Gomez,Eddie (b) | Chester,Gary (dr) | Gubin,Sol (dr) | Kahn,Leo (v) | Ockner,George (v) | Poliakin,Raoul (v) | Rosand,Aaron (v) | Jones,Karen (v) | Nadien,David (v) | Samaroff,Tosha (v) | Schwartz,David (v,viola) | Brown,Alfred (viola) | Forrest,Norman (viola) | Barab,Seymour (cello) | Ricci,George (cello) | Leonard,Mickey (cond,arr)

Bill Evans Quartet
Soirée | Soirée(alt.take 1) | Soirée(alt.take 2) | Lullaby For Helene | Lullaby For Helene(alt.take)
San Francisco,CA, rec. 26.3.1970
Evans,Bill (p,el-p) | Brown,Sam (g) | Gomez,Eddie (b) | Morell,Marty (dr) | Leonard,Mickey (arr)

Bill Evans Trio
Lullaby For Helene
Evans,Bill (p,el-p) | Brown,Sam (g) | Gomez,Eddie (b) | Leonard,Mickey (arr)

Bill Evans With Orchestra
NYC, rec. 23.4.1970
Evans,Bill (p,el-p) | Estrin,Harvey (fl,reeds) | Ashworth,Don (reeds) | Penque,Romeo (reeds) | Soldo,Joe (reeds) | Schwartz,David (v,viola) | Jones,Karen (v) | Kahn,Leo (v) | Nadien,David (v) | Ockner,George (v) | Poliakin,Raoul (v) | Samaroff,Tosha (v) | Forrest,Norman (viola) | Barab,Seymour (cello) | Brown,Sam (g) | Gomez,Eddie (b) | Chester,Gary (perc) | Leonard,Mickey (arr)
What Are You Doing The Rest Of Your Life | What Are You Doing The Rest Of Your Life(alt.take 1) | What Are You Doing The Rest Of Your Life(alt.take 2)
San Francisco,CA, rec. 26.3.1970
Evans,Bill (p,el-p) | Brown,Sam (g) | Gomez,Eddie (b) | Morell,Marty (dr) | Leonard,Mickey (arr)

Bill Evans Quartet With Orchestra
What Are You Doing The Rest Of Your Life
NYC, rec. April/May 1970
Evans,Bill (p,el-p) | Brown,Sam (g) | Gomez,Eddie (b) | Morell,Marty (dr) | Orchestra | details unknown | Leonard,Mickey (arr)

Bill Evans Quartet
The Dolphin-Before | The Dolphin-Before(alt.take 1) | The Dolphin-Before(alt.take 2) | The Dolphin-Before(alt.take 3) | The Dolphin-Before(alt.take 4) | The Dolphin-Before(alt.take 5)
San Francisco,CA, rec. 28.3.1970
Evans,Bill (p,el-p) | Brown,Sam (g) | Gomez,Eddie (b) | Morell,Marty (dr) | Leonard,Mickey (arr)
The Dolphin-Before
NYC, rec. 27.5.1970
Evans,Bill (p,el-p) | Brown,Sam (g) | Beal,John (el-b) | Morell,Marty (dr)

Bill Evans With Orchestra
The Dolphin-After
NYC, rec. 23.4.1970
Evans,Bill (p) | Estrin,Harvey (fl,reeds) | Ashworth,Don (reeds) | Penque,Romeo (reeds) | Soldo,Joe (reeds) | Schwartz,David (v,viola) | Jones,Karen (v) | Kahn,Leo (v) | Nadien,David (v) | Ockner,George (v) | Poliakin,Raoul (v) | Samaroff,Tosha (v) | Forrest,Norman (viola) | Barab,Seymour (cello) | Chester,Gary (perc) | Leonard,Mickey (cond,arr)

Bill Evans Quartet
Comrade Conrad | Comrade Conrad(alt.take 1) | Comrade Conrad(alt.take 2) | It Must Be Love | It Must Be Jelly(alt.take 1) | It Must Be Jelly(alt.take 2)
San Francisco,CA/Menlo Park,CA, rec. 25.3.1970
Evans,Bill (p,el-p) | Brown,Sam (g) | Gomez,Eddie (b) | Morell,Marty (dr)
Spoken Introduction | Dancing In The Dark | 'S Wonderful
Live at Newport,Rhode Island, rec. 6.7.1957
Evans,Bill (p) | Elliott,Don (vib,bongos,mellophone) | Furtado,Ernie (b) | Beldini,Al (dr)

Bill Evans Trio
I Love You
Evans,Bill (p) | Furtado,Ernie (b) | Beldini,Al (dr)

-> Note:Each recording was made by different groups and different dates!

528109-2 | CD | Verve Jazz Masters 44:Clifford Brown and Max Roach

Clifford Brown-Max Roach Quintet
Gertrude's Bounce
NYC, rec. 4.1.1956
Brown,Clifford (tp) | Rollins,Sonny (ts) | Powell,Richie (p) | Morrow,George (b) | Roach,Max (dr)
Flossie Lou
NYC, rec. 16.2.1956
Brown,Clifford (tp) | Rollins,Sonny (ts) | Powell,Richie (p) | Morrow,George (b) | Roach,Max (dr) | Dameron,Tadd (arr)

Clifford Brown With Strings
Stardust | What's New?
NYC, rec. 18.& 20.1.1955
Brown,Clifford (tp) | Powell,Richie (p) | Galbraith,Barry (g) | Morrow,George (b) | Roach,Max (dr) | Hefti,Neal (arr) | Strings | details unknown

Clifford Brown-Max Roach Quintet
Jordu | Stompin' At The Savoy | Joy Spring
Hollywood,CA, rec. 3./5.& 6.8.1954
Brown,Clifford (tp) | Land,Harold (ts) | Powell,Richie (p) | Morrow,George (b) | Roach,Max (dr)

Clifford Brown-Max Roach Quartet
It Might As Well Be Spring
Hollywood,CA, rec. 14.8.1954
Brown,Clifford (tp) | Powell,Richie (p) | Morrow,George (b) | Roach,Max (dr)

Clifford Brown-Max Roach Quintet
Cherokee | Blues Walk
NYC, rec. 24./25.2.1955
Brown,Clifford (tp) | Land,Harold (ts) | Powell,Richie (p) | Morrow,George (b) | Roach,Max (dr)

Helen Merrill With The Quincy Jones Orchestra
What's New?
NYC, rec. 24.12.1954
Merrill,Helen (voc) | Brown,Clifford (tp) | Bank,Danny (fl,bs) | Jones,Jimmy (p) | Galbraith,Barry (g) | Pettiford,Oscar (b) | Donaldson,Bobby (dr) | Jones,Quincy (arr,ld)

Clifford Brown All Stars
You Go To My Head
Los Angeles,CA, rec. 11.8.1954
Brown,Clifford (tp) | Geller,Herb (as) | Maini,Joe (as) | Benton,Walter (ts) | Drew,Kenny (p) | Counce,Curtis (b) | Roach,Max (dr)

528408-2 | 2 CD | Cannonball Adderley:Sophisticated Swing-The EmArCy Small Group Sessions

Nat Adderley Quartet
Sermonette
NYC, rec. 12.7.1956
Adderley,Nat (co) | Mance,Junior[Julian C.] (p) | Jones,Sam (b) | Wright,Charles 'Specs' (dr)

Cannonball Adderley Quintet
Bimini | Hoppin' John | Hayseed
Adderley,Julian \'Cannonball\' (as) | Adderley,Nat (co) | Mance,Junior[Julian C.] (p) | Jones,Sam (b) | Wright,Charles 'Specs' (dr)
Rattler's Groove | Jackleg
NYC, rec. 18.7.1956
Adderley,Julian \'Cannonball\' (as) | Adderley,Nat (co) | Mance,Junior[Julian C.] (p) | Jones,Sam (b) | Wright,Charles 'Specs' (dr)
Room No.251
Adderley,Julian \'Cannonball\' (as) | Adderley,Nat (co) | Mance,Junior[Julian C.] (p) | McKibbon,Al (b) | Wright,Charles 'Specs' (dr)
The Fat Man | The Nearness Of You
NYC, rec. 23.7.1956
Adderley,Julian \'Cannonball\' (as) | Adderley,Nat (co) | Mance,Junior[Julian C.] (p) | McKibbon,Al (b) | Wright,Charles 'Specs' (dr)
Yesterdays | Sam's Tune | Sam's Tune(alt.take)
Adderley,Julian \'Cannonball\' (as) | Adderley,Nat (co) | Mance,Junior[Julian C.] (p) | Jones,Sam (cello,b) | Wright,Charles 'Specs' (dr)
Spectacular | Miss Jackie's Delight | Tribute To Brownie | Cobbweb | 18th Century Ballroom | Lover Man(Oh,Where Can You Be?) | A Foggy Day(In London Town) | Hoppin' John | Jeannie | The Way You Look Tonight | Porky
NYC, rec. 6.-8.2.1957
Adderley,Julian \'Cannonball\' (as) | Adderley,Nat (co) | Mance,Junior[Julian C.] (p) | Jones,Sam (b) | Cobb,Jimmy (dr)
Another Kind Of Soul | Spring Is Here | That Funky Train | Edie McLin

NYC, rec. 11.2.1957
Adderley,Julian \'Cannonball\' (as) | Adderley,Nat (co) | Mance,Junior[Julian C.] (p) | Jones,Sam (b) | Cobb,Jimmy (dr)
Our Delight | Jubilation | What's New? | Straight No Chaser
NYC, rec. 4.3.1958
Adderley,Julian \'Cannonball\' (as) | Adderley,Nat (co) | Mance,Junior[Julian C.] (p) | Jones,Sam (b) | Cobb,Jimmy (dr)
If I Love Again | I'll Remember April | Fuller Bop Man | Fuller Bop Man(alt.take) | Stay On It
NYC, rec. 6.3.1958
Adderley,Julian \'Cannonball\' (as) | Adderley,Nat (co) | Mance,Junior[Julian C.] (p) | Jones,Sam (b) | Cobb,Jimmy (dr)

528783-2 | CD | Sarala
Hank Jones Meets Cheik-Tidiana Seck
Aly Kawélé | Sarala | Maningafoly | Tounia Kanibala | Komidiara | Fantaguè | Make! | Walidi Ya | Soundjata | Hank Miri | Hadja Fadima | Moriba Ka Foly
Paris,France, rec. April 1995
Jones,Hank (p) | Seck,Cheick-Tidiane (org,perc,ld,voc) | Mandinkas,The: | Wagué,Aly (fl) | Condé,Djely-Moussa (kora) | Kouyaté,Lansine (balafon) | Koita,Moriba (n'goni) | Kouyaté,Ousmane (g) | Kanté,Manflia (g) | Kouyaté,Diely-Moussa (g) | Diabaté,Sekou (b-g) | Anot,César (perc,b-g,voc) | Vinceno,Éric (b) | Sissoko,Moussa (djembe,tama) | Sanogo,Maré (doum-doum) | Amorin,Jorge (perc) | Annabi,Amina (voc) | Damba,Manian (voc) | Diabaté,Kassé-Mady (voc) | Diakité,Tom (perc,voc) | Keita,Assitan 'Mama' (perc,voc) | Koyaté,Fatoumata 'Mama' (voc)

529028-2 | CD | Modern Day Jazz Stories
Courtney Pine Group
Prelude- | The Water Of Life- | The 37th Chamber | Don't Explain | Dah Blessing | In The Garden Of Eden(Thinking Inside Of You) | Creative Stopper | After The Damaja | Absolution | Each One (Must) Teach One | The Unknown Warrior(Song For My Forefathers) | I've Known Rivers | Outro-Guiding Light | Prince Of Peace
NYC, rec. details unknown
Pine,Courtney (fl,ss,ts) | Henderson,Eddie (tp) | Whitfield,Mark (g) | Allen,Geri (p,org) | Moffett,Charnett (b) | Burrage,Ronnie (dr,perc) | Wilson,Cassandra (voc) | DJ Pogo (turntables)

529387-2 | CD | Forever Ella
Ella Fitzgerald With Orchestra
Someone To Watch Over Me | I Love Paris | Summertime | Misty | Gone With The Wind | I Can't Give You Anything But Love | Tenderly | I Only Have Eyes For You | These Foolish Things Remind Me On You | The Very Thought Of You | Love Me Or Leave Me | You Do Something To Me | I Won't Dance | Mountain Greenery | How Deep Is The Ocean | I've Got My Love To Keep Me Warm | Lullaby Of Birdland | On The Sunny Side Of The Street | Blue Skies | I Get A Kick Out Of You | One For My Baby(And One More For The Road)
different Places, rec. different Dates
Fitzgerald,Ella (voc) | details not on the cover

529555-2 | CD | The Main Ingredient
Shirley Horn Quintet
Blues For Sarge
Washington,DC, rec. 15.-18.5.1995
Horn,Shirley (p,voc) | Hill,Buck (ts) | Ables,Charles (g) | Novosel,Steve (b) | Williams,Stephen E. 'Steve' (dr)
All Or Nothing At All
Horn,Shirley (p,voc) | Henderson,Joe (ts) | Hill,Buck (ts) | Novosel,Steve (b) | Jones,Elvin (dr)
Shirley Horn Quartet
Come In From The Rain
Horn,Shirley (roland-p) | Ables,Charles (g) | Novosel,Steve (b) | Williams,Stephen E. 'Steve' (dr)
Keepin' Out Of Mischief Now
Horn,Shirley (p,voc) | Hill,Buck (ts) | Ables,Charles (b) | Williams,Stephen E. 'Steve' (dr)
The Meaning Of The Blues
Horn,Shirley (p,voc) | Hargrove,Roy (tp) | Ables,Charles (b) | Williams,Stephen E. 'Steve' (dr)
You Go To My Head
Horn,Shirley (p,voc) | Henderson,Joe (ts) | Ables,Charles (b) | Jones,Elvin (dr)
Shirley Horn Trio
The Look Of Love | Here's Looking At You! | Fever
Horn,Shirley (p,voc) | Ables,Charles (b) | Williams,Stephen E. 'Steve' (dr)
Peel Me A Grape
Horn,Shirley (p,voc) | Ables,Charles (b) | Hart,Billy (dr)

529578-2 | CD | Message From Home
Pharoah Sanders Orchestra
Our Roots(Began In Africa) | Nozipho | Tomoki | Ocean Song | Kumba | Country Mile
NYC/Brooklyn,NY, rec. 1995
Sanders,Pharoah (fl,ss,ts,bells,bowls,voc) | White,Michael (v) | Kanze,Dominic (g) | Henderson,William 'Bill' (p,el-p,voc) | Worrell,Bernie (electronic-keyboards) | Bova,Jeff (electronic-keyboards,programming) | Moffett,Charnett (b) | Neil,Steve (b,el-b) | Suso,Jali Foday Musa (dusungoni,kora,voc) | Drake,Hamid (dr,frame-dr,tablas,voc) | Dieng,Aib (congas,bells,chatan,gongs,voc) | Suso,Salie (voc) | Suso,Miriam (voc) | Mangasuba,Fanta (voc) | Sako,Fatoumata (voc)

529580-2 | CD | Talkin' Jazz:Roots Of Acid Jazz
Wes Montgomery With The Johnny Pate Orchestra
Movin' Wes(part 1) | Movin' Wes(part 2) | In And Out
Englewood Cliffs,NJ, rec. 18.11.1964
Montgomery,Wes (g) | Pate,Johnny (cond,arr) | Royal,Ernie (tp) | Terry,Clark (tp) | Young,Eugene 'Snooky' (tp) | Cleveland,Jimmy (tb) | Green,Urbie (tb) | Jackson,Quentin (tb) | Welsch,Chauncey (tb) | Butterfield,Don (tuba) | Richardson,Jerome (reeds) | Scott,Bobby (p) | Cranshaw,Bob (b) | Tate,Grady (dr) | Bobo,Willie (perc)
Wes Montgomery Quintet With The Claus Ogerman Orchestra
Bumpin' On Sunset
Englewood Cliffs,NJ, rec. 17.3.1966
Montgomery,Wes (g) | Devens,George (vib) | Carter,Ron (b) | Tate,Grady (dr) | Barretto,Ray (congas) | Eichen,Bernard (v) | Eidus,Arnold (v) | Gersham,Paul (v) | Green,Emmanuel (v) | Held,Julius (v) | Lookofsky,Harry (v) | Malin,Joe (v) | Orloff,Gene (v) | Kessler,Abe (cello) | McCracken,Charles (cello) | Ricci,George (cello) | Shapiro,Harvey (cello) | Ogerman,Claus (cond,arr)
Wes Montgomery With The Don Sebesky Orchestra
Green Peppers
Englewood Cliffs,NJ, rec. 15.9.1966
Montgomery,Wes (g) | Davis,Mel (tp) | Glow,Bernie (tp) | Nottingham,Jimmy (tp) | Andre,Wayne (tb) | Messner,John (tb) | Watrous,Bill (tb) | Buffington,Jimmy (fr-h) | Butterfield,Don (tuba) | Beckenstein,Ray (reeds) | Webb,Stanley (reeds) | Kane,Walter (reeds) | Casamenti,Al (g) | Pizzarelli,Bucky (g) | Jennings,Jack (vib,perc) | Davis,Richard (b) | Tate,Grady (dr,perc) | Barretto,Ray (perc)
Jimmy Smith-Wes Montgomery Quartet
OGD(Road Song)
NYC, rec. 28.9.1966
Montgomery,Wes (g) | Smith,Jimmy (org) | Tate,Grady (dr) | Barretto,Ray (congas)
Wes Montgomery Quartet
Impressions | Willow Weep For Me
Live at The Half Note Cafe,NYC, rec. 22./27.6.1965
Montgomery,Wes (g) | Kelly,Wynton (p) | Chambers,Paul (b) | Cobb,Jimmy (dr)
Jimmy Smith And Wes Montgomery With The Oliver Nelson Orchestra
13 (Death March) | Night Train
Englewood Cliffs,NJ, rec. 21./23.9.1966
Montgomery,Wes (g) | Terry,Clark (tp,fl-h) | Maxwell,Jimmy (tp) | Newman,Joe (tp) | Royal,Ernie (tp) | Cleveland,Jimmy (tb) | Hixon,Richard 'Dick' (tb) | Jackson,Quentin (tb) | Liston,Melba (tb) | Dodgion,Jerry (fl,cl,as) | Richardson,Jerome (fl,cl) | Woods,Phil (cl,as) | Ashton,Bob (fl,cl,ts) | Bank,Danny (fl,cl,b-cl,bs) | Smith,Jimmy (org) | Davis,Richard (b) | Tate,Grady (dr) | Barretto,Ray (congas) | Nelson,Oliver (arr,ld)
Wes Montgomery Quartet
The Thumb | Tequila
Englewood Cliffs,NJ, rec. 21.3.1966
Montgomery,Wes (g) | Carter,Ron (b) | Tate,Grady (dr) | Barretto,Ray (congas)
Wes Montgomery With The Oliver Nelson Orchestra
Boss City
Englewood Cliffs,NJ, rec. 20.11.1965
Montgomery,Wes (g) | Byrd,Donald (tp) | Newman,Joe (tp) | Royal,Ernie (tp) | Andre,Wayne (tb) | Cleveland,Jimmy (tb) | Jackson,Quentin (tb) | Moore,Danny (tp) | Studd,Tony (tb) | Ashton,Bob (reeds) | Woods,Phil (as) | Dodgion,Jerry (as) | Penque,Romeo (reeds) | Bank,Danny (reeds) | Hancock,Herbie (p) | Duvivier,George (b) | Tate,Grady (dr) | Nelson,Oliver (arr,ld)
Wes Montgomery With The Don Sebesky Orchestra
Sunny
Englewood Cliffs,NJ, rec. 16.9.1966
Montgomery,Wes (g) | Sebesky,Don (cond,arr) | Davis,Mel (tp) | Glow,Bernie (tp) | Nottingham,Jimmy (tp) | Andre,Wayne (tb) | Messner,John (tb) | Watrous,Bill (tb) | Butterfield,Don (tuba) | Buffington,Jimmy (fr-h) | Beckenstein,Ray (fl,as) | Webb,Stanley (cl,as) | Kane,Walter (ts) | Jennings,Jack (vib) | Casamenti,Al (g) | Pizzarelli,Bucky (g) | Davis,Richard (b) | Tate,Grady (dr) | Barretto,Ray (perc)
Mr.Walker
Montgomery,Wes (g) | Davis,Mel (tp) | Glow,Bernie (tp) | Nottingham,Jimmy (tp) | Andre,Wayne (tb) | Messner,John (tb) | Watrous,Bill (tb) | Buffington,Jimmy (fr-h) | Butterfield,Don (tuba) | Beckenstein,Ray (reeds) | Webb,Stanley (reeds) | Kane,Walter (reeds) | Casamenti,Al (g) | Pizzarelli,Bucky (g) | Jennings,Jack (vib,perc) | Davis,Richard (b) | Tate,Grady (dr,perc) | Barretto,Ray (perc)
Bumpin'
Englewood Cliffs,NJ, rec. 20.5.1965
Montgomery,Wes (g) | Kellaway,Roger (p) | Eidus,Arnold (v) | Eley,Lewis (v) | Gershman,Paul (v) | Haber,Louis (v) | Held,Julius (v) | Lookofsky,Harry (v) | Malignaggi,Joseph (v) | Orloff,Gene (v) | Shapiro,Sol (v) | Coletta,Harold (viola) | Schwartz,David (viola) | McCracken,Charles (cello) | Ricci,George (cello) | Cranshaw,Bob (b) | Ross,Margaret (harp) | Candido[Camero] (congas,bongos) | Milito,Helcio or Grady Tate (dr) | Sebesky,Don (cond,arr)

529581-2 | CD | Oh Lady Be Good:The Best Of The Gershwin Songbook
Ella Fitzgerald With The Nelson Riddle Orchestra
Fascinating Rhythm | Funny Face
Hollywood,CA, rec. 18.3.1959
Fitzgerald,Ella (voc) | Riddle,Nelson (cond,arr) | details unknown
'S Wonderful
Hollywood,CA, rec. 16.7.1959
Fitzgerald,Ella (voc) | Riddle,Nelson (cond,arr) | details unknown
Someone To Watch Over Me | Let's Call The Whole Thing Off | My One And Only | Nice Work If You Can Get It
Hollywood,CA, rec. 26.3.1959
Fitzgerald,Ella (voc) | Riddle,Nelson (cond,arr) | details unknown
He Loves And She Loves | A Foggy Day(In London Town) | The Man I Love
Hollywood,CA, rec. 5.1.1959
Fitzgerald,Ella (voc) | Lewis,Carroll (tp) | Mangano,Vito (tp) | McMickle,Dale (tp) | Sherock,Shorty (tp) | Bernhart,Milton 'Milt' (tb) | Noel,Richard (tb) | Pederson,Pullman 'Tommy' (tb) | Roberts,George (b-tb) | DeRosa,Vince (fr-h) | Nash,Ted (ts) | Collette,Buddy (reeds) | Klee,Harry (reeds) | Koch,Joe (reeds) | Webb,Champ (reeds) | Bay,Victor (v) | Beller,Alex 'Al' (v) | Gasselin,Jaques (v) | Getzoff,James (v) | Gill,Ben (v) | Kellner,Murray (v) | Ross,Nathan 'Nat' (v) | Shapiro,Eunice (v) | Slatkin,Felix (v) | Sosson,Marshall (v) | Dinkin,Alvin (viola) | Harris,Stan (viola) | Simons,Barbara (viola) | Kaproff,Armand (cello) | Reher,Kurt (cello) | Slatkin,Eleanor (cello) | Julyie,Katharine 'Kathryn' (harp) | Smith,Paul (p) | Bain,Robert 'Bob' (g) | Comfort,Joe (b) | Flynn,Fred (dr) | Stoller,Alvin (dr) | Riddle,Nelson (cond,arr)
Oh! Lady Be Good | But Not For Me | I've Got A Crush On You | Embraceable You
Hollywood,CA, rec. 8.1.1959
Fitzgerald,Ella (voc) | Riddle,Nelson (cond,arr) | details unknown
How Long Has This Been Going On | They Can't Take That Away From Me | I Got Rhythm
Hollywood,CA, rec. 5.1.1959
Fitzgerald,Ella (voc) | Riddle,Nelson (cond,arr) | details unknown

529698-2 | CD | Oscar Peterson:The Gershwin Songbooks
Oscar Peterson Trio
It Ain't Necessarily So | The Man I Love | Love Walked In | I Was Doing Alright | A Foggy Day(In London Town) | Oh! Lady Be Good | Our Love Is Here To Stay | They All Laughed | Let's Call The Whole Thing Off | Summertime | Nice Work If You Can Get It | Shall We Dance?
Chicago,Ill, rec. 21.7.-1.8.1959
Peterson,Oscar (p) | Brown,Ray (b) | Thigpen,Ed (dr)
The Man I Love | Fascinating Rhythm | It Ain't Necessarily So | Somebody Loves Me | Strike Up The Band | I've Got A Crush On You | I Was Doing Alright | 'S Wonderful | Oh! Lady Be Good | I Got Rhythm | A Foggy Day(In London Town) | Love Walked In
Los Angeles,CA, rec. 1.11.-4.12.1952
Peterson,Oscar (p) | Kessel,Barney (g) | Brown,Ray (b)

529700-2 | CD | Ella At Duke's Place
Ella Fitzgerald With The Duke Ellington Orchestra
Something To Live For | A Flower Is A Lovesome Thing | Passion Flower | I Like The Sunrise | Azure | Imagine My Frustration | Duke's Place(C Jam Blues) | Brown-Skinned Gal In The Calico Gown | What Am I Here For | Cotton Tail
Hollywood,CA, rec. 18.-20.10.1965
Fitzgerald,Ella (voc) | Ellington,Duke (p,ld) | Williams,Cootie (tp) | Jones,Herbie (tp) | Anderson,Cat (tp) | Brown,Lawrence (tb) | Cooper,Frank 'Buster' (tb) | Connors,Chuck (tb) | Hodges,Johnny (as) | Procope,Russell (as) | Hamilton,Jimmy (cl,ts) | Gonsalves,Paul (ts) | Carney,Harry (bs) | Lamb,John (b) | Woodyard,Sam (dr)

529828-2 | CD | The Promise
John McLaughlin Group
Django
London,GB, rec. details unknown
McLaughlin,John (el-g) | Beck,Jeff (el-g) | Hymas,Tony (keyboards) | Palladino,Pino (b) | Mondesir,Mark (dr)
Thelonius Melodius
Live at The Blue Note,Tokyo,Japan, rec. details unknown
McLaughlin,John (el-g) | DeFrancesco,Joey (org) | Chambers,Dennis (dr)
Amy And Joseph
Monaco, rec. details unknown
McLaughlin,John (g,keyboards) | Bimbi,Stephania (recitation) | Maresz,Yan (arr)
No Return
Milano,Italy, rec. details unknown
McLaughlin,John (g,keyboards) | DeFrancesco,Joey (tp)
El Ciego
Paris,France, rec. details unknown
McLaughlin,John (g) | De Lucia,Paco (g) | Di Meola,Al (g)
Jazz Jungle
NYC, rec. details unknown
McLaughlin,John (el-g) | Brecker,Michael (ts) | Beard,Jim (keyboards) | Genus,James (b-g) | Chambers,Dennis (dr) | Alias,Don (perc)
The Wish
London,GB, rec. details unknown
McLaughlin,John (el-g) | Khan,Nishat (sitar,voice) | Hussain,Zakir (tabla) | Gurtu,Trilok (perc)
English Jam
Witshire,GB, rec. details unknown
McLaughlin,John (el-g) | Sting (b) | Colaiuta,Vinnie (dr)
Tokyo Decadence
Milano,Italy, rec. details unknown
McLaughlin,John (midi-g) | Takahashi,Mariko (voice) | Costa,Max (arr)
Shin Jin Rui
NYC, rec. details unknown
McLaughlin,John (el-g) | Sanborn,David (as) | Beard,Jim (keyboards) | Genus,James (b-g) | Chambers,Dennis (dr) | Alias,Don (perc) | Toto (bird-songs) | Susanna (bird-songs) | John (bird-songs)
The Peacocks(with verse of Garcia Lorca)
Monaco, rec. details unknown
McLaughlin,John (g) | Loli,Philippe (g) | Maresz,Yan (b-g) | Beatrix,Ssana (recitation)

529849-2 | CD | Deep In The Blues
James Cotton Group
Down At You Buryin' | All Walks Of Life | Dealing With The Devil | Country Boy | Two Trains Runnin' | Sad Letter | Play With Your Poodle | Everbody's Fishin'
Los Angeles,CA, rec. 14./15.8.1995
Cotton,James (harm,voc) | Walker,Joe Louis (g,voc) | Haden,Charlie (b)
Blues In My Sleep
Cotton,James (harm) | Walker,Joe Louis (g) | Maxwell,David (p) | Haden,Charlie (b)
You Got My Nose Open
Cotton,James (harm,voc) | Walker,Joe Louis (g)
Strange Things Happen | Worried Life Blues
Cotton,James (harm) | Maxwell,David (p)
Joe Louis Walker
Vineyard Blues
Walker,Joe Louis (national-steel-g)
Charlie Haden
Ozark Mountain Railroad
Haden,Charlie (b-solo)

529866-2 | CD | Verve Jazz Masters Vol.60:The Collection
Quintet Du Hot Club De France
Sweet Georgia Brown
London,GB, rec. 31.1.1938
Quintet Du Hot Club De France | Grappelli,Stephane (v) | Reinhardt,Django (g) | Chaput,Roger (g) | Vees,Eugene (g) | Vola,Louis (b)
Norman Granz Jam Session
Jam Blues
NYC, rec. 2.9.1953
Norman Granz Jam Session | Eldridge,Roy (tp) | Gillespie,Dizzy (tp) | Harris,Bill (tb) | Phillips,Flip (ts) | Webster,Ben (ts) | Hampton,Lionel (vib) | Peterson,Oscar (p) | Brown,Ray (b) | Rich,Buddy (dr)
Ella Fitzgerald And Louis Armstrong With The Oscar Peterson Quartet
I've Got My Love To Keep Me Warm
Hollywood,CA, rec. 16.8.1956
Armstrong,Louis (tp,voc) | Fitzgerald,Ella (voc) | Peterson,Oscar (p) | Ellis,Herb (g) | Brown,Ray (b) | Bellson,Louie (dr)
Kenny Burrell With The Gil Evans Orchestra
Last Night When We Were Young
Englewood Cliffs,NJ, rec. 4.12.1964
Burrell,Kenny (g) | Evans,Gil (p,arr) | Coles,Johnny (tp) | Mucci,Louis (tp) | Cleveland,Jimmy (tb) | Knepper,Jimmy (tb) | Alonge,Ray (fr-h) | Watkins,Julius (fr-h) | Barber,Bill (tuba) | Fitzgerald,Andy (engl-h,fl) | Marge,George (engl-h,fl) | Beckenstein,Ray (fl,b-cl) | Lacy,Steve (ss) | Konitz,Lee (as) | Kamuca,Richie (ts,oboe) | Tricarico,Bob (fl,ts,bassoon) | Carter,Ron (b) | Persip,Charles (dr) | Jones,Elvin (dr)
Lester Young Quartet
Polka Dots And Moonbeams
NYC, rec. 17.9.1949
Young,Lester (ts) | Jones,Hank (p) | Brown,Ray (b) | Rich,Buddy (dr)
Oliver Nelson And His Orchestra
Ricardo's Dilemma
Englewood Cliffs,NJ, rec. 3./4.11.1966
Nelson,Oliver (as,arr,ld) | Collins,Bert (tp) | Royal,Ernie (tp) | Young,Eugene 'Snooky' (tp) | Wilder,Joe (tp) | Newman,Joe (tp) | Terry,Clark (tp,fl-h) | Brookmeyer,Bob (v-tb) | Cleveland,Jimmy (tb) | Johnson,J.J. (tb) | Studd,Tony (b-tb) | Woods,Phil (as) | Dodgion,Jerry (cl,as) | Sims,Zoot (ts) | Richardson,Jerome (reeds) | Bank,Danny (reeds) | Dailey,Albert (p) | Gale,Eric (g) | Carter,Ron (b) | Tate,Grady (dr) | Kraus,Phil (perc)
Jimmy Smith Trio
Organ Grinder's Swing
Englewood Cliffs,NJ, rec. 14./15.6.1965
Smith,Jimmy (org,voc) | Burrell,Kenny (g) | Tate,Grady (dr)
Billie Holiday And Her All Stars
Stormy Weather
NYC, rec. 27.7.1952
Holiday,Billie (voc) | Newman,Joe (tp) | Quinichette,Paul (ts) | Peterson,Oscar (p) | Green,Freddie (g) | Brown,Ray (b) | Johnson,Gus (dr)
Gerry Mulligan Concert Jazz Band
Ballad
NYC, rec. 18.-21.12.1962
Mulligan,Gerry (cl,bs) | Travis,Nick (tp) | Ferrara,Don (tp) | Severinsen,Doc (tp) | Terry,Clark (fl-h) | Brookmeyer,Bob (v-tb,p,arr) | Dennis,Willie (tb) | Studd,Tony (b-tb) | Quill,Gene (cl,as) | Caine,Eddie (as) | Reider,Jimmy (ts) | Allen,Gene (bs) | Hall,Jim (g) | Crow,Bill (b) | Johnson,Gus (dr)
Cal Tjader Group
Soul Sauce
NYC, rec. 20.11.1964
Tjader,Cal (vib) | Hewitt,Lonnie (p) | Hilliard,John (b) | Rae,Johnny (dr) | Bobo,Willie (perc) | Valdez,Alberto (perc) | Peraza,Armando (perc)
Roland Kirk Quartet
March On Swan Lake
Los Angeles,CA, rec. 22.7.1964
Kirk,Rahsaan Roland (ts,music-box) | Parlan,Horace (p) | Fleming,Michael (b) | Ellington,Steve (dr)
Sarah Vaughan And Her Trio
Words Can't Describe
NYC, rec. 14.2.1957
Vaughan,Sarah (voc) | Jones,Jimmie (p) | Davis,Richard (b) | Haynes,Roy (dr)
Coleman Hawkins And Ben Webster With The Oscar Peterson Quartet
Cocktails For Two
Hollywood,CA, rec. 16.10.1957
Hawkins,Coleman (ts) | Webster,Ben (ts) | Peterson,Oscar (p) | Ellis,Herb (g) | Brown,Ray (b) | Stoller,Alvin (dr)
Chet Baker Quartet
Summertime
Paris,France, rec. 24.10.1955
Baker,Chet (tp) | Goustin,Gerard (p) | Bond,Jimmy (b) | Dahlander,Nils-Bertil (dr)
Clifford Brown-Max Roach Quintet
Cherokee
NYC, rec. 24./25.2.1955
Brown,Clifford (tp) | Land,Harold (ts) | Powell,Richie (p) | Morrow,George (b) | Roach,Max (dr)
Herbie Mann Sextet
The Peanut Vendor
Hollywood,CA, rec. 10.8.1957
Mann,Herbie (fl) | Almeida,Laurindo (g,arr) | Rizzi,Tony (g) | Reyes,Tony (b) | Guerrero,Frank 'Chico' (perc) | Holland,Milt (perc)

529867-2 | CD | Verve Jazz Masters Vol.58:Nina Simone Sings Nina
Nina Simone Trio
Sugar In My Bowl | Four Women | If You Pray Right(Heaven Belongs To You) | Fodder On My Wings | If You Knew- | Let It Be Me- | Mississippi Goddam
Live at The Vine St.Bar,Los Angeles,CA, rec. 1987
Simone,Nina (p,voc) | Adams,Arthur (g,b) | McFadden,Cornell (dr)
Old Jim Crow
NYC, rec. 1./6.4.1964
Simone,Nina (p,voc) | Atkinson,Lisle (b) | Stevenson,Rudy prob. (bongos)
Nina Simone-Lisle Atkinson

Go Limp
Live at Carnegie Hall,NYC, rec. 21.3.1964
Simone,Nina (p,voc) | Atkinson,Lisle (b)

Nina Simone
Images
Simone,Nina (p,voc)

Nina Simone Quintet
Come Ye
details unknown, rec. August 1966
Simone,Nina (p,voc) | unkn. (4 perc)

Nina Simone With Hal Mooney's Orchestra
Take Me To The Water | I'm Going Back Home | The Last Rose Of Summer
Simone,Nina (p,voc) | Orchestra | Mooney,Hal (arr,ld) | details unknown

Nina Simone-Bobby Hamilton
Be My Husband
NYC, rec. 19./20.5.1965
Simone,Nina (p,voc) | Hamilton,Bobby (dr)

529900-2 | CD | Verve Jazz Masters 57:George Shearing

George Shearing Quintet
September In The Rain
NYC, rec. 17.2.1949
Shearing,George (p) | Hyams,Marjorie (vib) | Wayne,Chuck (g) | Levy,John (b) | Best,Denzil (dr)

I Didn't Know What Time It Was
NYC, rec. 28.6.1949
Shearing,George (p) | Hyams,Marjorie (vib) | Wayne,Chuck (g) | Levy,John (b) | Best,Denzil (dr)

George Shearing
Summertime
Shearing,George (p-solo)

George Shearing Quintet
East Of The Sun West Of The Moon | Conception
NYC, rec. 27.7.1949
Shearing,George (p) | Hyams,Marjorie (vib) | Wayne,Chuck (g) | Levy,John (b) | Best,Denzil (dr)

Jumpin' With Symphony Sid | I'll Remember April
NYC, rec. 12.12.1949
Shearing,George (p) | Hyams,Marjorie (vib) | Wayne,Chuck (g) | Levy,John (b) | Best,Denzil (dr)

Pick Yourself Up
NYC, rec. 5.7.1950
Shearing,George (p) | Hyams,Marjorie (vib) | Wayne,Chuck (g) | Levy,John (b) | Best,Denzil (dr)

I'll Be Around
NYC, rec. 5.2.1951
Shearing,George (p) | Elliott,Don (vib) | Wayne,Chuck (g) | Levy,John (b) | Best,Denzil (dr)

Easy Living
NYC, rec. 2.10.1951
Shearing,George (p) | Roland,Joe (vib) | Wayne,Chuck (g) | McKibbon,Al (b) | Best,Denzil (dr)

How High The Moon | Lonely Moments
NYC, rec. 18.12.1951
Shearing,George (p) | Roland,Joe (vib) | Wayne,Chuck (g) | McKibbon,Al (b) | Best,Denzil (dr)

I Wished On The Moon
NYC, rec. 10.7.1952
Shearing,George (p) | Roland,Joe (vib) | Garcia,Dick (g) | McKibbon,Al (b) | Foster,Marquis (dr) | King,Teddi (voc)

Lullaby Of Birdland
NYC, rec. 17.7.1952
Shearing,George (p) | Roland,Joe (vib) | Garcia,Dick (g) | McKibbon,Al (b) | Foster,Marquis (dr)

Love Is Just Around The Corner
Hollywood,CA, rec. 15.4.1953
Shearing,George (p) | Tjader,Cal (vib) | Thielemans,Jean 'Toots' (g) | McKibbon,Al (b) | Clark,Bill (dr)

George Shearing And His Quintet
Mambo Inn
Hollywood,CA, rec. 26.3.1954
Shearing,George (p) | Tjader,Cal (vib) | Thielemans,Jean 'Toots' (g) | McKibbon,Al (b) | Clark,Bill (dr) | Peraza,Armando (congas,bongos)

529901-2 | CD | Verve Jazz Masters 56:Herbie Mann

Herbie Mann With The Frank DeVol Orchestra
Oodles Of Noodles | Stardust
Hollywood,CA, rec. 9.8.1957
Mann,Herbie (fl) | Baker,Israel (v) | Frisina,Dave (v) | Lustgarten,Alfred (v) | Miller,Warren (v) | Ostrawsky,Robert (viola) | Thomas,Milton (viola) | DiTullio,Justin (cello) | Lustgarten,Edgar 'Ed' (cello) | Roberts,Howard (g) | Rowles,Jimmy (p) | Clark,Buddy (b) | Lewis,Mel (dr) | DeVol,Frank (cond,arr)

Herbie Mann Quartet
St.Louis Blues | Strike Up The Band
Hollywood,CA, rec. 10.8.1957
Mann,Herbie (fl) | Rowles,Jimmy (p) | Clark,Buddy (b) | Lewis,Mel (dr)

Herbie Mann Sextet
Baia | The Peanut Vendor
Mann,Herbie (fl) | Almeida,Laurindo (g,arr) | Rizzi,Tony (g) | Reyes,Tony (b) | Guerrero,Frank 'Chico' (perc) | Holland,Milt (perc)

Herbie Mann Trio
Evolution Of Mann
Mann,Herbie (fl) | Guerrero,Frank 'Chico' (perc) | Holland,Milt (perc)

Herbie Mann Sextet
Todos Locos | Cuban Patato Chip | Come On Mule | The Amazon River | Caravan
Live at Basin Street,NYC, rec. 30.9.1959
Mann,Herbie (fl,b-cl) | Rae,Johnny (vib,timbales) | Totah,Nabil 'Knobby' (b) | Miranda,Santo (dr) | Mangual,Jose (bongos) | Valdez,Carlos 'Patato' (congas)

Herbie Mann's Cuban Band
Fife 'N' Tambourine Corps
NYC, rec. 5.7.1960
Mann,Herbie (piccolo) | Ball,Leo (tp) | Kail,Jerry (tp) | Schatz,Ziggy (tp) | Rae,Johnny (vib) | Totah,Nabil 'Knobby' (b) | Collins,Rudy (dr) | Barretto,Ray (perc) | Mantilla,Ray (perc) | Olatunji,Babatunde (perc)

A Ritual | You Stepped Out Of A Dream
NYC, rec. 26.7.1960
Mann,Herbie (fl) | Ball,Leo (tp) | Kail,Jerry (tp) | Schatz,Ziggy (tp) | Rae,Johnny (vib) | Totah,Nabil 'Knobby' (b) | Collins,Rudy (dr) | Barretto,Ray (perc) | Mantilla,Ray (perc) | Olatunji,Babatunde (perc)

529903-2 | CD | Verve Jazz Masters 54:Woody Herman

Woody Herman And His Orchestra
Don't Get Around Much Anymore | Sister Sadie | Camel Walk
NYC, rec. 15./16.10.1962
Herman,Woody (cl,voc) | Harrell,Ziggy (tp) | Gale,Dave (tp) | Chase,Bill (tp) | Lamy,Gerald (tp) | Fontaine,Paul (tp) | Gale,Jack (tb) | Wilson,Phil (tb) | Morgan,Eddie (tb) | Nistico,Sal (ts) | Brisker,Gordon (ts) | Covelli,Larry (ts) | Allen,Gene (bs) | Pierce,Nat (p) | Andrus,Chuck (b) | Hanna,Jake (dr)

Body And Soul | Better Git It In Your Soul | Jazz Me Blues | Caldonia | The Good Earth
Live at Basin Street West,Hollywood,CA, rec. 19.-21.5.1963
Herman,Woody (cl,as,voc) | Hunt,Billy (tp) | Gale,Dave (tp) | Chase,Bill (tp) | Lamy,Gerald (tp) | Fontaine,Paul (tp) | Rudolph,Bob (tb) | Wilson,Phil (tb) | Southall,Henry (tb) | Nistico,Sal (ts) | Jones,Bobby (ts) | Perkins,Bill (ts) | Hittner,Frank (bs) | Pierce,Nat (p) | Andrus,Chuck (b) | Hanna,Jake (dr)

Deep Purple | Cousins
NYC, rec. 20.& 23.11.1963
Herman,Woody (cl,ss,as,voc) | Burke,Tim (tp) | Byrne,Billy (tp,fl-h) | Drews,Glenn (tp,fl-h) | Kennedy,Dave (tp,fl-h) | Powell,Jim (tp,fl-h) | Johnson,B. (tb) | Hinds,Nelson (tb) | Shunk,Larry (b-tb) | Ross,Bill (fl,ts) | Tiberi,Frank (fl,ts,bassoon) | Lovano,Joe (fl,ts) | Smulyan,Gary (bs) | Lalama,Dave (p) | Andersen,Jay (b) | Riley,John (dr)

Just Squeeze Me(But Don't Tease Me) | Dr. Wong's Bag | Dear John
Live at Harrah's Club,Lake Tahoe, rec. 9..9.1964
Herman,Woody (cl,as) | Chase,Bill (tp) | Ford,Larry (tp) | Goykovich,Dusko (tp) | Hunt,Billy (tp) | Lamy,Gerald (tp) | Southall,Henry (tb) | Stroup,Bob (tb) | Wilson,Phil (tb) | Klein,Gary (ts) | McGhee,Andy (ts) | Romero,Raoul (ts) | Anastas,Tom (bs) | Pierce,Nat (p) | Andrus,Chuck (b) | Hanna,Jake (dr) | Holman,Bill (arr) | Hammer,Bob (arr)

529904-2 | CD | Verve Jazz Masters 53:Stan Getz-Bossa Nova

Stan Getz Quintet Feat. Astrud Gilberto
Corcovado(Quiet Nights)
Englewood Cliffs,NJ, rec. 6.10.1964
Getz,Stan (ts) | Burton,Gary (vib) | Burrell,Kenny (g) | Cherico,Gene (b) | Milito,Helcio (dr) | Gilberto,Astrud (voc)

Only Trust Your Heart
Getz,Stan (ts) | Burton,Gary (vib) | Cherico,Gene (b) | Hunt,Joe (dr) | Gilberto,Astrud (voc)

Stan Getz-Laurindo Almeida Orchestra
Menina Moca(Young Lady) | Winter Moon
NYC, rec. 22.3.1963
Getz,Stan (ts) | Almeida,Laurindo (g) | Kuhn,Steve (p) | Duvivier,George (b) | Bailey,Dave (dr) | Machado,Edison (perc) | Parga,Luiz (perc) | Paulo,Jose (perc) | Soorez,Jose (perc)

Stan Getz Quintet
So Danco Samba(I Only Dance The Samba) | Doralice | Desafinado
NYC, rec. 18./19.3.1963
Getz,Stan (ts) | Gilberto,Joao (g,voc) | Jobim,Antonio Carlos (p) | Williams,Tommy (b) | Banana,Milton (dr)

Stan Getz With The Gary McFarland Orchestra
Manha De Carnaval(Morning Of The Carnival)
NYC, rec. 28.8.1962
Getz,Stan (ts) | Severinsen,Doc (tp) | Ferrante,Joe (tp) | Travis,Nick (tp) | Dennis,Willie (tb) | Studd,Tony (tb) | Alonge,Ray (fr-h) | Beckenstein,Ray (cl) | Clark,Babe (cl) | Levinsky,Walt (cl) | Caine,Eddie (fl) | Penque,Romeo (fl) | Jones,Hank (p) | Hall,Jim (g) | Williams,Tommy (b) | Rae,Johnny (dr) | Costa,Carmen (perc) | Paulo,Jose (perc)

Stan Getz-Charlie Byrd Sextet
Samba Da Una Nota So(One Note Samba) | Samba Triste
All Souls Unitarian Church,Washington,DC, rec. 13.2.1962
Getz,Stan (ts) | Byrd,Charlie (g) | Byrd,Gene (g) | Betts,Keter (b) | Reichenbach,Bill (perc) | Deppenschmidt,Buddy (perc)

Stan Getz Quintet Feat. Astrud Gilberto
Voce E Eu(You And I) | Girl From Ipanema(Garota De Ipanema)
Live at Carnegie Hall,NYC, rec. 9.10.1964
Getz,Stan (ts) | Burton,Gary (vib) | Gilberto,Joao (g) | Cherico,Gene (b) | Hunt,Joe (dr) | Gilberto,Astrud (voc)

Stan Getz Group
Insensatez(How Insensitive)
NYC, rec. 5.2.1963
Getz,Stan (ts) | Bonfa,Luiz (g) | Jobim,Antonio Carlos (p) | Duvivier,George (b) | Williams,Tommy (b) | Ferreira,Paulo (dr) | Carlos,Jose (perc) | Toledo,Maria (voc)

Stan Getz With The Gary McFarland Orchestra
Chega De Saudade(No More Blues)
NYC, rec. 27.8.1962
Getz,Stan (ts) | Severinsen,Doc (tp) | Glow,Bernie (tp) | Terry,Clark (tp) | Brookmeyer,Bob (tb) | Studd,Tony (tb) | Alonge,Ray (fr-h) | Beckenstein,Ray (cl) | Clark,Babe (cl) | Sanfino,Jerry (fl) | Caine,Eddie (fl) | Penque,Romeo (fl) | Jones,Hank (p) | Hall,Jim (g) | William,Tommy (sb) | Rae,Johnny (dr) | Costa,Carmen (perc) | Paulo,Jose (perc)

Stan Getz Quartet
O Grande Amor
Englewood Cliffs,NJ, rec. 21.3.1967
Getz,Stan (ts) | Corea,Chick (p) | Carter,Ron (b) | Tate,Grady (dr)

Menina Flor
NYC, rec. 9.2.1963
Getz,Stan (ts) | Bonfa,Luiz (g) | Payne,Don (b) | Ferreira,Paulo (dr) | Toledo,Maria (voc)

529905-2 | CD | Verve Jazz Masters 52:Maynard Ferguson

Ben Webster Sextet
King's Riff
Hollywood,CA, rec. 21.12.1951
Ferguson,Maynard (tp) | Webster,Ben (ts) | Carter,Benny (as,arr) | Wiggins,Gerald 'Gerry' (p) | Kirby,John (b) | Jenkins,George (dr)

Maynard Ferguson Band
Maiden Voyage | Hymn To Her | The Way You Look Tonight
Los Angeles,CA, rec. 19.2.1954
Ferguson,Maynard (tp) | Harper,Herbie (tb) | Shank,Bud (fl,as) | Cooper,Bob (ts,oboe) | Gordon,Bob (b-cl,bs) | Freeman,Russ (p) | Counce,Curtis (b) | Manne,Shelly (dr)

Willie Nillie
Ferguson,Maynard (tp) | Maiden,Willie (cl,arr) | Shank,Bud (fl,as) | Cooper,Bob (ts,oboe) | Gordon,Bob (b-cl,bs) | Freeman,Russ (p) | Counce,Curtis (b) | Manne,Shelly (dr)

Pete Rugolo And His Orchestra
Can't We Talk It Over
Los Angeles,CA, rec. 10.7.1956
Ferguson,Maynard (tp) | Palladino,Don (tp) | Linn,Ray (tp) | Candoli,Pete (tp) | Roberts,Howard (g) | Mondragon,Joe (b) | Manne,Shelly (dr) | Rugolo,Pete (cond,arr)

Maynard Ferguson Band
Egad,Martha
Los Angeles,CA, rec. 26.8.1955
Ferguson,Maynard (tp) | Candoli,Conte (tp) | Bernhart,Milton 'Milt' (tb) | Geller,Herb (as) | Tempo,Nino (ts) | Gordon,Bob (bs) | Geller,Lorraine (p) | Mitchell,Red (b) | Frommer,Gary (dr) | Holman,Bill (arr)

Maynard Ferguson And His Orchestra
Wildman
Los Angeles,CA, rec. 7.11.1955
Ferguson,Maynard (tp) | Childers,Buddy (tp) | Linn,Ray (tp) | Burgess,Bob 'Bobby' (tb) | Bernhart,Milton 'Milt' (tb) | Geller,Herb (as) | Holman,Bill (ts,arr) | Auld,Georgie (ts) | Shank,Bud (bs) | Geller,Lorraine (p) | Brown,Ray (b) | Stoller,Alvin (dr)

Dancing Nitely
Los Angeles,CA, rec. 10.11.1955
Ferguson,Maynard (tp) | Childers,Buddy (tp) | Linn,Ray (tp) | Burgess,Bob 'Bobby' (tb) | Bernhart,Milton 'Milt' (tb) | Geller,Herb (as) | Holman,Bill (ts,arr) | Auld,Georgie (ts) | Shank,Bud (bs) | Geller,Lorraine (p) | Brown,Ray (b) | Stoller,Alvin (dr)

Dream Boat | Never You Mind
Los Angeles,CA, rec. 7.5.1956
Ferguson,Maynard (tp) | Childers,Buddy (tp) | Linn,Ray (tp) | Burgess,Bob 'Bobby' (tb) | Bernhart,Milton 'Milt' (tb) | Geller,Herb (as) | Holman,Bill (ts,arr) | Auld,Georgie (ts) | Shank,Bud (bs) | Geller,Lorraine (p) | Clark,Buddy (b) | Stoller,Alvin (dr)

Pork Pie
Los Angeles,CA, rec. 12.5.1956
Ferguson,Maynard (tp) | Childers,Buddy (tp) | Linn,Ray (tp) | Burgess,Bob 'Bobby' (tb) | Bernhart,Milton 'Milt' (tb) | Geller,Herb (as) | Holman,Bill (ts,arr) | Auld,Georgie (ts) | Shank,Bud (bs) | Geller,Lorraine (p) | Clark,Buddy (b) | Stoller,Alvin (dr)

The Lamp Is Low | Easy To Love
NYC, rec. 2.8.1957
Ferguson,Maynard (tp) | Slaney,Tom (tp) | Bello,John (tp) | Burnett,Joe (tp) | Burgess,Bob 'Bobby' (tb) | Cleveland,Jimmy (tb) | Ford,Jimmy (as) | Ortega,Anthony (as) | Maiden,Willie (ts) | Houston,Tate (bs) | Timmons,Bobby (p) | Evans,Richard (b) | Bunker,Larry (vib,dr) | Holman,Bill (arr) | Wilkins,Ernie (arr)

Love Me Or Leave Me
Ferguson,Maynard (tp) | Slaney,Tom (tp) | Bello,John (tp) | Burnett,Joe (tp) | Burgess,Bob 'Bobby' (tb) | Cleveland,Jimmy (tb) | Ford,Jimmy (as) | Ortega,Anthony (as) | Maiden,Willie (ts) | Houston,Tate (bs) | Timmons,Bobby (p) | Evans,Richard (b) | Bunker,Larry (vib,dr) | Cohn,Al (arr)

Moonlight In Vermont
Ferguson,Maynard (tp) | Slaney,Tom (tp) | Bello,John (tp) | Burnett,Joe (tp) | Burgess,Bob 'Bobby' (tb) | Cleveland,Jimmy (tb) | Ford,Jimmy (as) | Ortega,Anthony (as) | Maiden,Willie (ts,arr) | Houston,Tate (bs) | Timmons,Bobby (p) | Evans,Richard (b) | Bunker,Larry (vib,dr) | Kral,Irene (voc)

529906-2 | CD | Verve Jazz Masters 51:Blossom Dearie

Blossom Dearie Quartet
I Want Dance
NYC, rec. 14.9.1956
Dearie,Blossom (p,voc) | Ellis,Herb (g) | Brown,Ray (b) | Jones,Jo (dr)

They Say It's Spring | Let Me Love You | Bang Goes The Drum | Give Him The Ooh-La-La
NYC, rec. 12./13.9.1957
Dearie,Blossom (p,voc) | Ellis,Herb (g) | Brown,Ray (b) | Jones,Jo (dr)

Once Upon A Summertime | The Surrey With The Fringe On Top | Down With Love
NYC, rec. 12./13.9.1958
Dearie,Blossom (p,voc) | Lowe,Mundell (g) | Brown,Ray (b) | Thigpen,Ed (dr)

Blossom Dearie Trio
Tea For Two | Manhattan
Dearie,Blossom (p,voc) | Brown,Ray (b) | Thigpen,Ed (dr)

Blossom Dearie Quartet
Dearie's Blues | The Party's Over
NYC, rec. 8./9.4.1959
Dearie,Blossom (p,voc) | Burrell,Kenny (g) | Brown,Ray (b) | Thigpen,Ed (dr)

Little Jazz Bird | Someone To Watch Over Me
NYC, rec. 21./22.4.1959
Dearie,Blossom (p,voc) | Burrell,Kenny (g) | Brown,Ray (b) | Thigpen,Ed (dr)

Blossom Dearie Quintet
L'Etang
NYC, rec. 21./22.5.1959
Dearie,Blossom (p,voc) | Jaspar,Bobby (fl) | Burrell,Kenny (g) | Brown,Ray (b) | Thigpen,Ed (dr)

Blossom Dearie With The Russ Garcia Orchestra
Rhode Island Is Famous For You
Hollywood,CA, rec. 19.2.1960
Dearie,Blossom (p,voc) | Orchestra | Garcia,Russell (cond,arr) | details unknown

531199-2 | CD | Gumbo Nouveau

Nicholas Payton Sextet
Whoopin' Blues | When The Saints Go Marching In | After You've Gone | Down In Honky Tonk Town | Lil' Liza Jane | St.James Infirmary
NYC, rec. 28.-30.11.1995
Payton,Nicholas (tp) | Davis,Jesse (as) | Warfield Jr.,Tim (ts) | Wonsey,Athony (p) | Rogers,Reuben (b) | Rose,Adonis (dr)

Nicholas Payton Quartet
Wild Man Blues | Way Down Yonder In New Orleans | I Gotta Right To Sing The Blues
Payton,Nicholas (tp) | Wonsey,Athony (p) | Rogers,Reuben (b) | Rose,Adonis (dr)

531232-2 | CD | Stan Getz Plays The Music Of Mickey One

Stan Getz With The Eddie Sauter Orchestra
Once Upon A Time | Mickey's Theme | On Stage(I'm A Polack Noel Coeard)- | Mickey's Flight- | The Crushout(Total Death)- | Is There Any Word From The Lord?- | Up From Limbo- | If You Ever Need Me- | A Taste Of Living- | Shaley's Neighborhood Sewer & The Pickle Club Rock- | The Agent- | The Stripper- | The Succuba | Mickey Polka | Where I Live- | The Apartment- | Cleaning Up For Jenny- | The Polish Landlady- | I Put My Live In Your Hands- | A Girl Named Jenny- | Yes-The Creature Machine- | Guilty Of Not Beeing Innocent- | Touching In Love- | A Five Day Live- | The Syndicate- | Ruby Lapp Is Dead- | Going To Who Owns Me- - (Going To) Who Owns Me- | The Big Fight- | Darkness Before The Day- | Morning Ecstasy(Under The Scaffold) | As Long As I Live | Is There Any Word? So This Is The Word | Mickey's Flight | Once Upon A Time | Mickey's Flight- | The Crushout- | Is There Any Word From The Lord?- | Up From Limbo- | If You Ever Need Me- | Shaley's Neighborhood Sewer & The Pickle Club Rock- | The Agent- | A Girl Named Jenny | Touching In Love | Going To Who Owns Me- - (Going To) Who Owns Me- | The Big Fight- | Morning Ecstasy(Under The Scaffold) | Is There Any Word? So This Is The Word
NYC, rec. 16./17.& 20.8.1965
Getz,Stan (ts) | DeRisi,Al (tp) | DiFalco,Ernie (tp) | Ferrante,Joe (tp) | Nichols,Bobby (tp) | Terry,Clark (tp,fl-h) | Bert,Eddie (tb) | Messner,John (tb) | Resnick,Eph (tb) | Russo,Sonny (tb) | Mitchell,Tom (b-tb) | Abernathy,Bob (fr-h) | Alonge,Ray (fr-h) | Berg,Richard (fr-h) | Buffington,Jimmy (fr-h) | Chapin,Earl (fr-h) | Phillips,Harvey (tuba) | Estrin,Harvey (fl,alto-fl,cl,piccolo) | Block,Al (fl,cl,ts,piccolo) | Shiner,Ray (engl-h,cl,ts,oboe) | Kane,Walter (cl,bs,bassoon) | Carmen,Eli (bassoon) | Ashworth,Don (woodwinds) | Russo,Charles (woodwinds) | Baumel,Herbert (v) | Carr,Norman (v) | Eichen,Bernard (v) | Finkelstein,Seymor (v) | Gabowitz,Louis (v) | Kruczek,Leo (v) | Libove,Charles (v) | Martin,Alan (v) | Nadien,David (v) | Ockner,George (v) | Pintavalle,John (v) | Raimondi,Matthew (v) | Simons,Ed (v) | Steinberg,Ben (v) | Barber,Julian (viola) | Brown,Alfred (viola) | Ferngut,Leon (viola) | Mankowitz,David (viola) | Shaier,Julius (viola) | Simons,Janet (viola) | McCracken,Charles (cello) | Ricci,George (cello) | Rogers,Bruce (cello) | Shapiro,Harvey (cello) | Agostini,Gloria (harp) | Newell,Laura (harp) | Kellaway,Roger (p) | Galbraith,Barry (g) | Davis,Richard (b) | Lewis,Mel (dr) | Bailey,Elden (perc) | Kraus,Phil (perc) | Rosenberger,Walter (perc) | Venuto,Joe (perc) | Sauter,Eddie (arr,ld)

531556-2 | CD | Antonio Carlos Jobim And Friends

Herbie Hancock
Prelude Medley: | Inutil Paisagem(Useless Landscape)- | Triste- | Esperanca Perdida-
Live at The Free Jazz Festival,Sao Paulo,Brazil, rec. 27.9.1993
Hancock,Herbie (p-solo)

Herbie Hancock Quartet
Ela E Carioca
Hancock,Herbie (p) | Carter,Ron (b) | Mason,Harvey (dr) | Acuna,Alejandro Neciosup (perc)

Shirley Horn Quintet
The Boy From Ipanema
Horn,Shirley (p,voc) | Castro-Neves,Oscar (g) | Carter,Ron (b) | Mason,Harvey (dr) | Acuna,Alejandro Neciosup (perc)

Shirley Horn Sextet
Once I Loved
Horn,Shirley (p,voc) | Castro-Neves,Oscar (g) | Hancock,Herbie (keyboards) | Carter,Ron (b) | Mason,Harvey (dr) | Acuna,Alejandro Neciosup (perc)

Joe Henderson Septet
O Grande Amor
Henderson,Joe (ts) | Rubalcaba,Gonzalo (p) | Castro-Neves,Oscar (g) | Jobim,Paulo (g) | Carter,Ron (b) | Mason,Harvey (dr) | Acuna,Alejandro Neciosup (perc)

Jon Hendricks With The Herbie Hancock Quintet
No More Blues
Hendricks,Jon (voc) | Hancock,Herbie (p) | Castro-Neves,Oscar (g) | Carter,Ron (b) | Mason,Harvey (dr) | Acuna,Alejandro Neciosup (perc)

Gonzalo Rubalcaba-Herbie Hancock Quintet
Agua De Beber(Water To Drink)
Rubalcaba,Gonzalo (p) | Hancock,Herbie (keyboards) | Carter,Ron (b) | Mason,Harvey (dr) | Acuna,Alejandro Neciosup (perc)

Gal Costa-Herbie Hancock
A Felicidade(Happiness)
Costa,Gal (voc) | Hancock,Herbie (p)

Gal Costa With The Herbie Hancock Sextet
Se Todos Fossem Iquais A Voce
Costa,Gal (voc) | Hancock,Herbie (p) | Castro-Neves,Oscar (g) | Jobim,Paulo (g) | Carter,Ron (b) | Mason,Harvey (dr) | Acuna,Alejandro Neciosup (perc)

Antonio Carlos Jobim
Luiza
Jobim,Antonio Carlos (p,voc)

Antonio Carlos Jobim With The Herbie Hancock Sextet
Wave
Jobim,Antonio Carlos (p) | Hancock,Herbie (p,keyboards) | Castro-Neves,Oscar (g) | Jobim,Paulo (g) | Carter,Ron (b) | Mason,Harvey (dr) | Acuna,Alejandro Neciosup (perc)

Antonio Carlos Jobim-Gal Costa Septet
Caminhos Cruzados
Jobim,Antonio Carlos (p) | Costa,Gal (voc) | Castro-Neves,Oscar (g) | Jobim,Paulo (g) | Carter,Ron (b) | Mason,Harvey (dr) | Acuna,Alejandro Neciosup (perc)
Antonio Carlos Jobim Group
Girl From Ipanema(Garota De Ipanema)
Jobim,Antonio Carlos (p,voc) | Costa,Gal (voc) | Hendricks,Jon (voc) | Henderson,Joe (ts) | Rubalcaba,Gonzalo (p) | Hancock,Herbie (keyboards) | Castro-Neves,Oscar (g) | Jobim,Paulo (g) | Carter,Ron (b) | Mason,Harvey (dr) | Acuna,Alejandro Neciosup (perc)

531558-2 | CD | The Song Is You-The Best Of The Verve Songbooks
Oscar Peterson Trio
Cheek To Cheek | It Ain't Necessarily So | Just A-Sittin' And A-Rockin' | What Is This Thing Called Love | Prelude To A Kiss | Fascinating Rhythm | Easter Parade | Night And Day
Los Angeles,CA, rec. December 1952
Peterson,Oscar (p) | Kessel,Barney (g) | Brown,Ray (b)
Tea For Two
Hollywood,CA, rec. December 1953
Peterson,Oscar (p) | Ellis,Herb (g) | Brown,Ray (b)
The Song Is You | Without A Song | The Lady Is A Tramp | Blue Moon | Lover
Hollywood,CA, rec. 7..12.1953
Peterson,Oscar (p) | Ellis,Herb (g) | Brown,Ray (b)
I Want To Be Happy
Hollywood,CA, rec. 10.12.1953
Peterson,Oscar (p) | Ellis,Herb (g) | Brown,Ray (b)
I Only Have Eyes For You | I Gotta Right To Sing The Blues | You Must Have Been A Beautiful Baby | Come Rain Or Come Shine | I Can't Give You Anything But Love | I'm In The Mood For Love
Hollywood,CA, rec. 15.11.1954
Peterson,Oscar (p) | Ellis,Herb (g) | Brown,Ray (b)
John Hardy's Wife | I Got It Bad And That Ain't Good | That Old Black Magic | A Foggy Day(In London Town) | I Couldn't Sleep A Wink Last Night | Blue Moon | Serenade In Blue | Love For Sale | The Song Is Ended | Yesterdays
Chicago,Ill, rec. 21.7.-1.8.1959
Peterson,Oscar (p) | Brown,Ray (b) | Thigpen,Ed (dr)

531562-2 | CD | Talkin Verve/Roots Of Acid Jazz:Cal Tjader
Cal Tjader's Orchestra
Los Jibaros | Picadillo
Englewood Cliffs,NJ, rec. 26.5.1966
Tjader,Cal (vib) | Priester,Julian (tb) | Rodriguez,Jose (tb) | Weinstein,Mark (tb) | Castro,George (fl,perc) | Palmieri,Eddie (p) | Rodriguez,Bobby (b) | Lopez,Tommy (dr) | Oquendo,Manny (dr) | Rogers,Barry (congas) | Quintana,Ismael (perc) | Ogerman,Claus (arr)
Manteca
Englewood Cliffs,NJ, rec. 11.2.1966
Tjader,Cal (vib) | Powell,Seldon (fl) | Dodgion,Jerry (fl) | Richardson,Jerome (fl) | Corea,Chick (p) | Zoller,Attila (g) | Davis,Richard (b) | Tate,Grady (dr) | Valdez,Carlos 'Patato' (congas) | Mangual,Jose (timbales) | Pantoja,Antonio (perc) | Nelson,Oliver (arr,ld)
Soul Burst
Tjader,Cal (vib) | Powell,Seldon (fl) | Dodgion,Jerry (fl) | Richardson,Jerome (fl) | Corea,Chick (p) | Davis,Richard (b) | Tate,Grady (dr) | Valdez,Carlos 'Patato' (congas) | Mangual,Jose (timbales) | Pantoja,Antonio (perc) | Nelson,Oliver (arr,ld)
Cal Tjader Quintet
Samba Do Suenho | Cuando,Cuando,Que Sera?
Englewood Cliffs,NJ, rec. 29.3.1967
Tjader,Cal (vib) | Corea,Chick (p) | Tate,Grady (dr) | Barretto,Ray (perc) | Peraza,Armando (perc) | O'Farrill,Chico (cond,arr)
Cal Tjader Sextet
Mambo In Miami | Triste
Hollywood,CA, rec. 28./29.8.1961
Tjader,Cal (vib) | Horn,Paul (fl) | Hewitt,Lonnie (p) | McKibbon,Al (b) | Rae,Johnny (dr) | Peraza,Armando (perc) | Vincente,Wilfredo (congas)
Cal Tjader Septet
Soul Sauce | Maramoor Mambo
NYC, rec. 20.11.1964
Tjader,Cal (vib) | Hewitt,Lonnie (p) | Hilliard,John (b) | Rae,Johnny (dr) | Bobo,Willie (perc,voc) | Peraza,Armando (perc) | Valdez,Alberto (perc)
Cal Tjader Quintet
Los Bandidos
Live at The El Matador Club,San Francisco,CA, rec. January 1967
Tjader,Cal (vib) | Zulaica,Al (p) | Gilbert,Stanley (b) | Burnett,Carl (dr) | Barretto,Ray (congas)
Insight
Hollywood,CA, rec. 29.1.1963
Tjader,Cal (vib) | Fischer,Clare (p) | Schreiber,Freddy (b) | Rae,Johnny (dr) | Fitch,Bill (congas)
Cal Tjader With The Lalo Schifrin Orchestra
Tokyo Blues
NYC, rec. 23.4.1963
Tjader,Cal (vib) | Schifrin,Lalo (cond,arr) | Royal,Ernie (tp) | Terry,Clark (tp) | Green,Urbie (tb) | Northern,Bob (fr-h) | Butterfield,Don (tuba) | Levinsky,Walt (fl,woodwinds) | Berg,George (b-cl,bassoon) | Cohen,Leon (oboe) | Horowitz,Irving (oboe) | Webb,Stanley (woodwinds) | Bodner,Phil (woodwinds) | Kraus,Phil (woodwinds) | Raney,Jimmy (g) | Duvivier,George (b) | Shaughnessy,Ed (dr) | Del Rio,Jack (congas,tambourine) | Rae,Johnny (perc,timbales)
Cal Tjader's Orchestra
Afro Blue
Englewood Cliffs,NJ, rec. 19.11.1964
Tjader,Cal (vib) | Byrd,Donald (tp) | Heath,Jimmy (ts) | Burrell,Kenny (g) | Bushnell,Bob (b) | Davis,Richard (b) | Tate,Grady (dr) | Peraza,Armando (perc) | Valdes,Alberto (perc)
Cal's Bluedo
Hollywood,CA, rec. 19.9.1967
Tjader,Cal (vib) | Donato,Joao (p) | Mitchell,Red (b) | Thigpen,Ed (dr) | Orchestra | details unknown
Fuji
NYC, rec. 25.11.1963
Tjader,Cal (vib) | Dodgion,Jerry (fl) | Hewitt,Lonnie (p) | Hyman,Dick (org) | Duvivier,George (b) | Strings | unkn. (g,dr,perc) | Applebaum,Stan (cond,arr,celeste)

531563-2 | CD | Jimmy Smith-Talkin' Verve
Jimmy Smith With The Oliver Nelson Orchestra
Hobo Flats
NYC, rec. 20.3.1963
Smith,Jimmy (org) | Terry,Clark (tp) | Newman,Joe (tp) | Royal,Ernie (tp) | Jackson,Quentin (tb) | Green,Urbie (tb) | Cleveland,Jimmy (tb) | Woods,Phil (as) | Dorsey,George (as) | Sims,Zoot (ts) | Cohn,Al (ts) | Duvivier,George (b) | Rodriguez,Bill (dr) | Nelson,Oliver (arr,ld)
Jimmy Smith With Orchestra
Ape Woman
Englewood Cliffs,NJ, rec. 17.7.1963
Smith,Jimmy (org) | Maxwell,Jimmy (tp) | Newman,Joe (tp) | Young,Eugene 'Snooky' (tp) | Cleveland,Jimmy (tb) | Liston,Melba (tb) | Winding,Kai (tb) | Faulise,Paul (b-tb) | Dodgion,Jerry (as) | Woods,Phil (as) | Johnson,Budd (ts) | Powell,Seldon (ts) | Halladay,Marvin (bs) | Burrell,Kenny (g) | Bushnell,Bob (b) | Lovelle,Herbie (dr) | Devens,George (perc)
Jimmy Smith Quartet
The Sermon
Englewood Cliffs,NJ, rec. 29.7.1963
Smith,Jimmy (org) | Burrell,Kenny (g) | Duvivier,George (b) | Lewis,Mel (dr)
Jimmy Smith With The Lalo Schifrin Orchestra
Blues In The Night
NYC, rec. 29.4.1964
Smith,Jimmy (org) | Schifrin,Lalo (cond,arr) | Royal,Ernie (tp) | Glow,Bernie (tp) | Maxwell,Jimmy (tp) | Jones,Thad (tp) | Markowitz,Irving 'Marky' (tp) | Young,Eugene 'Snooky' (tp) | Byers,Billy (tb) | Cleveland,Jimmy (tb) | Green,Urbie (tb) | Butterfield,Don (tuba) | Buffington,Jimmy (fr-h) | Chapin,Earl (fr-h) | Alonge,Ray (fr-h) | Correa,Bill (fr-h) | Burrell,Kenny (g) | Duvivier,George (b) | Tate,Grady (dr) | Kraus,Phil (perc)
Jimmy Smith Trio
Organ Grinder's Swing
Englewood Cliffs,NJ, rec. 14./15.6.1965
Smith,Jimmy (org,voc) | Burrell,Kenny (g) | Tate,Grady (dr)
Jimmy Smith Quartet
I Can't Get No Satisfaction
Englewood Cliffs,NJ, rec. 16.12.1965
Smith,Jimmy (org,voc) | Burrell,Kenny (g) | Tucker,Ben (b) | Tate,Grady (dr)
Jimmy Smith With The Oliver Nelson Orchestra
One Mint Julep | TNT
Englewood Cliffs,NJ, rec. 14.6.1966
Smith,Jimmy (org) | Newman,Joe (tp) | Royal,Ernie (tp) | Williams,Richard (tp) | Young,Eugene 'Snooky' (tp) | Jackson,Quentin (tb) | Liston,Melba (tb) | McIntosh,Tom (tb) | Woodman,Britt (tb) | Corrado,Donald (fr-h) | Ruff,Willie (fr-h) | Butterfield,Don (tuba) | Agee,Jack (reeds) | Ashton,Bob (reeds) | Dodgion,Jerry (reeds) | Richardson,Jerome (reeds) | Woods,Phil (reeds) | Burrell,Kenny (g) | Butler,Billy (g) | Galbraith,Barry (g) | Suyker,Willard 'Bill' (g) | Cranshaw,Bob (b) | Tate,Grady (dr) | Rosengarden,Bobby (perc) | Nelson,Oliver (arr,ld)
Jimmy Smith-Wes Montgomery Quartet
Mellow Mood
NYC, rec. 28.9.1966
Smith,Jimmy (org) | Montgomery,Wes (g) | Tate,Grady (dr) | Barretto,Ray (congas)
Jimmy Smith Quartet
Funky Broadway
NYC, rec. June 1967
Smith,Jimmy (org) | Schwartz,Thornel (g) | Bushnell,Bob (b) | Purdie,Bernard 'Pretty' (dr)
Jimmy Smith With The Oliver Nelson Orchestra
Burning Spear
Los Angeles,CA, rec. 13.5.1968
Smith,Jimmy (org) | Candoli,Conte (tp) | Childers,Buddy (tp) | Byers,Billy (tb) | Tack,Ernie (tb) | Johnson,Plas (reeds) | Scott,Tom (reeds) | unkn. (14 strings) | Roberts,Howard (g) | Kaye,Carol (b) | Bunker,Larry (dr) | unkn. (perc) | details unknown | Nelson,Oliver (arr,ld)
Jimmy Smith With The Johnny Pate Orchestra
Ode To Billy Joe
NYC, rec. 22.12.1969
Smith,Jimmy (org) | Markowitz,Irving 'Marky' (tp) | Royal,Ernie (tp) | Young,Eugene 'Snooky' (tp) | Andre,Wayne (tb) | Powell,Benny (tb) | Richardson,Jerome (reeds) | Bauer,Billy (g) | Carter,Ron (b) | unkn. (dr) | Pate,Johnny (arr,ld)
Jimmy Smith With Orchestra
Groove Drops
NYC, rec. 29.12.1969
Smith,Jimmy (org) | Berry,Bill (tp) | Royal,Ernie (tp) | Young,Eugene 'Snooky' (tp) | Andre,Wayne (tb) | Cleveland,Jimmy (tb) | Richardson,Jerome (reeds) | Carter,Ron (b) | Tate,Grady (dr)
Jimmy Smith Quartet
Blues For 3+1
Los Angeles,CA, rec. 11.9.1972
Smith,Jimmy (org) | Vinnegar,Leroy (b) | Dean,Donald (dr) | Pantoja,Victor (congas)

531762-2 | CD | Love Songs:The Best Of The Song Books
Ella Fitzgerald With The Buddy Bregman Orchestra
From This Moment On | Just One Of Those Things
Hollywood,CA, rec. 7.2.1956
Fitzgerald,Ella (voc) | Candoli,Pete (tp) | Edison,Harry 'Sweets' (tp) | Ferguson,Maynard (tp) | Gozzo,Conrad (tp) | Bernhart,Milton 'Milt' (tb) | Howard,Joe (tb) | Ulyate,Lloyd (tb) | Roberts,George (b-tb) | Geller,Herb (as) | Shank,Bud (as) | Cooper,Bob (ts) | Nash,Ted (ts) | Gentry,Chuck (bs) | Smith,Paul (p) | Kessel,Barney (g) | Mondragon,Joe (b) | Stoller,Alvin (dr) | Bregman,Buddy (cond,arr)
Lover
Hollywood,CA, rec. 21.8.1956
Fitzgerald,Ella (voc) | Candoli,Pete (tp) | Edison,Harry 'Sweets' (tp) | Lynn,Ray (tp) | Gozzo,Conrad (tp) | Bernhart,Milton 'Milt' (tb) | Howard,Joe (tb) | Ulyate,Lloyd (tb) | Roberts,George (b-tb) | Stein,Maurice (as) | Shank,Bud (as) | Cooper,Bob (ts) | Nash,Ted (ts) | Gentry,Chuck (bs) | Smith,Paul (p) | Kessel,Barney (g) | Mondragon,Joe (b) | Stoller,Alvin (dr) | Bregman,Buddy (cond,arr)
I Concentrate On You
Hollywood,CA, rec. 9.2.1956
Fitzgerald,Ella (voc) | Candoli,Pete (tp) | Edison,Harry 'Sweets' (tp) | Ferguson,Maynard (tp) | Gozzo,Conrad (tp) | Bernhart,Milton 'Milt' (tb) | Howard,Joe (tb) | Ulyate,Lloyd (tb) | Roberts,George (b-tb) | Geller,Herb (as) | Shank,Bud (as) | Cooper,Bob (ts) | Nash,Ted (ts) | Gentry,Chuck (bs) | Russell,Mischa (v) | unkn. (12 strings) | unkn. (4 cellos) | La Marchina,Robert 'Bob' (cello) | Lustgarten,Edgar 'Ed' (cello) | unkn. (2 cellos) | Hale,Corky (harp) | Smith,Paul (p) | Kessel,Barney (g) | Mondragon,Joe (b) | Stoller,Alvin (dr) | unkn. (perc) | Bregman,Buddy (cond,arr)
Ella Fitzgerald And Barney Kessel
Solitude
Hollywood,CA, rec. 4.9.1956
Fitzgerald,Ella (voc) | Kessel,Barney (g)
Ella Fitzgerald And Her All Stars
I Let A Song Go Out Of My Heart | Prelude To A Kiss
Fitzgerald,Ella (voc) | Webster,Ben (ts) | Smith,Stuff (v) | Smith,Paul (p) | Kessel,Barney (g) | Mondragon,Joe (b) | Stoller,Alvin (dr)
Love You Madly
NYC, rec. 17.10.1957
Fitzgerald,Ella (voc) | Webster,Ben (ts) | Peterson,Oscar (p) | Ellis,Herb (g) | Brown,Ray (b) | Stoller,Alvin (dr)
Ella Fitzgerald With The Nelson Riddle Orchestra
All The Things You Are
Fitzgerald,Ella (voc) | Fagerquist,Don (tp) | Lewis,Carroll (tp) | Seaberg,George (tp) | Sherock,Shorty (tp) | Nash,Dick (tb) | Pederson,Pullman 'Tommy' (tb) | Shepard,Tom (tb) | Roberts,George (b-tb) | Johnson,Plas (ts) | Klee,Harry (reeds) | Koch,Joe (reeds) | Schwartz,Wilbur (reeds) | Webb,Champ (reeds) | Arno,Victor (v) | Baker,Israel (v) | Bay,Victor (v) | Raderman,Lou (v) | Ross,Nathan 'Nat' (v) | Slatkin,Felix (v) | Sosson,Marshall (v) | Vinci,Gerry (v) | Neiman,Alex (viola) | Robyn,Paul (viola) | Simons,Barbara (viola) | Kaproff,Armand (cello) | Kramer,Ray (cello) | Lube,Dan (cello) | Smith,Paul (p) | Bain,Robert 'Bob' (g) | Comfort,Joe (b) | Flynn,Fred (dr) | Stoller,Alvin (dr) | Riddle,Nelson (cond,arr)
Ella Fitzgerald With The Billy May Orchestra
Out Of This World
Hollywood,CA, rec. 16.1.1961
Fitzgerald,Ella (voc) | Fagerquist,Don (tp) | Bernhart,Milton 'Milt' (tb) | Carter,Benny (as) | Gentry,Charles (bs) | Beau,Heinie (reeds) | Gordon,Justin (reeds) | Jacob,Julie (reeds) | Richards,Emil (marimba) | Levy,Lou (p) | Ellis,Herb (g) | Mondragon,Joe,(b) | Stoller,Alvin (dr) | May,Billy (cond,arr)
Ella Fitzgerald With Paul Weston And His Orchestra
Always
Hollywood,CA, rec. 13.3.1958
Fitzgerald,Ella (voc) | Fagerquist,Don (tp) | Stulce,Fred (cl) | Nash,Ted (ts) | Russin,Irving 'Babe' (ts) | Gentry,Chuck (bs) | Cipriano,Gene (reeds) | Smith,Paul (p) | Kessel,Barney (g) | Ryan,Jack (b) | Stoller,Alvin (dr) | Weston,Paul (cond,arr)
How About You
Hollywood,CA, rec. 17.3.1958
Fitzgerald,Ella (voc) | Levy,Lou (p) | Strings | Weston,Paul (cond,arr) | details unknown
Ella Fitzgerald With The Duke Ellington Orchestra
All Too Soon
NYC, rec. 26.6.1957
Fitzgerald,Ella (voc) | Ellington,Duke (p) | Anderson,Cat (tp) | Cook,Willie (tp) | Terry,Clark (tp) | Nance,Ray (tp) | Jackson,Quentin (tb) | Woodman,Britt (tb) | Sanders,John (tb) | Hamilton,Jimmy (cl,ts) | Procope,Russell (cl,as) | Hodges,Johnny (as) | Foster,Frank (ts) | Carney,Harry (cl,b-cl,bs) | Woode,Jimmy (b) | Woodyard,Sam (dr)
I'm Beginning To See The Light
NYC, rec. 27.6.1957
Fitzgerald,Ella (voc) | Ellington,Duke (p) | Anderson,Cat (tp) | Cook,Willie (tp) | Terry,Clark (tp) | Nance,Ray (tp) | Jackson,Quentin (tb) | Woodman,Britt (tb) | Sanders,John (tb) | Hamilton,Jimmy (cl,ts) | Procope,Russell (cl,as) | Hodges,Johnny (as) | Gonsalves,Paul (ts) | Carney,Harry (cl,b-cl,bs) | Woode,Jimmy (b) | Woodyard,Sam (dr)
Ella Fitzgerald With The Nelson Riddle Orchestra
The Man I Love
Hollywood,CA, rec. 5.1.1959
Fitzgerald,Ella (voc) | Lewis,Carroll (tp) | Mangano,Vito (tp) | McMickle,Dale (tp) | Sherock,Shorty (tp) | Bernhart,Milton 'Milt' (tb) | Noel,Richard (tb) | Pederson,Pullman 'Tommy' (tb) | Roberts,George (b-tb) | DeRosa,Vince (fr-h) | Nash,Ted (ts) | Collette,Buddy (reeds) | Klee,Harry (reeds) | Koch,Joe (reeds) | Webb,Champ (reeds) | Bay,Victor (v) | Beller,Alex 'Al' (v) | Gasselin,Jaques (v) | Getzoff,James (v) | Gill,Ben (v) | Kellner,Murray (v) | Ross,Nathan 'Nat' (v) | Shapiro,Eunice (v) | Slatkin,Felix (v) | Sosson,Marshall (v) | Dinkin,Alvin (viola) | Harris,Stan (viola) | Simons,Barbara (viola) | Kaproff,Armand (cello) | Reher,Kurt (cello) | Slatkin,Eleanor (cello) | Julyie,Katharine 'Kathryn' (harp) | Smith,Paul (p) | Bain,Robert 'Bob' (g) | Comfort,Joe (b) | Flynn,Fred (dr) | Stoller,Alvin (dr) | Riddle,Nelson (cond,arr)
I Remember You
Hollywood,CA, rec. 21.10.1964
Fitzgerald,Ella (voc) | Lewis,Carroll (tp) | Mangano,Vito (tp) | Seaberg,George (tp) | Sherock,Shorty (tp) | Bernhart,Milton 'Milt' (tb) | Pederson,Pullman 'Tommy' (tb) | Shepard,Tom (tb) | Roberts,George (b-tb) | Cave,John (fr-h) | Decker,James 'Jimmy' (fr-h) | Hinshaw,William 'Bill' (fr-h) | Collette,Buddy (fl) | Klee,Harry (fl) | DeFranco,Buddy (cl) | Smith,George (cl) | Johnson,Plas (ts) | Russin,Irving 'Babe' (ts) | Benno,Norman (oboe) | Schoneberg,Seymour (oboe) | Hildebrandt,Lloyd (bs) | Terry,Howard (bs) | Koch,Joe (reeds) | Schwartz,Wilbur (reeds) | Smith,Willie (as) | Julyie,Katharine 'Kathryn' (harp) | Smith,Paul (p) | Kessel,Barney (g) | Comfort,Joe (b) | Cottler,Irv (dr) | Richards,Emil (perc) | Riddle,Nelson (cond,arr) | details unknown

531763-2 | 2 CD | Art Tatum:20th Century Piano Genius
Art Tatum
Just Like A Butterfly | Tenderly | I Cover The Waterfront | Body And Soul | Someone To Watch Over Me | In A Sentimental Mood | Yesterdays | Willow Weep For Me | Wrap Your Troubles In Dreams | Makin' Whoopee | Memories Of You | September Song | Begin The Beguine | I'll Never Be The Same | Over The Rainbow | Love For Sale | My Heart Stood Still | Sweet Lorraine | Louise | Don't Blame Me | There'll Never Be Another You | Without A Song | Moon Song | You Took Advantage Of Me | Little Man You've Had A Busy Day | Danny Boy (Londonderry Air)
Ray Heindorf's Home,Beverly Hills, rec. 3.7.1955
Tatum,Art (p-solo)
Some Other Spring | Love For Sale | Mighty Like A Rose | Sweet Lorraine | Someone To Watch Over Me | Mine | Too Marvelous For Words | Jitterbug Waltz | Mr.Freddie Blues | Body And Soul | Yesterdays | Tea For Two- | Honeysuckle Rose- | Would You Like To Take A Walk- | After You've Gone-
Ray Heindorf's Home,Beverly Hills, rec. 16.4.1950(prob.)
Tatum,Art (p-solo)

533049-2 | 2 CD | Don Cherry-The Sonet Recordings:Eternal Now/Live Ankara
Don Cherry Group
Gamla Stan-The Old Town By Night
Stockholm,Sweden, rec. April/May 1973
Cherry,Don (dastar,gong,h'suan) | Berger,Bengt (african-finger-p,tibetan-bell)
Love Train
Cherry,Don (p,gong) | Bothen,Christer (p) | Rosengren,Bernt (taragot) | Ernström,Agneta (tibetan-bells)
Bass Figure For Ballatune(two pianos and three piano players)
Cherry,Don (p) | Bothen,Christer (p) | Berger,Bengt (p)
Moving Pictures For The Ear
Cherry,Don (harmonium,voice) | Bothen,Christer (dousso n'koni) | Berger,Bengt (mridangam) | Arnström,Agneta (dousso kynia)
Tibet
Cherry,Don (gamelan,gong,rkan-dung,voice) | Bothen,Christer (tibetan-bells) | Berger,Bengt (bells,tibetan-cymbals)
Gandalf's Travels | Omette's Concept | Omette's Tune | St.John And The Dragon | Efeler(turkish folk material) | Anadolu Havasi(turkish folk material) | The Discovery Of Bhupala | Water Boy | Yaz Geldi(turkish folk material) | Tamzara(turkish folk material) | Kara Deniz(turkish folk material) | Köcekce(turkish folk material) | Man On The Moon | The Creator Has A Master Plan | Two Flutes
US Ambassy,Ankara,Turkey, rec. 23.11.1969
Cherry,Don (tp,fl,p,trumpetzurna,voc) | Sümer,Irfan (ts,perc) | Sun,Selcuk (b) | Temiz,Okay (dr,perc)

533101-2 | CD | Talkin' Verve-Roots Of Acid Jazz:Roland Kirk
Roland Kirk Quartet
A Sack Full Of Soul
NYC, rec. 16.8.1961
Kirk,Rahsaan Roland (ts,manzello,stritch) | Wyands,Richard (p) | Davis,Art (b) | Persip,Charles (dr)
You Did It You Did It
NYC, rec. 17.8.1961
Kirk,Rahsaan Roland (fl) | Jones,Hank (p) | Marshall,Wendell (b) | Persip,Charles (dr)
Termini's Corner | When The Sun Comes Out
NYC, rec. 17./18.4.1962
Kirk,Rahsaan Roland (ts,manzello,strich) | Kelly,Wynton (p) | Martin,Vernon (b) | Haynes,Roy (dr)
Quincy Jones And His Orchestra
Dyna-Soar
NYC, rec. 15.6.1962
Kirk,Rahsaan Roland (fl,ts,strich) | Jones,Quincy (arr,ld) | Holley,Major (b) | details unknown
Roland Kirk Sextet
Limbo Boat
NYC, rec. 25.2.1963
Kirk,Rahsaan Roland (ts) | Jones,Virgil (tp) | Greenlee,Charles (tb) | Mabern,Harold (p) | Rafik,Abdullah (b) | Perkins,Walter (dr)
Roland Kirk Quartet
Get In The Basement
NYC, rec. 12.6.1963
Kirk,Rahsaan Roland (ts) | Mabern,Harold (p) | Rafik,Abdullah (b) | Brown,Sonny (dr)
Narrow Bolero
Live at The 'Jazzhus' Montmartre,Copenhagen, rec. October 1963
Kirk,Rahsaan Roland (fl,ts,manzello,stritch) | Montoliu,Tete (p) | Moore,Don prob. (b) | Moses,J.C. (dr)
Roland Kirk Quartet With Sonny Boy Williamson
Untitled Blues
Kirk,Rahsaan Roland (ts,strich) | Williamson,Sonny Boy [Rice Miller] (harm,voc) | Montoliu,Tete (p) | Orsted-Pedersen,Niels-Henning (b) | Moses,J.C. (dr)
Quincy Jones And His Orchestra
Theme From Peter Gunn
NYC, rec. 6.2.2964
Bello,John (tp) | Maxwell,Jimmy (tp) | Royal,Ernie (tp) | Young,Eugene 'Snooky' (tp) | Byers,Billy (tb) | Green,Urbie (tb) | Hixon,Richard 'Dick' (tb) | Jackson,Quentin (tb) | Studd,Tony (b-tb) | Kirk,Rahsaan Roland (fl,reeds) | Berg,George (reeds) | Penque,Romeo (reeds) | Powell,Seldon

LABELVERZEICHNIS

(reeds) | Richardson,Jerome (reeds) | Woods,Phil (reeds) | Burton,Gary (vib) | Scott,Bobby (p) | Bell,Vincent (g) | Hinton,Milt (b) | Holley,Major (b) | Johnson,Osie (dr) | Kraus,Phil (perc) | Jones,Quincy (arr,ld)

Roland Kirk And His Orchestra
Birkshire Blues
Los Angeles,CA, rec. 26.5.1964
Kirk,Rahsaan Roland (melodica,voc) | Bryant,Bobby (tp) | Callender,Red (tuba) | Fleming,Michael (b) | details unknown

Roland Kirk Quartet
Hip Chops | Jive Elephant
Los Angeles,CA, rec. 22.7.1964
Kirk,Rahsaan Roland (fl,ts,manzello,oboe,siren,stritch) | Parlan,Horace (p) | Fleming,Michael (b) | Ellington,Steve (dr)
Black Diamond
Englewood Cliffs,NJ, rec. 13.1.1965
Kirk,Rahsaan Roland (ts,manzello) | Byard,Jaki (p) | Davis,Richard (b) | Jones,Elvin (dr)
Blue Rol
Englewood Cliffs,NJ, rec. 2.5.1967
Kirk,Rahsaan Roland (cl,ts,manzello) | Smith,Lonnie Liston (p) | Boykins,Ronnie (b) | Tate,Grady (dr)

533108-2 | 2 CD | Return To The 7th Galaxy-Return To Forever:The Anthology

Return To Forever
500 Miles High | Captain Marvel | Light As A Feather
London,GB, rec. October 1972
Return To Forever | Farrell,Joe (fl,ts) | Corea,Chick (el-p) | Clarke,Stanley (el-b) | Moreira,Airto (dr,perc) | Purim,Flora (perc,voc)
Spain | After The Cosmic Rain | Bass Folk Song
Live at The Quiet Village,Long Island,NY, rec. 1973
Return To Forever | Connors,Bill (g) | Corea,Chick (el-p) | Clarke,Stanley (el-b) | Gadd,Steve (dr) | Lewis,Mingo (perc)
Hymn Of The Seventh Galaxy | Captain Senor Mouse | Theme To The Mothership
NYC, rec. August 1973
Return To Forever | Corea,Chick (p,el-p,org,gongs,harpsichord) | Connors,Bill (g,el-g) | Clarke,Stanley (bell-tree,el-b) | White,Lenny (dr,perc,congas,bongos)

533185-2 | CD | Quiet

John Scofield Groups
After The Fact | Tulle | Away With Words | Hold That Thought | Door | Beside Manner | Rolf And The Gang | But For Love | Away
NYC, rec. 3.-6.4.1996
Scofield,John (g) | Brecker,Randy (tp,fl-h) | Clark,John (fr-h) | Griffin,Fred (fr-h) | Pillow,Charles (engl-h,alto-fl,ts) | Feldman,Lawrence (fl,alto-fl,ts) | Rosenberg,Roger (b-cl) | Shorter,Wayne (ts) | Johnson,Howard (bs,tuba) | Swallow,Steve (b-g) | Stewart,Bill (dr) | Da Fonseca,Duduka (dr)

533215-2 | CD | Paco De Lucia-Al Di Meola-John McLaughlin

Paco De Lucia-Al Di Meola-John McLaughlin
La Estiba | Beyond The Mirage | Midsummer Night | Manha De Carnaval(Morning Of The Carnival) | Letter From India | Espiritu | Le Monastère Dans Les Montagnes | Azzura | Cardeosa
London,GB, rec. June/July 1996
De Lucia,Paco (g) | Di Meola,Al (g) | McLaughlin,John (g)

533232-2 | CD | Those Who Were

Niels-Henning Orsted-Pedersen Trio
With Respect | Friends Forever | Wishing And Hoping
Vanlose,Denmark, rec. May 1996
Orsted-Pedersen,Niels-Henning (b) | Wakenius,Ulf (g,el-g) | Lewis,Victor (dr)

Niels-Henning Orsted-Pedersen/Ulf Wakenius Duo
Our Love Is Here To Stay | Derfor Kan Vort Oje Glaedes
Orsted-Pedersen,Niels-Henning (b) | Wakenius,Ulf (g,el-g)

Niels-Henning Orsted-Pedersen Trio With Johnny Griffin
The Puzzle | You And The Night And The Music
Griffin,Johnny (ts) | Orsted-Pedersen,Niels-Henning (b) | Wakenius,Ulf (g,el-g) | Lewis,Victor (dr)

Niels-Henning Orsted-Pedersen Trio
Guilty,Your Honour
Orsted-Pedersen,Niels-Henning (b) | Wakenius,Ulf (g,el-g) | Riel,Alex (dr)

Niels-Henning Orsted-Pedersen/Ulf Wakenius Duo With Lisa Nilsson
Those Who Were
Orsted-Pedersen,Niels-Henning (b) | Wakenius,Ulf (g,el-g) | Nilsson,Lisa (voc)

533559-2 | CD | Who Used To Dance

Abbey Lincoln With Her Band
Who Used To Dance
NYC, rec. April/May 1996
Lincoln,Abbey (voc) | Cary,Marc Anthony (p) | Bowie,Michael (b) | Garnett,Alvester (dr) | Glover,Savion (tap-dance)
Love Has Gone Away | Street Of Dreams
Lincoln,Abbey (voc) | Coleman,Steve (as) | Cary,Marc Anthony (p) | Bowie,Michael (b) | Walker,Aaron (dr)
Mr.Tambourine Man
Lincoln,Abbey (voc) | Lourau,Julien (ts) | Cary,Marc Anthony (p) | Bowie,Michael (b) | Walker,Aaron (dr)
Love Lament | When Autumn Sings
Lincoln,Abbey (voc) | Morgan,Frank (as) | Cary,Marc Anthony (p) | Bowie,Michael (b) | Garnett,Alvester (dr)
Love What You Doin'
Lincoln,Abbey (voc) | Coleman,Steve (as) | Bandy,Riley T. (as) | Lake,Oliver (as) | Cary,Marc Anthony (p) | Bowie,Michael (b) | Garnett,Alvester (dr) | Noel,Randolph (horn-arr)
I Sing A Song
Lincoln,Abbey (voc) | Bandy,Riley T. (as) | Cary,Marc Anthony (p) | Bowie,Michael (b) | Walker,Aaron (dr)
The River
Lincoln,Abbey (voc) | Haynes,Graham (co) | Lake,Oliver (as) | Robinson,Justin (as) | Kendrick,Rodney (p) | Ormond,John (b) | Alexander,Taru (dr) | Gray,Bazzi Bartholomew (voc) | Green,Arthur (voc)

533825-2 | CD | The Best Of Bill Evans Live

Bill Evans Trio
Make Someone Happy | Spring Is Here | Walking Up
Live at Town Hall,NYC, rec. 21.2.1966
Evans,Bill (p) | Israels,Chuck (b) | Wise,Arnold (dr)
Wrap Your Troubles In Dreams | Polka Dots And Moonbeams | Turn Out The Stars
Live at The 'Village Vanguard',NYC, rec. 17.8.1967
Evans,Bill (p) | Gomez,Eddie (b) | Jones,Philly Joe (dr)
Emily
Live at The 'Village Vanguard',NYC, rec. 18.8.1967
Evans,Bill (p) | Gomez,Eddie (b) | Jones,Philly Joe (dr)
How Deep Is The Ocean | Nardis
Live at The Trident Club,Sausolito,CA, rec. 7.7.1964
Evans,Bill (p) | Israels,Chuck (b) | Bunker,Larry (dr)
The Touch Of Your Lips | Walkin' Up
Montreux,CH, rec. 15.6.1968
Evans,Bill (p) | Gomez,Eddie (b) | DeJohnette,Jack (dr)

Bill Evans
I Loves You Porgy
Evans,Bill (p-solo)

533846-2 | CD | Talking Verve:Dizzy Gillespie

Dizzy Gillespie And His Orchestra
Toccata-
NYC, rec. 16.11.1960
Gillespie,Dizzy (tp) | Frosk,John (tp) | Royal,Ernie (tp) | Terry,Clark (tp) | Wilder,Joe (tp) | Green,Urbie (tb) | Rehak,Frank (tb) | Woodman,Britt (tb) | Faulise,Paul (b-tb) | Lister,William (fr-h) | Scott,Morris (fr-h) | Schuller,Gunther (fr-h) | Watkins,Julius (fr-h) | Butterfield,Don (tuba) | Wright,Leo (fl,as) | Schifrin,Lalo (p,arr) | Davis,Art (b) | Lampkin,Chuck (dr) | Del Rio,Jack (bongos) | Candido[Camero] (congas) | Rodriguez,Willie (timbales)

Dizzy Gillespie Quintet
Theme From 'Cool World' | The Pusher
NYC, rec. 21.4.1964
Gillespie,Dizzy (tp) | Moody,James (ts) | Barron,Kenny (p) | White,Chris (b) | Collins,Rudy (dr)

Dizzy Gillespie Sextet
Jambo
Chicago,Ill, rec. 5.11.1964
Gillespie,Dizzy (tp,voc) | Moody,James (ts) | Barron,Kenny (p) | White,Chris (b) | Collins,Rudy (dr) | Fields,Kansas (perc)

Dizzy Gillespie Quintet
Taboo
NYC, rec. May 1962
Gillespie,Dizzy (tp) | Moody,James (ts) | Barron,Kenny (p) | White,Chris (b) | Collins,Rudy (dr)
Walk On The Wild Side
Chicago,Ill, rec. 14.9.1963
Gillespie,Dizzy (tp) | Moody,James (ts) | Barron,Kenny (p) | White,Chris (b) | Collins,Rudy (dr) | Byers,Billy (arr)

Dizzy Gillespie And His Orchestra
The Conquerors
Hollywood,CA, rec. September 1962
Gillespie,Dizzy (tp) | Candoli,Conte (tp) | Porcino,Al (tp) | Triscari,Ray (tp) | Williamson,Stu (tp) | Barone,Mike (tb) | Edmondson,Bob (tb) | Rosolino,Frank (tb) | Shroyer,Kenny (b-tb) | Kant,Luis, (fr-h) | Rensey,Stewart (fr-h) | Thompson,Ches (fr-h) | Callender,Red (tuba) | Kennedy,Charlie (as) | Woods,Phil (as) | Moody,James (ts) | Perkins,Bill (ts) | Hood,Bill (bs) | Schifrin,Lalo (p,arr) | Hendrickson,Al (g) | Clark,Buddy (b) | White,Chris (b) | Collins,Rudy (dr) | Lewis,Mel (dr) | Aquabella,Francisco (perc) | Bunker,Larry (perc) | Richards,Emil (perc) | Carter,Benny (cond)
Kush
Live at Carnegie Hall,NYC, rec. 4.3.1961
Gillespie,Dizzy (tp) | Frosk,John (tp) | Terry,Clark (tp) | Travis,Nick (tp) | Warwick,Carl (tp) | Matthews,George (tb) | Sparrow,Arnett (tb) | Woodman,Britt (tb) | Faulise,Paul (b-tb) | Buffington,Jimmy (fr-h) | Schuller,Gunther (fr-h) | Barrows,John (fr-h) | Berg,Richard (fr-h) | Butterfield,Don (tuba) | Wright,Leo (fl,as) | Schifrin,Lalo (p,arr) | Davis,Art (b) | Lampkin,Chuck (dr) | Barretto,Ray (congas) | Colazo,Julio (perc) | Mangual,Jose (perc)
Bang Bang
NYC, rec. 26.10.1966
Gillespie,Dizzy (tp) | Moody,James (as,voc) | Barron,Kenny (p,voc) | Butler,Billy (g,voc) | Schifano,Frank (b,voc) | Finch,Otis 'Candy' (dr,voc) | Candido[Camero] (congas,voc) | Francis,David 'Panama' (perc,voc)

Dizzy Gillespie Quintet
Swing Low Sweet Cadillac
NYC, rec. 17.2.1959
Gillespie,Dizzy (tp,voc) | Mance,Junior[Julian C.] (p,voc) | Spann,Les (g,voc) | Jones,Sam (b,voc) | Humphries,Lex (dr,voc)

535119-2 | CD | A Life In Jazz:A Musical Biography

Stan Getz With The Eddie Sauter Orchestra
Night Rider
NYC, rec. 28.7.1961
Getz,Stan (ts) | Neves,John (b) | Haynes,Roy (dr) | Strings | Kay,Hershy (ld) | Sauter,Eddie (arr) | details unknown

J.J.Johnson & Stan Getz With The Oscar Peterson Quartet
Billie's Bounce
Shrine Auditorium,LA, rec. 9.10.1957
Johnson,J.J. (tb) | Getz,Stan (ts) | Peterson,Oscar (p) | Ellis,Herb (g) | Brown,Ray (b) | Kay,Connie (dr)

Getz-Gilberto Quintet
Corcovado(Quiet Nights)
NYC, rec. 18./19.3.1963
Getz,Stan (ts) | Jobim,Antonio Carlos (p) | Gilberto,Joao (g,voc) | Williams,Tommy (b) | Banana,Milton (dr) | Gilberto,Astrud (voc)

Stan Getz Quartet
Litha
Englewood Cliffs,NJ, rec. 21.3.1967
Getz,Stan (ts) | Corea,Chick (p) | Carter,Ron (b) | Tate,Grady (dr)

Ella Fitzgerald With The Frank DeVol Orchestra
You're Blasé
Los Angeles,CA, rec. 15.10.1957
Fitzgerald,Ella (voc) | Getz,Stan (ts) | DeVol,Frank (cond,arr) | details unknown

Stan Getz Quartet
What Is This Thing Called Jazz
Live at The 'Jazzhus' Montmartre,Copenhagen, rec. 6.7.1987
Getz,Stan (ts) | Barron,Kenny (p) | Reid,Rufus (b) | Lewis,Victor (dr)

Stan Getz Quintet
Hymn Of The Orient
NYC, rec. 29.12.1952
Getz,Stan (ts) | Raney,Jimmy (g) | Jordan,Duke (p) | Crow,Bill (b) | Isola,Frank (dr)

Stan Getz New Quartet
Summertime
Englewood Cliffs,NJ, rec. 4.3.1964
Getz,Stan (ts) | Burton,Gary (vib) | Israels,Chuck (b) | Hunt,Joe (dr)

Abbey Lincoln With The Stan Getz Quartet
I'm In Love
NYC, rec. 25./26.2.1991
Lincoln,Abbey (voc) | Getz,Stan (ts) | Jones,Hank (p) | Haden,Charlie (b) | Johnson,Mark (dr)

Stan Getz-Bob Brookmeyer Quintet
Who Could Care
San Francisco,CA, rec. 11.9.1961
Brookmeyer,Bob (v-tb) | Getz,Stan (ts) | Kuhn,Steve (p) | Neves,John (b) | Haynes,Roy (dr)

Stan Getz-Kenny Barron
Night And Day
Live at The 'Jazzhus' Montmartre,Copenhagen, rec. 3.-6.3.1991
Getz,Stan (ts) | Barron,Kenny (p)

535271-2 | CD | Verve Jazz Masters Vol.59:Toots Thielemans

George Shearing Quintet
Undecided | Body And Soul
Los Angeles,CA, rec. 12./13.3.1953
Shearing,George (p) | Thielemans,Jean 'Toots' (harm) | Tjader,Cal (vib) | McKibbon,Al (b) | Clark,Bill (dr)

Quincy Jones And His Orchestra
Soldier In The Rain
NYC, rec. 5.2.1964
Royal,Ernie (tp) | Byers,Billy (tb) | Kane,Walter (reeds) | Richardson,Jerome (reeds) | Sims,Zoot (reeds) | Woods,Phil (reeds) | Burton,Gary (vib) | Thielemans,Jean 'Toots (harm,whistling) | Scott,Bobby (p) | Holley,Major (b) | Hinton,Milt (b) | Johnson,Osie (dr) | Grupp,Martin (perc) | Jones,Quincy (arr,ld)
Hummin'
Englewood Cliffs,NJ, rec. 25./26.3.1970
Royal,Ernie (tp) | Hubbard,Freddie (tp) | Moore,Danny (tp) | Stamm,Marvin (tp) | Young,Gene (tp,fl-h) | Andre,Wayne (tb) | Grey,Al (tb) | Powell,Benny (tb) | Studd,Tony (b-tb) | Laws,Hubert (fl) | Richardson,Jerome (ss) | Bank,Danny (bs) | Adams,Pepper (bs) | James,Bob (keyboards) | Gale,Eric (g) | Thielemans,Jean 'Toots' (g,whistling) | Brown,Ray (b) | Holley,Major (b) | Tate,Grady (dr) | Johnson,Jimmi (perc) | Simpson,Valerie (voc) | Jones,Quincy (arr,ld)
Brown Ballad
NYC, rec. 1971
Thielemans,Jean 'Toots' (g,harm) | Jackson,Milt (vib) | Scott,Bobby (p) | James,Bob (el-p) | Sample,Joe (el-p) | Alexander,Monty (tack-p) | Beaver,Paul (synth) | Kalehoff,Edd (synth) | Hall,Jim (g) | Brown,Ray (b) | Tate,Grady (dr) | Jones,Quincy (arr,ld)

Toots Thielemans-Cees Schrama
You're My Blues Machine
Laren,Holland, rec. 4.4.1974
Thielemans,Jean 'Toots' (g,harm) | Schrama,Cees (metronome)

Quincy Jones And His Orchestra
Bluesette
Los Angeles,CA, rec. 1975
Thielemans,Jean 'Toots' (g,harm) | Rosolino,Frank (tb) | Grusin,Dave (keyboards) | Rainey,Chuck (b) | Tate,Grady (dr) | Bahler,Tom (voc) | McWilliams,Paulette (voc) | Gilstrap,James (voc) | Greene,Joe (voc) | Kirkland,Jesse (voc) | Matthews,Myrna (voc) | Willis,Carolyn (voc) | Ware,Leon (voc) | Jones,Quincy (arr,ld)

Toots Thielemans And His Orchestra
Big Bossa
Weesp,NL, rec. September 1975
Thielemans,Jean 'Toots' (harm) | Bannet,John (tp) | Engels,Eddie (tp) | Kat,Wim (tp) | Van Lier,Bart (tb) | Van Wouw,J. (tb) | Voller,Bertil (b-tb) | Meijer,Joop (fr-h) | Soeteman,Iman (fr-h) | Van Woudenberg,A. (fr-h) | Povel,Ferdinand (ts) | Baan,Frans (bassoon) | Silberman,R. (v) | Beths,Gijsbert (v) | Blanket,F. (v) | Emmelot,H. (v) | Francois,Michel (v) | Hoekstra,P.E. (v) | Illes,J. (v) | Jansen-Engelen,M. (v) | Kroon,F. (v) | Lahota,A. (v) | Nederhorst,J. (v) | Nemeth,J.S. (v) | Sanders,H. (v) | Peeters-Goossens,G.F. (viola) | Schouten,K. (viola) | Chasson,Barbara (viola) | Lambooy,H.D. (cello) | Van Diercks,Rene (cello) | Franken,Rob (p) | Albers,Eef (g) | Langereis,Rob (b) | Castellucci,Bruno (dr) | Meyn,Rob (perc) | Bos,Ruud (cond,arr)

Toots Thielemans Quintet
Tenor Madness
Laren,Holland, rec. 10.4.1975
Thielemans,Jean 'Toots' (harm) | Overgaauw,Wim (g) | Franken,Rob (p) | Orsted-Pedersen,Niels-Henning (b) | Castellucci,Bruno (dr)

Toots Thielemans With Gals And Pals
Nocturne
Stockholm,Sweden, rec. 22./23.5.1978
Thielemans,Jean 'Toots' (harm) | Gals And Pals (voc-group) | Öhman,Kjell (p) | Dylag,Roman (b) | Bagge,Lasse (cond,arr)

Toots Thieleman And Sivuca
Vai Passar
Rio De Janeiro,Brazil, rec. 12.4.1985
Thielemans,Jean 'Toots' (harm) | Sivuca (accordeon,voc) | Avellar,Luiz (keyboards) | Silveira,Ricardo (g) | Maria,Luizano (b) | Braga,Paulo (dr) | Ohana (perc) | Marcal,Armando (perc)

Toots Thielemans-Marc Johnson
Killer Joe
NYC, rec. 17./18.4.1989
Thielemans,Jean 'Toots' (harm) | Johnson,Marc (b)

Toots Thielemans Quintet
The Peacocks
NYC, rec. 10./11.12.1989
Thielemans,Jean 'Toots' (harm) | Blanchard,Pierre (v) | Vander,Maurice (p) | Michelot,Pierre (b) | Higgins,Billy (dr)

Toots Thielemans Quartet
C To G Jam Blues
NYC, rec. 19./20.12.1989
Thielemans,Jean 'Toots' (harm) | Miller,Mulgrew (p) | Reid,Rufus (b) | Nash,Lewis (dr)

Toots Thielemans With The Shirley Horn Trio
For My Lady
Paris,France, rec. 3./4.4.1991
Thielemans,Jean 'Toots' (harm) | Horn,Shirley (p,voc) | Ables,Charles (el-b) | Williams,Stephen E. 'Steve' (dr)

535529-2 | CD | The Very Best Of Dixieland Jazz

Eddie Condon And His Chicagoans
Chicago
NYC, rec. 30.10.1961
Condon,Eddie (g) | McPartland,Jimmy (tp) | Teagarden,Jack (tb) | Russell,Pee Wee (cl) | Freeman,Bud (ts) | Sullivan,Joe (p) | Haggart,Bob (b) | Krupa,Gene (dr)

Jack Teagarden With The Red Allen Band
Basin Street Blues
Live at Newport,Rhode Island, rec. 4.7.1957
Allen,Henry Red (tp) | Teagarden,Jack (tb,voc) | Bailey,Buster (cl) | Hopkins,Claude (p) | Shaw,Arvell (b) | Cole,William 'Cozy' (dr)

Monty Sunshine Trio
Wild Cat Blues
London,GB, rec. 9.3.1955
Sunshine,Monty (cl) | Donegan,Tony 'Lonnie' (bj) | Barber,Chris (b)

Rita Reys With The Dutch Swing College Band
Up A Lazy River | Goody Goody
Den Haag,Holland, rec. 1.8.1963
Dutch Swing College Band | Kaart,Ray (tp) | Kaart,Dick (tb) | Schilperoort,Peter (cl) | Lighthart,Arie (g) | Van Oven,Bob (b) | De Lussanet,Louis (dr)

Kid Ory And His Band
Tiger Rag
Live at The Theatre Des Champs-Elysees,Paris,France, rec. 5.12.1956
Ory,Edward 'Kid' (tb) | Alcorn,Alvin (tp) | Gomez,Phil (cl) | Haywood,Cedric (p) | Davidson,Julian (g) | Braud,Wellman (b) | Fields,Kansas (dr)

The Six
Riverboat Shuffle
NYC, rec. April 1954
Six,The | Glasel,John (tp) | Cohen,Porky (tb) | Wilber,Bob (cl) | Goodman,Tommy (p) | Peterson,Bob (b) | Phyfe,Eddie (dr)

Ken Colyer's Jazzmen
Goin' Home
London,GB, rec. 4.11.1953
Colyer,Ken (tp,voc) | Barber,Chris (tb) | Sunshine,Monty (cl) | Donegan,Tony 'Lonnie' (bj) | Bray,Jim (b) | Bowden,Ron (dr)

Turk Murphy And His Jazz Band
Dippermouth Blues
San Francisco,CA, rec. 24.3.1958
Murphy,Turk (tb) | Conger,Larry (tp) | Helm,Bob (cl) | Clute,Pete (p) | Lammi,Dick (bj) | Conger,Al (b) | Vandon,Thad (dr)

Old Merrytale Jazz Band
Am Sonntag Will Mein Süsser Mit Mir Segeln Gehn
Hamburg, rec. 23.3.1961
Old Merrytale Jazzband | Nolte,Joachen (tp) | Münster,Jost 'Addi' (tb) | Schubert,Peter (cl) | Bock,Hans-Jürgen (p) | Grömmer,Rolf (bj) | Zaum,Reinhard (b,voc) | Wantjc,Peter (dr)

Roy Eldridge And His Central Plaza Dixielanders
Ja-Da | That's A Plenty
NYC, rec. 2.6.1956
Eldridge,Roy (tp) | Morton,Benny (tb) | Barefield,Eddie (cl) | Wellstood,Dick (p) | Page,Walter (b) | Jones,Jo (dr)

Mr.Acker Bilk And His Paramount Jazz Band
Summerset
London,GB, rec. 10.3.1959
Bilk,Bernhard 'Mr.Acker' (cl) | Collett,Dave (p) | James,Joy (bj) | Price,Ernest (b) | McKay,Ron (dr)

Chris Barber's Jazz Band
Ice Cream
Live at Royal Festival Hall,London,GB, rec. 20.10.1954
Barber,Chris (tb) | Halcox,Pat (co,voc) | Sunshine,Monty (cl) | Donegan,Tony 'Lonnie' (bj) | Bray,Jim (b) | Bowden,Ron (dr)

Eddie Condon And His Boys
St.Louis Blues
NYC, rec. 1958
Condon,Eddie (g) | Stewart,Rex (co) | Butterfield,Billy (tp) | Cary,Dick (alto-h) | Cutshall,Cutty (tb) | Hall,Herb (cl) | Freeman,Bud (ts) | Schroeder,Gene (p) | Gaskin,Leonard (b) | Wettling,George (dr)

Kid Ory And His Band
Atlanta Blues
Los Altos Hill,CA, rec. 31.3.1959
Ory,Edward 'Kid' (tb) | Buckner,Teddy (tp) | Roberts,Caughey (cl) | Haggerty,Frank (g) | Oden,Charles (b) | Sailes,Jesse (dr)

Henry Red Allen Band
Honeysuckle Rose
Los Angeles,CA, rec. 19.7.1959
Allen,Henry Red (tp) | Ory,Edward 'Kid' (tb) | McCracken,Bob (cl) | Haywood,Cedric (p) | Haggerty,Frank (g) | Corb,Morty (g) | Oden,Charles (b) | Redd,Alton (dr)

Louis Armstrong And Bing Crosby With Orchestra
Let's Sing Like A Dixieland Band
NYC, rec. 5.7.1960
Armstrong,Louis (tp,voc) | Crosby,Bing (voc) | Orchestra | May,Billy (arr,ld) | details unknown

Lu Watters' Yerba Buena Jazz Band
Blues My Naughty Sweetie Gives To Me

Live at Hambone Kelly's,El Cerrito,CA, rec. 1950
Watters,Lu (tp) | Smith,Warren (tb) | Helm,Bob (cl) | Rose,Wally (p) | Patton,Pat (bj) | Lammi,Dick (b) | Dart,Bill (dr)

537022-2 | CD | Loving You
Shirley Horn
Loving You | Should I Surrender | It Amazes Me
Hollywood,CA, rec. 17./18.5.1996
Horn,Shirley (p,voc)
Shirley Horn Quintet
The Man You Were | Love Dance | Someone To Light Up My Life
Horn,Shirley (p,voc) | Mesterhazy,George (g,el-p,synth,synth) | Novosel,Steve (b) | Williams,Stephen E. 'Steve' (dr) | Acuna,Alejandro Neciosup (perc)
Shirley Horn Quartet
Dreamy | In The Dark | Kiss And Run | All Of A Sudden My Heart Sings
Horn,Shirley (p,voc) | Mesterhazy,George (midi-orchestrations) | Novosel,Steve (b) | Williams,Stephen E. 'Steve' (dr)
Shirley Horn Trio
The Island
Horn,Shirley (voc) | Mesterhazy,George (g,midi-orchestrations) | Acuna,Alejandro Neciosup (perc)

537084-2 | CD | Best Of The West Coast Sessions
Stan Getz Quintet
Four
Hollywood,CA, rec. 9.8.1955
Getz,Stan (ts) | Candoli,Conte (tp) | Levy,Lou (p) | Vinnegar,Leroy (b) | Manne,Shelly (dr)
Suddenly It's Spring | East Of The Sun West Of The Moon | S-h-i-n-e
Hollywood,CA, rec. 15.8.1955
Getz,Stan (ts) | Candoli,Conte (tp) | Levy,Lou (p) | Vinnegar,Leroy (b) | Manne,Shelly (dr)
Stan Getz Quartet
Of Thee I Sing | A Handful Of Stars
Hollywood,CA, rec. 19.8.1955
Getz,Stan (ts) | Levy,Lou (p) | Vinnegar,Leroy (b) | Manne,Shelly (dr)
Blues For Mary Jane | You're Blasé | How About You
Hollywood,CA, rec. 24.11.1956
Getz,Stan (ts) | Levy,Lou (p) | Vinnegar,Leroy (b) | Levey,Stan (dr)
But Beautiful
Hollywood,CA, rec. 2.8.1957
Getz,Stan (ts) | Levy,Lou (p) | Vinnegar,Leroy (b) | Levey,Stan (dr)

537122-2 | CD | Junkanoo
Barbara Dennerlein Group
Visions
NYC, rec. October 1996
Dennerlein,Barbara (org,synth) | Lacy,Ku-umba Frank (tb) | Chapin,Thomas[Tom] (fl) | Sanchez,David (ss,ts) | Locke,Joe (vib) | Watkins,Mitch (g) | Plaxico,Lonnie (b,el-b) | Chambers,Dennis (dr) | Alias,Don (perc)
A Cat Strikes Back
Dennerlein,Barbara (synth,grand-p) | Brecker,Randy (tp,fl-h) | Murray,David (b-cl,ts) | Johnson,Howard (bs,tuba) | Watkins,Mitch (g) | Plaxico,Lonnie (b,el-b) | Chambers,Dennis (dr) | Alias,Don (perc)
Walk On Air
Dennerlein,Barbara (org,synth) | Brecker,Randy (tp,fl-h) | Murray,David (b-cl,ts) | Johnson,Howard (bs,tuba) | Watkins,Mitch (g) | Chambers,Dennis (dr) | Alias,Don (perc)
Just Play
Dennerlein,Barbara (org,synth) | Brecker,Randy (tp,fl-h) | Lacy,Ku-umba Frank (tb) | Sanchez,David (ss,ts) | Chambers,Dennis (dr) | Alias,Don (perc)
Nightowls
Dennerlein,Barbara (org,synth) | Brecker,Randy (tp,fl-h) | Lacy,Ku-umba Frank (tb) | Murray,David (b-cl,ts) | Johnson,Howard (bs,tuba) | Locke,Joe (vib) | Watkins,Mitch (g) | Plaxico,Lonnie (b,el-b) | Chambers,Dennis (dr) | Alias,Don (perc)
Samba And The Drum Stick
Dennerlein,Barbara (org,synth) | Sanchez,David (ss,ts) | Watkins,Mitch (g) | Plaxico,Lonnie (b,el-b) | Chambers,Dennis (dr) | Colon,Frank (perc)
Easy Going
Dennerlein,Barbara (org,synth) | Murray,David (b-cl,ts) | Watkins,Mitch (g) | Chambers,Dennis (dr) | Alias,Don (perc)
Andre's Mood
Dennerlein,Barbara (synth,grand-p) | Watkins,Mitch (g) | Plaxico,Lonnie (b,el-b) | Colon,Frank (perc)
Junkanoo
Dennerlein,Barbara (org,synth) | Brecker,Randy (tp,fl-h) | Murray,David (b-cl,ts) | Locke,Joe (vib) | Watkins,Mitch (g) | Plaxico,Lonnie (b,el-b) | Chambers,Dennis (dr) | Alias,Don (perc)

537130-2 | CD | Beyond The Missouri Sky
Charlie Haden-Pat Metheny
Waltz For Ruth | Our Spanish Love Song | Message To A Friend | Two For The Road | First Song(For Ruth) | The Moon Is A Harsh Mistress | The Precious Jewel | He's Gone Away | The Moon Song | Tears Of Rain | Cinema Paradiso(Love Theme) | Cinema Paradiso(Main Theme) | Spiritual
NYC, rec. 1996
Metheny,Pat (g,el-g,keyboards,perc,sitar) | Haden,Charlie (b)

537152-2 | CD | The Rosenberg Trio:The Collection
The Rosenberg Trio
Undecided | Minor Blues
Hilversum,NL, rec. August 1992
Rosenberg,Stochelo (g) | Rosenberg,Nou'che (g) | Rosenberg,Nonnie (b)
Chega De Saudade(No More Blues) | Valse A Rosental | Nuages | Troublant Bolero
Hilversum,NL, rec. October/November 1989
Rosenberg,Stochelo (g) | Rosenberg,Nou'che (g) | Rosenberg,Nonnie (b)
Anouman | Evocacao De Jacob
Hilversum,NL, rec. April 1991
Rosenberg,Stochelo (g) | Rosenberg,Nou'che (g) | Rosenberg,Nonnie (b)
Entre Dos Aguas | Gypsy Summer | Rio Ancho | For Sephora | Honeysuckle Rose
Rosenberg,Stochelo (g) | Rosenberg,Nou'che (g) | Rosenberg,Nonnie (b) | Conrad,Eddie (perc)
Tico Tico
Rosenberg,Stochelo (g) | Rosenberg,Nou'che (g) | Rosenberg,Nonnie (b) | Conrad,Eddie (perc) | Schimscheimer,Marcel (dr-programming)
The Rosenberg Trio With Stephane Grappelli
Tears
Paris,France, rec. January 1994
Grappelli,Stephane (v) | Rosenberg,Stochelo (g) | Rosenberg,Nou'che (g) | Rosenberg,Nonnie (b) | Conrad,Eddie (perc)
The Rosenberg Trio With Frits Landesbergen
Django
Hilversum,NL, rec. Spring 1995
Landesbergen,Frits (vib,dr) | Rosenberg,Stochelo (g) | Rosenberg,Nou'che (g) | Rosenberg,Nonnie (b) | Conrad,Eddie (perc)

537257-2 | 2 CD | Ella Fitzgerald Sings The Cole Porter Songbook
Ella Fitzgerald With The Buddy Bregman Orchestra
All Through The Night | Anything Goes | Miss Otis Regrets | Too Darn Hot | In The Still Of The Night | I Get A Kick Out Of You | Do I Love You | Always True To You In My Fashion | Let's Do It(Let's Fall In Love) | Let's Do It(Let's Fall In Love-alt.take) | Just One Of Those Things | Every Time We Say Goodbye | All Of You | Begin The Beguine | Get Out Of Town | I Am In Love | From This Moment On
Hollywood,CA, rec. 7.-9.2.1956
Fitzgerald,Ella (voc) | Candoli,Pete (tp) | Edison,Harry 'Sweets' (tp) | Ferguson,Maynard (tp) | Gozzo,Conrad (tp) | Bernhart,Milton 'Milt' (tb) | Howard,Joe (tb) | Ulyate,Lloyd (tb) | Roberts,George (b-tb) | Geller,Herb (as) | Shank,Bud (as) | Cooper,Bob (ts) | Nash,Ted (ts) | Gentry,Chuck (bs) | Smith,Paul (p) | Kessel,Barney (g) | Mondragon,Joe (b) | Stoller,Alvin (dr) | Bregman,Buddy (cond,arr)
I Love Paris | You Do Something To Me | Ridin' High | Easy To Love | It's All Right With Me | Why Can't You Behave | What Is This Thing Called Love | You're The Top | You're The Top(alt.take) | Love For Sale | It's De-Lovely | Night And Day | Ace In The Hole | So In Love | I've Got You Under My Skin | I Concentrate On You | I Concentrate On You(alt.take) | Don't Fence Me In
Hollywood,CA, rec. February/March 1956
Fitzgerald,Ella (voc) | Candoli,Pete (tp) | Edison,Harry 'Sweets' (tp) | Ferguson,Maynard (tp) | Gozzo,Conrad (tp) | Bernhart,Milton 'Milt' (tb) | Howard,Joe (tb) | Ulyate,Lloyd (tb) | Roberts,George (b-tb) | Geller,Herb (as) | Shank,Bud (as) | Cooper,Bob (ts) | Nash,Ted (ts) | Gentry,Chuck (bs) | Russell,Mischa (v) | unkn. (12 strings) | unkn. (4 cellos) | La Marchina,Robert 'Bob' (cello) | Lustgarten,Edgar 'Ed' (cello) | unkn. (2 cellos) | Hale,Corky (harp) | Smith,Paul (p) | Kessel,Barney (g) | Mondragon,Joe (b) | Stoller,Alvin (dr) | unkn. (perc) | Bregman,Buddy (cond,arr)

537258-2 | 2 CD | Ella Fitzgerald Sings The Rodgers And Hart Song Book
The Lady Is A Tramp | This Can't Be Love | Lover(Stereo Version) | Lover(Mono Version) | I've Got Five Dollars
Hollywood,CA, rec. 21.8.1956
Fitzgerald,Ella (voc) | Candoli,Pete (tp) | Edison,Harry 'Sweets' (tp) | Lynn,Ray (tp) | Gozzo,Conrad (tp) | Bernhart,Milton 'Milt' (tb) | Howard,Joe (tb) | Ulyate,Lloyd (tb) | Roberts,George (b-tb) | Stein,Maurice (as) | Shank,Bud (as) | Cooper,Bob (ts) | Nash,Ted (ts) | Gentry,Chuck (bs) | Smith,Paul (p) | Kessel,Barney (g) | Mondragon,Joe (b) | Stoller,Alvin (dr) | Bregman,Buddy (cond,arr)
Johnny One Note | I Wish I Were In Love Again | Give It Back To The Indians | Ten Cents A Dance | Mountain Greenery
Hollywood,CA, rec. 28.8.1956
Fitzgerald,Ella (voc) | Candoli,Pete (tp) | Ferguson,Maynard (tp) | Lynn,Ray (tp) | Gozzo,Conrad (tp) | Bernhart,Milton 'Milt' (tb) | Howard,Joe (tb) | Ulyate,Lloyd (tb) | Roberts,George (b-tb) | DeRosa,Vince (fr-h) | unkn. (fr-h) | Shank,Bud (as) | Schwartz,Willie (cl,as) | Cooper,Bob (ts) | Nash,Ted (ts) | Gentry,Chuck (bs) | Smith,Paul (p) | Kessel,Barney (g) | Mondragon,Joe (b) | Stoller,Alvin (dr) | unkn. (perc) | Russell,Mischa (concertmaster) | unkn. (12 strings) | unkn. (2 violas) | La Marchina,Robert 'Bob' (cello) | Lustgarten,Edgar 'Ed' (cello) | Bregman,Buddy (cond,arr)
Manhattan | Thou Swell | There's A Small Hotel | I Didn't Know What Time It Was | Blue Mood
Hollywood,CA, rec. 29.8.1956
Fitzgerald,Ella (voc) | DeRosa,Vince (fr-h) | unkn. (2 fr-h) | Shank,Bud (fl) | Schwartz,Willie (fl) | Nash,Ted (fl) | Koblenz,Arnold (engl-h,oboe) | Smith,Paul (p) | Kessel,Barney (g) | Mondragon,Joe (b) | Stoller,Alvin (dr) | Holland,Milt (vib,perc) | Russell,Mischa (concertmaster) | unkn. (12 strings) | unkn. (2 violas) | La Marchina,Robert 'Bob' (cello) | Lustgarten,Edgar 'Ed' (cello) | unkn. (2 cellos) | Bregman,Buddy (cond,arr)
Ella Fitzgerald With The Paul Smith Quartet
To Keep My Love Alive | With A Song In My Heart | Everything I've Got | Bewitched Bothered And Bewildered
Fitzgerald,Ella (voc) | Smith,Paul (p) | Kessel,Barney (g) | Mondragon,Joe (b) | Stoller,Alvin (dr)
Ella Fitzgerald And Barney Kessel
Wait 'Till You See Her
Fitzgerald,Ella (voc) | Kessel,Barney (g)
Ella Fitzgerald With The Buddy Bregman Orchestra
Have You Met Miss Jones | A Ship Without A Sail | Spring Is Here | It Never Entered My Mind | My Romance | Little Girl Blue | I Could Write A Book | My Funny Valentine | My Heart Stood Still
Hollywood,CA, rec. 30.8.1956
Fitzgerald,Ella (voc) | DeRosa,Vince (fr-h) | Nash,Ted (fl) | Cooper,Bob (engl-h,oboe) | Smith,Paul (p,celeste) | Kessel,Barney (g) | Mondragon,Joe (b) | Stoller,Alvin (dr) | Holland,Milt (vib,perc) | Russell,Mischa (concertmaster) | unkn. (9 strings) | unkn. (4 violas) | La Marchina,Robert 'Bob' (cello) | Lustgarten,Edgar 'Ed' (cello) | Bregman,Buddy (cond,arr)
Dancing On The Ceiling | The Blue Room | Isn't It Romantic
Hollywood,CA, rec. 31.8.1956
Fitzgerald,Ella (voc) | DeRosa,Vince (fr-h) | Kinzler,Jule (fl) | Most,Abe (cl) | Gentry,Chuck (b-cl,bass-sax) | Koblenz,Arnold (oboe) | Cooper,Bob (engl-h) | Smith,Paul (p,arr) | Kessel,Barney (g) | Mondragon,Joe (b) | Stoller,Alvin (dr) | Bregman,Buddy (cond)
Ella Fitzgerald With The Paul Smith Quartet
Here In My Arms
Fitzgerald,Ella (voc) | Smith,Paul (p,arr) | Kessel,Barney (g) | Mondragon,Joe (b) | Stoller,Alvin (dr)
Ella Fitzgerald With The Buddy Bregman Orchestra
You Took Advantage Of Me | Where Or When
Fitzgerald,Ella (voc) | Linn,Ray (tp) | DeRosa,Vince (fr-h) | Kinzler,Jule (fl) | Most,Abe (cl) | Gentry,Chuck (b-cl,bass-sax) | Koblenz,Arnold (oboe) | Cooper,Bob (engl-h) | Smith,Paul (p,arr) | Kessel,Barney (g) | Mondragon,Joe (b) | Stoller,Alvin (dr) | Bregman,Buddy (cond)

537284-2 | 3 CD | The Complete Ella Fitzgerald And Louis Armstrong On Verve
Ella Fitzgerald With Louis Armstrong And The All Stars
You Won't Be Satisfied Until You Break My Heart | Undecided
Hollywood Bowl,CA, rec. 15.8.1956
Fitzgerald,Ella (voc) | Armstrong,Louis (tp) | Young,Trummy (tb) | Hall,Edmond (cl) | Kyle,Billy (p) | Jones,Dale (b) | Deems,Barrett (dr)
Ella Fitzgerald And Louis Armstrong With The Oscar Peterson Quartet
Can't We Be Friends | Isn't It A Lovely Day | Moonlight In Vermont | They Can't Take That Away From Me | Under A Blanket Of Blue | Tenderly | A Foggy Day(In London Town) | Stars Fell On Alabama | Cheek To Cheek | The Nearness Of You | April In Paris
Hollywood,CA, rec. 16.8.1956
Fitzgerald,Ella (voc) | Armstrong,Louis (tp,voc) | Peterson,Oscar (p) | Ellis,Herb (g) | Brown,Ray (b) | Rich,Buddy (dr)
Don't Be That Way | I Won't Dance | I've Got My Love To Keep Me Warm | I'm Putting All My Eggs In One Basket | A Fine Romance
Hollywood,CA, rec. 13.8.1957
Fitzgerald,Ella (voc) | Armstrong,Louis (voc) | Peterson,Oscar (p) | Ellis,Herb (g) | Brown,Ray (b) | Bellson,Louie (dr)
They All Laughed | Comes Love | Autumn In New York | Stompin' At The Savoy | Gee Baby Ain't I Good To You | Let's Call The Whole Thing Off | These Foolish Things Remind Me On You | Ill Wind | Our Love Is Here To Stay | Learnin' The Blues
Hollywood,CA, rec. 23.7.1957
Fitzgerald,Ella (voc) | Armstrong,Louis (tp,voc) | Peterson,Oscar (p) | Ellis,Herb (g) | Brown,Ray (b) | Bellson,Louie (dr)
Makin' Whoopee | Let's Do It | Willow Weep For Me | I Get A Kick Out Of You
Hollywood,CA, rec. 31.7.1957
Armstrong,Louis (voc) | Peterson,Oscar (p) | Ellis,Herb (g) | Brown,Ray (b) | Bellson,Louie (dr)
Louis Armstrong And Ella Fitzgerald With Russell Garcia's Orchestra
Overture | Summertime | I Wants To Stay Here | My Man's Gone Now | I Got Plenty O'Nuttin' | Buzzard Song | Bess You Is My Woman Now | It Ain't Necessarily So | What You Want Wid Bess | A Woman Is A Sometime Thing | Oh Doctor Jesus | Here Comes De Honey Man- | Crab Man- | Oh Dey's So Fresh An' Fine (Strawberry Woman)- | There's A Boat Dat's Leavin' Soon For New York | Bess Oh Where's My Bess
NYC, rec. 18./19.8.& 14.10.1957
Armstrong,Louis (tp,voc) | Fitzgerald,Ella (voc) | Garcia,Russell (cond) | Orchestra | details unknown
Oh Lawd I'm On My Way
Los Angeles,CA, rec. 19.8.1957
Armstrong,Louis (tp,voc) | Fitzgerald,Ella (voc) | Garcia,Russell (cond) | Orchestra | Judd Conlon Singers,The | details unknown

537483-2 | CD | The Montreal Tapes
Charlie Haden Trio
Blues In Motion | Fiasco | First Song | Dolphy's Dance | For John Malachi | In The Year Of The Dragon
Live at The Jazzfestival Montreal, rec. 1.7.1989
Haden,Charlie (b) | Allen,Geri (p) | Motian,Paul (dr)

537555-2 | 3 CD | The Stockholm Concerts
Chet Baker-Stan Getz Quintet
Announcement | Stablemates | We'll Be Together Again | On The Up And Up | How Long Has This Been Going On | O Grande Amor | Just Friends | My Funny Valentine | Sippin' At Bells | Stella By Starlight | Airegin | Announcement | The Baggage Room Blues | We'll Be Together Again(2) | I'll Remember April | Just Friends | My Funny Valentine(2) | Just Friends(2) | Sippin' At Bells(2) | Blood Count | Milestones | Airegin | Dear Old Stockholm | Line For Lyons
Live at Södra Teatern,Stockholm, rec. 18.2.1983
Baker,Chet (tp) | Getz,Stan (ts) | McNeely,Jim (p) | Mraz,George 'Jiri' (b) | Lewis,Victor (dr)

537563-2 | CD | Habana
Roy Hargrove's Crisol
O My Seh Yeh | Una Mas | Dream Traveler | The Mountaincs | Afrodisia | Mambo For Roy | O My Seh Yeh(reprise)
Teatro Mancinelli,Orvieto,Italy, rec. 5./6.1.1997
Hargrove,Roy (tp,fl-h) | Lacy,Ku-umba Frank (tb) | Bartz,Gary (ss,as) | Sanchez,David (ss,ts) | Malone,Russell (g) | Valdes,Chucho (p) | Benitez,John (b) | Hernandez,Horacio 'El Negro' (dr) | Diaz,Miguel (congas) | Quintana,Jose Luis 'Chancuito' (timbales)
Nusia's Poem
Hargrove,Roy (tp,fl-h) | Lacy,Ku-umba Frank (tb) | Bartz,Gary (ss,as) | Sanchez,David (ss,ts) | Malone,Russell (g) | Valdes,Chucho (p) | Hicks,John (p) | Benitez,John (b) | Hernandez,Horacio 'El Negro' (dr) | Muhammad,Idris[Leo Morris] (dr) | Diaz,Miguel (congas) | Quintana,Jose Luis 'Chancuito' (timbales)
Mr.Bruce
Hargrove,Roy (tp,fl-h) | Lacy,Ku-umba Frank (tb) | Bartz,Gary (ss,as) | Sanchez,David (ss,ts) | Malone,Russell (g) | Valdes,Chucho (p) | Reyes,Jorge (b) | Hernandez,Horacio 'El Negro' (dr) | Diaz,Miguel (congas) | Quintana,Jose Luis 'Chancuito' (timbales)
Ballad For The Children
Hargrove,Roy (fl-h) | Valdes,Chucho (p) | Benitez,John (b) | Hernandez,Horacio 'El Negro' (dr) | Diaz,Miguel (congas)

537564-2 | CD | 1+1:Herbie Hancock-Wayne Shorter
Wayne Shorter-Herbie Hancock
Meridianne-A Wood Sylph | Aung San Suu Kyi | Sonrisa | Memory Of Enchantment | Visitor From Somewhere | Joanna's Theme | Visitor From Nowhere | Manhattan Lorelei | Hale-Bopp,Hip-Hop
Los Angeles,CA, rec. details unknown
Shorter,Wayne (ss) | Hancock,Herbie (p)

537670-2 | CD | The Montreal Tapes
Charlie Haden Trio
Vignette | Bay City | La Pasionaria | Silence | The Blessing | Solar
Live at The Jazzfestival Montreal, rec. 3.7.1989
Haden,Charlie (b) | Rubalcaba,Gonzalo (p) | Motian,Paul (dr)

537909-2 | CD | The Best Of Ella Fitzgerald And Louis Armstrong On Verve
Ella Fitzgerald With Louis Armstrong And The All Stars
You Won't Be Satisfied Until You Break My Heart
Hollywood Bowl,CA, rec. 15.8.1956
Fitzgerald,Ella (voc) | Armstrong,Louis (tp) | Young,Trummy (tb) | Hall,Edmond (cl) | Kyle,Billy (p) | Jones,Dale (b) | Deems,Barrett (dr)
Ella Fitzgerald And Louis Armstrong With The Oscar Peterson Quartet
They Can't Take That Away From Me | Under A Blanket Of Blue | Tenderly | Stars Fell On Alabama | The Nearness Of You
Hollywood,CA, rec. 16.8.1956
Fitzgerald,Ella (voc) | Armstrong,Louis (tp,voc) | Peterson,Oscar (p) | Ellis,Herb (g) | Brown,Ray (b) | Rich,Buddy (dr)
I've Got My Love To Keep Me Warm | I'm Putting All My Eggs In One Basket
Hollywood,CA, rec. 13.8.1957
Fitzgerald,Ella (voc) | Armstrong,Louis (voc) | Peterson,Oscar (p) | Ellis,Herb (g) | Brown,Ray (b) | Bellson,Louie (dr)
Autumn In New York | Stompin' At The Savoy | Gee Baby Ain't I Good To You | Let's Call The Whole Thing Off | Our Love Is Here To Stay
Hollywood,CA, rec. 23.7.1957
Fitzgerald,Ella (voc) | Armstrong,Louis (tp,voc) | Peterson,Oscar (p) | Ellis,Herb (g) | Brown,Ray (b) | Bellson,Louie (dr)
Louis Armstrong And Ella Fitzgerald With Russell Garcia's Orchestra
Summertime | I Wants To Stay Here
NYC, rec. 18./19.8.& 14.10.1957
Armstrong,Louis (tp,voc) | Fitzgerald,Ella (voc) | Garcia,Russell (cond) | Orchestra | details unknown

538328-2 | CD | Baby Breeze
Chet Baker Sextet
Baby Breeze | This Is The Thing | One With One | Pamela's Passion | Comin' Down
NYC, rec. 14.11.1964
Baker,Chet (fl-h) | Urso,Phil (ts) | Strozier,Frank (fl,as) | Galper,Hal (p) | Fleming,Michael (b) | Rice,Charlie (dr)
Chet Baker With Bobby Scott And Kenny Burrell
Born To Be Blue | Everything Depends On Me
Baker,Chet (voc) | Scott,Bobby (p,arr) | Burrell,Kenny (g)
Chet Baker With Kenny Burrell
You're Mine You | Sweet Sue Just You
Baker,Chet (voc) | Burrell,Kenny (g)
Chet Baker With Bobby Scott
A Taste Of Honey
Baker,Chet (voc) | Scott,Bobby (p,arr)
Chet Baker Quartet
I Wish You Love | The Touch Of Your Lips | Think Beautiful | I Wish You Love(alt.take) | Think Beautiful(alt.take)
NYC, rec. 20.11.1964
Baker,Chet (fl-h,voc) | James,Bob (p) | Fleming,Michael (b) | Rice,Charlie (dr)

538329-2 | CD | Down To Earth
Ramsey Lewis Trio
Dark Eyes | Come Back To Sorento | Soul Mist | Sometimes I Feel Like A Motherless Child | Sometimes I Feel Like A Motherless Child(alt.take) | Come Back To Sorento(alt.take)
Chicago,Ill, rec. 6.11.1958
Lewis,Ramsey (p) | Young,Eldee (b) | Holt,Red (dr)
John Henry | Greensleeves | We Blue It | Suzanne | Billy Boy | Decisions | John Henry(alt.take) | We Blue It(alt.take)
Chicago,Ill, rec. 4.12.1858
Lewis,Ramsey (p) | Young,Eldee (b) | Holt,Red (dr)

538620-2 | CD | In A New Setting
Milt Jackson Quartet
Project-S
NYC, rec. 9.12.1964
Jackson,Milt (vib) | Tyner,McCoy (p) | Cranshaw,Bob (b) | Kay,Connie (dr)
Milt Jackson Quintet
The Other Half Of Me
Jackson,Milt (vib) | Heath,Jimmy (ts) | Tyner,McCoy (p) | Cranshaw,Bob (b) | Kay,Connie (dr)
Clay's Blues | Lazy Melody | That's In
NYC, rec. 14.12.1964
Jackson,Milt (vib) | Heath,Jimmy (fl,ts) | Tyner,McCoy (p) | Cranshaw,Bob (b) | Kay,Connie (dr)
Milt Jackson Quartet
I'm Gonna Laugh You Out Of My Life | Every Time We Say Goodbye
NYC, rec. 28.12.1964
Jackson,Milt (vib) | Tyner,McCoy (p) | Cranshaw,Bob (b) | Kay,Connie (dr)
Sonny's Blues | Spanish Fly | No Moon At All | Slow Death | Inaffable
Jackson,Milt (vib) | Heath,Jimmy (ts) | Tyner,McCoy (p) | Cranshaw,Bob (b) | Kay,Connie (dr)

538635-2 | CD | Dinah Sings Bessie Smith
Dinah Washington With The Eddie Chamblee Orchestra
Send Me To The 'Lectric Chair | Trombone Butter(aka Trombone Chilly) | Careless Love Blues | Trombone Butter(aka Trombone Chilly-alt.take) | Careless Love Blues(alt.take)
Chicago,Ill, rec. 30.12.1957
Washington,Dinah (voc) | Chamblee,Eddie (ts) | Ricard,Fip (tp) |

Terry,Clark (tp) | Jackson,Quentin (tb) | Easton,McKinley (bs) | Craig,James (p) | Edmonson,Robare (b) | Slaughter,James (dr)
After You've Gone | Jailhouse Blues | You've Been A Good Old Wagon(Daddy But You Done Broke Down) | Me And My Gin
Chicago,Ill, rec. 7.1.1958
Washington,Dinah (voc) | Chamblee,Eddie (ts) | Ricard,Flip (tp) | Priester,Julian (tb) | Davis,Charles (bs) | Wilson,Jack (p) | Wilson,Robert (b) | Slaughter,James (dr) | Edmonson,Robare (arr)
Back Water Blues | If I Could Be With You One Hour Tonight | Fine Fat Daddy
Chicago,Ill, rec. 20.1.1958
Washington,Dinah (voc) | Chamblee,Eddie (ts) | Ricard,Flip (tp) | Priester,Julian (tb) | Davis,Charles (bs) | Wilson,Jack (p) | Wilson,Robert (b) | Slaughter,James (dr)
Dinah Washington With The Newport All Stars
Send Me To The 'Lectric Chair | Me And My Gin | Back Water Blues
Live at Newport,Rhode Island, rec. 6.7.1958
Washington,Dinah (voc) | Newport All Stars,The | Mitchell,Blue (tp) | Liston,Melba (tb) | Ousley,Harold (ts) | Shihab,Sahib (bs) | Kelly,Wynton (p) | West,Paul (b) | Roach,Max (dr)

538636-2 | CD | Charles Mingus:Pre-Bird(Mingus Revisited)
Charles Mingus Orchestra
Half-Mast Inhibition | Mingus Fingus No.2 | Bemoanable Lady
NYC, rec. 24.5.1960
Mingus,Charles (b) | Belgrave,Marcus (tp) | Curson,Ted (tp) | Dotson,Hobart (tp) | Terry,Clark (tp) | Williams,Richard (tp) | Bert,Eddie (tb) | Greenlee,Charles (tb) | Hampton,Slide (tb) | Knepper,Jimmy (tb) | Butterfield,Don (tuba) | Di Domenica,Bob (fl) | Schulman,Harry (oboe) | Dolphy,Eric (fl,b-cl,as) | LaPorta,John (as) | Lateef,Yusef (fl,ts) | Barron,Bill (ts) | Farrell,Joe (ts) | Bank,Danny (bs) | McCracken,Charles (cello) | Hanna,Sir Roland (p) | Richmond,Dannie (dr) | Evans,Sticks (perc) | Scott,George (perc) | Roach,Max (perc) | Schuller,Gunther (cond)
Weird Nightmare | Prayer For Passive Resistance | Eclipse | Do Nothin' Till You Hear From Me- | I Let A Song Go Out Of My Heart-
NYC, rec. 25.5.1960
Mingus,Charles (b) | Curson,Ted (tp) | Knepper,Jimmy (tb) | Dolphy,Eric (fl,cl,b-cl,as) | Farrell,Joe (ts) | Lateef,Yusef (fl,ts) | Ervin,Booker (ts) | Hanna,Sir Roland (p) | Richmond,Dannie (dr) | Cousins,Lorraine (voc)
Take The 'A' Train- | Exactly Like You-
Mingus,Charles (b) | Curson,Ted (tp) | Knepper,Jimmy (tb) | Dolphy,Eric (fl,cl,b-cl,as) | Farrell,Joe (ts) | Lateef,Yusef (fl,ts) | Ervin,Booker (ts) | Bley,Paul (p) | Richmond,Dannie (dr)

539030-2 | 2 CD | Ella & Duke At The Cote D'Azur
Ella Fitzgerald With The Jimmy Jones Trio
Jazz Samba | Goin' Out Of My Head | How Long Has This Been Going On | Misty | The More I See You | Lullaby Of Birdland
Live at Juan Les Pins,France, rec. 28./29.7.1966
Fitzgerald,Ella (voc) | Jones,Jimmy (p) | Hughart,Jim (b) | Tate,Grady (dr)
Duke Ellington And His Orchestra
Trombonia-Bustoso-Issimo | The Old Circus Train Turn-Around Blues
Live at Juan Les Pins,France, rec. 27./28.7.1966
Ellington,Duke (p) | Williams,Cootie (tp) | Anderson,Cat (tp) | Jones,Herbie (tp) | Ellington,Mercer (tp) | Bascomb,Dud (tp) | Brown,Lawrence (tb) | Cooper,Frank 'Buster' (tb) | Connors,Chuck (tb) | Hamilton,Jimmy (cl,ts) | Hodges,Johnny (as) | Procope,Russell (as) | Gonsalves,Paul (ts) | Carney,Harry (bs) | Lamb,John (b) | Woodyard,Sam (dr)
The Trip
Live at Juan Les Pins,France, rec. 28./29.7.1966
Ellington,Duke (p) | Anderson,Cat (tp) | Jones,Herbie (tp) | Ellington,Mercer (tp) | Bascomb,Dud (tp) | Brown,Lawrence (tb) | Cooper,Frank 'Buster' (tb) | Connors,Chuck (tb) | Hamilton,Jimmy (cl,ts) | Hodges,Johnny (as) | Procope,Russell (as) | Gonsalves,Paul (ts) | Carney,Harry (bs) | Lamb,John (b) | Woodyard,Sam (dr)
Things Ain't What They Used To Be
Ellington,Duke (p) | Williams,Cootie (tp) | Anderson,Cat (tp) | Jones,Herbie (tp) | Ellington,Mercer (tp) | Bascomb,Dud (tp) | Brown,Lawrence (tb) | Cooper,Frank 'Buster' (tb) | Connors,Chuck (tb) | Hamilton,Jimmy (cl,ts) | Hodges,Johnny (as) | Procope,Russell (as) | Gonsalves,Paul (ts) | Carney,Harry (bs) | Lamb,John (b) | Woodyard,Sam (dr)
Diminuendo And Crescendo In Blue
Live at Juan Les Pins,France, rec. 26.7.1966
Ellington,Duke (p) | Williams,Cootie (tp) | Anderson,Cat (tp) | Jones,Herbie (tp) | Ellington,Mercer (tp) | Bascomb,Dud (tp) | Brown,Lawrence (tb) | Cooper,Frank 'Buster' (tb) | Connors,Chuck (tb) | Hamilton,Jimmy (cl,ts) | Hodges,Johnny (as) | Procope,Russell (as) | Gonsalves,Paul (ts) | Carney,Harry (bs) | Lamb,John (b) | Woodyard,Sam (dr)
The Matador
Live at Juan Les Pins,France, rec. 27.7.1966
Williams,Cootie (tp) | Anderson,Cat (tp) | Jones,Herbie (tp) | Ellington,Mercer (tp) | Bascomb,Dud (tp) | Brown,Lawrence (tb) | Cooper,Frank 'Buster' (tb) | Connors,Chuck (tb) | Hamilton,Jimmy (cl,ts) | Hodges,Johnny (as) | Procope,Russell (as) | Gonsalves,Paul (ts) | Carney,Harry (bs) | Lamb,John (b) | Woodyard,Sam (dr)
Rose Of The Rio Grande
Live at Juan Les Pins,France, rec. 26.7.1966
Ellington,Duke (p) | Williams,Cootie (tp) | Anderson,Cat (tp) | Jones,Herbie (tp) | Ellington,Mercer (tp) | Bascomb,Dud (tp) | Brown,Lawrence (tb) | Cooper,Frank 'Buster' (tb) | Connors,Chuck (tb) | Hamilton,Jimmy (cl,ts) | Hodges,Johnny (as) | Procope,Russell (as) | Gonsalves,Paul (ts) | Carney,Harry (bs) | Lamb,John (b) | Woodyard,Sam (dr)
Jive Jam | All Too Soon
Live at Juan Les Pins,France, rec. 27./28.7.1966
Ellington,Duke (p) | Williams,Cootie (tp) | Anderson,Cat (tp) | Jones,Herbie (tp) | Ellington,Mercer (tp) | Nance,Ray (v,co) | Brown,Lawrence (tb) | Cooper,Frank 'Buster' (tb) | Connors,Chuck (tb) | Hamilton,Jimmy (cl,ts) | Hodges,Johnny (as) | Procope,Russell (as) | Gonsalves,Paul (ts) | Carney,Harry (bs) | Lamb,John (b) | Woodyard,Sam (dr)
Ella Fitzgerald With The Duke Ellington Orchestra And Jimmy Jones Trio
Mack The Knife(Moritat)
Live at Juan Les Pins,France, rec. 28.7.1966
Fitzgerald,Ella (voc) | Williams,Cootie (tp) | Anderson,Cat (tp) | Jones,Herbie (tp) | Ellington,Mercer (tp) | Brown,Lawrence (tb) | Cooper,Frank 'Buster' (tb) | Connors,Chuck (tb) | Hamilton,Jimmy (cl,ts) | Hodges,Johnny (as) | Procope,Russell (as) | Gonsalves,Paul (ts) | Carney,Harry (bs) | Jones,Jimmy (p) | Hughart,Jim (b) | Tate,Grady (dr)
Ella Fitzgerald With The Duke Ellington Orchestra
It Don't Mean A Thing If It Ain't Got That Swing
Live at Juan Les Pins,France, rec. 29.7.1966
Fitzgerald,Ella (voc) | Ellington,Duke (p) | Williams,Cootie (tp) | Anderson,Cat (tp) | Jones,Herbie (tp) | Ellington,Mercer (tp) | Brown,Lawrence (tb) | Cooper,Frank 'Buster' (tb) | Connors,Chuck (tb) | Hamilton,Jimmy (cl,ts) | Hodges,Johnny (as) | Procope,Russell (as) | Gonsalves,Paul (ts) | Carney,Harry (bs) | Lamb,John (b) | Woodyard,Sam (dr)
Just Squeeze Me(But Don't Tease Me)
Fitzgerald,Ella (voc) | Ellington,Duke (p) | Gonsalves,Paul (ts) | Webster,Ben (ts) | Lamb,John (b) | Woodyard,Sam (dr) | Nance,Ray (voc)

539033-2 | 8 CD | Ella Fitzgerald And Duke Ellington:Cote D'Azure Concerts on Verve
Duke Ellington And His Orchestra
Diminuendo And Crescendo In Blue | Rose Of The Rio Grande | Caravan | Tutti For Cootie | Skin Deep | Passion Flower | Things Ain't What They Used To Be | Wings And Things | The Star-Crossed Lovers | Such Sweet Thunder | Madness In Great Ones | Kinda Dukish- | Things Ain't What They Used To Be(2)
Live at Juan Les Pins,France, rec. 26.7.1966
Williams,Cootie (tp) | Anderson,Cat (tp) | Jones,Herbie (tp) | Ellington,Mercer (tp) | Brown,Lawrence (tb) | Cooper,Frank 'Buster' (tb,claves) | Connors,Chuck (tb,maracas) | Hamilton,Jimmy (cl,ts) | Hodges,Johnny (as) | Procope,Russell (as) | Gonsalves,Paul (ts) | Carney,Harry (bs) | Ellington,Duke (p) | Lamb,John (b) | Woodyard,Sam (dr)
Main Stem | Black And Tan Fantasy- | Creole Love Call- | The Mooche- | West Indian Pancake | El Viti(aka The Matador) | The Opener | La Plus Belle Africaine | Azure | Take The 'A' Train(theme) | Such Sweet Thunder | Half The Fun | Madness In Great Ones | The Star-Crossed Lovers | I Got It Bad And That Ain't Good | Things Ain't What They Used To Be | Wings And Things | Kinda Dukish- | Rockin' In Rhythm- | Chelsea Bridge | Skin Deep | Sophisticated Lady | Jam With Sam | Things Ain't What They Used To Be(2) | Take The 'A' Train
Live at Juan Les Pins,France, rec. 27.7.1966
Anderson,Cat (tp) | Ellington,Mercer (tp) | Jones,Herbie (tp) | Williams,Cootie (tp) | Brown,Lawrence (tb) | Cooper,Frank 'Buster' (tb) | Connors,Charles (b-tb) | Hodges,Johnny (as) | Procope,Russell (cl,as) | Hamilton,Jimmy (cl,ts) | Gonsalves,Paul (ts) | Carney,Harry (cl,b-cl,bs) | Ellington,Duke (p) | Lamb,John (b) | Woodyard,Sam (dr)
Ella Fitzgerald With The Duke Ellington Orchestra And Jimmy Jones Trio
Duke Ellington Introduces Ella Fitzgerald | Let's Do It | Satin Doll
Fitzgerald,Ella (voc) | Anderson,Cat (tp) | Ellington,Mercer (tp) | Jones,Herbie (tp) | Williams,Cootie (tp) | Brown,Lawrence (tb) | Cooper,Frank 'Buster' (tb) | Connors,Charles (b-tb) | Hodges,Johnny (as) | Procope,Russell (cl,as) | Hamilton,Jimmy (cl,ts) | Gonsalves,Paul (ts) | Carney,Harry (cl,b-cl,bs) | Jones,Jimmie (p) | Hughart,Jim (b) | Tate,Grady (dr)
Cotton Tail
Anderson,Cat (tp) | Ellington,Mercer (tp) | Jones,Herbie (tp) | Williams,Cootie (tp) | Brown,Lawrence (tb) | Cooper,Frank 'Buster' (tb) | Connors,Charles (b-tb) | Hodges,Johnny (as) | Procope,Russell (cl,as) | Hamilton,Jimmy (cl,ts) | Gonsalves,Paul (ts) | Carney,Harry (cl,b-cl,bs) | Ellington,Duke (p) | Hughart,Jim (b) | Tate,Grady (dr)
Duke Ellington And His Orchestra
Soul Call | West Indian Pancake | El Viti(aka The Matador) | The Opener | La Plus Belle Africaine | Take The 'A' Train | Trombonia-Bustoso-Issimo | Such Sweet Thunder | Half The Fun | Madness In Great Ones | The Star-Crossed Lovers | Prelude To A Kiss | Things Ain't What They Used To Be | The Old Circus Train Turn-Around Blues
Live at Juan Les Pins,France, rec. 28.7.1966
Fitzgerald,Ella (voc) | Anderson,Cat (tp) | Ellington,Mercer (tp) | Jones,Herbie (tp) | Williams,Cootie (tp) | Brown,Lawrence (tb) | Cooper,Frank 'Buster' (tb) | Connors,Charles (b-tb) | Hodges,Johnny (as) | Procope,Russell (cl,as) | Hamilton,Jimmy (cl,ts) | Gonsalves,Paul (ts) | Carney,Harry (cl,b-cl,bs) | Ellington,Duke (p) | Lamb,John (b) | Woodyard,Sam (dr)
Ella Fitzgerald With The Duke Ellington Orchestra And Jimmy Jones Trio
Thou Swell(incomplete) | Satin Doll | Wives And Lovers | Something To Live For | Let's Do It | Mack The Knife(Moritat)
Fitzgerald,Ella (voc) | Anderson,Cat (tp) | Ellington,Mercer (tp) | Jones,Herbie (tp) | Williams,Cootie (tp) | Brown,Lawrence (tb) | Cooper,Frank 'Buster' (tb) | Connors,Charles (b-tb) | Hodges,Johnny (as) | Procope,Russell (cl,as) | Hamilton,Jimmy (cl,ts) | Gonsalves,Paul (ts) | Carney,Harry (cl,b-cl,bs) | Jones,Jimmie (p) | Hughart,Jim (b) | Tate,Grady (dr)
Ella Fitzgerald With The Jimmy Jones Trio
The More I See You | Goin' Out Of My Head | How Long Has This Been Going On
Fitzgerald,Ella (voc) | Jones,Jimmie (p) | Hughart,Jim (b) | Tate,Grady (dr)
So Danco Samba(I Only Dance The Samba) | Lullaby Of Birdland
Fitzgerald,Ella (voc) | Jones,Jimmie (p) | Hughart,Jim (b) | Tate,Grady (dr) | Cooper,Frank 'Buster' (claves) | Connors,Chuck (maracas) | Williams,Cootie prob. (tp)
Duke Ellington And His Orchestra
Black And Tan Fantasy- | Creole Love Call- | The Mooche- | Soul Call | West Indian Pancake | El Viti(aka The Matador) | La Plus Belle Africaine | Such Sweet Thunder | Half The Fun | Madness In Great Ones | The Star-Crossed Lovers | Wings And Things | Things Ain't What They Used To Be
Live at Juan Les Pins,France, rec. 29.7.1966
Anderson,Cat (tp) | Ellington,Mercer (tp) | Jones,Herbie (tp) | Williams,Cootie (tp) | Brown,Lawrence (tb) | Cooper,Frank 'Buster' (tb) | Connors,Charles (b-tb) | Hodges,Johnny (as) | Procope,Russell (cl,as) | Hamilton,Jimmy (cl,ts) | Gonsalves,Paul (ts) | Carney,Harry (cl,b-cl,bs) | Ellington,Duke (p) | Lamb,John (b) | Woodyard,Sam (dr)
Ella Fitzgerald With The Duke Ellington Orchestra And Jimmy Jones Trio
Thou Swell | Satin Doll | Wives And Lovers | Something To Live For | Let's Do It | Sweet Georgia Brown | Mack The Knife(Moritat) | Cotton Tail
Fitzgerald,Ella (voc) | Anderson,Cat (tp) | Ellington,Mercer (tp) | Jones,Herbie (tp) | Williams,Cootie (tp) | Brown,Lawrence (tb) | Cooper,Frank 'Buster' (tb) | Connors,Charles (b-tb) | Hodges,Johnny (as) | Procope,Russell (cl,as) | Hamilton,Jimmy (cl,ts) | Gonsalves,Paul (ts) | Carney,Harry (cl,b-cl,bs) | Jones,Jimmie (p) | Hughart,Jim (b) | Tate,Grady (dr)
Ella Fitzgerald With The Jimmy Jones Trio
Goin' Out Of My Head | Lullaby Of Birdland | Moment Of Truth | Misty
Fitzgerald,Ella (voc) | Jones,Jimmie (p) | Hughart,Jim (b) | Tate,Grady (dr)
So Danco Samba(I Only Dance The Samba)
Fitzgerald,Ella (voc) | Jones,Jimmie (p) | Hughart,Jim (b) | Tate,Grady (dr) | Cooper,Frank 'Buster' (claves) | Connors,Chuck (maracas)
Duke Ellington And His Orchestra
The Trip | Jim Jam | All Too Soon | The Old Circus Train Turn-Around Blues
Anderson,Cat (tp) | Jones,Herbie (tp) | Ellington,Mercer (tp) | Nance,Ray (v,co) | Brown,Lawrence (tb) | Cooper,Frank 'Buster' (tb) | Connors,Chuck (b-tb) | Hodges,Johnny (as) | Procope,Russell (cl,as) | Hamilton,Jimmy (cl,ts) | Webster,Ben (ts) | Gonsalves,Paul (ts) | Carney,Harry (cl,b-cl,bs) | Ellington,Duke (p) | Lamb,John (b) | Woodyard,Sam (dr)
Ella Fitzgerald With The Duke Ellington Orchestra
It Don't Mean A Thing If It Ain't Got That Swing
Fitzgerald,Ella (voc) | Anderson,Cat (tp) | Jones,Herbie (tp) | Ellington,Mercer (tp) | Nance,Ray (co,voc) | Brown,Lawrence (tb) | Cooper,Frank 'Buster' (tb) | Connors,Chuck (tb) | Hamilton,Jimmy (cl,ts) | Procope,Russell (as) | Gonsalves,Paul (ts) | Carney,Harry (bs) | Ellington,Duke (p) | Lamb,John (b) | Woodyard,Sam (dr) | Jones,Jo (dr)
Just Squeeze Me(But Don't Tease Me)
Fitzgerald,Ella (voc) | Ellington,Duke (p) | Gonsalves,Paul (ts) | Webster,Ben (ts) | Lamb,John (b) | Woodyard,Sam (dr) | Nance,Ray (voc)
Duke Ellington And His Orchestra
The Old Circus Train Turn-Around Blues(rehersal) | Blue Fuse No.1(rehersal) | Blue Fuse No.2(rehersal) | The Shepherd(rehersal)
Juan Les Pins,France, rec. 26.-29.7.1966
Ellington,Duke (p) | Williams,Cootie (tp) | Anderson,Cat (tp) | Jones,Herbie (tp) | Ellington,Mercer (tp) | Bascomb,Dud (tp) | Brown,Lawrence (tb) | Cooper,Frank 'Buster' (tb) | Connors,Chuck (tb) | Hamilton,Jimmy (cl,ts) | Hodges,Johnny (as) | Procope,Russell (as) | Gonsalves,Paul (ts) | Carney,Harry (bs) | Lamb,John (b) | Woodyard,Sam (dr)

539048-2 | CD | Porgy And Bess
Joe Henderson Group
Introduction- | Jasbo Brown Blues-
NYC, rec. 25.-28.5.1997
Herwig,Conrad (tb) | Scofield,John (el-g) | Harris,Stefon (vib) | Flanagan,Tommy (p) | Holland,Dave (b) | DeJohnette,Jack (dr)
Summertime
Henderson,Joe (ts) | Herwig,Conrad (tb) | Scofield,John (el-g) | Harris,Stefon (vib) | Flanagan,Tommy (p) | Holland,Dave (b) | DeJohnette,Jack (dr) | Khan,Chaka (voc)
Here Comes De Honey Man- | They Pass By Singin'- | My Man's Gone Now | I Got Plenty O'Nuttin' | Oh Bess Where's My Bess | Summertime(Samba Version)
Henderson,Joe (ts) | Herwig,Conrad (tb) | Scofield,John (el-g) | Harris,Stefon (vib) | Flanagan,Tommy (p) | Holland,Dave (b) | DeJohnette,Jack (dr)
It Ain't Necessarily So
Henderson,Joe (ts) | Herwig,Conrad (tb) | Scofield,John (el-g) | Harris,Stefon (vib) | Flanagan,Tommy (p) | Holland,Dave (b) | DeJohnette,Jack (dr) | Sting (voc)
There's A Boat Dat's Leavin' Soon For New York
Henderson,Joe (ts) | Herwig,Conrad (tb) | Scofield,John (el-g) | Harris,Stefon (vib) | Holland,Dave (b) | DeJohnette,Jack (dr)
I Loves You Porgy
Henderson,Joe (ts) | Scofield,John (el-g) | Flanagan,Tommy (p) | Holland,Dave (b) | DeJohnette,Jack (dr)
Bess You Is My Woman Now
Henderson,Joe (ts) | Flanagan,Tommy (p)

539055-2 | 2 CD | The Complete Gerry Mulligan Meets Ben Webster Sessions
Gerry Mulligan-Ben Webster Quintet
Chelsea Bridge | Chelsea Bridge(alt.take) | Go Home | Go Home(alt.take) | Go Home(incompl.take 1) | Go Home(incompl.take 2) | Who's Got Rhythm
Los Angeles,CA, rec. 3.11.1959
Webster,Ben (ts) | Mulligan,Gerry (bs) | Rowles,Jimmy (p) | Vinnegar,Leroy (b) | Lewis,Mel (dr)
Tell Me When | Tell Me When(alt.take) | The Cat Walk | The Cat Walk(alt.take 1) | The Cat Walk(alt.take 2) | The Cat Walk(alt.take 3) | Sunday | Sunday(alt.take) | In A Mellow Tone | In A Mellow Tone(alt.take) | What Is This Thing Called Love | For Bessie | Fajista | Fajista(alt.take) | Fajista(incompl.take 1) | Fajista(incompl.take 2) | Blues In B Flat | Blues In B Flat(alt.take) | Blues In B Flat(incompl.take)
Los Angeles,CA, rec. 2.12.1959
Webster,Ben (ts) | Mulligan,Gerry (bs) | Rowles,Jimmy (p) | Vinnegar,Leroy (b) | Lewis,Mel (dr)

539056-2 | CD | Songs For Distingué Lovers
Billie Holiday And Her All Stars
A Foggy Day(In London Town) | I Wished On The Moon | Moonlight In Vermont
Los Angeles,CA, rec. 3.1.1957
Holiday,Billie (voc) | Edison,Harry 'Sweets' (tp) | Webster,Ben (ts) | Rowles,Jimmy (p) | Kessel,Barney (g) | Mitchell,Red (b) | Stoller,Alvin (dr)
I Didn't Know What Time It Was | Just One Of Those Things
Los Angeles,CA, rec. 4.1.1957
Holiday,Billie (voc) | Edison,Harry 'Sweets' (tp) | Webster,Ben (ts) | Rowles,Jimmy (p) | Kessel,Barney (g) | Mitchell,Red (b) | Stoller,Alvin (dr)
Day In Day Out | Body And Soul
Los Angeles,CA, rec. 7.1.1957
Holiday,Billie (voc) | Edison,Harry 'Sweets' (tp) | Webster,Ben (ts) | Rowles,Jimmy (p) | Kessel,Barney (g) | Mitchell,Red (b) | Stoller,Alvin (dr)
Stars Fell On Alabama | One For My Baby(And One More For The Road) | Our Love Is Here To Stay
Los Angeles,CA, rec. 8.1.1957
Holiday,Billie (voc) | Edison,Harry 'Sweets' (tp) | Webster,Ben (ts) | Rowles,Jimmy (p) | Kessel,Barney (g) | Mondragon,Joe (b) | Bunker,Larry (dr)
They Can't Take That Away From Me | Let's Call The Whole Thing Off
Los Angeles,CA, rec. 9.1.1957
Holiday,Billie (voc) | Edison,Harry 'Sweets' (tp) | Webster,Ben (ts) | Rowles,Jimmy (p) | Kessel,Barney (g) | Mitchell,Red (b) | Bunker,Larry (dr)

539057-2 | CD | Ella Fitzgerald Sings The Johnny Mercer Songbook
Ella Fitzgerald With The Nelson Riddle Orchestra
Early Autumn | Trav'lin' Light | Dream
Hollywood,CA, rec. 19.10.1954
Fitzgerald,Ella (voc) | Lewis,Carroll (tp) | Mangano,Vito (tp) | Seaberg,George (tp) | Sherock,Shorty (tp) | Nash,Dick (tb) | Pederson,Pullman 'Tommy' (tb) | Shepard,Tom (tb) | Roberts,George (b-tb) | Cave,Jack (fr-h) | Decker,James 'Jimmy' (fr-h) | Hinshaw,William 'Bill' (fr-h) | Collette,Buddy (fl) | Klee,Harry (fl) | Benno,Norman (oboe) | Schoneberg,Seymour (oboe) | DeFranco,Buddy (cl) | Most,Abe (cl) | Smith,Willie (as) | Johnson,Plas (ts) | Russin,Irving 'Babe' (ts) | Hildebrandt,Lloyd (bs) | Terry,Howard (bs) | Schwartz,Wilbur (reeds) | Koch,Joe (reeds) | Julyie,Katharine 'Kathryn' (harp) | Smith,Paul (p) | Kessel,Barney (g) | Comfort,Joe (b) | Cottler,Irv (dr) | Radocchia,Emil (perc) | Riddle,Nelson (cond,arr)
Too Marvelous For Words | Laura | Something's Gotta Give | I Remember | When A Woman Loves A Man
Hollywood,CA, rec. 21.10.1954
Fitzgerald,Ella (voc) | Lewis,Carroll (tp) | Mangano,Vito (tp) | Seaberg,George (tp) | Sherock,Shorty (tp) | Bernhart,Milton 'Milt' (tb) | Pederson,Pullman 'Tommy' (tb) | Shepard,Tom (tb) | Roberts,George (b-tb) | Cave,Jack (fr-h) | Decker,James 'Jimmy' (fr-h) | Hinshaw,William 'Bill' (fr-h) | Collette,Buddy (fl) | Klee,Harry (fl) | Benno,Norman (oboe) | Schoneberg,Seymour (oboe) | DeFranco,Buddy (cl) | Smith,George (cl) | Smith,Willie (as) | Johnson,Plas (ts) | Russin,Irving 'Babe' (ts) | Hildebrandt,Lloyd (bs) | Terry,Howard (bs) | Schwartz,Wilbur (reeds) | Koch,Joe (reeds) | Julyie,Katharine 'Kathryn' (harp) | Smith,Paul (p) | Kessel,Barney (g) | Comfort,Joe (b) | Cottler,Irv (dr) | Radocchia,Emil (perc) | Riddle,Nelson (cond,arr)
Day In Day Out | This Time The Dream's On Me | Skylark | Single 'O' | Midnight Sun
Hollywood,CA, rec. 20.10.1954
Fitzgerald,Ella (voc) | Lewis,Carroll (tp) | Mangano,Vito (tp) | Seaberg,George (tp) | Audino,Johnny (tp) | Bernhart,Milton 'Milt' (tb) | Falco,Gilbert (tb) | Shepard,Tom (tb) | Roberts,George (b-tb) | Perissi,Richard 'Dick' (fr-h) | Price,George (fr-h) | Hinshaw,William 'Bill' (fr-h) | Collette,Buddy (fl) | Klee,Harry (fl) | DeFranco,Buddy (cl) | Smith,George (cl) | Benno,Norman (oboe) | Schoneberg,Seymour (oboe) | Smith,Willie (as) | Cipriano,Gene (reeds) | Schwartz,Wilbur (reeds) | Koch,Joe (reeds) | Russin,Irving 'Babe' (ts) | Hildebrandt,Lloyd (bs) | Terry,Howard (bs) | Julyie,Katharine 'Kathryn' (harp) | Smith,Paul (p) | Bain,Bob (g) | Comfort,Joe (b) | Cottler,Irv (dr) | Flynn,Fred (perc) | Riddle,Nelson (cond,arr)

539058-2 | CD | Trio 64
Bill Evans Trio
Little Lulu | Little Lulu(alt.take 1) | Little Lulu(alt.take 2) | A Sleeping Bee | Always | Always(alt.take) | Always(incompl.take) | Santa Claus Is Coming To Town | I'll See You Again | I'll See You Again(alt.take) | I'll See You Again(incompl.take) | For Heaven's Sake | Dancing In The Dark | Everything Happens To Me | My Heart Stood Still | My Heart Stood Still(incompl.take)
NYC, rec. 18.12.1963
Evans,Bill (p) | Peacock,Gary (b) | Motian,Paul (dr)

539059-2 | CD | Ella And Basie
Ella Fitzgerald With The Count Basie Orchestra
Honeysuckle Rose | 'Deed I Do | Satin Doll | I'm Beginning To See The Light | On The Sunny Side Of The Street
NYC, rec. 15.7.1963
Fitzgerald,Ella (voc) | Basie,Count (p) | Newman,Joe (tp) | Al Aarons (tp) | Cohn[Cohen],Sonny (tp) | Rader,Don (tp) | Ricard,Fip (tp) | Coker,Henry (tb) | Mitchell,Grover (tb) | Powell,Benny (tb) | Green,Urbie (tb) | Royal,Marshall (cl,as) | Dixon,Eric (fl,ts) | Wess,Frank (fl,as,ts) | Foster,Frank (ts) | Fowlkes,Charlie (bs) | Green,Freddie (g) | Catlett,Buddy (b) | Payne,Sonny (dr) | Jones,Quincy (arr)

Into Each Life Some Rain Must Fall | Tea For Two | Shiny Stockings | My Last Affair | Ain't Misbehavin' | My Last Affair | My Last Affair(alt.take) | Robbin's Nest(incomplete take) | Robbin's Nest | Robbin's Nest(alt.take 1) | Robbin's Nest(alt.take 2)
NYC, rec. 16.7.1963
Fitzgerald,Ella (voc) | Basie,Count (p) | Newman,Joe (tp) | Al Aarons (tp) | Cohn[Cohen],Sonny (tp) | Rader,Don (tp) | Ricard,Fip (tp) | Coker,Henry (tb) | Mitchell,Grover (tb) | Powell,Benny (tb) | Green,Urbie (tb) | Royal,Marshall (cl,as) | Dixon,Eric (fl,ts) | Wess,Frank (fl,as,ts) | Foster,Frank (ts) | Fowlkes,Charlie (bs) | Green,Freddie (g) | Catlett,Buddy (b) | Payne,Sonny (dr) | Jones,Quincy (arr)
Ella Fitzgerald With The Count Basie Septet
Them There Eyes | Dream A Little Dream Of Me
Fitzgerald,Ella (voc) | Basie,Count (p) | Newman,Joe (tp) | Green,Urbie (tb) | Foster,Frank (ts) | Green,Freddie (g) | Catlett,Buddy (b) | Payne,Sonny (dr)

539060-2 | CD | Louis Armstrong Meets Oscar Peterson
Louis Armstrong With The Oscar Peterson Quartet
That Old Feeling | Let's Fall In Love | I'll Never Be The Same | Blues In The Night | How Long Has This Been Going On | I Was Doing Alright | What's New? | Moon Song | Just One Of Those Things | There's No You | You Go To My Head | Sweet Lorraine
Chicago,Ill, rec. 14.10.1957
Armstrong,Louis (tp,voc) | Peterson,Oscar (p) | Ellis,Herb (g) | Brown,Ray (b) | Bellson,Louie (dr)
I Get A Kick Out Of You | Makin' Whoopee | Willow Weep For Me | Let's Do It(Let's Fall In Love)
Los Angeles,CA, rec. 31.7.1957
Armstrong,Louis (tp,voc) | Peterson,Oscar (p) | Ellis,Herb (g) | Brown,Ray (b) | Bellson,Louie (dr)

539062-2 | CD | Bumpin'
Wes Montgomery With The Don Sebesky Orchestra
Here's That Rainy Day | Misty | Just Walkin' | Just Walkin'(alt.take)
Englewood Cliffs,NJ, rec. 16.5.1965
Montgomery,Wes (g) | Kellaway,Roger (p) | Eidus,Arnold (v) | Eley,Lewis (v) | Gershman,Paul (v) | Haber,Louis (v) | Held,Julius (v) | Lookofsky,Harry (v) | Malignaggi,Joseph (v) | Orloff,Gene (v) | Shapiro,Sol (v) | Coletta,Harold (viola) | Schwartz,David (viola) | McCracken,Charles (cello) | Ricci,George (cello) | Cranshaw,Bob (b) | Ross,Margaret (harp) | Candido[Camero] (congas,bongos) | Tate,Grady (dr) | Sebesky,Don (cond,arr)
The Shadow Of Your Smile
Englewood Cliffs,NJ, rec. 18.5.1965
Montgomery,Wes (g) | Kellaway,Roger (p) | Eidus,Arnold (v) | Eley,Lewis (v) | Gershman,Paul (v) | Haber,Louis (v) | Held,Julius (v) | Lookofsky,Harry (v) | Malignaggi,Joseph (v) | Orloff,Gene (v) | Shapiro,Sol (v) | Coletta,Harold (viola) | Schwartz,David (viola) | McCracken,Charles (cello) | Ricci,George (cello) | Cranshaw,Bob (b) | Ross,Margaret (harp) | Candido[Camero] (congas,bongos) | Tate,Grady (dr) | Sebesky,Don (cond,arr)
A Quiet Thing | Con Affetto
Englewood Cliffs,NJ, rec. 19.5.1965
Montgomery,Wes (g) | Kellaway,Roger (p) | Eidus,Arnold (v) | Eley,Lewis (v) | Gershman,Paul (v) | Haber,Louis (v) | Held,Julius (v) | Lookofsky,Harry (v) | Malignaggi,Joseph (v) | Orloff,Gene (v) | Shapiro,Sol (v) | Coletta,Harold (viola) | Schwartz,David (viola) | McCracken,Charles (cello) | Ricci,George (cello) | Cranshaw,Bob (b) | Ross,Margaret (harp) | Candido[Camero] (congas,bongos) | Milito,Helcio (dr) | Sebesky,Don (cond,arr)
Bumpin' | My One And Only Love
Englewood Cliffs,NJ, rec. 20.5.1965
Montgomery,Wes (g) | Kellaway,Roger (p) | Eidus,Arnold (v) | Eley,Lewis (v) | Gershman,Paul (v) | Haber,Louis (v) | Held,Julius (v) | Lookofsky,Harry (v) | Malignaggi,Joseph (v) | Orloff,Gene (v) | Shapiro,Sol (v) | Coletta,Harold (viola) | Schwartz,David (viola) | McCracken,Charles (cello) | Ricci,George (cello) | Cranshaw,Bob (b) | Ross,Margaret (harp) | Candido[Camero] (congas,bongos) | Tate,Grady (dr) | Sebesky,Don (cond,arr)
Mi Cosa
Montgomery,Wes (g) | Eidus,Arnold (v) | Eley,Lewis (v) | Gershman,Paul (v) | Haber,Louis (v) | Held,Julius (v) | Lookofsky,Harry (v) | Malignaggi,Joseph (v) | Orloff,Gene (v) | Shapiro,Sol (v) | Coletta,Harold (viola) | Schwartz,David (viola) | McCracken,Charles (cello) | Ricci,George (cello) | Cranshaw,Bob (b) | Ross,Margaret (harp) | Candido[Camero] (congas,bongos) | Sebesky,Don (cond,arr)
Wes Montgomery Quartet
Tear It Down
Englewood Cliffs,NJ, rec. 18.5.1965
Montgomery,Wes (g) | Kellaway,Roger (p) | Cranshaw,Bob (b) | Tate,Grady (dr)

539063-2 | CD | The Trio:Live From Chicago
Oscar Peterson Trio
I've Never Been In Love Before | In The Wee Small Hours Of The Morning | Chicago | The Night We Called It A Day | Sometimes I'm Happy | Whisper Not | Billy Boy | The Lonesome One | The Gravy Waltz | Woody'n You | Soon | Daahoud
Live at The London House,Chicago,Ill., rec. July 1961
Peterson,Oscar (p) | Brown,Ray (b) | Thigpen,Ed (dr)

539065-2 | CD | The Genius Of Coleman Hawkins
Coleman Hawkins With The Oscar Peterson Quartet
I'll Never Be The Same | You're Blasé | I Wished On The Moon | How Long Has This Been Going On | Like Someone In Love | My Melancholy Baby | Ill Wind | In A Mellow Tone | There's No You | The World Is Waiting For The Sunrise | Somebody Loves Me | Blues For René | Begin The Beguine | I Never Had A Chance(alt.take) | I Wished On The Moon(alt.take) | Like Someone In Love(alt.take) | Ill Wind(alt. take) | In A Mellow Tone(alt.take) | There's No You(alt.take) | Blues For René(alt.take)
Los Angeles,CA, rec. 16.10.1957
Hawkins,Coleman (ts) | Peterson,Oscar (p) | Ellis,Herb (g) | Brown,Ray (b) | Stoller,Alvin (dr)

539102-2 | CD | Dear Ella
Dee Dee Bridgewater With Big Band
A-Tisket A-Tasket | Undecided | Mr.Paganini | Cotton Tail | Oh! Lady Be Good
NYC, rec. 1./2.2.1997
Bridgewater,Dee Dee (voc) | Stripling,Byron (tp) | Tooley,Ron (tp) | Jones,Virgil (tp) | Urcola,Diego (tp) | Trowers,Robert (tb) | Banks,Clarence (tb) | Powell,Benny (tb) | Purviance,Don (b-tb) | Clayton,Jeff (as) | Hart,Antonio Maurice (as) | Easley,Bill (ts) | Avery,Teodross (ts) | Higgins,Patience (bs) | Levy,Lou (p) | Brown,Ray (b) | Tate,Grady (dr)
Dee Dee Bridgewater With Orchestra
Midnight Sun | Let's Do It | My Heart Belongs To Daddy | Stairway To The Stars
Los Angeles,CA, rec. 29.-30.1./6.18.& 19.2.1997
Bridgewater,Dee Dee (voc) | Levy,Lou (p) | Brown,Ray (b) | Ceccarelli,André (dr) | Winn,R. (fl) | Taylor,R. (fl) | Morgan,Richard (oboe) | Kelly,T. (cl) | Jowitt,R. (cl) | Wallbank,A. (b-cl) | Pignegny,John (fr-h) | Bissill,Richard (fr-h) | Grey,D. (fr-h) | Lloyd,Frank (fr-h) | Anderson,J. (tuba) | Kanga,Skaila (harp) | Rothstein,Jack (v) | Nolan,D. (v) | Ronayne,John (v) | Bradburry,J. (v) | Bunt,Belinda (v) | Georgiadis,J. (v) | Williams,Trevor (v) | Archer,Jim (v) | Oxer,P. (v) | Solomon,D. (v) | Solodchin,Galina (v) | Manning,P. (v) | Benson,Peter (v) | Cummings,Diana (v) | Jackson,G. (viola) | Essex,Kenneth (viola) | Underwood,John (viola) | Hawkins,Brian (viola) | Turnland,George (viola) | Graham,John (viola) | Harvey,Keith (cello) | Pleeth,Anthony (cello) | Willison,P. (cello) | Cummings,Diana (cello) | Laurence,Chris (b) | McTier,D. (b) | Ricotti,Frank (perc) | Hakin,A. (perc)
Dee Dee Bridgewater With Her Septet
How High The Moon
Los Angeles,CA, rec. 1./2.2.1997
Bridgewater,Dee Dee (voc) | Bridgewater,Cecil (tp) | Hampton,Slide (tb) | Hart,Antonio Maurice (as) | Jackson,Milt (vib) | Levy,Lou (p) | Brown,Ray (b) | Tate,Grady (dr)
Dee Dee Bridgewater With Her Trio
Mack The Knife(Moritat) | Slow Boat To China | Mack The Knife(Moritat-deutsch gesungen)
Los Angeles,CA, rec. 29./30.1.1997
Bridgewater,Dee Dee (voc) | Levy,Lou (p) | Brown,Ray (b) | Ceccarelli,André (dr)
Dee Dee Bridgewater-Kenny Burrell
Dear Ella
Bridgewater,Dee Dee (voc) | Burrell,Kenny (g)

539153-2 | CD | The Heart Of Things
John McLaughlin Group
Seven Sisters | Mr.D.C. | Fallen Angels | Healing Hands | When Love Is Far Away
Milano,Italy, rec. details unknown
McLaughlin,John (g,el-g,midi-g) | Thomas,Gary (fl,ss,ts) | Beard,Jim (p,synth) | Garrison,Matthew (b-g,fretles-b-g) | Chambers,Dennis (dr)
Acid Jazz
McLaughlin,John (g,el-g,midi-g) | Thomas,Gary (fl,ss,ts) | Beard,Jim (p,synth) | Celea,Jean-Paul (b) | Garrison,Matthew (b-g,fretles-b-g) | Chambers,Dennis (dr) | Williams,Victor (perc)

539299-2 | CD | The Sound Of Summer Running
Marc Johnson Group
Faith On You | Ghost Town | Summer Running | With My Boots On | Union Pacific | Porch Swing | Dingy-Dong Day | The Adventures Of Max And Ben | In A Quiet Place | For A Thousand Years
NYC, rec. 1997
Johnson,Marc (b) | Frisell,Bill (g,el-g) | Metheny,Pat (g,el-g,42-string-pikasso-g) | Baron,Joey (dr,tambourine)

539753-2 | CD | West Side Story
Oscar Peterson Trio
Something's Coming | Somewhere | Jet Song | Tonight | Maria | I Feel Pretty | Reprise
NYC, rec. 24./25.1.1962
Peterson,Oscar (p) | Brown,Ray (b) | Thigpen,Ed (dr)

539756-2 | CD | The Cat
Jimmy Smith With The Lalo Schifrin Orchestra
Theme From'Joy House' | Main Title From 'The Carpetbaggers' | Delon's Blues
Englewood Cliffs,NJ, rec. 27.4.1964
Smith,Jimmy (org) | Royal,Ernie (tp) | Glow,Bernie (tp) | Maxwell,Jimmy (tp) | Markowitz,Irving 'Marky' (tp) | Young,Eugene 'Snooky' (tp) | Jones,Thad (tp) | Cleveland,Jimmy (tb) | Green,Urbie (tb) | Studd,Tony (b-tb) | Alonge,Ray (fr-h) | Buffington,Jimmy (fr-h) | Chapin,Earl (fr-h) | Correa,Bill (fr-h) | Butterfield,Billy (tp) | Burrell,Kenny (g) | Duvivier,George (b) | Tate,Grady (dr) | Kraus,Phil (perc) | Schifrin,Lalo (cond,arr)
The Cat | Basin Street Blues | Chicago Serenade | St.Louis Blues | Blues In The Night
Englewood Cliffs,NJ, rec. 29.4.1964
Smith,Jimmy (org) | Royal,Ernie (tp) | Glow,Bernie (tp) | Maxwell,Jimmy (tp) | Markowitz,Irving 'Marky' (tp) | Young,Eugene 'Snooky' (tp) | Jones,Thad (tp) | Cleveland,Jimmy (tb) | Green,Urbie (tb) | Studd,Tony (b-tb) | Alonge,Ray (fr-h) | Buffington,Jimmy (fr-h) | Chapin,Earl (fr-h) | Correa,Bill (fr-h) | Butterfield,Billy (tp) | Burrell,Kenny (g) | Duvivier,George (b) | Tate,Grady (dr) | Kraus,Phil (perc) | Schifrin,Lalo (cond,arr)

539757-2 | CD | Charlie Parker
Charlie Parker Quartet
Now's The Time | I Remember You | Confirmation | Chi Chi | Chi Chi(alt.take 1) | Chi Chi(alt.take 2) | Chi Chi(alt.take 3) | Confirmation(2 false starts) | Chi Chi(2 false starts)
NYC, rec. 30.7.1953
Parker,Charlie (as) | Haig,Al (p) | Heath,Percy (b) | Roach,Max (dr)
The Song Is You | Laird Baird | Kim | Cosmic Rays | Kim(alt.take) | Cosmic Rays(alt.take)
NYC, rec. December 1952/January 1953
Parker,Charlie (as) | Jones,Hank (p) | Kotick,Teddy (b) | Roach,Max (dr)
Star Eyes | Blues(fast) | I'm In The Mood For Love
NYC, rec. March/April 1950
Parker,Charlie (as) | Jones,Hank (p) | Brown,Ray (b) | Rich,Buddy (dr)
The Bird
Live at Carnegie Hall,NYC, rec. December 1947
Parker,Charlie (as) | Jones,Hank (p) | Brown,Ray (b) | Manne,Shelly (dr)
Celebrity
NYC, rec. Fall 1950
Parker,Charlie (as) | Jones,Hank (p) | Brown,Ray (b) | Rich,Buddy (dr)
Charlie Parker Quintet
Ballade
Parker,Charlie (as) | Hawkins,Coleman (ts) | Jones,Hank (p) | Brown,Ray (b) | Rich,Buddy (dr)
Charlie Parker Septet
Cardboard | Visa
NYC
Parker,Charlie (as) | Dorham,Kenny (tp) | Turk,Tommy (tb) | Haig,Al (p) | Potter,Tommy (b) | Roach,Max (dr) | Vidal,Carlos (congas)

539758-2 | CD | At The Montreux Jazz Festival
Bill Evans Trio
Spoken Introduction | One For Helen | A Sleeping Bee | Mother Of Earl | Nardis | The Touch Of Your Lips | Embraceable You | Someday My Prince Will Come | Walkin' Up
Live at The Montreux Jazz Festival, rec. 15.6.1968
Evans,Bill (p) | Gomez,Eddie (b) | DeJohnette,Jack (dr)
Bill Evans
I Loves You Porgy | Quiet Now
Live at The Monterey Jazz Festival,CA, rec. 15.6.1968
Evans,Bill (p-solo)

539785-2 | CD | Soul Call
Duke Ellington And His Orchestra
Caravan
Juan Les Pins,France, rec. 26.7.1966
Ellington,Duke (p,ld) | Anderson,Cat (tp) | Ellington,Mercer (tp) | Jones,Herbie (tp) | Williams,Cootie (tp) | Brown,Lawrence (tb) | Cooper,Frank 'Buster' (tb) | Connors,Chuck (b-tb) | Hodges,Johnny (as) | Procope,Russell (cl,as) | Hamilton,Jimmy (cl,ts) | Gonsalves,Paul (ts) | Carney,Harry (cl,as,bs) | Lamb,John (b) | Woodyard,Sam (dr)
West Indian Pancake | Skin Deep | Jam With Sam | Sophisticated Lady | The Opener | Kinda Dukish- | Rockin' In Rhythm-
Juan Les Pins,France, rec. 27.7.1966
Ellington,Duke (p,ld) | Anderson,Cat (tp) | Ellington,Mercer (tp) | Jones,Herbie (tp) | Williams,Cootie (tp) | Brown,Lawrence (tb) | Cooper,Frank 'Buster' (tb) | Connors,Chuck (b-tb) | Hodges,Johnny (as) | Procope,Russell (cl,as) | Hamilton,Jimmy (cl,ts) | Gonsalves,Paul (ts) | Carney,Harry (cl,as,bs) | Lamb,John (b) | Woodyard,Sam (dr)
La Plus Belle Africaine | Such Sweet Thunder | Soul Call | Madness In Great Ones | Main Stem | Take The 'A' Train
Juan Les Pins,France, rec. 28.7.1966
Ellington,Duke (p,ld) | Anderson,Cat (tp) | Ellington,Mercer (tp) | Jones,Herbie (tp) | Williams,Cootie (tp) | Brown,Lawrence (tb) | Cooper,Frank 'Buster' (tb) | Connors,Chuck (b-tb) | Hodges,Johnny (as) | Procope,Russell (cl,as) | Hamilton,Jimmy (cl,ts) | Gonsalves,Paul (ts) | Carney,Harry (cl,as,bs) | Lamb,John (b) | Woodyard,Sam (dr)
Wings And Things
Juan Les Pins,France, rec. 29.7.1966
Ellington,Duke (p,ld) | Anderson,Cat (tp) | Ellington,Mercer (tp) | Jones,Herbie (tp) | Williams,Cootie (tp) | Brown,Lawrence (tb) | Cooper,Frank 'Buster' (claves) | Connors,Chuck (maracas) | Hodges,Johnny (as) | Procope,Russell (cl,as) | Hamilton,Jimmy (cl,ts) | Gonsalves,Paul (ts) | Carney,Harry (cl,as,bs) | Lamb,John (b) | Woodyard,Sam (dr) | Jones,Herbie (guiro)

539961-2 | CD | Night And The City
Charlie Haden-Kenny Barron
Twilight Song | For Heaven's Sake | Spring Is Here | Body And Soul | You Don't Know What Love Is | Waltz For Ruth | The Very Thought Of You
Live at The Iridium Jazz Club,NYC, rec. 20.-22.9.1996
Haden,Charlie (b) | Barron,Kenny (p)

539979-2 | CD | A Go Go
John Scofield Quartet
A Go Go | Chank | Boozer | Southern Pacific | Jeep On 35 | Kubrick | Green Tea | Hottentot | Chicken Dog | Deadzy
NYC, rec. details unknown
Scofield,John (g,el-g,whistle) | Medeski,John (p,org,clavinet,wurlitzer) | Wood,Chris (b,el-b) | Martin,Billy (dr,tambourine)

543042-2 | CD | The Enemies Of Energy
Kurt Rosenwinkel Quintet
The Enemies Og Enery | Grant | Cubism | Number Ten | The Polish Song | Point Of View | Christmas Song | Dream Of The Old | Synthetics | Hope And Fear
Brooklyn,NY, rec. 18.-20.11.1996
Rosenwinkel,Kurt (g,el-g,4-string-stella,voice) | Turner,Mark (ts) | Kinsey,Scott (p,keyboards) | Street,Ben (b) | Ballard,Jeff (dr)

543090-2 | CD | Monk's Dream
Steve Lacy-Roswell Rudd Quartet
Monk's Dream | The Bath | The Rent | Pannonia | Ko-Ko | Grey Blue | The Door
Paris,France, rec. 21./22.6.1999
Rudd,Roswell (tb) | Lacy,Steve (ss) | Avenel,Jean-Jacques (b) | Betsch,John (dr)
A Bright Pearl | Traces
Rudd,Roswell (tb) | Lacy,Steve (ss) | Avenel,Jean-Jacques (b) | Betsch,John (dr) | Aebi,Irene (voice)

543180-2 | CD | Spirit Song
Kenny Barron Group
The Pelican | Passion Dance | Sonja Braga | The Question Is | Cook's Bay
Brooklyn,NY, rec. 16./17.5.1999
Barron,Kenny (p) | Henderson,Eddie (tp) | Sanchez,David (ts) | Reid,Rufus (b) | Hart,Billy (dr)
Um Beijo(A Kiss) | Passion Flower
Barron,Kenny (p) | Henderson,Eddie (tp) | Sanchez,David (ts) | Carter,Regina (v) | Reid,Rufus (b) | Hart,Billy (dr)
The Wizard | And Then Again
Barron,Kenny (p) | Henderson,Eddie (tp) | Sanchez,David (ts) | Malone,Russell (g) | Reid,Rufus (b) | Hart,Billy (dr)
Spirit Song
Barron,Kenny (p) | Henderson,Eddie (tp) | Sanchez,David (ts) | Malone,Russell (g) | Reid,Rufus (b) | Hart,Billy (dr) | Grisby,Michael Wall (perc)

543256-2 | CD | Spirit! The Power Of Music | EAN 731454325622
Randy Weston African Rhythm Quintet and The Gnawa Master Musicians of Marocco
Receiving The Spirit | Introduction To Hag'Houge And String Bass | Chalabati | Who Knows Them? | El Wali Sidi Mimoun | Lalla Mira | Lalla Mira(part 2)
Brooklyn,NY, rec. 24.9.2000
Weston,Randy (p) | Powell,Benny (tb) | Kibwe,Talib (fl,as) | Blake,Alex (b) | Clarke,Neil (perc) | Othman,M'Barek Ben (karkaba,tbil,voc) | Othman,Ahmed Ben (karkaba,dancer,voc) | Saassaa.Ahmed (hag'houge,voc) | El Gourd,Addellah (hag'houge,voc) | Oubella,Abdemedi (karkaba,dancer,voc) | Oubella,Mostafa (karkaba,dancer,voc)

543300-2 | CD | What A Diff'rence A Day Makes!
Dinah Washington With The Belford Hendricks Orchestra
I Remember You | Nothing In The World(Could Make Me Love You More Than I Do) | Manhattan
NYC, rec. 1959
Washington,Dinah (voc) | Richardson,Jerome (fl) | Burrell,Kenny (g) | Zawinul,Joe (p) | Francis,Panama (dr) | Orchestra | details unknown | Hendricks,Belford (arr,ld)
I Thought About You | That's All There Is To That | I'm Thru With Love | Cry Me A River | Time After Time | It's Magic | A Sunday Kind Of Love | It Could Happen To You
Washington,Dinah (voc) | Zawinul,Joe (p) | Francis,Panama (dr) | Orchestra | details unknown | Hendricks,Belford (arr,ld)
I Won't Cry Anymore | What A Difference A Day Made | Time After Time(first version) | Come On Home
Washington,Dinah (voc) | Richardson,Jerome (sax) | Davis,Charles (bs) | Burrell,Kenny (g) | Zawinul,Joe (p) | Hinton,Milt (b) | Francis,Panama (dr) | Strings | Hendricks,Belford (arr,ld) | details unknown

543301-2 | CD | Laughin' To Keep From Cryin'
Lester Young Septet
Salute To Benny | They Can't Take That Away From Me | Romping | Gypsy In My Soul | Please Don't Talk About Me When I'm Gone | Ballad Medley: | The Very Thought Of You- | I Want A Little Girl- | Blue And Sentimental- | Mean To Me
NYC, rec. 8.2.1958
Young,Lester (cl,ts) | Eldridge,Roy (tp) | Edison,Harry 'Sweets' (tp) | Ellis,Herb (g) | Jones,Hank (p) | Duvivier,George (b) | Sheen,Mickey (dr)

543304-2 | CD | Ella And Louis
589598-2 SACD | SACD | Ella And Louis | EAN 731458959823
Ella Fitzgerald And Louis Armstrong With The Oscar Peterson Quartet
Can't We Be Friends | Isn't It A Lovely Day | Moonlight In Vermont | They Can't Take That Away From Me | Under A Blanket Of Blue | Tenderly | A Foggy Day(In London Town) | Stars Fell On Alabama | Cheek To Cheek | The Nearness Of You | April In Paris
Hollywood,CA, rec. 16.8.1956
Fitzgerald,Ella (voc) | Armstrong,Louis (tp,voc) | Peterson,Oscar (p) | Ellis,Herb (g) | Brown,Ray (b) | Rich,Buddy (dr)

543305-2 | CD | Sarah Vaughan
Sarah Vaughan With The Clifford Brown All Stars
Lullaby Of Birdland | You're Not The Kind | I'm Glad There Is You | September Song | Lullaby Of Birdland(alt.take)
NYC, rec. 16.12.1954
Vaughan,Sarah (voc) | Brown,Clifford (tp) | Mann,Herbie (fl) | Quinichette,Paul (ts) | Jones,Jimmy (p) | Benjamin,Joe (b) | Haynes,Roy (dr) | Wilkins,Rick (cond,arr)
April In Paris | He's My Guy | Jim | It's Crazy
NYC, rec. 18.12.1954
Vaughan,Sarah (voc) | Brown,Clifford (tp) | Mann,Herbie (fl) | Quinichette,Paul (ts) | Jones,Jimmy (p) | Benjamin,Joe (b) | Haynes,Roy (dr) | Wilkins,Rick (cond,arr)
Sarah Vaughan With The Jimmy Jones Trio
Embraceable You
Vaughan,Sarah (voc) | Jones,Jimmy (p) | Benjamin,Joe (b) | Haynes,Roy (dr)

543306-2 | CD | Clifford Brown And Max Roach
Clifford Brown-Max Roach Quintet
Delilah | Parisian Thoroughfare
Hollywood,CA, rec. 2.8.1954
Brown,Clifford (tp) | Land,Harold (ts) | Powell,Richie (p) | Morrow,George (b) | Roach,Max (dr)
Jordu
Hollywood,CA, rec. 3.8.1954
Brown,Clifford (tp) | Land,Harold (ts) | Powell,Richie (p) | Morrow,George (b) | Roach,Max (dr)
Daahoud | Joy Spring | Daahoud(alt.take) | Joyspring(alt.take)
Hollywood,CA, rec. 6.8.1954
Brown,Clifford (tp) | Land,Harold (ts) | Powell,Richie (p) | Morrow,George (b) | Roach,Max (dr)
The Blues Walk | What Am I Here For | The Blues Walk(alt.take)
NYC, rec. 24.2.1955
Brown,Clifford (tp) | Land,Harold (ts) | Powell,Richie (p) | Morrow,George (b) | Roach,Max (dr)

Max Roach Trio
These Foolish Things Remind Me On You
Hollywood,CA, rec. 6.8.1954
Roach,Max (dr) | Powell,Richie (p) | Morrow,George (b)

543320-2 | CD | Award Winner
Stan Getz Quartet
Where Or When | Woody'n You | Smiles | Three Little Words | Time After Time | This Can't Be Love | All God's Chillun Got Rhythm | But Beautiful | Woody'n You(alt.take) | Time After Time(alt.take) | All God's Chillun Got Rhythm(false start) | Smiles(false start) | Time After Time(2 false start) | Woody'n You(false start) | Woody'n You(inserts)
Hollywood,CA, rec. 2.8.1957
Getz,Stan (ts) | Levy,Lou (p) | Vinnegar,Leroy (b) | Levey,Stan (dr)

543321-2 | CD | The Sound Of The Trio
Oscar Peterson Trio
Tricotism | On Green Dolphin Street | Thag's Dance | Ill Wind | Kadota's Blues | Scrapple From The Apple | Jim | Band Call | The Night We Called It A Day | Billy Boy
Live at The London House,Chicago,Ill., rec. 27.7.-6.8.1961
Peterson,Oscar (p) | Brown,Ray (b) | Thigpen,Ed (dr)

543354-2 | CD | Live At Yoshi's | EAN 731454335423
Dee Dee Bridgewater With Her Trio
Undecided | Slow Boat To China | Stairway To The Stars | What A Little Moonlight Can Do | Sex Machine | Midnight Sun | Cherokee | Love For Sale | Cotton Tail
Live at Yoshi's Night Club,Oakland,CA, rec. 23.-25.4.1998
Bridgewater,Dee Dee (voc) | Eliez,Thierry (p,org) | Bramerie,Thomas (b) | Jackson,Ali 'Muhammed' (dr)

543477-2 | CD | Swing Is The Thing
Flip Phillips Quintet
I Hadn't Anyone 'Till You | Everything I Have Is Yours | Exactly Like You | Swing Is The Thing | For All We Know | Susan's Dream | Grand Rosé
NYC, rec. 12./13.10.1999
Phillips,Flip (ts) | Alden,Howard (g) | Green,Benny (p) | McBride,Christian (b) | Washington,Kenny (dr)

Flip Phillips Trio
Music Maestro Please
Phillips,Flip (ts) | Alden,Howard (g) | Green,Benny (p)

Flip Phillips-Christian McBride
In A Mellow Tone
Phillips,Flip (ts) | McBride,Christian (b)

Flip Phillips-Howard Alden
This Is All I Ask
Phillips,Flip (ts) | Alden,Howard (g)

Flip Phillips Sextet
Where Or When
Phillips,Flip (ts) | Carter,James (ts) | Alden,Howard (g) | Green,Benny (p) | McBride,Christian (b) | Washington,Kenny (dr)
Flip The Whip
Phillips,Flip (ts) | Lovano,Joe (ts) | Alden,Howard (g) | Green,Benny (p) | McBride,Christian (b) | Washington,Kenny (dr)

Flip Phillips Septet
The Mark Of Zoro(intro) | The Mark Of Zoro(outro)
Phillips,Flip (ts) | Carter,James (ts) | Lovano,Joe (ts) | Alden,Howard (g) | Green,Benny (p) | McBride,Christian (b) | Washington,Kenny (dr)

543487-2 | CD | From The Hot Afternoon
Paul Desmond Quartet With The Don Sebesby Orchestra
Outubro (October) | Gira Girou(Round 'N' Round) | Faithful Brother | To Say Goodbye | From The Hot Afternoon | Catavento | Canto Latino(Latin Chant) | Gira Girou(Round 'N' Round-alt.take) | Faithful Brother(alt.take) | From The Hot Afternoon(alt.take 1) | Catavento(alt.take) | Canto Latino(Latin Chant-alt.take) | From The Hot Afternoon(alt.take 2)
Englewood Cliffs,NJ, rec. 13./14.8.1969
Desmond,Paul (as) | Ferreira,Dorio (g) | Carter,Ron (b) | Moreira,Airto (dr,perc) | Markowitz,Irving 'Marky' (fl-h) | Stamm,Marvin (fl-h) | Faulise,Paul (b-tb) | Buffington,Jimmy (fr-h) | Hammond,Don (fl) | Laws,Hubert (fl) | Webb,Stanley (fl,alto-fl) | Bodner,Phil (cl,oboe,sax) | Marge,George (cl,oboe,sax) | Eley,Lewis (v) | Gershman,Paul (v) | Ockner,George (v) | Orloff,Gene (v) | Poliakin,Raoul (v) | Pollikoff,Max (v) | Raimondi,Matthew (v) | Shulman,Sylvan (v) | Weiss,Avram (v) | McCracken,Charles (cello) | Ricci,George (cello) | Ross,Margaret (harp) | Rebillot,Pat (p,el-p) | Jennings,Jack (perc) | Webb Jr.,Stan (perc) | De Sah,Wanda (voc) | Sebesky,Don (cond,arr)
Circles | Martha & Romao | Crystal Illusions
Desmond,Paul (as) | Lobo,Edu (g,voc) | Carter,Ron (b) | Moreira,Airto (dr,perc) | Markowitz,Irving 'Marky' (fl-h) | Stamm,Marvin (fl-h) | Faulise,Paul (b-tb) | Buffington,Jimmy (fr-h) | Hammond,Don (fl) | Laws,Hubert (fl) | Webb,Stanley (fl,alto-fl) | Bodner,Phil (cl,oboe,sax) | Marge,George (cl,oboe,sax) | Eley,Lewis (v) | Gershman,Paul (v) | Ockner,George (v) | Orloff,Gene (v) | Poliakin,Raoul (v) | Pollikoff,Max (v) | Raimondi,Matthew (v) | Shulman,Sylvan (v) | Weiss,Avram (v) | McCracken,Charles (cello) | Ricci,George (cello) | Ross,Margaret (harp) | Rebillot,Pat (p,el-p) | Jennings,Jack (perc) | Webb Jr.,Stan (perc) | De Sah,Wanda (voc) | Sebesky,Don (cond,arr)

543501-2 | CD | Live
Paul Desmond Quartet
Wendy | Wave | Things Ain't What They Used To Be | Nancy | Manha De Carnaval(Morning Of The Carnival) | Here's That Rainy Day | My Funny Valentine | Take Five | Line For Lyons
Toronto,Canada, rec. October/November 1975
Desmond,Paul (as) | Bickert,Ed (g) | Thompson,Don (b) | Fuller,Jerry (dr)

543534-2 | CD | The Roy Haynes Trio
Roy Haynes Trio
Wail | Question And Answer | Shulie A Bop | Dear Old Stockholm | It's Easy To Remember | Folk Song
NYC, rec. 23./24.11.1999
Haynes,Roy (dr) | Perez,Danilo (p) | Patitucci,John (b)
Sippin' At Bells | Bright Mississippi | Prelude To A Kiss | Green Chimneys
Live at Scullers Jazz Club,Boston,MA, rec. 10./11.9.1999
Haynes,Roy (dr) | Perez,Danilo (p) | Patitucci,John (b)

543536-2 | CD | Live In Paris
John McLaughlin Group
Seven Sisters | Mother Tongues | Fallen Angels | The Divide | Tony | Acid Jazz
Live at The Cigale,Paris,France, rec. 4./5.11.1998
McLaughlin,John (g) | Thomas,Gary (ss,ts) | Ruiz,Otmaro (p,keyboards) | Garrison,Matthew (el-b) | Chambers,Dennis (dr) | Williams,Victor (perc)

543543-2 | CD | Look Who's Here
Russell Malone Quartet
The Angle | Look Who's Here | Alfie | The Old Couple | Soulful Kisses | Get Out Of Town | You Will Know | The Heather On The Hill | An Affair To Remember | Be Careful It's My Heart
NYC, rec. 3.-5.5.1999
Malone,Russell (g,voc) | Wonsey,Athony (p) | Goods,Richie (b) | Landham,Byron (dr)

543747-2 | CD | I Love Jazz
Louis Armstrong And His All Stars
12th Street Rag
NYC, rec. 26.4.1950
Armstrong,Louis (tp) | Teagarden,Jack (tb) | Bigard,Barney (cl) | Hines,Earl 'Fatha' (p) | Shaw,Arvell (b) | Cole,William 'Cozy' (dr)
Tenderly- | You'll Never Walk Alone-
NYC, rec. 1.9.1954
Armstrong,Louis (tp,voc) | Young,Trummy (tb) | Bigard,Barney (cl) | Kyle,Billy (p) | Shaw,Arvell (b) | Deems,Barrett (dr)

Louis Armstrong And His Orchestra
Skokiaan(edited version without vocal)
NYC, rec. 13.8.1954
Armstrong,Louis (tp) | Jordan,Taft (tp) | Scott,William 'Chiefie'[Abdul Salaam] (tp) | Shavers,Charlie (tp) | Cobbs,Alfred (tb) | Crumbley,Elmer (tb) | Seiden,Paul (tb) | Bigard,Barney (cl) | Simeon,Omer (ss) | Martin,David (p) | Barker,Danny (g) | Shaw,Arvell (b) | Deems,Barrett (dr) | Oliver,Sy (arr)

Pretty Little Missy
NYC, rec. 25.4.1955
Armstrong,Louis (tp,voc) | Young,Trummy (tb,voc) | Bigard,Barney (cl,voc) | Kyle,Billy (p) | Shaw,Arvell (b) | Deems,Barrett (dr)
Frog-I-More
NYC, rec. 25.1.1957
Armstrong,Louis (tp) | Young,Trummy (tb) | Hall,Edmond (cl) | Kyle,Billy (p) | Barnes,George (g) | Gersh,Squire (b) | Deems,Barrett (dr)
Basin Street Blues | Otchi-Tchor-Ni-Ya
Hollywood,CA, rec. 8.10.1958
Armstrong,Louis (tp,voc) | Young,Trummy (tb) | Hucko,Peanuts (cl) | Miller,Eddie (ts) | Kyle,Billy (p) | Hendrickson,Al (g) | Herbert,Mort (b) | Barcelona,Danny (dr)
I Love Jazz | I Love Jazz(alt.take)
Armstrong,Louis (tp,voc) | Young,Trummy (tb) | Hucko,Peanuts (cl) | Miller,Eddie (ts) | Kyle,Billy (p) | Hendrickson,Al (g) | Herbert,Mort (b) | Barcelona,Danny (dr) | unkn. (voc-group)

543754-2 | CD | Giblet Gravy
George Benson Quintet
What's New? | Thunder Walk | Low Down And Dirty | Billie's Bounce | What's New?(alt.take 1) | What's New?(alt.take 2)
NYC, rec. 6.2.1968
Benson,George (g) | Hancock,Herbie (p) | Carter,Ron (b) | Cobham,Billy (dr) | Pacheco,Johnny (congas)

George Benson And His Orchestra
Along Came Mary
NYC, rec. 7.2.1968
Benson,George (g) | Royal,Ernie (tp) | Young,Eugene 'Snooky' (tp) | Owens,Jimmy (tp,fl-h) | Raph,Alan (b-tb) | Adams,Pepper (bs) | Lynch,Carl (g) | Carter,Ron (b) | Cobham,Billy (dr) | Pacheco,Johnny (congas) | McIntosh,Tom (cond,arr)
Groovin'
Benson,George (g) | Royal,Ernie (tp) | Young,Eugene 'Snooky' (tp) | Owens,Jimmy (tp,fl-h) | Raph,Alan (b-tb) | Adams,Pepper (bs) | Carter,Ron (b) | Cobham,Billy (dr) | Pacheco,Johnny (congas) | McIntosh,Tom (cond,arr)
Gilbet Gravy
NYC, rec. 5.2.1968
Benson,George (g) | Royal,Ernie (tp) | Young,Eugene 'Snooky' (tp) | Owens,Jimmy (tp,fl-h) | Raph,Alan (b-tb) | Adams,Pepper (bs) | Gale,Eric (g) | Cranshaw,Bob (b) | Cobham,Billy (dr) | Pacheco,Johnny (tambourine) | McIntosh,Tom (cond,arr)
Sack O'Woe
NYC, rec. 6.2.1968
Benson,George (g) | Royal,Ernie (tp) | Young,Eugene 'Snooky' (tp) | Owens,Jimmy (tp,fl-h) | Raph,Alan (b-tb) | Adams,Pepper (bs) | Gale,Eric (g) | Carter,Ron (b) | Cobham,Billy (dr) | Pacheco,Johnny (tambourine) | McIntosh,Tom (cond,arr)
Sunny | Walk On By
NYC, rec. 5.2.1968
Benson,George (g) | Owens,Jimmy (tp,fl-h) | Royal,Ernie (tp) | Young,Eugene 'Snooky' (tp) | Ralph,Alan (b-tb) | Adams,Pepper (bs) | Hancock,Herbie (p) | Gale,Eric (g) | Cranshaw,Bob (b) | Cobham,Billy (dr) | Gilbert,Eileen (voc) | Robinson,Albertine (voc) | Winter,Lois (voc)

543792-2 | CD | Satchmo Serenaders
Louis Armstrong With Sy Oliver And His Orchestra
Maybe It's Beacause | I'll Keep The Lovelight Burning(In My Heart)
Armstrong,Louis (tp,voc) | Clayton,Buck (tp) | Lloyd,Ivor (tp) | Chambers,Henderson (tb) | Baker,Artie (as) | Dorsey,George (as) | Johnson,Budd (ts) | Williams,Freddy (ts) | Henderson,Horace (p) | Barksdale,Everett (g) | Benjamin,Joe (b) | Bishop,Wallace (dr) | Oliver,Sy (cond,arr)
La Vie En Rose | C'Est Si Bon
NYC, rec. 26.6.1950
Armstrong,Louis (tp,voc) | Oliver,Sy (arr) | Solomon,Melvin (tp) | Privin,Bernie (tp) | Webster,Paul (tp) | Bullman,Morton (tb) | Schertzer,Hymie (as) | Yaner,Milt (as) | Drellinger,Art (ts) | Holcombe,Bill (ts) | Hines,Earl 'Fatha' (p) | Barksdale,Everett (g) | Duvivier,George (b) | Blowers,Johnny (dr)
I Get Ideas | A Kiss To Build A Dream On
NYC, rec. 24.6.1951
Armstrong,Louis (tp,voc) | Oliver,Sy (arr) | Cutshall,Cutty (tb) | Yaner,Milt (as) | Dorsey,George (as) | Williams,Freddy (ts) | Klink,Al (ts) | Kyle,Billy (p) | Block,Sandy (b) | Shawker,Norris 'Bunny' (dr)
Cold Cold Heart | Because Of You
NYC, rec. 17.9.1951
Armstrong,Louis (tp,voc) | Oliver,Sy (arr) | Holmes,Charlie (as) | Dorsey,George (as) | Clark,Harold (ts) | McRae,Dave (ts) | Abney,Don (p) | Barksdale,Everett (g) | Goodlette,Frank (b) | Parker,Jack 'The Bear' (dr)

Louis Armstrong And The Commanders under the Direction of Camarata
I Can't Afford To Miss This Dream | Someday You'll Be Sorry
NYC, rec. 22.10.1953
Armstrong,Louis (voc) | Camarata,Toots | Butterfield,Billy (tp) | Ferretti,Andy (tb) | Poole,Carl (tp) | McGarity,Lou (tb) | Cutshall,Cutty (tb) | Ciardina,Phil (tb) | Statterfield,Jack (tb) | Schertzer,Hymie (as) | Klink,Al (ts) | Leighton,Bernie (p) | Mastren,Carmen (g) | Block,Sandy (b) | Grady,Eddie (dr)

Louis Armstrong And His Orchestra
Ramona | April In Portugal
NYC, rec. 21.4.1953
Armstrong,Louis (tp) | Young,Trummy (tb) | Bigard,Barney (cl) | Yaner,Milt (as) | Jacobs,Dick (as) | Taylor,Sam 'The Man' (ts) | Bushkin,Joe (p) | Barksdale,Everett (g) | Shaw,Arvell (b) | Cole,William 'Cozy' (dr)

Louis Armstrong With Sy Oliver And His Orchestra
Takes Two To Tango | I Laughed At Love
NYC, rec. 25.8.1952
Armstrong,Louis (tp,voc) | Oliver,Sy (arr) | Schertzer,Hymie (cl,as) | Jacobs,Dick (cl,as) | Fresk,Livio 'Babe' (cl,ts) | Tax,Melvin (cl,ts) | Holcombe,Bill (bs) | Kyle,Billy (p) | Barksdale,Everett (g) | Benjamin,Joe (b) | Donaldson,Bobby (dr)
Congratulations To Someone | Your Cheatin' Heart
Detroit, rec. 23.2.1953
Armstrong,Louis (tp,voc) | Oliver,Sy (arr) | Young,Trummy (tb) | Bigard,Barney (cl) | Alois,Louis (as) | Van Deven,Everett (as) | Netting,Fred (ts) | Rozanoff,Abraham (bs) | Napoleon,Marty (p) | Rose,George (g) | Shaw,Arvell (b) | Cole,William 'Cozy' (dr)

Louis Armstrong And His All Stars
Kiss Of Fire | I'll Walk Alone
Denver,Colorado, rec. 19.4.1952
Armstrong,Louis (tp,voc) | Phillips,Russ (tb) | Bigard,Barney (cl) | Ruffell,Donald (ts) | Napoleon,Marty (p) | Jones,Duke (b) | Cole,William 'Cozy' (dr)

543795-2 | CD | My Kind Of Music
Mel Tormé With The Tony Osborne Orchestra
A Stranger In Town | Born To Be Blue | Dancing In The Dark
London,GB, rec. 18.7.1961
Tormé,Mel (voc) | Orchestra | Osborne,Tony (arr,cond) | details unknown

Mel Tormé With The Wally Stott Orchestra
I Guess I'll Have To Change My Plans | Country Fair | Welcome To The Club | The Christmas Song | Alone Together
London,GB, rec. 19.7.1961
Tormé,Mel (voc) | Orchestra | Scott,Wally (arr,cond) | details unknown

Mel Tormé With The Geoff Love Orchestra
You And The Night And The Music | By Myself | A Shine On Your Shoes
London,GB, rec. 21.7.1961
Tormé,Mel (voc) | Orchestra | Love,Geoff (arr,cond) | details unknown

543827-2 | CD | Sing A Song Of Basie
Lambert, Hendricks And Ross
It's Sand Man | Little Pony | Blues Backstage | Down For The Count
NYC, rec. 16.9.1957
Lambert,Hendricks & Ross | Lambert,Dave (voc) | Hendricks,Jon (voc) | Ross,Annie (voc) | Pierce,Nat (p) | Green,Freddie (g) | Jones,Eddie (b) | Payne,Sonny (dr)
Avenue C
NYC, rec. 11.10.1957
Lambert,Hendricks & Ross | Lambert,Dave (voc) | Hendricks,Jon (voc) | Ross,Annie (voc) | Pierce,Nat (p) | Green,Freddie (g) | Jones,Eddie (b) | Payne,Sonny (dr)
Down For Double | Fiesta In Blue | Two For The Blues | One O'Clock Jump | Everyday I Have The Blues
NYC, rec. 28.10.1957
Lambert,Hendricks & Ross | Lambert,Dave (voc) | Hendricks,Jon (voc) | Ross,Annie (voc) | Pierce,Nat (p) | Green,Freddie (g) | Jones,Eddie (b) | Payne,Sonny (dr)

John Hendricks WithThe Dave Lambert Singers
Cloudburst | Four Brothers | Standin' On The Corner(Whistlin' At The Pretty Girls)
NYC, rec. 12.5.1955
Hendricks,Jon (voc,whistling) | Lambert,Dave (voc) | Dave Lambert Singers,The | unkn. (g,p,b,dr)

543828-2 | CD | Introducing Nat Adderley | EAN 731454382823
Nat Adderley Quintet
Watermelon | Little Joanie Walks | Two Brothers | I Should Care | Crazy Baby | New Arrivals | Sun Dance | Fort Lauderdale | Friday Nite | Blues For Bohemia
NYC, rec. 6.9.1955
Adderley,Nat (co) | Adderley,Julian \'Cannonball\' (as) | Silver,Horace (p) | Chambers,Paul (b) | Haynes,Roy (dr)

543829-2 | CD | Blue Moon
Carmen McRae With The Tadd Dameron Orchestra
Blue Moon | I Was Doing Alright | I'm Putting All My Eggs In One Basket | Nowhere
NYC, rec. 28.3.1956
McRae,Carmen (voc) | Shavers,Charlie (tp) | Bryant,Ray (p) | Dameron,Tadd (arr,ld) | details unknown

Carmen McRae With The Jimmy Mundy Orchestra
My Foolish Heart | Until The Real Thing Comes Along | Lush Life | Laughing Boy
NYC, rec. 29.3.1956
McRae,Carmen (voc) | Mundy,Jimmy (arr,ld) | details unknown
Summer Is Gone | Even If It Breaks My Heart | Lilacs In The Rain | All This Could Lead To Love
NYC, rec. 30.3.1956
McRae,Carmen (voc) | Mundy,Jimmy (arr,ld) | details unknown

543830-2 | 2 CD | Ella Fitzgerald Sings The Irving Berlin Song Book
Ella Fitzgerald With Paul Weston And His Orchestra
Let's Face The Music And Dance | You're Laughing At Me | Let Yourself Go | You Can Have Him | Russian Lullaby | Puttin' On The Ritz | Get Thee Behind Me Satan | Alexander's Ragtime Band | Top Hat White Tie And Tails | How About Me | Cheek To Cheek | I Used To Be Colour Blind | Lazy | How Deep Is The Ocean | All By Myself | You Forgot To Remember | Blue Skies(Trumpets No End) | Suppertime | How's Chances | Heat Wave | Isn't This A Lovely Day | You Keep Coming Back Like A Song | Reaching For The Moon | Slumming On Park Avenue | The Song Is Ended | I'm Putting All My Eggs In One Basket | Now It Can Be Told | Always! | It's A Lovely Day Today | Change Partners | No Strings (I'm Fancy Free) | I've Got My Love To Keep Me Warm
rec. 16.-18.3.1958
Fitzgerald,Ella (voc) | Edison,Harry 'Sweets' (tp) | Best,John (tp) | Candoli,Pete (tp) | Fagerquist,Don (tp) | Klein,Manny (tp) | Kusby,Eddie (tb) | Noel,Dick (tb) | Schaefer,Bill (tb) | Tizol,Juan (v-tb) | Cipriano,Gene (reeds) | Gentry,Chuck (reeds) | Hartman,Leonard 'Lennie' (reeds) | Matlock,Matty (reeds) | Nash,Ted (reeds) | Russin,Irving 'Babe' (reeds) | Stulce,Fred (reeds) | Smith,Paul (p) | Kessel,Barney (g) | Mondragon,Joe (b) | Ryan,Jack (b) | Stoller,Alvin (dr) | Weston,Paul (cond)

543831-2 | CD | Organ Grinder Swing
Jimmy Smith Trio
Organ Grinder's Swing | Oh No Babe | Blues For J | Greensleeves | I'll Close My Eyes | Satin Doll
Englewood Cliffs,NJ, rec. 14./15.6.1965
Smith,Jimmy (org,voc) | Burrell,Kenny (g) | Tate,Grady (dr)

543832-2 | CD | Jazz Giant
Bud Powell Trio
Tempus Fugit | Celia | Cherokee | Strictly Confidential | All God's Chillun Got Rhythm
NYC, rec. 23.2.1949
Powell,Bud (p) | Brown,Ray (b) | Roach,Max (dr)
So Sorry Please | Get Happy | Sometimes I'm Happy | Sweet Georgia Brown | April In Paris | Body And Soul
NYC, rec. February 1950
Powell,Bud (p) | Russell,Curly (b) | Roach,Max (dr)

Bud Powell
I'll Keep Loving You
NYC, rec. 23.2.1949
Powell,Bud (p-solo)
Yesterdays
NYC, rec. February 1950
Powell,Bud (p-solo)

543833-2 | CD | Domino
Roland Kirk Quartet
Domino | Meeting On Termini's Corner | Time | Lament | A Strich In Time | 3-In-1 Without The Oil
Chicago,Ill, rec. 6.9.1962
Kirk,Rahsaan Roland (fl,ts,manzello,stritch) | Hill,Andrew (p,celeste) | Martin,Vernon (b) | Duncan,Henry (dr)
Get Out Of Town | Rolando | I Believe In You | E.D.
NYC, rec. 18.4.1962
Kirk,Rahsaan Roland (fl,ts,manzello,stritch) | Kelly,Wynton (p) | Martin,Vernon (b) | Haynes,Roy (dr)
Where Monk And Mingus Live- | Let's Call This- | Domino | I Didn't Know What Time It Was | I Didn't Know What Time It Was (alt.take-1) | I Didn't Know What Time It Was (alt.take-2) | Someone To Watch Over Me | Someone To Watch Over Me(alt.take) | Termini's Corner | Termini's Corner(alt.take) | Termini's Corner(6 breakdown takes) | When The Sun Comes Out | When The Sun Comes Out(alt.take 1) | When The Sun Comes Out(alt.take 2) | Time Races With Emit
NYC, rec. 17.4.1962
Kirk,Rahsaan Roland (fl,ts,manzello,stritch) | Hancock,Herbie (p) | Martin,Vernon (b) | Haynes,Roy (dr)

543834-2 | CD | On The Town
Oscar Peterson Trio
Sweet Georgia Brown | Should I | When Lights Are Low | Easy Listening Blues | Pennies From Heaven | The Champ | Moonlight In Vermont | Baby Baby All The Time | I Like To Recognize The Tune | Joy Spring | Gal In Calico | Our Love Is Here To Stay
Toronto,Canada, rec. 5.7.1958
Peterson,Oscar (p) | Ellis,Herb (g) | Brown,Ray (b)

547264-2 | CD | Peter & The Wolf
Jimmy Smith With The Oliver Nelson Orchestra
The Bird- | The Duck- | That Cat- | The Grandfather- | The Wolf- | The Hunter- | Peter- | Duck Theme- | Jimmy And The Duck- | Peter's Theme- | Meal Time- | Elegy For A Duck | Cat In A Tree | Capture Of The Wolf | Finale: | Parade- | Peter Plays Some Blues
Englewood Cliffs,NJ, rec. 11./12.5.1966
Smith,Jimmy (org) | Newman,Joe (tp) | Royal,Ernie (tp) | Williams,Richard (tp) | Young,Eugene 'Snooky' (tp) | Jackson,Quentin (tb) | McIntosh,Tom (tb) | Woodman,Britt (tb) | Hixon,Richard 'Dick' (b-tb) | Studd,Tony (b-tb) | Buffington,Jimmy (fr-h) | Ruff,Willie (fr-h) | Ashton,Bob (reeds) | Bank,Danny (reeds) | Dodgion,Jerry (reeds) | Richardson,Jerome (reeds) | Webb,Stanley (reeds) | Woods,Phil (reeds) | Butler,Billy (g) | Galbraith,Barry (g) | Davis,Richard (b) | Breuer,Harry (dr,perc) | Rosengarden,Bobby (dr,perc) | Tate,Grady (dr) | Nelson,Oliver (arr,ld)

547317-2 | CD | Stan Getz And The 'Cool' Sounds
Stan Getz Quintet
Rustic Hop
NYC, rec. 4.5.1953
Getz,Stan (ts) | Brookmeyer,Bob (v-tb) | Williams,John (p) | Crow,Bill (b) | Levitt,Al (dr)
Stan Getz Quartet
Nobody Else But Me | Down By The Sycamore Tree
Los Angeles,CA, rec. 23.1.1954
Getz,Stan (ts) | Rowles,Jimmy (p) | Whitlock,Bob (b) | Roach,Max (dr)
Stan Getz Quintet
Flamingo
Los Angeles,CA, rec. 9.11.1954
Getz,Stan (ts) | Brookmeyer,Bob (v-tb) | Williams,John (p) | Anthony,Bill (b) | Isola,Frank (dr)
Blue Bells | Roundup Time
NYC, rec. 31.1.1955
Getz,Stan (ts) | Fruscella,Tony (tp) | Williams,John (p) | Anthony,Bill (b) | Isola,Frank (dr)
Stan Getz Quartet
Of Thee I Sing | A Handful Of Stars | Our Love Is Here To Stay | Serenade In Blue
Los Angeles,CA, rec. 19.8.1955
Getz,Stan (ts) | Levy,Lou (p) | Vinnegar,Leroy (b) | Roach,Max (dr)

547403-2 | CD | The Art Of The Song
Charlie Haden Quartet West With Strings
Lonely Town | In Love In Vain | I'm Gonna Laugh You Out Of My Life | The Folks Who Live On The Hill
Hollywood,CA, rec. 19.-22.2.1999
Haden,Charlie (b) | Watts,Ernie (ts) | Broadbent,Alan (p) | Marable,Lawrence (dr) | Horn,Sheila (voc) | Adler,Murray (concertmaster) | Baker,Israel (v) | Bisharat,Charles (v) | Brosseau,Robert (v) | Bruce,Bobby (v) | Cantor,Russ (v) | Kentendijan,Joe (v) | Kronstadt,Gina (v) | Klinger,Ezra (v) | Palmer,Don (v) | Peterson,Robert (v) | Robinson,Kathleen (v) | Sanow,Robert (v) | Shure,Paul (v) | Sokolow,Rachel (v) | Vaj,Marcy (v) | Walsh,Francine (v) | Zelig,Tibor (v) | Mukogava,Carol (viola) | Giordana,Suzanna (viola) | Gordon,Steve (viola) | Granat,Mimi (viola) | Shirnian,Harry (viola) | Corbett,Larry (cello) | Katyama,Suzy (cello) | Kelley,Raymond J. (cello) | Kessler,Jerome (cello) | Madison,Earl (cello)
Why Did I Choose You | Ruth's Waltz | You My Love | Easy On The Heart
Haden,Charlie (b) | Watts,Ernie (ts) | Broadbent,Alan (p) | Marable,Lawrence (dr) | Henderson,Bill (voc) | Adler,Murray (concertmaster) | Baker,Israel (v) | Bisharat,Charles (v) | Brosseau,Robert (v) | Bruce,Bobby (v) | Cantor,Russ (v) | Kentendijan,Joe (v) | Kronstadt,Gina (v) | Klinger,Ezra (v) | Palmer,Don (v) | Peterson,Robert (v) | Robinson,Kathleen (v) | Sanow,Robert (v) | Shure,Paul (v) | Sokolow,Rachel (v) | Vaj,Marcy (v) | Walsh,Francine (v) | Zelig,Tibor (v) | Mukogava,Carol (viola) | Giordana,Suzanna (viola) | Gordon,Steve (viola) | Granat,Mimi (viola) | Shirnian,Harry (viola) | Corbett,Larry (cello) | Katyama,Suzy (cello) | Kelley,Raymond J. (cello) | Kessler,Jerome (cello) | Madison,Earl (cello)
Moment Musical Opus 16 No.3 In B Minor | Scenes From A Silver Screen | Prelude En La Mineur | Theme For Charlie
Haden,Charlie (b) | Watts,Ernie (ts) | Broadbent,Alan (p) | Marable,Lawrence (dr) | Adler,Murray (concertmaster) | Baker,Israel (v) | Bisharat,Charles (v) | Brosseau,Robert (v) | Bruce,Bobby (v) | Cantor,Russ (v) | Kentendijan,Joe (v) | Kronstadt,Gina (v) | Klinger,Ezra (v) | Palmer,Don (v) | Peterson,Robert (v) | Robinson,Kathleen (v) | Sanow,Robert (v) | Shure,Paul (v) | Sokolow,Rachel (v) | Vaj,Marcy (v) | Walsh,Francine (v) | Zelig,Tibor (v) | Mukogava,Carol (viola) | Giordana,Suzanna (viola) | Gordon,Steve (viola) | Granat,Mimi (viola) | Shirnian,Harry (viola) | Corbett,Larry (cello) | Katyama,Suzy (cello) | Kelley,Raymond J. (cello) | Kessler,Jerome (cello) | Madison,Earl (cello)
Charlie Haden With String Quartet
Wayfaring Stranger
Haden,Charlie (voc) | Adler,Murray (concertmaster) | Palmer,Don (v) | Mukogava,Carol (viola) | Corbett,Larry (cello)

547503-2 | CD | Outhipped
Barbara Dennerlein Group
Outhipped
NYC, rec. February 1999
Dennerlein,Barbara (org) | Barrett,Dan (tp) | Hart,Antonio Maurice (ss) | Handy,Craig (ts) | Nelson,Steve (marimba) | Watkins,Mitch (g) | Genus,James (b) | Watts,Jeff 'Tain' (dr) | Alias,Don (perc)
Bloody Mary
Dennerlein,Barbara (org) | Barrett,Dan (tp) | Anderson,Ray (tb) | Hart,Antonio Maurice (as) | Handy,Craig (ts,bs) | Nelson,Steve (vib) | Watkins,Mitch (g) | Genus,James (b) | Watts,Jeff 'Tain' (dr) | Alias,Don (perc)
In The Mud
Dennerlein,Barbara (org,synth) | Barrett,Dan (tp) | Anderson,Ray (tb) | Hart,Antonio Maurice (as) | Handy,Craig (ts) | Watkins,Mitch (g) | Genus,James (b) | Watts,Jeff 'Tain' (dr) | Alias,Don (perc) | Dyer,Ada (voc) | Smith,André (voc)
Satisfaction
Dennerlein,Barbara (org) | Anderson,Ray (tb,tuba) | Hart,Antonio Maurice (as) | Watkins,Mitch (g) | Genus,James (b) | Watts,Jeff 'Tain' (dr) | Alias,Don (perc)
Black And White
Dennerlein,Barbara (org) | Barrett,Dan (tp) | Handy,Craig (ts) | Watkins,Mitch (g) | Watts,Jeff 'Tain' (dr)
Frog Dance
Dennerlein,Barbara (org) | Sipiagin,Alex (tp) | Anderson,Ray (tb) | Slagle,Steve (fl) | Nelson,Steve (vib) | Watkins,Mitch (g) | Watts,Jeff 'Tain' (dr) | Alias,Don (perc)
Odd Blues
Dennerlein,Barbara (org) | Barrett,Dan (tp) | Anderson,Ray (tb) | Slagle,Steve (fl,alto-fl,piccolo) | Hart,Antonio Maurice (as) | Handy,Craig (ts,bs) | Watts,Jeff 'Tain' (dr)
Farewell To Old Friends
Dennerlein,Barbara (org) | Barrett,Dan (tp) | Handy,Craig (ts) | Watkins,Mitch (g) | Watts,Jeff 'Tain' (dr)
Mabuse
Dennerlein,Barbara (org,synth) | Sipiagin,Alex (fl-h) | Anderson,Ray (tb) | Hart,Antonio Maurice (ss) | Nelson,Steve (vib) | Watkins,Mitch (g) | Genus,James (b) | Watts,Jeff 'Tain' (dr) | Alias,Don (perc)
Sweet Poison
Dennerlein,Barbara (org) | Sipiagin,Alex (fl-h) | Nelson,Steve (vib) | Watts,Jeff 'Tain' (dr) | Alias,Don (perc)
Strange Passion
Dennerlein,Barbara (org) | Sipiagin,Alex (fl-h) | Anderson,Ray (tb) | Watkins,Mitch (g) | Genus,James (b) | Watts,Jeff 'Tain' (dr) | Alias,Don (perc)
Jammin'
Dennerlein,Barbara (org) | Watkins,Mitch (g)

547598-2 | CD | Nick@Night
Nicholas Payton Quintet
Beyond The Stars | Captain Crunch(Meets The Cereal Killer) | Faith(for Faith Evans) | Pleasant Dreams | Interlude No.1(Turn Up The Funk) | Nick@Night | Somnia | Interlude No.2(Turn Out The Burn Out) | Prince Of The Night | Blacker Black's Revenge | Little Angel(for Christopher) | Exquisite Tenderness | Sun Goddness
NYC, rec. 18.-20.5.1999
Payton,Nicholas (tp,fl-h,celeste,harpsichord) | Warfield Jr.,Tim (ss,ts) | Wonsey,Athony (p,celeste,harpsichord) | Rogers,Reuben (b) | Rose,Adonis (dr)

547769-2 | CD | Tequila
Wes Montgomery Quartet
Tequila | The Thumb | Tequila(alt.take)
Englewood Cliffs,NJ, rec. 21.3.1966
Montgomery,Wes (g) | Carter,Ron (b) | Tate,Grady (dr) | Barretto,Ray (congas)
Wes Montgomery Quintet With The Claus Ogerman Orchestra
The Big Hurt
Englewood Cliffs,NJ, rec. 17.3.1966
Montgomery,Wes (g) | Devens,George (vib) | Carter,Ron (b) | Tate,Grady (dr) | Eichen,Bernard (v) | Eidus,Arnold (v) | Gersham,Paul (v) | Green,Emmanuel (v) | Held,Julius (v) | Lookofsky,Harry (v) | Malin,Joe (v) | Orloff,Gene (v) | Kessler,Abe (cello) | McCracken,Charles (cello) | Ricci,George (cello) | Shapiro,Harvey (cello) | Ogerman,Claus (cond,arr)
Wes Montgomery Trio With The Claus Ogerman Orchestra
Little Child(Daddy Dear)
Montgomery,Wes (g) | Carter,Ron (b) | Tate,Grady (dr) | Eichen,Bernard (v) | Eidus,Arnold (v) | Gersham,Paul (v) | Green,Emmanuel (v) | Held,Julius (v) | Lookofsky,Harry (v) | Malin,Joe (v) | Orloff,Gene (v) | Kessler,Abe (cello) | McCracken,Charles (cello) | Ricci,George (cello) | Shapiro,Harvey (cello) | Ogerman,Claus (cond,arr)
Wes Montgomery Quartet With The Claus Ogerman Orchestra
Bumpin' On Sunset | How Insensitive(Insensatez)
Montgomery,Wes (g) | Carter,Ron (b) | Tate,Grady (dr) | Barretto,Ray (congas) | Eichen,Bernard (v) | Eidus,Arnold (v) | Gersham,Paul (v) | Green,Emmanuel (v) | Held,Julius (v) | Lookofsky,Harry (v) | Malin,Joe (v) | Orloff,Gene (v) | Kessler,Abe (cello) | McCracken,Charles (cello) | Ricci,George (cello) | Shapiro,Harvey (cello) | Ogerman,Claus (cond,arr)
Midnight Mood
Montgomery,Wes (g) | Devens,George (vib) | Carter,Ron (b) | Tate,Grady (dr) | Eichen,Bernard (v) | Eidus,Arnold (v) | Gersham,Paul (v) | Green,Emmanuel (v) | Held,Julius (v) | Lookofsky,Harry (v) | Malin,Joe (v) | Orloff,Gene (v) | Kessler,Abe (cello) | McCracken,Charles (cello) | Ricci,George (cello) | Shapiro,Harvey (cello) | Ogerman,Claus (cond,arr)
Wes Montgomery Trio
Wives And Lovers | Bumpin' On Sunset(alt.take)
Montgomery,Wes (g) | Carter,Ron (b) | Tate,Grady (dr)
Wes Montgomery Quartet
What The World Needs Now Is Love
Montgomery,Wes (g) | Devens,George (vib) | Carter,Ron (b) | Tate,Grady (dr)
Wes Montgomery Sextet
The Big Hurt(alt.take)
Montgomery,Wes (g) | Devens,George (vib) | unkn. (p) | Carter,Ron (b) | Tate,Grady (dr) | Barretto,Ray (congas)

547771-2 | CD | The Steamer
Stan Getz Quartet
Blues For Mary Jane | There'll Never Be Another You | You're Blasé | Too Close For Comfort | Like Someone In Love | How About You | How About You(alt.take) | There'll Never Be Another You(2 incomplete takes) | You're Blasé(false start) | Like Someone In Love(incomplete take) | How About You(2 false starts) | How About You(incomplete take)
Hollywood,CA, rec. 24.11.1956
Getz,Stan (ts) | Levy,Lou (p) | Vinnegar,Leroy (b) | Levey,Stan (dr)

547844-2 | CD | Time Is Of The Essence
Michael Brecker Group
Arc Of The Pendulum | Time Line | Outrance
NYC, rec. details unknown
Brecker,Michael (ts) | Metheny,Pat (g) | Goldings,Larry (org) | Jones,Elvin (dr)
Sound Off | The Morning Of This Night | Dr. Slate
Brecker,Michael (ts) | Metheny,Pat (g) | Goldings,Larry (org) | Watts,Jeff 'Tain' (dr)
Half Past Late | Renaissance Man | As I Am
Brecker,Michael (ts) | Metheny,Pat (g) | Goldings,Larry (org) | Stewart,Bill (dr)

549101-2 | CD | Over The Years
Abbey Lincoln And Her Trio
A Heart Is Not A Toy | Lucky To Be Me
NYC, rec. 18.-21.2.2000
Lincoln,Abbey (voc) | McCune,Brandon (p) | Ormond,John (b) | Sawyer,Jaz (dr)
Tender As A Rose
NYC, rec. 23.4.2000
Lincoln,Abbey (voc) | McCune,Brandon (p) | Ormond,John (b) | Sawyer,Jaz (dr)
Abbey Lincoln And Her Trio With Guests
Somos Novios(Impossible)
NYC, rec. 18.-21.2.2000
Lincoln,Abbey (voc) | Gonzalez,Jerry (tp) | McCune,Brandon (p) | Ormond,John (b) | Sawyer,Jaz (dr)
I'm Not Supposed To Know
Lincoln,Abbey (voc) | Gonzalez,Jerry (tp) | Lovano,Joe (ts) | McCune,Brandon (p) | Ormond,John (b) | Sawyer,Jaz (dr)
Blackberry Blossoms
Lincoln,Abbey (voc) | Lovano,Joe (ts) | Shank,Kendra (g) | McCune,Brandon (p) | Ormond,John (b) | Sawyer,Jaz (dr)
When Lights Are Low | What Will Tomorrow Bring
Lincoln,Abbey (voc) | Lovano,Joe (ts) | McCune,Brandon (p) | Vincent,Jennifer (cello) | Ormond,John (b) | Sawyer,Jaz (dr)
When The Lights Go On Again | I Could Sing It For A Song | Windmills Of Your Mind
Lincoln,Abbey (voc) | Lovano,Joe (ts) | McCune,Brandon (p) | Ormond,John (b) | Sawyer,Jaz (dr)

549111-2 | CD | Soul Bird | EAN 731454911122
Cal Tjader Sextet
The Wiffenproof Song | How High The Moon | That's All | Soul Motion | The Prophet | Sonny Boy | Doxy | Samba De Orfeu | Shiny Stockings | Daddy Longlegs
NYC, rec. 1./2.6.1965
Tjader,Cal (vib) | Griffin,Paul (p) | Davis,Richard (b) | Gubia,Sol (dr) | Tate,Grady (dr) | Peraza,Armando (perc)
Cal Tjader Quintet
Reza | Soul Bird(aka Tin Tin Deo)
Englewood Cliffs,NJ, rec. 21./22.7.1965
Tjader,Cal (vib) | Hewitt,Lonnie (p) | Williard,Terry (b) | Rae,Johnny (dr) | Peraza,Armando (perc)

549162-2 | CD | The Next Stop
Kurt Rosenwinkel Quartet
Zhivago | Minor Blues | A Shifting Design | Path Of The Heart | Filters | Use Of Light | The Next Stop | A Life Unfolds
NYC, rec. 12.-14.5.2000
Rosenwinkel,Kurt (g,p) | Turner,Mark (ts) | Street,Ben (b) | Ballard,Jeff (dr)

549281-2 | CD | Works For Me
John Scofield Quintet
I'll Catch You | Not You Again | Big J | Loose Canon | Love You Long Time | Hive | Heel To Toe | Do I Crazy? | Mrs. Scofield's Waltz | Six And Eight | Freepie
NYC, rec. 6.-8.1.2000
Scofield,John (g) | Garrett,Kenny (as) | Mehldau,Brad (p) | McBride,Christian (b) | Higgins,Billy (dr)

549366-2 | CD | Guys And Dolls Like Vives | EAN 731454936620
Eddie Costa Quartet
Guys And Dolls | I'll Know
NYC, rec. 15.1.1958
Costa,Eddie (vib) | Evans,Bill (p) | Marshall,Wendell (b) | Motian,Paul (dr)
Luck Be A Lady | I've Never Been In Love Before
NYC, rec. 16.1.1958
Costa,Eddie (vib) | Evans,Bill (p) | Marshall,Wendell (b) | Motian,Paul (dr)
Adeleide | If I Were A Bell
NYC, rec. 17.1.1958
Costa,Eddie (vib) | Evans,Bill (p) | Marshall,Wendell (b) | Motian,Paul (dr)

549371-2 | CD | Boss Tenors In Orbit!!!
Gene Ammons-Sonny Stitt Quintet
Long Ago And Far Away | Walkin' | Why Was I Born | John Brown's Body | Bye Bye Blackbird
NYC, rec. 18.2.1962
Ammons,Gene (ts) | Stitt,Sonny (ts) | Patterson,Don (org) | Weeden,Paul (g) | James,William 'Billy' (dr)

549373-2 | CD | Ella Sings Broadway | EAN 731454937320
Ella Fitzgerald With The Marty Paich Orchestra
Hernando's Hideaway | If I Were A Bell | Warm All Over | Almost Like Being In Love | Dites-Moi | I Could Have Danced All Night | Show Me | No Other Love | Steam Heat | Whatever Lola Wants | Guys And Dolls | Somebody Somewhere
Hollywood,CA, rec. 1.-4.10.1962
Fitzgerald,Ella (voc) | Orchestra | Paich,Marty (arr,ld) | details unknown

549433-2 | CD | Gratitude | EAN 731454943321
Chris Potter Quartet
The Source | Shadow | Sun King | High Noon | Eurydice | The Mind's Eye(Intro) | The Mind's Eye | Gratitude | The Visitor | Body And Soul | Star Eyes | Vox Humana
Avatar Studios,?, rec. 27./28.11.2000
Potter,Chris (wood-fl,alto-fl,b-cl,ss,as,ts) | Hays,Kevin (p,el-b) | Colley,Scott (b) | Blade,Brian (dr)
What's New?
Potter,Chris (ts-solo)

549592-2 | CD | Louis And The Angels | EAN 731454959223
Louis Armstrong With Sy Oliver And His Orchestra
When Did You Leave Heaven | You're A Heavenly Thing | I Married An Angel | A Sinner Kissed An Angel | Angel Child | Fools Rush In | Goodnight Angel
NYC, rec. 29.1.1957
Armstrong,Louis (tp,voc) | Dorsey,George (fl,as) | Urso,Phil (fl,as) | Thompson,Lucky (ts) | McRae,Dave (bs) | Kyle,Billy (p) | Barksdale,Everett (g) | Benjamin,Joe (b) | Trayler,Rudy (dr) | Clark,Lillian (voc) | unkn. (3 female, 3 male voc) | unkn. (strings) | Oliver,Sy (cond,arr)
Angela Mia | And The Angels Sing | I'll String Along With You | Angel | The Prisoner's Song
NYC, rec. 30.1.1957
Armstrong,Louis (tp,voc) | Dorsey,George (fl,as) | Urso,Phil (fl,as) | Thompson,Lucky (ts) | McRae,Dave (bs) | Kyle,Billy (p) | Barnes,George (g) | Block,Sid (b) | Trayler,Rudy (dr) | Clark,Lillian (voc) | unkn. (3 female, 3 male voc) | unkn. (strings) | Oliver,Sy (cond,arr)

549593-2 | CD | Louis And The Good Book | EAN 731454959322
Louis Armstrong With The Lyn Murray Chorus
Shadrack | Going To Shout All Over God's Heaven | Nobody Knows The Trouble I've Seen | Jonah And The Whale
NYC, rec. 14.6.1938
Armstrong,Louis (voc) | Lyn Murray Choir,The | unkn. (g,p,b,dr) | details unknown
Louis Armstrong With Harry Mills And Choir
Elder Eatmore's Sermon On Throwing Stones | Elder Eatmore's Sermon On Generosity
NYC, rec. 11.8.1938
Armstrong,Louis (talking) | Mills,Harry (org,talking) | Choir
Louis Armstrong With Sy Oliver's Choir And Orchestra
Sit Down, You're Rockin' The Boat | That's What The Man Said
NYC, rec. 31.8.1950
Armstrong,Louis (tp,voc) | Kyle,Billy (p) | Barksdale,Everett (g) | Benjamin,Joe (b) | Blowers,Johnny (dr) | Choir | Oliver,Sy (cond,arr)
Nobody Knows The Trouble I've Seen | Down By The Riverside | Jonah And The Whale | This Train
NYC, rec. 4.2.1958
Armstrong,Louis (tp,voc) | Oliver,Sy (cond,arr) | Young,Trummy (tb) | McRae,Dave (cl) | Tragg,Nickie (org) | Kyle,Billy (p) | Barnes,George (g) | Herbert,Mort (b) | Deems,Barrett (dr) | 10-voice-choir
Shadrack | On My Way
NYC, rec. 6.2.1958
Armstrong,Louis (tp,voc) | Oliver,Sy (cond,arr) | Young,Trummy (tb) | Hall,Edmond (cl) | Tragg,Nickie (org) | Kyle,Billy (p) | Barksdale,Everett (g)
Didn't Rain | Rock My Soul
Armstrong,Louis (voc) | Oliver,Sy (cond,arr) | Tragg,Nickie (org) | Kyle,Billy (p) | Barksdale,Everett (g) | Herbert,Mort (b) | Deems,Barrett (dr) | 10-voice-choir
Swing Low Sweet Chariot | Go Down Moses | Ezekiel Saw 'De Wheel | Sometimes I Feel Like A Motherless Child
NYC, rec. 7.2.1958
Armstrong,Louis (tp,voc) | Oliver,Sy (cond,arr) | Young,Trummy (tb) | D'Amico,Hank (cl) | Tragg,Nickie (org) | Kyle,Billy (p) | Barksdale,Everett (g) | Herbert,Mort (b) | Deems,Barrett (dr)

549594-2 | CD | Satchmo In Style | EAN 731454959421
Louis Armstrong With Gordon Jenkins And His Orchestra And Choir
Blueberry Hill | That Lucky Old Sun(Just Rolls Around Heaven)
NYC, rec. 6.9.1949
Armstrong,Louis (voc) | Butterfield,Billy (tp) | Poole,Carl (tp) | Lawson,Yank (tp) | Bradley,Will (tb) | Yaner,Milt (as) | Schertzer,Hymie (as) | Parshley,Tom (ts) | Drellinger,Art (ts) | Leighton,Bernie (p) | Kress,Carl (g) | Lesberg,Jack (b) | Blowers,Johnny (dr) | unkn. (choir) | Jenkins,Gordon (cond,arr)
Louis Armstrong With Gordon Jenkins And His Orchestra
You're Just In Love | If | I Want A Big Butter And Egg Man
Hollywood,CA, rec. 6.2.1951
Armstrong,Louis (voc) | Griffin,Chris (tp) | Ballard,Red (tb) | Songer,Wayne (as) | Eckels,Dent (ts) | LaVere,Charles (p) | Reuss,Allan (g) | Stephens,Phil (b) | Fatool,Nick (dr) | Middleton,Velma (voc) | Jenkins,Gordon (cond,arr)
Louis Armstrong With Gordon Jenkins And His Orchestra And Choir
It's All In The Game | Jeanine I Dream Of Lilac Time | Indian Love Call | When It's Sleepy Time Down South | When It's Sleepy Time Down South(alt.take)
Hollywood,CA, rec. 28.11.1951
Armstrong,Louis (voc) | Gifford,Charles (tp) | Hudson,Bruce (tp) | Thow,George (tp) | Eckels,Dent (ts) | Miller,Eddie (ts) | LaVere,Charles (p) | Reuss,Allan (g) | Stephens,Phil (b) | Fatool,Nick (dr) | unkn. (choir) | Jenkins,Gordon (cond,arr)
Chloe(Song Of The Swamp) | Listen To The Mockingbird
NYC, rec. 22.9.1952
Armstrong,Louis (tp,voc) | McCracken,Bob (as) | Yaner,Milt (as) | Ferguson,Stitz (ts) | Berg,George (woodwinds) | Penque,Romeo (woodwinds) | Napoleon,Marty (p) | Ryerson,Arthur 'Art' (g) | Shaw,Arvell (b) | Cole,William 'Cozy' (dr) | unkn. (strings) | unkn. (choir) | Jenkins,Gordon (cond,arr)
The Wiffenproof Song | Trees | Bye And Bye | Spooks
NYC, rec. 5.4.1954
Armstrong,Louis (tp,voc) | Yaner,Milt (cl) | details unknown | Parshley,Tom (as) | Greenberg,Jack (as) | Richmond,Abraham (ts) | Berg,George (ts) | Leighton,Bernie (p) | Barnes,George (g) | Lesberg,Jack (b) | Jaeger,Harry (dr) | unkn. (10 strings) | Chorus | Jenkins,Gordon (cond,arr)

549629-2 | CD | Pandora
Makoto Ozone Trio
You Never Be Anything | Lullaby For Rabbit | Reunion | Sofi | If I Had Known | Brazilian Sketch | Pennillium | Blessing The World | Pandora | Tiffany's Waltz | Around The Corner
NYC, rec. 2000
Ozone,Makoto (p) | Genus,James (b) | Penn,Clarence (dr)

549705-2 | CD | Nearness Of You-The Ballad Book
Michael Brecker Quintet
Chan's Song | Nascente | Midnight Mood | Incandescene | Sometimes I See | My Ship | Always | Seven Days | I Can See Your Dreams
Brecker,Michael (ts) | Metheny,Pat (g) | Hancock,Herbie (p) | Haden,Charlie (b) | DeJohnette,Jack (dr)
Don't Let Me Be Lonely Tonight | The Nearness Of You
Brecker,Michael (ts) | Metheny,Pat (g) | Hancock,Herbie (p) | Haden,Charlie (b) | DeJohnette,Jack (dr) | Taylor,James (voc)

549706-2 | CD | Freefall | EAN 731454970624
Kenny Barron-Regina Carter

Softly As In A Morning Sunrise | Fragile | Misterioso | Phantoms | What If
| Squatty Roo | Freefall | Shades Of Gray | Footprints | A Flower
Brooklyn,NY, rec. 19./20.12.2000
Carter,Regina (v) | Barron,Kenny (p)

549749-2 | CD | Diz And Getz | EAN 731454974929
Dizzy Gillespie-Stan Getz Sextet
Siboney(part 1) | Siboney(part 2) | It Don't Mean A Thing If It Ain't Got That Swing | Exactly Like You | Impromptu | I Let A Song Go Out Of My Heart | Girl Of My Dreams | It's The Talk Of The Town
Los Angeles,CA, rec. 9.12.1953
Gillespie,Dizzy (tp) | Getz,Stan (ts) | Peterson,Oscar (p) | Ellis,Herb (g) | Brown,Ray (b) | Roach,Max (dr)
Dizzy Gillespie Quintet
One Alone
NYC, rec. 25.5.1954
Gillespie,Dizzy (tp) | Mobley,Hank (ts) | Legge,Wade (p) | Hackney,Lou (b) | Persip,Charles (dr)

553780-2 | CD | Talkin' Verve:George Benson
George Benson And His Orchestra
Sunny
NYC, rec. 5.2.1968
Benson,George (g) | Owens,Jimmy (tp,fl-h) | Royal,Ernie (tp) | Young,Eugene 'Snooky' (tp) | Ralph,Alan (b-tb) | Adams,Pepper (bs) | Hancock,Herbie (p) | Gale,Eric (g) | Cranshaw,Bob (b) | Cobham,Billy (dr) | Gilbert,Eileen (voc) | Robinson,Albertine (voc) | Winter,Lois (voc)
Giblet Gravy
Benson,George (g) | Owens,Jimmy (tp,fl-h) | Royal,Ernie (tp) | Young,Eugene 'Snooky' (tp) | Ralph,Alan (b-tb) | Adams,Pepper (bs) | Hancock,Herbie (p) | Gale,Eric (g) | Cranshaw,Bob (b) | Cobham,Billy (dr)
George Benson Sextet
Thunder Walk | Low Down And Dirty Blues
NYC, rec. 6.2.1968
Benson,George (g) | Hancock,Herbie (p) | Gale,Eric (g) | Carter,Ron (b) | Cobham,Billy (dr) | Pacheco,Johnny (congas)
George Benson Orchestra
Groovin'
NYC, rec. 7.2.1968
Benson,George (g) | Owens,Jimmy (tp,fl-h) | Royal,Ernie (tp) | Young,Eugene 'Snooky' (tp) | Ralph,Alan (b-tb) | Adams,Pepper (bs) | Hancock,Herbie (p) | Gale,Eric (g) | Carter,Ron (b) | Cobham,Billy (dr)
Song For My Father | That Lucky Old Sun(Just Rolls Around Heaven)
NYC, rec. 18./19.11.1968
Benson,George (g) | Terry,Clark (tp) | Brown,Garnett (tb) | Clark,Arthur (fl,ts) | Marge,George (fl,ts) | Lucas,Buddy (harm) | Griffin,Paul (p,celeste) | Rainey,Chuck (b) | Muhammad,Idris[Leo Morris] (dr) | Jennings,Jack (vib,congas) | Winston Collymore Strings,The | Ott,Horace (cond,arr)
You Make Me Feel Like A Natural Woman - (You Make Me Feel) Like A Natural Woman | People Get Ready
NYC, rec. 18.11.1968
Benson,George (g) | Terry,Clark (tp) | Brown,Garnett (tb) | Clark,Arthur (fl,ts) | Marge,George (fl,ts) | Lucas,Buddy (harm) | Griffin,Paul (p,celeste) | Rainey,Chuck (b) | Muhammad,Idris[Leo Morris] (dr) | Jennings,Jack (vib,congas) | Winston Collymore Strings,The | Ott,Horace (cond,arr) | Sweet Inspirations,The (voc-group)
George Benson Quartet With The Sweet Inspirations
Doobie Doobie Blues
NYC, rec. 19.11.1968
Benson,George (g) | Griffin,Paul (p) | Cranshaw,Bob (b) | Johnson,Jimmy (dr) | Sweet Inspirations,The (voc-group)
George Benson Quartet
The Windmills Of You Mind
Benson,George (g) | Griffin,Paul (p) | Cranshaw,Bob (b) | Johnson,Jimmy (dr)
Jimmy Smith Trio
Some Of My Best Friends Are Blues
Live at Paschal's La Carousel Club,Atlanta,GA, rec. 1.11.1968
Smith,Jimmy (org) | Benson,George (g) | Bailey,Donald (dr)

557022-2 | CD | Noches Calientes
The Rosenberg Trio With Orchestra
Noches Calientes | Tango Op.165 Nr.2 | 2 The Night | Querer | El Noi De La Mare | Medley Paco De Lucia: | Entre Dos Aguas- | Rio Ancho- | Concierto D'Aranjuez(Adagio) | Noveleo | Rumba's Sunset | Chanson Anonyme | Sonata In D-Dur | El Testament D'Amelia
Amersfoort/Hilversum,NL, rec. details unknown
Rosenberg,Stochelo (g) | Rosenberg,Nou'che (g) | Rosenberg,Nonnie (b) | Oosthof,Jan (tp) | Hollander,Jan (tp) | Van Lier,Bart (tb) | Sohier,Martijn (tb) | Van Koten,Frank (engl-h,oboe) | Vorselen,Harry (fr-h) | Van Nes,Wendy (fl) | Benders,Mart (fl) | Micault,Gwénael (bandoneon) | De Vriend,Jan Willem (strings) | Hoogeven,Ronald (strings) | Haanstra,Jurre (p,el-p,dr,cond,arr) | Vroomans,Hans (el-p) | Amuedo,Leonardo (g) | Meulendijk,Bert (g) | Emmery,Harry (b) | Jacobs,Ruud (b) | Conrad,Eddie (perc) | De Rijk,Jeroen (perc)

557297-2 | CD | Save Our Children
Pharoah Sanders Group
Save Our Children | Midnight In Berkeley Square | Jewels Of Love | Kazuko | The Ancient Sound | Far-Off Sand
West Orange,NJ, rec. 1998
Sanders,Pharoah (ss,ts,perc,bells,double-reed,voice) | Henderson,William 'Bill' (p,harmonium) | Worrell,Bernie (el-p,org,synth) | Cedras,Tony (harmonium) | Bova,Jeff (synth,programming) | Blake,Alex (b) | Hussain,Zakir (mbira,tabla,voice,wooden-box) | Gurtu,Trilok (dr,perc,tabla) | M'boup,Abdou (talking-dr,voice) | Oyewole,Abiodun (voice) | Asante (voice)

557327-2 | CD | Payton's Place
Nicholas Payton Quintet
Zigaboogaloo | Back To The Source | Concentric Circle | Lil' Duke's Strut | Time Traveling | Paraphemalia | People Makes The World Go Round | The Last Goodbye
NYC, rec. 29./30.12 1997 & 6.1.1998
Payton,Nicholas (tp) | Warfield Jr.,Tim (ts) | Wonsey,Athony (p) | Rogers,Reuben (b) | Rose,Adonis (dr)
A Touch Of Silver
NYC, rec. 29./30.12.1997 & 6.1.1998
Payton,Nicholas (tp) | Redman,Joshua (ts) | Wonsey,Athony (p) | Rogers,Reuben (b) | Rose,Adonis (dr)
With A Song In My Heart
Payton,Nicholas (tp) | Hargrove,Roy (tp) | Wonsey,Athony (p) | Rogers,Reuben (b) | Rose,Adonis (dr)
Nicholas Payton Sextet
The Three Trumpeters
Payton,Nicholas (tp) | Marsalis,Wynton (tp) | Hargrove,Roy (tp) | Wonsey,Athony (p) | Rogers,Reuben (b) | Rose,Adonis (dr)

557351-2 | CD | Talkin' Verve:Les McCann
Les McCann Trio
Little Freak
Hollywood,CA, rec. December 1964
McCann,Les (p) | Gaskin,Victor (b) | Humphrey,Paul (dr)
Les McCann Quartet
Beaux J.Poo Boo | Green Green Rocky Road | The Great City
Los Angeles,CA, rec. July/August 1965
McCann,Les (p) | Corrao,Vinnie (g) | Gaskin,Victor (b) | Humphrey,Paul (dr)
Les McCann Trio
My Friends
Live at Shelly's Manne Hole,Los Angeles,CA, rec. 31.12.1965
McCann,Les (p) | Gaskin,Victor (b) | Humphrey,Paul (dr)
Les McCann Group
Guantanamera | Compared To What
NYC, rec. 9.9.1966
McCann,Les (p) | Powell,Seldon or Jerome Richardson (ts) | Chiasson,Warren (vib) | Bell,Vincent or Carl Lynch (g) | Vinnegar,Leroy (b) | Robinson,Booker T. (dr)
Sunny(part 1)
McCann,Les (p) | Bell,Vincent or Carl Lynch (g) | Vinnegar,Leroy (b) | Robinson,Booker T. (dr)
Sunny(part 2) | Sad Little Girl
McCann,Les (p) | Johnson,Plas (ts) | Blessing,Lyon (vib) | Georgantones,Jimmy (g) | Vinnegar,Leroy (b) | Robinson,Booker T. (dr) | Rich,Ron (congas)
Les McCann Orchestra
Watermelon Man | Red Top | La Brea | Boo-Go-Loo
Los Angeles,CA, rec. 27./28.12.1966
McCann,Les (p) | Katzman,Lee (tp) | Johnson,Plas (ts) | Blessing,Lyon (vib) | Georgantones,Jimmy (g) | Vinnegar,Leroy (b) | Robinson,Booker T. (dr) | Rich,Ron (congas) | Aleong,Aki (perc) | Torres,Joseph (perc) | DeSilva,Ric (perc)
Les McCann Trio
Goin' Out Of My Head | Colonel Rykken's Southern Fried Chicken
Live at The Bohemian Caverns,Washington,DC, rec. August 1967
McCann,Les (p) | Vinnegar,Leroy (b) | Severino,Frank (dr)

557446-2 | CD | Soul Burst
Cal Tjader's Orchestra
Soul Burst(Guajera)
Englewood Cliffs,NJ, rec. 9.2.1966
Tjader,Cal (vib) | Dodgion,Jerry (fl) | Powell,Seldon (fl) | Corea,Chick (p) | Rodriguez,Bobby (b) | Valdez,Carlos 'Patato' (congas,voc) | Mangual,Jose (timbales) | Pantoja,Victor (perc)
Curacao
Tjader,Cal (vib,cymbal) | Richardson,Jerome (fl) | Corea,Chick (p) | Rodriguez,Bobby (b) | Valdez,Carlos 'Patato' (congas,voc) | Mangual,Jose (timbales) | Pantoja,Victor (perc)
Descarga Cubana | Morning | It Didn't End(Nao Se Acabou)
Englewood Cliffs,NJ, rec. 10.2.1966
Tjader,Cal (vib,cymbal) | Richardson,Jerome (fl) | Corea,Chick (p,arr) | Rodriguez,Bobby (b) | Valdez,Carlos 'Patato' (congas) | Mangual,Jose (perc,timbales) | Pantoja,Victor (perc)
Oran
Tjader,Cal (vib,cabassa) | Richardson,Jerome (fl) | Corea,Chick (p) | Rodriguez,Bobby (b) | Valdez,Carlos 'Patato' (congas,voc) | Mangual,Jose (timbales) | Pantoja,Victor (perc)
Cuchy Frito Man | The Bilbao Song | Manteca | My Ship
Englewood Cliffs,NJ, rec. 11.2.1966
Tjader,Cal (vib,cymbal) | Richardson,Jerome (fl) | Powell,Seldon (fl) | Corea,Chick (p) | Zoller,Attila (g) | Davis,Richard (b) | Tate,Grady (dr) | Valdez,Carlos 'Patato' (congas) | Mangual,Jose (timbales) | Pantoja,Antonio (perc) | Nelson,Oliver (arr,ld)

557447-2 | CD | Any Number Can Win
Jimmy Smith With The Claus Ogerman Orchestra
You Came A Long Way From St. Louis | G'won Train | Tubs
Englewood Cliffs,NJ, rec. 10.7.1963
Smith,Jimmy (org) | Maxwell,Jimmy (tp) | Newman,Joe (tp) | Shavers,Charlie (tp) | Cleveland,Jimmy (tb) | Faulise,Paul (tb) | Liston,Melba (tb) | Winding,Kai (tb) | Dodgion,Jerry (reeds) | Halladay,Marvin (reeds) | Johnson,Budd (reeds) | Powell,Seldon (reeds) | Woods,Phil (reeds) | Davis,Art (b) | Shaughnessy,Ed (dr) | Devens,George (perc) | Byers,Billy (arr) | Ogerman,Claus (cond,arr)
The Ape Woman | Blues For C.A.
Englewood Cliffs,NJ, rec. 17.7.1963
Smith,Jimmy (org) | Maxwell,Jimmy (tp) | Newman,Joe (tp) | Young,Eugene Edward (tp) | Cleveland,Jimmy (tb) | Faulise,Paul (tb) | Liston,Melba (tb) | Winding,Kai (tb) | Dodgion,Jerry (reeds) | Halladay,Marvin (reeds) | Johnson,Budd (reeds) | Powell,Seldon (reeds) | Woods,Phil (reeds) | Davis,Art (b) | Bushnell,Bob (el-b) | Shaughnessy,Ed (dr) | Devens,George (perc) | Byers,Billy (arr) | Ogerman,Claus (cond,arr)
Georgia On My Mind | Ruby
Englewood Cliffs,NJ, rec. 25.7.1963
Smith,Jimmy (org) | Burrell,Kenny (g) | Mure,Billy (g) | Gambella,Vince (g) | Hinton,Milt (b) | Donaldson,Bobby (dr) | Allen,Doug (perc) | Marotti,Art (perc) | unkn. (chorus,overdubbed later) | Ogerman,Claus (arr)
Theme From Any Number Can Win
Smith,Jimmy (org) | Newman,Joe (tp) | Sedler,Jimmy (tp) | Johnson,Budd (reeds) | Richardson,Jerome (reeds) | Burrell,Kenny (g) | Mure,Billy (g) | Gambella,Vince (g) | Bushnell,Bob (el-b) | Donaldson,Bobby (dr) | Allen,Doug (perc) | Marotti,Art (perc) | Ogerman,Claus (arr)
Jimmy Smith Quartet
What'd I Say | The Sermon
Englewood Cliffs,NJ, rec. 26.& 29.7.1963
Smith,Jimmy (org) | Burrell,Kenny (g) | Duvivier,George (b) | Lewis,Mel (dr)

557449-2 | CD | A Certain Smile A Certain Sadness
Astrud Gilberto With The Walter Wanderley Quartet
A Certain Smile | Nega Do Cabelo Duro | So Nice(Summer Samba) | Voce Ja Foi Bahia | Portuguese Washerwoman | It's A Lovely Day Today
NYC, rec. 20.9.1966
Gilberto,Astrud (voc) | Wanderley,Walter (p,org) | Marino,Jose (b) | Slon,Claudio (dr) | Rosengarden,Bobby (perc)
Tu Mi Delirio
NYC, rec. 21.9.1966
Gilberto,Astrud (voc) | Wanderley,Walter (p,org) | Marino,Jose (b) | Slon,Claudio (dr) | Rosengarden,Bobby (perc)
Call Me | Here's That Rainy Day
NYC, rec. 23.9.1966
Gilberto,Astrud (voc) | Wanderley,Walter (p,org) | Marino,Jose (b) | Slon,Claudio (dr) | Rosengarden,Bobby (perc)
Astrud Gilberto With The Walter Wanderley Quintet
A Certain Sadness | Goodbye Sadness(Tristeza)
NYC, rec. 21.9.1966
Gilberto,Astrud (voc) | Gilberto,Joao prob. (g) | Wanderley,Walter (p,org) | Marino,Jose (b) | Slon,Claudio (dr) | Rosengarden,Bobby (perc)
Who Needs Forever?
NYC, rec. 23.9.1966
Gilberto,Astrud (voc) | Gilberto,Joao prob. (g) | Wanderley,Walter (p,org) | Marino,Jose (b) | Slon,Claudio (dr) | Rosengarden,Bobby (perc)
Astrud Gilberto-Walter Wanderley
The Sadness After
Gilberto,Astrud (voc) | Wanderley,Walter (p,org)

557450-2 | CD | What The World Needs Now-Stan Getz Plays Bacharach And David
Stan Getz With The Richard Evans Orchestra
Wives And Lovers | Windows Of The World | Any Old Time Of the Day | In Times Like These | A House Is Not A Home | Trains And Boats And Planes | Walk On By | A House Is Not A Home(alt.take)
Chicago,Ill, rec. 31.8.1967
Getz,Stan (ts) | Corea,Chick (p) | Upchurch,Phil (g) | Booker,Walter (b) | Haynes,Roy (dr) | unkn. (brass) | unkn. (strings) | Evans,Richard (cond,arr)
Stan Getz With The Claus Ogerman Orchestra
The Look Of Love | My Own True Love | Tara's Theme
Englewood Cliffs,NJ, rec. 27.10.1967
Getz,Stan (ts) | Hancock,Herbie (p) | Hall,Jim (g) | Carter,Ron (b) | Tate,Grady (dr) | Horwath,Bill (cymbalon) | Butler,Artie (perc) | Rosengarden,Bobby (perc) | unkn. (brass) | unkn. (strings) | unkn. (chorus) | Ogerman,Claus (cond,arr)
Stan Getz With The Richard Evans Orchestra
Alfie | What The World Needs Now Is Love | In Between The Heartaches | In Between The Heartaches(alt.take)
NYC, rec. 14.2.1968
Getz,Stan (ts) | Buffington,Jimmy (fr-h) | Richardson,Jerome (reeds) | Hancock,Herbie (p) | Carey David (vib) | Burrell,Kenny (g) | Carter,Ron (b) | Tate,Grady (dr) | Gershman,Paul (v) | Mankowitz,David (v) | Nadien,David (v) | Tarack,Gerald (v) | Zaslav,Bernard (viola) | McCracken,Charles (cello) | Agostini,Gloria (harp) | Evans,Richard (cond,arr)

557451-2 | CD | From Left To Right
Bill Evans Quartet With Orchestra
Why Did I Choose You
NYC, rec. April/May 1970
Evans,Bill (p,el-p) | Brown,Sam (g) | Gomez,Eddie (b) | Morell,Marty (dr) | Orchestra | Leonard,Mickey (cond,arr) | details unknown
I'm All Smiles | Like Someone In Love | Children's Play Song
NYC, rec. 23.& 29.4./1.5./14.& 21.10./13.11.1970
Evans,Bill (p,el-p) | Kait,Jerome (tp) | Triffon,George (tp,fr-h) | Andre,Wayne (tb) | Gravine,Mickey (tb) | Messner,John (tb) | Faulise,Paul (b-tb) | Alonge,Ray (fr-h) | D'Angelis,Joseph (fr-h) | Estrin,Harvey (fl) | Ashworth,Don (reeds) | Soldo,Joe (reeds) | Penque,Romeo (reeds) | Slapin,Bill (reeds) | Brown,Sam (g) | Gomez,Eddie (b) | Chester,Gary (dr) | Gubin,Sol (dr) | Kahn,Leo (v) | Ockner,George (v) | Poliakin,Raoul (v) | Rosand,Aaron (v) | Jones,Karen (v) | Nadien,David (v) | Samaroff,Tosha (v) | Schwartz,David (v,viola) | Brown,Alfred (viola) | Forrest,Norman (viola) | Barab,Seymour (cello) | Ricci,George (cello) | Leonard,Mickey (cond,arr)
Bill Evans Quartet
Soirée | Soirée(alt.take 1) | Lullaby For Helene | What Are You Doing The Rest Of Your Life | Why Did I Choose You
San Francisco,CA, rec. 26.3.1970
Evans,Bill (p,el-p) | Brown,Sam (g) | Gomez,Eddie (b) | Morell,Marty (dr) | Leonard,Mickey (arr)
Bill Evans With Orchestra
Lullaby For Helene
NYC, rec. 23.4.1970
Evans,Bill (p,el-p) | Estrin,Harvey (fl,reeds) | Ashworth,Don (reeds) | Penque,Romeo (reeds) | Soldo,Joe (reeds) | Schwartz,David (v,viola) | Jones,Karen (v) | Kahn,Leo (v) | Nadien,David (v) | Ockner,George (v) | Poliakin,Raoul (v) | Samaroff,Tosha (v) | Forrest,Norman (viola) | Barab,Seymour (cello) | Brown,Sam (g) | Gomez,Eddie (b) | Chester,Gary (perc) | Leonard,Mickey (arr)
Bill Evans Quartet With Orchestra
What Are You Doing The Rest Of Your Life
NYC, rec. April/May 1970
Evans,Bill (p,el-p) | Brown,Sam (g) | Gomez,Eddie (b) | Morell,Marty (dr) | Orchestra | details unknown | Leonard,Mickey (arr)
Bill Evans Quartet
The Dolphin-Before
NYC, rec. 27.5.1970
Evans,Bill (p,el-p) | Brown,Sam (g) | Beal,John (el-b) | Morell,Marty (dr)
Bill Evans With Orchestra
The Dolphin-After
NYC, rec. 23.4.1970
Evans,Bill (p) | Estrin,Harvey (fl,reeds) | Ashworth,Don (reeds) | Penque,Romeo (reeds) | Soldo,Joe (reeds) | Schwartz,David (v,viola) | Jones,Karen (v) | Kahn,Leo (v) | Nadien,David (v) | Ockner,George (v) | Poliakin,Raoul (v) | Samaroff,Tosha (v) | Forrest,Norman (viola) | Barab,Seymour (cello) | Chester,Gary (perc) | Leonard,Mickey (cond,arr)

-> Note:Each recording was made by different groups and different dates!

557453-2 | CD | Blue Bash
Kenny Burrell-Jimmy Smith Trio
Blue Bash | Kenny's Sound | Kenny's Sound(alt.take) | Easy Living | Kenny's Sound(alt.take-2)
Englewood Cliffs,NJ, rec. 16.7.1963
Burrell,Kenny (g) | Smith,Jimmy (org) | Lewis,Mel (dr)
Kenny Burrell-Jimmy Smith Quartet
Travelin' | Fever | Blues For Del | Soft Winds | Travelin'(alt.take) | Fever(alt.take) | Soft Winds(alt.take) | Travelin'(uncomplete take)
Englewood Cliffs,NJ, rec. 25.7.1963
Burrell,Kenny (g) | Smith,Jimmy (org) | Hinton,Milt (b) | English,Bill (dr)
Easy Living
NYC, rec. 29.7.1963
Burrell,Kenny (g) | Smith,Jimmy (org) | Duvivier,George (b) | Lewis,Mel (dr)

557454-2 | CD | Bold Conceptions
Bob James Trio
A Moment's Notice | Nardis | The Night We Called It A Day | Trilogy | Quest | My Love(from Candide) | Fly Me To The Moon | Birk's Works | Softly As In A Morning Sunrise | Ghost Riders In The Sky
Chicago,Ill, rec. 13.-15.8.1962
James,Bob (p) | Brooks,Ron (b) | Pozar,Robert 'Bob' (dr)

557455-2 | CD | Basie's Beatle Bag
Count Basie And His Orchestra
Help | Can't Buy Me Love | Michelle | I Wanna Be Your Man | Do You Want To Know A Secret? | A Hard Day's Night | All My Loving | Yesterday | And I Love Her | She Loves You | Kansas City
Hollywood,CA, rec. 3.-5.5.1966
Basie,Count (p,org) | Aarons,Albert 'Al' (tp) | Cohn[Cohen],Sonny (tp) | Davenport,Wallace (tp) | Guilbeau,Phil (tp) | Chambers,Henderson (tb) | Grey,Al (tb) | Mitchell,Grover (tb) | Hughes,Bill (b-tb) | Royal,Marshall (cl,as) | Plater,Bobby (fl,as) | Dixon,Eric (fl,ts) | Davis,Eddie 'Lockjaw' (ts) | Fowlkes,Charlie (fl,bs) | Green,Freddie (g) | Keenan,Norman (b) | Payne,Sonny (dr) | O'Farrill,Chico (arr)
Yesterday
Basie,Count (p,org) | Aarons,Albert 'Al' (tp) | Cohn[Cohen],Sonny (tp) | Davenport,Wallace (tp) | Guilbeau,Phil (tp) | Chambers,Henderson (tb) | Grey,Al (tb) | Mitchell,Grover (tb) | Hughes,Bill (b-tb) | Royal,Marshall (cl,as) | Plater,Bobby (fl,as) | Dixon,Eric (fl,ts) | Davis,Eddie 'Lockjaw' (ts) | Fowlkes,Charlie (fl,bs) | Green,Freddie (g) | Keenan,Norman (b) | Payne,Sonny (dr) | O'Farrill,Chico (arr) | Henderson,Bill (voc)

557486-2 | CD | With Respect To Nat
Oscar Peterson Trio
It's Only A Paper Moon | Sweet Lorraine | Little Girl | Gee Baby Ain't I Good To You | Straighten Up And Fly Right | What Can I Say After I Say I'm Sorry | Easy Listening Blues
Hollywood,CA, rec. 28.10.1965
Peterson,Oscar (p,voc) | Ellis,Herb (g) | Brown,Ray (b)
Oscar Peterson With Orchestra
When My Sugar Walks Down The Street | Walkin' My Baby Back Home | Unforgettable | Orange Coloured Sky | Calypso Blues
NYC, rec. 13.11.1965
Peterson,Oscar (voc) | Frosk,John (tp) | Newman,Joe (tp) | Royal,Ernie (tp) | Stiles,Danny (tp,fl-h) | Andre,Wayne (tb) | Cleveland,Jimmy (tb) | Johnson,J.J. (tb) | Studd,Tony (b-tb) | Powell,Seldon (fl,alto-fl) | Richardson,Jerome (fl,b-fl) | Dodgion,Jerry (as) | Woods,Phil (as) | Halladay,Marvin (bs) | Jones,Hank (p) | Galbraith,Barry (g) | Davis,Richard (b) | Lewis,Mel (dr,bongos) | Albam,Manny (cond,arr)

557492-2 | CD | Jambo Caribe
Dizzy Gillespie Sextet
Barbados Carnival | And Then She Stopped
Chicago,Ill, rec. 4.11.1964
Gillespie,Dizzy (tp) | Moody,James (fl,ts) | Barron,Kenny (p,voc) | White,Chris (g,b,voc) | Collins,Rudy (dr,perc) | Fields,Kansas (perc) | Henry,Ann (voc)
Jambo | Trinidad,Hello | Poor Joe
Chicago,Ill, rec. 5.11.1964
Gillespie,Dizzy (tp,voc) | Moody,James (ts) | Barron,Kenny (p) | White,Chris (b) | Collins,Rudy (dr) | Fields,Kansas (perc)
Don't Try To Keep Up With The Jones | Trinidad,Goodbye | Fiesta Mojo
Chicago,Ill, rec. 6.11.1964
Gillespie,Dizzy (tp,voc) | Moody,James (ts) | Barron,Kenny (p) | White,Chris (b) | Collins,Rudy (dr) | Fields,Kansas (perc)

557532-2 | CD | Ultimate Stan Getz selected by Joe Henderson
Stan Getz Quintet
The Way You Look Tonight | Stars Fell On Alabama
NYC, rec. 12.12.1952
Getz,Stan (ts) | Raney,Jimmy (g) | Jordan,Duke (p) | Crow,Bill (b) | Isola,Frank (dr)
Dizzy Gillespie-Stan Getz Sextet
Siboney(part 2) | It Don't Mean A Thing If It Ain't Got That Swing
Hollywood,CA, rec. 9.12.1953
Gillespie,Dizzy (tp) | Getz,Stan (ts) | Peterson,Oscar (p) | Ellis,Herb (g) | Brown,Ray (b) | Roach,Max (dr)

Stan Getz Quintet
Summertime | S-h-i-n-e
Hollywood,CA, rec. 15.8.1955
Getz,Stan (ts) | Candoli,Conte (tp) | Levy,Lou (p) | Vinnegar,Leroy (b) | Manne,Shelly (dr)
For Musicians Only
Wee(Allen's Alley)
Los Angeles,CA, rec. 16.10.1956
Gillespie,Dizzy (tp) | Stitt,Sonny (as) | Getz,Stan (ts) | Lewis,John (p) | Ellis,Herb (g) | Brown,Ray (b) | Levey,Stan (dr)
Stan Getz And J.J. Johnson With The Oscar Peterson Quartet
Billie's Bounce
Shrine Auditorium,LA, rec. 25.10.1957
Johnson,J.J. (tb) | Getz,Stan (ts) | Peterson,Oscar (p) | Ellis,Herb (g) | Brown,Ray (b) | Kay,Connie (dr)
Stan Getz With The Oscar Peterson Quartet
It Never Entered My Mind
Getz,Stan (ts) | Peterson,Oscar (p) | Ellis,Herb (g) | Brown,Ray (b) | Kay,Connie (dr)
Stan Getz With The Eddie Sauter Orchestra
Once Upon A Time
NYC, rec. 28.7.1961
Getz,Stan (ts) | Neves,John (b) | Haynes,Roy (dr) | Carr,Norman (v) | Martin,Alan (v) | Tarack,Gerald (v) | Glick,Jacob (viola) | Rogers,Bruce (cello) | unkn. (more strings) | unkn. (harp) | Kay,Hershy (ld) | Sauter,Eddie (arr)
Stan Getz-Charlie Byrd Sextet
Desafinado
Washington,DC, rec. 13.2.1962
Getz,Stan (ts) | Byrd,Charlie (g) | Byrd,Gene (g) | Betts,Keter (b) | Deppenschmidt,Buddy (perc) | Reichenbach,Bill (perc)
Stan Getz Quartet
Con Alma
Englewood Cliffs,NJ, rec. 30.3.1967
Getz,Stan (ts) | Corea,Chick (p) | Carter,Ron (b) | Tate,Grady (dr)

557534-2 | CD | Jazz At The Philharmonic:Best Of The 1940's Concerts
JATP All Stars
Bugle Call Rag
Hollywood,CA, rec. 2.7.1944
JATP All Stars | Sherock,Shorty (tp) | Jacquet,Illinois (ts) | McVea,Jack (ts) | Cole,Nat King (p) | Paul,Les (g) | Callender,Red (b) | Young,Lee (dr)
Oh! Lady Be Good
Hollywood,CA, rec. 28.1.1946
JATP All Stars | Killian,Al (tp) | McGhee,Howard (tp) | Parker,Charlie (as) | Smith,Willie (as) | Phillips,Flip (ts) | Ross,Arnold (p) | Hadnott,Billy (b) | Young,Lee (dr)
Gene Krupa Trio
Idaho
Krupa,Gene (dr) | Ventura,Charlie (ts) | Napoleon,Teddy (p)
JATP All Stars
Philharmonis Blues(Carnegie Blues)
NYC, rec. 27.5.1946
JATP All Stars | Clayton,Buck (tp) | Hawkins,Coleman (ts) | Jacquet,Illinois (ts) | Young,Lester (ts) | Kersey,Kenny (p) | McKibbon,Al (b) | Heard,J.C. (dr)
Billie Holiday With The JATP All Stars
Billie's Blues(aka I Love My Man)
Live at Carnegie Hall,NYC, rec. 3.6.1946
Holiday,Billie (voc) | JATP All Stars | Guy,Joe (tp) | Auld,Georgie (as) | Jacquet,Illinois (ts) | Young,Lester (ts) | Kersey,Kenny (p) | Grimes,Tiny prob. (g) | McKibbon,Al (b) | Heard,J.C. (dr)
JATP All Stars
How High The Moon
Live at Syria Mosque,Pittsburgh, rec. 5.3.1947
JATP All Stars | Clayton,Buck (tp) | Young,Trummy (tb) | Smith,Willie (as) | Hawkins,Coleman (ts) | Phillips,Flip (ts) | Kersey,Kenny (p) | Fonville,Benny (b) | Rich,Buddy (dr)
Perdido
Live at Carnegie Hall,NYC, rec. 27.9.1947
JATP All Stars | McGhee,Howard (tp) | Harris,Bill (tb) | Jacquet,Illinois (ts) | Phillips,Flip (ts) | Jones,Hank (p) | Brown,Ray (b) | Jones,Jo (dr)
Flying Home | Embraceable You
Live at Carnegie Hall,NYC, rec. 18.9.1949
JATP All Stars | Eldridge,Roy (tp) | Turk,Tommy (tb) | Parker,Charlie (as) | Phillips,Flip (ts) | Young,Lester (ts) | Jones,Hank (p) | Brown,Ray (b) | Rich,Buddy (dr)

557535-2 | CD | Ultimate Dizzy Gillespie
Dizzy Gillespie And His Orchestra
Birk's Works
NYC, rec. 7.4.1957
Gillespie,Dizzy (tp,arr,voc) | Dawud,Talib (tp) | Morgan,Lee (tp) | Perry,Ermit V. (tp) | Warwick,Carl (tp) | Grey,Al (tb) | Levitt,Rod (tb) | Liston,Melba (tb) | Powell,Jimmy (as) | Henry,Ernie (as) | Mitchell,Billy (ts) | Golson,Benny (ts) | Root,Billy (bs) | Kelly,Wynton (p) | West,Paul (b) | Persip,Charles (dr) | Wilkins,Ernie (arr)
Con Alma
Live at Newport,Rhode Island, rec. 6.7.1957
Gillespie,Dizzy (tp,arr,voc) | Dawud,Talib (tp) | Morgan,Lee (tp) | Perry,Ermit V. (tp) | Warwick,Carl (tp) | Grey,Al (tb) | Connors,Chuck (tb) | Liston,Melba (tb) | Powell,Jimmy (as) | Henry,Ernie (as) | Mitchell,Billy (ts) | Golson,Benny (ts) | Moore,Numa 'Pee Wee' (bs) | Kelly,Wynton (p) | West,Paul (b) | Persip,Charles (dr) | Golson,Benny (arr)
Charlie Parker Quintet
Bloomdido
NYC, rec. 6.6.1950
Parker,Charlie (as) | Gillespie,Dizzy (tp) | Monk,Thelonious (p) | Russell,Curly (b) | Rich,Buddy (dr)
Dizzy Gillespie-Roy Eldridge Sextet
Sometimes I'm Happy
Hollywood,CA, rec. 29.10.1954
Gillespie,Dizzy (tp) | Eldridge,Roy (tp,voc) | Peterson,Oscar (p) | Ellis,Herb (g) | Brown,Ray (b) | Bellson,Louie (dr)
For Musicians Only
Wee
Hollywood,CA, rec. 16.10.1956
Gillespie,Dizzy (tp) | Stitt,Sonny (as) | Getz,Stan (ts) | Lewis,John (p) | Ellis,Herb (g) | Brown,Ray (b) | Levey,Stan (dr)
Dizzy Gillespie And His Orchestra
Ool-Ya-Koo
Live at Carnegie Hall,NYC, rec. 4.3.1961
Gillespie,Dizzy (tp,voc) | Frosk,John (tp) | Terry,Clark (tp) | Travis,Nick (tp) | Warwick,Carl (tp) | Matthews,George (tb) | Sparrow,Arnett (tb) | Woodman,Britt (tb) | Faulise,Paul (b-tb) | Buffington,Jimmy (fr-h) | Schuller,Gunther (fr-h) | Barrows,John (fr-h) | Berg,Richard (fr-h) | Butterfield,Don (tuba) | Wright,Leo (fl,as) | Schifrin,Lalo (p,arr) | Davis,Art (b) | Lampkin,Chuck (dr) | Barretto,Ray (congas) | Colazo,Julio (perc) | Mangual,Jose (perc) | Carroll,Joe (voc)
Dizzy Gillespie Sextet
Umbrella Man
NYC, rec. 18.2.1958
Gillespie,Dizzy (tp,voc) | Spann,Les (fl) | Mance,Junior[Julian C.] (p) | Jones,Sam (b) | Humphries,Lex (dr) | Pozo,Chino (congas)
Fiesta Mojo
Chicago,Ill, rec. 6.11.1964
Gillespie,Dizzy (tp) | Moody,James (fl) | Barron,Kenny (p) | White,Chris (b) | Collins,Rudy (dr) | Fields,Kansas (perc,surdo)
Dizzy Gillespie Quintet
Bebop
NYC, rec. 23.4.1963
Gillespie,Dizzy (tp) | Moody,James (ts) | Barron,Kenny (p) | White,Chris (b) | Collins,Rudy (dr)
Dizzy Gillespie And His Orchestra
Chega De Saudade(No More Blues-part 2)
NYC, rec. 10.7.1962
Gillespie,Dizzy (tp) | Wright,Leo (fl,as) | Ventura,Charlie (ts,bass-sax) | Schifrin,Lalo (p,arr) | Sete,Bola (g) | Paula,Jose (g,tam) | White,Chris (b) | Collins,Rudy (dr) | Costa,Carmen (cabassa)
Come Sunday
NYC, rec. 27.4.1960
Gillespie,Dizzy (tp) | Green,Bennie (tb) | De Dominica,Robert (fl) | Webb,Stanley (sax) | Richie,Paul (woodwinds) | Murtauch,John (reeds) | Bright,Ernest (reeds) | Berg,Richard (fr-h) | Alonge,Ray (fr-h) | Singer,Joe (fr-h) | McAllister,Jay (tuba) | Devens,George (vib) | Jones,Hank (p) | Duvivier,George (b) | Persip,Charles (dr)

557536-2 | CD | Ultimate Bill Evans selected by Herbie Hancock
Bill Evans Trio
I Believe In You
NYC, rec. 20.8.1962
Evans,Bill (p) | Budwig,Monty (b) | Manne,Shelly (dr)
Bill Evans
N.Y.C.'s No Lark
NYC, rec. 6.2.1963
Evans,Bill (3-p-overdubbed)
Round About Midnight
NYC, rec. 9.2.1963
Evans,Bill (3-p-overdubbed)
Stan Getz With The Bill Evans Trio
Funkallero
Englewood Cliffs,NJ, rec. 6.5.1964
Getz,Stan (ts) | Evans,Bill (p) | Carter,Ron (b) | Jones,Elvin (dr)
Bill Evans Trio
What Is This Thing Called Love
Live at The Trident Club,Sausolito,CA, rec. 7./9.7.1964
Evans,Bill (p) | Israels,Chuck (b) | Bunker,Larry (dr)
I Should Care
Live at Town Hall,NYC, rec. 21.2.1966
Evans,Bill (p) | Israels,Chuck (b) | Wise,Arnold (dr)
Bill Evans-Jim Hall
Turn Out The Stars | Angel Face | Jazz Samba
Englewood Cliffs,NJ, rec. 7.& 10.4.1966
Evans,Bill (p) | Hall,Jim (g)
Bill Evans
I Loves You Porgy
Live at The Montreux Jazz Festival, rec. 15.6.1968
Evans,Bill (p-solo)
Bill Evans Trio
Walking Up | Mother Of Earl
Live at The Montreal Jazz Festival, rec. 15.6.1968
Evans,Bill (p) | Gomez,Eddie (b) | DeJohnette,Jack (dr)
Bill Evans
A Time For Love
NYC, rec. 23.9.1968
Evans,Bill (p-solo)

557537-2 | CD | Ultimate Ben Webster selected by James Carter
Dinah Washington With The Jimmy Cobb Orchestra
Trouble In Mind
Los Angeles,CA, rec. 18.1.1952
Washington,Dinah (voc) | Cobb,Jimmy (dr) | Webster,Ben (ts) | Gray,Wardell (ts) | Kelly,Wynton (p) | details unknown
The Ravens
Don't Mention My Name | I'll Be Back
details unknown, rec. December 1952
Ravens:,The | Van Loan,Joe (voc) | Puzie,Leonard (voc) | Suttles,Warren (voc) | Webster,Ben (ts) | Sanford,Bill (p) | Rucks,Jimmy (b,voc) | details unknown
Ben Webster With The Oscar Peterson Quartet
Cotton Tail
NYC, rec. 21.5.1953
Webster,Ben (ts) | Peterson,Oscar (p) | Kessel,Barney (g) | Brown,Ray (b) | Heard,J.C. (dr)
Tenderly
Hollywood,CA, rec. 8.12.1953
Webster,Ben (ts) | Peterson,Oscar (p) | Ellis,Herb (g) | Brown,Ray (b) | Stoller,Alvin (dr)
Ben Webster With Orchestra And Strings
Chelsea Bridge
NYC, rec. 28.5.1954
Webster,Ben (ts) | Scott,Tony (cl) | Ceppos,Mac (v) | Novales,David (v) | Russell,Mischa (v) | Dickler,Richard (viola) | Sims,Rudolph (cello) | Strayhorn,Billy (p,arr,ld) | Duvivier,George (b) | Bellson,Louie (dr)
There Is No Greater Love | Early Autumn
NYC, rec. 9.9.1955
Webster,Ben (ts) | Epstein[Young],Al (engl-h,cl,b-cl) | Bank,Danny (fl,cl) | Colletta,Harold (v) | Donegan,Martin (v) | Kruczek,Leo (v) | Lookofsky,Harry (v) | Orloff,Gene (v) | Samaroff,Tosha (v) | Winter,Paul (v) | Fish,Bert (viola) | Borodkin,Abram (cello) | Ricci,George (cello) | Schmit,Lucien (cello) | Jones,Hank (p) | Amsterdam,Chet (b) | Marshall,Wendell (b) | Johnson,Osie (dr) | Burns,Ralph (cond,arr)
Ben Webster Quartet
Boogie Woogie | Ill Wind
Hollywood,CA, rec. 15.10.1957
Webster,Ben (ts,p) | Ellis,Herb (g) | Brown,Ray (b) | Levey,Stan (dr)
Ben Webster-Stan Levey
Who?
Webster,Ben (p) | Levey,Stan (dr)
Ben Webster And His Associates
Time After Time
NYC, rec. 9.4.1959
Webster,Ben (ts) | Jones,Jimmy (p) | Spann,Les (g) | Brown,Ray (b) | Jones,Jo (dr)
Young Bean
Webster,Ben (ts) | Eldridge,Roy (tp) | Hawkins,Coleman (ts) | Johnson,Budd (ts) | Jones,Jimmy (p) | Spann,Les (g) | Brown,Ray (b) | Jones,Jo (dr)
Gerry Mulligan-Ben Webster Quintet
Sunday
Hollywood,CA, rec. 2.12.1959
Webster,Ben (ts) | Mulligan,Gerry (bs) | Rowles,Jimmy (p) | Vinnegar,Leroy (b) | Lewis,Mel (dr)

557538-2 | CD | Ultimate Coleman Hawkins selected by Sonny Rollins
Coleman Hawkins
Picasso
NYC, rec. 1948
Hawkins,Coleman (ts-solo)
Coleman Hawkins Quintet
Bean At The Met | I Only Have Eyes For You(alt.take) | I'm In The Mood For Love
NYC, rec. 31.1.1944
Hawkins,Coleman (ts) | Eldridge,Roy (tp) | Wilson,Teddy (p) | Taylor,Billy (b) | Cole,William 'Cozy' (dr)
Coleman Hawkins Quartet
Cattin' At Keynote | Night And Day
NYC, rec. 17.2.1944
Hawkins,Coleman (ts) | Wilson,Teddy (p) | Crosby,Israel (b) | Cole,William 'Cozy' (dr)
Cozy Cole All Stars
The Father Co-Operates | Just One More Chance | Thru For The Night
NYC, rec. 22.2.1944
Cole,William 'Cozy' (dr) | Thomas,Joe (tp) | Young,Trummy (tb) | Hawkins,Coleman (ts) | Hines,Earl 'Fatha' (p) | Walters,Teddy (g) | Taylor,Billy (b)
Coleman Hawkins Quartet
Just One Of Those Things | Don't Blame Me(alt.take) | Hallelujah
NYC, rec. 29.5.1944
Hawkins,Coleman (ts) | Wilson,Teddy (p) | Kirby,John (b) | Catlett,Big Sid (dr)
Coleman Hawkins Quintet
Under A Blanket Of Blue | Beyond The Blue Horizon
NYC, rec. 17.10.1944
Hawkins,Coleman (ts) | Clayton,Buck (tp) | Wilson,Teddy (p) | Stewart,Slam (b) | Best,Denzil (dr)
Coleman Hawkins With The Oscar Peterson Quartet
Like Someone In Love
Hollywood,CA, rec. 16.10.1957
Hawkins,Coleman (ts) | Peterson,Oscar (p) | Ellis,Herb (g) | Brown,Ray (b) | Stoller,Alvin (dr)
Coleman Hawkins And Ben Webster With The Oscar Peterson Quartet
La Rosita
Hawkins,Coleman (ts) | Webster,Ben (ts) | Peterson,Oscar (p) | Ellis,Herb (g) | Brown,Ray (b) | Stoller,Alvin (dr)

557543-2 | CD | Johnny Hodges With Billy Strayhorn And The Orchestra
Billy Strayhorn Orchestra
Don't Get Around Much Anymore | I Got It Bad And That Ain't Good | Gal From Joe's | Your Love Has Faded | Jeep's Blues | Day Dream | Juice A-Plenty | Stardust
Englewood Cliffs,NJ, rec. 11./12.12.1961
Strayhorn,Billy (arr,ld) | Anderson,Cat (tp) | Baker,Harold 'Shorty' (tp) | Berry,Bill (tp) | Mullens,Eddie (tp) | Brown,Lawrence (tb) | Jackson,Quentin (tb) | Connors,Chuck (b-tb) | Procope,Russell (cl,as) | Hodges,Johnny (as) | Hamilton,Jimmy (cl,as) | Gonsalves,Paul (ts) | Carney,Harry (b-cl,bs) | Jones,Jimmie (p) | Bell,Aaron (b) | Woodyard,Sam (dr)
Azure | Tailor Made
Strayhorn,Billy (arr,ld) | Anderson,Cat (tp) | Baker,Harold 'Shorty' (tp) | Berry,Bill (tp) | Mullens,Eddie (tp) | McGhee,Howard (tp) | Brown,Lawrence (tb) | Jackson,Quentin (tb) | Connors,Chuck (b-tb) | Procope,Russell (cl,as) | Hodges,Johnny (as) | Hamilton,Jimmy (cl,as) | Gonsalves,Paul (ts) | Carney,Harry (b-cl,bs) | Jones,Jimmie (p) | Bell,Aaron (b) | Woodyard,Sam (dr)
I'm Just A Lucky So-And-So
Strayhorn,Billy (arr,ld) | Anderson,Cat (tp) | Berry,Bill (tp) | Mullens,Eddie (tp) | McGhee,Howard (tp) | Brown,Lawrence (tb) | Jackson,Quentin (tb) | Connors,Chuck (b-tb) | Procope,Russell (cl,as) | Hodges,Johnny (as) | Hamilton,Jimmy (cl,as) | Gonsalves,Paul (ts) | Carney,Harry (b-cl,bs) | Jones,Jimmie (p) | Bell,Aaron (b) | Woodyard,Sam (dr)

557544-2 | CD | An Electrifying Evening With The Dizzy Gillespie Quintet
Dizzy Gillespie Quintet
Kush | Salt Peanuts | A Night In Tunisia | The Mooche
Live at The Museum Of Modern Art,NYC, rec. 9.2.1961
Gillespie,Dizzy (tp) | Wright,Leo (fl,as) | Schifrin,Lalo (p) | Cunningham,Bob (b) | Lampkin,Chuck (dr)
Dizzy Gillespie
Interview(18:03) by Charles Schwartz
Museum Of Modern Art,NYC, rec. 9.2.1961
Gillespie,Dizzy (talking)

557545-2 | CD | Sonny Rollins And The Big Brass
Sonny Rollins Orchestra
Who Cares | Love Is A Simple Thing | Grand Street | Far Out East | Grand Street(mono LP ending) | Grand Street(verve LP ending)
NYC, rec. 11.7.1958
Rollins,Sonny (ts) | Wilkins,Ernie (arr,ld) | Adderley,Nat (co) | Terry,Clark (tp) | Jones,Reunald (tp) | Royal,Ernie (tp) | Byers,Billy (tb) | Cleveland,Jimmy (tb) | Rehak,Frank (tb) | Thomas,Rene (g) | Katz,Dick (p) | Grimes,Henry (b) | Haynes,Roy (dr) | Butterfield,Don (tuba)
Sonny Rollins Trio
What's My Name? | If You Were The Only Girl In The World | Manhattan
NYC, rec. 10.7.1958
Rollins,Sonny (ts) | Grimes,Henry (b) | Wright,Charles 'Specs' (dr)
Body And Soul
Rollins,Sonny (ts-solo)
Sonny Rollins Quartet
Doxy | You Are Too Beautiful
Live at Music Inn,Lenox,Mass., rec. 3.8.1958
Rollins,Sonny (ts) | Lewis,John (p) | Heath,Percy (b) | Kay,Connie (dr)

557549-2 | CD | West Coast Jazz
Stan Getz Quintet
Four
Hollywood,CA, rec. 9.8.1955
Getz,Stan (ts) | Candoli,Conte (tp) | Levy,Lou (p) | Vinnegar,Leroy (b) | Manne,Shelly (dr)
East Of The Sun West Of The Moon | Suddenly It's Spring | A Night In Tunisia | Summertime | Shine | Split Kick
Hollywood,CA, rec. 15.8.1955
Getz,Stan (ts) | Candoli,Conte (tp) | Levy,Lou (p) | Vinnegar,Leroy (b) | Manne,Shelly (dr)
Stan Getz Quartet
Of Thee I Sing | A Handful Of Stars | Our Love Is Here To Stay | Serenade In Blue | Of Thee I Sing(alt.take) | Our Love Is Here To Stay(alt.take)
Hollywood,CA, rec. 19.8.1955
Getz,Stan (ts) | Levy,Lou (p) | Vinnegar,Leroy (b) | Manne,Shelly (dr)

557554-2 | CD | A Family Affair
Christian McBride Group
I'm Coming Home
North Hollywood,CA, rec. 27.-29.1.1998
McBride,Christian (b,voice) | Warfield Jr.,Tim (ts,voice) | Craig,Charles (el-p,voice) | Hutchinson,Gregory (dr,voice) | Jackson,Munyungo (tambourine,voice) | Duke,George (voice)
Brown Funk(for Ray)
McBride,Christian (el-b) | Warfield Jr.,Tim (ts) | Malone,Russell (el-g) | Craig,Charles (el-p,mini-moog) | Hutchinson,Gregory (dr) | Jackson,Munyungo (perc)
Theme From Our Fairytale
McBride,Christian (fretless-el-b) | Warfield Jr.,Tim (ts) | Malone,Russell (el-g) | Craig,Charles (p) | Hutchinson,Gregory (dr) | Jackson,Munyungo (perc)
Or So You Thought - ...Or So You Thought
McBride,Christian (keyboards,synth,fretless-el-b) | Warfield Jr.,Tim (ts) | Craig,Charles (el-p,mini-moog) | Hutchinson,Gregory (dr) | Jackson,Munyungo (perc) | Vesta (voc)
Summer Soft
McBride,Christian (fretless-el-b) | Warfield Jr.,Tim (ts) | Craig,Charles (el-p) | Hutchinson,Gregory (dr) | Jackson,Munyungo (perc)
A Dream Of You
McBride,Christian (b) | Warfield Jr.,Tim (ts) | Craig,Charles (p) | Hutchinson,Gregory (dr) | Downing,Will (voc)
Family Affair | Open Sesame
McBride,Christian (b) | Warfield Jr.,Tim (ts) | Craig,Charles (p,el-p) | Hutchinson,Gregory (dr)
Wayne's World
McBride,Christian (fretless-el-b) | Warfield Jr.,Tim (ts) | Craig,Charles (p,el-p) | Hutchinson,Gregory (dr)
I'll Write A Song For You
McBride,Christian (b) | Malone,Russell (g)

557567-2 | 2 CD | Sarah Vaughan Sings Gershwin
Sarah Vaughan With The Hal Mooney Orchestra
Isn't It A Pity | Someone To Watch Over Me | Bidin' My Time | The Man I Love | How Long Has This Been Going On | I've Got A Crush On You | Aren't You Kind Of Glad We Did | Looking For A Boy | He Loves And She Loves | A Foggy Day(In London Town) | Do It Again | Love Walked In
NYC, rec. 20.3.1957
Vaughan,Sarah (voc) | Jones,Jimmie (p) | Mooney,Hal (arr,ld) | details unknown
I'll Build A Stairway To Paradise | Lorelei | They All Laughed | Let's Call The Whole Thing Off
NYC, rec. 21.3.1957
Vaughan,Sarah (voc) | Jones,Jimmie (p) | Mooney,Hal (arr,ld) | details unknown
Of Thee I Sing | My One And Only | Summertime | I Won't Say I Will | Things Are Looking Up | Of Thee I Sing(stereo) | Summertime(alt.take) | Things Are Looking Up(rehersal) | I Won't Say I Will(rehersal) | I Won't Say I Will(alt.take) | Of Thee I Sing(alt.take 1) | Of Thee I Sing(alt.take 2) | Of Thee I Sing(alt.take 3) | Of Thee I Sing(alt.take 4) | Of Thee I Sing(alt.take 5) | My One And Only(rehersal) | My One And Only(alt.take 1) | My One And Only(alt.take 2)
NYC, rec. 24.4.1957
Vaughan,Sarah (voc) | Jones,Jimmie (p) | Mooney,Hal (arr,ld) | details unknown
My Man's Gone Now
NYC, rec. 25.4.1957
Vaughan,Sarah (voc) | Jones,Jimmie (p) | Mooney,Hal (arr,ld) | details unknown

LABELVERZEICHNIS

557821-2 | CD | Khepera
Randy Weston African Rhythm
Creation | Anu Anu | The Shrine | Prayer Blues | Niger Mambo | Mystery Of Love
NYC, rec. 23.-25.2.1998
Weston,Randy (p) | Powell,Benny (tb) | Kibwe,Talib (as) | Sanders,Pharoah (ts) | Blake,Alex (b) | Lewis,Victor (dr) | Bey,Chief (ashiko-dr,voc) | Clark,Neil (congas,african-perc,djimbe,gong)
Portrait Of Cheikh Anta Diop
Weston,Randy (p) | Powell,Benny (tb) | Kibwe,Talib (as) | Sanders,Pharoah (ts) | Blake,Alex (b) | Lewis,Victor (dr) | Bey,Chief (ashiko-dr,voc) | Clark,Neil (congas,african-perc,djimbe,gong) | Fen,Min Xiao (pipa)
Boram Xam Xam
Weston,Randy (p) | Blake,Alex (b) | Bey,Chief (ashiko-dr)
The Shang
Weston,Randy (p) | Fen,Min Xiao (gong,pipa)

557913-2 | CD | Big Band Bossa Nova
Quincy Jones And His Orchestra
Manha De Carnaval(Morning Of The Carnival)
NYC, rec. 4.9.1962
unkn. (tp,tb,woodwinds) | Richardson,Jerome (fl,alto-fl) | Gonsalves,Paul (ts) | Schifrin,Lalo (p) | White,Chris (b) | Collins,Rudy (dr)
Boogie Stop Shuffle
unkn. (tp,tb,woodwinds) | Terry,Clark (tp,fl-h) | Richardson,Jerome (fl,alto-fl) | Gonsalves,Paul (ts) | Schifrin,Lalo (p) | White,Chris (b) | Collins,Rudy (dr)
Samba Da Una Nota So(One Note Samba)
unkn. (tp,tb,woodwinds) | Richardson,Jerome (fl,alto-fl) | Woods,Phil (as) | Gonsalves,Paul (ts) | Schifrin,Lalo (p) | White,Chris (b) | Collins,Rudy (dr)
On The Street Where You Live | Lalo Bossa Nova | Serenata
NYC, rec. 7.9.1962
unkn. (tp,tb,woodwinds) | unkn. (3 fr-h) | Richardson,Jerome (fl,alto-fl) | Woods,Phil (as) | Hall,Jim (g) | Schifrin,Lalo (p) | White,Chris (b) | Collins,Rudy (dr)
Desafinado
NYC, rec. 8.9.1962
unkn. (tp,tb,woodwinds) | Richardson,Jerome (fl,alto-fl) | Hall,Jim (g) | Schifrin,Lalo (p) | White,Chris (b) | Collins,Rudy (dr)
Chega De Saudade(No More Blues)
unkn. (tp,tb,woodwinds) | Terry,Clark (fl-h) | Richardson,Jerome (fl,alto-fl) | Schifrin,Lalo (p) | White,Chris (b) | Collins,Rudy (dr)
So E Tarde Me Pardoa(Forgive Me If I'm Late) | A Taste Of Honey
NYC, rec. 13.9.1962
unkn. (tp,tb,woodwinds) | Richardson,Jerome (fl,alto-fl) | Schifrin,Lalo (p) | White,Chris (b) | Collins,Rudy (dr)
Soul Bossa Nova
unkn. (tp,tb,woodwinds) | Kirk,Rahsaan Roland (fl) | Richardson,Jerome (fl,alto-fl) | Schifrin,Lalo (p) | White,Chris (b) | Collins,Rudy (dr)

558074-2 | CD | The Swingin' Miss 'D'
Dinah Washington With The Quincy Jones Orchestra
They Didn't Believe Me
NYC, rec. 5.12.1956
Washington,Dinah (voc) | Glow,Bernie (tp) | Shavers,Charlie (tp) | Terry,Clark (tp) | Travis,Nick (tp) | Cleveland,Jimmy (tb) | Green,Urbie (tb) | Jackson,Quentin (tb) | Mitchell,Tom (b-tb) | Elliott,Don (vib,mellophone) | Anderson,Clarence 'Sleepy' (p) | Galbraith,Barry (g) | Hinton,Milt (b) | Johnson,Osie (dr) | Jones,Quincy (arr,ld)
Every Time We Say Goodbye | But Not For Me
Washington,Dinah (voc) | Glow,Bernie (tp) | Shavers,Charlie (tp) | Terry,Clark (tp) | Travis,Nick (tp) | Cleveland,Jimmy (tb) | Green,Urbie (tb) | Jackson,Quentin (tb) | Mitchell,Tom (b-tb) | McKusick,Hal (as) | Ortega,Anthony (as) | Richardson,Jerome (ts) | Thompson,Lucky (ts) | Bank,Danny (bs) | Elliott,Don (vib,mellophone) | Anderson,Clarence 'Sleepy' (p) | Galbraith,Barry (g) | Hinton,Milt (b) | Johnson,Osie (dr) | Wilkins,Ernie (arr) | Jones,Quincy (ld)
Bargain Day
NYC, rec. 6.12.1956
Washington,Dinah (voc) | Glow,Bernie (tp) | Shavers,Charlie (tp) | Terry,Clark (tp) | Travis,Nick (tp) | Cleveland,Jimmy (tb) | Green,Urbie (tb) | Jackson,Quentin (tb) | Mitchell,Tom (b-tb) | McKusick,Hal (as) | Ortega,Anthony (as) | Richardson,Jerome (ts) | Thompson,Lucky (ts) | Bank,Danny (bs) | Elliott,Don (vib,mellophone) | Anderson,Clarence 'Sleepy' (p) | Galbraith,Barry (g) | Hinton,Milt (b) | Johnson,Osie (dr) | Jones,Quincy (arr,ld)
Makin' Whoopee
Washington,Dinah (voc) | Shavers,Charlie (tp) | Terry,Clark (tp) | Severinsen,Doc (tp) | Maxwell,Jimmy (tp) | Cleveland,Jimmy (tb) | Green,Urbie (tb) | Jackson,Quentin (tb) | Mitchell,Tom (b-tb) | McKusick,Hal (as) | Ortega,Anthony (as) | Richardson,Jerome (ts) | Thompson,Lucky (ts) | Bank,Danny (bs) | Elliott,Don (xyl) | Anderson,Clarence 'Sleepy' (p) | Galbraith,Barry (g) | Hinton,Milt (b) | Johnson,Osie (dr) | Jones,Quincy (arr,ld)
Never Let Me Go
Washington,Dinah (voc) | Shavers,Charlie (tp) | Terry,Clark (tp) | Severinsen,Doc (tp) | Maxwell,Jimmy (tp) | Cleveland,Jimmy (tb) | Green,Urbie (tb) | Jackson,Quentin (tb) | Mitchell,Tom (b-tb) | McKusick,Hal (as) | Ortega,Anthony (as) | Richardson,Jerome (ts) | Thompson,Lucky (ts) | Bank,Danny (bs) | Elliott,Don (vib,bongos,mellophone) | Anderson,Clarence 'Sleepy' (p) | Galbraith,Barry (g) | Hinton,Milt (b) | Johnson,Osie (dr) | Golson,Benny (arr) | Jones,Quincy (ld)
I'll Close My Eyes
Washington,Dinah (voc) | Cleveland,Jimmy (tb) | Green,Urbie (tb) | Jackson,Quentin (tb) | Mitchell,Tom (b-tb) | Elliott,Don (vib,bongos,mellophone) | Anderson,Clarence 'Sleepy' (p) | Galbraith,Barry (g) | Hinton,Milt (b) | Johnson,Osie (dr) | Golson,Benny (arr) | Jones,Quincy (ld)
Caravan | Perdido | Is You Is Or Is You Ain't My Baby | Somebody Loves Me | I'll Drown In My Tears | You Let My Love Grow Old
NYC, rec. 4.12.1956
Washington,Dinah (voc) | Shavers,Charlie (tp) | Terry,Clark (tp) | Royal,Ernie (tp) | Wilder,Joe (tp) | Cleveland,Jimmy (tb) | Green,Urbie (tb) | Jackson,Quentin (tb) | Mitchell,Tom (b-tb) | Elliott,Don (vib,bongos,mellophone) | Anderson,Clarence 'Sleepy' (p) | Galbraith,Barry (g) | Hinton,Milt (b) | Crawford,Jimmy (dr) | Jones,Quincy (arr,ld)
Relax Max | Tears To Burn | The Kissing Way Home | I Know
NYC, rec. 25.6.1956
Washington,Dinah (voc) | Cleveland,Jimmy (tb) | Elliott,Don (tp,vib) | Ortega,Anthony (as) | Thompson,Lucky (ts) | Jones,Quincy (arr,ld) | details unknown

558075-2 | CD | Oscar Peterson Trio + One
Clark Terry With The Oscar Peterson Trio
Brotherhood Of Man | Jim | Blues For Smedley | Roundalay | Mumbles | Mack The Knife(Moritat) | They Didn't Believe Me | Squeaky's Blues | I Want A Little Girl | Incoherent Blues
Toronto,Canada, rec. 26.2.1964
Terry,Clark (tp,fl-h,voc) | Peterson,Oscar (p) | Brown,Ray (b) | Thigpen,Ed (dr)

558076-2 | CD | I Talk With The Spirits
Roland Kirk Group
Serenade To A Cuckoo
NYC, rec. 16./17.9.1964
Kirk,Rahsaan Roland (fl,african-fl) | Parlan,Horace (p) | Fleming,Michael (b) | Perkins,Walter (dr) | Albert,Miss C.J. (voc)
I Talk With The Spirits
Kirk,Rahsaan Roland (fl,african-fl) | Moses,Bobby (vib) | Parlan,Horace (p) | Fleming,Michael (b) | Perkins,Walter (dr) | Albert,Miss C.J. (voc)
Fugue'n And Alludin'
Kirk,Rahsaan Roland (fl,african-fl) | Moses,Bobby (vib)
We'll Be Together Again- | People- | My Ship
Kirk,Rahsaan Roland (fl,african-fl) | Parlan,Horace (p) | Fleming,Michael (b) | Perkins,Walter (dr)
Django | A Quote From Clifford Brown | Trees | The Business Ain't Nothin' But The Blues
Kirk,Rahsaan Roland (fl,african-fl) | Parlan,Horace (p,celeste) | Fleming,Michael (b) | Perkins,Walter (dr)
Ruined Castles
Kirk,Rahsaan Roland (fl,african-fl,music-box)

558077-2 | CD | Contrasts
Erroll Garner Trio
You Are My Sunshine | I've Got The World On A String | 7-11 Jump | Parti-Time Blues | Rosalie | In A Mellow Tone | Don't Worry 'Bout Me | All Of A Sudden My Heart Sings | There's A Small Hotel | Misty | I've Got To Be A Rug Cutter | Exactly Like You
Chicago,Ill, rec. 27.7.1954
Garner,Erroll (p) | Ruther,Wyatt (b) | Heard,Eugene 'Fats' (dr)
Erroll Garner Quartet
Sweet And Lovely
Garner,Erroll (p) | Ruther,Wyatt (b) | Heard,Eugene 'Fats' (dr) | Candido[Camero] (congas)

558078-2 | CD | Clifford Brown With Strings
Clifford Brown & The Neal Hefti Orchestra
Yesterdays | Laura | What's New? | Blue Moon | Can't Help Lovin' Dat Man | Embraceable You | Willow Weep For Me | Memories Of You | Smoke Gets In Your Eyes | Portrait Of Jenny | Where Or When | Stardust
NYC, rec. 18.-20.1.1955
Brown,Clifford (tp) | Powell,Richie (p) | Galbraith,Barry (g) | Morrow,George (b) | Roach,Max (dr) | unkn. (strings) | Hefti,Neal (cond,arr)

558079-2 | CD | Something Old Something New
Dizzy Gillespie Quintet
Bebop | Good Bait | I Can't Get Started- | Round About Midnight- | Dizzy Atmosphere | November Afternoon | This Lovely Feling | The Day After | Cup Bearers | Early Morning Blues
NYC, rec. 25.4.1963
Gillespie,Dizzy (tp) | Moody,James (fl,as,ts) | Barron,Kenny (p) | White,Chris (b) | Collins,Rudy (dr)

558401-2 | CD | Sarah Vaughan Sings The Mancini Songbook
Sarah Vaughan With Orchestra
How Soon? | Dear Heart | Too Little Time | Dreamsville | Peter Gunn | Moon River | I Love You And Don't You Forget It - (I Love You) And Don't You Forget It | Slow Hot Wind | It Had Better Be Tonight
NYC, rec. December 1964
Vaughan,Sarah (voc) | Orchestra | Shank,Bud (as) | James,Bob (p,arr) | Byers,Billy (arr) | Holman,Bill (arr) | details unknown
Days Of Wine And Roses | Charade
Copenhagen,Denmark, rec. 12.10.1963
Vaughan,Sarah (voc) | Orchestra | Svend Saaby Danish Choir | Farnon,Robert (cond,arr) | details unknown
Mr.Lucky
NYC, rec. 13.8.1964
Vaughan,Sarah (voc) | Andre,Wayne (tb) | Byers,Billy (tb) | Hixon,Richard 'Dick' (tb) | Powell,Benny (tb) | Woodman,Britt (tb) | Richardson,Jerome (fl) | Eichen,Bernard (v) | Eley,Lewis (v) | Green,Emmanuel (v) | Kruczek,Leo (v) | Libove,Charles (v) | Lookofsky,Harry (v) | Orloff,Gene (v) | Samaroff,Tosha (v) | James,Bob (p) | Galbraith,Barry (g) | Duvivier,George (b) | Donaldson,Bobby (dr) | Rodriguez,Willie (perc) | Foster,Frank (arr,ld)

559058-2 | CD | Love
Till Brönner Group
Where Do You Start | I Fall In Love Too Easily
NYC, rec. 1.-3.5.1998
Brönner,Till (tp) | Chastenier,Frank (p) | Lefebvre,Tim (b) | Haffner,Wolfgang (dr)
What Stays | Ich Hab Noch Einen Koffer In Berlin | Here's That Rainy Day | Our Game
Brönner,Till (fl-h,voc) | Chastenier,Frank (p,el-p) | Loeb,Chuck (g) | Lefebvre,Tim (b) | Haffner,Wolfgang (dr)
Brazil
Brönner,Till (tp) | Chastenier,Frank (p,el-p) | Loeb,Chuck (g) | Lefebvre,Tim (b) | Haffner,Wolfgang (dr) | Charles,David (perc)
We Fly Around The World
Brönner,Till (tp,voc) | Chastenier,Frank (el-p) | Loeb,Chuck (g) | Lefebvre,Tim (b) | Haffner,Wolfgang (dr) | Charles,David (perc) | Cuesta,Carmen (voc)
Time Will Tell
Brönner,Till (fl-h) | Chastenier,Frank (p)

559248-2 | 3 CD | Ella Fitzgerald Sings The Duke Ellington Songbook
Ella Fitzgerald With The Duke Ellington Orchestra
Rockin' In Rhythm | Drop Me Off In Harlem | Day Dream | Caravan | I Ain't Got Nothin' But The Blues | Clementine | I Didn't Know About You | I'm Beginning To See The Light | Lost In Meditation | Perdido
NYC, rec. 25.-27.6.1957
Fitzgerald,Ella (voc) | Ellington,Duke (p) | Anderson,Cat (tp) | Cook,Willie (tp) | Terry,Clark (tp) | Nance,Ray (tp,v) | Jackson,Quentin (tb) | Woodman,Britt (tb) | Sanders,John (tb) | Hamilton,Jimmy (cl,ts) | Procope,Russell (cl,as) | Hodges,Johnny (as) | Gonsalves,Paul (ts) | Foster,Frank (ts) | Carney,Harry (cl,b-cl,bs) | Woode,Jimmy (b) | Woodyard,Sam (dr)
Take The 'A' Train
Fitzgerald,Ella (voc) | Ellington,Duke (p) | Gillespie,Dizzy (tp) | Anderson,Cat (tp) | Cook,Willie (tp) | Terry,Clark (tp) | Nance,Ray (tp,v) | Jackson,Quentin (tb) | Woodman,Britt (tb) | Sanders,John (tb) | Hamilton,Jimmy (cl,ts) | Procope,Russell (cl,as) | Hodges,Johnny (as) | Gonsalves,Paul (ts) | Foster,Frank (ts) | Carney,Harry (cl,b-cl,bs) | Woode,Jimmy (b) | Woodyard,Sam (dr)
Ella Fitzgerald And Her All Stars
Cotton Tail | Do Nothin' Till You Hear From Me | Just A-Sittin' And A-Rockin' | Rocks In My Bed | Satin Doll | Sophisticated Lady | Just Squeeze Me(But Don't Tease Me) | It Don't Mean A Thing If It Ain't Got That Swing | I Let A Song Go Out Of My Heart | Don't Get Around Much Anymore | Prelude To A Kiss
Los Angeles,CA, rec. 4.& 16.9.1957
Fitzgerald,Ella (voc) | Webster,Ben (ts) | Smith,Stuff (v) | Smith,Paul (p) | Kessel,Barney (g) | Mondragon,Joe (b) | Stoller,Alvin (dr)
Ella Fitzgerald-Barney Kessel
In My Solitude | In A Sentimental Mood | Azure
Fitzgerald,Ella (voc) | Kessel,Barney (g)
Ella Fitzgerald And Her All Stars
Mood Indigo | In A Mellow Tone | Love You Madly | Lush Life | Squatty Roo
Los Angeles,CA, rec. 17.10.1957
Fitzgerald,Ella (voc) | Webster,Ben (ts) | Peterson,Oscar (p) | Ellis,Herb (g) | Brown,Ray (b) | Stoller,Alvin (dr)
Ella Fitzgerald With The Duke Ellington Orchestra
I'm Just A Lucky So-And-So | All Too Soon | Everything But You | I Got It Bad And That Ain't Good | Bli-Blip | Chelsea Bridge | The E And D Blues(E For Ella D For Duke)
NYC, rec. 25.-27.7.1957
Fitzgerald,Ella (voc) | Ellington,Duke (p) | Anderson,Cat (tp) | Cook,Willie (tp) | Terry,Clark (tp) | Nance,Ray (tp,v) | Jackson,Quentin (tb) | Woodman,Britt (tb) | Sanders,John (tb) | Hamilton,Jimmy (cl,ts) | Procope,Russell (cl,as) | Hodges,Johnny (as) | Gonsalves,Paul (ts) | Foster,Frank (ts) | Carney,Harry (cl,b-cl,bs) | Woode,Jimmy (b) | Woodyard,Sam (dr)
Portrait Of Ella Fitzgerald: | Royal Ancestry(First Movement) | All Heart(Second Movement) | Beyond Category(Third Movement) | Total Jazz(Fourth Movement)
NYC, rec. August/September 1957
Fitzgerald,Ella (voc) | Ellington,Duke (p,narration) | Anderson,Cat (tp) | Cook,Willie (tp) | Terry,Clark (tp) | Nance,Ray (tp,v) | Jackson,Quentin (tb) | Woodman,Britt (tb) | Sanders,John (tb) | Hamilton,Jimmy (cl,ts) | Procope,Russell (cl,as) | Hodges,Johnny (as) | Gonsalves,Paul (ts) | Foster,Frank (ts) | Carney,Harry (cl,b-cl,bs) | Strayhorn,Billy (p,narration) | Woode,Jimmy (b) | Woodyard,Sam (dr)

559512-2 | CD | Ego
Tony Williams Lifetime
Circa 45 | Lonesome Wells(Gwendy Trio) | Piskow's Filigree
NYC, rec. 22.2./2.3.1971
Williams,Tony (dr,voc) | Dunbar,Ted (g) | Young,Larry (org) | Carter,Ron (cello,b) | Alias,Don (perc) | Smith,Warren (perc)
There Comes A Time
NYC, rec. 23.2.1971
Williams,Tony (dr,voc) | Dunbar,Ted (g) | Young,Larry (org) | Carter,Ron (cello,b) | Alias,Don (perc) | Smith,Warren (perc)
Mom And Dad | The Urghins Of Shemese
NYC, rec. 25.2.1971
Williams,Tony (dr,voc) | Dunbar,Ted (g) | Young,Larry (org) | Carter,Ron (cello,b) | Alias,Don (perc) | Smith,Warren (perc)
Two Worlds
NYC, rec. February 1971
Williams,Tony (dr,voc) | Dunbar,Ted (g) | Young,Larry (org) | Carter,Ron (cello,b) | Alias,Don (perc) | Smith,Warren (perc) | Bruce,Jack (voc)
Clap City | Some Hip Drum Shit
NYC, rec. 23./25.2.1971
Williams,Tony (dr) | Alias,Don (perc) | Smith,Warren (perc)

559513-2 | CD | Rhythm Is My Business
Ella Fitzgerald With The Bill Doggett Orchestra
Broadway | You Can Depend On Me | Hallelujah I Love Him So | I Can't Face The Music | After You've Gone
NYC, rec. 30.1.1962
Fitzgerald,Ella (voc) | Doggett,Bill (org,arr) | Copeland,Ray (tp) | Jordan,Taft (tp) | Wilder,Joe (tp) | Royal,Ernie (tp) | Liston,Melba (tb) | Winding,Kai (tb) | Woodman,Britt (tb) | Davis,Carl (reeds) | Dodgion,Jerry (reeds) | Shakesnider,Wilmer (reeds) | Taylor,Les (reeds) | Woods,Phil (reeds) | Jones,Hank (p) | Lowe,Mundell (g) | Dixon,Lucille (b) | Johnson,Gus (dr)
Runnin' Wild | Show Me The Way To Go Out Of This World | I'll Always Be In Love With You | No Moon At All | Laughing On The Outside(Crying On The Inside) | Taking A Chance On Love | If I Could Be With You One Hour Tonight
NYC, rec. 31.1.1962
Fitzgerald,Ella (voc) | Doggett,Bill (org,arr) | Copeland,Ray (tp) | Jordan,Taft (tp) | Wilder,Joe (tp) | Royal,Ernie (tp) | Liston,Melba (tb) | Winding,Kai (tb) | Woodman,Britt (tb) | Davis,Carl (reeds) | Dodgion,Jerry (reeds) | Shakesnider,Wilmer (reeds) | Taylor,Les (reeds) | Woods,Phil (reeds) | Jones,Hank (p) | Lowe,Mundell (g) | Dixon,Lucille (b) | Johnson,Gus (dr)
Rough Ridin'
Fitzgerald,Ella (voc) | Doggett,Bill (org,arr) | Copeland,Ray (tp) | Jordan,Taft (tp) | Wilder,Joe (tp) | Royal,Ernie (tp) | Liston,Melba (tb) | Winding,Kai (tb) | Woodman,Britt (tb) | Davis,Carl (reeds) | Dodgion,Jerry (reeds) | Shakesnider,Wilmer (reeds) | Taylor,Les (reeds) | Woods,Phil (reeds) | Jones,Hank (p) | Lowe,Mundell (g) | Duvivier,George (b) | Johnson,Gus (dr)

559514-2 | CD | Swinging Kicks
Buddy Bregman And His Orchestra
Melody Room
Hollywood,CA, rec. 18.12.1956
Candoli,Conte (tp) | Shank,Bud (as) | Smith,Paul (p) | Mondragon,Joe (b) | Levey,Stan (dr) | Bregman,Buddy (cond,arr)
Kicks Swings
Candoli,Conte (tp) | Rosolino,Frank (tb) | Shank,Bud (as) | Giuffre,Jimmy (bs) | Smith,Paul (p) | Mondragon,Joe (b) | Levey,Stan (dr) | Bregman,Buddy (cond,arr)
Melody Lane | Melodyville
Candoli,Conte (tp) | Shank,Bud (as) | Smith,Paul (p) | Hendrickson,Al (g) | Mondragon,Joe (b) | Levey,Stan (dr) | Bregman,Buddy (cond,arr)
Go Kicks
Smith,Paul (p) | Hendrickson,Al (g) | Mondragon,Joe (b) | Levey,Stan (dr) | Bregman,Buddy (cond,arr)
Mulliganville
Candoli,Conte (tp) | Giuffre,Jimmy (bs) | Hendrickson,Al (g) | Mondragon,Joe (b) | Levey,Stan (dr) | Bregman,Buddy (cond,arr)
Honey Chile
Candoli,Conte (tp) | Rosolino,Frank (tb) | Shank,Bud (as) | Getz,Stan (ts) | Giuffre,Jimmy (bs) | Smith,Paul (p) | Hendrickson,Al (g) | Mondragon,Joe (b) | Levey,Stan (dr) | Bregman,Buddy (cond,arr)
Wild Party | Bada Blues | Lost Keys | Gage Flips | Derek's Blues | Terror Ride | The Flight | Tom's Idea | End Of Party
Hollywood,CA, rec. 20.12.1956
Candoli,Conte (tp) | Ferguson,Maynard (tp) | Gozzo,Conrad (tp) | Linn,Ray (tp) | Bernhart,Milton 'Milt' (tb) | Roberts,George (tb) | Rosolino,Frank (tb) | Ulyate,Lloyd (tb) | Shank,Bud (as) | Geller,Herb (as) | Auld,Georgie (ts) | Cooper,Bob (ts) | Webster,Ben (ts) | Giuffre,Jimmy (bs) | Smith,Paul (p) | Previn,André (p) | Hendrickson,Al (g) | Mondragon,Joe (b) | Stoller,Alvin (dr) | Bregman,Buddy (cond,arr)
Ben Webster-André Previn
Kicks In Love
Webster,Ben (ts) | Previn,André (p)

559515-2 | CD | The Swinging Guitar Of Tal Farlow
Tal Farlow Trio
Taking A Chance On Love | Yardbird Suite | You Stepped Out Of A Dream | They Can't Take That Away From Me | Like Someone In Love | Meteor | I Love You | Gone With The Wind | Taking A Chance On Love(alt.take) | Yardbird Suite(alt.take) | Gone With The Wind(alt.take)
NYC, rec. 31.5.1956
Farlow,Tal (g) | Costa,Eddie (p) | Burke,Vinnie (b)

559516-2 | CD | Samba '68
Marcos Valle With Orchestra
The Answer | Cricket Sing For Anamaria | So Nice(Summer Samba) | Chup Chup Away | If You Went Away | Pepino Beach | She Told Me,She Told Me | It's Time To Sing | Batucada(Nos E O Rio) | The Face I Love | Safely In Your Arms
NYC, rec. 23./25./26.10.& 10.11.1967
Valle,Marcos (g,voc) | Slon,Claudio (dr) | Valle,Anamaria (voc) | Deodato,Eumir (arr) | Strings | details unknown

559538-2 | CD | Wholly Earth
Abbey Lincoln With Her Band
And It's Supposed To Be Love | Caged Bird
NYC, rec. 3.-5.6.1998
Lincoln,Abbey (voc) | Brown,Maggie (voc) | Hutcherson,Bobby (vib,marimba) | Hurt,James (p) | Bowie,Michael (b) | Garnett,Alvester (dr) | Moreno,Daniel (perc)
Another World | Conversation With A Baby
Lincoln,Abbey (voc) | Hutcherson,Bobby (vib,marimba) | Cary,Marc Anthony (p) | Ormond,John (b) | Garnett,Alvester (dr) | Moreno,Daniel (perc)
Wholly Earth
Lincoln,Abbey (voc) | Cary,Marc Anthony (p) | Ormond,John (b) | Garnett,Alvester (dr) | Moreno,Daniel (perc)
If I Only Had A Brain
Lincoln,Abbey (voc) | Cary,Marc Anthony (p) | Ormond,John (b) | Garnett,Alvester (dr)
Look To The Stars | Another Time Another Place
Lincoln,Abbey (voc) | Payton,Nicholas (tp,fl-h) | Hutcherson,Bobby (vib) | Cary,Marc Anthony (p) | Ormond,John (b) | Garnett,Alvester (dr) | Moreno,Daniel (perc)
Midnight Sun | Learning How To Listen
Lincoln,Abbey (voc) | Hutcherson,Bobby (vib) | Cary,Marc Anthony (p) | Ormond,John (b) | Garnett,Alvester (dr) | Moreno,Daniel (perc)

559553-2 | CD | Margaret Whiting Sings The Jerome Kern Song Book | EAN 731455955323
Margaret Whiting With Russel Garcia And His Orchestra
Yesterdays | Why Was I Born | The Song Is You | Smoke Gets In Your Eyes | Can't Help Lovin' Dat Man
Los Angeles,CA, rec. 27.1.1960

Whiting,Margaret (voc) | Shank,Bud (fl,as) | Garcia,Russell (cond,arr) | details unknown
The Way You Look Tonight | All The Things You Are | Poor Pierrot | The Touch Of Your Hand
Los Angeles,CA, rec. 29.1.1960
Whiting,Margaret (voc) | Shank,Bud (fl,as) | Garcia,Russell (cond,arr) | details unknown
Dearly Beloved | Why Do I Love You | Don't Ever Leave Me | Remind Me
Los Angeles,CA, rec. 9.2.1960
Whiting,Margaret (voc) | Shank,Bud (fl,as) | Garcia,Russell (cond,arr) | details unknown
I Won't Dance | You Couldn't Be Cuter | A Fine Romance | Let's Begin | She Didn't Say Yes,She Didn't Say No | Look For The Silver Lining
Los Angeles,CA, rec. 11.2.1960
Whiting,Margaret (voc) | Shank,Bud (fl,as) | Garcia,Russell (cond,arr) | details unknown
Long Ago And Far Away | I'm Old Fashioned | Bill | D'ya Love Me? | All In Fun
Los Angeles,CA, rec. 15.2.1960
Whiting,Margaret (voc) | Shank,Bud (fl,as) | Garcia,Russell (cond,arr) | details unknown

559616-2 | CD | Skyline
Bobby Hutcherson Group
Who's Got You? | I Only Have Eyes For You | Pomponio | Tres Palabras | The Coaster
NYC, rec. 3.-5.8.1998
Hutcherson,Bobby (vib,marimba) | Garrett,Kenny (as) | Allen,Geri (p) | McBride,Christian (b) | Foster,Al (dr)
Delilah | Chan's Song
Hutcherson,Bobby (vib,marimba) | Allen,Geri (p) | McBride,Christian (b) | Foster,Al (dr)
Love Theme From Superman(Can You Read My Mind)
Hutcherson,Bobby (vib) | Allen,Geri (p) | McBride,Christian (b)
Candle
Hutcherson,Bobby (vib) | Allen,Geri (p)

559693-2 | CD | 4 By 4:Ella Fitzgerald/Sarah Vaughan/Billie Holiday/Dinah Washington
Ella Fitzgerald With The Lou Levy Quartet
A-Tisket A-Tasket | Mr.Paganini
NYC, rec. 12.5.1951
Fitzgerald,Ella (voc) | Levy,Lou (p) | Hall,Jim (g) | Middlebrooks,Wilfred (b) | Johnson,Gus (dr)
Ella Fitzgerald With The Paul Smith Quartet
Mack The Knife(Moritat) | How High The Moon
NYC, rec. 13.2.1960
Fitzgerald,Ella (voc) | Smith,Paul (p) | Hall,Jim (g) | Middlebrooks,Wilfred (b) | Johnson,Gus (dr)
Billie Holiday And Her All Stars
God Bless The Child | Strange Fruit | Good Morning Heartache
NYC, rec. 7.6.1956
Holiday,Billie (voc) | Shavers,Charlie (tp) | Scott,Tony (cl) | Quinichette,Paul (ts) | Kelly,Wynton (p) | Burrell,Kenny (g) | Bell,Aaron (b) | McBrowne,Lennie (dr)
What A Little Moonlight Can Do
NYC, rec. 14.4.1954
Holiday,Billie (voc) | Shavers,Charlie (tp) | Ellis,Herb (g) | Peterson,Oscar (p) | Brown,Ray (b) | Shaughnessy,Ed (dr)
Sarah Vaughan With The Quincy Jones Orchestra
Misty
NYC, rec. 7.7.1958
Vaughan,Sarah (voc) | Jones,Quincy (arr,ld) | Sims,Zoot (ts) | Hrasko,Joe (sax) | Boucaya,William (sax) | Hrasko,Marcel (sax) | Hausser,Michel (vib) | Bright,Ronnell (p) | Cullaz,Pierre (g) | Davis,Richard (b) | Clarke,Kenny (dr) | Strings
Sarah Vaughan With The Clifford Brown All Stars
Lullaby Of Birdland
NYC, rec. 16.12.1954
Vaughan,Sarah (voc) | Brown,Clifford (tp) | Mann,Herbie (fl) | Quinichette,Paul (ts) | Jones,Jimmy (p) | Benjamin,Joe (b) | Haynes,Roy (dr) | Wilkins,Rick (cond,arr)
Sarah Vaughan And Her Trio
Lover Man(Oh,Where Can You Be?)
NYC, rec. 12.4.1954
Vaughan,Sarah (voc) | Malachi,John (p) | Benjamin,Joe (b) | Haynes,Roy (dr)
Sarah Vaughan With The Hal Mooney Orchestra
Lush Life
NYC, rec. 1.4.1956
Vaughan,Sarah (voc) | Orchestra | Mooney,Hal (arr,ld) | details unknown
Dinah Washington With The Belford Hendricks Orchestra
This Bitter Earth | Unforgettable
NYC, rec. 6.10.1959
Washington,Dinah (voc) | Hendricks,Belford (arr,ld) | details unknown
What A Difference A Day Made
NYC, rec. 19.2.1959
Washington,Dinah (voc) | Richardson,Jerome (reeds) | Davis,Charles (bs) | Hinton,Milt (b) | Francis,Panama (dr) | Hendricks,Belford (arr,ld) | details unknown
Dinah Washington With The Quincy Jones Orchestra
Mad About The Boy
NYC, rec. 4.12.1961
Washington,Dinah (voc) | Orchestra | Jones,Quincy (arr,ld) | details unknown

559770-2 | CD | Cannonball & Coltrane
Cannonball Adderley Quintet In Chicago
Grand Central | The Sleeper | Wabash | Limehouse Blues
Chicago,Ill, rec. 3.2.1959
Adderley,Julian \'Cannonball\' (as) | Coltrane,John (ts) | Kelly,Wynton (p) | Chambers,Paul (b) | Cobb,Jimmy (dr)
Cannonball Adderley Quartet
Stars Fell On Alabama
Adderley,Julian \'Cannonball\' (as) | Kelly,Wynton (p) | Chambers,Paul (b) | Cobb,Jimmy (dr)
John Coltrane Quartet
You're A Weaver Of Dreams
Coltrane,John (ts) | Kelly,Wynton (p) | Chambers,Paul (b) | Cobb,Jimmy (dr)

559785-2 | CD | Oscar Peterson Plays The Duke Ellington Song Book
Oscar Peterson Trio
John Hardy's Wife | Sophisticated Lady | Things Ain't What They Used To Be | Just A-Sittin' And A-Rockin' | In A Mellow Tone | I Got It Bad And That Ain't Good | Prelude To A Kiss | Cotton Tail | Don't Get Around Much Anymore | Take The 'A' Train | Rockin' In Rhythm | Do Nothin' Till You Hear From Me
Hollywood,CA, rec. December 1952
Peterson,Oscar (p) | Kessel,Barney (g) | Brown,Ray (b)
Don't Get Around Much Anymore | Sophisticated Lady | Rockin' In Rhythm | Prelude To A Kiss | In A Mellow Tone | Cotton Tail | Just A-Sittin' And A-Rockin' | Things Ain't What They Used To Be | Take The 'A' Train | I Got It Bad And That Ain't Good | Do Nothin' Till You Hear From Me | John Hardy's Wife
Chicago,Ill, rec. 14.7.-9.8.1959
Peterson,Oscar (p) | Brown,Ray (b) | Thigpen,Ed (dr)

559797-2 | 5 CD | The Complete Lionel Hampton Quartets And Quintets With Oscar Peterson On Verve
Lionel Hampton Quartet
Always | 'S Wonderful | Air Mail Special | The Nearness Of You | Soft Winds | Stompin' At The Savoy
NYC, rec. 2.9.1953
Hampton,Lionel (vib) | Peterson,Oscar (p) | Brown,Ray (b) | Rich,Buddy (dr)
Love For Sale | April In Paris | Just One Of Those Things | Stardust | That Old Black Magic(part 1) | That Old Black Magic(part 2) | This Can't Be Love | Willow Weep For Me | How High The Moon | Blues For Norman | I Can't Get Started | Moonglow
NYC, rec. 12.4.1954
Hampton,Lionel (vib) | Peterson,Oscar (p) | Brown,Ray (b) | Rich,Buddy (dr)
Buddy DeFranco With The Oscar Peterson Trio
It's Only A Paper Moon
NYC, rec. 13.4.1954
DeFranco,Buddy (cl) | Peterson,Oscar (p) | Brown,Ray (b) | Rich,Buddy (dr)
Lionel Hampton Quintet
The Way You Look Tonight | Flying Home | These Foolish Things Remind Me On You | Don't Be That Way | Dinah | On The Sunny Side Of The Street | Je Ne Sais Pas
Hampton,Lionel (vib) | DeFranco,Buddy (cl) | Peterson,Oscar (p) | Brown,Ray (b) | Rich,Buddy (dr)
Lionel Hampton Quartet
It's A Blue World(false start) | It's A Blue World(alt.take) | It's A Blue World(LP master take) | It's A Blue World(78rpm master take)
Hampton,Lionel (vib) | DeFranco,Buddy (cl) | Peterson,Oscar (p) | Brown,Ray (b) | Rich,Buddy (dr)
Flying Home | Midnight Sun | Tenderly | Hallelujah | Back Home Again In Indiana(false start) | Back Home Again In Indiana | When The Saints Go Marching In
NYC, rec. 13.9.1954
Hampton,Lionel (vib) | Peterson,Oscar (p) | Brown,Ray (b) | Rich,Buddy (dr)
Lionel Hampton-Oscar Peterson Duo
The High And The Mighty
Hampton,Lionel (vib) | Peterson,Oscar (p)
Lionel Hampton Quintet
But Beautiful | Back Home Again In Indiana
NYC, rec. 15.9.1954
Hampton,Lionel (vib) | Ellis,Herb (g) | Peterson,Oscar (p) | Brown,Ray (b) | Rich,Buddy (dr)
Hamp's Boogie Woogie(LP master take) | Hamp's Boogie Woogie(78rpm master take) | Honeysuckle Rose | Honeysuckle Rose(short version) | China Boy | A Foggy Day(In London Town-LP master take) | A Foggy Day(In London Town-78rpm master take) | Our Love Is Here To Stay | Body And Soul | It's Only A Paper Moon | Sweethearts On Parade | Date With Oscar
Hampton,Lionel (vib,voc) | Ellis,Herb (g) | Peterson,Oscar (p) | Brown,Ray (b) | Rich,Buddy (dr)

559804-2 | CD | Round Trip
Phil Woods Quartet With Orchestra & Strings
Here's That Rainy Day | Solitude | Flowers
NYC, rec. 9.7.1969
Woods,Phil (as) | Jones,Thad (tp,fl-h) | Cleveland,Jimmy (tb) | Studd,Tony (b-tb) | Alonge,Ray (fr-h) | Buffington,Jimmy (fr-h) | Dodgion,Jerry (reeds) | Penque,Romeo (reeds) | Richardson,Jerome (reeds) | Hancock,Herbie (p) | Davis,Richard (b) | Tate,Grady (dr) | Aubert,Henri (v) | Brand,Julius (v) | Buldrini,Frederick (v) | Cahn,Max (v) | Gershman,Paul (v) | Green,Emmanuel (v) | Held,Julius (v) | Katzman,Harry (v) | Malin,Joe (v) | Raimondi,Matthew (v) | Samaroff,Tosha (v) | Van Dyke,Marcia (v) | Brown,Alfred (viola) | Coletta,Harold (viola) | Fleisig,Cal (viola) | Mankowitz,David (viola) | Barab,Seymour (cello) | McCracken,Charles (cello) | Moore,Kermit (cello) | Ricci,George (cello) | Swansen,Chris (cond)
Round Trip | I'm All Smiles | How Can I Be Sure | Come Out With Me
NYC, rec. 16.7.1969
Woods,Phil (as) | Jones,Thad (tp,fl-h) | Cleveland,Jimmy (tb) | Studd,Tony (b-tb) | Alonge,Ray (fr-h) | Buffington,Jimmy (fr-h) | Dodgion,Jerry (reeds) | Penque,Romeo (reeds) | Richardson,Jerome (reeds) | Hanna,Sir Roland (p) | Davis,Richard (b) | Tate,Grady (dr) | Aubert,Henri (v) | Brand,Julius (v) | Cahn,Max (v) | Green,Emmanuel (v) | Held,Julius (v) | Katzman,Harry (v) | Malin,Joe (v) | Samaroff,Tosha (v) | Ockner,George (v) | Poliakin,Raoul (v) | Pollikoff,Max (v) | Schachter,Julius (v) | Brown,Alfred (viola) | Coletta,Harold (viola) | Fleisig,Cal (viola) | Barber,Julian (viola) | Barab,Seymour (cello) | Sophos,Anthony (cello) | Moore,Kermit (cello) | Ricci,George (cello) | Swansen,Chris (cond)
Love Song For The Dead Che | Fill The Woods With Laughter | This Is All I Ask | Guess What
NYC, rec. late July 1969
Woods,Phil (as) | prob.personal: | Jones,Thad (tp,fl-h) | Cleveland,Jimmy (tb) | Studd,Tony (b-tb) | Alonge,Ray (fr-h) | Buffington,Jimmy (fr-h) | Dodgion,Jerry (reeds) | Penque,Romeo (reeds) | Richardson,Jerome (reeds) | Hancock,Herbie (p) | Davis,Richard (b) | Tate,Grady (dr) | Aubert,Henri (v) | Brand,Julius (v) | Buldrini,Frederick (v) | Cahn,Max (v) | Gershman,Paul (v) | Green,Emmanuel (v) | Held,Julius (v) | Katzman,Harry (v) | Malin,Joe (v) | Raimondi,Matthew (v) | Samaroff,Tosha (v) | Van Dyke,Marcia (v) | Brown,Alfred (viola) | Coletta,Harold (viola) | Fleisig,Cal (viola) | Mankowitz,David (viola) | Barab,Seymour (cello) | McCracken,Charles (cello) | Moore,Kermit (cello) | Ricci,George (cello) | Swansen,Chris (cond)

559805-2 | CD | Root Down
Jimmy Smith Quintet
Sagg Shootin' His Arrow | Foreveryone Under The Sun | Root Down(And Get It) | Let's Stay Together | Slow Down Sagg | Root Down(And Get It-alt.take)
Live at The Bombay Bicycle Club,Los Angeles,CA, rec. 9.2.1972
Smith,Jimmy (org) | Adams,Arthur (g) | Felder,Wilton (b) | Humphrey,Paul (dr) | Clark,Buck (congas,perc)
Jimmy Smith Sextet
After Hours
Smith,Jimmy (org) | Williams,Steve (harm) | Adams,Arthur (g) | Felder,Wilton (b) | Humphrey,Paul (dr) | Clark,Buck (congas,perc)

559806-2 | CD | One O'Clock Jump
Count Basie And His Orchestra
One O'Clock Jump | Jamboree | From Coast To Coast | One O'Clock Jump(alt.take) | One O'Clock Jump(EP version)
NYC/Holywood, rec. 27.6.& 23.-30.4.1957
Basie,Count (p) | Culley,Wendell (tp) | Jones,Reunald (tp) | Jones,Thad (tp) | Newman,Joe (tp) | Coker,Henry (tb) | Hughes,Bill (tb) | Powell,Benny (tb) | Royal,Marshall (cl,as) | Graham,Bill (as) | Wess,Frank (fl,ts) | Foster,Frank (ts) | Fowlkes,Charlie (bs) | Green,Freddie (g) | Jones,Eddie (b) | Payne,Sonny (dr)
Smack Dab In The Middle | Amazing Love | Only Forever | Don't Worry 'Bout Me | Stop Pretty Baby | I Don't Like You No More | Too Close For Comfort
NYC/Hollywood, rec. 25.-27.6.& 23.-30.4.1957
Basie,Count (p) | Culley,Wendell (tp) | Jones,Reunald (tp) | Jones,Thad (tp) | Newman,Joe (tp) | Coker,Henry (tb) | Hughes,Bill (tb) | Powell,Benny (tb) | Royal,Marshall (cl,as) | Graham,Bill (as) | Wess,Frank (fl,ts) | Foster,Frank (ts) | Fowlkes,Charlie (bs) | Green,Freddie (g) | Jones,Eddie (b) | Payne,Sonny (dr) | Williams,Joe (voc)
Too Close For Comfort
NYC, rec. 25.6.1957
Basie,Count (p) | Culley,Wendell (tp) | Jones,Reunald (tp) | Jones,Thad (tp) | Newman,Joe (tp) | Coker,Henry (tb) | Hughes,Bill (tb) | Powell,Benny (tb) | Royal,Marshall (cl,as) | Graham,Bill (as) | Wess,Frank (fl,ts) | Foster,Frank (ts) | Fowlkes,Charlie (bs) | Green,Freddie (g) | Jones,Eddie (b) | Payne,Sonny (dr) | Fitzgerald,Ella (voc) | Williams,Joe (voc)

559808-2 | CD | Time For 2
Anita O'Day With The Cal Tjader Quartet
Peel Me A Grape | The Party's Over | Spring Will Be A Little Late This Year
Hollywood,CA, rec. 26.2.1962
O'Day,Anita (voc) | Tjader,Cal (vib) | Corwin,Bob or Lonnie Hewitt (p) | Schreiber,Freddy (b) | Rae,Johnny (vib,dr)
Thanks For The Memory | It Shouldn't Happen To A Dream | Justin Time | Under A Blanket Of Blue | That's Your Red Wagon
Hollywood,CA, rec. 27.2.1962
O'Day,Anita (voc) | Tjader,Cal (vib) | Corwin,Bob or Lonnie Hewitt (p) | Schreiber,Freddy (b) | Rae,Johnny (vib,dr)
I Believe In You | Mr.Sandman | I'm Not Supposed To Be Blue Blues
Hollywood,CA, rec. 28.2.1962
O'Day,Anita (voc) | Tjader,Cal (vib) | Corwin,Bob or Lonnie Hewitt (p) | Schreiber,Freddy (b) | Rae,Johnny (vib,dr)

559810-2 | CD | The Drum Battle:Gene Krupa And Buddy Rich At JATP
JATP All Stars
Introduction by Norman Granz | Perdido
Live at Carnegie Hall,NYC, rec. 13.9.1952
JATP All Stars | Eldridge,Roy (tp) | Shavers,Charlie (tp) | Carter,Benny (as) | Young,Lester (ts) | Phillips,Flip (ts) | Peterson,Oscar (p) | Kessel,Barney (g) | Brown,Ray (b) | Rich,Buddy (dr) | Krupa,Gene (dr) | Fitzgerald,Ella (voc)
Gene Krupa Trio
Drum Boogie | Idaho | Flying Home | Sophisticated Lady
Krupa,Gene (dr) | Smith,Willie (as) | Jones,Hank (p)
Gene Krupa & Buddy Rich
The Drum Battle
Krupa,Gene (dr) | Rich,Buddy (dr)

559827-2 | CD | A Concert Of Contemporary Music
The Modern Jazz Society
Little David's Fugue | Django | Sun Dance
NYC, rec. 14.3.1955
Modern Jazz Society | Johnson,J.J. (tb) | Schuller,Gunther (fr-h,arr) | Politis,James (fl) | Sachs,Aaron (cl) | Thompson,Lucky (ts) | Zegler,Manuel (bassoon) | Putnam,Janet (harp) | Heath,Percy (b) | Kay,Connie (dr) | Lewis,John (arr)
Tumpike(rehersal take) | The Queen's Fancy(rehersal take)
Modern Jazz Society | Johnson,J.J. (tb) | Schuller,Gunther (fr-h,arr) | Politis,James (fl) | Sachs,Aaron (cl) | Thompson,Lucky (ts) | Zegler,Manuel (bassoon) | Putnam,Janet (harp) | Lewis,John (p) | Heath,Percy (b) | Kay,Connie (dr)
The Queen's Fancy | Midsömmer | Midsömmer(rehersal take)
Modern Jazz Society | Johnson,J.J. (tb) | Schuller,Gunther (fr-h,arr) | Politis,James (fl) | Scott,Tony (cl) | Getz,Stan (ts) | Zegler,Manuel (bassoon) | Putnam,Janet (harp) | Heath,Percy (b) | Kay,Connie (dr) | Lewis,John (arr)

559830-2 | CD | Very Tall
Oscar Peterson Trio With Milt Jackson
On Green Dolphin Street | Reunion Blues
NYC, rec. 15.9.1961
Jackson,Milt (vib) | Peterson,Oscar (p) | Brown,Ray (b) | Thigpen,Ed (dr)
Heart Strings | The Work Song | John Brown's Body | A Wonderful Guy
NYC, rec. 18.9.1961
Jackson,Milt (vib) | Peterson,Oscar (p) | Brown,Ray (b) | Thigpen,Ed (dr)

559832-2 | CD | Further Conversations With Myself
Bill Evans
Emily | Yesterdays | Santa Claus Is Coming To Town | Funny Man | The Shadow Of Your Smile | Little Lulu | Quiet Now
NYC, rec. 9.8.1967
Evans,Bill (p,overdubbed)

559833-2 | 2 CD | Woody Herman (And The Herd) At Carnegie Hall
Woody Herman And The Herd
Bijou | Sweet And Lovely | Superman With A Horn | Blowing Up A Storm | The Man I Love | Four Men And A Horse | The Good Earth | Introduction by Woody Herman | Your Father's Moustache | Everywhere | Mean To Me | Red Top | I'll Get By(As Long As I Have You) | Panacea | I Surrender Dear | Wildroot | With Someone New
Live at Carnegie Hall,NYC, rec. 25.3.1946
Herman,Woody (cl,as,voc) | Berman,Sonny (tp) | Candoli,Pete (tp) | Gozzo,Conrad (tp) | Markowitz,Irving 'Marky' (tp) | Rogers,Shorty (tp) | Harris,Bill (tb) | Kiefer,Ed (tb) | Pfeffner,Ralph (tb) | LaPorta,John (as) | Marowitz,Sam (as) | Folus,Mickey (ts) | Phillips,Flip (ts) | Rubinowitch,Sam (bs) | Norvo,Red (vib) | Aless,Tony (p) | Bauer,Billy (g) | Jackson,Chubby (b) | Lamond,Don (dr) | Burns,Ralph (arr) | Hefti,Neal (arr)
Summer Sequence(incomplete)
Herman,Woody (cl,as,voc) | Berman,Sonny (tp) | Candoli,Pete (tp) | Gozzo,Conrad (tp) | Markowitz,Irving 'Marky' (tp) | Rogers,Shorty (tp) | Harris,Bill (tb) | Kiefer,Ed (tb) | Pfeffner,Ralph (tb) | LaPorta,John (as) | Marowitz,Sam (as) | Folus,Mickey (ts) | Phillips,Flip (ts) | Rubinowitch,Sam (bs) | Norvo,Red (vib) | Burns,Ralph (p) | Bauer,Billy (g) | Jackson,Chubby (b) | Lamond,Don (dr) | Burns,Ralph (arr) | Hefti,Neal (arr)
Introduction by Woody Herman | Ebony Concerto(third movement)
Herman,Woody (cl) | Berman,Sonny (tp) | Candoli,Pete (tp) | Gozzo,Conrad (tp) | Markowitz,Irving 'Marky' (tp) | Rogers,Shorty (tp) | Harris,Bill (tb) | Kiefer,Ed (tb) | Pfeffner,Ralph (tb) | Barrows,John (fr-h) | LaPorta,John (as) | Marowitz,Sam (as) | Folus,Mickey (ts) | Phillips,Flip (ts) | Rubinowitch,Sam (b-cl,bs) | Norvo,Red (vib) | Rosen,Abe (harp) | Aless,Tony (p) | Bauer,Billy (g) | Jackson,Chubby (b) | Lamond,Don (dr) | Hendl,Walter (cond)
Woody Herman And His Woodshoppers
Hallelujah | Heads Up | 1-2-3-4-Jump
Herman,Woody (cl) | Berman,Sonny (tp) | Harris,Bill (tb) | Phillips,Flip (ts) | Norvo,Red (vib) | Aless,Tony (p) | Jackson,Chubby (b) | Lamond,Don (dr) | Rogers,Shorty (arr)

559834-2 | CD | The Modern Jazz Sextet
Modern Jazz Sextet
Tour De Force | Dizzy Meets Sonny | Old Folks- | What's New?- | How Deep Is The Ocean- | Mean To Me | Blues For Bird
NYC, rec. 12.1.1956
Modern Jazz Sextet,The | Gillespie,Dizzy (tp) | Stitt,Sonny (as) | Lewis,John (p) | Best,Skeeter (g) | Heath,Percy (b) | Persip,Charles (dr)

559835-2 | CD | Charlie Parker Big Band
Charlie Parker With The Joe Lipman Orchestra
Dancing In The Dark | Laura
NYC, rec. 5.7.1950
Parker,Charlie (as) | Singer,Joe (fr-h) | Brown,Eddie (oboe) | Caplan,Sam (v) | Kay,Howard (v) | Melnikoff,Harry (v) | Rand,Sam (v) | Smirnoff,Kelly (v) | Zir,Isadore (viola) | Brown,Maurice (cello) | Mills,Verley (harp) | Leighton,Bernie (p) | Brown,Ray (b) | Rich,Buddy (dr) | Lippman,Joe (cond,arr)
Temptation | Lover | Autumn In New York | Stella By Starlight
NYC, rec. 22./23.1.1952
Parker,Charlie (as) | Porcino,Al (tp) | Griffin,Chris (tp) | Privin,Bernie (tp) | Bradley,Will (tb) | Williams,Murray (as) | Mondello,Toots (as) | Ross,Hank (ts) | Webb,Stanley (bs) | Drellinger,Art (reeds) | unkn. (2 reeds) | Caplan,Sam prob. (v) | Shulman,Sylvan prob. (v) | Zayde,Jack prob. (v) | unkn. (5 v,2 viola,2 cello) | Mills,Verley (harp) | Stein,Lou (p) | Ryerson,Arthur 'Art' (g) | Haggart,Bob (b) | Lamond,Don (dr) | Lippman,Joe (cond,arr)
Night And Day | I Can't Get Started | What Is This Thing Called Love | Almost Like Being In Love
NYC, rec. 25.3.1952
Parker,Charlie (as) | Maxwell,Jimmy (tp) | Poole,Carl (tp) | Porcino,Al (tp) | Privin,Bernie (tp) | Harris,Bill (tb) | McGarity,Lou (tb) | Varsalona,Bart (tb) | Terrill,Harry (as) | Williams,Murray (as) | Phillips,Flip (ts) | Ross,Hank (ts) | Bank,Danny (bs) | Peterson,Oscar (p) | Green,Freddie (g) | Brown,Ray (b) | Lamond,Don (dr) | Lippman,Joe (cond,arr)
Charlie Parker With Orchestra
In The Still Of The Night | Old Folks | If I Love Again | In The Still Of The Night(alt.take 1) | In The Still Of The Night(alt.take 2) | In The Still Of The Night(alt.take 3) | Old Folks(alt.take 1) | Old Folks(alt.take 2) | Old Folks(alt.take 3) | In The Still Of The Night(3 false starts) | Old Folks(5 false starts)
NYC, rec. 25.5.1953
Parker,Charlie (as) | Collins,Junior (fr-h) | McKusick,Hal (cl) | Block,Al (fl) | Mace,Tommy (oboe) | Thaler,Manny (bassoon) | Aless,Tony (p) | Mingus,Charles (b) | Roach,Max (dr) | Dave Lambert Singers,The | Evans,Gil (cond,arr)

559859-2 | CD | Talkin' Bird

Charlie Parker Quintet
Bloomdido
NYC, rec. 6.6.1950
Parker,Charlie (as) | Gillespie,Dizzy (tp) | Monk,Thelonious (p) | Russell,Curly (b) | Rich,Buddy (dr)
K.C.Blues | Au Privave
NYC, rec. 17.1.1951
Parker,Charlie (as) | Davis,Miles (tp) | Bishop Jr.,Walter (p) | Kotick,Teddy (b) | Roach,Max (dr)
Charlie Parker Sextet
Tico Tico | My Little Suede Shoes
NYC, rec. 12.3.1951
Parker,Charlie (as) | Bishop Jr.,Walter (p) | Kotick,Teddy (b) | Haynes,Roy (dr) | Mangual,Jose (bongos) | Miranda,Luis (congas)
Charlie Parker Septet
La Cucaracha | La Paloma
NYC, rec. 23.1.1952
Parker,Charlie (as) | Harris,Benny (tp) | Bishop Jr.,Walter (p) | Kotick,Teddy (b) | Roach,Max (dr) | Miranda,Luis (congas) | Mangual,prob.Jose (bongo)
JATP All Stars
Lester Leaps In
Live at Carnegie Hall,NYC, rec. 18.9.1949
JATP All Stars | Eldridge,Roy (tp) | Turk,Tommy (tb) | Parker,Charlie (as) | Phillips,Flip (ts) | Young,Lester (ts) | Jones,Hank (p) | Brown,Ray (b) | Rich,Buddy (dr)
Charlie Parker Quartet
Confirmation | Now's The Time
NYC, rec. 30.7.1953
Parker,Charlie (as) | Haig,Al (p) | Heath,Percy (b) | Roach,Max (dr)
Charlie Parker With Machito And His Orchestra
Okiedoke
NYC, rec. January 1949
Parker,Charlie (as) | Machito (Raul Grillo) | Bauza,Mario (tp) | Davilla,Frank 'Paquito' (tp) | Woodlen,Bob (tp) | Johnson,Gene (as) | Skerritt,Fred (as) | Madera,Jose (ts) | Johnakins,Leslie (bs) | Fernandez,Rene (p) | Rodriguez,Roberto (b) | Mangual,Jose (bongos) | Miranda,Luis (dr,congas) | Nieto,Ubaldo (timbales)
Norman Granz Jam Session
Jam Blues
Hollywood,CA, rec. 17.1.952
Norman Granz Jam Session | Shavers,Charlie (tp) | Parker,Charlie (as) | Carter,Benny (as) | Hodges,Johnny (as) | Phillips,Flip (ts) | Webster,Ben (ts) | Peterson,Oscar (p) | Kessel,Barney (g) | Brown,Ray (b) | Heard,J.C. (dr)

559868-2 | 2 CD | Mr.Swing Harry Edison
Harry Sweets Edison Sextet
Pussy Willow | The Very Thought Of You | Nasty | The Strollers | Sunday | Fair Ground | How Am I To Know? | Our Love Is Here To Stay | Short Coat | Baby Won't You Please Come Home | Impressario | Ill Wind | Blues In The Closet
NYC, rec. 18.9.1958
Edison,Harry 'Sweets' (tp) | Forrest,Jimmy (ts) | Jones,Jimmy (p) | Green,Freddie (g) | Benjamin,Joe (b) | Persip,Charles (dr)

559872-2 | CD | Songs For Hip Lovers
Woody Herman And His Sextet
Makin' Whoopee | Willow Weep For Me | Moon Song | Alone Together | Bidin' My Time | Louise
Hollywood,CA, rec. 11./12.1.1957
Herman,Woody (voc) | Edison,Harry 'Sweets' (tp) | Webster,Ben (ts) | Kessel,Barney (g) | Rowles,Jimmy (p) | Mondragon,Joe (b) | Bunker,Larry (dr)
Woody Herman And His Orchestra
I Won't Dance | I Guess I'll Have To Change My Plans | Can't We Be Friends | Comes Love | Everything I've Got Belongs To You | Isn't This A Lovely Day
NYC, rec. 19.3.1957
Herman,Woody (voc) | Shavers,Charlie (tp) | Harris,Bill (tb) | McKusick,Hal (as) | Cook,Jerry (ts) | Newman,Bob (ts) | Nimitz,Jack or Sol Schlinger (bs) | Stein,Lou (p) | Bauer,Billy (g) | Hinton,Milt (b) | Jones,Jo (dr) | Paich,Marty (arr)

559930-2 | CD | Slide Trombone
Lawrence Brown Quintet
Rose Of The Rio Grande | Caravan | Down The Street, 'Round The Corner Blues | Where Or When
NYC, rec. 26.1.1955
Brown,Lawrence (tb,arr) | Taylor,Sam 'The Man' (ts) | Lovett,Leroy (p,voc) | Trottman,Lloyd (b) | Bellson,Louie (dr)
Lawrence Brown With The Ralph Burns Orchestra
Ill Wind | You Took Advantage Of Me | Blues For Duke | Just As Though You Were Here | Autumn In New York | Time After Time | For All We Know
NYC, rec. 14./17.9.1955
Brown,Lawrence (tb) | Royal,Ernie (tp) | Sunkel,Phil (tp) | Clarke,Arthur (ts) | Cohn,Al (ts) | Bank,Danny (bs) | Jones,Hank (p,celeste) | Marshall,Wendell (b) | Jones,Jo (dr) | Burns,Ralph (cond,arr)
Just One Of Those Things
NYC, rec. 17.9.1955
Brown,Lawrence (tb) | Royal,Ernie (tp) | Jones,Hank (p) | Marshall,Wendell (b) | Jones,Jo (dr) | unkn. (2 perc) | Burns,Ralph (cond,arr)

559944-2 | CD | Momentum Space
Dewey Redman-Cecil Taylor-Elvin Jones
Nine | Bekei | Spoonin' | Life As | It | Is | Dew And Mud
NYC, rec. 4./5.8.1998
Redman,Dewey (ts) | Taylor,Cecil (p) | Jones,Elvin (dr)

559945-2 | 2 CD | Remember Shakti
John McLaughlin Group
Chandrakauns | The Wish | Lotus Feet | Mukti | Zakir
Live in GB, rec. 24.-27.9.1997
McLaughlin,John (g,g-synth) | Chaurasia,Hariprasad (bansuri) | Metha,Uma (tanpura) | Hussain,Zakir (tabla) | Vinayakaram,T.H. (ghatam)

589100-2 | CD | The Lional Hampton Quintet | EAN 731458910022
Lionel Hampton Quartet
April In Paris
NYC, rec. 12.4.1954
Hampton,Lionel (vib) | Peterson,Oscar (p) | Brown,Ray (b) | Rich,Buddy (dr)
Lionel Hampton Quintet
Flying Home | Je Ne Sais Pas | On The Sunny Side Of The Street | The Way You Look Tonight | These Foolish Things Remind Me On You | Don't Be That Way
NYC, rec. 13.4.1954
Hampton,Lionel (vib) | DeFranco,Buddy (cl) | Peterson,Oscar (p) | Brown,Ray (b) | Rich,Buddy (dr)
It's Only A Paper Moon
DeFranco,Buddy (cl) | Peterson,Oscar (p) | Brown,Ray (b) | Rich,Buddy (dr)

589101-2 | CD | Blues-The Common Ground | EAN 731458910121
Kenny Burrell With The Don Sebesky Orchestra
Everydays | Everyday I Have The Blues | Wonder Why | See See Rider
NYC, rec. 12.2.1968
Burrell,Kenny (g) | Glow,Bernie (tp) | Owens,Jimmy (tp) | Young,Eugene 'Snooky' (tp) | Andre,Wayne (tb) | Cleveland,Jimmy (tb) | Faulise,Paul (tb) | Watrous,Bill (tb) | Butterfield,Don (tuba) | Richardson,Jerome (reeds) | Hancock,Herbie (p) | Carter,Ron (b) | McDonald,Donald (dr) | Pacheco,Johnny (perc) | Sebesky,Don (cond,arr)
The Preacher | Angel Eyes | The Common Ground | Burning Spear
NYC, rec. 15.12.1967
Burrell,Kenny (g) | Jones,Thad (tp) | Nottingham,Jimmy (tp) | Royal,Ernie (tp) | Andre,Wayne (tb) | Cleveland,Jimmy (tb) | Green,Urbie (tb) | Studd,Tony (tb) | Phillips,Harvey (tuba) | Richardson,Jerome (reeds) | Hancock,Herbie (p) | Carter,Ron (b) | Tate,Grady (dr) | Pacheco,Johnny (perc) | Sebesky,Don (cond,arr)
Kenny Burrell Quartet
Soulful Brothers | Sausalito Nights
NYC, rec. 19.2.1968
Burrell,Kenny (g) | Hancock,Herbie (p) | Carter,Ron (b) | Tate,Grady (dr)
Kenny Burrell
Where You There
Burrell,Kenny (g-solo)

589102-2 | CD | Blossom Dearie Sings Comden And Green | EAN 731458910220
Blossom Dearie Trio
Lucky To Be Me | Just In Time | Some Other Time | Dance Only With Me | I Like Myself
NYC, rec. 8.4.1959
Dearie,Blossom (p,voc) | Brown,Ray (b) | Thigpen,Ed (dr)
Blossom Dearie Quartet
The Party's Over | How Will He Know | It's Love | Hold Me Hold Me Hold Me | Lonely Town
NYC, rec. 9.4.1959
Dearie,Blossom (p,voc) | Burrell,Kenny (g) | Brown,Ray (b) | Thigpen,Ed (dr)

589103-2 | CD | Oscar Peterson Plays The Harold Arlen Song Book | EAN 731458910329
Oscar Peterson Trio
As Long As I Live | I Gotta Right To Sing The Blues | Come Rain Or Come Shine | Ac-Cent-Tchu-Ate The Positive | Between The Devil And The Deep Blue Sea | I've Got The World On A String | It's Only A Paper Moon | That Old Black Magic | Let's Fall In Love | Stormy Weather(Keeps Rainin' All The Time) | Blues In The Night
Hollywood,CA, rec. 15.11.1954
Peterson,Oscar (p) | Ellis,Herb (g) | Brown,Ray (b)
Over The Rainbow
Hollywood,CA, rec. 16.11.1954
Peterson,Oscar (p) | Ellis,Herb (g) | Brown,Ray (b)
Happiness Is A Thing Called Joe | Stormy Weather(Keeps Rainin' All The Time) | The Man That Got Away | Let's Fall In Love | As Long As I Live | Come Rain Or Come Shine | Ac-Cent-Tchu-Ate The Positive | Between The Devil And The Deep Blue Sea | I've Got The World On A String | That Old Black Magic
Chicago,Ill, rec. 21.7.1959
Peterson,Oscar (p) | Brown,Ray (b) | Thigpen,Ed (dr)
Oscar Peterson
Over The Rainbow | Ill Wind(You're Blowin' Me No Good)
Chicago,Ill, rec. 1.8.1959
Peterson,Oscar (p-solo)

589108-2 | 2 CD | Ella Fitzgerald Sings The Harold Arlen Song Book | EAN 731458910824
Ella Fitzgerald With The Billy May Orchestra
Hooray For Love | I've Got The World On A String | Let's Take A Walk Around The Block | Ac-Cent-Tchu-Ate The Positive | As Long As I Live | When The Sun Comes Out | It's Only A Paper Moon | The Man That Got Away
Los Angeles,CA, rec. 1.8.1960
Fitzgerald,Ella (voc) | May,Billy (arr,ld) | Fagerquist,Don (tp) | Bernhart,Milton 'Milt' (tb) | Nash,Dick (tb) | Carter,Benny (as) | Nash,Ted (as) | Johnson,Plas (ts) | Bunker,Larry (vib) | Smith,Paul (p) | Hendrickson,Al (g) | Collins,John (g) | Mondragon,Joe (b) | Stoller,Alvin (dr) | details unknown
Get Happy | Ding Dong! The Witch Is Dead | Sing My Heart | Let's Take A Walk Around The Block | Sing My Heart(alt.take)
Los Angeles,CA, rec. 2.8.1960
Fitzgerald,Ella (voc) | May,Billy (arr,ld) | Fagerquist,Don (tp) | Bernhart,Milton 'Milt' (tb) | Nash,Dick (tb) | Carter,Benny (as) | Nash,Ted (as) | Johnson,Plas (ts) | Bunker,Larry (vib) | Smith,Paul (p) | Hendrickson,Al (g) | Collins,John (g) | Mondragon,Joe (b) | Stoller,Alvin (dr) | details unknown
Blues In The Night | Stormy Weather(Keeps Rainin' All The Time) | That Old Black Magic | One For My Baby(And One More For The Road) | I Gotta Right To Sing The Blues
Hollywood,CA, rec. 14.1.1961
Fitzgerald,Ella (voc) | May,Billy (arr,ld) | Fagerquist,Don (tp) | Beach,Frank (tp) | Gozzo,Conrad (tp) | Triscari,Joe (tp) | Bernhart,Milton 'Milt' (tb) | Kusby,Eddie (tb) | Noel,Richard (tb) | Roberts,George (b-tb) | Carter,Benny (as) | Johnson,Plas (ts) | Gentry,Chuck (bs) | Gordon,Justin (reeds) | Schwartz,Wilbur (reeds) | Levy,Lou (p) | Ellis,Herb (g) | Middlebrooks,Wilfred (b) | Mondragon,Joe (b) | Stoller,Alvin (dr)
My Shining Hour | Hooray For Love | This Time The Dream's On Me | Ill Wind(You're Blowin' Me No Good) | It Was Written In The Stars | Over The Rainbow
Hollywood,CA, rec. 15.1.1961
Fitzgerald,Ella (voc) | May,Billy (arr,ld) | Fagerquist,Don (tp) | Bernhart,Milton 'Milt' (tb) | Carter,Benny (as) | Johnson,Plas (ts) | Gentry,Chuck (bs) | Baker,Israel (v) | Gasselin,Jaques (v) | Gill,Ben (v) | Kellner, | Lube,Dan (v) | Neufeld,Erno (v) | Raderman,Lou (v) | Ross,Nathan 'Nat' (v) | Russell,Mischa (v) | Sasson,Marshall (v) | Stepansky,Joe (v) | Vinci,Gerry (v) | Dinken,Alvin (viola) | Kievman,Louis (viola) | Majewski,Virginia (viola) | Robyn,Paul (viola) | Kaproff,Armand (cello) | Kramer,Ray (cello) | Lustgarten,Edgar 'Ed' (cello) | Slatkin,Eleanor (cello) | Brilhart,Verlye (harp) | Levy,Lou (p) | Ellis,Herb (g) | Middlebrooks,Wilfred (b) | Mondragon,Joe (b) | Stoller,Alvin (dr) | Sheet,Walter (arr)
Let's Fall In Love | Between The Devil And The Deep Blue Sea | Come Rain Or Come Shine | Happiness Is A Thing Called Joe
Hollywood,CA, rec. 16.1.1961
Fitzgerald,Ella (voc) | May,Billy (arr,ld) | Fagerquist,Don (tp) | Bernhart,Milton 'Milt' (tb) | Carter,Benny (as) | Gentry,Chuck (bs) | Beau,Henry (reeds) | Gordon,Justin (reeds) | Jacob,Julie (reeds) | Richards,Emil (vib) | Levy,Lou (p) | Ellis,Herb (g) | Middlebrooks,Wilfred (b) | Mondragon,Joe (b) | Stoller,Alvin (dr)

589307-2 | CD | Billy Eckstine Now Singing In 12 Great Movies | EAN 731458930723
Billy Eckstine With Hal Mooney And His Orchestra
Tonight
Hollywood,CA, rec. 1961
Eckstine,Billy (voc) | Orchestra | Mooney,Hal (arr,ld) | details unknown
Billy Eckstine With Bobby Tucker And His Orchestra
More (Theme From Mondo Cane) | The High And The Mighty | Moon River | Never On Sunday | Tender Is The Night | Manha De Carnaval(Morning Of The Carnival) | A Felicidade(Happiness) | Three Coins In The Fountain | Days Of Wine And Roses | On Green Dolphin Street | My Own True Love | The Good Life
Los Angeles,CA/Rio De Janeiro, rec. 1962/1963
Eckstine,Billy (voc) | Tucker,Bobby (p,cond) | Byers,Billy (arr) | Orchestra | details unknown

589318-2 | CD | You 'N' Me | EAN 731458931829
Al Cohn-Zoot Sims Quintet
The Note | You'd Be So Nice To Come Home To | You 'N' Me | On The Alamo | The Opener | Angel Eyes | Awful Lonely | Love For Sale
NYC, rec. 1.& 3.6.1960
Cohn,Al (ts) | Sims,Zoot (ts) | Allison,Mose (p) | Holley,Major (b) | Johnson,Osie (dr)
Al Cohn-Zoot Sims Duo
Improvisation For Two Unaccompanied Saxophones
Cohn,Al (ts) | Sims,Zoot (ts)

589486-2 | CD | Willow Weep For Me
Wes Montgomery Quartet With The Claus Ogerman Orchestra
Willow Weep For Me | Portrait Of Jenny | Surrey With The Fringe On Top
Live at The Half Note Cafe,NYC, rec. May/June 1963
Montgomery,Wes (g) | Kelly,Wynton (p) | Chambers,Paul (b) | Cobb,Jimmy (dr) | unkn. (brass + woodwinds) | Ogerman,Claus (cond,arr)
Impressions | Oh! You Crazy Moon | Four On Six | Misty
Live at The Half Note Cafe,NYC, rec. 13.8.1965
Montgomery,Wes (g) | Kelly,Wynton (p) | Chambers,Paul (b) | Cobb,Jimmy (dr) | unkn. (brass + woodwinds) | Ogerman,Claus (cond,arr)
-> Note: Brass + Woodwinds dubbed in on a later date!

589488-2 | CD | Gerry Mulligan And The Concert Band At The Village Vanguard | EAN 731458948827
Gerry Mulligan Concert Jazz Band
Lady Chatterley's Mother | Body And Soul | Let My People Be | Come Rain Or Come Shine | Blueport | Black Nightgown
Live at The 'Village Vanguard',NYC, rec. December 1960
Mulligan,Gerry (bs,p) | Travis,Nick (tp) | Ferrara,Don (tp) | Terry,Clark (tp) | Brookmeyer,Bob (v-tb) | Dennis,Willie (tb) | Ralph,Alan (tb) | Quill,Gene (cl,as) | Donovan,Bob (as) | Reider,Jimmy (ts) | Allen,Gene (b-cl,bs) | Crow,Bill (b) | Lewis,Mel (dr)

589516-2 | CD | Incomparable! Anita O'Day | EAN 731458951629
Anita O'Day With The Bill Holman Orchestra
It Could Happen To You | Blue Champagne | Avalon | Old Devil Moon | The Party's Over | Why Shouldn't I | Easy Living | Can't We Be Friends | Slaughter On 10th Avenue | If I Love Again | Speak Low | Indian Summer
Los Angeles,CA, rec. 23.8.1960
O'Day,Anita (voc) | Orchestra | Holman,Bill (arr,ld) | details unknown

589517-2 | CD | Mel Tormé Goes South Of The Border With Billy May | EAN 731458951728
Mel Tormé With The Billy May Orchestra
Vaya Con Dios | Six Lessons From Madame La Zonga | Nina | Frenesi | South Of The Border
Los Angeles,CA, rec. 21.3.1959
Tormé,Mel (voc) | Beach,Frank (tp) | Candoli,Pete (tp) | Gozzo,Conrad (tp) | Klein,Manny (tp) | Kusby,Eddie (tb) | Pederson,Pullman 'Tommy' (tb) | Wells,Dave (tb) | Zentner,Si (tb) | Callender,Red (tuba) | Cipriano,Gene (reeds) | Gentry,Chuck (reeds) | Gordon,Justin (reeds) | Nash,Ted (reeds) | Shank,Bud (reeds) | Rowles,Jimmy (p) | Mills,Verley (harp) | Gibbons,Bobby (g) | Pena,Ralph (b) | Bunker,Larry (dr) | Stoller,Alvin (dr) | May,Billy (arr,ld)
Pefidia | The Rhumba Jumps | Malaguena | Cuban Love Song | Rosita | Adios | Baia
Los Angeles,CA, rec. 2.4.1959
Tormé,Mel (voc) | Beach,Frank (tp) | Candoli,Pete (tp) | Gozzo,Conrad (tp) | Klein,Manny (tp) | Kusby,Eddie (tb) | Pederson,Pullman 'Tommy' (tb) | Wells,Dave (tb) | Zentner,Si (tb) | Callender,Red (tuba) | Cipriano,Gene (reeds) | Gentry,Chuck (reeds) | Gordon,Justin (reeds) | Nash,Ted (reeds) | Shank,Bud (reeds) | Pellegrini,Al (p) | Mills,Verley (harp) | Gibbons,Bobby (g) | Clark,Buddy (b) | Stoller,Alvin (dr) | Singer,Lou (perc) | May,Billy (arr,ld)

589595-2 SACD | CD | Getz/Gilberto | EAN 731458959526
Stan Getz Quintet Feat. Astrud Gilberto
Girl From Ipanema(Garota De Ipanema) | Doralice | Para Machucar Meu Coracao | Desafinado | Corcovado(Quiet Nights) | So Danco Samba(I Only Dance The Samba) | O Grande Amor | Vivo Sohando
NYC, rec. 18./19.3.1963
Getz,Stan (ts) | Gilberto,Joao (g,voc) | Jobim,Antonio Carlos (p) | Williams,Tommy (b) | Banana,Milton (dr) | Gilberto,Astrud (voc)

589654-2 | CD | Live at Massey Hall:Celebrating Miles Davis & John Coltrane | EAN 731458965428
Directions In Music
The Sorcerer | The Poet | So What- | Impressions- | Misstery | Naima | Transition | My Ship | D Trane
Live at Massey Hall,Toronto, rec. 25.10.2001
Directions In Music | Hargrove,Roy (tp,fl-h) | Brecker,Michael (ts) | Hancock,Herbie (p) | Patitucci,John (b) | Blade,Brian (dr)

589679-2 | CD | Footprints Live! | EAN 731458967927
Wayne Shorter Quartet
Juju
Live at The Umbria Jazz Festival,Perugia,Italy, rec. 14.7.2001
Shorter,Wayne (ss) | Perez,Danilo (p) | Patitucci,John (b) | Blade,Brian (dr)
Sanctuary | Masqualero | Footprints
Live at Festival De Jazz De Vitoria-Gastiez,Spain, rec. 20.7.2001
Shorter,Wayne (ts) | Perez,Danilo (p) | Patitucci,John (b) | Blade,Brian (dr)
Valse Triste | Go | Aung San Suu Kyi | Atlantis
Live at Jardins Palais Longchamps,Marseilles,France, rec. 24.7.2001
Shorter,Wayne (ss,ts) | Shorter,Wayne (ts) | Perez,Danilo (p) | Patitucci,John (b) | Blade,Brian (dr)

589764-2 | CD | At Newport | EAN 731458976424
Cecil Taylor Quartet
Johnny Comes Lately | Nona's Blues
Live at Newport,Rhode Island, rec. 6.7.1957
Taylor,Cecil (p) | Lacy,Steve (ss) | Neidlinger,Buell (b) | Charles,Dennis (dr)
Gigi Gryce-Donald Byrd Jazz Laboratory
Splittin' | Batland | Love For Sale
Live at Newport,Rhode Island, rec. 7.7.1957
Byrd,Donald (tp) | Gryce,Gigi (as) | Jones,Hank (p) | Marshall,Wendell (b) | Johnson,Osie (dr)

589826-2 | CD | Clifford Brown And Max Roach At Basin Street | EAN 731458982623
Clifford Brown-Max Roach Quintet
Powell's Prances | Gertrude's Bounce | Step Lightly(Junior's Arrival)
NYC, rec. 4.1.1956
Brown,Clifford (tp) | Rollins,Sonny (ts) | Powell,Richie (p) | Morrow,George (b) | Roach,Max (dr)
What Is This Thing Called Love | Love Is A Many-Splendored Thing | What Is This Thing Called Love(alt.take) | Love Is A Many-Splendored Thing(alt.take) | Love Is A Many-Splendored Thing(breakdown)
NYC, rec. 16.2.1956
Brown,Clifford (tp) | Rollins,Sonny (ts) | Powell,Richie (p) | Morrow,George (b) | Roach,Max (dr) | Dameron,Tadd (arr)
I'll Remember April | Time | The Scene Is Clean | Flossie Lou | I'll Remember April(alt.take) | I'll Remember April(breakdown) | Flossie Lou(alt.take)
NYC, rec. 17.2.1956
Brown,Clifford (tp) | Rollins,Sonny (ts) | Powell,Richie (p) | Morrow,George (b) | Roach,Max (dr) | Dameron,Tadd (arr)

589947-2 | CD | Whisper Not | EAN 731458947820
Ella Fitzgerald With The Marty Paich Orchestra
Sweet Georgia Brown | Whiser Not | I Said No | Thanks For The Memory | Spring Can Really Hang You Up The Most | Old McDonald
Los Angeles,CA, rec. 20.7.1966
Fitzgerald,Ella (voc) | personal included: | Edison,Harry 'Sweets' (tp) | Rowles,Jimmy (p) | Berghofer,Chuck (b) | Bellson,Louie (dr) | Paich,Marty (arr,ld) | details unknown
Time After Time | You've Changed | I've Got Your Number | Lover Man(Oh,Where Can You Be?) | Wives And Lovers | Matchmaker Matchmaker
Fitzgerald,Ella (voc) | personal included: | Williamson,Stu (tp) | Perkins,Bill (ts) | Rowles,Jimmy (p) | Viola,Al (g) | Mondragon,Joe (b) | Manne,Shelly (dr) | Paich,Marty (arr,ld) | details unknown

598319-2 | CD | Alone | EAN 731458931928
Bill Evans
All The Things You Are- | Midnight Mood-
NYC, rec. 23.9.1968
Evans,Bill (p-solo)
A Time For Love | Midnight Mood
NYC, rec. 9.10.1968
Evans,Bill (p-solo)
Here's That Rainy Day | Midnight Mood | On A Clear Day You Can See Forever | Never Let Me Go | The Two Lonely People(aka The Man And The Woman) | Here's That Rainy Day(alt.take) | A Time For Love | On A Clear Day You Can See Forever(alt.take) | Never Let Me Go(alt.take)
NYC, rec. 21.10.1968
Evans,Bill (p-solo)

821725-2 | CD | Getz Au Go Go
The New Stan Getz Quartet Feat. Astrud Gilberto
Samba Da Una Nota So(One Note Samba)
Cafe Au Go Go,NYC, rec. 19.8.1964
Getz,Stan (ts) | Burton,Gary (vib) | Israels,Chuck (b) | Hunt,Joe (dr) | Gilberto,Astrud (voc)

The New Stan Getz Quintet Feat. Astrud Gilberto
Corcovado(Quiet Nights) | It Might As Well Be Spring | Eu E Voce | The Telephone Song
Getz,Stan (ts) | Burton,Gary (vib) | Burrell,Kenny (g) | Israels,Chuck (b) | Milito,Helcio (dr) | Gilberto,Astrud (voc)
The New Stan Getz Quartet
The Singing Song | 6-Nix-Pix-Flix
Getz,Stan (ts) | Burton,Gary (vib) | Cherico,Gene (b) | Hunt,Joe (dr)
Summertime | Here's That Rainy Day
Getz,Stan (ts) | Burton,Gary (vib) | Israels,Chuck (b) | Hunt,Joe (dr)
The New Stan Getz Quartet Feat. Astrud Gilberto
Only Trust Your Heart
Getz,Stan (ts) | Burton,Gary (vib) | Cherico,Gene (b) | Hunt,Joe (dr) | Gilberto,Astrud (voc)

821983-2 | CD | Bill Evans Trio With Symphony Orchestra
Bill Evans Trio With The Claus Ogerman Orchestra
Granadas | Prelude | Pavane | Elegia(Elegy)
Englewood Cliffs,NJ, rec. 29.9.1965
Evans,Bill (p) | Israels,Chuck (b) | Bunker,Larry or Grady Tate (dr) | Orchestra | Ogerman,Claus (cond,arr) | details unknown
Valse | Blue Interlude
Englewood Cliffs,NJ, rec. 18.10.1965
Evans,Bill (p) | Israels,Chuck (b) | Bunker,Larry or Grady Tate (dr) | Orchestra | Ogerman,Claus (cond,arr) | details unknown
Time Remembered | My Bells
Englewood Cliffs,NJ, rec. 16.12.1965
Evans,Bill (p) | Israels,Chuck (b) | Bunker,Larry or Grady Tate (dr) | Orchestra | Ogerman,Claus (cond,arr) | details unknown

821987-2 | CD | Oscar Peterson Plays The Cole Porter Song Book
Oscar Peterson Trio
In The Still Of The Night | It's All Right With Me | Love For Sale | Just One Of Those Things | I've Got You Under My Skin | Every Time We Say Goodbye | Night And Day | Easy To Love | Why Can't You Behave? | I Love Paris | I Concentrate On You- | Moon River- | It's De-Lovely
Chicago,Ill, rec. 14.7.-9.8.1959
Peterson,Oscar (p) | Brown,Ray (b) | Thigpen,Ed (dr)

823149-2 | CD | Stan Getz With Guest Artist Laurindo Almeida
Stan Getz Group Feat.Laurindo Almeida
Menina Moca(Young Lady) | Once Again(Outra Vez) | Winter Moon | Do What You Do Do | Samba Da Sahra(Sahra's Samba) | Maracatu-Too | Corcovado(Quiet Nights)
Webster Hall, NYC, rec. March 1963
Getz,Stan (ts) | Almeida,Laurindo (g) | Duvivier,George (b) | Machado,Edison (dr) | Soorez,Jose (dr) | Bailey,Dave (dr) | Parga,Luiz (perc) | Paulo,Jose (perc)

823246-2 | CD | The Billie Holiday Song Book
Billie Holiday And Her All Stars
Good Morning Heartache | Lady Sings The Blues | God Bless The Child | Trav'lin' Light
NYC, rec. 7.6.1956
Holiday,Billie (voc) | Shavers,Charlie (tp) | Scott,Tony (cl) | Quinichette,Paul (ts) | Kelly,Wynton (p) | Burrell,Kenny (g) | Bell,Aaron (b) | McBrowne,Lennie (dr)
Strange Fruit
Holiday,Billie (voc) | Shavers,Charlie (tp) | Kelly,Wynton (p) | Burrell,Kenny (g) | McBrowne,Lennie (dr)
My Man
NYC, rec. 27.7.1952
Holiday,Billie (voc) | Newman,Joe (tp) | Quinichette,Paul (ts) | Peterson,Oscar (p) | Green,Freddie (g) | Brown,Ray (b) | Johnson,Gus (dr)
Billie's Blues
Live at Carnegie Hall,NYC, rec. 10.11.1956
Holiday,Billie (voc) | Drinkard,Carl (p) | Burrell,Kenny (g) | Smith,Carson (b) | Hamilton,Forrest 'Chico' (dr)
Don't Explain
Holiday,Billie (voc) | Eldridge,Roy (tp) | Hawkins,Coleman (ts) | Drinkard,Carl (p) | Burrell,Kenny (g) | Smith,Carson (b) | Hamilton,Forrest 'Chico' (dr) | Millstein,Gilbert (narration)
Fine And Mellow | I Cover The Waterfront
Holiday,Billie (voc) | Clayton,Buck (tp) | Scott,Tony (cl) | Cohn,Al (ts) | Drinkard,Carl (p) | Burrell,Kenny (g) | Smith,Carson (b) | Hamilton,Forrest 'Chico' (dr)
What A Little Moonlight Can Do | I Cried For You(Now It's Your Turn To Cry Over Me)
NYC, rec. 14.4.1954
Holiday,Billie (voc) | Shavers,Charlie (tp) | Ellis,Herb (g) | Peterson,Oscar (p) | Brown,Ray (b) | Shaughnessy,Ed (dr)
Lover Man(Oh,Where Can You Be?)
Live at Wallinford,Conn., rec. 26.9.1958
Holiday,Billie (voc) | Clayton,Buck (tp) | Waldron,Mal (p) | Hinton,Milt (b) | Lamond,Don (dr)
Stormy Blues
Los Angeles,CA, rec. 3.9.1954
Holiday,Billie (voc) | Edison,Harry 'Sweets' (tp) | Smith,Willie (as) | Tucker,Bobby (p) | Kessel,Barney (g) | Callender,Red (b) | Hamilton,Forrest 'Chico' (dr)

823250-2 | CD | The Cole Porter Songbook
Charlie Parker Quartet With Strings
Easy To Love
NYC, rec. 5.7.1950
Parker,Charlie (as) | Brown,Edwin C. (oboe) | Leighton,Bernie (p) | Brown,Ray (b) | Rich,Buddy (dr) | Caplan,Sam (v) | Kay,Howard (v) | Meinikoff,Harry (v) | Rand,Sam (v) | Smirnoff,Kelly (v) | Zor,Isadore (viola) | Brown,Maurice (cello) | Mills,Verley (harp) | Lippman,Joe (cond,arr)
Charlie Parker Sextet
Begin The Beguine
NYC, rec. 23.1.1952
Parker,Charlie (as) | Bishop Jr.,Walter (p) | Kotick,Teddy (b) | Roach,Max (dr) | Miranda,Luis (congas) | Mangual,Jose (bongos)
Charlie Parker And His Orchestra
Night And Day | What Is This Thing Called Love
NYC, rec. 25.3.1952
Parker,Charlie (as) | Maxwell,Jimmy (tp) | Poole,Carl (tp) | Porcino,Al (tp) | Privin,Bernie (tp) | Harris,Bill (tb) | McGarity,Lou (tb) | Varsalona,Bart (tb) | Terrill,Harry (as) | Williams,Murray (as) | Phillips,Flip (ts) | Ross,Hank (ts) | Bank,Danny (bs) | Peterson,Oscar (p) | Green,Freddie (g) | Brown,Ray (b) | Lamond,Don (dr) | Lippman,Joe (cond,arr)
In The Still Of The Night
NYC, rec. 22.5.1953
Parker,Charlie (as) | Collins,Junior (fr-h) | McKusick,Hal (cl) | Block,Al (fl) | Mace,Tommy (oboe) | Thaler,Manny (bassoon) | Aless,Tony (p) | Mingus,Charles (b) | Roach,Max (dr) | Dave Lambert Singers,The | Evans,Gil (cond,arr)
Charlie Parker Quintet
I Get A Kick Out Of You | Just One Of Those Things | My Heart Belongs To Daddy | I've Got You Under My Skin
NYC, rec. 31.3.1954
Parker,Charlie (as) | Bishop Jr.,Walter (p) | Darr,Jerome (g) | Kotick,Teddy (b) | Haynes,Roy (dr)
Love For Sale | I Love Paris
NYC, rec. 10.12.1954
Parker,Charlie (as) | Bishop Jr.,Walter (p) | Bauer,Billy (g) | Kotick,Teddy (b) | Taylor,Arthur 'Art' (dr)
JATP All Stars
What Is This Thing Called Love
Los Angeles,CA, rec. July 1952
JATP All Stars | Shavers,Charlie (tp) | Parker,Charlie (as) | Carter,Benny (as) | Hodges,Johnny (as) | Phillips,Flip (ts) | Webster,Ben (p) | Kessel,Barney (g) | Peterson,Oscar (p) | Brown,Ray (b) | Heard,J.C. (dr)

823445-2 PMS | CD | The Silver Collection: Ella Fitzgerald-The Songbooks
Ella Fitzgerald With The Nelson Riddle Orchestra
Oh! Lady Be Good | Nice Work If You Can Get It | Fascinating Rhythm
Los Angeles,CA, rec. Jan./March 1959
Fitzgerald,Ella (voc) | Riddle,Nelson (cond,arr) | details unknown
All The Things You Are | Yesterdays | Can't Help Lovin' Dat Man
Los Angeles,CA, rec. 1963
Fitzgerald,Ella (voc) | Riddle,Nelson (cond,arr) | details unknown
Laura | Skylark | This Time The Dream's On Me
Los Angeles,CA, rec. 20.10.1964
Fitzgerald,Ella (voc) | Riddle,Nelson (cond,arr) | details unknown
Ella Fitzgerald With The Billy May Orchestra
Come Rain Or Come Shine | It's Only A Paper Moon | Over The Rainbow
Los Angeles,CA, rec. 1.8.1960/14.& 16.1.1961
Fitzgerald,Ella (voc) | May,Billy (cond,arr) | details unknown
Ella Fitzgerald With The Paul Weston Orchestra
Puttin' On The Ritz | Alexander's Ragtime Band | Cheek To Cheek
Los Angeles,CA, rec. 18./19.3.1958
Fitzgerald,Ella (voc) | Weston,Paul (cond,arr) | details unknown
Ella Fitzgerald With The Buddy Bregman Orchestra
My Funny Valentine | Have You Met Miss Jones | The Lady Is A Tramp | Manhattan
Los Angeles,CA, rec. 27.-30.8.1956
Fitzgerald,Ella (voc) | Bregman,Buddy (cond,arr) | details unknown

823446-2 | CD | The Silver Collection: Louis Armstrong
Louis Armstrong With The Russell Garcia Orchestra
Top Hat White Tie And Tails | Have You Met Miss Jones | I Only Have Eyes For You | Stormy Weather | Home | East Of The Sun West Of The Moon | You're Blasé | Body And Soul | When Your Lover Has Gone | You're The Top | Nobody Knows The Trouble I've Seen | We'll Be Together Again | I've Got The World On A String | Do Nothin' Till You Hear From Me | I Gotta Right To Sing The Blues
Los Angeles,CA, rec. 14.8.1957
Armstrong,Louis (tp,voc) | Garcia,Russell (cond,arr) | details unknown

823447-2 PMS | CD | The Silver Collection: Oscar Peterson
Oscar Peterson Trio With The Nelson Riddle Orchestra
My Foolish Heart | Round About Midnight | Someday My Prince Will Come | Come Sunday | Nightingale | My Ship | A Sleeping Bee | Portrait Of Jenny | Good Bye
Los Angeles,CA, rec. 1963
Peterson,Oscar (p) | Brown,Ray (b) | Thigpen,Ed (dr) | Riddle,Nelson (cond,arr) | details unknown
Oscar Peterson Trio
Con Alma | Maidens Of Cadiz | My Heart Stood Still | Woody'n You
Chicago,Ill, rec. August 1959
Peterson,Oscar (p) | Brown,Ray (b) | Thigpen,Ed (dr)

823613-2 | CD | Jazz Samba Encore!
Stan Getz-Luiz Bonfa Orchestra
Sambalero | So Danco Samba(I Only Dance The Samba) | Insensatez(How Insensitive) | O Morro Nao Tem Vez(One I Loved) | Um Abraco No Getz(A Tribute To Getz)
Webster Hall, NYC, rec. 8.2.1963
Getz,Stan (ts) | Bonfa,Luiz (g) | Jobim,Antonio Carlos (g,p) | Duvivier,George (b) | Williams,Tommy (b) | Ferreira,Paulo (dr) | Carlos,Jose (dr) | Toledo,Maria (voc)
Stan Getz-Luiz Bonfa Quartet
Samba De Duas Notas | Menina Flor | Mania De Maria | Ebony Samba(first version)
Webster Hall, NYC, rec. 9.2.1963
Getz,Stan (ts) | Bonfa,Luiz (g) | Payne,Don (b) | Ferreira,Paulo (dr) | Toledo,Maria (voc)
Stan Getz-Luiz Bonfa Quintet
Saudade Vem Correndo | Ebony Samba(second version)
Webster Hall, NYC, rec. 27.2.1963
Getz,Stan (ts) | Bonfa,Luiz (g) | Payne,Don (b) | Bailey,Dave (dr) | Ferreira,Paulo (dr) | Toledo,Maria (voc)

825064-2 | CD | This Is Astrud Gilberto
Astrud Gilberto With Orchestra
Girl From Ipanema(Garota De Ipanema) | How Insensitive(Insensatez) | Beach Samba | Fly Me To The Moon | Without Him | The Face I Love | Parade | Bim Bom | The Shadow Of Your Smile | Haven't Got Anything Better To Do | Look To The Rainbow | Agua De Beber(Water To Drink) | Take Me To Aruanda
rec. 1964-1969
Gilberto,Astrud (voc) | details unknown
Astrud Gilberto With The Walter Wanderley Trio
It's A Lovely Day Today
rec. 1966
Gilberto,Astrud (voc) | Wanderley,Walter (org) | details unknown

825373-2 | CD | Ella & Louis
Ella Fitzgerald And Louis Armstrong With The Oscar Peterson Quartet
Can't We Be Friends | Isn't It A Lovely Day | Moonlight In Vermont | They Can't Take That Away From Me | Under A Blanket Of Blue | Tenderly | A Foggy Day(In London Town) | Stars Fell On Alabama | Cheek To Cheek | The Nearness Of You | April In Paris
Los Angeles,CA, rec. 16.8.1956
Fitzgerald,Ella (voc) | Armstrong,Louis (tp,voc) | Peterson,Oscar (p) | Ellis,Herb (g) | Brown,Ray (b) | Rich,Buddy (dr)

825374-2 | CD | Ella And Louis Again
Don't Be That Way | I Won't Dance | I've Got My Love To Keep Me Warm | I'm Putting All My Eggs In One Basket | A Fine Romance
Los Angeles,CA, rec. 13.8.1957
Fitzgerald,Ella (voc) | Armstrong,Louis (tp,voc) | Peterson,Oscar (p) | Ellis,Herb (g) | Brown,Ray (b) | Bellson,Louie (dr)
They All Laughed | Autumn In New York | Stompin' At The Savoy | Gee Baby Ain't I Good To You | Let's Call The Whole Thing Off | Our Love Is Here To Stay | Learnin' The Blues
Los Angeles,CA, rec. 23.8.1957
Fitzgerald,Ella (voc) | Armstrong,Louis (tp,voc) | Peterson,Oscar (p) | Ellis,Herb (g) | Brown,Ray (b) | Bellson,Louie (dr)

825769-2 | CD | A Jazz Portrait Of Frank Sinatra
Oscar Peterson Trio
You Make Me Feel So Young | Come Dance With Me | Learnin' The Blues | Witchcraft | The Tender Trap | Saturday Night Is The Loneliest Night Of The Week | Just In Time | It Happened In Monterey | I Get A Kick Out Of You | All Of Me | Birth Of The Blues | How About You
Paris,France, rec. 18.5.1959
Peterson,Oscar (p) | Brown,Ray (b) | Thigpen,Ed (dr)

825771-2 PMS | CD | Big Band Bossa Nova
Stan Getz With The Gary McFarland Orchestra
Chega De Saudade(No More Blues) | Noite Triste | Samba Dá Una Nota So(One Note Samba) | Bim Bom
NYC, rec. 27.8.1962
Getz,Stan (ts) | Severinsen,Doc (tp) | Glow,Bernie (tp) | Terry,Clark (tp) | Brookmeyer,Bob (tb) | Studd,Tony (tb) | Alonge,Ray (fr-h) | Beckenstein,Ray (cl) | Clark,Babe (cl) | Sanfino,Jerry (fl) | Caine,Eddie (fl) | Penque,Romeo (fl) | Jones,Hank (p) | Hall,Jim (g) | William,Tommy (sb) | Rae,Johnny (dr) | Costa,Carmen (perc) | Paulo,Jose (perc)
Manha De Carnaval(Morning Of The Carnival) | Melancolico | Entre Amigos | Balanco No Samba
NYC, rec. 28.8.1962
Getz,Stan (ts) | Severinsen,Doc (tp) | Ferrante,Joe (tp) | Travis,Nick (tp) | Dennis,Willie (tb) | Studd,Tony (tb) | Alonge,Ray (fr-h) | Beckenstein,Ray (cl) | Clark,Babe (cl) | Levinsky,Walt (cl) | Caine,Eddie (fl) | Penque,Romeo (fl) | Jones,Hank (p) | Hall,Jim (g) | Williams,Tommy (b) | Rae,Johnny (dr) | Costa,Carmen (perc) | Paulo,Jose (perc)

827475-2 | CD | Porgy And Bess
Louis Armstrong And Ella Fitzgerald With Russell Garcia's Orchestra
Overture | Summertime | I Wants To Stay Here | My Man's Gone Now | I Got Plenty O'Nuttin' | Buzzard Song | Bess You Is My Woman Now | It Ain't Necessarily So | What You Want Wid Bess | A Woman Is A Sometime Thing | Oh Doctor Jesus | Here Comes De Honey Man- | Crab Man- | Oh Dey's So Fresh An' Fine (Strawberry Woman)- | There's A Boat Dat's Leavin' Soon For New York | Bess Oh Where's My Bess | Oh Lawd I'm On My Way
NYC, rec. 18.8.1957
Armstrong,Louis (tp,voc) | Fitzgerald,Ella (voc) | Garcia,Russell (cond) | Orchestra | details unknown

827821-2 | CD | Very Tall
Oscar Peterson Trio With Milt Jackson
On Green Dolphin Street | Reunion Blues
NYC, rec. 15.9.1961
Jackson,Milt (vib) | Peterson,Oscar (p) | Brown,Ray (b) | Thigpen,Ed (dr)
Heart Strings | The Work Song | John Brown's Body | A Wonderful Guy
NYC, rec. 18.9.1961
Jackson,Milt (vib) | Peterson,Oscar (p) | Brown,Ray (b) | Thigpen,Ed (dr)

827826-2 | CD | The Silver Collection: Stan Getz And The Oscar Peterson Trio
Stan Getz And The Oscar Peterson Trio
I Want To Be Happy | Pennies From Heaven | Ballad Medley: | Bewitched Bothered And Bewildered | I Don't Know Why(I Just Do)- | How Long Has This Been Going On- | I Can't Get Started- | Polka Dots And Moonbeams- | I'm Glad There Is You | Tour's End | I Was Doing Alright | Bronx Blues | Three Little Words | Detour Ahead | Sunday | Blues For Henry
Los Angeles,CA, rec. 10.10.1957
Getz,Stan (ts) | Peterson,Oscar (p) | Ellis,Herb (g) | Brown,Ray (b)

827842-2 | CD | California Dreaming
Wes Montgomery With The Don Sebesky Orchestra
California Dreaming | Sundown | Oh! You Crazy Moon | More, More, Amor | Without You | Winds Of Barcelona | Sunny(alt.take) | Green Peppers | Mr.Walker | South Of The Border
Englewood Cliffs,NJ, rec. 14.-16.9.1966
Montgomery,Wes (g) | Davis,Mel (tp) | Glow,Bernie (tp) | Nottingham,Jimmy (tp) | Andre,Wayne (tb) | Messner,John (tb) | Watrous,Bill (tb) | Buffington,Jimmy (fr-h) | Butterfield,Don (tuba) | Beckenstein,Ray (reeds) | Webb,Stanley (reeds) | Kane,Walter (reeds) | Casamenti,Al (g) | Pizzarelli,Bucky (g) | Jennings,Jack (vib,perc) | Davis,Richard (b) | Tate,Grady (dr,perc) | Barretto,Ray (perc)

831271-2 | CD | Bill Evans At Town Hall
Bill Evans Trio
I Should Care | Spring Is Here | Who Can I Turn To | Make Someone Happy | Beautiful Love | My Foolish Heart | One For Helen
Live at Town Hall,NYC, rec. 21.2.1966
Evans,Bill (p) | Israels,Chuck (b) | Wise,Arnold (dr)
Bill Evans
In Memory Of My Father: | Prologue- | Story Line- | Turn Out The Stars- | Epilogue
Evans,Bill (p-solo)

831672-2 | CD | Hamp And Getz
Stan Getz-Lionel Hampton Quintet
Cherokee | Ballad Medley: | Tenderly- | Autumn In New York- | East Of The Sun West Of The Moon- | I Can't Get Started- | Louise | Jumpin' At The Woodside | Gladys
Los Angeles,CA, rec. 1.8.1955
Getz,Stan (ts) | Hampton,Lionel (vib) | Levy,Lou (p) | Vinnegar,Leroy (b) | Manne,Shelly (dr)
Stan Getz-Lionel Hampton Sextet
Gladys | Headache
Getz,Stan (ts) | Hampton,Lionel (vib) | unkn. (tb) | Levy,Lou (p) | Vinnegar,Leroy (b) | Manne,Shelly (dr)

831673-2 | CD | Quartet West
Charlie Haden Quartet West
Hermitage | Body And Soul | The Good Life | Bay City | My Foolish Heart | Passport | The Blessing | Passion Flower
Los Angeles,CA, rec. 22./23.12.1986
Haden,Charlie (b) | Watts,Ernie (ss,as,ts) | Broadbent,Alan (p) | Higgins,Billy (dr)
Charlie Haden Trio
In The Moment
Haden,Charlie (b) | Watts,Ernie (ts) | Higgins,Billy (dr)
Charlie Haden
Taney County
Haden,Charlie (b-solo)

833535-2 | CD | Stan Getz Plays
Stan Getz Quintet
Stella By Starlight | Time On My Hands | 'Tis Autumn | The Way You Look Tonight | Lover Come Back To Me | Body And Soul | Stars Fell On Alabama | You Turned The Tables On Me
NYC, rec. 12.12.1952
Getz,Stan (ts) | Raney,Jimmy (g) | Jordan,Duke (p) | Crow,Bill (b) | Isola,Frank (dr)
Thanks For The Memory | Hymn Of The Orient | These Foolish Things Remind Me On You | How Deep Is The Ocean
NYC, rec. 29.12.1952
Getz,Stan (ts) | Raney,Jimmy (g) | Jordan,Duke (p) | Crow,Bill (b) | Isola,Frank (dr)
Stan Getz Quartet
Nobody Else But Me | Down By The Sycamore Tree | I Hadn't Anyone 'Till You | With The Wind And The Rain In Your Hair
Los Angeles,CA, rec. 14.1.1954
Getz,Stan (ts) | Rowles,Jimmy (p) | Whitlock,Bob (b) | Roach,Max (dr)

833802-2 | CD | Stan Getz & Bill Evans
Stan Getz-Bill Evans Quartet
Night And Day | But Beautiful | Funkallero | Carpetbagger's Theme | WNEW(Theme Song) | Night And Day(alt.take)
Englewood Cliffs,NJ, rec. 6.5.1964
Getz,Stan (ts) | Evans,Bill (p) | Carter,Ron (b) | Jones,Elvin (dr)
My Heart Stood Still | Melinda | Grandfather's Waltz | My Heart Stood Still(alt.take) | Grandfather's Waltz(alt.take)
Englewood Cliffs,NJ, rec. 5.5.1964
Getz,Stan (ts) | Evans,Bill (p) | Davis,Richard (b) | Jones,Elvin (dr)

833804-2 | CD | The Individualism Of Gil Evans
Gil Evans Orchestra
Flute Song
NYC, rec. September 1963
Evans,Gil (p,arr) | Cleveland,Jimmy (tb) | Cohen,Gil (tb) | Corado,Donald (fr-h) | Watkins,Julius (fr-h) | Block,Al (fl) | Lacy,Steve (ss) | Dolphy,Eric (fl,b-cl) | Tricarico,Bob (reeds) | Ross,Margaret (harp) | Galbraith,Barry (g) | Chambers,Paul (b) | Tucker,Ben (b) | Davis,Richard (b) | Jones,Elvin (dr)
El Toreador
Evans,Gil (p,arr) | Coles,Johnny (tp) | Mucci,Louis (tp) | Royal,Ernie (tp) | Cleveland,Jimmy (tb) | Studd,Tony (tb) | Buffington,Jimmy (fr-h) | Northern,Bob (fr-h) | Richardson,Jerome (reeds) | Dolphy,Eric (fl,b-cl,as) | Lacy,Steve (ss) | Tricarico,Bob (reeds) | Chambers,Paul (b) | Tucker,Ben (b) | Davis,Richard (b) | Hinton,Milt (b) | Johnson,Osie (dr)
Las Vegas Tango | Hotel Me
NYC, rec. 6.4.1964
Evans,Gil (p,arr) | Coles,Johnny (tp) | Glow,Bernie (tp) | Cleveland,Jimmy (tb) | Studd,Tony (tb) | Alonge,Ray (fr-h) | Barber,Bill (tuba) | Bushell,Garvin (reeds) | Dolphy,Eric (fl,b-cl,as) | Tricarico,Bob (reeds) | Lacy,Steve (ss) | Burrell,Kenny (g) | Carter,Ron (b) | Chambers,Paul (b) | Jones,Elvin (dr)
Barbara Song
Englewood Cliffs,NJ, rec. 9.7.1964
Evans,Gil (p,arr) | Rehak,Frank (tb) | Alonge,Ray (fr-h) | Watkins,Julius (fr-h) | Barber,Bill (tuba) | Block,Al (reeds) | Fitzgerald,Andy (reeds) | Marge,George (reeds) | Tricarico,Bob (reeds) | Shorter,Wayne (ts) | Maxwell,Bob (harp) | Peacock,Gary (b) | Jones,Elvin (dr)
Time Of The Baracudas
Evans,Gil (p,arr) | Rehak,Frank (tb) | Alonge,Ray (fr-h) | Watkins,Julius (fr-h) | Barber,Bill (tuba) | Block,Al (reeds) | Fitzgerald,Andy (reeds) | Marge,George (reeds) | Tricarico,Bob (reeds) | Shorter,Wayne (ts) | Mackwell,Bob (harp) | Burrell,Kenny (g) | Peacock,Gary (b) | Jones,Elvin (dr)
Proclamation | Nothing Like You
Englewood Cliffs,NJ, rec. 29.10.1964
Evans,Gil (p,arr) | prob.personal: | Coles,Johnny (tp) | Rehak,Frank (tb) |

Alonge,Ray (fr-h) | Watkins,Julius (fr-h) | Barber,Bill (tuba) | Block,Al (reeds) | Fitzgerald,Andy (reeds) | Marge,George (reeds) | Tricarico,Bob (reeds) | Shorter,Wayne (ts) | Maxwell,Bob (harp) | Peacock,Gary (b) | Jones,Elvin (dr)
Concorde | Spoonful
NYC, rec. 25.5.1964
Evans,Gil (p,arr) | Jones,Thad (tp) | Glow,Bernie (tp) | Mucci,Louis (tp) | Cleveland,Jimmy (tb) | Knepper,Jimmy (tb) | Alonge,Ray (fr-h) | Watkins,Julius (fr-h) | Barber,Bill (tuba) | Fitzgerald,Andy (reeds) | Marge,George (reeds) | Tricarico,Bob (reeds) | Woods,Phil (reeds) | Lookofsky,Harry (v) | Burrell,Kenny (g) | Chambers,Paul (b) | Jones,Elvin (dr)

835254-2 | CD | Ben Webster And Associates
Ben Webster And His Associates
In A Mellow Tone | De-Dar | Young Bean | Time After Time | Budd Johnson
NYC, rec. 9.4.1959
Webster,Ben (ts) | Eldridge,Roy (tp) | Hawkins,Coleman (ts) | Johnson,Budd (ts) | Jones,Jimmy (p) | Spann,Les (g) | Brown,Ray (b) | Jones,Jo (dr)

835255-2 PMS | CD | Coleman Hawkins And Confreres
Coleman Hawkins And Confreres
Maria | Cocktails For Two
Los Angeles,CA, rec. 16.10.1957
Hawkins,Coleman (ts) | Webster,Ben (ts) | Peterson,Oscar (p) | Ellis,Herb (g) | Brown,Ray (b) | Stoller,Alvin (dr)
Sunday | Hanid | Honey Flower | Nabob | Honey Flower(alt.take)
NYC, rec. 7.2.1958
Hawkins,Coleman (ts) | Eldridge,Roy (tp) | Jones,Hank (p) | Duvivier,George (b) | Sheen,Mickey (dr)

835371-2 | CD | Music For Yoga Meditation And Other Joys
Tony Scott-Collin Walcott
Prahna-Life Force | Shiva-The Third Eye | Samandhi-Ultimate Bliss | Hare Krishna-Hail Krishna | Hatha-Sun And Moon | Kundalina-Serpent Power | Sahasrara-Highest Chakra | Triveni-Sacred Knot | Shanti-Peace
NYC, rec. 28.2.1968
Scott,Tony (cl,voc) | Walcott,Collin (sitar)

835418-2 | 2 CD | Peche Á La Mode-The Great Blue Star Sessions 1947/1953
Django Reinhardt And His Quintet
Peche A La Mouche
Paris,France, rec. 16.4.1947
Reinhardt,Django (g) | De Villers,Michel (as) | Bernard,Eddie (p) | Reinhardt,Joseph (g) | Lockwood,Willy (b) | Craig,Al (dr)
Django's Music
Minor Blues
Reinhardt,Django (g) | Casino,Vincent (tp) | Menardi,Louis (tp) | Boyer,Jo (tp) | Lafosse,André (tb) | Paquinet,Guy (tb) | De Villers,Michel (as) | Forenbach,Jean-Claude (ts) | Bernard,Eddie (p) | Reinhardt,Joseph (g) | Lockwood,Willy (b) | Craig,Al (dr) | Leveque,Gerard (arr)
Django Reinhardt And The Quintet Du Hot Club De France
I Love You For Sentimental Reasons | Danse Norvegienne | Blues For Barclay | Folie A Amphion | Vette | Anniversary Song | Swing '48
Paris,France, rec. 6.7.1947
Reinhardt,Django (g) | Rostaing,Hubert (cl) | Reinhardt,Joseph (g) | Czabancyk,Ladislas (b) | Jourdan,Andre (dr)
September Song | Brazil | I'll Never Smile Again | New York City | Django's Blues | Love's Mood | I Love You
Paris,France, rec. 18.7.1947
Reinhardt,Django (g) | Rostaing,Hubert (cl) | Vees,Eugene (g) | Soudieux,Emmanuel (b) | Jourdan,Andre (dr)
Topsy | Moppin' The Bride(Micro) | Insensiblement | Mano | Blues Primitif | Gypsy With A Song | Gypsy With A Song(alt.take)
Paris,France, rec. 4.10.1947
Reinhardt,Django (g) | Rostaing,Hubert (cl) | Reinhardt,Joseph (g) | Soudieux,Emmanuel (b) | Jourdan,Andre (dr)
Rex Stewart Quintet
Night And Day | Confessin'(That I Love You)
Paris,France, rec. 10.12.1947
Stewart,Rex (co) | Rostaing,Hubert (as) | Reinhardt,Django (g) | Czabancyk,Ladislas (b) | Curry,Ted (dr)
Django Reinhardt And His Rhythm
Blues For Ike | September Song | Night And Day | Insensiblement | Manoir De Mes Reves | Nuages | Brazil | Confessin'(That I Love You)
Paris,France, rec. 10.3.1953
Reinhardt,Django (g) | Vander,Maurice (p) | Michelot,Pierre (b) | Viale,Jean-Louis (dr)

835646-2 | CD | Clap Hands,Here Comes Charlie!
Ella Fitzgerald With The Lou Levy Quartet
A Night In Tunisia | You're My Thrill | My Reverie | Stella By Starlight | Round About Midnight | Jersey Bounce | Signing Off | Cry Me A River | This Year's Kisses | Good Morning Heartache | Born To Be Blue | Clap Hands Here Comes Charlie | Spring Can Really Hang You Up The Most | Music Goes 'Round And 'Round
Los Angeles,CA, rec. 22./23.6.1961
Fitzgerald,Ella (voc) | Levy,Lou (p) | Ellis,Herb (g) | Mondragon,Joe (b) | Levey,Stan (dr)
The One I Love Belongs To Somebody Else | I Got A Guy | This Could Be The Start Of Something Big
NYC, rec. 21.1.1961
Fitzgerald,Ella (voc) | Levy,Lou (p) | Ellis,Herb (g) | Middlebrooks,Wilfred (b) | Johnson,Gus (dr)

837031-2 | CD | In Angel City
Charlie Haden Quartet West
Sunday At The Hillcrest | First Song(For Ruth) | Blue In Green | Alpha | Live Your Dreams | Child's Play | Fortune's Fame | Tarantella | Lonely Woman
Hollywood,CA, rec. 30.5./1.6.1988
Haden,Charlie (b) | Watts,Ernie (ts,synth,shaker) | Broadbent,Alan (p) | Marable,Lawrence (dr)
The Red Wing
Haden,Charlie (b) | Watts,Ernie (ts) | Broadbent,Alan (p) | Cline,Alex (dr)

837141-2 | 10 CD | Bird: The Complete Charlie Parker On Verve
JATP All Stars
Blues For Norman | I Can't Get Started | Oh! Lady Be Good | After You've Gone
Philharmonic Auditorium,LA, rec. 28.1.1946
JATP All Stars | Killian,Al (tp) | McGhee,Howard (tp) | Parker,Charlie (as) | Smith,Willie (as) | Young,Lester (ts) | Ross,Arnold (p) | Hadnott,Billy (b) | Young,Lee (dr)
Sweet Georgia Brown
JATP All Stars | Killian,Al (tp) | Gillespie,Dizzy (tp) | Parker,Charlie (as) | Smith,Willie (as) | Young,Lester (ts) | Powell,Mel (p) | Hadnott,Billy (b) | Young,Lee (dr)
I Got Rhythm | Introduction by Norman Granz | JATP Blues
Embassy Theatre,Los Angeles,CA, rec. 22.4.1946
JATP All Stars | Clayton,Buck (tp) | Parker,Charlie (as) | Smith,Willie (as) | Hawkins,Coleman (ts) | Young,Lester (ts) | Kersey,Kenny (p) | Ashby,Irving (g) | Hadnott,Billy (b) | Rich,Buddy (dr)
Charlie Parker Quartet
The Bird
Carnegie Hall,NYC, rec. December 1947
Parker,Charlie (as) | Jones,Hank (p) | Brown,Ray (b) | Manne,Shelly (dr)
Charlie Parker With The Neal Hefti Orchestra
Repetition
Parker,Charlie (as) | Porcino,Al (tp) | Mettome,Doug (tp) | Wetzel,Ray (tp) | Harris,Bill (tb) | Varsalona,Bart (b-tb) | Jacobs,Vinnie (fr-h) | LaPorta,John (cl) | Williams,Murray (as) | Salad,Sonny (as) | Mondello,Pete (ts) | Phillips,Flip (ts) | Albam,Manny (bs) | Orloff,Gene (v) | Caplan,Sam (v) | Fidler,Manny (v) | Harris,Sid (v) | Katzman,Harry (v) | Smirnoff,Kelly (v) | Nathanson,Nat (viola) | Ruzilla,Fred (viola) | Benaventi,Joe (cello) | Aless,Tony (p) | Russell,Curly (b) | Manne,Shelly (dr) | Iborra,Diego (perc) | Hefti,Neal (cond,arr)
Charlie Parker With Machito And His Orchestra
No Noise(part 2) | Mango Mangue
NYC, rec. 20.12.1948
Parker,Charlie (as) | Bauza,Mario (tp) | Davilla,Frank 'Paquito' (tp) | Woodlen,Bob (tp) | Johnson,Gene (as) | Skerritt,Fred (as) | Madera,Jose (ts) | Johnakins,Leslie (bs) | Hernandez,Rene (p) | Rodriguez,Roberto (b) | Mangual,Jose (bongos) | Miranda,Luis (congas) | Nieto,Ubaldo (timbales) | Machito (Raul Grillo)
No Noise(part 1&2)
Parker,Charlie (as) | Bauza,Mario (tp) | Davilla,Frank 'Paquito' (tp) | Woodlen,Bob (tp) | Johnson,Gene (as) | Skerritt,Fred (as) | Phillips,Flip (ts) | Madera,Jose (ts) | Johnakins,Leslie (bs) | Hernandez,Rene (p) | Rodriguez,Roberto (b) | Mangual,Jose (bongos) | Miranda,Luis (congas) | Nieto,Ubaldo (timbales) | Machito (Raul Grillo)
Okidoki
NYC, rec. Jan.1949
Parker,Charlie (as) | Bauza,Mario (tp) | Davilla,Frank 'Paquito' (tp) | Woodlen,Bob (tp) | Johnson,Gene (as) | Skerritt,Fred (as) | Madera,Jose (ts) | Johnakins,Leslie (bs) | Hernandez,Rene (p) | Rodriguez,Roberto (b) | Mangual,Jose (bongos) | Miranda,Luis (congas) | Nieto,Ubaldo (timbales) | Machito (Raul Grillo)
Charlie Parker And His Orchestra
Cardboard | Visa
NYC, rec. ca.March 1949
Parker,Charlie (as) | Dorham,Kenny (tp) | Turk,Tommy (tb) | Haig,Al (p) | Potter,Tommy (b) | Roach,Max (dr) | Vidal,Carlos (congas)
Segment Tune X | Diverse Tune X(alternate) | Passport Tune Y(rare) | Passport Tune Z(common)
NYC, rec. 5.5.1949
Parker,Charlie (as) | Dorham,Kenny (tp) | Haig,Al (p) | Potter,Tommy (b) | Roach,Max (dr)
JATP All Stars
The Opener | Lester Leaps In | Embraceable You | The Closer
Carnegie Hall,NYC, rec. 18.9.1949
JATP All Stars | Eldridge,Roy (tp) | Turk,Tommy (tb) | Parker,Charlie (as) | Phillips,Flip (ts) | Young,Lester (ts) | Jones,Hank (p) | Brown,Ray (b) | Rich,Buddy (dr)
Introduction by Norman Granz | Flying Home | How High The Moon | Perdido
JATP All Stars | Eldridge,Roy (tp) | Turk,Tommy (tb) | Parker,Charlie (as) | Phillips,Flip (ts) | Young,Lester (ts) | Jones,Hank (p) | Brown,Ray (b) | Rich,Buddy (dr) | Fitzgerald,Ella (voc)
Charlie Parker With Strings
Just Friends | Everything Happens To Me | April In Paris | Summertime | I Didn't Know What Time It Was | If I Should Lose You
NYC, rec. 30.11.1949
Parker,Charlie (as) | Miller,Mitch (oboe,prob.engl-h) | Gimpel,Bronislaw (v) | Hollander,Max (v) | Lomask,Milt (v) | Brieff,Frank (viola) | Miller,Frank (cello) | Rosen,Meyer (harp) | Freeman,Stan (p) | Brown,Ray (b) | Rich,Buddy (dr) | Carroll,Jimmy (cond,arr)
Charlie Parker Quartet
Star Eyes | Blues(fast) | I'm In The Mood For Love
NYC, rec. early April 1950
Parker,Charlie (as) | Jones,Hank (p) | Brown,Ray (b) | Rich,Buddy (dr)
Charlie Parker And His Orchestra
Bloomdido | An Oscar For Treadwell(take 3) | An Oscar For Treadwell(take 4) | Mohawk(take 3) | Mohawk(take 6) | My Melancholy Baby(take 1) | My Melancholy Baby(take 2) | My Melancholy Baby(coda rehearsal) | Leap Frog(take 1-11) | Relaxin' With Lee(take 1-6)
NYC, rec. 6.6.1950
Parker,Charlie (as) | Gillespie,Dizzy (tp) | Monk,Thelonious (p) | Russell,Curly (b) | Rich,Buddy (dr)
Charlie Parker With Strings
Out Of Nowhere | Laura(take 1) | Laura(take 2) | East Of The Sun West Of The Moon | They Can't Take That Away From Me | Easy To Love | I'm In The Mood For Love(take 2) | I'm In The Mood For Love(take 3) | I'll Remember April(take 1) | I'll Remember April(take 2) | I'll Remember April(take 3)
NYC, rec. late Summer 1950
Parker,Charlie (as) | Singer,Joe (fr-h) | Brown,Eddie (oboe) | Caplan,Sam (v) | Kay,Howard (v) | Melnikoff,Harry (v) | Rand,Sam (v) | Smirnoff,Kelly (v) | Zir,Isadore (viola) | Brown,Maurice (viola) | Mills,Verley (harp) | Leighton,Bernie (p) | Brown,Ray (b) | Rich,Buddy (dr) | Lippman,Joe (cond,arr)
Dancing In The Dark
Parker,Charlie (as) | Singer,Joe (fr-h) | Brown,Eddie (oboe) | Caplan,Sam (v) | Kay,Howard (v) | Melnikoff,Harry (v) | Rand,Sam (v) | Smirnoff,Kelly (v) | Zir,Isadore (viola) | Brown,Maurice (viola) | Mills,Verley (harp) | Leighton,Bernie (p) | Brown,Ray (b) | Rich,Buddy (dr) | unkn. (xyl,chimes) | Lippman,Joe (cond,arr)
What Is This Thing Called Love | April In Paris | Repetition | Easy To Love | Rocker
Live at Carnegie Hall,NYC, rec. 17.9.1950
Parker,Charlie (as) | Mace,Tommy (oboe) | Blume,Teddy (v) | Caplan,Sam (v) | Karpenia,Stan (v) | Uchitel,Dave (viola) | unkn. (cello) | McManus,Wallace (harp) | Haig,Al (p) | Potter,Tommy (b) | Haynes,Roy (dr)
JATP All Stars
Celebrity
NYC, rec. ca.Fall 1950
JATP All Stars | Parker,Charlie (as) | Jones,Hank (p) | Brown,Ray (b) | Rich,Buddy (dr)
Ballad
JATP All Stars | Parker,Charlie (as) | Hawkins,Coleman (ts) | Jones,Hank (p) | Brown,Ray (b) | Rich,Buddy (dr)
Charlie Parker With Machito And His Orchestra
Afro-Cuban Jazz Suite
NYC, rec. 21.12.1950
Parker,Charlie (as) | Bauza,Mario (tp) | Davilla,Frank 'Paquito' (tp) | Edison,Harry 'Sweets' (tp) | Woodlen,Bob (tp) | Johnson,Gene (as) | Skerritt,Fred (as) | Madera,Jose (ts) | Phillips,Flip (ts) | Rabinowitz,Sol (ts) | Johnakins,Leslie (bs) | Hernandez,Rene (p) | Rodriguez,Roberto (b) | Rich,Buddy (dr) | Mangual,Jose (bongos) | Miranda,Rafael (congas) | Pozo,Chino (congas) | Nieto,Ubaldo (timbales) | Machito (Raul Grillo) | O'Farrill,Chico (cond,arr)
Charlie Parker And His Orchestra
Au Privave(take 2) | Au Privave(take 3) | She Rote(take 3) | She Rote(take 5) | K.C.Blues | Star Eyes
NYC, rec. 17.1.1951
Parker,Charlie (as) | Davis,Miles (tp) | Bishop Jr.,Walter (p) | Kotick,Teddy (b) | Roach,Max (dr)
Charlie Parker's Jazzers
My Little Suede Shoes | Un Poquito De Tu Amor | Tico Tico | Fiesta | Why Do I Love You(take 2) | Why Do I Love You(take 6) | Why Do I Love You(take 7)
NYC, rec. 12.3.1951
Parker,Charlie (as) | Bishop Jr.,Walter (p) | Kotick,Teddy (b) | Haynes,Roy (dr) | Mangual,Jose (bongos) | Miranda,Luis (congas)
Charlie Parker And His Orchestra
Blues For Alice | Si Si | Swedish Schnapps(take 3) | Swedish Schnapps(take 4) | Back Home Blues(take 1) | Back Home Blues(take 2) | Lover Man(Oh,Where Can You Be?)
NYC, rec. 8.8.1951
Parker,Charlie (as) | Rodney,Red (tp) | Lewis,John (p) | Brown,Ray (b) | Clarke,Kenny (dr)
Charlie Parker With Strings
Temptation | Lover | Autumn In New York | Stella By Starlight
NYC, rec. 22./23.1.1952
Parker,Charlie (as) | Porcino,Al (tp) | Griffin,Chris (tp) | Privin,Bernie (tp) | Bradley,Will (tb) | Harris,Bill (tb) | Williams,Murray (as) | Mondello,Toots (as) | Ross,Hank (ts) | Webb,Stanley (bs) | Drellinger,Art (reeds) | unkn. (reeds,oboe) | Caplan,Sam prob. (v) | Zayde,Sylvan prob. (v) | Zayde,Jack prob. (v) | unkn. (5 v) | unkn. (2 violas) | unkn. (2 cellos) | Mills,Verley (harp) | Stein,Lou (p) | Ryerson,Arthur 'Art' (g) | Haggart,Bob (b) | Lamond,Don (dr) | Lippman,Joe (cond,arr)
Charlie Parker Quintet
Mama Inez | La Cucaracha(take 1-4) | Estrellita(take 2,4-6) | La Paloma
NYC, rec. 23.1.1952
Parker,Charlie (as) | Harris,Benny (tp) | Bishop Jr.,Walter (p) | Kotick,Teddy (b) | Roach,Max (dr) | Mangual,Jose (bongos) | Miranda,Luis (congas)
Begin The Beguine
Parker,Charlie (as) | Bishop Jr.,Walter (p) | Kotick,Teddy (b) | Roach,Max (dr) | Mangual,Jose (bongos) | Miranda,Luis (congas)
Charlie Parker And His Orchestra
Night And Day | Almost Like Being In Love | I Can't Get Started | What Is This Thing Called Love
NYC, rec. 25.3.1952
Parker,Charlie (as) | Porcino,Al (tp) | Maxwell,Jimmy (tp) | Poole,Carl (tp) | Privin,Bernie (tp) | Harris,Bill (tb) | McGarity,Lou (tb) | Varsalona,Bart (tb) | Williams,Murray (as) | Terrill,Harry (as) | Phillips,Flip (ts) | Ross,Hank (ts) | Bank,Danny (bs) | Peterson,Oscar (p) | Green,Freddie (g) | Brown,Ray (b) | Lamond,Don (dr) | Lippman,Joe (cond,arr)
Norman Granz Jam Session
Jam Blues | What Is This Thing Called Love | Ballad Medley: | All The Things You Are- | Dearly Beloved- | The Nearness Of You- | I'll Get By(As Long As I Have You)- | Everything Happens To Me- | The Man I Love- | What's New?- | Someone To Watch Over Me- | Isn't It Romantic- | Funky Blues
Hollywood,CA, rec. June 1952
Norman Granz Jam Session | Shavers,Charlie (tp) | Parker,Charlie (as) | Carter,Benny (as) | Hodges,Johnny (as) | Phillips,Flip (ts) | Webster,Ben (ts) | Peterson,Oscar (p) | Kessel,Barney (g) | Brown,Ray (b) | Heard,J.C. (dr)
Charlie Parker Quartet
The Song Is You | Laird Baird | Kim(take 2) | Kim(take 4) | Cosmic Rays(take 2) | Cosmic Rays(take 5)
NYC, rec. December 1952/January 1953
Parker,Charlie (as) | Jones,Hank (p) | Kotick,Teddy (b) | Roach,Max (dr)
Charlie Parker And His Orchestra
In The Still Of The Night(take 1-7) | Old Folks(take 1-9) | If I Love Again
NYC, rec. 25.5.1953
Parker,Charlie (as) | Collins,Junior (fr-h) | McKusick,Hal (cl) | Mace,Tommy (oboe) | Thaler,Manny (bassoon) | Aless,Tony (p) | Mingus,Charles (b) | Roach,Max (dr) | Dave Lambert Singers,The | Lambert,Dave (voc) | Parker,Jerry (voc) | Birdsall,Butch (voc) | Ross,Annie (voc) | unkn. (2 voc) | Evans,Gil (cond,arr)
Charlie Parker Quartet
Chi Chi(take 1-6) | I Remember You | Now's The Time | Confirmation(take 1-3)
NYC, rec. 30.7.1953
Parker,Charlie (as) | Haig,Al (p) | Heath,Percy (b) | Roach,Max (dr)
Charlie Parker Quintet
I Get A Kick Out Of You(take 1-7) | Just One Of Those Things | My Heart Belongs To Daddy(take 1) | My Heart Belongs To Daddy(take 2) | I've Got You Under My Skin
NYC, rec. 31.3.1954
Parker,Charlie (as) | Bishop Jr.,Walter (p) | Darr,Jerome (g) | Kotick,Teddy (b) | Haynes,Roy (dr)
Love For Sale(take 1-5) | I Love Paris(take 2) | I Love Paris(take 3)
NYC, rec. 10.12.1954
Parker,Charlie (as) | Bishop Jr.,Walter (p) | Bauer,Billy (g) | Kotick,Teddy (b) | Taylor,Arthur 'Art' (dr)

837280-2 | CD | Que Alegria
John McLaughlin Trio
Belo Horizonte | Baba(for Ramana Maharashi) | Reincarnation | 1 Nite Stand | Marie | Hijacked | Mila Repa | Que Alegria | 3 Willows
Ludwigsburg, rec. 23.11.-3.12.1991
McLaughlin,John (g,g-synth) | Di Piazza,Dominique (4-string-b-g,5-string-b-g) | Gurtu,Trilok (perc)

837433-2 | CD | King Of Swing | EAN 042283743328
Count Basie And His Orchestra
Plymouth Rock
Los Angeles,CA, rec. 13.7.1953
Basie,Count (p) | Jones,Reunald (tp) | Campbell,Paul (tp) | Culley,Wendell (tp) | Newman,Joe (tp) | Coker,Henry (tb) | Mandell,Johnny (tb) | Powell,Benny (tb) | Royal,Marshall (as) | Wilkins,Ernie (as,ts) | Wess,Frank (fl,ts) | Foster,Frank (ts) | Fowlkes,Charlie (bs) | Green,Freddie (g) | Jones,Eddie (b) | Johnson,Gus (dr)
Bubbles | Cherry Point | The Blues Done Come Back | Right On
NYC, rec. 12.12.1953
Basie,Count (p) | Jones,Reunald (tp) | Culley,Wendell (tp) | Newman,Joe (tp) | Wilder,Joe (tp) | Chambers,Henderson (tb) | Coker,Henry (tb) | Mandell,Johnny (tb) | Powell,Benny (tb) | Royal,Marshall (as) | Wilkins,Ernie (as,ts) | Wess,Frank (fl,ts) | Foster,Frank (ts) | Fowlkes,Charlie (bs) | Green,Freddie (g) | Jones,Eddie (b) | Johnson,Gus (dr)
Slow But Shure | You For Me | Soft Drink | Two For The Blues | I Feel Like A New Man
NYC, rec. June 1954
Basie,Count (p) | Jones,Reunald (tp) | Culley,Wendell (tp) | Newman,Joe (tp) | Jones,Thad (tp) | Coker,Henry (tb) | Hughes,Bill (tb) | Powell,Benny (tb) | Royal,Marshall (as) | Wilkins,Ernie (as,ts) | Wess,Frank (fl,ts) | Foster,Frank (ts) | Fowlkes,Charlie (bs) | Green,Freddie (g) | Jones,Eddie (b) | Johnson,Gus (dr)

837435-2 | CD | For Musicians Only
For Musicians Only
Bebop | Dark Eyes | Wee(Allen's Alley) | Lover Come Back To Me | Dark Eyes(alt.take)
Los Angeles,CA, rec. 16.10.1956
Gillespie,Dizzy (tp) | Stitt,Sonny (as) | Getz,Stan (ts) | Lewis,John (p) | Ellis,Herb (g) | Brown,Ray (b) | Levey,Stan (dr)

837436-2 | CD | Stan Meets Chet
Chet Baker-Stan Getz Quintet
I'll Remember April | Ballad Medley: | Autumn In New York- | Embraceable You- | What's New?- | Jordu | Halfbreed Apache
Chicago,Ill, rec. 16.2.1958
Baker,Chet (tp) | Getz,Stan (ts) | Christian,Jodie (p) | Sproles,Victor (b) | Thompson,Marshall (dr)

839838-2 | CD | The Intimate Ella
Ella Fitzgerald And Paul Smith
Black Coffee | Angel Eyes | I Cried For You(Now It's Your Turn To Cry Over Me) | I Can't Give You Anything But Love | Then You've Never Been Blue | I Hadn't Anyone 'Till Now | My Melancholy Baby | Misty | September Song | One For My Baby(And One More For The Road) | Who's Sorry Now | I'm Getting Sentimental Over You | Reach For Tomorrow
Los Angeles,CA, rec. 1960
Fitzgerald,Ella (voc) | Smith,Paul (p)

841199-2 | CD | Victim Of Love | EAN 042284119924
Dee Dee Bridgewater With Band
Heartache Caravan | Wall Of Love | Love Takes Changes | I Go My Way | Precious Thing(Till The Next...Somewhere) | Mr.Guitar Man | Can't We Try Love Again | Sunset And Blue
different Places, rec. 1989
Bridgewater,Dee Dee (voc) | Bourree,Francis (ts) | Bjerkestrand,Kjetil (keyboards) | Arcadio,Bernard (keyboards) | Disley,Terry (keyboards) | Alnaes,Frode (g) | Raffaelli,Benjamin (g) | Chavanat,Joan-Claude (g) | KajdanJean Michael (g) | Leroux,Basile (g) | Bonfils,Tony (b) | Alvim,Cesarius (b) | Ceccarelli,André (dr) | Skorgan,Anita (voc) | Charles,Ray (voc) | Forward,Steve (voc)

841433-2 | CD | Buddy And Sweets | EAN 042284143325
Buddy Rich Quintet
Nice Work If You Can Get It | You're Getting To Be A Habit With Me | Now's

The Time | The Yellow Rose Of Brooklyn | All Sweets | Easy Does It | Barney's Bugle(Blues)
Los Angeles,CA, rec. 1.9.1955
Rich,Buddy (dr) | Edison,Harry 'Sweets' (tp) | Kessel,Barney (g) | Rowles,Jimmy (p) | Simmons,John (b)

841765-2 | 2 CD | For The Love Of Ella Fitzgerald
Ella Fitzgerald With The Lou Levy Quartet
A-Tisket A-Tasket | Mr.Paganini
Live at The Crescendo Club,Los Angeles,CA, rec. 11.or 21.5.1961
Fitzgerald,Ella (voc) | Levy,Lou (p) | Hall,Jim (g) | Middlebrooks,Wilfred (b) | Johnson,Gus (dr)
Ella Fitzgerald With The JATP All Stars
Oh! Lady Be Good | Stompin' At The Savoy
Live at Shrine Auditorium,Los Angeles,CA, rec. 25.10.1957
Fitzgerald,Ella (voc) | JATP All Stars | Eldridge,Roy (tp) | Johnson,J.J. (tb) | Stitt,Sonny (as) | Young,Lester (ts) | Jacquet,Illinois (ts) | Hawkins,Coleman (ts) | Getz,Stan (ts) | Phillips,Flip (ts) | Peterson,Oscar (p) | Ellis,Herb (g) | Brown,Ray (b) | Kay,Connie (dr)
Ella Fitzgerald With The Paul Smith Quartet
How High The Moon | Mack The Knife(Moritat) | Misty | Summertime
Live at The Deutschlandhalle, Berlin, rec. 13.2.1860
Fitzgerald,Ella (voc) | Smith,Paul (p) | Hall,Jim (g) | Middlebrooks,Wilfred (b) | Johnson,Gus (dr)
Ella Fitzgerald With The Marty Paich Orchestra
Sweet Georgia Brown
Los Angeles,CA, rec. 20.7.1966
Fitzgerald,Ella (voc) | Paich,Marty (cond,arr) | Edison,Harry 'Sweets' (tp) | Rowles,Jimmy (p) | Viola,Al (g) | Mondragon,Joe (b) | Manne,Shelly (dr) | details unknown
Ella Fitzgerald With The Lou Levy Trio
Caravan | I Loves You Porgy
Live at 'The Teatro Sistina',Rome, rec. 25.4.1958
Fitzgerald,Ella (voc) | Levy,Lou (p) | Bennett,Max (b) | Johnson,Gus (dr)
Ella Fitzgerald With The Lou Levy Quartet
A Night In Tunisia
Los Angeles,CA, rec. 24.6.1961
Fitzgerald,Ella (voc) | Levy,Lou (p) | Ellis,Herb (g) | Mondragon,Joe (b) | Levey,Stan (dr)
Ella Fitzgerald With The Duke Ellington Orchestra
Rockin' In Rhythm
NYC, rec. 26.6.1957
Fitzgerald,Ella (voc) | Ellington,Duke (p) | Anderson,Cat (tp) | Cook,Willie (tp) | Terry,Clark (tp) | Nance,Ray (tp,v) | Jackson,Quentin (tb) | Woodman,Britt (tb) | Sanders,John (tb) | Hamilton,Jimmy (cl,ts) | Procope,Russell (cl,as) | Hodges,Johnny (as) | Gonsalves,Paul (ts) | Foster,Frank (ts) | Carney,Harry (cl,b-cl,bs) | Woode,Jimmy (b) | Woodyard,Sam (dr)
Ella Fitzgerald With The Count Basie Orchestra
Honeysuckle Rose | On The Sunny Side Of The Street
Chicago,Ill(prob), rec. 15./16.7.1963
Fitzgerald,Ella (voc) | Basie,Count (p) | Minger,Pete (tp) | Cohn[Cohen],Sonny (tp) | Brown,Raymond (tp) | Smith,Nolan (tp) | Wanzo,Mel (tb) | Hughes,Bill (tb) | Wood,Booty (tb) | Wilson,Dennis (tb) | Plater,Bobby (as) | Turner,Danny (as) | Hing,Kenny (ts) | Dixon,Eric (ts) | Fowlkes,Charlie (bs) | Green,Freddie (g) | Clayton Jr.,John (b) | Miles,Butch (dr)
Ella Fitzgerald With The Nelson Riddle Orchestra
I Got Rhythm
Los Angeles,CA, rec. 5.1.1959
Fitzgerald,Ella (voc) | Fagerquist,Don (tp) | Cooper,Bob (ts) | Stoller,Alvin (dr) | Riddle,Nelson (cond,arr) | details unknown
Ella Fitzgerald And Louis Armstrong With The Oscar Peterson Quartet
A Fine Romance
Los Angeles,CA, rec. 13.8.1957
Fitzgerald,Ella (voc) | Armstrong,Louis (tp,voc) | Peterson,Oscar (p) | Ellis,Herb (g) | Brown,Ray (b) | Bellson,Louie (dr)
Autumn In New York
Los Angeles,CA, rec. 23.7.1957
Fitzgerald,Ella (voc) | Armstrong,Louis (tp,voc) | Peterson,Oscar (p) | Ellis,Herb (g) | Brown,Ray (b) | Bellson,Louie (dr)
Ella Fitzgerald And Joe Williams With The Count Basie Octet
Party Blues
NYC, rec. 25.6.1956
Fitzgerald,Ella (voc) | Basie,Count (p) | Newman,Joe (tp) | Jones,Thad (tp) | Coker,Henry (tb) | Wess,Frank (ts) | Green,Freddie (g) | Jones,Eddie (b) | Payne,Sonny (dr) | Williams,Joe (voc)
Ella Fitzgerald And Her All Stars
Cotton Tail | Sophisticated Lady
Los Angeles,CA, rec. 4.9.1956
Fitzgerald,Ella (voc) | Webster,Ben (ts) | Smith,Stuff (v) | Smith,Paul (p) | Kessel,Barney (g) | Mondragon,Joe (b) | Stoller,Alvin (dr)
Ella Fitzgerald With The Nelson Riddle Orchestra
Midnight Sun | Laura
Los Angeles,CA, rec. 20.10.1964
Fitzgerald,Ella (voc) | DeFranco,Buddy (cl) | Smith,Willie (as) | Johnson,Plas (ts) | Flynn,Frank (vib) | Smith,Paul (p) | Riddle,Nelson (cond,arr) | details unknown
Ella Fitzgerald And Barney Kessel
In My Solitude
Los Angeles,CA, rec. 4.9.1956
Fitzgerald,Ella (voc) | Kessel,Barney (g)
Ella Fitzgerald And Her All Stars
How Long How Long Blues | See See Rider
NYC, rec. 28.10.1963
Fitzgerald,Ella (voc) | Eldridge,Roy (tp) | Davis,Wild Bill (org) | Ellis,Herb (g) | Brown,Ray (b) | Johnson,Gus (dr)
Mood Indigo
Los Angeles,CA, rec. 17.10.1957
Fitzgerald,Ella (voc) | Webster,Ben (ts) | Peterson,Oscar (p) | Ellis,Herb (g) | Brown,Ray (b) | Stoller,Alvin (dr)
Ella Fitzgerald With The Billy May Orchestra
Stormy Weather | Blues In The Night
Los Angeles,CA, rec. 14.1.1961
Fitzgerald,Ella (voc) | May,Billy (arr,ld) | Fagerquist,Don (tp) | Bernhart,Milton 'Milt' (tb) | Nash,Dick (tb) | Carter,Benny (as) | Nash,Ted (as) | Johnson,Plas (ts) | Bunker,Larry (vib) | Smith,Paul (p) | Hendrickson,Al (g) | Collins,John (g) | Mondragon,Joe (b) | Stoller,Alvin (dr) | details unknown
Ella Fitzgerald With The Oscar Peterson Quartet
These Foolish Things Remind Me On You
Live at The 'Opera House',Chicago,Ill, rec. 19.10.1957
Fitzgerald,Ella (voc) | Peterson,Oscar (p) | Ellis,Herb (g) | Brown,Ray (b) | Bellson,Louie (dr)
Ella Fitzgerald With The Nelson Riddle Orchestra
I Can't Get Started
Los Angeles,CA, rec. 13.11.1961
Fitzgerald,Ella (voc) | Riddle,Nelson (cond,arr) | details unknown
Ella Fitzgerald With The Buddy Bregman Orchestra
I Love Paris
Los Angeles,CA, rec. 7.2.1957
Fitzgerald,Ella (voc) | Smith,Paul (p) | Mondragon,Joe (b) | Stoller,Alvin (dr) | Bregman,Buddy (cond,arr) | details unknown

843476-2 | CD | The World Is Falling Down
Abbey Lincoln And Her All Stars
The World Is Falling Down | First Song | You Must Believe In Spring And Love | I Got Thunder(And It Rings) | How High The Moon | When Love Was You And Me | Hi Fly | Live For Life
NYC, rec. 21./22.& 27.2.1990
Lincoln,Abbey (voc) | Terry,Clark (tp,fl-h) | McLean,Jackie (as) | Dodgion,Jerry (as) | Jean-Marie,Alain (p) | Haden,Charlie (b) | Higgins,Billy (dr)

844410-2 | CD | Verve Jazz Masters 33:Benny Goodman
Benny Goodman Sextet
If I Had You | Sweet Georgia Brown | Poor Butterfly
Live in Stockholm,Sweden, rec. 20.2.1970
Goodman,Benny (cl) | McGuffie,Bill (p) | Pizzarelli,Bucky (g) | Stewart,Louis (g) | Bush,Lennie (b) | Orr,Bobby (dr)
Benny Goodman And His Orchestra
A String Of Pearls
Goodman,Benny (cl) | Bowen,Gregg (tp) | McLevy,John (tp) | Watkins,Derek (tp) | Christie,Keith (tb) | Peck,Nat (tb) | Wilson,Jimmy (tb) | Burns,Bob (as) | Honeywell,Don (as) | Efford,Bob (ts) | Reidy,Frank (ts) | Willis,Dave (bs) | McGuffie,Bill (p) | Pizzarelli,Bucky (g) | Stewart,Louis (g) | Bush,Lennie (b) | Orr,Bobby (dr)
Benny Goodman And His All Star Sextet
I've Found A New Baby | After You've Gone | Honeysuckle Rose | Oh! Lady Be Good
Live in Copenhagen, rec. 13.3.1972
Goodman,Benny (cl) | Sims,Zoot (as,ts) | Appleyard,Peter (vib) | Pizzarelli,Bucky (g) | McGuffie,Bill (p) | Gaylor,Hal (b) | Alexander,Mousie (dr)
Benny Goodman Quintet
Memories Of You
Goodman,Benny (cl) | Pizzarelli,Bucky (g) | McGuffie,Bill (p) | Gaylor,Hal (b) | Alexander,Mousie (dr)
You Must Met My Wife
Stamford,CT, rec. 30.6.1976
Goodman,Benny (cl) | Fay,Tom (p) | Duran,Eddie (g) | Moore,Michael (b) | Kay,Connie (dr)
Benny Goodman Quartet
Please Be Kind
Stamford,CT, rec. January 1977
Goodman,Benny (cl) | Collins,Cal (g) | Heath,Percy (b) | Kay,Connie (dr)
Benny Goodman Sextet
Somebody Loves Me
Goodman,Benny (cl) | Vaché,Warren (tp) | Bunch,John (p) | Collins,Cal (g) | Heath,Percy (b) | Kay,Connie (dr)
Benny Goodman Septet
I Ain't Got Nobody
Goodman,Benny (cl) | Vaché,Warren (tp) | Hamilton,Scott (ts) | Bunch,John (p) | Collins,Cal (g) | Heath,Percy (b) | Kay,Connie (dr)
Benny Goodman And His Orchestra
That's A Plenty
Live at Carnegie Hall,NYC, rec. 17.1.1978
Goodman,Benny (cl) | Vaché,Warren (tp) | Andre,Wayne (tb) | Tate,Buddy (ts) | Collins,Cal (g) | Williams,Mary Lou (p) | Moore,Michael (b) | Kay,Connie (dr)
Stardust
Goodman,Benny (cl) | Paz,Victor (tp) | Vaché,Warren (tp) | Sheldon,Jack (tp) | Andre,Wayne (tb) | Masso,George (tb) | Messner,John (tb) | Young,George (as) | Rodnon,Mel (as) | Tate,Buddy (ts) | Wess,Frank (ts) | Schlinger,Sol (bs) | Collins,Cal (g) | Wright,Wayne (g) | Bunch,John (p) | Moore,Michael (b) | Kay,Connie (dr)

847408-2 | CD | Mr. Clarinet | EAN 042284740821
Buddy DeFranco Quartet
Buddy's Blues | Ferdinando | It Could Happen To Me | Autumn In New York | Left Field | Show Eyes | But Not For Me | Bass On Balls
NYC, rec. July 1953
DeFranco,Buddy (cl) | Drew,Kenny (p) | Hinton,Milt (b) | Blakey,Art (dr)

847430-2 | CD | Stan Getz Highlights
Stan Getz Quintet
Stella By Starlight
NYC, rec. 12.12.1952
Getz,Stan (ts) | Jordan,Duke (p) | Raney,Jimmy (g) | Crow,Bill (b) | Isola,Frank (dr)
Cool Mix
NYC, rec. 16.4.1953
Getz,Stan (ts) | Brookmeyer,Bob (v-tb) | Williams,Johnny (p) | Crow,Bill (b) | Levitt,Al (dr)
Dizzy Gillespie-Stan Getz Sextet
Exactly Like You
Los Angeles,CA, rec. 9.12.1953
Gillespie,Dizzy (tp) | Getz,Stan (ts) | Peterson,Oscar (p) | Ellis,Herb (g) | Brown,Ray (b) | Roach,Max (dr)
Stan Getz Quartet
With The Wind And The Rain In Your Hair
Los Angeles,CA, rec. 14.1.1954
Getz,Stan (ts) | Rowles,Jimmy (p) | Whitlock,Bob (b) | Roach,Max (dr)
Stan Getz Quintet
It Don't Mean A Thing If It Ain't Got That Swing
Los Angeles,CA, rec. 8.11.1954
Getz,Stan (ts) | Brookmeyer,Bob (v-tb) | Williams,Johnny (p) | Anthony,Bill (b) | Mardigan,Art (dr)
A Night In Tunisia
Los Angeles,CA, rec. 15.8.1955
Getz,Stan (ts) | Candoli,Conte (tp) | Levy,Lou (p) | Vinnegar,Leroy (b) | Manne,Shelly (dr)
Stan Getz Quartet
A Handful Of Stars
Los Angeles,CA, rec. 19.8.1955
Getz,Stan (ts) | Levy,Lou (p) | Vinnegar,Leroy (b) | Manne,Shelly (dr)
Over The Rainbow
Stockholm,Sweden, rec. 16.12.1955
Getz,Stan (ts) | Hallberg,Bengt (p) | Johnson,Gunnar (b) | Burman,Anders 'Andrew' (dr)
Dizzy Gillespie Septet
Wee(Allen's Alley)
Los Angeles,CA, rec. 16.10.1956
Gillespie,Dizzy (tp) | Getz,Stan (ts) | Stitt,Sonny (as) | Lewis,John (p) | Ellis,Herb (g) | Brown,Ray (b) | Levey,Stan (dr)
Stan Getz Quartet
Smiles
Hollywood,CA, rec. 2.8.1957
Getz,Stan (ts) | Levy,Lou (p) | Vinnegar,Leroy (b) | Levey,Stan (dr)
Stan Getz With The Oscar Peterson Trio
Blues For Henry
Los Angeles,CA, rec. 10.10.1957
Getz,Stan (ts) | Peterson,Oscar (p) | Ellis,Herb (g) | Brown,Ray (b)
Stan Getz-Gerry Mulligan Quintet
Ballad
Los Angeles,CA, rec. 22.10.1957
Getz,Stan (ts) | Mulligan,Gerry (bs) | Levy,Lou (p) | Brown,Ray (b) | Levey,Stan (dr)
Ella Fitzgerald With The Frank DeVol Orchestra
You're Blasé
Los Angeles,CA, rec. 15.10.1957
Fitzgerald,Ella (voc) | Getz,Stan (ts) | DeVol,Frank (cond,arr) | details unknown
J.J.Johnson & Stan Getz With The Oscar Peterson Quartet
My Funny Valentine
Los Angeles,CA, rec. 7.10.1957
Johnson,J.J. (tb) | Getz,Stan (ts) | Peterson,Oscar (p) | Ellis,Herb (g) | Brown,Ray (b) | Kay,Connie (dr)
Stan Getz And The Swedish All Stars
Gold Rush
Stockholm,Sweden, rec. 16.9.1958
Getz,Stan (ts) | Bailey,Benny (tp) | Persson,Ake (tb) | Nordstrom,Erik (ts) | Gullin,Lars (bs) | Johansson,Jan (p) | Johnson,Gunnar (b) | Schiöppfe,William (dr)
Stan Getz Quartet
Good Bye
Copenhagen,Denmark, rec. 14./15.1.1960
Getz,Stan (ts) | Johansson,Jan (p) | Jordan,Daniel (b) | Schiöppfe,William (dr)
Stan Getz With Orchestra
Round About Midnight
Baden-Baden, rec. March 1969
Getz,Stan (ts) | Johansson,Jan (p) | Dutton,Fred (b) | Karas,Sperie (dr) | Birdsong,Blanche (harp) | Garcia,Russell (cond,arr)
Stan Getz With The Eddie Sauter Orchestra
I'm Late, I'm Late
NYC, rec. 14.7.1961
Getz,Stan (ts) | Neves,John (b) | Haynes,Roy (dr) | Strings | Kay,Hershy (ld) | Sauter,Eddie (arr) | details unknown
Stan Getz-Charlie Byrd Sextet
Desafinado
Washington,DC, rec. 13.2.1962
Getz,Stan (ts) | Byrd,Charlie (g) | Byrd,Gene (g) | Betts,Keter (b) | Deppenschmidt,Buddy (perc) | Reichenbach,Bill (perc)
Stan Getz With The Gary McFarland Orchestra
Manha De Carnaval(Morning Of The Carnival)
NYC, rec. 28.8.1962
Getz,Stan (ts) | Severinsen,Doc (tp) | Ferrante,Joe (tp) | Travis,Nick (tp) | Dennis,Willie (tb) | Studd,Tony (tb) | Alonge,Ray (fr-h) | Beckenstein,Ray (cl) | Clark,Babe (cl) | Levinsky,Walt (cl) | Caine,Eddie (fl) | Penque,Romeo (fl) | Jones,Hank (p) | Hall,Jim (g) | Williams,Tommy (b) | Rae,Johnny (dr) | Costa,Carmen (perc) | Paulo,Jose (perc) | McFarland,Gary (cond,arr)
Stan Getz-Joao Gilberto Quintet
Girl From Ipanema(Garota De Ipanema)
NYC, rec. 18./19.3.1963
Getz,Stan (ts) | Gilberto,Joao (g,voc) | Jobim,Antonio Carlos (p) | Williams,Tommy (b) | Banana,Milton (dr) | Gilberto,Astrud (voc)
Stan Getz-Laurindo Almeida Orchestra
Corcovado(Quiet Nights)
NYC, rec. 21.3.1963
Getz,Stan (ts) | Almeida,Laurindo (g) | Kuhn,Steve (p) | Duvivier,George (b) | Bailey,Dave (dr) | Machado,Edison (perc) | Soorez,Jose (perc) | Parga,Luiz (perc) | Paulo,Jose (perc)
Stan Getz-Bill Evans Quartet
Melinda
Englewood Cliffs,NJ, rec. 5.5.1964
Getz,Stan (ts) | Evans,Bill (p) | Davis,Richard (b) | Jones,Elvin (dr)
Stan Getz With Orchestra And Voices
I Didn't Know What Time It Was
Englewood Cliffs,NJ, rec. 2.12.1966
Getz,Stan (ts) | Jones,Hank or Herbie Hancock (p) | Hall,Jim (g) | Carter,Ron (b) | Tate,Grady (dr) | Horwath,Bill (perc) | Butler,Artie (perc) | Rosengarden,Bobby (perc) | Chorus | Ogerman,Claus (cond,arr) | details unknown
Stan Getz Quartet
Sweet Rain
Englewood Cliffs,NJ, rec. 30.3.1967
Getz,Stan (ts) | Corea,Chick (p) | Carter,Ron (b) | Tate,Grady (dr)
I Remember Clifford
London,GB, rec. 15.-17.3.1971
Getz,Stan (ts) | Thomas,Rene (g) | Louiss,Eddie (org) | Lubat,Bernard (dr)
Stan Getz With The Michel Legrand Orchestra
Communications '72
Paris,France, rec. November 1971
Getz,Stan (ts) | Brass | Strings | Legrand,Michel (cond,arr) | details unknown

847482-2 | CD | You Won't Forget Me
Shirley Horn Trio
The Music That Makes Me Dance | Come Dance With Me | Too Late Now | I Just Found Out About Love | If You Go | All My Tomorrows
NYC, rec. 12./14.6.& 11.-13.8.1990
Horn,Shirley (p,voc) | Ables,Charles (b) | Williams,Stephen E. 'Steve' (dr)
Shirley Horn Trio with Wynton Marsalis
Don't Let The Sun Catch You Cryin'
Marsalis,Wynton (tp) | Horn,Shirley (p,voc) | Ables,Charles (b) | Williams,Stephen E. 'Steve' (dr)
Shirley Horn Trio with Branford Marsalis
It Had To Be You
Marsalis,Branford (ts) | Horn,Shirley (p,voc) | Ables,Charles (b) | Williams,Stephen E. 'Steve' (dr)
Shirley Horn Trio with Miles Davis
You Won't Forget Me
Davis,Miles (tp) | Horn,Shirley (p,voc) | Ables,Charles (b) | Williams,Stephen E. 'Steve' (dr)
Shirley Horn Trio with Toots Thielemans
Soothe Me
Thielemans,Jean 'Toots' (harm) | Horn,Shirley (p,voc) | Ables,Charles (b) | Williams,Stephen E. 'Steve' (dr)
Shirley Horn with Toots Thielemans
Beautiful Love
NYC, rec. 12./14.& 11.-13.8.1990
Horn,Shirley (voc) | Thielemans,Jean 'Toots' (g,harm)
Shirley Horn Trio
Come Back To Me
Horn,Shirley (p,voc) | Williams,Buster (b) | Hart,Billy (dr)
Shirley Horn Trio with Buck Hill
Foolin' Myself
Hill,Buck (ts) | Horn,Shirley (p,voc) | Williams,Buster (b) | Hart,Billy (dr)
Shirley Horn Quartet
You Stepped Out Of A Dream
Horn,Shirley (p,voc) | Ables,Charles (g) | Williams,Buster (b) | Hart,Billy (dr)

849392-2 | CD | Getz Meets Mulligan In Hi-Fi
Stan Getz-Gerry Mulligan Quintet
Scrapple From The Apple | I Didn't Know What Time It Was | A Ballad
NYC, rec. 12.10.1957
Getz,Stan (ts,bs) | Mulligan,Gerry (ts,bs) | Levy,Lou (p) | Brown,Ray (b) | Levey,Stan (dr)

940130-0 | CD | Louis And The Good Book
Louis Armstrong With Sy Oliver's Choir And Orchestra
Nobody Knows The Trouble I've Seen | Down By The Riverside | Jonah And The Whale | This Train
NYC, rec. 4.2.1958
Armstrong,Louis (tp,voc) | Oliver,Sy (cond,arr) | Young,Trummy (tb) | McRae,Dave (cl) | Tragg,Nickie (org) | Kyle,Billy (p) | Barnes,George (g) | Herbert,Mort (b) | Deems,Barrett (dr) | 10-voice-choir
Shadrack | On My Way
NYC, rec. 6.2.1958
Armstrong,Louis (tp,voc) | Oliver,Sy (cond,arr) | Young,Trummy (tb) | Hall,Edmond (cl) | Tragg,Nickie (org) | Kyle,Billy (p) | Barksdale,Everett (g)
Didn't Rain | Rock My Soul
Armstrong,Louis (voc) | Oliver,Sy (cond,arr) | Tragg,Nickie (org) | Kyle,Billy (p) | Barksdale,Everett (g) | Herbert,Mort (b) | Deems,Barrett (dr) | 10-voice-choir
Swing Low Sweet Chariot | Go Down Moses | Ezekiel Saw 'De Wheel | Sometimes I Feel Like A Motherless Child
NYC, rec. 7.2.1958
Armstrong,Louis (tp,voc) | Oliver,Sy (cond,arr) | Young,Trummy (tb) | D'Amico,Hank (cl) | Tragg,Nickie (org) | Kyle,Billy (p) | Barksdale,Everett (g) | Herbert,Mort (b) | Deems,Barrett (dr)

9513304 | CD | When I Look In Your Eyes
Diana Krall Group
Devil May Care | East Of The Sun West Of The Moon
NYC, rec. 1999
Krall,Diana (p,voc) | Malone,Russell (g) | Wolfe,Benjamin Jonah 'Ben' (b)
Popsicle Toes | The Best Thing For You
Krall,Diana (p,voc) | Malone,Russell (g) | Clayton,John (b) | Hamilton,Jeff (dr)
I Can't Give You Anything But Love
Krall,Diana (p,voc) | Malone,Russell (g)
Diana Krall Group With Orchestra
When I Look In Your Eyes
Krall,Diana (p,voc) | Malone,Russell (g) | Orchestra | details unknown
Let's Face The Music And Dance | Pick Yourself Up | Do It Again
Krall,Diana (p,voc) | Malone,Russell (g) | Clayton,John (b) | Hamilton,Jeff (dr) | Orchestra | details unknown
Let's Fall In Love
Krall,Diana (p,voc) | Bunker,Larry (vib) | Malone,Russell (g) | Clayton,John (b) | Hamilton,Jeff (dr) | Orchestra | details unknown
I've Got You Under My Skin
Krall,Diana (p,voc) | Bunker,Larry (vib) | Malone,Russell (g) | Wolfe,Benjamin Jonah 'Ben' (b) | Nash,Lewis (dr) | Orchestra | details unknown
I'll String Along With You
Krall,Diana (p,voc) | Malone,Russell (g) | Wolfe,Benjamin Jonah 'Ben' (b) | Nash,Lewis (dr) | Orchestra | details unknown

9801098 | CD | The Lost Sessions | EAN 602498010983
Stan Getz Quartet
Sunshower | Yours And Mine | Joanne Julia | Soul Eyes | Spiral | Beatrice | The Wind | El Sueno | Feijoada De Chocos
Hollywood,CA, rec. March 1989
Getz,Stan (ts) | Barron,Kenny (p) | Mraz,George 'Jiri' (b) | Lewis,Victor (dr)

9813132 | CD | The Montreal Tapes | EAN 602498131329
Charlie Haden-Joe Henderson-Al Foster
Round About Midnight | All The Things You Are | In The Moment | Passport
Live at The Festival International De Jazz De Montreal,Canada, rec. 30.6.1999
Haden,Charlie (b) | Henderson,Joe (sax) | Foster,Al (dr)

9860307 | CD | Snap Your Fingers | EAN 602498603079
Al Grey And His Allstars
Minor On Top | African Lady | Hi Fly
Live at 'Birdland',NYC, rec. 31.1.1962
Grey,Al (tb) | Byrd,Donald (tp) | Mitchell,Billy (ts) | Hutcherson,Bobby (vib) | Hancock,Herbie (p) | Wright,Herman (b) | Williams,Eddie (b)
Three-Fourth Blues | On Green Dolphin Street | Nothin' But The Truth | R.B.Q. | Just Waiting
Chicago,Ill, rec. 19.2.1962
Grey,Al (tb) | Burns,Dave (tp) | Mitchell,Billy (ts) | Hutcherson,Bobby (vib) | Morris,Floyd (p) | Wright,Herman (b) | Williams,Eddie (b)

9860308 | CD | J.J.'s Broadway | EAN 602498603086
J.J.Johnson's All Stars
Nobody's Heart | Who Will Buy
NYC, rec. 12.3.1963
Johnson,J.J. (tb) | McGarity,Lou (tb) | Green,Urbie (tb) | Mitchell,Tom (tb) | Faulise,Paul (tb) | Jones,Hank (p) | Israels,Chuck (b) | Perkins,Walter (dr)
Lovely | Mira | The Sweetest Sounds | A Sleepin' Bee
Johnson,J.J. (tb) | McGarity,Lou (tb) | Green,Urbie (tb) | Mitchell,Tom (tb) | Faulise,Paul (tb) | Israels,Chuck (b) | Perkins,Walter (dr)
J.J.Johnson Quartet
Put On A Happy Face | Make Someone Happy | My Favorite Things | Second Chance
NYC, rec. 6.4.1963
Johnson,J.J. (tb) | Jones,Hank (p) | Davis,Richard (b) | Perkins,Walter (dr)

9860309 | CD | GRRR | EAN 602498603093
Hugh Masekela Group
U-DWI(Smallpox) | Sharpville | Umaningi Bona(Long River) | Phatsha-Phatsha(Hurry-Hurry)
details unknown, rec. April 1965
Masekela,Hugh (tp,arr) | unkn. (tb,tuba,ts,p,b,dr,perc)
Zulu And The Mexican | Emavungwani(Green Home) | Ntyilo Ntyilo | Sipho | Kwa-Blaney | Mira
details unknown, rec. May 1965
Masekela,Hugh (tp,arr) | unkn. (tb,tuba,ts,p,b,dr,perc)

9860310 | CD | Mis'ry And The Blues | EAN 602498603109
Jack Teagarden And His Sextet
Don't Tell A Man About His Woman | Basin Street Blues | Froggie Moore | I Don't Want To Miss Mississippi | It's All In Your Mind | Mis'ry And The Blues | Original Dixieland One Step | Afternoon In August | Peaceful Valley
Chicago,Ill, rec. 18.-22.6.1961
Teagarden,Jack (tb,voc) | Goldie,Don (tp) | Cuesta,Henry (cl) | Ewell,Don (p) | Puls,Stan (b) | Deems,Barrett (dr)
Love Lies
Teagarden,Jack (tb,voc) | Goldie,Don (tp) | Cuesta,Henry (cl) | Ewell,Don (p) | Torrent,Shay (org) | Puls,Stan (b) | Deems,Barrett (dr)

9860417 | CD | Ella Fitzgerald Sings Sweet Songs For Swingers | EAN 602498604175
Ella Fitzgerald With The Frank DeVol Orchestra
East Of The Sun West Of The Moon | Lullaby Of Broadway | Let's Fall In | I Remember You | Sweet And Lovely | Can't We Be Friends | Out Of This World | Makin' Whoopee
Los Angeles,CA, rec. 24.11.1958
Fitzgerald,Ella (voc) | Edison,Harry 'Sweets' (tp) | DeVol,Frank (cond,arr) | details unknown
My Old Flame | Gone With The Wind | That Old Feeling
Los Angeles,CA, rec. 11.7.1959
Fitzgerald,Ella (voc) | DeVol,Frank (cond,arr) | details unknown

9860613 | 4 CD | The Complete Verve Gerry Mulligan Concert Band | EAN 602498606131
Gerry Mulligan Concert Jazz Band
I'm Gonna Go Fishin'
NYC, rec. 21.5.1960
Mulligan,Gerry (bs) | Stiles,Danny (tp) | Sunkel,Phil (tp) | Ferrara,Don (tp) | Brookmeyer,Bob (v-tb) | Andre,Wayne (tb) | Ralph,Alan (tb,b-tb) | Quill,Gene (cl,as) | Meldonian,Dick (as) | Reider,Jimmy (ts) | Allen,Gene (b-cl,bs) | Takas,Bill (b) | Bailey,Dave (dr)
Out Of This World | Sweet And Slow | Barbara's Theme | I Know Don't Know How
NYC, rec. 31.5.-3.6.1960
Mulligan,Gerry (bs) | Stiles,Danny (tp) | Sunkel,Phil (tp) | Ferrara,Don (tp) | Brookmeyer,Bob (v-tb) | Andre,Wayne (tb) | Ralph,Alan (tb,b-tb) | Quill,Gene (cl,as) | Meldonian,Dick (as) | Reider,Jimmy (ts) | Allen,Gene (b-cl,bs) | Takas,Bill (b) | Bailey,Dave (dr)
Manoir De Mes Reves(aka Django's Castle)[remake] | Bweebida Bwobbida(remake) | Sweet And Slow(remake) | Out Of This World(remake) | You Took Advantage Of Me | My Funny Valentine | Broadway
NYC, rec. 25.& 27.7.1960
Mulligan,Gerry (bs) | Travis,Nick (tp) | Candoli,Conte (tp) | Ferrara,Don (tp) | Brookmeyer,Bob (v-tb) | Andre,Wayne (tb) | Ralph,Alan (tb,b-tb) | Quill,Gene (cl,as) | Meldonian,Dick (as) | Sims,Zoot (ts) | Allen,Gene (b-cl,bs) | Clark,Buddy (b) | Lewis,Mel (dr)
Come Rain Or Come Shine | The Red Door | Go Home | As Catch Can | Young Blood | Blueport
Live at Santa Monica Civic Auditorium,CA, rec. 1.10.1960
Mulligan,Gerry (bs) | Travis,Nick (tp) | Candoli,Conte (tp) | Ferrara,Don (tp) | Brookmeyer,Bob (v-tb,p) | Dennis,Willie (tb) | Ralph,Alan (tb,b-tb) | Quill,Gene (cl,as) | Donovan,Bob (as) | Reider,Jimmy (ts) | Sims,Zoot (ts) | Allen,Gene (b-cl,bs) | Clark,Buddy (b) | Lewis,Mel (dr)
Theme From 'I Want To Live'
Live at Berliner Jazztage, rec. 4.11.1960
Mulligan,Gerry (bs) | Travis,Nick (tp) | Candoli,Conte (tp) | Ferrara,Don (tp) | Brookmeyer,Bob (v-tb) | Dennis,Willie (tb) | Ralph,Alan (tb,b-tb) | Quill,Gene (cl,as) | Donovan,Bob (as) | Reider,Jimmy (ts) | Sims,Zoot (ts) | Allen,Gene (b-cl,bs) | Clark,Buddy (b) | Lewis,Mel (dr)
Go Home | Apple Core | Barbara's Theme
Live in Milano, rec. 14.11.1960
Mulligan,Gerry (bs) | Travis,Nick (tp) | Candoli,Conte (tp) | Ferrara,Don (tp) | Brookmeyer,Bob (v-tb) | Dennis,Willie (tb) | Ralph,Alan (tb,b-tb) | Quill,Gene (cl,as) | Donovan,Bob (as) | Reider,Jimmy (ts) | Sims,Zoot (ts) | Allen,Gene (b-cl,bs) | Clark,Buddy (b) | Lewis,Mel (dr)
Lady Chatterley's Mother | Body And Soul | Let My People Be | Come Rain Or Come Shine | Blueport | Black Nightgown
Live at The 'Village Vanguard',NYC, rec. 11.12.1960
Mulligan,Gerry (bs,p) | Travis,Nick (tp) | Terry,Clark (tp) | Ferrara,Don (tp) | Brookmeyer,Bob (v-tb) | Dennis,Willie (tb) | Ralph,Alan (tb,b-tb) | Quill,Gene (cl,as) | Donovan,Bob (as) | Reider,Jimmy (ts) | Allen,Gene (cl,b-cl,bs) | Crow,Bill (b) | Lewis,Mel (dr)
All About Rosie(part 1&2) | Weep | Chuggin' | Israel | Summer's Over | All About Rosie(part 3) | I Know Don't Know How
NYC, rec. 10./11.7.1961
Mulligan,Gerry (bs,p) | Travis,Nick (tp) | Severinsen,Doc (tp) | Ferrara,Don (tp) | Brookmeyer,Bob (v-tb) | Dennis,Willie (tb) | Ralph,Alan (tb,b-tb) | Quill,Gene (cl,as) | Donovan,Bob (as) | Reider,Jimmy (ts) | Allen,Gene (cl,b-cl,bs) | Crow,Bill (b) | Lewis,Mel (dr)
Big City Blues | Pretty Little Gypsy | Little Rock Getaway | Ballad | Big City Life | Bridgehampton South | My Kinda Love | Bridgehampton Strut | Chant | Bridgehampton South(alt.take) | Bridgehampton Strut(alt.take)
NYC, rec. 18.-21.12.1962
Mulligan,Gerry (bs,cl) | Terry,Clark (tp,fl-h) | Travis,Nick (tp) | Severinsen,Doc (tp) | Ferrara,Don (tp) | Brookmeyer,Bob (v-tb,p) | Dennis,Willie (tb) | Studd,Tony (b-tb) | Quill,Gene (cl,as) | Caine,Eddie (alto-fl,as) | Reider,Jimmy (ts) | Allen,Gene (bs) | Hall,Jim (g) | Crow,Bill (b) | Johnson,Gus (dr)

9861050 | CD | Spanish Rice | EAN 602498610503
Clark Terry & Chico O'Farril Orchestra
Peanut Vendor | Angelitos Negros | El Cumbanchero | Joonji | Que Sera Sera | Mexican Hat Dance | Spanish Rice | Say Si Si | La Macarena(La Virchin De La Macarena) | Tin Tin Deo | Contigo En La Distancia | Happiness Is
NYC, rec. 18.-20.7.1966
Terry,Clark (tp,fl-h,voc) | Young,Eugene 'Snooky' (tp,fl-h) | Royal,Ernie (tp,fl-h) | Galbraith,Barry (g) | Barksdale,Everett (g) | Duvivier,George (b) | Tate,Grady (dr) | Cruz,Julie (perc) | Malabe,Frankie (perc) | Rosengarden,Bobby (perc) | Pozo,Chino (perc) | unkn. (voc-trio) | O'Farrill,Chico (cond,arr)

9861063 | CD | Tony Scott | EAN 602498610633
Tony Scott Trio
Sophisticated Lady
NYC, rec. 10.12.1969
Scott,Tony (bs) | Davis,Richard (b) | Lovelace,Jimmy (dr)
Tony Scott Group
Swara Sulina(The Beautiful Sound Of The Flute) | Ode To An Oud
Scott,Tony (cl) | Berberian,John (oud) | Zoller,Attila (g) | Hinton,Milt (b) | Lovelace,Jimmy (dr) | Baronian,Souren (dumbek) | Pumila,Steve (perc)
Homage To Lord Krishna
Scott,Tony (cl) | Walcott,Collin (sitar) | Zoller,Attila (g) | Hinton,Milt (b) | Lovelace,Jimmy (dr)
My Funny Valentine | Nina's Dance
Scott,Tony (cl) | Zoller,Attila (g) | Rubenstein,Bertil (p) | Davis,Richard (b) | Lovelace,Jimmy (dr)
Satin Doll | Blues For Charlie Parker | Brother Can You Spare A Dime
Scott,Tony (cl) | Rubenstein,Bertil (org) | Davis,Richard (b) | Lovelace,Jimmy (dr)

9861278 | 7 CD | The Complete Verve Roy Eldridge Studio Sessions | EAN 602498612781
Roy Eldridge And His Orchestra
Baby What's The Matter With You | Yard Dog | Sweet Lorraine | Jumbo The Elephant
NYC, rec. August 1951
Eldridge,Roy (tp,voc) | Tate,Buddy (ts) | Brannon,Teddy (p) | Lombardi,Clyde (b) | Smith,Charlie (dr)
Easter Parade | I See Everybody's Baby
NYC, rec. December 1951
Eldridge,Roy (tp) | unkn. (fl,fr-h,p,g,b,dr)
Roy Eldridge And His Orchestra With Strings
Basin Street Blues | I Remember Harlem
Eldridge,Roy (tp) | unkn. (fl,fr-h,p,g,b,dr) | Strings | Williams,George (ld)
Roy Eldridge Quintet
Roy's Riff | Wrap Your Troubles In Dreams | Rockin' Chair | Little Jazz
NYC, rec. 13.2.1953
Eldridge,Roy (tp,voc) | Kessel,Barney (g) | Peterson,Oscar (org) | Brown,Ray (b) | Heard,J.C. (dr)
Love For Sale | Dale's Wail | The Man I Love | Oscar's Arrangement | Dale's Wail(alt.take 1) | Dale's Wail(alt.take 2) | Dale's Wail(alt.take.3)
NYC, rec. 23.4.1953
Eldridge,Roy (tp) | Kessel,Barney (g) | Peterson,Oscar (org) | Brown,Ray (b) | Jones,Jo (dr)
Willow Weep For Me | Somebody Loves Me | When Your Lover Has Gone | When It's Sleepy Time Down South | When It's Sleepy Time Down South(alt.take) | Feeling A Draft | Don't Blame Me | Echoes Of Harlem | Echoes Of Harlem(10" LP-Master) | I Can't Get Started
Los Angeles,CA, rec. 10.12.1953
Eldridge,Roy (tp) | Ellis,Herb (g) | Peterson,Oscar (p) | Brown,Ray (b) | Stoller,Alvin (dr)
Roy Eldridge And His Orchestra
If I Had You | Blue Moon | Stormy Weather | Sweethearts On Parade | A Foggy Day(In London Town) | I Only Have Eyes For You | Sweet Georgia Brown | The Song Is Ended
NYC, rec. 15.9.1954
Eldridge,Roy (tp) | Ellis,Herb (g) | Peterson,Oscar (p) | Brown,Ray (b) | Rich,Buddy (dr)
Roy Eldridge-Dizzy Gillespie With The Oscar Peterson Quartet
Sometimes I'm Happy | Algo Bueno | Trumpet Blues | The Heat's On | Ballad Medley: | I'm Through With Love- | Can't We Be Friends- | Don't You Think- | I Don't Know Why(I Just Do)- | If I Had You- | Blue Moon | I've Found A New Baby | Pretty Eyed Baby | I Can't Get Started | Limehouse Blues
Los Angeles,CA, rec. 29.10.1955
Eldridge,Roy (tp,voc) | Gillespie,Dizzy (tp,voc) | Ellis,Herb (g) | Peterson,Oscar (p) | Brown,Ray (b) | Bellson,Louie (dr)
Ralph Burns And His Orchestra
Sprang
NYC, rec. 4.2.1955
Burns,Ralph (cond,arr) | DeRisi,Al (tp) | Eldridge,Roy (tp) | DiRisi,Al (tp) | Glow,Bernie (tp) | Oles,Lew (tp) | Porcino,Al (tp) | Marowitz,Sam (as) | McKusick,Hal (as) | Cohn,Al (ts) | Bank,Danny (bs) | Peterson,Oscar (p) | Brown,Ray (b) | Bellson,Louie (dr)
Music For A Stripteaser
Burns,Ralph (cond,arr) | DeRisi,Al (tp) | Eldridge,Roy (tp) | Glow,Bernie (tp) | Oles,Lew (tp) | Porcino,Al (tp) | Marowitz,Sam (as) | McKusick,Hal (as) | Phillips,Flip (ts) | Cohn,Al (ts) | Bank,Danny (bs) | Peterson,Oscar (p) | Brown,Ray (b) | Bellson,Louie (dr)
Roy Eldridge-Alvin Stoller
Where's Art? | I Don't Know | Striding | Wailing
Los Angeles,CA, rec. 21.3.1955
Eldridge,Roy (tp,fl-h,p) | Stoller,Alvin (dr) | Coe,Jimmy (bs)
Roy Eldridge-Benny Carter Quintet
I Still Love Him So | The Moon Is Low | The Moon Is Low(alt.take) | The Moon Is Low(78rpm-take) | Close Your Eyes | Close Your Eyes(78rpm-take) | I Missed My Hat | I Missed My Hat(alt.take) | Polite Blues | Ballad Medley: | I Remember You- | Chelsea Bridge- | I've Got The World On A String- | Ballad Medley: | I Remember You(alt.take)- | Chelsea Bridge(alt.take)- | I've Got The World On A String(alt.take)
Los Angeles,CA, rec. 23.3.1955
Eldridge,Roy (tp,fl-h) | Carter,Benny (as) | McDonald,Bruce (p) | Simmons,John (b) | Stoller,Alvin (dr)
Roy Eldridge-Dizzy Gillespie-Harry Edison With The Oscar Peterson Quartet
Tour De Force | Steeplechase
Los Angeles,CA, rec. 2.11.1955
Eldridge,Roy (tp) | Gillespie,Dizzy (tp) | Edison,Harry 'Sweets' (tp) | Ellis,Herb (g) | Peterson,Oscar (p) | Brown,Ray (b) | Rich,Buddy (dr)
Roy Eldridge And His Central Plaza Dixielanders
Royal Garden Blues | Royal Garden Blues(alt.take) | That's A Plenty | Tin Roof Blues | Jazz Me Blues | Ja-Da | Struttin' With Some Barbecue | Black And Blue | Bugle Call Rag
NYC, rec. 3.6.1956
Eldridge,Roy (tp) | Morton,Benny (tb) | Barefield,Eddie (cl) | Wellstood,Dick (p) | Page,Walter (b) | Jones,Jo (dr)
Dizzy Gillespie-Roy Eldridge Sextet
Ballad Medley: | I'm Through With Love- | The Nearness Of You- | Moonlight In Vermont- | Summertime-
Los Angeles,CA, rec. 16.10.1956
Gillespie,Dizzy (tp) | Eldridge,Roy (tp) | Ellis,Herb (g) | Lewis,John (p) | Brown,Ray (b) | Levey,Stan (dr)
Roy Eldridge With The Russell Garcia Orchestra
Have You Met Miss Jones | I Can't Get Started | Blue Moon | How Long Has This Been Going On | Our Love Is Here To Stay
Los Angeles,CA, rec. 10.10.1957
Eldridge,Roy (tp) | unkn. (g,p,b,dr) | unkn. (harp) | Strings | details unknown | Garcia,Russell (cond,arr)
Stars Fell On Alabama | You're Blasé | They Can't Take That Away From Me | Can't We Be Friends | It Never Entered My Mind | Cheek To Cheek | A Foggy Day(In London Town)
Los Angeles,CA, rec. 11.10.1957
Eldridge,Roy (tp) | unkn. (g,p,b,dr) | unkn. (harp) | Strings | details unknown | Garcia,Russell (cond,arr)
Roy Eldridge Quintet
Phil's Tune
Paris,France, rec. 1.5.1958
Eldridge,Roy (tp) | Ellis,Herb (g) | Peterson,Oscar (p) | Brown,Ray (b) | Johnson,Gus (dr)
Roy Eldridge Sextet
Les Tricheurs
Eldridge,Roy (tp) | Getz,Stan (ts) | Ellis,Herb (g) | Peterson,Oscar (p) | Brown,Ray (b) | Johnson,Gus (dr)
Roy 'Little Jazz' Eldridge Quartet
The Way You Look Tonight | I've Got A Crush On You | Song Of The Islands | Dreamy | Sweet Sue Just You | When I Grow Too Old To Dream | Easy Living | Honeysuckle Rose | But Not For Me | All The Things You Are | Bossa Nova | Misty
NYC, rec. 2./3.6.1960
Eldridge,Roy (tp) | Ball,Ronnie (p) | Moten,Benny (b) | Locke,Eddie (dr)
-> with tp overdubbing

9861357 | CD | En Route | EAN 602498613573
John Scofield Trio
Wee | Togs | Name That Tune | Hammock Soliloquy | Bag | It Is Written | Alfie | Travel John | Over Big Top
Live at The 'Blue Note',NYC, rec. December 2003
Scofield,John (g) | Swallow,Steve (el-b) | Stewart,Bill (dr)

9861487 | CD | Cat On A Hot Fiddle | EAN 602498614877
Stuff Smith Quartet
'S Wonderful | Somebody Loves Me | Oh! Lady Be Good | The Man I Love | They Can't Take That Away From Me | Nice Work If You Can Get It
Washington,DC, rec. 7.8.1959
Smith,Stuff (v,voc) | Horn,Shirley (p,voc) | Packer,Lewis (b) | Saunders,Harry (dr)
Strike Up The Band
Smith,Stuff (v) | Eaton,John (p) | Packer,Lewis (b) | Saunders,Harry (dr)
Blue Violin | Undecided | Nice And Warm | Take The 'A' Train
Los Angeles,CA, rec. 22.10.1959
Smith,Stuff (v) | Smith,Paul (p) | Mitchell,Red (b) | Bulkin,Sid (dr)

9861761 | CD | Count Basie At Newport | EAN 602498617618
Count Basie And His Orchestra
Introduction by John Hammond | Swingin' At Newport | Blee Blop Blues | Alright,Okay,You Win | The Comeback | Roll 'Em Pete | Smack Dab In The Middle
Live at Newport,Rhode Island, rec. 7.7.1957
Basie,Count (p) | Culley,Wendell (tp) | Jones,Reunald (tp) | Jones,Thad (tp) | Newman,Joe (tp) | Coker,Henry (tb) | Hughes,Bill (tb) | Powell,Benny (tb) | Royal,Marshall (as) | Graham,Bill (as) | Foster,Frank (ts) | Wess,Frank (fl,ts) | Fowlkes,Charlie (bs) | Green,Freddie (g) | Jones,Eddie (b) | Payne,Sonny (dr) | Williams,Joe (voc)
Polka Dots And Moonbeams | Lester Leaps In | Sent For You Yesterday And Here You Come Today | Boogie Woogie(I May Be Wrong) | Evenin'
Basie,Count (p) | Culley,Wendell (tp) | Jones,Reunald (tp) | Jones,Thad (tp) | Newman,Joe (tp) | Coker,Henry (tb) | Hughes,Bill (tb) | Powell,Benny (tb) | Royal,Marshall (as) | Graham,Bill (as) | Young,Lester (ts) | Foster,Frank (ts) | Wess,Frank (fl,ts) | Fowlkes,Charlie (bs) | Green,Freddie (g) | Jones,Eddie (b) | Jones,Jo (dr) | Rushing,Jimmy (voc)
One O'Clock Jump
Basie,Count (p) | Eldridge,Roy (tp) | Culley,Wendell (tp) | Jones,Reunald (tp) | Jones,Thad (tp) | Newman,Joe (tp) | Coker,Henry (tb) | Hughes,Bill (tb) | Powell,Benny (tb) | Royal,Marshall (as) | Graham,Bill (as) | Young,Lester (ts) | Jacquet,Illinois (ts) | Foster,Frank (ts) | Wess,Frank (fl,ts) | Fowlkes,Charlie (bs) | Green,Freddie (g) | Jones,Eddie (b) | Jones,Jo (dr)

9862246 | CD | The Girl In The Other Room | EAN 602498622469
Diana Krall Group
Temptation
NYC, rec. 2003
Krall,Diana (p,voc) | Wilson,Anthony (g) | Larsen,Neil (org) | McBride,Christian (b) | Carrington,Terri Lyne (dr)
Stop This World | Almost Blue | I'm Pulling Through | Black Crow | Narrow Daylight | Abandoned Masquerade | I'm Coming Through | Departure Bay
Krall,Diana (p,voc) | Wilson,Anthony (g) | McBride,Christian (b) | Erskine,Peter (dr)
The Girl In The Other Room | I've Changed My Adress | Love Me Like A Man
Krall,Diana (p,voc) | Wilson,Anthony (g) | Clayton,John (b) | Hamilton,Jeff (dr)

9901098 | CD | Bossas And Ballads:The Lost Sessions | EAN 602498010983
Stan Getz Quartet
Sunshower | Yours And Mine | Joanne Julia | Soul Eyes | Spiral | Beatrice | The Wind | El Sueno | Feijada
Hollywood,CA, rec. March 1989
Getz,Stan (ts) | Barron,Kenny (p) | Mraz,George 'Jiri' (b) | Lewis,Victor (dr)

Village | ZYX Music GmbH

VILCD 1015-2 | CD | Live | EAN 090204998173
Christian Wegscheider Trio
Besame Mucho | It Ain't Necessarily So | Bottle Blues | Am Berg | Understatement | How Deep Is The Ocean | Wohin?
Live at 'Jazz Im Studio', ORF,Studio Tirol, rec. 2.2.2000
Wegscheider,Christian (p) | Abrams,Marc (b) | Salfellner,Christian (dr)
Libed | Cajin
Live at 'Jazz Im Studio', ORF,Studio Tirol, rec. 15.3.2000
Wegscheider,Christian (p) | Abrams,Marc (b) | Salfellner,Christian (dr)

VILCD 1016-2 | CD | When I'm 64 | EAN 090204977833
Olaf Kübler Quartet
Hotel Ravel | Daughter's Waltz | Blues For Nothing | One For Eddie | Robbin's Nest | You Don't Know What Love Is | Knubbel Blues | Lover Man(Oh,Where Can You Be?) | Groove Passion | My Foolish Heart | Be Bop Salat I | Memories | Amazing Grace | Be Bop Salat II
Köln, rec. 8./9.10.2001
Kübler,Olaf (ts) | Spendel,Christoph (p) | Nendza,André (b) | Bilker,Kurt (dr)

VILCD 1020-2 | CD | Gentle | EAN 090204941117
Thomas Faist Sextet
Sisyphos | Gentle | Door To Freedom | Three | Nil | So Long | Say It | Talkin' To the Mirror | Relaxed Focus
Thorstadl,Obing, rec. July 2001
Faist,Thomas (as,ts) | Weyerer,Franz (tp) | Herrlich,Johannes (tb) | Lang,Walter (p) | Stabenow,Thomas (b) | Hollander,Rick (dr)

VILCD 1021-2 | CD | Full Moon Party | EAN 090204942862
Peter Materna Quartet
Nichts Muss,Alles Kann | Full Moon Party | Das Leben Ist Wie Ein Pfeifen | Safa | The Best To You | So Near So Far | Kabbelige See | Mittwoch Morgen | Thomey | Miss Cool | War Was?
Camarillo Sound Studio,?, rec. January-April 2002
Materna,Peter (sax) | Scholz,Martin (p) | Gerards,Michael (b) | Mokross,Benny (dr)

VILCD 1023-2 | CD | Live at Bird's Eye | EAN 090204962099
Klaus Ignatzek-Claudio Roditi Quintet
Joy Spring | Obrigado | Bag's Groove | Waltz For S. | I Miss You So | Speak Low | African Flower
Live at The Bird's Eye,Basel,CH, rec. 12.10.2001

Ignatzek,Klaus (p) | Roditi,Claudio (tp) | Bergalli,Gustavo (tp) | Rassinfosse,Jean-Louis (b) | Castellucci,Bruno (dr)

VILCD 1024-2 | CD | Midnight Soul | EAN 090204922895
Olaf Kübler Quartet
Sidewalk | Für Meine Söhne | Midnight Soul | Mack The Knife(Moritat) | Playing In The Yard | Reflection | Bouncing Baby | Red Nose | Guilty | Havanna Drive | Devil's Disciples | Almenrausch
Köln, rec. 15./16.2.2003
Kübler,Olaf (ts) | Spendel,Christoph (p) | Nendza,André (b) | Bonica,Joe (dr)

WLCD 1017-2 | CD | Let's Call It A Day
Markus Fleischer Quartet
Big Ears,Wet Nose | Elephant Song | Tomorrow Is Another Day | All The Things You Are | Let's Call It A Day | Blueth? | Hot Pants | Warme Melk Met Chokolade | You'd Be So Nice To Come Home To
Jazztronom,?, rec. 5.6.2001
Fleischer,Markus (g) | Jünemann,Uli (ss,as) | Schädlich,Johannes (b) | Copeland,Keith (dr)

Vogue | BMG-Ariola Classics GmbH

21409352 | CD | Jimmy Raney Visits Paris Vol.1
Jimmy Raney Quartet
Body And Soul | Once In A While | Pennies From Heaven | Stella By Starlight | There'll Never Be Another You | Yesterdays | You Go To My Head | Body And Soul(alt.take) | Stella By Starlight(alt.take-1) | Stella By Starlight(alt.take-2) | There'll Never Be Another You(alt.take) | Yesterdays(alt.take)
Paris,France, rec. 6.2.1954
Raney,Jimmy (g) | Clark,Sonny (p) | Mitchell,Red (b) | White,Bobby (dr)

21409362 | CD | Thelonious Monk Piano Solo
Thelonious Monk
Round About Midnight | Evidence | Smoke Gets In Your Eyes | Well You Needn't | Reflections | We See | Eronel | Off Minor | Hackensack
Paris,France, rec. 7.6.1954
Monk,Thelonious (p-solo)

21409392 | CD | Pleyel Jazz Concert 1953
Dizzy Gillespie Sextet
Intro | The Champ | Good Bait | Swing Low Sweet Cadillac | Oh! Lady Be Good | Mon Homme(My Man) | The Bluest Blues | Birk's Works | Oo-Shoo-Be-Doo-Bee | They Can't Take That Away From Me | I Can't Get Started | Tin Tin Deo | On The Sunny Side Of The Street | School Days
Live at Salle Pleyel,Paris,France, rec. 9.2.1953
Gillespie,Dizzy (tp,p,congas,voc) | Graham,Bill (bs,voc) | Legge,Wade (p) | Hackney,Lou (b) | Jones,Al (dr) | Carroll,Joe (voc)
Embraceable You
Gillespie,Dizzy (tp) | Graham,Bill (bs) | Legge,Wade (p) | Hackney,Lou (b) | Jones,Al (dr) | Vaughan,Sarah (voc)

21409412 | CD | Dizzy Gillespie:Pleyel Jazz Concert 1948 + Max Roach Quintet 1949
Dizzy Gillespie And His Orchestra
Oop-Pap-A-Da | Round About Midnight | Algo Bueno(Woody'n You) | I Can't Get Started | Two Bass Hit | Good Bait | Afro.Cuban Drum Suite | Ool-Ya-Koo | Things To Come
Live at Salle Pleyel,Paris,France, rec. 28.2.1948
Gillespie,Dizzy (tp,voc) | Bailey,Benny (tp) | Burns,Dave (tp) | Wright,Lammar (tp) | Wright,Elmon (tp) | Kelly,Ted (tb) | Shepherd,William 'Bill' (tb) | Johnson,Howard (as) | Brown,John (as) | Gayles,Joe (ts) | Nicholas,George 'Big Nick' (ts) | Payne,Cecil (bs) | Lewis,John (p) | McKibbon,Al (b) | Clarke,Kenny (dr) | Pozo,Chano (congas) | Hagood,Kenny (voc)
Max Roach Quintet
Prince Albert | Baby Sis | Tomorrow | Maximum
Paris,France, rec. 15.5.1949
Roach,Max (dr) | Dorham,Kenny (tp) | Moody,James (ts) | Haig,Al (p) | Potter,Tommy (b)

21409422 | CD | Gerry Mulligan:Pleyel Concert Vol.1
Gerry Mulligan Quartet
Bernie's Tune | Presentation Of The Musicians | Walking Shoes | The Nearness Of You | Motel | Love Me Or Leave Me | Soft Shoe | Bark For Barksdale | My Funny Valentine | Turnstile
Live at Salle Pleyel,Paris,France, rec. 1.6.1954
Mulligan,Gerry (bs) | Brookmeyer,Bob (v-tb) | Mitchell,Red (b) | Isola,Frank (dr)
I May Be Wrong(But I Think You're Wonderful) | Five Brothers | Gold Rush | Makin' Whoopee
Live at Salle Pleyel,Paris,France, rec. 3.6.1954
Mulligan,Gerry (bs) | Brookmeyer,Bob (v-tb) | Mitchell,Red (b) | Isola,Frank (dr)

21409432 | CD | Gerry Mulligan:Pleyel Concert Vol.2
The Lady Is A Tramp | Laura | Motel- | Utter Chaos-
Mulligan,Gerry (bs) | Brookmeyer,Bob (v-tb) | Mitchell,Red (b) | Isola,Frank (dr)
Five Brothers | Lullaby Of The Leaves | The Nearness Of You | Limelight
Live at Salle Pleyel,Paris,France, rec. 5.6.1954
Mulligan,Gerry (bs) | Brookmeyer,Bob (v-tb) | Mitchell,Red (b) | Isola,Frank (dr)
Come Out Wherever You Are | Makin' Whoopee | Love Me Or Leave Me | Laura | Line For Lyons | Moonlight In Vermont | Bark For Barksdale- | Utter Chaos-
Live at Salle Pleyel,Paris,France, rec. 7.6.1954
Mulligan,Gerry (bs) | Brookmeyer,Bob (v-tb) | Mitchell,Red (b) | Isola,Frank (dr)

21434802 | CD | Jimmy Raney Visits Paris Vol.2
Jimmy Raney Quartet
Love For Sale | Dinah
Paris,France, rec. 10.2.1954
Raney,Jimmy (g) | Vander,Maurice (p) | Ingrand,Jean-Marie (b) | Viale,Jean-Louis (dr)
Jimmy Raney Quintet
Fascinating Rhythm | Everything Happens To Me | Someone To Watch Over Me | Tres Chouette | Imagination | Have You Met Miss Jones
Raney,Jimmy (g) | Jaspar,Bobby (ts) | Vander,Maurice (p) | Ingrand,Jean-Marie (b) | Viale,Jean-Louis (dr)
What's New? | Night And Day | Too Marvelous For Words | Cherokee
Raney,Jimmy (g) | Guerin,Roger (tp) | Vander,Maurice (p) | Ingrand,Jean-Marie (b) | Viale,Jean-Louis (dr)

21511502 | CD | Lionel Hampton's Paris All Stars
Lionel Hampton Trio
September In The Rain | Always | I Only Have Eyes For You
Live at Salle Pleyel,Paris,France, rec. 28.9.1953
Hampton,Lionel (vib) | Mackel,Billy (g) | Montgomery William (el-b)
Lionel Hampton And His Orchestra
Blue Panassie | Free Press Qui
Hampton,Lionel (vib) | Williams,Walter (tp) | Cleveland,Jimmy (tb) | Hayse,Alvin (tb) | Mezzrow,Milton Mezz (cl) | Scott,Clifford (ts) | Combelle,Alix (ts) | Bolling,Claude (p) | Mackel,Billy (g) | Montgomery William (el-b) | Hamner,Curley (dr)
Walking At The Trocadero
Hampton,Lionel (p) | Williams,Walter (tp) | Cleveland,Jimmy (tb) | Hayse,Alvin (tb) | Mezzrow,Milton Mezz (cl) | Scott,Clifford (ts) | Combelle,Alix (ts) | Mackel,Billy (g) | Montgomery William (el-b) | Hamner,Curley (dr)
Real Crazy | More Crazy | More And More Crazy | Completely Crazy
Hampton,Lionel (vib) | Williams,Walter (tp) | Cleveland,Jimmy (tb) | Hayse,Alvin (tb) | Mezzrow,Milton Mezz (cl) | Scott,Clifford (ts) | Bolling,Claude (p) | Mackel,Billy (g) | Montgomery William (el-b) | Hamner,Curley (dr)

21559712 | CD | Coleman Hawkins/Johnny Hodges:The Vogue Recordings
Coleman Hawkins And His Rhythm
It's Only A Paper Moon | Shi-Sah | Bean's Talking Again | Bah U Bah
Paris,France, rec. 21.12.1949
Hawkins,Coleman (ts) | Peck,Nat (tb) | Fol,Hubert (as) | Mengeon,Jean-Pierre (p) | Michelot,Pierre (b) | Clarke,Kenny (dr)
I Surrender Dear | Sophisticated Lady
Hawkins,Coleman (ts) | Mengeon,Jean-Pierre (p) | Michelot,Pierre (b) | Clarke,Kenny (dr)
Johnny Hodges Orchestra
Jump That's All | Last Legs Blues(part 1) | Last Legs Blues(part 2) | Nix It Mix It | Time On My Hands
Paris,France, rec. 15.4.1950
Hodges,Johnny (as) | Baker,Harold 'Shorty' (tp) | Jackson,Quentin (tb) | Hamilton,Jimmy (cl) | Byas,Don (ts) | Fol,Raimond (p) | Marshall,Wendell (b) | Greer,William 'Sonny' (dr)
Run About | Wishing And Waiting | Get That Geet | That's Grand | Skip It
Paris,France, rec. 20.4.1950
Hodges,Johnny (as) | Baker,Harold 'Shorty' (tp) | Jackson,Quentin (tb) | Hamilton,Jimmy (cl) | Fol,Raimond (p) | Marshall,Wendell (b) | Ballard,Butch (dr)
Perdido | In The Shade Of The Old Apple Tree | Mood Indigo | Sweet Lorraine | Bean Bag Boogie | Hop Skip And Jump
Paris,France, rec. 20.6.1950
Hodges,Johnny (as) | Baker,Harold 'Shorty' (tp) | Jackson,Quentin (tb) | Fol,Raimond (p) | Marshall,Wendell (b) | Ballard,Butch (dr)

Warner | Warner Classics & Jazz Germany

2292-40132-2 | CD | Constellation
Klaus Doldinger
Constellation(part 1-5) | Skyscape | The Point | Dreamer's Tale | Timesignature
München-Grünwald, rec. details unknown
Doldinger,Klaus (electronics)

2292-40253-2 | CD | Man In The Mirror
Klaus Doldinger's Passport
Glass Culture | Evocation | Mango Tango | The Great Escape | Nightfall | In The Eye Of The Storm | Walkin' On The Air | Man In The Mirror
Passport | Doldinger,Klaus (ss,as,ts,keyboards,lyricon) | Mulligan,Kevin (g) | Weindorf,Hermann (keyboards) | Petereit,Dieter (b) | Cress,Curt (dr,perc)

2292-40458-2 | CD | Pili-Pili
Jasper Van't Hof
Kalungu Talks | Virgin Jungle | Afro Timento | Pili-Pili | Smiling Lingala
London GB & Blaricum,NL, rec. 1984
Van't Hof,Jasper (p,el-p,org,keyboards,synth,dr-computer) | Youle,Fode (voc) | Schellekens,Shell (dr) | Schoof,Manfred (tp) | Brooke,Paul (dr-computer) | Tagul Group,The Isaac (perc,voc)

2292-40633-2 | CD | Running In Real Time
Klaus Doldinger's Passport
Auryn
München-Grünwald, rec. details unknown
Passport | Doldinger,Klaus (as,ts,keyboards,bamboo-fl.ss) | Mulligan,Kevin (g) | Weindorf,Hermann (keyboards) | Petereit,Dieter (b) | Cress,Curt (dr,perc)
At Large | Joy Riding | Slap Shot
Passport | Doldinger,Klaus (as,ts,keyboards,bamboo-fl.ss) | Mulligan,Kevin (g) | Lang,Billy (g) | Weindorf,Hermann (keyboards) | Petereit,Dieter (b) | Cress,Curt (dr,perc)
Talisman | Help Me
Passport | Doldinger,Klaus (as,ts,keyboards,bamboo-fl.ss) | Mulligan,Kevin (g) | Lang,Billy (g) | Weindorf,Hermann (keyboards) | Petereit,Dieter (b) | Cress,Curt (dr,perc) | Miles,Victoria (voc)
Mr.Mystery
Passport | Doldinger,Klaus (as,ts,keyboards,bamboo-fl.ss) | Mulligan,Kevin (g) | Wydh,Roikey (g) | Weindorf,Hermann (keyboards) | Petereit,Dieter (b) | Cress,Curt (dr,perc) | Miles,Victoria (voc)
Running In Real Time
Passport | Doldinger,Klaus (as,ts,keyboards,bamboo-fl.ss) | Weyerer,Franz (tp) | Reichstaller,Claus (tp) | Mulligan,Kevin (g) | Wydh,Roikey (g) | Weindorf,Hermann (keyboards) | Petereit,Dieter (b) | Cress,Curt (dr,perc) | Miles,Victoria (voc)

2292-42006-2 | CD | Heavy Nights
Bahia Praia | Playing Games | Here Today | Forever | Heavy Nights | Easy Come Easy Go | Remembrance
Passport | Doldinger,Klaus (ss,ts,keyboards) | Mulligan,Kevin (g) | Weindorf,Hermann (keyboards) | Petereit,Dieter (b) | Cress,Curt (dr)
It's Magic
Passport | Doldinger,Klaus (ss,ts) | Mulligan,Kevin (g) | Weindorf,Hermann (keyboards) | Petereit,Dieter (b) | Cress,Curt (dr) | Miles,Victoria (voc)

2292-46478-2 | 2 CD | Lifelike
Klaus Doldinger & Passport
Introduction by Claude Nobbs | Shirokko
Live at The Montreux Jazz Festival, rec. 10.7.1980
Fairy Tale
Doldinger,Klaus (keyboards,synth) | Schaper,Hendrik (keyboards,synth)
Ostinato
Live at Liederhalle,Stuttgart, rec. 4.6.1980
Doldinger,Klaus (keyboards,synth) | Schaper,Hendrik (keyboards,synth)
Guna Guna | Bahia Do Sol
Doldinger,Klaus (ts,keyboards) | Mulligan,Kevin (g) | Schaper,Hendrik (keyboards) | Petereit,Dieter (b) | Crigger,Dave (dr)
Dreamware | Alegria
Doldinger,Klaus (ss,ts,keyboards) | Mulligan,Kevin (g) | Schaper,Hendrik (keyboards) | Petereit,Dieter (b) | Crigger,Dave (dr)
Ataraxia
Live at The Montreux Jazz Festival, rec. 10.7.1980
Doldinger,Klaus (ss,keyboards) | Mulligan,Kevin (g) | Schaper,Hendrik (keyboards) | Petereit,Dieter (b) | Crigger,Dave (dr)
Morning Sun
Live at Elzer Hof,Mainz, rec. 3.6.1980
Doldinger,Klaus (keyboards) | Mulligan,Kevin (g) | Petereit,Dieter (b)
Klaus Doldinger With Orchestra
Jadoo
Live at The Montreux Jazz Festival, rec. 10.7.1977
Doldinger,Klaus (ts) | Mann,Herbie (fl) | Jakubovic,Jaroslav (ss) | Fortune,Sonny (as) | Newman,David Fathead (as) | Morrissey,Dick (ts) | Duncan,Molly (ts) | McIntyre,Onnie (g) | Stuart,Hamish (g) | Mullen,Jim (g) | Ball,Roger (keyboards) | Gorrie,Alan (b) | Ferrone,Steve (dr) | Cruz,Rafael (perc) | Figueroa,Sammy (perc)
Sambukada
Doldinger,Klaus (ts) | Newman,David Fathead (ss) | Tee,Richard (p) | Berlin,Jeff (b) | Jordan,Steve (dr) | Cruz,Rafael (perc) | Figueroa,Sammy (perc)
Klaus Doldinger With Orchestra And Etta James
Stormy Monday Blues(They Call It Stormy Monday)
Doldinger,Klaus (ts) | Mann,Herbie (fl) | Newman,David Fathead (ss) | Ray,Brian (g) | Tee,Richard (p) | Berlin,Jeff (b) | Jordan,Steve (dr) | James,Etta (voc)

2292-46479-2 | CD | Oceanliner
Klaus Doldinger's Passport
Departure | Allegory | Ancient Saga | Oceanliner | Rub-A-Dub | Uptown Rendezvous | Bassride | Scope | Seaside
München-Grünwald, rec. details unknown
Passport | Doldinger,Klaus (sax,keyboards,lyricon,vocoder) | Mulligan,Kevin (g,voc) | Schaper,Hendrik (keyboards) | Petereit,Dieter (b) | Crigger,Dave (dr,perc)

2292-55069-2 | CD | The New Tango
Astor Piazzolla-Gary Burton Sextet
Milonga Is Coming | Vibraphonissina | Little Italy 1930 | Nuevo Tango | Laura's Dream | Operation Tango | La Muerta Del Angel
Live at The Montreux Jazz Festival, rec. July 1986
Piazzolla,Astor (bandoneon) | Burton,Gary (vib) | Suarez-Paz,Fernando (v) | Malviccino,Horacio (g) | Ziegler,Pablo (p) | Console,Hector (b)

4509-93207-2 | CD | Down To Earth
Klaus Doldinger & Passport
Wise Up | Lowdown And Flyin' High | Korako | Allemande Deux | Nighttime In
The City | Esperanto | Missing You | Ridin' On A Rainbow | Never Ending Blues
München, rec. details unknown
Passport | Doldinger,Klaus (fl,ss,ts) | O'Mara,Peter (g) | Di Gioia,Roberto (p,org,keyboards) | Schmidt,Jochen (b) | Haffner,Wolfgang (dr) | Ströer,Ernst (perc)
Passport's In The House
Passport | Doldinger,Klaus (fl,ss,ts) | O'Mara,Peter (g) | Di Gioia,Roberto (p,org,keyboards) | Schmidt,Jochen (b) | Haffner,Wolfgang (dr) | Ströer,Ernst (perc) | Cuffey,Allen C. (rap-voc)

7599-23525-2 | CD | Word Of Mouth
Jaco Pastorius With Orchestra
Crisis | 3 Views Of Secret | Liberty City | Chromatic Fantasy | Blackbird | Word Of Mouth | John And Mary
details unknown, rec. details unknown
Pastorius,Jaco (el-b) | personal included: | Findley,Chuck (tp) | Clark,John (fr-h) | Brecker,Michael (sax) | Laws,Hubert (fl) | Shorter,Wayne (sax) | Scott,Tom (sax) | Hancock,Herbie (keyboards) | DeJohnette,Jack (dr) | details unknown

7599-25490-2 | CD | Tutu
Miles Davis Group
Tutu | Tomaas | Portia | Splatch | Backyard Ritual | Perfect Way | Don't Lose You Mind | Full Nelson
NYC, rec. details unknown
Davis,Miles (tp) | Miller,Marcus (keyboards,synth,el-b) | Miles,Jason (synth-programming) | Da Costa,Paulinho (perc) | Reid,Steve (perc) | Holzman,Adam (synth,synth-programming) | Duke,George (tp,perc,b-g) | Hakim,Omar (dr,perc) | Bernard Wright (synth) | Urbaniak,Michal (el-v)

7599-25655-2 | CD | Siesta(Soundtrack)
Miles Davis-Marcus Miller Group
Lost In Madrid(part 1-5) | Siesta | Kitt's Kiss | Theme For Augustine | Wind | Seduction | Kiss | Submission | Conchita | Lament | Rat Dance | The Call | Claire | After Glow | Los Feliz
NYC, rec. ca.1987
Davis,Miles (tp) | Miller,Marcus (keyboards,synth,perc,el-b) | Walker,James (fl) | Miles,Jason (synth) | Scofield,John (g) | Klugh,Earl (g) | Hakim,Omar (dr)

7599-25873-2 | CD | Amandla
Miles Davis Group
Jo-Jo
NYC, rec. 1989
Davis,Miles (tp) | Garrett,Kenny (as) | Margitza,Rick (ts) | Bourelly,Jean-Paul (g) | Miller,Marcus (keyboards,synth,el-b) | Da Costa,Paulinho (perc)
Amandla
Davis,Miles (tp) | Garrett,Kenny (as) | Miller,Marcus (keyboards,synth,el-b) | Sample,Joe (p) | Hakim,Omar (dr) | Alias,Don (perc) | Johnson,Bashiri (perc)
Hannibal
Davis,Miles (tp) | Garrett,Kenny (as) | Miller,Marcus (b-cl,g,keyboards,el-b) | Foley,Keith (g) | Hakim,Omar (dr) | Da Costa,Paulinho (perc)
Jilli
Davis,Miles (tp) | Garrett,Kenny (as) | Foley,Keith (g) | Patterson,Billy (g) | Miller,Marcus (b-cl,keyboards,synth,el-b) | Wellman,Ricky (dr) | Bigham,John (g,keyboards,dr-programming)
Big Time
NYC, rec. details unknown
Davis,Miles (tp) | Garrett,Kenny (as) | Foley,Keith (g) | Bourelly,Jean-Paul (g) | Miller,Marcus (b-cl,ss,keyboards,synth,el-b) | Wellman,Ricky (dr) | Alias,Don (perc)
Cobra
NYC, rec. 1989
Davis,Miles (tp) | Garrett,Kenny (ss) | Miller,Marcus (b-cl,keyboards,el-b) | Duke,George (keyboards,synth) | Landau,Michael (g) | DeFrancesco,Joey (keyboards)
Catémbe
Davis,Miles (tp) | Garrett,Kenny (as) | Miller,Marcus (b-cl,ss,keyboards,el-b) | Alias,Don (perc) | Cinelu,Mino (perc)
Mr.Pastorius
Davis,Miles (tp) | Miller,Marcus (b-cl,keyboards,el-b) | Foster,Al (dr) | Miles,Jason (synth-programming)

7599-26318-2 | CD | Ashes To Ashes
Joe Sample Group
The Road Less Traveled | The Last Child | I'll Love You | Phoenix
NYC, rec. details unknown
Sample,Joe (p,synth) | Hey,Jerry (tp,fl-h) | Williams,Larry (fl,sax) | Landau,Michael (g) | Peterson,Ricky (synth) | Miller,Marcus (el-b) | Hakim,Omar (dr) | Castro,Lenny (perc) | Miles,Jason (synth-programming)
Ashes To Ashes | Mother's Eyes | Born In Trouble | Strike Two | Born To Be Bad
Sample,Joe (p,synth) | Hey,Jerry (tp,fl-h) | Williams,Larry (fl,sax) | Landau,Michael (g) | St.Paul (g) | Peterson,Ricky (synth) | Miller,Marcus (el-b) | Hakim,Omar (dr) | Castro,Lenny (perc) | Miles,Jason (synth-programming)

7599-26321-2 | CD | The Marksman
Mark Whitfield Quartet
The Marksman | In A Sentimental Mood | Medgar Evers Blues | Little Digi's Strut | The Very Thought Of You | Namu | There Is No Greater Love
Whitfield,Mark (g) | Roberts,Marcus (p) | Veal,Reginald (b) | Riley,Herlin (dr)
The Blues From Way Back | A Long Way From Home
Whitfield,Mark (g) | Roberts,Marcus (p) | Veal,Reginald (b) | Davis,Troy (dr)

7599-26656-2 | CD | Fourplay
Fourplay
Bali Run | 101 Eastbound | Moonjogger | Max-A-Man | Quadrille | Midnight Stroll | October Morning | Wish You Were Here | Rain Forest
Los Angeles,CA, rec. details unknown
Fourplay | James,Bob (keyboards) | Ritenour,Lee (g,el-g) | East,Nathan (b) | Mason,Harold (dr)
After The Dance
Fourplay | James,Bob (keyboards) | Ritenour,Lee (g,el-g) | East,Nathan (b,voc) | Mason,Harold (dr) | DeBarge,El (voc) | DeBarge,Darell (voc) | LaBelle,Patti (voc)

7599-26659-2 | CD | Patrice
Mark Whitfield Group
Go Down Moses | Dear Father | Lady Of The Day | Baby M's Bayou Blues | Midnight Sun | David's Theme | Brother Jack | Trouble At The South Bend | We'll Be Together Again
NYC, rec. details unknown
Whitfield,Mark (g) | Barron,Kenny (p) | Carter,Ron (b) | DeJohnette,Jack (dr) | Badrena,Manolo (perc)
Nobody Knows The Trouble I've Seen | Bee's Blues
Whitfield,Mark (g) | Batiste,Alvin (cl) | Barron,Kenny (p) | Carter,Ron (b) | DeJohnette,Jack (dr) | Badrena,Manolo (perc)
Patrice
Whitfield,Mark (g) | Group Five (voc)

7599-26750-2 | CD | The Earl Klugh Trio Volume One
Earl Klugh Trio
Bewitched Bothered And Bewildered | Days Of Wine And Roses | Insensatez(How Insensitive) | Love Theme From Spartacus | I'll Remember April | What Are You Doing The Rest Of Your Life | I Say A Little Prayer | Night And Day | Lonely Girl | Too Marvelous For Words | Samba Da Una Nota So(One Note Samba)
Dearborn Heights,Michigan, rec. details unknown
Klugh,Earl (g) | Armstrong,Ralphe (b) | Dunlap,Gene (dr)

7599-26938-2 | CD | Doo-Bop
Miles Davis Group
Mystery | The Doo Bop Song | Chocolate Chip | Night Speed Chase | Blow | Sonya | Fantasy | Duke Booty | Mystery(reprise)
details unknown, rec. details unknown

Davis,Miles (tp,keyboards) | Orchestra | details unknown

7599-26955-2 | CD | All The Way
(Little)Jimmy Scott And His Quintet
All The Way | Embraceable You | Angel Eyes | At Last | Someone To Watch Over Me | Every Time We Say Goodbye | I'll Be Around | My Foolish Heart | I'm Getting Sentimental Over You
NYC, rec. 1992
Scott,Jimmy[Little] (voc) | Newman,David Fathead (sax) | Pisano,John (g) | Barron,Kenny (p) | Carter,Ron (b) | Tate,Grady (dr)

7599-27362-2 | CD | All Fly Home
Al Jarreau With Band
Thinkin' About It Too | I'm Home | Brite 'N' Sunny Babe | I Do | Fly | Wait A Little While | She's Leaving Home | All | Sittin' On The Dock Of The Bay - (Sittin' On) The Dock Of The Bay
Hollywood,CA, rec. May/June 1978
Jarreau,Al (voice) | Hubbard,Freddie (fl-h) | Ritenour,Lee (g) | Canning,Tom (p,el-p,synth) | Blessing,Lyon (vib,org,keyboards,synth) | Williams,Larry (keyboards,synth) | Ryan,Jim (keyboards,synth) | McBride,Reggie (b) | Correro,Joe (dr) | Da Costa,Paulinho (perc)

7599-27387-2 | CD | Affinity
Bill Evans-Toots Thielemans Quintet
I Do It For Your Love | Sno' Peas | This Is All I Ask | Days Of Wine And Roses | Jesus' Last Ballad | Tomato Kiss | The Other Side Of Midnight(Noelle's Theme) | Blue And Green | Body And Soul
NYC, rec. 30.10.-2.11.1978
Thielemans,Jean 'Toots' (harm) | Evans,Bill (p) | Schneider,Larry (alto-fl,ss,ts) | Johnson,Marc (b) | Zigmund,Eliot (dr)

8122-75438-2 | CD | Comin' Home Baby!/Sings Sunday In New York
Mel Tormé With The Shorty Rogers Orchestra
Hi Fly | On Green Dolphin Street | Dat Dere | Moanin'
Los Angeles,CA, rec. 11.7.1962
Tormé,Mel (voc) | Orchestra | details unknown | Rogers,Shorty (arr,ld)
Walkin' | Whisper Not | Sidney's Soliloquy
Los Angeles,CA, rec. 13.7.1962
Tormé,Mel (voc) | Orchestra | details unknown | Rogers,Shorty (arr,ld)
The Lady's In Love With You | Sing You Sinners | Puttin' On The Ritz
Los Angeles,CA, rec. 16.7.1962
Tormé,Mel (voc) | Orchestra | details unknown | Rogers,Shorty (arr,ld)
Mel Tormé With The Claus Ogerman Orchestra
Comin' Home Baby | Right Now
Los Angeles,CA, rec. 13.9.1962
Tormé,Mel (voc) | Orchestra | details unknown | Ogerman,Claus (cond,arr)
Mel Tormé With Orchestra
Autumn In New York | Manhattan | Harlem Nocturne | Forty-Second Street | My Time Of Day
Los Angeles,CA, rec. 2.12.1963
Tormé,Mel (voc) | Orchestra | details unknown | Rogers,Shorty (arr,ld) | Williams,John (arr,ld) | Hazard,Dick (arr,ld)
Let Me Off Uptown | Sunday In New York | Broadway | Sidewalks Of New York
Los Angeles,CA, rec. 4.12.1963
Tormé,Mel (voc) | Orchestra | details unknown | Rogers,Shorty (arr,ld) | Williams,John (arr,ld) | Hazard,Dick (arr,ld)
Lullaby Of Birdland | New York New York | There's A Broken Heart For Every Light In Broadway | The Brooklyn Bridge
Los Angeles,CA, rec. 7.12.1963
Tormé,Mel (voc) | Orchestra | details unknown | Rogers,Shorty (arr,ld) | Williams,John (arr,ld) | Hazard,Dick (arr,ld)

8122-75439-2 | CD | Mose Alife!/Wild Man On The Loose
Mose Allison Trio
Wild Man On The Loose | No Trouble Livin' | What's With You | You Can Count On Me To Do My Part | Never More
NYC, rec. 26.1.1965
Allison,Mose (p,voc) | May,Earl (b) | Motian,Paul (dr)
That's The Stuff You Gotta Watch | War Horse | Power House | Night Watch
NYC, rec. 28.1.1965
Allison,Mose (p,voc) | May,Earl (b) | Motian,Paul (dr)
Smashed | Seventh Son | Fool's Paradise | I Love The Life I Live | Since I Fell For You | Love For Sale | Baby Please Don't Go | That's All Right | Parchman Farm | Tell Me Somethin' | The Chaser
Live at The Lighthouse,Hermosa Beach,CA, rec. 22.-31.10.1965
Allison,Mose (p,voc) | Gilbert,Stanley (b) | Lee,Mel (dr)

8122-76713-2 | CD | Breezin'
George Benson Group
Breezin' | This Masquerade | Six To Four | Affirmation | So This Is Love? | Lady | Down Here In The Ground | Shark Bite | This Masquerade(single-edit)
Hollywood,CA, rec. 6.-8.1.1976
Benson,George (g,voc) | Upchurch,Phil (g,b) | Foster,Ronnie (el-p,synth) | Dalto,George (p,el-p,clavinet) | Banks,Stanley (b) | Mason,Harvey (dr) | MacDonald,Ralph (perc)

8122-79934-2 | 2 CD | George Benson Anthology
George Benson Group/Orchestra
Shadow Dancer | Ain't That Peculiar | A Foggy Day(In London Town) | Ready And Able | What's New? | Chattanooga Choo Choo | White Rabbit | Summertime | Breezin' | This Masquerade | Shark Bite | Nature Boy | The Greatest Love Of All(single version) | We All Remember Wes | Love Ballad(single version) | Off Broadway | Moody's Mood | Give Me The Night(single version) | Turn Your Love Around | Love All The Hurt Away | Mimosa | Being With You | 20-20 | New Day | Kisses In The Moonlight(single version) | Mt.Airy Road | Let's Do It Again(single version) | Tenderly | Ready Now That You Are | The Long And Winding Road | C-Smooth
different Places, rec. 1964-1998
Benson,George (g,el-g,voc) | McDuff,Brother Jack (org) | Smith,Lonnie (org) | Laws,Hubert (fl) | Smith,Jimmy (org) | Klugh,Earl (g) | Franklin,Aretha (voc) | Count Basie Orchestra,The

8573-84132-2 | CD | Klaus Doldinger Passport Live
Klaus Doldinger's Passport
Green Lagoon | Blue Kind Of Mind | Happy Landing | Jungle Song
Live at Bayerischer Hof,München, rec. 12.5.1996
Passport | Doldinger,Klaus (fl,ss,ts) | O'Mara,Peter (el-g) | Di Gioia,Roberto (keyboards) | Scales,Patrick (el-b) | Haffner,Wolfgang (dr) | Ströer,Ernst (perc) | Darouiche,Biboul Ferkouzad (perc)
Liebling Kreuzberg
Live at The Nightclub,Bayerischer Hof,München, rec. 28.10.1998
Passport | Doldinger,Klaus (fl,ss,ts) | O'Mara,Peter (el-g) | Di Gioia,Roberto (keyboards) | Scales,Patrick (el-b) | Haffner,Wolfgang (dr) | Ströer,Ernst (perc) | Darouiche,Biboul Ferkouzad (perc)
Move | Escape | Tatort
Live at Centralstation,Darmstadt, rec. 27.1.2000
Passport | Doldinger,Klaus (fl,ss,ts) | O'Mara,Peter (el-g) | Di Gioia,Roberto (keyboards) | Scales,Patrick (el-b) | Haffner,Wolfgang (dr) | Ströer,Ernst (perc) | Darouiche,Biboul Ferkouzad (perc)
Sahara Sketches | Lucky Loser | Fifty Years Later
Live at Kammgarn,Kaiserslautern, rec. 28.1.2000
Passport | Doldinger,Klaus (fl,ss,ts) | O'Mara,Peter (el-g) | Di Gioia,Roberto (keyboards) | Scales,Patrick (el-b) | Haffner,Wolfgang (dr) | Ströer,Ernst (perc) | Darouiche,Biboul Ferkouzad (perc)

8573-84315-2 | CD | Time Change
Laurent De Wilde Sextet
Shuffle Boil | Time For Change | Battle In A Box | Out Of This World | Don't Axe Me | Jungle Hard Bop | Blues In The Background
Paris,France, rec. 28./29.11.1999
De Wilde,Laurent (el-p) | Boltro,Flavio (tp,fl-h) | Horellou,Gäel (as) | Imm,Paul (b) | Huchard,Stéphane (dr) | Garcia,Philippe (dr)
The Present
De Wilde,Laurent (el-p) | Boltro,Flavio (tp,fl-h) | Horellou,Gäel (as) | Imm,Paul (b) | Huchard,Stéphane (dr) | Garcia,Philippe (dr) | Bryant,Dana (voc)
Uno
De Wilde,Laurent (el-p) | Boltro,Flavio (tp,fl-h) | Horellou,Gäel (as) | Imm,Paul (b) | Huchard,Stéphane (dr) | Garcia,Philippe (dr) | Garay,Minino (voc)

8573-85268-2 | CD | Picture Perfect-70th Anniversary
Ahmad Jamal Trio
Building No.1 | Le Moment De Vérité-The Providing Ground | Le Rituel-The Ritual | It Always Happens | Spot One | Mystifying | The Blooming Flower | Ultra Violet
NYC, rec. 20.-24.5.2000
Jamal,Ahmad (p) | Cammack,James (b) | Muhammad,Idris[Leo Morris] (dr)
My Latin
Jamal,Ahmad (p) | Cammack,James (b) | Muhammad,Idris[Leo Morris] (dr) | Miller,L.Aziza (voc)
It's Only A Flower
Jamal,Ahmad (p) | Nasser,Jamil[George Joyner] (b) | Muhammad,Idris[Leo Morris] (dr)
Picture Perfect
Jamal,Ahmad (p) | Nasser,Jamil[George Joyner] (b) | Muhammad,Idris[Leo Morris] (dr) | Smith,O.C. (voc)
Whisperings
Jamal,Ahmad (p) | Cammack,James (b) | Muhammad,Idris[Leo Morris] (dr) | Cargill,Mark (v) | Smith,O.C. (voc)

9031-71233-2 | CD | Balance Of Happiness
Klaus Doldinger's Passport
Far Away | Balance Of Happiness | Horizon | Hope | The Traveller | Shapes Of Light | Goodbye To A Friend | Earthmusic | Mangrove
München-Grünwald, rec. details unknown
Passport | Doldinger,Klaus (ss,as,ts) | Shigihara,Paul (g) | Sendecki,Vladislaw (p,keyboards) | Schmidt,Jochen (b) | Haffner,Wolfgang (dr) | Ströer,Ernst (perc)

9031-75417-2 | CD | Blues Roots
Blues Roots | Louisiana Sunset | Time Signal | Blue Avenue | Goodbye Pork Pie Hat | How Did You Know
München, rec. details unknown
Passport | Doldinger,Klaus (ss,ts) | O'Mara,Peter (g) | Di Gioia,Roberto (p,keyboards) | Schmidt,Jochen (b) | Haffner,Wolfgang (dr) | Ströer,Ernst (perc)
Klaus Doldinger's Passport With Johnny 'Clyde' Copeland
Inner City Blues | Born Under A Bad Sign | Love Utopia | Idgo Now
Passport | Doldinger,Klaus (ss,ts) | Copeland,Johnny (g,voc) | O'Mara,Peter (g) | Di Gioia,Roberto (p,keyboards) | Schmidt,Jochen (b) | Haffner,Wolfgang (dr) | Ströer,Ernst (perc)

9362-45209-2 | CD | Invitation
Joe Sample Group
Black Is The Color Of My True Love's Hair | A House Is Not A Home | Come Rain Or Come Shine | Invitation | Summertime | Nica's Dream | Stormy Weather | Django | My One And Only | Mood Indigo
NYC, rec. details unknown
Sample,Joe (p,synth) | McBee,Cecil (b) | Lewis,Victor (dr) | Castro,Lenny (perc) | Mardin,Joe (synth-programming) | Williams,Larry (synth-programming) | Orchestra | Oehler,Dale (cond,arr) | details unknown

9362-45221-2 | CD | Miles & Quincy Live At Montreux
Miles Davis With Gil Evans Orchestra, The George Gruntz Concert Jazz Band And Guests
Introduction by Claude Nobbs And Quincy Jones | Boplicity | Introduction To Miles Ahead Medley | Springsville | Maids Of Cadiz | The Duke | My Ship | Miles Ahead | Blues For Pablo | Introduction To Porgy And Bess Medley | Orgone | Gone Gone Gone | Summertime | Here Comes De Honey Man | The Pan Piper | Solea
Live at The Montreux Jazz Festival, rec. 8.7.1991
Davis,Miles (tp) | Roney,Wallace (tp,fl-h) | Garrett,Kenny (as) | Soloff,Lew (tp) | Evans,Miles (tp) | Malone,Tom (tb) | Foster,Alex (fl,ss,as) | Adams,George (fl,ts) | Goldstein,Gil (keyboards) | Brown,Delmar (keyboards) | Dennard,Kenwood (dr,perc) | Stamm,Marvin (tp,fl-h) | D'Earth,John (tp,fl-h) | Walrath,Jack (tp,fl-h) | Clark,John (el-fr-h) | Varner,Tom (fr-h) | Bargeron,Dave (tb,euphonium) | McIntyre,Earl (tb,euphonium) | Taylor,Dave (b-tb) | Johnson,Howard (bs,tuba) | Giorgianni,Sal (as) | Malach,Bob (fl,cl,ts) | Schneider,Larry (fl,cl,ts,oboe) | Bergonzi,Jerry (ts) | Gruntz,George (p,ld) | Richmond,Mike (b) | Riley,John (dr,perc) | Bailey,Benny (tp,fl-h) | Schoof,Manfred (tp,fl-h) | Van Rooyen,Ack (tp,fl-h) | Dahinden,Roland (tb) | Herwig,Conrad (tb) | Brofsky,Alex (fr-h) | Pontiggia,Claudio (fr-h) | O'Brien,Anne (fl) | Crawdy,Julian (fl,alto-fl,piccolo) | Frehner,Hanspeter (fl,alto-fl,piccolo) | Weber,Michel (cl) | Gavillet,Christian (b-cl,bs) | Rosenberg,Roger (b-cl,bs) | Zahn,Tilman (oboe) | Seghezzo,Dave (oboe) | Duss,Xavier (oboe) | Wenziker,Judith (oboe) | Rabe,Christian (bassoon) | Erb,Reiner (bassoon) | Schindler,Xenia (harp) | Benavent,Carlos (b,el-b) | Tate,Grady (dr)

9362-45242-2 | CD | Joshua Redman
Joshua Redman Quartet
Body And Soul
NYC, rec. 27.5.1992
Redman,Joshua (ts) | LeDonne,Mike (p) | La Duca,Paul (b) | Washington,Kenny (dr)
Joshua Redman Trio
Trinkle Tinkle
NYC, rec. 4.6.1992
Redman,Joshua (ts) | McBride,Christian (b) | Penn,Clarence (dr)
Joshua Redman Quartet
Blues On Sunday | Wish | Echoes | I Got You (I Feel Good) | Tribalism | Groove X(By Any Means Necessary) | Salt Peanuts | On The Sunny Side Of The Street | Sublimation
NYC, rec. 15.9.1992
Redman,Joshua (ts) | Hays,Kevin (p) | McBride,Christian (b) | Hutchinson,Gregory (dr)

9362-45340-2 | CD | Between The Sheets
Fourplay
Chant | Monterey | Lil' Darlin' | Flying East | Once In Th A.M. | Gulliver | Amoroso | A Summer Child | Anthem | Song For Somalia
San Francisco,CA, rec. details unknown
Fourplay | Ritenour,Lee (g,el-g,synth) | James,Bob (keyboards,synth) | East,Nathan (el-b,fretless-b,voc) | Mason,Harvey (dr,dr-program)
Between The Sheets
Fourplay | Ritenour,Lee (g,el-g,synth) | James,Bob (keyboards,synth) | East,Nathan (el-b,fretless-b,voc) | Mason,Harvey (dr,dr-program) | Khan,Chaka (voc)

9362-45365-2 | CD | Wish
Joshua Redman Quartet
Touraround | Soul Dance | Make Sure You're Sure | The Deserving Many | We Had A Sister | Moose The Mooche | Tears In Heaven | Whittlin'
NYC, rec. 1993
Redman,Joshua (ts) | Metheny,Pat (g) | Haden,Charlie (b) | Higgins,Billy (dr)
Wish | Blues For Pat
Live at The 'Village Vanguard',NYC, rec. 1993
Redman,Joshua (ts) | Metheny,Pat (g) | Haden,Charlie (b) | Higgins,Billy (dr)

9362-45643-2 | CD | MoodSwing
Sweet Sorrow | Chill | Rejoice | Faith | Alone In The Morning | Mischief | Dialogue | The Oneness Of Two(In Three) | Past In The Present | Obsession | Headin' Home
NYC, rec. 8.-10.3.1994
Redman,Joshua (ts) | Mehldau,Brad (p) | McBride,Christian (b) | Blade,Brian (dr)

9362-45923-2 | 2 CD | Spirit Of The Moment:Live At The Village Vanguard
Jig-A-Jug | My One And Only Love | Count Me Out | Second Snow | Remember | Dialogue | St.Thomas | Herbs And Roots | Wait No Longer | Neverend | Justin Time | Mt. Zion | Slapstick | Lyric
Live at The 'Village Vanguard',NYC, rec. 21.-26.3.1995
Redman,Joshua (ss,as,ts) | Martin,Peter (p) | Thomas,Christopher (b) | Blade,Brian (dr)

9362-45997-2 | CD | Introducing Brad Mehldau
Brad Mehldau Trio
It Might As Well Be Spring | Countdown | My Romance | Angst | Young Werther
NYC, rec. 13.3.1995
Mehldau,Brad (p) | Grenadier,Larry (b) | Rossy,Jorge 'Jordi' (dr)
Prelude To A Kiss | London Blues | From This Moment On | Say Goodbye
NYC, rec. 3.4.1995
Mehldau,Brad (p) | McBride,Christian (b) | Blade,Brian (dr)

9362-46260-2 | CD | The Art Of The Trio Vol.1
Blame It On My Youth | I Didn't Know What Time It Was | Ron's Place | Blackbird | Lament For Linus | Mignon's Song | I Fall In Love Too Easily | Lucid | Nobody Else But Me
Live at The 'Village Vanguard',NYC, rec. 4./5.9.1996
Mehldau,Brad (p) | Grenadier,Larry (b) | Rossy,Jorge 'Jordi' (dr)

9362-46330-2 | CD | Freedom In The Goove
Joshua Redman Quintet
Hide And Seek | One Shining Soul | Streams Of Conciousness | When The Sun Comes Down | Home Fries | Invocation | Dare I Ask? | Cat Battles | Pantomime | Can't Dance
NYC, rec. 10.-13.4.1996
Redman,Joshua (ss,as,ts) | Bernstein,Peter (g) | Martin,Peter (p) | Thomas,Christopher (b) | Blade,Brian (dr)

9362-46791-2 | CD | Imaginary Day
Pat Metheny Group
Imaginary Day
NYC, rec. Spring 1997
Metheny,Pat (fretless-g) | Mays,Lyle (p,keyboards) | Rodby,Steve (b,el-b) | Wertico,Paul (dr) | Cinelu,Mino (perc) | Samuels,Dave (perc) | Alias,Don (perc)
Follow Me
Metheny,Pat (g,g-synth,sitar) | Ledford,Mark (tp,voc) | Blamires,David (tp,v,mellophone,voc) | Mays,Lyle (p,keyboards) | Rodby,Steve (b,el-b) | Wertico,Paul (dr) | Velez,Glen (perc) | Samuels,Dave (perc) | Alias,Don (perc)
Into The Dream
Metheny,Pat (42-string-pikasso-g)
A Story Within The Story
Metheny,Pat (el-g,pikasso-g) | Ledford,Mark (tp,voc) | Blamires,David (melodica,voc) | Mays,Lyle (p,keyboards) | Rodby,Steve (b,el-b) | Wertico,Paul (dr) | Cinelu,Mino (perc)
The Heat Of The Day | The Awakening
NYC, rec. 1997
Metheny,Pat (g,g-synth,sitar,tipple) | Ledford,Mark (tp,voc) | Blamires,David (tp,mellophone,recorder,voc) | Mays,Lyle (p,keyboards) | Rodby,Steve (b,el-b) | Wertico,Paul (dr) | Velez,Glen (perc) | Cinelu,Mino (perc) | Samuels,Dave (perc)
Across The Sky
NYC, rec. Spring 1997
Metheny,Pat (el-g) | Ledford,Mark (fl-h,voc) | Blamires,David (g,mellophone,voc) | Mays,Lyle (p,keyboards) | Rodby,Steve (b,el-b) | Wertico,Paul (dr) | Samuels,Dave (perc)
The Roots Of Coincidence
Metheny,Pat (el-g) | Ledford,Mark (tp) | Blamires,David (tp,el-g) | Mays,Lyle (p,keyboards) | Rodby,Steve (b,el-b) | Wertico,Paul (dr)
Too Soon Tomorrow
Metheny,Pat (g) | Ledford,Mark (fl-h) | Blamires,David (tp,mellophone,recorder,voc) | Mays,Lyle (p,keyboards) | Rodby,Steve (b,el-b) | Wertico,Paul (dr) | Cinelu,Mino (perc) | Samuels,Dave (perc)

9362-46848-2 | CD | The Art Of The Trio Vol.2
Brad Mehldau Trio
It's All Right With Me | Young And Foolish | Monk's Dream | The Way You Look Tonight | Moon River | Countdown
Live at The 'Village Vanguard',NYC, rec. 29.7.-3.8.1997
Mehldau,Brad (p) | Grenadier,Larry (b) | Rossy,Jorge 'Jordi' (dr)

9362-47025-2 | CD | My Romance
Kevin Mahogany With The Bob James Trio
Everything I Have Is Yours | Stairway To The Stars | I Apologize | How Did She Look | Lush Life
NYC, rec. 11.-13.5.1998
Mahogany,Kevin (voc) | James,Bob (p) | Fambrough,Charles (b) | Kilson,Billy (dr)
Kevin Mahogany With The Bob James Trio And Michael Brecker
I Know That You Know | May I Come In?
Mahogany,Kevin (voc) | Brecker,Michael (ts) | James,Bob (p) | Fambrough,Charles (b) | Kilson,Billy (dr)
Kevin Mahogany With The Bob James Trio And Kirk Whalum
Teach Me Tonight | My Romance | Don't Let Me Be Lonely Tonight
Mahogany,Kevin (voc) | Whalum,Kirk (ts) | James,Bob (p) | Fambrough,Charles (b) | Kilson,Billy (dr)
Kevin Mahogany With The Bob James Trio, Kirk Whalum And Strings
Wild Honey
Mahogany,Kevin (voc) | Whalum,Kirk (ts) | James,Bob (p) | Fambrough,Charles (b) | Kilson,Billy (dr) | Seaton,Laura (v) | Strenger,Yevgenia (v) | Pray,Sue (viola) | Cords,Nick (viola) | Seiver,Sarah (cello) | Moye,Eugene (cello)

9362-47051-2 | CD | Art Of The Trio Vol.3: Songs
Brad Mehldau Trio
Song-Song | Unrequited | Bewitched Bothered And Bewildered | Exit Music(for a Film) | At A Loss | Convalescent | For All We Know | River Man | Young At Heart | Sehnsucht
NYC, rec. 27./28.5.1998
Mehldau,Brad (p) | Grenadier,Larry (b) | Rossy,Jorge 'Jordi' (dr)

9362-47052-2 | CD | Timeless Tales
Joshua Redman Quartet
Summertime | Visions | Yesterdays | I Had A King | The Times They Are A-Changin' | It Might As Well Be Spring | How Deep Is The Ocean | Love For Sale | Eleanor Rigby | How Come U Don't Call Me Anymore
NYC, rec. 1998
Redman,Joshua (ss,as,ts) | Mehldau,Brad (p) | Grenadier,Larry (b) | Blade,Brian (dr)

9362-47284-2 | CD | Improvisations For Expanded Piano
Lyle Mays
This Moment | Let Me Count My Ways | We Are All Alone | The Imperative | Procession | Black Ice | Origami | Lightning Fields | Locked In Amber | Long Life
NYC, rec. August 1998
Mays,Lyle (p-solo,keyboards)

9362-47357-2 | CD | Elegiac Cycle
Brad Mehldau
Bard | Resignacion | Memory's Tricks | Elegy For William Burroughs And Allen Ginsberg | Lament For Linus | Trailer Park Ghost | Goodbye Storyteller(for Fred Myrow) | Rückblick | The Band Returns
Los Angeles,CA, rec. 1./2.2.1999
Mehldau,Brad (p-solo)

9362-47463-2 | CD | Art Of The Trio Vol.4: Back At The Vanguard
Brad Mehldau Trio
All The Things You Are | Sehnsucht | Nice Pass | Solar | London Blues | I'll Be Seeing You | Exit Music(for a Film)
Live at The 'Village Vanguard',NYC, rec. 5.1.1999
Mehldau,Brad (p) | Grenadier,Larry (b) | Rossy,Jorge 'Jordi' (dr)

9362-47465-2 | CD | Beyond
Joshua Redman Quartet
Courage(Assymetric Aria) | Belonging(Lopsided Lullaby) | Neverend | Balance | Twilight...And Beyond | Stoic Revolutions | Suspended Emanations | Last Rites Of Rock 'N Roll | A Life
NYC, rec. May 1999
Redman,Joshua (ss,ts) | Goldberg,Aaron (p) | Rogers,Ruben (b) | Hutchinson,Gregory (dr)
Joshua Redman Quartet feat. Mark Turner
Leap Of Faith
Redman,Joshua (ts) | Turner,Mark (ts) | Goldberg,Aaron (p) | Rogers,Ruben (b) | Hutchinson,Gregory (dr)

9362-47611-2 | CD | Tonight Take 6
Take 6
If We Never Needed The Lord Before | Walk On The Wild Side | How Sweet It Is(To Be Loved By You) | All Blues(Intro) | All Blues | Smile | Over The Hill Is Home(Intro) | Over The Hill Is Home | So Much 2 Say | I'm On My Way(intro) | I'm On My Way | Mary | I've Got Life- | Spread Love-

Live at The Blue Note,Tokyo,Japan, rec. 4.-6.10.1999
Take 6 (voc-group)

9362-47631-2 | CD | Ballad Session
Mark Turner Trio
Skylark
Turner,Mark (ts) | Grenadier,Larry (b) | Blade,Brian (dr)
Mark Turner Quartet
Nefertiti | No More | All Or Nothing At All | Late Lament
Turner,Mark (ts) | Rosenwinkel,Kurt (g) | Grenadier,Larry (b) | Blade,Brian (dr)
I Loves You Porgy | Jesus Maria
Turner,Mark (ts) | Hayes,Kevin (p) | Grenadier,Larry (b) | Blade,Brian (dr)
Mark Turner Quintet
Some Other Time | Visions | Alone And I
Turner,Mark (ts) | Rosenwinkel,Kurt (g) | Hayes,Kevin (p) | Grenadier,Larry (b) | Blade,Brian (dr)

9362-47632-2 | CD | Trio 99-00
Pat Metheny Trio
Go Get It - (Go) Get It | Giant Steps | Just Like The Day | Soul Cowboy | The Sun In Montreal | Capricorn | We Had A Sister | What Do You Want? | A Lot Of Livin' To Do | Lone Jack | Travels
NYC, rec. August 1999
Metheny,Pat (g) | Grenadier,Larry (b) | Stewart,Bill (dr)

9362-47693-2 | CD | Places
Brad Mehldau Trio
Los Angeles | Madrid | West Hartford | A Walk In The Park | Schloss Elmau | Los Angeles(reprise)
Los Angeles,CA, rec. 24./25.1.2000
Mehldau,Brad (p) | Grenadier,Larry (b) | Rossy,Jorge 'Jordi' (dr)
Brad Mehldau
Psalms | Amsterdam | Los Angeles | Airport Sadness | Perugia | Paris | Am Zauberberg
Los Angeles,CA, rec. 24./25.3.2000
Mehldau,Brad (p-solo)

9362-47694-2 | CD | Fourplay...Yes,Please!
Fourplay
Free Range | Double Trouble | Once Upon A Love | Robo Bop | Blues Force | Save Some Love For Me | Fortress | Go With Your Heart | Poco A Poco | A Little Fourplay | Lucky
Los Angeles,CA, rec. 1999
Fourplay | Carlton,Larry (g) | James,Bob (p) | East,Nathan (b,voc) | Mason,Harold (dr)
A Little Fourplay
Fourplay | Carlton,Larry (g) | James,Bob (p) | East,Nathan (b,voc) | Mason,Harold (dr) | Sherree (voc)

9362-47792-2 | CD | Basie & Beyond
The Quincy Jones-Sammy Nestico Orchestra
You Gotta Try...Harder!
Hollywood,CA, rec. 1999
Grant,Gary (tp) | Luening,Warren (tp) | Baptist,Rick (tp) | Brashear,Oscar (tp) | Bergeron,Wayne (tp) | Hey,Jerry (tp) | Loper,Charles (tb) | Bohanon,George (tb) | Watrous,Bill (tb) | Reichenbach,Bill (tb) | Young,Reginald (tb) | Folsom,Jerry (fr-h) | Warnaar,Brad (fr-h) | Williams,Gregory (fr-h) | Johnson,Tommy (tuba) | Laws,Hubert (fl) | Higgins,Dan (reeds) | Foster,Gary (reeds) | Watts,Ernie (reeds) | Christlieb,Pete (reeds) | Albright,Gerald (reeds) | Nimitz,Jack (reeds) | Kerber,Randy (p) | Phillinganes,Gregory (el-p) | Jackson Jr.,Paul (el-g) | Berghofer,Chuck (b) | Colaiuta,Vinnie (dr) | Richards,Emil (vib,perc)
How Sweet It Is
Grant,Gary (tp) | Luening,Warren (tp) | Baptist,Rick (tp) | Brashear,Oscar (tp) | Bergeron,Wayne (tp) | Hey,Jerry (tp) | Loper,Charles (tb) | Bohanon,George (tb) | Watrous,Bill (tb) | Reichenbach,Bill (tb) | Young,Reginald (tb) | Folsom,Jerry (fr-h) | Warnaar,Brad (fr-h) | Williams,Gregory (fr-h) | Johnson,Tommy (tuba) | Laws,Hubert (fl) | Higgins,Dan (reeds) | Foster,Gary (reeds) | Watts,Ernie (reeds) | Christlieb,Pete (reeds) | Albright,Gerald (reeds) | Nimitz,Jack (reeds) | Kerber,Randy (p) | Phillinganes,Gregory (el-p) | Jackson Jr.,Paul (el-g) | Berghofer,Chuck (b) | Colaiuta,Vinnie (dr) | Jones,Harold (dr) | Richards,Emil (vib,perc)
No Time Like The Present
Grant,Gary (tp) | Luening,Warren (tp) | Baptist,Rick (tp) | Brashear,Oscar (tp) | Bergeron,Wayne (tp) | Hey,Jerry (tp) | Loper,Charles (tb) | Bohanon,George (tb) | Watrous,Bill (tb) | Reichenbach,Bill (tb) | Young,Reginald (tb) | Folsom,Jerry (fr-h) | Warnaar,Brad (fr-h) | Williams,Gregory (fr-h) | Johnson,Tommy (tuba) | Whalum,Kirk (ss,ts) | Higgins,Dan (reeds) | Foster,Gary (reeds) | Watts,Ernie (reeds) | Christlieb,Pete (reeds) | Albright,Gerald (reeds) | Nimitz,Jack (reeds) | Kerber,Randy (p) | Phillinganes,Gregory (el-p) | Jackson Jr.,Paul (el-g) | Berghofer,Chuck (b) | Colaiuta,Vinnie (dr) | Jones,Harold (dr) | Richards,Emil (vib,perc)
Hard Rock Dance | The Witching Hour | For Lena And Lennie
Grant,Gary (tp) | Luening,Warren (tp) | Baptist,Rick (tp) | Brashear,Oscar (tp) | Bergeron,Wayne (tp) | Hey,Jerry (tp) | Loper,Charles (tb) | Bohanon,George (tb) | Watrous,Bill (tb) | Reichenbach,Bill (tb) | Young,Reginald (tb) | Folsom,Jerry (fr-h) | Warnaar,Brad (fr-h) | Williams,Gregory (fr-h) | Johnson,Tommy (tuba) | Higgins,Dan (reeds) | Foster,Gary (reeds) | Watts,Ernie (reeds) | Christlieb,Pete (reeds) | Albright,Gerald (reeds) | Nimitz,Jack (reeds) | Kerber,Randy (p) | Phillinganes,Gregory (el-p) | Jackson Jr.,Paul (el-g) | Berghofer,Chuck (b) | Colaiuta,Vinnie (dr) | Richards,Emil (vib,perc)
Grace
Grant,Gary (tp) | Luening,Warren (tp) | Baptist,Rick (tp) | Brashear,Oscar (tp) | Bergeron,Wayne (tp) | Hey,Jerry (tp) | Loper,Charles (tb) | Bohanon,George (tb) | Watrous,Bill (tb) | Reichenbach,Bill (tb) | Young,Reginald (tb) | Folsom,Jerry (fr-h) | Warnaar,Brad (fr-h) | Williams,Gregory (fr-h) | Johnson,Tommy (tuba) | Whalum,Kirk (ss,ts) | Higgins,Dan (reeds) | Foster,Gary (reeds) | Watts,Ernie (reeds) | Christlieb,Pete (reeds) | Albright,Gerald (reeds) | Nimitz,Jack (reeds) | Kerber,Randy (p) | Phillinganes,Gregory (el-p) | Jackson Jr.,Paul (el-g) | Stubenhaus,Neil (el-b) | Colaiuta,Vinnie (dr) | Richards,Emil (vib,perc) | Da Costa,Paulinho (perc)
The Joy Of Cookin'
Grant,Gary (tp) | Luening,Warren (tp) | Baptist,Rick (tp) | Brashear,Oscar (tp) | Bergeron,Wayne (tp) | Hey,Jerry (tp) | Loper,Charles (tb) | Bohanon,George (tb) | Watrous,Bill (tb) | Reichenbach,Bill (tb) | Young,Reginald (tb) | Folsom,Jerry (fr-h) | Warnaar,Brad (fr-h) | Williams,Gregory (fr-h) | Johnson,Tommy (tuba) | Whalum,Kirk (ss,ts) | Higgins,Dan (reeds) | Foster,Gary (reeds) | Watts,Ernie (reeds) | Christlieb,Pete (reeds) | Albright,Gerald (reeds) | Nimitz,Jack (reeds) | Kerber,Randy (p) | Phillinganes,Gregory (el-p) | Jackson Jr.,Paul (el-g) | Johnson,Jimmy (el-b) | Colaiuta,Vinnie (dr) | Richards,Emil (vib,perc)
Quintessence
Grant,Gary (tp) | Luening,Warren (tp) | Baptist,Rick (tp) | Brashear,Oscar (tp) | Bergeron,Wayne (tp) | Hey,Jerry (tp) | Loper,Charles (tb) | Bohanon,George (tb) | Watrous,Bill (tb) | Reichenbach,Bill (tb) | Young,Reginald (tb) | Folsom,Jerry (fr-h) | Warnaar,Brad (fr-h) | Williams,Gregory (fr-h) | Johnson,Tommy (tuba) | Higgins,Dan (reeds) | Foster,Gary (reeds) | Watts,Ernie (reeds) | Christlieb,Pete (reeds) | Albright,Gerald (reeds) | Nimitz,Jack (reeds) | Kerber,Randy (p) | Phillinganes,Gregory (el-p) | Jackson Jr.,Paul (el-g) | Johnson,Jimmy (el-b) | Colaiuta,Vinnie (dr) | Richards,Emil (vib,perc)
Lisette
Grant,Gary (tp) | Luening,Warren (tp) | Baptist,Rick (tp) | Brashear,Oscar (tp) | Bergeron,Wayne (tp) | Hey,Jerry (tp) | Loper,Charles (tb) | Bohanon,George (tb) | Watrous,Bill (tb) | Reichenbach,Bill (tb) | Young,Reginald (tb) | Folsom,Jerry (fr-h) | Warnaar,Brad (fr-h) | Williams,Gregory (fr-h) | Johnson,Tommy (tuba) | Higgins,Dan (reeds) | Foster,Gary (reeds) | Watts,Ernie (reeds) | Christlieb,Pete (reeds) | Albright,Gerald (reeds) | Nimitz,Jack (reeds) | Kerber,Randy (p) | Phillinganes,Gregory (el-p) | Jackson Jr.,Paul (el-g) | Stubenhaus,Neil (el-b) | Colaiuta,Vinnie (dr) | Richards,Emil (vib,perc)
Out Of The Night | Belly Roll
Grant,Gary (tp) | Luening,Warren (tp) | Baptist,Rick (tp) | Brashear,Oscar (tp) | Bergeron,Wayne (tp) | Hey,Jerry (tp) | Loper,Charles (tb) | Bohanon,George (tb) | Watrous,Bill (tb) | Reichenbach,Bill (tb) | Young,Reginald (tb) | Folsom,Jerry (fr-h) | Warnaar,Brad (fr-h) | Williams,Gregory (fr-h) | Johnson,Tommy (tuba) | Laws,Hubert (fl) | Higgins,Dan (reeds) | Foster,Gary (reeds) | Watts,Ernie (reeds) | Christlieb,Pete (reeds) | Albright,Gerald (reeds) | Nimitz,Jack (reeds) | Kerber,Randy (p) | Phillinganes,Gregory (el-p) | Jackson Jr.,Paul (el-g) | Stubenhaus,Neil (el-b) | Colaiuta,Vinnie (dr) | Richards,Emil (vib,perc) | Da Costa,Paulinho (perc)

9362-47813-2 | CD | Siblingity
The Clayton Brothers Quintet
Work Song- | Blues On Parade- | Runway | Filthy McNasty- | Silver Worth Gold- | Entrez Vous | Last Stop | You Bossa Nova Me | If This Isn't Love | The Night | Tricotism- | The Bop Be Bops- | Save Yourself For Me | Heavy Drama
Clayton,Jeff (fl,as) | Clayton,John (b) | Stafford,Terell (tp) | Cunliffe,Bill (p) | Hamilton,Jeff (dr)

9362-47874-2 | CD | With Strings Attached/The Three Faces Of Chico
Chico Hamilton Quintet
Andante | Modes | Fair Weather | Pottsville U.S.A. | Don's Delight
Los Angeles,CA, rec. 26.10.1958
Hamilton,Forrest 'Chico' (dr) | Dolphy,Eric (fl,as) | Gershman,Nathan (cello) | Budimir,Dennis (g) | Ruther,Wyatt (b)
Chico Hamilton Quintet With Strings
Something To Live For | Close Your Eyes | Strange | Everything I've Got | Speak Low
Los Angeles,CA, rec. 27.10.1958
Hamilton,Forrest 'Chico' (dr) | Dolphy,Eric (fl,b-cl,as) | Gershman,Nathan (cello) | Budimir,Dennis (g) | Ruther,Wyatt (b) | unkn. (strings) | Katz,Fred (arr,cond)
Chico Hamilton Quintet
More Than You Ever Know | Newport News | Miss Movement
Los Angeles,CA, rec. February 1959
Hamilton,Forrest 'Chico' (dr) | Dolphy,Eric (as) | Gershman,Nathan (cello) | Budimir,Dennis (g) | Ruther,Wyatt (b)
Chico Hamilton Orchestra
She's Funny That Way | The Best Things In Life Are Free | I Don't Know Why(I Just Do) | Where Or When
Hamilton,Forrest 'Chico' (dr,voc) | Dolphy,Eric (as) | Horn,Paul (as) | Collette,Buddy (ts) | Green,Bill (bs) | Gershman,Nathan (cello) | Budimir,Dennis (g) | Ruther,Wyatt (b)
Chico Hamilton
Trinkets | Happy Little Dance | No Speak No English,Man
Hamilton,Forrest 'Chico' (dr-solo)

9362-47875-2 | CD | Ella/Things Ain't What They Used To Be
Ella Fitzgerald With Orchestra
Get Ready | The Hunter Gets Captured By The Game | Yellow Man | I'll Never Fall In Love Again | Got To Get You Into My Life | I Wonder Why | Ooo Baby Baby | Savoy Truffle | Open Your Window | Knock On Wood
London,GB, rec. 26.-30.5.1969
Fitzgerald,Ella (voc) | Orchestra | details unknown | Perry,Richard (arr) | Vickers,Mike (arr) | Cameron,John (arr)
Sunny | Mas Que Nada | A Man And A Woman | Days Of Wine And Roses | Black Coffee | Tuxedo Junction | I Heard It Through The Grapevine | Don't Dream Of Anybody But Me | Things Ain't What They Used To Be | Willow Weep For Me | Manteca
Hollywood,CA, rec. 1970
Fitzgerald,Ella (voc) | Bryant,Bobby (tp) | McGuire,Larry (tp) | Rodriguez,Alex (tp) | Hubion,Paul (tp) | Edison,Harry 'Sweets' (tp) | Johnson,J.J. (tb) | Cleveland,Jimmy (tb) | Wimberley,Mike (tb) | Woodman,Britt (tb) | Tole,Bill (tb) | Thomas,Al (tb) | Green,Thurman (tb) | Maebe,Arthur (fr-h) | De Vega,Henri (as) | Ortega,Anthony (fl,piccolo) | Watts,Ernie (fl,piccolo) | Green,William (fl,piccolo) | Royal,Marshall (fl,cl,as) | Bojorquez,Ray (ts) | Land,Harold (ts) | Aplanalp,Richard (bs) | Flanagan,Tommy (p) | Sample,Joe (org,el-p) | Feldman,Victor (vib) | Hutcherson,Bobby (vib) | Ellis,Herb (g) | Budimir,Dennis (g) | Brown,Ray (b) | Bellson,Louie (dr) | Duran,Modesto (congas,bongos) | De Souza,Franzisco (congas,bongos)

9362-47906-2 | CD | Fictionary
Lyle Mays Trio
Bill Evans | Fictionary | Sienna | Lincoln Reviews His Notes | Hard Eights | Something Left Unsaid | Trio No.1 | Where Are You From Today | Trio No.2 | Falling Grace | On The Other Hand
NYC, rec. 23.4.1992
Mays,Lyle (p) | Johnson,Marc (b) | DeJohnette,Jack (dr)

9362-47907-2 | 2 CD | Part Metheny Trio Live
Pat Metheny Trio
Bright Size Life | Question And Answer | Giant Steps | Into A Dream | So May It Secretly Begin | The Beat | All The Things You Are | James | Unity Village | Soul Cowboy | Night Turns Into Day | Faith Healer | Counting Texas
different Places, rec. 1999/2000
Metheny,Pat (g,el-g,g-synth,fretless-12-string-g,42-string-picasso-g) | Grenadier,Larry (b) | Stewart,Bill (dr)

9362-47997-2 | CD | Passage Of Time
Joshua Redman Quartet
Before | Free Speech,Phase 1 | Free Speech,Phase 2 | Our Minuet | Bronze Dance | Time | Enemies Within | After
NYC, rec. October 2000
Redman,Joshua (ts) | Goldberg,Aaron (p) | Rogers,Reuben (b) | Hutchinson,Gregory (dr)

9362-47998-2 | CD | Dharma Days
Mark Turner Quartet
Iverson's Odyssey | Deserted Floor | Myron's World | We Three | Jacky's Place | Casa Oscura | Zürich | Dharma Days | Seven Points
NYC, rec. 29.1.-1.2.2001
Turner,Mark (ts) | Rosenwinkel,Kurt (g) | Anderson,Reid (b) | Waits,Nasheet (dr)

9362-48005-2 | 2 CD | Art Of The Trio Vol.5:Progression
Brad Mehldau Trio
The More I See You | Dream's Monk | The Folks Who Live On The Hill | Alone Together | It Might As Well Be Spring | Cry Me A River | River Man | Quit | Secret Love | Sublation | Resignation | Long Ago And Far Away | How Long Has This Been Going On
Live at The 'Village Vanguard',NYC, rec. 22.-24.9.2000
Mehldau,Brad (p) | Grenadier,Larry (b) | Rossy,Jorge 'Jordi' (dr)

9362-48278-2 | CD | Vertcal Vision | EAN 093624827825
Christian McBride Quartet
Circa 1990 | Technicolor Nightmare | Tahitian Pearl | The Wizard Of Montara | The Ballad Of Little Girl Dancer | Lejos De Usted | Precious One | Song For Maya | Boogie Woogie Waltz
NYC, rec. 14.-16.6.2002
McBride,Christian (b,el-b) | Blake,Ron (fl,ss,ts) | Keezer,Geoff (p,keyboards) | Gully,Terreon (dr)

9362-48404-2 | CD | KG Standard Of Language | EAN 093624840428
Kenny Garrett Quartet
What Is This Thing Called Jazz | Kurita Sensei | X Y Z | Native Tongue | Chief Blackwater | Doc Tone's Short Speech | Just A Second To Catch My Breath | Gendai
NYC/Los Angeles,CA, rec. details unknown
Garrett,Kenny (ss,as) | Brown,Vernell (p) | Moffett,Charnett (b) | Dave,Chris (dr)
Standard Of Language(I-III)
Garrett,Kenny (ss,as) | Brown,Vernell (p) | Moffett,Charnett (b) | Harland,Eric (dr)

9362-48445-2 | CD | You Are My Sunshine | EAN 093624844525
Cyrus Chestnut Trio
God Has Smiled On Me | It's All Right With Me | For The Saints | Precious | Lord Take My Hand | You Are My Sunshine | Erroling | Total Praise | Lighthearted Intelligence | Sweet Hour Of Prayer | Hope Song | Flipper | What A Fellowship | Pass Me Not O Gentle Savior
Tallahassee,FL, rec. 15./17.11.2002
Chestnut,Cyrus (p) | Hawkins,Michael (b) | Smith,Neal (dr)

9362-48473-2 | CD | One Quiet Night | EAN 093624847328
Pat Metheny
One Quiet Night | Song For The Boys | Don't Know Why | Another Chance | And Time Goes On | My Song | Peace Memory | Ferry Cross The Mersey | Over On 4th Street | I Will Find The Way | North To South,East To West | Last Train Home
NYC, rec. 24.11.2001
Metheny,Pat (bariton-g-solo)

9362-48608-2 | CD | Anything Goes | EAN 093624860822
Brad Mehldau Trio
Get Happy | Dreamsville | Anything Goes | Tres Palabras | Skippy | Nearness Of You | Still Crazy After All These Years | Everything In Its Right Place | Smile | I've Grown Accustomed To Her Face
NYC, rec. 8./9.10.2002
Mehldau,Brad (p) | Grenadier,Larry (b) | Rossy,Jorge 'Jordi' (dr)

Watt | ECM Export

1 | CD | Tropic Appetites
Carla Bley Group
What Will Be Left Between Us And The Moon Tonight | In India | Enormous Tots | Caucasian Bird Riffles | Funnybird Song | Indonesian Dock Sucking Supreme | Song Of The Jungle Stream | Nothing
NYC, rec. 1973/1974
Bley,Carla (marimba,p,el-p,org,perc,celeste,clavinet,recorder,voice) | Barbieri,Gato (ts,perc) | Mantler,Michael (tp,v-tb) | Johnson,Howard (cl,b-cl,bs,bass-s,tuba,voice) | Marcus,Toni (v,viola) | Holland,Dave (cello,b,b-g) | Motian,Paul (dr,perc) | Tippetts,Julie (voice)

12,5 | CD | I Hate To Sing
The Carla Bley Band
Murder | Very Very Simple | I Hate To Sing
Live at San Francisco,CA, rec. 19.-21.8.1981
Bley,Carla (p,org,glockenspiel,voice) | Mantler,Michael (tp) | Valente,Gary (tb) | Chancey,Vincent (fr-h) | McIntyre,Earl (b-tb,tuba,voice) | Slagle,Steve (as) | Dagradi,Tony (ts) | O'Farrill,Arturo (p,org,voice) | Swallow,Steve (dr,el-b) | Sharpe,D. (dr,voice)
The Piano Lesson | The Lone Arranger | Battleship
Live at NYC, rec. 11.-13.1.1983
Bley,Carla (org,glockenspiel,voice) | Mantler,Michael (tp) | Valente,Gary (tb) | Chancey,Vincent (fr-h) | Stewart,Robert 'Bob' (tuba) | Slagle,Steve (as) | Dagradi,Tony (ts) | O'Farrill,Arturo (p) | Swallow,Steve (el-b,voice) | Sharpe,D. (dr)

13 | CD | Something There
13 | LP | Something There
Michael Mantler Quintet With The London Symphony Orchestra
Twenty | Twenty One | Nineteen | Seventeen | Eighteen | Something There
rec. June/July 1982
Mantler,Michael (tp) | Stern,Mike (g) | Bley,Carla (p) | Swallow,Steve (b) | Mason,Nick (dr) | London Symphony Orchestra,The | Gibbs,Michael (cond,arr)

14 | CD | Heavy Heart
14 (817864-1) | LP | Heavy Heart
Carla Bley Band
Light Or Dark | Talking Hearts | Joyful Noise | Ending It | Starting Again | Heavy Heart
NYC, rec. Sept./Oct.1983
Bley,Carla (org,synth) | Mantler,Michael (tp) | Valente,Gary (tb) | McIntyre,Earl (tuba) | Slagle,Steve (fl,as,bs) | Bullock,Hiram (g) | Kirkland,Kenny (p) | Swallow,Steve (b) | Lewis,Victor (dr) | Badrena,Manolo (perc)

15 | CD | Alien
15 | LP | Alien
Michael Mantler-Don Preston
Alien(part 1-4)
NYC, rec. March/July 1985
Mantler,Michael (tp) | Preston,Don (synth)

16 | CD | Night-Glo
16 | LP | Night-Glo
Carla Bley Band
Pretend You're In Love | Night-Glo | Rut | Crazy With You | Wildlife: | Horns- | Paws Without Claws- | Sex With Birds-
NYC, rec. June-August 1985
Bley,Carla (org,synth) | Brecker,Randy (tp,fl-h) | Malone,Tom (tb) | Taylor,Dave (b-tb) | Clark,John (fr-h) | McCandless,Paul (engl-h,b-cl,bs,oboe,ss,ts) | Bullock,Hiram (g) | Willis,Larry (p,el-p) | Swallow,Steve (el-b) | Lewis,Victor (dr) | Badrena,Manolo (perc)

17 | CD | Sextet
17 | LP | Sextet
Carla Bley Sextet
More Brahms | Houses And People | The Girl Who Cried Champagne | Brooklyn Bridge | Lawns | Healing Power
NYC, rec. December 1986&January 1987
Bley,Carla (org) | Bullock,Hiram (g) | Willis,Larry (p) | Swallow,Steve (b) | Lewis,Victor (dr) | Alias,Don (perc)

18 | CD | Live
18 | LP | Live
Michael Mantler Quintet
Preview-No Answer | Slow Orchestra Piece No.3(Prisonnieres) | For Instance | Slow Orchestra Piece No.8(A L'abattoir) | When I Run | The Remembered Visit | Slow Orchestra Piece No.6 | The Hapless Child | The Doubtful Guest
Art Rock Festival,Frankfurt/M, rec. 8.2.1987
Mantler,Michael (tp) | Fenn,Rick (g) | Preston,Don (synth) | Greaves,John (p,b) | Mason,Nick (dr) | Bruce,Jack (voc)

21 | CD | Fleur Carnivore
21 | LP | Fleur Carnivore
Carla Bley Band
Fleur Carnivore | Song Of The Eternal Waiting Of Canute | Ups And Downs | The Girl Who Cried Champagne(part 1-3) | Healing Power
Live at The 'Jazzhus' Montmartre,Copenhagen, rec. 14.-16.11.1988
Bley,Carla (p) | Soloff,Lew (tp) | Winther,Jens (tp) | Lacy,Ku-umba Frank (fl-h,fr-h) | Valente,Gary (tb) | Stewart,Robert 'Bob' (tuba) | Beaussier,Daniel (fl,oboe) | Puschnig,Wolfgang (fl,as) | Sheppard,Andy (cl,ts) | Lauer,Christof (ss,ts) | Ottini,Roberto (ss,bs) | Mantler,Karen (vib,org,harm,chimes) | Swallow,Steve (b-g) | Williams,Buddy (dr) | Alias,Don (perc)

23 | CD | The Very Big Carla Bley Band
23 | LP | The Very Big Carla Bley Band
United States | Strange Arrangement | All Fall Down | Who Will Rescue You? | Lo Ultimo
Ludwigsburg, rec. 29./30.10.1990
Bley,Carla (p) | Soloff,Lew (tp) | Barker,Guy (tp) | Deppa,Claude (tp) | Bernstein,Steven (tp) | Valente,Gary (tb) | Edwards,Richard (tb) | Virji,Faez (tb) | Slater,Ashley (b-tb) | Jannotta,Roger (fl,cl,ss,oboe) | Puschnig,Wolfgang (fl,as) | Sheppard,Bob (ss,ts) | Hurt,Pete (cl,ts) | Calogero,Pablo (bs) | Mantler,Karen (org) | Swallow,Steve (b-g) | Lewis,Victor (dr) | Alias,Don (perc)

4 | CD | The Hapless Child
Michael Mantler Group
The Sinking Spell | The Object Lesson | The Insect God | The Doubtful Guest | The Remembered Visit | The Hapless Child
rec. July 1975-Jan.1976
Mantler,Michael (comp) | Rypdal,Terje (g) | Bley,Carla (p,synth,clavinet) | Swallow,Steve (b-g) | DeJohnette,Jack (dr,perc) | Wyatt,Robert (voc) | Benge,Alfreda (voice) | Caulder,Albert (voice) | Mason,Nick (voice)

XtraWatt/2 | CD | Carla

XtraWatt/2 | LP | Carla
Steve Swallow Group
Deep Trouble | Crab Alley | Fred And Ethel | Read My Lips | After Glow | Hold It Against Me | Count The Ways | Last Night
NYC, rec. 1986/1987
Swallow,Steve (el-b) | Bley,Carla (org) | Willis,Larry (p) | Bullock,Hiram (g) | Lewis,Victor (dr) | Alias,Don (perc) | Kavafian,Ida (v) | Bae,Ikwhan (viola) | Sherry,Fred (cello)

XtraWatt/3 | CD | My Cat Arnold
XtraWatt/3 | LP | My Cat Arnold
Karen Mantler Group
I Wanna Be Good | My Stove | Vacation | Breaking Up | People Die | My Cat Arnold | Best Of Friends | Fear Of Pain | Major Love | Green Beans
NYC, rec. Spring 1988
Mantler,Karen (p,org,harm,voc) | Bernstein,Steven (tp) | Calogero,Pablo (bs) | Muller,Marc (g) | Weisberg,Steve (synth) | Sanborn,Jonathan (b) | Winogrand,Ethan (dr) | Mingus,Eric (voc)

XtraWatt/5 | CD | Karen Mantler And Her Cat Arnold Get The Flu
The Flu | I Love Christmas | Let's Have A Baby | My Organ | Au Lait | Waiting | Call A Doctor | Good Luck | I'm Not Such A Bad Guy
NYC, rec. Summer 1990
Mantler,Karen (org,harm,voc) | Bernstein,Steven (tp) | Calogero,Pablo (fl,bs) | Muller,Marc (g) | Weisberg,Steve (keyboards) | Sanborn,Jonathan (b) | Winogrand,Ethan (dr) | Mingus,Eric (voc)
Mean To Me
Mantler,Karen (org,harm,voc) | Bernstein,Steven (tp) | Mantler,Michael (tp) | Swallow,Steve (fl-h) | Bley,Carla (c-mel-sax) | Calogero,Pablo (fl,bs) | Muller,Marc (g) | Weisberg,Steve (keyboards) | Sanborn,Jonathan (b) | Winogrand,Ethan (dr) | Mingus,Eric (voc)

XtraWatt/8 | CD | Farewell
Farewell | Mister E | Brain Dead | Arnold's Dead | I'm His Boss | My Life Is Hell | Help Me | I Hate Money | Beware
Willow,NY, rec. December 1995
Mantler,Karen (p,org,synth,harm,glockenspiel,voc) | Evans,Michael (as,vib,dr,perc,bell,tabla,voc,whistling)
On The Bill | Con Edison
Mantler,Karen (p,org,synth,harm,glockenspiel,voc) | Evans,Michael (as,vib,dr,perc,bell,tabla,voc,whistling) | Bley,Carla (c-mel-sax) | Williams,Scott (voc)

Watt | Universal Music Germany

11(831831-2) | CD | Social Studies
The Carla Bley Band
Reactionary Tango (In Three Parts) | Copyright Royalties | Utviklingssang | Valse Sinistre | Floater | Walking Batteriewoman
rec. December 1980
Bley,Carla (p,org) | Mantler,Michael (tp) | Ward,Carlos (ss,as) | Dagradi,Tony (cl,ts) | Valente,Gary (tb) | Daley,Joe (euphonium) | McIntyre,Earl (tuba) | Swallow,Steve (b) | Sharpe,D. (dr)

12(815730-2) | CD | Live!
12 (2313112) | LP | Live!
Carla Bley Band
Blunt Object | The Lord Is Listenin' To Ya Hallelujah | Time And Us | Still In The Room | Real Life Hits | Song Sung Long
rec. 19.-21.8.1981
Bley,Carla (p,org,glockenspiel) | Mantler,Michael (tp) | Valente,Gary (tb) | Chancey,Vincent (fr-h) | McIntyre,Earl (b-tb,tuba) | Slagle,Steve (fl,ss,as) | Dagradi,Tony (ts) | O'Farrill,Arturo (p,org) | Swallow,Steve (b) | Sharpe,D. (dr)

19(835580-2) | CD | Many Have No Speech
Michael Mantler Group With The Danish Concert Radio Orchestra
Introduction | Just As Someone | Ce Qu'a De Pis | Alles Scheint Rand | Imagine | In The End | Vieil Aller | Rien Nul | Tant De Temps | En Face | Chaque Jour | PSS | En Cadence | Something There | Comrade | Den Atem Ausgetauscht | A L'Abattoir | And What | D'Ou La Voix | Fous Qui Disiez | Merk, Jetzt | Son Ombre | Reve | Life Connects | Prisonniers | Silence | Viele Haben Keine Sprache
London,GB/Copenhagen,Denmark, rec. May-December 1987
Mantler,Michael (tp) | Fenn,Rick (g) | Bruce,Jack (voice) | Faithful,Marianne (voice) | Wyatt,Robert (voice) | Danish Radio Concert Orchestra | Kragerup,Peder (cond)

2/5(543374-2) | 2 CD | Michael Mantler: No Answer/Silence
Michael Mantler Group
Number Six(part 1-4) | Number Twelve(part 1-4)
NYC/London, rec. February/July & November 1973
Mantler,Michael (comp) | Cherry,Don (tp) | Bley,Carla (p,org,clavinet) | Bruce,Jack (b-g,voice)
I Walk With My Girl | I Watch The Clouds | It Is Curiously Hot | Whe I Run | Sometimes I See People | Around Me Sits The Night | She Was Looking Down | For Instance | A Long Way | After My Work Each Day | On Good Evening
NYC, rec. Januray-June 1976
Mantler,Michael (comp) | Bley,Carla (p,org,voice) | Spedding,Chris (g) | McClure,Ron (b,b-g) | Maher,Clare (cello) | Wyatt,Robert (perc,voice) | Coyne,Kevin (voice)

20(837345-2) | CD | Duets
20(837345-1) | LP | Duets
Carla Bley-Steve Swallow
Baby Baby | Walking Batteriewoman | Utviklingssang | Reactinary Tango(part 1-3) | Romantic Notions(No.3) | Remember | Ups And Downs | Ladies In Mercedes
NYC, rec. Summer 1988
Bley,Carla (p) | Swallow,Steve (el-b)

24(517673-2) | CD | Go Together
Sing Me Softly Of The Blues | Mother Of The Dead Man | Masquerade(in 3 parts): | Carnation- | Dark Glasses- | Mustache- | Ad Infinitum | Copyright Royalties | Peau Douce | Doctor | Fleur Carnivore
NYC, rec. Summer 1992
Bley,Carla (p) | Swallow,Steve (b-g)

25(519966-2) | CD | Big Band Theory
Carla Bley Band
On The Stage In Cages | Birds Of Paradise | Goodbye Pork Pie Hat | Fresh Impression
London,GB, rec. 2./3.7.1993
Bley,Carla (p) | Soloff,Lew (tp) | Barker,Guy (tp) | Deppa,Claude (tp) | Waterman,Steve (tp) | Valente,Gary (tb) | Edwards,Richard (tb) | Whitehead,Annie (tb) | Slater,Ashley (b-tb) | Jannotta,Roger (fl,ss) | Puschnig,Wolfgang (fl,as) | Sheppard,Bob (ss,ts) | Hurt,Pete (ts) | Argüelles,Julian (bs) | Mantler,Karen (org) | Swallow,Steve (b-g) | Mackrel,Dennis (dr)

26(527069) | CD | Song With Legs
Carla Bley/Andy Sheppard/Steve Swallow
Real Life Hits | The Lord Is Listenin' To Ya Hallelujah | Chicken | Misterioso | Wrong Key Donkey | Crazy Without You
Willow,NY, rec. May 1994
Bley,Carla (p) | Sheppard,Andy (ss,ts) | Swallow,Steve (b-g)

27(533682-2) | CD | The Carla Bley Big Band Goes To Church
Carla Bley Big Band
Setting Calvin's Waltz | Exaltation- | Religious Experience- | Major- | One Way | Beads | Permanent Way | Who Will Rescue You?
NYC, rec. 19.-21.7.1996
Bley,Carla (p) | Soloff,Lew (tp) | Barker,Guy (tp) | Deppa,Claude (tp) | Waterman,Steve (tp) | Valente,Gary (tb) | Beachill,Pete (tb) | Dean,Chris (tb) | Henry,Richard (b-tb) | Jannotta,Roger (fl,ss,as) | Puschnig,Wolfgang (as) | Sheppard,Andy (ts) | Underwood,Jerry (ts) | Argüelles,Julian (bs) | Mantler,Karen (org,harm) | Swallow,Steve (b-g) | Mackrel,Dennis (dr)

28(539937-2) | CD | Fancy Chamber Music
Carla Bley Band
Wolfgang Tango | Romantic Notion(No.4) | End Of Vienna | Tigers In Training | Romantic Notion(No.6) | JonBenet
London,GB, rec. 5./6.12.1997
Bley,Carla (p) | Hayhurst,Alison (fl) | Lee,Sarah (cl,glockenspiel) | Morris,Steve (v) | Byrt,Andrew (viola) | Black,Emma (cello) | Swallow,Steve (el-b) | Wells,Chris (perc)

29(547297) | CD | Are We There Yet?
Carla Bley-Steve Swallow
Major | A Dog's Life | Satie For Two | Lost In The Stars | King Korn | Playing With Water | Musique Mecanique(I) | Musique Mecanique(II-At Midnight) | Musique Mecanique(III)
?,Europe
Bley,Carla (p) | Swallow,Steve (el-b)

3 (2313103) | LP | 13-3/4
Carla Bley - Michael Mantler & Orchestra
13 For Piano And Two Orchestras | 3 | 4 For Piano And Orchestra
rec. August 1975
Mantler,Michael (comp) | Bley,Carla (p) | brass,Strings and woodwinds,details unkn.

30(159547-2) | CD | 4X4
Carla Bley Band
Blues In 12 Bars- | Blues In 12 Other Bars- | Sidewinder s In Paradise | Les Trois Lagons(D'apres Henri Matisse) | Plate XVII- | Plate XVIII- | Plate XIX- | Baseball | Utviklingssang
Oslo,N, rec. July 1999
Bley,Carla (p) | Soloff,Lew (tp) | Valente,Gary (tb) | Puschnig,Wolfgang (as) | Sheppard,Bob (ts) | Goldings,Larry (org) | Swallow,Steve (b-g) | Lewis,Victor (dr)

5 (2313105) | LP | Silence
Michael Mantler Group
I Walk With My Girl | I Watch The Clouds | It Is Curiously Hot | Whe I Run | Sometimes I See People | Around Me Sits The Night | She Was Looking Down | For Instance | A Long Way | After My Work Each Day | On Good Evening
NYC, rec. January-June 1976
Mantler,Michael (comp) | Bley,Carla (p,org,voice) | Spedding,Chris (g) | McClure,Ron (b,b-g) | Maher,Clare (cello) | Wyatt,Robert (perc,voice) | Coyne,Kevin (voice)

6(825815-2) | CD | Dinner Music
6 (2313106) | LP | Dinner Music
Carla Bley Band
Sing Me Softly Of The Blues | Dreams So Real | Ad Infinitum | Dining Alone | Song Sung Long | Ida Lupino | Funnybird Song | A New Hymn
rec. July-Sept.1976
Bley,Carla (ts,p,org,voc) | Mantler,Michael (tp) | Rudd,Roswell (tb) | Stewart,Robert 'Bob' (tuba) | Ward,Carlos (as,ts) | Tee,Richard (p,el-p) | Gale,Eric (g) | Dupree,Cornell (g) | Edwards,Gordon (b-g) | Gadd,Steve (dr)

7 (2313107) | LP | Movies
7 (543377-2) | CD | Movies
Michael Mantler Group
Movie One | Movie Two | Movie Three | Movie Four | Movie Five | Movie Six | Movie Seven | Movie Eight
NYC, rec. March 1977
Mantler,Michael (tp) | Coryell,Larry (g) | Bley,Carla (ts,p,synth) | Swallow,Steve (b-g) | Williams,Tony (dr)

7/10(543377-2) | 2 CD | Movies/More Movies
Mantler,Michael (tp) | Coryell,Larry (g) | Bley,Carla (ts,p,synth) | Swallow,Steve (b-g) | Williams,Tony (dr)
Michael Mantler Sextet
Movie Nine | The Sinking Spell | Movie Eleven | Will We Meet Tonight | Movie Thirteen | The Daubtful Quest | Movie Fourteen | Movie Fifteen | Movie Ten | Movie Twelve
NYC, rec. August 1979-March 1980
Mantler,Michael (tp) | Window,Gary (ts) | Catherine,Philip (g) | Bley,Carla (p,org) | Swallow,Steve (b-g) | Sharpe,D. (dr)

8 | CD | European Tour 1977
8 (2313108) | LP | European Tour 1977
Carla Bley Band
Rose And Sad Song | Wrong Key Donkey | Drinking Music | Spangled Banner Minor And Other Patriotic Songs
rec. September 1977
Bley,Carla (ts,org) | Mantler,Michael (tp) | Rudd,Roswell (tb) | Stewart,Robert 'Bob' (tuba) | Clark,John (fr-h) | Dean,Elton (as) | Window,Gary (ts) | Adams,Terry (p) | Hopper,Hugh (b-dr,b-g) | Cyrille,Andrew (dr,perc)

9 | CD | Musique Mecanique
440 | Musique Mecanique(I) | Musique Mecanique(II-At Midnight) | Musique Mecanique(III)
rec. August/November 1978
Bley,Carla (p,org,toy-p) | Mantler,Michael (tp) | Braufman,Alan (fl,cl,as) | Window,Gary (b-cl,ts) | Rudd,Roswell (tb,voc) | Clark,John (fr-h) | Stewart,Robert 'Bob' (tuba) | Adams,Terry (p,org) | Swallow,Steve (el-b) | Sharpe,D. (dr) | Mantler,Karen (glockenspiel)
Jesus Maria And Other Spanish Strains
Bley,Carla (p,org,toy-p) | Mantler,Michael (tp) | Braufman,Alan (fl,cl,as) | Window,Gary (b-cl,ts) | Rudd,Roswell (tb,voc) | Clark,John (fr-h) | Stewart,Robert 'Bob' (tuba) | Adams,Terry (p,org) | Swallow,Steve (el-b) | Sharpe,D. (dr) | Mantler,Karen (glockenspiel) | Chadbourne,Eugene (g,el-g,walkie-talkie) | Haden,Charlie (b)

XtraWatt/10(543506-2) | CD | Always Pack Your Uniform On Top
Steve Swallow Quintet
Bend Over Backwards | Dog With A Bone | Misery Loves Company | Reinventing The Wheel | Feet First | La Nostalgie De La Boue
Live at Ronnie Scott's,London,GB, rec. April 1999
Swallow,Steve (b-g) | Ries,Barry (tp) | Potter,Chris (ts) | Goodrick,Mick (g) | Nussbaum,Adam (dr)

XtraWatt/11(067792-2) | CD | Damaged In Transit | EAN 044006779225
Steve Swallow Trio
Item 1,D.I.T. | Item 2,D.I.T. | Item 3,D.I.T. | Item 4,D.I.T. | Item 5,D.I.T. | Item 6,D.I.T. | Item 7,D.I.T. | Item 8,D.I.T. | Item 9,D.I.T.
Live in France, rec. December 2001
Swallow,Steve (b-g) | Potter,Chris (ts) | Nussbaum,Adam (dr)

XtraWatt/4 | CD | Orchestra Jazz Siciliana Plays The Music Of Carla Bley
XtraWatt/4(843207-1) | LP | Orchestra Jazz Siciliana Plays The Music Of Carla Bley
Orchestra Jazz Siciliana
440 | The Lone Arranger | Dreams So Real | Baby Baby | Joyful Noise | Egyptian | Blunt Object
Live at Palermo,Sicily, rec. 11.-16.5.1989
Orchestra Jazz Siciliana | Riina,Nico (tp) | Greco,Massimo (tp) | Pedone,Pietro (tp) | Riina,Faro (tp) | Guttilla,Giovanni (tp) | Pizzo,Salvatore (tb) | Pizzurro,Salvatore (tb) | Valente,Gary (tb) | Persia,Maurizio (b-tb) | Maugeri,Orazio (as) | Montalbano,Claudio (ss,as) | D'Anna,Stefano (ts) | Palacino,Alessandro (ss,ts) | Pedone,Antonio (bs) | Garsia,Ignazio (p) | Greco,Pino (g) | Swallow,Steve (el-b) | Mappa,Paolo (dr) | Cammalleria,Sergio (perc)

XtraWatt/6 | CD | Swallow
XtraWatt/6 | LP | Swallow
Steve Swallow Group
Belles | Soca Symphony | Slender Thread | Thrills And Spills | William And Mary | Thirty Five | Ballroom | Playing With Water
NYC, rec. September-November 1991
Swallow,Steve (el-b) | Burton,Gary (vib) | Scofield,John (g) | Bullock,Hiram (g) | Kuhn,Steve (p) | Bley,Carla (org) | Mantler,Karen (synth,harm) | Ameen,Robert 'Robbie' (dr) | Alias,Don (perc)

XtraWatt/7(521637-2) | CD | Real Book
Bite Your Grandmother | Second Handy Motion | Wrong Together | Outfits | Thinkin' Out Loud | Let's Eat | Better Times | Willow | Muddy In The Bank | Ponytail
NYC, rec. December 1993
Swallow,Steve (el-b) | Harrell,Tom (tp,fl-h) | Lovano,Joe (ts) | Miller,Mulgrew (p) | DeJohnette,Jack (dr)

XtraWatt/9(537119-2) | CD | Deconstructed
Running In The Family | Babble On | Another Fine Mess | I Think My Wife Is A Hat | Bird World War | Bug In A Rug | Lost In Boston | Name That Tune | Viscous Consistency | Deconstructed
NYC, rec. December 1996
Swallow,Steve (b-g) | Kisor,Ryan (tp) | Potter,Chris (ts) | Goodrick,Mick (g) | Nussbaum,Adam (dr)

Wergo | sunny moon Musikvertrieb

SM 1067/68-50 | 2 CD | Improvisation IV
Herbert Henck
Improvisation IV für Klavier(Teil 1-3)
Bergisch Gladbach, rec. 2.-4.8.1986
Henck,Herbert (p-solo)

SM 1088-2 | CD | Wounded Knee-Lyrik Und Jazz
Okschila Tatanka
Traditional Song- | Interview- | Lauf Indianer Lauf(John Trudell) | Wounded Knee(Buddy Red Bow) | Das Ist Mein Leben(John Trudell) | Crying Song | Horcht(John Trudell) | Sie Haben Nicht Hingehört(Floyd Westermann) | Welt Ohne Morgen(Floyd Westermann) | Crying Song(II) | Caster Starb Für Eure Sünden(Floyd Westermann) | Black Elk(Buddy Red Bow) | Improvisationen(1-4)
details unknown, rec. details unknown
Tatanka,Okschila (hand-dr,voice) | Mangelsdorff,Albert (tb) | Böhlke,Edgar M. (narration) | Haindl,Hermann (narration)

SM 1531-2 | CD | Jazz Across The Border
Fairy Tale Trio
Karandila | Lastuna | The House Behind The River | Cadence In Green | Samotek | Sun Sanuvah | Chorovod | Marvellous Pig Stories | Shepherd's Baroque | Gornjak | Shuma
Berlin, rec. 22.6.1998
Fairy Tale Trio | Vapirov,Anatoly (ss) | Spassov,Theodossij (kaval,voice) | Yankoulov,Stoyan (perc,tupan)

WER 80007-50 | CD | Shadows & Smiles
Manfred Schoof/Rainer Brünninghaus
Smiles | Shadows | Sequence | Fire Side | Ingredience Of The Blues | Suggestion
Köln, rec. Oct.1987 & May 1988
Schoof,Manfred (tp,fl-h) | Brüninghaus,Rainer (p,keyboards)

WER 8008-2 | CD | Heloise
Michael Riessler Group
Ghigo | Wilhelm Von Champeaux | Und | Paraklet | Nocturne | Neulich | Bophal | Organistrum | Lais | Boscaglia | Sic Et Non | Comme Dans Un Train Pour Une Etoile | Quanta Qualia
Donaueschingen, rec. 17.10.1992
Riessler,Michael (cl,alto-cl,b-cl,contra-b-cl,sax) | Godard,Michel (serpent,tuba) | Clastrier,Valentin (drehleier) | Abou-Khalil,Rabih (oud) | Matinier,Jean-Louis (accordeon) | Sylvestre,Gaston (cymbal) | Sylvestre,Brigitte (harp) | Garcia-Fons,Renaud (b) | Siracusa,Gerard (dr,perc) | Rizzo,Carlo (perc)

WER 8009-2 | CD | Tentations D'Abélard
Sequentiae | St.Denis | S.D.F.-q.e.d. | Die Horen Des Astrolabius | Bulegria | Planctus- | Kanga- | La Chasse | Danse Brisée | Unstern | Grille | Cantus
Paris,France, rec. 3.-6.3.1994
Riessler,Michael (cl,sax) | Ambrosini,Marco (dudelsack,schlüsselfidel) | Clastrier,Valentin (drehleier) | Godard,Michel (serpent,tuba) | Matinier,Jean-Louis (accordeon) | Sylvestre,Brigitte (harp) | Sylvestre,Gaston (cymbal) | Garcia-Fons,Renaud (b) | Rizzo,Carlo (bendir,tambourin) | Siracusa,Gerard (perc)
Mr.J.D.(..sic!)
Riessler,Michael (cl,sax) | Ambrosini,Marco (dudelsack,schlüsselfidel) | Clastrier,Valentin (drehleier) | Godard,Michel (serpent,tuba) | Matinier,Jean-Louis (accordeon) | Sylvestre,Brigitte (harp) | Sylvestre,Gaston (cymbal) | Garcia-Fons,Renaud (b) | Rizzo,Carlo (bendir,tambourin) | Siracusa,Gerard (perc) | Ameen,Robert 'Robbie' (dr)

WER 8010-2 | CD | Palude
Trio Clastrier-Riessler-Rizzo
Palude | Larve | Laissez-Moi Tranquille | Zanza | Et La Roue De La Vie | Adrian | Esitazione | Sur Un Fil | Poliritmia | Toujours | Tredue
Köln, rec. 19.-21.12.1994
Riessler,Michael (cl,sax) | Clastrier,Valentin (drehleier) | Rizzo,Carlo (tambourin)

Windham Hill | BMG-Ariola Classics GmbH

34 10111-2 | CD | Tears Of Joy
Tuck And Patti
Tears Of Joy | Takes My Breath Away | I've Got Just About Everything | Time After Time | Everything's Gonna Be Alright | Better Than Anything | My Romance | Up And Ad It | Mad Mad Me | Love Is The Key
Menlo Park,CA, rec. details unknown
Tuck & Patti | Andress,Tuck (g) | Cathcart,Patti (voc)

34 10116-2 | CD | Love Warriors
Love Warriors | Honey Pie | They Can't Take That Away From Me | Hold Out, Hold Up And Hold On | Cantador(Like A Lover) | On A Clear Day You Can See Forever | Europa | Castles Made Of Sand- | Little Wing- | Glory Glory | If It's Magic
Tuck & Patti | Andress,Tuck (g) | Cathcart,Patti (voc)

34 10130-2 | CD | Dream
Dream | One Hand One Heart | Togethemess | Friends In High Places | The Voodoo Music | From Now On(We're One) | I Wish | Sitting In Limbo | High Heel Blues | All The Love | As Time Goes By
details unknown
Tuck & Patti | Andress,Tuck (g) | Cathcart,Patti (voc)

34 11032-2 | CD | Aerial Boundaries
Michael Hedges
Aerial Boundaries | Benusan | Rickover's Dream | Ragamuffin | Hot Type
West Townshend, rec. 1984
Hedges,Michael (g)
The Magic Farmer
San Francisco,CA, rec. 1984
Hedges,Michael (g)
Spare Change
Baltimore,MD, rec. 1984
Hedges,Michael (g)
After The Gold Rush
Hedges,Michael (g) | Manring,Michael (fretless-b)
Menage A Trois
San Francisco,CA, rec. 1984
Hedges,Michael (g) | Rosenfeld,Mindy (fl) | Manring,Michael (fretless-b)

34 11187-2 | CD | Linus & Lucy-The Music Of Vince Guaraldi
George Winston
Cast Your Fate To The Wind | Skating | Linus And Lucy | The Great Pumpkin Waltz | Monterey | A Charlie Brown Thanksgiving | Treat Street | Eight Five Five | The Masked Marvel | Charlie Brown And His All Stars | You're In Love,Charlie Brown | Peppermint Party | Bon Voyage | Young Man's Fancy | Remembrance | Theme To Grace- | Lament- | The Red Baron
Hollywood,CA, rec. 1996
Winston,George (p-solo)

Winter&Winter | Edel Contraire

910002-2 | CD | Found On Sordid Street
Gary Thomas Group
Spellbound | Treason | The Eternal Present | Exile's Gate | Hyperspace | Found On Sordid Streets | Peace Of The Korridor
Kensington,MD, rec. 19.-22.2.& 17./18.6.1996
Thomas,Gary (ts,pork-shop) | Bollenback,Paul (el-g) | Colligan,George (org) | Curtis,Howard (dr) | Moss,Steve (perc) | Rap Artist No Name

910003-2 | CD | Detail
Marc Ducret
Le Decor | Le Relief | Le Puits | Detail - (Detail) | Asile | Ma Plus Belle Histoire D'Amour | Septfamilles
Villa Medici-Giulini,Briosco,Italy, rec. 20.-23.1.1996
Ducret,Marc (g,12-string-g)

910004-2 | CD | Urlicht/Primal Light
Uri Caine Group
Funeral March(from Symphny No.5) | The Drummer Boy(from The Boy's Magic

Sollst Nicht Barfuß Geh'n | Schwesterlein,Schwesterlein,Wann Geh'n Wir Nach Haus? | Wie Schön Blüht Uns Der Maien | Guten Abend,Gute Nacht | Bunt Sind Schon Die Wälder | Der Hat Vergeben Das Ewig' Leben Der Nicht Die Musik Liebt | Guter Mond Du Gehst So Stille | Nun Komm Der Heiden Heiland
München, rec. 9.-11.10.2000
Kienemann,Joe (p) | Sieverts,Henning (b) | May,Guido (dr)
Joe Kienemann
Sah Ein Knab' Ein Röslein Steh'n | Hab' Oft Im Kreise Der Lieben Im Duftigen Grase Geruht | Leise Rieselt Der Schnee | Stille Nacht
Kienemann,Joe (p-solo)

CD 3097 | CD | Vitamin B 3
Barbara Jungfer Trio
Back Home | Open Window | Scones | Dawn Bird | Eloquence | God Bless The Child | Ginger Plant | Sereia | Snow Blues
Berlin, rec. 17./18.2.2001
Jungfer,Barbara (g) | Roggenkamp,Wolfgang (org) | Schlemmer,Christoph (dr)

CD 3114 | CD | New Life | EAN 4010207031147
Stefania Tallini Trio
Ulisse E L'Arco | Modmood | Trio Walk | New Life | Saudade | Eric Song | At Sunset | At Sunrise
Rome,Italy, rec. 18.-20.6.2003
Tallini,Stefania (p) | Cantarano,Stefano (b) | Marzi,Alessandro (dr)
Stefania Tallini Trio With Guests
Bolerepi | When All Was Chet
Tallini,Stefania (p) | Cantarano,Stefano (b) | Marzi,Alessandro (dr) | Bassi,Aldo (tp,fl-h)
Ics Dance
Tallini,Stefania (p) | Cantarano,Stefano (b) | Marzi,Alessandro (dr) | Girotto,Javier (ss)
Max Tango | Danza Sul Posta
Tallini,Stefania (p) | Cantarano,Stefano (b) | Marzi,Alessandro (dr) | Girotto,Javier (ss) | Rabbia,Michele (perc)

Zounds | PHONO-Spezial

CD 2700020089 | CD | Stanley Clarke Best
Stanley Clarke Groups
School Days | Rock'n Roll Jelly | Hello Jeff | Vulcan Princess | Desert Song | Danger Street | Born In The USA | Slow Dance | Justice's Groove | Wild Dog | Pit Bulls(An Endangered Species) | We Supply | Stories To Tell | Spanish Phrases For Strings And Bass | Hot Fun | Lords Of The Low Frequencies
different Places, rec. different Dates
Clarke,Stanley (b,el-b) | details not on the cover

CD 2700044001 | CD | Guitar Heroes Vol.1:Al Di Meola
Al Di Meola Groups
Dark Eye Tango | Egyptian Dance | Fantasy Suite For Two Guitars | Flight Over Rio | Land Of The Midnight Sun | Mediterranean Sundance | Race With Devil On Spanish Highway | Ritmo De La Noche | The Wizard | Kiss My Axe | Global Safari | Perpetual Emotion | Last Tango For Astor
Di Meola,Al (g,el-g,synth,12-string-g) | details not on the cover

CD 2700048 | CD | Classic Blues
Muddy Waters Blues Band
Hoochie Coochie Man
Chicago,Ill, rec. 1954
Muddy Waters[McKinley Morganfield] (g,voc) | details unknown
Robert Johnson
If I Had Possession Over Judgement Day
San Antonio,Texas, rec. 1936
Johnson,Robert (g,voc)
Willie Dixon
Since My Baby Gone
Chicago,Ill, rec. 1947
Dixon,Willie (b,voc) | details unknown
Pain In My Heart
Chicago,Ill, rec. 1951
Dixon,Willie (b,voc) | details unknown
Koko Taylor
Wang Wang Doodle
Chicago,Ill, rec. 1965
Taylor,Koko (voc) | details unknown
Son House
Death Letter
NYC, rec. 1965
House,Son (g,voc)
Blind Willie Johnson
God Moves On The Water
NYC, rec. 1929
Johnson,Blind Willie (g,voc) | Johnson,Angeline (voc)
B.B.King Blues Band
How Blue Can You Get
Chicago,Ill, rec. 1964
King,B.B. (g,voc) | details unknown
Sonny Boy Williamson Band
Bring It On Home
Chicago,Ill, rec. 1963
Williamson,Sonny Boy [Rice Miller] (harm,voc) | details unknown
Big Bill Broonzy
I Can't Be Satisfied
NYC, rec. 1930
Broonzy,Big Bill (g,voc)
Bukka White
Parchman Farm Blues
Chicago,Ill, rec. 1940
White,Bukka (g,voc)
Lonnie Johnson
She's Makin' Whoopee In Hell Tonight
NYC, rec. 1924
Johnson,Lonnie (g,voc)
Bessie Smith And Her Band
St.Louis Blues
Smith,Bessie (voc) | details unknown

CD 27100555 | CD | Jazzrock-Anthology Vol.3:Fusion
Paquito D'Rivera Orchestra
Just Kiddin'
D'Rivera,Paquito (as) | Roditi,Claudio (tp) | Camilo,Michel (p) | Freiberg,Daniel (keyboards) | Levy,Howard (harm) | Goines,Lincoln (b-g) | Brandao,Sergio (el-b) | Gadd,Steve (dr) | Portinho,Thelmo Martins Porto (perc) | Figueroa,Sammy (congas) | Bobadillis,Isidro (tambara) | Perez,Raymond (guiro)
Steve Khan Group
City Monsters
Khan,Steve (g) | Brecker,Randy (tp) | Sanborn,David (as) | Brecker,Michael (ts) | Mironov,Jeff (g) | Grolnick,Don (el-p) | Lee,Will (b) | Bennett,Errol 'Crusher' (perc)
Randy Brecker Group
Amandamena
Brecker,Randy (tp) | Brecker,Michael (alto-fl,voc) | Watanabe,Sadao (as) | Elias,Eliane (keyboards) | Lee,Will (b,voc) | Finnerty,Barry (g,voc) | Weckl,Dave (dr) | Badrena,Manolo (perc)
George Duke Group
Sugar Loaf Mountain
Duke,George (keyboards) | Hey,Jerry (tp) | Reichenbach,Bill (tb) | Williams,Larry (as) | Bautista,Roland (g) | Miller,Byron (b) | Lawson,Ricky (dr) | Escovedo,Sheila (timbales)
Azymuth
Partido Alto
Azymuth | Bertrami,Jose Roberto (keyboards,perc,voc) | Malheiros,Alex (b,voc) | Mamao,Ivan Conte (dr) | Aleuda (perc)
Caldera
Exaltation
Caldera | Del Barrio,Eddie (keyboards) | De Souza,Raoul (tb) | Tavaglione,Steve (ss) | Cortez,Dean (el-b) | Vega,Carlos (dr) | Azevedo,Mike (congas,perc) | Da Silva,Roberto (perc) | Dennis,Carol (voc)
Grover Washington Jr. Orchestra
Lover Man(Oh,Where Can You Be?)
Washington Jr.,Grover (as) | Frosk,John (tp) | Markowitz,Irving 'Marky' (tp) | Royal,Ernie (tp) | Rubin,Alan (tp) | Stamm,Marvin (tp) | Young,Eugene 'Snooky' (tp) | Andre,Wayne (tb) | Faulise,Paul (tb) | Studd,Tony (b-tb) | Alonge,Ray (fr-h) | Corrado,Donald (fr-h) | Klein,Fred (fr-h) | Tillotson,Brooks (fr-h) | Marge,George (engl-h,oboe) | Adams,Pepper (bs) | Clarke,Arthur (fl,bs) | James,Bob (keyboards,arr,ld) | Tee,Richard (org) | Gale,Eric (g) | Bertoncini,Gene (g) | Dupree,Cornell (g) | Spinozza,David (g) | Carter,Ron (b) | Cobham,Billy (dr) | Moreira,Airto (perc) | McDonald,Ralph (congas) | Cores,Alex (v) | Eichen,Bernard (v) | Ellen,Max (v) | Gershman,Paul (v) | Green,Emmanuel (v) | Kohon,Harold (v) | Lookofsky,Harry (v) | Malin,Joe (v) | Nadien,David (v) | Orloff,Gene (v) | Pintavalle,John (v) | Spice,Irving (v) | Dickler,Richard (viola) | Vardi,Emanuel 'Manny' (viola) | McCracken,Charles (cello) | Ricci,George (cello) | Ross,Margaret (harp)
Lee Ritenour Group
Sweet Syncopation
Ritenour,Lee (g) | Findley,Chuck (tp) | Rosolino,Frank (tb) | Scott,Tom (ts) | Richardson,Jerome (bs) | Grusin,Dave (keyboards) | Nash,Larry (clavinet) | Johnson,Louis (b) | Mason,Harold (dr) | Steinholtz,Jerry (perc)
Willie Bobo Group
Always There
Bobo,Willie (timbales) | Brashear,Oscar (tp) | King,Ron (tp) | Green,Thurman (tb) | Watts,Ernie (sax) | Herbig,Gary (sax) | Lyle,Bobby (keyboards) | Bautista,Roland (g) | Beck,Donny (b) | Phillips,Nathaniel (el-b) | Guiterrez,Steve (dr) | Pantoja,Antonio (perc)
Free Flight
El Pinero(The Pioneer)
Free Flight | Walker,Jim (fl) | Garson,Mike (keyboards) | Lacefield,Jim (b) | Humphrey,Ralph (dr)
Bobby Lyle Quintet
New Warrior
Lyle,Bobby (keyboards) | Phillips,Nathaniel (el-b) | Mason,Harold (dr) | Blocker,Joe (dr-synth) | Sunship (tympani)
Bob James And His Orchestra
One Mint Julep
James,Bob (keyboards) | Faddis,Jon (tp) | Frosk,John (tp) | Soloff,Lew (tp) | Stamm,Marvin (tp) | Andre,Wayne (tb) | Taylor,Dave (tb) | Bargeron,Dave (tb,tuba) | Laws,Hubert (fl) | Dodgion,Jerry (fl) | Daniels,Eddie (fl,ts) | Washington Jr.,Grover (ts) | Mironov,Jeff (g) | King,Gary (b) | Newmark,Andy (dr) | McDonald,Ralph (perc) | Buldrini,Frederick (v) | Cykman,Harry (v) | Eley,Lewis (v) | Ellen,Max (v) | Green,Emmanuel (v) | Kohon,Harold (v) | Nadien,David (v) | Raimondi,Matthew (v) | Brown,Alfred (viola) | Vardi,Emanuel 'Manny' (viola) | McCracken,Charles (cello) | Shulman,Alan (cello) | Agostini,Gloria (harp)
Al Di Meola Group
Roller Jubilee
Di Meola,Al (g) | Saisse,Phillippe (keyboards,marimba) | Cannarozzi,Pete (synth) | Jackson,Anthony (b) | Gadd,Steve (dr) | Lewis,Mingo (dr-synth,perc)

CD 2720007 | 2 CD | Jazz Zounds: Chris Barber
MC 2720009 | MC | Jazz Zounds: Chris Barber
Chris Barber's Jazzband & das Große Rundfunkorchester Berlin,DDR
A New Orleans Overture | Bourbon Street Parade | Lead Me On | Goin' Up The River | South Rampart Street Parade | Music From The Land Of Dreams | Mood Indigo | Harlem Rag | Wild Cat Blues | Concerto For Jazz Trombone And Orchestra: | Ragtime(Andante)- | Blues(Largo)- | Stomp(Presto)- | Reprise Stomp(Presto)- | Take Me Back To New Orleans | Under The Bamboo Tree | Das Gibt's Nur Einmal | Immigration Blues | Down By The Riverside | Ice Dream | Ice Cream(Reprise)
Rundfunk der DDR,Berlin, rec. details unknown
Barber,Chris (tb,voc) | Halcox,Pat (tp) | Wheeler,Ian (cl,sax,harm) | Crocker,John (cl,sax) | McCallum,Johnny (g,bj) | Slaughter,John (g) | Pitt,Vic (b) | Amberson,Norman (dr) | Rundfunkorchester Berlin | Hanell,Robert (ld)

CD 2730001 | CD | 7.Zelt-Musik-Festival:Jazz Events
VIBrations
Nice Talking To You
Freiburg,Brg., rec. 1989
VIBrations | Gronvad,Morten (vib) | Skipper,Ole (b) | Mutschler,Hermann (dr)
Adam Makowicz Trio
This Year's Kisses
Makowicz,Adam (p) | Ilg,Dieter (b) | Jones,Rusty (dr)
Adam Makowicz Trio With The Wilanow Quartet
Opus 57
Makowicz,Adam (p) | Ilg,Dieter (b) | Jones,Rusty (dr) | Wilanow String Quartet
Academic Jazz Band
Four Or Five Times | Plain Dirt
Academic Jazz Band | details unknown
Stephane Grappelli
Medley: | Time After Time- | Two Sleepy People- | Satin Doll-
Grappelli,Stephane (p-solo)
Stephane Grappelli Trio
Chattanooga Choo Choo
Grappelli,Stephane (v) | Fosset,Marc (g) | Sewing,Jack (b)
James Newton
Improvisation
Newton,James (fl)
Racine,Philippe (fl) | Ziegler,Matthias (fl) | Newton,James (fl)
Itchy Fingers
Dakhut
Itchy Fingers
Cab Calloway And His Hi De Ho Orchestra
Minnie The Moocher
Calloway,Cab (ld,voc) | details unknown
Dee Dee Bridgewater With Band
On A Clear Day You Can See Forever
Bridgewater,Dee Dee (voc) | details unknown
Dizzy Gillespie And The United Nation Orchestra
A Night In Tunisia
Gillespie,Dizzy (tp) | Sandoval,Arturo (tp,fl-h,piccolo-tp) | Roditi,Claudio (tp) | Hampton,Slide (tb) | Turre,Steve (b-tb,conch-shells) | D'Rivera,Paquito (cl,as) | Moody,James (fl,as,ts) | Rivera,Mario (ss,ts,perc) | Cherry,Ed (g) | Perez,Danilo (p) | Lee,John (b) | Berroa,Ignacio (dr) | Moreira,Airto (perc) | Hidalgo,Manenquito Giovanni (perc,congas) | Purim,Flora (voc)

zyx records | ZYX Music GmbH

FANCD 6076-2 | 3 CD | Thelonious Monk:85th Birthday Celebration | EAN 090204942589
Charlie Christian All Stars
Swing To Bop
Live at Minton's Play House,NYC, rec. 12.5.1941
Christian,Charlie (g) | Guy,Joe (tp) | Monk,Thelonious (p) | Fenton,Nick (b) | Clarke,Kenny (dr)
Coleman Hawkins Quartet
Flyin' Hawk
NYC, rec. 19.10.1944
Hawkins,Coleman (ts) | Monk,Thelonious (p) | Robinson,Edward 'Bass' (b) | Best,Denzil (dr)
Thelonious Monk Trio
Little Rootie Tootie | Monk's Dream
Hackensack,NJ, rec. 15.10.1952
Monk,Thelonious (p) | Mapp,Gary (b) | Blakey,Art (dr)
These Foolish Things Remind Me On You
Hackensack,NJ, rec. 18.12.1952
Monk,Thelonious (p) | Mapp,Gary (b) | Roach,Max (dr)
Thelonious Monk Quintet
Hackensack
Hackensack,NJ, rec. 1.5.1954
Monk,Thelonious (p) | Copeland,Ray (tp) | Foster,Frank (ts) | Russell,Curly (b) | Blakey,Art (dr)
Thelonious Monk
Just A Gigolo
Hackensack,NJ, rec. 22.9.1954
Monk,Thelonious (p-solo)
Thelonious Monk Quartet
I Want To Be Happy
Hackensack,NJ, rec. 25.10.1954
Rollins,Sonny (ts) | Monk,Thelonious (p) | Potter,Tommy (b) | Taylor,Arthur 'Art' (dr)
Miles Davis And The Modern Jazz Giants
Bemsha Swing
Hackensack,NJ, rec. 24.12.1954
Davis,Miles (tp) | Jackson,Milt (vib) | Monk,Thelonious (p) | Heath,Percy (b) | Clarke,Kenny (dr)
Thelonious Monk Trio
Mood Indigo
Hackensack,NJ, rec. 21.or 27.7.1955
Monk,Thelonious (p) | Pettiford,Oscar (b) | Clarke,Kenny (dr)
Honeysuckle Rose
Hackensack,NJ, rec. 17.3. or 3.4.1956
Monk,Thelonious (p) | Pettiford,Oscar (b) | Blakey,Art (dr)
Thelonious Monk Quintet
Pannonia | Brilliant Corners
NYC, rec. 9.10.1956
Monk,Thelonious (p,celeste) | Henry,Ernie (as) | Rollins,Sonny (ts) | Pettiford,Oscar (b) | Roach,Max (dr)
Thelonious Monk
Round About Midnight | I Should Care
NYC, rec. 5.4.1957
Monk,Thelonious (p-solo)
Thelonious Monk Trio
Monk's Mood
NYC, rec. 16.4.1957
Monk,Thelonious (p) | Coltrane,John (ts) | Ware,Wilbur (b)
Thelonious Monk Septet
Off Minor
NYC, rec. 26.6.1957
Monk,Thelonious (p) | Copeland,Ray (tp) | Gryce,Gigi (as) | Hawkins,Coleman (ts) | Coltrane,John (ts) | Ware,Wilbur (b) | Blakey,Art (dr)
Thelonious Monk Quartet
Ruby My Dear
Monk,Thelonious (p) | Hawkins,Coleman (ts) | Ware,Wilbur (b) | Blakey,Art (dr)
Trinkle Tinkle
NYC, rec. prob. July 1957
Monk,Thelonious (p) | Coltrane,John (ts) | Ware,Wilbur (b) | Wilson,Shadow (dr)
Thelonious Monk-Gerry Mulligan Quartet
Straight No Chaser | I Mean You
NYC, rec. 12.8.1957
Monk,Thelonious (p) | Mulligan,Gerry (bs) | Ware,Wilbur (b) | Wilson,Shadow (dr)
Clark Terry With The Thelonious Monk Trio
Let's Cool One
NYC, rec. 7.or 12.5.1958
Monk,Thelonious (p) | Terry,Clark (fl-h) | Jones,Sam (b) | Jones,Philly Joe (dr)
Thelonious Monk Quartet
Rhythm-A-Ning | Evidence | Epistrophy | Nutty
Live at The Five Spot Cafe,NYC, rec. 7.8.1958
Monk,Thelonious (p) | Griffin,Johnny (ts) | Abdul-Malik,Ahmed (b) | Haynes,Roy (dr)
In Walked Bud
Live at Town Hall,NYC, rec. 28.2.1959
Monk,Thelonious (p) | Rouse,Charlie (ts) | Jones,Sam (b) | Taylor,Arthur 'Art' (dr)
Thelonious Monk And His Orchestra
Friday The 13th | Thelonious
Monk,Thelonious (p) | Byrd,Donald (tp) | Bert,Eddie (tb) | Northern,Bob (fr-h) | Woods,Phil (as) | Rouse,Charlie (ts) | Adams,Pepper (bs) | McAllister,Jay (tuba) | Jones,Sam (b) | Taylor,Arthur 'Art' (dr) | Overton,Hal (arr)
Thelonious Monk Quintet
Ask Me Now
NYC, rec. 2.6.1959
Monk,Thelonious (p) | Jones,Thad (co) | Rouse,Charlie (ts) | Jones,Sam (b) | Taylor,Arthur 'Art' (dr)
Jackie-Ing
NYC, rec. 4.6.1959
Monk,Thelonious (p) | Jones,Thad (co) | Rouse,Charlie (ts) | Jones,Sam (b) | Taylor,Arthur 'Art' (dr)
Thelonious Monk
Blue Monk | Reflections
San Francisco,CA, rec. 21.10.1959
Monk,Thelonious (p-solo)
Thelonious Monk Quartet Plus Two
Four In One
Live at The Black Hawk,San Francisco,CA, rec. 29.4.1960
Monk,Thelonious (p) | Gordon,Joe (tp) | Rouse,Charlie (ts) | Land,Harold (ts) | Ore,John (b) | Higgins,Billy (dr)
Thelonious Monk Quartet
Well You Needn't
Live at The Olympia,Paris,France, rec. 18.4.1961
Monk,Thelonious (p) | Rouse,Charlie (ts) | Ore,John (b) | Dunlop,Frankie (dr)
Crepuscule With Nellie
Live at The Teatro Lirico,Milano,Italy, rec. 21.4.1961
Monk,Thelonious (p) | Rouse,Charlie (ts) | Ore,John (b) | Dunlop,Frankie (dr)

Winter&Winter | Edel Contraire

Horns] | Now Will The Sun Rise As Brightly(from Songs of The Death Children) | I Often Think They Have Merely Gon Out!(from Song of The Death Children) | Symphony No.1(Titan-3rd Movement) | Symphony No.2(Resurrection-Primal Light) | I Went Out This Morning Over The Countryside(from Songs of A Wayfarer)- | Symphony No.2(Resurrection-Andante Moderato)- | Symphony No.5(Adagietto) | The Drunkard In Spring(from The Song Of The Earth) | Who Throught Up This Song(from The Boy's Magic Horn) | The Farewell(from The Song Of The Earth)
Brooklyn,NY, rec. 11.-14./22.& 26.6.1996
Caine,Uri (p) | Douglas,Dave (tp) | Roseman,Joshua 'Josh' (tb) | Byron,Don (cl) | Binney,David 'Dave' (as) | Blume,Dave (g,electronics) | Feldman,Mark (v) | Gold,Larry (cello) | Formanek,Michael (b) | Baron,Joey (dr) | Bowman,Dean (voc) | Lindsay,Arto (voc) | Bensoussan,Aaron (cantor,hand-dr) | DJ Olive (turntables)

910005-2 | CD | Big Satan
Tim Berne-Marc Ducret-Tom Rainey
Bobby Raconte Une Histoire | Dialectes | The 12,5 % Solution | Scrap Metal | Yes Dear | Description Du Tunnel
Live at Montreuil/Paris,France, rec. 8.-10.12.1996
Berne,Tim (as,bs) | Ducret,Marc (el-g) | Rainey,Tom (dr)

910008-2 | CD | Sound Of Love
Paul Motian Trio
Misterioso | Duke Ellington's Sound Of Love | Mumbo Jumbo | Once Around The Park | Good Morning Heartache
Live at The 'Village Vanguard',NYC, rec. 14.9.1996
Motian,Paul (dr) | Lovano,Joe (ts) | Frisell,Bill (el-g)

910009-2 | CD | Flight Of The Blue Jay
Paul Motian Electric Bebop Band
Flight Of The Blue Jay | Pannonica | Brad's Bag | Celia | Blue Room | Light Blue | East Coast | Barbados | Work
NYC, rec. 20./21.8.1996
Motian,Paul (dr) | Potter,Chris (ts) | Cheek,Chris (ts) | Rosenwinkel,Kurt (el-g) | Schoeppach,Brad (el-g) | Swallow,Steve (el-b)

910012-2 | CD | Colla Parta
Ernst Reijseger
Colla Parta | Ricercare | Gwidza | Ritornello | Garbato Con Sordina | Violoncello Bastardo | Toccata | Divertimento | Giocoso | Rosa | Passaggio | Cello Di Buddha | La Madre Di Tutte Le Guerre
Villa Medici-Giulini,Briosco,Italy, rec. 26.-28.2.& 1.3.1997
Reijseger,Ernst (cello,voice)

910013-2 | CD | Wagner E Venezia
Uri Caine Ensemble
Liebestod(Tristan und Isolde) | Ouvertüre(Tannhäuser) | Ouvertüre(Lohengrin 3.Akt) | Prelude(Tristan und Isolde) | Ouvertüre(Die Meistersinger von Nürnberg) | Der Ritt Der Walküren | Ouvertüre(Lohengrin.1.Akt)
Live at Gran Caffè Quadri,Hotel Metropol, Venezia, rec. 6.-9.6.1997
Caine,Uri (p) | Feldman,Mark (v) | Hammann,Joyce (v) | Friedlander,Erik (cello) | Gress,Drew (b) | Cortese,Dominic (accordeon)

910015-2 | CD | Charms Of The Night Sky
Dave Douglas Quartet
Charms Of The Night Sky | Bal Masque | Sea Change | Facing West | Dance In Thy Soul | Little One | Mug Shots: | Wild Coffee- | The Girl With The Rose Hips- | Decafinata- | Poveri Fiori | Odyssey | Twisted | Codetta
NYC, rec. 18./19.9.1997
Douglas,Dave (tp) | Klucevsek,Guy (accordeon) | Feldman,Mark (v) | Cohen,Greg (b)

910016-2 | CD | Tethered Moon-First Meeting
Masabumi Kikuchi Trio
Tethered Moon | Misterioso | Intermezzo | So In Love | First Meeting | Solar | Open Trio | P.S.
NYC, rec. 20.10.1990&11.-13.3.1991
Kikuchi,Masabumi (p) | Peacock,Gary (b) | Motian,Paul (dr)

910019-2 | CD | Lust Corner
Noel Akchoté-Marc Ribot-Eugene Chadbourne
New York | Street Woman | Chadology | Body And Soul | Extensions | Free No.1 | Interlude No.2 | Chesire Hotel | Peace Warriors | Broken Shadows | Pas-Vous? | Dirt
Ludwigsburg, rec. 23./24.7.1997
Akchoté,Noel (el-g) | Ribot,Marc (el-g) | Chadbourne,Eugene (el-g,bj,voc)

910025-2 | CD | Tango Alla Baila
Tangata Rea
Felicia | Por Tu Culpa | La Mariposa | Garua | El Marne | El Amanecer | Comme Il Faut | Bahia Blanca | Danzarin | Pulentosa Baby | El Once | Tiempos Viejos | Pobre Pibe | El Monito | El Portenito(Milonga) | Ventarron | Romance De Barrio | Pumpa
Live at Club Del Vino,Buenos Aires,Argentina, rec. 19.-21.11.1997
Tangata Rea: Faulin,Rudi (p) | Longhi,Luis (bandoneon) | Linetzky,Andres (p) | Pujia,Victorio (g) | Horovitz,Lila (b)

910032-2 | CD | Paul Motian Trio 2000 + One
Paul Motian Trio With Chris Potter And Larry Grenadier
From Time To Time | Dance | One In Three | Pas De Deux | The Sunflower | Bend Over Backwards | Last Call | Protoplasm
NYC, rec. 11./12.8.1997
Motian,Paul (dr) | Potter,Chris (ts) | Kikuchi,Masabumi (p) | Grenadier,Larry (b) | Swallow,Steve (el-b)

910033-2 | CD | Pariah's Pariah
Gary Thomas Quartet
Who's In Control? | Only Hearsay | Pariah's Pariah | Zero Tolerance | Vanishing Time | For Those Who Still Hear The... | Is Everything Relative?
NYC, rec. 24./25.10.1997
Thomas,Gary (fl,ts) | Osby,Greg (as) | Formanek,Michael (b) | Arnold,John (dr)

910034-2 | CD | Blue Wail
Uri Caine Trio
Honeysuckle Rose | Loose Trade | The Face Of Space | Digature Of The Line | Blue Wail | Sweet Potato | Bones Don't Cry | Poem For Shulamit | Fireball | Honeysuckle Rose(2)
Ludwigsburg, rec. 9.2.1998
Caine,Uri (p) | Genus,James (b) | Peterson,Ralph (dr)

910037-2 | CD | Colla Voche
Ernst Reijseger & Tenore E Cuncordu De Orosei
Libra Me,Domine | Nanneddu Meu | Stabismo Di Venere | Armonica | A Una Rosa(Voche E Notte Antica) | Trumba | Colla Voche | Su Puddhu(Balla Turtumimu | Su Bolu É S'Astore | Dillu
Cattedrale Di S.Pietro,Galtelli,Sardinia, rec. September 1998
Reijseger,Ernst (cello,voice) | Purves,Alan (perc) | Tenore E Cuncordu De Orosei: Dessena,Salvatore (voc) | Siotto,Mario (voc) | Corimbi,Martino (voc) | Frau,Gianluca (voc) | Mura,Patrizio,Mura (harm,voc) | Flag,Jews-harp,voc) | Roych,Massimo (voc)

910038-2 | CD | Tin Pan Alley:The Sidewalks Of New York
The Sidewalks Of New York
Overture: | The Sidewalks Of New York- | I Wonder Who's Kissing Her Now- | Too Much Mustard | Has Anyone Here Seen Kelly? | Life's A Very Funny Proposition After All | Sidewalk Story: | Daisy Bell- | My Wild Irish Rose- | Gypsy Love Song- | Heliotrope Bouquet- | My Gal Sal- | Charleston Rag | Take Me Out To The Ballgame | Everybody's Doing I | How'd You Like To Spoon With Me? | Cohen Owes Me Ninety Seven Dollars | By The Light Of The Silver Moon | Nobody | Waiting For The Robert E.Lee | The Good Old Summertime | Some Of These Days(rehersal) | Some Of These Days(the show) | Castle Walk | They Didn't Believe Me | Memphis Blues | After The Ball | You're A Grand Old Flag | The Bowery | When I Leave This World Behind | The Sidewalks Of New York(finale) | The Sidewalks Of New York(coda)
NYC, rec. 4.-10.2.1999
Douglas,Dave (tp) | Alessi,Ralph (tp) | Roseman,Joshua 'Josh' (tb) | Stewart,Robert 'Bob' (tuba) | De Bellis,Richard (fl) | Byron,Don (cl) | Cortese,Dominic (accordeon) | Feldman,Mark (v) | Caine,Uri (p,voice)

Davis,Eddy (bj) | Genus,James (b) | Perowsky,Ben (dr) | Bey,Sadiq Galperin,Fay (voc) | Galperin,Saul (voc) | Hernandez,Philip (voc) | D'Arcy Jones,Brian (voc) | Opel,Nancy (voc) | The Romantchicks: Heafner,Susan (voc) | Walker,Barbara (voc) | Zagnit,Stuart (voc) | Morway-Baker,Renae (voc) | Anderson,Nancy (voc) | Sidewalks Of New York Choir, (the crowd)

910042-2 | CD | Wandering Souls
Dave Douglas Tiny Bell Trio
Sam Hill | At Dusk | Prolix | Loopy | One Shot | Brath-A-Thon | Nicht So Schnell,Mit Viel Mon Ton Zu Spielen | Gowanus | Wandering Souls | Ferrous
NYC, rec. 1./2.12.1998
Tiny Bell Trio: Douglas,Dave (tp) | Shepik,Brad (el-g) | Black,Jim (dr)

910044-2 | CD | Ensemble Modern-Fred Frith: Traffic Continues
Ensemble Modern
Traffic Continues: | Inadvertent Introduction | First Riddle | Traffic II | Third Riddle | Lourdement Gai | Traffic III- | Traffic I- | Freeway- | Shadow Of A Tree On Sand- | Fragile Finale
Frankfurt/M, rec. 14.-17.12.1998
Frith,Fred (g) | Ensemble Modern | Nockles,Bruce (tp) | Dierksen,Uwe (tb) | Ollu,Franck (fr-h,cond) | Wiesner,Dietmar (fl,bass-fl,piccolo) | Diry,Roland (cl) | Milliken,Catherine (oboe,bass-oboe,engl-h) | Shimada,Nariko (bassoon,contra-bassoon) | Stryi,Wolfgang (contra-b-cl,sax) | Kretzschmar,Hermann (p,sampler) | Kirby,Freya (v) | Sturt,Hilary (v) | Knight,Susan (viola) | Kasper,Michael M. (cello) | Fichter,Thomas (b,el-b) | Ogawa-Helferich,Rumi (cymbalon,perc) | Römer,Rainer (perc)
Traffic Continues II:Gusto(for Tom Cora) | Introduction: Limbo | Adage A- | At Your Earliest Hesitation- | Gyrate- | Adage B- | Not If I See You First | Any Other World | A Good Top Tongue | Nose At Nose | Will Cast Some Light On | Adage D- | Neither Fire Nor Place- | Monkey Lens Diphtong String | Howdwhoula | No Convenient Time | One Never Knows Do One- | Adage Coda- | Long Fade-
Frith,Fred (g) | Ensemble Modern | Nockles,Bruce (tp) | Dierksen,Uwe (tb) | Ollu,Franck (fr-h) | Wiesner,Dietmar (fl,bass-fl,piccolo) | Diry,Roland (cl) | Milliken,Catherine (oboe,bass-oboe,engl-h) | Shimada,Nariko (bassoon,contra-bassoon) | Stryi,Wolfgang (contra-b-cl,sax) | Kretzschmar,Hermann (p,sampler) | Parkins,Zeena (harp,el-harp) | Kirby,Freya (v) | Sturt,Hilary (v) | Knight,Susan (viola) | Kasper,Michael M. (cello) | Fichter,Thomas (b,el-b) | Ogawa-Helferich,Rumi (cymbalon,perc) | Römer,Rainer (perc) | Mori,Ikue (dr-machine)

910045-2 | CD | Monk And Powell
Paul Motian Electric Bebop Band
We See | I'll Keep Loving You | Brilliant Corners | Little Rootie Tootie | Blue Pearl | Boo Boo's Birthday | Wail | San Francisco Holiday | Parisian Thoroughfare
NYC, rec. 28./29.11.1998
Motian,Paul (dr) | Potter,Chris (ts) | Cheek,Chris (ts) | Rosenwinkel,Kurt (el-g) | Cadena,Steve (el-g) | Swallow,Steve (el-b)

910047-2 | CD | Chansons D'Edith Piaf
Tethered Moon
L'Accordeonniste | Que Nadie Sepa Mi Sufrir | Fais Comme Si | Sous Le Ciel De Paris | Le Petit Monsieur Triste | La Vie En Rose | Bravo Pour Le Clown | L'Homme De Berlin | Les Mois D'Amour
NYC, rec. May 1999
Tethered Moon | Kikuchi,Masabumi (p) | Peacock,Gary (b) | Motian,Paul (dr)

910049-2 | CD | Love Fugue-Robert Schumann
Uri Caine Ensemble
Dichterliebe(Robert Schumann op.48): | Im Wunderschönen Monat Mai | Aus Meinen Tränen Spriessen | Die Rose,Die Lilie,Die Taube | Wenn Ich In Deine Augen Seh' | Ich Will Meine Seele Tauchen | Im Rhein,Im Heiligen Strome | Ich Grolle Nicht | Und Wüsten's Die Blumen | Das Ist Ein Flöten Und Geigen | Hör' Ich Das Liedchen Klingen | Ein Jüngling Liebt Ein Mädchen | Am Leuchtenden Sommermorgen | Ich Hab Im Traum Geweint | Allnächtlich Im Traum | Aus Alten Märchen Winkt Es | Die Alten Bösen Lieder
Sala Gustav Mahler, Toblach,Italy, rec. 17./18.7.1999
Caine,Uri (p) | Gilmore,David (g) | Ledford,Mark (voc) | Moss,David (voc) | Caine,Shulamith Wechter (narration) | Patton,Julie (narration) | Takahashi,Mariko (narration)
La Gaia Scienza
Klavier-Quartett(Robert Schumann op.47) | Allegro | Scherzo | Andante | Finale
Villa Medici-Giulini,Briosco,Italy, rec. 10.-13.3.1999
La Gaia Scienza: Valli,Federica (p) | Barneschi,Stefano (v) | Bianchi,Marco (viola) | Beschi,Paolo (cello)

910057-2 | CD | Rien
Noel Akchoté Trio
Gifle | Peigne | Crache | Mords | Jette | Cesse | Coupe | Hurrle | Parle | Rien | Pousse
München, rec. 1.-3.10.1999
Akchoté,Noel (el-g) | Minkkinen,Erik (computer) | Sharpley,Andrew (sampler,turntable)

910058-2 | CD | Accordance
Guy Klucevsek-Alan Bern
Life,Liberty And The Prosciutto Happiness | Angel Blue | Information,Please: | Social Securities | Birthdays | Telephones | The Gunks | Bar Talk | Starting Over | Mr.Glime-Glide | Mug Shots: | Psychotina Nervosa(Wild Coffee) | The Girl With The Rose Hips | Decafinata | Astor Place | Scarlatti Fever | Hegel's Fantasy | Dueling Dovidls | Happy
Villa Medici-Giulini,Briosco,Italy, rec. 4.-6.6.2000
Klucevsek,Guy (accordeon) | Bern,Alan (accordeon)

910060-2 | CD | Winter Theme
Amsterdam String Trio
Wintertheme(1) | Le Tombeau De Jean Nicot | Only Trees | The Mousing Minuets: | Witte Bloemen- | Mousing- | Black Minuet- | Wintertheme(2) | Andreas Fleischmann | Nor Night,Nor Day,No Rest | Wedding Music | En Deuil | Blauwe Sliert | Winter | Een Kennis Vind Ik Niks | Die Viool Komt Wel Terug | En Schuifttrompet Voor Julius | Wintertheme(3)
Amsterdam String Trio | Horsthuis,Maurice (viola) | Reijseger,Ernst (cello) | Glerum,Ernst (b)

910061-2 | CD | Alasnoaxis
Jim Black Quartet
M m | Optical | Maybe | Ambacharm | Garden Frequency | Poet Staggered | Backfloatpedal | Icon | Luxuriate | Boombye | Auk And Dromedary | Trace | Nion | Melize | Angels And Artifice
Bearsville,NY, rec. 17./18.2.2000
Black,Jim (dr) | Speed,Chris (cl,ts) | Jensson,Hilmar (el-g) | Sverrisson,Skuli (el-b)

910063-2 | CD | Europe
Paul Motian Electric Bebop Band
Oska-T | Bird Feathers | Blue Midnight | Introspection | New Moon | Fiasco | Gallop's Gallop | If You Could See Me Now | 2300 Skiddoo
Ludwigsburg, rec. 2.-5.7.2000
Motian,Paul (dr) | Cheek,Chris (ts) | Tonolo,Pietro (ss,ts) | Monder,Ben (g) | Cardenas,Steve (g) | Christensen,Anders (el-b)

910068-2 | CD | Bedrock
Uri Caine Trio
Our Hour | Nymphomania | Fang | Skins | Humphrey Pass My Way | Flagrant Fragrant | Toe Jam | J.Edgar Hoover In A Dress
NYC, rec. 8.3.2001
Caine,Uri (p,el-p) | Lefebvre,Tim (b) | Danzinger,Zachary (dr,sampled-perc)
Lobby Daze
Caine,Uri (p,el-p) | Lefebvre,Tim (b) | Danzinger,Zachary (dr,sampled-perc) | System,Jessie (voc)
Red Eye
Caine,Uri (p,el-p) | Lefebvre,Tim (b) | Danzinger,Zachary (dr,sampled-perc) | D.J.Logic/Jason Kibler) (turntable)

Root Canal
Caine,Uri (p,el-p) | Lefebvre,Tim (b) | Danzinger,Zachary (dr,sampled-perc) | D.J.Logic/Jason Kibler) (turntable) | Davenport,Pete (voc)

910069-2 | CD | Holiday For Strings EAN 025091006922
Paul Motian E.B.B.B.
Arabesque | 5 Miles To Wrentham | Morpion | Luteous Pangolin | Look To The Black Wall | Holiday For Strings | Endgame | It Never Entered My Mind | Roundup | Oh What A Beautiful Mornin'
Ludwigsburg, rec. 10.-12.11.2001
Motian,Paul (dr) | Tonolo,Pietro (ss,ts) | Cheek,Chris (ts) | Monder,Ben (g) | Cardenas,Steve (g) | Christensen,Anders (el-b)

910071-2 | CD | Digital Wildlife EAN 025091007127
Fred Frith Maybe Monday
Close To Home | Touch- | Risk- | The Prisoner's Dilemma | Image In Atom | Digital Wildlife
Oakland,CA, rec. 1.-8.5.2001
Frith,Fred (g) | Ochs,Larry (ts,sopranino) | Jeanrenaud,Joan (cello) | Masaoka,Miya (koto,electronics)

910075-2 | CD | Solitaire
Uri Caine
Say It In French | As I Am | Roll On | Sonia Said | Beartoes | Inhaling You | Hamsin | Solitaire | The Call | Snort | All The Way | Twelve | Blackbird | Anaconda | Country Life
Schloss Elmau, rec. 22./23.11.2000
Caine,Uri (p-solo)

910076-2 | CD | Splay EAN 025091007622
Jim Black Alasnoaxis
Aloe Eva | Icratic | Cheepa Vs. Cheep | You Were Out | War Again Error | Ble | Myndir Now | Ant Work Song | Awkwarder | Blissed(Selfchatter Mix)
details unknown, rec. details unknown
Black,Jim (dr,perc) | Speed,Chris (cl,ts,perc) | Jensson,Hilmar (el-g,perc) | Sverrisson,Skuli (el-b,perc)

910081-2 | CD | Schumann's Bar Music EAN 025091008124
Fumio Yasuda
At Schumann's | Gone With The Wind | Emily | Someday My Prince Will Come | So Do I | Im 'Weissen Rössl' Am Wolfgang See | Somewhere Over The Rainbow | Keepin' Out Of Mischief Now | Try To Remember | Moon River | Edelweiss | Just Squeeze Me(But Don't Tease Me) | I've Grown Accustomed To Her Face | Amazing Grace | Charade | I Loves You Porgy | Bewitched Bothered And Bewildered | Smoke Gets In Your Eyes | Last Waltz
Ludwigsburg, rec. February & December 2001
Yasuda,Fumio (p-solo)

910086-2 | CD | Concerto Köln EAN 025091008629
Uri Caine With The Concerto Köln
Diabelli Variatios(Ludwig van Beethoven, Opus 120) | Variation 1-33
WDR Köln, rec. 23.-26.2.2002
Caine,Uri (p,arr) | Concerto Köln | Kothe,Hans (tp) | Baldin,Dileno (fr-h) | Breuer,Cordula (fl) | Fabretti,Pier Luigi (oboe) | Montes,Diego (cl) | Alpert,Lorenzo (bassoon) | Ehrhardt,Werner (v) | Buschhaus,Jörg (v) | Sänger,Steven (v) | Hoffmann,Markus (v) | Pöhl,Frauke (v) | Ehrhardt,Martin (v) | Van Der Linde,Hedwig (v) | Engel,Antje (v) | Hildebrand,Corinna (v) | Engelhardt,Godrun (v) | Tröger,Kathrin (v) | Abe,Chiharu (v) | Sabinski,Antje (viola) | Zordan,Giovanni (viola) | Haass,Lothar (viola) | Schmidt,Stefan (viola) | Matzke,Werner (cello) | Kunkel,Jan (cello) | Wahmhoff,Susanne (cello) | Esser,Johannes (b) | Wittulski,Miriam (cello) | Gawlick,Stefan (tympany)

910088-2 | CD | Tales From The Cryptic EAN 025091008827
Guy Klucevsek-Phillip Johnston
Spin Cycle | Tulips Are Better Than One | Am-Scray | The Gift | Trial By Error | Petite Ouverture A Danser(Erik Satie) | A Pear For Satie | Slippin' On A Star | No More Mr. Nice Guy | Der Leiermann | Diggin' Bones | A Goyish Kind Of Blues | The Road To Woy Woy | The Needless Kiss | Blue Window
Eysines,France, rec. 23./24.9.2002
Klucevsek,Guy (accordeon) | Johnston,Phillip (sax)

Woofy Productions | Fenn Music

WPCD 109 | CD | Las Vegar Late Night Sessions:Live At Capozzoli's | EAN 705973109025
Carl Saunders-Lanny Morgan Quintet
Blues For Buddy | You're So Cute | Just A Little | Looking Back | Dear Mr. Florence | I'm All For You
Live at Capozzoli's,Las Vegas, rec. 2./3.12.2000
Saunders,Carl (tp) | Morgan,Lanny (as) | Rainer,Tom (p) | Henry,Trey (b) | Savino,Santo (dr)

WPCD 116 | CD | Las Vegar Late Night Sessions:Live At Capozzoli's | EAN 705973116023
Don Menza Quintet
Robbin's Nest | Lee | Huckleberry Friend | Rubberneck | Brazilienza | Love Is For The Very Young | Motion
Live at Capozzoli's,Las Vegas, rec. 17./18.4.2001
Menza,Don (ts) | Lano,Joe (g) | Gordan,Christopher (b) | Marillo,Tony (dr)

WPCD 121 | CD | The Complete Phoenix Recordings Vol.1 | EAN 705973121027
Conte Candoli-Carl Fontana Quintet
Walkin' | Broadway | Poinciana | America The Beautiful | Lester Leaps In
details unknown, rec. 3.5.1993
Candoli,Conte (tp) | Fontana,Carl (tb) | Anderson,Bill (p) | Jones,Warren (b) | Wainwright,Rob (dr)

WPCD 122 | CD | The Complete Phoenix Recordings Vol.2 | EAN 705973122024
I Should Care | Emily | On The Trail(From The Grand Canyon Suite) | Girl Of My Dreams | Ow!
Candoli,Conte (tp) | Fontana,Carl (tb) | Anderson,Bill (p) | Jones,Warren (b) | Wainwright,Rob (dr)

WPCD 123 | CD | The Complete Phoenix Recordings Vol.3 | EAN 705973123021
Straight No Chaser | Bye Bye Blackbird | Lover Man(Oh,Where Can You Be?) | Honeysuckle I Love | Stella By Starlight
details unknown, rec. 4.5.1993
Candoli,Conte (tp) | Fontana,Carl (tb) | Anderson,Bill (p) | Jones,Warren (b) | Wainwright,Rob (dr)

WPCD 124 | CD | The Complete Phoenix Recordings Vol.4 | EAN 705973124028
All Of You | Girl Of My Dreams | Darn That Dream | The Night Has A Thousand Eyes | I Can't Get Started | Centerpiece
Candoli,Conte (tp) | Fontana,Carl (tb) | Anderson,Bill (p) | Jones,Warren (b) | Wainwright,Rob (dr)

WPCD 125 | CD | The Complete Phoenix Recordings Vol.5 | EAN 705973125025
Strollin' | A Day In The Life Of A Fool(Carnival) | I'm Getting Sentimental Over You | Nina Never Knew | Well You Needn't
details unknown, rec. 5.5.1993
Candoli,Conte (tp) | Fontana,Carl (tb) | Anderson,Bill (p) | Jones,Warren (b) | Wainwright,Rob (dr)

WPCD 126 | CD | The Complete Phoenix Recordings Vol.6 | EAN 705973125025
Surrey With The Fringe On Top | There'll Never Be Another You | I Should Care | Nardis | Lester Leaps In | Centerpiece
Candoli,Conte (tp) | Fontana,Carl (tb) | Anderson,Bill (p) | Jones,Warren (b) | Wainwright,Rob (dr)

yvp music | Fenn Music

CD 3095 | CD | Liedgut:Amsel,Drossel,Swing & Funk
Joe Kienemann Trio
Alle Vögel Sind Schon Da | Komm Lieber Mai Und Mache | Widele Wedele,Hinterm Städele Hält Der Bettelmann Hochzeit | Feins Liebchen,Du